A

GREEK-ENGLISH LEXICON

OF THE

NEW TESTAMENT

ἀρχὴ παιδεύσεως ἡ τῶν ὀνομάτων ἐπίσκεψις.

EPICTETUS, Diss. i. 17, 12.

maius quiddam atque divinius est sermo humanus quam quod totum mutis litterarum figuris comprehendi queat.

HERMANN, Opuscc. iii. 253.

ΤΑ ΡΗΜΑΤΑ Α ΕΓΩ ΛΕΛΑΛΗΚΑ ΥΜΙΝ ΠΝΕΥΜΑ ΕΣΤΙΝ ΚΑΙ ΖΩΗ ΕΣΤΙΝ

A

GREEK-ENGLISH LEXICON

OF THE

NEW TESTAMENT

BEING

Grimm's Wilke's Clavis Novi Testamenti

TRANSLATED REVISED AND ENLARGED

BY

JOSEPH HENRY THAYER, D.D.

NUMERICALLY CODED TO
STRONG'S EXHAUSTIVE CONCORDANCE

BAKER BOOK HOUSE
Grand Rapids, Michigan

PUBLISHER'S INTRODUCTION

———•———

How is the Bible student who does not read Greek to interpret some of the more difficult passages? Take, for example, this portion of II Thessalonians: "And now ye know what withholdeth that he [the man of sin] might be revealed in his time. For the mystery of iniquity doth already work: only he who now letteth will let, until he be taken out of the way" (2:6, 7). Unless one knows that the Greek verb translated "let" is the same as the one translated "withhold," and thus that *let* here means "hinder" or "restrain," one cannot possibly understand this passage. How is one to discover this who does not know Greek?

One way is through *Strong's Exhaustive Concordance*. This volume, first published in 1894, gives every word in the English Bible a number, and this number guides one to the proper Greek word in the brief Greek-English dictionary in the concordance itself. But can the student who does not read Greek avail himself of a full-fledged Greek-English lexicon (or dictionary)? Up until this edition of Thayer's lexicon, he could not. Now he can.

The numbers found in Strong's appear in this edition next to the appropriate Greek word. The student simply needs to look up an English word in Strong's concordance, find the number, look up that number in the margin of this volume, then see the appropriate Greek word and read its English meaning(s).

Having learned the basic steps, one will benefit by putting them into immediate use. Some examples follow.

In I Corinthians 2:14 the natural man is said to be unable to receive or know the things of God because these things are spiritually discerned. By looking up the word *natural,* one may gain a greater appreciation of the contrast Paul is making between the *natural* and the *spiritual* man (vv. 14, 15). Under *natural* on page 709 in Strong's concordance is a reference to I Corinthians 2:14, and on the right side of the column the code number *5591*. Now locate *5591* in this volume; it is on page 677. The first definition of ψυχικός is "having the nature and characteristics of the ψυχή, i.e. of the principle of animal life." The next definition (on page 678) is related but is more specific, drawing out the moral implications of ψυχικός: "governed by the ψυχή, i.e. the sensuous nature with its subjection to appetite and passion (as though made up of nothing but ψυχή). . . ." Further on it says that in the Authorized Version (i.e., the King James Version) ψυχικός is translated "sensual" in Jude 19. According to this verse and its context, "mockers . . . who . . . walk after their own ungodly lusts" are "*sensual,* having not the Spirit." Thus is confirmed the true character of the "*natural* man" of

I Corinthians 2:14: he is a helpless captive to his sensual or animal nature. "Having not the Spirit," he is unregenerate and unconverted.

It should be noted that by turning to *5591* in the Greek dictionary in Strong's concordance, one can discover the word from which ψυχικός was derived: ψυχή (*5590*). In both of these entries code numbers are given for other words from which these two words should be distinguished, and also for the Old Testament equivalents of each. Familiarity with related words that are both similar and different sheds much light and helps one avoid the theological pitfalls of basing one's interpretation only on the text of the English Bible.

A different study method may be illustrated by the word *letteth* in II Thessalonians 2:7. First, look up *letteth* in Strong's concordance. Locate the reference to II Thessalonians 2:7 and the code number, *2722*. Second, look up *2722* in the Greek dictionary in the concordance. The Greek word is κατέχω, and its root meaning is "to hold down (fast)." After this definition is an alphabetical list of every way in which κατέχω is translated in the KJV: "have, hold (fast), keep (in memory), let, x [i.e., a Greek idiom] make toward, possess, retain, seize on, stay, take, withhold." Third, look up each of these translations of κατέχω in the concordance, scanning the references under the various forms of each rendering for the code number *2722*. (Be sure to look only for italicized numbers; numbers that are not italicized refer to Hebrew words.) The following list should result:

have—had (John 5:4)

hold (fast)—hold (Rom. 1:18); hold fast (I Thess. 5:21; Heb. 3:6; 10:23); held (Rom. 7:6)

keep (in memory)—keep (Luke 8:15; I Cor. 11:2); keep in memory (I Cor. 13:2)

let—let (II Thess. 2:7); letteth (II Thess. 2:7)

make toward (Acts 27:40)

possess—possessed (I Cor. 7:30); possessing (II Cor. 6:10)

retain—retained (Philem. 13)

seize on (Matt. 21:38)

stay—stayed (Luke 4:42)

take (Luke 14:9)

withhold—withholdeth (II Thess. 2:6)

And fourth, look up *2722* in this edition of Thayer's lexicon and carefully note the various ways in which this word is defined. The two basic meanings are: (1) "to hold back, detain, retain"; and (2) "to get possession of, take, . . . to possess." Read the entire entry, including the Scripture references. The asterisk (*) at the end of the article means that all the places in the New Testament where κατέχω appears are here referred to.

The great value of this kind of word study is that it reveals the rich variety of meanings that a word can bear, as well as the technical precision with which it can be used in a certain context.

Another kind of word study vitally important to a correct interpretation of Scripture is the examination of Greek synonyms that are rendered by a single English word or verbal system (e.g., *faith* and *believe* belong to a single verbal system). An outstanding example is the words *repent* and *repentance*. These words are of great importance in New Testament teaching on the way of salvation, yet the word *repent* is occasionally used in the New Testament to designate actions other than (or less than) saving repentance. Matthew 27:3 says that "Judas, which had betrayed him, when he saw that he was condemned, *repented* himself. . . ." The word here is μεταμέλομαι (*3338*), which is more literally translated here, "having regretted (it)." The fate of Judas Iscariot, whom Christ had called "the son of perdition" (John 17:12) and "a devil" (John 6:70), is no secret. Μεταμέλομαι is also found in Matthew 21 in one of Christ's parables (v. 29) and its application (v. 32). In this context the word conveys the idea of a regret or remorse that could open the door for a thorough change of heart.

It is enlightening to see the contrasting use of the verb μετανοέω (*3340*), which means "repent," and its noun form μετάνοια (*3341*), which means "repentance." The verb is found thirty-four times in the New Testament, the noun twenty-four. Whenever men are commanded to repent in order to be saved, these are the words used. Thayer defines μετανοέω as "to change one's mind, i.e. to repent (to feel sorry that one has done this or that, John 3:9), of having offended some one, Luke 17:3 sq. . . . used especially of those who, conscious of their sins and with manifest tokens of sorrow, are intent on obtaining God's pardon . . . to change one's mind for the better, heartily to amend with abhorrence of one's past sins. . . ." He defines μετάνοια as "a change of mind: as it appears in one who repents of a purpose he has formed or of something he has done, Hebrews 12:17 . . . especially the change of mind of those who have begun to abhor their errors and misdeeds, and have determined to enter upon a better course of life, so that it embraces both a recognition of sin and sorrow for it and hearty amendment, the tokens and effects of which are good deeds. . . ." Though μετανοέω and μετάνοια were occasionally used interchangeably with μεταμέλομαι and its noun form in *secular* usage, the Holy Spirit clearly distinguished them in the New Testament Scriptures.

Upon close examination of all fifty-eight texts in which μετανοέω and μετάνοια occur, two things become apparent: (1) repentance (i.e., a radical alteration of mind and conduct) is an absolute necessity in the salvation of men from the dominion, love, practice, and eternal consequences of sin; (2) this saving repentance is such that the natural man cannot obtain it, though he seeks it with tears (Heb. 12:17), unless God's sovereign Spirit of grace gives it to him (Acts 5:31; 11:18; II Tim. 2:25).

One passage makes the distinction between μετανοέω (and derivatives) and μεταμέλομαι (and derivatives) crystal clear: II Corinthians 7:10. There Paul wrote: "For godly sorrow worketh repentance (μετάνοια) to salvation not to be repented of (ἀμεταμέλητος): but the sorrow of the world worketh death." R. C. H. Lenski translated this verse: "For the grief according to God's way works an unregrettable repentance for salvation; but the grief of the world works out death." This entire chapter, as none other in the New Testament, gives vital instruction on the distinctions between true repentance and regret (as in verse 8) and between godly sorrow (which always leads to repentance) and worldly sorrow (which produces death). Charles Hodge's famous commentary deals thoroughly with these distinctions.

A word of caution is necessary. Thayer was a Unitarian, and the errors of this sect occasionally come through in the explanatory notes. The reader should be alert for both subtle and blatant denials of such doctrines as the Trinity (Thayer regarded Christ as a mere man and the Holy Spirit as an impersonal force emanating from God), the inherent and total depravity of fallen human nature, the eternal punishment of the wicked, and Biblical inerrancy. When defining μεταμέλομαι, Thayer refuses to draw a clear distinction between this word and μετανοέω. Underlying this refusal is the view that man is inherently good, needing Christ not as a Savior but only as an example.

Also important to the careful student is the study of Greek words used only once in the New

Testament. (These words are called *hapax legomena,* "something said only once.") A few examples are ἀπαράβατος *(531),* ἀποκατάστασις *(605),* ἀποσκίασμα *(644),* κορβᾶν *(2878),* θεόπνευστος *(2315),* and νεωκόρος *(3511).* Though such words occur only once in the New Testament, Thayer often refers to places in the Septuagint (LXX—the most important ancient Greek version of the Old Testament) and in other ancient sources where these words occur.

The complete list of *hapax legomena* is a long one. Some are not especially important, like σχολή *(4981),* the "school" of Tyrannus in Acts 19:9. Others, however, occur in vitally important contexts. Θειότης *(2305)* and θεότης *(2320),* for example, are synonyms that occur only in Romans 1:20 and Colossians 2:9, respectively. They could almost be thought of as the same word, were it not for the letter iota (ι) in θειότης. Both are translated "Godhead." Thayer says that the two words are synonyms. Θειότης means "divinity, divine nature," and θεότης "deity, i.e. the state of being God, Godhead." He adds that "θεότης 'deity' differs from θειότης 'divinity,' as essence differs from quality or attribute. . . ." In Colossians 2:9, as Trench pointed out in *Synonyms of the New Testament,* "Paul is declaring that in the Son there dwells all the fulness of absolute Godhead [θεότης]; they were no mere rays of divine glory which gilded Him, lighting up His person for a season and with a splendour not His own; but He was, and is, absolute and perfect God. . . ." But in Romans 1:20, said Trench, "Paul is declaring how much of God may be known from the revelation of Himself which He has made in nature, from those vestiges of Himself which men may everywhere trace in the world around them. Yet it is not the personal God whom any man may learn to know by these aids: He can be known only by the revelation of Himself in His Son; but only His divine attributes, His majesty and glory."

This important distinction makes these two verses of particular value when dealing with cults that deny the essential deity of the Lord Jesus Christ. According to Colossians 2:9, ". . . in him [Christ] dwelleth all the fulness of the Godhead (θεότης) bodily." Whatever it is that makes God to be truly God, that divine essence dwells in its entirety in Jesus of Nazareth. Nor is this a vague godlikeness, an attribute that all gods have in common; Paul said in Romans 1:20 that the Creator's "eternal power and Godhead (θειότης)" are clearly seen from the creation of the world. A Jehovah's Witness, if taken first to Romans 1:20, will readily admit that *Godhead* (translated "godship" in the *New World Translation*) can only refer, in this context, to Jehovah Himself. Turn then to Colossians 2:9, which the *New World Translation* renders: ". . . in him . . . all the fullness of the divine quality dwells bodily." Is this all Paul meant to say? Obviously not, for θειότης in Romans 1:20 means "quality," the characteristic of Jehovah revealed in His creation, whereas θεότης in Colossians 2:9 means "essence," or, as Thayer puts it, "the state of being God." If there were no other proof in the Bible of the full deity of the Lord Jesus, every Christian should believe it on the strength of these two verses alone. You need only know how to use this volume to have such evidences at your fingertips.

Another important kind of word study is the examination of Greek words that occur frequently. Some of these encompass such a wealth of meaning that each requires a dozen or more different English terms or expressions to do it justice in its various contexts. Two examples follow.

Λόγος *(3056),* rendered "Word" in John 1:1, 14, is said by Thayer to have the following range of meanings: "the living voice"; "a saying"; "a decree, mandate, or order"; "a promise"; "a thought"; "a declaration"; "an aphorism"; "a maxim or weighty saying"; "a discourse, speech, or

instruction''; and various mental concepts such as ''reason''; ''an account, reckoning, or score'';
''relation'' (including a mathematical one); ''proportion''; ''a cause or ground.'' He adds that its
particular use in John's Gospel denotes the personal Wisdom of God. Because the English term *word*
fails to convey the fullness of the original, the Moffatt translation simply transliterates Λόγος
(''Logos'') instead of translating it (''Word'').

Ἀπόλλυμι (*622*) is translated ''destroy'' twenty-three times, ''lose'' twenty-eight times, and
''perish'' over thirty times. Since it is the main word referring to the destiny of the wicked after the
judgment, the question arises whether it should be translated ''annihilate.'' Thayer gives more than a
dozen meanings, none of them suggesting or requiring that the thing ''destroyed'' cease to exist. The
dominant meaning seems to be ''loss'' or ''ruin'' rather than ''cessation of existence.'' In fact, not
once does the context require the idea of annihilation, and many times the context does not allow that
connotation.

Thayer's Greek-English Lexicon and *Strong's Exhaustive Concordance* are based on different
Greek texts of the New Testament. Strong prefers the Received Text that underlies the King James
Version; Thayer, the critical text of Westcott and Hort that underlies the English Revised Version
(1881) and the American Standard Version (1901). Not all words in one Greek text are in the other,
and not all words are spelled the same in the two texts. The table below explains the symbols used to
mesh together Thayer's lexicon and Strong's concordance.

See *1234* St.	Indicates either (a) a Greek word not found in the Received Text (in which case the number refers one to the word that appears in place of this word in the Received Text) or (b) a Greek word spelled differently in the Received Text and the Westcott-Hort text. ''See *1234* St.'' means ''See the Greek word in Strong's concordance numbered *1234*.''
(*1234a*)	Indicates a Greek word omitted by Strong because it is not present in the Received Text. The number in parentheses is a place holder, and the lower-case letter indicates that it is not related to the preceding word with the same number.
1234a	Indicates either (a) an unusual form of the word with the number *1234* or (b) a word that Strong designates with a superscript mark—*1234'*.

The apostle Paul knew the difference between mere religious genius and the inspiration that is
from God. He explained what this difference means for the believer in Christ: ''Now we have
received, not the spirit of the world, but the spirit which is of God; that we might know the things that
are freely given to us of God. Which things also we speak, not in the words which man's wisdom
teacheth, but which the Holy Ghost teacheth; comparing spiritual things with spiritual'' (I Cor. 2:12,
13). It is the publisher's hope that this special edition of *Thayer's Greek-English Lexicon* will
encourage and enable the serious Bible student to seek out the Spirit's meaning by studying the ways
the Spirit uses His own vocabulary.

PREFACE

TOWARDS the close of the year 1862, the "Arnoldische Buchhandlung" in Leipzig published the First Part of a Greek-Latin Lexicon of the New Testament, prepared, upon the basis of the "Clavis Novi Testamenti Philologica" of C. G. Wilke (second edition, 2 vols. 1851), by Professor C. L. WILIBALD GRIMM of Jena. In his Prospectus Professor Grimm announced it as his purpose not only (in accordance with the improvements in classical lexicography embodied in the Paris edition of Stephen's Thesaurus and in the fifth edition of Passow's Dictionary edited by Rost and his coadjutors) to exhibit the historical growth of a word's significations and accordingly in selecting his vouchers for New Testament usage to show at what time and in what class of writers a given word became current, but also duly to notice the usage of the Septuagint and of the Old Testament Apocrypha, and especially to produce a Lexicon which should correspond to the present condition of textual criticism, of exegesis, and of biblical theology. He devoted more than seven years to his task. The successive Parts of his work received, as they appeared, the outspoken commendation of scholars diverging as widely in their views as Hupfeld and Hengstenberg; and since its completion in 1868 it has been generally acknowledged to be by far the best Lexicon of the New Testament extant.

An arrangement was early made with Professor Grimm and his publisher to reproduce the book in English, and an announcement of the same was given in the Bibliotheca Sacra for October 1864 (p. 886). The work of translating was promptly begun; but it was protracted by engrossing professional duties, and in particular by the necessity — as it seemed — of preparing the authorized translation of Lünemann's edition of Winer's New Testament Grammar, which was followed by a translation of the New Testament Grammar of Alexander Buttmann. Meantime a new edition of Professor Grimm's work was called for. To the typographical accuracy of this edition liberal contributions were made from this side the water. It appeared in its completed form in 1879. "Admirable", "unequalled", "invaluable", are some of the epithets it elicited from eminent judges in England; while as representing the estimate of the book by competent critics in Germany a few sentences may be quoted from Professor Schürer's review of it in the Theologische Literaturzeitung for January 5, 1878: "The use of Professor Grimm's book for years has convinced me that it is not only unquestionably the best among existing New Testament Lexicons, but that, apart from all comparisons, it is a work of the highest intrinsic merit, and one which is admirably adapted to initiate a learner into an acquaintance with the language of the New Testament. It ought to be regarded by every student as one of the first and most necessary requisites for the study of the New Testament, and consequently for the study of Theology in general."

Both Professor Grimm and his publisher courteously gave me permission to make such changes in his work as might in my judgment the better adapt it to the needs of English-speaking students. But the emphatic commendation it called out from all quarters, in a strain similar to the specimens just given, determined me to dismiss the thought of issuing a new book prepared on my predecessor's as a basis, and — alike in justice to him and for the satisfaction of students — to reproduce his second edition in its integrity (with only the silent correction of obvious oversights), and to introduce my additions in such a form as should render them distinguishable at once from Professor Grimm's work. (See [ ] in the list of "Explanations and Abbreviations" given below.) This decision has occasionally imposed on me some reserve and entailed some embarrassments. But notwithstanding all minor draw-backs the procedure will, I am sure, commend itself in the end, not only on the score of justice to the independent claims and responsibility of both authors, but also on account of the increased assurance (or, at least, the broader outlook) thus afforded the student respect-ing debatable matters, — whether of philology, of criticism, or of interpretation.

Some of the leading objects with the editor in his work of revision were stated in connection with a few specimen pages privately printed and circulated in 1881, and may here be repeated in substance as follows: to verify all references (biblical, classical, and — so far as practicable — modern) ; to note more generally the extra-biblical usage of words; to give the derivation of words in cases where it is agreed upon by the best etymologists and is of interest to the general student; to render complete the enumeration of (representative) verbal forms actually found in the New Testament (and exclude all others) ; to append to every verb a list of those of its compounds which occur in the Greek Testament; to supply the New Testament passages accidentally omitted in words marked at the end with an asterisk; to note more fully the variations in the Greek text of current editions; to introduce brief discussions of New Testament synonyms; to give the more noteworthy renderings not only of the "Authorized Version" but also of the Revised New Testament; to multiply cross references; references to grammatical works, both sacred (Winer, Buttmann, Green, etc.) and classical (Kühner, Krüger, Jelf, Donaldson, Goodwin, etc.) ; also to the best English and American Commentaries (Lightfoot, Ellicott, Westcott, Alford, Morison, Beet, Hackett, Alexander, The Speaker's Commentary, The New Testament Commentary, etc.), as well as to the latest exegetical works that have appeared on the Continent (Weiss, Heinrici, Keil, Godet, Oltramare, etc.) ; and to the recent Bible Dictionaries and Cyclopædias (Smith, Alexander's Kitto, McClintock and Strong, the completed Riehm, the new Herzog, etc.), besides the various Lives of Christ and of the Apostle Paul.

Respecting a few of these specifications an additional remark or two may be in place :

One of the most prominent and persistent embarrassments encountered by the New Testament lexicographer is occasioned by the diversity of readings in the current editions of the Greek text. A slight change in the form or even in the punctuation of a passage may entail a change in its construction, and consequently in its classification in the Lexicon. In the absence of an acknowledged consensus of scholars in favor of any one of the extant printed texts to the exclusion of its rivals, it is incumbent on any Lexicon which aspires after general currency to reckon alike with them all. Professor Grimm originally took account of the text of the 'Receptus', together with that of Griesbach, of Lachmann, and of Tischendorf. In his second edition, he made occasional reference also to the readings of Tregelles. In the present work not only have the textual statements of Grimm's second edition undergone thorough revision (see, for example, "Griesbach" in the list of "Explanations and Abbreviations"), but the readings (whether in the text or the margin) of the editions of Tregelles and of Westcott and Hort have also been carefully noted.

Again: the frequent reference, in the discussion of synonymous terms, to the distinctions holding in classic usage (as they are laid down by Schmidt in his voluminous work) must not be regarded as designed to modify the definitions given in the several articles. On the contrary, the exposition of classic usage is often intended merely to serve as a standard of comparison by which the direction and degree of a word's change in meaning can be measured. When so employed, the information given will often start suggestions alike interesting and instructive.

On points of etymology the statements of Professor Grimm have been allowed to stand, although, in form at least, they often fail to accord with modern philological methods. But they have been supplemented by references to the works of Curtius and Fick, or even more frequently, perhaps, to the Etymological Dictionary of Vaniček, as the most compendious digest of the views of specialists. The meaning of radical words and of the component parts of compounds is added, except when it is indubitably suggested by the derivative, or when such words may be found in their proper place in the Lexicon.

The nature and use of the New Testament writings require that the lexicographer should not be hampered by a too rigid adherence to the rules of scientific lexicography. A student often wants to know not so much the inherent meaning of a word as the particular sense it bears in a given context or discussion: — or, to state the same truth from another point of view, the lexicographer often cannot assign a particular New Testament reference to one or another of the acknowledged significations of a word without indicating his exposition of the passage in which the reference occurs. In such a case he is compelled to assume, at least to some extent, the functions of the exegete, although he can and should refrain from rehearsing the general arguments which support the interpretation adopted, as well as from arraying the objections to opposing interpretations.

Professor Grimm, in his Preface, with reason calls attention to the labor he has expended upon the explanation of doctrinal terms, while yet guarding himself against encroaching upon the province of the dogmatic theologian. In this particular the editor has endeavored to enter into his labors. Any one who consults such articles as αἰών, αἰώνιος, βασιλεία τοῦ θεοῦ etc., δίκαιος and its cognates, δόξα, ἐλπίς, ζωή, θάνατος, θεός, κόσμος, κύριος, πίστις, πνεῦμα, σάρξ, σοφία, σώζω and its cognates, υἱὸς τοῦ ἀνθρώπου, υἱὸς τοῦ θεοῦ, Χριστός, and the like, will find, it is believed, all the materials needed for a complete exposition of the biblical contents of those terms. On the comparatively few points respecting which doctrinal opinions still differ, references have been added to representative discussions on both sides, or to authors whose views may be regarded as supplementing or correcting those of Professor Grimm.

Convenience often prescribes that the archæological or historical facts requisite to the understanding of a passage be given the student on the spot, even though he be referred for fuller information to the works specially devoted to such topics.   In this particular, too, the editor has been guided by the example of his predecessor; yet with the constant exercise of self-restraint lest the book be encumbered with unnecessary material, and be robbed of that succinctness which is one of the distinctive excellences of the original.

In making his supplementary references and remarks the editor has been governed at different times by different considerations, corresponding to the different classes for whose use the Lexicon is designed.   Primarily, indeed, it is intended to satisfy the needs and to guide the researches of the a v e r a g e s t u d e n t; although the specialist will often find it serviceable, and on the other hand the beginner will find that he has not been forgotten. Accordingly, a caveat must be entered against the hasty inference that the mention of a different interpretation from that given by Professor Grimm always and of necessity implies dissent from him.   It may be intended merely to inform the student that the meaning of the passage is still in debate.   And the particular works selected for reference have been chosen — now because they seem best suited to supplement the statements or references of the original; now because they furnish the most copious references to other discussions of the same topic; now because they are familiar works or those to which a student can readily get access; now, again, because unfamiliar and likely otherwise to escape him altogether.

It is in deference, also, to the wants of the ordinary student that the references to grammatical works — particularly Winer and Buttmann — have been greatly multiplied.   The expert can easily train his eye to run over them; and yet even for him they may have their use, not only as giving him the opinion of eminent philologists on a passage in question, but also as continually recalling his attention to those philological considerations on which the decision of exegetical questions must mainly rest.

Moreover, in the case of a literature so limited in compass as the New Testament, it seems undesirable that even a beginner should be subjected to the inconvenience, expense, and especially the loss of facility, incident to a change of text-books.   He will accordingly find that not only have his wants been heeded in the body of the Lexicon, but that at the close of the Appendix a list of verbal forms has been added especially for his benefit.   The other portions of the Appendix will furnish students interested in the history of the New Testament vocabulary, or investigating questions — whether of criticism, authorship, or biblical theology — which involve its word-lists, with fuller and more trustworthy collections than can be found elsewhere.

Should I attempt, in conclusion, to record the names of all those who during the many years in which this work has been preparing have encouraged or assisted me by word or pen, by counsel or book, the list would be a long one.   Express acknowledgments, however, must be made to GEORGE B. JEWETT, D.D., of Salem and to Professor W. W. EATON now of Middlebury College, Vermont.   The former has verified and re-verified all the biblical and classical references, besides noting in the main the various readings of the critical texts, and rendering valuable aid in correcting many of the proofs; the latter has gathered the passages omitted from words marked with a final asterisk, completed and corrected the enumeration of verbal forms, catalogued the compound verbs, had an eye to matters of etymology and accentuation, and in many other particulars given the work the benefit of his conscientious and scholarly labor. To these names one other would be added were it longer written on earth. Had the lamented Dr. Abbot been spared to make good his generous offer to read the final proofs, every user of the book would doubtless have had occasion to thank him. He did, however, go through the manuscript and add with his own hand the variant verse-notation, in accordance with the results of investigation subsequently given to the learned world in his Excursus on the subject published in the First Part of the Prolegomena to Tischendorf's Editio Octava Critica Major.

To Dr. Caspar René Gregory of Leipzig (now Professor-elect at Johns Hopkins University, Baltimore) my thanks are due for the privilege of using the sheets of the Prolegomena just named in advance of their publication; and to the Delegates of the Clarendon Press, Oxford, for a similar courtesy in the case of the Seventh Edition of Liddell and Scott's Lexicon.

No one can have a keener sense than the editor has of the shortcomings of the present volume. But he is convinced that whatever supersedes it must be the joint product of several laborers, having at their command larger resources than he has enjoyed, and ampler leisure than falls to the lot of the average teacher. Meantime, may the present work so approve itself to students of the Sacred Volume as to enlist their co-operation with him in ridding it of every remaining blemish

— ἵνα ὁ λόγος τοῦ κυρίου τρέχῃ καὶ δοξάζηται.

J. H. THAYER

Cambridge, Massachusetts.

Dec. 25, 1885.

In issuing this "Corrected Edition" opportunity has been taken not only to revise the supplementary pages (725 sq.), but to add in the body of the work (as circumstances permitted) an occasional reference to special monographs on Biblical topics which have been published during the last three years, as well as to the Fourth Volume of Schmidt's Synonymik (1886), and also to works which (like Meisterhans) have appeared in an improved edition. The Third edition (1888) of Grimm, however, has yielded little new material; and Dr. Hatch's "Essays in Biblical Greek" comes to hand too late to permit references to its valuable discussions of words to be inserted.

To the correspondents, both in England and this country, who have called my attention to errata, I beg to express my thanks; and I would earnestly ask all who use the book to send me similar favors in time to come: — ἀτελὲς οὐδὲν οὐδενὸς μέτρον.

April 10, 1889.

LIST OF ANCIENT AUTHORS

QUOTED OR REFERRED TO IN THE LEXICON

N. B. In the preparation of this list, free use has been made of the lists in the Lexicons of Liddell and Scott and of Sophocles, also of Freund's Triennium Philologicum (1874) vols. i. and ii., of Smith's Dictionary of Greek and Roman Biography, of Smith and Wace's Dictionary of Christian Biography, of Engelmann's Bibliotheca Scriptorum Classicorum (8th ed. 1880), and of other current works of reference. An asterisk (*) before a date denotes birth, an obelisk (†) death.

	B.C.	A.D.
ACHILLES TATIUS		500 ?
Acts of Paul and Thecla, of Pilate, of Thomas, of Peter and Paul, of Barnabas, etc., at the earliest from . . .		2d cent. on
AELIAN		c. 180
AESCHINES	345	
AESCHYLUS	*525, †456	
AESOP [1]	570	
AETIUS		c. 500
AGATHARCHIDES	117 ?	
ALCAEUS MYTILENAEUS	610	
ALCIPHRON		200 ?
ALCMAN	610	
ALEXANDER APHRODISIENSIS . . .		200
ALEXIS	350	
AMBROSE, Bp. of Milan		374
AMMIANUS MARCELLINUS		† c. 400
AMMONIUS, the grammarian		390
ANACREON [2]	530	
ANAXANDRIDES	350	
ANAXIMANDER	580	
ANDOCIDES	405	
ANTIPHANES	380	
ANTIPHON	412	
ANTONINUS, M. AURELIUS		†180
APOLLODORUS of Athens	140	
APOLLONIUS DYSCOLUS		140
APOLLONIUS RHODIUS	200	
APPIAN		150
APPULEIUS		160
AQUILA (translator of the O. T.) . .		2d cent. (under Hadrian.)
ARATUS	270	
ARCHILOCHUS	700	
ARCHIMEDES, the mathematician . .	250	
ARCHYTAS	c. 400	

	B.C.	A.D.
ARETAEUS		80 ?
ARISTAENETUS		450 ?
ARISTEAS [1]	270	
ARISTIDES, P. AELIUS		160
ARISTOPHANES		*444, †380
ARISTOPHANES, the grammarian . . .		200
ARISTOTLE		*384, †322
ARRIAN (pupil and friend of Epictetus)		*c. 100
ARTEMIDORUS DALDIANUS (oneirocritica)		160
ATHANASIUS		†373
ATHENAEUS, the grammarian . . .		228
ATHENAGORAS of Athens		177 ?
AUGUSTINE, Bp. of Hippo		†430
AUSONIUS, DECIMUS MAGNUS . . .		† c. 390
BABRIUS (see *Rutherford*, Babrius, Intr. ch. i.) . . . . (some say 50 ?)		c. 225
BARNABAS, Epistle written		c. 100 ?
Baruch, Apocryphal Book of		c. 75 ?
Basilica, the [2]		c. 900
BASIL THE GREAT, Bp. of Cæsarea .		†379
BASIL of Seleucia		450
Bel and the Dragon	2d cent. ?	
BION	200	
CAESAR, GAIUS JULIUS . . . †March 15, 44		
CALLIMACHUS	260	
Canons and Constitutions, Apostolic . .	3d and 4th cent.	
CAPITOLINUS, JULIUS (one of the "Hist. August. scriptores sex")		c. 310
CEBES	399	
CEDRENUS		1050

[1] But his letter is spurious; see *Hody*, De Bibl. text. orig. l. i.; A. *Kurz*, Arist. ep. etc. (Bern 1872).

[2] The law-book of the Byzantine Empire, founded upon the work of Justinian and consisting of sixty books. It was begun under the emperor Basil of Macedonia (†886), completed under his son Leo, and revised in 945 under Constantine Porphyrogenitus; (ed. Heimbach, 6 vols. 1833-70)

[1] But the current Fables are not his; on the History of Greek Fable, see *Rutherford*, Babrius, Introd. ch. ii.

[2] Only a few fragments of the odes ascribed to him are genuine.

	B.C.	A.D.
LACTANTIUS		310
LAMPRIDIUS, the historian		310
LEO 'Philosophus', emperor		886
LIBANIUS, the rhetorician		350
LIVY	*59	†17
LONGINUS		250
LONGUS		400 ?
LUCAN, the epic poet		†65
LUCIAN of Samosata, the satirist . .		160 ?
LUCILIUS, the Roman satirist . . .	†103	
LUCRETIUS, the Roman poet	†55	
LYCOPHRON	c. 270	
LYCURGUS of Athens, the orator . .	†329	
LYNCEUS	300	
LYSIAS, the Athenian orator, opened his school	410	
LYSIPPUS	434	
MACARIUS		c. 350
Maccabees, First Book of	105–63 ?	
Maccabees, Second Book of	c. 75 ?	
Maccabees, Third Book of		c. 40 ?
Maccabees, Fourth Book of	1st. cent ?	
MACHON	280	
MACROBIUS		420
MALALAS, JOHN, the annalist . . .		600 ?
Manasses, Prayer of	1st cent. ?	
MANETHO, the Egyptian priest . . .	300	
MARCION		140
MAXIMUS TYRIUS	150	
MELA, POMPONIUS, the Roman geographer		45
MELEAGER, the founder of the epigram. anthologies	60	
MELITO, Bp. of Sardis		c. 175
MENANDER, the poet	325	
MENANDER, the Byzantine historian .		583
MIMNERMUS, the poet	c. 600	
MOERIS, the "Atticist" and lexicographer		2d cent.
MOSCHION		110 ?
MOSCHUS	200	
MUSONIUS RUFUS		66
NEMESIUS		400 ?
NEPOS	*90, †24	
NICANDER	160 ?	
NICEPHORUS, patriarch of Constantinople		†828
NICEPHORUS BRYENNIUS, the historian		†1137
NICEPHORUS GREGORAS, Byzantine historian		†1359
NICETAS ACOMINATUS (also Choniates), Byzantine historian		1200
Nicodemus, Gospel of, see Acts of Pilate		
NICOLAUS DAMASCENUS	14	
NICOMACHUS GERASENUS		50
NILUS, the pupil and friend of John Chrysostom		420
NONNUS of Panopolis in Upper Egypt, the poet		500 ?
NUMENIUS of Apameia, the philosopher (as quoted by Origen)		c. 150

	B.C.	A.D.
NUMENIUS (as quoted by Athen.) . .	c. 350	
OCELLUS LUCANUS	400 ?	
OECUMENIUS, Bp. of Tricca		950 ?
OLYMPIODORUS, the Neo-Platonic philosopher		525
OPPIAN of Anazarbus in Cilicia (auth. of the ἁλιευτικά)		180 ?
OPPIAN of Apameia in Syria (auth. of the κυνηγετικά)		210 ?
ORIGEN		† c. 254
OROSIUS PAULUS		415
Orphica, the		?
OVID		†17
PALAEPHATUS	?	
PAPIAS, Bp. of Hierapolis, first half of		2d cent.
PAUSANIAS		160
PETRUS ALEXANDRINUS		†311
PHALARIS, spurious epistles of . . .		?
PHAVORINUS, VARINUS [1]		
PHILEMON, COMICUS	330	
PHILO		39
PHILODEMUS	50	
PHILOSTRATUS		237
PHOCYLIDES	540	
PSEUDO-PHOCYLIDES (in the Sibyl. Orac., q. v.)		1st cent. ?
PHOTIUS (Patriarch of Constantinople)		850
PHRYNICHUS, the grammarian . . .		180
PHYLARCHUS	210	
PINDAR . . *521 (4 yrs. after Aeschylus), †441		
PLATO, COMICUS, contemporary of Aristophanes	427	
PLATO, the philosopher	*427, †347	
PLAUTUS	†184	
PLINY the elder, the naturalist . . .		†79
PLINY the younger, the nephew and adopted son of the preceding . . .		†113
PLOTINUS, the philosopher		†270
PLUTARCH		†120
POLLUX, author of the ὀνομαστικόν . .		180
POLYAENUS, author of the στρατηγήματα		163
POLYBIUS	†122	
POLYCARP		†155, Feb. 23
PORPHYRY, pupil of Plotinus		270
POSIDIPPUS	280	
POSIDONIUS, philosopher (teacher of Cicero and Pompey)	78	
PROCLUS, philosopher		450
PROPERTIUS	*48, †16	
Protevangelium Jacobi		2d cent.
Psalter of Solomon	63–48 ?	
PSELLUS the younger, philosopher . .		1050
PTOLEMY, the geographer		160
PYTHAGORAS	531	
QUINTILIAN, rhetorician, teacher of Pliny the younger		†95
QUINTUS SMYRNAEUS		380 ?

[1] The Latin name of the Italian Guarino Favorino, who died A. D. 1537, and was the author of a Greek Lexicon compiled mainly from Suïdas, Hesychius, Harpocration, Eustathius, and Phrynichus. 1st ed. Rome, 1523, and often elsewhere since.

LIST OF BOOKS

REFERRED TO MERELY BY THEIR AUTHOR'S NAME OR BY SOME EXTREME ABRIDGMENT OF THE TITLE

———•———

Alberti = *Joannes Alberti*, Observationes Philologicae in sacros Novi Foederis Libros. Lugd. Bat., 1725.

Aristotle: when p a g e s are cited, the reference is to the edition of the Berlin Academy (edited by Bekker and Brandis; index by Bonitz) 5 vols. 4to, 1831–1870. Of the Rhetoric, Sandys's edition of Cope (3 vols., Cambridge, 1877) has been used.

Bäumlein = *W. Bäumlein*, Untersuchungen über griechische Partikeln. Stuttgart, 1861.

B.D. = Dr. William Smith's Dictionary of the Bible, 3 vols. London, 1860–64. The American edition (4 vols., N. Y. 1868–1870), revised and edited by Professors Hackett and Abbot, has been the edition used, and is occasionally referred to by the abbreviation "Am. ed."

BB. DD. = Bible Dictionaries: — comprising especially the work just named, and the third edition of Kitto's Cyclopædia of Biblical Literature, edited by Dr. W. L. Alexander: 3 vols., Edinburgh, 1870.

Bnhdy. = *G. Bernhardy*, Wissenschaftliche Syntax der Griechischen Sprache. Berlin, 1829.

B. = *Alexander Buttmann*, Grammar of the New Testament Greek. (Authorized Translation with numerous Additions and Corrections by the Author: Andover, 1873.) Unless otherwise indicated, the reference is to the p a g e of the translation, with the corresponding page of the German original added in a parenthesis.

Bttm. Ausf. Spr. or Sprchl. = *Philipp Buttmann*, Ausführliche Griechische Sprachlehre. (2d ed., 1st vol. 1830, 2d vol. 1839.)

Bttm. Gram. = Philipp Buttmann's Griechische Grammatik. The edition used (though not the latest) is the twenty-first (edited by Alexander Buttmann: Berlin, 1863). Its sections agree with those of the eighteenth edition, translated by Dr. Robinson and published by Harper & Brothers, 1851. When the p a g e is given, the translation is referred to.

Bttm. Lexil. = Philipp Buttmann's Lexilogus u. s. w. (1st vol. 2d ed. and 2d vol. 1825.) The work was translated and edited by J. R. Fishlake, and issued in one volume by John Murray, London, 1836.

"Bible Educator" = a collection (with the preceding name) of miscellaneous papers on biblical topics by various writers under the editorship of Rev. Professor E. H. Plumptre, and published in 4 vols. (without date) by Cassell, Petter, and Galpin.

Chandler = *Henry W. Chandler*, A Practical Introduction to Greek Accentuation. Second edition, revised: Oxford, 1881.

Cremer = *Hermann Cremer*, Biblisch-theologisches Wörterbuch der Neutestamentlichen Gräcität. 'Third greatly enlarged and improved Edition': Gotha, 1883. Of the 'Fourth enlarged and improved Edition' nine parts (comprising nearly two thirds of the work) have come to hand, and are occasionally referred to. A translation of the second German edition was published in 1878 by the Messrs. Clark.

Curtius = *Georg Curtius*, Grundzüge der Griechischen Etymologie. Fifth edition, with the co-operation of Ernst Windisch: Leipzig, 1879.

De Wette, = *Wilhem Martin Leberecht De Wette*, Kurzgefasstes exegetisches Handbuch zum Neuen Testament. Leipzig: Weidmann'sche Buchhandlung, 1845-8.

Dict. of Antiq. = Dictionary of Greek and Roman Antiquities. Edited by Dr. William Smith. Second edition: Boston and London, 1869, also 1873.

Dict. of Biog. = Dictionary of Greek and Roman Biography and Mythology. Edited by Dr. William Smith. 3 vols. Boston and London, 1849.

Dict. of Chris. Antiq. = A Dictionary of Christian Antiquities, being a Continuation of the Dictionary of the Bible. Edited by Dr. William Smith and Professor Samuel Cheetham. 2 vols. 1875–1880.

Dict. of Chris. Biog. = A Dictionary of Christian Biography, Literature, Sects and Doctrines; etc. Edited by Dr. William Smith and Professor Henry Wace: vol. i. 1877; vol. ii. 1880; vol. iii. 1882; (not yet complete).

Dict. of Geogr. = Dictionary of Greek and Roman Geography. Edited by Dr. William Smith. 2 vols. 1854–1857.

Edersheim = *Alfred Edersheim*, The Life and Times of Jesus the Messiah. 2 vols. Second edition, stereotyped. London and New York, 1884.

Ellicott, = *Charles John Ellicott*, A Critical and Grammatical Commentary on the Pastoral Epistles with a Revised Translation. Andover: Warren F. Draper, 1865 (one volume of a comprehensive set).

Elsner = *J. Elsner*, Observationes sacrae in Novi Foederis libros etc. 2 vols., Traj. ad Rhen. 1720, 1728.

Etym. Magn. = the Etymologicum Magnum (see List of Ancient Authors, etc.) Gaisford's edition (1 vol. folio, Oxford, 1848) has been used.

Fick = *August Fick*, Vergleichendes Wörterbuch der Indogermanischen Sprachen. Third edition. 4 vols. Göttingen, 1874–1876.

Göttling = *Carl Goettling*, Allgemeine Lehre vom Accent der griechischen Sprache. Jena, 1835.

Goodwin = *W. W. Goodwin*, Syntax of the Moods and Tenses of the Greek Verb. 4th edition revised. Boston and Cambridge, 1871.

Graecus Venetus = the Greek version of the Pentateuch, Prov., Ruth, Canticles, Eccl., Lam., Dan., according to a unique MS. in the Library of St. Mark's, Venice; edited by O. v. Gebhardt. Lips. 1875, 8vo pp. 592.

Green = *Thomas Sheldon Green*, A Treatise on the Grammar of the New Testament etc. etc. A new Edition. London, Samuel Bagster and Sons, 1862.

    Also, by the same author, "Critical Notes on the New Testament, supplementary to his Treatise on the Grammar of the New Testament Dialect." London, Samuel Bagster and Sons, 1867.

Hamburger = *J. Hamburger*, Real-Encyclopädie für Bibel und Talmud. Strelitz. First Part 1870; Second Part 1883.

Herm. ad Vig., see Vig. ed. *Herm.*

Herzog = Real-Encyklopädie für Protestantische Theologie und Kirche. Edited by Herzog. 21 vols. with index, 1854–1868.

Herzog 2 or ed. 2 = a second edition of the above (edited by Herzog †, Plitt †, and Hauck), begun in 1877 and not yet complete.

Hesych. = Hesychius (see List of Ancient Authors, etc.) The edition used is that of M. Schmidt (5 vols. Jena, 1858–1868).

Jelf = *W. E. Jelf*, A Grammar of the Greek Language. Third edition. Oxford and London, 2 vols. 1861. (Subsequent editions have been issued, but without, it is believed, material alteration.)

Kautzsch = *E. Kautzsch*, Grammatik des Biblisch-Aramäischen. Leipzig, 1884.

Keim = *Theodor Keim*, Geschichte Jesu von Nazara u. s. w. 3 vols. Zürich, 1867–1872.

Klotz or Devar. = Matthaeus Devarius, Liber de Graecae Linguae Particulis, ed. R. Klotz, Lips., vol. i. 1835, vol. ii. sect. 1, 1840, vol. ii. sect. 2, 1842.

Krebs, Observv. = J. T. Krebsii Observationes in Nov. Test. e Flavio Josepho. Lips. 1755.

Krüger = *K. W. Krüger*, Griechische Sprachlehre für Schulen. Fourth improved and enlarged edition, 1861 sq.

Kypke, Observv. = *G. D. Kypke*, Observationes sacrae in Novi Foederis libros ex auctoribus potissimum Graecis et antiquitatibus. 2 vols. Wratisl. 1755.

L. and S. = *Liddell and Scott*, Greek-English Lexicon etc. Seventh edition, 1883.

Lob. ad Phryn., see Phryn. ed. *Lob.*

Loesner = C. F. Loesneri Observationes ad Novum Test. e Philone Alexandrino. Lips. 1777.

Lghtft. = Dr. John Lightfoot, the learned Hebraist of the 17th century.

Bp. Lghtft. = J. B. Lightfoot, D.D., Bishop of Durham; the 8th edition of his commentary on the Epistle to the Galatians is the one referred to, the 7th edition of his commentary on Philippians, the 7th edition of his commentary on Colossians and Philemon.

Lipsius = *K. H. A. Lipsius*, Grammatische Untersuchungen über die Biblische Gräcität (edited by Prof. R. A. Lipsius, the author's son). Leipzig, 1863.

Matthiae = *August Matthiä*, Ausführlich Griechische Grammatik. Third edition, 3 Pts., Leipz. 1835.

McC. and S. = McClintock and Strong's Cyclopædia of Biblical, Theological, and Ecclesiastical Literature. 10 vols. 1867–1881; with Supplement, vol. i. (1885), vol. ii. with Addenda (1887). New York : Harper and Brothers.

Meisterhans = *K. Meisterhans*, Grammatik der Attischen Inschriften. Berlin, 1885. (2d edition, 1888.)

Mullach = *F. W. A. Mullach*, Grammatik der Griechischen Vulgarsprache u. s. w. Berlin, 1856.

Munthe = *C. F. Munthe*, Observationes philolog. in sacros Nov. Test. libros ex Diod. Sic. collectae etc. (Hafn. et Lips. 1755.)

Palairet = *E. Palairet*, Observationes philol.-crit. in sacros Novi Foederis libros etc. Lugd. Bat. 1752.

Pape = *W. Pape*, Griechisch-Deutsches Handwörterbuch. Second edition. 2 vols. Brunswick, 1866. A continuation of the preceding work is the "Wörterbuch der Griechischen Eigennamen." Third edition, edited by G. E. Benseler. 1863–1870.

Passow = Franz Passow's Handwörterbuch der Griechischen Sprache as re-edited by Rost, Palm, and others. Leipz. 1841–1857.

Phryn. ed. *Lob.* = Phrynichi Eclogae Nominum et Verborum Atticorum etc. as edited by C. A. Lobeck. Leipzig, 1820. (Cf. Rutherford.)

Poll. = Pollux (see List of Ancient Authors, etc.) The edition used is that published at Amsterdam, 1 vol. folio, 1706. (The most serviceable is that of William Dindorf, 5 vols. 8vo, Leipzig, 1824.)

Pss. of Sol. = Psalter of Solomon ; see List of Ancient Authors, etc.

Raphel = G. Raphelii annotationes in Sacram Scripturam . . . ex Xen., Polyb., Arrian., et Herodoto collectae. 2 vols. Lugd. Bat. 1747.

Riddell, Platonic Idioms = A Digest of Idioms given as an Appendix to "The Apology of Plato" as edited by the Rev. James Riddell, M. A.; Oxford, 1867.

Riehm (or *Riehm*, HWB.) = Handwörterbuch des Biblischen Alterthums u. s. w. edited by Professor Edward C. A. Riehm in nineteen parts (2 vols.) 1875–1884.

Rutherford, New Phryn. = The New Phrynichus, being a revised text of the Ecloga of the Grammarian Phrynichus, etc., by W. Gunion Rutherford. London, 1881.

Schaff-Herzog = A Religious Encyclopædia etc. by Philip Schaff and associates. 3 vols. 1882–1884. Funk and Wagnalls, New York. Revised edition, 1887.

Schenkel (or *Schenkel*, BL.) = Bibel-Lexikon u. s. w. edited by Professor Daniel Schenkel. 5 vols. Leipz. 1869–1875.

Schmidt = *J. H. Heinrich Schmidt*, Synonymik der Griechischen Sprache. 4 vols. Leipz. 1876, 1878, 1879, 1886.

Schöttgen = Christiani Schoettgenii Horae Hebraicae et Talmudicae etc. 2 vols. Dresden and Leipzig, 1733, 1742.

Schürer = *Emil Schürer*, Lehrbuch der Neutestamentlichen Zeitgeschichte. Leipzig, 1874. The "Second Part" of a new and revised edition has already appeared under the title of Geschichte des Jüdischen Volkes im Zeitalter Jesu Christi, and to this new edition (for the portion of the original work which it covers) the references have been made, although for convenience the title of the first edition has been retained. An English translation is appearing at Edinburgh (T. and T. Clark).

Scrivener, F. H. A.: — A Plain Introduction to the Criticism of the New Testament etc. Third Edition. Cambridge and London, 1883.

Bezae Codex Cantabrigiensis etc. Cambridge and London, 1864.

A Full Collation of the Codex Sinaiticus with the Received Text of the New Testament etc. Second Edition, Revised. Cambridge and London, 1867.

Six Lectures on the Text of the New Testament etc. Cambridge and London, 1875.

Sept. = the translation of the Old Testament into Greek known as the Septuagint. Unless otherwise stated, the sixth edition of Tischendorf's text (edited by Nestle) is referred to; 2 vols. (with supplement), Leipzig, 1880. The double verse-notation occasionally given in the Apocryphal books has reference to the edition of the Apocrypha and select Pseudepigrapha by O. F. Fritzsche; Leipzig, 1871. Readings peculiar to the Complutensian, Aldine, Vatican, or Alexandrian form of the text are marked respectively by an appended Comp., Ald., Vat., Alex. For the first two the testimony of the edition of Lambert Bos, Franck. 1709, has been relied on.

The abbreviations Aq., Symm., Theod. or Theodot., appended to a reference to the O. T. denote respectively the Greek versions ascribed to Aquila, Symmachus, and Theodotion; see List of Ancient Authors, etc.

"Lag." designates the text as edited by Paul Lagarde, of which the first half appeared at Göttingen in 1883.

Soph. = E. A. Sophocles, Greek Lexicon of the Roman and Byzantine Periods (from B.C. 146 to A.D. 1100.) Boston: Little, Brown & Co. 1870. The forerunner (once or twice referred to) of the above work bears the title "A Glossary of Later and Byzantine Greek. Forming vol. vii. (new series) of the Memoirs of the American Academy." Cambridge, 1860.

Steph. Thes. = the "Thesaurus Graecae Linguae" of Henry Stephen as edited by Hase and the Dindorfs. 8 vols. Paris, 1831-1865. Occasionally the London (Valpy's) edition (1816-1826) of the same work has been referred to.

Suïd. = Suïdas (see List of Ancient Authors, etc.) Gaisford's edition (2 vols. folio, Oxford, 1834) has been followed.

'Teaching' = The Teaching of the Twelve Apostles (Διδαχὴ τῶν δώδεκα ἀποστόλων.) The edition of Harnack (in Gebhardt and Harnack's Texte und Untersuchungen u. s. w. Second vol., Pts. i. and ii., Leipzig 1884) has been followed, together with his division of the chapters into verses.

Thiersch = Friedrich Thiersch, Griechische Grammatik u. s. w. Third edition. Leipzig, 1826.

Trench = Abp. R. C. Trench's Synonyms of the New Testament. Ninth edition, improved. London, 1880.

Vaniček = Alois Vaniček, Griechisch-Lateinisches Etymologisches Wörterbuch. 2 vols. Leipz. 1877.

By the same author is "Fremdwörter im Griechischen und Lateinischen." Leipzig, 1878.

Veitch = William Veitch, Greek Verbs irregular and defective, etc. New Edition. Oxford, 1879.

Vig. ed. Herm. = Vigeri de praecipuis Graecae dictionis Idiotismis. Edited by G. Hermann. Fourth edition. Leipzig, 1834. A meagre abridgment and translation by Rev. John Seager was published at London in 1828.

Vulg. = the translation into Latin known as the Vulgate. Professor Tischendorf's edition (Leipzig, 1864) has been followed.

Wetst. or Wetstein = J. J. Wetstein's Novum Testamentum Graecum etc. 2 vols. folio. Amsterdam, 1751, 1752.

W. = G. B. Winer, Grammar of the Idiom of the New Testament etc. Revised and Authorized Translation of the seventh (German) edition of the original, edited by Lünemann; Andover, 1883. Unless otherwise indicated, it is referred to by pages, the corresponding page of the original being added in a parenthesis. When Dr. Moulton's translation of the sixth German edition is referred to, that fact is stated.

Win. RWB. = G. B. Winer, Biblisches Realwörterbuch u. s. w. Third edition. 2 vols., Leipzig and New York, 1849.

Win. De verb. Comp. etc. = G. B. Winer, De verborum cum praepositionibus compositorum in Novo Testamento usu. Five academic programs; Leipzig, 1843.

Other titles, it is believed, are so fully given as to be easily verifiable.

EXPLANATIONS AND ABBREVIATIONS

As respects PUNCTUATION — it should be noticed, that since only those verbal forms (or their representatives) are given in the Lexicon which actually occur in the Greek Testament, it becomes necessary to distinguish between a form of the Present Tense which is in use, and one which is given merely to secure for a verb its place in the alphabet. This is done by putting a semi-colon after a Present which actually occurs, and a colon after a Present which is a mere alphabetic locum tenens.

Further: a punctuation-mark inserted before a classic voucher or a reference to the Old Testament (whether such voucher or reference be included in a parenthesis or not) indicates that said voucher or reference applies to other passages, definitions, etc., besides the one which it immediately follows. The same principle governs the insertion or the omission of a comma after such abbreviations as "absol.", "pass.", etc.

A hyphen has been placed between the component parts of Greek compounds only in case each separate part is in actual use; otherwise the hyphen is omitted

[ ] Brackets have been used to mark additions by the American editor. To avoid, however, a complexity which might prove to the reader confusing, they have been occasionally dispensed with when the editorial additions serve only to complete a statement already made in part by Professor Grimm (as, in enumerating the forms of verbs, the readings of the critical editors, the verbs compounded with σύν which observe assimilation, etc. etc.); but in no instance have they been intentionally omitted where the omission might seem to attribute to Professor Grimm an opinion for which he is not responsible

* An asterisk at the close of an article indicates that all the instances of the word's occurrence in the New Testament are noticed in the article. Of the 5594 words composing the vocabulary of the New Testament 5300 are marked with an asterisk. To this extent, therefore, the present work may serve as a concordance as well as a lexicon.

A superior ᵃ or ᵇ or ᶜ etc. appended to a verse-numeral designates the first, second, third, etc., occurrence of a given word or construction in that verse. The same letters appended to a page-numeral designate respectively the first, second, third, columns of that page. A small a. b. c. etc. after a page-numeral designates the subdivision of the page.

The various forms of the GREEK TEXT referred to are represented by the following abbreviations:

R or Rec. = what is commonly known as the Textus Receptus. Dr. F. H. A. Scrivener's last edition (Cambridge and London 1877) has been taken as the standard.[1] To designate a particular form of this "Protean text" an abbreviation has been appended in superior type; as, ᵉˡᶻ for Elzevir, ˢᵗ for Stephen, ᵇᵉᶻ for Beza, ᵉʳᵃˢ for Erasmus.

G or Grsb. = the Greek text of Griesbach as given in his manual edition, 2 vols., Leipzig, 1805. Owing to a disregard of the signs by which Griesbach indicated his judgment respecting the various degrees of probability belonging to different readings, he is cited not infrequently, even in critical works, as supporting readings which he expressly questioned, but was not quite ready to expel from the text.

L or Lchm. = Lachmann's Greek text as given in his larger edition, 2 vols., Berlin, 1842 and 1850. When the text of his smaller or stereotyped edition (Berlin, 1831) is referred to, the abbreviation "min." or "ster." is added to his initial.

T or Tdf. = the text of Tischendorf's "Editio Octava Critica Major" (Leipzig, 1869-1872).

Tr or Treg. = "The Greek New Testament" etc. by S. P. Tregelles (London, 1857-1879).

WH = "The New Testament in the Original Greek. The Text Revised by Brooke Foss Westcott D.D. and Fenton John Anthony Hort D.D. Cambridge and London, Macmillan and Co. 1881."

KC = "Novum Testamentum ad Fidem Codicis Vaticani" as edited by Professors Kuenen and Cobet (Leyden, 1860).

The textual variations noticed are of course mainly those which affect the individual word or construction under discussion. Where an extended passage or entire section is textually debatable (as, for example, Mk. xvi. 9-20; Jn. v. 3 fin.-4; vii. 53 fin. — viii. 11), that fact is assumed to be known, or at least it is not stated under every word contained in the passage.

As respects the NUMBERING OF THE VERSES — the edition of Robert Stephen, in 2 vols. 16°, Geneva 1551, has been

---

[1] Respecting the edition issued by the Bible Society, which was followed by Professor Grimm, see Carl Bertheau in the Theologische Literaturzeitung for 1877, No. 5, pp. 103-106.

followed as the standard (as it is in the critical editions of Tregelles, Westcott and Hort, etc.). Variations from this standard are indicated by subjoining the variant verse-numeral within marks of parenthesis. The similar addition in the case of references to the Old Testament indicates the variation between the Hebrew notation and the Greek.

In quotations from the ENGLISH BIBLE —
A. V. = the current or so-called "Authorized Version ";
R. V. = the Revised New Testament of 1881. But when a rendering is ascribed to the former version it may be assumed to be retained also in the latter, unless the contrary be expressly stated. A translation preceded by R. V. is found in the Revision only.

A. S. = Anglo-Saxon.
Abp. = Archbishop.
absol. = absolutely.
acc. or accus. = accusative.
acc. to = according to.
ad l. or ad loc. = at or on the passage.
al. = others or elsewhere.
al. al. = others otherwise.
Ald. = the Aldine text of the Septuagint (see Sept. in List of Books).
Alex. = the Alexandrian text of the Septuagint (see Sept. in List of Books).
ap. = (quoted) in
App. = Appendix.
appos. = apposition.
Aq. = Aquila (see Sept. in List of Books).
art. = article.
augm. = augment.
auth. or author. = author or authorities.
B. or Bttm. see List of Books.
B. D. or BB. DD. see List of Books.
betw. = between.
Bibl. = Biblical.
Bp. = Bishop.
br. = brackets or enclose in brackets.
c. before a date = about.
Cantabr. = Cambridge
cf. = compare.
ch. = chapter.
cl. = clause.
cod., codd. = manuscript, manuscripts.
Com., Comm. = commentary, commentaries.
comp. = compound, compounded, etc.
compar. = comparative.
Comp. or Compl. = the Complutensian text of the Septuagint (see Sept. in List of Books).
contr. = contracted, contract.
dim. or dimin. = diminutive.
dir. disc. = direct discourse.
e. g. = for example.
esp. = especially.

ex., exx. = example, examples.
exc. = except.
excrpt. = an excerpt or extract.
fin. or ad fin. = at or near the end.
G or Grsb. = Griesbach's Greek text (see above).
Graec. Ven. = Graecus Venetus (see List of Books).
i. e. = that is.
ib. or ibid. = in the same place.
indir. disc. = indirect discourse.
init. or ad init. = at or near the beginning.
in l. or in loc. = in or on the passage.
i. q. = the same as, or equivalent to.
KC = Kuenen and Cobet's edition of the Vatican text (see above).
L or Lchm. = Lachmann's Greek text (see above).
L. and S. = Liddell and Scott (see List of Books).
l. or lib. = book.
l. c., ll. cc. = passage cited, passages cited.
Lag. = Lagarde's edition of the Septuagint (see Sept. in List of Books).
mrg. = the marginal reading (of a critical edition of the Greek Testament).
Opp. = Works.
opp. to = opposed to.
paral. = the parallel accounts (in the Synoptic Gospels).
Pt. or pt. = part.
q. v. = which see.
R or Rec. = the common Greek text (see above).
r. = root.
rel. or relat. = relative.
sc. = namely, to wit.
Skr. = Sanskrit.
sq., sqq. = following.
Steph. = Stephanus's Thesaurus (see List of Books).
Stud. u. Krit. = the Studien und Kritiken, a leading German Theological Quarterly.
s. v. = under the word.
Symm. = Symmachus, translator of the Old Testament into Greek (see Sept. in the List of Books).
T or Tdf. = Tischendorf's Greek text (see above).
Theod. or Theodot. = Theodotion (see Sept. in the List of Books).
Tr or Treg. = Tregelles's Greek text (see above).
u. i. = as below.
u. s. = as above.
v. = see.
var. = variant or variants (various readings).
Vat. = the Vatican Greek text (see above, and Sept. in the List of Books).
Vulg. = the Vulgate (see List of Books).
w. = with (especially before abbreviated names of cases).
writ. = writer, writers, writings.
WH = Westcott and Hort's Greek text (see above).

Other abbreviations will, it is hoped, explain themselves.

NEW TESTAMENT LEXICON

A

A, a, ἄλφα, τό, the first letter of the Greek alphabet, opening the series which the letter ω closes. Hence the expression ἐγώ εἰμι τὸ A [L T Tr WH ἄλφα] καὶ τὸ Ω ['Ω L WH], Rev. i. 8, 11 Rec., which is explained by the appended words ἡ ἀρχὴ καὶ τὸ τέλος, xxi. 6, and by the further addition ὁ πρῶτος καὶ ὁ ἔσχατος, xxii. 13. On the meaning of the phrase cf. Rev. xi. 17; Is. xli. 4; xliv. 6; xlviii. 12; [esp. B. D. Am. ed. p. 73]. *A*, when prefixed to words as an inseparable syllable, is **1. p r i v a t i v e** (στερητικόν), like the Lat. *in-*, the Eng. *un-*, giving a negative sense to the word to which it is prefixed, as ἀβαρής; or signifying what is contrary to it, as ἄτιμος, ἀτιμόω; before vowels generally ἀν-, as ἀναίτιος. **2. c o p u l a t i v e** (ἀθροιστικόν), akin to the particle ἅμα [cf. Curtius § 598], indicating community and fellowship, as in ἀδελφός, ἀκόλουθος. Hence it is **3. i n- t e n s i v e** (ἐπιτατικόν), strengthening the force of terms, like the Lat. *con* in composition; as ἀτενίζω fr. ἀτενής [yet cf. W. 100 (95)]. This use, however, is doubted or denied now by many [e. g. *Lob.* Path. Element. i. 34 sq.]. Cf. Kühner i. 741, § 339 Anm. 5; [Jelf § 342 δ]; *Bttm.* Gram. § 120 Anm. 11; [*Donaldson*, Gram. p. 334; New Crat. §§ 185, 213; L. and S. s. v.].*

'Ααρών, indecl. prop. **name** (ὁ 'Ααρών, -ῶ- : in Joseph.), אַהֲרֹן (fr. the unused Hebr. radical אָהַר, — Syr. ‎أهِر libidinosus, lascivus, — [*enlightened*, Fürst; acc. to Dietrich *wealthy*, or *fluent*, like אוֹכֵּר], acc. to Philo, de ebriet. § 32, fr. הַר *mountain* and equiv. to ὀρεινός), *Aaron*, the brother of Moses, the first high-priest of the Israelites and the head of the whole sacerdotal order: Lk. i. 5; Acts vii. 40; Heb. v. 4; vii. 11; ix. 4.*

'Αβαδδών, indecl., אֲבַדּוֹן, **1.** *ruin, destruction,* (fr. אָבַד to perish), Job xxxi. 12. **2.** *the place of destruction* i. q. *Orcus*, joined with שְׁאוֹל, Job xxvi. 6; Prov. xv. 11. **3.** as a proper name it is given to the angel-prince of the infernal regions, the minister of death and author of havoc on earth, and is rendered in Greek by 'Απολλύων *Destroyer*, Rev. ix. 11.*

ἀβαρής, -ές, (βάρος weight), *without weight, light; trop. not burdensome:* ἀβαρῆ ὑμῖν ἐμαυτὸν ἐτήρησα I have avoided burdening you with expense on my account, 2 Co. xi. 9; see 1 Th. ii. 9, cf. 6. (Fr. Aristot. down.)*

'Αββᾶ [WH -βά], Hebr. אַב *father*, in the Chald. emphatic state, אַבָּא i. e. ὁ πατήρ, a customary title of God in prayer. Whenever it occurs in the N. T. (Mk. xiv. 36; Ro. viii. 15; Gal. iv. 6) it has the Greek interpretation subjoined to it; this is apparently to be explained by the fact that the Chaldee אַבָּא, through frequent use in prayer, gradually acquired the nature of a most sacred proper name, to which the Greek-speaking Jews added the appellative from their own tongue.*

"Αβελ [WH "Αβ. (see their Intr. § 408)], indecl. prop. name (in Joseph. [e. g. antt. 1, 2, 1] "Αβελος, -ου), הֶבֶל (breath, vanity), *Abel*, the second son born to Adam (Gen. iv. 2 sqq.), so called from his short life and sudden death [cf. B. D. Am. ed. p. 5], (Job viii. 16; Ps. xxxix. 6): Mt. xxiii. 35; Lk. xi. 51; Heb. xi. 4; xii. 24.*

'Αβιά, indecl. prop. name (Joseph. antt. 7, 10, 3; 8, 10, 1 ὁ 'Αβίας [W. § 6, 1 m.], -α), אֲבִיָּה and אֲבִיָּהוּ (my father is Jehovah), *Abia* [or *Abijah*, cf. B. D. s. v.], **1.** a king of Judah, son of Rehoboam : Mt. i. 7 (1 K. xiv. 31; xv. 1). **2.** a priest, the head of a sacerdotal family, from whom, when David divided the priests into twenty-four classes (1 Chr. xxiv. 10), the class *Abia*, the eighth in order, took its name: Lk. i. 5.*

'Αβιάθαρ, indecl. prop. name (though in Joseph. antt. 6, 14, 6 'Αβιάθαρος, -ου), אֶבְיָתָר (father of abundance), *Abiathar*, a certain Hebrew high-priest: Mk. ii. 26, — where he is by mistake confounded with Ahimelech his father (1 S. xxi. 1 sqq.); [yet cf. 1 S. xxii. 20 with 1 Chr. xviii. 16; xxiv. 6, 31; also 2 S. xv. 24–29; 1 K. ii. 26, 27 with 2 S. viii. 17; 1 Chr. xxiv. 6, 31. It would seem that d o u b l e names were esp. common in the case of p r i e s t s (cf. 1 Macc. ii. 1–5; Joseph. vit. §§ 1, 2) and that father and son often bore the s a m e name (cf. Lk. i. 5, 59; Joseph. l. c. and antt. 20, 9, 1). See Mc-Clellan ad loc. and B. D. Am. ed. p. 7].*

9   'Αβιληνή [WH 'Αβειλ. (see s. v. ει)], -ῆς, ἡ, (sc. χώρα, the district belonging to the city Abila), *Abilene*, the name of a region lying between Lebanon and Hermon towards Phoenicia, 18 miles distant from Damascus and 37 [acc. to the Itin. Anton. 38] from Heliopolis: Lk. iii. 1. Cf. Λυσανίας [and B. D. s. v.].*

10   'Αβιούδ, ὁ, indecl. prop. name, אֲבִיהוּד (father of the Jews [al. of glory]), *Abiud*, son of Zorobabel or Zerubbabel: Mt. i. 13.*

11   'Αβραάμ [Rec.ˢᵗ 'Αβρ.; cf. *Tdf.* Proleg. p. 106] (Joseph. "Αβραμος, -ου), אַבְרָהָם (father of a multitude, cf. Gen. xvii. 5), *Abraham*, the renowned founder of the Jewish nation: Mt. i. 1 sq.; xxii. 32; Lk. xix. 9; Jn. viii. 33; Acts iii. 25; Heb. vii. 1 sqq., and elsewhere. He is extolled by the apostle Paul as a pattern of faith, Ro. iv. 1 sqq. 17 sqq.; Gal. iii. 6 (cf. Heb. xi. 8), on which account all believers in Christ have a claim to the title sons or posterity of Abraham, Gal. iii. 7, 29; cf. Ro. iv. 11.

12   ἄ-βυσσος, in classic Greek an adj., -ος, -ον, (fr. ὁ βυσσός i. q. βυθός), *bottomless* (so perhaps in Sap. x. 19), *unbounded* (πλοῦτος ἄβυσσος, Aeschyl. Sept. (931) 950). In the Scriptures ἡ ἄβυσσος (Sept. for תְּהוֹם) sc. χώρα, *the pit*, the immeasurable depth, *the abyss*. Hence of the 'deep' sea: Gen. i. 2; vii. 11; Deut. viii. 7; Sir. i. 3; xvi. 18, etc.; of *Orcus* (a very deep gulf or chasm in the lowest parts of the earth: Ps. lxx. (lxxi.) 21 ἐκ τῶν ἀβύσσων τῆς γῆς, Eur. Phoen. 1632 (1605) ταρτάρου ἄβυσσα χάσματα, Clem. Rom. 1 Cor. 20, 5 ἀβύσσων ἀνεξιχνίαστα κλίματα, ibid. 59, 3 ὁ ἐπιβλέπων ἐν ταῖς ἀβύσσοις, of God; [Act. Thom. 32 ὁ τὴν ἄβυσσον τοῦ ταρτάρου οἰκῶν, of the dragon]), both as the common receptacle of the dead, Ro. x. 7, and especially as the abode of demons, Lk. viii. 31; Rev. ix. 1 sq. 11; xi. 7; xvii. 8; xx. 1, 3. Among prof. auth. used as a subst. only by Diog. Laërt. 4, (5,) 27 κατῆλθες εἰς μέλαιναν Πλουτέως ἄβυσσον. Cf. *Knapp*, Scripta var. Arg. p. 554 sq.; [*J. G. Müller*, Philo's Lehre von der Weltschöpfung, p. 173 sq.; B. D. Am. ed. s. v. Deep].*

13   "Αγαβος [on the breathing see *WH.* Intr. § 408], -ου, ὁ, the name of a Christian prophet, *Agabus*: Acts xi. 28; xxi. 10. (Perhaps from עָגַב to love [cf. B. D. s. v.].)*

14   ἀγαθοεργέω, -ῶ; (fr. the unused ΕΡΓΩ — equiv. to ἔρδω, ἐργάζομαι — and ἀγαθόν); *to be beneficent* (towards the poor, the needy): 1 Tim. vi. 18 [A. V. *do good*]. Cf. ἀγαθουργέω. Found besides only in eccl. writ., but in the sense *to do well, act rightly*.*

15   ἀγαθο-ποιέω, -ῶ; 1 aor. inf. ἀγαθοποιῆσαι; (fr. ἀγαθοποιός);   **1.** *to do good, do something which profits others*: Mk. iii. 4 [Tdf. ἀγαθὸν ποιῆσαι; Lk. vi. 9]; *to show one's self beneficent*, Acts xiv. 17 Rec.; τινά, *to do some one a favor, to benefit*, Lk. vi. 33, 35, (equiv. to הֵיטִיב, Zeph. i. 12; Num. x. 32; Tob. xii. 13, etc.).   **2.** *to do well, do right*: 1 Pet. ii. 15, 20 (opp. to ἁμαρτάνω); iii. 6, 17; 3 Jn. 11. (Not found in secular authors, except in a few of the later in an astrological sense, *to furnish a good omen*.)*

16   ἀγαθοποιΐα [WH -ποιία (see I, ι)], -ας, ἡ, a course of right action, well-doing: ἐν ἀγαθοποιΐᾳ, 1 Pet. iv. 19 i. q. ἀγαθοποιοῦντες acting uprightly [cf. xii. Patr. Jos. § 18];*

if we read here with L Tr mrg. ἐν ἀγαθοποιΐαις we must understand it of single acts of rectitude [cf. W. § 27, 3; B. § 123, 2]. (In eccl. writ. ἀγαθοπ. denotes *beneficence*.)*

17   ἀγαθοποιός, -όν, *acting rightly, doing well*: 1 Pet. ii. 14. [Sir. xlii. 14; Plut. de Is. et Osir. § 42.]*

18   ἀγαθός, -ή, -όν, (akin to ἄγαμαι to wonder at, think highly of, ἀγαστός admirable, as explained by Plato, Crat. p. 412 c. [al. al.; cf. *Donaldson*, New Crat. § 323]), in general denotes "perfectus, . . . qui habet in se ac facit omnia quae habere et facere debet pro notione nominis, officio ac lege" (Irmisch ad H·lian. 1, 4, p. 134), *excelling in any respect, distinguished, good*. It can be predicated of persons, things, conditions, qualities and affections of the soul, deeds, times and seasons. To this general signif. can be traced back all those senses which the word gathers fr. the connection in which it stands;   **1.** *of a good constitution* or *nature*: γῆ, Lk. viii. 8; δένδρον, Mt. vii. 18, in sense equiv. to 'fertile soil,' 'a fruitful tree,' (Xen. oec. 16, 7 γῆ ἀγαθή, . . . γῆ κακή, an. 2, 4, 22 χώρας πολλῆς κ. ἀγαθῆς οὔσης). In Lk. viii. 15 ἀγαθὴ καρδία corresponds to the fig. expression "good ground", and denotes a soul inclined to goodness, and accordingly eager to learn saving truth and ready to bear the fruits (καρποὺς ἀγαθούς, Jas. iii. 17) of a Christian life.   **2.** *useful, salutary*: δόσις ἀγαθή (joined to δώρημα τέλειον) a gift which is truly a gift, salutary, Jas. i. 17; δόματα ἀγαθά, Mt. vii. 11; ἐντολὴ ἀγ. a commandment profitable to those who keep it, Ro. vii. 12, acc. to a Grk. scholium equiv. to εἰς τὸ συμφέρον εἰσηγουμένη, hence the question in vs. 13: τὸ οὖν ἀγαθὸν ἐμοὶ γέγονε θάνατος; ἀγ. μερίς the 'good part,' which insures salvation to him who chooses it, Lk. x. 42; ἔργον ἀγ. (differently in Ro. ii. 7, etc.) the saving work of God, i. e. substantially, the Christian life, due to divine efficiency, Phil. i. 6 [cf. the Comm. ad loc.]; εἰς ἀγαθόν *for good*, to advantage, Ro. viii. 28 (Sir. vii. 13; πάντα τοῖς εὐσεβέσι εἰς ἀγαθά, . . . τοῖς ἁμαρτωλοῖς εἰς κακά, Sir. xxxix. 27; τὸ κακὸν . . . γίγνεται εἰς ἀγαθόν, Theognis 162); *good for, suited to* something: πρὸς οἰκοδομήν, Eph. iv. 29 [cf. W. 363 (340)] (Xen. mem. 4, 6, 10).   **3.** of the feeling awakened by what is good, *pleasant, agreeable, joyful, happy*: ἡμέραι ἀγ. 1 Pet. iii. 10 (Ps. xxxiii. (xxxiv.) 13; Sir. xiv. 14; 1 Macc. x. 55); ἐλπίς, 2 Th. ii. 16 (μακαρία ἐλπίς, Tit. ii. 13); συνείδησις, a peaceful conscience, i. q. consciousness of rectitude, Acts xxiii. 1; 1 Tim. i. 5, 19; 1 Pet. iii. 16; reconciled to God, vs. 21.   **4.** *excellent, distinguished*: so τὶ ἀγαθόν, Jn. i. 46 (47).   **5.** *upright, honorable*: Mt. xii. 34; xix. 16; Lk. vi. 45; Acts xi. 24; 1 Pet. iii. 11, etc.; πονηροὶ κ. ἀγαθοί, Mt. v. 45; xxii. 10; ἀγαθ. καὶ δίκαιος, Lk. xxiii. 50; καρδία ἀγαθὴ κ. καλή, Lk. viii. 15 (see καλός, b.); fulfilling the duty or service demanded, δοῦλε ἀγαθὲ κ. πιστέ, Mt. xxv. 21, 23; upright, free from guile, particularly from a desire to corrupt the people, Jn. vii. 12; pre-eminently of God, as consummately and essentially good, Mt. xix. 17 (Mk. x. 18; Lk. xviii. 19); ἀγ. θησαυρός in Mt. xii. 35; Lk. vi. 45

denotes the soul considered as the repository of pure thoughts which are brought forth in speech; πίστις ἀγ. the fidelity due from a servant to his master, Tit. ii. 10 [WH mrg. om.]; on ἀγαθ. ἔργον, ἀγ. ἔργα, see ἔργον. In a narrower sense, *benevolent, kind, generous*: Mt. xx. 15; 1 Pet. ii. 18; μνεία, 1 Th. iii. 6 (cf. 2 Macc. vii. 20); *beneficent* (Xen. Cyr. 3, 3, 4; טוֹב, Jer. xxxiii. 11; Ps. xxxiv. 9; Cic. nat. deor. 2, 25, 64 "*optimus* i. e. beneficentissimus"), Ro. v. 7, where the meaning is, Hardly (on an innocent man does one encounter death; for if he even dares hazard his life for another, he does so for a benefactor (one from whom he has received favors); cf. W. 117 (111); [Gifford in the Speaker's Com. p. 123]. The neuter used substantively denotes 1. *a good thing, convenience, advantage*, and in partic. a. in the plur., external *goods, riches*: Lk. i. 53; xii. 18 sq. (Sir. xiv. 4; Sap. vii. 11); τὰ ἀγαθά σου comforts and delights which thy wealth procured for thee in abundance, Lk. xvi. 25 (opp. to κακά, as in Sir. xi. 14); outward and inward good things, Gal. vi. 6, cf. Wieseler ad loc. b. *the benefits of the Messianic kingdom*: Ro. x. 15; τὰ μέλλοντα ἀγ. Heb. ix. 11; x. 1. 2. *what is upright, honorable, and acceptable to God*: Ro. xii. 2; ἐργάζεσθαι τὸ ἀγ. Ro. ii. 10; Eph. iv. 28; πράσσειν, Ro. ix. 11; [2 Co. v. 10]; διώκειν, 1 Th. v. 15; μιμεῖσθαι, 3 Jn. 11; κολλᾶσθαι τῷ ἀγ. Ro. xii. 9; τί με ἐρωτᾷς περὶ τοῦ ἀγαθοῦ, Mt. xix. 17 G L T Tr WH, where the word expresses the general idea of right. Spec., what is *salutary, suited to the course of human affairs*: in the phrase διάκονος εἰς τὸ ἀγ. Ro. xiii. 4; of rendering service, Gal. vi. 10; Ro. xii. 21; τὸ ἀγ. σου the favor thou conferrest, Philem. 14.

[" It is to be regarded as a peculiarity in the usage of the Sept. that טוֹב *good* is predominantly [?] rendered by καλός. ... The translator of Gen. uses ἀγαθός only in the neut., *good, goods*, and this has been to a degree the model for the other translators. ... In the Greek O. T., where οἱ δίκαιοι is the technical designation of the pious, οἱ ἀγαθοί or ὁ ἀγαθός does not occur in so general a sense. The ἀνὴρ ἀγαθός is peculiar only to the Prov. (xiii. 22, 24; xv. 3); cf. besides the solitary instance in 1 Kings ii. 32. Thus even in the usage of the O. T. we are reminded of Christ's words, Mk. x. 18, οὐδεὶς ἀγαθὸς εἰ μὴ εἷς ὁ θεός. In the O. T. the term 'righteous' makes reference rather to a covenant and to one's relation to a positive standard; ἀγαθός would express the absolute idea of moral goodness" (Zezschwitz, Profangraec. u. bibl. Sprachgeist, Leipz. 1859, p. 60). Cf. Tittm. p. 19. On the comparison of ἀγαθός see B. 27 (24).]

(18α): see 14 & 15
ἀγαθουργέω, -ῶ; Acts xiv. 17 L T Tr WH for R ἀγαθοποιῶ. The contracted form is the rarer [cf. *WH*. App. p. 145], see ἀγαθοεργέω; but cf. κακοῦργος, ἱερουργέω.*

19
ἀγαθωσύνη, -ης, ἡ, [on its formation see W. 95 (90); *WH*. App. p. 152], found only in bibl. and eccl. writ., *uprightness of heart and life*, [A. V. *goodness*]: 2 Th. i. 11; Gal. v. 22 (unless here it denote *kindness, beneficence*); Ro. xv. 14; Eph. v. 9. [Cf. Trench § lxiii.; Ellic. and Bp. Lghtft. on Gal. l. c.]*

see 21
ἀγαλλιάομαι, see ἀγαλλιάω.

20
ἀγαλλίασις, -εως, ἡ, (ἀγαλλιάω), not used by prof. writ. but often by the Sept.; *exultation, extreme joy*: Lk. i.

14, 44; Acts ii. 46; Jude 24. Heb. i. 9 (fr. Ps. xliv. (xlv.) 8) *oil of gladness* with which persons were anointed at feasts (Ps. xxiii. 5), and which the writer, alluding to the inaugural ceremony of anointing, uses as an emblem of the divine power and majesty to which the Son of God has been exalted.*

21
ἀγαλλιάω, -ῶ, and -άομαι, (but the act. is not used exc. in Lk. i. 47 [ἠγαλλίασα], in Rev. xix. 7 [ἀγαλλιῶμεν] L T Tr WH [and in 1 Pet. i. 8 WH Tr mrg. (ἀγαλλιᾶτε), cf. *WH*. App. p. 169]); 1 aor. ἠγαλλιασάμην, and (with a mid. signif.) ἠγαλλιάθην (Jn. v. 35; Rec. ἠγαλλιάσθην); a word of Hellenistic coinage (fr. ἀγάλλομαι to rejoice, glory [yet cf. B. 51 (45)]), often in Sept. (for גִּיל, עָלַז, רָנַן, שׂוּשׂ), to exult, rejoice exceedingly: Mt. v. 12; Lk. x. 21; Acts ii. 26; xvi. 34; 1 Pet. i. 8; iv. 13; ἔν τινι, 1 Pet. i. 6, dat. of the thing in which the joy originates [cf. W. § 33 a.; B. 185 (160)]; but Jn. v. 35 means, 'to rejoice while his light shone' [i. e. *in* (the midst of) etc.]. ἐπί τινι, Lk. i. 47; foll. by ἵνα, Jn. viii. 56 *that he should see*, rejoiced because it had been promised him that he should see. This divine promise was fulfilled to him at length in paradise; cf. W. 339 (318); B. 239 (206). On this word see Gelpke in the Stud. u. Krit. for 1849, p. 645 sq.*

22
ἄ-γαμος, -ον, (γάμος), *unmarried*: 1 Co. vii. 8, 32; used even of women, 1 Co. vii. 11, 34 (Eur. Hel. 690 [and elsewhere]), where the Grks. commonly said ἄνανδρος.*

23
ἀγανακτέω, -ῶ; 1 aor. ἠγανάκτησα; (as πλεονεκτέω comes fr. πλοενέκτης, and this fr. πλέον and ἔχω, so through a conjectural ἀγανάκτης fr. ἄγαν and ἄχομαι to feel pain, grieve, [al. al.]); *to be indignant, moved with indignation*: Mt. xxi. 15; xxvi. 8; Mk. x. 14; xiv. 4; περί τινος [cf. W. § 33 a.], Mt. xx. 24; Mk. x. 41; foll. by ὅτι, Lk. xiii. 14. (From Hdt. down.)*

24
ἀγανάκτησις, -εως, ἡ, *indignation*: 2 Co. vii. 11. [(From Plat. on.)]*

25
ἀγαπάω, -ῶ; [impf. ἠγάπων]; fut. ἀγαπήσω; 1 aor. ἠγάπησα; pf. act. [1 pers. plur. ἠγαπήκαμεν 1 Jn. iv. 10 WH txt.], ptcp. ἠγαπηκώς (2 Tim. iv. 8); Pass., [pres. ἀγαπῶμαι]; pf. ptcp. ἠγαπημένος; 1 fut. ἀγαπηθήσομαι; (akin to ἄγαμαι [Fick, Pt. iv. 12; see ἀγαθός, init.]); *to love, to be full of good-will and exhibit the same*: Lk. vii. 47; 1 Jn. iv. 7 sq.; with acc. of the person, *to have a preference for, wish well to, regard the welfare of*: Mt. v. 43 sqq.; xix. 19; Lk. vii. 5; Jn. xi. 5; Ro. xiii. 8; 2 Co. xi. 11; xii. 15; Gal. v. 14; Eph. v. 25, 28; 1 Pet. i. 22, and elsewhere; often in 1 Ep. of Jn. of the love of Christians towards one another; of the benevolence which God, in providing salvation for men, has exhibited by sending his Son to them and giving him up to death, Jn. iii. 16; Ro. viii. 37; 2 Th. ii. 16; 1 Jn. iv. 11, 19; [noteworthy is Jude 1 L T Tr WH τοῖς ἐν θεῷ πατρὶ ἠγαπημένοις; see ἐν, I. 4, and cf. Bp. Lghtft. on Col. iii. 12]; of the love which led Christ, in procuring human salvation, to undergo sufferings and death, Gal. ii. 20; Eph. v. 2; of the love with which God regards Christ, Jn. iii. 35; [v. 20 L mrg.]; x. 17; xv. 9; Eph. i. 6. When used of love to a master, God or Christ, the word

involves the idea of affectionate reverence, prompt obedience, grateful recognition of benefits received: Mt. vi. 24; xxii. 37; Ro. viii. 28; 1 Co. ii. 9; viii. 3; Jas. i. 12; 1 Pet. i. 8; 1 Jn. iv. 10, 20, and elsewhere. With an acc. of the thing ἀγαπάω denotes *to take pleasure in the thing, prize it above other things, be unwilling to abandon it or do without it*: δικαιοσύνην, Heb. i. 9 (i. e. steadfastly to cleave to); τὴν δόξαν, Jn. xii. 43; τὴν πρωτοκαθεδρίαν, Lk. xi. 43; τὸ σκότος and τὸ φῶς, Jn. iii. 19; τὸν κόσμον, 1 Jn. ii. 15; τὸν νῦν αἰῶνα, 2 Tim. iv. 10, — both which last phrases signify to set the heart on earthly advantages and joys; τὴν ψυχὴν αὐτῶν, Rev. xii. 11; ζωήν, 1 Pet. iii. 10 (to derive pleasure from life, render it agreeable to himself); *to welcome with desire, long for*: τὴν ἐπιφάνειαν αὐτοῦ, 2 Tim. iv. 8 (Sap. i. 1; vi. 13; Sir. iv. 12, etc.; so of a person: ἠγαπήθη, Sap. iv. 10, cf. Grimm ad loc.). Concerning the unique proof of love which Jesus gave the apostles by washing their feet, it is said ἠγάπησεν αὐτούς, Jn. xiii. 1, cf. Lücke or Meyer ad loc. [but al. take ἠγάπ. here more comprehensively, see Weiss's Mey., Godet, Westcott, Keil]. The combination ἀγαπᾶν τινα occurs, when a relative intervenes, in Jn. xvii. 26; Eph. ii. 4, (2 S. xiii. 15 where τὸ μῖσος ὃ ἐμίσησεν αὐτήν is contrasted; cf. Gen. xlix. 25 εὐλόγησέ σε εὐλογίαν; Ps. Sal. xvii. 35 [in cod. Pseudepig. Vet. Test. ed. Fabric. i. p. 966; Libri Apocr. etc., ed. Fritzsche, p. 588] δόξαν ἣν ἐδόξασεν αὐτήν); cf. W. § 32, 2; [B. 148 sq. (129)]; Grimm on 1 Macc. ii. 54. On the difference betw. ἀγαπάω and φιλέω, see φιλέω. Cf. ἀγάπη, 1 fin.

ἀγάπη, -ης, ἡ, a purely bibl. and eccl. word (for Wyttenbach, following Reiske's conjecture, long ago restored ἀγαπήσων in place of ἀγάπης, ὧν in Plut. sympos. quaestt. 7, 6, 3 [vol. viii. p. 835 ed. Reiske]). Prof. auth. fr. [Aristot.], Plut. on used ἀγάπησις. "The Sept. use ἀγάπη for אַהֲבָה, Cant. ii. 4, 5, 7; iii. 5, 10; v. 8; vii. 6; viii. 4, 6, 7; [" It is noticeable that the word first makes its appearance as a current term in the Song of Sol.; — certainly no undesigned evidence respecting the idea which the Alex. translators had of the *love* in this Song" (*Zezschwitz*, Profangraec. u. bibl. Sprachgeist, p. 63)]; Jer. ii. 2; Eccl. ix. 1, 6; [2 S. xiii. 15]. It occurs besides in Sap. iii. 9; vi. 19. In Philo and Joseph. I do not remember to have met with it. Nor is it found in the N. T. in Acts, Mk., or Jas.; it occurs only once in Mt. and Lk., twice in Heb. and Rev., but frequently in the writings of Paul, John, Peter, Jude" (*Bretschn*. Lex. s. v.); [Philo, deus immut. § 14].

In signification it follows the verb ἀγαπάω; consequently it denotes   **1.** *affection, good-will, love, benevolence*: Jn. xv. 13; Ro. xiii. 10; 1 Jn. iv. 18. Of the love of men to men; esp. of that love of Christians towards Christians which is enjoined and prompted by their religion, whether the love be viewed as in the soul or as expressed: Mt. xxiv. 12; 1 Co. xiii. 1–4, 8; xiv. 1; 2 Co. ii. 4; Gal. v. 6; Philem. 5, 7; 1 Tim. i. 5; Heb. vi. 10; x. 24; Jn. xiii. 35; 1 Jn. iv. 7; Rev. ii. 4, 19, etc. Of the love of men towards God: ἡ ἀγάπη

τοῦ θεοῦ (obj. gen. [W. 185 (175)]), Lk. xi. 42; Jn. v. 42; 1 Jn. ii. 15 (τοῦ πατρός); iii. 17; iv. 12; v. 3. Of the love of God towards men: Ro. v. 8; viii. 39; 2 Co. xiii. 13 (14). Of the love of God towards Christ: Jn. xv. 10; xvii. 26. Of the love of Christ towards men: Jn. xv. 9 sq.; 2 Co. v. 14; Ro. viii. 35; Eph. iii. 19. In construction: ἀγ. εἴς τινα, 2 Co. ii. 8 [?]; Eph. i. 15 [L WH om. Tr mrg. br. τὴν ἀγάπην]; τῇ ἐξ ὑμῶν ἐν ἡμῖν i. e. love going forth from your soul and taking up its abode as it were in ours, i. q. your love to us, 2 Co. viii. 7 [W. 193 (181 sq.); B. 329 (283)]; μεθ᾽ ὑμῶν i. e. is present with (embraces) you, 1 Co. xvi. 24; μεθ᾽ ἡμῶν i. e. seen among us, 1 Jn. iv. 17. Phrases: ἔχειν ἀγάπην εἴς τινα, 2 Co. ii. 4; Col. i. 4 [L T Tr, but WH br.]; 1 Pet. iv. 8; ἀγάπην διδόναι to give a proof of love, 1 Jn. iii. 1; ἀγαπᾶν ἀγάπην τινά, Jn. xvii. 26; Eph. ii. 4 (v. in ἀγαπάω, sub fin.); ἀγ. τοῦ πνεύματος i. e. enkindled by the Holy Spirit, Ro. xv. 30; ὁ υἱὸς τῆς ἀγάπης the Son who is the object of love, i. q. ἀγαπητός, Col. i. 13 (W. 237 (222); [B. 162 (141)]); ὁ θεὸς τῆς ἀγ. the author of love, 2 Co. xiii. 11; κόπος τῆς ἀγ. troublesome service, toil, undertaken from love, 1 Th. i. 3; ἀγ. τῆς ἀληθείας love which embraces the truth, 2 Th. ii. 10; ὁ θεὸς ἀγάπη ἐστίν God is wholly love, his nature is summed up in love, 1 Jn. iv. 8, 16; φίλημα ἀγάπης a kiss as a sign among Christians of mutual affection, 1 Pet. v. 14; διὰ τὴν ἀγ. that love may have opportunity of influencing thee ('in order to give scope to the power of love' De W., Wies.), Philem. 9, cf. 14; ἐν ἀγάπῃ lovingly, in an affectionate spirit, 1 Co. iv. 21; on love as a basis [al. *in* love as the sphere or element], Eph. iv. 15 (where ἐν ἀγ. is to be connected not with ἀληθεύοντες but with αὐξήσωμεν), vs. 16; ἐξ ἀγάπης influenced by love, Phil. i. 17 (16); κατὰ ἀγάπην in a manner befitting love, Ro. xiv. 15. Love is mentioned together with faith and hope in 1 Co. xiii. 13; 1 Th. i. 3; v. 8; Col. i. 4 sq.; Heb. x. 22–24. On the words ἀγάπη, ἀγαπᾶν, cf. Gelpke in the Stud. u. Krit. for 1849, p. 646 sq.; on the idea and nature of Christian love see *Köstlin*, Lehrbgr. des Ev. Joh. etc. p. 248 sqq., 332 sqq.; *Rückert*, Theologie, ii. 452 sqq.; *Lipsius*, Paulin. Rechtfertigungsl. p. 188 sqq.; [*Reuss*, Théol. Chrét. livr. vii. chap. 13].   **2.** Plur. ἀγάπαι, -ῶν, *agapae, love-feasts*, feasts expressing and fostering mutual love which used to be held by Christians before the celebration of the Lord's supper, and at which the poorer Christians mingled with the wealthier and partook in common with the rest of food provided at the expense of the wealthy: Jude 12 (and in 2 Pet. ii. 13 L Tr txt. WH mrg.), cf. 1 Co. xi. 17 sqq.; Acts ii. 42, 46; xx. 7; Tertull. Apol. c. 39, and ad Martyr. c. 3; Cypr. ad Quirin. 3, 3; *Drescher*, De vet. christ. Agapis. Giess. 1824; *Mangold* in Schenkel i. 53 sq.; [B. D. s. v. Love-Feasts; Dict. of Christ. Antiq. s. v. Agapae; more fully in McC. and S. s. v. Agape].

ἀγαπητός, -ή, -όν, (ἀγαπάω), *beloved, esteemed, dear, favorite*; (opp. to ἐχθρός, Ro. xi. 28): ὁ υἱός μου (τοῦ Θεοῦ) ὁ ἀγαπητός, of Jesus, the Messiah, Mt. iii. 17

[here WH mrg. take ὁ ἀγ. absol., connecting it with what follows]; xii. 18; xvii. 5; Mk. i. 11; ix. 7; Lk. iii. 22; ix. 35 (where L mrg. T Tr WH ὁ ἐκλελεγμένος); 2 Pet. i. 17, cf. Mk. xii. 6; Lk. xx. 13; [cf. Ascensio Isa. (ed. Dillmann) vii. 23 sq.; viii. 18, 25, etc.]. ἀγαπητοὶ Θεοῦ [W. 194 (182 sq.); B. 190 (165)] is applied to Christians as being reconciled to God and judged by him to be worthy of eternal life: Ro. i. 7, cf. xi. 28; 1 Th. i. 4; Col. iii. 12, (Sept., Ps. lix. (lx.) 7; cvii. (cviii.) 7; cxxvi. (cxxvii.) 2, ἀγαπητοί σου and αὐτοῦ, of pious Israelites). But Christians, bound together by mutual love, are ἀγαπητοί also to one another (Philem. 16; 1 Tim. vi. 2); hence they are dignified with this epithet very often in tender address, both indirect (Ro. xvi. 5, 8; Col. iv. 14; Eph. vi. 21, etc.) and direct (Ro. xii. 19; 1 Co. iv. 14; [Philem. 2 Rec.]; Heb. vi. 9; Jas. i. 16; 1 Pet. ii. 11; 2 Pet. iii. 1; [1 Jn. ii. 7 G L T Tr WH], etc.). Generally foll. by the gen.; once by the dat. ἀγαπ. ἡμῖν, 1 Th. ii. 8 [yet cf. W. § 31, 2; B. 190 (165)]. ἀγαπητὸς ἐν κυρίῳ beloved in the fellowship of Christ, equiv. to dear fellow-Christian, Ro. xvi. 8. [Not used in the Fourth Gospel or the Rev. In class. Grk. fr. Hom. Il. 6, 401 on; cf. Cope on Aristot. rhet. 1, 7, 41.]

28

Ἄγαρ [WH Ἅγ. (see their Intr. § 408)], ἡ, indecl., (in Joseph. Ἀγάρα, -ης), הָגָר (flight), Hagar, a bondmaid of Abraham, and by him the mother of Ishmael (Gen. xvi.): Gal. iv. 24, [25 L txt. T om. Tr br.]. Since the Arabians according to Paul (who had formerly dwelt among them, Gal. i. 17) called the rocky Mt. Sinai by a name similar in sound to הגר (حَجَر i. e. rock), the apostle in the passage referred to employs the name Hagar allegorically to denote the servile sense of fear with which the Mosaic economy imbued its subjects. [Cf. B. D. Am. ed. pp. 978, 2366 note ᵃ; Bp. Lghtft.'s remarks appended to his Com. on Gal. l. c.]*

29

ἀγγαρεύω; fut. ἀγγαρεύσω; 1 aor. ἠγγάρευσα; to employ a courier, despatch a mounted messenger. A word of Persian origin [used by Menander, Sicyon. 4], but adopted also into Lat. (Vulg. angariare). Ἄγγαροι were public couriers (tabellarii), stationed by appointment of the king of Persia at fixed localities, with horses ready for use, in order to transmit royal messages from one to another and so convey them the more speedily to their destination. See Hdt. 8, 98 [and Rawlinscn's note]; Xen. Cyr. 8, 6, 17 (9); cf. Gesenius, Thesaur. s. v. אִגֶּרֶת; [B. D. s. v. Angareuo; Vaniček, Fremdwörter s. v. ἄγγαρος]. These couriers had authority to press into their service, in case of need, horses, vessels, even men they met, [cf. Joseph. antt. 13, 2, 3]. Hence ἀγγαρεύειν τινά denotes to compel one to go a journey, to bear a burden, or to perform any other service: Mt. v. 41 (ὅστις σε ἀγγαρεύσει μίλιον ἕν i. e. whoever shall compel thee to go one mile); xxvii. 32 (ἠγγάρευσαν ἵνα ἄρῃ i. e. they forced him to carry), so Mk. xv. 21.*

30

ἀγγεῖον, -ου, τό, (i. q. τὸ ἄγγος), a vessel, receptacle: Mt. xiii. 48 [R G L]; xxv. 4. (From Hdt. down.)*

ἀγγελία, -ας, ἡ, (ἄγγελος), a message, announcement, thing announced; precept declared, 1 Jn. i. 5 (where Rec. has ἐπαγγελία) [cf. Is. xxviii. 9]; iii. 11. [From Hom. down.]*

31

ἀγγέλλω; [1 aor. ἤγγειλα, Jn. iv. 51 T (for ἀπήγγ. R G L Tr br.)]; (ἄγγελος); to announce: ἀγγέλλουσα, Jn. xx. 18 L T Tr WH, for R G ἀπαγγέλλ. [From Hom. down. Comp.: ἀν-, ἀπ-, δι-, ἐξ-, ἐπ-, προ-επ-, κατ-, προ-κατ-, παρ-αγγέλλω.]*

see 31

ἄγγελος, -ου, ὁ, **1.** a messenger, envoy, one who is sent: Mt. xi. 10; Lk. vii. 24, 27; ix. 52; Mk. i. 2; Jas. ii. 25. [Fr. Hom. down.] **2.** In the Scriptures, both of the Old Test. and of the New, one of that host of heavenly spirits that, according alike to Jewish and Christian opinion, wait upon the monarch of the universe, and are sent by him to earth, now to execute his purposes (Mt. iv. 6, 11; xxviii. 2; Mk. i. 13; Lk. xvi. 22; xxii. 43 [L br. WH reject the pass.]; Acts vii. 35; xii. 23; Gal. iii. 19, cf. Heb. i. 14), now to make them known to men (Lk. i. 11, 26; ii. 9 sqq.; Acts x. 3; xxvii. 23; Mt. i. 20; ii. 13; xxviii. 5; Jn. xx. 12 sq.); hence the frequent expressions ἄγγελος (angel, messenger of God, מַלְאָךְ) and ἄγγελοι κυρίου or ἄγγ. τοῦ θεοῦ. They are subject not only to God but also to Christ (Heb. i. 4 sqq.; 1 Pet. iii. 22, cf. Eph. i. 21; Gal. iv. 14), who is described as hereafter to return to judgment surrounded by a multitude of them as servants and attendants: Mt. xiii. 41, 49; xvi. 27; xxiv. 31; xxv. 31; 2 Th. i. 7, cf. Jude 14. Single angels have the charge of separate elements; as fire, Rev. xiv. 18; waters, Rev. xvi. 5, cf. vii. 1 sq.; Jn. v. 4 [R L]. Respecting the ἄγγελος τῆς ἀβύσσου, Rev. ix. 11, see Ἀβαδδών, 3. Guardian angels of individuals are mentioned in Mt. xviii. 10; Acts xii. 15. 'The angels of the churches' in Rev. i. 20; ii. 1, 8, 12, 18; iii. 1, 7, 14 are not their presbyters or bishops, but heavenly spirits who exercise such a superintendence and guardianship over them that whatever in their assemblies is worthy of praise or of censure is counted to the praise or the blame of their angels also, as though the latter infused their spirit into the assemblies; cf. De Wette, Düsterdieck, [Alford,] on Rev. i. 20, and Lücke, Einl. in d. Offenb. d. Johan. ii. p. 429 sq. ed. 2; [Bp. Lghtft. on Philip. p. 199 sq.]. διὰ τοὺς ἀγγέλους that she may show reverence for the angels, invisibly present in the religious assemblies of Christians, and not displease them, 1 Co. xi. 10. ὤφθη ἀγγέλοις in 1 Tim. iii. 16 is probably to be explained neither of angels to whom Christ exhibited himself in heaven, nor of demons triumphed over by him in the nether world, but of the apostles, his messengers, to whom he appeared after his resurrection. This appellation, which is certainly extraordinary, is easily understood from the nature of the hymn from which the passage ἐφανερώθη ... ἐν δόξῃ seems to have been taken; cf. W. 639 sq. (594), [for other interpretations see Ellic. ad loc.]. In Jn. i. 51 (52) angels are employed, by a beautiful image borrowed from Gen. xxviii. 12, to represent the divine power that will aid Jesus in the discharge

32

of his Messianic office, and the signal proofs to appear in his history of a divine superintendence. Certain of the angels have proved faithless to the trust committed to them by God, and have given themselves up to sin, Jude 6; 2 Pet. ii. 4 (Enoch c. vi. etc., cf. Gen. vi. 2), and now obey the devil, Mt. xxv. 41; Rev. xii. 7, cf. 1 Co. vi. 3 [yet on this last passage cf. Meyer; he and others maintain that ἄγγ. without an epithet or limitation never in the N. T. signifies other than good angels]. Hence ἄγγελος Σατᾶν is trop. used in 2 Co. xii. 7 to denote a grievous bodily malady sent by Satan. See δαίμων; [Soph. Lex. s. v. ἄγγελος; and for the literature on the whole subject B. D. Am. ed. s. v. Angels, — and to the reff. there given add G. L. Hahn, Theol. des N. T., i. pp. 260–384; Delitzsch in Riehm s. v. Engel; Kübel in Herzog ed. 2, ibid.].

**(32α);
see 30**

ἄγγος, -εος, τό, (plur. ἄγγη), i. q. ἀγγεῖον q. v.: Mt. xiii. 48 T Tr WH. (From Hom. down; [cf. Rutherford, New Phryn. p. 23].) *

33

ἄγε, (properly impv. of ἄγω), come! come now! used, as it often is in the classics (W. 516 (481)), even when more than one is addressed: Jas. iv. 13; v. 1.*

34

ἀγέλη, -ης, ἡ, (ἄγω to drive), a herd: Mt. viii. 30 sqq.; Mk. v. 11, 13; Lk. viii. 32 sq. (From Hom. down.) *

35

ἀγενεαλόγητος, -ον, ὁ, (γενεαλογέω), of whose descent there is no account (in the O. T.), [R. V. without genealogy]: Heb. vii. 3 (vs. 6 μὴ γενεαλογούμενος). Nowhere found in prof. auth.*

36

ἀγενής, -ές (-οῦς), ὁ, ἡ, (γένος), opp. to εὐγενής, of no family, a man of base birth, a man of no name or reputation; often used by prof. writ., also in the secondary sense ignoble, cowardly, mean, base. In the N. T. only in 1 Co. i. 28, τὰ ἀγενῆ τοῦ κόσμου i. e. those who among men are held of no account; on the use of a neut. adj. in ref. to persons, see W. 178 (167); [B. 122 (107)].*

37

ἁγιάζω; 1 aor. ἡγίασα; Pass., [pres. ἁγιάζομαι]; pf. ἡγίασμαι; 1 aor. ἡγιάσθην; a word for which the Greeks use ἁγίζειν, but very freq. in bibl. (as equiv. to קָדַשׁ, הִקְדִּישׁ) and eccl. writ.; to make ἅγιον, render or declare sacred or holy, consecrate. Hence it denotes 1. to render or acknowledge to be venerable, to hallow: τὸ ὄνομα τοῦ θεοῦ, Mt. vi. 9 (so of God, Is. xxix. 23; Ezek. xx. 41; xxxviii. 23; Sir. xxxiii.) 4); [Lk. xi. 2]; τὸν Χριστόν, 1 Pet. iii. 15 (R G θεόν). Since the stamp of sacredness passes over from the holiness of God to whatever has any connection with God, ἁγιάζειν denotes 2. to separate from things profane and dedicate to God, to consecrate and so render inviolable; a. things (πᾶν πρωτότοκον, τὰ ἀρσενικά, Deut. xv. 19; ἡμέραν, Ex. xx. 8; οἶκον, 2 Chr. vii. 16, etc.): τὸν χρυσόν, Mt. xxiii. 17; τὸ δῶρον, vs. 19; σκεῦος, 2 Tim. ii. 21. b. persons. So Christ is said by undergoing death to consecrate himself to God, whose will he in that way fulfils, Jn. xvii. 19; God is said ἁγιάσαι Christ, i. e. to have selected him for his service (cf. ἀφορίζειν, Gal. i. 15) by having committed to him the office of Messiah, Jn. x. 36, cf. Jer. i. 5; Sir. xxxvi. 12 [ἐξ αὐτῶν ἡγίασε, καὶ πρὸς αὐτὸν ἤγγισεν, of his selection of men for the priesthood]; xlv

4; xlix. 7.   Since only what is pure and without blemish can be devoted and offered to God (Lev. xxii. 20; Deut. xv. 21; xvii. 1), ἁγιάζω signifies 3. to purify, (ἀπὸ τῶν ἀκαθαρσιῶν is added in Lev. xvi. 19; 2 S. xi. 4); and a. to cleanse externally (πρὸς τὴν τῆς σαρκὸς καθαρότητα), to purify levitically: Heb. ix. 13; 1 Tim. iv. 5. b. to purify by expiation, free from the guilt of sin: 1 Co. vi. 11; Eph. v. 26; Heb. x. 10, 14, 29; xiii. 12; ii. 11 (equiv. to כָּפַר, Ex. xxix. 33, 36); cf. Pfleiderer, Paulinismus, p. 340 sqq., [Eng. trans. ii. 68 sq.]. c. to purify internally by reformation of soul: Jn. xvii. 17, 19 (through knowledge of the truth, cf. Jn. viii. 32); 1 Th. v. 23; 1 Co. i. 2 (ἐν Χριστῷ Ἰησοῦ in the fellowship of Christ, the Holy One); Ro. xv. 16 (ἐν πνεύματι ἁγίῳ imbued with the Holy Spirit, the divine source of holiness); Jude 1 (L T Tr WH ἠγαπημένοις [q. v.]); Rev. xxii. 11.   In general, Christians are called ἡγιασμένοι [cf. Deut. xxxiii. 3], as those who, freed from the impurity of wickedness, have been brought near to God by their faith and sanctity, Acts xx. 32; xxvi. 18. In 1 Co. vii. 14 ἁγιάζεσθαι is used in a peculiar sense of those who, although not Christians themselves, are yet, by marriage with a Christian, withdrawn from the contamination of heathen impiety and brought under the saving influence of the Holy Spirit displaying itself among Christians; cf. Neander ad loc.*

38

ἁγιασμός, -οῦ, ὁ, a word used only by bibl. and eccl. writ. (for in Diod. 4, 39; Dion. Hal. 1, 21, ἁγισμός is the more correct reading), signifying 1. consecration, purification, τὸ ἁγιάζειν. 2. the effect of consecration: sanctification of heart and life, 1 Co. i. 30 (Christ is he to whom we are indebted for sanctification); 1 Th. iv. 7; Ro. vi. 19, 22; 1 Tim. ii. 15; Heb. xii. 14; ἁγιασμὸς πνεύματος sanctification wrought by the Holy Spirit, 2 Th. ii. 13; 1 Pet. i. 2. It is opposed to lust in 1 Th. iv. 3 sq. (It is used in a ritual sense, Judg. xvii. 3 [Alex.]; Ezek. xlv. 4; [Am. ii. 11]; Sir. vii. 31, etc.) [On its use in the N. T. cf. Ellic. on 1 Th. iv. 3; iii. 13.]*

39 & 40

ἅγιος, -α, -ον, (fr. τὸ ἄγος religious awe, reverence; ἄζω, ἄζομαι, to venerate, revere, esp. the gods, parents, [Curtius § 118]), rare in prof. auth.; very frequent in the sacred writ.; in the Sept. for קָדוֹשׁ; 1. properly reverend, worthy of veneration: τὸ ὄνομα τοῦ θεοῦ, Lk. i. 49; God, on account of his incomparable majesty, Rev. iv. 8 (Is. vi. 3, etc.), i. q. ἔνδοξος. Hence used a. of things which on account of some connection with God possess a certain distinction and claim to reverence, as places sacred to God which are not to be profaned, Acts vii. 33; τόπος ἅγιος the temple, Mt. xxiv. 15 (on which pass. see βδέλυγμα, c.); Acts vi. 13; xxi. 28; the holy land or Palestine, 2 Macc. i. 29; ii. 18; τὸ ἅγιον and τὰ ἅγια [W. 177 (167)] the temple, Heb. ix. 1, 24 (cf. Bleek on Heb. vol. ii. 2, p. 477 sq.); spec. that part of the temple or tabernacle which is called 'the holy place' (מִקְדָּשׁ, Ezek. xxxvii. 28; xlv. 18), Heb. ix. 2 [here Rec.⁰ reads ἁγία]; ἅγια ἁγίων [W. 246 (231), cf. Ex. xxix. 37; xxx. 10, etc.] the most hallowed portion of the temple, 'the holy of holies,' (Ex. xxvi. 33 [cf. Joseph.

antt. 3, 6, 4]), Heb. ix. 3, in ref. to which the simple τὰ ἅγια is also used : Heb. ix. 8, 25 ; x. 19 ; xiii. 11; fig. of heaven, Heb. viii. 2; ix. 8, 12 ; x. 19 ; ἁγία πόλις Jerusalem, on account of the temple there, Mt. iv. 5 ; xxvii. 53 ; Rev. xi. 2 ; xxi. 2 ; xxii. 19, (Is. xlviii. 2 ; Neh. xi. 1, 18 [Compl.], etc.) ; τὸ ὄρος τὸ ἅγιον, because Christ's transfiguration occurred there, 2 Pet. i. 18 ; ἡ (θεοῦ) ἁγία διαθήκη i. e. which is the more sacred because made by God himself, Lk. i. 72 ; τὸ ἅγιον, that worshipful offspring of divine power, Lk. i. 35 ; the blessing of the gospel, Mt. vii. 6 ; ἁγιωτάτη πίστις, faith (quae creditur i.e. the object of faith) which came from God and is therefore to be heeded most sacredly, Jude 20 ; in the same sense ἁγία ἐντολή, 2 Pet. ii. 21 ; κλῆσις ἁγία, because it is the invitation of God and claims us as his, 2 Tim. i. 9 ; ἅγιαι γραφαί (τὰ βιβλία τὰ ἅγια, 1 Macc. xii. 9), which came from God and contain his words, Ro. i. 2.   **b.** of persons whose services God employs; as for example, apostles, Eph. iii. 5 ; angels, 1 Th. iii. 13 ; Mt. xxv. 31 [Rec.] ; Rev. xiv. 10 ; Jude 14 ; prophets, Acts iii. 21 ; Lk. i. 70, (Sap. xi. 1); (οἱ) ἅγιοι (τοῦ) θεοῦ ἄνθρωποι, 2 Pet. i. 21 [R G L Tr txt.]; worthies of the O. T. accepted by God for their piety, Mt. xxvii. 52 ; 1 Pet. iii. 5.   **2.** set apart for God, to be, as it were, exclusively his ; foll. by a gen. or dat.: τῷ κυρίῳ, Lk. ii. 23 ; τοῦ θεοῦ (i. q. ἐκλεκτὸς τοῦ θεοῦ) of Christ, Mk. i. 24 ; Lk. iv. 34, and acc. to the true reading in Jn. vi. 69, cf. x. 36 ; he is called also ὁ ἅγιος παῖς τοῦ θεοῦ, Acts iv. 30, and simply ὁ ἅγιος, 1 Jn. ii. 20. Just as the Israelites claimed for themselves the title οἱ ἅγιοι, because God selected them from the other nations to lead a life acceptable to him and rejoice in his favor and protection (Dan. vii. 18, 22 ; 2 Esdr. viii. 28), so this appellation is very often in the N. T. transferred to Christians, as those whom God has selected ἐκ τοῦ κόσμου (Jn. xvii. 14, 16), that under the influence of the Holy Spirit they may be rendered, through holiness, partakers of salvation in the kingdom of God : 1 Pet. ii. 9 (Ex. xix. 6), cf. vs. 5 ; Acts ix. 13, 32, 41; xxvi. 10; Ro. i. 7; viii. 27; xii. 13; xvi. 15; 1 Co. vi. 1, 2 ; Phil. iv. 21 sq.; Col. i. 12 ; Heb. vi. 10; Jude 3 ; Rev. v. 8, etc.; [cf. B. D. Am. ed. s. v. Saints]. **3.** of sacrifices and offerings; prepared for God with solemn rite, pure, clean, (opp. to ἀκάθαρτος) : 1 Co. vii. 14, (cf. Eph. v. 3); connected with ἄμωμος, Eph. i. 4 ; v. 27 ; Col. i. 22 ; ἀπαρχή, Ro. xi. 16 ; θυσία, Ro. xii. 1. Hence   **4.** in a moral sense, pure, sinless, upright, holy : 1 Pet. i. 16 (Lev. xix. 2 ; xi. 44); 1 Co. vii. 34; δίκαιος κ. ἅγιος, of John the Baptist, Mk. vi. 20 ; ἅγιος κ. δίκαιος, of Christ, Acts iii. 14; distinctively of him, Rev. iii. 7; vi. 10; of God pre-eminently, 1 Pet. i. 15 ; Jn. xvii. 11 ; ἅγιαι ἀναστροφαί, 2 Pet. iii. 11 ; νόμος and ἐντολή, i. e. containing nothing exceptionable, Ro. vii. 12 ; φίλημα, such a kiss as is a sign of the purest love, 1 Th. v. 26 ; 1 Co. xvi. 20 ; 2 Co. xiii. 12 ; Ro. xvi. 16. On the phrase τὸ ἅγιον πνεῦμα and τὸ πνεῦμα τὸ ἅγιον, see πνεῦμα, 4 a.   Cf. *Diestel, Die Heiligkeit Gottes*, in Jahrbb. f. deutsch. Theol. iv. p. 1 sqq. ; [*Baudissin,*

Stud. z. Semitisch. Religionsgesch. Heft ii. p. 3 sqq.; *Delitzsch* in Herzog ed. 2, v. 714 sqq. ; esp.] *Cremer,* Wörterbuch, 4te Aufl. p. 32 sqq. [trans. of 2d ed. p. 34 sqq.; *Oehler* in Herzog xix. 618 sqq. ; *Zezschwitz,* Profangräcität u. s. w. p. 15 sqq.; Trench § lxxxviii.; *Campbell,* Dissertations, diss. vi., pt. iv.; esp. Schmidt ch. 181].

ἁγιότης, -ητος, ἡ, sanctity, in a moral sense; holiness: **41** 2 Co. i. 12 L T Tr WH; Heb. xii. 10. (Besides only in 2 Macc. xv. 2; [cf. W. 25, and on words of this termination *Lob.* ad Phryn. p. 350].) *

ἁγιωσύνη [on the ω see reff. in ἀγαθωσύνη, init.], -ης, ἡ,   **42** a word unknown to prof. auth. [B. 73 (64)];   **1.** (God's incomparable) majesty, (joined to μεγαλοπρέπεια, Ps. xcv. (xcvi.) 6, cf. cxliv. (cxlv.) 5) : πνεῦμα ἁγιωσύνης a spirit to which belongs ἁγιωσύνη, not equiv. to πνεῦμα ἅγιον, but the divine [?] spiritual nature in Christ as contrasted with his σάρξ, Ro. i. 4 ; cf. Rückert ad loc., and Zeller in his Theol. Jahrbb. for 1842, p. 486 sqq.; [yet cf. Mey. ad loc.; Gifford (in the Speaker's Com.). Most commentators (cf. e. g. Ellic. on Thess. as below) regard the word as uniformly and only signifying holiness]. **2.** moral purity : 1 Th. iii. 13 ; 2 Co. vii. 1.*

ἀγκάλη, -ης, ἡ, (ἀγκή, ἀγκάς [fr. r. ak to bend, curve,   **43** cf. Lat. uncus, angulus, Eng. angle, etc.; cf. Curtius § 1 ; Vaniček p. 2 sq.]), the curve or inner angle of the arm : δέξασθαι εἰς τὰς ἀγκάλας, Lk. ii. 28. The Greeks also said ἀγκὰς λαβεῖν, ἐν ἀγκάλαις περιφέρειν, etc., see ἐναγκαλίζομαι. [(From Aeschyl. and Hdt. down.)] *

ἄγκιστρον, -ου, τό, (fr. an unused ἀγκίζω to angle [see   **44** the preceding word]), a fish-hook : Mt. xvii. 27.*

ἄγκυρα, -ας, ἡ, [see ἀγκάλη], an anchor — [ancient an-   **45** chors resembled modern in form: were of iron, provided with a stock, and with two teeth-like extremities often but by no means always without flukes ; see *Roschach* in Daremberg and Saglio's Dict. des Antiq. (1873) p. 267; Guhl and Koner p. 258] : ῥίπτειν to cast (Lat. jacere), Acts xxvii. 29 ; ἐκτείνειν, vs. 30 ; περιαιρεῖν, vs. 40. Figuratively, any stay or safeguard : as hope, Heb. vi. 19 ; Eur. Hec. 78 (80) ; Heliod. vii. p. 352 (350).*

ἄγναφος, -ου, ὁ, ἡ, (γνάπτω to dress or full cloth, cf.   **46** ἄρραφος), unmilled, unfulled, undressed : Mt. ix. 16 ; Mk. ii. 21. [Cf. Moeris s. v. ἄκναπτον ; Thom. Mag. p. 12, 14.]*

ἁγνεία [WH ἁγνία (see I, ι)], -ας, ἡ, (ἁγνεύω), purity,   **47** sinlessness of life : 1 Tim. iv. 12 ; v. 2. (Of a Nazirite, Num. vi. 2, 21.) [From Soph. O. T. 864 down.] *

ἁγνίζω ; 1 aor. ἥγνισα ; pf. ptcp. act. ἡγνικώς ; pass.   **48** ἡγνισμένος ; 1 aor. pass. ἡγνίσθην [W. 252 (237)]; (ἁγνός); to purify ;   **1.** ceremonially : ἐμαυτόν, Jo. xi. 55 (to cleanse themselves from levitical pollution by means of prayers, abstinence, washings, sacrifices) ; the pass. has a reflexive force, to take upon one's self a purification, Acts xxi. 24, 26 ; xxiv. 18 (וְהִזִּיר, Num. vi. 3), and is used of Nazirites or those who had taken upon themselves a temporary or a life-long vow to abstain from wine and all kinds of intoxicating drink, from every defilement and from shaving the head [cf. BB. DD. s. v. Nazarite]. **2.** morally : τὰς καρδίας, Jas. iv. 8 ; τὰς ψυχάς, 1 Pet. i. 22 ; ἑαυτόν, 1 Jn. iii. 3. (Soph., Eur., Plut., al.)*

49 ἁγνισμός, -οῦ, ὁ, *purification, lustration*, [Dion. Hal. 3, 22, i. p. 469, 13; Plut. de defect. orac. 15]: Acts xxi. 26 (equiv. to נֵזֶר, Num. vi. 5), Naziritic; see ἁγνίζω, 1.*

50 ἀγνοέω (ΓΝΟ [cf. γινώσκω]), -ῶ, [impv. ἀγνοείτω 1 Co. xiv. 38 R G Tr txt. WH mrg.]; impf. ἠγνόουν; 1 aor. ἠγνόησα; [Pass., pres. ἀγνοοῦμαι, ptcp. ἀγνοούμενος; fr. Hom. down]; **a.** *to be ignorant, not to know*: absol., 1 Tim. i. 13; τινά, τί, Acts xiii. 27; xvii. 23; Ro. x. 3; ἔν τινι (as in [Test. Jos. § 14] Fabricii Pseudepigr. ii. p. 717 [but the reading ἠγνόουν ἐπὶ πᾶσι τούτοις is now given here; see Test. xii. Patr. ad fid. cod. Cant. etc., ed. Sinker, Cambr. 1869]), 2 Pet. ii. 12, unless one prefer to resolve the expression thus: ἐν τούτοις, ἃ ἀγνοοῦσι βλασφημοῦντες, W. 629 (584), [cf. B. 287 (246)]; foll. by ὅτι, Ro. ii. 4; vi. 3; vii. 1; 1 Co. xiv. 38 (where the antecedent clause ὅτι κτλ. is to be supplied again); οὐ θέλω ὑμᾶς ἀγνοεῖν, a phrase often used by Paul, [an emphatic] *scitote*: foll. by an acc. of the obj., Ro. xi. 25; ὑπέρ τινος, ὅτι, 2 Co. i. 8; περί τινος, 1 Co. xii. 1; 1 Th. iv. 13; foll. by ὅτι, Ro. i. 13; 1 Co. x. 1; in the pass. ἀγνοεῖται 'he is not known' i. e. acc. to the context 'he is disregarded,' 1 Co. xiv. 38 L T Tr mrg. WH txt.; ἀγνοούμενοι (opp. to ἐπιγινωσκόμενοι) men unknown, obscure, 2 Co. vi. 9; ἀγνοούμενός τινι unknown to one, Gal. i. 22; οὐκ ἀγνοεῖν to know very well, τί, 2 Co. ii. 11 (Sap. xii. 10). **b.** *not to understand*: τί, Mk. ix. 32; Lk. ix. 45. **c.** *to err, sin through mistake*, spoken mildly of those who are not high-handed or wilful transgressors (Sir. v. 15; 2 Macc. xi. 31): Heb. v. 2, on which see Delitzsch.*

51 ἀγνόημα, -τος, τό, *a sin*, (strictly, that committed through ignorance or thoughtlessness [A. V. *error*]): Heb. ix. 7 (1 Macc. xiii. 39; Tob. iii. 3; Sir. xxiii. 2); cf. ἀγνοέω, c. [and Trench § lxvi.].*

52 ἄγνοια, -ας, ἡ, [fr. Aeschyl. down], *want of knowledge, ignorance*, esp. of divine things: Acts xvii. 30; 1 Pet. i. 14; such as is inexcusable, Eph. iv. 18 (Sap. xiv. 22); of moral blindness, Acts iii. 17. [Cf. ἀγνοέω.]*

53 ἁγνός, -ή, -όν, (ἅζομαι, see ἅγιος); **1.** *exciting reverence, venerable, sacred*: πῦρ καὶ ἡ σποδός, 2 Macc. xiii. 8; Eur. El. 812. **2.** *pure* (Eur. Or. 1604 ἁγνὸς γάρ εἰμι χεῖρας, ἀλλ' οὐ τὰς φρένας, Hipp. 316 sq. ἁγνὰς ... χεῖρας αἵματος φέρεις, χεῖρες μὲν ἁγναί, φρὴν δ' ἔχει μίασμα); **a.** *pure from carnality, chaste, modest*: Tit. ii. 5; παρθένος an unsullied virgin, 2 Co. xi. 2 (4 Macc. xviii. 7). **b.** *pure from every fault, immaculate*: 2 Co. vii. 11; Phil. iv. 8; 1 Tim. v. 22; 1 Pet. iii. 2; 1 Jn. iii. 3 (of God [yet cf. ἐκεῖνος 1 b.]); Jas. iii. 17. (From Hom. down.) [Cf. reff. s. v. ἅγιος, fin.; Westc. on 1 Jn. iii. 3.]*

54 ἁγνότης, -ητος, ἡ, [ἁγνός], *purity, uprightness of life*: 2 Co. vi. 6; in 2 Co. xi. 3 some critical authorities add καὶ τῆς ἁγνότητος after ἁπλότητος (so L Tr txt., but Tr mrg. WH br.), others read τῆς ἁγνότητος καὶ before ἁπλότ. Found once in prof. auth., see *Boeckh*, Corp. Inscrr. i. p. 583 no. 1133 l. 15: δικαιοσύνης ἕνεκεν καὶ ἁγνότητος.*

55 ἁγνῶς, adv., *purely, with sincerity*: Phil. i. 16 (17).*

56 ἀγνωσία, -ας, ἡ, (γνῶσις), *want of knowledge, ignorance*: 1 Pet. ii. 15; 1 Co. xv. 34, (Sap. xiii. 1).*

57 ἄ-γνωστος, -ον, [fr. Hom. down], *unknown*: Acts xvii. 23 [cf. B. D. Am. ed. s. v. Altar].*

58 ἀγορά, -ᾶς, ἡ, (ἀγείρω, pf. ἤγορα, to collect), [fr. Hom. down]; **1.** *any collection of men, congregation, assembly*. **2.** *place where assemblies are held*; in the N. T. the forum or public place, — where trials are held, Acts xvi. 19; and the citizens resort, Acts xvii. 17; and commodities are exposed for sale, Mk. vii. 4 (ἀπ' ἀγορᾶς sc. ἐλθόντες on returning *from the market if they have not washed themselves they eat not*; W. § 66, 2 d. note); accordingly, the most frequented part of a city or village: Mt. xi. 16, (Lk. vii. 32); Mk. vi. 56; Mt. xx. 3; xxiii. 7; Mk. xii. 38; [Lk. xi. 43]; xx. 46. [See B. D. Am. ed. s. v. Market.]*

59 ἀγοράζω; [impf. ἠγόραζον; fut. ἀγοράσω]; 1 aor. ἠγόρασα; Pass., pf. ptcp. ἠγορασμένος; 1 aor. ἠγοράσθην; (ἀγορά); **1.** *to frequent the market-place*. **2.** *to buy* (properly, in the market-place), [Arstph., Xen., al.]; used **a.** literally: absol., Mt. xxi. 12; Mk. xi. 15; Lk. xix. 45 [not G T Tr WH]; τί, Mt. xiii. 44, 46; xiv. 15 and parallel pass., Jn. iv. 8; vi. 5; with παρά and gen. of the pers. fr. whom, Rev. iii. 18, [Sept., Polyb.]; ἐκ and gen. of price, Mt. xxvii. 7; simple gen. of price, Mk. vi. 37. **b.** figuratively: Christ is said to have purchased his disciples i. e. made them, as it were, his private property, 1 Co. vi. 20 [this is commonly understood of God; but cf. Jn. xvii. 9, 10]; 1 Co. vii. 23 (with gen. of price added; εεε τιμή, 1); 2 Pet. ii. 1. He is also said to have bought them for God ἐν τῷ αἵματι αὐτοῦ, by shedding his blood, Rev. v. 9; they, too, are spoken of as purchased ἀπὸ τῆς γῆς, Rev. xiv. 3, and ἀπὸ τῶν ἀνθρώπων, vs. 4, so that they are withdrawn from the earth (and its miseries) and from (wicked) men. But ἀγοράζω does not mean *redeem* (ἐξαγοράζω), — as is commonly said. [COMP.: ἐξ-αγοράζω.]

60 ἀγοραῖος (rarely -αία), -αῖον, (ἀγορά), *relating to the market-place*; **1.** *frequenting the market-place*, (either transacting business, as the κάπηλοι, or) *sauntering idly*, (Lat. *subrostranus, subbasilicanus*, Germ. *Pflastertreter*, our *loafer*): Acts xvii. 5, (Plat. Prot. 347 c. ἀγοραῖοι καὶ φαῦλοι, Arstph. ran. 1015, al.). **2.** *of affairs usually transacted in the market-place*: ἀγοραῖοι (sc. ἡμέραι [W. 590 (549)] or σύνοδοι [Mey. et al.]) ἄγονται, judicial days or assemblies, [A. V. mrg. *court-days*], Acts xix. 38 (τὰς ἀγοραίους ποιεῖσθαι, Strabo 13, p. 932), but many think we ought to read ἀγόραιοι here, so G L cf. W. 53 (52); but see [Alf. and Tdf. ad loc.; *Lipsius*, Gram. Untersuch. p. 26;] Meyer on Acts xvii. 5; Göttling p. 297; [Chandler ed. 1 p. 269].*

61 ἄγρα, -ας, ἡ, [ἄγω]; **1.** *a catching, hunting*: Lk. v. 4. **2.** *the thing caught*: ἡ ἄγρα τῶν ἰχθύων 'the catch or haul of fish' i. e. the fishes taken [A. V. *draught*], Lk. v. 9.*

62 ἀγράμματος, -ον, [γράμμα], *illiterate, without learning*: Acts iv. 13 (i. e. unversed in the learning of the Jewish schools; cf. Jn. vii. 15 γράμματα μὴ μεμαθηκώς).*

63 ἀγρ-αυλέω, -ῶ; *to be an ἄγραυλος* (ἀγρός, αὐλή), i. e. *to live in the fields, be under the open sky, even by night*: Lk. ii. 8, (Strabo p. 301 a.; Plut. Num. 4).*

64   ἀγρεύω : 1 aor. ἤγρευσα; (ἄγρα); *to catch* (properly, wild animals, fishes): fig., Mk. xii. 13 ἵνα αὐτὸν ἀγρεύσωσι λόγῳ in order to entrap him by some inconsiderate remark elicited from him in conversation, cf. Lk. xx. 20. (In Anthol. it often denotes *to ensnare in the toils of love, captivate*; cf. παγιδεύω, Mt. xxii. 15; σαγηνεύω, Lcian. Tim. 25.) *

65   ἀγρι-έλαιος, -ον, (ἄγριος and ἔλαιος or ἐλαία, like ἀγριάμπελος);   **1.** *of* or *belonging to the oleaster*, or *wild olive*, (σκυτάλην ἀγριέλαιον, Anthol. 9, 237, 4; [cf. Lob. Paralip. p. 376]); spoken of a scion, Ro. xi. 17.   **2.** As subst. ἡ ἀγριέλαιος *the oleaster, the wild olive;* (opp. to καλλιέλαιος [cf. Aristot. plant. 1, 6]), also called by the Greeks κότινος, Ro. xi. 24; cf. Fritzsche on Rom. vol. ii. 495 sqq. [See B. D. s. v. Olive, and *Tristram*, Nat. Hist. of the Bible, s. v. Olive. The latter says, p. 377, 'the wild olive must not be confounded with the Oleaster or Oil-tree'.]*

66   ἄγριος, -α, -ον, (ἀγρός), [fr. Hom. down];   **1.** *living* or *growing in the fields* or *the woods*, used of animals in a state of nature, and of plants which grow without culture : μέλι ἄγριον *wild honey*, either that which is deposited by bees in hollow trees, clefts of rocks, on the bare ground (1 S. xiv. 25 [cf. vs. 26]), etc., or more correctly that which distils from certain trees, and is gathered when it has become hard, (Diod. Sic. 19, 94 fin. speaking of the Nabathaean Arabians says φύεται παρ' αὐτοῖς μέλι πολὺ τὸ καλούμενον ἄγριον, ᾧ χρῶνται ποτῷ μεθ' ὕδατος; cf. Suid. and esp. Suicer s. v. ἀκρίς): Mt. iii. 4; Mk. i. 6.   **2.** *fierce, untamed*: κύματα θαλάσσης, Jude 13 (Sap. xiv. 1).*

67   Ἀγρίππας, -α (respecting this gen. see W. § 8, 1 p. 60 (59); B. 20 (18)), ὁ, see Ἡρώδης, (3 and) 4.

68   ἀγρός, -οῦ, ὁ, [fr. ἄγω; prop. a drove or driving-place, then, pasturage; cf. Lat. *ager*, Germ. *Acker*, Eng. *acre*; Fick, Pt. i. p. 8];   **a.** *a field, the country*: Mt. vi. 28; xxiv. 18; Lk. xv. 15; [Mk. xi. 8 T Tr WH], etc.   **b.** i. q. χωρίον, *a piece of land, bit of tillage*: Acts iv. 37; Mk. x. 29; Mt. xiii. 24, 27, etc.   **c.** οἱ ἀγροί *the farms, country-seats, neighboring hamlets*: Mk. v. 14 (opp. to πόλις; cf. vs. 36; Lk. ix. 12. [(From Hom. on.)]

69   ἀγρυπνέω, -ῶ; (ἄγρυπνος equiv. to ἄϋπνος) *to be sleepless, keep awake, watch*, (i. q. γρηγορέω [see below]); [fr. Theognis down]; trop. *to be circumspect, attentive, ready*: Mk. xiii. 33; Lk. xxi. 36; εἴς τι, to be intent upon a thing, Eph. vi. 18; ὑπέρ τινος, to exercise constant vigilance over something (an image drawn from shepherds), Heb. xiii. 17. [SYN. ἀγρυπνεῖν, γρηγορεῖν, νήφειν: "ἀγρυπνεῖν may be taken to express simply . . . absence of sleep, and, pointedly, the absence of it when due to nature, and thence a wakeful frame of mind as opposed to listlessness; while γρηγορεῖν (the offspring of ἐγρήγορα) represents a waking state as the effect of some arousing effort . . . i. e. a more stirring image than the former. The group of synonyms is completed by νήφειν, which signifies a state untouched by any slumberous or beclouding influences, and thence, one that is guarded against advances of drowsiness or

bewilderment. Thus it becomes a term for wariness (cf. νᾶφε καὶ μέμνασ' ἀπιστεῖν) against spiritual dangers and beguilements, 1 Pet. v. 8, etc." *Green*, Crit. Notes on the N. T. (note on Mk. xiii. 33 sq.).]*

70   ἀγρυπνία, -ας, ἡ, *sleeplessness, watching*: 2 Co. vi. 5; xi. 27. [From Hdt. down.]*

71   ἄγω; impf. ἦγον; fut. ἄξω; 2 aor. ἤγαγον, inf. ἀγαγεῖν, (more rarely 1 aor. ἦξα, in ἐπάγω 2 Pet. ii. 5); Pass., pres. ἄγομαι; impf. ἠγόμην; 1 aor. ἤχθην; 1 fut. ἀχθήσομαι; [fr. Hom. down]; *to drive, lead.*   **1.** properly [A. V. ordinarily, *to bring*];   **a.** *to lead by laying hold of*, and in this way to bring to the point of destination: of an animal, Mt. xxi. 7; Lk. xix. 35; Mk. xi. 7 (T Tr WH φέρουσιν); [Lk. xix. 30]; τινά foll. by εἰς with acc. of place, Lk. iv. 9 [al. refer this to 2 c.]; x. 34; (ἤγαγον κ. εἰσήγαγον, Lk. xxii. 54); Jn. xviii. 28; Acts vi. 12; ix. 2; xvii. 5 [R G]; xxi. 34; xxii. 5, 24 Rec.; xxiii. 10, 31; ἐπί with acc., Acts xvii. 19; ἕως, Lk. iv. 29; πρός τινα, to persons, Lk. [iv. 40]; xviii. 40; Acts ix. 27; Jn. viii. 3 [Rec.].   **b.** *to lead by accompanying* to (into) any place: εἰς, Acts xi. 26 (25); ἕως, Acts xvii. 15; πρός τινα, to persons, Jn. i. 42 (43); ix. 13; Acts xxiii. 18; foll. by dat. of pers. to whom, Acts xxi. 16 on which see W. 214 (201) at length, [cf. B. 284 (244)], (1 Macc. vii. 2 ἄγειν αὐτοὺς αὐτῷ).   **c.** *to lead with one's self*, attach to one's self as an attendant: τινά, 2 Tim. iv. 11; 1 Th. iv. 14, (Joseph. antt. 10, 9, 6 ἀπῆρεν εἰς τὴν Αἴγυπτον ἄγων καὶ Ἱερεμίαν). Some refer Acts xxi. 16 to this head, resolving it ἄγοντες Μνάσωνα παρ' ᾧ ξενισθῶμεν, but incorrectly, see W. [and B.] as above.   **d.** *to conduct, bring*: τινά, [Lk. xix. 27]; Jn. vii. 45; [xix. 4, 13]; Acts v. 21, 26, [27]; xix. 37; xx. 12; xxv. 6, 23; πῶλον, Mk. xi. 2 (where T Tr WH φέρετε); [Lk. xix. 30, see a. above]; τινά τινι or τί τινι, Mt. xxi. 2; Acts xiii. 23 G L T Tr WH.   **e.** *to lead away, to a court of justice, magistrate*, etc.: simply, Mk. xiii. 11; [Acts xxv. 17]; ἐπί with acc., Mt. x. 18; Lk. xxi. 12 (T Tr WH ἀπαγομένους); [Lk. xxiii. 1]; Acts [ix. 21]; xviii. 12; (often in Attic); [πρός with acc., Jn. xviii. 13 L T Tr WH]; to punishment: simply (2 Macc. vi. 29; vii. 18, etc.), Jn. xix. 16 Grsb. (R καὶ ἀπήγαγον, which L T Tr WH have expunged) with telic inf., Lk. xxiii. 32; [foll. by ἵνα, Mk. xv. 20 Lchm.]; ἐπὶ σφαγήν, Acts viii. 32, (ἐπὶ θανάτῳ, Xen. mem. 4, 4, 3; an. 1, 6, 10).   **2.** tropically   **a.** *to lead, guide, direct*: Jn. x. 16; εἰς μετάνοιαν, Ro. ii. 4.   **b.** *to lead through, conduct*, to something, become the author of good or of evil to some one: εἰς δόξαν, Heb. ii. 10, (εἰς [al. ἐπὶ] καλοκἀγαθίαν, Xen. mem. 1, 6, 14; εἰς δουλείαν, Dem. p. 213, 28).   **c.** *to move, impel*, of forces and influences affecting the mind: Lk. iv. 1 (where read ἐν τῇ ἐρήμῳ [with L txt. T Tr WH]); πνεύματι θεοῦ ἄγεσθαι, Ro. viii. 14; Gal. v. 18; ἐπιθυμίαις, 2 Tim. iii. 6; simply, *urged on by blind impulse*, 1 Co. xii. 2 — unless impelled by Satan's influence be preferable, cf. x. 20; Eph. ii. 2; [B. 383 (328) sq.].   **3.** *to pass a day, keep* or *celebrate* a feast, etc.: τρίτην ἡμέραν ἄγει sc. ὁ Ἰσραήλ, Lk. xxiv. 21 [others (see Meyer) supply αὐτός or ὁ Ἰησοῦς; still others take ἄγει as impers., *one passes*, Vulg. *tertia dies est*; see B. 134 (118)] ; γενεσίων ἀγομένων, Mt. xiv. 6 R G; ἀγοραῖοι (q. v. 2), Acts xix. 38; often in the O. T. Apocr. (cf. *Wahl*, Clavis Apocr. s. v. ἄγω, 3), in Hdt. and Attic writ. **4.** intrans. *to go, depart*, (W. § 38, 1, p. 251 (236) ; [B. 144 (126)]) : ἄγωμεν *let us go*, Mt. xxvi. 46; Mk. xiv. 42; Jn. xiv. 31; πρός τινα, Jn. xi. 15; εἰς with acc. of place, Mk. i. 38; Jn. xi. 7, (Epict. diss. 3, 22, 55 ἄγωμεν ἐπὶ τὸν ἀνθύπατον) ; [foll. by ἵνα, Jn. xi. 16. COMP.: ἀν-, ἐπ-αν-, ἀπ-, συν-απ-, δι-, εἰσ-, παρ-εισ-, ἐξ-, ἐπ-, παρ-, περι-, προ-, προσ-, συν-, ἐπι-συν-, ὑπ-άγω. SYN. cf. Schmidt ch. 105.]*

ἀγωγή, -ῆς, ἡ, (fr. ἄγω, like ἐδωδή fr. ἔδω) ; **1.** properly, *a leading.* **2.** figuratively, **a.** trans. *a conducting, training, education, discipline.* **b.** intrans. *the life led, way* or *course of life* (a use which arose from the fuller expression ἀγωγὴ τοῦ βίου, in Polyb. 4, 74, 1. 4 ; cf. Germ. *Lebensführung*) : 2 Tim. iii. 10 [R. V. *conduct*], (Esth. ii. 20 ; 2 Macc. iv. 16 ; ἡ ἐν Χριστῷ ἀγωγή, Clem. Rom. 1 Cor. 47, 6 ; ἀγνὴ ἀγωγή, ibid. 48, 1). Often in prof. auth. in all these senses.*

ἀγών, -ῶνος, ὁ, (ἄγω) ; **1.** *a place of assembly* (Hom. Il. 7, 298; 18, 376); spec. the place in which the Greeks assembled to celebrate solemn games (as the Pythian, the Olympian); hence **2.** *a contest*, of athletes, runners, charioteers. In a fig. sense, **a.** in the phrase (used by the Greeks, see τρέχω, b.) τρέχειν τὸν ἀγῶνα, Heb. xii. 1, that is to say ' Amid all hindrances let us exert ourselves to the utmost to attain to the goal of perfection set before the followers of Christ' ; any struggle with dangers, annoyances, obstacles, standing in the way of faith, holiness, and a desire to spread the gospel: 1 Th. ἰ̈. 2 ; Phil. i. 30 ; 1 Tim. vi. 12 ; 2 Tim. iv. 7. **b.** *intense solicitude, anxiety*: περί τινος, Col. ii. 1 [cf. Eur. Ph. 1350; Polyb. 4, 56, 4]. On the ethical use of figures borrowed from the Greek Games cf. Grimm on Sap. iv. 1; [*Howson*, Metaphors of St. Paul, Essay iv.; *Conyb. and Hows.* Life and Epp. of St. Paul, ch. xx.; *Mc. and S.* iii. 733ᵇ sq.; BB.DD. s. v. Games].*

ἀγωνία, -ας, ἡ ; **1.** i. q. ἀγών, which see. **2.** It is often used, from Dem. (on the Crown p. 236, 19 ἦν ὁ Φίλιππος ἐν φόβῳ καὶ πολλῇ ἀγωνίᾳ) down, of severe mental struggles and emotions, *agony, anguish* : Lk. xxii. 44 [L br. WH reject the pass.]; (2 Macc. iii. 14, 16 ; xv. 19 ; Joseph. antt. 11, 8, 4 ὁ ἀρχιερεὺς ἦν ἐν ἀγωνίᾳ καὶ δέει). [Cf. *Field*, Otium Norv. iii. on Lk. l. c.]*

ἀγωνίζομαι, impf. ἠγωνιζόμην ; pf. ἠγώνισμαι ; a depon. mid. verb [cf. W. 260 (244)] ; (ἀγών) ; **1.** *to enter a contest; contend in the gymnastic games* : 1 Co. ix. 25. **2.** univ. *to contend with adversaries, fight* : foll. by ἵνα μή, Jn. xviii. 36. **3.** fig. *to contend, struggle, with difficulties and dangers* antagonistic to the gospel: Col. i. 29; 1 Tim. iv. 10 (L T Tr txt. WH txt.; for Rec. ὀνειδιζόμεθα). ; ἀγωνίζομαι ἀγῶνα (often used by the Greeks also, esp. the Attic), 1 Tim. vi. 12; 2 Tim. iv. 7. **4.** *to endeavor with strenuous zeal, strive*, to obtain something ; foll. by an inf., Lk. xiii. 24 ; ὑπέρ τινος ἐν ταῖς

προσευχαῖς, ἵνα, Col. iv. 12. [COMP.: ἀντ-, ἐπ-, κατ-, συν-αγωνίζομαι.]*

Ἀδάμ, indecl. prop. name (but in Joseph. Ἄδαμος, -ου), Ἀδάμ (i. e. acc. to Philo, de leg. alleg. i. 29, Opp. i. p. 62 ed. Mang., γήϊνος ; acc. to Euseb. Prep. Ev. vii. 8 γηγενής ; acc. to Joseph. antt. 1, 1, 2 πυρρός, with which Gesenius agrees, see his Thesaur. i. p. 25) ; **1.** *Adam*, the first man and the parent of the whole human race : Lk. iii. 38; Ro. v. 14 ; 1 Co. xv. 22, 45 ; 1 Tim. ii. 13 sq.; Jude 14. In accordance with the Rabbinic distinction between the former Adam (אָדָם הָרִאשׁוֹן), the first man, the author of ' all our woe,' and the latter Adam (אָדָם הָאַחֲרוֹן), the Messiah, the redeemer, in 1 Co. xv. 45 Jesus Christ is called ὁ ἔσχατος Ἀδάμ (see ἔσχατος, 1) and contrasted with ὁ πρῶτος ἄνθρωπος ; Ro. v. 14 ὁ μέλλων sc. Ἀδάμ. [**2.** one of the ancestors of Jesus: Lk. iii. 33 WH mrg. (cf. Ἀδμείν).]*

ἀδάπανος, -ον, (δαπάνη), *without expense, requiring no outlay* : 1 Co. ix. 18 (ἵνα ἀδάπανον θήσω τὸ εὐαγγέλιον ' that I may make Christian instruction gratuitous ').*

Ἀδδί or Ἀδδεί T Tr WH [see *WH.* App. p. 155, and s. v. ει, ι], ὁ, the indecl. prop. name of one of the ancestors of Christ: Lk. iii. 28.*

ἀδελφή, -ῆς, ἡ, (see ἀδελφός), [fr. Aeschyl. down], *sister* ; **1.** a *full, own sister* (i. e. by birth) : Mt. xix. 29; Lk. x. 39 sq.; Jn. xi. 1, 3, 5; xix. 25 ; Ro. xvi. 15, etc.; respecting the sisters of Christ, mentioned in Mt. xiii. 56; Mk. vi. 3, see ἀδελφός, 1. **2.** *one connected by the tie of the Christian religion* : 1 Co. vii. 15; ix. 5 ; Philem. 2 L T Tr WH; Jas. ii. 15; with a subj. gen., a Christian woman especially dear to one, Ro. xvi. 1.

ἀδελφός, -οῦ, ὁ, (fr. α copulative and δελφύς, *from the same womb*; cf. ἀγάστωρ), [fr. Hom. down]; **1.** a *brother* (whether born of the same two parents, or only of the same father or the same mother) : Mt. i. 2; iv. 18, and often. That ' the brethren of Jesus,' Mt. xii. 46, 47 [but WH only in mrg.]; xiii. 55 sq.; Mk. vi. 3 (in the last two passages also *sisters*); Lk. viii. 19 sq.; Jn. ii. 12; vii. 3; Acts i. 14; Gal. i. 19; 1 Co. ix. 5, are neither sons of Joseph by a wife married before Mary (which is the account in the Apocryphal Gospels [cf. *Thilo*, Cod. Apocr. N. T. i. 362 sq.]), nor cousins, the children of Alphæus or Cleophas [i. e. Clopas] and Mary a sister of the mother of Jesus (the current opinion among the doctors of the church since Jerome and Augustine [cf. Bp. Lghtft. Com. on Gal., diss. ii.]), according to that use of language by which ἀδελφός like the Hebr. אָח denotes any blood-relation or kinsman (Gen. xiv. 16; 1 S. xx. 29; 2 K. x. 13; 1 Chr. xxiii. 2 ., etc.), but own brothers, born after Jesus, is clear principally from Mt. i. 25 [only in R G]; Lk. ii. 7 — where, had Mary borne no other children after Jesus, instead of υἱὸν πρωτότοκον, the expression υἱὸν μονογενῆ would have been used, as well as from Acts i. 14, cf. Jn. vii. 5, where the Lord's brethren are distinguished from the apostles. See further on this point under Ἰάκωβος, 3. [Cf. B. D. s. v. Brother; *Andrews*, Life of our Lord, pp. 104–116; Bib. Sacr. for 1864, pp. 855–869; for 1869 pp. 745–758; *Laurent*, N. T. Studien pp. 153–193; *Mc-Clellan*, note on Mt. xiii. 55.] **2.** according to a Hebr. use of אָח (Ex. ii. 11 ; iv. 18, etc.), hardly to be met with in prof. auth., *having the same national ancestor, belonging to the same people, countryman* ; so the Jews (as the σπέρμα Ἀβραάμ, υἱοὶ Ἰσραήλ, cf. Acts xiii. 26 ; [in Deut. xv. 3 opp. to ὁ ἀλλότριος, cf. xvii. 15 ; xv. 12 ; Philo de septen. § 9 init.]) are called ἀδελφοί : Mt. v. 47 ; Acts iii. 22 (Deut. xviii. 15) ; vii. 23 ; xxii. 5 ; xxviii. 15, 21; Ro. ix. 3 ; in address, Acts ii. 29 ; iii. 17 ; xxiii. 1 ; Heb. vii. 5. **3.** just as in Lev. xix. 17 the word אָח is used interchangeably with רֵעַ (but, as vss. 16, 18 show, in speaking of *Israelites*), so in the sayings of Christ, Mt. v. 22, 24 ; vii. 3 sqq., ἀδελφός is used for ὁ πλησίον to denote (as appears from Lk. x. 29 sqq.) *any fellow-man*, — as having one and the same father with others, viz. God (Heb. ii. 11), and as descended from the same first ancestor (Acts xvii. 26) ; cf. Epict. diss. 1, 13, 3. **4.** *a fellow-believer, united to another by the bond of affection* ; so most frequently of Christians, constituting as it were but a single family : Mt. xxiii. 8 ; Jn. xxi. 23 ; Acts vi. 3 [Lchm. om.] ; ix. 30 ; xi. 1 ; Gal. i. 2 ; 1 Co. v. 11 ; Phil. i. 14, etc. ; in courteous address, Ro. i. 13 ; vii. 1 ; 1 Co. i. 10 ; 1 Jn. ii. 7 Rec., and often elsewhere ; yet in the phraseology of John it has reference to the new life unto which men are begotten again by the efficiency of a common father, even God : 1 Jn. ii. 9 sqq. ; iii. 10, 14, etc., cf. v. 1. **5.** *an associate in employment* or *office* : 1 Co. i. 1 ; 2 Co. i. 1 ; ii. 13 (12) ; Eph. vi. 21 ; Col. i. 1. **6.** *brethren of Christ* is used of, **a.** his brothers by blood ; see 1 above. **b.** all men : Mt. xxv. 40 [Lchm. br.] ; Heb. ii. 11 sq. [al. refer these exx. to d.] **c.** apostles : Mt. xxviii. 10 : Jn. xx. 17. **d.** Christians, as those who are destined to be exalted to the same heavenly δόξα (q. v III. 4 b.) which he enjoys : Ro. viii. 29.

ἀδελφότης, -ητος, ἡ, *brotherhood* ; the abstract for the concrete, *a band of brothers* i. e. of Christians, *Christian brethren* : 1 Pet. ii. 17 ; v. 9. (1 Macc. xii. 10, 17, the connection of allied nations ; 4 Macc. ix. 23 ; x. 3, the connection of brothers ; Dio. Chrys. ii. 137 [ed. Reiske] ; often in eccl. writ.) *

ἄ-δηλος, -ον, (δῆλος), *not manifest* : Lk. xi. 44 ; *indistinct, uncertain, obscure* : φωνή, 1 Co. xiv. 8. (In Grk. auth. fr. Hes. down.) [Cf. δῆλος, fin. ; Schmidt ch. 130.] *

ἀδηλότης, -ητος, ἡ, *uncertainty* : 1 Tim. vi. 17 πλούτου ἀδηλότητι equiv. to πλούτῳ ἀδήλῳ, cf. W. § 34, 3 a. [Polyb., Dion. Hal., Philo.] *

ἀδήλως, adv., *uncertainly* : 1 Co. ix. 26 οὕτω τρέχω, ὡς οὐκ ἀδήλως i. e. not uncertain whither ; cf. Mey. ad loc. [(Thuc., al.)] *

ἀδημονέω, -ῶ ; (fr. the unused ἀδήμων, and this fr. α priv. and δῆμος ; accordingly uncomfortable, as *not at home*, cf. Germ. *unheimisch*, *unheimlich* ; cf. Bttm. Lexil. ii. 136 [Fishlake's trans. p. 29 sq. But Lob. (Pathol. Proleg. p. 238, cf. p. 160) et al. connect it with ἀδήμων, ἀδῆσαι ; see Bp. Lghtft. on Phil. ii. 26]) ; *to be troubled, distressed* : Mt. xxvi. 37 ; Mk. xiv. 33 ; Phil. ii. 26.

(Xen. Hell. 4, 4, 3 ἀδημονῆσαι τὰς ψυχάς, and often in prof. auth.) *

Ἅιδης, ᾅδης, -ου, ὁ, (for the older Ἀΐδης, which Hom. uses, and this fr. α priv. and ἰδεῖν, *not to be seen*, [cf. *Lob.* Path. Element. ii. 6 sq.]) ; in the classics **1.** a prop. name, *Hades, Pluto*, the god of the lower regions ; so in Hom. always. **2.** an appellative, *Orcus, the nether world, the realm of the dead* [cf. Theocr. idyll. 2, 159 schol. τὴν τοῦ ᾅδου κρούει πύλην· τοῦτ᾽ ἔστιν ἀποθανεῖται]. In the Sept. the Hebr. שְׁאוֹל is almost always rendered by this word (once by θάνατος, 2 S. xxii. 6) ; it denotes, therefore, in bibl. Grk. *Orcus, the infernal regions*, a dark (Job x. 21) and dismal place (but cf. γέεννα and παράδεισος) in the very depths of the earth (Job xi. 8 ; Is. lvii. 9 ; Am. ix. 2, etc. ; see ἄβυσσος), the common receptacle of disembodied spirits : Lk. xvi. 23 ; εἰς ᾅδου sc. δόμον, Acts ii. 27, 31, acc. to a very common ellipsis, cf. W. 592 (550) [B. 171 (149)] ; (but L T Tr WH in vs. 27 and T WH in both verses read εἰς ᾅδην ; so Sept. Ps. xv. (xvi.) 10) ; πύλαι ᾅδου, Mt. xvi. 18 (πυλωροὶ ᾅδου, Job xxxviii. 17 ; see πύλη) ; κλεῖς τοῦ ᾅδου, Rev. i. 18 ; Hades as a power is personified, 1 Co. xv. 55 (where L T Tr WH read θάνατε for R G ᾅδη [cf. Acts ii. 24 Tr mrg.]) ; Rev. vi. 8 ; xx. 13 sq. Metaph. ἕως ᾅδου [καταβαίνειν or] καταβιβάζεσθαι to [go or] be thrust down into the depth of misery and disgrace : Mt. xi. 23 [here L Tr WH καταβαίνειν] ; Lk. x. 15 [here Tr mrg. WH txt. καταβαίνειν]. [See esp. *Boettcher*, De Inferis, s. v. Ἅιδης in Grk. index. On the existence and locality of Hades cf. Greswell on the Parables, App. ch. x. vol. v. pt. ii. pp. 261–406 ; on the doctrinal significance of the word see the BB.DD. and E. R. Craven in Lange on Rev. pp. 364–377.] *

ἀ-διά-κριτος, -ον, (διακρίνω to distinguish) ; **1.** *undistinguished* and *undistinguishable* : φωνή, Polyb. 15, 12, 9 ; λόγος, Lcian. Jup. Trag. 25 ; for בֹּהוּ, Gen. i. 2 Symm. **2.** *without dubiousness, ambiguity*, or *uncertainty* (see διακρίνω, Pass. and Mid. 3 [al. *without variance*, cf. διακρίνω, 2]) : ἡ ἄνωθεν σοφία, Jas. iii. 17 (Ignat. ad Eph. 3, 2 Ἰησοῦς Χριστὸς τὸ ἀδιάκριτον ἡμῶν ζῆν [yet al. take the word here i. q. *inseparable*, cf. Zahn in Patr. Apost. Opp., ed. Gebh., Harn. and Zahn, fasc. ii. p. 7 ; see also in general Zahn, Ignatius, p. 429 note[1] ; Bp. Lghtft. on Ignat. l. c. ; *Soph.* Lex. s. v. Used from Hippocr. down.]). *

ἀδιάλειπτος, -ον, (διαλείπω to intermit, leave off), *unintermitted, unceasing* : Ro. ix. 2 ; 2 Tim. i. 3. [Tim. Locr. 98 e.] *

ἀδιαλείπτως, adv., *without intermission, incessantly, assiduously* : Ro. i. 9 ; 1 Th. i. 2 (3) ; ii. 13 ; v. 17. [Polyb., Diod., Strabo ; 1 Macc. xii. 11.] *

ἀ-δια-φθορία, -ας, ἡ, (fr. ἀδιάφθορος incorrupt, incorruptible ; and this from ἀδιαφθείρω), *incorruptibility, soundness, integrity* : of mind, ἐν τῇ διδασκαλίᾳ, Tit. ii. 7 (L T Tr WH ἀφθορίαν). Not found in the classics.*

ἀδικέω, -ῶ ; [fut. ἀδικήσω ;] 1 aor. ἠδίκησα ; Pass. [pres. ἀδικοῦμαι ; 1 aor. ἠδικήθην ; literally *to be ἄδικος*. **1.** absolutely ; **a.** *to act unjustly* or *wickedly, to sin* : Rev. xxii. 11 ; Col. iii. 25. **b.** *to be a criminal*, to have violated the laws in some way : Acts xxv. 11, (often so in Grk. writ. [cf. W. § 40, 2 c.]). **c.** *to do wrong*: 1 Co. vi. 8; 2 Co. vii. 12. **d.** *to do hurt*: Rev. ix. 19. **2.** transitively; **a.** τί, *to do some wrong, sin in some respect*: Col. iii. 25 (ὃ ἠδίκησε 'the wrong which he hath done'). **b.** τινά, *to wrong some one, act wickedly towards him*: Acts vii. 26 sq. (by blows); Mt. xx. 13 (by fraud); 2 Co. vii. 2; pass. ἀδικεῖσθαι to be wronged, 2 Co. vii. 12; Acts vii. 24; mid. ἀδικοῦμαι to suffer one's self to be wronged, take wrong [W. § 38, 3; cf. *Riddell*, Platonic Idioms, § 87 sq.]: 1 Co. vi. 7; τινὰ οὐδέν [B. § 131, 10; W. 227 (213)], Acts xxv. 10; Gal. iv. 12; τινά τι, Philem. 18; [ἀδικούμενοι μισθὸν ἀδικίας (R. V. *suffering wrong as the hire of wrong-doing*), 2 Pet. ii. 13 WH Tr mrg.]. **c.** τινά, *to hurt, damage, harm* (in this sense by Greeks of every period): Lk. x. 19; Rev. vi. 6; vii. 2 sq.; ix. 4, 10; xi. 5; pass. οὐ μὴ ἀδικηθῇ ἐκ τοῦ θανάτου shall suffer no violence from death, Rev. ii. 11.*

92   **ἀδίκημα**, -τος, τό, (ἀδικέω), [fr. Hdt. on], *a misdeed* [τὸ ἄδικον . . . ὅταν πραχθῇ, ἀδίκημά ἐστιν, Aristot. Eth. Nic. 5, 7]: Acts xviii. 14; xxiv. 20; Rev. xviii. 5.*

93   **ἀδικία**, -ας, ή, (ἄδικος), [fr. Hdt. down]; **1.** *injustice*, of a judge: Lk. xviii. 6; Ro. ix. 14. **2.** *unrighteousness of heart and life*; **a.** univ.: Mt. xxiii. 25 Grsb.; Acts viii. 23 (see σύνδεσμος); Ro. i. 18, 29; ii. 8; vi. 13; 2 Tim. ii. 19; opp. to ἡ ἀλήθεια, 1 Co. xiii. 6; 2 Th. ii. 12; opp. to ἡ δικαιοσύνη, Ro. iii. 5; Heb. i. 9 Tdf.; owing to the context, the *guilt* of unrighteousness, 1 Jn. i. 9; ἀπάτη τῆς ἀδικίας deceit which unrighteousness uses, 2 Th. ii. 10; μισθὸς ἀδικίας reward (i. e. penalty) due to unrighteousness, 2 Pet. ii. 13 [see ἀδικέω, 2 b. fin.]. **b.** spec., unrighteousness by which others are deceived: Jn. vii. 18 (opp. to ἀληθής); μαμωνᾶς τῆς ἀδικίας deceitful riches, Lk. xvi. 9 (cf. ἀπάτη τοῦ πλούτου, Mt. xiii. 22; others think 'riches wrongly acquired'; [others, riches apt to be used unrighteously; cf. vs. 8 and Mey. ad loc.]); κόσμος τῆς ἀδικίας, a phrase having reference to sins of the tongue, Jas. iii. 6 (cf. κόσμος, 8); *treachery*, Lk. xvi. 8 (οἰκονόμος τῆς ἀδικίας, [al. take it generally, 'acting unrighteously']). **3.** *a deed violating law and justice, act of unrighteousness*: πᾶσα ἀδικία ἁμαρτία ἐστί, 1 Jn. v. 17; ἐργάται τῆς ἀδικίας, Lk. xiii. 27; αἱ ἀδικίαι iniquities, misdeeds, Heb. viii. 12 (fr. Sept. Jer. xxxviii. (xxxi.) 34; cf. Dan. iv. 20 (24)); μισθὸς ἀδικίας reward obtained by wrong-doing, Acts i. 18; 2 Pet. ii. 15; spec., the wrong of depriving another of what is his, 2 Co. xii. 13 (where a favor is ironically called ἀδικία).*

94   **ἄδικος**, -ον, (δίκη), [fr. Hes. down]; descriptive of *one who violates* or *has violated justice*; **1.** *unjust*, (of God as judge): Ro. iii. 5; Heb. vi. 10. **2.** of one who breaks God's laws, *unrighteous, sinful*, (see ἀδικία, 2): [1 Co. vi. 9]; opp. to δίκαιος, Mt. v. 45; Acts xxiv. 15; 1 Pet. iii. 18; opp. to εὐσεβής, 2 Pet. ii. 9; in this sense acc. to Jewish speech the Gentiles are called ἄδικοι, 1 Co. vi. 1 (see ἁμαρτωλός, b. β.). **3.** spec., of one who deals fraudulently with others, Lk. xviii. 11; who is false to a trust, Lk. xvi. 10 (opp. to πιστός);

deceitful, μαμωνᾶς, ibid. vs. 11 (for other interpretations see ἀδικία, 2 b.).*

ἀδίκως, adv., *unjustly, undeservedly, without fault*: πάσχειν, 1 Pet. ii. 19 [A. V. *wrongfully*.   (Fr. Hdt. on.)] *   **95**

'Αδμείν, ὁ, *Admin*, the indecl. prop. name of one of   **see 689** the ancestors of Jesus: Lk. iii. 33, where Tdf. reads τοῦ 'Αδμείν τοῦ 'Αρνεί for Rec. τοῦ 'Αράμ (q. v.), [and WH txt. substitute the same reading for τοῦ 'Αμιναδάβ τοῦ 'Αράμ of R G, but in their mrg. 'Αδάμ (q. v. 2) for 'Αδμείν; on the spelling of the word see their App. p. 155].*

ἀ-δόκιμος, -ον, (δόκιμος), [fr. Eur. down], *not standing*   **96** *the test, not approved*; properly of metals and coin, ἀργύριον, Is. i. 22; Prov. xxv. 4; νόμισμα, Plat. legg. v. p. 742 a., al.; hence, *which does not prove itself to be such as it ought*: γῆ, of sterile soil, Heb. vi. 8; in a moral sense [A. V. *reprobate*], 1 Co. ix. 27; 2 Co. xiii. 5–7; νοῦς, Ro. i. 28; περὶ τὴν πίστιν, 2 Tim. iii. 8; hence, *unfit for something*: πρὸς πᾶν ἔργον ἀγαθὸν ἀδ. Tit. i. 16.*

ἄ-δολος, -ον, (δόλος), [fr. Pind. down], *guileless*; of   **97** things, *unadulterated, pure*: of milk, 1 Pet. ii. 2. [Cf. *Trench* § lvi.]*

'Αδραμυττηνός, -ή, -όν, adj., *of Adramyttium* ('Αδραμύτ-   **98** τιον, 'Αδραμύττειον, 'Αδραμμύττειον [also 'Ατραμυτ-, etc., cf. *Poppo*, Thuc. pt. i. vol. ii. p. 441 sq.; *Wetst.* on Acts, as below; WH 'Αδραμυντηνός, cf. their Intr. § 408 and App. p. 160]), a sea-port of Mysia: Acts xxvii. 2, [modern *Edremit, Ydramit, Adramiti*, etc.; cf. Mc. and S. s. v. Adramyttium].*

'Αδρίας [WH 'Αδρ.], -ου, ὁ, *Adrias, the Adriatic Sea*   **99** i. e., in a wide sense, the sea between Greece and Italy: Acts xxvii. 27, [cf. B. D. s. v. Adria; Dict. of Grk. & Rom. Geog. s. v. Adriaticum Mare].*

ἀδρότης [Rec.ˢᵗ ἀδρ.], -ητος, ή, or better (cf. *Bttm.* Ausf.   **100** Spr. ii. 417) ἀδροτής, -ῆτος, [on the accent cf. *Ebeling*, Lex. Hom. s. v.; *Chandler* §§ 634, 635], (fr. ἀδρός thick, stout, full-grown, strong, rich [2 K. x. 6, 11, etc.]; in Grk. writ. it follows the signif. of the adj. ἀδρός; once in the N. T.: 2 Co. viii. 20, *bountiful collection, great liberality*, [R. V. *bounty*]. (ἀδροσύνη, of an abundant harvest, Hes. ἔργ. 471.) *

ἀδυνατέω, -ῶ: fut. ἀδυνατήσω; (ἀδύνατος); **a.** *not to*   **101** *have strength, to be weak*; always so of persons in classic Grk. **b.** *a thing ἀδυνατεῖ, cannot be done, is impossible*; so only in the Sept. and N. T.: οὐκ ἀδυνατήσει παρὰ τῷ θεῷ [τοῦ θεοῦ L mrg. T Tr WH] πᾶν ῥῆμα, Lk. i. 37 (Sept. Gen. xviii. 14) [al. retain the act. sense here: *from God no word shall be without power*, see παρά, I. b. cf. *Field*, Otium Norv. pars iii. ad loc.]; οὐδὲν ἀδυνατήσει ὑμῖν, Mt. xvii. 20, (Job xlii. 2).*

ἀ-δύνατος, -ον, (δύναμαι), [fr. Hdt. down]; **1.** *without*   **102** *strength, impotent*: τοῖς ποσί, Acts xiv. 8; fig. of Christians whose faith is not yet quite firm, Ro. xv. 1 (opp. to δυνατός). **2.** *impossible* (in contrast with δυνατόν): παρά τινι, for (with) any one, Mt. xix. 26; Mk. x. 27; Lk. xviii. 27; τὸ ἀδύν. τοῦ νόμου 'what the law could not do' (this God effected by, etc.; [al. take τὸ ἀδύν. here as nom. absol., cf. B. 381 (326); W. 574 (534); Meyer or Gifford ad loc.]), Ro. viii. 3 ; foll. by acc. with inf., Heb. vi. 4, 18 ; x. 4 ; by inf., Heb. xi. 6.*

103 ᾄδω (ἀείδω) ; common in Grk. of every period ; in Sept. for שׁיר ; *to sing, chant* ; **1.** intrans. : τινί, to the praise of any one (Judith xvi. 1 (2)), Eph. v. 19 ; Col. iii. 16, (in both passages of the lyrical emotion of a devout and grateful soul). **2.** trans. : ᾠδήν, Rev. v. 9 ; xiv. 3 ; xv. 3.*

104 ἀεί, [see αἰών], adv., [fr. Hom. down], *always* ; **1.** *perpetually, incessantly* : Acts vii. 51 ; 2 Co. iv. 11 ; vi. 10 ; Tit. i. 12 ; Heb. iii. 10. **2.** *invariably, at any and every time* when according to the circumstances something is or ought to be done again : Mk. xv. 8 [T WH om.] (at every feast) ; 1 Pet. iii. 15 ; 2 Pet. i. 12.*

105 ἀετός, -οῦ, ὁ, (like Lat. *avis*, fr. ἄημι on account of its wind-like flight [cf. Curtius § 596]), [fr. Hom. down], in Sept. for נשׁר, *an eagle* : Rev. iv. 7 ; viii. 13 (Rec. ἀγγέλου) ; xii. 14. In Mt. xxiv. 28 ; Lk. xvii. 37 (as in Job xxxix. 30 ; Prov. xxx. 17) it is better, since eagles are said seldom or never to go in quest of carrion, to understand with many interpreters either the *vultur percnopterus*, which resembles an eagle (Plin. h. n. 10, 3 "quarti generis — viz. aquilarum — est percnopterus "), or the *vultur barbatus*. Cf. *Win.* RWB. s. v. Adler ; [*Tristram*, Nat. Hist. of the Bible, p. 172 sqq.]. The meaning of the proverb [cf. exx. in Wetst. on Mt. l. c.] quoted in both passages is, ʼwhere there are sinners (cf. πτῶμα), there judgments from heaven will not be wantingʼ.*

106 ἄζυμος, -ον, (ζύμη), Hebr. מַצָּה, *unfermented, free from leaven* ; properly : ἄρτοι, Ex. xxix. 2 ; Joseph. antt. 3, 6, 6 ; hence the neut. plur. τὰ ἄζυμα, מַצּוֹת, unleavened loaves ; ἡ ἑορτὴ τῶν ἀζύμων, חַג הַפְּצּוֹת the (paschal) festival at which for seven days the Israelites were accustomed to eat unleavened bread in commemoration of their exit from Egypt (Ex. xxiii. 15 ; Lev. xxiii. 6), Lk. xxii. 1 ; ἡ πρώτη (sc. ἡμέρα) τῶν ἀζ. Mt. xxvi. 17 ; Mk. xiv. 12 ; Lk. xxii. 7 ; αἱ ἡμέραι τῶν ἀζ. Acts xii. 3 ; xx. 6 ; the paschal festival itself is called τὰ ἄζυμα, Mk. xiv. 1, [cf. 1 Esdr. i. 10, 19 ; W. 176 (166) ; B. 23 (21)]. Figuratively : Christians, if such as they ought to be, are called ἄζυμοι i. e. devoid of the leaven of iniquity, free from faults, 1 Co. v. 7 ; and are admonished ἑορτάζειν ἐν ἀζύμοις εἰλικρινείας, to keep festival with the unleavened bread of sincerity and truth, vs. 8. (The word occurs twice in prof. auth., viz. Athen. 3, 74 (ἄρτον) ἄζυμος, Plat. Tim. p. 74 d. ἄζυμος σάρξ flesh not yet quite formed, [add Galen de alim. fac. 1, 2].)*

107 Ἀζώρ, Azor, the indecl. prop. name of one of the ancestors of Christ : Mt. i. 13 sq.*

108 Ἄζωτος, -ου, ἡ, אַשְׁדּוֹד, Azotus, *Ashdod*, one of the five chief cities of the Philistines, lying between Ashkelon and Jamnia [i. e. Jabneel] and near the Mediterranean : Acts viii. 40 ; at present a petty village, *Esdûd*. A succinct history of the city is given by *Gesenius*, Thesaur. iii. p. 1366 ; *Raumer*, Palästina, p. 174 ; [Alex.ʼs Kitto or Mc. and S. s. v. Ashdod].*

see 2237 & 2189 ἀηδία, -ας, ἡ, (fr. ἀηδής, and this fr. α priv. and ἦδος pleasure, delight), [fr. Lysip. down] ; **1.** *unpleasant-*

ness, annoyance. **2.** *dislike, hatred* : ἐν ἀηδίᾳ, cod. Cantabr. in Lk. xxiii. 12 for Rec. ἐν ἔχθρᾳ.*

109 ἀήρ, ἀέρος, ὁ, (ἄημι, ἄω, [cf. ἄνεμος, init.]), *the air* (particularly the lower and denser, as distinguished from the higher and rarer ὁ αἰθήρ, cf. Hom. Il. 14, 288), *the atmospheric region* : Acts xxii. 23 ; 1 Th. iv. 17 ; Rev. ix. 2 ; xvi. 17 ; ὁ ἄρχων τῆς ἐξουσίας τοῦ ἀέρος in Eph. ii. 2 signifies ʼ the ruler of the powers (spirits, see ἐξουσία 4 c. ββ.) in the air,ʼ i. e. the devil, the prince of the demons that according to Jewish opinion fill the realm of air (cf. Mey. ad loc. ; [B. D. Am. ed. s. v. Air ; Stuart in Bib. Sacr. for 1843, p. 139 sq.]). Sometimes indeed, ἀήρ denotes a hazy, obscure atmosphere (Hom. Il. 17, 644 ; 3, 381 ; 5, 356, etc. ; Polyb. 18, 3, 7), but is nowhere quite equiv. to σκότος, — the sense which many injudiciously assign it in Eph. l. c. ἀέρα δέρειν (cf. *verberat ictibus auras*, Verg. Aen. 5, 377, of pugilists who miss their aim) i. e. to contend in vain, 1 Co. ix. 26 ; εἰς ἀέρα λαλεῖν (*verba ventis profundere*, Lucr. 4, 929 (932)) ʼ to speak into the air ʼ i. e. without effect, used of those who speak what is not understood by the hearers, 1 Co. xiv. 9.*

110 ἀθανασία, -ας, ἡ, (ἀθάνατος), *immortality* : 1 Co. xv. 53 sq. ; 1 Tim. vi. 16 where God is described as ὁ μόνος ἔχων ἀθανασίαν, because he possesses it essentially — ʼ ἐκ τῆς οἰκείας οὐσίας, οὐκ ἐκ θελήματος ἄλλου, καθάπερ οἱ λοιποὶ πάντες ἀθάνατοι ʼ Justin, quaest. et resp. ad orthod. 61 p. 84 ed. Otto. (In Grk. writ. fr. Plato down.)*

111 ἀ-θέμιτος, -ον, a later form for the ancient and preferable ἀθέμιστος, (θέμιτος, θεμιστός, θεμίζω, θέμις law, right), *contrary to law and justice, prohibited by law, illicit, criminal* : 1 Pet. iv. 3 [here A. V. *abominable*] ; ἀθέμιτόν ἐστί τινι with inf., Acts x. 28.*

112 ἄ-θεος, -ον, (θεός), [fr. Pind. down], *without God, knowing and worshipping no God*, in which sense Ael. v. h. 2, 31 declares ὅτι μηδεὶς τῶν βαρβάρων ἄθεος ; in classic auth. generally *slighting the gods, impious, repudiating the gods recognized by the state*, in which sense certain Greek philosophers, the Jews (Joseph. c. Ap. 2, 14, 4), and subsequently Christians were called ἄθεοι by the heathen (Justin, apol. 1, 13, etc.). In Eph. ii. 12 of one who neither knows nor worships the true God ; so of the heathen (cf. 1 Th. iv. 5 ; Gal. iv. 8) ; Clem. Alex. protr. ii. 23 p. 19 Pott. ἀθέους . . . οἳ τὸν ὄντως ὄντα θεὸν ἠγνοήκασι, Philo, leg. ad Gai. § 25 αἰγυπτιακὴ ἀθεότης, Hos. iv. 15 Symm. οἶκος ἀθεΐας a house in which idols are worshipped, Ignat. ad Trall. 10 ἄθεοι τουτέστιν ἄπιστοι (of the Docetae) ; [al. understand Eph. l. c. passively *deserted of God*, Vulg. *sine Deo* ; on the various meanings of the word see Mey. (or Ellic.)].*

113 ἄ-θεσμος, -ον, (θεσμός), *lawless*, [A. V. *wicked*] ; of one who breaks through the restraints of law and gratifies his lusts : 2 Pet. ii. 7 ; iii. 17. [Sept., Diod., Philo, Joseph., Plut.]*

114 ἀθετέω, -ῶ ; fut. ἀθετήσω ; 1 aor. ἠθέτησα ; a word met with first (yet very often) in Sept. and Polyb. ; **a.** properly, *to render ἄθετον* ; *do away with* θετόν τι i. e. *something laid down, prescribed, established* : διαθήκην, Gal.

iii. 15, (1 Macc. xi. 36 ; 2 Macc. xiii. 25, etc.) ; acc. to the context, ʼto act towards anything as though it were annulledʼ; hence to deprive a law of force by opinions or acts opposed to it, to transgress it, Mk. vii. 9 ; Heb. x. 28, (Ezek. xxii. 26) ; πίστιν, to break oneʼs promise or engagement, 1 Tim. v. 12 ; (Polyb. 8, 2, 5 ; 11, 29, 3, al.; Diod. excerpt. [i. e. de virt. et vit.] p. 562, 67). Hence b. to thwart the efficacy of anything, nullify, make void, frustrate : τὴν βουλὴν τοῦ θεοῦ, Lk. vii. 30 (they rendered inefficacious the saving purpose of God); τὴν σύνεσιν to render prudent plans of no effect, 1 Co. i. 19 (Is. xxix. 14 [where κρύψω, yet cf. Bosʼs note]). c. to reject, refuse, slight : τὴν χάριν τοῦ θεοῦ, Gal. ii. 21 [al. refer this to b.]; of persons: Mk. vi. 26 (by breaking the promise given her) ; Lk. x. 16 ; Jn. xii. 48 ; 1 Th. iv. 8 ; Jude 8 (for which καταφρονεῖν is used in the parallel pass. 2 Pet. ii. 10). [For exx. of the use of this word see Soph. Lex. s. v.]*

115 ἀθέτησις, -εως, ἡ, (ἀθετέω, q. v.; like νουθέτησις fr. νουθετεῖν), abolition : Heb. vii. 18 ; ix. 26 ; (found occasionally in later authors, as Cicero ad Att. 6, 9 ; Diog. Laërt. 3, 39, 66 ; in the grammarians rejection ; more frequently in eccl. writ.).*

116 Ἀθῆναι, -ῶν, αἱ, (on the plur. cf. W. 176 (166)), Athens, the most celebrated city of Greece : Acts xvii. 15 sq. ; xviii. 1 ; 1 Th. iii. 1.*

117 Ἀθηναῖος, -αία, -αῖον, Athenian : Acts xvii. 21 sq.*
118 ἀθλέω, -ῶ; [1 aor. subjunc. 3 pers. sing. ἀθλήσῃ]; (ἆθλος a contest); to engage in a contest, contend in public games (e. g. Olympian, Pythian, Isthmian), with the poniard [?], gauntlet, quoit, in wrestling, running, or any other way : 2 Tim. ii. 5 ; (often in classic auth. who also use the form ἀθλεύω). [Comp.: συν-αθλέω.]*

119 ἄθλησις, -εως, ἡ, contest, combat, (freq. fr. Polyb. down); fig. ἄθλησις παθημάτων a struggle with sufferings, trials, Heb. x. 32 ; [of martyrdom, Ign. mart. 4 ; Clem. mart. 25].*

see 4867 ἀθροίζω: pf. pass. ptcp. ἠθροισμένος; (fr. ἀθρόος i. q. θρόος [a noisy crowd, noise], with a copulative [see A, a, 2]) ; to collect together, assemble; pass. to be assembled, to convene : Lk. xxiv. 33 L T Tr WH. ([Soph.,] Xen., Plat., Polyb., Plut., al.; O. T. Apocr.; sometimes in Sept. for קָבַץ.) [Comp.: ἐπ-, συν-αθροίζω.]*

120 ἀθυμέω, -ῶ; common among the Greeks fr. [Aeschyl.,] Thuc. down; to be ἄθυμος (θυμός spirit, courage), to be disheartened, dispirited, broken in spirit : Col. iii. 21. (Sept. 1 S. i. 6 sq., etc.; Judith vii. 22 ; 1 Macc. iv. 27.)*

121 ἄθωος [R G Tr], more correctly ἀθῷος (L WH and T [but not in his Sept. There is want of agreement among both the ancient gramm. and modern scholars ; cf. Steph. Thes. i. col. 875 c.; Lob. Path. Element. i. 440 sq. (cf. ii. 377) ; see I, ι]), -ον, (θωή [i. e. θωιή, cf. Etym. Mag. p. 26, 24] punishment), [fr. Plat. down], unpunished, innocent: αἷμα ἀθῷον, Mt. xxvii. 4 [Tr mrg. WH txt. δίκαιον], (Deut. xxvii. 25 ; 1 S. xix. 5, etc.; 1 Macc. i. 37 ; 2 Macc. i. 8) ; ἀπό τινος, after the Hebr. מִן נָקִי ([Num. xxxii. 22 ; cf. Gen. xxiv. 41 ; 2 S. iii. 28 ; W. 197 (185) ; B. 158 (138)]), ʼinnocent (and therefore far)

from,ʼ innocent of, Matt. xxvii. 24 (the guilt of the murder of this innocent man cannot be laid upon me) ; ἀπὸ τῆς ἁμαρτίας, Clem. Rom. 1 Cor. 59, 2 [cf. Num. v. 31]. The Greeks say ἀθῷός τινος [both in the sense of free from and unpunished for].*

αἴγειος [WH -γιος ; see their App. p. 154, and I, ι], -εία, -ειον, (αἴξ, gen. -γός goat, male or female), of a goat, **122** (cf. καμήλειος, ἵππειος, ὕειος, προβάτειος, etc.) : Heb. xi. 37. [From Hom. down.]*

αἰγιαλός, -οῦ, ὁ, the shore of the sea, beach, [fr. Hom. **123** down]: Mt. xiii. 2, 48 ; Jn. xxi. 4 ; Acts xxi. 5 ; xxvii. 39, 40. (Many derive the word from ἄγνυμι and ἅλς, as though equiv. to ἀκτή, the place where the sea breaks ; others fr. αἶγες billows and ἅλς [Curtius § 140 ; Vaniček p. 83] ; others fr. ἀΐσσω and ἅλς [Schenkl, L. and S., s. v.], the place where the sea rushes forth, bounds forward.)*

Αἰγύπτιος, -α, -ον, a gentile adjective, Egyptian : Acts **124** vii. 22, 24, 28 ; xxi. 38 ; Heb. xi. 29.*

Αἴγυπτος, -ου, ἡ, [always without the art., B. 87 (76) ; **125** W. § 18, 5 a.], the proper name of a well-known country, Egypt : Mt. ii. 13 sq. ; Acts ii. 10 ; Heb. iii. 16, etc.; more fully γῆ Αἴγυπτος, Acts vii. 36 [not L WH Tr txt.], 40 ; xiii. 17 ; Heb. viii. 9 ; Jude 5, (Ex. v. 12 ; vi. 26, etc. ; 1 Macc. i. 19 ; Bar. i. 19 sq., etc.) ; ἡ γῆ Αἰγύπτου, Acts vii. 11 ; ἐν Αἰγύπτου sc. γῆ, Heb. xi. 26 Lchm., but cf. Bleek ad loc.; B. 171 (149) ; [W. 384 (359)]. In Rev. xi. 8 Αἴγ. is figuratively used for Jerusalem i. e. for the Jewish nation viewed as persecuting Christ and his followers, and soʼto be likened to the Egyptians in their ancient hostility to the true God and their endeavors to crush his people.

ἀΐδιος, -ον, (for ἀείδιος fr. ἀεί), eternal, everlasting : **126** (Sap. vii. 26) Ro. i. 20 ; Jude 6. (Hom. hymn. 29, 3 ; Hes. scut. 310, and fr. Thuc. down in prose ; [freq. in Philo, e. g. de profug. § 18 (ζωὴ ἀΐδιος), § 31 ; de opif. mund. § 2, § 61 ; de cherub. § 1, § 2, § 3 ; de post. Cain. § 11 fin. Syn. see αἰώνιος].)*

αἰδώς, (-όος) -οῦς, ἡ ; fr. Hom. down ; a sense of shame, **127** modesty : 1 Tim. ii. 9 ; reverence, Heb. xii. 28 (λατρεύειν θεῷ μετὰ αἰδοῦς καὶ εὐλαβείας, but L T Tr WH εὐλαβείας καὶ δέους). [Syn. αἰδώς, αἰσχύνη: Ammonius distinguishes the words as follows, αἰδὼς καὶ αἰσχύνη διαφέρει, ὅτι ἡ μὲν αἰδώς ἐστιν ἐντροπὴ πρὸς ἕκαστον, ὡς σεβομένως τις ἔχει· αἰσχύνη δ᾽ ἐφ᾽ οἷς ἕκαστος ἁμαρτὼν αἰσχύνεται, ὡς μὴ δέον τι πράξας. καὶ αἰδεῖται μέν τις τὸν πατέρα· αἰσχύνεται δὲ ὃς μεθύσκεται, etc., etc.; accordingly αἰδ. is prominently objective in its reference, having regard to others; while αἰσχ. is subjective, making reference to oneʼs self and oneʼs actions. Cf. Schmidt ch. 140. It is often said that ʼ αἰδ. precedes and prevents the shameful act, αἰσχ. reflects upon its consequences in the shame it brings with itʼ (Cope, Aristot. rhet. 5, 6, 1). αἰδ. is the nobler word, αἰσχ. the stronger ; while " αἰδ. would always restrain a good man from an unworthy act, αἰσχ. would sometimes restrain a bad one." Trench §§ xix. xx.]*

Αἰθίοψ, -οπος, ὁ, (αἴθω to burn, and ὤψ [ὄψ] the face ; **128** swarthy), Ethiopian (Hebr. כּוּשִׁי) : Acts viii. 27, here the reference is to upper Ethiopia, called Habesh or Abyssinia, a country of Africa adjoining Egypt and including the island Meroë; [see Dillmann in Schenkel i. 285 sqq.; Alex.'s Kitto or Mc. and S. s. v. Ethiopia. Cf. Bib. Sacr. for 1866, p. 515].*

αἷμα, -τος, τό, *blood*, whether of men or of animals; **1.** **a.** simply and generally : Jn. xix. 34 ; Rev. viii. 7 sq. ; xi. 6 ; xvi. 3 sq. 6 [b] (on which passages cf. Ex. vii. 20 sqq.) ; xix. 13 ; ῥύσις αἵματος, Mk. v. 25, [(πηγὴ αἵμ. 29)] ; Lk. viii. 43 sq. ; θρόμβοι αἵματος, Lk. xxii. 44 [L br. WH reject the pass.]. So also in passages where the eating of blood (and of bloody flesh) is forbidden, Acts xv. 20, 29 ; xxi. 25 ; cf. Lev. iii. 17 ; vii. 16 (26) ; xvii. 10 ; see Knobel on Lev. vii. 26 sq. ; [Kalisch on Lev., Preliminary Essay § 1] ; *Rückert*, Abendmahl, p. 94. **b.** As it was anciently believed that the blood is the seat of the life (Lev. xvii. 11 ; [cf. *Delitzsch*, Bibl. Psychol. pp. 238–247 (Eng. trans. p. 281 sqq.)]), the phrase σὰρξ κ. αἷμα (בָּשָׂר וָדָם, a common phrase in Rabbinical writers), or in inverse order αἷμα κ. σάρξ, denotes man's living body compounded of flesh and blood, 1 Co. xv. 50 ; Heb. ii. 14, and so hints at the contrast between man and God (or even the more exalted creatures, Eph. vi. 12) as to suggest his feebleness, Eph. vi. 12 (Sir. xiv. 18), which is conspicuous as respects the knowledge of divine things, Gal. i. 16 ; Mt. xvi. 17. **c.** Since the first germs of animal life are thought to be in the blood (Sap. vii. 2 ; Eustath. ad Il. 6, 211 (ii. 104, 2) τὸ δὲ αἵματος ἀντὶ τοῦ σπέρματός φασιν οἱ σοφοί, ὡς τοῦ σπέρματος ὕλην τὸ αἷμα ἔχοντος), the word serves to denote generation and origin (in the classics also) : Jn. i. 13 (on the plur. cf. W. 177 (166)) ; Acts xvii. 26 [R G]. **d.** It is used of those things which by their redness resemble blood : αἱ. σταφυλῆς the juice of the grape [' the blood of grapes,' Gen. xlix. 11 ; Deut. xxxii. 14], Sir. xxxix. 26 ; l. 15 ; 1 Macc. vi. 34, etc. ; Achill. Tat. ii. 2 ; reference to this is made in Rev. xiv. 18–20. εἰς αἷμα, of the moon, Acts ii. 20 (Joel ii. 31 (iii. 4)), i. q. ὡς αἷμα Rev. vi. 12. **2.** *blood shed* or *to be shed by violence* (very often also in the classics) ; **a.** : Lk. xiii. 1 (the meaning is, whom Pilate had ordered to be massacred while they were sacrificing, so that their blood mingled with the blood [yet cf. W. 623 (579)] of the victims) ; αἱ. ἀθῷον [or δίκαιον Tr mrg. WH txt.] the blood of an innocent [or righteous] man viz. to be shed, Mt. xxvii. 4 ; ἐκχεῖν and ἐκχύνειν αἷμα, שָׁפַךְ דָּם, Gen. ix. 6 ; Is. lix. 7, etc.) *to shed blood, slay*, Mt. xxiii. 35 ; Lk. xi. 50 ; Acts xxii. 20 ; Ro. iii. 15 ; Rev. xvi. 6 [a] [here Tdf. αἵματα] ; hence αἷμα is used for the *bloody death* itself : Mt. xxiii. 30, 35 ; xxvii. 24 ; Lk. xi. 51 ; Acts [ii. 19, yet cf. 1 d. above;] xx. 26 ; Rev. xvii. 6 ; μέχρις αἵματος *unto blood* i. e. so as to undergo a bloody death, Heb. xii. 4, (τὸν αἴτιον τῆς . . . μέχρις αἵματος στάσεως, Heliod. 7, 8) ; τιμὴ αἵματος ' price of blood ' i. e. price received for murder, Mt. xxvii. 6 ; ἀγρὸς αἵματος field bought with the price of blood, Mt. xxvii. 8, i. q. χωρίον αἵματος, Acts i. 19 — unless in this latter passage we prefer the explanation, which agrees better with the

context, ' the field dyed with the blood of Judas ' ; *the guilt and punishment of bloodshed*, in the following Hebraistic expressions : ἐν αὐτῇ αἵματα (Rec. αἷμα [so L Tr WH]) εὑρέθη i. e. it was discovered that she was guilty of murders, Rev. xviii. 24 (cf. πόλις αἱμάτων, Ezek. xxiv. 6) ; τὸ αἷμα αὐτοῦ ἐφ' ἡμᾶς (sc. ἐλθέτω) let the penalty of the bloodshed fall on us, Mt. xxvii. 25 ; τὸ αἷμα ὑμῶν ἐπὶ τὴν κεφαλὴν ὑμῶν (sc. ἐλθέτω) let the guilt of your destruction be reckoned to your own account, Acts xviii. 6 (cf. 2 S. i. 16 ; Josh. ii. 19, etc.) ; ἐπάγειν τὸ αἷμά τινος ἐπί τινα to cause the punishment of a murder to be visited on any one, Acts v. 28 ; ἐκζητεῖν τὸ αἷμά τινος ἀπό τινος (בָּקַשׁ דָּם פ׳ מִיַד פ׳, 2 S. iv. 11 ; Ezek. iii. 18, 20 ; xxxiii. 8), to exact of any one the penalty for another's death, Lk. xi. 50 ; the same idea is expressed by ἐκδικεῖν τὸ αἷμά τινος, Rev. vi. 10 ; xix. 2. **b.** It is used specially *of the blood of sacrificial victims* having a purifying or expiating power (Lev. xvii. 11) : Heb. ix. 7, 12 sq. 18–22, 25 ; x. 4 ; xi. 28 ; xiii. 11. **c.** Frequent mention is made in the N. T. of *the blood of Christ* (αἷμα τοῦ Χριστοῦ, 1 Co. x. 16 ; τοῦ κυρίου, xi. 27 ; τοῦ ἀρνίου, Rev. vii. 14 ; xii. 11, cf. xix. 13) *shed on the cross* (αἱ. τοῦ σταυροῦ, Col. i. 20) for the salvation of many, Mt. xxvi. 28 ; Mk. xiv. 24, cf. Lk. xxii. 20 ; the pledge of redemption, Eph. i. 7 (ἀπολύτρωσις διὰ τοῦ αἱ. αὐτοῦ ; so too in Col. i. 14 Rec.) ; 1 Pet. i. 19 (see ἀγοράζω, 2 b.) ; having expiatory efficacy, Ro. iii. 25 ; Heb. ix. 12 ; by which believers are purified and are cleansed from the guilt of sin, Heb. ix. 14 ; xii. 24 ; [xiii. 12] ; 1 Jn. i. 7 (cf. 1 Jn. v. 6, 8) ; Rev. i. 5 ; vii. 14 ; 1 Pet. i. 2 ; are rendered acceptable to God, Ro. v. 9, and find access into the heavenly sanctuary, Heb. x. 19 ; by which the Gentiles are brought to God and the blessings of his kingdom, Eph. ii. 13, and in general all rational beings on earth and in heaven are reconciled to God, Col. i. 20; with which Christ purchased for himself the church, Acts xx. 28, and gathered it for God, Rev. v. 9. Moreover, since Christ's dying blood served to establish new religious institutions and a new relationship between men and God, it is likened also to a *federative* or *covenant sacrifice* : τὸ αἷμα τῆς διαθήκης the blood by the shedding of which the covenant should be ratified, Mt. xxvi. 28 ; Mk. xiv. 24, or has been ratified, Heb. x. 29 ; xiii. 20 (cf. ix. 20) ; add, 1 Co. xi. 25 ; Lk. xxii. 20 [WH reject this pass.] (in both which the meaning is, ' this cup containing wine, an emblem of blood, is rendered by the shedding of my blood an emblem of the new covenant '), 1 Co. xi. 27 ; (cf. Cic. pro Sestio 10, 24 foedus sanguine meo ictum sanciri, Liv. 23, 8 sanguine Hannibalis sanciam Romanum foedus). πίνειν τὸ αἷμα αὐτοῦ (i. e. of Christ), to appropriate the saving results of Christ's death, Jn. vi. 53 sq. 56. [*Westcott*, Epp. of Jn. p. 34 sq.]*

αἱματεκχυσία, -ας, ἡ, (αἷμα and ἐκχύνω), *shedding of blood* : Heb. ix. 22. Several times also in eccl. writ.*

αἱμορροέω, -ῶ ; *to be* αἱμόρροος (αἷμα and ῥέω), *to suffer from a flow of blood* : Mt. ix. 20. (Sept. Lev. xv. 33, where it means *menstruous*, and in medical writ.) *

132   **Αἰνέας, -ου, ὁ,** *Ae'neas,* the prop. name of the paralytic cured by Peter: Acts ix. 33 sq.*

133   **αἴνεσις, -εως, ἡ,** (αἰνέω), *praise:* θυσία αἰνέσεως (זֶבַח הַתּוֹדָה, Lev. vii. 13), Heb. xiii. 15 *a thank-offering,* [A. V. ' sacrifice of praise '], presented to God for some benefit received; see θυσία, b. (αἴνεσις often occurs in Sept., but not in prof. auth.) *

134   **αἰνέω, -ῶ**; (found in prof. auth. of every age [" only twice in good Attic prose " (where ἐπαιν. παραιν. etc. take its place), Veitch], but esp. freq. in Sept. and the Apocr. of the O. T.; from αἶνος); *to praise, extol:* τὸν θεόν, Lk. ii. 13, 20; xix. 37; xxiv. 53 [WH om. Tr txt. br.]; Acts ii. 47; iii. 8 sq.; Ro. xv. 11; with dat. of person, τῷ θεῷ, *to sing praises in honor of God,* Rev. xix. 5 L T Tr WH, as Sept. in 2 Chr. vii. 3 (for הוֹדוֹת לְ), 1 Chr. xvi. 36; xxiii. 5; Jer. xx. 13 etc. (for הַלֵּל לְ); [W. § 31, 1 f.; B. 176 (153). COMP. ἐπ-, παρ-αινέω.].*

135   **αἴνιγμα, -τος, τό,** (common fr. [Pind. frag. 165 (190),] Aeschyl. down; fr. αἰνίσσομαι or αἰνίττομαί τι to express something obscurely, [fr. αἶνος, q. v.]); **1.** *an obscure saying, an enigma,* Hebr. חִידָה (Judg. xiv. 13, Sept. πρόβλημα). **2.** *an obscure thing:* 1 Co. xiii. 12, where ἐν αἰνίγματι is not equiv. to αἰνιγματικῶς i. e. ἀμαυρῶς *obscurely,* but denotes the object in the discerning of which we are engaged, as βλέπειν ἔν τινι, Mt. vi. 4; cf. De Wette ad loc.; the apostle has in mind Num. xii. 8 Sept.: ἐν εἴδει καὶ οὐ δι' αἰνιγμάτων. [Al. take ἐν locally, of the sphere in which we are looking; al. refer the pass. to 1. and take ἐν instrumentally.] *

136   **αἶνος, -ου, ὁ,** (often used by the Grk. poets); **1.** *a saying, proverb.* **2.** *praise, laudatory discourse:* Mt. xxi. 16 (Ps. viii. 3); Lk. xviii. 43.*

137   **Αἰνών, ἡ,** (either a strengthened form of עַיִן and equiv. to עֵינָן, or a Chaldaic plur. i. q. עֲיָנִין springs; [al. al.]), *Aenon,* indecl. prop. name, either of a place, or of a fountain, not far from Salim: Jn. iii. 23, [thought to be Wâdy Fâr'ah, running from Mt. Ebal to the Jordan; see *Conder* in " Pal. Explor. Fund " for July 1874, p.191 sq.; Tent Work in Palestine, i. 91 sq.; esp. *Stevens* in Journ. of Exeget. Soc., Dec. 1883, pp. 128–141. Cf. B. D. Am. ed.].*

139   **αἵρεσις, -εως, ἡ**; **1.** (fr. αἱρέω), *act of taking, capture:* τῆς πόλεως, the storming of a city; in prof. auth. **2.** (fr. αἱρέομαι), *choosing, choice,* very often in prof. writ.: Sept. Lev. xxii. 18; 1 Macc. viii. 30. **3.** *that which is chosen,* a chosen course of thought and action; hence one's *chosen opinion, tenet;* acc. to the context, an opinion varying from the true exposition of the Christian faith (*heresy*): 2 Pet. ii. 1 (cf. De Wette ad loc.), and in eccl. writ. [cf. *Soph.* Lex. s. v.]. **4.** a body of men separating themselves from others and following their own tenets [*a sect* or *party*]: as the Sadducees, Acts v. 17; the Pharisees, Acts v. 5; xxvi. 5; the Christians, Acts xxiv. 5, 14 (in both instances with a suggestion of reproach); xxviii. 22, (in Diog. Laërt. 1 (13,) 18 sq., al., used of the schools of philosophy). **5.** *dissensions* arising from diversity of opinions and aims: Gal. v. 20; 1 Co. xi. 19. [Cf. Mey. ll. cc.; B.D.

Am. ed. s. v. Sects; *Burton,* Bampt. Lect. for 1829; *Campbell,* Diss. on the Gospels, diss. ix. pt. iv.] *

140   **αἱρετίζω** : 1 aor. ἡρέτισα [Treg. ἡρ., see I, ι]; (fr. αἱρετός, see αἱρέω); *to choose:* Mt. xii. 18. (Often in Sept. in O. T. Apocr. and in eccl. writ.; the mid. is found in Ctes. Pers. § 9 [cf. Hdt. ed. Schweig. vi. 2, p. 354]. Cf. *Sturz,* De dial. Maced. etc. p. 144.) *

141   **αἱρετικός, -ή, -όν,** [see αἱρέω]; **1.** *fitted* or *able to take* or *choose* a thing; rare in prof. auth. **2.** *schismatic, factious,* a follower of false doctrine: Tit. iii. 10.*

138   **αἱρέω, -ῶ** : [thought by some to be akin to ἄγρα, ἀγρέω, χείρ, Eng. *grip,* etc.; cf. *Bttm.* Lexil. i. 131 — but see Curtius § 117]; *to take.* In the N. T. in the mid. only: fut. αἱρήσομαι; 2 aor. εἱλόμην, but G L T Tr WH εἱλάμην, 2 Th. ii. 13, cf. [*Tdf.* Proleg. p. 123; *WH.* App. p. 165;] W. § 13, 1 a.; B. 40 (35), see ἀπέρχομαι init.; [ptcp. ἑλόμενος, Heb. xi. 25]; *to take for one's self, to choose, prefer*: Phil. i. 22; 2 Th. ii. 13; μᾶλλον foll. by inf. with ἤ (common in Attic), Heb. xi. 25. [COMP.: ἀν-, ἀφ-, δι-, ἐξ-, καθ-, περι-, προ-αιρέω.] *

142   **αἴρω** (contr. fr. poet. ἀείρω); fut. ἀρῶ; 1 aor. ἦρα, inf. ἆραι, impv ἆρον; pf. ἦρκα (Col. ii. 14); Pass., [pres. αἴρομαι]; pf. ἦρμαι (Jn. xx. 1); 1 aor. ἤρθην; (on the rejection of iota subscr. in these tenses see *Bttm.* Ausf. Spr. i. pp. 413, 439; [W. 47 (46)]); 1 fut. ἀρθήσομαι; [fr. Hom. down]; in the Sept. generally i. q. נָשָׂא; *to lift up, raise.* **1.** *to raise up;* **a.** *to raise from the ground, take up*: stones, Jn. viii. 59; serpents, Mk. xvi. 18; a dead body, Acts xx. 9. **b.** *to raise upwards, elevate, lift up*: the hand, Rev. x. 5; the eyes, Jn. xi. 41; the voice, i. e. speak in a loud tone, cry out, Lk. xvii. 13; Acts iv. 24, (also in prof. writ.); τὴν ψυχήν, to raise the mind, i. q. excite, affect strongly (with a sense of fear, hope, joy, grief, etc.); in Jn. x. 24 to hold the mind in suspense between doubt and hope, cf. Lücke [or Meyer] ad loc. **c.** *to draw up*: a fish, Mt. xvii. 27 (ἀνασπᾶν, Hab. i. 15); σκάφην, Acts xxvii. 17; anchors from the bottom of the sea, Acts xxvii. 13, where supply τὰς ἀγκύρας; cf. Kuinoel ad loc.; [W. 594 (552); B. 146 (127)]. **2.** *to take upon one's self and carry what has been raised, to bear*: τινὰ ἐπὶ χειρῶν, Mt. iv. 6; Lk. iv. 11, (Ps. xc. (xci.) 12); a sick man, Mk. ii. 3; ζυγόν, Mt. xi. 29 (Lam. iii. 27); a bed, Mt. ix. 6; Mk. ii. 9, 11 sq.; Lk. v. 24 sq.; Jn. v. 8–12; τὸν σταυρόν, Mt. [x. 38 Lchm. mrg.]; xvi. 24; xxvii. 32; Lk. ix. 23; Mk. viii. 34; x. 21 [in R Lbr.]; xv. 21; [λίθον,] Rev. xviii. 21; *to carry with one,* [A. V. *take*]: Mk. vi. 8; Lk. ix. 3; xxii. 36. Both of these ideas are expressed in class. Grk. by the mid. αἴρεσθαι. **3.** *to bear away what has been raised, carry off;* **a.** *to move from its place*: Mt. xxi. 21; Mk. xi. 23, (ἄρθητι be thou taken up, removed [B. 52 (45)], sc. from thy place); Mt. xxii. 13 [Rec.]; Jn. ii. 16; xi. 39, 41; xx. 1. **b.** *to take off* or *away* what is attached to anything: Jn. xix. 31, 38 sq.; to tear away, Mt. ix. 16; Mk. ii. 21; to rend away, cut off, Jn. xv. 2. **c.** *to remove*: 1 Co. v. 2 (cast out from the church, where ἀρθῇ should be read for Rec. ἐξαρθῇ); tropically: faults, Eph. iv. 31; τὴν ἁμαρτίαν, Jn. i. 29, [36 Lchm. in br.], to remove the guilt and punishment of sin by expiation, or to cause that sin be neither imputed nor punished (αἴρειν ἁμάρτημα, 1 S. xv. 25 ; ἀνόμημα, 1 S. xxv. 28, i. e. to grant pardon for an offence) ; but in 1 Jn. iii. 5 τὰς ἁμαρτίας ἡμῶν αἴρειν is to cause our sins to cease, i. e. that we no longer sin, while we enter into fellowship with Christ, who is free from sin, and abide in that fellowship, cf. vs. 6. **d.** *to carry off, carry away with one*: Mt. xiv. 12, 20 ; xv. 37 ; xx. 14 ; xxiv. 17 sq. ; Mk. vi. 29, 43 ; viii. 8, 19 sq. ; xiii. 15 sq. ; Lk. ix. 17 ; xvii. 31 ; Jn. xx. 2, 13, 15 ; Acts xx. 9. **e.** *to appropriate* what is taken : Lk. xix. 21 sq. ; Mk. xv. 24. **f.** *to take away from another what is his* or what is committed to him, *to take by force* : Lk. vi. 30 ; xi. 52 ; τὶ ἀπό with gen. of pers., Mt. xiii. 12 ; xxi. 43 ; xxv. 28 ; Lk. viii. 12, 18 ; xix. 24, 26 ; [Mt. xxv. 29] ; Mk. iv. (15), 25 ; Jn. x. 18 ; xvi. 22 ; perhaps also with the mere gen. of the pers. from whom anything is taken, Lk. vi. 29 ; xi. 22 ; Jn. xi. 48, unless one prefer to regard these as possessive gen. **g.** *to take and apply to any use*: Acts xxi. 11 ; 1 Co. vi. 15. **h.** *to take from among the living*, either by a natural death, Jn. xvii. 15 (ἐκ τοῦ κόσμου take away from intercourse with the world), or by violence, Mt. xxiv. 39 ; Lk. xxiii. 18 ; Jn. xix. 15 ; Acts xxi. 36 ; with the addition of ἀπὸ τῆς γῆς, Acts xxii. 22 ; αἴρεται ἀπὸ τῆς γῆς ἡ ζωὴ αὐτοῦ, of a bloody death inflicted upon one, Acts viii. 33 (Is. liii. 8). **i.** of things ; *to take out of the way, destroy* : χειρόγραφον, Col. ii. 14 ; *cause to cease* : τὴν κρίσιν, Acts viii. 33 (Is. liii. 8). [COMP. : ἀπ-, ἐξ-, ἐπ-, μετ-, συν-, ὑπερ-αίρω.]*

143   **αἰσθάνομαι** : 2 aor. ᾐσθόμην ; [fr. Aeschyl. down] ; depon. mid. *to perceive* ; **1.** by the bodily senses ; **2.** with the mind ; *to understand* : Lk. ix. 45.*

144   **αἴσθησις, -εως, ἡ,** (αἰσθάνομαι), [fr. Eurip. down], *perception*, not only by the senses but also by the intellect ; *cognition, discernment* ; (in the Sept., Prov. i. 22 ; ii. 10, etc., i. q. דַּעַת) : Phil. i. 9, of m o r al discernment, the understanding of e t h i c al matters, as is plain from what is added in vs. 10.*

145   **αἰσθητήριον, -ου, τό,** *an organ of perception, external sense,* [Hippoc.] ; Plat. Ax. 366 a. ; Aristot. polit. 4, 3, 9, al. ; *faculty of the m i nd* for perceiving, understanding, judging, Heb. v. 14, (Jer. iv. 19 αἰσθητ. τῆς καρδίας, 4 Macc. ii. 22 [com. text] τὰ ἔνδον αἰσθητήρια).*

146   **αἰσχροκερδής, -ές,** (αἰσχρός and κέρδος ; cf. αἰσχροπαθής in Philo [de merc. meretr. § 4]), *eager for base gain,* [*greedy of filthy lucre*] : 1 Tim. iii. 3 Rec., 8 ; Tit. i. 7. (Hdt. 1, 187 ; Xen., Plat., al. ; [cf. turpilucricupidus, Plaut. Trin. 1, 2, 63].) *

147   **αἰσχροκερδῶς,** adv., *from eagerness for base gain,* [*for filthy lucre*] : 1 Pet. v. 2, cf. Tit. i. 11. Not found elsewhere.*

148   **αἰσχρολογία, -ας, ἡ,** (fr. αἰσχρολόγος, and this fr. αἰσχρός and λέγω), *foul speaking* (Tertull. turpiloquium), *low and obscene speech,* [R. V. *shameful speaking*] : Col. iii. 8. (Xen., Aristot., Polyb.) [Cf. Bp. Lghtft. ad loc.; Trench § xxxiv.]*

αἰσχρός, -ά, -όν, (fr. αἶσχος baseness, disgrace), *base, dishonorable* : 1 Co. xi. 6 ; xiv. 35 ; Eph. v. 12 ; Tit. i. 11.* **149 & 150**

αἰσχρότης, -ητος, ἡ, *baseness, dishonor* : Eph. v. 4 [A. V. *filthiness*]. (Plat. Gorg. 525 a.)* **151**

αἰσχύνη, -ης, ἡ, (αἶσχος [cf. αἰσχρός]) ; **1.** subjectively, *the confusion of one who is ashamed of anything, sense of shame* : μετ᾽ αἰσχύνης suffused with shame, Lk. xiv. 9 ; τὰ κρυπτὰ τῆς αἰσχύνης those things which shame conceals, opp. to φανέρωσις τῆς ἀληθείας, 2 Co. iv. 2 (evil arts of which one ought to be ashamed). **2.** objectively, *ignominy* : visited on one by the wicked, Heb. xii. 2 ; which ought to arise from guilt, Phil. iii. 19 (opp. to δόξα). **3.** *a thing to be ashamed of* : ἡ αἰσχύνη τῆς γυμνότητος (gen. of appos.) nakedness to be ashamed of, Rev. iii. 18, cf. xvi. 15 ; plur. [cf. W. 176 (166)] αἱ αἰσχῦναι basenesses, disgraces, shameful deeds, Jude 13. [(Aeschyl., Hdt., al.) SYN. see αἰδώς, fin.]* **152**

αἰσχύνω : (αἶσχος [cf. αἰσχρός]) ; **1.** *to disfigure* : πρόσωπον, Hom. Il. 18, 24, and many others. **2.** *to dishonor* : Sept. Prov. xxix. 15. **3.** *to suffuse with shame, make ashamed* : Sir. xiii. 7. In the N. T. only pass., αἰσχύνομαι ; fut. αἰσχυνθήσομαι ; 1 aor. ᾐσχύνθην ; *to be suffused with shame, be made ashamed, be ashamed* : 2 Co. x. 8 ; Phil. i. 20 ; 1 Pet. iv. 16 ; μὴ αἰσχυνθῶμεν ἀπ᾽ αὐτοῦ that we may not in shame shrink from him, 1 Jn. ii. 28 (Sir. xxi. 22 αἰσχυνθήσεται ἀπὸ προσώπου [Is. i. 29 ; Jer. xii. 13 ; cf. B. § 147, 2]) ; foll. by inf. (on which see W. 346 (325)), Lk. xvi. 3. [COMP. : ἐπ-(-μαι), κατ-αισχύνω.]* **153**

αἰτέω, -ῶ ; fut. αἰτήσω ; 1 aor. ᾔτησα ; pf. ᾔτηκα ; Mid., pres. αἰτοῦμαι ; impf. ᾐτούμην ; fut. αἰτήσομαι ; 1 aor. ᾐτησάμην ; [fr. Hom. down] ; *to ask* ; mid. *to ask for one's self, request for one's self* ; absol. : Jas. i. 6 ; Mt. vii. 7 ; mid., Jas. iv. 3 ; Jn. xvi. 26 ; Mk. xv. 8 ; αἰτεῖσθαί τι, Jn. xv. 7 ; Mt. xiv. 7 ; Mk. vi. 24 ; x. 38 ; xi. 24 ; xv. 43 ; 1 Jn. v. 14 sq. ; Lk. xxiii. 52 ; Acts xxv. 3, 15, etc. ; αἰτεῖν with acc. of the pers. to whom the request is made : Mt. v. 42 ; vi. 8 ; Lk. vi. 30 ; αἰτεῖσθαι with acc. of the pers. asked for — whether to be released, Mt. xxvii. 20 ; Mk. xv. 6 [here T WH Tr mrg. παραιτ. q. v.] ; Lk. xxiii. 25 ; or bestowed as a gift, Acts xiii. 21 ; αἰτεῖν τι ἀπό τινος, Mt. xx. 20 L Tr txt. WH txt. ; [Lk. xii. 20 Tr WH] ; 1 Jn. v. 15 L T Tr WH ; (so αἰτεῖσθαι in Plut. Galb. 20) [cf. B. 149 (130)] ; τὶ παρά τινος, Acts iii. 2 ; Mt. xx. 20 R G T Tr mrg. WH mrg. ; Jas. i. 5 ; 1 Jn. v. 15 R G ; foll. by the inf., Jn. iv. 9 ; mid., Acts ix. 2 ; [αἰτεῖν τι ἐν τ. ὀνόματι Χριστοῦ, Jn. xiv. 13 ; xvi. 24 (see ὄνομα, 2 e.) ; τὶ ἐν τῇ προσευχῇ, Mt. xxi. 22] ; αἰτεῖν τινά τι, Mt. vii. 9 ; Lk. xi. 11 ; Mk. vi. 22 ; Jn. [xiv. 14 T but L WH Tr mrg. br.] ; xvi. 23 ; ὑπέρ τινος foll. by ἵνα, Col. i. 9 [cf. B. 237 (204)] ; αἰτεῖσθαι with the acc. and inf., Lk. xxiii. 23 ; Acts iii. 14 ; with inf. only, Acts vii. 46 (ᾐτήσατο εὑρεῖν he asked that he himself might find ; others wrongly translate ᾐτήσατο desired) ; Eph. iii. 13. With the idea of *demanding* prominent : αἰτεῖν τι, Lk. i. 63 ; 1 Co. i. 22 ; τινά τι, Lk. xii. 48 ; 1 Pet. iii. 15. **154**

[The constructions of this word in the Greek Bible, the

Apost. Fathers, etc., are exhibited in detail by Prof. Ezra Abbot in the No. Am. Rev. for Jan. 1872, p. 182 sq. He there shows also (in opposition to Trench, § xl., and others) that it is *not* " the constant word for the seeking of the inferior from the superior," and so differing from ἐρωτάω, which has been assumed to imply ' a certain equality or familiarity between the parties '; that the distinction between the words does not turn upon the relative dignity of the person asking and the person asked; but that αἰτέω signifies to ask for something to be g i v e n not d o n e, giving prominence to the t h i n g asked for rather than the p e r s o n, and hence is rarely used in exhortation. 'Ερωτάω, on the other hand, is to request a p e r s o n to do (rarely to give) something; referring more directly to the person, it is naturally used in exhortation, etc. The views of Trench are also rejected by Cremer, 4te Aufl. s. v. The latter distinguishes αἰτέω from similar words as follows: " αἰτέω denotes the request of the w i l l, ἐπιθυμέω that of the s e n s i b i l i t i e s, δέομαι the asking of n e e d, while ἐρωτάω marks the f o r m of the request, as does εὔχεσθαι also, which in classic Greek is the proper expression for a request directed to the gods and embodying itself in prayer." 'Ερωτάω, αἰτέω and δέομαι are also compared briefly by *Green, Critical Notes, etc.* (on Jn. xiv. 13, 16), who concludes of ἐρωτάω " it cannot serve to indicate directly any peculiar position, absolute or relative, of the agent. The use of the word may, therefore, be viewed as having relation to the manner and cast of the request, namely, when carrying a certain freedom of aim and bearing; a thing inseparable from the act of direct interrogation "; cf. further Schmidt ch. 7. COMP.: ἀπ-, ἐξ-, ἐπ-, παρ-(-μαι), προσ-αιτέω.]

155   **αἴτημα**, -τος, τό, (αἰτέω), [fr. Plato down], *what is or has been asked for*: Lk. xxiii. 24; plur. [A. V. *requests*], Phil. iv. 6 [cf. Ellic. ad loc.]; things asked for, 1 Jn. v. 15. [See the preceding word, and Trench § li.]*

156   **αἰτία**, -ας, ἡ;   1. *cause, reason*: Acts x. 21; xxii. 24; xxviii. 20; κατὰ πᾶσαν αἰτίαν *for every cause*, Mt. xix. 3; δι' ἢν αἰτίαν *for which cause, wherefore*, Lk. viii. 47; 2 Tim. i. 6, 12; Tit. i. 13; Heb. ii. 11; cf. Grimm on 2 Macc. iv. 28.   2. cause for which one is worthy of punishment; *crime* of which one is accused: Mt. xxvii. 37; Mk. xv. 26; Jn. xviii. 38; xix. 4, [6; Acts xxiii. 28]; αἰτία θανάτου [A. V. *cause of death*] crime deserving the punishment of death, Acts xiii. 28; xxviii. 18.   3. *charge of crime, accusation*: Acts xxv. 18, 27. (All these signif. in prof. writ. also; [but L. and S. now make signif. 3 the primary].) In Mt. xix. 10 the words εἰ οὔτως ἐστὶν ἡ αἰτία τοῦ ἀνθρώπου μετὰ τῆς γυναικός find a

157; see 157b next column   simple explanation in a Latinism (causa i. q. res: *si ita res se habet*, etc.) *if the case of the man with his wife is so*.*

αἰτίαμα, -τος, τό, see αἰτίωμα.

157α   [αἰτιάομαι, -ῶμαι: to accuse, bring a charge against; ἠτιασάμεθα is a various reading in Ro. iii. 9 for the προῃτιασάμεθα of the printed texts. (Prov. xix. 3; Sir. xxix. 5; freq. in prof. writ.) SYN. see κατηγορέω.*]

158 & 159   **αἴτιος**, -α, -ον, *that in which the cause of anything resides, causative, causing*. Hence   1. ὁ αἴτιος *the author*: σωτηρίας, Heb. v. 9 (the same phrase is freq. in prof. writ.; of the opp. αἱ. τῆς ἀπωλείας in Bel and the Dragon vs. 41; τῶν κακῶν, 2 Macc. xiii. 4; Lcian. Tim. 36 ed. Lips.; τῶν ἀγαθῶν, Isocr. ad Phil. 49 p. 106 a.; cf. Bleek on Heb. vol. ii. 2, p. 94 sq.).   2. τὸ

αἴτιον i. q. ἡ αἰτία;   a. *cause*: Acts xix. 40 [cf. B. 400 (342) n.].   b. *crime, offence*: Lk. xxiii. 4, 14, 22. (αἴτιος culprit.) [See αἰτία, 3.]*

157b; see 157α   **αἰτίωμα**, -τος, τό, (αἰτιάομαι); in Acts xxv. 7 the reading of the best codd. adopted by G L T Tr WH for Rec. αἰτίαμα: *accusation, charge of guilt*. (A form not found in other writ.; [yet Mey. notes αἰτίωσις for αἰτίασις, Eustath. p. 1422, 21; see B. 73; WH. App. p. 166].)*

160   **αἰφνίδιος**, -ον, (αἴφνης, ἀφανής, ἄφνω q. v.), *unexpected, sudden, unforeseen*: Lk. xxi. 34 [here WH ἐφνίδ., see their Intr. § 404 and App. p. 151]; 1 Th. v. 3. (Sap. xvii. 14; 2 Macc. xiv. 17; 3 Macc. iii. 24; Aeschyl., Thuc. 2, 61 τὸ αἰφνίδιον καὶ ἀπροσδόκητον, Polyb., Joseph., Plut., Dion. Hal., al.) *

161   **αἰχμαλωσία**, -ας, ἡ, (αἰχμάλωτος, q. v.), *captivity*: Rev. xiii. 10; abstr. for concr. i. q. αἰχμάλωτοι (cf. ἀδελφότης above), Eph. iv. 8 (fr. Ps. lxvii. (lxviii.) 19, [cf. B. 148 (129); W. 225 (211)]); also εἴ τις αἰχμαλωσίαν συνάγει (acc. to the common but doubtless corrupt text), Rev. xiii. 10 (as in Num. xxxi. 12, etc.). [Polyb., Diod., Joseph., Plut., al.]*

162   **αἰχμαλωτεύω**; 1 aor. ἠχμαλώτευσα; a later word (cf. Lob. ad Phryn. p. 442; [W. 92 (88)]); *to make captive, take captive*: 2 Tim. iii. 6 Rec.; freq. in the Sept. and O. T. Apocr.; *to lead captive*: Eph. iv. 8 (Ezek. xii. 3; [1 Esdr. vi. 15]).*

163   **αἰχμαλωτίζω**; 1 fut. pass. αἰχμαλωτισθήσομαι;   a. equiv. to αἰχμάλωτον ποιῶ, which the earlier Greeks use.   b. *to lead away captive*: foll. by εἰς with acc. of place, Lk. xxi. 24, (1 Macc. x. 33; Tob. i. 10).   c. fig. *to subjugate, bring under control*: 2 Co. x. 5 (on which passage see νόημα, 2); τινά τινι, Ro. vii. 23 [yet T Tr א etc. insert ἐν before the dat.]; *to take captive one's mind, captivate*: γυναικάρια, 2 Tim. iii. 6 [not Rec.], (Judith xvi. 9 τὸ κάλλος αὐτῆς ἠχμαλώτισε ψυχὴν αὐτοῦ). The word is used also in the Sept., Diod., Joseph., Plut., Arr., Heliod.; cf. Lob. ad Phryn. p. 442; [W. 91 (87); Ellic. on 2 Tim. l. c.].*

164   **αἰχμ-άλωτος**, -ον, (fr. αἰχμή a spear and ἁλωτός, verbal adj. fr. ἁλῶναι, prop. taken by the spear), [fr. Aeschyl. down], *captive*: Lk. iv. 18 (19).*

165   **αἰών**, -ῶνος, ὁ, (as if αἰὲν — poet. for ἀεὶ — ὤν, so teaches Aristot. de caelo 1, 11, 9, vol. i. p. 279ᵇ, 27; [so Proclus lib. iv. in Plat. Timaeo p. 241; et al.]; but more probable is the conjecture [cf. Etym. Magn. 41, 11] that αἰών is so connected with ἄημι to breathe, blow, as to denote properly *that which causes life, vital force*; cf. Harless on Eph. ii. 2). [But αἰών (= αἰϝών) is now generally connected with αἰεί, αἰεί, Skr. êvas (aivas), Lat. aevum, Goth. aivs, Germ. ewig, Eng. aye, ever; cf. Curtius § 585; Fick, Pt. i. p. 27; Vaniček p. 79; Benfey, Wurzellex. i. p. 7 sq.; Schleicher, Compend. ed. 2, p. 400; Pott, Etym. Forsch., ed. 2, ii. 2, p. 442; Ebeling, Lex. Hom. s. v.; L. and S. s. v. ἀεί; Cremer, edd. 2, 3, 4 (although in ed. 1 he agreed with Prof. Grimm); Pott and Fick, however, connect it with Skr. âyus rather than êvas, although both these forms are derived from i to go (see Pott, Schleicher, Fick, Vaniček, u. s.).)] In

Greek authors   1. *age* (Lat. *aevum*, which is αἰών with the Aeolic digamma), *a human lifetime* (in Hom., Hdt., Pind., Tragic poets), *life itself* (Hom. Il. 5, 685 μὲ καὶ λίποι αἰών etc.).   2. *an unbroken age, perpetuity of time, eternity*, (Plat. Tim. p. 37 d. 38 a.; Tim. Locr. p. 97 d. [quoted below]; Plut., al.). With this signification the Hebrew and Rabbinic idea of the word עוֹלָם (of which in the Sept. αἰών is the equiv.) combines in the bibl. and eccl. writ. Hence in the N. T. used 1. a. univ.: in the phrases εἰς τὸν αἰῶνα, לְעוֹלָם (Gen. vi. 3), *for ever*, Jn. vi. 51, 58; xiv. 16; Heb. v. 6; vi. 20, etc.; and strengthened εἰς τὸν αἰῶνα τοῦ αἰῶνος, Heb. i. 8 [fr. Ps. xliv. (xlv.) 7 Alex., cf. W. § 36, 2] (Tob. vi. 18; Ps. lxxxii. (lxxxiii.) 18, etc.); εἰς αἰῶνα, Jude 13; εἰς ἡμέραν αἰῶνος *unto the day which is eternity* (gen. of appos.), 2 Pet. iii. 18 [cf. Sir. xviii. 10 (9)]; with a negation: *never*, Jn. iv. 14 [Lchm. in br.]; viii. 51; x. 28; xi. 26; xiii. 8; 1 Co. viii. 13; or *not for ever, not always*, Jn. viii. 35; εἰς τοὺς αἰῶνας *unto the ages*, i. e. as long as time shall be (the plur. denotes the individual ages whose sum is eternity): [Lk. i. 33]; Ro. i. 25; ix. 5; xi. 36; [xvi. 27 R G Tr WH]; 2 Co. xi. 31; Heb. xiii. 8; εἰς πάντας τ. αἰῶνας, Jude 25; εἰς τοὺς αἰῶνας τῶν αἰώνων (in which expression the endless future is divided up into various periods, the shorter of which are comprehended in the longer [cf. W. § 36, 2; among the various phrases to express duration composed of this word with prep. or adjuncts, (which to the number of more than fifteen are to be found in the Sept., cf. Vaughan on Ro. i. 25), this combination of the double plural seems to be peculiar to the N. T.]): [Ro. xvi. 27 L T]; Gal. i. 5; [Phil. iv. 20]; 1 Tim. i. 17; [2 Tim. iv. 18; 1 Pet. iv. 11]; Rev. i. 6, 18; iv. 9 sq.; v. 13; vii. 12; x. 6; xi. 15; xv. 7; xix. 3; xx. 10; xxii. 5; εἰς αἰῶνας αἰώνων, Rev. xiv. 11; ὁ αἰὼν τῶν αἰώνων *the (whole) age embracing the (shorter) ages*, Eph. iii. 21 (cf. Mey. [or Ellic.] ad loc.); ἀπὸ τῶν αἰώνων *from the ages down, from eternity*, Col. i. 26; Eph. iii. 9; πρὸ τῶν αἰώνων *before time was, before the foundation of the world*, 1 Co. ii. 7; πρόθεσις τῶν αἰώνων *eternal purpose*, Eph. iii. 11.   b. in hyperbolic and popular usage: ἀπὸ τοῦ αἰῶνος (מֵעוֹלָם, Gen. vi. 4, cf. Deut. xxxii. 7) *from the most ancient time down, (within the memory of man), from of old*, Lk. i. 70; Acts iii. 21; xv. 18, (Tob. iv. 12 οἱ πατέρες ἡμῶν ἀπὸ τοῦ αἰῶνος; Longin. 34 τοὺς ἀπ᾽ αἰῶνος ῥήτορας); also ἐκ τοῦ αἰῶνος, Jn. ix. 32, (1 Esdr. ii. 19, 22 (23); Diod. iv. 83 of the temple of Venus τὴν ἐξ αἰῶνος ἀρχήν λαβόν, 17, 1 τοὺς ἐξ αἰῶνος βασιλεῖς, [excerpt. de legat. xl.] p. 632 τὴν ἐξ αἰῶνος παραδεδομένην ἐλευθερίαν).   2. by meton. of the container for the contained, οἱ αἰῶνες denotes *the worlds, the universe*, i. e. the aggregate of things contained in time, [on the plur. cf. W. 176 (166); B. 24 (21)]: Heb. i. 2; xi. 3; and (?) 1 Tim. i. 17; [Rev. xv. 3 WH txt., cf. Ps. cxliv. (cxlv.) 13; Tob. xiii. 6, cf. Sir. xxxvi. 22; Philo de plant. Noë § 12 bis; de mundo § 7; Joseph. antt. 1, 18, 7; Clem. Rom. 1 Cor. 61, 2; 35, 3 (πατὴρ τ. α.); 55, 6 (θεὸς τ. α.); Constt. Ap. 7, 34;

see Abbot in Journ. Soc. Bibl. Lit. etc. i. p. 106 n.]. So αἰών in Sap. xiii. 9; xiv. 6; xviii. 4; the same use occurs in the Talmud, Chaldee, Syriac, Arabic; cf. *Bleek*, Hebräerbr. ii. 1, p. 36 sqq.; *Gesenius*, Thesaur. ii. p. 1036; [cf. the use of οἱ αἰῶνες in the Fathers i. q. the world of mankind, e. g. Ignat. ad Eph. 19, 2].   3. As the Jews distinguished הָעוֹלָם הַזֶּה the time before the Messiah, and הָעוֹלָם הַבָּא the time after the advent of the Messiah (cf. *Riehm*, Lehrb. d. Hebräerbr. p. 204 sqq.; [Schürer § 29, 9]), so most of the N. T. writers distinguish ὁ αἰὼν οὗτος *this age* (also simply ὁ αἰών, Mt. xiii. 22; Mk. iv. 19 G L T Tr WH; ὁ ἐνεστὼς αἰών, Gal. i. 4; ὁ νῦν αἰών, 1 Tim. vi. 17; [2 Tim. iv. 10]; Tit. ii. 12), the time before the appointed return or truly Messianic advent of Christ (i. e. the παρουσία, q. v.), the period of instability, weakness, impiety, wickedness, calamity, misery, —and αἰὼν μέλλων *the future age* (also ὁ αἰὼν ἐκεῖνος, Lk. xx. 35; ὁ αἰὼν ὁ ἐρχόμενος, Lk. xviii. 30; Mk. x. 30; οἱ αἰῶνες οἱ ἐπερχόμενοι, Eph. ii. 7), i. e. the age after the return of Christ in majesty, the period of the consummate establishment of the divine kingdom and all its blessings: Mt. xii. 32; Eph. i. 21; cf. Fritzsche on Rom. vol. iii. 22 sq.   Hence the things of 'this age' are mentioned in the N. T. with censure: ὁ αἰὼν οὗτος, by meton. men controlled by the thoughts and pursuits of this present time, Ro. xii. 2, the same who are called υἱοὶ τοῦ αἰ. τούτου in Lk. xvi. 8; xx. 34; κατὰ τὸν αἰῶνα τοῦ κόσμου τούτου conformably to the age to which this (wicked) world belongs, Eph. ii. 2 [cf. Trench § lix. sub fin.]; ἀγαπᾶν τὸν νῦν αἰῶνα, 2 Tim. iv. 10 (see ἀγαπάω); ἄρχοντες τοῦ αἰ. τούτου, 1 Co. ii. 6 (see ἄρχων); ὁ θεὸς τοῦ αἰ. τούτου the devil, who rules the thoughts and deeds of the men of this age, 2 Co. iv. 4; αἱ μέριμναι τοῦ αἰῶνος the anxieties for the things of this age, Mk. iv. 19; πλούσιος ἐν τῷ νῦν αἰῶνι rich in worldly wealth, 1 Tim. vi. 17; σοφία τοῦ αἰ. τούτ. such wisdom as belongs to this age, — full of error, arrogant, hostile to the gospel, 1 Co. ii. 6; συζητητὴς τοῦ αἰ. τούτ. disputer, sophist, such as we now find him, 1 Co. i. 20; συντέλεια τοῦ αἰ. τούτ. the end, or rather consummation, of the age preceding Christ's return, with which will be connected the resurrection of the dead, the last judgment, the demolition of this world and its restoration to a more excellent condition [cf. 4 Esdr. vii. 43], Mt. xiii. 39 sq. 49; xxiv. 3; xxviii. 20; it is called συντέλεια τῶν αἰώνων in Heb. ix. 26 [so Test. xii. Patr., test. Levi 10, test. Benj. 11 (cf. Vorstman p. 133)]; τὰ τέλη τῶν αἰώνων the ends (last part) of the ages before the return of Christ, 1 Co. x. 11; δυνάμεις τοῦ μέλλοντος αἰῶνος powers which present themselves from the future or divine order of things, i. e. the Holy Spirit, Heb. vi. 5; τοῦ αἰῶνος ἐκείνου τυχεῖν to partake of the blessings of the future age, Lk. xx. 35.   Among the N. T. writers James does not use the word αἰών.

[On the word in its relation to κόσμος see Trench § lix. Its biblical sense and its relation to עוֹלָם are discussed by *Stuart*, Exeget. Essays on Words relating to Fut. Punishment, Andover, 1830 (and Presbyt. Publ. Committee, Phil.); Tayler Lewis in Lange's Com. on Eccl. pp. 44-51; *J. W. Hanson*, Aion-Aionios, (pp. 174), Chicago, 1880. See esp

E. *Abbot*, Literature of the Doctrine of a Future Life, etc., (New York, 1867), Index of subjects s. v. For its meanings in eccl. writ. see *Suicer*, Thesaur. Eccles. i. col. 140 sqq., cf. ii. col. 1609; *Huet*, Origeniana (App. to vol. iv. of De la Rue's Origen) lib. ii. c. ii. quaest. 11, § 26. Its use in Hom., Hes., Pind., Aeschyl., Soph., Eur., Aristot., Plato, Tim. Locr., is exhibited in detail by E. S. Goodwin in the Christ. Exam. for March and May, 1831, March and May, 1832. "On αἰών as *the complete period*, either of each particular life or of all existence, see Arist. cael. 1, 9, 15; on αἰών and χρόνος, cf. Philo [quis rer. div. her. § 34] i. 496, 18 sq., cf. mut. nom. § 47] i. 619, 10 sq." L. and S. ed. 6; see also Philo de alleg. leg. iii. 8; quod deus immut. § 6 fin.; de prof. § 11; de praem. et poen. § 15; and (de mund. opif. § 7) esp. *J. G. Müller*, Philo's Lehre v. d. Weltschöpfung, p. 168 (Berl. 1864). Schmidt (ch. 44) gives the distinction, for substance, as follows: both words denote the abstract idea of time and with special reference to its extent or duration; χρόνος is the general designation for time, which can be divided up into portions, each of which is in its turn a χρόνος; on the other hand, αἰών, which in the concrete and simple language of Homer (Pindar and the Tragedians) denotes the allotted lifetime, even the life, of the individual (Il. 4, 478 μινυνθάδιος δέ οἱ αἰών etc.), in Attic prose differs from χρόνος by denoting time unlimited and boundless, which is not conceived of as divisible into αἰῶνες (contrast here biblical usage and see below), but rather into χρόνοι. In philosophical speech it is without beginning also. Cf. Tim. Locr. 97 c. d. χρόνῳ δὲ τὰ μέρεα τάσδε τὰς περιόδως λέγοντι, ἃς ἐκόσμησεν ὁ θεὸς σὺν κόσμῳ· οὐ γὰρ ἦν πρὸ κόσμω ἄστρα· διόπερ οὐδ' ἐνιαυτὸς οὐδ' ὡρᾶν περίοδοι, αἷς μετρέεται ὁ γεννατὸς χρόνος οὗτος. ἐκὼν δέ ἐστι τῶ ἀγεννάτω χρόνω, ὃν αἰῶνα ποταγορεύομες· ὡς γὰρ ποτ' ἀΐδιον παράδειγμα, τὸν ἰδανικὸν κόσμον, ὅδε ὁ ὡρανὸς ἐγεννάθη, οὕτως ὡς πρὸς παράδειγμα, τὸν αἰῶνα, ὅδε ὁ χρόνος σὺν κόσμῳ ἐδαμιουργήθη — after Plato, Timaeus p. 37 d. (where see Stallbaum's note and reff.); Isocr. 8, 34 τοὺς δὲ μετ' εὐσεβείας κ. δικαιοσύνης ζῶντας (ὁρῶ) ἔν τε τοῖς παροῦσι χρόνοις ἀσφαλῶς διάγοντας καὶ περὶ τοῦ σύμπαντος αἰῶνος ἡδίους τὰς ἐλπίδας ἔχοντας. The adj. ἄχρονος independent of time, above and beyond all time, is synon. with αἰώνιος; where time (with its subdivisions and limitations) ends eternity begins: Nonnus, metaph. evang. Johan. i. 1, ἄχρονος ἦν, ἀκίχητος, ἐν ἀρρήτῳ λόγοις ἀρχῇ. Thoroughly Platonic in cast are the definitions of Gregory of Nazianzus (orat. xxxviii. 8) αἰὼν γὰρ οὔτε χρόνος οὔτε χρόνου τι μέρος· οὐδὲ γὰρ μετρητόν, ἀλλ' ὅπερ ἡμῖν ὁ χρόνος ἡλίου φορᾷ μετρούμενος, τοῦτο τοῖς ἀϊδίοις αἰών, τὸ συμπαρεκτεινόμενον τοῖς οὖσιν οἷον τι χρονικὸν κίνημα καὶ διάστημα (Suicer u. s.). So Clem. Alex. strom. i. 13, p. 756 a. ed. Migne, Ὁ γ' οὖν αἰὼν τοῦ χρόνου τὸ μέλλον καὶ τὸ ἐνεστὼς, αὐτὰρ δὴ καὶ τὸ παρῳχηκὸς ἀκαριαίως συνίστησεν. Instances from extra-biblical writ. of the use of αἰών in the plural are: τὸν ἀπ' αἰώνων μύθον, Anthol. vol. iii. pt. ii. p. 55 ed. Jacobs; εἰς αἰῶνας, ibid. vol. iv. epigr. 492; ἐκ περιτροπῆς αἰώνων, Joseph. b. j. 3, 8, 5; εἰς αἰῶνας διαμένει, Sext. Empir. adv. Phys. i. 62. The discussions which have been raised respecting the word may give interest to additional reff. to its use by Philo and Josephus. P h i l o : ὁ πᾶς (ἅπας, σύμπας) or πᾶς (etc.) ὁ αἰών: de alleg. leg. § 70; de cherub. § 1 (a noteworthy passage, cf. de congressu erud. § 11 and reff. s. v. θάνατος); de sacrif. Ab. et Caini § 11; quod det. pot. § 48; quod deus immut. § 1, § 24; de plantat. § 27; de sobrietate § 13; de migr. Abr. § 2; de prof. § 9; de mut. nom. § 34; de somn. ii. § 15, § 31, § 38; de legat. ad Gaium § 38; (ὁ) μακρὸς αἰ.: de sacrif. Ab. et Caini § 21; de ebrietate § 47; de prof. § 20; αἰ. μήκιστος:

de sobrietate § 5; de prof. § 21; ὁ ἄπειρος αἰ.: de legat. ad Gaium § 11; ὁ ἔμπροσθεν αἰ.: de praem. et. poen. § 6; αἰ. πολύς: de Abrah. § 46; τίς αἰ.: de merc. meretr. § 1; δι' αἰ.: de cherub. § 26; de plantat. § 27; εἰς τὸν αἰ.: de gigant. § 5; ἐν (τῷ) αἰ.: de mut. nom. § 2 (bis) (note the restriction); quod deus immut. § 6; ἐξ αἰ.: de somn. i. § 3; ἐπ' αἰ.: de plantat. § 12 (bis); de mundo § 7; πρὸ αἰ.: de mut. nom. § 2; πρὸς αἰ.: de mut. nom. § 11; (ὁ) αἰ.: de prof. § 18; de alleg. leg. iii. § 70; de cherub. § 22; de migr. Abr. § 22; de somn. i. § 18, § 22; de Josepho § 5; de vita Moys. ii. § 3; de decalogo § 14; de victimis § 3; frag. in Mang. ii. 660 (Richter vi. p. 219); de plantat. § 12 (bis); de mundo § 7. J o s e p h u s : (ὁ) πᾶς αἰών: antt. 1, 18, 7; 3, 8, 10; c. Ap. 2, 11, 3; 2, 22, 1; μακρὸς αἰ.: antt. 2, 7, 3; πολὺς αἰ.: c. Ap. 2, 31, 1; τοσοῦτος αἰ.: c. Ap. 1, 8, 4; πλῆθος αἰώνος: antt. prooem. § 3; ἀπ' αἰ.: b. j. prooem. § 4; δι' αἰ.: antt. 1, 18, 8; 4, 6, 4; b. j. 6, 2, 1; εἰς (τὸν) αἰ.: antt. 4, 8, 18; 5, 1, 27; 7, 9, 5; 7, 14, 5; ἐξ αἰ.: b. j. 5, 10, 5; (ὁ) αἰ.: antt. 19, 2, 2; b. j. 1, 21, 10; plur. (see above) 3, 8, 5. See αἰώνιος.]

αἰώνιος, -ον, and (in 2 Th. ii. 16; Heb. ix. 12; Num. xxv. 13; Plat. Tim. p. 38 b. [see below]; Diod. i. 1; [cf. *WH*. App. p. 157; W. 69 (67); B. 26 (23)]) -ος, -α, -ον, (αἰών); **1.** *without beginning or end, that which always has been and always will be*: θεός, Ro. xvi. 26, (ὁ μόνος αἰώνιος, 2 Macc. i. 25); πνεῦμα, Heb. ix. 14. **2.** *without beginning*: χρόνοις αἰωνίοις, Ro. xvi. 25; πρὸ χρόνων αἰωνίων, 2 Tim. i. 9; Tit. i. 2; εὐαγγέλιον a gospel whose subject-matter is eternal, i. e. the saving purpose of God adopted from eternity, Rev. xiv. 6. **3.** *without end, never to cease, everlasting*: 2 Co. iv. 18 (opp. to πρόσκαιρος); αἰώνιον αὐτόν, joined to thee forever as a sharer of the same eternal life, Philem. 15; βάρος δόξης, 2 Co. iv. 17; βασιλεία, 2 Pet. i. 11; δόξα, 2 Tim. ii. 10; 1 Pet. v. 10; ζωή (see ζωή, 2 b.); κληρονομία, Heb. ix. 15; λύτρωσις, Heb. ix. 12; παράκλησις, 2 Th. ii. 16; σκηναί, abodes to be occupied forever, Lk. xvi. 9 (the habitations of the blessed in heaven are referred to, cf. Jn. xiv. 2, [also, dabo eis tabernacula aeterna, quae praeparaveram illis, 4 Esdr. (*Fritzsche* 5 Esdr.) ii. 11]; similarly Hades is called αἰώνιος τόπος, Tob. iii. 6, cf. Eccl. xii. 5); σωτηρία, Heb. v. 9; [so Mk. xvi. WH, in the (rejected) 'Shorter Conclusion']. Opposite ideas are: κόλασις, Mt. xxv. 46; κρίμα, Heb. vi. 2; κρίσις, Mk. iii. 29 (Rec. [but L T WH Tr txt. ἁμαρτήματος; in Acta Thom. § 47, p. 227 Tdf., ἔσται σοι τοῦτο εἰς ἄφεσιν ἁμαρτιῶν καὶ λύτρον αἰωνίων παραπτωμάτων, it has been plausibly conjectured we should read λύτρον αἰώνιον (cf. Heb. ix. 12)]); ὄλεθρος [Lchm. txt. ὀλέθριος], 2 Th. i. 9, (4 Macc. x. 15); πῦρ, Mt. xxv. 41, (4 Macc. xii. 12 αἰωνίῳ πυρὶ κ. βασάνοις, αἳ εἰς ὅλον τὸν αἰῶνα οὐκ ἀνήσουσί σε).

[Of the examples of αἰώνιος from Philo (with whom it is less common than ἀΐδιος, q. v., of which there are some fifty instances) the following are noteworthy: de mut. nom. § 2; de caritate § 17; κόλασις αἰ. in Mang. ii. 667 fin. (Richter vi. 229 mid.); cf. de fragm. et poen. § 12. Other exx. are de alleg. leg. iii. § 70; de poster. Caini § 35; quod deus immut. § 30; quis rer. div. her. § 58; de congressu quaer. erud. § 19; de prof. § 38; de somn. ii. § 43; de Josepho § 24; quod omn. prob. lib. § 4, § 18; de ebrietate § 32; de Abrah. § 10; ζωὴ αἰ.: de prof. § 15; θεὸς (ὁ) αἰ.: de plantat. § 2, § 18 (bis), § 20 (bis); de mundo § 2. From Josephus: antt. 7, 14, 5; 12, 7, 3; 15, 10, 5; b. j. 1, 33, 2; 6, 2, 1; κλέος αἰ.: antt. 4, 6, 5; b. j. 3, 8, 5; μνήμη αἰ.: antt. 1, 13, 4; 6, 14, 4; 10, 11, 7; 15, 11, 1; οἶκον μὲν αἰώνιον ἔχεις (of God), antt. 8, 4, 2; ἐφυλάχθη ὁ Ἰωάννης δεσμοῖς αἰωνίοις, b. j. 6, 9, 4.

SYN. ἀΐδιος, αἰώνιος: ἀΐδ. covers the complete philosophic idea—without beginning and without end; also *either* without beginning *or* without end; as respects the past, it is applied to what has existed *time out of mind.* αἰώνιος (fr. Plato on) gives prominence to the immeasurableness of eternity (while such words as συνεχής continuous, unintermitted, διατελής perpetual, lasting to the end, are not so applicable to an abstract term, like αἰών); αἰώνιος accordingly is esp. adapted to supersensuous things, see the N. T. Cf. Tim. Locr. 96 c. θεὸν δὲ τὸν μὲν αἰώνιον νόος ὁρῇ μόνος etc.; Plat. Tim. 37 d. (and Stallbaum ad loc.); 38 b. c.; legg. x. p. 904 a. ἀνώλεθρον δὲ ὃν γενόμενον, ἀλλ' οὐκ αἰώνιον. Cf. also Plato's διαιώνιος (Tim. 38 b.; 39 e.). Schmidt ch. 45.]

167 ἀκαθαρσία, -ας, ἡ, (ἀκάθαρτος), [fr. Hippocr. down], *uncleanness*; **a.** physical: Mt. xxiii. 27. **b.** in a moral sense, the impurity of lustful, luxurious, profligate living: Ro. i. 24; vi. 19; 2 Co. xii. 21; Gal. v. 19; Eph. iv. 19; v. 3; Col. iii. 5; 1 Th. iv. 7; used of impure motives in 1 Th. ii. 3. (Dem. p. 553, 12.) Cf. Tittmann i. p. 150 sq.*

168 ἀκαθάρτης, -ητος, ἡ, *impurity*: Rev. xvii. 4,— not found elsewhere, and the true reading here is τὰ ἀκάθαρτα τῆς.*

169 ἀκάθαρτος, -ον, (καθαίρω), [fr. Soph. down], in the Sept. i. q. אָמֵא, *not cleansed, unclean*; **a.** in a ceremonial sense, that which must be abstained from according to the levitical law, lest impurity be contracted: Acts x. 14; xi. 8 (of food); Acts x. 28; 1 Co. vii. 14 (of men); 2 Co. vi. 17 (fr. Is. lii. 11, of things pertaining to idolatry); Rev. xviii. 2 (of birds). **b.** in a moral sense, *unclean in thought and life* (freq. in Plat.): Eph. v. 5; τὰ ἀκάθαρτα τῆς πορνείας, Rev. xvii. 4 (acc. to the true reading); πνεύματα, demons, bad angels, [in twenty-three pass. of the Gospels, Acts, Rev.]: Mt. x. 1; xii. 43; Mk. i. 23, 26; iii. 11, etc.; Lk. iv. 33, 36; vi. 18, etc.; Acts v. 16; viii. 7; Rev. xvi. 13; xviii. 2, (πνεύματα πονηρά in Mt. xii. 45; Lk. vii. 21; viii. 2; xi. 26; Acts xix. 12 sq. 15 sq.).

170 ἀκαιρέομαι, -οῦμαι: [impf. ἠκαιρούμην]; (ἄκαιρος inopportune); *to lack opportunity*, (opp. to εὐκαιρέω): Phil. iv. 10. (Phot., Suid., Zonar.: ἀκαιρεῖν, Diod. excerp. Vat. ed. Mai p. 30 [frag. l. x. § 7, ed. Dind.].)*

171 ἀκαίρως, (καιρός), adv., *unseasonably*, [A. V. *out of season*], (opp. to εὐκαίρως): 2 Tim. iv. 2 (whether seasonable for men or not). (Sir. xxxv. 4; [Aeschyl. Ag. 808]; Plat. de rep. x. p. 606 b.; Tim. 33 a.; 86 c.; Xen. Eph. 5, 7; Joseph. antt. 6, 7, 2, al.)*

172 ἄ-κακος, -ον, (κακός), **a.** *without guile* or *fraud, harmless*; *free from guilt*: Heb. vii. 26; [cf. Clement. frag. 8 ed. Jacobson, (Bp. *Lghtft.* S. Clement of Rome etc. p. 219): ἄκακος ὁ Πατὴρ πνεῦμα ἔδωκεν ἄκακον]. **b.** *fearing no evil from others, distrusting no one*, [cf. Eng. *guileless*]: Ro. xvi. 18. ([Aeschyl.,] Plat., Dem., Polyb., al.; Sept.) [Cf. Trench § lvi.; Tittmann i. p. 27 sq.]*

173 ἄκανθα, -ης, ἡ, (ἀκή a point [but see in ἀκμή]); **a.** *a thorn, bramble-bush, brier*: Mt. vii. 16; Lk. vi. 44; Heb. vi. 8; εἰς τὰς ἀκάνθας i. e. *among the* seeds of *thorns*, Mt. xiii. 22; Mk. iv. 7 [L mrg. ἐπί], 18 [Tdf. ἐπί]; Lk. viii. 14 (vs. 7 ἐν μέσῳ τῶν ἀκανθῶν); ἐπὶ τὰς ἀκ. i. e. upon ground in which seeds of thorns were lying hidden, Mt. xiii. 7. **b.** *a thorny plant*: στέφανον ἐξ ἀκανθῶν, Mt. xxvii. 29; Jn. xix. 2,—for bare thorns might have caused delirium or even death; what species of plant is referred to, is not clear. Some boldly read ἀκάνθων, from ἄκανθος, *acanthus, bear's-foot*; but the meaning of ἄκανθα is somewhat comprehensive even in prof. writ.; cf. the class. Grk. Lexx. s. v. [On the "Crown of thorns" see BB.DD. s. v., and for reff. Mc. and S.]*

174 ἀκάνθινος, -ον, (ἄκανθα; cf. ἀμαράντινος), *thorny, woven out of the twigs of a thorny plant*: Mk. xv. 17; Jn. xix. 5. (Is. xxxiv. 13.) Cf. the preceding word.*

175 ἄ-καρπος, -ον, (καρπός), [fr. Aeschyl. down], *without fruit, barren*, **1.** prop.: δένδρα, Jude 12. **2.** metaph. *not yielding what it ought to yield*, [A. V. *unfruitful*]: Mt. xiii. 22; Mk. iv. 19; destitute of good deeds, Tit. iii. 14; 2 Pet. i. 8; contributing nothing to the instruction, improvement, comfort, of others, 1 Co. xiv. 14; by litotes *pernicious*, Eph. v. 11, (Sap. xv. 4; cf. Grimm on Sap. i. 11).*

176 ἀ-κατά-γνωστος, -ον, (καταγινώσκω), *that cannot be condemned, not to be censured*: Tit. ii. 8. (2 Macc. iv. 47, and several times in eccl. writ.)*

177 ἀ-κατα-κάλυπτος, -ον, (κατακαλύπτω), *not covered, unveiled*: 1 Co. xi. 5, 13. (Polyb. 15, 27, 2; [Sept., Philo].)*

178 ἀ-κατά-κριτος, -ον, (κατακρίνω), *uncondemned; punished without being tried*: Acts xvi. 37; xxii. 25. (Not found in prof. writ.)*

179 ἀ-κατά-λυτος, -ον, (καταλύω), *indissoluble; not subject to destruction*, [A. V. *endless*]: ζωή, Heb. vii. 16. (4 Macc. x. 11; Dion. Hal. 10, 31.)*

see 180 ἀκατάπαστος, -ον,—found only in 2 Pet. ii. 14 in codd. A and B, from which L WH Tr mrg. have adopted it instead of the Rec. ἀκαταπαύστους, q. v. It may be derived fr. πατέομαι, pf. πέπασμαι, *to taste, eat*; whence ἀκατάπαστος *insatiable*. In prof. writ. κατάπαστος [which Bttm. conjectures may have been the original reading] signifies *besprinkled, soiled*, from καταπάσσω to besprinkle. For a fuller discussion of this various reading see B. 65 (57), [and *WH.* App. p. 170].*

180 ἀκατάπαυστος, -ον, (καταπαύω), *unable to stop, unceasing*; passively, *not quieted, that cannot be quieted*; with gen. of thing (on which cf. W. § 30, 4), 2 Pet. ii. 14 [R G T Tr txt.] (eyes not quieted with sin, sc. which they commit with adulterous look). (Polyb., Diod., Joseph., Plut.)*

181 ἀκαταστασία, -ας, ἡ, (ἀκατάστατος), *instability, a state of disorder, disturbance, confusion*: 1 Co. xiv. 33; Jas. iii. 16; [Clem. Rom. 1 Cor. 14, 1; [Prov. xxvi. 28; Tob. iv. 13]); plur. *disturbances, disorders*: of dissensions, 2 Co. xii. 20; of seditions, 2 Co. vi. 5 (cf. Mey. ad loc.); of the tumults or commotions of war, Lk. xxi. 9. (Polyb., Dion. Hal.)*

182 ἀ-κατά-στατος, -ον, (καθίστημι), unstable, inconstant, restless: Jas. i. 8, and L T Tr WH in iii. 8 also, but less fitly; [cf. Hermae Past. l. ii. mand. 2, 3 πονηρὸν πνεῦμά ἐστιν ἡ καταλαλιά, καὶ ἀκατάστατον δαιμόνιον, μηδέποτε εἰρηνεῦον, ἀλλά etc.]. ([Hippocr. et al.] Polyb. 7, 4, 6, al. [Sept. Is. liv. 11].) *

183 ἀ-κατάσχετος, -ον, (κατέχω to restrain, control), that cannot be restrained: Jas. iii. 8 R G. (Job xxxi. 11; 3 Macc. vi. 17; Diod. 17, 38 ἀκατ. δάκρυα, al.) *

184 Ἀκελδαμά, or Ἀκελδαμάχ (Lchm.), [or Ἀκελδ. WH (see their Intr. § 408)], or Ἀχελδαμάχ (T Tr), fr. Chald. חֲקַל דְּמָא (field of blood), Akeldama: Acts i. 19; see αἷμα, 2 a. [B. D. s. v.; esp. Kautzsch, Gram. pp. 8, 173].*

185 ἀκέραιος, -ον, (κεράννυμι); **a.** unmixed, pure, as wine, metals. **b.** of the mind, without admixture of evil, free from guile, innocent, simple: Mt. x. 16; Ro. xvi. 19; Phil. ii. 15; (and freq. in prof. writ.). [Cf. Ellic. on Phil. l. c.; Trench § lvi.; Tittmann i. 27 sq.]*

186 ἀκλινής, -ές, (κλίνω), not inclining, firm, unmoved: Heb. x. 23. (Freq. in prof. writ.) *

187 ἀκμάζω: 1 aor. ἤκμασα; (ἀκμή); to flourish, come to maturity: Rev. xiv. 18. (Very freq. in prof. writ.) *

see 188 St. ἀκμή, -ῆς, ἡ, (cf. ἀκή [on the accent cf. Chandler § 116; but the word is 'a mere figment of the grammarians,' Pape (yet cf. L. and S.) s. v.], αἰχμή, Lat. acies, acuo); among the Greeks **a.** prop. a point, to prick with (cf. [the classic] αἰχμή). **b.** extremity, climax, acme, highest degree. **c.** the present point of time. Hence accus. [W. 230 (216), 464 (432 sq.); B. 153 (134)] ἀκμήν with adverbial force, i. q. ἔτι, even now, even yet: Mt. xv. 16. (Theocr. id. 4, 60; Polyb. 4, 36, 8; Strat. epigr. 3 p. 101 ed. Lips.; Strabo l. i. [c. 3 prol.] p. 56; Plut. de glor. Athen. 2, 85, al.) Cf. Lob. ad Phryn. p. 123.*

189 ἀκοή, -ῆς, ἡ, (fr. an assumed pf. form ἤκοα, cf. ἀγορά above [but cf. Epic ἀκούή; Curtius p. 555]); **1.** hearing, by which one perceives sounds; sense of hearing: 1 Co. xii. 17; 2 Pet. ii. 8. Hebraistically, ἀκοῇ ἀκούειν by hearing to hear i. e. to perceive by hearing, Mt. xiii. 14; Acts xxviii. 26, (Is. vi. 9); cf. W. § 44, 8 Rem. 3 p. 339; § 54, 3 p. 466; [B. 183 sq. (159)]. **2.** the organ of hearing, the ear: Mk. vii. 35; Lk. vii. 1; 2 Tim. iv. 3, 4; Acts xvii. 20; Heb. v. 11. **3.** thing heard; **a.** instruction, namely o r a l; spec. the preaching of the gospel, [A. V. text. report]: Mt. xii. 38; Ro. x. 16 sq. (τίς ἐπίστευσε τῇ ἀκοῇ ἡμῶν; fr. Is. liii. 1, Hebr. שְׁמוּעָה, which in 2 S. iv. 4, etc., is rendered ἀγγελία; ἀκοὴ πίστεως preaching on the necessity of faith, (Germ. Glaubens-predigt), Gal. iii. 2, 5; λόγος ἀκοῆς i. q. λ. ἀκουσθείς [cf. W. 531 (494 sq.)]: 1 Th. ii. 13; Heb. iv. 2. **b.** hearsay, report, rumor; τινός, concerning any one: Mt. iv. 24; xiv. 1; xxiv. 6; Mk. i. 28; xiii. 7. (Freq. in Grk. writ.) *

190 ἀκολουθέω, -ῶ; fut. ἀκολουθήσω; impf. ἠκολούθουν; 1 aor. ἠκολούθησα; pf. ἠκολούθηκα (Mk. x. 28 L T Tr WH); (fr. ἀκόλουθος, and this fr. a copulative and κέλευθος road, prop. walking the same road); **1.** to follow one who precedes, join him as his attendant, accompany him: Mt. iv. 25; viii. 19; ix. 19; xxvii. 55; Mk. iii. 7;

v. 24, [37 Lchm.]; xiv. 51 [R G]; Lk. xxii. 39, 54; xxiii. 27; Jn. i. 37 sq. 43 (44); vi. 2; xviii. 15; xx. 6, etc.; Acts xii. 8; xiii. 43; xxi. 36; 1 Co. x. 4; distinguished fr. προάγειν in Mt. xxi. 9; Mk. xi. 9; trop. τὰ ἔργα αὐτῶν ἀκολουθεῖ μετ' αὐτῶν, their good deeds will accompany them to the presence of God the judge to be rewarded by him, Rev. xiv. 13; on the other hand, ἠκολούθησαν αὐτῆς αἱ ἁμαρτίαι ἄχρι τοῦ οὐρανοῦ, Rev. xviii. 5, but here for ἠκολούθησαν G L T Tr WH have restored ἐκολλήθησαν; [σημεῖα τοῖς πιστεύσασιν ἀκολουθήσει ταῦτα, Mk. xvi. 17 Tr WH txt. (where al. παρακολ. q. v.)]. to follow one in time, succeed one: Rev. xiv. 8 sq. (Hdian. 1, 14, 12 (6) τὰ γοῦν ἀκολουθήσαντα, al.)' Since among the ancients disciples were accustomed to accompany their masters on their walks and journeys — [al. derive the usage that follows from the figurative sense of the word directly; cf. e. g. 2 Macc. viii. 36 τὸ ἀκολουθεῖν τοῖς νόμοις; M. Antonin. l. vii. § 31 ἀκολούθησον θεῷ, and Gataker ad loc.], ἀκολουθέω denotes **2.** to join one as a disciple, become or be his disciple; side with his party, [A. V. follow him]: Mt. iv. 20, 22; ix. 9; xix. 27 sq.; Mk. i. 18; viii. 34; Lk. v. 11, 27, etc.; Jn. viii. 12 (where Jesus likens himself to a torch which the disciple follows); οὐκ ἀκολουθεῖ ἡμῖν he is not of our band of thy disciples, Mk. ix. 38. to cleave steadfastly to one, conform wholly to his example, in living and if need be in dying also: Mt. x. 38; xvi. 24; Jn. xii. 26; xxi. 22. This verb is not found in the Epp. exc. in 1 Co. x. 4. As in the classics, it is joined mostly with a dat. of the obj.; sometimes with μετά τινος, Lk. ix. 49; Rev. vi. 8 [Treg. mrg. dat.]; xiv. 13; (so also in Grk. writ.; cf. Lob. ad Phryn. p. 353 sq.; [Rutherford, New Phryn. p. 458 sq.]); ὀπίσω τινός, Mt. x. 38; Mk. viii. 34 (where R L WH Tr mrg. ἐλθεῖν), Hebr. הָלַךְ אַחֲרֵי פְּלֹנִי, cf. 1 K. xix. 21; see W. 234 (219); [B. 172 (150), cf. ἀκολ. κατόπιν τινός, Arstph. Plut. 13. COMP.: ἐξ-, ἐπ-, κατ-, παρ-, συν- ἀκολουθέω].

191 ἀκούω [on the use of the pres. in a pf. sense cf. W. 274 sq. (258); B. 203 (176)]; impf. ἤκουον; fut. (in best Grk. usage) ἀκούσομαι, Jn. v. 25 R G L, 28 R G L; Acts iii. 22; vii. 37 R G; xvii. 32; [xxi. 22]; xxv. 22; xxviii. 28; [Ro. x. 14 Tdf.], and (a later form) ἀκούσω, Mt. xii. 19; xiii. 14, (both fr. the Sept.); [Jn. x. 16; xvi. 13 Tr WH mrg.; Acts xxviii. 26]; Ro. x. 14 [R G]; and T Tr WH in Jn. v. 25, 28, (cf. W. 82 (79); B. 53 (46) [Veitch s. v.]); [1 aor. ἤκουσα, Jn. iii. 32, etc.]; pf. ἀκήκοα; Pass., [pres. ἀκούομαι; 1 fut. ἀκουσθήσομαι]; 1 aor. ἠκούσθην; [fr. Hom. down]; to hear. **I.** absol. **1.** to be endowed with the faculty of hearing (not deaf): Mk. vii. 37; Lk. vii. 22; Mt. xi. 5. **2.** to attend to (use the faculty of hearing), consider what is or has been said. So in exhortations: ἀκούετε, Mk. iv. 3; ἀκούσατε, Jas. ii. 5; ὁ ἔχων ὦτα ἀκούειν ἀκουέτω, Mt. xi. 15; xiii. 9, [in both T WH om. Tr br. ἀκούειν]; Mk. iv. 23; Lk. xiv. 35 (34); ὁ ἔχων οὖς ἀκουσάτω, Rev. ii. 7, 11, 17, 29; iii. 6, 13, 22, etc. **3.** trop. to understand, perceive the sense of what is said: Mt. xiii. 15 sq.; Mk. viii. 18; 1 Co. xiv. 2. **II.** with an object [B. § 132, 17; W. 199 (187 sq.)];

1. ἀκούω τι, *to hear something*;   **a.** *to perceive by the ear what is announced in one's presence*, (*to hear immediately*): τὴν φωνήν, Mt. xii. 19; Jn. iii. 8; Rev. iv. 1; v. 11; xviii. 4; Acts xxii. 9, etc.; τὸν ἀσπασμόν, Lk. i. 41 (cf. 44); Γαλιλαίαν, the name 'Galilee,' Lk. xxiii. 6 [T WH om. Tr mrg. br. Γαλ.; cf. B. 166 (145)]; ἀνάστασιν νεκρῶν, the phrase 'ἀνάστ. νεκρῶν,' Acts xvii. 32; τὸν λόγον, Mk. v. 36 [R G L] (on this pass. see παρακούω, 2); Mt. xix. 22; Jn. v. 24, etc.; τοὺς λόγους, Acts ii. 22; v. 24; Mt. vii. 24; ῥήματα, 2 Co. xii. 4; τί λέγουσιν, Mt. xxi. 16; pass., Mt. ii. 18; Rev. xviii. 22 sq.; τὶ ἔκ τινος, 2 Co. xii. 6 [R G]; foll. by ὅτι [B. 300 (257 sq.)], Acts xxii. 2; Mk. xvi. 11; Jn. iv. 42; xiv. 28.   **b.** *to get by hearing, learn* (from the mouth of the teacher or narrator): Acts xv. 17; Mt. x. 27 (ὃ εἰς τὸ οὖς ἀκούετε, what is taught you in secret); Ro. xv. 21; Eph. i. 13; Col. i. 6; Jn. xiv. 24; 1 Jn. ii. 7, 24; iii. 11; Χριστόν i. e. to become acquainted with Christ from apostolic teaching, Eph. iv. 21 (cf. μαθεῖν τὸν Χριστόν, vs. 20 [B. 166 (144) note; W. 199 (187) note]); pass., Lk. xii. 3; Heb. ii. 1; τὶ with gen. of pers. fr. whom one hears, Acts i. 4; τὶ παρά τινος, Jn. viii. 26, 40; xv. 15; Acts x. 22; xxviii. 22; 2 Tim. ii. 2, (Thuc. 6, 93; Xen. an. 1, 2, 5 [here Dind. om. παρά]; Plat. rep. vi. p. 506 d., al.; [B. 166 (145); W. 199 (188)]); [παρά τινος, without an obj. expressed, Jn. i. 40 (41)]; ἔκ τινος, Jn. xii. 34 (ἐκ τοῦ νόμου, from attendance on its public reading); ἀπό with gen. of pers., 1 Jn. i. 5; with περί τινος added, Acts ix. 13; foll. by ὅτι, Mt. v. 21, 27, 33, 38, 43.   **c.** ἀκούω τι, *a thing comes to one's ears, to find out* (*by hearsay*), *learn*, (*hear* [(*of*)] *mediately*): with acc. of thing, τὰ ἔργα, Mt. xi. 2; ὅσα ἐποίει, Mk. iii. 8 [Treg. txt. ποιεῖ]; πολέμους, Lk. xxi. 9; Mt. xxiv. 6; Mk. xiii. 7; *to learn*, absol. viz. what has just been mentioned: Mt. ii. 3; xxii. 7 [R L]; Mk. ii. 17; iii. 21; Gal. i. 13; Eph. i. 15; Col. i. 4; Philem. 5, etc. foll. by ὅτι, Mt. ii. 22; iv. 12; xx. 30; Mk. vi. 55; x. 47; Jn. iv. 47; ix. 35; xi. 6; xii. 12; Gal. i. 23; περί τινος, Mk. vii. 25; τὶ περί τινος, Lk. ix. 9; xvi. 2; xxiii. 8 [R G L]; foll. by an acc. with ptcp. [B. 303 (260)]: Lk. iv. 23; Acts vii. 12; 2 Th. iii. 11; 3 Jn. 4; foll. by acc. with inf. in two instances [cf. B. l. c.]: Jn. xii. 18; 1 Co. xi. 18. pass.: Acts xi. 22 (ἠκούσθη ὁ λόγος εἰς τὰ ὦτα τῆς ἐκκλησίας was brought to the ears); 1 Co. v. 1 (ἀκούεται πορνεία ἐν ὑμῖν); Mt. xxviii. 14 (ἐὰν ἀκουσθῇ τοῦτο ἐπὶ [L Tr WH mrg. ὑπὸ] τοῦ ἡγεμόνος); Mk. ii. 1; Jn. ix. 32 ἠκούσθη ὅτι.   **d.** *to give ear to* teaching or teacher: τοὺς λόγους, Mt. x. 14; *to follow with attentive hearing*, τὸν λόγον, Jn. viii. 43; τὰ ῥήματα τοῦ θεοῦ, 47.   **e.** *to comprehend, understand*, (like Lat. *audio*): Mk. iv. 33; Gal. iv. 21 [(Lchm. mrg. ἀναγινώσκετε) yet cf. Mey. ad loc.]; (Gen. xi. 7).   **2.** ἀκούειν is not joined with the g e n i t i v e of the obj. unless one hear the person or thing with his own ears [B. 166 (144)]; **a.** with gen. of a p e r s o n; simply;   **α.** *to perceive any one's voice*: οὗ i. e. of Christ, whose voice is heard in the instruction of his messengers (Lk. x. 16), Ro. x. 14, [W. 199 (187) note²].   **β.** *to give ear to one, listen,*

hearken, (Germ. *ihm zuhören, ihn anhören*): Mt. ii. 9; Mk. vii. 14; xii. 37; Lk. ii. 46; x. 16; xv. 1; xix. 48; xxi. 38; Acts xvii. 32; xxiv. 24 (in both these pass. τινὸς περί τινος); xxv. 22; Jn. vi. 60.   **γ.** *to yield to,* hear and obey, *hear to one,* (Germ. *auf einen hören*): Mt. xvii. 5, (Mk. ix. 7; Lk. ix. 35); Jn. iii. 29; x. 8; Acts iii. 22 sq.; iv. 19; vii. 37 [R G]; 1 Jn. iv. 5 sq. Hence **δ.** its use by John in the sense *to listen to, have regard to,* of God answering the prayers of men: Jn. ix. 31; xi. 41; 1 Jn. v. 14 sq. (the Sept. render שָׁמַע by εἰσακούω).   **ε.** with gen. of pers. and ptcp. [B. 301 (259)]: Mk. xiv. 58; Lk. xviii. 36; Jn. i. 37; vii. 32; Acts ii. 6, 11; Rev. xvi. 5; ἤκουσα τοῦ θυσιαστηρίου λέγοντος, Rev. xvi. 7 G L T [Tr WH cod. Sin.], a poetic personification; cf. De Wette ad loc., W. § 30, 11.   **b.** with gen. of a t h i n g: τῆς βλασφημίας, Mk. xiv. 64 (Lchm. τὴν βλασφημίαν, as in Mt. xxvi. 65; the acc. merely denotes the object; τῆς βλασφ. is equiv. in sense to αὐτοῦ βλασφημοῦντος, [cf. B. 166 (145)]); τῶν λόγων, Lk. vi. 47, (Mt. vii. 24 τοὺς λόγους); Jn. vii. 40 (L T Tr WH cod. Sin., but R G τὸν λόγον, [cf. B. u. s.]); συμφωνίας κ. χορῶν, Lk. xv. 25; τοῦ στεναγμοῦ, Acts vii. 34; τῆς ἀπολογίας, Acts xxii. 1. The frequent phrase ἀκούειν τῆς φωνῆς (i. q. שָׁמַע בְּקֹל, Ex. xviii. 19) means   **a.** *to perceive the distinct words of a voice*: Jn. v. 25, 28; Acts ix. 7; xi. 7; xxii. 7; Heb. iii. 7, 15; iv. 7; Rev. xiv. 13; xxi. 3.   **β.** *to yield obedience to the voice*: Jn. v. 25 (οἱ ἀκούσαντες sc. τῆς φωνῆς); x. 16, 27; xviii. 37; Rev. iii. 20. In Jn. xii. 47; xviii. 37; Lk. vi. 47; Acts xxii. 1, it is better to consider the pron. μοῦ which precedes as a possess. gen. rather than, with B. 167 (145 sq.), to assume a double gen. of the object, one of the pers. and one of the thing.   The Johannean phrase ἀκούειν παρὰ τοῦ θεοῦ, or τὶ παρὰ θεοῦ, signifies   **a.** *to perceive in the soul the inward communication of God*: Jn. vi. 45.   **b.** *to be taught by God's inward communication*: Jn. viii. 26, 40, (so, too, the simple ἀκούειν in v. 30); *to be taught by the d e v i l,* acc. to the reading of L T Tr WH, ἠκούσατε παρὰ τοῦ πατρός, in Jn. viii. 38. For the rest cf. B. 165 (144) sqq.; 301 (258) sqq. [COMP.: δι-, εἰσ-, ἐπ-, παρ-, προ-, ὑπ-ακούω.]

ἀκρασία, -ας, ἡ, (ἀκρατής), *want of self-control, incontinence, intemperance*: Mt. xxiii. 25 (Grsb. ἀδικία); 1 Co. vii. 5. Cf. *Lob.* ad Phryn. p. 524 sq. [(Aristot. on.)] *   **192**

ἀκρατής, -ές, gen. -έος, -οῦς, (κράτος), *without self-control, intemperate*: 2 Tim. iii. 3. (Freq. in prof. writ. fr. Plato and Xen. down.) *   **193**

ἄκρατος, -ον, (κεράννυμι), *unmixed, pure*: Rev. xiv. 10 (of wine undiluted with water, as freq. in prof. writ. and Jer. xxxii. 1 (xxv. 15)).*   **194**

ἀκρίβεια, -είας, ἡ, (ἀκριβής), *exactness, exactest care*: Acts xxii. 3 (κατὰ ἀκρίβειαν τοῦ νόμου in accordance with the strictness of the Mosaic law, [cf. Isoc. areop. p. 147 e.]). [From Thuc. down.]*   **195**

ἀκριβής, -ές, gen. -οῦς, *exact, careful*. The neut. compar.   **196 & 197** is used adverbially in Acts xviii. 26; xxiii. 15, 20; xxiv. 22; ἡ ἀκριβεστάτη αἵρεσις *the straitest sect* i. e. the most precise and rigorous in interpreting the Mosaic law, and

198

in observing even the more minute precepts of the law and of tradition, Acts xxvi. 5. [From Hdt. down.]*

ἀκριβόω, -ῶ: 1 aor. ἠκρίβωσα; (ἀκριβής); **1.** in prof. writ. *to know accurately, to do exactly.* **2.** *to investigate diligently*: Mt. ii. 7, 16, (ἀκριβῶς ἐξετάζειν, vs. 8); Aristot. gen. anim. 5, 1; Philo, m. opif. § 25 μετὰ πάσης ἐξετάσεως ἀκριβοῦντες. [Al. *to learn exactly, ascertain*; cf. Fritz. or Mey. on Mt. u. s.]*

199

ἀκριβῶς, adv., *exactly, accurately, diligently*: Mt. ii. 8; Lk. i. 3; Acts xviii. 25; 1 Th. v. 2; ἀκριβῶς περιπατεῖν to live carefully, circumspectly, deviating in no respect from the law of duty, Eph. v. 15. [Fr. Aeschyl. down.]*

200

ἀκρίς, -ίδος, ἡ, [fr. Hom. down], *a locust*, particularly that species which especially infests oriental countries, stripping fields and trees. Numberless swarms of them almost every spring are carried by the wind from Arabia into Palestine, and having devastated that country migrate to regions farther north, until they perish by falling into the sea. The Orientals are accustomed to feed upon locusts, either raw or roasted and seasoned with salt [or prepared in other ways], and the Israelites also (acc. to Lev. xi. 22) were permitted to eat them; (cf. Win. RWB. s. v. Heuschrecken; *Furrer* in Schenkel iii. p. 78 sq.; [BB.DD. s. v.; *Tristram*, Nat. Hist. of the Bible, p. 313 sqq.]): Mt. iii. 4; Mk. i. 6. A marvellous and infernal kind of locusts is described in Rev. ix. 3, 7, cf. 2, 5 sq. 8–12; see Düsterdieck ad loc.*

201

ἀκροατήριον, -ου, τό, (ἀκροάομαι to be a hearer), place of assemblage for hearing, *auditorium*; like this Lat. word in Roman Law, ἀκροατ. in Acts xxv. 23 denotes *a place set apart for hearing and deciding cases*, [yet cf. Mey. ad loc.]. (Several times in Plut. and other later writers.)*

202

ἀκροατής, -οῦ, ὁ, (ἀκροάομαι, [see the preceding word]), *a hearer*: τοῦ νόμου, Ro. ii. 13; τοῦ λόγου, Jas. i. 22 sq. 25. (Thuc., Isocr., Plat., Dem., Plut.)*

203

ἀκροβυστία, -ας, ἡ, (a word unknown to the Greeks, who used ἡ ἀκροποσθία and τὸ ἀκροπόσθιον, fr. πόσθη i. e. membrum virile. Accordingly it is likely that τὴν πόσθην of the Greeks was pronounced τὴν βύστην by the Alexandrians, and ἀκροβυστία said instead of ἀκροποσθία — i. e. τὸ ἄκρον τῆς πόσθης; cf. the acute remarks of Fritzsche, Com. on Rom. vol. i. 136, together with the opinion which Winer prefers 99 (94), [and Cremer, 3te Aufl. s. v.]), in the Sept. the equiv. of עָרְלָה *the prepuce*, the skin covering the glans penis; **a.** prop.: Acts xi. 3; Ro. ii. 25, 26ᵇ; 1 Co. vii. 19; Gal. v. 6; vi. 15; Col. iii. 11; (Judith xiv. 10; 1 Macc. i. 15); ἐν ἀκροβυστίᾳ ὤν having the foreskin (Tertull. *praeputiatus*), uncircumcised i. e. Gentile, Ro. iv. 10; ἐν ἀκρ. sc. ὤν, Co vii. 18; equiv. to the same is δι' ἀκροβυστίας, Ro. iv. 11; ἡ ἐν τῇ ἀκροβ. πίστις the faith which one has while he is uncircumcised, Ro. iv. 11 sq. **b.** by meton. of the abstr. for the concr., *having the foreskin* is equiv. to *a Gentile*: Ro. ii. 26*; iii. 30; iv. 9; Eph. ii. 11; ἡ ἐκ φύσεως ἀκροβ. one uncircumcised by birth or a Gentile, opp. to a Jew who shows himself a Gentile in c h a r a c t e r, Ro. ii. 27; εὐαγγέλιον τῆς ἀκροβ. gospel to be preached to the Gentiles, Gal.

ii. 7. **c.** in a transferred sense: ἡ ἀκροβ. τῆς σαρκός (opp. to the περιτομὴ ἀχειροποίητος or regeneration, Col. ii. 11), *the condition in which the corrupt desires rooted in the σάρξ were not yet extinct*, Col. ii. 13 (the expression is derived from the circumstance that the foreskin was the sign of impurity and alienation from God, [cf. B. D. s. v. Circumcision]).*

ἀκρο-γωνιαῖος, -αία, -αῖον, a word wholly bibl. and eccl., [W. 99 (94); 236 (221)], (ἄκρος extreme, and γωνία corner, angle), *placed at the extreme corner*; λίθος corner-stone; used of Christ, 1 Pet. ii. 6; Eph. ii. 20; Sept. Is. xxviii. 16 for אֶבֶן פִּנָּה. For as the corner-stone holds together two walls, so Christ joins together as Christians, into one body dedicated to God, those who were formerly Jews and Gentiles, Eph. ii. 20 [yet cf. Mey. ad loc.] compared with vss. 14, 16–19, 21 sq. And as a corner-stone contributes to sustain the edifice, but nevertheless some fall in going around the corner carelessly; so some are built up by the aid of Christ, while others stumbling at Christ perish, 1 Pet. ii. 6–8; see γωνία, a.*

204

ἀκροθίνιον, -ου, τό, (fr. ἄκρος extreme, and θίς, gen. θινός, a heap; extremity, topmost part of a heap), generally in plur. τὰ ἀκροθίνια *the first-fruits*, whether of *crops* or of *spoils* (among the Greeks customarily selected from the topmost part of the heaps and offered to the gods, Xen. Cyr. 7, 5, 35); in the Bible only once: Heb. vii. 4, of booty. (Pind., Aeschyl., Hdt., Thuc., Plut., al.)*

205

ἄκρος, -α, -ον, (ἀκή point [see ἀκμή]), [fr. Hom. down], *highest, extreme*; τὸ ἄκρον *the topmost point, the extremity* [cf. B. 94 (82)]: Lk. xvi. 24; Heb. xi. 21 [see προσκυνέω, a. fin.]; ἄκρα, ἄκρον γῆς, οὐρανοῦ, the farthest bounds, uttermost parts, end, of the earth, of heaven: Mt. xxiv. 31; Mk. xiii. 27; cf. Deut. iv. 32; xxviii. 64; Is. xiii. 5; Jer. xii. 12.*

206

'Ακύλας, -ου, [but no gen. seems to be extant, see B. 20 (18)], ὁ, *Aquila*, a Jew of Pontus, a tent-maker, convert to Christ, companion and ally of Paul in propagating the Christian religion: Acts xviii. 2, 18, 26; Ro. xvi. 3; 1 Co. xvi. 19; 2 Tim. iv. 19; [see B. D.].*

207

ἀκυρόω, -ῶ; 1 aor. ἠκύρωσα; (ἄκυρος without authority, not binding, void; fr. κῦρος force, authority), *to render void, deprive of force and authority*, (opp. to κυρόω to confirm, make valid): ἐντολήν, Mt. xv. 6 [R G]; νόμον, ibid. T WH mrg.]; λόγον [ibid. L Tr WH txt.]; Mk. vii. 13, (cf. ἀθετέω); διαθήκην, Gal. iii. 17. ([1 Esdr. vi. 31]; Diod., Dion. Hal., Plut.)*

208

ἀκωλύτως, adv., (κωλύω), *without hindrance*: Acts xxviii. 31. [Plato, Epict., Hdian.]*

209

ἄκων, ἄκουσα, ἄκον, (contr. fr. ἀέκων, a priv. and ἕκων willing), *not of one's own will, unwilling*: 1 Co. ix. 17. (Very freq. among the Greeks.)*

210

[ἅλα, τό, read by Tdf. in Mt. v. 13; Mk. ix. 50; Lk. xiv. 34; see ἅλας.] see 217

211

ἀλάβαστρον, -ου, τό, (in the plur. in Theocr. 15, 114; Anth. Pal. 9, 153; in other prof. writ. ὁ and ἡ ἀλάβαστρος; [the older and more correct spelling drops the ρ, cf. Steph. Thesaur. s. v. 1385 d.; L. and S. s. v. ἀλάβαστρος]), *a box made of alabaster*, in which unguents are preserved, (Plin. h. n. 13, 2 (3), [al. 13, 19,] "unguenta optime servantur in alabastris "); with the addition of μύρου (as in Lcian. dial. mer. 14, 2; [Hdt. 3, 20]): Lk. vii. 37; Mt. xxvi. 7; Mk. xiv. 3 (where L T adopt τὸν ἀλάβ., Tr WH [Mey.] τὴν ἀλ.; Mt. and Lk. do not add the article, so that it is not clear in what gender they use the word, [cf. Tdf.'s crit. note ad loc.]). Cf. *Win.* RWB. [or B. D.] s. v. Alabaster.*

212 ἀλαζονεία, and ἀλαζονία (which spelling, not uncommon in later Grk., T WH adopt [see I, ι]), -ας, ἡ, (fr. ἀλαζονεύομαι i. e. to act the ἀλαζών, q. v.); **a.** in prof. writ. [fr. Arstph. down] generally *empty, braggart talk*, sometimes also *empty display in act, swagger*. For illustration see Xen. Cyr. 2, 2, 12; mem. 1, 7; Aristot. eth. Nic. 4, 13, p. 1127 ed. Bekk.; [also Trench § xxix.]. **b.** *an insolent and empty assurance, which trusts in its own power and resources and shamefully despises and violates divine laws and human rights*: 2 Macc. ix. 8; Sap. v. 8. **c.** *an impious and empty presumption which trusts in the stability of earthly things*, [R. V. *vaunting*]: Jas. iv. 16 (where the plur. has reference to the various occasions on which this presumption shows itself; [cf. W. § 27, 3; B. 77 (67)]); τοῦ βίου, *display in one's style of living*, [R. V. *vainglory*], 1 Jn. ii. 16.*

213 ἀλαζών, -όνος, ὁ, ἡ, (ἄλη wandering), [fr. Arstph. on], *an empty pretender, a boaster*: Ro. i. 30; 2 Tim. iii. 2. [Trench § xxix.; Tittmann i. p. 73 sq.; Schmidt ch. 172, 2.]*

214 ἀλαλάζω; [fr. Pind. down]; **a.** prop. *to repeat frequently the cry ἀλαλά*, as soldiers used to do on entering battle. **b.** univ. *to utter a joyful shout*: Ps. xlvi. (xlvii.) 2; lxv. (lxvi.) 2; and in prof. writ. **c.** *to wail, lament*: Mk. v. 38, (הֵילִילוּ Jer. iv. 8; xxxii. 20 (xxv. 34)); cf. ὀλολύζω, Lat. *ululare*. [Syn. see κλαίω fin.] **d.** *to ring loudly, to clang*: 1 Co. xiii. 1, [cf. ἐν κυμβάλοις ἀλαλαγμοῦ, Ps. cl. 5].*

215 ἀ-λάλητος, -ον, (λαλητός fr. λαλέω; [cf. W. 23]), *not to be uttered, not to be expressed in words*: στεναγμοί mute *sighs*, the expression of which is suppressed by grief, Ro. viii. 26, [al. 'which (from their nature) **c a n n o t** be uttered'; cf. Mey. ad loc.; W. 97 (92)]. (Anth. Pal. 5, 4 συνίστορα ἀλαλήτων i. e. of love-secrets.) *

216 ἄ-λαλος, -ον, (λάλος talking, talkative), [fr. Aeschyl. on], *speechless, dumb, wanting the faculty of speech*: Mk. vii. 37; πνεῦμα, Mk. ix. 17, 25, because the defects of demoniacs were thought to proceed from the nature and peculiarities of the demons by which they were possessed. (Sept. Ps. xxxvii. (xxxviii.) 14; xxx. (xxxi.) 19; ἀλάλου καὶ κακοῦ πνεύματος πλήρης, Plut. de orac. def. 51 p. 438 b.) *

217 ἅλας, -ατος, τό, (a later form, found in Sept. and N. T. [Aristot. de mirab. ausc. § 138; Plut. qu. conv. iv. 4, 3, 3], cf. *Bttm.* Ausf. Spr. i. p. 220; dat. ἅλατι Col. iv. 6), and ἅλς, ἁλός, ὁ, (the classic form [fr. Hom. down]; Sir. xxii. 15 (13); xliii. 19; Sap. x. 7; 1 Macc. x. 29, etc.; Mk. ix. 49 ἁλί dat. [T WH Tr mrg. om. Tr txt. br.], and in vs. 50 L T Tr WH ἅλα acc. [yet without the art.] with nom. τὸ ἅλας), finally, nom. and acc. ἅλα Tdf.

in Mk. ix. 50 [also Mt. v. 13; Lk. xiv. 34 (where see his note)] (similar to γάλα, gen. γάλατος, a form noted by certain grammarians, see [*WH.* App. p. 158;] Kühner i. 353 sq.; but see what Fritzsche, Com. on Sir. (xxxix. 26) p. 226 sq., says in opposition); *salt*; **1.** Salt with which food is seasoned and sacrifices are sprinkled: Mk. ix. 49 R G; cf. ἁλίζω. **2.** ἅλας τῆς γῆς, those kinds of saline matter used to fertilize arable land, Mt. v. 13 ᵃ; here salt as a condiment cannot be understood, since this renders land sterile (Deut. xxix. 23; Zeph. ii. 9; Judg. ix. 45); cf. *Grohmann* in Käufer's Bibl. Studien, 1844, p. 82 sqq. The meaning is, 'It is your prerogative to impart to mankind (likened to arable land) the influences required for a life of devotion to God.' In the statement immediately following, ἐὰν δὲ ἅλας κτλ., the comparison seems to be drawn from salt as a condiment, so that two figures are blended; [but it is better to adopt this latter meaning throughout the pass., and take γῆ to denote the mass of mankind, see s. v. 4 b. and cf. Tholuck et al. ad loc.]. In Mk. ix. 50 ᵃ and Lk. xiv. 34 salt is a symbol of that health and vigor of soul which is essential to Christian virtue; [cf. Mey. on the former pass.]. **3.** Salt is a symbol of lasting concord, Mk. ix. 50 ᵉ, because it protects food from putrefaction and preserves it unchanged. Accordingly, in the solemn ratification of compacts, the Orientals were, and are to this day, accustomed to partake of salt together. Cf. *Win.* RWB. s. v. Salz; [BB.DD. s. v. Salt]; Knobel on Leviticus p. 370. **4.** Wisdom and grace exhibited in speech: Col. iv. 6 [where see Bp. Lghtft.].*

Ἅλασσα: Acts xxvii. 8; cf. Λασαία. ---------- see 2996

[ἀλεεύς, ὁ, T WH uniformly for ἁλιεύς, see Tdf.'s note -- see 231 on Mk. i. 16 and N. T. ed. 7, Proleg. p. l.; esp. ed. 8, Proleg. p. 82 sq.; *WH.* App. p. 151.]

218 ἀλείφω: impf. ἤλειφον; 1 aor. ἤλειψα; 1 aor. mid. impv. ἄλειψαι; [allied with λίπ-ος grease; cf. Curtius § 340; Vaniček p. 811; Peile p. 407; fr. Hom. down]; *to anoint*: τινά or τί, Mk. xvi. 1; Jn. xii. 3; τινά or τί τινι [W. 227 (213)], as ἐλαίῳ, Lk. vii. 46 ᵃ; Mk. vi. 13; Jas. v. 14; μύρῳ, Jn. xi. 2; Lk. vii. 38, 46 ᵇ; Mid.: Mt. vi. 17 (lit. 'anoint for thyself thy head,' *unge tibi caput tuum*; cf. W. 257 (242); B. 192 (166 sq.)). Cf. *Win.* RWB. s. v. Salbe; [B.D. or McC. and S. s. v. Anoint, etc. SYN.: "ἀλείφειν is the mundane and profane, χρίειν the sacred and religious, word." Trench § xxxviii. COMP.: ἐξ-αλείφω].*

219 ἀλεκτοροφωνία, -ας, ἡ, (ἀλέκτωρ and φωνή [W. 25]), *the crowing of a cock, cock-crowing*: Aesop. fab. 79 [44]. Used of the third watch of the night: Mk. xiii. 35; in this passage the watches are enumerated into which the Jews, following the Roman method, divided the night; [cf. *Win.* RWB. s. v. Nachtwachen; B. D. s. v. Watches of Night; Alex.'s Kitto s. v. Cock-crowing; Wetst. on Mt. xiv. 25; *Wieseler*, Chron. Syn. p. 406 note]. (For writ. who use this word see *Lob.* ad Phryn. p. 229, [and add (fr. *Soph.* Lex. s. v.) Strab. 7, frag. 35 p. 83, 24; Orig. i. 825 b.; Constt. Ap. 5, 18; 5, 19; 8, 34].) *

220 ἀλέκτωρ, -ορος, ὁ, a cock, (Lat. gallus gallinaceus): Mt. xxvi. 34, 74 sq.; Mk. xiv. 30, 68 [Lchm. br.], 72; Lk. xxii. 34, 60 sq.; Jn. xiii. 38; xviii. 27. Cf. Lob. ad Phryn. p. 229; [Rutherford, New Phryn. p. 307; W. 23; see also BB.DD. s. v.; Tristram, Nat. Hist. of the Bible, p. 221 sq.; esp. Egli, Zeitschr. f. wiss. Theol., 1879 p. 517 sqq.].*

221 Ἀλεξανδρεύς, -έως, ὁ, an Alexandrian, a native or a resident of Alexandria (a celebrated city of Egypt): Acts vi. 9; xviii. 24. [(Plut. Pomp. 49, 6; al.)]*

222 Ἀλεξανδρινός [cf. Tdf.'s note on Acts xxvii. 6; G L Tr Cobet, al. -δρῖνος; Chandler § 397 note], -ή, -όν, Alexandrian: Acts xxvii. 6; xxviii. 11. [(Polyb. 34, 8, 7.)]*

223 Ἀλέξανδρος [i. e. defender of men], -ου, ὁ, Alexander; **1.** a son of that Simon of Cyrene who carried the cross of Jesus: Mk. xv. 21. **2.** a certain man of the kindred of the high priest: Acts iv. 6. **3.** a certain Jew: Acts xix. 33. **4.** a certain coppersmith, an opponent of the apostle Paul: 1 Tim. i. 20; 2 Tim. iv. 14; [al. doubt whether both these passages relate to the same man; cf. e. g. Ellic. on the former].*

224 ἄλευρον, -ου, τό, (ἀλέω to grind), wheaten flour, meal: Mt. xiii. 33; Lk. xiii. 21. Hesych. ἄλευρα κυρίως τὰ τοῦ σίτου, ἄλφιτα δὲ τῶν κριθῶν. (Hdt., Xen., Plat., Joseph., al.)*

225 ἀλήθεια, -ας, ἡ, (ἀληθής), [fr. Hom. down], verity, truth. **I.** objectively; **1.** univ. what is true in any matter under consideration (opp. to what is feigned, fictitious, false): Jas. iii. 14; ἀλήθειαν λέγειν, ἐρεῖν, Jn. viii. 45 sq.; xvi. 7; Ro. ix. 1; 1 Co. xii. 6; 1 Tim. ii. 7; εἶπεν αὐτῷ πᾶσαν τὴν ἀλήθειαν, everything as it really was, Mk. v. 33, (so in classics); μαρτυρεῖν τῇ ἀληθείᾳ to testify according to the true state of the case, Jn. v. 33; in a broader sense, λαλεῖν ἀλήθειαν to speak always according to truth, Eph. iv. 25; [ἀληθείας ῥήματα ἀποφθέγγομαι, as opp. to the vagaries of madness, Acts xxvi. 25]; ἀλήθεια ἐγένετο, was shown to be true by the event, 2 Co. vii. 14. ἐν ἀληθείᾳ in truth, truly, as the case is, according to fact: Mt. xxii. 16; Jn. iv. 23 sq. (as accords with the divine nature); 2 Co. vii. 14; Col. i. 6; ἐπ' ἀληθείας **a.** truly, in truth, according to truth: Mk. xii. 32; Lk. iv. 25, (Job ix. 2 Sept.; Philo, vit. Moys. i. § 1). **b.** of a truth, in reality, in fact, certainly: Mk. xii. 14; Lk. xx. 21; [xxii. 59]; Acts iv. 27; x. 34, (Clem. Rom. 1 Cor. 23, 5 and 47, 3); [cf. W. § 51, 2 f.; B. 336 (289)]; κατ' ἀλήθειαν in accordance with fact, i. e. (acc. to the context) justly, without partiality: Ro. ii. 2; εἴτε προφάσει, εἴτε ἀληθείᾳ, Phil. i. 18; ἐν ἔργῳ κ. ἀληθείᾳ, 1 Jn. iii. 18 [Rec. om. ἐν; so Eph. iv. 21 WH mrg.]. **2.** In reference to religion, the word denotes what is true in things appertaining to God and the duties of man, ('moral and religious truth'); and that **a.** with the greatest latitude, in the sceptical question τί ἐστιν ἀλήθεια, Jn. xviii. 38; **b.** the true notions of God which are open to human reason without his supernatural intervention: Ro. i. 18; also ἡ ἀλήθεια θεοῦ the truth of which God is the author, Ro. i. 25, cf. 19, (ἡ ἀλήθεια τοῦ Χριστοῦ, Evang. Nicod. c. 5, 2); accordingly it is not, as many interpret the phrase, the true nature of God [yet

see Mey. ad loc.]); truth, the embodiment of which the Jews sought in the Mosaic law, Ro. ii. 20. **c.** the truth, as taught in the Christian religion, respecting God and the execution of his purposes through Christ, and respecting the duties of man, opposed alike to the superstitions of the Gentiles and the inventions of the Jews, and to the corrupt opinions and precepts of false teachers even among Christians: ἡ ἀλήθεια τοῦ εὐαγγ. the truth which is the gospel or which the gospel presents, Gal. ii. 5, 14, [cf. W. § 34, 3 a.]; and absol. ἡ ἀλήθεια and ἀλήθεια: Jn. i. 14, 17; viii. 32, 40; [xvi. 13]; xvii. 19; 1 Jn. i. 8; ii. 4, 21; 2 Jn. 1–3; Gal. iii. 1 (Rec.); v. 7; 2 Co. iv. 2; xiii. 8; Eph. iv. 24; 2 Th. ii. 10, 12; 1 Tim. ii. 7 (ἐν πίστει κ. ἀληθείᾳ in faith and truth, of which I became a partaker through faith); iii. 15; iv. 3; vi. 5; 2 Tim. ii. 18; iii. 8; iv. 4; Tit. i. 14; 2 Pet. i. 12; [3 Jn. 8, 12]; ὁ λόγος τῆς ἀληθείας, Col. i. 5; Eph. i. 13; 2 Tim. ii. 15; λόγος ἀληθείας, 2 Co. vi. 7; Jas. i. 18; ὁδὸς τῆς ἀλ. 2 Pet. ii. 2; πίστις ἀληθείας, 2 Th. ii. 13 [W. 186 (175)]; ὑπακοὴ τῆς ἀλ. 1 Pet. i. 22; ἐπίγνωσις τῆς ἀλ. Heb. x. 26; 1 Tim. ii. 4; 2 Tim. ii. 25; iii. 7; [Tit. i. 1]; πνεῦμα τῆς ἀλ. the Spirit (of God) which is truth (1 Jn. v. 6) and imbues men with the knowledge of the truth, Jn. xiv. 17; [xvi. 13]; xv. 26; 1 Jn. iv. 6; ἐγώ εἰμι ἡ ἀλήθεια I am he in whom the truth is summed up and impersonated, Jn. xiv. 6; ἡ ἀλήθειά σου [Rec.] (i. e. θεοῦ) the truth which is in thee and proceeds from thee, Jn. xvii. 17; [ἔστιν ἀλήθεια Χριστοῦ ἐν ἐμοί i. e. controls, actuates, me, 2 Co. xi. 10]; εἶναι ἐκ τῆς ἀληθείας to be eager to know the truth, Jn. xviii. 37 (see ἐκ, II. 7, and εἰμί, V. 3 d.); to proceed from the truth, 1 Jn. ii. 21; to be prompted and controlled by the truth, 1 Jn. iii. 19; μαρτυρεῖν τῇ ἀληθ. to give testimony in favor of the truth in order to establish its authority among men, Jn. xviii. 37; ἀλήθειαν ποιεῖν to exemplify truth in the life, to express the form of truth in one's habits of thought and modes of living, Jn. iii. 21; 1 Jn. i. 6, (Tob. xiii. 6; iv. 6; cf. Neh. ix. 33; ὁδὸν ἀληθείας αἱρετίζεσθαι, Ps. cxviii. (cxix.) 30); so also περιπατεῖν ἐν τῇ ἀλ. 2 Jn. 4; 3 Jn. 3 sq.; ἀπειθεῖν τῇ ἀλ. is just the opposite, Ro. ii. 8; so also πλανηθῆναι ἀπὸ τῆς ἀλ. Jas. v. 19. **II.** subjectively; truth as a personal excellence; that candor of mind which is free from affectation, pretence, simulation, falsehood, deceit: Jn. viii. 44; sincerity of mind and integrity of character, or a mode of life in harmony with divine truth: 1 Co. v. 8; xiii. 6 (opp. to ἀδικία); Eph. iv. 21 [see I. 1 b. above]; v. 9; [vi. 14]; σοῦ ἡ ἀλήθεια the truth as it is discerned in thee, thy habit of thinking and acting in congruity with truth, 3 Jn. 3; ἡ ἀλήθεια τοῦ θεοῦ which belongs to God, i. e. his holiness [but cf. περισσεύω, 1 b. fin.], Ro. iii. 7; spec. veracity (of God in keeping his promises), Ro. xv. 8; ἐν ἀληθείᾳ sincerely and truthfully, 2 Jn. 1; 3 Jn. 1. The word is not found in Rev. ([nor in 1 Thess., Philem., Jude]). Cf. Hölemann, "Bibelstudien ", (Lpz. 1859) 1te Abth. p. 8 sqq.; [Wendt in Stud. u. Krit., 1883, p. 511 sqq]*

ἀληθεύω; in prof. writ. ([Aeschyl.], Xen., Plat., Aristot., al.) to speak the truth; **a.** to teach the truth: τιν.

Gal. iv. 16. **b.** to profess the truth (true doctrine):
Eph. iv. 15. [R. V. mrg. in both pass. *to deal truly.*] *

ἀληθής, -ές, (*a* priv. and λήθω, λαθεῖν [λανθάνω], τὸ
λῆθος, — cf. *ἀμαθής*; lit. *not hidden, unconcealed*), [fr.
Hom. down]; **1.** *true:* Jn. iv. 18; x. 41; xix. 35;
1 Jn. ii. 8, 27; Acts xii. 9 (an actual occurrence, opp.
to ὄραμα); Phil. iv. 8; μαρτυρία, Jn. v. 31 sq.; viii.
13 sq. 17; xxi. 24; 3 Jn. 12; Tit. i. 13; κρίσις, just,
Jn. viii. 16 (L T Tr WH ἀληθινή); παροιμία, 2 Pet. ii.
22; χάρις, grace which can be trusted, 1 Pet. v. 12.
2. *loving the truth, speaking the truth, truthful:* Mt. xxii.
16; Mk. xii. 14; Jn. viii. 14; 2 Co. vi. 8 (opp. to
πλάνος); of God, Jn. iii. 33; viii. 26; Ro. iii. 4 (opp. to
ψεύστης). **3.** i. q. ἀληθινός, 1: Jn. vi. 55 (L T Tr
WH; for Rec. ἀληθῶς), as in Sap. xii. 27, where ἀληθὴς
θεός is contrasted with οὓς ἐδόκουν θεούς. Cf. *Rückert,*
Abendmahl, p. 266 sq. [On the distinction betw. this
word and the next, see Trench § viii.; Schmidt ch. 178, 6.] *

ἀληθινός, -ή, -όν, (freq. in prof. writ. fr. Plato down;
[twenty-three times in Jn.'s writ.; only five (acc. to
Lchm. six) times in the rest of the N. T.]); **1.** "*that
which has not only the name and semblance, but the real
nature corresponding to the name*" (Tittmann p. 155;
["particularly applied to express that which is all that it
pretends to be, for instance, pure gold as opp. to adulterated metal" *Donaldson,* New Crat. § 258; see, at
length, Trench § viii.]), *in every respect corresponding to
the idea signified by the name, real and true, genuine;*
a. opp. to what is fictitious, counterfeit, imaginary,
simulated, pretended: θεός (אֱלֹהֵי אֱמֶת, 2 Chr. xv. 3),
1 Th. i. 9; Heb. ix. 14 Lchm.; Jn. xvii. 3; 1 Jn. v. 20.
(ἀληθινοὶ φίλοι, Dem. Phil. 3, p. 113, 27.) **b.** it contrasts realities with their semblances: σκηνή, Heb. viii.
2; the sanctuary, Heb. ix. 24. (ὁ ἵππος contrasted
with ὁ ἐν τῇ εἰκόνι, Ael. v. h. 2, 3.) **c.** opp. to what is
imperfect, defective, frail, uncertain: Jn. iv. 23, 37; vii.
28; used without adjunct of Jesus as the true Messiah,
Rev. iii. 7; φῶς, Jn. i. 9; 1 Jn. ii. 8; κρίσις, Jn. viii. 16
(L T Tr WH; Is. lix. 4); κρίσεις, Rev. xvi. 7; xix. 2;
ἄρτος, as nourishing the soul unto life everlasting, Jn.
vi. 32; ἄμπελος, Jn. xv. 1; μαρτυρία, Jn. xix. 35; μάρτυς,
Rev. iii. 14; δεσπότης, Rev. vi. 10; ὁδοί, Rev. xv. 3;
coupled with πιστός, Rev. iii. 14; xix. 11; substantively,
τὸ ἀληθινόν the genuine, real good, opp. to external
riches, Lk. xvi. 11, ([οἷς μὲν γὰρ ἀληθινὸς πλοῦτος ἐν
οὐρανῷ, Philo de praem. et poen. § 17, p. 425 ed.
Mang.; cf. Wetst. on Lk. l. c.]; ἀθληταί, Polyb. 1, 6, 6).
2. i. q. ἀληθής, true, veracious, sincere, (often so in Sept.):
καρδία, Heb. x. 22 (μετ' ἀληθείας ἐν καρδίᾳ ἀληθινῇ, Is.
xxxviii. 3); λόγοι, Rev. [xix. 9]; xxi. 5; xxii. 6, (Plut.
apoph. p. 184 e.). [Cf. Cremer 4te Aufl. s. v. ἀλήθεια.]*

ἀλήθω; (a com. Grk. form for the Attic ἀλέω, cf. *Lob.*
ad Phryn. p. 151); *to grind:* Mt. xxiv. 41; Lk. xvii.
35. It was the custom to send women and female slaves
to the mill-houses [?] to turn the hand-mills (Ex. xi. 5),
who were called by the Greeks γυναῖκες ἀλετρίδες (Hom.
Od. 20, 105); [cf. B. D. s. v. Mill].*

ἀληθῶς, adv., [fr. Aeschyl. down], *truly, of a truth, in*

reality; most certainly: Jn. i. 47 (48); iv. 42; vi. 14, 55
Rec.; vii. 26, 40; viii. 31; xvii. 8; Mt. xiv. 33; xxvi.
73; [Mk. xiv. 70; Mt.] xxvii. 54; [Mk. xv. 39]; Lk.
ix. 27; xii. 44; xxi. 3; Acts xii. 11; 1 Th. ii. 13; 1 Jn.
ii. 5.*

ἀλιεύς, -έως, ὁ, (ἅλς, ἁλός, the sea), [fr. Hom. down];
a fisherman, fisher: Mt. iv. 18 sq.; Mk. i. 16 sq.; Lk.
v. 2, — in all which pass. T and WH have ἁλιεῖς fr. the
form ἁλεεύς, q. v.*

ἁλιεύω; (ἁλιεύς); *to fish:* Jn. xxi. 3. [Philo, Plut.]*

ἁλίζω: (ἅλς, ἁλός, salt); *to salt, season with salt, sprinkle with salt;* only the fut. pass. is found in the N. T.:
ἐν τίνι ἁλισθήσεται; by what means can its saltness be
restored? Mt. v. 13; θυσία ἁλὶ ἁλισθήσεται, the sacrifice
is sprinkled with salt and thus rendered acceptable to
God, Mk. ix. 49 [R G L Tr txt. br.], (Lev. ii. 13; Ezek.
xliii. 24; Joseph. antt. 3, 9, 1; cf. Knobel on Lev.
p. 369 sq.; *Win.* RWB. s. v. Salz; [BB.DD. s. v. Salt]);
πᾶς πυρὶ ἁλισθήσεται, every true Christian is rendered
ripe for a holy and happy association with God in his
kingdom by fire, i. e. by the pain of afflictions and
trials, which if endured with constancy tend to purge
and strengthen the soul, Mk. ix. 49. But this extremely difficult passage is explained differently by
others; [cf. Meyer, who also briefly reviews the history
of its exposition]. (Used by the Sept., Aristot., [cf.
Soph. Lex.]; Ignat. ad Magnes. 10 [shorter form] ἁλί-
σθητε ἐν Χριστῷ, ἵνα μὴ διαφθαρῇ τις ἐν ὑμῖν.) [COMP.:
συν-αλίζω, — but see the word.]*

ἁλίσγημα, -τος, τό, (ἁλισγέω to pollute, which occurs
Sir. xl. 29; Dan. i. 8; Mal. i. 7, 12; akin to ἀλίνω, ἀλινέω
to besmear [Lat. *linere,* cf. *Lob.* Pathol. Element. p. 21;
Rhemat. p. 123; Steph., Hesych., *Sturz,* De Dial. Alex.
p. 145]), *pollution, contamination:* Acts xv. 20 (τοῦ
ἀπέχεσθαι κτλ. to beware of pollution from the use
of meats left from the heathen sacrifices, cf. vs. 29).
Neither ἀλισγέω nor ἁλίσγημα occurs in Grk. writ.*

ἀλλά, an adversative particle, derived from ἄλλα,
neut. of the adj. ἄλλος, which was originally pronounced
ἀλλός (cf. *Klotz* ad Devar. ii. p. 1 sq.), hence properly,
other things sc. than those just mentioned. It differs
from δέ, as the Lat. *at* and *sed* from *autem*, [cf. W. 441
sq. (411)]. **I.** *But.* So related to the preceding words
that it serves to introduce **1.** an opposition to concessions; *nevertheless, notwithstanding:* Mt. xxiv. 6;
Mk. xiii. 20; xiv. 28; Jn. xvi. 7, 20; Acts iv. 17; vii.
48; Ro. v. 14 sq.; x. 16; 1 Co. iv. 4; 2 Co. vii. 6;
Phil. ii. 27 (ἀλλ' ὁ θεός etc.), etc. **2.** an objection:
Jn. vii. 27; Ro. x. 18 sq.; 1 Co. xv. 35; Jas. ii. 18.
3. an exception: Lk. xxii. 53; Ro. iv. 2; 1 Co. i. 7;
x. 23. **4.** a restriction: Jn. xi. 42; Gal. iv. 8; Mk.
xiv. 36. **5.** an ascensive transition or gradation,
nay rather, yea moreover: Jn. xvi. 2; 2 Co. i. 9; esp.
with καί added, Lk. xii. 7; xvi. 21; xxiv. 22. ἀλλ' οὐδέ,
but . . . not even (Germ. *ja nicht einmal*): Lk. xxiii. 15;
Acts xix. 2; 1 Co. iii. 2 [Rec. οὔτε]; cf. Fritzsche on
Mk. p. 157. **6.** or forms a transition to the cardinal
matter, especially before imperatives: Mt. ix. 18; Mk.

ix. 22; xvi. 7; Lk. vii. 7; Jn. viii. 26; xvi. 4; Acts ix. 6 [not Rec.]; x. 20; xxvi. 16. **7.** it is put elliptically: ἀλλ' ἵνα, i. e. ἀλλὰ τοῦτο γέγονεν, ἵνα, Mk. xiv. 49; Jn. xiii. 18; xv. 25; 1 Jn. ii. 19. **8.** after a conditional or concessive protasis it signifies, at the beginning of the apodosis, *yet* [cf. W. 442 (411)]: after καὶ εἰ, 2 Co. xiii. 4 [R G]; Mk. xiv. 29 R G L, (2 Macc. viii. 15); after εἰ καί, Mk. xiv. 29 [T Tr WH]; 2 Co. iv. 16; v. 16; xi. 6; Col. ii. 5, (2 Macc. vi. 26); after εἰ, 1 Co. ix. 2; Ro. vi. 5, (1 Macc. ii. 20); after ἐάν, 1 Co. iv. 15; after εἴπερ, 1 Co. viii. 6 [L Tr mrg. WH br. ἀλλ']; cf. *Klotz* ad Devar. ii. p. 93 sq.; Kühner i. p. 827, § 535 Anm. 6. **9.** after a preceding μέν: Mk. ix. 13 [T om. Tr br. μέν]; Acts iv. 16; Ro. xiv. 20; 1 Co. xiv. 17. **10.** it is joined to other particles; ἀλλά γε [Grsb. ἀλλάγε] (twice in the N. T.): *yet at least*, 1 Co. ix. 2; *yet surely* (*aber freilich*), Lk. xxiv. 21 [L T Tr WH add καί *yea and* etc.], cf. Bornemann ad loc. In the more elegant Greek writers these particles are not combined without the interposition of the most emphatic word between them; cf. Bornemann l. c.; *Klotz* ad Devar. ii. pp. 15 sq. 24 sq.; *Ast*, Lex. Plat. i. p. 101; [W. 444 (413)]. ἀλλ' ἤ (arising from the blending of the two statements οὐδὲν ἄλλο ἤ and οὐδὲν ἄλλο, ἀλλά) *save only*, *except*: 1 Co. iii. 5 (where ἀλλ' ἤ omitted by G L T Tr WH is spurious); Lk. xii. 51, (Sir. xxxvii. 12; xliv. 10); and after ἄλλα itself, 2 Co. i. 13 [here Lchm. br. ἀλλ' before ἤ]; cf. Klotz u. s. ii. 31 sqq.; Kühner ii. p. 824 sq. § 535, 6; W. 442 (412); [B. 374 (320)]. ἀλλ' οὐ *but not*, *yet not*: Heb. iii. 16 (if punctuated παρεπίκραναν; ἀλλ' οὐ for 'but why do I ask? did not all,' etc.; cf. Bleek ad loc. [W. 442 (411)]. ἀλλ' οὐχί *will he not rather*? Lk. xvii. 8. **II.** preceded by a negation: *but* (Lat. *sed*, Germ. *sondern*); **1.** οὐκ (μή) ... ἀλλά: Mt. xix. 11; Mk. v. 39; Jn. vii. 16; 1 Co. i. 17; vii. 10, 19 [οὐδέν]; 2 Co. vii. 9; 1 Tim. v. 23 [μηκέτι], etc. By a rhetorical construction οὐκ ... ἀλλά sometimes is logically equiv. to *not so much* ... *as*: Mk. ix. 37 (οὐκ ἐμὲ δέχεται, ἀλλὰ τὸν ἀποστείλαντά με); Mt. x. 20; Jn. xii. 44; Acts v. 4; 1 Co. xv. 10; 1 Th. iv. 8; by this form of speech the emphasis is laid on the second member; cf. Fritzsche on Mk. p. 773 sqq.; W. § 55, 8 b.; [B. 356 (306)]. οὐ μόνον ... ἀλλὰ καί *not only* ... *but also*: Jn. v. 18; xi. 52 [ἀλλ' ἵνα καί, etc.]; Ro. i. 32, and very often. When καί is omitted (as in the Lat. *non solum ... sed*), the gradation is strengthened: Acts xix. 26 [Lchm. adds καί]; 1 Jn. v. 6; ἀλλὰ πολλῷ μᾶλλον, Phil. ii. 12; cf. Fritzsche l. c. p. 786 sqq.; W. 498 (464); [B. 369 sq. (317)]. **2.** The negation to which ἀλλά pertains is suppressed, but can easily be supplied upon reflection [W. 442 (412)]: Mt. xi. 7–9; Lk. vii. 24–26, (in each passage, before ἀλλά supply 'you will say you did not go out into the wilderness for this purpose'); Acts xix. 2 (we have not received the Holy Spirit, but . . .); Gal. ii. 3 (they said not one word in opposition to me, but . . .); 2 Co. vii. 11 (where before ἀλλά, repeated six times by anaphora, supply οὐ μόνον with the accus. of the preceding

word). It is used in answers to questions having the force of a negation [W. 442 (412)]: Jn. vii. 49; Acts xv. 11; 1 Co. x. 20. ἀλλὰ ἵνα [or ἀλλ' ἵνα, cf. W. 40; B. 10] elliptical after a negation [W. 316 sq. (297); 620 (576); Fritzsche on Mt. p. 840 sq.]: Jn. i. 8 (supply ἀλλὰ ἦλθεν, ἵνα); ix. 3 (ἀλλὰ τυφλὸς ἐγένετο [or ἐγεννήθη], ἵνα]; Mk. iv. 22 (ἀλλὰ τοιοῦτο ἐγένετο, ἵνα). ["The best Mss. seem to elide the final a before nouns, but not before verbs" *Scrivener*, Plain Introduction, etc., p. 14; but see Dr. Gregory's full exhibition of the facts in *Tdf.* Proleg. p. 93 sq., from which it appears that "elision is commonly or almost always omitted before a, almost always before v, often before ε and η, rarely before o and ω, never before ι; and it should be noticed that this coincides with the fact that the familiar words ἐν, ἵνα, ὅτι, οὐ, ὡς, prefer the form ἀλλ'"; see also WH. App. p. 146. Cf. W. § 5, 1 a.; B. p. 10.]

ἀλλάσσω: fut. ἀλλάξω; 1 aor. ἤλλαξα; 2 fut. pass. ἀλλαγήσομαι; (ἄλλος); [fr. Aeschyl. down]; *to change*: to cause one thing to cease and another to take its place, τὰ ἔθη, Acts vi. 14; τὴν φωνήν to vary the voice, i. e. to speak in a different manner according to the different conditions of minds, to adapt the matter and form of discourse to mental moods, to treat them now severely, now gently, Gal. iv. 20 [but see Meyer ad loc.]. *to exchange one thing for another*: τὶ ἔν τινι, Ro. i. 23 (בְּ הֵמִיר Ps. cv. (cvi.) 20); the Greeks say ἀλλάσσειν τί τινος [cf. W. 206 (194), 388 (363); Vaughan on Rom. l. c.]). *to transform*: 1 Co. xv. 51 sq.; Heb. i. 12. [Comp.: ἀπ-, δι-, κατ-, ἀπο-κατ-, μετ-, συν-αλλάσσω.]*

ἀλλαχόθεν, adv., *from another place*: Jn. x. 1 (i. q. ἄλλοθεν [which the grammarians prefer, Thom. Mag. ed. Ritschl p. 10, 13; Moeris ed. Piers. p. 11]; cf. ἑκασταχόθεν, πανταχόθεν). [(Antiph., al.)]*

ἀλλαχοῦ, adv., i. q. ἄλλοθι, *elsewhere*, *in another place*: Mk. i. 38 (T Tr txt. WH Tr mrg. br.). Cf. Bornemann in the Stud. u. Krit. for 1843, p. 127 sq. [Soph., Xen., al.; see Thom. M. and Moer. as in the preced. word.]*

ἀλληγορέω, -ῶ: [pres. pass. ptcp. ἀλληγορούμενος]; i. e. ἄλλο μὲν ἀγορεύω, ἄλλο δὲ νοέω, "aliud verbis, aliud sensu ostendo" (Quint. instt. 8, 6, 44), *to speak allegorically* or *in a figure*: Gal. iv. 24. (Philo, Joseph., Plut., and gram. writ.; [cf. Mey. on Gal. l. c.].)*

ἀλληλούϊα, [WH. Ἀλλ. and -ά; see Intr. § 408], Hebr. הַלְלוּ־יָהּ, *praise ye the Lord*, *Hallelujah*: Rev. xix. 1, 3 sq. 6. [Sept. Pss. *passim*; Tob. xiii. 18; 3 Macc. vii. 13.]*

ἀλλήλων, gen. plur. [no nom. being possible]; dat. -οις, -αις, -οις; acc. -ους, -ας, -α, *one another*; *reciprocally*, *mutually*: Mt. xxiv. 10; Jn. xiii. 35; Acts xxviii. 25; Ro. i. 12; Jas. v. 16; Rev. vi. 4, and often. [Fr. Hom. down.]

ἀλλογενής, -ές, (ἄλλος and γένος), *sprung from another race*, *a foreigner*, *alien*: Lk. xvii. 18. (In Sept. [Gen. xvii. 27; Ex. xii. 43, etc.], but nowhere in prof. writ.)*

ἄλλομαι, impf. ἡλλόμην; aor. ἡλάμην and ἡλόμην [Bttm. Ausf. Spr. ii. p. 108; [W. 82 (79); B. 54 (47)]]; *to leap* (Lat. *salio*): Acts iii. 8; xiv. 10 (Rec. ἥλλετο;

236

237

see 237

238

239

240

241

242

G L T Tr WH ἥλατο); *to spring up, gush up,* of water, Jn. iv. 14, (as in Lat. *salire,* Verg. ecl. 5, 47; Suet. Octav. 82). [Comp.: ἐξ-, ἐφ-άλλομαι.]*

243   ἄλλος, -η, -ο, [cf. Lat. *alius,* Germ. *alles,* Eng. *else*; fr. Hom. down], *another, other*; **a.** absol.: Mt. xxvii. 42; xx. 3; Mk. vi. 15; Acts xix. 32; xxi. 34 (ἄλλοι μὲν ἄλλο), and often.   **b.** as an adj.: Mt. ii. 12; iv. 21; Jn. xiv. 16; 1 Co. x. 29 (ἄλλη συνείδησις i. e. ἡ συν. ἄλλου τινός).   **c.** with the art.: ὁ ἄλλος *the other* (of two), Mt. v. 39; xii. 13, etc. [cf. B. 32 (28), 122 (107)]; οἱ ἄλλοι *all others, the remainder, the rest*: Jn. xxi. 8; 1 Co. xiv. 29.

[Syn. ἄλλος, ἕτερος: ἄλ. as compared with ἕτ. denotes numerical in distinction from qualitative difference; ἄλ. adds (' one besides '), ἕτ. distinguishes (' one of two '); every ἕτ. is an ἄλ., but not every ἄλ. is a ἕτ.; ἄλ. generally ' denotes simply distinction of i n d i v i d u a l s, ἕτερος involves the secondary idea of difference of k i n d '; e. g. 2 Co. xi. 4; Gal. i. 6, 7. See Bp. Lghtft. and Mey. on the latter pass.; Trench § xcv.; Schmidt ch. 198.]

244   ἀλλοτριο-επίσκοπος (L T Tr WH ἀλλοτριεπ.), -ου, ὁ, (ἀλλότριος and ἐπίσκοπος), *one who takes the supervision of affairs pertaining to others and in no wise to himself,* [*a meddler in other men's matters*]: 1 Pet. iv. 15 (the writer seems to refer to those who, with holy but intemperate zeal, meddle with the affairs of the Gentiles — whether public or private, civil or sacred — in order to make them conform to the Christian standard). [Hilgenfeld (cf. Einl. ins N. T. p. 630) would make it equiv. to the Lat. *delator.*] The word is found again only in Dion. Areop. ep. 8 p. 783 (of one who intrudes into another's office), and [Germ. of Const. ep. 2 ad Cypr. c. 9, in] Coteler. Eccl. Graec. Mon. ii. 481 b.; [cf. W. 25, 99 (94)].*

245   ἀλλότριος, -α, -ον; **1.** *belonging to another* (opp. to ἴδιος), *not one's own*: Heb. ix. 25; Ro. xiv. 4; xv. 20; 2 Co. x. 15 sq.; 1 Tim. v. 22; Jn. x. 5. in neut., Lk. xvi. 12 (opp. to τὸ ὑμέτερον). **2.** *foreign, strange*: γῆ, Acts vii. 6; Heb. xi. 9; *not of one's own family, alien,* Mt. xvii. 25 sq.; *an enemy,* Heb. xi. 34, (Hom. Il. 5, 214; Xen. an. 3, 5, 5).*

246   ἀλλόφυλος, -ον, (ἄλλος, and φῦλον race), *foreign,* (in prof. auth. fr. [Aeschyl.,] Thuc. down); when used in Hellenistic Grk. in opp. to a J e w, it signifies *a Gentile,* [A. V. *one of another nation*]: Acts x. 28.   (Philo, Joseph.)*

247   ἄλλως, adv., (ἄλλος), [fr. Hom. down], *otherwise*: 1 Tim. v. 25 (τὰ ἄλλως ἔχοντα, which are of a different sort i. e. which are not καλὰ ἔργα, [al. which are not πρόδηλα]).*

248   ἀλοάω, -ῶ; (connected with ἡ ἅλως or ἡ ἁλωή, the floor on which grain is trodden or threshed out); *to thresh,* (Ammon. τὸ ἐπὶ τῇ ἅλῳ πατεῖν καὶ τρίβειν τὰς στάχυας): 1 Co. ix. [9], 10; 1 Tim. v. 18 (Deut. xxv. 4). In prof. auth. fr. Arstph., Plato down.*

249   ἄ-λογος, -ον, (λόγος reason); **1.** *destitute of reason, brute*: ζῷα, brute animals, Jude 10; 2 Pet. ii. 12, (Sap. xi. 16; Xen. Hier. 7, 3, al.).   **2.** *contrary to reason, absurd*: Acts xxv. 27, (Xen. Ages. 11, 1; Thuc. 6, 85; often in Plat., Isocr., al.).*

ἀλόη [on the accent see Chandler § 149], -ης, ἡ, (commonly ξυλαλόη, ἀγάλλοχον), Plut., *the aloe, aloes*: Jn. xix. 39. The name of an aromatic tree which grows in eastern India and Cochin China, and whose soft and bitter wood the Orientals used in fumigation and in embalming the dead (as, acc. to Hdt., the Egyptians did), Hebr. אֲהָלִים and אֲהָלוֹת [see Mühlau and Volck s. vv.], Num. xxiv. 6; Ps. xlv. 9; Prov. vii. 17; Cant. iv. 14. Arab. *Alluwe*; Linn.: *Excoecaria Agallochum.* Cf. Win. RWB. s. v. Aloë [Löw § 235; BB.DD] **250, 251; see 217**

ἅλς, ἁλός, ὁ, see ἅλας. — — — — — — — — — — see 217

ἁλυκός, -ή, -όν, *salt* (i. q. ἁλμυρός): Jas. iii. 12. ([Hippocr., Arstph.,] Plat. Tim. p. 65 e.; Aristot., Theophr., al.)*   **252**

ἄλυπος, -ον, (λύπη), *free from pain* or *grief*: Phil. ii. 28. (Very often in Grk. writ. fr. Soph. and Plat. down.)*   **see 253 St.**

ἅλυσις, or as it is com. written ἄλυσις [see WH. App. p. 144], -εως, ἡ, (fr. a priv. and λύω, because a chain is ἄλυτος i. e. not to be loosed [al. fr. r. val, and allied w. εἰλέω to restrain, ἁλίζω to collect, crowd; Curtius § 660; Vaniček p. 898]), *a chain, bond,* by which the body, or any part of it (the hands, feet), is bound: Mk. v. 3; Acts xxi. 33; xxviii. 20; Rev. xx. 1; ἐν ἁλύσει in chains, a prisoner, Eph. vi. 20; οὐκ ἐπαισχύνθη τὴν ἅλ. μου he was not ashamed of my bonds i. e. did not desert me because I was a prisoner, 2 Tim. i. 16. spec. used of *a manacle* or *hand-cuff,* the chain by which the hands are bound together [yet cf. Mey. on Mk. u. i.; per contra esp. Bp. Lghtft. on Phil. p. 8]: Mk. v. 4; [Lk. viii. 29]; Acts xii. 6 sq. (From Hdt. down.)*   **254**

ἀ-λυσιτελής, -ές, (λυσιτελής, see λυσιτελέω), *unprofitable,* (Xen. vectig. 4, 6); by litotes, *hurtful, pernicious*: Heb. xiii. 17. (From [Hippocr.,] Xen. down.)*   **255**

ἄλφα, τό, indecl.: Rev. i. 8; xxi. 6; xxii. 13. See A   **see 1**

Ἀλφαῖος [WH Ἀλφ., see their Intr. § 408], -αίου, ὁ, (חַלְפַּי, cf. חַגַּי Ἀγγαῖος, Hag. i. 1), *Alphæus* or *Alpheus*; **1.** the father of Levi the publican: Mk. ii. 14, see Λευΐ, 4.   **2.** the father of James the less, so called, one of the twelve apostles: Mt. x. 3; Mk. iii. 18; Lk. vi. 15; Acts i. 13. He seems to be the same person who in Jn. xix. 25 (cf. Mt. xxvii. 56; Mk. xv. 40) is called Κλωπᾶς after a different pronunciation of the Hebr. חלפי acc. to which ח was changed into κ, as פֶּסַח φασέκ, 2 Chr. xxx. 1. Cf. Ἰάκωβος, 2; [B. D. Am. ed. s. v. Alphæus; also Bp. Lghtft. Com. on Gal. pp. 256, 267 (Am. ed. pp. 92, 103); *Wetzel* in Stud. u. Krit. for 1883, p. 620 sq.].*   **256**

ἅλων, -ωνος, ἡ, (in Sept. also ὁ, cf. Ruth iii. 2; Job xxxix. 12), i. q. ἅλως, gen. ἅλω, *a ground-plot* or *threshing-floor,* i. e. a place in the field itself, made hard after the harvest by a roller, where the grain was threshed out: Mt. iii. 12; Lk. iii. 17. In both these pass., by meton. of the container for the thing contained, ἅλων is the heap of grain, *the flooring,* already indeed threshed out, but still mixed with chaff and straw, like Hebr. גֹּרֶן, Ruth iii. 2; Job xxxix. 12 (Sept. in each place ἅλωνα); [al. adhere to the primary meaning. Used by Aristot. de vent. 3, Opp. ii. 973ᵃ, 14].*   **257**

ἀλώπηξ, -εκος, ἡ, *a fox*: Mt. viii. 20; Lk. ix. 58.   **258**

Metaph. a sly and crafty man: Lk. xiii. 32; (in the same sense often in the Grk. writ., as Solon in Plut. Sol. 30, 2; Pind. Pyth. 2, 141; Plut. Sulla 28, 5).*

259 ἅλωσις, -εως, ἡ, (ἁλόω, ἁλίσκομαι to be caught), a catching, capture: 2 Pet. ii. 12 εἰς ἅλωσιν to be taken, [some would here take the word actively: to take]. (Fr. Pind. and Hdt. down.) *

260 ἅμα [Skr. sa, sama; Eng. same; Lat. simul; Germ. sammt, etc.; Curtius § 449; Vaniček p. 972. Fr. Hom. down]; **1.** adv., at the same time, at once, together: Acts xxiv. 26; xxvii. 40; Col. iv. 3; 1 Tim. v. 13; Philem. 22; all to a man, every one, Ro. iii. 12. **2.** prep. [W. 470 (439)], together with, with dat.: Mt. xiii. 29. ἅμα πρωΐ early in the morning: Mt. xx. 1, (in Grk. writ. ἅμα τῷ ἡλίῳ, ἅμα τῇ ἡμέρᾳ). In 1 Th. iv. 17 and v. 10, where ἅμα is foll. by σύν, ἅμα is an adv. (at the same time) and must be joined to the verb.*

[Syn. ἅμα, ὁμοῦ: the distinction given by Ammonius (de diff. voc. s. v.) et al., that ἅμα is temporal, ὁμοῦ local, seems to hold in the main; yet see Ro. iii. 12, and cf. Hesych. s. v.]

261 ἀμαθής, -ές, gen. -οῦς, (μανθάνω, whence ἔμαθον, τὸ μάθος, cf. ἀληθής), unlearned, ignorant: 2 Pet. iii. 16. (In Grk. writ. fr. Hdt. down.)*

262 ἀμαράντινος, -ον, (fr. ἀμάραντος, as ῥόδινος made of roses, fr. ῥόδον a rose; cf. ἀκάνθινος), composed of amaranth (a flower, so called because it never withers or fades, and when plucked off revives if moistened with water; hence it is a symbol of perpetuity and immortality, [see Paradise Lost iii. 353 sqq.]; Plin. h. n. 21 (15), 23 [al. 47]): στέφανος, 1 Pet. v. 4. (Found besides only in Philostr. her. 19, p. 741; [and (conjecturally) in Boeckh, Corp. Inscr. 155, 39, c. B. C. 340].) *

263 ἀμάραντος, -ον, (fr. μαραίνω; cf. ἀμίαντος, ἄφαντος, etc.), not fading away, unfading, perennial; Vulg. immarcescibilis; (hence the name of the flower, [Diosc. 4, 57, al.]; see ἀμαράντινος): 1 Pet. i. 4. Found elsewhere only in Sap. vi. 13; [ζωὴ ἀμαρ. Sibyll. 8, 411; Boeckh, Corp. Inscr. ii. p. 1124, no. 2942 c, 4; Lcian. Dom. c. 9].*

264 ἁμαρτάνω; fut. ἁμαρτήσω (Mt. xviii. 21; Ro. vi. 15; in the latter pass. LTTrWH give ἁμαρτήσωμεν for RG ἁμαρτήσομεν), in class. Grk. ἁμαρτήσομαι; 1 aor. (later) ἡμάρτησα, Mt. xviii. 15; Ro. v. 14, 16 (cf. W. 82 (79); B. 54 (47)); 2 aor. ἥμαρτον; pf. ἡμάρτηκα; (acc. to a conjecture of Bttm., Lexil. i. p. 137, fr. a priv. and μείρω, μείρομαι, μέρος, prop. to be without a share in, sc. the mark); prop. to miss the mark, (Hom. Il. 8, 311, etc.; with gen. of the thing missed, Hom. Il. 10, 372; 4, 491; τοῦ σκοποῦ, Plat. Hipp. min. p. 375 a.; τῆς ὁδοῦ, Arstph. Plut. 961, al.); then to err, be mistaken; lastly to miss or wander from the path of uprightness and honor, to do or go wrong. ["Even the Sept., although the Hebr. חטא also means primarily to miss, endeavor to reserve ἁμαρτ. exclusively for the idea of sin; and where the Hebr. signifies to miss one's aim in the literal sense, they avail themselves of expressive compounds, in particular ἐξαμαρτάνειν, Judg. xx. 16." Zezschwitz, Profangraec. u. bibl. Sprachgeist, p. 63 sq.] In the N. T.

to wander from the law of God, violate God's law, sin; **a.** absol.: Mt. xxvii. 4; Jn. v. 14; viii. 11; ix. 2 sq.; 1 Jn. i. 10; ii. 1; iii. 6, 8 sq.; v. 18; Ro. ii. 12; iii. 23; v. 12, 14, 16; vi. 15; 1 Co. vii. 28, 36; xv. 34; Eph. iv. 26; 1 Tim. v. 20; Tit. iii. 11; Heb. iii. 17; x. 26 (ἑκουσίως); [2 Pet. ii. 4]; of the violation of civil laws, which Christians regard as also the transgression of divine law, 1 Pet. ii. 20. **b.** ἁμαρτάνειν ἁμαρτίαν to commit (lit. sin) a sin, 1 Jn. v. 16, (μεγάλην ἁμαρτίαν, Ex. xxxii. 30 sq. Hebr. חֲטָאָה חָטָא; αἰσχρὰν ἁμ. Soph. Phil. 1249; μεγάλα ἁμαρτήματα ἁμαρτάνειν, Plat. Phaedo p. 113 e.); cf. ἀγαπάω, sub fin. ἁμαρτάνειν εἴς τινα [B. 173 (150); W. 233 (219)]: Mt. xviii. 15 (LTWH om. Tr mrg. br. εἰς σέ), 21; Lk. xv. 18, 21; xvii. 3 Rec., 4; 1 Co. viii. 12; τὶ εἰς Καίσαρα, Acts xxv. 8; εἰς τὸ ἴδιον σῶμα, 1 Co. vi. 18, (εἰς αὑτούς τε καὶ εἰς ἄλλους, Plat. rep. 3, p. 396 a.; εἰς τὸ θεῖον, Plat. Phaedr. p. 242 c.; εἰς θεούς, Xen. Hell. 1, 7, 19, etc.; [cf. ἁμ. κυρίῳ θεῷ, Bar. i. 13; ii. 5]); Hebraistically, ἐνώπιόν (לִפְנֵי) τινος [B. § 146, 1] in the presence of, before any one, the one wronged by the sinful act being, as it were, present and looking on: Lk. xv. 18, 21, (1 S. vii. 6; Tob. iii. 3, etc.; [cf. ἔναντι κυρίου, Bar. i. 17]). [For reff. see ἁμαρτία. Comp.: προ-αμαρτάνω.]*

265 ἁμάρτημα, -τος, τό, (fr. ἁμαρτέω i. q. ἁμαρτάνω, cf. ἀδίκημα, ἀλίσγημα), a sin, evil deed, ["Differunt ἡ ἁμαρτία et τὸ ἁμάρτημα ut Latinorum peccatus et peccatum. Nam τὸ ἁμάρτημα et peccatum proprie malum facinus indicant; contra ἡ ἁμαρτία et peccatus primum peccationem, τὸ peccare, deinde peccatum, rem consequentem, valent." Fritzsche; see ἁμαρτία, fin.; cf. also Trench § lxvi.]: Mk. iii. 28, and (LTTr txt. WH) 29; iv. 12 (where GTTr txt. WH om. LTr mrg. br. τὰ ἁμαρτ.); Ro. iii. 25; 1 Co. vi. 18; 2 Pet. i. 9 (R [LWH txt. Tr mrg.] ἁμαρτιῶν). In prof. auth. fr. Soph. and Thuc. down; [of bodily defects, Plato, Gorg. 479 a.; ἁμ. μνημονικόν, Cic. ad Att. 13, 21; ἁμ. γραφικόν, Polyb. 34, 3, 11; ὅταν μὲν παραλόγως ἡ βλάβη γένηται, ἀτύχημα· ὅταν δὲ μὴ παραλόγως, ἄνευ δὲ κακίας, ἁμάρτημα· ὅταν δὲ εἰδὼς μὲν μὴ προβουλεύσας δέ, ἀδίκημα, Aristot. eth. Nic. 5, 10 p. 1135ᵇ, 16 sq.].*

266 ἁμαρτία, -ας, ἡ, (fr. 2 aor. ἁμαρτεῖν, as ἀποτυχία fr. ἀποτυχεῖν), a failing to hit the mark (see ἁμαρτάνω). In Grk. writ. (fr. Aeschyl. and Thuc. down). 1st, an error of the understanding (cf. Ackermann, Das Christl. im Plato, p. 59 Anm. 3 [Eng. trans. (S. R. Asbury, 1861) p. 57 n. 99]). 2d, a bad action, evil deed. In the N. T. always in an ethical sense, and **1.** equiv. to τὸ ἁμαρτάνειν a sinning, whether it occurs by omission or commission, in thought and feeling or in speech and action (cf. Cic. de fin. 3, 9): Ro. v. 12 sq. 20; ὑφ' ἁμαρτίαν εἶναι held down in sin, Ro. iii. 9; ἐπιμένειν τῇ ἁμαρτίᾳ, Ro. vi. 1; ἀποθνήσκειν τῇ ἁμ. and ζῆν ἐν αὐτῇ, Ro. vi. 2; τὴν ἁμ. γινώσκειν, Ro. vii. 7; 2 Co. v. 21; νεκρὸς τῇ ἁμ. Ro. vi. 11; περὶ ἁμαρτίας to break the power of sin, Ro. viii. 3 [cf. Mey.]; σῶμα τῆς ἁμ. the body as the instrument of sin, Ro. vi. 6; ἀπάτη τῆς ἁμ. the craft by which sin is accustomed to deceive, Heb. iii. 13; ἄνθρωπος τῆς ἁμ. [ἀνομίας TTr txt. WH txt.] the man so possessed by sin that he seems unable to exist without it, the man utterly given up to sin, 2 Th. ii. 3 [W. § 34, 3 Note 2]. In this sense ἡ ἁμαρτία (i. q. τὸ ἁμαρτάνειν) as a power exercising dominion over men (*sin as a principle and power*) is rhetorically represented as an imperial personage in the phrases ἡ ἁμ. βασιλεύει, κυριεύει, κατεργάζεται, Ro. v. 21; vi. 12, 14; vii. 17, 20; δουλεύειν τῇ ἁμ. Ro. vi. 6; δοῦλος τῆς ἁμ. Jn. viii. 34 [WH br. Gom. τῆς ἁμ.]; Ro. vi. 17; νόμος τῆς ἁμ. the dictate of sin or an impulse proceeding from it, Ro. vii. 23; viii. 2; δύναμις τῆς ἁμ. 1 Co. xv. 56; (the prosopopœia occurs in Gen. iv. 7 and, acc. to the reading ἁμαρτία, in Sir. xxvii. 10). Thus ἁμαρτία in sense, but not in signification, is the source whence the several evil acts proceed; but it never denotes *vitiosity*. **2.** *that which is done wrong*, committed or resultant *sin*, *an offence, a violation of the divine law in thought or in act* (ἡ ἁμαρτία ἐστὶν ἡ ἀνομία, 1 Jn. iii. 4); **a.** generally: Jas i. 15; Jn. viii. 46 (where ἁμαρτ. must be taken to mean neither *error*, nor *craft* by which Jesus is corrupting the people, but *sin* viewed generally, as is well shown by Lücke ad loc. and Ullmann in the Stud. u. Krit. for 1842, p. 667 sqq. [cf. his Sündlosigkeit Jesu p. 66 sqq. (Eng. trans. of 7th ed. p. 71 sq.)]; the thought is, 'If any one convicts me of sin, then you may lawfully question the truth and divinity of my doctrine, for sin hinders the perception of truth'); χωρὶς ἁμαρτίας so that he did not commit sin, Heb. iv. 15; ποιεῖν ἁμαρτίαν and τὴν ἁμ. Jn. viii. 34; 1 Jn. iii. 8; 2 Co. xi. 7; 1 Pet. ii. 22; ἔχειν ἁμαρτίαν to have sin as though it were one's odious private property, or to have done something needing expiation, i. q. to have committed sin, Jn. ix. 41; xv. 22, 24; xix. 11; 1 Jn. i. 8, (so αἷμα ἔχειν, of one who has committed murder, Eur. Or. 514); very often in the plur. ἁμαρτίαι [in the Synopt. Gospels the sing. occurs but once: Mt. xii. 31] 1 Th. ii. 16; [Jas. v. 16 L T Tr WH]; Rev. xviii. 4 sq., etc.; πλῆθος ἁμαρτιῶν, Jas. v. 20; 1 Pet. iv. 8; ποιεῖν ἁμαρτίας, Jas. v. 15; also in the expressions ἄφεσις ἁμαρτιῶν, ἀφιέναι τὰς ἁμ., (see ἀφίημι, 1 d.), in which the word does not of itself denote the *guilt* or *penalty of sins*, but the sins are conceived of as removed so to speak from God's sight, regarded by him as not having been done, and therefore are not punished. ἐν ἁμαρτ. σὺ ἐγεννήθης ὅλος thou wast covered all over with sins when thou wast born, i. e. didst sin abundantly before thou wast born, Jn. ix. 34; ἐν ταῖς ἁμ. ἀποθνῄσκειν to die loaded with evil deeds, therefore unreformed, Jn. viii. 24; ἔτι ἐν ἁμαρτίαις εἶναι still to have one's sins, sc. unexpiated, 1 Co. xv. 17. **b.** *some particular evil deed*: τὴν ἁμ. ταύτην, Acts vii. 60; πᾶσα ἁμαρτία, Mt. xii. 31; ἁμαρτία πρὸς θάνατον, 1 Jn. v. 16 (an offence of such gravity that a Christian lapses from the state of ζωή received from Christ into the state of θάνατος (cf. θάνατος, 2) in which he was before he became united to Christ by faith; cf. Lücke, DeWette, [esp. Westcott, ad L]). **3.** collectively, *the complex or aggregate of sins committed either by a single person or by many*: αἴρειν τὴν ἁμ. τοῦ κόσμου, Jn. i. 29 (see αἴρω, 3 c.); ἀποθνῄσκειν ἐν τῇ ἁμ. Jn. viii. 21 (see 2 a. sub fin.); περὶ ἁμαρτίας, sc. θυσίας [W. 583 (542); B. 393 (336)],

expiatory sacrifices, Heb. x. 6 (acc. to the usage of the Sept., who sometimes so translate the Hebr. חַטָּאָה and חַטָּאת, e. g. Lev. v. 11; vii. 27 (37); Ps. xxxix. (xl.) 7); χωρὶς ἁμαρτίας having no fellowship with the sin which he is about [?] to expiate, Heb. ix. 28. **4.** abstract for the concrete, i. q. ἁμαρτωλός: Ro. vii. 7 (ὁ νόμος ἁμαρτία, opp. to ὁ νόμος ἅγιος, vs. 12); 2 Co. v. 21 (τὸν ... ἁμαρτίαν ἐποίησεν he treated him, who knew not sin, as a sinner). Cf. Fritzsche on Rom. vol. i. 289 sqq.; [see ἁμάρτημα; Trench § lxvi.].

ἁμάρτυρος, -ον, (μάρτυς), *without witness* or *testimony, unattested*: Acts xiv. 17. (Thuc., Dem., Joseph., Plut., Lcian., Hdian.) *   **267**

ἁμαρτωλός, -όν, (fr. the form ἅμαρτω, as φειδωλός from φείδομαι), *devoted to sin, a* (masc. or fem.) *sinner.* In the N. T. distinctions are so drawn that one is called ἁμαρτωλός who is **a.** *not free from sin.* In this sense all men are sinners: as, Mt. ix. 13; Mk. ii. 17; Lk. v. 8, 32; xiii. 2; xviii. 13; Ro. iii. 7; v. [8], 19; 1 Tim. i. 15; Heb. vii. 26. **b.** *pre-eminently sinful, especially wicked*; **α.** univ.: 1 Tim. i. 9; Jude 15; Mk. viii. 38; Lk. vi. 32–34; vii. 37, 39; xv. 7, 10; Jn. ix. 16, 24 sq. 31; Gal. ii. 17; Heb. xii. 3; Jas. iv. 8; v. 20; 1 Pet. iv. 18; ἁμαρτία itself is called ἁμαρτωλός, Ro. vii. 13. **β.** spec., of men stained with certain definite vices or crimes, e. g. the tax-gatherers: Lk. xv. 2; xviii. 13; xix. 7; hence the combination τελῶναι καὶ ἁμαρτωλοί, Mt. ix. 10 sq.; xi. 19; Mk. ii. 15 sq.; Lk. v. 30; vii. 34; xv. 1. heathen, called by the Jews sinners κατ' ἐξοχήν (1 Macc. i. 34; ii. 48, 62; Tob. xiii. 6): Mt. xxvi. 45 [?]; Mk. xiv. 41; Lk. xxiv. 7; Gal. ii. 15. (The word is found often in Sept., as the equiv. of חַטָּא and רָשָׁע, and in the O. T. Apocr.; very seldom in Grk. writ., as Aristot. eth. Nic. 2, 9 p. 1109ᵃ, 33; Plut. de audiend. poët. 7, p. 25 c.)*   **268**

ἄμαχος, -ον, (μάχη), in Grk. writ. [fr. Pind. down] commonly *not to be withstood, invincible*; more rarely *abstaining from fighting*, (Xen. Cyr. 4, 1, 16; Hell. 4, 4, 9); in the N. T. twice metaph. *not contentious*: 1 Tim. iii. 3; Tit. iii. 2.*   **269**

ἀμάω, -ῶ: 1 aor. ἤμησα; (fr. ἅμα together; hence *to gather together*, cf. Germ. *sammeln*; [al. regard the init. *a* as euphonic and the word as allied to Lat. *meto*, Eng. *mow*, thus making the sense of *cutting* primary, and that of *gathering in* secondary; cf. Vaníček p. 673]); freq. in the Grk. poets, *to reap, mow down*: τὰς χώρας, Jas. v. 4.*   **270**

ἀμέθυστος, -ου, ἡ, *amethyst*, a precious stone of a violet and purple color (Ex. xxviii. 19; acc. to Phavorinus so called διὰ τὸ ἀπείργειν τῆς μέθης [so Plut. quaest. conviv. iii. 1, 3, 6]): Rev. xxi. 20. [Cf. B. D. s. v.]*   **271**

ἀμελέω, -ῶ; fut. ἀμελήσω; 1 aor. ἠμέλησα; (fr. ἀμελής, and this fr. ἀ priv. and μέλω to care for); very com. in prof. auth.; *to be careless of, to neglect*: τινός, Heb. ii. 3; viii. 9; 1 Tim. iv. 14; foll. by inf., 2 Pet. i. 12 R G; without a case, ἀμελήσαντες (not caring for what had just been said [A. V. they made light of it]), Mt. xxii. 5.*   **272**

ἄμεμπτος, -ον, (μέμφομαι to blame), *blameless, deserving no censure* (Tertull. *irreprehensibilis*), *free from fault* or *defect*: Lk. i. 6; Phil. ii. 15; iii. 6; 1 Th. iii. 13 [WH   **273** mrg. ἀμέμπτως]; Heb. viii. 7 (in which nothing is lacking); in Sept. i. q. תָּם, Job i. 1, 8 etc. Com. in Grk. writ. [Cf. Trench § ciii.] *

274 ἀ-μέμπτως, adv., *blamelessly, so that there is no cause for censure*: 1 Th. ii. 10; [iii. 13 WH mrg.]; v. 23. [Fr. Aeschyl. down. Cf. Trench § ciii.] *

275 ἀμέριμνος, -ον, (μέριμνα), *free from anxiety, free from care*: Mt. xxviii. 14; 1 Co. vii. 32 (free from earthly cares). (Sap. vi. 16; vii. 23; Hdian. 2, 4, 3; 3, 7, 11; Anth. 9, 359, 5; [in pass. sense, Soph. Ajax 1206].) *

276 ἀ-μετάθετος, -ον, (μετατίθημι), *not transposed, not to be transferred; fixed, unalterable*: Heb. vi. 18; τὸ ἀμετάθετον as subst., *immutability*, Heb. vi. 17. (3 Macc. v. 1; Polyb., Diod., Plut.) *

277 ἀ-μετα-κίνητος, -ον, (μετακινέω), *not to be moved from its place, unmoved*; metaph. *firmly persistent*, [A. V. *unmovable*]: 1 Co. xv. 58. (Plat. ep. 7, p. 343 a.; Dion. Hal. 8, 74; [Joseph. c. Ap. 2, 16, 9; 2, 32, 3; 2, 35, 4].) *

278 ἀ-μεταμέλητος, -ον, (μεταμέλομαι, μεταμέλει), *not repented of, unregretted*: Ro. xi. 29; σωτηρία, by litotes, salvation affording supreme joy, 2 Co. vii. 10 [al. connect it with μετάνοιαν]. (Plat., Polyb., Plut.) *

279 ἀμετανόητος, -ον, (μετανοέω, q. v.), *admitting no change of mind* (amendment), *unrepentant, impenitent*: Ro. ii. 5. (In Lcian. Abdic. 11 [passively], i. q. ἀμεταμέλητος, q. v.; [Philo de praem. et poen. § 3].) *

280 ἄμετρος, -ον, (μέτρον a measure), *without measure, immense*: 2 Co. x. 13, 15 sq. (εἰς τὰ ἄμετρα καυχᾶσθαι to boast to an immense extent, i. e. beyond measure, excessively). (Plat., Xen., Anthol. iv. p. 170, and ii. 206, ed. Jacobs.) *

281 ἀμήν, Hebr. אָמֵן; **1.** verbal adj. (fr. אָמַן to prop; Niph. to be firm), *firm*, metaph. *faithful*: ὁ ἀμήν, Rev. iii. 14 (where is added ὁ μάρτυς ὁ πιστὸς κ. ἀληθινός). **2.** it came to be used as an adverb by which something is asserted or confirmed: **a.** at the beginning of a discourse, *surely, of a truth, truly*; so freq. in the discourses of Christ in Mt. and Lk.: ἀμὴν λέγω ὑμῖν 'I solemnly declare unto you,' e. g. Mt. v. 18; Mk. iii. 28; Lk. iv. 24. The repetition of the word (ἀμὴν ἀμήν), employed by John alone in his Gospel (twenty-five times), has the force of a superlative, *most assuredly*: Jn. i. 51 (52); iii. 3. **b.** at the close of a sentence; *so it is, so be it, may it be fulfilled* (γένοιτο, Sept. Num. v. 22; Deut. xxvii. 15, etc.): Ro. i. 25; ix. 5; Gal. i. 5; Eph. iii. 21; Phil. iv. 20; 1 Tim. i. 17; Heb. xiii. 21; 1 Pet. iv. 11; Rev. i. 6, and often; cf. Jer. xi. 5; xxxv. (xxviii.) 6; 1 K. i. 30. It was a custom, which passed over from the synagogues into the Christian assemblies, that when he who had read or discoursed had offered up a solemn prayer to God, the others in attendance responded *Amen*, and thus made the substance of what was uttered their own: 1 Co. xiv. 16 (τὸ ἀμήν, the well-known response *Amen*), cf. Num. v. 22; Deut. xxvii. 15 sqq.; Neh. v. 13; viii. 6. 2 Co. i. 20 αἱ ἐπαγγελίαι . . . τὸ ναί, καὶ . . . τὸ ἀμήν, i. e. had shown themselves most sure. [Cf. B. D. s. v. Amen.]

282 ἀμήτωρ, -ορος, ὁ, ἡ, (μήτηρ), *without a mother, motherless*; in Grk. writ. **1.** *born without a mother*, e. g.

Minerva, Eur. Phoen. 666 sq., al.; God himself, inasmuch as he is without origin, Lact. instt. 4, 13, 2. **2.** bereft of a mother, Hdt. 4, 154, al. **3.** born of a base or unknown mother, Eur. Ion 109 cf. 837. **4.** unmotherly, unworthy of the name of mother: μήτηρ ἀμήτωρ, Soph. El. 1154. Cf. Bleek on Heb. vol. ii. 2, p. 305 sqq. **5.** in a signif. unused by the Greeks, 'whose mother is not recorded in the genealogy': of Melchizedek, Heb. vii. 3; (of Sarah by Philo in de temul. § 14, and rer. div. haer. § 12; [cf. Bleek u. s.]); cf. the classic ἀνολυμπιάς.*

283 ἀμίαντος, -ον, (μιαίνω), *not defiled, unsoiled; free from that by which the nature of a thing is deformed and debased, or its force and vigor impaired*: κοίτη pure, free from adultery, Heb. xiii. 4; κληρονομία (without defect), 1 Pet. i. 4; θρησκεία, Jas. i. 27; pure from sin, Heb. vii. 26. (Also in the Grk. writ.; in an ethical sense, Plat. legg. 6, p. 777 e.; Plut. Pericl. c. 39 βίος καθαρὸς καὶ ἀμίαντος.)*

284 Ἀμιναδάβ, ὁ, עַמִּינָדָב (servant of the prince, [al. my people are noble; but cf. B. D. s. v.]), [A. V. *Aminadab*], the prop. name of one of the ancestors of Christ (1 Chr. ii. 10 [A. V. Amminadab]): Mt. i. 4; Lk. iii. 33 [not WH. See B. D. s. v.].*

285 ἄμμος, -ον, ἡ, *sand*; acc. to a Hebr. comparison ἄμ. τῆς θαλάσσης and ἄμ. παρὰ τὸ χεῖλος τῆς θαλ. are used for an innumerable multitude, Ro. ix. 27; Heb. xi. 12; Rev. xx. 8, equiv. to xii. 18 (xiii. 1). Acc. to the context *sandy ground*, Mt. vii. 26. (Xen., Plat., Theophr. often, Plut., Sept. often.)*

286 ἀμνός, -οῦ, ὁ, [fr. Soph. and Arstph. down], *a lamb*: Acts viii. 32; 1 Pet. i. 19; τοῦ θεοῦ, consecrated to God, Jn. i. 29, 36. In these passages Christ is likened to a sacrificial lamb on account of his death, innocently and patiently endured, to expiate sin. See ἀρνίον.*

287 ἀμοιβή, -ῆς, ἡ, (fr. ἀμείβω, as ἀλοιφή fr. ἀλείφω, στοιβή fr. στείβω), a very com. word with the Greeks, *requital, recompense*, in a good and a bad sense (fr. the signif. of the mid. ἀμείβομαι to requite, return like for like): in a good sense, 1 Tim. v. 4.*

288 ἄμπελος, -ον, ἡ, [fr. Hom. down], *a vine*: Mt. xxvi. 29; Mk. xiv. 25; Lk. xxii. 18; Jas. iii. 12. In Jn. xv. 1, 4 sq. Christ calls himself a vine, because, as the vine imparts to its branches sap and productiveness, so Christ infuses into his followers his own divine strength and life. ἄμπ. τῆς γῆς in Rev. xiv. 18 [Recˢᵗ om. τῆς ἀμπ.], 19, signifies the enemies of Christ, who, ripe for destruction, are likened to clusters of grapes, to be cut off, thrown into the wine-press, and trodden there.*

289 ἀμπελουργός, -οῦ, ὁ, ἡ, (fr. ἄμπελος and ΕΡΓΩ), *a vinedresser*: Lk. xiii. 7. (Arstph., Plut., Geopon., al.; Sept. for כֹּרֵם.)*

290 ἀμπελών, -ῶνος, ὁ, *a vineyard*: Mt. xx. 1 sqq.; xxi. 28, [33], 39 sqq.; Mk. xii. 1 sqq.; Lk. [xiii. 6]; xx. 9 sqq.; 1 Co. ix. 7. (Sept.; Diod. 4, 6; Plut. pro nobilit. c. 3.)*

291 Ἀμπλίας [T Ἀμπλίατος, Tr WH L mrg. Ἀμπλιᾶτος; hence accent Ἀμπλιᾶς; cf. Lob. Pathol. Proleg. p. 505; Chandler § 32], -ον, ὁ, *Amplias* (a contraction from the Lat. *Ampliatus*, which form appears in some authorities,

cf. W. 102 (97)), a certain Christian at Rome : Ro. xvi.
8. [See Bp. Lghtft. on Phil. p. 174 ; cf. *The Athenæum*
for March 4, 1882, p. 289 sq.]*

(291α);   'Αμπλίατος (Tdf.) or more correctly 'Αμπλιᾶτος (L
see 291   mrg. Tr WH) i. q. 'Αμπλίας, q. v.

see ----- ἀμύνω : 1 aor. mid. ἠμυνάμην ; [allied w. Lat. *munio*,
292 St.   *moenia*, etc., Vaniček p. 731; Curtius § 451] ; in Grk.
writ. [fr. Hom. down] *to ward off*, *keep off* any thing
from any one, τί τινι, acc. of the thing and dat. of pers. ;
hence, with a simple dat. of the pers., *to aid*, *assist any
one* (Thuc. 1, 50 ; 3, 67, al.). Mid. ἀμύνομαι, with acc.
of pers., *to keep off*, *ward off*, *any one from one's self; to
defend one's self against any one* (so also 2 Macc. x. 17 ;
Sap. xi. 3 ; Sept. Josh. x. 13) ; *to take vengeance on any
one* (Xen. an. 2, 3, 23 ; Joseph. antt. 9, 1, 2) : Acts vii.
24, where in thought supply τὸν ἀδικοῦντα [cf. B. 194
(168) note ; W. 258 (242)].*

see 294   ἀμφιάζω ; [fr. ἀμφί, lit. to put around] ; *to put on*,
clothe : in Lk. xii. 28 L WH ἀμφιάζει for Rec. ἀμφιέννυσι.
(A later Grk. word; Sept. [2 K. xvii. 9 Alex.] ; Job
xxix. 14 ; [xxxi. 19] ; xl. 5 ; Ps. lxxii. 6 Symm. ; several
times in Themist. ; cf. Bttm. Ausf. Spr. ii. p. 112 ; [Veitch
s. v. ; B. 49 (42 sq.). Steph. s. v. col. 201 c. quotes from
Cram. Anecdot. Ox. vol. ii. p. 338, 31 τὸ μὲν ἀμφιέζω ἐστὶ
κοινῶς, τὸ δὲ ἀμφιάζω Δωρικόν, ὥσπερ τὸ ὑποπιέζω καὶ
ὑποπιάζω].) Cf. ἀμφιέζω.*

see 293   ἀμφι-βάλλω ; *to throw around*, i. q. περιβάλλω, of a garment (Hom. Od. 14, 342) ; *to cast to and fro now to one
side now to the other* : a net, Mk. i. 16 G L T Tr WH [acc.
to T Tr WH used absol. ; cf. οἱ ἀμφιβολεῖς, Is. xix. 8].
(Hab. i. 17.)*

293   ἀμφίβληστρον, -ου, τό, (ἀμφιβάλλω), in Grk. writ. *anything thrown around one to impede his motion*, as chains,
a garment ; spec. *a net for fishing*, [*casting-net*] : Mk. i.
16 R G L ; Mt. iv. 18. (Sept. ; Hes. scut. 215 ; Hdt. 1,
141 ; Athen. 10, 72, p. 450.) [SYN. see δίκτυον, and cf.
Trench § lxiv. ; B. D. s. v. net.]*

see 294   ἀμφιέζω, i. q. ἀμφιέννυμι ; in Lk. xii. 28 ἀμφιέζει T Tr.
Cf. ἀμφιάζω.

294   ἀμφι-έννυμι ; pf. pass. ἠμφίεσμαι ; (ἔννυμι) ; [fr. Hom.
down] ; *to put on*, *to clothe* : Lk. xii. 28 (R G ; cf. ἀμφιέζω) ;
Mt. vi. 30 ; ἔν τινι [B. 191 (166)], Lk. vii. 25 ; Mt. xi. 8.*

295   'Αμφίπολις, -εως, ἡ, *Amphipolis*, the metropolis of
Macedonia Prima [cf. B. D. s. v. Macedonia] ; so called,
because the Strymon flowed around it [Thuc. 4, 102] ;
formerly called Ἐννέα ὁδοί (Thuc. 1,100) : Acts xvii. 1
[see B. D.].*

296   ἄμφοδον, -ου, τό, (ἀμφί, ὁδός), prop. *a road round anything*, *a street*, [Hesych. ἄμφοδα· αἱ ῥύμαι. ἀγυιαί. δίοδοι
(al. διέξοδοι διορυγμαί, al. ἡ πλατεία) ; Lex. in Bekk. An-
ecdota i. p. 205, 14 "Αμφοδον· ἡ ὥσπερ ἐκ τετραγώνου
διαγεγραμμένη ὁδός. For exx. see *Soph. Lex.* ; Wetst. on
Mk. l. c. ; cod. D in Acts xix. 28 (where see Tdf.'s
note)] : Mk. xi. 4. (Jer. xvii. 27 ; xxx. 16 (xlix. 27), and
in Grk. writ.) *

see   ἀμφότεροι, -αι, -α, [fr. Hom. down], *both of two*, *both the
297 St.   one and the other* : Mt. ix. 17, etc. ; τὰ ἀμφότερα, Acts
xxiii. 8 ; Eph. ii. 14.

ἀ-μώμητος, -ον, (μωμάομαι), *that cannot be censured*,   298
blameless : Phil. ii. 15 R G (cf. τέκνα μωμητά, Deut.
xxxii. 5) ; 2 Pet. iii. 14. (Hom. Il. 12, 109 ; [Hesiod,
Pind., al. ;] Plut. frat. amor. 18 ; often in Anthol.)*

ἄμωμον, -ου, τό, *amomum*, a fragrant plant of India,   see 2368
having the foliage of the white vine [al. ampeloleuce]
and seed, in clusters like grapes, from which ointment
was made (Plin. h. n. 12, 13 [28]) : Rev. xviii. 13 G L
T Tr WH. [See B. D. Am. ed. s. v.]*

ἄ-μωμος, -ον, (μῶμος), *without blemish*, free from faulti-   299
ness, as a victim without spot or blemish : 1 Pet. i. 19
(Lev. xxii. 21) ; Heb. ix. 14 ; in both places allusion is
made to the sinless life of Christ. Ethically, *without
blemish*, *faultless*, *unblamable* : Eph. i. 4 ; v. 27 ; Col. i.
22 ; Phil. ii. 15 L T Tr WH ; Jude 24 ; Rev. xiv. 5.
(Often in Sept. ; [Hesiod, Simon., Iambl.], Hdt. 2, 177 ;
Aeschyl. Pers. 185 ; Theocr. 18, 25.) [SYN. see Trench
§ ciii. ; Tittmann i. 29 sq.]*

'Αμών, ὁ, indecl., *Amon*, (אָמוֹן artificer [but cf. B. D.]),   300
king of Judah, son of Manasseh, and father of Josiah :
Mt. i. 10, [L T Tr WH -μώς. Cf. B. D.].*

'Αμώς, ὁ, *Amos*, (אָמוֹץ strong), indecl. prop. name of one   301
of Christ's ancestors : [Mt. i. 10 L T Tr WH]; Lk. iii. 25.*

ἄν, a particle indicating that something can or could   302
occur on certain conditions, or by the combination of
certain fortuitous causes. In Lat. it has no equivalent ;
nor do the Eng. *haply*, *perchance*, Germ. *wohl* (*wol*),
etwa, exactly and everywhere correspond to it. The
use of this particle in the N. T., illustrated by copious
exx. fr. Grk. writ., is shown by W. § 42 ; [cf. B. 216
(186) sqq. Its use in classic Grk. is fully exhibited (by
Prof. Goodwin) in L. and S. s. v.].

It is joined   I. in the apodoses of hypothetical sentences   1. with the Impf., where the Lat. uses the
impf. subjunctive, e. g. Lk. vii. 39 (ἐγίνωσκεν ἄν, sciret,
he would know) ; Lk. xvii. 6 (ἐλέγετε ἄν ye would say) ; Mt.
xxiii. 30 (non essemus, we should not have been) ; Jn.
v. 46 ; viii. 42 ; ix. 41 ; xv. 19 ; xviii. 36 ; 1 Co. xi. 31 ;
Gal. i. 10 ; iii. 21 [but WH mrg. br.] ; Heb. iv. 8 ; viii. 4,
7.   2. with the indic. A o r. (where the Lat. uses the
plpf. subj. like the fut. pf. subj., *I would have done it*),
to express what would have been, if this or that either
were (εἰ with the impf. in the protasis preceding), or
had been (εἰ with the aor. or plpf. preceding) : Mt. xi.
21 and Lk. x. 13 (ἂν μετενόησαν they would have re-
pentⴰ, , Mt. xi. 23 ; xii. 7 (ye would not have condemned) ; Mt. xxiv. 43 (he would have watched), 22 and
Mk. xiii. 20 (no one would have been saved, i. e. all even now
would have to be regarded as those who had perished ;
cf. W. 304 (286)) ; Jn. iv. 10 (thou wouldst have asked) ;
xiv. 2 (εἶπον ἄν I would have said so) ; 28 (ye would have
rejoiced) ; Ro. ix. 29 (we should have become) ; 1 Co. ii.
8 ; Gal. iv. 15 (R G) ; Acts xviii. 14. Sometimes the
condition is not expressly stated, but is easily gathered
from what is said : Lk. xix. 23 and Mt. xxv. 27 (*I should
have received it back with interest*, sc. if thou hadst given
it to the bankers).   3. with the Plupf. : Jn. xi. 21
[R Tr mrg.] (οὐκ ἄν ἐτεθνήκει [L T Tr txt. WH ἀπέθανεν]

would not have died, for which, in 32, the aor. οὐκ ἂν ἀπέθανε); Jn. xiv. 7 [not Tdf.] (εἰ with the plpf. preceding); 1 Jn. ii. 19 (*they would have remained with us*). Sometimes (as in Grk. writ., esp. the later) ἄν is omitted, in order to intimate that the thing wanted but little (impf.) or had wanted but little (plpf. or aor.) of being done, which yet was not done because the condition was not fulfilled (cf. *Alex. Bttm.* in the Stud. u. Krit. for 1858, p. 489 sqq.; [N. T. Gram. p. 225 (194)]; Fritzsche on Rom. vol. ii. 33; W. § 42, 2 p. 305 (286)), e. g. Jn. viii. 39 (where the ἄν is spurious); xv. 22, 24; xix. 11; Acts xxvi. 32; Ro. vii. 7; Gal. iv. 15 (ἄν before ἐδώκατε has been correctly expunged by L T Tr WH). **II.** Joined to relative pronouns, relative adverbs, and adverbs of time and quality, it has the same force as the Lat. *cumque* or *cunque, -ever, -soever*, (Germ. *irgend, etwa*). **1.** foll. by a past tense of the I n d i c a t i v e, when some matter of fact, something certain, is spoken of; where, "when the thing itself which is said to have been done is certain, the notion of uncertainty involved in ἄν belongs rather to the relative, whether pronoun or particle" (*Klotz* ad Dev. p. 145) [cf. W. § 42, 3 a.]; ὅσοι ἄν as many as: Mk. vi. 56 (ὅσοι ἂν ἥπτοντο [ἥψαντο L txt. T Tr txt. WH] αὐτοῦ as many as touched him [cf. B. 216 (187)]); Mk. xi. 24 (ὅσα ἂν προσευχόμενοι αἰτεῖσθε [Grsb. om. ἄν], but L txt. T Tr WH have rightly restored ὅσα προσεύχεσθε κ. αἰτεῖσθε). καθότι ἄν *in so far* or *so often as, according as*, (Germ. *je nachdem gerade*): Acts ii. 45; iv. 35. ὡς ἄν: 1 Co. xii. 2 (in whatever manner ye were led [cf. B. § 139, 13; 383 (329) sq.]). **2.** foll. by a S u b - j u n c t i v e, **a.** the P r e s e n t, concerning that which may have been done, or is usually or constantly done (where the Germ. uses *mögen*); ἡνίκα ἄν *whensoever, as often as:* 2 Co. iii. 15 L T Tr WH; ὃς ἄν *whoever, be he who he may:* Mt. xvi. 25 (L T Tr WH ἐάν); [Mk. viii. 35 (where T Tr WH fut. indic.; see *WH.* App. p. 172)]; Lk. x. 5 (L T Tr WH aor.), 8; Gal. v. 17 (L T Tr WH ἐάν, L br. ἐάν); 1 Jn. ii. 5; iii. 17; Ro. ix. 15 (Ex. xxxiii. 19); xvi. 2; 1 Co. xi. 27, etc. ὅστις ἄν: 1 Co. xvi. 2 [Tr WH ἐάν; WH mrg. aor.]; Col. iii. 17 (Ltxt. Tr WH ἐάν). ὅσοι ἄν: Mt. vii. 12 (T WH ἐάν); xxii. 9 (L T Tr WH ἐάν). ὅπου ἄν *whithersoever:* Lk. ix. 57 (L Tr ἐάν); Rev. xiv. 4 (L Tr [T ed. 7 not 8, WH] have adopted ὑπάγει, defended also by B. 228 (196)); Jas. iii. 4 (R G L Tr mrg. in br.). ὁσάκις ἄν *how often soever:* 1 Co. xi. 25 sq. (where L T Tr WH ἐάν). ὡς ἄν *in what way soever:* 1 Th. ii. 7 ([cf. Ellic. ad loc.; B. 232 (200)], L T Tr WH ἐάν). **b.** the A o r i s t, where the Lat. uses the fut. pf.; ὃς ἄν: Mt. v. 21, 22 (εἴπῃ whoever, if ever any one shall have said); 31 sq. [in vs. 32 L T Tr WH read πᾶς ὁ ἀπολύων]; x. 11; xxvi. 48 (Tdf. ἐάν); Mk. iii. 29, 35; ix. 41, etc. ὅστις ἄν: Mt. x. 33 [L Tr WH txt. om. ἄν]; xii. 50; Jn. xiv. 13 [Tr mrg. WH pres.]; Acts iii. 23 (Tdf. ἐάν), etc. ὅσοι ἄν: Mt. xxi. 22 (Treg. ἐάν); xxiii. 3 (T WH ἐά''); Mk. iii. 28 (Tr WH ἐάν); Lk. ix. 5 (L T Tr WH pres.); Jn. xi. 22; Acts ii. 39 (Lchm. οὖς); iii. 22. ὅπου ἄν: Mk. xiv. 9 (T WH ἐάν); ix. 18 (L T Tr WH ἐάν). ἄχρις οὖ ἄν *until (donec):* 1 Co. xv. 25 Rec.; Rev. ii. 25. ἕως ἄν

until (usque dum): Mt. ii. 13; x. 11; xxii. 44; Mk. vi. 10; Lk. xxi. 32; 1 Co. iv. 5, etc. ἡνίκα ἄν, of fut. time, *not until then, when . . . or then at length, when . . . :* 2 Co. iii. 16 (T W H txt. ἐάν) [cf. Kühner ii. 951; Jelf ii. 565]. ὡς ἄν *as soon as* [B. 232 (200)]: 1 Co. xi. 34; Phil. ii. 23. ἀφ' οὖ ἂν ἐγερθῇ, Lk. xiii. 25 (from the time, whatever the time is, when he shall have risen up). But ἐάν (q. v.) is also joined to the pronouns and adverbs mentioned, instead of ἄν; and in many places the Mss. and edd. fluctuate between ἄν and ἐάν, (exx. of which have already been adduced); [cf. *Tdf.* Proleg. p. 96; *WH.* App. p. 173 "predominantly is found after consonants, and ἐάν after vowels"]. Finally, to this head must be referred ὅταν (i. q. ὅτε ἄν) with the indic. and much oftener with the subj. (see ὅταν), and ὅπως ἄν, although this last came to be used as a final conjunction in the sense, *that, if it be possible:* Lk. ii. 35; Acts iii. 20 (19); xv. 17; Ro. iii. 4; see ὅπως, II. 1 b. [Cf. W. 309 (290 sq.); B. 234 (201).] **III.** ἄν is joined to the O p t a t. [W. 303 (284); B. 217 (188)]; when a certain condition is laid down, as in wishes, *I would that* etc.: Acts xxvi. 29 (εὐξαίμην [Tdf. εὐξάμην] ἄν *I could pray*, sc. did it depend on me); in d i r e c t questions [W. l. c.; B. 254 (219)]: Acts viii. 31 (πῶς ἂν δυναίμην; *i. e.* on what condition, by what possibility, could I? cf. Xen. oec. 11, 5); Acts xvii. 18 (τί ἂν θέλοι . . . λέγειν *what would he say?* it being assumed that he wishes to utter some definite notion or other); Acts ii. 12 R G; in d e p e n d e n t sentences and i n d i r e c t questions in which the narrator introduces another's thought [W. § 42, 4; B. l. c.]: Lk. i. 62; vi. 11; ix. 46; [xv. 26 L br. Tr WH; cf. xviii. 36 L br. Tr br. WH mrg.]; Acts v. 24; x. 17; xvii. 20 R G. **IV.** ἄν is found without a mood in 1 Co. vii. 5 (εἰ μή τι ἄν [WH br. ἄν], *except perhaps*, sc. γένοιτο, [but cf. Bttm. as below]). ὡς ἄν, adverbially, *tanquam* (so already the Vulg.), *as if:* 2 Co. x. 9 (like ὥσπερ ἄν in Grk. writ.; cf. Kühner ii. 210 [§ 398 Anm. 4; Jelf § 430]; B. 219 (189); [L. and S. s. v. D. III.]).

ἄν, contr. from ἐάν, *if;* foll. by the subjunc.: Jn. xx. 23 [Lchm. ἐάν. Also by the (pres.) indic. in 1 Jn. v. 15 Lchm.; see B. 223 (192); W. 295 (277)]. Further, L T Tr WH have received ἄν in Jn. xiii. 20; xvi. 23; [so WH Jn. xii. 32; cf. W. 291 (274); B. 72 (63)].*

ἀνά, prep., prop. *upwards, up,* (cf. the adv. ἄνω, opp. to κατά and κάτω), denoting motion from a lower place to a higher [cf. W. 398 (372) n.]; rare in the N. T. and only with the accus. **1.** in the expressions ἀνὰ μέσον (or jointly ἀνάμεσον [so R*ᵗ* Tr in Rev. vii. 17]) *into the midst, in the midst, amidst, among, between,*—with gen. of place, Mt. xiii. 25; Mk. vii. 31; Rev. vii. 17 [on this pass. see μέσος, 2 sub fin.]; of pers., 1 Co. vi. 5, with which cf. Sir. xxv. 18(17) ἀνὰ μέσον τοῦ (Fritz. τῶν) πλησίον αὐτοῦ; cf. W. § 27, 1 fin. [B. 332 (285)], (Sir. xxvii. 2; 1 Macc. vii. 28; xiii. 40, etc.; in Sept. for בְּתוֹךְ, Ex. xxvi. 28; Josh. xvi. 9; xix. 1; Diod. 2, 4 ἀνὰ μέσον τῶν χειλέων [see μέσος, 2]); ἀνὰ μέρος, (Vulg. *per partes*), *in turn, one after another, in succession:* 1 Co. xiv. 27 [where Rec*ᵗ* writes ἀναμέρος], (Polyb. 4, 20, 10 ἀνὰ μέρος ᾄδειν). **2.** joined to

303

numerals, it has a *distributive* force [W. 398 (372); B. 331 sq. (285)]: Jn. ii. 6 (ἀνὰ μετρητὰς δύο ἢ τρεῖς two or three metretæ apiece); Mt. xx. 9 sq. (ἔλαβον ἀνὰ δηνάριον they received each a denarius); Lk. ix. 3 [Tr br. WH om. ἀνά; ix. 14]; x. 1 (ἀνὰ δύο [WH ἀνὰ δύο [δύο]] two by two); Mk. vi. 40 (L T Tr WH κατά); [Rev. iv. 8]; and very often in Grk. writ.; cf. W. 398 (372). It is used adverbially in Rev. xxi. 21 (ἀνὰ εἷς ἕκαστος, like ἀνὰ τέσσαρες, Plut. Aem. 32; cf. W. 249 (234); [B. 30 (26)]). **3.** Prefixed to verbs ἀνά signifies,   **a.** *upwards, up, up to*, (Lat. *ad*, Germ. *auf*), as in ἀνακρούειν, ἀναβαίνειν, ἀναβάλλειν, ἀνακράζειν, etc.   **b.** it corresponds to the Lat. *ad* (Germ. *an*), *to* [indicating the goal], as in ἀναγγέλλειν [al. would refer this to d.], ἀνάπτειν.   **c.** it denotes repetition, renewal, i. q. *denuo, anew, over again*, as in ἀναγεννᾶν.   **d.** it corresponds to the Lat. *re, retro, back, backwards*, as in ἀνακάμπτειν, ἀναχωρεῖν, etc. Cf. Win. De verb. comp. Pt. iii. p. 3 sq.*

304   **ἀνα-βαθμός**, -οῦ, ὁ, (βαθμός, and this fr. βαίνω);   **1.** *an ascent.*   **2.** *a means of going up, a flight of steps, a stair*: Acts xxi. 35, 40. Exx. fr. Grk. writ. in Lob. ad Phryn. p. 324 sq.*

305   **ἀνα-βαίνω**; [impf. ἀνέβαινον Acts iii. 1; fut. ἀναβήσομαι Ro. x. 6, after Deut. xxx. 12]; pf. ἀναβέβηκα; 2 aor. ἀνέβην, ptcp. ἀναβάς, impv. ἀνάβα Rev. iv. 1 (ἀνάβηθι Lchm.), plur. ἀνάβατε (for R G ἀνάβητε) Rev. xi. 12 L T Tr [WH; cf. WH. App. p. 168ᵇ]; W. § 14, 1 h.; [B. 54 (47); fr. Hom. down]; Sept. for עָלָה;   **a.** *to go up, move to a higher place, ascend*: a tree (ἐπί), Lk. xix. 4; upon the roof of a house (ἐπί), Lk. v. 19; into a ship (εἰς), Mk. vi. 51; [Mt. xv. 39 G Tr txt.; Acts xxi. 6 Tdf.]; εἰς τὸ ὄρος, Mt. v. 1; Lk. ix. 28; Mk. iii. 13; εἰς τὸ ὑπερῷον, Acts i. 13; εἰς τὸν οὐρανόν, Ro. x. 6; Rev. xi. 12; εἰς τὸν οὐρ. is omitted, but to be supplied, in Jn. i. 51 (52); vi. 62, and in the phrase ἀναβ. πρὸς τὸν πατέρα, Jn. xx. 17. (It is commonly maintained that those persons are fig. said ἀναβεβηκέναι εἰς τὸν οὐρανόν, who have penetrated the heavenly mysteries: Jn. iii. 13, cf. Deut. xxx. 12; Prov. xxiv. 27 (xxx. 4); Bar. iii. 29. But in these latter pass. also the expression is to be understood literally. And as respects Jn. iii. 13, it must be remembered that Christ brought his knowledge of the divine counsels with him from heaven, inasmuch as he had dwelt there prior to his incarnation. Now the natural language was οὐδεὶς ἦν ἐν τῷ οὐρανῷ; but the expression ἀναβέβηκεν is used because none but Christ could get there except by ascending. Accordingly εἰ μή refers merely to the idea, involved in ἀναβέβηκεν, of a past residence in heaven. Cf. Meyer [or Westcott] ad loc.) Used of travelling to a higher place: εἰς Ἱεροσόλ. Mt. xx. 17 sq.; Mk. x. 32 sq., etc.; εἰς τὸ ἱερόν, Jn. vii. 14; Lk. xviii. 10. Often the place to or into which the ascent is made is not mentioned, but is easily understood from the context: Acts viii. 31 (into the chariot); Mk. xv. 8 (to the palace of the governor, acc. to the reading ἀναβάς restored by L T Tr txt. WH for R G ἀναβοήσας), etc.; or the place alone is mentioned from which (ἀπό, ἐκ) the ascent is made: Mt. iii. 16; Acts viii. 39; Rev. xi. 7.   **b.** in a wider sense

of things rising up, *to rise, mount, be borne up, spring up*: of a fish swimming up, Mt. xvii. 27; of smoke rising up, Rev. viii. 4; ix. 2; of plants springing up from the ground, Mt. xiii. 7; Mk. iv. 7, 32, (as in Grk. writ.; Theophr. hist. plant. 8, 3, and Hebr. עָלָה); of things which come up in one's mind (Lat. *suboriri*): ἀναβαίν. ἐπὶ τὴν καρδ. or ἐν τῇ καρδίᾳ, Lk. xxiv. 38; 1 Co. ii. 9; Acts vii. 23 (ἀνέβη ἐπὶ τὴν κ. it came into his mind i. e. he resolved, foll. by inf.), after the Hebr. עָלָה אֶל לֵב, Jer. iii. 16, etc. [B. 135 (118)]. Of messages, prayers, deeds, brought up or reported to one in a higher place: Acts x. 4; xxi. 31 (tidings came up to the tribune of the cohort, who dwelt in the tower Antonia). [COMP.: προσ-, συν-αναβαίνω.]

ἀνα-βάλλω: 2 aor. mid. ἀνεβαλόμην;   **1.** *to throw or toss up.*   **2.** *to put back* or *off, delay, postpone*, (very often in Grk. writ.); often in mid. (prop. *to defer for one's self*): τινά, *to hold back, delay*; in a forensic sense *to put off any one* (Lat. *ampliare*, Cic. Verr. act. 2, 1, 9 § 26) i. e. *to defer hearing and deciding* (*adjourn*) *any one's case*: Acts xxiv. 22; cf. Kypke [or Wetst.] ad loc.*   **see 306 St.**

ἀνα-βιβάζω: 1 aor. ἀνεβίβασα; *to cause to go up* or *ascend, to draw up*, (often in Sept. and Grk. writ.): Mt. xiii. 48, (Xen. Hell. 1, 1, 2 πρὸς τὴν γῆν ἀνεβίβαζε τὰς ἑαυτοῦ τριήρεις).*   **307**

ἀνα-βλέπω: 1 aor. ἀνέβλεψα; [fr. Hdt. down];   **1.** *to look up*: Mk. viii. 24, [25 R G L]; xvi. 4; Lk. xix. 5; xxi. 1; Acts xxii. 13; εἰς τινα, ibid.; εἰς τὸν οὐρανόν, Mt. xiv. 19; Mk. vi. 41; vii. 34, (Plat. Axioch. p. 370 b.; Xen. Cyr. 6, 4, 9).   **2.** *to recover* (lost) *sight*: Mt. xi. 5; xx. 34; Lk. xviii. 41 sqq., etc. ([Hdt. 2, 111;] Plat. Phaedrus p. 234 b. παραχρῆμα ἀνέβλεψα, Arstph. Plut. 126); used somewhat loosely also of the man blind from birth who was cured by Christ, Jn. ix. 11 (12) (cf. Meyer ad loc.), 17 sq. (Paus. 4, 12, 7 (10) συνέβη τὸν Ὀφιονέα . . . τὸν ἐκ γενετῆς τυφλὸν ἀναβλέψαι). Cf. Win. De verb. comp. etc. Pt. iii. p. 7 sq.   **308**

ἀνά-βλεψις, -εως, ἡ, *recovery of sight*: Lk. iv. 18 (19), (Sept. Is. lxi. 1). [Aristot.]*   **309**

ἀνα-βοάω, -ῶ: 1 aor. ἀνεβόησα; [fr. Aeschyl. and Hdt. down]; *to raise a cry, to cry out* anything, say it shouting: Lk. ix. 38 (L T Tr WH ἐβόησε); Mk. xv. 8 (where read ἀναβάς, see ἀναβαίνω, a. sub fin.); with the addition of φωνῇ μεγάλῃ, Mt. xxvii. 46 [Tr WH L mrg. ἐβόησε], (as Gen. xxvii. 38; Is. xxxvi. 13, etc.). Cf. Win. De verb. comp. Pt. iii. p. 6 sq.; [and see βοάω, fin.].*   **310**

ἀνα-βολή, -ῆς, ἡ, (ἀναβάλλω, q. v.), often in Grk. writ., *a putting off, delay*: ποιεῖσθαι ἀναβολήν *to interpose* (lit. make) *delay*, Acts xxv. 17, (as in Thuc. 2, 42; Dion. Hal. 11, 33; Plut. Camill. c. 35).*   **311**

ἀνάγαιον, -ου, τό, (fr. ἀνά and γαῖα i. e. γῆ), prop. *anything above the ground*; hence *a room in the upper part of a house*: Mk. xiv. 15; Lk. xxii. 12, (in G L T Tr WH). Also written ἀνώγαιον (which Tdf. formerly adopted; cf. Xen. an. 5, 4, 29 [where Dind. ἀνακείων]), ἀνώγεον (Rec.), ἀνώγεων; on this variety in writing cf. Lob. ad Phryn. p. 297 sq.; [Rutherford, New Phryn. p. 358];   **(311α); see 508 St.**

Fritzsche on Mk. p. 611 sq.; B. 13 (12); [*WH.* App. p. 151].*

312   ἀν-αγγέλλω; impf. ἀνήγγελλον; [fut. ἀναγγελῶ]; 1 aor. ἀνήγγειλα; 2 aor. pass. ἀνηγγέλην, Ro. xv. 21; 1 Pet. i. 12 (several times in Sept.; 1 Macc. ii. 31; W. 82 (78); [Veitch s. v. ἀγγέλλω]); *to announce, make known,* [cf. ἀνά, 3 b.]: τί, Acts xix. 18; foll. by ὅτι, Jn. v. 15 [L mrg. WH txt. Τ εἶπεν]; ὅσα κτλ. Acts xiv. 27; [Mk. v. 19 R G L mrg.]; [absol. with εἰς, Mk. v. 14 Rec.]; equiv. to *disclose*: τί τινι, Jn. iv. 25; xvi. 13–15; used of the formal proclamation of the Christian religion: Acts xx. 20; 1 Pet. i. 12; 1 Jn. i. 5; περί τινος, Ro. xv. 21 (Is. lii. 15); *to report, bring back tidings, rehearse,* used as in Grk. writers (Aeschyl. Prom. 664 (661); Xen. an. 1, 3, 21; Polyb. 25, 2, 7) of messengers reporting what they have seen or heard, [cf. ἀνά u. s.]: τί, Acts xvi. 38 (where L T Tr WH ἀπήγγ.); 2 Co. vii. 7.

313   ἀνα-γεννάω, -ῶ: 1 aor. ἀνεγέννησα; pf. pass. ἀναγεγέννημαι; *to produce again, beget again, beget anew;* metaph.: τινά, thoroughly to change the mind of one, so that he lives a new life and one conformed to the will of God, 1 Pet. i. 3; passively ἔκ τινος, ibid. i. 23. (In the same sense in eccl. writ. [cf. *Soph.* Lex. s. v.]. Among prof. auth. used by Joseph. antt. 4, 2, 1 τῶν ἐκ τοῦ στασιάζειν αὐτοῖς ἀναγεννωμένων [yet Bekker ἄν γενομένων] δεινῶν *which originated.*)*

314   ἀνα-γινώσκω; [impf. ἀνεγίνωσκεν Acts viii. 28]; 2 aor. ἀνέγνων, [inf. ἀναγνῶναι Lk. iv. 16], ptcp. ἀναγνούς; Pass., [pres. ἀναγινώσκομαι]; 1 aor. ἀνεγνώσθην; in prof. auth. **1.** *to distinguish between, to recognize, to know accurately, to acknowledge;* hence **2.** *to read,* (in this signif. ["first in Pind. O. 10 (11). 1"] fr. [Arstph.,] Thuc. down): τί, Mt. xxii. 31; Mk. xii. 10; Lk. vi. 3; Jn. xix. 20; Acts viii. 30, 32; 2 Co. i. 13; [Gal. iv. 21 Lchm. mrg.]; Rev. i. 3; v. 4 Rec.; τινά, one's book, Acts viii. 28, 30; ἐν with dat. of the book, Mt. xii. 5; xxi. 42; Mk. xii. 26; with ellipsis of ἐν τῷ νόμῳ, Lk. x. 26; foll. by ὅτι [objective], Mt. xix. 4; [foll. by ὅτι recitative, Mt. xxi. 16]; τί ἐποίησε, Mt. xii. 3; Mk. ii. 25. The obj. not mentioned, but to be understood from what precedes: Mt. xxiv. 15; Mk. xiii. 14; Acts xv. 31; xxiii. 34; Eph. iii. 4; pass. 2 Co. iii. 2. *to read to others, read aloud:* 2 Co. iii. 15; Acts xv. 21, (in both places Μωϋσῆς i. q. the books of Moses); [Lk. iv. 16; Acts xiii. 27]; 1 Th. v. 27; Col. iv. 16.*

315   ἀναγκάζω; [impf. ἠνάγκαζον]; 1 aor. ἠνάγκασα; 1 aor. pass. ἠναγκάσθην; (fr. ἀνάγκη); [fr. Soph. down]; *to necessitate, compel, drive to, constrain,* whether by force, threats, etc., or by persuasion, entreaties, etc., or by other means: τινά, 2 Co. xii. 11 (by your behavior towards me); τινά foll. by inf., Acts xxvi. 11; xxviii. 19; Gal. ii. 3, 14 (by your example); vi. 12; Mt. xiv. 22; Mk. vi. 45; Lk. xiv. 23.*

316   ἀναγκαῖος, -αία, -αῖον, (ἀνάγκη), [fr. Hom. down (in various senses)], *necessary*; **a.** what one cannot do without, *indispensable*: 1 Co. xii. 22 (τὰ μέλη); Tit. iii. 14 (χρεῖαι). **b.** *connected by the bonds of nature or of friendship*: Acts x. 24 (ἀναγκαῖοι [A. V. *near*] φίλοι).

c. *what ought according to the law of duty to be done, what is required by the condition of things*: Phil. i. 24. ἀναγκαῖόν ἐστι foll. by acc. with inf., Acts xiii. 46; Heb. viii. 3. ἀναγκαῖον ἡγεῖσθαι to deem necessary, foll. by inf., Phil. ii. 25; 2 Co. ix. 5.*

317   ἀναγκαστῶς, adv., *by force or constraint*; opp. to ἑκουσίως, 1 Pet. v. 2. (Plat. Ax. p. 366 a.)*

318   ἀνάγκη, -ης, ἡ; **1.** *necessity,* imposed either by the external condition of things, or by the law of duty, regard to one's advantage, custom, argument: κατ᾽ ἀνάγκην perforce (opp. to κατὰ ἑκούσιον), Philem. 14; ἐξ ἀνάγκης of necessity, compelled, 2 Co. ix. 7; Heb. vii. 12 (*necessarily*); ἔχω ἀνάγκην I have (am compelled by) necessity, (also in Grk. writ.): 1 Co. vii. 37; Heb. vii. 27; foll. by inf., Lk. xiv. 18; xxiii. 17 R L br.; Jude 3; ἀν. μοι ἐπίκειται necessity is laid upon me, 1 Co. ix. 16; ἀνάγκη (i. q. ἀναγκαῖόν ἐστι) foll. by inf.: Mt. xviii. 7; Ro. xiii. 5; Heb. ix. 16, 23, (so Grk. writ.). **2.** in a sense rare in the classics (Diod. 4, 43), but very common in Hellenistic writ. (also in Joseph. b. j. 5, 13, 7, etc.; see W. 30), *calamity, distress, straits*: Lk. xxi. 23; 1 Co. vii. 26; 1 Th. iii. 7; plur. ἐν ἀνάγκαις, 2 Co. vi. 4; xii. 10.*

see 319 St.   ἀνα-γνωρίζω: 1 aor. pass. ἀνεγνωρίσθην; *to recognize*: Acts vii. 13 [Tr txt. WH txt. ἐγνωρίσθη] was recognized by his brethren, cf. Gen. xlv. 1. (Plat. politic. p. 258 a. ἀναγνωρίζειν τοὺς συγγενεῖς.)*

320   ἀνά-γνωσις, -εως, ἡ, (ἀναγινώσκω, q. v.); **a.** *a knowing again, owning.* **b.** *reading,* [fr. Plato on]: Acts xiii. 15; 2 Co. iii. 14; 1 Tim. iv. 13. (Neh. viii. 8 i. q. מִקְרָא.)*

321   ἀν-άγω: 2 aor. ἀνήγαγον, inf. ἀναγαγεῖν, [ptcp. ἀναγαγών]; Pass., [pres. ἀνάγομαι]; 1 aor. [cf. sub fin.] ἀνήχθην; [fr. Hom. down]; *to lead up, to lead or bring into a higher place*; foll. by εἰς with acc. of the place: Lk. ii. 22; iv. 5 [T T Tr WH om. L br. the cl.]; xxii. 66 [T Tr WH ἀπήγαγον]; Acts xvi. 39; xvi. 34; Mt. iv. 1 (εἰς τ. ἔρημον, sc. fr. the low bank of the Jordan). τινὰ ἐκ νεκρῶν fr. the dead in the world below, to the upper world, Heb. xiii. 20; Ro. x. 7; τινὰ τῷ λαῷ to bring one forth who has been detained in prison (a lower place), and set him before the people to be tried, Acts xii. 4; θυσίαν τῷ εἰδώλῳ to offer sacrifice to the idol, because the victim is lifted up on the altar, Acts vii. 41. Navigators are κατ᾽ ἐξοχήν said ἀνάγεσθαι (pass. [or mid.]) when they *launch out,* set sail, *put to sea,* (so ἀναγωγή in Justin. Mart. dial. c. Tr. c. 142 [and in the classics]): Lk. viii. 22; Acts xiii. 13; xvi. 11; xviii. 21; xx. 3, 13; xxi. [1], 2; xxvii. 2, 4, 12, 21; xxviii. 10 sq. (Polyb. 1, 21, 4; 23, 3, etc.) [COMP.: ἐπ-ανάγω.]*

322   ἀνα-δείκνυμι: 1 aor. ἀνέδειξα, [impv. ἀνάδειξον; fr. Soph. down]; *to lift up anything on high and exhibit* it for all to behold (Germ. *aufzeigen*); hence to show accurately, clearly, to disclose what was hidden, (2 Macc. ii. 8 cf. 6): Acts i. 24 (show which of these two thou hast chosen). Hence ἀναδ. τινά to proclaim any one as elected to an office, to announce as appointed (king, general, etc., messenger): Lk. x. 1, (2 Macc. ix. 14, 23, 25; x. 11; xiv. 12, 26; 1 Esdr. i. 35; viii. 23; Polyb. 4, 48,

3; 51, 3; Diod. i. 66; 13, 98; Plut. Caes. 37, etc.; Hdian. 2, 12, 5 (3), al.). Cf. Win. De verb. comp. Pt. iii. p. 12 sq.*

323 ἀνά-δειξις, -εως, ἡ, (ἀναδείκνυμι, q. v.), *a pointing out, public showing forth; τῶν χρόνων,* Sir. xliii. 6. *a proclaiming, announcing, inaugurating,* of such as are elected to office (Plut. Mar. 8 ὑπάτων ἀνάδειξις [cf. Polyb. 15, 26, 7]): Lk. i. 80 (until the day when he was announced [A. V. *of his shewing*] to the people as the forerunner of the Messiah; this announcement he himself made at the command of God, Lk. iii. 2 sqq.).*

324 ἀνα-δέχομαι: 1 aor. ἀνεδεξάμην; fr. Hom. down; *to take up, take upon one's self, undertake, assume;* hence *to receive, entertain any one hospitably:* Acts xxviii. 7; *to entertain in one's mind: τὰς ἐπαγγελίας,* i. e. to embrace them with faith, Heb. xi. 17.*

325 ἀνα-δίδωμι: 2 aor. ptcp. ἀναδούς; **1.** *to give forth, send up,* so of the earth producing plants, of plants yielding fruit, etc.; in prof. auth. **2.** acc. to the second sense which ἀνά has in composition [see ἀνά, 3 b.], *to deliver up, hand over: ἐπιστολήν,* Acts xxiii. 33, (the same phrase in Polyb. [29, 10, 7] and Plut.).*

326 ἀνα-ζάω, -ῶ: 1 aor. ἀνέζησα; a word found only in the N. T. and eccl. writ.; *to live again, recover life;* **a.** prop., in Rec. of Ro. xiv. 9; Rev. xx. 5. **b.** trop. one is said ἀναζῆν who has been νεκρός in a trop. sense; **a.** *to be restored to a correct life:* of one who returns to a better moral state, Lk. xv. 24 [WH mrg. ἔζησεν] ([A. V. *is alive again*], cf. Mey. ad loc.), 32 (T Tr WH ἔζησε). **β.** *to revive, regain strength and vigor:* Ro. vii. 9; sin is alive, indeed, and vigorous among men ever since the fall of Adam; yet it is destitute of power (νεκρά ἐστι) in innocent children ignorant of the law; but when they come to a knowledge of the law, sin recovers its power in them also. Others less aptly explain ἀνέζησε here *began to live, sprang into life,* (Germ. *lebte auf*).*

327 ἀνα-ζητέω, -ῶ; [impf. ἀνεζήτουν] 1 aor. ἀνεζήτησα; 'to run through with the eyes any series or succession of men or things, and so *to seek out, search through, make diligent search,* Germ. *daran hinsuchen, aufsuchen*' (Win. De verb. comp. etc. Pt. iii. p. 14); τινά, Lk. ii. 44, (and 45 L txt. T Tr WH); Acts xi. 25. (See exx. fr. Grk. writ. [fr. Plato on] in Win. l. c.)*

328 ἀνα-ζώννυμι: *to gird up;* mid. *to gird up one's self or for one's self: ἀναζωσάμενοι τὰς ὀσφύας,* 1 Pet. i. 13, i. e. *prepared,* — a metaphor derived from the practice of the Orientals, who in order to be unimpeded in their movements were accustomed, when about to start on a journey or engage in any work, to bind their long and flowing garments closely around their bodies and fasten them with a leathern girdle; cf. περιζώννυμι. (Sept. Judg. xviii. 16; Prov. xxix. 35 (xxxi. 17); Dio Chrys. or. 72, 2, ed. Emp. p. 729; Didym. ap. Athen. 4, (17) p. 139 d., al.)*

329 ἀνα-ζωπυρέω, -ῶ; (τὸ ζώπυρον i. e. *a.* the remains of a fire, embers; *b.* that by which the fire is kindled anew or lighted up, a pair of bellows); *to kindle anew, rekindle, resuscitate,* [yet on the force of ἀνα- cf. Ellic.

on 2 Tim. as below]; generally trop., *to kindle up, inflame, one's mind, strength, zeal,* (Xen. de re equest. 10, 16 of a horse roused to his utmost; Hell. 5, 4, 46; Antonin. 7, 2 φαντασίας; Plut. Pericl. 1, 4; Pomp. 41, 2; 49, 5; Plat. Charm. p. 156 d.; etc.): τὸ χάρισμα, 2 Tim. i. 6, i. e. τὸ πνεῦμα, vs. 7. Intrans. *to be enkindled, to gain strength:* Gen. xlv. 27; 1 Macc. xiii. 7, and in prof. auth.; ἀναζωπυρησάτω ἡ πίστις, Clem. Rom. 1 Cor. 27, 3 [see Gebh. and Harn. ad loc.].*

330 ἀνα-θάλλω: 2 aor. ἀνέθαλον; (Ps. xxvii. (xxviii.) 7; Sap. iv. 4; very rare in Grk. writ. and only in the poets, cf. Bttm. Ausf. Spr. ii. p. 195; [Veitch s. v. θάλλω; W. 87 (83); B. 59 (52)]); *to shoot up, sprout again, grow green again, flourish again,* (Hom. Il. 1, 236; Ael. v. h. 5, 4); trop. of those whose condition and affairs are becoming more prosperous: Phil. iv. 10 ἀνεθάλετε τὸ ὑπὲρ ἐμοῦ φρονεῖν ye have revived so as to take thought for me [the inf. being the Grk. accus., or accus. of specification, W. 317 (298); cf. Ellic. ad loc.]. Others, acc. to a trans. use of the verb found only in the Sept. (Ezek. xvii. 24; Sir. i. 18, etc.), render ye have revived (allowed to revive) your thought for me [the inf. being taken as an object-acc., W. 323 (303); B. 263 (226); cf. Bp. Lghtft. ad loc.]; against whom see Meyer ad loc.*

331 ἀνά-θεμα, -τος, τό, (i. q. τὸ ἀνατεθειμένον); **1.** prop. *a thing set up or laid by* in order to be kept; spec. a votive offering, which after being consecrated to a god was hung upon the walls or columns of his temple, or put in some other conspicuous place: 2 Macc. ii. 13, (Plut. Pelop. c. 25); Lk. xxi. 5 in L T, for ἀναθήμασι R G Tr WH; for the two forms are sometimes confounded in the codd.; Moeris, ἀνάθημα ἀττικῶς, ἀνάθεμα ἑλληνικῶς. Cf. ἐπίθημα, ἐπίθεμα, etc., in Lob. ad Phryn. p. 249 [cf. 445; Paral. 417; see also Lipsius, Gram. Unters. p. 41]. **2.** ἀνάθεμα in the Sept. is generally the translation of the Heb. חֵרֶם, *a thing devoted to God* without hope of being redeemed, and, if an animal, to be slain [Lev. xxvii. 28, 29]; therefore a person or thing doomed to destruction, Josh. vi. 17; vii. 12, etc. [W. 32]; a thing abominable and detestable, an accursed thing, Deut. vii. 26. Hence in the N. T. ἀνάθεμα denotes **a.** *a curse:* ἀναθέματι ἀναθεματίζειν, Acts xxiii. 14 [W. 466 (434); B. 184 (159)]. **b.** *a man accursed, devoted to the direst woes* (i. q. ἐπικατάρατος): ἀνάθεμα ἔστω, Gal. i. 8 sq.; 1 Co. xvi. 22; ἀνάθεμα λέγειν τινά to execrate one, 1 Co. xii. 3 (R G, but L T Tr WH have restored ἀνάθεμα Ἰησοῦς, sc. ἔστω); ἀνάθεμα εἶναι ἀπὸ τοῦ Χριστοῦ, Ro. ix. 3 (pregnantly i. q. *doomed* and so separated *from Christ*). Cf. the full remarks on this word in Fritzsche on Rom. vol. ii. 247 sqq.; Wieseler on Gal. p. 39 sqq.; [a trans. of the latter by Prof. *Riddle* in Schaff's Lange on Rom. p. 302 sqq.; see also Trench § v.; Bp. Lightfoot on Gal. l. c.; Ellicott ibid.; Tholuck on Rom. l. c.; BB.DD. s. vv. Anathema, Excommunication].*

332 ἀνα-θεματίζω; 1 aor. ἀνεθεμάτισα; (ἀνάθεμα, q. v.); a purely bibl. and eccl. word, *to declare anathema or accursed;* in the Sept. i. q. הַחֲרִים *to devote to destruction,* (Josh. vi. 21, etc.; 1 Macc. v. 5); ἑαυτόν to declare one's self liable to the severest divine penalties, Acts xxiii. 12, 21; ἀναθέματι ἀναθεματίζειν (Deut. xiii. 15; xx. 17, [W. § 54, 3; B. 184 (159)]) ἑαυτόν foll. by inf., to bind one's self under a curse to do something, Acts xxiii. 14. absol., to asseverate with direful imprecations: Mk. xiv. 71. [COMP.: κατ-αναθεματίζω.]*

ἀνα-θεωρέω, -ῶ; prop. 'to survey a series of things from the lowest to the highest, Germ. *daran hinsehen, längs durchsehen*', [*to look along up* or *through*], (*Win.* De verb. comp. Pt. iii. p. 3); hence *to look at attentively, to observe accurately, consider well*: τί, Acts xvii. 23; Heb. xiii. 7. (Diod. Sic. 12, 15 ἐξ ἐπιπολῆς μὲν θεωρούμενος....ἀναθεωρούμενος δὲ καὶ μετ' ἀκριβείας ἐξεταζόμενος; 14, 109; 2, 5; Lcian. vit. auct. 2; necyom. 15; Plut. Aem. P. 1 [uncertain]; Cat. min. 14; [adv. Colot. 21, 2].)*

ἀνά-θημα, -τος, τό, (ἀνατίθημι), a *gift consecrated and laid up in a temple, a votive offering* (see ἀνάθεμα, 1): Lk. xxi. 5 [R G Tr WH]. (3 Macc. iii. 17; cf. Grimm on 2 Macc. iii. 2; κοσμεῖν ἀναθήμασι occurs also in 2 Macc. ix. 16; Plato, Alcib. ii. § 12, p. 148 e. ἀναθήμασί τε κεκοσμήκαμεν τὰ ἱερὰ αὐτῶν, Hdt. 1, 183 τὸ μὲν δὴ ἱερὸν οὕτω κεκόσμηται· ἔστι δὲ καὶ ἴδια ἀναθήματα πολλά.)*

ἀναίδεια (T WH ἀναιδία; see I, ι), -ας, ἡ, (ἀναιδής, and this fr. ἡ αἰδώς a sense of shame); fr. Hom. down; *shamelessness, impudence*: Lk. xi. 8 (of an importunate man, persisting in his entreaties; [A. V. *importunity*]).*

ἀν-αίρεσις, -εως, ἡ, (fr. ἀναιρέω, 2, q. v.), a *destroying, killing, murder,* 'taking off': Acts viii. 1; xxii. 20 Rec. (Sept. only in Num. xi. 15; Judg. xv. 17; Jud. xv. 4; 2 Macc. v. 13. Xen. Hell. 6, 3, 5; Hdian. 2, 13, 1.)*

ἀν-αιρέω, -ῶ; fut. ἀνελῶ, 2 Th. ii. 8 (L T Tr WH txt. cf. Jud. vii. 13; Dion. Hal. 11, 18; Diod. Sic. 2, 25; cf. W. 82 (78); [B. 53 (47); Veitch s. v. αἱρέω, "perh. late ἑλῶ"]), for the usual ἀναιρήσω; 2 aor. ἀνεῖλον; 2 aor. mid. ἀνειλόμην (but ἀνείλατο Acts vii. 21, ἀνεῖλαν Acts x. 39, ἀνείλατε Acts ii. 23, in G L T Tr WH, after the Alex. form, cf. W. 73 (71) sq.; B. 39 (34) sq. [see αἱρέω]); Pass., pres. ἀναιροῦμαι; 1 aor. ἀνῃρέθην; **1.** *to take up, to lift up* (from the ground); mid. *to take up for myself as mine, to own,* (an exposed infant): Acts vii. 21; (so ἀναιρεῖσθαι, Arstph. nub. 531; Epict. diss. 1, 23, 7; [Plut. Anton. 36, 3; fortuna Rom. 8; fratern. am. 18, etc.]). **2.** *to take away, abolish;* **a.** ordinances, established customs, (to abrogate): Heb. x. 9: **b.** a man, *to put out of the way, slay, kill,* (often so in Sept. and Grk. writ. fr. [Hdt. 4, 66] Thuc. down): Mt. ii. 16; Lk. xxii. 2; xxiii. 32; Acts ii. 23; v. 33, 36; vii. 28; ix. 23 sq. 29; x. 39; xii. 2; xiii. 28; xxii. 20; xxiii. 15, 21, 27; xxv. 3; xxvi. 10; 2 Th. ii. 8 L T Tr WH txt.; ἑαυτόν, to kill one's self, Acts xvi. 27.*

ἀν-αίτιος, -ον, (αἰτία) *guiltless, innocent*: Mt. xii. 5, 7. Often in Grk. writ.; Deut. xxi. 8 sq. i. q. נָקִי; Sus. 62.)*

ἀνα-καθ-ίζω: 1 aor. ἀνεκάθισα; *to raise one's self and sit upright; to sit up, sit erect*: Lk. vii. 15 [Lchm. mrg. WH mrg. ἐκάθισεν]; Acts ix. 40. (Xen. cyn. 5, 7, 19; Plut. Alex. c. 14; and often in medical writ.; with ἑαυτόν, Plut. Philop. c. 20; mid. in same sense, Plat. Phaedo c. 3 p. 60 b.)*

ἀνα-καινίζω; (καινός); *to renew, renovate,* (cf. Germ. *auffrischen*): τινὰ εἰς μετάνοιαν so to renew that he shall repent, Heb. vi. 6. (Isocr. Areop. 3; Philo, leg. ad Gaium § 11; Joseph. antt. 9, 8, 2; Plut. Marcell. c. 6; Lcian. Philop. c. 12; Sept. Ps. cii. (ciii.) 5; ciii. (civ.) 30, etc.; eccl. writ.) Cf. *Win.* De verb. comp. Pt. iii. p. 10.*   **340**

ἀνα-καινόω, -ῶ: [pres. pass. ἀνακαινοῦμαι]; a word peculiar to the apostle Paul; prop. *to cause to grow up* (ἀνά) *new, to make new*; pass., new strength and vigor is given to me, 2 Co. iv. 16; to be changed into a new kind of life, opposed to the former corrupt state, Col. iii. 10. Cf. *Win.* De verb. comp. Pt. iii. p. 10 [or Mey. on Col. l. c.; Test. xii. Patr., test. Levi 16, 17 ἀνακαινοποιέω. Cf. *Köstlin* in Herzog ed. 2, i. 477 sq.]*   **341**

ἀνα-καίνωσις, -εως, ἡ, a *renewal, renovation, complete change for the better,* (cf. ἀνακαινόω): τοῦ νοός, object. gen., Ro. xii. 2; πνεύματος ἁγίου, effected by the Holy Spirit, Tit. iii. 5. (Etym. Magn., Suid.; [Herm. vis. 3, 8, 9; other eccl. writ.]; the simple καίνωσις is found only in Joseph. antt. 18, 6, 10.) [Cf. Trench § xviii.]*   **342**

ἀνα-καλύπτω: [Pass., pres. ptcp. ἀνακαλυπτόμενος; pf. ptcp. ἀνακεκαλυμμένος]; *to unveil, to uncover* (by drawing back the veil), (i. q. גָּלָה, Job xii. 22; Ps. xvii. (xviii.) 16): κάλυμμα ... μὴ ἀνακαλυπτόμενον the veil ... *not being lifted* (lit. *unveiled*) [so WH punctuate, see W. 534 (497); but L T Alf. etc. take the ptcp. as a neut. acc. absol. referring to the clause that follows with ὅτι: *it not being revealed that,* etc.; (for ἀνακαλ. in this sense see Polyb. 4, 85, 6; Tob. xii. 7, 11); see Meyer ad loc.], is used allegor. of a hindrance to the understanding, 2 Co. iii. 14, (ἀνακαλύπτειν συγκάλυμμα, Deut. xxii. 30 Alex.;) ἀνακεκαλυμμένῳ προσώπῳ *with unveiled face,* 2 Co. iii. 18, is also used allegor. of a mind not blinded, but disposed to perceive the glorious majesty of Christ. (The word is used by Eur., Xen., [Aristot. de sens. 5, vol. i. p. 444ᵇ, 25], Polyb., Plut.)*   **343**

ἀνα-κάμπτω: fut. ἀνακάμψω; 1 aor. ἀνέκαμψα; *to bend back, turn back.* In the N. T. (as often in prof. auth.; in Sept. i. q. שׁוּב) intrans. *to return*: Mt. ii. 12; Lk. x. 6 (where the meaning is, 'your salutation shall return to you, as if not spoken'); Acts xviii. 21; Heb. xi. 15.*   **344**

ἀνά-κειμαι; [impf. 3 pers. sing. ἀνέκειτο]; depon. mid. *to be laid up, laid*: Mk. v. 40 R L br. [cf. Eng. *to lay out*]. In later Grk. *to lie at table* (on the *lectus tricliniaris* [cf. B.D. s. v. Meals]; the earlier Greeks used κεῖσθαι, κατακεῖσθαι, cf. *Lob.* ad Phryn. p. 216 sq.; Fritzsche [or Wetst.] on Mt. ix. 10): Mt. ix. 10; xxii. 10 sq.; xxvi. 7, 20; Mk. [vi. 26 T Tr WH]; xiv. 18; xvi. 14; Lk. vii. 37 (L T Tr WH κατάκειται); xxii. 27; Jn. xii. 2 (Rec. συνανακειμ.); xiii. 23, 28. Generally, *to eat together, to dine*: Jn. vi. 11. [Cf. ἀναπίπτω, fin. COMP.: συν-ανάκειμαι.]*   **345**

ἀνα-κεφαλαιόω, -ῶ: [pres. pass. ἀνακεφαλαιοῦμαι; 1 aor. mid. inf. ἀνακεφαλαιώσασθαι]; (fr. κεφαλαιόω, q. v., and this fr. κεφάλαιον, q. v.): *to sum up* (*again*), *to repeat summarily* and so *to condense into a summary* (as, the substance of a speech; Quintil. 6. 1 'rerum repetitio et congregatio, quae graece ἀνακεφαλαίωσις dicitur', [ἔργον   **see 346 St.**

ῥητορικῆς . . . ἀνακεφαλαιώσασθαι πρὸς ἀνάμνησιν, Aristot. frag. 123, vol. v. p. 1499ᵃ, 33]); so in Ro. xiii. 9. In Eph. i. 10 God is said ἀνακεφαλαιώσασθαι τὰ πάντα ἐν τῷ Χριστῷ, to bring together again for himself (note the mid.) all things and beings (hitherto disunited by sin) into one combined state of fellowship in Christ, the universal bond, [cf. Mey. or Ellic. on Eph. l. c.]; (Protev. Jac. 13 εἰς ἐμὲ ἀνεκεφαλαιώθη ἡ ἱστορία ᾿Αδάμ, where cf. Thilo).*

347   ἀνα-κλίνω: fut. ἀνακλινῶ; 1 aor. ἀνέκλινα; Pass., 1 aor. ἀνεκλίθην; fut. ἀνακλιθήσομαι; [fr. Hom. down]; to lean against, lean upon;   **a.** to lay down: τινά, Lk. ii. 7 (ἐν (τῇ) φάτνῃ).   **b.** to make or bid to recline: Mk. vi. 39 (ἐπέταξεν αὐτοῖς, sc. the disciples, ἀνακλῖναι [-κλιθῆναι L WΗ txt.] πάντας i. e. the people); Lk. ix 15 (T Tr WH κατέκλιναν); xii. 37. Pass. to lie back, recline, lie down: Mt. xiv. 19; of those reclining at table and at feasts, Lk. vii. 36 (R G); xiii. 29; Mt. viii. 11, — in the last two pass. used fig. of participation in future blessedness in the Messiah's kingdom.*

348   ἀνα-κόπτω: 1 aor. ἀνέκοψα; to beat back, check, (as the course of a ship, Theophr. char. 24 (25), 1 [var.]). τινά foll. by an inf. [A. V. hinder], Gal. v. 7 Rec., where the preceding ἐτρέχετε shows that Paul was thinking of an obstructed road; cf. ἐγκόπτω.*

349   ἀνα-κράζω: 1 aor. [" rare and late," Veitch s. v. κράζω; B. 61 (53)] ἀνέκραξα; 2 aor. ἀνέκραγον (Lk. xxiii. 18 T Tr txt. WH); to raise a cry from the depth of the throat, to cry out: Mk. i. 23; vi. 49; Lk. iv. 33; viii. 28; xxiii. 18. Exx. fr. prof. auth. in Win. De verb. comp. etc. Pt. iii. p. 6 sq.*

350   ἀνα-κρίνω; 1 aor. ἀνέκρινα; Pass., [pres. ἀνακρίνομαι]; 1 aor. ἀνεκρίθην; (freq. in Grk. writ., esp. Attic); prop. by looking through a series (ἀνά) of objects or particulars to distinguish (κρίνω) or search after. Hence   **a.** to investigate, examine, inquire into, scrutinize, sift, question: Acts xvii. 11 (τὰς γραφάς); 1 Co. x. 25, 27 (not anxiously questioning, sc. whether the meat set before you be the residue from heathen sacrifices). Spec. in a forensic sense (often also in Grk. writ.) of a judge, to hold an investigation; to interrogate, examine, the accused or the witnesses; absol.: Lk. xxiii. 14; Acts xxiv. 8. τινά, Acts xii. 19; xxviii. 18; pass., Acts iv. 9. Paul has in mind this judicial use (as his preceding term ἀπολογία shows) when in 1 Co. ix. 3 he speaks of τοῖς ἐμὲ ἀνακρίνουσι, investigating me, whether I am a true apostle.   **b.** univ. to judge of, estimate, determine (the excellence or defects of any person or thing): τί, 1 Co. ii. 15; τινά, 1 Co. iv. 3 sq.; pass., 1 Co. ii. [14], 15; xiv. 24. [Cf. Lghtft. Fresh Revision, etc. iv. § 3 (p. 67 sq. Am. ed.).]*

351   ἀνά-κρισις, -εως, ἡ, an examination; as a law-term among the Greeks, the preliminary investigation held for the purpose of gathering evidence for the information of the judges (Meier and Schömann, Att. Process. pp. 27, [622; cf. Dict. of Antiq. s. v.]); this seems to be the sense of the word in Acts xxv. 26.*

see
617 St.

ἀνα-κυλίω: **1.** to roll up.   **2.** to roll back: ἀνακε-

κύλισται ὁ λίθος, Mk. xvi. 4 T Tr WH. (Alexis in Athen. vi. p. 237 c.; Lcian. de luctu 8; Dion. Hal., Plut., al.)*

352   ἀνα-κύπτω: 1 aor. ἀνέκυψα; to raise or lift one's self up;   **a.** one's body: Lk. xiii. 11; Jn. viii. 7, 10; (Xen. de re equ. 7, 10, al.; Sept. Job x. 15).   **b.** one's soul; to be elated, exalted: Lk. xxi. 28; (Xen. oec. 11, 5 ; Joseph. b. j. 6, 8, 5, al.).*

353   ἀνα-λαμβάνω; 2 aor. ἀνέλαβον; 1 aor. pass. ἀνελήφθην (ἀνελήμφθην L T Tr WH; cf. W. p. 48 [B. 62 (54); Veitch (s. v. λαμβάνω); see λαμβάνω, and s. v. M, μ]); [fr. Hdt. down];   **1.** to take up, raise: εἰς τὸν οὐρανόν, Mk. xvi. 19; Acts i. 11; x. 16, (Sept. 2 K. ii. 11) without case, Acts i. 2, 22; 1 Tim. iii. 16 [cf. W. 413 (385)], (Sir. xlviii. 9).   **2.** to take up (a thing in order to carry or use it): Acts vii. 43; Eph. vi. 13, 16. to take to one's self: τινά, in order to conduct him, Acts xxiii. 31; or as a companion, 2 Tim. iv. 11; or in Acts xx. 13 sq. to take up sc. into the ship.*

354   ἀνά-ληψις (ἀνάλημψις L T Tr WH; see M, μ), -εως, ἡ, (ἀναλαμβάνω), [fr. Hippocr. down], a taking up: Lk. ix. 51 (sc. εἰς τὸν οὐρανόν of the ascension of Jesus into heaven; [cf. Test. xii. Patr. test. Levi § 18; Suicer, Thesaur. Eccles. s. v.; and Meyer on Lk. l. c.]).*

355   ἀν-αλίσκω: fr. the pres. ἀναλόω [3 pers. sing. ἀναλοῖ, 2 Th. ii. 8 WH mrg.] come the fut. ἀναλώσω; 1 aor. ἀνήλωσα and ἀνάλωσα [see Veitch]; 1 aor. pass. ἀνηλώθην; (the simple verb is found only in the pass. ἁλίσκομαι to be taken; but a ἀλίσκομαι is short, in ἀναλίσκω long; cf. Bttm. Ausf. Spr. ii. p. 113; [Veitch s. vv.; "the diff. quantity, the act. form, the trans. sense of the pf., and above all the difference of sense, indicate a diff. origin for the two verbs." L. and S.]); [fr. Pind. down];   **1.** to expend; to consume, e. g. χρήματα (to spend money; very often in Xen.).   **2.** to consume, use up, destroy: Lk. ix. 54; Gal. v. 15; 2 Th. ii. 8 R G WH mrg. (Sept. Jer. xxvii. (l.) 7; Prov. xxiii. 28; Gen. xli. 30, etc.) [Comp.: κατ-, προσ-αναλίσκω.]*

356   ἀναλογία, -ας, ἡ, (ἀνάλογος conformable, proportional), proportion: κατὰ τὴν ἀναλογίαν τῆς πίστεως, i. q. κατὰ τὸ μέτρον πίστεως received from God, Ro. xii. 6, cf. 3. (Plat., Dem., Aristot., Theophr., al.)*

357   ἀνα-λογίζομαι: 1 aor. ἀνελογισάμην; dep. mid. to think over, ponder, consider: commonly with acc. of the thing, but in Heb. xii. 3 with acc. of the pers. 'to consider by weighing, comparing,' etc. (3 Macc. vii. 7. Often in Grk. writ. fr. Plat. and Xen. down.)*

358   ἄναλος, -ον, (ἅλς salt), saltless, unsalted, (ἄρτοι ἄναλοι, Aristot. probl. 21, 5, 1; ἄρτος ἄναλος, Plut. symp. v. quaest. 10 § 1): ἅλας ἄναλον salt destitute of pungency, Mk. ix. 50.*

[ἀναλόω, see ἀναλίσκω.]

359   ἀνά-λυσις, -εως, ἡ, (ἀναλύω, q. v.);   **1.** an unloosing (as of things woven), a dissolving (into separate parts).   **2.** departure, (a metaphor drawn from loosing from moorings preparatory to setting sail, cf. Hom. Od. 15, 548; [or, acc. to others, fr. breaking up an encampment; cf. Bp. Lghtft. on Phil. i. 23]), Germ. Aufbruch: 2 Tim. iv. 6 (departure from life; Philo in Flacc. § 21 [p. 544

ed. Mang.] ἡ ἐκ τοῦ βίου τελευταία ἀνάλυσις; [Clem. Rom. 1 Cor. 44, 5 ἔγκαρπον κ. τελείαν ἔσχον τὴν ἀνάλυσιν; Euseb. h. e. 3, 32, 1 μαρτυρίῳ τὸν βίον ἀναλῦσαι, cf. 3, 34]. Cf. ἀνάλυσις ἀπὸ συνουσίας, Joseph. antt. 19, 4, 1).*

360   ἀνα-λύω: fut. ἀναλύσω; 1 aor. ἀνέλυσα; **1.** *to un-loose, undo again*, (as, woven threads). **2.** *to depart*, Germ. *aufbrechen, break up* (see ἀνάλυσις, 2), so very often in Grk. writ.; *to depart from life*: Phil. i. 23, (Lcian. Philops. c. 14 ὀκτωκαιδεκαέτης ὢν ἀνέλυεν; add Ael. v. h. 4, 23; [ἀνέλυσεν ὁ ἐπίσκοπος Πλάτων ἐν κυρίῳ, Acta et mart. Matth. § 31]). *to return*, ἐκ τῶν γάμων, Lk. xii. 36 [B. 145 (127); for exx.] cf. Kuinoel [and Wetstein] ad loc.; Grimm on 2 Macc. viii. 25.*

361   ἀναμάρτητος, -ον, (fr. ἀν priv. and the form ἁμαρτέω), *sinless*, both *one who has not sinned*, and *one who cannot sin*. In the former sense in Jn. viii. 7; Deut. xxix. 19; 2 Macc. viii. 4; xii. 42; [Test. xii. Patr. test. Benj. § 3]. On the use of this word fr. Hdt. down, cf. *Ull-mann*, Sündlosigkeit Jesu, p. 91 sq. [(abridged in) Eng. trans. p. 99; Cremer s. v.].*

362   ἀνα-μένω; [fr. Hom. down]; τινά, *to wait for one* (Germ. *erharren*, or rather *heranharren* [i. e. to await one whose coming is known or foreseen]), with the added notion of patience and trust: 1 Th. i. 10 [cf. Ellicott ad loc.]. Good Greek; cf. *Win.* De verb. comp. etc. Pt. iii. p. 15 sq.*

[ἀνα-μέρος, i. e. ἀνὰ μέρος, see ἀνά, 1.]

[ἀνά-μεσον, i. e. ἀνὰ μέσον, see ἀνά, 1.]

363   ἀνα-μιμνήσκω; fut. ἀναμνήσω (fr. the form μνάω); Pass., [pres. ἀναμιμνήσκομαι]; 1 aor. ἀνεμνήσθην; [fr. Hom. down]; *to call to remembrance, to remind*: τινά τι one of a thing [W. § 32, 4 a.], 1 Co. iv. 17; *to admonish*, τινά foll. by inf., 2 Tim. i. 6. Pass. *to recall to one's own mind, to remember*; absol.: Mk. xi. 21. with gen. of the thing, Mk. xiv. 72 Rec. τί, Mk. xiv. 72 L T Tr WH; contextually, *to (remember and) weigh well, consider*: 2 Co. vii. 15; Heb. x. 32; cf. W. § 30, 10 c.; [B. § 132, 14]; Matth. ii. p. 820 sq. [COMP.: ἐπ-αναμιμνήσκω. SYN. see ἀνάμνησις fin.]*

364   ἀνάμνησις, -εως, ἡ, (ἀναμιμνήσκω), *a remembering, recol-lection*: εἰς τ. ἐμὴν ἀνάμνησιν *to call me* (affectionately) *to remembrance*, Lk. xxii. 19 [WH reject the pass.]; 1 Co. xi. 24 sq. ἐν αὐταῖς (sc. θυσίαις) ἀνάμνησις ἁμαρτιῶν in offering sacrifices there is a remembrance of sins, i. e. the memory of sins committed is revived by the sacri-fices, Heb. x. 3. In Grk. writ. fr. Plat. down.*

[SYN. ἀνάμνησις, ὑπόμνησις: The distinction between these words as stated by Ammonius et al. — viz. that ἀνάμν. denotes an unassisted recalling, ὑπόμν. a remembrance prompted by another, — seems to be not wholly without warrant; note the force of ὑπό (cf. our 'sug-gest'). But even in class. Grk. the words are easily interchangeable. Schmidt ch. 14; Trench § cvii. 6, cf. p. 61 note; Ellic. or Holtzm. on 2 Tim. i. 5.]

365   ἀνα-νεόω, -ῶ: *to renew*, (often in Grk. writ.); Pass. [W. § 39, 3 N. 3; for the mid. has an act. or reciprocal force, cf. 1 Macc. xii. 1 and Grimm ad loc.] ἀνανεοῦσθαι τῷ πνεύματι *to be renewed in mind*, i. e. to be spiritually transformed, to take on a new mind [see νοῦς, 1 b. fin.;

πνεῦμα, fin.], Eph. iv. 23. Cf. Tittmann i. p. 60; [Trench §§ lx. xviii.], and ἀνακαινόω above.*

366   ἀνα-νήφω: ['in good auth. apparently confined to the pres.'; 1 aor. ἀνένηψα]; *to return to soberness* (ἐκ μέθης, which is added by Grk. writ.); metaph.: 2 Tim. ii. 26 ἐκ τῆς τοῦ διαβόλου παγίδος [W. § 66, 2 d.] to be set free from the snare of the devil and to return to a sound mind ['one's sober senses']. (Philo, legg. alleg. ii. § 16 ἀνα-νήφει, τοῦτ' ἔστι μετανοεῖ; add Joseph. antt. 6, 11, 10; Ceb. tab. 9; Antonin. 6, 31; Charit. 5, 1.) [See ἀγρυ-πνέω, fin.]*

367   Ἀνανίας [WH. Ἀναν., see their Intr. § 408], -α [but on the gen. cf. B. 20 (18)], ὁ, *Ananias* (חֲנַנְיָה, fr. חָנַן to be gracious, and יָהּ Jehovah, [cf. Mey. on Acts v. 1]): **1.** a certain Christian [at Jerusalem], the husband of Sapphira: Acts v. 1-6. **2.** a Christian of Damascus: Acts ix. 10-18; xxii. 12 sqq. **3.** a son of Nedebaeus, and high priest of the Jews c. A. D. 47-59. In the year 66 he was slain by the Sicarii: Acts xxiii. 2 sq.; xxiv. 1 sq.; Joseph. antt. 20, 5, 2; 6, 2; 9, 2-4; b. j. 2, 17, 6; 9. [Cf. B. D. s. v.]*

368   ἀν-αντί-ρρητος [WH ἀναντίρητος; see P, ρ], -ον, (a priv., ἀντί, and ῥητός fr. ΡΕΩ to say), *not contradicted* and *not to be contradicted; undeniable*, [*not to be gainsaid*]; in the latter sense, Acts xix. 36. (Occasionally in Grk. writ. fr. Polyb. down.)*

369   ἀναντιρρήτως [WH ἀναντιρήτως, see their App. p. 163, and P, ρ], adv., *without contradiction*: Acts x. 29 (I came without gainsaying). Polyb. 23, 8, 11, [al.].*

370   ἀν-άξιος, -ον, (a priv. and ἄξιος), [fr. Soph. down], *un-worthy* (τινός): *unfit for a thing*, 1 Co. vi. 2.*

371   ἀν-αξίως, adv., [fr. Soph. down], *in an unworthy man-ner*: 1 Co. xi. 27, and 29 Rec. [Cf. W. 463 (431).]*

372   ἀνά-παυσις, -εως, ἡ, (ἀναπαύω), [fr. Mimnerm., Pind. down]; **1.** *intermission, cessation*, of any motion, busi-ness, labor: ἀνάπαυσιν οὐκ ἔχουσι λέγοντες [Rec. λέγοντα] equiv. to οὐκ ἀναπαύονται λέγοντες they incessantly say, Rev. iv. 8. **2.** *rest, recreation*: Mt. xii. 43; Lk. xi. 24; Rev. xiv. 11, (and often in Grk. writ.); blessed tranquillity of soul, Mt. xi. 29, (Sir. vi. [27] 28]; li. 27; Sap. iv. 7). [The word denotes a t e m p o r a r y rest, a respite, e. g. of soldiers; cf. Schmidt ch. 25; Bp. Lghtft. on Philem. 7; Trench § xli.] *

373   ἀνα-παύω: fut. ἀναπαύσω; 1 aor. ἀνέπαυσα; pf. pass. ἀναπέπαυμαι; Mid., [pres. ἀναπαύομαι]; fut. ἀναπαύσομαι (Rev. vi. 11 [Lchm. ed. min., Tdf. edd. 2, 7, WH; but G L T Tr with R -σωνται]), and in the colloquial speech of inferior Grk. ἀναπαήσομαι (Rev. xiv. 13 L T Tr WH, cf. Bttm. (57) esp. Eng. trans. p. 64 sq.; Kühner i. 886; [Tdf. Proleg. p. 123; WH. App. p. 170]; see also in ἐπαναπαύω); 1 aor. ἀνεπαυσάμην; (a common verb fr. Hom. down): *to cause or permit one to cease from any movement or labor in order to recover and collect his strength* (note the prefix ἀνά and distinguish fr. κατα-παύω, [see ἀνάπαυσις, fin.]), *to give rest, refresh*; mid. *to give one's self rest, take rest*. So in mid. absol. of rest after travelling, Mk. vi. 31; and for taking sleep, Mt. xxvi. 45; Mk. xiv. 41; of the sweet repose one enjoys after

toil, Lk. xii. 19; *to keep quiet,* of calm and patient expectation, Rev. vi. 11; of the blessed rest of the dead, Rev. xiv. 13 (ἐκ τῶν κόπων exempt from toils [cf. B. 158 (138)]; Plat. Critias in. ἐκ μακρᾶς ὁδοῦ). By a Hebraism (נוּחַ עַל, Isa. xi. 2) τὸ πνεῦμα ἐφ᾽ ὑμᾶς ἀναπαύεται rests upon you, to actuate you, 1 Pet. iv. 14. Act. *to refresh,* the soul of any one: τινά, Mt. xi. 28; τὸ πνεῦμά τινος, 1 Co. xvi. 18; τὰ σπλάγχνα τινός, Philem. 20. In pass., Philem. 7; 2 Co. vii. 13 (ἀπὸ πάντων ὑμῶν from your sight, attentions, intercourse). [COMP.: ἐπ-, συν- (-μαι).]*

374   **ἀνα-πείθω**; *to stir up by persuasion* (cf. Germ. *aufreizen*), *to solicit, incite*: τινά τι ποιῆσαι, Acts xviii. 13. So also in Hdt., Thuc., Plat., Xen., al.*

see 376   **ἀνάπειρος,** a false spelling (arising from itacism, [cf. Phryn. in *Bekker,* Anecd. i. p. 9, 22: διὰ τοῦ η τὴν τρίτην, οὐ διὰ τῆς ει διφθόγγου ὡς οἱ ἀμαθεῖς]) in some Mss. in Lk. xiv. 13, 21 (and adopted by L Tr WH; [see *WH.* App. p. 151]) for ἀνάπηρος, q. v.

375   **ἀνα-πέμπω** : 1 aor. ἀνέπεμψα; [fr. Pind. and Aeschyl. down]; **1.** *to send up*; i. e. **a.** to a higher place; **b.** to a person higher in office, authority, power, (Plut. Marius c. 17; [Philo de creat. princip. § 8; Joseph. b. j. 2, 20, 5]): τινὰ πρός τινα, Lk. xxiii. 7, 15; Acts xxv. 21 L T Tr WH. **2.** *to send back*: τινά, Philem. 12 (11); τινά τινι, Lk. xxiii. 11.*

see 450   **ἀνα-πηδάω**: [1 aor. ptcp. ἀναπηδήσας]; (Hom. Il. 11, 379; often in Plat., Xen., Dem.); *to leap up, spring up, start up*: ἀναπηδήσας, Mk. x. 50 L T Tr WH; cf. Fritzsche ad loc. (1 S. xx. 34; Prov. xviii. 4 [Ald. etc.]; Tob. ii. 4; vi. 3; vii. 6.)*

376   **ἀνά-πηρος,** -ον, (prop. πηρός fr. the lowest part to the highest — ἀνά; hence Suid. ὁ καθ᾽ ὑπερβολὴν πεπηρωμένος, [cf. *Lob.* Path. Elementa i. 195]), *disabled in the limbs, maimed, crippled*; injured in, or bereft of, some member of the body: Lk. xiv. 13, 21 ἀναπήρους, χωλούς, τυφλούς. In both these pass. L Tr WH have adopted with certain Mss. the spelling ἀναπείρους — manifestly false, as arising from itacism. (Plat. Crito p. 53 a. χωλοὶ καὶ τυφλοὶ καὶ ἄλλοι ἀνάπηροι; Aristot. h. a. 7, 6 [vol. i. p. 585ᵇ, 29] γίνονται ἐξ ἀναπήρων ἀνάπηροι; Lys. ap. Suid. ῥῖνα καὶ ὦτα ἀνάπηρος; 2 Macc. viii. 24 τοῖς μέλεσιν ἀναπήρους.)*

377   **ἀνα-πίπτω**: 2 aor. ἀνέπεσον, 3 pers. plur. ἀνέπεσον Mk. vi. 40 (T Tr WH ἀνέπεσαν), Jn. vi. 10 (L T Tr WH ἀνέπεσαν), inf. ἀναπεσεῖν, impv. ἀνάπεσε Lk. xiv. 10 (Rec. ἀνάπεσον fr. 1 aor. ἀνέπεσα, [(Grsb. ἀνάπεσαι i. e. 1 aor. mid. impv.)]); Lk. xvii. 7 [R G ἀνάπεσαι, cf. *WH.* App. p. 164; *Tdf.* Proleg. p. 123; see πίπτω], ptcp. ἀναπεσών; cf. W. § 13, 1 p. 73 (71); [B. 39 (34) sq., 67 (59); fr. Eur. down]; *to lie back, lie down*: absol., Mk. vi. 40; Jn. vi. 10, (sc. on the ground); ἐπὶ τὴν γῆν, Mt. xv. 35; ἐπὶ τῆς γῆς, Mk. viii. 6. In later Grk. (cf. *Lob.* ad Phryn. p. 216; [W. 23 (22)]) for ἀνακλίνομαι to recline at table: Lk. xi. 37; xiv. 10; xvii. 7; xxii. 14; Jn. xiii. 12; xxi. 20 [al. refer this to the following signif.]. *to lean back,* Jn. xiii. 25 L Tr WH. [It denotes an act rather than a state, and in the last pass. differs from ἀνάκειμαι, vs. 23, by indicating a change of position.]*

378   **ἀνα-πληρόω,** -ῶ; fut. ἀναπληρώσω; 1 aor. ἀνεπλήρωσα;

[pres. pass. ἀναπληροῦμαι]; (ἀνά to, up to, e. g. to fill a vessel up to the brim; up to the appointed measure or standard, Germ. *anfüllen*); [fr. Eurip. down]; **1.** *to fill up, make full,* e. g. a ditch (Strabo 5, 6 p. 223); hence trop. ἁμαρτίας, 1 Th. ii. 16 (to add what is still wanting to complete the number of their sins; on the meaning, cf. Gen. xv. 16; Dan. viii. 23; ix. 24; Mt. xxiii. 32; 2 Macc. vi. 14). ἀναπληροῦται ἡ προφητεία the prophecy is fully satisfied, the event completely corresponds to it, Mt. xiii. 14. τὸν νόμον to fulfil i. e. observe the law perfectly, Gal. vi. 2, (Barn. ep. 21 ἀναπλ. πᾶσαν ἐντολήν); τὸν τόπον τινός to fill the place of any one, 1 Co. xiv. 16 (after the rabbin. מָלֵא מָקוֹם to hold the position of any one, [yet cf. Mey. ad loc.]). **2.** *to supply*: τὸ ὑστέρημα, Phil. ii. 30, (Col. i. 24); 1 Co. xvi. 17 (they by their presence supplied your place in your absence); cf. Plat. symp. p. 188 e. ἀλλ᾽ εἴ τι ἐξέλιπον, σὸν ἔργον (sc. ἐστίν) ἀναπληρῶσαι. Cf. *Win.* De verb. comp. etc. Pt. iii. p. 11 sq.; [Ellic. on Phil. l. c., or Mey. on Gal. l. c. COMP.: ἀντ-, προσ-αναπληρόω].*

379   **ἀναπολόγητος,** -ον, *without defence or excuse,* Ro. i. 20; also *that cannot be defended, inexcusable,* Ro. ii. 1. (Polyb., Dion. Hal. antt. 7, 46; Plut. Brut. 46, al.)*

380   **ἀνα-πτύσσω**: 1 aor. ἀνέπτυξα; (ἀνά — cf. the Germ. *auf* i. q. *auseinander,* see ἀναλύω — and πτύσσω to fold up, roll together); *to unroll,* [i. e. open for reading]: τὸ βιβλίον (as in Hdt. 1, 48 and 125), Lk. iv. 17 [R G T], (2 K. xix. 14). The books of the Hebrews were rolls (מְגִלּוֹת) fastened to [one or] two smooth rods and furnished with handles, so that they could be rolled up and unrolled; [cf. B. D. s. v. Writing].*

381   **ἀν-άπτω**; 1 aor. ἀνῆψα; 1 aor. pass. ἀνήφθην; *to light up, kindle:* Lk. xii. 49; Acts xxviii. 2 [R G]; Jas. iii. 5. [From Hdt. down.]*

382   **ἀν-αρίθμητος,** -ον, (α priv. and ἀριθμέω), *innumerable:* Heb. xi. 12. [From Pind. down.]*

383   **ἀνα-σείω**; 1 aor. ἀνέσεισα; *to shake up;* trop. *to stir up, excite, rouse:* τὸν ὄχλον, Mk. xv. 11; τὸν λαόν, Lk. xxiii. 5. (So in Diod. 13, 91; 14, 10; Dion. Hal. antt. 8, 81.)*

384   **ἀνα-σκευάζω**; (σκευάζω, fr. σκεῦος a vessel, utensil); **1.** *to pack up baggage* (Lat. *vasa colligere*) *in order to carry it away to another place:* Xen. an. 5, 10, (6, 2) 8. Mid. *to move one's furniture* (when setting out for some other place, Xen. Cyr. 8, 5, 4 ὅταν δὲ ἀνασκευάζωνται, συντίθησι μὲν ἕκαστος τὰ σκεύη); hence **2.** of an enemy *dismantling, plundering,* a place (Thuc. 4, 116); *to overthrow, ravage, destroy,* towns, lands, etc.; trop. ψυχάς, *to turn away violently from a right state, to unsettle, subvert:* Acts xv. 24.*

385   **ἀνα-σπάω,** -ῶ: ἀνασπάσω; 1 aor. pass. ἀνεσπάσθην; *to draw up:* Lk. xiv. 5; Acts xi. 10. [From Hom. down.]*

386   **ἀνά-στασις,** -εως, ἡ, (ἀνίστημι), [fr. Aeschyl. down]; **1.** *a raising up, rising,* (e. g. fr. a seat): Lk. ii. 34 (opp. to πτῶσις; the meaning is 'It lies [or 'is set' A. V.] like a stone, which some will lay hold of in order to climb; but others will strike against it and fall'). **2.** *a rising from the dead* (eccl. Lat. *resurrectio*), [Aeschyl.

Eum. 648];   **a.** that of **Christ**: Acts i. 22; ii. 31; iv. 33; Ro. vi. 5; Phil. iii. 10; 1 Pet. iii. 21; with the addition of νεκρῶν, Ro. i. 4 (a generic phrase: *the resurrection-of-the-dead*, although it has come to pass as yet only in the case of Christ alone; cf. Acts xvii. 32; W. § 30, 2 *a.* fin.); *ἐκ νεκρῶν*, 1 Pet. i. 3.   **b.** that of all men at the end of the present age. This is called simply *ἀνάστασις* or *ἡ ἀνάστασις*, Mt. xxii. 23, [28], 30; Mk. xii. 18, 23; Lk. xx. 27, 33, 36; Jn. xi. 24; Acts xvii. 18; xxiii. 8; 2 Tim. ii. 18; by meton. i. q. the author of resurrection, Jn. xi. 25; with the addition of *ἡ ἐκ νεκρῶν*, Lk. xx. 35; Acts iv. 2; or simply of *τῶν νεκρῶν* [on the distinction which some (e. g. Van Hengel on Ro. i. 4; Van Hengel and Bp. Lghtft. on Phil. iii. 11; Cremer s. v.) would make between these phrases, see W. 123 (117); B. 89 (78)], Mt. xxii. 31; Acts xvii. 32; xxiii. 6; xxiv. 15 [Rec.], 21; xxvi. 23; 1 Co. xv. 12 sq. 21, 42; Heb. vi. 2. *ἀνάστ. ζωῆς* resurrection to life (*ἀν. εἰς ζωήν*, 2 Macc. vii. 14 [cf. Dan. xii. 2]), and *ἀν. τῆς κρίσεως* resurrection to judgment, Jn. v. 29, (on the genitives cf. W. 188 (177)); the former is *ἡ ἀνάστ. τῶν δικαίων*, Lk. xiv. 14; *κρείττων ἀνάστασις*, Heb. xi. 35 (so called in comparison with a continuance of life on earth, which is spoken of as an *ἀνάστασις* by a kind of license; [cf. W. 460 (429)]). *ἡ ἀνάστ. ἡ πρώτη* in Rev. xx. 5 sq. will be that of true Christians, and at the end of a thousand years will be followed by a second resurrection, that of all the rest of mankind, Rev. xx. 12 sqq. On the question whether and in what sense Paul also believed in two resurrections, separated from each other by a definite space of time, cf. *Grimm* in the Zeitschr. für wissenschaftl. Theol., 1873, p. 388 sq.   **c.** the resurrection of certain in ancient Jewish story who were restored to life before burial: Heb. xi. 35.*

387   **ἀναστατόω, -ῶ**; 1 aor. *ἀνεστάτωσα*; a verb found nowhere in prof. auth:, but [in Dan. vii. 23 Sept.; Deut. xxix. 27 Graec. Venet.] several times in the O. T. fragments of Aquila [e. g. Ps. x. 1] and Symmachus [e. g. Ps. lviii. 11; Is. xxii. 3], and in Eustathius, (fr. *ἀνάστατος*, driven from one's abode, outcast, or roused up from one's situation; accordingly equiv. to *ἀνάστατον ποιῶ*), *to stir up, excite, unsettle*; foll. by an acc.   **a.** to excite tumults and seditions in the State: Acts xvii. 6; xxi. 38.   **b.** to upset, unsettle, minds by disseminating religious error: Gal. v. 12.*

388   **ἀνα-σταυρόω, -ῶ**; *to raise up upon a cross, crucify*, (*ἀνά* as in *ἀνασκολοπίζω*): Heb. vi. 6, (very often in Grk. writ. fr. Hdt. down). Cf. *Win.* De verb. comp. etc. Pt. iii. p. 9 sq.; [Winer admits that in Heb. l. c. the meaning to crucify *again*, or *afresh*, may also be assigned to this verb legitimately, and that the absence of a precedent in prof. writ. for such a sense is, from the nature of the case, not surprising.]*

389   **ἀνα-στενάζω**: 1 aor. *ἀνεστέναξα*; *to draw sighs up from the bottom of the breast, to sigh deeply*: Mk. viii. 12. (Lam. i. 4; Sir. xxv. 18 (17); 2 Macc. vi. 30, and in Grk. writ. fr. [Aeschyl. choëph. 335,] Hdt. 1, 86 down.)*

390   **ἀνα-στρέφω**: fut. *ἀναστρέψω*; [1 aor. *ἀνέστρεψα*; Pass., pres. *ἀναστρέφομαι*]; 2 aor. *ἀνεστράφην*;   **1.** *to turn*

upside down, overturn: *τὰς τραπέζας*, Jn. ii. 15, (*δίφρους*, Hom. Il. 23, 436).   **2.** *to turn back*; intrans. [W. 251 (236)] *to return*, like the Lat. *reverto* i. q. *revertor*, (as in Grk. writ.; in Sept. i. q. שׁוּב): Acts v. 22; xv. 16 (here *ἀναστρέψω καί* has not like the Hebr. שׁוּב the force of an adverb, *again*, but God in the Messiah's advent returns to his people, whom he is conceived of as having previously abandoned; cf. W. 469 (437)).   **3.** *to turn hither and thither*; pass. reflexively, *to turn one's self about, sojourn, dwell, ἐν in a place*;   **a.** literally: Mt. xvii. 22, where L T WH Tr txt. *συστρεφομένων*, cf. Keim ii. p. 581 [Eng. trans. iv. p. 303]. (Josh. v. 5; Ezek. xix. 6, and in Grk. writ.)   **b.** like the Hebr. הָלַךְ to walk, of the manner of life and moral character, *to conduct one's self, behave one's self, live*: 2 Co. i. 12 (*ἐν τῷ κόσμῳ*); 1 Tim. iii. 15 (*ἐν οἴκῳ θεοῦ*); Eph. ii. 3 (*ἐν οἷς* among whom); 2 Pet. ii. 18 (*ἐν πλάνῃ*). simply *to conduct or behave one's self, 'walk'*, (Germ. *wandeln*): 1 Pet. i. 17; Heb. x. 33; (*καλῶς*) xiii. 18. [Cf. its use e. g. in Xen. an. 2, 5, 14; Polyb. 1, 9, 7; 74, 13; 86, 5 etc., (see *ἀναστροφή*, fin.); Prov. xx. 7 Sept.; Clem. Rom. 1 Cor. 1, 21, 8; etc.]*

391   **ἀνα-στροφή, -ῆς, ἡ**, (fr. the pass. *ἀναστρέφομαι*, see the preceding word), prop. 'walk,' i. e. *manner of life, behavior, conduct*, (Germ. *Lebenswandel*): Gal. i. 13; Eph. iv. 22; 1 Tim. iv. 12; Jas. iii. 13; 1 Pet. i. 15, 18; ii. 12; iii. 1 sq. 16; 2 Pet. ii. 7; plur. *ἅγιαι ἀναστροφαί* the ways in which holy living shows itself, 2 Pet. iii. 11. Hence *life* in so far as it is comprised in conduct, Heb. xiii. 7. (This word, in the senses given, is found in Grk. writ. fr. Polyb. 4, 82, 1 down; in the Scriptures first in Tob. iv. 14; 2 Macc. v. 8; add Epict. diss. 1, 9, 5; 4, 7, 5, [and fr. *Soph.* Lex. s. v.] Agatharchides 134, 12; 153, 8; Aristeas 16].)*

392   **ἀνα-τάσσομαι**; [1 aor. mid. inf. *ἀνατάξασθαι*]; (mid. of *ἀνατάσσω*), *to put together in order, arrange, compose*: *διήγησιν*, Lk. i. 1 (so to construct [R. V. *draw up*] a narrative that the sequence of events may be evident. Found besides only in Plut. de sollert. anim. c. 12, where it denotes to go regularly through a thing again, rehearse it; [in Eccl. ii. 20 Ald., and in eccl. writ. e. g. Iren. 3, 21, 2 sub fin.]).*

393   **ἀνα-τέλλω**; 1 aor. *ἀνέτειλα*; pf. *ἀνατέταλκα*;   **a.** trans. *to cause to rise*: *τὸν ἥλιον*, Mt. v. 45, (of the earth bringing forth plants, Gen. iii. 18; of a river producing something, Hom. Il. 5, 777).   **b.** intrans. *to rise, arise*: light, Mt. iv. 16, (Is. lviii. 10); the sun, Mt. xiii. 6; Mk. iv. 6; xvi. 2; Jas. i. 11; the clouds, Lk. xii. 54; *φωσφόρος*, 2 Pet. i. 19. trop. *to rise from, be descended from*, Heb. vii. 14. The earlier Greeks commonly used *ἀνατέλλειν* of the sun and moon, and *ἐπιτέλλειν* of the stars; but Aelian., Paus., Stob. and other later writ. neglect this distinction; see *Lob.* ad Phryn. p. 124 sq. [COMP.: *ἐξ-ανατέλλω*.]*

see   **ἀνα-τίθημι**: 2 aor. mid. *ἀνεθέμην*; [in various senses fr.
394 St.   Hom. down]; in the mid. voice *to set forth* a thing drawn forth, as it were, from some corner (*ἀνά*), *to set forth* [in words], *declare*, [R. V. *lay before*]: *τινί τι*, Acts

xxv. 14; Gal. ii. 2, (2 Macc. iii. 9; [Mic.ˌvii. 5]; Artem. oneir. 2, 64 τινὶ τὸ ὄναρ; Diog. Laërt. 2, 17, 16 p. 191 ed. Heubn.; Plut. amat. narr. p. 772 d.) Cf. *Fritzschiorum* Opusc. p. 169; [*Holsten*, Zum Evang. des Paulus u. d. Petrus p. 256 sq. COMP.: *προσ-ανατίθημι*.] *

395 ἀνατολή, -ῆς, ἡ, (fr. ἀνατέλλω, q. v.), as in Grk. writ.; **1.** *a rising* (of the sun and stars); *light rising* ἐξ ὕψους, Lk. i. 78. **2.** *the east* (the quarter of the sun's rising): Mt. ii. 2, 9; Rev. xxi. 13 (Grsb. ἀνατολῶν); Hdian. 2, 8, 18 (10); 3, 5, 1; Joseph. c. Ap. 1, 14, 3, [6; 1, 26, 6; Mk. xvi. WH (rejected) 'Shorter Conclusion']; Clem. Rom. 1 Cor. 5, 6; Ignat. ad Ro. 2, 2; Melito ap. Euseb. h. e. 4, 26, 14; with ἡλίου added, Rev. vii. 2 [R G T Tr WH txt.]; Plur. eastern regions, *the east*, [W. 176 (166)]: Mt. ii. 1; viii. 11; xxiv. 27; Lk. xiii. 29, (Sept., Hdt., Plat., Polyb., Plut., al.; Philo in Flacc. § 7); with the addition of ἡλίου, Rev. xvi. 12 [-λῆς T Tr txt. WH txt.; vii. 2 L WH mrg.].*

396 ἀνα-τρέπω; *to overthrow, overturn, destroy*; ethically, *to subvert*: οἴκους families, Tit. i. 11. τήν τινων πίστιν, 2 Tim. ii. 18. (Common in Grk. writ., and in the same sense.)*

397 ἀνα-τρέφω; 2 aor. pass. ἀνετράφην; pf. pass. ptcp. ἀνατεθραμμένος; 1 aor. mid. ἀνεθρεψάμην; *to nurse up, nourish up*, (Germ. *aufnähren, auffüttern*); prop. of young children and animals nourished to promote their growth (Xen. mem. 4, 3, 10, etc.; Sap. vii. 4); *to bring up*: Lk. iv. 16 T WH mrg.; Acts vii. 20 sq.; with the predominant idea of forming the mind, Acts xxii. 3, (4 Macc. x. 2, and often in Grk. writ.). Cf. *Win.* De verb. comp. etc. Pt. iii. p. 4.*

398 ἀνα-φαίνω; 1 aor. ἀνέφανα, Doric for the more com. ἀνέφηνα, (Acts xxi. 3 R T WH [with Erasm., Steph., Mill]; cf. Passow p. 2199; [Veitch, and L. and S., s. v. φαίνω; W. 89 (85); B. 41 (35)]; see ἐπιφαίνω); Pass., [pres. ἀναφαίνομαι]; 2 aor. ἀνεφάνην; [fr. Hom. down]; *to bring to light, hold up to view, show*; Pass. *to appear, be made apparent*: Lk. xix. 11. An unusual phrase is ἀναφανέντες τὴν Κύπρον *having sighted Cyprus*, for ἀναφανείσης ἡμῖν τῆς Κύπρου, Acts xxi. 3; cf. B. 190 (164); W. § 39, 1 a. p. 260 (244); here Rˢᵗ T WH [see above] read ἀναφάναντες τὴν K. after we had rendered Cyprus visible (to us); [R. V. *had come in sight of Cyprus*.]*

399 ἀνα-φέρω; fut. ἀνοίσω (Lev. xiv. 20; Num. xiv. 33, etc.); 1 aor. ἀνήνεγκα; 2 aor. ἀνήνεγκον; [see reff. s. v. φέρω]; impf. pass. ἀνεφερόμην; fr. Hom. down]; **1.** *to carry* or *bring up, to lead up*; men to a higher place: Mt. xvii. 1; Mk. ix. 2; pass., Lk. xxiv. 51 [Tdf. om. WH reject the cl.]. ἀναφέρειν τὰς ἁμαρτίας ἐπὶ τὸ ξύλον, 1 Pet. ii. 24 (to bear sins up on the cross, sc. in order to expiate them by suffering death, [cf. W. 428 sq. (399)]). **2.** *to put upon the altar, to bring to the altar, to offer*, (Sept. for הֶעֱלָה of presentation as a priestly act, cf. Kurtz on Hebr. p. 154 sq.), θυσίας, θυσίαν, etc., (Isa. lvii. 6, etc.): Heb. vii. 27; xiii. 15; 1 Pet. ii. 5; with ἐπὶ τὸ θυσιαστήριον added, Jas. ii. 21, (Gen. viii. 20; Lev. xiv. 20; [Bar. i. 10; 1 Macc. iv. 53]); [ἑαυτόν, Heb. vii. 27, T Tr mrg. WH mrg. προσενέγκας]. Cf. Kurtz u. s. **3.**

to lift up on one's self, to take upon one's self, i. e. to place on one's self anything as a load to be upborne, *to sustain*: τὰς ἁμαρτίας i. e. by meton. their *punishment*, Heb. ix. 28 (Is. liii. 12; τὴν πορνείαν, Num. xiv. 33); cf. *Win.* De verb. comp. etc. Pt. iii. p. 5 sq.*

400 ἀνα-φωνέω, -ῶ; 1 aor. ἀνεφώνησα; *to cry out with a loud voice, call aloud, exclaim*: Lk. i. 42. (1 Chr. xv. 28; xvi. 4; [Aristot. de mund. 6, vol. i. p. 400ᵃ, 18]; Polyb., often in Plut.)*

401 ἀνά-χυσις, -εως, ἡ, (ἀναχέω [to pour forth]), rare in Grk. writ. [Strabo, Philo, Plut.; ἀν. ψυχῆς, in a good sense, Philo de decal. § 10 mid.]; *an overflowing, a pouring out*: metaph., 1 Pet. iv. 4 ἀσωτίας ἀνάχυσις *the excess* (flood) *of riot* in which a dissolute life pours itself forth.*

402 ἀνα-χωρέω, -ῶ; 1 aor. ἀνεχώρησα; (freq. in Grk. writ.); **1.** *to go back, return*: Mt. ii. 12 sq. [al. refer this to next head]. **2.** *to withdraw*: **a.** univ., so as to leave room: Mt. ix. 24. **b.** of those who through fear seek some other place, or shun sight: Mt. ii. 14, 22; iv. 12; xii. 15; xiv. 13; xv. 21; xxvii. 5; Mk. iii. 7; Jn. vi. 15 [Tdf. φεύγει]; Acts xxiii. 19 (κατ' ἰδίαν); xxvi. 31.*

403 ἀνά-ψυξις, -εως, ἡ, (ἀναψύχω, q. v.), *a cooling, refreshing*: Acts iii. 20 (19), of the Messianic blessedness to be ushered in by the return of Christ from heaven; Vulg. *refrigerium*. (Ex. viii. 15; Philo de Abr. § 29; Strabo 10, p. 459: and in eccl. writ.)*

404 ἀνα-ψύχω; 1 aor. ἀνέψυξα; *to cool again, to cool off, recover from the effects of heat*, (Hom. Od. 4, 568; Il. 5, 795; Plut. Aem. P. 25, etc.); trop. *to refresh*: τινά, one's spirit, by fellowship, consolation, kindnesses, 2 Tim. i. 16. (intrans. *to recover breath, take the air, cool off, revive, refresh one's self*, in Sept. [Ps. xxxviii. (xxxix.) 14; 2 S. xvi. 14; Ex. xxiii. 12; 1 S. xvi. 23; etc., in] 2 Macc. iv. 46; xiii. 11; and in the later Grk. writ.)*

405 ἀνδραποδιστής, -οῦ, ὁ, (fr. ἀνδραποδίζω, and this fr. τὸ ἀνδράποδον—fr. ἀνήρ and πούς—a slave, a man taken in war and sold into slavery), *a slave-dealer, kidnapper, man-stealer*, i. e. as well one who unjustly reduces free men to slavery, as one who steals the slaves of others and sells them: 1 Tim. i. 10. (Arstph., Xen., Plat., Dem., Isocr., Lys., Polyb.)*

406 Ἀνδρέας, -ου, ὁ, *Andrew*, (a Grk. name [meaning *manly*; for its occurrence, see *Pape*, Eigennamen, s. v.; B. D. s. v. Andrew, init.]), a native of Bethsaida in Galilee, brother of Simon Peter, a disciple of John the Baptist, afterwards an apostle of Christ: Jn. i. 40, 44 (41, 45); vi. 8; xii. 22; Mt. iv. 18; x. 2; Mk. i. 16, 29; iii. 18; xiii. 3; Lk. vi. 14; Acts i. 13.*

see 407 St. ἀνδρίζω: (ἀνήρ); *to make a man* of or *make brave*, (Xen. oec. 5, 4). Mid. pres. ἀνδρίζομαι; *to show one's self a man, be brave*: 1 Co. xvi. 13 [A. V. *quit you like men*]. (Often in Sept.; Sir. xxxiv. 25; 1 Macc. ii. 64; Xen., Plat., App., Plut., al.)*

408 Ἀνδρόνικος, -ου, ὁ, *Androni'cus*, (a Grk. name, [lit. man of victory; for its occurrence see *Pape*, Eigennamen, s. v.]), a Jewish Christian and a kinsman of Paul: Ro. xvi. 7.*

409   ἀνδρο-φόνος, -ου, ὁ, a manslayer : 1 Tim. i. 9. (2 Macc. ix. 28 ; Hom., Plat., Dem., al.) [Cf. φονεύς.] *

410   ἀν-έγκλητος, -ον, (a priv. and ἐγκαλέω, q. v.), that cannot be called to account, unreprovable, unaccused, blameless : 1 Co. i. 8 ; Col. i. 22 ; 1 Tim. iii. 10 ; Tit. i. 6 sq. (3 Macc. v. 31 ; Xen., Plat., Dem., Aristot., al.) [Cf. Trench § ciii.] *

411   ἀν-εκδιήγητος, -ον, (a priv. and ἐκδιηγέομαι, q. v.), unspeakable, indescribable : 2 Co. ix. 15 δωρεά, to describe and commemorate which words fail. (Only in eccl. writ. [Clem. Rom. 1 Cor. 20, 5 : 49, 4 ; Athenag., Theoph., al.].)*

412   ἀν-εκ-λάλητος, -ον, (a priv. and ἐκλαλέω), unspeakable : 1 Pet. i. 8 (to which words are inadequate). ([Diosc. medicam. p. 93 ed. Kühn] ; Heliod. 6, 15 p. 252 (296) ; and in eccl. writ.)*

413   ἀνέκλειπτος, -ον, (a priv. and ἐκλείπω to fail), unfailing : Lk. xii. 33. ([Hyperid. p. 58ᵃ ed. Teubner] ; Diod. 4, 84 ; 1, 36, cf. 3, 16 ; Plut. de orac. defect. p. 438 d., and in eccl. writ.)*

see 414 St.   ἀν-εκτός, -όν, and in later Grk. also -ός, -ή, -όν [cf. W. 68 (67) ; B. 25 (22)], (ἀνέχομαι to bear, endure) ; fr. Hom. down ; bearable, tolerable : ἀνεκτότερον ἔσται the lot will be more tolerable, Mt. x. 15 ; xi. 22, 24 ; Mk. vi. 11 R L br. ; Lk. x. 12, 14. (In Grk. writ. fr. Hom. down.)*

415   ἀν-ελεήμων, -ον, gen. -ονος, (a priv. and ἐλεήμων), without mercy, merciless : Ro. i. 31. ([Aristot. rhet. Alex. 37 p. 1442ᵃ, 13] ; Prov. v. 9, etc. ; Sir. xiii. 12, etc. ; Sap. xii. 5 ; xix. 1.)*

see 448; 415   ἀν-έλεος, -ον, without mercy, merciless : Jas. ii. 13 L T Tr WH, unusual form for ἀνίλεως R G. The Greeks said ἀνηλεής and ἀνελεής, cf. Lob. ad Phryn. p. 710 sq. ; W. 100 (95).*

416   ἀνεμίζω : (ἄνεμος) ; to agitate or drive by the wind ; pres. pass. ptcp. ἀνεμιζόμενος, Jas. i. 6. Besides only in schol. on Hom. Od. 12, 336 ἔνθα ἦν σκέπη πρὸς τὸ μὴ ἀνεμίζεσθαι, [Hesych. s. v. ἀναψύξαι· ἀνεμίσαι ; Joannes Moschus (in Patr. Graec. lxxxvii. p. 3044 a.) ἀνεμίζοντος τοῦ πλοίου velificante nave]. The Greeks said ἀνεμόω. Cf. κλυδωνίζομαι.*

417   ἄνεμος, -ου, ὁ, (ἄω, ἄημι to breathe, blow, [but etymologists connect ἄω with Skr. vâ, Grk. ἀήρ, Lat. ventus, Eng. wind, and ἄνεμος with Skr. an to breathe, etc. ; cf. Curtius §§ 419, 587 ; Vaniček p. 28]), [fr. Hom. down], wind, a violent agitation and stream of air, [cf. (Trench § lxxiii.) πνεῦμα, 1 fin.] : Mt. xi. 7 ; xiv. 24 ; Jas. iii. 4, etc. ; of a very strong and tempestuous wind : Mt. vii. 25 ; Mk. iv. 39 ; Lk. viii. 24, etc. οἱ τέσσαρες ἄνεμοι, the four principal or cardinal winds (Jer. xxv. 15 (xlix. 36)), τῆς γῆς, Rev. vii. 1 ; hence the four quarters of the heavens (whence the cardinal winds blow) : Mt. xxiv. 31 ; Mk. xiii. 27 ; (Ezek. xxxvii. 9 ; 1 Chr. ix. 24). Metaph. ἄνεμος τῆς διδασκαλίας, variability and emptiness [?] of teaching, Eph. iv. 14.

418   ἀν-ένδεκτος, -ον, (a priv. and ἔνδεκτος, and this fr. ἐνδέχομαι, q. v.), that cannot be admitted, inadmissible, unallowable, improper : ἀνένδεκτόν ἐστι τοῦ μὴ ἐλθεῖν it cannot be but that they will come, Lk. xvii. 1 [W. 328 (308) ;

B. 269 (231)]. (Artem. oneir. 2, 70 ὁ ἀριθμὸς πρὸς τὸν μέλλοντα χρόνον ἀνένδεκτος, [Diog. Laërt. 7, 50], and several times in eccl. and Byzant. writ.) *

419   ἀνεξερεύνητος, T Tr WH -ραύνητος [cf. Tdf. Proleg. p. 81 ; B. 58 (50) ; Sturz, De dial. Maced. et Alex. p. 117 ; see ἐραυνάω], -ον, (a priv. and ἐξ-ερευνάω), that cannot be searched out : Ro. xi. 33. (Symm. Prov. xxv. 3 ; Jer. xvii. 9. Dio Cass. 69, 14.)*

420   ἀνεξί-κακος, -ον, (fr. the fut. of ἀνέχομαι, and κακόν ; cf. classic ἀλεξίκακος, ἀμνησίκακος), patient of ills and wrongs, forbearing : 2 Tim. ii. 24. (Lcian. jud. voc. 9 ; [Justin M. apol. 1, 16 init. ; Pollux 5, 138].)*

421   ἀνεξιχνίαστος, -ον, (a priv. and ἐξιχνιάζω to trace out), that cannot be traced out, that cannot be comprehended, [A. V. unsearchable] : Ro. xi. 33 ; Eph. iii. 8. (Job v. 9 ; ix. 10 ; [xxxiv. 24] ; Or. Manass. 6 [see Sept. ed. Tdf., Proleg. § xxix.] ; several times in eccl. writ.)*

422   ἀν-επ-αίσχυντος, -ον, (a priv. and ἐπαισχύνω), (Vulg. inconfusibilis), having no cause to be ashamed : 2 Tim. ii. 15. ([Joseph. antt. 18, 7, 1] ; unused in Grk. writ. [W. 236 (221)].)*

423   ἀν-επί-ληπτος [L T Tr WH -λημπτος ; see M, μ], -ον, (a priv. and ἐπιλαμβάνω), prop. not apprehended, that cannot be laid hold of ; hence that cannot be reprehended, not open to censure, irreproachable, [Tittmann i. p. 31 ; Trench § ciii.] : 1 Tim. iii. 2 ; v. 7 ; vi. 14. (Freq. in Grk. writ. fr. [Eur. and] Thuc. down.)*

424   ἀν-έρχομαι : 2 aor. ἀνῆλθον ; [fr. Hom. down] ; to go up : Jn. vi. 3 ; to a higher place ; to Jerusalem, Gal. i. 17 [L Tr mrg. ἀπῆλθον], 18 ; (1 K. xiii. 12). [Comp. : ἐπ-ανέρχομαι.] *

425   ἄν-εσις, -εως, ἡ, (ἀνίημι to let loose, slacken, anything tense, e. g. a bow), a loosening, relaxing ; spoken of a more tolerable condition in captivity : ἔχειν ἄνεσιν to be held in less rigorous confinement [R. V. have indulgence], Acts xxiv. 23, (Joseph. antt. 18, 6, 10 φυλακὴ μὲν γὰρ καὶ τήρησις ἦν, μετὰ μέντοι ἀνέσεως τῆς εἰς δίαιταν). relief, rest, from persecutions, 2 Th. i. 7 ; from the troubles of poverty, 2 Co. viii. 13 ; relief from anxiety, quiet, 2 Co. ii. 13 (12) ; vii. 5. (Sept. ; in Grk. writ. fr. Thuc. [Hdt. 5, 28] down.) [Syn. see ἀνάπαυσις, fin.]

426   ἀν-ετάζω ; pres. pass. ἀνετάζομαι ; (ἐτάζω to examine, test) ; to investigate, examine ; τινά, to examine judicially : Acts xxii. 24, 29. (Judg. vi. 29 cod. Alex. ; Sus. [i. e. Dan. (Theod.) init.] 14 ; [Anaph. Pilati A 6 p. 417 ed. Tdf.]. Not found in prof. auth.)*

427   ἄνευ, prep. with gen., without : 1 Pet. iii. 1 ; iv. 9. with gen. of the pers. without one's will or intervention, (often so in Grk. writ. fr. Hom. down) : Mt. x. 29. [Compared with χωρίς, see Tittm. i. p. 93 sq. ; Ellic. on Eph. ii. 12 ; Green, Crit. Notes, etc. (on Ro. iii. 28).]*

428   ἀν-εύ-θετος, -ον, not convenient, not commodious, not fit : Acts xxvii. 12. (Unused by Grk. writ. ; [Moschion 53].)*

429   ἀν-ευρίσκω : 2 aor. ἀνεῦρον, 3 pers. plur. ἀνεῦραν, Lk. ii. 16 [T Tr WH ἀνεῦρον] ; to find out by search : τινά, Lk. ii. 16 ; Acts xxi. 4. (In Grk. writ. fr. Hdt. down.) Cf. Win. De verb. comp. etc. Pt. iii. p. 13 sq.*

ἀν-έχω : in the N. T. only in the mid. ἀνέχομαι ; fut.

see 430 St.

ἀνέξομαι (W. 83 (79)); impf. ἠνειχόμην 2 Co. xi. [1 Rec.ᵉˡᶻ].
'4 [Rec.] (G T Tr WH mrg. ἀνειχόμην [cf. Moeris ed.
Piers. p. 176; (but L WH txt. in vs. 4 ἀνέχ.); cf. WH.
App. p. 162; W. 72 (70); B. 35 (31)]); 2 aor. ἠνεσχόμην Acts xviii. 14 (L T Tr WH ἀνεσχόμην, reff. u. s.);
to hold up, (e. g. κεφαλήν, χεῖρας, Hom. et al.); hence in
mid. to hold one's self erect and firm (against any pers.
or thing), to sustain, to bear (with equanimity), to bear
with, endure, with a gen. of the pers. (in Grk. writ. the
accus. is more com., both of the pers. and of the thing),
of his opinions, actions, etc.: Mt. xvii. 17; Mk. ix. 19;
Lk. ix. 41; 2 Co. xi. 19; Eph. iv. 2; Col. iii. 13. foll. by
gen. of the thing: 2 Th. i. 4 [WH mrg. ἐνεχ.] (αἶς by
attraction for ὧν, unless ἅς be preferred [B. 161 (140);
cf. W. 202 (190)]). foll. by μικρόν τι with gen. of both
pers. and thing, 2 Co. xi. 1 (acc. to the reading μου
μικρόν τι ἀφροσύνης [Rᵇᵉᶻ ᵉˡᶻ L T Tr WH]; cf. Meyer
ad loc.). without a case, 1 Co. iv. 12 (we endure). foll.
by εἴ τις, 2 Co. xi. 20. Owing to the context, to bear
with i. e. to listen: with gen. of the pers., Acts xviii. 14;
of the thing, 2 Tim. iv. 3; Heb. xiii. 22. [Comp.: προσανέχω.] *

431   ἀνεψιός, -οῦ, ὁ, [for ἀ-νεπτ-ιός con-nepot-ius, cf. Lat. ne-
pos, Germ. nichte, Eng. nephew, niece; Curtius § 342], a
cousin: Col. iv. 10. (Num. xxxvi. 11; Tob. vii. 2.) [Cf.
Lob. ad Phryn. p. 306; but esp. Bp. Lghtft. on Col. l. c.;
also B. D. Am. ed. s. v. Sister's Son.] *

432   ἄνηθον, -ου, τό, dill, anise [(?); cf. BB.DD. s. v.; Tristram, Nat. Hist. of the Bible, p. 419 sq.]: Mt. xxiii. 23.
(Arstph. nub. 982; [Aristot., al.]; often in Theophr.
hist. pl.) *

433   ἀν-ήκω; [impf. ἀνῆκεν]; in Grk. writ. to have come up
to, arrived at, to reach to, pertain to, foll. generally by
εἴς τι; hence in later writ. ἀνήκει τί τινι something apper-
tains to one, is due to him sc. to be rendered or performed
by others (1 Macc. x. 42; xi. 35; 2 Macc. xiv. 8), and
then ethically τὸ ἀνῆκον what is due, duty, [R. V. befitting],
Philem. 8; τὰ οὐκ ἀνήκοντα unbecoming, discreditable,
Eph. v. 4 (L T Tr WH ἃ οὐκ ἀνῆκεν, W. 486 (452); [B.
350 (301)]); impers. ὡς ἀνῆκε as was fitting, sc. ever
since ye were converted to Christ, Col. iii. 18, [W. 270
(254); cf. B. 217 (187) and Bp. Lghtft. ad loc.].*

434   ἀν-ήμερος, -ον (ἀ priv. and ἥμερος), not tame, savage,
fierce: 2 Tim. iii. 3. (In Grk. writ. fr. [Anacr. 1, 7]
Aeschyl. down.)*

435   ἀνήρ, ἀνδρός, ὁ, a man, Lat. vir. The meanings of this
word in the N. T. differ in no respect fr. classic usage;
for it is employed **1.** with a reference to sex, and
so to distinguish a man from a woman; either **a.** as a
male: Acts viii. 12; xvii. 12; 1 Tim. ii. 12; or **b.** as a
husband: Mt. i. 16; Mk. x. 2; Jn. iv. 16 sqq.; Ro. vii. 2
sqq.; 1 Co. vii. 2 sqq.; Gal. iv. 27; 1 Tim. iii. 2, 12; Tit.
i. 6, etc.; a betrothed or future husband: Mt. i. 19; Rev.
xxi. 2, etc. **2.** with a reference to age, and to distinguish an adult man from a boy: Mt. xiv. 21; xv. 38
(where ἄνδρες, γυναῖκες and παιδία are discriminated);
with the added notion also of intelligence and virtue:
1 Co. xiii. 11 (opp. to νήπιος); Eph. iv. 13; Jas. iii. 2, (in

the last two pass. τέλειος ἀνήρ). **3.** univ. any male
person, a man; so where τις might have been used:
Lk. viii. 41; ix. 38; Acts vi. 11; x. 5, etc. where ἀνήρ
and τις are united: Lk. viii. 27; Acts v. 1; x. 1. or
ἀνήρ and ὅς he who, etc.: Ro. iv. 8; Jas. i. 12. where
mention is made of something usually done by men, not
by women: Lk. xxii. 63; Acts v. 36. where angels or
other heavenly beings are said to have borne the forms
of men: Lk. ix. 30; xxiv. 4; Acts x. 30. where it is so
connected with an adjective as to give the adj. the force
of a substantive: ἀνὴρ ἁμαρτωλός a sinner, Lk. v. 8;
λεπροὶ ἄνδρες, Lk. xvii. 12; or is joined to appellatives:
ἀνὴρ φονεύς, Acts iii. 14; ἀν. προφήτης, Lk. xxiv. 19,
(נָבִיא אִישׁ, Judg. vi. 8; [cf. W. 30; § 59, 1; B. 82 (72);
other reff. s. v. ἄνθρωπος, 4 a. fin.]); or to gentile names:
ἄνδρες Νινευῖται, Mt. xii. 41; ἀνὴρ Ἰουδαῖος, Acts xxii. 3;
ἀν. Αἰθίοψ, Acts viii. 27; ἀνδ. Κύπριοι, Acts xi. 20; esp.
in addresses of honor and respect [W. § 65, 5 d.; B.
82 (72)], Acts i. 11; ii. 14; xiii. 16; xvii. 22, etc.; even
ἄνδρες ἀδελφοί, Acts i. 16; [ii. 29, 37; vii. 2]; xiii. [15],
26, etc. **4.** when persons of either sex are included,
but named after the more important: Mt. xiv. 35; Acts
iv. 4; [Meyer seems inclined (see his com. on Acts
l. c.) to dispute even these examples; but al. would refer
several other instances (esp. Lk. xi. 31; Jas. i. 20) to
the same head].

ἀνθ-ίστημι: pf. ἀνθέστηκα; 2 aor. ἀντέστην, [impv. ἀν- **436**
τίστητε], inf. ἀντιστῆναι; Mid., pres. ἀνθίσταμαι; impf.
ἀνθιστάμην; (ἀντί and ἵστημι); to set against; as in Grk.
writ., in the mid., and in the pf. plpf. [having pres. and
impf. force, W. 274 (257)] and 2 aor. act., to set one's
self against, to withstand, resist, oppose: pf. act., Ro. ix.
19; xiii. 2; 2 Tim. iv. 15 [R G]. 2 aor. act., Mt. v. 39;
Lk. xxi. 15; Acts vi. 10; Gal. ii. 11; Eph. vi. 13; 2 Tim.
iii. 8; [iv. 15 L T Tr WH]. impv., Jas. iv. 7; 1 Pet. v.
9. Mid.: pres., 2 Tim. iii. 8. impf., Acts xiii. 8.*

ἀνθ-ομολογέομαι, -οῦμαι: [impf. ἀνθωμολογούμην]; (ἀντί **437**
and ὁμολογέομαι); in Grk. writ. (fr. Dem. down) **1.**
to reply by professing or by confessing. **2.** to agree
mutually (in turn), to make a compact. **3.** to acknowledge in the presence of (ἀντί before, over against; cf.
ἐξομολογεῖσθαι ἔναντι κυρίου, 2 Chr. vii. 6) any one, (see
Win. De verb. comp. etc. Pt. iii. p. 19 sq.): τὰς ἁμαρτίας
to confess sins, Joseph. antt. 8, 10, 3 [Bekk. reads ἀνομο-
λογουμένους]; cf. 1 Esdr. viii. 88 (90). τινί, to declare
something in honor of one, to celebrate his praises, give
thanks to him, Lk. ii. 38; (for הוֹדָה in Ps. lxxviii. (lxxix.)
13; 3 Macc. vi. 33; [Dan. iv. 31 (34) Sept.; Test. xii.
Patr. test. Jud. § 1]).*

ἄνθος, -εος, τό, [fr. Hom. down]; a flower: Jas. i. 10 **438**
sq.; 1 Pet. i. 24.*

ἀνθρακιά [on accent cf. Etym. Magn. 801, 21; Chand- **439**
ler § 95], -ᾶς, ἡ, a heap of burning coals: Jn. xviii. 18;
xxi. 9. (Sir. xi. 32; 4 Macc. ix. 20; Hom. Il. 9, 213,
etc.) [Cf. BB.DD. s. v. Coal.]*

ἄνθραξ, -ακος, ὁ, coal, (also, fr. Thuc. and Arstph. down, **440**
a live coal), ἄνθρ. πυρός a coal of fire i. e. a burning or
live coal; Ro. xii. 20 ἄνθο. πυρὸς σωρεύειν ἐπὶ τὴν κεφαλήν

τινος, a proverbial expression, fr. Prov. xxv. 22, signifying to call up, by the favors you confer on your enemy,
the memory in him of the wrong he has done you (which
shall pain him as if live coals were heaped on his head),
that he may the more readily repent. The Arabians
call things that cause very acute mental pain *burning
coals of the heart* and *fire in the liver*; cf. *Gesenius* in
Rosenmüller's Bibl.-exeg. Repert. i. p. 140 sq. [or in his
Thesaurus i. 280; cf. also BB.DD. s. v. Coal].*

441   ἀνθρωπ-άρεσκος, -ον, (ἄνθρωπος and ἄρεσκος agreeable,
pleasing, insinuating; cf. εὐάρεσκος, δυσάρεσκος, αὐτά-
ρεσκος in *Lob.* ad Phryn. p. 621); only in bibl. and
eccl. writ. [W. 25]: *studying to please men, courting the
favor of men*: Eph. vi. 6; Col. iii. 22. (Ps. lii. (liii.) 6;
[Ps. Sal. iv. 8, 10].)*

442   ἀνθρώπινος, -ίνη, -ινον, (ἄνθρωπος), [fr. Hdt. down],
human; applied to things belonging to men: χεῖρες,
Acts xvii. 25 L T Tr WH; φύσις, Jas. iii. 7; or instituted by men: κτίσις, [q. v. 3], 1 Pet. ii. 13; adjusted to
the strength of man: πειρασμός [R. V. *a temptation such
as man can bear*], 1 Co. x. 13 (cf. Neander [and Heinrici]
ad loc.; Pollux 3, 27, 131 ὃ οὐκ ἄν τις ὑπομένειεν, ὃ οὐκ ἄν
τις ἐνέγκῃ . . . τὸ δὲ ἐναντίον, κουφόν, εὔφορον, οἰστόν, ἀνθρώπινον, ἀνεκτόν). Opp. to divine things, with the implied idea of defect or weakness: 1 Co. ii. 4 Rec.; 13
(σοφία, originating with man); iv. 3 (ἀνθρωπίνη ἡμέρα
the judicial day of men, i. e. human judgment). ἀνθρώπινον λέγω, Ro. vi. 19 (I say what is human, speak as
is usual among men, who do not always suitably weigh
the force of their words; by this expression the apostle apologizes for the use of the phrase δουλωθῆναι τῇ
δικαιοσύνῃ).*

443   ἀνθρωποκτόνος, -ον, (κτείνω to kill), a *manslayer, murderer*: Jn. viii. 44. contextually, to be deemed equal to
a murderer, 1 Jn. iii. 15. (Eur. Iph. T. (382) 389.) [Cf.
Trench § lxxxiii. and φονεύς.]*

444   ἄνθρωπος, -ου, ὁ, [perh. fr. ἀνήρ and ὤψ, i. e. man's face;
Curtius § 422; Vaniček p. 9. From Hom. down]; *man*.
It is used   **1.** univ., with ref. to the genus or nature,
without distinction of sex, *a human being, whether male
or female*: Jn. xvi. 21. And in this sense **a.** with the
article, generically, so as to include all human individuals: Mt. iv. 4 (ἐπ' ἄρτῳ ζήσεται ὁ ἄνθρωπος); Mt. xii. 35
(ὁ ἀγαθὸς ἄνθ. every good person); Mt. xv. 11, 18; Mk.
ii. 27; vii. 15, 18, 20; Lk. iv. 4; Jn. ii. 25 [W. § 18, 8];
vii. 51; Ro. vii. 1, etc. **b.** so that a man is distinguished
from beings of a different race or order; **α.** from animals, plants, etc.: Lk. v. 10; Mt. iv. 19; xii. 12; 2 Pet.
ii. 16; Rev. ix. 4, 7, 10, 15, 18; xi. 13, etc. **β.** from
God, from Christ as divine, and from angels: Mt. x. 32;
xix. 6; Mk. x. 9; Lk. ii. 15 [T WH om., L Tr br.] (opp.
to angels); Jn. x. 33; Acts x. 26; xiv. 11; 1 Th. ii. 13;
Gal. i. 10, 12; 1 Co. iii. 21; vii. 23; Phil. ii. 7, 7 (8); 1 Tim.
ii. 5; Heb. viii. 2; xiii. 6; 1 Pet. ii. 4, etc. **c.** with
the added notion of w e a k n e s s, by which man is led
into mistake or prompted to sin: οὐκ ἄνθρωποί (R G
σαρκικοί) ἐστε; 1 Co. iii. 4; σοφία ἀνθρώπων, 1 Co. iii. 5;
ἀνθρώπων ἐπιθυμίαι, 1 Pet. iv. 2; κατὰ ἄνθρωπον περιπατεῖτε

ye conduct yourselves as men, 1 Co. iii. 3; λαλεῖν or
λέγειν κατὰ ἄνθρωπον, to speak according to human modes
of thinking, 1 Co. ix. 8; Ro. iii. 5; κατὰ ἄνθρωπον λέγω,
I speak as a man to whom analogies from human affairs
present themselves, while I illustrate divine things by an
example drawn from ordinary human life, Gal. iii. 15;
κατὰ ἄνθρ. θηριομαχεῖν, as man is wont to fight, urged on by
the desire of gain, honor and other earthly advantages,
1 Co. xv. 32; οὐκ ἔστι κατὰ ἄνθρ. is not accommodated
to the opinions and desires of men, Gal. i. 11; [for exx.
of κατὰ ἀνθ. in prof. auth. see Wetstein on Rom. u. s.];
with the accessory notion of m a l i g n i t y: προσέχετε
ἀπὸ τῶν ἀνθρώπων, Mt. x. 17; εἰς χεῖρας ἀνθρώπων, Mt.
xvii. 22; Lk. ix. 44. **d.** with the adjunct notion of
c o n t e m p t, (as sometimes in Grk. writ.): Jn. v. 12; the
address ὦ ἄνθρωπε, or ἄνθρωπε, is one either of contempt
and disdainful pity, Ro. ix. 20 (Plat. Gorg. p. 452 b. σὺ
δὲ . . . τίς εἶ, ὦ ἄνθρωπε), or of gentle rebuke, Lk. xxii.
58, 60. The word serves to suggest commiseration: ἴδε
[T Tr WH ἰδοὺ] ὁ ἄνθρ. behold the man in question, maltreated, defenceless, Jn. xix. 5. **e.** with a reference
to the twofold nature of man, ὁ ἔσω and ὁ ἔξω ἄνθρωπος,
soul and body: Ro. vii. 22; Eph. iii. 16; 2 Co. iv. 16,
(Plat. rep. 9, 589 a. ὁ ἐντὸς ἄνθρωπος; Plotin. Enn. 5, 1,
10 ὁ εἴσω ἄνθρ.; cf. Fritzsche on Rom. vol. ii. 61 sq. [Mey.
on Ro. l. c.; Ellic. on Eph. l. c.]); ὁ κρυπτὸς τῆς καρδίας
ἄνθρ. 1 Pet. iii. 4. **f.** with a reference to the twofold
moral condition of man, ὁ παλαιός (the corrupt) and ὁ
καινὸς (ὁ νέος) ἄνθρ. (the truly Christian man, conformed
to the nature of God): Ro. vi. 6; Eph. ii. 15; iv. 22, 24;
Col. iii. 9 sq. **g.** with a reference to the sex, (contextually) *a male*: Jn. vii. 22 sq. **2.** indefinitely, without
the article, ἄνθρωπος, **a.** *some one, a* (certain) *man*,
when w h o he is either is not known or is not important: i. q. τὶς, Mt. xvii. 14; xxi. 28; xxii. 11; Mk. xii. 1;
xiv. 13; Lk. v. 18; xiii. 19, etc. with the addition of τὶς,
Mt. xviii. 12; Lk. x. 30; xiv. 2, 16; xv. 11; xvi. 1, 19;
Jn. v. 5. in address, where the speaker either cannot
or will not give the name, Lk. v. 20; or where the writer
addresses any and every reader, Ro. ii. 1, 3. **b.** where
what is said holds of every man, so that ἄνθρ. is equiv.
to the Germ. indef. *man, one*: Ro. iii. 28; 1 Co. iv. 1;
vii. 1; xi. 28; Gal. ii. 16. So also where opp. to domestics, Mt. x. 36; to a wife, Mt. xix. 10; to a father, Mt.
x. 35; to the master of a household, Lk. xii. 36 sq.,—in
which passages many, confounding s e n s e and s i g n i f i-
c a t i o n, incorrectly say that the word ἄνθρ. signifies *father
of a family, husband, son, servant*. **3.** in the plur. οἱ
ἄνθρ. is sometimes (the) *people*, Germ. *die Leute*: Mt.
v. 13, 16; vi. 5, 18; viii. 27; xvi. 13; Lk. xi. 44; Mk.
viii. 24, 27; Jn. iv. 28; οὐδεὶς ἀνθρώπων (nemo homi-
num) no one, Mk. xi. 2; 1 Tim. vi. 16. **4.** It is joined
 a. to another substantive,— a quasi-predicate of office,
or employment, or characteristic,— the idea of the predicate predominating [W. § 59, 1]: ἄνθρωπος ἔμπορος *a
merchant* (-man), Mt. xiii. 45 [WH txt. om. ἄνθρ.]; οἰκοδεσπότης, Mt. xiii. 52; xx. 1; xxi. 33; βασιλεύς, Mt.
xviii. 23; xxii. 2; φάγος, Mt. xi. 19. (So in Hebr.

אִישׁ סָרִיס a eunuch, Jer. xxxviii. 7 sq., אִישׁ כֹּהֵן a priest, Lev. xxi. 9; also in Grk. writ.: ἄνθ. ὁδίτης, Hom. Il. 16, 263, al.; cf. Matthiae § 430, 6; [Krüger § 57, 1, 1]; but in Attic this combination generally has a contemptuous force; cf. Bnhdy. p. 48; in Lat. *homo gladiator*, Cic. epp. ad diversos 12, 22, 1). **b.** to a gentile noun: ἄνθ. Κυρηναῖος, Mt. xxvii. 32; Ἰουδαῖος, Acts xxi. 39; Ῥωμαῖος, Acts xvi. 37; xxii. 25, (acc. to the context, *a Roman citizen*). **5.** ὁ ἄνθρ., with the article, the particular man under consideration, w h o he is being plain from the context: Mt. xii. 13; xxvi. 72; Mk. iii. 5; Lk. xxiii. 6; Jn. iv. 50. οὗτος ὁ ἄνθ., Lk. xiv. 30; Jn. ix. 16, 24 [L Tr mrg. WH]; xi. 47; ὁ ἄνθ. οὗτος, Mk. xiv. 71; Lk. xxiii. 4, 14, 47; Jn. ix. 24 [R G T Tr txt.]: xviii. 17; Acts vi. 13; xxii. 26; xxvi. 31, 32. ὁ ἄνθ. ἐκεῖνος, Mt. xii. 45; xxvi. 24; Mk. xiv. 21. **6.** Phrases: ὁ ἄνθ. τῆς ἁμαρτίας (or with T Tr txt. WH txt. τῆς ἀνομίας), 2 Th. ii. 3, see ἁμαρτία, 1 p. 30 sq. ἄνθ. τοῦ θεοῦ a man devoted to the service of God, God's minister: 1 Tim. vi. 11; 2 Tim. iii. 17, (of the evangelists, the associates of the apostles); 2 Pet. i. 21 (of prophets, like אִישׁ אֱלֹהִים often in the O. T.; cf. *Gesenius*, Thesaur. i. p. 85). For ὁ υἱὸς τοῦ ἀνθρώπου and υἱοὶ τῶν ἀνθρ., see under υἱός.

445   ἀνθ-υπατεύω; (ἀντί for i. e. in lieu or stead of any one, and ὑπατεύω to be ὕπατος, to be supreme, to be consul); *to be proconsul*: Acts xviii. 12 [R G; cf. B. 169 (147)]. (Plut. comp. Dem. c. Cic. c. 3; Hdian. 7, 5, 2.) *

446   ἀνθ-ύπατος, -ου, ὁ, [see the preceding word], *proconsul*: Acts xiii. 7, 8, 12; xviii. 12 L T Tr WH; xix. 38. The emperor Augustus divided the Roman provinces into senatorial and imperial. The former were presided over by proconsuls; the latter were administered by legates of the emperor, sometimes called also propraetors. (Polyb., Dion. H., Lcian., Plut., and often in Dio Cass.) [B. D. s. v. Proconsul; Alex.'s Kitto s. v. Province; esp. Bp. Lghtft. in The Contemp. Rev. for 1878, p. 289 sq.] *

447   ἀν-ίημι, [ptcp. plur. ἀνιέντες]; 2 aor. subj. ἀνῶ, ptcp. plur. ἀνέντες; 1 aor. pass. ἀνέθην; *to send back*; *to relax*; contextually, *to loosen*: τί, Acts xvi. 26, (τοὺς δεσμούς, Plut. Alex. M. 73); xxvii. 40. trop. τὴν ἀπειλήν, *to give up, omit, calm* [?], Eph. vi. 9; (τὴν ἔχθραν, Thuc. 3, 10; τὴν ὀργήν, Plut. Alex. M. 70). *to leave, not to uphold, to let sink*: Heb. xiii. 5, (Deut. xxxi. 6).*

448   ἀν-ίλεως, -ων, gen. -ω, (ἵλεως, Attic for ἵλαος), *without mercy, merciless*: Jas. ii. 13 [R G]. Found nowhere else [exc. Hdian. epim. 257]. Cf. ἀνέλεος.*

449   ἄνιπτος, -ον, (νίπτω to wash), *unwashed*: Mt. xv. 20; Mk. vii. 2, and R L mrg. in 5. (Hom. Il. 6, 266, etc.)*

450   ἀν-ίστημι; fut. ἀναστήσω; 1 aor. ἀνέστησα and (Acts xii. 7; Eph. v. 14 and L WH txt. in Acts ix. 11) ἀνάστα (W. § 14, 1 h.; [B. 47 (40)]); Mid., pres. ἀνίσταμαι; fut. ἀναστήσομαι; [fr. Hom. down]; **I. Transitively**, in the pres. 1 aor. and fut. act., *to cause to rise, raise up*, (הֵקִים): **a.** prop. of one lying down: Acts ix. 41. **b.** *to raise up* from death: Jn. vi. 39 sq. 44, 54; Acts ii. 32; xiii. 34, (so in Grk. writ.). **c.** *to raise up, cause to be born*:

σπέρμα offspring (Gen. xxxviii. 8), Mt. xxii. 24, [cf. W. 33 (32)]; τὸν Χριστόν, Acts ii. 30 Rec. *to cause to appear, bring forward*, τινά τινι one for any one's succor: προφήτην, Acts iii. 22; vii. 37; τὸν παῖδα αὐτοῦ, Acts iii. 26. **II. Intransitively**, in the pf. plpf. and 2 aor. act., and in the mid.; **1.** *to rise, stand up*; used **a.** of persons lying down (on a couch or bed): Mk. i. 35; v. 42; Lk. viii. 55; xi. 7; Acts ix. 34, 40. of persons lying on the ground: Mk. ix. 27; Lk. xvii. 19; xxii. 46; Acts ix. 6. **b.** of persons seated: Lk. iv. 16 (ἀνέστη ἀναγνῶναι); Mt. xxvi. 62; Mk. xiv. 60; Acts xxiii. 9. **c.** of those who leave a place to go elsewhere: Mt. ix. 9; Mk. ii. 14; [x. 50 R G]; Lk. iv. 38; xxiii. 1; Acts ix. 39. Hence of those who prepare themselves for a journey, (Germ. *sich aufmachen*): Mk. vii. 24; x. 1; Lk. i. 39; xv. 18, 20; Acts x. 20; xxii. 10. In the same way the Hebr. קוּם (esp. וַיָּקָם) is put before verbs of going, departing, etc., according to the well known oriental custom to omit nothing contributing to the full pictorial delineation of an action or event; hence formerly וַיָּקָם and ἀναστάς were sometimes incorrectly said to be redundant; cf. W. 608 (565). ἀναστῆναι ἀπό to rise up from something, i. e. from what one has been doing while either sitting or prostrate on the ground: Lk. xxii. 45. **d.** of the dead; 2 aor., with ἐκ νεκρῶν added: Mt. xvii. 9 R G WH mrg.; Mk. ix. 9 sq.; xii. 25; Lk. xvi. 31; xxiv. 46; Jn. xx. 9; Eph. v. 14 (here fig.); with ἐκ νεκρῶν omitted: Mk. viii. 31; xvi. 9; Lk. ix. 8, 19, [22 L Tr mrg. WH mrg.]; xxiv. 7; Ro. xiv. 9 Rec.; so (without ἐκ νεκρ.) in the fut. mid. also: Mt. xii. 41; [xvii. 23 L WH mrg.]; xx. 19 [R G L Tr mrg. WH mrg.]; Mk. x. 34; Lk. xi. 32; xviii. 33; Jn. xi. 23 sq.; 1 Th. iv. 16. **2.** *to arise, appear, stand forth*; of kings, prophets, priests, leaders of insurgents: Acts v. 36 sq.; vii. 18. mid., Ro. xv. 12; Heb. vii. 11, 15. of those about to enter into conversation or dispute with any one, Lk. x. 25; Acts vi. 9; or to undertake some business, Acts v. 6; or to attempt something against others, Acts v. 17. Hence ἀναστῆναι ἐπί τινα to rise up against any one: Mk. iii. 26, (קוּם עַל). [Syn. see ἐγείρω, fin. Comp.: ἐπ-, ἐξ-ανίστημι.]

451   Ἅννα [WH Ἅννα, see their Intr. § 408], -ας [on this gen. cf. B. 17 (15); *Ph. Bttm.* Ausf. Spr. i. p. 138], ἡ, *Anna*, (חַנָּה grace), the prop. name of a woman (so in 1 S. i. 2 sqq.; ii. 1 Alex.; Tob. i. 9, 20, etc.), a prophetess, in other respects unknown: Lk. ii. 36.*

452   Ἅννας [WH Ἅννας, see their Intr. § 408], -α (on this gen. cf. W. § 8, 1 p. 60 (59)), ὁ, (in Joseph. Ἅνανος; fr. Hebr. חָנָן to be gracious), a high-priest of the Jews, elevated to the pontificate by Quirinius the governor of Syria c. A. D. 6 or 7; but afterwards, A. D. 15, deposed by Valerius Gratus, the procurator of Judæa, who put in his place, first Ismael, son of Phabi, and shortly after Eleazar, son of Annas. From the latter, the office passed to Simon; from Simon c. A. D. 18 to Caiaphas, (Joseph. antt. 18, 2, 1 sq.); but Annas, even after he had been put out of office, continued to have great influence: Jn. xviii. 13, 24. This explains the mistake [but see reff. below (esp. to Schürer), and cf. ἀρχιερεύς, 2] by which Luke, in his Gospel iii. 2 (acc. to the true reading ἀρχιερέως) and in Acts iv. 6, attributes to him the pontificate long after he had been removed from office. Cf. Win. RWB. s. v. Annas; Keim in Schenkel i. p. 135 sq.; Schürer in the Zeitschr. für wissensch. Theol. for 1876, p. 580 sq. [also in his Neutest. Zeitgesch. § 23 iv.; and BB.DD. s. v.].*

453 ἀ-νόητος, -ον, (νοητός fr. νοέω); **1.** not understood, unintelligible; **2.** generally active, not understanding, unwise, foolish: Ro. i. 14 (opp. to σοφοί); Lk. xxiv. 25; Gal. iii. 1, 3; Tit. iii. 3. ἐπιθυμίαι ἀνόητοι, 1 Tim. vi. 9. (Prov. xvii. 28; Ps. xlviii. (xlix.) 13; and often in Attic writ.; [cf. Trench § lxxv.; Ellic. on Gal. iii. 1; Schmidt ch. 147 § 20].)*

454 ἄνοια, -ας, ἡ, (ἄνους [i. e. ἄνοος without understanding]), want of understanding, folly: 2 Tim. iii. 9. madness expressing itself in rage, Lk. vi. 11, [δύο δ᾽ ἀνοίας γένη, τὸ μὲν μανίαν, τὸ δὲ ἀμαθίαν, Plato, Tim. p. 86 b.]. ([Theogn. 453]; Hdt. 6, 69; Attic writ. fr. Thuc. down.)*

455 ἀν-οίγω, (ἀνά, οἴγω i. e. οἴγνυμι) ; fut. ἀνοίξω; 1 aor. ἤνοιξα and (Jn. ix. 14 and as a var. elsewh. also) ἀνέῳξα (an earlier form) [and ἠνέῳξα WH in Jn. ix. 17, 32 (cf. Gen. viii. 6), so Tr (when corrected), but without iota subscr.; see I, ι]; 2 pf. ἀνέῳγα (to be or stand open; cf. Bttm. Ausf. Spr. ii. p. 250 sq.; [Rutherford, New Phryn. p. 247; Veitch s. v.]; the Attic writ. give this force mostly to the pf. pass.); Pass., [pres. ἀνοίγομαι Mt. vii. 8 L Tr txt. WH mrg.; xi. 10 Tr mrg. WH mrg.]; pf. ptcp. ἀνεῳγμένος and ἠνεῳγμένος, (ἠνοιγμένος Acts ix. 8 Tdf.); 1 aor. ἀνεῴχθην, ἠνεῴχθην, and ἠνοίχθην, inf. ἀνεῳχθῆναι (with double augm. Lk. iii. 21); 2 aor. ἠνοίγην (the usual later form); 1 fut. ἀνοιχθήσομαι (Lk. xi. 9 Tdf., 10 L T); 2 fut. ἀνοιγήσομαι; (on these forms, in the use of which both codd. and edd. differ much, cf. [Tdf. Proleg. p. 121 sq.]; WH. App. pp. 161, 170; Bttm. Gram. p. 280 [21st Germ. ed.]; Bttm. N. T. Gr. 63 (55); W. 72 (70) and 83 (79); [Veitch s. v.]); to open: a door, a gate, Acts v. 19; xii. 10, 14; xvi. 26 sq.; Rev. iv. 1; very often in Grk. writ. Metaph., to give entrance into the soul, Rev. iii. 20; to furnish opportunity to do something, Acts xiv. 27; Col. iv. 3; pass., of an opportunity offered, 1 Co. xvi. 9; 2 Co. ii. 12; Rev. iii. 8; cf. θύρα. simply ἀνοίγειν τινί to open (the door [B. 145 (127)]) to one; prop.: Lk. xii. 36; Acts v. 23; xii. 16; Jn. x. 3; in a proverbial saying, to grant something asked for, Mt. vii. 7 sq.; Lk. xi. 9 sq.; parabolically, to give access to the blessings of God's kingdom, Mt. xxv. 11; Lk. xiii. 25; Rev. iii. 7. τοὺς θησαυρούς, Mt. ii. 11, (Sir. xliii. 14; Eur. Ion 923); τὰ μνημεῖα, Mt. xxvii. 52; τάφος, Ro. iii. 13; τὸ φρέαρ, Rev. ix. 2. heaven is said to be opened and something to descend fr. it, Mt. iii. 16; Lk. iii. 21; Jn. i. 51 (52); Acts x. 11; or something is said to be seen there, Acts vii. 56 R G; Rev. xi. 19 (ὁ ναὸς . . . ὁ ἐν τῷ οὐρανῷ); [xv. 5]; xix. 11. ἀνοίγ. τὸ στόμα: of a fish's mouth, Mt. xvii. 27; Hebraistically, of those who begin to speak [W. 33 (32), 608 (565)], Mt. v. 2; Acts viii. 32, 35; x. 34; xviii. 14; foll. by εἰς βλασφημίαν [-μίας

L T Tr WH], Rev. xiii. 6; ἐν παραβολαῖς, i. e. to make use of (A. V. in), Mt. xiii. 35, (Ps. lxxvii. (lxxviii.) 2; ἐν ἔπεσι Lcian. Philops. § 33); πρός τινα, 2 Co. vi. 11 (τὸ στόμα ἡμῶν ἀνέῳγε πρὸς ὑμᾶς our mouth is open towards you, i. e. we speak freely to you, we keep nothing back); the mouth of one is said to be opened who recovers the power of speech, Lk. i. 64; of the earth yawning, Rev. xii. 16. ἀν. ἀκοάς τινος i. e. to restore the faculty of hearing, Mk. vii. 35 (L T Tr WH). ἀν. τοὺς ὀφθαλμούς [W. 33 (32)], to part the eyelids so as to see, Acts ix. 8, 40; τινός, to restore one's sight, Mt. ix. 30; xx. 33; Jn. ix. 10, 14, 17, 21, 26, 30, 32; x. 21; xi. 37; metaph., Acts xxvi. 18 (to open the eyes of one's mind). ἀνοίγω τὴν σφραγίδα, to unseal, Rev. v. 9; vi. 1, 3, 5, 7, 9, 12; viii. 1; ἀν. τὸ βιβλίον, βιβλαρίδιον, to unroll, Lk. iv. 17 L Tr WH; Rev. v. 2–5; x. 2, 8; xx. 12. [COMP.: δι-ανοίγω.] *

456 ἀν-οικο-δομέω, -ῶ: fut. ἀνοικοδομήσω; to build again, (Vulg. reaedifico): Acts xv. 16. ([Thuc. 1, 89, 3]; Diod. 11, 39; Plut. Them. 19; Cam. 31; Hdian. 8, 2, 12 [5 ed. Bekk.].)*

457 ἄνοιξις, -εως, ἡ, (ἀνοίγω, q. v.), an opening: ἐν ἀνοίξει τοῦ στόματός μου as often as I open my mouth to speak, Eph. vi. 19. (Thuc. 4, 68, 4; τῶν πυλῶν, id. 4, 67, 3; χειλῶν, Plut. mor. [symp. l. ix. quaest. 2, 3] p. 738 c.)*

458 ἀνομία, -ας, ἡ, (ἄνομος); **1.** prop. the condition of one without law, — either because ignorant of it, or because violating it. **2.** contempt and violation of law, iniquity, wickedness: Mt. xxiii. 28; xxiv. 12; 2 Th. ii. 3 (T Tr txt. WH txt.; cf. ἁμαρτία, 1 p. 30 sq.), 7; Tit. ii. 14; 1 Jn. iii. 4. opp. to ἡ δικαιοσύνη, 2 Co. vi. 14; Heb. i. 9 [not Tdf.], (Xen. mem. 1, 2, 24 ἀνομίᾳ μᾶλλον ἢ δικαιοσύνῃ χρώμενοι); and to ἡ δικαιοσύνη and ὁ ἁγιασμός, Ro. vi. 19 (τῇ ἀνομίᾳ εἰς τὴν ἀνομίαν to iniquity — personified — in order to work iniquity); ποιεῖν τὴν ἀνομίαν to do iniquity, act wickedly, Mt. xiii. 41; 1 Jn. iii. 4; in the same sense, ἐργάζεσθαι τὴν ἀν. Mt. vii. 23; plur. αἱ ἀνομίαι manifestations of disregard for law, iniquities, evil deeds: Ro. iv. 7 (Ps. xxxi. (xxxii.) 1); Heb. viii. 12 [R G L]; x. 17. (In Grk. writ. fr. [Hdt. 1, 96] Thuc. down; often in Sept.) [SYN. cf. Trench § lxvi.; Tittm. i. 48; Ellic. on Tit. ii. 14.]*

459 ἄ-νομος, -ον, (νόμος); **1.** destitute of (the Mosaic) law: used of Gentiles, 1 Co. ix. 21, (without any suggestion of 'iniquity'; just as in Add. to Esth. iv. 42, where ἄνομοι ἀπερίτμητοι and ἀλλότριοι are used together). **2.** departing from the law, a violator of the law, lawless, wicked; (Vulg. iniquus; [also injustus]): Mk. xv. 28 [R L Tr br.]; Lk. xxii. 37; Acts ii. 23, (so in Grk. writ.); opp. to ὁ δίκαιος, 1 Tim. i. 9; ὁ ἄνομος (κατ᾽ ἐξοχήν), he in whom all iniquity has as it were fixed its abode, 2 Th. ii. 8; ἄν. ἔργον an unlawful deed, 2 Pet. ii. 8; free from law, not subject to law, [Vulg. sine lege]: μὴ ὢν ἄνομος θεοῦ [B. 169 (147)] (Rec. θεῷ), 1 Co. ix. 21. (Very often in Sept.) [SYN. see ἀνομία, fin.] *

460 ἀνόμως, adv., without the law (see ἄνομος, 1), without a knowledge of the law: ἀν. ἁμαρτάνειν to sin in ignorance of the Mosaic law, Ro. ii. 12; ἀπόλυσθαι to perish, but not by sentence of the Mosaic law, ibid. (ἀνόμως ζῆν τε live ignorant of law and discipline, Isoc. panegyr. c. 10

§ 39; ἀνόμως ἀπόλλυσθαι to be slain contrary to law, as in wars, seditions, etc., ibid. c. 44 § 168. In Grk. writ. generally *unjustly, wickedly*, as 2 Macc. viii. 17.)*

461   ἀν-ορθόω, -ῶ: fut. ἀνορθώσω; 1 aor. ἀνώρθωσα; 1 aor. pass. ἀνωρθώθην (Lk. xiii. 13; without the aug. ἀνορθώθην L T Tr; cf. [*WH*. App. p. 161]; B. 34 (30); [W. 73] (70)); **1.** *to set up, make erect*: a crooked person, Lk. xiii. 13 (*she was made straight, stood erect*); drooping hands and relaxed knees (to raise them up by restoring their strength), Heb. xii. 12. **2.** *to rear again, build anew*: σκηνήν, Acts xv. 16 (Hdt. 1, 19 τὸν νηὸν . . . τὸν ἐνέπρησαν; 8, 140; Xen. Hell. 4, 8, 12, etc.; in various senses in Sept.).*

462   ἀν-όσιος, -ον, (a priv. and ὅσιος, q. v.), *unholy, impious, wicked*: 1 Tim. i. 9; 2 Tim. iii. 2. (In Grk. writ. from [Aeschyl. and] Hdt. down.)*

463   ἀνοχή, -ῆς, ἡ, (compare ἀνέχομαι τινος, s. v. ἀνέχω p. 45), *toleration, forbearance*; in this sense only in Ro. ii. 4; iii. 26 (25). (In Grk. writ. a h o l d i n g b a c k, d e l a y i n g, fr. ἀνέχω to hold back, hinder.) [Cf. Trench § liii.]*

464   ἀντ-αγωνίζομαι; *to struggle, fight*; πρός τι, against a thing, Heb. xii. 4 [cf. W. § 52, 4, 3]. (Xen., Plat., Dem., etc.)*

465   ἀντ-άλλαγμα, -τος, τό, (ἀντί in place of, in turn, and ἄλλαγμα see ἀλλάσσω), *that which is given in place of another thing by way of exchange; what is given either in order to keep or to acquire anything*: Mt. xvi. 26; Mk. viii. 37, where the sense is, 'nothing equals in value the soul's salvation.' Christ transfers a proverbial expression respecting the supreme value of the natural life (Hom. Il. 9, 401 οὐ γὰρ ἐμοὶ ψυχῆς ἀντάξιον) to the life eternal. (Ruth iv. 7; Jer. xv. 13; Sir. vi. 15, etc.; Eur. Or. 1157; Joseph. b. j. 1, 18, 3.)*

466   ἀντ-ανα-πληρόω, -ῶ; (ἀντί and ἀναπληρόω, q. v.); *to fill up in turn*: Col. i. 24 (the meaning is, 'what is wanting of the afflictions of Christ to be borne by me, that I supply in order to repay the benefits which Christ conferred on me by filling up the measure of the afflictions laid upon him'); [Mey., Ellic., etc., explain the word (with Wetst.) by 'ἀντὶ ὑστερήματος succedit ἀναπλήρωμα'; but see Bp. Lghtft. ad loc., who also q u o t e s the passages where the word occurs]. (Dem. p. 182, 22; Dio Cass. 44, 48; Apollon. Dysc. de constr. orat. i. pp. 14, 1 [cf. Bttm. ad loc.]; 114, 8; 258, 3; 337, 4.)*

467   ἀντ-απο-δίδωμι: fut. ἀνταποδώσω; 2 aor. inf. ἀνταποδοῦναι; 1 fut. pass. ἀνταποδοθήσομαι; (ἀντί for something received, in return, ἀποδίδωμι to give back); *to repay, requite*; **a.** in a good sense: Lk. xiv. 14; Ro. xi. 35; εὐχαριστίαν τινί, 1 Th. iii. 9. **b.** in a bad sense, of penalty and vengeance; absol.: Ro. xii. 19; Heb. x. 30, (Deut. xxxii. 35); θλίψιν τινί, 2 Th. i. 6. (Very often in the Sept. and Apocr., in both senses; in Grk. writ. fr. [Hdt.] Thuc. down.)*

468   ἀντ-από-δομα, -τος, τό, (see ἀνταποδίδωμι), *the thing paid back, requital*; **a.** in a good sense: Lk. xiv. 12. **b.** in a bad sense: Ro. xi. 9. (In Sept. i. q. גְּמוּל, Judg. ix. 16 [Alex.], etc.; the Greeks say ἀνταπόδοσις [cf. W. 25].)*

469   ἀντ-από-δοσις, -εως, ἡ, *recompense*: Col. iii. 24. (In

Sept. i. q. גְּמוּל, Is. lix. 18, etc.; in Grk. writ. fr. Thuc. down.)*

ἀντ-απο-κρίνομαι; 1 aor. pass. ἀνταπεκρίθην [see ἀποκρίνω, ii.]; *to contradict in reply, to answer by contradicting, reply against*: τινί πρός τι, Lk. xiv. 6; (Sept. Judg. v. 29 [Alex.]; Job xvi. 8; xxxii. 12; Aesop. fab. 172 ed. de Furia, [p. 353 ed. Coray]). Hence i. q. *to altercate, dispute*: with dat. of pers. Ro. ix. 20. (In a mathematical sense, *to correspond to each other* or *be parallel*, in Nicomach. arithm. 1, 8, 11 p. 77 a. [p. 17 ed. Hoche].) Cf. *Win*. De verb. comp. etc. Pt. iii. p. 17.*   **470**

ἀντ-εῖπον, a 2 aor. used instead of the verb ἀντιλέγειν, *to speak against, gainsay*; [fr. Aeschyl. down]: Lk. xxi. 15; Acts iv. 14. Cf. εἶπον.*   **see 471 St.**

ἀντ-έχω: Mid., [pres. ἀντέχομαι]; fut. ἀνθέξομαι; *to hold before* or *against, hold back, withstand, endure*; in the N. T. only in Mid. *to keep one's self directly opposite to any one, hold to him firmly, cleave to*, paying heed to him: τινός, Mt. vi. 24; Lk. xvi. 13; τῶν ἀσθενῶν, to aid them, care for them, 1 Th. v. 14; τοῦ λόγου, to hold to, hold it fast, Tit. i. 9. (Deut. xxxii. 41; Is. lvi. 4, 6; Prov. iii. 18, etc., and often in Grk. writ.) Cf. Kühner § 520 b. [2te Aufl. § 416, 2; cf. Jelf § 536]; W. 202 (190); [B. 161 (140)].*   **see 472 St.**

ἀντί [before ὧν, ἀνθ'; elsewhere neglecting elision] a preposition foll. by the gen. (answering to the Lat. *ante* and the Germ. prefixes *ant-, ent-*), in the use of which the N. T. writ. coincide with the Greek (W. 364 (341)); **1.** prop. it seems to have signified *over against, opposite to, before*, in a local sense (*Bttm.* Gram. p. 412; [cf. Curtius § 204]). Hence **2.** indicating exchange, succession, *for, instead of, in place of* (something). **a.** univ. *instead of*: ἀντὶ ἰχθύος ὄφιν, Lk. xi. 11; ἀντὶ περιβολαίου to serve as a covering, 1 Co. xi. 15; ἀντὶ τοῦ λέγειν, Jas. iv. 15, (ἀντὶ τοῦ with inf. often in Grk. writ. [W. 329 (309); B. 263 (226)]). **b.** of that *for* which any thing is given, received, endured: Mt. v. 38; xvii. 27 (to release me and thyself from obligation); Heb. xii. 2 (to obtain the joy; cf. Bleek, Lünemann, or Delitzsch ad loc.); of the price of sale (or purchase): Heb. xii. 16; λύτρον ἀντὶ πολλῶν, Mt. xx. 28; Mk. x. 45. Then **c.** of recompense: κακὸν ἀντὶ κακοῦ ἀποδιδόναι, Ro. xii. 17; 1 Th. v. 15; 1 Pet. iii. 9, (Sap. xi. 16 (15)). ἀνθ' ὧν equiv. to ἀντὶ τούτων, ὅτι *for that, because*: Lk. i. 20; xix. 44; Acts xii. 23; 2 Th. ii. 10, (also in prof. auth. [exx. in Wetst. on Luke i. 20]; cf. *Herm*. ad Vig. p. 710; [W. 364 (342), cf. 162 (153); B. 105 (92)]; Hebr. תַּחַת אֲשֶׁר, Deut. xxi. 14; 2 K. xxii. 17). **d.** of the cause: ἀνθ' ὧν *wherefore*, Lk. xii. 3; ἀντὶ τούτου *for this cause*, Eph. v. 31. **e.** of succession to the place of another: Ἀρχ. βασιλεύει ἀντὶ Ἡρώδου in place of Herod, Mt. ii. 22, (1 K. xi. 44; Hdt. 1, 108; Xen. an. 1, 1, 4). χάριν ἀντὶ χάριτος grace in the place of grace, grace succeeding grace perpetually, i. e. the richest abundance of grace, Jn. i. 16, (Theogn. vs. 344 ἀντ' ἀνιῶν ἀνίας [yet cf. the context vs. 342 (vss. 780 and 778 ed. Welcker); more appropriate are the reff. to Philo, i. 254 ed. Mang. (de poster. Caini § 43, vol. ii. 39 ed. Richter), and Chrys. de sacer-   **473** dot. l. vi. c. 13 § 622]). **3.** As a prefix, it denotes **a.** *opposite, over against* : ἀντιπέραν, ἀντιπαρέρχεσθαι. **b.** the mutual efficiency of two : ἀντιβάλλειν, ἀντικαλεῖν, ἀντιλοιδορεῖν. **c.** requital : ἀντιμισθία, ἀνταποδίδωμι. **d.** hostile opposition : ἀντίχριστος. **e.** official substitution, *instead of* : ἀνθύπατος.*

474   **ἀντι-βάλλω** ; *to throw in turn,* (prop. Thuc. 7, 25 ; Plut. Nic. 25) : λόγους πρὸς ἀλλήλους to exchange words with one another, Lk. xxiv. 17, [cf. 2 Macc. xi. 13].*

see 475 St.   **ἀντι-δια-τίθημι** : [pres. mid. ἀντιδιατίθεμαι] ; in mid. *to place one's self in opposition, to oppose* : of heretics, 2 Tim. ii. 25, cf. De Wette [or Holtzm.] ad loc. ; (several times in eccl. writ. ; in the act. *to dispose in turn, to take in hand in turn* : τινά, Diod. exc. p. 602 [vol. v. p. 105, 24 ed. Dind. ; absol. *to retaliate,* Philo de spec. legg. § 15 ; de concupisc. § 4]).*

476   **ἀντί-δικος, -ον,** (δίκη) ; as subst. ὁ ἀντίδικος **a.** *an opponent in a suit at law* : Mt. v. 25 ; Lk. xii. 58 ; xviii. 3, (Xen., Plat., often in the Attic orators). **b.** univ. *an adversary, enemy,* (Aeschyl. Ag. 41 ; Sir. xxxiii. 9 ; 1 S. ii. 10 ; Is. xli. 11, etc.) : 1 Pet. v. 8 (unless we prefer to regard the devil as here called ἀντίδικος because he accuses men before God).*

477   **ἀντί-θεσις,** [(τίθημι), fr. Plato down], -εως, ἡ ; **a.** *opposition.* **b.** *that which is opposed* : 1 Tim. vi. 20 (ἀντιθέσεις τῆς ψευδών. γνώσ. the inventions of false knowledge, either mutually oppugnant, or opposed to true Christian doctrine).*

478   **ἀντι-καθ-ίστημι** : 2 aor. ἀντικατέστην ; [fr. Hdt. down] ; in the trans. tenses **1.** *to put in place of another.* **2.** *to place in opposition* ; *to dispose troops, set an army in line of battle*) ; in the intrans. tenses, *to stand against, resist* : Heb. xii. 4, (Thuc. 1, 62. 71).*

479   **ἀντι-καλέω, -ῶ** : 1 aor. ἀντεκάλεσα ; *to invite in turn* : τινά, Lk. xiv. 12. [Xen. conviv. 1, 15.]*

480   **ἀντί-κειμαι** ; **1.** *to be set over against, lie opposite to,* in a local sense, ([Hippocr. de aëre p. 282 Foes. (191 Chart.) ; Strab. 7, 7, 5] ; Hdian. 6, 2, 4 (2 Bekk.) ; 3, 15, 17 (8 Bekk.) ; [cf. Aristot. de caelo 1, 8 p. 277ᵃ, 23]). **2.** *to oppose, be adverse to, withstand* : τινί, Lk. xiii. 17 ; xxi. 15 ; Gal. v. 17 ; 1 Tim. i. 10. simply (ὁ) ἀντικείμενος, *an adversary,* [Tittmann ii. 9] : 1 Co. xvi. 9 ; Phil. i. 28 ; 2 Th. ii. 4 ; 1 Tim. v. 14. (Dio Cass. 39, 8. Ex. xxiii. 22 ; 2 Macc. x. 26, etc. ; [see *Soph.* Lex. s. v.].) *

481   **ἀντικρύ** (L T WH ἄντικρυς [Chandler § 881 ; Treg. ἀντικρύς. Cf. *Lob.* Path. Elementa ii. 283] ; ad Phryn. p. 444 ; [*Rutherford*, New Phryn. p. 500 sq.] ; Bttm. Ausf. Spr. ii. 366), adv. of place, *over against, opposite* : with gen., Acts xx. 15. (Often in Grk. writ. ; Philo de vict. off. § 3 ; de vit. Moys. iii. § 7 ; in Flacc. § 10.) *

see 482 St.   **ἀντι-λαμβάνω** : Mid., [pres. ἀντιλαμβάνομαι] ; 2 aor. ἀντελαβόμην ; *to take in turn* or *in return, to receive one thing for another given, to receive instead of* ; in mid. freq. in Attic prose writ., **1.** *to lay hold of, hold fast to,* anything : τινός. **2.** *to take a person* or *thing in order as it were to be held, to take to, embrace* ; with a gen. of the pers., *to help, succor* : Lk. i. 54 ; Acts xx. 35, (Diod. 11, 13 ; Dio Cass. 40, 27 ; 46, 45 ; often in Sept.).

with a gen. of the thing, *to be a partaker, partake of* : τῆς εὐεργεσίας of the benefit of the services rendered by the slaves, 1 Tim. vi. 2 ; cf. De Wette ad loc. (μήτε ἐσθίων πλειόνων ἡδονῶν ἀντιλήψεται, Porphyr. de abstin. 1, 46 ; [cf. Euseb. h. e. 4, 15, 37 and exx. in *Field,* Otium Norv. pars. iii. ad l. c.]) [COMP. : συν-αντι-λαμβάνομαι.] *

ἀντι-λέγω ; [impf. ἀντέλεγον] ; *to speak against, gainsay, contradict* ; absol. : Acts xiii. 45 [L Tr WH om.] ; xxviii. 19 ; Tit. i. 9. τινί, Acts xiii. 45. foll. by μή and acc. with inf. : Lk. xx. 27 [L mrg. Tr WH λέγοντες], (as in Grk. writ. ; see Passow [or L. and S.] s. v. ; [W. § 65, 2 β. ; B. 355 (305)]). *to oppose one's self to one, decline to obey him, declare one's self against him, refuse to have anything to do with him,* [cf. W. 23 (22)] : τινί, Jn. xix. 12, (Lcian. dial. inferor. 30, 3) ; absol. Ro. x. 21 [cf. Meyer] ; Tit. ii. 9, (Achill. Tat. 5, 27). Pass. ἀντιλέγομαι *I am disputed, assent* or *compliance is refused me,* (W. § 39, 1) : Lk. ii. 34 ; Acts xxviii. 22.*   **483**

ἀντί-ληψις [L T Tr WH -λημψις ; see M, μ], -εως, ἡ, (ἀντιλαμβάνομαι), in prof. auth. *mutual acceptance* (Thuc. 1, 120), *a laying hold of, apprehension, perception, objection of a disputant,* etc. In bibl. speech *aid, help,* (Ps. xxi. 20 [cf. vs. 1] ; 1 Esdr. viii. 27 ; Sir. xi. 12 ; li. 7 ; 2 Macc. xv. 7, etc.) ; plur., 1 Co. xii. 28, the ministrations of the deacons, who have care of the poor and the sick.*   **484**

ἀντιλογία, -ας, ἡ, (ἀντίλογος, and this fr. ἀντιλέγω), [fr. Hdt. down] ; **1.** *gainsaying, contradiction* : Heb. vii. 7 ; with the added notion of *strife,* Heb. vi. 16, (Ex. xviii. 16 ; Deut. xix. 17, etc.). **2.** *opposition* in act, [this sense is disputed by some, e. g. Lün. on Heb. as below, Mey. on Ro. x. 21 (see ἀντιλέγω) ; contra cf. Fritzsche on Ro. l. c.] : Heb. xii. 3 ; *rebellion,* Jude 11, (Prov. xvii. 11).*   **485**

ἀντι-λοιδορέω -ῶ : [impf. ἀντελοιδόρουν] ; *to revile in turn, to retort railing* : 1 Pet. ii. 23. (Lcian. conviv. 40 ; Plut. Anton. 42 ; [de inimic. util. § 5].)*   **486**

ἀντί-λυτρον, -ου, τό, *what is given in exchange for another as the price of his redemption, ransom* : 1 Tim. ii. 6. (An uncert. translator in Ps. xlviii. (xlix.) 9 ; Orph. lith. 587 ; [cf. W. 25].)*   **487**

ἀντι-μετρέω, -ῶ : fut. pass. ἀντιμετρηθήσομαι ; *to measure back, measure in return* : Mt. vii. 2 Rec. ; Lk. vi. 38 [L. mrg. WH mrg. μετρέω], (in a proverbial phrase, i. q. *to repay* ; Lcian. amor. c. 19).*   **488**

ἀντιμισθία, -ας, ἡ, (ἀντίμισθος remunerating) *a reward given in compensation, requital, recompense* ; **a.** in a good sense : 2 Co. vi. 13 (τὴν αὐτὴν ἀντιμισθίαν πλατύνθητε καὶ ὑμεῖς, a concise expression for *Be ye also enlarged* i. e. enlarge your hearts, just as I have done (vs. 11), *that so ye may recompense me,* — for τὸ αὐτό, ὅ ἐστιν ἀντιμισθία ; cf. W. 530 (493), and § 66, 1 b. ; [B. 190 (164) ; 396 (339)]). **b.** in a bad sense : Ro. i. 27. (Found besides only in Theoph. Ant. ; Clem. Al. ; [Clem. Rom. 2 Cor. 1, 3. 5 ; 9, 7 ; 11, 6], and other Fathers.)*   **489**

Ἀντιόχεια, -ας, ἡ, *Antioch,* the name (derived fr. various monarchs) of several Asiatic cities, two of which are mentioned in the N. T. ; **1.** The most celebrated of all, and the capital of Syria, was situated on the river Orontes, founded by Seleucus [I. sometimes (cf. Suidas s. v.   **490**

Σέλευκος, col. 3277 b. ed. Gaisf.) called] Nicanor [elsewhere (cf. id. col. 2137 b. s. v. Κολασσαεύς) son of Nicanor; but commonly Nicator (cf. Appian de rebus Syr. § 57; Spanh. de numis. diss. vii. § 3, vol. i. p. 413)], and named in honor of his father Antiochus. Many Ἑλληνισταί, Greek-Jews, lived in it; and there those who professed the name of Christ were first called Christians : Acts xi. 19 sqq.; xiii. 1; xiv. 26; xv. 22 sqq.; Gal. ii. 11; cf. Reuss in Schenkel i. 141 sq.; [BB. DD. s. v.; Conyb. and Howson, St. Paul, i. 121–126; also the latter in the Dict. of Geogr. s. v.; Renan, Les Apôtres, ch. xii.]. **2.** A city of Phrygia, but called in Acts xiii. 14 Antioch of Pisidia [or acc. to the crit. texts the Pisidian Antioch (see Πισίδιος)] because it was on the confines of Pisidia, (more exactly ἡ πρὸς Πισιδίᾳ, Strabo 12, p. 577, 8): Acts xiv. 19, 21; 2 Tim. iii. 11. This was founded also by Seleucus Nicator, [cf. BB. DD. s. v.; Conyb. and Howson, St. Paul, i. 168 sqq.].*

491   'Αντιοχεύς, -έως, ὁ, an Antiochian, a native of Antioch : Acts vi. 5.*

492   ἀντι-παρ-έρχομαι : 2 aor. ἀντιπαρῆλθον; to pass by opposite to, [A. V. to pass by on the other side]: Lk. x. 31 sq. (where the meaning is, 'he passed by on the side opposite to the wounded man, showing no compassion for him'). (Anthol. Pal. 12, 8; to come to one's assistance against a thing, Sap. xvi. 10. Found besides in eccl. and Byzant. writ.) *

493   'Αντίπας [Tdf. 'Αντείπας, see s. v. ει, ι], -α (cf. W. § 8, 1; [B. 20 (18)]), ὁ, Antipas (contr. fr. 'Αντίπατρος W. 103 (97)), a Christian of Pergamum who suffered martyrdom, otherwise unknown: Rev. ii. 13. On the absurd interpretations of this name, cf. Düsterd. [Alf., Lee, al.] ad loc. Fr. Görres in the Zeitschr. f. wissensch. Theol. for 1878, p. 257 sqq., endeavors to discredit the opinion that he was martyred, but by insufficient arguments.*

494   'Αντιπατρίς, -ίδος, ἡ, Antipatris, a city situated between Joppa and Cæsarea, in a very fertile region, not far from the coast; formerly called Χαβαρζαβᾶ [al. Καφαρσαβᾶ (or -σάβα)] (Joseph. antt. 13, 15, 1), and afterwards rebuilt by Herod the Great and named Antipatris in honor of his father Antipater (Joseph. b. j. 1, 21, 9): Acts xxiii. 31. Cf. Robinson, Researches etc. iii. 45 sq.; Later Researches, iii. 138 sq., [also Bib. Sacr. for 1843 pp. 478–498; and for 1853 p. 528 sq.].*

495   ἀντι-πέραν, or (acc. to the later forms fr. Polyb. down) ἀντίπερα [T WH], ἀντιπέρα [L Tr; cf. B. 321; Lob. Path. Elem. ii. 206; Chandler § 867], adv. of place, over against, on the opposite shore, on the other side, with a gen.: Lk. viii. 26.*

496   ἀντι-πίπτω; **a.** to fall upon, run against, [fr. Aristot. down]; **b.** to be adverse, oppose, strive against: τινί, Acts vii. 51. (Ex. xxvi. 5; xxxvi. 12 ed. Compl.; Num. xxvii. 14; often in Polyb., Plut.)*

497   ἀντι-στρατεύομαι; **1.** to make a military expedition, or take the field, against any one: Xen. Cyr. 8, 8, 26. **2.** to oppose, war against: τινί, Ro. vii. 23. (Aristaenet. 2, 1, 13.)*

498   ἀντι-τάσσω or -ττω : [pres. mid. ἀντιτάσσομαι]; to range

in battle against; mid. to oppose one's self, resist: τινί, Ro. xiii. 2; Jas. iv. 6; v. 6; 1 Pet. v. 5; cf. Prov. iii. 34. absol., Acts xviii. 6. (Used by Grk. writ. fr. Aeschyl. down.) *

ἀντί-τυπος, -ον, (τύπτω), in Grk. writ. **1.** prop. **a.** actively, repelling a blow, striking back, echoing, reflecting light; resisting, rough, hard. **b.** passively, struck back, repelled. **2.** metaph. rough, harsh, obstinate, hostile. In the N. T. language ἀντίτυπον as a subst. means **1.** a thing formed after some pattern (τύπος [q. v. 4 a.]), (Germ. Abbild): Heb. ix. 24 [R. V. like in pattern]. **2.** a thing resembling another, its counterpart; something in the Messianic times which answers to the type (see τύπος, 4 γ.) prefiguring it in the O. T. (Germ. Gegenbild, Eng. antitype), as baptism corresponds to the deluge : 1 Pet. iii. 21 [R. V. txt. after a true likeness].*   **499**

ἀντί-χριστος, -ον, ὁ, (ἀντί against and Χριστός, like ἀντίθεος opposing God, in Philo de somn. l. ii. § 27, etc., Justin, quaest. et resp. p. 463 c. and other Fathers; [see Soph. Lex. s. v., cf. Trench § xxx.]), the adversary of the Messiah, a most pestilent being, to appear just before the Messiah's advent, concerning whom the Jews had conceived diverse opinions, derived partly fr. Dan. xi. 36 sqq.; vii. 25; viii. 25, partly fr. Ezek. xxxviii. xxxix. Cf. Eisenmenger, Entdecktes Judenthum, ii. 704 sqq.; Gesenius in Ersch and Gruber's Encycl. iv. 292 sqq. s. v. Antichrist; Böhmer, Die Lehre v. Antichrist nach Schneckenburger, in the Jahrbb. f. deutsche Theol. vol. iv. p. 405 sqq. The name ὁ ἀντίχριστος was formed perhaps by John, the only writer in the N. T. who uses it, [five times]; he employs it of the corrupt power and influence hostile to Christian interests, especially that which is at work in false teachers who have come from the bosom of the church and are engaged in disseminating error: 1 Jn. ii. 18 (where the meaning is, 'what ye have heard concerning Antichrist, as about to make his appearance just before the return of Christ, is now fulfilled in the many false teachers, most worthy to be called antichrists,' [on the om. of the art. cf. B. 89 (78)]); 1 Jn. iv. 3; and of the false teachers themselves, 1 Jn. ii. 22; 2 Jn. 7. In Paul and the Rev. the idea but not the name of Antichrist is found; yet the conception differs from that of John. For Paul teaches that Antichrist will be an individual man [cf. B. D. as below], of the very worst character (τὸν ἄνθρ. τῆς ἁμαρτίας; see ἁμαρτία, 1), instigated by the devil to try to palm himself off as God : 2 Th. ii. 3–10. The author of the Apocalypse discovers the power of Antichrist in the sway of imperial Rome, and his person in the Emperor Nero, soon to return from the dead: Rev. xiii. and xvii. (Often in eccl. writ.) [See B. D. s.v. (Am. ed. for additional reff.), also B. D. s. v. Thess. 2d Ep. to the; Kähler in Herzog ed. 2, i. 446 sq.; Westcott, Epp. of St. John, pp. 68, 89.] *   **500**

ἀντλέω, -ῶ; 1 aor. ἤντλησα; pf. ἤντληκα; (fr. ὁ ἄντλος, or τὸ ἄντλον, bilge-water, [or rather, the place in the hold where it settles, Eustath. com. in Hom. 1728, 58 ὁ τόπος ἔνθα ὕδωρ συρρέει, τό τε ἄνωθεν καὶ ἐκ τῶν ἁρμονιῶν]); **a.** prop. to draw out a ship's bilge-water, to bale or pump   **501** out. **b.** univ. *to draw* water : Jn. ii. 8 ; iv. 15 ; ὕδωρ, Jn. ii. 9 ; iv. 7. (Gen. xxiv. 13, 20 ; Ex. ii. 16, 19 ; Is. xii. 3. In Grk. writ. fr. Hdt. down.)*

502 ἄντλημα, -τος, τό ; **a.** prop. *what is drawn*, (Dioscor. 4, 64). **b.** *the act of drawing* water, (Plut. mor. [de solert. an. 21, 1] p. 974 e. [but this example belongs rather under c.]). **c.** *a thing to draw with* [cf. W. 93 (89)], *bucket and rope let down into a well* : Jn. iv. 11.*

503 ἀντοφθαλμέω, -ῶ ; (ἀντόφθαλμος looking in the eye) ; **1.** prop. *to look against* or *straight at*. **2.** metaph. *to bear up against, withstand* : τῷ ἀνέμῳ, of a ship, [cf. our 'look the wind in the eye,' 'face' (R. V.) the wind] : Acts xxvii. 15. (Sap. xii. 14 ; often in Polyb. ; in eccl. writ.)*

504 ἄνυδρος, -ον, (a priv. and ὕδωρ), *without water* : πηγαί, 2 Pet. ii. 17 ; τόποι, desert places, Mt. xii. 43 ; Lk. xi. 24, (ἡ ἄνυδρος the desert, Is. xliii. 19 ; Hdt. 3, 4, etc. ; in Sept. often γῆ ἄνυδρος), [desert places were believed to be the haunts of demons ; see Is. xiii. 21 ; xxxiv. 14 (in Sept.), and Gesen. or Alex. on the former pass. ; cf. further, Bar. iv. 35 ; Tob. viii. 3 ; 4 Macc. xviii. 8 ; (Enoch x. 4) ; Rev. xviii. 2 ; cf. d. Zeitschr. d. deutsch. morgenl. Gesell. xxi. 609] ; νεφέλαι, *waterless clouds* (Verg. georg. 3, 197 sq. *arida nubila*), which promise rain but yield none, Jude 12. (In Grk. writ. fr. Hdt. down.)*

505 ἀν-υπόκριτος, -ον, (a priv. and ὑποκρίνομαι), *unfeigned, undisguised* : Ro. xii. 9 ; 2 Co. vi. 6 ; 1 Tim. i. 5 ; 2 Tim. i. 5 ; 1 Pet. i. 22 ; Jas. iii. 17. (Sap. v. 19 ; xviii. 16. Not found in prof. auth., except the adv. ἀνυποκρίτως in Antonin. 8, 5.)*

506 ἀν-υπότακτος, -ον, (a priv. and ὑποτάσσω) ; **1.** [passively] *not made subject, unsubjected* : Heb. ii. 8, [Artem. oneir. 2, 30]. **2.** [actively] *that cannot be subjected to control, disobedient, unruly, refractory* : 1 Tim. i. 9 ; Tit. i. 6, 10, ([Epict. 2, 10, 1 ; 4, 1, 161 ; Philo, quis rer. div. her. § 1] ; διήγησις ἀνυπ. a narrative which the reader cannot classify, i. e. *confused*, Polyb. 3, 36, 4 ; 3, 38, 4 ; 5, 21, 4).*

507 ἄνω, adv., [fr. Hom. down] ; **a.** *above, in a higher place*, (opp. to κάτω) : Acts ii. 19 ; with the article, ὁ, ἡ, τὸ ἄνω : Gal. iv. 26 (ἡ ἄνω Ἰερουσαλήμ the upper i. e. the heavenly Jerusalem) ; Phil. iii. 14 (ἡ ἄνω κλῆσις the calling made in heaven, equiv. to ἐπουράνιος, Heb. iii. 1) ; the neut. plur. τὰ ἄνω as subst., heavenly things, Col. iii. 1 sq. ; ἐκ τῶν ἄνω from heaven, Jn. viii. 23. ἕως ἄνω, Jn. ii. 7 (up to the brim). **b.** *upwards, up, on high* : Jn. xi. 41 (αἴρω) ; Heb. xii. 15 (ἄνω φύει).*

see 508 Sh. & (311α) above ‾‾‾‾‾‾‾

ἀνώγαιον and ἀνώγεον, see under ἀνάγαιον.

509 ‾‾‾‾‾ ἄνωθεν, (ἄνω), adv. ; **a.** *from above, from a higher place* : ἀπὸ ἄνωθεν (W. § 50, 7 N. 1), Mt. xxvii. 51 [Tdf. om. ἀπό] ; Mk. xv. 38 ; ἐκ τῶν ἄνωθεν from the upper part, from the top, Jn. xix. 23. Often (also in Grk. writ.) used of things which come *from heaven*, or from God as dwelling in heaven : Jn. iii. 31 ; xix. 11 ; Jas. i. 17 ; iii. 15, 17. **b.** *from the first* : Lk. i. 3 ; then, *from the beginning on, from the very first* : Acts xxvi. 5. Hence **c.** *anew, over again*, indicating repetition, (a use somewhat rare, but wrongly denied by many [Mey. among them ; cf. his comm. on Jn. and Gal. as below]) : Jn. iii. 3,

7 ἄν. γεννηθῆναι, where others explain it *from above*, i. e. from heaven. But, acc. to this explanation, Nicodemus ought to have wondered how it was possible for any one to be born *from heaven* ; but this he did n o t say ; [cf. Westcott, Com. on Jn. p. 63]. Of the repetition of p h y s-i c a l birth, we read in Artem. oneir. 1, 13 (14) p. 18 [i. p. 26 ed. Reiff] (ἀνδρὶ) ἔτι τῷ ἔχοντι ἐγκύον γυναῖκα σημαίνει παῖδα αὐτῷ γεννήσεσθαι ὅμοιον κατὰ πάντα. οὕτω γὰρ ἄνωθεν αὐτὸς δόξειε γεννᾶσθαι ; cf. Joseph. antt. 1, 18, 3 φιλίαν ἄνωθεν ποιεῖσθαι, where a little before stands προτέρα φιλία ; add, Martyr. Polyc. 1, 1 ; [also Socrates in Stob. flor. cxxiv. 41, iv. 135 ed. Meineke (iii. 438 ed. Gaisf.) ; Harpocration, Lex. s. vv. ἀναδικάσασθαι, ἀναθέσθαι, ἀναποδιζόμενα, ἀνασύνταξις ; Canon. apost. 46 (al. 39, Coteler. patr. apost. opp. i. 444) ; Pseudo-Basil, de bapt. 1, 2, 7 (iii. 1537) ; Origen in Joann. t. xx. c. 12 (opp. iv. 322 c. De la Rue). See *Abbot*, Authorship of the Fourth Gospel, etc. (Boston 1880) p. 34 sq.]. πάλιν ἄνωθεν (on this combination of synonymous words cf. Kühner § 534, 1 ; [Jelf § 777, 1] ; Grimm on Sap. xix. 5 (6)) : Gal. iv. 9 (*again, since ye were in bondage once before*).*

ἀνωτερικός, -ή, -όν, (ἀνώτερος), *upper* : τὰ ἀνωτερικὰ μέρη, 　　　　**510** Acts xix. 1 (i. e. the part of Asia Minor more remote from the Mediterranean, farther east). (The word is used by [Hippocr. and] Galen.)*

ἀνώτερος, -έρα, -ερον, (compar. fr. ἄνω, cf. κατώτερος, 　　**511** see W. § 11, 2 c. ; [B. 28 (24 sq.)]), *higher*. The neut. ἀνώτερον as adv., *higher* ; **a.** of motion, *to a higher place*, (*up higher*) : Lk. xiv. 10. **b.** of rest, *in a higher place, above* i. e. in the immediately preceding part of the passage quoted, Heb. x. 8. Similarly Polyb. 3, 1, 1 τρίτῃ ἀνώτερον βίβλῳ. (In Lev. xi. 21, with gen.)*

ἀν-ωφελής, -ές, (a priv. and ὄφελος) ; fr. Aeschyl. down ; 　　**512** *unprofitable, useless* : Tit. iii. 9. Neut. as subst. in Heb. vii. 18 (διὰ τὸ αὐτῆς ἀνωφελές on account of its unprofitableness).*

ἀξίνη, -ης, ἡ, ([perh. fr.] ἄγνυμι, fut. ἄξω, to break), *an* 　　**513** *axe* : Lk. iii. 9 ; Mt. iii. 10. (As old as Hom. and Hdt.)*

ἄξιος, -α, -ον, (fr. ἄγω, ἄξω ; therefore prop. *drawing* 　　**514** *down the scale* ; hence) **a.** *weighing, having weight* ; with a gen. *having the weight of* (weighing as much as) *another thing, of like value, worth as much* : βοὸς ἄξιος, Hom. Il. 23, 885 ; with gen. of price [W. 206 (194)], as ἄξ. δέκα μνῶν, common in Attic writ. ; πᾶν τίμιον οὐκ ἄξιον αὐτῆς (σοφίας) ἐστι, Prov. iii. 15 ; viii. 11 ; οὐκ ἔστι σταθμὸς πᾶς ἄξιος ἐγκρατοῦς ψυχῆς, Sir. xxvi. 15 ; οὐκ ἄξια πρὸς τ. δόξαν are of no weight in comparison with the glory, i. e. are not to be put on an equality with the glory, Ro. viii. 18 ; cf. Fritzsche ad loc. and W. 405 (378) ; [B. 340 (292)]. **b.** *befitting, congruous, corresponding, τινός, to a thing* : τῆς μετανοίας, Mt. iii. 8 ; Lk. iii. 8 ; Acts xxvi. 20 ; ἄξια τῶν ἐπράξαμεν, Lk. xxiii. 41. ἄξιόν ἐστι it is befitting : **α.** *it is meet*, 2 Th. i. 3 (4 Macc. xvii. 8) ; **β.** *it is worth the while*, foll. by τοῦ with acc. and inf., 1 Co. xvi. 4 ; — (in both senses very com. in Grk. writ. fr. Hom. and Hdt. down, and often with ἐστί omitted). **c.** of one who has merited anything, *worthy,* — both in a good reference and a bad ;

a. in a good sense; with a gen. of the thing: Mt. x. 10; Lk. vii. 4; [x. 7]; Acts xiii. 46; 1 Tim. i. 15; iv. 9; v. 18; vi. 1. foll. by the aor. inf.: Lk. xv. 19, 21; Acts xiii. 25; Rev. iv. 11; v. 2, 4, 9, 12; foll. by ἵνα: Jn. i. 27 (ἵνα λύσω, a construction somewhat rare; cf. Dem. pro cor. p. 279, 9 ἀξιοῦν, ἵνα βοηθήσῃ [(dubious); see s. v. ἵνα, II. 2 init. and c.]); foll. by ὅς with a finite verb (like Lat. dignus, qui): Lk. vii. 4 [B. 229 (198)]. It stands alone, but so that the context makes it plain of what one is said to be worthy: Mt. x. 11 (to lodge with); Mt. x. 13 (sc. τῆς εἰρήνης); Mt. xxii. 8 (sc. of the favor of an invitation); Rev. iii. 4 (sc. to walk with me, clothed in white). with a gen. of the person, — worthy of one's fellowship, and of the blessings connected with it: Mt. x. 37 sq.; Heb. xi. 38, (τοῦ θεοῦ, Sap. iii. 5; Ignat. ad Eph. 2). β. in a bad sense; with a gen. of the thing: πληγῶν, Lk. xii. 48; θανάτου, Lk. xxiii. 15; Acts [xxiii. 29]; xxv. 11, [25]; xxvi. 31; Ro. i. 32; absol.: Rev. xvi. 6 (sc. to drink blood).*

515 ἀξιόω, -ῶ; impf. ἠξίουν; 1 aor. ἠξίωσα; Pass., pf. ἠξίωμαι; 1 fut. ἀξιωθήσομαι; (ἄξιος); as in Grk. writ. **a.** to think meet, fit, right: foll. by an inf., Acts xv. 38; xxviii. 22. **b.** to judge worthy, deem deserving: τινά with an inf. of the object, Lk. vii. 7; τινά τινος, 2 Th. i. 11; pass. with gen. of the thing, 1 Tim. v. 17; Heb. iii. 3; x. 29. [Comp.: κατ-αξιόω.]*

516 ἀξίως, adv., suitably; worthily, in a manner worthy of: with the gen., Ro. xvi. 2; Phil. i. 27; Col. i. 10; 1 Th. ii. 12; Eph. iv. 1; 3 Jn. 6. [From Soph. down.]*

517 ἀ-όρατος, -ον, (ὁράω), either, not seen i. e. unseen, or that cannot be seen i. e. invisible. In the latter sense of God in Col. i. 15; 1 Tim. i. 17; Heb. xi. 27; τὰ ἀόρατα αὐτοῦ his (God's) invisible nature [perfections], Ro. i. 20; τὰ ὁρατὰ καὶ τὰ ἀόρατα, Col. i. 16. (Gen. i. 2; Is. xlv. 3; 2 Macc. ix. 5; Xen., Plat., Polyb., Plut., al.)*

518 ἀπ-αγγέλλω; impf. ἀπήγγελλον; fut. ἀπαγγελῶ; 1 aor. ἀπήγγειλα; 2 aor. pass. ἀπηγγέλην (Lk. viii. 20); [fr. Hom. down]; **1.** ἀπό τινος to bring tidings (from a person or thing), bring word, report: Jn. iv. 51 [R G L Tr br.]; Acts iv. 23; v. 22; [xv. 27]; with dat. of the pers., Mt. ii. 8; xiv. 12; xxviii. 8, [8 (9) Rec.], 10; Mk. xvi. [10], 13; Acts v. 25; xi. 13; [xxiii. 16, 19]; τινί τι, [Mt. xi. 4; xxviii. 11 (here Tdf. ἀναγγ.)]; Mk. [v. 19 (L mrg. R G ἀναγγ.)]; vi. 30; Lk. [vii. 22; ix. 36]; xiv. 21; xxiv. 9; Acts xi. 13; [xii. 17; xvi. 38 L T Tr WH; xxiii. 17]; τινί foll. by ὅτι, Lk. xviii. 37; [Jn. xx. 18 R G]; foll. by πῶς, Lk. viii. 36]; τὶ πρός τινα, Acts xvi. 36; τινὶ περί τινος, Lk. viii. 18; xiii. 1; τὶ περί τινος, Acts xxviii. 21; [foll. by λέγων and direct disc., Acts xxii. 26]; foll. by acc. with inf., Acts xii. 14; εἰς with acc. of place, to carry tidings to a place, Mk. v. 14 (Rec. ἀνήγγ.); Lk. viii. 34; with addition of an acc. of the thing announced, Mt. viii. 33, (Xen. an. 6, 2 (4), 25; Joseph. antt 5, 11, 3; εἰς τοὺς ἀνθρώπους, Am. iv. 13 Sept.). **2.** to proclaim (ἀπό, because what one announces he openly lays, as it were, off from himself, cf. Germ. abkündigen), to make known openly, declare: univ., περί τινος, 1 Th. i. 9; [τινὶ περί τ. Jn. xvi. 25 L T Tr WH]; by teaching, τί, 1 Jn.

i. 2 sq.; by teaching and commanding, τινί τι, Mt. viii. 33; τινί, with inf., Acts xxvi. 20; [xvii. 30 T WH Tr mrg.]; by avowing and praising, Lk. viii. 47; τινί τι, Heb. ii. 12 (Ps. xxi. (xxii.) 23 [yet Sept. διηγήσομαι]); [Mt. xii. 18]; foll. by ὅτι, 1 Co. xiv. 25.*

see
519 St.
ἀπ-άγχω [cf. Lat. angustus, anxius, Eng. anguish, etc.; Curtius § 166]: 1 aor. mid. ἀπηγξάμην; to throttle, strangle, in order to put out of the way (ἀπό away, cf. ἀποκτείνω to kill off), Hom. Od. 19, 230; mid. to hang one's self, to end one's life by hanging: Mt. xxvii. 5. (2 S. xvii. 23; Tob. iii. 10; in Attic from Aeschyl. down.)*

520 ἀπ-άγω; [impf. ἀπῆγον (Lk. xxiii. 26 Tr mrg. WH mrg.)]; 2 aor. ἀπήγαγον; Pass., [pres. ἀπάγομαι]; 1 aor. ἀπήχθην; [fr. Hom. down]; to lead away: Lk. xiii. 15 (sc. ἀπὸ τῆς φάτνης); Acts xxiii. 10 (Lchm. [ed. min.]); 17 (sc. hence); xxiv. 7 [R G] (away, ἐκ τῶν χειρῶν ἡμῶν); 1 Co. xii. 2 (led astray πρὸς τὰ εἴδωλα. Used esp. of those led off to trial, prison, punishment: Mt. xxvi. 57; xxvii. 2, 31; Mk. xiv. 44, 53; xv. 16; Lk. xxi. 12 (T Tr WH); [xxii. 66 T Tr WH]; xxiii. 26; Jn. xviii. 13 R G [ἤγαγον L T Tr WH]; xix. 16 Rec.; Acts xii. 19; (so also in Grk. writ.). Used of a way leading to a certain end: Mt. vii. 13, 14 (εἰς τὴν ἀπώλειαν, εἰς τὴν ζωήν). [Comp.: συν-απάγω.]*

521 ἀ-παίδευτος, -ον, (παιδεύω), without instruction and discipline, uneducated, ignorant, rude, [W. 96 (92)]: ζητήσεις, stupid questions, 2 Tim. ii. 23. (In classics fr. [Eurip.,] Xen. down; Sept.; Joseph.)*

522 ἀπ-αίρω; 1 aor. pass. ἀπήρθην; to lift off, take or carry away; pass., ἀπό τινος to be taken away from any one: Mt. ix. 15; Mk. ii. 20; Lk. v. 35. (In Grk. writ. fr. Hdt. down.) *

523 ἀπ-αιτέω, -ῶ; to ask back, demand back, exact something due (Sir. xx. 15 (14) σήμερον δανειεῖ καὶ αὔριον ἀπαιτήσει): Lk. vi. 30; τὴν ψυχήν σου ἀπαιτοῦσιν [Tr WH αἰτοῦσιν] thy soul, intrusted to thee by God for a time, is demanded back, Lk. xii. 20, (Sap. xv. 8 τὸ τῆς ψυχῆς ἀπαιτηθεὶς χρέος). (In Grk. writ. fr. Hdt. down.)*

524 ἀπ-αλγέω, -ῶ: [pf. ptcp. ἀπηλγηκώς]; to cease to feel pain or grief; **a.** to bear troubles with greater equanimity, cease to feel pain at: Thuc. 2, 61 etc. **b.** to become callous, insensible to pain, apathetic: so those who have become insensible to truth and honor and shame are called ἀπηλγηκότες [A. V. past feeling] in Eph. iv. 19. (Polyb. 1, 35, 5 ἀπηλγηκυίας ψυχάς dispirited and useless for war, [cf. Polyb. 16, 12, 7].)*

525 ἀπ-αλλάσσω: 1 aor. ἀπήλλαξα; Pass., [pres. ἀπαλλάσσομαι]; pf. inf. ἀπηλλάχθαι; (ἀλλάσσω to change; ἀπό, sc. τινός); com. in Grk. writ.; to remove, release; pass. to be removed, to depart: ἀπ᾽ αὐτῶν τὰς νόσους, Acts xix. 12 (Plat. Eryx. 401 c. εἰ αἱ νόσοι ἀπαλλαγείησαν ἐκ τῶν σωμάτων); in a transferred and esp. in a legal sense, ἀπό with gen. of pers., to be set free, the opponent being appeased and withdrawing the suit, to be quit of one: Lk. xii. 58, (so with a simple gen. of pers. Xen. mem. 2, 9, 6). Hence univ. to set free, deliver: τινά, Heb. ii. 15; (in prof. auth. the gen. of the thing freed fr. is often added; cf. Bleek on Heb. vol. ii. 1, p. 339 sq.).*

526 ἀπ-αλλοτριόω, -ῶ: pf. pass. ptcp. ἀπηλλοτριωμένος; to alienate, estrange; pass. to be rendered ἀλλότριος, to be shut out from one's fellowship and intimacy: τινός, Eph. ii. 12; iv. 18; sc. τοῦ θεοῦ, Col. i. 21, (equiv. to זוּר, used of those who have estranged themselves fr. God, Ps. lvii. (lviii.) 4; Is. i. 4 [Ald. etc.]; Ezek. xiv. 5, 7; [Test. xii. Patr. test. Benj. § 10]; τῶν πατρίων δογμάτων, 3 Macc. i. 3; ἀπαλλοτριοῦν τινα τοῦ καλῶς ἔχοντος, Clem. Rom. 1 Cor. 14, 2). (In Grk. writ. fr. [Hippocr.,] Plato down.)*

527 ἀπαλός, -ή, -όν, tender: of the branch of a tree, when full of sap, Mt. xxiv. 32; Mk. xiii. 28. [From Hom. down.]*

528 ἀπ-αντάω, -ῶ: fut. ἀπαντήσω (Mk. xiv. 13; but in better Grk. ἀπαντήσομαι, cf. W. 83 (79); [B. 53 (46)]); 1 aor. ἀπήντησα; to go to meet; in past tenses, to meet: τινί, Mt. xxviii. 9 [T Tr WH ὑπ-]; Mk. v. 2 R G; xiv. 13; Lk. xvii. 12 [L WH om. Tr br. dat.; T WH mrg. read ὑπ-]; Jn. iv. 51 R G; Acts xvi. 16 [R G L]. In a military sense of a hostile meeting: Lk. xiv. 31 R G, as in 1 S. xxii. 17; 2 S. i. 15; 1 Macc. xi. 15, 68 and often in Grk. writ.*

529 ἀπάντησις, -εως, ἡ, (ἀπαντάω), a meeting; εἰς ἀπάντησίν τινος or τινι to meet one: Mt. xxv. 1 R G; vs. 6; Acts xxviii. 15; 1 Th. iv. 17. (Polyb. 5, 26, 8; Diod. 18, 59; very often in Sept. equiv. to לִקְרַאת [cf. W. 30].) *

530 ἅπαξ, adv., once, one time, [fr. Hom. down]; **a.** univ.: 2 Co. xi. 25; Heb. ix. 26 sq.; 1 Pet. iii. 20 Rec.; ἔτι ἅπαξ, Heb. xii. 26 sq.; ἅπαξ τοῦ ἐνιαυτοῦ, Heb. ix. 7, [Hdt. 2, 59, etc.]. **b.** like Lat. semel, used of what is so done as to be of perpetual validity and never need repetition, once for all: Heb. vi. 4; x. 2; 1 Pet. iii. 18; Jude vss. 3, 5. **c.** καὶ ἅπαξ καὶ δίς indicates a definite number [the double καί emphasizing the repetition, both once and again i. e.] twice: 1 Th. ii. 18; Phil. iv. 16; on the other hand, ἅπαξ καὶ δίς means [once and again i. e.] several times, repeatedly: Neh. xiii. 20; 1 Macc. iii. 30. Cf. Schott on 1 Th. ii. 18, p. 86; [Meyer on Phil. l. c.].*

531 ἀ-παρά-βατος, -ον, (παραβαίνω), fr. the phrase παραβαίνειν νόμον to transgress i. e. to violate, signifying either unviolated, or not to be violated, inviolable: ἱερωσύνη unchangeable and therefore not liable to pass to a successor, Heb. vii. 24; cf. Bleek and Delitzsch ad loc. (A later word, cf. Lob. ad Phryn. p. 313; in Joseph., Plut., al.)*

532 ἀ-παρα-σκεύαστος, -ον, (παρασκευάζω), unprepared: 2 Co. ix. 4. (Xen. Cyr. 2, 4, 15; an. 1, 1, 6 [var.]; 2, 3, 21; Joseph. antt. 4, 8, 41; Hdian. 3, 9, 19 [(11) ed. Bekk.]; adv. ἀπαρασκευάστως, [Aristot. rhet. Alex. 9 p. 1430ᵃ 3]; Clem. hom. 32, 15.) *

533 ἀπ-αρνέομαι, -οῦμαι: depon. verb; fut. ἀπαρνήσομαι; 1 aor. ἀπηρνησάμην; 1 fut. pass. ἀπαρνηθήσομαι with a pass. signif. (Lk. xii. 9, as in Soph. Phil. 527, [cf. B. 53 (46)]); to deny (ab nego): τινά, to affirm that one has no acquaintance or connection with him; of Peter denying Christ: Mt. xxvi. 34 sq. 75; Mk. xiv. 30 sq. 72; [Lk. xxii. 61]; Jn. xiii. 38 R G L mrg.; more fully ἀπ. μὴ εἰδέναι Ἰησοῦν, Lk. xxii. 34 (L Tr WH om. μή, concerning which cf. Kühner ii. p. 761; [Jelf § 749, 1; W. § 65, 2 β.; B. 355 (305)]). ἑαυτόν to forget one's self, lose sight of one's self and one's own interests: Mt. xvi. 24; Mk. viii. 34; Lk. ix. 23 R WH mrg.*

534 ἀπάρτι [so Tdf. in Jn., T and Tr in Rev.], or rather ἀπ' ἄρτι (cf. W. § 5, 2 p. 45, and 422 (393); [B. 320 (275); Lipsius p. 127]; see ἄρτι), adv., from now, henceforth: Mt. xxiii. 39; xxvi. 29, 64 (in Lk. xxii. 69 ἀπὸ τοῦ νῦν); Jn. i. 51 (52) Rec.; xiii. 19; xiv. 7; Rev. xiv. 13 (where connect ἀπ' ἄρτι with μακάριοι). In the Grk. of the O. T. it is not found (for the Sept. render מֵעַתָּה by ἀπὸ τοῦ νῦν), and scarcely [yet L. and S. cite Arstph. Pl. 388; Plat. Com. Σοφ. 10] in the earlier and more elegant Grk. writ. For the similar term which the classic writ. require is to be written as one word, and oxytone (viz. ἀπαρτί), and has a different signif. (viz. completely, exactly); cf. Knapp, Scripta var. Arg. i. p. 296; Lob. ad Phryn. p. 20 sq.*

535 ἀπαρτισμός, -οῦ, ὁ, (ἀπαρτίζω to finish, complete), completion: Lk. xiv. 28. Found besides only in Dion. Hal. de comp. verb. c. 24; [Apollon. Dysc. de adv. p. 532, 7, al.; cf. W. p. 24].*

536 ἀπ-αρχή, -ῆς, ἡ, (fr. ἀπάρχομαι: a. to offer firstlings or first-fruits; b. to take away the first-fruits; cf. ἀπό in ἀποδεκατόω), in Sept. generally equiv. to רֵאשִׁית; the first-fruits of the productions of the earth (both those in a natural state and those prepared for use by hand), which were offered to God; cf. Win. R W B. s. v. Erstlinge, [BB.DD. s. v. First-fruits]: ἡ ἀπαρχή sc. τοῦ φυράματος, the first portion of the dough, from which sacred loaves were to be prepared (Num. xv. 19–21), Ro. xi. 16. Hence, in a transferred use, employed **a.** of persons consecrated to God, leading the rest in time: ἀπ. τῆς Ἀχαΐας the first person in Achaia to enroll himself as a Christian, 1 Co. xvi. 15; with εἰς Χριστόν added, Ro. xvi. 5; with a reference to the moral creation effected by Christianity all the Christians of that age are called ἀπαρχή τις (a kind of first-fruits) τῶν τοῦ θεοῦ κτισμάτων, Jas. i. 18 (see Huther ad loc.), [noteworthy is εἵλατο ὑμᾶς ὁ θεὸς ἀπαρχήν etc. as first-fruits] 2 Th. ii. 13 L Tr mrg. WH mrg.; Christ is called ἀπ. τῶν κεκοιμημένων the first one recalled to life of them that have fallen asleep, 1 Co. xv. 20, 23 (here the phrase seems also to signify that by his case the future resurrection of Christians is guaranteed; because the first-fruits forerun and are, as it were, a pledge and promise of the rest of the harvest). **b.** of persons superior in excellence of others of the same class: so in Rev. xiv. 4 of a certain class of Christians sacred and dear to God and Christ beyond all others, (Schol. ad Eur. Or. 96 ἀπαρχὴ ἐλέγετο οὐ μόνον τὸ πρῶτον τῇ τάξει, ἀλλὰ καὶ τὸ πρῶτον τῇ τιμῇ). **c.** οἱ ἔχοντες τὴν ἀπ. τοῦ πνεύματος who have the first-fruits of future blessings in the Spirit (τοῦ πν. is gen. of apposition), Ro. viii. 23; cf. what Winer § 59, 8 a. says in opposition to those [e. g. Meyer, but see Weiss in ed. 6] who take τοῦ πν. as a partitive gen., so that οἱ ἔχ. τ. ἀπ. τοῦ πν. are distinguished from the great multitude who will receive the Spirit subsequently. (In Grk. writ. fr. [Soph.,] Hdt. down.) *

537 ἅ-πας, -ασα, -αν, (fr. ἅμα [or rather ἁ (Skr. sa; cf. a copulative), see Curtius § 598; Vaniček p. 972] and πᾶς; stronger than the simple πᾶς), [fr. Hom. down]; quite all, the whole, all together, all; it is either placed before a subst. having the art., as Lk. iii. 21; viii. 37; xix. 37; or placed after, as Mk. xvi. 15 (εἰς τὸν κόσμον ἅπαντα into all parts of the world); Lk. iv. 6 (this dominion whole-ly i. e. all parts of this dominion which you see); xix. 48. used absolutely, — in the masc., as Mt. xxiv. 39; Lk. iii. 16 [T WH Tr mrg. πᾶσιν]; [iv. 40 WH txt. Tr mrg.]; v. 26; ix. 15 [WH mrg. πάντας]; Mk. xi. 32 [Lchm. πάντες]; Jas. iii. 2; — in the neut., as Mt. xxviii. 11; Lk. v. 28 [R G]; Acts ii. 44; iv. 32 [L WH Tr mrg. πάντα]; x. 8; xi. 10; Eph. vi. 13; once in John viz. iv. 25 T Tr WH; [ἅπαντες οὗτοι, Acts ii. 7 L T; ἅπαντες ὑμεῖς, Gal. iii. 28 T Tr; cf. πᾶς, II. 1 fin. Rarely used by Paul; most frequently by Luke. On its occurrence, cf. Alford, Grk. Test. vol. ii. Proleg. p. 81; Ellicott on 1 Tim. i. 16].

(537α):
see 782

ἀπ-ασπάζομαι: 1 aor. ἀπησπασάμην; to salute on leaving, bid farewell, take leave of: τινά, Acts xxi. 6 L T Tr WH. (Himer. eclog. ex Phot. 11, p. 194.)*

538

ἀπατάω,- ῶ; 1 aor. pass. ἠπατήθην; (ἀπάτη); fr. Hom. down; to cheat, deceive, beguile: τὴν καρδίαν αὐτοῦ [R T Tr WH mrg., αὑτ. G, ἑαυτ. L WH txt.], Jas. i. 26; τινά τινι, one with a thing, Eph. v. 6; pass. 1 Tim. ii. 14 (where L T Tr WH ἐξαπατηθεῖσα), cf. Gen. iii. 13. [COMP.: ἐξ-απατάω.]*

539

ἀπάτη, -ης, ἡ, [fr. Hom. down], deceit, deceitfulness: Col. ii. 8; τοῦ πλούτου, Mt. xiii. 22; Mk. iv. 19; τῆς ἀδικίας, 2 Th. ii. 10; τῆς ἁμαρτίας, Heb. iii. 13; αἱ ἐπιθυμίαι τῆς ἀπάτης the lusts excited by deceit, i. e. by deceitful influences seducing to sin, Eph. iv. 22, (others, 'deceitful lusts'; but cf. Mey. ad loc.). Plur. ἀπάται: 2 Pet. ii. 13 (where L Tr txt. WH mrg. ἐν ἀγάπαις), by a paragram (or verbal play) applied to the agapae or love-feasts (cf. ἀγάπη, 2), because these were transformed by base men into seductive revels.*

540

ἀπάτωρ, -ορος, ὁ, ἡ, (πατήρ), a word which has almost the same variety of senses as ἀμήτωρ, q. v.; [fr. Soph. down]; [without father i. e.] whose father is not recorded in the genealogies: Heb. vii. 3.*

541

ἀπ-αύγασμα, -τος, τό, (fr. ἀπαυγάζω to emit brightness, and this fr. αὐγή brightness; cf. ἀποσκίασμα, ἀπείκασμα, ἀπεικόνισμα, ἀπήχημα), reflected brightness: Christ is called in Heb. i. 3 ἀπαύγ. τῆς δόξης τοῦ θεοῦ, inasmuch as he perfectly reflects•the majesty of God; so that the same thing is declared here of Christ metaphysically, which he says of himself in an ethical sense in Jn. xii. 45 (xiv. 9): ὁ θεωρῶν ἐμὲ θεωρεῖ τὸν πέμψαντά με. (Sap. vii. 26; Philo, mund. opif. § 51; plant. Noë § 12; de concup. § 11; and often in eccl. writ.; see more fully in Grimm on Sap. l. c., p. 161 sq.) [Some interpreters still adhere to the signif. effulgence or radiance (as distinguished from refulgence or reflection), see Kurtz ad loc.; Soph. Lex. s. v.; Cremer s. v.]*

see
542 St.

ἀπ-εῖδον (ἀπό and εἶδον, 2 aor. of obsol. εἴδω), serves as 2 aor. of ἀφοράω, (cf. Germ. absehen); 1. to look away from one thing and at another. 2. to look at from somewhere, either from a distance or from a certain present condition of things; to perceive: ὡς ἂν ἀπίδω (L T Tr WH ἀφίδω [see ἀφεῖδον]) τὰ περὶ ἐμέ as soon as I shall have seen what issue my affairs will have [A. V.

how it will go with me], Phil. ii. 23. (In Sept., Jon. iv. 5, etc.)*

ἀπείθεια [WH -θία, exc. in Heb. as below (see I, ι)], -ας, ἡ, (ἀπειθής), disobedience, (Jerome, inobedientia), obstinacy, and in the N. T. particularly obstinate opposition to the divine will: Ro. xi. 30, 32; Heb. iv. 6, 11; υἱοὶ τ. ἀπειθείας, those who are animated by this obstinacy (see υἱός, 2), used of the Gentiles: Eph. ii. 2; v. 6; Col. iii. 6 [R G L br.]. (Xen. mem. 3, 5, 5; Plut., al.)*

543

ἀπειθέω, -ῶ; impf. ἠπείθουν; 1 aor. ἠπείθησα; to be ἀπειθής (q. v.); not to allow one's self to be persuaded; not to comply with; a. to refuse or withhold belief (in Christ, in the gospel; opp. to πιστεύω): τῷ υἱῷ, Jn. iii. 36; τῷ λόγῳ, 1 Pet. ii. 8; iii. 1; absol. of those who reject the gospel, [R. V. to be disobedient; cf. b.]: Acts xiv. 2; xvii. 5 [Rec.]; xix. 9; Ro. xv. 31; 1 Pet. ii. 7 (T Tr WH ἀπιστοῦσιν). b. to refuse belief and obedience: with dat. of thing or pers., Ro. ii. 8 (τῇ ἀληθείᾳ); xi. 30 sq. (τῷ θεῷ); 1 Pet. iv. 17; absol., Ro. x. 21 (Is. lxv. 2); Heb. iii. 18; xi. 31; 1 Pet. iii. 20. (In Sept. com. equiv. to מָרָה, סָרַר; in Grk. writ. often fr. Aeschyl. Ag. 1049 down; in Hom. et al. ἀπιθεῖν.)*

544

ἀπειθής, -ές, gen. -οῦς, (πείθομαι), impersuasible, uncompliant, contumacious, [A. V. disobedient]: absol. Lk. i. 17; Tit. i. 16; iii. 3; 2 Tim. iii. 2; Ro. i. 30; Acts xxvi. 19. (Deut. xxi. 18; Num. xx. 10; Is. xxx. 9; Zech. vii. 12; in Grk. writ. fr. Thuc. down; [in Theogn. 1235 actively not persuasive].)*

545

ἀπειλέω, -ῶ; impf. ἠπείλουν; 1 aor. mid. ἠπειλησάμην; to threaten, menace: 1 Pet. ii. 23; in mid., acc. to later Grk. usage [App. bell. civ. 3, 29]; Polyaen. 7, 35, 2), actively [B. 54 (47)]: Acts iv. 17 (ἀπειλῇ [L T Tr WH om.] ἀπειλείσθαι, with dat. of pers. foll. by μή with inf., with sternest threats to forbid one to etc., W. § 54, 3; [B. 183 (159)]). (From Hom. down.) [COMP.: προσαπειλέω.]*

546

ἀπειλή, -ῆς, ἡ, a threatening, threat: Acts iv. 17 R G (cf. ἀπειλέω), 29; ix. 1; Eph. vi. 9. (From Hom. down.)*

547

ἄπ-ειμι, (εἰμί to be); [fr. Hom. down]; to be away, be absent: 1 Co. v. 3; 2 Co. x. 1, 11; xiii. 2, 10; Col. ii. 5; Phil. i. 27; [in all cases exc. Col. l. c. opp. to πάρειμι].*

548

ἄπ-ειμι; impf. 3 pers. plur. ἀπῄεσαν; (εἶμι to go); [fr. Hom. down]; to go away, depart: Acts xvii. 10.*

549

ἀπ-εῖπον (εἶπον, 2 aor. fr. obsol. ἔπω); 1. to speak out, set forth, declare, (Hom. Il. 7, 416 ἀγγελίην ἀπέειπεν, 9, 309 τὸν μῦθον ἀποειπεῖν). 2. to forbid: 1 K. xi. 2, and in Attic writ. 3. to give up, renounce: with acc. of the thing, Job x. 3 (for מָאַס), and often in Grk. writ. fr. Hom. down. In the same sense 1 aor. mid. ἀπειπάμην, 2 Co. iv. 2 [see WH. App. p. 164], (cf. αἰσχύνη, 1); so too in Hdt. 1, 59; 5, 56; 7, 14, [etc.], and the later writ. fr. Polyb. down.*

see
550 St.

ἀπείραστος, -ον, (πειράζω), as well untempted as untemptable: ἀπείραστος κακῶν that cannot be tempted by evil, not liable to temptation to sin, Jas. i. 13; cf. the full remarks on this pass. in W. § 30, 4 [cf. § 16, 3 α.; B. 170 (148)]. (Joseph. b. j. 5, 9, 3; 7, 8, 1, and eccl. writ. The Greeks said ἀπείρατος, fr. πειράω.)*

551

552 ἄπειρος, -ον, (πεῖρα trial, experience), *inexperienced in, without experience of*, with gen. of the thing (as in Grk. writ.) : Heb. v. 13. [(Pind. and Hdt. down.)] *

553 ἀπ-εκ-δέχομαι ; [impf. ἀπεξεδεχόμην]; *assiduously and patiently to wait for*, [cf. Eng. wait it out] : absol., 1 Pet. iii. 20 (Rec. ἐκδέχομαι) ; τί, Ro. viii. 19, 23, 25 ; 1 Co. i. 7 ; Gal. v. 5 (on this pass. cf. ἐλπίς sub fin.) ; with the acc. of a pers., Christ in his return from heaven : Phil. iii. 20 ; Heb. ix. 28. Cf. C. F. A. Fritzsche in *Fritzschiorum Opuscc.* p. 155 sq. ; *Win.* De verb. comp. etc. Pt. iv. p. 14 ; [Ellic. on Gal. l. c.]. (Scarcely found out of the N. T. ; Heliod. Aeth. 2, 35 ; 7, 23.)*

554 ἀπ-εκ-δύομαι : 1 aor. ἀπεκδυσάμην ; **1.** *wholly to put off from one's self* (ἀπό denoting separation fr. what is put off) : τὸν παλαιὸν ἄνθρωπον, Col. iii. 9. **2.** *wholly to strip off for one's self* (for one's own advantage), *despoil, disarm* : τινά, Col. ii. 15. Cf. *Win.* De verb. comp. etc. Pt. iv. p. 14 sq., [esp. Bp. Lghtft. on Col. ii. 15]. (Joseph. antt. 6, 14, 2 ἀπεκδὺς [but ed. Bekk. μετεκδὺς] τὴν βασιλικὴν ἐσθῆτα.)*

555 ἀπ-έκ-δυσις, -εως, ἡ, (ἀπεκδύομαι, q. v.), *a putting off, laying aside* : Col. ii. 11. (Not found in Grk. writ.) *

556 ἀπ-ελαύνω : 1 aor. ἀπήλασα ; *to drive away, drive off* : Acts xviii. 16. (Com. in Grk. writ.)*

557 ἀπ-ελεγμός, -οῦ, ὁ, (ἀπελέγχω to convict, expose, refute ; ἐλεγμός conviction, refutation, in Sept. for ἔλεγξις), *censure, repudiation of a thing shown to be worthless* : ἐλθεῖν εἰς ἀπελεγμόν to be proved to be worthless, to be disesteemed, come into contempt [R. V. *disrepute*], Acts xix. 27. (Not used by prof. auth.)*

558 ἀπ-ελεύθερος, -ου, ὁ, ἡ, *a manumitted slave, a freedman*, (ἀπό, cf. Germ. *los*, [set free f r o m bondage]) : τοῦ κυρίου, presented with (spiritual) freedom by the Lord, 1 Co. vii. 22. (In Grk. writ. fr. Xen. and Plat. down.)*

559 Ἀπελλῆς [better -λλῆς (so all edd.) ; see Chandler §§ 59, 60], -οῦ, ὁ, *Apelles*, the prop. name of a certain Christian : Ro. xvi. 10. [Cf. Bp. Lghtft. on Philip. p. 174.]*

560 ἀπ-ελπίζω (Lchm. ἀφελπίζω, [cf. gram. reff. s. v. ἀφεῖδον]) ; *to despair* [W. 24] : μηδὲν ἀπελπίζοντες *nothing despairing* sc. of the hoped-for recompense from God the requiter, Lk. vi. 35, [T WH mrg. μηδένα ἀπελπ.; if this reading is to be tolerated it may be rendered *despairing of no one*, or even *causing no one to despair* (cf. the Jerus. Syriac). Tdf. himself seems half inclined to take μηδένα as neut. plur., a form thought to be not wholly unprecedented ; cf. *Steph.* Thesaur. v. col. 962]. (Is. xxix. 19 ; 2 Macc. ix. 18 ; Sir. xxii. 21 ; [xxvii. 21 ; Judith ix. 11]; often in Polyb. and Diod. [cf. *Soph.* Lex. s. v.].)*

561 ἀπ-έναντι, adv., with gen. [B. 319 (273)]; **1.** *over against, opposite* : τοῦ τάφου, Mt. xxvii. 61 ; [τοῦ γαζοφυλακίου, Mk. xii. 41 Tr txt. WH mrg.]. **2.** *in sight of, before* : Mt. xxi. 2 R G ; xxvii. 24 (here L Tr WH txt. κατέναντι) ; Acts iii. 16 ; Ro. iii. 18 (Ps. xxxv. (xxxvi.) 2). **3.** *in opposition to, against* : τῶν δογμάτων Καίσαρος, Acts xvii. 7. (Common in Sept. and Apocr. ; Polyb. 1, 86, 3.)*

562 ἀπέραντος, -ον, (περαίνω to go through, finish ; cf. ἀμά-

ραντος), *that cannot be passed through, boundless, endless* : γενεαλογίαι, protracted interminably, 1 Tim. i. 4. (Job xxxvi. 26 ; 3 Macc. ii. 9 ; in Grk. writ. fr. Pind. down.)*

563 ἀπερισπάστως, adv., (περισπάω, q. v.), *without distraction, without solicitude* : 1 Co. vii. 35. (The adjective occurs in Sap. xvi. 11 ; Sir. xli. 1 ; often in Polyb. [the adv. in 2, 20, 10 ; 4, 18, 6 ; 12, 28, 4 ; cf. W. 463 (431)] and Plut.) *

564 ἀ-περί-τμητος, -ον, (περιτέμνω), *uncircumcised* ; metaph. ἀπερίτμητοι τῇ καρδίᾳ (Jer. ix. 26 ; Ezek. xliv. 7) καὶ τ. ὠσί (Jer. vi. 10) whose heart and ears are covered, i. e. whose soul and senses are closed to divine admonitions, *obdurate*, Acts vii. 51. (Often in Sept. for עָרֵל ; 1 Macc. i. 48 ; ii. 46 ; [Philo de migr. Abr. § 39] ; Plut. am. prol. 3.)*

565 ἀπ-έρχομαι ; fut. ἀπελεύσομαι (Mt. xxv. 46 ; Ro. xv. 28 ; W. 86 (82)) ; 2 aor. ἀπῆλθον (ἀπῆλθα in Rev. x. 9 [where R G Tr -θον], ἀπῆλθαν L T Tr WH in Mt. xxii. 22 ; Rev. xxi. 1, 4 [(but here WH txt. only), etc., and WH in Lk. xxiv. 24]; cf. W. § 13, 1 ; Mullach p. 17 sq. [226] ; B. 39 (34) ; [*Soph.* Lex. p. 38 ; *Tdf.* Proleg. p. 123 ; *WH.* App. p. 164 sq. ; *Kuenen and Cobet*, N. T. p. lxiv.; *Scrivener*, Introd. p. 563 ; Collation, etc., p. liv. sq.]) ; pf. ἀπελήλυθα (Jas. i. 24) ; plpf. ἀπεληλύθειν (Jn. iv. 8) ; [fr. Hom. down] ; *to go away* (fr. a place), *to depart* ; **1.** *properly*, **a.** absol.: Mt. xiii. 25 ; xix. 22 ; Mk. v. 20 ; Lk. viii. 39 ; xvii. 23 ; Jn. xvi. 7, etc. Ptcp. ἀπελθών with indic. or subj. of other verbs in past time *to go* (away) and etc.: Mt. xiii. 28, 46 ; xviii. 30 ; xxv. 18, 25 ; xxvi. 36 ; xxvii. 5 ; Mk. vi. 27 (28), 37 ; Lk. v. 14. **b.** with specification of the place into which, or of the person to whom or from whom one departs : εἰς with acc. of place, Mt. v. 30 L T Tr WH ; xiv. 15 ; xvi. 21 ; xxii. 5 ; Mk. vi. 36 ; ix. 43 ; Jn. iv. 8 ; Ro. xv. 28, etc.; εἰς ὁδὸν ἐθνῶν, Mt. x. 5 ; εἰς τὸ πέραν, Mt. viii. 18 ; Mk. viii. 13 ; [δι᾽ ὑμῶν εἰς Μακεδ. 2 Co. i. 16 Lchm. txt.] ; ἐπί with acc. of place, Lk. [xxiii. 33 R G T] ; xxiv. 24 ; ἐπί with acc. of the business which one goes to attend to : ἐπί (the true reading for R G εἰς) τὴν ἐμπορίαν αὐτοῦ, Mt. xxii. 5 ; ἐκεῖ, Mt. ii. 22 ; ἔξω with gen., Acts iv. 15 ; πρός τινα, Mt. xiv. 25 [Rec.] ; Rev. x. 9 ; ἀπό τινος, Lk. i. 38 ; viii. 37. Hebraistically (cf. הָלַךְ אַחֲרֵי) ἀπέρχ. ὀπίσω τινός *to go away in order to follow any one, go after him* figuratively, i. e. *to follow his party, follow him as a leader* : Mk. i. 20 ; Jn. xii. 19 ; in the same sense ἀπέρχ. πρός τινα, Jn. vi. 68 ; Xen. an. 1, 9, 16 (29) ; used also of those who seek any one for vile purposes, Jude 7. Lexicographers (following Suidas, ᾽ἀπέλθη· ἀντὶ τοῦ ἐπανέλθη᾽) incorrectly ascribe to ἀπέρχεσθαι also the idea of *returning, going back*, — misled by the fact that a going *away* is often at the same time a going *back*. But where this is the case, it is made evident either by the connection, as in Lk. vii. 24, or by some adjunct, as εἰς τὸν οἶκον αὐτοῦ, Mt. ix. 7 ; Mk. vii. 30, (οἴκαδε, Xen. Cyr. 1, 3, 6) ; πρὸς ἑαυτόν [Treg. πρ. αὐτόν] home, Lk. xxiv. 12 [R G, but L Tr br. TWH reject the vs.]. Jn. xx. 10 [here T Tr πρὸς αὐτούς, WH π. αὐτ. (see αὐτοῦ)] ; εἰς τὰ ὀπίσω, Jn. vi. 66 (to return home) ; xviii. 6 (to draw back, retreat).   **2.** trop.: of departing evils and sufferings, Mk. i. 42; Lk. v. 13 (ἡ λέπρα ἀπῆλθεν ἀπ' αὐτοῦ); Rev. ix. 12; xi. 14; of good things taken away from one, Rev. xviii. 14 [R G]; of an evanescent state of things, Rev. xxi. 1 (Rec. παρῆλθε), 4; of a report going forth or spread εἰς, Mt. iv. 24 [Treg. mrg. ἐξῆλθεν].

566.
567.
& 568

ἀπ-έχω; [impf. ἀπεῖχον Mt. xiv. 24 Tr txt. WH txt.; pres. mid. ἀπέχομαι];   **1.** trans. **a.** *to hold back, keep off, prevent,* (Hom. Il. 1, 97 [Zenod.]; 6, 96; Plat. Crat. c. 23 p. 407 b.).   **b.** *to have wholly* or *in full, to have received* (what one had a right to expect or demand; cf. ἀποδιδόναι, ἀπολαμβάνειν, [*Win.* De verb. comp. etc. Pt. iv. p. 8; Gram. 275 (258); B. 203 (176); acc. to Bp. Lghtft. (on Phil. iv. 18) ἀπό denotes correspondence, i. e. of the contents to the capacity, of the possession to the desire, etc.]): τινά, Philem. 15; μισθόν, Mt. vi. 2, 5, 16; παράκλησιν, Lk. vi. 24; πάντα, Phil. iv. 18; (often so in Grk. writ. [cf. Bp. Lghtft. on Phil. l. c.]).   Hence **c.** ἀπέχει, impers., *it is enough, sufficient*: Mk. xiv. 41, where the explanation is 'ye have slept now long enough'; so that Christ takes away the permission, just given to his disciples, of sleeping longer; cf. Meyer ad loc.; (in the same sense in (Pseudo-) Anacr. in Odar. (15) 28, 33; Cyril Alex. on Hag. ii. 9 [but the true meaning here seems to be ἀπέχω, see P. E. Pusey's ed. Oxon. 1868]).   **2.** intrans. *to be away, absent, distant,* [B. 144 (126)]: absol., Lk. xv. 20; ἀπό, Lk. vii. 6; xxiv. 13; Mt. [xiv. 24 Tr txt. WH txt.]; xv. 8; Mk. vii. 6, (Is. xxix. 13).   **3.** Mid. *to hold one's self off, abstain*: ἀπό τινος, from any thing, Acts xv. 20 [R G]; 1 Th. iv. 3; v. 22, (Job i. 1; ii. 3; Ezek. viii. 6); τινός, Acts xv. 29; 1 Tim. iv. 3; 1 Pet. ii. 11.   (So in Grk. writ. fr. Hom. down.) *

569

ἀπιστέω, -ῶ; [impf. ἠπίστουν]; 1 aor. ἠπίστησα; (ἄπιστος);   **1.** *to betray a trust, be unfaithful*: 2 Tim. ii. 13 (opp. to πιστὸς μένει); Ro. iii. 3; [al. deny this sense in the N. T.; cf. Morison or Mey. on Rom. l. c.; Ellic. on 2 Tim. l. c.].   **2.** *to have no belief, disbelieve*: in the news of Christ's resurrection, Mk. xvi. 11; Lk. xxiv. 41; with dat. of pers., Lk. xxiv. 11; in the tidings concerning Jesus the Messiah, Mk. xvi. 16 (opp. to πιστεύω), [so 1 Pet. ii. 7 T Tr WH]; Acts xxviii. 24.   (In Grk. writ. fr. Hom. down.)*

570

ἀπιστία, -ας, ἡ, (fr. ἄπιστος), *want of faith and trust*;   **1.** *unfaithfulness, faithlessness,* (of persons betraying a trust): Ro. iii. 3 [cf. reff. s. v. ἀπιστέω, 1].   **2.** *want of faith, unbelief*: shown in withholding belief in the divine power, Mk. xvi. 14, or in the power and promises of God, Ro. iv. 20; Heb. iii. 19; in the divine mission of Jesus, Mt. xiii. 58; Mk. vi. 6; by opposition to the gospel, 1 Tim. i. 13; with the added notion of obstinacy, Ro. xi. 20, 23; Heb. iii. 12. contextually, *weakness of faith*: Mt. xvii. 20 (where L T Tr WH ὀλιγοπιστίαν]; Mk. ix. 24.   (In Grk. writ. fr. Hes. and Hdt. down.)*

571

ἄ-πιστος, -ον, (πιστός), [fr. Hom. down], *without faith* or *trust*;   **1.** *unfaithful, faithless,* (not to be trusted, perfidious): Lk. xii. 46; Rev. xxi. 8.   **2.** *incredible,* of things: Acts xxvi. 8; (Xen. Hiero 1, 9; symp. 4,

49; Cyr. 3, 1, 26; Plat. Phaedr. 245 c.; Joseph. antt. 6, 10, 2, etc.).   **3.** *unbelieving, incredulous*: of Thomas disbelieving the news of the resurrection of Jesus, Jn. xx. 27; of those who refuse belief in the gospel, 1 Co. vi. 6; vii. 12–15; x. 27; xiv. 22 sqq.; [1 Tim. v. 8]; with the added idea of impiety and wickedness, 2 Co. iv. 4; vi. 14 sq. of those among the Christians themselves who reject the true faith, Tit. i. 15. *without trust* (in God), Mt. xvii. 17; Mk. ix. 19; Lk. ix. 41.*

572

ἁπλότης, -ητος, ἡ, *singleness, simplicity, sincerity, mental honesty*; the virtue of one who is free from pretence and dissimulation, (so in Grk. writ. fr. Xen. Cyr. 1, 4, 3; Hell. 6, 1, 18, down): ἐν ἁπλότητι (L T Tr WH ἁγιότητι) καὶ εἰλικρινείᾳ θεοῦ i. e. infused by God through the Spirit [W. § 36, 3 b.], 2 Co. i. 12; ἐν ἁπλ. τῆς καρδίας (שֶׁר לֵבָב, 1 Chr. xxix. 17), Col. iii. 22; Eph. vi. 5, (Sap. i. 1); εἰς Χριστόν, sincerity of mind towards Christ, i. e. single-hearted faith in Christ, as opp. to false wisdom in matters pertaining to Christianity, 2 Co. xi. 3; ἐν ἁπλότητι in simplicity, i. e. without self-seeking, Ro. xii. 8.   *openness of heart manifesting itself by benefactions, liberality,* [Joseph. antt. 7, 13, 4; but in opposition see Fritzsche on Rom. vol. iii. 62 sq.]: 2 Co. viii. 2; ix. 11, 13 (τῆς κοινωνίας, manifested by fellowship).   Cf. *Kling* s. v. 'Einfalt' in Herzog iii. p. 723 sq.*

573

ἁπλοῦς, -ῆ, -οῦν, (contr. fr. -όος, -όη, -όον), [fr. Aeschyl. down], *simple, single,* (in which there is nothing complicated or confused; without folds, [cf. Trench § lvi.]); *whole*; of the eye, *good,* fulfilling its office, *sound*: Mt. vi. 22; Lk. xi. 34, — [al. contend that the moral sense of the word is the only sense lexically warranted; cf. Test. xii. Patr. test. Isach. § 3 οὐ κατελάλησά τινος, etc. πορευόμενος ἐν ἁπλότητι ὀφθαλμῶν, ibid. § 4 πάντα ὁρᾷ ἐν ἁπλότητι, μὴ ἐπιδεχόμενος ὀφθαλμοῖς πονηρίας ἀπὸ τῆς πλάνης τοῦ κόσμου; yet cf. Fritzsche on Ro. xii. 8].*

574

ἁπλῶς, adv., [fr. Aeschyl. down], *simply, openly, frankly, sincerely*: Jas. i. 5 (led solely by his desire to bless).*

575

ἀπό, [fr. Hom. down], preposition with the Genitive, (Lat. *a, ab, abs,* Germ. *von, ab, weg,* [cf. Eng. *of, off*]), *from,* signifying now Separation, now Origin.   On its use in the N. T., in which the influence of the Hebr. מִן is traceable, cf. W. 364 sq. (342), 369 (346) sqq.; B. 321 (276) sqq.   [On the neglect of elision before words beginning with a vowel see *Tdf.* Proleg. p. 94; cf. W. § 5, 1 a.; B. p. 10 sq.; *WH.* App. p. 146.]   In order to avoid repetition we forbear to cite all the examples, but refer the reader to the several verbs followed by this preposition.   ἀπό, then, is used

I. of Separation; and   **1.** of local separation, after verbs of motion fr. a place, (of *departing, fleeing, removing, expelling, throwing,* etc., see αἴρω, ἀπέρχομαι, ἀποτινάσσω, ἀποχωρέω, ἀφίστημι, φεύγω, etc.): ἀπεσπάσθη ἀπ' αὐτῶν, Lk. xxii. 41; βάλε ἀπὸ σοῦ, Mt. v. 29 sq.; ἐκβάλω τὸ κάρφος ἀπὸ [L T Tr WH ἐκ] τοῦ ὀφθαλμοῦ, Mt. vii. 4; ἀφ' [L WH Tr txt. παρ' (q. v. I. a.)] ἧς ἐκβεβλήκει δαιμόνια, Mk. xvi. 9; καθεῖλε ἀπὸ θρόνων, Lk. i. 52.   **2.** of the separation of a part from the whole; where of a whole some part is taken: ἀπὸ τοῦ ἱματίου, Mt. ix. 16;

ἀπὸ μελισσίου κηρίου, Lk. xxiv. 42 [R G, but Tr br. the clause]; ἀπὸ τῶν ὀψαρίων, Jn. xxi. 10; τὰ ἀπὸ τοῦ πλοίου fragments of the ship, Acts xxvii. 44; ἐνοσφίσατο ἀπὸ τῆς τιμῆς, Acts v. 2; ἐκχεῶ ἀπὸ τοῦ πνεύματος, Acts ii. 17; ἐκλεξάμενος ἀπ' αὐτῶν, Lk. vi. 13; τίνα ἀπὸ τῶν δύο, Mt. xxvii. 21; ὃν ἐτιμήσαντο ἀπὸ υἱῶν Ἰσραήλ, sc. τινές [R. V. whom certain of the children of Israel did price (cf. τὶς, 2 c.); but al. refer this to II. 2 d. aa. fin. q. v.], Mt. xxvii. 9, (ἐξῆλθον ἀπὸ τῶν ἱερέων, sc. τινές, 1 Macc. vii. 33); after verbs of eating and drinking (usually joined in Grk. to the simple gen. of the thing [cf. B. 159 (139); W. 198 (186) sq.]): Mt. xv. 27; Mk. vii. 28; πίνειν ἀπό, Lk. xxii. 18 (elsewhere in the N. T. ἐκ). **3.** of any kind of separation of one thing from another by which the union or fellowship of the two is destroyed; **a.** after verbs of averting, loosening, liberating, ransoming, preserving: see ἀγοράζω, ἀπαλλάσσω, ἀποστρέφω, ἐλευθερόω, θεραπεύω, καθαρίζω, λούω, λυτρόω, λύω, ῥύομαι, σώζω, φυλάσσω, etc. **b.** after verbs of desisting, abstaining, avoiding, etc.: see ἀπέχω, παύω, καταπαύω, βλέπω, προσέχω, φυλάσσομαι, etc. **c.** after verbs of concealing and hindering: see κρύπτω, κωλύω, παρακαλύπτω. **d.** Concise constructions, [cf. esp. B. 322 (277)]: ἀνάθεμα ἀπὸ τοῦ Χριστοῦ, Ro. ix. 3 (see ἀνάθεμα sub fin.); λούειν ἀπὸ τῶν πληγῶν to wash away the blood from the stripes, Acts xvi. 33; μετανοεῖν ἀπὸ τῆς κακίας by repentance to turn away from wickedness, Acts viii. 22; ἀποθνήσκειν ἀπό τινος by death to be freed from a thing, Col. ii. 20; φθείρεσθαι ἀπὸ τῆς ἁπλότητος to be corrupted and thus led away from singleness of heart, 2 Co. xi. 3; εἰσακουσθεὶς ἀπὸ τ. εὐλαβείας heard and accordingly delivered from his fear, Heb. v. 7 (al. heard for i. e. on account of his godly fear [cf. II. 2 b. below]). **4.** of a state of separation, i. e. of distance; and **a.** of distance of Place,—of the local terminus from which: Mt. xxiii. 34; xxiv. 31, etc.; after μακράν, Mt. viii. 30; Mk. xii. 34; Jn. xxi. 8; after ἀπέχειν, see ἀπέχω, 2; ἀπὸ ἄνωθεν ἕως κάτω, Mk. xv. 38; ἀπὸ μακρόθεν, Mt. xxvii. 55, etc. [cf. B. 70 (62); W. § 65, 2]. Acc. to later Grk. usage it is put before nouns indicating local distance: Jn. xi. 18 (ἦν ἐγγὺς ὡς ἀπὸ σταδίων δεκαπέντε about fifteen furlongs off); Jn. xxi. 8; Rev. xiv. 20, (Diod. i. 51 ἐπάνω τῆς πόλεως ἀπὸ δέκα σχοίνων λίμνην ὤρυξε, [also 1, 97; 4, 56; 16, 46; 17, 112; 18, 40; 19, 25, etc.; cf. Soph. Lex. s. v. 5]: Joseph. b. j. 1, 3, 5 τοῦτο ἀφ' ἑξακοσίων σταδίων ἐντεῦθέν ἐστιν, Plut. Aem. Paul. c. 18, 5 ὥστε τοὺς πρώτους νεκροὺς ἀπὸ δυοῖν σταδίων καταπεσεῖν, vit. Oth. c. 11, 1 κατεστρατοπέδευσεν ἀπὸ πεντήκοντα σταδίων, vit. Philop. c. 4, 3 ἦν γὰρ ἀγρὸς αὐτῷ ἀπὸ σταδίων εἴκοσι τῆς πόλεως); cf. W. 557 (518) sq.; [B. 153 (133)]. **b.** of distance of Time,—of the temporal terminus from which, (Lat. inde a): ἀπὸ τῆς ὥρας ἐκείνης, Mt. ix. 22; xvii. 18; Jn. xix. 27; ἀπ' ἐκ τῆς ἡμέρας, Mt. xxii. 46; Jn. xi. 53; [ἀπὸ πρώτης ἡμέρας,] Acts xx. 18; Phil. i. 5 [L Tr Tr WH τῆς πρ. ἡμ.]; ἀφ' ἡμερῶν ἀρχαίων, Acts xv. 7; ἀπ' ἐτῶν, Lk. viii. 43; Ro. xv. 23; ἀπ' αἰῶνος and ἀπὸ τ. αἰώνων, Lk. i. 70, etc.; ἀπ' ἀρχῆς, Mt. xix. 4, 8, etc.; ἀπὸ καταβολῆς κόσμου, Mt. xiii. 35 [L T Tr WH om. κοσμ.], etc.; ἀπὸ κτίσεως

κόσμου, Ro. i. 20; ἀπὸ βρέφους from a child, 2 Tim. iii. 15; ἀπὸ τῆς παρθενίας, Lk. ii. 36; ἀφ' ἧς (sc. ἡμέρας) since, Lk. vii. 45; Acts xxiv. 11; 2 Pet. iii. 4; ἀφ' ἧς ἡμέρας, Col. i. 6, 9; ἀφ' οὗ equiv. to ἀπὸ τούτου ὅτε [cf. B. 82 (71); 105 (92)], Lk. xiii. 25; xxiv. 21; Rev. xvi. 18, (Hdt. 2, 44; and in Attic); ἀφ' οὗ after τρία ἔτη, Lk. xiii. 7 T Tr WH; ἀπὸ τοῦ νῦν from the present, henceforth, Lk. i. 48; v. 10; xii. 52; xxii. 69; Acts xviii. 6; 2 Co. v. 16; ἀπὸ τότε, Mt. iv. 17; xvi. 21; xxvi. 16; Lk. xvi. 16; ἀπὸ πέρυσι since last year, a year ago, 2 Co. viii. 10; ix. 2; ἀπὸ πρωΐ, Acts xxviii. 23; cf. W. 422 (393); [B. 320 (275)]; Lob. ad Phryn. pp. 47, 461. **c.** of distance of Order or Rank,—of the terminus from which in any succession of things or persons: ἀπὸ διετοῦς (sc. παιδός) καὶ κατωτέρω, Mt. ii. 16, (τοὺς Λευΐτας ἀπὸ εἰκοσαετοῦς καὶ ἐπάνω, Num. i. 20; 2 Esdr. iii. 8); ἀπὸ Ἀβραὰμ ἕως Δαυείδ, Mt. i. 17; ἀπὸ βδομος ἀπὸ Ἀδάμ, Jude 14; ἀπὸ μικροῦ ἕως μεγάλου, Acts viii. 10; Heb. viii. 11; ἄρχεσθαι ἀπὸ τινος, Mt. xx. 8; Lk. xxiii. 5; xxiv. 27; Jn. viii. 9; Acts viii. 35; x. 37.

II. of Origin; whether of local origin, the place whence; or of causal origin, the cause from which. **1.** of the Place whence anything is, comes, befalls, is taken; **a.** after verbs of coming; see ἔρχομαι, ἥκω, etc.: ἀπὸ [L Tr WH ἀπ'] ἀγορᾶς sc. ἐλθόντες, Mk. vii. 4; ἄγγελος ἀπ' (τοῦ) οὐρανοῦ, Lk. xxii. 43 [L br. WH reject the pass.]; τὸν ἀπ' οὐρανῶν sc. λαλοῦντα, Heb. xii. 25, etc.; of the country, province, town, village, from which any one has originated or proceeded [cf. W. 364 (342); B. 324 (279)]: Mt. ii. 1; iv. 25; Jn. i. 44 (45); xi. 1; μία ἀπὸ ὄρους Σινᾶ, Gal. iv. 24. Hence ὁ or οἱ ἀπό τινος a native of, a man of, some place: ὁ ἀπὸ Ναζαρέθ the Nazarene, Mt. xxi. 11; ὁ ἀπὸ Ἀριμαθαίας, Mk. xv. 43; Jn. xix. 38 [here G L Tr WH om. ὁ]; οἱ ἀπὸ Ἰόππης, Acts x. 23; οἱ ἀπὸ Ἰταλίας the Italians, Heb. xiii. 24 [cf. W. § 66, 6]. A great number of exx. fr. prof. writ. are given by Wieseler, Untersuch. üb. d. Hebräerbr. 2te Hälfte, p. 14 sq. **b.** of the party or society from which one has proceeded, i. e. a member of the sect or society, a disciple or votary of it: οἱ ἀπὸ τῆς ἐκκλησίας, Acts xii. 1; οἱ ἀπὸ τῆς αἱρέσεως τῶν Φαρισαίων, Acts xv. 5, (as in Grk. writ.: οἱ ἀπὸ τῆς Στοᾶς, οἱ ἀπὸ τῆς Ἀκαδημίας, etc.). **c.** of the material from which a thing is made: ἀπὸ τριχῶν καμήλου, Mt. iii. 4 [W. 370 (347); B. 324 (279)]. **d.** trop. of that from or by which a thing is known: ἀπὸ τῶν καρπῶν ἐπιγινώσκειν, Mt. vii. 16, 20 [here Lchm. ἐκ τ. κ. etc.] (Lys. in Andoc. § 6; Aeschin. adv. Tim. p. 69 ed. Reiske); μανθάνειν ἀπό τινος to learn from the example of any one, Mt. xi. 29; xxiv. 32; Mk. xiii. 28; but in Gal. iii. 2; Col. i. 7; Heb. v. 8, μανθ. ἀπό τινος means to learn from one's teaching or training [cf. B. 324 (279) c.; W. 372 (348)]. **e.** after verbs of seeking, inquiring, demanding: ἀπαιτεῖν, Lk. xii. 20 [Tr WH αἰτ.]; ζητεῖν, 1 Th. ii. 6 (alternating there with ἐκ [cf. W. § 50, 2]); ἐκζητεῖν, Lk. xi. 50 sq.; see αἰτέω. **2.** of causal origin, or the Cause; and **a.** of the material cause, so called, or of that which supplies the material for the maintenance of the action expressed by the verb: so γεμίζεσθαι, χορτάζεσθαι, πλουτεῖν, διακονεῖν ἀπό τινος, — see those verbs. b. of the cause on account of which anything is or is done, where commonly it can be rendered *for* (Lat. *prae*, Germ. *vor*): οὐκ ἠδύνατο ἀπὸ τοῦ ὄχλου, Lk. xix. 3; οὐκέτι ἴσχυσαν ἀπὸ τοῦ πλήθους, Jn. xxi. 6, (Judith ii. 20); ἀπὸ τ. δόξης τοῦ φωτός, Acts xxii. 11; [here many would bring in Heb. v. 7 (W. 371 (348); B. 322 (276)), see I. 3 d. above]. c. of the moving or impelling cause (Lat. *ex*, *prae*; Germ. *aus*, *vor*), *for*, *out of*: ἀπὸ τῆς χαρᾶς αὐτοῦ ὑπάγει, Mt. xiii. 44; ἀπὸ τοῦ φόβου *for fear*, Mt. xiv. 26; xxviii. 4; Lk. xxi. 26. Hebraistically: φοβεῖσθαι ἀπό τινος (יָרֵא מִן), Mt. x. 28; Lk. xii. 4; φεύγειν ἀπό τινος (נוּס מִן), to flee for fear of one, Jn. x. 5; Mk. xiv. 52 (R G, but L Tr mrg. br. ἀπ’ αὐτῶν); Rev. ix. 6; cf. φεύγω and W. 223 (209 sq.). d. of the efficient cause, viz. of things from the force of which anything proceeds, and of persons from whose will, power, authority, command, favor, order, influence, direction, anything is to be sought; aa. in general: ἀπὸ τοῦ ὕπνου by force of the sleep, Acts xx. 9; ἀπὸ σοῦ σημεῖον, Mt. xii. 38; ἀπὸ δόξης εἰς δόξαν, 2 Co. iii. 18 (from the glory which we behold for ourselves [cf. W. 254 (238)] in a mirror, goes out a glory in which we share, cf. Meyer ad loc.); ἀπὸ κυρίου πνεύματος by the Spirit of the Lord [yet cf. B. 343 (295)], ibid.; ὄλεθρον ἀπὸ προσώπου τοῦ κυρίου destruction proceeding from the (incensed, wrathful) countenance of the Lord, 2 Th. i. 9 (on this passage, to be explained after Jer. iv. 26 Sept., cf. Ewald); on the other hand, ἀνάψυξις ἀπὸ προσώπου τ. κ. Acts iii. 20 (19); ἀπεκτάνθησαν ἀπὸ (Rec. ὑπό) τῶν πληγῶν, Rev. ix. 18. ἀφ’ ἑαυτοῦ, ἀφ’ ἑαυτῶν, ἀπ’ ἐμαυτοῦ, an expression esp. com. in John, *of himself* (*myself*, etc.), *from his own disposition* or *judgment*, as distinguished from another’s instruction, [cf. W. 372 (348)]: Lk. xii. 57; xxi. 30; Jn. v. 19, 30; xi. 51; xiv. 10; xvi. 13; xviii. 34 [L Tr WH ἀπὸ σεαυτ.]; 2 Co. iii. 5; x. 7 [T Tr WH ἐφ’ ἑ. (see ἐπί A. I. 1 c’.)]; *of one’s own will and motion*, as opp. to the command and authority of another: Jn. vii. 17 sq. 28; viii. 42; x. 18, (Num. xvi. 28); *by one’s own power* Jn. xv. 4; *by one’s power and on one’s own judgment*: Jn. viii. 28; exx. fr. prof. auth. are given in *Kypke*, Observ. i. p. 391. [Cf. εὐχὴν ἔχοντες ἀφ’ (al. ἐφ’ see ἐπί A. I. 1 f.) ἑαυτῶν, Acts xxi. 23 WH txt.] after verbs *of learning, knowing, receiving*, ἀπό is used of him to whom we are indebted for what we know, receive, possess, [cf.W. 370 (347) n., also De verb. comp. etc. Pt. ii. p.7 sq.; B. 324 (279); Mey. on 1 Co. xi. 23; per contra Bp. Lghtft. on Gal. i. 12]: ἀκούειν, Acts ix. 13; 1 Jn. i. 5; γινώσκειν, Mk. xv. 45; λαμβάνειν, Mt. xvii. 25 sq.; 1 Jn. ii. 27; iii. 22 L T Tr WH; ἔχειν, 1 Jn. iv. 21; 2 Co. iii. 3, etc.; παραλαμβάνειν, 1 Co. xi. 23; δέχεσθαι, Acts xxviii. 21; respecting μανθάνειν see above, II. 1 d.; λατρεύω τῷ θεῷ ἀπὸ προγόνων after the manner of the λατρεία received from my forefathers [cf. W. 372 (349); B. 322 (277)], 2 Tim. i. 3. γίνεταί μοι, 1 Co. i. 30; iv. 5; χάρις ἀπὸ θεοῦ or τοῦ θεοῦ, from God, the author, bestower, Ro. i. 7; 1 Co. i. 3; Gal. i. 3, and often; καὶ τοῦτο ἀπὸ θεοῦ, Phil. i. 28. ἀπόστολος ἀπό etc., constituted an apostle by authority

and commission, etc. [cf. W. 418 (390)], Gal. i. 1. after πάσχειν, Mt. xvi. 21; [akin to this, acc. to many, is Mt. xxvii. 9 ὃν ἐτιμήσαντο ἀπὸ τῶν υἱῶν Ἰσραήλ, R. V. mrg. *whom they priced on the part of the sons of Israel*; but see in I. 2 above]. bb. When ἀπό is used after passives (which is rare in the better Grk. auth., cf. Bnhdy. p. 222 sqq.; [B. 325 (280); W. 371 (347 sq.)]), the connection between the cause and the effect is conceived of as looser and more remote than that indicated by ὑπό, and may often be expressed by *on the part of* (Germ. *von Seiten*), [A. V. generally *of*]: ἀπὸ τοῦ θεοῦ ἀποδεδειγμένον approved (by miracles) according to God’s will and appointment, Acts ii. 22; ἀπὸ θεοῦ πειράζομαι the cause of my temptation is to be sought in God, Jas. i. 13; ἀπεστερημένος [T Tr WH ἀφυστερ.] ἀφ’ ὑμῶν by your fraud, Jas. v. 4; ἀποδοκιμάζεσθαι, Lk. xvii. 25; [ἐδικαιώθη ἡ σοφία ἀπὸ τῶν τέκνων, Lk. vii. 35 acc. to some; see δικαιόω, 2]; τόπον ἡτοιμασμένον ἀπὸ τοῦ θεοῦ by the will and direction of God, Rev. xii. 6; ὀχλούμενοι ἀπὸ (Rec. ὑπό, [see ὀχλέω]) πνευμάτων ἀκαθάρτ. Lk. vi. 18 (whose annoyance by diseases [(?) cf. vs. 17] proceeded from unclean spirits [A. V. vexed (troubled) *with* etc.]); ἀπὸ τ. σαρκὸς ἐσπιλωμένον by touching the flesh, Jude 23; [add Lk. i. 26 T Tr WH ἀπεστάλη ὁ ἄγγελος ἀπὸ (R G L ὑπό) τοῦ θεοῦ]. As in prof. auth. so also in the N. T. the Mss. sometimes vary between ἀπό and ὑπό: e. g. in Mk. viii. 31; [Lk. viii. 43]; Acts iv. 36; [x. 17, 33; xv. 4]; Ro. xiii. 1; [xv. 24]; Rev ix. 18; see W. 370 (347) sq.; B. 325 (280) sq.; [cf. *Vincent and Dickson*, Mod. Grk. 2d ed. App. § 41].

III. Phrases having a quasi-adverbial force, and indicating the manner or degree in which anything is done or occurs, are the following: ἀπὸ τ. καρδιῶν ὑμῶν from your hearts, i. e. willingly and sincerely, Mt. xviii. 35; ἀπὸ μέρους in part, 2 Co. i. 14; ii. 5; Ro. xi. 25; xv. 24; ἀπὸ μιᾶς sc. either φωνῆς *with one voice*, or γνώμης or ψυχῆς *with one consent, one mind*, Lk. xiv. 18 (cf. Kuinoel ad loc.; [W. 423 (394); 591 (549 sq.); yet see *Lob.* Paralip. p. 363]).

IV. The extraordinary construction ἀπὸ ὁ ὢν (for Rec. ἀπὸ τοῦ ὁ) καὶ ὁ ἦν καὶ ὁ ἐρχόμενος, Rev. i. 4, finds its explanation in the fact that the writer seems to have used the words ὁ ὢν κτλ. as an indeclinable noun, for the purpose of indicating the meaning of the proper name יהוה; cf. W. § 10, 2 fin.; [B. 50 (43)].

V. In composition ἀπό indicates separation, liberation, cessation, departure, as in ἀποβάλλω, ἀποκόπτω, ἀποκυλίω, ἀπολύω, ἀπολύτρωσις, ἀπαλγέω, ἀπέρχομαι; finishing and completion, as in ἀπαρτίζω, ἀποτελέω; refers to the pattern from which a copy is taken, as in ἀπογράφειν, ἀφομοιοῦν, etc.; or to him from whom the action proceeds, as in ἀποδείκνυμι, ἀποτολμάω, etc.

ἀπο-βαίνω: fut. ἀποβήσομαι; 2 aor. ἀπέβην; **1.** *to come down from*: a ship (so even in Hom.), ἀπό, Lk. v. 2 [Tr mrg. br. ἀπ’ αὐτῶν]; εἰς τὴν γῆν, Jn. xxi. 9. **2.** trop. *to turn out*, ‘*eventuate*,’ (so fr. Hdt. down): ἀποβήσεται ὑμῖν εἰς μαρτύριον *it will issue, turn out*, Lk. xxi. 13; εἰς σωτηρίαν, Phil. i. 19. (Job xiii. 16; Artem. oneir. 3, 66.) •

577   **ἀπο-βάλλω** : 2 aor. ἀπέβαλον; [fr. Hom. down]; *to throw off, cast away* : a garment, Mk. x. 50. trop. confidence, Heb. x. 35.*

578   **ἀπο-βλέπω** : [impf. ἀπέβλεπον]; *to turn the eyes away from other things and fix them on some one thing* ; *to look at attentively* : εἴς τι (often in Grk. writ.); trop. *to look with steadfast mental gaze* : εἰς τ. μισθαποδοσίαν, Heb. xi. 26 [W. § 66, 2 d.].*

579   **ἀπό-βλητος, -ον,** *thrown away, to be thrown away, rejected, despised, abominated* : as unclean, 1 Tim. iv. 4, (in Hos. ix. 3 Symm. equiv. to טָמֵא unclean; Hom. Il. 2, 361; 3, 65; Lcian., Plut.).*

580   **ἀπο-βολή, -ῆς, ἡ,** *a throwing away*;   **1.** *rejection, repudiation,* (ἀποβάλλεσθαι *to throw away from one's self, cast off, repudiate*): Ro. xi. 15 (opp. to πρόσλημψις αὐτῶν, objec. gen.).   **2.** *a losing, loss,* (fr. ἀποβάλλω in the sense of *lose*): Acts xxvii. 22 ἀποβολὴ ψυχῆς οὐδεμία ἔσται ἐξ ὑμῶν no one of you shall lose his life [W. § 67, 1 e.]. (Plat., Plut., al.)*

see 581 St.   **ἀπο-γίνομαι** : [2 aor. ἀπεγενόμην];   **1.** *to be removed from, depart.*   **2.** *to die,* (often so in Grk. writ. fr. Hdt. down); hence trop. ἀπογ. τινί *to die to any thing* : ταῖς ἁμαρτίαις ἀπογενόμενοι i. e. become utterly alienated from our sins, 1 Pet. ii. 24 [W. § 52, 4, 1 d.; B. 178 (155)].*

582   **ἀπο-γραφή, -ῆς, ἡ,** (ἀπογράφω);   **a.** *a writing off, transcript* (from some pattern).   **b.** *an enrolment* (or *registration*) *in the public records of persons together with their property and income,* as the basis of an ἀποτίμησις (census or valuation), i. e. that it might appear how much tax should be levied upon each one: Lk. ii. 2; Acts v. 37; on the occurrence spoken of in both pass. cf. *Schürer,* Ntl. Zeitgesch. § 17, pp. 251, 262–286, and books there mentioned; [McClellan i. 392–399; B. D. s. v. Taxing].*

583   **ἀπο-γράφω** : Mid., [pres. inf. ἀπογράφεσθαι]; 1 aor. inf. ἀπογράψασθαι; [pf. pass. ptcp. ἀπογεγραμμένος; fr. Hdt. down];   **a.** *to write off, copy* (from some pattern).   **b.** *to enter in a register* or *records*; spec. *to enter in the public records the names of men, their property and income, to enroll,* (cf. ἀπογραφή, b.); mid. *to have one's self registered, to enroll one's self* [W. § 38, 3]: Lk. ii. 1, 3, 5; pass. οἱ ἐν οὐρανοῖς ἀπογεγραμμένοι those whose names are inscribed in the heavenly register, Heb. xii. 23 (the reference is to the dead already received into the heavenly city, the figure being drawn from civil communities on earth, whose citizens are enrolled in a register).*

584   **ἀπο-δείκνυμι** ; 1 aor. ἀπέδειξα; [pf. pass. ptcp. ἀποδεδειγμένος; (freq. in Grk. writ. fr. Pind. Nem. 6, 80 down];   **1.** prop. *to point away from one's self, to point out, show forth*; *to expose to view, exhibit,* (Hdt. 3, 122 and often) : 1 Co. iv. 9. Hence   **2.** *to declare* : τινά, *to show, prove what kind of a person any one is,* Acts ii. 22 (where cod. D gives the gloss [δεδοκιμ]ασμένον) ; 2 Th. ii. 4 [Lchm. mrg. ἀποδεικνύοντα]. *to prove by arguments, demonstrate* : Acts xxv. 7. Cf. *Win.* De verb. comp. etc. Pt. iv. p. 16 sq.*

585   **ἀπό-δειξις, -εως, ἡ,** (ἀποδείκνυμι, q. v.), [fr. Hdt. down] ;   **a.** *a making manifest, showing forth.*   **b.** *a demonstration, proof*: ἀπόδειξις πνεύματος καὶ δυνάμεως a proof by the Spirit and power of God, operating in me, and stirring in

the minds of my hearers the most holy emotions and thus persuading them, 1 Co. ii. 4 (contextually opposed to proof by rhetorical arts and philosophic arguments, — the sense in which the Greek philosophers use the word ; [see *Heinrici,* Corinthierbr. i. p. 103 sq.]).*

see 586   **ἀπο-δεκατεύω,** Lk. xviii. 12, for ἀποδεκατόω q. v.; [cf. WH. App. p. 171].

586   **ἀπο-δεκατόω, -ῶ,** inf. pres. ἀποδεκατοῖν, Heb. vii. 5 T Tr WH (cf. Delitzsch ad loc.; B. 44 (38); [Tdf.'s note ad loc.; WH. Intr. § 410]); (δεκατόω q. v.); a bibl. and eccl. word; Sept. for עָשַׂר; *to tithe* i. e.   **1.** with acc. of the thing, *to give, pay, a tenth of any thing* : Mt. xxiii. 23; Lk. xi. 42; xviii. 12 where T WH, after codd. א* B only, have adopted ἀποδεκατεύω, for which the simple δεκατεύω is more common in Grk. writ.; (Gen. xxviii. 22; Deut. xiv. 21 (22)).   **2.** τινά, *to exact, receive, a tenth from any one* : Heb. vii. 5; (1 S. viii. 15, 17). [B. D. s. v. Tithe.]*

587   **ἀπό-δεκτος** [so L T WH accent (and Rec. in 1 Tim. ii. 3); al. ἀποδεκτός, cf. *Lob.* Paralip. p. 498; Göttling p. 313 sq.; Chandler § 529 sq.], -ον, (see ἀποδέχομαι), a later word, *accepted, acceptable, agreeable* : 1 Tim. ii. 3; v. 4.*

588   **ἀπο-δέχομαι**; depon. mid.; impf. ἀπεδεχόμην; 1 aor. ἀπεδεξάμην; 1 aor. pass. ἀπεδέχθην; common in Grk. writ., esp. the Attic, fr. Hom. down; in the N. T. used only by Luke; *to accept what is offered from without* (ἀπό, cf. Lat. *ex cipio*), *to accept from, receive* : τινά, simply, *to give one access to one's self,* Lk. ix. 11 L T Tr WH; Acts xxviii. 30; with emphasis [cf. Tob. vii. 17 and Fritzsche ad loc.], *to receive with joy,* Lk. viii. 40; *to receive to hospitality,* Acts xxi. 17 L T Tr WH; *to grant one access to one's self in the capacity in which he wishes to be regarded,* e. g. as the messenger of others, Acts xv. 4 (L T Tr WH παρεδέχθησαν) ; as a Christian, Acts xviii. 27; metaph. τί, *to receive into the mind* with assent : *to approve,* Acts xxiv. 3; *to believe,* τὸν λόγον, Acts ii. 41; (so in Grk. writ. esp. Plato; cf. *Ast,* Lex. Plat. i. p. 232).*

589   **ἀποδημέω, -ῶ** ; 1 aor. ἀπεδήμησα; (ἀπόδημος, q. v.); *to go away to foreign parts, go abroad* : Mt. xxi. 33; xxv. 14 sq.; Mk. xii. 1; Lk. xv. 13 (εἰς χώραν); xx. 9. (In Grk. writ. fr. Hdt. down.)*

590   **ἀπό-δημος, -ον,** (fr. ἀπό and δῆμος the people), *away from one's people, gone abroad* : Mk. xiii. 34 [R. V. *sojourning in another country*]. [From Pind. down.]*

591   **ἀπο-δίδωμι,** pres. ptcp. neut. ἀποδιδοῦν (fr. the form -διδόω, Rev. xxii. 2, where T Tr WH mrg. -διδούς [see WH. App. p. 167]); impf. 3 pers. plur. ἀπεδίδουν (for the more com. ἀπεδίδοσαν, Acts iv. 33; cf. W. § 14, 1 c.) ; fut. ἀποδώσω ; 1 aor. ἀπέδωκα ; 2 aor. ἀπέδων, impv. ἀπόδος, subj. 3 pers. sing. ἀποδῷ and in 1 Thess. v. 15 Tdf. ἀποδοῖ (see δίδωμι), opt. 3 pers. sing. ἀποδώῃ [or rather, -δῴη; for -δῴη is a subjunctive form] (2 Tim. iv. 14, for ἀποδοίη, cf. W. § 14, 1 g.; B. 46 (40) ; yet L T Tr WH ἀποδώσει); Pass., 1 aor. inf. ἀποδοθῆναι; Mid., 2 aor. ἀπεδόμην, 3 pers. sing. ἀπέδοτο (Heb. xii. 16, where L WH ἀπέδετο; cf. B. 47 (41) ; Delitzsch on Hebr. p. 632 note ; [WH. App. p. 167]); a common verb in Grk. writ. fr. Hom. down, and the N. T. does not deviate at all from their use of it; prop. *to put away by giving, to give up, give over,* (Germ.

abgeben, [cf. *Win.* De verb. ccmp. etc. Pt. iv. p. 12 sq. who regards ἀπό as denoting to give *from* some reserved store, or to give *over* something which might have been retained, or to lay *off* some burden of debt or duty; cf. Cope on Aristot. rhet. 1, 1, 7]); **1.** *to deliver*, relinquish what is one's own: τὸ σῶμα τοῦ Ἰησοῦ, Mt. xxvii. 58; hence in mid. *to give away for one's own profit what is one's own*, i. e. *to sell* [W. 253 (238)]: τί, Acts v. 8; Heb. xii. 16; τινά, Acts vii. 9, (often in this sense in Grk. writ., esp. the Attic, fr. Hdt. 1, 70 down; in Sept. for כָּכַר, Gen. xxv. 33 etc.; Bar. vi. [i. e. Ep. Jer.] 27 (28)). **2.** *to pay off*, *discharge*, what is due, (because a debt, like a burden, is thrown *off*, ἀπό, by being paid): a debt (Germ. *abtragen*), Mt. v. 26; xviii. 25-30, 34; Lk. vii. 42; x. 35; xii. 59; wages, Mt. xx. 8; tribute and other dues to the government, Mt. xxii. 21; Mk. xii. 17; Lk. xx. 25; Ro. xiii. 7; produce due, Mt. xxi. 41; Heb. xii. 11; Rev. xxii. 2; ὅρκους things promised under oath, Mt. v. 33, cf. Num. xxx. 3, (εὐχήν a vow, Deut. xxiii. 21, etc.); conjugal duty, 1 Co. vii. 3; ἀμοιβάς grateful requitals, 1 Tim. v. 4; λόγον *to render account*: Mt. xii. 36; Lk. xvi. 2; Acts xix. 40; Ro. xiv. 12 L txt. Tr txt.; Heb. xiii. 17; 1 Pet. iv. 5; μαρτύριον to give testimony (as something officially due), Acts iv. 33. Hence **3.** *to give back*, *restore*: Lk. iv. 20; [vii. 15 Lchm. mrg.]; ix. 42; xix. 8. **4.** *to requite*, *recompense*, in a good or a bad sense: Mt. vi. 4, 6, 18; xvi. 27; Ro. ii. 6; 2 Tim. iv. [8], 14; Rev. xviii. 6; xxii. 12; κακὸν ἀντὶ κακοῦ, Ro. xii. 17; 1 Th. v. 15; 1 Pet. iii. 9. [COMP.: ἀντ-αποδίδωμι.]*

ἀπο-δι-ορίζω ; (διορίζω, and this fr. ὅρος a limit); by drawing boundaries *to disjoin, part, separate* from another: Jude 19 (οἱ ἀποδιορίζοντες ἑαυτούς those who by their wickedness separate themselves from the living fellowship of Christians; if ἑαυτ. be dropped, with Rec.ᵘᵗ G L T Tr WH, the rendering is *making divisions* or *separations*). (Aristot. pol. 4, 4, 13 [p. 1290ᵇ, 25].)*

ἀπο-δοκιμάζω : (see δοκιμάζω); 1 aor. ἀπεδοκίμασα; Pass., 1 aor. ἀπεδοκιμάσθην; pf. ptcp. ἀποδεδοκιμασμένος; *to disapprove, reject, repudiate*: Mt. xxi. 42; Mk. viii. 31; xii. 10; Lk. ix. 22; xvii. 25; xx. 17; 1 Pet. ii. 4, 7; Heb. xii. 17. (Equiv. to מָאַס in Ps. cxvii. (cxviii.) 22; Jer. viii. 9, etc.; in Grk. writ. fr. Hdt. 6, 130 down.)*

ἀπο-δοχή, -ῆς, ἡ, [ἀποδέχομαι, q. v.), *reception, admission, acceptance, approbation*, [A. V. *acceptation*]: 1 Tim. i. 15; iv. 9. (Polyb. 2, 56, 1; 6, 2, 13, etc.; ὁ λόγος ἀποδοχῆς τυγχάνει id. 1, 5, 5; Diod. 4, 84; Joseph. antt. 6, 14, 4; al. [cf. *Field*, Otium Norv. pars iii. p. 124].)*

ἀπό-θεσις, -εως, ἡ, [ἀποτίθημι], *a putting off* or *away*: 2 Pet. i. 14; 1 Pet. iii. 21. [In various senses fr. Hippoc. and Plato down.]*

ἀπο-θήκη, -ης, ἡ, (ἀποτίθημι), *a place in which any thing is laid by* or *up*; *a storehouse, granary*, [A. V. *garner, barn*]: Mt. iii. 12; vi. 26; xiii. 30; Lk. iii. 17; xii. 18, 24. (Jer. xxvii. (l.) 26; Thuc. 6, 97.)*

ἀπο-θησαυρίζω ; *to put away, lay by in store, to treasure away*, [seponendo thesaurum colligere, *Win.* De verb. comp. etc. Pt. iv. p. 10]; *to store up abundance for future use*: 1 Tim. vi. 19. [Sir. iii. 4; Diod., Joseph., Epict.. al.]*

ἀπο-θλίβω ; *to press on all sides, squeeze, press hard*: Lk. viii. 45. (Num. xxii. 25; used also of pressing out grapes and olives, Diod. 3, 62; Joseph. antt. 2, 5, 2; [al.].) *

ἀπο-θνήσκω, impf. ἀπέθνησκον (Lk. viii. 42); 2 aor. ἀπέθανον ; fut. ἀποθανοῦμαι, Ro. v. 7; Jn. viii. 21, 24, (see θνήσκω); found in Grk. writ. fr. Hom. down; *to die* (ἀπό, so as to be no more; [cf. Lat. *emorior*; Eng. *die off* or *out*, *pass away*]; Germ. *absterben*, *versterben*); **I.** used properly **1.** of the natural death of men: Mt. ix. 24; xxii. 24; Lk. xvi. 22; Jn. iv. 47; Ro. vii. 2, and very often; ἀποθνήσκοντες ἄνθρωποι subject to death, mortal, Heb. vii. 8 [B. 206 (178)]. **2.** of the violent death — both of animals, Mt. viii. 32, and of men, Mt. xxvi. 35; Acts xxi. 13 etc.; 1 Pet. iii. 18 L T Tr WH txt.; ἐν φόνῳ μαχαίρας, Heb. xi. 37; of the punishment of death, Heb. x. 28; often of the violent death which Christ suffered, as Jn. xii. 33; Ro. v. 6, etc. **3.** Phrases: ἀποθνήσκω. ἔκ τινος to perish by means of something, [cf. Eng. *to die of*], Rev. viii. 11; ἐν τῇ ἁμαρτίᾳ, ἐν ταῖς ἁμαρτίαις, fixed in sin, hence to die unreformed, Jn. viii. 21, 24; ἐν τῷ Ἀδάμ by connection with Adam, 1 Co. xv. 22; ἐν κυρίῳ in fellowship with, and trusting in, the Lord, Rev. xiv. 13; ἀποθνήσκ. τι to die a certain death, Ro. vi. 10, (θάνατον μακρόν, Charit. p. 12 ed. D'Orville [l. i. c. 8 p. 17, 6 ed. Beck; cf. W. 227 (213); B. 149 (130)]); τῇ ἁμαρτίᾳ, used of Christ, 'that he might not have to busy himself more with the sin of men,' Ro. vi. 10; ἑαυτῷ to become one's own master, independent, by dying, Ro. xiv. 7 [cf. Meyer]; τῷ κυρίῳ to become subject to the Lord's will by dying, Ro. xiv. 8 [cf. Mey.]; διά τινα i. e. to save one, 1 Co. viii. 11; on the phrases ἀποθνήσκ. περί and ὑπέρ τινος, see περί I. c. δ. and ὑπέρ I. 2 and 3. Oratorically, although the proper signification of the verb is retained, καθ᾿ ἡμέραν ἀποθνήσκω I meet death daily, live daily in danger of death, 1 Co. xv. 31, cf. 2 Co. vi. 9. **4.** of trees which *dry up*, Jude 12; of seeds, which while being resolved into their elements in the ground seem *to perish by rotting*, Jn. xii. 24; 1 Co. xv. 36. **II.** tropically, in various senses; **1.** of eternal death, as it is called, i. e. to be subject to eternal misery, and that, too, already beginning on earth: Ro. viii. 13; Jn. vi. 50; xi. 26. **2.** of moral death, in various senses; **a.** to be deprived of real life, i. e. esp. of the power of doing right, of confidence in God and the hope of future blessedness, Ro. vii. 10; of the spiritual torpor of those who have fallen from the fellowship of Christ, the fountain of true life, Rev. iii. 2. **b.** with dat. of the thing [cf. W. 210 (197); 428 (398); B. 178 (155)], to become wholly alienated from a thing, and freed from all connection with it: τῷ νόμῳ, Gal. ii. 19, which must also be supplied with ἀποθανόντες (for so we must read for Rec.ᵉˡᶻ ἀποθανόντος) in Ro. vii. 6 [cf. W. 159 (150)]; τῇ ἁμαρτίᾳ, Ro. vi. 2 (in another sense in vs. 10; see I. 3 above); ἀπὸ τῶν στοιχείων τοῦ κόσμου so that your relation to etc. has passed away, Col. ii. 20, (ἀπὸ τῶν παθῶν, Porphyr. de abst. animal. 1, 41 [cf. B. 322 (277); W. 370 (347)]); true Christians are said simply ἀποθανεῖν, as having put off all sensibility to worldly things that draw them away from God, Col. iii. 3 ; since they owe this habit of mind to the death of Christ, they are said also ἀποθανεῖν σὺν Χριστῷ, Ro. vi. 8 ; Col. ii. 20. [COMP.: συν-απο-θνῄσκω.]

600

ἀπο-καθ-ίστημι, ἀποκαθιστάω (Mk. ix. 12 ἀποκαθιστᾷ R G), and ἀποκαθιστάνω (Mk. ix. 12 L T Tr [but WH ἀποκατιστάνω, see their App. p. 168]; Acts i. 6 ; cf. W. 78 (75) ; [B. 44 sq. (39)]) ; fut. ἀποκαταστήσω ; 2 aor. ἀπεκατέστην (with double augm., [cf. Ex. iv. 7 ; Jer. xxiii. 8], Mk. viii. 25 T Tr WH) ; 1 aor. pass. ἀποκατεστάθην or, acc. to the better reading, with double augm. ἀπεκατε-στάθην, Mt. xii. 13 ; Mk. iii. 5 ; Lk. vi. 10 (Ignat. ad Smyrn. 11 ; cf.[WH. App. p. 162]; W. 72 (69 sq.) ; [B. 35 (31)]; Mullach p. 22) ; as in Grk. writ. to restore to its former state ; 2 aor. act. to be in its former state : used of parts of the body restored to health, Mt. xii. 13 ; Mk. iii. 5 ; Lk. vi. 10 ; of a man cured of blindness, Mk. viii. 25 ; of the restoration of dominion, Acts i. 6 (1 Macc. xv. 3) ; of the restoration of a disturbed order of affairs, Mt. xvii. 11 ; Mk. ix. 12 ; of a man at a distance from his friends and to be restored to them, Heb. xiii. 19.*

601

ἀπο-καλύπτω : fut. ἀποκαλύψω ; 1 aor. ἀπεκάλυψα ; [Pass., pres. ἀποκαλύπτομαι] ; 1 aor. ἀπεκαλύφθην ; 1 fut. ἀπο-καλυφθήσομαι ; in Grk. writ. fr.[Hdt. and] Plat. down ; in Sept. equiv. to גָּלָה ; 1. prop. to uncover, lay open what has been veiled or covered up ; to disclose, make bare : Ex. xx. 26 ; Lev. xviii. 11 sqq.; Num. v. 18 ; Sus. 32 ; τὰ στήθη, Plat. Prot. p. 352 a.; τὴν κεφαλήν, Plut. Crass. 6. 2. metaph. to make known, make manifest, disclose, what before was unknown ; a. pass. of any method whatever by which something before unknown becomes evident : Mt. x. 26 ; Lk. xii. 2. b. pass. of matters which come to light from things done : Lk. ii. 35 [some make the verb mid. here] ; Jn. xii. 38 (Is. liii. 1) ; Ro. i. 18 ; from the gospel : Ro. i. 17. c. ἀποκαλύπτειν τί τινι is used of God revealing to men things unknown [Dan. ii. 19 Theod., 22, 28 ; Ps. xcvii. (xcviii.) 2 ; 1 S. ii. 27, cf. iii. 21], especially those relating to salvation :— whether by deeds, Mt. xi. 25 ; xvi. 17 ; Lk. x. 21 (by in-timacy with Christ, by his words and acts) ; — or by the Holy Spirit, 1 Co. ii. 10 ; xiv. 30 ; Eph. iii. 5 ; Phil. iii. 15 ; 1 Pet. i. 12 ; τὸν υἱὸν αὐτοῦ ἐν ἐμοί who, what, how great his Son is, in my soul, Gal. i. 16. Of Christ teaching men : Mt. xi. 27 ; Lk. x. 22. d. pass. of things, previously non-existent, coming into being and to view : as, ἡ δόξα, Ro. viii. 18 (εἰς ἡμᾶς to be conferred on us) ; 1 Pet. v. 1 ; ἡ σωτηρία, 1 Pet. i. 5 ; ἡ πίστις, Gal. iii. 23 ; the day of judgment, 1 Co. iii. 13. e. pass. of persons, previ-ously concealed, making their appearance in public : of Christ, who will return from heaven where he is now hidden (Col. iii. 3) to the earth, Lk. xvii. 30 ; of Anti-christ, 2 Th. ii. 3, 6, 8.*

[On this word (and the foll.) cf. Westcott, Introd. to the Study of the Gospels, p. 9 sq. (Am. ed. 34 sq.) ; Lücke, Einl. in d. Offenb. d. Johan. 2d ed. p. 18 sqq.; esp. F. G. B. van Bell, Disput. theolog. de vocabulis φανεροῦν et ἀποκαλύπτειν in N. T., Lugd. Bat., 1849. φανερόω is thought to describe an ex-ternal manifestation, to the senses and hence open to all, but single or isolated ; ἀποκαλύπτω an internal disclosure, to the

believer, and abiding. The ἀποκάλυψις or unveiling precedes and produces the φανέρωσις or manifestation ; the former looks toward the object revealed, the latter toward the persons to whom the revelation is made. Others, however, seem to question the possibility of discrimination ; see e. g. Fritz-sche on Rom. vol. ii. 149. Cf. 1 Co. iii. 13.]

ἀπο-κάλυψις, -εως, ἡ, (ἀποκαλύπτω, q. v.), an uncovering ;   602
1. prop. a laying bare, making naked (1 S. xx. 30).
2. tropically, in N. T. and eccl. language [see end], a. a disclosure of truth, instruction, concerning divine things before unknown — esp. those relating to the Christian salvation — given to the soul by God himself, or by the ascended Christ, esp. through the operation of the Holy Spirit (1 Co. ii. 10), and so to be distinguished from other methods of instruction ; hence, κατὰ ἀποκά-λυψιν γνωρίζεσθαι, Eph. iii. 3. πνεῦμα ἀποκαλύψεως, a spirit received from God disclosing what and how great are the benefits of salvation, Eph. i. 17, cf. 18. with gen. of the obj., τοῦ μυστηρίου, Ro. xvi. 25. with gen. of the subj., κυρίου, Ἰησοῦ Χριστοῦ, 2 Co. xii. 1 (revelations by ecstasies and visions, [so 7]) ; Gal. i. 12 ; Rev. i. 1 (revel-ation of future things relating to the consummation of the divine kingdom) ; κατ᾽ ἀποκάλυψιν, Gal. ii. 2 ; λαλεῖν ἐν ἀποκ. to speak on the ground of [al. in the form of] a revelation, agreeably to a revelation received, 1 Co. xiv. 6 ; equiv. to ἀποκεκαλυμμένον, in the phrase ἀποκά-λυψιν ἔχειν, 1 Co. xiv. 26. b. equiv. to τὸ ἀποκαλύ-πτεσθαι as used of events by which things or states or persons hitherto withdrawn from view are made visible to all, manifestation, appearance, cf. ἀποκαλύπτω, 2, d. and e.: φῶς εἰς ἀποκάλ. ἐθνῶν a light to appear to the Gentiles [al. render 'a light for a revelation (of divine truth) to the Gentiles,' and so refer the use to a. above], Lk. ii. 32 ; ἀποκ. δικαιοκρισίας θεοῦ, Ro. ii. 5 ; τῶν υἱῶν τοῦ θεοῦ, the event in which it will appear who and what the sons of God are, by the glory received from God at the last day, Ro. viii. 19 ; τῆς δόξης τοῦ Χριστοῦ, of the glory clothed with which he will return from heaven, 1 Pet. iv. 13 ; of this return itself the phrase is used ἀπο-κάλυψις τοῦ κυρίου Ἰ. Χριστοῦ : 2 Th. i. 7 ; 1 Co. i. 7 ; 1 Pet. i. 7, 13. (Among Grk. writ. Plut. uses the word once, Cat. maj. c. 20, of the denudation of the body, [also in Paul. Aemil. 14 ἀ. ὑδάτων ; in Quomodo adul. ab amic. 32 ἀ. ἁμαρτίας ; cf. Sir. xi. 27 ; xxii. 22 etc. See Trench § xciv. and reff. s. v. ἀποκαλύπτω, fin.]) *

ἀπο-καραδοκία, -ας, ἡ, (fr. ἀποκαραδοκεῖν, and this fr. ἀπό,   603
κάρα the head, and δοκεῖν in the Ion. dial. to watch ; hence καραδοκεῖν [Hdt. 7. 163, 168 ; Xen. mem. 3, 5, 6 ; Eur., al.] to watch with head erect or outstretched, to direct attention to anything, to wait for in suspense ; ἀποκαραδοκεῖν (Polyb. 16, 2, 8 ; 18, 31, 4 ; 22, 19, 3 ; [Plut. parall. p. 310, 43, vol. vii. p. 235 ed. Reiske] ; Joseph. b. j. 3, 7, 26, and in Ps. xxxvi. (xxxvii.) 7 Aq. for הִתְהוֹלֵל), anxiously [?] to look forth from one's post. But the prefix ἀπό refers also to time (like the Germ. ab in abwarten, [cf. Eng. wait it out]), so that it signifies constancy in expecting ; hence the noun, found in Paul alone and but twice, denotes), anxious[?] and persistent expectation : Ro. viii. 19 ; Phil. i. 20. This word is very

fully discussed by C. F. A. Fritzsche in Fritzschiorum Opuscc. p. 150 sqq.; [cf. Ellic. and Lghtft. on Phil. l. c.].*

604   ἀπο-κατ-αλλάσσω or -ττω : 1 aor. ἀποκατήλλαξα ; 2 aor. pass. ἀποκατηλλάγητε (Col. i. 22 (21) L Tr mrg. WH mrg.); *to reconcile completely* (ἀπό), [al. *to reconcile back again*, bring back to a former state of harmony ; Ellic. on Eph. ii. 16 ; Bp. Lghtft. or Bleek on Col. i. 20 ; Win. De verb. comp. etc. Pt. iv. p. 7 sq.; yet see Mey. on Eph. l. c.; Fritzsche on Rom. vol. i. p. 278 ; (see ἀπό V.)], (cf. καταλλάσσω) : Col. i. 22 (21) [cf. Bp. Lghtft. ad loc.]; τινά τινι, Eph. ii. 16 ; concisely, πάντα εἰς αὐτόν [better αὐτόν with edd.; cf. B. p. 111 (97) and s. v. αὐτοῦ], to draw to himself by reconciliation, or so to reconcile that they should be devoted to himself, Col. i. 20 [W. 212 (200) but cf. § 49, a. c. δ.]. (Found neither in prof. auth. nor in the Grk. O. T.) *

605   ἀπο-κατά-στασις, -εως, ἡ, (ἀποκαθίστημι, q. v.), *restoration* : τῶν πάντων, the restoration not only of the true theocracy but also of that more perfect state of (even physical) things which existed before the fall, Acts iii. 21 ; cf. Meyer ad loc. (Often in Polyb., Diod., Plut., al.)*

[ἀπο-κατ-ιστάνω, see ἀποκαθίστημι.]

606   ἀπό-κειμαι ; *to be laid away, laid by, reserved,* (ἀπό as in ἀποθησαυρίζω [q. v.], ἀποθήκη) ; **a.** prop.: Lk. xix. 20. **b.** metaph., with dat. of pers., *reserved for one, awaiting him* : Col. i. 5 (ἐλπίς hoped-for blessedness) ; 2 Tim. iv. 8 (στέφανος) ; Heb. ix. 27 (ἀποθανεῖν, as in 4 Macc. viii. 10). (In both senses in Grk. writ. fr. Xen. down.)*

607   ἀποκεφαλίζω : 1 aor. ἀπεκεφάλισα ; (κεφαλή) ; *to cut off the head, behead, decapitate* : Mt. xiv. 10 ; Mk. vi. 16, 27 (28) ; Lk. ix. 9. A later Grk. word : [Sept. Ps. fin.]; Epict. diss. 1, 1, 19 ; 24 ; 29 ; Artem. oneir. 1, 35 ; cf. *Fischer*, De vitiis lexx. N. T. p. 690 sqq. ; *Lob.* ad Phryn. p. 341.*

608   ἀπο-κλείω : 1 aor. ἀπέκλεισα ; *to shut up* : τὴν θύραν, Lk. xiii. 25. (Gen. xix. 10 ; 2 S. xiii. 17 sq.; often in Hdt.; in Attic prose writ. fr. Thuc. down.) *

609   ἀπο-κόπτω : 1 aor. ἀπέκοψα ; fut. mid. ἀποκόψομαι ; *to cut off, amputate* : Mk. ix. 43, [45] ; Jn. xviii. 10, 26 ; Acts xxvii. 32 ; ὄφελον καὶ ἀποκόψονται I would that they (who urge the necessity of circumcision would not only circumcise themselves, but) would even mutilate themselves (or cut off their privy parts), Gal. v. 12. ἀποκόπτεσθαι occurs in this sense in Deut. xxiii. 1; [Philo de alleg. leg. iii. 3 ; de vict. off. § 13 ; cf. de spec. legg. i.§7]; Epict. diss. 2, 20, 19 ; Lcian. Eun. 8 ; [Dion Cass. 79, 11 ; Diod. Sic. 3, 31], and other pass. quoted by Wetst. ad loc. [and *Soph.* Lex. s. v.]. Others incorrectly : I would that they would cut themselves off from the society of Christians, quit it altogether ; [cf. Mey. and Bp. Lghtft. ad loc.].*

610   ἀπό-κριμα, -τος, τό, (ἀποκρίνομαι, q. v. in ἀποκρίνω), *an answer* : 2 Co. i. 9, where the meaning is, 'On asking myself whether I should come out safe from mortal peril, I answered, "I must die."' (Joseph. antt. 14, 10, 6 of an answer (rescript) of the Roman senate ; [similarly in Polyb. except. Vat. 12, 26ᵇ, 1].)*

see 611 St.   ἀπο-κρίνω : [Pass., 1 aor. ἀπεκρίθην ; 1 fut. ἀποκριθήσο-

μαι] ; **i.** *to part, separate* ; Pass. *to be parted, separated,* (1 aor. ἀπεκρίθην *was separated*, Hom. Il. v. 12 ; Thuc. 2, 49 ; [4, 72] ; Theoph. de caus. plant. 6, 14, 10 ; [other exx. in Veitch s. v.]). **ii.** *to give sentence against one, decide that he has lost* ; hence Mid., [pres. ἀποκρίνομαι ; 1 aor. 3 pers. sing. ἀπεκρίνατο] ; (*to give forth a decision from myself* [W. 253 (238)]), *to give answer, to reply* ; so from Thuc. down (and even in Hdt. 5, 49 [Gaisf.]; 8, 101 [Gaisf., Bekk.], who generally uses ὑ π ο κρίνομαι). But the earlier and more elegant Grk. writ. do not give this sense to the pass. tenses ἀπεκρίθην, ἀποκριθήσομαι. "The example adduced from Plat. Alcib. Secund. p. 149 b. [cf. Stallb. p. 388] is justly discredited by *Sturz*, De dial. Alex. p. 148, since it is without parallel, the author of the dialogue is uncertain, and, moreover, the common form is sometimes introduced by copyists." *Lobeck* ad Phryn. p. 108 ; [cf. *Rutherford*, New Phryn. p. 186 sq. ; Veitch s. v. ; W. 23 (22)]. But from Polyb. down ἀποκριθῆναι and ἀποκρίνασθαι are used indiscriminately, and in the Bible the pass. forms are by far the more common. In the N. T. the aor. m i d d l e ἀπεκρίνατο is found only in Mt. xxvii. 12 ; Mk. xiv. 61 ; Lk. iii. 16 ; xxiii. 9 ; Jn. v. 17, 19 ; xii. 23 [R G L Tr mrg.] ; Acts iii. 12 ; in the great majority of places ἀπεκρίθη is used ; cf. W. § 39, 2 ; [B. 51 (44)]. **1.** *to give an answer* to a question proposed, *to answer* ; **a.** simply : καλῶς, Mk. xii. 28 ; νουνεχῶς, 34 ; ὀρθῶς, Lk. x. 28 ; πρός τι, Mt. xxvii. 14. **b.** with acc. : λόγον, Mt. xxii. 46 ; οὐδέν, Mt. xxvii. 12 ; Mk. xiv. 61 ; xv. 4 sq. **c.** with dat. etc. : ἑνὶ ἑκάστῳ, Col. iv. 6 ; together with the words which the answerer uses, Jn. v. 7, 11 ; vi. 7, 68, etc. ; the dat. omitted : Jn. vii. 46 ; viii. 19, 49, etc. πρός τινα, Acts xxv. 16. joined with φάναι, or λέγειν, or εἰπεῖν, in the form of a ptcp., as ἀποκριθεὶς εἶπε or ἔφη or λέγει : Mt. iv. 4 ; viii. 8 ; xv. 13 ; Lk. ix. 19 ; xiii. 2 ; Mk. x. 3, etc. ; or ἀπεκρίθη λέγων : Mt. xxv. 9, 37, 44 ; Lk. iv. 4 [R G L] ; viii. 50 [R G Tr mrg. br.] ; Jn. i. 26 ; x. 33 [Rec.] ; xii. 23. But John far more frequently says ἀπεκρίθη καὶ εἶπε : Jn. i. 48 (49) ; ii. 19 ; iv. 13 ; vii. 16, 20 [R G], 52, etc. **d.** foll. by the inf. : Lk. xx. 7 ; foll. by the acc. with inf. : Acts xxv. 4 ; foll. by ὅτι : Acts xxv. 16. **2.** In imitation of the Hebr. עָנָה (*Gesenius,* Thesaur. ii. p. 1047) *to begin to speak,* but always where something has preceded (either said or done) to which the remarks refer [W. 19] : Mt. xi. 25 ; xii. 38 ; xv. 15 ; xvii. 4 ; xxii. 1 ; xxviii. 5 ; Mk. ix. 5, [6 T Tr WH] ; x. 24 ; xi. 14 ; xii. 35 ; Lk. xiv. 3 ; Jn. ii. 18 ; v. 17 ; Acts iii. 12 ; Rev. vii. 13. (Sept. [Deut. xxvi. 5] ; Is. xiv. 10 ; Zech. i. 10 ; iii. 4, etc. ; 1 Macc. ii. 17 ; viii. 19 ; 2 Macc. xv. 14.) [COMP. : ἀντ-αποκρίνομαι.]

612   ἀπό-κρισις, -εως, ἡ, (ἀποκρίνομαι, see ἀποκρίνω), *a replying, an answer* : Lk. ii. 47 ; xx. 26 ; Jn. i. 22 ; xix. 9. (From [Theognis, 1167 ed. Bekk., 345 ed. Welck., and] Hdt. down.) *

613   ἀπο-κρύπτω : 1 aor. ἀπέκρυψα ; pf. pass. ptcp. ἀποκεκρυμμένος ; **a.** *to hide* : τί, Mt. xxv. 18 (L T Tr WH ἔκρυψε). **b.** Pass. in the sense of *concealing, keeping secret* : σοφία, 1 Co. ii. 7 ; μυστήριον, Col. i. 26 (opp. to φανεροῦσθαι) ; with the addition of ἐν τῷ θεῷ, Eph. iii. 9 ; τὶ ἀπό τινος,

Lk. x. 21; **Mt. xi. 25** (L T Tr WH ἔκρυψας), in imitation of the Hebr. מִן, Ps. xxxvii. (xxxviii.) 10; cxviii. (cxix.) 19; Jer. xxxix. (xxxii.) 17; cf. κρύπτω, [B. 149 (130); 189 (163); W. 227 (213)]. (In Grk. writ. fr. Hom. down.)*

614   **ἀπόκρυφος,-ον,** (ἀποκρύπτω), *hidden, secreted*: Mk. iv. 22; Lk. viii. 17. *stored up*: Col. ii. 3. (Dan. xi. 43 [Theod.]; Is. xlv. 3; 1 Macc. i. 23; Xen., Eur.; [cf. Bp. Lghtft. on the word, Col. l. c.].)*

615   **ἀπο-κτείνω,** and Aeol. -κτέννω (Mt. x. 28 L T Tr; Mk. xii. 5 G L T Tr; Lk. xii. 4 L T Tr; 2 Co. iii. 6 T Tr; cf. Fritzsche on Mk. p. 507 sq.; [*Tdf.* Proleg. p. 79]; W. 83 (79); [B. 61 (54)]), ἀποκτένω (Grsb. in Mt. x. 28; Lk. xii. 4), ἀποκταίνω (Lchm. in 2 Co. iii. 6; Rev. xiii. 10), ἀποκτέννυντες (Mk. xii. 5 WH); fut. ἀποκτενῶ; 1 aor. ἀπέκτεινα; Pass., pres. inf. ἀποκτέννεσθαι (Rev. vi. 11 G L T Tr WH); 1 aor. ἀπεκτάνθην (Bttm. Ausf. Spr. ii. 227; W. l. c.; [B. 41 (35 sq.)]); [fr. Hom. down]; **1.** prop. *to kill* in any way whatever, (ἀπό i. e. so as to put out of the way; cf. [Eng. to kill *off*], Germ. *abschlachten*): Mt. xvi. 21; xxii. 6; Mk. vi. 19; ix. 31; Jn. v. 18; viii. 22; Acts iii. 15; Rev. ii. 13, and very often; [ἀποκτ. ἐν θανάτῳ, Rev. ii. 23; vi. 8, cf. B. 184 (159); W. 339 (319)]. *to destroy* (allow to perish): Mk. iii. 4 [yet al. take it here absol., *to kill*]. **2.** metaph. *to extinguish, abolish*: τὴν ἔχθραν, Eph. ii. 16; *to inflict moral death*, Ro. vii. 11 (see ἀποθνήσκω, II. 2); *to deprive of spiritual life and procure eternal misery*, 2 Co. iii. 6 [Lchm. ἀποκταίνει; see above].

616   **ἀπο-κυέω, -ῶ,** or ἀποκύω, (hence 3 pers. sing. pres. either ἀποκυεῖ [so WH] or ἀποκύει, Jas. i. 15; cf. W. 88 (84); B. 62 (54)); 1 aor. ἀπεκύησα; (κύω, or κυέω, to be pregnant; cf. ἔγκυος); *to bring forth* from the womb, give birth to: τινά, Jas. i. 15; *to produce*, ibid. 18. (4 Macc. xv. 17; Dion. Hal. 1, 70; Plut., Lcian., Ael. v. h. 5, 4; Hdian. 1, 5, 13 [5 ed. Bekk.]; 1, 4, 2 [1 ed. Bekk.].)*

617   **ἀπο-κυλίω;** fut. ἀποκυλίσω; 1 aor. ἀπεκύλισα; pf. pass. [3 pers. sing. ἀποκεκύλισται Mk. xvi. 4 R G L but T Tr WH ἀνακεκ.], ptcp. ἀποκεκυλισμένος; *to roll off* or *away*: Mt. xxviii. 2; Mk. xvi. 3; Lk. xxiv. 2. (Gen. xxix. 3, 8, 10; Judith xiii. 9; Joseph. antt. 4, 8, 37; 5, 11, 3; Lcian. rhet. praec. 3.) But see ἀνακυλίω.*

618   **ἀπο-λαμβάνω;** fut. ἀπολήψομαι (Col. iii. 24; L T Tr WH ἀπολήμψεσθε; see λαμβάνω) 2 aor. ἀπέλαβον; 2 aor. mid. ἀπελαβόμην; fr. Hdt. down; **1.** *to receive* (from another, ἀπό [cf. Mey. on Gal. iv. 5; Ellic. ibid. and Win. De verb. comp. etc. as below]) *what is due* or *promised* (cf. ἀποδίδωμι, 2): τ. υἱοθεσίαν the adoption promised to believers, Gal. iv. 5; τὰ ἀγαθά σου thy good things, "which thou couldst expect and as it were demand, which seemed due to thee" (*Win.* De verb. comp. etc. Pt. iv. p. 13), Lk. xvi. 25. Hence **2.** *to take again* or *back, to recover*: Lk. vi. 34 [T Tr txt. WH λαβεῖν]; xv. 27; and *to receive by way of retribution*: Lk. xviii. 30 (L txt. Tr mrg. WH txt. λάβῃ); xxiii. 41; Ro. i. 27; 2 Jn. 8; Col. iii. 24. **3.** *to take from others, take apart* or *aside*; Mid. τινά, *to take a person with one aside out of the view of others*: with the addition of ἀπὸ τοῦ ὄχλου κατ᾽ ἰδίαν in Mk. vii.

33, (Joseph. b. j. 2, 7, 2; and in the Act., 2 Macc. vi. 21; Ὑστάσπεα ἀπολαβὼν μοῦνον, Hdt. 1, 209; Arstph. ran. 78; ἰδίᾳ ἕνα τῶν τριῶν ἀπολαβών, App. b. civ. 5, 40). **4.** *to receive* any one hospitably: 3 Jn. 8, where L T Tr WH have restored ὑπολαμβάνειν.*

619   **ἀπόλαυσις, -εως, ἡ,** (fr. ἀπολαύω to enjoy), *enjoyment* (Lat. *fructus*): 1 Tim. vi. 17 (εἰς ἀπόλαυσιν to enjoy); Heb. xi. 25 (ἁμαρτίας ἀπόλ. pleasure born of sin). (In Grk. writ. fr. [Eur. and] Thuc. down.)*

620   **ἀπο-λείπω:** [impf. ἀπέλειπον, WH txt. in 2 Tim. iv. 13, 20; Tit. i. 5]; 2 aor. ἀπέλιπον; [fr. Hom. down]; **1.** *to leave, leave behind*: one in some place, Tit. i. 5 L T Tr WH; 2 Tim. iv. 13, 20. Pass. ἀπολείπεται *it remains, is reserved*: Heb. iv. 9; x. 26; foll. by acc. and inf., Heb. iv. 6. **2.** *to desert, forsake*: a place, Jude 6.*

621   **ἀπο-λείχω:** [impf. ἀπέλειχον]; *to lick off, lick up*: Lk. xvi. 21 R G; cf. ἐπιλείχω. ([Apollon. Rhod. 4, 478]; Athen. vi. c. 13 p. 250 a.)*

622   **ἀπ-όλλυμι** and ἀπολλύω ([ἀπολλύει Jn. xii. 25 T TrWH], impv. ἀπόλλυε Ro. xiv. 15, [cf. B. 45 (39); *WH.* App. p. 168 sq.]); fut. ἀπολέσω and (1 Co. i. 19 ἀπολῶ fr. a pass. in the O. T., where often) ἀπολῶ (cf. W. 83 (80); [B. 64 (56)]); 1 aor. ἀπώλεσα; *to destroy*; Mid., pres. ἀπόλλυμαι; [impf. 3 pers. plur. ἀπώλλυντο 1 Co. x. 9 T Tr WH]; fut. ἀπολοῦμαι; 2 aor. ἀπωλόμην; (2 pf. act. ptcp. ἀπολωλώς); [fr. Hom. down]; *to perish*. **1.** *to destroy* i. e. *to put out of the way entirely, abolish, put an end to, ruin*: Mk. i. 24; Lk. iv. 34; xvii. 27, 29; Jude 5; τὴν σοφίαν *render useless, cause its emptiness to be perceived*, 1 Co. i. 19 (fr. Sept. of Is. xxix. 14); *to kill*: Mt. ii. 13; xii. 14; Mk. ix. 22; xi. 18; Jn. x. 10, etc.; contextually, *to declare that one must be put to death*: Mt. xxvii. 20; metaph. *to devote* or *give over to eternal misery*: Mt. x. 28; Jas. iv. 12; contextually, *by one's conduct to cause another to lose eternal salvation*: Ro. xiv. 15. Mid. *to perish, to be lost, ruined, destroyed*; **a.** of persons; **α.** properly: Mt. viii. 25; Lk. xiii. 3, 5, 33; Jn. xi. 50; 2 Pet. iii. 6; Jude 11, etc.; ἀπόλλυμαι λιμῷ, Lk. xv. 17; ἐν μαχαίρᾳ, Mt. xxvi. 52; καταβαλλόμενοι, ἀλλ᾽ οὐκ ἀπολλύμενοι, 2 Co. iv. 9. **β.** tropically, *to incur the loss of true* or *eternal life; to be delivered up to eternal misery*: Jn. iii. 15 [R L br.], 16; x. 28; xvii. 12, (it must be borne in mind, that acc. to John's conception eternal life begins on earth, just as soon as one becomes united to Christ by faith); Ro. ii. 12; 1 Co. viii. 11; xv. 18; 2 Pet. iii. 9. Hence οἱ σωζόμενοι they to whom it belongs to partake of salvation, and οἱ ἀπολλύμενοι those to whom it belongs to perish or to be consigned to eternal misery, are contrasted by Paul: 1 Co. i. 18; 2 Co. ii. 15; iv. 3; 2 Th. ii. 10, (on these pres. ptcps. cf. W. 342 (321); B. 206 (178)). **b.** of things; *to be blotted out, to vanish away*: ἡ εὐπρέπεια, Jas. i. 11; the heavens, Heb. i. 11 (fr. Ps. ci. (cii.) 27); *to perish*,—of things which on being thrown away are decomposed, as μέλος τοῦ σώματος, Mt. v. 29 sq.; remnants of bread, Jn. vi. 12; — or which perish in some other way, as βρῶσις, Jn. vi. 27; χρυσίον, 1 Pet. i. 7; — or which are ruined so that they can no longer subserve the use for which they were designed, as οἱ ἀσκοί: Mt.

ix. 17 ; Mk. ii. 22 ; Lk. v. 37.   **2.** *to destroy* i. e. *to lose* ; a. prop. : Mt. x. 42 ; Mk. ix. 41 (τὸν μισθὸν αὐτοῦ) ; Lk. xv. 4, 8, 9 ; ix. 25 ; xvii. 33 ; Jn. xii. 25 ; 2 Jn. 8, etc. b. metaph. Christ is said *to lose any one* of his followers (whom the Father has drawn to discipleship) if such a one becomes wicked and fails of salvation : Jn. vi. 39, cf. xviii. 9. Mid. *to be lost* : θρὶξ ἐκ τῆς κεφαλῆς, Lk. xxi. 18 ; θ. ἀπὸ τῆς κεφαλῆς, Acts xxvii. 34 (Rec. πεσεῖται) ; τὰ λαμπρὰ ἀπώλετο ἀπό σου, Rev. xviii. 14 (Rec. ἀπῆλθε). Used of sheep, straying from the flock : prop. Lk. xv. 4 (τὸ ἀπολωλός, in Mt. xviii. 12 τὸ πλανώμενον). Metaph. in accordance with the O. T. comparison of the people of Israel to a flock (Jer. xxvii. (l.) 6 ; Ezek. xxxiv. 4, 16), the Jews, neglected by their religious teachers, left to themselves and thereby in danger of losing eternal salvation, wandering about as it were without guidance, are called τὰ πρόβατα τὰ ἀπολωλότα τοῦ οἴκου Ἰσραήλ : Mt. x. 6 ; xv. 24, (Is. liii. 6 ; 1 Pet. ii. 25) ; and Christ, reclaiming them from wickedness, is likened to a shepherd and is said ζητεῖν καὶ σώζειν τὸ ἀπολωλός : Lk. xix. 10 ; Mt. xviii. 11 Rec. [Comp. : συν-απόλλυμι.]

623   'Απολλύων, -οντος, ὁ, (ptcp. fr. ἀπολλύω), *Apollyon* (a prop. name, formed by the author of the Apocalypse), i. e. *Destroyer* : Rev. ix. 11 ; cf. 'Αβάδδων, [and B. D. s. v.].*

624   'Απολλωνία, -ας, ἡ, *Apollonia*, a maritime city of Macedonia, about a day's journey [acc. to the Antonine Itinerary 32 Roman miles] from Amphipolis, through which Paul passed on his way to Thessalonica [36 miles further] : Acts xvii. 1. [See B. D. s. v.]*

625   'Απολλώς [acc. to some, contr. fr. 'Απολλώνιος, W. 102 (97) ; acc. to others, the *o* is lengthened, cf. *Fick*, Griech. Personennamen, p. xxi.], gen. -ώ (cf. B. 20 (18) sq. ; [W. 62 (61)]), accus. -ώ (Acts xix. 1) and -ών (1 Co. iv. 6 T Tr WH ; Tit. iii. 13 T WH ; cf. [*WH.* App. p. 157]; Kühner i. p. 315), ὁ, *Apollos*, an Alexandrian Jew who became a Christian and a teacher of Christianity, attached to the apostle Paul : Acts xviii. 24 ; xix. 1 ; 1 Co. i. 12 ; iii. 4 sqq. 22 ; iv. 6 ; xvi. 12 ; Tit. iii. 13.*

626   ἀπολογέομαι, -οῦμαι ; impf. ἀπελογούμην (Acts xxvi. 1) ; 1 aor. ἀπελογησάμην ; 1 aor. pass. inf. ἀπολογηθῆναι, in a reflex. sense (Lk. xxi. 14) ; a depon. mid. verb (fr. λόγος), prop. *to speak so as to absolve* (ἀπό) *one's self*, talk one's self *off* of a charge etc. ;   **1.** *to defend one's self, make one's defence* : absol., Lk. xxi. 14 ; Acts xxvi. 1 ; foll. by ὅτι, Acts xxv. 8 ; τί, to bring forward something in defence of one's self, Lk. xii. 11 ; Acts xxvi. 24, (often so in Grk. writ. also) ; τὰ περὶ ἐμαυτοῦ ἀπ. either *I bring forward what contributes to my defence* [?], or *I plead my own cause* [R. V. *make my defence*], Acts xxiv. 10 ; περί with gen. of the thing and ἐπί with gen. of pers., *concerning a thing before* one's tribunal, Acts xxvi. 2 ; with dat. of the person whom by my defence I strive to convince that I am innocent or upright, *to defend* or *justify myself in one's eyes* [A. V. *unto*], Acts xix. 33 ; 2 Co. xii. 19, (Plat. Prot. p. 359 a. ; often in Lcian., Plut. ; [cf. B. 172 (149)]). **2.** *to defend a person* or *a thing* (so not infreq. in prof. auth.) : Ro. ii. 15 (where acc. to the context the deeds of men must be understood as defended) ; τὰ περὶ ἐμοῦ, Acts xxvi. 2 (but see under 1).*

ἀπολογία, -ας, ἡ, (see ἀπολογέομαι), *verbal defence, speech in defence* : Acts xxv. 16 ; 2 Co. vii. 11 ; Phil. i. 7, 17 (16) ; 2 Tim. iv. 16 ; with a dat. of the pers. who is to hear the defence, to whom one labors to excuse or to make good his cause : 1 Co. ix. 3 ; 1 Pet. iii. 15 ; in the same sense ἡ ἀπολ. ἡ πρός τινα, Acts xxii. 1, (Xen. mem. 4, 8, 5).*   **627**

ἀπο-λούω : *to wash off* or *away* ; in the N. T. twice in 1 aor. mid. figuratively [cf. Philo de mut. nom. § 6, i. p. 585 ed. Mang.] : ἀπελούσασθε, 1 Co. vi. 11 ; βάπτισαι καὶ ἀπόλουσαι τὰς ἁμαρτίας σου, Acts xxii. 16. For the sinner is unclean, polluted as it were by the filth of his sins. Whoever obtains remission of sins has his sins put, so to speak, out of God's sight, — is cleansed from them in the sight of God. Remission is [represented as] obtained by undergoing baptism ; hence those who have gone down into the baptismal bath [*lavacrum*, cf. Tit. iii. 5 ; Eph. v. 26] are said ἀπολούσασθαι *to have washed themselves*, or τὰς ἁμαρτ. ἀπολούσασθαι *to have washed away their sins*, i. e. to have been cleansed from their sins.*   **628**

ἀπο-λύτρωσις, -εως, ἡ, (fr. ἀπολυτρόω signifying a. to redeem one by paying the price, cf. λύτρον : Plut. Pomp. 24 ; Sept. Ex. xxi. 8 ; Zeph. iii. 1 ; b. to let one go free on receiving the price : Plat. legg. 11 p. 919 a. ; Polyb. 22, 21, 8 ; [cf.] Diod. 13, 24), *a releasing effected by payment of ransom* ; *redemption, deliverance, liberation procured by the payment of a ransom* ;   **1.** prop. : πόλεων αἰχμαλώτων, Plut. Pomp. 24 (the only pass. in prof. writ. where the word has as yet been noted ; [add, Joseph. antt. 12, 2, 3 ; Diod. frag. l. xxxvii. 5, 3 p. 149, 6 Dind. ; Philo, quod omn. prob. lib. § 17]). **2.** everywhere in the N. T. metaph., viz. deliverance effected through the death of Christ from the retributive wrath of a holy God and the merited penalty of sin : Ro. iii. 24 ; Eph. i. 7 ; Col. i. 14, (cf. ἐξαγοράζω, ἀγοράζω, λυτρόω, etc. [and Trench § lxxvii.]) ; ἀπολύτρ. τῶν παραβάσεων deliverance from the penalty of transgressions, effected through their expiation, Heb. ix. 15, (cf. Delitzsch ad loc. and Fritzsche on Rom. vol. ii. p. 178) ; ἡμέρα ἀπολυτρώσεως, the last day, when consummate liberation is experienced from the sin still lingering even in the regenerate, and from all the ills and troubles of this life, Eph. iv. 30 ; in the same sense the word is apparently to be taken in 1 Co. i. 30 (where Christ himself is said to be redemption, i. e. the author of redemption, the one without whom we could have none), and is to be taken in the phrase ἀπολύτρ. τῆς περιποιήσεως, Eph. i. 14, the redemption which will come to his possession, or to the men who are God's own through Christ, (cf. Meyer ad loc.) ; τοῦ σώματος, deliverance of the body from frailty and mortality, Ro. viii. 23 [W. 187 (176)]; deliverance from the hatred and persecutions of enemies by the return of Christ from heaven, Lk. xxi. 28, cf. xviii. 7 sq. ; deliverance or release from torture, Heb. xi. 35.*   **629**

ἀπο-λύω ; [impf. ἀπέλυον] ; fut. ἀπολύσω ; 1 aor. ἀπέλυσα ; Pass., pf. ἀπολέλυμαι ; 1 aor. ἀπελύθην ; [fut. ἀπο-   **630** λυθήσομαι]; impf. mid. ἀπελυόμην (Acts xxviii. 25); used in the N. T. only in the historical books and in Heb. xiii. 23; *to loose from, sever by loosening, undo,* [see ἀπό, V.]; **1.** *to set free* : τινά τινος (so in Grk. writ. even fr. Hom. down), to liberate one from a thing (as from a bond), Lk. xiii. 12 (ἀπολέλυσαι [thou hast been loosed i. e.] be thou free from [cf. W. § 40, 4] τῆς ἀσθενείας [L T ἀπὸ τ. ἀσθ.]). **2.** *to let go, dismiss,* (to detain no longer); τινά, **a.** a suppliant to whom liberty to depart is given by a decisive answer: Mt. xv. 23; Lk. ii. 29 ('me whom thou hadst determined to keep on earth until I had seen the salvation prepared for Israel, cf. vs. 26, thou art now dismissing with my wish accomplished, and this dismission is at the same time dismission also from life' — in reference to which ἀπολύειν is used in Num. xx. 29; Tob. iii. 6; [cf. Gen. xv. 2; 2 Macc. vii. 9; Plut. consol. ad Apoll. § 13 cf. 11 fin.]); [Acts xxiii. 22]. **b.** *to bid depart, send away* : Mt. xiv. 15, 22 sq.; xv. 32, 39; Mk. vi. 36, 45; viii. 3, 9; Lk. viii. 38; ix. 12; xiv. 4; Acts xiii. 3; xix. 41 (τὴν ἐκκλησίαν); pass. Acts xv. 30, 33. **3.** *to let go free, to release*; **a.** a captive, i. e. to loose his bonds and bid him depart, to give him liberty to depart: Lk. xxii. 68 [R G L Tr in br.]; xxiii. 22; Jn. xix. 10; Acts xvi. 35 sq.; xxvi. 32 (ἀπολελύσθαι ἐδύνατο [might have been set at liberty, cf. B. 217 (187), § 139, 27 c.; W. 305 (286) i. e.] *might be free*; pf. as in Lk. xiii. 12 [see 1 above, and W. 334 (313)]); Acts xxviii. 18; Heb. xiii. 23; ἀπολ. τινά τινι to release one to one, grant him his liberty: Mt. xxvii. 15, 17, 21, 26; Mk. xv. 6, 9, 11, 15; Lk. xxiii. [16], 17 [R L in br.], 18, 20, 25; [Jn. xviii. 39]. **b.** to acquit one accused of a crime and set him at liberty: Jn. xix. 12; Acts iii. 13. **c.** indulgently to grant a prisoner leave to depart: Acts iv. 21, 23; v. 40; xvii. 9. **d.** to release a debtor, i. e. not to press one's claim against him, to remit his debt: Mt. xviii. 27; metaph. to pardon another his offences against me: Lk. vi. 37, (τῆς ἁμαρτίας ἀπολύεσθαι, 2 Macc. xii. 45). **4.** used of d i v o r c e, as ἀπολύω τὴν γυναῖκα to dismiss from the house, to repudiate: Mt. i. 19; v. 31 sq.; xix. 3, 7–9; Mk. x. 2, 4, 11; Lk. xvi. 18; [1 Esdr. ix. 36]; and improperly a wife deserting her husband is said τὸν ἄνδρα ἀπολύειν in Mk. x. 12 [cf. Diod. 12, 18] (unless, as is more probable, Mark, contrary to historic accuracy [yet cf. Joseph. antt. 15, 7, 10], makes Jesus speak in accordance with Greek and Roman usage, acc. to which wives also repudiated their husbands [reff. in Mey. ad l.]); (cf. רְלַשׁ, Jer. iii. 8; Deut. xxi. 14; xxii. 19, 29). **5.** Mid. ἀπολύομαι, prop. to send one's self away; *to depart* [W. 253 (238)]: Acts xxviii. 25 (returned home; Ex. xxxiii. 11).*

see 631 St. ἀπο-μάσσω : (μάσσω to touch with the hands, handle, work with the hands, knead), *to wipe off*; Mid. ἀπομάσσομαι *to wipe one's self off, to wipe off for one's self* : τὸν κονιορτὸν ὑμῖν, Lk. x. 11. (In Grk. writ. fr. Arstph. down.)*

632 ἀπο-νέμω ; (νέμω to dispense a portion, to distribute), *to assign, portion out,* (ἀπό as in ἀποδίδωμι [q. v., cf. ἀπό, V.]): τινί τι viz. τιμήν, showing honor, 1 Pet. iii. 7, (so Hdian. 1, 8, 1; τὴν τιμὴν καὶ τὴν εὐχαριστίαν, Joseph. antt. 1, 7,

1; τῷ ἐπισκόπῳ πᾶσαν ἐντροπήν, Ignat. ad Magnes. 3; first found in [Simon. 97 in Anthol. Pal. 7, 253, 2 (vol. i. p. 64 ed. Jacobs)]; Pind. Isthm. 2, 68; often in Plat., Aristot., Plut., al.).*

633 ἀπο-νίπτω : *to wash off*; 1 aor. mid. ἀπενιψάμην; in mid. *to wash one's self off, to wash off for one's self* : τὰς χεῖρας, Mt. xxvii. 24, cf. Deut. xxi. 6 sq. (The earlier Greeks say ἀπονίζω — but with fut. ἀπονίψω, 1 aor. ἀπένιψα; the later, as Theophr. char. 25 [30 (17)]; Plut. Phoc. 18; Athen. iv. c. 31 p. 149 c., ἀπονίπτω, although this is found [but in the mid.] even in Hom. Od. 18, 179.)*

634 ἀπο-πίπτω : 2 aor. ἀπέπεσον; [(cf. πίπτω); fr. Hom. down]; *to fall off, slip down from* : Acts ix. 18 [W. § 52, 4, 1 a.].*

635 ἀπο-πλανάω, -ῶ ; 1 aor. pass. ἀπεπλανήθην; *to cause to go astray,* trop. *to lead away from the truth to error* : τινά, Mk. xiii. 22; pass. *to go astray, stray away from* : ἀπὸ τῆς πίστεως, 1 Tim. vi. 10. ([Hippocr.]; Plat. Ax. p. 369 d.; Polyb. 3, 57, 4; Dion. Hal., Plut., al.)*

636 ἀπο-πλέω ; 1 aor. ἀπέπλευσα; [fr. Hom. down]; *to sail away, depart by ship, set sail* : Acts xiii. 4; xiv. 26; xx. 15; xxvii. 1.*

637 ἀπο-πλύνω : [1 aor. ἀπέπλυνα (?)]; *to wash off* : Lk. v. 2 (where L Tr WH txt. ἔπλυνον, T WH mrg. -αν, for R G ἀπέπλυναν [possibly an impf. form, cf. B. 40 (35); Soph. Glossary, etc. p. 90]). (Hom. Od. 6, 95; Plat., Plut., and subseq. writ.; Sept. 2 S. xix. 24, [cf. Jer. ii. 22; iv. 14; Ezek. xvi. 9 var.].)*

638 ἀπο-πνίγω : 1 aor. ἀπέπνιξα; 2 aor. pass. ἀπεπνίγην; (ἀπό as in ἀποκτείνω q. v. [cf. to choke off]); *to choke* : Mt. xiii. 7 (T WH mrg. ἔπνιξαν); Lk. viii. 7 (of seed overlaid by thorns and killed by them); to suffocate with water, to drown, Lk. viii. 33 (as in Dem. 32, 6 [i. e. p. 883, 28 etc.; schol. ad Eur. Or. 812]).*

639 ἀπορέω, -ῶ : impf. 3 pers. sing. ἠπόρει [Mk. vi. 20 T WH Tr mrg.]; [pres. mid. ἀπορούμαι]; *to be ἄπορος* (fr. α priv. and πόρος a transit, ford, way, revenue, resource), i. e. *to be without resources, to be in straits, to be left wanting, to be embarrassed, to be in doubt, not to know which way to turn* ; [impf. in Mk. vi. 20 (see above) πολλὰ ἠπόρει *he was in perplexity about many things* or *much perplexed* (cf. Thuc. 5, 40, 3; Xen. Hell. 6, 1, 4; Hdt. 3, 4; 4, 179; Aristot. meteorolog. 1, 1)]; elsewhere] Mid. *to be at a loss with one's self, be in doubt; not to know how to decide* or *what to do, to be perplexed* : absol. 2 Co. iv. 8; περί τινος, Lk. xxiv. 4 L T Tr WH; περί τίνος τις λέγει, Jn. xiii. 22; ἀπορούμαι ἐν ὑμῖν I am perplexed about you, I know not how to deal with you, in what style to address you, Gal. iv. 20; ἀπορούμενος ἐγὼ εἰς [T Tr WH om. εἰς] τὴν περὶ τούτου [-των L T Tr WH] ζήτησιν I being perplexed how to decide in reference to the inquiry concerning him [or these things], Acts xxv. 20. (Often in prof. auth. fr. Hdt. down; often also in Sept.) [Comp. : δι-, ἐξ-απορέω.]*

640 ἀπορία, -ας, ἡ, (ἀπορέω, q. v.), *the state of one who is ἄπορος, perplexity* : Lk. xxi. 25. (Often in Grk. writ. fr. [Pind. and] Hdt. down; Sept.)*

641 ἀπο-ρρίπτω : 1 aor. ἀπέρριψα [T WH write with one ρ;

see P,ρ]; [fr. Hom. down]; *to throw away, cast down*; reflexively, *to cast one's self down*: Acts xxvii. 43 [R.V. *cast themselves overboard*]. (So in Lcian. ver. hist. 1, 30 var.; [Chariton 3, 5, see D'Orville ad loc.]; cf. W. 251 (236); [B. 145 (127)].)*

642 ἀπ-ορφανίζω: [1 aor. pass. ptcp. ἀπορφανισθείς]; (fr. ὀρφανός bereft, and ἀπό sc. τινός), *to bereave of a parent or parents*, (so Aeschyl. choëph. 247 (249)); hence metaph. ἀπορφανισθέντες ἀφ' ὑμῶν bereft of your intercourse and society, 1 Th. ii. 17 [here Rec^elz (by mistake) ἀποφανισθέντες].*

643 ἀπο-σκευάζω: 1 aor. mid. ἀπεσκευασάμην; (σκευάζω to prepare, provide, fr. σκεῦος a utensil), *to carry off goods and chattels*; *to pack up and carry off*; mid. *to carry off one's personal property* or *provide for its carrying away*, (Polyb. 4, 81, 11; Diod. 13, 91; Dion. Hal. 9, 23, etc.): ἀποσκευασάμενοι having collected and removed our baggage, Acts xxi. 15; but L T Tr WH read ἐπισκευασάμενοι q. v.).*

644 ἀπο-σκίασμα, -τος, τό, (σκιάζω, fr. σκιά), *a shade cast by one object upon another, a shadow*: τροπῆς ἀποσκίασμα shadow caused by revolution, Jas. i. 17. Cf. ἀπαύγασμα.*

645 ἀπο-σπάω, -ῶ; 1 aor. ἀπέσπασα; 1 aor. pass. ἀπεσπάσθην; *to draw off, tear away*: τ. μάχαιραν to draw one's sword, Mt. xxvi. 51 (ἐκσπᾶν τ. μάχ. (or ῥομφαίαν), 1 S. xvii. 51 [Alex. etc.]; σπᾶν, 1 Chr. xi. 1; Mk. xiv. 47); ἀποσπᾶν τοὺς μαθητὰς ὀπίσω ἑαυτῶν to draw away the disciples to their own party, Acts xx. 30, (very similarly, Ael. v. h. 13, 32). Pass. reflexively: ἀποσπασθέντες ἀπ' αὐτῶν having torn ourselves from the embrace of our friends, Acts xxi. 1; ἀπεσπάσθη ἀπ' αὐτῶν he parted, tore himself, from them about a stone's cast, Lk. xxii. 41; cf. Meyer ad loc. (In prof. auth. fr. [Pind. and] Hdt. down.)*

646 ἀποστασία, -ας, ἡ, (ἀφίσταμαι), *a falling away, defection, apostasy*; in the Bible sc. from the true religion: Acts xxi. 21; 2 Th. ii. 3; ([Josh. xxii. 22; 2 Chr. xxix. 19; xxxiii. 19]; Jer. ii. 19; xxxvi. (xxix.) 32 Compl.; 1 Macc. ii. 15). The earlier Greeks say ἀπόστασις; see *Lob.* ad Phryn. p. 528; [W. 24].*

647 ἀποστάσιον, -ου, τό, very seldom in native Grk. writ., *defection*, of a freedman from his patron, Dem. 35, 48 [940, 16]; in the Bible **1.** *divorce, repudiation*: Mt. xix. 7; Mk. x. 4 (βιβλίον ἀποστασίου, equiv. to כֵּפֶר כְּרִיתֻת book or bill of divorce, Deut. xxiv. 1, 3; [Is. l. 1; Jer. iii. 8]). **2.** *a bill of divorce*: Mt. v. 31. Grotius ad loc. and *Lightfoot*, Horae Hebr. ad loc., give a copy of one.*

648 ἀπο-στεγάζω: 1 aor. ἀπεστέγασα; (στεγάζω, fr. στέγη) *to uncover, take off the roof*: Mk. ii. 4 (Jesus, with his hearers, was in the ὑπερῷον q. v., and it was the roof of this which those who were bringing the sick man to Jesus are said to have 'dug out'; [cf. B. D. s. v. House, p. 1104]). (Strabo 4, 4, 6, p. 303; 8, 3, 30, p. 542.) *

649 ἀπο-στέλλω; fut. ἀποστελῶ; 1 aor. ἀπέστειλα; pf. ἀπέσταλκα, [3 pers. plur. ἀπέσταλκαν Acts xvi. 36 L T Tr WH (see γίνομαι init.)]; Pass., pres. ἀποστέλλομαι; pf. ἀπέσταλμαι; 2 aor. ἀπεστάλην; [fr. Soph. down]; prop. *to send off, send away*; **1.** *to order* (one) *to go to a place appointed*;

pointed; **a.** either **persons** sent with commissions, or **things** intended for some one. So, very frequently, Jesus teaches that God sent him, as Mt. x. 40; Mk. ix. 37; Lk. x. 16; Jn. v. 36, etc. he, too, is said to have sent his apostles, i. e. to have appointed them: Mk. vi. 7; Mt. x. 16; Lk. xxii. 35; Jn. xx. 21, etc. messengers are sent: Lk. vii. 3; ix. 52; x. 1; servants, Mk. vi. 27; xii. 2; Mt. xxi. 36; xxii. 3; an embassy, Lk. xiv. 32; xix. 14; angels, Mk. xiii. 27; Mt. xxiv. 31, etc. Things are said to be sent, which are ordered to be led away or conveyed to any one, as Mt. xxi. 3; Mk. xi. 3; τὸ δρέπανον i. e. reapers, Mk. iv. 29 [al. take ἀποστέλλω here of the "putting forth" of the sickle, i. e. of the act of reaping; cf. Joel (iii. 18) iv. 13; Rev. xiv. 15 (s. v. πέμπω, b.)]; τὸν λόγον, Acts x. 36; xiii. 26 (L T Tr WH ἐξαπεστάλη); τὴν ἐπαγγελίαν (equiv. to τὸ ἐπηγγελμένον, i. e. the promised Holy Spirit) ἐφ' ὑμᾶς, Lk. xxiv. 49 [T Tr WH ἐξαποστέλλω]; τὶ διὰ χειρός τινος, after the Hebr. בְּיַד, Acts xi. 30. **b.** The Place of the sending is specified: ἀποστ. εἴς τινα τόπον, Mt. xx. 2; Lk. i. 26; Acts vii. 34; x. 8; xix. 22; 2 Tim. iv. 12; Rev. v. 6, etc. God sent Jesus εἰς τὸν κόσμον: Jn. iii. 17; x. 36; xvii. 18; 1 Jn. iv. 9. εἰς [unto i.e.] among: Mt. xv. 24; Lk. xi. 49; Acts [xxii. 21 WH mrg.]; xxvi. 17; [ἐν (by a pregnant or a Lat. construction) cf. W. § 50, 4; B. 329 (283): Mt. x. 16; Lk. x. 3; yet see 1 a. above]; ὀπίσω τινός, Lk. xix. 14; ἔμπροσθέν τινος, Jn. iii. 28; and πρὸ προσώπου τινός, after the Hebr. לִפְנֵי, *before* (to precede) one: Mt. xi. 10; Mk. i. 2; Lk. vii. 27; x. 1. πρός τινα, to one: Mt. xxi. 34, 37; Mk. xii. 2 sq.; Lk. vii. 3, 20; Jn. v. 33; Acts viii. 14; 2 Co. xii. 17, etc. Whence, or by or from whom, one is sent: ὑπὸ τοῦ θεοῦ, Lk. i. 26 (T Tr WH ἀπό); παρὰ θεοῦ, Jn. i. 6 (Sir. xv. 9); ἀπό with gen. of pers., from the house of any one: Acts x. 17 [T WH Tr mrg. ὑπό], 21 Rec.; ἐκ with gen. of place: Jn. i. 19. **c.** The Object of the mission is indicated by an infin. following: Mk. iii. 14; Mt. xxii. 3; Lk. i. 19; iv. 18 (Is. lxi. 1, [on the pf. cf. W. 272 (255); B. 197 (171)]); Lk. ix. 2; Jn. iv. 38; 1 Co. i. 17; Rev. xxii. 6. [foll. by εἰς for: εἰς διακονίαν, Heb. i. 14. foll. by ἵνα: Mk. xii. 2, 13; Lk. xx. 10, 20; Jn. i. 19; iii. 17; vii. 32; 1 Jn. iv. 9. [foll. by ὅπως: Acts ix. 17.] foll. by an acc. with inf.: Acts v. 21. foll. by τινά with a pred. acc.: Acts iii. 26 (εὐλογοῦντα ὑμᾶς to confer God's blessing on you [cf. B. 203 (176) sqq.]); Acts vii. 35 (ἄρχοντα, to be a ruler); 1 Jn. iv. 10. **d.** ἀποστέλλω by itself, without an acc. [cf. W. 594 (552); B. 146 (128)]: as ἀποστέλλειν πρός τινα, Jn. v. 33; with the addition of the ptcp. λέγων, λέγουσα, λέγοντες, *to say through a messenger*: Mt. xxvii. 19; Mk. iii. 31 [here φωνοῦντες αὐτόν R G, καλοῦντες αὐτ. L T Tr WH]; Jn. xi. 3; Acts xiii. 15; [xxi. 25 περὶ τῶν πεπιστευκότων ἐθνῶν ἡμεῖς ἀπεστείλαμεν (L Tr txt. WH txt.) κρίναντες etc. *we sent word, giving judgment*, etc.]. When one accomplished anything through a messenger, it is expressed thus: ἀποστείλας or πέμψας he did so and so; as, ἀποστείλας ἀνεῖλε, Mt. ii. 16; Mk. vi. 17; Acts vii. 14; Rev. i. 1; (so also the Greeks, as Xen. Cyr. 3, 1, 6 πέμψας ἠρώτα, Plut. de liber. educ. c. 14 πέμψας ἀνεῖλε τὸν Θεό-

κριτον; and Sept. 2 K. vi. 13 ἀποστείλας λήψομαι αὐτόν).
2. *to send away* i. e. *to dismiss*; **a.** *to allow one to depart*: τινὰ ἐν ἀφέσει, that he may be in a state of liberty, Lk. iv. 18 (19), (Is. lviii. 6). **b.** *to order one to depart, send off*: Mk. viii. 26; τινὰ κενόν, Mk. xii. 3. **c.** *to drive away*: Mk. v. 10. [COMP.: ἐξ-, συν-αποστέλλω. SYN. see πέμπω, fin.]

650 **ἀπο-στερέω, -ῶ**; 1 aor. ἀπεστέρησα; [Pass., pres. ἀποστεροῦμαι]; pf. ptcp. ἀπεστερημένος; *to defraud, rob, despoil*: absol., Mk. x. 19; 1 Co. vi. 8; ἀλλήλους to withhold themselves from one another, of those who mutually deny themselves cohabitation, 1 Co. vii. 5. Mid. *to allow one's self to be defrauded* [W. § 38, 3]: 1 Co. vi. 7; τινά τινος (as in Grk. writ.), *to deprive one of a thing*; pass. ἀπεστερημένοι τῆς ἀληθείας, 1 Tim. vi. 5 [W. 196 (185); B. 158 (138)]; τί to defraud of a thing, to withdraw or keep back a thing by fraud: pass. μισθὸς ἀπεστερημένος, Jas. v. 4 (T Tr WH ἀφυστερημένος, see ἀφυστερέω; [cf. also ἀπό, II. 2 d. bb. p. 59ᵇ]), (Deut. xxiv. 14 [(16) Alex.]; Mal. iii. 5).*

651 **ἀπο-στολή, -ῆς, ἡ**, (ἀποστέλλω) ; **1.** *a sending away*: Τιμολέοντος εἰς Σικελίαν, Plut. Timol. 1, etc.; of the sending off of a fleet, Thuc. 8, 9; also of consuls with an army, i. e. of an expedition, Polyb. 26, 7, 1. **2.** *a sending away* i. e. *dismission*, release: Sept. Eccl. viii. 8. **3.** *a thing sent*, esp of gifts: 1 K. ix. 16 [Alex.]; 1 Macc. ii. 18 etc. cf. Grimm ad loc. **4.** in the N. T. *the office and dignity of the apostles of Christ*, (Vulg. *apostolatus*), *apostolate, apostleship*: Acts i. 25; Ro. i. 5; 1 Co. ix. 2; Gal. ii. 8.*

652 **ἀπόστολος, -ου, ὁ**; **1.** *a delegate, messenger, one sent forth with orders*, (Hdt. 1, 21; 5, 38; for שָׁלוּחַ in 1 K. xiv. 6 [Alex.]; rabbin.): שְׁלִיחַ): Jn. xiii. 16 (where ὁ ἀπόστ. and ὁ πέμψας αὐτόν are contrasted); foll. by a gen., as τῶν ἐκκλησιῶν, 2 Co. viii. 23; Phil. ii. 25; ἀπόστ. τῆς ὁμολογίας ἡμῶν the apostle whom we confess, of Christ, God's chief messenger, who has brought the κλῆσις ἐπουράνιος, as compared with Moses, whom the Jews confess, Heb. iii. 1. **2.** Specially applied to the twelve disciples whom Christ selected, out of the multitude of his adherents, to be his constant companions and the heralds to proclaim to men the kingdom of God: Mt. x. 1-4; Lk. vi. 13; Acts i. 26; Rev. xxi. 14, and often, but nowhere in the Gospel and Epistles of John; ["the word ἀπόστολος occurs 79 times in the N. T., and of these 68 instances are in St. Luke and St. Paul." Bp. Lghtft.]. With these apostles Paul claimed equality, because through a heavenly intervention he had been appointed by the ascended Christ himself to preach the gospel among the Gentiles, and owed his knowledge of the way of salvation not to man's instruction but to direct revelation from Christ himself, and moreover had evinced his apostolic qualifications by many signal proofs: Gal. i. 1, 11 sq.; ii. 8; 1 Co. i. 17; ix. 1 sq.; xv. 8-10; 2 Co. iii. 2 sqq.; xii. 12; 1 Tim. ii. 7; 2 Tim. i. 11, cf. Acts xxvi. 12-20. According to Paul, apostles surpassed as well the various other orders of Christian teachers (cf. διδάσκαλος, εὐαγγελιστής, προφήτης), as also the rest of those on whom the special gifts (cf. χάρισμα) of the Holy Spirit had been bestowed, by receiving a richer and more copious conferment of the Spirit: 1 Co. xii. 28 sq.; Eph. iv. 11. Certain false teachers are rated sharply for arrogating to themselves the name and authority of apostles of Christ: 2 Co. xi. 5, 13; Rev. ii. 2. **3.** In a broader sense the name is transferred to other eminent Christian teachers; as Barnabas, Acts xiv. 14, and perhaps also Timothy and Silvanus, 1 Th. ii. 7 (6), cf. too Ro. xvi. 7 (?). But in Lk. xi. 49; Eph. iii. 5; Rev. xviii. 20, 'apostles' is to be taken in the narrower sense. [On the application of the term see esp. Bp. Lghtft. on Gal. pp. 92-101; Harnack on 'Teaching' etc. 11, 3; cf BB.DD. s. v.]

653 **ἀποστοματίζω**; (στοματίζω—not extant—from στόμα); prop. *to speak ἀπὸ στόματος*, (cf. ἀποστηθίζω); **1.** *to recite from memory*: Themist. or. 20 p. 238 ed. Hard.; *to repeat to a pupil* (anything) *for him to commit to memory*: Plat. Euthyd. p. 276 c., 277 a.; used of a Sibyl prophesying, Plut. Thes. 24. **2.** *to ply with questions, catechize*, and so *to entice to* [off-hand] *answers*: τινά, Lk. xi. 53.*

654 **ἀπο-στρέφω**; fut. ἀποστρέψω; 1 aor. ἀπέστρεψα; 2 aor. pass. ἀπεστράφην; [pres. mid. ἀποστρέφομαι; fr. Hom. down]; **1.** *to turn away*: τινὰ or τὶ ἀπό τινος, 2 Tim. iv. 4 (τὴν ἀκοὴν ἀπὸ τῆς ἀληθείας); *to remove* anything from any one, Ro. xi. 26 (Is. lix. 20); ἀποστρέφειν τινά simply, *to turn him away from allegiance* to any one, tempt to defection, [A. V. *pervert*], Lk. xxiii. 14. **2.** *to turn back, return, bring back*: Mt. xxvi. 52 (put back thy sword into its sheath); Mt. xxvii. 3, (of Judas bringing back the shekels, where T Tr WH ἔστρεψε, [cf. Test. xii. Patr. test. Jos. § 17]. (In the same sense for הֵשִׁיב, Gen. xiv. 16; xxviii. 15; xliii. 11 (12), 20 (21), etc.; Bar. i. 8; ii. 34, etc.) **3.** intrans. *to turn one's self away, turn back, return*: ἀπὸ τῶν πονηριῶν, Acts iii. 26, cf. 19, (ἀπὸ ἁμαρτίας, Sir. viii. 5; xvii. 21 [26 Tdf.]; to return from a place, Gen. xviii. 33; 1 Macc. xi. 54, etc.; [see Kneucker on Bar. i. 13]; Xen. Hell. 3, 4, 12); cf. Meyer on Acts l. c.; [al. (with A. V.) take it actively here: *in turning away every one of you*, etc.]. **4.** Mid., with 2 aor. pass., *to turn one's self away from*, with acc. of the obj. (cf. [Jelf § 548 obs. 1; Krüg. § 47, 23, 1]; B. 192 (166)); *to reject, refuse*: τινά, Mt. v. 42; Heb. xii. 25; τὴν ἀλήθειαν, Tit. i. 14; in the sense of *deserting*, τινά, 2 Tim. i. 15.*

655 **ἀπο-στυγέω, -ῶ**; *to dislike, abhor, have a horror of*: Ro. xii. 9; (Hdt. 2, 47; 6, 129; Soph., Eur., al.). The word is fully discussed by Fritzsche ad loc. [who takes the ἀπο- as expressive of separation (cf. Lat. reformidare), al. regard it as intensive; (see ἀπό, V.)].*

656 **ἀποσυνάγωγος, -ον**, (συναγωγή, q. v.), *excluded from the sacred assemblies of the Israelites; excommunicated*, [A. V. *put out of the synagogue*]: Jn. ix. 22; xii. 42; xvi. 2. Whether it denotes also exclusion fr. all intercourse with Israelites (2 Esdr. x. 8), must apparently be left in doubt; Win. [or *Riehm*] R W B. s. v. Bann; Wieseler on Gal. i. 8, p. 45 sqq. [reproduced by Prof. *Riddle* in Schaff's Lange's Romans pp. 304-306; cf. B. D. s. v. Excommunication]. (Not found in prof. auth.)*

see
657 St.

ἀπο-τάσσω : *to set apart, to separate* ; in the N. T. only in Mid. ἀποτάσσομαι ; 1 aor. ἀπεταξάμην ; **1.** prop. *to separate one's self, withdraw one's self* from any one, i. e. *to take leave of, bid farewell to*, (Vulg. *valefacio* [etc.]) : τινί, Mk. vi. 46 ; Lk. ix. 61 ; Acts xviii. 18, 21 [here L T Tr om. the dat.] ; 2 Co. ii. 13. (That the early Grk. writ. never so used the word, but said ἀσπάζεσθαί τινα, is shown by *Lobeck* ad Phryn. p. 23 sq. ; [cf. W. 23 (22) ; B. 179 (156)].) **2.** trop. *to renounce, forsake*: τινί, Lk. xiv. 33. (So also Joseph. antt. 11, 6, 8 ; Phil. alleg. iii. § 48 ; ταῖς τοῦ βίου φροντίσι, Euseb. h. e. 2, 17, 5 ; [τῷ βίῳ, Ignat. ad Philadelph. 11, 1 ; cf. Herm. mand. 6, 2, 9 ; Clem. Rom. 2 Cor. 6, 4 and 5 where see Gebh. and Harn. for other exx., also *Soph.* Lex. s. v.].) *

658
ἀπο-τελέω, -ῶ ; [1 aor. pass. ptcp. ἀποτελεσθείς] ; *to perfect*; *to bring quite to an end* : ἰάσεις, *accomplish*, Lk. xiii. 32 (L T Tr WH for R G ἐπιτελῶ) ; ἡ ἁμαρτία ἀποτελεσθεῖσα having come to maturity, Jas. i. 15. (Hdt., Xen., Plat., and subseq. writ.) *

659
ἀπο-τίθημι : 2 aor. mid. ἀπεθέμην ; [fr. Hom. down] ; *to put off* or *aside* ; in the N. T. only mid. *to put off from one's self* : τὰ ἱμάτια, Acts vii. 58 ; [*to lay up* or *away, ἐν τῇ φυλακῇ* (i. e. *put*), Mt. xiv. 3 L T Tr WH (so εἰς φυλακήν, Lev. xxiv. 12 ; Num. xv. 34 ; 2 Chr. xviii. 26 ; Polyb. 24, 8, 8 ; Diod. 4, 49, etc.)] ; trop. those things are said *to be put off* or *away* which any one gives up, renounces : as τὰ ἔργα τοῦ σκότους, Ro. xiii. 12 ; — Eph. iv. 22 [cf. W. 347 (325) ; B. 274 (236)], 25 ; Col. iii. 8 ; Jas. i. 21 ; 1 Pet. ii. 1 ; Heb. xii. 1 ; (τὴν ὀργήν, Plut. Coriol. 19 ; τὸν πλοῦτον, τὴν μαλακίαν, etc. Luc. dial. mort. 10, 8 ; τ. ἐλευθερίαν κ. παρρησίαν, ibid. 9, etc.).*

660
ἀπο-τινάσσω ; 1 aor. ἀπετίναξα ; [1 aor. mid. ptcp. ἀποτιναξάμενος, Acts xxviii. 5 Tr mrg.] ; *to shake off* : Lk. ix. 5 ; Acts xxviii. 5. (1 S. x. 2 ; Lam. ii. 7 ; Eur. Bacch. 253 ; [ἀποτιναχθῇ, Galen 6, 821 ed. Kühn].) *

661
ἀπο-τίνω and ἀπο-τίω : fut. ἀποτίσω ; (ἀπό as in ἀποδίδωμι [cf. also ἀπό, V.]), *to pay off, repay* : Philem. 19. (Often in Sept. for שִׁלֵּם ; in prof. auth. fr. Hom. down.) *

662
ἀπο-τολμάω, -ῶ ; prop. *to be bold of one's self* (ἀπό [q. v. V.]), i. e. *to assume boldness, make bold* : Ro. x. 20 ; cf. *Win.* De verb. comp. etc. Pt. iv. p. 15. (Occasionally in Thuc., Plat., Aeschin., Polyb., Diod., Plut.) *

663
ἀποτομία, -ας, ἡ, (the nature of that which is ἀπότομος, cut off, abrupt, precipitous like a cliff, rough ; fr. ἀποτέμνω), prop. *sharpness*, (differing fr. ἀποτομή a cutting off, a segment) ; *severity, roughness, rigor* : Ro. xi. 22 (where opp. to χρηστότης, as in Plut. de lib. educ. c. 18 to πραότης, in Dion. Hal. 8, 61 to τὸ ἐπιεικές, and in Diod. p. 591 [except. lxxxiii. (frag. l. 32, 27, 3 Dind.)] to ἡμερότης).*

664
ἀποτόμως, adv., (cf. ἀποτομία) ; a. *abruptly, precipitously*. b. trop. *sharply, severely*, [cf. our *curtly*] : Tit. i. 13 ; 2 Co. xiii. 10. On the adj. ἀπότομος cf. Grimm on Sap. p. 121 [who in illustration of its use in Sap. v. 20, 22 ; vi. 5, 11 ; xi. 10 ; xii. 9 ; xviii. 15, refers to the similar metaph. use in Diod. 2, 57 ; Longin. de sublim. 27 ; and the use of the Lat. *abscisus* in Val. Max. 2, 7, 14, etc. ; see also Polb. 17, 11, 2 ; Polyc. ad Phil. 6, 1].*

ἀπο-τρέπω : [fr. Hom. down] ; *to turn away* ; Mid. [pres. ἀποτρέπομαι, impv. ἀποτρέπου] *to turn one's self away from, to shun, avoid* : τινά or τί (see ἀποστρέφω sub fin.), 2 Tim. iii. 5. (4 Macc. i. 33 ; Aeschyl. Sept. 1060 ; Eur. Iph. Aul. 336 ; [Aristot. plant. 1, 1 p. 815ᵇ, 18 ; Polyb. al.].)* 665

ἀπ-ουσία, -ας, ἡ, (ἀπεῖναι), *absence* : Phil. ii. 12. [From Aeschyl. down.] * 666

ἀπο-φέρω : 1 aor. ἀπήνεγκα ; 2 aor. inf. ἀπενεγκεῖν ; Pass., [pres. inf. ἀποφέρεσθαι] ; 1 aor. inf. ἀπενεχθῆναι ; [fr. Hom. down] ; *to carry off, take away* : τινά, with the idea of violence included, Mk. xv. 1 ; εἰς τόπον τινά, Rev. xvii. 3 ; xxi. 10 ; pass. Lk. xvi. 22. *to carry* or *bring away* (Lat. *defero*) : τὶ εἰς with acc. of place, 1 Co. xvi. 3 ; τὶ ἀπό τινος ἐπί τινα, with pass., Acts xix. 12 (L T Tr WH for Rec. ἐπιφέρεσθαι).* 667

ἀπο-φεύγω [ptcp. in 2 Pet. ii. 18 L T Tr WH ; W. 342 (321)] ; 2 aor. ἀπέφυγον ; [fr. (Hom.) batrach. 42, 47 down] ; *to flee from, escape*; with acc., 2 Pet. ii. 18 (where L T wrongly put a comma after ἀποφ. [W. 529 (492)]), 20 ; with gen., by virtue of the prep. [B. 158 (138) ; W. § 52, 4, 1 c.], 2 Pet. i. 4.* 668

ἀπο-φθέγγομαι ; 1 aor. ἀπεφθεγξάμην ; *to speak out, speak forth, pronounce*, not a word of every-day speech, but one "belonging to dignified and elevated discourse, like the Lat. *profari, pronuntiare* ; properly it has the force of *to utter* or *declare one's self, give one's opinion*, (*einen Ausspruch thun*), and is used not only of prophets (see Kypke on Acts ii. 4,— adding from the Sept. Ezek. xiii. 9 ; Mic. v. 12 ; 1 Chr. xxv. 1), but also of wise men and philosophers (Diog. Laërt. 1, 63 ; ‛73 ; 79 ; whose pointed sayings the Greeks call ἀποφθέγματα, Cic. off. 1, 29) " ; [see φθέγγομαι]. Accordingly, "it is used of the utterances of the Christians, and esp. Peter, on that illustrious day of Pentecost after they had been fired by the Holy Spirit, Acts ii. 4, 14 ; and also of the disclosures made by Paul to [before] king Agrippa concerning the ἀποκάλυψις κυρίου that had been given him, Acts xxvi. 25." *Win.* De verb. comp. etc. Pt. iv. p. 16.* 669

ἀπο-φορτίζομαι ; (φορτίζω to load ; φόρτος a load), *to disburden one's self*, τί, *to lay down a load, unlade, discharge* : τὸν γόμον, of a ship, Acts xxi. 3 ; cf. Meyer and De Wette ad loc. ; W. 349 (328) sq. (Elsewhere also used of sailors lightening ship during a storm in order to avoid shipwreck : Philo de praem. et poen. § 5 κυβερνήτης, χειμώνων ἐπιγινομένων, ἀποφορτίζεται ; Athen. 2, 5, p. 37 c. sq. where it occurs twice.) * 670

ἀπό-χρησις, -εως, ἡ, (ἀποχράομαι to use to the full, to abuse), *abuse, misuse* : Col. ii. 22 ἅ ἐστιν πάντα εἰς φθορὰν τῇ ἀποχρήσει "all which (i. e. things forbidden) tend to destruction (bring destruction) by abuse " ; Paul says this from the standpoint of the false teachers, who in any use of those things whatever saw an "abuse," i. e. a blameworthy use. In opposition to those who treat the clause as parenthetical and understand ἀπόχρησις to mean *consumption by use* (*a being used up*, as in Plut. moral. p. 267 f. [quaest. Rom. 18]), so that the words do not give the sentiment of the false teachers but Paul's 671

judgment of it, very similar to that set forth in Mt. xv.
17; 1 Co. vi. 13, cf. De Wette ad loc. [But see Meyer,
Ellicott, Lightfoot.]*

672 ἀπο-χωρέω, -ῶ; 1 aor. ἀπεχώρησα; [fr. Thuc. down];
to go away, depart: ἀπό τινος, Mt. vii. 23; Lk. ix. 39;
Acts xiii. 13; [absol. Lk. xx. 20 Tr mrg.].*

673 ἀπο-χωρίζω: [1 aor. pass. ἀπεχωρίσθην]; *to separate,
sever*, (often in Plato); *to part asunder*: pass. ὁ οὐρανὸς
ἀπεχωρίσθη, Rev. vi. 14; reflexively, *to separate one's
self, depart from*: ἀποχωρισθῆναι αὐτοὺς ἀπ' ἀλλήλων, Acts
xv. 39.*

674 ἀπο-ψύχω; *to breathe out life, expire*; *to faint* or *swoon
away*: Lk. xxi. 26. (So Thuc. 1, 134; Bion 1, 9, al.;
4 Macc. xv. 18.)*

675 Ἄππιος, -ου, ὁ, *Appius*, a Roman praenomen; Ἀππίου
φόρον *Appii Forum* (Cic. ad Att. 2, 10; Hor. sat. 1, 5,
3), [R. V. *The Market of Appius*], the name of a town
in Italy, situated 43 Roman miles from Rome on the
Appian way, — (this road was paved with square [(?)]
polygonal] stone by the censor Appius Claudius Caecus,
b. c. 312, and led through the *porta Capena* to Capua,
and thence as far as Brundisium): Acts xxviii. 15. [Cf.
BB.DD.]*

676 ἀ-πρόσ-ιτος, -ον, (προσιέναι to go to), *unapproachable, inaccessible*: φῶς ἀπρόσιτον, 1 Tim. vi. 16. (Polyb., Diod.,
[Strabo], Philo, Lcian., Plut.; φέγγος ἀπρόσιτον, Tatian
c. 20; δόξα [φῶς], Chrys. [vi. 66 ed. Montf.] on Is.
vi. 2.)*

677 ἀπρόσκοπος, -ον, (προσκόπτω, q. v.); **1.** actively,
having nothing for one to strike against; *not causing to
stumble*; **a.** prop.: ὁδός, a smooth road, Sir. xxxv.
(xxxii.) 21. **b.** metaph. *not leading others into sin by
one's mode of life*: 1 Co. x. 32. **2.** passively, **a.** *not
striking against* or *stumbling*; metaph. *not led into sin*;
blameless: Phil. i. 10 (joined with εἰλικρινεῖς). **b.** *without offence*: συνείδησις, not troubled and distressed by a
consciousness of sin, Acts xxiv. 16. (Not found in prof.
auth. [exc. Sext. Emp. 1, 195 (p. 644, 13 Bekk.)].)*

678 ἀπροσωπολήπτως [-λήμπτως L T Tr WH; cf. reff. s. v.
Μ, μ], a word of Hellenistic origin, (α priv. and προσω-
πολήπτης, q. v.), *without respect of persons*, i. e. impartially: 1 Pet. i. 17, (Ep. of Barn. 4, 12; [Clem. Rom. 1
Cor. 1, 3]). (The adj. ἀπροσωπόληπτος occurs here and
there in eccl. writ.)*

679 ἀ-πταιστος, -ον, (πταίω, q. v.), *not stumbling, standing
firm, exempt from falling*, (prop., of a horse, Xen. de re
eq. 1, 6); metaph.: Jude 24. [Cf. W. 97 (92); B. 42
(37).]*

680 & 681 ἅπτω; 1 aor. ptcp. ἅψας; (cf. Lat. *apto*, Germ. *heften*);
[fr. Hom. down]; **1.** prop. *to fasten to, make adhere
to*; hence, spec. to fasten fire to a thing, *to kindle, set on
fire*, (often so in Attic): λύχνον, Lk. viii. 16; xi. 33; xv.
8, (Arstph. nub. 57; Theophr. char. 20 (18); Joseph.
antt. 4, 3, 4); πῦρ, Lk. xxii. 55 [T Tr txt. WH π ε ρ ι-
αψάντων]; πυράν, Acts xxviii. 2 L T Tr WH. **2.** Mid.,
[pres. ἅπτομαι]; impf. ἡπτόμην [Mk. vi. 56 R G Tr mrg.];
1 aor. ἡψάμην; in Sept. generally for נָגַע, הִגִּיעַ; prop.
to fasten one's self to, adhere to, cling to, (Hom. Il. 8, 67);

a. *to touch,* foll. by the obj. in gen. [W. § 30, 8 c.; B. 167
(146); cf. Donaldson p. 483]: Mt. viii. 3; Mk. iii. 10;
vii. 33; viii. 22, etc.; Lk. xviii. 15; xxii. 51, — very
often in Mt., Mk. and Lk. In Jn. xx. 17, μή μου ἅπτου is
to be explained thus: Do not handle me to see whether
I am still clothed with a body; there is no need of such
an examination, "*for not yet*" etc.; cf. Baumg.- Crusius and
Meyer ad loc. [as given by *Hackett* in Bib. Sacr. for
1868, p. 779 sq., or B. D. Am. ed. p. 1813 sq.]. **b.** γυναικός, of carnal intercourse with a woman, or cohabitation,
1 Co. vii. 1, like the Lat. *tangere*, Hor. sat. 1, 2, 54: Ter.
Heaut. 4, 4, 15, and the Hebr. נָגַע, Gen. xx. 6; Prov. vi.
29, (Plat. de legg. viii. 840 a.; Plut. Alex. Magn. c. 21).
c. with allusion to the levitical precept ἀκαθάρτου μὴ
ἅπτεσθε, have no intercourse with the Gentiles, no fellowship in their heathenish practices, 2 Co. vi. 17 (fr.
Is. lii. 11); and in the Jewish sense, μὴ ἅψῃ, Col. ii. 21
(the things not to be touched appear to be both women
and certain kinds of food, so that celibacy and abstinence
from various kinds of food and drink are recommended;
cf. De Wette ad loc. [but also Meyer and Bp. Lghtft.;
on the distinction between the stronger term ἅπτεσθαι
(*to handle?*) and the more delicate θιγεῖν (*to touch?*) cf.
the two commentators just named and Trench § xvii. In
classic Grk. also ἅπτεσθαι is the stronger term, denoting
often *to lay hold of, hold fast, appropriate*; in its carnal
reference differing from θιγγάνειν by suggesting unlaw-
fulness. θιγγάνειν is used of touching by the hand as a
means of knowledge, handling for a purpose; ψηλαφᾶν
signifies *to feel around with the fingers* or *hands*, esp. in
searching for something, often *to grope, fumble*, cf. ψηλα-
φίνδα *blindman's buff.* Schmidt ch. 10.]). **d.** *to touch* i. e.
assail: τινός, any one, 1 Jn. v. 18, (1 Chr. xvi. 22, etc.).
[Comp.: ἀν-, καθ-, περι-άπτω.]

682 Ἀπφία, -ας, ἡ, *Apphia*, name of a woman: Philem. 2.
[Apparently a Phrygian name expressive of endearment,
cf. Suïdae Lex. ed. Gaisf. col. 534 a. Ἀπφά: ἀδελφῆς κ.
ἀδελφοῦ ὑποκόρισμα, etc. cf. Ἀπφύς. See fully in Bp.
Lghtft.'s Com. on Col. and Philem. p. 306 sqq.]*

**see
683 St.** ἀπ-ωθέω, -ῶ: *to thrust away, push away, repel*; in the
N. T. only Mid., pres. ἀπωθέομαι (-οῦμαι); 1 aor. ἀπωσάμην
(for which the better writ. used ἀπεωσάμην, cf. W 90 (86);
B. 69 (61)); *to thrust away from one's self, to drive away
from one's self*, i. e. *to repudiate, reject, refuse*: τινά, Acts
vii. 27, 39; xiii. 46; Ro. xi. 1 sq.; 1 Tim. i. 19. (Jer.
ii. 36 (37); iv. 30; vi. 19; Ps. xciii. (xciv.) 14 and often.
In Grk. writ. fr. Hom. down.) *

684 ἀπώλεια, -ας, ἡ, (fr. ἀπόλλυμι, q. v.); **1.** actively, *a
destroying, utter destruction*: as, of vessels, Ro. ix. 22;
τοῦ μύρου, *waste*, Mk. xiv. 4 (in Mt. xxvi. 8 without a
gen.), (in Polyb. 6, 59, 5 consumption, opp. to τήρησις);
the putting of a man to death, Acts xxv. 16 Rec.; by
meton. a destructive thing or opinion: in plur. 2
Pet. ii. 2 Rec.; but the correct reading ἀσελγείαις was
long ago adopted here. **2.** passively, *a perishing, ruin,
destruction*; **a.** in general: τὸ ἀργύριόν σου σὺν σοι εἴη εἰς
ἀπ. let thy money perish with thee, Acts viii. 20; βυθίζειν
τινὰ εἰς ὄλεθρον κ. ἀπώλειαν, with the included idea of

---

* For 685 see p. 71.

misery, 1 Tim. vi. 9; αἱρέσεις ἀπωλείας destructive opinions, 2 Pet. ii. 1; ἐπάγειν ἑαυτοῖς ἀπώλειαν, ibid. cf. vs. 3. **b.** in particular, *the destruction which consists in the loss of eternal life, eternal misery, perdition,* the lot of those excluded from the kingdom of God: Rev. xvii. 8, 11, cf. xix. 20; Phil. iii. 19; 2 Pet. iii. 16; opp. to ἡ περιποίησις τῆς ψυχῆς, Heb. x. 39; to ἡ ζωή, Mt. vii. 13; to σωτηρία, Phil. i. 28. ὁ υἱὸς τῆς ἀπωλείας, a man doomed to eternal misery (a Hebraism, see υἱός, 2): 2 Th. ii. 3 (of Antichrist); Jn. xvii. 12 (of Judas, the traitor); ἡμέρα κρίσεως κ. ἀπωλείας τῶν ἀσεβῶν, 2 Pet. iii. 7. (In prof. auth. fr. Polyb. u. s. [but see Aristot. probl. 17, 3, 2, vol. ii. p. 916ᵃ, 26; 29,14, 10 ibid. 952ᵇ, 26; Nicom. eth. 4, 1 ibid. 1120ᵃ, 2, etc.]; often in the Sept. and O. T. Apocr.)*

ἄρα, an illative particle (akin, as it seems, to the verbal root ΑΡΩ to join, to be fitted, [cf. Curtius § 488; Vaniček p. 47]), whose use among native Greeks is illustrated fully by Kühner ii. §§ 509, 545; [Jelf §§ 787–789], and *Klotz* ad Devar. ii. pp. 160–180, among others; [for a statement of diverse views see *Bäumlein*, Griech. Partikeln, p. 19 sq.]. It intimates that, "under these circumstances something either is so or becomes so" (Klotz l. c. p. 167): Lat. *igitur, consequently*, [differing from οὖν in 'denoting a subjective impression rather than a positive conclusion.' L. and S. (see 5 below)]. In the N. T. it is used frequently by Paul, but in the writings of John and in the so-called Catholic Epistles it does not occur. On its use in the N. T. cf. W. §§ 53, 8 a. and 61, 6. It is found   **1.** subjoined to another word: Ro. vii. 21; viii. 1; Gal. iii. 7; ἐπεὶ ἄρα since, if it were otherwise, 1 Co. vii. 14; [v. 10, cf. B. § 149, 5]. When placed after pronouns and interrogative particles, it refers to a preceding assertion or fact, or even to something existing only in the mind: τίς ἄρα *who then?* Mt. xviii. 1 (i. e. one certainly will be the greater, *who then?*); Mt. xix. 25 (i. e. certainly one will be saved; you say that the rich will not; *who then?*); Mt. xix. 27; xxiv. 45 (I bid you be ready; *who then* etc.? the question follows from this command of mine); Mk. iv. 41; Lk. i. 66 (from all these things doubtless something follows; *what, then?*); Lk. viii. 25; xii. 42; xxii. 23 (it will be one of us, *which then?*); Acts xii. 18 (Peter has disappeared; *what, then,* has become of him?). εἰ ἄρα, Mk. xi. 13 (whether, since the tree had leaves, he might also find some fruit on it); Acts vii. 1 [Rec.] (ἄρα equiv. to 'since the witnesses testify thus'); Acts viii. 22 (if, since thy sin is so grievous, perhaps the thought etc.); εἴπερ ἄρα, 1 Co. xv. 15, (אִם־נָא), εἰ ἄρα, Gen. xviii. 3). οὐκ ἄρα, Acts xxi. 38 (thou hast a knowledge of Greek; art thou not then the Egyptian, as I suspected?); μήτι ἄρα (Lat. *num igitur*), did I then etc., 2 Co. i. 17.   **2.** By a use doubtful in Grk. writ. (cf. B. 371 (318); [W. 558 (519)]) it is placed at the beginning of a sentence; *and so, so then, accordingly,* equiv. to ὥστε with a finite verb: ἄρα μαρτυρεῖτε [μάρτυρές ἐστε T Tr WH], Lk. xi. 48 (Mt. xxiii. 31 ὥστε μαρτυρεῖτε); Ro. x. 17; 1 Co. xv. 18; 2 Co. v. 14 (15) (in L T Tr WH no conditional protasis preceding); 2 Co. vii. 12; Gal. iv. 31 (L T Tr WH διό); Heb. iv. 9.   **3.** in an

apodosis, after a protasis with εἰ, in order to bring out what follows as a matter of course, (Germ. *so ist ja* the obvious inference is): Lk. xi. 20; Mt. xii. 28; 2 Co. v. 14 (15) (R G, a protasis with εἰ preceding); Gal. ii. 21; iii. 29; v. 11; Heb. xii. 8; joined to another word, 1 Co. xv. 14.   **4.** with γέ, rendering it more pointed, ἄραγε [L Tr uniformly ἄρα γε; so R WH in Acts xvii. 27; cf. W. p. 45; *Lips.* Gram. Untersuch. p. 123], *surely then, so then*, (Lat. *itaque ergo*): Mt. vii. 20; xvii. 26; Acts xi. 18 (L T Tr WH om. γέ); and subjoined to a word, Acts xvii. 27 [W. 299 (281)].   **5.** ἄρα οὖν, a combination peculiar to Paul, at the beginning of a sentence (W. 445 (414); B. 371 (318), ["ἄρα ad internam potius caussam spectat, οὖν magis ad externam." *Klotz* ad Devar. ii. p. 717; ἄρα is the more l o g i c a l, οὖν the more f o r m a l connective; "ἄρα is illative, οὖν continuative," Win. l. c.; cf. also Kühner § 545, 3]), [R. V.] *so then*, (Lat. *hinc igitur*): Ro. v. 18; vii. 3, 25; viii. 12; ix. 16, 18; xiv. 12 (L Tr om. WH br. οὖν); 19 [L mrg. ἄρα]; Gal. vi. 10; Eph. ii. 19; 1 Th. v. 6; 2 Th. ii. 15.*

ἄρα, an interrogative particle ["implying a n x i e t y or i m p a t i e n c e on the part of the questioner." L. and S. s. v.], (of the same root as the preceding ἄρα, and only differing from it in that more vocal stress is laid upon the first syllable, which is therefore circumflexed);   **1.** *num igitur*, i. e. marking an inferential question to which a negative answer is expected: Lk. xviii. 8; with γε rendering it more pointed, ἄρά γε [G T ἄράγε]: Acts viii. 30; [ἄρα οὖν ... διώκομεν Lchm. ed. min. also maj. mrg. *are we then pursuing* etc. Ro. xiv. 19].   **2.** *ergone* i. e. a question to which an affirmative answer is expected, in an interrogative apodosis, (Germ. *so ist also wohl?*), *he is then?* Gal. ii. 17 (where others [e. g. Lchm.] write ἄρα, so that this example is referred to those mentioned under ἄρα, 3, and is rendered *Christ is then a minister of sin*; but μὴ γένοιτο, which follows, is everywhere by Paul opposed to a question). Cf. W. 510 (475) sq. [also B. 247 (213), 371 (318); *Herm.* ad Vig. p. 820 sqq.; *Klotz* ad Devar. ii. p. 180 sqq.; speaking somewhat loosely, it may be said "ἄρα expresses bewilderment as to a possible conclusion... ἄρα hesitates, while ἄρα concludes." Bp. Lghtft. on Gal. l. c.].*

ἀρά, -ᾶς, ἡ,   **1.** *a prayer; a supplication*; much oftener   **2.** *an imprecation, curse, malediction,* (cf. κατάρα); so in Ro. iii. 14 (cf. Ps. ix. 28 (x. 7)), and often in Sept. (In both senses in native Grk. writ. fr. Hom. down.)*

Ἀραβία, -ας, ἡ, [fr. Hdt. down], *Arabia,* a well-known peninsula of Asia, lying towards Africa, and bounded by Egypt, Palestine, Syria, Mesopotamia, Babylonia, the Gulf of Arabia, the Persian Gulf, the Red Sea [and the Ocean]: Gal. i. 17; iv. 25.*

Ἀράμ, *Aram* [or *Ram*], indecl. prop. name of one of ---- the male ancestors of Christ: Mt. i. 3 sq.; Lk. iii. 33 [not T WH Tr mrg.; see Ἀδμείν and Ἀρνεί].*

ἄραφος T Tr for ἄρραφος, q. v.

687

685

688

see 728
see 686
see 687

---- 689

(689a);
see 729

690 Ἄραψ, -αβος, ὁ, an Arabian: Acts ii. 11.*

691 ἀργέω, -ῶ; (to be ἀργός, q. v.); to be idle, inactive; contextually, to linger, delay: 2 Pet. ii. 3 οἷς τὸ κρίμα ἔκπαλαι οὐκ ἀργεῖ, i. e. whose punishment has long been impending and will shortly fall.   (In Grk. writ. fr. Soph. down.) [COMP.: κατ-αργέω.] *

692 ἀργός, -όν, and in later writ. fr. Aristot. hist. anim. 10, 40 [vol. i. p. 627ᵃ, 15] on and consequently also in the N. T. with the fem. ἀργή, which among the early Greeks Epimenides alone is said to have used, Tit. i. 12; cf. Lob. ad Phryn. p. 104 sq.; id. Paralip. p. 455 sqq.; W. 68 (67), [cf. 24; B. 25 (23)], (contr. fr. ἄεργος which Hom. uses, fr. ἀ priv. and ἔργον without work, without labor, doing nothing), inactive, idle; **a.** free from labor, at leisure, (ἀργὸν εἶναι, Hdt. 5, 6): Mt. xx. 3, 6 [Rec.]; 1 Tim. v. 13. **b.** lazy, shunning the labor which one ought to perform, (Hom. Il. 9, 320 ὅ, τ' ἀεργὸς ἀνήρ, ὅ, τε πολλὰ ἐοργώς): πίστις, Jas. ii. 20 (L T Tr WH for R G νεκρά); γαστέρες ἀργαί i. e. idle gluttons, fr. Epimenides, Tit. i. 12 (Nicet. ann. 7, 4, 135 d. εἰς ἀργὰς γαστέρας ὀχετηγήσας); ἀργὸς καὶ ἄκαρπος εἴς τι, 2 Pet. i. 8. **c.** of things from which no profit is derived, although they can and ought to be productive; as of fields, trees, gold and silver, (cf. Grimm on Sap. xiv. 5; [L. and S. s. v. I. 2]); unprofitable, ῥῆμα ἀργόν, by litotes i. q. pernicious (see ἄκαρπος): Mt. xii. 36.*
[SYN. ἀργός, βραδύς, νωθρός: ἀργ. idle, involving blameworthiness; βρ. slow (tardy), having a purely temporal reference and no necessary bad sense; νωθρ. sluggish, descriptive of constitutional qualities and suggestive of censure. Schmidt ch. 49; Trench § civ.]

693 ἀργύρεος -οῦς, -έα -ᾶ, -εον -οῦν, of silver; in the contracted form in Acts xix. 24 [but WH br.]; 2 Tim. ii. 20; Rev. ix. 20. [From Hom. down.] *

694 ἀργύριον, -ου, τό, (fr. ἄργυρος, q. v.), [fr. Hdt. down]; **1.** silver: Acts iii. 6; vii. 16; xx. 33; 1 Pet. i. 18; [1 Co. iii. 12 T Tr WH].   **2.** money: simply, Mt. xxv. 18, 27; Mk. xiv. 11; Lk. ix. 3; xix. 15, 23; xxii. 5; Acts viii. 20; plur., Mt. xxviii. [12], 15.   **3.** Spec. a silver coin, silver-piece, (Luther, Silberling), כֶּסֶף, σίκλος, shekel [see B. D. s. v.], i. e. a coin in circulation among the Jews after the exile, from the time of Simon (c. B. C. 141) down (cf. 1 Macc. xv. 6 sq. [yet see B. D. s. v. Money, and reff. in Schürer, N. T. Zeitgesch. § 7]); according to Josephus (antt. 3, 8, 2) equal to the Attic tetradrachm or the Alexandrian didrachm (cf. στατήρ [B. D. s. v. Piece of Silver]): Mt. xxvi. 15; xxvii. 3, 5 sq. 9. In Acts xix. 19, ἀργυρίου μυριάδες πέντε fifty thousand pieces of silver (Germ. 50,000 in Silber i. q. Silbergeld), doubtless drachmas [cf. δηνάριον] are meant; cf. Meyer [et al.] ad loc.*

695 ἀργυροκόπος, -ου, ὁ, (ἄργυρος and κόπτω to beat, hammer; a silver-beater), a silversmith: Acts xix. 24. (Judg. xvii. 4; Jer. vi. 29. Plut. de vitand. aere alien. c. 7.) *

696 ἄργυρος, -ου, ὁ, (ἀργός shining), [fr. Hom. down], silver: 1 Co. iii. 12 [T Tr WH ἀργύριον] (reference is made to the silver with which the columns of noble buildings were covered and the rafters adorned); by meton. things made of silver, silver-work, vessels, images of the gods, etc.: Acts xvii. 29; Jas. v. 3; Rev. xviii. 12. silver coin: Mt. x. 9.*

697 Ἄρειος [Tdf. Ἄριος] πάγος, -ου, ὁ, Areopagus (a rocky height in the city of Athens not far from the Acropolis toward the west; πάγος a hill, Ἄρειος belonging to (Ares) Mars, Mars' Hill; so called, because, as the story went, Mars, having slain Halirrhothius, son of Neptune, for the attempted violation of his daughter Alcippe, was tried for the murder here before the twelve gods as judges; Pausan. Attic. 1, 28, 5), the place where the judges convened who, by appointment of Solon, had jurisdiction of capital offences, (as wilful murder, arson, poisoning, malicious wounding, and breach of the established religious usages). The court itself was called Areopagus from the place where it sat, also Areum judicium (Tacit. ann. 2, 55), and curia Martis (Juv. sat. 9, 101). To that hill the apostle Paul was led, not to defend himself before the judges, but that he might set forth his opinions on divine subjects to a greater multitude of people, flocking together there and eager to hear something new: Acts xvii. 19–22; cf. vs. 32. Cf. J. H. Krause in Pauly's Real-Encycl. 2te Aufl. i. 2 p. 1497 sqq. s. v. Areopag; [Grote, Hist. of Greece, index s. v.; Dicts. of Geogr. and Antiq.; BB.DD. s. v. Areopagus; and on Paul's discourse, esp. B. D. Am. ed. s. v. Mars' Hill].*

698 Ἀρεοπαγίτης, Tdf. -γείτης [see s. v. ει, ι], -ου, ὁ, (fr. the preceding [cf. Lob. ad Phryn. 697 sq.]), a member of the court of Areopagus, an Areopagite: Acts xvii. 34.*

699 ἀρεσκεία (T WH -κία [see I, ι]), -ας, ἡ, (fr. ἀρεσκεύω to be complaisant; hence not to be written [with R G L Tr] ἀρέσκεια, [cf. Chandler § 99; W. § 6, 1 g; B. 12 (11)]), desire to please: περιπατεῖν ἀξίως τοῦ κυρίου εἰς πᾶσαν ἀρεσκείαν, to please him in all things, Col. i. 10; (of the desire to please God, in Philo, opif. § 50; de profug. § 17; de victim. § 3 sub fin. In native Grk. writ. commonly in a bad sense: Theophr. char. 3 (5); Polyb. 31, 26, 5; Diod. 13, 53; al. [cf. Bp. Lghtft. on Col. l. c.]).*

700 ἀρέσκω; impf. ἤρεσκον; fut. ἀρέσω; 1 aor. ἤρεσα; (ΑΡΩ [see ἄρα init.]); [fr. Hom. down]; **a.** to please: τινί, Mt. xiv. 6; Mk. vi. 22; Ro. viii. 8; xv. 2; 1 Th. ii. 15; iv. 1; 1 Co. vii. 32–34; Gal. i. 10; 2 Tim. ii. 4; ἐνώπιόν τινος, after the Hebr. בְּעֵינֵי, Acts vi. 5, (1 K. iii. 10; Gen. xxxiv. 18, etc.). **b.** to strive to please; to accommodate one's self to the opinions, desires, interests of others: τινί, 1 Co. x. 33 (πάντα πᾶσιν ἀρέσκω); 1 Th. ii. 4. ἀρέσκειν ἑαυτῷ, to please one's self and therefore to have an eye to one's own interests: Ro. xv. 1, 3.*

701 ἀρεστός, -ή, -όν, (ἀρέσκω), pleasing, agreeable: τινί, Jn. viii. 29; Acts xii. 3; ἐνώπιόν τινος, 1 Jn. iii. 22 (cf. ἀρέσκω, a.); ἀρεστόν foll. by acc. with inf. it is fit, Acts vi. 2 [yet cf. Meyer ad loc.]. (In Grk. writ. fr. [Soph.] Hdt. down.) *

702 Ἀρέτας [WH 'Ἀρ., see their Intr. § 408], -α (cf. W. § 8, 1; [B. 20 (18)]), ὁ, Aretas, (a name common to many of the kings of Arabia Petraea or Nabathaean Arabia [cf. B. D. s. v. Nebaioth]; cf. Schürer, Neutest. Zeitgesch. § 17 b p. 233 sq.); an Arabian king who made war (A. D. 36) on his son-in-law Herod Antipas for having repudiated his daughter; and with such success as completely to destroy his army (Joseph. antt. 18, 5). In consequence of this, Vitellius, governor of Syria, being ordered by Tiberius to march an army against Aretas, prepared for the war. But Tiberius meantime having died [March 16, A. D. 37], he recalled his troops from the march, dismissed them to their winter quarters, and departed to Rome. After his departure Aretas held sway over the region of Damascus (how acquired we do not know), and placed an ethnarch over the city: 2 Co. xi. 32. Cf. Win. RWB. s. v.; Wieseler in Herzog i. p. 488 sq.; Keim in Schenkel i. p. 238 sq.; Schürer in Riehm p. 83 sq.; [B. D. Am. ed. s. v. Aretas; Meyer on Acts, Einl. § 4 (cf. ibid. ed. Wendt)].*

703   **ἀρετή**, -ῆς, ἡ, [see ἄρα init.], a word of very wide signification in Grk. writ.; *any excellence of a person* (in body or mind) or *of a thing*, an eminent endowment, property or quality. Used of the human mind and in an ethical sense, it denotes **1.** a virtuous course of thought, feeling and action; *virtue, moral goodness*, (Sap. iv. 1; v. 13; often in 4 Macc. and in Grk. writ.): 2 Pet. i. 5 [al. take it here specifically, viz. moral *vigor*; cf. next head]. **2.** any particular moral excellence, as modesty, purity; hence (plur. αἱ ἀρεταί, Sap. viii. 7; often in 4 Macc. and in the Grk. philosophers) τὶς ἀρετή, Phil. iv. 8. Used of God, it denotes **a.** his power: 2 Pet. i. 3. **b.** in the plur. his excellences, perfections, ‘which shine forth in our gratuitous calling and in the whole work of our salvation’ (Jn. Gerhard): 1 Pet. ii. 9. (In Sept. for הוֹד splendor, glory, Hab. iii. 3, of God; Zech. vi. 13, of the Messiah; in plur. for תְּהִלּוֹת praises, of God, Is. xliii. 21; xlii. 12; lxiii. 7.) *

704   **ἀρήν**, ὁ, nom. not in use; the other cases are by syncope ἀρνός (for ἀρένος), ἀρνί, ἄρνα, plur. ἄρνες, ἀρνῶν, ἀρνάσι, ἄρνας, a sheep, a lamb: Lk. x. 3. (Gen. xxx. 32; Ex. xxiii. 19, etc.; in Grk. writ. fr. Hom. down.) *

705   **ἀριθμέω**, -ῶ: 1 aor. ἠρίθμησα; pf. pass. ἠρίθμημαι; (ἀριθμός); [fr. Hom. down]; *to number*: Mt. x. 30; Lk. xii. 7; Rev. vii. 9. [COMP.: κατ-αριθμέω.] *

706   **ἀριθμός**, -οῦ, ὁ, [fr. Hom. down], a number. **a.** a fixed and definite number: τὸν ἀριθμὸν πεντακισχίλιοι, in number, Jn. vi. 10, (2 Macc. viii. 16; 3 Macc. v. 2, and often in Grk. writ.; W. 230 (216); [B. 153 (134)]); ἐκ τοῦ ἀριθμοῦ τῶν δώδεκα, Lk. xxii. 3; ἀρ. ἀνθρώπου, a number whose letters indicate a certain man, Rev. xiii. 18. **b.** an indefinite number, i. q. a multitude: Acts vi. 7; xi. 21; Rev. xx. 8.

707   **Ἀριμαθαία** [WH Ἁρ., see their Intr. § 408], -ας, ἡ, Arimathæa, Hebr. רָמָה (a height), the name of several cities of Palestine; cf. Gesenius, Thesaur. iii. p. 1275. The one mentioned in Mt. xxvii. 57; Mk. xv. 43; Lk. xxiii. 51; Jn. xix. 38 appears to have been the same as that which was the birthplace and residence of Samuel, in Mount Ephraim: 1 S. i. 1, 19, etc. Sept. Ἀρμαθαίμ, and without the art. Ῥαμαθέμ, and acc. to another reading Ῥαμαθαίμ, 1 Macc. xi. 34; Ῥαμαθά in Joseph. antt. 13, 4, 9. Cf. Grimm on 1 Macc. xi. 34; Keim, Jesus von Naz. iii. 514; [B. D. Am. ed.].*

708   **Ἀρίσταρχος**, -ου, ὁ, [lit. best-ruling], Aristarchus, a certain Christian of Thessalonica, a ‘fellow-captive’ with Paul [cf. B. D. Am. ed.; Bp. Lghtft. and Mey. on Col. as below]: Acts xix. 29; xx. 4; xxvii. 2; Col. iv. 10; Philem. 24.*

709   **ἀριστάω**, -ῶ: 1 aor. ἠρίστησα; (τὸ ἄριστον, q. v.); **a.** *to breakfast*: Jn. xxi. 12, 15; (Xen. Cyr. 6, 4, 1; and often in Attic). **b.** by later usage *to dine*: παρά τινι, Lk. xi. 37; (Gen. xliii. 24; Ael. v. h. 9, 19).*

710   **ἀριστερός**, -ά, -όν, left: Mt. vi. 3; Lk. xxiii. 33; [Mk. x. 37 T Tr WH, on the plur. cf. W. § 27, 3]; ὅπλα ἀριστερά i. e. carried in the left hand, defensive weapons, 2 Co. vi. 7. [From Hom. down.] *

711   **Ἀριστόβουλος**, -ου, ὁ, [lit. best-counselling], Aristobulus a certain Christian [cf. B. D. Am. ed. s. v. and Bp. Lghtft on Phil. p. 174 sq.]: Ro. xvi. 10.*

712   **ἄριστον**, -ου, τό, [fr. Hom. down]; **a.** the first food, taken early in the morning before work, breakfast; dinner was called δεῖπνον. But the later Greeks called breakfast τὸ ἀκράτισμα, and dinner ἄριστον i. e. δεῖπνον μεσημβρινόν, Athen. 1, 9, 10 p. 11 b.; and so in the N. T. Hence **b.** dinner: Lk. xiv. 12 (ποιεῖν ἄριστον ἢ δεῖπνον, to which others are invited); Lk. xi. 38; Mt. xxii. 4 (ἑτοιμάζειν). [B. D. s. v. Meals; Becker's Charicles, sc. vi. excurs. i. (Eng. trans. p. 312 sq.).] *

713   **ἀρκετός**, -ή, -όν, (ἀρκέω), sufficient: Mt. vi. 34 (where the meaning is, ‘Let the present day's trouble suffice for a man, and let him not rashly increase it by anticipating the cares of days to come’; [on the neut. cf. W. § 58, 5; B. 127 (111)]); ἀρκετόν τῷ μαθητῇ [A.V. it is enough for the disciple i.e.] let him be content etc., foll. by ἵνα, Mt. x. 25; foll. by an inf., 1 Pet. iv. 3. (Chrysipp. ap. Athen. 3, 79 p. 113 b.) *

714   **ἀρκέω**, ῶ; 1 aor. ἤρκεσα; [Pass., pres. ἀρκοῦμαι]; 1 fut. ἀρκεσθήσομαι; *to be possessed of unfailing strength; to be strong, to suffice, to be enough* (as against any danger; hence *to defend, ward off*, in Hom.; [al. make this the radical meaning, cf. Lat arceo; Curtius § 7]): with dat. of pers., Mt. xxv. 9; Jn. vi. 7; ἀρκεῖ σοι ἡ χάρις μου my grace is sufficient for thee, sc. to enable thee to bear the evil manfully; there is, therefore, no reason why thou shouldst ask for its removal, 2 Co. xii. 9; impersonally, ἀρκεῖ ἡμῖν 'tis enough for us, we are content, Jn. xiv. 8. Pass. (as in Grk. writ.) to be satisfied, contented: τινί, with a thing, Lk. iii. 14; Heb. xiii. 5; 1 Tim. vi. 8; (2 Macc. v. 15); ἐπί τινι, 3 Jn. 10. [COMP.: ἐπ-αρκέω.] *

715   **ἄρκτος**, -ου, ὁ, ἡ, or [so GLTTrWH] ἄρκος, -ου, ὁ, ἡ, a bear: Rev. xiii. 2. [From Hom. down.] *

716   **ἅρμα**, -ατος, τό, (fr. ΑΡΩ to join, fit; a team), a chariot: Acts viii. 28 sq. 38; of war-chariots (i. e. armed with scythes) we read ἅρματα ἵππων πολλῶν chariots drawn by many horses, Rev. ix. 9, (Joel ii. 5. In Grk. writ. fr. Hom. down).*

717   **Ἁρμαγεδών** [Grsb. Ἁρμ., WH Ἁρ Μαγεδών, see their Intr. § 408; Tdf. Proleg. p. 106] or (so Rec.) Ἁρμαγεδδών, Har-Magedon or Armageddon, indecl. prop. name of an imaginary place: Rev. xvi. 16. Many, following Beza and Glassius, suppose that the name is compounded of

הַר mountain, and מְגִדּוֹן or מְגִדּוֹן, Sept. Μαγεδώ, Μαγεδδώ. Megiddo was a city of the Manassites, situated in the great plain of the tribe of Issachar, and famous for a double slaughter, first of the Canaanites (Judg. v. 19), and again of the Israelites (2 K. xxiii. 29 sq.; 2 Chr. xxxv. 22, cf. Zech. xii. 11); so that in the Apocalypse it would signify the place where the kings opposing Christ were to be destroyed with a slaughter like that which the Canaanites or the Israelites had experienced of old. But since these two overthrows are said to have taken place ἐπὶ ὕδατι Μαγ. (Judg. l. c.) and ἐν τῷ πεδίῳ Μαγ. (2 Chr. l. c.), it is not easy to perceive what can be the meaning of the mountain of Megiddo, which could be none other than Carmel. Hence, for one, I think the conjecture of L. Capellus [i. e. Louis Cappel (akin to that of Drusius, see the Comm.)] to be far more easy and probable, viz. that Ἁρμαγεδών is for Ἁρμαμεγεδών, compounded of חרמא destruction, and מגידון. [Wieseler (Zur Gesch. d. N. T. Schrift, p. 188), Hitzig (in Hilgenf. Einl. p. 440 n.), al., revive the derivation (cf. Hiller, Simonis, al.) fr. מְ עָר city of Megiddo.]*

718   ἁρμόζω, Attic ἁρμόττω: 1 aor. mid. ἡρμοσάμην; (ἁρμός, q. v.);   **1.** to join, to fit together; so in Hom. of carpenters, fastening together beams and planks to build houses, ships, etc.   **2.** of marriage: ἁρμόζειν τινὶ τὴν θυγατέρα (Hdt. 9, 108) to betroth a daughter to any one; pass. ἁρμόζεται γυνὴ ἀνδρί, Sept. Prov. xix. 14; mid. ἁρμόσασθαι τὴν θυγατέρα τινός (Hdt. 5, 32; 47; 6, 65) to join to one's self, i. e. to marry, the daughter of any one; ἁρμόσασθαί τινί τινα to betroth, to give one in marriage to any one: 2 Co. xi. 2, and often in Philo, cf. Loesner ad loc.; the mid. cannot be said to be used actively, but refers to him to whom the care of betrothing has been committed; [cf. B. 193 (167); per contra Mey. ad loc.; W. 258 (242)].*

719   ἁρμός, -οῦ, ὁ, (ΑΡΩ to join, fit), a joining, a joint: Heb. iv. 12. (Soph., Xen., al.; Sir. xxvii. 2.) *

see 704   ἄρνας, see ἀρήν.

see 689   Ἀρνεί, ὁ, indecl. prop. name of one of the ancestors of Jesus: Lk. iii. 33 T WH Tr mrg.*

720   ἀρνέομαι, -οῦμαι; fut. ἀρνήσομαι; impf. ἠρνούμην; 1 aor. ἠρνησάμην (rare in Attic, where generally ἠρνήθην, cf. Matth. i. p. 538 [better Veitch s. v.]); pf. ἤρνημαι; a depon. verb [(fr. Hom. down)] signifying   **1.** to deny, i. e. εἰπεῖν ... οὐκ [to say ... not, contradict]: Mk. xiv. 70; Mt. xxvi. 70; Jn. i. 20; xviii. 25, 27; Lk. viii. 45; Acts iv. 16; foll. by ὅτι οὐ instead of simple ὅτι, in order to make the negation more strong and explicit: Mt. xxvi. 72; 1 Jn. ii. 22; (on the same use in Grk. writ. cf. Kühner ii. p. 761; [Jelf ii. 450; W. § 65, 2 β.; B. 355 (305)]).   **2.** to deny, with an acc. of the pers., in various senses: **a.** ἀρν. Ἰησοῦν is used of followers of Jesus who, for fear of death or persecution, deny that Jesus is their master, and desert his cause, [to disown]: Mt. x. 33; Lk. xii. 9; [Jn. xiii. 38 L txt. T Tr WH]; 2 Tim. ii. 12, (ἀρν. τὸ ὄνομα αὐτοῦ, Rev. iii. 8, means the same); and on the other hand, of Jesus, denying that one is his follower: Mt. x. 33; 2 Tim. ii. 12.

b. ἀρν. God and Christ, is used of those who by cherishing and disseminating pernicious opinions and immorality are adjudged to have apostatized from God and Christ: 1 Jn. ii. 22 (cf. iv. 2; 2 Jn. 7-11); Jude 4; 2 Pet. ii. 1.   **c.** ἀρν. ἑαυτόν to deny himself, is used in two senses,   **α.** to disregard his own interests: Lk. ix. 23 [R WH mrg. ἀπαρν.]; cf. ἀπαρνέομαι.   **β.** to prove false to himself, act entirely unlike himself: 2 Tim. ii. 13.   **3.** to deny i. e. abnegate, abjure; τί, to renounce a thing, forsake it: τὴν ἀσέβειαν κ. τὰς ἐπιθυμίας, Tit. ii. 12; by act to show estrangement from a thing: τὴν πίστιν, 1 Tim. v. 8; Rev. ii. 13; τὴν δύναμιν τῆς εὐσεβείας, 2 Tim. iii. 5.   **4.** not to accept, to reject, refuse, something offered: τινά, Acts iii. 14; vii. 35; with an inf. indicating the thing, Heb. xi. 24. [Comp.: ἀπ-αρνέομαι.]

ἀρνίον, -ου, τό, (dimin. fr. ἀρήν, q. v.), [fr. Lys. down],   **721** a little lamb, a lamb: Rev. xiii. 11; Jesus calls his followers τὰ ἀρνία μου in Jn. xxi. 15; τὸ ἀρνίον is used of Christ, innocently suffering and dying to expiate the sins of men, very often in Rev., as v. 6, 8, 12, etc. (Jer. xi. 19; xxvii. (l.) 45; Ps. cxiii. (cxiv.) 4, 6; Joseph. antt. 3, 8, 10.) *

ἀροτριάω, -ῶ; (ἄροτρον, q. v.); to plough: Lk. xvii. 7;   **722** 1 Co. ix. 10. (Deut. xxii. 10; [1 K. xix. 19]; Mic. iii. 12. In Grk. writ. fr. Theophr. down for the more ancient ἀρόω; cf. Lob. ad Phryn. p. 254 sq. [W. 24].) *

ἄροτρον, -ου, τό, (ἀρόω to plough), a plough: Lk. ix. 62.   **723** (In Grk. writ. fr. Hom. down.)*

ἁρπαγή, -ῆς, ἡ, (ἁρπάζω), rapine, pillage;   **1.** the act   **724** of plundering, robbery: Heb. x. 34.   **2.** plunder, spoil: Mt. xxiii. 25; Lk. xi. 39. (Is. iii. 14; Nah. ii. 12. In Grk. writ. fr. Aeschyl. down.) *

ἁρπαγμός, -οῦ, ὁ, (ἁρπάζω);   **1.** the act of seizing, rob-   **725** bery, (so Plut. de lib. educ. c. 15 (al. 14, 37), vol. ii. 12 a. the only instance of its use noted in prof. auth.)   **2.** a thing seized or to be seized, booty: ἁρπαγμὸν ἡγεῖσθαί τι to deem anything a prize, — a thing to be seized upon or to be held fast, retained, Phil. ii. 6; on the meaning of this pass. see μορφή; (ἡγεῖσθαι or ποιεῖσθαί τι ἅρπαγμα, Euseb. h. e. 8, 12, 2; vit. Const. 2, 31; [Comm. in Luc. vi., cf. Mai, Nov. Bibl. Patr. iv. p. 165]; Heliod. 7, 11 and 20; 8, 7; [Plut. de Alex. virt. 1, 8 p. 330 d.]; ut omnium bona praedam tuam duceres, Cic. Verr. ii. 5, 15, 39; [see Bp. Lghtft. on Phil. p. 133 sq. (cf. p. 111); Wetstein ad loc.; Cremer 4te Aufl. p. 153 sq.]).*

ἁρπάζω; fut. ἁρπάσω [Veitch s. v.; cf. Rutherford, New   **726** Phryn. p. 407]; 1 aor. ἥρπασα; Pass., 1 aor. ἡρπάσθην; 2 aor. ἡρπάγην (2 Co. xii. 2, 4; Sap. iv. 11; cf. W. 83 (80); [B. 54 (47); WH. App. p. 170]); 2 fut. ἁρπαγήσομαι; [(Lat. rapio; Curtius § 331); fr. Hom. down]; to seize, carry off by force: τί, [Mt. xii. 29 not RG, (see διαρπάζω)]; Jn. x. 12; to seize on, claim for one's self eagerly: τὴν βασιλείαν τοῦ θεοῦ, Mt. xi. 12, (Xen. an. 6, 5, 18, etc.); to snatch out or away: τί, Mt. xiii. 19; τὶ ἐκ χειρός τινος, Jn. x. 28 sq.; τινὰ ἐκ πυρός, proverbial, to rescue from the danger of destruction, Jude 23, (Am. iv. 11; Zech. iii. 2); τινά, to seize and carry off speedily, Jn. vi. 15; Acts xxiii. 10; used of divine power transferring a person marvellously and swiftly from one place to another, *to snatch* or *catch away* : Acts viii. 39 ; pass. πρὸς τ. θεόν, Rev. xii. 5 ; foll. by ἕως with gen. of place, 2 Co. xii. 2 ; εἰς τ. παράδεισον, 2 Co. xii. 4 ; εἰς ἀέρα, 1 Th. iv. 17. [COMP. : δι-, συν-αρπάζω.]*

727   **ἄρπαξ**, -αγος, ὁ, adj., *rapacious, ravenous* : Mt. vii. 15 ; Lk. xviii. 11 ; as subst. *a robber, an extortioner* : 1 Co. v. 10 sq.; vi. 10. (In both uses fr. [Arstph.], Xen. down.)*

728   **ἀρραβών** [Tdf. ἀραβών: 2 Co. i. 22 (to Lchm.) ; v. 5, (but not in Eph. i. 14), see his Proleg. p. 80 ; *WH.* App. p. 148; cf. W. 48 (47 sq.) ; B. 32 (28 sq.) , cf. P, ρ],-ῶνος, ὁ, (Hebr. עֵרָבוֹן, Gen. xxxviii. 17 sq. 20 ; fr. עָרַב to pledge; a word which seems to have passed from the Phœnicians to the Greeks, and thence into Latin), *an earnest*, i. e. money which in purchases is given as a pledge that the full amount will subsequently be paid [Suid. s. v. ἀραβών], (cf. [obs. Eng. *earlespenny* ; *caution-money*], Germ. *Kaufschilling, Haftpfennig*) : 2 Co. i. 22; v. 5, τὸν ἀρραβῶνα τοῦ πνεύματος i. e. τὸ πνεῦμα ὡς ἀρραβῶνα sc. τῆς κληρονομίας, as is expressed in full in Eph. i. 14 [cf. W. § 59, 8 a.; B. 78 (68)] ; for the gift of the Holy Spirit, comprising as it does the δυνάμεις τοῦ μέλλοντος αἰῶνος (Heb. vi. 5), is both a foretaste and a pledge of future blessedness ; cf. s. v. ἀπαρχή, c. [B.D. s. v. Earnest.] (Isae. 8, 23 [p. 210 ed. Reiske] ; Aristot. pol. 1, 4, 5 [p. 1259ᵃ, 12] ; al.)*

729   **ἄρραφος**, T Tr WH ἄραφος (cf. W. 48 ; B. 32 (29); [*WH.* App. p. 163 ; *Tdf.* Proleg. p. 80 ; cf. P, ρ]), -ον, (ῥάπτω to sew together), *not sewed together, without a seam* : Jn. xix. 23.*

730; see 730α below   **ἄρρην**, see ἄρσην.

731   **ἄρ-ρητος**, -ον, (ῥητός, fr. ΡΕΩ) ; a. *unsaid, unspoken* : Hom. Od. 14, 466, and often in Attic. b. *unspeakable* (on account of its sacredness), (Hdt. 5, 83, and often in other writ.) : 2 Co. xii. 4, explained by what follows: ἃ οὐκ ἐξὸν ἀνθρώπῳ λαλῆσαι.*

732   **ἄρρωστος**, -ον, (ῥώννυμι, q. v.), *without strength, weak; sick* : Mt. xiv. 14; Mk. vi. 5, 13; xvi. 18 ; 1 Co. xi. 30. ([Hippocr.], Xen., Plut.) *

733   **ἀρσενοκοίτης**, -ου, ὁ, (ἄρσην a male ; κοίτη a bed), *one who lies with a male as with a female, a sodomite* : 1 Co. vi. 9 ; 1 Tim. i. 10. (Anthol. 9, 686, 5 ; eccl. writ.) *

730α   **ἄρσην**, -ενος, ὁ, ἄρσεν, τό, also (acc. to R G in Rev. xii. 5, 13, and in many edd., that of Tdf. included, in Ro. i. 27ᵃ ; cf. Fritzsche on Rom. vol. i. p. 78; [W. 22]) ἄρρην, -ενος, ὁ, ἄρρεν, τό, [fr. Hom. down], *male* : Mt. xix. 4 ; Mk. x. 6 ; Lk. ii. 23 ; Ro. i. 27 ; Gal. iii. 28 ; Rev. xii. 5, 13 (where Lchm. reads ἄρσεναν ; on which Alex. form of the acc. cf. W. 48 (47 sq.); 66 (64) ; Mullach p. 22 [cf. p. 162]; B. 13 (12) ; [*Soph.* Lex., Intr. p. 36; *Tdf.* Proleg. p. 118; Müller's note on Barn. ep. 6, 2 p. 158 ; *WH.* App. p. 157; *Scrivener*, Collation etc. p. liv.]).*

734   **Ἀρτεμᾶς**, -ᾶ, ὁ, (abbreviated fr. Ἀρτεμίδωρος [i. e. gift of Artemis], cf. W. 102 (97) ; [B. 20 (17 sq.) ; *Lob.* Pathol. Proleg. p. 505 sq. ; Chandler § 32]), *Artemas*, a friend of Paul the apostle: Tit. iii. 12. [Cf. B. D. s. v.]*

735   **Ἄρτεμις**, -ιδος and -ιος, ἡ, *Artemis*, that is to say, the so-called Tauric or Persian or Ephesian Ar-

temis, the goddess of many Asiatic peoples, to be distinguished from the Artemis of the Greeks, the sister of Apollo ; cf. Grimm on 2 Macc. p. 39 ; [B. D. s. v. Diana]. A very splendid temple was built to her at Ephesus, which was set on fire by Herostratus and reduced to ashes ; but afterwards, in the time of Alexander the Great, it was rebuilt in a style of still greater magnificence : Acts xix. 24, 27 sq. 34 sq. Cf. *Stark* in Schenkel i. p. 604 sq. s. v. Diana ; [*Wood*, Discoveries at Ephesus, Lond. 1877].*

736   **ἀρτέμων**, -ονος (L T Tr WH -ωνος, cf. W. § 9, 1 d. ; [B. 24 (22)]), ὁ, *top-sail* [or *foresail?*] of a ship : Acts xxvii. 40 ; cf. Meyer ad loc. ; [esp. *Smith*, Voyage and Shipwr. of St. Paul, p. 192 sq. ; *Graser* in the Philologus, 3d suppl. 1865, p. 201 sqq.].*

737   **ἄρτι**, adv., acc. to its deriv. (fr. ΑΡΩ to draw close together, to join, Lat. *arto* ; [cf. Curtius § 488]) denoting time closely connected ;   **1.** in Attic *"just now, this moment*, (Germ. *gerade, eben*), marking something begun or finished even now, just before the time in which we are speaking" (*Lobeck* ad Phryn. p. 20) : Mt. ix. 18; 1 Th. iii. 6, and perhaps Rev. xii. 10.   **2.** acc. to later Grk. usage univ. *now, at this time*; opp. to past time : Jn. ix. 19, 25 ; xiii. 33 ; 1 Co. xvi. 7 ; Gal. i. 9 sq. opp. to future time : Jn. xiii. 37 ; xvi. 12, 31 ; 2 Th. ii. 7 ; opp. to fut. time subsequent to the return of Christ : 1 Co. xiii. 12 ; 1 Pet. i. 6, 8. of present time most closely limited, *at this very time, this moment* : Mt. iii. 15 ; xxvi. 53 ; Jn. xiii. 7 ; Gal. iv. 20. ἄχρι τῆς ἄρτι ὥρας, 1 Co. iv. 11 ; ἕως ἄρτι, *hitherto* ; *until now, up to this time* : Mt. xi. 12 ; Jn. ii. 10 ; v. 17 ; xvi. 24 ; 1 Co. iv. 13 ; viii. 7 ; xv. 6 ; 1 Jn. ii. 9. ἀπ᾽ ἄρτι, see ἀπάρτι above. Cf. *Lobeck* ad Phryn. p. 18 sqq. ; [*Rutherford*, New Phryn. p. 70 sq.].*

[SYN. ἄρτι, ἤδη, νῦν : Roughly speaking, it may be said that ἄρτι *just now, even now*, properly marks time closely connected with the present ; later, strictly present time, (see above, and compare in Eng. "just now" i. e. *a moment ago*, and "just now" (emphat.) i. e. *at this precise time*). νῦν *now*, marks a definite point (or period) of time, the (objective) immediate present. ἤδη *now (already)* with a suggested reference to some other time or to some expectation, the subjective present (i. e. so regarded by the writer). ἤδη and ἄρτι are associated in 2 Thess. ii. 7 ; νῦν and ἤδη in 1 Jn. iv. 3. See Kühner §§ 498, 499 ; Bäumlein, Partikeln, p. 138 sqq. ; Ellic. on 1 Thess. iii. 6 ; 2 Tim. iv. 6.]

738   **ἀρτι-γέννητος**, -ον, (ἄρτι and γεννάω), *just born, new-born* : 1 Pet. ii. 2. (Lcian. Alex. 13 ; Long. past. 1, (7) 9 ; 2, (3) 4.) *

739   **ἄρτιος**, -α, -ον, (ΑΡΩ to fit, [cf. Curtius § 488]) ;   **1.** *fitted*.   **2.** *complete, perfect*, [having reference apparently to 'special aptitude for given uses'] ; so 2 Tim. iii. 17, [cf. Ellicott ad loc. ; Trench § xxii.]. (In Grk. writ. fr. Hom. down.) *

740   **ἄρτος**, -ου, ὁ, (fr. ΑΡΩ to fit, put together, [cf. Etym. Magn. 150, 36 — but doubtful]), *bread* ; Hebr. לֶחֶם ;   **1.** *food composed of flour mixed with water and baked*; the Israelites made it in the form of an oblong or round cake, as thick as one's thumb, and as large as a plate or platter (cf. *Win.* R W B. s. v. Backen ; [BB.DD.]);

hence it was not cut, but broken (see κλάσις and κλάω) : Mt. iv. 3 ; vii. 9 ; xiv. 17, 19 ; Mk. vi. 36 [T Tr WH om. L br.], 37 sq. ; Lk. iv. 3 ; xxiv. 30 ; Jn. vi. 5 sqq. ; Acts xxvii. 35, and often ; ἄρτοι τῆς προθέσεως, loaves consecrated to Jehovah, see πρόθεσις ; on the bread used at the love-feasts and the sacred supper [W. 35], cf. Mt. xxvi. 26 ; Mk. xiv. 22 ; Lk. xxii. 19 ; Acts ii. 42, 46 ; xx. 7 ; 1 Co. x. 16 sq. ; xi. 26–28. **2.** As in Grk. writ., and like the Hebr. לֶחֶם, *food of any kind* : Mt. vi. 11 ; Mk. vi. 8 ; Lk. xi. 3 ; 2 Co. ix. 10 ; ὁ ἄρτος τῶν τέκνων the food served to the children, Mk. vii. 27 ; ἄρτον φαγεῖν or ἐσθίειν *to take food, to eat* (אָכַל לֶחֶם) [W. 33 (32)] : Mk. iii. 20 ; Lk. xiv. 1, 15 ; Mt. xv. 2 ; ἄρτον φαγεῖν παρά τινος to take food supplied by one, 2 Th. iii. 8 ; τὸν ἑαυτοῦ ἄρτ. ἐσθίειν to eat the food which one has procured for himself by his own labor, 2 Th. iii. 12 ; μήτε ἄρτον ἐσθίων, μήτε οἶνον πίνων, abstaining from the usual sustenance, or using it sparingly, Lk. vii. 33 ; τρώγειν τὸν ἄρτον μετά τινος to be one's table-companion, his familiar friend, Jn. xiii. 18 (Ps. xl. (xli.) 10). In Jn. vi. 32–35 Jesus calls himself τὸν ἄρτον τοῦ θεοῦ, τ. ἄ. ἐκ τοῦ οὐρανοῦ, τ. ἄ. τῆς ζωῆς, as the divine λόγος, come from heaven, who containing in himself the source of heavenly life supplies celestial nutriment to souls that they may attain to life eternal.

741 ἀρτύω : fut. ἀρτύσω ; Pass., pf. ἤρτυμαι ; 1 fut. ἀρτυθήσομαι ; (ΑΡΩ to fit) ; *to prepare, arrange* ; often so in Hom. In the comic writers and epigrammatists used of preparing food, *to season, make savory,* ([τὰ ὄψα, Aristot. eth. Nic. 3, 13 p. 1118ᵃ, 29] ; ἠρτυμένος οἶνος, Theophr. de odor. § 51 [frag. 4, c. 11]) ; so Mk. ix. 50 ; Lk. xiv. 34 ; metaph. ὁ λόγος ἅλατι ἠρτυμένος, full of wisdom and grace and hence pleasant and wholesome, Col. iv. 6.*

742 Ἀρφαξάδ, ὁ, Arphaxad, (אַרְפַּכְשַׁד), son of Shem (Gen. x. 22, 24 ; xi. 10, 12, [cf. Jos. antt. 1, 6, 4]) : Lk. iii. 36.*

743 ἀρχ-άγγελος, -ου, ὁ, (fr. ἄρχι, q. v., and ἄγγελος), a bibl. and eccl. word, *archangel,* i. e. chief of the angels (Hebr. שַׂר chief, prince, Dan. x. 20 ; xii. 1), or one of the princes and leaders of the angels (הַשָּׂרִים הָרִאשֹׁנִים, Dan. x. 13) : 1 Th. iv. 16 ; Jude 9. For the Jews after the exile distinguished several orders of angels, and some (as the author of the book of Enoch, ix. 1 sqq. ; cf. Dillmann ad loc. p. 97 sq.) reckoned f o u r angels (answering to the four sides of the throne of God) of the highest rank ; but others, and apparently the majority (Tob. xii. 15, where cf. Fritzsche ; Rev. viii. 2), reckoned s e v e n (after the pattern of the seven *Amshaspands,* the highest spirits in the religion of Zoroaster). See s. vv. Γαβριήλ and Μιχαήλ.*

744 ἀρχαῖος, -αία, -αῖον, (fr. ἀρχή beginning, hence) prop. *that has been from the beginning, original, primeval, old, ancient,* used of men, things, times, conditions : Lk. ix. 8, 19 ; Acts xv. 7, 21 ; xxi. 16 ; 2 Pet. ii. 5 ; Rev. xii. 9 ; xx. 2 ; οἱ ἀρχαῖοι the ancients, the early Israelites : Mt. v. 21, 27 [Rec.], 33 ; τὰ ἀρχαῖα the man's previous moral condition : 2 Co. v. 17. (In Grk. writ. fr. Pind. and Hdt. down.)*

[Syn. ἀρχαῖος, παλαιός : in παλ. the simple idea of time dominates, while ἀρχ. ("σημαίνει καὶ τὸ ἀρχῆς ἔχεσθαι,"

and so) often carries with it a suggestion of nature or original character. Cf. Schmidt ch. 46 ; Trench § lxvii.]

745 Ἀρχέ-λαος, -ου, ὁ, *Archelaus,* (fr. ἄρχω and λαός, ruling the people), a son of Herod the Great by Malthace, the Samaritan. He and his brother Antipas were brought up with a certain private man at Rome (Joseph. antt. 17, 1, 3). After the death of his father he ruled ten years as ethnarch over Judæa, Samaria, and Idumæa, (with the exception of the cities Gaza, Gadara, and Hippo). The Jews and Samaritans having accused him at Rome of tyranny, he was banished by the emperor (Augustus) to Vienna of the Allobroges, and died there (Joseph. antt. 17, 9, 3 ; 11, 4 ; 13, 2 ; b. j. 2, 7, 3) : Mt. ii. 22. [See B. D. s. v. and cf. Ἡρώδης.] *

746 ἀρχή, -ῆς, ἡ, [fr. Hom. down], in Sept. mostly equiv. to רֹאשׁ, רֵאשִׁית, תְּחִלָּה ; **1.** *beginning, origin* ; **a.** used absolutely, of the beginning of all things : ἐν ἀρχῇ, Jn. i. 1 sq. (Gen. i. 1) ; ἀπ᾽ ἀρχῆς, Mt. xix. 4 (with which cf. Xen. mem. 1, 4, 5 ὁ ἐξ ἀρχῆς ποιῶν ἀνθρώπους), 8 ; Jn. viii. 44 ; 1 Jn. i. 1 ; ii. 13 sq. ; iii. 8 ; more fully ἀπ᾽ ἀρχῆς κτίσεως or κόσμου, Mt. xxiv. 21 ; Mk. x. 6 ; xiii. 19 ; 2 Th. ii. 13 (where L [Tr mrg. WH mrg.] ἀπαρχήν, q. v.) ; 2 Pet. iii. 4 ; κατ᾽ ἀρχάς, Heb. i. 10 (Ps. ci. (cii.) 26). **b.** in a relative sense, of the beginning of the thing spoken of : ἐξ ἀρχῆς, fr. the time when Jesus gathered disciples, Jn. vi. 64 ; xvi. 4 ; ἀπ᾽ ἀρχῆς, Jn. xv. 27 (since I appeared in public) ; as soon as instruction was imparted, 1 Jn. ii. [7], 24 ; iii. 11 ; 2 Jn. 5 sqq. ; more fully ἐν ἀρχῇ τοῦ εὐαγγελίου, Phil. iv. 15 (Clem. Rom. 1 Cor. 47, 2 [see note in Gebh. and Harn. ad loc. and cf.] Polyc. ad Philipp. 11, 3) ; from the beginning of the gospel history, Lk. i. 2 ; from the commencement of life, Acts xxvi. 4 ; ἐν ἀρχῇ, in the beginning, when the church was founded, Acts xi. 15. The acc. ἀρχήν [cf. W. 124 (118) ; Bp. Lghtft. on Col. i. 18] and τὴν ἀρχήν in the Grk. writ. (cf. Lennep ad Phalarid. p. 82 sqq. and p. 94 sqq. ed. Lips. ; Brückner in De Wette's Hdbch. on John p. 151) is often used adverbially, i. q. ὅλως *altogether,* (properly an acc. of ‘direction towards’ : *usque ad initium,* [cf. W. 230 (216) ; B. 153 (134)]), commonly followed by a negative, but not always [cf. e. g. Dio Cass. frag. 101 (93 Dind.) ; xlv. 34 (Dind. vol. ii. p. 194) ; lix. 20 ; lxii. 4 ; see, further, Lycurg. § 125 ed. Mätzner] ; hence that extremely difficult passage, Jn. viii. 25 τὴν . . . ὑμῖν, must in my opinion be interpreted as follows : *I am altogether* or *wholly* (i. e. in all respects, precisely) *that which I even speak to you* (I not only am, but also declare to you what I am ; therefore you have no need to question me), [cf. W. 464 (432) ; B. 253 (218)]. ἀρχὴν λαμβάνειν to take beginning, to begin, Heb. ii. 3. with the addition of the gen. of the thing spoken of : ὠδίνων, Mt. xxiv. 8 ; Mk. xiii. 8 (9) [(here R G plur.) τῶν σημείων, Jn. ii. 11] ; ἡμερῶν, Heb. vii. 3 ; τοῦ εὐαγγελίου, that from which the gospel history took its beginning, Mk. i. 1 ; τῆς ὑποστάσεως, the confidence with which we have made a beginning, opp. to μέχρι τέλους, Heb. iii. 14. τὰ στοιχεῖα τῆς ἀρχῆς, Heb. v. 12 (τῆς ἀρχῆς is added for greater explicitness, as in Lat. *rudimenta prima,* Liv. 1, 3 ; Justin. hist. 7, 5 ; and *prima* *elementa*, Horat. sat. 1, 1, 26, etc.) ; ὁ τῆς ἀρχῆς τοῦ Χριστοῦ λόγος equiv. to ὁ τοῦ Χριστοῦ λόγος ὁ τῆς ἀρχῆς, i. e. the instruction concerning Christ such as it was at the very outset [cf. W. 188 (177) ; B. 155 (136)], Heb. vi. 1. **2.** *the person* or *thing that commences, the first person* or *thing in a series, the leader* : Col. i. 18 ; Rev. i. 8 Rec. ; xxi. 6 ; xxii. 13 ; (Deut. xxi. 17 ; Job xl. 14 (19), etc.). **3.** *that by which anything begins to be, the origin*, active cause (a sense in which the philosopher Anaximander, 8th cent. B. C., is said to have been the first to use the word ; cf. Simpl. on Aristot. phys. f. 9 p. 326 ed. Brandis and 32 p. 334 ed. Brandis, [cf. *Teichmüller*, Stud. zur Gesch. d. Begriffe, pp. 48 sqq. 560 sqq.]) : ἡ ἀρχὴ τῆς κτίσεως, of Christ as the divine λόγος, Rev. iii. 14 (cf. Düsterdieck ad loc. ; Clem. Al. protrept. 1, p. 6 ed. Potter, [p. 30 ed. Sylb.] ὁ λόγος ἀρχὴ θεία τῶν πάντων ; in Evang. Nicod. c. 23 [p. 308 ed. Tdf., p. 736 ed. Thilo] the devil is called ἡ ἀρχὴ τοῦ θανάτου καὶ ῥίζα τῆς ἁμαρτίας). **4.** *the extremity* of a thing : of the corners of a sail, Acts x. 11 ; xi. 5 ; (Hdt. 4, 60 ; Diod. 1, 35 ; al.). **5.** *the first place, principality, rule, magistracy*, [cf. Eng. '*authorities*'], (ἄρχω τινός) : Lk. xii. 11 ; xx. 20 ; Tit. iii. 1 ; office given in charge (Gen. xl. 13, 21 ; 2 Macc. iv. 10, etc.), Jude 6. Hence the term is transferred by Paul to angels and demons holding dominions entrusted to them in the order of things (see ἄγγελος, 2 [cf. Bp. Lghtft. on Col. i. 16 ; Mey. on Eph. i. 21]) : Ro. viii. 38 ; 1 Co. xv. 24 ; Eph. i. 21 ; iii. 10 ; vi. 12 ; Col. i. 16 ; ii. 10, 15. See ἐξουσία, 4 c. ββ. *

ἀρχηγός, -όν, adj., *leading, furnishing the first cause* or *occasion* : Eur. Hipp. 881 ; Plat. Crat. p. 401 d. ; chiefly used as subst. ὁ, ἡ, ἀρχηγός, (ἀρχή and ἄγω) ; **1.** *the chief leader, prince* : of Christ, Acts v. 31 ; (Aeschyl. Ag. 259 ; Thuc. 1, 132 ; Sept. Is. iii. 5 sq. ; 2 Chr. xxiii. 14, and often). **2.** *one that takes the lead in any thing* (1 Macc. x. 47 ἀρχ. λόγων εἰρηνικῶν) and thus *affords an example, a predecessor in a matter* : τῆς πίστεως, of Christ, Heb. xii. 2 (who in the pre-eminence of his faith far surpassed the examples of faith commemorated in ch. xi.), [al. bring this under the next head ; yet cf. Kurtz ad loc.]. So ἀρχηγὸς ἁμαρτίας, Mic. i. 13 ; ζήλους, Clem. Rom. 1 Cor. 14, 1 ; τῆς στάσεως καὶ διχοστασίας, ibid. 51, 1 ; τῆς ἀποστασίας, of the devil, Iren. 4, 40, 1 ; τοιαύτης φιλοσοφίας, of Thales, Aristot. met. 1, 3, 7 [p. 983^b 20]. Hence **3.** *the author* : τῆς ζωῆς, Acts iii. 15 ; τῆς σωτηρίας, Heb. ii. 10. (Often so in prof. auth. : τῶν πάντων, of God, [Plato] Tim. Locr. p. 96 c. ; τοῦ γένους τῶν ἀνθρώπων, of God, Diod. 5, 72 ; ἀρχηγὸς καὶ αἴτιος, leader and author, are often joined, as Polyb. 1, 66, 10 ; Hdian. 2, 6, 22 [14 ed. Bekk.]). Cf. Bleek on Heb. vol. ii. 1, p. 301 sq. *

see 746 & 756

ἀρχι, (fr. ἄρχω, ἀρχός), an inseparable prefix, usually to names of office or dignity, to designate the one who is placed over the rest that hold the office (Germ. *Ober-, Erz-,* [Eng. *arch-* (*chief-, high-*)]), as ἀρχάγγελος, ἀρχιποίμην [q. v.], ἀρχιερεύς, ἀρχίατρος, ἀρχιευνοῦχος, ἀρχυπηρέτης (in Egypt. inscriptions), etc., most of which belong to Alexand. and Byzant. Grk. Cf. *Thiersch*, De Pentateuchi versione Alex. p. 77 sq.

ἀρχ-ιερατικός, -ή, -όν, (ἄρχι and ἱερατικός, and this fr. ἱεράομαι [to be a priest]), *high-priestly, pontifical* : γένος, Acts iv. 6, [so Corp. Inscrr. Graec. no. 4363 ; see Schürer as cited s. v. ἀρχιερεύς, 2 fin.]. (Joseph. antt. 4, 4, 7 ; 6, 6, 3 ; 15, 3, 1.) *

ἀρχ-ιερεύς, -έως, ὁ, *chief priest, high-priest.* **1.** He who above all others was honored with the title of priest, the chief of the priests, כֹּהֵן הַגָּדוֹל (Lev. xxi. 10 ; Num. xxxv. 25, [later כֹּהֵן הָרֹאשׁ, 2 K. xxv. 18 ; 2 Chr. xix. 11, etc.]) : Mt. xxvi. 3, and often in the Gospels, the Acts, and the Ep. to the Heb. It was lawful for him to perform the common duties of the priesthood ; but his chief duty was, once a year on the day of atonement, to enter the Holy of holies (from which the other priests were excluded) and offer sacrifice for his own sins and the sins of the people (Lev. xvi. ; Heb. ix. 7, 25), and to preside over the Sanhedrin, or supreme Council, when convened for judicial deliberations (Mt. xxvi. 3 ; Acts xxii. 5 ; xxiii. 2). According to the Mosaic law no one could aspire to the high-priesthood unless he were of the tribe of Aaron, and descended moreover from a high-priestly family ; and he on whom the office was conferred held it till death. But from the time of Antiochus Epiphanes, when the kings of the Seleucidæ and afterwards the Herodian princes and the Romans arrogated to themselves the power of appointing the high-priests, the office neither remained vested in the pontifical family nor was conferred on any one for life ; but it became venal, and could be transferred from one to another according to the will of civil or military rulers. Hence it came to pass, that during the one hundred and seven years intervening between Herod the Great and the destruction of the holy city, twenty-eight persons held the pontifical dignity (Joseph. antt. 20, 10 ; see Ἄννας). Cf. *Win.* RWB. s. v. Hoherpriester ; *Oehler* in Herzog vi. p. 198 sqq. ; [BB.DD. s. vv. Highpriest, Priest, etc. The names of the 28 (27?) above alluded to are given, together with a brief notice of each, in an art. by Schürer in the Stud. u. Krit. for 1872, pp. 597–607]. **2.** The plur. ἀρχιερεῖς, which occurs often in the Gospels and Acts, as Mt. ii. 4 ; xvi. 21 ; xxvi. 3 ; xxvii. 41 ; Mk. viii. 31 ; xiv. 1 ; xv. 1 ; Lk. xix. 47 ; xxii. 52, 66 ; xxiii. 4 ; xxiv. 20 ; Jn. vii. 32 ; xi. 57 ; xviii. 35 ; Acts iv. 23 ; v. 24 ; ix. 14, 21 ; xxii. 30 ; xxiii. 14, etc., and in Josephus, comprises, in addition to the one actually holding the high-priestly office, both those who had previously discharged it and although deposed continued to have great power in the State (Joseph. vita 38 ; b. j. 2, 12, 6 ; 4, 3, 7 ; 9 ; 4, 4, 3 ; see Ἄννας above), as well as the members of the families from which high-priests were created, provided they had much influence in public affairs (Joseph. b. j. 6, 2, 2). See on this point the learned discussion by *Schürer*, Die ἀρχιερεῖς im N. T., in the Stud. u. Krit. for 1872, p. 593 sqq. and in his Neutest. Zeitgesch. § 23 iii. p. 407 sqq. [Prof. Schürer, besides reviewing the opinions of the more recent writers, contends that in no instance where indubitable reference to the heads of the twenty-four classes is made (neither in the Sept. 1 Chr. xxiv.

3 sq.; 2 Chr. xxxvi. 14; Ezra x. 5; Neh. xii. 7; nor in Joseph. antt. 7, 14, 7) are they called ἀρχιερεῖς; that the nearest approximations to this term are periphrases such as ἄρχοντες τῶν ἱερέων, Neh. xii. 7, or φύλαρχοι τῶν ἱερέων, Esra apocr. (1 Esdr.) viii. 92 (94); Joseph. antt. 11, 5, 4; and that the word ἀρχιερεῖς was restricted in its application to those who actually held, or had held, the high-priestly office, together with the members of the few prominent families from which the high-priests still continued to be selected, cf. Acts iv. 6; Joseph. b. j. 4, 3, 6.] **3.** In the Ep. to the Heb. Christ is called 'high-priest,' because by undergoing a bloody death he offered himself as an expiatory sacrifice to God, and has entered the heavenly sanctuary where he continually intercedes on our behalf: ii. 17; iii. 1; iv. 14; v. 10; vi. 20; vii. 26; viii. 1; ix. 11; cf. *Winzer*, De sacerdotis officio, quod Christo tribuitur in Ep. ad Hebr. (three Programs), Leips. 1825 sq.; *Riehm*, Lehrbegriff des Hebräerbriefes, ii. pp. 431–488. In Grk. writ. the word is used by Hdt. 2, [(37), 142,] 143 and 151; Plat. legg. 12 p. 947 a.; Polyb. 23, 1, 2; 32, 22, 5; Plut. Numa c. 9, al.; [often in Inscrr.]; once (viz. Lev. iv. 3) in the Sept., where ἱερεὺς μέγας is usual, in the O. T. Apocr. 1 Esdr. v. 40; ix. 40, and often in the bks. of Macc.

750   ἀρχι-ποίμην, -ενος [so L T Tr WH KC (after Mss.), but Grsb. al. -μήν, -μένος; cf. *Lob.* Paralip. p 195 sq.; *Steph.* Thesaur. s. v.; Chandler § 580], ὁ, a bibl. word [Test. xii. Patr. test. Jud. § 8], *chief shepherd*: of Christ the head of the church, 1 Pet. v. 4; see ποιμήν, b.*

751   Ἄρχιππος [Chandler § 308], -ου, ὁ, [i. e. master of the horse], *Archippus*, a certain Christian at Colossæ: Col. iv. 17; Philem. 2. [Cf. B. D. s. v.; Bp. Lghtft. on Col. and Philem. p. 308 sq.]*

752   ἀρχισυνάγωγος, -ου, ὁ, (συναγωγή), *ruler of a synagogue*, רֹאשׁ הַכְּנֶסֶת: Mk. v. 22, 35 sq. 38; Lk. viii. 49; xiii. 14; Acts xiii. 15; xviii. 8, 17. It was his duty to select the readers or teachers in the synagogue, to examine the discourses of the public speakers, and to see that all things were done with decency and in accordance with ancestral usage; [cf. Alex.'s Kitto s. v. Synagogue]. (Not found in prof. writ.; [yet Schürer (Theol. Literatur-Zeit., 1878, p. 5) refers to Corp. Inscrr. Graec. no 2007 f. ⟨Addenda ii. p. 994), no. 2221ᵉ (ii. p. 1031), nos. 9894, 9906; *Mommsen*, Inscrr. Regni Neap. no. 3657; *Garrucci*, Cimitero degli antichi Ebrei, p. 67; *Lampridius*, Vita Alexandr. Sever. c. 28; *Vopiscus*, Vit. Saturnin. c. 8; Codex Theodos. xvi. 8, 4, 13, 14; also Acta Pilat. in Tdf.'s Ev. Apocr. ed. 2, pp. 221, 270, 275, 284; Justin. dial. c. Tryph. c. 137; Epiph. haer. 30, 18; Euseb. h. e. 7, 10, 4; see fully in his Gemeindeverfassung der Juden in Rom in d. Kaiserzeit nach d. Inschriften dargestellt (Leips. 1879), p. 25 sq.].)*

753   ἀρχι-τέκτων, -ονος, ὁ, (τέκτων, q. v.), *a master-builder, architect*, the superintendent in the erection of buildings: 1 Co. iii. 10. (Hdt., Xen., Plat. and subseq. writ.; Is. iii. 3; Sir. xxxviii. 27; 2 Macc. ii. 29.)*

754   ἀρχι-τελώνης, -ου, ὁ, *a chief of the tax-collectors, chief publican*: Lk. xix. 2. [See τελώνης.]*

ἀρχι-τρίκλινος, -ου, ὁ, (τρίκλινον [or -νος (sc. οἶκος), a room with three couches]), *the superintendent of a dining-room*, a τρικλινάρχης, *table-master*: Jn. ii. 8 sq. [cf. B.D. s. v. Governor]. It differs from "the master of a feast," συμποσιάρχης, *toast-master*, who was one of the guests selected by lot to prescribe to the rest the mode of drinking; cf. Sir. xxxv. (xxxii.) 1. But it was the duty of the ἀρχιτρίκλινος to place in order the tables and couches, arrange the courses, taste the food and wine beforehand, etc. (Heliod. 7, 27.) [Some regard the distinction between the two words as obliterated in later Grk.; cf. Soph. Lex. s. v., and Schaff's Lange's Com. on Jn. l. c.]*   **755**

ἄρχομαι, see ἄρχω.   756; see 757

ἄρχω; [fr. Hom. down]; *to be first*. **1.** *to be the first to do* (anything), *to begin*,—a sense not found in the Grk. Bible. **2.** *to be chief, leader, ruler*: τινός [B. 169 (147)], Mk. x. 42; Ro. xv. 12 (fr. Is. xi. 10). See ἄρχων. Mid., pres. ἄρχομαι; fut. ἄρξομαι (once [*twice*], Lk. xiii. 26 [but not Tr mrg. WH mrg.; xxiii. 30]); 1 aor. ἠρξάμην; *to begin, make a beginning*: ἀπό τινος, Acts x. 37 [B. 79 (69); cf. Matth. § 558]; 1 Pet. iv. 17; by brachylogy ἀρξάμενος ἀπό τινος ἕως τινός for, having begun from some person or thing (and c o n t i n u e d or continuing) to some person or thing: Mt. xx. 8; Jn. viii. 9 [i. e. Rec.]; Acts i. 22; cf. W. § 66, 1 c.; [B. 374 (320)]; ἀρξάμενον is used impers. and absol. *a beginning being made*, Lk. xxiv. 27 (so in Hdt. 3, 91; cf. W. 624 (580); [B. 374 sq. (321)]); carelessly, ἀρξάμενος ἀπὸ Μωυσέως καὶ ἀπὸ πάντων προφητῶν διηρμήνευεν for, beginning from Moses he went through all the prophets, Lk. xxiv. 27; W. § 67, 2; [B. 374 (320 sq.)]. ὧν ἤρξατο ποιεῖν τε καὶ διδάσκειν, ἄχρι ἧς ἡμέρας *which he began* and continued *both to do and to teach*, until etc., Acts i. 1 [W. § 66, 1 c.; B. u. s.]. Ἄρχομαι is connected with an inf. and that so often, esp. in the historical books, that formerly most interpreters thought it constituted a periphrasis for the finite form of the verb standing in the inf., as ἤρξατο κηρύσσειν for ἐκήρυξε. But through the influence principally of Fritzsche (on Mt. p. 539 sq.), cf. W. § 65, 7 d., it is now conceded that the theory of a periphrasis of this kind was a rash assumption, and that there is scarcely an example which cannot be reduced to one of the following classes: **a.** the idea of *beginning* has more or less weight or importance, so that it is brought out by a separate word: Mt. xi. 7 (the disciples of John having retired, Christ began to speak concerning John, which he did not do while they were present); Lk. iii. 8 (do not even begin to say; make not even an attempt to excuse yourselves); Lk. xv. 14 (the *beginning* of want followed hard upon the squandering of his goods); Lk. xxi. 28; 2 Co. iii. 1; esp. when the beginning of an action is contrasted with its continuance or its repetition, Mk. vi. 7; viii. 31 (cf. ix. 31; x. 33 sq.); or with the end of it, Lk. xiv. 30 (opp. to ἐκτελέσαι); Jn. xiii. 5 (cf. 12). **b.** ἄρχ. denotes something as begun by some one, others following: Acts xxvii. 35 sq. [W. § 65, 7 d.]. **c.** ἄρχ. indicates that a thing was but just begun when it was interrupted by something else: Mt. xii. 1 (they had begun to pluck ears of corn,   **757** but they were prevented from continuing by the interference of the Pharisees); Mt. xxvi. 22 (Jesus answered before all had finished), 74 ; Mk. ii. 23; iv. 1 (he had scarcely begun to teach, when a multitude gathered unto him) ; Mk. vi. 2 ; x. 41 ; Lk. v. 21 ; xii. 45 sq. ; xiii. 25 ; Acts xi. 15 (cf. x. 44) ; xviii. 26, and often. d. the action itself, instead of its beginning, might indeed have been mentioned ; but in order that the more attention may be given to occurrences which seem to the writer to be of special importance, their initial stage, their beginning, is expressly pointed out : Mk. xiv. 65 ; Lk. xiv. 18 ; Acts ii. 4, etc. e. ἄρχ. occurs in a sentence which has grown out of the blending of two statements : Mt. iv. 17 ; xvi. 21 (fr. ἀπὸ τότε ἐκήρυξε . . . ἔδειξε, and τότε ἤρξατο κηρύσσειν . . . δεικνύειν). The inf. is wanting when discoverable from the context : ἀρχόμενος, sc. to discharge the Messianic office, Lk. iii. 23 [W. 349 (328)] ; ἀρξάμενος sc. λέγειν, Acts xi. 4. [COMP.: ἐν-(-μαι), προ-εν-(-μαι), ὑπ-, προ-ὑπ -άρχω.]

758 ἄρχων, -οντος, ὁ, (pres. ptcp. of the verb ἄρχω), [fr. Aeschyl. down], *a ruler, commander, chief, leader* : used of Jesus, ἄρχων τῶν βασιλέων τῆς γῆς, Rev. i. 5 ; of the rulers of nations, Mt. xx. 25 ; Acts iv. 26 ; vii. 35 ; univ. of magistrates, Ro. xiii. 3 ; Acts xxiii. 5 ; especially judges, Lk. xii. 58 ; Acts vii. 27, 35 (where note the antithesis : whom they refused as ἄρχοντα καὶ δικαστήν, him God sent as ἄρχοντα— *leader, ruler*— καὶ λυτρωτήν) ; Acts xvi. 19. οἱ ἄρχοντες τοῦ αἰῶνος τούτου, those who in the present age (see αἰών, 3) by nobility of birth, learning and wisdom, power and authority, wield the greatest influence, whether among Jews or Gentiles, 1 Co. ii. 6, 8 ; cf. Neander ad loc. p. 62 sqq. Of the members of the Jewish Sanhedrin : Lk. xxiii. 13, 35 ; xxiv. 20 ; Jn. iii. 1 ; vii. 26, 48 ; xii. 42 ; Acts iii. 17 ; iv. 5, 8 ; xiii. 27 ; xiv. 5. of the officers presiding over synagogues : Mt. ix. 18, 23 ; Lk. viii. 41 (ἄρχων τῆς συναγωγῆς, cf. Mk. v. 22 ἀρχισυνάγωγος), and perhaps also Lk. xviii. 18 ; ἄρχων τῶν Φαρισαίων, one who has great influence among the Pharisees, Lk. xiv. 1. of the devil, the prince of evil spirits: (ὁ) ἄρχων τῶν δαιμονίων, Mt. ix. 34 ; xii. 24 ; Mk. iii. 22 ; Lk. xi. 15 ; ὁ ἀρχ. τοῦ κόσμου, the ruler of the irreligious mass of mankind, Jn. xii. 31 ; xiv. 30 ; xvi. 11, (in rabbin. writ. שַׂר הָעוֹלָם ; ἄρχ. τοῦ αἰῶνος τούτου, Ignat. ad Eph. 19, 1 [ad Magn. 1, 3] ; ἄρχων τοῦ καιροῦ τῆς ἀνομίας, Barn. ep. 18, 2) ; τῆς ἐξουσίας τοῦ ἀέρος, Eph. ii. 2 (see ἀήρ). [See Hort in Dict. of Chris. Biog., s.v. Archon.]*

759 ἄρωμα, -τος, τό, (fr. ΑΡΩ to prepare, whence ἀρτύω to season ; [al. connect it w. r. ar (ἀρόω) to plough (cf. Gen. xxvii. 27) ; al. al.]), *spice, perfume* : Mk. xvi. 1 ; Lk. xxiii. 56 ; xxiv. 1 ; Jn. xix. 40. (2 K. xx. 13 ; Esth. ii. 12 ; Cant. iv. 10, 16. [Hippocr.], Xen., Theophr. and subseq. writ.) *

760 Ἀσά, ὁ, (Chald. אָסָא to cure), *Asa*, king of Judah, son of king Abijah (1 K. xv. 8 sqq.) : Mt. i. 7 sq. [L T Tr WH read Ἀσάφ q. v.] *

see 4525 ἀσαίνω: in 1 Th. iii. 3, Kuenen and Cobet (in their N. T. ad fidem cod. Vat., Lugd. 1860 [pref. p. xc.]), following Lchm. [who followed Valckenaer in following J.

J. Reiske (Animad. ad Polyb. p. 68) ; see *Valck.* Opuscc. ii. 246–249] in his larger edit., conjectured and received into their text μηδὲν ἀσαίνεσθαι, which they think to be equiv. to ἄχθεσθαι, χαλεπῶς φέρειν. But there is no necessity for changing the Rec. (see σαίνω, 2 b. β.), nor can it be shown that ἀσαίνω is used by Grk. writ. for ἀσάω.*

ἀ-σάλευτος, -ον, (σαλεύω), *unshaken, unmoved* : prop.   **761** Acts xxvii. 41 ; metaph. βασιλεία, not liable to disorder and overthrow, firm, stable, Heb. xii. 28. (Eur. Bacch. 391 ; ἐλευθερία, Diod. 2; 48 ; εὐδαιμονία, ibid. 3, 47 ; ἡσυχία, Plat. Ax. 370 d. ; Plut., al.) *

Ἀσάφ, ὁ, (אָסָף collector), a man's name, a clerical   **see 760** error for R G Ἀσά (q. v.), adopted by L T Tr WH in Mt. i. 7 sq.*

ἄ-σβεστος, -ον, (σβέννυμι), *unquenched* (Ovid, *inexstinc-*   **762** *tus*), *unquenchable* (Vulg. *inexstinguibilis*) : πῦρ, Mt. iii. 12 ; Lk. iii. 17 ; Mk. ix. 43, and R G L br. in 45. (Often in Hom. ; πῦρ ἄσβ. of the perpetual fire of Vesta, Dion. Hal. antt. 1, 76 ; [of the fire on the altar, Philo de ebriet. § 34 (Mang. i. 378) ; de vict. off. § 5 (Mang. ii. 254) ; of the fire of the magi, Strabo 15, (3) 15 ; see also Plut. symp. l. vii. probl. 4 ; Aelian. nat. an. 5, 3 ; cf. Heinichen on Euseb. h. e. 6, 41, 15].) *

ἀσέβεια, -ας, ἡ, (ἀσεβής, q. v.), *want of reverence towards*   **763** *God, impiety, ungodliness* : Ro. i. 18 ; 2 Tim. ii. 16 ; Tit. ii. 12 ; plur. ungodly thoughts and deeds, Ro. xi. 26 (fr. Is. lix. 20) ; τὰ ἔργα ἀσεβείας [Treg. br. ἀσεβ.] *works of ungodliness*, a Hebraism, Jude 15, cf. W. § 34, 3 b. ; [B. § 132, 10] ; αἱ ἐπιθυμίαι τῶν ἀσεβειῶν their desires to do ungodly deeds, Jude 18. (In Grk. writ. fr. [Eur.], Plat. and Xen. down ; in the Sept. it corresponds chiefly to רֶשַׁע.) *

ἀσεβέω, -ῶ ; 1 aor. ἠσέβησα ; (ἀσεβής, q. v.) ; from   **764** [Aeschyl.], Xen. and Plato down ; *to be ungodly, act impiously* : 2 Pet. ii. 6 ; ἀσεβεῖν ἔργα ἀσεβείας [Treg. br. ἀσεβείας], Jude 15, cf. W. 222 (209) ; [B. 149 (130)]. (Equiv. to רֶשַׁע, Zeph. iii. 11 ; רָשַׁע, Dan. ix. 5.) *

ἀσεβής, -ές, (σέβω to reverence) ; fr. Aeschyl. and   **765** Thuc. down, Sept. for רָשָׁע ; *destitute of reverential awe towards God, contemning God, impious* : Ro. iv. 5 ; v. 6 ; 1 Tim. i. 9 (joined here with ἁμαρτωλός, as in 1 Pet. iv. 18) ; 2 Pet. ii. 5 ; iii. 7 ; Jude 4, 15.*

ἀσέλγεια, -ας, ἡ, the conduct and character of one who   **766** is ἀσελγής (a word which some suppose to be compounded of α priv. and Σέλγη, the name of a city in Pisidia whose citizens excelled in strictness of morals [so Etym. Magn. 152, 38 ; per contra cf. Suidas 603 d.] : others of α intens. and σαλαγεῖν to disturb, raise a din ; others, and now the majority, of α priv. and σέλγω i. q. θέλγω, not affecting pleasantly, exciting disgust), *unbridled lust, excess, licentiousness, lasciviousness, wantonness, outrageousness, shamelessness, insolence* : Mk. vii. 22 (where it is uncertain what particular vice is spoken of) ; of gluttony and venery, Jude 4 ; plur., 1 Pet. iv. 3 ; 2 Pet. ii. 2 (for Rec. ἀπωλείαις) ; 18 ; of carnality, *lasciviousness* : 2 Co. xii. 21 ; Gal. v. 19 ; Eph. iv. 19 ; 2 Pet. ii. 7 ; plur. "*wanton* (acts or) *manners*, as filthy words, indecent bodily movements, unchaste handling of males and females, etc." (Fritzsche), Ro. xiii. 13. (In bibl. Grk. besides only in Sap. xiv. 26 and 3 Macc. ii. 26. Among Grk. writ. used by Plat., Isocr. et sqq.; at length by Plut. [Lucull. 38] and Lcian. [dial. meretr. 6] of the wantonness of w o m e n [Lob. ad Phryn. p. 184 n.].) Cf. Tittmann i. p. 151 sq.; [esp. Trench § xvi.].*

767   ἄσημος, -ον, (σῆμα a mark), unmarked or unstamped (money); unknown, of no mark, insignificant, ignoble : Acts xxi. 39. (3 Macc. i. 3; in Grk. writ. fr. Hdt. down; trop. fr. Eur. down.) *

768   'Ασήρ, ό, an indecl. Hebr. prop. name, (אָשֵׁר [i. e. happy, Gen. xxx. 13]), (in Joseph. "Ασηρος, -ου, ό), Asher, the eighth son of the patriarch Jacob : Lk. ii. 36 ; Rev. vii. 6.*

769   ἀσθένεια, -ας, ἡ, (ἀσθενής), [fr. Hdt. down], want of strength, weakness, infirmity ; **a.** of B o d y ; **α.** its native weakness and frailty : 1 Co. xv. 43 ; 2 Co. xiii. 4. **β.** feebleness of health ; sickness : Jn. v. 5 ; xi. 4 ; Lk. xiii. 11, 12 ; Gal. iv. 13 (ἀσθένεια τῆς σαρκός) ; Heb. xi. 34 ; in plur. : Mt. viii. 17 ; Lk. v. 15 ; viii. 2 ; Acts xxviii. 9 ; 1 Tim. v. 23. **b.** of S o u l ; want of the strength and capacity requisite **α.** to understand a thing : Ro. vi. 19 (where ἀσθ. σαρκός denotes the weakness of human nature). **β.** to do things great and glorious, as want of human wisdom, of skill in speaking, in the management of men : 1 Co. ii. 3. **γ.** to restrain corrupt desires ; proclivity to s̄in : Heb. v. 2 ; vii. 28 ; plur. the various kinds of this proclivity, Heb. iv. 15. **δ.** to bear trials and troubles : Ro. viii. 26 (where read τῇ ἀσθενείᾳ for Rec. ταῖς ἀσθενείαις) ; 2 Co. xi. 30 ; xii. 9 ; plur. the mental [?] states in which this weakness manifests itself : 2 Co. xii. 5, 9 sq.*

770   ἀσθενέω, -ῶ ; impf. ἠσθένουν ; pf. ἠσθένηκα (2 Co. xi. 21 L T TrWH) ; 1 aor. ἠσθένησα ; (ἀσθενής) ; [fr. Eur. down] ; to be weak, feeble ; univ. to be without strength, powerless : Ro. viii. 3 ; rhetorically, of one who purposely abstains from the use of his strength, 2 Co. xiii. 4 ; and of one who has no occasion to prove his strength, 2 Co. xiii. 9 ; contextually, to be unable to wield and hold sway over others, 2 Co. xi. 21 ; by oxymoron, ὅταν ἀσθενῶ, τότε δυνατός εἰμι when I am weak in human strength, then am I strong in strength divine, 2 Co. xii. 10 ; εἰς τινα to be weak towards one, 2 Co. xiii. 3 ; with a dat. of the respect added : πίστει, to be weak in faith, Ro. iv. 19 ; πίστει, to be doubtful about things lawful and unlawful to a Christian, Ro. xiv. 1 ; simple ἀσθενεῖν with the same idea suggested, Ro. xiv. 2, 21 [T WH om. Tr mrg. br.] ; 1 Co. viii. 9 Rec., 11 sq. ; τίς ἀσθενεῖ, καὶ οὐκ ἀσθενῶ ; who is weak (in his feelings and conviction about things lawful), and I am not filled with a compassionate sense of the same weakness ? 2 Co. xi. 29. contextually, to be weak in means, needy, poor : Acts xx. 35 (so [Arstph. pax 636] ; Eur. in Stob. 145 vol. ii. 168 ed. Gaisf.), cf. De Wette [more fully Hackett, per contra Meyer] ad loc. Specially of debility in health : with νόσοις added, Lk. iv. 40 ; simply, to be feeble, sick : Lk. vii. 10 [R G Tr mrg. br.] ; Mt. xxv. 36, 39 L txt. T Tr WH ; Jn. iv. 46 ; xi. 1–3, 6 ; Acts ix. 37 ; Phil. ii. 26 sq. ; 2 Tim. iv. 20 ; Jas. v. 14 ; οἱ ἀσθενοῦντες, and ἀσθενοῦντες, the sick, sick

folks : Mt. x. 8 ; Mk. vi. 56 ; Lk. ix. 2 Rec. ; Jn. v. 3, 7, 13 Tdf. ; vi. 2 ; Acts xix. 12.*

ἀσθένημα, -ατος, τό, (ἀσθενέω), infirmity : Ro. xv. 1   **771** (where used of error arising from weakness of mind). [In a physical sense in Aristot. hist. an. 11, 7 vol. i. 638ᵇ, 37 ; gen. an. 1, 18 ibid. p. 726ᵃ 15.] *

ἀσθενής, -ές, (τὸ σθένος strength), weak, infirm, feeble ;   **772** [fr. Pind. down] ; **a.** univ. : Mt. xxvi. 41 ; Mk. xiv. 38 ; 1 Pet. iii. 7 ; τὸ ἀσθενὲς τοῦ θεοῦ, the act of God in which weakness seems to appear, viz. that the suffering of the cross should be borne by the Messiah, 1 Co. i. 25. **b.** spec. : contextually, unable to achieve anything great, 1 Co. iv. 10 ; destitute of power among men, 1 Co. i. 27 [Lchm. br.] ; weaker and inferior, μέλος, 1 Co. xii. 22 ; sluggish in doing right, Ro. v. 6 ; wanting in manliness and dignity, 2 Co. x. 10 ; used of the religious systems anterior to Christ, as having no power to promote piety and salvation, Gal. iv. 9 ; Heb. vii. 18 ; wanting in decision about things lawful and unlawful (see ἀσθενέω), 1 Co. viii. 7, 9 L T Tr WH, 10 ; ix. 22 ; 1 Th. v. 14. **c.** of the body, feeble, sick : Mt. xxv. 39 R G L mrg., 43 sq. ; Lk. ix. 2 L Tr br. ; x. 9 ; Acts iv. 9 ; v. 15 sq. ; 1 Co. xi. 30.*

'Ασία, -ας, ἡ, Asia ;   **1.** Asia proper, ἡ ἰδίως καλου-   **773** μένη 'Ασία (Ptol. 5, 2), or proconsular Asia[often so called from the 16th cent. down ; but correctly speaking it was a provincia c o nsularis, although the ruler of it was vested with ' proconsular power.' The ' Asia ' of the N. T. must not be confounded with the ' Asia proconsularis ' of the 4th cent.], embracing Mysia, Lydia, Phrygia and Caria [cf. Cic. pro Flac. c. 27] : Acts vi. 9 [L om. Tr mrg. br.] ; xvi. 6 sqq. ; 1 Pet. i. 1 ; Rev. i. 4 ; and, apparently, Acts xix. 26 ; xx. 16 ; 2 Co. i. 8 ; 2 Tim. i. 15, etc. Cf. Win. R W B. s. v. Asien ; Stark in Schenkel i. p. 261 sq. ; [BB. DD. s. v. Asia ; Conyb. and Howson, St. Paul, ch. viii. ; Wieseler, Chron. d. apost. Zeit. p. 31 sqq.]. **2.** A part of proconsular Asia, embracing Mysia, Lydia, and Caria, (Plin. h. n. 5, 27, (28) [al. 5, 100]) : Acts ii. 9.

'Ασιανός, -οῦ, ό, a native of Asia, Asian, Asiatic : Acts   **774** xx. 4. [(Thuc., al.)]*

'Ασιάρχης, -ου, ό, an Asiarch, President of Asia : Acts   **775** xix. 31. Each of the cities of proconsular Asia, at the autumnal equinox, assembled its most honorable and opulent citizens, in order to select one to preside over the games to be exhibited that year, at his expense, in honor of the gods and the Roman emperor. Thereupon each city reported the name of the person selected to a general assembly held in some leading city, as Ephesus, Smyrna, Sardis. This general council, called τὸ κοινόν, selected t e n out of the number of candidates, and sent them to the proconsul ; and the proconsul, apparently, chose one of these ten to preside over the rest. This explains how it is that in Acts l. c. s e v e r a l Asiarchs are spoken of, while Eusebius h. e. 4, 15, 27 mentions only o n e ; [perhaps also the t i t l e outlasted the s e r v i c e]. Cf. Meyer on Acts l. c. ; Win. RWB. s. v. Asiarchen ; [BB.DD. s. v. ; but esp. Le Bas et Waddington, Voyage Archéol. Inscr. part. v. p. 244 sq. ; Kuhn,

Die städtische u. bürgerl. Verf. des röm. Reichs, i. 106 sqq.; *Marquardt*, Röm. Staatsverwalt. i. 374 sqq.; *Stark* in Schenkel i. 263; esp. Bp. *Lghtft*. Polycarp, p. 987 sqq.].*

776 **ἀσιτία, -ας, ἡ,** (ἄσιτος q. v.), *abstinence from food* (whether voluntary or enforced) : πολλή long, Acts xxvii. 21. (Hdt. 3, 52; Eur. Suppl. 1105; [Aristot. probl. 10, 35; cth. Nic. 10 p. 1180ᵇ, 9]; Joseph. antt. 12, 7; al.)*

777 **ἄ-σιτος, -ον,** (σῖτος), *fasting*; without having eaten : Acts xxvii. 33. (Hom. Od. 4, 788; then fr. Soph. and Thuc. down.)*

778 **ἀσκέω, -ῶ;** 1. *to form by art, to adorn*; in Homer. 2. *to exercise* (one's self), *take pains, labor, strive*; foll. by an inf. (as in Xen. mem. 2, 1, 6; Cyr. 5, 5, 12, etc.) : Acts xxiv. 16.*

779 **ἀσκός, -οῦ, ὁ,** a *leathern bag* or *bottle*, in which water or wine was kept : Mt. ix. 17; Mk. ii. 22; Lk. v. 37 sq. (Often in Grk. writ. fr. Hom. down; Sept.) [BB.DD. s. v. Bottle; *Tristram*, Nat. Hist. of the Bible, p. 92.]*

780 **ἀσμένως,** adv., (for ἡσμένως; fr. ἥδομαι), *with joy, gladly* : Acts ii. 41 [Rec.]; xxi. 17. (In Grk. writ. fr. Hom. [the adv. fr. Aeschyl.] down.)*

781 **ἄ-σοφος, -ον,** (σοφός), *unwise, foolish* : Eph. v. 15. [From Theogn. down.]*

782 **ἀσπάζομαι;** [impf. ἠσπαζόμην]; 1 aor. ἠσπασάμην; (fr. σπάω with a intensive [q. v., but cf. Vaniček p. 1163; *Curtius*, Das Verbum, i. 324 sq.]; hence prop. *to draw to one's self* [W. § 38, 7 fin.]; cf. ἀσκαίρω for σκαίρω, ἀσπαίρω for σπαίρω, ἀσπαρίζω for σπαρίζω); [fr. Hom. down]; a. with an acc. of the pers., *to salute one, greet, bid welcome, wish well to*, (the Israelites, on meeting and at parting, generally used the formula שָׁלוֹם לְךָ); used of those accosting any one : Mt. x. 12; Mk. ix. 15; xv. 18; Lk. i. 40; Acts xxi. 19. of those who visit one to see him a little while, departing almost immediately afterwards : Acts xviii. 22; xxi. 7; like the Lat. *salutare*, our '*pay one's respects to*,' of those who show regard for a distinguished person by visiting him : Acts xxv. 13, (Joseph. antt. 1, 19, 5; 6, 11, 1). of those who greet one whom they meet in the way : Mt. v. 47 (in the East even now Christians and Mohammedans do not salute each other); Lk. x. 4 (as a salutation was made not merely by a slight gesture and a few words, but generally by embracing and kissing, a journey was retarded by saluting frequently). of those departing and bidding farewell : Acts xx. 1; xxi. 6 [R G]. of the absent, saluting by letter : Ro. xvi. 3, 5–23; 1 Co. xvi. 19; 2 Co. xiii. 12 (13); Phil. iv. 21 sq.; Col. iv. 10–12, 14 sq.; 1 Th. v. 26, etc. ἐν φιλήματι : Ro. xvi. 16; 1 Co. xvi. 20; 2 Co. xiii. 12; 1 Pet. v. 14. b. with an acc. of the thing, *to receive joyfully, welcome* : τὰς ἐπαγγελίας, Heb. xi. 13, (τὴν συμφοράν, Eur. Ion 587; τὴν εὔνοιαν, Joseph. antt. 6, 5, 3; τοὺς λόγους, ibid. 7, 8, 4; so *saluto*, Verg. Aen. 3, 524). [COMP.: ἀπ-ασπάζομαι.]

783 **ἀσπασμός, -οῦ, ὁ,** (ἀσπάζομαι), a *salutation*, — either oral : Mt. xxiii. 7; Mk. xii. 38; Lk. i. 29, 41, 44; xi. 43; xx. 46; or written : 1 Co. xvi. 21; Col. iv. 18; 2 Th. iii. 17. [From Theogn. down.]*

784 **ἄ-σπιλος, -ον,** (σπίλος a spot), *spotless* : ἀμνός, 1 Pet. i.

19; (ἵππος, Hdian. 5, 6, 16 [7 ed. Bekk.]; μῆλον, Anthol. Pal. 6, 252, 3). metaph. *free from censure, irreproachable*, 1 Tim. vi. 14; *free from vice, unsullied*, 2 Pet. iii. 14; ἀπὸ τοῦ κόσμου, Jas. i. 27 [B. § 132, 5]. (In eccl. writ.)*

785 **ἀσπίς, -ίδος, ἡ,** an *asp*, a small and most venomous serpent, the bite of which is fatal unless the part bitten be immediately cut away : Ro. iii. 13. (Deut. xxxii. 33; Is. xxx. 6 [etc. Hdt., Aristot., al.] Ael. nat. an. 2, 24; 6, 38; Plut. mor. p. 380 f. i. e. de Isid. et Osir. § 74; Oppian. cyn. 3, 433.) [Cf. BB.DD. s. v. Asp; *Tristram*, Nat. Hist. of the Bible, p. 270 sqq.]*

786 **ἄσπονδος, -ον,** (σπονδή a libation, which, as a kind of sacrifice, accompanied the making of treaties and compacts; cf. Lat. *spondere*); [fr. Thuc. down]; 1. *without a treaty* or *covenant*; of things not mutually agreed upon, e. g. abstinence from hostilities, Thuc. 1, 37, etc. 2. *that cannot be persuaded to enter into a covenant, implacable*, (in this sense fr. Aeschyl. down; esp. in the phrase ἄσπονδος πόλεμος, Dem. pro cor. p. 314, 16; Polyb. 1, 65, 6; [Philo de sacrif. § 4]; Cic. ad Att. 9, 10, 5; [cf. Trench § lii.]) : joined with ἄστοργος, Ro. i. 31 Rec.; 2 Tim. iii. 3.*

787 **ἀσσάριον, -ου, τό,** an *assarium* or *assarius*, the name of a coin equal to the tenth part of a drachma [see δηνάριον], (dimin. of the Lat. *as*, Rabbin. אִיסָּר), [*a penny*] : Mt. x. 29; Lk. xii. 6. (Dion. Hal., Plut., al.) [Cf. BB.DD. s. v. Farthing.]*

788 **ἆσσον,** adv., *nearer*, (compar. of ἄγχι *near* [cf. ἐγγύς]) : Acts xxvii. 13 [here Rec.ˢᵗ Ἄσσον (or Ἄσσ. q. v.), Recᵇᵉᶻ ᵉˡᶻ ἆσσ., (cf. Tdf. ad loc.); but see Meyer]. (Hom., Hdt., tragic poets; Joseph. antt. 19, 2, 4.)*

789 **Ἄσσος** [so all edd., perh. better -σός; Chandler § 317, cf. § 319; *Pape*, Eigennamen s. v.], -ου, ἡ, *Assos*, a maritime city in Asia Minor, on the Ægean Sea [Gulf of Adramyttium], and nine [acc. to Tab. Peuting. (ed. Fortia d'Urban, Paris 1845, p. 170) 20 to 25] miles [see Hackett on Acts as below] distant [to the S.] from Troas, a city of Lesser Phrygia : Acts xx. 13 sq.; [formerly read also in Acts xxvii. 13 after the Vulg.; cf. ἆσσον. See Papers of the Archæol. Inst. of America, Classical Series i. (1882) esp. pp. 60 sqq.].*

790 **ἀστατέω, -ῶ;** (ἄστατος unstable, strolling about; cf. ἀκατάστατος); *to wander about, to rove without a settled abode*, [A. V. *to have no certain dwelling-place*] : 1 Co. iv. 11. (Anthol. Pal. appendix 39, 4.)*

791 **ἀστεῖος, -ον,** (ἄστυ a city); 1. *of the city*; *of polished manners* (opp. to ἄγροικος rustic), *genteel*, (fr. Xen. and Plat. down). 2. *elegant* (of body), *comely, fair*, (Judith xi. 23; Aristaenet. 1, 4, 1 and 19, 8) : of Moses (Ex. ii. 2), Heb. xi. 23; with τῷ θεῷ added, *unto God*, God being judge, i. e. truly fair, Acts vii. 20; cf. W. § 31, 4 a. p. 212 (199); [248 (232)]; B. 179 (156); (Philo, vit. Moys. i. § 3, says of Moses γεννηθεὶς ὁ παῖς εὐθὺς ὄψιν ἐνέφηνεν ἀστειοτέραν ἢ κατ' ἰδιώτην). [Cf. Trench § cvi.]*

792 **ἀστήρ, -έρος, ὁ,** [fr. r. star (prob. as *strewn* over the sky), cf. ἄστρον, Lat. *stella*, Germ. *Stern*, Eng. *star*; Fick, Pt. i. 250; Curtius § 205; Vaniček p. 1146; fr. Hom.

down]; *a star*: Mt. ii. 7, 9, 10 [acc. -έραν א* C; see ἄρσην fin.]; xxiv. 29; Mk. xiii. 25; 1 Co. xv. 41; Rev. vi. 13; viii. 10–12; ix. 1; xii. 1, 4; ὁ ἀστὴρ αὐτοῦ, the star betokening his birth, Mt. ii. 2 (i. e. 'the star of the Messiah,' on which cf. *Bertholdt*, Christologia Judaeorum § 14; *Anger*, Der Stern der Weisen, in Niedner's Zeitschr. f. d. histor. Theol. for 1847, fasc. 3; [B. D. s. v. Star of the Wise Men]); by the figure of the seven stars which Christ holds in his right hand, Rev. i. 16; ii. 1; iii. 1, are signified the angels of the seven churches, under the direction of Christ, ibid. i. 20; see what was said s. v. ἄγγελος, 2. ἀστὴρ ὁ πρωϊνός the morning star, Rev. xxii. 16 [Rec. ὀρθρινός]; ii. 28 (δώσω αὐτῷ τὸν ἀστέρα τ. πρωϊνόν I will give to him the morning star, that he may be irradiated with its splendor and outshine all others, i. e. I will cause his heavenly glory to excel that of others). ἀστέρες πλανῆται, wandering stars, Jude 13 (these are not *planets*, the motion of which is scarcely noticed by the commonalty, but far more probably *comets*, which Jude regards as stars which have left the course prescribed them by God, and wander about at will — cf. Enoch xviii. 15, and so are a fit symbol of men πλανῶντες καὶ πλανώμενοι, 2 Tim. iii. 13).*

793   ἀ-στήρικτος, -ον, (στηρίζω), *unstable, unsteadfast*: 2 Pet. ii. 14; iii. 16. (Anthol. Pal. 6, 203, 11.)*

794   ἄστοργος, -ον, (στοργή love of kindred), *without natural affection*: Ro. i. 31; 2 Tim. iii. 3. (Aeschin., Theocr., Plut., al.)*

795   ἀστοχέω, -ῶ: 1 aor. ἠστόχησα; (to be ἄστοχος, fr. στόχος a mark), *to deviate from, miss,* (the mark): with gen. [W. § 30, 6], to deviate from anything, 1 Tim. i. 6 (Sir. vii. 19; viii. 9); περί τι, 1 Tim. vi. 21; 2 Tim. ii. 18. (Polyb., Plut., Lcian., [al.].)*

796   ἀστραπή, -ῆς, ἡ, *lightning*: Lk. x. 18; xvii. 24; Mt. xxiv. 27; xxviii. 3; plur., Rev. iv. 5; viii. 5; xi. 19; xvi. 18; of the gleam of a lamp, Lk. xi. 36 [so Aeschyl. frag. (fr. schol. on Soph. Oed. Col. 1047) 188 Ahrens, 372 Dind.].*

797   ἀστράπτω; (later form στράπτω, see ἀσπάζομαι init. [prob. allied with ἀστήρ q. v.]); *to lighten,* (Hom. Il. 9, 237; 17, 595, and often in Attic): Lk. xvii. 24. Of dazzling objects: ἐσθής (R G ἐσθήσεις), Lk. xxiv. 4 (and very often in Grk. writ. fr. Soph. Oed. Col. 1067; Eur. Phoen. 111, down). [Comp.: ἐξ-, περι-αστράπτω.]*

798   ἄστρον, -ου, τό, [(see ἀστήρ init.), fr. Hom. down]; 1. *a group of stars, a constellation*; but not infreq. also 2. i. q. ἀστήρ *a star*: Lk. xxi. 25; Acts xxvii. 20; Heb. xi. 12; the image of a star, Acts vii. 43.*

799   Ἀ-σύγ-κριτος [TWH Ἀσύνκρ.], -ου, ὁ, (a priv. and συγκρίνω to compare; incomparable); *Asyncritus*, the name of an unknown Christian at Rome: Ro. xvi. 14.*

800   ἀ-σύμφωνος, -ον, *not agreeing in sound, dissonant, inharmonious, at variance*: πρὸς ἀλλήλους (Diod. 4, 1), Acts xxviii. 25. (Sap. xviii. 10; [Joseph. c. Ap. 1, 8, 1]; Plat., Plut., [al.].)*

801   ἀ-σύνετος, -ον, *unintelligent, without understanding*: Mt. xv. 16; Mk. vii. 18; *stupid*: Ro. i. 21; x. 19. In imitation of the Hebr. נָבָל, *ungodly* (Sap. i. 5; Sir. xv. 7 sq. [cf. ἀσυνετεῖν, Ps. cxviii. (cxix.) 158]), because a wicked man has no mind for the things which make for salvation: Ro. i. 31 [al. adhere here to the Grk. usage; cf. Fritzsche ad loc.]. (In Grk. writ. fr. Hdt. down.) [Cf. σοφός, fin.]*

ἀ-σύν-θετος, -ον,   1. *uncompounded, simple,* (Plat.,   802 Aristot., al.).   2. (συντίθεμαι to covenant), *covenantbreaking, faithless*: Ro. i. 31 (so in Jer. iii. 8, 11; Dem. de falsa leg. p. 383, 6; cf. Pape and Passow s. v.; ἀσυνθετεῖν to be faithless [Ps. lxxii. (lxxiii.) 15; 2 Esdr. x. 2; Neh. i. 8, etc.]; ἀσυνθεσία transgression, 1 Chr. ix. 1 [Ald., Compl.; 2 Esdr. ix. 2, 4; Jer. iii. 7]; εὐσυνθετεῖν to keep faith; [cf. Trench § lii.]).*

ἀσφάλεια, -ας, ἡ, (ἀσφαλής), [fr. Aeschyl. down]; a.   803 *firmness, stability*: ἐν πάσῃ ἀσφ. most securely, Acts v. 23. trop. *certainty, undoubted truth*: λόγων (see λόγος, I. 7), Lk. i. 4, (τοῦ λόγου, the certainty of a proof, Xen. mem. 4, 6, 15). b. *security from enemies and dangers, safety*: 1 Th. v. 3 (opp. to κίνδυνος, Xen. mem. 3, 12, 7).*

ἀσφαλής, -ές, (σφάλλω to make to totter or fall, to   804 cheat, [cf. Lat. *fallo*, Germ. *fallen*, etc., Eng. *fall, fail*], σφάλλομαι to fall, to reel, [fr. Hom. down]; a. *firm* (that can be relied on, confided in): ἄγκυρα, Heb. vi. 19 (where L and Tr have received as the form of acc. sing. ἀσφαλήν [Tdf. 7 -λὴν; cf. Tdf. ad loc.; *Delitzsch*, Com. ad loc.] see ἄρσην). trop. *certain, true*: Acts xxv. 26; τὸ ἀσφαλές, Acts xxi. 34; xxii. 30. b. *suited to confirm*: τινί, Phil. iii. 1 (so Joseph. antt. 3, 2, 1).*

ἀσφαλίζω: 1 aor. pass. inf. ἀσφαλισθῆναι; 1 aor. mid.   805 ἠσφαλισάμην; (ἀσφαλής); esp. freq. fr. Polyb. down; *to make firm, to make secure* against harm; pass. *to be made secure*: Mt. xxvii. 64 (ὁ τάφος) [B. 52 (46)]; mid. prop. to make secure for one's self or for one's own advantage, (often in Polyb.): Mt. xxvii. 65 sq.; to make fast τοὺς πόδας εἰς τὸ ξύλον, Acts xvi. 24 [W. § 66, 2 d.; B. § 147, 8].*

ἀσφαλῶς, adv., [fr. Hom. down], *safely* (so as to prevent   806 escape): Mk. xiv. 44; Acts xvi. 23. *assuredly*: γινώσκειν, Acts iii. 36 (εἰδότες, Sap. xviii. 6).*

ἀσχημονέω, -ῶ: (to be ἀσχήμων, deformed; τὴν κεφα   807 λὴν ἀσχημονεῖν, of a bald man, Ael. v. h. 11, 4); *to act unbecomingly* ([Eur.], Xen., Plat., al.): 1 Co. xiii. 5; ἐπί τινα, towards one, i. e. contextually, to prepare disgrace for her, 1 Co. vii. 36.*

ἀσχημοσύνη, -ης, ἡ, (ἀσχήμων); fr. Plato down; *un   808 seemliness, an unseemly deed*: Ro. i. 27; of the pudenda, one's *nakedness, shame*: Rev. xvi. 15, as in Ex. xx. 26; Deut. xxiii. 14, etc. (In Grk. writ. fr. Plat. down.)*

ἀσχήμων, -ονος, neut. ἄσχημον, (σχῆμα); a. *deformed.*   809 b. *indecent, unseemly*: 1 Co. xii. 23, opp. to εὐσχήμων. ([Hdt.], Xen., Plat., and subseq. writ.)*

ἀσωτία, -ας, ἡ, (the character of an ἄσωτος, i. e. of an   810 abandoned man, one that cannot be saved, fr. σαόω, σόω i. q. σώζω, [ἀ-σω-το-s, Curtius § 570]; hence prop. *incorrigibleness*), *an abandoned, dissolute, life*; *profligacy, prodigality*, [R. V. *riot*]: Eph. v. 18; Tit. i. 6; 1 Pet. iv. 4; (Prov. xxviii. 7; 2 Macc. vi. 4. Plat. rep. 8, p. 560 e.; Aristot. eth. Nic. 4, 1, 5 (3) p. 1120ᵇ, 3; Polyb. 32, 20, 9; 40, 12, 7; cf. Cic. Tusc. 3, 8; Hdian. 2, 5, 2 (1 ed.

Bekk.), and elsewhere). Cf. Tittmann i. p. 152 sq.; [Trench § xvi.].*

811   ἀσώτως, adv., (adj. ἄσωτος, on which see ἀσωτία), *dissolutely, profligately*: ζῆν (Joseph. antt. 12, 4, 8), Lk. xv. 13 [A. V. *riotous living*].*

812   ἀτακτέω, -ῶ: 1 aor. ἠτάκτησα; *to be ἄτακτος, to be disorderly*; a. prop. of soldiers marching out of order or quitting the ranks: Xen. Cyr. 7, 2, 6, etc. Hence b. *to be neglectful of duty, to be lawless*: Xen. Cyr. 8, 1, 22; oec. 5, 15; Lys. 141, 18 [i. e. c. Alcib. or. 1 § 18], al. c. *to lead a disorderly life*: 2 Th. iii. 7, cf. 11.*

813   ἄ-τακτος, -ον, (τάσσω), *disorderly, out of the ranks*, (often so of soldiers); *irregular, inordinate* (ἄτακτοι ἡδοναί immoderate pleasures, Plat. legg. 2, 660 b.; Plut. de lib. educ. c. 7), *deviating from the prescribed order or rule*: 1 Th. v. 14, cf. 2 Th. iii. 6. (In Grk. writ. fr. [Hdt. and] Thuc. down; often in Plat.) *

814   ἀ-τάκτως, adv., *disorderly*: 2 Th. iii. 6 ἀτάκτως περιπατεῖν, which is explained by the added καὶ μὴ κατὰ τὴν παράδοσιν ἣν παρέλαβε παρ' ἡμῶν; cf. ibid. 11, where it is explained by μηδὲν ἐργαζόμενοι, ἀλλὰ περιεργαζόμενοι. (Often in Plato.) *

815   ἄτεκνος, -ον, (τέκνον), *without offspring, childless*: Lk. xx. 28–30. (Gen. xv. 2; Sir. xvi. 3. In Grk. writ. fr. Hesiod opp. 600 down.)*

816   ἀτενίζω; 1 aor. ἠτένισα; (fr. ἀτενής stretched, intent, and this fr. τείνω and a intensive; [yet cf. W. § 16, 4 B. a. fin., and s. v. A, a, 3]); *to fix the eyes on, gaze upon*: with dat. of pers., Lk. iv. 20; xxii. 56; Acts iii. 12; x. 4; xiv. 9; xxiii. 1; foll. by εἰς with acc. of pers., Acts iii. 4; vi. 15; xiii. 9; metaph. to fix one's mind on one as an example, Clem. Rom. 1 Cor. 9, 2; εἴς τι, Acts i. 10; vii. 55; 2 Co. iii. 7, 13; εἴς τι, *to look into anything*, Acts xi. 6. (3 Macc. ii. 26. [Aristot.], Polyb. 6, 11, 5 [i. e. 6, 11ᵃ, 12 Dind.]; Diod. 3, 39 [Dind. ἐνατ.]; Joseph. b. j. 5, 12, 3; Lcian. cont. 16, al.) *

817   ἄτερ, prep., freq. in the poets [fr. Hom. down], rare in prose writ. fr. Plat. [?] down; *without, apart from*: with gen. [Dion. Hal. 3, 10; Plut. Num. 14, Cat. min. 5]; in the Bible only in 2 Macc. xii. 15; Lk. xxii. 6 (ἄτερ ὄχλου in the absence of the multitude; hence, without tumult), 35. ['Teaching' 3, 10; Herm. sim. 5, 4, 5.]*

818   ἀτιμάζω; 1 aor. ἠτίμασα; [Pass., pres. ἀτιμάζομαι; 1 aor. inf. ἀτιμασθῆναι; (fr. ἄτιμος; hence) *to make ἄτιμος, to dishonor, insult, treat with contumely*, whether in word, in deed, or in thought: [Mk. xii. 4 T Tr mrg. WH (cf. ἀτιμάω and -μόω)]; Lk. xx. 11; Jn. viii. 49; Acts v. 41; Ro. ii. 23; Jas. ii. 6 [W. § 40, 5, 2; B. 202 (175)]. Pass.: Ro. i. 24, on which cf. W. 326 (305 sq.); [and § 39, 3 N. 3]. (In Grk. writ. fr. Hom. down; Sept.) *

see 818   ἀ-τιμάω, -ῶ: [1 aor. ἠτίμησα]; (τιμή); *to deprive of honor, despise, treat with contempt or contumely*: τινά, Mk. xii. 4 L Tr txt. ἠτίμησαν (see ἀτιμάζω and -μόω). (In Grk. writ. [chiefly Epic] fr. Hom. down.) *

819   ἀτιμία, -ας, ἡ, (ἄτιμος), *dishonor, ignominy, disgrace*, [fr. Hom. down]: 1 Co. xi. 14; opp. to δόξα, 2 Co. vi. 8; 1 Co xv. 43 (ἐν ἀτιμίᾳ sc. ὄν, in a state of disgrace, used of the unseemliness and offensiveness of a dead body);

κατ' ἀτιμίαν equiv. to ἀτίμως, with contempt sc. of myself, 2 Co. xi. 21 [R. V. *by way of disparagement*, cf. κατά, II. fin.]; πάθη ἀτιμίας base lusts, vile passions, Ro. i. 26, cf. W. § 34, 3 b.; [B. § 132, 10]. εἰς ἀτιμίαν for a dishonorable use, of vessels, opp. to τιμή: Ro. ix. 21; 2 Tim. ii. 20.*

820   ἄτιμος, -ον, (τιμή); fr. Hom. down; *without honor, unhonored, dishonored*: Mt. xiii. 57; Mk. vi. 4; 1 Co. iv. 10 (opp. to ἔνδοξος); *base, of less esteem*: 1 Co. xii. 23 [here the neut. plur. of the compar., ἀτιμότερα (Rec.ᵉˡᶻ ἀτιμώτερα)].*

821   ἀτιμόω, -ῶ: [pf. pass. ptcp. ἠτιμωμένος]; (ἄτιμος); fr. Aeschyl. down; *to dishonor, mark with disgrace*: Mk. xii. 4 R G, see ἀτιμάω [and ἀτιμάζω].*

822   ἀτμίς, -ίδος, ἡ, *vapor*: Jas. iv. 14; καπνοῦ (Joel ii. 30 [al. iii. 3]), Acts ii. 19 [opp. to καπνός in Aristot. meteor. 2, 4 p. 359ᵇ, 29 sq., to νέφος ibid. 1, 9 p. 346ᵇ, 32]. (In Grk. writ. fr. [Hdt. 4, 75 and] Plat. Tim. p. 86 e. down.) *

823   ἄτομος, -ον, (τέμνω to cut), *that cannot be cut in two or divided, indivisible*, [Plat. Soph. 229 d.; of time, Aristot. phys. 8, 8 p. 263ᵇ, 27]: ἐν ἀτόμῳ *in a moment*, 1 Co. xv. 52.*

824   ἄ-τοπος, -ον, (τόπος), *out of place; not befitting, unbecoming*, (so in Grk. writ. fr. Thuc. down); *very often in* Plato); in later Grk. in an ethical sense, *improper, wicked*: Lk. xxiii. 41 (ἄτοπόν τι πράσσειν, as in Job xxvii. 6; 2 Macc. xiv. 23); Acts xxv. 5 L T Tr WH; (Sept. for אָוֶן Job iv. 8; xi. 11, etc. Joseph. antt. 6, 5, 6; Plut. de aud. poët. c. 3 φαυλά and ἄτοπα) ; of men : 2 Th. iii. 2 (ἄτοποι καὶ πονηροί). Luth. *unartig*, more correctly *unrighteous* [(*iniquus*), A. V. *unreasonable*, cf. Ellic. ad loc.]). *inconvenient, harmful*: Acts xxviii. 6 μηδὲν ἄτοπον εἰς αὐτὸν γινόμενον, no injury, no harm coming to him, (Thuc. 2, 49; Joseph. antt. 11, 5, 2; Hdian. 4, 11, 7 [4, ed. Bekk.]).*

825   Ἀττάλεια [-λία T WH (see I, ι)], -ας, ἡ, *Attalia*, a maritime city of Pamphylia in Asia, very near the borders of Lycia, built and named by Attalus Philadelphus, king of Pergamum; now *Antali* [or *Adalia*; cf. Dict. of Geog.]: Acts xiv. 25.*

826   αὐγάζω; 1 aor. inf. αὐγάσαι; (αὐγή); **1.** in Grk. writ. transitively, *to beam upon, irradiate*. **2.** in the Bible intrans. *to be bright, to shine forth*: 2 Co. iv. 4 [L mrg. Tr mrg. καταυγ. see φωτισμός, b.], (Lev. xiii. 24–28, [etc.]). [Comp.: δι-, κατ-αυγάζω.]*

827   αὐγή, -ῆς, ἡ, *brightness, radiance*, (cf. Germ. *Auge* [*eye*], of which the tragic poets sometimes use αὐγή, see Pape [or L. and S.; cf. Lat. *lumina*]), especially *of the sun*; hence ἡλίου is often added (Hom. and sqq.), *daylight*; hence ἄχρις [-ρι T Tr WH] αὐγῆς even till break of day, Acts xx. 11 (Polyaen. 4, 18 p. 386 κατὰ τὴν πρώτην αὐγὴν τῆς ἡμέρας). [Syn. see φέγγος, fin.]*

828   Αὔγουστος, -ου, ὁ, *Augustus* [cf. Eng. *Majesty*; see σεβαστός, 2], the surname of G. Julius Caesar Octavianus, the first Roman emperor: Lk. ii. 1.*

829   αὐθάδης, -ες, (fr. αὐτός and ἥδομαι), *self-pleasing, self-willed, arrogant*: Tit. i. 7; 2 Pet. ii. 10. (Gen. xlix. 3, 7;

Prov. xxi. 24. In Grk. writ. fr. Aeschyl. and Hdt. down.) [Trench § xciii.]*

830   αὐθ-αίρετος, -ον, (fr. αὐτός and αἱρέομαι), self-chosen; in Grk. writ. esp. of states or conditions, as δουλεία, Thuc. 6, 40, etc., more rarely of persons; voluntary, of free choice, of one's own accord, (as στρατηγός, Xen. an. 5, 7, 29, explained § 28 by ὃς ἑαυτὸν ἔληται): 2 Co. viii. 3, 17.*

831   αὐθεντέω, -ῶ; (a bibl. and eccl. word; fr. αὐθέντης contr. fr. αὐτοέντης, and this fr. αὐτός and ἔντεα arms [al. ἔντης, cf. Hesych. συνέντης· συνεργός; cf. Lobeck, Technol. p. 121]; hence a. acc. to earlier usage, one who with his own hand kills either others or himself. b. in later Grk. writ. one who does a thing himself, the author (τῆς πράξεως, Polyb. 23, 14, 2, etc.); one who acts on his own authority, autocratic, i. q. αὐτοκράτωρ an absolute master; cf. Lobeck ad Phryn. p. 120 [also as above; cf. W. § 2, 1 c.]); to govern one, exercise dominion over one: τινός, 1 Tim. ii. 12.*

832   αὐλέω, -ῶ: 1 aor. ηὔλησα; [pres. pass. ptcp. τὸ αὐλούμενον]; (αὐλός); to play on the flute, to pipe: Mt. xi. 17; Lk. vii. 32; 1 Co. xiv. 7. (Fr. [Alcm., Hdt.,] Xen. and Plat. down.)*

833   αὐλή, -ῆς, ἡ, (ἄω to blow; hence) prop. a place open to the air (διαπνεόμενος τόπος αὐλὴ λέγεται, Athen. 5, 15 p. 189 b.);   1. among the Greeks in Homer's time an uncovered space around the house, enclosed by a wall, in which the stables stood (Hom. Od. 9, 185; Il. 4, 433); hence among the Orientals that roofless enclosure in the open country in which flocks were herded at night, a sheep-fold: Jn. x. 1, 16. 2. the uncovered court-yard of the house, Hebr. חָצֵר, Sept. αὐλή, Vulg. atrium. In the O. T. particularly of the courts of the tabernacle and of the temple at Jerusalem; so in the N. T. once: Rev. xi. 2 (τὴν αὐλὴν τὴν ἔξωθεν [Rec.ˢᵗ ἔσωθεν] τοῦ ναοῦ). The dwellings of the higher classes usually had two αὐλαί, one exterior, between the door and the street, called also προαύλιον (q. v.); the other interior, surrounded by the buildings of the dwelling itself. The latter is mentioned Mt. xxvi. 69 (where ἔξω is opp. to the room in which the judges were sitting); Mk. xiv. 66; Lk. xxii. 55. Cf. Win. RWB. s. v. Häuser; [B. D. Am. ed. s. v. Court; BB.DD. s. v. House]. 3. the house itself, a palace: Mt. xxvi. 3, 58; Mk. xiv. 54; xv. 16; Lk. xi. 21; Jn. xviii. 15, and so very often in Grk. writ. fr. Hom. Od. 4, 74 down [cf. Eustath. 1483, 39 τῷ τῆς αὐλῆς ὀνόματι τὰ δώματα δηλοῖ, Suid. col. 652 c. αὐλή· ἡ τοῦ βασιλέως οἰκία. Yet this sense is denied to the N. T. by Meyer et al.; see Mey. on Mt. l. c.].*

834   αὐλητής, -οῦ, ὁ, (αὐλέω), a flute-player: Mt. ix. 23; Rev. xviii. 22. (In Grk. writ. fr. [Theogn. and] Hdt. 6, 60 down.)*

835   αὐλίζομαι: depon.; impf. ηὐλιζόμην; 1 aor. ηὐλίσθην [Veitch s. v.; B. 51 (44); W. § 39, 2]; (αὐλή); in Sept. mostly for לוּן; 1. prop. to lodge in the court-yard esp. at night; of flocks and shepherds. 2. to pass the night in the open air, bivouac. 3. univ. to pass the night, lodge: so Mt. xxi. 17; Lk. xxi. 37 (ἐξερχόμενος ηὐλίζετο εἰς τὸ ὄρος, going out to pass the night he retired

to the mountain; cf. B. § 147, 15). (In Grk. writ. fr. Hom. down.)*

836   αὐλός, -οῦ, ὁ, (ἄω, αὔω), [fr. Hom. down], a pipe: 1 Co. xiv. 7. [Cf. Stainer, Music of the Bible, ch. v.]*

837   αὐξάνω, and earlier (the only form in Pind. and Soph. [Veitch s. v. says, 'Hes. Mimnerm. Soph. Thuc. always have αὔξω or αὔξομαι, and Pind. except αὐξάνοι Fr. 130 (Bergk)']) αὔξω (Eph. ii. 21; Col. ii. 19); impf. ηὔξανον; fut. αὐξήσω; 1 aor. ηὔξησα; [Pass., pres. αὐξάνομαι]; 1 aor. ηὐξήθην; 1. trans. to cause to grow, to augment: 1 Co. iii. 6 sq.; 2 Co. ix. 10. Pass. to grow, increase, become greater: Mt. xiii. 32; Mk. iv. 8 L T Tr WH; 2 Co. x. 15; Col. i. 6 [not Rec.]; εἰς τὴν ἐπίγνωσιν τοῦ θεοῦ unto the knowledge of God, Col. i. 10 (G L T Tr WH τῇ ἐπιγνώσει τοῦ θεοῦ); εἰς σωτηρίαν [not Rec.] to the attaining of salvation, 1 Pet. ii. 2. 2. acc. to later usage (fr. Aristot. an. post. 1, 13 p. 78ᵇ, 6, etc., down; but nowhere in Sept. [cf. B. 54 (47); 145 (127); W. § 38, 1]) intrans. to grow, increase: of plants, Mt. vi. 28; Mk. iv. 8 Rec.; Lk. xii. 27 [not Tdf.; Tr mrg. br. αὔξ.]; Lk. xiii. 19; of infants, Lk. i. 80; ii. 40; of a multitude of people, Acts vii. 17. of inward Christian growth: εἰς Χριστόν, in reference to [W. 397 (371); yet cf. Ellic. ad loc.] Christ, Eph. iv. 15; εἰς ναόν, so as to form a temple, Eph. ii. 21; ἐν χάριτι, 2 Pet. iii. 18; with an acc. of the substance, τὴν αὔξησιν, Col. ii. 19 [cf. W. § 32, 2; B. § 131, 5, also Bp. Lghtft.'s note ad loc.]; of the external increase of the gospel it is said ὁ λόγος ηὔξανε: Acts vi. 7; xii. 24; xix. 20; of the growing authority of a teacher and the number of his adherents (opp. to ἐλαττοῦσθαι), Jn. iii. 30. [ΣΟΜΡ.: συν-, ὑπερ-αυξάνω.]*

838   αὔξησις, -εως, ἡ, (αὔξω), increase, growth: Eph. iv. 16; τοῦ θεοῦ, effected by God, Col. ii. 19; cf. Meyer ad loc. ([Hdt.], Thuc., Xen., Plat., and subseq. writ.)*

see 837   αὔξω, see αὐξάνω.

839   αὔριον, adv., (fr. αὔρα the morning air, and this fr. ἄω to breathe, blow; [acc. to al. akin to ἠώς, Lat. aurora; Curtius § 613, cf. Vaniček p. 944]), to-morrow (Lat. cras): Mt. vi. 30; Lk. xii. 28; Acts xxiii. 15 Rec., 20; xxv. 22; 1 Co. xv. 32 (fr. Is. xxii. 13); σήμερον καὶ αὔριον, Lk. xiii. 32 sq.; Jas. iv. 13 [Rec.ˢᵗ G, al. σήμ. ἢ αὔρ.]. ἡ αὔριον sc. ἡμέρα [W. § 64, 5; B. § 123, 8] the morrow, Mt. vi. 34; Acts iv. 3; ἐπὶ τὴν αὔριον, on the morrow, i. e. the next morning, Lk. x. 35; Acts iv. 5; τὸ [L τὰ; WH om.] τῆς αὔριον, what the morrow will bring forth, Jas. iv. 14. [From Hom. down.]*

840   αὐστηρός, -ά, -όν, (fr. αὔω to dry up), harsh (Lat. austerus), stringent of taste, αὐστηρὸν καὶ γλυκὺ (καὶ πικρόν), Plat. legg. 10, 897 a.; οἶνος, Diog. Laërt. 7, 117. of mind and manners, harsh, rough, rigid, [cf. Trench § xiv.]: Lk. xix. 21, 22; (Polyb. 4, 20, 7; Diog. Laërt. 7, 26, etc. 2 Macc. xiv. 30).*

841   αὐτάρκεια, -ας, ἡ, (αὐτάρκης, q. v.), a perfect condition of life, in which no aid or support is needed; equiv. to τελειότης κτήσεως ἀγαθῶν, Plat. def. p. 412 b.; often in Aristot. [defined by him (pol. 7, 5 init. p. 1326ᵇ, 29) as follows: τὸ πάντα ὑπάρχειν κ. δεῖσθαι μηθενὸς αὐτάρκες; cf. Bp. Lghtft. on Phil. iv. 11]; hence, a sufficiency of the *necessaries of life*: 2 Co. ix. 8; subjectively, *a mind contented with its lot, contentment*: 1 Tim. vi. 6; (Diog. Laërt. 10, 130).*

842 **αὐτάρκης** [on the accent see Chandler § 705], -ες, (αὐτός, ἀρκέω), [fr. Aeschyl. down], *sufficient for one's self, strong enough* or *possessing enough to need no aid or support; independent of external circumstances*; often in Grk. writ. fr. [Aeschyl. and] Hdt. 1, 32 down. Subjectively, *contented with one's lot, with one's means, though the slenderest*: Phil. iv. 11, (so Sir. xl. 18; Polyb. 6, 48, 7; Diog. Laërt. 2, 24 of Socrates, αὐτάρκης καὶ σεμνός). [Cf. αὐτάρκεια.] *

843 **αὐτο-κατά-κριτος**, -ον, (αὐτός, κατακρίνω), *self-condemned*: Tit. iii. 11; (eccl. writ. [cf. W. § 34, 3]).*

844 **αὐτόματος**, -ον, and -η, -ον, (fr. αὐτός and μέμαα to desire eagerly, fr. obsol. theme μάω), *moved by one's own impulse*, or *acting without the instigation* or *intervention of another*, (fr. Hom. down); often of the earth producing plants of itself, and of the plants themselves and fruits growing without culture; [on its a d v e r b i a l use cf. W. § 54, 2]: Mk. iv. 28; (Hdt. 2, 94; 8, 138; Plat. polit. p. 272 a.; [Theophr. h. p. 2, 1]; Diod. 1, 8, etc. Lev. xxv. 5, 11). of gates opening of their own accord: Acts xii. 10, (so in Hom. Il. 5, 749; Xen. Hell. 6, 4, 7; Apoll. Rh. 4, 41; Plut. Timol. 12; Nonn. Dion. 44, 21; [Dion Cass. 44, 17]).*

845 **αὐτόπτης**, -ου, ὁ, (αὐτός, ΟΠΤΩ), *seeing with one's own eyes, an eye-witness*, (cf. αὐτήκοος one who has himself heard a thing): Lk. i. 2. (In Grk. writ. fr. Hdt. down.)*

846 **αὐτός**, -ή, -ό, pron. ("derived from the particle αὖ with the added force of a demonstrative pronoun. In itself it signifies nothing more than *again*, applied to what has either been previously mentioned or, when the whole discourse is looked at, must necessarily be supplied." *Klotz* ad Devar. ii. p. 219; [see Vaniček p. 268]). It is used by the bibl. writ. both of the O. T. and of the N. T. far more frequently than the other pronouns; and in this very frequent and almost inordinate use of it, they deviate greatly from prof. auth.; cf. B. § 127, 9. [On classic usage cf. *Hermann*, Opusc. i. 308 sqq., of which dissertation a summary is given in his edition of Viger pp. 732–736.]
I. *self*, as used (in all persons, genders, numbers) to distinguish a person or thing from or contrast it with another, or to give him (it) emphatic prominence. **1.** When used to express O p p o s i t i o n or D i s t i n c t i o n, it is added **a.** to the subjects implied in the verb, the personal pronouns ἐγώ, ἡμεῖς, σύ, etc., being omitted: Lk. v. 37 (αὐτὸς ἐκχυθήσεται the wine, as opp. to the skins); Lk. xxii. 71 (αὐτοὶ γὰρ ἠκούσαμεν we ourselves, opp. to witnesses whose testimony could have been taken); Jn. ii. 25 (αὐτὸς ἐγίνωσκεν, opp. to testimony he might have called for); Jn. iv. 42 (we ourselves, not thou only); Jn. ix. 21 [T WH om. παι]; Acts xviii. 15 (ὄψεσθε αὐτοί); xx. 34; xxii. 19; 1 Th. i. 9, etc.; with a negative added, 'he does not himself do this or that,' i. e. he leaves it to others: Lk. vi. 42 (αὐτός, viz. *thou*, οὐ βλέπων); Lk. xi. 46 (αὐτοί, viz. *ye*, οὐ προσψαύετε), 52; Jn. xviii. 28; 3

Jn. 10. With the addition of καί to indicate that a thing is ascribed to one equally with others: Lk. xiv. 12 (μήποτε καὶ αὐτοί σε ἀντικαλέσωσι); xvi. 28; Acts ii. 22 [G L T Tr WH om. καί]; Jn. iv. 45; xvii. 19, 21; Phil. ii. 24, etc. In other pass. καὶ αὐτός is added to a subject expressly mentioned, and is placed after it; and in translation may be joined to the predicate and rendered *likewise*: Lk. i. 36 (ἡ συγγενής σου καὶ αὐτὴ συνειληφυῖα υἱόν thy kinswoman *herself* also, i. e. as well as thou); Mt. xxvii. 57 (ὃς καὶ αὐτὸς ἐμαθήτευσε [L T Tr WH txt. -τεύθη] τῷ Ἰησοῦ); Lk. xxiii. 51 [R G]; Mk. xv. 43; Acts viii. 13 (ὁ δὲ Σίμων καὶ αὐτὸς ἐπίστευσεν); xv. 32; xxi. 24; 1 Jn. ii. 6; Gal. ii. 17; Heb. xiii. 3. **b.** it is added to subjects expressed, whether to pronouns personal or demonstrative, or to nouns proper or common: Jn. iii. 28 (αὐτοὶ ὑμεῖς ye yourselves bear witness, not only have I affirmed); Acts xx. 30 (ἐξ ὑμῶν αὐτῶν from among your own selves, not only from other quarters); Ro. xv. 14 (καὶ αὐτὸς ἐγώ I of myself also, not only assured by report, cf. i. 8); 1 Co. v. 13 (ἐξ ὑμῶν αὐτῶν from your own society, opp. to them that are without, of whose character God must be the judge); 1 Co. vii. 35; xi. 13; 1 Th. iv. 9; αὐτοὶ οὗτοι, Acts xxiv. 20; αὐτοῦ τούτου (masc.), Acts xxv. 25; Ἰησοῦς αὐτός Jesus himself, personally, opp. to those who baptized by his command, Jn. iv. 2; αὐτὸς Ἰησοῦς, opp. to those who believed on him on account of his miracles, Jn. ii. 24; Jesus himself, not others only, Jn. iv. 44; αὐτ. Δαυείδ, opp. to the doctors of the law, whose decision did not seem quite to agree with the words of David, Mk. xii. 36 sq.; Lk. xx. 42; αὐτὸς ὁ Σατανᾶς, opp. to his ministers, 2 Co. xi. 14; αὐτὸς ὁ θεός, God himself, not another, Rev. xxi. 3; αὐτὰ τὰ ἐπουράνια, the heavenly things themselves [i. e. sanctuary], opp. to its copies, Heb. ix. 23 [see ἐπουράνιος, 1 c.]. **c.** it is used to distinguish one not only from his companions, disciples, servants, — as Mk. ii. 25 (αὐτὸς καὶ οἱ μετ' αὐτοῦ); Jn. ii. 12; iv. 53; xviii. 1,— but also from t h i n g s done by him or belonging to him, as Jn. vii. 4 (τὶ ποιεῖ καὶ ζητεῖ αὐτός [L Tr mrg. WH mrg. αὐτό]); 1 Co. iii. 15 (τινὸς τὸ ἔργον κατακαήσεται, αὐτὸς δὲ σωθήσεται); Lk. xxiv. 15 (αὐτὸς (ὁ) Ἰησοῦς, Jesus himself in person, opp. to their previous conversation about him). **d.** *self* to the exclusion of others, i. e. he etc. *alone, by one's self*: Mk. vi. 31 (ὑμεῖς αὐτοί ye alone, unattended by any of the people; cf. Fritzsche ad loc.); Jn. xiv. 11 (διὰ τὰ ἔργα αὐτά [WH mrg. αὐτοῦ]); Ro. vii. 25 (αὐτὸς ἐγώ I alone, unaided by the Spirit of Christ; cf. viii. 2); 2 Co. xii. 13 (αὐτὸς ἐγώ, unlike the other preachers of the gospel); Rev. xix. 12; cf. *Herm.* ad Vig. p. 733 iii.; Matth. § 467, 5; Kühner § 468 Anm. 2; [Jelf § 656, 3]; with the addition of μόνος (as often in Attic writ.): Jn. vi. 15. **e.** *self, not prompted* or *influenced by another*, i. e. *of one's self, of one's own accord*: Jn. xvi. 27 (so even Hom. Il. 17, 254; and among Attic writ. esp. Xen.). **2.** When it gives P r o m i n e n c e, it answers **a.** to our emphatic *he, she, it*: Mt. i. 21 (αὐτὸς σώσει HE and no other); Mt. v. 4–10 (αὐτοί); vi. 4 [R G]; xvii. 5 (αὐτοῦ ἀκούετε); Lk. vi. 35; xvii. 16; xxiv. 21; Jn. ix. 21 (αὐτὸς [T Tr WH om.] . . .

αὐτόν . . . αὐτός); Acts x. 42 [L txt. Tr txt. WH οὗτος]; Gal. iv. 17 (αὐτούς); Eph. ii. 10 (αὐτοῦ); Col. i. 17 ; 1 Jn. ii. 2 ; iv. 5 ; Jas. ii. 6 sq. So in Grk. writ. also fr. Hom. down ; cf. *Herm.* ad Vig. p. 734 v. It is used with the same force after relative sentences, where Greek prose uses οὗτος : Mt. xii. 50 (ὅστις ἂν ποιήσῃ . . . , αὐτός μου ἀδελφός ἐστιν, where in Mk. iii. 35 οὗτος); Mt. xxvi. 48 ; Mk. xiv. 44 ; cf. B. 107 (94) sq. Less emphatically, αὐτός is put before subjects, serving to recall them again : Mt. iii. 4 (αὐτὸς δὲ 'Ιωάννης now he, whom I spoke of, John) ; Mk. vi. 17 (αὐτὸς γὰρ Ἡρῴδης) ; Ro. viii. 16 (αὐτὸ τὸ πνεῦμα). **b.** it points out some one as c h i e f, l e a d e r, m a s t e r of the rest (often so in Grk., as in the well-known phrase of the Pythagoreans αὐτὸς ἔφα [cf. W. § 22, 3, 4 and p. 150 (142)]) : of Christ, Mt. viii. 24 ; Mk. iv. 38 ; vi. 47 ; viii. 29 ; Lk. v. 16 sq.; ix. 51 ; x. 38 ; of God, Lk. vi. 35 ; Heb. xiii. 5 ; 1 Jn. iv. 19 [not Lchm.]. **c.** it answers to our *very, just, exactly,* (Germ. *eben, gerade*) : Ro. ix. 3 (αὐτὸς ἐγώ I myself, the very man who seems to be inimical to the Israelites) ; 2 Co. x. 1 (I myself, who bore myself lowly in your presence, as ye said) ; αὐτὰ τὰ ἔργα, Jn. v. 36 ; often in Luke ἐν αὐτῇ τῇ ἡμέρᾳ or ὥρᾳ, αὐτῷ τῷ καιρῷ, in that very day, hour, season : Lk. ii. 38 ; x. 21 ; xii. 12 ; xiii. 1, 31 ; xx. 19 ; xxiii. 12 ; xxiv. 13, 33 ; Acts xvi. 18. In the writings of Paul αὐτὸ τοῦτο this very thing : Gal. ii. 10 ; 2 Co. vii. 11 ; Phil. i. 6 ; εἰς αὐτὸ τοῦτο for this very purpose, on this very account : Ro. ix. 17 ; xiii. 6 ; 2 Co. v. 5 ; Eph. vi. 22 ; Col. iv. 8 ; and in the same sense [for this very thing] the simple accus. (as in Attic, cf. Matth. § 470, 7 ; Kühner ii. 267 Anm. 5) : W. § 21 N. 2) τοῦτο αὐτό, 2 Co. ii. 3 [but see Mey. ad loc.], and αὐτὸ τοῦτο, 2 Pet. i. 5 [Lchm. reads here αὐτοί]. **d.** *even,* Lat. *vel, adeo,* (in Hom. ; cf. *Herm.* ad Vig. p. 733 ii.) : καὶ αὐτὴ ἡ κτίσις, Ro. viii. 21 ; οὐδὲ ἡ φύσις αὐτή, 1 Co. xi. 14 ; καὶ [Tr om. L WH br. καὶ] αὐτὸς ὁ υἱός, 1 Co. xv. 28 ; καὶ αὐτὴ Σάρρα even Sarah herself, although a feeble old woman, Heb. xi. 11 [yet WH mrg. reads the dat. αὐτῇ Σάρρᾳ ; see καταβολή, 1].

II. αὐτός has the force of a simple personal pronoun of the third person, answering to our unemphatic *he, she, it* ; and that   **1.** as in classic Grk., in the o b l i q u e c a s e s, *him, her, it, them,* etc. : numberless instances, — as in the gen. absolute, e. g. αὐτοῦ ἐλθόντος, λαλήσαντος, etc.; or in the acc. with inf., εἰς τὸ εἶναι αὐτοὺς ἀναπολογήτους, Ro. i. 20 ; or after prepositions, ἐξ αὐτοῦ, ἐν αὐτῷ, etc.; or where it indicates the possessor, ὁ πατὴρ αὐτοῦ ; or a person as the (dir. or indir.) object of an active verb, as ἐπιδώσει αὐτῷ, Mt. vii. 9 ; ἀσπάσασθε αὐτήν, Mt. x. 12 ; ἀφεὶς αὐτούς, Mt. xxvi. 44 ; ἣν διανεύων αὐτοῖς, Lk. i. 22 ; οὐκ εἴα αὐτὰ λαλεῖν, Lk. iv. 41 ; ἡ σκοτία αὐτὸ οὐ κατέλαβε, Jn. i. 5. But see αὐτοῦ below.   **2.** Contrary to Grk. usage, in the N. T. even in the N o m i n a t i v e it is put for a simple personal pronoun of the third person, where the Greeks say οὗτος or ὁ δέ, or use no pronoun at all. This has been convincingly shown by B. 107 (93) sqq.; and yet some of the examples adduced by him are not decisive, but either must be or can be referred to the usage illustrated under I. 1 ; — those in which αὐτός is used of

Christ, apparently to I. 1 b. But, in my opinion, the question is settled even by the following : αὐτός, Mt. xiv. 2 ; Mk. xiv. 15 ; Lk. i. 22 ; xv. 14 ; so too in the Sept. (cf. *Thiersch,* De Pentat. vers. Alex. p. 98) ; Sir. xlix. 7 ; Tob. vi. 11 ; αὐτοί, Mk. ii. 8 (οὕτως αὐτοὶ διαλογίζονται in Grsb.); Lk. ix. 36 ; xiv. 1 ; xxii. 23 ; αὐτό, Lk. xi. 14 [Tr mrg. WH om., Tr txt. br.]. Whether αὐτή and αὐταί also are so used, is doubtful ; cf. B. 109 (95).   **3.** Sometimes in the oblique cases the pron. is omitted, being evident from the context : Mk. vi. 5 (ἐπιθείς, sc. αὐτοῖς); Jn. iii. 34 (δίδωσι, sc. αὐτῷ); Jn. x. 29 (δέδωκέ μοι, sc. αὐτούς) ; Acts xiii. 3 (ἀπέλυσαν, sc. αὐτούς) ; Rev. xviii. 21 (ἔβαλεν, sc. αὐτόν), etc.   **4.** Not infrequently αὐτός in the oblique cases is a d d e d to the v e r b, although the case belonging to this very verb has preceded : Mt. viii. 1 (καταβάντι δὲ αὐτῷ [L Tr WH gen. absol.] ἀπὸ τοῦ ὄρους ἠκολούθησαν αὐτῷ) ; Mt. iv. 16 ; v. 40 ; viii. 23, 28 [R G] ; ix. 28 ; xxv. 29 (ἀπὸ [om. by L T Tr WH] τοῦ μὴ ἔχοντος . . . ἀπ' αὐτοῦ) ; xxvi. 71 [R G Lbr. T] ; Mk. v. 2 [R G] ; ix. 28 [R G] ; Jn. xv. 2 (πᾶν κλῆμα . . . αἴρει αὐτό) ; Acts vii. 21 [R G] ; Jas. iv. 17 ; Rev. ii. 7 ; vi. 4 [L Tr mrg. br.] ; cf. W. § 22, 4 a.; B. 142 (125). Doubtless the writer, while writing the earlier words with the intention of joining them to the leading verb to follow, marked off these very words as a clause by themselves, as if they formed a protasis ; and so, when he came to the leading verb, he construed it just as though it were to form an apodosis.   **5.** By a Hebraism αὐτός is used r e d u n d a n t l y in relative sentences : ἧς εἶχε τὸ θυγάτριον αὐτῆς, Mk. vii. 25 ; οὗ τῷ μώλωπι αὐτοῦ, 1 Pet. ii. 24 (R G T, but Tr mrg. br. αὐτοῦ) ; esp. in the Apocalypse : ἦν οὐδεὶς δύναται κλεῖσαι αὐτήν, Rev. iii. 8 (acc. to the true text) ; οἷς ἐδόθη αὐτοῖς, Rev. vii. 2 ; add vs. 9 ; xiii. 12 ; xvii. 9 ; far oftener in the Sept. ; rare in Grk. writ. [fr. Callim. ep. 44] ; cf. *Herm.* ad Vig. p. 709 ; [B. § 143, 1] ; W. § 22, 4 a. where add to the exx. Hdian. 8, 6, 10 [5 Bekk.] οἷς ἐπιφοιτῶσιν αὐτοῖς τὰς λοιπὰς πόλεις πύλας ἀνοίγνυντο. But to this construction must not be referred Mt. iii. 12 οὗ τὸ πτύον ἐν τῇ χειρὶ αὐτοῦ, nor 1 Pet. ii. 24 ὃς τὰς ἁμαρτίας ἡμῶν αὐτὸς ἀνήνεγκεν. For in the latter passage αὐτός is in contrast with us, who must otherwise have paid the penalty of our sins ; and in the former the sense is, 'he holds his winnowing-shovel in his hand.'   **6.** Very often αὐτός is used rather l a x l y, where the subject or the object to which it must be referred is not expressly indicated, but must be gathered especially from some preceding name of a province or city, or from the context : Mt. iv. 23 (περιῆγεν τὴν Γαλιλαίαν διδάσκων ἐν ταῖς συναγωγαῖς αὐτῶν, i. e. of the Galilæans) ; Acts viii. 5 (Σαμαρείας ἐκήρυσσεν αὐτοῖς, i. e. τοῖς Σαμαρείταις) ; xx. 2 (αὐτούς, i. e. the inhabitants τῶν μερῶν ἐκείνων) ; 2 Co. ii. 13 (αὐτοῖς, i. e. the Christians of Troas) ; Mt. xix. 2 (ὄχλοι πολλοὶ καὶ ἐθεράπευσεν αὐτούς, i. e. their sick) ; 1 Pet. iii. 14 (φόβον αὐτῶν, i. e. of those who may be able κακῶσαι you, vs. 13) ; Lk. xxiii. 51 (τῇ βουλῇ αὐτῶν, i. e. of those with whom he had been a βουλευτής) ; Heb. viii. 8 (αὐτοῖς [L T WH Tr mrg. αὐτούς; see μέμφομαι] i. e. τοῖς ἔχουσι τὴν διαθήκην τὴν πρώτην) ; Lk. ii. 22 (τοῦ καθαρισμοῦ αὐτῶν.

of the purification prescribed by the law of Moses to women in child-bed); Jn. viii. 44 (ψεύστης ἐστὶν καὶ ὁ πατὴρ αὐτοῦ, i. e. of the liar; cf. Baumg.-Crusius and Meyer ad loc.). By this rather careless use of the pronoun it came about that at length αὐτοί alone might be used for ἄνθρωποι: Mt. viii. 4; Mk. i. 44; Lk. v. 14, 17 [here T WH Tr mrg. αὐτόν]; cf. W. § 22, 3; B. § 127, 8. **7.** Sometimes, in relative sentences consisting of several members, the second member is not joined to the first by the relative ὅς, but by a loose connection proceeds with καὶ αὐτός; as, Lk. xvii. 31; Acts iii. 13 (ὃν ὑμεῖς παρεδώκατε καὶ ἠρνήσασθε αὐτόν [L T WH om. Tr br. αὐτόν]); 1 Co. viii. 6 (ἐξ οὗ τὰ πάντα καὶ ἡμεῖς εἰς αὐτόν, for καὶ εἰς ὃν ἡμεῖς); 2 Pet. ii. 3. This is the usage likewise of Greek as well as of Hebrew; cf. W. 149 (141); [B. 283 (243)]; Bnhdy. p. 304.

III. ὁ αὐτός, ἡ αὐτή, τὸ αὐτό, with the article, *the same*; **1.** without a noun: ὁ αὐτός, immutable, Heb. i. 12; xiii. 8, (Thuc. 2, 61); τὸ αὐτό: — ποιεῖν, Mt. v. 46 [R G T WH txt., 47 L T Tr WH]; Lk. vi. 33; λέγειν, to profess the same opinion, 1 Co. i. 10; ὀνειδίζειν, not *in the same manner* but reproached him with *the same*, cast on him *the same reproach*, Mt. xxvii. 44, (ὀνειδίζειν τοιαῦτα, Soph. Oed. Col. 1002). τὰ αὐτά: Acts xv. 27; Ro. ii. 1; Eph. vi. 9. ἐπὶ τὸ αὐτό [Rec. passim ἐπιτοαυτό] (Hesych. ὁμοῦ, ἐπὶ τὸν αὐτὸν τόπον), to the same place, in the same place: Mt. xxii. 34; Acts i. 15; ii. 1; 1 Co. xi. 20; xiv. 23, (Ps. ii. 2; 2 S. ii. 13; 3 Macc. iii. 1; Sus. 14); *together*: Lk. xvii. 35; Acts iii. 1 [L T Tr WH join it to ch. ii.; 1 Co. vii. 5]; κατὰ τὸ αὐτό, (Vulg. simul), together: Acts xiv. 1 (for יַחַד, Ex. xxvi. 24; 1 K. iii. 18; exx. fr. Grk. writ. are given by Kypke, Observv. ii. p. 69 sqq.). Like adj. of equality ὁ αὐτός is foll. by the dat.: ἐν καὶ τὸ αὐτὸ τῇ ἐξυρημένῃ, 1 Co. xi. 5, (Sap. xviii. 11; 4 Macc. viii. 5; x. 2, 13, and often in Grk. writ., cf. W. 150 (141)). **2.** With a noun added: Mt. xxvi. 44; Mk. xiv. 39 (τὸν αὐτὸν λόγον); Lk. vi. 38 [R G L mrg.] (τῷ αὐτῷ μέτρῳ); Phil. i. 30; 1 Co. i. 10 (ἐν τῷ αὐτῷ νοΐ); 1 Co. xii. 4 (τὸ δὲ αὐτὸ πνεῦμα), etc. τὰ αὐτά (with the force of a subst.: *the same kind*) τῶν παθημάτων, 1 Pet. v. 9. [Cf. ταὐτά.]

847　αὐτοῦ, prop. neuter genitive of the pron. αὐτός, *in that place, there, here*: Mt. xxvi. 36; [Lk. ix. 27 (R L ὧδε)]; Acts xv. 34 (a spurious vs. [see WH. App. ad loc.]); xviii. 19 [L Tr mrg. ἐκεῖ); xxi. 4 (Lchm. αὐτοῖς).*

848　αὑτοῦ, -ῆς, -οῦ, of himself, herself, itself, i. q. ἑαυτοῦ, q. v. It is very common in the edd. of the N. T. by the Elzevirs, Griesbach, Knapp, al.; but Bengel, Matthaei, Lchm., Tdf., Trg. have everywhere substituted αὐτοῦ, αὐτῷ, etc. for αὑτοῦ, αὑτῷ, etc. "For I have observed that the former are used almost constantly [not always then? Grimm] not only in uncial codd. of the viii. ix. and x. cent., but also in many others (and not N. T. codd. alone). That this is the correct mode of writing is proved also by numerous examples where the pron. is joined to prepositions; for these last are often found written not ἐφ, αφ, μεθ, καθ, ανθ, etc., but επ, απ, μετ, κατ, αντ." *Tdf.* Proleg. ad N. T., ed. 2 p. xxvi. [ed. 8 p. 126]; cf. his Proleg. ad Sept., ed. 1 p. lxx. [ed. 4 p. xxxiii. (not in

---

ed. 6)]. Bleek entertains the same opinion and sets it forth at length in his note on Heb. i. 3, vol. ii. 1 p. 67 sqq. The question is hard to decide, not only because the breathings and accents are wanting in the oldest codd., but also because it often depends upon the mere preference of the writer or speaker whether he will speak in his own person, or acc. to the thought of the person spoken of. Certainly in the large majority of the passages in the N. T. αὐτοῦ is correctly restored; but apparently we ought to write δι' αὐτοῦ (Rec. ἑαυτοῦ [so L mrg. T WH]), Ro. xiv. 14 [L txt. Tr δι' αὐτ.]; εἰς αὐτόν, Col. i. 20 [al. εἰς αὐτ.]; αὐτὸς περὶ αὐτοῦ [T Tr txt. WH ἑαυτοῦ], Jn. ix. 21. Cf. W. 151 (143); [B. 111 (97) sq.; Bp. Lghtft. on Col. l. c., and see esp. *Hort* in Westcott and Hort's Grk. Test., App. p. 144 sq.; these editors have introduced the aspirated form into their text "nearly twenty times" (e. g. Mt. vi. 34; Lk. xii. 17, 21; xxiii. 12; xxiv. 12; Jn. ii. 24; xiii. 32; xix. 17; xx. 10; Acts xiv. 17; Ro. i. 27; 2 Co. iii. 5; Eph. ii. 15; Phil. iii. 21; 1 Jn. v. 10; Rev. viii. 6, etc.). Cf. *Rutherford*, New Phryn. p. 432].

αὐτόφωρος, -ον, (αὐτός and φώρ a thief, φωρά a theft),　(848a); [fr. Soph. down]; prop. *caught in the act of theft*; then　see 1888 univ. *caught in the act of perpetrating any other crime*; very often in the phrases ἐπ' αὐτοφώρῳ (as one word ἐπαυτοφώρῳ) τινὰ λαμβάνειν, pass. λαμβάνεσθαι, καταλαμβάνεσθαι, ἁλίσκεσθαι, (fr. Hdt. 6, 72 on), the crime being specified by a participle: μοιχευομένη, Jn. viii. 4 [R G], as in Ael. nat. an. 11, 15; Plut. mor. vi. p. 446 ed. Tauchn. [x. p. 723 ed. Reiske, cf. Nicias 4, 5; Eumen. 2, 2]; Sext. Empir. adv. Rhet. 65 [p. 151 ed. Fabric.].*

αὐτό-χειρ, -ρος, ὁ, (αὐτός and χείρ, cf. μακρόχειρ, ἀδικό-　849 χειρ), doing a thing *with one's own hand*: Acts xxvii. 19. (Often in the tragedians and Attic orators.) *

αὐχέω; (in pres. and impf. fr. Aeschyl. and Hdt. down,　see 3166 but rare in prose); prop. *to lift up the neck*, hence *to boast*: μεγάλα αὐχεῖ, Jas. iii. 5 L T Tr WH for R G μεγαλαυχεῖ. q. v.*

αὐχμηρός, -ά, -όν, (αὐχμέω to be squalid), *squalid, dirty*,　850 (Xen., Plat., sqq.), and since dirty things are destitute of brightness, *dark*: 2 Pet. i. 19, Aristot. de color. 3 τὸ λαμπρὸν ἢ στίλβον . . . ἢ τοὐναντίον αὐχμηρὸν καὶ ἀλαμπές. (Hesych., Suidas, Pollux.) *

ἀφ-αιρέω, -ῶ; fut. ἀφαιρήσω (Rev. xxii. 19 Rec. [fr.　851 Erasmus, apparently on *no* Ms. authority; see Tdf.'s note]), and ἀφελῶ (ibid. G L T Tr WH; on this rarer fut. cf. *Bttm.* Ausf. Spr. ii. p. 100); 2 aor. ἀφεῖλον; 1 fut. pass. ἀφαιρεθήσομαι; Mid., pres. ἀφαιροῦμαι; 2 aor. ἀφειλόμην; [see αἱρέω]; in Grk. writ. fr. Hom. down; *to take from, take away, remove, carry off*: τί, Lk. i. 25; *to cut off*, τὸ ὠτίον, Mt. xxvi. 51; Mk. xiv. 47 [L T Tr WH τὸ ὠτάριον]; Lk. xxii. 50 [τὸ οὖς], (τὴν κεφαλήν τινος, 1 Macc. vii. 47; for כרת, 1 S. xvii. 51); *to take away*, τὶ ἀπό with gen. of a thing, Rev. xxii. 19; τὶ ἀπό with gen. of pers. Lk. x. 42 [T WH om. L Tr br. ἀπό], (Gen. xxxi. 31; Job xxxvi. 7; Prov. iv. 16 [Alex.], etc.); mid. (prop. to take away or bear off *for one's self*), Lk. xvi. 3, (Lev. iv. 10; Mic. ii. 8; in Grk. writ. with a simple gen. for ἀπό τινος); ἀφαιρεῖν τὰς ἁμαρτίας *to take away sins*, of victims expiating them, Heb. x. 4, (Jer. xi. 15; Sir. xlvii. 11); mid. of God putting out of his sight, remembering no more, the sins committed by men, i. e. granting pardon for sins (see ἁμαρτία, 2 a.): Ro. xi. 27.*

852 ἀφανής, -ές, (φαίνω), not manifest, hidden: Heb. iv. 13. (Often in Grk. writ. fr. [Aeschyl. and] Hdt. down.) [Cf. δῆλος, and Schmidt ch. 130.]*

853 ἀφανίζω; [Pass., pres. ἀφανίζομαι]; 1 aor. ἠφανίσθην; (ἀφανής); a. to snatch out of sight, to put out of view, to make unseen, (Xen. an. 3, 4, 8 ἥλιον νεφέλη παρακαλύψασα ἠφάνισε sc. τὴν πόλιν, Plat. Phil. 66 a. ἀφανίζοντες κρύπτομεν). b. to cause to vanish away, to destroy, consume: Mt. vi. 19 sq. (often so in Grk. writ. and Sept. [cf. B. § 130, 5]); Pass. to perish: Acts xiii. 41 (Luth. vor Schrecken vergehen); to vanish away, Jas. iv. 14, (Hdt. 7, 6; 167; Plat. et sqq.). c. to deprive of lustre, render unsightly; to disfigure: τὸ πρόσωπον, Mt. vi. 16.*

854 ἀφανισμός, -οῦ, ὁ, (ἀφανίζω, q. v.), disappearance; destruction: Heb. viii. 13. (Theophr., Polyb., Diod., Plut., Lcian., al.; often in Sept., particularly for שַׁמָּה and שְׁמָמָה.)*

855 ἄ-φαντος, -ον, (fr. φαίνομαι), taken out of sight, made invisible: ἄφαντος ἐγένετο ἀπ' αὐτῶν, he departed from them suddenly and in a way unseen, he vanished, Lk. xxiv. 31. (In poets fr. Hom. down; later in prose writ. also; Diod. 4, 65 ἐμπεσὼν εἰς τὸ χάσμα . . . ἄφαντος ἐγένετο, Plut. orac. def. c. 1. Sometimes angels, withdrawing suddenly from human view, are said ἀφανεῖς γίνεσθαι: 2 Macc. iii. 34; Acta Thom. §§ 27 and 43.)*

856 ἀφεδρών, -ῶνος, ὁ, apparently a word of Macedonian origin, which Suidas calls 'barbarous'; the place into which the alvine discharges are voided; a privy, sink; found only in Mt. xv. 17; Mk. vii. 19. It appears to be derived not from ἀφ' ἑδρῶν a podicibus, but from ἄφεδρος, the same Macedon. word which in Lev. xii. 5; xv. 19 sqq. answers to the Hebr. נִדָּה sordes menstruorum. Cf. Fischer's full discussion of the word in his De vitiis lexx. N. T. p. 698 sqq.*

857 ἀφειδία (ἀφείδεια Lchm., see s. v. ει, ι), -ας, ἡ, (the disposition of a man who is ἀφειδής, unsparing), unsparing severity: with gen. of the object, τοῦ σώματος, Col. ii. 23 (τῶν σωμάτων ἀφειδεῖν, Lys. 2, 25 (193, 5); Diod. 13, 60; 79 etc. [see Bp. Lghtft. on Col. l. c.]; in Plat. defin. p. 412 d. ἀφειδία means liberality).*

see 542 ἀφ-εῖδον, i. q. ἀπεῖδον, q. v. Cf. B. 7; Mullach p. 22; W. 45 (44); [Tdf. Proleg. p. 91 sq., Sept. ed. 4 Proleg. p. xxxiii.; Scrivener's ed. of cod. Cantab. Intr. p. xlvii. (11); esp. WH. App. p. 143 sq., Meisterhans § 20, and Bp. Lghtft. on Phil. ii. 23; Curtius p. 687 sq.].

858 ἀφελότης, -ητος, ἡ, (fr. ἀφελής without rock, smooth, plain, and this fr. φελλεύς rocky land), simplicity, [A.V. singleness]: καρδίας, Acts ii. 46, (found only here [and in eccl. writ.]. The Greeks used ἀφέλεια).*

see 560 ἀφ-ελπίζω, i. q. ἀπελπίζω, q. v.; cf. ἀφεῖδον.

859 ἄφ-εσις, -εως, ἡ, (ἀφίημι). 1. release, as from bondage, imprisonment, etc.: Lk. iv. 18 (19), (Is. lxi. 1 sq.; Polyb. 1, 79, 12, etc.). 2. ἄφεσις ἁμαρτιῶν forgiveness, pardon, of sins (prop. the letting them go, as if they had

not been committed [see at length Trench § xxxiii.]), remission of their penalty: Mt. xxvi. 28; Mk. i. 4; Lk. i. 77; iii. 3; xxiv. 47; Acts ii. 38; v. 31; x. 43; xiii. 38; xxvi. 18; Col. i. 14; τῶν παραπτωμάτων, Eph. i. 7; and simply ἄφεσις: Mk. iii. 29; Heb. ix. 22; x. 18, (φόνου, Plat. legg. 9 p. 869 d.; ἐγκλημάτων, Diod. 20, 44 [so Dion. Hal. l. 8 § 50, see also 7, 33; 7, 46; esp. 7, 64; ἁμαρτημάτων, Philo, vit. Moys. iii. 17; al.]).*

860 ἀφή, -ῆς, ἡ, (ἅπτω to fasten together, to fit), (Vulg. junctura [and nexus]), bond, connection, [A. V. joint (see esp. Bp. Lghtft. on Col. as below)]: Eph. iv. 16; Col. ii. 19. (Plut. Anton. c. 27.)*

861 ἀφθαρσία, -ας, ἡ, (ἄφθαρτος, cf. ἀκαθαρσία), (Tertull. and subseq. writ. incorruptibilitas, Vulg. incorruptio [and incorruptela]), incorruption, perpetuity: τοῦ κόσμου, Philo de incorr. mund. § 11; it is ascribed to τὸ θεῖον in Plut. Arist. c. 6; of the body of man exempt from decay after the resurrection, 1 Co. xv. 42 (ἐν ἀφθ. sc. ὄν), 50, 53 sq.; of a blessed immortality (Sap. ii. 23; vi. 19; 4 Macc. xvii. 12), Ro. ii. 7; 2 Tim. i. 10. τινὰ ἀγαπᾶν ἐν ἀφθαρσίᾳ to love one with never diminishing love, Eph. vi. 24 [cf. Mey. ad loc. The word seems to have the meaning purity, sincerity, incorruptness in Tit. ii. 7 Rec.ˢᵗ].*

862 ἄ-φθαρτος, -ον, (φθείρω), uncorrupted, not liable to corruption or decay, imperishable: of things, 1 Co. ix. 25; 1 Pet. i. 4, 23; iii. 4; [ἀφθ. κήρυγμα τῆς αἰωνίου σωτηρίας, Mk. xvi. WH in (rejected) 'Shorter Conclusion']. immortal: of the risen dead, 1 Co. xv. 52; of God, Ro. i. 23; 1 Tim. i. 17. (Sap. xii. 1; xviii. 4. [Aristot.], Plut., Lcian., al. [Cf. Trench § lxviii.])*

see 90 ἀ-φθορία, -ας, ἡ, (ἄφθορος uncorrupted, fr. φθείρω), uncorruptness: Tit. ii. 7 L T Tr WH; see ἀδιαφθορία.*

863 ἀφ-ίημι; pres. 2 pers. sing. ἀφεῖς (fr. the form ἀφέω, Rev. ii. 20 for Rec. ἐᾷς), [3 pers. plur. ἀφιοῦσιν Rev. xi. 9 Tdf. edd. 2, 7, fr. a form ἀφιέω; cf. B. 48 (42)]; impf. 3 pers. sing. ἤφιε, with the augm. before the prep., Mk. i. 34; xi. 16, fr. the form ἀφίω; whence also pres. 1 pers. plur. ἀφίομεν Lk. xi. 4 L T Tr WH for ἀφίεμεν Rec. and 3 pers. ἀφίουσιν Rev. xi. 9 L T Tr WH; [see WH. App. p. 167]; fut. ἀφήσω; 1 aor. ἀφῆκα, 2 pers. sing. -κες Rev. ii. 4 T Tr WH [cf. κοπιάω]; 2 aor. impv. ἄφες, ἄφετε, subj. 3 pers. sing. ἀφῇ, 2 pers. plur. ἀφῆτε, [inf. ἀφεῖναι (Mt. xxiii. 23 L T Tr WH; Lk. v. 21 L txt. T Tr WH)], ptcp. ἀφείς, ἀφέντες; Pass., pres. ἀφίεμαι, [yet 3 pers. plur. ἀφίονται Jn. xx. 23 WH mrg. etc.; cf. ἀφίω above]; pf. 3 pers. plur. ἀφέωνται (a Doric form [cf. W. § 14, 3 a.; B 49 (42); Kühner § 285, 4], Mt. ix. 2, 5; Mk. ii. 5, [9] — in both these Gospels L [exc. in Mk. mrg.] T Tr WH have restored the pres. 3 pers. plur. ἀφίενται; Lk. v. 20, 23; vii. 47, [48]; Jn. xx. 23 L txt. T Tr txt. WH txt.; 1 Jn. ii. 12); 1 aor. ἀφέθην; fut. ἀφεθήσομαι; cf. W. § 14, 3; B. 48 (42); [WH. App. p. 167]; Veitch s. v. ἵημι]; (fr. ἀπό and ἵημι); [fr. Hom. down]; to send from (ἀπό) one's self; 1. to send away; a. to bid go away or depart: τοὺς ὄχλους, Mt. xiii. 36 [al. refer this to 3 below]; τὴν γυναῖκα, of a husband putting away his wife, 1 Co. vii. 11–13, (Hdt. 5, 39; and subst. ἄφεσις, Plut. Pomp. c. 42, 6). b. to send forth, yield up, emit: τὸ

πνεῦμα, to expire, Mt. xxvii. 50 (τὴν ψυχήν, Gen. xxxv. 18; Hdt. 4, 190 and often in other Grk. writ. [see πνεῦμα, 2]), φωνήν to utter a cry (emittere vocem, Liv. 1, 58), Mk. xv. 37 (Gen. xlv. 2 and often in Grk. writ.; [cf. Heinichen on Euseb. h. e. 8, 14, 17]). c. to let go, let alone, let be; a. to disregard: Mt. xv. 14. β. to leave, not to discuss now, a topic, used of teachers, writers, speakers, etc.: Heb. vi. 1, (Eur. Andr. 392; Theophr. char. praef. § 3; for other examples fr. Grk. writ. see Bleek on Heb. vol. ii. 2 p. 144 sq.), [al. take the word in Heb. l. c. as expressive of the duty of the readers, rather than the purpose of the writer; and consequently refer the passage to 3 below]. γ. to omit, neglect: Mt. xxiii. 23, [Lk. xi. 42 R G]; Mk. vii. 8; Ro. i. 27. d. to let go, give up, a debt, by not demanding it (opp. to κρατεῖν, Jn. xx. 23), i. e. to remit, forgive: τὸ δάνειον, Mt. xviii. 27; τὴν ὀφειλήν, Mt. xviii. 32; τὰ ὀφειλήματα, Mt. vi. 12; τὰ παραπτώματα, vi. 14 sq.; Mk. xi. 25 sq. [T Tr WH om. verse 26]; τὰς ἁμαρτίας, τὰ ἁμαρτήματα, τὰς ἀνομίας, Mt. ix. 2, 5 sq.; xii. 31; Mk. ii. 5, 7; iii. 28; Lk. v. 20 sq. 23; Ro. iv. 7 (fr. Ps. xxxi. (xxxii. 1); 1 Jn. i. 9; Jas. v. 15, (Is. xxii. 14; xxxiii. 24, etc.); τ. ἐπίνοιαν τῆς καρδίας, Acts viii. 22, (τὴν αἰτίαν, Hdt. 6, 30; τὰ χρέα, Ael. v. h. 14, 24); absolutely, ἀφιέναι τινί to forgive one: Mt. xii. 32; xviii. 21, 35; Mk. iv. 12; Lk. xi. 4; xii. 10; xvii. 3 sq.; xxiii. 34 [L br. WH reject the pass.]. e. to give up, keep no longer: τὴν πρώτην ἀγάπην, Rev. ii. 4. 2. to permit, allow, not to hinder b. foll. by a pres. inf. [B. 258 (222)]: Mk. x. 14; Lk. xviii. 16 ἄφετε ἔρχεσθαι καὶ μὴ κωλύετε αὐτά, Mt. xiii. 30; Mk. i. 34; Jn. xi. 44; xviii. 8. by the aor. inf.: Mt. viii. 22; xxiii. 13 (14); Mk. v. 37; vii. 12, 27; Lk. viii. 51; ix. 60; xii. 39; Rev. xi. 9. b. without an inf.: Mt. iii. 15 (ἄφες ἄρτι permit it just now). with acc. of the pers. or thing permitted: Mt. iii. 15 τότε ἀφίησιν αὐτόν, Mk. v. 19; xi. 6; xiv. 6; Lk. xiii. 8; Jn. xii. 7 R G; xi. 48; Acts v. 38 (L T Tr WH; R G ἐάσατε); Rev. ii. 20 (Rec. ἐᾷς). c. ἀφίημι τινί τι, to give up a thing to one: Mt. v. 40 (ἄφες αὐτῷ καὶ τὸ ἱμάτιον). d. foll. by ἵνα: Mk. xi. 16; Jn. xii. 7 L T Tr WH, a later construction, cf. W. § 44, 8; B. 238 (205). e. foll. by the simple hortative subjunc.: Mt. vii. 4; Lk. vi. 42 (ἄφες ἐκβάλω); Mt. xxvii. 49; Mk. xv. 36, (ἄφετε ἴδωμεν); Epict. diss. 1, 9, 15 ἄφες δείξωμεν, 3, 12, 15 ἄφες ἴδω. Cf. B. 209 (181) sq.; W. 285 (268). 3. to leave, go away from one; to depart from any one, a. in order to go to another place: Mt. xxii. 22; xxvi. 44; Mk. viii. 13 (Mt. xvi. 4 καταλιπών); xii. 12; xiii. 34; Jn. iv. 3; xvi. 28. b. to depart from one whom one wishes to quit: Mt. iv. 11; so of diseases departing, ἀφῆκέν τινα ὁ πυρετός, Mt. viii. 15; Mk. i. 31; Lk. iv. 39; Jn. iv. 52. c. to depart from one and leave him to himself, so that all mutual claims are abandoned: τὸν πατέρα, Mt. iv. 22; Mk. i. 20; Mt. xviii. 12 (Lk. xv. 4 καταλείπει). Thus also ἀφιέναι τὰ ἑαυτοῦ to leave possessions, home, etc.: Mt. iv. 20; xix. 27, 29; Mk. i. 18; x. 28 sq.; Lk. v. 11; xviii. 28 sq. d. to desert one (wrongfully): Mt. xxvi. 56; Mk. xiv. 50; Jn. x. 12. e. to go away leaving something behind: Mt. v. 24; Jn. iv. 28. f. to leave one by not taking him as a companion: opp. to παραλαμβάνειν, Mt. xxiv. 40 sq.:

Lk. xvii. 34 sq. g. to leave on dying, leave behind one: τέκνα, γυναῖκα, Mt. xxii. 25; Mk. xii. 20, 22, (Lk. xx. 31 καταλείπω). h. to leave so that what is left may remain, leave remaining: οὐ μὴ ἀφεθῇ ὧδε λίθος ἐπὶ λίθον [or λίθῳ], Mt. xxiv. 2; Mk. xiii. 2; Lk. xxi. 6. i. ἀφιέναι foll. by the acc. of a noun or pron. with an acc. of the predicate [B. § 144, 18]: Lk. x. 30 (ἡμιθανῆ); Jn. xiv. 18 (τινὰ ὀρφανόν); Mt. xxiii. 38; Lk. xiii. 35, (but Lchm. om. ἔρημος in both pass., WH txt. om. in Mt., G T Tr WH om. in Luke; that being omitted, ἀφιέναι means to abandon, to leave destitute of God's help); Acts xiv. 17 (ἀμάρτυρον ἑαυτόν [L T Tr αὐτόν (WH αὑτ. q. v.)]).

ἀφ-ικνέομαι, -οῦμαι: 2 aor. ἀφικόμην; (ἱκνέομαι to come); very often in Grk. writ. fr. Hom. down; to come from (ἀπό) a place (but often the prep. has almost lost its force); to come to, arrive at; in the N. T. once, tropically: Ro. xvi. 19 (ὑμῶν ὑπακοὴ εἰς πάντας ἀφίκετο your obedience has reached the ears of [A. V. is come abroad unto] all men; Sir. xlvii. 16 εἰς νήσους ἀφίκετο τὸ ὄνομά σου. Joseph. antt. 19, 1, 16 εἰς τὸ θέατρον . . . ἀφίκετο ὁ λόγος).*   **864**

ἀ-φιλ-άγαθος, -ον, (a priv. and φιλάγαθος), opposed to goodness and good men, [R. V. no lover of good]; found only in 2 Tim. iii. 3.*   **865**

ἀ-φιλ-άργυρος, -ον, (a priv. and φιλάργυρος), not loving money, not avaricious; only in the N. T., twice viz. 1 Tim. iii. 3; Heb. xiii. 5. [Cf. Trench § xxiv.]*   **866**

ἄφ-ιξις, -εως, ἡ, (ἀφικνέομαι), in Grk. writ. generally arrival; more rarely departure, as Hdt. 9, 17; Dem. 1463, 7; [1484, 8]; Joseph. antt. 4, 8, 47; 3 Macc. vii. 18; and so in Acts xx. 29.*   **867**

ἀφ-ίστημι: 1 aor. ἀπέστησα; 2 aor. ἀπέστην; Mid., pres. ἀφίσταμαι, impv. ἀφίστασο (1 Tim. vi. 5 Rec.; cf. W. § 14, 1 e.); [impf. ἀφιστάμην;] fut. ἀποστήσομαι; 1. transitively, in pres., impf., fut., 1 aor. active, to make stand off, cause to withdraw, to remove; trop. to excite to revolt: Acts v. 37 (ἀπέστησε λαὸν . . . ὀπίσω αὐτοῦ drew away after him; τινὰ ἀπό τινος, Deut. vii. 4, and in Grk. writ. fr. Hdt. 1, 76 down). 2. intransitively, in pf., plpf., 2 aor. active, to stand off, stand aloof, in various senses [as in Grk. writ.] acc. to the context: ἀπό with gen. of pers. to go away, depart, from any one, Lk. xiii. 27 (fr. Ps. vi. 9; cf. Mt. vii. 23 ἀποχωρεῖτε ἀπ᾽ ἐμοῦ); Acts xii. 10; xix. 9; to desert, withdraw from, one, Acts xv. 38; to cease to vex one, Lk. iv. 13; Acts v. 38; xxii. 29; 2 Co. xii. 8; to fall away, become faithless, ἀπὸ θεοῦ, Heb. iii. 12; to shun, flee from, ἀπὸ τῆς ἀδικίας, 2 Tim. ii. 19. Mid. to withdraw one's self from: absol. to fall away, Lk. viii. 13; [τῆς πίστεως, 1 Tim. iv. 1, cf. W. 427, 428 (398)]; to keep one's self away from, absent one's self from, Lk. ii. 37 (οὐκ ἀφίστατο ἀπὸ [T Tr WH om. ἀπὸ] τοῦ ἱεροῦ, she was in the temple every day); from any one's society or fellowship, 1 Tim. vi. 5 Rec.*   **868**

ἄφνω, adv., (akin to αἴφνης, see in αἰφνίδιος above), suddenly: Acts ii. 2; xvi. 26; xxviii. 6. (Sept.; [Aeschyl.], Thuc. and subseq. writ.)*   **869**

ἀ-φόβως, adv., (φόβος), without fear, boldly: Lk. i. 74; Phil. i. 14; 1 Co. xvi. 10; Jude 12. [From Xen. down.]*   **870**

ἀφ-ομοιόω, -ῶ: [pf. pass. ptcp. ἀφωμοιωμένος (on augm.   **871** see *WH.* App. p. 161)]; *to cause a model to pass off* (ἀπό) *into an image* or *shape like it,* — *to express itself in it,* (cf. ἀπεικάζειν, ἀπεικονίζειν, ἀποπλάσσειν, ἀπομιμεῖσθαι); *to copy; to produce a fac-simile:* τὰ καλὰ εἴδη, of painters, Xen. mem. 3, 10, 2; often in Plato. Pass. *to be made like, rendered similar:* so Heb. vii. 3. (Ep. Jer. 4 (5), 62 (63), 70 (71); and in Plato.) *

872 ἀφ-οράω, -ῶ; *to turn the eyes away from other things and fix them on something;* cf. ἀποβλέπω. trop. to turn one's mind to: εἴς τινα, Heb. xii. 2 [W. § 66, 2 d.], (εἰς θεόν, 4 Macc. xvii. 10; for exx. fr. Grk. writ. cf. Bleek on Heb. vol. ii. 2 p. 862). Further, cf. ἀπεῖδον.*

873 ἀφ-ορίζω; impf. ἀφώριζον; Attic fut. ἀφοριῶ Mt. xxv. 32 (T WH ἀφορίσω); xiii. 49, [W. § 13, 1 c.; B. 37 (32)]; 1 aor. ἀφώρισα; Pass., pf. ptcp. ἀφωρισμένος; 1 aor. impv. ἀφορίσθητε; (ὁρίζω to make a ὅρος or boundary); *to mark off from* (ἀπό) *others by boundaries, to limit, to separate:* ἑαυτόν, from others, Gal. ii. 12; τοὺς μαθητάς, from those unwilling to obey the gospel, Acts xix. 9; ἐκ μέσου τινῶν, Mt. xiii. 49; ἀπό τινος, xxv. 32. Pass. in a reflex. sense: 2 Co. vi. 17. absol.: in a bad sense, *to exclude as disreputable,* Lk. vi. 22; in a good sense, τινὰ εἴς τι, *to appoint, set apart, one for some purpose* (to do something), Acts xiii. 2; Ro. i. 1; τινά foll. by a telic inf., Gal. i. 15 [(?) see the Comm. ad loc.]. ([Soph.], Eur., Plat., Isocr., Dem., Polyb., al.; very often in Sept. esp. for הִבְדִּיל, הֵנִיף, הֵרִים, סָגַר, etc.) *

874 ἀφ-ορμή, -ῆς, ἡ, (ἀπό and ὁρμή q. v.); **1.** prop. *a place from which a movement* or *attack is made, a base of operations:* Thuc. 1, 90 (τὴν Πελοπόννησον πᾶσιν ἀναχώρησίν τε καὶ ἀφορμὴν ἱκανὴν εἶναι); Polyb. 1, 41, 6. **2.** metaph. *that by which endeavor is excited and from which it goes forth; that which gives occasion and supplies matter for an undertaking, the incentive; the resources we avail ourselves of in attempting* or *performing anything:* Xen. mem. 3, 12, 4 (τοῖς ἑαυτῶν παισὶ καλλίους ἀφορμὰς εἰς τὸν βίον καταλείπουσι), and often in Grk. writ.; λαμβάνειν, to take occasion, find an incentive, Ro. vii. 8, 11; διδόναι, 2 Co. v. 12; 1 Tim. v. 14, (3 Macc. iii. 2; both phrases often also in Grk. writ.); 2 Co. xi. 12; Gal. v. 13. On the meanings of this word see Viger. ed. *Herm.* p. 81 sq.; Phryn. ed. *Lob.* p. 223 sq.; [*Rutherford*, New Phryn. p. 304].*

875 ἀφρίζω; (ἀφρός); *to foam:* Mk. ix. 18, 20. (Soph. El. 719; Diod. 3, 10; Athen. 11, 43 p. 472 a.; [al.].) [COMP.: ἐπ-αφρίζω.]*

876 ἀφρός, -οῦ, ὁ, *foam:* Lk. ix. 39. (Hom. Il. 20, 168; [al.].) *

877 ἀφροσύνη, -ης, ἡ, (ἄφρων), *foolishness, folly, senselessness:* 2 Co. xi. 1, 17, 21; *thoughtlessness, recklessness,* Mk. vii. 22. [From Hom. down.] *

878 ἄφρων, -ονος, ὁ, ἡ, -ον, τό, (fr. a priv. and φρήν, cf. εὔφρων, σώφρων), [fr. Hom. down], prop. *without reason* ([εἴδωλα, Xen. mem. 1, 4, 4]; of beasts, ibid. 1, 4, 14), *senseless, foolish, stupid; without reflection* or *intelligence, acting rashly:* Lk. xi. 40; xii. 20; Ro. ii. 20; 1 Co. xv. 36; 2 Co. xi. 16, 19 (opp. to φρόνιμος, as in Prov. xi. 29); 2 Co. xii. 6, 11; Eph. v. 17 (opp. to συνιέντες); 1 Pet. ii. 15. [A strong term; cf. Schmidt ch. 147 § 17.]*

ἀφ-υπνόω, -ῶ: 1 aor. ἀφύπνωσα; (ὑπνόω to put to sleep, to sleep); **a.** *to awaken from sleep* (Anthol. Pal. 9, 517, 5). **b.** *to fall asleep, to fall off to sleep:* Lk. viii. 23; for this the ancient Greeks used καθυπνόω; see Lobeck ad Phryn. p. 224. [Herm. vis. 1, 1.] * **879**

ἀφ-υστερέω, -ῶ: (a later Grk. word); **1.** *to be behindhand, come too late* (ἀπό so as to be far from, or to fail, a person or thing); used of persons not present at the right time: Polyb. 22, 5, 2; Posidon. ap. Athen. 4, 37 (i. e. 4 p. 151 e.); [al.]; ἀπὸ ἀγαθῆς ἡμέρας to fail (to make use of) a good day, to let the opportunity pass by, Sir. xiv. 14. **2.** transitively, *to cause to fail, to withdraw, take away from, defraud:* τὸ μάννα σου οὐκ ἀφυστέρησας ἀπὸ στόματος αὐτῶν, Neh. ix. 20 (for מָנַע to withhold); pf. pass. ptcp. ἀφυστερημένος (μισθός), Jas. v. 4 T Tr WH after א B*, [Rec. ἀπεστερημένος, see ἀποστερέω, also s. v. ἀπό, II. 2 d. bb., p. 59ᵇ].* **see 650**

ἄφωνος, -ον, (φωνή), *voiceless, dumb; without the faculty of speech;* used of idols, 1 Co. xii. 2 (cf. Ps. cxv. 5 (cxiii. 13); Hab. ii. 18); of beasts, 2 Pet. ii. 16. 1 Co. xiv. 10 τοσαῦτα γένη φωνῶν καὶ οὐδὲν αὐτῶν [L T Tr WH om. αὐτ.] ἄφωνον, i. e. there is no language destitute of the power of language, [R. V. txt. *no kind (of voice) is without signification*], (cf. the phrases βίος ἀβίωτος a life unworthy of the name of life, χάρις ἄχαρις). used of one that is patiently silent or dumb: ἀμνός, Acts viii. 32 fr. Is. liii. 7. (In Grk. writ. fr. [Theog.], Pind., Aeschyl. down.)* **880**

Ἄχαξ [WH Ἄχας], ὁ, (so Sept. for אָחָז possessing, possessor; in Joseph. Ἀχάζης, -ου, ὁ), *Ahaz,* king of Judah, [fr. c. B. C. 741 to c. B. C. 725; cf. B. D. s. v. Israel, kingdom of], (2 K. xvi. 1 sqq.; 2 Chr. xxviii. 16 sqq.; Is. vii. 1 sqq.): Mt. i. 9.* **881**

Ἀχαΐα [WH Ἀχαία (see I, ι)], -ας, ἡ, *Achaia;* **1.** in a restricted sense, the maritime region of northern Peloponnesus. **2.** in a broader sense, fr. B. C. 146 on [yet see Dict. of Geog. s. v.], a Roman province embracing all Greece except Thessaly. So in the N. T.: Acts xviii. 12, 27; xix. 21; Ro. xv. 26; xvi. 5 Rec.; 1 Co. xvi. 15; 2 Co. i. 1; ix. 2; xi. 10; 1 Th. i. 7 sq. [B. D. s. v.]* **882**

Ἀχαϊκός, -οῦ, ὁ, *Achaicus,* the name of a Christian of Corinth: 1 Co. xvi. 17.* **883**

ἀχάριστος, -ον, (χαρίζομαι), *ungracious;* **a.** *unpleasing* (Hom. Od. 8, 236; 20, 392; Xen. oec. 7, 37; al.). **b.** *unthankful* (so in Grk. writ. fr. Hdt. 1, 90 down): Lk. vi. 35; 2 Tim. iii. 2. (Sir. xxix. 17; Sap. xvi. 29.)* **884**

[Ἄχας, Mt. i. 9 WH; see Ἄχαξ.] **see 881**

Ἀχείμ, ὁ, *Achim,* prop. name of one of the ancestors of Christ, not mentioned in the O. T.: Mt. i. 14.* **885**

ἀ-χειρο-ποίητος, -ον, (χειροποίητος, q. v.), *not made with hands:* Mk. xiv. 58; 2 Co. v. 1; Col. ii. 11 [where cf. Bp. Lghtft.]. (Found neither in prof. auth. nor in the Sept. [W. § 34, 3].)* **886**

[Ἀχελδαμάχ: Acts i. 19 T Tr for R G Ἀκελδαμά q. v.] **see 184**

ἀχλύς, -ύος, ἡ, *a mist, dimness,* (Lat. *caligo*), esp. over the eyes, (a poetic word, often in Hom.; then in Hesiod, Aeschyl.; in prose writ. fr. [Aristot. meteor. 2, 8 p. 367ᵇ, **887**

17 etc. and] Polyb. 34, 11, 15 on; [of a cataract, Dioscor. Cf. Trench § c.]) : Acts xiii. 11. (Joseph. antt. 9, 4, 3 τὰς τῶν πολεμίων ὄψεις ἀμαυρῶσαι τὸν θεὸν παρεκάλει ἀχλὺν αὐταῖς ἐπιβαλόντα. Metaph. of the mind, Clem. Rom. 2 Cor. 1, 6 ἀχλύος γέμειν.) *

888 **ἀχρεῖος, -ον**, (χρεῖος useful), *useless, good for nothing* : Mt. xxv. 30 (δοῦλος, cf. Plat. Alc. i. 17 p. 122 b. τῶν οἰκετῶν τὸν ἀχρειότατον) ; by an hyperbole of pious modesty in Lk. xvii. 10 'the servant' calls himself ἀχρεῖον, because, although he has done all, yet he has done nothing except what he o u g h t to have done; accordingly he possesses no m e r i t, and could only claim to be called '*profitable*,' should he do more than what he is bound to do; cf. Bengel ad loc. (Often in Grk. writ. fr. Hom. down; Xen. mem. 1, 2, 54 ἀχρεῖον καὶ ἀνωφελές. Sept. 2 S. vi. 22 equiv. to רָקִיק *low, base.*) [Syn. cf. Tittmann ii. p. 11 sq.; Ellic. on Philem. 11.] *

889 **ἀχρειόω, -ῶ** : 1 aor. pass. ἠχρειώθην ; (ἀχρεῖος, q. v.) ; *to make useless, render unserviceable* : of character, Ro. iii. 12 (fr. Ps. xiii. (xiv.) 3), where L mrg. T Tr WH read ἠχρεώθησαν fr. the rarer ἄχρεος i. q. ἀχρεῖος. (Several times prop. in Polyb.) *

890 **ἄ-χρηστος, -ον**, (χρηστός, and this fr. χράομαι), *useless, unprofitable* : Philem. 11 (here opp. to εὔχρηστος). (In Grk. writ. fr. Hom. [i. e. Batrach. 70 ; Theogn.] down.) [Syn. cf. Tittmann ii. 11 sq. ; Trench § c. 17 ; Ellic. on Philem. 11.] *

891 **ἄχρι and ἄχρις** (the latter of which in the N. T. is nowhere placed before a consonant, but the former before both vowels and consonants, although euphony is so far regarded that we almost constantly find ἄχρι ἧς ἡμέρας, ἄχρις οὗ, cf. B. 10 (9) ; [W. 42] ; and ἄχρις οὗ is not used except in Acts vii. 18 and Rev. ii. 25 by L T Tr WH and Lk. xxi. 24 by T Tr WH ; [to these instances must now be added 1 Co. xi. 26 T WH ; xv. 25 T WH ; Ro. xi. 25 WH (see their App. p. 148) ; on the usage in secular authors ('where -ρι is the only Attic form, but in later auth. the Epic -ρις prevailed', L. and S. s. v.) cf. *Lobeck*, Pathol. Elementa, vol. ii. p. 210 sq. ; *Rutherford*, New Phryn. p. 64 ; further, *Klotz* ad Devar. vol. ii. 1 p. 230 sq.]) ; a particle indicating the t e r m i n u s a d q u e m. (On its use in the Grk. writ. cf. Klotz u. s. p. 224 sqq.) It has the force now of a prep. now of a conj., *even to* ; *until, to the time that* ; (on its derivation see below). **1.** as a Preposition it takes the gen. [cf. W. § 54, 6], and is used **a.** of P l a c e : Acts xi. 5 ; xiii. 6 ; xx. 4 [T Tr mrg. WH om., Tr txt. br.] ; xxviii. 15 ; 2 Co. x. 13 sq. ; Heb. iv. 12 (see μερισμός, 2) ; Rev. xiv. 20 ; xviii. 5. **b.** of T i m e : ἄχρι καιροῦ, until a season that seemed to him opportune, Lk. iv. 13 [but cf. καιρός, 2 a.] ; until a certain time, *for a season*, Acts xiii. 11 ; [ἄχρι (vel μέχρι, q. v. 1 a.) τοῦ θερισμοῦ, Mt. xiii. 30 WH mrg. cf. ἕως, II. 5] ; ἄχρι ἧς ἡμέρας until the day that etc. Mt. xxiv. 38 ; Lk. i. 20 ; xvii. 27 ; Acts i. 2 ; [ἄχρι (Rec. et al. ἕως) τῆς ἡμέρας ἧς, Acts i. 22 Tdf.] ; ἄχρι ταύτης τῆς ἡμέρας and ἄχρι τῆς ἡμέρας ταύτης, Acts

ii. 29 ; xxiii. 1 ; xxvi. 22 ; ἄχρι [-ρις R G] ἡμερῶν πέντε even to the space of five days, i. e. after [A. V. *in*] five days, Acts xx. 6 ; ἄχρις [-ρι T Tr WH] αὐγῆς, Acts xx. 11 ; ἄχρι τοῦ νῦν, Ro. viii. 22 ; Phil. i. 5 ; ἄχρι τέλους, Heb. vi. 11 ; Rev. ii. 26 ; see besides, Acts iii. 21 ; [xxii. 22] ; Ro. i. 13 ; v. 13 ; 1 Co. iv. 11 ; 2 Co. iii. 14 ; Gal. iv. 2 ; Phil. i. 6 [-ρι L T WH]. **c.** of M a n n e r and D e g r e e : ἄχρι θανάτου, Acts xxii. 4 (even to delivering unto death) ; Rev. ii. 10 (to the enduring of death itself) ; Rev. xii. 11 ; and, in the opinion of many interpreters, Heb. iv. 12 [see μερισμός, 2]. **d.** joined to the rel. οὗ (ἄχρις οὗ for ἄχρι τούτου, ᾧ) it has the force of a c o n j u n c - t i o n, *until, to the time that* : foll. by the indic. pret., of things that actually occurred and up to the beginning of which something continued, Acts vii. 18 (ἄχρις οὗ ἀνέστη βασιλεύς) ; xxvii. 33. foll. by a subj. aor. having the force of a fut. pf., Lk. xxi. 24 L T Tr WH ; Ro. xi. 25 ; 1 Co. xi. 26 [Rec. ἄχρις οὗ ἄν] ; Gal. iii. 19 [not WH txt. (see 2 below)] ; iv. 19 [T Tr WH μέχρις] ; Rev. vii. 3 Rec.elz G ; ἄχρις οὗ ἄν until, whenever it may be [cf. W. § 42, 5 b.], 1 Co. xv. 25 [Rec.] ; Rev. ii. 25. with indic. pres. *as long as* : Heb. iii. 13 ; cf. Bleek ad loc. and B. 231 (199). **2.** ἄχρις without οὗ has the force of a s i m p l e C o n j u n c t i o n, *until, to the time that* : foll. by subj. aor., Lk. xxi. 24 R G ; Rev. vii. 3 L T Tr WH ; viii. 8 ; [xvii. 17 Rec.] ; xx. 3, [5 G L T Tr WH] ; with indic. fut., Rev. xvii. 17 [L T Tr WH] ; [ἄχρις ἄν foll. by subj. aor., Gal. iii. 19 WH txt. (see 1 d. above)]. Since ἄχρι is akin to ἀκή and ἀκρός [but cf. Vaniček p. 22 ; Curtius § 166], and μέχρι to μῆκος, μακρός, by the use of the former particle the reach to which a thing is said to extend is likened to a h e i g h t, by the use of μέχρι, to a l e n g t h ; ἄχρι, indicating ascent, signifies *up to* ; μέχρι, indicating extent, is *unto, as far as* ; cf. Klotz u. s. p. 225 sq. But this primitive distinction is often disregarded, and each particle used of the same thing ; cf. ἄχρι τέλους, Heb. vi. 11 ; μέχρι τέλους, ibid. iii. 6, 14 ; Xen. symp. 4, 37 περίεστί μοι καὶ ἐσθίοντι ἄχρι τοῦ μὴ πεινῆν ἀφικέσθαι καὶ πίνοντι μ έ χ ρ ι τοῦ μὴ διψῆν. Cf. Fritzsche on Ro. v. 13, vol. i. p. 308 sqq. ; [Ellic. on 2 Tim. ii. 9. Ἄχρι occurs 20 times in the writings of Luke ; elsewhere in the four Gospels only in Mt. xxiv. 38.]. *

892 **ἄχυρον, -ου, τό**, *a stalk of grain from which the kernels have been beaten out ; straw broken up by a threshing-machine, chaff* : Mt. iii. 12 ; Lk. iii. 17. (In Grk. writ. fr. Hdt. 4, 72 ; Xen. oec. 18. 1, 2, 6 down ; mostly in plur. τὰ ἄχυρα ; in Job xxi. 18 Sept. also of the chaff wont to be driven away by the wind.) *

893 **ἀ-ψευδής, -ές**, (ψεῦδος), *without lie, truthful* : Tit. i. 2. (In Grk. writ. fr. Hes. theog. 233 down.) *

894 **ἄψινθος, -ου, ἡ**, *wormwood, Absinthe* : Rev. viii. 11 ; ὁ ἄψινθος ibid. is given as a prop. name to the star which fell into the waters and made them bitter. *

895 **ἄψυχος, -ον**, (ψυχή), *without a soul, lifeless* : 1 Co. xiv. 7. (In Grk. writ. from [Archil., Simon. and] Aeschylus down.) *

B

896   **Βαάλ** [so accented also by Pape (Eigenn. s. v.), Kuenen and Cobet (Ro. as below); but L T (yet the name of the month, 1 K. vi. 5 (38), Βαάλ) Tr WH etc. Βάαλ; so Etym. Magn. 194, 19; Suid. 1746 a. etc. *Dind.* in Steph. Thesaur. s. v. Βάαλ or Βαάλ], ὁ, ἡ, an indecl. noun (Hebr. בַּעַל, Chald. בֵּל contr. fr. בְּעֵל), *lord*: Ro. xi. 4. This was the name of the supreme heavenly divinity worshipped by the Shemitic nations (the Phœnicians, Canaanites, Babylonians, Assyrians), often also by the Israelites themselves, and represented by the Sun: τῇ Βαάλ, Ro. xi. 4. Cf. *Win.* RWB. [and BB.DD.] s. v. and *J. G. Müller* in Herzog i. p. 637 sqq.; *Merx* in Schenkel i. 322 sqq.; *Schlottmann* in Riehm p. 126 sq. Since in this form the supreme power of nature generating all things, and consequently a male deity, was worshipped, with which the female deity Astarte was associated, it is hard to explain why the Sept. in some places say ὁ Βαάλ (Num. xxii. 41; Judg. ii. 13; 1 K. xvi. 31; xix. 18, etc.), in others ἡ Βαάλ (Hos. ii. 8; 1 S. vii. 4, etc. [yet see Dillmann, as below, p. 617]). Among the various conjectures on this subject the easiest is this: that the Sept. called the deity ἡ Βαάλ in derision, as weak and impotent, just as the Arabs call idols goddesses and the Rabbins אֱלֹהוֹת; so *Gesenius* in Rosenmüller's Repert. i. p. 139 and Tholuck on Ro. l. c.; [yet cf. Dillmann, as below, p. 602; for other opinions and reff. see Meyer ad loc.; cf. W. § 27, 6 N. 1. But Prof. Dillmann shows (in the Monatsbericht d. Akad. zu Berlin, 16 Juni 1881, p. 601 sqq.), that the Jews (just as they abstained from pronouncing the word Jehovah) avoided uttering the abhorred name of Baal (Ex. xxiii. 13). As a substitute in Aramaic they read מְעוּת דחלא or פתכרא, and in Greek αἰσχύνη (cf. 1 K. xviii. 19, 25). This substitute in Grk. was suggested by the use of the fem. article. Hence we find in the Sept. ἡ B. everywhere in the prophetic bks. Jer., Zeph., Hos., etc., while in the Pentateuch it does not prevail, nor even in Judges, Sam., Kings, (exc. 1 S. vii. 4; 2 K. xxi. 3). It disappears, too, (when the worship of Baal had died out) in the later versions of Aq., Sym., etc. The apostle's use in Ro. l. c. accords with the sacred custom; cf. the substitution of the Hebr. בֹּשֶׁת in Ish-bosheth, Mephi-bosheth, etc. 2 S. ii. 8, 10; iv. 4 with 1 Chr. viii. 33, 34, also 2 S. xi. 21 with Judg. vi. 32; etc.]*

897   **Βαβυλών**, -ῶνος, ἡ, (Hebr. בָּבֶל fr. בָּלַל to confound, acc. to Gen. xi. 9; cf. Aeschyl. Pers. 52 Βαβυλὼν δ' ἡ πολύχρυσος πάμμικτον ὄχλον πέμπει σύρδην. But more correctly, as it seems, fr. בָּאב בֵּל the gate i. e. the court or city of Belus [Assyr. *Bâb-Il* the Gate of God; (perh. of Il, the supreme God); cf. *Schrader*, Keilinschr. u. d. Alt. Test. 2te Aufl. p. 127 sq.; *Oppert* in the Zeitsch. d. Deutsch. Morg. Gesellschaft, viii. p. 595]), *Babylon*, formerly a very celebrated and large city, the residence of the Babylonian kings, situated on both banks of the Euphrates. Cyrus had formerly captured it, but Darius Hystaspis threw down its gates and walls, and Xerxes destroyed [?] the temple of Belus. At length the city was reduced almost to a solitude, the population having been drawn off by the neighboring Seleucia, built on the Tigris by Seleucus Nicanor. [Cf. Prof. Rawlinson in B. D. s. v. and his Herodotus, vol. i. Essays vi. and viii., vol. ii. Essay iv.] The name is used in the N. T. **1.** of the city itself: Acts vii. 43; 1 Pet. v. 13 (where some have understood Babylon, a small town in Egypt, to be referred to; but in opposition cf. *Mayerhoff*, Einl. in die petrin. Schriften, p. 126 sqq.; [cf. 3 fin. below]). **2.** of *the territory*, Babylonia: Mt. i. 11 sq. 17; [often so in Grk. writ.]. **3.** allegorically, of *Rome* as the most corrupt seat of idolatry and the enemy of Christianity: Rev. xiv. 8 [here Rec.ᵉˡᶻ Βαβουλών]; xvi. 19; xvii. 5; xviii. 2, 10, 21, (in the opinion of some 1 Pet. v. 13 also; [cf. 1 fin. above]).*

βαθέως, adv., *deeply*: ὄρθρου βαθέως sc. ὄντος (cf. Bnhdy. p. 338), deep in the morning, *at early dawn*, Lk. xxiv. 1 L T Tr WH; so Meyer ad loc. But βαθέως here is more correctly taken as the Attic form of the gen. fr. βαθύς, q. v.; cf. B. 26 (23); [*Lob.* Phryn. p. 247].*   **see 901**

βαθμός, -οῦ, ὁ, (fr. obsol. βάω i. q. βαίνω, like σταθμός [fr. ἵστημι]), *threshold, step*; of a grade of dignity and wholesome influence in the church, [R. V. *standing*], 1 Tim. iii. 13 [cf. Ellic. ad loc.]. (Used by [Sept.? S. v. 5; 2 K. xx. 9; also Sir. vi. 36]; Strabo, [Plut.], Lcian., Appian, Artemid., [al.]; cf. *Lob.* ad Phryn. p. 324.) *   **898**

βάθος, -εος (-ους), τό, (connected with the obsol. verb βάζω, βάω [but cf. Curtius § 635; Vaniček p. 195]; cf. βαθύς, βάσσων, and ὁ βυθός, ὁ βυσσός; Germ. *Boden*), *depth, height*, — [acc. as measured down or up]; **1.** prop.: Mt. xiii. 5; Mk. iv. 5; Ro. viii. 39 (opp. to ὕψωμα); Eph. iii. 18 (opp. to ὕψος); of '*the deep*' sea (the 'high seas'), Lk. v. 4. **2.** metaph.: ἡ κατὰ βάθους πτωχεία αὐτῶν, *deep*, extreme, *poverty*, 2 Co. viii. 2; τὰ βάθη τοῦ θεοῦ *the deep things of God*, things hidden and above man's scrutiny, esp. the divine counsels, 1 Co. ii. 10 (τοῦ Σατανᾶ, Rev. ii. 24 Rec.; καρδίας ἀνθρώπου, Judith viii. 14; [τὰ β. τῆς θείας γνώσεως, Clem. Rom. 1 Cor. 40, 1 (cf. Lghtft. ad loc.)]); inexhaustible abundance, immense amount, πλούτου, Ro. xi. 33 (so also Soph. Aj. 130; βαθὺς πλοῦτος, Ael. v. h. 3, 18; κακῶν, [Aeschyl. Pers. 465, 712]; Eur. Hel. 303; Sept. Prov. xviii. 3).*   **899**

βαθύνω: [impf ἐβάθυνον]; (βαθύς); *to make deep*: Lk.   **900**

vi. 48, where ἔσκαψε καὶ ἐβάθυνε is not used for βαθέως ἔσκαψε, but ἐβάθυνε expresses the continuation of the work, [he dug and *deepened* i. e. *went deep*]; cf. W. § 54, 5. (In Grk. writ. fr. Hom. down.) *

βαθύς, -εῖα, -ύ, [cf. βάθος], *deep*; prop.: Jn. iv. 11. metaph.: ὕπνος, a deep sleep, Acts xx. 9 (Sir. xxii. 7; often also in Grk. writ.); ὄρθρος (see βαθέως), Lk. xxiv. 1 ([Arstph. vesp. 215]; Plat. Crito 43 a.; Polyaen. 4, 9, 1; ἔτι βαθέος ὄρθρου, Plat. Prot. 310 a. [cf. also Philo de mutat. nom. § 30; de vita Moys. i. § 32]); τὰ βαθέα τοῦ Σατανᾶ, Rev. ii. 24 (G L T Tr WH; cf. βάθος).*

βαΐον [al. also βάϊον (or even βαῖον, Chandler ed. 1 p. 272); on its deriv. (fr. the Egyptian) cf. *Steph.* Thesaur. s. v. βαΐς], -ου, τό, *a palm-branch*; with τῶν φοινίκων added [so Test. xii. Patr. test. Naph. § 5] (after the fashion of οἰκοδεσπότης τῆς οἰκίας, ὑποπόδιον τῶν ποδῶν, [cf. W. 603 (561)]), Jn. xii. 13. (A bibl. and eccles. word: 1 Macc. xiii. 51; Cant. vii. 8 Symm.; Lev. xxiii. 40 unknown trans. In the Grk. church Palm-Sunday is called ἡ κυριακὴ τῶν βαΐων. Cf. *Fischer,* De vitiis Lexx. N. T. p. 18 sqq.; [*Sturz,* Dial. Maced. etc. p. 88 sq.; esp. *Soph.* Lex. s. v.].)*

Βαλαάμ, ὁ, indecl., (in Sept. for בִּלְעָם, acc. to Gesenius ["perhaps"] fr. בַּל and עָם *non-populus,* i. e. foreign; acc. to Jo. Simonis equiv. to בָּלַע עָם a swallowing up of the people; in Joseph. ὁ Βάλαμος), *Balaam* (or *Bileam*), a native of Pethor a city of Mesopotamia, endued by Jehovah with prophetic power. He was hired by Balak (see Βαλάκ) to curse the Israelites; and influenced by the love of reward, he wished to gratify Balak; but he was compelled by Jehovah's power to bless them (Num. xxii.-xxiv.; Deut. xxiii. 5 sq.; Josh. xiii. 22; xxiv. 9; Mic. vi. 5). Hence the later Jews saw in him a most abandoned deceiver: Rev. ii. 14; 2 Pet. ii. 15; Jude 11. Cf. *Win.* RWB. [and BB.DD.] s. v.*

Βαλάκ, ὁ, indecl., (בָּלָק empty [so Gesen. in his Thesaur. but in his later works he adopts (with Fürst et al.) an act. sense 'one who makes empty,' 'a devastator,' 'spoiler'; see BD. Am. ed. s. v.]), *Balak,* king of the Moabites (Num. xxii. 2 sq. and elsewhere): Rev. ii. 14.*

βαλάντιον and **βαλλάντιον** (so L T Tr WH; cf. [Tdf. Proleg. p. 79]; Fritzsche on Mk. p. 620; W. p. 43; *Passow,* Lex. [also L. and S.] s. v.), -ου, τό, *a money-bag, purse*: Lk. x. 4; xii. 33; xxii. 35 sq. (Sept. Job xiv. 17 cf. [Simon. 181]; Arstph. ran. 772; Xen. symp. 4, 2; Plat. Gorg. p. 508 e.; Hdian. 5, 4, 4 [3 ed. Bekk.], and other writ.) *

βάλλω; fut. βαλῶ; pf. βέβληκα; 2 aor. ἔβαλον (3 pers. plur. ἔβαλον in Lk. xxiii. 34; Acts xvi. 23, ἔβαλαν, the Alex. form, in Acts xvi. 37 L T Tr WH; [Rev. xviii. 19 Lchm., see WH. App. p. 165 and] for reff. ἀπέρχομαι init.); Pass., [pres. βάλλομαι]; pf. βέβλημαι; plpf. ἐβεβλήμην; 1 aor. ἐβλήθην; 1 fut. βληθήσομαι; *to throw,*— either with force, or without force yet with a purpose, or even carelessly; **1.** with f o r c e and effort: βάλλειν τινὰ ῥαπίσμασι to smite one with slaps, to buffet, Mk. xiv. 65 Rec. (an imitation of the phrases, τινὰ βάλλειν λίθοις, βέλεσι, τόξοις, etc., κακοῖς, ψόγῳ, σκώμμασι, etc., in Grk. writ.; cf. Passow i. p. 487; [L. and S. s. v. I. 1 and 3]; for the Rec. ἔβαλλον we must read with

Fritzsche and Schott ἔβαλον, fr. which arose ἔλαβον, adopted by L T Tr WH; βαλεῖν and λαβεῖν are often confounded in codd.; cf. Grimm on 2 Macc. v. 6; [*Scrivener,* Introd. p. 10]); βάλλειν λίθους ἐπί τινι or τινα, Jn. viii. (7), 59; χοῦν ἐπὶ τὰς κεφαλάς, Rev. xviii. 19 [WH mrg. ἐπέβ.]; κονιορτὸν εἰς τὸν ἀέρα, Acts xxii. 23; τὶ εἰς τὴν θάλασσαν, Mk. ix. 42; Rev. viii. 8; xviii. 21; εἰς τὸ πῦρ, Mt. iii. 10; xviii. 8; Lk. iii. 9; Mk. ix. 22; Jn. xv. 6; εἰς κλίβανον, Mt. vi. 30; Lk. xii. 28; εἰς γέεννα, Mt. v. [29], 30 [R G]; Mk. ix. 47; εἰς τ. γῆν, Rev. viii. 5, 7; xii. 4, 9, 13; εἰς τ. ληνόν, Rev. xiv. 19; εἰς τ. λιμνήν, Rev. xix. 20; xx. 10, 14 sq.; εἰς τ. ἄβυσσον, Rev. xx. 3; absol. and in the pass. *to be violently displaced from a position gained,* Rev. xii. 10 L T Tr WH. *an attack of disease* is said βάλλειν τινὰ εἰς κλίνην, Rev. ii. 22; Pass. *to lie sick abed, be prostrated by sickness*: βέβλημαι ἐπὶ κλίνης, Mt. ix. 2; Mk. vii. 30 [R G L mrg.]; with ἐπὶ κλίνης omitted, Mt. viii. 6, 14, cf. Lk. xvi. 20; τινὰ εἰς φυλακήν, to cast one into prison, Mt. v. 25; xviii. 30; Lk. xii. 58; xxiii. 19 [R G L], 25; Jn. iii. 24; Acts xvi. 23 sq. 37; Rev. ii. 10; [β. ἐπί τινα τὴν χεῖρα or τὰς χεῖρας *to lay hand* or *hands on one,* apprehend him, Jn. vii. 44 L T Tr WH, also 30 L mrg.]; δρέπανον εἰς γῆν to apply with force, *thrust in,* the sickle, Rev. xiv. 19; μάχαιραν βάλλειν (*to cast,* send) ἐπὶ τ. γῆν, Mt. x. 34, which phrase gave rise to another found in the same passage, viz. εἰρήνην βάλλ. ἐπὶ τ. γῆν to cast (send) peace; ἔξω, to cast out or forth: Mt. v. 13; xiii. 48; Lk. xiv. 35 (34); 1 Jn. iv. 18; Jn. xv. 6; ἑαυτὸν κάτω to cast one's self down: Mt. iv. 6; Lk. iv. 9; ἑαυτὸν εἰς τ. θάλασσαν, Jn. xxi. 7; pass. in a reflex. sense [B. 52 (45)], βλήθητι, Mt. xxi. 21; Mk. xi. 23; τὶ ἀφ' ἑαυτοῦ to cast a thing from one's self, throw it away: Mt. v. 29 sq.; xviii. 8; ὕδωρ ἐκ τοῦ στόματος, Rev. xii. 15 sq. (*cast out of his mouth,* Luther *schoss aus ihrem Munde*); ἐνώπιον before, in gen. of place, to cast before (eagerly lay down), Rev. iv. 10; of a tree casting its fruit because violently shaken by the wind, Rev. vi. 13. Intrans. *to rush* (*throw one's self* [cf. W. 251 (236); 381 (357) note[1]; B. 145 (127)]): Acts xxvii. 14; (Hom. Il. 11, 722; 23, 462, and other writ.; [cf. L. and S. s. v. III. 1]). **2.** w i t h o u t force and effort; *to throw* or *let go of a thing without caring where it falls*: κλῆρον to cast a lot into the urn [B. D. s. v. Lot], Mt. xxvii. 35; Mk. xv. 24; Lk. xxiii. 34; Jn. xix. 24 fr. Ps. xxi. (xxii.) 19; (κύβους, Plat. legg. 12 p. 968 e. and in other writ.). *to scatter:* κόπρια [Rec.st κοπρίαν], Lk. xiii. 8; seed ἐπὶ τῆς γῆς, Mk. iv. 26; εἰς κῆπον, Lk. xiii. 19. *to throw, cast, into:* ἀργύριον εἰς τὸν κορβανᾶν [L mrg. Tr mrg. κορβᾶν], Mt. xxvii. 6; χαλκόν, δῶρα, etc., εἰς τὸ γαζοφυλάκιον, Mk. xii. 41–44; Lk. xxi. 1–4, cf. Jn. xii. 6. βάλλειν τί τινι, *to throw, cast, a thing to*: τὸν ἄρτον τοῖς κυναρίοις, Mt. xv. 26; Mk. vii. 27; ἔμπροσθέν τινος, Mt. vii. 6; ἐνώπιόν τινος, Rev. ii. 14 (see σκάνδαλον, b. β.); *to give over to one's care uncertain about the result*: ἀργύριον τοῖς τραπεζίταις, to deposit, Mt. xxv. 27. of fluids, *to pour, to pour in*: foll. by εἰς, Mt. ix. 17; Mk. ii. 22; Lk. v. 37; Jn. xiii. 5, (οἶνον εἰς τὸν πίθον, Epictet. 4, 13, 12; of rivers, ῥόον εἰς ἅλα, Ap. Rhod. 2, 401, etc.; Sept. Judg. vi. 19 [Ald., Compl.]); *to pour* *out*, ἐπί τινος, Mt. xxvi. 12.   **3**. to move, give motion to, not with force yet with attention and for a purpose; εἴς τι, *to put into, insert*: Mk. vii. 33 (τοὺς δακτύλους εἰς τὰ ὦτα); Jn. xx. 25, 27; xviii. 11; χαλίνους εἰς τὸ στόμα, Jas. iii. 3; *to let down, cast down*: Jn. v. 7; Mt. iv. 18 [cf. Mk. i. 16 Rec.]; Mt. xvii. 27. Metaph.: εἰς τὴν καρδίαν τινός, *to suggest*, Jn. xiii. 2 (τὶ ἐν θυμῷ τινος, Hom. Od. 1, 201; 14, 269; εἰς νοῦν, schol. ad Pind. Pyth. 4, 133; al.; ἐμβάλλειν εἰς νοῦν τινι, Plut. vit. Timol. c. 3). [COMP.: ἀμφι-, ἀνα-, ἀντι-, ἀπο-, δια-, ἐκ-, ἐμ-, παρ-εμ-, ἐπι-, κατα-, μετα-, παρα-, περι-, προ-, συμ-, ὑπερ-, ὑπο-βάλλω.]

βαπτίζω; [impf. ἐβάπτιζον]; fut. βαπτίσω; 1 aor. ἐβάπτισα; Pass., [pres. βαπτίζομαι]; impf. ἐβαπτιζόμην; pf. ptcp. βεβαπτισμένος; 1 aor. ἐβαπτίσθην; 1 fut. βαπτισθήσομαι; 1 aor. mid. ἐβαπτισάμην; (frequent. [?] fr. βάπτω, like βαλλίζω fr. βάλλω); here and there in Plat., Polyb., Diod., Strab., Joseph., Plut., al. **I. 1.** prop. *to dip repeatedly, to immerge, submerge*, (of vessels sunk, Polyb. 1, 51, 6; 8, 8, 4; of animals, Diod. 1, 36). **2.** *to cleanse by dipping* or *submerging, to wash, to make clean with water*; in the mid. and the 1 aor. pass. *to wash one's self, bathe*; so Mk. vii. 4 [where WH txt. ῥαντίσωνται]; Lk. xi. 38, (2 K. v. 14 ἐβαπτίσατο ἐν τῷ Ἰορδάνῃ, for מָבַל; Sir. xxxi. (xxxiv.) 30; Judith xii. 7). **3.** metaph. *to overwhelm*, as ἰδιώτας ταῖς εἰσφοραῖς, Diod. 1, 73; ὀφλήμασι, Plut. Galba 21; τῇ συμφορᾷ βεβαπτισμένος, Heliod. Aeth. 2, 3; and alone, *to inflict great and abounding calamities on one*: ἐβάπτισαν τὴν πόλιν, Joseph. b. j. 4, 3, 3; ἡ ἀνομία με βαπτίζει, Is. xxi. 4 Sept. hence βαπτίζεσθαι βάπτισμα (cf. W. 225 (211); [B. 148 (129)]; cf. λούεσθαι τὸ λουτρόν, Ael. de nat. an. 3, 42), *to be overwhelmed with calamities*, of those who must bear them, Mt. xx. 22 sq. Rec.; Mk. x. 38 sq.; Lk. xii. 50, (cf. the Germ. *etwas auszubaden haben*, and the use of the word e. g. respecting those who cross a river with difficulty, ἕως τῶν μαστῶν οἱ πεζοὶ βαπτιζόμενοι διέβαινον, Polyb. 3, 72, 4; [for exx. see Soph. Lex. s. v.; also *T. J. Conant*, Baptizein, its meaning and use, N. Y. 1864 (printed also as an App. to their revised version of the Gosp. of Mt. by the "Am. Bible Union"); and esp. four works by J. W. Dale entitled Classic, Judaic, Johannic, Christic, Baptism, Phil. 1867 sqq.; *D. B. Ford*, Studies on the Bapt. Quest. (including a review of Dr. Dale's works), Bost. 1879]). **II.** In the N. T. it is used particularly of the rite of sacred ablution, first instituted by John the Baptist, afterwards by Christ's command received by Christians and adjusted to the contents and nature of their religion (see βάπτισμα, 3), viz. an immersion in water, performed as a sign of the removal of sin, and administered to those who, impelled by a desire for salvation, sought admission to the benefits of the Messiah's kingdom; [for patristic reff. respecting the mode, ministrant, subjects, etc. of the rite, cf. Soph. Lex. s. v.; Dict. of Chris. Antiq. s. v. Baptism]. **a.** The word is used absolutely, *to administer the rite of ablution, to baptize*, (Vulg. *baptizo*; Tertull. *tingo, tinguo*, [cf. *mergito*, de corona mil. § 3]): Mk. i. 4; Jn. i. 25 sq. 28; iii. 22 sq. 26; iv. 2; x. 40; 1 Co. i. 17; with the cognate noun τὸ βάπτισμα, Acts xix. 4; ὁ βαπτίζων substantively

i. q. ὁ βαπτιστής, Mk. vi. 14, [24 T Tr WH]. τινά, Jn. iv. 1; Acts viii. 38; 1 Co. i. 14, 16. Pass. *to be baptized*: Mt. iii. 13 sq. 16; Mk. xvi. 16; Lk. iii. 21; Acts ii. 41; viii. 12, 13, [36]; x. 47; xvi. 15; 1 Co. i. 15 L T Tr WH; x. 2 L T Tr mrg. WH mrg. Pass. in a reflex. sense [i. e. Mid. cf. W. § 38, 3], *to allow one's self to be initiated by baptism, to receive baptism*: Lk. [iii. 7, 12]; vii. 30; Acts ii. 38; ix. 18; xvi. 33; xviii. 8; with the cognate noun τὸ βάπτισμα added, Lk. vii. 29; 1 aor. mid., 1 Co. x. 2 (L T Tr mrg. WH mrg. ἐβαπτίσθησαν [cf. W. § 38, 4 b.]); Acts xxii. 16. foll. by a dat. of the thing with which baptism is performed, ὕδατι, see bb. below. **b.** with Prepositions; **aa.** εἰς, to mark the element into which the immersion is made: εἰς τὸν Ἰορδάνην, Mk. i. 9. to mark the end: εἰς μετάνοιαν, to bind one to repentance, Mt. iii. 11; εἰς τὸ Ἰωάννου βάπτισμα, to bind to the duties imposed by John's baptism, Acts xix. 3 [cf. W. 397 (371)]; εἰς ὄνομά τινος, to profess the name (see ὄνομα, 2) of one whose follower we become, Mt. xxviii. 19; Acts viii. 16; xix. 5; 1 Co. i. 13, 15; εἰς ἄφεσιν ἁμαρτιῶν, to obtain the forgiveness of sins, Acts ii. 38; εἰς τὸν Μωϋσῆν, to follow Moses as a leader, 1 Co. x. 2. to indicate the effect: εἰς ἓν σῶμα, to unite together into one body by baptism, 1 Co. xii. 13; εἰς Χριστόν, εἰς τὸν θάνατον αὐτοῦ, to bring by baptism into fellowship with Christ, into fellowship in his death, by which fellowship we have died to sin, Gal. iii. 27; Ro. vi. 3, [cf. Mey. on the latter pass., Ellic. on the former]. **bb.** ἐν, with dat. of the thing in which one is immersed: ἐν τῷ Ἰορδάνῃ, Mk. i. 5; ἐν τῷ ὕδατι, Jn. i. 31 (L T Tr WH ἐν ὕδ., but cf. Mey. ad loc. [who makes the art. deictic]). of the thing used in baptizing: ἐν ὕδατι, Mt. iii. 11; Mk. i. 8 [T WH Tr mrg. om. Tr txt. br. ἐν]; Jn. i. 26, 33; cf. B. § 133, 19; [cf. W. 412 (384); see ἐν, I. 5 d. a.]; with the simple dat., ὕδατι, Lk. iii. 16; Acts i. 5; xi. 16. ἐν πνεύματι ἁγίῳ, to imbue richly with the Holy Spirit, (just as its large bestowment is called an *outpouring*): Mt. iii. 11; Mk. i. 8 [L Tr br. ἐν]; Lk. iii. 16; Jn. i. 33; Acts i. 5; xi. 16; with the addition καὶ πυρί to overwhelm with fire (those who do not repent), i. e. to subject them to the terrible penalties of hell, Mt. iii. 11. ἐν ὀνόματι τοῦ κυρίου, by the authority of the Lord, Acts x. 48. **cc.** Pass. ἐπὶ [L Tr WH ἐν] τῷ ὀνόματι Ἰησοῦ Χριστοῦ, relying on the name of Jesus Christ, i. e. reposing one's hope on him, Acts ii. 38. **dd.** ὑπὲρ τῶν νεκρῶν on behalf of the dead, i. e. to promote their eternal salvation by undergoing baptism in their stead, 1 Co. xv. 29; cf. [W. 175 (165); 279 (262); 382 (358); Meyer (or Beet) ad loc.]; esp. Neander ad loc.; *Rückert*, Progr. on the passage, Jen. 18 47; *Paret* in Ewald's Jahrb. d. bibl. Wissensch. ix. p. 247; [cf. B. D. s. v. Baptism XII. Alex.'s Kitto ibid. VI.].*

βάπτισμα, -τος, τό. (βαπτίζω), a word peculiar to N. T. and eccl writ., *immersion, submersion*; **1.** used trop. of calamities and afflictions with which one is quite overwhelmed: Mt. xx. 22 sq. Rec.; Mk. x. 38 sq.; Lk. xii. 50, (see βαπτίζω, I. 3). **2.** of John's baptism, that purificatory rite by which men on confessing their sins were bound to a spiritual reformation, obtained the pardon of their past sins and became qualified for the benefits of the Messiah's kingdom soon to be set up: Mt. iii. 7; xxi. 25; Mk. xi. 30; Lk. vii. 29; xx. 4; Acts i. 22; x. 37; xviii. 25; [xix. 3]; *βάπτ. μετανοίας*, binding to repentance [W. 188 (177)], Mk. i. 4; Lk. iii. 3; Acts xiii. 24; xix. 4. 3. of Christian baptism; this, according to the view of the apostles, is a rite of sacred immersion, commanded by Christ, by which men confessing their sins and professing their faith in Christ are born again by the Holy Spirit unto a new life, come into the fellowship of Christ and the church (1 Co. xii. 13), and are made partakers of eternal salvation; [but see art. "Baptism" in BB.DD., McC. and S., Schaff-Herzog]: Eph. iv. 5; Col. ii. 12 [L mrg. Tr -μῷ q. v.]; 1 Pet. iii. 21; *εἰς τὸν θάνατον*, Ro. vi. 4 (see *βαπτίζω*, II. b. aa. fin.). [Trench § xcix.]*

909 **βαπτισμός**, -οῦ, ὁ, (*βαπτίζω*), a washing, purification effected by means of water: Mk. vii. 4, 8 [R G L Tr in br.] (*ξεστῶν καὶ ποτηρίων*); of the washings prescribed by the Mosaic law, Heb. ix. 10. *βαπτισμῶν διδαχῆς* equiv. to *διδαχῆς περὶ βαπτισμῶν*, Heb. vi. 2 [where L txt. WH txt. *βαπτ. διδαχήν*], which seems to mean an exposition of the difference between the washings prescribed by the Mosaic law and Christian baptism. (Among prof. writ. Josephus alone, antt. 18, 5, 2, uses the word, and of John's baptism; [respecting its interchange with *βάπτισμα* cf. exx. in *Soph*. Lex. s. v. 2 and Bp. Lghtft. on Col. ii. 12, where L mrg. Tr read *βαπτισμός*; cf. Trench § xcix.].) *

910 **βαπτιστής**, -οῦ, ὁ, (*βαπτίζω*), a baptizer; one who administers the rite of baptism; the surname of John, the forerunner of Christ: Mt. iii. 1; xi. 11 sq.; [xiv. 2, 8; xvi. 14; xvii. 13]; Mk. vi. 24 [T Tr WH *τοῦ βαπτίζοντος*], 25; viii. 28; Lk. vii. 20, 28 [T Tr WH om.], 33; ix. 19; also given him by Josephus, antt. 18, 5, 2, and found in no other prof. writ. [Joh. d. Täufer by Breest (1881), Köhler ('84).]*

911 **βάπτω**: [fut. *βάψω*, Jn. xiii. 26 T Tr WH]; 1 aor. *ἔβαψα*; pf. pass. ptcp. *βεβαμμένος*; in Grk. writ. fr. Hom. down; in Sept. for מָבַל; **a.** to dip, dip in, immerse: *τί*, Jn. xiii. 26 [but in 26ᵇ Lchm. *ἐμβάψας*, as in 26ᵇ L txt. R G]; foll. by a gen. of the thing into which the object is dipped (because only a part of it is touched by the act of dipping), Lk. xvi. 24 (cf. *ἅπτεσθαί τινος, λούεσθαι ποταμοῖο*, Hom. Il. 5, 6; 6, 508; cf. B. § 132, 25; [W. § 30, 8 c.]). **b.** to dip into dye, to dye, color: *ἱμάτιον αἵματι*, Rev. xix. 13 [Tdf. *περιρεραμμένον*, see s. v. *περιρραίνω*; WH *ῥεραντισμένον*, see *ῥαντίζω*]. (Hdt. 7, 67; Anth. 11, 68; Joseph. antt. 3, 6, 1.) [COMP.: *ἐμ-βάπτω*.]*

βάρ, Chald. בַּר [cf. Ps. ii. 12; Prov. xxxi. 2]; *βὰρ Ἰωνᾶ* son of Jonah (or Jonas): Mt. xvi. 17, where L T WH *Βαριωνᾶ* (q. v.) Barjonah (or Barjonas), as if a surname, like *Βαρνάβας*, etc. [R. V. Bar-Jonah. Cf. *Ἰωνᾶς*, 2.]*

912 **Βαραββᾶς**, -ᾶ, ὁ, (fr. בַּר son, and אַבָּא father, hence son of a father i. e. of a master [cf. Mt. xxiii. 9]), a captive robber whom the Jews begged Pilate to release instead of Christ: Mt. xxvii. 16 sq. (where codd. mentioned by Origen, and some other authorities, place *Ἰησοῦν* before *βαραββᾶν*, approved by Fritzsche, De Wette, Meyer, Bleek, al.; [cf. WH. App. and Tdf.'s note ad loc.; also

Treg. Printed Text, etc. p. 194 sq.]), 20 sq. 26; Mk. xv. 7, 11, 15; Lk. xxiii. 18; Jn. xviii. 40.*

Βαράκ, ὁ, indecl., (בָּרָק lightning), *Barak*, a commander of the Israelites (Judg. iv. 6, 8): Heb. xi. 32. [BB.DD.] * **913**

Βαραχίας, -ου, ὁ, [בֶּרֶכְיָה Jehovah blesses], *Barachiah*: in Mt. xxiii. 35 said to have been the father of the Zachariah slain in the temple; cf. *Ζαχαρίας*.* **914**

βάρβαρος, -ον; **1.** prop. one whose speech is rude, rough, harsh, as if repeating the syllables *βαρβάρ* (cf. Strabo 14, 2, 28 p. 662; *ὠνοματοπεποίηται ἡ λέξις*, Etym. Magn. [188, 11 (but Gaisf. reads *βράγχος* for *βάρβαρος*); cf. Curtius § 394; Vaniček p. 561]); hence **2.** one who speaks a foreign or strange language which is not understood by another (Hdt. 2, 158 *βαρβάρους πάντας οἱ Αἰγύπτιοι καλέουσι τοὺς μὴ σφίσι ὁμογλώσσους*, Ovid. trist. 5, 10, 37 barbarus hic ego sum, quia non intelligor ulli); so 1 Co. xiv. 11. **3.** The Greeks used *βάρβαρος* of any foreigner ignorant of the Greek language and the Greek culture, whether mental or moral, with the added notion, after the Persian war, of rudeness and brutality. Hence the word is applied in the N. T., but not reproachfully, in Acts xxviii. 2, 4, to the inhabitants of Malta [i. e. *Μελίτη*, q. v.], who were of Phœnician or Punic origin; and to those nations that had, indeed, some refinement of manners, but not the opportunity of becoming Christians, as the Scythians, Col. iii. 11 [but cf. Bp. Lghtft. ad loc.]. But the phrase *Ἕλληνές τε καὶ βάρβαροι* forms also a periphrasis for all peoples, or indicates their diversity yet without reproach to foreigners (Plat. Theaet. p. 175 a.; Isocr. Euag. c. 17 p. 192 b.; Joseph. antt. 4, 2, 1 and in other writ.); so in Ro. i. 14. (In Philo de Abr. § 45 sub fin. of all nations not Jews. Josephus b. j. prooem. 1 reckons the Jews among barbarians.) Cf. Grimm on 2 Macc. ii. 21 p. 61; [Bp. Lghtft. on Col. u. s.; B. D. s. v. Barbarian].* **915**

βαρέω, -ῶ: to burden, weigh down, depress; in the N. T. found only in Pass., viz. pres. ptcp. *βαρούμενοι*, impv. *βαρείσθω*; 1 aor. *ἐβαρήθην*; pf. pass. *βεβαρημένος*; the better writ. do not use the pres.; they use only the ptcps. *βεβαρηώς* and *βεβαρημένος*; see Matth. § 227; W. 83 (80); [B. 54 (47); Veitch s. v.]. Used simply: to be weighed down, oppressed, with external evils and calamities, 2 Co. i. 8; of the mental oppression which the thought of inevitable death occasions, 2 Co. v. 4; *ὀφθαλμοὶ βεβαρημένοι*, sc. *ὕπνῳ*, weighed down with sleep, Mk. xiv. 40 (L T Tr WH *καταβαρυνόμενοι*); Mt. xxvi. 43; with *ὕπνῳ* added, Lk. ix. 32; *ἐν* (בְּ) *κραιπάλῃ*, Lk. xxi. 34 Rec. *βαρυνθῶσιν*, [see *βαρύνω*], (Hom. Od. 19, 122 οἴνῳ *βεβαρηότες*, Diod. Sic. 4, 38 *τῇ νόσῳ*); *μὴ βαρείσθω* let it not be burdened, sc. with their expense, 1 Tim. v. 16, (*εἰσφοραῖς*, Dio Cass. 46, 32). [COMP.: *ἐπι-, κατα-βαρέω*.]* **916**

βαρέως, adv., (*βαρύς*, q. v.), heavily, with difficulty: Mt. xiii. 15; Acts xxviii. 27, (Is. vi. 10). [From Hdt. on.]* **917**

Βαρθολομαῖος, -ου, ὁ, (בַּר תַּלְמַי son of Tolmai), *Bartholomew*, one of the twelve apostles of Christ: Mt. x. 3; Mk. iii. 18; Lk. vi. 14; Acts i. 13. [See *Ναθαναήλ* and BB.DD.] * **918**

919   **Βαρ-ιησοῦς**, ὁ, (בַּר son, יְשׁוּעַ Jesus), *Bar-Jesus*, a certain false prophet: Acts xiii. 6 [where Tdf. -σοῦ; see his note. Cf. Ἐλύμας].*

920   **Βαρ-ιωνᾶς**, -ᾶ [cf. B. 20 (17 sq.)], ὁ, (fr. בַּר son, and יוֹנָה Jonah [al. יוֹחָנָן i. e. Johanan, Jona, John; cf. Mey. on Jn. i. 42 (43) and Lghtft. as below]), *Bar-Jonah* [or *Bar-Jonas*], the surname of the apostle Peter: Mt. xvi. 17 [L T WH; in Jn. i. 42 (43); xxi. 15 sqq. son of *John*; see Lghtft. Fresh Revision, etc., p. 159 note (Am. ed. p. 137 note)]; see in βάρ and Ἰωνᾶς, 2.*

921   **Βαρνάβας**, -α [B. 20 (18)], ὁ, (בַּר son, and נְבָא; acc. to Luke's interpretation υἱὸς παρακλήσεως, i. e. excelling in the power τῆς παρακλήσεως, Acts iv. 36; see παράκλησις, 5), *Barnabas*, the surname of Joses [better J o s e p h], a Levite, a native of Cyprus. He was a distinguished teacher of the Christian religion, and a companion and colleague of Paul: Acts ix. 27; xi. 22, [25 Rec.], 30; xii. 25; xiii.–xv.; 1 Co. ix. 6; Gal. ii. 1, 9, 13; Col. iv. 10.*

922   **βάρος**, -εος, τό, *heaviness, weight, burden, trouble*: load, ἐπιτιθέναι τινί (Xen. oec. 17, 9), to impose upon one difficult requirements, Acts xv. 28; βάλλειν ἐπί τινα, Rev. ii. 24 (where the meaning is, 'I put upon you no other injunction which it might be difficult to observe'; cf. Düsterdieck ad loc.); βαστάζειν τὸ βάρος τινός, i. e. either the burden of a thing, as τὸ βάρος τῆς ἡμέρας the wearisome labor of the day Mt. xx. 12, or that which a person bears, as in Gal. vi. 2 (where used of troublesome moral faults; the meaning is, 'bear one another's faults'). αἰώνιον βάρος δόξης a weight of glory never to cease, i. e. vast and transcendent glory (blessedness), 2 Co. iv. 17; cf. W. § 34, 3; (πλούτου, Plut. Alex. M. 48). *weight* i. q. *authority*: ἐν βάρει εἶναι to have authority and influence, 1 Th. ii. 7 (6), (so also in Grk. writ.; cf. Wesseling on Diod. Sic. 4, 61; [exx. in Suidas s. v.]). [Syn. see ὄγκος.] *

923   **Βαρσαβᾶς** [-σαββᾶς L T Tr WH; see WH. App. p. 159], -ᾶ [B. 20 (18)], ὁ, *Barsabas* [or *Barsabbas*] (i. e. son of Saba [al. Zaba]);   **1.** the surname of a certain Joseph: Acts i. 23, [B. D. s. v. Joseph Barsabas].   **2.** the surname of a certain Judas: Acts xv. 22, [B. D. s. v. Judas Barsabas].*

924   **Βαρ-τίμαιος** [Tdf. -μαῖος, yet cf. Chandler § 253], -ον, ὁ, (son of Timæus), *Bartimæus*, a certain blind man: Mk. x. 46.*

925   **βαρύνω**: *to weigh down, overcharge*: Lk. xxi. 34 (1 aor. pass. subj.) βαρυνθῶσιν Rec. [cf. W. 83 (80); B. 54 (47)], for βαρηθῶσιν; see βαρέω. [Comp.: κατα-βαρύνω.] *

926   **βαρύς**, -εῖα, -ύ, *heavy*;   **1.** prop. i. e. heavy in weight: φορτίον, Mt. xxiii. 4 (in xi. 30 we have the opposite, ἐλαφρόν).   **2.** metaph.   **a.** *burdensome*: ἐντολή, the keeping of which is grievous, 1 Jn. v. 3.   **b.** *severe, stern*: ἐπιστολή, 2 Co. x. 10 [al. *imposing, impressive*, cf. Wetstein ad loc.].   **c.** *weighty*, i. e. *of great moment*: τὰ βαρύτερα τοῦ νόμου the weightier precepts of the law, Mt. xxiii. 23; αἰτιάματα [better αἰτιώματα (q. v.)], Acts xxv. 7.   **d.** *violent, cruel, unsparing*, [A. V. *grievous*]: λύκοι, Acts xx. 29 (so also Hom. Il. i. 89; Xen. Ages. 11, 12).*

927   **βαρύτιμος**, -ον, (βαρύς and τιμή), *of weighty* (i. e. *great*) *value, very precious, costly*: Mt. xxvi. 7 [R G Tr txt. WH], (so Strabo 17 p. 798; selling at a great price, Heliod. 2, 30 [var.]; possessed of great honor, Aeschyl. suppl. 25 [but Dindorf (Lex. s. v.) gives here (after a schol.) *severely punishing*]).*

928   **βασανίζω**: [impf. ἐβασάνιζον]; 1 aor. ἐβασάνισα; Pass., [pres. βασανίζομαι]; 1 aor. ἐβασανίσθην; 1 fut. βασανισθήσομαι; (βάσανος);   **1.** prop. *to test* (metals) *by the touchstone*.   **2.** *to question by applying torture*.   **3.** *to torture* (2 Macc. vii. 13); hence   **4.** univ. *to vex with grievous pains* (of body or mind), *to torment*: τινά, Mt. viii. 29; Mk. v. 7; Lk. viii. 28; 2 Pet. ii. 8; Rev. xi. 10; passively, Mt. viii. 6; Rev. ix. 5; xx. 10; of the pains of child-birth, Rev. xii. 2 (cf. Anthol. 2, p. 205 ed. Jacobs); with ἐν and the dat. of the material in which one is tormented, Rev. xiv. 10.   **5.** Pass. *to be harassed, distressed*; of those who at sea are struggling with a head wind, Mk. vi. 48; of a ship tossed by the waves, Mt. xiv. 24. (In Grk. writ. fr. Hdt. down. Often in O. T. Apocr.) *

929   **βασανισμός**, -οῦ, ὁ, (βασανίζω, q. v.);   **1.** *a testing by the touchstone* or *by torture*.   **2.** *torment, torture*;   **a.** the act of tormenting: Rev. ix. 5.   **b.** the state or condition of those tormented: Rev. xviii. 7, 10, 15; ὁ κάπνος τοῦ βασανισμοῦ αὐτῶν the smoke of the fire by which they are tormented, Rev. xiv. 11. (4 Macc. ix. 6; xi. 2; [al.]; bad wine is called βασανισμός by Alexis in Athen. 1, 56 p. 30 f.) *

930   **βασανιστής**, -οῦ, ὁ, (βασανίζω), one who elicits the truth by the use of the rack, an inquisitor, torturer, ([Antiphon; al.]; Dem. p. 978, 11; Philo in Flacc. § 11 end; [de concupisc. § 1; quod omn. prob. lib. 16; Plut. an vitios. ad infel. suff. § 2]); used in Mt. xviii. 34 of a jailer (δεσμοφύλαξ Acts xvi. 23), doubtless because the business of torturing was also assigned to him.*

931   **βάσανος**, -ον, ἡ, [Curtius p. 439];   **a.** *the touchstone*, [called also *basanite*, Lat. *lapis Lydius*], by which gold and other metals are tested.   **b.** *the rack* or *instrument of torture by which one is forced to divulge the truth*.   **c.** *torture, torment, acute pains*: used of the pains of disease, Mt. iv. 24; of the torments of the wicked after death, ἐν βασάνοις ὑπάρχειν, Lk. xvi. 23 (Sap. iii. 1; 4 Macc. xiii. 14); hence ὁ τόπος τῆς βασάνου is used of Gehenna, Lk. xvi. 28. (In Grk. writ. fr. [Theogn.], Pind. down.) *

932   **βασιλεία**, -ας, ἡ, (fr. βασιλεύω; to be distinguished fr. βασίλεια a queen; cf. ἱερεία priesthood fr. ἱερεύω, and ἱέρεια a priestess fr. ἱερεύς), [fr. Hdt. down];   **1.** *royal power, kingship, dominion, rule*: Lk. i. 33; xix. 12, 15; xxii. 29; Jn. xviii. 36; Acts i. 6; Heb. i. 8; 1 Co. xv. 24; Rev. xvii. 12; of the royal power of Jesus as the triumphant Messiah, in the phrase ἔρχεσθαι ἐν τῇ βασ. αὐτοῦ, i. e. to come in his kingship, clothed with this power: Mt. xvi. 28; Lk. xxiii. 42 [εἰς τὴν β. L mrg. Tr mrg. WH txt.]; of the royal power and dignity conferred on Christians in the Messiah's kingdom: Rev. i. 6 (acc. to Tr txt. WH mrg. ἐποίησεν ἡμῖν or L ἡμῶν [yet R G T WH txt. Tr mrg. ἡμᾶς] βασιλείαν [Rec. βασιλεῖς]); τοῦ θεοῦ, the royal power and dignity belonging to God, Rev. xii.

10.   **2.** *a kingdom* i. e. the territory subject to the rule of a king: Mt. xii. 25 sq.; xxiv. 7; Mk. iii. 24; vi. 23; xiii. 8; Lk. xi. 17; xxi. 10; plur.: Mt. iv. 8; Lk. iv. 5; Heb. xi. 33.   **3.** Frequent in the N. T. in reference to the Reign of the Messiah are the following phrases: ἡ βασιλεία τοῦ θεοῦ (מַלְכוּתָא דֶאֱלָהָא, Targ. Is. xl. 9; Mic. iv. 7), prop. *the kingdom over which God rules*; ἡ βασιλεία τοῦ Χριστοῦ (מַלְכוּת דִמְשִׁיחָא, Targ. Jonath. ad Is. liii. 10), *the kingdom of the Messiah*, which will be founded by God through the Messiah and over which the Messiah will preside as God's vicegerent; ἡ βασ. τῶν οὐρανῶν, only in Matthew, but very frequently [some 33 times], *the kingdom of heaven*, i. e. the kingdom which is of heavenly or divine origin and nature (in rabbin. writ. מַלְכוּת שָׁמַיִם is *the rule of God, the theocracy* viewed universally, not the Messianic kingdom); sometimes simply ἡ βασιλεία: Mt. iv. 23, etc.; Jas. ii. 5; once ἡ βασ. τοῦ Δαυείδ, because it was supposed the Messiah would be one of David's descendants and a king very like David, Mk. xi. 10; once also ἡ βασ. τοῦ Χριστοῦ καὶ θεοῦ, Eph. v. 5. Relying principally on the prophecies of Daniel — who had declared it to be the purpose of God that, after four vast and mighty kingdoms had succeeded one another and the last of them shown itself hostile to the people of God, at length its despotism should be broken, and the empire of the world pass over for ever to the holy people of God (Dan. ii. 44; vii. 14, 18, 27) — the Jews were expecting a kingdom of the greatest felicity, which *God through the Messiah* would set up, raising the dead to life again and renovating earth and heaven; and that in this kingdom they would bear sway for ever over all the nations of the world. This kingdom was called *the kingdom of God* or *the kingdom of the Messiah*; and in this sense must these terms be understood in the utterances of the Jews and of the disciples of Jesus when conversing with him, as Mt. xviii. 1; xx. 21; Mk. xi. 10; Lk. xvii. 20; xix. 11. But Jesus employed the phrase *kingdom of God* or *of heaven* to indicate *that perfect order of things which he was about to establish, in which all those of every nation who should believe in him were to be gathered together into one society, dedicated and intimately united to God, and made partakers of eternal salvation.* This kingdom is spoken of as now begun and actually present, inasmuch as its foundations have already been laid by Christ and its benefits realized among men that believe in him: Mt. xi. 12; xii. 28; xiii. 41 (in this pass. its earthly condition is spoken of, in which it includes bad subjects as well as good); Lk. xvii. 21; 1 Co. iv. 20; Ro. xiv. 17 (where the meaning is, 'the essence of the kingdom of God is not to be found in questions about eating and drinking') ; Col. i. 13. But far more frequently the kingdom of heaven is spoken of as a future blessing, since its consummate establishment is to be looked for on Christ's solemn return from the skies, the dead being called to life again, the ills and wrongs which burden the present state of things being done away, the powers hostile to God being vanquished: Mt. vi. 10; viii. 11; xxvi. 29; Mk. ix. 1; xv. 43; Lk. ix.

27; xiii. 28 sq.; xiv. 15; xxii. 18; 2 Pet. i. 11; also in the phrases εἰσέρχεσθαι εἰς τ. βασ. τ. οὐρανῶν or τ. θεοῦ: Mt. v. 20; vii. 21; xviii. 3; xix. 23, 24; Mk. ix. 47; x. 23, 24, 25; Lk. xviii. 24 [T Tr txt. WH εἰσπορεύονται], 25; Jn. iii. 5; Acts xiv. 22; κληρονόμος τῆς βασιλείας, Jas. ii. 5; κληρονομεῖν τ. β. τ. θ.; see d. below. By a singular use ἡ βασ. τοῦ κυρίου ἡ ἐπουράνιος *God's heavenly kingdom*, in 2 Tim. iv. 18, denotes the exalted and perfect order of things which already exists in heaven, and into which true Christians are ushered immediately after death; cf. Phil. i. 23; Heb. xii. 22 sq. The phrase βασ. τῶν οὐρανῶν or τοῦ θεοῦ, while retaining its meaning *kingdom of heaven* or *of God*, must be understood, according to the requirements of the context, **a.** of the beginning, growth, potency, of the divine kingdom: Mt. xiii. 31–33; Mk. iv. 30; Lk. xiii. 18. **b.** of its fortunes: Mt. xiii. 24; Mk. iv. 26. **c.** of the conditions to be complied with in order to reception among its citizens: Mt. xviii. 23; xx. 1; xxii. 2; xxv. 1. **d.** of its blessings and benefits, whether present or future: Mt. xiii. 44 sq.; Lk. vi. 20; also in the phrases ζητεῖν τὴν βασ. τ. θεοῦ, Mt. vi. 33 [L T WH om. τ. θεοῦ]; Lk. xii. 31 [αὐτοῦ L txt. T Tr WH]; δέχεσθαι τ. βασ. τ. θ. ὡς παιδίον, Mk. x. 15; Lk. xviii. 17; κληρονομεῖν τ. β. τ. θ. Mt. xxv. 34; 1 Co. vi. 9 sq.; xv. 50; Gal. v. 21; see in κληρονομέω, 2. **e.** of the congregation of those who constitute the royal 'city of God': ποιεῖν τινας βασιλείαν, Rev. i. 6 G T WH txt. Tr mrg. [cf. 1 above]; v. 10 (here R G βασιλεῖς, so R in the preceding pass.), cf. Ex. xix. 6. Further, the foll. expressions are noteworthy: of persons fit for admission into the divine kingdom it is said αὐτῶν or τοιούτων ἐστὶν ἡ βασ. τῶν οὐρ. or τοῦ θεοῦ: Mt. v. 3, 10; xix. 14; Mk. x. 14; Lk. xviii. 16. διδόναι τινὶ τ. βασ. is used of God, making men partners of his kingdom, Lk. xii. 32; παραλαμβάνειν of those who are made partners, Heb. xii. 28. διὰ τὴν βασ. τ. οὐρ. to advance the interests of the heavenly kingdom, Mt. xix. 12; ἕνεκεν τῆς βασ. τ. θ. for the sake of becoming a partner in the kingdom of God, Lk. xviii. 29. Those who announce the near approach of the kingdom, and describe its nature, and set forth the conditions of obtaining citizenship in it, are said διαγγέλλειν τ. βασ. τ. θ. Lk. ix. 60; εὐαγγελίζεσθαι τὴν β. τ. θ. Lk. iv. 43; viii. 1; xvi. 16; περὶ τῆς βασ. τ. θ. Acts viii. 12; κηρύσσειν τὴν βασ. τ. θ. Lk. ix. 2; Acts xx. 25; xxviii. 31; τὸ εὐαγγέλιον τῆς βασ. Mt. iv. 23; ix. 35; xxiv. 14; with the addition of τοῦ θεοῦ, Mk. i. 14 R L br. ἤγγικεν ἡ βασ. τ. οὐρ. or τοῦ θεοῦ, is used of its institution as close at hand: Mt. iii. 2; iv. 17; Mk. i. 15; Lk. x. 9, 11. it is said ἔρχεσθαι i. e. *to be established*, in Mt. vi. 10; Lk. xi. 2; xvii. 20; Mk. xi. 10. In accordance with the comparison which likens the kingdom of God to a palace, the power of admitting into it and of excluding from it is called κλεῖς τῆς β. τ. οὐρ. Mt. xvi. 19; κλείειν τὴν β. τ. οὐρ. to keep from entering, Mt. xxiii. 13 (14). υἱοὶ τῆς βασ. are those to whom the prophetic promise of the heavenly kingdom extends: used of the Jews, Mt. viii. 12; of those gathered out of all nations who have shown themselves worthy of a share in this kingdom, Mt. xiii. 38. (In the O. T.

Apocr. ἡ βασ. τοῦ θεοῦ denotes *God's rule, the divine administration*, Sap. vi. 5; x. 10; Tob. xiii. 1; so too in Ps. cii. (ciii.) 19; civ. (cv.) 11–13; Dan. iv. 33; vi. 26; *the universe subject to God's sway, God's royal domain*, Song of the Three Children 32; ἡ βασιλεία, simply, *the O. T. theocratic commonwealth*, 2 Macc. i. 7.) Cf. *Fleck*, De regno divino, Lips. 1829; *Baumg.-Crusius*, Bibl. Theol. p. 147 sqq.; *Tholuck*, Die Bergrede Christi, 5te Aufl. p. 55 sqq. [on Mt. v. 3]; *Cölln*, Bibl. Theol. i. p. 567 sqq., ii. p. 108 sqq.; *Schmid*, Bibl. Theol. des N. T. p. 262 sqq. ed. 4; *Baur*, Neutest. Theol. p. 69 sqq.; *Weiss*, Bibl. Theol. d. N. T. § 13; [also in his Leben Jesu, bk. iv. ch. 2]; *Schürer*, [Neutest. Zeitgesch. § 29 (esp. par. 8) and reff. there; also] in the Jahrbb. für protest. Theol., 1876, pp. 166–187 (cf. Lipsius ibid. 1878, p. 189); [B.D. Am. ed. s. v. Kingdom of Heaven, and reff. there].

933 & 934 βασίλειος, (rarely -εία), -ειον, *royal, kingly, regal*: 1 Pet. ii. 9. As subst. τὸ βασίλειον (Xen. Cyr. 2, 4, 3; Prov. xviii. 19 Sept.; Joseph. antt. 6, 12, 4), and much oftener (fr. Hdt. 1, 30 down) in plur. τὰ βασίλεια (Sept. Esth. i. 9, etc.), *the royal palace*: Lk. vii. 25 [A. V. *kings' courts*].*

935 βασιλεύς, -έως, ὁ, *leader of the people, prince, commander, lord of the land, king*; univ.: οἱ βασιλεῖς τῆς γῆς, Mt. xvii. 25; Rev. xvi. 14 [L T Tr WH om. τῆς γῆς], etc.; τῶν ἐθνῶν, Lk. xxii. 25; of the king of Egypt, Acts vii. 10, 18; Heb. xi. 23, 27; of David, Mt. i. 6; Acts xiii. 22; of Herod the Great and his successors, Mt. ii. 1 sqq.; Lk. i. 5; Acts xii. 1; xxv. 13; of a tetrarch, Mt. xiv. 9; Mk. vi. 14, 22, (of the son of a king, Xen. oec. 4, 16; "reges Syriae, regis Antiochi pueros, scitis Romae nuper fuisse," Cic. Verr. ii. 4, 27, cf. de senectute 17, 59; [Verg. Aen. 9, 223]); of a Roman emperor, 1 Tim. ii. 2; 1 Pet. ii. 17, cf. Rev. xvii. 9 (10), (so in prof. writ. in the Roman age, as in Joseph. b. j. 5, 13, 6; Hdian. 2, 4, 8 [4 Bekk.]; of the son of the emperor, ibid. 1, 5, 15 [5 Bekk.]); of the Messiah, ὁ βασιλεὺς τῶν Ἰουδαίων, Mt. ii. 2, etc.; τοῦ Ἰσραήλ, Mk. xv. 32; Jn. i. 49 (50); xii. 13; of Christians, as to reign over the world with Christ in the millennial kingdom, Rev. i. 6; v. 10 (Rec. in both pass. and Grsb. in the latter; see βασιλεία, 3 e.); of God, the supreme ruler over all, Mt. v. 35; 1 Tim. i. 17 (see αἰών, 2); Rev. xv. 3; βασιλεὺς βασιλέων, Rev. xvii. 14 [but here as in xix. 16 of the victorious Messiah]; ὁ βασ. τῶν βασιλευόντων, 1 Tim. vi. 15, (2 Macc. xiii. 4; 3 Macc. v. 35; Enoch 9, 4; [84, 2; Philo de decal. § 10]; cf. [κύριος τῶν βασ. Dan. ii. 47]; κύριος τ. κυρίων, Deut. x. 17; Ps. cxxxv. (cxxxvi.) 3; [so of the king of the Parthians, Plut. Pomp. § 38, 1]).

936 βασιλεύω; fut. βασιλεύσω; 1 aor. ἐβασίλευσα; (βασιλεύς); — in Grk. writ. [fr. Hom. down] with gen. or dat., in the sacred writ., after the Hebr. (עַל מָשַׁל), foll. by ἐπί with gen. of place, Mt. ii. 22 (where L T WH om. Tr br. ἐπί); Rev. v. 10; foll. by ἐπί with acc. of the pers., Lk. i. 33; xix. 14, 27; Ro. v. 14; [cf. W. 206 (193 sq.); B. 169 (147)]—*to be king, to exercise kingly power, to reign*: univ., 1 Tim. vi. 15; Lk. xix. 14, 27; of the governor of a country, although not possessing kingly

rank, Mt. ii. 22; of God, Rev. xi. 15, 17; xix. 6; of the rule of Jesus, the Messiah, Lk. i. 33; 1 Co. xv. 25; Rev. xi. 15; of the reign of Christians in the millennium, Rev. v. 10; xx. 4, 6; xxii. 5; hence Paul transfers the word to denote the supreme moral dignity, liberty, blessedness, which will be enjoyed by Christ's redeemed ones: Ro. v. 17 (cf. De Wette and Thol. ad loc.); 1 Co. iv. 8. Metaph. *to exercise the highest influence, to control*: Ro. v. 14, 17, 21; vi. 12. The aor. ἐβασίλευσα denotes *I obtained royal power, became king, have come to reign*, in 1 Co. iv. 8 [cf. W. 302 (283); B. 215 (185)]; Rev. xi. 17; xix. 6, (as often in Sept. and prof. writ.; cf. Grimm on 1 Macc. p. 11; Breitenbach or Kühner on Xen. mem. 1, 1, 18; on the aor. to express entrance into a state, see Bnhdy. p. 382; Krüger § 53, 5, 1; [Kühner § 386, 5; Goodwin § 19 N. 1]). [COMP.: συμ-βασιλεύω.]*

937 βασιλικός, -ή, -όν, *of* or *belonging to a king, kingly, royal, regal*; of a man, *the officer* or *minister of a prince, a courtier*: Jn. iv. 46, 49, (Polyb. 4, 76, 2; Plut. Sol. 27; often in Joseph.). *subject to a king*: of a country, Acts xii. 20. *befitting* or *worthy of a king, royal*: ἐσθής, Acts xii. 21. Hence metaph. *principal, chief*: νόμος, Jas. ii. 8 (Plat. Min. p. 317 c. τὸ ὀρθὸν νόμος ἐστὶ βασιλικός, Xen. symp. 1, 8 βασιλικὸν κάλλος; 4 Macc. xiv. 2).*

see 935 [βασιλίσκος, -ου, ὁ, (dimin. of βασιλεύς), *a petty king*; a reading noted by WH in their (rejected) marg. of Jn. iv. 46, 49. (Polyb., al.)*]

938 βασίλισσα, -ης, ἡ, *queen*: Mt. xii. 42; Lk. xi. 31; Acts viii. 27; Rev. xviii. 7. (Xen. oec. 9, 15; Aristot. oec. 9 [in *Bekker*, Anecd. i. p. 84; cf. frag. 385 (fr. Poll. 8, 90) p. 1542ᵃ, 25]; Polyb. 23, 18, 2 [excrpt. Vales. 7], and often in later writ.; Sept.; Joseph.; the Atticists prefer the forms βασιλίς and βασίλεια; cf. *Lob.* ad Phryn. p. 225; [on the termination, corresponding to Eng. *-ess*, cf. W. 24; B. 73; *Soph.* Lex. p. 37; *Sturz*, De dial. Maced. et Alex. p. 151 sqq.; Curtius p. 653].)*

939 βάσις, -εως, ἡ, (ΒΑΩ, βαίνω); **1.** *a stepping, walking*, (Aeschyl., Soph., al.). **2.** *that with which one steps, the foot*: Acts iii. 7, (Plat. Tim. p. 92 a. et al.; Sap. xiii. 18).*

940 βασκαίνω: 1 aor. ἐβάσκανα, on which form cf. W. [75 (72)]; 83 (80); [B. 41 (35); *Lob.* ad Phryn. p. 25 sq.; Paralip. p. 21 sq.]; (βάζω, βάσκω [φάσκω] to speak, talk); τινά [W. 223 (209)]; **1.** *to speak ill of one, to slander, traduce him*, (Dem. 8, 19 [94, 19]; Ael. v. h. 2, 13, etc.). **2.** *to bring evil on one by feigned praise or an evil eye, to charm, bewitch one*, (Aristot. probl. 20, 34 [p. 926ᵇ, 24]; Theocr. 6, 39; Ael. nat. an. 1, 35); hence, of those who lead away others into error by wicked arts (Diod. 4, 6): Gal. iii. 1. Cf. Schott [or Bp. Lghtft.] ad loc.; *Lob.* ad Phryn. p. 462.*

941 βαστάζω; fut. βαστάσω; 1 aor. ἐβάστασα; **1.** *to take up with the hands*: λίθους, Jn. x. 31, (λᾶαν, Hom. Od. 11, 594; τὴν μάχαιραν ἀπὸ τῆς γῆς, Joseph. antt. 7, 11, 7). **2.** *to take up in order to carry* or *bear*; *to put upon one's self* (something) *to be carried*; *to bear* what is burdensome: τὸν σταυρόν, Jn. xix. 17; Lk. xiv. 27, (see σταυρός

2 a. and b.) ; Metaph.: βαστάζειν τι, to be equal to understanding a matter and receiving it calmly, Jn. xvi. 12 (Epict. ench. 29, 5); φορτίον, Gal. vi. 5; βαστάσει τὸ κρίμα, must take upon himself the condemnation of the judge, Gal. v. 10 (אֵשָׂא מְשַׁפֵּט, Mic. vii. 9). Hence to bear, endure: Mt. xx. 12; Acts xv. 10 (ζυγόν); Ro. xv. 1; Gal. vi. 2; Rev. ii. 2 sq. (Epict. diss. 1, 3, 2; Anthol. 5, 9, 3; in this sense the Greeks more commonly use φέρειν.)   3. simply to bear, carry: Mt. iii. 11; Mk. xiv. 13; Lk. vii. 14; xxii. 10; Rev. xvii. 7; pass., Acts iii. 2; xxi. 35. τὸ ὄνομά μου ἐνώπιον ἐθνῶν, so to bear it that it may be in the presence of Gentiles, i. e. by preaching to carry the knowledge of my name to the Gentiles, Acts ix. 15.   to carry on one's person: Lk. x. 4; Gal. vi. 17 [cf. Ellic. ad loc.]; of the womb carrying the foetus, Lk. xi. 27; to sustain, i. e. uphold, support: Ro. xi. 18.   4. by a use unknown to Attic writ., to bear away, carry off: νόσους, to take away or remove by curing them, Mt. viii. 17 (Galen de compos. medicam. per gen. 2, 14 [339 ed. Bas.] ψώρας τε θεραπεύει καὶ ὑπώπια βαστάζει) [al. refer the use in Mt. l. c. to 2; cf. Meyer]. Jn. xii. 6 (ἐβάσταζε used to pilfer [R. V. txt. took away; cf. our 'shoplifting', though perh. this lift is a diff. word, see Skeat s. v.]); Jn. xx. 15, (Polyb. 1, 48, 2 ὁ ἄνεμος τοὺς πύργους τῇ βίᾳ βαστάζει, Apollod. bibl. 2, 6, 2; 3, 4, 3; Athen. 2, 26 p. 46 f.; 15, 48 p. 693 e.; very many instances fr. Joseph. are given by Krebs, Observv. p. 152 sqq.). [SYN. cf. Schmidt ch. 105.] *

942   βάτος, -ου, ἡ and (in Mk. xii. 26 G L T Tr WH) ὁ, (the latter acc. to Moeris, Attic; the former Hellenistic; cf. Fritzsche on Mk. p. 532; W. 63 (62) [cf. 36; B. 12 (11)]), [fr. Hom. down], a thorn or bramble-bush [cf. B. D. s. v. Bush]: Lk. vi. 44; Acts vii. 30, 35; ἐπὶ τοῦ (τῆς) βάτου at the Bush, i. e. where it tells about the Bush, Mk. xii. 26; Lk. xx. 37; cf. Fritzsche on Ro. xi. 2; [B.D. s. v. Bible IV. 1].*

943   βάτος, -ου, ὁ, Hebr. בַּת a bath, [A. V. measure], a Jewish measure of liquids containing 72 sextarii [between 8 and 9 gal.], (Joseph. antt. 8, 2, 9): Lk. xvi. 6 [see B.D. s. v. Weights and Measures II. 2].*

944   βάτραχος, -ου, ὁ, a frog, (fr. Hom. [i. e. Batrach., and Hdt.] down): Rev. xvi. 13.*

945   βαττολογέω [T WH βατταλ. (with א B, see WH. App. p. 152)], -ῶ: 1 aor. subj. βαττολογήσω;   a. to stammer, and, since stammerers are accustomed to repeat the same sounds,   b. to repeat the same things over and over, to use many and idle words, to babble, prate; so Mt. vi. 7, where it is explained by ἐν τῇ πολυλογίᾳ, (Vulg. multum loqui; [A. V. to use vain repetitions]); cf. Tholuck ad loc.   Some suppose the word to be derived from Battus, a king of Cyrene, who is said to have stuttered (Hdt. 4, 155); others from Battus, an author of tedious and wordy poems; but comparing βατταρίζειν, which has the same meaning, and βάρβαρος (q. v.), it seems far more probable that the word is onomatopoetic. (Simplic. in Epict. [ench. 30 fin.] p. 340 ed. Schweigh.) *

946   βδέλυγμα, -τος, τό, (βδελύσσομαι), a bibl. and eccl. word; in Sept. mostly for תּוֹעֵבָה, also for שִׁקּוּץ and שֶׁקֶץ, a foul thing (loathsome on acct. of its stench), a detestable thing; (Tertull. abominamentum); Luth. Greuel; [A. V. abomination]; a. univ.: Lk. xvi. 15.   b. in the O. T. often used of idols and things pertaining to idolatry, to be held in abomination by the Israelites; as 1 K. xi. 6 (5); xx. (xxi.) 26; 2 K. xvi. 3; xxi. 2; 1 Esdr. vii. 13; Sap. xii. 23; xiv. 11; hence in the N. T. in Rev. xvii. 4 sq. of idol-worship and its impurities; ποιεῖν βδέλυγμα κ. ψεῦδος, Rev. xxi. 27.   c. the expression τὸ βδ. τῆς ἐρημώσεως the desolating abomination [al. take the gen. al.; e. g. Mey. as gen. epex.] in Mt. xxiv. 15; Mk. xiii. 14, (1 Macc. i. 54), seems to designate some terrible event in the Jewish war by which the temple was desecrated, perh. that related by Joseph. b. j. 4, 9, 11 sqq. (Sept. Dan. xi. 31; xii. 11, βδ. (τῆς) ἐρημώσεως for שִׁקּוּץ מְשֹׁמֵם and שֹׁמֵם "זְ, Dan. ix. 27 βδ. τῶν ἐρημώσεων for שִׁקּוּצִים מְשֹׁמֵם the abomination (or abominations) wrought by the desolator, i. e. not the statue of Jupiter Olympius, but a little idol-altar placed upon the altar of whole burnt-offerings; cf. Grimm on 1 Macc. p. 31; Hengstenberg, Authentie des Daniel, p. 85 sq.; [the principal explanations of the N. T. phrase are noticed in Dr. Jas. Morison's Com. on Mt. l. c.].) *

947   βδελυκτός, -ή, όν, (βδελύσσομαι), abominable, detestable: Tit. i. 16. (Besides only in Prov. xvii. 15; Sir. xli. 5; 2 Macc. i. 27; [cf. Philo de victim. offer. § 12 sub fin.].)*

948   βδελύσσω: (βδέω quietly to break wind, to stink);   1. to render foul, to cause to be abhorred: τὴν ὀσμήν, Ex. v. 21; to defile, pollute: τὰς ψυχάς, τ. ψυχήν, Lev. xx. 25; 1 Macc. i. 48; pf. pass. ptcp. ἐβδελυγμένος abominable, Rev. xxi. 8, (Lev. xviii. 30; Prov. viii. 7; Job xv. 16; 3 Macc. vi. 9; βδελυσσόμενος, 2 Macc. v. 8). In native Grk. writ. neither the act. nor the pass. is found.   2. βδελύσσομαι; depon. mid. (1 aor. ἐβδελυξάμην often in Sept. [Joseph. b. j. 6, 2, 10]; in Grk. writ. depon. passive, and fr. Arstph. down); prop. to turn one's self away from on account of the stench; metaph. to abhor, detest: τί, Ro. ii. 22.*

949   βέβαιος, -αία (W. 69 (67); B. 25 (22)), -αιον, (ΒΑΩ, βαίνω), [fr. Aeschyl. down], stable, fast, firm; prop.: ἄγκυρα, Heb. vi. 19; metaph. sure, trusty: ἐπαγγελία, Ro. iv. 16; κλῆσις καὶ ἐκλογή, 2 Pet. i. 10; λόγος προφητικός, 2 Pet. i. 19; unshaken, constant, Heb. iii. 14; ἐλπίς, 2 Co. i. 7 (6), (4 Macc. xvii. 4); παρρησία, Heb. iii. 6 (but WH Tr mrg. in br.); valid and therefore inviolable, λόγος, Heb. ii. 2; διαθήκη, Heb. ix. 17. (With the same meanings in Grk. writ. fr. IIdt. down.) *

950   βεβαιόω, -ῶ; fut. βεβαιώσω; 1 aor. ἐβεβαίωσα; Pass., [pres. βεβαιοῦμαι]; 1 aor. ἐβεβαιώθην; (βέβαιος) ; to make firm, establish, confirm, make sure: τὸν λόγον, to prove its truth and divinity, Mk. xvi. 20; τὰς ἐπαγγελίας make good the promises by the event, i. e. fulfil them, Ro. xv. 8 (so also in Grk. writ. as Diod. 1, 5); Pass.: τὸ μαρτύριον τοῦ Χριστοῦ, 1 Co. i. 6; ἡ σωτηρία ... εἰς ἡμᾶς ἐβεβαιώθη, a constructio praegnans [W. § 66, 2 d.] which may be resolved into εἰς ἡμᾶς παρεδόθη καὶ ἐν ἡμῖν βέβαιος ἐγένετο, Heb. ii. 3 cf. 2; see βέβαιος. of men made steadfast and constant in soul: Heb. xiii. 9; 1 Co. i. 8 (βεβ.ιώσει ὑμᾶς

ἀνεγκλήτους will so confirm you that ye may be unreprovable [W. § 59, 6 fin.]); 2 Co. i. 21 (βεβαιῶν ἡμᾶς εἰς Χριστόν, causing us to be steadfast in our fellowship with Christ; cf. Meyer ad loc.); ἐν τῇ πίστει, Col. ii. 7 [L T Tr WH om. ἐν]. (In Grk. writ. fr. Thuc. and Plat. down.) [Comp.: δια-βεβαιόομαι.]*

951 βεβαίωσις, -εως, ἡ, (βεβαιόω), confirmation: τοῦ εὐαγγελίου, Phil. i. 7; εἰς βεβαίωσιν to produce confidence, Heb. vi. 16. (Sap. vi. 19. Thuc., Plut., Dio Cass., [al.])*

952 βέβηλος, -ον, (ΒΑ͂Ω, βαίνω, βηλός threshold); 1. accessible, lawful to be trodden; prop. used of places; hence 2. profane, equiv. to חֹל [i. e. unhallowed, common], Lev. x. 10; 1 S. xxi. 4; opp. to ἅγιος (as in [Ezek. xxii. 26]; Philo, vit. Moys. iii. § 18): 1 Tim. iv. 7; vi. 20; 2 Tim. ii. 16; of men, profane i. e. ungodly: 1 Tim. i. 9; Heb. xii. 16. (Often in Grk. writ. fr. Aeschyl. down.) [Cf. Trench § ci.]*

953 βεβηλόω, -ῶ; 1 aor. ἐβεβήλωσα; (βέβηλος); to profane, desecrate: τὸ σάββατον, Mt. xii. 5; τὸ ἱερόν, Acts xxiv. 6. (Often in Sept. for חָלַל; Judith ix. 8; 1 Macc. ii. 12, etc.; Heliod. 2, 25.)*

954 Βεελζεβούλ and, as written by some [yet no G r e e k] authorities, Βεελζεβούβ [cod. B Βεεζεβούλ, so cod. א exc. in Mk. iii. 22; adopted by WH, see their App. p. 159; cf. B. 6], ὁ, indecl., Beelzebul or Beelzebub, a name of Satan, the prince of evil spirits: Mt. x. 25; xii. 24, 27; Mk. iii. 22; Lk. xi. 15, 18, 19. The form Βεελζεβούλ is composed of זְבוּל (rabbin. for זֶבֶל dung) and בַּעַל, lord of dung or of filth, i. e. of idolatry; cf. Lightfoot on Mt. xii. 24. The few who follow Jerome in preferring the form Βεελζεβούβ derive the name fr. זְבוּב בַּעַל, lord of flies, a false god of the Ekronites (2 K. i. 2) having the power to drive away troublesome flies, and think the Jews transferred the name to Satan in contempt. Cf. Win. RWB. s. v. Beelzebub: and J. G. M(üller) in Herzog vol. i. p. 768 sqq.; [BB.DD.; cf. also Meyer and Dr. Jas. Morison on Mt. x. 25; some, as Weiss (on Mk. l. c.; Bibl. Theol. § 23 a.), doubt alike whether the true derivation of the name has yet been hit upon, and whether it denotes Satan or only some subordinate ‘Prince of demons’]. (Besides only in eccl. writ., as Ev. Nicod. c. 1 sq.)*

955 Βελίαλ, ὁ, (בְּלִיַּעַל worthlessness, wickedness), Belial, a name of Satan, 2 Co. vi. 15 in Rec.bez elz L. But Βελίαρ (q. v.) is preferable, [see WH. App. p. 159; B. 6].*

see 955 Βελίαρ, ὁ, indecl., Beliar, a name of Satan in 2 Co. vi. 15 Rec.st G T Tr WH, etc. This form is either to be ascribed (as most suppose) to the harsh Syriac pronunciation of the word Βελίαλ (q. v.), or must be derived from יַעַר בַּל lord of the forest, i. e. who rules over forests and deserts, (cf. Sept. Is. xiii. 21; Mt. xii. 43; [BB.DD. s. v. Belial, esp. Alex.'s Kitto]). Often in eccl. writ.*

see 956 βελόνη, -ης, ἡ, (βέλος); a. the point of a spear. b. a needle: Lk. xviii. 25 L T Tr WH; see ῥαφίς. ([Batr. 130], Arstph., Aeschin., Aristot., al.; cf. Lob. ad Phryn. p. 90.)*

956 βέλος, -εος, τό, (βάλλω), a missile, a dart, javelin, arrow: Eph. vi. 16. [From Hom. down.]*

957 βελτίων, -ον, gen. -ονος, better; neut. adverbially in 2 Tim. i. 18 [W. 242 (227); B. 27 (24). Soph., Thuc., al.].*

Βενιαμίν [-μείν L T Tr WH; see WH. App. 155, and s. v. ει,ι],ὁ, (בֶּנְיָמִין, i. e. יָמִין בֶּן son of the right hand, i. e. of good fortune, Gen. xxxv. 18), Benjamin, Jacob's twelfth son; φυλὴ Βενιαμίν the tribe of Benjamin: Acts xiii. 21; Ro. xi. 1; Phil. iii. 5; Rev. vii. 8.* **958**

Βερνίκη, -ης, ἡ, (for Βερενίκη, and this the Macedonic form [cf. Sturz, De dial. Mac. p. 31] of Φερενίκη [i. e. victorious]), Bernice or Berenice, daughter of Herod Agrippa the elder. She married first her uncle Herod, king of Chalcis, and after his death Polemon, king of Cilicia. Deserting him soon afterwards, she returned to her brother Agrippa, with whom previously when a widow she was said to have lived incestuously. Finally she became for a time the mistress of the emperor Titus (Joseph. antt. 19, 5, 1; 20, 7, 1 and 3; Tacit. hist. 2, 2 and 81; Suet. Tit. 7): Acts xxv. 13, 23; xxvi. 30. Cf. Hausrath in Schenkel i. p. 396 sq.; [Farrar, St. Paul, ii. 599 sq.].* **959**

Βέροια, -ας, ἡ, (also Βέρροια [i. e. well-watered]), Berœa, a city of Macedonia, near Pella, at the foot of Mount Bermius: Acts xvii. 10, 13.* **960**

Βεροιαῖος, -α, -ον, Berœan: Acts xx. 4.*

[Βηδσαϊδά, given by L mrg. Tr mrg. in Lk. x. 13 where Rec. etc. Βηθσαϊδά, q. v.] **961**

Βηθαβαρά, -ᾶς, [-ρᾶ Rec.bez st, indecl.], ἡ, (בֵּית עֲבָרָה place of crossing, i. e. where there is a crossing or ford, cf. Germ. Furthhausen), Bethabara: Jn. i. 28 Rec. [in Rec.elz of 1st decl., but cf. W. 61 (60)]; see [WH. App. ad loc. and] Βηθανία, 2.* **962**

Βηθανία, -ας, ἡ, (בֵּית עֲנִיָּה house of depression or misery [cf. B.D. Am. ed.]), Bethany; 1. a town or village beyond the Mount of Olives, fifteen furlongs from Jerusalem: Jn. xi. 1, 18; xii. 1; Mt. xxi. 17; xxvi. 6; Lk. xix. 29 [here WH give the accus. -νά (see their App. p. 160), cf. Tr mrg.]; xxiv. 50; Mk. xi. 1, 11 sq.; xiv. 3; now a little Arab hamlet, of from ‘20 to 30 families, called el-'Azirîyeh or el-'Azir (the Arabic name of Lazarus); cf. Robinson i. 431 sq.; [BB.DD. s. v.]. 2. a town or village on the east bank of the Jordan, where John baptized: Jn. i. 28 L T Tr WH, [see the preceding word]. But Origen, although confessing that in his day nearly all the codd. read ἐν Βηθανίᾳ, declares that when he journeyed through those parts he did not find any place of that name, but that Bethabara was pointed out as the place where John had baptized; the statement is confirmed by Eusebius and Jerome also, who were well acquainted with the region. Hence it is most probable that Bethany disappeared after the Apostles' time, and was restored under the name of Bethabara; çf. Lücke ad loc. p. 391 sqq. [Cf. Prof. J. A. Paine in Phila. S. S. Times for Apr. 16, 1881, p. 243 sq.]* **963**

Βηθεσδά, ἡ, indecl., (Chald. חֶסְדָּא בֵּית, i. e. house of mercy, or place for receiving and caring for the sick), Bethesda, the name of a pool near the sheep-gate at Jerusalem, the waters of which had curative powers: Jn. v. 2 [here L mrg. WH mrg. read Βηθσαϊδά, T WH txt. Βηθζαθά (q. v.)]. What locality in the modern city is its representative is not clear; cf. Win. RWB. s. v.; **964**

Arnold in Herzog ii. p. 117 sq.; Robinson i. 330 sq. 342 sq.; [B.D. s. v.; "The Recovery of Jerusalem" (see index)].*

Βηθζαθά, ἡ, (perh. fr. Chald. בֵּית זֵיתָא house of olives; not, as some suppose, בֵּית חֲדָתָא house of newness, Germ. Neuhaus, since it cannot be shown that the Hebr. ח is ever represented by the Grk. ζ), Bethzatha: Jn. v. 2 T [WH txt.] after codd. א L D and other authorities (no doubt a corrupt reading, yet approved by Keim ii. p. 177, [see also WH. App. ad loc.]), for Rec. Βηθεσδά, q. v. [Cf. Kautzsch, Gram. d. Bibl.-Aram. p. 9.]*

965   **Βηθλεέμ**, ἡ, [indecl.], (in Joseph. not only so [antt. 8, 10, 1], but also Βηθλεέμη, -ης, antt. 6, 8, 1; 11, 7; [7, 1, 3]; ἀπὸ Βηθλέμων, 5, 2, 8; ἐκ Βηθλεέμων, 5, 9, 1; [cf. 7, 13; 9, 2]), Bethlehem, (בֵּית לֶחֶם house of bread), a little town, named from the fertility of its soil, six Roman miles south of Jerusalem, now Beit Lachm, with about 3000 [" 5000 ", Baedeker] inhabitants: Mt. ii. 1, 5 sq. 8, 16; Lk. ii. 4, 15; Jn. vii. 42. Cf. Win. RWB. s. v.; Robinson i. p. 470 sqq.; Raumer p. 313 sqq.; Tobler, Bethlehem in Palästina u.s.w. 1849; [Socin (i. e. Baedeker), Hdbk. etc., s. v.; Porter (i. e. Murray) ib.; BB.DD.].*

966   **Βηθσαϊδά** [WH -σαϊδά; see I, ι] and (Mt. xi. 21 R G T WH) -δάν, ἡ, indecl. but with acc. [which may, however, be only the alternate form just given; cf. WH. App. p. 160] Βηθσαϊδάν [B. 17 (16 sq.); Win. 61 (60); Tdf. Proleg. p. 119 sq.], (Syr. ܒܝܬ ܨܝܕܐ i. e. house or place of hunting or fishing), Bethsaida: **1.** a small city (πόλις, Jn. i. 44 (45)) or a village (κώμη, Mk. viii. 22, 23) on the western shore of the Lake of Gennesaret: Jn. i. 44 (45); Mt. xi. 21; Mk. vi. 45; Lk. x. 13 [here L mrg. Tr mrg. Βηθσαϊδά; cf. Tdf. Proleg. u. s.]; Jn. xii. 21 (where τῆς Γαλιλαίας is added).   **2.** a village in lower Gaulanitis on the eastern shore of Lake Gennesaret, not far from the place where the Jordan empties into it. Philip the tetrarch so increased its population that it was reckoned as a city, and was called Julias in honor of Julia, the daughter of the emperor Augustus (Joseph. antt. 18, 2, 1; Plin. h. n. 5, 15). Many think that this city is referred to in Lk. ix. 10, on account of Mk. vi. 32, 45; Jn. vi. 1; others that the Evangelists disagree. Cf. Win. RWB. s. v.; Raumer p. 122 sq.; [BB.DD. s. v.   **3.** In Jn. v. 2 Lchm. mrg. WH mrg. read Βηθσαϊδά; see s. v. Βηθεσδά.]*

967   **Βηθφαγή** [but Lchm. uniformly, Treg. in Mt. and Mk. and R G in Mt. -γῆ (B. 15; W. 52 (51); cf. Tdf. Proleg. p. 103); in Mt. xxi. 1 Tdf. ed. 7 -σφαγή], ἡ, indecl., (fr. בֵּית and פַּג house of unripe figs), Bethphage, the name of a country-seat or hamlet (Euseb. calls it κώμη, Jerome villula), on the Mount of Olives, near Bethany: Mt. xxi. 1; Mk. xi. 1 R G Tr txt. WH txt., but Tr mrg. in br.; Lk. xix. 29. [BB.DD. s. v.]*

968   **βῆμα**, -τος, τό, (fr. ΒΑΩ, βαίνω), [fr. Hom. (h. Merc.), Pind. down];   **1.** a step, pace: βῆμα ποδός (a space which the foot covers, a foot-breadth, Acts vii. 5 (for כַּף־רֶגֶל Deut. ii. 5, cf. Xen. an. 4, 7, 10; Cyr. 7, 5, 6).   **2.** a raised place mounted by steps; a platform, tribune:

used of the official seat of a judge, Mt. xxvii. 19; Jn. xix. 13; Acts xviii. 12, 16 sq.; xxv. 6, 10, [17]; of the judgment-seat of Christ, Ro. xiv. 10 (L T Tr WH τοῦ θεοῦ); 2 Co. v. 10; of the structure, resembling a throne, which Herod built in the theatre at Cæsarea, and from which he used to view the games and make speeches to the people, Acts xii. 21; (of an orator's pulpit, 2 Macc. xiii. 26; Neh. viii. 4. Xen. mem. 3, 6, 1; Hdian. 2, 10, 2 [1 ed. Bekk.]).*

969   **βήρυλλος**, -ου, ὁ, ἡ, beryl, a precious stone of a pale green color (Plin. h. n. 37, 5 (20) [i. e. 37, 79]): Rev. xxi. 20. (Tob. xiii. 17; neut. βηρύλλιον equiv. to שֹׁהַם, Ex. xxviii. 20; xxxvi. 20 (xxxix. 13)). Cf. Win. RWB. s. v. Edelsteine, 11; [esp. Riehm, HWB. ib. 3 and 12].*

970   **βία**, -ας, ἡ;   **1.** strength, whether of body or of mind: Hom. and subseq. writ.   **2.** strength in violent action, force: μετὰ βίας by the use of force, with violence, Acts v. 26; xxiv. 7 [Rec.]; shock τῶν κυμάτων, Acts xxvii. 41 [R G, but Tr txt. br. al. om. τῶν κυμάτων]; διὰ τ. βίαν τοῦ ὄχλου, the crowd pressing on so violently, Acts xxi. 35. [SYN. see δύναμις, fin.]*

971   **βιάζω**: (βία); to use force, to apply force; τινά, to force, inflict violence on, one; the Act. is very rare and almost exclusively poetic, [fr. Hom. down]; Pass. [B. 53 (46)] in Mt. xi. 12 ἡ βασιλεία τ. οὐρ. βιάζεται, the king-dom of heaven is taken by violence, carried by storm, i. e. a share in the heavenly kingdom is sought for with the most ardent zeal and the intensest exertion; cf. Xen. Hell. 5, 2, 15 (23) πόλεις τὰς βεβιασμένας; [but see Weiss, Jas. Morison, Norton, in loc.]. The other explanation: the kingdom of heaven suffereth violence sc. from its ene-mies, agrees neither with the time when Christ spoke the words, nor with the context; cf. Fritzsche, De Wette, Meyer, ad loc. Mid. βιάζομαι foll. by εἴς τι to force one's way into a thing, (ἐς τὴν Ποτίδαιαν, Thuc. 1, 63; ἐς τὸ ἔξω, 7, 69; εἰς τὴν παρεμβολήν, Polyb. 1, 74, 5; εἰς τὸ ἐντός, Philo, vit. Moys. i. § 19; εἰς τὸ στρατόπεδον, Plut. Otho 12, etc.): εἰς τ. βασιλείαν τοῦ θεοῦ, to get a share in the kingdom of God by the utmost earnestness and effort, Lk. xvi. 16.   [COMP.: παραβιάζομαι.]*

972   **βίαιος**, -α, -ον, (βία), violent, forcible: Acts ii. 2 [A. V. mighty]. (In Grk. writ. fr. Hom. down.)*

973   **βιαστής**, -οῦ, ὁ, (βιάζω);   **1.** strong, forceful: Pind. Ol. 9, 114 [75]; Pyth. 4, 420 [236]; but Pind. only uses the form βιατάς, so al.].   **2.** using force, violent: Philo, agric. § 19. In Mt. xi. 12 those are called βιασταί by whom the kingdom of God βιάζεται, i. e. who strive to obtain its privileges with the utmost eagerness and effort.*

974   **βιβλαρίδιον**, -ου, τό, (dimin. of the dimin. βιβλάριον fr. ἡ βίβλος), a little book: Rev. x. 2, 8 [L Tr WH βιβλίον, Tdf. 2 and 7 βιβλιδάριον, q. v.], 9, 10. Not found in prof. auth. [Herm. vis. 2, 4, 3]; cf. W. 96 (91).*

see 974   **βιβλιδάριον**, -ου, τό, (fr. βιβλίδιον, like ἱματιδάριον fr. ἱματίδιον), a little book: Rev. x. 8 Tdf. [edd. 2 and] 7. (Arstph. frag. 596.)*

975   **βιβλίον**, -ου, τό, (dimin. of βίβλος), a small book, a scroll: Lk. iv. 17, 20; Jn. xx. 30; Gal. iii. 10; 2 Tim. iv.

13, etc.; a written document; a sheet on which something has been written, β. ἀποστασίου [bill of divorcement]: Mt. xix. 7; Mk. x. 4; see ἀποστάσιον, 1. βιβλίον ζωῆς, the list of those whom God has appointed to eternal salvation: Rev. xiii. 8 [Rec. τῇ βίβλῳ]; xvii. 8; xx. 12; xxi. 27; see ζωή, 2 b. [From Hdt. down.]

976   βίβλος, -ου, ἡ, (or rather ἡ βύβλος [but the form βίβλ. more com. when it denotes a writing], the plant called papyrus, Theophr. hist. plant. 4, 8, 2 sq.; [Plin. h. n. 13, 11 sq. (21 sq.)]; fr. its bark [rather, the cellular substance of its stem (for it was an endogenous plant)] paper was made [see Tristram, Nat. Hist. etc. p. 433 sq.; esp. Dureau de la Malle in the Mémoires de l'Acad. d. Inscrr. etc. tom. 19 pt. 1 (1851) pp. 140–183, and (in correction of current misapprehensions) Prof. E. Abbot in the Library Journal for Nov. 1878, p. 323 sq., where other reff. are also given]), a written book, a roll or scroll: Mt. i. 1; Lk. iii. 4; Mk. xii. 26; Acts i. 20; τῆς ζωῆς, Phil. iv. 3; Rev. iii. 5, etc.; see βιβλίον. [From Aeschyl. down.]

977   βιβρώσκω: pf. βέβρωκα; to eat: Jn. vi. 13. (In Grk. writ. fr. Hom. down; often in Sept.) *

978   Βιθυνία, -ας, ἡ, Bithynia, a province of Asia Minor, bounded by the Euxine Sea, the Propontis, Mysia, Phrygia, Galatia, Paphlagonia: Acts xvi. 7; 1 Pet. i. 1. [Cf. B. D. s. v.; Dict. of Grk. and Rom. Geog. s. v.; Conybeare and Howson, St. Paul, etc. ch. viii.] *

979   βίος, -ου, ὁ, [fr. Hom. down.] a. life extensively, i. e. the period or course of life [see below and Trench § xxvii.]: Lk. viii. 14; 1 Tim. ii. 2; 2 Tim. ii. 4; 1 Jn. ii. 16; 1 Pet. iv. 3 [Rec.]. b. (as often in Grk. writ. fr. Hes. opp. 230, 575; Hdt., Xen.) that by which life is sustained, resources, wealth, [A. V. living]: Mk. xii. 44; Lk. viii. 43 [WH om. Tr mrg. br. cl.]; xv. 12, 30; xxi. 4; 1 Jn. iii. 17 [goods]. (For לֶחֶם in Prov. xxxi. 14 (xxix. 32).) *

[SYN. βίος, ζωή: ζ. existence (having death as its antithesis); β. the period, means, manner, of existence. Hence the former is more naturally used of animals, the latter of men; cf. zoology, biography. N. T. usage exalts ζωή, and so tends to debase βίος. But see Bp. Lghtft. Ign. ad Rom. 7.]

980   βιόω, -ῶ: 1 aor. inf. βιῶσαι; for which in Attic the 2 aor. inf. βιῶναι is more common, cf. W. 84 (80); [B. 54 (48); Veitch or L. and S. s. v.]; (βίος); [fr. Hom. down]; to spend life, to live: τὸν χρόνον, to pass the time, 1 Pet. iv. 2; (Job xxix. 18; ἡμέρας, Xen. mem. 4, 8, 2). [SYN. see βίος, fin.] *

981   βίωσις, -εως, ἡ, manner of living and acting, way of life: Acts xxvi. 4. (Sir. prolog. 10 διὰ τῆς ἐννόμου βιώσεως; not found in prof. auth.) *

982   βιωτικός, -ή, -όν, pertaining to life and the affairs of this life: Lk. xxi. 34; 1 Co. vi. 3 sq. (The word, not used in Attic, first occurs in Aristot. h. a. 9, 17, 2 [p. 616ᵇ, 27]; χρεῖαι βιωτικαί is often used, as Polyb. 4, 73, 8; Philo, vit. Moys. iii. § 18 fin.; Diod. 2, 29; Artemid. oneir. 1, 31. Cf. Lob. ad Phryn. p. 354 sq.) *

983   βλαβερός, -ά, -όν, (βλάπτω), hurtful, injurious, (Xen. mem. 1, 5, 3 opp. to ὠφέλιμος): 1 Tim. vi. 9 ἐπιθυμίαι

βλαβεραί, cf. ἡδοναὶ βλ. Xen. mem. 1, 3, 11. (Often in Grk. writ. fr. Hom. [i. e. h. Merc. 36 (taken fr. Hes. opp. 365)] down; once in Sept., Prov. x. 26.) *

984   βλάπτω: fut. βλάψω; 1 aor. ἔβλαψα; to hurt, harm, injure: τινά, Mk. xvi. 18; Lk. iv. 35. (Very often in Grk. writ. fr. Hom. down; Tob. xii. 2; 2 Macc. xii. 22, etc.) *

985   βλαστάνω, 3 pers. sing. pres. subj. βλαστᾷ fr. the form βλαστάω, Mk. iv. 27 L T Tr WH (cf. B. 55 (48); [Eccl. ii. 6; Herm. sim. 4, 1 sq.]); 1 aor. ἐβλάστησα (cf. W. 84 (80); [B. l. c.]); 1. intransitively, to sprout, bud, put forth leaves: Mk. iv. 27; Mt. xiii. 26; Heb. ix. 4; (Num. xvii. 8; Joel ii. 22, etc.; in Grk. writ. fr. Pind. down). 2. in later Grk. writ. transitively, to produce: τὸν καρπόν, Jas. v. 18. (Gen. i. 11, etc.) *

986   Βλάστος [i. e. a sprout], -ου, ὁ, Blastus, the chamberlain of king Herod Agrippa I.: Acts xii. 20 [cf. Mey. ad loc.].*

987   βλασφημέω, -ῶ; impf. ἐβλασφήμουν; 1 aor. ἐβλασφήμησα; Pass., [pres. βλασφημοῦμαι]; 1 fut. βλασφημηθήσομαι; (βλάσφημος, q. v.); to speak reproachfully, rail at, revile, calumniate, (Vulg. blasphemo); absol.: Lk. xxii. 65; Acts xiii. 45; xviii. 6; xxvi. 11; 1 Tim. i. 20; 1 Pet. iv. 4; with acc. of pers. or thing (as in later Grk., Joseph., Plut., Appian, etc.): Mt. xxvii. 39; Mk. iii. 28 L T Tr WH; xv. 29; Lk. xxiii. 39; Tit. iii. 2; Jas. ii. 7; Jude 10; with the cognate noun βλασφημίαν, to utter blasphemy (Plat. legg. 7 p. 800 c.; see ἀγαπάω ad fin.), Mk. iii. 28 R G (where L T Tr WH ὅσα for ὅσας, see above); [foll. by ἐν, 2 Pet. ii. 12; cf. Bttm. as at end, and see ἀγνοέω, a.]. Pass. βλασφημοῦμαι to be evil spoken of, reviled, railed at: Ro. iii. 8; xiv. 16; 1 Co. iv. 13 (T WH Tr mrg. δυσφημούμενοι); x. 30; Tit. ii. 5; 2 Pet. ii. 2; τὸ ὄνομά τινος, Ro. ii. 24; 1 Tim. vi. 1. Spec. of those who by contemptuous speech intentionally come short of the reverence due to God or to sacred things (for חָרַף, 2 K. xix. 6, 22 cf. 4; cf. Grimm on 2 Macc. x. 34); absol.: Mt. ix. 3; xxvi. 65; Mk. ii. 7 L T Tr WH; [Jn. x. 36]; τὸν θεόν, Rev. xvi. 11, 21; τὴν θεάν, Acts xix. 37 (G L T Tr WH τὴν θεόν); τὸ ὄνομα τοῦ θεοῦ, Rev. xiii. 6; xvi. 9; τὸ πνεῦμα τοῦ θεοῦ (βλασφημεῖται), 1 Pet. iv. 14 Rec.; δόξας, Jude 8; 2 Pet. ii. 10 (see δόξα, III. 3 b. γ.); εἰς τὸ πνεῦμα τὸ ἅγ. Mk. iii. 29; Lk. xii. 10, (εἰς θεούς, Plat. rep. 2 p. 381 e.). The earlier Grks. say βλασφ. εἴς τινα, περί or κατά τινος; [on the N. T. constructions cf. W. 222 (208); 629 (584); B. 146 (128)].*

988   βλασφημία, -ας, ἡ, railing, reviling, (Vulg. blasphemia); a. univ. slander, detraction, speech injurious to another's good name: Mt. xii. 31; xv. 19; Mk. iii. 28; vii. 22; Eph. iv. 31; Col. iii. 8; 1 Tim. vi. 4; Jude 9 (κρίσις βλασφημίας, i. q. κρίσις βλάσφημος in 2 Pet. ii. 11, a judgment pronounced in reproachful terms); Rev. ii. 9. b. specifically, impious and reproachful speech injurious to the divine majesty: Mt. xxvi. 65; Mk. ii. 7 [R G]; xiv. 64; Lk. v. 21; Jn. x. 33; Rev. xiii. 5 [not Lchm.]; ὄνομα or ὀνόματα βλασφημίας i. q. βλάσφημα (cf. W. § 34, 3 b.; [B. § 132, 10]): Rev. xiii. 1; xvii. 3 [R G Tr, see γέμω]; τοῦ πνεύματος, gen. of obj., Mt. xii. 31; πρὸς τὸν θεόν, Rev. xiii. 6. (Eur., Plat., Dem., al.; for נְאָצָה Ezek. xxxv.

989

12.) [BB.DD. s. v. Blasphemy; *Campbell*, Diss. on the Gospels, diss. ix. pt. ii.] *

βλάσφημος, -ον, (βλάξ sluggish, stupid, and φήμη speech, report, [al. βλάπτω (q. v.) and φ.]), *speaking evil, slanderous, reproachful, railing, abusive* : Acts vi. 11 (ῥήματα βλάσφημα εἰς Μωϋσῆν καὶ τὸν θεόν) ; [vi. 13 Rec. (ῥ. βλ. κατὰ τοῦ τόπου τοῦ ἁγίου)] ; 2 Pet. ii. 11 (see βλασφημία, a.) ; Rev. xiii. 5 [Lchm.] ; βλάσφημος as subst. *a blasphemer* : 1 Tim. i. 13 ; 2 Tim. iii. 2. (Is. lxvi. 3 ; Sap. i. 6 ; Sir. iii. 16 ; 2 Macc. ix. 28 ; [x. 36 (cf. 4)]) ; in Grk. writ. fr. Dem. down.) *

990

βλέμμα, -τος, τό, (βλέπω) ; *a look, glance* : βλέμματι κ. ἀκοῇ *in seeing and hearing*, 2 Pet. ii. 8 [cf. *Warfield* in Presbyt. Rev. for 1883 p. 629 sqq.]. (Eur., Arstph., Dem., Plut., al.) *

991

βλέπω ; [impf. ἔβλεπον] ; fut. βλέψω ; 1 aor. ἔβλεψα ; [pres. pass. βλέπομαι] ; Sept. for רָאָה, פָּנָה, חָזָה, הִבִּיט ; in Grk. writ. fr. Aeschyl. down ; *to see, discern.* **1.** with the b o d i l y eye ; **a.** *to be possessed of sight, have the power of seeing*, opp. to τυφλός : Mt. xii. 22 ; xiii. 16 ; xv. 31 ; Jn. ix. 7, 15, 19, 25 ; Acts ix. 9 ; Ro. xi. 8, 10 ; Rev. iii. 18, etc. (Soph. Oed. Col. 73 ; Arstph. Plut. 15 ; Xen. mem. 1, 3, 4 ; Ael. v. h. 6, 12, etc. Ex. iv. 11 ; xxiii. 8, etc. Tob. xi. 15). τὸ βλέπειν sight, the power of seeing, Lk. vii. 21 (G L T Tr WH om. τό). **b.** to perceive by the use of the eyes, *to see, look, descry* ; **α.** absol. : βλεπόντων αὐτῶν *while they were looking*, Acts i. 9 ; [xxii. 11 Tr mrg. WH mrg.] ; ἔρχου καὶ βλέπε, Rec. in Rev. vi. 1, 3, 5, 7. **β.** with acc. of pers. or thing : Mt. vii. 3 ; xi. 4 ; xxiv. 2 ; Mk. v. 31 ; viii. 23 sq. ; xiii. 2 ; Lk. vi. 41 ; xxiv. 12 [T om. L Tr br. WH reject the vs.] ; Jn. i. 29 ; Acts iv. 14, etc. ; [Rev. xviii. 18 Rec. ὁρῶντες ;] τὴν φωνήν, him who uttered the voice, Rev. i. 12 ; ὅραμα, Acts xii. 9 ; he who has free access to one, as princes, ministers, and personal friends have to a king, is said βλ. τὸ πρόσωπόν τινος (רֹאֵי פְּנֵי הַמֶּלֶךְ), 2 K. xxv. 19 ; Jer. lii. 25 ; Esth. i. 14) ; hence in Mt. xviii. 10 angels of closest access or of highest rank are referred to (see ἀρχάγγελος). Pass. τὰ βλεπόμενα the things that are seen : 2 Co. iv. 18 ; Heb. xi. 3 (L T Tr WH τὸ βλεπόμενον, the sum-total or complex of things seen) ; ἐλπὶς βλεπομένη hope of things that are seen, i. e. that are present, Ro. viii. 24. **c.** to turn the eyes to anything, *to look at, look upon, gaze at* : γυναῖκα, Mt. v. 28 ; εἰς τι or τινα [W. § 33 g.], Lk. ix. 62 ; Jn. xiii. 22 ; Acts iii. 4 ; εἰς τὸν οὐρανόν, Acts i. 11 T Tr WH ; in the sense of *looking into* (i. e. in order to read), βιβλίον, Rev. v. 3 sq. **d.** univ. *to perceive by the senses, to feel* : τὸν ἄνεμον ἰσχυρόν [T WH om. ἰσχ.], Mt. xiv. 30, (κτύπον δέδορκα, Aeschyl. sept. 104). **e.** *to discover by use, to know by experience* : τί, Ro. vii. 23 ; foll. by ὅτι, 2 Co. vii. 8 ; by attract. τὸ θηρίον, ὅτι κτλ. Rev. xvii. 8 ; ὑπὲρ ὃ βλέπει με for ὑπὲρ τοῦτο, ὃ βλέπει με ὄντα, lest he think me greater than on personal knowledge he finds me to be, 2 Co. xii. 6. **2.** metaph. to see with the m i n d 's eye ; **a.** *to have* (the power of) *understanding* : βλέποντες οὐ βλέπουσι, though endued with understanding they do not understand, Mt. xiii. 13 ; Lk. viii. 10. **b.** *to discern mentally, observe, perceive, discover, understand* ; absol. : δι' ἐσόπτρου, 1 Co. xiii. 12 ; of

the omniscient God βλέπων ἐν τῷ κρυπτῷ *seeing in secret*, where man sees nothing, Mt. vi. 4, 6, 18 [here L T Tr WH βλ. ἐν τ. κρυφαίῳ] ; ἐγγίζουσαν τὴν ἡμέραν, Heb. x. 25 (fr. certain external signs) ; Ἰησοῦν . . . ἐστεφανωμένον, we see (from his resurrection and from the effects and witness of the Holy Spirit) Jesus crowned, Heb. ii. 9 ; foll. by ὅτι, Heb. iii. 19 ; Jas. ii. 22. **c.** *to turn the thoughts* or *direct the mind to* a thing, *to consider, contemplate, look :ο ;* absol. βλέπετε take heed : Mk. xiii. 23, 33 ; with an acc. of the thing or pers., 1 Co. i. 26 ; x. 18 ; 2 Co. x. 7 ; Phil. iii. 2 ; Col. ii. 5 ; foll. by πῶς with indic. [W. 300 (282) ; B. 255 (219)], Lk. viii. 18 ; 1 Co. iii. 10 ; Eph. v. 15 ; *to weigh carefully, examine*, foll. by interrog. τί with indic. Mk. iv. 24 ; εἰς πρόσωπόν τινος, *to look at* i. e. have regard to one's external condition, —used of those who are influenced by partiality : Mt. xxii. 16 ; Mk. xii. 14. By a use not found in Grk. auth. ἑαυτὸν βλέπειν *to look to one's self* (i. q. *sibi cavere*) : Mk. xiii. 9 ; foll. by ἵνα μή [cf. B. 242 (209)], 2 Jn. 8 ; βλέπειν ἀπό τινος (i. q. *sibi cavere ab aliquo*) *to beware of* one [W. 223 (209), cf. 39 (38) ; B. 242 (209), cf. 323 (278)], Mk. viii. 15 ; xii. 38 ; *look to* in the sense of *providing, taking care* : foll. by ἵνα, 1 Co. xvi. 10 ; foll. by μή with subj. aor., Mt. xxiv. 4 ; Mk. xiii. 5 ; Lk. xxi. 8 ; Acts xiii. 40 ; 1 Co. viii. 9 (μήπως) ; x. 12 ; Gal. v. 15 ; Heb. xii. 25 ; foll. by μή with fut. indic., Col. ii. 8 ; Heb. iii. 12. The Grks. say ὁρᾶν μή, etc. [cf. W. 503 (468 sq.) ; B. 242 sq. (209)]. **3.** in a geographical sense, like Lat. *specto* [Eng. *look*], of places, mountains, buildings, etc., turned towards any quarter, as it were *facing* it : foll. by κατά with acc., Acts xxvii. 12 [cf. B. D. Am. ed. s. v. Phenice], (Sept. [Num. xxi. 20] ; Ezek. xi. 1 ; [xliv. 1 ; xlvii. 1] ; πρός, Xen. Hell. 7, 1, 17 ; mem. 3, 8, 9 ; Hdian. 6, 5, 2 ; Diog. Laërt. 1, 2, 48 ; Sept. Ezek. ix. 2 ; xl. 24 ; [xlvi. 1] ; εἰς, viii. 3, etc. [for other exx. see *Soph.* Lex. s. v.]). [SYN. see s. v. ὁράω. COMP. : ἀνα-, ἀπο-, δια-, ἐμ-, ἐπι-, περι-, προ-βλέπω.]

992

βλητέος, -α, -ον, (βάλλω), *which must be thrown* or *put*, (see βάλλω, 2) ; found only in neut. : Mk. ii. 22 (WH T om. Tr br.) ; Lk. v. 38 βλητέον ἐστί foll. by acc. τὸν οἶνον, cf. Matth. § 447, 3 a. ; [B. 190 (165)]. (Besides only in Basil i. p. 137 c. ed. Benedict.) *

993

Βοανεργές ([RG, so Suid. (ed. Gaisf. 751 a.) ; but] L T Tr WH Βοανηργές), *Boanerges*, Hebr. רְגֶשׁ בְּנֵי i. e. sons of thunder (as Mark himself explains it), [the name given by our Lord to James and John the sons of Zebedee] : Mk. iii. 17 ; בְּ pronounced Boa as Noabhyim for Nebhyim ; see *Lghtft.* Horae Hebr. ad loc. ; רְגֶשׁ, in Ps. lv. 15 *a tumultuous crowd*, seems in Syriac to have signified *thunder* ; so that the name Βοανηργές seems to denote fiery and destructive zeal that may be likened to a thunder-storm, and to make reference to the occurrence narrated in Lk. ix. 54. [Cf. Dr. Jas. Morison's Com. on Mk. l. c. ; *Kautzsch*, Gram. d. Bibl.-Aram. p. 9.] *

994

βοάω, -ῶ ; [impf. ἐβόων Acts xxi. 34 Rec.] ; 1 aor. ἐβόησα ; (βοή) ; fr. Hom. down ; in Sept. mostly for קָרָא, זָעַק, צָעַק, *to cry aloud, shout*, (Lat. *boo*) ; **1.** *to raise a cry* : of joy, Gal. iv. 27 (fr. Is. liv. 1) ; of pain,

Mt. xxvii. 46 L mrg. Tr WH; Acts viii. 7. **2.** *to cry*
i. e. *speak with a high, strong voice*: Mt. iii. 3, Mk. i. 3, Lk.
iii. 4, Jn. i. 23, (all fr. Is. xl. 3); Mk. xv. 34; Lk. ix. 38
(R G ἀναβ.); [xviii. 38]; Acts xvii. 6; xxi. 34 Rec.;
xxv. 24 (R G ἐπιβ.). **3.** πρός τινα *to cry to one for
help, implore his aid*: Lk. xviii. 7 [T Tr WH αὐτῷ; cf.
W. 212 (199)], (1 S. vii. 8; 1 Chr. v. 20; Hos. vii. 14,
etc. for אֶל זָעַק). [Comp. : ἀνα-, ἐπι-βοάω.] *

[Syn. βοάω, καλέω, κράζω, κραυγάζω: It is not un-
instructive to notice that in classic usage καλεῖν denotes
'to cry out' for a purpose, *to call*; βοᾶν to cry out as a manifestation of feeling; κράζειν to cry out harshly, often of
an inarticulate and brutish sound; thus καλεῖν suggests intelligence; βοᾶν sensibilities; κράζειν instincts;
hence, βοᾶν esp. a cry for help. κραυγάζειν, intensive of
κράζω, denotes to cry coarsely, in contempt, etc. Cf. Schmidt
ch. 3.]

(994α)
see 1003 ⟶ Βοές, ὁ, Mt. i. 5 T WH, for Rec. Βοόζ, q. v.

995 βοή, -ῆς, ἡ, *a cry*: Jas. v. 4 (of those imploring vengeance). From Hom. down.*

996 βοήθεια, -ας, ἡ, (see βοηθέω), *help*: Heb. iv. 16, (often
in Sept., chiefly for עֶזְרָה and עֵזֶר; in Grk. writ. fr.
Thuc. and Xen. down); plur. *helps*: Acts xxvii. 17
[see Hackett ad loc.; B.D. s. v. Ship 4; *Smith*, Voyage
and Shipwr. of St. Paul, pp. 106 sq. 204 sq.; cf. ὑποζών-
νυμι].*

997 βοη-θέω, -ῶ; 1 aor. ἐβοήθησα; (fr. βοή a cry and θέω
to run); in Sept. chiefly for עֵזֶר; in Grk. writ. fr.
[Aeschyl. and] Hdt. down; prop. *to run to the cry* (of
those in danger); hence univ. *to help, succor, bring aid*:
τινί, Mt. xv. 25; Mk. ix. 22, 24 (βοήθει μου τῇ ἀπιστίᾳ,
"quod fiduciae meae deest bonitate tua supple," Grotius); Acts xvi. 9; xxi. 28; 2 Co. vi. 2; Heb. ii. 18;
Rev. xii. 16.*

998 βοηθός, -όν, *helping*, (νῆες, Hdt. 5, 97; στήριγμα, Tob.
viii. 6); mostly as subst. [so fr. Hdt. down] *a helper*:
Heb. xiii. 6 (of God, fr. Ps. cxvii. (cxviii.) 7, as often
in Sept.).*

999 βόθυνος, -ου, ὁ, *a pit, a ditch*: Mt. xii. 11; xv. 14; Lk.
vi. 39. (Solon in Bekker's Anecd. i. 85; Xen. oec. 19,
3; Theophr. hist. pl. 4, 2, 2 [(var.); al.]; Sept. 2 S.
xviii. 17, etc.) *

1000 βολή, -ῆς, ἡ, (βάλλω), *a throw*: ὡσεὶ λίθου βολήν *about
a stone's throw*, as far as a stone can be cast by the hand,
Lk. xxii. 41, (ὡσεὶ τόξου βολήν, Gen. xxi. 16; μέχρι λίθου
κ. ἀκοντίου βολῆς, Thuc. 5, 65; ἐξ ἀκοντίου βολῆς, Xen.
Hell. 4, 5, 15).*

1001 βολίζω: 1 aor. ἐβόλισα; (βολίς a missile, dart; a line
and plummet with which mariners sound the depth of
the sea, a sounding-lead); *to heave the lead, take sound-
ings*: Acts xxvii. 28. (Besides only in Eustath.; [Mid.
intrans. *to sink* in water, Geopon. 6, 17].) *

1002 βολίς, -ίδος, ἡ, (βάλλω), *a missile, dart, javelin*: Heb.
xii. 20 Rec. fr. Ex. xix. 13. (Neh. iv. 17; Num. xxiv.
8; [Sap. v. 22]; Hab. iii. 11]; Plut. Demetr. 3.) *

1003 Βοόζ, ὁ, (בֹּעַז fleetness [but see B.D. Am. ed.]), *Booz*,
[more commonly] *Boaz*, a kinsman of Ruth, afterwards
her (second) husband, (Ruth ii. 1 sqq.; 1 Chr. ii. 11):

Mt. i. 5 [Βοός L Tr, Βοές T WH]; Lk. iii. 32 [L T Tr
WH Βοός].*

1004 βόρβορος, -ου, ὁ, *dung, mire*: 2 Pet. ii. 22. (Sept.;
Aeschyl., Arstph., Plat., sqq.; ἐν βορβόρῳ κυλίεσθαι, of
the vicious, Epict. diss. 4, 11, 29.) *

1005 βορρᾶς, -ᾶ [W. § 8, 1; B. 20 (18)], ὁ, (equiv. to
βορέας, -έου), often [in Attic writ.], in Sept. for צָפוֹן;
1. *Boreas; the north-north-east wind*. **2.** *the north*:
Lk. xiii. 29; Rev. xxi. 13, [cf. W. 121 (115) s. v. με-
σημβρία].*

1006 βόσκω; as in Grk. writ. fr. Hom. down, *to feed*: Mk.
v. 14; Lk. xv. 15; ἀρνία, πρόβατα, Jn. xxi. 15, 17, (in a
fig. disc. portraying the duty of a Christian teacher to
promote in every way the spiritual welfare of the members of the church); ὁ βόσκων a herdsman: Mt. viii. 33;
Lk. viii. 34. In Pass. and Mid. [pres. ptcp. βοσκόμενος,
cf. W. § 38, 2 note] of flocks or herds, *to feed, graze*:
Mt. viii. 30; Mk. v. 11; Lk. viii. 32. (In Sept. for
רָעָה.) *

[Syn. βόσκειν, ποιμαίνειν: π. is the wider, β. the narrower term; the former includes oversight, the latter denotes nourishment; π. may be rendered *tend*, β. specifically
feed. See Trench § xxv.; Mey. on Jn. u. s.; Schmidt ch. 200.]

1007 Βοσόρ, ὁ, (בְּעוֹר a torch, a lamp; Sept. Βεώρ, Num.
xxii. 5; xxxi. 8; Deut. xxiii. 4; by change of ע into σ,
Βοσόρ), *Bosor*, the father of Balaam: 2 Pet. ii. 15 [WH
txt. Βεώρ].*

1008 βοτάνη, -ης, ἡ, (βόσκω), *an herb fit for fodder, green
herb, growing plant*: Heb. vi. 7. (Hom., Pind., Plat.,
Eur., Diod., Ael., al. Sept. for עֵשֶׂב, חָצִיר, דֶּשֶׁא. [Met-
aph. of men, Ignat. ad Eph. 10, 3; ad Trall. 6, 1; ad
Philad. 3, 1].) *

1009 βότρυς, -υος, ὁ, *a bunch* ο. *cluster of grapes*: Rev. xiv.
18 [cf. B. 14 (13)]. (Gen. xl. 10; Num. xiii. 24 sq.
Grk. writ. fr. Hom. down.) *

1010 βουλευτής, -οῦ, ὁ, *a councillor, senator*, (buleuta, Plin.
epp.): first in Hom. Il. 6, 114; of a member of the
Sanhedrin, Mk. xv. 43; Lk. xxiii. 50. (Job iii. 14;
xii. 17.) *

1011 βουλεύω: **1.** *to deliberate, take counsel, resolve, give
counsel*, (Is. xxiii. 8; [fr. Hom. down]). **2.** *to be a
councillor or senator, discharge the office of a senator*:
Xen. mem. 1, 1, 18; Plat. Gorg. p. 473 e.; [al.]. In the
N. T. Mid., [pres. βουλεύομαι; impf. ἐβουλευόμην; fut.
βουλεύσομαι, Lk. xiv. 31 L mrg. T WH; 1 aor. ἐβουλευσά-
μην]; **1.** *to deliberate with one's self, consider*: foll.
by εἰ, Lk. xiv. 31, (Xen. mem. 3, 6, 8). **2.** *to take
counsel, resolve*: foll. by inf., Acts v. 33 [RG T Tr
mrg.]; xv. 37 [Rec.]; xxvii. 39; τί, 2 Co. i. 17; foll.
by ἵνα, Jn. xi. 53 L T Tr txt. WH; xii. 10 [cf. W. § 38,
3]. [Comp. : παρα- (-μαι), συμ-βουλεύω.] *

1012 βουλή, -ῆς, ἡ, (βούλομαι), fr. Hom. down; often in
Sept. for עֵצָה; *counsel, purpose*: Lk. xxiii. 51 (where
distinguished fr. ἡ πρᾶξις); Acts v. 38; xxvii. 12 (see
τίθημι, 1 a.), 42; plur. 1 Co. iv. 5; ἡ βουλὴ τοῦ θεοῦ, Acts
xiii. 36; esp. of the purpose of God respecting the salvation of men through Christ: Lk. vii. 30; Acts ii. 23;
iv. 28; [Heb. vi. 17]; πᾶσαν τὴν βουλὴν τοῦ θεοῦ all the

contents of the divine plan, Acts xx. 27; ἡ βουλὴ τοῦ θελήματος αὐτοῦ the counsel of his will, Eph. i. 11.*

1013 βούλημα, -τος, τό, (βούλομαι), will, counsel, purpose: Acts xxvii. 43; Ro. ix. 19; 1 Pet. iv. 3 (Rec. θέλημα). (2 Macc. xv. 5; in Grk. writ. fr. Plat. down.) [SYN. cf. θέλω, fin.]*

1014 βούλομαι, 2 pers. sing. βούλει Lk. xxii. 42 (Attic for βούλῃ, cf. W. § 13, 2 a.; B. 42 (37)); impf. ἐβουλόμην (Attic [(cf. Veitch), yet commonly] ἠβουλόμην); 1 aor. ἐβουλήθην (Mt. i. 19) and ἠβουλήθην (2 Jn. 12 R G; but al. ἐβουλήθ. cf. [WH. App. p. 162]; W. § 12, 1 c.; B. 33 (29)); Sept. for אָבָה, חָפֵץ; [fr. Hom. down]; to will, wish; and   1. commonly, to will deliberately, have a purpose, be minded: foll. by an inf., Mk. xv. 15; Acts v. 28, 33 (L WH Tr txt. for R G T ἐβουλεύοντο); xii. 4; xv. 37 (L T Tr WH for R ἐβουλεύσατο); xviii. 27; xix. 30; xxii. 30; xxiii. 28; xxvii. 43; xxviii. 18; 2 Co. i. 15; Heb. vi. 17; 2 Jn. 12; 3 Jn. 10 (τοὺς βουλομένους sc. ἐπιδέχεσθαι τοὺς ἀδελφούς); Jude 5; Jas. i. 18 (βουληθεὶς ἀπεκύησεν ἡμᾶς of his own free will he brought us forth, with which will it ill accords to say, as some do, that they are tempted to sin by God). with an acc. of the obj. τοῦτο, 2 Co. i. 17 (L T Tr WH for R βουλευόμενος); foll. by an acc. with inf. 2 Pet. iii. 9. of the will electing or choosing between two or more things, answering to the Lat. placet mihi: Mt. i. 19 (cf. ἐνθυμεῖσθαι, 20); xi. 27 [not L mrg.]; Lk. x. 22; xxii. 42; Acts xxv. 20; [1 Co. xii. 11]; Jas. iii. 4; iv. 4; foll. by the subj. βούλεσθε, ὑμῖν ἀπολύσω; is it your will I should release unto you? (cf. W. § 41 a. 4 b.; B. § 139, 2), Jn. xviii. 39. of the will prescribing, foll. by an acc. with inf.: Phil. i. 12 (γινώσκειν ὑμᾶς βούλομαι I would have you know, know ye); 1 Tim. ii. 8; v. 14; Tit. iii. 8.   2. of willing as an affection, to desire: foll. by an inf., 1 Tim. vi. 9 (οἱ βουλόμενοι πλουτεῖν); Acts xvii. 20; xviii. 15; ἐβουλόμην (on this use of the impf. see B. 217 (187) sq.; [cf. W. 283 (266); Bp. Lghtft. on Philem. 13]), Acts xxv. 22; Philem. 13. On the difference between βούλομαι and θέλω, see θέλω, fin.*

1015 βουνός, -οῦ, ὁ, a Cyrenaic word acc. to Hdt. 4, 199, which Eustath. [831, 33] on Il. 11, 710 says was used by Philemon [Noθ. 1], a comic poet (of the 3d cent. B. C.). It was rejected by the Atticists, but from Polyb. on [who (5, 22, 1 sq.) uses it interchangeably with λόφος] it was occasionally received by the later Grk. writ. (Strabo, Pausan., Plut., al.); in Sept. very often for נִבְעָה; (perh. fr. ΒΑΩ to ascend [cf. Hesych. βουνοί· βωμοί, and βωμίδες in Hdt. 2, 125 (Schmidt ch. 99, 11)]); a hill, eminence, mound: Lk. iii. 5 (Is. xl. 4); xxiii. 30 (Hos. x. 8). Cf. Sturz, De dial. Maced. etc. p. 153 sq.; Lob. ad Phryn. p. 355 sq.; [Donaldson, New Crat. § 469].*

1016 βοῦς, βοός, acc. sing. βοῦν, [acc. plur. βόας, B. 14 (13)], ὁ, ἡ, an ox, a cow: Lk. xiii. 15; xiv. 5, 19; Jn. ii. 14 sq.; 1 Co. ix. 9; 1 Tim. v. 18. [From Hom. down.]*

1017 βραβεῖον, -ου, τό, (βραβεύς the arbiter and director of a contest, who awards the prize; called also βραβευτής, Lat. designator), the award to the victor in the games, a prize, (in eccl. Lat. brabeum, brabium), (Vulg. bravium):

1 Co. ix. 24; metaph. of the heavenly reward for Christian character, Phil. iii. 14. (Oppian, cyn. 4, 197; Lycophr. 1154; ὑπομονῆς βρ. Clem. Rom. 1 Cor. 5, 5 [where see Lghtft., Gebh. and Harn.]; ἀφθαρσίας, Mart. Polyc. 17.) *

1018 βραβεύω; in Grk. writ. fr. Isoc. and Dem. down;   1. to be a βραβεύς or umpire (see βραβεῖον).   2. to decide, determine.   3. to direct, control, rule: Col. iii. 15 [where see Meyer; contra, Bp. Lghtft. COMP.: κατα-βραβεύω.]*

1019 βραδύνω; (βραδύς); to delay, be slow;   1. rarely trans. to render slow, retard: τὴν σωτηρίαν, Sept. Is. xlvi. 13; pass. ὁδός, Soph. El. 1501 [cf. O. C. 1628]. Mostly   2. intrans. to be long, to tarry, loiter, (so fr. Aeschyl. down): 1 Tim. iii. 15; unusually, with gen. of the thing which one delays to effect, 2 Pet. iii. 9 τῆς ἐπαγγελίας [A. V. is not slack concerning his promise] i. e. to fulfil his promise; cf. W. § 30, 6 b. (Sir. xxxii. (xxxv.) 22.)*

1020 βραδυπλοέω, -ῶ; (βραδύς and πλοῦς); to sail slowly: pres. ptcp. in Acts xxvii. 7. (Artem. oneir. 4, 30.) *

1021 βραδύς -εῖα, -ύ, slow;   a. prop.: εἴς τι, Jas. i. 19.   b. metaph. dull, inactive, in mind; stupid, slow to apprehend or believe, (so Hom. Il. 10, 226; opp. to συνετός, Polyb. 4, 8, 7; τὸν νοῦν, Dion. Hal. de Att. oratt. 7 [de Lys. judic.]; δυσμαθία· βραδυτὴς ἐν μαθήσει, Plat. defin. p. 415 e.): with a dat. of respect, τῇ καρδίᾳ, Lk. xxiv. 25. [SYN. see ἀργός, fin.] *

1022 βραδυτής (on accent cf. Bttm. Ausf. Spr. ii. p. 417 sq.; [Chandler §§ 634, 635; W. 52 sq. (52)]), -ῆτος, ἡ, (βραδύς), slowness, delay: 2 Pet. iii. 9. (From Hom. down.) *

1023 βραχίων, -ονος, ὁ, [fr. Hom. down], the arm: the βραχίων of God is spoken of Hebraistically for the might, the power of God, Lk. i. 51 (cf. Deut. iv. 34; v. 15; xxvi. 8); Jn. xii. 38 (Is. liii. 1); Acts xiii. 17.*

1024 βραχύς, -εῖα, -ύ, short, small, little, (fr. Pind., Hdt., Thuc. down);   a. of place; neut. βραχύ adverbially, a short distance, a little: Acts xxvii. 28 (2 S. xvi. 1; Thuc. 1, 63).   b. of time; βραχύ τι a short time, for a little while: Heb. ii. 7, 9, (where the writer transfers to time what the Sept. in Ps. viii. 6 says of rank); Acts v. 34 [here L T Tr WH om. τι]; μετὰ βραχύ shortly after, Lk. xxii. 58.   c. of quantity and measure; βραχύ τι [Tr txt. WH om. L Tr mrg. br. τι] some little part, a little: Jn. vi. 7 (βραχύ τι τοῦ μέλιτος, 1 S. xiv. 29; ἔλαιον βραχύ, Joseph. antt. 9, 4, 2; βραχύτατος λιβανωτός, Philo de vict. off. § 4); διὰ βραχέων in few sc. words, briefly, Heb. xiii. 22 (so [Plat., Dem., al. (cf. Bleek on Heb. l. c.)] Joseph. b. j. 4, 5, 4; ἐν βραχυτάτῳ δηλοῦν to show very briefly, Xen. Cyr. 1, 2, 15).*

1025 βρέφος, -ους, τό;   a. an unborn child, embryo, fœtus: Lk. i. 41, 44; (Hom. Il. 23, 266; Plut. rep. Stoic. 41 τὸ βρ. ἐν τῇ γαστρί).   b. a new-born child, an infant, a babe, (so fr. Pind. down): Lk. ii. 12, 16; xviii. 15; Acts vii. 19; 1 Pet. ii. 2; ἀπὸ βρέφους from infancy, 2 Tim. iii. 15 (so ἐκ βρέφους, Anth. Pal. 9, 567).*

1026 βρέχω; 1 aor. ἔβρεξα; fr. Pind. and Hdt. down;   1. to moisten, wet, water: Lk. vii. 38 (τ. πόδας δάκρυσι, cf. Ps. vi. 7), 44.   2. in later writ. (cf. Lob. ad Phryn. p. 291 [W. 23]) to water with rain (Polyb. 16, 12, 3), to cause to rain, to pour the rain, spoken of God : ἐπί τινα, Mt. v. 45 ; to send down like rain : κύριος ἔβρεξε θεῖον κ. πῦρ, Gen. xix. 24 ; χάλαζαν, Ex. ix. 23 ; [μάννα, Ps. lxxvii. (lxxviii.) 24] ; impers. βρέχει it rains (cf. W. § 58, 9 b. β.) : Jas. v. 17 ; with added acc., πῦρ κ. θεῖον, Lk. xvii. 29 ; with added subject, ὑετός, Rev. xi. 6.*

1027 βροντή, -ῆς, ἡ, thunder : Mk. iii. 17 (on which see Βοανεργές) ; Jn. xii. 29 ; Rev. iv. 5 ; vi. 1 ; viii. 5 ; x. 3 sq. ; xi. 19 ; xiv. 2 ; xvi. 18 ; xix. 6. [From Hom. down.]*

1028 βροχή, -ῆς, ἡ, (βρέχω, q. v.), a later Grk. word (cf. Lob. ad Phryn. p. 291), a besprinkling, watering, rain : used of a heavy shower or violent rainstorm, Mt. vii. 25, 27 ; Ps. lxvii. (lxviii.) 10 ; civ. (cv.) 32, for גֶּשֶׁם.*

1029 βρόχος, -ου, ὁ, a noose, slip-knot, by which any person or thing is caught, or fastened, or suspended, (fr. Hom. down) : βρόχον ἐπιβάλλειν τινί to throw a noose upon one, a fig. expression borrowed from war [or the chase] (so βρ. περιβάλλειν τινί, Philo, vit. Moys. iii. § 34 ; Joseph. b. j. 7, 7, 4), i. e. by craft or by force to bind one to some necessity, to constrain him to obey some command, 1 Co. vii. 35.*

1030 βρυγμός, -οῦ, ὁ, (βρύχω, q. v.), a gnashing of teeth : with τῶν ὀδόντων added, a phrase denoting the extreme anguish and utter despair of men consigned to eternal condemnation, Mt. viii. 12 ; xiii. 42, 50 ; xxii. 13 ; xxiv. 51 ; xxv. 30 ; Lk. xiii. 28. (In Sir. li. 3 βρυγμός is attributed to beasts, which gnash the teeth as they attack their prey ; in Prov. xix. 12 Sept. for נַהַם snarling, growling ; in the sense of biting, Nic. th. 716, to be derived fr. βρύκω to bite ; cf. Fritzsche on Sir. as above, p. 308.)*

1031 βρύχω : [impf. ἔβρυχον] ; to grind, gnash, with the teeth : ὀδόντας ἐπί τινα, Acts vii. 54, (Job xvi. 9 ; Ps. xxxiv. (xxxv.) 16 ; xxxvi. (xxxvii.) 12 for חָרַק בְּשִׁנַּיִם and חָרַק שֵׁנַּיִם ; intrans. without ὀδόντας, [Hermipp. ap.] Plut. Pericl. 33 fin. ; [Hipp. (see L. and S.)]). Of the same origin as βρύκω (cf. δέχω and δέκω), to bite, chew ; see Hermann on Soph. Philoct. 735 ; [Ellendt, Lex. Soph. s. v. βρύκω].*

1032 βρύω ; 1. intrans. to abound, gush forth, teem with juices, ([akin to βλύω, φλύω ; see Lob. Techn. p. 22 sq. ; Curtius p. 531], cf. Germ. Brust, Brühe) ; often so fr. Hom. down (Il. 17, 56 ἔρνος ἄνθεϊ βρύει). 2. more rarely trans. to send forth abundantly : absol. to teem, ἡ γῆ βρύει, Xen. venat. 5, 12 ; with an acc. of flowers, fruits, Χάριτες ῥόδα βρύουσι, Anacr. 44, 2 (37, 2) ; to send forth water, Jas. iii. 11.*

1033 βρῶμα, -τος, τό, (βρόω i. q. βιβρώσκω), that which is eaten, food ; (fr. Thuc. and Xen. down) : 1 Co. viii. 8, 13 ; x. 3 ; Ro. xiv. 15, 20 ; plur. : Mt. xiv. 15 ; Mk. vii. 19 ; Lk. iii. 11 ; ix. 13 ; 1 Co. vi. 13 ; 1 Tim. iv. 3 ; Heb. xiii. 9 ; βρώματα κ. πόματα meats and drinks, Heb. ix. 10 (as in Plat. legg. 11 p. 932 e. ; 6 p. 782 a. ; Critias p. 115 b. ; in sing. Xen. Cyr. 5, 2, 17). of the soul's aliment, i. e. either instruction, 1 Co. iii. 2 (as solid food opp. to τὸ

γάλα), or that which delights and truly satisfies the mind, Jn. iv. 34.*

1034 βρώσιμος, -ον, (βρῶσις), eatable : Lk. xxiv. 41. (Lev. xix. 23 ; Ezek. xlvii. 12. Aeschyl. Prom. 479 ; [Antiatt. in Bekker, Anecd. p. 84, 25].)*

1035 βρῶσις, -εως, ἡ, (βρόω, βιβρώσκω) ; 1. the act of eating, (Tertull. esus) : βρῶσις κ. πόσις, Ro. xiv. 17 (on which see βασιλεία, 3) ; with gen. of the obj. 1 Co. viii. 4 (Plat. de rep. 10 p. 619 c. παίδων αὑτοῦ) ; in a wider sense, corrosion : Mt. vi. 19 sq. 2. as almost everywhere in Grk. writ. that which is eaten, food, aliment : Heb. xii. 16 ; εἰς βρῶσιν for food, 2 Co. ix. 10 (Sap. iv. 5) ; βρῶσις καὶ [so WH txt. Tr mrg. ; al. ἢ] πόσις, Col. ii. 16, (Hom. Od. 1, 191 ; Plat. legg. 6, 783 c. ; Xen. mem. 1, 3, 15 ; [cf. Fritzsche on Rom. iii. p. 200 note ; per contra Mey. or Ellic. on Col. l. c.]). used of the soul's aliment — either that which refreshes it, Jn. iv. 32, or nourishes and supports it unto life eternal, Jn. vi. 27, 55.*

βρώσκω, unused pres. whence pf. βέβρωκα ; see βι-   **see 977**
βρώσκω.

1036 βυθίζω ; [pres. pass. βυθίζομαι] ; (βυθός, q. v.) ; to plunge into the deep, to sink : ὥστε βυθίζεσθαι αὐτά, of ships (as Polyb. 2, 10, 5 ; 16, 3, 2 ; [Aristot., Diod., al.]), so that they began to sink, Lk. v. 7 ; metaph. τινὰ εἰς ὄλεθρον [A. V. drown], 1 Tim. vi. 9.*

1037 βυθός, -οῦ, ὁ, the bottom (of a ditch or trench, Xen. oec. 19, 11) ; the bottom or depth of the sea, often in Grk. writ. fr. Aeschyl. Prom. 432 down ; the sea itself, the deep sea : 2 Co. xi. 25, as in Ps. cvi. (cvii.) 24 ; so Lat. profundum in Lucan, Phars. 2, 680 "profundi ora videns."*

1038 βυρσεύς, -έως, ὁ, (βύρσα a skin stripped off, a hide), a tanner : Acts ix. 43 ; x. 6, 32. (Artem. oneir. 4, 56.) [Cf. B.D. Am. ed. s. v. Tanner.]*

1039 βύσσινος, -η, -ον, (ἡ βύσσος, q. v. ; cf. ἀκάνθινος, ἀμαράντινος), made of fine linen ; neut. βύσσινον sc. ἱμάτιον (W. 591 (550) ; [B. 82 (72)]), (a) fine linen (garment) : Rev. xviii. 12 (Rec. βύσσου), 16 ; xix. 8, 14 [WH mrg. λευκοβύσσινον (for βύσσινον λευκόν)]. (Gen. xli. 42 ; 1 Chr. xv. 27. Aeschyl., Hdt., Eur., Diod. 1, 85 ; Plut., al.)*

1040 βύσσος, -ου, ἡ, [Vaniček, Fremdwörter, s. v.], byssus, a species of Egyptian flax (found also in India and Achaia) — or linen made from it — very costly, delicate, soft, white, and also of a yellow color, (see respecting it Pollux, onomast. l. 7 c. 17 § 75) : Lk. xvi. 19 ; Rev. xviii. 12 Rec. (In Sept. generally for שֵׁשׁ, also בּוּץ, cf. 1 Chr. xv. 27 ; 2 Chr. v. 12 ; cf. Win. RWB. s. v. Baumwolle ; [BB.DD. s. vv. Byssus and Linen]. Joseph. antt. 3, 6, 1 sq. ; 3, 7, 2 ; Philostr. vit. Apoll. 2, 20 [p. 71 ed. Olear.] ; on the flax of Achaia growing about Elis, cf. Pausan. 5, 5, 2 ; 7, 21, 7.)*

1041 βωμός, -οῦ, ὁ, (see βουνός), an elevated place ; very freq. in Grk. writ. fr. Hom. down, a raised place on which to offer sacrifice, an altar : Acts xvii. 23. (Often in Sept. for מִזְבֵּחַ.)*

Γ

Γαββαθᾶ 1042   1049 γαζοφυλάκιον

1042 Γαββαθᾶ [-θά WH], ἡ, indecl., *Gabbatha*, Chald. גַּבְּתָא, (Hebr. גַב the back); hence *a raised place, an elevation*, (cf. *C. F. A. Fritzsche*, Ueber die Verdienste Tholucks u.s.w. p. 102 sq.; *Delitzsch* in the Zeitschr. f. luth. Theol. for 1876, p. 605; [*Wünsche*, Neue Beiträge u.s.w. p. 560]; but see the somewhat diff. opinion of *Keim*, Jesu von Nazara, iii. 365): Jn. xix. 13, where is added the rather loose interpretation λιθόστρωτον, i. e. *a stone pavement*, which some interpreters think was a portable pavement, or the square blocks such as the Roman generals carried with them, to be laid down not only under their seats in general, but also under those they occupied in administering justice (cf. Suet. Jul. Caes. 46 and *Casaubon* ad loc.). This opinion is opposed by the circumstance that John is not accustomed to add a Greek interpretation except to the Hebr. names of fixed Jewish localities, cf. v. 2; ix. 7; xix. 17; and that this is so in the present case is evident from the fact that he has said εἰς τόπον, i. e. in a definite locality which had that name. Besides, it cannot be proved that that custom of the military commanders was followed also by the governors of provinces residing in cities. Doubtless the C h a l d a i c name was given to the spot from its s h a p e, the G r e e k name from the nature of its p a v e m e n t. Cf. below under λιθόστρωτον; *Win.* RWB. s. v. Lithostroton; [BB. DD. s. v. Gabbatha; *Tholuck*, Beiträge zur Spracherklärung u.s.w. p. 119 sqq.].*

1043 Γαβριήλ, ὁ, (נַבְרִיאֵל, fr. גֶבֶר strong man, hero, and אֵל God), indecl., *Gabriel*, one of the angel-princes or chiefs of the angels (Dan. viii. 16; ix. 21): Lk. i. 19, 26; see ἀρχάγγελος [and reff. s. v. ἄγγελος, fin.; BB.DD. s. v.].*

1044 γάγγραινα, -ης, ἡ, (γράω or γραίνω to gnaw, eat), *a gangrene*, a disease by which any part of the body suffering from inflammation becomes so corrupted that, unless a remedy be seasonably applied, the evil continually spreads, attacks other parts, and at last eats away the bones: 2 Tim. ii. 17 [where cf. Ellic.]. (Medical writ. [cf. Wetst. ad l. c.]; Plut. discr. am. et adulat. c. 36.)*

1045 Γάδ, ὁ, (נָד fortune, cf. Gen. xxx. 11; [xlix. 19; on the meaning of the word see B.D. s. v.]), indecl., *Gad*, the seventh son of the patriarch Jacob, by Zilpah, Leah's maid: Rev. vii. 5.*

1046 Γαδαρηνός, -ή, -όν, (fr. the prop. name Γαδαρά; cf. the adj. Ἀβιληνή, Μαγδαληνή), *of Gadara, a Gadarene*. Gadara was the capital of Peræa (Joseph. b. j. 4, 7, 3), situated opposite the southern extremity of the Lake of Gennesaret to the south-east, but at some distance from the lake on the banks of the river Hieromax (Plin. h. n. 5, 16), 60 stadia from the city Tiberias (Joseph. vita 65), inhabited chiefly by Gentiles (Joseph. antt. 17,

11, 4); cf. *Win.* RWB. s. v. Gadara; *Rüetschi* in Herzog iv. p. 636 sq.; *Kneucker* in Schenkel ii. 313 sq.; *Riehm*, HWB. p. 454; [BB.DD. s. v.]. χώρα τῶν Γαδαρηνῶν *the country of the Gadarenes, Gadaris*: Mk. v. 1 Rec.; Lk. viii. 26 Rec., 37 R G [but here ἡ περίχωρος τῶν Γ.], and in Mt. viii. 28 T Tr WH; but the Mss. differ in these pass.; see Γερασηνοί and Γεργεσηνοί.*

1047 γάζα, -ης, ἡ, a Persian word, adopted by the Greeks and Latins (Cic. off. 2, 22), *the royal treasury, treasure, riches,* (Curt. 3, 13, 5 pecuniam regiam, quam *gazam* Persae vocant): Acts viii. 27. ([Theophr.], Polyb., Diod. 17, 35 and 64; Plut., al. Sept. 2 Esdr. v. 17; vii. 20.)*

1048 Γάζα, -ης [B. 17 (15)], ἡ, (עַזָּה i. e. strong, fortified, (cf. *Valentia*); the ע being represented by γ, cf. עֲמֹרָה Γομόρρα), formerly a celebrated city of the Philistines, situated on a hill near the southern border of the land of Israel, between Raphia and Ascalon, twenty stadia ['at the most,' Arrian. exp. Alex. 2, 26; "seven," Strabo 16, 30] from the sea and eleven geographical miles from Jerusalem. It was fortified and surrounded by a massive wall. Although held by a Persian garrison, Alexander the Great captured it after a siege of two months, but did not destroy it ([Joseph. antt. 11, 8, 4]; Diod. 17, 48; Plut. Alex. 25; Curt. 4, 6 sq.). Afterwards, in the year B. c. 96, Alexander Jannæus, king of the Jews, took it after a year's siege and destroyed it (Joseph. antt. 13, 13, 3). Gabinius rebuilt it B. c. 58 (Joseph. l. c. 14, 5, 3). Finally the emperor Augustus gave it [B. c. 30] to Herod the Great (Joseph. l. c. 15, 7, 3), after whose death it was annexed to Syria (Joseph. l. c. 17, 11, 4). Modern *Ghuzzeh* [or *Ghazzeh*], an unfortified town, having an area of two English miles, with fifteen and sixteen thousand inhabitants. Mentioned in the N. T. in Acts viii. 26, where the words αὕτη ἐστὶν ἔρημος refer to ἡ ὁδός; Philip is bidden to take the way which is ἔρημος, solitary; cf. Meyer ad loc.; [W. § 18, 9 N. 3; B. 104 (91)]. A full history of the city is given by *Stark*, Gaza u. d. philistäische Küste. Jena, 1852; a briefer account by *Win.* RWB. [see also BB. DD.] s. v. Gaza; *Arnold* in Herzog iv. p. 671 sqq.*

1049 γαζο-φυλάκιον, -ου, τό, (fr. γάζα, q. v., and φυλακή; hence i. q. θησαυροφυλάκιον, Hesych.), *a repository of treasure*, esp. of public treasure, *a treasury*: Esth. iii. 9; 1 Esdr. viii. 18, 44; 1 Macc. iii. 28. In Sept. used for לִשְׁכָּה and נִשְׁכָּה of apartments constructed in the courts of the temple, in which not only the sacred offerings and things needful for the temple service were kept, but in which also the priests, etc., dwelt: Neh. xiii. 7; x. 37 sqq.; of the sacred treasury, in which not only treasure but also the public records (1 Macc. xiv. 49; cf. Grimm ad loc.) were stored, and the property of widows and orphans was deposited (2 Macc. iii. 10; cf. Grimm ad loc.) : 1 Macc. xiv. 49; 2 Macc. iii. 6, 28, 40; iv. 42; v. 18. Josephus speaks of both γαζοφυλάκια (plur.) in the women's court of Herod's temple, b. j. 5, 5, 2; 6, 5, 2; and τὸ γαζοφ., antt. 19, 6, 1. In the N. T., in Mk. xii. 41, 43; Lk. xxi. 1; Jn. viii. 20 (ἐν τῷ γαζοφ. at, near, the treasury [yet cf. W. § 48, a. 1 c.]), τὸ γαζ. seems to be used of that receptacle mentioned by the Rabbins to which were fitted thirteen chests or boxes, שׁוֹפָרוֹת i. e. trumpets, so called from their shape, and into which were put the contributions made voluntarily or paid yearly by the Jews for the service of the temple and the support of the poor; cf. Lightfoot, Horae Hebr. et Talm. p. 536 sq.; Lücke [Tholuck, or Godet] on Jn. viii. 20; [B.D. Am. ed. s. v. Treasury]. (Strabo 2 p. 319 [i. e. 7, 6, 1].) *

1050 Γάιος [WH Γαῖος (cf. I, ι)], -ου, ὁ, Gaius or Caius; the name of a Christian   **1.** of Derbe: Acts xx. 4.   **2.** of Macedonia: Acts xix. 29.   **3.** of Corinth, Paul's host during his [second] sojourn there: Ro. xvi. 23; 1 Co. i. 14.   **4.** of an unknown Christian, to whom the third Ep. of John was addressed: 3 Jn. vs. 1. [B.D. Am. ed. s. v. Gaius; Farrar, Early Days of Christianity, ii. 506.] *

1051 γάλα, -λακτος [cf. Lat. lac; Curtius § 123], τό, [from Hom. down], milk: 1 Co. ix. 7. Metaph. of the less difficult truths of the Christian religion, 1 Co. iii. 2; Heb. v. 12 sq. (Quintil. 2, 4, 5 "doctoribus hoc esse curae velim, ut teneras adhuc mentes more nutricum mollius alant et satiari velut quodam jucundioris disciplinae lacte patiantur," [cf. Siegfried, Philo von Alex. p. 329, cf. p. 261]); of the word of God, by which souls newly regenerate are healthfully nourished unto growth in the Christian life, 1 Pet. ii. 2.*

1052 Γαλάτης, -ου, ὁ, a Galatian, (see Γαλατία): Gal. iii. 1. (1 Macc. viii. 2; 2 Macc. viii. 20.) *

1053 Γαλατία, -ας, ἡ, Galatia, Gallograecia, a region of Asia Minor, bounded by Paphlagonia, Pontus, Cappadocia, Lycaonia, Phrygia, and Bithynia. It took its name from those Gallic tribes that crossed into Asia Minor B. C. 278, and after roaming about there for a time at length settled down permanently in the above-mentioned region, and intermarried with the Greeks. From B. C. 189 on, though subject to the Romans, they were governed by their own chiefs; but B. C. 24 [al. 25] their country was formally reduced to a Roman province, (cf. Liv. 37, 8; 38, 16 and 18; Joseph. antt. 16, 6; Strabo 12, 5, 1 p. 567; Flor. 2, 11 [i. e. 1, 27]): Gal. i. 2; 1 Co. xvi. 1; 2 Tim. iv. 10 [T Tr mrg. Γαλλίαν]; 1 Pet. i. 1. Cf. Grimm, Ueb. d. (keltische) Nationalität der kleinasiat. Galater, in the Stud. u. Krit. for 1876, p. 199 sqq.; replied to by K. Wieseler, Die deutsche Nationalität d. kleinas. Galater. Gütersl. 1877; [but see Hertzberg in the Stud. u. Krit. for 1878, pp. 525–541; Bp. Lghtft. in his Com. on Gal., Dissertation i. also Intr. § 1].*

1054 Γαλατικός, -ή, -όν, Galatian, belonging to Galatia: Acts xvi. 6; xviii. 23.*

1055 γαλήνη, -ης, ἡ, (adj. ὁ, ἡ, γαληνός calm, cheerful), calm-

ness, stillness of the sea, a calm: Mt. viii. 26; Mk. iv. 39; Lk. viii. 24. (From Hom. down.) *

1056 Γαλιλαία, -ας, ἡ, Galilee, (fr. הַגָּלִילָה, 2 K. xv. 29; הַגָּלִיל, Josh. xx. 7; xxi. 32; אֶרֶץ גְּלִיל, 1 K. ix. 11, i. e. the circle or circuit, by which name even before the exile a certain district of northern Palestine was designated; Sept. Γαλιλαία); the name of a region of northern Palestine, bounded on the north by Syria, on the west by Sidon, Tyre, Ptolemais and their territories and the promontory of Carmel, on the south by Samaria and on the east by the Jordan. It was divided into Upper Galilee (extending from the borders of Tyre and Sidon to the sources of the Jordan), and Lower Galilee (which, lower and more level, embraced the lands of the tribes of Issachar and Zebulun and the part of Naphtali bordering on the Sea of Galilee): ἡ ἄνω καὶ ἡ κάτω Γαλιλαία (Joseph. b. j. 3, 3, 1, where its boundaries are given). It was a very fertile region, populous, having 204 towns and villages (Joseph. vit. 45), and inasmuch as it had, esp. in the upper part, many Gentiles among its inhabitants (Judg. i. 30–33; Strabo 16, 34 p. 760), it was called, Mt. iv. 15, Γαλιλαία τῶν ἐθνῶν (Is. viii. 23 (ix. 1)), and, 1 Macc. v. 15, Γαλιλαία ἀλλοφύλων. Often mentioned in the Gospels, and three times in the Acts, viz. ix. 31; x. 37; xiii. 31. [Cf. Merrill, Galilee in the Time of Christ, Boston 1881.]

1057 Γαλιλαῖος, -αία, -αῖον, Galilæan, a native of Galilee: Mt. xxvi. 69; Mk. xiv. 70; Lk. xiii. 1 sq.; xxii. 59; xxiii. 6; Jn. iv. 45; Acts i. 11; ii. 7; v. 37.*

see 1053 Γαλλία, -ας, ἡ, Gallia: 2 Tim. iv. 10 T Tr mrg., by which is to be understood Galatia in Asia Minor or Γαλλία ἡ ἑῴα, App. b. civ. 2, 49. [See esp. Bp. Lghtft. Com. on Gal. pp. 3, 31 (Am. ed. pp. 11, 37).]*

1058 Γαλλίων, -ωνος, ὁ, Gallio, proconsul of Achaia, elder brother of L. Annaeus Seneca the philosopher. His original name was Marcus Annaeus Novatus, but after his adoption into the family of Junius Gallio the rhetorician, he was called Gallio: Acts xviii. 12, 14, 17. [Cf. B.D. Am. ed.; Farrar, St. Paul, i. 566 sq.]*

1059 Γαμαλιήλ, ὁ, (גַּמְלִיאֵל recompense of God [God the avenger, Fürst]; Num. i. 10; ii. 20), indecl., Gamaliel (distinguished by the Jews from his grandson of the same name by the title הַזָּקֵן, the elder), a Pharisee and doctor of the law, son of R. Simeon, grandson of Hillel, and teacher of the apostle Paul. He is said to have had very great influence in the Sanhedrin, and to have died eighteen years before the destruction of Jerusalem. A man of permanent renown among the Jews: Acts v. 34; xxii. 3. Cf. Grätz, Gesch. d. Juden, iii. p. 289 sqq.; Schenkel, BL. ii. p. 328 sqq.; [esp. Alex.'s Kitto s. v. Gamaliel I. (cf. Farrar, St. Paul, i. 44 and exc. v.)].*

1060 γαμέω, -ῶ; impf. ἐγάμουν (Lk. xvii. 27); 1 aor. ἔγημα (the classic form, [Mt. xxii. 25 L T Tr WH]; Lk. xiv. 20; 1 Co. vii. 28ᵃ R G, 28ᵇ) and ἐγάμησα (the later form, Mt. v. 32; [xxii. 25 R G]; Mk. vi. 17; x. 11; 1 Co. vii. 9, [28ᵃ L T Tr WH], 33); pf. γεγάμηκα; 1 aor. pass. ἐγαμήθην; (cf. W. 84 (80); B. 55 (48); Bttm. Ausf. Spr. ii. 134; Lob. ad Phryn. p. 742; [Veitch s. v.]);   **1.** used of the man, as in Grk. writ. fr. Hom. down, to lead in marriage, take to wife; **a.** with the addition of γυναῖκα or other acc. : Mt. v. 32 [here WH br. the cl.]; xix. 9; Mk. vi. 17; x. 11; Lk. xiv. 20; xvi. 18. **b.** without a case, absol. *to get married, to marry*, [cf. B. 145 (127)]: Mt. xix. 10; xxii. 25, 30; xxiv. 38; Mk. xii. 25; Lk. xvii. 27; xx. 34 sq.; 1 Co. vii. 28, 33; (Ael. v. h. 4, 1; οἱ γεγαμηκότες, Xen. Cyr. 1, 2, 4; opp. to ἄγαμοι, Xen. symp. 9, 7). Pass. and Mid. γαμέομαί τινι, of women [Lat. *nubere alicui*, cf. B. § 133, 8], *to give one's self in marriage* [W. § 38, 3]: 1 aor. pass., Mk. x. 12 (where L T Tr WH γαμήσῃ ἄλλον for R G γαμηθῇ ἄλλῳ); 1 Co. vii. 39.   **2.** contrary to Grk. usage, the Act. γαμεῖν is used of women, *to give one's self in marriage*; and **a.** with the acc.: Mk. x. 12 L T Tr WH (see above); **b.** absol.: 1 Co. vii. 28, 34 (ἡ γαμήσασα, opp. to ἡ ἄγαμος); 1 Tim. v. 11, 14.   **3.** absol. of both sexes: 1 Tim. iv. 3; 1 Co. vii. 9 sq. 36 (γαμείτωσαν, sc. the virgin and he who seeks her to wife). In the O. T. γαμεῖν occurs only in 2 Macc. xiv. 25.*

(1060α): see 1547   γαμίζω; [Pass., pres. γαμίζομαι; impf. ἐγαμιζόμην] (γάμος); *to give* a daughter *in marriage*: 1 Co. vii. 38ᵃ [L T Tr WH, 38ᵇ] G L T Tr WH; Pass.: Mt. xxii. 30 L T Tr WH; [xxiv. 38 T WH]; Mk. xii. 25; Lk. xvii. 27; xx. 35 [WH mrg. γαμίσκονται]. (The word is mentioned in Apoll. de constr. 3, 31 p. 280, 10 ed. Bekk.) [COMP.: ἐκ-γαμίζω.]*

1061; see 1060α   γαμίσκω, i. q. γαμίζω, q. v. [Mt. xxiv. 38 Lchm.]; Pass. [pres. γαμίσκομαι]; Mk. xii. 25 R G; Lk. xx. 34 L T Tr WH, [35 WH mrg.; cf. W. 92 (88); and Tdf.'s note on Mt. xxii. 30]. (Aristot. pol. 7, 14, 4 etc.) [COMP.: ἐκ-γαμίσκω.]*

1062   γάμος, -ου, ὁ, [prob. fr. r. *gam* to bind, unite; Curtius p. 546 sq.], as in Grk. writ. fr. Hom. down;   **1.** *a wedding* or *marriage-festival*: Jn. ii. 1 sq.; Rev. xix. 7 (under the figure of a marriage here is represented the intimate and everlasting union of Christ, at his return from heaven, with his church); τὸ δεῖπνον τοῦ γάμου, ibid. 9 (a symbol of the future blessings of the Messiah's kingdom); esp. *a wedding-banquet, a marriage-feast*: Mt. xxii. 8, 10 [here T WH Tr mrg. νυμφῶν], 11, 12; plur. (referring apparently to the several acts of feasting), Mt. xxii. 2 sqq. 9; xxv. 10; Lk. xii. 36; xiv. 8, (cf. W. § 27, 3; B. 23 (21)).   **2.** *marriage, matrimony*: Heb. xiii. 4.*

1063   γάρ, a conjunction, which acc. to its composition, γέ and ἄρα (i. q. ἄρ), is properly a particle of affirmation and conclusion, denoting *truly therefore, verily as the case stands*, "the thing is first affirmed by the particle γέ, and then is referred to what precedes by the force of the particle ἄρα" (*Klotz* ad Devar. ii. 1, p. 232; cf. Kühner ii. p. 724; [Jelf § 786; W. 445 (415) sq.]). Now since by a new affirmation not infrequently the reason and nature of something previously mentioned are set forth, it comes to pass that, by the use of this particle, either the reason and cause of a foregoing statement is added, whence arises the causal or argumentative force of the particle, *for* (Lat. *nam, enim*; Germ. *denn*); or some previous declaration is explained, whence γάρ takes on an explicative force:

for, the fact is, namely (Lat. *videlicet*, Germ. *nämlich*). Thus the force of the particle is either conclusive, or demonstrative, or explicative and declaratory; cf. *Rost* in Passow's Lex. i. p. 535 sqq.; Kühner ii. pp. 724 sqq. 852 sqq.; [cf. L. and S. s. v.]. The use of the particle in the N. T. does not differ from that in the classics.

I. Its primary and original Conclusive force is seen in questions (in Grk. writ. also in exclamations) and answers expressed with emotion; where, acc. to the connexion, it may be freely represented by *assuredly, verily, forsooth, why, then,* etc.: ἐν γὰρ τούτῳ etc. ye profess not to know whence he is; herein then is assuredly a marvellous thing, *why, herein* etc. Jn. ix. 30; οὐ γάρ, ἀλλά etc. by no means in this state of things, *nay verily, but* etc. Acts xvi. 37; certainly, if that is the case, 1 Co. viii. 11 L T Tr WH. It is joined to interrogative particles and pronouns: μὴ γὰρ etc. Jn. vii. 41 (do ye then suppose that the Christ comes out of Galilee? *What*, doth the Christ, etc. ?); μὴ γὰρ . . . οὐκ, 1 Co. xi. 22 (*what! since ye are so eager to eat and drink, have ye not*, etc. ?); τίς γάρ, τί γάρ: Mt. xxvii. 23 (τί γὰρ κακὸν ἐποίησεν, ye demand that he be crucified like a malefactor, *Why, what evil hath he done?*); Mt. ix. 5 (your thoughts are evil; *which then do ye suppose to be the easier*, etc. ?); Mt. xvi. 26; xxiii. 17, 19; Lk. ix. 25; Acts xix. 35; τί γάρ; for τί γάρ ἐστι, *what then?* i. e. what, under these circumstances, ought to be the conclusion? Phil. i. 18 [cf. Ellic. ad loc.]; πῶς γάρ, Acts viii. 31; cf. Klotz l. c. p. 245 sqq.; Kühner ii. p. 726; [Jelf ii. p. 608]; W. 447 (416). Here belongs also the vexed passage Lk. xviii. 14 ἢ γὰρ ἐκεῖνος (so G T Tr mrg., but L WH Tr txt. παρ' ἐκεῖνον) *or* do ye suppose *then* that *that man* went down approved of God? cf. W. 241 (226).

II. It adduces the Cause or gives the Reason of a preceding statement or opinion;   **1.** univ.: Mt. ii. 5; vi. 24; Mk. i. 22; ix. 6; Lk. i. 15, 18; xxi. 4; Jn. ii. 25; Acts ii. 25; Ro. i. 9, 11; 1 Co. xi. 5; Heb. ii. 8; 1 Jn. ii. 19; Rev. i. 3, and very often. In Jn. iv. 44 γάρ assigns the reason why now at length Jesus betook himself into Galilee; for the authority denied to a prophet in his own country (Galilee), he had previously to seek and obtain among strangers; cf. 45; Meyer [yet see ed. 6 (Weiss)] ad loc.; *Strauss*, Leben Jesu, i. 725 ed. 3; *Neander*, Leben Jesu, p. 385 sq. ed. 1 [Am. trans. pp. 100, 168]; *Ewald*, Jahrbb. d. bibl. Wissensch. x. p. 108 sqq.   **2.** Often the sentences are connected in such a way that either some particular statement is established by a general proposition ('the particular by the universal'), as in Mt. vii. 8; xiii. 12; xxii. 14; Mk. iv. 22, 25; Jn. iii. 20; 1 Co. xii. 12; Heb. v. 13, etc.; or what has been stated generally, is proved to be correctly stated by a particular instance ('the universal by the particular'): Mk. vii. 10; Lk. xii. 52, 58; Ro. vii. 2; 1 Co. i. 26; xii. 8.   **3.** To sentences in which something is commanded or forbidden, γάρ annexes the reason why the thing must either be done or avoided: Mt. i. 20 sq.; ii. 20; iii. 9; vii. 2; Ro. xiii. 11; Col. iii. 3;

1 Th. iv. 3 ; Heb. ii. 2, and very often. In Phil. ii. 13 γάρ connects the verse with vs. 12 thus : work out your salvation with most intense earnestness, for nothing short of this accords with God's saving efficiency within your souls, to whom you owe both the good desire and the power to execute that desire.   **4.** To questions, γάρ annexes the reason why the question is asked : Mt. ii. 2 (we ask this with good reason, for we have seen the star which announces his birth); Mt. xxii. 28 ; Ro. xiv. 10 ; 1 Co. xiv. 9 ; Gal. i. 10.   **5.** Frequently the statement which contains the cause is interrogative ; τίς, τί γάρ : Lk. xxii. 27 ; Ro. iv. 3 ; xi. 34 ; 1 Co. ii. 16 ; vii. 16 ; Heb. i. 5 ; xii. 7 ; τί γάρ for τί γάρ ἐστι, Ro. iii. 3 (cf. Fritzsche ad loc. ; [Ellic. on Phil. i. 18]) ; ἵνα τί γάρ, 1 Co. x. 29 ; ποία γάρ, Jas. iv. 14 [WH txt. om. Tr br. γάρ]. **6.** Sometimes in answers it is so used to make good the substance of a preceding question that it can be rendered *yea, assuredly* : 1 Co. ix. 10 ; 1 Th. ii. 20 ; cf. Kühner ii. p. 724.   **7.** Sometimes it confirms, not a single statement, but the point of an entire discussion : Ro. ii. 25 (it is no advantage to a wicked Jew, *for* etc.).   On the other hand, it may so confirm but a single thought as to involve the force of asseveration and be rendered *assuredly, yea* : Ro. xv. 27 (εὐδόκησαν γάρ) ; so also καὶ γάρ, Phil. ii. 27.   **8.** It is often said that the sentence of which γάρ introduces the cause, or renders the reason, is n o t e x p r e s s e d, but must be gathered from the context and supplied in thought.   But that this ellipsis is wholly imaginary is clearly shown by *Klotz* ad Devar. ii. 1 p. 236 sq., cf. W. 446 (415) sq.   The particle is everywhere used in reference to something expressly stated.   Suffice it to append a very few examples ; the true nature of many others is shown under the remaining heads of this article :   In Mt. v. 12 before γάρ some supply 'nor does this happen to you alone' ; but the reason is added why a great reward in heaven is reserved for those who suffer persecution, which reason consists in this, that the prophets also suffered persecution, and that their reward is great no one can doubt.   In Ro. viii. 18 some have supplied 'do not shrink from this *suffering with Christ*' ; but on the use of γάρ here, see III. a. below.   On Mk. vii. 28 [T Tr WH om. L br. γάρ], where before καὶ γάρ some supply 'but help me,' or 'yet we do not suffer even the dogs to perish with hunger,' see 10 b. below.   In Acts ix. 11 before γάρ many supply 'he will listen to thee' ; but it introduces the reason for the preceding command.   **9.** When in successive statements γάρ is repeated twice or thrice, or even four or five times, either   **a.** one and the same thought is confirmed by as many arguments, each having its own force, as there are repetitions of the particle [Mey. denies the coördinate use of γάρ in the N. T., asserting that the first is argumentative, the second e x p l i c a t i v e, see his Comm. on the pass. to follow, also on Ro. viii. 6] : Mt. vi. 32 ; Ro. xvi. 18 sq. ; or   **b.** every succeeding statement contains the reason for its immediate predecessor, so that the statements are subordinate one to another : Mk. vi. 52 ; Mt. xvi. 25–27 ; Jn. iii. 19 sq. ; v. 21 sq. ; Acts ii. 15 ; Ro. iv.

13–15 ; viii. 2 sq. 5 sq. ; 1 Co. iii. 3 sq. ; ix. 15–17 (where five times in G L T Tr WH) ; 1 Co. xvi. 7 ; Jas. ii. 10, etc. ; or   **c.** it is repeated in a different sense : Mk. ix. 39–41 ; Ro. v. 6 sq. (where cf. W. 453 (422)) ; x. 2–5 (four times) ; Jas. iv. 14 [WH txt. om. Tr br. the first γάρ, L WH mrg. om. the second].   **10.** καὶ γάρ (on which cf. Kühner ii. p. 854 sq. ; W. 448 (417) ; [Ellic. on 2 Thess. iii. 10]) is   **a.** *for, and truly,* (*etenim, namque,* [the simple rendering *for* is regarded as inexact by many ; cf. Mey. on 2 Co. xiii. 4 and see *Hartung,* Partikeln, i.137 sq. ; Krüger § 69, 32, 21]) : Mk. xiv. 70 ; Lk. xxii. 37 [L Tr br. γάρ] ; 1 Co. v. 7 ; xi. 9 ; xii. 13.   **b.** *for also, for even,* (*nam etiam*) : Mt. viii. 9 ; Mk. x. 45 ; Lk. vi. 32 ; Jn. iv. 45 ; 1 Co. xii. 14, etc.   In Mk. vii. 28 καὶ γὰρ [R G L br.] τὰ κυνάρια etc. the woman, by adducing an example, confirms what Christ had said, but the example is of such a sort as also to prove that her request ought to be granted. τὲ γάρ *for indeed* (Germ. *denn ja*) : Ro. vii. 7 ; cf. Fritzsche ad loc. ; W. 448 (417). ἰδοὺ γάρ, see under ἰδού.

III. It serves to e x p l a i n, make c l e a r, illus-t r a t e, a preceding thought or word : *for* i. q. *that is, namely* ;   **a.** so that it begins an exposition of the thing just announced [cf. W. 454 (423) sq.] : Mt. i. 18 [R G] ; xix. 12 ; Lk. xi. 30 ; xviii. 32.   In Ro. viii. 18 γάρ introduces a statement setting forth the nature of the συνδοξασθῆναι just mentioned.   **b.** so that the explanation is intercalated into the discourse, or even added by way of appendix : Mt. iv. 18 ; Mk. i. 16 ; ii. 15 ; v. 42 ; Ro. vii. 1 ; 1 Co. xvi. 5.   In Mk. xvi. 4 the information ἦν γὰρ μέγας σφόδρα is added to throw light on all that has been previously said (in vs. 3 sq.) about the stone.

IV. As respects P o s i t i o n : γάρ never occupies the first place in a sentence, but the second, or third, or even the fourth (ὁ τοῦ θεοῦ γὰρ υἱός, 2 Co. i. 19 — acc. to true text).   Moreover, "not the n u m b e r but the n a t u r e of the word after which it stands is the point to be noticed," *Hermann* on Soph. Phil. 1437.

γαστήρ, -ρός (poet. -έρος), ή, in Grk. auth. fr. Hom. down ; in Sept. for בֶּטֶן ;   **1.** *the belly* ; by meton. of the whole for a part,   **2.** Lat. *uterus, the womb* : ἐν γαστρὶ ἔχειν *to be with child* [see ἔχω, I. 1 b.] : Mt. i. 18, 23 ; xxiv. 19 ; Mk. xiii. 17 ; Lk. xxi. 23 ; 1 Th. v. 3 ; Rev. xii. 2 ; (in Sept. for הָרָה, Gen. xvi. 4 sq. ; xxxviii. 25 ; Is. vii. 14, etc. ; Hdt. 3, 32 and vit. Hom. 2 ; Artem. oneir. 2, 18 p. 105 ; 3, 32 p. 177 ; Pausan., Hdian., al.) ; συλλαμβάνεσθαι ἐν γαστρί to conceive, become pregnant, Lk. i. 31.   **3.** *the stomach* ; by synecdoche *a glutton, gormandizer,* a man who is as it were all stomach, Hes. theog. 26 (so also γάστρις, Arstph. av. 1604 ; Ael. v. h. 1, 28 ; and Lat. *venter* in Lucil. sat. 2, 24 ed. Gerl. 'vivite ventres') : γαστέρες ἀργαί, Tit. i. 12 ; see ἀργός, b.*

γέ, an enclitic particle, answering exactly to no one word in Lat. or Eng. ; used by the bibl. writ. much more rarely than by Grk. writ.   How the Greeks use it, is shown by (among others) *Hermann* ad Vig. p. 822 sqq. ; *Klotz* ad Devar. ii. 1 p. 272 sqq. ; *Rost* in Passow's Lex. i. p. 538 sqq. ; [L. and S. s. v. ; *T. S. Evans* in Journ. of class. and sacr. Philol. for 1857, p. 187 sqq.].   It indicates that the meaning of the word to which it belongs has especial prominence, and therefore that that word is to be distinguished from the rest of the sentence and uttered with greater emphasis. This distinction " can be made in two ways, by mentioning either the least important or the most; thus it happens that γέ seems to have contrary significations: *at least* and *even*" (Hermann l. c. p. 822). **1.** where what is least is indicated; *indeed, truly, at least*: διὰ γε τὴν ἀναίδειαν, Lk. xi. 8 (where, since the force of the statement lies in the substantive not in the preposition, the Greek should have read διὰ τήν γε ἀναίδ., cf. Klotz l. c. p. 327; Rost l. c. p. 542; [L. and S. s. v. IV.]); διά γε τὸ παρέχειν μοι κόπον, at least for this reason, that she troubleth me [A. V. *yet because* etc.], Lk. xviii. 5 (better Greek διὰ τό γε etc.). **2.** where what is most or greatest is indicated; *even*: ὅς γε the very one who etc., *precisely he who* etc. (Germ. *der es ja ist, welcher* etc.), Ro. viii. 32; cf. Klotz l. c. p. 305; *Matthiae,* Lex. Euripid. i. p. 613 sq. **3.** joined to other particles it strengthens their force; **a.** ἀλλά γε [so most edd.] or ἀλλά γε [Grsb.] (cf. W. § 5, 2): Lk. xxiv. 21; 1 Co. ix. 2; see ἀλλά, I. 10. **b.** ἄρα γε or ἄραγε, see ἄρα, 4. ἀρά γε, see ἄρα, 1. **c.** εἴγε [so G T, but L Tr WH εἴ γε; cf. W. u. s.; *Lips.* Gram. Unters. p. 123], foll. by the indic. *if indeed, seeing that,* "of a thing believed to be correctly assumed" (*Herm.* ad Vig. p. 831; cf. *Fritzsche,* Praeliminarien u.s.w. p. 67 sqq.; *Anger,* Laodicenerbrief, p. 46; [W. 448 (417 sq.). Others hold that Hermann's statement does not apply to the N. T. instances. Acc. to Meyer (see notes on 2 Co. v. 3; Eph. iii. 2; Gal. iii. 4) the certainty of the assumption resides not in the particle but in the context; so Ellicott (on Gal. l. c., Eph. l. c.); cf. Bp. Lghtft. on Gal. l. c.; Col. i. 23. Hermann's canon, though assented to by Bornemann (Cyrop. 2, 2, 3 p. 132), Stallbaum (Meno p. 36), al., is qualified by *Bäumlein* (Partikeln, p. 64 sq.), who holds that γέ often has no other effect than to emphasize the condition expressed by εἰ; cf. also Winer ed. Moulton p. 561]), *if, that is to say; on the assumption that,* (see εἴπερ s. v. εἰ, III. 13): Eph. iii. 2; iv. 21; Col. i. 23; with καί added, *if that also, if it be indeed,* (Germ. *wenn denn auch*): εἴγε [L Tr WH mrg. εἴ περ] καὶ ἐνδυσάμενοι, οὐ γυμνοὶ εὑρεθ. if indeed we shall be found actually clothed (with a new body), not naked, 2 Co. v. 3 (cf. Meyer ad loc.); εἴγε καὶ εἰκῆ sc. τοσαῦτα ἐπάθετε, if indeed, as I believe, ye have experienced such benefits *in vain,* and have not already received h a r m from your inclination to Judaism, Gal. iii. 4 [yet cf. Mey., Ellic., Bp. Lghtft., al. ad loc.]. **d.** εἰ δὲ μήγε [or εἰ δὲ μή γε Lchm. Treg.] (also in Plat., Arstph., Plut., al.; cf. *Bornemann,* Scholia ad Luc. p. 95; *Klotz* ad Devar. ii. 1 p. 319), stronger than εἰ δὲ καὶ μή [B. 393 (336 sq.); cf. W. 583 (543); 605 (563); Mey. on 2 Cor. xi. 16], **a.** after affirmative sentences, *but unless perchance, but if not*: Mt. vi. 1; Lk. x. 6; xiii. 9. **β.** after negative sentences, *otherwise, else, in the contrary event*: Mt. ix. 17; Lk. v. 36 sq.; xiv. 32; 2 Co. xi. 16. **e.** καίγε [so G T, but L Tr WH καί γε; cf. reff. under εἴγε above], (cf. *Klotz* ad Devar. ii. 1 p. 319; [W. 438 (408)]), **a.** *and at*

least: Lk. xix. 42 [Tr txt. WH om. L Tr mrg. br.]. **β.** *and truly, yea indeed, yea and*: Acts ii. 18; xvii. 27 L T Tr WH. **f.** καίτοιγε [so G T WH, but L καίτοι γε, Tr καί τοι γε; cf. reff. under c. above. Cf. *Klotz* ad Devar. ii. 2 p. 654; W. 444 (413)], *although indeed, and yet indeed*: Jn. iv. 2; also in Acts xiv. 17 [R G]; xvii. 27 Rec. **g.** μενοῦνγε see in its place. **h.** μήτιγε, see μήτι, [and in its place].*

Γεδεών, ὁ, indecl. [in the Bible (cf. B. p. 15 (14)), and in Suidas (e. g. 1737 a.); but] in Joseph. antt. 5, 6, [3 and] 4 Γεδεών, -ῶνος, (גִּדְעוֹן cutting off, [al. tree-feller i. e. mighty warrior], fr. גָּדַע), *Gideon,* a leader of the Israelites, who delivered them from the power of the Midianites (Judg. vi.–viii.): Heb. xi. 32 [where A. V. unfortunately follows the Grk. spelling *Gedeon*].*　　　　　　　**1066**

γέεννα [al. would accent γεέννα, deriving it through the Chaldee. In Mk. ix. 45 Rec.[st] γέενα], -ης [B. 17 (15)], ἡ, (fr. הִנֹּם גֵּי, Neh. xi. 30; more fully גֵיא בֶּן־הִנֹּם, Josh. xv. 8; xviii. 16; 2 Chr. xxviii. 3; Jer. vii. 32; גֵי בְנֵי־הִנֹּם, 2 K. xxiii. 10 K'thibh; Chald. גֵּיהִנָּם, the valley of the son of lamentation, or of the sons of lamentation, the valley of lamentation, הִנֹּם being used for נָהַם lamentation; see *Hiller,* Onomasticum; cf. Hitzig [and Graf] on Jer. vii. 31; [*Böttcher,* De Inferis, i. p. 82 sqq.]; acc. to the com. opinion הִנֹּם is the name of a man], *Gehenna,* the name of a valley on the S. and E. of Jerusalem [yet apparently beginning on the W., cf. Josh. xv. 8; *Press₁ l* in Herzog s. v.], which was so called from the cries of the little children who were thrown into the fiery arms of Moloch [q. v.], i. e. of an idol having the form of a bull. The Jews so abhorred the place after these horrible sacrifices had been abolished by king Josiah (2 K. xxiii. 10), that they cast into it not only all manner of refuse, but even the dead bodies of animals and of unburied criminals who had been executed. And since fires were always needed to consume the dead bodies, that the air might not become tainted by the putrefaction, it came to pass that the place was called γέεννα τοῦ πυρός [this common explanation of the descriptive gen. τοῦ πυρός is found in Rabbi David Kimchi (fl. c. A.D. 1200) on Ps. xxvii. 13. Some suppose the gen. to refer not to purifying fires but to the fires of Moloch; others regard it as the natural symbol of penalty (cf. Lev. x. 2; Num. xvi. 35; 2 K. i. 2; Ps. xi. 6; Mt. iii. 11; xiii. 42; 2 Th. i. 8, etc.). See *Böttcher,* u. s. p. 84; Mey., (Thol.,) Wetst. on Mt. v. 22]; and then this name was transferred to that place in Hades where the wicked after death will suffer punishment: Mt. v. 22, 29 sq.; x. 28; Lk. xii. 5; Mk. ix. 43, 45; Jas. iii. 6; γέεννα τοῦ πυρός, Mt. v. 22; xviii. 9; Mk. ix. 47 [R G Tr mrg. br.]; κρίσις τῆς γεέννης, Mt. xxiii. 33; υἱὸς τῆς γεέννης, worthy of punishment in Gehenna, Mt. xxiii. 15. Further, cf. *Dillmann,* Buch Henoch, 27, 1 sq. p. 131 sq.; [B. D. Am. ed.; *Böttcher,* u. s. p. 80 sqq.; *Hamburger,* Real-Encycl., Abth. I. s. v. Hölle; *Bartlett,* Life and Death eternal, App. II.].*　**1067**

Γεθσημανῆ, or **Γεθσημανεί** (T WH), or **Γεθσημανεί** (L Tr.); [on the accent in codd. see *Tdf.* Proleg. p. 103; W. § 6, 1 m.; indecl. B. 15 (14)], (fr. גַּת press, and שֶׁמֶן oil),　**1068**

Gethsemane, the name of a 'place' (χωρίον [an enclosure or landed property]) at the foot of the Mount of Olives, beyond the torrent Kidron: Mt. xxvi. 36; Mk. xiv. 32. [B. D. Am. ed. s. v.]*

1069 γείτων, -ονος, ὁ, ἡ, [fr. γῆ, hence originally 'of the same land,' cf. Curtius § 132], fr. Hom. down, *a neighbor*: Lk. xiv. 12; xv. 6, 9; Jn. ix. 8.*

1070 γελάω, -ῶ; fut. γελάσω (in Grk. writ. more com. γελάσομαι [B. 53 (46); W. 84 (80)]); [fr. Hom. down]; *to laugh*: Lk. vi. 21 (opp. to κλαίω), 25. [COMP.: κατα-γελάω.]*

1071 γέλως, -ωτος, ὁ, *laughter*: Jas. iv. 9. [From Hom. down.]*

1072 γεμίζω: 1 aor. ἐγέμισα; Pass., [pres. γεμίζομαι]; 1 aor. ἐγεμίσθην; (γέμω, q. v.); *to fill, fill full*; a. absol. in pass.: Mk. iv. 37; Lk. xiv. 23. b. τί τινος, to fill a thing full of something: Mk. xv. 36; Jn. ii. 7; vi. 13; Rev. xv. 8, (Aeschyl. Ag. 443; al.); τὶ ἀπό τινος, of that which is used for filling, Lk. xv. 16 [not WH Tr mrg.]; also in the same sense τὶ ἔκ τινος, Rev. viii. 5; [cf. Lk. xv. 16 in WH mrg.], (בָּלָא כִי, Ex. xvi. 32; Jer. li. 34, etc. [cf. W. § 30, 8 b.; B. 163 (143)]).*

1073 γέμω, defect. verb, used only in pres. and impf., [in N. T. only in pres. indic. and ptcp.]; *to be full, filled full*; a. τινός (as generally in Grk. writ.): Mt. xxiii. 25 Lchm., 27; Lk. xi. 39; Ro. iii. 14 (fr. Ps. ix. 28 (x.7)); Rev. iv. 6, 8; v. 8; xv. 7; xvii. 3 R G (see below), 4; xxi. 9. b. ἔκ τινος: Mt. xxiii. 25 (γέμουσιν ἐξ ἁρπαγῆς [L om. Tr br. ἐξ] their contents are derived from plunder; see γεμίζω, b. [and reff. there]). c. Hebraistically (see πληρόω, 1 [cf. B. 164 (143); W. § 30, 8 b.]), with acc. of the material, γέμοντα [Treg. γέμον τὰ] ὀνόματα βλασφημίας, Rev. xvii. 3 [L T Tr WH (see above and cf. B. 80 (70))].*

1074 γενεά, -ᾶς, ἡ, (ΓΕΝΩ, γίνομαι [cf. Curtius p. 610]); Sept. often for דּוֹר; in Grk. writ. fr. Hom. down; **1.** *a begetting, birth, nativity*: Hdt. 3, 33; Xen. Cyr. 1, 2, 8, etc.; [others make the c o l l e c t i v e sense the primary signif., see Curtius u. s.]. **2.** passively, *that which has been begotten, men of the same stock, a family*; a. prop. as early as Hom.; equiv. to מִשְׁפָּחָה, Gen. xxxi. 3, etc.; σώζειν Ῥαχάβην κ· τὴν γενεὰν αὐτῆς, Joseph. antt. 5, 1, 5. *the several ranks in a natural descent, the successive members of a genealogy*: Mt. i. 17, (ἑβδόμη γενεὰ οὗτός ἐστιν ἀπὸ τοῦ πρώτου, Philo, vit. Moys. i. § 2). b. metaph. *a race of men very like each other in endowments, pursuits, character*; and esp. in a bad sense *a perverse race*: Mt. xvii. 17; Mk. ix. 19; Lk. ix. 41; xvi. 8; [Acts ii. 40]. **3.** *the whole multitude of men living at the same time*: Mt. xxiv. 34; Mk. xiii. 30; Lk. i. 48 (πᾶσαι αἱ γενεαί); xxi. 32; Phil. ii. 15; used esp. of the Jewish race living at one and the same period: Mt. xi. 16; xii. 39, 41 sq. 45; xvi. 4; xxiii. 36; Mk. viii. 12, 38; Lk. xi. 29 sq. 32, 50 sq.; xvii. 25; Acts xiii. 36; Heb. iii. 10; ἄνθρωποι τῆς γενεᾶς ταύτης, Lk. vii. 31; ἄνδρες τῆς γεν. ταύ. Lk. xi. 31; τὴν δὲ γενεὰν αὐτοῦ τίς διηγήσεται, who can describe the wickedness of the present generation, Acts viii. 33 (fr. Is. liii. 8 Sept.) [but cf. Mey. ad loc.]. **4.** *an age* (i. e. the time ordinarily occupied by each successive generation), the space of from 30 to 33 years (Hdt. 2, 142 et al.; Heraclit. in Plut. def. orac. c. 11), or ὁ χρόνος, ἐν ᾧ γεν-

νῶντα παρέχει τὸν ἐξ αὐτοῦ γεγεννημένον ὁ γεννήσας (Plut. l. c.); in the N. T. com. in plur.: Eph. iii. 5 [W. § 31, 9 a.; B. 186 (161)]; παρῳχημέναις γενεαῖς in ages gone by, Acts xiv. 16; ἀπὸ τῶν γενεῶν for ages, since the generations began, Col. i. 26; ἐκ γενεῶν ἀρχαίων from the generations of old, from ancient times down, Acts xv. 21; εἰς γενεὰς γενεῶν unto generations of generations, through all ages, for ever, (a phrase which assumes that the longer ages are made up of shorter; see αἰών, 1 a.): Lk. i. 50 R L (לְדֹר דֹּרִים, Is. li. 8); εἰς γενεὰς κ. γενεὰς unto generations and generations, ibid. T Tr WH equiv. to לְדוֹר וָדֹר, Ps. lxxxix. 2 sq.; Is. xxxiv. 17; very often in Sept.; [add, εἰς πάσας τὰς γενεὰς τοῦ αἰῶνος τῶν αἰώνων, Eph. iii. 21, cf. Ellic. ad loc.] (γενεά is used of a century in Gen. xv. 16, cf. Knobel ad loc., and on the senses of the word see the full remarks of Keim iii. 206 [v. 245 Eng. trans.]).*

1075 γενεαλογέω, -ῶ: [pres. pass. γενεαλογοῦμαι]; *to act the genealogist* (γενεά and λέγω), *to recount a family's origin and lineage, trace ancestry*, (often in Hdt.; Xen., Plat., Theophr., Lcian., Ael., al.; [Sept. 1 Chr. v. 2]); pass. *to draw one's origin, derive one's pedigree*: ἔκ τινος, Heb. vii. 6.*

1076 γενεαλογία, -ας, ἡ, *a genealogy, a record of descent* or *lineage*, (Plat. Crat. p. 396 c.; Polyb. 9, 2, 1; Dion. Hal. antt. 1, 11; [al.]. Sept. [edd. Ald., Compl.] 1 Chr. vii. 5, 7; ix. 22; [iv. 33 Compl.; Ezra viii. 1 ib.]); in plur. of the orders of æons, according to the doctrine of the Gnostics: 1 Tim. i. 4; Tit. iii. 9; cf. De Wette on Tit. i. 14 [substantially reproduced by Alf. on 1 Tim. l. c.; see also Holtzmann, Pastoralbriefe, pp. 126 sq. 134 sq. 143].*

1077 γενέσια, -ων, τά [cf. W. 176 (166)], (fr. the adj. γενέσιος fr. γένεσις), *a birth-day celebration, a birth-day feast*: Mk. vi. 21; Mt. xiv. 6; (Alciphr. epp. 3, 18 and 55; Dio Cass. 47, 18, etc.; ἡ γενέσιος ἡμέρα, Joseph. antt. 12, 4, 7). The earlier Greeks used γενέσια of *funeral commemorations*, a festival commemorative of a d e c e a s e d friend (Lat. feriae denicales), see Lob. ad Phryn. p. 103 sq.; [Rutherford, New Phryn. p. 184; W. 24 (23)]. Cf. Keim ii. p. 516 [iv. 223 Eng. trans.].*

1078 γένεσις, -εως, ἡ, (ΓΕΝΩ [Curtius § 128]), in Grk. writ. for the first time in Hom. Il. 14, 201 [cf. 246]; **1.** *source, origin*: βίβλος γενέσεώς τινος a book of one's lineage, i. e. in which his ancestry or his progeny are enumerated (i. q. סֵפֶר תּוֹלְדֹת, Gen. v. 1, etc.), [Mt. i. 1]. **2.** used of *birth, nativity*, in Mt. i. 18 and Lk. i. 14, for Rec. γέννησις (ἡμέραι τῆς γενέσεώς μου equiv. to ἀφ' οὗ ἐγεννήθην, Judith xii. 18 cf. 20); πρόσωπον τῆς γενέσεως his *native* (natural) face, Jas. i. 23. **3.** of that which follows origin, viz. *existence, life*: ὁ τροχὸς τῆς γενέσεως the wheel [cf. Eng. "machinery"] of life, Jas. iii. 6 (cf. Grimm on Sap. vii. 5); but others explain it *the wheel of human origin* which as soon as men are born begins to run, i. e. the course [cf. Eng. "round"] of life.*

1079 γενετή, -ῆς, ἡ, (ΓΕΝΩ, γίνομαι), (cf. Germ. *die Gewordenheit*), *birth*; hence very often ἐκ γενετῆς *from birth* on (Hom. Il. 24, 535; Aristot. eth. Nic. 6, 13, 1 p. 1144b, 6 etc.; Polyb. 3, 20, 4; Diod. 5, 32, al.; Sept. Lev. xxv. 47): Jn. ix. 1.*

(1079α);
see 1081

γένημα, -ατος, τό, (fr. γίνομαι), a form supported by the best Mss. in Mt. xxvi. 29; Mk. xiv. 25; Lk. xii. 18; xxii. 18; 2 Co. ix. 10, and therefore adopted by T [see his Proleg. p. 79] Tr [L WH (see *WH.* App. p. 148 and below)], printed by Grsb. only in Lk. xii. 18; 2 Co. ix. 10, but given by no grammarian, and therefore attributed by Fritzsche (on Mk. p. 619 sq.) to the carelessness of transcribers, — for Rec. [but in Lk. l. c. Rˢᵗ reads γένημ.] γένημα, q. v. In Mk. xiv. 25 Lchm. has retained the common reading; [and in Lk. xii. 18 Tr txt. WH have σῖτον. In Ezek. xxxvi. 30 codd. A B read γενήματα].*

1080

γεννάω, -ῶ; fut. γεννήσω; 1 aor. ἐγέννησα; pf. γεγέννηκα; [Pass., pres. γεννάομαι, -ῶμαι]; pf. γεγέννημαι; 1 aor. ἐγεννήθην; (fr. γέννα, poetic for γένος); in Grk. writ. fr. Pind. down; in Sept. for יָלַד; *to beget*; **1.** properly: of men begetting children, Mt. i. 1–16; Acts vii. 8, 29; foll. by ἐκ with gen. of the mother, Mt. i. 3, 5, 6; more rarely of women giving birth to children, Lk. i. 13, 57; xxiii. 29; Jn. xvi. 21; εἰς δουλείαν to bear a child unto bondage, that will be a slave, Gal. iv. 24, ([Xen. de rep. Lac. 1, 3]; Lcian. de sacrif. 6; Plut. de liber. educ. 5; al.; Sept. Is. lxvi. 9; 4 Macc. x. 2, etc.). Pass. *to be begotten*: τὸ ἐν αὐτῇ γεννηθέν that which is begotten in her womb, Mt. i. 20; *to be born*: Mt. ii. 1, 4 [W. 266 (250); B. 203 (176)]; xix. 12; xxvi. 24; Mk. xiv. 21; Lk. i. 35; Jn. iii. 4; [Acts vii. 20]; Ro. ix. 11; Heb. xi. 23; with the addition εἰς τὸν κόσμον, Jn. xvi. 21; foll. by ἐν with dat. of place, Acts xxii. 3; ἀπό τινος, to spring from one as father, Heb. xi. 12 [Tr WH mrg. ἐγενήθ. see Tdf. ad loc.]; ἐκ τινος to be born of a mother, Mt. i. 16; ἐκ πορνείας, Jn. viii. 41; ἐξ αἱμάτων, ἐκ θελήματος ἀνδρός, Jn. i. 13; ἐκ τῆς σαρκός, Jn. iii. 6 [Rec.ᵉˡᶻ γεγενημ.]; ἐν ἁμαρτίαις ὅλος, Jn. ix. 34 (see ἁμαρτία, 2 a.); εἴς τι, to be born for something, Jn. xviii. 37; 2 Pet. ii. 12 [Tdf. γεγενημ. so Rec.ˢᵗ ᵇᵉᶻ]; with an adj.: τυφλὸς γεγέννημαι, Jn. ix. 2, 19 sq. 32; ʽΡωμαῖος to be supplied, Acts xxii. 28; τῇ διαλέκτῳ, ἐν ᾗ ἐγεννήθημεν, Acts ii. 8; γεννηθεὶς κατὰ σάρκα begotten or born according to (by) the working of natural passion; κατὰ πνεῦμα according to (by) the working of the divine promise, Gal. iv. 29, cf. 23. **2.** metaph. **a.** univ. *to engender, cause to arise, excite*: μάχας, 2 Tim. ii. 23 (βλάβην, λύπην, etc. in Grk. writ.). **b.** in a Jewish sense, of one who brings others over to his way of life: ὑμᾶς ἐγέννησα I am the author of your Christian life, 1 Co. iv. 15; Philem. 10, (Sanhedr. fol. 19, 2 "If one teaches the son of his neighbor the law, the Scripture reckons this the same as though he had begotten him"; [cf. Philo, leg. ad Gaium § 8]). **c.** after Ps. ii. 7, it is used of God making Christ his son: **a.** formally to show him to be the Messiah (υἱὸν τοῦ θεοῦ), viz. by the resurrection: Acts xiii. 33. **β.** to be the author of the divine nature which he possesses [but cf. the Comm. on the pass. that follow]: Heb. i. 5; v. 5. **d.** peculiarly, in the Gospel and 1 Ep. of John, of God conferring upon men the nature and disposition of his sons, imparting to them spiritual life, i. e. by his own holy power prompting and persuading souls to put faith in Christ and live a new life consecrated to himself; absol.: 1 Jn. v. 1:

mostly in pass., ἐκ θεοῦ or ἐκ τοῦ θεοῦ ἐγεννήθησαν, γεγέννηται, γεγεννημένος, etc.: Jn. i. 13; 1 Jn. ii. 29 [Rec.ˢᵗ γεγένηται]; iii. 9; iv. 7; v. 1, 4, 18; also ἐκ τοῦ πνεύματος γεννᾶσθαι, Jn. iii. 6 [Rec.ᵉˡᶻ γεγενημ.], 8; ἐξ ὕδατος καὶ πνεύματος (because that moral generation is effected in receiving baptism [(?) cf. Schaff's Lange, Godet, Westcott, on the words, and reff. s. v. βάπτισμα, 3]), Jn. iii. 5; ἄνωθεν γεννᾶσθαι, Jn. iii. 3, 7 (see ἄνωθεν, c.) equiv. to τέκνον θεοῦ γίνεσθαι, i. 12. [Comp.: ἀνα-γεννάω.] *

γέννημα, -τος, τό, (fr. γεννάω), *that which has been begotten or born*; **a.** as in the earlier Grk. writ. fr. Soph. down, *the offspring, progeny*, of men or of animals: ἐχιδνῶν, Mt. iii. 7; xii. 34; xxiii. 33; Lk. iii. 7; (γυναικῶν, Sir. x. 18). **b.** fr. Polyb. [1, 71, 1 etc.] on [cf. W. 23], *the fruits of the earth, products of agriculture*, (in Sept. often γεννήματα τῆς γῆς): Lk. xii. 18 (where Tr [txt. WH] τὸν σῖτον); τῆς ἀμπέλου, Mt. xxvi. 29; Mk. xiv. 25; Lk. xxii. 18; cf. Lob. ad Phryn. p. 286. Metaph. *fruit, reward, profit*: τῆς δικαιοσύνης, 2 Co. ix. 10, (Hos. x. 12; τῆς σοφίας, Sir. i. 17; vi. 19). Further, see γένημα.*   1081

Γεννησαρέτ [so G T Tr WH], -ρέθ [Lchm. in Mt. xiv. 34], [Γεννσαρέτ Rec. in Mk. vi. 53; cf. Tdf. ed. 2 Proleg. p. xxxv., ed. 7 Proleg. p. liv. note³], (Targums גִּנֵיסַר or גִּנּוֹסַר [acc. to *Delitzsch* (Römerbr. in d. Hebr. übers. p. 27) גִּנּוֹסַר, גְּנֵיסַר]; Γεννησάρ, 1 Macc. xi. 67; Joseph. b. j. 2, 20, 6 etc.; *Genesara*, Plin. 5, 15), *Gennesaret*, a very lovely and fertile region on the Sea of Galilee (Joseph. b. j. 3, 10, 7): ἡ γῆ Γεννησ. Mt. xiv. 34; Mk. vi. 53; ἡ λίμνη Γεννησ. Lk. v. 1, anciently כִּנֶּרֶת יָם, Num. xxxiv. 11, or כִּנְּרוֹת יָם, Josh. xii. 3, fr. the city כִּנֶּרֶת, Deut. iii. 17, which was near by; called in the Gospels ἡ θάλασσα τῆς Γαλιλαίας, Mk. i. 16; Mt. iv. 18; ἡ θάλασσα τῆς Τιβεριάδος, Jn. vi. 1; xxi. 1. The lake, acc. to Joseph. b. j. 3, 10, 7, is 140 stadia long and 40 wide; [its extreme dimensions now are said to average 12¼ m. by 6¾ m., and its level to be nearly 700 ft. below that of the Mediterranean]. Cf. *Rüetschi* in Herzog v. p. 6 sq.; *Furrer* in Schenkel ii. p. 322 sqq.; [*Wilson* in "The Recovery of Jerusalem," Pt. ii.; *Robinson*, Phys. Geog. of the Holy Land, p. 199 sqq.; BB.DD. For conjectures respecting the derivation of the word cf. Alex.'s Kitto sub fin.; *Merrill*, Galilee in the Time of Christ, § vii.].*   1082

γέννησις, -εως, ἡ, (γεννάω), *a begetting, engendering*, (often so in Plat.); *nativity, birth*: Rec. in Mt. i. 18 and Lk. i. 14; see γένεσις, 2.*   1083

γεννητός, -ή, -όν, (γεννάω), *begotten, born*, (often in Plat.; Diod. 1, 6 sqq.); after the Hebr. (אִשָּׁה יְלוּד, Job xiv. 1, etc.), γεννητοὶ γυναικῶν [B. 169 (147), *born of women*] is a periphrasis for *men*, with the implied idea of weakness and frailty: Mt. xi. 11; Lk. vii. 28.*   1084

γένος, -ους, τό, (ΓΕΝΩ, γίνομαι), *race*; **a.** *offspring*: τινός, Acts xvii. 28 sq. (fr. the poet Aratus); Rev. xxii. 16. **b.** *family*: Acts [iv. 6, see ἀρχιερεύς, 2 fin.]; vii. 13 [al. refer this to c.]; xiii. 26. **c.** *stock, race*: Acts viii. 19; 2 Co. xi. 26; Phil. iii. 5; Gal. i. 14; 1 Pet. ii. 9; (Gen. xi. 6; xvii. 14, etc. for עַם); *nation* (i. e. *nationality* or *descent from a particular people*): Mk. vii. 26; Acts iv. 36; xviii. 2, 24. **d.** concr. *the aggregate of many indi-*   1085 *viduals of the same nature, kind, sort, species*: Mt. xiii. 7; xvii. 21 [T WH om. Tr br. the vs.]; Mk. ix. 29; 1 Co. xii. 10, 28; xiv. 10. (With the same significations in Grk. writ. fr. Hom. down.) *

(1085α);
see 1086

Γερασηνός, -οῦ, ὁ, *Gerasene*, i. e. belonging to the city Gerasa (τὰ Γέρασα, Joseph. b. j. 3, 3, 3): Mt. viii. 28 [Lchm.]; Mk. v. 1 [L T WH Tr txt.]; Lk. viii. 26 and 37 [L Tr WH] acc. to very many codd. seen by Origen. But since Gerasa was a city situated in the southern part of Peræa (Joseph. l. c., cf. 4, 9, 1), or in Arabia (Orig. opp. iv. 140 ed. De la Rue), that cannot be referred to here; see Γαδαρηνός, and the next word.*

1086   **Γεργεσηνός, -ή, -όν,** *Gergesene*, belonging to the city Gergesa, which is assumed to have been situated on the eastern shore of Lake Gennesaret: Mt. viii. 28 Rec. But this reading depends on the authority and opinion of Origen, who thought the variants found in his Mss. Γαδαρηνῶν and Γερασηνῶν (see these words) must be made to conform to the testimony of those who said that there was formerly a certain city Gergesa near the lake. But Josephus knows nothing of it, and states expressly (antt. 1, 6, 2), that no trace of the ancient Gergesites [A. V. Girgashites, cf. B. D. s. v.] (mentioned Gen. xv. 20; Josh. xxiv. 11) had survived, except the names preserved in the O. T. Hence in Mt. viii. 28 we must read Γαδαρηνῶν [so T Tr WH] and suppose that the jurisdiction of the city Gadara extended quite to the Lake of Gennesaret; but that Matthew (viii. 34) erroneously thought that this city was situated on the lake itself. For in Mk. v. 14 sq.; Lk. viii. 34, there is no objection to the supposition that the men came to Jesus from the rural districts alone. [But for the light thrown on this matter by modern research, see B. D. Am. ed. s. v. Gadara; *Thomson*, The Land and the Book, ii. 34 sqq.; Wilson in "The Recovery of Jerusalem" p. 286 sq.]*

1087   **γερουσία, -ας, ἡ,** (adj. γερούσιος, belonging to old men, γέρων), *a senate, council of elders*; used in prof. auth. of the chief council of nations and cities (ἐν ταῖς πόλεσι αἱ γερουσίαι, Xen. mem. 4, 4, 16; in the O. T. of the chief council not only of the whole people of Israel, Ex. iii. 16, etc.; 1 Macc. xii. 6, etc.; but also of cities, Deut. xix. 12, etc.); of the Great Council, the Sanhedrin of the Jews: Acts v. 21, where to τὸ συνέδριον is added καὶ πᾶσαν τὴν γερουσίαν τῶν υἱῶν Ἰσραήλ *and indeed* (καί explicative) *all the senate*, to signify the full Sanhedrin. [Cf. *Schürer*, Die Gemeindeverfassung d. Juden in Rom in d. Kaiserzeit nach d. Inschriften dargestellt. Leips. 1879, p. 18 sq.; *Hatch*, Bamp. Lects. for 1880, p. 64 sq.]*

1088   **γέρων, -οντος, ὁ,** [fr. Hom. down], *an old man*: Jn. iii. 4. [SYN. cf. Augustine in Trench § cvii. 2.] *

see
1089 St.

γεύω: [cf. Lat. *gusto*, Germ. *kosten*; Curtius § 131]; *to cause to taste, to give one a taste of*, τινά (Gen. xxv. 30). In the N. T. only Mid. γεύομαι: fut. γεύσομαι; 1 aor. ἐγευσάμην. **1.** *to taste, try the flavor of*: Mt. xxvii. 34; contrary to better Grk. usage (cf. W. § 30, 7 c. [and p. 36; Anthol. Pal. 6, 120]) with acc. of the obj.: Jn. ii. 9. **2.** *to taste*, i. e. *perceive the flavor of, partake of, enjoy*: τινός, Lk. xiv. 24 (γεύσεταί μου τοῦ δείπνου, i. e. shall par-

take of my banquet); hence, as in Grk. writ. fr. Hom. down, i. q. *to feel, make trial of, experience*: τινός, Heb. **vi.** 4; ῥῆμα θεοῦ, ib. 5, (τῆς γνώσεως, Clem. Rom. 1 Cor. 36, 2). as in Chald., Syr. and Rabbin. writers, γεύεσθαι τοῦ θανάτου [W. 33 (32)]: Mt. xvi. 28; Mk. ix. 1; Lk. ix. 27; Jn. viii. 52; Heb. ii. 9; [cf. Wetstein on Mt. l. c.; Meyer on Jn. l. c.; Bleek, Lünem., Alf. on Heb. l. c.]. foll. by ὅτι: 1 Pet. ii. 3 (Ps. xxxiii. (xxxiv.) 9). **3.** *to take food, eat*: absol., Acts x. 10; xx. 11; cf. *Kypke*, Observv. ii. p. 47; *to take nourishment, eat* — [but substantially as above], with gen. μηδενός, Acts xxiii. 14; with the ellipsis of a gen. denoting unlawful food, Col. ii. 21.*

1090   **γεωργέω, -ῶ:** [pres. pass. γεωργοῦμαι]; (γεωργός, q. v.); *to practise agriculture, to till the ground*: τὴν γῆν (Plat. Theag. p. 121 b.; Eryx. p. 392 d.; [al.]; 1 Esdr. iv. 6; 1 Macc. xiv. 8); Pass.: Heb. vi. 7.*

1091   **γεώργιον, -ου, τό,** *a* (cultivated) *field*: 1 Co. iii. 9 [A. V. *husbandry* (with marg. *tillage*)]. (Prov. xxiv. 45 (30); xxxi. 16 (xxix. 34); Theag. in schol. Pind. Nem. 3, 21; Strabo 14, 5, 6 p. 671; [al.].) *

1092   **γεωργός, -οῦ, ὁ,** (fr. γῆ and ΕΡΓΩ), fr. [Hdt.], Xen. and Plat. down; *a husbandman, tiller of the soil*: 2 Tim. ii. 6; Jas. v. 7; several times in Sept.; used of *a vine-dresser* (Ael. nat. an. 7, 28; [Plat. Theaet. p. 178 d.; al.]) in Mt. xxi. 33 sqq.; Mk. xii. 1 sq. 7, 9; Lk. xx. 9 sq. 14, 16; Jn. xv. 1.*

1093   **γῆ,** gen. γῆς, ἡ, (contr. fr. γέα, poet. γαῖα), Sept. very often for אֶרֶץ and אֲדָמָה, *earth*; **1.** *arable land*: Mt. xiii. 5, 8, 23; Mk. iv. 8, 20, 26, 28, 31; Lk. xiii. 7; xiv. 35 (34); Jn. xii. 24; Heb. vi. 7; Jas. v. 7; Rev. ix. 4; of the earthy material out of which a thing is formed, with the implied idea of frailty and weakness: ἐκ γῆς χοϊκός, 1 Co. xv. 47. **2.** *the ground, the earth* as a standing-place, (Germ. *Boden*): Mt. x. 29; xv. 35; xxiii. 35; xxvii. 51; Mk. viii. 6; ix. 20; xiv. 35; Lk. xxii. 44 [L br. WH reject the pass.]; xxiv. 5; Jn. viii. 6, 8, [i. e. Rec.]; Acts ix. 4, 8. **3.** *the main land*, opp. to sea or water: Mk. iv. 1; vi. 47; Lk. v. 3; viii. 27; Jn. vi. 21; xxi. 8 sq. 11; Rev. xii. 12. **4.** *the earth* as a whole, *the world* (Lat. *terrarum orbis*); **a.** *the earth* as opp. *to the heavens*: Mt. v. 18, 35; vi. 10; xvi. 19; xviii. 18; xxiv. 35; Mk. xiii. 31; Lk. ii. 14; Jn. xii. 32; Acts ii. 19; iv. 24; 2 Pet. iii. 5, 7, 10, 13; Rev. xxi. 1; τὰ ἐπὶ τῆς γῆς the things and beings that are on the earth, Eph. i. 10; Col. i. 16 [T WH om. L Tr br. τά]; involving a suggestion of mutability, frailty, infirmity, alike in thought and in action, Mt. vi. 19; τὰ ἐπὶ τῆς γῆς (equiv. to τὰ ἐπίγεια, Phil. iii. 19) terrestrial goods, pleasures, honors, Col. iii. 2 (opp. to τὰ ἄνω); τὰ μέλη ὑμῶν τὰ ἐπὶ τῆς γῆς the members of your earthly body, as it were the abode and instruments of corrupt desires, Col. iii. 5; ὁ ὢν ἐκ τῆς γῆς ... λαλεῖ (in contrast with Christ as having come from heaven) he who is of earthly (human) origin, has an earthly nature, and speaks as his earthly origin and nature prompt, Jn. iii. 31. **b.** *the inhabited earth*, the abode of men and animals: Lk. xxi. 35; Acts i. 8; x. 12; xi. 6; xvii. 26; Heb. xi. 13; Rev. iii. 10; αἴρειν ζωήν τινος or τινὰ ἀπὸ τῆς γῆς, Acts viii. 33; xxii. 22; κληρονομεῖν τὴν γῆν (see κληρονομέω, 2), Mt. v. 5 (4); πῦρ βάλλειν ἐπὶ [Rec. εἰς] τὴν γῆν, i. e. among men, Lk. xii. 49, cf. 51 and Mt. x. 34; ἐπὶ τῆς γῆς among men, Lk. xviii. 8; Jn. xvii. 4.   **5.** *a country, land enclosed within fixed boundaries, a tract of land, territory, region*; simply, when it is plain from the context what land is meant, as that of the Jews: Lk. iv. 25; xxi. 23; Ro. ix. 28; Jas. v. 17; with a gentile noun added [then, as a rule, anarthrous, W. 121 (114 sq.)]: γῆ Ἰσραήλ, Mt. ii. 20 sq.; Ἰούδα, Mt. ii. 6; Γεννησαρέτ, Mt. xiv. 34; Mk. vi. 53; Σοδόμων κ. Γομόρρων, Mt. x. 15; xi. 24; Χαλδαίων, Acts vii. 4; Αἴγυπτος, (see Αἴγυπτος); ἡ Ἰουδαία γῆ, Jn. iii. 22; with the addition of an adj.: ἀλλοτρία, Acts vii. 6; ἐκείνη, Mt. ix. 26, 31; with gen. of pers. *one's country*, native land, Acts vii. 3.

γῆρας, -αος (-ως), Ion. γήρεος, dat. γήρεϊ, γήρει, τό, [fr. Hom. down], *old age*: Lk. i. 36 ἐν γήρει G L T Tr WH for Rec. ἐν γήρᾳ, a form found without var. in Sir. xxv. 3; [also Ps. xci. (xcii.) 15; cf. Gen. xv. 15 Alex.; xxi. 7 ib.; xxv. 8 ib.; 1 Chr. xxix. 28 ib.]; Clem. Rom. 1 Cor. 10, 7 var.; cf. *Tdf.* Proleg. p. 117]; Fritzsche on Sir. iii. 12; *Sturz*, De dial. Maced. etc. p. 155; W. [36 and] 64 (62); [B. 15 (14)].*

γηράσκω or **γηράω**: 1 aor. ἐγήρασα; fr. Hom. down; [cf. W. 92 (88); *Donaldson*, New Crat. § 387]; *to grow old*: Jn. xxi. 18; of things, institutions, etc., *to fail from age, be obsolescent*: Heb. viii. 13 (to be deprived of force and authority; [here associated with παλαιούμενος — the latter (used only of things) marking the lapse of time, while γηράσκων carries with it a suggestion of the waning strength, the decay, incident to old age (cf. Schmidt ch. 46, 7; Theophr. caus. pl. 6, 7, 5): "that which *is becoming old* and *faileth for age*" etc.]).*

γίνομαι (in Ionic prose writ. and in com. Grk. fr. Aristot. on for Attic γίγνομαι); [impf. ἐγινόμην]; fut. γενήσομαι; 2 aor. ἐγενόμην (often in 3 pers. sing. optat. γένοιτο; [ptcp. γενάμενος, Lk. xxiv. 22 Tdf. ed. 7]), and, with no diff. in signif., 1 aor. pass. ἐγενήθην, rejected by the Atticists (cf. *Lob.* ad Phryn. p. 108 sq.; [Thom. Mag. ed. Ritschl p. 75, 6 sq.]), not rare in later Grk., common in Sept. (Acts iv. 4; 1 Th. ii. 14; 1 Co. xv. 10, etc.); impv. γενηθήτω (Mt. vi. 10; xv. 28, etc.); pf. γεγένημαι and γέγονα, 3 pers. plur. γέγοναν L T Tr WH in Ro. xvi. 7 and Rev. xxi. 6 (cf. [*Tdf.* Proleg. p. 124; *WH.* App. p. 166; *Soph.* Lex. p. 37 sq.; *Curtius*, Das Verbum, ii. 187]; W. 36 and 76 (73) sq.; Mullach p. 16; B. 43 (37 sq.)), [ptcp. γεγονώς]; plpf. 3 pers. sing. ἐγεγόνει (Jn. vi. 17 [not Tdf.]; Acts iv. 22 [where L T Tr WH γεγόνει, W. § 12, 9; B. 33 (29); Tdf.'s note on the pass.]); *to become*, and

1. *to become*, i. e. *to come into existence, begin to be, receive being*: absol., Jn. i. 15, 30 (ἔμπροσθέν μου γέγονεν); Jn. viii. 58 (πρὶν Ἀβραὰμ γενέσθαι); 1 Co. xv. 37 (τὸ σῶμα τὸ γενησόμενον); ἔκ τινος, *to be born*, Ro. i. 3 (ἐκ σπέρματος Δαυίδ); Gal. iv. 4 (ἐκ γυναικός); Mt. xxi. 19 (μηκέτι ἐκ σοῦ καρπὸς γένηται, *come from*); of the origin of all things, Heb. xi. 3; διά τινος, Jn. i. 3, 10. *to rise, arise, come on, appear*, of occurrences in nature or in life: as γίνεται βροντή, Jn. xii. 29; ἀστραπή, Rev. viii. 5; σεισμός, Rev.

[vi. 12; xi. 13]; xvi. 18; γαλήνη, Mt. viii. 26; Mk. iv. 39; Lk. viii. 24; λαῖλαψ, Mk. iv. 37; γογγυσμός, Acts vi. 1; ζήτησις, Jn. iii. 25 [foll. by ἐκ of origin; στάσις καὶ ζήτησις], Acts xv. 2 [Grsb. questions ζήτ., Rec. reads συζήτ.]; πόλεμος, Rev. xii. 7; ἡ βασιλεία [or αἱ β.] κτλ. Rev. xi. 15; xii. 10; χαρά, Acts viii. 8, and in many other exx. Here belong also the phrases γίνεται ἡμέρα *it becomes day, day comes on*, Lk. iv. 42; vi. 13; xxii. 66; Acts xii. 18; xvi. 35; xxiii. 12; xxvii. 29, 33, 39; γ. ὀψέ *evening comes*, Mk. xi. 19, i. q. γ ὀψία, Mt. viii. 16, xiv. 15, 23; xvi. 2 [T br. WH reject the pass.]; xxvi. 20; Mk. xiv. 17; Jn. vi. 16, etc.; πρωΐα, Mt. xxvii. 1; Jn. xxi. 4; νύξ, Acts xxvii. 27 [cf. s. v. ἐπιγίν. 2]; σκοτία, Jn. vi. 17 [not Tdf.].

2. *to become* i. q. *to come to pass, happen*, of events; **a.** univ.: Mt. v. 18; xxiv. 6, 20, 34; Lk. i. 20; xii. 54; xxi. 28; Jn. i. 28; xiii. 19, etc.; τοῦτο γέγονεν, ἵνα etc. *this hath come to pass* that etc., Mt. i. 22; xxi. 4; xxvi. 56; τὰ γενόμενα or γινόμενα, Mt. xviii. 31; xxvii. 54; xxviii. 11; Lk. xxiii. 48; [cf. τὰ γενόμενα ἀγαθά, Heb. ix. 11 L WH txt. Tr mrg.]; τὸ γενόμενον, Lk. xxiii. 47; τὸ γεγονός, Mk. v. 14; Lk. xxiv. 12 [T om. L Tr br. WH reject the s.]; Acts iv. 21; τὸ ῥῆμα τὸ γεγονός, Lk. ii. 15; τὰ μέλλοντα γίνεσθαι, Lk. xxi. 36; Acts xxvi. 22; τὴν ἀνάστασιν ἤδη γεγονέναι, 2 Tim. ii. 18; θανάτου γενομένου *a death having taken place* (Germ. *nach erfolgtem Tode*), Heb. ix. 15. μὴ γένοιτο, a formula esp. freq. in Paul (and in Epictetus, cf. *Schweigh.* Index Graec. in Epict. p. 392), *far be it! God forbid!* [cf. *Morison*, Exposition of Rom. iii., p. 31 sq.]: Lk. xx. 16; Ro. iii. 4, 6, 31; vi. 2, 15; vii. 7, 13; ix. 14; xi. 1, 11; 1 Co. vi. 15; Gal. ii. 17; iii. 21 (equiv. to חָלִילָה, Josh. xxii. 29, etc.); cf. *Sturz*, De dial. Maced. etc. p. 204 sq.; τί γέγονεν, ὅτι etc. *what has come to pass, that* i. q. *for what reason, why*? Jn. xiv. 22 (τί ἐγένετο, ὅτι ... Eccles. vii. 11 (10); τί ἐστιν, ὡς etc., Eur. Troad. 889). **b.** Very common in the first three Gospels, esp. that of Luke, and in the Acts, is the phrase καὶ ἐγένετο (וַיְהִי foll. by וְ); cf. W. § 65, 4 e. [also § 44, 3 c.], and esp. B. § 141, 6. **α.** καὶ ἐγένετο καί with a finite verb: Mk. ii. 15 ([Tr txt. καὶ γίνεται], T WH καὶ γίν. [foll. by acc. and inf.]); Lk. ii. 15 [R G L br. Tr br.]; viii. 1; xiv. 1; xvii. 11; xix. 15; xxiv. 15 [WH br. καί]; foll. by καὶ ἰδού, Mt. ix. 10 [T om. καί before ἰδ.]; Lk. xxiv. 4. **β.** much oftener καί is not repeated: Mt. vii. 28; Mk. iv. 4; Lk. i. 23; ii. [15 T WH], 46; vi. 12; vii. 11; ix. 18, 33; xi. 1; xix. 29; xxiv. 30. **γ.** καὶ ἐγέν. foll. by acc. with inf.: Mk. ii. 23 [W. 578 (537) note]; Lk. vi. 1, 6 [R G ἐγέν. δὲ καί]. **c.** In like manner ἐγένετο δέ **a.** foll. by καί with a finite verb: Lk. v. 1; ix. 28 [WH txt. om. L br. καί, 51; x. 38 R G T, L Tr mrg. br. καί]; Acts v. 7. **β.** ἐγένετο δέ foll. by a fin. verb without καί: Lk. i. 8; ii. 1, 6; [vi. 12 R G L]; viii. 40 [WH Tr txt. om. ἐγέν.]; ix. 37; xi. 14, 27. **γ.** ἐγένετο δέ foll. by acc. with inf.: Lk. iii. 21; [vi. 1, 6 L T Tr WH, 12 T Tr WH]; xvi. 22; Acts iv. 5; ix. 3 [without δέ], 32, 37; xi. 26 R G; xiv. 1; [xvi. 16; xix. 1]; xxviii. 8, [17]. **δ.** ἐγέν. δὲ [ὡς δὲ ἐγέν.] foll. by τοῦ with inf.: Acts x. 25 (Rec. om. τοῦ), cf. Mey. ad loc. and W. 328 (307); [B. 270 (232)]. **d.** with dat. of pers. *to occur* or *happen to one, befall one*: foll. by inf., Acts xx. 16; ἐὰν γένηται (sc. αὐτῷ) εὑρεῖν αὐτό, if it happen to him, Mt. xviii. 13; ἐμοὶ δὲ μὴ γένοιτο καυχᾶσθαι *far be it from me to glory*, Gal. vi. 14, (Gen. xliv. 7, 17; 1 K. xx. (xxi.) 3; Alciphr. epp. 1, 26); foll. by acc. with inf. *it happened to me, that* etc.: Acts xi. 26 L T Tr WH [but acc. implied]; xxii. 6, 17, [cf. W. 323 (303); B. 305 (262)]; with adverbs, *go, fare*, (Germ. *ergehen*): εὖ, Eph. vi. 3, (μὴ γένοιτό σοι οὕτω κακῶς, Ael. v. h. 9, 36). with specification of the thing befalling one: τί γέγονεν [L T Tr txt. WH ἐγέν.] αὐτῷ, Acts vii. 40 (fr. Ex. xxxii. 1); ἐγένετο [L T Tr WH ἐγίνετο] πάσῃ ψυχῇ φόβος fear came upon, Acts ii. 43. — Mk. iv. 11; ix. 21; Lk. xix. 9; Jn. v. 14; xv. 7; Ro. xi. 25; 1 Co. iv. 5; 2 Co. i. 8 [G L T Tr WH om. dat.]; 2 Tim. iii. 11; 1 Pet. iv. 12; with the ellipsis of ἡμῖν, Jn. i. 17. ἐγένετο (αὐτῷ) γνώμη a purpose occurred to him, he determined, Acts xx. 3 [B. 268 (230), but T Tr WH read ἐγέν. γνώμης; see below, 5 e. *a*.]. foll. by prepositions: ἐπ᾽ αὐτῷ *upon* (Germ. *bei* or *an*) *her*, Mk. v. 33 [R G L br.]; εἴς τινα, Acts xxviii. 6.

3. *to arise, appear in history, come upon the stage*: of men appearing in public, Mk. i. 4; Jn. i. 6, [on which two pass. cf. W. 350 (328); B. 308 (264) sq.]; 2 Pet. ii. 1; γεγόνασι, have arisen and now exist, 1 Jn. ii. 18.

4. *to be made, done, finished*: τὰ ἔργα, Heb. iv. 3; διὰ χειρῶν, of things fabricated, Acts xix. 26; of miracles *to be performed, wrought*: διὰ τῶν χειρῶν τινος, Mk. vi. 2; διά τινος, Acts ii. 43; iv. 16, 30; xii. 9; ὑπό τινος, Lk. ix. 7 (R L [but the latter br. ὑπ᾽ αὐτοῦ]); xiii. 17; xxiii. 8; γενόμενα εἰς Καφαρν. done unto (on) Capernaum i. e. for its benefit (W. 416 (388); [cf. B. 333 (286)]), Lk. iv. 23 [Rec. ἐν τῇ Κ.]. of commands, decisions, purposes, requests, etc. *to be done, executed*: Mt. vi. 10; xxi. 21; xxvi. 42; Mk. xi. 23; Lk. xiv. 22; xxiii. 24; Acts xxi. 14; γενήσεται ὁ λόγος will be accomplished the saying, 1 Co. xv. 54. joined to nouns implying a certain action: ἡ ἀπώλεια γέγονε, Mk. xiv. 4; ἀπογραφή, Lk. ii. 2; ἐπαγγελία γενομένη ὑπὸ θεοῦ given by God, Acts xxvi. 6; ἀνάκρισις, Acts xxv. 26; νόμου μετάθεσις, Heb. vii. 12; ἄφεσις, Heb. ix. 22. of institutions, laws, etc. *to be established, enacted*: τὸ σάββατον ἐγένετο, the institution of the Sabbath, Mk. ii. 27; ὁ νόμος, Gal. iii. 17; οὐ γέγονεν οὕτως hath not been so ordained, Mt. xix. 8. of feasts, marriages, entertainments, *to be kept, celebrated*: τὸ πάσχα, Mt. xxvi. 2 (i. q. נַעֲשֶׂה, 2 K. xxiii. 22); τὸ σάββατον, Mk. vi. 2; τὰ ἐγκαίνια, Jn. x. 22; [γενεσίοις γενομένοις (cf. W. § 31, 9 b.; R G γενεσίων ἀγομένων), Mt. xiv. 6], (τὰ Ὀλύμπια, Xen. Hell. 7, 4, 28; Ἴσθμια, 4, 5, 1); γάμος, Jn. ii. 1. οὕτως γένηται ἐν ἐμοί so done with me, in my case, 1 Co. ix. 15.

5. *to become, be made*, "in passages where it is specified who or what a person or thing is or has been rendered, as respects quality, condition, place, rank, character" (*Wahl*, Clavis Apocr. V. T. p. 101). **a.** with a predicate added, expressed by a subst. or an adj.: οἱ λίθοι οὗτοι ἄρτοι γένωνται, Mt. iv. 3; Lk. iv. 3; ὕδωρ οἶνον γεγενημένον, Jn. ii. 9; ἀρχιερεὺς γενόμενος, Heb. vi. 20; διάκονος, Col. i. 25; ὁ λόγος σὰρξ ἐγένετο, Jn. i. 14; ἀνήρ, 1 Co. xiii. 11, and many other exx.; χάρις οὐκέτι γίνεται χάρις grace

ceases to have the nature of grace, can no longer be called grace, Ro. xi. 6; ἄκαρπος γίνεται, Mt. xiii. 22; Mk. iv. 19; — in Mt. xvii. 2; Lk. viii. 17; Jn. v. 6, and many other places. contextually, *to show one's self, prove one's self*: Lk. x. 36; xix. 17; xxiv. 19; Ro. xi. 34; xvi. 2; 2 Co. i. 18 Rec.; 1 Th. i. 6; ii. 7; Heb. xi. 6, etc.; esp. in exhortations: γίνεσθε, Mt. x. 16; xxiv. 44; Lk. vi. 36; Eph. iv. 32; Col. iii. 15; μὴ γίνου, Jn. xx. 27; μὴ γίνεσθε, Mt. vi. 16; Eph. v. 7, 17; 1 Co. x. 7; μὴ γινώμεθα, Gal. v. 26; hence used declaratively, i. q. *to be found, shown*: Lk. xiii. 2 (that it was shown by their fate that they were sinners); Ro. iii. 4; 2 Co. vii. 14; — γίνομαί τινί τις to show one's self (to be) some one to one: 1 Co. ix. 20, 22. **b.** with an interrog. pron. as predicate: τί ὁ Πέτρος ἐγένετο what had become of Peter, Acts xii. 18 [cf. use of τί ἐγέν. in Act. Phil. in Hell. § 23, *Tdf.* Acta apost. apocr. p. 104]. **c.** γίνεσθαι ὡς or ὡσεί τινα *to become as* or *like to one*: Mt. x. 25; xviii. 3; xxviii. 4; Mk. ix. 26; Lk. xxii. 44 [L br. WH reject the pass.]; Ro. ix. 29 (fr. Is. i. 9); 1 Co. iv. 13; Gal. iv. 12. **d.** γίνεσθαι εἴς τι *to become* i. e. be changed *into something, come to be, issue in, something* (Germ. *zu etwas werden*): ἐγενήθη εἰς κεφαλὴν γωνίας, Mt. xxi. 42; Mk. xii. 10; Lk. xx. 17; Acts iv. 11; 1 Pet. ii. 7, — all after Ps. cxvii. (cxviii.) 22. Lk. xiii. 19 (εἰς δένδρον μέγα); Jn. xvi. 20; Acts v. 36; Ro. ix. 29 (fr. Ps. lxviii. (lxix.) 23); 1 Th. iii. 5; Rev. viii. 11; xvi. 19, etc. (equiv. to הָיָה לְ; but the expression is also classic; cf. W. § 29, 3 a.; B. 150 (131)). **e.** γίνεσθαι with Cases: **a.** with the gen. *to become the property of any one, to come into the power of a person* or *thing*, [cf. W. § 30, 5; esp. B. 162 (142)]: Lk. xx. 14 [L mrg. ἔσται], 33; Rev. xi. 15; [γνώμης, Acts xx. 3 T Tr WH (cf. ἐλπίδος μεγάλης γίν. Plut. Phoc. 23, 4)]; προφητεία ἰδίας ἐπιλύσεως οὐ γίνεται no one can explain prophecy by his own mental power (it is not a matter of subjective interpretation), but to explain it one needs the same illumination of the Holy Spirit in which it originated, for etc. 2 Pet. i. 20. γενέσθαι with a gen. indicating one's age, (to be) so many years old: Lk. ii. 42; 1 Tim. v. 9. **β.** with the dat. [cf. W. 210 sq. (198)]: γίνεσθαι ἀνδρί *to become a man's wife*, Ro. vii. 3 sq. (הָיָה לְאִישׁ, Lev. xxii. 12; Ruth i. 12, etc.). **f.** joined to prepositions with their substantives; ἔν τινι, *to come* or *pass into a certain state* [cf. B. 330 (284)]: ἐν ἀγωνίᾳ, Lk. xxii. 44 [L br. WH reject the pass.]; ἐν ἐκστάσει, Acts xxii. 17; ἐν πνεύματι, Rev. i. 10; iv. 2; ἐν δόξῃ [R. V. came with (in) glory], 2 Co. iii. 7; ἐν παραβάσει, 1 Tim. ii. 14; ἐν ἑαυτῷ, to come to himself, recover reason, Acts xii. 11 (also in Grk. writ.; cf. *Hermann* ad Vig. p. 749); ἐν Χριστῷ, to be brought to the fellowship of Christ, to become a Christian, Ro. xvi. 7; ἐν ὁμοιώματι ἀνθρώπων, to become like men, Phil. ii. 7; ἐν λόγῳ κολακείας [R. V. were we found using] flattering speech, 1 Th. ii. 5. ἐπάνω τινός *to be placed over a thing*, Lk. xix. 19. μετά τινος or σύν τινι *to become one's companion, associate with him*: Mk. xvi. 10; Acts vii. 38; xx. 18; ὑπό τινα *to be made subject to one*, Gal. iv. 4. [Cf. h. below.] **g.** with specification of the *terminus of motion* or *the place of rest*: εἰς with acc. of place, to come to some place, arrive at some thing, Acts xx. 16; xxi. 17; xxv. 15; ὡς ἐγένετο ... εἰς τὰ ὦτά μου when the voice came into my ears, Lk. i. 44; εἰς with acc. of pers., of evils coming upon one, Rev. xvi. 2 R G; of blessings, Gal. iii. 14; 1 Th. i. 5 [Lchm. πρός; Acts xxvi. 6 L T Tr WH]; γενέσθαι ἐπὶ τοῦ τόπου, Lk. xxii. 40; ἐπὶ τῆς γῆς, Jn. vi. 21 [Tdf. ἐπὶ τὴν γ.]; ὧδε, ib. 25 (ἐκεῖ, Xen. an. 6, 3 [5], 20; [cf. B. 71]); ἐπί with acc. of place, Lk. xxiv. 22; Acts xxi. 35; [Jn. vi. 21 Tdf.]; ἐγένετο διωγμὸς ἐπὶ τὴν ἐκκλησίαν, Acts viii. 1; ἐγένετο φόβος or θάμβος ἐπὶ πάντας, Lk. i. 65; iv. 36; Acts v. 5, 11; [ἔκστασις, Acts x. 10 (Rec. ἐπέπεσεν)]; ἕλκος κακὸν κ. πονηρὸν ἐπὶ τ. ἀνθρώπους, Rev. xvi. 2 L T Tr WH; ἐγένετο ῥῆμα ἐπί τινα, λόγος or φωνὴ πρός τινα (came to): Lk. iii. 2; Jn. x. 35; Acts vii. 31 [Rec.]; x. 13, (Gen. xv. 1, 4; Jer. i. 2, 11; xiii. 8; Ezek. vi. 1; Hos. i. 1); [ἐπαγγελία, Acts xiii. 32; xxvi. 6 Rec.]; κατά with acc. of place, Lk. x. 32 [Tr WH om.]; Acts xxvii. 7, (Xen. Cyr. 7, 1, 15); κατά with gen.: τὸ γενόμενον ῥῆμα καθ' ὅλης τῆς Ἰουδαίας the matter the report of which spread throughout all Judæa, Acts x. 37; πρός τινα, 2 Jn. 12 (Rec. ἐλθεῖν); 1 Co. ii. 3; σύν τινι, to be joined to one as an associate, Lk. ii. 13, (Xen. Cyr. 5, 3, 8); ἐγγὺς γίνεσθαι, Eph. ii. 13; τινός, Jn. vi. 19;   h. [with ἐκ of the source (see 1 above): Mk. i. 11 (Tdf. om. ἐγέν.); ix. 7 (T Tr mrg. WH); Lk. iii. 22; ix. 35; Acts xix. 34]; γίνεσθαι ἐκ μέσου, to be taken out of the way, 2 Th. ii. 7; γενέσθαι ὁμοθυμαδόν, of many come together in one place, Acts xv. 25 cf. ii. 1 [but only in R G; γενομένοις ὁμοθυμαδόν in xv. 25 may mean either having become of one mind, or possibly having come together with one accord. On the alleged use of γίνομαι in the N. T. as interchangeable with εἰμί see Fritzschior. Opuscc. p. 284 note. COMP.: ἀπο-, δια-, ἐπι-, παρα-, συμ- παρα-, προ-γίνομαι.]

1097   γινώσκω (Attic γιγνώσκω; fr. ΓΝΟΩ, as βιβρώσκω fr. ΒΡΟΩ); [impf. ἐγίνωσκον; fut. γνώσομαι; 2 aor. ἔγνων (fr. ΓΝΟΜΙ), impv. γνῶθι, γνώτω, subj. γνῶ (3 pers. sing. γνοῖ, Mk. v. 43; ix. 30; Lk. xix. 15 L T Tr WH, for R G γνῷ [B. p. 46 (40); cf. δίδωμι init.]), inf. γνῶναι, ptcp. γνούς; pf. ἔγνωκα (Jn. xvii. 7; 3 pers. plur. ἔγνωκαν for ἐγνώκασι, see reff. in γίνομαι init.); plpf. ἐγνώκειν; Pass., [pres. 3 pers. sing. γινώσκεται (Mk. xiii. 28 Tr mrg.)]; pf. ἔγνωσμαι; 1 aor. ἐγνώσθην; fut. γνωσθήσομαι; in Grk. writ. fr. Hom. down; Sept. for יָדַע; Lat. nosco, novi (i. e. gnosco, gnovi);

I. univ.   **1.** to learn to know, come to know, get a knowledge of; pass. to become known: with acc., Mt. xxii. 18; Mk. v. 43; Acts xxi. 34; 1 Co. iv. 19; 2 Co. ii. 4; Col. iv. 8; 1 Th. iii. 5, etc. Pass., Mt. x. 26; Acts ix. 24; Phil. iv. 5, etc.; [impers. γινώσκεται, Mk. xiii. 28 Tr mrg. T 2, 7]; τὶ ἐκ τινος, Mt. xii. 33; Lk. vi. 44; 1 Jn. iv. 6; τινὰ or τὶ ἔν τινι, to find a sign in a thing by which to know, to recognize in or by something, Lk. xxiv. 35; Jn. xiii. 35; 1 Jn. iv. 2; κατὰ τί γνώσομαι τοῦτο, the truth of this promise, Lk. i. 18 (Gen. xv. 8); περὶ τῆς διδαχῆς, Jn. vii. 17. often the object is not added, but is readily understood from what precedes: Mt. ix. 30; xii. 15 (the consultation held by the Pharisees); Mk. vii. 24 (he would have no one know that he was present); Mk. ix. 30; Ro. x. 19, etc.;

foll. by ὅτι, Mt. xxi. 45; Jn. iv. 1; v. 6; xii. 9, etc.; foll. by the interrog. τί, Mt. vi. 3; Lk. xvi. 4; ἀπό τινος, to learn from one, Mk. xv. 45.   with acc. of pers. to recognize as worthy of intimacy and love, to own; so those whom God has judged worthy of the blessings of the gospel are said ὑπὸ τοῦ θεοῦ γινώσκεσθαι, 1 Co. viii. 3; Gal. iv. 9, [on both cf. W. § 39, 3 Note 2; B. 55 (48)]; negatively, in the sentence of Christ οὐδέποτε ἔγνων ὑμᾶς, I never knew you, never had any acquaintance with you, Mt. vii. 23.   to perceive, feel: ἔγνω τῷ σώματι, ὅτι etc. Mk. v. 29; ἔγνων δύναμιν ἐξελθοῦσαν ἀπ' ἐμοῦ, Lk. viii. 46.   **2.** to know, understand, perceive, have knowledge of;   a. to understand: with acc., τὰ λεγόμενα, Lk. xviii. 34; ἃ ἀναγινώσκεις, Acts viii. 30; foll. by ὅτι, Mt. xxi. 45; Jn. viii. 27 sq.; 2 Co. xiii. 6; Gal. iii. 7; Jas. ii. 20; foll. by interrog. τί, Jn. x. 6; xiii. 12, 28; ὃ κατεργάζομαι οὐ γινώσκω I do not understand what I am doing, my conduct is inexplicable to me, Ro. vii. 15.   b. to know: τὸ θέλημα, Lk. xii. 47; τὰς καρδίας, Lk. xvi. 15; τὸν μὴ γνόντα ἁμαρτίαν ignorant of sin, i. e. not conscious of having committed sin, 2 Co. v. 21; ἐπιστολὴ γινωσκομένη καὶ ἀναγινωσκομένη, 2 Co. iii. 2; τινά, to know one, his person, character, mind, plans: Jn. i. 48 (49); ii. 24; Acts xix. 15; 2 Tim. ii. 19 (fr. Num. xvi. 5); foll. by ὅτι, Jn. xxi. 17; Phil. i. 12; Jas. i. 3; 2 Pet. i. 20; foll. by acc. with inf. Heb. x. 34; foll. by an indirect question, Rev. iii. 3; ἑλληνιστὶ γινώσκ. to know Greek (graece scire, Cic. de fin. 2, 5): Acts xxi. 37, (ἐπίστασθαι συριστί, Xen. Cyr. 7, 5, 31; graece nescire, Cic. pro Flac. 4, 10); ἴστε (Rec. ἐστε) γινώσκοντες ye know, understanding etc. [R. V. ye know of a surety, etc.], Eph. v. 5; see W. 355 (333); [cf. B. 51 (44); 314 (269)]. impv. γινώσκετε know ye: Mt. xxiv. 32 sq. 43; Mk. xiii. 29; Lk. x. 11; Jn. xv. 18; Acts ii. 36; Heb. xiii. 23; 1 Jn. ii. 29.   **3.** by a Hebraistic euphemism [cf. W. 18], found also in Grk. writ. fr. the Alexandrian age down, γινώσκω is used of the carnal connection of male and female, rem cum aliquo or aliqua habere (cf. our have a [criminal] intimacy with): of a husband, Mt. i. 25; of the woman, Lk. i. 34; (Gen. iv. 1, 17; xix. 8; 1 S. i. 19, etc.; Judith xvi. 22; Callim. epigr. 58, 3; often in Plut.; cf. Vögelin, Plut. Brut. p. 10 sqq.; so also Lat. cognosco, Ovid. met. 4, 596; novi, Justin. hist. 27, 3, 11).

II. In particular γινώσκω, to become acquainted with, to know, is employed in the N. T. of the knowledge of God and Christ, and of the things relating to them or proceeding from them;   a. τὸν θεόν, the one, true God, in contrast with the polytheism of the Gentiles: Ro. i. 21; Gal. iv. 9; also τὸν μόνον ἀληθινὸν θεόν, Jn. xvii. 3 cf. 1 Jn. v. 20; τὸν θεόν, the nature and will of God, in contrast with the false wisdom of both Jews and Gentiles, 1 Co. i. 21; τὸν πατέρα, the nature of God the Father, esp. the holy will and affection by which he aims to sanctify and redeem men through Christ, Jn. viii. 55; xvi. 3; 1 Jn. ii. 3 sq. 14 (13); iii. 1, 6; iv. 8; a peculiar knowledge of God the Father is claimed by Christ for himself, Jn. x. 15; xvii. 25; γνῶθι τὸν κύριον, the precepts of the Lord, Heb. viii. 11; τὸ θέλημα (of God), Ro. ii. 18; νοῦν κυρίου, Ro. xi. 34; 1 Co. ii. 16; τὴν σοφίαν τοῦ θεοῦ, 1 Co. ii. 8; τὰς ὁδοὺς τοῦ θεοῦ, Heb. iii. 10 (fr. Ps. xciv. (xcv.) 10). **b.** Χριστόν, his blessings, Phil. iii. 10; in Χριστὸν ἐγνωκέναι κατὰ σάρκα, 2 Co. v. 16, Paul speaks of that knowledge of Christ which he had before his conversion, and by which he knew him merely in the form of a servant, and therefore had not yet seen in him the Son of God. Acc. to J o h n's usage, γινώσκειν, ἐγνωκέναι Χριστόν denotes *to come to know, to know,* his Messianic dignity (Jn. xvii. 3; vi. 69); his divinity (τὸν ἀπ' ἀρχῆς, 1 Jn. ii. 13 sq. cf. Jn. i. 10), his consummate kindness towards us, and the benefits redounding to us from fellowship with him (in Christ's words γινώσκομαι ὑπὸ τῶν ἐμῶν, Jn. x. 14 [acc. to the crit. texts γινώσκουσίν με τὰ ἐμά]); his love of God (Jn. xiv. 31); his sinless holiness (1 Jn. iii. 6). John unites πιστεύειν and γινώσκειν, at one time putting πιστεύειν first: vi. 69 [cf. Schaff's Lange or Mey. ad loc.]; but at another time γινώσκειν: x. 38 (acc. to R G, for which L T Tr WH read ἵνα γνῶτε καὶ γινώσκητε [R. V. *know and understand*]); xvii. 8 [L br. κ. ἔγν.]; 1 Jn. iv. 16 (the love of God). **c.** γ. τὰ τοῦ πνεύματος the things which proceed from the Spirit, 1 Co. ii. 14; τὸ πνεῦμα τ. ἀληθείας καὶ τὸ πν. τῆς πλάνης, 1 Jn. iv. 6; τὰ μυστήρια τῆς βασιλείας τῶν οὐρανῶν, Mt. xiii. 11; τὴν ἀλήθειαν, Jn. viii. 32; 2 Jn. 1; absol., of the knowledge of divine things, 1 Co. xiii. 12; of the knowledge of things lawful for a Christian, 1 Co. viii. 2.

[SYN. γ ι ν ώ σ κ ε ι ν, ε ἰ δ έ ν α ι, ἐ π ί σ τ α σ θ α ι, σ υ ν ι έ ν α ι : In classic usage (cf. Schmidt ch. 13), γινώσκειν, distinguished from the rest by its original i n c h o a t i v e force, denotes a discriminating apprehension of external impressions, a knowledge grounded in personal experience. εἰδέναι, lit. ' to have seen with the mind's eye,' signifies a clear and purely mental perception, in contrast both to conjecture and to knowledge derived from others. ἐπίστασθαι primarily expresses the knowledge obtained by p r o x i m i t y to the thing known (cf. our *understand,* Germ. *verstehen*); then knowledge viewed as the result of prolonged practice, in opposition to the process of learning on the one hand, and to the uncertain knowledge of a dilettante on the other. συνιέναι implies native insight, the soul's capacity of itself not only to lay hold of the phenomena of the outer world through the senses, but by combination (σύν and ἰέναι) to arrive at their underlying laws. Hence συνιέναι may mark an a n t i t h e s i s to sense-perception; whereas γινώσκειν marks an a d v a n c e upon it. As applied e. g. to a work of literature, γινώσκειν expresses an acquaintance with it; ἐπίστασθαι the knowledge of its contents; συνιέναι the understanding of it, a comprehension of its meaning. γινώσκειν and εἰδέναι most readily come into contrast with each other; if εἰδέναι and ἐπίστασθαι are contrasted, the former refers more to n a t u r a l, the latter to a c q u i r e d knowledge. In the N. T., as might be expected, these distinctions are somewhat less sharply marked. Such passages as John i. 26, 31, 48 (49); vii. 27 sq.; xxi. 17; 2 Co. v. 16; 1 Jn. v. 20 may seem to indicate that, sometimes at least, γινώσκω and οἶδα are nearly interchangeable; yet see Jn. iii. 10, 11; viii. 55 (yet cf. xvii. 25); 1 Jn. ii. 29 (*know . . . perceive*), and the characteristic use of εἰδέναι by John to describe our Lord's direct insight into divine things: iii. 11; v. 32 (contrast 42); vii. 29; viii. 55; xii. 50, etc; cf. Bp. Lghtft.'s note on Gal. iv. 9; *Green,* 'Critical Notes' etc. p. 75 (on Jn. viii. 55); Westcott on John ii. 24. γινώσκω and ἐπίσταμαι are associated in Acts xix. 15 (cf. Green, as above, p. 97); οἶδα and γινώσκω in 1 Co. ii. 11; Eph v. 5; οἶδα and ἐπίσταμαι in Jude 10. COMP.: ἀνα-, δια-, ἐπι-, κατα-, προ-γινώσκω.]

γλεῦκος, -ους, τό, *must,* the sweet juice pressed from the   **1098** grape; Nicand. alex. 184, 299; Plut., al.; Job xxxii. 19; *sweet wine:* Acts ii. 13. [Cf. BB. DD. s. v. Wine.]*

γλυκύς, -εῖα, -ύ, *sweet:* Jas. iii. 11 (opp. to πικρόν); 12   **1099** (opp. to ἁλυκόν); Rev. x. 9, [10]. [From Hom. down.]*

γλῶσσα, -ης, ἡ, [fr. Hom. down], *the tongue;* **1.** *the*   **1100** *tongue,* a member of the body, the organ of speech: Mk. vii. 33, 35; Lk. i. 64; xvi. 24; 1 Co. xiv. 9; Jas. i. 26; iii. 5, 6, 8; 1 Pet. iii. 10; 1 Jn. iii. 18; [Rev. xvi. 10]. By a poetical and rhetorical usage, esp. Hebraistic, that member of the body which is chiefly engaged in some act has ascribed to it what belongs to the man; the *tongue* is so used in Acts ii. 26 (ἠγαλλιάσατο ἡ γλῶσσά μου); Ro. iii. 13; xiv. 11; Phil. ii. 11 (the tongue of every man); of the little tongue-like flames symbolizing the gift of foreign tongues, in Acts ii. 3. **2.** *a tongue,* i. e. the *language* used by a particular people in distinction from that of other nations: Acts ii. 11; hence in later Jewish usage (Is. lxvi. 18; Dan. iii. 4; v. 19 Theod.; vi. 25; vii. 14 Theod.; Jud. iii. 8) joined with φυλή, λαός, ἔθνος, it serves to designate people of various languages [cf. W. 32], Rev. v. 9; vii. 9; x. 11; xi. 9; xiii. 7; xiv. 6; xvii. 15. λαλεῖν ἑτέραις γλώσσαις *to speak with other* than their native i. e. in f o r e i g n *tongues,* Acts ii. 4 cf. 6–11; γλώσσαις λαλεῖν καιναῖς *to speak with new tongues* which the speaker has not learned previously, Mk. xvi. 17 [but Tr txt. WH txt. om. Tr mrg. br. καιναῖς]; cf. De Wette on Acts p. 27 sqq. [correct and supplement his reff. by Mey. on 1 Co. xii. 10; cf. also B. D. s. v. *Tongues, Gift of*]. From both these expressions must be carefully distinguished the simple phrases λαλεῖν γλώσσαις, γλώσσαις λαλεῖν, λαλεῖν γλώσσῃ, γλώσσῃ λαλεῖν (and προσεύχεσθαι γλώσσῃ, 1 Co. xiv. 14), *to speak with* (in) *a tongue* (the organ of speech), *to speak with tongues*; this, as appears from 1 Co. xiv. 7 sqq., is the gift of men who, rapt in an ecstasy and no longer quite masters of their own reason and consciousness, pour forth their glowing spiritual emotions in strange utterances, rugged, dark, disconnected, quite unfitted to instruct or to influence the minds of others: Acts x. 46; xix. 6; 1 Co. xii. 30; xiii. 1; xiv. 2, 4–6, 13, 18, 23, 27, 39. The origin of the expression is apparently to be found in the fact, that in Hebrew the tongue is spoken of as the leading instrument by which the praises of God are proclaimed (ἡ τῶν θείων ὕμνων μελῳδός, 4 Macc. x. 21, cf. Ps. xxxiv. (xxxv.) 28; lxv. (lxvi.) 17; lxx. (lxxi.) 24; cxxv. (cxxvi.) 2; Acts ii. 26; Phil. ii. 11; λαλεῖν ἐν γλώσσῃ, Ps. xxxviii. (xxxix.) 4), and that according to the more rigorous conception of inspiration nothing human in an inspired man was thought to be active except the tongue, put in motion by the Holy Spirit (καταχρῆται ἕτερος αὐτοῦ τοῖς φωνητηρίοις ὀργάνοις, στόματι καὶ γλώττῃ πρὸς μήνυσιν ὧν ἂν θέλῃ, Philo, rer. div. haer. § 53, [i. 510 ed. Mang.]); hence the contrast δ ι ὰ τ ο ῦ ν ο ὸ ς [crit. edd. τῷ νοΐ] λαλεῖν, 1 Co. xiv. 19 cf. 9. The plur. in the phrase γλώσσαις λαλεῖν, used even of a single person (1 Co. xiv. 5 sq.), refers to the various motions of the tongue. By meton. of the cause for the effect, γλῶσσαι tongues are equiv. to λόγοι ἐν γλώσση (1 Co. xiv. 19) words spoken in a tongue (Zungenvorträge): xiii. 8; xiv. 22; γένη γλωσσῶν, 1 Co. xii. 10, 28, of which two kinds are mentioned viz. προσευχή and ψαλμός, 1 Co. xiv. 15; γλῶσσαν ἔχω, something to utter with a tongue, 1 Co. xiv. 26. [On 'Speaking with Tongues' see, in addition to the discussions above referred to, Wendt in the 5th ed. of Meyer on Acts (ii. 4); Heinrici, Korinthierbriefe, i. 372 sqq.; Schaff, Hist. of the Chr. Church, i. 234–245 (1882); Farrar, St. Paul, i. 95 sqq.]*

1101 γλωσσόκομον, -ου, τό, (for the earlier γλωσσοκομεῖον or γλωσσοκόμιον [W. 24 (23), 94 (90); yet see Boeckh, Corp. inscrr. 2448, viii. 25, 31], fr. γλῶσσα and κομέω to tend); **a.** a case in which to keep the mouth-pieces of wind instruments. **b.** a small box for other uses also; esp. a casket, purse to keep money in: Jn. xii. 6; xiii. 29; cf. Lob. ad Phryn. p. 98 sq. (For אֲרוֹן a chest, 2 Chr. xxiv. 8, 10 sq.; Joseph. antt. 6, 1, 2; Plut., Longin., al.)*

1102 γναφεύς, -έως, ὁ, (also [earlier] κναφεύς, fr. γνάπτω or κνάπτω to card), a fuller: Mk. ix. 3. (Hdt., Xen., and sqq.; Sept. Is. vii. 3; xxxvi. 2; 2 K. xviii. 17.)*

1103 γνήσιος, -α, -ον, (by syncope for γενήσιος fr. γίνομαι, γεν-, [cf. Curtius § 128]), legitimately born, not spurious; genuine, true, sincere: Phil. iv. 3; 1 Tim. i. 2; Tit. i. 4; τὸ τῆς ἀγάπης γνήσιον i. q. τὴν γνησιότητα [A. V. the sincerity], 2 Co. viii. 8. (From Hom. down.)*

1104 γνησίως, adv., genuinely, faithfully, sincerely: Phil. ii. 20. [From Eur. down.]*

1105 γνόφος, -ου, ὁ, (for the earlier [and poetic] δνόφος, akin to νέφος [so Bttm. Lexil. ii. 266; but see Curtius pp. 704 sq. 706, cf. 535; Vaniček p. 1070]), darkness, gloom: Heb. xii. 18. (Aristot. de mund. c. 2 fin. p. 392ᵇ, 12; Lcian. de mort. Peregr. 43; Dio Chrys.; Sept. also for עֲנָן a cloud, Deut. iv. 11, etc. and for עֲרָפֶל 'thick cloud,' Ex. xx. 21, etc.; [Trench § c.].)*

1106 γνώμη, -ης, ἡ, (fr. γινώσκω); **1.** the faculty of knowing, mind, reason. **2.** that which is thought or known, one's mind; **a.** view, judgment, opinion: 1 Co. i. 10; Rev. xvii. 13. **b.** mind concerning what ought to be done, **aa.** by one's self, resolve, purpose, intention: ἐγένετο γνώμη [T Tr WH γνώμης, see γίνομαι 5 e. a.] τοῦ ὑποστρέφειν, Acts xx. 3 [B. 268 (230)]. **bb.** by others, judgment, advice: διδόναι γνώμην, 1 Co. vii. 25, [40]; 2 Co. viii. 10. **cc.** decree: Rev. xvii. 17; χωρὶς τῆς σῆς γνώμης, without thy consent, Philem. 14. (In the same senses in Grk. writ.; [cf. Schmidt, ch. 13, 9; Mey. on 1 Co. i. 10].)*

1107 γνωρίζω; fut. γνωρίσω (Jn. xvii. 26; Eph. vi. 21; Col. iv. 7), Attic -ιῶ (Col. iv. 9 [L WH -ίσω; B. 37 (32); WH. App. p. 163]); 1 aor. ἐγνώρισα; Pass., [pres. γνωρίζομαι]; 1 aor. ἐγνωρίσθην; in Grk. writ. fr. Aeschyl. down [see ad fin.]; Sept. for יָדַע and Chald. יְדַע; **1.** trans. to make known: τί, Ro. ix. 22 sq.; τί τινι, Lk. ii. 15; Jn. xv. 15; xvii. 26; Acts ii. 28; 2 Co. viii. 1; Eph. iii. 5, 10, [pass. in these two exx.]; Eph. vi. 21; Col. iv. 7, 9; 2 Pet. i. 16; τινὶ τὸ μυστήριον, Eph. i. 9; iii. 3 [G L T Tr WH read the pass.]; vi. 19; τινὶ ὅτι, 1 Co. xii. 3; τινί τι, ὅτι i. q. τινὶ ὅτι τι, Gal. i. 11; foll. by τί interrog. Col. i. 27; περί τινος, Lk. ii. 17 L T Tr WH;

γνωριζέσθω πρὸς τὸν θεόν be brought to the knowledge of God, Phil. iv. 6; γνωρίζεσθαι εἰς πάντα τὰ ἔθνη to be made known unto all the nations, Ro. xvi. 26; contextually and emphatically i. q. to recall to one's mind, as though what is made known had escaped him, 1 Co. xv. 1; with acc. of pers. [(Plut. Fab. Max. 21, 6)], in pass., to become known, be recognized: Acts vii. 13 Tr txt. WH txt. **2.** intrans. to know: τί αἱρήσομαι, οὐ γνωρίζω, Phil. i. 22 [WH mrg. punctuate τί αἱρ.; οὐ γν.; some refer this to 1 (R. V. mrg. I do not make known), cf. Mey. ad loc. In earlier Grk. γνωρίζω signifies either 'to gain a knowledge of,' or 'to have thorough knowledge of.' Its later and N. T.) causative force seems to be found only in Aeschyl. Prom. 487; cf. Schmidt vol. i. p. 287; Bp. Lghtft. on Phil. l. c. COMP.: ἀνα-, δια-γνωρίζω].*

1108 γνῶσις, -εως, ἡ, (γινώσκω), [fr. Thuc. down], knowledge: with gen. of the obj., σωτηρίας, Lk. i. 77; τοῦ θεοῦ, the knowledge of God, such as is offered in the gospel, 2 Co. ii. 14, esp. in Paul's exposition of it, 2 Co. x. 5; τῆς δόξης τοῦ θεοῦ ἐν προσώπῳ Χριστοῦ, 2 Co. iv. 6; Ἰησοῦ Χριστοῦ, of Christ as a saviour, Phil. iii. 8; 2 Pet. iii. 18; with subj. gen. τοῦ θεοῦ, the knowledge of things which belongs to God, Ro. xi. 33. γνῶσις, by itself, signifies in general intelligence, understanding: Eph. iii. 19; the general knowledge of the Christian religion, Ro. xv. 14; 1 Co. i. 5; the deeper, more perfect and enlarged knowledge of this religion, such as belongs to the more advanced, 1 Co. xii. 8; xiii. 2, 8; xiv. 6; 2 Co. vi. 6; viii. 7; xi. 6; esp. of things lawful and unlawful for Christians, 1 Co. viii. 1, 7, 10 sq.; the higher knowledge of Christian and divine things which false teachers boast of, ψευδώνυμος γνῶσις, 1 Tim. vi. 20 [cf. Holtzmann, Pastoralbriefe, p. 132 sq.]; moral wisdom, such as is seen in right living, 2 Pet. i. 5; and in intercourse with others: κατὰ γνῶσιν, wisely, 1 Pet. iii. 7. objective knowledge: what is known concerning divine things and human duties, Ro. ii. 20; Col. ii. 3; concerning salvation through Christ, Lk. xi. 52. Where γνῶσις and σοφία are used together the former seems to be knowledge regarded by itself, the latter wisdom as exhibited in action: Ro. xi. 33; 1 Co. xii. 8; Col. ii. 3. ["γν. is simply intuitive, σοφ. is ratiocinative also; γν. applies chiefly to the apprehension of truths, σοφ. superadds the power of reasoning about them and tracing their relations." Bp. Lghtft. on Col. l. c. To such the same effect Fritzsche (on Ro. l. c.), "γν. perspicientia veri, σοφ. sapientia aut mentis sollertia, quae cognita intellectaque veritate utatur, ut res efficiendas efficiat." Meyer (on 1 Co. l. c.) nearly reverses Lghtft.'s distinction; elsewhere, however (e. g. on Col. l. c., cf. i. 9), he and others regard σοφ. merely as the more general, γν. as the more restricted and special term. Cf. Lghtft. u. s.; Trench § lxxv.]*

1109 γνώστης, -ου, ὁ, (a knower), an expert; a connoisseur: Acts xxvi. 3. (Plut. Flam. c. 4; θεὸς ὁ τῶν κρυπτῶν γνώστης, Hist. Sus. vs. 42; of those who divine the future, 1 S. xxviii. 3, 9, etc.)*

1110 γνωστός, -ή, -όν, known: Acts ix. 42; τινί, Jn. xviii. 15 sq.; Acts i. 19; xv. 18 R L; xix. 17; xxviii. 22; γνωστὸν ἔστω ὑμῖν *be it known to you*: Acts ii. 14; iv. 10; xiii. 38; xxviii. 28; contextually, *notable*, Acts iv. 16; γνωστὸν ποιεῖν *to make known, disclose*: Acts xv. 17 sq. G T Tr WH [al. construe γνωστ. as pred. of ταῦτα: R. V. mrg. *who doeth these things* which were *known*; cf. Mey. ad loc.]. τὸ γνωστὸν τοῦ θεοῦ, either *that which may be known of God*, or i. q. γνῶσις τοῦ θεοῦ, for both come to the same thing: Ro. i. 19; cf. Fritzsche ad loc. and W. 235 (220), [and Meyer (ed. Weiss) ad loc.]. plur. of γνωστοί *acquaintance, intimates*, (Ps. xxx. (xxxi.) 12; [lxxxvii. (lxxxviii.) 9, 19]; Neh. v. 10): Lk. ii. 44; xxiii. 49. (In Grk. writ. fr. Aeschyl. down.)*

1111 γογγύζω; impf. ἐγόγγυζον; 1 aor. ἐγόγγυσα; *to murmur, mutter, grumble, say anything in a low tone*, (acc. to Pollux and Phavorinus used of the cooing of doves, like the τονθρύζω and τονθορύζω of the more elegant Grk. writ.; cf. *Lob.* ad Phryn. p. 358; [W. 22; Bp. Lghtft. on Phil. ii. 14]); hence of those who confer together secretly, τὶ περί τινος, Jn. vii. 32; of those who discontentedly complain: 1 Co. x. 10; πρός τινα, Lk. v. 30; μετ' ἀλλήλων, Jn. vi. 43; κατά τινος, Mt. xx. 11; περί τινος, Jn. vi. 41, 61; (Sept.; Antonin. 2, 3; Epict. diss. 1, 29, 55; 4, 1, 79; [al.].) [COMP.: δια-γογγύζω.]*

1112 γογγυσμός, -οῦ, ὁ, (γογγύζω, q. v.), *a murmur, murmuring, muttering*; applied to **a.** *secret debate*: περί τινος, Jn. vii. 12. **b.** *secret displeasure, not openly avowed*: πρός τινα, Acts vi. 1; in plur. χωρὶς or ἄνευ γογγυσμῶν *without querulous discontent, without murmurings*, i. e. with a cheerful and willing mind, Phil. ii. 14; 1 Pet. iv. 9 (where L T Tr WH read the sing.). (Ex. xvi. 7 sqq.; Sap. i. 10 sq.; Antonin. 9, 37.)*

1113 γογγυστής, -οῦ, ὁ, *a murmurer*, (Vulg., Augustine, *murmurator*), one who discontentedly complains (against God; for μεμψίμοιροι is added): Jude 16. [Prov. xxvi. 21 Theod., 22 Symm.; xxvi. 20, 22 Graec. Ven.]*

1114 γόης, -ητος, ὁ, (γοάω to bewail, howl); **1.** *a wailer, howler*: Aeschyl. choëph. 823 [Hermann et al. γοητής]. **2.** *a juggler, enchanter*, (because incantations used to be uttered in a kind of howl). **3.** *a deceiver, impostor*: 2 Tim. iii. 13; (Hdt., Eur., Plat., and subseq. writ.).*

1115 Γολγοθά [Tr WH, or -θᾶ R G L T (see *Tdf.* Proleg. p. 102; Kautzsch p. 10); also -θθ L WH mrg. in Jn. xix. 17; acc. -ᾶν Tdf. in Mk. xv. 22 (WH -άν, see their App. p. 160), elsewhere indecl., W. 61 (60)], Golgotha, Chald. גָּלְגַּלְתָּא Heb. גֻּלְגֹּלֶת (fr. גָּלַל *to roll*), i. e. κρανίον, *a skull* [Lat. *calvaria*], the name of a place outside of Jerusalem where Jesus was crucified; so called, apparently, because its form resembled a skull: Mt. xxvii. 33; Mk. xv. 22; Jn. xix. 17. Cf. *Tobler*, Golgatha. St. Gall. 1851; *Furrer* in Schenkel ii. 506 sqq.; *Keim*, Jesus von Naz. iii. 404 sq.; [*Porter* in Alex.'s Kitto s. v.; *F. Howe*, The true Site of Calvary, N. Y., 1871].*

1116 Γόμορρα [or Γομόρρα, cf. Chandler §167], -ας, ἡ, and -ων, τά, [cf. B. 18 (16); *Tdf.* Proleg. p. 116; *WH*. App. p. 156], *Gomorrah*, (עֲמֹרָה, cf. עַזָּה *Gaza*), the name of a city in the eastern part of Judæa, destroyed by the same earthquake [cf. B. D. s. v. Sea, The Salt] with Sodom and its neighbor cities: Gen. xix. 24. Their site is now occupied by the Asphaltic Lake or Dead Sea [cf. BB. DD. s. vv. Gomorrah and Sodom]: Mt. x. 15; Mk. vi. 11 R L in br.; Ro. ix. 29; 2 Pet. ii. 6; Jude 7.*

1117 γόμος, -ου, ὁ, (γέμω); **a.** *the lading* or *freight of a ship, cargo, merchandise conveyed in a ship*: Acts xxi. 3, (Hdt. 1, 194; [Aeschyl.], Dem., al.; [in Sept. the *load* of a beast of burden, Ex. xxiii. 5; 2 K. v. 17]). **b.** any *merchandise*: Rev. xviii. 11 sq.*

1118 γονεύς, -έως, ὁ, (ΓΕΝΩ, γέγονα), [Hom. h. Cer., Hes., al.]; *a begetter, parent*; plur. οἱ γονεῖς *the parents*: Lk. ii. 41, 43 L txt. T Tr WH; [viii. 56]; xxi. 16; Jn. ix. 2, 3, 20, 22, 23; 2 Co. xii. 14; Ro. i. 30; Eph. vi. 1; Col. iii. 20; 2 Tim. iii. 2; acc. plur. γονεῖς: Mt. x. 21; [xix. 29 Lchm. mrg.]; Lk. ii. 27; [xviii. 29]; Mk. xiii. 12; [Jn. ix. 18]; on this form cf. W. § 9, 2; [B. 14 (13)].*

1119 γόνυ, γόνατος, τό, [fr. Hom. down], *the knee*: Heb. xii. 12; τιθέναι τὰ γόνατα *to bend the knees, kneel down*, of persons supplicating: Lk. xxii. 41; Acts vii. 60; ix. 40; xx. 36; xxi. 5; of [mock] worshippers, Mk. xv. 19, so also προσπίπτειν τοῖς γόνασί τινος, Lk. v. 8 (of a suppliant in Eur. Or. 1332); κάμπτειν τὰ γόνατα *to bow the knee*, of those worshipping God or Christ: τινί, Ro. xi. 4; πρός τινα, Eph. iii. 14; reflexively, γόνυ κάμπτει τινί, to i. e. in honor of one, Ro. xiv. 11 (1 K. xix. 18); ἐν ὀνόματι Ἰησοῦ, Phil. ii. 10 (Is. xlv. 23).*

1120 γονυπετέω, -ῶ; 1 aor. ptcp. γονυπετήσας; (γονυπετής, and this fr. γόνυ and ΠΕΤΩ i. q. πίπτω); *to fall on the knees*, the act of one imploring aid, and of one expressing reverence and honor: τινί, Mt. xvii. 14 Rec.; τινά, ibid. G L T Tr WH; Mk. i. 40 R G Tr txt. br. WH br.; x. 17; cf. W. 210 (197); [B. 147 sq. (129)]; ἔμπροσθέν τινος, Mt. xxvii. 29. (Polyb., Heliod.; eccl. writ.)*

1121 γράμμα, -τος, τό, (γράφω), *that which has been written*; **1.** *a letter* i. e. the character: Lk. xxiii. 38 [R G L br. Tr mrg. br.]; Gal. vi. 11. **2.** *any writing, a document* or *record*; **a.** *a note of hand, bill, bond, account, written acknowledgment of debt*, (as *scriptio* in Varr. sat. Men. 8, 1 [cf. Edersheim ii. 268 sqq.]): Lk. xvi. 6 sq. ([Joseph. antt. 18, 6, 3], in L txt. T Tr WH plur. τὰ γράμματα; so of one document also in Antiph. p. 114, (30); Dem. p. 1034, 16; Vulg. *cautio*). **b.** *a letter, an epistle*: Acts xxviii. 21; (Hdt. 5, 14; Thuc. 8, 50; Xen. Cyr. 4, 5, 26, etc.). **c.** τὰ ἱερὰ γράμματα *the sacred writings* (of the O. T.; [so Joseph. antt. prooem. § 3; 10, 10, 4 fin.; c. Ap. 1, 10; Philo, de vit. Moys. 3, 39; de praem. et poen. § 14; leg. ad Gai. § 29, etc.— but always τὰ ἱ. γ.]): 2 Tim. iii. 15 [here T WH om. L Tr br. τά]; γράμμα i. q. the written law of Moses, Ro. ii. 27; Μωϋσέως γράμματα, Jn. v. 47. Since the Jews so clave to the letter of the law that it not only became to them a mere letter but also a hindrance to true religion, Paul calls it γράμμα in a disparaging sense, and contrasts it with τὸ πνεῦμα i. e. the divine S p i r i t, whether operative in the Mosaic law, Ro. ii. 29, or in the gospel, by which Christians are governed, Ro. vii. 6; 2 Co. iii. 6 sq. [but in vs. 7 R G T WH read the plur. *written in letters*, so L mrg. Tr mrg.]. **3.** τὰ γράμματα, like the Lat. *litterae*, Eng. *letters*, i. q. *learning*: Acts xxvi. 24; εἰδέναι, μεμαθηκέναι γρ. (cf. Germ. *studirt* *haben*), of sacred learning, Jn. vii. 15. (μανθάνειν, ἐπίστασθαι, etc., γράμματα are used by the Greeks of the rudiments of learning; cf. Passow i. p. 571; [L. and S. s. v. II. a.].) *

1122 γραμματεύς, -έως, (acc. plur. -εῖς, W. § 9, 2; [B. 14 (13)]), ὁ, (γράμμα), Sept. for סֹפֵר and שֹׁטֵר; **1.** in prof. auth. and here and there in the O. T. [e. g. 2 S. viii. 17; xx. 25; 2 K. xix. 2; xxv. 19; Ps. xliv. (xlv.) 2], *a clerk, scribe*, esp. *a public scribe, secretary, recorder*, whose office and influence differed in different states : Acts xix. 35, (Sir. x. 5); [cf. *Lghtft.* in The Contemp. Rev. for 1878, p. 294; *Wood*, Discoveries at Ephesus, App. Inscrr. fr. the Great Theatre, p. 49 n.]. **2.** in the Bible, *a man learned in the Mosaic law and in the sacred writings, an interpreter, teacher* : Mt. xxiii. 34; 1 Co. i. 20, (called also νομικός in Lk. x. 25, and νομοδιδάσκαλος in Lk. v. 17; [Meyer (on Mt. xxii. 35), while denying any essential diff. betw. γραμματεύς and νομικός (cf. Lk. xi. 52, 53 — yet see crit. txts.), regards the latter name as the more specific (*a jurisconsult*) and Classic, γρ. as the more general (*a learned man*) and Hebraistic; it is also the more common in the Apocr., where νομ. occurs only 4 Macc. v. 3. As *teachers* they were called νομοδιδάσκαλοι. Cf. B. D. s. v. Lawyer, also s. v. Scribes I. 1 note]); Jer. viii. 8 (cf. ii. 8); Neh. viii. 1 sq.; xii. 26, 36; 2 Esdr. vii. 6, 11, and esp. Sir. xxxviii. 24, 31 sqq.; xxxix. 1–11. The γραμματεῖς explained the meaning of the sacred oracles, Mt. ii. 4 [γρ. τοῦ λαοῦ, Josh. i. 10; 1 Macc. v. 42; cf. Sir. xliv. 4]; xvii. 10; Mk. ix. 11; xii. 35; examined into the more difficult and subtile questions of the law, Mt. ix. 3; Mk. ii. 6 sq.; xii. 28; added to the Mosaic law decisions of various kinds thought to elucidate its meaning and scope, and did this to the detriment of religion, Mt. v. 20; xv. 1 sqq.; xxiii. 2 sqq.; Mk. vii. 1 sqq.; cf. Lk. xi. 46. Since the advice of men skilled in the law was needed in the examination of causes and the solution of difficult questions, they were enrolled in the Sanhedrin; and accordingly in the N. T. they are often mentioned in connection with the priests and elders of the people : Mt. xxi. 15; xxvi. 3 R G; Mk. xi. 18, 27; xiv. 1; xv. 1; Lk. xix. 47; xx. 1; xxii. 2. Cf. *Schürer*, Neutest. Zeitgesch. § 25 ii.; *Klöpper* in Schenkel v. 247 sqq.; [and thorough articles in BB.DD. s. v. Scribes; cf. *W. Robertson Smith*, The O. T. in the Jewish Ch., Lect. iii.]. **3.** univ. *a religious teacher* : γραμματεὺς μαθητευθεὶς εἰς τὴν βασιλ. τῶν οὐρ. a teacher so instructed that from his learning and ability to teach advantage may redound to the kingdom of heaven, Mt. xiii. 52 [but G T Tr WH read μαθ. τῇ βασιλείᾳ (L ἐν τ. β.); and many interpret *made a disciple unto the k. of h.* (which is personified); see μαθητεύω, fin.].

1123 γραπτός, -ή, -όν, *written* : Ro. ii. 15. [Gorg. apol. Palam. p. 190 sub fin.; Sept.; al.] *

1124 γραφή, -ῆς, ἡ, (γράφω, cf. γλυφή and γλύφω); **a.** *a writing, thing written*, [fr. Soph. down] : πᾶσα γραφή *every scripture* sc. of the O. T., 2 Tim. iii. 16; plur. γραφαὶ ἅγιαι, *holy scriptures, the sacred books* (of the O. T.), Ro. i. 2; προφητικαί, Ro. xvi. 26; αἱ γραφαὶ τῶν προφητῶν,

Mt. xxvi. 56. **b.** ἡ γραφή, *the Scripture* κατ᾽ ἐξοχήν, *the holy scripture* (of the O. T.), — and used to denote either the book itself, or its contents [some would restrict the sing. γραφή always to *a particular passage*; see Bp. Lghtft. on Gal. iii. 22] : Jn. vii. 38; x. 35; Acts viii. 32; Ro. iv. 3; Gal. iii. 22; iv. 30; Jas. ii. 8; 1 Pet. ii. 6, 2 Pet. i. 20; also in plur. αἱ γραφαί : Mt. xxi. 42; xxvi. 54; Mk. xiv. 49; Lk. xxiv. 27; Jn. v. 39; Acts xvii. 2, 11; xviii. 24, 28; 1 Co. xv. 3 sq.; once αἱ γραφαί comprehends also the books of the N. T. already begun to be collected into a canon, 2 Pet. iii. 16; by meton. ἡ γραφή is used for God speaking in it : Ro. ix. 17; Gal. iv. 30; ἡ γραφή is introduced as a person and distinguished from God in Gal. iii. 8. εἰδέναι τὰς γραφάς, Mt. xxii. 29; Mk. xii. 24; συνιέναι, Lk. xxiv. 45. **c.** *a certain portion* or *section of holy Scripture* : Mk. xii. 10; Lk. iv. 21; Jn. xix. 37; Acts i. 16. [Cf. B. D. s. v. Scripture.]

1125 γράφω; [impf. ἔγραφον]; fut. γράψω; 1 aor. ἔγραψα; pf. γέγραφα; Pass., [pres. γράφομαι]; pf. γέγραμμαι; [plpf. 3 pers. sing. ἐγέγραπτο, Rev. xvii. 8 Lchm.]; 2 aor. ἐγράφην; (prop. *to grave, scrape, scratch, engrave*; cf. Germ. *graben, eingraben*; γράψεν δὲ οἱ ὀστέον ἄχρις αἰχμή, Hom. Il. 17, 599; σήματα γράψας ἐν πίνακι, ib. 6, 169; hence *to draw letters*), *to write*; **1.** With reference to the f o r m of the letters; *to delineate* (or *form*) *letters* on a tablet, parchment, paper, or other material : τῷ δακτύλῳ ἔγραφεν εἰς τὴν γῆν made figures on the ground, Jn. viii. 6 Rec.; οὕτω γράφω so am I accustomed to form my letters, 2 Thess. iii. 17; πηλίκοις γράμμασι ἔγραψα with how large (and so, ill-formed [?]) letters I have written, Gal. vi. 11; cf. Winer, Rückert, Hilgenfeld ad loc. [for the views of those who regard ἔγρ. as covering the close of the Ep. only, see Bp. Lghtft. and Mey.; cf. W. 278 (261); B. 198 (171 sq.)]. **2.** with reference to the c o n t e n t s of the writing; **a.** *to express in written characters*, foll. by the words expressed : ἔγραψε λέγων Ἰωάννης ἐστὶ τὸ ὄνομα αὐτοῦ, Lk. i. 63; μὴ γράφε· ὁ βασιλεὺς τῶν Ἰουδαίων κτλ. Jn. xix. 21; γράψον· μακάριοι κτλ. Rev. xiv. 13. γράφω τι, Jn. xix. 22; pass. Rev. i. 3; τὶ ἐπί τι, Rev. ii. 17; xix. 16; τὶ ἐπί τινα, iii. 12; ἐπί τινος, xiv. 1. **b.** *to commit to writing* (things not to be forgotten), *write down, record* : Rev. i. 19 (γράψον ἃ εἶδες); x. 4; γράφειν εἰς βιβλίον, Rev. i. 11; ἐπὶ τὸ βιβλίον τῆς ζωῆς, Rev. xvii. 8; γεγραμμ. ἐν τ. βιβλίῳ (on τῇ βίβλῳ), ἐν τοῖς βιβλίοις, Rev. xiii. 8; xx. 12, 15; xxi. 27; xxii. 18, 19; τὰ ὀνόματα ὑμῶν ἐγράφη [ἐν-(ἐγ- Tr see N, ν)γέγρ. T Tr WH] ἐν τοῖς οὐρανοῖς, i. e. that ye have been enrolled with those for whom eternal blessedness has been prepared, Lk. x. 20; γράφειν τί τινι, to record something for some one's use, Lk. i. 3. **c.** ἐγράφη and γέγραπται (in the Synoptists and Paul), and γεγραμμένον ἐστί (in John), are used of those things which stand written in the sacred books (of the O. T.); absol. γέγραπται, foll. by the quotation fr. the sacred vol. : Mt. iv. 4, 6 sq. 10; xxi. 13; Mk. vii. 6; xi. 17; xiv. 27; Lk. iv. 8; xix. 46; καθὼς γέγραπται, Acts xv. 15, very often in Paul, as Ro. i. 17; ii. 24; iii. 4 [see below]; 1 Co. i. 31; ii. 9; 2 Co. viii. 15; ix. 9; καθάπερ γέγρ. Ro. xi. 8 T Tr WH; [iii. 4 T Tr

WH]; γέγραπται γάρ, Mt. xxvi. 31; Lk. iv. 10; Acts xxiii. 5; Ro. xii. 19; xiv. 11; 1 Co. iii. 19; Gal. iii. 10, 13 Rec.; iv. 22, 27; ὁ λόγος ὁ γεγραμμένος, 1 Co. xv. 54; κατὰ τὸ γεγραμμένον, 2 Co. iv. 13; γεγραμμένον ἐστί, Jn. ii. 17; vi. 31; xii. 14; ἐγράφη δὲ πρὸς νουθεσίαν ἡμῶν, 1 Co. x. 11; ἐγράφη δι᾽ ἡμᾶς for our sake, Ro. iv. 24; 1 Co. ix. 10; with the name of the author of the written words or of the books in which they are found: γέγραπται ἐν βίβλῳ ψαλμῶν, Acts i. 20; ἐν βίβλῳ τῶν προφητῶν, Acts vii. 42; ἐν τῷ πρώτῳ [R WH δευτέρῳ] ψαλμῷ, Acts xiii. 33; ἐν Ἡσαΐᾳ, Mk. i. 2 [not Rec.], etc. τινά or τί to write of i. e. in writing to mention or refer to a person or a thing: ὃν ἔγραψε Μωϋσῆς whom Moses had in mind in writing of the Messiah, or whose likeness Moses delineated, Jn. i. 45 (46); Μωϋσῆς γράφει τὴν δικαιοσύνην τὴν ἐκ νόμου, Moses, writing the words ὅτι ὁ ποιήσας αὐτά κτλ., points out the righteousness which is of the law, Ro. x. 5. γέγραπται, γράφειν, etc. περί τινος, concerning one: Mt. xxvi. 24; Mk. xiv. 21; Jn. v. 46; Acts xiii. 29; ἐπὶ τὸν υἱὸν τοῦ ἀνθρώπου, that it should find fulfilment in him, Mk. ix. 12 sq. [cf. ἵνα, II. 2 b.]; ἐπ᾽ αὐτῷ, on him i. e. of him (cf. W. 393 (368) [and ἐπί, B. 2 f. β.]), Jn. xii. 16; τὰ γεγραμμένα τῷ υἱῷ τοῦ ἀνθρ. written for him, allotted to him in Scripture, i. e. to be accomplished in his career, Lk. xviii. 31; cf. W. § 31, 4; [yet cf. B. 178 (154)]; Μωϋσῆς ἔγραψεν ὑμῖν ἵνα etc. Moses in the Scripture commanded us that etc. [cf. B. 237 (204)], Mk. xii. 19; Lk. xx. 28. d. γράφειν τινί to write to one i. e. by writing (in a written epistle) to give information, directions, etc. to one: Ro. xv. 15; 2 Co. ii. 4, 9 [dat. implied]; vii. 12; Philem. 21; 2 Pet. iii. 15; 1 Jn. ii. 12 sqq.; δι᾽ ὀλίγων, 1 Pet. v. 12; διὰ μέλανος καὶ καλάμου, 3 Jn. 13; foll. by the words written or to be written in the letter: Acts xv. 23; Rev. ii. 1, 8, 12, 18; iii. 1, 7, 14; γράφειν τινί τι, 1 Co. xiv. 37; 2 Co. i. 13; ii. 3 [L T Tr WH om. the dat.]; Gal. i. 20; 1 Tim. iii. 14; 1 Jn. i. 4 [R G L]; ii. 1; περί τινος, 1 Jn. ii. 26; Acts xxv. 26; 2 Co. ix. 1; 1 Th. iv. 9; v. 1; Jude 3; διὰ χειρός τινος, to send a letter by one, Acts xv. 23 [see χείρ]; γράφειν τινί, foll. by an inf., by letter to bid one do a thing, Acts xviii. 27; foll. by μή with inf. (to forbid, write one not to etc.), 1 Co. v. 9, 11. 3. to fill with writing, (Germ. beschreiben): βιβλίον γεγραμμένον ἔσωθεν καὶ ὄπισθεν a volume written within and behind, on the back, hence on both sides, Rev. v. 1 (Ezek. ii. 10); cf. Düsterdieck, [Alford, al.] ad loc. 4. to draw up in writing, compose: βιβλίον, Mk. x. 4; Jn. xxi. 25 [Tdf. om. the vs.; see WH. App. ad loc.]; τίτλον, Jn. xix. 19; ἐπιστολήν, Acts xxiii. 25; 2 Pet. iii. 1; ἐντολήν τινι to write a commandment to one, Mk. x. 5; 1 Jn. ii. 7 sq.; 2 Jn. 5. [Comp.: ἀπο-, ἐγ-, ἐπι-, κατα-, προ-γράφω.]

γραώδης, -ες, (fr. γραῦς an old woman, and εἶδος), old-womanish, anile, [A. V. old wives']: 1 Tim. iv. 7. (Strabo 1 p. 32 [p. 44 ed. Sieben.]; Galen; al.)*

γρηγορέω, -ῶ; 1 aor. ἐγρηγόρησα; (fr. ἐγρήγορα, to have been roused from sleep, to be awake, pf. of ἐγείρω; cf. Lob. ad Phryn. p. 118 sq.; Bttm. Ausf. Spr. ii. p. 158; [W. 26 (25); 92 (88)]); to watch; 1. prop.: Mt. xxiv. 43; xxvi. 38, 40; Mk. xiii. 34; xiv. 34, 37; Lk. xii.

1126

1127

37, 39 R G L Tr txt. WH txt. As to sleep is often i. q. to die, so once, 1 Th. v. 10, γρηγ. means to live, be alive on earth. 2. Metaph. to watch i. e. give strict attention to, be cautious, active: — to take heed lest through remissness and indolence some destructive calamity suddenly overtake one, Mt. xxiv. 42; xxv. 13; Mk. xiii. 35, [37]; Rev. xvi. 15; or lest one be led to forsake Christ, Mt. xxvi. 41; Mk. xiv. 38; or lest one fall into sin, 1 Th. v. 6; 1 Co. xvi. 13; 1 Pet. v. 8; Rev. iii. 2 sq.; or be corrupted by errors, Acts xx. 31; ἔν τινι, to be watchful in, employ the most punctilious care in a thing: Col. iv. 2. (Sept.; [Bar. ii. 9; 1 Macc. xii. 27; Aristot. plant. 1, 2 p. 816ᵇ, 29. 37]; Joseph. antt. 11, 3, 4; Achill. Tat.; al.) [Syn. see ἀγρυπνέω. Comp.: δια- γρηγορέω.]*

γυμνάζω; [pf. pass. ptcp. γεγυμνασμένος]; (γυμνός); com. in Grk. writ. fr. Aeschyl. down; 1. prop. to exercise naked (in the palæstra). 2. to exercise vigorously, in any way, either the body or the mind: ἑαυτὸν πρὸς εὐσέβειαν, of one who strives earnestly to become godly, 1 Tim. iv. 7; γεγυμνασμένος exercised, Heb. v. 14; xii. 11; καρδίαν γεγυμν. πλεονεξίας (Rec. πλεονεξίαις), a soul that covetousness or the love of gain has trained in its crafty ways, 2 Pet. ii. 14; cf. W. § 30, 4.* 1128

γυμνασία, -ας, ἡ, (γυμνάζω); a. prop. the exercise of the body in the palæstra. b. any exercise whatever: σωματικὴ γυμνασία, the exercise of conscientiousness relative to the body, such as is characteristic of ascetics and consists in abstinence from matrimony and certain kinds of food, 1 Tim. iv. 8. (4 Macc. xi. 19. In Grk. writ. fr. Plat. legg. i. p. 648 c. down.)* 1129

γυμνητεύω (γυμνῖτεύω L T Tr WH; [cf. Tdf. Proleg. p. 81; W. 92 (88)]); (γυμνήτης); [A. V. literally to be naked i. e.] to be lightly or poorly clad: 1 Co. iv. 11. (So in Dio Chrys. 25, 3 and other later writ.; to be a light-armed soldier, Plut. Aem. 16; Dio Cass. 47, 34, 2.)* 1130

γυμνός, -ή, -όν, in Sept. for עֵירֹם and עָרוֹם, naked, not covered; 1. prop. a. unclad, without clothing: Mk. xiv. 52; Rev. iii. 17; xvi. 15; xvii. 16; τὸ γυμνόν, substantively, the naked body: ἐπὶ γυμνοῦ, Mk. xiv. 51; cf. Fritzsche ad loc.; (τὰ γυμνά, Lcian. nav. 33). b. ill-clad: Mt. xxv. 36, 38, 43 sq.; Acts xix. 16 (with torn garments); Jas. ii. 15; (Job xxii. 6; xxiv. 10; xxvi. 6). c. clad in the undergarment only (the outer garment or cloak being laid aside): Jn. xxi. 7; (1 S. xix. 24; Is. xx. 2; Hes. opp. 389; often in Attic; so nudus, Verg. Georg. 1, 299). d. of the soul, whose garment is the body, stript of the body, without a body: 2 Co. v. 3, (Plat. Crat. c. 20 p. 403 b. ἡ ψυχὴ γυμνὴ τοῦ σώματος). 2. metaph. a. naked, i. e. open, laid bare: Heb. iv. 13, (γυμνὸς ὁ ᾅδης ἐνώπιον αὐτοῦ, Job xxvi. 6; exx. fr. Grk. auth. see in Bleek on Heb. vol. ii. 1 p 585). b. only, mere, bare, i. q. ψιλός (like Lat. nudus): γυμνὸς κόκκος, mere grain, not the plant itself, 1 Co. xv. 37, (Clem. Rom. 1 Cor. 24, 5 σπέρματα πεσόντα εἰς τὴν γῆν ξηρὰ καὶ γυμνὰ διαλύεται).* 1131

γυμνότης, -ητος, ἡ, (γυμνός), nakedness: of the body, Rev. iii. 18 (see αἰσχύνη, 3); used of want of clothing, Ro. viii. 35; 2 Co. xi. 27. (Deut. xxviii. 48; Antonin. 11, 27.)* 1132

1133 γυναικάριον, -ου, τό, (dimin. fr. γυνή), *a little woman*; used contemptuously in 2 Tim. iii. 6 [A. V. *silly women*; cf. Lat. *muliercula*]. (Diocles. com. in *Bekk*. Anecd. p. 87, 4; Antonin. 5, 11; occasionally in Epictet.) On dimin. ending in άριον see *Lob.* ad Phryn. p. 180; Fritzsche on Mk. p. 638; [cf. W. 24, 96 (91)].*

1134 γυναικεῖος, -εία, -εῖον, *of* or *belonging to a woman, feminine, female*: 1 Pet. iii. 7. (From Hom. down; Sept.) *

1135 γυνή, -αικός, ἡ; **1.** univ. *a woman* of any age, whether a virgin, or married, or a widow: Mt. ix. 20; xiii. 33; xxvii. 55; Lk. xiii. 11; Acts v. 14, etc.; ἡ μεμνηστευμένη τινὶ γυνή, Lk. ii. 5 R G; ἡ ὕπανδρος γυνή, Ro. vii. 2; γυνὴ χήρα, Lk. iv. 26 (1 K. vii. 2 (14); xvii. 9; *femina vidua*, Nep. praef. 4). **2.** *a wife*: 1 Co. vii. 3 sq. 10, 13 sq.; Eph. v. 22, etc.; γυνή τινος, Mt. v. 31 sq.; xix. 3, 5; Acts v. 1, 7; 1 Co. vii. 2; Eph. v. 28; Rev. ii. 20 [G L WH mrg.], etc. *of a betrothed* woman: Mt. i. 20, 24. ἡ γυνὴ τοῦ πατρός *his step-mother*: 1 Co. v. 1 (אֵשֶׁת אָב, Lev. xviii. 8). ἔχειν γυναῖκα: Mt. xiv. 4; xxii. 28; Mk. vi. 18; xii. 23; Lk. xx. 33; see ἔχω, I. 2 b. fin. γύναι, as a form of address, may be used — either in indignation, Lk. xxii. 57; or in admiration, Mt. xv. 28; or in kindness and favor, Lk. xiii. 12; Jn. iv. 21; or in respect, Jn. ii. 4; xix. 26, (as in Hom. Il. 3, 204; Od. 19, 221; Joseph. antt. 1, 16, 3).

1136 Γώγ, ὁ, (גּוֹג), indecl. prop. name, *Gog*, king of the land of *Magog* [q. v. in BB.DD.], who it is said in Ezek. xxxviii. sq. will come from the remote north, with innumerable hosts of his own nation as well as of allies, and will attack the people of Israel, reëstablished after the exile; but by divine interposition he will be utterly destroyed. Hence in Rev. xx. 8 sq. ὁ Γώγ and ὁ Μαγώγ are used collectively to designate the nations that at the close of the millennial reign, instigated by Satan, will break forth from the four quarters of the earth against the Messiah's kingdom, but will be destroyed by fire from heaven.*

1137 γωνία, -ας, ἡ, [fr. Hdt. down], *an angle*, i. e. **a.** an external angle, *corner* (Germ. *Ecke*): τῶν πλατειῶν, Mt. vi. 5; κεφαλὴ γωνίας, Mt. xxi. 42; Mk. xii. 10; Lk. xx. 17; Acts iv. 11; 1 Pet. ii. 7, (רֹאשׁ פִּנָּה, Ps. cxvii. (cxviii.) 22), the head of the corner, i. e. the corner-stone, (ἀκρογωνιαῖος, q. v.); αἱ τέσσαρες γωνίαι τῆς γῆς, the four extreme limits of the earth, Rev. vii. 1; xx. 8. **b.** like Germ. *Winkel*, Lat. *angulus*, Eng. (internal) *corner*, i. q. *a secret place*: Acts xxvi. 26, (so Plat. Gorg. p. 485 d. βίον βιῶναι ἐν γωνίᾳ, Epict. diss. 2, 12, 17; [for other examples see Wetstein on Acts l. c.; Stallbaum on Plato l. c.]).*

Δ

1138 Δαβίδ (the form in Rec. after the more recent codd. [minuscules, cf. Tdf. on Mt. i. 1, and Treg. on Lk. iii. 31]), Δαυίδ (Grsb., Schott, Knapp, Theile, al.), and Δαυείδ (L T Tr WH [on the ει see *WH*. App. p. 155 and s. v. ει, ι]; cf. W. p. 44; Bleek on Heb. vol. ii. 1 p. 538; in Joseph. [antt. 6, 8, 1 sqq. also Nicol. of Damasc. fr. 31 p. 114] Δαυίδης, -ου), ὁ, (דָּוִד, and esp. after the exile דָּוִיד, [i. e. beloved]), *David*, indecl. name of by far the most celebrated king of the Israelites: Mt. i. 1, 6, 17, etc. ἡ σκηνὴ Δ. Acts xv. 16; ἡ κλεὶς τοῦ Δ. Rev. iii. 7; ὁ θρόνος Δ. Lk. i. 32; ὁ υἱὸς Δ., a name of the Messiah, viz. the descendant of David and heir to his throne (see υἱός, 1 b.); ἡ ῥίζα Δ. the offspring of David, Rev. v. 5; xxii. 16; ἡ βασιλεία τοῦ Δ. Mk. xi. 10 (see βασιλεία, 3); ἐν Δαυίδ, in the book of the Psalms of David, Heb. iv. 7 [al. take it personally, cf. i. 1 sq.; yet see ἐν, I. 1 d.].

1139 δαιμονίζομαι; 1 aor. pass. ptcp. δαιμονισθείς; (δαίμων); *to be under the power of a demon*: ἄλλος κατ' ἄλλην δαιμονίζεται τύχην, Philem. in Stob. ecl. phys. 1 p. 196; of the insane, Plut. symp. 7, 5, 4, and in other later auth. In the N. T. δαιμονιζόμενοι are persons afflicted with especially severe diseases, either bodily or mental (such as paralysis, blindness, deafness, loss of speech, epilepsy,

melancholy, insanity, etc.), whose bodies in the opinion of the Jews demons (see δαιμόνιον) had entered, and so held possession of them as not only to afflict them with ills, but also to dethrone the reason and take its place themselves; accordingly the possessed were wont to express the mind and consciousness of the demons dwelling in them; and their cure was thought to require the expulsion of the demon — [but on this subject see B.D. Am. ed. s. v. Demoniacs and reff. there; *Weiss*, Leben Jesu bk. iii. ch. 6]: Mt. iv. 24; viii. 16, 28, 33; ix. 32; xii. 22; xv. 22; Mk. i. 32; v. 15 sq.; Jn. x. 21; δαιμονισθείς, that had been possessed by a demon [demons], Mk. v. 18; Lk. viii. 36. They are said also to be ὀχλούμενοι ὑπὸ or ἀπὸ πνευμάτων ἀκαθάρτων, Lk. vi. 18 [T Tr WH ἐνοχλ.]; Acts v. 16; καταδυναστευόμενοι ὑπὸ τοῦ διαβόλου i. e. by his ministers, the demons, Acts x. 38.*

1140 δαιμόνιον, -ου, τό, (neut. of adj. δαιμόνιος, -α, -ον, divine, fr. δαίμων; equiv. to τὸ θεῖον); **1.** *the divine Power, deity, divinity*; so sometimes in prof. auth. as Joseph. b. j. 1, 2, 8; Ael. v. h. 12, 57; in plur. καινὰ δαιμόνια, Xen. mem. 1, 1, 1 sq., and once in the N. T. ξένα δαιμόνια, Acts xvii. 18. **2.** *a spirit, a being inferior to God, superior to men* [πᾶν τὸ δαιμόνιον μεταξύ ἐστι θεοῦ τε καὶ θνητοῦ, Plat. symp. 23 p. 202 e. (where see Stallbaum)], in both a good sense and a bad; thus Jesus, after his resurrection, said to his disciples οὐκ εἰμὶ δαιμόνιον ἀσώματον, as Ignat. (ad Smyrn. 3, 2) records it; πνεῦμα δαιμονίου ἀκαθάρτου (gen. of apposition), Lk. iv. 33; (πονηρόν, Tob. iii. 8, 17; δαιμόνιον ἢ πνεῦμα πονηρόν, ibid. vi. 8). But elsewhere in the Scriptures used, without an adjunct, of evil spirits or the messengers and ministers of the devil [W. 23 (22)]: Lk. iv. 35; ix. 1, 42; x. 17; Jn. x. 21; Jas. ii. 19; (Ps. xc. (xci.) 6; Is. xiii. 21; xxxiv. 14; Tob. vi. 18; viii. 3; Bar. iv. 35); πνεύματα δαιμονίων (Rec. δαιμόνων) i. e. of that rank of spirits that are demons (gen. of appos.), Rev. xvi. 14; ἄρχων τῶν δαιμονίων, the prince of the demons, or the devil: Mt. ix. 34; xii. 24; Mk. iii. 22; Lk. xi. 15; they are said εἰσέρχεσθαι εἴς τινα, to enter into (the body of) one to vex him with diseases (see δαιμονίζομαι): Lk. viii. 30, 32 sq.; ἐκβληθῆναι and ἐξέρχεσθαι ἔκ τινος or ἀπό τινος, when they are forced to come out of one to restore him to health: Mt. ix. 33; xvii. 18; Mk. vii. 29, 30; Lk. iv. 35, 41; viii. 2, 33, 35. ἐκβάλλειν δαιμόνια, is used of those who compel demons to come out: Mt. vii. 22; xii. 27 sq.; Mk. i. 34, 39; Lk. ix. 49, etc. ἔχειν δαιμόνιον, to have a demon, possessed by a demon, is said of those who either suffer from some exceptionally severe disease, Lk. iv. 33; viii. 27 (ἐχ. δαιμόνια); or act and speak as though they were mad, Mt. xi. 18; Lk. vii. 33; Jn. vii. 20; viii. 48 sq. 52; x. 20. According to a Jewish opinion which passed over to the Christians, the demons are the gods of the Gentiles and the authors of idolatry; hence δαιμόνια stands for אֱלִילִים Ps. xcv. (xcvi.) 5, and שֵׁדִים Deut. xxxii. 17; Ps. cv. (cvi.) 37, cf. Bar. iv. 7: προσκυνεῖν τὰ δαιμόνια καὶ τὰ εἴδωλα, Rev. ix. 20. The apostle Paul, though teaching that the gods of the Gentiles are a fiction (1 Co. viii. 4; x. 19), thinks that the conception of them has been put into the minds of men by demons, who appropriate to their own use and honor the sacrifices offered to idols. Hence what the Gentiles θύουσι, he says δαιμονίοις θύουσιν καὶ οὐ θεῷ, 1 Co. x. 20 (fr. the Sept. of Deut. xxxii. 17, cf. Bar. iv. 7), and those who frequent the sacrificial feasts of the Gentiles come into fellowship with demons, 1 Co. x. 20 sq.; [cf. Baudissin, Stud. zur semit. Religionsgesch. vol. i. (St. ii. 4) p. 110 sqq.]. Pernicious errors are disseminated by demons even among Christians, seducing them from the truth, 1 Tim. iv. 1. Josephus also makes mention of δαιμόνι ι taking possession of men, antt. 6, 11, 2 sq.; 6, 8, 2; 8, 2, 5; but he sees in them, not as the N. T. writers do, bad angels, but the spirits of wicked men deceased, b. j. 7, 6, 3.

1141 δαιμονιώδης, -ες, (δαιμόνιον, q. v., and εἶδος), resembling or proceeding from an evil spirit, demon-like: Jas. iii. 15. [Schol. Arstph. ran. 295; Ps. xc. 6 Symm.]*

1142 δαίμων, -ονος, ὁ, ἡ; 1. in Grk. auth. a god, a goddess; an inferior deity, whether good or bad; hence ἀγαθοδαίμονες and κακοδαίμονες are distinguished [cf. W. 23 (22)]. 2. In the N. T. an evil spirit (see δαιμόνιον, 2): Mt. viii. 31; Mk. v. 12 [R L]; Lk. viii. 29 [R G L

mrg.]; Rev. xvi. 14 (Rec.); xviii. 2 (where L T Tr WII δαιμονίων). [B. D. (esp. Am. ed.) s. v. Demon; cf. δαιμονίζομαι.]*

1143 δάκνω; to bite; a. prop. with the teeth. b. metaph. to wound the soul, cut, lacerate, rend with reproaches: Gal. v. 15. So even in Hom. Il. 5, 493 μῦθος δάκε φρένας, Menand. ap. Athen. 12, 77 p. 552 e., and times without number in other auth.*

1144 δάκρυ, -υος, τό, and τὸ δάκρυον, -ου, [fr. Hom. down], a tear: Mk. ix. 24 R G; Acts xx. 19, 31; 2 Co. ii. 4; 2 Tim. i. 4; Heb. v. 7; xii. 17. The (nom.) form τὸ δάκρυον in Rev. vii. 17; xxi. 4, (Is. xxv. 8). dat. plur. δάκρυσι in Lk. vii. 38, 44, (Ps. cxxv. (cxxvi.) 5; Lam. ii. 11).*

1145 δακρύω: 1 aor. ἐδάκρυσα; to weep, shed tears: Jn. xi. 35. [From Hom. down. SYN. see κλαίω, fin.]*

1146 δακτύλιος, -ου, ὁ, (fr. δάκτυλος, because decorating the fingers), a ring: Lk. xv. 22. (From Hdt. down.)*

1147 δάκτυλος, -ου, ὁ, [fr. Batrach. 45 and Hdt. down], a finger: Mt. xxiii. 4; Lk. xi. 46; xvi. 24; Mk. vii. 33; Jn. viii. 6 Rec.; xx. 25, 27; ἐν δακτύλῳ θεοῦ, by the power of God, divine efficiency by which something is made visible to men, Lk. xi. 20 (Mt. xii. 28 ἐν πνεύματι θεοῦ); Ex. viii. 19, [cf. xxxi. 18; Ps. viii. 4].*

1148 Δαλμανουθά [on the accent cf. Tdf. Proleg. p. 103], ἡ, Dalmanutha, the name of a little town or village not far from Magdala [better Magadan (q. v.)], or lying within its territory: Mk. viii. 10 (cf. Mt. xv. 39), see Fritzsche ad loc. [B. D. Am. ed. s. v.]. Derivation of the name uncertain; cf. Keim ii. 528 [(Eng. trans. iv. 238), who associates it with Zalmonah, Num. xxxiii. 41 sq., but mentions other opinions. Furrer in the Zeitschr. des Deutsch. Palaestin.-Vereins for 1879, p. 58 sqq. identifies it with Minyeh (abbrev. Manutha, Lat. mensa)].*

1149 Δαλματία [Lchm. Δελμ. (" prob. Alexandrian but possibly genuine," Hort)], -ας, ἡ, Dalmatia, a part of Illyricum on the Adriatic Sea; on the east adjoining Pannonia and upper Moesia, on the north separated from Liburnia by the river Titius, and extending southwards as far as to the river Drinus and the city Lissus [cf. Dict. of Geog. s. v.; Conyb. and Hows. St. Paul, ii. 126 sq.; Lewin, St. Paul, ii. 357]: 2 Tim. iv. 10.*

1150 δαμάζω: 1 aor. ἐδάμασα; Pass., [pres. δαμάζομαι]; pf. δεδάμασμαι; [akin to Lat. domo, dominus, Goth. gatamjan; Eng. tame; cf. Curtius § 260]; com. fr. Hom. down; to tame: Mk. v. 4; Jas. iii. 7; to restrain, curb, τὴν γλῶσσαν, Jas. iii. 8.*

1151 δάμαλις, -εως, ἡ, (fem. of ὁ δαμάλης a young bullock or steer), a young cow, heifer, (Aeschyl., Dion. Hal., Lcian., al.) used in Num. xix. 2, 6, 9 sq. for פָּרָה and in Heb. ix. 13 of the red heifer with whose ashes, by the Mosaic law, those were to be sprinkled who had become defiled. (Besides in Sept. chiefly for עֶגְלָה.) *

1152 Δάμαρις, -ιδος, ἡ, Damaris, a woman of Athens converted by Paul: Acts xvii. 34; [cf. Mey. ad loc.; B. D. s. v.].*

1153 Δαμασκηνός, -ή, -όν, of Damascus, Damascene; substantively οἱ Δαμασκηνοί: 2 Co. xi. 32.*

1154   **Δαμασκός**, -οῦ, ἡ, *Damascus*, (Hebr. דַּמֶּשֶׂק), a very ancient (Gen. xiv. 15), celebrated, flourishing city of Syria, lying in a most lovely and fertile plain at the eastern base of Antilibanus. It had a great number of Jews among its inhabitants (Joseph. b. j. 2, 20, 2 cf. 7, 8, 7). Still one of the most opulent cities of western Asia, having about 109,000 inhabitants ["in 1859 about 150,000; of these 6,000 were Jews, and 15,000 Christians" (Porter)]: Acts ix. 2 sqq.; xxii. 5 sqq.; 2 Co. xi. 32; Gal. i. 17. [Cf. BB.DD. s. v., esp. Alex.'s Kitto.]*

1155   **δανείζω** (T WH δανίζω [see I, ι]); 1 aor. ἐδάνεισα (Lk. vi. 34 L txt. T WH Tr mrg.); 1 aor. mid. ἐδανεισάμην; (δάνειον, q. v.); [fr. Arstph. down]; *to lend money*: Lk. vi. 34 sq.; Mid. *to have money lent to one's self, to take a loan, borrow* [cf. W. § 38, 3; *Riddell*, Platon. idioms, § 87]: Mt. v. 42. (Deut. xv. 6, 8; Prov. xix. 17; in Grk. auth. fr. Xen. and Plat. down.)*

[SYN.: δανείζω, κίχρημι: δ. *to lend on interest*, as a business transaction; κίχρ. *to lend*, grant the use of, as a friendly act.]

1156   **δάνειον** [WH δάνιον, see I, ι], -είου, τό, (δάνος a gift), *a loan*: Mt. xviii. 27. (Deut. xxiv. 8; xxiv. 13 (11); Aristot. eth. Nic. 9, 2, 3; Diod. 1, 79; Plut.; al.)*

1157   **δανειστής** (T WH δανιστής [see I, ι]), -οῦ, ὁ, (δανείζω, q. v.), *a money-lender, creditor*: Lk. vii. 41. (2 K. iv. 1; Ps. cviii. (cix.) 11; Prov. xxix. 13; Sir. xxix. 28. Dem. p. 885, 18; Plut. Sol. 13, 5; de vitand. aere, etc. 7, 8; [al.].)*

see 1155 **──δανίζω**, see δανείζω.

1158   **Δανιήλ**, ὁ, דָּנִיֵּאל and דָּנִאֵל i. e. judge of God [or God is my judge]), *Daniel*, prop. name of a Jewish prophet, conspicuous for his wisdom, to whom are ascribed the well-known prophecies composed between B. C. 167–164; [but cf. BB.DD.]: Mt. xxiv. 15; Mk. xiii. 14 Rec.*

see 1156 **─[δάνιον**, see δάνειον.]

see 1157 **── δανιστής**, see δανειστής.

1159   **δαπανάω**, -ῶ; fut. δαπανήσω; 1 aor. ἐδαπάνησα; (δαπάνη); fr. [Hdt. and] Thuc. down; *to incur expense, expend, spend*: τί, Mk. v. 26 (1 Macc. xiv. 32); ἐπί with dat. of pers., for one, in his favor, Acts xxi. 24; ὑπέρ τινος, 2 Co. xii. 15. in a bad sense, *to waste, squander, consume*: πάντα, Lk. xv. 14; ἵνα ἐν ταῖς ἡδοναῖς ὑμῶν δαπανήσητε, that ye may consume, waste what ye receive, in luxurious indulgence ─ [ἐν marking the realm *in* rather than the object *on*]: Jas. iv. 3. [COMP.: ἐκ-, προσ- δαπανάω.]*

1160   **δαπάνη**, -ης, ἡ, (fr. δάπτω to tear, consume, [akin are δεῖπνον, Lat. *daps*; Curtius § 261]), *expense, cost*: Lk. xiv. 28. (2 Esdr. vi. 4; 1 Macc. iii. 30, etc. Among Grk. writ. Hes. opp. 721, Pind., Eur., Thuc., et sqq.)*

see 1138 **──Δαυείδ and Δαυίδ**, see Δαβίδ.

1161   **δέ** (related to δή, as μέν to μήν, cf. *Klotz* ad Devar. ii. 2 p. 355), a particle adversative, distinctive, disjunctive, *but, moreover*, (W. § 53, 7 and 10, 2); it is much more freq. in the historical parts of the N. T. than in the other books, very rare in the Epp. of John and the Apocalypse. [On its general neglect of elision (when the next word begins with a vowel) cf. *Tdf.* Proleg. p. 96; *WH*. App. p. 146; W. § 5, 1 a.] It is used   **1.**

univ. by way of **opposition and distinction**; it is added to statements opp. to a preceding statement: ἐὰν γὰρ ἀφῆτε . . . ἐὰν δὲ μὴ ἀφῆτε, Mt. vi. 14 sq.; ἐὰν δὲ ὁ ὀφθαλμός κτλ. Mt. vi. 23; ἐλεύσονται δὲ ἡμέραι, Mk. ii. 20; it opposes persons to persons or things previously mentioned or thought of, ─ either with strong emphasis: ἐγὼ δέ, Mt. v. 22, 28, 32, 34, 39, 44; ἡμεῖς δέ, 1 Co. i. 23; 2 Co. x. 13; σὺ δέ, Mt. vi. 6; ὑμεῖς δέ, Mk. viii. 29; οἱ δὲ υἱοὶ τῆς βασιλείας, Mt. viii. 12; αἱ ἀλώπεκες, Mt. viii. 20; Lk. ix. 58; πᾶς ὁ λαὸς . . . οἱ δὲ Φαρισαῖοι, Lk. vii. 29 sq.; ὁ δὲ πνευματικός, 1 Co. ii. 15, and often; ─ or with a slight discrimination, ὁ δέ, αὐτὸς δέ: Mk. i. 45; v. 34; vi. 37; vii. 6; Mt. xiii. 29, 37, 52; xv. 23 sqq.; Lk. iv. 40, 43; v. 16; vi. 8; viii. 10, 54; xv. 29; οἱ δέ, Mt. ii. 5; Mk. iii. 4; viii. 28, etc., etc.; with the addition also of a prop. name, as ὁ δὲ Ἰησοῦς: Mt. viii. 22 [Tdf. om. Ἰ.]; ix. 12 [R G Tr br.], 22 [Tdf. om. Ἰ.]; xiii. 57; Mk. i. 41 [R G L mrg. Tr mrg.]; ἀποκρ. δὲ (ὁ) Σίμων, Lk. vii. 43 R G L br.; ἡ δὲ Μαρία, Lk. ii. 19, etc. **2.** μέν . . . δέ, see μέν. **3.** after negative sentences, *but, but rather* (Germ. *wohl aber*): Mt. vi. 19 sq. (μὴ θησαυρίζετε . . . θησαυρίζετε δέ); x. 5 sq.; Acts xii. 9, 14; Ro. 28; 1 Co. i. 10; vii. 37; 1 Th. v. 21 [not Rec.]; Eph. iv. 14 sq.; Heb. ii. 5 sq.; iv. 13, 15; ix. 12; x. 26 sq.; xii. 13; 1 Pet. i. 12 (οὐχ ἑαυτοῖς ὑμῖν [Rec. ἡμ.] δέ); Jas. i. 13 sq.; ii. 11. **4.** it is joined to terms which are repeated with a certain emphasis, and with such additions as tend to explain and establish them more exactly; in this use of the particle we may supply a suppressed negative clause [and give its force in Eng. by inserting *I say, and that, so then*, etc.]: Ro. iii. 21 sq. (not that common δικαιοσύνη which the Jews boast of and strive after, but δικαιοσ. διὰ πίστεως); Ro. ix. 30; 1 Co. ii. 6 (σοφίαν δὲ οὐ τοῦ αἰῶνος τούτου); Gal. ii. 2 (I went up, not of my own accord, but etc.); Phil. ii. 8; cf. *Klotz* ad Dev. ii. 2 p. 361 sq.; *L. Dindorf* in Steph. Thes. ii. col. 928; [cf. W. 443 (412)]. **5.** it serves to mark a transition to something new (δέ metabatic); by this use of the particle, the new addition is distinguished from and, as it were, opposed to what goes before: Mt. i. 18; ii. 19; x. 21; Lk. xii. 13; xiii. 1; Jn. vii. 14, 37; Acts vi. 1; Ro. viii. 28; 1 Co. 1, etc., etc.; so also in the phrase ἐγένετο δέ, see γίνομαι, 2 c. **6.** it introduces explanations and separates them from the things to be explained: Jn. iii. 19; vi. 39; 1 Co. i. 12; vii. 6, 29; Eph. v. 32, etc.; ─ esp. remarks and explanations intercalated into the discourse, or added, as it were, by way of appendix: Mk. v. 13 (ἦσαν δέ etc. R L br.); xv. 25; xvi. 8 [R G]; Jn. vi. 10; ix. 14; xii. 3; τοῦτο δὲ γέγονε, Mt. i. 22; xxi. 4. Owing to this use, the particle not infrequently came to be confounded in the Mss. (of prof. writ. also) with γάρ; cf. Winer on Gal. i. 11; Fritzsche on Mk. xiv. 2; also his Com. on Rom. vol. i. pp. 234, 265; ii. p. 476; iii. p. 196; [W. 452 (421); B. 363 (312)]. **7.** after a parenthesis or an explanation which had led away from the subject under discussion, it serves to take up the discourse again [cf. W. 443 (412)]: Mt. iii. 4; Lk. iv. 1; Ro. v. 8; 2 Co. ii. 12; v. 8; x. 2; Eph. ii. 4; cf. *Klotz* ad Devar.

ii. 2 p. 376 sq.   **8.** it introduces the apodosis and, as it were, opposes it to the protasis: Acts xi. 17 R G (1 Macc. xiv. 29; 2 Macc. i. 34) after a participial construction which has the force of a protasis: Col. i. 22 (21); cf. Matthiae ii. 1470; Kühner ii. 818; [Jelf § 770]; Klotz u. s. p. 370 sq.; [B. 364 (312)].   **9.** καὶ ... δέ, but ... also, yea and, moreover also: Mt. x. 18; xvi. 18; Lk. ii. 35 [WH txt. om. L Tr br. δέ]; Jn. vi. 51; xv. 27; Acts iii. 24; xxii. 29; Ro. xi. 23; 2 Tim. iii. 12; 1 Jn. i. 3; 2 Pet. i. 5; cf. Klotz u. s. p. 645 sq.; B. 364 (312); [also W. 443 (413); Ellic. on 1 Tim. iii. 10; Mey. on Jn. vi. 51]. καὶ ἐὰν δέ yea even if: Jn. viii. 16.   **10.** δέ never stands as the first word in the sentence, but generally second; and when the words to which it is added cannot be separated, it stands third (as in Mt. x. 11; xviii. 25; Mk. iv. 34; Lk. x. 31; Acts xvii. 6; xxviii. 6; Gal. iii. 23; 2 Tim. iii. 8, etc.; in οὐ μόνον δέ, Ro. v. 3, 11, etc.), or even in the fourth place, Mt. x. 18; Jn. vi. 51; viii. 16 sq.; 1 Jn. i. 3; 1 Co. iv. 18; [Lk. xxii. 69 L T Tr WH].

1162   δέησις, -εως, ἡ, (δέομαι);   **1.** need, indigence, (Ps. xxi. (xxii.) 25; Aeschin. dial. 2, 39 sq.; [Plato, Eryx. 405 e. bis]; Aristot. rhet. 2, 7 [ii. p. 1385ᵃ, 27]).   **2.** a seeking, asking, entreating, entreaty, (fr. Plat. down); in the N. T. requests addressed by men to G o d (Germ. Bittgebet, supplication); univ.: Jas. v. 16; 1 Pet. iii. 12; as often in the Sept., joined with προσευχή (i. e. any pious address to God [see below]): Acts i. 14 Rec.; Eph. vi. 18; Phil. iv. 6; plur. 2 Tim. i. 3; joined with προσευχαί, 1 Tim. v. 5; with νηστείαι, Lk. ii. 37; ποιεῖσθαι δέησιν, Phil. i. 4; π. δεήσεις, Lk. v. 33; 1 Tim. ii. 1.   contextually, of prayers imploring God's aid in some particular matter: Lk. i. 13; Phil. i. 19; plur. Heb. v. 7; supplication for others: [2 Co. i. 11]; περί τινος, Eph. vi. 18; ὑπέρ τινος, 2 Co. ix. 14; Phil. i. 4; with the addition πρὸς τὸν θεόν, Ro. x. 1.*

[Syn. δέησις, προσευχή, ἔντευξις: πρ., as Prof. Grimm remarks, is unrestricted as respects its contents, while δ. is petitionary; moreover πρ. is a word of s a c r e d character, being limited to prayer to God, whereas δ. may also be used of a request addressed to man. In Byzantine Grk. it is used of a w r i t t e n supplication (like our petition); cf. Soph. Lex. s. v. See more at length Trench § li.; also Bp. Lghtft. on Phil. iv. 6; Ellic. on Eph. vi. 18; cf. Schmidt ch. vii. In 1 Tim. ii. 1 to these two words is added ἔντευξις, which expresses confiding access to God; thus, in combination, δέησις gives prominence to the expression of personal n e e d, προσευχή to the element of d e v o t i o n, ἔντευξις to that of childlike c o n f i d e n c e, by representing prayer as the heart's converse with God. See Huther's extended note ad loc.; Ellic. ad loc.; Trench u. s.]

1163   δεῖ; subjunc. pres. δέῃ; impf. ἔδει; an impers. verb [cf. B. § 132, 12; cf. § 131, 3; fr. Hom. down]; (δέω, sc. τινός, to have need of, be in want of; cf. Germ. es bedarf), it is necessary, there is need of, it behooves, is right and proper; foll. either by the inf. alone (cf. our one ought), or by the acc. with inf. [cf. B. 147 (129)], it denotes any sort of necessity; as   **a.** necessity lying in the nature of the case: Jn. iii. 30; 2 Tim. ii. 6.   **b.** necessity brought on by circumstances or by

the conduct of others toward us: Mt. xxvi. 35 (κἂν δέῃ με ἀποθανεῖν), cf. Mk. xiv. 31; Jn. iv. 4; Acts xxvii. 21; 2 Co. xi. 30; [xii. 1 L T Tr WH txt.]; or imposed by a condition of mind: Lk. ii. 49; xix. 5.   **c.** necessity in reference to what is required to attain some end: Lk. xii. 12; Jn. iii. 7; Acts ix. 6; xvi. 30; 1 Co. xi. 19; Heb. ix. 26 (on this cf. W. 283 (266); [also B. 216 (187); 225 (195)]); Heb. xi. 6.   **d.** a necessity of law and command, of duty, equity: Mt. xviii. 33; xxiii. 23; Lk. xi. 42; xiii. 14; xv. 32; xviii. 1; xxii. 7; Jn. iv. 20; Acts v. 29; xv. 5; Ro. i. 27 (ἀντιμισθίαν, ἣν ἔδει, sc. ἀπολαμβάνεσθαι, the recompense due by the law of God); Ro. viii. 26; xii. 3; 1 Co. viii. 2, etc. or of office: Lk. iv. 43; xiii. 33; Jn. ix. 4; x. 16; Eph. vi. 20; Col. iv. 4; 2 Tim. ii. 24.   **e.** necessity established by the counsel and decree of God, esp. by that purpose of his which relates to the salvation of men by the intervention of Christ and which is disclosed in the O. T. prophecies: Mt. xvii. 10; xxiv. 6; Mk. ix. 11; Acts iv. 12; 1 Co. xv. 53; in this use, esp. of what Christ was destined finally to undergo, his sufferings, death, resurrection, ascension: Lk. xxiv. 46 [R G L br.]; Mt. xxvi. 54; Jn. iii. 14; Acts iii. 21, etc. (of the necessity of fate in Hdt. 5, 33; with the addition κατὰ τὸ θεοπρόπιον, 8, 53; Thuc. 5, 26.)

[Syn.: δεῖ, χρή: δεῖ seems to be more suggestive of m o r a l obligation, denoting esp. that constraint which arises from divine appointment; whereas χρή signifies rather the necessity resulting from time and circumstance. Schmidt ch. 150.]

δεῖγμα, -τος, τό, (δείκνυμι);   **a.** prop. thing shown.   **b.** a specimen of any thing, example, pattern: πυρὸς αἰωνίου, set forth as a warning, Jude 7. (From Xen., Plat., Isocr. down.) *   **1164**

δειγματίζω: 1 aor. ἐδειγμάτισα; (δεῖγμα); to make an example of, to show as an example; τινά, to expose one to disgrace (cf. παραδειγματίζω, θεατρίζω): Mt. i. 19 L T Tr WH; Col. ii. 15. A word unknown to Grk. writ. [Cf. Act. Petr. et Paul. § 33; W. 25 (24); 91 (87); δειγματισμός occurs on the Rosetta stone, line 30; Boeckh, Inscrr. 4697. Comp.: παρα-δειγματίζω.]*   **1165**

δεικνύω (δεικνύειν, Mt. xvi. 21; δεικνύεις, Jn. ii. 18; τοῦ δεικνύοντος, Rev. xxii. 8 [not Tdf.]) and δείκνυμι (1 Co. xii. 31; Mt. iv. 8; Jn. v. 20; cf. B. 45 (39)); fut. δείξω; 1 aor. ἔδειξα; 1 aor. pass. ptcp. δειχθείς (Heb. viii. 5); Sept. mostly for הִרְאָה; to show, exhibit;   **1.** prop. to show i. e. expose to the eyes: τινί τι, Mt. iv. 8; Lk. iv. 5; xx. 24 (for Rec. ἐπιδείξ.); xxii. 12; xxiv. 40 [R G L, but Tom. Tr br. WH reject the vs.]; Mk. xiv. 15; Jn. xx. 20; Acts vii. 3; ὁδόν τινι, metaph., in which one ought to go, i. e. to teach one what he ought to do, 1 Co. xii. 31; κατὰ τὸν τύπον τὸν δειχθέντα σοι, Heb. viii. 5; ἑαυτὸν δεικνύαι τινί to expose one's self to the view of one, Mt. viii. 4; Mk. i. 44; Lk. v. 14; δεῖξον ἡμῖν τὸν πατέρα render the Father visible to us, Jn. xiv. 8 sq.; of things presented to one in a vision: τινί τι, Rev. xvii. 1; xxi. 9 sq.; xxii. 1, 8; δεῖξαί τινι, ἃ δεῖ γενέσθαι, Rev. i. 1; iv. 1; xxii. 6.   to show, i. q. to bring to pass, produce what can be seen (Germ. sehen lassen); of miracles per-   **1166**

formed in presence of others to be seen by them: σημεῖον, Jn. ii. 18, (Bar. vi. [i. e. ep. Jer.] 66; σῆμα, Hom. Od. 3, 174; Il. 13, 244); ἔργα ἔκ τινος, works done by the aid of one, Jn. x. 32; τὴν ἐπιφάνειαν Ἰησοῦ Χριστοῦ, spoken of God, as the author of Christ's visible return, 1 Tim. vi. 15; ἔργα δεικνύειν is used differently in Jn. v. 20, to show works to one for him to do.   2. metaph.   a. with acc. of the thing, to give the evidence or proof of a thing: πίστιν, Jas. ii. 18; τὶ ἔκ τινος, as τὴν πίστιν ἐκ τῶν ἔργων, ibid.; τὰ ἔργα ἐκ τῆς καλῆς ἀναστροφῆς, Jas. iii. 13.   b. to show by words, to teach: foll. by ὅτι, Mt. xvi. 21 (διδάσκειν in Mk. viii. 31 for δεικνύειν); foll. by an inf. Acts x. 28. [COMP.: ἀνα-, ἀπο-, ἐν-, ἐπι-, ὑπο-δείκνυμι.] *

1167   **δειλία, -ας, ἡ,** (δειλός), timidity, fearfulness, cowardice: 2 Tim. i. 7. (Soph., [Hdt.], Eur., [Arstph.], Thuc., and subseq. writ.) *

[SYN. δ ε ι λ ί α, φ ό β ο ς, ε ὐ λ ά β ε ι α: "of these three words the first is used always in a bad sense; the second is a middle term, capable of a good interpretation, capable of an evil, and lying pretty evenly between the two; the third is quite predominantly used in a good sense, though it too has not altogether escaped being employed in an evil." Trench § x. q. v.; cf. δέος.]

1168   **δειλιάω, -ῶ;** (δειλία, q. v.); to be timid, fearful: Jn. xiv. 27. (Deut. xxxi. 6; i. 21 and often in Sept.; Sir. xxii. 16; xxxi. (xxxiv.) 16; 4 Macc. xiv. 4. Diod. 20, 78. The Greeks prefer the comp. ἀποδειλιῶ.) *

1169   **δειλός, -ή, -όν,** (δείδω to fear), timid, fearful: Mt. viii. 26; Mk. iv. 40; in Rev. xxi. 8 of Christians who through cowardice give way under persecutions and apostatize. (From Hom. down) *

1170   **δεῖνα, ὁ, ἡ, τό;** gen. δεῖνος; dat. δεῖνι; acc. χὸν, τὴν, τὸ δεῖνα (cf. Matthiae § 151), such a one, a certain one, i. e. one whose name I cannot call on the instant, or whose name it is of no importance to mention; once in the Scriptures, viz. Mt. xxvi. 18. (Arstph., Dem., al.) *

1171   **δεινῶς,** adv., (δεινός), terribly, grievously: Mt. viii. 6; Lk. xi. 53. [From Hdt. down.] *

1172   **δειπνέω, -ῶ:** [fut. δειπνήσω]; 1 aor. ἐδείπνησα; (δεῖπνον); to sup: Lk. xvii. 8; xxii. 20 [WH reject the whole pass., see their App.]; 1 Co. xi. 25; in an allegory, δειπνήσω μετ᾽ αὐτοῦ, I will make him to share in my most intimate and blissful intercourse: Rev. iii. 20.*

1173   **δεῖπνον, -ου, τό,** and acc. to a rare and late form ὁ δεῖπνος in Lk. xiv. 16 Lchm. [cf. Tdf. on Rev. xix. 9, 17, also W. 65 (64); on deriv. cf. δαπάνη], (in Hom. the morning meal or breakfast, cf. Passow [more fully L. and S.] s. v.; this the Greeks afterwards call τὸ ἄριστον q. v. [and reff. there], designating as τὸ δεῖπνον the evening meal or supper);   1. supper, esp. a formal meal usually held at evening: Lk. xiv. 17, 24; Jn. xiii. 2, 4; xxi. 20; plur.: Mt. xxiii. 6; Mk. xii. 39; Lk. (xi. 43 Lchm. in br.); xx. 46; used of the Messiah's feast, symbolizing salvation in the kingdom of heaven: Rev. xix. 9, 17; κυριακὸν δεῖπνον (see κυριακός, 1), 1 Co. xi. 20; ποιεῖν δεῖπνον, Lk. xiv. 12 (ἄριστον ἢ δεῖπνον); 16 (Dan. v. 1 [Theodot.]); with the addition τινί, Mk. vi. 21; Jn. xii. 2.   2. univ. food taken at evening: 1 Co. xi. 21.*

δεισιδαιμονία, -ας, ἡ, (δεισιδαίμων), fear of the gods;   1. in a good sense, reverence for the gods, piety, religion: Polyb. 6, 56, 7; Joseph. antt. 10, 3, 2; καὶ θεοφιλὴς βίος, Diod. 1, 70.   2. i. q. ἡ δειλία πρὸς τὸ δαιμόνιον (Theophr. char. 16 (22) init. [cf. Jebb p. 263 sq.]); superstition: [Polyb. 12, 24, 5]; Plut. [Sol. 12, 4]; Alex. 75, 1; de adulat. et am. 25, and in his Essay περὶ τῆς δεισιδαιμονίας; Antonin. 6, 30 θεοσεβὴς χωρὶς δεισιδαιμονίας.   3. religion, in an objective sense; in which sense Josephus, antt. 19, 5, 3, says Claudius commanded the Jews μὴ τὰς τῶν ἄλλων ἐθνῶν δεισιδαιμονίας ἐξουδενίζειν. Festus in the presence of Agrippa the Jewish king employs the word ambiguously and cautiously, in Acts xxv. 19, of the Jewish religion, viz. so as to leave his own judgment concerning its truth in suspense. Cf. Zezschwitz, Profangräcität u. bibl. Sprachgeist, p. 59; [K. F. Hermann, Lehrb. d. gottesdienstl. Alterthümer, § 8 note 6; Trench § xlviii.; (cf. Kenrick, Bibl. Essays, 1864, p. 108 sqq.; Field, Otium Norv. iii. p. 80 sq.).]*

δεισι-δαίμων, -ον, gen. -ονος, (δείδω to fear, and δαίμων deity), fearing the deity or deities, like the Lat. religiosus: used either   1. in a good sense, reverencing god or the gods, pious, religious: Xen. Cyr. 3, 3, 58; Ages. 11, 8; Aristot. pol. 5, 11 [p. 1315ᵃ, 1]; or   2. in a bad sense, superstitious: Theophr. char. 16 (22); Diod. 1, 62; 4, 51; Plut. de adul. c. 16; de superstit. c. 10 sq. Paul in the opening of his address to the Athenians, Acts xvii. 22, calls them, with kindly ambiguity, κατὰ πάντα δεισιδαιμονεστέρους (sc. than the rest of the Greeks [W. 244 (229)], cf. Meyer ad loc.), as being devout without the knowledge of the true God; cf. Bengel ad loc.*

δέκα, οἱ, αἱ, τά, [fr. Hom. down], ten: Mt. xx. 24, etc. θλίψις ἡμερῶν δέκα, i. e. to last a short time: Rev. ii. 10; cf. Dan. i. 12, 14; Num. xi. 19; Ter. heaut. 5, 1, 36 decem dierum vix mi est familia.

δεκα-δύο, rare in the earlier writ., frequent in the later (see Passow s. v. δέκα [esp. Soph. Lex. s. v.; cf. W. 23 (22); Bp. Lghtft. on Gal. i. 18]), and in Sept.; i. q. δώδεκα, twelve: Acts xix. 7 and xxiv. 11, in both places L T Tr WH δώδεκα; [Rev. xxi. 16 Tdf. edd. 2, 7].*

[**δεκα-έξ,** sixteen: Rev. xiii. 18 Lmrg. (Sept., al.) *]
[**δεκα-οκτώ** for δέκα καὶ ὀκτώ, eighteen: Tdf. in Lk. xiii. 4, 11, but WH om. L Tr br. καί; cf. s. v. καί, I. 1 b.*]

δεκα-πέντε, for the earlier πεντεκαίδεκα, fifteen: Jn. xi. 18; Acts xxvii. 28; Gal. i. 18; [Gen. vii. 20 Ald., Compl.; Ex. xxvii. 15; 1 Macc. x. 40; Polyb. 3, 56, 3 var.; Diod. 2, 13; Plut. Dion 38, 1; al.; cf. δεκαδύο].*

Δεκά-πολις, -εως, ἡ, Decapolis (regio decapolitana, Plin. h. n. 5, 16. 17), i. e. a region embracing ten cities. This name is borne by a district of the tribe of Manasseh beyond the Jordan and bordering upon Syria, embracing ten principal cities with smaller towns also scattered in among them. But the ancient geographers vary in their enumeration of these ten cities. Pliny l. c. reckons Damascus among them, which Josephus seems to have excluded, calling Scythopolis μεγίστην τῆς δεκαπόλεως, b. j. 3, 9, 7. All seem to agree in this, that Gadara, Hippo, Pella and Scythopolis were of the number. Cf.

1175

see 1174 St.

1176

1177

1178

1179

Win. RWB. s. v. Decapolis; *Vaihinger* in Herzog iii. 325 sq.; *Riehm*, HWB. 266 sq.; [BB.DD. s. v.]: Mt. iv. 25; Mk. v. 20; vii. 31.*

1180   δεκα-τέσσαρες, -ων, οἱ, αἱ, -σαρα, τά, *fourteen*: Mt. i. 17; 2 Co. xii. 2; Gal. ii. 1. [Gen. xxxi. 41; Tob. viii. 19; x. 7; Polyb. 1, 36, 11; cf. δεκαδύο.] *

1181   δεκάτη, -ης, ἡ, (δέκατος), the tenth part of any thing, *a tithe*; specially the tenth part of booty taken from the enemy: Heb. vii. 2, 4; the tithes of the fruits of the earth and of the flocks, which, by the law of Moses, were presented to the Levites in the congregation of Israel: Heb. vii. 8 sq. (In Grk. writ. fr. [Simon. 133 Bgk.; Hdt. 2, 135]; 4, 152 down; Sept. for מַעֲשֵׂר.) [Cf. BB.DD. s. v. Tithe.] *

1182   δέκατος, -η, -ον, (δέκα), [fr. Hom. down], *the tenth*: Jn. i. 39 (40); Rev. xxi. 20; τὸ δέκατον, subst., the tenth part: Rev. xi. 13.*

1183   δεκατόω, -ῶ: pf. δεδεκάτωκα; pf. pass. δεδεκάτωμαι; (δέκατος); *to exact* or *receive the tenth part* (for which Grk. writ. use δεκατεύω [W. 24]): with acc. of pers. from whom, Heb. vii. 6 [on the pf. cf. W. § 40, 4 a.; *Lghtft.* St. Clement, App. p. 414]; Pass. *to pay tithes* (Vulg. *decimor*): Heb. vii. 9. (Neh. x. 37.) [COMP.: ἀπο-δεκατόω.] *

1184   δεκτός, -ή, -όν, (δέχομαι), *accepted, acceptable*: Lk. iv. 24; Phil. iv. 18; τινί, Acts x. 35; the phrases καιρὸς δεκτός, 2 Co. vi. 2 (Is. xlix. 8 for עֵת רָצוֹן), and ἐνιαυτὸς δεκτός, Lk. iv. 19 (Is. lxi. 2 for שְׁנַת רָצוֹן), denote that most blessed time when salvation and the free favors of God profusely abound. (Ex. xxviii. 34; Is. lvi. 7, [etc.]. Among prof. auth. used by Jambl. protr. symb. § 20 p. 350.) *

1185   δελεάζω; [pres. pass. δελεάζομαι]; (δέλεαρ a bait);   **1.** prop. *to bait, catch by a bait*: Xen. mem. 2, 1, 4, et al. **2.** as often in prof. auth., metaph. *to beguile by blandishments, allure, entice, deceive*: τινά, 2 Pet. ii. 14, 18; Jas. i. 14, on this pass. cf. Philo, quod omn. prob. lib. § 22 πρὸς ἐπιθυμίας ἐλαύνεται ἢ ὑφ' ἡδονῆς δελεάζεται.*

[Δελματία see Δαλματία.]

1186   δένδρον, -ου, τό, *a tree*: Mt. vii. 17, etc.; γίνεσθαι δένδρον or εἰς δένδρον, to grow to the shape and size of a tree, Mt. xiii. 32; Lk. xiii. 19. [(Hom., Hdt.), Arstph., Thuc. down.]

see 1187   δεξιο-βόλος, -ου, ὁ, (fr. δεξιός and βάλλω), *throwing with the right hand, a slinger, an archer*: Acts xxiii. 23 in Lchm. ed. min.; cf. the foll. word.*

1187   δεξιολάβος, -ου, ὁ, (δεξιός and λαμβάνω), a word unknown to the earlier writ., found in Constant. Porphyrogenitus (10th cent.) de them. 1, 1, who speaks of δεξιολάβοι, as a kind of soldiers, in company with bow-men (τοξοφόροι) and peltasts; [they are also mentioned by Theoph. Simoc. (hist. 4, 1) in the 7th cent.; see the quotations in Meyer]. Since in Acts xxiii. 23 two hundred of them are ordered to be ready, apparently *spearmen* are referred to (carrying a lance in the right hand); and so the Vulg. has taken it. The great number spoken of conflicts with the interpretation of those who suppose them to be soldiers whose duty it was

to guard captives bound by a chain on the right hand. Meyer ad loc. understands them to be [either] *javelin-men* [or *slingers*].*

1188   δεξιός, -ά, -όν, (fr. δέχομαι, fut. δέξομαι, or fr. δέκω, which is akin to δείκνυμι; prop. of that hand which is wont to *take hold of* as well as to *point out*; just as ἄξιος comes fr. ἄξω, fut. of ἄγω; [cf. Curtius §§ 11, 266]), *the right*: Mt. v. 29, 39; Lk. xxii. 50; Jn. xviii. 10; Rev. x. 2; ἡ δεξιὰ χείρ, Mt. v. 30; Lk. vi. 6; Acts iii. 7; Rev. i. 16; xiii. 16; and (with χείρ omitted) ἡ δεξιά (like ἡ ἀριστερά), Mt. vi. 3; xxvii. 29; Rev. i. 20; ii. 1; v. 7; ἐπὶ τὴν δεξιάν [on the right hand i. e.] at the right side, Rev. v. 1 [but al. take it more closely, *in* the right hand; cf. vs. 7 and xx. 1]; διδόναι τὴν δεξιάν or τὰς δεξιάς, to pledge either a mutual friendship, or a compact, by joining the right hands: Gal. ii. 9 (1 Macc. vi. 58; xi. 50, 62, 66; xiii. 50; 2 Macc. xi. 26; xii. 11; xiii. 22; cf. *Gesenius*, Thesaur. ii. pp. 566 and 599; and in prof. auth. as Xen. an. 1, 6, 6; 2, 5, 3; Joseph. antt. 18, 9, 3 δεξιάν τε καὶ πίστιν δοῦναι τινί); God is said to have done something τῇ δεξιᾷ αὐτοῦ with his right hand i. e., acc. to Hebr. idiom, *by his own power* [cf. W. 214 (201)]: Acts ii. 33; v. 31; τὰ ὅπλα τὰ δεξιά, arms carried in the right hand and used for attack, as the sword, the spear, καὶ ἀριστερά those carried in the left hand, for the purpose of defence, as the shield: 2 Co. vi. 7; τὰ δεξιὰ μέρη τοῦ πλοίου, Jn. xxi. 6. τὰ δεξιά the right side [W. 176 (166)]: Mk. xvi. 5; ἐκ δεξιῶν τινος *on one's right hand* (Lat. *ad alicuius dextram*), Mt. xxv. 33 sq.; xxvii. 38; Mk. xv. 27; Lk. i. 11; xxiii. 33; εἶναι, Acts ii. 25 (fr. Ps. xv. (xvi.) 8, he is at my right hand, sc. as a leader, to sustain me). As in this expression the Greeks use the prep. ἐκ, so the Hebrews sometimes use מִן (מִימִין from i. e. at the right, מֵאֵצַל פֹּ from i. e. at the side of any one) and the Romans ab (*sedere a dextra alicuius*, proximum esse ab aliquo), because they define the position of one standing or sitting next another by proceeding *from* the one next to whom he is said to stand or sit [cf. W. 367 (344)]. καθίσαι ἐκ δεξιῶν κ. ἐξ εὐωνύμων τινὸς βασιλέως, to occupy the places of honor nearest to the king, Mt. xx. 21, 23; Mk. x. 37, 40; (יָשַׁב לִימִין פֹּ, 1 K. ii. 19; Ps. xliv. (xlv.) 10). Hence, after Ps. cix. (cx.) 1 as applied to the Messiah (Mt. xxii. 44; Mk. xii. 36; Lk. xx. 42), Christ is said to have ascended καθῆσθαι or καθίσαι ἐκ δεξιῶν (at or on the right hand) of God, Mt. xxvi. 64; Mk. xiv. 62; xvi. 19; Lk. xxii. 69; Acts ii. 34; Heb. i. 13; εἶναι or καθίσαι ἐν δεξιᾷ τ. θεοῦ, Ro. viii. 34; Eph. i. 20; Col. iii. 1; Heb. i. 3; viii. 1; x. 12; xii. 2, — to indicate that he has *become a partner in God's universal government* (cf. *Knapp*, De J. Chr. ad dextram dei sedente, in his Scripta var. arg. p. 41 sqq.; [*Stuart*, Com. on Heb., excurs. iv.]). That these expressions are to be understood in this figurative sense, and not of a fixed and definite place in the highest heavens (as *Chr. Fr. Fritzsche* in Nov. Opusc. acad. p. 209 sqq. tries to prove, after the orthodox theologians of the reformed church), will be questioned by no one who carefully considers Rev. iii. 21. Christ is once spoken of as ἑστὼς ἐκ δεξιῶν τοῦ θεοῦ, as though in indignation at his adversaries [acc.

to others, to welcome his martyred servant] he had risen from his heavenly throne, Acts vii. 55 sq.

1189   δέομαι; 3 pers. sing. impf. ἐδέετο (cf. Lob. ad Phryn. p. 220; W. 46; [Veitch s. v. δέω to need fin.]), Lk. viii. 38 (where Lchm. ἐδεεῖτο, Tr WH ἐδεῖτο; cf. Mey. ad loc.; [WH. App. p. 166]; B. 55 (48)); 1 aor. ἐδεήθην; (fr. δέω to want, need; whence mid. δέομαι to stand in need of, want for one's self); [fr. Hdt. down]; **1.** to want, lack: τινός. **2.** to desire, long for: τινός. **3.** to ask, beg, (Germ. bitten); a. univ.— the thing asked for being evident from the context: with gen. of the pers. from whom, Gal. iv. 12; the thing sought being specified in direct discourse: Lk. v. 12; viii. 28; ix. 38 (acc. to the reading ἐπίβλεψον R L); Acts viii. 34 (δέομαί σου, περὶ τίνος ὁ προφήτης λέγει τοῦτο; of whom, I pray thee, doth the prophet say this?); Acts xxi. 39; 2 Co. v. 20; foll. by the inf., Lk. viii. 38; ix. 38 (acc. to the reading ἐπιβλέψαι Tr WH); Acts xxvi. 3 (where G L T Tr WH om. σοῦ after δέομαι); foll. by ἵνα, Lk. ix. 40 (cf. W. 335 (315); [B. 258 (222)]); foll. by τό with inf. 2 Co. x. 2 [cf. B. 263 (226), 279 (239); W. 321, 322 (301 sq.)]; with gen. of pers. and acc. of thing, 2 Co. viii. 4 (G L T Tr WH; for Rec. adds δέξασθαι ἡμᾶς without warrant), [cf. B. 164 (143); W. 198 (186)]. **b.** spec. of requests addressed to God; absol. to pray, make supplication: Acts iv. 31; τοῦ θεοῦ, Acts x. 2; foll. by εἰ ἄρα, Acts viii. 22 [B. 256 (220); W. 300 (282)]; τοῦ κυρίου, ὅπως etc. Mt. ix. 38; Lk. x. 2; without the gen. θεοῦ,— foll. by εἴ πως, Ro. i. 10 [cf. W. and B. ll. cc.]; by ἵνα, Lk. xxi. 36; xxii. 32; by the telic εἰς τό, 1 Th. iii. 10 [cf. B. 265 (228)]; ὑπέρ τινος πρὸς τὸν κύριον, ὅπως, Acts viii. 24. [SYN. see αἰτέω and δέησις. COMP.: προσ-δέομαι.]*

see 1163   δέον, -οντος, τό, (ptcp. of δεῖ, q. v.), fr. [Soph. and] Hdt. down, that of which there is need, which is requisite, due, proper: δέον ἐστί there is need, 1 Pet. i. 6 [T Tr txt. WH om. Tr mrg. br. ἐ.]; foll. by acc. with inf. Acts xix. 36; τὰ μὴ δέοντα the things that are not proper, 1 Tim. v. 13.*

see 127,   δέος, -ους, τό, (δείδω), [fr. Hom. down], fear, awe: μετὰ
2124 &   εὐλαβείας καὶ δέους, Heb. xii. 28 L T Tr WH.*
5401   [SYN. δ έ ο ς (apprehension), φ ό β ο ς (fear): Ammonius s. v. δ. says δέος καὶ φόβος διαφέρει· δέος μὲν γὰρ ἐστι πολυχρόνιος κακοῦ ὑπόνοια. φόβος δὲ ἡ παραυτίκα πτόησις. Plato (Laches p. 198 b.): δέος γὰρ εἶναι προσδοκίαν μέλλοντος κακοῦ. Cf. Stallbaum on Plato's Protag. p. 167; Schmidt ch. 139; and see s. v. δειλία.]

1190   Δερβαῖος, -ον, ὁ, of Derbe, a native of Derbe: Acts xx. 4.*
1191   Δέρβη, -ης, ἡ, Derbe, a city of Lycaonia, on the confines of Isauria, [on its supposed site see Lewin, St. Paul, i. 151 sq.; B.D. s. v.; cf. Conyb. and Hows. St. Paul, Index s. v.]: Acts xiv. 6, 20; xvi. 1.*

1192   δέρμα, -τος, τό, (fr. δέρω or δείρω, as κέρμα fr. κείρω), a skin, hide, leather: Heb. xi. 37. (Hom. et sqq.)*

1193   δερμάτινος, -η, -ον, (δέρμα), made of skin, leathern (Vulg. pelliceus): Mt. iii. 4; Mk. i. 6; cf. 2 K. i. 8. (Hom., Hdt., Plat., Strab., al.)*

1194   δέρω; 1 aor. ἔδειρα; 2 fut. pass. δαρήσομαι; **1.** to flay, skin: Hom. Il. 1, 459; 23, 167, etc. **2.** to beat, thrash, smite, (cf. Germ. durchgerben, [low Eng. hide]), so sometimes in prof. auth. fr. Arstph. ran. 619 [cf. vesp.

485] down: τινά, Mt. xxi. 35; Mk. xii. 3, 5; Lk. xx. 10 sq.; xxii. 63; Jn. xviii. 23; Acts v. 40; xvi. 37; xxii. 19; εἰς πρόσωπον δέρειν τινά, 2 Co. xi. 20; ἀέρα δέρειν (see ἀήρ), 1 Co. ix. 26; Pass.: Mk. xiii. 9; Lk. xii. 47 (δαρήσεται πολλάς, sc. πληγάς, will be beaten with many stripes); 48, (ὀλίγας, cf. Xen. an. 5, 8, 12 παίειν ὀλίγας, Soph. El. 1415 παίειν διπλῆν, Arstph. nub. 968 (972) τύπτεσθαι πολλάς, Plat. legg. 8 p. 845 a. μαστιγοῦσθαι πληγάς; cf. [W. 589 (548)]; B. [82 (72)]; § 134, 6).*

1195   δεσμεύω; [impf. pass. 3 pers. sing. ἐδεσμεύετο (Lk. viii. 29 T Tr WH)]; (δεσμός); **a.** to put in chains: Lk. viii. 29 T Tr WH; Acts xxii. 4; (Sept. Judg. xvi. 11; Eur. Bacch. 616; Xen. Hier. 6, 14; Plat. legg. 7 p. 808 d.). **b.** to bind up, bind together: φορτία, Mt. xxiii. 4; (δράγματα, Gen. xxxvii. 7; Judith viii. 3. [Hes. opp. 479, al.]).*

1196   δεσμέω, -ῶ: [impf. pass. 3 pers. sing. ἐδεσμεῖτο]; to bind, tie: Lk. viii. 29 R G L; see δεσμεύω. ([Aristot. de plant. 1, 2 p. 817ᵇ, 21; al.]; Heliod. 8, 9.)*

1197   δέσμη, -ης, or as others write it [e. g. Rec.ˢᵗ T; yet cf. Lob. Paralip. p. 396; Chandler § 132] δεσμή, -ῆς, ἡ, (δέω), a bundle: Mt. xiii. 30. (Ex. xii. 22. Dem., Dion. Hal., al.)*

1198   δέσμιος, -ον, ὁ, bound, in bonds, a captive, a prisoner, [fr. Soph. down]: Mt. xxvii. 15 sq.; Mk. xv. 6; Acts xvi. 25, 27; xxiii. 18; xxv. 14, 27; xxviii. 16 [R G], 17; Heb. x. 34 G L T Tr txt. WH; xiii. 3; ὁ δέσμιος τοῦ Χριστοῦ Ἰησοῦ, whom Christ, i. e. his truth which I have preached, has put in bonds (W. 189 (178); [B. 169 (147)]), Eph. iii. 1; 2 Tim. i. 8; Philem. 1, 9; in the same sense ὁ δέσμιος ἐν κυρίῳ, Eph. iv. 1; [cf. Bp. Lghtft. on Philem. 13].*

1199   δεσμός, -οῦ, ὁ, (δέω), [fr. Hom. down], a band or bond: Mk. vii. 35 (ἐλύθη ὁ δεσμὸς τῆς γλώσσης αὐτοῦ, i. e. the impediment in his speech was removed); Lk. xiii. 16 (λυθῆναι ἀπὸ τοῦ δεσμοῦ, of a woman bowed together, held fast as it were by a bond). The plur. form τὰ δεσμά, the more com. form in Grk. writ. (W. 63 (62) [cf. B. 23 (21); see below]), is found in Lk. viii. 29; Acts xvi. 26; xx. 23; the other form οἱ δεσμοί in Phil. i. 13 (ὥστε τοὺς δεσμούς μου φανεροὺς ἐν Χριστῷ γενέσθαι, so that my captivity became manifest as made for the cause of Christ), ["δεσμά sunt vincula quibus quis constringitur, sed δεσμός est in carcerem conjectio et captivitas in vinculis ... Utraque forma et ceteri Graeci omnes et Attici utuntur, sed non promiscue ut inter se permutari possint." Cobet as quoted in Rutherford, New Phryn. p. 353]; the gen. and dat. in Acts xxii. 30 Rec.; xxiii. 29; xxvi. 29, 31; Phil. i. 7, 14, 16 (17); Col. iv. 18; 2 Tim. ii. 9; Philem. 10; Heb. x. 34 R Tr mrg.; xi. 36; Jude 6; ἐν τοῖς δεσμοῖς τοῦ εὐαγγελίου, in the captivity into which the preaching of the gospel has thrown me, Philem. 13 [W. 189 (178); cf. ref. s. v. δέσμιος, fin.].*

1200   δεσμο-φύλαξ, -κος, ὁ, (δεσμός and φύλαξ, like θησαυροφύλαξ [cf. W. 100 (95)]), a keeper of a prison, a jailer: Acts xvi. 23, 27, 36. (Joseph. antt. 2, 5, 1; Lcian. Tox. 30; [Artem. oneir. 3, 60; al.]; ἀρχιδεσμοφύλαξ, Gen. xxxix. 21–23.)*

1201   δεσμωτήριον, -ου, τό, *a prison, jail*: Mt. xi. 2; Acts v. 21, 23; xvi. 26. (Gen. xl. 3; [Hdt.], Thuc., Plat., Dem., al.) *

1202   δεσμώτης, -ου, ὁ, *one bound, a prisoner*: Acts xxvii. 1, 42. (Gen. xxxix. 20; Bar. i. 9; Hdt., Aeschyl., Soph., Thuc., subseq. writ.)*

1203   δεσπότης, -ου, ὁ, [fr. Pind. down], *a master, lord* (as of δοῦλοι, οἰκέται): 1 Tim. vi. 1, [2]; 2 Tim. ii. 21; Tit. ii. 9; 1 Pet. ii. 18; God is thus addressed by one who calls himself his δοῦλος: Lk. ii. 29, cf. Acts iv. 24, 29, (δεσπότης τῶν πάντων, Job v. 8; Sap. vi. 8); Christ is so called, as one who has bought his servants, 2 Pet. ii. 1; rules over his church, Jude 4 [some take δ. here as designating God; cf. R. V. mrg.]; and whose prerogative it is to take vengeance on those who persecute his followers, Rev. vi. 10.*

[Syn. δεσπότης, κύριος: δ. was strictly the correlative of slave, δοῦλος, and hence denoted absolute ownership and uncontrolled power; κύριος had a wider meaning, applicable to the various ranks and relations of life, and not suggestive either of property or of absolutism. Ammonius s. v. δεσπότης says δ. ὁ τῶν ἀργυρωνήτων · κύριος δὲ καὶ πατὴρ υἱοῦ καὶ αὐτός τις ἑαυτοῦ. So Philo, quis rer. div. heres § 6 ὥστε τὸν δεσπότην κύριον εἶναι καὶ ἔτι ὡσανεὶ φοβερὸν κύριον, οὐ μόνον τὸ κῦρος καὶ τὸ κράτος ἁπάντων ἀνημμένον, ἀλλὰ καὶ δέος καὶ φόβον ἱκανὸν ἐμποιῆσαι. Cf. Trench § xxviii.; Woolsey, in Bib. Sacr. for 1861, p. 599 sq.; Schmidt ch. 161, 5.]

1204   δεῦρο, adv., fr. Hom. down; **1.** of place, **a.** *hither*; *to this place*. **b.** in urging and calling, *here! come!* (Sept. esp. for לְךָ and לְכָה): Mt. xix. 21; Mk. x. 21; Lk. xviii. 22; Jn. xi. 43 (δεῦρο ἔξω *come forth*). Acts vii. 34; Rev. xvii. 1; xxi. 9; δεῦρο εἰς γῆν, ἣν κτλ. Acts iii. 3 (δεῦρο εἰς τὸν οἶκόν σου, 1 K. i. 53; εἰς Πτολεμαΐδα, 1 Macc. xii. 45). **2.** of time, *hitherto, now*: ἄχρι τοῦ δεῦρο up to this time, Ro. i. 13 (μέχρι δεῦρο, [Plat. legg. 7 p. 811 c.]; Athen. 1, 62 p. 34 c.; Plut. vit. Num. 4; Pomp. 24).*

1205   δεῦτε, adv., used when two or more are addressed [cf. B. 70 (61)]; perhaps fr. δεῦρ' ἴτε [yet see Bttm. Gram. 21te Aufl. § 115 Anm. 8], see δεῦρο, 1; **1.** fr. Hom. down, *come hither, come here, come*: foll. by an impv., δεῦτε, κληρονομήσατε, Mt. xxv. 34; δεῦτε, ἴδετε, Mt. xxviii. 6; Jn. iv. 29; δεῦτε, ἀριστήσατε, Jn. xxi. 12; δεῦτε, συνάχθητε (Rec. δ. καὶ συνάγεσθε), Rev. xix. 17. δεῦτε ὀπίσω μου *come after me*, be my disciples: Mt. iv. 19; Mk. i. 17, (equiv. to לְכוּ אַחֲרַי, 2 K. vi. 19); δεῦτε εἰς τ. γάμους, Mt. xxii. 4; εἰς ἔρημον τόπον, Mk. vi. 31; δεῦτε πρός με, Mt. xi. 28. **2.** It gets the force of an interjection, *come! come now!* foll. by a hortat. subj.: δεῦτε, ἀποκτείνωμεν, Mt. xxi. 38; Mk. xii. 7 and R G in Lk. xx. 14. (Sept. mostly for לְכוּ, sometimes for בֹּאוּ.) *

1206   δευτεραῖος, -αία, -αῖον, (δεύτερος), [Hdt., Xen., al.], *of* or *belonging to the second*; of one who comes, or does a thing, *on the second day* (cf. τριταῖος, τεταρταῖος, etc.): δευτεραῖοι ἤλθομεν, Acts xxviii. 13; cf. W. § 54, 2; [B. § 123, 9].*

1207   δευτερό-πρωτος, -ον, *second-first* (cf. δευτερέσχατος *second-last, last but one*): ἐν σαββάτῳ δευτεροπρώτῳ in Lk. vi. 1 seems to be, *the second of the first sabbaths after the feast of the Passover*; cf. Redslob in the Intelligenzblatt

zur Hall. Lit. Zeit. 1847, N. 70; *Ewald*, Jahrbb. d. bibl. Wissensch. i. p. 72; [*WH.* App. ad loc.]. The various opinions of others are reviewed by Meyer [and McClellan] ad loc. and Lübkert in the Stud. und Krit. for 1835, p. 664 sqq. (Eustrat. in vita Eutych. n. 95 calls the first Sunday after Easter δευτεροπρώτην κυριακήν). [But the genuineness of the word is questionable. It is wanting in אBL1, 33, 69 and some other authorities. Hence Tr txt. WH om. the word, L Tr mrg. br. it. Tischendorf, after expunging it in his 2d ed., restored it in his 7th, subsequently put it in brackets, and finally (ed. 8) inserted it again. It is questioned or discarded, by Mey., Bleek, Alf., Weiss (on Mk. p. 101), Holtz., Hilgenf., Volkm., Farrar (Com. ad loc. and Life of Christ i. 435), al. For the evidence see Tdf.'s note, and for discussions of it see *WH.* App. ad loc.; *Scrivener*, Intr. p. 515 sq.; *Green*, "Developed Criticism" ad loc.] *

1208   δεύτερος, -έρα, -ερον, [fr. Hom. down; Curtius § 277], *second*: Mt. xxii. 26; Mk. xii. 21; Lk. xii. 38; Jn. iv. 54; Rev. iv. 7, etc.; *the second*, the other of two: Mt. xxii. 39; Mk. xii. 31; 1 Co. xv. 47; Tit. iii. 10; 2 Pet. iii. 1; Heb. viii. 7; x. 9; δεύτερος θάνατος (see θάνατος, 3), Rev. ii. 11; xx. 14; xxi. 8; δευτέρα χάρις in 2 Co. i. 15 is not *a double* benefit, but *a second*, opp. to the former which the Corinthians would have had if Paul in passing through Achaia into Macedonia had visited them πρότερον, [WH txt. Tr mrg. read δευτ. χαράν, q. v.]. The neuter δεύτερον is used adverbially *in the second place, a second time* [cf. W. § 37, 5 Note 1]: Jn. iii. 4; Rev. xix. 3; πάλιν is added, as often in Grk. writ. (see ἄνωθεν, fin.): Jn. xxi. 16; also τὸ δεύτερον, 2 Co. xiii. 2; Jude 5; ἐκ δευτέρου (1 Macc. ix. 1), Mk. xiv. 72; Jn. ix. 24; Acts xi. 9; Heb. ix. 28; cf. W. § 51, 1 d.; with πάλιν added, Mt. xxvi. 42; Acts x. 15, (Hom. Od. 3, 161 ἐπὶ δεύτερον αὖτις); ἐν τῷ δευτέρῳ *at the second time*, Acts vii. 13 (when they had come the second time); δεύτερον *in a partition, then, in the second place*: 1 Co. xii. 28.

1209   δέχομαι; [fut. 2 pers. plur. δέξεσθε, Eph. vi. 17 Rec.bez]; 1 aor. ἐδεξάμην; pf. δέδεγμαι (Acts viii. 14); depon. mid.; Sept. mostly for לקח; **1.** *to take with the hand*: τὸ γράμμα [L txt. T Tr WH τὰ γράμματα], Lk. xvi. 6 sq.; τὸ ποτήριον, Lk. xxii. 17; *to take hold of, take up*, τ. περικεφαλαίαν, τ. μάχαιραν, Eph. vi. 17; τὸ παιδίον εἰς τὰς ἀγκάλας, Lk. ii. 28. **2.** *to take up, receive*, (Germ. *aufnehmen, annehmen*) **a.** used of a place receiving one: ὃν δεῖ οὐρανὸν δέξασθαι (οὐρ. is subject), Acts iii. 21, (Plat. Theaet. p. 177 a. τελευτήσαντας αὐτοὺς . . . ὁ τῶν κακῶν καθαρὸς τόπος οὐ δέξεται). **b.** with acc. of pers. *to receive, grant access to, a visitor; not to refuse intercourse* or *friendship*: Lk. ix. 11 R G; Jn. iv. 45; 2 Co. vii. 15; Gal. iv. 14; Col. iv. 10; *to receive to hospitality*, Mt. x. 14, 40 sq.; Mk. vi. 11; Lk. ix. 5, 53; x. 8, 10; Acts xxi. 17 Rec.; Heb. xi. 31, (often in Grk. writ. fr. Hom. down); παιδίον, *to receive* into one's family in order to bring up and educate, Mt. xviii. 5; Mk. ix. 37; Lk. ix. 48; *to receive* εἰς τ. οἴκους, τὰς σκηνάς, Lk. xvi. 4, 9; δέξαι τὸ πνεῦμά μου, *to* thyself in heaven, Acts vii. 59. **c.** with acc. of the thing offered in speaking, teaching, instructing; *to receive fa-*

vorably, give ear to, embrace, make one's own, approve, not to reject: τὸν λόγον, Lk. viii. 13; Acts viii. 14; xi. 1; xvii. 11; 1 Th. i. 6; ii. 13; Jas. i. 21; τὰ τοῦ πνεύματος, 1 Co. ii. 14; τὴν παράκλησιν, 2 Co. viii. 17; τὴν ἀγάπην τῆς ἀληθείας sc. commended to them, 2 Th. ii. 10; [add the elliptical constr. in Mt. xi. 14], (often in Grk. writ.); to receive a benefit offered, not to reject it, 2 Co. viii. 4 Rec. **d.** to receive i. q. to take upon one's self, sustain, bear, endure: τινά, his bearing and behavior, 2 Co. xi. 16, (τὴν ἀδικίαν, Hebr. אָשָׂא, Gen. l. 17; πᾶν, ὅ ἐὰν ἐπαχθῇ, Sir. ii. 4; μῦθον χαλεπόν, Hom. Od. 20, 271, and often in Grk. writ.). **3.** to receive, get, (Germ. empfangen): ἐπιστολάς, Acts xxii. 5; γράμματα, Acts xxviii. 21; τὴν βασιλείαν τοῦ θεοῦ, to become a partaker of the benefits of God's kingdom, Mk. x. 15; Lk. xviii. 17; λόγια ζῶντα, Acts vii. 38; εὐαγγέλιον, 2 Co. xi. 4; τὴν χάριν τοῦ θεοῦ, 2 Co. vi. 1; — i. q. to learn: Phil. iv. 18 [(?) see the Comm. ad loc.].

[SYN. δέχομαι, λαμβάνω: The earlier classic use of these verbs sustains in the main the distinction laid down in the glossaries (e. g. Ammonius s. v. λαβεῖν: λαβεῖν μέν ἐστι, τὸ κείμενόν τι ἀνελέσθαι· δέξασθαι δέ, τὸ διδόμενον ἐκ χειρός), and the suggestion of a self-prompted taking still adheres to λ. in many connexions (cf. λαβεῖν τινα γυναῖκα, ἀρχὴν λαβεῖν) in distinction from a receiving of what is offered; in use, however, the words overlap and distinctions disappear; yet the suggestion of a welcoming or an appropriating reception generally cleaves to δ. See Schmidt ch. 107, who treats of the comp. of δ. in detail. COMP.: ἀνα-, ἀπο-, δια-, εἰσ-, ἐκ-, ἀπ-ἐκ-, ἐν-, ἐπι-, παρα-, προσ-, ὑπο-δέχομαι.]

1210

δέω; [fut. δήσω]; 1 aor. ἔδησα; pf. ptcp. δεδεκώς (Acts xxii. 29); Pass., pf. δέδεμαι; 1 aor. inf. δεθῆναι (Acts xxi. 33); Sept. chiefly for אָסַר; [fr. Hom. down]; to bind, tie, fasten; **1.** prop.: τί, εἰς δεσμάς, Mt. xiii. 30 [Tr WH br. G prob. om. εἰς, cf. B. 150 (131); W. 225 (211)]; ὀθόνη τέσσαρσιν ἀρχαῖς δεδεμ. a sheet bound by the four corners (to the sky), Acts x. 11 (G L T Tr WH om. δεδεμ. καί); an animal, to prevent it from straying about, ὄνος δεδεμένη, πῶλος δεδεμένος, Mt. xxi. 2; Mk. xi. 2; Lk. xix. 30; with πρὸς τ. θύραν added, Mk. xi. 4; with acc. of pers. to bind, to fasten with chains, to throw into chains: ἀγγέλους, Rev. ix. 14; a madman, πέδαις καὶ ἁλύσεσι, Mk. v. 3 sq.; captives, Mt. [xii. 29]; xiv. 3; xxii. 13; xxvii. 2; Mk. [iii. 27]; vi. 17; xv. 1; Jn. xviii. 12; Acts ix. 14; xxi. 11; xxii. 29; Rev. xx. 2; Pass., Mk. xv. 7; Jn. xviii. 24; Acts ix. 2, 21 (in the last two pass. δεδεμένον ἄγειν τινά); Acts xxi. 13; xxii. 5; xxiv. 27; Col. iv. 3; ἁλύσεσι, Acts xii. 6; xxi. 33; ὁ λόγος τοῦ θεοῦ οὐ δέδεται, fig. for these bonds of mine in no way hinder its course, i. e. the preaching, extension, and efficacy of the gospel, 2 Tim. ii. 9; the bodies of the dead, which were wont to be bound with bandages and linen cloths: ὁ τεθνηκὼς δεδεμένος τοὺς πόδας κ. τὰς χεῖρας κειρίαις, bound hand and foot with grave-cloths, Jn. xi. 44; τὸ σῶμα ὀθονίοις (Tdf. 2, 7 ἐν ὀθον.), to swathe in linen cloths, Jn. xix. 40. **2.** metaph. **a.** Satan is said δῆσαι a woman bent together, i. e. by means of a demon, as his messenger, taking possession of the woman and preventing her from standing upright, Lk. xiii. 16 cf. 11. **b.** to bind, i. e. put under

obligation, sc. of law, duty, etc.: δεδεμένος τῷ πνεύματι, bound or constrained in my spirit, i. e. compelled by my convictions, Acts xx. 22 (so not infreq. in Grk. auth. as Plat. rep. 8 p. 567 d. ἀνάγκῃ δέδεται ἢ προστάττει αὐτῷ); with dat. of pers. δεδέσθαι τινί to be bound to one: ἀνδρί, of a wife, Ro. vii. 2; γυναικί, of a husband, 1 Co. vii. 27; δέδεται absol., opp. to ἐλευθέρα ἐστί, ibid. 39; (Achill. Tat. 1, 11 p. 41 ἄλλη δέδεμαι παρθένῳ, Jambl. vit. Pyth. 11, 56 τὴν μὲν ἄγαμον, . . . τὴν δὲ πρὸς ἄνδρα δεδεμένην). **c.** by a Chald. and rabbin. idiom (equiv. to אָסַר) to forbid, prohibit, declare to be illicit: Mt. xvi. 19; xviii. 18. [COMP.: κατα-, περι-, συν-, ὑπο-δέω.] *

δή, (shortened fr. ἤδη [al. al.]), a particle which, the Epic phrases δὴ τότε, δὴ γάρ excepted, is never placed at the beginning of a sentence, but is joined to some preceding word, and indicates that "what it introduces can be taken as something settled, laid down in deed and in truth" (Klotz ad Devar. ii. 2 p. 392): now therefore, then, verily, in truth, (Lat. jam, igitur, sane, etc.—although neither Lat., Germ., [nor Eng.] has a word precisely equiv. to δή). **1.** added to relative pronouns: ὃς δή who is such a one as, who preëminently, who then, Mt. xiii. 23. **2.** joined to imperatives and hortatory subjunctives it signifies that the thing enjoined must be done forthwith, at once [cf. W. § 43, 3 a.], so that it may be evident that it is being done (cf. Passow i. p. 612ᵇ), where the Lat. says agedum, jam, Germ. doch, nur, [Eng. now, only, but]: Lk. ii. 15; Acts [vi. 3 L WH mrg. br.]; xiii. 2; xv. 36; 1 Co. vi. 20, (Sir. xliv. 1). **3.** surely, certainly: 2 Co. xii. 1 R G.*

1211

δηλαυγῶς, (fr. δῆλος and αὐγή), radiantly, in full light, clearly: Mk. viii. 25 T WH mrg. with codd. ℵ*CLΔ for Rec. τηλαυγῶς. Hesych. says δηλαυγῶς· ἄγαν φανερῶς; add δηλαυγέςι τεκμηρίοις, Democrit. in Fabricius, Biblioth. Gr. iv. p. 333. With the exception of this word [δηλοποιέω, (Plut. Pericl. 33, 8; al.)] and the very rare δηλοφανής, δῆλος is not found in composition.*

see 5081

δῆλος, -η, -ον, [fr. Hom. down], clear, evident, manifest: Mt. xxvi. 73; δῆλον sc. ἐστίν it is manifest, evident, foll. by ὅτι (4 Macc. ii. 7; Xen. an. 1, 3, 9; al.): 1 Co. xv. 27 [here some would take the words adverbially and parenthetically i. e. δηλονότι manifestly cf. W. § 64, 2 a.]; Gal. iii. 11; 1 Tim. vi. 7 (here L T Tr WH om. δῆλον).*

[SYN. δῆλος, φανερός: δ. evident, what is known and understood, φ. manifest, as opp. to what is concealed or invisible; δ. points rather to inner perception, φ. to outward appearance. Cf. Schmidt ch. 129.]

1212

δηλόω, -ῶ; [impf. ἐδήλουν; fut. δηλώσω]; 1 aor. ἐδήλωσα; Pass., [impf. 3 pers. sing. ἐδηλοῦτο (1 Pet. 11 WH mrg.)]; 1 aor. ἐδηλώθην; (δῆλος); Sept. for הֹורִיעַ and sometimes for הֹורָה; in Grk. auth. fr. [Aeschyl. and] Hdt. down; to make manifest: τί, 1 Co. iii. 13; to make known by relating, to declare: τί, Col. i. 8; τινὶ περί τινος, ὅτι, 1 Co. i. 11; to give one to understand, to indicate, signify: τί, Heb. xii. 27; 2 Pet. i. 14; foll. by acc. with inf. Heb. ix. 8; εἴς τι, point unto, 1 Pet. i. 11.*

[SYN. δηλόω, ἐμφανίζω: ἐμφ. to manifest to the sight, make visible; δ. to render evident to the mind, of such disclosures as exhibit character or suggest inferences; hence

1213

esp. of prophetical, typical, or other supernatural disclosures. Cf. Schmidt ch. 129 § 6; Bleek on Heb. ix. 8.]

1214   . **Δημᾶς**, ὁ, *Demas*, (prop. name, contracted apparently fr. Δημήτριος, cf. W. 103 (97); [on its declension, cf. B. 20 (18)]), a companion of Paul, who deserted the apostle when he was a prisoner at Rome and returned to Thessalonica: Col. iv. 14; Philem. 24; 2 Tim. iv. 10.*

1215   **δημηγορέω**, -ῶ: [impf. ἐδημηγόρουν]; (to be a δημηγόρος, fr. δῆμος and ἀγορεύω to harangue the people); *to address a public assembly, make a speech to the people*: ἐδημηγόρει πρὸς αὐτούς [A. V. made an oration], Acts xii. 21. (Arstph., Xen., Plat., Dem., al. Prov. xxx. 31 (xxiv. 66); 4 Macc. v. 15.) *

1216   **Δημήτριος**, -ου, ὁ, *Demetrius*; **1.** a silversmith of Ephesus, a heathen: Acts xix. 24, 38. **2.** a certain Christian: 3 Jn. 12.*

1217   **δημιουργός**, -οῦ, ὁ, (δῆμιος public, belonging to the people, and ΕΡΓΩ; cf. ἱερουργός, ἀμπελουργός, etc.), often in Grk. writ. fr. Hom. down; **a.** prop. *a workman for the public.* **b.** univ. *the author of any work, an artisan, framer, builder*: τεχνίτης κ. δημιουργός, Heb. xi. 10; (Xen. mem. 1, 4, 7 [cf. 9] σοφοῦ τινος δημιουργοῦ τέχνημα. God is called ὁ τοῦ οὐρανοῦ δημιουργός in Plat. rep. 7 p. 530 a.; ὁ δημ. τῶν ὅλων in Joseph. antt. 1, 7, 1, and often in eccl. writ. from Clem. Rom. 1 Cor. 20, 11; 26, 1; 33, 2 on; [cf. Philo, de mut. nom. § 4; de opif. mund. ed. Müller p. 133; *Piper*, Einl. in monument. Theol. § 26; *Soph.* Lex. s. v.]. In the Scriptures, besides, only in 2 Macc. iv. 1 κακῶν δημ.). [Cf. Trench § cv.]*

1218   **δῆμος**, -ου, ὁ, *the people, the mass of the people assembled in a public place*: Acts xii. 22; xix. 33; ἄγειν [R G], εἰσελθεῖν εἰς τὸν δῆμον: Acts xvii. 5 [L T Tr WH προαγ.]; xix. 30. [From Hom. down.]*

[Syn. δῆμος, λαός: in classic Grk. δῆμος denotes the people as organized into a body politic, λαός the unorganized people at large. But in biblical Grk. λαός is used esp. of the chosen people of God; δῆμος on the other hand (found only in Acts) denotes the people of a heathen city. Cf. Trench § xcviii.; Schmidt ch. 199.]

1219   **δημόσιος**, -α, -ον, esp. freq. in Attic; *belonging to the people* or *state, public* (opp. to ἴδιος): Acts v. 18; in dat. fem. δημοσίᾳ used adverbially (opp. to ἰδίᾳ) [cf. W. 591 (549) note], *publicly, in public places, in view of all*: Acts xvi. 37; xviii. 28; δημ. καὶ κατ᾽ οἴκους, Acts xx. 20; (2 Macc. vi. 10; 3 Macc. ii. 27; in Grk. writ. also *by public authority, at the public expense*).*

1220   **δηνάριον**, -ου, τό, [Plut., Epict., al.], a Lat. word, *a denarius*, a silver coin, originally consisting of ten [whence its name], afterwards [fr. B. c. 217 on] of sixteen asses; about [3.898 grams, i. e. 8½ pence or 16⅔ cents; rapidly debased fr. Nero on; cf. BB.DD. s. v. Denarius]: Mt. xviii. 28; xx. 2, 9, 13; xxii. 19; Mk. vi. 37; xii. 15; xiv. 5; Lk. vii. 41; x. 35; xx. 24; Jn. vi. 7; xii. 5; Rev. vi. 6 [cf. W. 587 (546); B. 164 (143)]; τὸ ἀνὰ δηνάριον sc. ὄν the pay of a denarius apiece promised to each workman, Mt. xx. 10 T Tr [txt., Tr mrg. WH br. τό].*

1221   **δήποτε** (fr. δή and ποτέ), adv., *now at length (jam aliquando); at any time; at last,* etc., *just exactly*; [hence .it generalizes a relative, like the Lat. *cumque*; see *Lob.*

ad Phryn. p. 373]: ᾧ δήποτε νοσήματι, with whatsoever disease, Jn. v. 4 [R G, but L οἰῳδηποτοῦν].*

δή-που [L WH δή που; cf. *Lipsius*, Gram. Untersuch. p.   **1222** 123 sq.], adv., (fr. δή and πού), prop. *now in some way, whatever that way is*; it is used when something is affirmed in a slightly ironical manner, as if with an affectation of uncertainty, *perhaps, doubtless, verily*: οὐ δήπου *not surely* (Germ. *doch nicht etwa*), *hardly I trow*; (cf. *Rost* in Passow i. p. 613ᵇ; *Klotz* ad Devar. ii. 2 p. 427 sq.). Once in Scripture: Heb. ii. 16.*

[**Δία**, see Ζεύς.]   **see 2203**

διά, [" written δι᾽ before a vowel, exc. in prop. names   **1223** and 2 Co. v. 7; Ro. viii. 10 " *Tdf.* Proleg. p. 94], akin to δίς and Lat. *dis* in composition, prop. denoting a division into two or more parts; a preposition taking the gen. and the acc. In its use the bibl. writ. differ in no respect fr. the Grk.; cf. W. 377 (353) sqq.; 398 (372) sq.

A. with the Genitive: *through*;   **I.** of Place; **1.** prop. after verbs denoting an extension, or a motion, or an act, that occurs through any place: δι᾽ ἄλλης ὁδοῦ ἀναχωρεῖν, Mt. ii. 12; δι᾽ ἀνύδρων τόπων, Mt. xii. 43; διὰ τῆς Σαμαρείας, Jn. iv. 4; διὰ τῆς θύρας, Jn. x. 1 sq.; add, Mt. xix. 24; Mk. ii. 23; x. 25; xi. 16; Lk. iv. 30; v. 19; xviii. 25; 2 Co. xi. 33; Heb. ix. 11 sq.; xi. 29, etc.; δι᾽ ὑμῶν, through your city, Ro. xv. 28; [on διὰ πάντων, Acts ix. 32, see πᾶς, II. 1]; ὁ διὰ πάντων, diffusing his saving influence through all, Eph. iv. 6; σῴζεσθαι διὰ πυρός, 1 Co. iii. 15; διασῴζ. δι᾽ ὕδατος, 1 Pet. iii. 20 (Ev. Nicod. c. 9 p. 568 sq. ed. Thilo [p. 228 ed. Tdf.] διὰ θαλάσσης ὡς διὰ ξηρᾶς); βλέπειν δι᾽ ἐσόπτρου, 1 Co. xiii. 12 [cf. W. 380 (356)]. Add the adverbial phrase δι᾽ ὅλου from top to bottom, throughout, Jn. xix. 23 (metaph. *in every way*, 1 Macc. vi. 18). From this use of the preposition has come **2.** its tropical use of a state or condition in which (prop. passing through which as through a space) one does or suffers something, where we, with a different conception, employ *with, in,* etc. (Germ. *bei, unter, mit*): ὁ διὰ γράμματος κ. περιτομῆς παραβάτης νόμου, Ro. ii. 27 [W. 380 (355)]; οἱ πιστεύοντες δι᾽ ἀκροβυστίας who believe though uncircumcised (see ἀκροβυστία, a.), Ro. iv. 11; διὰ προσκόμματος ἐσθίειν, with offence, or so as to be an offence [cf. W. 380 (356), and see πρόσκομμα], Ro. xiv. 20; διὰ πίστεως περιπατεῖν, οὐ διὰ εἴδους (see εἶδος, 1), 2 Co. v. 7; τὰ διὰ [Lchm. mrg. (cf. Tr mrg.) τὰ ἴδια (see Mey. ad loc.)] τοῦ σώματος, done in the body (i. e. while we were clothed with our earthly body [al. take διά here instrumentally; see III. 2 below], 2 Co. v. 10; διὰ πολλῶν δακρύων, 2 Co. ii. 4; διὰ δόξης, clothed with glory, 2 Co. iii. 11; ἔρχεσθαι, εἰσέρχ. διά τινος *with a thing*, Heb. ix. 12; 1 Jn. v. 6, [but cf. W. 380 (355)]; δι᾽ ὑπομονῆς, Ro. viii. 25, (διὰ πένθους τὸ γῆρας διάγειν, Xen. Cyr. 4, 6, 6; cf. Matthiae ii. p. 1353).

II. of Time [cf. W. 380 (356); Ellic. or Mey. on Gal. ii. 1; Fritzsche as below]; **1.** of continued time; hence **a.** of the time throughout (*during*) which anything is done: Mt. xxvi. 61; Mk. xiv. 58; δι᾽ ὅλης (τῆς R G) νυκτός, Lk. v. 5; διὰ παντὸς τοῦ ζῆν, Heb. ii. 15;

διὰ παντός [so L WH Tr (exc. Mk. v. 5; Lk. xxiv. 53)], or written together διαπαντός [so G T (exc. in Mt.); cf. W. 46 (45); *Lipsius*, Gram. Unters. p. 125], *continually, always*: Mt. xviii. 10; Mk. v. 5; Lk. xxiv. 53; Acts ii. 25 (fr. Ps. xv. (xvi.) 8); x. 2; xxiv. 16; Ro. xi. 10 (fr. Ps. lxviii. (lxix.) 24); 2 Th. iii. 16; Heb. ix. 6; xiii. 15, (often in Grk. writ.). **b.** of the time *within* which a thing is done: διὰ τῆς νυκτός (L T Tr WH διὰ νυκτός), by night, Acts v. 19; xvi. 9; xvii. 10; xxiii. 31, (Palaeph. 1, 10); δι' ἡμερῶν τεσσαράκοντα, repeatedly within the space of forty days, Acts i. 3; — (denying this use of the prep., *C. F. A. Fritzsche* in Fritzschiorum Opuscc. p. 164 sq. would refer these instances to the use noted under a. [see Win., Ellic., Mey. u. s.]). **2.** of time e l a p s e d, and which has, so to say, been passed t h r o u g h: Gal. ii. 1 [cf. W. 380 (356)]; δι' ἡμερῶν, (some) days having intervened, *after* (some) days, Mk. ii. 1; δι' ἐτῶν πλειόνων, Acts xxiv. 17; exx. fr. Grk. auth. in Fritzsche on Mk. p. 50; [W. 380 (356); L. and S. s. v. A. II. 2; *Soph.* Lex. s. v. 2; *Field*, Otium Norv. iii p. 14].

III. of the M e a n s or I n s t r u m e n t by which anything is effected; because what is done by means of a person or thing seems to pass as it were *through* the same [cf. W. 378 (354)]. **1.** of one who is the author of the action as well as its instrument, or of the e f f i-c i e n t c a u s e: δι' αὐτοῦ (i. e. τοῦ θεοῦ) τὰ πάντα sc. ἐστίν or ἐγένετο, Ro. xi. 36; also δι' οὗ, Heb. ii. 10; δι' οὗ ἐκλή-θητε, 1 Co. i. 9; add [Gal. iv. 7 L T Tr WH, see below]; Heb. vii. 21 (ἡ ἰατρικὴ πᾶσα διὰ τοῦ θεοῦ τούτου, i. e. Aes-culapius, κυβερνᾶται, Plat. symp. p. 186 e.; cf. Fritzsche on Rom. vol. i. p. 15, [and for exx. *Soph.* Lex. s. v. 1]); of him to whom that is due which any one has or has done; hence i. q. *by the fault of* any one: δι' οὗ τὸ σκάνδαλον ἔρχεται, Mt. xviii. 7; δι' ἑνὸς ἀνθρ. ἡ ἁμαρτία ... εἰσῆλθε, Ro. v. 12, cf. 16–19; ἠσθένει διὰ τῆς σαρκός, Ro. viii. 3; *by the merit, aid, favor of* any one: ἐν ζωῇ βασιλεύσουσι διά etc. Ro. v. 17, cf. 18 sq.; 1 Co. xv. 21; διὰ τοῦ Χριστοῦ, and the like: Ro. v. 1 sq. 11; Acts x. 43; Gal. iv. 7 [Rec., but see above]; δοξάζειν τ. θεὸν διὰ Ἰησοῦ Χριστοῦ, 1 Pet. iv 11, and εὐχαριστεῖν τῷ θεῷ διὰ Ἰησ. Χρ. Ro. i. 8; vii. 25 (where L T Tr WH txt. χάρις τῷ θεῷ); Col. iii. 17,—because the possibility both of glorifying God and of giving thanks to him is due to the kindness of Christ; καυχᾶσθαι ἐν τῷ θεῷ διὰ Ἰησ. Χρ. Ro. v. 11; ἀναπαύεσθαι διά τινος, Philem. 7; οἱ πεπιστευκότες διὰ τῆς χάριτος, Acts xviii. 27; πολλῆς εἰρήνης τυγχάνοντες διὰ σοῦ ... διὰ τῆς σῆς προνοίας, Acts xxiv. 2 (3); ὑπερνικᾶν διὰ τοῦ ἀγαπή-σαντος ἡμᾶς, Ro. viii. 37; περισσεύειν διά τινος, by the increase which comes from one, Phil. i. 26; 2 Co. i. 5; ix. 12; διὰ τῆς ὑμῶν δεήσεως, Phil. i. 19; add, Philem. 22; Ro. i. 12; 2 Co. i. 4; Gal. iv. 23; 1 Pet. i. 5. **2.** of the instrument used to accomplish a thing, or of the i n s t r u-m e n t a l c a u s e in the stricter sense: — with gen. of pers. *by the service, the intervention of, any one*; with gen. of thing, *by means of, with the help of, any thing*; **a.** in passages where a subject expressly mentioned is said to do or to have done a thing by some person or by some thing: Mk. xvi. 20 (τοῦ κυρίου τὸν λόγον βεβαιοῦντος διὰ

τ. σημείων); Lk. i. 70; Acts i. 16; ii. 22 (τέρασι κ. σημεί-οις, οἷς ἐποίησε δι' αὐτοῦ ὁ θεός); viii. 20; x. 36; xv. 23 (γράψαντες διὰ χειρὸς αὐτῶν); xx. 28; xxi. 19; xxviii. 25; Ro. ii. 16; iii. 31; vii. 13; [viii. 11 Rec.bez elz L ed. min. TWH txt.]; xv. 18; xvi. 18; 1 Co. i. 21 [cf. W. 381 (357)]; ii. 10; iv. 15; vi. 14; xiv. 9, 19 [R G]; xv. 57; 2 Co. i. 4; iv. 14 R G; v. 18, 20; ix. 13 [cf. W. 381 (357)]; x. 9; xii. 17; Eph. i. 5; ii. 16; Col. i. 20, 22; ii. 8; 1 Th. iv. 14; 2 Th. ii. 14; Tit. iii. 5; Heb. i. 2, 3 [R G]; ii. 14; vi. 12; vii. 19; ix. 26; xiii. 2, 12, 15, 21; Rev. i. 1; γῆ ἐξ ὕδατος (material cause) κ. δι' ὕδατος συνε-στῶσα τῷ τοῦ θεοῦ λόγῳ, 2 Pet. iii. 5 [W. 419 (390) cf. 217 (204)]. **b.** in passages in which the author or prin-cipal cause is not mentioned, but is easily understood from the nature of the case, or from the context: Ro. i. 12; 1 Co. xi. 12 [cf. W. 381 (357)]; Phil. i. 20; 1 Th. iii. 7; 2 Th. ii. 2, 15; Heb. xi. 39 [cf. W. u. s., also § 50, 3]; xii. 11, 15; 1 Pet. i. 7; διὰ πολλῶν μαρτύρων, by the me-diation (intervention) of many witnesses, they being summoned for that purpose [cf. W. 378 (354); A. V. *among*], 2 Tim. ii. 2. Where it is evident from the relig-ious conceptions of the Bible that G o d is the author or first cause: Jn. xi. 4; Acts v. 12; Eph. iii. 10; iv. 16; Col. ii. 19; 2 Tim. i. 6; Heb. x. 10; 2 Pet. iii. 6; σώζε-σθαι διὰ τ. πίστεως, Eph. ii. 8; συνεγείρεσθαι διὰ τ. πίστ. Col. ii. 12; δικαιοῦσθαι διὰ τ. πίστ. Gal. ii. 16, cf. Ro. iii. 30; in the phrases διὰ τοῦ Ἰησ. Χριστοῦ, and the like: Jn. i. 17; iii. 17; Acts xiii. 38; Ro. i. 5; v. 9; 1 Co. xv. 57; 1 Jn. iv. 9; Phil. i. 11; διὰ τοῦ εὐαγγελίου, 1 Co. xv. 2; Eph. iii. 6; διὰ λόγου θεοῦ, 1 Pet. i. 23, cf. 3; διὰ νόμου, Ro. iii. 27; iv. 13; δι' ἀποκαλύψεως Ἰησ. Χρ. Gal. i. 12, cf. 15 sq.; διὰ τοῦ (ἁγίου) πνεύματος, Ro. v. 5; 1 Co. xii. 8; Eph. iii. 16; πιστεύειν διά τινος (see πιστεύω, 1 b. γ.), Jn. i. 7; 1 Co. iii. 5; σημεῖον γέγονε δι' αὐτῶν, Acts iv. 16; ὁ λόγος ὁ δι' ἀγγέλων λαληθείς, Heb. ii. 2, cf. Gal. iii. 19; ὁ νόμος διὰ Μωϋσέως ἐδόθη, Jn. i. 17; in pas-sages in which something is said to have been spoken through the O. T. prophets, or some one of them [cf. *Lghtft.* Fresh Revision etc. p. 121 sq.]: Mt. ii. 5, 17 L T Tr WH, 23; [iii. 3 L T Tr WH]; iv. 14; viii. 17; xii. 17; xxi. 4; xxiv. 15; xxvii. 9; Acts iii. 16; or to have been so written: Lk. xviii. 31; with the added mention of the first cause: ὑπὸ τοῦ κυρίου διὰ τοῦ προφ. Mt. i. 22; ii. 15, cf. Lk. i. 70; Acts i. 16; xxviii. 25; Ro. i. 2; in passages relating to the Logos: πάντα δι' αὐτοῦ (i. e. through the divine Logos [cf. W. 379 (355)]) ἐγένετο or ἐκτίσθη: Jn. i. 3; 1 Co. viii. 6 (where he is expressly distinguished from the first cause: ἐξ αὐτοῦ [W. 419 (391)]; Col. i. 16 [W. l. c.], cf. Heb. i. 2, (Philo de cherub. § 35). The instrumental cause and the princi-pal are distinguished in 1 Co. xi. 12 (διὰ τῆς γυναικός ... ἐκ τοῦ θεοῦ); Gal. i. 1 (ἀπ' ἀνθρώπων ... δι' ἀνθρώπου [cf. W. 418 (390)]). **3.** with the gen. of a thing διά is used to denote the manner in which a thing is done, or the f o r m a l c a u s e: εἶπε διὰ παραβολῆς, Lk. viii. 4; εἶπε δι' ὁράματος, Acts xviii. 9; ἀπαγγέλλειν διὰ λόγου, by word of mouth, Acts xv. 27; τῷ λόγῳ δι' ἐπιστολῶν, 2 Co. x. 11, cf. 2 Th. ii. 15; πίστις ἐνεργουμένη δι' ἀγάπης, Gal. v. 6;

κεχάρισται δι᾽ ἐπαγγελίας, Gal. iii. 18; δουλεύειν διὰ τῆς ἀγάπης, Gal. v. 13; ἐπιστέλλειν διὰ βραχέων, Heb. xiii. 22; γράφειν δι᾽ ὀλίγων, 1 Pet. v. 12, (Plat. Gorg. p. 449 b. διὰ μακρῶν λόγους ποιεῖσθαι [see ὀλίγος, fin.; cf. W. § 51, 1 b.]); διὰ χάρτου καὶ μέλανος, 2 Jn. 12; διὰ μέλανος κ. καλάμου, 3 Jn. 13, (Plut. Sol. 17, 3). To this head I should refer also the use of διά τινος in exhortations etc., where one seeks to strengthen his exhortation by the mention of a thing or a person held sacred by those whom he is admonishing (διά equiv. to *by an allusion to, by reminding you of* [cf. W. 381 (357)]): Ro. xii. 1; xv. 30; 1 Co. i. 10; 2 Co. x. 1; 1 Th. iv. 2 [yet cf. W. 379 (355) note]; 2 Th. iii. 12 R G.

B. with the ACCUSATIVE [W. 398 (372) sq.]. **I.** of Place; *through*; often so in the Grk. poets, once in the N. T. acc. to L T Tr WH viz. Lk. xvii. 11 διὰ μέσον Σαμαρείας, for R G διὰ μέσου Σαμ. [but see μέσος, 2].

II. of the Ground or Reason on account of which anything is or is not done; *by reason of, because of* (Germ. *aus Grund*). **1.** of the reason for which a thing is done, or of the efficient reason, when for greater perspicuity it may be rendered *by* [cf. Kühner § 434 Anm.]; **a.** with acc. of the thing: δι᾽ ἥν, viz. τὴν τοῦ θεοῦ ἡμέραν (prop. by reason of which day i. e. because it will come [cf. W. 400 (373)]), 2 Pet. iii. 12; διὰ τ. λόγον (prop. by reason of the word i. e. because the word has cleansing power), Jn. xv. 3; διὰ τὸ θέλημά σου (Vulg. *propter voluntatem tuam* i. e. because thou didst will it), Rev. iv. 11; add, Rev. xii. 11; xiii. 14, (ἀναβιώσκεται διὰ τὴν τοῦ πατρὸς φύσιν, Plato, symp. p. 203 e.); cf. Grimm on 2 Macc. iii. 1. **b.** with acc. of the person, by whose will, agency, favor, fault, anything is or is done: διὰ τὸν πατέρα ... δι᾽ ἐμέ (prop. because the father lives ... because I live [cf. W. 399 (373)]), Jn. vi. 57; διὰ τὸν ὑποτάξαντα, by the will of him who subjected it, opp. to οὐχ ἑκοῦσα, Ro. viii. 20 [cf. Win. 399 (373) note]; μὴ εἴπῃς ὅτι διὰ κύριον ἀπέστην, Sir. xv. 11; so too in the Grk. writ. of every age; cf. Krüger § 68, 23; Grimm on 2 Macc. vi. 25. Much oftener **2.** of the reason or cause on account of which anything is or is done, or ought to be done; *on account of, because of*; **a.** in the phrases διὰ τοῦτο *for this cause; for this reason; therefore; on this account; since this is so*: Mt. vi. 25; xii. 27, 31; xiii. 13, etc.; Mk. vi. 14; xi. 24; Lk. xi. 49; xiv. 20; Jn. vi. 65; ix. 23; Acts ii. 26; Ro. i. 26; v. 12; xiii. 6; xv. 9; 1 Co. iv. 17; xi. 10, 30; 2 Co. iv. 1; Eph. i. 15; v. 17; vi. 13; Col. i. 9; 1 Th. ii. 13; iii. 5, 7; 2 Th. ii. 11; 2 Tim. ii. 10; Heb. i. 9; ii. 1; 1 Jn. iv. 5; 3 Jn. 10; Rev. vii. 15; xii. 12; xviii. 8. foll. by ὅτι, *for this cause ... because, therefore ... because*: Jn. v. 16, 18; viii. 47; x. 17; xii. 18, 39; 1 Jn. iii. 1; cf. Tholuck 7 on Jn x. 17, [he questions, at least for x. 17 and xii. 39, the canon of Meyer (on xii. 39), Luthardt (on x. 17), al., that in this phrase in Jn. the τοῦτο always looks backwards]. in the opposite order (when the words that precede with ὅτι are to be emphasized): Jn. xv. 19. It indicates the end and purpose, being foll. either by ἵνα, 2 Co. xiii. 10; 1

Tim. i. 16; Philem. 15, (in the opp. order, Jn. i. 31); or by ὅπως, Heb. ix. 15. διὰ τί [so L Tr WH] and written together διατί [so G T; cf. W. 45; *Lipsius*, Gram. Unters. p. 126], *why? wherefore?* Mt. ix. 11, 14; xiii. 10; xvii. 19; Mk. ii. 18; Lk. v. 30; Jn. vii. 45; Acts v. 3; Ro. ix. 32; 1 Co. vi. 7; Rev. xvii. 7. δι᾽ ἣν αἰτίαν, see αἰτία, 1. τίς ἡ αἰτία, δι᾽ ἥν, Acts x. 21; xxiii. 28; διὰ ταύτην τὴν αἰτίαν, Acts xxviii. 20; διὰ ταῦτα, Eph. v. 6, etc. **b.** used, with the acc. of any noun, of the mental affection by which one is impelled to some act [Eng. *for*; cf. W. 399 (372)]: διὰ φθόνον, because prompted by envy, *for* envy, Mt. xxvii. 18; Mk. xv. 10; διὰ τὸν φόβον τινός, Jn. vii. 13; xix. 38; xx. 19; Rev. xviii. 10, 15; διὰ τὴν πολλὴν ἀγάπην, Eph. ii. 4. of any other cause on account of which one is said to do or to have done something, — as in Mt. xiv. 3, 9; xv. 3, 6; Jn. iv. 39, 41 sq.; xii. 11; xiv. 11; Acts xxviii. 2; Ro. iii. 25 (διὰ τὴν πάρεσιν τῶν προγεγ. ἁμαρτημ. because of the pretermission etc., i. e. because he had left the sins unpunished); Ro. vi. 19; xv. 15; 2 Co. ix. 14; Gal. iv. 13 (δι᾽ ἀσθένειαν τῆς σαρκός, on account of an infirmity of the flesh, i. e. detained among you by sickness; cf. Wieseler [or Bp. Lghtft.] ad loc.); — or to suffer or have suffered something, Mt. xxiv. 9; xxvii. 19; Lk. xxiii. 19, 25; Acts xxi. 35; 2 Co. iv. 11; Col. iii. 6; 1 Pet. iii. 14; Rev. i. 9; vi. 9; — or to have obtained something, Heb. ii. 9; v. 14; 1 Jn. ii. 12; — or to be or to become something, Ro. viii. 10; xi. 28; Eph. iv. 18; Heb. v. 12 [W. 399 (373)]; vii. 18. of the impeding cause, where by reason of some person or thing something is said to have been impossible: Mt. xiii. 58; xvii. 20; Mk. ii. 4; Lk. v. 19; viii. 19; Acts xxi. 34; Heb. iii. 19; iv. 6. διά with the acc. of a pers. is often i. q. *for the benefit of*, [Eng. *for the sake of*]: Mk. ii. 27; Jn. xi. 42; xii. 30; 1 Co. xi. 9; Heb. i. 14; vi. 7; διὰ τοὺς ἐκλεκτούς, Mt. xxiv. 22; Mk. xiii. 20; 2 Tim. ii. 10; διὰ Χριστόν for Christ's sake, to promote his cause, 1 Co. iv. 10; δι᾽ ὑμᾶς, Jn. xii. 30; 2 Co. iv. 15; viii. 9; Phil. i. 24; 1 Th. i. 5. διά τινα, because of the example set by one: 2 Co. ii. 10; Ro. ii. 24; 2 Pet. ii. 2; διὰ τὸν Χριστόν *for Christ*, to become a partner of Christ, Phil. iii. 7 (equiv. to ἵνα Χριστὸν κερδήσω, vs. 8). **c.** διὰ τό, *because that, for that*, is placed before the inf. — either standing alone, as Lk. ix. 7; Heb. vii. 23; — or having a subject acc. expressed, as Mt. xxiv. 12; Mk. v. 4; Lk. ii. 4; xix. 11; Acts iv. 2; xii. 20; xviii. 2; xxvii. 4, 9; xxviii. 18; Phil. i. 7; Heb. vii. 24; x. 2; Jas. iv. 2; — or with its subject acc. evident from the context, as Mt. xiii. 6; Mk. iv. 6; Lk. xi. 8; xviii. 5; xxiii. 8; Acts viii. 11; xviii. 3.

C. In Composition διά indicates **1.** a passing through space or time, *through*, (διαβαίνω, διέρχομαι, διϋλίζω, etc.); hence **2.** continuity of time (διαμένω, διατελέω, διατηρέω), and completeness of action (διακαθαρίζω, διαζώννυμι). **3.** distribution (διαδίδωμι, διαγγέλλω, διαφημίζω). **4.** separation (διαλύω, διαιρέω). **5.** rivalry and endeavor (διαπίνω, διακατελέγχομαι; cf. *Herm.* ad Vig. p. 854; [Winer, as below, p. 6]). **6.** transition from one state to another (διαλλάσσω, διορθόω). [Cf. *Winer*, De verb. comp. etc. Pt. v.; Valckenaer on Hdt. 5, 18; *Cattier*. Gazophyl. ed. Abresch, Cant. 1810, p. 39; *A.*

Rieder, Ueb. d. mit mehr als ein. präp. zusammeng. verba im N. T. p. 17 sq.] No one of the N. T. writers makes more freq. use of verbs compounded with διά than Luke, [see the list in Winer, u. s. p. 3 note; on their constr. W. § 52, 4, 8].

1224   δια-βαίνω : 2 aor. διέβην, inf. διαβῆναι, ptcp. διαβάς; as in Grk. writ. fr. Hom. down; (Plin. *pertranseo*); *to pass through, cross over*; **a.** transitively : τὴν θάλασσαν ὡς διὰ ξηρᾶς, Heb. xi. 29. **b.** intrans.: πρός τινα, Lk. xvi. 26; εἰς with acc. of place, Acts xvi. 9; (for עָבַר, 1 S. xiii. 7).*

1225   δια-βάλλω : 1 aor. pass. διεβλήθην; **1.** prop. *to throw over* or *across, to send over*, (τὶ διά τινος). **2.** very often, fr. Hdt. down, *to traduce, calumniate, slander, accuse, defame* (cf. Lat. *perstringere*, Germ. *durchziehen*, [διά as it were from one to another; see *Winer*, De verb. comp. etc. Pt. v. p. 17]), not only of those who bring a false charge against one (διέβλητο πρὸς αὐτὸν ἀδίκως, Joseph. antt. 7, 11, 3), but also of those who disseminate the truth concerning a man, but do so maliciously, insidiously, with hostility [cf. Lucian's Essay de calumn. non temere credend.], (Dan. iii. 8 Sept.; Dan. vi. 24 Theodot.); so διεβλήθη αὐτῷ ὡς διασκορπίζων, Lk. xvi. 1 (with dat. of pers. to whom the charge is made, also in Hdt. 5, 35, et al.; τινὰ πρός τινα, Hdt. 5, 96, et al.; foll. by ὡς with ptcp., Xen. Hell. 2, 3, 23; Plat. epp. 7 p. 334 a.). [SYN. see κατηγορέω.]*

1226   δια-βεβαιόομαι (-οῦμαι); mid. *to affirm strongly, assert confidently,* [cf. W. 253 (238)]: περί τινος (Polyb. 12, 11 (12), 6), 1 Tim. i. 7 [cf. *WH*. App. p. 167]; Tit. iii. 8. (Dem. p. 220, 4; Diod., Dion. Hal., Plut., Ael.) *

1227   δια-βλέπω : fut. διαβλέψω; 1 aor. διέβλεψα; *to look through, penetrate by vision*; **a.** *to look fixedly, stare straight before one* (Plat. Phaedo p. 86 d.) : διέβλεψε, of a blind man recovering sight, Mk. viii. 25 T WH Tr txt. [some refer this to b.]. **b.** *to see clearly* : foll. by an inf. expressing the purpose, Mt. vii. 5 ; Lk. vi. 42. (Aristot., Plut.) *

1228   διάβολος, -ον, (διαβάλλω, q. v.), *prone to slander, slanderous, accusing falsely,* (Arstph., Andoc., Plut., al.) : 1 Tim. iii. 11 ; 2 Tim. iii. 3 ; Tit. ii. 3 ; as subst. ὁ διάβολος, *a calumniator, false accuser, slanderer,* [see κατηγορέω, fin.], (Xen. Ages. 11, 5 ; [Aristot., al.]) : Sept. Esth. vii. 4 ; viii. 1. In the Bible and in eccl. writ. ὁ διάβολος [also διάβ. without the art.; cf. W. 124 (118) ; B. 89 (78)] is applied κατ' ἐξοχήν to the one called in Hebr. הַשָּׂטָן, ὁ σατανᾶς (q. v.), viz. *Satan,* the prince of demons, the author of evil, persecuting good men (Job i. ; Zech. iii. 1 sqq., cf. Rev. xii. 10), estranging mankind from God and enticing them to sin, and afflicting them with diseases by means of demons who take possession of their bodies at his bidding; the malignant enemy of God and the Messiah : Mt. iv. 1, 5, [8, 11] ; xiii. 39 ; xxv. 41 ; Lk. iv. 2, [3, 5 R L, 6, 13] ; viii. 12 ; Jn. xiii. 2 ; Acts x. 38 ; Eph. iv. 27 ; vi. 11 ; 1 Tim. iii. 6 sq. ; 2 Tim. ii. 26 ; Heb. ii. 14 ; Jas. iv. 7 ; 1 Pet. v. 8 ; Jude 9 ; Rev. ii. 10 ; xii. 9, 12 ; xx. 2, 10 ; (Sap. ii. 24 ; [cf. Ps. cviii. (cix.) 6 ; 1 Chr. xxi. 1]). Men who resemble the devil in mind and will are said εἶναι ἐκ τοῦ διαβόλου *to be of the devil,* prop. *to de-rive their origin from the devil,* trop. *to depend upon the devil in thought and action, to be prompted and governed by him* : Jn. viii. 44 ; 1 Jn. iii. 8 ; the same are called τέκνα τοῦ διαβ. *children of the devil,* 1 Jn. iii. 10 ; υἱοὶ τοῦ δ. *sons of the devil,* Acts xiii. 10, cf. Mt. xiii. 38 ; Jn. viii. 38 ; 1 Jn. iii. 10. The name διάβολος is fig. applied to a man who, by opposing the cause of God, may be said to act the part of the devil or to side with him : Jn. vi. 70, cf. Mt. xvi. 23 ; Mk. viii. 33. [Cf. σατᾶν fin.]*

1229   δι-αγγέλλω ; 2 aor. pass. διηγγέλην ; fr. Pind. down ; *to carry a message through, announce everywhere, through places, through assemblies of men,* etc. ; *to publish abroad, declare,* [see διά, C. 3] : τί, Lk. ix. 60 ; Acts xxi. 26 (διαγγέλλων, sc. to all who were in the temple and were knowing to the affair) ; with the addition ἐν πάσῃ τῇ γῇ, Ro. ix. 17 fr. Ex. ix. 16. (Lev. xxv. 9 ; Josh. vi. 10 ; Ps. ii. 7 ; [lviii. (lix.) 13] ; Sir. xliii. 2 ; 2 Macc. iii. 34.) *

δια-γε, see γέ, 1. ----------------------- see **1065**

1230   δια-γίνομαι : 2 aor. διεγενόμην ; **1.** *to be through, continue.* **2.** *to be between, intervene* ; hence in Grk. writ. fr. Isaeus (p. 84, 14, 9 [or. de Hagn. hered.] χρόνων διαγενομένων) down, the aor. is used of time, *to have intervened, elapsed, passed meanwhile,* [cf. χρόνου μεταξὺ διαγενομένου Lys. 93, 6] : ἡμερῶν διαγενομένων τινῶν, Acts xxv. 13 ; ἱκανοῦ χρόνου διαγενομένου, Acts xxvii. 9 ; διαγενομένου τοῦ σαββάτου, Mk. xvi. 1.*

1231   δια-γινώσκω ; fut. διαγνώσομαι ; **1.** *to distinguish* (Lat. *dignosco*), i. e. *to know accurately, ascertain exactly* : τί, Acts xxiii. 15 ; (so in Grk. writ. fr. Hom. down). **2.** in a legal sense, *to examine, determine, decide,* (cf. Cic. *cognosco*) : τὰ καθ' ὑμᾶς *your case,* Acts xxiv. 22 ; (2 Macc. ix. 15 ; Dem. p. 629, 25 ; p. 545, 9 ; al.).*

1232   δια-γνωρίζω : 1 aor. διεγνώρισα ; *to publish abroad, make known thoroughly* : περί τινος, Lk. ii. 17 R G. Besides, only in [Philo, quod det. pot. § 26, i. 210, 16 ed. Mang. and] in Schol. in *Bekk.* Anecd. p. 787, 15 *to discriminate.*

1233   δια-γνωσις, -εως, ἡ, (see διαγινώσκω) ; **1.** *a distinguishing.* **2.** in a legal sense (Lat. *cognitio*), *examination, opinion, decision,* (Sap. iii. 18 ; Plat. legg. 9 p. 865 c.): Acts xxv. 21.*

1234   δια-γογγύζω : impf. διεγόγγυζον ; *to murmur* (διά i. e. either through a whole crowd, or ' among one another,' Germ. *durch einander* [cf. διά, C.]); hence it is always used of many indignantly complaining (see γογγύζω): Lk. xv. 2 ; xix. 7. (Ex. xvi. 2, 7, 8 ; [Num. xiv. 2] ; Josh. ix. 24 (18), etc. ; Sir. xxxiv. (xxxi.) 24 ; Clem. Alex. i p. 528 ed. Pott. ; Heliod. 7, 27, and in some Byzant. writ.) Cf. *Win.* De verb. comp. etc. Pt. v. p. 16 sq.*

1235   δια-γρηγορέω, -ῶ : 1 aor. διεγρηγόρησα ; *to watch through,* (Hdian. 3, 4, 8 [4 ed. Bekk.] πάσης τῆς νυκτὸς . . . διαγρηγορήσαντες, Niceph. Greg. Hist. Byz. p. 205 f. and 571 a.) ; *to remain awake* : Lk. ix. 32 (for they had overcome the force of sleep, with which they were weighed down, βεβαρημ. ὕπνῳ) ; [al. (e. g. R. V. txt.) *to be fully awake,* cf. Niceph. u. s. p. 205 f. δόξαν ἀπεβαλόμην ὥσπερ οἱ διαγρηγορήσαντες τὰ ἐν τοῖς ὕπνοις ὀνείρατα ; *Win.* De verb. comp. etc. Pt. v. p. 11 sq.].*

1236   δι-άγω ; **1.** *to lead through, lead across, send across.*

2. with τὸν βίον, τὸν χρόνον, etc., added or understood, to pass: βίον, 1 Tim. ii. 2 (very often in Grk. writ.); διάγειν ἔν τινι, sc. τὸν βίον to live [W. 593 (551 sq.); B. 144 (126)], Tit. iii. 3 (ἐν φιλοσοφίᾳ, Plat. Phaedr. p. 259 d.; ἐν εἰρήνῃ καὶ σχολῇ, Plut. Timol. 3).*

1237 δια-δέχομαι: 1 aor. διεδεξάμην; prop. *to receive through another* anything left or bequeathed by him, *to receive in succession, receive in turn, succeed to*: τὴν σκηνήν the tabernacle, Acts vii. 45. (τὴν ἀρχήν, τὴν βασιλείαν, etc., in Polyb., Diod., Joseph., al.) [Cf. δέχομαι.]*

1238 διάδημα, -τος, τό, (διαδέω to bind round), *a diadem*, i. e. the blue band marked with white with which Persian kings used to bind on the turban or tiara; the kingly ornament for the head: Rev. xii. 3; xiii. 1; xix. 12. (Xen. Cyr. 8, 3, 13; Esth. i. 11; ii. 17 for כֶּתֶר; 1 Macc. i. 9.)* [SYN. διά η μα, στέφανος: στ. like the Lat. *corona* is a crown in the sense of a chaplet, wreath, or garland — the badge of "victory in the games, of civic worth, of military valor, of nuptial joy, of festal gladness"; διάδημα is a crown as the badge of royalty, βασιλείας γνώρισμα (Lucian, Pisc. 35). Cf. Trench § xxiii.; Bp. Lghtft. on Phil. iv. 1; Dict. of Christ. Antiq. s. v. Coronation p. 464 sq.; B. D. Am. ed. s. v. Diadem; but cf. στέφανος, a.]

1239 δια-δίδωμι; fut. διαδιδώσω (Rev. xvii. 13 Rec.); 1 aor. διέδωκα; 2 aor. impv. διάδος; Pass., impf. 3 pers. sing. διεδίδοτο (Acts iv. 35), for which L T Tr WH read διεδίδετο (see ἀποδίδωμι); **1.** *to distribute, divide among several* [cf. διά, C. 3]: τί, Lk. xi. 22; τί τινι, Lk. xviii. 22 (Lchm. δός); Jn. vi. 11 (Tdf. ἔδωκεν); pass. Acts iv. 35. Its meaning is esp. illustrated by Xen. Cyr. 1, 3, 7 τὸν Κῦρον λαβόντα τῶν κρεῶν διαδιδόναι τοῖς ... θεραπευταῖς ... τοιαῦτα ἐποίει, ἕως διεδίδου πάντα ἃ ἔλαβε κρέα. **2.** *to give over, deliver*: τί τινι, Rev. xvii. 13; but here G L T Tr WH have restored διδόασι (cf. δίδωμι, init.).*

1240 διά-δοχος, -ον, ὁ, ἡ, (διαδέχομαι), *succeeding, a successor*: Acts xxiv. 27. (Sir. xlvi. 1; [xlviii. 8]; 2 Macc. xiv. 26; often in Grk. writ. fr. [Aeschyl. and] Hdt. 5, 26 down.)*

1241 δια-ζώννυμι or διαζώννυω: 1 aor. διέζωσα; 1 aor. mid. διεζωσάμην; pf. pass. ptcp. διεζωσμένος; *to bind* or *gird all around* (διά; this force of the prep. appears in the trop. use of the verb in Plut. Brut. 31, 2 ὡς δ' ἡ φλὸξ ῥυεῖσα καὶ διαζώσασα πανταχόθεν τὴν πόλιν διέλαμψε πολλή) τι αὐτόν, Jn. xiii. 4; Pass. διαζώννυμαί τι *to be girded*: ἑαυτόν, Jn. xiii. 5; Mid. διαζώννυμαί τι *to gird one's self with a thing, gird a thing around one's self*: Jn. xxi. 7; (Ezek. xxiii. 15 [Alex.]. in Grk. writ. occasionally fr. Thuc. on). Cf. Win. De verb. comp. etc. Pt. v. p. 13.*

1242 διαθήκη, -ης, ἡ, (διατίθημι); **1.** *a disposition, arrangement, of any sort*, which one wishes to be valid, (Germ. *Verordnung, Willensverfügung*): Gal. iii. 15, where under the name of *a man's disposition* is meant specifically *a testament*, so far forth as it is a specimen and example of that disposition [cf. Mey. or Bp. Lghtft. ad loc.]; esp. *the last disposal* which one makes of his earthly possessions after his death, *a testament* or *will* (so in Grk. writ. fr. [Arstph.], Plat. legg. 11 p. 922 c. sqq. down): Heb. ix. 16 sq. **2.** *a compact, covenant* (Arstph. av. 440), very often in the Scriptures for בְּרִית (Vulg. *testamen-*

tum). For the word *covenant* is used to denote the close relationship which God entered into, first with Noah (Gen. vi. 18; ix. 9 sqq. [cf. Sir. xliv. 18]), then with Abraham, Isaac and Jacob and their posterity (Lev. xxvi. 42 [cf. 2 Macc. i. 2]), but esp. with Abraham (Gen. xv. and xvii.), and afterwards through Moses with the people of Israel (Ex. xxiv.; Deut. v. 2; xxviii. 69 (xxix. 1)). By this last covenant the Israelites are bound to obey God's will as expressed and solemnly promulged in the Mosaic law; and he promises them his almighty protection and blessings of every kind in this world, but threatens transgressors with the severest punishments. Hence in the N. T. we find mention of αἱ πλάκες τῆς διαθήκης (לוּחֹת הַבְּרִית, Deut. ix. 9, 15), *the tables of the law*, on which *the duties of the covenant* were inscribed (Ex. xx.); of ἡ κιβωτὸς τῆς διαθ. (אֲרוֹן הַבְּרִית, Deut. x. 8; xxxi. 9; Josh. iii. 6, etc.), *the ark of the covenant* or *law*, in which those tables were deposited, Heb. ix. 4; Rev. xi. 19; of ἡ διαθήκη περιτομῆς the covenant of circumcision, made with Abraham, whose sign and seal was circumcision (Gen. xvii. 10 sqq.), Acts vii. 8; of τὸ αἷμα τῆς διαθήκης the blood of the victims, by the shedding and sprinkling of which the Mosaic covenant was ratified, Heb. ix. 20 fr. Ex. xxiv. 8; of αἱ διαθῆκαι the covenants, one made with Abraham, the other through Moses with the Israelites, Ro. ix. 4 [L txt. Tr mrg. ἡ διαθήκη] (Sap. xviii. 22; Sir. xliv. 11; 2 Macc. viii. 15; Ep. of Barn. 9; [cf. W. 177 (166)]); of αἱ διαθῆκαι τῆς ἐπαγγελίας, the covenants to which the promise of salvation through the Messiah was annexed, Eph. ii. 12 (συνθῆκαι ἀγαθῶν ὑποσχέσεων, Sap. xii. 21); for Christian salvation is the fulfilment of the divine promises annexed to those covenants, esp. to that made with Abraham: Lk. i. 72 sq.; Acts iii. 25; Ro. xi. 27; Gal. iii. 17 (where διαθήκη is God's *arrangement* i. e. *the promise* made to Abraham). As the new and far more excellent bond of friendship which God in the Messiah's time would enter into with the people of Israel is called בְּרִית חֲדָשָׁה, καινὴ διαθήκη (Jer. xxxviii. (xxxi.) 31),—which divine promise Christ has made good (Heb. viii. 8–10; x. 16),— we find in the N. T. two distinct covenants spoken of, δύο διαθῆκαι (Gal. iv. 24), viz. the Mosaic and the Christian, with the former of which (τῇ πρώτῃ διαθήκῃ, Heb. ix. 15, 18, cf. viii. 9) the latter is contrasted, as καινὴ διαθήκη, Mt. xxvi. 28; Mk. xiv. 24 (in both pass. in R G L [in Mt. in Tr also]); Lk. xxii. 20 [WH reject the pass.]; 1 Co. xi. 25; 2 Co. iii. 6; Heb. viii. 8; κρείττων διαθήκη, Heb. vii. 22; αἰώνιος διαθήκη, Heb. xiii. 20; and Christ is called κρείττονος or καινῆς or νέας διαθήκης μεσίτης: Heb. viii. 6; ix. 15; xii. 24. This new covenant binds men to exercise faith in Christ, and God promises them grace and salvation eternal. This covenant Christ set up and ratified by undergoing d e a t h; hence the phrases τὸ αἷμα τῆς καινῆς διαθήκης, τὸ αἷμα τῆς διαθήκης, (see αἷμα sub fin.), [Heb. x. 29]; τὸ αἷμά μου τῆς διαθήκης, my blood by the shedding of which the covenant is established, Mt. xxvi. 28 T WH and Mk. xiv. 24 T Tr WH (on two gen. after one noun cf. Matthiae § 380, Anm. 1; Kühner ii. p. 288 sq.;

[.Jelf § 543, 1, cf. § 466; W. § 30, 3 Note 3; B. 155 (136)]).
By metonymy of the contained for the container ἡ παλαιὰ
διαθήκη is used in 2 Co. iii. 14 of *the sacred books of the
O. T.* because in them the conditions and principles of
the older covenant were recorded. Finally must be
noted the amphiboly or twofold use [cf. Philo de mut.
nom. § 6] by which the writer to the Hebrews, in ix. 16
sq., substitutes for the meaning *covenant* which διαθήκη
bears elsewhere in the Ep. that of *testament* (see 1 above),
and likens Christ to a testator, — not only because the
author regards eternal blessedness as an inheritance bequeathed by Christ, but also because he is endeavoring
to show, both that the attainment of eternal salvation is
made possible for the disciples of Christ by his *death*
(ix. 15), and that even the Mosaic covenant had been
consecrated by blood (18 sqq.). This, apparently, led
the Latin Vulgate to render διαθήκη wherever it occurs
in the Bible [i. e. in the New Test., not always in the
Old; see B. D. s. v. Covenant, and B. D. Am. ed. s. v.
Testament] by the word *testamentum.**

1243   **δι-αίρεσις**, -εως, ἡ, (διαιρέω, q. v.);   **1.** *division, distribution*, (Hdt., Xen., Plat., al.).   **2.** *distinction, difference*, (Plat. Soph. p. 267 b. τίνα διαίρεσιν ἀγνωσίας τε καὶ
γνώσεως θήσομεν; al.); in particular, *a distinction arising
from a different distribution to different persons*, [A. V.
diversity] : 1 Co. xii. 4–6, cf. 11 διαιροῦν ἰδίᾳ ἑκάστῳ καθὼς
βούλεται.*

1244   **δι-αιρέω**, -ῶ; 2 aor. διεῖλον;   **1.** *to divide into parts,
to part, to tear, cleave* or *cut asunder*, (Hom. and subseq.
writ.; Gen. xv. 10; 1 K. iii. 25).   **2.** *to distribute* : τί
τινι (Xen. Cyr. 4, 5, 51; Hell. 3, 2, 10) : Lk. xv. 12; 1
Co. xii. 11; (Josh. xviii. 5; 1 Chr. xxiii. 6, etc.).*

see 1245   [**δια-καθαίρω**: 1 aor. διεκάθαρα (un-Attic and later form ;
cf. Moeris, ed. Piers. p. 137; *Lob.* ad Phryn. p. 25; Veitch
s. v. καθαίρω), inf. διακαθᾶραι; *to cleanse* (throughly cf. διά,
C. 2 i.e.) *thoroughly* : Lk. iii. 17 T WH L mrg. Tr mrg.;
for R G διακαθαρίζω. (Fr. Arstph. and Plat. down.) *]

1245   **δια-καθαρίζω**: fut. διακαθαριῶ [B. 37 (32); W. § 13, 1 c.;
WH. App. p. 163]; *to cleanse thoroughly*, (Vulg. *per-
mundo*) : τὴν ἅλωνα, Mt. iii. 12; Lk. iii. 17 [T WH etc.
διακαθᾶραι, q. v.]. (Not found in prof. auth., who use
διακαθαίρω, as τὴν ἅλω, Alciphr. ep. 3, 26.) *

1246   **δια-κατ-ελέγχομαι**: impf. διακατηλεγχόμην; *to confute
with rivalry and effort* or *in a contest* (on this use of the
prep. διά in compos. cf. *Herm.* ad Vig. p. 854; [al. give
it here the sense of completeness; see διά, C. 2]) : with
dat. of pers. [W. § 31, 1 f.; B. 177 (154)]; not found exc.
in Acts xviii. 28 [R. V. *powerfully confuted*].*

1247   **διακονέω**, -ῶ; impf. διηκόνουν (as if the verb were compounded of διά and ἀκονέω, for the rarer and earlier form
ἐδιακόνουν, cf. B. 35 (31); *Ph. Bttm.* Ausf. Spr. § 86 Anm.
6; Krüger § 28, 14, 13); [fut. διακονήσω]; 1 aor. διηκό-
νησα (for the peculiar ἐδιακόνησα); Pass., pres. ptcp. δια-
κονούμενος; 1 aor. inf. διακονηθῆναι, ptcp. διακονηθείς;
(διάκονος, q. v.); in Grk. writ. fr. [Soph.], Hdt. down; *to
be a servant, attendant, domestic; to serve, wait upon* ;   **1.**
univ.: [absol. ὁ διακονῶν, Lk. xxii. 26]; with dat. of
pers. *to minister to one*; *render ministering offices to* : Jn.

xii. 26; Acts xix. 22; Philem. 13; Pass. *to be served,
ministered unto* (W. § 39, 1; [B. 188 (163)]) : Mt. xx.
28; Mk. x. 45.   **2.** Like the Lat. *ministrare, to wait
at table and offer food and drink to the guests*, [cf. W. 593
(552)] : with dat. of pers., Mt. iv. 11; viii. 15; Mk. i. 13,
31; Lk. iv. 39; xii. 37; xvii. 8; absol. ὁ διακονῶν, Lk.
xxii. 27; so also of women preparing food, Lk. x. 40; Jn.
xii. 2; (Menand. ap. Athen. 6 c. 46, p. 245 c.; Anacr.
4, 6; al.; pass. διακονεῖσθαι ὑπό τινος, Diod. 5, 28; Philo,
vit. contempl. § 9).   **3.** *to minister* i. e. *supply food and
the necessaries of life* : with dat. of pers., Mt. xxv. 44;
xxvii. 55; Mk. xv. 41; διηκόνουν αὐτοῖς ἐκ (Rec. ἀπὸ)
τῶν ὑπαρχόντων αὐταῖς, Lk. viii. 3; *to relieve one's necessities* (e. g. by collecting alms) : Ro. xv. 25; Heb. vi. 10;
τραπέζαις , to provide, take care of, distribute, the things
necessary to sustain life, Acts vi. 2. absol., those are
said διακονεῖν, i. e. to take care of the poor and the sick,
who administer the office of *deacon* (see διάκονος, 2) in
the Christian churches, *to serve as deacons* : 1 Tim. iii.
10, 13; 1 Pet. iv. 11 [many take this last ex. in a general rather than an official sense].   **4.** with acc.
of the thing, *to minister* i. e. *attend to, anything*, that may
serve another's interests: χάρις διακονουμένη ὑφ᾽ ἡμῶν, 2
Co. viii. 19; [ἁδρότης, ibid. 20]; ὅσα διηκόνησε, how many
things I owe to his ministration, 2 Tim. i. 18; ἐπιστολὴ
διακονηθεῖσα ὑφ᾽ ἡμῶν, an epistle written, as it were, by
our serving as amanuenses, 2 Co. iii. 3. with acc. of the
thing and dat. of pers., *to minister a thing unto one, to
serve one with* or *by supplying any thing* : 1 Pet. i. 12; τὶ
εἰς ἑαυτούς, i. e. εἰς ἀλλήλους *to one another*, for mutual
use, 1 Pet. iv. 10.*

διακονία, -ας, ἡ, (διάκονος), [fr. Thuc., Plat. down], *service, ministering*, esp. of those who execute the commands
of others;   **1.** univ.: 2 Tim. iv. 11; Heb. i. 14.   **2.**
of those who by the command of God proclaim and promote religion among men;   **a.** of the office of Moses:
ἡ διακ. τοῦ θανάτου, concisely for the ministration by
which the law is promulgated that threatens and brings
death, 2 Co. iii. 7; τῆς κατακρίσεως, the ministration by
which condemnation is caused, ibid. 9.   **b.** of the
office of the apostles and its administration : Acts i.
17, 25; xx. 24; xxi. 19; Ro. xi. 13; 2 Co. iv. 1; vi. 3;
1 Tim. i. 12; τοῦ λόγου, Acts iv. 4; τοῦ πνεύματος, the
ministry whose office it is to cause men to obtain and
be governed by the Holy Spirit, 2 Co. iii. 8; τῆς δικαιοσύνης, by which men are taught how they may become
righteous with God, ibid. 9; τῆς καταλλαγῆς, the ministry
whose work it is to induce men to embrace the offered
reconciliation with God, 2 Co. v. 18; πρὸς τὴν ὑμῶν διακονίαν, that by preaching the gospel I might minister
unto you, 2 Co. xi. 8.   **c.** of the ministration or service
of all who, endowed by God with powers of mind and
heart peculiarly adapted to this end, endeavor zealously
and laboriously to promote the cause of Christ among
men, as apostles, prophets, evangelists, elders, etc.: 1 Co.
xii. 5; Eph. iv. 12; 2 Tim. iv. 5. What ministry is referred to in Col. iv. 17 is not clear.   **3.** *the ministration of those who render to others the offices of Christian*

1248

affection: 1 Co. xvi. 15 ; Rev. ii. 19, esp. of those who succor need by either collecting or bestowing benefactions [Acts xii. 25] ; the care of the poor, the supplying or distributing of charities, (Luther uses *Handreichung*): Acts vi. 1 ; 2 Co. ix. 13 ; ἡ διακονία ἡ εἰς τοὺς ἁγίους, 2 Co. viii. 4 ; ix. 1 ; ἡ διακονία τῆς λειτουργίας, the ministration rendered through this λειτουργία, 2 Co. ix. 12 ; πέμπειν εἰς διακονίαν τινί, to send a thing to one for the relief of his want [A. V. *to send relief unto*], Acts xi. 29 (κομίζειν χρήματα πολλὰ εἰς διακονίαν τῶν χηρῶν, Acta Thomae § 56, p. 233 ed. Tdf.) ; ἡ διακονία μου ἡ εἰς Ἱερουσαλ. "my ministration in bringing the money collected by me, a ministration intended for Jerusalem" (Fritzsche), Ro. xv. 31 [here L Tr mrg. read ἡ δωροφορία . . . ἐν etc.]. **4.** the office of deacon in the primitive church (see διάκονος, 2) : Ro. xii. 7. **5.** the service of those who prepare and present food : Lk. x. 40 (as in Xen. oec. 7, 41).*

διάκονος, -ου, ὁ, ἡ, (of uncert. origin, but by no means, as was formerly thought, compounded of διά and κόνις, so as·to mean prop. 'raising dust by hastening' ; cf. ἐγκονεῖν ; for *a* in the prep. διά is short, in διάκονος long. *Bttm.* Lexil. i. p. 218 sqq. [Eng. trans. p. 231 sq.] thinks it is derived fr. obsol. διάκω i. q. διήκω [allied with διώκω ; cf. Vaniček p. 363]) ; *one who executes the commands of another*, esp. *of a master* ; *a servant, attendant, minister* ; **1.** univ.: of the servant of a king, Mt. xxii. 13 ; with gen. of the pers. served, Mt. xx. 26 ; xxiii. 11 ; Mk. ix. 35 ; x. 43, (in which pass. it is used fig. of those who advance others' interests even at the sacrifice of their own) ; τῆς ἐκκλησίας, of one who does what promotes the welfare and prosperity of the church, Col. i. 25 ; διάκονοι τοῦ θεοῦ, those through whom God carries on his administration on earth, as magistrates, Ro. xiii. 4 ; teachers of the Christian religion, 1 Co. iii. 5 ; 2 Co. vi. 4 ; 1 Th. iii. 2 R T Tr WH txt. L mrg. ; the same are called διάκονοι (τοῦ) Χριστοῦ, 2 Co. xi. 23 ; Col. i. 7 ; 1 Tim. iv. 6 ; ἐν κυρίῳ, in the cause of the Lord, Col. iv. 7 ; [Eph. vi. 21] ; ὁ διάκ. μου my follower, Jn. xii. 26 ; τοῦ Σατανᾶ, whom Satan uses as a servant, 2 Co. xi. 15 ; [ἁμαρτίας, Gal. ii. 17] ; διάκ. περιτομῆς (abstr. for concr.), of Christ, who labored for the salvation of the circumcised i. e. the Jews, Ro. xv. 8 ; with gen. of the thing to which service is rendered, i. e. to which one is devoted : καινῆς διαθήκης, 2 Co. iii. 6 ; τοῦ εὐαγγελίου, Eph. iii. 7 ; Col. i. 23 ; δικαιοσύνης, 2 Co. xi. 15. **2.** *a deacon*, one who, by virtue of the office assigned him by the church, cares for the poor and has charge of and distributes the money collected for their use, [cf. BB.DD., Dict. of Christ. Antiq., Schaff-Herzog s. v. Deacon ; Bp. *Lghtft.* Com. on Phil. dissert. i. § i. ; *Julius Müller*, Dogmatische Abhandlungen, p. 560 sqq.] : Phil. i. 1 ; 1 Tim. iii. 8, 12, cf. Acts vi. 3 sqq. ; ἡ διάκονος, *a deaconess* (*ministra*, Plin. epp. 10, 97), a woman to whom the care of either poor or sick women was entrusted, Ro. xvi. 1 [cf. Dicts. as above, s. v. Deaconess ; Lghtft. as above p. 191 ; B. D. s. v. Phœbe]. **3.** *a waiter*, one who serves food and drink : Jn. ii. 5, 9, as in Xen. mem. 1, 5, 2 ; Hier. 3, 11 (4, 2) ; Polyb. 31, 4, 5 ; Lcian. de merced. § 26 ; Athen. 7, p. 291 a. ; 10,

420 e. ; see διακονέω, 2 and -νία, 5 ; [also Wetst. on Mt. iv. 11].*

[Syn. **διάκονος, δοῦλος, θεράπων, ὑπηρέτης**: "διάκονος represents the servant in his activity for the work ; not in his relation, either servile, as that of the δοῦλος, or more voluntary, as in the case of the θεράπων, to a person" Trench ; [yet cf. e. g. Ro. xiii. 4 ; 2 Cor. vi. 4 etc.]. δοῦλος opp. to ἐλεύθερος, and correlate to δεσπότης or κύριος, denotes a *bondman*, one who sustains a permanent servile relation to another. θεράπων is the voluntary performer of services, whether as a freeman or a slave ; it is a nobler, tenderer word than δοῦλος. ὑπηρ. acc. to its etymol. suggests subordination. Cf. Trench § ix. ; B. D. s. v. Minister ; Mey. on Eph. iii. 7 ; Schmidt ch. 164.]

διακόσιοι, -αι, -α, *two hundred* : Mk. vi. 37 ; Jn. vi. 7, etc.   **1250**

δι-ακούω: fut. διακούσομαι ; prop. *to hear* one *through,* *hear to the end, hear with care, hear fully,* [cf. διά, C. 2] (Xen., Plat., sqq.) : of a judge trying a cause, Acts xxiii. 35 ; so in Deut. i. 16 ; Dio Cass. 36, 53 (36).*   **see 1251 St.**

δια-κρίνω ; impf. διέκρινον ; 1 aor. διέκρινα ; Mid., [pres. διακρίνομαι] ; impf. διεκρινόμην ; 1 aor. διεκρίθην (in prof. auth. in a pass. sense, *to be separated* ; cf. W. § 39, 2 ; [B. 52 (45)]) ; in Grk. writ. fr. Hom. down ; in Sept. chiefly for שָׁפַט, also for הָרִין etc. **1.** *to separate, make a distinction, discriminate,* [cf. διά, C. 4] : οὐδὲν διέκρινε μεταξὺ ἡμῶν τε καὶ αὐτῶν, Acts xv. 9 ; μηδὲν διακρίναντα, making no difference, sc. between Jews and Gentiles, Acts xi. 12 L T Tr WH ; like the Lat. *distinguo*, used emphatically : to distinguish or separate a person or thing from the rest, in effect i. q. *to prefer*, yield to him the preference or honor : τινά, 1 Co. iv. 7 [cf. W. 452 (421)] ; τὸ σῶμα (τοῦ κυρίου), 1 Co. xi. 29. **2.** *to learn by discrimination,* *to try, decide* : Mt. xvi. 3 [T br. WH reject the pass.] ; 1 Co. xiv. 29 ; ἑαυτόν, 1 Co. xi. 31 ; *to determine, give judgment, decide a dispute* : 1 Co. vi. 5. **Pass. and Mid.** *to be* *parted, to separate one's self from* ; **1.** *to withdraw from one, desert him* (Thuc. 1, 105 ; 3, 9) ; of heretics withdrawing from the society of true Christians (Sozom. 7, 2 [p. 705 ed. Vales.] ἐκ τούτου οἱ μὲν διακριθέντες ἰδίᾳ ἐκκλησίαζον) : Jude 22 acc. to the (preferable) reading of L T Tr txt. ἐλέγχετε διακρινομένους, *those who separate themselves* from you, i. e. *who apostatize* ; instead of the Rec. ἐλεεῖτε διακρινόμενοι, which is to be rendered, *making for yourselves a selection* ; cf. Huther ad loc. ; [others though adopting the reading preferred above, refer διακρ. to the following head and translate it *while they dispute* with you ; but WH (see their App.) Tr mrg. follow codd. אB and a few other author. in reading ἐλεᾶτε διακρινομένους acc. to which διακρ. is probably to be referred to signification 3 : R. V. txt. "on some have mercy, *who are in doubt*"]. **2.** to separate one's self in a hostile spirit, *to oppose, strive with, dispute, contend* : with dat. of pers. Jude 9, (Polyb. 2, 22, 11 [cf. W. § 31, 1 g. ; B. 177 (154)]) ; πρός τινα, Acts xi. 2, (Hdt. 9, 58). **3.** in a sense not found in prof. auth. *to be at variance with one's self, hesitate, doubt* : Mt. xxi. 21 ; Ro. xiv. 23 ; Jas. i. 6 ; ἐν τῇ καρδίᾳ αὐτοῦ, Mk. xi. 23 ; ἐν ἑαυτῷ [i. e. -τοῖς], Jas. ii. 4 [al. refer this to 1 : *do ye not make distinctions among yourselves*] ; μηδὲν διακρινόμενος, nothing doubting i. e. wholly free from doubt, **1252**

1249

Jas. i. 6; without any hesitation as to whether it be lawful or not, Acts x. 20 and acc. to R G in xi. 12; οὐ διεκρίθη τῇ ἀπιστίᾳ he did not hesitate through want of faith, Ro. iv. 20.*

1253   διά-κρισις, -εως, ἡ, (διακρίνω), a distinguishing, discerning, judging: πνευμάτων, 1 Co. xii. 10; καλοῦ τε καὶ κακοῦ, Heb. v. 14; μὴ εἰς διακρίσεις διαλογισμῶν not for the purpose of passing judgment on opinions, as to which one is to be preferred as the more correct, Ro. xiv. 1 [see διαλογισμός, 1]. (Xen., Plat., al.)*

1254   διὰ-κωλύω: impf. διεκώλυον; (διά in this compound does not denote effort as is com. said, but separation, Lat. dis, cf. Germ. verhindern, Lat. prohibere; cf. διακλείω, to separate by shutting, shut out; cf. Win. De verb. comp. etc. Pt. v. p. 17 sq.); to hinder, prevent: τινά, Mt. iii. 14 [on the tense cf. W. § 40, 3 c.; B. 205 (178)]. (From Soph. and Thuc. down.)*

1255   δια-λαλέω: impf. διελάλουν; impf. pass. διελαλούμην; to converse together, to talk with, (διά denoting by turns, or one with another; see διακατελέγχομαι), τί, pass. [were talked of], Lk. i. 65; πρὸς ἀλλήλους (as Polyb. 23, 9, 6), τί ἂν ποιήσειαν [-σαιεν al.], of the conference of men deliberating, Lk. vi. 11. (Eur. Cycl. 175.)*

1256   δια-λέγομαι; impf. διελεγόμην; [1 aor. 3 pers. sing. διελέξατο (L T Tr WH in Acts xvii. 2; xviii. 19)]; 1 aor. διελέχθην; (mid. of διαλέγω, to select, distinguish); 1. to think different things with one's self, mingle thought with thought (cf. διαλογίζομαι); to ponder, revolve in mind; so in Hom. 2. as very freq. in Attic, to converse, discourse with one, argue, discuss: absol., Acts [xviii. 4]; xix. 8 sq.; [xx. 9]; περί τινος, Acts xxiv. 25; τινί, with one, Acts xvii. 17; xviii. 19; xx. 7; Heb. xii. 5; ἀπὸ τῶν γραφῶν, drawing arguments from the Scriptures, Acts xvii. 2; πρός τινα, Acts xvii. 17; xxiv. 12; with the idea of disputing prominent: πρὸς ἀλλήλους, foll. by interrog. τίς, Mk. ix. 34; περί τινος, Jude 9.*

1257   δια-λείπω: [2 aor. διέλιπον]; to interpose a delay, to intermit, leave off for a time something already begun: οὐ διέλιπε [T WH mrg. διέλειπεν] καταφιλοῦσα (on the ptcp. cf. W. § 45, 4 a.; [B. 300 (257)]), she has not ceased kissing, has continually kissed, Lk. vii. 45. (Is. v. 14; Jer. xvii. 8; often in Grk. writ. fr. Hdt. down.)*

1258   διά-λεκτος, -ου, ἡ, (διαλέγω); 1. conversation, speech, discourse, language (Plat., Dem., al.). 2. fr. Polyb. [cf. Aristot. probl. 10, 38 τοῦ ἀνθρώπου μία φωνή, ἀλλὰ διάλεκτοι πολλαί] down, the tongue or language peculiar to any people: Acts i. 19; ii. 6, 8; xxi. 40; xxii. 2; xxvi. 14. (Polyb. 1, 80, 6; 3, 22, 4; 40, 6, 3 sq.; μεθερμηνεύειν εἰς τὴν Ἑλλήνων διάλεκτον, Diod. 1, 37; πᾶσα μὲν διάλεκτος, ἡ δ' ἑλληνικὴ διαφερόντως ὀνομάτων πλουτεῖ, Philo, vit. Moys. ii. § 7; [cf. Müller on Joseph. c. Ap. 1, 22, 4 fin.].)*

[δια-λιμπάνω (or -λυμπάνω): impf. διελίμπανον; to intermit, cease: κλαίων οὐ διελίμπανεν, Acts viii. 24 WH (rejected) mrg.; cf. W. 345 sq. (323 sq.); B. 300 (257). (Tobit x. 7; Galen in Hippocr. Epid. 1, 3; cf. Bornem. on Acts l. c.; Veitch s. v. λιμπάνω.)*]

1259   δι-αλλάσσω: 2 aor. pass. διηλλάγην; (see διά, C. 6); 1. to change: τὶ ἀντί τινος [cf. W. 206 (194)]. 2. to

change the mind of any one, to reconcile (so fr. [Aeschyl.] Thuc. down): τινά τινι. Pass. to be reconciled, τινί, to renew friendship with one: Mt. v. 24; (1 S. xxix. 4; 1 Esdr. iv. 31). See Fritzsche's learned discussion of this word in his Com. on Rom. vol. i. p. 276 sqq. [in opp. to Tittmann's view that it implies mutual enmity; see καταλλάσσω, fin.]; cf. Win. De verb. comp. etc. Pt. v. pp. 7, 10; [Tholuck, Bergrede Christi, p. 171 (on Mt. v. 24)].*

1260   δια-λογίζομαι; dep. mid.; impf. διελογιζόμην; [1 aor. διελογισάμην, Lk. xx. 14 Lchm.]; (διά as in διαλέγομαι); to bring together different reasons, to reckon up the reasons, to reason, revolve in one's mind, deliberate: simply, Lk. i. 29; v. 21; ἐν τῇ καρδίᾳ, Mk. ii. 6, 8; Lk. v. 22; with addition of περί τινος, Lk. iii. 15; ἐν ἑαυτῷ [or -τοῖς], within himself, etc., Mk. ii. 8; Lk. xii. 17; ἐν ἑαυτοῖς i. q. ἐν ἀλλήλοις among themselves, Mt. xvi. 7 sq.; πρὸς ἑαυτούς i. q. πρὸς ἀλλήλους, one turned towards another, one with another, Mk. ix. 33 Rec.; xi. 31 L T Tr WH; Lk. xx. 14; πρὸς ἀλλήλους, Mk. viii. 16; παρ' ἑαυτοῖς [see παρά, II. c.], Mt. xxi. 25 [L Tr WH txt. ἐν ἑ.]; ὅτι, Jn. xi. 50 Rec.; ὅτι equiv. to περὶ τούτου ὅτι, Mk. viii. 17. (For חָשַׁב several times in the Psalms; 2 Macc. xii. 43; in Grk. writ. fr. Plat. and Xen. down.)*

1261   δια-λογισμός, -οῦ, ὁ, (διαλογίζομαι), Sept. for מַחֲשָׁבָה and Chald. רַעְיוֹן, in Grk. writ. fr. Plat. down, the thinking of a man deliberating with himself; hence 1. a thought, inward reasoning: Lk. ii. 35; v. 22; vi. 8; ix. 46 sq.; Ro. xiv. 1 [yet some bring this under 2]; the reasoning of those who think themselves to be wise, Ro. i. 21; 1 Co. iii. 20; an opinion: κριταὶ διαλογισμῶν πονηρῶν judges with evil thoughts, i. e. who follow perverse opinions, reprehensible principles, Jas. ii. 4 [cf. W. 187 (176)]; purpose, design: Mt. xv. 19; Mk. vii. 21. 2. a deliberating, questioning, about what is true: Lk. xxiv. 38; when in reference to what ought to be done, hesitation, doubting: χωρὶς γογγυσμῶν καὶ διαλογισμῶν, Phil. ii. 14 ['γογγ. is the moral, διαλ. the intellectual rebellion against God' Bp. Lghtft.]; χωρὶς ὀργῆς κ. διαλογισμοῦ, 1 Tim. ii. 8; [in the last two pass. al. still advocate the rendering disputing; yet cf. Mey. on Phil. l. c.].*

1262   δια-λύω: 1 aor. pass. διελύθην; to dissolve [cf. διά, C. 4]: in Acts v. 36 of a body of men broken up and dispersed, as often in Grk. writ.*

1263   δια-μαρτύρομαι; dep. mid.; impf. διεμαρτυρόμην (Acts ii. 40 Rec.); 1 aor. διεμαρτυράμην; in Sept. mostly for הֵעִיד; often in Grk. writ. fr. Xen. down; see a multitude of exx. fr. them in Win. De verb. comp. etc. Pt. v. p. 20 sqq.; to call gods and men to witness [διά, with the interposition of gods and men; cf. Ellic. (after Win.) on 1 Tim. v. 21]; 1. to testify, i. e. earnestly, religiously to charge: foll. by an impv. Acts ii. 40; ἐνώπιον τοῦ θεοῦ κ. Χριστοῦ Ἰησοῦ, 2 Tim. iv. 1, (2 K. xvii. 13; Xen. Cyr. 7, 1, 17 σὺ μὴ πρότερον ἔμβαλλε τοῖς πολεμίοις, διαμαρτύρομαι, πρίν etc.); also with ἐνώπιον τοῦ θεοῦ κτλ. foll. by ἵνα [cf. B. 237 (204)], 1 Tim. v. 21, (foll. by μή, Ex. xix. 21); foll. by the inf. 2 Tim. ii. 14 [not Lchm., Mk. xiii. 26]. 2. to attest, testify to, solemnly affirm: Acts xx. 23; 1 Th. iv. 6; Heb. ii. 6; foll. by ὅτι, Acts x. 42; with dat. of pers.

to give solemn testimony to one, Lk. xvi. 28 ; with acc. of the obj. *to confirm a thing by* (the interposition of) *testimony, to testify, cause it to be believed* : τὸν λόγον τοῦ κυρίου, Acts viii. 25 ; τὸ εὐαγγέλιον, Acts xx. 24 ; τὴν βασιλείαν τοῦ θεοῦ, Acts xxviii. 23 ; for all the apostolic instruction came back finally to testimony respecting things which they themselves had seen or heard, or which had been disclosed to them by divine revelation, (Acts i. 21 sq. ; v. 32 ; x. 41 ; xxii. 18) ; with the addition of εἰς and an acc. of the place unto which the testimony is borne : τὰ περὶ ἐμοῦ εἰς Ἰερουσ. Acts xxiii. 11 ; with the addition of a dat. of the pers. to whom the testimony is given : τοῖς Ἰουδαίοις τὸν Χριστὸν Ἰησοῦν, the Messianic dignity of Jesus, Acts xviii. 5 ; Ἰουδ. τὴν μετάνοιαν καὶ πίστιν, the necessity of repentance and faith, Acts xx. 21, (τῇ Ἰερουσ. τὰς ἀνομίας, into what sins she has fallen, Ezek. xvi. 2).*

1264   **δια-μάχομαι** : impf. διεμαχόμην ; *to fight it out ; contend fiercely* : of disputants, Acts xxiii. 9. (Sir. viii. 1, 3 ; very freq. in Attic writ.) *

1265   **δια-μένω** ; [impf. διέμενον] ; 2 pers. sing. fut. διαμενεῖς (Heb. i. 11 Knapp, Bleek, al., for Rec. [G L T Tr WH al.] διαμένεις) ; 1 aor. διέμεινα ; pf. διαμεμένηκα ; *to stay permanently, remain permanently, continue*, [cf. *perdure* ; διά, C. 2] (Philo de gigant. § 7 πνεῦμα θεῖον μένειν δυνατὸν ἐν ψυχῇ, διαμένειν δὲ ἀδύνατον) : Gal. ii. 5 ; opp. to ἀπόλλυμαι, Heb. i. 11 fr. Ps. ci. (cii.) 27 ; with an adj. or adv. added denoting the condition : διέμεινε κωφός, Lk. i. 22 ; οὕτω, as they are, 2 Pet. iii. 4 ; *to persevere* : ἔν τινι, Lk. xxii. 28. (Xen., Plat. and subseq. writ.) *

1266   **δια-μερίζω** : impf. διεμέριζον ; 1 aor. impv. 2 pers. plur. διαμερίσατε ; Pass., [pres. διαμερίζομαι] ; pf. ptcp. διαμεμερισμένος ; 1 aor. διεμερίσθην ; fut. διαμερισθήσομαι ; [Mid., pres. διαμερίζομαι ; 1 aor. διεμερισάμην ;] *to divide* ; **1.** *to cleave asunder, cut in pieces* : ζῷα διαμερισθέντα sc. by the butcher, Plat. legg. 8 p. 849 d. ; acc. to a use peculiar to Lk. in pass. *to be divided into opposing parts, to be at variance, in dissension* : ἐπί τινα, against one, Lk. xi. 17 sq. ; ἐπί τινι, xii. 52 sq. **2.** *to distribute* (Plat. polit. p. 289 c. ; in Sept. chiefly for חָלַק) : τί, Mk. xv. 24 Rec. ; τί τινι, Lk. xxii. 17 (where L T Tr WH εἰς ἑαυτούς for R G ἑαυτοῖς) ; Acts ii. 45 ; Pass. Acts ii. 3 ; Mid. *to distribute among themselves* : τί, Mt. xxvii. 35 ; Mk. xv. 24 G L T Tr WH ; Lk. xxiii. 34 ; with ἑαυτοῖς added, [Mt. xxvii. 35 Rec.] ; Jn. xix. 24 fr. Ps. xxi. (xxii.) 19.*

1267   **δια-μερισμός**, -οῦ, ὁ, (διαμερίζω), *division* ; **1.** *a parting, distribution* : Plat. legg. 6 p. 771 d. ; Diod. 11, 47 ; Joseph. antt. 10, 11, 7 ; Sept. Ezek. xlviii. 29 ; Mic. vii. 12. **2.** *disunion, dissension* : opp. to εἰρήνη, Lk. xii. 51 ; see διαμερίζω, 1.*

1268   **δια-νέμω** : 1 aor. pass. διενεμήθην ; *to distribute, divide*, (Arstph., Xen., Plat., sqq.) : pass. εἰς τὸν λαόν to be disseminated, spread, among the people, Acts iv. 17.*

1269   **δια-νεύω** ; *to express one's meaning by a sign, nod to, beckon to, wink at*, (διά, because "the sign is conceived of as passing *through* the intervening space to him to whom it is made" Win. De verb. comp. etc. Pt. v. p. 4) : Lk. i. 22. (Ps. xxxiv. (xxxv.) 19 ; Sir. xxvii. 22 ; Diod. 3, 18 ; 17, 37 ; Lcian. ver. hist. 2, 44 ; Icarom. 15 ; [al.].)*

δια-νόημα, -τος, τό, (διανοέω to think), *a thought* : Lk. xi. 17. (Sept. ; Sir. ; often in Plat.) *   **1270**

διάνοια, -ας, ἡ, (διά and νοός), Sept. for לֵב and לְבָב ; very freq. in Grk. writ. fr. [Aeschyl.] Hdt. down ; **1.** *the mind as the faculty of understanding, feeling, desiring* : Mt. xxii. 37 ; Mk. xii. 30 [Tr mrg. br.] ; Lk. x. 27 ; Eph. i. 18 Rec. ; iv. 18 ; Heb. viii. 10 ; x. 16 ; 1 Pet. i. 13. **2.** *understanding* : 1 Jn. v. 20. **3.** *mind* i. e. *spirit* (Lat. *animus*), *way of thinking and feeling* : Col. i. 21 ; Lk. i. 51 ; 2 Pet. iii. 1. **4.** *thought* ; plur. contextually in a bad sense, *evil* thoughts : Eph. ii. 3, as in Num. xv. 39 μνησθήσεσθε πασῶν τῶν ἐντολῶν κυρίου . . καὶ οὐ διαστραφήσεσθε ὀπίσω τῶν διανοιῶν ὑμῶν.*   **1271**

δι-αν-οίγω ; impf. διήνοιγον ; 1 aor. διήνοιξα ; Pass., 1 aor. διηνοίχθην ; [2 aor. διηνοίγην] ; pf. ptcp. διηνοιγμένος (Acts vii. 56 L T Tr WH) ; [on variations of augm. see reff. s. v. ἀνοίγω] ; Sept. chiefly for פָּקַח and פָּתַח ; occasionally in prof. auth. fr. Plat. Lys. p. 210 a. down ; *to open by dividing or drawing asunder* (διά), *to open thoroughly* (what had been closed) ; **1.** prop. : ἄρσεν διανοῖγον μήτραν, a male opening the womb (the closed matrix), i. e. the first-born, Lk. ii. 23 (Ex. xiii. 2, etc.) ; οὐρανούς, pass., Acts vii. 56 L T Tr WH ; *the ears, the eyes*, i. e. *to restore or to give hearing, sight* : Mk. vii. 34, 35 R G ; Lk. xxiv. 31, (Gen. iii. 5, 7 ; Is. xxxv. 5 ; 2 K. vi. 17, etc.). **2.** trop. : τὰς γραφάς, to open the sense of the Scriptures, explain them, Lk. xxiv. 32 ; τὸν νοῦν τινος to open the mind of one, i. e. cause him to understand a thing, Lk. xxiv. 45 ; τὴν καρδίαν to open one's soul, i. e. to rouse in one the faculty of understanding or the desire of learning, Acts xvi. 14, (2 Macc. i. 4 ; Themist. orat. 2 de Constantio imp. [p. 29 ed. Harduin] διανοίγεταί μου ἡ καρδία κ. διανγεστέρα γίνεται ἡ ψυχή) ; absol., foll. by ὅτι, *to explain, expound* sc. αὐτάς, i. e. τὰς γραφάς, Acts xvii. 3. Cf. Win. De verb. comp. etc. Pt. v. p. 19 sq.*   **1272**

δια-νυκτερεύω ; (opp. to διημερεύω) ; *to spend the night, to pass the whole night*, [cf. διά, C. 1] : ἔν τινι, in any employment, Lk. vi. 12. (Diod. 13, 62 ; Antonin. 7, 66 ; Plut. mor. p. 950 b. ; Hdian. 1, 16, 12 [5 Bekk.] ; Joseph. antt. 6, 13, 9 ; b. j. 2, 14, 7 [Job ii. 9 ; Phil. incorr. mund. § 2 ; in Flac. § 6] ; with τὴν νύκτα added, Xen. Hell. 5, 4, 3.)*   **1273**

δι-ανύω : 1 aor. ptcp. διανύσας ; *to accomplish fully, bring quite to an end, finish* : τὸν πλοῦν, Acts xxi. 7. (2 Macc. xii. 17 ; fr. Hom. down.) [Cf. *Field*, Otium Norv. iii. p. 85 sq.] *   **1274**

δια-παντός, see διά, A. II. 1. a.   ------------------ **1275**

δια-παρα-τριβή, -ῆς, ἡ, *constant contention, incessant wrangling* or *strife*, (παρατριβή attrition ; contention, wrangling) ; a word justly adopted in 1 Tim. vi. 5 by G L T Tr WH (for Rec. παραδιατριβαί, q. v.) ; not found elsewhere [exc. Clem. Al. etc.] ; cf. W. 102 (96). Cf. the double compounds διαπαρατηρεῖν, 2 S. iii. 30 ; also (doubtful, it must be confessed), διαπαρακύπτομαι, 1 K. vi. 4 Ald. ; διαπαροξύνω, Joseph. antt. 10, 7, 5. [Steph. gives also διαπαράγω, Greg. Nyss. ii. 177 b. ; διαπαραλαμβάνω ; διαπαρασιωπάω, Joseph. Genes. p. 9 a. ; διαπαρασύρω, Schol. Lucian. ii. 796 Hemst.] *   (1275a): see 3859

δια-περάω, -ῶ ; 1 aor. διεπέρασα ; *to pass over, cross over* ;   **1276**

e. g. a river, a lake : Mt. ix. 1 ; xiv. 34 ; Mk. vi. 53 [here T WH follow with ἐπὶ τὴν γῆν *for* (to) *the land* (cf. R. V. mrg.)] ; foll. by εἰς with acc. of place, Mk. v. 21 ; Acts xxi. 2 ; πρός with acc. of pers. Lk. xvi. 26. ([Eur.], Arstph., Xen., subseq. writ. ; Sept. for עָבַר.) *

1277   **δια-πλέω** : 1 aor. ptcp. διαπλεύσας ; (Plin. *pernavigo*), *to sail across* : πέλαγος (as often in Grk. writ.), Acts xxvii. 5 [W. § 52, 4, 8].*

1278   **δια-πονέω** : *to work out laboriously, make complete by labor.* Mid. [pres. διαπονοῦμαι] ; with 1 aor. pass. διεπονήθην (for which Attic writ. διεπονησάμην) ; **a.** *to exert one's self, strive* ; **b.** *to manage with pains, accomplish with great labor* ; in prof. auth. in both senses [fr. Aeschyl. down]. **c.** *to be troubled, displeased, offended, pained,* [cf. colloq. Eng. to be *worked up* ; W. 23 (22)] : Acts iv. 2 ; xvi. 18. (Aquila in Gen. vi. 6 ; 1 S. xx. 30 ; Sept. in Eccl. x. 9 for נָצַב ; Hesych. διαπονηθείς · λυπηθείς.) *

see 1279 St.   **δια-πορεύω** : *to cause one to pass through a place* ; to *carry across* ; Pass., [pres. διαπορεύομαι] ; impf. διεπορευόμην] ; with fut. mid. [(not found in N. T.) ; fr. Hdt. down] ; *to journey through a place, go through* : as in Grk. writ. foll. by διά with gen. of place, Mk. ii. 23 L Tr WH txt. ; Lk. vi. 1 ; foll. by acc. [W. § 52, 4, 8] *to travel through* : Acts xvi. 4 ; absol. : Lk. xviii. 36 ; Ro. xv. 24 ; with the addition κατὰ πόλεις καὶ κώμας, Lk. xiii. 22. [SYN. see ἔρχομαι.] *

1280   **δι-απορέω, -ῶ** : impf. διηπόρουν ; Mid., [pres. inf. διαπορεῖσθαι (Lk. xxiv. 4 R G)] ; impf. διηπορούμην (Acts ii. 12 T Tr WH) ; in the Grk. Bible only in [Dan. ii. 3 Symm. and] Luke ; prop. *thoroughly* (δια)ἀπορέω (q. v.), *to be entirely at a loss, to be in perplexity* : absol. Acts ii. 12 ; foll. by διὰ τό with inf. Lk. ix. 7 ; περί τινος, Lk. xxiv. 4 (here the mid. is to be at a loss *with one's self,* for which L T Tr WH read the simple ἀπορεῖσθαι) ; Acts v. 24 ; ἐν ἑαυτῷ foll. by indir. discourse, Acts x. 17. (Plat., Aristot., Polyb., Diod., Philo, Plut., al.) *

1281   **δια-πραγματεύομαι** : 1 aor. διεπραγματευσάμην ; *thoroughly, earnestly* (διά) *to undertake a business,* Dion. Hal. 3, 72 ; contextually, *to undertake a business for the sake of gain* : Lk. xix. 15. (In Plat. Phaedo p. 77 d. 95 e. *to examine thoroughly.*) *

1282   **δια-πρίω** : impf. pass. διεπριόμην ; *to saw asunder or in twain, to divide by a saw* : 1 Chr. xx. 3 ; Plat. conv. p. 193 a. ; Arstph. eqq. 768, and elsewhere. Pass. trop. *to be sawn through mentally,* i. e. to be rent with vexation, [A. V. *cut to the heart*], Acts v. 33 ; with the addition ταῖς καρδίαις αὐτῶν, Acts vii. 54 (cf. Lk. ii. 35) ; μεγάλως ἐχαλέπαινον καὶ διεπρίοντο καθ' ἡμῶν, Euseb. h. e. 5, 1, 6 [15 ed. Heinich. ; cf. *Gataker,* Advers. misc. col. 916 g.].*

1283   **δι-αρπάζω** : fut. διαρπάσω ; 1 aor. [subj. 3 pers. sing. διαρπάσῃ], inf. διαρπάσαι ; *to plunder* : Mt. xii. 29ᵃ (where L T Tr WH ἁρπάσαι), 29ᵇ (R T Tr WH) ; Mk. iii. 27. [From Hom. down.] *

1284   **δια-ρρήγνυμι** and διαρρήσσω (Lk. viii. 29 [R G ; see below]) ; 1 aor. διέρρηξα ; impf. pass. 3 pers. sing. διερρήγνυτο (Lk. v. 6, where Lchm. txt. διερήγνυτο and T Tr WH διερρήσσετο (L mrg. διερρ.), also L T Tr WH διαρρήσσων in Lk. viii. 29 ; [WH have διέρηξεν in Mt. xxvi. 65, and διαρήξας in Mk. xiv. 63 ; see their App. p. 163, and

s. v. P, ρ]) ; *to break asunder, burst through, rend asunder* : τὰ δεσμά, Lk. viii. 29 ; τὸ δίκτυον, pass., Lk. v. 6 ; τὰ ἱμάτια, χιτῶνας, *to rend,* which was done by the Jews in extreme indignation or in deep grief [cf. B. D. s. v. Dress, 4] : Mt. xxvi. 65 ; Mk. xiv. 63 ; Acts xiv. 14, cf. Gen. xxxvii. 29, 34, etc. ; 1 Macc. xi. 71 ; Joseph. b. j. 2, 15, 4. (Sept. [Hom.], Soph., Xen., subseq. writ.) *

1285   **διασαφέω, -ῶ** : 1 aor. διεσάφησα ; (σαφής clear) ; **1.** *to make clear or plain, to explain, unfold, declare* : τὴν παραβολήν, Mt. xiii. 36 L Tr txt. WH ; (Eur. Phoen. 398 ; Plat. legg. 6, 754 a. ; al. ; Polyb. 2, 1, 1 ; 3, 52, 5). **2.** of things done, to declare i. e. *to tell, announce, narrate* : Mt. xviii. 31 ; (2 Macc. 1, 18 ; Polyb. 1, 46, 4 ; 2, 27, 3). Cf. *Fischer,* De vitiis lexx. N. T. p. 622 sqq. ; *Win.* De verb. comp. etc. Pt. v. p. 11.*

1286   **δια-σείω** : 1 aor. διέσεισα ; in Grk. writ. fr. Hdt. down ; *to shake thoroughly* ; trop. *to make to tremble, to terrify* (Job iv. 14 for הִפְחִיד), *to agitate* ; like *concutio* in juridical Latin, *to extort* from one *by intimidation* money or other property : τινά, Lk. iii. 14 [A. V. *do violence to*] ; 3 Macc. vii. 21 ; the Basilica ; [Heinichen on Euseb. h. e. 7, 30, 7].*

1287   **δια-σκορπίζω** ; 1 aor. διεσκόρπισα ; Pass., pf. ptcp. διεσκορπισμένος ; 1 aor. διεσκορπίσθην ; 1 fut. διασκορπισθήσομαι ; often in Sept., more rarely in Grk. writ. fr. Polyb. 1, 47, 4 ; 27, 2, 10 on (cf. *Lob.* ad Phryn. p. 218 ; [W. 25]) ; *to scatter abroad, disperse* : Jn. xi. 52 (opp. to συνάγω) ; of the enemy, Lk. i. 51 ; Acts v. 37, (Num. x. 35, etc. ; Joseph. antt. 8, 15, 4 ; Ael. v. h. 13, 46 (1, 6) ὁ δράκων τοὺς μὲν διεσκόρπισε, τοὺς δὲ ἀπέκτεινε). of a flock of sheep : Mt. xxvi. 31 (fr. Zech. xiii. 7) ; Mk. xiv. 27 ; of property, *to squander, waste* : Lk. xv. 13 ; xvi. 1, (like διασπείρω in Soph. El. 1291). like the Hebr. זָרָה (Sept. Ezek. v. 2, 10, 12 [Ald.], etc.) of grain, *to scatter* i. e. *to winnow* (i. e. to throw the grain a considerable distance, or up into the air, that it may be separated from the chaff ; opp. to συνάγω, to gather the wheat, freed from the chaff, into the granary [cf. BB.DD. s. v. Agriculture]) : Mt. xxv. 24, 26.*

1288   **δια-σπάω** : Pass., [pf. inf. διεσπάσθαι] ; 1 aor. διεσπάσθην ; *to rend asunder, break asunder* : τὰς ἁλύσεις, Mk. v. 4 (τὰς νευράς, Judg. xvi. 9) ; of a man, *to tear in pieces* : Acts xxiii. 10, (τοὺς ἄνδρας κρεουργηδόν, Hdt. 3, 13).*

1289   **δια-σπείρω** : 2 aor. pass. διεσπάρην ; *to scatter abroad, disperse* ; Pass. of those who are driven to different places, Acts viii. 1, 4 ; xi. 19. (In Grk. writ. fr. [Soph. and] Hdt. down ; very often in Sept.) *

1290   **δια-σπορά, -ᾶς, ἡ,** (διασπείρω, cf. such words as ἀγορά, διαφθορά), (Vulg. *dispersio*), *a scattering, dispersion* : ἀτόμων, opp. to σύμμιξις κ. παράξευξις, Plut. mor. p. 1105 a. ; in the Sept. used of the Israelites dispersed among foreign nations, Deut. xxviii. 25 ; xxx. 4 ; esp. of their Babylonian exile, Jer. xli. (xxxiv.) 17 ; Is. xlix. 6 ; Judith v. 19 ; abstr. for concr. of the exiles themselves, Ps. cxlvi. (cxlvii.) 2 (i. q. נִדָּחִים expelled, outcasts) ; 2 Macc. i. 27 ; εἰς τ. διασπορὰν τῶν Ἑλλήνων unto those dispersed among the Greeks [W. § 30, 2 a.], Jn. vii. 35. Transferred to *Christians* [i. e. *Jewish* Christians (?)] scattered abroad among the Gentiles: Jas. i. 1 (ἐν τῇ διασπορᾷ, sc. οὖσι); παρεπίδημοι διασπορᾶς Πόντου, sojourners far away from home, in Pontus, 1 Pet. i. 1 (see παρεπίδημος). [BB.DD. s. v. Dispersion; esp. Schürer, N. T. Zeitgesch. § 31.]*

see 1291 St.   **δια-στέλλω**: *to draw asunder, divide, distinguish, dispose, order*, (Plat., Polyb., Diod., Strab., Plut.; often in Sept.); Pass. τὸ διαστελλόμενον, *the injunction*: Heb. xii. 20, (2 Macc. xiv. 28). Mid., [pres. διαστέλλομαι]; impf. διεστελλόμην; 1 aor. διεστειλάμην; *to open one's self* i. e. *one's mind, to set forth distinctly*, (Aristot., Polyb.); hence in the N. T. [so Ezek. iii. 18, 19; Judith xi. 12] *to admonish, order, charge*: τινί, Mk. viii. 15; Acts xv. 24; foll. by ἵνα [cf. B. 237 (204)], Mt. xvi. 20 R T Tr WH mrg.; Mk. vii. 36; ix. 9; διεστείλατο πολλά, ἵνα etc. Mk. v. 43.*

1292   **διάστημα**, -τος, τό, [(διαστῆναι)], *an interval, distance*; *space* of time: ὡς ὡρῶν τριῶν διάστ. Acts v. 7, ([ἐκ πολλοῦ διαστήματος, Aristot. de audib. p. 800b, 5 etc.]; τετραετὲς δ. Polyb. 9, 1, 1; [σύμπας ὁ χρόνος ἡμερῶν κ. νυκτῶν ἐστι διάστημα, Philo, alleg. leg. i. § 2 etc., see Siegfried s. v. p. 66]).*

1293   **δια-στολή**, -ῆς, ἡ, (διαστέλλω, cf. ἀνατολή), *a distinction, difference*: Ro. iii. 22; x. 12; of the difference of the sounds made by musical instruments, 1 Co. xiv. 7. ([Aristot., Theophr.], Polyb., Plut., al.) *

1294   **δια-στρέφω**; 1 aor. inf. διαστρέψαι; pf. pass. ptcp. διεστραμμένος [cf. WH. App. p. 170 sq.]; fr. Aeschyl. down; **a.** *to distort, turn aside*: τὰς ὁδοὺς κυρίου τὰς εὐθείας, figuratively (Prov. x. 10), to oppose, plot against, the saving purposes and plans of God, Acts xiii. 10. Hence **b.** *to turn aside from the right path, to pervert, corrupt*: τὸ ἔθνος, Lk. xxiii. 2 (Polyb. 5, 41, 1; 8, 24, 3); τινὰ ἀπό τινος, to corrupt and so turn one aside from etc. Acts xiii. 8, (Ex. v. 4; voluptates animum *detorquent* a virtute, Cic.); διεστραμμένος *perverse, corrupt, wicked*: Mt. xvii. 17; Lk. ix. 41; Acts xx. 30; Phil. ii. 15.*

1295   **δια-σώζω**: 1 aor. διέσωσα; 1 aor. pass. διεσώθην; in Grk. writ. fr. Hdt. down; often in Sept., esp. for מָלַט and הוֹשִׁיעַ; *to preserve through* danger, *to bring safe through*; *to save* i. e. *cure* one who is sick (cf. our colloq. *bring him through*): Lk. vii. 3; pass. Mt. xiv. 36; *to save* i. e. *keep safe, keep from perishing*: Acts xxvii. 43; *to save out of danger, rescue*: Acts xxviii. 1; ἐκ τῆς θαλάσσης, ibid. 4; — as very often in Grk. writ. (see exx. in Win. De verb. comp. etc. Pt. v. p. 9 sq.) with specification of the person to whom or of the place to which one is brought safe through: πρὸς Φήλικα, Acts xxiii. 24; ἐπὶ τὴν γῆν, Acts xxvii. 44; εἴς τι, 1 Pet. iii. 20.*

1296   **δια-ταγή**, -ῆς, ἡ, (διατάσσω), *a* purely bibl. [2 Esdr. iv. 11] and eccl. word (for which the Greeks use διάταξις), *a disposition, arrangement, ordinance*: Ro. xiii. 2; ἐλάβετε τὸν νόμον εἰς διαταγὰς ἀγγέλων, Acts vii. 53, ye received the law, influenced by the authority of the ordaining angels, or because ye thought it your duty to receive what was enjoined by angels (*at the ministration of angels* [nearly i. q. as being the ordinances etc.], similar to εἰς ὄνομα δέχεσθαι, Mt. x. 41; see εἰς, B. II. 2 d.; [W. 398 (372), cf. 228 (214), also B. 151 (131)]). On the

Jewish opinion that angels were employed as God's assistants in the solemn proclamation of the Mosaic law, cf. Deut. xxxiii. 2 Sept.; Acts vii. 38; Gal. iii. 19; Heb. ii. 2; Joseph. antt. 15, 5, 3; [Philo de somn. i. § 22; Bp. Lghtft. Com. on Gal. l. c.].*

1297   **διά-ταγμα**, -τος, τό, (διατάσσω), *an injunction, mandate*: Heb. xi. 23 [Lchm. δόγμα]. (2 Esdr. vii. 11; Add. Esth. iii. 14 [in Tdf. ch. iii. fin., line 14]; Sap. xi. 8; Philo, decal. § 4; Diod. 18, 64; Plut. Marcell. c. 24 fin.; [al.].) *

1298   **δια-ταράσσω**, or -ττω: 1 aor. pass. διεταράχθην; *to agitate greatly, trouble greatly*, (Lat. *perturbare*): Lk. i. 29. (Plat., Xen., al.) *

1299   **δια-τάσσω**; 1 aor. διέταξα; pf. inf. διατεταχέναι (Acts xviii. 2 [not Tdf.]); Pass., pf. ptcp. διατεταγμένος; 1 aor. ptcp. διαταχθείς; 2 aor. ptcp. διαταγείς; Mid., pres. διατάσσομαι; fut. διατάξομαι; 1 aor. διεταξάμην; (on the force of διά cf. Germ. *v e r ordnen*, [Lat. *d i s ponere*, Win. De verb. comp. etc. Pt. v. p. 7 sq.]); *to arrange, appoint, ordain, prescribe, give order*: τινί, Mt. xi. 1; 1 Co. xvi. 1; foll. by acc. with inf., Lk. viii. 55; Acts xviii. 2 [here T τεταχ. Tr mrg. br. δια-; τινί foll. by inf. 1 Co. ix. 14]; τί, pass., ὁ νόμος διαταγεὶς δι᾽ ἀγγέλων (see διαταγή): Gal. iii. 19, (Hes. opp. 274); τινί τι, pass.: Lk. iii. 13; xvii. 9 [Rec.], 10; Acts xxiii. 31. Mid.: 1 Co. vii. 17; οὕτω ἦν διατεταγμένος (cf. W. 262 (246); [B. 193 (167)]), Acts xx. 13; τινί, Tit. i. 5; τί, 1 Co. xi. 34; τινί, foll. by inf.: Acts vii. 44; xxiv. 23; [Comp.: ἐπι-διατάσσομαι.] *

1300   **δια-τελέω**, -ῶ; *to bring thoroughly to an end, accomplish*, [cf. διά, C. 2]; with the addition of τὸν βίον, τὸν χρόνον, etc., it is joined to participles or adjectives and denotes the continuousness of the act or state expressed by the ptcp. or adj. (as in Hdt. 6, 117; 7, 111; Plat. apol. p. 31 a.); oftener, however, without the accus. it is joined with the same force simply to the ptcps. or adjs.: thus ἄσιτοι διατελεῖτε ye continue fasting, constantly fast, Acts xxvii. 33 (so ἀσφαλέστερος [al. -τατος] διατελεῖ, Thuc. 1, 34; often in Xen.; W. 348 (326); [B. 304 (261)]).*

1301   **δια-τηρέω**, -ῶ; 3 pers. sing. impf. διετήρει; *to keep continually or carefully* (see διά, C. 2): Lk. ii. 51, (Gen. xxxvii. 11); ἐμαυτὸν ἔκ τινος (cf. τηρεῖν ἔκ τινος, Jn. xvii. 15), to keep one's self (pure) from a thing, Acts xv. 29; ἀπό τινος for שָׁמַר foll. by מִן, Ps. xi. (xii.) 8. (Plat., Dem., Polyb., al.) *

δια-τί, see διά, B. II. 2 a. p. 134b.   see 1223

1302; see 1223

see 1303 St.   **δια-τίθημι**: *to place separately, dispose, arrange, appoint*, [cf. διά, C. 3]. In the N. T. only in Mid., pres. διατίθεμαι; 2 aor. διεθέμην; fut. διαθήσομαι; **1.** *to arrange, dispose of, one's own affairs*; **a.** τί, of something that belongs to one (often so in prof. auth. fr. Xen. down); with dat. of pers. added, *in one's favor, to one's advantage*; hence *to assign a thing to another as his possession*: τινὶ βασιλείαν (to appoint), Lk. xxii. 29. **b.** *to dispose of by will, make a testament*: Heb. ix. 16 sq.; (Plat. legg. 11 p. 924 e.; with διαθήκην added, ibid. p. 923 c., etc.). **2.** διατίθεμαι διαθήκην τινί (כָּרַת בְּרִית אֶת פ׳), Jer. xxxviii. (xxxi.) 31 sqq.), *to make a covenant, enter into covenant, with one*, [cf. W. 225 (211); B. 148 (129 sq.)]:

Heb. viii. 10, (Gen. xv. 18); πρός τινα, Acts iii. 25; Heb. x. 16, (Deut. vii. 2); μετά τινος, 1 Macc.˜ i. 11. The Grks. said συντίθεμαι πρός τινα, αἱ πρός τινα συνθῆκαι, Xen. Cyr. 3, 1, 21. [Comp.: ἀντι-διατίθημι.]*

1304 δια-τρίβω; impf. διέτριβον; 1 aor. διέτριψα; to rub between, rub hard, (prop. Hom. Il. 11, 847, al.); to wear away, consume; χρόνον or ἡμέρας, to spend, pass time: Acts xiv. 3, 28; xvi. 12; xx. 6; xxv. 6, 14, (Lev. xiv. 8; Arstph., Xen., Plat., al.); simply to stay, tarry, [cf. B. 145 (127); W. 593 (552)]: Jn. iii. 22; xi. 54 [WH Tr txt. ἔμεινεν]; Acts xii. 19; xiv. 18 (Lchm. ed. min.); xv. 35; (Judith x. 2; 2 Macc. xiv. 23, and often in prof. auth. fr. Hom. Il. 19, 150 down).*

1305 δια-τροφή, -ῆς, ἡ, (διατρέφω to support), sustenance: 1 Tim. vi. 8. (Xen. vect. 4, 49; Menand. ap. Stob. floril. 61, 1 [vol. ii. 386 ed. Gaisf.]; Diod. 19, 32; Epict. ench. 12; Joseph. antt. 2, 5, 7; 4, 8, 21; often in Plut.; 1 Macc. vi. 49.)*

1306 δι-αυγάζω: 1 aor. διηύγασα; to shine through, (Vulg. elucesco), to dawn; of daylight breaking through the darkness of night (Polyb. 3, 104, 5, [cf. Act. Andr. 8 p. 116 ed. Tdf.]): 2 Pet. i. 19. [Plut. de plac. philos. 3, 3, 2; al. (see Soph. Lex. s. v.).]*

see 1307 & 1306 διαυγής, -ές, (αὐγή), translucent, transparent: Rev. xxi. 21, for the Rec. διαφανής. ([Aristot.], Philo, Apoll. Rh., Lcian., Plut., Themist.; often in the Anthol.) *

1307 διαφανής, -ές, (διαφαίνω to show through), transparent, translucent: Rev. xxi. 21 Rec.; see διαυγής. (Hdt., Arstph., Plat., al.) *

1308 δια-φέρω; 2 aor. διήνεγκον [but the subj. 3 pers. sing. διενέγκῃ (Mk. xi. 16), the only aor. form which occurs, can come as well fr. 1 aor. διήνεγκα; cf. Veitch s. v. φέρω, fin.]; Pass., [pres. διαφέρομαι]; impf. διεφερόμην; [fr. Hom. (h. Merc. 255), Pind. down]; **1.** to bear or carry through any place: σκεῦος διὰ τοῦ ἱεροῦ, Mk. xi. 16. **2.** to carry different ways, i. e. **a.** trans. to carry in different directions, to different places: thus persons are said διαφέρεσθαι, who are carried hither and thither in a ship, driven to and fro, Acts xxvii. 27, (Strab. 3, 2, 7 p. 144; σκάφος ὑπ᾽ ἐναντίων πνευμάτων διαφερόμενον, Philo, migr. Abr. § 27; Lcian. Hermot. 28; often in Plut.); metaph. to spread abroad: διεφέρετο ὁ λόγος τοῦ κυρίου δι᾽ ὅλης τῆς χώρας, Acts xiii. 49, (ἀγγελίας, Lcian. dial. deor. 24, 1; φήμη διαφέρεται, Plut. mor. p. 163 d.). **b.** intrans. (like the Lat. differo) to differ: δοκιμάζειν τὰ διαφέροντα to test, prove, the things that differ, i. e. to distinguish between good and evil, lawful and unlawful, Ro. ii. 18; Phil. i. 10, (διάκρισις καλοῦ τε καὶ κακοῦ, Heb. v. 14); cf. Thol. Com. on Rom. p. 111 ed. 5.; Theoph. Ant. ad Autol. p. 6 ed. Otto δοκιμάζοντες τὰ διαφέροντα, ἤτοι φῶς, ἢ σκότος, ἢ λευκὸν, ἢ μέλαν κτλ.); [al., adopting a secondary sense of each verb in the above passages, translate (cf. A. V.) to approve the things that excel; see Mey. (yet cf. ed. Weiss) on Ro. l. c.; Ellic. on Phil. l. c.]. διαφέρω τινός, to differ from one, i. e. to excel, surpass one: Mt. vi. 26; x. 31; xii. 12; Lk. xii. 7, 24, (often so in Attic auth.); τινὸς ἔν τινι, 1 Co. xv. 41; [τινὸς ουδέν, Gal. iv. 1]. **c.** impersonally, διαφέρει it makes a differ-

ence, it matters, is of importance: οὐδέν μοι διαφέρει it matters nothing to me, Gal. ii. 6, (Plat. Prot. p. 316 b. ἡμῖν οὐδὲν διαφέρει, p. 358 e.; de rep. 1 p. 340 c.; Dem. 124, 3 (in Phil. 3, 50); Polyb. 3, 21, 9; Ael. v. h. 1, 25; al.; [cf. Lob. ad Phryn. p. 394; Wetst. on Gal. l. c.]).*

1309 δια-φεύγω: [2 aor. διέφυγον]; fr. Hdt. down; to flee through danger, to escape: Acts xxvii. 42, (Prov. xix. 5; Josh. viii. 22).*

1310 δια-φημίζω; 1 aor. διεφήμισα; 1 aor. pass. διεφημίσθην; to spread abroad, blaze abroad: τὸν λόγον, Mk. i. 45; Mt. xxviii. 15 [T WH mrg. ἐφημίσθ.]; τινά, to spread abroad his fame, verbally diffuse his renown, Mt. ix. 31; in Lat. diffamare aliquem, but in a bad sense. (Rarely in Grk. writ., as Arat. phaen. 221; Dion. Hal. 11, 46; Palaeph. incred. 14, 4; [cf. Win. De verb. comp. etc. Pt. v. p. 14 sq.].) *

1311 δια-φθείρω; 1 aor. διέφθειρα; Pass., [pres. διαφθείρομαι]; pf. ptcp. διεφθαρμένος; 2 aor. διεφθάρην; Sept. very often for שָׁחַת, occasionally for חָבַל; in Grk. writ. fr. Hom. down; **1.** to change for the worse, to corrupt: minds, morals; τὴν γῆν, i. e. the men that inhabit the earth, Rev. xi. 18; διεφθαρμένοι τὸν νοῦν, 1 Tim. vi. 5, (τὴν διάνοιαν, Plat. legg. 10 p. 888 a.; τὴν γνώμην, Dion. Hal. antt. 5, 21; τοὺς ὀφθαλμούς, Xen. an. 4, 5, 12). **2.** to destroy, ruin, (Lat. perdere); **a.** to consume, of bodily vigor and strength: ὁ ἔξω ἡμῶν ἄνθρωπος διαφθείρεται [is decaying], 2 Co. iv. 16; of the worm or moth that eats provisions, clothing, etc. Lk. xii. 33. **b.** to destroy (Lat. delere): Rev. viii. 9; to kill, διαφθείρειν τοὺς etc. Rev. xi. 18.*

1312 δια-φθορά, -ᾶς, ἡ, (διαφθείρω), corruption, destruction: in the N. T. that destruction which is effected by the decay of the body after death: Acts ii. 27, 31; xiii. 34–37 [cf. W. § 65, 10], see εἴδω, I. 5 and ὑποστρέφω, 2. (Sept. for שַׁחַת; in Grk. writ. fr. Aeschyl. down.)*

1313 διά-φορος, -ον, (διαφέρω); **1.** different, varying in kind, (Hdt. and sqq.): Ro. xii. 6; Heb. ix. 10. **2.** excellent, surpassing, ([Diod.], Polyb., Plut., al.): compar. διαφορώτερος, Heb. i. 4; viii. 6.*

δια-φυλάσσω: 1 aor. inf. διαφυλάξαι; fr. Hdt. down; to guard carefully: τινά, Lk. iv. 10 fr. Ps. xc. (xci.) 11. "The seventy chose to employ this term esp. of God's providential care; cf. Gen. xxviii. 15; Josh. xxiv. 17; Ps. xl. (xli.) 3. Hence it came to pass that the later writers at the close of their letters used to write διαφυλάττοι, διαφυλάξαι ὑμᾶς ὁ θεός, cf. Theodoret. iii. pp. 800, 818, 826, (edd. Schulze, Nösselt, etc. Hal.)." Win. De verb. comp. etc. Pt. v. p. 16.*

see 1315 St. δια-χειρίζω: 1 aor. mid. διεχειρισάμην; to move by the use of the hands, take in hand, manage, administer, govern, (fr. [Andoc., Lys.], Xen. and Plato down). Mid. to lay hands on, slay, kill [with one's own hand]: τινά (Polyb. 8, 23, 8; Diod. 18, 46; Joseph., Dion. Hal., Plut., Hdian.), Acts v. 30; xxvi. 21.*

(1315α); see 5512 δια-χλευάζω; to deride, scoff, mock, ["deridere i. e. ridendo exagitare" Win.]: Acts ii. 13 G L T Tr WH. (Plat. Ax. p. 364 b.; Dem. p. 1221, 26 [adv. Polycl. 49]; Aeschin. dial. 3, 2; Polyb. 17, 4, 4; al.; eccles. writ.) Cf. Win. De verb. comp. etc. Pt. v. p. 17.*

**see
1316 St.**

δια-χωρίζω: *to separate thoroughly* or *wholly* (cf. διά, C. 2), (Arstph., Xen., Plat., al.; Sept.). Pass. pres. διαχωρίζομαι ([in reflex. sense] cf. ἀποχωρίζω) *to separate one's self, depart*, (Gen. xiii. 9, 11, 14; Diod. 4, 53): ἀπό τινος, Lk. ix. 33.*

1317   **διδακτικός, -ή, -όν,** (i. q. διδασκαλικός in Grk. writ.), *apt and skilful in teaching*: 1 Tim. iii. 2; 2 Tim. ii. 24. (διδακτικὴ ἀρετή, the virtue which renders one teachable, docility, Philo, praem. et poen. § 4; [de congressu erud. § 7].) *

1318   **διδακτός, -ή, -όν,** (διδάσκω);   1. *that can be taught* (Pind., Xen., Plat., al.).   2. *taught, instructed*, foll. by gen. *by* one [cf. W. 189 (178); 194 (182); B. 169 (147)]: τοῦ θεοῦ, by God, Jn. vi. 45 fr. Is. liv. 13; πνεύματος ἁγίου [G L T Tr WH om. ἁγίου], by the (Holy) Spirit, 1 Co. ii. 13. (νουθετήματα κείνης διδακτά, Soph. El. 344.)*

1319   **διδασκαλία, -ας, ἡ,** (διδάσκαλος), [fr. Pind. down];   1. *teaching, instruction*: Ro. xii. 7; xv. 4 (εἰς τὴν ἡμετέραν διδασκαλίαν, that we might be taught, [A. V. *for our learning*]); 1 Tim. iv. 13, 16; v. 17; 2 Tim. iii. 10, 16; Tit. ii. 7.   2. *teaching* i. e. *that which is taught, doctrine*: Eph. iv. 14; 1 Tim. i. 10; iv. 6; vi. 1, 3; 2 Tim. iv. 3; Tit. i. 9; ii. 1, 10; plur. διδασκαλίαι *teachings, precepts*, (fr. Is. xxix. 13), Mt. xv. 9; Mk. vii. 7; ἀνθρώπων, Col. ii. 22; δαιμονίων, 1 Tim. iv. 1.*

1320   **διδάσκαλος, -ου, ὁ,** (διδάσκω), *a teacher*; in the N. T. one who teaches concerning the things of God, and the duties of man;   1. of one who is fitted to teach, or thinks himself so: Heb. v. 12; Ro. ii. 20.   2. of the teachers of the Jewish religion: Lk. ii. 46; Jn. iii. 10; hence the Hebr. רַב is rendered in Greek διδάσκαλος: Jn. i. 38 (39); xx. 16; cf. below, under ῥαββί, and Pressel in Herzog xii. p. 471 sq.; [Campbell, Dissert. on the Gospels, diss. vii. pt. 2].   3. of those who by their great power as teachers drew crowds about them;   a. of John the Baptist: Lk. iii. 12.   b. of Jesus: Jn. i. 38 (39); iii. 2; viii. 4; xi. 28; xiii. 13 sq.; xx. 16; often in the first three Gospels.   4. by preëminence used of Jesus by himself, as the one who showed men the way of salvation: Mt. xxiii. 8 L T Tr WH.   5. of the apostles: ὁ διδάσκαλος τῶν ἐθνῶν, of Paul, 1 Tim. ii. 7; 2 Tim. i. 11.   6. of those who in the religious assemblies of Christians undertook the work of teaching, with the special assistance of the Holy Spirit: 1 Co. xii. 28 sq.; Eph. iv. 11; Acts xiii. 1, cf. Jas. iii. 1.   7. of false teachers among Christians: 2 Tim. iv. 3. [Hom. (h. Merc. 556), Aeschyl., al.]

1321   **διδάσκω,** impf. ἐδίδασκον; fut. διδάξω; 1 aor. ἐδίδαξα; 1 aor. pass. ἐδιδάχθην; (ΔΑΩ [cf. Vaniček p. 327]); [fr. Hom. down]; Sept. for הוֹרָה, הוֹרֵי, and esp. for לִמֵּד; *to teach*;   1. absol.   a. *to hold discourse with others in order to instruct them, deliver didactic discourses*: Mt. iv. 23; xxi. 23; Mk. i. 21; vi. 6; xiv. 49; Lk. iv. 15; v. 17; vi. 6; Jn. vi. 59; vii. 14; xviii. 20, and often in the Gospels; 1 Tim. ii. 12.   b. *to be a teacher* (see διδάσκαλος, 6): Ro. xii. 7.   c. *to discharge the office of teacher, conduct one's self as a teacher*: 1 Co. iv. 17.   2. in construction;   a. either in imitation of the Hebr. לְ לִמֵּד (Job xxi. 22), or by an irregular use of the later Greeks

(of which no well-attested example remains exc. one in Plut. Marcell. c. 12), with dat. of person : τῷ Βαλάκ, Rev. ii. 14 (acc. to the reading now generally accepted for the Rec.^bez elz τὸν Βαλ.) ; cf. B. 149 (130) ; W. 223 (209), cf. 227 (213).   b. acc. to the regular use, with acc. of pers., *to teach one*: used of Jesus and the apostles uttering in public what they wished their hearers to know and remember, Mt. v. 2; Mk. i. 22; ii. 13; iv. 2; Lk. v. 3; Jn. viii. 2; Acts iv. 2; v. 25; xx. 20; τοὺς Ἕλληνας, to act the part of a teacher among the Greeks, Jn. vii. 35; used of those who enjoin upon others to observe some ordinance, to embrace some opinion, or to obey some precept: Mt. v. 19; Acts xv. 1; Heb. viii. 11; with esp. reference to the addition which the teacher makes to the knowledge of the one he teaches, *to impart instruction, instil doctrine into one*: Acts xi. 26; xxi. 28; Jn. ix. 34; Ro. ii. 21; Col. iii. 16; 1 Jn. ii. 27; Rev. ii. 20.   c. the thing taught or enjoined is indicated by a foll. ὅτι: Mk. viii. 31; 1 Co. xi. 14; by a foll. infin., Lk. xi. 1; Mt. xxviii. 20; Rev. ii. 14; περί τινος, 1 Jn. ii. 27; ἐν Χριστῷ διδαχθῆναι, to be taught in the fellowship of Christ, Eph. iv. 21; foll. by an acc. of the thing, to teach i. e. *prescribe a thing*: διδασκαλίας, ἐντάλματα ἀνθρώπων, precepts which are commandments of men (fr. Is. xxix. 13), Mt. xv. 9; Mk. vii. 7, [B. 148 (129)]; τὴν ὁδὸν τοῦ θεοῦ, Mt. xxii. 16; Mk. xii. 14; Lk. xx. 21; ταῦτα, 1 Tim. iv. 11; ἃ μὴ δεῖ, Tit. i. 11; *to explain, expound*, a thing: Acts xviii. 11, 25; xxviii. 31; ἀποστασίαν ἀπὸ Μωϋσέως, the necessity of forsaking Moses, Acts xxi. 21.   d. with acc. of pers. and of thing, *to teach one something* [W. 226 sq. (212); B. 149 (130)]: [ἐκεῖνος ὑμᾶς διδάξει πάντα, Jn. xiv. 26]; τοῦ διδάσκειν ὑμᾶς τινα τὰ στοιχεῖα, Heb. v. 12 (where R G T Tr and others read — not so well — τίνα; [but cf. B. 260 (224) note, 268 (230) note]); ἑτέρους διδάξαι, sc. αὐτά, 2 Tim. ii. 2; hence pass. διδαχθῆναί τι [B. 188 (163); W. 229 (215)]: Gal. i. 12 (ἐδιδάχθην, sc. αὐτό), 2 Th. ii. 15.

1322   **διδαχή, -ῆς, ἡ,** (διδάσκω), [fr. Hdt. down];   1. *teaching, viz. that which is taught*: Mk. i. 27; Jn. vii. 16; Acts xvii. 19; Ro. [vi. 17]; xvi. 17; 2 Jn. 10; Rev. ii. 24; ἡ διδ. τινος, one's doctrine, i. e. what he teaches: Mt. vii. 28; xvi. 12; xxii. 33; Mk. i. 22; xi. 18; Lk. iv. 32; Jn. xviii. 19; Acts v. 28; Rev. ii. 14 sq.; ἡ διδαχή of God, τοῦ κυρίου, τοῦ Χριστοῦ, the doctrine which has God, Christ, the Lord, for its author and supporter: Jn. vii. 17; Acts xiii. 12; 2 Jn. 9; with the gen. of the object, *doctrine, teaching, concerning something*: Heb. vi. 2 [W. 187 (176); 192 (181); 551 (513)]; plur. Heb. xiii. 9.   2. [the act of] *teaching, instruction*, (cf. διδασκαλία [on the supposed distinction betw. the two words and their use in the N. T. see Ellic. on 2 Tim. iv. 2; they are associated in 2 Tim. iv. 2, 3; Tit. i. 9]): Acts ii. 42; 2 Tim. iv. 2; ἐν τῇ διδαχῇ, while he was teaching, a phrase by which the Evangelist indicates that he is about to cite some of the many words which Jesus spoke at that time, Mk. iv. 2; xii. 38; τοῦ κατὰ τὴν διδαχὴν πιστοῦ λόγου, the faithful word which is in accordance with the received (2 Tim. iii. 14) instruction, Tit. i. 9; in particular, the teaching of the διδάσκαλος (q. v. 6) in the religious assemblies of Christians: λαλεῖν ἐν διδαχῇ to speak in the way of *teaching*, in distinction from other modes of speaking in public, 1 Co. xiv. 6 ; ἔχω διδαχήν, to have something to teach, ibid. 26.*

1323   **δίδραχμον**, -ου, τό, (neut. of the adj. δίδραχμος, -ον, sc. νόμισμα; fr. δίς and δραχμή), *a didrachmon* or *doubledrachma*, a silver coin equal to two Attic drachms or one Alexandrian, or half a shekel, [about one third of a dollar] (see in ἀργύριον, 3) : Mt. xvii. 24. (Sept. often for שֶׁקֶל; [Poll., Galen].) *

1324   **δίδυμος**, -η, -ον, and -ος, -ον, *twofold, twain*, (double, Hom. Od. 19, 227; as τρίδυμος triple, τετράδυμος quadruple, ἑπτάδυμος); hence *twin* (sc. παῖς, as τρίδυμοι παῖδες, υἱοί, Germ. *Drillinge*, three born at a birth), Hebr. תְּאֹם, a surname of the apostle Thomas [cf. Luthardt on the first of the foll. pass.; B. D. s. v. Thomas] : Jn. xi. 16 ; xx. 24 ; xxi. 2. (Hom. Il. 23, 641.) *

1325   **δίδωμι** (διδῶ, Rev. iii. 9 L T WH ; [δίδω Tr, yet see *WH*. App. p. 167]), 3 pers. plur. διδόασι (Rev. xvii. 13 [not Rec.]), impv. δίδου (Mt. v. 42 R G) ; impf. 3 pers. sing. ἐδίδου, 3 pers. plur. ἐδίδουν (ἐδίδοσαν, Jn. xix. 3 L T Tr WH [see ἔχω]) ; fut. δώσω ; 1 aor. ἔδωκα [2 pers. sing. -κες, Jn. xvii. 7 Tr mrg., 8 Tr mrg.; cf. reff. s. v. κοπιάω], subjunc. δώσῃ [and δώσωμεν] fr. an imaginary indic. form ἔδωσα, [Mk. vi. 37 T Tr mrg.]; Jn. xvii. 2 (Tr mrg. WH δώσει) ; Rev. viii. 3 (L T Tr WH δώσει ; cf. *Lob.* ad Phryn. p. 720 sq.; B. 36 (31) ; W. 79 (76) ; [Veitch s. v. δίδ. fin., also *Soph.* Lex. s. v. and esp. Intr. p. 40 ; *WH*. App. p. 172]) ; pf. δέδωκα [on the interchange between the forms of the pf. and of the aor. in this verb cf. B. 199 (172)]; plpf. ἐδεδώκειν and without augm. [W. § 12, 9 ; B. 33 (29)] δεδώκειν, Mk. xiv. 44 ; and L txt. T Tr WH in Lk. xix. 15 ; 3 pers. plur. δεδώκεισαν, Jn. xi. 57; 2 aor. subjunc. 3 pers. sing. δῷ [δώῃ, Jn. xv. 16 Tr mrg.; Eph. i. 17 WH mrg. ; 2 Tim. ii. 25 L WH mrg.; δοῖ, Mk. viii. 37 T Tr WH; cf. B. 46 (40)]. *WH*. App. p. 168; *Kuenen and Cobet*, praef. p. lxi.], plur. δῶμεν, δῶτε, δῶσιν, optat. 3 pers. sing. δῴη for δοίη, Ro. xv. 5 ; [2 Th. iii. 16] ; 2 Tim. i. 16, 18 ; [ii. 25 T Tr WH txt.; Eph. i. 17 R G ; iii. 16 R G] and elsewhere among the variants ([cf. W. § 14, 1 g.; B. 46 (40), cf. § 139, 37 and 62]; see [*WH*. App. u. s.; *Tdf.* Proleg. p. 122;] *Lob.* ad Phryn. p. 346; [*Kühner* § 282 Anm. 2; *Veitch* s. v. δίδωμι ad fin.]), impv. δός, δότε, inf. δοῦναι, ptcp. δούς ; Pass., pf. δέδομαι ; 1 aor. ἐδόθην ; 1 fut. δοθήσομαι ; cf. B. 45 (39) sq.; [WH u. s.]. In the Sept. times without number for נָתַן, sometimes for שׂוּם; and for Chald. יְהַב; [fr. Hom. down]; *to give*;

A. absolutely and generally : μακάριόν ἐστι μᾶλλον διδόναι, ἢ λαμβάνειν, Acts xx. 35.

B. In construction;   **I.** τινί τι, *to give something to some one*, — in various senses;   **1.** *of one's own accord to give one something*, to his advantage; *to bestow, give as a gift* : Mt. iv. 9 ; Lk. i. 32 ; xii. 32, and often ; δόματα [cf. B. 148 (129)], Mt. vii. 11 ; Lk. xi. 13 ; Eph. iv. 8 (Ps. lxvii. (lxviii.) 19) ; τὰ ὑπάρχοντα what thou hast τοῖς πτωχοῖς, Mt. xix. 21 ; χρήματα, Acts xxiv. 26.

2. *to grant, give to one asking, let have* : Mt. xii. 39 ; xiv. 7 sq.; xvi. 4 ; xx. 23 ; Mk. vi. 22, 25 ; viii. 12 ; x. 40 ; Lk. xi. 29 ; xv. 16 ; Jn. xi. 22 ; xiv. 16 ; xv. 16 ; xvi. 23 ; Acts iii. 6 ; Jas. i. 5 ; [noteworthy is 1 Jn. v. 16 δώσει (sc. prob. ὁ θεός) αὐτῷ ζωὴν τοῖς ἁμαρτάνουσιν etc., where αὐτῷ seems to be an ethical dat. and τ. ἁμαρ. dependent on the verb; see B. 133 (116) note, cf. 179 (156) ; W. 523 (487), cf. 530 (494)] ; in contradistinction from what one claims: Jn. iii. 27 ; xix. 11.   **3.** *to supply, furnish*, necessary things : as ἄρτον τινί, Mt. vi. 11 ; Lk. xi. 3 ; Jn. vi. 32, 51 ; τροφήν, Mt. xxiv. 45 ; βρῶσιν, Jn. vi. 27 ; besides in Mt. xxv. 15, 28 sq.; Mk. ii. 26 ; iv. 25 ; Lk. v. 4 ; viii. 18 ; xii. 42 ; xix. 24, 26 ; Jn. iv. 10, 14, 15 ; Eph. vi. 19.   **4.** *to give over, deliver*, i. e. **a.** *to reach out, extend, present* : as Mt. xiv. 19 ; xvii. 27 ; Mk. vi. 41 ; xiv. 22 sq.; Lk. ix. 16 ; xxii. 19 ; τὸ ψωμίον, Jn. xiii. 26 ; τὸ ποτήριον, Jn. xviii. 11 ; Rev. xvi. 19 ; τὰς χεῖρας διδόναι to give one the hand, Acts ix. 41 ; Gal. ii. 9. **b.** of a writing : ἀποστάσιον, Mt. v. 31. **c.** *to give to one's care, intrust, commit*; **aa.** something to be administered ; univ.: παντὶ ᾧ ἐδόθη πολύ, Lk. xii. 48 ; property, money, Mt. xxv. 15 ; Lk. xix. 13, 15 ; ἀμπελῶνα, a vineyard to be cultivated, Mk. xii. 9 ; Lk. xx. 9 ; τὰς κλεῖς [κλείδας] τῆς βασ. Mt. xvi. 19 ; τὴν κρίσιν, Jn. v. 22 ; κρίμα, Rev. xx. 4 ; τὴν ἐξουσίαν ἑαυτῶν, Rev. xvii. 13 [not Rec.]; τὰ ἔργα, ἵνα τελειώσω αὐτά, Jn. v. 36 ; τὸ ἔργον, ἵνα ποιήσω, Jn. xvii. 4 ; τὸ ὄνομα τοῦ θεοῦ, to be declared, Jn. xvii. 11 [not Rec., 12 T Tr WH]. **bb.** *to give* or *commit to some one something to be religiously observed* : διαθήκην περιτομῆς, Acts vii. 8 ; τὴν περιτομήν, the ordinance of circumcision, Jn. vii. 22 ; τὸν νόμον, ibid. vs. 19 ; λόγια ζῶντα, Acts vii. 38.   **5.** *to give what is due* or *obligatory, to pay* : wages or reward, Mt. xx. 4, 14 ; xxvi. 15 ; Rev. xi. 18 ; ἀργύριον, as a reward, Mk. xiv. 11 ; Lk. xxii. 5 ; taxes, tribute, tithes, etc.: Mt. xvii. 27 ; xxii. 17 ; Mk. xii. 14 (15) ; Lk. xx. 22 ; xxiii. 2 ; Heb. vii. 4 ; θυσίαν sc. τῷ κυρίῳ, Lk. ii. 24 (θυσίαν ἀποδοῦναι τῷ θεῷ, Joseph. antt. 7, 9, 1) ; λόγον, render account, Ro. xiv. 12 [L txt. Tr txt. ἀποδ.].   **6.** δίδωμι is joined with nouns denoting an act or an effect ; and **a.** the act or effect of him who gives, in such a sense that what he is said διδόναι (either absolutely or with dat. of pers.) he is conceived of as e f f e c t i n g, or as becoming its a u t h o r. Hence δίδωμι joined with a noun can often be changed into an active verb expressing the effecting of that which the noun denotes. Thus διδόναι αἶνον τῷ θεῷ is equiv. to αἰνεῖν τὸν θεόν, Lk. xviii. 43 ; ἀπόκρισίν τινι i. q. ἀποκρίνεσθαι, Jn. i. 22 ; xix. 9 ; ἐγκοπὴν δοῦναι τῷ εὐαγγελίῳ i. q. ἐγκόπτειν τὸ εὐαγγ. to hinder (the progress of) the gospel, 1 Co. ix. 12 ; ἐντολήν τινι i. q. ἐντέλλεσθαί τινι, Jn. xi. 57 ; xii. 49 ; xiii. 34 ; 1 Jn. iii. 23 ; δόξαν τινί i. q. δοξάζειν τινά (see δόξα, II.) ; ἐργασίαν, after the Lat. *operam dare, take pains*, [A. V. *give diligence*], i. q. ἐργάζεσθαι, Lk. xii. 58 ; [συμβούλιον, cf. the Lat. *consilium dare*, i. q. συμβουλεύεσθαι, Mk. iii. 6 Tr txt. WH txt.]; διαστολήν τινι i. q. διαστέλλειν τι, 1 Co. xiv. 7 ; παραγγελίαν, 1 Th. iv. 2 ; παράκλησιν, 2 Th. ii. 16 ; ἔλεος i. q. ἐλεεῖν, 2 Tim. i. 16, 18 ; ἀγάπην, show [A. V. *bestow*], 1 Jn. iii. 1 ; ἐκδίκησιν,

2 Th. i. 8; βασανισμόν, Rev. xviii. 7; ῥάπισμα i. q. ῥαπίζειν τινά, Jn. xviii. 22; xix. 3; φίλημα i. q. φιλεῖν τινα, Lk. vii. 45. or   b. the noun denotes something to be done by him to whom it is said to be given: διδόναι τινὶ μετάνοιαν, to cause him to repent, Acts v. 31; xi. 18; γνῶσιν σωτηρίας, Lk. i. 77; ἐλπίδα τινί, 2 Th. ii. 16.   7. Joined with nouns denoting strength, faculty, power, virtue, δίδωμι (τινί τι) is equiv. to to furnish, endue, (one with a thing): Lk. xxi. 15 (δώσω ὑμῖν στόμα κ. σοφίαν); Acts vii. 10; ἐξουσίαν, Mt. ix. 8; x. 1; Lk. x. 19; Jn. xvii. 2; Rev. ii. 26; vi. 8; xiii. 7; διάνοιαν, 1 Jn. v. 20; σύνεσιν, 2 Tim. ii. 7; and in the very common phrase διδόναι τὸ πνεῦμα.   [Ι΄. δ. τινί τινος to give to one (a part) of etc.: Rev. ii. 17 (G L T Tr WH) δώσω αὐτῷ τοῦ μάννα, cf. W. 198 (186); B. 159 (139).]

II. δίδωμί τι without a dative, δίδωμί τινα.   1. δίδωμί τι;   a. with the force of to cause, produce, give forth from one's self: ὑετόν, from heaven, Jas. v. 18; καρπόν, Mt. xiii. 8; Mk. iv. 7, 8 sq., (Deut. xxv. 19; Sir. xxiii. 25); σημεῖα, Mt. xxiv. 24; Mk. xiii. 22 [not Tdf.]; Acts ii. 19, (Ex. vii. 9; Deut. xiii. 1, etc.); ὑπόδειγμα, Jn. xiii. 15; φέγγος, Mt. xxiv. 29; Mk. xiii. 24, (φῶς, Is. xiii. 10); φωνήν, 1 Co. xiv. 7 sq.; διὰ τῆς γλώσσης λόγον, ibid. 9; γνώμην, to give one's opinion, to give advice, 1 Co. vii. 25; 2 Co. viii. 10.   b. διδόναι κλήρους (נָתַן גּוֹרָל, Lev. xvi. 8), to give i. e. hand out lots, sc. to be cast into the urn [see κλῆρος, 1], Acts i. 26.   c. δίδωμί τι with pred. acc.: Mt. xx. 28; Mk. x. 45, (to give up as a λύτρον), Mt. xvi. 26; Mk. xiv. 37, (to pay as an equivalent).   2. δίδωμί τινα;   a. where the noun refers to the office one bears, to appoint: κριτάς, Acts xiii. 20.   b. to cause to come forth: δίδωμι ἐκ τῆς συναγωγῆς τοῦ Σατανᾶ τῶν λεγόντων (sc. τινάς [cf. B. 158 (138); W. § 59, 4 b.]), Rev. iii. 9; so also the sea, death, Hades, are said to give (up) the dead who have been engulfed or received by them, Rev. xx. 13.   3. δίδωμί τινά τινι;   a. to give one to some one as his own: as the object of his saving care, Heb. ii. 13; to give one to some one, to follow him as a leader and master, Jn. vi. 37, 39; x. 29; xvii. 6, 9, 12 [but see B. I. 4. c. aa. above], 24; xviii. 9; in these pass. God is said to have given certain men to Christ, i. e. to have disposed them to acknowledge Christ as the author and medium of their salvation, and to enter into intimate relations with him, hence Christ calls them 'his own' (τὰ ἐμά, Jn. x. 14).   b. to give one to some one to care for his interests: Jn. iii. 16 (ἔδωκεν sc. αὐτῷ, i. e. τῷ κόσμῳ); Acts xiii. 21.   c. to give one to some one to whom he already belonged, to return: Lk. vii. 15 (ix. 42 ἀπέδωκε [so L mrg. in vii. 15]).   d. δίδωμι ἐμαυτόν τινι, to one demanding of me something, I give myself up as it were; an hyperbole for disregarding entirely my private interests, I give as much as ever I can: 2 Co. viii. 5.   4. δίδωμί τινα with a predicate acc.: ἑαυτὸν τύπον, to render or set forth one's self as an example, 2 Th. iii. 9; with a predicate of dignity, office, function, and a dat. of the person added for whose benefit some one invested with said dignity or office is given, that is, is bestowed: αὐτὸν ἔδωκεν κεφαλὴν ὑπὲρ πάντα τῇ ἐκκλησίᾳ, head over

all things to the church, Eph. i. 22; ἔδωκεν τοὺς μὲν ἀποστόλους κτλ. sc. τῇ ἐκκλησίᾳ, Eph. iv. 11. For in neither of these passages are we obliged, with many interpreters, to translate the word appointed, made, after the use of the Hebr. נָתַן; esp. since in the second Paul seems to wish to confirm the words quoted in vs. 8, ἔδωκε δόματα τοῖς ἀνθρώποις. Those in the church whom Christ has endued with gifts and functions for the common advantage the apostle reckons among the δόματα given by him after his ascension to heaven.

III. Phrases in which to the verb δίδωμι, either standing alone or joined to cases, there is added   1. an infinitive, either alone or with an accusative; δίδωμί τινι foll. by an infin. denoting the object: δίδωμί τινι φαγεῖν, give, supply, something to eat, give food [B. 261 (224); W. 318 sq. (299)], Mt. xiv. 16; xxv. 35, 42; Mk. vi. 37; v. 43; Lk. viii. 55; ix. 13; Rev. ii. 7; πιεῖν, Jn. iv. 7, 10; with the addition of an object acc. depending on the φαγεῖν or πιεῖν: Mt. xxvii. 34; Mk. xv. 23 [R G L]; with an acc. added depending on the verb δίδωμι: Jn. vi. 31; Rev. xvi. 6; foll. by an infin. indicating design [cf. B. u. s.], to grant or permit one to etc.: Lk. i. 73 sq. (δοῦναι ἡμῖν ἀφόβως λατρεύειν αὐτῷ); Jn. v. 26; Acts iv. 29; Ro. xv. 5; Eph. iii. 16; Rev. iii. 21; vi. 4; vii. 2; [foll. by εἰς with the infin.: Ro. xv. 16, cf. B. 265 (228)]; by a constr. borrowed from the Hebrew, καὶ δώσω τοῖς ... καὶ προφητεύσουσι, Rev. xi. 3; in the passive, Mt. xiii. 12; Mk. iv. 11 (ὑμῖν δέδοται γνῶναι [G L T Tr WH om. γνῶναι] to you it has been granted etc.); foll. by the acc. and inf.: δῴη [L T Tr WH δῷ] ὑμῖν ... κατοικῆσαι τὸν Χριστὸν ἐν ταῖς καρδίαις ὑμῶν, Eph. iii. 16 sq.; ἔδωκεν αὐτὸν ἐμφανῆ γενέσθαι, Acts x. 40; οὐ δώσεις τὸν ὅσιόν σου ἰδεῖν διαφθοράν (fr. Ps. xv. (xvi.) 10), Acts ii. 27; xiii. 35.   2. δίδωμί τινι, foll. by ἵνα, to grant or permit, that etc. [B. 238 (205); W. 337 (316), cf. 545 (507)]: Mk. x. 37; Rev. xix. 8. to commission, Rev. ix. 5.

IV. δίδωμί τι, or τινί τι, or τινί or τινά, foll. by a preposition with a noun (or pronoun);   1. τινὶ ἔκ τινος [cf. W. § 28, 1; B. 159 (139)]: δότε ἡμῖν (a part) ἐκ τοῦ ἐλαίου ὑμῶν, Mt. xxv. 8; ἐκ τῶν ἄρτων, easily to be supplied from the context, Mk. ii. 26; Lk. vi. 4; ἐκ τοῦ πνεύματος αὐτοῦ ἔδωκεν ἡμῖν, 1 Jn. iv. 13; otherwise in Jn. iii. 34 ὁ θεὸς οὐ δίδωσι τὸ πνεῦμα ἐκ μέτρου, by measure i. e. according to measure, moderately, [cf. W. § 51, 1 d.]; otherwise in Rev. iii. 9 δίδωμι ἐκ τῆς συναγωγῆς, (see II. 2 b. above). τινὶ ἀπό τινος: Lk. xx. 10 ἵνα ἀπὸ τοῦ καρποῦ τοῦ ἀμπελῶνος δῶσιν [L T Tr WH δώσουσιν] αὐτῷ, sc. the portion due. τί foll. by εἰς with a noun, to give something to be put into, Lk. vi. 38 μέτρον δώσουσιν εἰς τὸν κόλπον ὑμῶν (shall they give i. e. pour into your bosom), or upon, Lk. xv. 22 δότε δακτύλιον εἰς τὴν χεῖρα αὐτοῦ (put a ring on his hand); εἰς τὸν ἀγρόν for the field, to pay its price, Mt. xxvii. 10; τινί τι εἰς τὰς χεῖρας, to commit a thing to one, deliver it into one's power: Jn. xiii. 3 (Hebr. נָתַן בְּיַד פ׳, Gen. ix. 2; xiv. 20; Ex. iv. 21); εἰς τ. διάνοιαν, or ἐπὶ τὰς καρδίας (Jer. xxxviii. (xxxi.) 33), put into the mind, fasten upon the heart, Heb. viii. 10; x. 16; or εἰς τ. καρδίας with inf. of the thing, Rev. xvii. 17; (Xen. Cyr. 8, 2, 20 διδόναι τινί τι εἰς τὴν ψυχήν). ἑαυτὸν διδόναι εἰς with acc. of place, to betake one's self somewhere, to go into some place: Acts xix. 31, (εἰς τόπους παραβόλους, Polyb. 5, 14, 9; εἰς τόπους τραχεῖς, Diod. 14, 81; εἰς τὰς ἐρημίας, Diod. 5, 59; Joseph. antt. 15, 7, 7; εἰς κώμην τινά, Joseph. antt. 7, 9, 7). **2.** δίδωμί τι ἔν τινι, i. e. to be or remain in, so that it is in, [cf. W. 414 (386); B. 329 (283)]: ἐν τῇ χειρί τινος, Jn. iii. 35; ἐν ταῖς καρδίαις, 2 Co. i. 22; ἐν τῇ καρδ. τινός, 2 Co. viii. 16, (cf. 1 K. x. 24); εἰρήνην δοῦναι ἐν τῇ γῇ to bring peace to be on earth, Lk. xii. 51. **3.** δίδωμί τι ὑπέρ τινος, give up for etc. [cf. W. 383 (358) sq.]: Jn. vi. 51; ἑαυτὸν ὑπέρ τινος, Tit. ii. 14; ἑαυτὸν ἀντίλυτρον ὑπέρ τινος, 1 Tim. ii. 6; ἑαυτὸν περὶ [R W H txt. ὑπέρ; cf. περί, I. c. δ.] τῶν ἁμαρτιῶν, for sins, i. e. to expiate them, Gal. i. 4. **4.** διδόναι τινὶ κατὰ τὰ ἔργα, τὴν πρᾶξιν, to give one acc. to his works, to render to one the reward of his deeds: Rev. ii. 23 [Ps. xxvii. (xxviii.) 4]; (cf. ἀποδώσει, Mt. xvi. 27; Ro. ii. 6). **5.** Hebraistically, δέδωκα ἐνώπιόν σου θύραν ἀνεῳγμένην I have set before thee a door opened i. e. have caused the door to be open to thee, Rev. iii. 8.

[SYN. διδόναι, δωρεῖσθαι: διδ. to give in general, antithetic to λαμβάνειν; δωρ. specific, to bestow, present; διδ. might be used even of evils, but δωρ. could be used of such things only ironically; see δῶμα, fin. COMP.: ἀνα-, ἀπο-, ἀντ-απο-, δια-, ἐκ-, ἐπι-, μετα-, παρα-, προ- δίδωμι.]

1326　δι-εγείρω; 1 aor. διήγειρα; Pass., impf. διηγειρόμην [but Tr WH (T edd. 2, 7) διεγείρετο in Jn. vi. 18, cf. B. 34 (30); WH. App. p. 161]; 1 aor. ptcp. διεγερθείς; to wake up, awaken, arouse (from repose; differing from the simple ἐγείρω, which has a wider meaning): from sleep: τινά, Mk. iv. 38 [here T Tr WH ἐγείρουσιν]; Lk. viii. 24; pass., Lk. viii. 24 T Tr txt. WH; Mk. iv. 39; with the addition ἀπὸ τοῦ ὕπνου, Mt. i. 24 (L T Tr WH ἐγερθείς); from repose, quiet: in pass. of the sea, which begins to be agitated, to rise, Jn. vi. 18. Metaph. to arouse the mind; stir up, render active: 2 Pet. i. 13; iii. 1, as in 2 Macc. xv. 10, τινὰ τοῖς θυμοῖς. (Several times in the O. T. Apocr. [cf. W. 102 (97)]; Hippocr., [Aristot.], Hdian.; occasionally in Anthol.)*

see 1760　δι-ενθυμέομαι, -οῦμαι; to weigh in the mind, consider: περί τινος, Acts x. 19, for Rec. ἐνθυμ. (Besides, only in eccl. writ.)*

see 1831　δι-εξ-έρχομαι: [2 aor. διεξῆλθον]; to go out through something: διεξελθοῦσα, sc. διὰ φρυγάνων, Acts xxviii. 3 Tdf. edd. 2, 7. (Sept.; in Grk. writ. fr. [Soph., Hdt.], Eur. down.)*

1327　δι-έξ-οδος, -ου, ἡ; fr. Hdt. down; a way out through, outlet, exit: διέξοδοι τῶν ὁδῶν, Mt. xxii. 9, lit. ways through which ways go out, i. e. acc. to the context and the design of the parable places before the city where the roads from the country terminate, therefore outlets of the country highways, the same being also their entrances; [cf. Ob. 14; Ezek. xxi. 21]; the R. V. renders it partings of the highways]. The phrase figuratively represents the territory of heathen nations, into which the apostles were about to go forth, (as is well shown by Fischer, De vitiis lexx. N. T. p. 634 sqq.). Used of the boundaries of countries, it is equiv. to the Hebr. תּוֹצָאֹת, Num. xxxiv. 4 sq. 8 sq., and

often in the book of Joshua, [cf. Rieder, Die zusammengesetzten Verba u. s. w. p. 18. Others understand the crossings or thoroughfares here to represent the most frequented spots.]*

see 2058　δι-ερμηνεία, -ας, ἡ, (διερμηνεύω, q. v.), interpretation: of obscure utterances, 1 Co. xii. 10 L txt. (Not yet found elsewhere.)*

1328　δι-ερμηνευτής, -οῦ, ὁ, (διερμηνεύω, q. v.), an interpreter: 1 Co. xiv. 28 [L Tr WH mrg. ἑρμην.]. (Eccles. writ.)*

1329　δι-ερμηνεύω; impf. διηρμήνευον and (without augm. cf. B. 34 (30)) διερμήνευον (Lk. xxiv. 27 L Tr mrg.]; 1 aor. (also without augm.; so "all early Mss." Hort) διερμήνευσα (Lk. l. c. T Tr txt. WH); [pres. pass. διερμηνευόμαι]; to interpret [διά intensifying by marking transition, (cf. Germ. verdeutlichen); Win. De verb. comp. etc. Pt. v. p. 10 sq.]; **1.** to unfold the meaning of what is said, explain, expound: τί, Lk. xxiv. 27; absolutely, 1 Co. xii. 30; xiv. 5, 13, 27. **2.** to translate into one's native language: Acts ix. 36, (2 Macc. i. 36; Polyb. 3, 22, 3, and several times in Philo [cf. Siegfried, Glossar. Phil. s. v.]).*

1330　δι-έρχομαι; impf. διηρχόμην; fut. διελεύσομαι (Lk. ii. 35; see W. 86 (82); [cf. B. 58 (50)]); 2 aor. διῆλθον; pf. ptcp. διεληλυθώς (Heb. iv. 14); [fr. Hom. down]; **1.** where διά has the force of through (Lat. per; [cf. διά, C.]): to go through, pass through, [on its constructions cf. W. § 52, 4, 8]; **a.** διά τινος, to go, walk, journey, pass through a place (Germ. den Durchweg nehmen): Mt. xii. 43; xix. 24 R L Tr mrg. WH mrg.; Mk. x. 25 [Rec.st εἰσελθεῖν]; Lk. xi. 24; xviii. 25 L Tr mrg.; Jn. iv. 4; 1 Co. x. 1; διὰ μέσου αὐτῶν, through the midst of a crowd, Lk. iv. 30; Jo. viii. 59 Rec.; [διὰ μέσου (L T Tr WH δ. μέσον, see διά, B. I.) Σαμαρείας, Lk. xvii. 11]; δι᾽ ὑμῶν, i. e. διὰ τῆς χώρας ὑμῶν, 2 Co. i. 16 (where Lchm. txt. ἀπελθεῖν); [διὰ πάντων sc. τῶν ἁγίων (see πᾶς, II. 1), Acts ix. 32]. **b.** with acc. to travel the road which leads through a place, go, pass, travel through a region: Lk. xix. 1; Acts xii. 10; xiii. 6; xiv. 24; xv. 3, 41; xvi. 6; xvii. 23 (τὰ σεβάσματα); xviii. 23; xix. 1, 21; xx. 2; 1 Co. xvi. 5; Heb. iv. 14; of a thing: τὴν ψυχὴν διελεύσεται ῥομφαία, penetrate, pierce, Lk. ii. 35, (of a spear, dart, with gen. Hom. Il. 20, 263; 23, 876). **c.** absolutely: ἐκείνης sc. ὁδοῦ (δι᾽ before ἐκείνης in Rec. is spurious) ἤμελλε διέρχεσθαι, for he was to pass that way, Lk. xix. 4. **d.** with specification of the goal or limit, so that the prefix διά makes reference to the intervening space to be passed through or gone over: ἐνθάδε, Jn. iv. 15 T WH Tr mrg.; [εἰς τὴν Ἀχαίαν, Acts xviii. 27]; εἰς τὸ πέραν, to go, cross, over to the farther shore, Mk. iv. 35; Lk. viii. 22; ὁ θάνατος διῆλθεν εἰς πάντας ἀνθρώπους, passed through unto all men, so that no one could escape its power, Ro. v. 12; ἕως τινός, go even unto, etc. Lk. ii. 15; Acts ix. 38; xi. 19, 22 R G [W. 609 (566)]. **2.** where διά answers to the Latin dis [cf. διά, C.]; to go to different places (2 Chr. xvii. 9; Am. vi. 2): Acts viii. 4, 40; [x. 38]; διελθόντες ἀπὸ τῆς Πέργης having departed from Perga sc. to various places, Acts xiii. 14 [al. refer this to 1, understanding διελθόντες of passing through the extent of country]; ἐν οἷς διῆλθον *among whom* i. e. in whose country *I went about*, or visited different places, Acts xx. 25; διήρχοντο κατὰ τὰς κώμας they went about in various directions from one village to another, Lk. ix. 6; of a report, *to spread, go abroad*: διέρχεται ὁ λόγος, Lk. v. 15; Thuc. 6, 46; Xen. an. 1, 4, 7. [Syn. see ἔρχομαι.] *

1331   δι-ερωτάω : 1 aor. ptcp. διερωτήσας; *to ask through* (i. e. ask many, one after another) : τί, to find out by asking, to inquire out, Acts x. 17. (Xen., Plat., Dem., Polyb., Dio Cass. 43, 10; 48, 8.) Cf. Win. De verb. comp. etc. Pt. v. p. 15.*

1332   διετής, -ές, (δίς and ἔτος), [fr. Hdt. down], *of two years, two years old* : ἀπὸ διετοῦς sc. παιδός, Mt. ii. 16, cf. Fritzsche ad loc.; [others take διετοῦς here as neut.; see Meyer].*

1333   διετία, -ας, ἡ, (from διετής, cf. τριετία, τετραετία), *the space of two years* : Acts xxiv. 27; xxviii. 30. (Philo in Flacc. § 16; [Graec. Ven. Gen. xli. 1; xlv. 5].) *

1334   δι-ηγέομαι, -οῦμαι, [impv. 2 pers. sing. διηγοῦ, ptcp. διηγούμενος]; fut. διηγήσομαι; 1 aor. διηγησάμην; *to lead or carry a narration through to the end*, (cf. the fig. use of Germ. *durchführen*); *set forth, recount, relate in full* : absol. Heb. xi. 32; τί, *describe*, Acts viii. 33 (see γενεά, 3); τινί foll. by indir. disc., πῶς etc., Mk. v. 16; Acts ix. 27; xii. 17 [here T om. Tr br. the dat.]; foll. by ἃ εἶδον, Mk. ix. 9; ὅσα ἐποίησε or ἐποίησαν, Lk. viii. 39; ix. 10. (Arstph., Thuc., Xen., Plat., al.; Sept. often for סָפַר.) [Comp. : ἐκ-διηγέομαι.] *

see 1335 St.   δι-ήγησις, -εως, ἡ, (διηγέομαι), *a narration, narrative* : Lk. i. 1; used of the Gospel narratives also in Euseb. h. e. 3, 24, 7; 3, 39, 12; cf. *Grimm* in the Jahrbb. f. deutsche Theol. 1871, p. 36. (Plat., Aristot., Polyb.; Sir. vi. 35 (34); ix. 15, etc.; 2 Macc. ii. 32; vi. 17.) *

1336   δι-ηνεκής, -ές, (fr. διήνεγκα, διαφέρω, as the simple ἠνεκής fr. ἤνεγκα, φέρω), fr. Hom. down, *continuous* : εἰς τὸ διηνεκές, *continually*, Heb. vii. 3; x. 1, 12, 14, (δικτάτωρ ἐς τὸ διηνεκὲς ᾑρέθη, App. b. c. 1, 4).*

1337   διθάλασσος, -ον, (δίς and θάλασσα);   **1.** *resembling* [or *forming*] *two seas* : thus of the Euxine Sea, Strab. 2, 5, 22; Dion. Per. 156.   **2.** *lying between two seas*, i. e. washed by the sea on both sides (Dio Chrys. 5 p. 83) : τόπος διθάλασσος, *an isthmus* or *tongue of land*, the extremity of which is covered by the waves, Acts xxvii. 41; al. understand here a projecting reef or bar against which the waves dash on both sides; in opposition cf. Meyer ad loc. (In Clem. hom. p. 20, ed. Dressel [Ep. Petr. ad Jacob. § 14], men ἀλόγιστοι κ. ἐνδοιάζοντες περὶ τῶν τῆς ἀληθείας ἐπαγγελμάτων are allegorically styled τόποι διθάλασσοι δὲ καὶ θηριώδεις.) *

1338   δι-ικνέομαι [L WH διικν. (see I, ι)], -οῦμαι; *to go through, penetrate, pierce* : Heb. iv. 12. (Ex. xxvi. 28; Thuc., Theophr., Plut., al.; in Homer transitively, *to go through in narrating*.)*

1339   δι-ίστημι : 1 aor. διέστησα; 2 aor. διέστην; [fr. Hom. down]; *to place separately, put asunder, disjoin* ; in the mid. [or pass.] and the pf. and 2 aor. act. *to stand apart, to part, depart* : βραχὺ δὲ διαστήσαντες, sc. ἑαυτούς or τὴν ναῦν (cf. B. 47 (41)), when they had gone a little distance

viz. from the place before mentioned, i. e. having gone a little farther, Acts xxvii. 28; of time : διαστάσης ὥρας μιᾶς one hour having intervened, Lk. xxii. 59; διέστη ἀπ' αὐτῶν parted, withdrew from them, Lk. xxiv. 51.*

1340   δι-ισχυρίζομαι [L WH δισχ. (see I, ι)] : impf. διϊσχυριζόμην;   **1.** *to lean upon*.   **2.** *to affirm stoutly, assert confidently* : Lk. xxii. 59; Acts xii. 15. (Lys., Isae., Plat., Dem., Joseph. antt. 2, 6, 4; Ael. hist. an. 7, 18; Dio Cass. 57, 23; al.) *

see 2613   [δικάζω; 1 aor. pass. ἐδικάσθην; fr. Hom. down; *to judge, pass judgment* : absol. Lk. vi. 37 Tr mrg. (al. καταδικ.).*]

1341   δικαιοκρισία, -ας, ἡ, *righteous judgment* : Ro. ii. 5. (an uncert. trans. in Hos. vi. 5 [where Sept. κρίμα]; Test. xii. patr. [test. Levi § 3] p. 547, and [§ 15] p. 581, ed. Fabric.; Justin. Mart. resp. de resurrect. xi. (15) 28 p. 360 ed. tent. Otto; [Hippol. p. 801 a. ed. Migne]; Basil iii. p. 476 d. ed. Garn. or p. 694 ed. Par. alt. 1839. [Cf. W. 25; 99 (94)].) *

1342   δίκαιος, -αία, -αιον, (fr. δίκη right), [fr. Hom. down], prop. the Hebr. צַדִּיק, *observant of ἡ δίκη, righteous, observing divine and human laws* ; one who is such as he ought to be ; (Germ. *rechtbeschaffen* ; in the earlier language, whence appropriated by Luther, *gerecht* in a broad sense ; in Grk. writ. used even of physical things, as ἵππος, Xen. mem. 4, 4, 5; γῄδιον δικαιότατον, most fertile, Xen. Cyr. 8, 3, 38; [ἅρμα δίκαιον, ib. 2, 2, 26]);   **1.** in a wide sense, *upright, righteous, virtuous, keeping the commands of God*;   **a.** univ. : Mt. i. 19 (the meaning is, it was not consistent with his uprightness to expose his betrothed to public reproach); Mt. x. 41; xiii. 43, 49; xxiii. 28; xxv. 37, 46; Lk. i. 6, 17; xiv. 14; xviii. 9; xx. 20; Ro. v. 7 [cf. W. 117 (111)]; 1 Tim. i. 9; Jas. v. 6, 16; 1 Pet. iii. 12; 1 Jn. iii. 7, [10 Lchm.]; Rev. xxii. 11; opp. to ἁμαρτωλοὶ καὶ ἀσεβεῖς, 1 Pet. iv. 18; δίκαιοι καὶ ἄδικοι, Mt. v. 45; Acts xxiv. 15; used of O. T. characters noted for piety and probity : Mt. xiii. 17; [xxiii. 29]; Heb. xii. 23; thus of Abel, Mt. xxiii. 35; Heb. xi. 4; of Lot, 2 Pet. ii. 7 sq. (Sap. x. 4 sq.); of those who seem to themselves to be righteous, who pride themselves on their virtues, whether real or imaginary : Mt. ix. 13; Mk. ii. 17; Lk. v. 32; xv. 7, (Eccl. vii. 17 (16)). Joined with εὐλαβής, Lk. ii. 25 (ἤθη εὐλαβῆ κ. δίκαια, τὸ δίκαιον κ. εὐλαβές, Plat. polit. p. 311 a. b.); with ἅγιος, Mk. vi. 20; with ἀγαθός, Lk. xxiii. 50; with φοβούμενος τὸν θεόν, Acts x. 22; ἔργα δίκαια, opp. to πονηρά, 1 Jn. iii. 12. Neut. τὸ δίκαιον, *that which regard for duty demands, what is right* : 2 Pet. i. 13; plur. Phil. iv. 8; δίκαιόν ἐστι, Eph. vi. 1; Phil. i. 7; with the addition of ἐνώπιον τοῦ θεοῦ, God being judge, Acts iv. 19.   **b.** the negative idea predominating : *innocent, faultless, guiltless*, (for נָקִי, Prov. i. 11; Job ix. 23, etc.); thus used of Christ in the speech of Gentiles : Mt. xxvii. 19, 24 R G L br. Tr br. WH mrg.; Lk. xxiii. 47; αἷμα δίκαιον (Prov. vi. 17; Joel iii. 19 (24); Jon. i. 14), Mt. xxiii. 35; [xxvii. 4 Tr mrg. WH txt.]; ἡ ἐντολὴ ἁγία κ. δικαία (having no fellowship with sin [al. al., see the Comm. ad loc.]) κ. ἀγαθή, Ro. vii. 12.   **c.** preëminently, of him whose way of thinking, feeling, and acting is wholly conformed to the will of God, and who therefore needs no rectification in heart or life; in this sense Christ alone can be called δίκαιος : Acts vii. 52; xxii. 14; 1 Pet. iii. 18; 1 Jn. ii. 1; ἅγιος κ. δίκαιος, Acts iii. 14; among the rest of mankind it is rightly denied that one δίκαιος can be found, Ro. iii. 10 (Eccl. vii. 21 (20) ἄνθρωπος οὐκ ἔστι δίκαιος ἐν τῇ γῇ, ὃς ποιήσει ἀγαθὸν καὶ οὐχ ἁμαρτήσεται). of God: holy, Ro. iii. 26 (where it is to be closely rendered just or righteous, on account of the following καὶ τὸν δικαιοῦντα and the justifier or who pronounces righteous, but the substantial m e a n i n g is holy, that quality by virtue of which he hates and punishes sin); 1 Jn. ii. 29. d. contextually, approved of God, acceptable to God, (Germ. gottwohlgefällig): Ro. v. 19; with the addition ἐκ πίστεως, acceptable to God by faith [W. 136 (129)]: Ro. i. 17; Gal. iii. 11; Heb. x. 38; δίκ. παρὰ τῷ θεῷ, Ro. ii. 13.   2. In a narrower sense, rendering to each his due; and that in a judicial sense, passing just judgment on others, whether expressed in words or shown by the manner of dealing with them: Tit. i. 8; so of God recompensing men impartially according to their deeds, Rev. xvi. 5; in the same sense also in Jn. xvii. 25 (who does not award the same fate to the loving and faithful disciples of Christ and to 'the world'); 1 Jn. i. 9 (who executes the laws of his government, and therefore also the law concerning the pardon of sins); ὁ δίκαιος κριτής, of Christ, 2 Tim. iv. 8; κρίσις δικαία, Jn. v. 30; vii. 24; 2 Th. i. 5; plur., Rev. xvi. 7; xix. 2; αἱ ὁδοὶ τ. θεοῦ δίκαιαι κ. ἀληθιναί, Rev. xv. 3; neut. τὸ δίκαιον, what is due to others, Col. iv. 1; what is agreeable to justice and law, Lk. xii. 57; δίκαιον sc. ἐστίν, it is agreeable to justice, 2 Th. i. 6; accordant with deserts, Mt. xx. 4, and 7 Rec. [See reff. s. v. δικαιόω, fin.; cf. ἀγαθός, fin.] *

1343

δικαιοσύνη, -ης, ἡ, (δίκαιος); most frequently in Sept. for צֶדֶק and צְדָקָה, rarely for חֶסֶד; the virtue or quality or state of one who is δίκαιος;   1. in the broad sense, the state of him who is such as he ought to be, righteousness (Germ. Rechtbeschaffenheit); the condition acceptable to God (Germ. Gottwohlgefälligkeit);   a. univ.: λόγος τῆς δικαιοσύνης (like λόγος τῆς καταλλαγῆς, λ. τοῦ σταυροῦ), the doctrine concerning the way in which man may attain to a state approved of God, Heb. v. 13; βασιλεὺς δικαιοσύνης, the king who himself has the approbation of God, and who renders his subjects acceptable to God, Heb. vii. 2; cf. Bleek ad loc. b. integrity, virtue, purity of life, uprightness, correctness in thinking, feeling, and acting: Mt. iii. 15; v. 6, 10, 20; vi. 1 G L T Tr WH; Acts xiii. 10; xxiv. 25; Ro. vi. 13, 16, 18–20 (opp. to ἁμαρτία, ἀνομία, and ἀκαθαρσία); Ro. viii. 10 (opp. to ἁμαρτία); Ro. xiv. 17 (? [see c.]); 2 Co. vi. 7, 14 (opp. to ἀνομία, as in Xen. mem. 1, 2, 24); 2 Co. xi. 15; Eph. v. 9; vi. 14; Phil. i. 11; 1 Tim. vi. 11; 2 Tim. ii. 22; iii. 16; iv. 8; Tit. iii. 5; Heb. i. 9; xii. 11; Jas. iii. 18; 1 Pet. iii. 14; 2 Pet. ii. 5, 21; iii. 13, and very often in the O. T.; ἐν ὁδῷ δικαιοσύνης, walking in the way of righteousness i. q. an upright, righteous, man, Mt. xxi. 32; τοῦ θεοῦ, the righteousness which God demands, Mt. vi. 33; Jas. i. 20; of righteousness which manifests itself in beneficence: 2 Co. ix. 9 sq.

(cf. Tob. xiv. 11; Gesenius, Thesaur. iii. p. 1151; so Chald. צִדְקָה, Dan. iv. 24, and in the Talmud and rabbin. writ. [Buxtorf. col. 1891 (p. 941 ed. Fischer); cf.W. 32]); where δικ. καὶ ὁσιότης are connected, — Lk. i. 75; Eph. iv. 24, (Sap. ix. 3; Clem. Rom. 1 Cor. 48, 4 and occasionally in prof. writ.), — the former denotes right conduct towards men, the latter piety towards God (cf. Plat. Gorg. p. 507 b.; Grimm on Sap. p. 181 sq.; [cf. Trench § lxxxviii. p. 328 sq.; for additional exx. see Wetst. on Eph. l. c.; cf. ὅσιος]; εὐσέβεια κ. δικαιοσύνη, Diod. 1, 2); ποιεῖν τὴν δικαιοσ. to do righteousness, to live uprightly: 1 Jn. ii. 29; iii. 7; iii. 10 [not Lchm.]; and in Rev. xxii. 11 acc. to the text now accepted; in like manner ἐργάζεσθαι δικαιοσύνην, Acts x. 35; Heb. xi. 33; ζῆν τῇ δικαιοσύνῃ, to live, devote the life, to righteousness, 1 Pet. ii. 24; πληροῦν πᾶσαν δικαιοσύνην, to perform completely whatever is right, Mt. iii. 15. When affirmed of Christ, δικαιοσύνη denotes his perfect moral purity, integrity, sinlessness: Jn. xvi. 8, 10; when used of God, his holiness: Ro. iii. 5, 25 sq. c. in the writings of PAUL ἡ δικαιοσύνη has a peculiar meaning, opposed to the views of the Jews and Judaizing Christians. To understand this meaning, the foll. facts esp. must be kept in view: the Jews as a people, and very many who had become converts from among them to Christianity, supposed that they s e c u r e d the favor of God by w o r k s conformed to the requirements of the Mosaic law, as though by way of merit; and that they would thus attain to eternal salvation. But this law demands p e r f e c t obedience to all its precepts, and threatens condemnation to those who do not render such obedience (Gal. iii. 10, 12). Obedience of this kind no one has rendered (Ro. iii. 10), neither Jews nor Gentiles (Ro. i. 24 — ii. 1), — for with the latter the natural law of right written on their souls takes the place of the Mosaic law (Ro. ii. 14 sq.). On this account Paul proclaims the love of God, in that by giving up Christ, his Son, to die as an expiatory sacrifice for the sins of men he has attested his grace and good-will to mankind, so that they can hope for salvation as if they had not sinned. But the way to obtain this hope, he teaches, is only through faith (see πίστις [esp. 1 b. and d.]), by which a man appropriates that grace of God revealed and pledged in Christ; and this faith is reckoned by God to the man as δικαιοσύνη; that is to say, δ. denotes the state acceptable to God which becomes a sinner's possession through that faith by which he embraces the grace of God offered him in the expiatory death of Jesus Christ (see δικαιόω, 3 b.). In this sense ἡ δικαιοσύνη is used without an adjunct in Ro. iv. 5 sq. 11; v. 17, 21; ix. 30 sq.; Ro. xiv. 17 (? [see b.]); 1 Co. i. 30; Gal. v. 5; δικαιοσύνη θεοῦ, ἡ τοῦ θεοῦ δικαιοσύνη, the righteousness which God ascribes, what God declares to be righteousness [W. 186 (175)], Ro. i. 17; iii. 21; x. 3; by a pregnant use, equiv. to that divine arrangement by which God leads men to a state acceptable to him, Ro. x. 4; as abstract for concrete, equiv. to those whom God accounts righteous, 2 Co. v. 21; δικ. θεοῦ διὰ πίστεως, Ro. iii. 22; ἡ δικ. τῆς πίστεως, which is acquired by faith, or seen in faith, Ro.

iv. 11, 13; ἡ ἐκ θεοῦ δικαιοσ. which comes from God, i. e. is adjudged, imputed, Phil. iii. 9 (where the addition ἐπὶ τῇ πίστει depends on ἔχων, having . . . founded upon faith [cf. W. 137 (130); 392 (367); yet cf. Ellic. ad loc.]); ἡ ἐκ πίστεως δικαιοσ. which comes from faith, Ro. ix. 30; x. 6; ἡ διὰ πίστεως Χριστοῦ, Phil. iii. 9; ἡ κατὰ πίστιν δικαιοσ. according to, appropriate to, faith, Heb. xi. 7 (but it should be kept in mind that the conception of 'faith' in the Ep. to the Heb. is broader than in Paul's writings [cf. e. g. Kurtz ad loc.]); Christ is called δικαιοσύνη, as being the one without whom there is no righteousness, as the author of righteousness, 1 Co. i. 30; εἰς δικαιοσύνην, unto righteousness as the result, to obtain righteousness, Ro. x. 4, 10; ἡ πίστις λογίζεταί τινι εἰς δικαιοσύνην faith is reckoned to one for righteousness, i. e. is so taken into account, that righteousness is ascribed to it or recognized in it: Ro. iv. 3, 6, 9, 22; Gal. iii. 6; Jas. ii. 23; ἡ διακονία τῆς δικαιοσ. (see διακονία, 2 b.), 2 Co. iii. 9. Opposed to this δικαιοσύνη arising from faith is ἡ ἐκ νόμου δικαιοσ., a state acceptable to God which is supposed to result from obedience to the law, Ro. x. 5 sq.; ἡ δικ. ἐν νόμῳ relying on the law, i. e. on imaginary obedience to it, Phil. iii. 6; ἡ ἰδία δικαιοσ. and ἡ ἐμὴ δικ., such as one supposes that he has acquired for himself by his own works, Ro. x. 3; Phil. iii. 9, cf. Gal. ii. 21; iii. 21. **2.** in a closer sense, *justice*, or *the virtue which gives each one his due*; it is said to belong to God and Christ, as bestowing ἰσότιμον πίστιν upon all Christians impartially, 2 Pet. i. 1; of judicial justice, Ro. ix. 28 R G Tr mrg. in br.; κρίνειν ἐν δικαιοσύνῃ, Acts xvii. 31; Rev. xix. 11. [See reff. s. v. δικαιόω, fin.]*

1344

δικαιόω, -ῶ; fut. δικαιώσω; 1 aor. ἐδικαίωσα; Pass., [pres. δικαιοῦμαι]; pf. δεδικαίωμαι; 1 aor. ἐδικαιώθην; fut. δικαιωθήσομαι; (δίκαιος); Sept. for צָדֵק and הִצְדִּיק; **1.** prop. (acc. to the analogy of other verbs ending in όω, as τυφλόω, δουλόω) *to make δίκαιος*; *to render righteous* or *such as he ought to be*; (Vulg. *justifico*); but this meaning is extremely rare, if not altogether doubtful; ἐδικαίωσα τὴν καρδίαν μου stands for וָאֶזְכֶּה לְבָבִי in Ps. lxxii. (lxxiii.) 13 (unless *I have shown my heart to be upright* be preferred as the rendering of the Greek there). **2.** τινά, *to show*, *exhibit*, *evince*, one *to be righteous, such as he is and wishes himself to be considered* (Ezek. xvi. 51 sq.; τὴν ψυχὴν αὐτοῦ, Jer. iii. 11, and, probably, δικαιοῦν δίκαιον, Is. liii. 11); ἡ σοφία ἐδικαιώθη ἀπὸ τῶν τέκνων αὐτῆς, the wisdom taught and exemplified by John the Baptist, and by Jesus, gained from its disciples (i. e. from their life, character, and deeds) the benefit of being shown to be righteous, i. e. true and divine [cf. B. 322 (277); al. interpret, was acknowledged to be righteous on the part of (nearly i. q. by) her children; cf. B. 325 (280); see ἀπό, II. 2 d. bb.], Lk. vii. 35; Mt. xi. 19 [here T Tr txt. WH read ἔργων i. e. by her works]; Pass., of Christ: ἐδικαιώθη ἐν πνεύματι, evinced to be righteous as to his spiritual (divine [(?) cf. e. g. Ellic. ad loc., or Mey. on Ro. i. 4]) nature, 1 Tim. iii. 16; of God: ὅπως δικαιωθῇς ἐν τοῖς λόγοις σου, Ro. iii. 4 fr. Ps. l. (li.) 6 (κύριος μόνος δικαιωθήσεται, Sir. xviii. 2); pass. used re-

flexively, *to show one's self righteous*: of men, Rev. xxii. 11 Rec.; (τί δικαιωθῶμεν; Gen. xliv. 16). **3.** τινά, *to declare*, *pronounce*, one *to be just, righteous*, or *such as he ought to be*, (cf. ὁμοιόω to declare to be like, liken i. e. compare; ὁσιόω, Sap. vi. 11; ἀξιόω, which never means *to make* worthy, but *to judge* worthy, *to declare* worthy, *to treat as* worthy; see also κοινόω, 2 b.); **a.** with the negative idea predominant, *to declare guiltless* one accused or who may be accused, *acquit of a charge* or *reproach*, (Deut. xxv. 1; Sir. xiii. 22 (21), etc.; an unjust judge is said δικαιοῦν τὸν ἀσεβῆ in Ex. xxiii. 7; Is. v. 23): ἑαυτόν, Lk. x. 29; pass. οὐ δεδικαίωμαι, sc. with God, 1 Co. iv. 4; pregnantly with ἀπὸ τῶν ἁμαρτιῶν added, to be declared innocent and therefore to be absolved from the charge of sins [cf. B. 322 (277)], Acts xiii. 38 (39) (so ἀπὸ ἁμαρτίας, Sir. xxvi. 29; simply, *to be absolved*, sc. from the payment of a vow, Sir. xviii. 22 (21)); hence figuratively, by a usage not met with elsewhere, *to be freed*, ἀπὸ τῆς ἁμαρτίας, from *its dominion*, Ro. vi. 7, where cf. Fritzsche or [(less fully) Meyer]. **b.** with the positive idea predominant, *to judge, declare, pronounce, righteous and therefore acceptable*, (God is said δικαιοῦν δίκαιον, 1 K. viii. 32): ἑαυτόν, Lk. xvi. 15; ἐδικαίωσαν τὸν θεόν declared God to be righteous, i. e. by receiving the baptism declared that it had been prescribed by God rightly, Lk. vii. 29; pass. by God, Ro. ii. 13; ἐξ ἔργων ἐδικαιώθη, got his reputation for righteousness (sc. with his countrymen [but see Mey. (ed. Weiss) ad loc.]) by works, Ro. iv. 2; ἐκ τῶν λόγων, by thy words, in contrast with καταδικάζεσθαι, sc. by God, Mt. xii. 37. Especially is it so used, in the technical phraseology of Paul, respecting God who judges and declares such men as put faith in Christ to be righteous and acceptable to him, and accordingly fit to receive the pardon of their sins and eternal life (see δικαιοσύνη, 1 c.): thus absolutely, δικαιοῦν τινα, Ro. iii. 26; iv. 5; viii. 30, 33 (sc. ἡμᾶς, opp. to ἐγκαλεῖν); with the addition of ἐκ (in consequence of) πίστεως, Ro. iii. 30; Gal. iii. 8; of διὰ τῆς πίστεως, Ro. iii. 30; men are said δικαιοῦσθαι, δικαιωθῆναι, τῇ χάριτι τοῦ θεοῦ, Tit. iii. 7; δωρεὰν τῇ χάρ. τ. θεοῦ, Ro. iii. 24; πίστει, Ro. iii. 28; ἐκ πίστεως, by means of faith, Ro. v. 1; Gal. ii. 16; iii. 24; ἐν τῷ αἵματι τοῦ Χριστοῦ (as the meritorious cause of their acceptance, as the old theologians say, *faith* being the apprehending or subjective cause), Ro. v. 9; ἐν τῷ ὀνόματι τοῦ κυρίου Ἰησοῦ καὶ ἐν τῷ πνεύματι τοῦ θεοῦ ἡμῶν, by confessing the name of the Lord (which implies faith in him, Ro. x. 10, cf. 2 Co. iv. 13), and by the Spirit of God (which has awakened faith in the soul), 1 Co. vi. 11; ἐν Χριστῷ through Christ, Gal. ii. 17; Acts xiii. 39; it is vehemently denied by Paul, that a man δικαιοῦται ἐξ ἔργων νόμου, Gal. ii. 16,—with the addition ἐνώπιον αὐτοῦ, i. e. of God, Ro. iii. 20, cf. vs. 28; iv. 2, (see δικαιοσύνη, 1 c. sub fin.);—a statement which is affirmed by James in ii. 21, 24 sq. (though he says simply ἐξ ἔργων δικαιοῦται, significantly omitting νόμου); to the same purport Paul denies that a man δικαιοῦται ἐν νόμῳ, in obeying the law, or by keeping it, Gal. v. 4; with the addition παρὰ τῷ θεῷ, in the sight of God, Gal. iii. 11. **Lk.** xviii. 14 teaches that a man δικαιοῦται by deep sorrow for his sins, which so humbles him that he hopes for salvation only from divine grace.

The Pauline conceptions of δίκαιος, δικαιοσύνη, δικαιόω, are elucidated esp. by *Winzer*, De vocabulis δίκαιος, etc., in Ep. ad Rom., Lips. 1831 ; *Usteri*, Paulin. Lehrbegriff p. 86 sq. ed. 4 etc.; *Neander*, Gesch. der Pflanzung u.s.w. ii. p. 567 sqq. et passim, ed. 3, [Robinson's trans. of ed. 4, pp. 382 sqq., 417 sqq.]; *Baur*, Paulus p. 572 sqq. [(Zeller's) ed. 2, vol. ii. 145–183 ; Eng. trans. vol. ii. p. 134 sqq.]; *Rauwenhoff*, Disquisitio etc., Lugd. Bat. 1852 ; *Lipsius*, Die paulin. Rechtfertigungslehre, Lpz. 1853 ; *Schmid*, Bibl. Theologie des N. T. p. 562 sqq. ed. 2, [p. 558 sqq. ed. 4 ; Eng. trans. p. 495 sq.]; *Ernesti*, Vom Ursprung der Sünde u.s.w. i. p. 152 sqq.; *Messner*, Lehre der Apostel, p. 256 sqq., [summary by S. R. Asbury in Bib. Sacr. for 1870, p. 140 sq.]; *Jul.* Köstlin in the Jahrbb. für deutsche Theol. 1856 fasc. 1 p. 85 sqq.; *Wieseler*, Commentar ü. d. Br. an d. Galater, p. 176 sqq. [see in Schaff's Lange's Rom. p. 122 sq.]; *Kahnis*, Lutherische Dogmatik, Bd. i. p. 592 sqq.; *Philippi*, Dogmatik, v. 1 p. 208 sqq.; *Weiss*, Bibl. Theol. des N. T. § 65 ; *Ritschl*, Die christl. Lehre v. d. Versöhnung u. Rechtf. ii. 318 sqq.; *Pfleiderer*, Paulinismus, p. 172 sqq. [Eng. trans. vol. i. p. 171 sqq.; but esp. Dr. *Jas.* Morison, Crit. Expos. of the Third Chap. of the Ep. to the Rom. pp. 163–198. On the patristic usage see *Reithmayr*, Galaterbrief, p. 177 sq.; *Cremer*, Wörterbuch, 4te Aufl. p. 285 ; *Suicer*, Thesaur. s. v.].

In classic Grk. δικαιόω (Ionic δικαιέω, Hdt.) is 1. i. q. δίκαιον νομίζω, to deem right or fair: τί, often foll. by the inf.; to choose what is right and fair, hence univ. to choose, desire, decide : Hdt., Soph., Thuc., al. 2. with acc. of person, τὸ δίκαιον ποιῶ τινα to do one justice, in a bad sense, viz. to condemn, punish, one : Hdt., Thuc., Plat., al.; hence δικαιοῦσθαι, to have justice done one's self, to suffer justice, be treated rightly, opp. to ἀδικεῖσθαι, Aristot. eth. Nic. 5, 9, 11 p. 1136ᵃ, 18 sqq. (In like manner the German rechtfertigen in its early forensic use bore a bad sense viz. to try judicially (so for ἀνακρίνειν, Acts xii. 19 Luther), then condemn; execute judgment, esp. put to death.) *

1345　δικαίωμα, -τος, τό, (fr. δικαιόω ; ὃ δεδικαίωται or τὸ δεδικαιωμένον), Sept. very often for חֹק, חֻקָּה, and מִשְׁפָּט ; for מִצְוָה, Deut. xxx. 16 ; 1 K. ii. 3 ; plur. occasionally for פִּקּוּדִים ; 1. that which has been deemed right so as to have the force of law; a. what has been established and ordained by law, an ordinance : univ. of an appointment of God having the force of law, Ro. i. 32 ; plur. used of the divine precepts of the Mosaic law : τοῦ κυρίου, Lk. i. 6 ; τοῦ νόμου, Ro. ii. 26 ; τὸ δικαίωμα τοῦ νόμου, collectively, of the (moral) precepts of the same law, Ro. viii. 4 ; δικαιώματα λατρείας, precepts concerning the public worship of God, Heb. ix. 1 ; δικαιώματα σαρκός, laws respecting bodily purity [(?) cf. vii. 16], ibid. vs. 10. b. a judicial decision, sentence ; of G o d — either the favorable judgment by which he acquits men and declares

them acceptable to him, Ro. v. 16 ; or unfavorable: sentence of condemnation, Rev. xv. 4, (punishment, Plat. legg. 9, 864 e.). 2. a righteous act or deed : τὰ δικαιώματα τῶν ἁγίων, Rev. xix. 8 (τῶν πατέρων, Bar. ii. 19) ; ἑνὸς δικαίωμα, the righteous act of one (Christ) in his giving himself up to death, opp. to the first sin of Adam, Ro. v. 18, (Aristot. eth. Nic. 5, 7, 7 p. 1135ᵃ, 12 sq. καλεῖται δὲ μᾶλλον δικαιοπράγημα τὸ κοινόν, δικαίωμα δὲ τὸ ἐπανόρθωμα τοῦ ἀδικήματος, [cf. rhet. 1, 13, 1 and Cope's note on 1, 3, 9]). [Cf. reff. in δικαιόω.] *

δικαίως, adv., [fr. Hom. down]; 1. justly, agreeably **1346** to right: κρίνειν (see δίκαιος, 2), 1 Pet. ii. 23 ; to suffer, Lk. xxiii. 41. 2. properly, as is right : 1 Co. xv. 34. 3. uprightly, agreeably to the law of rectitude : 1 Th. ii. 10 (ὁσίως καὶ δικαίως, as Plat. rep. 1 p. 331 a. [cf. Trench § lxxxviii. p. 328]) ; Tit. ii. 12.*

δικαίωσις, -εως, ἡ, (fr. δικαιόω, equiv. to τὸ δικαιοῦν, the **1347** act τοῦ δικαιοῦντος ; in extra-bibl. writ. fr. Thuc. on, the justification or defence of a cause ; sentence of condemnation ; judgment in reference to what is just), the act of God's declaring men free from guilt and acceptable to him ; adjudging to be righteous, [A. V. justification]: διὰ τὴν δικαίωσιν ἡμῶν, because God wished to declare us righteous, Ro. iv. 25 ; εἰς δικαίωσιν ζωῆς, unto acquittal, which brings with it the bestowment of life, Ro. v. 18. [Cf. reff. in δικαιόω.] *

δικαστής, -οῦ, ὁ, (δικάζω), a judge, arbitrator, umpire : **1348** Lk. xii. 14 [here crit. texts κριτήν] ; Acts vii. 27 (fr. Ex. ii. 14) ; Acts vii. 35. (Sept. for שֹׁפֵט ; in Grk. writ. fr. [Aeschyl. and] Hdt. on.) *

[SYN. δικαστής, κριτής: acc. to etymol. and classic usage δ. is the more dignified and official term ; κ. gives prominence to the mental process, whether the ' judge ' be a magistrate or not. Schmidt ch. 18, 6.]

δίκη, -ης, ἡ, [allied with δείκνυμι, Curtius § 14], fr. **1349** Hom. down ; 1. custom, usage, [cf. Schmidt ch. 18, 4 cf. 3]. 2. right, justice. 3. a suit at law. 4. a judicial hearing, judicial decision, esp. a sentence of condemnation ; so in Acts xxv. 15 [L T Tr WH καταδίκην]. 5. execution of the sentence, punishment, (Sap. xviii. 11 ; 2 Macc. viii. 11) : δίκην ὑπέχειν, Jude 7 ; δίκην τίνειν (Soph. El. 298 ; Aj. 113 ; Eur. Or. 7), to suffer punishment, 2 Th. i. 9. 6. the goddess Justice, avenging justice : Acts xxviii. 4, as in Grk. writ. often fr. Hes. theog. 902 on ; (of the avenging justice of God, personified, Sap. i. 8, etc.; cf. Grimm ad loc. and Com. on 4 Macc. p. 318, [he cites 4 Macc. iv. 13, 21 ; viii. 13, 21 ; ix. 9 ; xi. 3 ; xii. 12 ; xviii. 22 ; Philo adv. Flacc. § 18 ; Euseb. h. e. 2, 6, 8]).*

δίκτυον, -ου, τό, [perhaps fr. ΔΙΚΕΙΝ to cast, cf. Etym. **1350** Magn. col. 275, 21], a net : Mt. iv. 20 sq.; Mk. i. 18 sq.; Lk. v. 2, 4–6 ; Jn. xxi. 6, 8, 11. (Hom. et sqq.)*

[SYN. δίκτυον, ἀμφίβληστρον, σαγήνη : δ. seems to be the general name for nets of all kinds ; whereas ἀμφ. and σαγ. designate specifically nets for fishing : — the former a casting-net, generally pear-shaped ; the latter a seine or drag-net. Cf. Trench § lxiv.; B.D. s. v. Net.]

δίλογος, -ον, (δίς and λέγω) ; 1. saying the same thing **1351** twice, repeating : Poll. 2, 118 p. 212 ed. Hemst.; whence διλογεῖν and διλογία, Xen. de re equ. 8, 2. **2.** *double-tongued, double in speech, saying one thing with one person, another with another* (with intent to deceive): 1 Tim. iii. 8.*

1352 **διό,** conjunction i. q. δι' ὅ, [fr. Thuc. and Plato down], *wherefore, on which account*: Mt. xxvii. 8; Lk. i. 35; vii. 7; Acts x. 29; Ro. i. 24; ii. 1; 1 Co. xii. 3; 2 Co. vi. 17; Heb. iii. 7; Jas. i. 21; 1 Pet. i. 13, and often. [Cf. W. 445 (414); B. 233 (200); on Paul's use, see Ellic. on Gal. iv. 31.]

1353 **δι-οδεύω**: impf. διώδευον; [1 aor. διώδευσα]; **1.** *to pass* or *travel through*: τόπον τινά, Acts xvii. 1; (Sept., Polyb., Plut., al.). **2.** *to travel hither and thither, go about*: with κατὰ πόλιν καὶ κώμην added, *through city and village*, Lk. viii. 1.*

1354 **Διονύσιος, -ου, ὁ,** *Dionysius,* an Athenian, a member of the Areopagus, converted to Christianity by Paul's instrumentality: Acts xvii. 34. [Cf. B.D. s. v.]*

1355 **διό-περ,** conjunction, (fr. διό and the enclitic particle πέρ [q. v.]), [fr. Thuc. down]; *on which very account,* [A. V. *wherefore*]: 1 Co. viii. 13 [Treg. διό περ]; x. 14; xiv. 13 where L T Tr WH διό.*

1356 **διοπετής, -ές,** (fr. Διός of Zeus, and πέτω for πίπτω; in prof. writ. also διϊπετής), *fallen from Zeus,* i. e. *from heaven*: τὸ διοπετές, sc. ἄγαλμα (which is expressed in Eur. Iph. T. 977; Hdian. 1, 11, 2 [1 ed. Bekk.; cf. W. 234 (219); 592 (551)]), an image of the Ephesian Artemis which was supposed to have fallen from heaven, Acts xix. 35; [cf. Meyer ad loc.; Farrar, St. Paul, ii. 13 sq.].*

see 2735 **διόρθωμα, -τος, τό,** (fr. διορθόω to set right); *correction, amendment, reform*: Acts xxiv. 2 (3) L T Tr WH for R G κατορθωμάτων. (Hippocr., Aristot., Polyb. 3, 13; Plut. Num. 17; Diog. Laërt. 10, 121; [cf. *Lob.* ad Phryn. p. 250 sq.].) *

1357 **δι-όρθωσις, -εως, ἡ,** (fr. διορθόω); **1.** prop. in a physical sense, *a making straight,* restoring to its natural and normal condition something which in some way protrudes or has got out of line, as (in Hippocr.) broken or misshapen limbs. **2.** of acts and institutions, *reformation*: καιρὸς διορθώσεως a season of reformation, or the perfecting of things, referring to the times of the Messiah, Heb. ix. 10. (Aristot. Pol. 3, 1, 4 [p. 1275ᵇ, 13]; νόμου, de mund. 6 p. 400ᵇ, 29; [cf. Joseph. c. Ap. 2, 20, 2]; Polyb. 3, 118, 12 τῶν πολιτευμάτων, Diod. 1, 75 τῶν ἁμαρτημάτων, Joseph. antt. 2, 4, 4; b. j. 1, 20, 1; al.; [cf. *Lob.* ad Phryn. p. 250 sq.].) *

1358 **δι-ορύσσω**; Pass., 1 aor. inf. διορυχθῆναι (Mt. xxiv. 43 T Tr WH; Lk. xii. 39 T WH Tr mrg.); 2 aor. inf. διορυγῆναι, [cf. WH. App. p. 170; fr. Hom. down]; *to dig through*: a house (Xen. symp. 4, 30; Job xxiv. 16 Sept.), Mt. xxiv. 43; Lk. xii. 39; absol. Mt. vi. 19 sq. [W. 594 (552); B. 146 (127)].*

see 2203 ~-[Διός, see Δίς.]

1359 **Διόσ-κουροι** (Phrynichus prefers the form Διόσκοροι; in earlier Attic the dual τὼ Διοσκόρω was more usual, cf. *Lob.* ad Phryn. p. 235), **-ων, οἱ,** (fr. Διός of Zeus, and κοῦρος or κόρος boy, as κόρη girl), *Dioscuri,* the name

given to Castor and [(Polydeuces, the Roman)] Pollux, the twin sons of Zeus and Leda, tutelary deities of sailors: Acts xxviii. 11 [R. V. *The Twin Brothers*; cf. B.D. s. v. Castor and Pollux].*

1360 **δι-ότι,** conjunction, equiv. to διὰ τοῦτο, ὅτι; **1.** *on this account that, because,* [cf. W. 445 (415)]: Lk. ii. 7; xxi. 28; Acts [xiii. 35, where R G διό]; xvii. 31 Rec.; xx. 26 T WH Tr mrg.; xxii. 18; 1 Co. xv. 9; Gal. ii. 16 (L T Tr WH ὅτι); Phil. ii. 26; 1 Th. ii. 8; iv. 6; Heb. xi. 5, 23; Jas. iv. 3; 1 Pet. i. 16, 24; ii. 6 [Rec. διὸ καί]. **2.** *for* (cf. Fritzsche on Ro. i. 19, vol. i. p. 57 sq.; [per contra Mey. ad loc.; Ellic. on Gal. ii. 16; (cf. Jebb in Vincent and Dickson, Modern Greek etc. ed. 2, App. § 80, 3)]): Lk. i. 13; Acts x. 20 Rec.; xviii. 10; Ro. i. 19, 21; iii. 20; viii. 7; (1 Th. ii. 18 L T Tr WH for R G διό); [1 Pet. i. 16ᵇ Tdf. From Hdt. down.]*

1361 **Διοτρεφής** [L WH -τρέφης; cf. Chandler §§ 634, 637], **ὁ,** (fr. Διός and τρέφω, nourished by Zeus, or foster-child of Zeus), *Diotrephes,* a Christian man, but proud and arrogant: 3 Jn. vs. 9 sq. [Cf. B. D. (esp. Am. ed.) s. v.]*

1362 **διπλόος (-οῦς), -όη (-ῆ), -όον (-οῦν),** [fr. Hom. down], *twofold, double*: 1 Tim. v. 17; Rev. xviii. 6; διπλότερος (a compar. found also in Appian. hist. praef. § 10, from the positive form διπλός [B. 27 (24)]) ὑμῶν, *twofold more than yourselves,* Mt. xxiii. 15 [(cf. Just. M. dial. 122)].*

1363 **διπλόω, -ῶ:** [1 aor. ἐδίπλωσα]; (διπλόος); *to double*: διπλώσατε αὐτῇ [only R G] διπλᾶ [τὰ δ. T Tr WH br.] i. e. *return to her double, repay in double measure the evils she has brought upon you,* Rev. xviii. 6 [R.V. *double unto her the double*]. (Xen. Hell. 6, 5, 19; Plut. Cam. 41; Diog. Laërt. 6, 22.) *

1364 **δίς,** adv., [Curtius § 277; fr. Hom. down], *twice*: Mk. xiv. 30, 72; δὶς τοῦ σαββάτου twice in the week, Lk. xviii. 12; καὶ ἅπαξ καὶ δίς (see ἅπαξ, c.), Phil. iv. 16; 1 Th. ii. 18. In the phrase δὶς ἀποθανόντα, Jude 12, δίς is not equiv. to *completely, absolutely*; but the figure is so adjusted to the fact, that men are represented as twice dead in a moral sense, first as not having yet been regenerated, and secondly as having fallen from a state of grace; see ἀποθνήσκω, I. 4; [but cf. the various interp. as given in (Mey.) Huther or in Schaff's Lange (Fronm.) ad loc. In the Babyl. Talm. (Ber. 10 a.) we read, 'Thou art dead here below, and thou shalt have no part in the life to come'].*

see 2203 **Δίς,** an unused nominat. for Ζεύς, gen. Διός, acc. Δία (Δίαν, Acts xiv. 12 Tdf. ed. 7; see in ἄρρην and B. 14 (373)), *Zeus, Jupiter,* the supreme divinity in the belief of Greeks and Romans; the father of gods and men: Acts xiv. 12 sq. (2 Macc. vi. 2.) [Cf. Ζεύς.] *

see 3461 **δισ-μυριάς, -άδος, ἡ,** *twice ten thousand, two myriads*: Rev. ix. 16 L T (WH δὶς μυριάδες), for R G δύο μυριάδες.*

1365 **διστάζω:** 1 aor. ἐδίστασα; (δίς); *to doubt, waver*: Mt. xiv. 31; xxviii. 17. (Plat., [Soph.], Aristot., Plut., al.) *

1366 **δί-στομος, -ον,** (δίς and στόμα), *having a double mouth,* as a river, Polyb. 34, 10, 5; [ὁδοί i. e. branching, Soph. O. C. 900]. As στόμα is used of the edge of a sword and of other weapons, so δίστομος has the meaning *two-edged*: used of a sword in Heb. iv. 12; Rev. i. 16; ii. 12, and

acc. to Schott in xix. 15 ; also Judges iii. 16 ; Prov. v. 4 ;
Ps. cxlix. 6 ; Sir. xxi. 3 ; ξίφος, Eur. Hel. 983.*

1367   **δισ-χίλιοι**, -αι, -α, *two thousand* : Mk. v. 13. [From
Hdt. down.] *

1368   **δι-υλίζω** [R G T Tr διϋλ. (see Υ, υ)] ; (ὑλίζω to defecate,
cleanse from dregs or filth) ; *to filter through, strain thoroughly, pour through a filter* : τὸν κώνωπα, to rid wine of a
gnat by filtering, *strain out*, Mt. xxiii. 24. (Amos vi. 6
διυλισμένος οἶνος, Artem. oneir. 4, 48 ἔδοξαν διυλίζειν
πρότερον τὸν οἶνον, Dioscor. 2, 86 διὰ ῥάκους λινοῦ διυλισθέν
[et passim ; Plut. quaest. conviv. 6, 7, 1, 5] ; Archyt. ap.
Stob. floril. i. p. 13, 40 metaph. θεὸς εἰλικρινῆ καὶ διυλι-
σμέναν ἔχει τὴν ἀρετάν.) *

1369   **διχάζω** : 1 aor. inf. διχάσαι ; (δίχα) ; *to cut into two parts,
cleave asunder, dissever* : Plat. polit. p. 264 d. ; metaph.
διχάζω τινὰ κατά τινος, to set one at variance with [lit.
against] another : Mt. x. 35. [Cf. *Fischer*, De vitiis
lexx. etc. p. 334 sq.] *

1370   **διχοστασία**, -ας, ἡ, (διχοστατέω to stand apart), *dissension, division* ; plur. : Ro. xvi. 17 ; 1 Co. iii. 3 [Rec.] ;
Gal. v. 20. (Occasionally in Grk. writ. fr. Solon in Dem.
p. 423, 4 and Hdt. 5, 75 on ; [1 Macc. iii. 29].) *

1371   **διχοτομέω**, -ῶ : fut. διχοτομήσω ; (διχοτόμος cutting in
two) ; *to cut into two parts* (Ex. xxix. 17) : Mt. xxiv. 51 ;
Lk. xii. 46, — in these passages many suppose reference
to be made to that most cruel mode of punishment, in use
among the Hebrews (1 S. xv. 33) and other ancient nations
(see *Win.* RWB. s. v. Lebensstrafen ; [B. D. s. v. Punishments, III. b. 3 ; esp. Wetstein on Mt. l. c.]), by which
criminals and captives were cut in two. But in the text
the words which follow, and which imply that the one
thus *'cut asunder'* is still surviving, oppose this interpretation ; so that here the word is more fitly translated *cut
up by scourging, scourge severely*, [but see Meyer on Mt.
l. c.]. (Occasionally in Grk. writ. fr. Plato down.) *

1372   **διψάω**, -ῶ, subjunc. pres. 3 pers. sing. διψᾷ (Jn. vii. 37 ;
Ro. xii. 20 ; often so fr. the Maced. age on for the Attic
διψῇ, cf. W. § 13, 3 b. ; [B. 44 (38)] ; *Lob.* ad Phryn. p.
61) ; fut. διψήσω ; 1 aor. ἐδίψησα ; (δίψα thirst) ; [fr.
Hom. down] ; *to thirst* ; **1.** absolutely, *to suffer thirst ;
suffer from thirst* : prop., Mt. xxv. 35, 37, 42, 44 ; Jn. iv.
15 ; xix. 28 ; Ro. xii. 20 ; 1 Co. iv. 11 ; figuratively, those
are said *to thirst* who painfully feel their want of, and
eagerly long for, those things by which the soul is re-
freshed, supported, strengthened : Jn. iv. 13 sq. ; vi. 35 ;
vii. 37 ; Rev. vii. 16 ; xxi. 6 ; xxii. 17 ; (Sir. xxiv. 21 (20) ;
li. 24). **2.** with an acc. of the thing desired : τὴν δικαιοσύνην, Mt. v. 6, (Ps. lxii. (lxiii.) 2 ; in the better Grk.
writ. with gen. ; cf. W. § 30, 10 b. ; [B. 147 (129)] ; ἐλευθερίας, Plat. rep. 8 p. 562 c. ; τιμῆς, Plut. Cat. maj. 11 ; al. ;
cf. W. 17).*

1373   **δίψος**, -εος (-ους), τό, *thirst* : 2 Co. xi. 27. [From Thuc.
down, for the older δίψα.] *

1374   **δίψυχος**, -ον, (δίς and ψυχή), *double-minded* ; **a.** *wavering, uncertain, doubting* : Jas. i. 8, (οἱ δίψυχοι καὶ οἱ
διστάζοντες περὶ τῆς τοῦ θεοῦ δυνάμεως, Clem. Rom. 1 Cor.
11, 2 ; ταλαίπωροί εἰσιν οἱ δίψυχοι, οἱ διστάζοντες τὴν ψυχήν
[al. τῇ ψυχῇ], ibid. 23, 3 ; μὴ γίνου δίψυχος ἐν προσευχῇ

σου, εἰ ἔσται ἢ οὐ, Constt. apostol. 7, 11 ; μὴ γίνου δίψυχος
ἐν προσευχῇ σου, μακάριος γὰρ ὁ μὴ διστάσας, Ignat. ad
Heron. 7 ; [cf. reff. in Müller's note on Barn. ep. 19, 5]).
b. *divided in interest* sc. between God and the world :
Jas. iv. 8. Not found in prof. writ. [Philo, frag. ii. 663].*

1375   **διωγμός**, -οῦ, ὁ, (διώκω), *persecution* : Mt. xiii. 21 ; Mk. iv.
17 ; x. 30 ; Acts viii. 1 ; xiii. 50 ; Ro. viii. 35 ; plur., 2 Co.
xii. 10 ; 2 Th. i. 4 ; 2 Tim. iii. 11. [Fr. Aeschyl. down.] *

1376   **διώκτης**, -ου, ὁ, (διώκω), *a persecutor* : 1 Tim. i. 13.
Not found in prof. writ.*

1377   **διώκω** ; impf. ἐδίωκον ; fut. διώξω (Mt. xxiii. 34 ; Lk.
xxi. 12 ; Jn. xv. 20 ; 2 S. xxii. 38 ; Sap. xix. 2 ; a rarer
form for the more com. Attic διώξομαι, cf. Bttm. Ausf.
Spr. ii. 154 ; W. 84 (80) ; [B. 53 (46) ; esp. Veitch s. v. ;
Rutherford, New Phryn. p. 377]) ; 1 aor. ἐδίωξα ; Pass.,
[pres. διώκομαι] ; pf. ptcp. δεδιωγμένος ; 1 fut. διωχθήσομαι ;
(fr. δίω to flee) ; Sept. commonly for רָדַף ; **1.** *to make
to run or flee, put to flight, drive away* : (τινὰ) ἀπὸ πόλεως
εἰς πόλιν, Mt. xxiii. 34, cf. x. 23 Grsb. **2.** *to run swiftly
in order to catch some person* or *thing, to run after* ; absol.
(Hom. Il. 23, 344 ; Soph. El. 738, etc. ; διώκειν δρόμῳ,
Xen. an. 6, 5, 25 ; cf. 7, 2, 20), *to press on* : fig. of one
who in a race runs swiftly to reach the goal, Phil. iii. 12
(where distinguished fr. καταλαμβάνειν, [cf. Hdt. 9, 58 ;
Lcian. Hermot. 77]), vs. 14. *to pursue* (in a hostile
manner) : τινά, Acts xxvi. 11 ; Rev. xii. 13. Hence,
3. in any way whatever *to harass, trouble, molest* one ;
to persecute, (cf. Lat. *persequor*, Germ. *verfolgen*) : Mt.
v. 10–12, 44 ; x. 23 ; Lk. xxi. 12 ; [xi. 49 WH Tr mrg.] ;
Jn. v. 16 ; xv. 20 ; Acts vii. 52 ; ix. 4 sq. ; xxii. 4, 7 sq. ;
xxvi. 14 sq. ; Ro. xii. 14 ; 1 Co. iv. 12 ; xv. 9 ; 2 Co. iv.
9 ; Gal. i. 13, 23 ; iv. 29 ; v. 11 ; Phil. iii. 6 ; 2 Tim. iii.
12 ; Pass. with a dat. denoting the cause, *to be maltreated,
suffer persecution on account of something*, Gal. vi. 12
[here L mrg. T read διώκονται (al. -κωνται), see *WH.* App.
p. 169 ; on the dat. see W. § 31, 6 c. ; B. 186 (161)].
4. without the idea of hostility, *to run after, follow after* :
some one, Lk. xvii. 23. **5.** metaph. with acc. of thing,
to pursue i. e. *to seek after eagerly, earnestly endeavor to
acquire* : Ro. ix. 30 (distinguished here fr. καταλαμβάνειν) ; 1 Tim. vi. 11 ; 2 Tim. ii. 22, (in both pass. opp. to
φεύγειν) ; νόμον δικαιοσύνης, Ro. ix. 31, (Prov. xv. 9 ; τὸ δίκαιον, Deut. xvi. 20 ; Sir. xxvii. 8, where distinguished fr.
καταλαμβάνειν) ; τ. φιλοξενίαν, Ro. xii. 13 ; τὰ τῆς εἰρήνης,
Ro. xiv. 19 [here L mrg. Tr mrg. WH mrg. T read διώκομεν (for the διώκωμεν of al.), see *WH.* App. p. 169] ; τ.
ἀγάπην, 1 Co. xiv. 1 ; τὸ ἀγαθόν, 1 Th. v. 15 ; εἰρήνην, Heb.
xii. 14 ; 1 Pet. iii. 11 (here joined with ζητεῖν τι) ; times
without number in Grk. writ. (fr. Hom. Il. 17, 75 διώκειν
ἀκίχητα on ; as τιμάς, ἀρετήν, τὰ καλά, [cf. W. 30.]).
[Comp. : *ἐκ-, κατα-διώκω*.] *

1378   **δόγμα**, -τος, τό, (fr. δοκέω, and equiv. to τὸ δεδογμένον),
an opinion, a judgment (Plat., al.), *doctrine, decree, ordinance* ; **1.** of public *decrees* (as τῆς πόλεως, Plat. legg.
1 p. 644 d. ; of the Roman Senate, [Polyb. 6, 13, 2] ;
Hdian. 7, 10, 8 [5 ed. Bekk.]) : of rulers, Lk. ii. 1 ; Acts
xvii. 7 ; Heb. xi. 23 Lchm., (Theodot. in Dan. ii. 13 ; iii.
10 ; iv. 3 ; vi. 13, etc., — where the Sept. use other words).

2. of the rules and requirements of the law of Moses, 3 Macc. i. 3; διατήρησις τῶν ἁγίων δογμάτων, Philo, alleg. legg. i. § 16; carrying a suggestion of severity, and of threatened punishment, τὸν νόμον τῶν ἐντολῶν ἐν δόγμασι, the law containing precepts in the form of decrees [A. V. *the law of commandments* contained *in ordinances*], Eph. ii. 15; τὸ καθ' ἡμῶν χειρόγραφον τοῖς δόγμασι equiv. to τὸ τοῖς δόγμασι (dat. of instrument) ὃν καθ' ἡμῶν, the bond against us by its decrees, Col. ii. 14; cf.W. § 31, 10 Note 1, [B. 92 (80); on both pass. see Bp. Lghtft. on Col. l. c.]. 3. of certain decrees of the apostles relative to right living: Acts xvi. 4. (Of all the precepts of the Christian religion: βεβαιωθῆναι ἐν τοῖς δόγμασιν τοῦ κυρίου καὶ τῶν ἀποστόλων, Ignat. ad Magnes. 13, 1; of the precepts ('sentences' or tenets) of philosophers, in the later prof. writ.: Cic. acad. 2, 9, 27 de suis decretis, quae philosophi vocant *dogmata*.) [On the use of the word in general, see Bp. Lghtft. as above; (cf. 'Teaching' etc. 11, 3).]*

δογματίζω: *to decree, command, enjoin, lay down an ordinance*: Diod. 4, 83, etc.; Esth. iii. 9; 2 Macc. x. 8 [etc.]; Sept. (not Theodot.) Dan. ii. 13; Pass. [pres. δογματίζομαι]; *ordinances are imposed upon me, I suffer ordinances to be imposed upon me*: Col. ii. 20 [R. V. *do ye subject yourselves to ordinances*]; cf. W. § 39, 1 a.; B. 188 (163); Mey. or Bp. Lghtft. ad loc.].*

δοκέω, -ῶ; impf. ἐδόκουν; 1 aor. ἔδοξα; (akin to δέχομαι or δέκομαι, whence δόκος an assumption, opinion, [cf. Lat. *decus, decet, dignus*; Curtius § 15; cf. his Das Verbum, i. pp. 376, 382]); [fr. Hom. down]. 1. *to be of opinion, think, suppose*: foll. by acc. with inf., Mk. vi. 49 [R G L Tr]; 2 Co. xi. 16; 1 Co. xii. 23; with an inf. relating to the same subject as that of δοκέω itself, Lk. viii. 18 (ὃ δοκεῖ ἔχειν); xxiv. 37 (ἐδόκουν πνεῦμα θεωρεῖν); Jn. v. 39; xvi. 2; Acts xii. 9; xxvii. 13; 1 Co. iii. 18; vii. 40; viii. 2; x. 12; xiv. 37; Gal. vi. 3; Phil. iii. 4; Jas. i. 26; μὴ δόξητε λέγειν ἐν ἑαυτοῖς do not suppose that ye may think, Mt. iii. 9; cf. Fritzsche ad loc. foll. by ὅτι, Mt. vi. 7; xxvi. 53; [Mk. vi. 49 T WH]; Lk. xii. 51; xiii. 2, 4; xix. 11; Jn. v. 45; xi. 13, [31 T Tr WH]; xiii. 29; xx. 15; 1 Co. iv. 9; 2 Co. xii. 19; Jas. iv. 5. so used that the object is easily understood from the context: Mt. xxiv. 44 (ᾗ ὥρᾳ οὐ δοκεῖτε ὁ υἱὸς τοῦ ἀνθρώπου ἔρχεται); Lk. xii. 40; xvii. 9 [R G L br. Tr mrg. br.]; forming a parenthesis in the midst of a question: πόσῳ, δοκεῖτε, χείρονος ἀξιωθήσεται τιμωρίας; Heb. x. 29; (Arstph. Acharn. 12 πῶς τοῦτ' ἔσεισέ μου, δοκεῖς, τὴν καρδίαν; Anacr. 40, 15 [i. e. 35 (33), 16] πόσον, δοκεῖς, πονοῦσιν, ἔρως, ὅσους σὺ βάλλεις;). [Syn. see ἡγέομαι, fin.] 2. intrans. *to seem, be accounted, reputed*: Lk. x. 36; xxii. 24; Acts xvii. 18; xxv. 27; 1 Co. xii. 22; 2 Co. x. 9; Heb. xii. 11; ἔδοξα ἐμαυτῷ δεῖν πρᾶξαι, I seemed to myself, i. e. I thought, Acts xxvi. 9 [cf. B. 111 (97)]; οἱ δοκοῦντες ἄρχειν those that are accounted to rule, who are recognized as rulers, Mk. x. 42; οἱ δοκοῦντες εἶναί τι those who are reputed to be somewhat (of importance), and therefore have influence, Gal. ii. 6, [9], (Plat. Euthyd. p. 303 c.); simply, οἱ δοκοῦντες those highly esteemed, of repute, looked up to, influential, Gal. ii. 2 (often in Grk.

writ. as Eur. Hec. 295, where cf. Schäfer; [cf. W. § 45, 7]). By way of courtesy, things certain are sometimes said δοκεῖν, as in Heb. iv. 1 (cf. Cic. offic. 3, 2, 6 ut tute tibi defuisse *videare*); 1 Co. xi. 16 [but cf. Mey. ad loc.]; cf. W. § 65, 7 c. 3. impers. δοκεῖ *it seems to me*; i. e. a. *I think, judge*: thus in questions, τί σοι (ὑμῖν) δοκεῖ; Mt. xvii. 25; xviii. 12; xxi. 28; xxii. 17, 42; xxvi. 66; Jn. xi. 56; κατὰ τὸ δοκοῦν αὐτοῖς as seemed good to them, Heb. xii. 10, (Lcian. Tim. § 25, and παρὰ τὸ δοκοῦν ἡμῖν, Thuc. 1, 84). b. ἔδοξέ μοι *it seemed good to, pleased, me*; *I determined*: foll. by inf., Lk. i. 3; Acts xv. 22, 25, 28, 34 Rec.; also often in Grk. writ. COMP.: εὐ-, συν- εὐ- δοκέω.*

[SYN. δοκεῖν 2, φαίνεσθαι: φαίν. (primarily of luminous bodies) makes reference to the actual external appearance, generally correct but possibly deceptive; δοκ. refers to the subjective judgment, which may or may not conform to the fact. Hence such a combination as δοκεῖ φαίνεσθαι is no pleonasm. Cf. Trench § lxxx.; Schmidt ch. 15.]

δοκιμάζω; [fut. δοκιμάσω]; 1 aor. ἐδοκίμασα; Pass., [pres. δοκιμάζομαι]; pf. δεδοκίμασμαι; (δόκιμος); Sept. chiefly for בָּחַן; as in Grk. writ. fr. [Hdt., Thuc.], Xen. and Plat. on, *to try*; 1. *to test, examine, prove, scrutinize* (to see whether a thing be genuine or not), as metals: χρυσίον διὰ πυρός (Isocr. p. 240 d. [i. e. Panathen. § 14]; ad Demon. p. 7 b. [here Bekk. βασανίζομεν]; Sept., Prov. viii. 10; Sir. ii. 5; Sap. iii. 6; ἄργυρον, Prov. xvii. 3, [cf. Zech. xiii. 9]), 1 Pet. i. 7; other things: Lk. xii. 56; xiv. 19; 2 Co. viii. 8; Gal. vi. 4; 1 Th. ii. 4; v. 21; τὰ διαφέροντα, Ro. ii. 18; Phil. i. 10, [al. refer these pass. to 2; see διαφέρω, 2 b.]; men, 1 Tim. iii. 10 (in the pass.); ἑαυτόν, 1 Co. xi. 28; 2 Co. xiii. 5, (cf. ἐξετάζειν ἑαυτόν, Xen. mem. 2, 5, 1 and 4); θεόν, Heb. iii. 9 (R G, fr. Ps. xciv. (xcv.) 9; on the sense of the phrase see πειράζω, 2 d. β.); τὰ πνεύματα, foll. by εἰ *whether* etc. 1 Jn. iv. 1; foll. by indir. disc., Ro. xii. 2; 1 Co. iii. 13; Eph. v. 10. 2. *to recognize as genuine* after examination, *to approve, deem worthy*: 1 Co. xvi. 3; τινὰ σπουδαῖον ὄντα, 2 Co. viii. 22; ἐν ᾧ δοκιμάζει for ἐν τούτῳ, ὃ δοκιμάζει in that which he approves, deems right, Ro. xiv. 22; δεδοκιμάσμεθα ὑπὸ τοῦ θεοῦ πιστευθῆναι τὸ εὐαγγέλιον we have been approved by God to be intrusted with the business of pointing out to men the way of salvation, 1 Th. ii. 4; οὐκ ἐδοκίμασαν τὸν θεὸν ἔχειν ἐν ἐπιγνώσει they did not think God worthy to be kept in knowledge, Ro. i. 28. [On δοκιμάζω (as compared with πειράζω) see Trench § lxxiv.; Cremer s. v. πειράζω. COMP.: ἀποδοκιμάζω.]*

δοκιμασία, -ας, ἡ, *a proving, putting to the proof*: πειράζειν ἐν δοκιμασίᾳ to tempt by proving, Heb. iii. 9 L T Tr WH. ([Lys.], Xen., Plat., Dem., Polyb., Plut., al.; λίθος δοκιμασίας, Sir. vi. 21.)*

δοκιμή, -ῆς, ἡ, (δόκιμος); 1. in an active sense, *a proving, trial*: θλίψεως, through affliction, 2 Co. viii. 2. 2. *approvedness, tried character*: Ro. v. 4; 2 Co. ii. 9; Phil. ii. 22; τῆς διακονίας, exhibited in the contribution, 2 Co. ix. 13. 3. *a proof* [objectively], *a specimen of tried worth*: 2 Co. xiii. 3. (Diosc. 4, 186 (183); occasionally in eccl. writ.)*

1379

1380

1381

see 1381

1382

1383   δοκίμιον, -ου, τό, (δοκιμή);   **1.** i. q. τὸ δοκιμάζειν, *the proving*: τῆς πίστεως, Jas. i. 3.   **2.** *that by which something is tried* or *proved, a test*: Dion. Hal. ars rhet. 11; γλῶσσα γεύσεως δοκίμιον, Longin. de sublim. 32, 5; δοκίμιον δὲ στρατιωτῶν κάματος, Hdian. 2, 10, 12 [6 ed. Bekk.]; in Sept. of a crucible or furnace for smelting: Prov. xxvii. 21; Ps. xi. (xii.) 7.   **3.** equiv. to δοκιμή, 2: ὑμῶν τῆς πίστεως, your proved faith, 1 Pet. i. 7. This word is treated of fully by Fritzsche in his Präliminarien u.s.w. pp. 40, 44.*

1384   δόκιμος, -ον, (δέχομαι); fr. Hdt. down;   **1.** prop. *accepted*, particularly of coins and metals, Gen. xxiii. 16; 2 Chr. ix. 17; Lcian. Herm. 68, etc.; hence univ. *proved, tried*: in the N. T. one who is of tried faith and integrity [R. V. *approved*], Ro. xvi. 10 (τὸν δόκιμον ἐν Χριστῷ, the approved servant of Christ); 1 Co. xi. 19; 2 Co. x. 18; xiii. 7; 2 Tim. ii. 15 (παριστάναι ἑαυτὸν δόκιμον τῷ θεῷ); Jas. i. 12.   **2.** *accepted* i. q. *acceptable, pleasing*: εὐάρεστος τῷ θεῷ κ. δόκιμος [L mrg. -μοις] τοῖς ἀνθρώποις, Ro. xiv. 18.*

1385   δοκός, -οῦ, ἡ, (fr. δέκομαι for δέχομαι, in so far as it has the idea of bearing [cf. Curtius § 11]); fr. Hom. down; *a beam*: Mt. vii. 3–5; Lk. vi. 41 sq.*

1386   δόλιος, -α, -ον, (δόλος); fr. Hom. on; *deceitful*: 2 Co. xi. 13.*

1387   δολιόω: (δόλιος); *to deceive, use deceit*: in Ro. iii. 13, fr. Ps. v. 10, impf. ἐδολιοῦσαν an Alexandrian form for ἐδολίουν, see Lob. ad Phryn. p. 349; W. § 13, 2 f.; Mullach p. 16; B. 43 (37); [cf. ἔχω]. (Not found in prof. writ.; [Numb. xxv. 18; Ps. civ. (cv.) 25. Cf. W. 26 (25)].) *

1388   δόλος, -ου, ὁ, (fr. δέλω to catch with a bait [(?)]; Lat. *dolus*, cf. Curtius § 271]; see δελεάζω above); prop. *bait*, Hom. Od. 12, 252; a lure, snare; hence *craft, deceit, guile*: Mt. xxvi. 4; Mk. xiv. 1; vii. 22; Jn. i. 47 (48); Acts xiii. 10; 2 Co. xii. 16; Ro. i. 29; 1 Th. ii. 3 (οὐκ ἔστι ἐν δόλῳ, there is no deceit under it); 1 Pet. ii. [1], 22, and Rev. xiv. 5 Rec., after Is. liii. 9; λαλεῖν δόλον to speak deceitfully (Ps. xxxiii. (xxxiv.) 14), 1 Pet. iii. 10.*

1389   δολόω, -ῶ; (δόλος);   **1.** *to ensnare*: Hes., Hdt. and succeeding writers.   **2.** *to corrupt*, ([βδέλλιον and λίβανον, Dioscor. 1, 80. 81]; τὸν οἶνον, Lcian. Hermot. 59): τὸν λόγον τοῦ θεοῦ, divine truth by mingling with it wrong notions, 2 Co. iv. 2. [Cf. Trench § lxii. and see καπηλεύω.] *

1390   δόμα, -τος, τό, (δίδωμι), *a gift*: Mt. vii. 11; Lk. xi. 13; Eph. iv. 8; Phil. iv. 17. (Plat. def. p. 415 b.; Plut.; often in Sept., chiefly for מַתָּנָה.) Cf. Fritzsche on Mt. p. 291 sq. [who quotes Varro de ling. Lat. l. iv. p. 48 ed. Bip. "dos erit pecunia si nuptiarum causa data: haec Graece δωτίνη, ita enim hoc Siculi: ab eodem Donum. Nam Graece ut ipsi δῶρον, ut alii δόμα, et ut Attici δόσις."].*

[SYN. δόμα, δόσις, δῶρον, δωρεά: δόσ. act. a giving, pass. thing given, cf. medical "dose"; δῶρ. specific "present," yet not always a gratuitous or wholly unsuggestive of recompense; but δωρεά differs from δῶρ. in denoting a gift which is also a gratuity, hence of the benefactions of a sover-

eign; a δόσις θεοῦ is what God confers as possessor of all things; a δωρεὰ θεοῦ is an expression of his favor; a δῶρον θεοῦ is something which becomes the recipient's abiding possession. Philo de cherub. § 25, says πάνυ ἐκδήλως παριστάς (Num. xxviii. 2), ὅτι τῶν ὄντων τὰ μὲν χάριτος μέσης ἠξίωται, ἡ καλεῖται δόσις, τὰ δὲ ἀμείνονος, ἧς ὄνομα οἰκεῖον δωρεά. Again, de leg. alleg. iii. § 70 (on the same bibl. pass.), διατηρήσεις ὅτι δῶρα δομάτων διαφέρουσι· τὰ μὲν γὰρ ἔμφασιν μεγέθους τελείων ἀγαθῶν δηλοῦσιν ... τὰ δὲ εἰς βραχύτατον ἔσταλται κτλ. Hence δόμα, δόσις, *gift*; δωρεά, δῶρον, *benefaction, bounty*, etc.; yet cf. e. g. Test. xii. Patr. test. Zab. § 1 ἐγώ εἰμι Ζαβουλών, δόσις ἀγαθὴ τοῖς γονεῦσί μου, with Gen. xxx. 20 δεδώρηται ὁ θεός μοι δῶρον καλὸν ... κ. ἐκάλεσε τὸ ὄνομα αὐτοῦ Ζαβουλών. Cf. Schmidt ch. 106.]

1391   δόξα, -ης, ἡ, (δοκέω), [fr. Hom. down], Sept. most freq. for כָּבוֹד, several times for הוֹד, הָדָר, etc.;

I. *opinion, judgment, view*: in this sense very often in prof. writ.; but in the Bible only in 4 Macc. v. 17 (18).

II. *opinion, estimate*, whether good or bad, concerning some one; but (like the Lat. *existimatio*) in prof. writ. generally, in the sacred writ. always, *good opinion* concerning one, and as resulting from that, *praise, honor, glory*: Lk. xiv. 10; Heb. iii. 3; 1 Pet. v. 4; opp. to ἀτιμία, 2 Co. vi. 8; opp. to αἰσχύνη, Phil. iii. 19; joined with τιμή, Ro. ii. 7, 10; 1 Pet. i. 7; 2 Pet. i. 17; δόξα τινός, praise or honor coming to some one, Lk. ii. 32; Eph. iii. 13; coming from some one, Jn. viii. 54; xii. 43; τῶν ἀνθρώπων, τοῦ θεοῦ, Jn. xii. 43; Ro. iii. 23; persons whose excellence is to redound to the glory of others are called their δόξα: thus, ὑμεῖς ἐστε ἡ δόξα ἡμῶν, 1 Th. ii. 20; ἀδελφοὶ ἡμῶν δόξα Χριστοῦ, 2 Co. viii. 23. ζητεῖν τὴν ἰδίαν δόξαν, or τ. δόξ. αὐτοῦ, Jn. vii. 18; viii. 50; of God, to endeavor to promote the glory of God, Jn. vii. 18; ζητεῖν δόξαν ἐξ ἀνθρώπων, 1 Th. ii. 6; τὴν δόξαν τ. παρὰ τοῦ θεοῦ, Jn. v. 44; λαμβάνειν δόξαν (Lat. *captare* honorem) to seek to receive, catch at glory, Jn. v. 41, 44; to receive glory, 2 Pet. i. 17; Rev. v. 12; ἡ δόξαν, the glory due [cf. W. 105 (100) sq.; B. 88 (77)]; Ellic. on Gal. i. 5, cf. B. 89 (78)], Rev. iv. 11; διδόναι δόξαν τῷ θεῷ, שׂוּם כָּבוֹד לַיהֹוָה or (Jer. xiii. 16) נָתַן, to give or ascribe glory to God, why and how being evident in each case from the context: thus, by declaring one's gratitude to God for a benefit received, Lk. xvii. 18; by not distrusting God's promises, Ro. iv. 20; by celebrating his praises, Rev. iv. 9; xi. 13; xiv. 7; [xvi. 9]; xix. 7 (τὴν δόξαν the glory due); by rendering its due honor to God's majesty, Acts xii. 23; δὸς δόξαν τῷ θεῷ, acknowledge that God knows all things, and show that you believe it by the confession you are about to make, Jn. ix. 24, cf. 1 S. vi. 5; Josh. vii. 19; Ev. Nicod. c. 14 [p. 622 ed. Thilo, 296 ed. Tdf.]; cf. Grimm on 4 Macc. i. 12. εἰς δόξαν θεοῦ, so as to honor God, to promote his glory (among men): Ro. xv. 7; 1 Co. x. 31; Phil. i. 11; ii. 11; εἰς τὴν δόξ. τ. θεοῦ, Ro. iii. 7; 2 Co. iv. 15; τῷ θεῷ πρὸς δόξαν, 2 Co. i. 20; πρὸς τὴν τοῦ κυρίου δόξαν, 2 Co. viii. 19; ὑπὲρ τῆς δόξης τοῦ θεοῦ, Jn. xi. 4; in doxologies: δόξα ἐν ὑψίστοις θεῷ, Lk. ii. 14, cf. xix. 38; αὐτῷ ἡ δόξα, Ro. xi. 36; Eph. iii. 21; 2 Pet. iii. 18; ᾧ ἡ δόξα, Ro. xvi. 27; Gal. i. 5; 2 Tim. iv. 18; Heb. xiii. 21; τῷ θεῷ ἡ δόξα, Phil. iv.

20; τιμὴ καὶ δόξα, 1 Tim. i. 17. [Even in classic Grk. δόξα is a word of wide signif., ranging from one's private opinion, fancy, to public opinion, repute, renown (κλέος; cf. the relation of φήμη to φάναι). Coupled with τιμή it denotes rather the splendid condition (evident glory), τιμή the estimate and acknowledgment of it (paid honor).]

III. As a translation of the Hebr. כָּבוֹד, in a use foreign to Grk. writ. [W. 32], splendor, brightness; **1.** properly: τοῦ φωτός, Acts xxii. 11; of the sun, moon, stars, 1 Co. xv. 40 sq.; used of the heavenly brightness, by which God was conceived of as surrounded, Lk. ii. 9; Acts vii. 55, and by which heavenly beings were surrounded when they appeared on earth, Lk. ix. 31; Rev. xviii. 1; with which the face of Moses was once made luminous, 2 Co. iii. 7, and also Christ in his transfiguration, Lk. ix. 32; δόξα τοῦ κυρίου, in Sept. equiv. to כְּבוֹד יְהוָה, in the targ. and talm. שְׁכִינָה, Shekinah or Shechinah [see BB.DD. s. v.], the glory of the Lord, and simply ἡ δόξα, a bright cloud by which God made manifest to men his presence and power on earth (Ex. xxiv. 17; xl. 28 (34) sqq., etc.): Ro. ix. 4; Rev. xv. 8; xxi. 11, 23; hence, ὁ θεὸς τῆς δόξης (God to whom belongs δόξα) ὤφθη, Acts vii. 2; Χερουβεὶν δόξης, on whom the divine glory rests (so δόξα without the article, Ex. xl. 28 (34); 1 S. iv. 22; Sir. xlix. 8), Heb. ix. 5. **2.** magnificence, excellence, preëminence, dignity, grace: βασιλείαι τοῦ κόσμου κ. ἡ δόξα αὐτῶν, i. e. their resources, wealth, the magnificence and greatness of their cities, their fertile lands, their thronging population, Mt. iv. 8; Lk. iv. 6; ἡ δόξα τῶν βασιλειῶν τῆς γῆς, Rev. xxi. [24; τῶν ἐθνῶν, ibid.] 26; used of royal state, splendid apparel, and the like: Mt. vi. 29; Lk. xii. 27, (Esth. v. 1; Joseph. antt. 8, 6, 5); glorious form and appearance: e. g. of human bodies restored to life, opp. to ἡ ἀτιμία which characterized them when they were buried, 1 Co. xv. 43; ἡ δόξα τῆς σαρκός "omne id, quod in rebus humanis magnificum dicitur" (Calvin), 1 Pet. i. 24; εἶναί τινι δόξα to be a glory, ornament, to one, 1 Co. xi. 15; univ. preëminence, excellence: 2 Co. iii. 8–11. **3.** majesty; **a.** that which belongs to God; and **α.** the kingly majesty which belongs to him as the supreme ruler; so in pass. where it is joined with βασιλεία, δύναμις, κράτος, ἐξουσία, and the like: Mt. vi. 13 Rec.; esp. in doxologies, 1 Pet. iv. 11; v. 11 R G; Jude 25; Rev. i. 6; these pass. I have preferred to distinguish fr. those cited above, II. fin., and yet in pass. similar to each other in form it is not always clear whether δόξα is used to denote praise and honor, or regal majesty, as in Rev. vii. 12 ἡ εὐλογία κ. ἡ δόξα κ. ἡ σοφία κ. ἡ εὐχαριστία κ. ἡ τιμὴ κ. ἡ ἰσχύς, Rev. xix. 1 ἡ σωτηρία κ. ἡ δόξα κ. ἡ τιμὴ κ. ἡ δύναμις; likewise in Rev. v. 12, [13]. of the judicial majesty of God as exhibited at the last day, Jude vs. 24. ἀνὴρ εἰκὼν κ. δόξα θεοῦ ὑπάρχων, whose function of government reflects the majesty of the divine ruler, 1 Co. xi. 7; (ἡ) γυνὴ δόξα ἀνδρός, because in her the preëminence and authority of her husband are conspicuous, ibid. **β.** majesty in the sense of the absolute perfection of the deity: Ro. i. 23; 2 Co. iv. 6; Heb. i. 3; 2 Pet. i. 17; 1 Pet.

iv. 14; ἐν δόξῃ i. q. ἐνδόξως, i. e. as accords with his divine perfection, Phil. iv. 19 [cf. Mey. and Bp. Lghtft. ad loc.]; of the majesty of his saving grace: Ro. ix. 23; Eph. i. 12, 14, 18; iii. 16; 1 Tim. i. 11; 2 Pet. i. 3 [W. 381 (356)]; more fully δόξα τῆς χάριτος, Eph. i. 6; ὁ πατὴρ τῆς δόξης, the Father whose characteristic is majesty, Eph. i. 17; the majesty of God as exhibited in deeds of power: Jn. xi. 40; Ro. vi. 4 (whence δόξα for יָד, Sept. Is. xii. 2; xlv. 24); hence τὸ κράτος τῆς δόξης αὐτοῦ, the might in which his majesty excels, Col. i. 11. **b.** majesty which belongs to Christ; and **α.** the kingly majesty of the Messiah, to which belongs his kingly state, the splendor of his external appearance, the retinue of angels, and the like (see in III. 1): Mk. x. 37; in this sense it is said that Christ will come hereafter to set up the Messianic kingdom ἐν τῇ δόξῃ τοῦ πατρός, clothed by the Father in kingly array, Mt. xvi. 27; Mk. viii. 38; Lk. ix. 26; μετὰ δυνάμεως κ. δόξης πολλῆς, Mt. xxiv. 30; Mk. xiii. 26; Lk. xxi. 27 cf. Mt. xxv. 31; Tit. ii. 13; 1 Pet. iv. 13; also καθίσαι ἐπὶ θρόνου δόξης αὐτοῦ, Mt. xix. 28; xxv. 31, cf. 1 S. ii. 8; ἡ δόξα τῆς ἰσχύος αὐτοῦ, the majesty of his Messianic power with which he will punish his adversaries, 2 Th. i. 9. **β.** the absolutely perfect inward or personal excellence of Christ: 2 Co. iii. 18; iv. 4; in which he excels by virtue of his nature as ὁ θεῖος λόγος, Jn. i. 14; xii. 41; of which majesty he gave tokens in the miracles he performed, Jn. ii. 11 cf. xi. 40; ὁ κύριος τῆς δόξης, 1 Co. ii. 8; Jas. ii. 1. **γ.** the majesty (glory) of angels, as apparent in their exterior brightness, Lk. ix. 26; in a wider sense, in which angels are called δόξαι as being spiritual beings of preëminent dignity: Jude vs. 8; 2 Pet. ii. 10. **4.** a most glorious condition, most exalted state; **a.** of that condition with God the Father in heaven to which Christ was raised after he had achieved his work on earth: Lk. xxiv. 26; Jn. xvii. 5 (where he is said to have been in the same condition before his incarnation, and even before the beginning of the world); ib. 22, 24; Heb. ii. 7, 9; 1 Pet. i. 11, 21; τὸ σῶμα τῆς δόξης αὐτοῦ, the body in which his glorious condition is manifested, Phil. iii. 21; ἀνελήφθη ἐν δόξῃ, was taken up (into heaven) so that he is now ἐν δόξῃ, 1 Tim. iii. 16 [cf. W. 413 (385); B. 328 (283)]. **b.** the glorious condition of blessedness into which it is appointed and promised that true Christians shall enter after their Saviour's return from heaven: Ro. viii. 18, 21; ix. 23; 2 Co. iv. 17; Col. i. 27 (twice; cf. Meyer ad loc.); iii. 4; 2 Tim. ii. 10; Heb. ii. 10; 1 Pet. v. 1; which condition begins to be enjoyed even now through the devout contemplation of the divine majesty of Christ, and its influence upon those who contemplate it, 2 Co. iii. 18; and this condition will include not only the blessedness of the soul, but also the gain of a more excellent body (1 Co. xv. 43; Phil. iii. 21); cf. Lipsius, Paulin. Rechtfertigungslehre, p. 203 sqq.; ἡ δόξα τοῦ θεοῦ, which God bestows, Ro. v. 2; 1 Th. ii. 12; δόξα τοῦ κυρ. ἡμ. Ἰησ. Χρ. the same in which Christ rejoices, 2 Th. ii. 14 (cf. Ro. viii. 17, etc.); εἰς δόξαν ἡμῶν, to render us partakers of δόξα, 1 Co. ii. 7. Cf. Weiss, Bibl. Theol. des N. T. § 76 d.*

1392   **δοξάζω**, [impf. ἐδόξαζον] ; fut. δοξάσω ; 1 aor. ἐδόξασα ; Pass., [pres. δοξάζομαι] ; pf. δεδόξασμαι ; 1 aor. ἐδοξάσθην ; (δόξα) ; Vulg. *honorifico, glorifico, clarifico* ; Sept. chiefly for כָּבֵד, several times for פָּאַר, (in Ex. xxxiv. 29 sq. 35 δοξάζεσθαι stands for קָרַן to shine) ; **1.** *to think, suppose, be of opinion,* (Aeschyl., Soph., Xen., Plat., Thuc., et sqq. ; nowhere in this sense in the sacred writings). **2.** fr. Polyb. (6, 53, 10 δεδοξασμένοι ἐπ' ἀρετῇ) on *to praise, extol, magnify, celebrate* : τινά, pass., Mt. vi. 2 ; Lk. iv. 15 ; ἑαυτόν, to glorify one's self, Jn. viii. 54 ; Rev. xviii. 7 ; τὸν λόγον τοῦ κυρίου, Acts xiii. 48 ; τὸ ὄνομα τοῦ κυρίου, Rev. xv. 4 ; τὸν θεόν, Mt. v. 16 ; ix. 8 ; xv. 31 ; Mk. ii. 12 ; Lk. v. 25 sq. ; vii. 16 ; xiii. 13 ; xvii. 15 ; xviii. 43 ; xxiii. 47 ; Acts xi. 18 ; xxi. 20 [Rec. κύριον] ; Ro. xv. 6, 9 [W. § 44, 3 b. ; 332 (311)] ; 1 Pet. ii. 12 ; iv. 14 Rec. ; with the addition of ἐπί τινι, for something, Lk. ii. 20 ; Acts iv. 21 ; 2 Co. ix. 13 ; ἐν ἐμοί, on account of me (properly, finding in me matter for giving praise [cf. W. 387 (362) sq.]), Gal. i. 24 ; ἐν τῷ ὀνόματι τούτῳ, 1 Pet. iv. 16 L T Tr WH. **3.** *to honor, do honor to, hold in honor* : τὴν διακονίαν μου, by the most devoted administration of it endeavoring to convert as many Gentiles as possible to Christ, Ro. xi. 13 ; a member of the body, 1 Co. xii. 26 ; θεόν, to worship, Ro. i. 21 ; with the adjunct ἐν τῷ σώματι, by keeping the body pure and sound, 1 Co. vi. 20 ; τῷ θανάτῳ, to undergo death for the honor of God, Jn. xxi. 19. **4.** By a use not found in prof. writ. *to make glorious, adorn with lustre, clothe with splendor* ; **a.** *to impart glory* to something, *render* it *excellent* : pf. pass. δεδόξασμαι to excel, be preëminent ; δεδοξασμένος excelling, eminent, glorious, 2 Co. iii. 10 ; δεδοξασμένη χάρα surpassing i. e. heavenly joy, [A. V. *full of glory*], 1 Pet. i. 8. **b.** *to make renowned, render illustrious,* i. e. *to cause the dignity and worth of some person* or *thing to become manifest and acknowledged* : τὸν λόγον τοῦ θεοῦ, 2 Th. iii. 1 ; Christ, the Son of God, Jn. viii. 54 ; xi. 4 ; xvi. 14 ; xvii. 10 ; God the Father, Jn. xiii. 31 sq. ; xiv. 13 ; xv. 8 ; xvii. 1, 4 ; 1 Pet. iv. 11 ; τὸ ὄνομα τοῦ θεοῦ, Jn. xii. 28. **c.** *to exalt to a glorious rank* or *condition* (Is. xliv. 23 ; lv. 5, etc. ; joined to ὑψοῦν, Is. iv. 2 ; Esth. iii. 1) : οὐχ ἑαυτὸν ἐδόξασε did not assume to himself the dignity (equiv. to οὐχ ἑαυτῷ τὴν τιμὴν ἔλαβε, vs. 4), the words γενηθῆναι ἀρχιερέα being added epexegetically (W. § 44, 1), Heb. v. 5 ; of God exalting, or rather restoring, Christ his Son to a state of glory in heaven : Jn. vii. 39 ; xii. 16, [23] ; xiii. 31 sq. ; xvii. 1, 5 ; Acts iii. 13 ; (see δόξα, III. 4 a.) ; of God bringing Christians to a heavenly dignity and condition, (see δόξα, III. 4 b.) : Ro. viii. 30. [COMP. : ἐν-, συν-δοξάζω.]*

1393   **Δορκάς**, -άδος, ἡ, (prop. a wild she-goat, a gazelle, "παρὰ τὸ δέρκω, τὸ βλέπω· ὀξυδερκὲς γὰρ τὸ ζῷον κ. εὐόμματον " Etym. Magn. [284, 6]), *Dorcas*, a certain Christian woman : Acts ix. 36, 39 ; see Ταβιθά.*

1394   **δόσις**, -εως, ἡ, (δίδωμι) ; **1.** *a giving,* [fr. Hdt. down] : λόγος δόσεως κ. λήψεως, an account of giving and receiving [i. e. debit and credit accounts ; cf. λόγος II. 3], Phil. iv. 15 ; here Paul, by a pleasant euphemism, refers to the pecuniary gifts, which the church bestow-

ing them enters in the account of expenses, but he himself in the account of receipts ; cf. Van Hengel ad loc. ; so δόσις καὶ λῆψις, of money given and received, Sir. xli. 19 ; xlii. 7 ; [Herm. mand. 5, 2, 2], and plur. Epict. diss. 2, 9, 12. **2.** *a gift,* [fr. Hom. down] : Jas. i. 17. [SYN. see δόμα, fin.]*

1395   **δότης**, -ου, ὁ, (δίδωμι), for the more usual δοτήρ, *a giver, bestower* : 2 Co. ix. 7 fr. Prov. xxii. 8. Not found elsewhere.*

1396   **δουλαγωγέω** [Rec.st -αγαγ-], -ῶ ; (δουλάγωγος, cf. παιδάγωγος) ; *to lead away into slavery, claim as one's slave,* (Diod. Sic. 12, 24, and occasionally in other later writ.) ; *to make a slave* and *to treat as a slave* i. e. *with severity, to subject to stern and rigid discipline* : 1 Co. ix. 27. Cf. Fischer, De vitiis lexicorum N. T. p. 472 sq.*

1397   **δουλεία** (Tdf. -ία, [see I, ι]), -ας, ἡ, (δουλεύω) ; *slavery, bondage, the condition of a slave* : τῆς φθορᾶς, the bondage which consists in decay [W. § 59, 8 a., cf. B. 78 (68)], equiv. to the law, the necessity, of perishing, Ro. viii. 21 ; used of the slavish sense of fear, devoid alike of buoyancy of spirit and of trust in God, such as is produced by the thought of death, Heb. ii. 15, as well as by the Mosaic law in its votaries, Ro. viii. 15 (πνεῦμα δουλείας) ; the Mosaic system is said to cause δουλεία on account of the grievous burdens its precepts impose upon its adherents : Gal. iv. 24 ; v. 1. [From Pind. down.]*

1398   **δουλεύω**, fut. δουλεύσω ; 1 aor. ἐδούλευσα ; pf. δεδούλευκα ; (δοῦλος) ; Sept. for עָבַד ; **1.** prop. *to be a slave, serve, do service* : absol., Eph. vi. 7 ; 1 Tim. vi. 2 ; τινί, Mt. vi. 24 ; Lk. xvi. 13 ; Ro. ix. 12 ; said of nations in subjection to other nations, Jn. viii. 33 ; Acts vii. 7 ; men are said δουλεύειν who bear the yoke of the Mosaic law, Gal. iv. 25 (see δουλεία). **2.** metaph. *to obey, submit to* ; **a.** in a good sense : absol. *to yield obedience,* Ro. vii. 6 ; τινί, *to obey one's commands and render to him the services due,* Lk. xv. 29 ; God : Mt. vi. 24 ; Lk. xvi. 13 ; 1 Th. i. 9 ; κυρίῳ and τῷ κυρίῳ, Acts xx. 19 ; Ro. xii. 11 (not Rec.st, see below) ; Eph. vi. 7 ; Christ : Ro. xiv. 18 ; Col. iii. 24 ; νόμῳ θεοῦ, acc. to the context, *feel myself bound to,* Ro. vii. 25 ; τοῖς θεοῖς, to worship gods, Gal. iv. 8 ; τῷ καιρῷ (Anth. 9, 441, 6), wisely adapt one's self to, Ro. xii. 11 Rec.st (see above), cf. Fritzsche ad loc. ; perform services of kindness and Christian love : ἀλλήλοις, Gal. v. 13 ; used of those who zealously advance the interests of anything : ὡς πατρὶ τέκνον σὺν ἐμοὶ ἐδούλευσεν εἰς τὸ εὐαγγέλιον equiv. to ὡς πατρὶ τέκνον δουλεύει, ἐμοὶ ἐδούλευσεν καὶ οὕτω σὺν ἐμοὶ ἐδούλ. etc. Phil. ii. 22 [W. 422 (393) ; 577 (537)]. **b.** in a bad sense, of those who become slaves to some base power, *to yield to, give one's self up to* : τῇ ἁμαρτίᾳ, Ro. vi. 6 ; νόμῳ ἁμαρτίας, Ro. vii. 25 ; ἐπιθυμίαις κ. ἡδοναῖς, Tit. iii. 3, (Xen. mem. 1, 5, 5 ; apol. Socr. 16 ; Plat. Phaedrus p. 238 e. ; Polyb. 17, 15, 16 ; Hdian. 1, 17, 22 [9 ed. Bekk.]) ; τῇ κοιλίᾳ, Ro. xvi. 18, (γαστρί, Anthol. 11, 410, 4 ; Xen. mem. 1, 6, 8 ; *abdomini servire,* Sen. de benef. 7, 26, 4 ; *ventri obedire,* Sall. [Cat. i. 1]) ; μαμωνᾷ, to devote one's self to getting wealth : Mt. vi. 24 ; Lk. xvi. 13. τοῖς στοιχείοις τοῦ κόσμου, Gal. iv. 9.*

1399, 1400 & 1401   **δοῦλος**, -η, -ον, (derived by most fr. δέω to tie, bind ;

by some fr. ΔΕΛΩ to ensnare, capture, [(?) al. al.; cf. Vaniček p. 322]); *serving, subject to*: παρεστήσατε τὰ μέλη ὑμῶν δοῦλα τῇ ἀκαθαρσίᾳ, Ro. vi. 19. Then substantively, ἡ δούλη *a female slave, bondmaid, handmaid*: τοῦ θεοῦ, τοῦ κυρίου, one who worships God and submits to him, Acts ii. 18 (fr. Joel ii. 29 (iii. 2)); Lk. i. 38, 48. ὁ δοῦλος, Sept. for עֶבֶד; **1.** *a slave, bondman, man of servile condition*; **a.** properly: opp. to ἐλεύθερος, 1 Co. vii. 21; xii. 13; Gal. iii. 28; Eph. vi. 8; Col. iii. 11; Rev. vi. 15; xiii. 16; xix. 18; opp. to κύριος, δεσπότης, οἰκοδεσπότης, Mt. x. 24; xiii. 27 sq.; Lk. xii. 46; Jn. xv. 15; Eph. vi. 5; Col. iii. 22; iv. 1; 1 Tim. vi. 1; Tit. ii. 9, and very often. **b.** metaph. **α.** *one who gives himself up wholly to another's will*, 1 Co. vii. 23; or dominion, τῆς ἁμαρτίας, Jn. viii. 34; Ro. vi. 17, 20; τῆς φθορᾶς, 2 Pet. ii. 19, (τῶν ἡδονῶν, Athen. 12 p. 531 c.; τῶν χρημάτων, Plut. Pelop. c. 3; τοῦ πίνειν, Ael. v. h. 2, 41). **β.** the δοῦλοι Χριστοῦ, τοῦ Χριστοῦ, Ἰησοῦ Χριστοῦ, are those whose service is used by Christ in extending and advancing his cause among men: used of apostles, Ro. i. 1; Gal. i. 10; Phil. i. 1; 2 Tim. ii. 24; Tit. i. 1; Jas. i. 1; 2 Pet. i. 1; of other preachers and teachers of the gospel, Col. iv. 12; 2 Tim. ii. 24; Jude vs. 1; of the true worshippers of Christ (who is κύριος πάντων, Acts x. 36), Eph. vi. 6. the δοῦλοι τοῦ θεοῦ, עַבְדֵי יְהֹוָה, are those whose agency God employs in executing his purposes: used of apostles, Acts iv. 29; xvi. 17; of Moses (Josh. i. 1), Rev. xv. 3; of prophets (Jer. vii. 25; xxv. 4), Rev. i. 1; x. 7; xi. 18; of all who obey God's commands, his true worshippers, Lk. ii. 29; Rev. ii. 20; vii. 3; xix. 2, 5; xxii. 3, 6; (Ps. xxxiii. (xxxiv.) 23; lxviii. (lxix.) 37; lxxxviii. (lxxxix.) 4, 21). **γ.** δοῦλός τινος, devoted to another to the disregard of one's own interests: Mt. xx. 27; Mk. x. 44; strenuously laboring for another's salvation, 2 Co. iv. 5. **2.** *a servant, attendant*, (of a king): Mt. xviii. 23, 26 sqq. [SYN. see διάκονος.]

1402 δουλόω, -ῶ: fut. δουλώσω; 1 aor. ἐδούλωσα; pf. pass. δεδούλωμαι; 1 aor. pass. ἐδουλώθην; (δοῦλος); [fr. Aeschyl. and Hdt. down]; *to make a slave of, reduce to bondage*; **a.** prop.: τινά, Acts vii. 6; [τούτῳ καὶ [yet T WH om. Tr br. καὶ] δεδούλωται to him he has also been made a bondman, 2 Pet. ii. 19. **b.** metaph.: ἐμαυτόν τινι give myself wholly to one's needs and service, make myself a bondman to him, 1 Co. ix. 19; δουλοῦσθαί τινι, to be made subject to the rule of some one, e. g. τῇ δικαιοσύνῃ, τῷ θεῷ, Ro. vi. 18, 22; likewise ὑπό τι, Gal. iv. 3; δεδουλωμένος οἴνῳ, wholly given up to, enslaved to, Tit. ii. 3 (δουλεύειν οἴνῳ, Liban. epist. 319); δεδούλωμαι ἔν τινι, to be under bondage, held by constraint of law or necessity, in some matter, 1 Co. vii. 15. [COMP.: κατα-δουλόω.]*

1403 δοχή, -ῆς, ἡ, (δέχομαι to receive as a guest), *a feast, banquet*, [cf. our *reception*]: δοχὴν ποιῶ, Lk. v. 29; xiv. 13. (i. q. מִשְׁתֶּה, Gen. [xxi. 8]; xxvi. 30; Esth. i. 3; v. 4 sqq.; Athen. 8 p. 348 f.; Plut. moral. p. 1102 b. [i. e. non posse suav. vivi etc. 21, 9].)*

1404 δράκων, -οντος, ὁ, (apparently fr. δέρκομαι, 2 aor. ἔδρακον; hence δράκων prop. equiv. to ὀξὺ βλέπων [Etym. Magn. 286, 7; cf. Curtius § 13]); Sept. chiefly for תַּנִּין,

a dragon, a great serpent, a fabulous animal, (so as early as Hom. Il. 2, 308 sq., etc.). From it, after Gen. iii. 1 sqq., is derived the fig. description of the devil in Rev. xii. 3–17; xiii. 2, 4, 11; xvi. 13; xx. 2. [Cf. *Baudissin*, Studien zur semitisch. Religionsgesch. vol. i. (iv. 4) p. 281 sqq.]*

δράμω, to run, see τρέχω.   see 5143

1405 δράσσομαι; *to grasp with the hand, to take*: τινά, 1 Co. iii. 19 [B. 291 (250); W. 352 (330)]. (In Grk. writ. fr. Hom. down; Sept.)*

1406 δραχμή, -ῆς, ἡ, (δράσσομαι, [hence prop. a grip, a handful]), [fr. Hdt. down], *a drachma, a silver coin of* [nearly] *the same weight as the Roman denarius* (see δηνάριον): Lk. xv. 8 sq.*

1407 δρέπανον, -ου, τό, (i. q. δρεπάνη, fr. δρέπω to pluck, pluck off), *a sickle, a pruning-hook, a hooked vine-knife*, such as reapers and vine-dressers use: Mk. iv. 29; Rev. xiv. 14–19. (Hom. and subseq. writ.; Sept.)*

1408 δρόμος, -ου, ὁ, (fr. ΔΡΑΜΩ [q. v.]; cf. νόμος, τρόμος, and the like), *a course* (Hom. et sqq.); in the N. T. fig., *the course of life* or *of office*: πληροῦσθαι τὸν δρόμον, Acts xiii. 25; τελειοῦν, Acts xx. 24; τελεῖν, 2 Tim. iv. 7.*

1409 Δρούσιλλα [al. Δρούσιλλα, cf. Chandler § 120], -ης, ἡ, *Drusilla*, daughter of Agrippa the elder, wife of Felix, the governor of Judæa, a most licentious woman (Joseph. antt. 20, 7, 1 sq.): Acts xxiv. 24; cf. *Win.* RWB. [and B. D.] s. v.; *Schürer*, Neutest. Zeitgesch. § 19, 4.*

1410 δύναμαι, depon. verb, pres. indic. 2 pers. sing. δύνασαι and, acc. to a rarer form occasional in the poets and fr. Polyb. on to be met with in prose writ. also (cf. *Lob.* ad Phryn. p. 359; [*WH.* App. p. 168; W. § 13, 2 b.; Veitch s. v.]), δύνῃ (Mk. ix. 22 sq. L T Tr WH; [Lk. xvi. 2 T WH Tr txt.]; Rev. ii. 2); impf. ἐδυνάμην and Attic ἠδυνάμην, between which forms the Mss. and editions are almost everywhere divided, [in Mk. vi. 19; xiv. 5; Lk. viii. 19; xix. 3; Jn. ix. 33; xii. 39 all edd. read ἠδ., so R G in Mt. xxvi. 9; Lk. i. 22; Jn. xi. 37; Rev. xiv. 3; on the other hand, in Mt. xxii. 46; Lk. i. 22; Jn. xi. 37; Rev. xiv. 3, L T Tr WH all read ἐδ., so T WH in Mt. xxvi. 9; R G in Mt. xxii. 46. Cf. *WH.* App. p. 162; W. § 12, 1 b.; B. 33 (29)]; fut. δυνήσομαι; 1 aor. ἠδυνήθην and (in Mk. vii. 24 T WH, after codd. אB only; in Mt. xvii. 16 cod. B) ἠδυνάσθην (cf. [WH u. s. and p. 169]; Kühner § 343 s. v.; [Veitch s. v.; W. 84 (81); B. 33 (29); *Curtius*, Das Verbum, ii. 402]); Sept. for יָכֹל; *to be able, have power*, whether by virtue of one's own ability and resources, or of a state of mind, or through favorable circumstances, or by permission of law or custom; **a.** foll. by an inf. [W. § 44, 3] pres. or aor. (on the distinction between which, cf. W. § 44, 7). **a.** foll. by a pres. inf.: Mt. vi. 24; ix. 15; Mk. ii. 7; iii. 23; Lk. vi. 39; Jn. iii. 2; v. 19; Acts xxvii. 15; 1 Co. x. 21; Heb. v. 7; 1 Jn. iii. 9; Rev. ix. 20, and often. **β.** foll. by an aor. inf.: Mt. iii. 9; v. 14; Mk. i. 45; ii. 4; v. 3; Lk. viii. 19; xiii. 11; Jn. iii. 3 sq.; vi. 52; viii. 36; Acts iv. 16 [R G]; v. 39; x. 47; Ro. viii. 39; xvi. 25; 1 Co. iii. 1; vi. 5; 2 Co. iii. 7; Gal. iii. 21; Eph. iii. 4, 20; 1 Th. iii. 9; 1 Tim. vi. 7, 16; 2 Tim. iii. 13; iii. 7, 15; Heb. ii.

18; iii. 19; [xi. 19 Lchm.]; Jas. i. 21; Rev. iii. 8; v. 3; vi. 17, and very often. **b.** with Inf. omitted, as being easily supplied from the context: Mt. xvi. 3 [here T br. WH reject the pass.]; xx. 22; Mk. vi. 19; x. 39; Lk. ix. 40; xvi. 26; xix. 3; Ro. viii. 7. **c.** joined with an accus. δύναμαί τι, *to be able to do something* (cf. Germ. *ich vermag etwas*): Mk. ix. 22; Lk. xii. 26; 2 Co. xiii. 8, (and in Grk. writ. fr. Hom. on). **d.** absol., like the Lat. *possum* (as in Caes. b. gall. 1, 18, 6), i. q. *to be able, capable, strong, powerful*: 1 Co. iii. 2; x. 13. (2 Chr. xxxii. 13; 1 Macc. v. 40 sq.; in 2 Macc. xi. 13 cod. Alex., and often in Grk. writ. as Eur. Or. 889; Thuc. 4, 105; Xen. an. 4, 5, 11 sq.; Isoc., Dem., Aeschin.)

δύναμις, -εως, ἡ; [fr. Hom. down]; Sept. for חַיִל, גְּבוּרָה, עֹז, כֹּחַ, צָבָא (an army, a host); *strength, ability, power*; **a.** univ. *inherent power, power residing in a thing by virtue of its nature, or which a person or thing exerts and puts forth*: Lk. i. 17; Acts iv. 7; 1 Co. iv. 20; 2 Co. iv. 7; xii. 9 (ἡ δύναμις ἐν ἀσθενείᾳ τελεῖται [R G τελειοῦται]); xiii. 4; 1 Th. i. 5; Heb. vii. 16; xi. 34; Rev. i. 16; xvii. 13; ἰδίᾳ δυνάμει, Acts iii. 12; μεγάλῃ δυνάμει, Acts iv. 33; ἑκάστῳ κατὰ τὴν ἰδίαν δύναμιν, Mt. xxv. 15; ὑπὲρ δύναμιν, beyond our power, 2 Co. i. 8; ἐν δυνάμει sc. ὤν, endued with power, Lk. iv. 36; 1 Co. xv. 43; so in the phrase ἔρχεσθαι ἐν δυνάμει, Mk. ix. 1; *powerfully*, Col. i. 29; 2 Th. i. 11; contextually i. q. *evidently*, Ro. i. 4; ἐν δυνάμει σημείων κ. τεράτων, through the power which I exerted upon their souls by performing miracles, Ro. xv. 19; δύν. εἴς τι, Heb. xi. 11; δύν. ἐπὶ τὰ δαιμόνια καὶ νόσους θεραπεύειν, Lk. ix. 1; ἡ δύναμις τῆς ἁμαρτίας ὁ νόμος, sin exercises its power (upon the soul) through the law, i. e. through the abuse of the law, 1 Co. xv. 56; τῆς ἀναστάσεως τοῦ Χριστοῦ, the power which the resurrection of Christ has, for instructing, reforming, elevating, tranquillizing, the soul, Phil. iii. 10; τῆς εὐσεβείας, inhering in godliness and operating upon souls, 2 Tim. iii. 5; δυνάμεις μέλλοντος αἰῶνος (see αἰών, 3), Heb. vi. 5; τὸ πνεῦμα τῆς δυνάμεως (see πνεῦμα, 5), 1 Pet. iv. 14 Lchm.; 2 Tim. i. 7; δύναμις is used of the power of angels: Eph. i. 21 [cf. Mey. ad loc.]; 2 Pet. ii. 11; of the power of the devil and evil spirits, 1 Co. xv. 24; τοῦ ἐχθροῦ, i. e. of the devil, Lk. x. 19; τοῦ δράκοντος, Rev. xiii. 2; angels, as excelling in power, are called δυνάμεις [cf. (Philo de mutat. nom. § 8 δυνάμεις ἀσώματοι) Mey. as above; Bp. Lghtft. on Col. i. 16; see ἄγγελος]: Ro. viii. 38; 1 Pet. iii. 22. ἡ δύναμις τοῦ θεοῦ, univ. *the power of God*: Mt. xxii. 29; Mk. xii. 24; Lk. xxii. 69; Acts viii. 10; Ro. i. 20; ix. 17; 1 Co. vi. 14; δύναμις ὑψίστου, Lk. i. 35; ἡ δύναμις, esp. in doxologies, the kingly power of God, Mt. vi. 13 Rec.; Rev. iv. 11; vii. 12; xi. 17; xii. 10; xv. 8; xix. 1; and the abstract for the concrete (as הַגְּבוּרָה in Jewish writ.; cf. *Buxtorf*, Lex. talm. col. 385 [p. 201 sq. ed. Fischer]) equiv. to ὁ δυνατός, Mt. xxvi. 64; Mk. xiv. 62; δύναμις τοῦ θεοῦ is used of the divine power considered as acting upon the minds of men, 1 Co. ii. 5; 2 Co. vi. 7; Eph. iii. 7, 20; [2 Tim. i. 8; 1 Pet. i. 5]; εἴς τινα, 2 Co. xiii. 4 [but WH in br.]; Eph. i. 19; ἐνδύεσθαι δύναμιν ἐξ ὕψους, Lk. xxiv. 49; by meton. t h i n g s or p e r s o n s in

which God's saving power shows its efficacy are called δυνάμεις θεοῦ: thus ὁ Χριστός, 1 Co. i. 24; ὁ λόγος τοῦ σταυροῦ, 1 Co. i. 18; τὸ εὐαγγέλιον, with the addition εἰς σωτηρίαν παντὶ etc. Ro. i. 16 [cf. W. § 36, 3 b.]. δύναμις is ascribed to Christ, now in one sense and now in another: a power to heal disease proceeds from him, Mk. v. 30; Lk. v. 17; vi. 19; viii. 46; the kingly power of the Messiah is his, Mt. xxiv. 30; [Mk. xiii. 26]; Lk. xxi. 27; 2 Pet. i. 16; Rev. v. 12; ἄγγελοι τῆς δυνάμεως αὐτοῦ (see ἄγγελος, 2), ministering to his power, 2 Thess. i. 7 [W. § 34, 3 b. note]; m e t a p h y s i c a l [or e s s e n t i a l] power, viz. that which belongs to him as ὁ θεῖος λόγος, in the expression τὸ ῥῆμα τῆς δυνάμ. αὐτοῦ the word uttered by his power, equiv. to his most powerful will and energy, Heb. i. 3; m o r a l power, operating on the soul, 2 Co. xii. 9 R G; and called ἡ θεία αὐτοῦ δύναμις in 2 Pet. i. 3; ἡ δύναμις τοῦ κυρίου, the power of Christ invisibly present and operative in a Christian church formally assembled, 1 Co. v. 4. δύναμις τοῦ ἁγίου πνεύματος: Acts i. 8 [W. 125 (119)]; πν. ἅγιον κ. δύναμις, Acts x. 38; ἀπόδειξις πνεύματος καὶ δυνάμεως (see ἀπόδειξις, b.), 1 Co. ii. 4; ἐν τῇ δυνάμει τοῦ πνεύματος, under or full of the power of the Holy Spirit, Lk. iv. 14; ἐν δυνάμει πνεύματος ἁγίου, by the power and influence of the Holy Spirit, Ro. xv. 13; by the power which, under the influence of the Holy Spirit, I exerted upon their souls, Ro. xv. 19. **b.** specifically, *the power of performing miracles*: Acts vi. 8; πᾶσα δύναμις, every kind of power of working miracles (with the addition καὶ σημείοις κ. τέρασι), 2 Th. ii. 9; plur.: [Mt. xiii. 54; xiv. 2; Mk. vi. 14]; 1 Co. xii. 28 sq.; Gal. iii. 5; ἐνεργήματα δυνάμεων, 1 Co. xii. 10; by meton. of the cause for the effect, *a mighty work* [cf. W. 32; Trench § xci.]: δύναμιν ποιεῖν, Mk. vi. 5; ix. 39; so in the plur., Mk. vi. 2; Lk. xix. 37; joined with σημεῖα, Acts viii. 13; with σημεῖα κ. τέρατα, Acts ii. 22; 2 Co. xii. 12; Heb. ii. 4 [?]; ποιεῖν δυνάμεις, Mt. vii. 22; [xiii. 58]; Acts xix. 11; γίνονται δυνάμεις, Mt. xi. 20 sq. 23; Lk. x. 13. **c.** *m o r a l power and excellence of soul*: 1 Co. iv. 19; 2 Co. iv. 7; Eph. iii. 16; Col. i. 11. **d.** *the power and influence which belong to r i c h e s*; (pecuniary ability), *wealth*: τοῦ στρήνους, 'riches ministering to luxury' (Grotius), Rev. xviii. 3; κατὰ δύναμιν καὶ ὑπὲρ [al. παρὰ] δύναμιν, according to their means, yea, beyond their means, 2 Co. viii. 3; (in this sense, of חַיִל, Sept. Deut. viii. 17 sq.; Ruth iv. 11; not infreq. in Grk. writ., as Xen. Cyr. 8, 4, 34; an. 7, 7, 21 (36)). **e.** *power* and resources arising from numbers: Rev. iii. 8. **f.** *power consisting in* or *resting upon a r m i e s, forces, hosts*, (so, both in sing. and in plur., often in Grk. writ. fr. Hdt., Thuc., Xen. on; in the Sept. and in Apocr.); hence δυνάμεις τοῦ οὐρανοῦ *the hosts of heaven*, Hebraistically the stars: Mt. xxiv. 29; Lk. xxi. 26; and δ. ἐν τοῖς οὐρανοῖς, Mk. xiii. 25; equiv. to צְבָא הַשָּׁמַיִם, 2 K. xvii. 16; xxiii. 4; Is. xxxiv. 4; Jer. viii. 2; Dan. viii. 10, etc. [cf. σαβαώθ]. **g.** Like the Lat. *vis* and *potestas*, equiv. to the (*force* i. e.) *meaning of a word or expression*: 1 Co. xiv. 11; (Plat. Crat. p. 394 b.; Polyb. 20, 9, 11; Dion. Hal. 1, 68; Dio Cass. 55, 3; al.).*

[SYN. βία, δύναμις, ἐνέργεια, ἐξουσία, ἰσχύς, κράτος:

βία *force*, effective, often oppressive power, exhibiting itself in single deeds of violence; **δύν.** *power*, natural ability, general and inherent; **ἐνέργ.** *working*, power in exercise, operative power; **ἐξουσ.** primarily liberty of action; then, *authority* —either as delegated power, or as unrestrained, arbitrary power; **ἰσχ.** *strength*, power (esp. physical) as an endowment; **κράτος**, *might*, relative and manifested power — in the N. T. chiefly of God; τὸ κράτος τῆς ἰσχ. Eph. vi. 10, ἡ ἐνέργ. τῆς δυν. Eph. iii. 7, ἡ ἐνέργ. τοῦ κρ. τῆς ἰσχ. Eph. i. 19. Cf. Schmidt ch. 148; Bp. Lghtft. on Col. i. 16; Mey. on Eph. i. 19.]

1412 **δυναμόω, -ῶ**: [pres. pass. δυναμοῦμαι]; *to make strong, confirm, strengthen*: Col. i. 11; [Eph. vi. 10 WH mrg.]; 1 aor. ἐδυναμώθησαν, Heb. xi. 34 (R G ἐνεδ.). (Ps. lxvii. (lxviii.) 29; Eccl. x. 10; Dan. ix. 27 [Theod.; Ps. lxiv. (lxv.) 4 Aq.; Job xxxvi. 9 Aq.] and occasionally in eccl. and Byz. writ.; cf. *Lob.* ad Phryn. p. 605; [W. 26 (25)].) [Comp.: ἐν-δυναμόω.]*

1413 **δυνάστης, -ου, ὁ**, fr. [Soph. and] Hdt. on; *powerful*; **1.** *a prince, potentate*: Lk. i. 52; used of God (Sir. xlvi. 5; 2 Macc. xv. 3, 23, etc.; of Zeus, Soph. Ant. 608), 1 Tim. vi. 15. **2.** *a courtier, high officer, royal minister*: Acts viii. 27 [A. V. (*a eunuch*) *of great authority*; but see Meyer ad loc.], (δυνάσται Φαραώ, Gen. l. 4).*

1414 **δυνατέω, -ῶ**; (δυνατός); *to be powerful* or *mighty*; *show one's self powerful*: 2 Co. xiii. 3 (opp. to ἀσθενῶ); *to be able, have power*: foll. by an inf., Ro. xiv. 4 L T Tr WH; 2 Co. ix. 8 L T Tr WH. Not found in prof. writ. nor in the Sept.*

1415 **δυνατός, -ή, -όν**, (δύναμαι); [fr. Pind. down], Sept. for גִּבּוֹר; *able, powerful, mighty, strong*; **1.** absolutely; *a. mighty in wealth and influence*: 1 Co. i. 26; (Rev. vi. 15 Rec.); οἱ δυνατοί, *the chief men*, Acts xxv. 5, (Joseph. b. j. 1, 12, 4 ἧκον Ἰουδαίων οἱ δυνατοί; Xen. Cyr. 5, 4, 1; Thuc. 1, 89; Polyb. 9, 23, 4). ὁ δυνατός, *the preëminently mighty one, almighty God*, Lk. i. 49. **b.** *strong in soul*: *to bear calamities and trials with fortitude and patience*, 2 Co. xii. 10; *strong in Christian virtue*, 2 Co. xiii. 9; firm in conviction and faith, Ro. xv. 1. **2.** in construction; **a.** δυνατός εἰμι with inf., *to be able* (*to do something*); [B. 260 (224); W. 319 (299)]): Lk. xiv. 31; Acts xi. 17; Ro. iv. 21; xi. 23; xiv. 4 R G; 2 Co. ix. 8 R G; 2 Tim. i. 12; Tit. i. 9; Heb. xi. 19 (Lchm. δύναται); Jas. iii. 2. **b.** δυνατὸς ἔν τινι, *mighty* i. e. *excelling in something*: ἐν ἔργῳ κ. λόγῳ, Lk. xxiv. 19; ἐν λόγοις καὶ ἔργοις, Acts vii. 22; ἐν γραφαῖς, *excelling in knowledge of the Scriptures*, Acts xviii. 24. **c.** πρός τι, *mighty* i. e. *having power for something*: 2 Co. x. 4. **d.** neuter δυνατόν [in pass. sense, cf. B. 190 (165)] *possible*: εἰ δυνατόν (ἐστι), Mt. xxiv. 24; xxvi. 39; Mk. xiii. 22; xiv. 35; Ro. xii. 18; Gal. iv. 15; οὐκ ἦν δυνατόν foll. by inf. Acts ii. 24; δυνατόν τί ἐστι τινι [B. 190 (165)], Mk. ix. 23; xiv. 36; Acts xx. 16; παρὰ θεῷ πάντα δυνατά ἐστι, Mt. xix. 26; Mk. x. 27; Lk. xviii. 27. τὸ δυνατὸν αὐτοῦ, *what his power could do*, equiv. to τὴν δύναμιν αὐτοῦ, Ro. ix. 22, cf. W. § 34, 2.*

1416 **δύνω** or **δύω**; 2 aor. ἔδυν; 1 aor. (in Grk. writ. transitively) ἔδυσα (Mk. i. 32 L Tr WH), cf. *Bttm.* Ausf. Spr. ii. p. 156 sq.; W. p. 84 (81); B. 56 (49); [Veitch s. vv.];

to go into, enter; *go under, be plunged into, sink in* : in the N. T. twice of the setting sun (sinking as it were into the sea), Mk. i. 32; Lk. iv. 40. So times without number in Grk. writ. fr. Hom. on; Sept., Gen. xxviii. 11; Lev. xxii. 7, etc.; Tob. ii. 4; 1 Macc. x. 50. [Comp.: ἐκ-, ἀπ-εκ- (-μαι), ἐν-, ἐπ-εν-, παρ-εισ-, ἐπι-δύνω.]*

1417 **δύο**, genit. indecl. δύο (as in Epic, and occasionally in Hdt., Thuc., Xen., Polyb., al. for δυοῖν, more common in Attic [see *Rutherford*, New Phryn. p. 289 sq.]); dat. δυσί, δυσίν, ([-σί in Mt. vi. 24; Lk. xvi. 13; Acts xxi. 33 (Tr -σίν), -σίν in Mt. xxii. 40; Mk. xvi. 12; Lk. xii. 52 (R G -σί); Acts xii. 6 (R G L -σί); Heb. x. 28; Rev. xi. 3 (R G -σί); cf. *Tdf.* Proleg. p. 98; *WH.* App. p. 147]—a form not found in the older and better writ., met with in Hippocr., Aristot., Theophr., frequent fr. Polyb. on, for the Attic δυοῖν; acc. δύο (cf. *Lob.* ad Phryn. p. 210; *Bttm.* Ausf. Spr. i. p. 276 sq.; W. § 9, 2 b.; Passow i. p. 729); *two*: absol., οὐκ ἔτι εἰσὶ δύο, ἀλλὰ σὰρξ μία, Mt. xix. 6; Mk. x. 8; δύο ἢ τρεῖς, Mt. xviii. 20; 1 Co. xiv. 29; τρεῖς ἐπὶ δυσὶ κ. δύο ἐπὶ τρισί, Lk. xii. 52; ἀνὰ and κατὰ δύο, *two by two* [W. 398 (372); 401 (374); B. 30 (26)], Lk. ix. 3 [WH om. Tr br. ἀνά]; x. 1 [WH ἀνὰ δύο [δύο]; cf. Acta Philip. § 36, ed. Tdf. p. 92]; Jn. ii. 6 [apiece]; 1 Co. xiv. 27; δύο δύο *two and two*, Mk. vi. 7 (so, after the Hebr., in Gen. vi. 19, 20; but the phrase is not altogether foreign even to the Grk. poets, as Aeschyl. Pers. 981 μυρία μυρία for κατὰ μυριάδας, cf. W. 249 (234), [cf. 39 (38)]); neut. εἰς δύο *into two parts*, Mt. xxvii. 51; Mk. xv. 38; with gen. δύο τῶν μαθητῶν (αὐτοῦ), Mk. xi. 1; xiv. 13; Lk. xix. 29; [Mt. xi. 2 R G]; τῶν οἰκετῶν, Acts x. 7. δύο ἐξ αὐτῶν, Lk. xxiv. 13 [cf. Bttm. 158 (138); Win. 203 (191)]. with a noun or pronoun: δύο δαιμονιζόμενοι, Mt. viii. 28. δύο μάχαιραι, Lk. xxii. 38; ἐπὶ στόματος δύο μαρτύρων, Mt. xviii. 16; 2 Co. xiii. 1; δυσὶ κυρίοις, Mt. vi. 24; Lk. xvi. 13; εἶδε δύο ἀδελφούς, Mt. iv. 18; preceded by the article, οἱ δύο *the two, the twain*: Mt. xix. 5; Mk. x. 8; 1 Co. vi. 16; Eph. v. 31; τοὺς δύο, Eph. ii. 15; αἱ [Rec. only] δύο διαθῆκαι, Gal. iv. 24; οὗτοι [Lchm. br. οὗτ.] οἱ δύο υἱοί μου, Mt. xx. 21; περὶ τῶν δύο ἀδελφῶν, Mt. xx. 24; ἐν ταύταις ταῖς δυσὶν ἐντολαῖς, Mt. xxii. 40; τοὺς δύο ἰχθύας, Mt. xiv. 19; Mk. vi. 41; Lk. ix. 16; δύο δηνάρια, Lk. x. 35.

1418 **δυς**, an inseparable prefix conveying the idea of difficulty, opposition, injuriousness or the like, and corresponding to our *mis-, un-* [Curtius § 278]; opp. to εὖ.

1419 **δυσ-βάστακτος, -ον**, (βαστάζω), *hard* [A. V. *grievous*] *to be borne*: Mt. xxiii. 4 [T WH txt. om. Tr br. δυσβάστ.] and Lk. xi. 46 φορτία δυσβάστακτα, said of precepts hard to obey, and irksome. (Sept. Prov. xxvii. 3; Philo, omn. prob. lib. § 5; Plut. quaest. nat. c. 16, 4 p. 915 f.)*

1420 **δυσεντερία, -ας, ἡ**, (ἔντερον *intestine*), *dysentery*, (Lat. *tormina intestinorum*, bowel-complaint): Acts xxviii. 8 R G; see the foll. word. (Hippocr. and med. writ.; Hdt., Plat., Aristot., Polyb., al.)*

see 1420 **δυσεντέριον, -ου, τό**, a later form for δυσεντερία, q. v.: Acts xxviii. 8 L T Tr WH. Cf. *Lob.* ad Phryn. p. 518.*

1421 **δυσερμήνευτος, -ον**, (ἑρμηνεύω), *hard to interpret, difficult of explanation*: Heb. v. 11. (Diod. 2, 52; Philo de somn. § 32 fin.; Artem. oneir. 3, 66.)*

[δύσις, -εως, ἡ;   1. *a sinking* or *setting*, esp. of the heavenly bodies;   2. of the quarter in which the sun sets, *the west*: Mk. xvi. WH (rejected) 'Shorter Conclusion.' (So both in sing. and in plur.: Aristot. de mund. 3 p. 393ᵃ, 17 ; 4 p. 394ᵇ, 21 ; Polyb. 1, 42, 5 etc.)*]

1422   δύσκολος, -ον, (κόλον food) ;   1. prop. *hard to find agreeable food for, fastidious about food.*   2. *difficult to please, always finding fault*; (Eur., Arstph., Xen., Plat., al.).   3. univ. *difficult* (Xen. oec. 15, 10 ἡ γεωργία δύσκολός ἐστι μαθεῖν) : πῶς δύσκολόν ἐστι, foll. by acc. with inf., Mk. x. 24.*

1423   δυσκόλως, adv., (δύσκολος), [fr. Plato down], *with difficulty*: Mt. xix. 23 ; Mk. x. 23 ; Lk. xviii. 24.*

1424   δυσμή, -ῆς, ἡ, [fr. Aeschyl. and Hdt. down], much oftener in plur. [W. § 27, 3] δυσμαί, αἱ, (δύω or δύνω, q. v.), sc. ἡλίου, *the setting of the sun*: Lk. xii. 54 [acc. to the reading of T WH Tr mrg. ἐπὶ δ. may possibly be understood of *time* (cf. W. 375 sq. (352)) ; see ἐπί, A. II. ; al. take the prep. locally, *over, in,* and give δυσμ. the meaning which follows ; see ἐπί, A. I. 1 b.] ; *the region of sunset, the west*, [anarthrous, W. 121 (115)] : Rev. xxi. 13 ; ἀπὸ ἀνατολῶν καὶ δυσμῶν, from all regions or nations, Mt. viii. 11 ; xxiv. 27 ; Lk. xiii. 29 ; in Hebr. מְבוֹא הַשֶּׁמֶשׁ, Josh. i. 4. Often in prof. writ. fr. Hdt. on, both with and without ἡλίου.*

1425   δυσνόητος, -ον, (νοέω), *hard to be understood* : 2 Pet. iii. 16. (χρησμός, Lcian. Alex. 54 ; Diog. Laërt. 9, 13 δυσνόητόν τε καὶ δυσεξήγητον; [Aristot. plant. 1, 1 p. 816ᵃ, 3].)

see 987   δυσφημέω, -ῶ : [pres. pass. δυσφημοῦμαι] ; (δύσφημος) ; *to use ill words, defame* ; pass. *to be defamed*, 1 Co. iv. 13 T WH Tr mrg. (1 Macc. vii. 41 ; in Grk. writ. fr. Aeschyl. Agam. 1078 down.) *

1426   δυσφημία, -ας, ἡ, both *the condition of a δύσφημος,* i. e. *of one who is defamed*, viz. *ill-repute*, and *the action of one who uses opprobrious language*, viz. *defamation, reproach* : διὰ δυσφημίας κ. εὐφημίας [A. V. *by evil report and good report*], 2 Co. vi. 8. (1 Macc. vii. 38 ; 3 Macc. ii. 26. Dion. H. 6, 48 ; Plut. de gen. Socr. § 18 p. 587 f.) *

see 1416   δύω, see δύνω.
1427   δώδεκα, οἱ, αἱ, τά, [fr. Hom. down], *twelve* : Mt. ix. 20 ; x. 1 ; [L T Tr WH in Acts xix. 7 ; xxiv. 11 for δεκαδύο] ; Rev. vii. 5 [R G ιβ′] ; xxi. 21, etc. ; οἱ δώδεκα, *the twelve* apostles of Jesus, so called by way of eminence : Mk. ix. 35 ; x. 32 ; xi. 11 ; Mt. xxvi. 14, 20 ; Lk. xxii. 3, etc.

1428   δωδέκατος, -η, -ον, (νοέω), *twelfth* : Rev. xxi. 20. [Fr. Hom. on.]*
1429   δωδεκά-φυλον, -ον, τό, (fr. δώδεκα, and φυλή tribe), *the twelve tribes,* used collectively of the Israelitish people, as consisting of twelve tribes : Acts xxvi. 7. (Clem. Rom. 1 Cor. 55, 6 ; Prot. Jac. c. 1, 3 ; λαὸς ὁ δωδεκάφυλος, Orac. Sibyll. Cf. δεκάφυλος, τετράφυλος, Hdt. 5, 66 ; [W. 100 (95)].)*

δῶμα, -τος, τό, (δέμω to build) ;   1. *a building, house,* (Hom. et sqq.).   2. *a part of a building, dining-room, hall,* (Hom. et sqq.).   3. in the Script. equiv. to גַּג, *house-top, roof* [W. 23] : Mt. xxiv. 17 ; Mk. xiii. 15 ; Lk. v. 19 ; xvii. 31. The house-tops of the Orientals were (and still are) level, and were frequented not only for walking but also for meditation and prayer : Acts x. 9 ; hence ἐπὶ δωμάτων, *on the house-tops,* i. e. *in public* : Mt. x. 27 ; Lk. xii. 3 ; ἐπὶ τὸ δῶμα . . . κατ' ὀφθαλμοὺς παντὸς Ἰσραήλ, 2 S. xvi. 22.*   **1430**

δωρεά, -ᾶς, ἡ, (δίδωμι) ; from [Aeschyl. and] Hdt. down ; *a gift* : Jn. iv. 10 ; Acts viii. 20 ; xi. 17 ; Ro. v. 15 ; 2 Co. ix. 15 ; Heb. vi. 4 ; ἡ χάρις ἐδόθη κατὰ τὸ μέτρον τῆς δωρεᾶς τοῦ Χριστοῦ, according to the measure in which Christ gave it, Eph. iv. 7 ; with an epexegetical gen. of the thing given, viz. τοῦ ἁγίου πνεύματος, Acts ii. 38 ; x. 45 ; δικαιοσύνης, Ro. v. 17 [L WH Tr mrg. br. τ. δωρ.] ; τῆς χάριτος τοῦ θεοῦ, Eph. iii. 7. The acc. δωρεάν (prop. *as a gift, gift-wise* [cf. W. 230 (216) ; B. 153 (134)]) is used adverbially ; Sept. for חִנָּם ;   a. *freely, for naught, gratis, gratuitously* : Mt. x. 8 ; Ro. iii. 24 ; 2 Co. xi. 7 ; 2 Th. iii. 8 ; Rev. xxi. 6 ; xxii. 17, (Polyb. 18, 17, 7 ; Ex. xxi. 11 ; δωρεὰν ἄνευ ἀργυρίου, Is. lii. 3).   b. *by a usage of which as yet no example has been noted fr. Grk. writ., without just cause, unnecessarily* : Jn. xv. 25 (Ps. lxviii. (lxix.) 5 ; xxxiv. (xxxv.) 19) ; Gal. ii. 21, (Job i. 9 [?]) ; Ps. xxxiv. (xxxv.) 7 [where Symm. ἀναιτίως] ; so the Lat. *gratuitus* : Liv. 2, 42 *gratuitus furor*, Sen. epp. 105, 3 [bk. xviii. ep. 2, § 3] *odium aut est ex offensa . . . aut gratuitum.* [Syn. see δόμα, fin.]*   **1431**

δωρεάν, see δωρεά.   --- **1432;**   **see 1431**

δωρέω, -ῶ : *to present, bestow,* (Hes., Pind., Hdt., al.) ; pass. Lev. vii. 5 (Heb. text vs. 15). But much more frequently as depon. mid. δωρέομαι, -οῦμαι (Hom. et sqq.) : 1 aor. ἐδωρησάμην ; pf. δεδώρημαι ; τινί τι, Mk. xv. 45 ; 2 Pet. i. 3, 4.*   ---- see **1433 St.**

δώρημα, -τος, τό, (δωρέομαι) ; *a gift, bounty, benefaction* : Ro. v. 16 ; Jas. i. 17. ([Aeschyl.], Soph., Xen., al.) [Cf. δόμα, fin.]*   **1434**

δῶρον, -ου, τό, [fr. Hom. down], Sept. generally for קָרְבָּן, often also for מִנְחָה and שֹׁחַד ; *a gift, present*: Eph. ii. 8 ; Rev. xi. 10 ; of gifts offered as an expression of honor, Mt. ii. 11 ; of sacrifices and other gifts offered to God, Mt. v. 23 sq. ; viii. 4 ; xv. 5 ; xxiii. 18 sq. ; Mk. vii. 11 ; Heb. v. 1 ; viii. 3 sq. ; ix. 9 ; xi. 4 ; of money cast into the treasury for the purposes of the temple and for the support of the poor, Lk. xxi. 1, [4]. [SYN. see δόμα, fin.] *   **1435**

δωροφορία, -ας, ἡ, (δωροφόρος bringing gifts), *the offering of a gift* or *of gifts* : Ro. xv. 31 L Tr mrg. cf. διακονία, 3. (Alciphr. 1, 6 ; Pollux 4, 47 [p. 371 ed. Hemst.] ; several times in eccles. writ.) *   **(1435α)**   **see 1248**

E

1436 ἔα, an interjection expressive of indignation, or of wonder mixed with fear, (derived apparently from the impv. pres. of the verb ἐάω [acc. to others a natural, instinctive, sound]), freq. in the Attic poets, rare in prose writ. (as Plat. Prot. p. 314 d.), *ha ! ah !*: Mk. i. 24 R G; Lk. iv. 34; cf. Fritzsche on Mk. p. 32 sq.*

1437 ἐάν; I. a conditional particle (derived fr. εἰ ἄν), which makes reference to time and to experience, introducing something future, but not determining, before the event, whether it is certainly to take place; *if, in case*, (Lat. *si*; Germ. *wenn*; *im Fall, dass*; *falls*; *wofern*); cf., among others, *Hermann* ad Viger. p. 832; *Klotz* ad Devar. ii. 2 p. 450 sqq.; W. 291 (273) sq. It is connected **1.** with the S u b j u n c t i v e, according to the regular usage of the more ancient and elegant classic writers. **a.** with the subjunc. P r e s e n t: Mt. vi. 22 (ἐὰν οὖν ὁ ὀφθαλμός σου ἁπλοῦς ᾖ, if it be the case, as to which I do not know, that thine eye etc.); ibid. 23; xvii. 20; Lk. x. 6; Jn. vii. 17; viii. 54 [R G L mrg.]; ix. 31; xi. 9, 10; Acts v. 38; xiii. 41; Ro. ii. 25 sq.; 1 Co. ix. 16; Gal. v. 2; 1 Tim. i. 8 [not Lchm.]; Heb. xiii. 23; Jn. i. 9; ii. 3, 15 etc. **b.** with the subjunc. A o r i s t, corresponding to the Lat. fut. perf.: Mt. iv. 9 (ἐὰν προσκυνήσῃς μοι if thou shalt have worshipped me); v. 46; ix. 21; Mk. iii. 24; ix. 50; Lk. xiv. 34; xvii. 4; xx. 28; Jn. v. 43; xi. 57; Ro. vii. 2; x. 9; 1 Co. vii. 8, 39; viii. 10; xvi. 10 (ἐὰν ἔλθῃ Τιμό-θεος; for although he was already on his way to Cor-inth, yet some hindrance might still prevent his arriv-ing); 2 Co. ix. 4; Gal. vi. 1; Jas. ii. 2; 1 Jn. v. 16 [Lchm. pres.]; Rev. iii. 20, and often; also in the oratio obliqua, where the better Grk. writ. use the Optative: Jn. ix. 22; xi. 57; Acts ix. 2 (W. 294 (276); [cf. B. 224 (193)]). The difference between the Pres. and the Aor. may be seen especially from the following passages: 2 Tim. ii. 5 ἐὰν δὲ καὶ ἀθλῇ τις, οὐ στεφανοῦται, ἐὰν μὴ νομίμως ἀθλήσῃ, 1 Co. xiv. 23 ἐὰν οὖν συνέλθῃ ἡ ἐκκλησία . . . καὶ πάντες γλώσ-σαις λαλῶσιν, εἰσέλθωσι δὲ ἰδιῶται ἢ ἄπιστοι, vs. 24 ἐὰν δὲ πάντες προφητεύωσιν, εἰσέλθῃ δέ τις ἄπιστος, Mt. xxi. 21 ἐὰν ἔχητε πίστιν καὶ μὴ διακριθῆτε. Also εἰ ("quod per se nihil significat praeter conditionem," Klotz l. c. p. 455) and ἐάν are distinguished in propositions subjoined the one to the other [W. 296 (277 sq.)]: Jn. xiii. 17 εἰ ταῦτα οἴδατε, μακάριοί ἐστε, ἐὰν ποιῆτε αὐτά, Jn. iii. 12; 1 Co. vii. 36; in statements antithetic, Acts v. 38 sq.; or parallel, Mk. iii. 24–26. Finally, where one of the evan-gelists uses εἰ another has ἐάν, but so that each particle retains its own force, inasmuch as one and the same thing is differently conceived of by the different minds: Mk. ix. 43 ἐὰν σκανδαλίζῃ [-λίσῃ L mrg.] T WH txt.] ἡ χείρ σου, and vs. 47 ἐὰν ὁ ὀφθαλμός σου σκανδαλίζῃ σε, i. e. if so

be that etc.; on the other hand, Matthew, in xviii. 8 sq. and v. 29 sq. concerning the same thing says εἰ. **c.** irreg-ularly, but to be explained as an imitation of the Hebr. אִם which is also a particle of time (cf. *Gesenius*, Thesaur. s. v. 4), ἐάν with the Subjunc. Aor. is used of things which the speaker or writer thinks will certainly take place, where ὅταν *when, whenever*, should have been used: ἐὰν ὑψωθῶ, Jn. xii. 32; ἐὰν πορευθῶ, Jn. xiv. 3; ἐὰν φανερωθῇ, 1 Jn. ii. 28 (L T Tr WH, for ὅταν R G); iii. 2; ἐὰν ἀκούσητε, Heb. iii. 7 fr. Ps. xciv. (xcv.) 8; (ἐὰν εἰσέλθῃς εἰς τὸν νυμφῶνα, Tob. vi. 17 (16) [al. ὅταν]; ἐὰν ἀποθάνω, θάψον με, Tob. iv. 3, cf. vs. 4 ὅταν ἀποθάνῃ, θάψον αὐτήν; for אִם *when*, Is. xxiv. 13; Am. vii. 2). **d.** sometimes when the particle is used with the Subj. Aor. the futurity of a thing is not so much affirmed as imagined, it being known to be something which never could happen: ἐὰν εἴπῃ ὁ πούς, if the foot should say, or were to say, 1 Co. xii. 15; ἐὰν ἔλθω πρὸς ὑμᾶς γλώσσαις λαλῶν, 1 Co. xiv. 6. **2.** By a somewhat negligent use, met with from the time of Aristotle on, ἐάν is connected also with the I n-d i c a t i v e, [cf. Klotz l. c. p. 468 sqq.; Kühner § 575 Anm. 5; W. 295 (277); B. 221 (191) sq.; *Tdf.* Proleg. p. 124 sq.; *WH.* App. p. 171; *Soph.* Lex. s. v.; *Vin-cent and Dickson*, Mod. Grk. 2d ed. App. § 77]; and **a.** with the indic. F u t u r e, in meaning akin, as is well known, to the subjunc.: [ἐὰν δύο συμφωνήσουσιν, Mt. xviii. 19 T Tr]; ἐὰν οὗτοι σιωπήσουσι, Lk. xix. 40 L T Tr WH; ἐὰν . . . ὁδηγήσει, Acts viii. 31 T Tr WH, (ἐὰν βεβη-λώσουσιν αὐτά, Lev. xxii. 9); but also **b.** with the indic. P r e s e n t: ἐὰν δανείζετε, Lk. vi. 34 L mrg. Tr txt.; ἐὰν στήκετε, 1 Th. iii. 8 T Tr txt. WH; ἐάν τε ἀποθνήσκομεν, Ro. xiv. 8 Lchm. with an indic. P r e t e r i t e, but one having the force of a Pres.: ἐὰν [Lchm. ἄν] οἴδαμεν, 1 Jn. v. 15 without var. **3.** ἐάν joined with other particles; **a.** ἐὰν δὲ καί *but if also, but even if*, [A. V. *but and if* (re-tained by R. V. in 1 Co.)]; with the Subjunc.: Mt. xviii. 17; 1 Co. vii. 11, 28; 2 Tim. ii. 5. **b.** ἐὰν καί: Gal. vi. 1. **c.** ἐὰν μή *if not, unless, except*; with the subjunc. Present: Mt. x. 13; Lk. xiii. 3 [Lchm. txt. aor.]; Acts xv. 1 [Rec.]; 1 Co. viii. 8; ix. 16 [R G L mrg. T WH mrg.]; Jas. ii. 17; 1 Jn. iii. 21; with the subjunc. Aorist: Mt. vi. 15; xviii. 35; Mk. iii. 27; Jn. iii. 3; viii. 24; 1 Co. xiv. 6 sq. 9; Ro. x. 15; [xi. 23 R L]; 2 Tim. ii. 5; Rev. ii. 5, 22 [R L], and often. with the Indicative pres.: ἐὰν μὴ πιστεύετε, Jn. x. 38 Tdf. In some passages, although the particles ἐὰν μή retain their native force of *unless, if not*, yet so far as the s e n s e is concerned one may translate them *but that, without*: Mt. xxvi. 42 (the cup cannot pass by without my drinking it); οὐ γάρ ἐστιν κρυπτόν, ἐὰν μὴ φανερωθῇ (Treg.), there is nothing hid, but that it shall be made manifest (properly, nothing whatever is hid, except that it should be made manifest), Mk. iv. 22; οὐδείς ἐστιν, ὃς ἀφῆκεν οἰκίαν ... ἐὰν μὴ λάβῃ, but that shall receive (properly, unless he shall receive ... it cannot be said that any one has left), Mk. x. 29, 30, [cf. B. § 149, 6. On the supposed use of ἐὰν μή (εἰ μή) as equiv. to ἀλλά, cf. Mey. on Mt. xii. 4; Gal. i. 7; ii. 16; Fritzsche on Ro. xiv. 14 fin.; Ellic. and Bp. Lghtft. on Gal. ll. cc. See εἰ, III. 8 c. β.] **d.** ἐάνπερ [L Tr separately, ἐάν περ] if only, if indeed: Heb. iii. 6 (where L br. περ, and T Tr WH read ἐάν), 14; vi. 3; it occurs neither in the Sept. nor in the O. T. Apocr.; on its use in Grk. writ. cf. Klotz, l. c. p. 483 sq. **e.** ἐάν τε ... ἐάν τε, sive ... sive, whether ... or: Ro. xiv. 8; (often in Sept. for אִם ... אִם, as Ex. xix. 13; Lev. iii. 1; Deut. xviii. 3). Cf. Klotz, l. c. p. 479 sq.; Kühner § 541; [B. 221 (191)]. **f.** κάν for καὶ ἐάν, see κάν. **II.** The classic use of the conditional particle ἐάν also in the contracted form ἄν (see p. 34ᵇ above) seems to have led the biblical writers of both Testaments to connect ἐάν with relative pronouns and adverbs instead of the potential particle ἄν, as ὃς ἐάν [so Tdf. in 12 places], ὃ ἐάν [so Tdf. uniformly], etc. (this use among prof. writ. is very doubtful, cf. W. p. 310 (291); B. 72 (63)]: Mt. v. 19; x. 14 [R G]; xv. 5; Mk. vi. 22 sq.; Lk. ix. 48 [WH ἄν]; xvii. 33; Acts vii. 7 [R G T]; 1 Co. vi. 18; Eph. vi. 8 [R G L txt.]; 3 Jn. 5, etc.; ὅπου ἐάν, Mt. viii. 19; xxvi. 13; Mk. vi. 10 [L Tr ἄν]. ὁσάκις ἐάν, Rev. xi. 6. οὗ ἐάν, 1 Co. xvi. 6 (1 Macc. vi. 36). καθὸ ἐάν, 2 Co. viii. 12 [Tdf. ἄν; ὅστις ἐάν, Gal. v. 10 T Tr WH]; ἥτις ἐάν, Acts iii. 23 Tdf. For many other exx. see Soph. Lex. s. v. ἐάν, 3.] In many places the codd. vary between ἐάν and ἄν; cf. ἄν, II. p. 34; [and esp. Tdf. Proleg. p. 96].

(1437a); see 1437

ἐάν-περ, see ἐάν, I. 3 d.

1438 ἑαυτοῦ, -ῆς, -οῦ, etc. or (contracted) αὑτοῦ, -ῆς, -οῦ, (see p. 87); plur. ἑαυτῶν; dat. -οῖς, -αῖς, -οῖς, etc.; reflexive pronoun of the 3d person. It is used **1.** of the 3d pers. sing. and plur., to denote that the agent and the person acted on are the same; as, σώζειν ἑαυτόν, Mt. xxvii. 42; Mk. xv. 31; Lk. xxiii. 35; ὑψοῦν ἑαυτόν, Mt. xxiii. 12, etc. ἑαυτῷ, ἑαυτόν are also often added to middle verbs: διεμερίσαντο ἑαυτοῖς, Jn. xix. 24 (Xen. mem. 1, 6, 13 ποιεῖσθαι ἑαυτῷ φίλον); cf. W. § 38, 6; [B. § 135, 6]. Of the phrases into which this pronoun enters we notice the following: ἀφ' ἑαυτοῦ, see ἀπό, II. 2 d. aa.; δι' ἑαυτοῦ of itself, i. e. in its own nature, Ro. xiv. 14 [Tr L txt. read αὑτ.]; ἐν ἑαυτῷ, see in διαλογίζεσθαι, λέγειν, εἰπεῖν. εἰς ἑαυτὸν ἔρχεσθαι to come to one's self, to a better mind, Lk. xv. 17 (Diod. 13, 95). καθ' ἑαυτόν by one's self, alone: Acts xxviii. 16; Jas. ii. 17. παρ' ἑαυτῷ, by him i. e. at his home, 1 Co. xvi. 2 (Xen. mem. 3, 13, 3). πρὸς ἑαυτόν, to himself i. e. to his home, Lk. xxiv. 12 [R G; T om., WH (but with αὑτ.) reject, L Tr (but the latter with αὑτ.) br., the verse]; Jn. xx. 10 [T Tr αὑτ. (see αὑτοῦ)]; with [cf. our to] himself, i. e. in his own mind, προσεύχεσθαι, Lk. xviii. 11 [Tdf. om.], (2 Macc. xi. 13); in the gen., joined with a noun, it has the force of a possessive pronoun, as τοὺς ἑαυτῶν νεκρούς: Mt. viii. 22; Lk.

---

ix. 60. **2.** It serves as reflexive also to the 1st and 2d pers., as often in classic Greek, when no ambiguity is thereby occasioned; thus, ἐν ἑαυτοῖς equiv. to ἐν ἡμῖν αὐτοῖς, Ro. viii. 23; ἑαυτούς equiv. to ἡμᾶς αὐτούς, 1 Co. xi. 31; ἀφ' ἑαυτοῦ i. q. ἀπὸ σεαυτοῦ [read by L Tr WH], Jn. xviii. 34; ἑαυτόν i. q. σεαυτόν [read by L T Tr WH], Ro. xiii. 9; ἑαυτοῖς for ὑμῖν αὐτοῖς, Mt. xxiii. 31, etc.; cf. Matthiae § 489 II.; W. § 22, 5; [B. § 127, 15]. **3.** It is used frequently in the plural for the reciprocal pronoun ἀλλήλων, ἀλλήλοις, ἀλλήλους, reciprocally, mutually, one another: Mt. xvi. 7; xxi. 38; Mk. x. 26 [Tr mrg. WH αὑτόν]; xvi. 3; Lk. xx. 5; Eph. iv. 32; Col. iii. 13, 16; 1 Pet. iv. 8, 10; see Matthiae § 489 III.; Kühner ii. p. 497 sq.; Bnhdy. p. 273; [Bp. Lghtft. on Col. iii. 13].

1439 ἐάω, -ῶ; impf. εἴων; fut. ἐάσω; 1 aor. εἴασα; fr. Hom. down; **1.** to allow, permit, let: foll. by the inf., οὐκ ἂν εἴασε διορυγῆναι [T Tr WH -χθῆναι], Mt. xxiv. 43; by the acc. of the person and the inf., Lk. iv. 41 (οὐκ εἴα αὐτὰ λαλεῖν); Acts xiv. 16; xxiii. 32; xxvii. 32; xxviii. 4; 1 Co. x. 13; by the acc. alone, when the inf. is easily supplied from the context, οὐκ εἴασεν αὐτούς, sc. πορευθῆναι, Acts xvi. 7; οὐκ εἴων αὐτόν, sc. εἰσελθεῖν, Acts xix. 30; [cf. W. 476 (444)]. **2.** τινά, to suffer one to do what he wishes, not to restrain, to let alone: Rev. ii. 20 Rec.; Acts v. 38 R G; ἐᾶτε sc. αὐτούς, is spoken by Christ to the apostles, meaning, 'do not resist them, let them alone,' (the following ἕως τούτου is to be separated from what precedes; [al. connect the words closely, and render ' suffer them to go even to this extreme'; but cf. Mey. ad loc. ed. Weiss]), Lk. xxii. 51. **3.** To give up, let go, leave: τὰς ἀγκύρας ... εἴων εἰς τὴν θάλασσαν, they let down into the sea [i. e. abandoned; cf. B. D. Am. ed. p. 3009ᵃ bot.], Acts xxvii. 40. [COMP.: προσ-εάω.]*

1440 ἑβδομήκοντα, οἱ, αἱ, τά, [fr. Hdt. down], seventy: Acts vii. 14 [here Rec.ᵉˡᶻ ἑβδομηκονταπέντε]; xxiii. 23; xxvii. 37; οἱ ἑβδομήκοντα [ἑβδ. δύο L br. WH br.], the seventy disciples whom Jesus sent out in addition to the twelve apostles: Lk. x. 1, 17. [B. D. Am. ed. s. v. Seventy Disciples.]*

1440a [ἑβδομήκοντα-ἓξ for ἑβδομήκοντα ἕξ, seventy-six: Acts xxvii. 37 Rec.*]

1441 ἑβδομηκοντάκις, [Gen. iv. 24], seventy times: ἑβδομηκοντάκις ἑπτά, seventy times seven times, i. e. countless times, Mt. xviii. 22 [cf. W. § 37, 5 Note 2; B. 30 (26) and see ἑπτά, fin.; al. (cf. R. V. mrg.) seventy-seven times, see Mey. ad loc.].*

1440b [ἑβδομηκοντα-πέντε, seventy-five: Acts vii. 14 Rec.ᵉˡᶻ (Gen. xxv. 7; Ex. xxxix. 6 (xxxviii. 27); 1 Esdr. v. 12).*]

1442 ἕβδομος, -η, -ον, seventh: Jn. iv. 52; Heb. iv. 4; Jude 14; Rev. viii. 1; xi. 15, etc. [From Hom. down.]

1443 Ἑβέρ [Rᵗ G], more correctly [L T WH] Ἕβερ [on the accent in codd. see Tdf. Proleg. p. 103; Treg. Ἕβ., cf. Tdf. Proleg. p. 107; WH. Intr. § 408; cf. B. D. s. v. Heber], ὁ, Eber or Heber, indeclinable proper name of a Hebrew: Lk. iii. 35 (Gen. x. 24 sq.).*

1444 Ἑβραϊκός, -ή, -όν, Hebrew: Lk. xxiii. 38 (R G L br. Tr mrg. br.).*

1445 Ἑβραῖος [WH Ἑβρ., see their Intr. § 408], -ου, ὁ, a

Hebrew (עֵבֶר) a name first given to Abraham, Gen. xiv. 13, afterwards transferred to his posterity descended from Isaac and Jacob; by it in the O. T. the Israelites are both distinguished from and designated by foreigners, as afterwards by Pausan., Plutarch, al. The name is now generally derived from עֵבֶר for עֵבֶר הַנָּהָר i. e. *of the region beyond the Euphrates*, whence עִבְרִי equiv. to *one who comes from the region beyond the Euphrates*; Gen. xiv. 13 Sept. ὁ περάτης. Cf. *Gesenius*, Gesch. d. hebr. Sprache u. Schrift, p. 11 sq.; Thesaurus, ii. p. 987; *Knobel*, Völkertafel der Genesis, p. 176 sqq.; *Bleek*, Einl. in d. A. T. ed. 1, p. 73 sq. [Eng. trans. i. 76 sq.]; [B. D. s. v. Hebrew. For Syn. see 'Ιουδαῖος.]). In the N. T. **1.** any one of the Jewish or Israelitish nation : 2 Co. xi. 22; Phil. iii. 5. (In this sense Euseb. h. e. 2, 4, 3 calls Philo, the Alexandrian Jew, 'Εβραῖος, although his education was Greek, and he had little [if any] knowledge even of the Hebrew language; and in Praep. evang. 8, 8, 34 he applies the same word to Aristobulus, who was both an Alexandrian, and a Greek-speaking Jew.) **2.** In a narrower sense those are called 'Εβραῖοι who lived in Palestine and used the language of the country, i. e. Chaldee; from whom are distinguished οἱ Ἑλληνισταί, q. v. That name adhered to them even after they had gone over to Christianity : Acts vi. 1. (Philo in his de conf. lingg. § 26 makes a contrast between 'Εβραῖοι and ἡμεῖς; and in his de congr. erud. grat. § 8 he calls Greek ἡ ἡμετέρα διάλεκτος. Hence in this sense he does not reckon himself as a Hebrew.) **3.** All Jewish Christians, whether they spoke Aramaic or Greek, equiv. to πιστοὶ ἐξ Ἑβραίων; so in the heading of the Epistle to the Hebrews; called by Euseb. h. e. 3, 4, 2 οἱ ἐξ Ἑβραίων ὄντες. [Cf. *K. Wieseler*, Unters. ü. d. Hebräerbrief, 2te Hälfte. Kiel, 1861, pp. 25–30.] *

1446   'Εβραΐς [WH 'Εβρ., see their Intr. § 408], -ίδος, ἡ, *Hebrew*, the Hebrew language ; not that however in which the O. T. was written, but the Chaldee (not Syro-Chaldaic, as it is commonly but incorrectly called ; cf. *A. Th. Hoffmann*, Grammat. Syriac. p. 14), which at the time of Jesus and the apostles had long superseded it in Palestine: Acts xxi. 40; xxii. 2; xxvi. 14; 'Εβραΐς φωνή, 4 Macc. xii. 7; xvi. 15. [Cf. B. D. s. v. Shemitic Languages etc.; ib. Am. ed. s. v. Lang. of the New Test.] *

1447   'Εβραϊστί [WH 'Εβρ., see their Intr. § 408], adv., (ἑβραΐζω), *in Hebrew*, i. e. *in Chaldee* (see the foregoing word and reff.) : Jn. v. 2; xix. 13, 17, 20; [xx. 16 T Tr WH L br.]; Rev. ix. 11; xvi. 16. [Sir. prol. line 13.] *

1448   ἐγγίζω; impf. ἤγγιζον; Attic fut. ἐγγιῶ (Jas. iv. 8 [Bttm. 37 (32); W. § 13, 1 c.]); 1 aor. ἤγγισα; pf. ἤγγικα; (ἐγγύς); in Grk. writ. fr. Polyb. and Diod. on; Sept. for נגשׁ and קרב. **1.** trans. *to bring near, to join* one thing to another : Polyb. 8, 6, 7; Sept., Gen. xlviii. 10; Is. v. 8. **2.** intrans. *to draw* or *come near, to approach*; absol., Mt. xxi. 34; Lk. xviii. 40; [xix. 41]; xxi. 28; xxii. 1; xxiv. 15; Acts vii. 17; xxi. 33; xxiii. 15; [Heb. x. 25]; pf. ἤγγικε has come nigh, is at hand : ἡ βασιλ. τοῦ θεοῦ, Mt. iii. 2; iv. 17; x. 7; Mk. i. 15; Lk. x. 11; with the addition ἐφ' ὑμᾶς, vs. 9; ἡ ἐρήμωσις, Lk. xxi. 20; ἡ ὥρα, Mt. xxvi. 45; ὁ παραδιδούς με, Mt. xxvi. 46; [Mk.

xiv. 42 (where Tdf. ἤγγισεν)]; ὁ καιρός, Lk. xxi. 8; ἡ ἡμέρα, Ro. xiii. 12; τὸ τέλος, 1 Pet. iv. 7; ἡ παρουσία τοῦ κυρίου, Jas. v. 8. Construed with the dat. of the person or the place approached : Lk. vii. 12; xv. 1, 25; xxii. 47; Acts ix. 3; x. 9; xxii. 6; ἐγγίζειν τῷ θεῷ (in Sept. used esp. of the priests entering the temple to offer sacrifices or to perform other ministrations there, Ex. xix. 22; xxxiv. 30; Lev. x. 3, etc.) : to worship God, Mt. xv. 8 Rec., fr. Is. xxix. 13; to turn one's thoughts to God, to become acquainted with him, Heb. vii. 19; Jas. iv. 8; ὁ θεὸς ἐγγίζει τινί, God draws near to one in the bestowment of his grace and help, Jas. iv. 8. Foll. by εἰς and the acc. of the place : Mt. xxi. 1; Mk. xi. 1; Lk. xviii. 35; xix. 29; xxiv. 28; [foll. by πρός w. the dat., Lk. xix. 37, see B. § 147, 28; al. regard this as a pregn. constr., cf. W. §§ 48, e.; 66, 2 d.]; μέχρι θανάτου ἤγγισε, to draw nigh unto, be at the point of, death, Phil. ii. 30 (ἐγγίζειν εἰς θάνατον, Job xxxiii. 22); with an adv. of place, ὅπου κλέπτης οὐκ ἐγγίζει, Lk. xii. 33. [COMP.: προσ-εγγίζω.] *

[ἔγγιστα, neut. plur. superl. (fr. ἐγγύς) as adv., *nearest*, see 2945 *next* : WH (rejected) mrg. in Mk. vi. 36 (al. κύκλῳ).*]

1449   ἐγ-γράφω [T WH ἐνγρ., see ἐν, III. 3] : pf. pass. ἐγγέγραμμαι; [fr. Aeschyl. and Hdt. down]; *to engrave*; *inscribe, write in* or *on* : τί, pass. with dat. of the means [*with*] and foll. by ἐν with dat. of the place (in minds, tablets), 2 Co. iii. 2, 3; *to record, enrol* : τὰ ὀνόματα, pass. Lk. x. 20 T Tr WH. *

1450   ἔγγυος, -ου, ὁ, ἡ, *a surety*, (Cic. and Vulg. *sponsor*) : κρείττονος διαθήκης ἔγγυος, he by whom we get full assurance of the more excellent covenant made by God with us, and of the truth and stability of the promises connected with it, Heb. vii. 22. (2 Macc. x. 28; Sir. xxix. 15 sq. Xen. vect. 4, 20; Aeschin. Epp. 11, 12 p. 128 a.; Aristot. oec. 2, 22 [vol. ii. p. 1350ᵃ, 19], Polyb., Diod., al.)*

1451   ἐγγύς, adv., (fr. ἐν and γυῖον [limb, hand], at hand; [but rather allied w. ἄγχι, ἄγχω, *anxius, anguish*, etc.; see Curtius § 166; Vaniček p. 22]), [fr. Hom. down], Sept. for קָרוֹב; *near*; **1.** of Place and position; **a.** prop. : absol. Jn. xix. 42, [cf. also 20 G L T Tr WH (but see below)]; with gen. (Matthiae § 339, 1 p. 812; W. 195 (183); [471 (439); B. § 132, 24]), Lk. xix. 11; Jn. iii. 23; vi. 19, 23; xi. 18, 54; xix. 20 [Rec., but see above]; Acts i. 12; with dat. (Matthiae § 386, 6; Kühner § 423, 13; [Jelf § 592, 2]), Acts ix. 38; xxvii. 8. **b.** tropically; οἱ ἐγγύς, those who are near of access to God i. e. Jews, and οἱ μακράν, those who are alien from the true God and the blessings of the theocracy, i. e. Gentiles : Eph. ii. 17 (cf. Is. lvii. 19); ἐγγὺς γίνεσθαι, *to be brought near*, sc. to the blessings of the kingdom of God, Eph. ii. 13, (so with the Rabbins not infrequently *to make nigh* is equiv. to *to make a proselyte*, cf. Wetstein ad l. c.; [*Schöttgen*, Horae etc. i. 761 sq.; *Valck*. Schol. i. 363]); ἐγγύς σου τὸ ῥῆμά ἐστιν, near thee i. e. at hand, already, as it were, in thy mind, Ro. x. 8 fr. Deut. xxx. 14, [cf. B. § 129, 11; W. 465 (434)]. **2.** of Time; concerning things imminent and soon to come to pass : Mt. xxiv. 32; xxvi. 18; Mk. xiii. 28; Lk. xxi. 30, 31; Jn. ii. 13; vi. 4; vii. 2; xi. 55; Rev. i. 3; xxii. 10; of the near advent of persons: ὁ κύριος ἐγγύς, of Christ's return from heaven, Phil. iv. 5 (in another sense, of God in Ps. cxliv. (cxlv.) 18); with the addition ἐπὶ θύραις, at the door, Mt. xxiv. 33; Mk. xiii. 29; ἐγγὺς κατάρας, near to being cursed, Heb. vi. 8; ἀφανισμοῦ, soon to vanish, Heb. viii. 13.*

1452   ἐγγύτερον, neut. of the compar. ἐγγύτερος (fr. ἐγγύς), used adverbially, *nearer*: Ro. xiii. 11.*

1453   ἐγείρω; fut. ἐγερῶ; 1 aor. ἤγειρα; Pass., pres. ἐγείρομαι, impv. 2 pers. sing. ἐγείρου (Mk. ii. 9 T WH), Lk. viii. 54 (where L Tr WH ἔγειρε), 2 pers. plur. ἐγείρεσθε; pf. ἐγήγερμαι; 1 aor. ἠγέρθην [cf. B. 52 (45); W. § 38, 1]; 1 fut. ἐγερθήσομαι; Mid., 1 aor. impv. ἔγειραι Rec.; but, after good codd., Grsb. has in many pass. and lately L T Tr WH have everywhere in the N. T. restored ἔγειρε, pres. act. impv. used intransitively and employed as a formula for arousing; properly, *rise*, i. e. *up! come!* cf. ἄγε; so in Eur. Iph. A. 624; Arstph. ran. 340; cf. Fritzsche on Mk. p. 55; [B. 56 (49), 144 (126) sq.; Kühner § 373, 2]; Sept. generally for הֵעִיר and הֵקִים; *to arouse, cause to rise*;   **1.** as in Grk. writ. fr. Homer down, *to arouse from sleep, to awake*: Acts xii. 7; [Mk. iv. 38 T Tr WH]; pass. *to be awaked, wake up*, [A. V. *arise*, often including thus the subseq. action (cf. 3 below)]: Mt. xxv. 7; Mk. iv. 27; [ἀπὸ τοῦ ὕπνου, Mt. i. 24 L T Tr WH]; ἐγερθείς with the impv. Mt. ii. 13, 20; with a finite verb, Mt. ii. 14, 21; viii. 26; [Lk. viii. 24 R G L Tr mrg.]; ἐγείρεσθε, Mt. xxvi. 46; Mk. xiv. 42. Metaph. ἐξ ὕπνου ἐγερθῆναι, to arise from a state of moral sloth to an active life devoted to God, Ro. xiii. 11; likewise ἔγειρε [Rec. -ραι] *arise*, ὁ καθεύδων, Eph. v. 14.   **2.** *to arouse from the sleep of death, to recall the dead to life*: with νεκρούς added, Jn. v. 21; Acts xxvi. 8; 2 Co. i. 9. ἔγειρε [Rec. -ραι] *arise*, Mk. v. 41; pass. ἐγείρου, Lk. viii. 54 [R G T]; ἐγέρθητι, *arise from death*, Lk. vii. 14; ἐγείρονται οἱ νεκροί, Mt. xi. 5; Lk. viii. 22; xx. 37; 1 Co. xv. 15, 16, 29, 32, (Is. xxvi. 19); ἐγείρειν ἐκ νεκρῶν, from the company of the dead [cf. W. 123 (117); B. 89 (78)], Jn. xii. 1, 9; Acts iii. 15; iv. 10; xiii. 30; Ro. iv. 24; viii. 11; x. 9; Gal. i. 1; Eph. i. 20; Col. ii. 12; 1 Th. i. 10; Heb. xi. 19; 1 Pet. i. 21; pass., Ro. vi. 4, 9; vii. 4; 1 Co. xv. 12, 20; Jn. ii. 22; xxi. 14; Mk. vi. 16 [T WH om. Tr br. ἐκ νεκρ.]; Lk. ix. 7; [Mt. xvi. 9 L T Tr WH txt.]; ἀπὸ τῶν νεκρῶν, Mt. xiv. 2; xxvii. 64; xxviii. 7, (νεκρὸν ἐκ θανάτου καὶ ἐξ ᾄδου, Sir. xlviii. 5; for הֵקִים, 2 K. iv. 31); ἐγείρειν simply: Acts v. 30; x. 40; xiii. 37; 1 Co. vi. 14; 2 Co. iv. 14; pass., Mt. xvi. 21; xvii. 23 [L WH mrg. ἀναστήσεται]; [xx. 19 T Tr txt. WH txt.]; xxvi. 32; xxvii. 63; Mk. [vi. 16 T WH (see above)]; xvi. 6; Lk. xxiv. 6 [WH reject the clause], 34; Ro. iv. 25; 1 Co. xv. 4, etc.   **3.** in later usage generally *to cause to rise, raise*, from a seat, bed, etc.; pass. and mid. *to rise, arise*; used   **a.** of one sitting: ἐγείρεται [L Tr WH ἠγέρθη] ταχύ, Jn. xi. 29, cf. vs. 20; pres. act. imperative ἔγειρε (see above), Mk. x. 49 [not Rec.], cf. vs. 46; hence (like the Hebr. קוּם, Gen. xxii. 3; 1 Chr. xxii. 19), in the redundant manner spoken of s. v. ἀνίστημι, II. 1 c. it is used before verbs of going, etc.: ἐγερθεὶς ἠκολούθει [-ησεν R G] αὐτῷ, Mt. ix. 19; ἔγειρε [R G -ραι]

καὶ μέτρησον, Rev. xi. 1.   **b.** of one reclining: ἐγείρεται ἐκ τοῦ δείπνου, Jn. xiii. 4; ἐγείρεσθε, Jn. xiv. 31.   **c.** of one lying, *to raise up*: ἤγειρεν αὐτόν, Acts x. 26; ἐγέρθητε *arise*, Mt. xvii. 7; ἔγειρε (see above) Acts iii. 6 [L Tr txt. br.]; ἠγέρθη ἀπὸ τῆς γῆς he rose from the earth, Acts ix. 8; *to* [raise up i. e.] *draw out* an animal from a pit, Mt. xii. 11.   **d.** of one 'down' with disease, lying sick: act., Mk. ix. 27; Acts iii. 7; ἐγερεῖ αὐτὸν ὁ κύριος, will cause him to recover, Jas. v. 15; pass. Mt. viii. 15; ἔγειρε ([Rec. -ραι, so Grsb. (doubtfully in Mt.)], see above) arise: Mt. ix. 5; Jn. v. 8; Acts iii. 6 [T WH om. Tr br.].   **4.** *To raise up, produce, cause to appear*:   **a.** *to cause to appear, bring before the public* (any one who is to attract the attention of men): ἤγειρε τῷ Ἰσραὴλ σωτῆρα, Acts xiii. 23 Rec.; ἤγειρεν αὐτοῖς τὸν Δαυεὶδ εἰς βασιλέα, Acts xiii. 22 (so הֵקִים, Judg. ii. 18; iii. 9, 15); pass. ἐγείρομαι, *to come before the public, to appear, arise*: Mt. xi. 11; xxiv. 11, 24; Mk. xiii. 22; Lk. vii. 16; Jn. vii. 52 [cf. W. 266 (250); B. 204 (177)]; contextually, *to appear before a judge*: Mt. xii. 42; Lk. xi. 31.   **b.** ἐπί τινα *to raise up, incite, stir up, against one*; pass. *to rise against*: Mt. xxiv. 7; Mk. xiii. 8; Lk. xxi. 10.   **c.** *to cause to be born*: τέκνα τινί, Mt. iii. 9; Lk. iii. 8; κέρας σωτηρίας, Lk. i. 69 (see ἀνίστημι, I. c. ἐξανίστημι, 1); θλῖψιν τοῖς δεσμοῖς μου, to cause affliction to arise to my bonds, i. e. the misery of my imprisonment to be increased by tribulation, Phil. i. 16 (17) L T Tr WH.   **d.** of buildings, *to raise, construct, erect*: τὸν ναόν, Jn. ii. 19 sq. (so הֵקִים, Deut. xvi. 22; 1 K. xvi. 32. Aelian. de nat. an. 11, 10; Joseph. antt. 4, 6, 5; Hdian. 3, 15, 6 [3d. Bekk.]; 8, 2, 12 [5 ed. Bekk.]; Lcian. Pseudomant. § 19; Anthol. 9, 696. 1 Esdr. v. 43; Sir. xlix. 13; Lat. *excito turrem*, Caes. b. g. 5, 40; *sepulcrum*, Cic. legg. 2, 27, 68). [Ammonius: ἀναστῆναι καὶ ἐγερθῆναι διαφέρει· ἀναστῆναι μὲν γὰρ ἐπὶ ἔργον· ἐγερθῆναι δὲ ἐξ ὕπνου; cf. also Thom. Mag. ed. Ritschl p. 14, 10 sq. But see exx. above. Comp.: δι-, ἐξ-, ἐπ-, συν-εγείρω.]

ἔγερσις, -εως, ἡ, (ἐγείρω), *a rousing, excitation*: τοῦ θυμοῦ,   **1454** Plat. Tim. p. 70 c.; *a rising up*, Ps. cxxxviii. (cxxxix.) 2; *resurrection* from death: Mt. xxvii. 53.*

ἐγκάθετος [T WH ἐνκ., see ἐν, III. 3], -ου, ὁ, ἡ, (ἐγκαθί-   **1455** ημι [to send down in (secretly)]), *suborned to lie in wait; a lier-in-wait, spy*, [cf. Lat. *insidiator*; Eng. *insidious*]: used in Lk. xx. 20 of one who is suborned by others to entrap a man by crafty words. (Plat. Ax. p. 368 e.; Dem. p. 1483, 1; Joseph. b. j. 6, 5, 2; Polyb. 13, 5, 1, al.; Sept., Job [xix. 12]; xxxi. 9.)*

ἐγκαίνια [T WH ἐνκ., see ἐν, III. 3], -ων, τά, (fr. ἐν and   **1456** καινός); only in bibl. and eccl. writ., (on the plur. cf. W. § 27, 3; B. 23 (21)]; *dedication, consecration*; thus in 2 Esdr. vi. 16, 17; Neh. xii. 27 for חֲנֻכָּה; in particular, [Vulg. *encaenium* i. e. *renovation*], an annual feast celebrated eight days beginning on the 25th of Chislev (middle of our December), instituted by Judas Maccabaeus [B. c. 164] in memory of the cleansing of the temple from the pollutions of Antiochus Epiphanes (αἱ ἡμέραι ἐγκαινισμοῦ τοῦ θυσιαστηρίου, 1 Macc. iv. 59): Jn. x. 22. Cf. Win. RWB. [also Riehm, HWB.] s. v. Kirchweihfest;

Oehler in Herzog iv. p. 389; Grimm on 1 Macc. i. 54; iv. 52; *Dillmann* in Schenkel iii. 534 sq.; [BB.DD. (esp. Kitto) s. v. Dedication, Feast of the].*

1457 ἐγ-καινίζω [T WH ἐνκ., see ἐν, III. 3] : 1 aor. ἐνεκαίνισα; pf. pass. ἐγκεκαίνισμαι; a word exclusively bibl. and eccl. [W. 33]; *to innovate*, i. e. **1.** *to renew* : 2 Chr. xv. 8. **2.** *to do anew, again* : σημεῖα, Sir. xxxiii. (xxxvi.) 6. **3.** *to initiate, consecrate, dedicate,* (Deut. xx. 5; 1 K. viii. 63; 1 S. xi. 14, etc.) : διαθήκην, Heb. ix. 18; ὁδόν, Heb. x. 20.*

see 1573 ἐγ-κακέω, -ῶ [(see below) ; 1 aor. ἐνεκάκησα] ; (κακός) ; [prop. to behave badly in; hence] *to be weary in* anything, or *to lose courage, flag, faint* : adopted by L T Tr WH in place of R G ἐκκακέω (q. v.) in Lk. xviii. 1; 2 Co. iv. 1, 16; Gal. vi. 9; Eph. iii. 13; 2 Th. iii. 13 — except that T WH write ἐνκ. in Lk. xviii. 1; Gal. vi. 9; Eph. iii. 13; so WH in 2 Th. iii. 13, also; see ἐν, III. 3; [cf. Tdf.'s note on 2 Co. iv. 1 ; Meyer ibid., who thinks that ἐκκ. may have been a colloquial form. See the full exhibition of the usage of the Mss. given by Dr. *Gregory* in his Proleg. to Tdf. ed. 8, p. 78.] (Found a few times in Symmachus [Gen. xxvii. 46 ; Num. xxi. 5 ; Is. vii. 16 ; also Prov. iii. 11 Theod.] ; Clem. Rom. 2 Cor. 2, 2 ; in prof. writ. only in Polyb. 4, 19, 10 τὸ πέμπειν τὰς βοηθείας ἐνεκάκησαν they culpably neglected to send aid, [add Philo de confus. lingg. §13 (Mang. i. 412, 36) οὐκ ἐκκακούμενος ἐκνάμφθην].)*

1458 ἐγ-καλέω [see ἐν, III. 3] -ῶ ; fut. ἐγκαλέσω ; impf. ἐνεκάλουν ; [pres. pass. ἐγκαλοῦμαι] ; prop. *to call* (something) *in* some one (ἐν [i. e. prob. *in his case* ; or possibly, as rooted *in* him]) ; hence, *to call to account, bring a charge against, accuse* : as in classic Grk. foll. by dat. of the person [cf. W. § 30, 9 a.], Acts xix. 38 ; xxiii. 28, (Sir. xlvi. 19) ; κατά with gen. of the pers. *to come forward as accuser against, bring a charge against* : Ro. viii. 33. Pass. *to be accused* (cf. B. § 134, 4, [§ 133, 9 ; yet cf. Mey. on Acts as below, W. u. s.]) ; with gen. of the thing : στάσεως, Acts xix. 40, (ἀσεβείας ἐς τὸν Τιβέριον ἐγκληθείς, Dio Cass. 58, 4 ; act. with dat. of the pers. and gen. of the thing, Plut. Arist. 10, 9 ; see W. u. s.; Matthiae § 369) ; περὶ τούτων, ὧν ἐγκαλοῦμαι, unless this is to be resolved into περὶ τούτων ἅ etc., acc. to the well-known construction ἐγκαλεῖν τινί τι, Acts xxvi. 2 ; περί τινος (act. Diod. 11, 83) Acts xxiii. 29 ; xxvi. 7, [B. § 133, 9]. (In Grk. writ. fr. Soph. and Xen. down.) [SYN. see κατηγορέω, fin.]*

1459 ἐγ-κατα-λείπω [Acts ii. 27, 31, T WH ἐνκ.; T also in Ro. ix. 29, see his note and cf. ἐν, III. 3] ; [impf. ἐγκατέλειπον (WH txt. in 2 Tim. iv. 10, 16)] ; fut. ἐγκαταλείψω ; 2 aor. ἐγκατέλιπον ; Pass., [pres. ἐγκαταλείπομαι] ; 1 aor. ἐγκατελείφθην ; Sept. for עָזַב ; **1.** *to abandon, desert,* (ἐν equiv. to ἔν τινι, in some place or condition), i. e. *to leave in straits, leave helpless,* (colloq. *leave in the lurch*) : τινά, Mt. xxvii. 46 and Mk. xv. 34 fr. Ps. xxi. (xxii.) 2 ; Heb. xiii. 5 ; pass. 2 Co. iv. 9 ; after the Hebr. עָזַב with לְ, τινὰ εἰς ᾅδου [or ᾅδην], by forsaking one to let him go into Hades, abandon unto Hades, Acts ii. 27, 31 (not R). *to desert, forsake* : τινά, 2 Tim. iv. 10, 16 ; τὴν ἐπισυναγωγήν, Heb. x. 25. **2.** *to leave behind among, to leave surviv-*

ing : ἡμῖν σπέρμα, Ro. ix. 29 fr. Is. i. 9. (Hes. opp. 376 ; Thuc., sqq.)*

1460 ἐγ-κατ-οικέω [T WH ἐνκ., see ἐν, III. 3], -ῶ ; *to dwell among* : ἐν αὐτοῖς among them, 2 Pet. ii. 8. (Very rare in prof. writ. as [Hdt. 4, 204] ; Eur. frag. [188] ap. Dion Chrys. or. 73 fin. ; Polyb. 18, 26, 13.)*

see 2744 ἐγ-καυχάομαι [T WH ἐνκ., see ἐν, III. 3] ; *to glory in* : foll. by ἐν with dat. of the obj. (Ps. li. (lii.) 3 ; xcvi. (xcvii.) 7 ; cv. (cvi.) 47), 2 Th. i. 4 L T Tr WH. (With simple dat. of thing in eccl. writ. and Aesop's Fables.)*

1461 ἐγ-κεντρίζω [T WH ἐνκ., see ἐν, III. 3] : 1 aor. ἐνεκέντρισα ; Pass., 1 aor. ἐνεκεντρίσθην ; 1 fut. ἐγκεντρισθήσομαι ; *to cut into for the sake of inserting a scion ; to inoculate, ingraft, graft in,* (Aristot. ap. Athen. 14, 68 [p. 653 d.] ; Theophr. h. p. 2, 2, 5 ; Antonin. 11, 8) : τινά, Ro. xi. 17, 19, 23, 24 [cf. W. § 52, 4, 5] ; in these pass. Paul likens the heathen who by becoming Christians have been admitted into fellowship with the people for whom the Messianic salvation is destined, to scions from wild trees inserted into a cultivated stock ; [cf. Beet on vs. 24 ; B. D. s. v. Olive].*

1462 ἔγκλημα [see ἐν, III. 3], -τος, τό, (ἐγκαλέω), *accusation* : the *crime* of which one is accused, Acts xxv. 16 ; ἔγκλημα ἔχειν, to have laid to one's charge, be accused of a crime, Acts xxiii. 29. (Often in Attic writ. fr. Soph. and Thuc. on.)*

[SYN. see κατηγορέω ; cf. Isoc. 16, 2 τὰς μὲν γὰρ δίκας ὑπὲρ τῶν ἰδίων ἐγκλημάτων λαγχάνουσι, τὰς δὲ κατηγορίας ὑπὲρ τῶν τῆς πόλεως πραγμάτων ποιοῦνται, καὶ πλείω χρόνον διατρίβουσι τὸν πατέρα μου διαβάλλοντες ἢ κτλ.]

1463 ἐγ-κομβόομαι [see ἐν, III. 3], -οῦμαι : [1 aor. mid. ἐνεκομβωσάμην] ; (fr. ἐν and κομβόω to knot, tie, and this fr. κόμβος knot, band, (Germ. *Schleife*), by which two things are fastened together), *to fasten* or *gird on one's self* ; the ἐγκόμβωμα was the white scarf or apron of slaves, which was fastened to the girdle of the vest [ἐξωμίς], and distinguished slaves from freemen ; hence 1 Pet. v. 5 τὴν ταπεινοφρ. ἐγκομβώσασθε, gird yourselves with humility as your servile garb (ἐγκόμβωμα) i. e. by putting on humility show your subjection one to another. That this idea lies in the phrase is shown by *C. F. A. Fritzsche*, with his usual learning, in Fritzschiorum Opusc. p. 259 sqq.*

1464 ἐγ-κοπή [WH ἐνκ. T ἐκκ., see ἐν, III. 3], -ῆς, ἡ, (ἐγκόπτω), properly, *a cutting* (made in the road to impede an enemy in pursuit [(?)], hence), *a hindrance* : 1 Co. ix. 12. (Diod. 1, 32 ; Dion. Hal. de comp. verb. p. 157, 15 (22) ; Longin. de sublim. 41, 3 ; [al.].)*

1465 ἐγ-κόπτω [in Acts T WH ἐνκ., so T in 1 Pet. where R ἐκκ. ; see ἐν, III. 3] ; 1 aor. ἐνέκοψα ; Pass., [pres. ἐγκόπτομαι] ; impf. ἐνεκοπτόμην ; *to cut into, to impede one's course by cutting off his way* ; hence univ. *to hinder* (Hesych. : ἐμποδίζω, διακωλύω) ; with dat. of the obj., Polyb. 24, 1, 12 ; in the N. T. with acc. of the obj., 1 Th. ii. 18 ; foll. by inf., Gal. v. 7 (see ἀνακόπτω) ; inf. preceded by τοῦ, Ro. xv. 22 ; εἰς τὸ μὴ ἐγκόπτεσθαι τὰς προσευχὰς ὑμῶν, that ye be not hindered from praying (together), 1 Pet. iii. 7 ; i. q. *to detain* [A. V. *to be tedious unto*] one, Acts xxiv. 4 [cf. Valcken. Schol. i. 600 sq.].*

1466 ἐγκράτεια [see ἐν, III. 3], -ας, ἡ, (ἐγκρατής), *self-control,*

Lat. *continentia, temperantia*, (the virtue of one who masters his desires and passions, especially his sensual appetites): Acts xxiv. 25; Gal. v. 23 (22); 2 Pet. i. 6. (Xen., Plat., sqq.; Sir. xviii. 29; 4 Macc. v. 34.)*

1467 ἐγκρατεύομαι [see ἐν, III. 3]; depon. mid.; *to be self-controlled, continent* (ἐγκρατής); *to exhibit self-government, conduct one's self temperately*: [used absol. Gen. xliii. 30]; with dat. of respect, τῇ γλώσσῃ, Sir. xix. 6 var.; πάντα, in everything, every way, 1 Co. ix. 25 (in a figure drawn from athletes, who in preparing themselves for the games abstained from unwholesome food, wine, and sexual indulgence); οὐκ ἐγκρατεύεσθαι, said of those who cannot curb sexual desire, 1 Co. vii. 9. Though this word does not occur in the earlier Grk. writ. that have come down to us [exc. in Aristot. eth. Eudem. 2, 7 p. 1223ᵇ, 13 ed. Bekk.], yet its use is approved of by Phrynichus; cf. *Lob.* ad Phryn. p. 442; [W. 25].*

1468 ἐγκρατής [see ἐν, III. 3], -ές, (κράτος); **1.** prop. equiv. to ὁ ἐν κράτει ὤν, *strong, robust*: Aeschyl., Thuc., sqq. **2.** *having power over, possessed of* (a thing), with a gen. of the object; so fr. [Soph. and] Hdt. down. **3.** *mastering, controlling, curbing, restraining*: ἀφροδισίων, Xen. mem. 1, 2, 1; ἡδονῆς, ibid. 4, 5, 10; ἑαυτοῦ, Plat.; absol. (without a gen.), *controlling one's self, temperate, continent*, ([Aristot. eth. Nic. 7, 4 p. 1146ᵇ, 10 sqq.]; Sir. xxvi. 15; Sap. viii. 21; Philo de Jos. § 11]: Tit. i. 8.*

1469 ἐγ-κρίνω [T WH ἐνκ., see ἐν, III. 3]: [1 aor. ἐνέκρινα]; *to reckon among, judge among*: τινά τινι, *to judge one worthy of being admitted to* a certain class [A. V. *to number with*], 2 Co. x. 12. (From Xen. and Plato down.)*

1470 ἐγ-κρύπτω: 1 aor. ἐνέκρυψα; *to conceal in* something, τὶ εἴς τι (Diod. 3, 63; Apollod. 1, 5, 1 § 4); contextually, *to mingle one thing with another*: Mt. xiii. 33; Lk. xiii. 21 here T Tr WH ἔκρυψεν. (τί τινι, Hom. Od. 5, 488.)*

1471 ἔγκυος [WH ἔνκ., see ἐν, III. 3], -ον, for the more usual ἐγκύμων, (fr. ἐν and κύω), *big with child, pregnant*: Lk. ii. 5. (Hdt. 1, 5 etc.; Diod. 4, 2; Joseph. antt. 4, 8, 33.)*

1472 ἐγ-χρίω [see ἐν, III. 3]: 1 aor. act. impv. ἔγχρισον, mid. (in T Tr) ἔγχρισαι [but L WH 1 aor. act. infin. ἐγχρῖσαι (Grsb. ἐγχρῖσαι; cf. Veitch s. v. χρίω, fin.)]; *to rub in, besmear, anoint*; Mid. *to anoint for one's self*: τοὺς ὀφθαλμούς, Rev. iii. 18 [cf. Bttm. 149 sq. (131); W. § 32, 4 a.]. (Tob. vi. 9; xi. 7; Strab., Anthol., Epict., al.)*

1473 ἐγώ, gen. ἐμοῦ, enclitic μοῦ; dat. ἐμοί, enclitic μοί; acc. ἐμέ, enclitic μέ; plur. ἡμεῖς, etc.; personal pronoun, *I*. **1.** The nominatives ἐγώ and ἡμεῖς, when joined to a verb, generally have force and emphasis, or indicate antithesis, as Mt. iii. 11; Mk. i. 8; Lk. iii. 16 (ἐγὼ μὲν ... ὁ δέ; Mt. iii. 14 (ἐγὼ ... ἔχω, καὶ σύ); v. 22, 28, 39, and often; ἡμεῖς, contrasted with God, Mt. vi. 12; ἡμεῖς κ. οἱ Φαρισαῖοι, Mt. ix. 14; cf. W. § 22, 6. But sometimes they are used where there is no emphasis or antithesis in them, as Mt. x. 16; Jn. x. 17; and in many edd. in Mk. i. 2; Lk. vii. 27; cf. B. § 129, 12. ἰδοὺ ἐγώ, הִנֵּנִי, *behold me, here am I*: Acts ix. 10 (1 S. iii. 8). ἐγώ, like אָנֹכִי, *I am*: Jn. i. 23; Acts vii. 32, [cf. W. 585 (544); B. 125 (109)]. **2.** The enclitic (and monosyllabic) gen., dat., and acc.

are connected with nouns, verbs, adverbs, but not with prepositions: ἔμπροσθέν μου, Jn. i. 15; ὀπίσω μου, Mt. iii. 11; ἰσχυρότερός μου, ibid.; τίς μου ἥψατο, Mk. v. 31; λέγει μοι, Rev. v. 5; ἀρνήσηταί με, Mt. x. 33; Lk. xii. 9, (on the accent in these expressions cf. W. § 6, 3; [*Lipsius*, Gram. Untersuch. p. 59 sqq.; *Lob.* Path. Elementa ii. p. 323 sq.; *Tdf.* N. T. ed. 7, Proleg. p. lxi. sq.; ed. 8 p. 104]); but δι' ἐμοῦ, κατ' ἐμοῦ, πρὸ ἐμοῦ, etc., σὺν ἐμοί, περὶ, δι', ἐπ', κατ', εἰς ἐμέ. The only exception is πρός, to which the enclitic μέ is generally joined, Mt. xxv. 36; Mk. ix. 19, and very often; very rarely πρὸς ἐμέ, Jn. vi. 37ᵃ, and acc. to L T Tr WH in Acts xxii. 8, 13; xxiv. 19; [also Acts xxiii. 22 T Tr WH; Jn. vi. 35 and 45 T WH txt. WH; Lk. i. 43 T WH; Mt. xix. 14; Jn. vi. 37ᵇ, 65, Tdf.; Jn. vi. 44 Tr txt. WH mrg.; 1 Co. xvi. 11 L Tr; but πρὸς μέ, Mt. iii. 14 Tdf. and xi. 28 Grsb.; cf. Lipsius u. s. p. 61 note]. Moreover, the full forms ἐμοῦ, ἐμοί, ἐμέ are used in case of emphasis or antithesis; thus, ἐμοῦ, Lk. x. 16; ἐμοί, Jn. vii. 23; x. 38, etc.; ἐμέ, Mk. xiv. 7; Jn. vii. 7, etc. **3.** As in classic Greek, μου and ἡμῶν are very often used for the possessive pronouns ἐμός and ἡμέτερος [B. § 127, 21]; and when so used, **a.** they are generally placed after their substantives, as ὁ οἶκός μου, ἡ ζωὴ ἡμῶν, etc. — the fuller form ἐμοῦ only for the sake of distinction or antithesis [cf. B. § 127, 22], as μητέρα αὐτοῦ καὶ ἐμοῦ, Ro. xvi. 13; πίστεως ὑμῶν τε καὶ ἐμοῦ, Ro. i. 12. But **b.** they are sometimes placed before substantives, even which have the article, when no emphasis resides in the pron. or antithesis is involved in its use [W. § 22, 7 N. 1; B. u. s.]: μου τοὺς λόγους, Mt. vii. 24, 26; even before prepositions, μου ὑπὸ τὴν στέγην, Mt. viii. 8; less frequently ἡμῶν, as ἡμῶν τὴν πόλιν, Acts xvi. 20; it is prefixed for emphasis in ἡμῶν τὸ πολίτευμα, Phil. iii. 20, cf. W. u. s.; Rost § 99, 4 p. 452 sqq. 7th ed. adduces a multitude of exx. fr. Grk. auth.; [cf. Krüger, § 47, 9, 12 who states the rule as follows: when joined to a subst. having the art. the **reflexive** gen., with αὐτοῦ *ipsius*, and ἀλλήλων, requires the **attributive** position, the **personal** gen., and αὐτοῦ *ejus*, the **partitive** position]. **4.** τί ἐμοί (ἡμῖν) καὶ σοί (ὑμῖν); *what have I (we) to do with thee (you)?* [cf. B. 138 (121); W. 211 (198); 585 (544)]: Mt. viii. 29; Mk. i. 24; v. 7; Lk. viii. 28; Jn. ii. 4; Heb. מַה־לִּי וָלָךְ, Judg. xi. 12; 2 K. iii. 13; 2 S. xvi. 10; 2 Chr. xxxv. 21; 1 Esdr. i. 24; also in classic Greek; cf. Gell. n. a. 1, 2; Epict. diss. 2, 9, 16; τί ἡμῖν κ. αὐτῷ, ibid. 1, 1, 16; τί ἐμοὶ καὶ αὐτοῖς, ibid. 1, 27, 13; 22, 15. τί γάρ μοι, *what does it concern me? what have I to do etc.*: 1 Co. v. 12; cf. *Bos*, Ellipses Graec. p. 599, ed. Schaefer; Bnhdy. p. 98; Krüger § 48, 3, 9; Kühner ii. 364 sq.; [B. as above, also 394 (337); W. 586 (545)].

1474 ἐδαφίζω: Attic fut. ἐδαφιῶ [B. 37 (32); W. § 13, 1 c.]; (see ἔδαφος); *to throw to the ground*, — both of cities, buildings, *to raze, level with the earth*, and of men; in both applications in Lk. xix. 44 [by zeugma (?) cf. W. § 66, 2 e.]. (Ps. cxxxvi. (cxxxvii.) 9; Is. iii. 26; Ezek. xxxi. 12; Hos. xiv. 1 (xiii. 16); Am. ix. 14 [Ald.]; rare in prof. writ., as [Aristot. probl. 23, 29]; Polyb. 6, 33, 6.)*

1475   **ἔδαφος**, -εος (-ους), τό, *bottom, base, ground*: πίπτειν εἰς τὸ ἔδαφος, Acts xxii. 7. (Sept.; in class. writ. fr. Hom. down.) *

1476   **ἑδραῖος**, (rarely fem. -αία [W. § 11, 1]), -αῖον, (ἕδρα seat, chair);   **1.** *sitting, sedentary*, (Xen., Plat., al.).   **2.** *firm, immovable, steadfast*, (Eur., Plat., al.); in the N. T. metaph., of those who are fixed in purpose: 1 Co. xv. 58; Col. i. 23; ἕστηκεν ἐν τῇ καρδίᾳ, 1 Co. vii. 37.*

1477   **ἑδραίωμα**, -τος, τό, (ἑδραιόω to make stable, settle firmly), *a stay, prop, support*, (Vulg. *firmamentum*) : 1 Tim. iii. 15 [A.V. *ground*]. (Eccl. writ.) *

1478   **Ἐζεκίας** [WH Ἐζ-; L -κείας, see *Tdf.* Proleg. p. 85], (חִזְקִיָּה strength of Jehovah, i. e. strength given by Jehovah; Germ. *Gotthard*; Sept. Ἐζεκίας), [gen. -ου, cf. B. 17 (16) no. 8], *Hezekiah*, king of Judah (2 K. xviii. 1 sqq.; xx. 1 sqq.; Is. xxxviii. 1 sqq.): Mt. i. 9, 10. *

1479   **ἐθελο-θρησκεία** [T WH -κία, see I, ι], -ας, ἡ, (fr. ἐθέλω and θρησκεία, q. v. [cf. W. 100 (95)]), *voluntary, arbitrary worship*, (Vulg. *superstitio*), [A. V. *will-worship*], i. e. worship which one devises and prescribes for himself, contrary to the contents and nature of the faith which ought to be directed to Christ; said of the misdirected zeal and practices of ascetics: Col. ii. 23; Suid. ἐθελοθρησκεῖ· ἰδίῳ θελήματι σέβει τὸ δοκοῦν. Cf. ἐθελόδουλος, ἐθελοδουλεία, ἐθελοπρόξενος one who acts the part of a *proxenus* without having been appointed to the office, etc. The explanation of others: *simulated, counterfeit religion* (cf. in Greek lexicons ἐθελοφιλόσοφος, ἐθελόκωφος, etc.), does not square so well with the context. (The word is found besides in *Mansi*, Collect. Concil. vol. iv. p. 1380, and in Theodoret, vol. iv. ep. clxi. p. [1460 b. ed. Migne] 1331, Halle ed.; [Euseb. h. e. 6, 12, 1; Jerome ep. cxxi. vol. i. 1034 ed. Migne]. Epiph. haer. 1, 16 [i. p. 318, 3 ed. Dind.] attributes ἐθελοπερισσοθρησκεία to the Pharisees.)*

see **2309** — — **ἐθέλω**, see θέλω.

1480   **ἐθίζω**, (ἔθος q. v.); *to accustom*; Pass. *to be accustomed*; pf. ptcp. τὸ εἰθισμένον *usage, custom*: τοῦ νόμου, prescribed by the law, Lk. ii. 27. (Eur., [Arstph.], Thuc., Xen., Plat., al.) *

1481   **ἐθνάρχης**, -ου, ὁ, (fr. ἔθνος and ἄρχω), [i. q. founder of a nation, Philo, quis rer. div. her. § 56], *an ethnarch*, one set over a people as ruler, but without the authority and name of king (Lcian. in Macrob. § 17 ἀντὶ ἐθνάρχου βασιλεὺς ἀναγορευθεὶς Βοσπόρου; so the governor whom the Alexandrian Jews used to have was called ἐθνάρχης, of whom Josephus says, antt. 14, 7, 2, ὃς διοικεῖ τε τὸ ἔθνος καὶ διαιτᾷ κρίσεις καὶ συμβολαίων ἐπιμελεῖται καὶ προσταγμάτων, ὡς ἂν πολιτείας ἄρχων αὐτοτελοῦς; likewise Simon Maccabaeus, 1 Macc. xiv. 47; xv. 1, 2; Joseph. antt. 13, 6, 6; cf. [19, 5, 2]; b. j. 2, 6, 3): 2 Co. xi. 32 ὁ ἐθνάρχης Ἀρέτα τοῦ βασιλέως, the governor of Damascene Syria, ruling in the name of king Aretas [(q. v.); cf. B. D. s. v. Governor, 11].*

1482   **ἐθνικός**, -ή, -όν, (ἔθνος);   **1.** *adapted to the genius or customs of a people, peculiar to a people, national*: Polyb., Diod., al.   **2.** *suited to the manners or language of foreigners, strange, foreign*; so in the grammarians [cf. our

'gentile'].   **3.** in the N. T. *savoring of the nature of pagans, alien to the worship of the true God, heathenish*; substantively, ὁ ἐθνικός *the pagan, the Gentile* : Mt. xviii. 17; plur., Mt. v. 47 G L T Tr WH; vi. 7; and 3 Jn. 7 L T Tr WH.*

ἐθνικῶς, adv., (see ἐθνικός), *like the Gentiles* : Gal. ii. 14, [W. 463 (431). Apollon. Dysk. p. 190, 5; Diog. Laërt. 7, 56].*   **1483**

ἔθνος, -ους, τό;   **1.** *a multitude* (whether of men or   **1484** of beasts) *associated* or *living together* ; *a company, troop, swarm*: ἔθνος ἑταίρων, ἔθνος Ἀχαιῶν, ἔθνος λαῶν, Hom. Il.; ἔθνος μελισσάων, 2, 87; μυιάων ἔθνεα, ib. 469.   **2.** *a multitude of individuals of the same nature* or *genus*, (τὸ ἔθνος τὸ θῆλυ ἢ τὸ ἄρρεν, Xen. oec. 7, 26): πᾶν ἔθνος ἀνθρώπων, *the human race*, Acts xvii. 26 [but this seems to belong under the next head].   **3.** *race, nation* : Mt. xxi. 43; Acts x. 35, etc.; ἔθνος ἐπὶ ἔθνος, Mt. xxiv. 7; Mk. xiii. 8; οἱ ἄρχοντες, οἱ βασιλεῖς τῶν ἐθνῶν, Mt. xx. 25; Lk. xxii. 25; used [in the sing.] of the Jewish people, Lk. vii. 5; xxiii. 2; Jn. xi. 48, 50–53; xviii. 35; Acts x. 22; xxiv. 2 (3), 10; xxvi. 4; xxviii. 19.   **4.** (τὰ) ἔθνη, like גּוֹיִם in the O. T., *foreign nations not worshipping the true God, pagans, Gentiles*, [cf. Trench § xcviii.] : Mt. iv. 15 (Γαλιλαία τῶν ἐθνῶν), vi. 32; [3 Jn. 7 R G; cf. Rev. xv. 3 G L T Tr WH mrg. after Jn. x. 7], and very often; in plain contradistinction to the Jews: Ro. iii. 29; ix. 24; [1 Co. i. 23 G L T Tr WH]; Gal. ii. 8, etc.; ὁ λαός (τοῦ θεοῦ, Jews) καὶ τὰ ἔθνη, Lk. ii. 32; Acts xxvi. 17, 23; Ro. xv. 10.   **5.** Paul uses τὰ ἔθνη even of Gentile *Christians* : Ro. xi. 13; xv. 27; xvi. 4; Gal. ii. 12 (opp. vs. 13 to οἱ Ἰουδαῖοι i. e. Jewish Christians), vs. 14; Eph. iii. 1, cf. iv. 17 [W. § 59, 4 a.; B. 130 (114)].

ἔθος, -εος (-ους), [cf. ἦθος], τό, fr. Aeschyl. [Agam.   **1485** 728 (?); better fr. Soph.] down, *custom*: Lk. xxii. 39; ἔθος ἐστί τινι foll. by an inf., Jn. xix. 40; Acts xxv. 16; Heb. x. 25; contextually, *usage prescribed by law, institute, prescription, rite* : Lk. i. 9; ii. 42; Acts xxi. 21; xxvi. 3; xxviii. 17; περιτέμνεσθαι τῷ ἔθει Μωϋσέως, Acts xv. 1; ἀλλάξει τὰ ἔθη ἃ παρέδωκε Μωϋσῆς, Acts vi. 14.*

ἔθω (of the pres. only the ptcp. ἔθων is used, in Hom.):   **1486** pf. εἴωθα, *to be accustomed, used, wont* ; [plpf. as impf. (W. 274 (257 sq.)) εἰώθειν] ; foll. by inf.: Mt. xxvii. 15; Mk. x. 1. Ptcp. τὸ εἰωθός in a pass. sense, *that which is wont* ; *usage, custom*: κατὰ τὸ εἰωθός τινι as one's custom is, as is his wont, Lk. iv. 16; Acts xvii. 2.*

[εἰ, ι: εἰ and ι are freq. interchanged in N. T. spelling. This is due partly to itacism, partly to the endeavor to mark the ι sound as long or short. See the remarks on this subject in WH. App. p. 152 sq. (cf. Intr. § 399); *Tdf.* Proleg. p. 83 sq.; *Soph.* Lex. s. v. εἰ. The use of ι for εἰ is noticed s. v. I, ι; instances in which εἰ is substituted for ι are the foll. : Ἀβειληνή WH; Ἀδδεί T Tr WH; Ἀντείπας T; Ἀρεοπαγείτης T; Βενιαμείν L T Tr WH; Δαυείδ L T Tr WH; Ἐζεκείας L; Ἐλαμείτης T WH; Ἐλεισάβετ WH; Ἐσλεί T Tr WH; Εὐνείκη Rec.ˢᵗ; Ἠλεί T Tr WH; Ἠλείας T WH; Ἰερειχώ T WH; Ἱεροσολυμείτης T WH; Ἰσραηλείτης T WH, so Tr in Jn. i. 47 (48); Ἰωσείας L T Tr WH; Κείς L T Tr WH; Κυρεῖνος Tr mrg. WH mrg.; Λευείς T WH, so Tr exc. in Mk. ii. 14; Λευείτης T WH, so Tr exc. in Acts iv. 36; Λευειτικός T WH; Μελχεί T T Tr WH; Νηρεί T Tr WH; Νινευείτης T

1487

WH, so Tr in Mt. xii. 41; Ὀζείας L T Tr WH; Πειλᾶτος T WH; Σεμεεΐν T Tr WH; Ταβειθά WH; Χερουβεΐν L T Tr WH (-βίμ R G); Χοραζεΐν T Tr WH; ἀφειδεια L; εἰδέα T Tr WH; ἐπαρχεία T WH; ἐπιπόθεια WH; ἠλεί T; πανοικεί T WH; ῥαββεί T WH; ῥαββουνεί WH; σαβαχθανεί T Tr WH; ταλειθά WH; τάχειον WH; τραπεζείτης T WH.]

εἰ, is first a conditional particle, *if* (Lat. *si*); secondly, an interrogative particle, *whether*, (Lat. *an, num, ne*).

I. εἰ CONDITIONAL (on the difference between it and ἐάν, see ἐάν, I. 1 b.) is connected, according to the variety of conditions, with various tenses and moods; viz. **1.** with the Indicative of all tenses, when anything is simply and generally assumed to be, or to be done, or to have been done, or to be about to be, (W. § 41 b., 2; cf. 42, 2; [B. 220 (190)]). **a.** with the Ind. Present **a.** foll. in the apodosis by the ind. pres.: Mt. xix. 10 (εἰ οὕτως ἐστὶν ἡ αἰτία . . . οὐ συμφέρει γαμῆσαι); xi. 14; Ro. vii. 16, 20; viii. 25; xiv. 15; 1 Co. ix. 17, Gal. ii. 18; v. 18; Heb. xii. 8; Jas. ii. 8 sq., etc. **β.** foll. by an Imperative in the apodosis, — either the pres., as [Mt. xix. 17 L Tr txt. WH txt.]; Mk. iv. 23; vii. 16 R G L; Jn. xv. 18; Acts xiii. 15; xxv. 5; 1 Co. vii. 12, 15; Jas. iii. 14, etc.; or the aor., as Mt. v. 29, 30; viii. 31; xix. 17 [R G T Tr mrg. WH mrg.]; Mk. ix. 22 [cf. B. 55 (48)]; Lk. xxii. 67 (66); 1 Co. vii. 9. **γ.** foll. by the Future in the apodosis: Lk. xvi. 31; Acts v. 39 L T Tr WH; xix. 39; Ro. viii. 11, 13; 2 Co. xi. 30, etc. **δ.** foll. by the Perfect or the Aorist in the apodosis, where it is declared that, if this or that is, something else has or has not occurred: Mt. xii. 26, 28; Lk. xi. 20; 1 Co. xv. 16; Gal. ii. 21; Ro. iv. 14; 2 Pet. ii. 20. **ε.** foll. by the Imperfect, either with or without ἄν, where in the protasis something is simply assumed to be, but the apodosis shows that what has been assumed cannot be the case. Three passages falling under this head have a doubtful or disputed text: εἰ ἔχετε (T Tr WH, for the R G L εἴχετε) . . . ἐλέγετε ἄν etc. Lk. xvii. 6; εἰ . . . μνημονεύουσιν (T Tr, for R G L WH ἐμνημόνευον) . . . εἶχον ἄν, Heb. xi. 15 (where by the pres. tense the writer refers to the language of the Jewish Fathers as at present recorded in the sacred Scriptures; cf. τοιαῦτα λέγοντες vs. 14); εἰ τέκνα τοῦ Ἀβρ. ἐστε (G L T Tr WH, for R ἦτε) . . . ἐποιεῖτε ([WH txt. ποι.] R L add ἄν), Jn. viii. 39; cf. *Bttm.* in Stud. u. Krit. for 1858 p. 474 sqq. [N. T. Gram. § 139, 26; but cf. Mey. on Lk. l. c.]. But 2 Co. xi. 4 εἰ . . . κηρύσσει . . . ἀνείχεσθε G T Tr WH mrg. (ἀνέχεσθε L WH txt.) must not be referred to this head; here Paul in the protasis supposes something which actually occurred, in the apodosis censures a thing which actually occurred viz. the readiness with which his readers gave ear continually (this is indicated by the impf.) to false teachers. On the difficulty of the passage cf. *Holsten* in the Zeitschr. f. wissensch. Theol. for 1874, p. 1 sqq.; [cf. also B. 226 (195); but W. 306 (287) and Mey. ad loc.]. **ζ.** with a question as the apodosis: Mt. vi. 23; Jn. v. 47; vii. 23; viii. 46; 1 Pet. ii. 20. **b.** with the Ind. Future: Mt. xxvi. 33; Jas. ii. 11 R G; 1 Pet. ii. 20. **c.** with the Ind. Perfect: Jn. xi. 12; Acts xvi. 15; Ro. vi. 5; xi. 6 (where after εἰ supply λεῖμμα γέγονεν fr. what precedes), 2 Co. ii. 5; v. 16; vii. 14. **d.** with the Ind. Aorist, — foll. by the

Pres. in the apodosis, Lk. xix. 8; Ro. iv. 2; xv. 27; foll. by a question in the apodosis, Lk. xvi. 11, 12; Jn. xviii. 23; 1 Co. iv. 7; ix. 11; foll. by the Aor. in the apodosis, Rev. xx. 15; by the Impv. in the apodosis, Jn. xviii. 23; xx. 15; Ro. xi. 17 sq.; 1 Tim. v. 9, 10; Philem. 18; by the Fut. in the apodosis, Jn. xiii. 32; xv. 20; Heb. xii. 25 (where supply οὐκ ἐκφευξόμεθα in the apodosis). **2.** Not infrequently, when a conclusion is drawn from something that is quite certain, εἰ with the Indic. is used argumentatively so as to be equiv. in sense to ἐπεί, (cf. the use of Germ. *wenn*) [cf. W. 448 (418)]: Mt. xii. 28; Lk. xxiii. 31; Jn. vii. 4; Ro. v. 17; vi. 5; viii. 31; xi. 6, 12; Col. ii. 20; iii. 1, etc. **3.** When it is said what would have been, or what would be now or in the future, if something else were or had been, εἰ is used with the Impf., Plpf., and Aor. ind.; in the apodosis it is followed in direct disc. by ἄν with the impf. or the plpf. or the aor.; sometimes ἄν is omitted, (on the causes of the omission, see B. § 139, 27); sometimes the apodosis is made a question, [cf. W. 304 (285) sq.]. **a.** εἰ with the Impf., foll. in the apodosis by ἄν with the impf.: Mt. xxiii. 30; Lk. vii. 39 (εἰ οὗτος ἦν προφήτης, ἐγίνωσκεν ἄν if this man were a prophet, he would know); Jn. v. 46; viii. 42; ix. 41; xv. 19; 1 Co. xi. 31; Gal. i. 10; Heb. viii. 4, 7 (if . . . were etc. there would not be sought etc. viz. in the O. T. passage quoted vs. 8); by a question in the apodosis: 1 Co. xii. 19; Heb. vii. 11; by ἄν with the aor., where the Latin uses the plupf. subjunc.: Jn. xi. 32 (εἰ ἦς ὧδε if thou hadst been here, οὐκ ἄν ἀπέθανέ μου ὁ ἀδελφός my brother would not have died [when he did (cf. below); B. § 139, 25 regards the impf. in prot. as expressing duration]); Jn. iv. 10; xviii. 30 (εἰ μὴ ἦν οὗτος κακοποιός, οὐκ ἄν σοι παρεδώκαμεν αὐτόν, we would not have delivered him to thee); Acts xviii. 14; by ἄν with the plupf.: Jn. xi. 21 (εἰ ἦς ὧδε . . . οὐκ ἄν ἐτεθνήκει, would not have died [and be now dead]; cf. W. 304 (285)] and see above; but L T Tr txt. WH read the aor. here also]); 1 Jn. ii. 19. **b.** εἰ with the Plpf., foll. in the apodosis by ἄν with the plpf. or the aor., in the sense of the Latin plpf. subj.: Mt. xii. 7 (εἰ ἐγνώκειτε if ye had understood i. e. if ye knew, οὐκ ἄν κατεδικάσατε τοὺς ἀναιτίους ye would not have condemned the guiltless); Mt. xxiv. 43 and Lk. xii. 39, (εἰ ᾔδει if he had perceived i. e. if he knew, ἐγρηγόρησεν ἄν he would have watched, sc. before the thief had approached [Tr txt. WH om. ἄν in Lk. l. c.]); Jn. iv. 10; viii. 19; xiv. 7 [R G L]. **c.** with the Aor. in the same sense as the Lat. plpf. subjunc.: εἰ ἐδόθη νόμος . . . ὄντως ἄν ἐκ νόμου ἦν ἡ δικαιοσύνη if a law had been given, righteousness would in truth come from the law, Gal. iii. 21; εἰ αὐτοὺς Ἰησοῦς κατέπαυσεν if Joshua had given them rest, οὐκ ἄν περὶ ἄλλης ἐλάλει he would not be speaking, sc. in the passage quoted, Heb. iv. 8; apodosis without ἄν, Jn. xv. 22, see ἄν I. 3 p. 33 sq. **4.** As in classic Greek, εἰ with the Ind. is often joined to verbs expressing wonder, surprise, or other strong emotion (where ὅτι might have been expected), when the thing spoken of is either not quite certain, or, although certain, yet in accordance with the well-known Greek urbanity is represented as not quite free from doubt (Matthiae ii. p. 1474 sq.; Kühner ii. p. 887 sq.; [Jelf § 804, 9]; W. § 60, 6; [B. § 139, 52]). Thus it is joined – to the verb θαυμάζω : ἐθαύμαζεν, εἰ ἤδη τέθνηκε, for the matter had not yet been investigated; hence it is added ἐπηρώτησεν αὐτόν, εἰ ἤδη [R G T Tr mrg. WH mrg. πάλαι) ἀπέθανεν, Mk. xv. 44; μὴ θαυμάζετε, εἰ μισεῖ ὑμᾶς ὁ κόσμος (the thing is certain) 1 Jn. iii. 13 ; to the phrase ἄπιστον κρίνεται: Acts xxvi. 8, (with παράδοξον preceding, Lcian. dial. mort. 13, 1); to καλόν ἐστιν and λυσιτελεῖ : Mk. ix. 42 and Lk. xvii. 2 (Mt. xviii. 6 has συμφέρει, ἵνα); Mt. xxvi. 24 and Mk. xiv. 21; to μέγα ἐστί : 1 Co. ix. 11 (on which see 8 below); 2 Co. xi. 15 ; τί θέλω, εἰ ἤδη ἀνήφθη (τὸ πῦρ), how would I if (i. e. that) it were already kindled (but it has not yet been kindled), Lk. xii. 49 (al. al., but cf. Meyer ad loc.; [so B. l. c.; cf. W. 448 (418) ; see τίς, 1 e. γ. fin.]; Sir. xxiii. 14 ἐπίστευσεις, εἰ μὴ ἐγεννήθης; [in addition to the other interpretations noticed by Win. and Mey. ll. cc. mention may be made of that which takes θέλω as subjunc. : *what am I to choose if* (as I may well assume) *it has already been kindled*; cf. Green, 'Crit. Notes' ad loc.]).   **5.** Contrary to Greek usage, in imitation of the Hebr. אִם, εἰ with the Indic. is so used in oaths and asseverations that by aposiopesis the formula of imprecation [constituting the apodosis] is suppressed (W. § 55 fin.; B. § 149, 4) : ἀμὴν λέγω ὑμῖν, εἰ δοθήσεται . . . σημεῖον (fully expressed, 'may God punish me, if it shall be given,' i. e. it shall by no means be given), Mk. viii. 12; ὤμοσα, εἰ εἰσελεύσονται εἰς τὴν κατάπαυσίν μου (fully, 'let my name no longer be Jehovah, if they shall enter' etc.), Heb. iii. 11 ; iv. 3, fr. Ps. xciv. (xcv.) 11 Sept. (Hebr. אִם, Gen. xiv. 23 ; Num. xiv. 30; 1 S. xiv. 45, etc.; we have the full expression in 1 S. iii. 17; Cant. ii. 7, etc.).   **6.** Sometimes, as in classic Grk., after a protasis with εἰ and the Indic., the apodosis is suppressed on account of mental agitation and left to be supplied by the reader or the hearer from the context, (cf. W. 599 sq. (557)) : εἰ βούλει παρενεγκεῖν τὸ ποτήριον τοῦτο (sc. παρένεγκε [but here L Tr WH adopt the impv. in place of the inf.; yet cf. B. 396 (339)]), Lk. xxii. 42 ; εἰ δὲ πνεῦμα ἐλάλησεν αὐτῷ ἢ ἄγγελος, supply in place of an apodosis the question *what then?* Acts xxiii. 9 (the apod. added in Rec., μὴ θεομαχῶμεν, is spurious) ; εἰ ἔγνως . . . τὰ πρὸς εἰρήνην σου, sc. ἐπίστευες ἂν ἐμοί, Lk. xix. 42 [B. 396 (339)].   **7.** The conditional εἰ is joined with the Optative, to indicate that the condition is merely thought of or stated as a possibility, (cf. *Klotz* ad Devar. ii. 2 p. 491 sqq.; W. 293 (275) sq.; B. § 139, 24). No example of this construction is found in the Gospels; very few in the rest of the N. T.   **a.** univ. in short intercalated clauses : εἰ τύχοι if it so chance, it may be, (see τυγχάνω, 2), 1 Co. xiv. 10; xv. 37; εἰ θέλοι τὸ θέλημα τοῦ θεοῦ, 1 Pet. iii. 17 (Rec. θέλει).   **b.** where it indicates that something may occur repeatedly (cf. Klotz l. c. p. 492 sq.) : εἰ καὶ πάσχοιτε, 1 Pet. iii. 14 [cf. W. u. s.].   **c.** where the condition represents the mind and judgment of others : εἰς ὃν ἐβουλεύοντο [R G -σαντο], εἰ δύναιντο ἐξῶσαι [WH txt. ἐκσῶσαι (q. v.)] τὸ πλοῖον, into which

bay [or rather 'upon which beach'; see ἐξωθέω] they determined to run the ship, if they could ; as though the navigators had said among themselves, ἐξώσαμεν, εἰ δυνάμεθα, Acts xxvii. 39 ; so also εἴ τι ἔχοιεν πρός με, if they think they have anything against me, Acts xxiv. 19.   **8.** with the Subjunctive, when it is assumed that something may take place, but whether it will in reality is unknown before the event, in order to make the event seem to be more certain than if ἐάν were used (Klotz l. c. p. 500 sqq.; W. 294 (276) sq.; B. § 139, 22) : εἰ θερίσωμεν, 1 Co. ix. 11 Tdf. edd. 2, 7, [Lchm. mrg. ; al. -σομεν]; (Sept. Gen. xliii. 3 sq.; Sir. xxii. 26 ; 4 Macc. vi. 20). But see III. below, under εἰ μή, εἰ μήτι, εἴ πως, εἴτε . . . εἴτε, εἴ τις.

     II. εἰ INTERROGATIVE, *whether.* "The conditional particle gets this force if a question is asked about anything, whether it is or is not so, and that about which the question is put is uttered as it were conditionally " (Klotz l. c. p. 508; [W. § 57, 1; Bttm. 248 (214) sqq.; 254 (218) sq.]).   **1.** As in Grk. writ. in an indirect question after verbs of seeing, asking, deliberating, knowing, saying, etc.   **a.** with the Indic. Present: as οὐδ᾽ εἰ πνεῦμα ἅγιον ἔστιν, ἠκούσαμεν (prop., acc. to the conditional force of the particle, ' if there is [i. e. has appeared, been given; cf. εἰμί, I. 2] a Holy Spirit, we did not even hear'), Acts xix. 2 ; ἴδωμεν, εἰ ἔρχεται, Mt. xxvii. 49; Mk. xv. 36; βουλεύεται [T WH L mrg. -σεται], εἰ δυνατός ἐστιν, Lk. xiv. 31 ; ἵνα εἴπῃς, εἰ σὺ εἶ, Mt. xxvi. 63 ; [ἵνα γνῶ τὴν δοκιμὴν ὑμῶν εἰ (WH mrg. ῇ) . . ὑπήκοοί ἐστε, 2 Co. ii. 9 (see WH. Intr. § 404)]; after οὐκ οἶδα, Jn. ix. 25; after κρίνατε, Acts iv. 19; δοκιμάζετε [(?), πειράζετε], 2 Co. xiii. 5.   **b.** with the Indic. Future [cf. W. 300 (282); B. § 139, 61 b.]: δεήθητι, εἰ ἄρα ἀφεθήσεταί σοι, Acts viii. 22; τί οἶδας, εἰ . . . σώσεις, 1 Co. vii. 16 ; παρετήρουν, εἰ θεραπεύσει [Tdf. -πεύει], Mk. iii. 2 and in Lk. vi. 7 [R G WH mrg.]; ἦλθεν (sc. to see), εἰ ἄρα τι εὑρήσει, Mk. xi. 13.   **c.** with the Indic. Aorist : οὐκ οἶδα, εἴ τινα ἄλλον ἐβάπτισα, whether I baptized, 1 Co. i. 16 ; ἐπηρώτησαν, εἰ πάλαι [L Tr txt. WH txt. ἤδη] ἀπέθανεν, whether he were long dead, Mk. xv. 44 ; εἰπέ μοι, εἰ . . . ἀπέδοσθε, Acts v. 8.   **d.** with the Subjunctive Aorist [cf. B. 255 sq. (220) ; W. 298 (280) sq.]: διώκω, εἰ καὶ καταλάβω I press on (sc. πειρώμενος or σκοπῶν, trying to see), whether I may also lay hold, Phil. iii. 12. So *si* is used in Latin, e. g. Nep. vit. Hann. 8 Hannibal . . . Africam accessit in finibus Cyrenaeorum (sc. experturus), si forte Carthaginienses ad bellum possent induci ; Caes. b. g. 1, 8, 4 si perrumpere possent, conati; add Caes. b. g. 2, 9, 1. Cf. Kühner ii. p. 1032 sq.; [Jelf § 877 b.].   **2.** Contrary to the usage of Grk. auth., like the Hebr. אִם and interrog. הֲ, it is used in the Sept. and the N. T. (esp. by Luke) also in direct questions (cf. the colloq. use of the Germ. *ob*; e. g. *ob ich's wohl thun soll?*) ; cf. W. § 57, 1; B. 248 (214), and, in opposition to those who have striven to absolve the sacred writers from this misuse of the particle (esp. Fritzsche and Meyer [see the latter's note on Mt. xii. 10 and Lk. xiii. 23]; he quotes with approval the language of

Ast (Lexicon Platon. vol. i. 601), 'dubitanter interrogat, ita ut interrogatio videatur directa esse ']), cf. *Lipsius*, Paulin. Rechtfertigungslehre, p. 30 sqq.: — εἰπέ τις αὐτῷ, κύριε, εἰ ὀλίγοι οἱ σωζόμενοι; Lk. xiii. 23; κύριε, εἰ πατάξομεν ἐν μαχαίρᾳ [-ρῃ T Tr WH]; Lk. xxii. 49; κύριε, εἰ ... ἀποκαθιστάνεις τ. βασιλείαν; Acts i. 6; cf. besides, Mt. xii. 10; xix. 3; Mk. viii. 23 (acc. to the reading of [Tdf. 2, 7] Tr [mrg. WH txt.] εἴ τι βλέπεις for R G L T Tr txt. WH mrg. βλέπει); Acts xix. 2, etc. (Gen. xvii. 17; xliii. 6; 1 S. x. 24, etc.; in the O. T. Apocr. 2 Macc. vii. 7; xv. 3; 4 Macc. xviii. 17 fr. Ezek. xxxvii. 3 Sept.; Tob. v. 5).

III. εἰ with other particles and with the indef. pron. τὶς, τὶ. **1.** εἰ ἄρα, see ἄρα, 1. **2.** εἴγε, see γέ, 3 c. **3.** εἰ δὲ καί, **a.** *but if also*, so that καί belongs to some word that follows: Lk. xi. 18 (but if Satan also). **b.** *but though, but even if*, so that καί belongs to εἰ : 1 Co. iv. 7; 2 Co. iv. 3; v. 16 [R G; al. om. δέ]; xi. 6; see 6 below. **4.** εἰ δὲ μή, *but if not*; *if it is or were otherwise*, [B. 393 (336 sq.), cf. 345 (297); W. as below]: Jn. xiv. 2 (εἰ δὲ μή, sc. οὕτως ἦν), 11 (εἰ δὲ μή, sc. ἐμοὶ πιστεύετε, i. e. my words). As in these passages so generally the phrase stands where a word or clause must be repeated in thought from what immediately precedes; it thus has the force of the Lat. *alioquin, otherwise, or else*, [W. 583 (543)]: Rev. ii. 5, 16; also after negative declarations, Mk. ii. 21 sq.; cf. Matthiae § 617 b. **5.** εἰ δὲ μήγε, see γέ, 3 d. **6.** εἰ καί, **a.** *if even, if also*, (cf. εἰ δὲ καί, 3 a., [and 7 below]): 1 Co. vii. 21 [cf. Mey. ad loc.; Bp. Lghtft. on Philem. p. 324]; 2 Co. xi. 15. **b.** *though, although*: Lk. xi. 8; 2 Co. iv. 16; vii. 8, 12; Phil. ii. 17; Col. ii. 5 [εἰ γὰρ καί]; Heb. vi. 9; with the optat. 1 Pet. iii. 14; see I. 7 b. above. **7.** καὶ εἰ, *even if*: Mk. xiv. 29 [T Tr WH εἰ καί]; 1 Pet. iii. 1; cf. Klotz l. c. p. 519 [who says, "In εἰ καί the conditional particle εἰ has the greater force; in καὶ εἰ the conjunctive particle καί. Hence καὶ εἰ is used of what is only assumed to be true; εἰ καί, on the other hand, of what is as it is said to be." Bäumlein (Griech. Partikeln, p. 151) says, "In εἰ καί the καί naturally belongs to the conditional clause and is taken up into it, *if even*; in the combination καὶ εἰ the καί belongs to the consequent clause, *even if*. Sometimes however the difference disappears." Krüger (§ 65, 5, 15): "with καὶ εἰ, the leading clause is regarded as holding under every condition, even the one stated, which appears to be the most extreme; with εἰ καί the condition, which may also come to pass, is regarded as a matter of indifference in reference to the leading clause;" Sauppe (on Dem. Ol. ii. § 20) is very explicit: "καὶ εἰ and εἰ καί both indicate that something conflicts with what is expressed in the leading clause, but that that is (or is done) notwithstanding. καὶ εἰ, however, represents the thing adduced in the conditional sentence to be the only thing conflicting; but when the conditional particle precedes (εἰ καί), the representation is that something which is (or may be) accompanied by many others (καί) conflicts ineffectually. Accordingly the phrase καὶ εἰ greatly augments the force of

what follows, εἰ καί lays less emphasis upon it; although it is evident that εἰ καί can often be substituted for καὶ εἰ." Cf. *Herm.* Vig. p. 829 sq.; W. 444 (413); Ellic. on Phil. ii. 17; *Schmalfeld*, Griech. Syntax, § 41; *Paley*, Grk. Particles, p. 31]. **8.** εἰ μή, **a.** in a conditional protasis, with the same sequence of moods and tenses as the simple εἰ, see I. above, *if not, unless, except*, [W. 477 (444) sqq.; B. 345 (297)]: Mt. xxiv. 22; Jn. ix. 33; xv. 22, 24; Ro. vii. 7, etc. **b.** it serves, with the entire following sentence, to limit or correct what has just been said, *only, save that*, (Lat. *nisi quod*), [B. 359 (308)]: Mk. vi. 5; 1 Co. vii. 17 (where Paul by the addition εἰ μὴ ἑκάστῳ κτλ. strives to prevent any one in applying what had been said a little while before, viz. οὐ δεδούλωται ... ἐν τοιούτοις to his own case, from going too far); in ironical answers, *unless perchance, save forsooth that*, (Kühner § 577, 7; [Jelf § 860, 5 Obs.]): εἰ μὴ χρῄζομεν κτλ. 2 Co. iii. 1 Rec. **c.** εἰ μή very often coalesce into one particle, as it were, which takes the same verb as the preceding negation: *unless*, i. q. *except, save*, [Kühner § 577, 8; B. 359 (308)]; **a.** univ.: Mt. xi. 27; xii. 39; Mk. ii. 26; viii. 14; Jn. iii. 13; Ro. vii. 7; xiii. 1, 8; 1 Co. viii. 4; xii. 3; 2 Co. xii. 5, etc. as in classic Greek, μόνος, μόνον, is added pleonastically: Mt. xviii. 8; xxi. 19; xxiv. 36; Acts xi. 19; Phil. iv. 15; Rev. xiii. 17, etc. **β.** after negatives joined to nouns it is so used as to refer to the negative alone (hence many have regarded it as used for ἀλλά [i. e. as being not exceptive but adversative]), and can be rendered in Lat. *sed tantum, but only*: Mt. xii. 4 (οὐκ ἐξὸν ἦν αὐτῷ φαγεῖν οὐδὲ τοῖς μετ' αὐτοῦ, εἰ μὴ τοῖς ἱερεῦσι μόνοις, as if οὐκ ἐξὸν ἦν φαγεῖν alone preceded); Lk. iv. 26 sq.; Ro. xiv. 14; Rev. ix. 4; xxi. 27 (ἐὰν μή is so used in Gal. ii. 16; on Gal. i. 19 see Ἰάκωβος, 3); cf. Fritzsche on Rom. vol. iii. p. 195; [see ἐάν, I. 3 c. and reff.]. **γ.** when preceded by the interrogative τίς in questions having a negative force: Mk. ii. 7; Lk. v. 21; Ro. xi. 15; 1 Co. ii. 11; 2 Co. ii. 2; xii. 13; Heb. iii. 18; 1 Jn. ii. 22; v. 5; (Xen. oec. 9, 1; Arstph. eqq. 615). **δ.** with other conjunctions: εἰ μὴ ἵνα, Jn. x. 10; εἰ μὴ ὅταν, Mk. ix. 9; τί ἐστιν, εἰ μὴ ὅτι etc., 2 Co. xii. 13; Eph. iv. 9. **ε.** it has its own verb, and makes a phrase by itself: ὃ οὐκ ἔστιν ἄλλο, εἰ μή τινές εἰσιν οἱ ταράσσοντες ὑμᾶς which means nothing else, save that there are some who trouble you, Gal. i. 7 [so Winer (Com. ad loc.) et al.; but see Meyer]. **d.** ἐκτὸς εἰ μή, arising from the blending of the two expressions εἰ μή and ἐκτὸς εἰ, like the Lat. *nisi si* equiv. to *praeterquam si, except in case, except*: 1 Tim. v. 19; with the indic. aor. 1 Co. xv. 2; with the subjunc. pres. 1 Co. xiv. 5; [Lcian. de luctu c. 19; dial. meret. 1, 2, etc.). Cf. *Lob.* ad Phryn. p. 459; W. § 65, 3 c.; [B. index s. v. ἐκτὸς εἰ μή]. **9.** εἰ μήν, *assuredly, surely*, in oaths: Heb. vi. 14 L T Tr WH (for R G ἦ μήν [q. v.]) and several times in Sept. as Ezek. xxxiii. 27; xxxiv. 8; [cf. xxxvi. 5; xxxviii. 19]; 1 K. xxi. (xx.) 23], etc.; here, if εἰ did not come from ἦ by itacism, εἰ μήν must be explained as a confusion of the Hebraistic εἰ μή (see I. 5 above) and the Grk. formula of asseveration ἦ μήν; cf. Bleek on Heb.

vol. ii. 2 p. 248 sqq., and what Fritzsche says on the other side, Com. on Bar. ii. 29; Judith i. 12; [cf. Kneucker on Bar. l. c.; B. 359 (308); *Tdf.* Proleg. p. 59; *WH*. App. p. 151; B. D. s. v. New Testament, I. 31]. **10.** εἰ μή τι or μήτι, *unless in some respect, unless perchance, unless indeed*: ironically, with the indic. pres. 2 Co. xiii. 5; hesitatingly, with the subjunc. aor. Lk. ix. 13; cf. Meyer ad loc. [also W. 294 (276); B. 221 (191)]; εἰ μή τι ἄν: 1 Co. vii. 5, see ἄν, IV. **11.** εἰ οὐ (fully discussed by W. § 55, 2 c. and B. 345 (297) sqq.), *if not*; this combination is used much more frequently in the N. T. than in the more elegant Grk. auth.; it differs from εἰ μή in this, that in the latter μή belongs to the particle εἰ, while in εἰ οὐ the οὐ refers to some following word and denies it emphatically, not infrequently even coalescing with it into a single idea. **a.** when the idea to which οὐ belongs is antithetic **α.** to a p o s i t i v e term, either preceding or following: εἰ δὲ οὐ μοιχεύεις φονεύεις δέ, Jas. ii. 11 [in R G the fut.]; εἰ γὰρ ὁ θεὸς . . . οὐκ ἐφείσατο, . . . ἀλλὰ . . . παρέδωκεν εἰς κρίσιν, 2 Pet. ii. 4 sq.; εἰ καὶ οὐ δώσει . . . διά γε . . . δώσει, Lk. xi. 8; εἰ οὐ ποιῶ . . . εἰ δὲ ποιῶ, Jn. x. 37 sq.; εἰ γὰρ ἐπιστεύετε . . . , εἰ δὲ . . . οὐ πιστεύετε, Jn. v. 46 sq.; add, Mk. xi. 26 R G L; Ro. viii. 9; 1 Co. ix. 2; xi. 6; Jas. iii. 2. **β.** to some other idea which is n e g a t i v e (formally or virtually): εἰ . . . οὐκ ἀκούουσιν, οὐδὲ . . . πεισθήσονται, Lk. xvi. 31; εἰ . . . οὐκ ἐφείσατο, οὐδὲ σοῦ φείσεται [Rec. -σηται], Ro. xi. 21; add, 1 Co. xv. 13, 15–17; 2 Th. iii. 10; foll. in the apodosis by a question having the force of a negative: Lk. xvi. 11 sq.; Jn. iii. 12; 1 Tim. iii. 5. **γ.** the οὐ denies with emphasis the idea to which it belongs: καλὸν ἦν αὐτῷ, εἰ οὐκ ἐγεννήθη, good were it for him not to have been born, Mt. xxvi. 24; Mk. xiv. 21. **δ.** the whole emphasis is placed on the negative itself: εἰ σὺ οὐκ εἶ ὁ Χριστός, Jn. i. 25. **b.** the οὐ coalesces, as it were, with the word to which it belongs into a single idea: εἰ δὲ οὐκ ἐγκρατεύονται, if they are *incontinent*, 1 Co. vii. 9; εἴ τις τῶν ἰδίων οὐ προνοεῖ [or -εῖται T Tr txt. WH mrg.], *neglects*, 1 Tim. v. 8; add, Lk. xiv. 26; 1 Co. xvi. 22; Rev. xx. 15, etc. **12.** εἰ οὖν, *if then*: Mt. vi. 23; vii. 11; Lk. xi. 13, 36; Jn. xiii. 14; xviii. 8; Acts xi. 17; Col. iii. 1; Philem. 17. [On εἰ μὲν οὖν see μέν II. 4.] **13.** εἴπερ [so T WH (exc. in 2 Co. v. 3 mrg.), but L Tr εἴ περ; cf. W. 45; *Lipsius*, Gram. Unters. p. 123], (εἰ and πέρ, and this apparently from περί), prop. *if on the whole; if only, provided that*, is used "of a thing which is assumed to be, but whether rightly or wrongly is left in doubt" (*Herm.* ad Vig. p. 831, [so W. 448 (417); but cf. *Bäumlein*, Griech. Partikeln, p. 202 (cf. 64 bot.); *Klotz* ad Devar. ii. 2 p. 528, and esp. s. v. εἴγε (in γέ, 3 c.) and the reff. to Mey., Lghtft., Ellic., there given]): Ro. viii. 9, 17; 1 Co. viii. 5; xv. 15; 1 Pet. ii. 3 (where L T Tr WH εἰ); by a species of rhetorical politeness it is used of that about which there is no doubt: 2 Th. i. 6; Ro. iii. 30 L T Tr WH; 2 Co. v. 3 L Tr WH mrg. **14.** εἴ πως [L Tr WH] or εἴπως [G T], *if in any way, if by any means, if possibly*: with the optat. pres. (see I. 7 above), Acts xxvii. 12; interrogatively, with the indic. fut. Ro. i. 10;

with the subjunc. aor., so that before εἰ the word σκοπῶν or πειρώμενος must be mentally supplied (see II. 1 d. above): Ro. xi. 14; Phil. iii. 11. **15.** εἴτε . . . εἴτε, **a.** *whether . . . or* [as disjunc. conjunc., *sive . . . sive*; cf. W. 440 (409 sq.); B. 221 (191)], without a verb following: Ro. xii. 6–8; 1 Co. iii. 22; viii. 5; 2 Co. v. 9 sq.; Phil. i. 18, 20, 27; 2 Th. ii. 15; Col. i. 16, 20; 1 Pet. ii. 13 sq.; εἴτε οὖν . . . εἴτε, 1 Co. xv. 11; foll. by the indic. pres., 1 Co. xii. 26; xiii. 8; 2 Co. i. 6; foll. by the subjunc. pres. 1 Th. v. 10, where the use of the subjunc. was occasioned by the subjunc. ζήσωμεν in the leading clause; cf. W. 294 (276); B. 221 (191). **b.** *whether . . . or* [as indirect interrogatives, *utrum . . . an*; cf. B. 250 (215)] (see exx. fr. Grk. auth. in Matthiae p. 1476 sq.): after οὐκ οἶδα, 2 Co. xii. 2 sq. **16.** εἴ τις, εἴ τι: exx. of this combination have already been given among the preceding; here may be added εἴ τις ἕτερος, εἴ τι ἕτερον, *and if* (there be) *any other* person or thing, — a phrase used as a conclusion after the mention or enumeration of several particulars belonging to the same class (in the classics εἴ τις ἄλλος, εἰ καί τις ἄλλος, καὶ εἴ τι ἄλλο, etc., in Hdt., Xen., Plat., al.): Ro. xiii. 9; 1 Tim. i. 10; εἴ τις with subjunc. pres. Rev. xi. 5 Rec.; with the subjunc. aor., ibid. T Tr WH txt.

[εἴγε, see γέ, 3 c.] --------------------------------

εἰδέα, -ας, ἡ, Mt. xxviii. 3 T Tr WH, a poet. form for ἰδέα, q. v. [cf. *WH*. App. p. 153], (Bar. vi. [ep. Jer.] 62; Arstph. Thesm. 438 var.). Cf. B. 5; [W. 48 (47); see εἰ, ι].*

εἶδος, -ους, τό, (ΕΙΔΩ), in Sept. chiefly for מַרְאֶה and רֹאַה; prop. that which strikes the eye, which is exposed to view; **1.** *the external appearance, form, figure, shape,* (so fr. Hom. down): Jn. v. 37; σωματικῷ εἴδει, Lk. iii. 22; τὸ εἶδος τοῦ προσώπου αὐτοῦ, Lk. ix. 29; διὰ εἴδους, as encompassed with the visible appearance (of eternal things), (see διά, A. I. 2), 2 Co. v. 7, — com. explained, *by sight* i. e. *beholding* (Luth.: *im Schauen*); but no ex. has yet been adduced fr. any Grk. writ. in which εἶδος is used actively, like the Lat. *species*, of *vision*; (στόμα κατὰ στόμα, ἐν εἴδει, καὶ οὐ δι' ὁραμάτων καὶ ἐνυπνίων, Clem. homil. 17, 18; cf. Num. xii. 8 Sept.). **2.** *form, kind*: ἀπὸ παντὸς εἴδους πονηροῦ ἀπέχεσθε, i. e. from every kind of evil or wrong, 1 Th. v. 22 [cf. πονηρός, sub fin.]; (Joseph. antt. 10, 3, 1 πᾶν εἶδος πονηρίας. The Grks., esp. Plato, oppose τὸ εἶδος to τὸ γένος, as the Lat. does *species* to *genus*. Cf. Schmidt ch. 182, 2).*

εἴδω, ἴδω, Lat. *video*, [Skr. vid, pf. vêda *know*, vind-ámi *find*, (cf. Vedas); Curtius § 282], an obsol. form of the present tense, the place of which is supplied by ὁράω. The tenses coming from εἴδω and retained by usage form two families, of which one signifies *to see*, the other *to know*.

I. 2 aor. εἶδον, the com. form, with the term. of the 1 aor. (see reff. s. v. ἀπέρχομαι, init.) εἶδα, Rev. xvii. 3 L, 6 L T Tr; 1 pers. plur. εἴδαμεν, L T Tr WH in Acts iv. 20; Mk. ii. 12; Tr WH in Mt. xxv. 37; WH in Mt. xxv. 38; Mk. ix. 38; Lk. ix. 49; 3 pers. plur. εἶδαν, T WH in Lk. ix. 32; Tr WH in Lk. x. 24; Acts vi. 15; xxviii. 4; T Tr WH in Mk. vi. 50; L T Tr WH in Jn.

1489; see 1487 & 1065

see 2397

1491

1492

i. 39 (40); Acts ix. 35; xii. 16; WH in Mk. vi. 33; add ἴδαν Tdf. in Mt. xiii. 17; Lk. x. 24; ἴδον (an Epic form, cf. Matthiae i. p. 564; [Veitch p. 215]; very freq. in Sept. and in 1 Macc., cf. Grimm on 1 Macc. p. 54; on the freq. interchange of ἴδον and εἶδον in codd., cf. Jacobs ad Achill. Tat. 2, 24; [WH. App. pp. 162, 164; Tdf. Sept. Proleg. p. lx.; N. T. Proleg. p. 89; B. 39 (34)]), Tdf. in Rev. iv. 1; vi. 1, 2, 5, 8, 9, 12; vii. 1, etc.; 3 pers. sing. ἴδεν, Tdf. in Lk. v. 2; Rev. i. 2; 2 pers. plur. ἴδετε, Phil. i. 30 Rec.; 3 pers. plur. ἴδον, Tdf. in [Lk. ii. 20]; Jn. xix. 6; subjunc. ἴδω; impv. ἴδε (Attic ἰδέ, cf. W. § 6, 1 a.; [B. 62 (54); Göttling, Accentl. 52]), [2 pers. plur. ἴδετε, Jn. i. 39 (40) R G L]; inf. ἰδεῖν; ptcp. ἰδών; (Sept. mostly for רָאָה, sometimes for חָזָה and יָדַע); to see (have seen), be seeing (saw), i. e. **1.** to perceive (with the eyes; Lat. conspicere, Germ. erblicken); **a.** univ. τινά or τί: Mt. ii. 2; iv. 16; xiv. 14; xxviii. 6; Mk. i. 10, 16; ii. 14; Lk. v. 26; vii. 22; Jn. i. 47 (48) sq.; vi. 26; xix. 6; Acts ix. 35; xii. 16; Gal. i. 19; 1 Tim. vi. 16, and very often. οὐδέποτε οὕτως εἴδομεν we never saw in such fashion, i. e. such a sight never befell us, Mk. ii. 12, old Germ. also hat man nicht gesehen, seit etc.; cf. Kuinoel ad Mat. p. 280 ed. 4. ἰδεῖν τι and ἀκοῦσαί τι are conjoined in Lk. vii. 22; Acts xxii. 14; 1 Co. ii. 9; Jas. v. 11; ἰδεῖν and ἰδεῖν τι are also used by those to whom something is presented in vision, as the author of the Apocalypse relates that he saw this or that: Rev. i. 12, 17; iv. 1 [here εἶδον κ. ἰδού a formula peculiar to Rev.; see ἰδού, sub fin.]; v. 1 sq. 6, 11; vi. 9; vii. 1, 9, etc.; Jn. xii. 41; ἰδεῖν ὅραμα, Acts x. 17; xvi. 10; ἰδεῖν ἐν ὁράματι, Acts ix. 12 [R G]; x. 3; ἐν τῇ ὁράσει, Rev. ix. 17; elliptically ἰδεῖν τι ἔκ τινος sc. ἐκπορευθέν, Rev. xvi. 13, cf. i. 16; Hebraistically (on which see W. § 45, 8; B. § 144, 30) ἰδὼν εἶδον I have surely seen: Acts vii. 34 after Ex. iii. 7. Frequent in the historical books of the N. T. is the ptcp. ἰδών, ἰδόντες, continuing the narrative, placed before a finite verb, and either having an acc. added, as in Mt. ii. 10; iii. 7; v. 1; viii. 34; Mk. v. 22; ix. 20; Lk. ii. 48; vii. 13; Jn. v. 6; vi. 14; Acts xiii. 12; xiv. 11, etc.; or the acc. is omitted, as being evident from the context: Mt. ix. 8, 11; xxi. 20; Mk. x. 14; Lk. i. 12; ii. 17; Acts iii. 12; vii. 31, etc. **b.** with the acc. of a pers. or a thing, and a ptcp. [cf. W. § 45, 4 a.]: Mt. iii. 7, 16; viii. 14; Mk. i. 16; vi. 33; Lk. ix. 49; xxi. 2; Jn. i. 33, 47 (48) sq.; Acts iii. 9; xi. 13; 1 Co. viii. 10; 1 Jn. v. 16; Rev. ix. 1, and often. **c.** foll. by ὅτι: Mk. ii. 16 L T Tr WH; ix. 25; Jn. vi. 22, 24, etc. **d.** foll. by an indirect question with the indic.: with τίς, Lk. xix. 3; with τί, Mk. v. 14; with πηλίκος, Gal. vi. 11. **e.** ἔρχου καὶ ἴδε, a formula of invitation, the use of which leaves the object of the seeing to be inferred by the hearers from the matter under consideration: Jn. xi. 34 (35); i. 46 (47) (here ἴδε is equiv. to by seeing learn, sc. that Jesus is the Messiah), and Grsb. in Rev. vi. 1, 5; plur. Jn. i. 39 (40) (where T Tr WH ἔρχ. κ. ὄψεσθε). The Rabbins use the phrases הא וחזי and בא וראה to command attention. **f.** ἰδεῖν used absol. and πιστεύειν are contrasted in Jn. xx. 29. **2.** like the Lat. video, to perceive by any of the senses: Mt.

xxvii. 54; Mk. xv. 39; Lk. xvii. 15. **3.** univ. to perceive, notice, discern, discover: τὴν πίστιν αὐτῶν, Mt. ix. 2; τὰς ἐνθυμήσεις αὐτῶν, ib. 4 (where L Tr WH txt. εἰδὼς for ἰδών); τ. διαλογισμὸν τῆς καρδίας αὐτῶν, Lk. ix. 47 [T WH txt. Tr mrg. εἰδώς]; ἴδε with acc. of the thing, Ro. xi. 22; foll. by ὅτι, Mt. xxvii. 3, 24; Acts xii. 3; xiv. 9; xvi. 19; Gal. ii. 7, 14; ἴδε, ὅτι, Jn. vii. 52; ἰδεῖν τινα, ὅτι, Mk. xii. 34 [Tr br. the acc.]. **4.** to see, i. e. to turn the eyes, the mind, the attention to anything; **a.** to pay attention, observe: foll. by εἰ interrog. Mt. xxvii. 49; by ποταπός, 1 Jn. iii. 1. **b.** περί τινος (cf. Lat. videre de aliqua re), to see about something [A. V. to consider of], i. e. to ascertain what must be done about it, Acts xv. 6. **c.** to inspect, examine: τί, Lk. xiv. 18. **d.** τινά, to look at, behold: Jn. xxi. 21; Mk. viii. 33. **5.** to experience, τί, any state or condition [cf. W. 17]: as τὸν θάνατον, Lk. ii. 26; Heb. xi. 5, (Joseph. antt. 9, 2, 2 [οἶδεν]), cf. Jn. viii. 51 (Ps. lxxxviii. (lxxxix.) 49); τὴν διαφθοράν, to pass into a state of corruption, be dissolved, Acts ii. 27, 31; xiii. 35-37, (Ps. xv. (xvi.) 10); τὴν βασιλ. τ. θεοῦ, to partake of salvation in the kingdom of God, Jn. iii. 3; πένθος, Rev. xviii. 7; τὴν δόξαν τοῦ θεοῦ, by some marvellous event get a signal experience of the beneficent power of God, Jn. xi. 40; στενοχωρίας, 1 Macc. xiii. 3, (ἀλόχου χάριν, Hom. Il. 11, 243); on the same use of the verb רָאָה and the Lat. videre, cf. Gesenius, Thesaur. iii. p. 1246. ἡμέραν, to live to see a day (a time) and enjoy the blessings it brings: ἡμέρας ἀγαθάς, 1 Pet. iii. 10 fr. Ps. xxxiii. (xxxiv.) 13; τὴν ἡμέραν ἐμήν (Christ's language) the time when I should exercise my saving power on earth, Jn. viii. 56; εἶδε sc. τ. ἡμ. ἐμήν, from the abode of the blessed in paradise he in spirit saw my day, ibid. (see ἀγαλλιάω, sub fin.); ἐπιθυμήσετε μίαν τῶν ἡμερῶν . . . ἰδεῖν, ye will wish that even a single day of the blessed coming age of the Messiah may break upon your wretched times, Lk. xvii. 22; so in Grk. writ., esp. the poets, ἦμαρ, ἡμέραν ἰδεῖν, in Latin videre diem; cf. Kuinoel on Jn. viii. 56. **6.** with acc. of pers. to see i. e. have an interview with, to visit: Lk. viii. 20; Jn. xii. 21; Acts xvi. 40; xxviii. 20; Ro. i. 11; 1 Co. xvi. 7; Phil. i. 27; 1 Th. iii. 6; 2 Tim. i. 4; 3 Jn. 14; τὸ πρόσωπόν τινος; 1 Th. ii. 17; iii. 10, (Lcian. dial. d. 24, 2 [cf. Rutherford on Babr. 11, 9]); with an acc. of place, to visit, go to: Acts xix. 21.

[SYN.: 'When εἶδον, ἰδεῖν are called "momentary preterites," it must not be supposed that thereby a quickly-past action is designated; these forms merely present the action without reference to its duration.... The unaugmented moods, too, are not exclusively past, but present or future as well, — the last most decidedly in the imperative. Now it is obvious that when a perception is stated without regard to its duration, its form or mode cannot have prominence; hence ἰδεῖν is much less physical than ὁρᾶν. ἰδεῖν denotes to perceive with the eyes; ὁρᾶν [q. v.], on the other hand, to see, i. e. it marks the use and action of the eye as the principal thing. Perception as denoted by ἰδεῖν, when conceived of as completed, permits the sensuous element to be forgotten and abides merely as an activity of the soul; for οἶδα, εἰδέναι, signifies not "to have seen," but "to know."' Schmidt ch. xi. COMP.: ἀπ-, ἐπ-, προ-, συν-, ὑπερ-εἶδον.]

II. 2 pf. οἶδα, οἶδας (1 Co. vii. 16; Jn. xxi. 15, for the more com. οἶσθα), οἴδαμεν (for ἴσμεν, more com. in Grk.), οἴδατε (ἴστε, the more usual classic form, is found only in Eph. v. 5 G L T Tr WH and Heb. xii. 17, [prob. also in Jas. i. 19 acc. to the reading of L T Tr WH; but see below]), οἴδασι (and once the Attic ἴσασι, Acts xxvi. 4), impv. ἴστε, once, Jas. i. 19 L T Tr WH, [but see above], subjunc. εἰδῶ, inf. εἰδέναι, ptcp. εἰδώς, εἰδυῖα (Mk. v. 33; Acts v. 7); plpf. ᾔδειν, 2 pers. everywhere ᾔδεις, 3 pers. ᾔδει, plur. 2 pers. ᾔδειτε, 3 pers. ᾔδεισαν (for the more com. ᾔδεσαν [Veitch p. 218; B. 43 (38)]); fut. εἰδήσω (Heb. viii. 11); cf. W. 84 (81); B. 51 (44); Sept. chiefly for יָדַע; like the Lat. *novi* it has the signification of a present *to know, understand*; and the plpf. the signif. of an impf.; [cf. W. 274 (257)].

1. *to know*: with acc. of the thing, Mt. xxv. 13; Mk. x. 19; Jn. x. 4; xiii. 17; xiv. 4; Acts v. 7; Ro. vii. 7; 1 Co. ii. 2; Rev. ii. 2, 9, etc.; τοῦτο [Rec.; al. πάντα] foll. by ὅτι etc. Jude 5; with acc. of pers., Mt. xxvi. 72, 74; Jn. i. 31; vi. 42; Acts iii. 16; 2 Co. v. 16, etc.; τὸν θεόν, Tit. i. 16, cf. Jn. viii. 19; xv. 21; Gentiles are called οἱ μὴ εἰδότες τ. θεόν in 1 Th. iv. 5; 2 Th. i. 8, cf. Gal. iv. 8; the predicate of the person is added (as often in Attic), εἰδὼς αὐτὸν ἄνδρα δίκαιον, sc. ὄντα, Mk. vi. 20 [B. 304 (261)]; in the form of a ptcp. 2 Co. xii. 2. to an accus. of the object by attraction (W. § 66, 5 a.; B. 377 (323)) an epexegetical clause is added [cf. esp. B. 301 (258)], with ὅτι, 1 Co. xvi. 15; 2 Co. xii. 3 sq.; Acts xvi. 3; or an indirect question [B. 250 (215) sq.], Mk. i. 24; Lk. iv. 34; xiii. 25, 27; Jn. vii. 27; ix. 29. εἰδέναι is used with the acc. and inf. in Lk. iv. 41; 1 Pet. v. 9; foll. by ὅτι, Mt. ix. 6; Jn. xix. 35; Acts ii. 30; Ro. v. 3, and very often; οἴδαμεν foll. by ὅτι is not infrequently, so far as the sense is concerned, equiv. to *it is well known, acknowledged*: Mt. xxii. 16; Lk. xx. 21; Jn. iii. 2; ix. 31; Ro. ii. 2; iii. 19; vii. 14; viii. 22, 28; 2 Co. v. 1; 1 Tim. i. 8; 1 Jn. iii. 2; v. 20; cf. Lightfoot [in his Horae Hebr. et Talm.] and Baumg.-Crusius on Jn. iii. 2. freq., esp. in Paul, is the interrog. formula οὐκ οἴδατε and ἢ οὐκ οἴδατε ὅτι, by which something well known is commended to one for his thoughtful consideration: Ro. xi. 2; 1 Co iii. 16; v. 6; vi. 2 sq. 9, 15 sq. 19; ix. 13, 24; οὐκ οἴδατε foll. by an indir. quest. Lk. ix. 55 [Rec.]; οὐκ οἶδας ὅτι, Jn. xix. 10; οὐκ ᾔδειτε, Lk. ii. 49; εἰδέναι foll. by an indir. quest. [cf. B. u. s.], Mt. xxvi. 70; Jn. ix. 21, 25, 30; xiv. 5; xx. 13; 1 Co. i. 16; vii. 16; 2 Co. xii. 2 sq.; Ro. viii. 26; Eph. vi. 21; 1 Tim. iii. 15, and very often. **2.** *to know* i. e. *get knowledge of, understand, perceive*; **a.** any fact: as, τὰς ἐνθυμήσεις, Mt. xii. 25; τὴν ὑπόκρισιν, Mk. xii. 15; τοὺς διαλογισμοὺς αὐτῶν, Lk. vi. 8; xi. 17; with the addition of ἐν ἑαυτῷ foll. by ὅτι, Jn. vi. 61. **b.** the force and meaning of something, which has a definite meaning: 1 Co. ii. 11 sq.; τὴν παραβολήν, Mk. iv. 13; μυστήρια, 1 Co. xiii. 2; foll. by an indir. quest. Eph. i. 18. **c.** as in class. Grk., foll. by an inf. in the sense of *to know how* (Lat. *calleo, to be skilled in*): Mt. vii. 11; Lk. xi. 13; xii. 56; Phil. iv. 12; 1 Th. iv. 4; 1 Tim. iii. 5; Jas. iv. 17; 2 Pet. ii. 9; ὡς οἴδατε, sc. ἀσφαλίσασθαι, Mt. xxvii.

65. **3.** Hebraistically, εἰδέναι τινά *to have regard for one, cherish, pay attention to*: 1 Th. v. 12, (Sept. Gen. xxxix. 6 for יָדַע). [SYN. see γινώσκω.]

εἰδωλεῖον [-λιον T WH; see I, ι], -ου, τό, (εἴδωλον, q. v.; cf. Ἀσκληπεῖον, Ἀπολλωνεῖον, Ἡρακλεῖον, etc. [W. 95 (90)]), *an idol's temple, temple consecrated to idols*: 1 Co. viii. 10, (1 Macc. i. 47; x. 83; 1 Esdr. ii. 9; not found in prof. auth.; for in the frag. fr. Soph. [152 Dind.] in Plut. de amico et adul. c. 36 ἐδώλια has of late been restored).*   **1493**

εἰδωλόθυτος, -ον, (εἴδωλον and θύω), a bibl. and eccl. word [W. 26; 100 (94)], *sacrificed to idols*; τὸ εἰδωλόθυτον and τὰ εἰδωλόθυτα denote the flesh left over from the heathen sacrifices; it was either eaten at feasts, or sold (by the poor and the miserly) in the market: Acts xv. 29; xxi. 25; 1 Co. viii. 1, 4, 7, 10; x. 19, 28 (here L txt. T Tr WH read ἱερόθυτον, q. v.); Rev. ii. 14, 20. [Cf. Bp. Lghtft. on Gal. p. 308 sq.]*   **1494**

εἰδωλο-λατρεία [-τρία WH; see I, ι], -ας, ἡ, (εἴδωλον, q. v., and λατρεία), (Tertull. al. *idololatria*), *the worship of false gods, idolatry*: Gal. v. 20; used of the formal sacrificial feasts held in honor of false gods, 1 Co. x. 14; or of avarice, as a worship of Mammon [q. v.], Col. iii. 5 [Bp. Lghtft. ad loc.]; in plur., the vices springing from idolatry and peculiar to it, 1 Pet. iv. 3. (Eccl. writ. [cf. W. 26].)*   **1495**

εἰδωλολάτρης, -ου, ὁ, (εἴδωλον, and λάτρις i. e. a hireling, servant, slave), *a worshipper of false gods, an idolater*, (Tertull. *idololatres*): 1 Co. v. 10; Rev. xxi. 8; xxii. 15; any one, even a Christian, participant in any way in the worship of heathen, 1 Co. v. 11; vi. 9; esp. one who attends their sacrificial feasts and eats of the remains of the offered victims, 1 Co. x. 7; a covetous man, as a worshipper of Mammon, Eph. v. 5; cf. Meyer ad loc. (Eccl. writ. [cf. W. 100 (94 sq.)].)*   **1496**

εἴδωλον, -ου, τό, (εἶδος [cf. W. 96 (91)]; Etym. Magn. 296, 9]), in Grk. writ. fr. Hom. down, *an image, likeness*, i. e. whatever represents the form of an object, either real or imaginary; used of the shades of the departed (in Hom.), of apparitions, spectres, phantoms of the mind, etc.; in bibl. writ. [*an idol*, i. e.] **1.** *the image of a heathen god*: Acts vii. 41; 1 Co. xii. 2; Rev. ix. 20, (Is. xxx. 22; 2 Chr. xxiii. 17, etc.; θεῶν ἢ δαιμόνων εἴδωλα, Polyb. 31, 3, 13); **2.** *a false god*: Acts xv. 20 (on which see ἀλίσγημα); Ro. ii. 22; 1 Co. viii. 4, 7; x. 19; 2 Co. vi. 16; 1 Th. i. 9, (often in Sept.); φυλάσσειν ἑαυτὸν ἀπὸ τ. εἰδώλων, to guard one's self from all manner of fellowship with heathen worship, 1 Jn. v. 21.*   **1497**

εἰκῆ (L WH Rᵉˡˢ εἰκῇ; cf. Bttm. Ausf. Spr. ii. p. 342; B. 69 (61); [W. § 5, 4 e.; Jelf § 324 Obs. 6; Kühner § 336 Anm. 7; esp. Etym. Magn. 78, 26 sq.; and reff. s. v. I, ι]), adv.; in Grk. writ. fr. Aeschyl. down; **1.** *inconsiderately, without purpose, without just cause*: Mt. v. 22 R G Tr br.; Ro. xiii. 4 (i. e. 'not to hide it in the scabbard, but to draw it' Fritzsche); Col. ii. 18. **2.** *in vain; without success or effect*: 1 Co. xv. 2; Gal. iii. 4; iv. 11. [From Xenophon, Aeschyl. down.]*   **1500**

εἴκοσι [or -σιν; Tdf. uses σι ten times before a consonant, and says -σι "etiam ante vocalem fere semper in   **1501**

---

*For 1498 & 1499 see Strong.

codd. antiquiss." Proleg. p. 98 ; WH everywhere -σι,
cf. their App. p. 148 ; B. 9], οἰ, αἰ, τά, twenty : Lk. xiv.
31 ; Acts i. 15, etc. [From Hom. down.]

1502   εἴκω : 1 aor. εἶξα ; to yield, [A. V. give place] : τινί, Gal.
ii. 5. (From Hom. down.) [Comp. : ὑπ-είκω.] *

1503   ΕΙΚΩ : whence 2 pf. ἔοικα with the force of a pres.
[W. 274 (257)] ; to be like : τινί, Jas. i. 6, 23. [From
Hom. down.]*

1504   εἰκών, -όνος, (acc. εἰκόναν, Rev. xiii. 14 Lchm. ; see
ἄρσην), ἡ, (ΕΙΚΩ, q. v.) ; [fr. Aeschyl. and Hdt. down] ;
Sept. mostly for צֶלֶם ; an image, figure, likeness ; a. Mt.
xxii. 20 ; Mk. xii. 16 ; Lk. xx. 24 ; Ro. i. 23 ; 1 Co. xv. 49 ;
Rev. xiii. 14 sq. ; xiv. 9, 11 ; xv. 2 ; xvi. 2 ; xix. 20 ; xx. 4 ;
ἡ εἰκὼν τῶν πραγμάτων, the image of the things (sc. the
heavenly things), in Heb. x. 1, is opp. to ἡ σκιά, just as
in Cic. de off. 3, 17 solida et expressa effigies is opp. to
umbra ; εἰκὼν τ. θεοῦ is used of the moral likeness of renewed men to God, Col. iii. 10 ; εἰκὼν τοῦ υἱοῦ τοῦ θεοῦ
the image of the Son of God, into which true Christians
are transformed, is likeness not only to the heavenly
body (cf. 1 Co. xv. 49 ; Phil. iii. 21), but also to the most
holy and blessed state of mind, which Christ possesses :
Ro. viii. 29 ; 2 Co. iii. 18. b. metonymically, εἰκών τινος,
the image of one ; one in whom the likeness of any one
is seen : εἰκὼν θεοῦ is applied to man, on account of his
power of command (see δόξα, III. 3 a. ά.), 1 Co. xi. 7 ; to
Christ, on account of his divine nature and absolute
moral excellence, Col. i. 15 ; 2 Co. iv. 4 ; [cf. Bp. Lghtft.
and Mey. on Col. l. c.].*

[Syn. εἰκών, ὁμοίωμα : ὁμ. denotes often not mere
similarity but likeness (see ὁμοίωμα, b. and cf. Mey. on Ro. i.
23), visible conformity to its object ; εἰκ. adds to the idea of
likeness the suggestions of representation (as a derived likeness) and manifestation. Cf. Trench § xv. ;
Lghtft. u. s.]

1505   εἰλικρίνεια (-ία T [WH, see I, ι ; on the breathing see
WH. App. p. 144]), -ας, ἡ, (εἰλικρινής, q. v.), purity, sincerity, ingenuousness : 1 Co. v. 8 ; 2 Co. ii. 17 ; τοῦ θεοῦ,
which God effects by the Holy Spirit, 2 Co. i. 12 [W.
§ 36, 3 b.]. (Theophr., Sext. Empir., Stob.) *

1506   εἰλικρινής, -ές, ([on the breathing see WH. App. p.
144 ; L. and S. s. v. fin.] ; com. supposed to be fr. εἴλη or
ἕλη sunlight, and κρίνω, prop. found pure when unfolded
and examined by the sun's light ; hence some write εἰλ.
[see reff. above] ; acc. to the conjecture of others fr.
εἴλος, εἰλεῖν, prop. sifted and cleansed by rapid movement or rolling to and fro), pure, unsullied, sincere ; of the
soul, an εἰλικρινής man : Phil. i. 10 ; διάνοια, 2 Pet. iii. 1.
(Sap. vii. 25, where cf. Grimm, Exgt. Hdb. ; [see, on the
word, also Trench § lxxxv.] ; [Hippocr.], Xen., Plat.,
[Aristot., Plut.], Polyb., Philo, [al.].) *

[Syn. εἰλικρινής, καθαρός : Acc. to Trench u. s. the
former word expresses freedom from the falsehoods, the
latter from the defilements, of the flesh and of the world.]

1507   εἰλίσσω, Ionic and poetic and occasional in later prose
for ἑλίσσω [W. § 2, 1 a.] : [pres. pass. εἰλίσσομαι ; (εἴλω
to press close, to roll up, [cf. L. and S. s. v. fin.]), to roll
up or together : Rev. vi. 14 R G ; but L T Tr WH have
restored ἑλισσόμ. (From Hom. down.) *

*For 1508 & 1509 see Strong.

εἰμί (fr. ἔω, whence ἐμί in inscriptions [?] ; Aeol. ἐμμί   1510
[Curtius (yet ἔμμι, so G. Meyer) § 564 ; Veitch p. 228]),
impv. ἴσθι, ἔστω, less usual ἤτω, 1 Co. xvi. 22 ; Jas. v. 12 ;
Clem. Rom. 1 Cor. 48, 5 ; [1 Macc. x. 31 ; Ps. ciii. (civ.)
31] ; Plat. rep. 2 p. 361 c. [here it has given place to ἔστω
(or ἴτω), see Stallb. ad loc. ; Veitch p. 200 sq. ; 3 pers.
plur. ἔστωσαν, Lk. xii. 35 ; 1 Tim. iii. 12], inf. εἶναι ; impf.
—acc. to the more ancient and elegant form, ἦν, 2 pers.
ἦσθα (Mt. xxvi. 69 ; Mk. xiv. 67), rarer form ἦς (Mt.
xxv. 21, 23 ; Jn. xi. 21, 32 ; xxi. 18 ; Rev. iii. 15 G L T
Tr WH), 3 pers. ἦν, 1 pers. plur. ἦμεν, — acc. to the mid.
form, com. in later Grk. [cf. Veitch p. 226], ἤμην (Mt. xxv.
35 sq. ; [on Acts xi. 11 cf. WH. Intr. § 404]) ; Gal. i. 10,
etc.), plur. ἤμεθα (Mt. xxiii. 30 G L T Tr WH) ; Acts
xxvii. 37 L T Tr WH ; [Gal. iv. 3 T WH Tr mrg.] ; Eph.
ii. 3 T Tr WH ; Bar. i. 19]) ; cf. Lob. ad Phryn. pp.
149, 152 ; fut. ἔσομαι ; cf. W. § 14, 2 ; B. 49 sq. (43) ; to
be ;

I. εἰμί has the force of a predicate [i. e. is the substantive verb : to be, i. e. 1. to exist ; a. passages
in which the idea of the verb preponderates, and some
person or thing is said to exist by way of distinction
from things non-existent : ἔστιν ὁ θεός, Heb. xi. 6 ; ὁ
ὢν καὶ ὁ ἦν [W. 68 (66), cf. 182 (172) ; B. 50 (43)], Rev.
i. 4, [8 ; iv. 8] ; xi. 17 ; xvi. 5 ; ἐν ἀρχῇ ἦν ὁ λόγος, Jn. i. 1 ;
πρὶν Ἀβραὰμ γενέσθαι, ἐγὼ εἰμί, Jn. viii. 58 [so WH mrg.
in 24, 28 ; xiii. 19 (see II. 5 below)] ; πρὸ τοῦ τὸν κόσμον
εἶναι, Jn. xvii. 5 ; ἦν, καὶ οὐκ ἔστι καίπερ ἐστίν Rec., acc.
to the better reading καὶ πάρεσται [G Tr WH, but L T
παρέσται, correctly ; cf. Bttm. Ausf. Spr. § 108 Anm. 20 ;
Chandler § 803], Rev. xvii. 8 ; ἐσμέν, Acts xvii. 28 ; τὰ
μὴ ὄντα and τὰ ὄντα things that are not, things that are,
Ro. iv. 17 ; things that have some or have no influence,
of some or of no account, 1 Co. i. 28, (ἐκάλεσεν ἡμᾶς οὐκ
ὄντας καὶ ἠθέλησεν ἐκ μὴ ὄντος εἶναι ἡμᾶς, Clem. Rom. 2
Cor. i. 8 [cf. Gebh. and Harn. ad loc. and esp. on Herm.
vis. 1, 1, 6]). Hence b. i. q. to live : εἰ ἤμεθα [or ἦμεν
Rec.] ἐν ταῖς ἡμέραις τῶν πατέρων ἡμῶν if we had been
(viz. living) in the days of our fathers, Mt. xxiii. 30 ;
οὐκ εἶναι is used (as in class. Grk., cf. Passow i. p. 792,
[L. and S. s. v. A. I. 1]) of the dead [who are not, are no
more] : Mt. ii. 18. c. i. q. to stay, remain, be in a place :
Mt. ii. 13, 15 ; Mk. i. 45 [L WH br. ἦν] ; v. 21 ; Lk. i. 80 ;
see V. 4 below. d. i. q. to be found, the subject being
anarthrous ; as, ἦν ἄνθρωπος there was (found, Germ. es
gab) a man, etc. : Lk. xvi. 1, 19 ; xviii. 23 ; Jn. iii. 1 ;
iv. 6 ; v. 2 ; vi. 10 ; 1 Co. viii. 5 ; xii. 4–6 ; xiv. 10 ; xv.
44 ; 1 Jn. v. 16, and often ; ἔσονται ἐμπαῖκται, Jude 18 ;
ἔστι, ἦν, ἔσται with a negative : οὐκ ἔστι δίκαιος there is
not (sc. found) a righteous man, Ro. iii. 10 ; add 12, 18 ;
χρόνος οὐκ ἔσται ἔτι there shall be no longer time, Rev. x.
6 ; add, Rev. xxii. 3, 5 [Rec. adds ἐκεῖ] ; xxi. 25 [here ἐκεῖ
stands] ; ἀνάστασις νεκρῶν οὐκ ἔστιν, 1 Co. xv. 12 ; μὴ εἶναι
ἀνάστασιν, Mt. xxii. 23 and its parall. ; Acts xxiii. 8. Here
belong also the phrases εἰσίν, οἱ etc., οἵτινες etc., there are
(some) who etc. : Mt. xvi. 28 ; xix. 12 ; Mk. ix. 1 ; Lk. ix.
27 ; Jn. vi. 64 ; Acts xi. 20 ; οὐδείς ἐστιν, ὅς, Mk. ix. 39
sq. ; x. 29 ; Lk. i. 61 ; xviii. 29 ; with a noun added, ἐξ

ἡμέραι εἰσίν, ἐν αἷς etc. Lk. xiii. 14; τίς ἐστιν, ὅς, Mt. vii. 9 [L Tr WH om. ἐστ.]; xii. 11 [Tr om. WH br. ἐστ.]: ἔστιν ὁ with a ptcp. *there is* (viz. is not wanting) *one that* etc. Jn. v. 32 [?], 45; viii. 50. **e.** when used of **things**, events, facts, etc., εἶναι is i. q. *to happen, take place*: νῦν κρίσις ἐστίν, Jn. xii. 31; γογγυσμὸς ἦν, Jn. vii. 12; θόρυβος τοῦ λαοῦ. Mk. xiv. 2; σχίσμα, σχίσματα, Jn. ix. 16; 1 Co. i. 10; xii. 25; ἔριδες, 1 Co. i. 11; αἱρέσεις, 1 Co. xi. 19; πένθος, πόνος, κραυγή, Rev. xxi. 4; ἔσονται λιμοὶ κ. λοιμοί [R G Tr mrg. in br., al. om. κ. λοιμ.] κ. σεισμοί, Mt. xxiv. 7; ἀνάγκη μεγάλη, Lk. xxi. 23; ἀνάστασιν μέλλειν ἔσεσθαι, Acts xxiv. 15. of times and seasons: χειμών ἐστιν, Jn. x. 22; νύξ, Jn. xiii. 30; ψῦχος, Jn. xviii. 18; καύσων, Lk. xii. 55; ἑσπέρα, Acts iv. 3; πρωΐα, Jn. xviii. 28 [Rec.]; σκοτία, Jn. xx. 1: ἔστι, ἦν ὥρα, — as ἕκτη, Lk. xxiii. 44; Jn. iv. 6; xix. 14 [L Tr WH]; i. 39 (40), etc.; also of feasts: Jn. v. 1, 10; ix. 14; Acts xii. 3; Lk. xxiii. 54; Mk. xv. 42. univ. τὸ ἐσόμενον what will be, follow, happen: Lk. xxii. 49; πότε ταῦτα ἔσται; Mt. xxiv. 3; πῶς ἔσται τοῦτο; Lk. i. 34; after the Hebr., καὶ ἔσται (equiv. to וְהָיָה) foll. by the fut. of another verb: Acts ii. 17 (fr. Joel ii. 28 (iii. 1)); 21 (fr. Joel ii. 32 (iii. 5)); Acts iii. 23; Ro. ix. 26 (fr. Hos. i. 10 (ii. 1)). τί οὖν ἐστιν; *what then is it?* i. e. *how stands the case? what follows therefore?* Acts xxi. 22; 1 Co. xiv. 15, 26. **2.** i. q. πάρειμι, *to be present; to be at hand; to be in store*: οἶνος οὐκ ἔστιν, Jn. ii. 3 Tdf.; παμπόλλου [Rec.] ὄχλου ὄντος, when there was present, Mk. viii. 1; add, ii. 15; Mt. xii. 10 R G; Heb. viii. 4; οὔπω γὰρ ἦν πνεῦμα (ἅγιον), *was not yet* present, i. e. had not yet been *given* [which some authorities add], Jn. vii. 39; so also in the words εἰ πνεῦμα ἅγιον ἔστιν [but R G Tr accent ἅγιόν ἐστ., cf. Chandler § 938], Acts xix. 2; ἀκούσας ... ὄντα σῖτα, *that there was an abundance of grain*, Acts vii. 12; δύναμις κυρίου ἦν εἰς τὸ ἰᾶσθαι αὐτούς, was present to heal them, Lk. v. 17. **3.** ἔστιν with inf., as in Grk. writ. fr. Hom. down (see Passow i. p. 792 sq.; [L. and S. s. v. A. VI.]; see exx. fr. the O. T. Apocr. in *Wahl*, Clavis apocryph. p. 155), *it is possible to* etc.; with a negative (as more com. in classic Grk. also), *it is impossible*: Heb. ix. 5; 1 Co. xi. 20, [cf. W. § 44, 2 b.].

II. εἰμί [as a copula] connects the subject with the predicate, where the sentence shows who or what a person or thing is as respects character, nature, disposition, race, power, dignity, greatness, age, etc. **1.** univ.: ἐγώ εἰμι πρεσβύτης, Lk. i. 18; ἐγώ εἰμι Γαβριήλ, Lk. i. 19; ἔρημός ἐστιν ὁ τόπος, Mt. xiv. 15; προφήτης εἶ σύ, Jn. iv. 19; σὺ εἶ ὁ Χριστός, Mt. xxvi. 63; καθαροί ἐστε, Jn. xiii. 10; ὑμεῖς ἐστε τὸ ἅλας τῆς γῆς, Mt. v. 13; Ἰουδαίους εἶναι ἑαυτούς, Rev. iii. 9, cf. ii. 9, and countless other exx. **2.** εἰμί, as a copula, indicates that the subject is or is to be compared to the thing expressed by the predicate: ἡ σφραγίς μου τῆς ἀποστολῆς ὑμεῖς ἐστε, ye are, as it were, the seal attesting my apostleship, i. e. your faith is proof that the name of apostle is given me rightfully, 1 Co. ix. 2; ἡ ἐπιστολὴ (sc. συστατική, cf. vs. 1) ὑμεῖς ἐστε, i. e. ye yourselves are like a letter of recommendation for me, or ye serve as a substitute for a letter of recommenda-

tion, 2 Co. iii. 2; τοῦτό ἐστι τὸ σῶμά μου, this which I now hand to you is, as it were, my body, Mt. xxvi. 26; Mk. xiv. 22; Lk. xxii. 19; ὑμεῖς ναὸς θεοῦ ἐστέ [L txt. T Tr txt. WH ἡμεῖς ... ἐσμέν] ye [we] are to be regarded as the temple of God, 2 Co. vi. 16, cf. 1 Co. vi. 19; ὁ θεὸς ναὸς αὐτῆς ἐστιν [ἐστι(ν) R G Tr], κ. τὸ ἀρνίον, they are to be regarded as its temple, they occupy the place of a temple in the city because present with every one in it, Rev. xxi. 22. Hence **3.** εἶναι, getting an **explicative** force, is often i. q. *to denote, signify, import*, as ὁ ἀγρός ἐστιν ὁ κόσμος, Mt. xiii. 37–39, 19 sq. 22 sq.; Lk. viii. 11 sq. 14 sq.; Gal. iv. 24 sq.; Rev. xvii. 15; xix. 8, (Sept. Gen. xli. 26 sq.; Ezek. xxxvii. 11); τοῦτ' ἔστιν [so T WH uniformly, exc. that WH om. ν ἐφελκ. in Heb. ii. 14], Lchm. τουτέστιν [exc. in Ro. x. 6, 7, 8; also Treg. exc. in Mt. xxvii. 46; Mk. vii. 2; Acts i. 19; Ro. ix. 8; x. 6, 7, 8; sometimes written τοῦτο ἐστιν, see *Tdf.* Proleg. p. 111; cf. W. 45; B. 11 (10)], an explanatory formula (equiv. to τοῦτο σημαίνει) which is either inserted into the discourse as a parenthesis, or annexed to words as an apposition [cf. W. 530 (493); B. 400 (342). It is to be distinguished from τοῦτο δέ ἐστιν: τοῦτ' ἔστιν introduces an incidental explanation for the most part of the **language**; τοῦτο δέ ἐστιν subjoins an explanatory statement, relating generally to the **thought**; (cf. our "*that is to say*," and "*that is*"); see Ro. i. 12 and Fritzsche ad loc.]: Mt. xxvii. 46; Mk. vii. 2; Acts i. 19; Ro. vii. 18; x. 6–8; Philem. 12; Heb. ii. 14; vii. 5, etc.; likewise ὅ ἐστι, Mk. iii. 17; vii. 11, 34; Heb. vii. 2; ὅ ἐστι μεθερμηνευόμενον, *this signifies, when interpreted*, etc. Mk. xv. 34; Acts iv. 36; see 6 c. below. **4.** In the Bible far more frequently than in prof. auth., and in the N. T. much oftener in the historical than in the other books, a participle **without the article** serves as the predicate, being connected with the subject by the verb εἶναι (cf. W. § 45, 5 and esp. B. 309 (265) sqq.); and **a.** so as to form a mere periphrasis of the finite verb; **α.** with the Present ptcp. is formed — a periphrasis of the pres.: ἐστὶ προσαναπληροῦσα ... καὶ περισσεύουσα, 2 Co. ix. 12; — a periph. of the impf. or of the aor., mostly in Mark and Luke [B. 312 (268)]: ἦν καθεύδων, Mk. iv. 38; ἦν προάγων, x. 32; ἦν συγκαθήμενος, xiv. 54; ἦν διανεύων, Lk. i. 22; ἦσαν καθήμενοι, v. 17; ἦν ἐκβάλλων, xi. 14; ἦσαν καθεζόμενοι [Lchm., al. καθήμενοι], Acts ii. 2, and other exx.; once in Paul, Phil. ii. 26 ἐπιποθῶν ἦν; — a periph. of the fut.: ἔσονται πίπτοντες [ἐκπ. R G], Mk. xiii. 25. **β.** with the Perfect ptcp. is formed — a periph. of the aor. [impf. (?)]: ἦν ἑστηκότες, Lk. v. 1; — a periph. of the plpf.: ἦσαν ἐληλυθότες, συνεληλυθυῖαι, Lk. v. 17; xxiii. 55; esp. with the pf. pass. ptcp.: ἦν ἡ ἐπιγραφὴ ἐπιγεγραμμένη, Mk. xv. 26; ἦν αὐτῷ κεχρηματισμένον, Lk. ii. 26; ἦν τεθραμμένος, Lk. iv. 16; add, viii. 2; xxiii. 51; Acts i. 17, etc. **γ.** once with an Aorist ptcp. a periph. of the plpf. is formed: ἦν ... βληθείς (R G L Tr mrg. βεβλημένος) ἐν τῇ φυλακῇ, Lk. xxiii. 19 T Tr txt. WH; on the same use of the aor. sometimes in Grk. writ. cf. Passow i. p. 793; [L and S. s. v. B. 2; yet cf. B. § 144, 24 fin.]. **b.** so as to indicate **continuance** in any act or state [B. 310 sq.

(266)] : ἦν διδάσκων was wont to teach, Mk. i. 22 ; Lk. iv. 31 ; xix. 47 ; ἦν [T Tr txt. WH ἦλθεν] κηρύσσων, Mk. i. 39 ; Lk. iv. 44 ; ἦσαν νηστεύοντες held their fast, Mk. ii. 18 ; ἦσαν συλλαλοῦντες were talking, Mk. ix. 4 ; ἦν συγκύπτουσα, Lk. xiii. 11 ; ἦν θέλων, Lk. xxiii. 8 ; ἦν προσδεχόμενος, Mk. xv. 43 (Lk. xxiii. 51 προσεδέχετο) ; once in Paul, Gal. i. 23 ἦσαν ἀκούοντες. with the Future [cf. B. 311 (267)] : ἔσται δεδεμένον, ἔσται λελυμένον, i. q. shall remain bound, shall remain loosed, Mt. xvi. 19 ; ἔσται πατουμένη shall continue to be trodden down, Lk. xxi. 24, and other exx. c. to signify that one is in the act of doing something : ἦν ἐρχόμενον was in the act of coming, Jn. i. 9 [cf. Mey. ed. Weiss ad loc.] ; ἦν ὑποστρέφων, Acts viii. 28. d. the combination of εἶναι with a ptcp. seems intended also to give the verbal idea more force and prominence by putting it in the form of a noun [see B. and W. u. s.] : ἦν ἔχων κτήματα πολλά (Germ. wohlhabend, [Eng. was one that had]), Mt. xix. 22 ; Mk. x. 22 ; ἔση σιωπῶν, Lk. i. 20 ; ἦν ὑποτασσόμενος (obedient, in subjection), Lk. ii. 51 ; ἴσθι ἐξουσίαν ἔχων, be thou ruler over, Lk. xix. 17 ; ἦν συνευδοκῶν, Acts viii. 1 ; ζῶν εἰμι, Rev. i. 18, and in other exx. three times in Paul : εἰ . . . ἠλπικότες ἐσμὲν μόνον if we are those who have only hoped, or to whom nothing is left but hope, 1 Co. xv. 19 ; ἦν . . . καταλλάσσων, the reconciler, 2 Co. v. 19 ; ἅτινά ἐστι λόγον ἔχοντα σοφίας, are things having a reputation of wisdom, Col. ii. 23, (Matthiae § 560 [(so Kühner § 353 Anm. 3)] gives exx. fr. prof. auth. in which several words intervene between εἶναι and the ptcp.). e. Of quite another sort are those exx. in which εἶναι has its own force, being equiv. to to be found, to be present, to stay, (see I. above), and the ptcp. is added to express an act or condition of the subject (cf. B. § 144, 27) : ἐν τοῖς μνήμασι . . . ἦν (was i. e. stayed) κράζων, Mk. v. 5 ; ἦν δὲ ἐκεῖ (was kept there) . . . βοσκομένη, Mk. v. 11 ; Mt. viii. 30 ; ἦσαν ἐν τῇ ὁδῷ ἀναβαίνοντες, Luther correctly, they were in the road, going up etc. Mk. x. 32 ; εἰσὶν ἄνδρες . . . εὐχὴν ἔχοντες, Acts xxi. 23 ; add, Mt. xii. 10 [R G] ; xxvii. 55 ; Mk. ii. 6, (in the last two exx. ἦσαν were present) ; Lk. iv. 33 ; Jn. i. 28 ; iii. 23 ; Acts xxv. 14 ; Ro. iii. 12, etc. ; ἄνωθέν ἐστιν, καταβαῖνον etc. (insert a comma after ἐστίν), is from above, καταβαῖνον etc. being added by way of explanation, Jas. i. 17 [cf. B. 310 (266)]. 5. The formula ἐγώ εἰμι (I am he), freq. in the Gospels, esp. in John, must have its predicate supplied mentally, inasmuch as it is evident from the context (cf. Krüger § 60, 7) ; thus, ἐγώ εἰμι, sc. Ἰησοῦς ὁ Ναζ. Jn. xviii. 5 [here L mrg. expresses ὁ Ἰησοῦς, WH mrg. Ἰησ.], 6, 8 ; it is I whom you see, not another, Mt. xiv. 27 ; Mk. vi. 50 ; Lk. xxiv. 36 [Lchm. in br.) ; Jn. vi. 20 ; sc. ὁ καθήμενος κ. προσαιτῶν, Jn. ix. 9 ; simply εἰμί, I am teacher and Lord, Jn. xiii. 13 ; οὐκ εἰμί sc. ἐξ αὐτῶν, Lk. xxii. 58 ; Jn. xviii. 25 ; I am not Elijah, Jn. i. 21 ; spec. I am the Messiah, Mk. xiii. 6 ; xiv. 62 ; Lk. xxi. 8 ; Jn. iv. 26 ; viii. 24, 28 ; xiii. 19 ; I am the Son of God, Lk. xxii. 70 (like אֲנִי הוּא, Deut. xxxii. 39 ; Is. xlii. 10) ; cf. Keim iii. 320 [Eng. trans. vi. 34 ; Hofmann, Schriftbeweis, i. 63 sq.]. The third pers. is used in the same way : ἐκεῖνός ἐστιν, sc. ὁ υἱὸς τοῦ θεοῦ,

Jn. ix. 37 ; sc. ὁ παραδώσων ἐμέ, Jn. xiii. 26. 6. Of the phrases having a pronoun in place of a predicate, the following deserve notice : a. τίς εἰμι, εἶ, ἐστίν, a formula of inquiry, used by those desiring — either to know what sort of a man one is whom they see, or what his name is, Jn. i. 19 ; viii. 25 ; xxi. 12 ; Acts xxvi. 15 ; — or that they may see the face of some one spoken of, and that he may be pointed out to them, Lk. xix. 3 ; Jn. ix. 36 ; σὺ τίς εἶ ὁ with a ptcp., who (i. e. how petty) art thou, that etc. ? the question of one administering a rebuke and contemptuously denying another's right to do a thing, Ro. ix. 20 ; xiv. 4, (Strabo 6, 2, 4 p. 271 σὺ τίς (εἶ ὁ τὸν Ὅμηρον ψέγων ὡς μυθόγραφον;) ; ἐγὼ τίς εἰμι ; who (how small) am I ? the language of one holding a modest opinion of himself and recognizing his weakness, Acts xi. 17, cf. Ex. iii. 11. b. εἰμὶ τὶς, like sum aliquis in Lat., to be somebody (eminent) : Acts v. 36 ; εἶναί τι, like the Lat. aliquid esse, to be something (i. e. something excellent) : Gal. ii. 6 ; vi. 3 ; in these phrases τὶς and τὶ are emphatic ; cf. Kühner § 470, 3 ; [W. 170 (161) ; B. 114 (100)] ; εἶναί τι after a negative, to be nothing, 1 Co. iii. 7, cf. Mey. ad loc. ; also in questions having a negative force, 1 Co. x. 19 [cf. W. § 6, 2]. οὐδέν εἰμι, 1 Co. xiii. 2 ; 2 Co. xii. 11 ; οὐδέν ἐστιν, it is nothing, is of no account, Mt. xxiii. 16, 18 ; Jn. viii. 54 ; Acts xxi. 24 ; 1 Co. vii. 19. c. τίς ἐστι, e. g. ἡ παραβολή, what does it mean ? what is the explanation of the thing ? Lk. viii. 9 τίς εἴη ἡ παραβολὴ αὕτη ; Acts x. 17 τί ἂν εἴη τὸ ὅραμα ; Mk. i. 27 τί ἐστι τοῦτο ; what is this ? expressive of astonishment, Lk. xv. 26 τί εἴη ταῦτα ; what might be the cause of the noise he heard ? Lk. xviii. 36 ; Jn. x. 6 τίνα ἦν, ἃ ἐλάλει αὐτοῖς. τί ἐστι what does it mean ? Mt. ix. 13 ; xii. 7 ; Lk. xx. 17 ; Jn. xvi. 17 sq. ; τί ἐστιν εἰ μὴ ὅτι, Eph. iv. 9 ; see II. 3 above. d. οὗτος, αὕτη, τοῦτό ἐστιν foll. by a noun, equiv. to in this is seen, is contained, etc. a. is so employed that the pronoun refers to something which has just been said : οὗτος γάρ ἐστι ὁ νόμος, the law is summed up in what I have just mentioned, comes to this, Mt. vii. 12. β. in John's usage it is so employed that the pronoun serves as the subject, which is defined by a noun that follows, and this noun itself is a substitute as it were for the predicate : αὕτη ἐστὶν ἡ νίκη . . . ἡ πίστις ἡμῶν, 1 Jn. v. 4 ; αὕτη ἐστὶν ἡ μαρτυρία τοῦ θεοῦ, ἣν etc. 1 Jn. v. 9 Rec. οὗτος, αὕτη, τοῦτό ἐστι foll. by ὅτι [B. 105 (92) ; cf. W. 161 (152)] : Jn. iii. 19 ; 1 Jn. i. 5 ; v. 11, 14 ; foll. by ἵνα (to say that something ought to be done, or that something is desired or demanded [cf. W. 338 (317) ; B. 240 (207)]) : Jn. vi. 29, 39 sq. ; xv. 12 ; 1 Jn. iii. 11, 23 ; v. 3 ; foll. by ὅτε etc. Jn. i. 19 [W. 438 (408)]. 7. The participle ὤν, οὖσα, ὄν, ὄντες, ὄντα, joined to a substantive or an adjective, has the force of an intercalated clause, and may be translated since or although I am, thou art, etc., [here the Eng. use of the ptcp. agrees in the main with the Grk.]: εἰ οὖν ὑμεῖς, πονηροὶ ὄντες, οἴδατε, Mt. vii. 11 ; add, xii. 34 ; Lk. xx. 36 ; Jn. iii. 4 ; iv. 9 ; Acts xvi. 21 ; Ro. v. 10 ; 1 Co. viii. 7 ; Gal. iii. 3 ; Jas. iii. 4, and often ; twice with other participles, used adjectively [B. 310 (266)] : ὄντες ἀπηλλοτριωμένοι, Col. i. 21 ; ἐσκοτισμένοι

[R G, al. -τωμενοι], Eph. iv. 18.   **8.** Sometimes the copula ἔστιν (with the accent [see Chandler § 938]) stands at the beginning of a sentence, to emphasize the truth of what the sentence affirms or denies: Lk. viii. 11 ; 1 Tim. vi. 6 ; ἔστι δὲ πίστις etc. Heb. xi. 1 (although some explain it here [as a subst. verb], 'but faith *exists*' or '*is found*,' to wit in the examples adduced immediately after [see W. § 7, 3]) ; several times so used in Philo in statements (quoted by Delitzsch on Heb. xi. 1) resembling definitions. οὐκ ἔστιν: Mt. xiii. 57 ; Mk. xii. 27 ; Acts x. 34 ; 1 Co. xiv. 33 ; Jas. iii. 15.

III. εἰμί joined with Adverbs; **1.** with adverbs of place; **a.** where? *to be, be busy, somewhere* : ἐκεῖ, Mt. ii. 15 ; xxvii. 55 ; Mk. iii. 1 [L om. Tr br. ἦν], etc. ; ἐνθάδε, Acts xvi. 28 ; ἔσω, Jn. xx. 26 ; οὗ, Mt. ii. 9 ; xviii. 20 ; Acts xvi. 13 ; ὅπου, Mk. ii. 4 ; v. 40 ; Jn. vi. 62 ; Acts xvii. 1, etc. ; πού, Mt. ii. 2 ; Jn. vii. 11, etc. ; ὧδε, Mt. xxviii. 6 ; Mk. ix. 5, etc. **b.** with adverbs of distance : ἀπέναντί τινος, Ro. iii. 18 (Ps. xxxv. (xxxvi.) 2) ; ἐκτός τινος, 2 Co. xii. 2, [3 χωρίς τ. L T Tr WH] ; ἔμπροσθέν τινος, Lk. xiv. 2 ; ἐντός τινος. Lk. xvii. 21 ; ἐνώπιόν τινος, Rev. i. 4 ; vii. 15 ; μακρὰν ἀπό τινος, Jn. xxi. 8 ; Mk. xii. 34 ; πόρρω, Lk. xiv. 32 ; ἐπάνω, Jn. iii. 31ᵃ, [31ᵇ G T WH mrg. om. the cl.] ; of the situation of regions and places : ἀντιπέρα [or -τίπερα etc. see s. v.] τινός, Lk. viii. 26 ; ἐγγύς, — now standing absol. Jn. xix. 42 ; now with gen., Jn. xi. 18 ; xix. 20, etc. ; now with dat., Acts ix. 38 ; xxvii. 8. **c.** whence? *to be from some quarter*, i. e. *to come, originate, from* : πόθεν, Mt. xxi. 25 ; Lk. xiii. 25, 27 ; Jn. vii. 27 ; ix. 29 ; xix. 9 ; ii. 9 (πόθεν ἐστίν sc. ὁ οἶνος, whence the wine was procured) ; ἐντεῦθεν, Jn. xviii. 36. **2.** with adverbs of quality; οὕτως εἰμί, *to be thus* or *so, to be such* ; absol. Mt. xiii. 49 ; with ἐν ὑμῖν added, Mt. xx. 26 [here R G T ἔσται] ; οὕτως ἔσται, so will it be i. e. come to pass, Mt. xiii. 40, (49 [see above]) ; οὕτως ἐστίν or ἔσται, of things, events, etc., *such is* or *will be the state of the case* [W. 465 (434)] : Mt. xix. 10 ; xxiv. 27, 37, 39 ; Mk. iv. 26 ; Ro. iv. 18 (Gen. xv. 5) ; so of persons, Jn. iii. 8. καθὼς ἐστιν as, even as, he etc. is, 1 Jn. iii. 2, 7 ; iv. 17 ; εἰμί ὥσπερ τις to be, to do as one, to imitate him, be like him, Mt. vi. 5 [R G] ; Lk. xviii. 11 [R G T WH txt.] ; ἔστω σοι ὥσπερ etc. regard him as a heathen and a publican, i. e. have no fellowship with him, Mt. xviii. 17 ; εἰμί ὡς or ὡσεί τις, to be as i. e. like or equal to any one, Mt. [vi. 5 L T Tr WH] ; xxii. 30 ; xxviii. 3 ; Lk. xi. 44 ; [xviii. 11 L Tr WH mrg.] ; xxii. 27 ; 1 Co. vii. 29 sq. ; τὰ σπλάγχνα περισσοτέρως εἰς ὑμᾶς ἐστιν he is moved with the more abundant love toward you, 2 Co. vii. 15. — But see each adverb in its place.

IV. εἰμί with the oblique cases of substantives or of pronouns; **1.** εἶναί τινος, like the Lat. *alicuius esse*, i. q. *to pertain to* a person or a thing, denotes any kind of possession or connection (Possessive Genitive) ; cf. Krüger § 47, 6,4 sqq. ; W. § 30, 5 b. ; B. § 132, 11. **a.** of things which one owns : ἔσται σοῦ πᾶσα [Rec. πάντα], Lk. iv. 7 ; οὗ ἐστιν ἡ ζώνη αὕτη, Acts xxi. 11 ; add, Mk. xii. 7 ; Jn. x. 12 ; xix. 24 ; — or for the possession of which he is fitted : τινός ἐστιν ἡ βασιλεία τ. οὐρ. or τοῦ θεοῦ, he is fit

for a share in the kingdom of God, Mt. v. 3, 10 ; xix. 14 ; Mk. x. 14 ; Lk. xviii. 16. πάντα ὑμῶν ἐστι, all things serve your interests and promote your salvation, 1 Co. iii. 21. **b.** of things which proceed from one : 2 Co. iv. 7. **c.** *to be of one's party, be devoted to one* : 1 Co. i. 12 ; 2 Tim. ii. 19 ; τοῦ Χριστοῦ, Mk. ix. 41 ; Ro. viii. 9 ; 1 Co. i. 12 ; 2 Co. x. 7 ; hence also τῆς ὁδοῦ (sc. τοῦ κυρίου) εἶναι, Acts ix. 2 [cf. B. 163 (142)]. **d.** *to be subject to one ; to be in his hands* or *power* : Mt. xxii. 28 ; Acts xxvii. 23 ; Ro. ix. 16 ; xiv. 8 ; 1 Co. iii. 23 ; vi. 19, 20 Rec. ; πνεύματος, Lk. ix. 55 Rec. Hence **e.** *to be suitable, fit, for one* : Acts i. 7. **f.** *to be of a kind* or *class* : εἶναι νυκτός, σκότους, ἡμέρας, 1 Th. v. 5, 8 ; or *to be of the number of* [a partit. gen., cf. B. 159 (139)] : Acts xxiii. 6 ; 1 Tim. i. 20 ; 2 Tim. i. 15. **g.** with a gen. *of quality* : Heb. x. 39 ; xii. 11. **h.** with a gen. *of age* : Mk. v. 42 ; Lk. iii. 23 ; Acts iv. 22, (Tob. xiv. 11). With this use (viz. 1) of εἶναι, those examples must not be confounded in which a predicate nominative is to be repeated from the subject (cf. Krüger § 47, 6, 1) : οὐκ ἔστιν ὁ θεὸς νεκρῶν, ἀλλὰ ζώντων, sc. θεός, Mt. xxii. 32, cf. Mk. xii. 27 ; Lk. xx. 38 ; ταῦτα τὰ ῥήματα οὐκ ἔστι δαιμονιζομένου, sc. ῥήματα, Jn. x. 21 ; οὐκ ἔστιν ἀκαταστασίας ὁ θεός, ἀλλὰ εἰρήνης, 1 Co. xiv. 33 ; ἄλλο βιβλίον, ὅ ἐστι τῆς ζωῆς, Rev. xx. 12 ; add, 2 Co. ii. 3 ; 1 Pet. iii. 3. **2.** εἰμί with the dative (cf. Krüger § 48, 3 [who appears to regard the dat. as expressing a less close or necessary relationship than the gen.] ; W. § 31, 2) ; **a.** ἔστι μοι, ἡμῖν, etc. *it is mine, ours, etc., I, we, etc., have* : Lk. i. 7 ; ii. 7, 10 ; xiv. 10 ; Jn. xviii. 10, 39 ; xix. 40 ; Acts vii. 5 ; viii. 21 ; x. 6 ; Ro. ix. 2, 9 ; 1 Co. ix. 16 ; 1 Pet. iv. 11, and often. οὐκ ἔστι ἡμῖν [al. ὑμ.] ἡ πάλη πρός etc. we have not a struggle against etc. Eph. vi. 12 ; εἰσὶν ἡμῖν we have here etc. Acts xxi. 23 ; τί ἔσται ἡμῖν what shall we have? what will be given us? Mt. xix. 27 ; ὑμῖν ἐστιν ἡ ἐπαγγελία the promise belongs to you, Acts ii. 39. **b.** εἶναί τινί τι *to be something to* (or *for*) *some one*, used of various relations, as of service, protection, etc. : σκεῦος ἐκλογῆς ἐστί μοι οὗτος, sc. τοῦ with inf. Acts ix. 15 ; ἔσεσθέ μοι μάρτυρες, Acts [i. 8 R G, cf.] xxii. 15 ; ἔσομαι αὐτῷ θεὸς κ. αὐτὸς ἔσται μοι υἱός, Rev. xxi. 7 ; ἔσονται μοι λαός, 2 Co. vi. 16 [R G] ; εἰς τὸ εἶναι αὐτὸν . . . πατέρα . . . τοῖς etc. Ro. iv. 11. **c.** εἶναι τινί τι, to be to one as or for something, to pass for etc. : 1 Co. i. 18 ; ii. 14 ; ix. 2, cf. Mt. xviii. 17. **d.** εἶναί τινί τι, *to be* i. e. *conduce, redound to* one *for* (or *as*) *something* (cf. Krüger § 48, 3, 5) : 1 Co. xi. 14 sq. ; 2 Co. ii. 15 ; Phil. i. 28 ; οὐαὶ δέ μοί ἐστι, 1 Co. ix. 16 (Hos. ix. 12). **e.** ἔσται τινί, *will come upon, befall, happen to, one* : Mt. xvi. 22 ; Lk. i. 45. **f.** Acts xxiv. 11 οὐ πλείους εἰσί μοι ἡμέραι ἢ δεκαδύο [L T Tr WH om. ἢ and read δώδεκα] not more than twelve days are (sc. passed) to me i. e. it is not more than twelve days. Lk. i. 36 οὗτος μὴν ἔκτος ἐστὶν αὐτῇ this is the sixth month to (with) her. Those passages must not be brought under this head in which the dative does not belong to the verb but depends on an adjective, as καλός, κοινωνός, φίλος, etc.

V. εἰμί with Prepositions and their cases. **1.** ἀπό τινος (τόπου), *to come from, be a native of* : Jn. i. 44

(45) [cf. ἀπό, II. 1 a.]. **2.** εἴς τι, **a.** to have betaken one's self to some place and *to be* there, to have gone *into* (cf. W. § 50, 4 b.; [B. 333 (286)]): εἰς οἶκον, Mk. ii. 1 [R G; al. ἐν]; εἰς τὸν ἀγρόν, Mk. xiii. 16 [R G]; εἰς τ. κοίτην, Lk. xi. 7; εἰς τὸν κόλπον, Jn. i. 18, where cf. Tholuck, [W. 415 (387); B. u. s.]; (on Acts viii. 20 see ἀπώλεια, 2 a.). metaph. *to come to*: εἰς χολὴν πικρίας (hast fallen into), Acts viii. 23. **b.** *to be directed towards* a thing: ὥστε τὴν πίστιν ὑμῶν . . . εἶναι εἰς θεόν, 1 Pet. i. 21; *to tend to* anything: Ro. xi. 36 [W. § 50, 6]. **c.** *to be for* i. e. conduce or inure to, serve for, [B. 150 (131) sq.; W. § 29, 3 a.]: 1 Co. xiv. 22; Col. ii. 22; Jas. v. 3; ἐμοὶ εἰς ἐλάχιστόν ἐστι, it results for me in, i. e. I account it, a very small thing, 1 Co. iv. 3, (εἰς ὠφέλειαν, Aesop. fab. 124, 2). **d.** In imitation of the Hebr. הָיָה foll. by לְ, εἶναι εἴς τινα or τι stands where the Greeks use a nominative [W. and B. u. s.; esp. *Soph.* Lex. s. v. εἰς, 3]: Mt. xix. 5 and Mk. x. 8 and 1 Co. vi. 16 and Eph. v. 31 ἔσονται εἰς σάρκα μίαν (fr. Gen. ii. 24); 1 Jn. v. 8 εἰς τὸ ἔν εἰσιν, unite, conspire, towards one and the same result, agree in one; 2 Co. vi. 18 (Jer. xxxviii. (xxxi.) 1); Heb. i. 5 (2 S. vii. 14); viii. 10. **3.** ἔκ τινος, **a.** *to be of* i. e. *a part of any thing, to belong to*, etc. [W. 368 (345); cf. B. 159 (139)]: 1 Co. xii. 15 sq.; ἔκ τινων, *of the number of*: Mt. xxvi. 73; Mk. xiv. 69 sq.; Lk. xxii. 58; Jn. i. 24; vi. 64, 71 [R T]; vii. 50; x. 26; xviii. 17, 25; Acts xxi. 8; 2 Tim. iii. 6; 1 Jn. ii. 19; Rev. xvii. 11, (Xen. mem. 3, 6, 17); ἐκ τοῦ ἀριθμοῦ τινων, Lk. xxii. 3. **b.** *to be of* i. e. *to have originated, sprung, come, from* [W. § 51, 1 d.; B. 327 (281 sq.)]: Lk. xxiii. 7; Jn. i. 46 (47); iii. 31 (ὁ ὢν ἐκ τῆς γῆς); iv. 22; vii. 52; viii. 23; xviii. 36; Acts iv. 6; xix. 5; xxiii. 34; Gal. iii. 21; 1 Jn. iv. 7; ὅς ἐστιν ἐξ ὑμῶν, your fellow-countryman, Col. iv. 9. **c.** *to be of* i. e. *proceed from one as the author* [W. 366 (344) sq.; B. 327 (281)]: Mt. v. 37; Jn. vii. 17; Acts v. 38 sq.; 2 Co. iv. 7; 1 Jn. ii. 16; Heb. ii. 11; εἶναι ἐξ οὐρανοῦ, ἐξ ἀνθρώπων, to be instituted by the authority of God, by the authority of men, Mt. xxi. 25; Mk. xi. 30; Lk. xx. 4; to be begotten of one, Mt. i. 20. **d.** *to be of* i. e. *to be connected with one; to be related to*, [cf. Win. § 51, 1 d.; cf. in ἐκ, II. 1 a. and 7]: ὁ νόμος οὐκ ἔστιν ἐκ πίστεως, has no connection with faith, Gal. iii. 12; ἐξ ἔργων νόμου εἶναι (Luth. *mit Werken umgehen*), Gal. iii. 10; esp. in John's usage, *to depend on the power of one, to be prompted and governed by one, and reflect his character*: thus εἶναι ἐκ τοῦ διαβόλου, Jn. viii. 44; 1 Jn. iii. 8; ἐκ τοῦ πονηροῦ, 1 Jn. iii. 12; ἐκ τοῦ κόσμου, Jn. xv. 19; xvii. 14, 16; 1 Jn. iv. 5; when this expression is used of wickedness, it is equiv. to produced by the world and pertaining to it, 1 Jn. ii. 16; opp. to ἐκ τοῦ θεοῦ εἶναι, Jn. viii. 47; 1 Jn. iv. 1–3; this latter phrase is used esp. of true Christians, as begotten anew by the Spirit of God (see γεννάω, 2 d.): 1 Jn. iv. 4, 6; v. 19; 3 Jn. 11; ἐκ τῆς ἀληθείας εἶναι, either to come from the love of truth as an effect, as 1 Jn. ii. 21, or, if used of a man, to be led and governed by the love and pursuit of truth, as Jn. xviii. 37; 1 Jn. iii. 19; ὁ ὢν ἐκ τῆς γῆς ἐκ τῆς γῆς ἐστί, he who is from the earth as respects origin bears the nature of this his earth-

ly origin, is earthly, Jn. iii. 31. **e.** *to be of* i. e. *formed from*: Rev. xxi. 21; 1 Co. xi. 8. **4.** ἔν τινι, **a.** with dat. of place, *to be in* i. e. *be present, to stay, dwell*; **α.** prop.: Mt. xxiv. 26; Lk. ii. 49, etc.; on the surface of a place (Germ. *auf*), as ἐν τῇ ὁδῷ, Mk. x. 32 and elsewhere; ἐν τῷ ἀγρῷ, Lk. xv. 25. *at*: ἐν δεξιᾷ τοῦ θεοῦ, Ro. viii. 34; *to live, dwell*, as in a city: Lk. xviii. 3; Acts ix. 10; Phil. i. 1; 1 Co. i. 2, etc.; of God, ἐν οὐρανοῖς, Eph. vi. 9; of things which are found, met with, in a place: 2 Tim. ii. 20, etc. **β.** things so pertaining to locality that one can, in a proper sense, *be in* them or be surrounded by them, are spoken of in the same way metaph. and improp., as εἶναι ἐν τῷ φωτί, ἐν τῇ σκοτίᾳ: 1 Jn. ii. 9, 11; 1 Th. v. 4; ἐν σαρκί, Ro. vii. 5; viii. 8, (see σάρξ, 4). **b.** *to be in a state* or *condition* [see B. 330 (284); cf. W. § 29, 3 b. and ἐν, I. 5 e.]: ἐν εἰρήνῃ, Lk. xi. 21; ἐν ἐχθρᾷ, xxiii. 12; ἐν κρίματι, ibid. 40; ἐν περιτομῇ, ἐν ἀκροβυστίᾳ, Ro. iv. 10; ἐν δόξῃ, 2 Co. iii. 8, etc.; hence spoken of ills which one is afflicted with: ἐν ῥύσει αἵματος, Mk. v. 25; Lk. viii. 43, (ἐν τῇ νόσῳ, Soph. Aj. 271; *in morbo esse*, Cic. Tusc. 3, 4, 9); of wickedness in which one is, as it were, merged, ἐν ταῖς ἁμαρτίαις, 1 Co. xv. 17; of holiness, in which one perseveres, ἐν πίστει, 2 Co. xiii. 5. **c.** *to be in possession of, provided with a thing* [W. 386 (361)]: Phil. iv. 11; ἐν ἐξουσίᾳ, Lk. iv. 32; ἐν βάρει (see βάρος, fin.), 1 Th. ii. 7 (6). **d.** *to be occupied in* a thing (Bnhdy. p. 210; [see ἐν, I. 5 g.]): ἐν τῇ ἑορτῇ, in celebrating the feast, Jn. ii. 23; *to be sedulously devoted to* [A. V. *give one's self wholly to*] a thing, 1 Tim. iv. 15, (Hor. epp. 1, 1, 11 omnis in hoc sum). **e.** a person or thing is said *to be in one*, i. e. *in his soul*: thus, God (by his power and influence) in the prophets, 1 Co. xiv. 25; Christ (i. e. his holy mind and power) in the souls of his disciples or of Christians, Jn. xvii. 26; 2 Co. xiii. 5; τὸ πνεῦμα τῆς ἀληθείας, Jn. xiv. 17; friends are said to be ἐν τῇ καρδίᾳ of one who loves them, 2 Co. vii. 3. vices, virtues, and the like, are said to be in one: as δόλος, Jn. i. 47 (48); ἀδικία, Jn. vii. 18; ἄγνοια, Eph. iv. 18; ἁμαρτία, 1 Jn. iii. 5; ἀλήθεια, Jn. viii. 44; 2 Co. xi. 10; Eph. iv. 21; 1 Jn. i. 8; ii. 4, (ἀλήθεια καὶ κρίσις, 1 Macc. vii. 18); ἀγάπη, Jn. xvii. 26; 1 Jn. ii. 15; ὁ λόγος αὐτοῦ (τ. θεοῦ) οὐκ ἔστιν ἐν ἡμῖν, God's word has not left its impress on our souls, 1 Jn. i. 10; τὸ φῶς οὐκ ἔστιν ἐν αὐτῷ, the efficacy or influence of the light is not in his soul, [rather, an obvious physical fact is used to suggest a spiritual truth: *the light is not in him*, does not shine from within outwards], Jn. xi. 10; σκοτία, 1 Jn. i. 5; σκάνδαλον, 1 Jn. ii. 10 i. e. there is nothing within him to seduce him to sin (cf. Düsterdieck and Huther ad loc.). Acts xiii. 15 (if ye have in mind any word of exhortation etc. [W. 218 (204 sq.)]). **f.** ἐν τῷ θεῷ εἶναι is said **a.** of Christians, as being rooted, so to speak, in him, i. e. intimately united to him, 1 Jn. ii. 5; v. 20; **β.** of all men, because the ground of their creation and continued being is to be found in him alone, Acts xvii. 28. **g.** with a dat. of the pers. *to be in*, — [i. e. either] *among the number of*: Mt. xxvii. 56; Mk. xv. 40; Lk. ii. 44; Ro. i. 6; — [or, *in the midst of*: Acts ii. 29; vii. 44 Rec., etc.]

h. noteworthy, further, are the following: ἔστι τι ἔν τινι there is something (to blame) in one, Acts xxv. 5; something is (founded [A. V. *stand*]) in a thing, 1 Co. ii. 5; οὐκ ἔστιν ἐν οὐδενὶ ἄλλῳ ἡ σωτηρία salvation is (laid up, embodied) in none other, can be expected from none, Acts iv. 12; with dat. of the thing, *is* (contained, wrapped up) *in* something: Eph. v. 18; Heb. x. 3; 1 Jn. iv. 18. **5.** εἰμὶ ἐπί a. τινός, to be *on*: ἐπὶ τοῦ δώματος, Lk. xvii. 31; ἐπὶ τῆς κεφαλῆς, Jn. xx. 7; to be (set) over a thing, Acts viii. 27; to preside, rule, over, Ro. ix. 5. b. τινί, *to be at* [W. 392 (367)]: ἐπὶ θύραις, Mt. xxiv. 33; Mk. xiii. 29. c. τινά, *to be upon* one: χάρις ἦν ἐπί τινα, was with him, assisted him, Lk. ii. 40; Acts iv. 33; πνεῦμα ἦν ἐπί τινα, had come upon one, was impelling him, Lk. ii. 25, cf. Lk. iv. 18; Sept. Is. lxi. 1; add, Gal. vi. 16; εἶναι ἐπὶ τὸ αὐτό, *to be* (assembled) *together* [cf. αὐτός, III. 1], Acts i. 15; ii. 1, 44; of cohabitation, 1 Co. vii. 5 (acc. to the reading ἦτε for Rec. συνέρχεσθε). **6.** εἰμί κατά a. τινός, to be *against* one, to oppose him: Mt. xii. 30; Lk. ix. 50; xi. 23; Gal. v. 23; Ro. viii. 31 (opp. to ὑπέρ τινος, as in Mk. ix. 40). b. κατά τι, *according to something*: κατὰ σάρκα, κατὰ πνεῦμα, to bear the character, have the nature, of the flesh or of the Spirit, Ro. viii. 5; εἶναι κατ' ἄνθρωπον, Gal. i. 11; κατ' ἀλήθειαν, Ro. ii. 2. **7.** μετά τινος, a. *to be with* (i. e. to associate with) one: Mt. xvii. 17; Mk. iii. 14; v. 18; Lk. vi. 3; Jn. iii. 26; xii. 17; xvi. 32; Acts ix. 39, and often in the Gospels; Rev. xxi. 3; of ships accompanying one, Mk. iv. 36; of what is present with one for his profit, 2 Jn. 2; Ro. xvi. 20; Hebraistically, *to be with one* i. e. as a help, (of God, becoming the companion, as it were, of the righteous): Lk. i. 66; Jn. iii. 2; viii. 29; xvi. 32; Acts vii. 9; x. 38; xi. 21; xviii. 10; 2 Co. xiii. 11; Phil. iv. 9; 2 Jn. 3, cf. Mt. xxviii. 20, (Gen. xxi. 20; Judg. vi. 12, etc.). b. *to be* (i. e. to coöperate) *with*: Mt. xii. 30; Lk. xi. 23, (Xen. an. 1, 3, 5 [al. ἰέναι]). **8.** εἰμὶ παρά a. τινός, *to* (have come and) *be from one*: Christ is said εἶναι παρὰ τοῦ θεοῦ, Jn. vi. 46; vii. 29; ix. 16, 33; τὶ παρά τινος, is from i. e. given by one, Jn. xvii. 7. b. τινί, *to be with one*: Mt. xxii. 25; οὐκ εἶναι παρὰ τῷ θεῷ is used to describe qualities alien to God, as προσωπολημψία, Ro. ii. 11; Eph. vi. 9; ἀδικία, Ro. ix. 14. c. τινά (τόπον), *by, by the side of*: Mk. v. 21; Acts x. 6. **9.** πρός τινα [cf. W. 405 (378)], a. *towards*: πρὸς ἑσπέραν ἐστί it is towards evening, Lk. xxiv. 29. b. *by* (turned towards): Mk. iv. 1. c. *with one*: Mt. xiii. 56; Mk. vi. 3; ix. 19; Lk. ix. 41; Jn. i. 1 [cf. Mey. ad loc.]. **10.** σύν τινι, a. *to associate with one*: Lk. xxii. 56; xxiv. 44; Acts xiii. 7; Phil. i. 23; Col. ii. 5; 1 Th. iv. 17. b. *to be the companion of one, to accompany him*: Lk. vii. 12 [Rᵉˡᶻ T Tr br. WH]; viii. 38; Acts iv. 13; xxii. 9; 2 Pet. i. 18. c. *to be an adherent of one, be on his side*: Acts v. 17; xiv. 4 [A. V. *to hold with*], (Xen. Cyr. 5, 4, 37). **11.** εἰμὶ ὑπέρ a. τινός, *to be for one, to favor his side*: Mk. ix. 40; Lk. ix. 50; Ro. viii. 31, (opp. to εἰμὶ κατά τινος). b. τινά, *to be above one, to surpass, excel him*: Lk. vi. 40. **12.** ὑπό τινα [cf. B. 341 (293)], a. *to be under* (i. e. subject to) *one*: Mt. viii. 9 R G T Tr; Ro.

iii. 9; vi. 14 sq.; Gal. iii. 10, 25; v. 18; 1 Tim. vi. 1. b. *to be* (locally) *under a thing*: e. g. under a tree, Jn. i. 48 (49); a cloud, 1 Co. x. 1. Further, see each preposition in its own place.

VI. As in classical Greek, so also in the N. T. εἰμί is very often omitted (cf. Winer § 64, I. 2, who gives numerous exx. [cf. 596 (555); 350 (328 sq.)]; B. 136 (119) sq.), ἐστίν most frequently of all the parts: Lk. iv. 18; Ro. xi. 36; 1 Co. iv. 20; 2 Tim. iii. 16; Heb. v. 13, etc.; in exclamations, Acts xix. 28, 34; in questions, Ro. ix. 14; 2 Co. vi. 14–16; τί γάρ, Phil. i. 18; Ro. iii. 3; τί οὖν, Ro. iii. 9; vi. 15; also εἴ, Rev. xv. 4; εἰμί, 2 Co. xi. 6; ἐσμέν, ἐστέ, 1 Co. iv. 10; εἰσί, Ro. iv. 14; 1 Co. xiii. 8, etc.; the impv. ἔστω, Ro. xii. 9; Heb. xiii. 4 sq.; ἔστε, Ro. xii. 9; 1 Pet. iii. 8; εἴη in wishes, Mt. xvi. 22; Gal. vi. 16, etc.; even the subjunc. ᾖ after ἵνα, Ro. iv. 16; 2 Co. viii. 11 [after ὅπως], 13; often the ptcp. ὤν, ὄντες, as (see B. § 144, 18) in Mk. vi. 20; Acts xxvii. 33; in the expressions οἱ ἐκ περιτομῆς, ὁ ἐκ πίστεως, οἱ ὑπὸ νόμον, etc. [COMP.: ἀπ-, ἔν-, (ἔξ-εστι,) πάρ-, συμ-πάρ-, σύν-ειμι.]

εἰμι, *to go*, approved of by some in Jn. vii. 34, 36, for the ordinary εἰμί, but cf. W. § 6, 2; [B. 50 (43). COMP.: ἀπ-, εἴσ-, ἐξ-, ἐπ-, σύν-ειμι.]*

ἕνεκεν, see ἕνεκα, ἕνεκεν.

εἴ-περ, see εἰ, III. 13.

εἶπον, 2 aor. act. fr. an obsol. pres. ΕΠΩ [late Epic and in composition; see Veitch] (cf. ἔπος [Curtius § 620]), Ion. ΕΙΠΩ (like ἐρωτάω, ἔρωτ.; ἐλίσσω, εἰλίσσ.); subjunc. εἴπω, impv. εἰπέ, inf. εἰπεῖν, ptcp. εἰπών; 1 aor. εἶπα (Jn. x. 34 R G T Tr WH, fr. Ps. lxxxi. (lxxxii.) 6; Acts xxvi. 15 L T Tr WH; Heb. iii. 10 Lchm. fr. Ps. xciv. (xcv.) 10; add [Mk ix. 18 T WH Tr txt.]; Job xxix. 18; xxxii. 8, etc.; Sir. xxiv. 31 (29); 1 Macc. vi. 11, etc.; cf. Kühner i. 817, [esp. Veitch s. v. pp. 232, 233]), 2 pers. εἶπας (Mt. xxvi. 25, [64]; Mk. xii. 32 [not T WH; Jn. iv. 17 where T WH again -πες; Lk. xx. 39]), 3 pers. plur. εἶπαν (often in L T Tr WH [i. e. out of the 127 instances in which the choice lies between 3 pers. plur. -πον of the Rec. and -παν, the latter ending has been adopted by L in 56, by T in 82, by Tr in 74, by WH in 104, cf. Tdf. Proleg. p. 123], e. g. Mt. xii. 2; xxvii. 6; Jn. xviii. 30, etc.); impv. εἰπόν (Mk. xiii. 4 L T Tr WH; Lk. x. 40 T WH Tr mrg.; Acts xxviii. 26 G L T Tr WH, [also Mt. iv. 3 WH]; xviii. 17 T WH; xxii. 17 T WH Tr mrg.; xxiv. 3 WH; Lk. xx. 2 T Tr WH; xxii. (66) 67 T Tr WH; Jn. x. 24 T WH], for the Attic εἰπόν, cf. W. § 6, 1 k.; [Chandler § 775]; Fritzsche on Mk. p. 515 sqq.; [but Win. (p. 85 (81)) regards εἰπόν as impv. of the 2nd aor.; cf., too, Lob. ad Phryn. p. 348; B. 57 (50); esp. Fritz. l. c.]), in the remaining persons εἰπάτω (Rev. xxii. 17), εἴπατε (Mt. [x. 27; xxi. 5]; xxii. 4; xxvi. 18, etc.; Mk. [xi. 3]; xiv. 14; xvi. 7; [Lk. x. 10]; xiii. 32; xx. 3; Col. iv. 17]), εἰπάτωσαν (Acts xxiv. 20) also freq. in Attic, [Veitch s. v.; WH. App. p. 164; Rutherford, New Phryn. p. 219]; ptcp., after the form chiefly Ion., εἴπας ([Jn. xi. 28 Tr WH]; Acts vii. 37 L T Tr WH [also xxii. 24; xxiv. 22; xxvii. 35]); the fut. ἐρῶ is from the Epic pres. εἴρω [cf. Lob. Technol. p. 137]; on the other

(1510α); see 548, 549, 1524, 1826 & 4896

see 1752

1512; see 1487 & 4007

(1512α); see 2036 St.

*For 1511 see 1510.

hand, from PEΩ come pf. εἴρηκα, 3 pers. plur. εἰρήκασιν (Acts xvii. 28), εἴρηκαν (Rev. xix. 3; see γίνομαι), inf. εἰρηκέναι, Heb. x. 15 L T Tr WH; Pass., pf. 3 pers. sing. εἴρηται, ptcp. εἰρημένον; plpf. εἰρήκειν; 1 aor. ἐρρέθην (Rev. vi. 11; ix. 4 and R G T WH in Mt. v. 21 sqq.; L T Tr WH in Ro. ix. 12, 26; Gal. iii. 16), [" strict" (cf. Veitch p. 575)] Attic ἐρρήθην (Mt. v. 21 sqq. L Tr; R G in Ro. ix. 12, 26; Gal. iii. 16; [cf. B. 57 (50); WH. App. p. 166]), ptcp. ῥηθείς, ῥηθέν; Sept. for אָמַר; to speak, say, whether orally or by letter;

1. with an accus. of the obj.; **a.** with acc. of the thing: εἰπεῖν λόγον, Mt. viii. 8 Rec.; Jn. ii. 22 [L T Tr WH]; vii. 36; xviii. 9, 32; ῥῆμα, Mk. xiv. 72 [Knapp et al.]; εἰπεῖν λόγον εἴς τινα, i. q. βλασφημεῖν, Lk. xii. 10; also κατά τινος, Mt. xii. 32; ὡς ἔπος εἰπεῖν, so to say (a phrase freq. in class. Grk., cf. Weiske, De pleonasmis gr. p. 47; Matthiae § 545; Delitzsch on Heb. as below; [Kühner § 585, 3; Krüger § 55, 1, 2; Goodwin § 100; W. 449 (419); 317 (298)]), Heb. vii. 9, (opp. to ἀκριβεῖ λόγω, Plat. rep. 1, 341 b.); τὴν ἀλήθειαν, Mk. v. 33; ἀλήθειαν ἐρῶ, 2 Co. xii. 6; τοῦτο ἀληθὲς εἴρηκας, Jn. iv. 18 [W. 464 (433) n.]; τί εἴπω; what shall I say? (the expression of one who is in doubt what to say), Jn. xii. 27; πῶς ἐρεῖ τὸ ἀμήν . . .; 1 Co. xiv. 16; τί ἐροῦμεν; or τί οὖν ἐροῦμεν; what shall we say? i. e. what reply can we make? or, to what does that bring us? only in the Ep. to the Ro. [W. § 40, 6] viz. iii. 5; vi. .1; vii. 7; ix. 14, 30; with πρὸς ταῦτα added, viii. 31; εἰπεῖν τι περί τινος, Jn. vii. 39; x. 41. Sayings from the O. T. which are quoted in the New are usually introduced as follows: τὸ ῥηθὲν ὑπὸ τοῦ [L T Tr WH om. τοῦ] κυρίου διὰ τοῦ προφήτου, Mt. i. 22; ii. 15; ὑπὸ τοῦ θεοῦ, Mt. xxii. 31; ὑπὸ τοῦ προφήτου Rec. Mt. xxvii. 35, cf. ii. 17; τὸ ῥηθὲν διά τινος, Mt. ii. 17 L T Tr WH, 23; iv. 14; viii. 17; xiii. 17; xxi. 4; xxvii. 9; τὸ εἰρημένον διὰ τοῦ προφ. Acts ii. 16; τὸ εἰρημένον, Lk. ii. 24; Acts xiii. 40; Ro. iv. 18; ἐρρέθη, Mt. v. 21, etc.; καθὼς εἴρηκεν, Heb. iv. 3. **b.** with acc. of the pers. to speak of, designate by words: ὃν εἶπον, Jn. i. 15 [(not WH txt.); B. 377 (323); cf. Ro. iv. 1 WH txt. (say of)]; ὁ ῥηθείς, Mt. iii. 3. εἰπεῖν τινα καλῶς, to speak well of one, praise him, Lk. vi. 26, (εὖ εἰπεῖν τινα, Hom. xii. 302); κακῶς, to speak ill of one, Acts xxiii. 5 fr. Ex. xxii. 28; cf. Kühner § 409, 2; 411, 5; [W. § 32, 1 b. β.; B. 146 (128)]. **c.** with an ellipsis of the acc. αὐτό (see αὐτός, II. 3): Lk. xxii. 67; Jn. ix. 27; xvi. 4, etc. σὺ εἶπας (sc. αὐτό), i. e. you have just expressed it in words; that's it; it is just as you say: Mt. xxvi. 25, 64, [a rabbinical formula; for exx. cf. Schoettgen or Wetstein on vs. 25; al. seem to regard the answer as non-committal, e. g. Origen on vs. 64 (opp. iii. 910 De la Rue); Wünsche, Erläut. der Evang. aus Talmud usw. on vs. 25; but cf. the ἐγώ εἰμι of Mk. xiv. 62; in Mt. xxvi. 64 WH mrg. take it interrogatively]. **2.** the person, to whom a thing is said, is indicated **a.** by a dat.: εἰπεῖν τί τινι, Lk. vii. 40, and very often; εἶπον ὑμῖν sc. αὐτό, I (have just) told it you; this is what I mean; let this be the word: Mt. xxviii. 7; cf. Bnhdy. p. 381; [Jelf § 403, 1; Goodwin § 19, 5; esp. (for exx.) Herm. Vig. p. 746]. τινὶ περί

τινος [cf. W. § 47, 4], Mt. xvii. 13; Jn. xviii. 34. to say anything to one by way of censure, Mt. xxi. 3; to cast in one's teeth, ἐρεῖτέ μοι τὴν παραβολήν, Lk. iv. 23. to tell what anything means, e. g. τὸ μυστήριον, Rev. xvii. 7. **b.** by the use of a prep.: πρός τινα [cf. B. 172 (150); Krüger § 48, 7, 13], to say (a thing) to one, as Lk. iv. 23; v. 4; xii. 16, and many other places in Luke; to say a thing in reference to one [W. 405 (378)], Mk. xii. 12; Lk. xviii. 9; xx. 19. **3.** εἶπον, to say, speak, simply and without an acc. of the obj., i. e. merely to declare in words, to use language; **a.** with the addition of an adverb or of some other adjunct: ὁμοίως, Mt. xxvi. 35; ὡσαύτως, Mt. xxi. 30; καθώς, Mt. xxviii. 6; Lk. xxiv. 24; Jn. i. 23; vii. 38; εἶπε διὰ παραβολῆς, making use of a parable [see διά, A. III. 3] he spake, Lk. viii. 4; ἐν παραβολαῖς, Mt. xxii. 1; with an instrumental dative: εἰπὲ λόγῳ, say in (using only) a (single) word, sc. that my servant shall be healed, Mt. viii. 8 (where Rec. λόγον); Lk. vii. 7. **b.** with the words spoken added in direct discourse; so a hundred times in the historical books of the N. T., as Mt. ix. 4 sq.; viii. 32; [xv. 4 L Tr WH], etc.; i Co. xii. 15; [2 Co. iv. 6 L txt. T Tr WH, (cf. 4 below)]; Heb. i. 5; iii. 10; x. 7, [15 L T Tr WH], 30; xii. 21; Jas. ii. 3, 11; Jude 9; Rev. vii. 14; πέμψας εἶπεν he said by a messenger or messengers, Mt. xi. 2 sq. The following and other phrases are freq. in the Synoptic Gospels: ὁ δὲ ἀποκριθεὶς εἶπεν, as Mt. iv. 4; xv. 13; καὶ ἀποκριθεὶς εἶπεν, Mt. xxiv. 4; ἀποκριθεῖσα ἡ μήτηρ εἶπεν, Lk. i. 60; ἀποκριθεὶς ὁ Σίμων εἶπεν, Lk. vii. 43, etc.; ἀποκριθέντες δὲ εἶπον [-παν T Tr WH], Lk. xx. 24; but John usually writes ἀπεκρίθη καὶ εἶπεν: Jn. i. 48 (49); ii. 19; iii. 10; iv. 10, 13, 17; vi. 26, 29; vii. 16, 20 [R G], 52; ix. 11 [R G L br.], 30, 36 [L Tr mrg. om. WH br. κ. εἶπ.]; xiii. 7; xviii. 23; xviii. 30; — εἶπαν αὐτῷ λέγοντες, Mk. viii. 28 T WH Tr mrg., cf. xii. 26]. **c.** foll. by ὅτι: Mt. xxviii. 7; Mk. xvi. 7; Jn. vi. 36; vii. 42; viii. 55; xi. 40; xvi. 15; xviii. 8; 1 Jn. i. 6, 8, 10; 1 Co. i. 15; xiv. 23; xv. 27 [L br. WH mrg. om. ὅτι]. **d.** foll. by acc. and inf.: τί οὖν ἐροῦμεν Ἀβραὰμ τὸν πατέρα ἡμῶν εὑρηκέναι [WH txt. om. Tr mrg. br. εὑρηκ.; cf. 1 b. above] κατὰ σάρκα; Ro. iv. 1. **4.** εἰπεῖν sometimes involves in it the idea of commanding [cf. B. 275 sq. (237)]: foll. by the inf., εἶπε δοθῆναι αὐτῇ φαγεῖν, Mk. v. 43; εἶπε τῷ ἀδελφῷ μου μερίσασθαι μετ' ἐμοῦ τὴν κληρονομίαν, Lk. xii. 13; ὅσα ἂν εἴπωσιν ὑμῖν (sc. τηρεῖν [inserted in R G]), τηρεῖτε, Mt. xxiii. 3, (Sap. ix. 8). foll. by the acc. and inf., ὁ εἰπὼν ἐκ σκότους φῶς λάμψαι, 2 Co. iv. 6 [R G L mrg., cf. B. 273 sq. (235); but L txt. T Tr WH read λάμψει, thus changing the construction fr. the acc. with infin. to direct discourse, see 3 b. above]; εἶπεν αὐτῷ (for ἑαυτῷ, see αὐτοῦ) φωνηθῆναι τοὺς δούλους τούτους, he commanded to be called for him (i. e. to him) these servants, Lk. xix. 15; cf. W. § 44, 3 b.; Krüger § 55, 3, 13. foll. by ἵνα with the subjunc.: Mt. iv. 3; xx. 21; Lk. iv. 3; to εἰπεῖν is added a dat. of the pers. bidden to do something, Mk. iii. 9; Lk. x. 40 cf. iv. 3; Rev. vi. 11; ix. 4. "Moreover, notice that ἵνα and ὄφρα are often used by the later poets after verbs of commanding;" Hermann ad Vig. p. 849; cf. W. § 44, 8; [B. 237

(204)].   **5.** By a Hebraism εἰπεῖν ἐν ἑαυτῷ (like אָמַר בְּלִבּוֹ, Deut. viii. 17; Ps. x. 6 (ix. 27); xiii. (xiv.) 1; Esth. vi. 6) is equiv. to *to think* (because thinking is a silent soliloquy): Mt. ix. 3; Lk. vii. 39; xvi. 3; xviii. 4 (elsewhere also λέγειν ἐν ἑαυτῷ); and εἰπεῖν ἐν τῇ καρδίᾳ αὐτοῦ amounts to the same, Lk. xii. 45; Ro. x. 6; but in other passages εἶπον, ἔλεγον, ἐν ἑαυτοῖς is i. q. ἐν ἀλλήλοις: Mt. xxi. 38; see λέγω, II. 1 d.   **6.** εἰπεῖν τινα with a predicate accus. *to call, style, one*: ἐκείνους εἶπε θεούς, Jn. x. 35; ὑμᾶς εἴρηκα φίλους, Jn. xv. 15; (Hom. Od. 19, 334; Xen. apol. Socr. § 15; Lcian. Tim. § 20). [COMP.: ἀντ-, ἀπ-, προ-εἶπον.]

1513; see 1487 & 4458

εἴ-πως, see εἰ, III. 14.

1514————— εἰρηνεύω; (εἰρήνη); **1.** *to make peace*: 1 Macc. vi. 60; Dio Cass. 77, 12, etc.   **2.** *to cultivate* or *keep peace*, i. e. harmony; *to be at peace, live in peace*: 2 Co. xiii. 11; ἐν ἀλλήλοις, Mk. ix. 50; ἐν ἑαυτοῖς [T Tr αὐτοῖς], 1 Th. v. 13; μετά τινος, Ro. xii. 18; (Plat. Theaet. p. 180 b.; Dio Cass. 42, 15, etc.; Sept.).*

1515 εἰρήνη, -ης, ἡ, (apparently fr. εἴρω to join; [al. fr. εἴρω i. q. λέγω; Etym. Magn. 303, 41; Vaniček p. 892; Lob. Path. Proleg. p. 194; Benfey, Wurzellex. ii. p. 7]), Sept. chiefly for שָׁלוֹם; [fr. Hom. down]; *peace*, i. e.   **1.** *a state of national tranquillity*; *exemption from the rage and havoc of war*: Rev. vi. 4; πολλὴ εἰρήνη, Acts xxiv. 2 (3); τὰ [WH txt. om. τά] πρὸς εἰρήνην, things that look towards peace, as an armistice, conditions for the restoration of peace, Lk. xiv. 32; αἰτεῖσθαι εἰρήνην, Acts xii. 20; ἔχειν εἰρήνην, of the church free from persecutions, Acts ix. 31.   **2.** *peace between individuals*, i. e. *harmony, concord*: Mt. x. 34; Lk. xii. 51; Acts vii. 26; Ro. xiv. 17; 1 Co. vii. 15; Gal. v. 22; Eph. ii. 17; iv. 3; i. q. the author of peace, Eph. ii. 14 [cf. B. 125 (109)]; ἐν εἰρήνῃ, where harmony prevails, in a peaceful mind, Jas. iii. 18; ὁδὸς εἰρήνης, way leading to peace, a course of life promoting harmony, Ro. iii. 17 (fr. Is. lix. 8); μετ᾽ εἰρήνης, in a mild and friendly spirit, Heb. xi. 31; ποιεῖν εἰρήνην, to promote concord, Jas. iii. 18; to effect it, Eph. ii. 15; ζητεῖν, 1 Pet. iii. 11; διώκειν, 2 Tim. ii. 22; with μετὰ πάντων added, Heb. xii. 14; τὰ τῆς εἰρήνης διώκειν, Ro. xiv. 19 [cf. B. 95 (83); W. 109 (103 sq.)]. spec. *good order*, opp. to ἀκαταστασία, 1 Co. xiv. 33.   **3.** after the Hebr. שָׁלוֹם, *security, safety, prosperity, felicity*, (because peace and harmony make and keep things safe and prosperous): Lk. xix. 42; Heb. vii. 2; εἰρήνη κ. ἀσφάλεια, opp. to ὄλεθρος, 1 Th. v. 3; ἐν εἰρήνῃ ἐστὶ τὰ ὑπάρχοντα αὐτοῦ, his goods are secure from hostile attack, Lk. xi. 21; ὕπαγε εἰς εἰρήνην, Mk. v. 34, and πορεύου εἰς εἰρ. Lk. vii. 50; viii. 48, a formula of wishing well, blessing, addressed by the Hebrews to departing friends (לֵךְ לְשָׁלוֹם, 1 S. i. 17; xx. 42, etc.; properly, *depart into a place* or *state of peace*; [cf. B. 184 (160)]); πορεύεσθαι ἐν εἰρήνῃ, Acts xvi. 36, and ὑπάγετε ἐν εἰρήνῃ, Jas. ii. 16, *go in peace* i. e. *may happiness attend you*; ἀπολύειν τινὰ μετ᾽ εἰρήνης, to dismiss one with good wishes, Acts xv. 33; ἐν εἰρ. with my wish fulfilled, and therefore happy, Lk. ii. 29 (see ἀπολύω, 2 a.); προπέμπειν τινὰ ἐν εἰρ. free from danger, safe, 1 Co. xvi. 11 [al. take it of inward peace or

of *harmony*; cf. Mey. ad loc.].   The Hebrews in invoking blessings on a man called out שָׁלוֹם לְךָ (Judg. vi. 23; Dan. x. 19); from this is to be derived the explanation of those expressions which refer apparently to the Messianic blessings (see 4 below): εἰρήνη τῷ οἴκῳ τούτῳ, let peace, blessedness, come to this household, Lk. x. 5; υἱὸς εἰρήνης, worthy of peace [cf. W. § 34, 3 N. 2; B. 161 sq. (141)], Lk. x. 6; ἐλθέτω ἡ εἰρήνη ἐπ᾽ αὐτόν, let the peace which ye wish it come upon it, i. e. be its lot, Mt. x. 13; to the same purport ἐπαναπ. ἡ εἰρ. ὑμ. ἐπ᾽ αὐτόν, Lk. x. 6; ἡ εἰρ. ὑμ. πρὸς ὑμᾶς ἐπιστραφήτω, let your peace return to you, because it could not rest upon it, i. e. let it be just as if ye had not uttered the wish, Mt. x. 13.   **4.** spec. *the Messiah's peace*: Lk. ii. 14; ὁδὸς εἰρήνης, the way that leads to peace (salvation), Lk. i. 79; εἰρ. ἐν οὐρανῷ, peace, salvation, is prepared for us in heaven, Lk. xix. 38; εὐαγγελίζεσθαι εἰρήνην, Acts x. 36.   **5.** acc. to a conception distinctly peculiar to Christianity, *the tranquil state of a soul assured of its salvation through Christ, and so fearing nothing from God and content with its earthly lot, of whatsoever sort that is*: Ro. viii. 6; ἐν εἰρήνῃ sc. ὄντες is used of those who, assured of salvation, tranquilly await the return of Christ and the transformation of all things which will accompany that event, 2 Pet. iii. 14; [πληροῦν πάσης . . . εἰρήνης ἐν τῷ πιστεύειν, Ro. xv. 13 (where L mrg. ἐν π. εἰρήνῃ)]; ἔχειν ἐν Χριστῷ εἰρήνην (opp. to ἐν τῷ κόσμῳ θλίψιν ἔχειν), Jn. xvi. 33; ἔχειν εἰρ. πρὸς τ. θεόν, with God, Ro. v. 1, (εἰρ. πρός τινα, Plat. rep. 5 p. 465 b.; cf. Diod. 21, 12; cf Mey. on Ro. l. c.; W. 186 (175); 406 (379)]); εὐαγγελίζεσθαι εἰρήνην, Ro. x. 15 [R G Tr mrg. in br.]; τὸ εὐαγγέλιον τῆς εἰρήνης, Eph. vi. 15; in the expression εἰρήνην ἀφίημι κτλ. Jn. xiv. 27, in which Christ, with allusion to the usual Jewish formula at leave-taking (see 3 above), says that he not merely wishes, but gives peace; ἡ εἰρήνη τοῦ Χριστοῦ, which comes from Christ, Col. iii. 15 [Rec. θεοῦ]; τοῦ θεοῦ, Phil. iv. 7, [cf.W. 186 (175)].   Comprehensively of every kind of peace (blessing), yet with a predominance apparently of the notion of *peace with God*, εἰρήνη is used —in the salutations of Christ after his resurrection, εἰρήνη ὑμῖν (לָכֶם שָׁלוֹם), Lk. xxiv. 36 [T om. WH reject the cl.]; Jn. xx. 19, 21, 26; in the phrases ὁ κύριος τῆς εἰρήνης, the Lord who is the author and promoter of peace, 2 Th. iii. 16; ὁ θεὸς τῆς εἰρ. Ro. xv. 33; xvi. 20; 2 Co. xiii. 11; Phil. iv. 9; 1 Th. v. 23; Heb. xiii. 20; in the salutations at the beginning and the close of the apostolic Epp.: Ro. i. 7; 1 Co. i. 3; 2 Co. i. 2; Gal. i. 3; vi. 16; Eph. i. 2; vi. 23; Phil. i. 2; Col. i. 2; 1 Th. i. 1; 2 Th. i. 2; iii. 16; 1 Tim. i. 2; 2 Tim. i. 2; Tit. i. 4; [Philem. 3]; 1 Pet. i. 2; v. 14; 2 Pet. i. 2; 2 Jn. 3; 3 Jn. 15 (14); [Jude 2]; Rev. i. 4.   Cf. *Kling* in Herzog iv. p. 596 sq. s. v. *Friede mit Gott*; *Weiss*, Bibl. Theol. d. N. T. § 83 b.; [*Otto* in the Jahrbb. für deutsch. Theol. for 1867, p. 678 sqq.; cf. W. 549 (511)].   **6.** of *the blessed state* of devout and upright men *after death* (Sap. iii. 3): Ro. ii. 10.*

εἰρηνικός, -ή, -όν, **1.** *relating to peace*: ἐπιστῆμαι, the arts of peace, Xen. oec. 1, 17; ἔργα, ibid. 6, 1; χρείαι,

Diod. 5, 31; often in 1 Macc.   **2.** *peaceable, pacific, loving peace*: Jas. iii. 17; (Plat., Isoc., al. ; Sept.).   **3.** *bringing peace with it, peaceful, salutary,* (see εἰρήνη, 3): Heb. xii. 11.*

1517 εἰρηνο-ποιέω, -ῶ: [1 aor. εἰρηνοποίησα]; (εἰρηνοποιός); *to make peace, establish harmony*: Col. i. 20. (Prov. x. 10; in Mid., Hermes ap. Stob. eclog. ph. 1, 52 [984].)*

1518 εἰρηνοποιός, -όν, masc. *a peace-maker* (Xen. Hell. 6, 3, 4; Dio Cass.); *pacific, loving peace*: Mt. v. 9; [others (cf. A. V.) dispute this secondary meaning; see Meyer ad loc.].*

see
(1512a) εἴρω, fut. ἐρῶ, see εἶπον.

1519 εἰς, a Prep. governing the Accusative, and denoting entrance into, or direction and limit: *into, to, towards, for, among.* It is used

A. Properly **I.** of Place, after verbs of going, coming, sailing, flying, falling, living, leading, carrying, throwing, sending, etc. ;   **1.** of a place entered, or of entrance into a place, *into*; and   **a.** it stands before nouns designating an open place, a hollow thing, or one in which an object can be hidden: as εἰς (τὴν) πόλιν, Mt. xxvi. 18; xxviii. 11; Mk. i. 45, and often; εἰς τ. οἶκον, Mt. ix. 7; συναγωγήν, Acts xvii. 10; πλοῖον, Mt. viii. 23; Jn. vi. 17; Acts xxi. 6; θάλασσαν, Mt. xvii. 27; ἄβυσσον, Lk. viii. 31; οὐρανόν, Lk. ii. 15; κόσμον, Jn. i. 9; iii. 19, etc.; τὰ ἴδια, Jn. i. 11; xvi. 32; Acts xxi. 6; ἀποθήκην, Mt. iii. 12; εἰς τὰ ὦτα, Lk. i. 44; εἰς τὰς ζώνας or ζώνην, Mt. x. 9; Mk. vi. 8, etc.; εἰς τὸν ἀέρα, 1 Co. xiv. 9; εἰς πῦρ, Mk. ix. 22, etc.; εἰς αὐτόν, of a demon entering the body of a man, Mk. ix. 25. with acc. of pers. (Germ. *zu jemand hinein*), *into* the house of one (cf. Kühner § 432, 1, 1 a. ; [Jelf § 625, 1 a.]) : εἰς τὴν Λυδίαν, Acts xvi. 40 Rec., but here more correctly πρός with G L T Tr WH; cf. W. § 49, a, a. (εἰς ἑαυτόν, Sap. viii. 18). γίνομαι εἰς with acc. of place, see γίνομαι, 5 g. **b.** before names of cities, villages, and countries, εἰς may be rendered simply *to, towards*, (Germ. *nach* ; as if it indicated merely motion towards a destination; [cf. W. § 49, a, a.]); as εἰς Ἱεροσόλυμα, εἰς Δαμασκόν, εἰς Βέροιαν, etc. ; εἰς Σπανίαν, Αἴγυπτον, Γαλιλαίαν, etc. ; but it is not to be so translated in such phrases as εἰς τὴν Ἰουδαίαν γῆν, etc., Jn. iii. 22; Mt. ii. 12 cf. 20, 21; εἰς τὰ μέρη τῆς Γαλιλαίας, Mt. ii. 22, etc. **c.** elliptical expressions are — εἰς ᾅδου, sc. δόμον, Acts ii. 27 [Rec.], 31 [not T WH]; see ᾅδης, 2. ἐπιστολαὶ εἰς Δαμασκόν, to be carried to D., Acts ix. 2; ἡ διακονία μου ἡ εἰς [L Tr mrg. ἐν] Ἱερουσ. (see in διακονία, 3), Ro. xv. 31; cf. Bnhdy. p. 216. **d.** εἰς means *among (in among)* before nouns comprising a multitude; as, εἰς τοὺς λῃστάς, Lk. x. 36; εἰς [L mrg. ἐπὶ] τὰς ἀκάνθας, Mk. iv. 7 (for which Lk. viii. 7 gives ἐν μέσῳ τῶν ἀκανθῶν); or before persons, Mk. viii. 19 sq.; Lk. xi. 49; Jn. xxi. 23; Acts xviii. 6; xx. 29; xxii. 21, 30; xxvi. 17; see ἀποστέλλω, 1 b.; or before a collective noun in the singular number, as εἰς τὸν δῆμον, Acts xvii. 5; xix. 30; εἰς τὸν ὄχλον, Acts xiv. 14; εἰς τὸν λαόν, Acts iv. 17. **2.** If the surface only of the place entered is touched or occupied, εἰς, like the Lat. *in*, may [often] be rendered *on, upon*, (Germ. *auf*), [sometimes by *unto*, — (idioms

vary)], to mark the limit reached, or where one sets foot. Of this sort are εἰς τὸ πέραν [A. V. *unto*], Mt. viii. 18; xiv. 22; Mk. iv. 35; εἰς τὴν γῆν, Lk. xii. 49 (L T Tr WH ἐπί); Acts xxvi. 14; Rev. viii. 5, 7; ix. 3; xii. 4, 9; εἰς τὴν κλίνην, Rev. ii. 22; εἰς ὁδόν, Mt. x. 5; Mk. vi. 8; Lk. i. 79; εἰς τὴν ὁδόν, Mk. xi. 8ª [L mrg. ἐν w. dat., 8ᵇ R G L]; εἰς τ. ἀγρόν, Mt. xxii. 5; Mk. xiii. 16; εἰς τὸ ὄρος [or εἰς ὄρ.; here A. V. uses *into*], Mt. v. 1; xiv. 23; xv. 29; xvii. 1; Mk. iii. 13; ix. 2; Lk. ix. 28; Jn. vi. 3, etc.; εἰς τὰ δεξιά, Jn. xxi. 6; σπείρειν εἰς τι (τὴν σάρκα), Gal. vi. 8 [here A. V. *unto*; cf. Ellic. ad loc.]; ἀναπίπτειν εἰς τόπον, Lk. xiv. 10; δέχομαι εἰς τὰς ἀγκάλας, Lk. ii. 28; τύπτειν εἰς τὴν κεφαλήν, Mt. xxvii. 30, [εἰς τὴν σιαγόνα, Lk. vi. 29 Tdf.; ῥαπίζειν εἰς τ. σιαγόνα, Mt. v. 39 L T Tr txt. WH, where R G ἐπί], and in other phrases. **3.** of motion (not into a place itself, but) into the vicinity of a place; where it may be rendered *to, near, towards,* (cf. Fritzsche on Mk. p. 81 sq. [for exx. only]): εἰς τ. θάλασσαν, Mk. iii. 7 G L T Tr mrg.; εἰς πόλιν, Jn. iv. 5 cf. 28; εἰς τὸ μνημεῖον, Jn. xi. 31, 38; xx. 1, 3 sq. 8; ἐγγίζειν εἰς etc. Mt. xxi. 1; Mk. xi. 1; Lk. xviii. 35; xix. 29; εἰς τοὺς φραγμούς, Lk. xiv. 23; πίπτειν εἰς τ. πόδας, at, Jn. xi. 32 [T Tr WH πρός]; κλίνειν τὸ πρόσωπον εἰς τ. γῆν, Lk. xxiv. 5; εἰς τὴν χεῖρα, on, Lk. xv. 22. **4.** of the limit to which; with acc. of place, *as far as, even to*: λάμπειν ἐκ . . . εἰς, Lk. xvii. 24; with acc. plur. of pers. *to, unto*: Acts xxiii. 15 (εἰς ὑμᾶς, for R G πρός); Ro. v. 12; xvi. 19; 2 Co. ix. 5 [L Tr πρός]; x. 14. **5.** of local direction; **a.** after verbs of *seeing*: ἐπαίρειν τοὺς ὀφθαλμοὺς εἴς τι, τινα, Lk. vi. 20; βλέπειν, Lk. ix. 62; Jn. xiii. 22; Acts iii. 4; ἀναβλέπειν, Mk. vi. 41; Lk. ix. 16; Acts xxii. 13; ἐμβλέπειν, Mt. vi. 26; ἀτενίζειν, q. v. **b.** after verbs of saying, teaching, announcing, etc. (cf. Germ. *die Rede richten an* etc. ; Lat. *dicere ad* or *coram*; [Eng. *direct one's remarks to* or *towards*]; exx. fr. Grk. auth. are given by Bnhdy. p. 217; Passow i. p. 802ᵇ; [L. and S. s. v. I. b. 3]; Krüger § 68, 21, 6): κηρύσσειν, as ἦν κηρύσσων εἰς τὰς συναγωγὰς αὐτῶν εἰς ὅλην τὴν Γαλιλ. *preaching to the synagogues throughout all Galilee*, Mk. i. 39 (Rec. ἐν ταῖς συναγ., as Lk. iv. 44 [where T WH Tr txt. now εἰς; cf. W. 416 (387); B. 333 (287)]; but in Mk. l. c. T Tr txt. WH now read ἦλθεν κηρύσσων κτλ.]); τὸ εὐαγγ. εἰς ὅλον τ. κόσμον, Mk. xiv. 9; εἰς πάντα τὰ ἔθνη, Mk. xiii. 10; Lk. xxiv. 47; εἰς ὑμᾶς 1 Th. ii. 9; ἀπαγγέλλειν [Rec. ἀναγγ.] τι εἰς, Mk. v. 14; Lk. viii. 34; γνωρίζειν, Ro. xvi. 26; εὐαγγελίζεσθαι, 2 Co. x. 16; εἰς ὑμᾶς, 1 Pet. i. 25; λέγειν [Rec.; al. λαλεῖν] εἰς τὸν κόσμον, Jn. viii. 26; [λαλεῖν τὸν λόγον εἰς τὴν Πέργην, Acts xiv. 25 T WH mrg.]; διαμαρτύρεσθαι and μαρτυρεῖν, Acts xxiii. 11.

II. of Time;   **1.** it denotes entrance into a period which is penetrated, as it were, i. e. duration *through* a time, (Lat. *in*; Germ. *hinein, hinaus*): εἰς τὸν αἰῶνα, and the like, see αἰών, 1 a.; εἰς τὸ διηνεκές, Heb. vii. 3; x. 1, 12, 14; εἰς ἔτη πολλά, Lk. xii. 19; τῇ ἐπιφωσκούσῃ (ἡμέρᾳ) εἰς μίαν σαββάτων, dawning into [A. V. *towards*] the first day of the week, Mt. xxviii. 1.   Hence **2.** of the time in which a thing is done; because he who does or experiences a thing at any time is conceived of as, so to speak, entering into that time: εἰς τὸν καιρὸν αὐτῶν, in their season, Lk. i. 20; εἰς τὸ μέλλον sc. ἔτος, the next year, [but s. v. μέλλω, 1. Grimm seems to take the phrase indefinitely, *thenceforth* (cf. Grk. txt.)], Lk. xiii. 9; εἰς τὸ μεταξὺ σάββατον, *on the next sabbath*, Acts xiii. 42; εἰς τὸ πάλιν, again (*for* the second, third, time), 2 Co. xiii. 2.   **3.** of the (temporal) limit **for which** anything is or is done; Lat. *in*; our *for, unto*: Rev. ix. 15; εἰς τὴν αὔριον sc. ἡμέραν, for the morrow, Mt. vi. 34; Acts iv. 3; εἰς ἡμέραν κρίσεως, 2 Pet. ii. 9; iii. 7; εἰς ἡμέραν Χριστοῦ, Phil. i. 10; ii. 16; εἰς ἡμέραν ἀπολυτρώσεως, Eph. iv. 30.   **4.** of the (temporal) limit **to which**; *unto* i. e. *even to, until*: Acts xxv. 21; 1 Th. iv. 15; εἰς ἐκείνην τὴν ἡμέραν, 2 Tim. i. 12. On the phrase εἰς τέλος, see τέλος, 1 a.

B. Used METAPHORICALLY, εἰς   **I.** retains the force of entering into anything,   **1.** where one thing is said to be changed into another, or to be separated into parts, or where several persons or things are said to be collected or combined into one, etc.: ἀποβαίνειν εἰς τι, Phil. i. 19; γίνεσθαι εἰς τι, see γίνομαι, 5 d.; εἶναι εἰς τι, see εἰμί, V. 2 [a. fin.] c. and d.; στρέφειν τι εἰς τι, Rev. xi. 6; μεταστρέφειν, Acts ii. 20; Jas. iv. 9; μεταλλάσσειν, Ro. i. 26; μετασχηματίζεσθαι, 2 Co. xi. 13 sq.; συνοικοδομεῖσθαι, Eph. ii. 22; κτίζειν τινὰ εἰς, Eph. ii. 15; λαμβάνειν τι εἰς, Heb. xi. 8; λογίζεσθαι εἰς τι, see λογίζομαι, 1 a. ἐσχίσθη εἰς δύο, Mt. xxvii. 51; Mk. xv. 38, (Polyb. 2, 16, 11 σχίζεται εἰς δύο μέρη); δέειν εἰς δεσμάς, Mt. xiii. 30 [G om. Tr WH br. εἰς]; εἰς ἓν τελειοῦσθαι, Jn. xvii. 23; συνάγειν εἰς ἕν, Jn. xi. 52.   **2.** after verbs of going, coming, leading, etc., εἰς is joined to nouns designating the condition or state into which one passes, falls, etc.: εἰσέρχεσθαι εἰς τὴν βασιλ. τῶν οὐραν. or τοῦ θεοῦ, see βασιλεία, 3 p. 97ᵇ; εἰς τ. ζωήν, Mt. xviii. 8; xix. 17; xxv. 46; εἰς τ. χαράν, Mt. xxv. 21, 23; εἰς κόλασιν αἰώνιον, ib. 46; ἔρχεσθαι εἰς κρίσιν, Jn. v. 24; εἰσφέρειν, εἰσέρχ. εἰς πειρασμόν, Mt. vi. 13; xxvi. 41; Mk. xiv. 38 [T WH ἔλθητε]; ἔρχεσθαι εἰς τὸ χεῖρον, Mk. v. 26; εἰς ἀπελεγμόν, Acts xix. 27; εἰς προκοπήν, Phil. i. 12; μεταβαίνειν εἰς τ. ζωήν, Jn. v. 24; 1 Jn. iii. 14; πορεύεσθαι εἰς θάνατον, Lk. xxii. 33; ὑπάγειν εἰς ἀπώλειαν, Rev. xvii. 8, 11; ὑπάγειν or πορεύεσθαι εἰς εἰρήνην, see εἰρήνη, 3; ὑποστρέφειν εἰς διαφθοράν, Acts xiii. 34; συντρέχειν εἰς ἀνάχυσιν, 1 Pet. iv. 4; βάλλειν εἰς θλίψιν, Rev. ii. 22; περιτρέπειν εἰς μανίαν, Acts xxvi. 24; μεταστρέφειν and στρέφειν εἴς τι, Acts ii. 20; Rev. xi. 6; ὁδηγεῖν εἰς τ. ἀλήθειαν [T ἐν τῇ ἀλ.], Jn. xvi. 13; αἰχμαλωτίζειν εἰς ὑπακοήν, 2 Co. x. 5; παραδιδόναι εἰς θλίψιν, Mt. xxiv. 9; εἰς θάνατον, 2 Co. iv. 11; εἰς κρίμα θανάτου, Lk. xxiv. 20; συγκλείειν εἰς ἀπείθειαν, Ro. xi. 32; ἐμπίπτειν εἰς κρίμα, εἰς ὀνειδισμὸν καὶ παγίδα, εἰς πειρασμόν, 1 Tim. iii. 6 sq.; vi. 9.   **3.** it is used of the business which one enters into, i. e. of what he undertakes: εἰσέρχεσθαι εἰς τ. κόπον τινός, to take up and carry on a labor begun by another, Jn. iv. 38; τρέχειν εἰς πόλεμον, Rev. ix. 9; ἔρχομαι εἰς ἀποκαλύψεις, I come, in my narrative, to revelations i. e. to the mention of them, 2 Co. xii. 1.

II. εἰς after words indicating motion or direction or end;   **1.** it denotes motion to something, after verbs of going, coming, leading, calling, etc., and answers to the Lat. *ad, to*: καλεῖν τινα εἰς γάμον, γάμους, δεῖπνον, etc. *to invite to*, etc., Mt. xxii. 3; Lk. xiv. 8, 10; Jn. ii. 2; καλεῖν τινα εἰς μετάνοιαν, etc., Lk. v. 32; 2 Th. ii. 14; ἄγειν τινὰ εἰς μετάνοιαν, Ro. ii. 4; ἐπιστρέφειν εἰς τὸ φῶς, Acts xxvi. 18; ἐκτρέπεσθαι εἰς ματαιολογίαν, 1 Tim. i. 6; μετατίθεσθαι εἰς ἕτερον εὐαγγέλ. Gal. i. 6; χωρῆσαι εἰς μετάνοιαν, 2 Pet. iii. 9, etc.   **2.** of ethical direction or reference;   **a.** univ. of acts in which the mind is directed *towards*, or looks *to*, something: βλέπειν εἰς πρόσωπόν τινος (see βλέπω, 2 c.); ἀποβλέπειν εἰς τ. μισθαποδοσίαν, Heb. xi. 26; ἀφορᾶν εἰς . . . Ἰησοῦν, ib. xii. 2 (see A. I. 5 a. above); πιστεύειν εἰς τινα, and the like, cf. under πιστεύω, πίστις, ἐλπίζω, [ἐλπίς], etc.; ἐπιθυμίαν ἔχειν εἰς τι, directed towards etc. Phil. i. 23; λέγειν εἰς τινα, to speak with reference to one, Acts ii. 25 (Diod. Sic. 11, 50); λέγειν τι εἴς τι, to say something in reference to something, Eph. v. 32; λαλεῖν τι εἴς τι, to speak something relating to something, Heb. vii. 14; ὀμνύειν εἴς τι, to swear with the mind directed towards, Mt. v. 35; εὐδοκεῖν εἴς τινα, Mt. xii. 18 [R G]; 2 Pet. i. 17.   **b.** for one's advantage or disadvantage;   **α.** *for, for the benefit of, to the advantage of*: εἰς ἡμᾶς, Eph. i. 19; εἰς ὑμᾶς, 2 Co. xiii. 4 [but WH br.]; Eph. iii. 2; Col. i. 25; πλουτεῖν εἰς θεόν, to abound in riches made to subserve God's purposes and promote his glory, Lk. xii. 21 [so too W. 397 (371); but cf. Mey. ed. Weiss ad loc.]; Christ is said πλουτεῖν εἰς πάντας, to abound in riches redounding to the salvation of all men, Ro. x. 12; πλεονάζειν εἴς τι, Phil. iv. 17; ἐλεημοσύνην ποιεῖν εἰς τὸ ἔθνος, Acts xxiv. 17; εἰς τοὺς πτωχούς, for the benefit of the poor, Ro. xv. 26; εἰς τοὺς ἁγίους, 2 Co. viii. 4; ix. 1, cf. 13; κοπιᾶν εἰς τινα, Ro. xvi. 6; Gal. iv. 11; εἰς Χριστόν, to the advantage and honor of Christ, Philem. 6; ἐργάζεσθαί τι εἴς τινα, Mk. xiv. 6 Rec.; 3 Jn. 5; λειτουργὸς εἰς τὰ ἔθνη, Ro. xv. 16; γενόμενα εἰς Καφαρναούμ (for Rec. ἐν Καπερναούμ [cf. W. 416 (388); B. 333 (286)]), Lk. iv. 23.   **β.** *unto* in a disadvantageous sense, (*against*): μηδὲν ἄτοπον εἰς αὐτὸν γενόμενον, Acts xxviii. 6.   **c.** of the mood or inclination, affecting one towards any person or thing; of one's mode of action towards;   **α.** in a good sense: ἀγάπη εἴς τινα, unto, towards, one, Ro. v. 8; 2 Co. ii. 4, 8; Col. i. 4; 1 Th. iii. 12; τὸ αὐτὸ εἰς ἀλλήλους φρονεῖν, Ro. xii. 16; φιλόστοργος, ib. 10; φιλόξενος, 1 Pet. iv. 9; χρηστός, Eph. iv. 32; ἀποκαταλλάσσειν εἰς αὐτόν [al. αὐτ. see αὐτοῦ], Col. i. 20 [cf. W. 397 (371)].   **β.** in a bad sense: ἁμαρτάνειν εἴς τινα (see ἁμαρτάνω, b.); λόγον εἰπεῖν and βλασφημεῖν εἴς τινα, Lk. xii. 10; Mk. iii. 29; βλάσφημος εἴς τινα, Acts vi. 11; βλασφημῶν λέγω εἴς τινα, Lk. xxii. 65; ἐπιβουλὴ εἴς τινα, Acts xxiii. 30; ἔχθρα, Ro. viii. 7; ἀντιλογία, Heb. xii. 3; θαρρεῖν εἴς τινα, 2 Co. x. 1.   **d.** of reference or relation; *with respect to, in reference to; as regards*, (cf. Kühner ii. 408 c.; [Jelf § 625, 3 e.]): Lk. vii. 30; Acts xxv. 20 [T Tr WH om. εἰς]; Ro. iv. 20; xv. 2; 2 Co. x. 16; xiii. 3; Gal. vi. 4; Eph. iii. 16; Phil. i. 5; ii.

22; 1 Th. v. 18; εἰς τί ἐδίστασας; '(looking) unto what (i. e. *wherefore*) didst thou doubt? Mt. xiv. 31; cf. *Hermann* ad Oed. C. 528' (Fritzsche). of the consideration influencing one to do anything: μετανοεῖν εἰς κήρυγμά τινος, at the preaching of one, i. e. out of regard to the substance of his preaching, Mt. xii. 41; δέχεσθαί τινα εἰς ὄνομά τινος, Mt. x. 41 sq.; εἰς διαταγὰς ἀγγέλων (see διαταγή), Acts vii. 53. **e.** with acc. of the pers. *towards* (Germ. *nach einem hin*), but in sense nearly equiv. to the simple dat. *to*, *unto*, after verbs of approving, manifesting, showing one's self: ἀποδεδειγμένος εἰς ὑμᾶς, Acts ii. 22; ἔνδειξιν ἐνδείκνυσθαι, 2 Co. viii. 24; φανερωθέντες εἰς ὑμᾶς, 2 Co. xi. 6 (L T Tr WH φανερώσαντες sc. τὴν γνῶσιν). **3.** it denotes the end; and **a.** the end to which a thing reaches or extends, i. e. measure or degree: [ἔφερεν εἰς τριάκοντα, Mk. iv. 8 T Tr txt. WH; cf. B. 30 (27); L. and S. s. v. A. III. 2]; εἰς τὰ ἄμετρα, 2 Co. x. 13; εἰς περισσείαν, 2 Co. x. 15; εἰς ὑπερβολήν (often in Grk. writ., as Eur. Hipp. 939; Aeschin. f. leg. § 4), 2 Co. iv. 17. of the limit: εἰς τὸ σωφρονεῖν, unto moderation, modesty, i. e. not beyond it, Ro. xii. 3. **b.** the end which a thing is adapted to attain (a use akin to that in B. II. 2 b.; [cf. W. 213 (200)]): ἀργὸς κ. ἄκαρπος εἴς τι, 2 Pet. i. 8; εὔθετος, Lk. ix. 62 R G; xiv. 35 (34); εὔχρηστος, 2 Tim. iv. 11; χρήσιμος, 2 Tim. ii. 14 R G, δυναμούμενος, Col. i. 11; θεοδίδακτος, 1 Th. iv. 9; βραδύς, Jas. i. 19; σοφός, Ro. xvi. 19; φῶς εἰς ἀποκάλυψιν, Lk. ii. 32; δύναμις εἰς etc. Ro. i. 16; Heb. xi. 11; ἀναγεννᾶν εἰς, 1 Pet. i. 3 sq.; ἀνακαινόω, Col. iii. 10; σοφίζειν τινὰ εἰς, 2 Tim. iii. 15; ἰσχύειν εἰς, Mt. v. 13. **c.** the end which one has in view, i. e. object, purpose; **α.** associated with other prepositions [cf. W. § 50,5]: ἐκ πίστεως εἰς πίστιν, to produce faith, Ro. i. 17, cf. Fritzsche, Meyer, Van Hengel, ad loc.; ἐξ αὐτοῦ καὶ δι' αὐτοῦ καὶ εἰς αὐτόν, answering to his purposes (the final cause), Ro. xi. 36; ἐξ οὗ τὰ πάντα καὶ ἡμεῖς εἰς αὐτόν, 1 Co. viii. 6; δι' αὐτοῦ καὶ εἰς αὐτόν (see διά, A. III. 2 b. sub fin.), Col. i. 16; δι' αὐτοῦ εἰς αὐτόν, Col. i. 20. **β.** shorter phrases: εἰς τοῦτο, to this end, Mk. i. 38; [Lk. iv. 43 R G Tr mrg.]; εἰς αὐτὸ τοῦτο [R. V. *for this very thing*], 2 Co. v. 5; εἰς τοῦτο ... ἵνα etc. Jn. xviii. 37; 1 Jn. iii. 8; Ro. xiv. 9; 2 Co. ii. 9; 1 Pet. iv. 6; εἰς αὐτὸ τοῦτο ... ὅπως etc. Ro. ix. 17; ἵνα, Col. iv. 8; Eph. vi. 22; εἰς τί, to what purpose, Mt. xxvi. 8; Mk. xiv. 4; εἰς ὅ, to which end, for which cause, 2 Th. i. 11; Col. i. 29. **γ.** univ.: βαπτίζω εἴς τινα, τι (see βαπτίζω, II. b. aa.); παιδαγωγὸς εἰς τὸν Χριστόν, Gal. iii. 24; συγκεκλεισμένοι εἰς τ. πίστιν, that we might the more readily embrace the faith when its time should come, Gal. iii. 23; φρουρούμενοι εἰς τὴν σωτηρίαν, that future salvation may be yours, 1 Pet. i. 5; ἀγοράζειν εἰς τ. ἑορτήν, Jn. xiii. 29; εἰς ὄλεθρον σαρκός, 1 Co. v. 5; εἰς τ. ἡμετέραν διδασκαλίαν, Ro. xv. 4, and in many other exx. esp. after verbs of appointing, choosing, preparing, doing, coming, sending, etc.: κεῖμαι, Lk. ii. 34; Phil. i. 17 (16); 1 Th. iii. 3; τάσσω, 1 Co. xvi. 15; τάσσομαι, Acts xiii. 48; ἀφορίζω, Ro. i. 1; Acts xiii. 2; προορίζω, Eph. i. 5; 1 Co. ii. 7; αἱρέομαι, 2 Th. ii. 13; τίθεμαι, 1 Tim. i. 12; 1 Pet. ii. 8; καταρτίζω, Ro. ix. 22 sq.; ἀποστέλλω,

Heb. i. 14; πέμπω, 1 Th. iii. 2, 5; Col. iv. 8; Phil. iv. 16 [L br. εἰς]; 1 Pet. ii. 14; ἔρχομαι, Jn. ix. 39; ποιεῖν τι εἰς, 1 Co. x. 31; xi. 24. Modelled after the Hebr. are the phrases, ἐγείρειν τινὰ εἰς βασιλέα, *to be* king, Acts xiii. 22; ἀνατρέφεσθαί τινα εἰς υἱόν, Acts vii. 21; τέθεικά σε εἰς φῶς ἐθνῶν, Acts xiii. 47 (fr. Is. xlix. 6 Alex.); cf. *Gesenius*, Lehrgeb. p. 814; B. 150 (131); [W. § 32, 4 b.]. **δ.** εἴς τι, indicating purpose, often depends not on any one preceding word with which it coalesces into a single phrase, but has the force of a telic clause added to the already complete preceding statement; thus, εἰς δόξαν τοῦ θεοῦ, Ro. xv. 7; Phil. i. 11; ii. 11; εἰς φόβον, that ye should fear, Ro. viii. 15; εἰς ἔνδειξιν, that he might show, Ro. iii. 25; εἰς ζωὴν αἰώνιον, to procure eternal life (sc. for those mentioned), Jn. iv. 14; vi. 27, (in which passages the phrase is by many interpp. [e. g. De Wette, Mey., Lange; cf. W. 397 (371) note] incorrectly joined with ἅλλεσθαι and μένειν [cf. Thol., Luthardt, al.]); Ro. v. 21; 1 Tim. i. 16; Jude 21; add, Mt. viii. 4; xxvii. 7; Mk. vi. 11; Acts xi. 18; Ro. x. 4; Phil. i. 25; ii. 16; 2 Tim. ii. 25; Rev. xxii. 2, etc. **ε.** εἰς τό foll. by an inf., a favorite construction with Paul (cf. B. 264 (227) sq.; *Harmsen* in the Zeitschr. f. wissensch. Theol. for 1874, pp. 345–360), is like the Lat. *ad* with the gerundive. It is of two kinds; either **aa.** εἰς τό combines with the verb on which it depends into a single sentence, as παραδώσουσιν αὐτὸν ... εἰς τὸ ἐμπαῖξαι, (Vulg. *ad deludendum*), Mt. xx. 19; εἰς τὸ σταυρωθῆναι, Mt. xxvi. 2; οἰκοδομηθήσεται εἰς τὸ τὰ εἰδωλόθυτα ἐσθίειν, (Vulg. *aedificabitur ad manducandum idolothyta*), 1 Co. viii. 10; μὴ οἰκίας οὐκ ἔχετε εἰς τὸ ἐσθίειν κ. πίνειν, 1 Co. xi. 22; εἰς τὸ προσφέρειν δῶρά τε καὶ θυσίας καθίσταται, (Vulg. *ad offerenda munera et hostias*), Heb. viii. 3; add, Heb. ix. 28; 1 Th. ii. 16; iv. 9; Phil. i. 23; or **ββ.** εἰς τό with the inf. has the force of a separate telic clause (equiv. to ἵνα with the subjunc.), [Meyer (on Ro. i. 20) asserts that this is its uniform force, at least in Ro. (cf. his note on 2 Co. viii. 6); on the other hand, Harmsen (u. s.) denies the telic force of εἰς τό before an inf. Present; cf. also W. 329 (309); esp. B. as above and p. 265 note; Ellic. on 1 Thess. ii. 12; and see below, d. fin.]: Lk. xx. 20 R G; Acts iii. 19 [T WH πρός]; Ro. i. 11; iv. 16, 18; xi. 11; xii. 2; xv. 8, 13; 1 Co. ix. 15; x. 6; Gal. iii. 17; Eph. i. 12, 18; 1 Th. ii. 12, 16; iii. 5; 2 Th. i. 5; ii. 2, 10; Jas. i. 18; Heb. ii. 17; vii. 25; ix. 14, 28; xii. 10; xiii. 21; εἰς τὸ μή, *lest*, 2 Co. iv. 4; 1 Pet. iii. 7. **d.** the end by which a thing is completed, i. e. the result or effect: Acts x. 4; Ro. vi. 19 (εἰς τ. ἀνομίαν [but WH br.], so that iniquity was the result); x. 10; xiii. 14; 1 Co. xi. 17; 2 Co. ii. 16; Eph. v. 2, etc.; εἰς τό with inf. *so that* [cf. ββ. above]: Ro. i. 20; 2 Co. viii. 6.

C. CONSTRUCTIONS in some respects PECULIAR. **1.** Various forms of pregnant and brachylogical construction (W. § 66, 2; [less fully, B. 327 (282)]; Bnhdy. p. 348 sq.): σώζειν τινὰ εἰς etc. to save by translating into etc. 2 Tim. iv. 18 [see σώζω, b. sub fin.]; διασώζειν, 1 Pet. iii. 20 (Sept. Gen. xix. 19, and often in Grk. writ.); μισθοῦσθαι ἐργάτας εἰς τ. ἀμπελῶνα, to go into etc. Mt. xx. 1 ; ἐλευθεροῦν εἰς etc. Ro. viii. 21 ; ἀποδιδόναι τινὰ εἰς Αἴγυπτον, Acts vii. 9 ; ἔνοχος εἰς γέενναν, to depart into etc. [cf. B. 170 (148) note], Mt. v. 22 ; κλᾶν εἴς τινας, to break and distribute among etc. Mk. viii. 19 ; ἀσφαλίζεσθαι εἰς τὸ ξύλον, Acts xvi. 24 ; κτᾶσθαι χρυσὸν εἰς τ. ζώνας, Mt. x. 9 ; ἐντετυλιγμένον εἰς ἕνα τόπον, rolled up and laid away in etc. Jn. xx. 7.   **2.** Akin to this is the very common use of εἰς after verbs signifying r e s t or c o n t i n u a n c e in a place, because the idea of a previous motion into the place spoken of is involved (cf. W. § 50, 4 b.; B. 332 (286) sq.; Kühner ii. p. 317; [Jelf § 646, 1]; Bnhdy. p. 215; [yet cf. also exx. in *Soph.* Lex. s. v. εἰς, 1]) : εὑρέθη εἰς Ἄζωτον, sc. transferred or carried off to, Acts viii. 40, cf. 39 πνεῦμα κυρίου ἥρπασε τὸν Φίλιππον, (Esth. i. 5 τοῖς ἔθνεσι τοῖς εὑρεθεῖσιν εἰς τ. πόλιν ; so φανεῖσθαι is foll. by εἰς in 2 Macc. i. 33 ; vii. 22). δεῖ με τὴν ἑορτὴν ποιῆσαι εἰς Ἱεροσ. sc. by going, Acts xviii. 21 Rec.; likewise ἑτοίμως ἔχω ἀποθανεῖν εἰς Ἱεροσ. Acts xxi. 13 ('Ηφαιστίων εἰς Ἐκβάτανα ἀπέθανε, Ael. v. h. 7, 8) ; συνέβαλεν ἡμῖν εἰς Ἄσσον, Acts xx. 14 ; ἡ μέλλουσα δόξα εἰς ἡμᾶς ἀποκαλυφθῆναι, which shall be revealed (and conferred) on us, Ro. viii. 18. κατοικεῖν εἰς πόλιν, εἰς γῆν, to come into a city and dwell there, Mt. ii. 23 ; iv. 13 ; Acts vii. 4, [cf. Num. xxxv. 33 ; 2 Chr. xix. 4 etc.]; also παροικεῖν, Heb. xi. 9 (ἐνοικεῖν, Xen. an. 1, 2, 24) ; στῆναι, ἑστηκέναι (because it is nearly equiv. to *to have placed one's self*) εἴς τι, Lk. vi. 8 ; Jn. xx. 19, 26 ; 1 Pet. v. 12 ; καθῆσθαι, to have gone unto a place and to be sitting there, Mk. xiii. 3 ; 2 Th. ii. 4, (on this use of these two verbs in Grk. auth. cf. Matthiae ii. p. 1344 sq.; [cf. W. and B. u. s.]). εἶναι εἰς with acc. of place see εἰμί, V. 2 a.; οἱ εἰς τ. οἶκόν μου sc. ὄντες, Lk. ix. 61 ; τοῖς εἰς μακράν sc. οὖσι (Germ. *ins Ferne hin befindlich*), Acts ii. 39. συνάγεσθαι foll. by εἰς with acc. of place : to go to a place and assemble there, Mt. xxvi. 3 and Acts iv. 5 R T, (1 Esdr. v. 46 (47) ; ix. 3). Sometimes a word implying m o t i o n, occurring in the same sentence, seems to have occasioned the connection of a verb of r e s t with εἰς, as it were by a kind of attraction [B. u. s.] : ἐξερχόμενος ηὐλίζετο εἰς τὸ ὄρος, Lk. xxi. 37 ; ἀκούσας . . . ὄντα σιτία εἰς Αἴγυπτον [Rec. σῖτα ἐν Αἰγ.] ἐξαπέστειλεν etc. Acts vii. 12 ; παραδώσουσιν ὑμᾶς εἰς συνέδρια κ. εἰς συναγωγὰς δαρήσεσθε, Mk. xiii. 9 [W. 416 (387), B. 333 (287)] ; ὕπαγε, νίψαι [but L br.] εἰς τ. κολυμβήθραν, Jn. ix. 7, although νίπτεσθαι εἴς τι can also be used (as λούεσθαι εἰς τὸ βαλανεῖον, Alciphr. epp. 3, 43 ; εἰς λουτρῶνας, Athen. 10 p. 438 e.; λούειν τινὰ εἰς σκάφην, Epict. diss. 3, 22, 71), since the water with which one bathes flows down into the pool. Cf. *Beyer*, De praepositt. εἰς et ἐν in N. T. permutatione. Lips. 1824, 4to.

   D. Adverbial Phrases (cf. Matthiae § 578 d.) : εἰς τέλος (see τέλος, 1 a.) ; εἰς τὸ πάλιν, see A. II. 2 above ; εἰς τὸ παντελές, perfectly, utterly, Lk. xiii. 11 [cf. W. § 51, 1 c.]; εἰς κενόν (see κενός, 3) ; εἰς ὑπάντησιν and εἰς ἀπάντησιν, see each subst.

   In composition εἰς is equiv. to the Lat. *in* and *ad*.

1520   **εἷς, μία, ἕν,** gen. ἑνός, μιᾶς, ἑνός, a cardinal numeral, *one.* Used   **1.** univ.   **a.** in opp. to m a n y ; and

α. added to nouns after the manner of an adjective : Mt. xxv. 15 (opp. to πέντε, δύο) ; Ro. v. 12 (opp. to πάντες) ; Mt. xx. 13 ; xxvii. 15 ; Lk. xvii. 34 [but L WH br.] ; Acts xxviii. 13 ; 1 Co. x. 8 ; Jas. iv. 13 [R G], and often ; παρὰ μίαν sc. πληγήν [W. 589 (548) ; B. 82 (72)], save one [W. § 49, g.], 2 Co. xi. 24 ; with the article, ὁ εἷς ἄνθρωπος, the one man, of whom I have spoken, Ro. v. 15. **β.** substantively, with a partit. gen.,— to denote one, whichever it may be : μίαν τῶν ἐντολῶν, one commandment, whichever of the whole number it may be, Mt. v. 19 ; add, Mt. vi. 29 ; xviii. 6 ; Mk. ix. 42 ; Lk. xii. 27 ; xvii. 2, 22 ; or, that one is required to be singled out from a certain number : Lk. xxiii. 39 ; Jn. xix. 34, etc. foll. by ἐκ with the gen. of a noun signifying a whole, to denote that one of (*out of*) a company did this or that : Mt. xxii. 35 ; xxvi. 21 ; xxvii. 48 ; Mk. xiv. 18 ; Lk. xvii. 15 ; Jn. i. 40 (41) ; vi. 8, 70 ; xii. 2 [T WH Tr mrg. in br.], 4 [Tr om. ἐκ] ; xiii. 21, 23 [Rec. om. ἐκ] ; xviii. 26 ; Rev. v. 5 ; vii. 13 ; ix. 13 ; xiii. 3 [Rec. om. ἐκ]. **γ.** absol. : Mt. xxiii. 8–10 ; Heb. ii. 11 ; xi. 12 ; and where it takes the place of a predicate, Gal. iii. 20 [cf. W. 593 (551), 28 (ye that adhere to Christ make one person, just as the Lord himself) ; συνάγειν εἰς ἕν, to gather together into one, Jn. xi. 52 ; ποιεῖν τὰ ἀμφότερα ἕν, Eph. ii. 14 ; with the article, ὁ εἷς, the one, whom I have named, Ro. v. 15, 19. **b.** in opp. to a d i v i s i o n i n t o p a r t s, and in ethical matters to d i s s e n s i o n s : ἐν σῶμα, πολλὰ μέλη, Ro. xii. 4 sq.; 1 Co. xii. 12, 20 ; ἐν εἶναι, to be united most closely (in will, spirit), Jn. x. 30 ; xvii. 11, 21–23 ; ἐν ἐνὶ πνεύματι, μιᾷ ψυχῇ, Phil. i. 27 cf. Acts iv. 32, (cf. Cic. Lael. 25 (92) amicitiae vis est in eo, ut unus quasi animus fiat ex pluribus) ; ἀπὸ μιᾶς (see ἀπό, III. p. 59ᵇ), Lk. xiv. 18. **c.** with a negative following joined to the verb, εἷς . . . οὐ or μή, (one . . . not, i. e.) no one, (more explicit and emphatic than οὐδείς) : ἓν ἐξ αὐτῶν οὐ πεσεῖται, Mt. x. 29 ; besides, Mt. v. 18 ; Lk. xi. 46 ; xii. 6 ; this usage is not only Hebraistic (as that language has no particular word to express the notion of *none*), but also Greek (Arstph. eccl. 153 ; thesm. 549 ; Xen. an. 5, 6, 12 ; Dion. Hal. verb. comp. 18, etc.), cf. W. 172 (163) ; [B. 121 (106)]. **2.** emphatically, so that others are excluded, and εἷς is the same as   **a.** *a single* (Lat. *unus* i. q. *unicus*) ; joined to nouns : Mt. xxi. 24 ; Mk. viii. 14 (οὐκ . . . εἰ μὴ ἕνα ἄρτον) ; Mk. xii. 6 ; Lk. xii. 52 ; Jn. xi. 50 ; vii. 21 ; 1 Co. xii. 19 ; Eph. iv. 5, etc.; absol. : 1 Co. ix. 24 ; 2 Co. v. 14 (15) ; 1 Tim. ii. 5 ; Jas. iv. 12, etc.; οὐδὲ εἷς, *not even one* : Mt. xxvii. 14 ; Jn. i. 3 ; Acts iv. 32 ; Ro. iii. 10 ; 1 Co. vi. 5 [R G] ; οὐκ ἔστιν ἕως ἑνός [there is not so much as one], Ro. iii. 12 fr. Ps. xiii. (xiv.) 3 ; cf. Lat. *omnes ad unum, all to a man.* Neut. ἕν, one thing, *exclusive of the rest* ; *one thing before all others* : Mk. x. 21 ; Lk. xviii. 22 ; x. 42 [but WH only txt.] ; Jn. ix. 25 ; Phil. iii. 13 (14) ; Jas. ii. 10. **b.** *alone* : οὐδεὶς . . . εἰ μὴ εἷς ὁ θεός, Mk. ii. 7 (for which in Lk. v. 21 μόνος ὁ θεός) ; Mk. x. 18 ; Lk. xviii. 19. **c.** *one and the same* (not at variance with, in accord with one's self) : Ro. iii. 30 ; Rev. xvii. 13, 17 [L om.] ; xviii. 8 ; τὸ ἓν φρονεῖν, Phil. ii. 2 [WH mrg. αὐτό] ; ἕν εἶναι *are one*, i. e. are of the same importance and esteem, 1 Co. iii. 8; εἰς τὸ ἐν εἶναι (see εἰμί, V. 2 d.), 1 Jn. v. 8; more fully τὸ ἐν καὶ τὸ αὐτό, 1 Co. xii. 11; ἐν καὶ τὸ αὐτό τινι, 1 Co. xi. 5. **3.** the numerical force of εἰς is often so weakened that it hardly differs from the indef. pron. τὶς, or from our indef. article (W. 117 (111), [cf. 29 note 2; B. 85 (74)]): Mt. viii. 19 (εἰς γραμματεύς); xix. 16; xxvi. 69; Jn. vi. 9 (παιδάριον ἕν, where T Tr WH om. and L br. ἕν); Rev. viii. 13; ix. 13, (Arstph. av. 1292; Xen. mem. 3, 3, 12; Plat. de rep. 6 p. 494 d.; legg. 9 p. 855 d., etc.; esp. later writ.; [Tob. i. 19; ii. 3; 3 Esdr. iv. 18; Gen. xxi. 15; 2 S. ii. 18; Judith xiv. 6]; so the Hebr. אֶחָד, Dan. viii. 3; Gen. xxii. 13; 1 S. i. 2; 1 K. xxi. (xx.) 13; see *Gesenius*, Lehrgeb. p. 655); εἰς τις (Lat. *unus aliquis*), a *certain one*; one, I know not who; one who need not be named: with a subst. Mk. xiv. 51 (L Tr WH om. εἰς); or foll. by a gen. Mk. xiv. 47 where L Tr om. WH br. τὶς; foll. by ἐκ, ἐξ, with gen.: Lk. xxii. 50; Jn. xi. 49, (ἔν τι τῶν ῥημάτων, Judith ii. 13, and often in Grk. writ.; cf. Wetstein on Mk. xiv. 51; Matthiae § 487). **4.** it is used distributively [W. § 26, 2; esp. B. 102 (90)]; **a.** εἰς . . . καὶ εἰς, *one . . . and one*: Mt. xvii. 4; xx. 21; xxiv. 40 L T Tr WH, 41; xxvii. 38; Mk. iv. 8 [R G L WH mrg.], 20 [R G L Tr mrg. WH mrg. in br.]; ix. 5; x. 37; xv. 27; Lk. ix. 33; Jn. xx. 12; Gal. iv. 22; (in Grk. auth. εἰς μὲν . . . εἰς δέ, as Aristot. eth. 6, 1, 5; Xen. Cyr. 1, 2, 4); with the art. prefixed, ὁ εἰς *the one*, Lk. xxiv. 18 R G; foll. by ὁ εἰς, *the one . . . the other*, Mt. xxiv. 40 R G; foll. by ὁ ἕτερος, Mt. vi. 24; Lk. vii. 41; xvi. 13ᵇ; xvii. 34 R WH; xviii. 10 R G T WH mrg.; Acts xxiii. 6; εἰς (without the art.) . . . ὁ ἕτερος: Lk. xvi. 13ᶜ; xvii. 34 G L T Tr; xviii. 10 L Tr WH txt.; πέντε . . . ὁ εἰς . . . ὁ ἄλλος, Rev. xvii. 10. **b.** εἰς ἕκαστος, *every one*: Acts ii. 6; xx. 31; Eph. iv. 16; Col. iv. 6; foll. by a partit. gen.: Lk. iv. 40; xvi. 5; Acts ii. 3; xvii. 27; xxi. 26; 1 Co. xii. 18; Eph. iv. 7; 1 Th. ii. 11; cf. B. 102 (89) sq.; ἀνὰ εἰς ἕκαστος (see ἀνά, 2), Rev. xxi. 21. **c.** a solecism, com. in later Grk. (cf. Lcian. soloec. [Pseudosoph.] § 9; W. § 37, 3; B. 30 (26) sq.; Fritzsche on Mk. p. 613 sq.; [Soph. Lex. s. v. καθεῖς]), is καθ' εἰς, and in combination καθεῖς, (so that either κατά is used adverbially, or εἰς as indeclinable): ὁ καθ' εἰς, i. q. εἰς ἕκαστος, Ro. xii. 5 (where L T Tr WH τὸ καθ' εἰς, as *respects each one, severally*; cf. what is said against this reading by Fritzsche, Com. iii. p. 44 sq., and in its favor by Meyer); with a partit. gen. 3 Macc. v. 34; εἰς καθ' [T WH Tr mrg. κατὰ] εἰς, *every one, one by one*, Mk. xiv. 19; Jn. viii. 9; καθ' ἕνα, καθ' ἕν, (as in Grk. writ.), of a series, *one by one, successively*: καθ' ἕν, *all in succession*, Jn. xxi. 25 [not Tdf.]; καθ' ἕνα πάντες, 1 Co. xiv. 31 (Xen. venat. 6, 14); καθ' ἕν ἕκαστον, Acts xxi. 19 (Xen. Cyr. 1, 6, 22 (27); Ages. 7, 1); ὑμεῖς οἱ καθ' ἕνα ἕκαστος, *ye severally, every one*, Eph. v. 33. **5.** like the Hebr. אֶחָד, εἰς is put for the ordinal πρῶτος, *first* [W. § 37, 1; B. 29 (26)]: μία σαββάτων the first day of the week, Mt. xxviii. 1; Mk. xvi. 2; Lk. xxiv. 1; Jn. xx. 1, 19; Acts xx. 7; 1 Co. xvi. 2 [L T Tr WH μίᾳ σαββάτου]; (in Grk. writ. so used only when joined with other ordinal numbers, as εἰς καὶ τριηκοστός, Hdt. 5, 89: Diod. 16, 71. Cic.

de senect. 5 *uno et octogesimo anno*. [Cf. Soph. Lex. s. v.]).

εἰσ-άγω: 2 aor. εἰσήγαγον; [pres. pass. εἰσάγομαι]; [fr. Hom. down]; Sept. chiefly for הֵבִיא; **1.** *to lead in*: τινά foll. by εἰς with acc. of place, Lk. xxii. 54 [Tr mrg. br.]; Acts ix. 8; xxi. 28, 29, 37; xxii. 24 (for Rec. ἄγεσθαι); ὧδε, Lk. xiv. 21; the place into which not being expressly noted: Jn. xviii. 16 (sc. εἰς τὴν αὐλήν); Heb. i. 6 ὅταν . . . εἰσαγάγῃ, λέγει, God, having in view the time *when he shall have again brought into the first-born into the world* (i. e. at the time of the παρουσία) says etc. **2.** *to bring in*, the place into which not being expressly stated: Acts vii. 45 (sc. εἰς τὴν γῆν); Lk. ii. 27 (sc. εἰς τὸ ἱερόν). [COMP. : παρ-εισάγω.]*   **1521**

εἰσ-ακούω: fut. εἰσακούσομαι; Pass., 1 aor. εἰσηκούσθην; 1 fut. εἰσακουσθήσομαι; Sept. very often for שָׁמַע, but also for עָנָה to answer; in Grk. writ. fr. Hom. Il. 8, 97 down; *to hearken unto, to give ear to*; i. e. **1.** *to give heed to, comply with*, admonition; *to obey* (Lat. *obedio* i. e. *ob-audio*) : τινός, 1 Co. xiv. 21, (Deut. i. 43; ix. 23; Sir. iii. 6, etc.). **2.** *to listen to, assent to*, a request; pass. *to be heard*, to have one's request granted; **a.** of persons offering up prayers to God: Heb. v. 7 (on which see ἀπό, I. 3 d. fin.); Mt. vi. 7. **b.** of the prayers offered up: Lk. i. 13; Acts x. 31, (Ps. iv. 2; Sir. xxxi. (xxxiv.) 29 (26), etc.).*   **1522**

εἰσ-δέχομαι: fut. εἰσδέξομαι; *to receive kindly*, i. e. contextually, *to treat with favor*: τινά, 2 Co. vi. 17. [From Pind. and Soph. down. SYN. cf. δέχομαι, fin.]*   **1523**

εἰσ-ειμι, inf. εἰσιέναι; impf. εἰσῄειν; [cf. B. 50 (43)]); [fr. Hom. down]; *to go into, enter*: foll. by εἰς with the name of the place (cf. Win. De verb. comp. etc. Pt. ii. p. 11), Acts iii. 3; xxi. 26; Heb. ix. 6 [W. 267 (251)]; πρός τινα, Acts xxi. 18.*   **1524**

εἰσ-έρχομαι; fut. εἰσελεύσομαι; 2 aor. εἰσῆλθον, 2 pers. plur. εἰσήλθατε (Lk. xi. 52, but Rec. -θετε), impv. εἰσέλθατε (Mt. vii. 13 but R G -θετε, [3d pers. sing. -θάτω Mk. xiii. 15, R G -θέτω]); see ἀπέρχομαι, init.; pf. εἰσελήλυθα, 3 pers. plur. εἰσελήλυθαν (Jas. v. 4, for R G εἰσεληλύθασιν, see γίνομαι, init.); Sept. mostly for בּוֹא; *to go or come into or in*; *to enter*; **1.** prop., of men and of animals: foll. by εἰς with specification of the place (cf. Win. De verb. comp. etc. Pt. ii. p. 12 sq.), as into a house, into a city, Mt. viii. 5; x. 12; Mk. ii. 1; xi. 11; Acts xxiii. 16, 33, and often. without specification of place, — when mention of it has already been made, as Mt. ix. 25; [Mk. vii. 25 Tdf.]; Lk. vii. 45; xiv. 23; xv. 28 cf. 25; xxiv. 3; Acts i. 13; v. 7, 10; x. 25; 1 Co. xiv. 23 sq.; 24; xvii. 7; εἰς is also added to signify *among*: Acts xix. 30; xx. 29; εἰσέρχ. διά τινος, to enter (a place) through something: διὰ τῆς πύλης, to enter the kingdom of God (compared to a palace) through the gate, Mt. vii. 13; Lk. xiii. 24; διὰ τῆς θύρας εἰς τ. αὐλήν, Jn. x. 1 sq.; add, Mt. xix. 24 G T Tr txt. WH txt.; [Mk. x. 25 Rᵃᵗ L mrg. Tr mrg.]; Lk. xviii. 25 R G T Tr txt. WH; εἰσέρχ. ὑπὸ τὴν στέγην, by entering to come under the roof. i. e. enter my house, Mt. viii. 8; with adverbs:

ὅπου, Mk. xiv. 14; Heb. vi. 20; ὧδε, Mt. xxii. 12; ἔσω, Mt. xxvi. 58; εἰς with acc. of pers., into one's house, Acts xvi. 40, but on this pass. see εἰς, A. I. 1 a. εἰσέρχ. πρός τινα, to one, i. e. into his house, visit, Mk. xv. 43; Lk. i. 28; Acts x. 3; xi. 3; xvi. 40 G L T Tr WH; xxviii. 8; Rev. iii. 20; to an assembly of persons, Acts xvii. 2. Moreover the following deserve notice: a. the phrase εἰσέρχεσθαι καὶ ἐξέρχεσθαι, to go in and out, (the Hebr. זֵאצֵא בֹּא, or reversed בּוֹא זֵאצֵא, usually denotes one's whole mode of living and acting, Deut. xxviii. 6; 1 S. xxix. 6, etc.; cf. Gesenius, Thesaur. i. p. 184 sq.), is used of familiar intercourse with one: ἐν παντὶ χρόνῳ ᾧ εἰσῆλθε κ. ἐξῆλθεν ἐφ' ἡμᾶς ὁ κύριος, equiv. to εἰσῆλθε ἐφ' ἡμᾶς κ. ἐξῆλθε ἀφ' ἡμ. Acts i. 21, (Eur. Phoen. 536 ἐς οἴκους εἰσῆλθε κ. ἐξῆλθ' [W. 624 sq. (580); but cf. B. 390 (334)]); figuratively, of moral pursuits unimpeded by difficulties, Jn. x. 9. b. εἰσέρχ. εἰς is joined with nouns designating not a place, but what occurs in a place: εἰς τοὺς γάμους, Mt. xxv. 10; εἰς τὴν χαρὰν τοῦ κυρίου, 21, 23. c. εἰσελθεῖν εἴς τινα is used of demons or of Satan taking possession of the body of a person: Mk. ix. 25; Lk. viii. 30; xxii. 3; Jn. xiii. 27. d. of things:—as of food, that enters into the eater's mouth, Mt. xv. 11; Acts xi. 8; figuratively, hope is called ἄγκυρα εἰσερχομένη εἰς τὸ ἐσώτερον τοῦ καταπετάσματος, i. e. we firmly rely on the hope that we shall be received into heaven, Heb. vi. 19; cries of complaint are said εἰσέρχ. εἰς τὰ ὦτά τινος, i. e. to be heard, Jas. v. 4; of forces and influences: πνεῦμα ζωῆς εἰσῆλθεν ἐν αὐτοῖς (Tr om. WH br. ἐν; Rec. ἐπ' αὐτούς [B. 338 (291)]), a pregnant construction, the breath of life entered into and remained in them, Rev. xi. 11 [W. § 50, 4; B. 329 (283)]. 2. Metaph. used, a. of entrance into any condition, state of things, society, employment: εἰς τ. ζωήν, Mt. xviii. 8 sq.; xix. 17; Mk. ix. 43, 45; εἰς τ. βασιλ. τῶν οὐρανῶν or τοῦ θεοῦ (see βασιλεία, 3 p. 97b); τοὺς εἰσερχομένους, that are trying to enter, or rather, that have taken the road to enter, are (engaged in) entering, Mt. xxiii. 13 (14); Lk. xi. 52; used absol. of those who come into (i. e. become members of) the Christian church, Ro. xi. 25, (hence in 1 Co. v. 12 sq. οἱ ἔσω and οἱ ἔξω are distinguished); εἰς τ. κατάπαυσιν, Heb. iii. 11, 18; iv. 1, 3, 5 sq. 10 sq.; εἰς τὴν δόξαν, Lk. xxiv. 26; εἰς πειρασμόν, to come (i. e. fall) into temptation, Mt. xxvi. 41; Mk. xiv. 38 [T WH ἔλθητε]; Lk. xxii. 40, 46; εἰς τὸν κόπον τινός (see εἰς, B. I. 3), Jn. iv. 38. εἰσέρχεσθ. εἰς τ. κόσμον, to enter the world [cf. W. 18], is a. i. q. to arise, come into existence, begin to be [i. e. among men]: used thus of sin and death, Ro. v. 12; of death, Sap. ii. 24; Clem. Rom. 1 Cor. 3, 4; of idols, Sap. xiv. 14. β. of men, to come into life: whether by birth, Antonin. 6, 56; or by divine creation, Philo, opif. mund. § 25. γ. to come before the public: 2 Jn. 7 [Rec.]; to come to men, of Christ, Jn. xviii. 37; εἰσερχόμ. εἰς τ. κόσμον, when he cometh into the world, i. e. when he was on the point of entering it, viz. at his incarnation, Heb. x. 5. b. of thoughts coming into the mind: εἰσῆλθε διαλογισμὸς ἐν αὐτοῖς, a pregnant construction, there came in and established itself within [al. take ἐν outwardly: among (cf.

διαλογ. fin.)] them, Lk. ix. 46 [cf. W. 413 (385)]. The Grks. fr. Hom. down use εἰσέρχεσθαί τινα of thoughts and feelings, as φόβος, μένος, πόθος, etc. [cf. W. 427 (398).

ComP. ἐπ-, παρ-, συν- εἰσέρχομαι.]

εἰσ-καλέομαι, -οῦμαι, (mid. of εἰσκαλέω): 1 aor. ptcp. εἰσκαλεσάμενος; to call in unto one's self, to invite in to one's house: τινά, Acts x. 23. [Polyb., al.]*

εἰσ-οδος, -ου, ἡ, (ὁδός), [fr. Hom. on], an entrance, i. e. both the place or way leading into a place (as, a gate), and the act of entering; only in the latter sense in the N. T. With gen. of place, τῶν ἁγίων, entrance into the holy place, i. e. reception into heaven, Heb. x. 19 [but in 20 apparently called ὁδός]; εἰς τ. βασιλείαν τοῦ κυρίου, 2 Pet. i. 11; of the act of coming forward to administer an office, Acts xiii. 24; with πρός τινα added, 1 Th. i. 9; ii. 1.*

εἰσ-πηδάω, -ῶ: 1 aor. εἰσεπήδησα; to spring in: εἰς τὸν ὄχλον, Acts xiv. 14 Rec. (see ἐκπηδάω); to rush in impetuously, Acts xvi. 29. (Xen., Dem., al.; Sept. Am. v. 19.)*

εἰσ-πορεύομαι (pass. of εἰσπορεύω to lead into, Eur. El. 1285); impf. εἰσεπορευόμην (Mk. vi. 56); to go into, enter; 1. prop. a. of persons: foll. by εἰς with acc. of place, Mk. i. 21; vi. 56; xi. 2; Acts iii. 2; ὅπου, Mk. v. 40; οὗ, Lk. xxii. 10 [R G, cf. B. 71 (62); W. § 54, 7]; without specification of place where that is evident from the context, Lk. viii. 16; xi. 33; xix. 30; κατὰ τοὺς οἴκους, to enter house after house [A. V. every house, see κατά, II. 3 a. a.], Acts viii. 3; πρός τινα, to visit one at his dwelling, Acts xxviii. 30; εἰσπορεύεσθαι κ. ἐκπορεύεσθαι μετά τινος, to associate with one, Acts ix. 28 (ἐνώπιόν τινος, Tob. v. 18; see εἰσέρχομαι, 1 a.). b. when used of things it is i. q. to be carried into or put into: so of food, which is put into the mouth, Mk. vii. 15, 18, [19]; Mt. xv. 17, (see εἰσέρχομαι, 1 d.). 2. metaph.: [εἰς τὴν βασιλείαν τοῦ θεοῦ, Lk. xviii. 24 T Tr txt. WH; see βασιλεία, 3 p. 97b]; of affections entering the soul, Mk. iv. 19; see εἰσέρχομαι, 2 b. (Of the earlier Grk. writ. Xen. alone uses this verb, Cyr. 2, 3, 21; Sept. often for בּוֹא.) *

εἰσ-τρέχω: 2 aor. εἰσέδραμον; to run in: Acts xii. 14. [Thuc., Xen., al.] *

εἰσ-φέρω; 1 aor. εἰσήνεγκα; 2 aor. εἰσήνεγκον; [pres. pass. εἰσφέρομαι; fr. Hom. down]; to bring into, in or to; a. τί, foll. by εἰς with acc. of place, 1 Tim. vi. 7; pass. Heb. xiii. 11; τινά sc. εἰς τ. οἰκίαν, Lk. v. 18 sq.; [τινὰ ἐπὶ τ. συναγωγάς etc. Lk. xii. 11 T Tr txt. WH]; τὶ εἰς τὰς ἀκοάς τινος, i. e. to tell one a thing, Acts xvii. 20 (φέρειν τι εἰς τὰ ὦτά τινος, Soph. Aj. 149). b. to lead into: τινὰ εἰς πειρασμόν, Mt. vi. 13; Lk. xi. 4. [ComP.: παρ-εισφέρω.] *

εἶτα, adv. of time, then; next; after that: Mk. viii. 25; Lk. viii. 12; Jn. xiii. 5; xix. 27; xx. 27; Jas. i. 15; with the addition of a gen. absol. to define it more precisely, Mk. iv. 17; as in classic Grk., it stands in enumerations, to mark a sequence depending either on temporal succession, as Mk. iv. 28 (see εἶτεν); 1 Co. xv. 5–7 (εἶτα [T ἔπειτα, so in mrg. Tr WH] . . . ἔπειτα . . . ἔπειτα . . . εἶτα [T ἔπειτα, so in mrg. L Tr WH]); 1 Co. xv. 24 (ἔπειτα . . . εἶτα); 1 Tim. ii. 13; or on the nature of the

see 1528 St.

1529

1530

1531

1532

1533

1534

things enumerated, 1 Co. xii. 28 (πρῶτον . . . δεύτερον
. . . τρίτον . . . ἔπειτα . . . εἶτα for which L T Tr WH
ἔπειτα); [1 Tim. iii. 10]; in arguments it serves to add
(1534a); a new reason, *furthermore* (Germ. *sodann*) : Heb. xii. 9.*
see 1487 — εἴτε, see εἰ, III. 15.
see 1534 — εἴτεν a very rare [Ionic] form for εἶτα (q. v.) : Mk. iv.
* 28 T WH. [Cf. *Kuenen et Cobet*, Nov. Test. etc. praef.
p. xxxiii.; *Lob.* Phryn. p. 124, also Pathol. Gr. Element.
ii. 155; *Steph.* Thesaur. s. v. and s. v. ἔπειτεν.] *
see 1486 — εἴωθα, see ἔθω.
1537 — ἐκ, before a vowel ἐξ, a preposition governing the genitive. It denotes as well exit or emission out of, as
separation from, something with which there has been
close connection; opp. to the prepositions εἰς into and ἐν
in : *from out of, out from, forth from, from*, (Lat. *e, ex*), [cf.
W. 364, 366 (343) sq.; B. 326 sq. (281)]. It is used
I. of PLACE, and 1. univ. of the place from
which; from a surrounding or enclosing place,
from the interior of : ἄρτος, ἄγγελος, φῶς ἐξ οὐρανοῦ,
Jn. vi. 31 sq.; Acts ix. 3 [here R G ἀπό]; Gal. i. 8;
ἀνατολή, δύναμις ἐξ ὕψους, Lk. i. 78; xxiv. 49; esp. after
verbs of going, fleeing, leading, calling, freeing, removing, releasing, etc.; ἥκειν ἐκ τῆς Ἰουδαίας
εἰς τ. Γαλιλαίαν, Jn. iv. 47; ἐξέρχεσθαι ἔκ τινος out of the
body of one (spoken of demons), Mk. i. 25; v. 8 [here
L mrg. ἀπό]; vii. 29; of power emanating from the
body, Mk. v. 30 [cf. B. 301 (258); W. 346 (324); Mey.
ed. Weiss ad loc.]; ἐκπορεύεσθαι ἐκ τῶν μνημείων, Mt. viii. 28; xxvii.
53; ἐκπορεύεσθαι, Mt. xv. 11, 18 sq.; καταβαίνειν ἐκ
τοῦ οὐρανοῦ, Mt. xxviii. 2; iii. 16; iii. 32; iii. 13; vi. 33; ἐξάγειν, Acts xii. 17; φεύγειν, Acts xxvii. 30; καλεῖν, Mt. ii.
15; metaph. ἐκ τοῦ σκότους εἰς τὸ φῶς, 1 Pet. ii. 9; ἐκβάλλειν τὸ κάρφος ἐκ τοῦ ὀφθαλμοῦ, Mt. vii. [4 (R G ἀπό)], 5;
Lk. vi. 42 (opp. to ἐν τῷ ὀφθαλμῷ); τὶ ἐκ τοῦ θησαυροῦ, Mt.
xii. 35 [but see under II. 9 below]; xiii. 52; τὸ δαιμόνιον
ἔκ τινος, out of the body of one, Mk. vii. 26; ἀποκυλίειν
τὸν λίθον ἐκ [L Tr txt. ἀπό; cf. W. 364 (342) note] τῆς
θύρας, Mk. xvi. 3; αἴρειν, Jn. xx. 1 sq.; κινέω, Rev. vi. 14;
σώζειν ἐκ γῆς Αἰγύπτου, Jude 5; διασώζειν ἐκ τῆς θαλάσσης,
Acts xxviii. 4. Metaph. ἐκ τῆς χειρός τινος, out of the
power of one [cf. B. 182 (158)] : after ἐξέρχεσθαι, Jn. x.
39; after ἀπάγειν, Acts xxiv. 7 [Rec.]; after ἁρπάζειν, Jn.
x. 28 sq.; after ἐξαιρεῖσθαι, Acts xii. 11; after ῥύεσθαι,
Lk. i. 74; after σωτηρία, Lk. i. 71. after πίνειν, of the
thing out of which one drinks [differently in II. 9 below] :
ἐκ τοῦ ποτηρίου, Mt. xxvi. 27; Mk. xiv. 23; 1 Co. xi. 28; ἐκ
πέτρας, 1 Co. x. 4; ἐκ τοῦ φρέατος, Jn. iv. 12; after ἐσθίειν,
of the place whence the food is derived, ἐκ τοῦ ἱεροῦ, 1 Co.
ix. 13 [but T Tr WH read τὰ ἐκ κτλ.]. of the place forth
from which one does something : διδάσκειν ἐκ τοῦ πλοίου,
Lk. v. 3 [here Tdf. ἐν etc.]. It is joined also to nouns
designating not a place, but what is done in a place :
ἐγείρεσθαι ἐκ τοῦ δείπνου, Jn. xiii. 4; ἀναλύειν ἐκ τῶν
γάμων, Lk. xii. 36. 2. from the midst (of a group,
number, company, community) of many; a. after
verbs of going, leading, choosing, removing,
etc. a. before collective nouns, as ἐξολεθρεύω ἐκ τοῦ
λαοῦ, Acts iii. 23; προβιβάζω or συμβιβάζω ἐκ τοῦ ὄχλου,

Acts xix. 33; ἐκλέγειν ἐκ τοῦ κόσμου, Jn. xv. 19. ἐκ
μέσου τινῶν ἀφορίζειν, Mt. xiii. 49; ἐξέρχεσθαι, Acts xvii.
33; ἁρπάζειν, Acts xxiii. 10; ἐξαίρειν, 1 Co. v. 13; ἐκ
πάσης φυλῆς κ. γλώσσης ἀγοράζειν, Rev. v. 9; ἐκ παντὸς
γένους συνάγειν, Mt. xiii. 47. β. before plurals : ἀνιστάναι
τινὰ ἔκ τινων, Acts iii. 22; ἐκ νεκρῶν, Acts xvii. 31; ἀνί-
σταταί τις ἐκ νεκρῶν, Acts x. 41; xvii. 3; ἐγείρειν τινὰ ἐκ
νεκρῶν, Jn. xii. 1, 9, 17; Acts iii. 15; iv. 10; xiii. 30;
Heb. xi. 19, etc.; ἡ ἀνάστασις ἐκ νεκρῶν, Lk. xx. 35; 1 Pet.
i. 3; ἀνάγειν τινὰ ἐκ νεκρῶν, Ro. x. 7; ἐκλέγειν, Acts i. 24;
xv. 22; καλεῖν, Ro. ix. 24; ἐγένετο ζήτησις ἐκ τῶν etc. Jn.
iii. 25 [but cf. II. 1 b.; W. 368 (345)]. b. before words
signifying quantity: after εἷς, as Mt. x. 29; xxvi. 21;
Lk. xvii. 15, and often; πολλοί, Jn. xi. 19, 45, etc.; οἱ
πλείους (πλείονες), 1 Co. xv. 6; οὐδείς, Jn. vii. 19; xvi.
5, and elsewhere; χιλιάδες ἐκ πάσης φυλῆς, Rev. vii. 4;
after the indef. τὶς, Lk. xi. 15; xii. 13; Jn. iv. 64; vii.
48; τὶς γυνὴ ἐκ τοῦ ὄχλου, Lk. xi. 27; with τινές to be
added mentally [cf. W. 203(191); B. 158 (138)] : Jn. ix.
40 [(?) better, vii. 40]; xvi. 17; Rev. xi. 9, (1 Esdr. v.
45 (44)); τινάς : Mt. xxiii. 34; Lk. xi. 49; xxi. 16; 2 Jn.
4; Rev. ii. 10; cf. *Fritzsche*, Conjectanea in N. T. p. 36
note; after the interrog. τίς, *who* ? Mt. vi. 27; Lk. xi.
5, etc.; τίς πατήρ, Lk. xi. 11 [L T Tr WH]; preceded
by a generic noun : ἄνθρωπος ἐκ τῶν etc. Jn. iii. 1. c.
εἶναι ἔκ τινων, to be of the number, company, fellowship,
etc., of; see εἰμί, V. 3 a. 3. from a local surface,
as sometimes the Lat. *ex* for *de*; *down from* : καταβαίνειν
ἐκ τοῦ ὄρους (Hom. Il. 13, 17; Xen. an. 7, 4, 12; Sept.
Ex. xix. 14; xxxii. 1; Deut. ix. 15; x. 5; Josh. ii. 23),
Mt. xvii. 9 (for the more com. ἀπὸ τοῦ ὄρ. of Rec. and the
parallel pass. Mk. ix. 9 [here L WH txt. Tr mrg. ἐκ];
Lk. ix. 37; [cf. Mt. viii. 1]); θρὶξ ἐκ τῆς κεφαλῆς ἀπόλ-
λυται (unless we prefer to regard ἐκ as prompted here
by the conception of the hair as fixed in the skin),
Lk. xxi. 18; Acts xxvii. 34 [here L T Tr WH ἀπό; cf.
W. 364 (342) note]; ἐκπίπτειν ἐκ τῶν χειρῶν, of the chains
with which the hands had been bound, Acts xii. 7;
κρέμασθαι ἔκ τινος, Acts xxviii. 4, (1 Macc. i. 61; 2 Macc.
vi. 10; so the Grks. fr. Hom. down); φαγεῖν ἐκ τοῦ
θυσιαστηρίου, the things laid upon the altar, Heb. xiii.
10. Akin to this is ἐξελθεῖν ἐκ τοῦ θεοῦ, from an abode
with God (for the more usual ἀπὸ τ. θεοῦ), Jn. viii. 42.
4. of the direction whence; ἐκ δεξιῶν, Lat. *a dex-
tra*, lit. *from* i. e. (Germ. *zu*) *on the right*, see δεξιός; so
ἐκ δεξιᾶς, ἐξ ἀριστερᾶς, sc. χώρας [or χειρός which is
sometimes expressed; W. 592 cf. 591; B. 82 (72)], (also
in Grk. writ., as Xen. Cyr. 8, 5, 15); ἐξ ἐναντίας, over
against, Mk. xv. 39 (Hdt. 8, 6; Sir. xxxvii. 9; 1 Macc.
iv. 34; Sap. iv. 20); metaph. [W. § 51, 1 d.] ὁ ἐξ ἐναντίας [A. V. *he that is of the contrary part*], our *opponent*,
adversary, Tit. ii. 8; ἐκ ῥιζῶν, from the roots, i. e. utterly,
Mk. xi. 20 (Job xxviii. 9; xxxi. 12). 5. of the condition or state out of which one comes or is brought :
σώζειν ἐκ θανάτου, Heb. v. 7; Jas. v. 20; ἔρχεσθαι ἐκ
[Lchm. ἀπὸ] θλίψεως, Rev. vii. 14; μεταβαίνειν ἐκ τοῦ
θανάτου εἰς τ. ζωήν, Jn. v. 24; 1 Jn. iii. 14; ἐγερθῆναι ἐξ
ὕπνου, Ro. xiii. 11 [cf. W. 366 (344) note]; ζῶντες ἐκ

*For 1535 & 1536 see Strong.

νεκρῶν, alive from being dead (i. e. who had been dead and were alive again), Ro. vi. 13; ζωὴ ἐκ νεκρῶν i. e. of those that had been νεκροί, Ro. xi. 15, (ἐλεύθερος ἐκ δούλου καὶ πλούσιος ἐκ πτωχοῦ γεγονώς, Dem. p. 270 fin.; ἐκ πλουσίου πένητα γενέσθαι καὶ ἐκ βασιλέως ἰδιώτην φανῆναι, Xen. an. 7, 7, 28; γίγνομαι τυφλὸς ἐκ δεδορκότος, Soph. O. T. 454; ἔλαφον ἐξ ἀνδρὸς γενέσθαι, Palaeph. 3, 2; add, Lys. adv. Ergocl. init.; Tac. ann. 1, 74 ex pauperibus divites, ex contemtis metuendi). Also of the state out of the midst of which one does something: ἐκ πολλῆς θλίψεως γράφειν, 2 Co. ii. 4. **6.** of any kind of separation or dissolution of connection with a thing or person [cf. B. 157 (138)]: ἀναπαύεσθαι ἐκ (released from) τῶν κόπων, Rev. xiv. 13; ἀνανήφειν ἐκ (set free from) τῆς τοῦ διαβόλου παγίδος, 2 Tim. ii. 26; μετανοῶν ἐκ etc. Rev. ii. 21 sq.; ix. 20 sq.; xvi. 11; ἐπιστρέφειν [L T Tr WH ὑποστρ.] ἐκ ([L ἀπό], by severing their connection with) τῆς ἐντολῆς, 2 Pet. ii. 21; τηρεῖν τινα ἐκ etc. to keep one at a distance from etc. [cf. B. 327 (281)], Jn. xvii. 15; Rev. iii. 10; also διατηρεῖν, Acts xv. 29; νικᾶν ἔκ τινος, by conquest to free one's self from the power of one [cf. B. 147 (128); W. 367 (344)], Rev. xv. 2; ὑψοῦσθαι ἐκ τῆς γῆς, to be so lifted up as to dissolve present relations to the earth ['taken out of the sphere of earthly action' Westcott], Jn. xii. 32; ἐλεύθερος ἐκ πάντων (elsewhere always ἀπό τινος), 1 Co. ix. 19. **7.** Hebraistically: ἐκδικεῖν τὸ αἷμά τινος ἐκ χειρός τινος (נָקַם דָּם מִיָד, 2 K. ix. 7), to avenge the blood (murder) of one at the hand of (on) the slayer, Rev. xix. 2 [B. 182 (158)]; κρίνειν τὸ κρίμα τινὸς ἔκ τινος, to judge one's judgment on one, vindicate by vengeance on [cf. B. u. s.], Rev. xviii. 20 (cf. Sept. Ps. cxviii. (cxix.) 84).

II. of the ORIGIN, SOURCE, CAUSE; **1.** of generation, birth, race, lineage, nativity; **a.** after verbs of begetting, being born, etc.: ἐν γαστρὶ ἔχειν ἔκ τινος, Mt. i. 18 cf. 20; κοίτην ἔχειν ἔκ τ. Ro. ix. 10; γεννᾶν τινα ἐκ with gen. of the woman, Mt. i. 3, 5 sq. 16; γίνεσθαι ἐκ γυναικός, to be born of a woman, Gal. iv. 4 cf. 22 sq.; γεννᾶσθαι ἐξ αἱμάτων, ἐκ θελήματος σαρκός, Jn. i. 13; ἐκ τῆς σαρκός, Jn. iii. 6; ἐκ πορνείας, Jn. viii. 41; ἐγείρειν τινὶ τέκνα ἐκ, Mt. iii. 9; Lk. iii. 8; (τὶς) ἐκ καρποῦ τῆς ὀσφύος αὐτοῦ, Acts ii. 30 (Ps. cxxxi. (cxxxii.) 11); ἡ ἐκ φύσεως ἀκροβυστία, Ro. ii. 27. In a supernatural sense: τὸ πνεῦμα τὸ ἐκ θεοῦ sc. ὄν, from the divine nature [cf. W. 193 (182)], 1 Co. ii. 12 cf. Rev. ii. 11; men are said γεννᾶσθαι ἐκ πνεύματος, Jn. iii. 5 sq. 8; γεγεννημένοι εἶναι ἐκ θεοῦ (see γεννάω, 2 d.), and to the same purport εἶναι ἐκ θεοῦ, 1 Jn. iv. 4, 6; v. 19, (see εἰμί, V. 3 d. [and cf. 7 below]). **b.** εἶναι, γενέσθαι, ἔρχεσθαι, etc., ἐκ with the name of the city, race, people, tribe, family, etc., to spring or originate from, come from: ἐκ Ναζαρὲτ εἶναι, Jn. i. 46 (47); ἐκ πόλεως, i. 44 (45); ἐξ ὧν, sc. πατέρων [?], Ro. ix. 5; ἐξ οἴκου τινός, Lk. i. 27; ii. 4; ἐκ γένους, Phil. iii. 5; Acts iv. 6; Ἑβραῖος ἐξ Ἑβραίων, Phil. iii. 5; ἐκ φυλῆς, Lk. ii. 36; Acts xiii. 21; Ro. xi. 1; ἐξ Ἰούδα, Heb. vii. 14; ἐκ σπέρματός τινος, Jn. vii. 42; Ro. i. 3; xi. 1; without a verb: ἐξ ἐθνῶν ἁμαρτωλοί, sinners of Gentile birth, Gal. ii. 15; of the country to which any one belongs: εἶναι

ἐκ τῆς ἐξουσίας Ἡρώδου, Lk. xxiii. 7; ἐξ ἐπαρχίας, Acts xxiii. 34; ὁ ὢν ἐκ τῆς γῆς, Jn. iii. 31. **2.** of any other kind of origin: καπνὸς ἐκ τῆς δόξης τοῦ θεοῦ, Rev. xv. 8; ἐκ τῶν Ἰουδαίων ἐστί, comes from the Jews, Jn. iv. 22; εἶναι ἔκ τινος, to proceed from any one as the author, Mt. v. 37; Jn. vii. 17, 22; Ro. ii. 29; 2 Co. iv. 7; 1 Jn. ii. 16, 21, etc.; with ἐστίν to be mentally supplied: Ro. xi. 36; 1 Co. viii. 6, (see εἰς, B. II. 3 c. a.); 1 Co. xi. 12; 2 Co. iii. 5; v. 18; Gal. v. 8; ἔργα ἐκ τοῦ πατρός μου, works of which my father is the author, i. e. which I, endued with my father's power, have wrought, Jn. x. 32; οἰκοδομὴ ἐκ θεοῦ, whose author is God, 2 Co. v. 1; χάρισμα, 1 Co. vii. 7; δεδομένον ἐκ τοῦ πατρός, Jn. vi. 65; add, Jn. xviii. 3; 1 Co. vii. 7. ἡ ἐκ θεοῦ δικαιοσύνη, that comes from God, i. e. is adjudged by him, Phil. iii. 9; ἡ ἐξ ὑμῶν ἐν ἡμῖν [WH txt. ἡμ. ἐν ὑμ.] ἀγάπη, love proceeding from you and taking up its abode in us, i. e. your love the influence of which we feel [W. 193 (181 sq.); B. 157 (137)], 2 Co. viii. 7; ὁ ἐξ ὑμῶν ζῆλος, your zeal, 2 Co. ix. 2 [R G; cf. W. u. s. note; B. u. s.]; βλασφημία ἔκ τινος, calumny from i. e. disseminated by, Rev. ii. 9 [not Rec.]; εἶναι ἐξ οὐρανοῦ, ἐξ ἀνθρώπων, see εἰμί, V. 3 c.; with the suggested idea of a nature and disposition derived from one's origin: οὐκ ἔστιν ἐκ τοῦ κόσμου τούτου, is not of earthly origin nor of earthly nature, Jn. xviii. 36; ἐκ τῆς γῆς ἐστιν, is of an earthly nature, Jn. iii. 31; ἐκ τῆς γῆς λαλεῖν, to speak as an earthly origin prompts, ibid.; human virtues are said *to be from God*, as having their prototype in God and being wrought in the soul by his power, ἡ ἀγάπη ἐκ τοῦ θεοῦ ἐστιν, 1 Jn. iv. 7. **3.** of the material out of which a thing is made, etc.: ἡ γυνὴ ἐκ τοῦ ἀνδρός, from "one of his ribs," 1 Co. xi. 12; στέφανον ἐξ ἀκανθῶν, Mt. xxvii. 29; Jn. xix. 2; add, Jn. ii. 15; ix. 6; Ro. ix. 21; 1 Co. xv. 47; Rev. xviii. 12; xxi. 21. Akin is **4.** its use to note the price, because the money is, as it were, changed into that which is bought, (the simple gen. of price is more common, cf. W. 206 (194); [B. § 132, 13]): ἀγοράζειν τι ἔκ τινος, Mt. xxvii. 7, (Bar. vi. [i. e. ep. Jer.] 24); κτᾶσθαι ἐκ, Acts i. 18, (ὠνεῖσθαι ἐκ, Palaeph. 46, 3 sq.); συμφωνεῖν ἐκ δηναρίου (because the agreement comes from the promised denary [cf. W. 368 (345); B. u. s.]), Mt. xx. 2. Cognate to this is the phrase ποιεῖν ἑαυτῷ φίλους ἐκ τοῦ μαμωνᾶ, Lk. xvi. 9. **5.** esp. after neut. and pass. verbs, ἐκ is used of the cause (whether thing or person) by which the act expressed by the accompanying verb is aided, sustained, effected: ὠφελεῖσθαι ἔκ τινος, Mt. xv. 5; Mk. vii. 11; ζημιοῦσθαι, 2 Co. vii. 9; λυπεῖσθαι, 2 Co. ii. 2; esp. in the Apocalypse: ἀδικεῖσθαι, Rev. ii. 11; ἀποθανεῖν, viii. 11; [ἀποκτείνεσθαι], ix. 18; φωτίζεσθαι, xviii. 1; σκοτίζεσθαι [L T WH σκοτοῦσθαι], ix. 2; πυροῦσθαι, iii. 18; γεμίζεσθαι, xv. 8 (cf. Is. vi. 4); Jn. vi. 13; γέμειν, Mt. xxiii. 25 (where L om. Tr br. ἐξ); πληροῦσθαι, Jn. xii. 3 [Treg. marg. ἐπλήσθη]; χορτάζεσθαι, Rev. xix. 21; πλουτεῖν, xviii. 3, 19; μεθύσκεσθαι, μεθύειν, xvii. 2, 6 [not Treg. marg.]; ζῆν, Ro. i. 17; 1 Co. ix. 14; Gal. iii. 11; αὔξησιν ποιεῖσθαι, Eph. iv. 16; Col. ii. 19; τελειοῦσθαι, Jas. ii. 22; κεκοπιακώς, Jn. iv. 6, (Ael. v. h. 3, 23 ἐκ τοῦ πότου ἐκάθευδεν). Also after active verbs: γεμίζειν, Jn. vi. 13; Rev. viii. 5; ποτίζειν, Rev. xiv. 8; [on ἐκ with the gen. after verbs of fulness, cf. B. 163 (142 sq.); W. 201 (189)]. **6.** of that on which a thing depends, or from which it results: οὐκ ἔστιν ἡ ζωὴ ἐκ τῶν ὑπαρχόντων, does not depend upon possessions, i. e. possessions cannot secure life, Lk. xii. 15; εὐπορία ἡμῶν ἐστι ἐκ τῆς ἐργασίας ταύτης, Acts xix. 25; τὸ ἐξ ὑμῶν, as far as depends on you, Ro. xii. 18; in the Pauline phrases δίκαιος, δικαιοσύνη, δικαιοῦν ἐκ πίστεως, ἐξ ἔργων, see [the several words, esp.] p. 150; ἐξ (as the result of, in consequence of) ἔργων λαβεῖν τὸ πνεῦμα, Gal. iii. 2, 5; ἐξ ἀναστάσεως λαβεῖν τοὺς νεκρούς, Heb. xi. 35; ἐσταυρώθη ἐξ ἀσθενείας, 2 Co. xiii. 4; add, Ro. xi. 6; Gal. iii. 18, 21 sq.; Eph. ii. 8 sq. **7.** of the power on which any one depends, by which he is prompted and governed, whose character he reflects: ἐκ θεοῦ (equiv. to θεόπνευστον) λαλεῖν, 2 Co. ii. 17; in the Johannean expressions, εἶναι ἐκ θεοῦ, Jn. viii. 47 (in a different sense above, II. 1 a.); ἐκ τοῦ διαβόλου, ἐκ τοῦ πονηροῦ, ἐκ τοῦ κόσμου, see εἰμί, V. 3 d.; ἐκ τῆς ἀληθείας εἶναι, to be led by a desire to know the truth, be a lover of the truth, Jn. xviii. 37; 1 Jn. iii. 19; οἱ ἐκ νόμου, the subjects of the law, Ro. iv. 14; οἱ ἐξ ἐριθείας equiv. to οἱ ἐριθευόμενοι [cf. ἐριθεία], Ro. ii. 8; ὁ ἐκ πίστεως equiv. to ὁ πιστεύων, Ro. iii. 26; iv. 16. εἶναι ἔκ τινος also means *to be bound to one, connected with him; to have relations with him*; see εἰμί, V. 3 d.; hence the periphrasis οἱ ἐκ περιτομῆς, *the circumcised*: Acts xi. 2; Ro. iv. 12; Gal. ii. 12; οἱ ὄντες ἐκ περιτομῆς, Col. iv. 11; οἱ ἐκ περιτομῆς πιστοί, Jewish Christians, Acts x. 45. **8.** of the cause for which: ἐκ τοῦ πόνου, *for pain*, Rev. xvi. 10; of the reason for (because of) which: Rev. viii. 13; xvi. 11; ἐκ τούτου, Jn. vi. 66; xix. 12; cf. Meyer on these pass. [who urges that ἐκ τούτου used of time denotes "the point of departure of a temporal series" (W. 367 (344)): *from this time on, thenceforth*. This argument seems not to be decisive in the second example (Jn. xix. 12), for there the verb is in the imperfect. On the use of the phrase in classic Grk. see L. and S. s. v. ἐκ, II. 1; Krüger § 68, 17, 7. Cf. our Eng. *upon this, hereupon*, in which the temporal sense and the causal often seem to blend. See below, IV. 1 fin.]. **9.** of the supply out of (from) which a thing is taken, given, received, eaten, drunk, etc. [cf. W. § 30, 7 and 8; B. 159 (139) sqq.]: λαμβάνειν ἐκ, Jn. i. 16; xvi. 14 sq.; διδόναι, διαδιδόναι, Mt. xxv. 8; Jn. vi. 11; 1 Jn. iv. 13; ἐσθίειν, 1 Co. ix. 7; xi. 28; φαγεῖν, Jn. vi. 26, 50 sq.; Rev. ii. 7; μετέχειν, 1 Co. x. 17 (but see μετέχω); πίνειν, Mt. xxvi. 29; Mk. xiv. 25; Jn. iv. 13 sq.; Rev. xiv. 10; xviii. 3, (differently in I. 1 above); λαλεῖν ἐκ τῶν ἰδίων, Jn. viii. 44; ἐκ τοῦ περισσεύματος τῆς καρδίας, Mt. xii. 34; ἐκβάλλειν, ib. 35 [this belongs here only in case θησαυρός is taken in the sense of *treasure* not *treasury* (the contents as distinguished from the repository); cf. I. 1 above, and s. v. θησαυρός]; βάλλειν ἐκ (a part), Mk. xii. 44; Lk. xxi. 4. **10.** of that from which any thing is obtained: συλλέγειν ἐξ ἀκανθῶν, τρυγᾶν ἐκ βάτου, Lk. vi. 44; θερίζειν ἐκ, Gal. vi. 8. **11.** of the whole of which anything

is a part: 1 Co. xii. 15 sq. [cf. W. 368 (345)]. **12.** of the source; **a.** univ.: ἐξ ἐμαυτοῦ οὐκ ἐλάλησα, Jn. xii. 49, (οὐδὲν ἐκ σαυτῆς λέγεις, Soph. El. 344). **b.** of the source of conduct, as to be found in the state of the soul, its feelings, virtues, vices, etc.: ἐκ καρδίας, Ro. vi. 17; ἐκ ψυχῆς, Eph. vi. 6; Col. iii. 23, (1 Macc. viii. 27; ἐκ τῆς ψυχῆς ἀσπάζεσθαι, Xen. oec. 10, 4); ἐκ καθαρᾶς καρδίας, 1 Tim. i. 5; 2 Tim. ii. 22; 1 Pet. i. 22 [L T Tr WH om. καθ.]; ἐξ ὅλης τῆς καρδίας … ψυχῆς … διανοίας κτλ. Mk. xii. 30 sqq. (Sap. viii. 21; 4 Macc. vii. 18); ἐκ πίστεως, Ro. xiv. 23; ἐξ εἰλικρινείας, 2 Co. ii. 17; ἐξ ἐριθείας, Phil. i. 16 (17) [yet see ἐριθεία]. **c.** of the source of knowledge: κατηχεῖσθαι ἐκ, Ro. ii. 18; ἀκούειν ἐκ, Jn. xii. 34; γινώσκειν, Mt. xii. 33; Lk. vi. 44; 1 Jn. iv. 6; ἐποπτεύειν, 1 Pet. ii. 12. δεικνύναι, Jas. ii. 18; ὁρίζειν, to declare, prove to be, Ro. i. 4 [cf. s. v. ὁρίζω, 2 and Mey. ad loc.]. **13.** of that from which a rule of judging or acting is derived; *after, according to*, [cf. W. 368 (345)]: κρίνειν ἐκ, Lk. xix. 22 [A. V. *out of* thine own mouth, etc.]; Rev. xx. 12 (Xen. Cyr. 2, 2, 21 ἐκ τῶν ἔργων κρίνεσθαι); δικαιοῦν, καταδικάζειν, Mt. xii. 37; ὀνομάζειν ἐκ, Eph. iii. 15 (Hom. Il. 10, 68; Soph. O. T. 1036, etc.); ἐκ τοῦ ἔχειν, according to your ability, 2 Co. viii. 11.

III. By ATTRACTION, common in classic Grk. (cf. W. § 66, 6; [B. 377 sq. (323)]), two prepositions coalesce as it were into one, so that ἐκ seems to be used for ἐν, thus ἆραι τὰ ἐκ τῆς οἰκίας αὐτοῦ concisely for τὰ ἐν τῇ οἰκίᾳ αὐτοῦ ἐξ αὐτῆς, Mt. xxiv. 17; ὁ πατὴρ ὁ ἐξ οὐρανοῦ δώσει for ὁ πατὴρ ὁ ἐν οὐρανῷ δώσει ἐκ τοῦ οὐρανοῦ, Lk. xi. 13; τὴν ἐκ Λαοδικείας ἐπιστολὴν for τὴν εἰς Λαοδίκ. γεγραμμένην καὶ ἐκ Λαοδικείας κομιστέαν, Col. iv. 16, (2 Macc. iii. 18). [To this constr. some would refer ἐπιγνοὺς ἐν ἑαυτῷ τὴν ἐξ αὐτοῦ δύναμιν ἐξελθοῦσαν, Mk. v. 30, resolving τὴν ἐν αὐτῷ δύναμιν ἐξελθοῦσαν ἐξ αὐτοῦ; cf. Field, Otium Norvicense, pars iii. ad loc.]

IV. of TIME [W. 367 (344)]; **1.** of the (temporal) point from which; Lat. *ex, inde a*; *from, from … on, since*: ἐκ χρόνων ἱκανῶν, Lk. viii. 27 [R G Tr mrg.]; ἐκ γενετῆς, Jn. ix. 1 (Hom. Il. 24, 535; Od. 18, 6); ἐκ κοιλίας μητρός (see κοιλία, 4); ἐκ νεότητος, Mt. xix. 20 [R G]; Mk. x. 20; Lk. xviii. 21; Acts xxvi. 4 (Hom. Il. 14, 86); ἐκ τοῦ αἰῶνος (see αἰών, 1 b.), Jn. ix. 32 (Ael. v. h. 6, 13; 12, 64 ἐξ αἰῶνος); ἐξ ἀρχῆς, Jn. vi. 64; xvi. 4; ἐκ γενεῶν ἀρχαίων, Acts xv. 21; ἐξ ἐτῶν ὀκτώ, Acts ix. 33; ἐκ πολλῶν ἐτῶν, Acts xxiv. 10; ἐξ αὐτῆς (sc. ὥρας), *forthwith, instantly* (see ἐξαυτῆς); ἐξ ἱκανοῦ [(sc. χρόνου); but L T Tr WH here ἐξ ἱκανῶν χρόνων], of a long time, Lk. xxiii. 8, (Thuc. 1, 68; 2, 88); with an adverb: ἐκ παιδιόθεν, Mk. ix. 21 L T Tr WH, (ἐκ πρωΐθεν, 1 Macc. x. 80), cf. W. § 65, 2; [B. 70 (62)]. Many interpreters translate ἐκ τούτου, Jn. vi. 66; xix. 12, *from this time*, but cf. II. 8 above. **2.** of succession in time, a temporal series: ἐκ δευτέρου (as it were, *proceeding from, beginning from the second*), *a second time* (see δεύτερος); ἐκ τρίτου, Mt. xxvi. 44 [L Tr mrg. br. ἐκ τρίτ.]; ἡμέραν ἐξ ἡμέρας (*diem ex die*, Cic. ad Att. 7, 26; Caes. b. g. 1, 16, 4; *diem de die*, Liv. 5, 48) *from day to day*,

day after day, 2 Pet. ii. 8, (Gen. xxxix. 10; Num. xxx. 15; [2 Chr. xxiv. 11]; Sir. v. 7; Eur. Rhes. 437 (445) etc.; ἔτος ἐξ ἔτους, Lev. xxv. 50; ἐνιαυτὸν ἐξ ἐνιαυτοῦ, Deut. xv. 20).

V. ADVERBIAL PHRASES [cf. W. § 51, 1 d.], in which lies the idea **1.** of direction whence: ἐξ ἐναντίας, cf. I. 4 above. **2.** of source: ἐκ συμφώνου, by consent, by agreement, 1 Co. vii. 5; ἐξ ἀνάγκης of necessity, i. e. by compulsion, 2 Co. ix. 7; necessarily, Heb. vii. 12. **3.** of the measure or standard: ἐκ μέρους, so that each is a part of the whole, proportionately, [R. V. mrg. each in his part], 1 Co. xii. 27, cf. Meyer ad loc.; in part, partly, 1 Co. xiii. 9 sqq.; ἐκ μέτρου i. q. μετρίως, by measure, moderately, sparingly, Jn. iii. 34; ἐξ ἰσότητος, by equality, in equal proportion, 2 Co. viii. 13 (14) (ἐξ ἴσου, Hdt. 7, 135); ἐκ περισσοῦ, beyond measure, Mk. vi. 51 [WH om. Tr. br.].

VI. In COMPOSITION ἐκ denotes **1.** egress ἐκβαίνω, ἐξέρχομαι. **2.** emission, removal, separation: ἐκβάλλω, ἐκπέμπω, ἐξαιρέω. **3.** origin: ἔκγονος. **4.** publicity: ἐξαγγέλλω. **5.** the unfolding, opening out, of something tied together or rolled up: ἐκτείνω, ἐκπετάννυμι. **6.** is i. q. utterly, entirely, παντελῶς, [cf. Eng. out and out], denoting completion and perfection: ἐκπληρόω, ἐκτελέω. Cf. Fritzsche on Matt. p. 120 sq.

1538 ἕκαστος, -η, -ον, Sept. for אִישׁ, [fr. Hom. down], each, every; **a.** joined to a substantive: ἕκαστον δένδρον, Lk. vi. 44; ἑκάστῳ στρατιώτῃ, Jn. xix. 23; κατὰ μῆνα ἕκαστον, every month, Rev. xxii. 2 [not Rec.]; καθ' ἑκάστην ἡμέραν, Heb. iii. 13; cf. W. 111 (106); B. § 127, 30. preceded by εἷς, Lat. unusquisque, every one: with a substantive, Eph. iv. 16; Rev. xxii. 2 Rec. **b.** used substantively: Jn. vii. 53 [Rec.]; Acts iv. 35; Ro. ii. 6; Gal. vi. 4, etc.; once plur. ἕκαστοι: Rev. vi. 11 Rec. With a partitive genitive added: ἡμῶν, Ro. xiv. 12; ὑμῶν, Lk. xiii. 15; 1 Co. i. 12; Heb. vi. 11; αὐτῶν, Jn. vi. 7 [R G]; τῶν σπερμάτων, 1 Co. xv. 38. εἷς ἕκαστος, every one (see εἷς, 4 b.): without a partit. gen., Acts xx. 31; Col. iv. 6; with a partit. gen., Lk. iv. 40; Acts ii. 3; xvii. 27; 1 Co. xii. 18, etc. ἕκαστος, when it denotes individually, every one of many, is often added appositively to nouns and pronouns and verbs in the plural number, (Matthiae ii. p. 764 sq.; [W. 516 (481); B. 131 (114)]): ἡμεῖς ἀκούομεν ἕκαστος, Acts ii. 8; σκορπισθῆτε ἕκαστος, Jn. xvi. 32; ἐπορεύοντο πάντες . . . , ἕκαστος . . . , Lk. ii. 3; add, Acts iii. 26; 1 Pet. iv. 10; Rev. v. 8; xx. 13; likewise εἷς ἕκαστος, Acts ii. 6; xxi. 26; ὑμεῖς οἱ καθ' ἕνα ἕκαστος τὴν ἑαυτοῦ γυναῖκα ἀγαπάτω, you one by one, each one of you severally, Eph. v. 33. In imitation of the Hebr., ἕκαστος τῷ ἀδελφῷ αὐτοῦ (אִישׁ לְאָחִיו, Gen. xxvi. 31), Mt. xviii. 35; μετὰ τοῦ πλησίον αὐτοῦ (אִישׁ אֶל-רֵעֵהוּ, Judg. vi. 29, etc.), Eph. iv. 25, cf. Heb. viii. 11 Rec.

1539 ἑκάστοτε, adv., at every time, always: 2 Pet. i. 15. (Hdt., Thuc., Xen., Plat., al.) *

1540 ἑκατόν, οἱ, αἱ, τά, [fr. Hom. down], a hundred: Mt. xiii. 8 (sc. καρπούς); xviii. 12; Jn. xix. 39, etc.

1541 ἑκατονταέτης [R G T], -ες, and ἑκατονταετής [L Tr WH],

-ές, (fr. ἑκατόν and ἔτος; on the want of uniformity in accentuation among authors, copyists, and grammarians see Lob. ad Phryn. p. 406 sq.; W. § 6, 1 b.; B. 29 (26); [Tdf. Proleg. p. 102; Ellendt, Lex. Soph. s. v. δεκέτης; esp. Chandler §§ 703, 709; Göttling p. 323 sq.]), centenarian, a hundred years old: Ro. iv. 19. (Pind. Pyth. 4, 502.) *

ἑκατονταπλασίων, -ον, a hundredfold, a hundred times 1542
as much: Mt. xix. 29 [R G]; Mk. x. 30; Lk. viii. 8. (2 S. xxiv. 3; Xen. oec. 2, 3.) *

ἑκατοντάρχης, -ου, ὁ, (ἑκατον and ἄρχω; on the termi- 1543
nations ἄρχης and ἄρχος see the full exposition in W. 61 (60); cf. B. 73 (64); Bornemann, Schol. ad Luc. p. 151 sq.; [Tdf. Proleg. p. 117; WH. App. p. 156 sq.]), a centurion: Mt. viii. [5 and 8 Tdf.], 13 G L T Tr WH; [xxvii. 54 T]; Lk. vii. [2 (?)], 6 T WH; [xxiii. 47 T Tr WH]; Acts x. 1, 22; xxi. 32 L T Tr WH; [xxii. 26 L T WH]; xxiv. 23; xxvii. 1, 6 L T Tr WH, 11 G L T Tr WH, 31, 43 L T Tr WH; gen. plur. T WH in Acts xxiii. 17, 23. (Aeschyl. ap. Athen. 1 p. 11 d.; Hdt. 7, 81; Dion. Hal., Plut., al.). See the foll. word.*

ἑκατόνταρχος, -ου, ὁ, i. q. ἑκατοντάρχης, q. v.: Mt. viii. 5, see 1543
8 [in 5, 8, Tdf. -άρχης], 13 Rec.; xxvii. 54 [Tdf. -άρχης]; Lk. vii. 2, 6 [T WH -άρχης]; xxiii. 47 [T Tr WH -άρχης]; Acts xxi. 32 R G; xxii. 25, 26 [L T WH -άρχης]; xxvii. 6 [R G, 11 Rec., 43 R G], also xxviii. 16 Rec.; gen. plur., Acts xxiii. 17 and 23 R G L Tr. (Xen. Cyr. 5, 3, 41; Plut., al.) [Cf. Meisterhans p. 53 sq.] *

ἐκ-βαίνω: 2 aor. ἐξέβην; [fr. Hom. down]; to go out: see 1831
Heb. xi. 15 L T Tr WH.*

ἐκ-βάλλω; impf. 3 pers. plur. ἐξέβαλλον (Mk. vi. 13 1544
[Tr mrg. aor.]); fut. ἐκβαλῶ; plpf. ἐκβεβλήκειν (without augm., Mk. xvi. 9; cf. W. § 12, 9; B. 33 (29)); 2 aor. ἐξέβαλον; [Pass. and Mid. pres. ἐκβάλλομαι]; 1 aor. pass. ἐξεβλήθην; fut. pass. ἐκβληθήσομαι; [fr. Hom. down]; Sept. generally for גֵּרַשׁ, occasionally for הוֹצִיא, הוֹרִישׁ, הִשְׁלִיךְ; to cast out; to drive out; to send out; **1.** with the included notion of more or less violence; **a.** to drive out, (cast out): a person, Mt. xxi. 12; Mk. ix. 15; Jn. ii. 15 (ἐκ); Lk. xx. 12, etc.; pass. Mt. viii. 12 [T WH (rejected) mrg. ἐξελεύσονται]; δαιμόνια, Mt. vii. 22; viii. 16, 31; ix. 33; Mk. i. 34, 39; Lk. xi. 20; xiii. 32, etc.; ἐκ τινος, Mk. viii. 26; ἀπό, Mk. xvi. 9 [L WH Tr txt. παρά], Mt. ix. 34; xii. 24, 27 sq.; Mk. iii. 22; Lk. xi. 15, 19 sq.; τῷ ὀνόματί τινος, Mt. vii. 22; [Mk. ix. 38 Rᵃ G]; ἐπὶ τῷ ὀν. τινος, Lk. ix. 49 [WH Tr mrg. ἐν; ἐν τῷ ὀν. Mk. ix. 38 Rᵉˡᶻ L T Tr WH]; λόγῳ, Mt. viii. 16; τινὰ ἔξω τῆς πόλεως, Lk. iv. 29; Acts vii. 58. **b.** to cast out: τινά foll. by ἔξω, Jn. vi. 37; ix. 34 sq.; xii. 31 (sc. out of the world, i. e. be deprived of the power and influence he exercises in the world); Lk. xiii. 28; ἔξω with gen., Mt. xxi. 39; Mk. xii. 8; Lk. xx. 15. a thing: excrement from the belly into the sink, Mt. xv. 17; mid. ἐκβαλλόμενοι (i. e. for themselves, that they might the more easily save the ship and thereby their lives) τὸν σῖτον εἰς τ. θάλασσαν, Acts xxvii. 38. **c.** to expel a person from a society: to banish from a family, Gal. iv. 30 (Gen. xxi. 10); ἐκ [Tdf. om. ἐκ] τῆς ἐκκλησίας, 3

Jn. 10. **d.** *to compel one to depart*: ἀπὸ τῶν ὁρίων, Acts xiii. 50; *to bid one depart*, in stern though not violent language, Mt. ix. 25; Mk. v. 40; Acts ix. 40; xvi. 37 (where distinguished fr. ἐξάγειν); to bid one go forth to do some business, Mt. ix. 38; Lk. x. 2. **e.** so employed that the rapid motion of the one going is transferred to the one sending forth; *to command* or *cause one to depart in haste*: Mk. i. 43; Jas. ii. 25; τὰ πάντα (sc. πρόβατα), to let them out of the fold so that they rush forth, [al. to thrust them forth by laying hold of them], Jn. x. 4. **f.** *to draw out with force, tear out*: τί, Mk. ix. 47. **g.** with the implication of force overcoming opposing force; *to cause a thing to move straight on to its intended goal*: τὴν κρίσιν εἰς νῖκος, Mt. xii. 20. **h.** *to reject with contempt*; *to cast off* or *away*: τὸ ὄνομά τινος ὡς πονηρόν, Lk. vi. 22, (Plat. Crito p. 46 b.; de rep. 2 p. 377 c.; Soph. O. C. 636, 646; of actors driven from the stage, hissed and hooted off, Dem. p. 449, 19). **2.** without the notion of violence; **a.** *to draw out, extract*, one thing inserted in another: τὸ κάρφος τὸ ἐν τῷ ὀφθαλμῷ, Lk. vi. 42; ἐκ τοῦ ὀφθαλμοῦ, ibid. and Mt. vii. 5; ἀπὸ τοῦ ὀφθ. 4 (where L T Tr WH ἐκ). **b.** *to bring out of, to draw* or *bring forth*: τὶ ἐκ τοῦ θησαυροῦ, Mt. xii. 35; xiii. 52; money from a purse, Lk. x. 35. **c.** *to except, to leave out*, i. e. *not receive*: τί, foll. by ἔξω [or ἔξωθεν], Rev. xi. 2 (leave out from the things to be measured, equiv. to μὴ αὐτὴν μετρήσῃς). **d.** foll. by εἰς with acc. of place, *to lead one forth* or *away somewhere with a force which he cannot resist*: Mk. i. 12. [On the pleonastic phrase ἐκβ. ἔξω (or ἔξωθεν) cf. W. § 65, 2.]

ἔκ-βασις, -εως, ἡ, (ἐκβαίνω); **1.** *an egress, way out*, (Hom., et al.): applied fig. to the way of escape from temptation into which one εἰσέρχεται or εἰσφέρεται (see these words), 1 Co. x. 13. **2.** in a sense foreign to prof. auth., *the issue* [(cf. its objective sense e. g. Epict. diss. 2, 7, 9)] i. q. *end*: used of the end of life, Sap. ii. 17; ἐκβ. τῆς ἀναστροφῆς τινων, in Heb. xiii. 7, is not merely the end of their physical life, but the manner in which they closed a well-spent life as exhibited by their spirit in dying; cf. Delitzsch ad loc.*

ἐκ-βολή, -ῆς, ἡ, (ἐκβάλλω); **a.** *a casting out.* **b.** spec. *the throwing overboard* of goods and lading whereby sailors lighten a ship in a storm to keep her from sinking, (Aeschyl. sept. 769; Aristot. eth. Nic. 3, 1, 5 [p. 1110ᵃ, 9]; Lcian. de merc. cond. 1): ποιεῖσθαι ἐκβολήν, Lat. *jacturam facere, to throw* the cargo *overboard*, Acts xxvii. 18; with τῶν σκευῶν added, Sept. Jon. i. 5; τῶν φορτίων, Poll. 1, 99 p. 70 ed. Hemsterh.*

ἐκ-γαμίζω; Pass., [pres. ἐκγαμίζομαι]; impf. ἐξεγαμιζόμην; *to give away* [ἐκ out of the house [cf. W. 102 (97)]] *in marriage*: a daughter, 1 Co. vii. 38ᵃ R G, [ibid.ᵇ Rec.]; Mt. xxiv. 38 R G Tr txt. Pass. *to marry, to be given in marriage*, Mt. xxii. 30 R G [cf. Tdf.'s note ad loc.]; Lk. xvii. 27 R G; see γαμίζω. Not found elsewhere.*

ἐκ-γαμίσκω, i. q. ἐκγαμίζω, q. v.: Pass. [pres. ἐκγαμίσκομαι]; Lk. xx. 34 sq. R G; cf. γαμίσκω and Fritzsche on Mk. p. 529 sqq. Not found elsewhere.*

ἔκ-γονος, -ον, (ἐκγίνομαι), *sprung from one, born, begotten,* (Hom. and sqq.); commonly as a subst. ὁ, ἡ ἔκγονος, οἱ ἔκγονοι, a son, daughter, offspring, children, descendants; in Sept. com. in neut. plur. ἔκγονα and τὰ ἔκγονα, for פְּרִי, Deut. vii. 13 [Alex.]; xxviii. 4, etc.; צֶאֱצָאִים, Is. xlviii. 19; lxi. 9; נִין, Is. xlix. 15; also in Sir. xliv. 11, etc. In the N. T. once: 1 Tim. v. 4 τέκνα ἢ ἔκγονα, *grandchildren*, [(A. V. renders it by the obsol. *nephews*; cf. *Eastwood and Wright*, Bible Word-Book, or B.D. Am. ed. s. v. Nephew)].* **1549**

ἐκ-δαπανάω: [fut. ἐκδαπανήσω]; 1 fut. pass. ἐκδαπανηθήσομαι; *to exhaust by expending, to spend wholly, use up*: τὰς προσόδους, Polyb. 25, 8, 4. Pass. reflexively, *to spend one's self wholly*: foll. by ὑπέρ τινος, of one who consumes strength and life in laboring for others' salvation, 2 Co. xii. 15; cf. Kypke ad loc.; [Soph. Lex. s. v.].* **1550**

ἐκ-δέχομαι; impf. ἐξεδεχόμην; (ἐκ *from* some person or quarter); **1.** *to receive, accept*, ([Hom.], Aeschyl., Hdt., sqq.). **2.** *to look for, expect, wait for, await*: τί, Jn. v. 3 R L; Heb. xi. 10; Jas. v. 7; τινά, Acts xvii. 16; 1 Co. xvi. 11; ἀλλήλους ἐκδέχεσθε wait for one another, sc. until each shall have received his food, 1 Co. xi. 33, cf. 21; foll. by ἕως etc. Heb. x. 13; [absol. 1 Pet. iii. 20 Rec., but see Tdf.'s note ad loc.]. Rarely with this meaning in prof. auth., as Soph. Phil. 123; Apollod. 1, 9, 27 § 3; ἕως ἂν γένηταί τι, Dion. Hal. 6, 67. [COMP.: ἀπ-εκδέχομαι. Cf. δέχομαι, fin.]* **1551**

ἔκ-δηλος, -ον, (δῆλος), *evident, clear, conspicuous*: 2 Tim. iii. 9. (Hom. Il. 5, 2; Dem. p. 24, 10; Polyb.)* **1552**

ἐκδημέω, -ῶ; 1 aor. inf. ἐκδημῆσαι; (ἔκδημος *away from home*); **1.** *to go abroad* (Hdt., Soph., Plat., Joseph., al.); hence univ. *to emigrate, depart*: ἐκ τοῦ σώματος, from the body as the earthly abode of the spirit, 2 Co. v. 8. **2.** *to be* or *live abroad*: 2 Co. v. 9; ἀπὸ τοῦ κυρίου, abode with whom is promised us, 2 Co. v. 6; in these exx. opp. to ἐνδημέω, q. v.* **1553**

ἐκ-δίδωμι: Mid., fut. ἐκδώσομαι; 2 aor. 3 pers. sing. ἐξέδοτο, T WH ἐξέδετο (see ἀποδίδωμι); a com. word in Grk. auth. fr. Hom. Il. 3, 459 on; *to give out of one's house, power, hand, stores*; *to give out, give up, give over*; hence also *to let out for hire, to farm out*, Hdt. 1, 68; γεωργίαι δὲ ἐκδεδομέναι δούλοις, Plat. legg. 7 p. 806 d.; al. In the N. T., Mid. *to let out for one's advantage*: Mt. xxi. 33, 41 [Rec. ἐκδόσεται, cf. Tdf.'s note; B. 47 (41)]; Mk. xii. 1; Lk. xx. 9.* **1554**

ἐκ-δι-ηγέομαι, -οῦμαι; dep. mid.; prop. *to narrate in full* or *wholly*; univ. *to relate, tell, declare*: τί, Acts xiii. 41 (Hab. i. 5); xv. 3. ([Aristot. rhet. Alex. 23 p. 1434ᵇ, 4]; Joseph., [Philo], Galen, [al.]; Sept.)* **1555**

ἐκδικέω, -ῶ; fut. ἐκδικήσω; 1 aor. ἐξεδίκησα; (ἔκδικος, q. v.); Sept. for נָקַם, פָּקַד, שָׁפַט; **a.** τινά, *to vindicate one's right, do one justice*, [A. V. *avenge*]: Lk. xviii. 5 (1 Macc. vi. 22); τινὰ ἀπό τινος, *to protect, defend, one person from another*, Lk. xviii. 3; ἑαυτόν, *to avenge one's self*, Ro. xii. 19. **b.** τί, *to avenge a thing* (i. e. *to punish* a person for a thing): τὴν παρακοήν, 2 Co. x. 6; τὸ αἷμά τινος ἀπό or ἔκ τινος, to demand in punishment the blood of one from another, i. e. to exact of the murderer **1556** the penalty of his crime, [A. V. *avenge one's blood on or at the hand of*]: Rev. vi. 10; xix. 2; see ἐκ, I. 7. (In Grk. auth. fr. [Apollod.], Diod. down.) *

1557   ἐκ-δίκησις, -εως, ἡ, (ἐκδικέω, q. v.), Sept. for נְקָמָה and נָקָם, פְּקֻדָּה, מִשְׁפָּט (Ezek. xvi. 38; xxiii. 45) and שְׁפָטִים; *a revenging; vengeance, punishment*: Ro. xii. 19 and Heb. x. 30 fr. Deut. xxxii. 35; 2 Co. vii. 11; Lk. xxi. 22; ποιεῖν τὴν ἐκδίκησίν τινος, to vindicate one from wrongs, accomplish the avenging of, Lk. xviii. 7 sq.; τινί, to avenge an injured person, Acts vii. 24 (Judg. xi. 36); ἐκδίκησίς τινος, objec. gen., *the punishment of one*, 1 Pet. ii. 14; διδόναι ἐκδίκησίν τινι, to inflict punishment on, [render vengeance to] one, 2 Th. i. 8; cf. [Sir. xii. 6]; Ezek. xxv. 14. (Polyb. 3, 8, 10.) *

1558   ἔκδικος, -ον, (δίκη right, justice, penalty); **1.** *without law and justice* (cf. Lat. *exlex*), *unjust*: Aeschyl., Soph., Eur., Ael. n. an. 16, 5. **2.** *exacting penalty from* (ἐκ) one; *an avenger, punisher*: Ro. xiii. 4; περί τινος, 1 Th. iv. 6; (Sap. xii. 12; Sir. xxx. 6; 4 Macc. xv. 26 (29); [Plut. de garrul. § 14 p. 509 f.]; Hdian. 7, 4, 10 [5 ed. Bekk.; al.]).*

1559   ἐκ-διώκω: fut. ἐκδιώξω; 1 aor. ἐξεδίωξα; **1.** *to drive out, banish*: τινά, Lk. xi. 49 [here WH Tr mrg. διώξουσιν; some refer this to 2]; (Thuc. 1, 24; Lcian. Tim. 10; Sept. 1 Chr. viii. 13; Joel ii. 20, etc.). **2.** *to pursue* i. q. *to persecute, oppress with calamities*: τινά, 1 Th. ii. 15 [some refer this to 1]; (Ps. cxviii. (cxix.) 157; Sir. xxx. 19; Dem. 883, 27).*

1560   ἔκ-δοτος, -ον, (ἐκδίδωμι), *given over, delivered up*, (to enemies, or to the power, the will, of some one): λαμβάνειν τινὰ ἔκδοτον, Acts ii. 23 (but λαβόντες is rejected by G L T Tr WH); διδόναι or ποιεῖν τινα ἐκδ. Hdt. 3, 1; Dem. 648, 25; Joseph. antt. 6, 13, 9; Palaeph. 41, 2; al.; Bel and the Dragon vs. 22; ἑαυτὸν ἔκδ. διδόναι τῷ θανάτῳ, Ignat. ad Smyrn. 4, 2.*

1561   ἐκ-δοχή, -ῆς, ἡ, (ἐκδέχομαι), *the act or manner of receiving from*; hence in prof. auth. **1.** *reception.* **2.** *succession.* **3.** [a taking in a certain sense, i. e.] *interpretation.* **4.** once in the sacred writings, *expectation, awaiting*, [cf. ἐκδέχομαι, 2]: Heb. x. 27.*

1562   ἐκ-δύω: 1 aor. ἐξέδυσα; 1 aor. mid. ἐξεδυσάμην; (δύω); *to take off*: τινά, *to strip one of his garments*, Mt. xxvii. 28 [L WH mrg. ἐνδύσ.]; Lk. x. 30; τινά τι (as in Grk. fr. Hom. down), [a thing *from* a person]: Mt. xxvii. 31; Mk. xv. 20; Mid. *to take off from one's self, to put off one's raiment*, (Xen. Ag. 1, 28; Hell. 3, 4, 19); fig. *to put off the body, the clothing of the soul*, [A. V. *be unclothed*]: 2 Co. v. 4; the reading ἐκδυσάμενοι, adopted in vs. 3 by certain critics [e. g. Mill, Tdf. 7, Reiche, al.], is due to a correction by the copyists; see γυμνός, 1 d. [COMP.: ἀπ-εκδύομαι.] *

1563   ἐκεῖ, adv. of place, *there*; **a.** properly: Mt. ii. 13, 15; v. 24, and freq. In Lk. xiii. 28 ἐκεῖ is not used for ἐν ἐκείνῳ τῷ καιρῷ foll. by ὅταν (at that time . . . when etc.), but means *in that place whither ye have been banished*; cf. Meyer ad loc. οἱ ἐκεῖ, sc. ὄντες, standing there, Mt. xxvi. 71 [Tr mrg. αὐτοὶ ἐκεῖ]. It answers to a relative adv.: οὗ τὸ πνεῦμα, ἐκεῖ ἐλευθερία, 2 Co. iii. 17

Rec.; Mt. vi. 21; xviii. 20; xxiv. 28; Mk. vi. 10; Lk. xii. 34; Hebraistically, where a preceding adv. or rel. pron. has already attracted the verb, ἐκεῖ is added to this verb pleonastically: Rev. xii. 6 G T Tr WH (ὅπου ἔχει ἐκεῖ τόπον), 14 (ὅπου τρέφεται ἐκεῖ); cf. Deut. iv. 5, 14, 26; 1 Macc. xiv. 34, and what was said p. 86ᵇ, 5 on the pron. αὐτός after a relative. **b.** by a negligent use common also in the classics it stands after verbs of motion to ἐκεῖσε, *thither*: so after ἀπέρχομαι, Mt. ii. 22; μεταβαίνω, Mt. xvii. 20; ὑπάγω, Jn. xi. 8; ἔρχομαι, Jn. xviii. 3; προπέμπομαι, Ro. xv. 24; cf. Lob. ad Phryn. pp. 43 sq. 128; *Hermann* on Soph. Antig. 515; Trachin. 1006; *Bttm.* on Philoct. 481; W. § 54, 7; B. 71 (62) and 378 (324).

1564   ἐκεῖθεν, adv. of place, *thence, from that place*, [A. V. sometimes *from thence*]: Mt. iv. 21; Mk. vi. 1; Lk. ix. 4; Jn. iv. 43; Acts xiii. 4; and often in the historical bks. of the N. T. οἱ ἐκεῖθεν elliptically for οἱ ἐκεῖθεν διαβῆναι θέλοντες, Lk. xvi. 26 (where L WH om. οἱ).

1565   ἐκεῖνος, -η, -ο, (fr. ἐκεῖ, prop. *the one there*, cf. Germ. *dortig, der dort*), demonst. pron., *that* man, woman, thing (Lat. *ille, illa, illud*); properly of persons, things, times, places somewhat remote from the speaker. **1.** used absolutely, **a.** in antithesis, referring to the more remote subject: opp. to οὗτος, Lk. xviii. 14; Jas. iv. 15; ὑμῖν . . . ἐκείνοις, Mt. xiii. 11; Mk. iv. 11; ἐκεῖνοι . . . ἡμεῖς, Heb. xii. 25; ἄλλοι . . . ἄλλοι . . . ἐκεῖνος, Jn. ix. 9; ἐκεῖνον . . . ἐμέ, Jn. iii. 30; οἱ Ἰουδαῖοι . . . ἐκεῖνος δέ, Jn. ii. 20 sq.; ὁ μὲν κύριος Ἰησοῦς [R G T om. Ἰ. WH Tr mrg. br.] . . . ἐκεῖνοι δέ, Mk. xvi. 19 sq., etc. **b.** of noted persons (as in classic Grk.): in a bad sense, *that notorious man*, Jn. vii. 11; ix. 28; in a good sense, — of the Lord Jesus, 1 Jn. ii. 6; iii. 3, 5, 7, 16; iv. 17; of the Holy Spirit, with an apposition added, ἐκεῖνος, τὸ πνεῦμα τῆς ἀληθείας, Jn. xvi. 13. **c.** referring to a noun immediately preceding, *he, she, it*, (Lat. *is, ea, id*, Germ. *selbiger*): Jn. viii. 45; v. 46; Mk. xvi. 11; Acts iii. 13, etc.; cf. W. § 23, 1; [B. 104 (91). Here perhaps may be noticed its use together with αὐτός of the same subject in the same sentence: ἐζωγρημένοι ὑπ' αὐτοῦ (i. e. the devil) εἰς τὸ ἐκείνου θέλημα, 2 Tim. ii. 26; cf. Thuc. 1, 132, 6; 4, 29, 3; Xen. Cyr. 4, 5, 20; see *Riddell*, Apol. of Plato, App. § 49; Kühner § 467, 12; cf. ζωγρέω, 2]; equiv. to an emphatic (Germ. *er*) *he*, etc., Mt. xvii. 27; Jn. i. 8; v. 43; Tit. iii. 7; equiv. to the forcibly uttered Germ. *der* (that one etc.), in which sense it serves to recall and lay stress upon nouns just before used [cf. our resumptive *the same*; W. § 23, 4]: Jn. i. 18; v. 39; xii. 48; xiv. 26; xv. 26; esp. is it thus resumptive of a subject expressed participially [B. 306 (262 sq.)]: Mk. vii. 15 [T WH om. Tr br. the pron.], 20; Jn. i. 33; ix. 37 (ἐκεῖνός ἐστιν, sc. ὁ υἱὸς τοῦ θεοῦ, see εἰμί, II. 5); Jn. x. 1; xiv. 21; Ro. xiv. 14; 2 Co. x. 18; (Xen. Cyr. 6, 2, 33 ὁ γὰρ λόγχην ἀκονῶν, ἐκεῖνος καὶ τὴν ψυχήν τι παρακονᾷ). **d.** foll. by ὅτι, Mt. xxiv. 43; foll. by ὅς, Jn. xiii. 26; Ro. xiv. 15. **2.** joined with nouns, and then the noun with the article either precedes, or (somewhat more rarely) follows it (W. 162 (153)), [B. 119 (104) sq.]; **a.** in contrasts:

ἡ πρώτη ἐκείνη, Heb. viii. 7. **b.** used to distinguish accurately from others the things or the persons spoken of, (Germ. *selbig*): Mt. vii. 25, 27; x. 15; xviii. 32; Mk. iii. 24 sq.; Lk. vi. 48 sq.; Jn. xviii. 15, and often; esp. of T i m e, — and of time p a s t: ἐν ταῖς ἡμέραις ἐκείναις, בַּיָּמִים הָהֵם, at that time which has been spoken of; said of time which the writer either cannot or will not define more precisely and yet wishes to be connected with the time of the events just narrated: Mt. iii. 1; Mk. i. 9; viii. 1; Lk. ii. 1, (Ex. ii. 11; Judg. xviii. 1; 1 S. xxviii. 1); cf. Fritzsche on Mt. p. 106 sq.; *at the time under consideration*: Lk. iv. 2; ix. 36; the same phrase is used of time f u t u r e: Mt. xxiv. 19; Acts ii. 18 (fr. Joel ii. 29 (iii. 2)); Rev. ix. 6; likewise in the singular, ἐν ἐκείνῃ τῇ ἡμέρᾳ, Lk. xvii. 31; Jn. xvi. 23, 26. But the solemn phrase ἐκείνη ἡ ἡμέρα, or ἡ ἡμέρα ἐκείνη, simply sets future time in opposition to the present, *that fateful day*, that decisive day, when the Messiah will come to judge: Mt. vii. 22; Lk. vi. 23; x. 12; 2 Th. i. 10; 2 Tim. i. 12, 18; Rev. xvi. 14 (where L T Tr WH om. ἐκείνης); so in the phrase ὁ αἰὼν ἐκεῖνος, Lk. xx. 35. **3.** ἐκείνης (in Rec. δι' ἐκείνης), scil. ὁδοῦ, adverbially, *(by) that way*: Lk. xix. 4; W. § 64, 5; [B. 171 (149); see ποῖος, fin.]. John's use of the pronoun ἐκεῖνος is discussed by *Steitz* in the Stud. u. Krit. for 1859, p. 497 sqq.; 1861, p. 267 sqq., and by *Alex*. Buttmann, ibid. 1860, p. 505 sqq. and in Hilgenfeld's Zeitsch. für wissenschaftl. Theol. 1862, p. 204 sqq.; Buttmann clearly proves in opp. to Steitz that John's usage deviates in no respect from the Greek; Steitz, however, resorts to psychological considerations in the case of Jn. xix. 35, [regarding ἐκ there as expressing the writer's inward assurance. But Steitz is now understood to have modified his published views.]

1566　ἐκεῖσε, adv. of place, *thither, towards that place*: Acts xxi. 3, on which see W. 349 (328); used for ἐκεῖ in the pregn. constr. τοὺς ἐκεῖσε ὄντας, collected there, Acts xxii. 5, (Acta Thomae § 8); cf. W. § 54, 7.*

1567　ἐκ-ζητέω, -ῶ; 1 aor. ἐξεζήτησα; Pass., 1 aor. ἐξεζητήθην; 1 fut. ἐκζητηθήσομαι; (ἐκ out from a secret place, from all sides); Sept. very often for דָּרַשׁ, also for בָּקַשׁ, etc.; **a.** *to seek out, search for*: properly, τινά, 1 Macc. ix. 26; figuratively: τὸν κύριον, τὸν θεόν, to seek the favor of God, worship him, Acts xv. 17; Ro. iii. 11 [Tr mrg. WH mrg. ζητῶν]; Heb. xi. 6, (Ps. xiii. (xiv.) 2; xxxiii. (xxxiv.) 5; lxviii. (lxix.) 33; Amos v. 4, etc.). **b.** *to seek out i. e. investigate, scrutinize*: τί, Sir. xxxix. 1, 3; περί τινος, to examine into anything, 1 Pet. i. 10, where it is joined with ἐξερευνᾶν [to *seek out* and *search out*], as in 1 Macc. ix. 26. **c.** *to seek out for one's self, beg, crave*: Heb. xii. 17. **d.** *to demand back, require*: τὸ αἷμα τῶν προφητῶν ἀπὸ τῆς γενεᾶς ταύτης, to take vengeance on this generation for the slaughter of the prophets (after the Hebr., cf. 2 S. iv. 11; Ezek. iii. 18; see ἐκ, I. 7): Lk. xi. 50, [51]. (In prof. auth. thus far only a single passage has been noted in which this word appears, Aristid. or. 8, i. p. 488 [i. e. orat. 38, i. p. 726 ed. Dind.].) *

ἐκ-ζήτησις, (ἐκζητέω, q. v.), -εως, ἡ; **1.** *an investigating*. **2.** *a subject of subtle inquiry and dispute*, [R. V. *questioning*]: 1 Tim. i. 4 T Tr [WH; see Ellic. ad loc. and cf. οἰκονομία]. (Basil Caes., Didym. Al.) * — see 1567 & 2214

ἐκ-θαμβέω, -ῶ: Pass., [pres. ἐκθαμβοῦμαι]; 1 aor. ἐξεθαμβήθην; (ἔκθαμβος, q. v.); **1.** trans. *to throw into amazement* or *terror*; *to alarm thoroughly, to terrify*: Sir. xxx. 9; [Job xxxiii. 7 Aq., Compl.]. **2.** intrans. *to be struck with amazement*; *to be thoroughly amazed, astounded*; in Grk. writ. once, Orph. Arg. 1217. In the N. T. only in the pass. and by Mark: *to be amazed, for joy* at the unexpected coming of Christ, ix. 15; *to be struck with terror*, xvi. 5 sq.; joined with ἀδημονεῖν, xiv. 33.* — **1568**

ἔκ-θαμβος, -ον, (θάμβος, cf. ἔκφοβος), *quite astonished, amazed*: Acts iii. 11. (Polyb. 20, 10, 9. Eccl. and Byzant. writ.; *terrifying, dreadful*, Dan. vii. 7 Theod.) * — **1569**

ἐκ-θαυμάζω; [impf. ἐξεθαύμαζον]; *to wonder* or *marvel greatly* (see ἐκ, VI. 6): ἐπί τινι, at one, Mk. xii. 17 T WH. (Sir. xxvii. 23; xliii. 18; Dion. Hal., Longin., al.) * — see 2296

ἔκ-θετος, -ον, (ἐκτίθημι), *cast out, exposed*: ποιεῖν ἔκθετα (equiv. to ἐκτιθέναι) τὰ βρέφη, Acts vii. 19. (Eur. Andr. 70; [Manetho, apoteles. 6, 52].)* — **1570**

ἐκ-καθαίρω: 1 aor. ἐξεκάθαρα [on the a cf. B. 41 (35)]; (ἐκ either i. q. *utterly* or for ἔκ τινος); in Grk. writ. fr. Hom. Il. 2, 153 down; *to cleanse out, clean thoroughly*: ἐμαυτὸν ἀπό τινος, to avoid defilement from one and so keep one's self pure, 2 Tim. ii. 21; with acc. of the thing by the removal of which something is made clean, [A. V. *purge out*], 1 Co v. 7. (For צָרַף i. q. *to cleanse*, Judg. vii. 4 var.; for בָּעַר i. q. *to take away*, Deut. xxvi. 13.) * — **1571**

ἐκ-καίω: 1 aor. pass. ἐξεκαύθην; **1.** *to burn out*. **2.** *to set on fire*. pass. *to be kindled, to burn*, (Hdt. and sqq.; often in Sept.): properly, of fire; metaph. of the fire and glow of the passions (of anger, Job iii. 17; Sir. xvi. 6, and often in Plut.); of lust, Ro. i. 27, (Alciphr. 3, 67 οὕτως ἐξεκαύθην εἰς ἔρωτα).* — **1572**

ἐκκακέω, -ῶ; [1 aor. ἐξεκάκησα]; (κακός); *to be utterly spiritless, to be wearied out, exhausted*; see ἐγκακέω [cf. W. 25]. — **1573**

ἐκ-κεντέω, -ῶ: 1 aor. ἐξεκέντησα; **1.** *to put out, dig out*: τὰ ὄμματα, Aristot. h. a. 2, 17 [p. 508b, 6]; 6, 5. **2.** *to dig through, transfix, pierce*: τινά, Rev. i. 7; ὄψονται εἰς ὃν (i. e. εἰς τοῦτον, ὃν [cf. W. 158 (150)]) ἐξεκέντησαν, Jn. xix. 37. (Polyb. 5, 56, 12; Polyaen. 5, 3, 8; for דָּקַר, Judg. ix. 54; הָרַג to kill, Num. xxii. 29. 2 Macc. xii. 6. Cf. *Fischer*, De vitiis lexicc. etc. p. 540 sq.)* — **1574**

ἐκ-κλάω: 1 aor. pass. ἐξεκλάσθην; *to break off*; *to cut off*: Ro. xi. 17, 19, 20 R G T WH (on this vs. see κλάω). (Sept. Lev. i. 17; Plat. rep. 10 p. 611 d.; Plut., Alciphr., al.) * — **1575**

ἐκ-κλείω: 1 aor. inf. ἐκκλεῖσαι; 1 aor. pass. ἐξεκλείσθην; [fr. (Hdt.) Eur. down]; *to shut out*: Gal. iv. 17 (viz. from intercourse with me and with teachers coöperating with me); i. q. *to turn out of doors*: to prevent the approach of one, pass. in Ro. iii. 27.* — **1576**

ἐκκλησία, -ας, ἡ, (fr. ἔκκλητος called out or forth, and this fr. ἐκκαλέω); prop. *a gathering of citizens called out* — **1577** *from their homes into some public place; an assembly*; so used   **1.** among the Greeks from Thuc. [cf. Hdt. 3, 142] down, *an assembly of the people* convened at the public place of council for the purpose of deliberating: Acts xix. 39.   **2.** in the Sept. often equiv. to קָהָל, *the assembly of the Israelites*, Judg. xxi. 8; 1 Chr. xxix. 1, etc., esp. when gathered for sacred purposes, Deut. xxxi. 30 (xxxii. 1); Josh. viii. 35 (ix. 8), etc.; in the N. T. thus in Acts vii. 38; Heb. ii. 12.   **3.** *any gathering or throng of men assembled by chance or tumultuously*: Acts xix. 32, 41.   **4.** in the Christian sense, **a.** *an assembly of Christians gathered for worship*: ἐν ἐκκλησίᾳ, in the religious meeting, 1 Co. xiv. 19, 35; ἐν ταῖς ἐκκλησίαις, ib. 34; συνέρχεσθαι ἐν ἐκκλησίᾳ, 1 Co. xi. 18; cf. W. § 50, 4 a.   **b.** *a company of Christians*, or of those who, hoping for eternal salvation through Jesus Christ, observe their own religious rites, hold their own religious meetings, and manage their own affairs according to regulations prescribed for the body for order's sake; **aa.** those who anywhere, in city or village, constitute such a company and are united into one body: Acts v. 11; viii. 3; 1 Co. iv. 17; vi. 4; Phil. iv. 15; 3 Jn. 6 [cf. W. 122 (116)]; with specification of place, Acts viii. 1; xi. 22; Ro. xvi. 1; 1 Co. iv. 17; vi. 4; Rev. ii. 1, 8, etc.; Θεσσαλονικέων, 1 Th. i. 1; 2 Th. i. 1; Λαοδικέων, Col. iv. 16; with gen. of the possessor, τοῦ θεοῦ (equiv. to קָהָל יְהוָה, Num. xvi. 3; xx. 4), 1 Co. xi. 22; and mention of the place, 1 Co. i. 2; 2 Co. i. 1. Plur. αἱ ἐκκλησίαι: Acts xv. 41; 1 Co. vii. 17; 2 Co. viii. 19; Rev. i. 4; iii. 6, etc.; with τοῦ θεοῦ added, 1 Th. ii. 14; 2 Th. i. 4; τοῦ Χριστοῦ, Ro. xvi. 16; with mention of the place, as τῆς Ἀσίας, Γαλατίας, etc.: 1 Co. xvi. 1, 19; 2 Co. viii. 1; Gal. i. 2; τῆς Ἰουδαίας ταῖς ἐν Χριστῷ, joined to Christ [see ἐν, I. 6 b.], i. e. Christian assemblies, in contrast with those of the Jews, Gal. i. 22; ἐκκλησίαι τῶν ἐθνῶν, gathered from the Gentiles, Ro. xvi. 4; τῶν ἁγίων, composed of the saints, 1 Co. xiv. 33. ἡ ἐκκλησία κατ' οἶκόν τινος, *the church in one's house*, i. e. the company of Christians belonging to a person's family; others less aptly understand the phrase of the Christians accustomed to meet for worship in the house of some one (for as appears from 1 Co. xiv. 23, the whole Corinthian church was accustomed to assemble in one and the same place; [but see Bp. Lghtft. on Col. iv. 15]): Ro. xvi. 5; 1 Co. xvi. 19; Col. iv. 15; Philem. 2.   The name ἡ ἐκκλησία is used even by Christ while on earth of the company of his adherents in any city or village: Mt. xviii. 17.   **bb.** the whole body of Christians scattered throughout the earth; collectively, all who worship and honor God and Christ in whatever place they may be: Mt. xvi. 18 (where perhaps the Evangelist employs τὴν ἐκκλησίαν although Christ may have said τὴν βασιλείαν μου); 1 Co. xii. 28; Eph. i. 22; iii. 10; v. 23 sqq. 27, 29, 32; Phil. iii. 6; Col. i. 18, 24; with gen. of the possessor: τοῦ κυρίου, Acts xx. 28 [R Tr mrg. WH τ. θεοῦ]; τοῦ θεοῦ, Gal. i. 13; 1 Co. xv. 9; 1 Tim. iii. 15.   **cc.** the name is transferred to the assembly of faithful Christians already dead and received into heaven: Heb. xii. 23 (on this pass. see in ἀπογράφω, b. and πρωτότοκος,

fin.). [In general, see Trench § 1, and B. D. s. v. Church, esp. Am. ed.; and for patristic usage *Soph.* Lex. s. v.]

ἐκ-κλίνω [Ro. xvi. 17 T Tr WH]; 1 aor. ἐξέκλινα; in Grk. writ. fr. Thuc. down; Sept. chiefly for סוּר and נָטָה; intrans. *to turn aside, deviate* (from the right way and course, Mal. ii. 8, [cf. Deut. v. 32]); metaph. and absol. *to turn (one's self) away* [B. 144 (126) sq.; W. 251 (236)], either from the path of rectitude, Ro. iii. 12 (Ps. xiii. (xiv.) 3); or from evil (*a malis declinare*, Cic. Tusc. 4, 6): ἀπὸ κακοῦ, 1 Pet. iii. 11; Ps. xxxiii. (xxxiv.) 15; xxxvi. (xxxvii.) 27; Prov. iii. 7); ἀπό with gen. of pers. *to turn away from, keep aloof from, one's society; to shun one*: Ro. xvi. 17, (οὕς, Ignat. ad Eph. 7, 1).*   **1578**

ἐκ-κολυμβάω, -ῶ: 1 aor. ptcp. ἐκκολυμβήσας; *to swim out of*: Acts xxvii. 42. (Eur. Hel. 1609; Diod., Dion. Hal.)*   **1579**

ἐκ-κομίζω: impf. pass. ἐξεκομιζόμην; *to carry out*; a dead man for burial (Polyb. 35, 6, 2; Plut. Agis 21; Hdian. 2, 1, 5 [2 ed. Bekk.], etc.; in Lat. *efferre*): Lk. vii. 12.*   **1580**

ἐκ-κοπή, -ῆς, ἡ, [Polyb., Plut., al.], see ἐγκοπή.   **see 1464**

ἐκ-κόπτω: fut. ἐκκόψω; 1 aor. impv. ἔκκοψον, subjunc. ἐκκόψω; [Pass., pres. ἐκκόπτομαι]; 2 aor. ἐξεκόπην; 2 fut. ἐκκοπήσομαι; *to cut out, cut off*; **a.** properly: of a tree, Mt. iii. 10; vii. 19; Lk. iii. 9; xiii. 7, 9, (Hdt. 9, 97, etc.); a hand, an eye: Mt. v. 30; xviii. 8, (τὸν ὀφθαλμόν, Dem. p. 744, (13) 17); pass. ἔκ τινος, a branch from a tree, Ro. xi. 22, 24. **b.** figuratively: τὴν ἀφορμήν, to cut off occasion, 2 Co. xi. 12, (τὴν ἐλπίδα, Job xix. 10). In 1 Pet. iii. 7 read ἐγκόπτεσθαι; see ἐγκόπτω.*   **1581**

ἐκ-κρέμαμαι (mid. of ἐκκρεμάννυμι, cf. *Bttm.* Ausf. Spr. ii. 224 sq.; [Veitch s. v. κρέμαμαι]; B. 61 (53)): [impf. ἐξεκρεμάμην]; *to hang from*: ἐξεκρέματο αὐτοῦ ἀκούων, hung upon his lips (Verg. Aen. 4, 79), Lk. xix. 48, where T WH ἐξεκρέμετο, after codd. אB, a form which T conjectures "a vulgari usu haud alienum fuisse;" [cf. B. u. s.; WH. App. p. 168]. (Plat., Philo, Plut., al.)*   **1582**

ἐκ-κρέμομαι, see the preceding word. ----------- **see 1582**

ἐκ-λαλέω, -ῶ: 1 aor. inf. ἐκλαλῆσαι; *to speak out, divulge*: τινί, foll. by ὅτι, Acts xxiii. 22. (Judith xi. 9; Demosth., Philo, Dio Cass., al.) *   **1583**

ἐκ-λάμπω: fut. ἐκλάμψω; *to shine forth*: Mt. xiii. 43; Dan. xii. 3 var. (Grk. writ. fr. Aeschyl. down.)*   **1584**

ἐκ-λανθάνω: *to cause to forget*; Mid. *to forget*; pf. ἐκλέλησμαι, foll. by gen.: Heb. xii. 5. (Hom. et sqq.) *   **see 1585 St.**

ἐκ-λέγω: pf. pass. ptcp. ἐκλελεγμένος, once in Lk. ix. 35 L mrg. T Tr WH; Mid., impf. ἐξελεγόμην (Lk. xiv. 7); 1 aor. ἐξελεξάμην; in Grk. writ. fr. Hdt. down; Sept. for בָּחַר; *to pick out, choose*; in the N. T. (exc. Lk. ix. 35, where the reading is doubtful) always mid., ἐκλέγομαι, *to pick or choose out for one's self*: τί, Lk. x. 42; xiv. 7; τινά, one from among many (of Jesus choosing his disciples), Jn. vi. 70; xiii. 18; xv. 16; Acts i. 2; ἀπό τινων, from a number of persons (Sir. xlv. 16), Lk. vi. 13; ἐκ τοῦ κόσμου, Jn. xv. 19; used of choosing one for an office, Acts vi. 5; foll. by ἔκ τινων, Acts i. 24; *to discharge some business*, Acts xv. 22, 25; ἐν ἡμῖν (al. ὑμῖν) ἐξελέξατο ὁ θεός, foll. by the acc. and inf. denoting the end,   **see 1586 St.**

God made choice among us i. e. *in our ranks*, Acts xv. 7, where formerly many, misled by the Hebr. בָּחַר בְּ (1 S. xvi. 9; 1 K. viii. 16, etc., and the Sept. of these pass.), wrongly regarded ἐν ἡμῖν as the object on which the mind of the chooser was as it were fixed; [W. § 32, 3 a.; B. 159 (138)]. Especially is G o d said ἐκλέξασθαι those whom he has judged fit to receive his favors and separated from the rest of mankind to be peculiarly his own and to be attended continually by his gracious oversight: thus of t h e I s r a e l i t e s, Acts xiii. 17 (Deut. xiv. 2, [cf. iv. 37]; 2 Macc. v. 19); of C h r i s t i a n s, as those whom he has set apart from among the irreligious multitude as dear unto himself, and whom he has rendered, through faith in Christ, citizens in the Messianic kingdom: Mk. xiii. 20; 1 Co. i. 27 sq.; with two acc. one of the object, the other of the predicate [W. § 32, 4 b.], Jas. ii. 5; τινὰ ἐν Χριστῷ, *so that the ground of the choice lies in Christ and his merits*, foll. by acc. with inf. denoting the end, Eph. i. 4. In Lk. ix. 35 L mrg. T Tr WH Jesus is called ὁ υἱὸς τοῦ θεοῦ ὁ ἐκλελεγμένος (R G L txt. ἀγαπητός), as being dear to God beyond all others and exalted by him to the preëminent dignity of Messiah; but see ἐκλεκτός, 1 b.*

1587 ἐκ-λείπω; fut. ἐκλείψω; 2 aor. ἐξέλιπον; **1.** trans. **a.** *to leave out, omit, pass by*. **b.** *to leave, quit*, (a place): τὸ ζῆν, τὸν βίον, *to die*, 2 Macc. x. 13; 3 Macc. ii. 23; Soph. Electr. 1131; Polyb. 2, 41, 2, al.; Dion. Hal. 1, 24; Luc. Macrob. 12; Alciphr. 3, 28. **2.** intrans. *to fail*; i. e. *to leave off, cease, stop*: τὰ ἔτη, Heb. i. 12 fr. Ps. ci. (cii.) 28 (where for תָּכֵם), ἡ πίστις, Lk. xxii. 32; riches, acc. to the reading ἐκλίπῃ (L txt. T Tr WH), Lk. xvi. 9 (often so in Grk. writ., and the Sept. as Jer. vii. 28; xxviii. (li.) 30). as often in classic Grk. fr. Thuc. down, it is used of the failing or eclipse of the light of the sun and the moon: τοῦ ἡλίου ἐκλιπόντος [WH ἐκλείποντος], *the sun having failed* [or *failing*], Lk. xxiii. 45 Tdf.; on this (without doubt the true) reading [see esp. WH. App. ad loc., and] cf., besides Tdf.'s note, Keim iii. 440 [Eng. trans. vi. 173] (Sir. xvii. 31 (26)). *to expire, die*; so acc. to R G L mrg. ἐκλίπητε in Lk. xvi. 9, (Tob. xiv. 11; Sap. v. 13; Sept. for גָּוַע, Gen. xxv. 8, etc.; Ps. ciii. (civ.) 29; Lam. i. 19; for מוּת, Jer. xlix. (xlii.) 17, 22. Plat. legg. 6, 759 e.; 9, 856 e.; Xen. Cyr. 8, 7, 26).*

1588 ἐκ-λεκτός, -ή, -όν, (ἐκλέγω), *picked out, chosen*; rare in Grk. writ., as Thuc. 6, 100; Plat. legg. 11 p. 938 b.; 12, 948 a., etc.; Sept. for בָּחוּר and בָּחִיר; in the N. T. **1.** *chosen b y G o d*, and **a.** *to obtain salvation through Christ* (see ἐκλέγω); hence C h r i s t i a n s are called οἱ ἐκλεκτοὶ τοῦ θεοῦ, *the chosen* or *elect of God*, [cf. W. 35 (34); 234 (219)], בְּחִירֵי יְהֹוָה, said of pious Israelites, Is. lxv. 9, 15, 23; Ps. civ. (cv.) 43, cf. Sap. iv. 15): Lk. xviii. 7; Ro. viii. 33; Col. iii. 12; Tit. i. 1; without the gen. θεοῦ, Mt. xxiv. 22, 24; Mk. xiii. 20, 22; 1 Pet. i. 1; with the addition of τοῦ Χριστοῦ, as gen. of possessor, Mt. xxiv. 31; Mk. xiii. 27 [T Tr om. gen.]; κλητοὶ καὶ ἐκλεκτοὶ κ. πιστοί, Rev. xvii. 14; γένος ἐκλεκτόν, 1 Pet. ii. 9 (fr. Is. xliii. 20, cf. Add. to Esth. viii. 40 [vi. 17, p. 64

ed. Fritz.]); ἐκλεκτοί, those who have become true partakers of the Christian salvation are contrasted with κλητοί, those who have been invited but who have not shown themselves fitted to obtain it, [al. regard the 'called' and the 'chosen' here as alike partakers of salvation, but the latter as the '*choice* ones' (see 2 below), distinguished above the former; cf. Jas. Morison or Meyer ad loc.], Mt. xx. 16 [here T W'H om. Tr br. the cl.]; xxii. 14; finally, those are called ἐκλεκτοί who are destined for salvation but have not yet been brought to it, 2 Tim. ii. 10 [but cf. Huther or Ellic. ad loc.]. **b.** The M e s s i a h is called preëminently ὁ ἐκλεκτὸς τοῦ θεοῦ, as appointed by God to the most exalted office conceivable : Lk. xxiii. 35, cf. ix. 35 L mrg. T Tr WH; cf. *Dillmann, Das Buch Henoch* [übers. u. erklärt; allgem. Einl.], p. xxiii. **c.** A n g e l s are called ἐκλεκτοί, as those whom God has chosen out from other created beings to be peculiarly associated with him, and his highest ministers in governing the universe: 1 Tim. v. 21; see ἅγιος, 1 b.; μαρτύρομαι δὲ ἐγὼ μὲν ὑμῶν τὰ ἅγια καὶ τοὺς ἱ ε ρ ο ὺ ς ἀ γ γ έ λ ο υ ς τοῦ θεοῦ, Joseph. b. j. 2, 16, 4 sub fin.; [yet al. explain by 2 Pet. ii. 4; Jude 6; cf. Ellic. on 1 Tim. l. c.]. **2.** univ. *choice, select*, i. e. the best of its kind or class, *excellent, preëminent*: applied to certain individual Christians, 2 Jn. 1, 13; with ἐν κυρίῳ added, eminent as a Christian (see ἐν, I. 6 b.), Ro. xvi. 13; of things: λίθος, 1 Pet. ii. 4, [6], (Is. xxviii. 16; 2 Esdr. v. 8; Enoch c. 8 Grk. txt., ed. Dillmann p. 82 sq.).*

1589 ἐκλογή, -ῆς, ἡ, (ἐκλέγω), *election, choice*; **a.** *the act* *of picking out, choosing*: σκεῦος ἐκλογῆς (gen. of quality; cf. W. § 34, 3 b.; [B. 161 (140 sq.)]), i. q. ἐκλεκτόν, sc. τοῦ θεοῦ, Acts ix. 15; spec. used of that act of God's free will by which before the foundation of the world he decreed his blessings to certain persons;— ἡ κατ᾽ ἐκλογὴν πρόθεσις, the decree made from choice [A. V. *the purpose acc. to election*, cf. W. 193 (182)], Ro. ix. 11 (cf. Fritzsche ad loc. p. 298 sqq.);— particularly that by which he determined to bless certain persons through Christ, Ro. xi. 28; κατ᾽ ἐκλογὴν χάριτος, according to an election which is due to grace, or a gracious election, Ro. xi. 5; with gen. of the pers. elected, 1 Th. i. 4; 2 Pet. i. 10. **b.** *the thing* or *person chosen*: i. q. ἐκλεκτοί, Ro. xi. 7. (Plat., Aristot., Polyb., Diod., Joseph., Dion. Hal., al.)*

1590 ἐκ-λύω: [Pass., pres. ἐκλύομαι;] pf. ptcp. ἐκλελυμένος; 1 aor. ἐξελύθην; 1 fut. ἐκλυθήσομαι; often in Grk. writ. fr. [Hom.], Aeschyl. down; **1.** *to loose, unloose* (cf. Germ. *auslösen*), *to set free*: τινά τινος and ἔκ τινος. **2.** *to dissolve*; metaph. *to weaken, relax, exhaust*, (Sept. Josh. x. 6; Jer. xlv. (xxxviii.) 4; Aristot. h. an. 9, 1 sub fin. [p. 610ᵃ, 27]; Joseph. antt. 8, 11, 3; 13, 8, 1). Commonly in the Pass. **a.** *to have one's strength relaxed, to be enfeebled through exhaustion, to grow weak, grow weary, be tired out*, (often so in Grk. writ.): of the body, Mt. ix. 36 Rec.; xv. 32; Mk. viii. 3; thus for יָעֵף, 1 S. xiv. 28; 2 S. xvii. 29; for רָפָה, 2 S. iv. 1 etc.; of the mind, Gal. vi. 9 (μὴ ἐκλυόμενοι *if we faint not*, sc. in well-doing). Cf. Grimm on 1 Macc. iii. 17. **b.** *to despond, become faint-hearted*: Heb. xii. 5, (Deut. xx. 3; Prov.

iii. 11); with ταῖς ψυχαῖς added, Heb. xii. 3; τοῖς σώμασι, ταῖς ψυχαῖς, Polyb. 20, 4, 7; τῇ ψυχῇ, 29, 6, 14; 40, 12, 7; cf. Grimm on 1 Macc. ix. 8; 2 Macc. iii. 24.*

1591   ἐκ-μάσσω; impf. ἐξέμασσον; 1 aor. ἐξέμαξα; *to wipe off, to wipe away*: with acc. of object and dat. of instrument, Lk. vii. 38, 44; Jn. xi. 2; xii. 3; xiii. 5. (Soph., Eur., Hippocr., Aristot., al. Sir. xii. 11; Bar. vi. (ep. Jer.) 12, 23 (13, 24).) *

1592   ἐκ-μυκτηρίζω: impf. ἐξεμυκτήριζον; *to deride by turning up the nose, to sneer at, scoff at*: τινά, Lk. xvi. 14; xxiii. 35. (For לָעַג, Ps. ii. 4; [xxxiv. (xxxv.) 16]; 2 K. xix. 21 [here the simple verb]; 1 Esdr. i. 49 Alex.; Ev. Nicod. c. 10. Prof. writ. use the simple verb (fr. μυκτήρ the nose); [cf. W. 25].) *

1593   ἐκ-νεύω: 1 aor. ἐξένευσα; **1.** *to bend to one side* (τῇ κεφαλῇ, Xen. ven. 10, 12). **2.** *to take one's self away, withdraw*: Jn. v. 13, where Chrysostom says that ἐξένευσε is equiv. to ἐξέκλινε; but others derive the form from ἐκνέω, q. v. (Sept. for סוּר, Judg. iv. 18 Alex.; פָּנָה, *to turn one's self*, Judg. xviii. 26 Alex.; 2 K. ii. 24; xxiii. 16; [add 3 Macc. iii. 22; Joseph. antt. 7, 4, 2]. In ref. auth. also transitively, *to avoid a thing*; as τὰ βέλη, Diod. 15, 87; πληγήν, ib. 17, 100.) *

see 1593   ἐκ-νέω: **1.** properly, *to swim away, escape by swimming*, (Thuc. 2, 90). **2.** *to escape, slip away secretly*, ([Pind. Ol. 13, 163]; Eur. Hipp. 470, etc.); in this sense many interpp. take ἐξένευσε in Jn. v. 13. But Jesus withdrew not to avoid danger but the admiration of the people; for the danger first arose after his withdrawal.*

1594   ἐκ-νήφω: 1 aor. ἐξένηψα; **a.** prop. *to return to one's self from drunkenness, become sober*, (Gen. ix. 24; [1 S. xxv. 37]; Joel i. 5; [Sir. xxxiv. (xxxi.) 2]; Lynceus ap. Ath. 4, 5 p. 130 b.). **b.** metaph. *to return to soberness of mind* (cf. ἀνανήφω): 1 Co. xv. 34, (Plut. Dem. 20).*

1595   ἑκούσιος, -ον, (ἑκών), *voluntary*: κατὰ ἑκούσιον, *of free will*, Philem. 14. (Num. xv. 3; καθ' ἑκουσίαν, Thuc. 8, 27 — [" The word understood in the one case appears to be τρόπον (Porphyr. de abst. 1, 9 καθ' ἑκούσιον τρόπον, comp. Eur. Med. 751 ἑκουσίῳ τρόπῳ); in the other, γνώμην so ἑκουσίᾳ [doubtful, see L. and S.], ἐξ ἑκουσίας, etc.; " cf. Lobeck, Phryn. p. 4; Bp. Lghtft. on Philem. l. c.; cf. W. 463 (432)].) *

1596   ἑκουσίως, adv., [fr. Eur. down], *voluntarily, willingly, of one's own accord*: Heb. x. 26 (ἑκ. ἁμαρτάνειν [A. V. to sin wilfully] is tacitly opposed to sins committed inconsiderately, and from ignorance or from weakness); 1 Pet. v. 2.*

1597   ἔκ-παλαι, adv., (fr. ἐκ and πάλαι, formed like ἔκτοτε [cf. W. 24 (23); 422 (393); B. 321 (275)]), *from of old; of a long time*: 2 Pet. ii. 3; iii. 5. (A later Grk. word, fr. Philo down; see *Lob.* ad Phryn. p. 45 sqq.) *

1598   ἐκ-πειράζω; fut. ἐκπειράσω; [1 aor. ἐξεπείρασα, 1 Co. x. 9ᵇ L mrg. T WH mrg.]; a word wholly biblical [put by Philo (de congr. erud. grat. §30, Mang. i. 543) for Sept. πειράζ. in quoting Deut. viii. 2]; *to prove, test, thoroughly* [A. V. tempt]: τινά, his mind and judgment, Lk. x. 25; τὸν θεόν, to put to proof God's character and power: Mt. iv. 7; Lk. iv. 12, after Deut. vi. 16, where for נִסָּה;

τὸν Χριστόν, by irreligion and immorality to test the patience or the avenging power of Christ (exalted to God's right hand), 1 Co. x. 9ᵃ [(yet L T WH Tr txt. κύριον), 9ᵇ L mrg. T WH mrg. Cf. Ps. lxxvii. (lxxviii.) 18].*

ἐκ-πέμπω: 1 aor. ἐξέπεμψα; 1 aor. pass. ptcp. ἐκπεμφθείς; *to send forth, send away*: Acts xiii. 4; xvii. 10. [From Hom. down.] *   **1599**

ἐκ-περισσῶς, adv., *exceedingly, out of measure, the more*: used of intense earnestness, Mk. xiv. 31 L T Tr WH (for Rec. ἐκ περισσοῦ); not found elsewhere. But see ὑπερεκπερισσῶς.*   **(1599α); see 1537 & 4053**

ἐκ-πετάννυμι: 1 aor. ἐξεπέτασα; *to spread out, stretch forth*: τὰς χεῖρας πρός τινα, Ro. x. 21 fr. Is. lxv. 2. (Eur., Polyb., Plut., Anthol., al.) *   **1600**

ἐκ-πηδάω, -ῶ: 1 aor. ἐξεπήδησα; *to spring out, leap forth*: εἰς τ. ὄχλον, Acts xiv. 14 G L T Tr WH. (εἰς τὸν λαόν, Judith xiv. 17; in Grk. writ. fr. [Soph. and] Hdt. down. Deut. xxxiii. 22.) *   **see 1530**

ἐκ-πίπτω; pf. ἐκπέπτωκα; 2 aor. ἐξέπεσον; 1 aor. ἐξέπεσα (Acts xii. 7 L T Tr WH; Gal. v. 4; on this aor. see [πίπτω and] ἀπέρχομαι); [fr. Hom. down]; *to fall out of, to fall down from*; **1.** prop.: αἱ ἁλύσεις ἐκ τῶν χειρῶν (see ἐκ, I. 3 [cf. W. 427 (398) and De verb. comp. etc. Pt. ii. p. 11]), Acts xii. 7 (ἐκ τῆς θήκης, Is. vi. 13; ἐκ τοῦ οὐρανοῦ, Is. xiv. 12); absol.: Mk. xiii. 25 R G; Acts xxvii. 32; Jas. i. 11; 1 Pet. i. 24; of navigators, ἐκπ. εἰς (i. e. from a straight course) *to fall off* i. e. *be driven into* [cf. Stallbaum on Plato's Phileb. p. 106 sq.; al. supply 'from deep water,' and render ἐκπ. *to be cast away*], Acts xxvii. 17, 26, 29, in this last vs. L T Tr WH have adopted ἐκπ. κατά; (often in Grk. writ., as εἰς γῆν, Eur. Hel. 409; εἰς τὸν λιμένα, Thuc. 2, 92). **2.** metaph. **a.** τινός [W. 427 (398), and De verb. comp. etc. u. s.], *to fall from a thing, to lose it*: τῆς χάριτος, Gal. v. 4; τοῦ ἰδίου στηριγμοῦ, 2 Pet. iii. 17, (τῆς πρὸς τὸν δῆμον εὐνοίας, Plut. Tib. Gracch. 21; βασιλείας, Joseph. antt. 7, 9, 2; also with prepositions, ἐκ τῶν ἐόντων, Hdt. 3, 14; ἀπὸ τῶν ἐλπίδων, Thuc. 8, 81); πόθεν, Rev. ii. 5 Rec. (ἐκεῖθεν, Ael. v. h. 4, 7). **b.** absol. *to perish*; *to fail*, (properly, *to fall from a place which one cannot keep, fall from its position*): ἡ ἀγάπη, 1 Co. xiii. 8 R G; *to fall powerless, fall to the ground, be without effect*: of the divine promise of salvation by Christ, Ro. ix. 6.*   **1601**

ἐκ-πλέω: [impf. ἐξέπλεον]; 1 aor. ἐξέπλευσα; *to sail from, sail away, depart by ship*: ἀπό with gen. of place, Acts xx. 6; εἰς with acc. of place, Acts xv. 39; xviii. 18. [Soph., Hdt., Thuc., al.] *   **1602**

ἐκ-πληρόω: pf. ἐκπεπλήρωκα; *to fill full, to fill up completely*; metaph. τὴν ἐπαγγελίαν, *to fulfil* i. e. *make good*: Acts xiii. 33 (32), as in Polyb. 1, 67, 1. [From Hdt. down.]*   **1603**

ἐκ-πλήρωσις, -εως, ἡ, *a completing, fulfilment*: τ. ἡμερῶν τ. ἁγνισμοῦ, the time when the days of purification are to end, Acts xxi. 26. [Dion. Hal., Strab., Philo, al.] *   **1604**

ἐκ-πλήσσω, -ττω: Pass., [pres. ἐκπλήσσομαι or -ττομαι (so R G Mt. xiii. 54; Tr WH Acts xiii. 12)]; impf. ἐξεπλησσόμην; 2 aor. ἐξεπλάγην; com. in Grk. fr. Hom.   **1605** down; prop. *to strike out, expel by a blow, drive out or away*; *to cast off by a blow, to drive out*; commonly, *to strike one out of self-possession, to strike with panic, shock, astonish*; Pass. *to be struck with astonishment, astonished, amazed*; absol.: Mt. xiii. 54; xix. 25; Mk. vi. 2; x. 26; Lk. ii. 48; used of the glad amazement of the wondering people, Mk. vii. 37; ἐπὶ τῇ διδαχῇ, Mt. vii. 28; xxii. 33; Mk. i. 22; xi. 18; Lk. iv. 32; Acts xiii. 12; [ἐπὶ τῇ μεγαλειότητι, Lk. ix. 43], (ἐπὶ τῷ κάλλει, Xen. Cyr. 1, 4, 27; ἐπὶ τῇ θέᾳ, Ael. v. h. 12, 41; [W. § 33, b.]; by the Greeks also with simple dat. and with acc. of the thing, as Sap. xiii. 4; 2 Macc. vii. 12). [Syn. see φοβέω, fin.] *

1606   ἐκ-πνέω: 1 aor. ἐξέπνευσα; *to breathe out, breathe out one's life, breathe one's last, expire*: Mk. xv. 37, 39; Lk. xxiii. 46, and often in Grk. writ., both without an object (fr. [Soph. Aj. 1026] Eur. down), and with βίον or ψυχήν added (fr. Aeschyl. down).*

1607   ἐκ-πορεύομαι; impf. ἐξεπορευόμην; fut. ἐκπορεύσομαι; (pass. [mid., cf. πορεύω] of ἐκπορεύω *to make to go forth, to lead out*, with fut. mid.); [fr. Xen. down]; Sept. for אָצָא; *to go forth, go out, depart*; **1.** prop.; with mention of the place whence: ἀπό, Mt. xx. 29; Mk. x. 46; ἔξω (τῆς πόλεως), Mk. xi. 19; ἐκ, Mk. xiii. 1; ἐκεῖθεν, Mk. vi. 11; παρά τινος, from one's abode, one's vicinity, Jn. xv. 26, (ἀκούσωμεν τὰ ἐκπορευόμενα παρὰ κυρίου, Ezek. xxxiii. 30); without mention of the place whence or whither, which must be learned from the context: Lk. iii. 7; Acts xxv. 4; with mention of the end to which: ἐπί τινα, Rev. xvi. 14; πρός τινα, Mt. iii. 5; Mk. i. 5; ἐκπορεύεσθαι εἰς ὁδόν, *to go forth* from some place *into the road* [or *on his way*, cf. ὁδός, 1 b.], Mk. x. 17; on Acts ix. 28 see εἰσπορεύομαι, 1 a. demons, when expelled, are said *to go out* (sc. from the human body): Mt. xvii. 21 R G L; Acts xix. 12 G L T Tr WH. [food (excrement)] *to go out* i. e. *be discharged*, Mk. vii. 19. *to come forth*, ἐκ τῶν μνημείων, of the dead who are restored to life and leave the tomb, Jn. v. 29. **2.** fig. *to come forth, to issue, to proceed*: with the adjuncts ἐκ τοῦ ἀνθρώπου, ἐκ τῆς καρδίας, ἐκ τοῦ στόματος, of feelings, affections, deeds, sayings, Mt. xv. 11, 18; Mk. vii. 15 L T Tr WH, 20; Lk. iv. 22; Eph. iv. 29; [ἔσωθεν ἐκ τῆς καρδίας, Mk. vii. 21; with ἔσωθεν alone, ibid. 23]; πᾶν ῥῆμα ἐκπορ. διὰ στόματος θεοῦ, every appointment whereby God bids a man to be nourished and preserved, Mt. iv. 4, fr. Deut. viii. 3. *to break forth*: of lightnings, flames, etc., ἔκ τινος, Rev. iv. 5; ix. 17 sq.; xi. 5. *to flow forth*: of a river (ἔκ τ.), Rev. xxii. 1. *to project*, from the mouth of one: of a sword, Rev. i. 16; xix. 15, 21 Rec. *to spread abroad*, of a rumor: foll. by εἰς, Lk. iv. 37. [Syn. cf. ἔρχομαι, fin.] *

1608   ἐκ-πορνεύω: 1 aor. ptcp. fem. ἐκπορνεύσασα; (the prefix ἐκ seems to indicate a lust that gluts itself, satisfies itself completely); Sept. often for זָנָה; *to go a whoring*, 'give one's self over to fornication' A. V.: Jude 7. Not found in prof. writ. [Test. xii. Patr. test. Dan § 5; Poll. 6, 30 (126).] *

1609   ἐκ-πτύω: 1 aor. ἐξέπτυσα; *to spit out* (Hom. Od. 5, 322, etc.); trop. *to reject, spurn, loathe*: τί, Gal. iv. 14, in which sense the Greeks used καταπτύειν, προσπτύειν,

πτύειν, and Philo παραπτύειν; cf. Kypke and Loesner [or Ellic.] on Gal. l. c.; *Lob.* ad Phryn. p. 17.*

1610   ἐκ-ριζόω, -ῶ: 1 aor. ἐξερίζωσα; Pass., 1 aor. ἐξεριζώθην; 1 fut. ἐκριζωθήσομαι; *to root out, pluck up by the roots*: τί, Mt. xiii. 29; xv. 13; Lk. xvii. 6; Jude 12. (Jer. i. 10; Zeph. ii. 4; Sir. iii. 9; [Sap. iv. 4]; 1 Macc. v. 51 [Alex.]; 2 Macc. xii. 7; [Sibyll. frag. 2, 21; al.]; Geopon.) *

1611   ἔκ-στασις, -εως, ἡ, (ἐξίστημι); **1.** univ. in Grk. writ. *any casting down of a thing from its proper place* or *state*; *displacement*, (Aristot., Plut.). **2.** *a throwing of the mind out of its normal state, alienation of mind*, whether such as makes a lunatic (διανοίας, Deut. xxviii. 28; τῶν λογισμῶν, Plut. Sol. 8), or that of the man who by some sudden emotion is transported as it were out of himself, so that in this rapt condition, although he is awake, his mind is so drawn off from all surrounding objects and wholly fixed on things divine that he sees nothing but the forms and images lying within, and thinks that he perceives with his bodily eyes and ears realities shown him by God, (Philo, quis rerum divin. heres § 53 [cf. 51; B. D. s.v. Trance; *Delitzsch*, Psychol. v. 5]): ἐπέπεσεν [Rec., al. ἐγένετο] ἐπ' αὐτὸν ἔκστασις, Acts x. 10; εἶδεν ἐν ἐκστάσει ὅραμα, Acts xi. 5; γενέσθαι ἐν ἐκστάσει, Acts xxii. 17, cf. 2 Co. xii. 2 sq. **3.** In the O. T. and the New *amazement* [cf. Longin. 1, 4; Stob. flor. tit. 104, 7], the state of one who, either owing to the importance or the novelty of an event, is thrown into a state of blended fear and wonder: εἶχεν αὐτὰς τρόμος καὶ ἔκστασις, Mk. xvi. 8; ἐξέστησαν ἐκστάσει μεγάλῃ, Mk. v. 42 (Ezek. xxvi. 16); ἔκστασις ἔλαβεν ἅπαντας, Lk. v. 26; ἐπλήσθησαν θάμβους κ. ἐκστάσεως, Acts iii. 10; (for חֲרָדָה, trembling, Gen. xxvii. 33; 1 S. xiv. 15, etc.; פַּחַד, fear, 2 Chr. xiv. 14, etc.).*

1612   ἐκ-στρέφω: pf. pass. ἐξέστραμμαι; **1.** *to turn* or *twist out, tear up*, (Hom. Il. 17, 58). **2.** *to turn inside out, invert*; trop. *to change for the worse, pervert, corrupt*, (Arstph. nub. 554; Sept. Deut. xxxii. 20): Tit. iii. 11.*

see 1856   [ἐκ-σώζω: 1 aor. ἐξέσωσα; *to save from*, either to keep or to rescue from danger (fr. Aeschyl. and Hdt. down): εἰς αἰγιαλὸν ἐκσῶσαι τὸ πλοῖον to bring the ship safe to shore, Acts xxvii. 39 WH txt.; al. ἐξῶσαι, see ἐξωθέω, and εἰ I. 7 c.*]

1613   ἐκ-ταράσσω; post-classical; *to agitate, trouble, exceedingly*: τ. πόλιν, Acts xvi. 20. (τ. δῆμον, Plut. Coriol. 19, and the like often in Dion Cass. Ps. xvii. (xviii.) 5; Sap. xvii. 3, etc.) *

1614   ἐκ-τείνω; fut. ἐκτενῶ; 1 aor. ἐξέτεινα; [fr. Aeschyl., Soph., Hdt. down]; Sept. com. for נָטָה פָּרַשׂ and שָׁלַח; *to stretch out, stretch forth*: τὴν χεῖρα (often in Sept.), Mt. viii. 3; xii. 13; xiv. 31; xxvi. 51; Mk. i. 41; iii. 5; Lk. v. 13; vi. 10; Jn. xxi. 18; Acts xxvi. 1; with the addition of ἐπί τινα, *over, towards, against one* — either to point out something, Mt. xii. 49, or to lay hold of a person in order to do him violence, Lk. xxii. 53; ἐκτ. τ. χεῖρα εἰς ἴασιν, spoken of God, Acts iv. 30; ἀγκύρας, properly, *to carry forward* [R. V. *lay out*] the cable to which the anchor is fastened, i. e. *to cast anchor*, ["the idea of extending the cables runs into that of carrying out and dropping the anchors" (Hackett); cf. B. D.

Am. ed. p. 3009ᵃ last par.], Acts xxvii. 30. [COMP.: ἐπ-, ὑπερ-εκτείνω.]*

1615   ἐκ-τελέω, -ῶ: 1 aor. inf. ἐκτελέσαι; to finish, complete: Lk. xiv. 29 sq. (From Hom. down; i. q. בְּלָה, Deut. xxxii. 45.)*

1616   ἐκ-τένεια, -ας, ἡ, (ἐκτενής), a later Grk. word, (cf. Lob. ad Phryn. p. 311); **a.** prop. extension. **b.** intentness (of mind), earnestness: ἐν ἐκτενείᾳ, earnestly, Acts xxvi. 7. (2 Macc. xiv. 38; Judith iv. 9. Cf. Grimm on 3 Macc. vi. 41 [where he refers to Cic. ad Att. 10, 17, 1].)*

1617 & 1618   ἐκτενής, -ές, (ἐκτείνω), prop. stretched out; fig. intent, earnest, assiduous: προσευχή, Acts xii. 5 R G (εὐχή, Ignat. [interpol.] ad Eph. 10; δέησίς κ. ἱκεσία, Clem. Rom. 1 Cor. 59, 2); ἀγάπη, 1 Pet. iv. 8. Neut. of the compar. ἐκτενέστερον, as adv., more intently, more earnestly, Lk. xxii. 44 [L br. WH reject the pass.]. (ἐκτενὴς φίλος, Aeschyl. suppl. 983; Polyb. 22, 5, 4; then very often fr. Philo on; cf. Lob. ad Phryn. p. 311.)*

1619   ἐκτενῶς, adv., earnestly, fervently: Acts xii. 5 L T Tr WH; ἀγαπᾶν, 1 Pet. i. 22. (Jonah iii. 8; Joel i. 14; 3 Macc. v. 9. Polyb. etc. Cf. Lob. ad Phryn. p. 311; [W. 25; 463 (431)].)*

1620   ἐκ-τίθημι: 1 aor. pass. ptcp. ἐκτεθείς; Mid., impf. ἐξετιθέμην; 2 aor. ἐξεθέμην; to place or set out, expose; **1.** prop.: an infant, Acts vii. 21; (Sap. xviii. 5; [Hdt. 1, 112]; Arstph. nub. 531; Ael. v. h. 2, 7; Lcian. de sacrif. 5, and often). **2.** Mid. metaph. to set forth, declare, expound: Acts xi. 4; τί, Acts xviii. 26; xxviii. 23; ([Aristot. passim]; Diod. 12, 18; Joseph. antt. 1, 12, 2; Athen. 7 p. 278 d.; al.).*

1621   ἐκ-τινάσσω: 1 aor. impv. ἐκτινάξατε; 1 aor. mid. ptcp. ἐκτιναξάμενος; to shake off, so that something adhering shall fall: τὸν χοῦν, Mk. vi. 11; τὸν κονιορτόν, Mt. x. 14 (where the gen. τῶν ποδῶν does not depend on the verb but on the subst. [L T WH mrg., however, insert ἐκ]); by this symbolic act a person expresses extreme contempt for another and refuses to have any further intercourse with him [B. D. Am. ed. s. v. Dust]; Mid. to shake off for (the cleansing of) one's self: τ. κονιορτὸν . . . ἐπί τινα, against one, Acts xiii. 51; τὰ ἱμάτια, dust from garments, Acts xviii. 6; [cf. B. D. u. s.; Neh. v. 13]. (to knock out, τοὺς ὀδόντας, Hom. Il. 16, 348; Plut. Cat. maj. 14.)*

1623   ἕκτος, -η, -ον, the sixth: Mt. xx. 5, etc. [From Hom. down.]

1622   ἐκτός, adv., (opp. to ἐντός, q. v.), outside, beyond; **a.** τὸ ἐκτός, the outside, exterior, with possess. gen., Mt. xxiii. 26 (cf. τὸ ἔξωθεν τοῦ ποτηρίου, 25). On the pleonastic phrase ἐκτὸς εἰ μή, see εἰ, III. 8 d. **b.** It has the force of a prep. [cf. W. § 54, 6], and is foll. by the gen. [so even in Hom.]; **α.** outside of: ἐκτὸς τοῦ σώματος out of the body, i. e. freed from it, 2 Co. xii. 2 sq. (in vs. 3 L T Tr WH read χωρίς for ἐκτός); εἶναι ἐκτὸς τοῦ σώμ. [A. V. without the body i. e.], does not pertain to the body, 1 Co. vi. 18. **β.** beyond, besides, except: Acts xxvi. 22 (where the constr. is οὐδὲν λέγων ἐκτὸς τούτων, ἅτε οἱ . . . ἐλάλησαν etc. [cf. B. 287 (246); W. 158 (149) sq.]); 1 Co. xv. 27. (Sept. for לְבַד foll. by מִן, Judg. viii. 26; , 1 K. x. 13; 2 Chr. ix. 12; xvii. 19.)*

ἐκ-τρέπω: Pass., [pres. ἐκτρέπομαι]; 2 aor. ἐξετράπην; 2 fut. ἐκτραπήσομαι; **1.** to turn or twist out; pass. in a medical sense, in a fig. of the limbs: ἵνα μὴ τὸ χωλὸν ἐκτραπῇ, lest it be wrenched out of (its proper) place, dislocated, [R. V. mrg. put out of joint], (see exx. of this use fr. med. writ. in Steph. Thesaur. iii. col. 607 d.), i. e. lest he who is weak in a state of grace fall therefrom, Heb. xii. 13 [but Lünem., Delitzsch, al., still adhere to the meaning turn aside, go astray; cf. A. V., R. V. txt.]. **2.** to turn off or aside; pass. in a mid. sense [cf. B. 192 (166 sq.)], to turn one's self aside, to be turned aside: (intrans.) to turn aside; Hesych.: ἐξετράπησαν· ἐξέκλιναν, (τῆς ὁδοῦ, Lcian. dial. deor. 25, 2; Ael. v. h. 14, 49 [48]; ἔξω τῆς ὁδοῦ, Arr. exp. Al. 3, 21, 7 [4]; absol. Xen. an. 4, 5, 15; Arstph. Plut. 837; with mention of the place to which, Hdt. 6, 34; Plat. Soph. p. 222 a.; al.); figuratively: εἰς ματαιολογίαν, 1 Tim. i. 6; ἐπὶ τοὺς μύθους, 2 Tim. iv. 4; ὀπίσω τινός, to turn away from one in order to follow another, 1 Tim. v. 15, (εἰς ἀδίκους πράξεις, Joseph. antt. 8, 10, 2). with acc. to turn away from, to shun a thing, to avoid meeting or associating with one: τὰς κενοφωνίας, 1 Tim. vi. 20, (τὸν ἔλεγχον, Polyb. 35, 4, 14; Γάλλους ἐκτρέπεσθαι καὶ σύνοδον φεύγειν τὴν μετ' αὐτῶν, Joseph. antt. 4, 8, 40).*

ἐκ-τρέφω; fr. Aeschyl. down; **1.** to nourish up to maturity; then univ. to nourish: τὴν ἑαυτοῦ σάρκα, Eph. v. 29. **2.** to nurture, bring up: τὰ τέκνα, Eph. vi. 4.*   **1625**

[ἔκτρομος, adj., (cf. ἔκφοβος), trembling exceedingly, exceedingly terrified: Heb. xii. 21 Tr mrg. WH mrg., after codd. Sin. and Clarom. (al. ἔντρομος, q. v.). Not found elsewhere.*]   **see 1630**

ἔκ-τρωμα, -τος, τό, (ἐκτιτρώσκω to cause to or to suffer abortion; like ἔκβρωμα fr. ἐκβιβρώσκω), an abortion, abortive birth; an untimely birth: 1 Co. xv. 8, where Paul likens himself to an ἔκτρωμα, and in vs. 9 explains in what sense: that he is as inferior to the rest of the apostles as an immature birth comes short of a mature one, and is no more worthy of the name of an apostle than an abortion is of the name of a child. (Num. xii. 12; Eccl. vi. 3; Job iii. 16; in Grk. first used by Aristot. de gen. an. 4, 5, 4 [p. 773ᵇ, 18]; but, as Phrynichus shows, p. 208 sq. ed. Lob., [288 sq. ed. Rutherford], ἄμβλωμα and ἐξάμβλωμα are preferable; [Huxtable in "Expositor" for Apr. 1882 p. 277 sqq.; Bp. Lghtft. Ignat. ad Rom. 9 p. 230 sq.].)*   **1626**

ἐκ-φέρω; fut. ἐξοίσω; 1 aor. ἐξήνεγκα; 2 aor. ἐξήνεγκον; **1.** to carry out, to bear forth: τινά, Acts v. 15; the dead for burial, Acts v. 6, 9 sq. (often so in Grk. writ. fr. Hom. Il. 24, 786 down; see ἐκκομίζω); τί, Lk. xv. 22; 1 Tim. vi. 7. **2.** to (bring i. e.) lead out: τινά, Mk. viii. 23 T Tr txt. WH. **3.** to bring forth i. e. produce: of the earth bearing plants, Heb. vi. 8 [cf. W. § 45, 6 a.]; (Hdt. 1, 193; Xen. oec. 16, 5; Ael. v. h. 3, 18 and often; Sept., Gen. i. 12; Hag. i. 11; Cant. ii. 13).*   **1627**

ἐκ-φεύγω: fut. ἐκφεύξομαι; pf. ἐκπέφευγα; 2 aor. ἐξέφυγον; [fr. Hom. down]; to flee out of, flee away; **a.** to seek safety in flight; absol. Acts xvi. 27; ἐκ τοῦ οἴκου, Acts xix. 16. **b.** to escape: 1 Th. v. 3; Heb. ii. 3; τί, Lk. xxi. 36; Ro. ii. 3; τινά, Heb. xii. 25 L T Tr WH;   **1628** [τὰς χεῖράς τινος, 2 Co. xi. 33. Cf. W. § 52, 4, 4 ; B. 146 (128) sq.].*

1629 ἐκ-φοβέω, -ῶ ; to frighten away, to terrify ; to throw into violent fright : τινά, 2 Co. x. 9. (Deut. xxviii. 26 ; Zeph. iii. 13, etc. ; Thuc., Plat., al.) *

1630 ἔκφοβος, -ον, stricken with fear or terror, exceedingly frightened, terrified : Mk. ix. 6 ; Heb. xii. 21 fr. Deut. ix. 19. (Aristot. physiogn. 6 [p. 812ᵇ, 29] ; Plut. Fab. 6.) *

1631 ἐκ-φύω ; 2 aor. pass. ἐξεφύην (W. 90 (86) ; B. 68 (60) ; Krüger § 40, s. v. φύω ; [Veitch ibid.]) ; [fr. Hom. down] ; to generate or produce from ; to cause to grow out : ὅταν ὁ κλάδος . . . τὰ φύλλα ἐκφύῃ (subj. pres.), when the branch has become tender and puts forth leaves, R (not Rˢᵗ) G T WH in Mt. xxiv. 32 and Mk. xiii. 28 ; [al., retaining the same accentuation, regard it as 2 aor. act. subj. intrans., with τὰ φύλ. as subject ; but against the change of subject see Meyer or Weiss]. But Fritzsche, Lchm., Treg., al. have with reason restored [after Erasmus] ἐκφυῇ (2 aor. pass. subj.), which Grsb. had approved : when the leaves have grown out,—so that τὰ φύλλα is the subject.*

1632 ἐκ-χέω and (a form censured by the grammarians, see Lob. ad Phryn. p. 726) ἐκχύνω (whence pres. pass. ptcp. ἐκχυνόμενος and, in L T Tr WH after the Aeolic form, ἐκχυννόμενος [cf. B. 69 (61) ; W. § 2, 1 d. ; Tdf. Proleg. p. 79] : Mt. xxiii. 35 ; xxvi. 28 ; Mk. xiv. 24 ; Lk. xi. 50 [where Tr txt. WH txt. ἐκκεχυμένον for ἐκχυννόμενον] ; xxii. 20 [WH reject the pass.]) ; impv. plur. ἐκχέετε (Rev. xvi. 1 L T WH ; on which uncontr. form cf. Bttm. Gram. p. 196 [p. 174 Robinson's trans.] ; B. 44 (38) ; [some would make it a 2 aor., see WH. App. p. 165]) ; fut. ἐκχεῶ (Acts ii. 17 sq. ; Ex. xxix. 12), for which the earlier Greek used ἐκχεύσω (W. 77 (74) ; [cf. 85 (82) ; esp. B. 68 (60)]) ; 1 aor. ἐξέχεα, 3 pers. sing. ἐξέχεε ([whereas the 3 sing. of the impf. is c o n t r. -έχεε -έχει, cf. Rutherford, New Phryn. p. 299 sq.] ; cf. Bttm. Gram. p. 196 note *** [Eng. trans. u. s. note †]), inf. ἐκχέαι (Ro. iii. 15 ; Is. lix. 7 ; Ezek. ix. 8) ; Pass., [pres. ἐκχεῖται, Mk. ii. 22 R G L Tr mrg. br. ; impf. 3 pers. ἐξεχεῖτο, Acts xxii. 20 R G, ἐξεχύννετο L T Tr WH] ; pf. ἐκκέχυμαι ; 1 aor. ἐξεχύθην ; 1 fut. ἐκχυθήσομαι (see B. 69 (60) sq.) ; [fr. Hom. down] ; Sept. for שָׁפַךְ ; to pour out ; **a.** prop. : φιάλην, by meton. of the container for the contained, Rev. xvi. 1–4, 8, 10, 12, 17 ; of wine, which when the vessel is burst runs out and is lost, Mt. ix. 17 ; Mk. ii. 22 [R G L Tr mrg. in br.] ; Lk. v. 37 ; used of other things usually guarded with care which are poured forth or cast out : of money, Jn. ii. 15 ; ἐξεχύθη τὰ σπλάγχνα, of the ruptured body of a man, Acts i. 18 (ἐξεχύθη ἡ κοιλία αὐτοῦ εἰς τ. γῆν, of a man thrust through with a sword, 2 S. xx. 10). The phrase αἷμα ἐκχεῖν or ἐκχύν(ν)ειν is freq. used of bloodshed : [Mt. xxiii. 35 ; Lk. xi. 50 ; Acts xxii. 20 ; Ro. iii. 15 ; Rev. xvi. 6ᵃ (where Tdf. αἵματα)] ; see αἷμα, 2 a. **b.** metaph. i. q. to bestow or distribute largely (cf. Fritzsche on Tob. iv. 17 and Sir. i. 8) : τὸ πνεῦμα τὸ ἅγιον or ἀπὸ τοῦ πνεύματος, i. e. the abundant bestowal of the Holy Spirit, Acts ii. 33 fr. Joel ii. 28, 29 (iii. 1, 2) ; ἐπί τινα, Acts ii. 17 sq. ; x. 45 ; Tit. iii. 6 ; ἡ ἀγάπη τοῦ θεοῦ ἐκκέχυται ἐν ταῖς καρδίαις

ἡμῶν διὰ πν. ἁγίου, the Holy Spirit gives our souls a rich sense of the greatness of God's love for us, Ro. v. 5 ; (ὀργην, Sir. xxxiii. (xxxvi.) 8, [cf. xvi. 11]). The pass., like the Lat. effundor, me effundo, is used of those who give themselves up to a thing, rush headlong into it, (γέλωτι, Alciphr. ; εἰς ἑταίρας, Polyb. 32, 11, 4) : absol. τῇ πλάνῃ τοῦ Βαλαὰμ μισθοῦ ἐξεχύθησαν, led astray by the hire of Balaam (i. e. by the same love of reward as Balaam) they gave themselves up, sc. to wickedness, Jude 11, (so ἐκχυθῆναι in Arstph. vesp. 1469 is used absol. of one giving himself up to joy. The passage in Jude is generally explained thus : "for hire they gave themselves up to [R. V. ran riotously in] the error of Balaam" ; cf. W. 206 (194) [and De Wette (ed. Brückner) ad loc.]).*

ἐκ-χύνω, and (L T Tr WH) ἐκχύννω, see ἐκχέω. **see 1632** [Comp. : ὑπερ- εκχύνω.]

ἐκ-χωρέω, -ῶ ; [fr. Soph. and Hdt. on] ; to depart from ; **1633** to remove from in the sense of fleeing from : Lk. xxi. 21. (For בָּרַח, Am. vii. 12.) *

ἐκ-ψύχω : 1 aor. ἐξέψυξα ; to expire, to breathe out one's **1634** life (see ἐκπνέω) : Acts v. 5, 10 ; xii. 23. (Hippocr., Jambl.) *

ἑκών, -οῦσα, -όν, unforced, voluntary, willing, of one's **1635** own will, of one's own accord : Ro. viii. 20 ; 1 Co. ix. 17. [From Hom. down.]*

ἐλαία, -ας, ἡ, [fr. Hom. down], Sept. for זַיִת ; **1.** an **1636** olive tree : Ro. xi. 17, 24 ; plur. Rev. xi. 4. τὸ ὄρος τῶν ἐλαιῶν (for הַר הַזֵּיתִים, Zech. xiv. 4), the Mount of Olives, so called from the multitude of olive-trees which grew upon it, distant from Jerusalem (Joseph. antt. 20, 8, 6) five stadia eastward (cf. Win. RWB. s. v. Oelberg ; Arnold in Herzog x. p. 549 sqq. ; Furrer in Schenkel iv. 354 sq. ; [Grove and Porter in BB.DD.]) : Mt. xxi. **1** ; xxiv. 3 ; xxvi. 30 ; Mk. xi. 1 ; xiii. 3 ; xiv. 26 ; Lk. xix. 37 ; xxii. 39 ; Jn. viii. 1 Rec. ; (on Lk. xix. 29 ; xxi. 37, see ἐλαιών). **2.** an olive, the fruit of the olive-tree : Jas. iii. 12.*

ἔλαιον, -ου, τό, [fr. Hom. down], Sept. chiefly for שֶׁמֶן, **1637** also for יִצְהָר ; olive-oil : used for feeding lamps, Mt. xxv. 3 sq. 8 ; for healing the sick, Mk. vi. 13 ; Lk. x. 34 ; Jas. v. 14 ; for anointing the head and body at feasts (Athen. 15, c. 11) [cf. s. v. μύρον], Lk. vii. 46 ; Heb. i. 9 (on which pass. see ἀγαλλίασις) ; mentioned among articles of commerce, Lk. xvi. 6 ; Rev. vi. 6 ; xviii. 13. Cf. Win. RWB. s. v. Oel ; Furrer in Schenkel iv. 354 ; Schnedermann, Die bibl. Symbolik des Oelbaumes u. d. Oeles, in the Zeitschr. f. d. luth. Theol. for 1874, p. 4 sqq. ; [B. D. s. v. Oil, II. 4 ; and Mey. ed. Weiss on Mk. vi. 13].*

ἐλαιών, -ῶνος, ὁ, (the ending ών in derivative nouns in- **1638** dicating a place set with trees of the kind designated by the primitive, as δαφνών, ἰτεών, δρυμών, κεδρών, cf. Bttm. Ausf. Spr. ii. p. 422 sqq. ; Kühner i. p. 711 ; [Jelf § 335 d.]) ; an olive-orchard, a place planted with olive trees, i. e. the Mount of Olives [A.V. Olivet] (see ἐλαία, 1) : Acts i. 12 (διὰ τοῦ ἐλαιῶνος ὄρους, Joseph. antt. 7, 9, 2). In Lk. xix. 29 ; xxi. 37 also we should write τὸ ὄρος τὸ καλούμενον ἐλαιών (so L T Tr, [but WH with R G -ῶν]) ; likewise in Joseph. antt. 20, 8, 6 πρὸς ὄρος τὸ προσαγορευόμενον ἐλαιών; b. j. 2, 13, 5 and 5, 2, 3 εἰς (κατὰ) ἐλαιῶν καλούμενον ὄρος; 6, 2, 8 κατὰ τὸ ἐλαιῶν ὄρος; [but in Joseph. ll. cc. Bekker edits -ῶν]. Cf. Fritzsche on Mk. p. 794 sq.; B. 22 (19 sq.); W. 182 (171) n. 1; [but see WH. App. p. 158ᵇ]. (The Sept. sometimes render זַיִת freely by ἐλαιών, as Ex. xxiii. 11; Deut. vi. 11; 1 S. viii. 14, etc.; not found in Grk. writ.) *

1639   'Ελαμίτης (T WH 'Ελαμείτης, [see s. v. ει, ι]), -ου, ὁ, an Elamite, i. e. an inhabitant of the province of Elymais, a region stretching southwards to the Persian Gulf, but the boundaries of which are variously given (cf. Win. RWB. s. v. Elam; Vaihinger in Herzog iii. p. 747 sqq.; Dillmann in Schenkel ii. p. 91 sq.; Schrader in Riehm p. 358 sq.; Grimm on 1 Macc. vi. 1; [BB.DD. s. vv. Elam, Elamites]): Acts ii. 9. (Is. xxi. 2; in Grk. writ. 'Ελυμαῖος, and so Judith i. 6.) *

1640   ἐλάσσων [in Jn., Ro.] or -ττων [in Heb., 1 Tim.; cf. B. 7], -ον, (compar. of the Epic adj. ἐλαχύς equiv. to μικρός, [fr. Hom. down], less, — either in age (younger), Ro. ix. 12; or in rank, Heb. vii. 7; or in excellence, worse (opp. to καλός), Jn. ii. 10. Neuter ἔλαττον, adverbially, less [sc. than etc., A. V. under; cf. W. 239 (225); 595 sq. (554); B. 127 sq. (112)]: 1 Tim. v. 9.*

1641   ἐλαττονέω [B. 7], -ῶ: 1 aor. ἠλαττόνησα; (ἔλαττον); not found in prof. auth. [yet see Aristot. de plant. 2, 3 p. 825ᵃ, 23]; to be less, inferior, (in possessions): 2 Co. viii. 15 fr. Ex. xvi. 18. (Prov. xi. 24; Sir. xix. (5) 6; also transitively, to make less, diminish: Gen. viii. 3; Prov. xiv. 34; 2 Macc. xiii. 19, etc.) *

1642   ἐλαττόω [B. 7], -ῶ: 1 aor. ἠλάττωσα; Pass., [pres. ἐλαττοῦμαι]; pf. ptcp. ἠλαττωμένος; (ἐλάττων); to make less or inferior: τινά, in dignity, Heb. ii. 7; Pass. to be made less or inferior: in dignity, Heb. ii. 9; to decrease (opp. to αὐξάνω), in authority and popularity, Jn. iii. 30. (Many times in Sept.; in Grk. writ. fr. Thuc. on.) *

1643   ἐλαύνω; pf. ptcp. ἐληλακώς; Pass., [pres. ἐλαύνομαι]; impf. ἠλαυνόμην; to drive: of the wind driving ships or clouds, Jas. iii. 4; 2 Pet. ii. 17; of sailors propelling a vessel by oars, to row, Mk. vi. 48; to be carried in a ship, to sail, Jn. vi. 19, (often so in Grk. writ. fr. Hom. down; often also with νῆα or ναῦν added); of demons driving to some place the men whom they possess, Lk. viii. 29. [COMP.: ἀπ-, συν-ελαύνω.] *

1644   ἐλαφρία, -ας, ἡ, (ἐλαφρός), lightness; used of levity and fickleness of mind, 2 Co. i. 17; a later word, cf. Lob. ad Phryn. p. 343.*

1645   ἐλαφρός, -ά, -όν, light in weight, quick, agile; a light φορτίον is used fig. concerning the commandments of Jesus, easy to be kept, Mt. xi. 30; neut. τὸ ἐλαφρόν, substantively, the lightness: τῆς θλίψεως [A. V. our light affliction], 2 Co. iv. 17. (From Hom. down.) *

1646   ἐλάχιστος, -η, -ον, (superl. of the adj. μικρός, but coming fr. ἐλαχύς, [(Hom. h. Merc. 573), Hdt. down], smallest, least, — whether in size: Jas. iii. 4; in amount: of the management of affairs, πιστὸς ἐν ἐλαχίστῳ, Lk. xvi. 10 (opp. to ἐν πολλῷ); xix. 17; ἐν ἐλαχίστῳ ἄδικος, Lk. xvi. 10; in importance: what is of the least moment, 1 Co. vi. 2; in authority: of commandments, Mt. v. 19;

in the estimation of men: of persons, Mt. xxv. 40, 45; in rank and excellence: of persons, Mt. v. 19; 1 Co. xv. 9; of a town, Mt. ii. 6. οὐδὲ [R G οὔτε] ἐλάχιστον, not even a very small thing, Lk. xii. 26; ἐμοὶ εἰς ἐλάχιστόν ἐστι (see εἰμί, V. 2 c.), 1 Co. iv. 3.*

1647   ἐλαχιστότερος, -α, -ον, (compar. formed fr. the superl. ἐλάχιστος; there is also a superl. ἐλαχιστότατος; "it is well known that this kind of double comparison is common in the poets; but in prose, it is regarded as faulty." Lob. ad Phryn. p. 136; cf. W. § 11, 2 b., [also 27 (26); B. 28 (25)]), less than the least, lower than the lowest: Eph. iii. 8.*

ἐλάω, see ἐλαύνω.

1648   'Ελεάζαρ, (אֶלְעָזָר whom God helps), ὁ, indecl., Eleazar, one of the ancestors of Christ: Mt. i. 15.*

see 1653   ἐλεάω, adopted for the more com. ἐλεέω (q. v.) by L T Tr WH in Ro. ix. 16 and Jude 23, [also by WH Tr mrg. in 22]; (Prov. xxi. 26 cod. Vat.; 4 Macc. ix. 3 var.; Clem. Rom. 1 Cor. 13, 2; Polyc. ad Philip. 2, 2). Cf. W. 85 (82); B. 57 (50); [Mullach p. 252; WH. App. p. 166; Tdf. Proleg. p. 122].*

see 1650   ἐλεγμός, -οῦ, ὁ, (ἐλέγχω), correction, reproof, censure: 2 Tim. iii. 16 L T Tr WH for R G ἔλεγχον. (Sir. xxi. 6; xxxv. (xxxii.) 17, etc.; for תּוֹכֵחָה chastisement, punishment, 2 K. xix. 3; Ps. cxlix. 7; [Is. xxxvii. 3; etc.]. Not found in prof. writ.)*

1649   ἔλεγξις, -εως, ἡ, (ἐλέγχω, q. v.), refutation, rebuke; (Vulg. correptio; Augustine, convictio): ἔλεγξιν ἔσχεν ἰδίας παρανομίας, he was rebuked for his own transgression, 2 Pet. ii. 16. (Philostr. vit. Apoll. 2, 22 [p. 74 ed. Olear.]; Sept., Job xxi. 4; xxiii. 2, for שִׂיחַ complaint; [Protevangel. Jacob. 16, 1 τὸ ὕδωρ τῆς ἐλέγξεως κυρίου (Sept. Num. v. 18 τὸ ὕδωρ τοῦ ἐλεγμοῦ)].) *

1650   ἔλεγχος, -ου, ὁ, (ἐλέγχω); 1. a proof, that by which a thing is proved or tested, (τὸ πρᾶγμα τὸν ἔλεγχον δώσει, Dem. 44, 15 [i. e. in Phil. 1, 15]; τῆς εὐψυχίας, Eur. Herc. fur. 162; ἐνθάδ' ὁ ἔλεγχος τοῦ πράγματος, Epict. diss. 3, 10, 11; al.): τῶν [or rather, πραγμάτων] οὐ βλεπομένων, that by which invisible things are proved (and we are convinced of their reality), Heb. xi. 1 (Vulg. argumentum non apparentium [Tdf. rerum arg. non parentum]); [al. take the word here (in accordance with the preceding ὑπόστασις, q. v.) of the inward result of proving viz. a conviction; see Lünem. ad loc.]. 2. conviction (Augustine, convictio): πρὸς ἔλεγχον, for convicting one of his sinfulness, 2 Tim. iii. 16 R G. (Eur., Plat., Dem., al.; Sept. chiefly for תּוֹכֵחַ.

1651   ἐλέγχω; fut. ἐλέγξω; 1 aor. inf. ἐλέγξαι, impv. ἔλεγξον; [Pass., pres. ἐλέγχομαι; 1 aor. ἐλέγχθην]; Sept. for הוֹכִיחַ; 1. to convict, refute, confute, generally with a suggestion of the shame of the person convicted, [" ἐλέγχειν hat eigentlich nicht die Bedeutung 'tadeln, schmähen, zurechtweisen,' welche ihm die Lexika zuschreiben, sondern bedeutet nichts als überführen" (Schmidt ch. iv. § 12)]: τινά, of crime, fault, or error; of sin, 1 Co. xiv. 24; ἐλεγχόμενοι ὑπὸ τοῦ νόμου ὡς παραβάται, Jas. ii. 9; ὑπὸ τῆς συνειδήσεως, Jn. viii. 9 R G (Philo, opp. ii. p. 649 [ed. Mang., vi. 203 ed. Richter, frag. περὶ ἀναστάσεως καὶ κρίσεως] τὸ συνειδὸς ἔλεγχος ἀδέκαστος καὶ πάντων ἀψευδέστατος); foll. by περί with gen. of thing, Jn. viii. 46; xvi. 8, and L T Tr WH in Jude 15, (Arstph. Plut. 574); contextually, *by conviction to bring to light, to expose*: τί, Jn. iii. 20, cf. 21; Eph. v. 11, 13, (Arstph. eccl. 485; τὰ κρυπτά, Artem. oneir. 1, 68; ἐπιστάμενος, ὡς εἰ καὶ λάθοι ἡ ἐπιβουλὴ κ. μὴ ἐλεγχθείη, Hdian. 3, 12, 11 [4 ed. Bekk.]; al.); used of the exposure and confutation of false teachers of Christianity, Tit. i. 9, 13; ταῦτα ἔλεγχε, utter these things by way of refutation, Tit. ii. 15. **2.** *to find fault with, correct*; **a.** by word; *to reprehend severely, chide, admonish, reprove*: Jude 22 L T Tr txt.; 1 Tim. v. 20; 2 Tim. iv. 2; τινὰ περί τινος, Lk. iii. 19; contextually, *to call to account, show one his fault, demand an explanation*: τινά, from some one, Mt. xviii. 15. **b.** by deed; *to chasten, punish*, (acc. to the trans. of the Hebr. הוֹכִיחַ, Ps. xxxvii. (xxxviii.) 2, etc.; Sap. xii. 2): Heb. xii. 5 (fr. Prov. iii. 11); Rev. iii. 19. [On this word cf. *J. C. Hare*, The Mission of the Comforter, note L; Trench § iv. Comp.: ἐξ-, δια-κατ-(-μαι).] *

1652   ἐλεεινός, -ή, -όν, (ἔλεος), fr. Hom. down, *to be pitied, miserable*: Rev. iii. 17, [where WH have adopted the Attic form ἐλεινός, see their App. p. 145]; compar. 1 Co. xv. 19. [Cf. W. 99 (94).] *

1653   ἐλεέω, -ῶ; fut. ἐλεήσω; 1 aor. ἠλέησα; Pass., 1 aor. ἠλεήθην; 1 fut. ἐλεηθήσομαι; pf. ptcp. ἠλεημένος; (ἔλεος) fr. Hom. down; Sept. most freq. for חָנַן to be gracious, also for רָחַם to have mercy; several times for חָמַל to spare, and נָחַם to console; *to have mercy on*: τινά [W. § 32, 1 b. a.], *to succor* one afflicted or seeking aid, Mt. ix. 27; xv. 22; xvii. 15; xviii. 33; xx. 30 sq.; Mk. v. 19 [here, by zeugma (W. § 66, 2 e, the ὅσα is brought over with an adverbial force (W. 463 (431 sq.), *how*]; x. 47 sq.; Lk. xvi. 24; xvii. 13; xviii. 38 sq.; Phil. ii. 27; Jude 22 Rec.; absol. *to succor the afflicted, to bring help to the wretched*, [A. V. *to show mercy*], Ro. xii. 8; pass. *to experience* [A. V. *obtain*] *mercy*, Mt. v. 7. Spec. of God granting even to the u n w o r t h y favor, benefits, opportunities, and particularly salvation by Christ: Ro. ix. 15,16 R G (see ἐλεάω), 18; xi. 32; pass., Ro. xi. 30 sq.; 1 Co. vii. 25; 2 Co. iv. 1; 1 Tim. i. 13, 16; 1 Pet. ii. 10.*

[Syn. ἐ λ ε έ ω, ο ἰ κ τ ε ί ρ ω: ἐλ. to feel sympathy with the misery of another, esp. such sympathy as manifests itself in act, less freq. in word; whereas οἰκτ. denotes the inward feeling of compassion which abides in the heart. A criminal begs ἔλεος of his judge; but h o p e l e s s suffering is often the object of οἰκτιρμός. Schmidt ch. 143. On the other hand, Fritzsche (Com. on Rom. vol. ii. p. 315) makes οἰκτ. and its derivatives the stronger terms: ἐλ. the generic word for the feeling excited by another's misery; οἰκτ. the same, esp. when it calls (or is suited to call) out exclamations and tears.]

1654   ἐλεημοσύνη, -ης, ἡ, (ἐλεήμων), Sept. for חֶסֶד and צְדָקָה (see δικαιοσύνη, 1 b.), **1.** *mercy, pity* (Callim. in Del. 152; Is. xxxviii. 18; Sir. xvii. 22 (24), etc.), esp. *as exhibited in giving alms, charity*: Mt. vi. 4; ποιεῖν ἐλεημοσύνην, to practise the virtue of mercy or beneficence, to show one's compassion, [A. V. *do alms*], (cf. the similar phrases δικαιοσύνην, ἀλήθειαν, etc. ποιεῖν, Mt. vi. 1 Rec.,

2, 3, (Sir. vii. 10; Tob. iv. 7; xii. 8, etc.; for עָשָׂה חֶסֶד Gen. xlvii. 29); ἐλεημοσύνας, acts of beneficence, benefactions [cf. W. 176 (166); B. 77 (67)], Acts x. 2; εἰς τινα, Acts xxiv. 17.   Hence **2.** *the benefaction itself, a donation to the poor, alms*, (the Germ. *Almosen* [and the Eng. *alms*] being [alike] a corruption of the Grk. word): ἐλεημοσύνην διδόναι [(Diog. Laërt. 5, 17)], Lk. xi. 41; xii. 33; αἰτεῖν, Acts iii. 2; λαμβάνειν, ib. 3; πρὸς τὴν ἐλεημοσ. for (the purpose of asking) alms, Acts iii. 10; plur., Acts ix. 36; x. 4, 31.*

ἐλεήμων, -ον, *merciful*: Mt. v. 7; Heb. ii. 17. [From   **1655** Hom. Od. 5, 191 on; Sept.] *

[ἐλεινός, see ἐλεεινός.] ------------------ see 1652

ἔλεος, -ου, ὁ, *mercy*: that of G o d towards sinners, Tit.   **1656** iii. 5; ἔλεον λαμβάνειν, to receive i. e. experience, Heb. iv. 16; that of m e n: readiness to help those in trouble, Mt. ix. 13 and xii. 7 (fr. Hos. vi. 6); Mt. xxiii. 23. But in all these pass. L T Tr WH have adopted the neut. form τὸ ἔλεος (q. v.), much more com. in Hellenistic writ. than the masc. ὁ ἔλεος, which is the only form in classic Grk. [Soph. (Lex. s. v.) notes τὸ ἔλ. in Polyb. 1, 88, 2; and Pape in Diod. Sic. 3, 18 var.]. The Grk. Mss. of the O. T. also freq. waver between the two forms. Cf. [WH. App. p. 158]; W. 66 (64); B. 22 (20).*

ἔλεος, -ους, τό, (a form more common in Hellenistic   **1656** Grk. than the classic ὁ ἔλεος, q. v.), *mercy; kindness or good will towards the miserable and afflicted, joined with a desire to relieve them*; **1.** of m e n towards men: Mt. ix. 13; xii. 7; xxiii. 23, (in these three pass. acc. to L T Tr WH); Jas. ii. 13; iii. 17; ποιεῖν ἔλεος, to exercise the virtue of mercy, show one's self merciful, Jas. ii. 13; with the addition of μετά τινος (in imitation of the very com. Hebr. phrase עָשָׂה חֶסֶד עִם פ׳, Gen. xxi. 23; xxiv. 12; Judg. i. 24, etc.; cf. *Thiersch*, De Pentateuchi vers. Alex. p. 147; [W. 33 (32); 376 (353)]), to show, afford, mercy to one, Lk. x. 37. **2.** of G o d towards men; **a.** univ.: Lk. i. 50; in benedictions: Gal. vi. 16; 1 Tim. i. 2; 2 Tim. i. 2; [(prob.) Tit. i. 4 R L]; 2 Jn. 3; Jude 2. ἐμεγάλυνε κύριος τὸ ἔλεος αὐτοῦ μετ' αὐτῆς, magnified his mercy towards her, i. e. showed distinguished mercy to her, (after the Hebr., see Gen. xix. 19), Lk. i. 58. **b.** esp. the mercy and clemency of God in providing and offering to men salvation by Christ: Lk. i. 54; Ro. xv. 9; Eph. ii. 4; [Tit. iii. 5 L T Tr WH; Heb. iv. 16 L T Tr WH]; 1 Pet. i. 3; σπλάγχνα ἐλέους (gen. of quality [cf. W. 611 (568)]), wherein mercy dwells, — as we should say, *the heart of mercy*, Lk. i. 78; ποιεῖν ἔλεος μετά τινος (see 1 above), Lk. i. 72; σκεύη ἐλέους, vessels (fitted for the reception) of mercy, i. e. men whom God has made fit to obtain salvation through Christ, Ro. ix. 23; τῷ ὑμετέρῳ ἐλέει, by (in consequence of, moved by) the mercy shown you in your conversion to Christ, Ro. xi. 31 [cf. W. § 22, 7 (cf. § 61, 3 a.); B. 157 (137)]. **3.** the mercy of C h r i s t, whereby at his return to judgment he will bless true Christians with eternal life: Jude 21; [2 Tim. i. 16, 18, (on the repetition of κύριος in 18 cf. Gen. xix. 24; 1 S. iii. 21; xv. 22; 2 Chr. vii. 2; Gen. i. 27, etc. W. § 22, 2)]; but Prof.

Grimm understands κύριος here as referring to God; see κύριος, c. a.]. [Cf. Trench § xlvii.; and see ἐλεέω fin.]*

1657   **ἐλευθερία**, -ας, ἡ, (ἐλεύθερος), *liberty*, [fr. Pind., Hdt. down]; in the N. T. **a.** liberty to do or to omit things having no relation to salvation, 1 Co. x. 29; from the yoke of the Mosaic law, Gal. ii. 4; v. 1, 13; 1 Pet. ii. 16; from Jewish errors so blinding the mental vision that it does not discern the majesty of Christ, 2 Co. iii. 17; freedom from the dominion of corrupt desires, so that we do by the free impulse of the soul what the will of God requires: ὁ νόμος τῆς ἐλευθερίας, i. e. the Christian religion, which furnishes that rule of right living by which the liberty just mentioned is attained, Jas. i. 25; ii. 12; freedom from the restraints and miseries of earthly frailty: so in the expression ἡ ἐλευθερία τῆς δόξης (epexeget. gen. [W. 531 (494)]), manifested in the glorious condition of the future life, Ro. viii. 21. **b.** fancied liberty, i. e. license, the liberty to do as one pleases, 2 Pet. ii. 19. J. C. Erler, Commentatio exeg. de libertatis christianae notione in N. T. libris obvia, 1830, (an essay I have never had the good fortune to see).*

1658   **ἐλεύθερος**, -έρα, -ερον, (ΕΛΕΥΘΩ i. q. ἔρχομαι [so Curtius, p. 497, after Etym. Magn. 329, 43; Suid. col. 1202 a. ed. Gaisf.; but al. al., cf. Vaniček p. 61]; hence, prop. one who can go whither he pleases, [fr. Hom. down], Sept. for חָפְשִׁי, *free*, **1.** *freeborn*; in a civil sense, *one who is not a slave*: Jn. viii. 33; 1 Co. vii. 22; xii. 13; Gal. iii. 28; Eph. vi. 8; Col. iii. 11; Rev. vi. 15; xiii. 16; xix. 18; fem., Gal. iv. 22 sq. 30 sq. (opp. to ἡ παιδίσκη): *of one who ceases to be a slave, freed, manumitted*: γίνεσθαι ἐλεύθερον, 1 Co. vii. 21. **2.** *free, exempt, unrestrained, not bound by an obligation*: 1 Co. ix. 1; ἐκ πάντων (see ἐκ, I. 6 fin.), 1 Co. ix. 19; ἀπό τινος, *free from* i. e. no longer under obligation to, so that one may now do what was formerly forbidden by the person or thing to which he was bound, Ro. vii. 3 [cf. W. 196 sq. (185); B. 157 sq. (138), 269 (231)], foll. by an inf. [W. 319 (299); B. 260 (224)], ἐλευθέρα ἐστὶν . . . γαμηθῆναι she is free to be married, has liberty to marry, 1 Co. vii. 39; exempt from paying tribute or tax, Mt. xvii. 26. **3.** in an ethical sense: free from the yoke of the Mosaic law, Gal. iv. 26; 1 Pet. ii. 16; from the bondage of sin, Jn. viii. 36; left to one's own will and pleasure, with dat. of respect, τῇ δικαιοσύνῃ, so far as relates to righteousness, as respects righteousness, Ro. vi. 20 (W. ἰ 31, 1 k.; B. § 133, 12).*

1659   **ἐλευθερόω**, -ῶ: fut. ἐλευθερώσω; 1 aor. ἠλευθέρωσα; Pass., 1 aor. ἠλευθερώθην; 1 fut. ἐλευθερωθήσομαι; (ἐλεύθερος); [fr. Aeschyl. down]; *to make free, set at liberty*: from the dominion of sin, Jn. viii. 32, 36; τινὰ ἀπό τινος, one from another's control [W. 196 sq. (185); B. 157 sq. (138)]: ἀπὸ τοῦ νόμου τ. ἁμαρτίας κ. τοῦ θανάτου (see νόμος, 1), Ro. viii. 2; ἀπὸ τ. ἁμαρτίας, from the dominion of sin, Ro. vi. 18, 22; ἀπὸ τ. δουλείας τ. φθορᾶς εἰς τ. ἐλευθερίαν, to liberate from bondage (see δουλεία) and to bring (transfer) into etc. (see εἰς, C. 1), Ro. viii. 21; with a dat. commodi, τῇ ἐλευθερίᾳ, that we might be pos-

sessors of liberty, Gal. v. 1; cf. B. § 133, 12 [and Bp. Lghtft. ad loc.].*

ἔλευσις, -εως, ἡ, (ἔρχομαι), *a coming, advent*, (Dion. **1660** Hal. 3, 59): Acts vii. 52. (ἐν τῇ ἐλεύσει αὐτοῦ, i. e. of Christ, καὶ ἐπιφανείᾳ τῇ ὑστέρᾳ, Act. Thom. 28; plur. αἱ ἐλεύσεις, of the first and the second coming of Christ to earth, Iren. 1, 10.) *

ἐλεφάντινος, -ίνη, -ινον, (ἐλέφας), *of ivory*: Rev. xviii. **1661** 12. [Alcae., Arstph., Polyb., al.]*

Ἐλιακείμ, (אֶלְיָקִים whom *God set up*), *Eliakim*, one of **1662** the ancestors of Christ: Mt. i. 13; Lk. iii. 30.*

[**ἔλιγμα**, -ατος, τό, (ἑλίσσω), *a roll*: Jn. xix. 39 WH txt., **see 1667** where al. read μίγμα, q. v. (Athen., Anth. P., al.)*] **& 3395**

Ἐλιέζερ, (אֱלִיעֶזֶר my *God* is *help*), *Eliezer*, one of the **1663** ancestors of Christ: Lk. iii. 29.*

Ἐλιούδ, (fr. אֵל and הוֹד *glory*, [?]), *Eliud*, one of the **1664** ancestors of Christ: Mt. i. 14 sq.*

Ἐλισάβετ [WH Ἐλεισ-, see *WH*. App. p. 155, and **1665** s. v. ει, ι], (אֱלִישֶׁבַע my *God* is *my oath*, i. e. *a worshipper of God*), *Elisabeth*, wife of Zacharias the priest and mother of John the Baptist: Lk. i. 5 sqq.*

Ἐλισσαῖος and (so L T) **Ἐλισαῖος** [cf. Tdf. Proleg. p. **1666** 107; Tr WH Ἐλισαῖος, cf. *WH*. App. p. 159], -ου, ὁ, (אֱלִישָׁע my *God* is *salvation*), *Elisha*, a distinguished O. T. prophet, the disciple, companion, and successor of Elijah (1 K. xix. 16 sq.; 2 K. i.–xiii.): Lk. iv. 27.*

ἑλίσσω: fut. ἑλίξω [Rec.st ἑλ.]; [pres. pass. ἑλίσσομαι; **1667** fr. Hom. down]; *to roll up, fold together*: Heb. i. 12 [where T Tr mrg. ἀλλάξεις], and Rev. vi. 14 L T Tr WH; see εἱλίσσω.*

ἕλκος, -εος (-ους), [cf. Lat. ulcus, ulcerare; perh. akin **1668** to ἕλκω (Etym. Magn. 331, 3; 641, 3), yet cf. Curtius § 23], τό; **1.** *a wound*, esp. *a suppurated wound*; so in Hom. and earlier writ. **2.** fr. [Thuc.], Theophr., Polyb. on, *a sore, an ulcer*: Rev. xvi. 2; plur., Lk. xvi. 21; Rev. xvi. 11. (for שְׁחִין, Ex. ix. 9; Job ii. 7, etc.) *

ἑλκόω, -ῶ: *to make sore, cause to ulcerate* (Hippocr. **1669** and Med. writ.); Pass. *to be ulcerated*; pf. ptcp. pass. ἡλκωμένος (L T Tr WH εἱλκωμ. [*WH*. App. p. 161; W. § 12, 8; B. 34 (30)]), *full of sores*: Lk. xvi. 20, (Xen. de re. eq. 1, 4; 5, 1).*

ἑλκύω, see ἕλκω.   **see 1670**

ἕλκω (and in later writ. ἑλκύω also [Veitch s. v.; W. **1670** 86 (82)]); impf. εἷλκον (Acts xxi. 30); fut. ἑλκύσω [ἑλκ. Rec.elz Jn. xii. 32]; 1 aor. εἵλκυσα ([inf. (Jn. xxi. 6) ἑλκύσαι Rbez elz L T WH, -κῦσαι Rs GTr]; cf. Bttm. Ausf. Spr. § 114, vol. ii. p. 171; Krüger § 40 s. v.; [Lob. Paralip. p. 35 sq.; Veitch s. v.]); fr. Hom. down; Sept. for מָשַׁךְ; *to draw*; **1.** prop.: τὸ δίκτυον, Jn. xxi. 6, 11; μάχαιραν, i. e. unsheathe, Jn. xviii. 10 (Soph. Ant. 1208 (1233), etc.); τινά, a person forcibly and against his will (our *drag, drag off*), ἔξω τοῦ ἱεροῦ, Acts xxi. 30; εἰς τὴν ἀγοράν, Acts xvi. 19; εἰς κριτήρια, Jas. ii. 6 (πρὸς τὸν δῆμον, Arstph. eqq. 710; and in Latin, as Caes. b. g. 1, 53 (54, 4) cum trinis catenis vinctus traheretur, Liv. 2, 27 cum a lictoribus jam traheretur). **2.** metaph. *to draw by inward power, lead, impel*: Jn. vi. 44 (so in Grk. also; as ἐπιθυμίας . . . ἑλκούσης ἐπὶ ἡδονάς, Plat.

Phaedr. p. 238 a.; ὑπὸ τῆς ἡδονῆς ἑλκόμενοι, Ael. h. a. 6, 31; likewise 4 Macc. xiv. 13; xv. 8 (11). *trahit sua quemque voluptas*, Vergil, ecl. 2, 65); πάντας ἑλκύσω πρὸς ἐμαυτόν, I by my moral, my spiritual, influence will win over to myself the hearts of all, Jn. xii. 32. Cf. Mey. on Jn. vi. 44; [Trench § xxi. COMP.: ἐξ-έλκω.] *

1671 Ἑλλάς, -άδος, ἡ, *Greece* i. e. Greece proper, as opp. to Macedonia, i. q. Ἀχαΐα (q. v.) in the time of the Romans: Acts xx. 2 [cf. Wetstein ad loc.; Mey. on xviii. 12].*

1672 Ἕλλην, -ηνος, ὁ; **1.** *a Greek* by nationality, whether a native of the main land or of the Greek islands or colonies: Acts xviii. 17 Rec.; Ἕλληνές τε καὶ βάρβαροι, Ro. i. 14.   **2.** in a wider sense the name embraces all nations not Jews that made the language, customs, and learning of the Greeks their own; so that where Ἕλληνες are opp. to Jews, the primary reference is to a difference of religion and worship: Jn. vii. 35 (cf. Meyer ad loc.); Acts xi. 20 G L T Tr [cf. B.D. Am. ed. p. 967]; Acts xvi. 1, 3; [xxi. 28]; 1 Co. i. 22, 23 Rec.; Gal. ii. 3, (Joseph. antt. 20, 11, 2); Ἰουδαῖοί τε καὶ Ἕλληνες, and the like: Acts xiv. 1; xviii. 4; xix. 10, 17; xx. 21; Ro. i. 16; ii. 9, 10; iii. 9; x. 12; 1 Co. i. 24; x. 32; xii. 13; Gal. iii. 28; Col. iii. 11. The word is used in the same wide sense by the Grk. church Fathers, cf. *Otto* on Tatian p. 2; [*Soph.* Lex. s. v.]. The Ἕλληνες spoken of in Jn. xii. 20 and Acts xvii. 4 are Jewish proselytes from the Gentiles; see προσήλυτος, 2. [Cf. B. D. s. v. Greece etc. (esp. Am. ed.)] *

1673 Ἑλληνικός, -ή, -όν, *Greek, Grecian*: Lk. xxiii. 38 [T WH Tr txt. om. L Tr mrg. br. the cl.]; Rev. ix. 11. [From Aeschyl., Hdt. down.]*

1674 Ἑλληνίς, -ίδος, ἡ;   **1.** *a Greek woman.* **2.** a Gentile woman; not a Jewess (see Ἕλλην, 2): Mk. vii. 26; Acts xvii. 12.*

1675 Ἑλληνιστής, -οῦ, ὁ, (fr. ἑλληνίζω to copy the manners and worship of the Greeks or to use the Greek language [W. 94 (89 sq.), cf. 28]), *a Hellenist*, i. e. one who imitates the manners and customs or the worship of the Greeks, and uses the Greek tongue; employed in the N. T. of Jews born in foreign lands and speaking Greek, [*Grecian Jews*]: Acts xi. 20 R [WH; see in Ἕλλην, 2]; ix. 29; the name adhered to them even after they had embraced Christianity, Acts vi. 1, where it is opp. to οἱ Ἑβραῖοι, q. v. Cf. *Win.* RWB. s. v. Hellenisten; *Reuss* in Herzog v. p. 701 sqq.; [BB.DD. s. v. Hellenist; *Farrar*, St. Paul, ch. vii.; Wetst. on Acts vi. 1].*

1676 Ἑλληνιστί, adv., (ἑλληνίζω), *in Greek*, i. e. in the Greek language: Jn. xix. 20; Acts xxi. 37. [Xen. an. 7, 6, 8; al.] *

see 1677 ἐλλογάω, i. q. ἐλλογέω, q. v.

1677 ἐλλογέω [see ἐν, III. 3], -ῶ; [Pass., 3 pers. sing. pres. ἐλλογεῖται R G L txt T Tr; impf. ἐλλογᾶτο L mrg. WH; cf. *WH.* App. p. 166; *Tdf.* Proleg. p. 122; Mullach p. 252; B. 57 sq. (50); W. 85 (82)]; (λόγος a reckoning, account); *to reckon in*, set to one's account, lay to one's *charge, impute*: τοῦτο ἐμοὶ ἐλλόγει (L T Tr WH ἐλλόγα [see reff. above]), charge this to my account, Philem.

18; sin the penalty of which is under consideration, Ro. v. 13, where cf. Fritzsche p. 311. (Inscr. ap. Boeckh i. p. 850 [no. 1732 a.; Bp. Lghtft. adds Edict. Diocl. in Corp. Inscrr. Lat. iii. p. 836; see further his note on Philem. 18; cf. B. 57 sq. (50)].) *

Ἐλμωδάμ (Lchm. Ἐλμαδάμ, T Tr WH Ἐλμαδάμ [on the   **1678** breathing in codd. see *Tdf.* Proleg. p. 107]), ὁ, *Elmodam* or *Elmadam*, proper name of one of the ancestors of Christ: Lk. iii. 28.*

ἐλπίζω; impf. ἤλπιζον; Attic fut. ἐλπιῶ (Mt. xii. 21,   **1679** and often in Sept. [(whence in Ro. xv. 12); cf. B. 37 (32); W. § 13, 1 c.]; the com. form ἐλπίσω does not occur in bibl. Grk.); 1 aor. ἤλπισα; pf. ἤλπικα; [pres. pass. ἐλπίζομαι]; (ἐλπίς, q. v.); Sept. for בָּטַח to trust; חָסָה to flee for refuge; יָחַל to wait, to hope; *to hope* (in a religious sense, *to wait for salvation with joy and full of confidence*): τί, Ro. viii. 24 sq.; 1 Co. xiii. 7; (τὰ) ἐλπιζόμενα, things hoped for, Heb. xi. 1 [but WH mrg. connect ἐλπ. with the foll. πραγμ.]; once with dat. of the obj. on which the hope rests, *hopefully to trust in*: τῷ ὀνόματι αὐτοῦ (as in prof. auth. once τῇ τύχῃ, Thuc. 3, 97, 2), Mt. xii. 21 G L T Tr WH [cf. B. 176 (153)]; καθώς, 2 Co. viii. 5. foll. by an inf. relating to the subject of the verb ἐλπίζω [cf. W. 331 (311); B. 259 (223)]: Lk. vi. 34; xxiii. 8; Acts xxvi. 7; Ro. xv. 24; 1 Co. xvi. 7; Phil. ii. [19], 23; 1 Tim. iii. 14; 2 Jn. 12; 3 Jn. 14; foll. by a pf. inf. 2 Co. v. 11; foll. by ὅτι with a pres. Lk. xxiv. 21; ὅτι with a fut., Acts xxiv. 26; 2 Co. i. 13; xiii. 6; Philem. 22. Peculiar to bibl. Grk. is the constr. of this verb with prepositions and a case of noun or pron. (cf. B. 175 (152) sq. [cf. 337 (290); W. § 33, d.; Ellic. on 1 Tim. iv. 10]): εἴς τινα, to direct hope unto one, Jn. v. 45 (pf. ἠλπίκατε, in whom you have put your hope, and rely upon it [W. § 40, 4 a.]); 1 Pet. iii. 5 L T Tr WH; with addition of ὅτι with fut. 2 Co. i. 10 [L txt. Tr WH br. ὅτι, and so detach the foll. clause]; ἐπί τινι, to build hope on one, as on a foundation, (often in Sept.), Ro. xv. 12 (fr. Is. xi. 10); 1 Tim. iv. 10; vi. 17; ἔν τινι, to repose hope in one, 1 Co. xv. 19; foll. by inf. Phil. ii. 19; ἐπί with acc. to direct hope *towards* something: ἐπί τι, to hope to receive something, 1 Pet. i. 13; ἐπὶ τὸν θεόν, of those who hope for something from God, 1 Pet. iii. 5 R G; 1 Tim. v. 5, (and often in Sept.). [COMP.: ἀπ-, προ-ελπίζω.] *

ἐλπίς [sometimes written ἐλπὶς; so WH in Ro. viii.   **1680** 20; Tdf. in Acts ii. 26; see (in 2 below, and) the reff. s. v. ἀφειδον], -ίδος, ἡ, (ἔλπω to make to hope), Sept. for בֶּטַח and בִּטְחָה, trust; מַחֲסֶה that in which one confides or to which he flees for refuge; תִּקְוָה expectation, hope; in the classics a vox media, i. e. *expectation* whether of good or of ill;   **1.** rarely in a bad sense, *expectation of evil, fear*; as, ἡ τῶν κακῶν ἐλπίς, Lcian. Tyrannic. c. 3; τοῦ φόβου ἐλπίς, Thuc. 7, 61; κακὴ ἐλπίς, Plat. rep. 1 p. 330 e. [cf. legg. 1 p. 644 c. fin.]; πονηρὰ ἐλπ. Is. xxviii. 19 Sept.   **2.** much more freq. in the classics, and always in the N. T., in a good sense: *expectation of good, hope*; and in the Christian sense, *joyful and confident expectation of eternal salvation*: Acts xxiii. 6;

xxvi. 7; Ro. v. 4 sq.; xii. 12; xv. 13; 1 Co. xiii. 13; 1 Pet. i. 3; iii. 15; ἀγαθὴ ἐλπίς (often in prof. auth., as Plat. Phaedo 67 c.; plur. ἐλπίδες ἀγαθαί, legg. 1 p. 649 b.; Xen. Ages. 1, 27), 2 Th. ii. 16; ἐλπὶς βλεπομένη, hope whose object is seen, Ro. viii. 24; ὁ θεὸς τῆς ἐλπίδος, God, the author of hope, Ro. xv. 13; ἡ πληροφορία τῆς ἐλπίδος, fulness i. e. certainty and strength of hope, Heb. vi. 11; ἡ ὁμολογία τῆς ἐλπ· the confession of those things which we hope for, Heb. x. 23; τὸ καύχημα τῆς ἐλπ. hope wherein we glory, Heb. iii. 6; ἐπεισαγωγὴ κρείττονος ἐλπίδος, the bringing in of a better hope, Heb. vii. 19; ἐλπίς with gen. of the subj., Acts xxviii. 20; 2 Co. i. 7 (6); Phil. i. 20; with gen. of the obj., Acts xxvii. 20; Ro. v. 2; 1 Co. ix. 10; 1 Th. v. 8; Tit. iii. 7; with gen. of the thing on which the hope depends, ἡ ἐλπὶς τῆς ἐργασίας αὐτῶν, Acts xvi. 19; τῆς κλήσεως, Eph. i. 18; iv. 4; τοῦ εὐαγγελίου, Col. i. 23; with gen. of the pers. in whom hope is reposed, 1 Th. i. 3 [cf. B. 155 (136)]. ἐπ' [or ἐφ' — so Acts ii. 26 LT; Ro. iv. 18 L; viii. 20 (21) T WH; cf. Scrivener, Introd. etc. p. 565; (but see above, init.)] ἐλπίδι, relying on hope, having hope, in hope, (Eur. Herc. fur. 804; Diod. Sic. 13, 21; ἐπ' ἐλπίδι ἀγαθῇ, Xen. mem. 2, 1, 18) [W. 394 (368), cf. 425 (396); B. 337 (290)]: Acts ii. 26 (of a return to life); Ro. iv. 18; with gen. of the thing hoped for added: ζωῆς αἰωνίου, Tit. i. 2; τοῦ μετέχειν, 1 Co. ix. 10 [G L T Tr WH]; in hope, foll. by ὅτι, Ro. viii. 20 (21) [but Tdf. reads διότι]; on account of the hope, for the hope [B. 165 (144)], with gen. of the thing on which the hope rests, Acts xxvi. 6. παρ' ἐλπίδα, beyond, against, hope [W. 404 (377)]: Ro. iv. 18 (i. e. where the laws of nature left no room for hope). ἔχειν ἐλπίδα (often in Grk. writ.): Ro. xv. 4; 2 Co. iii. 12; with an inf. belonging to the person hoping, 2 Co. x. 15; ἐλπίδα ἔχειν εἰς [Tdf. πρὸς] foll. by acc. with inf. Acts xxiv. 15, (εἰς Χριστὸν ἔχειν τὰς ἐλπίδας, Acta Thomae § 28; [τ. ἐλπίδα εἰς τ. Ἰησοῦν ἐν τ. πνεύματι ἔχοντες, Barn. ep. 11, 11]); ἐπί with dat. of pers. 1 Jn. iii. 3; ἐλπίδα μὴ ἔχοντες, (of the heathen) having no hope (of salvation), Eph. ii. 12; 1 Th. iv. 13; ἡ ἐλπὶς ἐστιν εἰς θεόν, directed unto God, 1 Pet. i. 21. By meton. it denotes   a. the author of hope, or he who is its foundation, (often so in Grk. auth., as Aeschyl. choëph. 776; Thuc. 3, 57; [cf. Ignat. ad Eph. 21, 2; ad Magn. 11 fin.; ad Philad. 11, 2; ad Trall. inscr. and 2, 2, etc.]): 1 Tim. i. 1; 1 Th. ii. 19; with gen. of obj. added, τῆς δόξης, Col. i. 27.   b. the thing hoped for: προσδέχεσθαι τὴν μακαρίαν ἐλπίδα, Tit. ii. 13; ἐλπίδα δικαιοσύνης ἀπεκδέχεσθαι, the thing hoped for, which is righteousness [cf. Mey. ed. Sieffert ad l.], Gal. v. 5, (προσδοκῶν τὰς ὑπὸ θεοῦ ἐλπίδας, 2 Macc. vii. 14); διὰ ἐλπίδα τὴν ἀποκειμένην ἐν τοῖς οὐρανοῖς, Col. i. 5; κρατῆσαι τῆς προκειμένης ἐλπίδος, Heb. vi. 18 (cf. Bleek ad loc.). — Zöckler, De vi ac notione vocis ἐλπίς in N. T. Gissae 1856.*

1681   Ἐλύμας, ὁ, [B. 20 (18)], Elymas, an appellative name which Luke interprets as μάγος, — derived either, as is commonly supposed, fr. the Arabic عَلِيم (elymon), i. e. wise; or, acc. to the more probable opinion of De-litzsch (Zeitschrift f. d. Luth. Theol. 1877, p. 7), fr. the Aramaic אֱלִימָא powerful: Acts xiii. 8. [BB.DD. s. v.]*

ἐλωΐ (L T Ἑλωΐ, [WH ἐλωΐ; see I, ι]), Eloi, Syriac form (ܐܰܠܳܗܝ, אֱלֹהִי) for Hebr. אֵל (Ps. xxi. (xxii.) 2): Mk. xv. 34. [Cf. Kautzsch, Gram. d. Bibl.-Aram. p. 11.]*   see 1682 St.

1683   ἐμαυτοῦ, -ῆς, -οῦ, (fr. ἐμοῦ and αὐτοῦ), reflexive pronoun of 1st pers., of myself, used only in gen., dat., and acc. sing. [cf. B. 110 (96) sqq.]: ἀπ' ἐμαυτοῦ, see ἀπό, II. 2 d. aa.; ὑπ' ἐμαυτόν, under my control, Mt. viii. 9; Lk. vii. 8; ἐμαυτόν, myself, as opp. to Christ, the supposed minister of sin (vs. 17), Gal. ii. 18; tacitly opp. to an animal offered in sacrifice, Jn. xvii. 19; negligently for αὐτὸς ἐμέ, 1 Co. iv. 3 [yet cf. Mey. ad loc.]. As in Grk. writers (Matthiae § 148 Anm. 2, i. p. 354; Passow s. v. p. 883), its force is sometimes so weakened that it scarcely differs from the simple pers. pron. of the first person [yet denied by Meyer], as Jn. xii. 32; xiv. 21; Philem. 13.

1684   ἐμ-βαίνω [see ἐν, III. 3]; 2 aor. ἐνέβην, inf. ἐμβῆναι, ptcp. ἐμβάς; [fr. Hom. down]; to go into, step into: Jn. v. 4 R L; εἰς τὸ πλοῖον, to embark, Mt. viii. 23, and often.

1685   ἐμ-βάλλω [see ἐν, III. 3]; 2 aor. inf. ἐμβαλεῖν; to throw in, cast into: εἰς, Lk. xii. 5. [From Hom. down. Comp.: παρ-εμβάλλω.]*

1686   ἐμ-βάπτω [see ἐν, III. 3]; 1 aor. ptcp. ἐμβάψας; to dip in: τί, Jn. xiii. 26a Lchm., 26b R G L txt.; ὁ ἐμβάπτων τὴν χεῖρα ἐν τῷ τρυβλίῳ, Mt. xxvi. 23; mid. ὁ ἐμβαπτόμενος μετ' ἐμοῦ [Lchm. adds τὴν χεῖρα] εἰς τὸ [WH add ἓν in br.] τρυβλίον, Mk. xiv. 20. (Arstph., Xen., al.)*

1687   ἐμβατεύω [see ἐν, III. 3]; (ἐμβάτης stepping in, going in); to enter;   1. prop.: πόλιν, Eur. El. 595; πατρίδος, Soph. O. T. 825; εἰς τὸ ὄρος, Joseph. antt. 2, 12, 1; to frequent, haunt, often of gods frequenting favorite spots, as νῆσον, Aeschyl. Pers. 449; τῷ χωρίῳ, Dion. Hal. antt. 1, 77; often to come into possession of a thing; thus εἰς ναῦν, Dem. p. 894, 7 [6 Dind.]; τὴν γῆν, Josh. xix. 51 Sept.; to invade, make a hostile incursion into, εἰς with acc. of place, 1 Macc. xii. 25, etc.   2. tropically, (cf. Germ. eingehen);   a. to go into details in narrating: absol. 2 Macc. ii. 30.   b. to investigate, search into, scrutinize minutely: ταῖς ἐπιστήμαις, Philo, plant. Noë § 19; ἃ μὴ ἑώρακε ἐμβατεύων, things which he has not seen, i. e. things denied to the sight (cf. 1 Jn. iv. 20), Col. ii. 18, — where, if with G L [in ed. min., but in ed. maj. reinserted, yet in br.] T Tr WH Huther, Meyer, we expunge μή, we must render, "going into curious and subtile speculation about things which he has seen in visions granted him"; but cf. Baumg.-Crusius ad loc. and W. § 55, 3 e.; [also Reiche (Com. crit.), Bleek, Hofm., al., defend the μή. But see Tdf. and WH. ad loc., and Bp. Lghtft.'s 'detached note'; cf. B. 349 (300). Some interpret "(conceitedly) taking his stand on the things which" etc.; see under 1]; Phavor. ἐμβατεῦσαι· ἐπιβῆναι τὰ ἔνδον ἐξερευνῆσαι ἢ σκοπῆσαι; [similarly Hesych. 2293, vol. ii. p. 73 ed. Schmidt, cf. his note; further see reff. in Suidas, col. 1213 d.].*

1688　ἐμ-βιβάζω: 1 aor. ἐνεβίβασα; *to put in* or *on, lead in, cause to enter*; as often in the Greek writ. τινὰ εἰς τὸ πλοῖον: Acts xxvii. 6.*

1689　ἐμ-βλέπω [see ἐν, III. 3]; impf. ἐνέβλεπον; 1 aor. ἐνέβλεψα, ptcp. ἐμβλέψας; *to turn one's eyes on*; *look at*; 1. prop.: with acc. Mk. viii. 25, (Anth. 11, 3; Sept. Judg. xvi. 27 [Alex.]); τινί (Plat. rep. 10, 608 d.; Polyb. 15, 28, 3, and elsewhere), Mt. xix. 26; Mk. x. 21, 27; xiv. 67; Lk. xx. 17; xxii. 61; Jn. i. 36, 42 (43), (in all these pass. ἐμβλέψας αὐτῷ or αὐτοῖς λέγει or εἶπεν, cf. Xen. Cyr. 1, 3, 2 ἐμβλέπων αὐτῷ ἔλεγεν). εἰς τ. οὐρανόν Acts i. 11 R G L, (εἰς τ. γῆν, Is. v. 30; viii. 22; εἰς ὀφθαλμόν, Plat. Alc. 1 p. 132 e.). Absol., οὐκ ἐνέβλεπον I beheld not, i. e. the power of looking upon (sc. surrounding objects) was taken away from me, Acts xxii. 11 [Tr mrg. WH mrg. ἔβλεπ.], (2 Chr. xx. 24 [Ald.]; Xen. mem. 3, 11, 10). 2. fig. *to look at with the mind, to consider*: Mt. vi. 26, (Is. li. 1 sq.; Sir. ii. 10; xxxvi. (xxxiii.) 15; with acc. only, Is. v. 12; with dat., 2 Macc. xii. 45).*

1690　ἐμ-βριμάομαι [see ἐν, III. 3], -ῶμαι, depon. verb, pres. ptcp. ἐμβριμώμενος (Jn. xi. 38, where Tdf. ἐμβριμούμενος; see ἐρωτάω, init.); impf. 3 pers. plur. ἐνεβριμῶντο (Mk. xiv. 5, where Tdf. -μοῦντο, cf. ἐρωτάω u. s.); 1 aor. ἐνεβριμησάμην, and (Mt. ix. 30 L T Tr WH) ἐνεβριμήθην [B. 52 (46)]; (βριμάομαι, fr. βρίμη, to be moved with anger); *to snort in* (of horses; Germ. *darein schnauben*): Aeschyl. sept. 461; *to be very angry, to be moved with indignation*: τινί (Liban.), Mk. xiv. 5 (see above); absol., with addition of ἐν ἑαυτῷ, Jn. xi. 38; with dat. of respect, ib. 33. In a sense unknown to prof. auth. *to charge with earnest admonition, sternly to charge, threateningly to enjoin*: Mt. ix. 30; Mk. i. 43.*

1692　ἐμέω, -ῶ [(cf. Skr. *vam*, Lat. *vom-ere*; Curtius § 452; Vaniček p. 886 sq.)]: 1 aor. inf. ἐμέσαι; *to vomit, vomit forth, throw up*, fr. Hom. down; τινὰ ἐκ τοῦ στόματος, i. e. to reject with extreme disgust, Rev. iii. 16.*

1693　ἐμ-μαίνομαι [see ἐν, III. 3]; τινί, *to rage against* [A. V. *to be exceedingly mad against*] one: Acts xxvi. 11; besides only in Joseph. antt. 17, 6, 5.*

1694　Ἐμμανουήλ, ὁ, *Immanuel*, (fr. עִמָּנוּ and אֵל; God with us), i. q. *savior*, a name given to Christ by Matthew, i. 23, after Is. vii. 14. Acc. to the orthodox interpretation the name denotes the same as θεάνθρωπος, and has reference to the personal union of the human nature and the divine in Christ. [See BB. DD. s. v.]*

1695　Ἐμμαούς (in Joseph. also Ἀμμαούς), ἡ, *Emmaus* (Lat. gen. *-untis*), a village 30 stadia from Jerusalem (acc. to the true reading [so Dind. and Bekk.] in Joseph. b. j. 7, 6, 6; not, as is com. said, foll. the authority of Luke, 60 stadia), apparently represented by the modern *Kulonieh* (cf. *Ewald*, Gesch. des Volkes Israel, 2te Ausg. vi. p. 675 sq.; [*Caspari*, Chronolog. and Geograph. Intr. to the Life of Christ § 191; *Sepp*, Jerus. u. d. heil. Land, i. 52]): Lk. xxiv. 13. There was a town of the same name in the level country of Judæa, 175 stadia from Jerusalem, noted for its hot springs and for the slaughter of the Syrians routed by Judas Maccabaeus, 1 Macc. iii. 40, 57; afterwards fortified by Bacchides,

the Syrian leader, 1 Macc. ix. 50, and from the 3d cent. on called *Nicopolis* [B. D. s. v. Emmaus or Nicopolis]. A third place of the same name was situated near Tiberias, and was famous for its medicinal springs. Cf. Keim iii. p. 555 sq. (Eng. trans. vi. 306 sq.); *Wolff* in Riehm p. 376 sq.; [esp. *Hackett* in B. D. Am. ed. p. 731].*

1696　ἐμμένω [Tdf. ἐνμένω, Acts xiv. 22; see ἐν, III. 3]; 1 aor. ἐνέμεινα; fr. Aeschyl. and Hdt. down; (Augustine, *immaneo*), *to remain in, continue*; a. prop. in a place: ἔν τινι, Acts xxviii. 30 T Tr WH. b. *to persevere* in anything, a state of mind, etc.; *to hold fast, be true to, abide by, keep*: τῇ πίστει, Acts xiv. 22 (νόμῳ, ὅρκοις, etc. in the Grk. writ.); ἔν τινι (more rarely so in the classics, as ἐν ταῖς σπονδαῖς, Thuc. 4, 118; ἐν τῇ πίστει, Polyb. 3, 70, 4): ἐν [so R G only] τοῖς γεγραμμένοις, Gal. iii. 10·fr. Deut. xxvii. 26; ἐν τῇ διαθήκῃ, Heb. viii. 9 fr. Jer. xxxviii. (xxxi.) 32. [Cf. W. § 52, 4, 5.]*

see 3319　ἐμμέσῳ, i. q. ἐν μέσῳ, (see μέσος, 2): Rev. i. 13; ii. 1; iv. 6; v. 6; xxii. 2, in Tdf. ed. 7; [see his Proleg. p. xlviii., (but nowhere in ed. 8, see the Proleg. p. 76 sq.); cf. WH. App. p. 150; B. 8].

1697　Ἐμμόρ (Ἐμμώρ L T Tr, [but WH Ἑμμώρ, see their Intr. § 408]), ὁ, (חֲמוֹר i. e. ass), *Emmor* [or *Hamor*, acc. to the Hebr.], proper name of a man: Acts vii. 16; see concerning him, Gen. xxxiii. 19; xxxiv. 2 sq.*

1698, 1699 & 1700　ἐμός, -ή, -όν, (fr. ἐμοῦ), possess. pron. of the first pers., *mine*; a. *that which I have*; *what I possess*: Jn. iv. 34; xiii. 35; [xv. 11 ἡ χαρὰ ἡ ἐμή (see μένω, I. 1 b. a.)]; xviii. 36; Ro. x.·1; Philem. 12, and often; τῇ ἐμῇ χειρί, with my own hand [B. 117 (102) note], 1 Co. xvi. 21; Gal. vi. 11; Col. iv. 18; as a predicate, Jn. vii. 16; xiv. 24; xvi. 15; substantively, τὸ ἐμόν that which is mine, mine own, esp. my money, Mt. xxv. 27; divine truth, in the knowledge of which I excel, Jn. xvi. 15; univ. in plur. τὰ ἐμά my goods, Mt. xx. 15; Lk. xv. 31. b. *proceeding from me*: οἱ ἐμοὶ λόγοι, Mk. viii. 38; Lk. ix. 26 [here Tr mrg. br. λόγ.]; ὁ λόγος ὁ ἐμός, Jn. viii. 37; ἡ ἐντολὴ ἡ ἐμή, Jn. xv. 12; ἡ ἐμὴ διδαχή, Jn. vii. 16, and in other exx. c. *pertaining* or *relating to me*; a. *appointed for me*: ὁ καιρὸς ὁ ἐμός, Jn. vii. 6. β. equiv. to a gen. of the object: ἡ ἐμὴ ἀνάμνησις, Lk. xxii. 19; 1 Co. xi. 24; exx. fr. Grk. writ. are given by W. § 22, 7; [Kühner § 454, Anm. 11; Krüger § 47, 7, 8]. γ. ἔστιν ἐμόν *it is mine*, equiv. to, it rests with me: Mt. xx. 23; Mk. x. 40. In connecting the article with this pron. the N. T. writ. do not deviate fr. Attic usage; cf. B. § 124, 6.

see 1702 & 1703　ἐμπαιγμονή [see ἐν, III. 3], -ῆς, ἡ, (ἐμπαίζω), *derision, mockery*: 2 Pet. iii. 3 G L T Tr WH. Not found elsewhere.*

1701　ἐμ-παιγμός [see ἐν, III. 3], -οῦ, ὁ, (ἐμπαίζω), unknown to prof. auth., *a mocking, scoffing*: Heb. xi. 36; Ezek. xxii. 4; Sir. xxvii. 28; Sap. xii. 25; [Ps. xxxvii. (xxxviii.) 8]; torture inflicted in mockery, 2 Macc. vii. 7 [etc.].*

1702　ἐμ-παίζω [see ἐν, III. 3]; impf. ἐνέπαιζον; fut. ἐμπαίξω (Mk. x. 34 for the more com. -ξοῦμαι and -ξομαι); 1 aor. ἐνέπαιξα (for the older ἐνέπαισα); Pass., 1 aor. ἐνεπαίχθην (Mt. ii. 16, for the older ἐνεπαίσθην); 1 fut. ἐμπαιχθήσομαι;

*For 1691 see Strong.

(cf. *Lob.* ad Phryn. p. 240 sq.; Krüger § 40 s. v. παίζω; [Veitch ibid.]; B. 64 (56) sq.); *to play in*, τινί, Ps. ciii. (civ.) 26; Eur. Bacch. 867. *to play with, trifle with*, (Lat. *illudere*) i. e. **a.** *to mock*: absol., Mt. xx. 19; xxvii. 41; Mk. x. 34; xv. 31; Lk. xxiii. 11; τινί (Hdt. 4, 134), Mt. xxvii. 29, [31]; Mk. xv. 20; Lk. xiv. 29; xxii. 63; xxiii. 36; in pass. Lk. xviii. 32. **b.** *to delude, deceive*, (Soph. Ant. 799); in pass. Mt. ii. 16, (Jer. x. 15).*

1703 ἐμ-παίκτης [see ἐν, III. 3], -ου, ὁ, (ἐμπαίζω), *a mocker, a scoffer*: 2 Pet. iii. 3; Jude 18; playing like children, Is. iii. 4. Not used by prof. auth.*

1704 ἐμ-περι-πατέω [TWH ἐν-, see ἐν, III. 3], -ῶ: fut. ἐμπεριπατήσω; *to go about in, walk in*: ἔν τισι, among persons, 2 Co. vi. 16 fr. Lev. xxvi. 12. (Job i. 7; Sap. xix. 20; [Philo, Plut.], Lcian., Achill. Tat., al.)*

1705 ἐμ-πίπλημι [not ἐμπιμπλ. (see ἐν, III. 3); for euphony's sake, *Lob.* ad Phryn. p. 95; Veitch p. 536] and ἐμπιπλάω (fr. which form comes the pres. ptcp. ἐμπιπλῶν, Acts xiv. 17 [W. § 14, 1 f.; B. 66 (58)]); 1 aor. ἐνέπλησα; 1 aor. pass. ἐνεπλήσθην; pf. pass. ptcp. ἐμπεπλησμένος; Sept. for מָלֵא and in pass. often for שָׂבַע to be satiated; in Grk. writ. fr. Hom. down; *to fill up, fill full*: τινά τινος, to bestow something bountifully on one, Lk. i. 53; Acts xiv. 17, (Jer. xxxviii. (xxxi.) 14; Ps. cvi. (cvii.) 9; Is. xxix. 19; Sir. iv. 12); *to fill with food*, i. e. *satisfy, satiate*; pass., Lk. vi. 25; Jn. vi. 12, (Deut. vi. 11; viii. 10; Ruth ii. 14; Neh. ix. 25, etc.); *to take one's fill of, glut one's desire for*: pass. with gen. of pers., one's intercourse and companionship, Ro. xv. 24; cf. Kypke ad loc.; τοῦ κάλλους αὐτῆς, gazing at her beauty, Sus. 32.*

see 4092 ἐμ-πιπράω [see ἐν, III. 3], (for the more com. ἐμπίπρημι, fr. πίμπρημι to burn; on the dropping of the μ cf. ἐμπίπλημι, init.); fr. Hdt. down; *to burn, set on fire*; pres. infin. pass. ἐμπιπρᾶσθαι *to be* (inflamed, and so) *swollen* (Hesych. πιμπρᾶν ... φυσᾶν; Etym. Magn. 672, 23 πιμπρᾶσαι· φυσῶσαι; Joseph. antt. 3, 11, 6; etc.) of the human body *to swell up*: from the bite of a viper, Acts xxviii. 6 Tdf., for R G etc. πίμπρασθαι, q. v. [and Veitch s. v. πίμπρημι].*

1706 ἐμ-πίπτω [see ἐν, III. 3]; fut. ἐμπεσοῦμαι; 2 aor. ἐνέπεσον; [fr. Hom. down]; *to fall into*: εἰς βόθυνον, Mt. xii. 11, and L txt. T Tr WH in Lk. vi. 39; εἰς φρέαρ, Lk. xiv. 5 [R G]; *to fall among robbers*, εἰς τοὺς λῃστάς, Lk. x. 36, and in metaph. phrases, 1 Tim. iii. 6 sq.; vi. 9; εἰς χεῖράς τινος, into one's power: τοῦ θεοῦ, to incur divine penalties, Heb. x. 31, as in 2 S. xxiv. 14; 1 Chr. xxi. 13; Sir. ii. 18.*

1707 ἐμ-πλέκω [see ἐν, III. 3]: Pass., [pres. ἐμπλέκομαι]; 2 aor. ptcp. ἐμπλακείς; *to inweave*; trop. in pass., with dat. of thing, *to entangle, involve in*: 2 Tim. ii. 4; 2 Pet. ii. 20. (From Aeschyl. down.)*

1708 ἐμ-πλοκή [see ἐν, III. 3], -ῆς, ἡ, (ἐμπλέκω), *an interweaving, braiding, a knot*: τριχῶν [Lchm. om.], an elaborate gathering of the hair into knots, Vulg. *capillatura*, [A. V. *plaiting*], 1 Pet. iii. 3 (κόμης, Strab. 17 p. 828).*

1709 ἐμ-πνέω [TWH ἐν-, see ἐν, III. 3]; **1.** *to breathe in* or *on*, [fr. Hom. down]. **2.** *to inhale*, (Aeschyl.,

Plat., al.); with partitive gen., ἀπειλῆς κ. φόνου, threatening and slaughter were so to speak the element from which he drew his breath, Acts ix. 1; see Meyer ad loc., cf. W. § 30, 9 c.; [B. 167 (146)]; ἐμπνέον ζωῆς, Sept. Josh. x. 40.*

1710 ἐμ-πορεύομαι [see ἐν, III. 3]: depon. pass. with fut. mid. ἐμπορεύσομαι; (fr. ἔμπορος, q. v.); *to go a trading, to travel for business, to traffic, trade*, (Thuc. et sqq.; Sept.): Jas. iv. 13 [Rˢᵗ G here give the 1 aor. subj. -σώμεθα]; with the acc. of a thing, *to import for sale* (as ἔλαιον εἰς Αἴγυπτον, Sept. Hos. xii. 1; πορφύραν ἀπὸ Φοινίκης, Diog. Laërt. 7, 2; γλαῦκας, Lcian. Nigrin. init.); *to deal in*; *to use a thing* or *a person for gain*, [A. V. *make merchandise of*], (ὥραν τοῦ σώματος, Joseph. antt. 4, 6, 8; Ἀσπασία ἐνεπορεύετο πλήθη γυναικῶν, Athen. 13 p. 569 f.): 2 Pet. ii. 3; cf. W. 223 (209); [B. 147 (129)].*

1711 ἐμπορία [see ἐν, III. 3], -ας, ἡ, (ἔμπορος), *trade, merchandise*: Mt. xxii. 5. (Hesiod, sqq.; Sept.)*

1712 ἐμπόριον [see ἐν, III. 3], -ου, τό, (ἔμπορος), *a place where trade is carried on*, esp. *a seaport*; *a mart, emporium*; (Plin. *forum nundinarium*): οἶκος ἐμπορίου a market house (epexeget. gen. [W. § 59, 8 a.; A. V. *a house of merchandise*]), Jn. ii. 16. (From Hdt. down; Sept.)*

1713 ἔμ-πορος [see ἐν, III. 3], -ου, ὁ, (πόρος); **1.** i. q. ὁ ἐπ' ἀλλοτρίας νεὼς πλέων μισθοῦ, ὁ ἐπιβάτης; so Hesych., with whom agree Phavorinus and the Schol. ad Arstph. Plut. 521; and so the word is used by Homer. **2.** after Hom. one on a journey, whether by sea or by land, esp. *for traffic*; hence **3.** *a merchant*, (opp. to κάπηλος a retailer, petty tradesman): Rev. xviii. 3, 11, 15, 23; ἄνθρωπος ἔμπορος (see ἄνθρωπος, 4 a.), Mt. xiii. 45 [WH txt. om. ἄνθρ.]. (Sept. for סֹחֵר and רֹכֵל.)*

1714 ἐμ-πρήθω: 1 aor. ἐνέπρησα; fr. Hom. down; Sept. for הִצִּית and שָׂרַף; *to burn*; *destroy by fire*: τὴν πόλιν, Mt. xxii. 7.*

1715 ἔμ-προσθεν [Tdf. in Rev. iv. 6 ἔνπρ. [see ἐν, III. 3; cf. Bttm. 8]], adv. of place and of time, (fr. ἐν and πρόσθεν, prop. in the fore part); [fr. Hdt. down]; Sept. chiefly for לִפְנֵי before. In the N. T. used only of place; **1.** adverbially, *in front, before*: Rev. iv. 6 (opp. to ὄπισθεν, as in Palaeph. 29, 2). *before*: πορεύεσθαι, to precede, to go before, Lk. xix. 28; προδραμὼν ἔμπροσθεν, ib. 4 [TWH εἰς τὸ ἔμπρ., cf. Hdt. 4, 61 (8, 89)], like προπορεύεσθαι ἔμπροσθεν, Xen. Cyr. 4, 2, 23 [fig. Plato, Gorg. p. 497 a. πρόϊθι εἰς τὸ ἔμπρ.]. τὰ ἔμπροσθεν the things which lie *before* one advancing, the goal set before me, Phil. iii. 13 (14) (opp. to τὰ ὀπίσω). **2.** it serves as a prep., with the gen. [B. 319 (274); W. § 54, 6]; **a.** *before*, i. e. in that local region which is in front of a person or a thing: Mt. v. 24; vii. 6; Lk. v. 19; xiv. 2; to prostrate one's self ἔμπροσθεν τῶν ποδῶν τινος, Rev. xix. 10; xxii. 8; γονυπετεῖν ἔμπρ. τινος, Mt. xxvii. 29; πορεύεσθαι ἔμπρ. τινος, to go before one, Jn. x. 4; ἀποστέλλεσθαι ἔμπρ. τινος, to be sent before one, Jn. iii. 28; σαλπίζειν ἔμπρ. τινος, Mt. vi. 2; τὴν ὁδὸν κατασκευάσαι, where ἔμπρ. τινος is nearly equiv. to a dat. [cf. B. 172 (150)], Mt. xi. 10; Mk. i. 2 Rec.; Lk. vii. 27. **b.** *before, in the presence of*, i. q. *opposite to, over against* one: στῆναι, Mt. xxvii. 11; ὁμολογεῖν and ἀρνεῖσθαι [B. 176 (153)], Mt. x. 32 sq.; xxvi. 70; Lk. xii. 8, [9 Lchm.]; also Gal. ii. 14; 1 Th. i. 3; ii. 19; iii. 9, 13; *before one*, i. e. *at his tribunal*: Mt. xxv. 32; xxvii. 11; Lk. xxi. 36; Acts xviii. 17; 2 Co. v. 10; 1 Th. ii. 19; [1 Jn. iii. 19]. Here belong the expressions εὐδοκία, θέλημά ἐστι ἔμπροσθεν θεοῦ, *it is the good pleasure, the will of God*, Mt. xi. 26; xviii. 14; Lk. x. 21, formed after Chald. usage; for in 1 S. xii. 22 the words הוֹאִיל יְחוָה, *God wills*, Jonathan the targumist renders רְעָוא קְדָם יי; cf. *Fischer*, De vitiis lexx. N. T. etc. p. 329 sq.; [cf. B. 172 (150)]. **c.** *before* i. e. *in the sight of* one: Mt. v. 16; vi. 1; xvii. 2; xxiii. 13 (14); Mk. ii. 12 T Tr mrg. WH; ix. 2; Lk. xix. 27; Jn. xii. 37; Acts x. 4 L T Tr WH. **d.** *before*, denoting r a n k: γεγονέναι ἔμπρ. τινος, to have obtained greater dignity than another, Jn. i. 15, 30, also 27 R L br.; (Gen. xlviii. 20 ἔθηκε τὸν Ἐφραὶμ ἔμπροσθεν τοῦ Μανασσῆ; [cf. Plat. legg. 1, 631 d.; 5, 743 e.; 7, 805 d.]).*

1716 **ἐμ-πτύω** [see ἐν, III. 3]; impf. ἐνέπτυον; fut. ἐμπτύσω; 1 aor. ἐνέπτυσα; fut. pass. ἐμπτυσθήσομαι; [fr. Hdt. down]; *to spit upon*: τινί, Mk. x. 34; xiv. 65; xv. 19; εἰς τὸ πρόσωπόν τινος, Mt. xxvi. 67 (Num. xii. 14; Plut. ii. p. 189 a. [i. e. reg. et imper. apotheg. Phoc. 17]; κατὰ τὸ πρόσωπ. τινι, Deut. xxv. 9); εἴς τινα, Mt. xxvii. 30; Pass. *to be spit upon*: Lk. xviii. 32. Muson. ap. Stob. floril. 19, 16. Cf. *Lob.* ad Phryn. x. 17; [*Rutherford*, New Phryn. p. 66].*

1717 **ἐμφανής** [see ἐν, III. 3], -ές, (ἐμφαίνω to show in, exhibit), *manifest*: γίνομαι τινι, in its literal sense, Acts x. 40; fig., of God giving proofs of his saving grace and thus manifesting himself, Ro. x. 20 fr. Is. lxv. 1. [From Aeschyl. down.]*

1718 **ἐμφανίζω** [see ἐν, III. 3]; fut. ἐμφανίσω [B. 37 (32)]; 1 aor. ἐνεφάνισα; 1 aor. pass. ἐνεφανίσθην; fr. Xen. and Plato down; (ἐμφανής); **1.** *to manifest, exhibit to view*: ἑαυτόν τινι, prop. to present one's self to the sight of another, manifest one's self to (Ex. xxxiii. 13), Jn. xiv. 22; metaph. of Christ giving evidence by the action of the Holy Spirit on the souls of the disciples that he is alive in heaven, Jn. xiv. 21. Pass. *to show one's self, come to view, appear, be manifest*: τινί (of spectres, Sap. xvii. 4; αὐτοῖς θεοὺς ἐμφανίζεσθαι λέγοντες, Diog. Laërt. prooem. 7; so of God, Joseph. antt. 1, 13, 1), Mt. xxvii. 53; τῷ προσώπῳ τοῦ θεοῦ, of Christ appearing before God in heaven, Heb. ix. 24; (of God imparting to souls the knowledge of himself, Sap. i. 2; Theoph. Ant. ad Autol. 1, 2, 4). **2.** *to indicate, disclose, declare, make known*: foll. by ὅτι, Heb. xi. 14; with dat. of pers. Acts xxiii. 15; τὶ πρός τινα, ib. 22; τὶ κατά τινος, to report or declare a thing against a person, to inform against one, Acts xxiv. 1; xxv. 2; περί τινος, about one, Acts xxv. 15. [Syn. see δηλόω.]*

1719 **ἔμ-φοβος** [see ἐν, III. 3], -ον, (φόβος), *thrown into fear, terrified, affrighted*: Lk. xxiv. 5, [37]; Acts x. 4; (xxii. 9 Rec.); xxiv. 25; Rev. xi. 13. Theophr. char. 25 (24), 1; [1 Macc. xiii. 2; in a good sense, Sir. xix. 24 (21)]. (Actively, *inspiring fear, terrible*, Soph. O. C. 39.)*

1720 **ἐμ-φυσάω**, -ῶ [see ἐν, III. 3]: 1 aor. ἐνεφύσησα; *to blow*

or *breathe on*: τινά, Jn. xx. 22, where Jesus, after the manner of the Hebrew prophets, expresses by the symbolic act of breathing upon the apostles the communication of the Holy Spirit to them, — having in view the primary meaning of the words רוּחַ and πνεῦμα [cf. e. g. Ezek. xxxvii. 5]. (Sept.; Diosc., Aret., Geop., al.; [to *inflate*, Aristot., al.].) *

1721 **ἔμ-φυτος** [see ἐν, III. 3], -ον, (ἐμφύω to implant), in prof. auth. [fr. Hdt. down] *inborn, implanted by nature*; cf. *Grimm*, Exeget. Hdb. on Sap. [xii. 10] p. 224; *implanted by others' instruction*: thus Jas. i. 21 τὸν ἔμφυτον λόγον, the doctrine implanted by your teachers [al. by G o d; cf. *Brückner* in De Wette, or Huther ad loc.], δέξασθε ἐν πραΰτητι, receive like mellow soil, as it were.*

1722 **ἐν**, a preposition taking the dative after it; Hebr. בְ; Lat. *in* with abl.; Eng. *in, on, at, with, by, among*. [W. § 48 a.; B. 328 (282) sq.] It is used

I. L o c a l l y; **1.** of P l a c e proper; **a.** in the interior of some whole; *within the limits of some space*: ἐν γαστρί, Mt. i. 18; ἐν Βηθλεέμ, Mt. ii. 1; ἐν τῇ πόλει, Lk. vii. 37; ἐν τῇ Ἰουδαίᾳ, ἐν τῇ ἐρήμῳ, ἐν τῷ πλοίῳ, ἐν τῷ οὐρανῷ, and innumerable other exx. **b.** *in* (on) t h e s u r f a c e of a place, (Germ. *auf*): ἐν τῷ ὄρει, Mt. iv. 20 sq.; Heb. viii. 5; ἐν πλαξί, 2 Co. iii. 3; ἐν τῇ ἀγορᾷ, Mt. xx. 3; ἐν τῇ ὁδῷ, Mt. v. 25, etc. **c.** of proximity, *at, near, by*: ἐν ταῖς γωνίαις τῶν πλατειῶν, Mt. vi. 5; ἐν τῷ Σιλωάμ, at the fountain Siloam, Lk. xiii. 4; ἐν τῷ γαζοφυλακίῳ, Jn. viii. 20 [see B.D. Am. ed. s. v. Treasury; and on this pass. and the preceding cf. W. 385 (360)]; καθίζειν ἐν τῇ δεξιᾷ θεοῦ etc., at the right hand: Heb. i. 3; viii. 1; Eph. i. 20. **d.** of the contents of a writing, book, etc.: ἐν τῇ ἐπιστολῇ, 1 Co. v. 9; ἐν κεφαλίδι βιβλίου γράφειν, Heb. x. 7; ἐν τῇ βίβλῳ, τῷ βιβλίῳ, Rev. xiii. 8; Gal. iii. 10; ἐν τῷ νόμῳ, Lk. xxiv. 44; Jn. i. 45 (46); ἐν τοῖς προφήταις, in the book of the prophets, Acts xiii. 40; ἐν Ἠλίᾳ, in that portion of Scripture which treats of Elijah, Ro. xi. 2, cf. Fritzsche ad loc.; [*Delitzsch*, Brief a. d. Römer, p. 12; W. 385 (360); B. 331 (285)]; ἐν Δαυίδ, in the Psalms of David, Heb. iv. 7 [see Δαβίδ, fin.]; ἐν τῷ Ὡσηέ, in the prophecies of Hosea, Ro. ix. 25. **e.** trop. applied to things not perceived by the senses, as ἐν τῇ καρδίᾳ, ἐν ταῖς καρδίαις, Mt. v. 28; xiii. 19; 2 Co. vi. 6, and often; ἐν ταῖς συνειδήσεσι, 2 Co. v. 11. **2.** with dat. of a P e r s o n, *in the person, nature, soul, thought of any one*: thus ἐν τῷ θεῷ κέκρυπται ἡ ζωὴ ὑμῶν, it lies hidden as it were in the bosom of God until it shall come forth to view, Col. iii. 3, cf. Eph. iii. 9; ἐν αὐτῷ, i. e. in the person of Christ, κατοικεῖ πᾶν τὸ πλήρωμα etc., Col. i. 19; iii. 3 [(?), 9]. phrases in which ἡ ἁμαρτία is said to dwell in men, Ro. vii. 17 sq.; or ὁ Χριστὸς (the mind, power, life of Christ) εἶναι, [Jn. xvii. 26]; Ro. viii. 10; 2 Co. xiii. 5; μένειν, Jn. vi. 56; [xv. 4, 5]; ζῆν, Gal. ii. 20; μορφοῦσθαι, Gal. iv. 19; λαλεῖν, 2 Co. xiii. 3; ὁ λόγος τοῦ θεοῦ εἶναι, 1 Jn. i. 10; μένειν, Jn. v. 38; ἐνοικεῖν or οἰκεῖν ὁ λόγος τοῦ Χριστοῦ, Col. iii. 16; τὸ πνεῦμα (of God, of Christ), Ro. viii. 9, 11; 1 Co. iii. 16; 2 Tim. i. 14; τὸ ἔν τινι χάρισμα, 1 Tim. iv. 14; 2 Tim. i. 6; ἐνεργεῖν ἔν τινι, Mt. xiv. 2; Eph. ii. 2; 1 Co.

xii. 6, etc.; ἐνεργεῖσθαι, Col. i. 29; κατεργάζεσθαι, Ro. vii. 8. after verbs of revealing, manifesting: ἀποκαλύψαι ἐν ἐμοί, in my soul, Gal. i. 16; φανερόν ἐστιν ἐν αὐτοῖς, Ro. i. 19. ἐν ἑαυτῷ, ἐν ἑαυτοῖς, within one's self i. e. *in the soul, spirit, heart*: after the verbs εἰδέναι, Jn. vi. 61; εἰπεῖν, Lk. vii. 39; xviii. 4; ἐμβριμᾶσθαι, Jn. xi. 38; στενάζειν, Ro. viii. 23; διαλογίζεσθαι, Mk. ii. 8 (alternating there with ἐν ταῖς καρδίαις, cf. vs. 6); Lk. xii. 17; διαπορεῖν, Acts x. 17; λέγειν, Mt. iii. 9; ix. 21; Lk. vii. 49; also 2 Co. i. 9; for other exx. of divers kinds, see εἰμί, V. 4 e.   3. it answers to the Germ. *an* [*on*; often freely to be rendered *in the case of, with*, etc. W. § 48, a. 3 a.], when used   a. of the person or thing on whom or on which some power is operative: ἵνα οὕτω γένηται ἐν ἐμοί, 1 Co. ix. 15; ποιεῖν τι ἔν τινι, Mt. xvii. 12; Lk. xxiii. 31; cf. Matthiae ii. p. 1341; [W. u. s. and 218 (204 sq.); B. 149 (130)].   b. of that in which something is manifest [W. u. s.]: μανθάνειν ἔν τινι, 1 Co. iv. 6; γινώσκειν, Lk. xxiv. 35; Jn. xiii. 35; 1 Jn. iii. 19 (exx. fr. the classics are given by Passow i. 2 p. 908ᵇ; [cf. L. and S. s. v. A. III.]); likewise of that in which a thing is sought: ζητεῖν ἔν τινι, 1 Co. iv. 2.   c. after verbs of stumbling, striking: προσκόπτειν, Ro. xiv. 21; πταίειν, Jas. ii. 10; σκανδαλίζεσθαι, q. v. in its place.   4. *with, among, in the presence of*, with dat. of pers. (also often in the classics; cf. Matthiae ii. p. 1340; W. 385 (360) and 217 sq. (204)): 1 Co. ii. 6; ἐν ὀφθαλμοῖς ἡμῶν, Mt. xxi. 42; ἐν ἐμοί, in my judgment, 1 Co. xiv. 11; [perh. add Jude 1 L T Tr WH; but cf. 6 b. below]. To this head some refer ἐν ὑμῖν, 1 Co. vi. 2, interpreting it *in your assembly*, cf. Meyer ad loc.; but see 5 d. γ.   5. used of that with which a person is surrounded, equipped, furnished, assisted, or acts, [W. § 48, a. 1 b.]; a. *in* i. q. *among*, with collective nouns: ἐν τῷ ὄχλῳ, Mk. v. 30 [W. 414 (386)]; ἐν τῇ γενεᾷ ταύτῃ, among the men of this age, Mk. viii. 38; ἐν τῷ γένει μου, in my nation i. e. among my countrymen, Gal. i. 14; esp. with dat. plur. of persons, as ἐν ἡμῖν, ἐν ὑμῖν, among us, among you, ἐν ἀλλήλοις, among yourselves, one with another: Mt. ii. 6; xi. 11; Mk. ix. 50; Lk. i. 1; Jn. i. 14; xiii. 35; Acts ii. 29; 1 Co. iii. 18; v. 1, and often.   b. of the garments with (*in*) which one is clad: ἐν ἐνδύμασι and the like, Mt. vii. 15; Mk. xii. 38; Lk. xxiv. 4; Jn. xx. 12; Acts x. 30; Heb. xi. 37; Jas. ii. 2; Rev. iii. 4; ἠμφιεσμένον ἐν ἱματίοις, Mt. xi. 8 [T Tr WH om. L br. ἱματ.]; Lk. vii. 25; περιβάλλεσθαι ἐν ἱματίοις, Rev. iii. 5; iv. 4 [L WH txt. om. ἐν].   c. of that which one either leads or brings with him, or with which he is furnished or equipped; esp. after verbs of coming, (ἐν of accompaniment), where we often say *with*: ἐν δέκα χιλιάσιν ὑπαντᾶν, Lk. xiv. 31; ἦλθεν ἐν μυριάσι, Jude 14; cf. Grimm on 1 Macc. i. 17; εἰσέρχεσθαι ἐν αἵματι, Heb. ix. 25; ἐν τῷ ὕδατι κ. τῷ αἵματι, 1 Jn. v. 6 (i. e. with the water of baptism and the blood of atonement, by means of both which he has procured the pardon of our sins, of which fact we are assured by the testimony of the Holy Spirit); ἐν ῥάβδῳ, 1 Co. iv. 21; ἐν πληρώματι εὐλογίας, Ro. xv. 29; φθάνειν

ἐν τῷ εὐαγγελίῳ, 2 Co. x. 14; ἐν πνεύματι κ. δυνάμει Ἠλίου, imbued or furnished with the spirit and power of Elijah, Lk. i. 17; ἐν τῇ βασιλείᾳ αὐτοῦ, furnished with the regal power of the Messiah, possessed of his kingly power, [B. 330 (284)]: Mt. xvi. 28; Lk. xxiii. 42 [WH txt. L mrg. Tr mrg. εἰς τὴν β.]. Akin is its use   d. of the instrument or means by or with which anything is accomplished, owing to the influence of the Hebr. prep. בְּ much more common in the sacred writ. than in prof. auth. (cf. W. § 48, a. 3 d.; B. 181 (157) and 329 (283) sq.), where we say *with, by means of, by (through)*; a. in phrases in which the primitive force of the prep. is discernible, as ἐν πυρὶ κατακαίειν, Rev. xvii. 16 [T om. WH br. ἐν]; ἐν ἅλατι ἁλίζειν or ἀρτύειν, Mt. v. 13; Mk. ix. 50; Lk. xiv. 34; ἐν τῷ αἵματι λευκάνειν, Rev. vii. 14; ἐν τῷ αἵματι καθαρίζειν, Heb. ix. 22; ἐν ὕδατι βαπτίζειν, Mt. iii. 11, etc. (see βαπτίζω, II. b. bb.).   β. with the dat., where the simple dat. of the instrument might have been used, esp. in the Revelation: ἐν μαχαίρᾳ, ἐν ῥομφαίᾳ ἀποκτείνειν, Rev. vi. 8; xiii. 10; πατάσσειν, Lk. xxii. 49; ἀπόλλυσθαι, Mt. xxvi. 52; καταπατεῖν ἐν τοῖς ποσίν, Mt. vii. 6; ἐν βραχίονι αὐτοῦ, Lk. i. 51; ἐν δακτύλῳ θεοῦ, Lk. xi. 20, and in other exx.; of things relating to the soul, as ἐν ἁγιασμῷ, 2 Th. ii. 13 [W. 417 (388)]; 1 Pet. i. 2; ἐν τῇ παρακλήσει, 2 Co. vii. 7; ἐν προσευχῇ, Mt. xvii. 21 [T WH om. Tr br. the vs.]; εὐλογεῖν ἐν εὐλογίᾳ, Eph. i. 3; δικαιοῦσθαι ἐν τῷ αἵματι, Ro. v. 9.   γ. more rarely with dat. of pers., meaning *aided by one, by the intervention* or *agency of some one, by (means of) one*, [cf. W. 389 (364); B. 329 (283) sq.]: ἐν τῷ ἄρχοντι τῶν δαιμονίων, Mt. ix. 34; ἐν ἑτερογλώσσοις, 1 Co. xiv. 21; κρίνειν τ. οἰκουμένην ἐν ἀνδρί, Acts xvii. 31; ἐν ὑμῖν κρίνεται ὁ κόσμος (preceded by οἱ ἅγιοι τὸν κόσμον κρινοῦσιν), 1 Co. vi. 2; ἐργάζεσθαι ἔν τινι, Sir. xiii. 4; xxx. 13, 34.   δ. foll. by an inf. with the article, *in that* (Germ. *dadurch dass*), or like the Lat. gerund [or Eng. participial noun; cf. B. 264 (227)]: Acts iii. 26; iv. 30; Heb. ii. 8; viii. 13.   e. of the state or condition in which anything is done or any one exists, acts, suffers; out of a great number of exx. (see also in γίνομαι, 5 f., and εἰμί, V. 4 b.) it is sufficient to cite: ἐν βασάνοις, Lk. xvi. 23; ἐν τῷ θανάτῳ, 1 Jn. iii. 14; ἐν ζωῇ, Ro. v. 10; ἐν τοῖς δεσμοῖς, Philem. 13; ἐν πειρασμοῖς, 1 Pet. i. 6; ἐν ὁμοιώματι σαρκός, Ro. viii. 3; ἐν πολλῷ ἀγῶνι, 1 Th. ii. 2; ἐν δόξῃ, Phil. iv. 19; 2 Co. iii. 7 sq.; σπείρεται ἐν φθορᾷ κτλ. it (sc. that which is sown) is sown in a state of corruption, sc. ὄν, 1 Co. xv. 42 sq.; ἐν ἑτοίμῳ ἔχειν, to be prepared, in readiness, 2 Co. x. 6; ἐν ἐκστάσει, Acts xi. 5; xxii. 17; very often so used of virtues and vices, as ἐν εὐσεβείᾳ κ. σεμνότητι, 1 Tim. ii. 2; ἐν ἁγιασμῷ, 1 Tim. ii. 15; ἐν καινότητι ζωῆς, Ro. vi. 4; ἐν τῇ ἀνοχῇ τοῦ θεοῦ, Ro. iii. 26 (25); ἐν κακίᾳ καὶ φθόνῳ, Tit. iii. 3; ἐν πανουργίᾳ, 2 Co. iv. 2; also with an adverbial force: as ἐν δυνάμει, powerfully, with power [W. § 51, 1 e.; B. 330 (284)], Mk. ix. 1; Ro. i. 4; Col. i. 29; 2 Th. i. 11; κρίνειν ἐν δικαιοσύνῃ, Acts xvii. 31; Rev. xix. 11; ἐν χαρᾷ, in joy, joyful, Ro. xv. 32; ἐν ἐκτενείᾳ, Acts xxvi. 7; ἐν σπουδῇ, Ro. xii. 8; ἐν χάριτι, Gal. i. 6; 2 Th. ii. 16; ἐν τάχει, Lk.

xviii. 8; Ro. xvi. 20; Rev. i. 1. [Here perh. may be introduced the noteworthy adv. phrase ἐν πᾶσι τούτοις, with all this, Lk. xvi. 26 Lmrg. T Trmrg. WH for R G ἐπὶ π. τ. (see ἐπί, B. 2 d.); also ἐν πᾶσιν, in all things [R. V. withal], Eph. vi. 16 Ltxt. T Tr WH.] A similar use occurs in speaking   **f.** of the form in which anything appears or is exhibited, where ἐν may be represented by the Germ. als [Eng. as]; twice so in the N. T.: σοφίαν λαλεῖν ἐν μυστηρίῳ (as a mystery [here A. V. in]), 1 Co. ii. 7; ἐν τῷ αὐτῷ ὑποδείγματι πίπτειν, Heb. iv. 11 [(A. V. after); al. regard this as a pregnant constr., the ἐν marking rest after motion (R. V.mrg. into); cf. Kurtz or Lünem. ad loc.; B. 329 (283); and 7 below]; (διδόναι τι ἐν δωρεᾷ, 2 Macc. iv. 30; Polyb. 23, 3, 4; 26, 7, 5; ἐν μερίδι, Sir. xxvi. 3; λαμβάνειν τι ἐν φέρνῃ, Polyb. 28, 17, 9; exx. fr. Plato are given by Ast, Lex. Plat. i. p. 702; Lat. in mandatis dare i. e. to be considered as orders, Caes. b. g. 1, 43). [Here perhaps may be noticed the apparent use of ἐν to denote "the measure or standard" (W. § 48, a. 3 b.; Bnhdy. p. 211): ἐν μέτρῳ, Eph. iv. 16 (see μέτρον, 2); ἔφερεν ἐν ἑξήκοντα etc. Mk. iv. 8 WH txt. (note the εἰς, q. v. B. II. 3 a.); καρποφοροῦσιν ἐν τριάκοντα etc. ibid. 20 T Tr txt. WH txt.; but some would take ἐν here distributively, cf. Fritzsche on Mk. iv. 8.]   **g.** of the things in (with) which one is busied: 1 Tim. iv. 15; Col. iv. 2; ἐν οἷς, Acts xxvi. 12; ἐν αὐτῷ, in preaching the gospel, Eph. vi. 20; ἐν τῇ ἑορτῇ, in celebrating the feast, Jn. ii. 23 [L Tr br. ἐν]; ἐν τῇ διδαχῇ, in giving instruction, while teaching, Mk. iv. 2; xii. 38; see εἰμί, V. 4 d.; Passow i. p. 910ᵇ; [L. and S. s. v. II. 1].   **h.** of that in which anything is embodied or summed up: ἐν αὐτῷ ζωὴ ἦν, i. e. that life of which created beings were made partakers was comprehended in him, Jn. i. 4; ἐν τούτῳ τῷ λόγῳ ἀνακεφαλαιοῦται, Ro. xiii. 9, (on Eph. i. 10 see ἀνακεφαλαιόω); πᾶσαν τ. συγγένειαν ἐν ψυχαῖς ἑβδομήκοντα πέντε, comprised in, consisting of, seventy-five souls, Acts vii. 14 [W. 391 (366)].   **6.** of that in which any person or thing is inherently fixed, implanted, or with which it is intimately connected: **a.** of the whole in which a part inheres: prop., μένειν ἐν τῇ ἀμπέλῳ, Jn. xv. 4; ἐν ἑνὶ σώματι μέλη πολλά, Ro. xii. 4; fig. κρεμᾶσθαι ἔν τινι, Mt. xxii. 40.   **b.** of a person to whom another is wholly joined and to whose power and influence he is subject, so that the former may be likened to the place in which the latter lives and moves. So used in the writings of Paul and of John particularly of intimate relationship with God or with Christ, and for the most part involving contextually the idea of power and blessing resulting from that union; thus, εἶναι or μένειν ἐν τῷ πατρί or ἐν τῷ θεῷ, of Christ, Jn. x. 38; xiv. 10 sq.; of Christians, 1 Jn. iii. 24; iv. 13, 15 sq.; εἶναι or μένειν in Christ, of his disciples and worshippers, Jn. xiv. 20; xv. 4 sq.; μένειν ἐν τῷ υἱῷ κ. ἐν τῷ πατρί, 1 Jn. ii. 24; ἐν θεῷ, i. e. amplified and strengthened in the fellowship of God and the consciousness of that fellowship, ἐργάζεσθαί τι, Jn. iii. 21; παρρησιάζεσθαι, 1 Th. ii. 2.   Of frequent use by Paul are the phrases

ἐν Χριστῷ, ἐν Χριστῷ Ἰησοῦ, ἐν κυρίῳ, (cf. Fritzsche, Com. on Rom. vol. ii. p. 82 sqq.; W. 389 (364); Weiss, Bibl. Theol. des N. T. §§ 84 b., 149 c.), ingrafted as it were in Christ, in fellowship and union with Christ, with the Lord: Ro. iii. 24; vi. 11, 23; viii. 39; 1 Co. i. 4; 2 Co. iii. 14; Gal. ii. 4; iii. 14, 26, 28; v. 6; Eph. i. 3 [Rec. om. ἐν]; ii. 6 sq. 10, 13; 1 Tim. i. 14; 2 Tim. i. 1, 13; ii. 1; 1 Pet. iii. 16; v. 10; στήκειν ἐν κυρίῳ, Phil. iv. 1; ἵνα εὑρεθῶ ἐν αὐτῷ, that I may be found (by God and Christ) most intimately united to him, Phil. iii. 9; εἶναι ἐν Χριστῷ Ἰησ. 1 Co. i. 30; οἱ ἐν Χρ. Ἰησ. Ro. viii. 1; 1 Pet. v. 14; κοιμᾶσθαι ἐν Χριστῷ, θνήσκειν ἐν κυρίῳ, to fall asleep, to die, mindful of relationship to Christ and confiding in it [W. u. s.], 1 Co. xv. 18; Rev. xiv. 13.   Since such union with Christ is the basis on which actions and virtues rest, the expression is equivalent in meaning to by virtue of spiritual fellowship or union with Christ; in this sense it is joined to the following words and phrases: πέπεισμαι, Ro. xiv. 14 [W. u. s. and 390 note]; πεποιθέναι, Gal. v. 10; Phil. i. 14; 2 Th. iii. 4; παρρησίαν ἔχειν, Philem. 8; ἐλπίζειν, Phil. ii. 19; καύχησιν ἔχειν, Ro. xv. 17; 1 Co. xv. 31; ἀνῆκεν, Col. iii. 18; τὸ αὐτὸ φρονεῖν, Phil. iv. 2; ὑπακούειν, Eph. vi. 1 [L om. Tr WH br. ἐν κ.]; φῶς, Eph. v. 8; αὔξει, ii. 21; ζωοποιεῖσθαι, 1 Co. xv. 22; ὁ κόπος οὐκ ἔστι κενός, ib. 58; ἅγιος, Phil. i. 1; ἡγιασμένος, 1 Co. i. 2; λαλεῖν, 2 Co. ii. 17; xii. 19; ἀλήθειαν λέγειν, Ro. ix. 1; λέγειν κ. μαρτύρεσθαι, Eph. iv. 17.   Hence it denotes the Christian aim, nature, quality of any action or virtue; thus, εὐάρεστον ἐν κυρίῳ, Col. iii. 20 G L T Tr WH; προσδέχεσθαί τινα, Ro. xvi. 2; Phil. ii. 29; ἀσπάζεσθαί τινα, Ro. xvi. 8, 22; 1 Co. xvi. 19; κοπιᾶν, Ro. xvi. 12 [W. 390 note; L br. the cl.]; γαμηθῆναι, 1 Co. vii. 39; χαίρειν, Phil. iii. 1; iv. 4, 10; παρακαλεῖν, 1 Th. iv. 1; προΐστασθαί τινος, 1 Th. v. 12;—or is equiv. to in things pertaining to Christ, in the cause of Christ: νήπιος, 1 Co. iii. 1; φρόνιμος, 1 Co. iv. 10; παιδαγωγοί, 15; ὁδοί μου, 17; θύρας μοι ἀνεῳγμένης ἐν κυρίῳ, in the kingdom of the Lord, 2 Co. ii. 12.   δικαιοῦσθαι ἐν Χριστῷ, by faith in Christ, Gal. ii. 17.   Finally, it serves as a periphrasis for Christian (whether person or thing): τοὺς ἐκ τῶν Ναρκίσσου τοὺς ὄντας ἐν κυρίῳ (opp. to those of the family of Narcissus who were not Christians), Ro. xvi. 11; ἄνθρωπος ἐν Χρ. a Christian, 2 Co. xii. 2; αἱ ἐκκλησίαι αἱ ἐν Χρ. Gal. i. 22; 1 Th. ii. 14; οἱ νεκροὶ ἐν Χρ. those of the dead who are Christians, 1 Th. iv. 16; ἐκλεκτὸς ἐν κ. a Christian of mark, Ro. xvi. 13; δόκιμος ἐν Χρ. an approved Christian, Ro. xvi. 10; δέσμιος ἐν κυρ. a Christian prisoner (tacitly opp. to prisoners of another sort [W. 388 (363)]), Eph. iv. 1; πιστὸς διάκονος ἐν κ. Eph. vi. 21; Col. iv. 7; διακονία, 17; ἐν Χρ. γεννᾶν τινα, to be the author of one's Christian life or life devoted to Christ, 1 Co. iv. 15; δεσμοὶ ἐν Χρ. bonds occasioned by one's fellowship with Christ, Phil. i. 13 [al. connect ἐν Χρ. here with φανερούς]; it might be freely rendered as Christians, as a Christian, in 1 Co. ix. 1 sq.; Philem. 16.   ἐν πνεύματι (ἁγίῳ) εἶναι, to be in the power of, be actuated by, inspired by, the Holy Spirit: Ro. viii. 9 (here in opp. to ἐν σαρκί); γίνεσθαι, Rev. i.

10; iv. 2; ἐν πνεύματι θεοῦ λαλεῖν, 1 Co. xii. 3; ἐν πνεύματι or ἐν πν. τῷ ἁγίῳ or ἐν πν. θεοῦ sc. ὤν, (being) *in* i. e. under the power of the Spirit, moved by the Spirit [cf. B. 330 (283 sq.); W. 390 (364 sq.)]: Mt. xxii. 43; Mk. xii. 36; Lk. ii. 27; 1 Co. xii. 3; Rev. xvii. 3; xxi. 10. ἄνθρωπος ἐν πνεύματι ἀκαθάρτῳ, sc. ὤν, in the power of an unclean spirit, possessed by one, Mk. i. 23; ἐν τῷ πονηρῷ κεῖσθαι, to be held in the power of Satan, 1 Jn. v. 19. οἱ ἐν νόμῳ, subject to the control of the law, Ro. iii. 19. ἐν τῷ Ἀδὰμ ἀποθνήσκειν, through connection with Adam, 1 Co. xv. 22. **c.** of that in which other things are c o n t a i n e d and u p h e l d, as their c a u s e and o r i g i n: ἐν αὐτῷ (i. e. in God) ζῶμεν κτλ. in God is found the cause why we live, Acts xvii. 28; ἐν αὐτῷ (in Christ, as the divine hypostatic λόγος) ἐκτίσθη τὰ πάντα, in him resides the cause why all things were originally created, Col. i. 16 (the cause both i n s t r u m e n t a l and f i n a l as well, for ἐν αὐτῷ is immediately afterwards resolved into δι’ αὐτοῦ κ. εἰς αὐτόν [cf. W. § 50, 6 and Bp. Lghtft. ad loc.]); τὰ πάντα ἐν αὐτῷ συνέστηκε, Col. i. 17; ἐν Ἰσαὰκ κληθήσεταί σοι σπέρμα, Ro. ix. 7; Heb. xi. 18, fr. Gen. xxi. 12; ἁγιάζεσθαι ἐν with dat. of thing, Heb. x. 10, cf. 1 Co. vi. 11; ἐν τούτῳ πιστεύομεν, in this lies the reason why we believe, Jn. xvi. 30, cf 1 Co. iv. 4; ἐν ᾧ equiv. to ἐν τούτῳ, ὅτι, [*in that*], *since*: Ro. viii. 3; Heb. ii. 18; vi. 17, [see 8 e. below]. Closely related is the use of ἐν **d.** of that which gives opportunity, t h e o c c a s i o n: ἔφυγεν ἐν τῷ λόγῳ τούτῳ (*on* i. e. *after* this word; cf. W. § 48, a. 3 e.), Acts vii. 29. **e.** after certain verbs denoting an a f f e c t i o n, because the affection inheres or resides, as it were, in that to which it relates, [cf. B. 185 (160 sq.); W. 232 (217 sq.)]; see εὐδοκέω, εὐδοκία, εὐφραίνομαι, καυχάομαι, χαίρω, etc.; likewise sometimes after ἐλπίζω, πιστεύω, πίστις, (which see in their prop. places), because faith and hope are placed in what is believed or hoped for. **7.** after verbs implying m o t i o n ἐν w. the dat. is so used as to seem, according to our laws of speech, to be employed for εἰς with the acc.; but it indicates the idea of rest and continuance succeeding the motion; cf. W. § 50, 4; B. 328 (282) sq.: thus after ἀποστέλλω, Mt. x. 16; Lk. x. 3; εἰσέρχεσθαι, Lk. ix. 46; Rev. xi. 11 [not R Tr; WH br. ἐν]; ἐξέρχεσθαι, Lk. vii. 17; 1 Th. i. 8, (but not after ἔρχεσθαι in Lk. xxiii. 42, on which pass. see 5 c. above); καταβαίνειν, Jn. v. 4 [R L; cf. W. § 50, 4 a.]; ἐπιστρέψαι ἀπειθεῖς ἐν φρονήσει δικαίων, that they may abide *in* etc. Lk. i. 17; καλεῖν ἐν εἰρήνῃ, ἐν ἁγιασμῷ, ἐν μιᾷ ἐλπίδι, equiv. to εἰς τὸ εἶναι ἡμᾶς (ὑμᾶς) ἐν etc.: 1 Co. vii. 15; 1 Th. iv. 7; Eph. iv. 4; esp. after τιθέναι and ἱστάναι, which words see in their places. On the same use of the prep., common in Homer, somewhat rare in the classic auth., but recurring freq. in writ. of a later age, see W. l. c.; Passow i. 2 p. 909ᵃ; [cf. L. and S. s. v. I. 8]. **8.** Constructions somewhat p e c u l i a r: **a.** ἐν Αἰγύπτου sc. γῇ (by an ellipsis com. in Grk. writ., cf. Passow i. 2 p. 908ᵇ; [L. and S. s. v. I. 2]; W. 384 (359); [B. 171 (149)]): Heb. xi. 26 [Lchm.]; but see Αἴγυπτος. **b.** expressions shaped by the Hebr. idiom: ἀγοράζειν ἐν with dat. of price (for the price is

the means by which a thing is bought [cf. W. § 48, a. 3 e.]), Rev. v. 9, (ἐν ἀργυρίῳ, 1 Chr. xxi. 24). ἀλλάσσειν τι ἐν τινι (see ἀλλάσσω), *to exchange one thing for another* (prop. to change something and have the exchange *in* [cf. W. 388 (363) note; 206 (194)]): Ro. i. 23, 25 [here μετήλλαξαν]. ὄμνυμι ἔν τινι (בְּ‎ נִשְׁבַּע), cf. *Gesenius,* Thesaur. iii. p. 1355; [W. § 32, 1 b.; B. 147 (128)]), *to swear by* (i. e. the name of some one being interposed), or as it were relying *on*, supported by, some one [cf. W. 389 (364)]: Mt. v. 34–36; xxiii. 16, 18–22; Rev. x. 6. **c.** ὁμολογῶ ἔν τινι after the Syriac ( ) [not the Hebr., see Fritzsche on Mt. p. 386; B. 176 (153); W. § 32, 3 b., yet cf. § 4, a.]), prop. *to confess in one's case* (or *when one's cause is at stake* [cf. W. l. c.; Fritzsche l. c.; *Weiss,* Das Matthäus-evang. p. 278 note [1] (and in Mey. on Mt. ed. 7)]), the nature of the confession being evident from the context; as, *to confess one to be my master and lord,* or *to be my worshipper*: Mt. x. 32; Lk. xii. 8; [cf. *Westcott,* Canon, p. 305 note [1]]. **d.** on the very com. phrase ἐν ὀνόματι τινος, see ὄνομα (esp. 2). **e.** the phrase ἐν ᾧ varies in meaning acc. to the varying sense of ἐν. It may be, **a.** local, *wherein* (i. q. ἐν τούτῳ ἐν ᾧ): Ro. ii. 1; xiv. 22; 2 Co. xi. 12. **β.** temporal, *while* (cf. II. below; W. § 48, a. 2): Mk. ii. 19; Lk. v. 34; Jn. v. 7; Lk. xix. 13 (Rec. ἕως, q. v.). **γ.** instrumental, *whereby*: Ro. xiv. 21. **δ.** causal, Eng. *in that* (see *Mätzner,* Eng. Gram., trans. by Grece, iii. 452, — concomitance passing over into causal dependence, or the substratum of the action being regarded as that on which its existence depends; cf. 'in those circumstances I did so and so'), *on the ground of this that, because*: Ro. viii. 3, etc.; see in 6 c. above. Acc. to the last two uses, the phrase may be resolved into ἐν τούτῳ ὅτι or ἐν τούτῳ ὅ (cf. W. § 23, 2 b. and b.); on its use see W. 387 (362) note; B. 331 (284 sq.); Bnhdy. p. 211; esp. Fritzsche on Rom. vol. ii. p. 93 sq.]

II. With the notion of T I M E ἐν marks **a.** periods and portions of time in which anything occurs, *in, on, at, during*: ἐν τῇ ἡμέρᾳ, ἐν τῇ νυκτί, Jn. xi. 9 sq., etc.; ἐν ταῖς ἡμέραις ἐκείναις, Mt. iii. 1, etc.; ἐν σαββάτῳ, Mt. xii. 2, and in many other exx.; ἐν τῷ δευτέρῳ, at the second time, Acts vii. 13; ἐν τῷ καθεξῆς, Lk. viii. 1; ἐν τῷ μεταξύ, in the meantime [W. 592 sq. (551)], Jn. iv. 31; [ἐν ἐσχάτῳ χρόνῳ, Jude 18 Rec.]. **b.** before substantives signifying an event, it is sometimes equiv. to *at the time of* this or that event, (Germ. *bei*): thus ἐν τῇ παλιγγενεσίᾳ, Mt. xix. 28; ἐν τῇ παρουσίᾳ αὐτοῦ or μου, 1 Co. xv. 23; 1 Th. ii. 19; iii. 13 [W. § 50,5]; Phil. ii. 12; 1 Jn. ii. 28; ἐν τῇ ἀναστάσει, Mt. xxii. 28; Mk. xii. 23; Lk. xiv. 14; xx. 33; ἐν τῇ ἐσχάτῃ σάλπιγγι, at (the sounding of) the last trumpet, 1 Co. xv. 52; ἐν τῇ ἀποκαλύψει of Christ, 2 Th. i. 7; 1 Pet. i. 7, 13; iv. 13. **c.** before infinitives with the article [B. 263 (226) sq.; W. § 44, 6]; before the inf. p r e s e n t it signifies *while, as*: Mt. xiii. 4 (ἐν τῷ σπείρειν), 25 (ἐν τ. καθεύδειν τοὺς ἀνθρώπους); Mt. xxvii. 12; Mk. vi. 48; Lk. i. 21 [cf. B. l. c.]; xxiv. 51;

1 Co. xi. 21; Gal. iv. 18, etc.; before the inf. aorist, when, after that: Lk. ix. 36; xix. 15, etc. **d.** within, in the course of: ἐν τρισὶν ἡμέραις, Mt. xxvii. 40; Mk. xv. 29 [L T Tr om. WH br. ἐν]; Jn. ii. 19 [Tr WH br. ἐν], 20; cf. W. § 48, a. 2; [B. § 133, 26].

III. In COMPOSITION. Prefixed to Adjectives ἐν denotes lying or situated in some place or condition, possessed of or noted for something; as in ἐνάλιος, ἔνδοξος, ἔμφοβος. Prefixed to Verbs it signifies **1.** remaining, staying, continuing in some place, state, or condition; as, ἔνειμι, ἐμμένω, ἐνοικέω. **2.** motion into something, entering into, mingling in; as, ἐμβαίνω, ἐμβατεύω, ἐγκαλέω (summon to court), ἐγγράφω, ἐγκρύπτω. **3.** in ἐμφυσάω, ἐμπρήθω, ἐμπτύω it answers to Germ. an (on).

Before β, μ, π, φ, ψ, ἐν changes to ἐμ-, before γ, κ, ξ, χ, to ἐγ-, before λ to ἐλ-, although this assimilation is neglected also in the older codd. [in א "not often changed," Scrivener, Collation etc. p. lvi.; "in some words assimilation is constant acc. to all or at least all primary Mss. while in a comparatively small number of cases authority is divided. Speaking generally, assimilation is the rule in compounds of ἐν, retention of ν in those of σύν" (Prof. Hort). Following manuscript authority T WH write ἐγγράφω, ἐγκάθετος, ἐγκαίνια, ἐγκαινίζω, ἐγκατοικέω, ἐγκαυχάομαι, ἐγκεντρίζω, ἐγκρίνω, ἐνπεριπατέω, ἐννεύω; T ἔγκοπτω; but L T Tr WH retain ἐγκαλέω, ἔγκλημα, ἐγκομβόομαι, ἐγκράτεια, ἐγκρατεύομαι, ἐγκρατής, ἐγχρίω, ἐλλογέω (-άω), ἐμβαίνω, ἐμβάλλω, ἐμβάπτω, ἐμβατεύω, ἐμβλέπω, ἐμβριμάομαι, ἐμμαίνομαι, ἐμπαιγμονή, ἐμπαιγμός, ἐμπαίζω, ἐμπαίκτης, ἐμπίπλημι, ἐμπίπτω, ἐμπλέκω, ἐμπλοκή, ἐμπορεύομαι, ἐμπορία, ἐμπόριον, ἔμπορος, ἐμπτύω, ἐμφανής, ἐμφανίζω, ἔμφοβος, ἔμφυτος; L T Tr ἔγκυος; L Tr WH ἐμμένω, ἔμπροσθεν; L Tr ἐγγράφω, ἐγκάθετος, ἐγκαίνια, ἐγκαινίζω, ἐγκακέω, ἐγκαταλείπω, ἐγκατοικέω, ἐγκαυχάομαι, ἐγκεντρίζω, ἐγκοπή, ἐγκόπτω, ἐγκρίνω, ἐμπεριπατέω, ἐμπνέω; T ἐμπιπράω; T WH are not uniform in ἐγκακέω, ἐγκαταλείπω; nor T in ἐμμένω, ἔμπροσθεν; nor WH in ἔγκοπτω.—Add L T Tr WH ἀνέγκλητος, παρεμβάλλω, παρεμβολή. See Gregory in the Proleg. to Tdf. ed. 8, p. 76 sqq.; Hort in WH. App. p. 149; Bttm. in Stud. u. Krit. for 1862, p. 179 sq.; esp. Meisterhans p. 46]

1723   **ἐν-αγκαλίζομαι:** 1 aor. ptcp. ἐναγκαλισάμενος; (mid. i. q. εἰς τὰς ἀγκάλας δέχομαι, Lk. ii. 28); to take into the arms, embrace: τινά, Mk. ix. 36; x. 16. (Prov. vi. 10; xxiv. 48 (33); Meleag. in Anth. 7, 476, 10; Plut.; Alciphr. epp. 2, 4; al.) *

1724   **ἐν-άλιος, -ον,** or ἐνάλιος, -α, -ον, [cf. W. § 11, 1],)ἅλς the sea), that which is in the sea, marine; plur. τὰ ἐνάλια marine animals, Jas. iii. 7. (Often in Grk. writ.; the Epic form εἰνάλιος as old as Hom.) *

1725   **ἔν-αντι,** adv., (ἐν and ἀντί, prop. in that part of space which is opposite), before: as a prep. foll. by a gen. [B. 319 (273)]; ἔναντι τοῦ θεοῦ, לִפְנֵי יְהוָה, before God, i. e. in the temple, Lk. i. 8 [Tr mrg. ἐναντίον]; in the judgment of God, Acts viii. 21 G L T Tr WH; [ἔναντι Φαραώ, Acts vii. 10 Tdf.; cf. B. 180 (156)]. (Very often in Sept., and in the Palestin. Apocr. of the O. T.; but nowhere in prof. auth.) *

1726 & 1727   **ἐν-αντίος, -α, -ον,** (ἀντίος set against), [fr. Hom. down], prop. that which is over against; opposite; used **1.**

primarily of place; opposite, contrary: of the wind (Xen. an. 4, 5, 3), Mt. xiv. 24; Mk. vi. 48; Acts xxvii. 4; ἐξ ἐναντίας [W. 591 (550); B. 82 (71)], opposite, over against (see ἐκ, I. 4), with gen. Mk. xv. 39. **2.** metaph. opposed as an adversary, hostile, antagonistic in feeling or act: 1 Th. ii. 15 (on which pass. [for confirmatory reff. to anc. auth.] cf. Grimm on 3 Macc. vii. 4 [on the other hand, see Lünem. on 1 Thess. l. c.]); ὁ ἐξ ἐναντίας, an opponent [A. V. he that is of the contrary part], Tit. ii. 8; ἐναντίον ποιεῖν τί τινι, to do something against one, Acts xxviii. 17; ἐναντία πράττειν πρὸς τὸ ὄνομά τινος, Acts xxvi. 9. Neutr. ἐναντίον, adv., as a prep. is constr. with the gen. [B. 319 (273)], before, in the sight of, in the presence of, one (so in Grk. writ. fr. Hom. down); Sept. often for לִפְנֵי and בְּעֵינֵי also for לְעֵינֵי): Mk. ii. 12 (T Tr mrg. WH ἔμπροσθεν); Lk. xx. 26; Acts vii. 10 (ἐναντίον Φαραώ, when he stood before Pharaoh [here Tdf. ἔναντι, q. v.]); Acts viii. 32; Hebraistically, in the judgment, estimation, of one, Lk. xxiv. 19; [i. 6 T Tr WH], (Gen. x. 9, etc.). [τὸ ἐναντίον i. e. τοὐναντίον see in its place.] *

ἐν-άρχομαι: 1 aor. ἐνηρξάμην; to begin, make a beginning: with dat. of the thing fr. which the beginning is made, Gal. iii. 3; τί, Phil. i. 6; 2 Co. viii. 6 Lchm. ed. min. (Polyb., Dion. Hal., Plut., Lcian.; generally with gen. of the thing begun, as in Sir. xxxvi. 29 (26); xxxviii. 16; 1 Macc. ix. 54. in Eur. with acc., of beginning sacrificial rites; at length, to govern, rule, with gen. Josh. x. 24 Sept.) [COMP.: προ-ενάρχομαι.] *   **1728**

ἔνατος, see ἔννατος. ———————————————— see **1766**
ἐν-γράφω, see ἐν, III. 2 and 3. ——————————— see **1722** & **1125**

ἐνδεής, -ές, (fr. ἐνδέω to lack, mid. to be in need of), needy, destitute: Acts iv. 34. (From [Soph.], Hdt. down; Sept.) *   **1729**

ἔν-δειγμα, -τος, τό, (ἐνδείκνυμι), token, evidence, proof, [A. V. manifest token]: 2 Th. i. 5 [cf. B. 153 (134)]. (Plat. Critias p. 110 b.; Dem. 423, 13.) *   **1730**

ἐν-δείκνυμι: to point out, (Lat. indicare; Germ. anzeigen), fr. Pind. down; in mid. first in Hom.; in the N. T. only in Mid.; [pres. ἐνδείκνυμαι]; 1 aor. ἐνεδειξάμην; prop. to show one's self in something, show something in one's self [cf. B. 192 (166)]; **1.** to show, demonstrate, prove, whether by arguments or by acts: τί, Ro. ix. 22 (joined with γνωρίσαι); Eph. ii. 7; Tit. ii. 10; iii. 2; Heb. vi. 11; with two acc., the one of the object, the other of the predicate, Ro. ii. 15; τὶ ἔν τινι, dat. of the pers., Ro. ix. 17 [cf. Ex. ix. 16 [cf. W. 254 (238)]); 1 Tim. i. 16; τὶ εἰς τὸ ὄνομά τινος, Heb. vi. 10; τὴν ἔνδειξιν ἐνδείκνυσθαι (as in Plat. legg. 12 p. 966 b.; cf. W. 225 (211)); εἰς τινα, 2 Co. viii. 24. **2.** to manifest, display, put forth: τινὶ (dat. of pers.) κακά, 2 Tim. iv. 14; Gen. l. 15, 17.*   **1731**

ἔν-δειξις, -εως, ἡ, (ἐνδείκνυμι), demonstration, proof: i. e. manifestation, made in act, τῆς δικαιοσύνης, Ro. iii. 25 sq.; τῆς ἀγάπης, 2 Co. viii. 24; i. q. sign, evidence, [A. V. evident token], ἀπωλείας, Phil. i. 28. [Plat., al.] *   **1732**

ἔν-δεκα, οἱ, αἱ, τά, eleven: οἱ ἔνδεκα, the eleven apostles of Christ remaining after the death of Judas the traitor, Mt. xxviii. 16; Mk. xvi. 14; Lk. xxiv. 9, 33; Acts i. 26; ii. 14. [From Hom. down.] *   **1733**

1734   ἐν-δέκατος, -άτη, -ατον, *eleventh* : Mt. xx. 6, 9 ; Rev. xxi. 20. [From Hom. down.] *

see   ἐν-δέχομαι ; *to receive, approve of, admit, allow,* (as τὸν **1735 St.** λόγον, Hdt. 1, 60). Impersonally, *ἐνδέχεται it can be allowed, is possible, may be,* (often thus in Grk. prose fr. Thuc. down) : foll. by acc. w. inf. Lk. xiii. 33, cf. xvii. 1. [Cf. δέχομαι, fin.] *

1736   ἐνδημέω, -ῶ ; 1 aor. inf. ἐνδημῆσαι ; (ἔνδημος one who is among his own people or in his own land, one who does not travel abroad ; opp. to ἔκδημος), prop. *to be among one's own people, dwell in one's own country, stay at home* (opp. to ἐκδημέω, ἀποδημέω ; see those words) ; i. q. *to have a fixed abode, be at home,* ἐν τῷ σώματι, of life on earth, 2 Co. v. 6, 9 ; πρὸς τὸν κύριον, of life in heaven, ib. 8. (Rare in the classics, as Lys. p. 114, 36.) *

1737   ἐνδιδύσκω (i. q. ἐνδύω [cf. B. 56 (49)]) ; impf. mid. ἐνεδιδυσκόμην ; *to put on, clothe* : τινὰ πορφύραν, Mk. xv. 17 L T Tr WH ; mid. *to put on one's self, be clothed in* [w. acc. B. 191 (166)] ; W. § 32,5] ; ἱμάτιον, Lk. viii. 27 [R G L Tr mrg.] ; πορφύραν, βύσσον, Lk. xvi. 19 ; (2 S. i. 24 ; xiii. 18 ; Prov. xxix. 39 (xxxi. 21) ; Judith ix. 1 ; Sir. l. 11 ; Joseph. b. j. 7, 2).*

1738   ἔνδικος, -ον, (δίκη), *according to right, righteous, just* : Ro. iii. 8 ; Heb. ii. 2. (Pind., Trag., Plat.) *

1739   ἐν-δόμησις (ἐνδομέω to build in), and ἐνδώμησις T Tr WH ([see WH. App. p. 152] δωμάω to build), -εως, ἡ, *that which is built in,* (Germ. *Einbau*) : τοῦ τείχους, the material built into the wall, i. e. of which the wall was composed, Rev. xxi. 18 ; elsewhere only in Joseph. antt. 15, 9, 6, of a mole built into the sea to form a breakwater, and so construct a harbor.*

1740   ἐν-δοξάζω : 1 aor. pass. ἐνεδοξάσθην ; *to make ἔνδοξος, to glorify, adorn with glory,* (Vulg. *glorifico, clarifico*) : in pass. 2 Th. i. 12 ; ἐνδοξασθῆναι ἐν τοῖς ἁγίοις, that his glory may be seen in the saints, i. e. in the glory, blessedness, conferred on them, 2 Th. i. 10. (Ex. xiv. 4 ; Ezek. xxviii. 22, etc. ; Sir. xxxviii. 6. Not found in prof. auth.) *

1741   ἔνδοξος, -ον, (δόξα), held *in good* or *in great esteem, of high repute* ; **a.** *illustrious, honorable, esteemed,* (Xen., Plat., sqq.) : 1 Co. iv. 10, (thus in Sept. for נִכְבָּד, 1 S. ix. 6 ; xxii. 14 ; Is. xxiii. 8, etc. ; Sir. xi. 5 ; xliv. 1, etc.). **b.** *notable, glorious* : τὰ ἔνδοξα, wonderful deeds, [A. V. glorious things], Lk. xiii. 17 ; (for נִפְלָאוֹת, Ex. xxxiv. 10). **c.** *splendid* : of clothing, [A. V. gorgeous], Lk. vii. 25 ; figuratively i. q. *free from sin,* Eph. v. 27.*

1742   ἔνδυμα, -τος, τό, (ἐνδύω), *garment, raiment,* (Gell., Lact. *indumentum*) : Mt. vi. 25, 28 ; Lk. xii. 23 ; spec. *a cloak, an outer garment* : Mt. iii. 4 ; xxii. 11 sq. (ἐνδ. γάμου a wedding garment) ; Mt. xxviii. 3 ; ἐνδ. προβάτων, sheep's clothing, i. e. the skins of sheep, Mt. vii. 15 [al. take the phrase figuratively : 'with a lamb-like exterior ']. ([Strab. 3, 3, 7] ; Joseph. b. j. 5, 5, 7 ; [antt. 3, 7, 2] ; Plut. Sol. 8 ; Sept. for לְבוּשׁ).*

1743   ἐν-δυναμόω, -ῶ ; 1 aor. ἐνεδυνάμωσα ; Pass., [pres. impv. 2 pers. sing. ἐνδυναμοῦ, 2 pers. plur. ἐνδυναμοῦσθε] ; impf. 3 pers. sing. ἐνεδυναμοῦτο ; 1 aor. ἐνεδυναμώθην ; (fr. ἐνδύναμος equiv. to ὁ ἐν δυνάμει ὤν) ; *to make strong, endue with strength, strengthen* : τινά, Phil. iv. 13 ; 1 Tim. i. 12 ; 2

Tim. iv. 17 ; passively, *to receive strength, be strengthened, increase in strength* : Acts ix. 22 ; ἔν τινι, in anything, 2 Tim. ii. 1 ; ἐν κυρίῳ, in union with the Lord, Eph. vi. 10 ; with dat. of respect, τῇ πίστει, Ro. iv. 20 ; ἀπὸ ἀσθενείας, to recover strength from weakness or disease, Heb. xi. 34 R G ; (in a bad sense, *be bold, headstrong,* Ps. li. (lii.) 9 ; [Judg. vi. 34 Alex., Ald., Compl. ; 1 Chr. xii. 18 Alex. ; Gen. vii. 20 Aq.] ; elsewhere only in eccl. writ.).*

1744   ἐν-δύω [2 Tim. iii. 6] and ἐν-δύω [Mk. xv. 17 R G] ; 1 aor. ἐνέδυσα ; 1 aor. mid. ἐνεδυσάμην ; pf. ptcp. mid. or pass. ἐνδεδυμένος ; Sept. for לָבַשׁ ; as in the classics, **1.** trans. (prop. *to envelop in, to hide in*), *to put on* : τινά τι, **a.** in a literal sense, *to put on, clothe with* a garment : Mt. xxvii. 31 ; [with τινά alone, ib. 28 L WH mrg.] ; Mk. xv. 17 R G, 20 ; Lk. xv. 22. Mid. *to put on one's self, be clothed with* : τί [B. 191 (166)] ; cf. W. § 32,5] ; Mt. vi. 25 ; Lk. xii. 22 ; [viii. 27 T WH Tr txt.] ; Mk. vi. 9 ; Acts xii. 21 ; ἐνδεδυμένος with acc. of a thing, Mk. i. 6 ; Mt. xxii. 11 [B. 148 (129) ; cf. W. § 32, 2] ; Rev. i. 13 ; xv. 6 ; xix. 14 ; ἐνδυσάμενος (opp. to γυμνός) *clothed* with a body, 2 Co. v. 3, on which pass. see γέ, 3 c., (Aristot. de anima 1, 3 fin. p. 407ᵇ, 23 ψυχὴν . . . ἐνδύεσθαι σῶμα). **b.** in metaphorical phrases : of armor fig. so called, ἐνδύεσθαι τὰ ὅπλα [L mrg. ἔργα] τοῦ φωτός, Ro. xiii. 12 ; τὴν πανοπλίαν τοῦ θεοῦ, τὸν θώρακα τῆς δικαιοσύνης, Eph. vi. 11, 14 ; θώρακα πίστεως, 1 Th. v. 8 (with double acc. ; of obj. and pred., θώρακα δικαιοσύνην, Sap. v. 19 (18), [cf. Is. lix. 17] ; prop. ὅπλα, Xen. Cyr. 1, 4, 18 ; τὸν θώρακα, an. 1,8,3). *to be furnished with anything, adorned* with a virtue, as if *clothed* with a garment, ἐνδύεσθαι ἀφθαρσίαν, ἀθανασίαν, 1 Co. xv. 53 sq. ; σπλάγχνα οἰκτιρμοῦ, Col. iii. 12] ; δύναμιν, Lk. xxiv. 49, (ἰσχύν, Is. li. 9 ; [lii.] δύναμιν, εὐπρέπειαν, Ps. xcii. (xciii.) 1 ; αἰσχύνην, Ps. xxxiv. (xxxv.) 26 ; cxxxi. (cxxxii.) 18 ; 1 Macc. i. 29 ; δικαιοσύνην, Job xxix. 14 ; Ps. cxxxi. (cxxxii.) 9 ; σωτηρίαν, ibid. 16 ; etc.] ; δύειν ἀλκήν, Hom. Il. [9, 231] ; 19, 36 ; ἕννυσθαι and ἐπιέννυσθαι ἀλκήν, Il. 20, 381 ; Od. 9, 214 etc. ; many similar exx. in Hebr. and Arabic, cf. Gesenius, Thesaur. ii. 742 ; Lat. *induere novum ingenium,* Liv. 3, 33) ; τὸν καινὸν ἄνθρωπον, i. e. a new purpose and life, Eph. iv. 24 ; Col. iii. 10 ; Ἰησοῦν Χριστόν, to become so possessed of the mind of Christ as in thought, feeling, and action to resemble him and, as it were, reproduce the life he lived, Ro. xiii. 14 ; Gal. iii. 27 ; (similarly the Greeks and Romans said [cf. W. 30], τὸν Ταρκύνιον ἐνδύεσθαι, Dion. Hal. 11, 5, 5 ; ῥίψας τὸν στρατιώτην ἐνέδυ τὸν σοφιστήν, Liban. ep. 968 ; *proditorem et hostem induere,* Tac. ann. 16, 28 ; cf. Fritzsche on Rom. iii. p. 143 sq. ; Wieseler on Gal. p. 317 sqq. ; [Gataker, Advers. misc. 1, 9 p. 223 sqq.]). **2.** intrans. *to creep into, insinuate one's self into ; to enter* : ἐνδύνοντες εἰς τὰς οἰκίας, 2 Tim. iii. 6. [COMP. : ἐπ-ενδύω.] *

1745   ἐν-δυσις, -εως, ἡ, (ἐνδύω), *a putting on,* (Germ. *das Anziehen, der Anzug*) : τῶν ἱματίων, 1 Pet. iii. 3 ; (*clothing,* Job xli. 4 ; Athen. 12 p. 550 c. ; Dio Cass. 78, 3 ; *an entering,* Plat. Crat. p. 419 c.).*

— — — — 1746; ἐν-δύω, see ἐνδύνω.— — — — — — — — — — — see 1744 ἐν-δώμησις, see ἐνδόμησις. — — — — — — — — (1746α); see 1739 ἐνέγκω, see φέρω.

1747 ——————ἐν-έδρα, -ας, ἡ, (fr. ἐν and ἕδρα a seat), a lying in wait, ambush : Acts xxiii. 16 [Rec.ˢᵗ τὸ ἔνεδρον, q. v.] ; ἐνέδραν ποιεῖν, Acts xxv. 3. (Sept. ; Thuc., sqq.) *

1748   ἐνεδρεύω ; (ἐνέδρα) ; to lie in wait for, to lay wait for, prepare a trap for : τινά, a person, Lk. xi. 54 [G om. ἐνεδ. αὐτ., T om. αὐτόν] ; Acts xxiii. 21. (Thuc., Xen., sqq. ; Sept.) *

1749   ἔνεδρον, -ου, τό, i. q. ἐνέδρα, a lying in wait, an ambush : Acts xxiii. 16 Rec.ˢᵗ (Sept. ; Sap. xiv. 21 ; Sir. xi. 29 ; 1 Macc. ix. 40, etc. ; not found in prof. auth.) *

1750   ἐν-ειλέω, -ῶ : 1 aor. ἐνείλησα ; to roll in, wind in : τινά τινι, one in anything, Mk. xv. 46. (1 S. xxi. 9 ; [Aristot. mund. 4 p. 396ᵃ, 14 ; Philo] Plut., Artemid., Philostr., al.) *

1751   ἔν-ειμι ; (εἰμί) ; [fr. Hom. down] ; to be in : τὰ ἐνόντα what is within, i. e. the soul, Lk. xi. 41 (equiv. to τὸ ἔσωθεν ὑμῶν, vs. 39) ; this is to be regarded as an ironical exhortation (similar to that in Amos iv. 4) adjusted to the Pharisees' own views : 'as respects your soul (τὰ ἐνόντα acc. absol.), give alms (to the needy), and behold all things are clean unto you (in your opinion)' ; cf. Bornemann ad loc. Most interpreters think τὰ ἐνόντα to be the things that are within the cup and the platter [obj. acc. after δότε, with ἐλεημ. as pred. acc.], and to be spoken of unjustly acquired riches to be expended in charity. [Still others (following the same construction) take τὰ ἐνόντα (sc. δοῦναι) in the sense of the things within your power, (R. V. mrg. which ye can) ; cf. Steph. Thesaur. s. v. col. 1055 a. ; but see Mey. ed. Weiss ad loc.] Moreover, in the opinion of many ἔνι, [1 Co. vi. 5 G L T Tr WH ; Jas. i. 17 ;] Gal. iii. 28 ; Col. iii. 11 etc., is contracted from ἔνεστι ; but see below under ἔνι.*

1752   ἕνεκα (only before consonants [Rec. three times (Grsb. twice) out of twenty-five]), and ἕνεκεν [R G 19 times, L (out of 26) 21 times, Tr 20, WH 18, T 17], or in a form at first Ionic εἵνεκεν (Lk. iv. 18 [Rec. ἕν. ; xviii. 29 T WH ; Acts xxviii. 20 T WH] ; 2 Co. iii. 10 [R G L mrg. ἕν.] ; vii. 12 [R G], both the last forms alike before consonants and vowels [cf. s. v. N, ν ; W. § 5, 1 d. 1 ; B. 10 (9) ; Krüger (dialects) § 68, 19, 1 ; WH. App. p. 173]), a prep. foll. by the genitive, on account of, for the sake of, for : Mt. v. 10 sq. ; xvi. 25 ; xix. 29 ; Mk. viii. 35 ; Lk. vi. 22 ; Acts xxviii. 20 ; Ro. viii. 36 ; 2 Co. iii. 10 ; ἕνεκεν τούτου, for this cause, therefore, Mt. xix. 5 ; τούτων, Acts xxvi. 21 ; τίνος ἕνεκεν, for what cause, wherefore, Acts xix. 32 ; before τοῦ with inf. expressing purpose [W. 329 (309) ; B. 266 (228)], 2 Co. vii. 12 ; οὗ εἵνεκεν, because, Lk. iv. 18 ; cf. Meyer ad loc.

see 1768   ἐνενήκοντα, see ἐννενήκοντα.
see 1769   ἐνεός, see ἐννεός.

1753   ἐνέργεια, -ας, ἡ, (ἐνεργής, q. v.), working, efficiency ; in the N. T. used only of superhuman power, whether of God or of the devil : of God : Eph. iii. 7 ; Col. ii. 12 ; ἡ ἐνέργεια ἡ ἐνεργουμένη, Col. i. 29 ; with a relative intervening, ἐνεργεῖν ἐνέργειαν, Eph. i. 19 sq. ; κατ' ἐνέργειαν ἐν μέτρῳ ἑνὸς ἑκάστου μέρους, acc. to the working which agrees with the measure of (is commensurate with)

every single part, Eph. iv. 16 ; κατὰ τ. ἐνέργειαν τοῦ δύνασθαι αὐτόν κτλ. according to the efficiency by which he is able to subject all things to himself, Phil. iii. 21. ἐνέργ. τοῦ Σατανᾶ, 2 Th. ii. 9 ; πλάνης, the power with which error works, vs. 11. (Sap. vii. 17, etc. ; 2 Macc. iii. 29 ; τῆς προνοίας, 3 Macc. iv. 21 ; not found in Sept. ; in the classics first in Aristot. ; [on ἐνέργεια, ἐνεργεῖν, of diabolic influences, cf. Müller on Barn. ep. 19, 6].) [SYN. see δύναμις, fin.] *

ἐνεργέω, -ῶ ; 1 aor. ἐνήργησα ; pf. ἐνήργηκα (Eph. i. 20   1754
L T WH txt. Tr mrg.) ; (ἐνεργός [see ἐνεργής]) ;   1. intrans. to be operative, be at work, put forth power : foll. by ἐν with dat. of pers., Mt. xiv. 2 ; Mk. vi. 14 ; Eph. ii. 2 ; foll. by the dat. of advantage (dat. com. ; [cf. Bp. Lghtft. on Gal. as below]), to work for one, aid one, εἴς τι, unto (the accomplishing of) something [W. 397 (371) : εἰς ἀποστολήν, unto the assumption [or discharge] of the apostolic office ; εἰς τὰ ἔθνη, i. q. εἰς ἀποστολὴν [cf. W. § 66, 2 d. ; B. § 147, 8] τῶν ἐθνῶν, Gal. ii. 8.   2. trans. to effect : τί, 1 Co. xii. 11 ; [Eph. i. 11] ; ἐνεργεῖν ἐνέργειαν, Eph. i. 19 sq. ; τὶ ἔν τινι, dat. of pers., 1 Co. xii. 6 [B. 124 (109)] ; Gal. iii. 5 ; Phil. ii. 13.   3. Mid., pres. ἐνεργοῦμαι ; [impf. ἐνηργούμην] ; (not found in the O. T. or in prof. auth., and in the N. T. used only by Paul and James [cf. Bp. Lghtft. on Gal. as below]) ; it is used only of things (cf. W. § 38, 6 fin. ; [B. 193 (167)]), to display one's activity, show one's self operative : [2 Th. ii. 7 (see μυστήριον, 2 fin.)] ; foll. by ἐν with dat. of the thing, where, Ro. vii. 5 ; ἐν with dat. of the condition, 2 Co. i. 6 ; ἐν with dat. of pers. in whose mind a thing shows itself active, 2 Co. iv. 12 ; Eph. iii. 20 ; Col. i. 29 ; 1 Th. ii. 13 ; foll. by διά with gen. of thing, Gal. v. 6. In Jas. v. 16 ἐνεργουμένη does not have the force of an adj., but gives the reason why the δέησις of a righteous man has outward success, viz. as due to the fact that it exhibits its activity ["works"] (inwardly), i. e. is solemn and earnest. (The act. [and pass.] in Grk. writ. fr. Aristot. down.) [On this word cf. (besides Bp. Lghtft. on Gal. ii. 8 ; v. 6) Fritzsche and Vaughan on Ro. vii. 5 ; Ellic. on Gal. ii. 8.] *

ἐνέργημα, -τος, τό, (ἐνεργέω), thing wrought ; effect, op-   1755
eration : plur. [R. V. workings], 1 Co. xii. 6 ; with the addition of the epexeget. gen. δυνάμεων, ibid. 10. (Polyb., Diod., Antonin., [al.].) *

ἐνεργής, -ές, (i. q. ἐνεργός, equiv. to ὁ ὢν ἐν τῷ ἔργῳ   1756
[Eng. at work]), active : Heb. iv. 12 ; by a somewhat incongruous fig., in 1 Co. xvi. 9 a θύρα ἐνεργής is spoken of, 'an opportunity for the working of the gospel' ; ἐνεργ. γίνομαι ἔν τινι, in something, Philem. vs. 6. ([Aristot.], Polyb., Diod., Plut., al.) *

ἐν-εστώς, see ἐνίστημι.   see 1764

ἐν-ευλογέω, -ῶ : 1 fut. pass. ἐνευλογηθήσομαι ; (the prep.   1757
seems to refer to the pers. on whom the blessing is conferred ; cf. Germ. e in segnen) ; to confer benefits on, to bless : pass. foll. by ἐν with dat. of that in which lies the ground of the blessing received or expected, Acts iii. 25 (where the Rec. gives τῷ σπέρμ., dat. of the instrument ; [WH read the simple εὐλογ.]) ; Gal. iii. 8,

where Rec.ᵇᵉᶻ ᵉˡᶻ has the simple εὐλογ. (Gen. xii. 3; xviii. 18; xxvi. 4 Alex.; [Ps. lxxi. (lxxii.) 17 Ald., Compl.]; Sir. xliv. 21; not found in prof. auth.)*

1758 **ἐν-έχω**; impf. ἐνεῖχον; [pres. pass. ἐνέχομαι]; *to have within, to hold in*; a. pass. *to be held, be entangled, be held ensnared*, with a dat. of the thing in which one is held captive, — very often in Grk. writ., both lit. (as τῇ πάγῃ, Hdt. 2, 121, 2) and fig. (as ἀγγελίᾳ, Pind. Pyth. 8, 69; φιλοτιμίᾳ, Eur. Iph. A. 527; κακῷ, Epict. diss. 3, 22, 93): ζυγῷ δουλείας, Gal. v. 1; [θλίψεσιν, 2 Th. i. 4 WH mrg.], (ἀσεβείαις, 3 Macc. vi. 10). b. ἐνέχω τινί, *to be enraged with, set one's self against, hold a grudge against some one*: Mk. vi. 19; Lk. xi. 53, (Gen. xlix. 23); the expression is elliptical, and occurs in full (χόλον τινί *to have anger in one's self against another*) in Hdt. 1, 118; 8, 27; 6, 119; see a similar ellipsis under προσέχω. [In this last case the ellipsis supplied is τὸν νοῦν, W. 593 (552); B. 144 (126); Meyer et al. would supply the same after ἐνέχειν in Mk. and Lk. ll. cc. and render the phrase *to have* (an eye) *on, watch* with hostility; but De Wette, Bleek, al. agree with Grimm. Many take the expression in Lk. l. c. outwardly, *to press upon* (R. V. txt.); see Steph. Thes. s. v.; L. and S. s. v.; Hesych. ἐνέχει· μηνσικακεῖ. ἔγκειται.]*

1759 **ἐνθά-δε**, adv., (fr. ἔνθα and the enclitic δέ; Krüger § 9, 8, 1 and 2; [cf. W. 472 (440); B. 71 (62)]), [fr. Hom. down]; a. *here*: Lk. xxiv. 41; Acts x. 18; xvi. 28; xvii. 6; xxv. 24. b. *hither*: Jn. iv. 15 sq.; Acts xxv. 17.*

see 1782 **ἔνθεν**, adv., (fr. ἐν and the syllable θεν, indicating the place whence), *hence*: Mt. xvii. 20 L T Tr WH; Lk. xvi. 26 G L T Tr WH. [From Hom. down.]*

1760 **ἐνθυμέομαι**, -οῦμαι; a depon. pass.; 1 aor. ptcp. ἐνθυμηθείς; fr. Aeschyl. down, with the object now in the gen. now in the acc.; cf. Matthiae § 349, ii. p. 823; Kühner § 417 Anm. 9, ii. p. 310; [Jelf § 485]; Krüger § 47, 11, 1 and 2; (fr. ἐν and θυμός); *to bring to mind, revolve in mind, ponder*: τί, Mt. i. 20; ix. 4; *to think, to deliberate*: περί τινος, about anything, Acts x. 19 Rec. (So also Sap. vi. 16; Plat. rep. 10 p. 595 a.; Isoc. ep. 9 p. 614, § 9 Bekk.) [Comp.: δι-ενθυμέομαι.]*

1761 **ἐνθύμησις**, -εως, ἡ, *a thinking, consideration*: Acts xvii. 29 [A. V. *device*]; plur. *thoughts*: Mt. ix. 4; xii. 25; Heb. iv. 12 [here L mrg. sing.]. (Rare in the classics; Hippocr., Eur., Thuc., Lcian.)*

1762 **ἔνι** i. q. ἐνί, the accent being thrown back, same as ἐν, used adverbially [W. § 50, 7 N. 2] for ἔνεστι, *is in, is among, has place, is present*, (Hom. Od. 21, 218; Thuc. 2, 40): Gal. iii. 28 (three times); Col. iii. 11; Jas. i. 17; with addition of ἐν ὑμῖν, 1 Co. vi. 5 (where Rec. ἔστιν); in prof. auth. fr. Soph. and Thuc. on very often, *it can be, is possible, is lawful*; [here some would place Jas. l. c.]. The opinion of many [e. g. Fritzsche on Mk. p. 642; Meyer on Gal. l. c.; cf. Ellic. ibid.] that ἔνι is a contracted form for ἔνεστι is opposed by the like use of πάρα, ἄνα, which can hardly be supposed to be contracted from πάρεστι, ἄνεστι; cf. Krüger § 9, 11, 4; W. 80 (77); Göttling, Lehre v. Accent etc. p. 380; [Chandler § 917 sq.; B. 72 (64); Lob. Path. Element. ii. 315].*

1763 **ἐνιαυτός**, -οῦ, ὁ, *a year*: Jn. xi. 49, 51; xviii. 13; Acts xi. 26; xviii. 11; Jas. v. 17; Rev. ix. 15; plur., of the Jewish years of Jubilee, Gal. iv. 10 [cf. Ellic. ad loc.]; ποιεῖν ἐνιαυτόν, to spend a year, Jas. iv. 13; ἅπαξ τοῦ ἐνιαυτοῦ, Heb. ix. 7 (like ἑπτάκις τῆς ἡμέρας, Lk. xvii. 4), [cf. W. § 30, 8 N. 1; Krüger § 47, 10, 4]; κατ' ἐνιαυτόν, *yearly*, Heb. ix. 25; x. 1, 3, (Thuc. 1, 93; Xen. oec. 4, 6; an. 3, 2, 12); in a wider sense, for some fixed and definite period of time: Lk. iv. 19 (fr. Is. lxi. 2), on which pass. see δεκτός. [From Hom. down.]*

[Syn. ἐνιαυτός, ἔτος: originally ἐν. seems to have denoted (yet cf. Curtius § 210) a year viewed as a cycle or period of time, ἔτ. as a division or sectional portion of time.]

1764 **ἐν-ίστημι**: pf. ἐνέστηκα, ptcp. ἐνεστηκώς (Heb. ix. 9), and by syncope ἐνεστώς; fut. mid. ἐνστήσομαι; *to place in or among*; *to put in*; in pf., plpf., 2 aor., and in mid. (prop. as it were *to stand in sight, stand near*) *to be upon, impend, threaten*: 2 Th. ii. 2; fut. mid. 2 Tim. iii. 1. pf. ptcp. *close at hand*, 1 Co. vii. 26; as often in Grk. writ. (in the grammarians ὁ ἐνεστώς sc. χρόνος is the *present* tense [cf. Philo de plant. Noë § 27 τριμερὴς χρόνος, ὃς εἰς τὸν παρεληλυθότα καὶ ἐνεστῶτα καὶ μέλλοντα τέμνεσθαι πέφυκεν]), *present*: ὁ καιρὸς ὁ ἐνεστώς, Heb. ix. 9; τὰ ἐνεστῶτα opp. to τὰ μέλλοντα, Ro. viii. 38; 1 Co. iii. 22; ὁ ἐνεστὼς αἰὼν πονηρός in tacit contrast with τῷ μέλλοντι αἰῶνι, Gal. i. 4, (Basil. ep. 57 ad Melet. [iii. p. 151 c. ed. Benedict.] ὠφέλιμα διδάγματα ἢ ἐφόδια πρός τε τὸν ἐνεστῶτα αἰῶνα καὶ τὸν μέλλοντα). [Many (so R. V.) would adopt the meaning *present* in 2 Th. ii. 2 and 1 Co. vii. 26 also; but cf. Mey. on Gal. l. c.]*

1765 **ἐν-ισχύω**; 1 aor. ἐνίσχυσα; [cf. B. 145 (127)]; 1. intrans. *to grow strong, to receive strength*: Acts ix. 19 [here WH Tr mrg. ἐνισχύθη]; (Aristot., Theophr., Diod., Sept.). 2. trans. *to make strong, to strengthen*, (2 S. xxii. 40; Sir. l. 4; Hippocr. leg. p. 2, 26 ὁ χρόνος ταῦτα πάντα ἐνισχύει); to strengthen one in soul, *to inspirit*: Lk. xxii. 43 [L br. WH reject the pass.].*

see 1722 ἐνκ- see ἐγκ- and s. v. ἐν, III. 3.

see 1696 & 1722 [ἐν-μένω, see ἐμμένω and s. v. ἐν, III. 3.]

1766 **ἔννατος** or **ἔνατος** (which latter form, supported by the authority alike of codd. and of inscrr., has been everywhere restored by L T Tr WH; cf. [s. v. Ν, ν; Tdf. Proleg. p. 80]; Krüger § 24, 2, 12; W. 43; [found once (Rev. xxi. 20) in Rec.ˢᵗ]), -άτη, -ατον, [fr. Hom. down], *ninth*: Rev. xxi. 20; ἡ ἐνάτη ὥρα, spoken of in Mt. xx. 5; xxvii. 45 sq.; Mk. xv. 33 sq.; Lk. xxiii. 44; Acts iii. 1; x. 3, 30, corresponds to our 3 o'clock in the afternoon; for the sixth hour of the Jews coincides with the twelfth of the day as divided by our method, and the first hour of the day with them is the same as the sixth with us. [Cf. BB.DD. s. v. Hour.]*

1767 **ἐννέα**, οἱ, αἱ, τά, [fr. Hom. down], *nine*: Lk. xvii. 17; see the foll. word.*

1768 **ἐννενηκοντα-εννέα**, more correctly ἐνενήκοντα ἐννέα (i. e. written separately, and the first word with a single ν, as by L T Tr WH; cf. [s. v. Ν, ν; Tdf. Proleg. p. 80; WH. App. p. 148]; W. 43 sq.; Bornemann, Scholia ad Luc. p. 95), *ninety-nine*: Mt. xviii. 12 sq.; Lk. xv. 4, 7.*

1769   ἐννεός, more correctly ἐνεός (L T Tr WH [cf. the preceding word]), -οῦ, ὁ, (it seems to be identical with ἄνεως i. q. unused ἄναυος, ἄναος, fr. ἄω, αὔω to cry out, hence *without sound, mute*), dumb, mute, destitute of the power of speech, (Plat., Aristot.) : Is. lvi. 10, cf. Prov. xvii. 28; ἐνεὸν μὴ δυνάμενον λαλῆσαι, of an idol, Bar. vi. (Ep. Jer.) 40; *unable to speak for terror, struck dumb, astounded*: so εἰστήκεισαν ἐνεοί, stood speechless (Vulg. stabant stupefacti), Acts ix. 7; Hesych. ἐμβροντηθέντες· ἐνεοὶ γενόμενοι. Cf. Alberti, Glossar. in N. T. p. 69. In the same sense ἀπηνεώθη, Dan. iv. 16 Theodot., fr. ἀπενεόω.*

1770   ἐν-νεύω: impf. ἐνένευον; to nod to, signify or express by a nod or sign : τινί τι, Lk. i. 62. (Arstph. in Babyloniis frag. 58 [i. e. 22 ed. Brunck, 16 p. 455 Didot]; Lcian. dial. meretr. 12, 1; with ὀφθαλμῷ added, Prov. vi. 13; x. 10.)*

1771   ἔννοια, -ας, ἡ, (νοῦς);   1. the act of *thinking, consideration, meditation*; (Xen., Plat., al.).   2. *a thought, notion, conception*; (Plat. Phaedo p. 73 c., etc.; esp. in philosoph. writ., as Cic. Tusc. 1, 24, 57; Acad. 2, 7 and 10; Epict. diss. 2, 11, 2 sq., etc.; Plut. plac. philos. 4, 11, 1; Diog. Laërt. 3, 79).   3. *mind, understanding, will; manner of thinking and feeling*; Germ. Gesinnung, (Eur. Hel. 1026; Diod. 2, 30 var.; τοιαύτην ἔννοιαν ἐμποιεῖν τινι, Isoc. p. 112 d.; τήρησον τὴν ἐμὴν βουλὴν καὶ ἔννοιαν, Prov. iii. 21; φυλάσσειν ἔννοιαν ἀγαθήν, v. 2) : so 1 Pet. iv. 1; plur. with καρδίας added (as in Prov. xxiii. 19), Heb. iv. 12 [A. V. *intents* of the heart], cf. Sap. ii. 14.*

1772   ἔν-νομος, -ον, (νόμος)   1. *bound to the law; bound by the law*: Χριστῷ, or more correctly Χριστοῦ L T Tr WH, 1 Co. ix. 21 [cf. B. § 132, 23].   2. as in Grk. writ. fr. [Pind.], Aeschyl. down, *lawful, regular*: Acts xix. 39 [on which see Bp. Lghtft. in The Contemp. Rev. for 1878, p. 295; Wood, Ephesus etc., App. p. 38].*

1773   ἔννυχος, -ον, (νύξ), *nightly, nocturnal*, (Hom., Pind., Tragg.). Neut. adverbially, *by night*: Mk. i. 35, where L T Tr WH have neut. plur. ἔννυχα [cf. W. 463 (432); B. § 128, 2].*

1774   ἐν-οικέω, -ῶ; fut. ἐνοικήσω; 1 aor. ἐνῴκησα; Sept. for בׁשֵׁי; *to dwell in*; in the N. T. with ἔν τινι, dat. of pers. *in one*, everywhere metaphorically, *to dwell in one and influence him (for good)*: ἔν τινι, in a person's soul, of the Holy Spirit, Ro. viii. 11; 2 Tim. i. 14; of πίστις, 2 Tim. i. 5; [of sin, Ro. vii. 17 T WH (for simple οἰκεῖν)]; ἐν ὑμῖν, in your assembly, of Christian truth, Col. iii. 16; ἐν αὐτοῖς, in a Christian church, of God, 2 Co. vi. 16, cf. 1 Co. iii. 16; [al. understand the phrase in Col. and Co. ll. cc. *internally*, "in your hearts"; but see Meyer].*

see 1751   ἐν-όντα, τά, see ἔνειμι.

see 3726   ἐν-ορκίζω; *to adjure, put under oath, solemnly entreat*, with two acc., one of him who is adjured, one of him by whom he is adjured [B. 147 (128)] : 1 Th. v. 27 L T Tr WH, for R G ὁρκίζω, [on the inf. foll. cf. B. 276 (237)]. Elsewhere not found except once [twice] in mid. ἐνορκίζομαι in Boeckh, Inscrr. ii. p. 42, no. 1933; [and Joseph. antt. 8, 15, 4 Dind., also Bekk.]; the subst. ἐνορκισμός occurs in Synes. [1413 b. Migne]; once also ἐνορκέω in Schol. ad Lcian. Catapl. c. 23 ἐνορκῶ σε κατὰ τοῦ πατρός;

[to which Soph. Lex. s. v. adds Porph. Adm. 208, 18 ἐνορκῶ σε εἰς τὸν θεὸν ἵνα ἀπέλθῃς].*

1775   ἑνότης, -ητος, ἡ, (fr. εἷς, ἑνός, one), *unity* (Aristot., Plut.) ; i. q. *unanimity, agreement* : with gen. τῆς πίστεως, Eph. iv. 13; τοῦ πνεύματος, ib. vs. 3.*

1776   ἐν-οχλέω, -ῶ; [pres. pass. ptcp. ἐνοχλούμενος]; (ὀχλέω, fr. ὄχλος a crowd, annoyance) ; in the classics fr. Arstph., Xen., Plat. on; *to excite disturbance, to trouble, annoy*, (ἐν, *in* a person) ; in Grk. writ. foll. by both τινά and τινί; pass. with ἀπό τινος, Lk. vi. 18 T Tr WH; absol. of the growth of a poisonous plant, fig. representing the man who corrupts the faith, piety, character, of the Christian church : Heb. xii. 15 fr. Deut. xxix. 18 after cod. Alex. which gives ἐνοχλῇ for ἐν χολῇ, which agreeably to the Hebr. text is the reading of cod. Vat. (Gen. xlviii. 1; 1 S. xix. 14, etc.)   [COMP.: παρ-ενοχλέω.]*

1777   ἔνοχος, -ον, i. q. ὁ ἐνεχόμενος, one who is *held in anything, so that he cannot escape; bound, under obligation, subject to, liable* : with gen. of the thing by which one is bound, δουλείας, Heb. ii. 15; used of one who is held by, possessed with, love and zeal for anything; thus τῶν βιβλίων, Sir. prolog. 9; with dat. τοῖς ἐρωτικοῖς, Plut.; [on supposed distinctions in meaning betw. the constr. w. the gen. and w. the dat. (e. g. 'the constr. with the dat. expresses liability, that with the gen. carries the meaning further and implies either the actual or the rightful hold.' Green) see Schäfer on Demosth. v. p. 323; cf. W. § 28, 2; B. 170 (148)]. As in Grk. writ., chiefly in a forensic sense, denoting the connection of a person either with his crime, or with the penalty or trial, or with that against whom or which he has offended; so   a. absol. *guilty, worthy of punishment*: Lev. xx. 9, 11, 13, 16, 27; 1 Macc. xiv. 45.   b. with gen. of the thing by the violation of which guilt is contracted, *guilty of anything*: τοῦ σώματος κ. τοῦ αἵματος τοῦ κυρίου, guilty of a crime committed against the body and blood of the Lord, 1 Co. xi. 27 [see Meyer; W. 202 (190 sq.)]; πάντων, sc. ἐνταλμάτων, Jas. ii. 10; οἱ ἔνοχοί σου, Is. liv. 17.   c. with gen. of the crime : αἰωνίου ἁμαρτήματος [*an eternal sin*], Mk. iii. 29 L T Tr txt. WH; (τῶν βιαίων, Plat. legg. 11, 914 e.; κλοπῆς, Philo de Jos. § 37; ἱεροσυλίας, 2 Macc. xiii. 6; Aristot. oec. 2 [p. 1349ᵃ, 19], and in other exx.; but much oftener in the classics with dat. of the crime; cf. Passow or [L. and S.] s. v.).   d. with gen. of the penalty : θανάτου, Mk. xiv. 64; Mt. xxvi. 66; Gen. xxvi. 11; αἰωνίου κρίσεως, Mk. iii. 29 Rec.; δεσμοῦ [al. dat.], Dem. p. 1229, 11.   e. with dat. of the tribunal; *liable to this* or *that tribunal* i. e. to punishment to be imposed by this or that tribunal : τῇ κρίσει, τῷ συνεδρίῳ, Mt. v. 21 sq.; ἔνοχος γραφῇ, to be indicted, Xen. mem. 1, 2, 64; cf. Bleek, Br. an d. Hebr. ii. 1 p. 340 sq.; [W. 210 (198)].   f. by a use unknown to Grk. writ. it is connected with εἰς and the acc. of the place where the punishment is to be suffered : εἰς τ. γέενναν τοῦ πυρός, a pregn. constr. [W. 213 (200); 621 (577)] (but cf. B. 170 (148) [who regards it as a vivid circumlocution for the dat.]; cf. Green, Crit. Notes (ad loc.) 'liable as far' in respect of penal consequence 'as the fiery G.']) viz. to go away or be cast *into* etc. Mt. v. 22.*

ἐνπ- see ἐμπ- and s. v. ἐν, III. 3 fine print.

1778 ἔνταλμα, -τος, τό, (ἐντέλλομαι [see ἐντέλλω]), a precept: plur., Mt. xv. 9; Mk. vii. 7; Col. ii. 22. (Is. xxix. 13 διδάσκοντες ἐντάλματα ἀνθρώπων; [Job xxiii. 11, 12]. Not found in prof. auth.; [W. 25].) *

1779 ἐνταφιάζω; 1 aor. inf. ἐνταφιάσαι; to see to τὰ ἐντάφια (fr. ἐν and τάφος), i. e. to prepare a body for burial, by the use of every requisite provision and funereal adornment, to wit, baths, vestments, flowers, wreaths, perfumes, libations, etc.; to lay out a corpse (Lat. pollingere): Mt. xxvi. 12; Jn. xix. 40. (Gen. l. 2 sq.; Anthol. 11, 125, 5; Plut. de esu carn. 1, 5, 7 mor. p. 995 c.) *

1780 ἐνταφιασμός, -οῦ, ὁ, (ἐνταφιάζω, q. v.), preparation of a body for burial: Mk. xiv. 8; Jn. xii. 7. (Schol. ad Eur. Phoen. 1654; [Schol. ad Arstph. Plut. 1009].) *

see 1781 St. ἐν-τέλλω: (τέλλω equiv. to τελέω); several times in the poets (Pind. Olymp. 7, 73) and the later writers (ἐντέταλκε, Joseph. antt. 7, 14, 5 [but Bekk. ἐντετάλθαι]; καθὼς ἐντέταλταί σοι, passively, Sir. vii. 31); generally, and so always in the N. T., depon. mid. ἐντέλλομαι; fut. ἐντελοῦμαι; 1 aor. ἐνετειλάμην; pf. 3 pers. sing. ἐντέταλται (Acts xiii. 47); Sept. very often for צִוָּה; to order, command to be done, enjoin: περί τινος, Heb. xi. 22; ἐνετείλατο λέγων, Mt. xv. 4 [R T]; τινί, Acts i. 2; [with λέγων added, Mt. xvii. 9]; with οὕτω added, Acts xiii. 47; καθώς, [Mk. xi. 6 R L mrg.]; Jn. xiv. 31 R G T; foll. by inf. Mt. xix. 7; τινί, foll. by inf. [B. § 141, 2; 275 (237)], Jn. viii. 5 Rec.; τινί, ἵνα [cf. B. 237 (204)], Mk. xiii. 34 (Joseph. antt. 7, 14, 5; 8, 14, 2); τινί τι, Mt. xxviii. 20; Mk. x. 3; Jn. xv. 14, 17; τινὶ περί τινος, gen. of pers., Mt. iv. 6; Lk. iv. 10, fr. Ps. xc. (xci.) 11 sq. διαθήκην ἐντέλλεσθαι πρός τινα, to command to be delivered to one, Heb. ix. 20; cf. ἐνετείλατο αὐτῷ πρὸς τὸν αὐτοῦ, Sir. xlv. 3; the phrase ἐντέλλεσθαι (τινί) διαθήκην occurs also in Josh. xxiii. 16; Judg. ii. 20; Jer. xi. 4; Ps. cx. (cxi.) 9, but in another sense, as appears from the full expression διαθήκην, ἣν ἐνετείλατο ὑμῖν ποιεῖν, Deut. iv. 13. [SYN. see κελεύω, fin.] *

1782 ἐντεῦθεν, adv. of place, from this place, hence, (as ἐκεῖθεν thence): Mt. xvii. 20 R G; Lk. iv. 9; xiii. 31; xvi. 26 Rec.; Jn. ii. 16; [vii. 3]; xiv. 31; xviii. 36; ἐντεῦθεν κ. ἐντεῦθεν, on the one side and the other, on each side: Jn. xix. 18; Rev. xxii. 2 Rec. [cf. Num. xxii. 24; Dan. xii. 5 Theodot.]; metaph. hence, i. e. from that cause or origin, from this source, i. q. ἐκ τούτου [see ἐκ, II. 8], Jas. iv. 1 [W. 161 (152); B. 400 (342)].*

1783 ἔν-τευξις, -εως, ἡ, (ἐντυγχάνω, q. v.), a falling in with, meeting with, (αἱ τοῖς λησταῖς ἐντεύξεις, Plat. politic. p. 298 d.); an interview, a coming together, to visit, converse, or for any other cause; that for which an interview is held, a conference or conversation (Polyb., Diod., al.), a petition, supplication (Diod. 16, 55; Joseph. antt. 15, 3, 8; Plut. Tib. Gracch. 11); used of prayer to God: 1 Tim. iv. 5; plur. [A. V. intercessions], 1 Tim. ii. 1, (Plut. Num. 14 ποιεῖσθαι τὰς πρὸς τὸ θεῖον ἐντεύξεις). [SYN. see δέησις, fin.] *

1784 ἔντιμος, -ον, (τιμή), held in honor, prized; hence, precious: λίθος, 1 Pet. ii. 4, 6, (Is. xxviii. 16); honorable,

noble, Lk. xiv. 8; τινί, dear to one, Lk. vii. 2; ἔντιμον ἔχειν τινά to hold one dear or in honor, to value highly, Phil. ii. 29. [(Soph., Plat., al.)]*

1785 ἐντολή, -ῆς, ἡ, (ἐντέλλω or ἐντέλλομαι, q. v.), fr. Pind. and Hdt. down; Sept. often for מִצְוָה, in the Pss. the plur. ἐντολαί also for פִּקּוּדִים; an order, command, charge, precept; **1.** univ. a charge, injunction: Lk. xv. 29; ἐντολὴν λαμβάνειν παρά τινος, Jn. x. 18; πρός τινα, Acts xvii. 15; λαβεῖν ἐντολὰς περί τινος, Col. iv. 10; that which is prescribed to one by reason of his office, ἐντολὴν ἔχειν foll. by inf., Heb. vii. 5; ἐντολὴν διδόναι τινί, Jn. xiv. 31 L Tr WH; with τί εἴπῃ added, of Christ, whom God commanded what to teach to men, Jn. xii. 49; ἡ ἐντολὴ αὐτοῦ, of God, respecting the same thing, vs. 50. **2.** a commandment, i. e. a prescribed rule in accordance with which a thing is done; a. univ. ἐντολὴ σαρκική [-ίνη G L T Tr WH], a precept relating to lineage, Heb. vii. 16; of the Mosaic precept concerning the priesthood, Heb. vii. 18; of a magistrate's order or edict: ἐντολὴν διδόναι, ἵνα, Jn. xi. 57. b. ethically; a. used of the commandments of the Mosaic law: ἡ ἐντολὴ τοῦ θεοῦ, what God prescribes in the law of Moses, Mt. xv. 3, (and R G in vs. 6); Mk. vii. 8 sq.; esp. of particular precepts of this law as distinguished from ὁ νόμος (the law) their body or sum: Mt. xxii. 36, 38; Mk. x. 5; xii. 28 sqq.; Ro. vii. 8–13; xiii. 9; Eph. vi. 2; Heb. ix. 19; κατὰ τ. ἐντολήν, according to the precept of the law, Lk. xxiii. 56; plur., Mt. [v. 19]; xxii. 40; Mk. x. 19; [Lk. xviii. 20]; τηρεῖν τὰς ἐντολάς, Mt. xix. 17; πορεύεσθαι ἐν τ. ἐντολαῖς, Lk. i. 6; ὁ νόμος τῶν ἐντολῶν, the law containing the precepts, Eph. ii. 15 (see δόγμα, 2). β. of the precepts of Jewish tradition: ἐντολαὶ ἀνθρώπων, Tit. i. 14. γ. univ. of the commandments of God, esp. as promulgated in the Christian religion: 1 Jn. iii. 23; iv. 21; v. 3; ἐντολὴν διδόναι, 1 Jn. iii. 23; ἐντολὴν ἔχειν, ἵνα, 1 Jn. iv. 21; ἐντολὴν λαβεῖν παρὰ τοῦ πατρός, 2 Jn. 4; τήρησις ἐντολῶν θεοῦ, 1 Co. vii. 19; τηρεῖν τὰς ἐντολὰς αὐτοῦ, 1 Jn. ii. 3 sq.; iii. 22, 24; v. 2 [here L T Tr WH ποιῶμεν], 3; or τοῦ θεοῦ, Rev. xii. 17; xiv. 12; ποιεῖν τὰς ἐντολὰς αὐτοῦ, Rev. xxii. 14 R G; περιπατεῖν κατὰ τὰς ἐντολὰς αὐτοῦ, 2 Jn. 6; of those things which God commanded to be done by Christ, Jn. xv. 10ᵇ; of the precepts of Christ relative to the orderly management of affairs in religious assemblies, 1 Co. xiv. 37 R G L Tr WH; of the moral precepts of Christ and his apostles: ἐντολὴν διδόναι, ἵνα, Jn. xiii. 34; ἐντολὴν γράφειν, 1 Jn. ii. 7 sq.; [2 Jn. 5]; τὰς ἐντολὰς τηρεῖν, Jn. [xiv. 15]; xv. 10ᵃ; ἔχειν τὰς ἐντ. κ. τηρεῖν αὐτάς, "habere in memoria et servare in vita" (Augustine), Jn. xiv. 21; αὕτη ἐστὶν ἡ ἐντ. ἵνα, Jn. xv. 12, cf. 1 Jn. iii. 23. ἡ ἐντολή, collectively, of the whole body of the moral precepts of Christianity: 1 Tim. vi. 14; 2 Pet. ii. 21; iii. 2, (thus ἡ ἐντολὴ τοῦ θεοῦ, Polyc. ad Phil. 5).*

1786 ἐντόπιος, -ον, (τόπος), a dweller in a place; a resident or native of a place: Acts xxi. 12. (Soph. [?], Plat., al.) *

1787 ἐντός, adv., ([fr. ἐν], opp. to ἐκτός), within, inside: with gen. ἐντὸς ὑμῶν, within you, i. e. in the midst of you, Lk. xvii. 21, (ἐντὸς αὐτῶν, Xen. an. 1, 10, 3 [but see the pass.]; ἐντὸς τούτων, Hell. 2, 3, 19. al.); others, within you (i. e. *in your souls*), a meaning which the use of the word permits (ἐντός μου, Ps. xxxviii. (xxxix.) 4; cviii. (cix.) 22, etc.; [Hippol. ref. haer. 5, 7. 8; Petrus Alex. ep· can. 5]), but not the context; τὸ ἐντός, the inside, Mt. xxiii. 26.*

1788 ἐν-τρέπω; [Mid., pres. ἐντρέπομαι; impf. ἐνετρεπόμην]; 2 aor. pass. ἐνετράπην; 2 fut. mid. [i. e. pass. with mid. force, B. 52 (45)] ἐντραπήσομαι; prop. *to turn about*, so in pass. even in Hom.; τινά, prop. to turn one upon himself, i. e. *to shame one*, 1 Co. iv. 14 (Diog. Laërt. 2, 29; Ael. v. h. 3, 17; Sept.); pass. *to be ashamed*: 2 Th. iii. 14; Tit. ii, 8. Mid., τινά, *to reverence a person*: Mt. xxi. 37; Mk. xii. 6; Lk. xviii. 2, 4; xx. 13; Heb. xii. 9; Ex. x. 3; Sap. ii. 10; Polyb. 9, 36, 10; 30, 9, 2; θεούς, Diod. 19, 7; so in Grk. writ., esp. fr. Plut. on; the earlier Greeks said ἐντρέπεσθαί τινος; so also Polyb. 9, 31, 6; [cf. W. § 32, 1 b. *a.*; B. 192 (166)].*

1789 ἐν-τρέφω; [pres. pass. ptcp. ἐντρεφόμενος]; *to nourish in*: τινά τινι, *a person in a thing*; metaph. *to educate, form the mind*: τοῖς λόγοις τῆς πίστεως, 1 Tim. iv. 6; τοῖς νόμοις, Plat. legg. 7 p. 798 a.; Philo, vict. offer. § 10 sub fin.; τοῖς ἱεροῖς γράμμασι, Phil. leg. ad Gai. § 29 sub fin.*

1790 ἔν-τρομος, -ον, (τρόμος, cf. ἔμφοβος), *trembling, terrified*: Acts vii. 32 and xvi. 29 ἔντρ. γενόμενος, becoming tremulous, made to tremble; Heb. xii. 21 [Tr mrg. WH mrg. ἔκτρομος, q. v.]. (Sept.; 1 Macc. xiii. 2; Plut. Fab. 3.) *

1791 ἐν-τροπή, -ῆς, ἡ, (ἐντρέπω, q. v.), *shame*: πρὸς ἐντροπὴν ὑμῖν λέγω [or λαλῶ], *to arouse your shame*, 1 Co. vi. 5; xv. 34. (Ps. xxxiv. (xxxv.) 26; lxviii. (lxix.) 8, 20; *respect, reverence*, Soph., Polyb., Joseph., al.) *

1792 ἐν-τρυφάω, -ῶ; (see τρυφάω and τρυφή); *to live in luxury, live delicately* or *luxuriously, to revel in*: ἐν ταῖς ἀπάταις [L Tr txt. WH mrg. ἀγάπαις, see ἀγάπη, 2] αὐτῶν, (on the meaning see ἀπάτη), 2 Pet. ii. 13 [cf. W. § 52, 4, 5]. (Xen. Hell. 4, 1, 30; Diod. 19, 71; also *to take delight in*: ἐν ἀγαθοῖς, Is. lv. 2; *that* of thing, 4 Macc. viii. 7; Hdian. 3, 5, 4 [2 ed. Bekk.].) *

1793 ἐν-τυγχάνω; 2 aor. ἐνέτυχον; generally with a dat. either of pers. or of thing; **1.** *to light upon a person* or *a thing, fall in with, hit upon, a person* or *a thing*; so often in Attic. **2.** *to go to* or *meet a person*, esp. *for the purpose of conversation, consultation,* or *supplication*, (Polyb., Plut., Aelian, al.): with the addition περί τινος, gen. of person, *for the purpose of consulting about a person*, Acts xxv. 24 [R. V. *made suit*]; *to make petition*: ἐνέτυχον τῷ κυρίῳ καὶ ἐδεήθην αὐτοῦ, Sap. viii. 21; ἐνέτυχον τῷ βασιλεῖ τὴν ἀπόλυσιν ... αἰτούμενοι, 3 Macc. vi. 37; hence, *to pray, entreat*: ὑπέρ with gen. of pers. *to make intercession for* any one (the dat. of the pers. approached in prayer being omitted, as evident from the context), Ro. viii. 27, 34; Heb. vii. 25, (foll. by περί with gen. of person, Clem. Rom. 1 Cor. 56, 1); τινὶ κατά τινος, [*to plead with one against any one*], *to accuse one to any one*, Ro. xi. 2, cf. 1 Macc. viii. 32; x. 61, 63 sq.; xi. 25. (Not found in Sept.) [COMP.: ὑπερ-εντυγχάνω.] *

1794 ἐν-τυλίσσω; 1 aor. ἐνετύλιξα; pf. pass. ptcp. ἐντετυλιγμένος; *to roll in, wrap in*: τινὰ σινδόνι, Mt. xxvii. 59 (ἐν σ. Tr, [ἐν] σ. WH); Lk. xxiii. 53; Ev. Nicod. c. 11 fin. *to*

roll up, wrap together: pass. Jn. xx. 7. (Arstph. Plut. 692; nub. 987; Athen. 3 p. 106 sq.) *

ἐν-τυπόω, -ῶ: pf. pass. ptcp. ἐντετυπωμένος; *to engrave, imprint* (a figure): [foll. by dat. (Rec. with ἐν)], 2 Co. iii. 7 [cf. W. 634 sq. (589)]. (Aristot., Dio Cass., Plut., and in earlier frag. in Athen.)*   **1795**

ἐν-υβρίζω: 1 aor. ptcp. ἐνυβρίσας; *to treat with contumely*: Heb. x. 29. (From Soph. on.) *   **1796**

ἐνυπνιάζω (ἐνύπνιον, q. v.): *to dream* (Aristot. h. an. 4, 10, etc.), and dep. ἐνυπνιάζομαι (Hippocr., Plut. Brut. c. 24); so always in the Bible, for חָלַם, with fut. pass. ἐνυπνιασθήσομαι, and com. with aor. pass. ἐνυπνιάσθην, more rarely mid. ἐνυπνιασάμην (Gen. xxxvii. 9; Judg. vii. 13); ἐνύπνια ἐνυπνιάζεσθαι (in Sept. for חָלַם חֲלוֹמֹת), *to dream* (divinely suggested) *dreams*: Acts ii. 17 fr. Joel iii. 1 (ii. 28); but the reading ἐνυπνίοις (ἐνυπνιάζεσθαι) was long ago restored, which reading also cod. Alex. gives in Joel. Metaph. *to be beguiled with sensual images* and *carried away to an impious course of conduct*: Jude 8.*   **1797**

ἐνύπνιον, -ου, τό, (ἐν and ὕπνος, what appears *in sleep*; fr. Aeschyl. down), *a dream* (Lat. *insomnium*), a vision which presents itself to one in sleep: Acts ii. 17, on which pass. see ἐνυπνιάζω. (Sept. for חֲלוֹם.) *   **1798**

ἐνώπιον, neut. of the adj. ἐνώπιος, -ον, (i. q. ὁ ἐν ὠπὶ ὤν, one who is *in sight*, Theocr. 22, 152; Sept. Ex. xxxiii. 11; ἄρτοι ἐνώπιοι, Ex. xxv. 29); used adverbially it gets the force of a preposition [W. § 54, 6; B. 319 (274)], and is joined with the gen. (hardly to be found so in any prof. auth.), *before, in sight of* any one; time and again in Sept. for עֵינֵי and לִפְנֵי, also for נֶגֶד and לְנֶגֶד; among N. T. writ. used most freq. by Luke and the auth. of the Rev., but never by Matthew and Mark. It is used **1.** of occupied place: *in that place which is before*, or *over against, opposite*, any one and towards which another turns his eyes; **a.** prop.: εἶναι ἐνώπ. τινος, Rev. i. 4; vii. 15; [xiv. 5 Rec.]; so that εἶναι must be mentally supplied before ἐνώπιον, Rev. iv. 5 sq.; viii. 3; ix. 13; after στῆναι, Acts x. 30; ἑστηκέναι, Rev. vii. 9; viii. 2; xi. 4; xii. 4; xx. 12; παρεστηκέναι, Lk. i. 19; Acts iv. 10; ἱστάναι, Acts vi. 6; καθῆσθαι, Rev. xi. 16; θύρα ἀνεῳγμένη ἐν τινος, i. q. a door opened for one (see θύρα, c. γ. [B. 173 (150)]), Rev. iii. 8; after verbs signifying motion to a place: τιθέναι, Lk. v. 18; ἀναβαίνειν, Rev. viii. 4; βάλλειν, Rev. iv. 10; πίπτειν or πεσεῖν (of worshippers), Rev. iv. 10; v. 8; [vii. 11]; προσκυνεῖν, Lk. iv. 7; Rev. iii. 9; xv. 4, [cf. B. u. s.; 147 (129); W. 214 (201)]. **b.** in metaphorical phrases after verbs signifying motion: βαστάζειν τὸ ὄνομα ... ἐνώπιον ἐθνῶν (see βαστάζω, 3), Acts ix. 15; σκάνδαλα βάλλειν ἐνώπ. τινος, to cast stumbling-blocks (incitements to sin) before one, Rev. ii. 14; after προέρχεσθαι, to go before one like a herald, Lk. i. 17; [after προπορεύεσθαι, Lk. i. 76 WH]. in phrases in which something is supposed to be done by one while standing or appearing in the presence of another [cf. B. 176 (153)]: after ἀρνεῖσθαι, Lk. xii. 9 [Lchm. ἔμπροσθεν]; [ἀπαρνεῖσθαι, ibid.]; ὁμολογεῖν, Rev. iii. 5 [Rec. ἐξομ.]; κατηγορεῖν, Rev. xii. 10; [ᾄδειν, Rev. xiv. 3];

καυχᾶσθαι, to come before God and glory, 1 Co. i. 29 ; δικαιοῦν ἑαυτόν, Lk. xvi. 15. c. i. q. *apud* (*with*) ; *in the soul* of any one : χαρὰ γίνεται ἐνώπιον τῶν ἀγγέλων, Lk. xv. 10 [al. understand this of God's joy, by reverent suggestion described as *in the presence of* the angels ; cf. ἐν οὐρ. vs. 7] ; ἔσται σοι δόξα ἐνώπ. τῶν συνανακειμένων, Lk. xiv. 10 [al. take this outwardly ; cf. 2 below] ; after verbs of r e m e m b e r i n g and f o r g e t t i n g : εἰς μνημόσυνον ἐνώπ. (L T Tr WH ἔμπροσθεν) τοῦ θεοῦ, Acts x. 4 ; μνησθῆναι ἐνώπ. τ. θεοῦ, Acts x. 31 ; Rev. xvi. 19 ; ἐπιλελησμένον ἐνώπ. τ. θεοῦ, Lk. xii. 6 [cf. B. § 134, 3]. 2. *before one's eyes ; in one's presence and sight* or *hearing ;* a. prop. : φαγεῖν ἐνώπ. τινος, Lk. xxiv. 43 ; this same phrase signifies a living together in Lk. xiii. 26 (2 S. xi. 13 ; 1 K. i. 25) ; σημεῖα ποιεῖν, Jn. xx. 30 ; ἀνακρίνειν, Lk. xxiii. 14 ; ἐνώπ. πολλῶν μαρτύρων, 1 Tim. vi. 12 ; add Lk. [v. 25] ; viii. 47 ; Acts xix. 9, 19 ; xxvii. 35 ; [1 Tim. v. 20] ; 3 Jn. 6 ; Rev. iii. 5 ; [xiii. 13 ; xiv. 10]. b. metaph. : πίστιν ἔχε ἐνώπιον τοῦ θεοῦ, have faith, satisfied with this that it is not hidden from the sight of God, Ro. xiv. 22 ; ἁμαρτάνειν ἐν τινος (see ἁμαρτάνω ad fin.), Lk. xv. 18, 21 ; esp. in affirmations, oaths, adjurations : ἐνώπιον τοῦ θεοῦ, τοῦ κυρίου, etc., Gal. i. 20 ; 1 Tim. v. 21 ; vi. 13 ; 2 Tim. ii. 14 ; iv. 1. Hence those are said to do something *in the presence of* one who have him present to their thought, who set him before their mind's eye : προωρώμην [προορ. L T Tr WH] τὸν κύριον ἐνώπ. μου, Acts ii. 25 ; ταπεινοῦσθαι ἐν. τοῦ κυρίου, Jas. iv. 10, (Sir. ii. 17). c. *at the instance of* any one, *by his power and authority :* Rev. xiii. 12, 14 ; xix. 20. d. *before the eyes of* one, i. e. *if he turns his eyes thither :* Heb. iv. 13 (where οὐκ ἀφανὴς αὐτοῦ is explained by the following γυμνὰ . . . τοῖς ὀφθαλμοῖς αὐτοῦ ; cf. Job xxvi. 6 γυμνὸς ὁ ᾅδης ἐνώπιον αὐτοῦ, *before his look, to his view*). e. *before one* i. e. *he looking on and judging, in one's judgment* [W. 32 ; B. 172 (150) ; § 133, 14] : ἐφάνησαν ἐνώπ. αὐτῶν ὡσεὶ λῆρος, Lk. xxiv. 11 (cf. Greek Ἡρακλείδῃ λῆρος πάντα δοκεῖ εἶναι.) : so esp. ἐνώπιον τοῦ θεοῦ, τοῦ κυρίου, after the foll. words : τὰ ἀρεστά, 1 Jn. iii. 22 ; βδέλυγμα, Lk. xvi. 15 ; δίκαιος, Lk. i. 6 (T Tr WH ἐναντίον) ; Acts iv. 19 ; δικαιοῦσθαι, Ro. iii. 20 ; εὐάρεστος, Heb. xiii. 21 ; εὐθύς, Acts viii. 21 Rec. ; καλόν, ἀπόδεκτον, 1 Tim. ii. 3 ; v. 4 ; Ro. xii. 17 ; 2 Co. viii. 21 ; μέγας, Lk. i. 15 ; πολυτελές, 1 Pet. iii. 4 ; πεπληρωμένος, Rev. iii. 2 ; ἀρέσκειν, Acts vi. 5 (Deut. i. 23 [Alex.] ; 2 S. iii. 36 ; [W. § 33, f.]) ; *in the sight of God* i. e. *God looking on and approving :* Lk. i. 75 ; Acts x. 33 ; 2 Co. iv. 2 ; vii. 12. *in the sight of God*, or *with God :* εὑρίσκειν χάριν מָצָא חֵן often in the O. T.), to be approved by God, please him, Acts vii. 46.*

'Ενώς (אֱנוֹשׁ [i. e. man, mortal]), *Enos*, son of Seth (Gen. iv. 26) : Lk. iii. 38.*

ἐνωτίζομαι : in bibl. writ. depon. mid. ; 1 aor. impv. 2 pers. plur. ἐνωτίσασθε ; i. q. ἐν ὠτίοις δέχομαι (Hesych.), *to receive into the ear ; give ear to :* τί, Acts ii. 14 ; Sept. for הֶאֱזִין ; elsewhere only in eccl. and Byzant. writ., and in these also as depon. pass. Cf. *Fischer*, De vitiis lexicc. p. 693 sq. ; [*Sturz*, Dial. Alex. p. 166 ; W. 33].*

'Ενώχ [WH 'Ενώχ, see their Intr. § 408], ("Ανωχος, -ου, ὁ, Joseph. antt. 1, 3, 4 ; Hebr. חֲנוֹךְ initiated or initiating, [cf. B. D. s. v.]), *Enoch*, father of Methuselah (Lk. iii. 37) ; on account of his extraordinary piety taken up alive by God to heaven (Gen. v. 18–24 ; Heb. xi. 5 ; [cf. Sir. xliv. 16 ; Joseph. antt. 1, 3, 4]) ; in the opinion of later Jews the most renowned antediluvian prophet ; to whom, towards the end of the second century before Christ, was falsely attributed an apocalyptical book which was afterwards combined with fragments of other apocryphal books, and preserved by the Fathers in Greek fragments and entire in an Ethiopic translation. This translation, having been found among the Abyssinian Christians towards the close of the last century, has been edited by Richard Laurence, archbishop of Cashel (" Libri Henoch versio aethiopica." Oxon. 1838), and by A. Dillmann (" Liber Henoch, aethiopice." Lips. 1851) ; it was translated into English by R. Laurence (1st ed. 1821 ; 3d ed. 1838 [reprinted (Scribners, N. Y.) 1883 ; also (with notes) by G. H. Schodde (Andover, 1882)], into German by A. G. Hoffman (Jen. 1833–38, 2 vols.) and by A. Dillmann (Lips. 1853) ; each of the last two translators added a commentary. From this book is taken the 'prophecy' in Jude 14 sq. ; [cf. B.D. (Am. ed.), also Dict. of Chris. Biog., s. v. Enoch, The Book of].*

ἐξ, see ἐκ. ————————————————— see 1537

ἕξ, οἱ, αἱ, τά, indecl. numeral, *six* : Mt. xvii. 1 ; Lk. xiii. 14, etc. ——— 1803

ἐξ-αγγέλλω : 1 aor. subjunc. 2 pers. plur. ἐξαγγείλητε ; first in Hom. Il. 5, 390 ; properly, *to tell out* or *forth* [see ἐκ, VI. 4], *to declare abroad, divulge, publish :* [Mk. xvi. WH (rejected) 'Shorter Conclusion'] ; with Hebraistic emphasis, *to make known by praising* or *proclaiming, to celebrate*, [A. V. *show forth*] : 1 Pet. ii. 9. (For סָפַר, Ps. lxxii. (lxxiii.) 28 ; lxxviii. (lxxix.) 13, cf. Sir. xliv. 15.) *

ἐξ-αγοράζω : 1 aor. ἐξηγόρασα ; [pres. mid. ἐξαγοράζομαι] ; 1. *to redeem* i. e. by payment of a price to recover from the power of another, *to ransom, buy off*, [cf. ἐκ, VI. 2] : prop. θεραπαινίδα, Diod. 36, 1 p. 530 ; metaph. of Christ freeing men from the dominion of the Mosaic law at the price of his vicarious death (see ἀγοράζω, 2 b.), τινά, Gal. iv. 5 ; with addition of ἐκ τῆς κατάρας τοῦ νόμου, Gal. iii. 13. 2. *to buy up*, Polyb. 3, 42, 2 ; Plut. Crass. 2 ; Mid. τί, *to buy up for one's self, for one's use* [W. § 38, 2 b.; B. 192 (166 sq.)] : trop. in the obscure phrase ἐξαγ. τὸν καιρόν, Eph. v. 16 and Col. iv. 5, where the meaning seems to be *to make a wise and sacred use of every opportunity for doing good*, so that zeal and well-doing are as it were the purchase-money by which we make the time our own ; (act. ἐξαγοράζειν καιρόν, *to seek [to gain time* (A. V.) i. e.] *delay*, Dan. ii. 8 ; mid. with acc. of thing, 'by ransom to avert evil from one's self', 'to buy one's self off or deliver one's self from evil' : διὰ μιᾶς ὥρας τὴν αἰώνιον κόλασιν ἐξαγοραζόμενοι, of the martyrs, Mart. Polyc. 2, 3).*

ἐξ-άγω ; 2 aor. ἐξήγαγον ; Sept. often for הוֹצִיא ; *to lead out* [cf. ἐκ, VI. 1] : τινά (the place whence being supplied in thought), Mk. xv. 20 (of the city to punishment [but Lchm. ἄγουσιν]); Acts xvi. 37, 39; v. 19 and xvi. 39 (from prison); Acts vii. 36 (from Egypt); Jn. x. 3 (sheep from the fold); with ἔξω added [in R G L br.], Lk. xxiv. 50; ἔξω τῆς κώμης, Mk. viii. 23 R G L Tr mrg. [cf. W. 603 (561)]; with the addition of ἐκ w. gen. of place, Acts vii. 40; xii. 17; xiii. 17; Heb. viii. 9; foll. by εἰς with acc. of place, Acts xxi. 38.*

1807　ἐξ-αιρέω, -ῶ: 2 aor. impv. ἔξελε; Mid., [pres. ptcp. ἐξαιρούμενος]; 2 aor. ἐξειλόμην and in Alex. form (L T Tr WH) ἐξειλάμην (Acts vii. 10 [so Grsb.]; xii. 11 [so Grsb.]; xxiii. 27; see reff. in [αἱρέω and] ἀπέρχομαι), inf. ἐξελέσθαι (Acts vii. 34); Sept. usually for הִצִּיל; *to take out* [cf. ἐκ, VI. 2]; **1.** *to pluck out, draw out,* i. e. *to root out:* τὸν ὀφθαλμόν, Mt. v. 29; xviii. 9. **2.** Mid. **a.** *to choose out (for one's self), select,* one person from many: Acts xxvi. 17 (so for בָּחַר in Is. xlix. 7 [but there the Sept. has ἐξελεξάμην; perh. Is. xlviii. 10 is meant] and sometimes in Grk. writ.; first in Hom. Od. 14, 232) [al. refer Acts l. c. to the next head; (see Hackett ad loc.)]. **b.** *to rescue, deliver,* (prop. *to cause to be rescued,* but the middle force is lost [cf. W. 253 (238)]): τινά, Acts vii. 34; xxiii. 27; τινὰ ἔκ τινος, Acts vii. 10; xii. 11; Gal. i. 4; (Ex. iii. 8, etc.; Aeschyl. suppl. 924; Hdt. 3, 137; Dem. 256, 3; Polyb. 1, 11, 11).*

1808　ἐξ-αίρω: fut. ἐξαρῶ (1 Co. v. 13 Rec.); 1 aor. impv. 2 pers. plur. ἐξάρατε (ib. G L T Tr WH); 1 aor. pass. ἐξῆρθην, *to lift up* or *take away out of* a place; *to remove* [cf. ἐκ, VI. 2]: τινὰ ἐκ, one from a company, 1 Co. v. 2 Rec. [see αἴρω, 3 c.]; vs. 13 fr. Deut. [xix. 19 or] xxiv. 9.*

see
1809 St.　ἐξ-αιτέω, -ῶ: 1 aor. mid. ἐξῃτησάμην; *to ask from, demand of,* [cf. ἐκ, VI. 2]. Mid. *to ask from* (or *beg*) *for one's self:* τινά, *to ask that one be given up to one from the power of another,* — in both senses, either for good, *to beg one from another, ask for the pardon, the safety, of some one,* (Xen. an. 1, 1, 3; Dem. p. 546, 22; Plut. Per. 32; Palaeph. 41, 2); or in a bad sense, *for torture, for punishment,* (Plut. mor. p. 417 d. de defect. orac. 14; in prof. auth. often with this sense in the act.); so of Satan asking the apostles out of the power and keeping of God to be tried by afflictions (allusion being made to Job i. 1-12): Lk. xxii. 31 (Test. xii. Patr. p. 729 [test. Benj. § 3] ἐὰν τὰ πνεύματα τοῦ Βελίαρ εἰς πᾶσαν πονηρίαν θλίψεως ἐξαιτήσωνται ὑμᾶς).*

1810　ἐξ-αίφνης [WH ἐξέφνης (exc. in Acts xxii. 6), see their App. p. 151], adv., (αἴφνης, ἄφνω, ἄφνως suddenly), *of a sudden, suddenly, unexpectedly:* Mk. xiii. 36; Lk. ii. 13; ix. 39; Acts ix. 3; xxii. 6. (Hom. et al.; Sept.)*

1811　ἐξ-ακολουθέω, -ῶ: fut. ἐξακολουθήσω; 1 aor. ptcp. ἐξακολουθήσας; *to follow out* or *up, tread in one's steps;* **a.** τῇ ὁδῷ τινος, metaph., *to imitate one's way of acting:* 2 Pet. ii. 15, cf. Is. lvi. 11. **b.** *to follow one's authority:* μύθοις, 2 Pet. i. 16; Joseph. antt. prooem. 4, (ἀρχηγοῖς, Clem. Rom. 1 Cor. 14, 1; δυσὶ βασιλεῦσι, Test. xii. Patr. p. 643 [test. Zeb. § 9]). **c.** *to comply with, yield to:* ἀσελγείαις [Rec. ἀπωλείαις], 2 Pet. ii. 2, (πνεύμασι πλάνης, Test. xii. Patr. p. 665 [test. Napht. § 3; τοῖς πονηροῖς διαβουλίοις, xii. Patr. p. 628 test. Is. § 6]; cf.

also Am. ii. 4; Job xxxi. 9; Sir. v. 2). Among prof. auth. Polyb., Plut. occasionally use the word; [add Dion. Hal. de comp. verb. § 24 p. 188, 7; Epictet. diss. 1, 22, 16].*

1812　ἐξακόσιοι, -αι, -α, *six hundred:* Rev. [xiii. 18]; xiv. 20.*

1813　ἐξ-αλείφω: fut. ἐξαλείψω; 1 aor. ptcp. ἐξαλείψας; 1 aor. pass. infin. ἐξαλειφθῆναι [(WH -λιφθῆναι; see their App. p. 154, and s. v. I, ι below)]; **1.** (ἐξ- denoting completeness [cf. ἐκ, VI. 6]), *to anoint* or *wash in every part,* hence *to besmear:* i. q. *cover with lime* (to whitewash or plaster), τὸ τεῖχος, Thuc. 3, 20; τοὺς τοίχους τοῦ ἱεροῦ [here to *overlay* with gold etc.], 1 Chr. xxix. 4; τὴν οἰκίαν, Lev. xiv. 42 (for טוּחַ). **2.** (ἐξ- denoting removal [cf. ἐκ, VI. 2]), *to wipe off, wipe away:* δάκρυον ἀπὸ [G L T Tr WH ἐκ] τῶν ὀφθαλμῶν, Rev. vii. 17; xxi. 4 [R G WH mrg., al. ἐκ]; *to obliterate, erase, wipe out, blot out,* (Aeschyl., Hdt., al.; Sept. for מָחָה): τί, Col. ii. 14; τὸ ὄνομα ἐκ τῆς βίβλου, Rev. iii. 5 (Ps. lxviii. (lxix.) 29, cf. Deut. ix. 14; xxv. 6); τὰς ἁμαρτίας, the guilt of sins, Acts iii. 19, (Ps. cviii. (cix.) 13; τὸ ἀνόμημα, τὰς ἀνομίας, Is. xliii. 25; Ps. l. (li.) 11; Sir. xlvi. 20; τ. ἁμαρτίας ἀπαλείφειν, 3 Macc. ii. 19).*

1814　ἐξ-άλλομαι; *to leap up:* Acts iii. 8. (Xen. Cyr. 7, 1, 27, et al.; Sept. Is. lv. 12.) *

1815　ἐξ-ανάστασις, -εως, ἡ, (ἐξανίστημι, q. v.), *a rising up* (Polyb. 3, 55, 4); *a rising again, resurrection:* τῶν νεκρῶν or (L T Tr WH) ἡ ἐκ τῶν νεκρῶν, Phil. iii. 11.*

1816　ἐξ-ανα-τέλλω: 1 aor. ἐξανέτειλα; **1.** trans. *to make spring up, cause to shoot forth:* Gen. ii. 9, etc. **2.** intrans. *to spring up:* Mt. xiii. 5; Mk. iv. 5. (Rare in prof. auth. [cf. W. 102 (97)].) *

1817　ἐξ-αν-ίστημι: 1 aor. ἐξανέστησα; 2 aor. ἐξανέστην; **1.** *to make rise up, to raise up, to produce:* σπέρμα, Mk. xii. 19; Lk. xx. 28, (Hebr. הֵקִים זֶרַע, Gen. xxxviii. 8). **2.** 2 aor. act. *to rise in an assembly to speak* (as in Xen. an. 6, 1, 30): Acts xv. 5.*

1818　ἐξ-απατάω, -ῶ; 1 aor. ἐξηπάτησα; 1 aor. pass. ptcp. fem. ἐξαπατηθεῖσα; (ἐξ- strengthens the simple verb [cf. ἐκ, VI. 6]), *to deceive:* Ro. vii. 11; xvi. 18; 1 Co. iii. 18; 2 Co. xi. 3; 2 Th. ii. 3; pass. 1 Tim. ii. 14 [L T Tr WH]. (From Hom. down; twice in the O. T. viz. Ex. viii. 29; Sus. vs. 56.) *

1819　ἐξάπινα, (a somewhat rare later Grk. form for ἐξαπίνης, ἐξαίφνης, q. v. [W. § 2, 1 d.]), adv., *suddenly:* Mk. ix. 8. (Sept.; Jambl., Zonar., al.; Byzant.) *

see
1820 St.　ἐξ-απορέω and (so in the Bible) depon. pass. ἐξαπορέομαι, -οῦμαι; 1 aor. ἐξηπορήθην; *to be utterly at a loss, be utterly destitute of measures* or *resources, to renounce all hope, be in despair,* [cf. ἐκ, VI. 6], (Polyb., Diod., Plut., al.): 2 Co. iv. 8 (where it is distinguished fr. the simple ἀπορέομαι); τινός of anything: τοῦ ζῆν, 2 Co. i. 8, on this gen. cf. Matthiae ii. p. 828 sq. (τοῦ ἀργυρίου, to be utterly in want of, Dion. Hal. 7, 18; act. with dat. of respect: τοῖς λογισμοῖς, Polyb. 1, 62, 1; once in the O. T. absol. Ps. lxxxvii. (lxxxviii.) 16).*

1821　ἐξ-απο-στέλλω: fut. ἐξαποστελῶ; 1 aor. ἐξαπέστειλα; [2 aor. pass. ἐξαπεστάλην]; Sept. very often for שָׁלַח; prop. *to send away* from one's self (ἀπό) *out of* the place or out of doors (ἐκ [q. v. VI. 2]);   **1.** *to send forth* : τινά, with commissions, Acts vii. 12 ; [xii. 11] ; Gal. iv. 4 ; foll. by inf. of purpose, Acts xi. 22 (but L T Tr WH om. the inf.) ; εἰς ἔθνη, unto the Gentiles, Acts xxii. 21 [WH mrg. ἀποστ.] ; used also of powers, influences, things, (see ἀποστέλλω, 1 a.) : τὴν ἐπαγγελίαν, the promised blessing, Lk. xxiv. 49 T Tr WH ; τὸ πνεῦμα εἰς τὰς καρδίας, to send forth i. e. impart the Spirit to our hearts, Gal. iv. 6 ; [τὸ . . . κήρυγμα τῆς αἰωνίου σωτηρίας, Mk. xvi. WH in (rejected) ' Shorter Conclusion '] ; ὑμῖν ὁ λόγος . . . ἐξαπεστάλη, the message was sent forth, i. e. commanded to be announced, to you, Acts xiii. 26 L T Tr WH.   **2.** *to send away* : τινὰ εἰς etc. Acts ix. 30 ; foll. by inf. of purpose, Acts xvii. 14 ; τινὰ κενόν, Lk. i. 53 ; xx. 10, 11. (Dem., Polyb., Diod.) *

1822   **ἐξαρτίζω** : 1 aor. inf. ἐξαρτίσαι ; pf. pass. ptcp. ἐξηρτισμένος ; (see ἄρτιος, 2) ; rare in prof. auth. ; *to complete, finish* ;   **a.** *to furnish perfectly* : τινά, pass., πρός τι, 2 Tim. iii. 17 (πολεμεῖν . . . τοῖς ἅπασι καλῶς ἐξηρτισμένοι, Joseph. antt. 3, 2, 2).   **b.** τὰς ἡμέρας, *to finish, accomplish,* (as it were, to render the days complete) : Acts xxi. 5 (so ἀπαρτίζειν τὴν ὀκτάμηνον, Hipp. epid. ii. 180 [cf. *Lob.* ad Phryn. p. 447 sq.]).*

1823   **ἐξ-αστράπτω**.   **1.** prop. *to send forth lightning, to lighten.*   **2.** *to flash out like lightning, to shine, be radiant* : of garments, Lk. ix. 29 ; (of gleaming arms, Nah. iii. 3 ; Ezek. i. 4, 7 ; φόβῳ κ. κάλλεῖ πολλῷ Tryphiodor. 103 ; [cf. W. 102 (97)]).*

1824   **ἐξ-αυτῆς** and **ἐξ αὐτῆς** [so Rec. Mk. vi. 25], (scil. ὥρας [W. 591 sq. (550) ; B. 82 (71)]), *on the instant ; forthwith* : Mk. vi. 25 ; Acts x. 33 ; xi. 11 ; xxi. 32 ; xxiii. 30 [R G WH] ; Phil. ii. 23. (Cratin. in Bekk. anecd. i. p. 94 ; Theogn., Arat., Polyb., Joseph., al.) *

1825   **ἐξ-εγείρω** [1 Co. vi. 14 Lchm. txt.] ; fut. ἐξεγερῶ ; 1 aor. ἐξήγειρα ; *to arouse, raise up* (from sleep) ; Soph., Eur., Xen., al.) ; *from the dead* (Aeschyl. cho. 495), 1 Co. vi. 14. *to rouse up, stir up, incite* : τινά, to resistance, Ro. ix. 17 (τὸν θυμόν τινος, 2 Macc. xiii. 4, cf. 2 Chr. xxxvi. 22), where some explain the words ἐξήγειρά σε *I have raised thee up into life, caused thee to exist,* or *I have raised thee to a public position, set thee up as king* (Joseph. antt. 8, 11, 1 βασιλεὺς γὰρ ἐξεγείρεται ὑπ' ἐμοῦ) ; but the objection to these interpretations lies in the fact that Paul draws from vs. 17 what he says in vs. 18, and therefore ἐξεγείρειν must be nearly synonymous with σκληρύνειν, [but see Meyer].*

1826   **ἔξ-ειμι** ; impf. ἐξῄεσαν ; (εἶμι) ; *to go out, go forth* : foll. in Rec. by ἐκ with gen. of place, Acts xiii. 42 ; without mention of the place, that being known from the context, Acts xvii. 15 ; xx. 7 ; ἐπὶ τὴν γῆν (from the water), to escape to the land, Acts xxvii. 43.*

see 1832   **ἔξ-ειμι** from εἰμί, see ἔξεστι.

1827   **ἐξ-ελέγχω** : 1 aor. inf. ἐξελέγξαι ; (ἐξ strengthens the simple verb [cf. ἐκ, VI. 6]) ; *to prove to be in the wrong, convict,* (chiefly in Attic writ.) : by punishing, τινὰ περὶ τινος, Jude 15 Rec. (see ἐλέγχω, 1) of God as judge, as in Is. ii. 4 ; Mic. iv. 3 for הוֹכִיחַ.*

1828   **ἐξ-έλκω** : [pres. pass. ptcp. ἐξελκόμενος] ; *to draw out,*

(Hom., Pind., Attic writ.) ; metaph. i. q. *to lure forth,* [A. V. *draw away*] : ὑπὸ τῆς . . . ἐπιθυμίας ἐξελκόμενος, Jas. i. 14, where the metaphor is taken from hunting and fishing : as game is lured from its covert, so man by lust is allured from the safety of self-restraint to sin. [The language of hunting seems to be transferred here (so elsewhere, cf. Wetst. ad loc.) to the seductions of a h a r l o t, personated by ἐπιθυμία ; see τίκτω.]*

ἐξ-έλω, see ἐξαιρέω.   see 1807

ἐξ-έραμα, -τος, τό, (fr. ἐξεράω to eject, cast forth, vomit   1829
forth ; cf. *Lob.* ad Phryn. p. 64), *vomit ; what is cast out by vomiting* : 2 Pet. ii. 22, cf. Prov. xxvi. 11. (Dioscor. de venenis c. 19 (p. 29 ed. Spreng.) [an example of the verb. Cf. Wetst. on Pet. l. c., and esp. *Gataker,* Advers. miscell. col. 853 sq.].) *

[**ἐξ-ερaυνάω** T Tr WH for ἐξερευνάω, q. v. ; see ἐραυνάω.]   see 2045

ἐξ-ερευνάω, -ῶ : 1 aor. ἐξηρεύνησα ; *to search out, search*   1830
anxiously and diligently : περί τινος, 1 Pet. i. 10 [where T Tr WH ἐξεραυν. q. v.]. (1 Macc. iii. 48 ; ix. 26 ; Sept. ; Soph., Eur., Polyb., Plut., al.) *

ἐξ-έρχομαι ; impf. ἐξηρχόμην ; fut. ἐξελεύσομαι ; 2 aor.   1831
ἐξῆλθον, plur. 2 pers. ἐξήλθετε, 3 pers. ἐξῆλθον, and in L T Tr WH the Alex. forms (see ἀπέρχομαι, init.) ἐξήλθατε (Mt. xi. 7, 8, 9 ; xxvi. 55 ; Mk. xiv. 48, etc.), ἐξῆλθαν (1 Jn. ii. 19 ; 2 Jn. 7 [here Tdf. -θον ; 3 Jn. 7, etc.]) ; pf. ἐξελήλυθα ; plpf. ἐξεληλύθειν (Lk. viii. 38, etc.) ; Sept. for יָצָא times without number ; *to go* or *come out of* ;   **1.** properly ;   **a.** with mention of the place out of which one goes, or of the point from which he departs ;   **α.** of those who leave a place of their own accord : with the gen. alone, Mt. x. 14 (L T Tr WH insert ἔξω) ; Acts xvi. 39 R G. foll. by ἐκ : Mk. v. 2 ; vii. 31 ; Jn. iv. 30 ; viii. 59 ; Acts vii. 3 sq. ; 1 Co. v. 10 ; Rev. xviii. 4, etc. foll. by ἔξω with gen. — with addition of εἰς and acc. of place, Mt. xxi. 17 ; Mk. xiv. 68 ; or παρά with acc. of place, Acts xvi. 13 ; or πρός τινα, acc. of pers., Heb. xiii. 13. ἐξέρχ. ἀπό with gen. of place, Mt. xiii. 1 R G ; Mk. xi. 12 ; Lk. ix. 5 ; Phil. iv. 15 ; [Heb. xi. 15 R G] ; ἐξέρχ. ἐκεῖθεν, Mt. xv. 21 ; Mk. vi. 1, 10 ; Lk. ix. 4 ; [xi. 53 T Tr txt. WH txt.] ; Jn. iv. 43 ; ὅθεν ἐξῆλθον, Mt. xii. 44 ; Lk. xi. 24 [yet see β. below]. ἐξέρχ. ἐκ etc. *to come forth from, out of, a place* : Mt. viii. 28 ; Rev. xiv. 15, 17, 18 [L om. WH br. ἐξῆλ.] ; xv. 6 ; ἐξελθεῖν ἀπό, *to come out* (towards one) *from,* Mt. xv. 22. In the Gospel of John Christ, who by his incarnation left his place with God in heaven, is said ἐξελθεῖν παρὰ τοῦ θεοῦ : xvi. 27 and R G L mrg. in vs. 28 ; ἀπὸ τοῦ θεοῦ, xiii. 3 ; xvi. 30 ; ἐκ τοῦ θεοῦ, from his place with God, from God's abode, viii. 42 and L txt. T Tr WH in xvi. 28.   **β.** of those expelled or cast out (esp. of demons driven forth from a body of which they have held possession) : ἔκ τινος, gen. of pers. : Mk. i. 25 sq. ; v. 8 [L mrg. ἀπό] ; vii. 29 ; Lk. iv. 35 R Tr mrg. ; or ἀπό τινος, Mt. xii. 43 ; xvii. 18 ; Lk. iv. 35 L T Tr txt. WH ; viii. 29, 33, 35 ; xi. 24 [yet see *a.* above] ; Acts xvi. 18 ; [xix. 12 Rec.].   **γ.** of those who come forth, or are let go, from confinement in which they have been kept (e. g. from prison) : Mt. v. 26 ; Acts xvi. 40.   **b.** without mention of the place from which one goes out ;

a. where the place from which one goes forth (as a house, city, ship) has just been mentioned: Mt. [viii. 12 Tdf.]; ix. 31 sq. (from the house, vs. 28); x. 11 (sc. ἐκεῖθεν, i. e. ἐκ τῆς πόλεως ἢ κώμης ἐκείνης); xii. 14 (cf. 9); xviii. 28 (cf. 24); xiv. 14; Mk. i. 45 (cf. 43 ἐξέβαλεν αὐτόν); Lk. i. 22 (from the temple); viii. 27; x. 35 [Rec.]; Jn. xiii. 30, 31 (30), etc.; so also when the verb ἐξέρχεσθαι refers to the departure of demons: Mt. viii. 32; Mk. v. 13; vii. 30; ix. 29; Acts viii. 7; xvi. 19 (where for the name of the demon itself is substituted the descriptive clause ἡ ἐλπὶς τ. ἐργασίας αὐτῶν; see 2 e. δ.). **β.** where one is said to have gone forth to do something, and it is obvious that he has gone forth from his home, or at least from the place where he has been staying: foll. by an inf., Mt. xi. 8; xiii. 3 [inf. w. τοῦ]; xx. 1; Mk. iii. 21; iv. 3 [R G inf. w. τοῦ (Tr br. τοῦ)]; v. 14 Rec.; Lk. vii. 25 sq.; Acts xx. 1; Rev. xx. 8; with the addition of ἐπί τινα (against), Mt. xxvi. 55; Mk. xiv. 48; Lk. xxii. 52; εἰς τοῦτο, Mk. i. 38; ἵνα, Rev. vi. 2; also without any inf. or conjunction indicating the purpose: Mk. vi. 12; viii. 11; xiv. 16; xvi. 20; Lk. v. 27; ix. 6; Jn. xxi. 3; Acts x. 23; xx. 11; 2 Co. viii. 17; foll. by εἰς with acc. of place: Mt. xxii. 10; xxvi. 30, 71; Mk. viii. 27; xi. 11; Lk. vi. 12; vii. 21, 23; Jn. i. 43 (44); Acts xi. 25; xiv. 20; 2 Co. ii. 13; the place to which one goes forth being evident either from what goes before or from the context: Mt. xxiv. 26 (sc. εἰς τὴν ἔρημον); xxvii. 32 (from the city to the place of crucifixion); ἐξέρχ. alone is used of a people quitting the land which they had previously inhabited, Acts vii. 7, cf. Heb. xi. 8; of angels coming forth from heaven, Mt. xiii. 49. ἐξέρχ. εἰς ἀπάντησίν τινος, to meet one, Mt. xxv. 1 [L Tr WH ὑπάντ.], 6; [εἰς ἀπάντ. or ὑπάντ.] τινί, Jn. xii. 13; Acts xxviii. 15 R G; εἰς συνάντησίν τινι, Mt. viii. 34 [L T Tr WH ὑπάντ.]. Agreeably to the oriental redundancy of style in description (see ἀνίστημι, II. 1 c.), the participle ἐξελθών is often placed before another finite verb of departure: Mt. viii. 32; xv. 21; xxiv. 1 (ἐξελθών [from the temple, see xxi. 23] ἐπορεύετο ἀπὸ τοῦ ἱεροῦ, he departed from its vicinity); Mk. xvi. 8; Lk. xxii. 39; Acts xii. 9, 17; xvi. 36, 40; xxi. 5, 8. **2.** figuratively: **a.** ἔκ τινων, ἐκ μέσου τινῶν, to go out from some assembly, i. e. to forsake it: 1 Jn. ii. 19 (opp. to μεμενήκεισαν μεθ᾽ ἡμῶν); 2 Co. vi. 17. **b.** to come forth from physically, arise from, to be born of: ἐκ with gen. of the place from which one comes by birth, Mt. ii. 6 (fr. Mic. v. 2); ἐκ τῆς ὀσφύος τινός, Hebr. יָצָא מֵחֲלָצִים (Gen. xxxv. 11; 1 K. viii. 19; [cf. W. 33 (32)]), Heb. vii. 5. **c.** ἐκ χειρός τινος, to go forth from one's power, escape from it in safety: Jn. x. 39. **d.** εἰς τὸν κόσμον, to come forth (from privacy) into the world, before the public, (of those who by novelty of opinion attract attention): 1 Jn. iv. 1. **e.** of things: **a.** of report, rumors, messages, precepts, etc., i. q. to be uttered, to be heard: φωνή, Rev. xvi. 17; xix. 5; i. q. to be made known, declared: ὁ λόγος τοῦ θεοῦ foll. by ἀπό τινων, from their city or church, 1 Co. xiv. 36; i. q. to spread, be diffused: ἡ φήμη, Mt. ix. 26; Lk. iv. 14; ἡ ἀκοή, Mk. i. 28; [Mt. iv. 24 Tr mrg.]; ὁ φθόγγος, τὰ ῥήματα, Ro. x. 18; ὁ λόγος the word, saying, Jn. xxi. 23; Lk. vii. 17;

ἡ πίστις τινός, the report of one's faith, 1 Th. i. 8; i. q. to be proclaimed: δόγμα, an imperial edict, παρά τινος, gen. pers., Lk. ii. 1. **β.** to come forth i. q. be emitted, as from the heart, the mouth, etc.: Mt. xv. 18 sq.; Jas. iii. 10; [cf. ῥομφαία ἐκ τοῦ στόματος, Rev. xix. 21 G L T Tr WH]; i. q. to flow forth from the body: Jn. xix. 34; i. q. to emanate, issue: Lk. viii. 46; Rev. xiv. 20. **γ.** ἐξέρχεσθαι (ἀπ᾽ ἀνατολῶν), used of a sudden flash of lightning, Mt. xxiv. 27. **δ.** that ἐξέρχεσθαι in Acts xvi. 19 (on which see 1 b. a. above) is used also of a thing's vanishing, viz. of a hope which has disappeared, arises from the circumstance that the demon that had gone out had been the hope of those who complain that their hope has gone out. On the phrase εἰσέρχεσθαι κ. ἐξέρχεσθαι see in εἰσέρχομαι, 1 a. [COMP.: δι-εξέρχομαι.]

ἔξ-εστι, impers. verb, (fr. the unused ἔξειμι), it is lawful; **a.** foll. by the pres. inf.: Mt. xii. 2, 10 [Tdf. inf. aor.], 12; xiv. 4; Lk. vi. 2 [R G T]; xx. 3 [L T Tr WH inf. aor.]; with the aor. inf.: Mt. [xv. 26 L T]; xxii. 17; xxvii. 6; Mk. iii. 4; xii. 14; Lk. vi. 9; Acts ii. 29 (ἐξὸν εἰπεῖν scil. ἔστω, allow me, [al. supply ἐστί, B. 318 (273); W. § 64, I. 2 a., cf. § 2, 1 d.]); with the inf. omitted because readily suggested by the context, Mk. ii. 24 and Rec. in Acts viii. 37. **b.** foll. by dat. of pers. and a pres. inf.: Mk. vi. 18; Acts xvi. 21; xxii. 25; and an aor. inf.: Mt. xix. 3 [L T WH om. dat.]; xx. 15; Mk. ii. 26 [R G L Tr txt.]; x. 2; Lk. xx. 22 R G L; Jn. v. 10; xviii. 31; Acts xxi. 37; ἐξὸν ἦν, Mt. xii. 4; ἃ οὐκ ἐξόν, sc. ἐστί, 2 Co. xii. 4; with the inf. omitted, as being evident from the context: πάντα (μοι) ἔξεστιν, sc. ποιεῖν, 1 Co. vi. 12; x. 23. **c.** foll. by the acc. and inf.: Lk. vi. 4; xx. 22 T Tr WH; so here and there even in classic writ.; cf. Rost § 127 Anm. 2; Kühner § 475 Anm. 2; [B. § 142, 2].*

ἐξ-ετάζω: 1 aor. impv. 2 pers. plur. ἐξετάσατε, inf. ἐξετάσαι; to search out; to examine strictly, inquire: περί τινος and with the adv. ἀκριβῶς added, Mt. ii. 8; foll. by an indir. quest. Mt. x. 11; τινά inquire of some one, foll. by a direct question, Jn. xxi. 12. (Sept.; often in Grk. writ. fr. Thuc. down.) *

[ἐξέφνης, see ἐξαίφνης.] ‑‑‑‑‑‑‑‑‑‑‑‑‑‑ see 1810

ἐξ-ηγέομαι, -οῦμαι; impf. ἐξηγούμην; 1 aor. ἐξηγησάμην; **1.** prop. to lead out, be leader, go before, (Hom. et al.). **2.** metaph. (cf. Germ. ausführen) to draw out in narrative, unfold in teaching: **a.** to recount, rehearse: [w. acc. of the thing and dat. of pers., Acts x. 8]; w. acc. of thing, Lk. xxiv. 35; Acts xxi. 19; without an acc., foll. by rel. pron. or adv., ὅσα ἐποίησεν, Acts xv. 12; καθώς, 14, (so in Grk. writ. fr. Hdt. down; Sept. for סָפַר, Judg. vii. 13, etc.). **b.** to unfold, declare: Jn. i. 18 (sc. the things relating to God; also used in Grk. writ. of the interpretation of things sacred and divine, oracles, dreams, etc.; cf. Meyer ad loc.; Alberti, Observationes etc. p. 207 sq.).*

ἑξήκοντα, οἱ, αἱ, τά, sixty: Mt. xiii. 8, 23, etc.

ἑξῆς, adv., (fr. ἔχω, fut. ἕξω; cf. ἔχομαί τινος to cleave to, come next to, a thing), successively, in order, (fr. Hom. down); ὁ, ἡ, τὸ ἑξῆς the next following, the next in succession: so ἡ ἑξῆς ἡμέρα, Lk. ix. 37; elliptically ἐν τῇ ἑξῆς, sc. ἡμέρᾳ, Lk. vii. 11 (here WH txt. Tr txt. L mrg. ἐν τῷ ἑξῆς sc. χρόνῳ, soon afterwards); τῇ ἑξῆς, sc. ἡμέρᾳ, Acts xxi. 1; xxv. 17; xxvii. 18.*

**see
1837 St.** ἐξ-ηχέω, -ῶ: to sound forth, emit sound, resound; pass. ἐξηχεῖταί τι the sound of something is borne forth, is propagated: ἀφ' ὑμῶν ἐξήχηται ὁ λόγος τοῦ κυρίου, from your city or from your church the word of the Lord has sounded forth i. e. has been disseminated by report, 1 Th. i. 8, cf. De Wette ad loc. (Joel iii. 14 (iv. 19); Sir. xl. 13; 3 Macc. iii. 2. Polyb. 30, 4, 7 [not Dind.]; Philo in Flacc. § 6; [quis rer. div. her. § 4]; Byzant.) *

1838 ἕξις, -εως, ἡ, (ἔχω, fut. ἕξω), a habit, whether of body or of mind (Xen., Plat., Aristot., al.); a power acquired by custom, practice, use, ("firma quaedam facilitas, quae apud Graecos ἕξις nominatur," Quint. 10, 1 init.); so Heb. v. 14, (ἐν τούτοις ἱκανὴν ἕξιν περιποιησάμενος, Sir. prol. 7; ἕξιν ἔχειν γραμματικῆς, Polyb. 10, 47, 7; ἐν τοῖς πολεμικοῖς, 21, 7, 3; ἐν ἀστρολογίᾳ μεγίστην ἕξιν ἔχειν, Diod. 2, 31; λογικὴν ἕξιν περιποιούμενος, Philo, alleg. legg. 1, 4).*

1839 ἐξ-ίστημι: likewise ἐξιστάω and ἐξιστάνω. (Acts viii. 9 ptcp. ἐξιστῶν R G, ἐξιστάνων L T Tr WH [see ἵστημι]); 1 aor. ἐξέστησα; 2 aor. ἐξέστην; pf. inf. ἐξεστακέναι; Mid., [pres. inf. ἐξίστασθαι]; impf. 3 pers. plur. ἐξίσταντο; **1.** In pres., impf., fut., 1 aor. act. to throw out of position, to displace: τινὰ τοῦ φρονεῖν, to throw one out of his mind, drive one out of his senses, Xen. mem. 1, 3, 12; φρενῶν, Eur. Bacch. 850; hence simply to amaze, astonish, throw into wonderment: τινά, Lk. xxiv. 22; Acts viii. 9. **2.** In perf., pluperf., 2 aor. act. and also the mid., **a.** to be amazed, astounded: Mt. xii. 23; Mk. ii. 12; Lk. viii. 56; Acts ii. 7, 12; viii. 13; ix. 21; xii. 16, (Sept. for חָרֵד, to tremble, Ex. xix. 18; Ruth iii. 8, etc.); ἐξέστησαν ἐκστάσει μεγάλῃ, they were amazed with a great amazement (see ἔκστασις, 3), Mk. v. 42; ἐν ἑαυτοῖς ἐξίσταντο, Mk. vi. 51; with dat. of the thing: μαγείαις ἐξεστακέναι, had been put beside themselves with magic arts, carried away with wonder at them, Acts viii. 11 [but this form of the perf. is transitive; cf. B. 48 (41)]; Veitch 339]; ἐξίσταντο ἐπί with dat. of thing, Lk. ii. 47 (Ex. xix. 18; Sap. v. 2). **b.** to be out of one's mind, beside one's self, insane: 2 Co. v. 13 (opp. to σωφρονεῖν); Mk. iii. 21 [cf. B. 198 (171); W. § 40, 5 b.]; (Grk. writ., where they use the word in this sense, generally add τοῦ φρονεῖν, τῶν φρενῶν: Isoc., Eur., Polyb., al.).*

1840 ἐξ-ισχύω: 1 aor. subjunc. 2 pers. plur. ἐξισχύσητε, to be eminently able, to have full strength, [cf. ἐκ, VI. 6]: foll. by an inf. Eph. iii. 18. (Sir. vii. 6; rare in Grk. writ., as Dioscor., Strab., Plut.) *

1841 ἔξ-οδος, -ου, ἡ, (ὁδός), exit, i. e. departure: Heb. xi. 22; metaph. ἡ ἔξοδός τινος the close of one's career, one's final fate, Lk. ix. 31; departure from life, decease: 2 Pet. i. 15, as in Sap. iii. 2; vii. 6; [Philo de caritate § 4]; with addition of τοῦ ζῆν, Joseph. antt. 4, 8, 2; [of τοῦ βίου, Just. dial. c. Tryph. § 105].*

1842 ἐξ-ολοθρεύω and (acc. to the reading best attested by the oldest Mss. of the Sept. and received by L T Tr WH [see ὀλοθρεύω]) ἐξολεθρεύω: fut. pass. ἐξολοθρευθήσομαι; to destroy out of its place, destroy utterly, to extirpate: ἐκ τοῦ λαοῦ, Acts iii. 23. (Often in the Sept., and in the

O. T. Apocr., and in Test. xii. Patr.; Joseph. antt. 8, 11, 1; 11, 6, 6; hardly in native Grk. writ.) *

1843 ἐξ-ομολογέω, -ῶ: 1 aor. ἐξωμολόγησα; Mid., [pres. ἐξομολογοῦμαι]; fut. ἐξομολογήσομαι; [1 aor. subj. 3 pers. sing. -γήσηται, Phil. ii. 11 R G L txt. Tr txt. WH]; (ἐξ either forth from the heart, freely, or publicly, openly [cf. W. 102 (97)]); act. and depon. mid. to confess, to profess; **1.** to confess: τὰς ἁμαρτίας, Mt. iii. 6; Mk. i. 5; [Jas. v. 16 L T Tr WH], (Joseph. antt. 8, 4, 6; [cf. b. j. 5, 10, 5; Clem. Rom. 1 Cor. 51, 3; Barn. ep. 19, 12]); τὰς πράξεις, Acts xix. 18; τὰ παραπτώματα, Jas. v. 16 R G; (ἧτταν, Plut. Eum. c. 17; τὴν ἀλήθειαν ἄνευ βασάνων, id. Anton. c. 59). **2.** to profess i. e. to acknowledge openly and joyfully: τὸ ὄνομά τινος, Rev. iii. 5 Rec.; foll. by ὅτι, Phil. ii. 11; with dat. of pers. [cf. W. § 31, 1 f.; B. 176 (153)] to one's honor, i. e. to celebrate, give praise to (so Sept. for הוֹדָה לְ, Ps. xxix. (xxx.) 5; cv. (cvi.) 47; cxxi. (cxxii.) 4, etc.; [W. 32]): Ro. xiv. 11; xv. 9 fr. Ps. xvii. (xviii.) 50, (Clem. Rom. 1 Cor. 61, 3); τινί (dat. of pers.) foll. by ὅτι: Mt. xi. 25; Lk. x. 21. to profess that one will do something, to promise, agree, engage: Lk. xxii. 6 [Lchm. om.]; (in this sense the Greeks and Josephus use ὁμολογεῖν).*

see 1832 ἐξ-όν, see ἔξεστι.

1844 ἐξ-ορκίζω; **1.** to exact an oath, to force to an oath, (Dem., Polyb., Apollod., Diod., Plut., al.), for which the earlier Grks. used ἐξορκόω, [cf. W. 102 (97)]. **2.** to adjure: τινὰ κατά τινος, one by a person [cf. κατά, I. 2 a.], foll. by ἵνα [B. 237 (205)], Mt. xxvi. 63; (Gen. xxiv. 3).*

1845 ἐξ-ορκιστής, -οῦ, ὁ, (ἐξορκίζω); **1.** he who exacts an oath of another. **2.** an exorcist, i. e. one who employs a formula of conjuration for expelling demons: Acts xix. 13. (Joseph. antt. 8, 2, 5; Lcian. epigr. in Anthol. 11, 427; often in the church Fathers.) *

1846 ἐξ-ορύσσω: 1 aor. ptcp. ἐξορύξαντες; fr. Hdt. down; **1.** to dig out: τοὺς ὀφθαλμούς (prop. to pluck out the eyes; so Judg. xvi. 21 [Alex.]; 1 S. xi. 2; Hdt. 8, 116; Joseph. antt. 6, 5, 1; Lcian. dial. deor. 1, 1; al.) καὶ διδόναι τινί, metaph. to renounce the most precious things for another's advantage, Gal. iv. 15 (similar expressions see in Ter. adelph. 4, 5, 67; Hor. sat. 2, 5, 35; [Wetstein ad loc.]); in opposition to a very few interp. who, assuming that Paul suffered from a weakness of the eyes, understand the words literally, "Ye would have plucked out your sound eyes and have put them into me," see Meyer ad loc.; [cf. reff. s. v. σκόλοψ, fin.]. **2.** to dig through: τὴν στέγην, Mk. ii. 4.*

**1847α;
see 1847** ἐξ-ουδενέω, -ῶ: 1 aor. pass. subjunc. 3 pers. sing. ἐξουδενηθῇ; pf. pass. ptcp. ἐξουδενημένος; to hold and treat as of no account, utterly to despise: τὸν λόγον, pass., 2 Co. x. 10 Lchm. to set at nought, treat with contumely: a person, pass., Mk. ix. 12 L Tr WH, (Ezek. xxi. 10). Cf. Lob. ad Phryn. p. 182; [B. 28 (25); W. 91 (87); Soph. Lex. s. v.; WH. App. p. 166].*

**1847;
see 1847α** ἐξ-ουδενόω, -ῶ: [1 aor. pass. subjunc. 3 pers. sing. ἐξουδενωθῇ]; i. q. ἐξουδενέω, q. v.: Mk. ix. 12 R G; often in Sept., esp. for בּוּז and מָאַס. [Cf. reff. in the preceding word.]*

1848   ἐξουθενέω, -ῶ; 1 aor. ἐξουθένησα; Pass., pf. ptcp. ἐξουθενημένος; [1 aor. ptcp. ἐξουθενηθείς]; (see οὐδείς); to make of no account, to despise utterly: τινά, Lk. xviii. 9; Ro. xiv. 3, 10; 1 Co. xvi. 11; τί, 1 Th. v. 20; Gal. iv. 14 (where it is coupled with ἐκπτύω); in pass. οἱ ἐξουθενημένοι, 1 Co. vi. 4; τὰ ἐξουθενημένα, 1 Co. i. 28 (see ἀγενής); ὁ λόγος ἐξουθενημένος, 2 Co. x. 10 [here Lchm. ἐξουδ.]; ὁ (λίθος ὁ) ἐξουθενηθεὶς ὑπὸ τῶν οἰκοδομούντων, set at nought, i. e. rejected, cast aside, Acts iv. 11. *To treat with contempt* (i. e. acc. to the context, *with mockery*): Lk. xxiii. 11; (for בּוּז, Prov. i. 7; בָּזָה, Ezek. xxii. 8, etc.; כָּאַס, 1 S. viii. 7. Sap. iv. 18; 2 Macc. i. 27; Barn. ep. 7, 9; and other eccl. writ.). Cf. *Lob.* ad Phryn. p. 182; [and reff. s. v. ἐξουδενέω, fin.].*

see 1848   ἐξουθενόω, i. q. ἐξουθενέω, q. v.: Mk. ix. 12 Tdf.*

1849   ἐξουσία, -ας, ἡ, (fr. ἔξεστι, ἐξόν, q. v.), fr. Eur., Xen., Plato down; Sept. for מֶמְשָׁלָה and Chald. שָׁלְטָן; *power*. **1.** *power of choice, liberty of doing as one pleases; leave or permission*: 1 Co. ix. 12, 18; ἔχειν ἐξουσίαν, 2 Th. iii. 9; with an inf. added indicating the thing to be done, Jn. x. 18; 1 Co. ix. 4 sq.; Heb. xiii. 10 [WH br. ἐξ.]; foll. by an inf. with τοῦ, 1 Co. ix. 6 (L T Tr WH om. τοῦ); with a gen. of the thing or the pers. with regard to which one has the power to decide: Ro. ix. 21 (where an explanatory infin. is added [B. 260 (224)]); 1 Co. ix. 12; ἐπὶ τὸ ξύλον τῆς ζωῆς, permission to use the tree of life, Rev. xxii. 14 [see ἐπί, C. I. 2 e.]; ἐξουσίαν ἔχειν περὶ τοῦ ἰδίου θελήματος (opp. to ἀνάγκην ἔχειν [cf. W. § 30, 3 N. 5]), 1 Co. vii. 37; ἐν τῇ ἰδίᾳ ἐξουσίᾳ, [appointed, see τίθημι, 1 a. sub fin.] according to his own choice, Acts i. 7; ἐν τῇ σῇ ἐξουσίᾳ ὑπῆρχεν, i. e. at thy free disposal, Acts v. 4; used of liberty under the gospel, as opp. to the yoke of the Mosaic law, 1 Co. viii. 9. **2.** *physical and mental power; the ability or strength with which one is endued, which he either possesses or exercises*: Mt. ix. 8; Acts viii. 19; Rev. ix. 3, 19; xiii. 2, 4; xviii. 1; foll. by an inf. of the thing to be done, Mk. iii. 15; Lk. xii. 5; Jn. i. 12; Rev. ix. 10; xi. 6; xiii. 5; foll. by τοῦ with the inf. Lk. x. 19; αὕτη ἐστὶν ἡ ἐξουσία τοῦ σκότους, this is the power that darkness exerts, Lk. xxii. 53; ποιεῖν ἐξουσίαν to exert power, give exhibitions of power, Rev. xiii. 12; ἐν ἐξουσίᾳ εἶναι, to be possessed of power and influence, Lk. iv. 32; also ἐξουσίαν ἔχειν (both expressions refer to the ability and weight which Jesus exhibited in his teaching) Mt. vii. 29; [Mk. i. 22]; κατ' ἐξουσίαν *powerfully*, Mk. i. 27; also ἐν ἐξουσίᾳ, Lk. iv. 36. **3.** *the power of authority* (influence) *and of right*: Mt. xxi. 23; Mk. xi. 28; Lk. xx. 2; spoken of the authority of an apostle, 2 Co. x. 8; xiii. 10; of the divine authority granted to Jesus as Messiah, with the inf. of the thing to be done, Mt. ix. 6; Mk. ii. 10; Lk. v. 24; Jn. v. 27; ἐν ποίᾳ ἐξουσίᾳ; clothed in what authority (i. e. thine own or God's?), Mt. xxi. 23, 24, 27; Mk. xi. 28, 29, 33; Lk. xx. 2, 8; *delegated authority* (Germ. *Vollmacht*, authorization): παρά τινος, with gen. of the pers. by whom the authority is given, or received, Acts ix. 14; xxvi. 10, 12 [R G]. **4.** *the power of rule* or *government* (the power of him whose will

and commands must be submitted to by others and obeyed, [generally translated *authority*]); **a.** univ.: Mt. xxviii. 18; Jude 25; Rev. xii. 10; xvii. 13; λαμβάνειν ἐξουσίαν ὡς βασιλεύς, Rev. xvii. 12; εἰμὶ ὑπὸ ἐξουσίαν, I am under authority, Mt. viii. 9; with τασσόμενος added, [Mt. viii. 9 L WH br.]; Lk. vii. 8; ἐξουσία τινός, gen. of the object, *authority* (to be exercised) *over*, as τῶν πνευμάτων τῶν ἀκαθάρτων, Mk. vi. 7; with ὥστε ἐκβάλλειν αὐτά added, Mt. x. 1; ἐξουσίαν πάσης σαρκός, authority over all mankind, Jn. xvii. 2, (πάσης σαρκὸς κυρείαν, Bel and the Drag. vs. 5); [gen. of the subject, τοῦ Σατανᾶ, Acts xxvi. 18]; ἐπί τινα, power over one, so as to be able to subdue, drive out, destroy, Rev. vi. 8; ἐπὶ τὰ δαιμόνια, Lk. ix. 1; or to hold submissive to one's will, Rev. xiii. 7; ἐπὶ τὰς πληγάς, the power to inflict plagues and to put an end to them, Rev. xvi. 9; ἐπὶ τῶν ἐθνῶν, over the heathen nations, Rev. ii. 26; ἐπί τινος, to destroy one, Rev. xx. 6; ἔχειν ἐξουσίαν ἐπὶ τοῦ πυρός, to preside, have control, over fire, to hold it subject to his will, Rev. xiv. 18; ἐπὶ τῶν ὑδάτων, xi. 6; ἐπάνω τινὸς ἐξουσίαν ἔχειν, to be ruler over a thing, Lk. xix. 17. **b.** specifically, **a.** of the power of judicial decision; ἐξουσίαν ἔχειν with an inf. of the thing decided: σταυρῶσαι and ἀπολῦσαί τινα, Jn. xix. 10; foll. by κατά τινος, the power of deciding against one, ibid. 11; παραδοῦναί τινα . . . τῇ ἐξουσίᾳ τοῦ ἡγεμόνος, Lk. xx. 20. **β.** of authority to manage domestic affairs: Mk. xiii. 34. **c.** metonymically, **a.** *a thing subject to authority or rule*: Lk. iv. 6; *jurisdiction*: ἐκ τῆς ἐξουσίας Ἡρώδου ἐστίν, Lk. xxiii. 7 (1 Macc. vi. 11 [cf. Ps. cxiii. (cxiv.) 2; Is. xxxix. 2]). **β.** *one who possesses authority*; (cf. the Lat. use of *honestates, dignitates, auctoritates* [so the Eng. *authorities, dignities*, etc.] in reference to persons); **aa.** a *ruler, human magistrate*, (Dion. Hal. 8, 44; 11, 32): Ro. xiii. 1–3; plur.: Lk. xii. 11; Ro. xiii. 1; Tit. iii. 1. **ββ.** *the leading and more powerful among created beings superior to man, spiritual potentates*; used in the plur. of a certain class of angels (see ἀρχή, δύναμις, θρόνος, κυριότης): Col. i. 16; 1 Pet. iii. 22, (cf. Fritzsche on Rom. vol. ii. p. 226 sq.; [Bp. Lghtft. on Col. l. c.]); with ἐν τοῖς ἐπουρανίοις added, Eph. iii. 10; πᾶσα ἐξουσία, 1 Co. xv. 24; Eph. i. 21; Col. ii. 10; used also of demons: in the plur., Eph. vi. 12; Col. ii. 15; collectively [cf. *Lob.* ad Phryn. p. 469], ἡ ἐξουσία τοῦ ἀέρος (see ἀήρ), Eph. ii. 2; τοῦ σκότους, Col. i. 13 [al. refer this to 4 a. (or c. a.) above (cf. Lk. xxii. 53 in 2), and regard σκότος as personified; see σκότος, b.]. **d.** *a sign of the husband's authority over his wife*, i. e. the veil with which propriety required a woman to cover herself, 1 Co. xi. 10 (as βασιλεία is used by Diodorus 1, 47 for the sign of regal power, i. e. a crown). [SYN. see δύναμις, fin. On the inf. after ἐξ. and ἐξ. ἔχειν cf. B. 260 (223 sq.).] *

1850   ἐξουσιάζω; 1 fut. pass. ἐξουσιασθήσομαι; (ἐξουσία); i. q. ἐξουσίαν ἔχω, to have power or authority, use power: [ἐν πλείοσι ἐξ. πολλῶν μοναρχίων, Aristot. eth. Eud. 1, 5 p. 1216ᵃ, 2]; ἐν ἀτίμοις, Dion. Hal. antt. 9, 44; τινός, to be master of any one, exercise authority over one, Lk. xxii. 25; τοῦ σώματος, to be master of the body, i. e. to have full and entire authority over the body, to hold the body subject to one's will, 1 Co. vii. 4. Pass. foll. by ὑπό τινος, to be brought under the power of any one, 1 Co. vi. 12. (Sept. several times in Neh. and Eccl., chiefly for מֶשֶׁל and שֶׁלֶט.) [Comp.: κατ-εξουσιάζω.]*

1851 ἐξοχή, -ῆς, ἡ, (fr. ἐξέχω to stand out, be prominent; cf. ὑπεροχή); **1.** prop. in Grk. writ. any prominence or projection, as the peak or summit of a mountain (ἐπ' ἐξοχῇ πέτρας, Job xxxix. 28 Sept.); in medical writ. a protuberance, swelling, wart, etc. **2.** metaph. eminence, excellence, superiority, (Cic. ad Att. 4, 15, 7 ἐξοχή in nullo est, pecunia omnium dignitatem exaequat); ἄνδρες οἱ κατ' ἐξοχὴν ὄντες τῆς πόλεως, the prominent men of the city, Acts xxv. 23.*

1852 ἐξ-υπνίζω: 1 aor. subjunc. ἐξυπνίσω; (ὕπνος); to wake up, awaken out of sleep: [trans. αὐτόν], Jn. xi. 11. ([Judg. xvi. 14]; 1 K. iii. 15; Job xiv. 12; Antonin. 6, 31; Plut. [de solert. anim. 29, 4]; Test. xii. Patr. [Levi § 8; Jud. § 25, etc.]; the better Grks. said ἀφυπνίζω, see Lob. ad Phryn. p. 224; [W. § 2, 1 d.].)*

1853 ἐξ-υπνος, -ον, (ὕπνος), roused out of sleep: Acts xvi. 27. (1 Esdr. iii. 3; [Joseph. antt. 11, 3, 2].)*

1854 ἔξω, adv., (fr. ἐξ, as ἔσω and εἴσω fr. ἐς and εἰς); **1.** without, out of doors; **a.** adverbially: Mk. xi. 4; joined with verbs: ἑστάναι, Mt. xii. 46, 47 [WH txt. om. the vs.]; Mk. iii. 31; Lk. viii. 20; xiii. 25; Jn. xviii. 16; xx. 11 [Lchm. om.]; καθῆσθαι, Mt. xxvi. 69; or with some other verb declaring that the person without is doing something, Mk. iii. 31. Preceded by the art. ὁ ἔξω, absol. he who is without, prop. of place; metaph., in plur., those who do not belong to the Christian church [cf. Bp. Lghtft. on Col. as below; Mey. on Mk. as below]: 1 Co. v. 12, 13; Col. iv. 5; 1 Th. iv. 12; those who are not of the number of the apostles, Mk. iv. 11[cf. Meyer; WH mrg. ἔξωθεν, q. v.]. With a noun added: αἱ ἔξω πόλεις, foreign, Acts xxvi. 11; ὁ ἔξω ἄνθρωπος, the outer man, i. e. the body (see ἄνθρωπος, 1 e.), 2 Co. iv. 16. **b.** it takes the place of a prep. and is joined with the gen., without i. e. out of, outside of, [W. § 54, 6]: Lk. xiii. 33; Acts xxi. 5; Heb. xiii. 11, 12. **2.** after the verbs of going, sending, placing, leading, drawing, etc., which commonly take prepositions or adverbs signifying rest in a place rather than those expressive of motion toward a place, ἔξω has the force of the Lat. foras (Germ. hinaus, heraus), forth out, out of; **a.** adverbially: after the verbs ἐξέρχομαι, Mt. xxvi. 75; Mk. xiv. 68; Lk. xxii. 62; Jn. xix. 4, 5; Rev. iii. 12; ἄγω, Jn. xix. 4, 13; προάγω, Acts xvi. 30; ἐξάγω, Lk. xxiv. 50 [R G L br.]; βάλλω and ἐκβάλλω, Mt. v. 13; xiii. 48; Lk. viii. 54 R G; xiii. 28; xiv. 35 (34); Jn. vi. 37; ix. 34, 35; xii. 31; xv. 6; Acts ix. 40; 1 Jn. iv. 18; Rev. xi. 2 R G; δεῦρο ἔξω, Jn. xi. 43; ἔξω ποιεῖν τινα, Acts v. 34. **b.** as a prep. with the gen.: after ἀπελθεῖν, Acts iv. 15; ἀποστέλλειν, Mk. v. 10; ἐκβάλλειν, Mk. xii. 8; Lk. iv. 29; xx. 15; Acts vii. 58; ἐξέρχεσθαι, Mt. xxi. 17; Acts xvi. 13; Heb. xiii. 13; ἐκπορεύεσθαι, Mk. xi. 19; ἐξάγειν, Mk. viii. 23 [R G L Tr mrg.]; σύρειν τινά, Acts xiv. 19; ἕλκειν τινά, Acts xxi. 30.

1855 ἔξωθεν, adv., (fr. ἔξω, opp. to ἔσωθεν fr. ἔσω); cf.

ἄνωθεν, πόρρωθεν), from without, outward, [cf. W. 472 (440)]; **1.** adverbially: (outwardly), Mt. xxiii. 27 sq.; Mk. vii. 18; 2 Co. vii. 5; τὸ ἔξωθεν, the outside, the exterior, Mt. xxiii. 25; Lk. xi. 39 sq.; ἐκβάλλειν ἔξωθεν (for R G ἔξω), Rev. xi. 2[b] L T Tr WH; οἱ ἔξωθεν for οἱ ἔξω, those who do not belong to the Christian church, 1 Tim. iii. 7; [cf. Mk. iv. 11 WH mrg. and s. v. ἔξω, 1 a.]; ὁ ἔξωθεν κόσμος the outward adorning, 1 Pet. iii. 3. **2.** as a preposition with the gen. [cf. W. § 54, 6]: Mk. vii. 15; Rev. xi. 2[a] [R[bcz els] G L T Tr WH; xiv. 20 where Rec. ἔξω].*

1856 ἐξ-ωθέω, -ῶ: 1 aor. ἔξωσα [so accented by G T ed. 7 Tr, but L WH ἐξέωσα] and in Tdf. ἐξέωσα [WH. App. p. 162] (cf. W. p. 90 (86); [B. 69 (61); Steph. Thesaur. and Veitch s. v. ὠθέω]); to thrust out; expel from one's abode: Acts vii. 45, (Thuc., Xen., al.). to propel, drive: τὸ πλοῖον εἰς αἰγιαλόν, Acts xxvii. 39 [WH txt. ἐκσῶσαι; see ἐκσώζω], (the same use in Thuc., Xen., al.).*

1857 ἐξώτερος, -έρα, -ερον, (a comparative fr. ἔξω, cf. ἐσώτερος, ἀνώτερος, κατώτερος), outer: τὸ σκότος τὸ ἐξώτερον, the darkness outside the limits of the lighted palace (to which the Messiah's kingdom is here likened), Mt. viii. 12; xxii. 13; xxv. 30. [(Sept.; Strabo, al.)]*

ἔοικα, see ΕΙΚΩ.   **see 1503**

1858 ἑορτάζω; (ἑορτή); to keep a feast-day, celebrate a festival: 1 Co. v. 8, on which pass. see ἄζυμος. (Sept. חָגַג; Eur., Arstph., Xen., Plato, al.; ὁρτάζω, Hdt.) *

1859 ἑορτή, -ῆς, ἡ, Sept. for חָג; Grk. writ. fr. Hom. down; in Hdt. ὁρτή; a feast-day, festival: Lk. ii. 42; Jn. v. 1; vi. 4; vii. 2, 37; Col. ii. 16; ἡ ἑορτὴ τοῦ πάσχα: Lk. ii. 41 [W. 215 (202); B. 186 (161)]; Jn. xiii. 1; i. q. ἡ ἑορτὴ τῶν ἀζύμων, Lk. xxii. 1; ἐν τῇ ἑορτῇ, during the feast, Mt. xxvi. 5; Mk. xiv. 2; Jn. iv. 45; vii. 11; xii. 20; εἶναι ἐν τῇ ἑορτῇ, to be engaged in celebrating the feast, Jn. ii. 23, cf. Baumg.-Crusius and Meyer ad loc.; εἰς τὴν ἑορτήν, for the feast, Jn. xiii. 29; ἀναβαίνειν (to Jerusalem) εἰς τὴν ἑορτήν, Jn. vii. 8, 10; ἔρχεσθαι εἰς τὴν ἑορτήν, Jn. iv. 45; xi. 56; xii. 12; τῆς ἑορτῆς μεσούσης, in the midst of the feast, Jn. vii. 14; κατὰ ἑορτήν, at every feast [see κατά, II. 3 a. β.], Mt. xxvii. 15; Mk. xv. 6; Lk. xxiii. 17 [Rec.]; τὴν ἑορτὴν ποιεῖν to keep, celebrate, the feast, Acts xviii. 21 [Rec.]; κατὰ τὸ ἔθος τῆς ἑορτῆς, after the custom of the feast, Lk. ii. 42.*

1860 ἐπ-αγγελία, -ας, ἡ, (ἐπαγγέλλω); **1.** announcement: 1 Jn. i. 5 (Rec., where ἀγγελία was long since restored); κατ' ἐπαγγελίαν ζωῆς τῆς ἐν Χριστῷ Ἰησοῦ, to proclaim life in fellowship with Christ, 2 Tim. i. 1 [W. 402 (376); cf. κατά, II. fin. But others give ἐπαγγ. here as elsewhere the sense of promise, cf. 2 below]. **2.** promise; **a.** the act of promising, a promise given or to be given: προσδέχεσθαι τὴν ἀπό τινος ἐπαγγελίαν (assent; the reference is to a promise to surrender Paul to the power and sentence of the Jews), Acts xxiii. 21; [add, ἐπαγγελίας ὁ λόγος οὗτος, Ro. ix. 9]. It is used also of the divine promises of blessing, esp. of the benefits of salvation by Christ, [cf. Bp. Lghtft. on Gal. iii. 14]: Acts vii. 17; Ro. iv. 14, 16; [plur. Ro. ix. 4]; Gal. iii. 17 sq. 21; iv. 23; Heb. xi. 17; 2 Pet. iii. 9 (on which see βραδύνω, 2); Heb. viii. 6; xi. 9; foll. by the inf. Heb. iv. 1; γίνεται τινι, Ro. iv. 13; πρός τινα, Acts xiii. 32; xxvi. 6; ἐρρήθη τινί, Gal. iii. 16; ἐστί τινι, belongs to one, Acts ii. 39; ἐπαγγέλλεσθαι τὴν ἐπ. 1 Jn. ii. 25; ἔχειν ἐπαγγελίας, to have received, Heb. vii. 6; 2 Co. vii. 1, [cf. W. 177 (166)]; to have linked to it, 1 Tim. iv. 8; εἶναι ἐν ἐπαγγελίᾳ, joined with a promise [al. al.; cf. W. 391 (366)], Eph. vi. 2; ἡ γῆ τῆς ἐπαγγελίας, the promised land, Heb. xi. 9; τὰ τέκνα τῆς ἐπαγγελίας, born in accordance with the promise, Ro. ix. 8; Gal. iv. 28; τὸ πνεῦμα τῆς ἐπαγγελίας τὸ ἅγιον, the promised Spirit, Eph. i. 13; αἱ διαθῆκαι τῆς ἐπαγγελίας, covenants to which was united the promise (of salvation through the Messiah), Eph. ii. 12; ἡ ἐπαγγελία τοῦ θεοῦ, given by God, Ro. iv. 20; in the plur. 2 Co. i. 20; αἱ ἐπαγγελίαι τῶν πατέρων, the promises made to the fathers, Ro. xv. 8; with the gen. of the object, τῆς ζωῆς, 1 Tim. iv. 8; τῆς παρουσίας αὐτοῦ, 2 Pet. iii. 4; κατ᾽ ἐπαγγελίαν according to promise, Acts xiii. 23; Gal. iii. 29; δι᾽ ἐπαγγελίας, Gal. iii. 18.　b. by meton. a promised good or blessing (cf. ἐλπίς, sub fin.): Gal. iii. 22; Eph. iii. 6 [yet here cf. Mey. or Ellic.]; ἀποστέλλειν τὴν ἐπαγγελίαν τοῦ πατρός μου, the blessing promised by my Father, Lk. xxiv. 49; περιμένειν, Acts i. 4; κομίζεσθαι τὴν ἐπαγγελίαν, Heb. x. 36; xi. [13 T Tr WH, προσδέχεσθαι L], 39; λαμβάνειν τὰς ἐπαγγελίας, Heb. xi. 13 [R G]; ἐπιτυγχάνειν ἐπαγγελιῶν, ib. vs. 33; κληρονομεῖν τὰς ἐπαγγελίας, Heb. vi. 12; ἐπιτυγχάνειν τῆς ἐπαγγελίας, ib. 15; κληρονόμοι τῆς ἐπαγγελίας, vs. 17 — (to reconcile Heb. vi. 12, 15, 17 with xi. 13, 39, which at first sight seem to be in conflict, we must hold, in accordance with xii. 22–24, that the O. T. saints, after the expiatory sacrifice offered at length to God by Christ, were made partakers of the heavenly blessings before Christ's return from heaven; [al. explain the apparent contradiction by the difference between the initial and the consummate reception of the promise; see the Comm. ad l.]); with the epexeget. gen. λαβεῖν τὴν ἐπαγγελίαν τοῦ ἁγίου πνεύματος, the promised blessing, which is the Holy Spirit, Acts ii. 33; Gal. iii. 14, [cf. W. § 34, 3 a. fin.]; τὴν ἐπαγγελίαν τῆς αἰωνίου κληρονομίας, Heb. ix. 15. ([Dem. 519, 8; Aristot. eth. Nic. 10, 1 p. 1164ᵃ, 29]; Polyb. 1, 43, 6, and often; Diod. 1, 5; Joseph. antt. 3, 5, 1; 5, 8, 11; 1 Macc. x. 15.) *

1861 ἐπ-αγγέλλω: [pres. mid. ἐπαγγέλλομαι]; pf. pass. and mid. ἐπήγγελμαι; 1 aor. mid. ἐπηγγειλάμην; from Hom. down; **1.** to announce. **2.** to promise: pass. ᾧ ἐπήγγελται, to whom the promise hath been made, Gal. iii. 19. **Mid.** to announce concerning one's self; i. e. **1.** to announce that one is about to do or furnish something, i. e. to promise (of one's own accord), to engage (voluntarily): ὁ ἐπαγγειλάμενος, Heb. x. 23; xi. 11; ἐπήγγελται, he hath promised, foll. by λέγων, Heb. xii. 26; τινί, to give a promise to one, Heb. vi. 13; τί, Ro. iv. 21; Tit. i. 2; τινί τι, Jas. i. 12; ii. 5; 2 Pet. ii. 19; ἐπαγγελίαν, to give a promise, 1 Jn. ii. 25 (Esth. iv. 7; [cf. W. 225 (211); B. 148 (129)]); foll. by the inf. [cf. W. § 44, 7 c.]: Mk. xiv. 11; Acts vii. 5. **2.** to profess: τί, e. g. an art, to profess one's self skilled in it (τὴν ἀρετήν, Xen. mem. 1, 2, 7; τὴν στρατιάν, Hell. 3, 4, 3; σοφίαν, Diog. Laërt.

prooem. 12; σωφροσύνην, Clem. Al. paedag. 3, 4 p. 299, 27 ed. Klotz; [cf. L. and S. s. v. 5]): θεοσέβειαν, 1 Tim. ii. 10; γνῶσιν, vi. 21. [ΣΟΜΡ. προ-επαγγέλλω.] *

1862 ἐπ-άγγελμα, -τος, τό, (ἐπαγγέλλω), a promise: 2 Pet. i. 4; iii. 13. (Dem., Isoc., al.) *

1863 ἐπ-άγω, [pres. ptcp. ἐπάγων]; 1 aor. ptcp. ἐπάξας (W. p. 82 (78); [Veitch s. v. ἄγω]); 2 aor. inf. ἐπαγαγεῖν; fr. Hom. down; Sept. chiefly for הֵבִיא; to lead or bring upon: τινί τι, to bring a thing on one, i. e. to cause something to befall one, usually something evil, 2 Pet. ii. 1, 5, (πῆμα, Hesiod. opp. 240; ἄταν, Soph. Ajax 1189; γῆρας νόσους ἐπάγει, Plat. Tim. 33 a.; ἑαυτοῖς δουλείαν, Dem. p. 424, 9; δεινά, Palaeph. 6, 7; κακά, Bar. iv. 29; ἀμέτρητον ὕδωρ, 3 Macc. ii. 4, and in other exx.; in the Sept. ἐπί τινά τι, as κακά, Jer. vi. 19; xi. 11, etc.; πληγήν, Ex. xi. 1; also in a good sense, as ἀγαθά, Jer. xxix. (xxxii.) 42; τινὶ εὐφροσύνην, Bar. iv. 29). ἐπάγειν τὸ αἷμά τινος ἐπί τινα, to bring the blood of one upon any one, i. e. lay upon one the guilt of, make him answerable for, the violent death inflicted on another: Acts v. 28, (like ἐπάγειν ἁμαρτίαν ἐπί τινα, Gen. xx. 9; Ex. xxxii. 21, 34; ἁμαρτίας πατέρων ἐπὶ τέκνα, Ex. xxxiv. 7).*

1864 ἐπ-αγωνίζομαι; to contend: τινί, for a thing, Jude 3. (τῷ Ἀννίβᾳ, against Hannibal, Plut. Fab. 23, 2; ταῖς νίκαις, added a new contest to his victories, id. Cim. 13, 4; by others in diff. senses.) *

1865 ἐπ-αθροίζω: [pres. pass. ptcp. ἐπαθροιζόμενος]; to gather together (to others already present): pass. in Lk. xi. 29. (Plut. Anton. 44, 1.) *

1866 Ἐπαίνετος [so W. § 6, 1 l. (cf. Chandler § 325); Ἐπαινετός Recᵗ T; see Tdf. Proleg. p. 103; Lipsius, Gram. Unters. p. 30 sq.; Roehl, Inscr. index iii.], (ἐπαινέω), -ου, ὁ, Epænetus, the name of a Christian mentioned in Ro. xvi. 5.*

1867 ἐπ-αινέω, -ῶ; fut. ἐπαινέσω (1 Co. xi. 22, for the more com. ἐπαινέσομαι, cf. W. 86 (82); [B. 53 (46)]; L txt. Tr mrg. ἐπαινῶ); 1 aor. ἐπῄνεσα (ἔπαινος); fr. Hom. down; Sept. for הָלַל and שָׁבַח; to approve, to praise, (with the ἐπί cf. Germ. be- in beloben [Passow s. v. ἐπί, IV. C. 3 cc.]): τινά, Ro. xv. 11; 1 Co. xi. 22; τινά, foll. by ὅτι [cf. W. § 30, 9 b.], Lk. xvi. 8; 1 Co. xi. 2; absol., foll. by ὅτι, 1 Co. xi. 17.*

1868 ἔπ-αινος, -ου, ὁ, (ἐπί and αἶνος [as it were, a tale for another; cf. Bttm. Lexil. § 83, 4; Schmidt ch. 155]); approbation, commendation, praise: Phil. iv. 8; ἔκ τινος, bestowed by one, Ro. ii. 29; ἔπαινον ἔχειν ἔκ τινος, gen. of pers., Ro. xiii. 3; ὁ ἔπαινος γενήσεται ἑκάστῳ ἀπὸ τοῦ θεοῦ, 1 Co. iv. 5; with gen. of the pers. to whom the praise is given, Ro. ii. 29; 2 Co. viii. 18; εἰς ἔπαινον, to the obtaining of praise, 1 Pet. i. 7; εἰς ἔπαινόν τινος, that a pers. or thing may be praised, Eph. i. 6, 14; Phil. i. 11; [πέμπεσθαι εἰς ἔπ. τινος, 1 Pet. ii. 14]; εἶναι εἰς ἔπαινόν τινος to be a praise to a pers. or thing, Eph. i. 12.*

1869 ἐπ-αίρω; 1 aor. ἐπῆρα, ptcp. ἐπάρας, impv. 2 pers. plur. ἐπάρατε, inf. ἐπᾶραι; pf. ἐπῆρκα (Jn. xiii. 18 Tdf.); [Pass. and Mid., pres. ἐπαίρομαι]; 1 aor. pass. ἐπήρθην; (on the om. of iota subscr. see αἴρω init.); fr. Hdt. down; Sept. chiefly for נָשָׂא, also for הֵרִים; to lift up, raise up, raise *on high*: τὸν ἀρτέμονα, to hoist up, Acts xxvii. 40 (τὰ ἱστία, Plut. mor. p. 870 [de Herod. malign. § 39]); τὰς χεῖρας, in offering prayer, 1 Tim. ii. 8 (Neh. viii. 6; Ps. cxxxiii. (cxxxiv.) 2); in blessing, Lk. xxiv. 50 [cf. W. § 65, 4 c.] (Lev. ix. 22 [yet here ἐξάρας]; Sir. l. 20); τὰς κεφαλάς, of the timid and sorrowful recovering spirit, Lk. xxi. 28 (so αὐχένα, Philo de prof. § 20); τοὺς ὀφθαλμούς, to look up, Mt. xvii. 8; Lk. xvi. 23; Jn. iv. 35; vi. 5; εἰς τινα, Lk. vi. 20; εἰς τὸν οὐρανόν, Lk. xviii. 13; Jn. xvii. 1; τὴν φωνήν, Lk. xi. 27; Acts ii. 14; xiv. 11; xxii. 22, (Dem. 449, 13; Sept. Judg. ii. 4; ix. 7; 2 S. xiii. 36); τὴν πτέρναν ἐπί τινα, to lift the heel against one (see πτέρνα), Jn. xiii. 18. Pass. ἐπήρθη, was taken up (of Christ, taken up into heaven), Acts i. 9; reflex. and metaph. *to be lifted up with pride, to exalt one's self*: 2 Co. xi. 20 (Jer. xiii. 15; Ps. xlvi. (xlvii.) 10; Sir. xi. 4; xxxv. (xxxii.) 1; 1 Macc. i. 3; ii. 63; Arstph. nub. 810; Thuc. 4, 18; Aeschin. 87, 24; with dat. of the thing of which one is proud, Prov. iii. 5; Zeph. i. 11; Hdt. 9, 49; Thuc. 1, 120; Xen. Cyr. 8, 5, 24); — on 2 Co. x. 5 see ὕψωμα.*

1870 ἐπ-αισχύνομαι; fut. ἐπαισχυνθήσομαι; 1 aor. ἐπησχύνθην, and with neglect of augm. ἐπαισχύνθην (2 Tim. i. 16 L T Tr WH; cf. [WH. App. p. 161]; B. 34 (30); [W. § 12 fin.]); fr. Aeschyl. down; *to be ashamed* (ἐπί on account of [cf. Is. i. 29 Alex.]; Ellic. on 2 Tim. i. 8]; see αἰσχύνω): absol. 2 Tim. i. 12; τινά [on the accus. cf. W. § 32, 1 b. a.; B. 192 (166)], of a person, Mk. viii. 38; Lk. ix. 26; τί, of a thing, Ro. i. 16; 2 Tim. i. 8, 16; ἐπί τινι, dat. of a thing, Ro. vi. 21; foll. by the inf. Heb. ii. 11; with the acc. of a pers. and the inf. of a thing, Heb. xi. 16. (Twice in the Sept.: Is. i. 29 [Alex.]; Job xxxiv. 19.) *

1871 ἐπ-αιτέω, -ῶ; **1.** *to ask besides, ask for more*: Hom. Il. 23, 593. **2.** *to ask again and again, importunately*: Soph. Oed. Tyr. 1416; *to beg, to ask alms*: Lk. xvi. 3; [xviii. 35 L T Tr WH]; (Ps. cviii. (cix.) 10; Sir. xl. 28; Soph. Oed. Col. 1364).*

1872 ἐπ-ακολουθέω, -ῶ; 1 aor. ἐπηκολούθησα; *to follow* (close) *upon, follow after*; in the N. T. only metaph. τοῖς ἴχνεσί τινος, to tread in one's footsteps, i. e. to imitate his example, 1 Pet. ii. 21; with the dat. of a pers. 1 Tim. v. 24 (opp. to προάγω, to go before; the meaning is, ' the sins of some men are manifest now, even before they are called to account, but the misdeeds of others are exposed when finally judgment is held '; cf. Huther [or Ellic.] ad loc.); ἔργῳ ἀγαθῷ, to be devoted to good works, 1 Tim. v. 10; used, with the dat. of the pers. to be mentally supplied, of the miracles accompanying the preaching of Christ's ministers, Mk. xvi. 20. (Arstph., Thuc., Xen., Plato, sqq.; occasionally in Sept.) *

1873 ἐπ-ακούω; 1 aor. ἐπήκουσα; fr. Hom. down; Sept. often for עָנָה and שָׁמַע; **1.** *to give ear to, listen to*; *to perceive by the ear.* **2.** *to listen to* i. e. *hear with favor, grant one's prayer*, (Aeschyl. choëph. 725; τῶν εὐχῶν, Lcian. Tim. 34): τινός, *to hearken to one*, 2 Co. vi. 2 fr. Is. xlix. 8; often so in Sept.*

1874 ἐπ-ακροάομαι, -ῶμαι; 3 pers. plur. impf. ἐπηκροῶντο; *to listen to*: with the gen. of a pers. Acts xvi. 25. (Plat.

comic. in Bekk. anecd. p. 360; Lcian. Icarom. 1; Test. xii. Patr. p. 710, test. Jos. § 8.) *

1875 ἐπ-άν, conj. (fr. ἐπεί and ἄν), *after, when*: with the subjunc. pres. Lk. xi. 34; with the subjunc. aor., answering to the Lat. fut. exact. (fut. perf.), Mt. ii. 8; Lk. xi. 22. Cf. *Klotz* ad Devar. ii. 2, p. 547.*

1876 ἐπάναγκες, (ἀνάγκη, [hence lit. *on compulsion*]), *necessarily*: πλὴν τῶν ἐπάναγκες τούτων, besides these things which are necessarily imposed, Acts xv. 28 [B. 27 (24)]. (Hdt., Andoc., Plato, Dem., Aristot., Dion. Hal., Plut., Aelian, Epict.) *

1877 ἐπ-αν-άγω; 2 aor. inf. ἐπαναγαγεῖν, impv. ἐπανάγαγε, [ptcp. ἐπαναγαγών, Mt. xxi. 18 T WH txt. Tr mrg.]; **1.** lit. *to lead up upon*, sc. τὸ πλοῖον, a ship upon the deep, i. e. *to put out*, Lk. v. 3 (Xen. Hell. 6, 2, 28; 2 Macc. xii. 4); with εἰς τὸ βάθος added, into the deep, ibid. 4. **2.** *to lead back*; intrans. *to return* [cf. B. 144 (126)]: Mt. xxi. 18; (2 Macc. ix. 21; Xen. Cyr. 4, 1, 3; Polyb., Diod., Joseph., Hdian., al.).*

1878 ἐπ-ανα-μιμνήσκω; *to recall to mind again*: τινά, reminding one, Ro. xv. 15. (Rare; Plato, legg. 3 p. 688 a.; Dem. 74, (7) 9; [Aristot.].) *

see 1879 St. ἐπ-ανα-παύω: **1.** *to cause to rest upon anything*: Sept. in Judg. xvi. 26 acc. to cod. Alex.; Greg. Nyss. **2.** Mid., [pres. ἐπαναπαύομαι]; fut. ἐπαναπαύσομαι, and (Lk. x. 6 T WH after codd. אB) ἐπαναπαήσομαι (see ἀναπαύω); *to rest upon anything*: τινί, metaph. τῷ νόμῳ, to lean upon, trust to, Ro. ii. 17 (Mic. iii. 11; 1 Macc. viii. 12). *to settle upon, fix its abode upon*: ἐπί τινα, with the included idea of antecedent motion towards (see εἰς, C. 2 p. 186ᵃ): ἡ εἰρήνη ἐπ᾽ αὐτόν i. e. shall rest, remain, upon him or it, Lk. x. 6 (τὸ πνεῦμα ἐπί τινα, Num. xi. 25; 2 K. ii. 15; ἐπί τινι, Num. xi. 26 var.).*

1880 ἐπ-αν-έρχομαι; 2 aor. ἐπανῆλθον; *to return, come back again*: Lk. x. 35; xix. 15. (Hdt.; freq. in Attic writ.)*

see 1881 St. ἐπ-αν-ίστημι: fut. mid. ἐπαναστήσομαι; *to cause to rise up against, to raise up against*; Mid. *to rise up against* (Hdt., Arstph., Thuc., Polyb., al.): ἐπί τινα, Mt. x. 21; Mk. xiii. 12, as in Sept. Mic. vii. 6; xxii. 26; Mic. vii. 6.*

1882 ἐπ-αν-όρθωσις, -εως, ἡ, (ἐπανορθόω), *restoration to an up-right or a right state*; *correction, improvement*, (in Grk. writ. fr. Dem. down): of life and character, 2 Tim. iii. 16 [cf. τὸν θεὸν . . . χρόνον γε πρὸς ἐπανόρθωσιν (αὐτοῖς) προσιζάνειν, Plut. de sera num. vind. 6]; with τοῦ βίου added, Polyb. 1, 35, 1; Epict. diss. 3, 21, 15; σεαυτοῦ, id. ench. 51, 1; [ἠθικὴ δὲ τὰ πρὸς ἀνθρωπίνων ἐπανόρθωσιν ἠθῶν, Philo de ebriet. § 22; cf. de confus. lingg. § 36 fin.]; (cf. ἐπανορθοῦν καὶ εἰς μετάνοιαν ἀπάγειν, Joseph. antt. 4, 6, 10).*

1883 ἐπ-άνω, adv., (ἐπί and ἄνω [cf. W. 102 (97); B. 319 (273)]), Hdt. et sqq.; often in the Sept.; *above*; **1.** adverbially, **a.** of place: Lk. xi. 44; **b.** of number; *beyond, more than*: πραθῆναι ἐπάνω τριακοσίων δηναρίων, sold for more than three hundred denaries, Mk. xiv. 5; ὤφθη ἐπάνω πεντακοσίοις ἀδελφοῖς, by more than five hundred brethren, 1 Co. xv. 6; cf. W. § 37, 5; [B. 168 (146)]. **2.** as a preposition it is joined with the gen. [W. § 54, 6], **a.** of place: Mt. ii. 9; v. 14; xxi. 7 R G;

xxiii. 18, 20, [22]; xxvii. 37; xxviii. 2; Lk. iv. 39; [x. 19]; Rev. vi. 8 [WH br. the gen.]; xx. 3, [11 Tr txt.]. **b.** of dignity and power: ἐξουσίαν ἔχειν ἐπάνω τινός, Lk. xix. 17, [19]; ἐπάνω πάντων ἐστί, Jn. iii. 31ᵃ, [31ᵇ (but here G T WH mrg. om. the cl.)].*

(1883α);
see 1944
ἐπ-άρατος, -ον, (ἐπαράομαι [to call down curses upon]), *accursed*: Jn. vii. 49 L T Tr WH. (Thuc., Plato, Aeschin., Dio Cass., al.) *

1884
ἐπ-αρκέω, -ῶ; 1 aor. [ἐπήρκεσα], subjunc. ἐπαρκέσω; properly, *to avail* or *be strong enough for* . . . (see ἀρκέω); hence **a.** *to ward off* or *drive away*, τί τινι, a thing for another's advantage i. q. *a thing from* any one (Hom.), *to defend.* **b.** *to aid, give assistance, relieve*, (Hdt., Aeschyl., al.): τινί, 1 Tim. v. 10; Mid. *to give aid from one's own resources*, 1 Tim. v. 16 acc. to the reading ἐπαρκείσθω (L txt. T Tr WH mrg.) for ἐπαρκείτω (R G L mrg. WH txt.); (κατὰ δύναμιν ἀλλήλοις ἐπαρκεῖν, Xen. mem. 2, 7, 1).*

see 1885
ἐπάρχειος, -ον, *belonging to an* ἔπαρχος *or prefect*; ἡ ἐπάρχειος sc. ἐξουσία, i. q. ἡ ἐπαρχία (see the foll. word), *a prefecture, province*: Acts xxv. 1 T WH mrg. So ἡ ἐπάρχιος, Euseb. h. e. 2, 10, 3 (with the var. ἐπάρχειον); 2, 26, 2; 3, 33, 3; de mart. Pal. 8, 1; 13, 11.*

1885
ἐπαρχία [-χεία T WH (see ει, ι)], -ας, ἡ, (fr. ἔπαρχος i. e. ὁ ἐπ' ἀρχῇ ὤν from one in command, prefect, governor), *prefecture*; i. e. **1.** the office of ἔπαρχος or prefect. **2.** *the region subject to a prefect; a province* of the Roman empire, either a larger province, or an appendage to a larger province, as Palestine was to that of Syria [cf. *Schürer*, Zeitgesch. p. 144 sqq.]: Acts xxiii. 34; xxv. 1 [see the preced. word]; (Polyb., Diod., Plut., Dio Cass.). Cf. *Krebs*, Observv. etc. p. 256 sqq.; *Fischer*, De vitiis Lexx. N. T. p. 432 sqq.; [BB.DD. (esp. Kitto) s. v. Province].*

1886
ἔπ-αυλις, -εως, ἡ, (ἐπί and αὖλις tent, place to pass the night in; hence a country-house, cottage, cabin, fold), *a farm; a dwelling*, [A. V. *habitation*]: Acts i. 20 fr. Ps. lxviii. (lxix.) 26. (Diod., Plut., al.; also *a camp*, military quarters, Plato, Polyb.) *

1887
ἐπ-αύριον, adv. of time, i. q. ἐπ' αὔριον, *on the morrow*; in the N. T. τῇ ἐπαύριον, sc. ἡμέρᾳ, the next day, on the morrow: Mt. xxvii. 62; Mk. xi. 12; Jn. i. 29; Acts x. 9, etc.; Sept. for מִמָּחֳרָת.

1888;
see (848α)
ἐπ-αυτοφώρῳ, see αὐτόφωρος, p. 87ᵇ.

1889
Ἐπαφρᾶς, -ᾶ [B. 20 (17 sq.)], ὁ, *Epaphras*, a Christian man mentioned in Col. i. 7; iv. 12; Philem. 23. The conjecture of some that the name is contracted from Ἐπαφρόδιτος (q. v. [cf. W. 103 (97)]) and hence that these two names belong to one and the same man, is not probable; [see B. D. Am. ed. s. v. Epaphras; Bp. Lghtft. Com. on Phil. p. 61 note ⁴]. The name is com. in inscriptions.*

1890
ἐπ-αφρίζω; *to foam up* (Mosch. 5, 5); *to cast out as foam, foam out*: τί, Jude 13 calls the godless and graceless set of whom he speaks κύματα ἐπαφρίζοντα τὰς ἑαυτῶν αἰσχύνας, i. e. (dropping the figure) impelled by their restless passions, they unblushingly exhibit, in word and deed, their base and abandoned spirit; cf. Is. lvii. 20.*

Ἐπαφρόδιτος, -ον, ὁ, (fr. Ἀφροδίτη, prop. 'charming '), *Epaphroditus*, an associate with Paul in the ministry: Phil. ii. 25; iv. 18. See Ἐπαφρᾶς above.* **1891**

ἐπ-εγείρω: 1 aor. ἐπήγειρα; *to raise* or *excite against*: τὶ ἐπί τινα, Acts xiii. 50 (διωγμόν); κατά τινος, to stir up against one: τὰς ψυχὰς . . . κατὰ τῶν ἀδελφῶν, Acts xiv. 2.* **1892**

ἐπεί, [fr. temporal ἐπί and εἰ, lit. thereupon when; *Curtius*, Erläut. etc. p. 182; cf. Etym. Magn. 356, 7], conjunction, (Lat. *cum*), *when, since*, [cf. W. § 53, 1]; used **1.** of time, *after*; so once in the N. T.: Lk. vii. 1 (where L T Tr txt. WH txt. ἐπειδή). **2.** of cause, etc., *since, seeing that, because*: Mt. xviii. 32; [xxi. 46 T Tr WH]; xxvii. 6; Mk. xv. 42; Lk. i. 34; Jn. xiii. 29; xix. 31; 1 Co. xiv. 12; 2 Co. xi. 18; xiii. 3; Heb. v. 2, 11; vi. 13; ix. 17; xi. 11; ἐπεὶ οὖν *since then*, Heb. ii. 14; iv. 6. Agreeably to a very common abbreviation of speech, we must often supply in thought between ἐπεί and the proposition depending upon it some such phrase as *if it is* (or *were*) *otherwise*; so that the particle, although retaining the force of *since*, is yet to be rendered *otherwise, else*, or *for then*, (Germ. *sonst*); so in Ro. xi. 6, 22; Heb. ix. 26; ἐπεὶ ἄρα, 1 Co. v. 10; vii. 14, [cf. W. § 53, 8 a.]; ἐπεί alone before a question [cf. W. 480 (447)]. B. 233 (201): Ro. iii. 6; 1 Co. xiv. 16; xv. 29; Heb. x. 2; (4 Macc. i. 33; ii. 7, 19; vi. 34 (35); vii. 21; viii. 8). Cf. Matthiae § 618; [B. § 149, 5].* **1893**

ἐπει-δή, conjunction, (fr. ἐπεί and δή), Lat. *cum jam, when now, since now*, [cf. W. 434 (404), 448 (417); Ellic. on Phil. ii. 26]; **1.** of time; *when now, after that*; so once in the N. T.: Lk. vii. 1 L T Tr txt. WH txt. **2.** of cause; *since, seeing that, forasmuch as*: Mt. xxi. 46 [R G L]; Lk. xi. 6; Acts xiii. 46; xiv. 12; xv. 24; 1 Co. i. 21, 22; xiv. 16; xv. 21; [2 Co. v. 4 Rec.ˢᵗ]; Phil. ii. 26.* **1894**

ἐπει-δή-περ [ἐπειδή περ Lchm.], conjunction, (fr. ἐπεί, δή and πέρ), *seeing that, forasmuch as*; Itala and Vulg. *quoniam quidem, since now*, [cf. W. 448 (417)]: Lk. i. 1. (Aristot. phys. 8, 5 [p. 256ᵇ, 25]; Dion. Hal. 2, 72; Philo ad Gai. § 25, and Attic writ. fr. Thuc. down.) * **1895**

ἐπ-εῖδον [Tdf. 7 ἐφεῖδον]; impv. ἔπιδε (Lchm. ἔφιδε, cf. W. § 5, 1 d. 14; B. 7; [reff. s. v. ἀφεῖδον]; besides see εἴδω, I.); *to look upon, to regard*: foll. by a telic inf., ἐπεῖδεν ἀφελεῖν τὸ ὄνειδός μου ([R. V. *looked upon* me to take away etc.], Germ. *hat hergeblickt*), Lk. i. 25; ἐπί τι, *to look upon* [for the purpose of punishing, cf. Lat. *animadvertere*], Acts iv. 29.* **1896**

ἔπ-ειμι; (ἐπί, and εἶμι to go); *to come upon, approach*; of time, *to come on, be at hand*; ptcp. ἐπιών, -οῦσα, -όν, *next, following*: τῇ ἐπιούσῃ, sc. ἡμέρα, on the following day, Acts xvi. 11; xx. 15; xxi. 18, (Polyb. 2, 25, 11; 5, 13, 10; Joseph. antt. 3, 1, 6; [Prov. xxvii. 1]; etc.); with ἡμέρα added (as in the earlier writ. fr. Hdt. down), Acts vii. 26; τῇ ἐπιούσῃ νυκτί, Acts xxiii. 11. Cf. *Lob.* ad Phryn. p. 464.* **(1896α);**
see 1966

ἐπεί-περ, conjunction, (ἐπεί, πέρ), *since indeed, since at all events*; [it introduces a "known and unquestioned certainty"]: Ro. iii. 30 R G (but L Tr εἴ περ, T WH εἴπερ). Cf. *Hermann* ad Vig. p. 784; [Bäumlein p. 204; W. 448 (417). Fr. the Tragg. down.]* **1897**

1898   ἐπ-εισ-αγωγή, -ῆς, ἡ, a bringing in besides or in addition to what is or has been brought in: κρείττονος ἐλπίδος, Heb. vii. 19. (In Joseph. antt. 11, 6, 2 used of the introduction of a new wife in place of one repudiated; ἑτέρων ἰητρῶν, Hippocr. p. 27 [vol. i. p. 81 ed. Kühn]; προσώπων, of characters in a play, Dion. Hal. scr. cens. 2, 10; in the plur. of places for letting in the enemy, Thuc. 8, 92.) *

see 1904   ἐπ-εισ-έρχομαι: fut. ἐπεισελεύσομαι;   **1.** to come in besides or to those who are already within; to enter afterwards, (Hdt., Thuc., Plato, al.).   **2.** to come in upon, come upon by entering; to enter against: ἐπί τινα, acc. of pers., Lk. xxi. 35 L T Tr txt. WH; with simple dat. of pers. 1 Macc. xvi. 16.*

1899   ἔπειτα, adv., (ἐπί, εἶτα), thereupon, thereafter, then, afterwards; used **a.** of time: Mk. vii. 5 R G; Lk. xvi. 7; Gal. i. 21; Jas. iv. 14; μετὰ τοῦτο is added redundantly in Jn. xi. 7 (cf. Meyer ad loc.; W. § 65, 2; [B. 397 (340)]); a more definite specification of time is added epexegetically, μετὰ ἔτη τρία, Gal. i. 18; διὰ δεκατεσσάρων ἐτῶν, Gal. ii. 1. **b.** in enumerations it is used **a.** of time and order: πρῶτον . . . ἔπειτα, 1 Co. xv. 46; 1 Th. iv. 17; πρότερον . . . ἔπειτα, Heb. vii. 27; ἀπαρχὴ . . . ἔπειτα, 1 Co. xv. 23; εἶτα [but T Tr mrg. WH mrg. ἔπειτα] . . . ἔπειτα, 1 Co. xv. 5, 6; ἔπειτα . . . ἔπειτα, ib. 7 L mrg. T Tr mrg. WH mrg. **β.** of order alone: πρῶτον . . . ἔπειτα, Heb. vii. 2; τρίτον . . . ἔπειτα . . . ἔπειτα (R G εἶτα), 1 Co. xii. 28.*

1900   ἐπ-έκεινα (i. q. ἐπ' ἐκεῖνα sc. μέρη [cf. W. § 6, 1 l. fin.]), adv., beyond: with the gen., Βαβυλῶνος, Acts vii. 43. (Often in Grk. writ. fr. Hdt. down both with and without the gen.; in the Sept. Am. v. 27; Gen. xxxv. 16; Jer. xxii. 19.)*

1901   ἐπ-εκ-τείνω: [pres. mid. ptcp. ἐπεκτεινόμενος]; to stretch out to or towards; Mid. to stretch (one's self) forward to: with dat. of thing indicating the direction [W. § 52, 4, 7], Phil. iii. 13 (14), (see ἔμπροσθεν, 1 fin.).*

1903   ἐπενδύτης, -ου, ὁ, (ἐπενδύνω or ἐπενδύω, q. v., [cf. W. 25; 94 (90)]), an upper garment, (Tertull. superindumentum): Jn. xxi. 7, where it seems to denote a kind of linen blouse or frock which fishermen used to wear at their work. (Soph. frag. 391 Dind. [(248 Ahrens); Poll. 7, 45 p. 717]; Sept. twice [thrice] for מְעִיל, 1 S. xviii. 4 [Alex.]; 2 S. xiii. 18; [add Lev. viii. 7 Alex.].) *

see 1902 St.   ἐπ-εν-δύω: 1 aor. mid. inf. ἐπενδύσασθαι; to put on over [A. V. to be clothed upon]: 2 Co. v. 2, 4. (Plut. Pelop. 11; actively, Joseph. antt. 5, 1, 12.) *

1904   ἐπ-έρχομαι; fut. ἐπελεύσομαι; 2 aor. ἐπῆλθον (3 pers. plur. ἐπῆλθαν, Acts xiv. 19 L T Tr WH); Sept. chiefly for בּוֹא; **1.** to come to, to arrive; **a.** univ., foll. by ἀπό with a gen. of place, Acts xiv. 19. **b.** of time; to come on, be at hand, be future: ἐν τοῖς αἰῶσι τοῖς ἐπερχομένοις, Eph. ii. 7, (Is. xli. 4, 22, 23; in Grk. writ. fr. Hom. down); of that which time will bring, to impend: ἡ ταλαιπωρία ἡ ἐπερχομένη, Jas. v. 1; τινί, Lk. xxi. 26, (Is. lxiii. 4; also of things favorable, ἡ εὐλογία, Sir. iii. 8). **2.** to come upon, overtake, one; so even in Hom., as of sleep, τινά, Od. 4, 793; 10, 31; τινί, 12, 311; of disease, 11, 200: ἐπί τινα, **a.** of calamities: Lk. xxi. 35 R G;

Acts viii. 24; xiii. 40 [L T Tr txt. WH om. Tr mrg. br. ἐφ' ὑ.], (Gen. xlii. 21; Mic. iii. 11; Zeph. ii. 2; 2 Ch. xx. 9; Jer. v. 12 [here ἥξει]). **b.** of the Holy Spirit, descending and operating in one: Lk. i. 35; Acts i. 8. **c.** of an enemy attacking one: ἐπελθὼν νικήσῃ αὐτόν, Lk. xi. 22; (Hom. Il. 12, 136; 1 S. xxx. 23; w. dat. of pers. Hdian. 1, 8, 12 [6 Bekk.]).*

1905   ἐπ-ερωτάω, -ῶ; impf. ἐπηρώτων; fut. ἐπερωτήσω; 1 aor. ἐπηρώτησα; 1 aor. pass. ptcp. ἐπερωτηθείς; Sept. mostly for שָׁאַל, sometimes for דָּרַשׁ; **1.** to accost one with an inquiry, put a question to, inquire of, ask, interrogate, [ἐπί directive, uniformly in the N. T.; Mey. on Mk. xi. 29 (cf. ἐπί, D. 2)]: τινά, Mk. ix. 32; xii. 34; Mt. xxii. 46; Lk. ii. 46; 1 Co. xiv. 35; Jn. xviii. 21 R G; τινά τι, ask one any thing, Mk. vii. 17 L T Tr WH; xi. 29; Lk. xx. 40; τινὰ περί τινος, one about a thing, Mk. vii. 17 R G; [Lk. ix. 45 Lchm.], (Hdt. 1, 32; Dem. 1072, 12); foll. by λέγων with the words used by the questioner, Mt. xii. 10; xvii. 10; Mk. ix. 11; xii. 18; Lk. iii. 10, 14; xx. 27; xxiii. 3 [R G L], and often in the Synoptic Gospels; foll. by εἰ, whether, Mk. viii. 23; xv. 44; Lk. xxiii. 6; or some other form of the indirect question, Acts xxiii. 34; ἐπηρώτων λέγοντες [L T Tr WH om. λέγ.], τίς εἴη, Lk. viii. 9; ἐπερωτᾶν θεόν to consult God (Num. xxiii. 3; Josh. ix. 20 (14); Judg. i. 1; xviii. 5; 1 S. xix. 3, etc.; Thuc. 1, 118, [etc.]), hence to seek to know God's purpose and to do his will, Ro. x. 20 fr. Is. lxv. 1. **2.** by a usage foreign to the Greeks, to address one with a request or demand; to ask of or demand of one: foll. by the inf. Mt. xvi. 1 (so ἐπερ. τινά τι, Hebr. שָׁאַל, in Ps. cxxxvi. (cxxxvii.) 3; [this sense is disputed by some; see Zezschwitz as referred to at end of next word; cf. Weiss on Mt. l. c., and see ἐρωτάω, 2]).

1906   ἐπ-ερώτημα, -τος, τό, (ἐπερωτάω); **1.** an inquiry, a question: Hdt. 6, 67; Thuc. 3, 53. 68. **2.** a demand; so for the Chald. שְׁאֵלָא in Dan. iv. 14 Theod.; see ἐπερωτάω, 2. **3.** As the terms of inquiry and demand often include the idea of desire, the word thus gets the signification of earnest seeking, i. e. a craving, an intense desire (so ἐπερωτᾶν εἴς τι, to long for something, 2 S. xi. 7 — [but surely the phrase here (like שָׁאַל לְ) means simply to ask in reference to, ask about]). If this use of the word is conceded, it affords us the easiest and most congruous explanation of that vexed passage 1 Pet. iii. 21: "which (baptism) now saves us [you] not because in receiving it we [ye] have put away the filth of the flesh, but because we [ye] have earnestly sought a conscience reconciled to God" (συνειδήσεως ἀγαθῆς gen. of the obj., as opp. to σαρκὸς ῥύπου). It is doubtful, indeed, whether εἰς θεόν is to be joined with ἐπερώτημα, and signifies a craving directed unto God [W. 194 (182) — yet less fully and decidedly than in ed. 5, p. 216 sq.], or with συνείδησις, and denotes the attitude of the conscience towards (in relation to) God; the latter construction is favored by a comparison of Acts xxiv. 16 ἀπρόσκοπον συνείδησιν ἔχειν πρὸς τὸν θεόν. The signification of ἐπερ. which is approved by others, viz. stipulation, agreement, is first met with in the Byzantine writers on law: "moreover, the formula κατὰ τὸ ἐπερώτημα τῆς σεμνοτάτης βουλῆς, common in inscriptions of the age of the Antonines and the following Cæsars, exhibits no new sense of the word ἐπερώτημα; for this formula does not mean ' acc. to the decree of the senate' (ex senatus consulto, the Grk. for which is κατὰ τὰ δόξαντα τῇ βουλῇ), but 'after inquiry of or application to the senate,' i. e. 'with government sanction.'" Zezschwitz, Petri ap. de Christi ad inferos descensu sententia (Lips. 1857) p. 45; [Farrar, Early Days of Christianity, i. 138 n.; Kähler, Das Gewissen, i. 1 (Halle 1878) pp. 331-338. Others would adhere to the (more analogical) passive sense of ἐπερ. viz. 'the thing asked (the demand) of a good conscience towards God' i. q. the avowal of consecration unto him].*

1907　ἐπ-έχω; impf. ἐπεῖχον; 2 aor. ἐπέσχον;　　1. to have or hold upon, apply: sc. τὸν νοῦν, to observe, attend to, foll. by an indir. quest., Lk. xiv. 7; τινί, dat. of pers., to give attention to one, Acts iii. 5; 1 Tim. iv. 16, (with dat. of a thing, Sir. xxxi. (xxxiv.) 2; 2 Macc. ix. 25; Polyb. 3, 43, 2, etc.; fully ὀφθαλμόν τινι, Lcian. dial. mar. 1, 2).　　2. to hold towards, hold forth, present: λόγον ζωῆς, as a light, by which illumined ye are the lights of the world, Phil. ii. 16 [al. al., cf. Mey. or Ellic. ad loc.].　　3. to check ([cf. Eng. hold up], Germ. anhalten): sc. ἐμαυτόν, to delay, stop, stay, Acts xix. 22, and in Grk. writ. fr. Hom. down; [cf. W. § 38, 1; B. 144 (126); Fritzsche on Sir. v. 1].*

1908　ἐπηρεάζω; (ἐπήρεια [spiteful abuse, cf. Aristot. rhet. 2, 2, 4]); to insult; to treat abusively, use despitefully; to revile: τινά, Mt. v. 44 R G; Lk. vi. 28, (with dat. of pers., Xen. mem. 1, 2, 31; 3, 5, 16); in a forensic sense, to accuse falsely: with the acc. of a thing, 1 Pet. iii. 16. (Xen., Isaeus, Dem., Philo, Plut., Lcian., Hdian.; to threaten, Hdt. 6, 9 [but cf. Cope on Aristot. u. s.].)*

1909　ἐπί, [before a rough breathing ἐφ' (occasionally in Mss. ἐπ'; see e. g. Ps. cxlv. (cxlvi.) 3), and also in some instances before a smooth breathing (as ἐφ' ἐλπίδι, Acts ii. 26 L; Ro. viii. 20 (21) Tdf.); see ἀφείδον. It neglects elision before proper names beginning with a vowel (exc. Αἴγυπτον Acts vii. 10, 18) and (at least in Tdf.'s txt.) before some other words, see the Proleg. p. 94 sq.; cf. W. § 5, 1 a.; B. p. 10], a preposition [fr. the Skr. local prefix ápi; Curtius § 335], joined to the gen., the dat., and the acc.; its primary signification is upon (Lat. super; [cf. W. 374 (350) note]).

A. with the GENITIVE [cf. W. § 47, g.; B. 336 (289)];　I. of Place; and　1. of the place on which; a. upon the surface of (Lat. in or super with the abl., Germ. auf with the dat.); after verbs of abiding, remaining, standing, going, coming, etc.; of doing anything: ἐπὶ κλίνης, Mt. ix. 2; Lk. xvii. 34; ἐπὶ τοῦ δώματος, Mt. xxiv. 17; Lk. xvii. 31; ἐπ' ἐρημίας (cf. on a desert), Mk. viii. 4; ἐπὶ τῶν νεφελῶν, Mt. xxiv. 30; xxvi. 64; ἐπὶ (τῆς) γῆς, Mt. vi. 10; ix. 6; xxiii. 9; xxviii. 18; Lk. xxi. 25; Acts ii. 19, and very often; ἐπὶ τῆς θαλάσσης, on (the surface of) the sea, Mt. xiv. 25 R G; 26 L T Tr WH; Mk. vi. 48, [49]; Rev. v. 13, and, acc. to the interp. of many, Jn. vi. 19; but cf. Baumg.-Crusius ad loc. [per contra, cf. Lücke ad loc.; Meyer on

Mt. l. c.], (Job ix. 8; βαδίζειν ἐφ' ὕδατος, Lcian. philops. 13; ἐπὶ τοῦ πελάγους διαθέοντες, v. h. 2, 4; [Artem. oneir. 3, 16]; on a different sense of the phrase ἐπὶ τῆς θαλάσσης see 2 a. below [W. 374 (351)]); ποιεῖν σημεῖα ἐπὶ τῶν ἀσθενούντων, to be seen upon the bodies of men, externally, (on the sick [cf. W. 375 (351)]), Jn. vi. 2; ἐκάθισα and κάθημαι [καθέζομαι] ἐπί, Mt. xix. 28; xxiii. 2; xxiv. 3; xxv. 31; xxvii. 19; Jn. xix. 13; Acts xx. 9; Rev. ix. 17, etc.; ἔστην, ἕστηκα ἐπί, Lk. vi. 17; Acts xxi. 40; Rev. v. 5, 8; where parts of the body are spoken of: ἐπὶ χειρῶν, Mt. iv. 6; Lk. iv. 11; ἐπὶ τῆς κεφαλῆς, Jn. xx. 7; 1 Co. xi. 10; Rev. x. 1 R G [al. acc.]; xii. 1; σινδόνα ἐπὶ γυμνοῦ, Mk. xiv. 51; ἐπὶ τοῦ μετώπου [or -πων], Rev. vii. 3; ix. 4; xiii. 16 [Rec., al. acc.]; xiv. 9.　b. Like the prep. ἐν (see the exposition s. v. ἐν, I. 7 p. 212ᵃ), so also ἐπί with the gen. is used after verbs expressing motion to indicate the rest following the motion; thus after βάλλειν, Mk. iv. 26; Mt. xxvi. 12; σπείρειν, Mk. iv. 31; τιθέναι, Jn. xix. 19; Acts v. 15; [Lk. viii. 16 L T Tr WH]; ἐπιτιθέναι, Lk. viii. 16 [R G]; καθιέναι, Acts x. 11; πίπτειν, Mk. ix. 20; xiv. 35; ἐπιγράφειν, Heb. x. 16 R G; ἑλκύειν, Jn. xxi. 11 R G; ἔρχεσθαι, Heb. vi. 7; Rev. iii. 10; [ἀνατέλλειν, Lk. xii. 54 T Tr mrg. WH]; γενόμενος ἐπὶ τοῦ τόπου (cf. our having arrived on the spot), Lk. xxii. 40, [cf. W. p. 376 (352) and see below, C. I. 1 b. fin.]. κρεμᾶν τινα ἐπί (Hebr. עַל תָּלָה, Gen. xl. 19; Deut. xxi. 22, etc.), for which the Latin has suspendere ex, de, a, and alicui, Acts v. 30; x. 39; Gal. iii. 13.　c. fig. used of that upon which any thing rests, (like our upon) [cf. W. 375 (351)]; B. 336 (289); Ellic. on 1 Tim. as below]: ἵνα σταθῇ ἐπὶ στόματος etc. (עַל־פִּי יָקוּם, Deut. xix. 15), resting on the declaration, etc., Mt. xviii. 16; 2 Co. xiii. 1; more simply ἐπὶ μαρτύρων, 1 Tim. v. 19; in the adv. phrase ἐπ' ἀληθείας (on the ground of truth), see ἀλήθεια, I. 1. [c'. akin is its use (with a personal or a reflex. pron.) to denote dependence, as in λογιζέσθω ἐφ' (al. ἀφ' q. v. II. 2 d. aa.) ἑαυτοῦ, 2 Co. x. 7 T Tr WH (for himself, i. e. apart from and independently of others; R. V. with himself); cf. Kühner ii. 432; L. and S. s. v. A. I. 1 d.]　d. fig. used of things, affairs, persons, which one is set over, over which he exercises power; Lat. supra, our over [cf. below, B. 2 b. and C. I. 2 e.]: ἐπὶ πάντων, Ro. ix. 5; Eph. iv. 6 (where ἐπί, διά and ἐν are distinguished); καθίστημι τινα ἐπὶ τινος, Mt. xxiv. 45; xxv. 21, 23; Lk. xii. 42; Acts vi. 3, (Gen. xxxix. 4, 5; 1 Macc. vi. 14; x. 37, etc.; Plat. rep. 5 p. 460 b., etc.); δίδωμι τινι ἐξουσίαν ἐπί τινος, Rev. ii. 26; ἔχω ἐξουσίαν ἐπί τινος, Rev. xx. 6; βασιλεύειν ἐπί τινος, Mt. ii. 22 R G Tr br.; Rev. v. 10; ἔχειν ἐφ' ἑαυτοῦ βασιλέα, Rev. xi. 1; ἔχειν βασιλείαν ἐπὶ τῶν βασιλέων, Rev. xvii. 18; ὃς ἦν ἐπ' τῆς γάζης, who was over the treasury, Acts viii. 27; ὁ ἐπὶ τοῦ κοιτῶνος, he who presided over the bed-chamber, the chamberlain, Acts xii. 20 (Passow i. 2 p. 1035ᵃ gives many exx. fr. Grk. auth. [cf. L. and S. s. v. A. III. 1; Lob. ad Phryn. p. 474; Soph. Lex. s. v.]; for exx. fr. the O. T. Apocr. see Wahl, Clavis Apocr. p. 218ᵇ).　e. of that to which the mental act looks or refers: λέγειν ἐπί τινος, to speak upon (of) a thing, Gal. iii. 16 (Plato,

Charm. p. 155 d.; legg. 2 p. 662 d.; Ael. v. h. 1, 30; scribere super re, Cic. ad Att. 16, 6 ; disserere super, Tac. ann. 6, 28; cf. W. 375 (351) ; [B. 336 (289)]). **f.** of one on whom an obligation has been laid : εὐχὴν ἔχειν ἐφ᾿ ἑαυτοῦ, have (taken) on themselves a vow, have bound themselves by a vow, Acts xxi. 23 [WH txt. ἀφ᾿ ἑαυτ. (see ἀπό, II. 2 d. aa.)]. **2.** used of vicinity, i. e. of the place at, near, hard by, which, (Germ. bei, an) ; **a.** prop. κόλπος ὁ ἐπὶ ποσιδηΐου, Hdt. 7, 115 ; ἐπὶ τῶν θυρῶν, [Acts v. 23 L T Tr WH] (1 Macc. i. 55 ; [Plut. G. Gracch. 14, 3 p. 841 c.]) ; cf. Matthiae ii. p. 1366 § 584; Passow s. v. p. 1034ᵇ; [L. and S. s. v. I. 1 a. sub fin.]. But the exx. of this signification adduced from the N. T. [with the exception of Acts l. c.] (and most of those fr. Grk. auth. also) are such as to allow the rendering of ἐπί by super also, over or above [so W. 374 sq. (351)] : ἐπὶ τῆς θαλάσσης at the sea, upon the shore, or above the sea, for the shore overhung the sea, Jn. vi. 19 (? [cf. 1 a. above]) ; xxi. 1, (Ex. xiv. 2 ; Deut. i. 40 ; 1 Macc. xiv. 34 ; xv. 11 ; Polyb. 1, 44, 4 ; cf. the French Boulogne sur mer, Châlons sur Marne, [Eng. Stratford on Avon], etc. ; ἐπὶ τοῦ ποταμοῦ, Ezek. i. 1 ; [Xen. an. 4, 3, 28] ; ἐπὶ τοῦ Ἰορδάνου, 2 K. ii. 7) ; ἐσθίειν ἐπὶ τῆς τραπέζης (Germ. über Jemands Tische essen, [cf. Eng. over one's food, over one's cups, etc.]), food and drink placed upon the table, Lk. xxii. 30 cf. 21 ; συκῆν ἐπὶ τῆς ὁδοῦ, a fig-tree above (i. e. higher than) the way, Mt. xxi. 19. **b.** before, with gen. of a pers., in the presence of one as spectator, or auditor, [W. 375 (351) ; B. 336 (289)] : Mt. xxviii. 14 [L Tr WH mrg. ὑπό] ; Mk. xiii. 9 ; Acts xxiv. 19, 20 ; xxv. 9 ; xxvi. 2 ; 1 Co. vi. 1, 6 ; 2 Co. vii. 14 ; 1 Tim. vi. 13 [some bring this under II. below ; see μαρτυρέω] ; ἐπὶ τοῦ βήματος Καίσαρος, Acts xxv. 10. **c.** ἐπὶ τοῦ (Rec. τῆς) βάτου at the bush, i. e. at the place in the sacred volume where the bush is spoken of, Mk. xii. 26 (see ἐν, I. 1 d.). **II.** of Time when; with gen. of a pers. in the time or age of a man, ["in the days of"] ; at the time when an office was held by one ; under the administration of, [cf. W. 375 (352) ; B. 336 (289)] : Mk. ii. 26 ; Lk. iii. 2 ; iv. 27 ; Acts xi. 28 ; (1 Macc. xiii. 42 ; xiv. 27, [for other exx. in which this phrase is equiv. to "in or of the reign etc. of," and is preceded by a specification of the year etc., see B. D. Am. ed. p. 651 noteᵇ] ; 2 Macc. xiii. 19 ; xv. 22 ; for numerous exx. fr. Grk. writ. see Passow i. 2 p. 1035, [less fully in L. and S. s. v. A. II.]). with the gen. of a thing, at the time of any occurrence : ἐπὶ τῆς μετοικεσίας Βαβυλῶνος, at the time of the deportation to Babylon, Mt. i. 11 ; [on Lk. xii. 54 T Tr mrg. WH see δυσμή] ; of the time when any occupation is (or was) carried on : ἐπὶ τῶν προσευχῶν μου, Lat. in precibus meis, at my prayers, when I am praying, Ro. i. 10 (9) ; Eph. i. 16 ; 1 Th. i. 2 ; Philem. 4. of time itself, ἐπ᾿ ἐσχάτων and (acc. to another reading) ἐσχάτου τῶν ἡμερῶν (lit. at the end of the days) : 2 Pet. iii. 3 ; Heb. i. 2 (1), (for the Hebr. בְּאַחֲרִית הַיָּמִים, Gen. xlix. 1 ; Num. xxiv. 14 ; Jer. xxxvii. (xxx.) 24 ; Mic. iv. 1 ; Dan. x. 14) ; ἐπ᾿ ἐσχάτου τοῦ χρόνου, Jude 18 L T TrWH ; [τῶν χρόνων, 1 Pet. i. 20 L T TrWH].

B. with the DATIVE, used of Place [W. 392 (366) sq. ; B. 336 (289) sq.] ; and **1.** properly ; **a.** of the place where or in which (Lat. in with the abl., Germ. auf with the dat.) [Eng. on, etc.], where continuance, position, situation, etc., are spoken of : ἐφ᾿ ᾧ (L txt. T Tr WH ὅπου) κατέκειτο, Mk. ii. 4 ; λίθος ἐπὶ λίθῳ [-θον T Tr WH], Mk. xiii. 2 ; ἐπὶ πίνακι, Mt. xiv. 8, 11 ; Mk. vi. 25 ; ἐπὶ τοῖς κραββάτοις, Mk. vi. 55 ; ἀνακλῖναι πάντας ἐπὶ τῷ χόρτῳ, Mk. vi. 39 ; ἐπέκειτο ἐπ᾿ αὐτῷ, lay upon it, Jn. xi. 38 ; ἐφ᾿ ἵπποις, Rev. xix. 14. **b.** of the place in which (Lat. in with the abl., Germ. auf with the acc.), after verbs expressing motion towards a place, to denote a remaining in the place after the motion, [Eng. upon, at, etc.] : βάλλειν λίθον ἐπί τινι, dat. of pers., Jn. viii. 7 Rec. ; οἰκοδομεῖν, Mt. xvi. 18 ; ἐποικοδομεῖν, Eph. ii. 20 ; ἐπιβάλλειν, Mt. ix. 16 (Lk. v. 36 ἐπιβάλλειν ἐπί τι) ; ἐπιρράπτειν, Mk. ii. 21 (where L T Tr WH have ἐπί with acc.) ; ἐπιπίπτειν, Acts viii. 16. **c.** of the place above which (Lat. super, Germ. über, [Eng. over]) : ἐπ᾿ αὐτῷ, over his head, Lk. xxiii. 38 (for which Mt. xxvii. 37 ἐπάνω τῆς κεφαλῆς αὐτοῦ). **d.** of the place at, or by, or near which : ἐπὶ θύραις and ἐπὶ τῇ θύρᾳ, Mt. xxiv. 33 ; Mk. xiii. 29 ; Acts v. 9, (and often in Grk. writ. ; cf. Passow s. v. p. 1037ᵃ ; [L. and S. s. v. B. I. 1 a. ; cf. A. I. 2 a. above]) ; ἐπὶ τῇ προβατικῇ, Jn. v. 2 ; ἐπὶ τῷ ποταμῷ, Rev. ix. 14 ; ἐπὶ τῇ στοᾷ, Acts iii. 11 ; ἐπ᾿ [L T Tr WH παρ᾿] αὐτοῖς ἐπιμεῖναι, Acts xxviii. 14. **2.** Metaph.; **a.** of that upon which any action, effect, condition, rests as a basis or support ; prop. upon the ground of ; and **α.** of that upon which anything is sustained or upheld : ζῆν ἐπί τινι, to sustain life on (by) a thing, Mt. iv. 4 (where L Tr, the second time, ἐν ; [cf. W. 389 (364) note]) ; Lk. iv. 4, (Deut. viii. 3 for יִחְיֶה עַל ; Plat. Alcib. 1 p. 105 c.; Plut. de cup. divit. 7 p. 526 d.; Alciphr. epp. 3, 7, etc.) ; συνιέναι ἐπὶ τοῖς ἄρτοις, to understand by reasoning built upon the loaves, Mk. vi. 52 [cf. W. 392 (367) ; B. 337 (290)]. **β.** of that upon which anything rests (our upon) : ἐπ᾿ ἐλπίδι [see in ἐλπίς, 2], supported by hope, in hope, [cf. W. § 51, 2 f.], Acts ii. 26 ; Ro. iv. 18 ; 1 Co. ix. 10, [differently in ε. below] ; to do any thing ἐπὶ τῷ ὀνόματί τινος, relying upon the name i. e. the authority of any one [cf. W. 393 (367)] : ἐλεύσονται ἐπὶ τῷ ὀνόματί μου, appropriating to themselves the name of Messiah, which belongs to me, Mt. xxiv. 5 ; Mk. xiii. 6 ; Lk. xxi. 8, (in which pass. λέγοντες, ὅτι ἐγώ εἰμι ὁ Χριστός is added by way of explanation) ; βαπτίζεσθαι ἐπὶ [L Tr WH ἐν] τῷ ὀν. Χριστοῦ, so as to repose your hope and confidence in his Messianic authority, Acts ii. 38 ; δέχεσθαί τινα ἐπὶ τῷ ὀν. μου, to receive one because he bears my name, is devoted to my authority and instruction, Mt. xviii. 5 ; Mk. ix. 37 ; Lk. ix. 48. to do anything upon the name of Christ, his name being introduced, appeal being made to his authority and command : as κηρύσσειν, διδάσκειν, etc., Lk. xxiv. 47 ; Acts iv. 17, 18 ; v. 28, 40 ; δύναμιν ποιεῖν, δαιμόνια ἐκβάλλειν, using his name as a formula of exorcism, [cf. W. 393 (367)], Mk. ix. 39 ; Lk. ix. 49 [WH Tr mrg. ἐν]. **γ.** of that upon which as a foundation any superstructure is reared : νομοθετεῖσθαι, Heb. vii. 11 (ἐπ᾿ αὐτῇ, for which L T Tr WH have ἐπ᾿ αὐτῆς); viii. 6 ; after verbs of trusting, believing, hoping, etc.: ἀρκεῖσθαι ἐπί τινι, 3 Jn. 10 ; παρρησιάζεσθαι, Acts xiv. 3 ; πεποιθέναι, Mt. xxvii. 43 L txt. WH mrg. ; Lk. xi. 22 ; xviii. 9 ; Mk. x. 24 [T WH om. Tr mrg. br. the cl.] ; 2 Co. i. 9 ; Heb. ii. 13 ; πιστεύειν, Lk. xxiv. 25 ; Ro. ix. 33 ; x. 11, etc.; ἐλπίζειν (see ἐλπίζω), [cf. C. I. 2 g. a. below]. δ. of the reason or motive underlying words and deeds, so that ἐπί is equiv. to *for, on account of*, [W. 394 (368) ; B. 337 (290)] : Mt. xix. 9 R G T Tr WH txt. ; Lk. v. 5 (ἐπὶ τῷ ῥήματί σου, *at thy word*, Germ. *auf*; [cf. W. §48, c. d. ; in reliance *on*]) ; Acts iii. 16 [WH om.] ; iv. 9 ; xi. 19 [L Tr mrg. have the gen.] ; xxi. 24 ; 1 Co. viii. 11 (ἀπόλλυσθαι ἐπί τινι, Germ. *zu Grunde gehen über* etc. [cf. W. 394 (368) note, but L T Tr WH read ἐν]) ; Phil. iii. 9 ; after αἰνεῖν, Lk. ii. 20 ; δοξάζειν, Acts iv. 21 ; 2 Co. ix. 13 [cf. W. 381 (357)] ; μαρτυρεῖν, Heb. xi. 4 ; εὐχαριστεῖν etc. to give thanks *for*, 1 Co. i. 4 ; 2 Co. ix. 15 ; Phil. i. 5 ; 1 Th. iii. 9. ἐφ᾿ ᾧ (equiv. to ἐπὶ τούτῳ, ὅτι *for that, on the ground of this, that*) *because that, because*, Ro. v. 12 (on the various interrp. of this pass. see *Dietzsch*, Adam und Christus. Bonn 1871, p. 50 sqq.) ; 2 Co. v. 4 [Rec^st ἐπειδή] ; Phil. iii. 12, (ἐφ᾿ ᾧ — ὁ σατανᾶς — οὐκ ἴσχυσε θανατῶσαι αὐτούς, Theoph. ad Autol. 2, 29 p. 138 ed. Otto ; ἐφ᾿ ᾧ Γεννάδιον ἔγραψεν, *for the reason that he had accused Gennadius*, Synes. ep. 73 ; cf. *Hermann* ad Vig. p. 710 ; the better Greeks commonly used ἐφ᾿ οἷς in the same sense, cf. W. 394 (368) ; [Fritzsche or Mey. on Ro. l. c. ; Ellic. on Phil. l. c.]). Used esp. after verbs signifying a mental affection or emotion, where we also often say *over* (for exx. fr. Grk. writ. see Passow i. 2, p. 1039^b ; Krüger § 68, 41, 6 ; [cf. W. 393 (368) c.]): as ἀγαλλιᾶν, Lk. i. 47 ; χαίρειν, Mt. xviii. 13 ; Lk. i. 14 ; xiii. 17 ; Ro. xvi. 19, etc. ; χαρὰ ἔσται, Lk. xv. 7 ; χαρὰν (Rec. χαράν) ἔχω, Philem. 7 ; παρακαλεῖν, παρακαλεῖσθαι, 2 Co. i. 4 ; vii. 13 ; 1 Th. iii. 7 ; κλαίειν, Lk. xix. 41 R G ; κοπετὸν ποιεῖν, Acts viii. 2 ; κόπτεσθαι, Rev. xviii. 9 [T Tr WH txt. the acc.] ; ὀδυνᾶσθαι, Acts xx. 38 ; ὀλολύζειν, Jas. v. 1 ; στυγνάζειν, Mk. x. 22 ; συλλυπεῖσθαι, Mk. iii. 5 ; μετανοεῖν ἐπί, to grieve over, *repent of*, 2 Co. xii. 21 ; σπλαγχνίζεσθαι, Mt. xiv. 14 G L T Tr WH ; Mk. vi. 34 R G ; Lk. vii. 13 [Tdf. the acc.] ; μακροθυμεῖν, Mt. xviii. 26 [Tr the acc.], 29 [L Tr the acc.] ; Lk. xviii. 7 [see μακροθυμέω, 2] ; Jas. v. 7 ; ὀργίζεσθαι, Rev. xii. 17 [Lchm. om. ἐπί] ; ἐκπλήσσεσθαι, Mt. vii. 28 ; Mk. i. 22 ; Lk. iv. 32 ; Acts xiii. 12 ; διαταράσσεσθαι, Lk. i. 29 ; ἐξίστασθαι, Lk. ii. 47 ; θαμβεῖσθαι, Mk. x. 24 ; θάμβος, Lk. v. 9 ; Acts iii. 10 ; θαυμάζειν, Mk. xii. 17 ; Lk. ii. 33 ; iv. 22 ; ix. 43 ; xx. 26 ; Acts iii. 12 ; καυχᾶσθαι, Ro. v. 2 ; ἐπαισχύνεσθαι, Ro. vi. 21 ; παραζηλοῦν and παροργίζειν τινὰ ἐπί τινι, Ro. x. 19. ε. of the rule, or condition [W. 394 (368) d.] : ἐπ᾿ ἐλπίδι, a hope being held out or given, Ro. viii. 20 ; Tit. i. 2, (differently in β. above) ; ἐπὶ δυσὶν . . . μάρτυσιν, on condition that two witnesses testify to the matter in question, [*at* (the mouth of) *two* etc. ; cf. W. 392 (367)], Heb. x. 28 ; ἐπὶ νεκροῖς, equiv. to *ὄντων νεκρῶν* (*in the case of the dead*), if any one has died, Heb. ix. 17. ζ. of the purpose

and end [*unto, for* ; W. 394 (368) e.] : ἐπ᾿ ὀνόματι αὐτοῦ, to worship and profess his name, Acts xv. 14 Rec. ; καλεῖν τινα ἐπί τινι, Lat. *ad aliquid*, Gal. v. 13 ; 1 Th. iv. 7, (ἐπὶ ξενίᾳ, Xen. an. 7, 6, 3 ; cf. W. u. s.) ; κτισθέντες ἐπὶ ἔργοις ἀγαθοῖς, Eph. ii. 10 ; φρονεῖν ἐπί τινι to take thought for a thing, Phil. iv. 10 ; ἐφ᾿ ᾧ (by a later Grk. impropriety for ἐπὶ τίνι, cf. W. § 24, 4 ; [B. § 139, 59 ; but on the extreme doubtfulness of this alleged use of ὅς in direct questions, see Pres. T. D. Woolsey in the Bibliotheca Sacra for Apr. 1874, p. 314 sqq.]) πάρει ; for what purpose art thou come ? Vulg. *ad quid* [al. *quod*] *venisti?* Mt. xxvi. 50 R [but G L T Tr WH ἐφ᾿ ὅ, see C. I. 2 g. γ. aa. below] (Theoph. ἐπὶ ποίῳ σκοπῷ ; cf. Hdt. 7, 146 πυθόμενος, ἐπ᾿ οἷσι ἦλθον ; [but the view of many ancient expositors which explains the passage by an aposiopesis: "*that for which thou hast come* — do " is thoroughly established by Dr. Woolsey u. s.]). of the issue or undesigned result: λογομαχεῖν ἐπὶ καταστροφῇ τῶν ἀκουόντων, 2 Tim. ii. 14 ; (τοῖς ἐπὶ ὠφελείᾳ πεποιημένοις ἐπὶ βλάβῃ χρῆσθαι, Xen. mem. 2, 3, 19). η. of the pattern or standard [A. V. *after*; W. 394 (368) f.] : καλεῖν τινα ἐπὶ τῷ ὀνόματί τινος, to call one after the name of another, Lk. i. 59 (Neh. vii. 63 [W. 410 (382)]) ; ἐπὶ τῷ ὁμοιώματί τινος after the likeness of a thing, Ro. v. 14. b. of that over which one is placed, for its care or administration : ἐπὶ τοῖς ὑπάρχουσί τινα καθιστάναι, Lk. xii. 44 (cf. A. I. 1 d. above, [also C. I. 2 e. below] ; *Lob.* ad Phryn. p. 474 sq. ; Bnhdy. p. 249 ; [W. 393 (367) a.]). c. used of a hostile aim, *against* (for exx. fr. Grk. writ. fr. Hom. down, see Passow i. 2 p. 1036^a ; [cf. L. and S. s. v. B. I. 1 c. ; W. 392 (367) ; B. 337 (290)]) : Lk. xii. 52 sq. ; θλίψις γενομένη ἐπὶ Στεφάνῳ [-νου, L Tr mrg.], Acts xi. 19 [A. V. *about*]. d. of that to which anything is added (so that it is, as it were, *upon* it) ; *in addition to; over and above*, [W. 393 (367 sq.) b.] : 2 Co. vii. 13 (L T Tr WH ἐπὶ δὲ τῇ παρακλήσει ὑμῶν [but L T Tr WH ἡμῶν] περισσοτέρως κτλ. but in addition to the comfort given (us) by you, we rejoiced the more exceedingly etc. [A. V. *in* etc. (of condition)]) ; κερδαίνειν τι ἐπί τινι, Mt. xxv. 20, 22 R G ; ἔχειν λύπην ἐπὶ λύπῃ, Phil. ii. 27 Rec. (Eur. Iph. T. 197 φόνος ἐπὶ φόνῳ, Troad. 596 ἐπὶ δ᾿ ἄλγεσιν ἄλγεα, Soph. O. C. 544 ἐπὶ νόσῳ νόσον ; [cf. Mey. on Phil. l. c. ; but G L T Tr WH give the acc., see C. I. 2 c. below]) ; προστιθέναι ἐπί, Lk. iii. 20 ; ἐπὶ πᾶσι τούτοις, besides all this, Lk. xvi. 26 [L mrg. T Tr mrg. WH ἐν ; see ἐν, I. 5 e. p. 211^a] ; Eph. vi. 16 [L txt. T Tr WH ἐν (and there is no τούτοις) ; see ἐν, u. s.] ; Col. iii. 14, (Sir. xxxvii. 15 ; 1 Macc. x. 42 ; [classic exx. in Wetst. on Lk. l. c.]) ; add also Heb. viii. 1 [see Lünem. ad loc.] ; ix. 10 ; 1 Co. xiv. 16. e. of that which is connected as an adjunct (esp. of time) with the principal matter under consideration, (in Germ. generally *bei*, i. e. *at, on*, etc.) [W. 392 (367)] : εὐχαριστῶ τῷ θεῷ μου ἐπὶ πάσῃ τῇ μνείᾳ ὑμῶν, at every mention of you, as often as I call you to mind, Phil. i. 3 [but see Mey., Ellic., Bp. Lghtft. ad l., and s. v. πᾶς, I. 2] ; σπένδομαι ἐπὶ τῇ θυσίᾳ, while engaged in (busied over) the sacrifice, Phil. ii. 17 ; ἐπὶ συντελείᾳ τῶν αἰώνων, Heb. ix. 26 ; ἐπὶ τῇ πρώτῃ διαθήκῃ, ib. 15 ; σπείρειν and θερίζειν ἐπ᾿ εὐλογίαις, so that blessings attend, i. e. bountifully, freely, 2 Co. ix. 6 ; ἐπὶ πάσῃ τῇ ἀνάγκῃ, 1 Th. iii. 7 ; ἐπὶ τῷ παροργισμῷ ὑμῶν while your anger lasts, Eph. iv. 26 ; ἐπὶ τούτῳ meanwhile, i. e. while this was going on [(?), upon this], Jn. iv. 27. **f.** of the object of an action, and **a.** where the Germ. uses an, [Eng. on (nearly i. q. to)]: πράσσειν τι ἐπί τινι, Acts v. 35 (like δρᾶν τι ἐπί τινι, Hdt. 3, 14 ; Ael. n. an. 11, 11) ; cf. Bnhdy. p. 250 bot. ; [but see B. 337 (290)] ; ὃ γέγονεν ἐπ᾿ αὐτῇ, Mk. v. 33 [T Tr WH om. L br. ἐπί] ; ἀναπληροῦσθαι, Mt. xiii. 14 Rec. **β.** where the Germ. says über, [Eng. upon, of, concerning], after verbs of writing, speaking, thinking: γεγραμμένα ἐπ᾿ αὐτῷ, Jn. xii. 16 (Hdt. 1, 66) ; προφητεύειν, Rev. x. 11 ; μαρτυρεῖν, xxii. 16 R G T Tr txt. WH txt. [see μαρτυρέω, a.], (δόξα ἐπὶ τῇ εὐσεβείᾳ, an opinion about, on, piety, 4 Macc. v. 17 (18)).

C. with the ACCUSATIVE [W. § 49, l. ; B. 337 (290) sq.] ; **I.** of Place ; **1.** properly ; **a.** of the place above, over, which, our up on, on to: after verbs signifying motion and continuance, ἐλθεῖν, περιπατεῖν ἐπὶ τὰ ὕδατα, Mt. xiv. 28 sq. ; ἐπὶ τὴν θάλασσαν, ib. 25 L T Tr WH, 26 R G, (πλεῖν ἐπὶ πόντον, Hom. Od. 1, 183) ; ἀναπεσεῖν ἐπὶ τὴν γῆν, Mt. xv. 35 ; ἐπὶ τὸ στῆθός τινος, Jn. xxi. 20 ; ἀνακλιθῆναι ἐπὶ τοὺς χόρτους, Mt. xiv. 19 R G ; κατοικεῖν ἐπὶ πᾶν τὸ πρόσωπον (L T Tr WH παντὸς προσώπου [cf. πᾶς, I. 1 c.]) τῆς γῆς, Acts xvii. 26 ; καθῆσθαι, Lk. xxi. 35 ; ἦλθε λιμὸς ἐφ᾿ ὅλην τὴν γῆν, Acts vii. 11 ; σκότος ἐγένετο ἐπὶ πᾶσαν τὴν γῆν, Mt. xxvii. 45. over i. e. along: εἱστήκει ἐπὶ τὸν αἰγιαλόν, Mt. xiii. 2 [W. 408 (380) ; differently in d. below]. **b.** of motion to a place whose surface is occupied or touched (Germ. auf with the acc.), upon, unto, on to ; after verbs of going, coming, ascending, descending, falling, etc.: πορεύεσθαι ἐπὶ τὴν ὁδόν, Acts viii. 26 ; ix. 11 ; ἐπὶ τὰς διεξόδους, Mt. xxii. 9 ; προέρχεσθαι, Acts xx. 13 [here Tr WH mrg. προσέρχ.] ; φεύγειν, Mt. xxiv. 16 (where L Tr WH txt. εἰς) ; ἐξέρχεσθαι, Lk. viii. 27 ; ἐξιέναι, Acts xxvii. 43 ; ἐπιβαίνειν, Mt. xxi. 5 ; ἀναβαίνειν, Lk. v. 19 ; xix. 4 ; Acts x. 9 ; Rev. xx. 9 ; καταβαίνειν, Lk. xxii. 44 [L br. WH reject the pass.] ; Rev. xvi. 21 ; ἀπέρχεσθαι, Lk. xxiii. 33 [L Tr WH ἔρχεσθαι] ; πίπτειν ἐπὶ τοὺς πόδας, Acts x. 25 ; ἐπὶ πρόσωπον, to fall upon the face, Mt. xvii. 6 ; xxvi. 39 ; Lk. v. 12 ; xvii. 16 ; 1 Co. xiv. 25 ; Rev. vii. 11. After verbs of placing, leading, bringing, building, laying, throwing, etc.: τιθέναι, Mt. v. 15 ; Lk. xi. 33 ; ἐπιτιθέναι, Mt. xxiii. 4 ; Lk. xv. 5 ; Acts xv. 10, etc. ; τιθέναι τὰ γόνατα ἐπί, Acts xxi. 5 ; οἰκοδομεῖν, Mt. vii. 24, 26 ; Lk. vi. 49 ; Ro. xv. 20 ; ἐποικοδομεῖν, 1 Co. iii. 12 ; θεμελιοῦν, Lk. vi. 48 ; βάλλειν, Jn. viii. 59 ; Rev. ii. 24 ; xiv. 16 ; xviii. 19 ; ἐπιβάλλειν, Lk. v. 36 (ἐπιβ. ἐπί τινι, Mt. ix. 16) ; ἐπιβάλλειν τὰς χεῖρας ἐπί τινα, Mt. xxvi. 50, etc. (see ἐπιβάλλω, 1 a.) ; ἐπιρρίπτειν, Lk. xix. 35 and tropically 1 Pet. v. 7 ; ῥαπίζειν, Mt. v. 39 [L T Tr txt. WH εἰς] ; τύπτειν, Lk. vi. 29 [Tdf. εἰς] ; ἀναβιβάζειν, Mt. xiii. 48 [not Lchm. txt.] ; ἐπιβιβάζειν, Lk. x. 34 ; κατάγειν, Lk. v. 11 ; σωρεύειν, Ro. xii. 20 ; διδόναι, Lk. vii. 44 ; xix. 23 ; Rev. viii. 3 ; ἀναφέρειν, 1 Pet. ii. 24 ; κρεμᾶν, Mt. xviii. 6 [L T Tr WH περί] ; γράφειν, Rev. ii. 17 ; iii. 12 ; xix. 16 ;

ἐπιγράφειν, Heb. viii. 10. After verbs which include another verb signifying motion, or transfer, or entrance into, (where Germ. uses auf or über ; our on, to, etc.) : ἀνατέλλειν, Mt. v. 45 ; βρέχειν, ibid. ; πνέειν, Rev. vii. 1 (here we see the difference betw. ἐπί with the gen. to blow over a thing, Germ. über, and ἐπί with the acc. to blow on a thing, to come blowing upon it, Germ. einen anwehen, wehend auf einen kommen) ; [apparently nearly the same view of the distinction betw. the cases is taken by Thiersch § 274, 6 ; Hermann on Eur. Alcest. 845. But Krüger (§ 68, 40, 3), Kühner (ii. § 438, I. 1 b.), al., regard ἐ. with the acc. as denoting merely movement towards a place, while ἐ. with the gen. involves the idea of actual or intended arrival ; cf. L. and S. s. v. A. I. 1. Still others hold the two expressions to be substantially synonymous : e. g. Bttm. Gram. § 147 (p. 417 Eng. trans.) ; Matthiae § 584 ; Passow p. 1034ᵃ ; — esp. in the N. T., see W. 409 sq. (382) ; 408 (381) note ; B. 338 (291). On the variations of case with this prep. in the Rev. cf. Alford on iv. 2] ; διασωθῆναι ἐπὶ τὴν γῆν, Acts xxvii. 44. **c.** It is used of persons over whom anything is done, that thereby some benefit may accrue to them, (Germ. über with the dat.) [W. 408 (381) note] : ὀνομάζειν τὸ ὄνομα Ἰησοῦ ἐπί τινα, to name the name of Jesus (as a spell, a magic formula) over one, sc. that help may come to him from that name, Acts xix. 13 ; προσεύχεσθαι ἐπί τινα, Jas. v. 14. **d.** As εἰς (q. v. C. 2 p. 186ᵃ), so ἐπί also stands after verbs of rest and continuance [B. 337 (290) sq. ; W. § 49, l. 1] : καθεύδειν ἐπί τι, Mk. iv. 38 ; στῆναι, Rev. xi. 11 ; σταθῆναι ἐπί τι, Rev. xii. 18 (xiii. 1) ; ἑστηκέναι, Jn. xxi. 4 (ἐπὶ τὸν αἰγιαλὸν L T Tr mrg. WH mrg. ; otherwise where many are spoken of ; see a. fin. above) ; Rev. xiv. 1 ; καθῆσθαι, Jn. xii. 15 ; Rev. iv. 4 ; vi. 2 [Rec. dat.] ; xi. 16 ; xiv. 14, 16 [L T Tr WH txt. gen.] ; xvii. 3 ; xix. 11 ; κεκαθικέναι, καθίσαι, Mk. xi. 2 ; Lk. xix. 30 ; Jn. xii. 14 ; Rev. xx. 4 ; καθίσεσθαι, Mt. xix. 28 ; σκηνοῦν, Rev. vii. 15 ; κεῖσθαι, 2 Co. iii. 15 ; κατακεῖσθαι, Lk. v. 25 T Tr WH ; εἶναι ἐπὶ τὸ αὐτό, to be together, assembled, in the same place : Lk. xvii. 35 ; Acts i. 15 ; ii. 1, 44, — to come together, of sexual intercourse, 1 Co. vii. 5 G L T Tr WH ; συνελθεῖν ἐπὶ τὸ αὐτό have convened, come together, to the same place, 1 Co. xiv. 23 [L txt. ἐλθεῖν] ; simply ἐπὶ τὸ αὐτό sc. ὄντες, together, Acts iii. 1 [but L T Tr WH (so R. V.) connect ἐπὶ τ. α. here with ii. 47] ; 2 S. ii. 13 [cf. B. 338 (291)]. **e.** used of motion or arrival into the vicinity of a place (not to the place itself) ; near ; to, as far as ; (Germ. an, bei, zu, hin . . . zu) : ἐπὶ τὸ μνημεῖον [or μνῆμα], Mk. xvi. 2 ; Lk. xxiv. 12 [L Tr br. T om. WH reject the vs.], 22, 24 ; ἐπὶ τοὺς ἀναβαθμούς, Acts xxi. 35 ; ἔρχεσθαι ἐπί τι ὕδωρ, Acts viii. 36 ; ἐπὶ τὴν πύλην, Acts xii. 10 ; ἐπιστῆναι ἐπὶ τὸν πυλῶνα, Acts x. 17 ; καταβαίνειν ἐπὶ τὴν θάλασσαν, Jn. vi. 16, etc., etc. : with the acc. of a pers. to, near to one : Jn. xix. 33 ; Acts xxv. 12 ; 2 Th. ii. 1 ; Rev. xvi. 14 ; esp. to judges, kings, etc., i. q. to their tribunal : Mt. x. 18 ; Lk. xii. 58 ; xxi. 12 ; xxiii. 1 ; Acts ix. 21 ; xvi. 19. also in pregn. constr. after verbs of sitting, standing, etc. : καθῆσθαι ἐπὶ τὸ τελώνιον, Mt. ix.

9; Mk. ii. 14; ἐστηκέναι ἐπί, Rev. iii. 20; xv. 2; ἐπιστῆναι ἐπί, Acts x. 17; xi. 11; ἐπὶ τὴν δεξιάν on the right hand, Rev. v. 1. **f.** of mere direction towards a terminus (so that the terminus itself is not reached): πορεύεσθαι ἐπὶ τὸ ἀπολωλός, to recover it (where we say *after*), Lk. xv. 4; ἐκτείνειν τὰς χεῖρας ἐπί, *against* one, to take him, Lk. xxii. 53; *towards* one, in pointing him out, Mt. xii. 49; ἐξέρχεσθαι ἐπὶ λῃστήν, to take a robber, Mt. xxvi. 55; Mk. xiv. 48; Lk. xxii. 52, cf. Lk. xiv. 31. **2.** It is used metaphorically, **a.** with the acc. of a pers. after verbs of coming, falling, bringing, etc. **α.** of evils befalling (falling 'upon') one, and of perturbations coming upon the mind: τὸ αἷμά τινος (the penalty for slaying him) ἥκει or ἔρχεται ἐπί τινα, Mt. xxiii. 35 sq.; xxvii. 25; ἐπάγειν τὸ αἷμά τινος ἐπί τινα, Acts v. 28; ἔρχεσθαι and ἥκειν ἐπί τινα, of other evils, Jn. xviii. 4; Eph. v. 6; Rev. iii. 3; after γίνεσθαι, Lk. i. 65; iv. 36; Acts v. 5; ἐπέρχεσθαι [ἐπεισέρχ. L T Tr WH], Lk. xxi. 35; ἐπιπίπτειν, Lk. i. 12; Acts xiii. 11 [L T Tr WH πίπτειν]; xix. 17 [L Tr πίπτειν]; Rev. xv. 3 (fr. Ps. lxviii. (lxix.) 10); Rev. xi. 11 [Rec. πίπτειν]; ἐπιστῆναι, Lk. xxi. 34. **β.** of blessings coming upon one: after ἔρχεσθαι, Mt. x. 13; ἐπιπίπτειν, of a trance, Acts x. 10 [L T Tr WH γίνεσθαι]; ἐπισκηνοῦν, 2 Co. xii. 9; ἔφθασεν and ἤγγικεν ἐφ' ὑμᾶς (upon you sc. fr. heaven, [cf. W. 407 (380) note]) ἡ βασιλεία τοῦ θεοῦ, Mt. xii. 28; Lk. x. 9; xi. 20. the Holy Spirit is said at one time ἐπί τινα ἐκχεῖσθαι, Acts ii. 17 sq.; x. 45; Tit. iii. 6; at another, ἀποστέλλεσθαι [or ἐξαποστέλ. T Tr WH], Lk. xxiv. 49; again, ἐπέρχεσθαι, Acts i. 8; once more, καταβαίνειν, Mk. i. 10 [L txt. T Tr WH εἰς]; Lk. iii. 22; Jn. i. 33; ἔπεσεν ὁ κλῆρος ἐπί τινα, Acts i. 26; after words of rest and continuance: χάρις ἦν ἐπί τινα, Lk. ii. 40; Acts iv. 33; ἐπαναπαύεσθαι, Lk. x. 6; the Holy Spirit is said at one time ἐπί τινα μένειν, descending upon one to remain on him, Jn. i. 32 sq. [B. 338 (291)]; and again ἀναπαύεσθαι, 1 Pet. iv. 14. **b.** of one upon whom anything is imposed, as a burden, office, duty, etc.: τὴν μέριμναν ἐπιρρίπτειν ἐπὶ θεόν, 1 Pet. v. 7; συντελεῖν διαθήκην ἐπί τινα, to put a covenant upon one, to be kept by him, Heb. viii. 8, (in Ps. lxxxii. (lxxxiii.) 6 וְעָלֶיךָ כָּרַת בְּרִית is to make a covenant *against* one). **c.** of that to which anything is added, [Eng. upon (nearly i. q. *after*)]: λύπη ἐπὶ λύπην, Phil. ii. 27 G L T Tr WH (Ps. lxviii. (lxix.) 27; Ezek. vii. 26; [esp. Is. xxviii. 10, 13; cf. Lat. *super* in Liv. 1, 50; 22, 54 etc.]; see above, B. 2 d.); [so some take οἶκος ἐπ' οἶκον, Lk. xi. 17, B. 338 (291); see above, 2]; ἐπικαλεῖν ὄνομα ἐπί τινα (see ἐπικαλέω, 2 [and B. 338 (291)]), to call (put) a name upon one, Acts xv. 17; Jas. ii. 7. **d.** of the number or degree reached; Lat. *usque ad* [W. § 49, l. 3 a.]: ἐπὶ σταδίους δώδεκα, Rev. xxi. 16 [Rᵉ T Tr WH txt. gen.] (Xen. mem. 1, 4, 17; an. 1, 7, 15; Polyb. 3, 54, 7; Song of the Three 23); ἐπὶ τρίς, Vulg. *per ter*, for three times, thrice; Acts x. 16 (so εἰς τρίς, Hdt. 1, 86; Xen. an. 6, 4, 16. 19; Cyr. 7, 1, 4 etc. [cf. W. 422 (394)]); ἐπὶ πλεῖον more widely, to a greater degree, further, the more, [differently below, II. 1]: Acts iv. 17; [xx. 9 WH mrg.]; 2 Tim. ii. 16; iii. 9; ἐφ'

ὅσον, *forasmuch as, inasmuch as*, [differently II. 1 below]: Mt. xxv. 40, 45; Ro. xi. 13. **e.** of care, power, control over anything, (Germ. *über* with the acc.) [W. § 49, l. 3 b.], (cf. above, A. I. 1 d. and B. 2 b.): βασιλεύειν ἐπί τινα (Hebr. עַל מָשַׁל), Lk. i. 33; xix. 14, 27; Ro. v. 14; ἡγούμενον ἐπ' Αἴγυπτον, Acts vii. 10; καθίστημι, Heb. ii. 7 R [(fr. Ps. viii. 7), L Tr WH br.]; ἐπὶ τὸν οἶκον αὐτοῦ sc. [Heb. iii. 6; ἱερέα μέγαν ἐπὶ τὸν οἶκον τοῦ θεοῦ sc. καθεστηκότα, Heb. x. 21; καθιστάναι δικαστὴν ἐπί, Lk. xii. 14 (ἄρχοντα, Xen. Cyr. 4, 5 fin.); ἐξουσία, Lk. x. 19; Rev. vi. 8; xvi. 9; xxii. 14; φυλάσσειν φυλακάς, Lk. ii. 8; of usurped dignity: ὑπεραίρεσθαι ἐπὶ πάντα λεγόμενον θεόν, 2 Th. ii. 4 cf. Dan. xi. 36 sq. [al. refer the use in Th. l. c. to g. γ. ββ. below]. Akin to this is the expression πιστὸς ἐπί τι (because fidelity is as it were spread over the things intrusted to its care), Mt. xxv. 21. **f.** of the end which the mind reaches or to which it is led; Lat. *ad, to, unto*: ἐπιστρέφειν, ἐπιστρέφεσθαι ἐπί τινα, esp. to God, Lk. i. 17; Acts ix. 35; xi. 21; xiv. 15; xxvi. 20; Gal. iv. 9; 1 Pet. ii. 25. **g.** of direction towards a person or a thing, (Germ. *auf, upon*; see above, B. 2 a. γ.): after verbs of trusting and hoping, (Germ. *auf, upon*; see above, B. 2 a. γ.): after ἐλπίζειν, 1 Pet. i. 13; iii. 5 R G; 1 Tim. v. 5, (and often in Sept.); πιστεύειν, Acts ix. 42; xi. 17; xvi. 31; xxii. 19; Ro. iv. 24; πίστις, Heb. vi. 1; πεποιθέναι, Mt. xxvii. 43 (where L txt. WH mrg. ἐπί with dat.). **β.** of the feelings, affections, emotions, Germ. *über, over*: κόπτομαι, Rev. i. 7; xviii. 9 [R G L WH mrg. w. dat.]; κλαίω, Lk. xxiii. 28; Rev. xviii. 9; εὐφραίνεσθαι, Rev. xviii. 20 [G L T Tr WH w. dat.]. *unto, towards*, Lat. *erga*: σπλαγχνίζομαι, Mt. xv. 32; Mk. viii. 2; ix. 22; [μακροθυμέω, Mt. xviii. 26 Tr, 29 L Tr]; χρηστός, Lk. vi. 35; χρηστότης, Ro. xi. 22; Eph. ii. 7. **γ.** of the direction of the will and action; **αα.** of purpose and end [W. § 49, l. 3 d.]: ἐπὶ τὸ βάπτισμα αὐτοῦ, to receive his baptism, Mt. iii. 7; ἐπὶ θεωρίαν ταύτην, Lk. xxiii. 48; ἐφ' ὃ πάρει, Mt. xxvi. 50 G L T Tr WH (see above, B. 2 a. ζ.); where aim and result coalesce: ἐπὶ τὸ συμφέρον, Heb. xii. 10. **ββ.** of things done with hostility; *against*: after ἀπορία, Ro. xi. 22; ἀναστῆναι, Mk. iii. 26; ἐγείρεσθαι, Mt. xxiv. 7; Mk. xiii. 8; Lk. xxi. 10; ἐπεγείρειν διωγμόν, Acts xiii. 50; μερισθῆναι, Mt. xii. 26; Mk. iii. 24 sq.; ἐπαίρειν τι ἐπί, Jn. xiii. 18; μάρτυρ, 2 Co. i. 23; μαρτύριον, Lk. ix. 5; ἀσχημονεῖν, 1 Co. vii. 36 (εἰς τινα, Dion. Hal. 2, 26); μοιχᾶσθαι, Mk. x. 11; τολμᾶν, 2 Co. x. 2; βρύχειν ὀδόντας, Acts vii. 54. **γγ.** of that to which one refers in writing or speaking [cf. W. § 49, l. 3 d.]: after λέγειν, Heb. vii. 13; ὁ οὖν μακαρισμὸς . . . ἀκροβυστίαν, sc. λέγεται [W. 587 (546), cf. B. 394 (338)], Ro. iv. 9; προφητεία, 1 Tim. i. 18; on Mk. ix. 12 sq. see γράφω, 2 c. **δδ.** upon i. e. *in reference to*; *for*: after βάλλειν κλῆρον, Mk. xv. 24; Jn. xix. 24; cf. Fritzsche on Mark p. 686 [who compares Ps. xxi. (xxii.) 19, and remarks that an Attic writ. would have said ἐπί τινι]. **II.** of Time [W. § 49, l. 2]. **1.** of time *during* or *for* ['for the space of'] which (Germ. *auf, während*): ἐπὶ ἔτη τρία, Lk. iv. 25 [R G T WH mrg.]; ἐπὶ ἡμέρας πλείους, Acts xiii. 31; add also xvi. 18; xvii. 2; xviii. 20; xix. 10; Heb. xi. 30, etc., and often in Grk. writ. fr. Hom. down; cf. Passow s. v. p. 1044, [L. and S. s. v. C. II.]; ἐφ' ὅσον χρόνον *for so long time as*, Ro. vii. 1; 1 Co. vii. 39; Gal. iv. 1; and simply ἐφ' ὅσον *as long as* [differently in I. 2 d. above], Mt. ix. 15; 2 Pet. i. 13; ἐφ' ἱκανόν *long enough*, for a considerable time, Acts xx. 11; ἐπὶ πλεῖον *somewhat long, too long* [differently in I. 2 d. above]: Acts xx. 9 [not WH mrg., see u. s.]; xxiv. 4. **2.** *about, towards,* (Germ. *gegen*): ἐπὶ τὴν αὔριον *on the morrow*, Lk. x. 35; Acts iv. 5; ἐπὶ τὴν ὥραν τῆς προσευχῆς, Acts iii. 1; ἐπὶ τὸ πρωΐ, Mk. xv. 1 [R G]; rarely so in Grk. writ., as Arr. exp. Al. 3, 18, 11 (7) ἐπὶ [al. ὑπὸ] τὴν ἕω.

D. In COMPOSITION ἐπί denotes **1.** continuance, rest, influence upon or over any person or thing: ἐπίγειος, ἐπουράνιος, ἐπιδημέω, ἐπαναπαύομαι, etc. **2.** motion, approach, direction towards or to anything: ἐπακούω, ἐπιβοάω, ἐπιβλέπω, ἐπεκτείνω, etc. **3.** imposition: ἐπικαθίζω, ἐπιτίθημι, ἐπιβιβάζω, ἐπιβαρέω, ἐπιγράφω, ἐπιρρίπτω, ἐπιτάσσω, etc. **4.** accumulation, increase, addition: ἐπεισαγωγή, ἐπισυνάγω, ἐπισωρεύω (by a cognomen), etc. **5.** repetition: ἐπαιτέω, ἐπαναμιμνήσκω, etc. **6.** up, upward: ἐπαίρω, ἐπανάγω, ἐπαφρίζω, etc. **7.** against: ἐπιβουλή, ἐπανίστημι, ἐπίορκος, ἐπιορκέω, etc. **8.** superintendence: ἐπιστάτης.

1910 ἐπι-βαίνω; 2 aor. ἐπέβην; pf. ptcp. ἐπιβεβηκώς; **1.** *to get upon, mount*: ἐπί τι, Mt. xxi. 5 (Xen. Hell. 3, 4, 1, etc.; Gen. xxiv. 61); τῷ πλοίῳ [*to embark in*], Acts xxvii. 2 (Thuc. 7, 70); εἰς τὸ πλοῖον, Acts xxi. 6 R G; used without a case, of *going aboard* (a ship), Acts xxi. 2; *to go up*: εἰς Ἱεροσόλ. Acts xxi. 4 L T Tr WH, [yet al. refer this to 2]. **2.** *to set foot in, enter*: εἰς with the acc. of place, Acts xx. 18; with the dat. of place (as also in Grk. writ.), Acts xxv. 1.*

1911 ἐπι-βάλλω; impf. ἐπέβαλλον; fut. ἐπιβαλῶ; 2 aor. ἐπέβαλον, [3 pers. plur. -λαν, Acts xxi. 27 T Tr WH; Mk. xiv. 46 T WH, (see ἀπέρχομαι, init.)]; **1.** Transitively, **a.** *to cast upon*: τινὶ βρόχον, 1 Co. vii. 35; τινὶ τὰ ἱμάτια, Mk. xi. 7; [χοῦν ἐπὶ τὰς κεφ. Rev. xviii. 19 WH mrg.]; *to lay upon*, ἐπί τινα τὴν χεῖρα or τὰς χεῖρας, used of seizing one to lead him off as a prisoner: Mt. xxvi. 50; Mk. xiv. 46 R G L; Lk. xx. 19; xxi. 12; Jn. vii. 30 [L mrg. ἔβαλεν], 44 (L Tr WH the simple βάλλειν); Acts v. 18; xxi. 27, (for the Hebr. בְּ יָד שָׁלַח, Gen. xxii. 12); also τὰς χεῖράς τινι, Mk. xiv. 46 T Tr WH; Acts iv. 3, (Polyb. 3, 2, 8; 5, 5; Lcian. Tim. 4); ἐπιβάλλειν τὰς χεῖρας foll. by the inf. indicating the purpose, Acts xii. 1; τὴν χεῖρα ἐπ' ἄροτρον, to put the hand to the plough (to begin work), Lk. ix. 62. **b.** *to put* (i. e. sew) *on*: ἐπίβλημα ἐπὶ ἱμάτιον, Lk. v. 36; ἐπὶ ἱματίῳ, Mt. ix. 16. **2.** Intrans. (as in Grk. writ. fr. Hom. down, [cf. W. 251 (236); B. 144 (126) sq.]) *to throw one's self upon, rush upon*: εἰς τὸ πλοῖον, of waves rushing into a ship, Mk. iv. 37; *to put one's mind upon a thing, attend to*, with the dat. of the thing: τούτῳ γὰρ ἐπιβάλλω, Antonin. 10, 30; μηδενὶ γὰρ ἐπιβάλλειν μηδετέραν (i. e. τὴν αἴσθησιν καὶ τὴν νόησιν) χωρὶς τοῦ προσπίπτοντος εἰδώλου, Plut. plac. phil. 4, 8; absol. ἐπιβαλών, sc. τῷ ῥήματι τοῦ Ἰησοῦ, when he had considered the utterance of

Jesus, Mk. xiv. 72; cf. Kypke, [Wetst., McClellan] ad loc.; B. 145 (127); [and for the diff. interpp. see Mey. and esp. Morison ad loc.]. **3.** Impersonally, ἐπιβάλλει μοι *it belongs to me, falls to my share*: τὸ ἐπιβάλλον (sc. μοί) μέρος τῆς οὐσίας, Lk. xv. 12 (κτημάτων τὸ ἐπιβάλλον, Hdt. 4, 115; τὸ ἐπιβάλλον αὐτοῖς μέρος, Diod. 14, 17, and the like often in other writ. [see Meyer; σοὶ ἐπιβάλλει ἡ κληρονομία, Tob. vi. 12 (cf. iii. 17; 1 Macc. x. 30, etc.)]).*

1912 ἐπι-βαρέω, -ῶ; 1 aor. inf. ἐπιβαρῆσαι; *to put a burden upon, to load*, [cf. ἐπί, D. 3]; trop. *to be burdensome*; so in the N. T.: τινά, 1 Th. ii. 9; 2 Th. iii. 8; absol. ἵνα μὴ ἐπιβαρῶ 'that I press not too heavily' i. e. lest I give pain by too severe language, 2 Co. ii. 5. (Dion. Hal., Appian.)*

1913 ἐπι-βιβάζω; 1 aor. ἐπεβίβασα; *to cause to mount; to place upon*, [cf. ἐπί, D. 3]: τινά or τὶ ἐπί τι, Lk. x. 34; xix. 35; Acts xxiii. 24. (Thuc., Plat., Diod., al.; Sept. several times for הִרְכִּיב.)*

1914 ἐπι-βλέπω; 1 aor. ἐπέβλεψα; in the Sept. often for הִבִּיט and פָּנָה, also for רָאָה; *to turn the eyes upon, to look upon, gaze upon,* (ἐπί τινα [cf. ἐπί, D. 2]): ἐπί τινα, contextually, to look upon one with a feeling of admiration and respect, *to look up to, regard*, Jas. ii. 3; contextually, to look upon in pity for the sake of giving aid, i. q. *to have regard for, to regard*, Lk. ix. 38 (where for ἐπίβλεψον [R L] and ἐπιβλέψαι [G T] write [with Tr WH] ἐπιβλέψαι, 1 aor. act. inf.; cf. Bornemann, Schol. ad loc., and above in δέομαι, 3 a., [also B. 273 (234) note]); ἐπὶ τὴν ταπείνωσίν τινος, Lk. i. 48; often in the O. T. in the same sense, as 1 S. i. 11; ix. 16; Ps. xxiv. (xxv.) 16; lxviii. (lxix.) 17; Tob. iii. 3, etc. (In Grk. writ. fr. Soph. and Plato down, both lit. and fig.)*

1915 ἐπί-βλημα, -τος, τό, (ἐπιβάλλω), *that which is thrown or put upon a thing,* or *that which is added to it*; *an addition*; spec. *that which is sewed on to cover a rent, a patch*; Vulg. *assumentum* [(also *commissura*)], (i. q. ἐπίρραμα): Mt. ix. 16; Mk. ii. 21; Lk. v. 36. [Sept., Plut., Arr.]*

1916 ἐπι-βοάω, -ῶ; *to cry out to* [cf. ἐπί, D. 2], *cry out*: foll. by acc. with inf. Acts xxv. 24 R G, [but L T Tr WH βοάω, q. v. 2, and fin. From Hom., Hdt. down].*

1917 ἐπι-βουλή, -ῆς, ἡ, *a plan* formed *against* one [cf. ἐπί, D. 7], *a plot*: Acts ix. 24; γίνεταί τινι ἐπιβουλὴ ὑπό τινος, Acts xx. 3; εἴς τινα, Acts xxiii. 30; plur. Acts xx. 19. (From [Hdt.], Thuc. down.)*

1918 ἐπι-γαμβρεύω; fut. ἐπιγαμβρεύσω; *to be related to by marriage, enter into affinity with*; **1.** Sept. for הִתְחַתֵּן, *to become* any one's *father-in-law* or *son-in-law*: τινί, Gen. xxxiv. 9; 1 S. xviii. 22 sqq.; 2 Chr. xviii. 1; 2 Esdr. ix. 14; 1 Macc. x. 54, 56. **2.** τινά, for יָבַם, *to marry the widow of a brother who has died childless*: Gen. xxxviii. 8; Mt. xxii. 24, where allusion is made to the levirate law recorded in Deut. xxv. 5–10; cf. Win. RWB. s. v. Leviratsehe; [BB. DD. s. v. Marriage]. (Not found in native Grk. auth. [exc. schol. ad Eur. Or. 574 sqq.; cf. W. 26].)*

1919 ἐπί-γειος, -ον, (ἐπί and γῆ), existing *upon the earth, earthly, terrestrial*: οἰκία, the house we live in on earth, spoken of the body with which we are clothed in this world, 2 Co. v. 1; σώματα ἐπίγεια, opp. to ἐπουράνια, 1

Co. xv. 40; absolutely, οἱ ἐπίγειοι (opp. to οἱ ἐπουράνιοι and οἱ καταχθόνιοι), those who are on earth, the inhabitants of the earth, men, Phil. ii. 10; τὰ ἐπίγεια, things done on earth, spoken of the new birth wrought by the Holy Spirit, Jn. iii. 12; cf. Knapp, Scripta var. Arg. p. 212 sq.; τὰ ἐπίγεια φρονεῖν, to set the mind on the pleasures and good things of earth, Phil. iii. 19; σοφία ἐπίγειος (opp. to ἡ ἄνωθεν κατερχομένη), the wisdom of man, liable to error and misleading, Jas. iii. 15. (From Plato down; nowhere in the O. T.) *

1920   ἐπι-γίνομαι : 2 aor. ἐπεγενόμην;   **1.** to become or happen afterwards; to be born after.   **2.** to come to, arrive : of time, τεσσαρεσκαιδεκάτη νὺξ ἐπεγένετο, Acts xxvii. 27 L [ed. ster.], T [edd. 2, 7]; (ἔαρος ἐπιγίγνεται ὥρη, Hom. Il. 6, 148).   **3.** to arise, spring up, come on : ἐπιγενομένου νότου, a south wind having sprung up, Acts xxviii. 13; (Thuc. 3, 74; 4, 30).*

1921   ἐπι-γινώσκω; [impf. ἐπεγίνωσκον]; fut. ἐπιγνώσομαι; 2 aor. ἐπέγνων; pf. ἐπέγνωκα; [Pass., pres. ἐπιγινώσκομαι; 1 aor. ἐπεγνώσθην]; (ἐπί denotes mental direction towards, application to, that which is known); in the Sept. chiefly for ידע and נכר‎, הכיר‎;   **1.** to become thoroughly acquainted with, to know thoroughly; to know accurately, know well, [see reff. s. v. ἐπίγνωσις, init.] : 1 Co. xiii. 12 (where γινώσκω ἐκ μέρους and ἐπιγιν. i. e. to know thoroughly, know well, divine things, are contrasted [W. § 39, 3 N. 2]); with an acc. of the thing, Lk. i. 4; 2 Co. i. 13; τὴν χάριν τοῦ θεοῦ, Col. i. 6; τὴν ἀλήθειαν, 1 Tim. iv. 3; τὴν ὁδὸν τῆς δικαιοσύνης, 2 Pet. ii. 21 [cf. B. 305 (262)]; τὸ δικαίωμα τοῦ θεοῦ, Ro. i. 32; τὶ foll. by ὅτι (by the familiar attraction [W. 626 (581); B. 376 (322)]; some bring this ex. under 2 a. in the sense of acknowledge]), 1 Co. xiv. 37; τινά, one's character, will, deeds, deserts, etc., 1 Co. xvi. 18; 2 Co. i. 14; [pass. opp. to ἀγνοούμενοι, 2 Co. vi. 9]; τινὰ ἀπό τινος (gen. of thing), Mt. vii. 16, 20 [Lchm. ἐκ] ("a Gallicis armis atque insignibus cognoscere," for the more common ex, Caes. b. g. 1, 22, 2 [cf. B. 324 (278 sq.); W. 372 (348)]); by attraction τινά, ὅτι etc. 2 Co. xiii. 5; ἐπιγινώσκει ὃν υἱόν, τὸν πατέρα, Mt. xi. 27.   **2.** univ. to know;   **a.** to recognize : τινά, i. e. by sight, hearing, or certain signs, to perceive who a person is, Mt. xiv. 35; Mk. vi. 54; Lk. xxiv. 16, 31; Mk. vi. 33 [R T, but G WH mrg. without the accus.]; by attraction, τινά, ὅτι, Acts iii. 10; iv. 13; τινά, his rank and authority, Mt. xvii. 12; with acc. of the thing, to recognize a thing to be what it really is : τὴν φωνὴν τοῦ Πέτρου, Acts xii. 14; τὴν γῆν, Acts xxvii. 39.   **b.** to know i. q. to perceive : τί, Lk. v. 22; ἐν ἑαυτῷ, foll. by acc. of the thing with a ptcp. [B. 301 (258)], Mk. v. 30; foll. by ὅτι, Lk. i. 22; τῷ πνεύματι foll. by ὅτι, Mk. ii. 8.   **c.** to know i. e. to find out, ascertain : acc. αὐτό, Acts ix. 30; foll. by ὅτι, Lk. vii. 37; xxiii. 7; Acts xix. 34; xxii. 29; xxiv. 11 L T R Tr WH; xxviii. 1; τί, foll. by an indirect quest., Acts xxiii. 28 L T Tr WH; [δι᾽ ἣν αἰτίαν etc. Acts xxii. 24]; παρά τινος (gen. of pers.). περί τινος (gen. of thing), Acts xxiv. 8.   **d.** to know i. e. to understand : Acts xxv. 10. [From Hom. down.]*

1922   ἐπί-γνωσις, -εως, ἡ, (ἐπιγινώσκω, q. v. [cf. also Bp. Lghtft.

on Col. i. 9; Trench § lxxv. ad fin.]), precise and correct knowledge; used in the N. T. of the knowledge of things ethical and divine : absol., Phil. i. 9; Col. iii. 10; κατ᾽ ἐπίγνωσιν, Ro. x. 2; with gen. of the thing known, Col. i. 9; ii. 2; Philem. 6; τῆς ἀληθείας, 1 Tim. ii. 4; 2 Tim. ii. 25; iii. 7; Tit. i. 1; Heb. x. 26; τῆς ἁμαρτίας, Ro. iii. 20; with gen. of the person known; — of God, esp. the knowledge of his holy will and of the blessings which he has bestowed and constantly bestows on men through Christ : Eph. i. 17; Col. i. 10; 2 Pet. i. 2; of Christ, i. e. the true knowledge of Christ's nature, dignity, benefits : Eph. iv. 13; 2 Pet. i. 8; ii. 20; of God and Christ : 2 Pet. i. 2; θεὸν ἔχειν ἐν ἐπιγνώσει, i. e. to keep the knowledge of the one true God which has illumined the soul, Ro. i. 28. (Polyb., Plut., Hdian., [al.]; Sept. occasionally for דַעַת‎; 2 Macc. ix. 11.) *

1923   ἐπι-γραφή, -ῆς, ἡ, (ἐπιγράφω), an inscription, title : in the N. T. of an inscription in black letters upon a whitened tablet [B. D. s. v. Cross], Lk. xxiii. 38; with the gen. τῆς αἰτίας, i. e. of the accusation, Mk. xv. 26, (γράμματα τὴν αἰτίαν τῆς θανατώσεως αὐτοῦ δηλοῦντα, Dio Cass. 54, 3; cf. Sueton. Calig. 32; Domit. 10); of the inscription on a coin : Mt. xxii. 20; Mk. xii. 16; Lk. xx. 24. (From Thuc. down.) *

1924   ἐπι-γράφω; fut. ἐπιγράψω; pf. pass. ptcp. ἐπιγεγραμμένος; plpf. 3 pers. sing. ἐπεγέγραπτο; to write upon, inscribe : ἐπιγραφήν, Mk. xv. 26 and L Tr br. in Lk. xxiii. 38; ὀνόματα, Rev. xxi. 12; ἔν τινι, Acts xvii. 23; fig. to write upon the mind, i. e. to fix indelibly upon it, cause to cleave to it and to be always vividly present to it : νόμους ἐπὶ καρδίας [-δίαν T WH mrg.], Heb. viii. 10; ἐπὶ τῶν διανοιῶν, Heb. x. 16 R G, ἐπὶ τὴν διάνοιαν, ibid. L T Tr WH, (τοὺς λόγους ἐπὶ τὸ πλάτος τῆς καρδίας, Prov. vii. 3). [From Hom. down.] *

1925   ἐπι-δείκνυμι; 1 aor. ἐπέδειξα; [pres. mid. ἐπιδείκνυμαι]; to exhibit, show, [as though for e x p o s i t i o n or e x a m i n a t i o n (Schmidt ch. 127, 5); fr. Pind., Hdt. down.];   **a.** to bring forth to view : τί, Mt. xxii. 19; Lk. xx. 24 Rec.; τί τινι, Lk. xxiv. 40 R G; ἑαυτόν τινι, Lk. xvii. 14; to show i. e. bid to look at, τί τινι, Mt. xxiv. 1; to show i. e. furnish to be looked at, produce what may be looked at : σημεῖον, Mt. xvi. 1; Mid. with acc. of the thing, to display something belonging to one's self : χιτῶνας, the tunics as their own, Acts ix. 39 [see Meyer].   **b.** to prove, demonstrate, set forth to be known and acknowledged : Heb. vi. 17; foll. by the acc. and inf. Acts xviii. 28.*

1926   ἐπι-δέχομαι; [fr. Hdt. down];   **1.** to receive hospitably : τινά, 3 Jn. 10 (Polyb. 22, 1, 3).   **2.** to admit, i. e. not to reject : τινά, one's authority, 3 Jn. 9 (τοὺς λόγους, 1 Macc. x. 46; παιδείαν, Sir. li. 26). [Cf. δέχομαι, fin.] *

1927   ἐπιδημέω, -ῶ; (ἐπίδημος);   **1.** to be present among one's people, in one's city or in one's native land, [cf. ἐπί D. 1], (Thuc., Plato, al.; opp. to ἀποδημεῖν, Xen. Cyr. 7, 5, 69; ἐπιδημεῖν ἐν τῷδε τῷ βίῳ, Theoph. ad Autol. 2, 12 [p. 88 ed. Otto]).   **2.** to be a sojourner, a foreign resident, among any people, in any country : Acts ii. 10; οἱ ἐπιδημοῦντες ξένοι, Acts xvii. 21; (Xen., Plato, Theophr., Lcian., Aelian, al.).*

1928 **ἐπι-δια-τάσσομαι**; *to ordain besides, to add something to what has been ordained,* [cf. ἐπί, D. 4]: Gal. iii. 15. Not found elsewhere.*

1929 **ἐπι-δίδωμι**: 3 pers. sing. impf. ἐπεδίδου; fut. ἐπιδώσω; 1 aor. ἐπέδωκα; 2 aor. ptcp. plur. ἐπιδόντες; 1 aor. pass. ἐπεδόθην; [fr. Hom. down]; *to give over;* **1.** *to hand, give by handing:* τινί τι, Mt. vii. 9 sq.; Lk. xi. 11 sq.; xxiv. 30, 42; Jn. xiii. 26 [R G L]; Acts xv. 30; pass. Lk. iv. 17. **2.** *to give over, i. e. give up to the power or will of one* (Germ. *preisgeben*): Acts xxvii. 15 (sc. ἑαυτούς or τὸ πλοῖον τῷ ἀνέμῳ).*

1930 **ἐπι-δι-ορθόω** (see διόρθωσις): *to set in order besides or further* (what still remains to be set in order, [cf. ἐπί, D. 4]): Tit. i. 5, where, for the common reading ἐπιδιορθώσῃ (1 aor. mid. subjunc.), Lchm. has adopted ἐπιδιορθώσῃς (1 aor. act. subjunc.). Found also in inscriptions (Boeckh ii. 409, 9), and in eccl. writ.*

1931 **ἐπι-δύω**; *to go down, set* (of the sun): Eph. iv. 26, on which see ἐπί, B. 2 e. (Deut. xxiv. 17 (15); Jer. xv. 9; [Philo de spec. legg. 28]; and with tmesis, Hom. Il. 2, 413.)*

1932 **ἐπιείκεια** [WH -κία, see I, ι], -ας, ἡ, (ἐπιεικής, q. v.), *mildness, gentleness, fairness,* ['*sweet reasonableness*' (Matthew Arnold)]: Acts xxiv. 4; joined with πραότης [q. v.], 2 Co. x. 1; Plut. Pericl. 39; with φιλανθρωπία, Polyb. 1, 14, 4; Philo, vit. Moys. i. § 36; with χρηστότης, Hdian. 5, 1, 12 [6 ed. Bekk.]. Cf. Plato, defin. p. 412 b.; Aristot. eth. Nic. 5, 10. (Bar. ii. 27; Sap. ii. 19; xii. 18; 2 Macc. ii. 22; 3 Macc. iii. 15.)*

[Syn. ἐπιείκεια, πραότης: "πρ. magis ad animum, ἐπι. vero magis ad exteriorem conversationem pertinet" (Estius on 2 Co. x. 1). "πρ. virtus magis absoluta; ἐπι. magis refertur ad alios" (Bengel, ibid.). See at length Trench § xliii.]

1933 **ἐπιεικής**, -ές, (εἰκός, what is reasonable); **1.** *seemly, suitable,* (fr. Hom. down). **2.** *equitable, fair, mild, gentle*: 1 Tim. iii. 3; Tit. iii. 2; 1 Pet. ii. 18; Jas. iii. 17. Neut. τὸ ἐπιεικές (as often in Grk. writ. fr. Thuc. down) ὑμῶν i. q. ἡ ἐπιείκεια ὑμῶν, Phil. iv. 5. [See ἐπιείκεια, fin.]*

1934 **ἐπι-ζητέω**, -ῶ; impf. ἐπεζήτουν; 1 aor. ἐπεζήτησα; fr. Hdt. down; Sept. for שָׁרַשׁ and in 1 S. xx. 1; Eccl. vii. 29 (28) for בָּקַשׁ; *to inquire for, seek for, search for, seek diligently,* (Germ. *herbeisuchen* [the ἐπι- seems to be directive rather than intensive]): τινά, Lk. iv. 42 (for Rec. ἐζήτουν); Acts xii. 19; i. q. *to desire, wish for, crave*: τί, Mt. vi. 32; Lk. xii. 30; Ro. xi. 7; Phil. iv. 17; Heb. xi. 14; xiii. 14; περί τινος, Acts xix. 39 [R G T] (but if your inquiry or desire has reference to other matters); with the inf. Acts xiii. 7 (as in Polyb. 3, 57, 7; Diod. 19, 8); i. q. *to demand, clamor for*: σημεῖον, Mt. xii. 39; xvi. 4; Mk. viii. 12 R G; Lk. xi. 29 (where T Tr WH ζητεῖ [as L T Tr WH in Mk. l. c.]).*

1935 **ἐπιθανάτιος**, -ον, (θάνατος), *doomed to death*: 1 Co. iv. 9. (Dion. Hal. antt. 7, 35.)*

1936 **ἐπί-θεσις**, -εως, ἡ, (ἐπιτίθημι), *a laying on, imposition*: τῶν χειρῶν, Acts viii. 18; 1 Tim. iv. 14; 2 Tim. i. 6; Heb. vi. 2. The imposition of hands, χειροθεσία, was a sacred rite transmitted by the Jews to the Christians, and employed in praying for another, or in conferring upon him divine blessings, especially bodily health, or the Holy Spirit (at the administration of baptism and the inauguration to their office of the teachers and ministers of the church): Gen. xlviii. 14; Num. xxvii. 18, 23; Deut. xxxiv. 9; 2 K. v. 11, etc.; Mt. xix. 13; Mk. xvi. 18; Acts vi. 6; xiii. 3; xix. 6, etc. [See B. D. s. v. Baptism (supplement); McCl. and Strong and Dict. of Chris. Antiq. s. v. Imposition of Hands.]*

1937 **ἐπιθυμέω**, -ῶ; [impf. ἐπεθύμουν]; fut. ἐπιθυμήσω; 1 aor. ἐπεθύμησα; (θυμός); fr. Aeschyl. down; Sept. for אָוָה and חָמַד; prop. *to keep the θυμός turned upon a thing,* hence [cf. our *to set one's heart upon*] *to have a desire for, long for*; absol. *to desire* [A. V. *lust*], Jas. iv. 2; *to lust after, covet,* of those who seek things forbidden, Ro. vii. 7; xiii. 9 (fr. Ex. xx. 17); 1 Co. x. 6, (4 Macc. ii. 6); κατά τινος, to have desires opposed to [A.V. *lust against*] a thing, Gal. v. 17 [B. 335 (288)]; τινός, to long for, covet a thing, Acts xx. 33; 1 Tim. iii. 1; of sexual desire, γυναικός, Mt. v. 28 Rec. [see below] (παιδὸς ἢ γυναικός, Xen. an. 4, 1, 14; with the gen. also in Ex. xxxiv. 24; Prov. xxi. 26; xxiii. 3, 6; Sap. vi. 12; Sir. xxiv. 19 (18), etc.); contrary to the usage of the better Grk. writ. with the acc. of the object, Mt. v. 28 L Tr (WH br.), and without an obj. Tdf. (Ex. xx. 17; Deut. v. 21; Mic. ii. 2; Sap. xvi. 3; Sir. i. 26 (23), etc.; cf. W. § 30, 10 b.); as often in Grk. writ., foll. by the inf.: Mt. xiii. 17; Lk. xv. 16; [xvi. 21]; xvii. 22; 1 Pet. i. 12; Rev. ix. 6; foll. by the acc. with the inf. Heb. vi. 11; ἐπιθυμίᾳ ἐπεθύμησα I have greatly desired, Lk. xxii. 15; cf. W. § 54, 3; B. § 133, 22 a.*

1938 **ἐπιθυμητής**, -οῦ, ὁ, (ἐπιθυμέω), *one who longs for, a craver, lover, one eager for*: κακῶν, 1 Co. x. 6 (Num. xi. 4). In Grk. writ. fr. Hdt. down.*

1939 **ἐπιθυμία**, -ας, ἡ, (ἐπιθυμέω), [fr. Hdt. on], Sept. chiefly for חֶמֶד, אַוָּה, תַּאֲוָה; *desire, craving, longing*: Lk. xxii. 15 (on which see in ἐπιθυμέω, fin.); Rev. xviii. 14; τὴν ἐπιθυμίαν ἔχειν εἴς τι, the desire directed towards, Phil. i. 23; ἐν πολλῇ ἐπιθυμίᾳ with great desire, 1 Th. ii. 17; plur. αἱ περὶ τὰ λοιπὰ ἐπιθυμίαι, Mk. iv. 19 [W. § 30, 3 N. 5]; spec. *desire for what is forbidden, lust,* (Vulg. *concupiscentia*): Ro. vii. 7 sq.; Jas. i. 14 sq.; 2 Pet. i. 4; πάθος ἐπιθυμίας, 1 Th. iv. 5; ἐπιθυμία κακή, Col. iii. 5, (Prov. xxi. 26; [xii. 12]; Plat. legg. 9 p. 854 a.; πονηρά, Xen. mem. 1, 2, 64; ἀγαθή, Sir. xiv. 14 where see Fritzsche, [who cites also Prov. xi. 23; xiii. 12]); plur., Gal. v. 24; 1 Tim. vi. 9; 2 Tim. ii. 22; iv. 3; 1 Pet. i. 14; iv. 2; with a gen. of the object, ἐπιθυμία μιασμοῦ, for unclean intercourse, 2 Pet. ii. 10 [al. with W. § 34, 3 b. take μιασμ. as gen. of quality; with a gen. of the subject, αἱ ἐπιθυμίαι τῶν καρδιῶν, Ro. i. 24; with a gen. of the thing by which the desire is excited, ἡ ἐπιθυμία τοῦ κόσμου, 1 Jn. ii. 17; τοῦ σώματος, Ro. vi. 12; τῆς ἀπάτης (see ἀπάτη), Eph. iv. 22; τῆς σαρκός, τῶν ὀφθαλμῶν, 1 Jn. ii. 16 (cf. Huther ad loc.); 2 Pet. ii. 18; τελεῖν ἐπιθυμίαν σαρκός, Gal. v. 16; αἱ σαρκικαὶ ἐπιθυμίαι, 1 Pet. ii. 11 (ψυχικαί, σωματικαί, 4 Macc. i. 32); αἱ κοσμικαὶ ἐπιθυμίαι, Tit. ii.

12; εἰς ἐπιθυμίας to arouse lusts, Ro. xiii. 14; ποιεῖν τὰς ἐπιθυμίας, Jn. viii. 44; ὑπακούειν ταῖς ἐπιθυμίαις, Ro. vi. 12 [L T Tr WH]; δουλεύειν ἐπιθυμίαις (see δουλεύω, 2 b.), Tit. iii. 3; ἄγεσθαι ἐπιθυμίαις, 2 Tim. iii. 6; πορεύεσθαι ἐν ἐπιθυμίαις, 1 Pet. iv. 3; πορεύεσθαι κατὰ τὰς ἐπιθυμίας, Jude 16, 18; 2 Pet. iii. 3; ἀναστρέφεσθαι ἐν ταῖς ἐπιθυμίαις τῆς σαρκός, Eph. ii. 3. [SYN. cf. πάθος, and see Trench § lxxxvii.] *

1940

ἐπι-καθ-ίζω : 1 aor. ἐπεκάθισα; **1.** *to cause to sit upon, to set upon* : Mt. xxi. 7 Rec.ᵉˡᶻ **2.** intrans. *to sit upon* : Matt. l. c. [Rec.ˢᵗ] G L T Tr WH al.*

see 1941 St.

ἐπι-καλέω, -ῶ : 1 aor. ἐπεκάλεσα; [Pass. and Mid., pres. ἐπικαλοῦμαι]; pf. pass. ἐπικέκλημαι; plpf. 3 pers. sing. ἐπεκέκλητο, and with neglect of augm. [cf. W. § 12, 9; B. 33 (29)] ἐπίκέκλητο (Acts xxvi. 32 Lchm.); 1 aor. pass. ἐπεκλήθην; fut. mid. ἐπικαλέσομαι; 1 aor. mid. ἐπεκαλεσάμην; Sept. very often for קָרָא; **1.** *to put a name upon, to surname* : τινά (Xen., Plato, al.), Mt. x. 25 G T Tr WH (Rec. ἐκάλεσαν); pass. ὁ ἐπικαλούμενος, he who is surnamed, Lk. xxii. 3 R G L; Acts x. 18; xi. 13; xii. 12; xv. 22 R G; also ὃς ἐπικαλεῖται, Acts x. 5, 32; ὁ ἐπικληθείς, Mt. x. 3 [R G]; Acts iv. 36; xii. 25; i. q. ὃς ἐπεκλήθη, Acts i. 23. Pass. with the force of a mid. [cf. W. § 38, 3], *to permit one's self to be surnamed* : Heb. xi. 16; Mid. w. τινά : 1 Pet. i. 17 εἰ πατέρα ἐπικαλεῖσθε τὸν etc. i. e. if ye call (for yourselves) on him as father, i. e. if ye surname him your father. ἐπικαλεῖται τὸ ὄνομά τινος ἐπί τινα, after the Hebr. עַל פּ׳ שֵׁם נִקְרָא, *the name of one is named upon some one*, i. e. *he is called by his name* or *declared to be dedicated to him* (cf. Gesenius, Thesaur. iii. p. 1232ᵃ) : Acts xv. 17 fr. Am. ix. 12 (the name referred to is *the people of God*); Jas. ii. 7 (the name οἱ τοῦ Χριστοῦ). **3.** τινί with the acc. of the object; prop. *to call something to one* [cf. Eng. *to cry out upon* (or *against*) *one*]; *to charge something to one as a crime* or *reproach*; *to summon one on any charge, prosecute one for a crime*; *to blame one for, accuse one of*, (Arstph. pax 663; Thuc. 2, 27; 3, 36; Plat. legg. 6, 761 e.; 7, 809 e.; Dio Cass. 36, 28; 40, 41 and often in the orators [cf. s. v. κατηγορέω]) : εἰ τῷ οἰκοδεσπότῃ Βεελζεβοὺλ ἐπεκάλεσαν (i. e. accused of commerce with Beelzebul, of receiving his help, cf. Mt. ix. 34; xii. 24; Mk. iii. 22; Lk. xi. 15), πόσῳ μᾶλλον τοῖς οἰκιακοῖς αὐτοῦ, Mt. x. 25 L WH mrg. after cod. Vat. (see 1 above), a reading defended by Rettig in the Stud. u. Krit. for 1838, p. 477 sqq. and by Alex. Bttm. in the same journal for 1860, p. 343, and also in his N. T. Gram. 151 (132); [also by Weiss in Mey. ed. 7 ad loc.]. But this expression (Beelzebul for the help of Beelzebul) is too hard not to be suggestive of the emendation of some ignorant scribe, who took offence because (with the exception of this passage) the enemies of Jesus are nowhere in the Gospels said to have called him by the name of Beelzebul. **4.** *to call upon* (like Germ. *anrufen*), *to invoke*; Mid. *to call upon for one's self*, in one's behalf : any one as a helper, Acts vii. 59, where supply τὸν κύριον Ἰησοῦν (βοηθόν), Plat. Euthyd. p. 297 c.; Diod. 5, 79); τινὰ μάρτυρα, as my witness, 2 Co. i. 23 (Plat. legg. 2, 664 c.);

as a judge, i. e. *to appeal to one, make appeal unto*: Καίσαρα, Acts xxv. 11 sq.; xxvi. 32; xxviii. 19; [τὸν Σεβαστόν, Acts xxv. 25]; foll. by the inf. pass. Acts xxv. 21 (to be reserved). **5.** Hebraistically (like בְּשֵׁם יְהֹוָה קָרָא to call upon by pronouncing the name of Jehovah, Gen. iv. 26; xii. 8; 2 K. v. 11, etc.; cf. *Gesenius*, Thesaur. p. 1231ᵇ [or Hebr. Lex. s. v. קָרָא]; an expression finding its explanation in the fact that prayers addressed to God ordinarily began with an invocation of the divine name: Ps. iii. 2; vi. 2; vii. 2, etc.) ἐπικαλοῦμαι τὸ ὄνομα τοῦ κυρίου, *I call upon* (on my behalf) *the name of the Lord*, i. e. *to invoke, adore, worship*, the Lord, i. e. Christ: Acts ii. 21 (fr. Joel ii. 32 (iii. 5)); ix. 14, 21; xxii. 16; Ro. x. 13 sq.; 1 Co. i. 2; τὸν κύριον, Ro. x. 12; 2 Tim. ii. 22; (often in Grk. writ. ἐπικαλεῖσθαι τοὺς θεούς, as Xen. Cyr. 7, 1, 35; Plat. Tim. p. 27 c.; Polyb. 15, 1, 13).*

ἐπι-κάλυμμα, -τος, τό, (ἐπικαλύπτω), *a covering, veil*; prop. in Sept.: Ex. xxvi. 14; xxxvi. 19 Compl. [cf. xxxix. 21 Tdf.]; metaph. i. q. *a pretext, cloak*: τῆς κακίας, 1 Pet. ii. 16 (πλοῦτος δὲ πολλῶν ἐπικάλυμμ᾽ ἐστὶ κακῶν, Menand. ap. Stob. flor. 91, 19 [iii. 191 ed. Gaisf.]; "quaerentes libidinibus suis patrocinium et velamentum," Seneca, vita beata 12).*

see 1942 St.

ἐπι-καλύπτω : [1 aor. ἐπεκαλύφθην]; *to cover over*: αἱ ἁμαρτίαι ἐπικαλύπτονται, are covered over so as not to come to view, i. e. are pardoned, Ro. iv. 7 fr. Ps. xxxi. (xxxii.) 1.*

1943

ἐπι-κατ-άρατος, -ον, (ἐπικαταράομαι to imprecate curses upon), only in bibl. and eccl. use, *accursed, execrable, exposed to divine vengeance, lying under God's curse*: Jn. vii. 49 R G; Gal. iii. 10 (Deut. xxvii. 26); ibid. 13 (Deut. xxi. 23); (Sap. iii. 12 (13); xiv. 8; 4 Macc. ii. 19; in Sept. often for אָרוּר).*

1944

ἐπί-κειμαι; impf. ἐπεκείμην; *to lie upon* or *over, rest upon, be laid* or *placed upon*; **a.** prop.: ἐπί τινι, Jn. xi. 38; sc. on the burning coals, Jn. xxi. 9. **b.** figuratively, **α.** of things: of the pressure of a violent tempest, χειμῶνος ἐπικειμένου, Acts xxvii. 20 (Plut. Timol. 28, 7); ἀνάγκη μοι ἐπίκειται, is laid upon me, 1 Co. ix. 16 (Hom. Il. 6, 458); ἐπικείμενα, of observances imposed on a man by law, Heb. ix. 10 [cf. W. 635 (589)]. **β.** of men; *to press upon, to be urgent*: with dat. of pers. Lk. v. 1; ἐπέκειντο αἰτούμενοι, Lk. xxiii. 23 (πολλῷ μᾶλλον ἐπέκειτο ἀξιῶν, Joseph. antt. 18, 6, 6; μᾶλλον ἐπέκειντο βλάσφημοῦντες, 20, 5, 3).*

1945

ἐπι-κέλλω : [1 aor. ἐπέκειλα]; *to run a ship ashore, to bring to land*; so fr. Hom. Od. 9, 148 down; ἐπέκειλαν (R G ἐπώκειλαν) τὴν ναῦν, Acts xxvii. 41 L T Tr WH; but in opposition see Meyer ad loc. [Cf. B. D. Am. ed. p. 3009.] *

see 2027

[ἐπι-κεφάλαιον, -ου, τό, head-money, poll-tax, (Aristot. oec. 2 p. 1346ᵃ, 4 and 1348ᵃ, 32): Mk. xii. 14 WH (rejected) mrg. for κῆνσον (al.).*]

see 2778

Ἐπικούρειος [-ριος T WH; see I, ι], -ου, ὁ, *Epicurean*, belonging to the sect of Epicurus, the philosopher: Acts xvii. 18.*

1946

ἐπικουρία, -ας, ἡ, (ἐπικυρέω to aid), *aid, succor*: Acts xxvi. 22. (Sap. xiii. 18; fr. Thuc. and Eur. down.) *

1947

1948   ἐπι-κρίνω : 1 aor. ἐπέκρινα; *to adjudge, approve by one's decision, decree, give sentence* : foll. by the acc. with inf., Lk. xxiii. 24. (Plato, Dem., Plut., Hdian., al.) *

see 1949 St.   ἐπι-λαμβάνω ; 2 aor. mid. ἐπελαβόμην ; *to take in addition* [cf. ἐπί, D. 4], *to take, lay hold of, take possession of, overtake, attain to.* In the Bible only in the mid. ; Sept. for אָחַז and הֶחֱזִיק ; **a.** prop. *to lay hold of* or *to seize upon anything with the hands* (Germ. *sich an etwas anhalten*) : τῶν ἀφλάστων νηός, Hdt. 6, 114 ; hence, univ. *to take hold of, lay hold of* : with gen. of pers., Mt. xiv. 31 ; Lk. ix. 47. [Tr WH acc.] ; (xxiii. 26 R G) ; Acts xvii. 19 ; xxi. 30, 33 ; with acc. of pers., Lk. xxiii. 26 L T Tr WH, but in opposition see Meyer ; for where the ptcp. ἐπιλαβόμενος is in this sense joined with an acc., the acc., by the σχῆμα ἀπὸ κοινοῦ, depends also upon the accompanying finite verb (cf. B. § 132, 9 ; [so W. (ed. Lünem.) 202 (190)]) : Acts ix. 27 ; xvi. 19 ; xviii. 17, cf. Lk. xiv. 4. with the gen. of a thing : τῆς χειρός τινος, Mk. viii. 23 ; Acts xxiii. 19 ; of a leader, and thus metaph. of God, Heb. viii. 9 [cf. W. 571 (531) ; B. 316 (271)] ; with gen. of a pers. and of a thing : ἐπιλ. τινος λόγου, ῥήματος, to take any one in his speech, i. e. to lay hold of something said by him which can be turned against him, Lk. xx. 20 [Tr λόγον], 26 [WH Tr mrg. τοῦ for αὐτοῦ] ; ἐπιλ. τῆς αἰωνίου [al. ὄντως] ζωῆς, to seize upon, lay hold of, i. e. to struggle to obtain eternal life, 1 Tim. vi. 12, 19, [cf. W. 312 (293)]. **b.** by a metaph. drawn from laying hold of another to rescue him from peril, *to help, to succor*, (cf. Germ. *sich eines annehmen*) : τινός, Heb. ii. 16 ; in this sense used besides only in Sir. iv. 11 and Schol. ad Aeschyl. Pers. 739. In Appian. bel. civ. 4, 96 the act. is thus used with the dat.: ἡμῖν τὸ δαιμόνιον ἐπιλαμβάνει.*

1950   ἐπι-λανθάνομαι ; pf. pass. ἐπιλέλησμαι ; 2 aor. mid. ἐπελαθόμην ; Sept. often for שָׁכַח ; *to forget* : foll. by the inf., Mt. xvi. 5 ; Mk. viii. 14 ; foll. by an indir. quest. Jas. i. 24 ; in the sense of *neglecting, no longer caring for* : with the gen., Heb. vi. 10 ; xiii. 2, 16 ; with the acc. (cf. W. § 30, 10 c.; Matthiae § 347 Anm. 2, ii. p. 820 sq.), Phil. iii. 13 (14) ; with a pass. signification (Is. xxiii. 16 ; Sir. iii. 14 ; xxxii. (xxxv.) 9 ; Sap. ii. 4, etc. [cf. B. 52 (46)]) : ἐπιλελησμένος *forgotten*, given over to oblivion, i. e. *uncared for*, ἐνώπιον τοῦ θεοῦ before God i. e. by God (Sir. xxiii. 14), Lk. xii. 6. [(From Hom. on.)]*

see 1951 St.   ἐπι-λέγω : [pres. pass. ptcp. ἐπιλεγόμενος] ; 1 aor. mid. ptcp. ἐπιλεξάμενος ; **1.** *to say besides* [cf. ἐπί, D. 4], (Hdt. et al.) ; *to surname* (Plato, legg. 3 p. 700 b.): in pass. Jn. v. 2 [Tdf. τὸ λεγ.], unless the meaning *to name* (put a name upon) be preferred here ; cf. ἐπονομάζω. **2.** *to choose for* (Hdt. et sqq. ; Sept.) ; mid. *to choose for one's self* : Acts xv. 40 (2 S. x. 9 ; Hdt. 3, 157 ; Thuc. 7, 19 ; Diod. 3, 73 (74) ; 14, 12 ; Joseph. antt. 4, 2, 4, and others).*

1952   ἐπι-λείπω : fut. ἐπιλείψω; *to fail, not to suffice for* (any purpose, for the attainment of an end) : τινὰ ὁ χρόνος, time fails one, Heb. xi. 32 and many like exx. in Grk. writ. fr. Dem. down; see *Bleek*, Brief an d. Hebr. ii. 2 p. 818.*

ἐπι-λείχω : impf. ἐπέλειχον; *to lick the surface of, lick over* ([cf. ἐπί, D. 1] ; Germ. *belecken*) : with the acc. of a thing, Lk. xvi. 21 L T Tr WH ; (in Long. past. 1, 24 (11) a var. for ἐπιτρέχω).*   **see 621**

ἐπιλησμονή, -ῆς, ἡ, (ἐπιλήσμων forgetful [W. 93 (89)]), *forgetfulness* : ἀκροατὴς ἐπιλησμονῆς, a forgetful hearer [cf. W. § 34, 3 b.; B. 161 (140)], Jas. i. 25. (Sir. xi. 27 (25).) *   **1953**

ἐπί-λοιπος, -ον, (λοιπός), *remaining besides, left over*, [cf. ἐπί, D. 4] : 1 Pet. iv. 2. (Sept. ; Grk. writ. fr. Hdt. down.) *   **1954**

ἐπί-λυσις, -εως, ἡ, (ἐπιλύω, q. v.), *a loosening, unloosing* (Germ. *Auflösung*) ; metaph. *interpretation* : 2 Pet. i. 20, on which pass. see γίνομαι, 5 e. *a.* (Gen. xl. 8 Aq.; Heliod. 1, 18 ; but not Philo, vita contempl. § 10, where ἐπιδείξεως was long ago restored.) *   **1955**

ἐπι-λύω ; impf. ἐπέλυον ; 1 fut. pass. ἐπιλυθήσομαι ; **a.** properly, *to unloose, untie* (Germ. *auflösen*) anything knotted or bound or sealed up; (Xen., Theocr., Hdian.). **b.** *to clear* (a controversy), *to decide, settle* : Acts xix. 39 ; *to explain* (what is obscure and hard to understand) : Mk. iv. 34 (as in Gen. xli. 12 var. ; Philo, vita contempl. § 10 ; de agricult. § 3 ; Sext. Empir. 2, 246 ; γρίφους, Athen. 10 p. 449 e.; also in mid., Athen. 10 p. 450 f.; Joseph. antt. 8, 6, 5, and often by the Scholiasts).*   **1956**

ἐπι-μαρτυρέω, -ῶ ; *to bear witness to, establish by testimony* : foll. by the acc. with inf., 1 Pet. v. 12. (Plato, Joseph., Plut., Lcian., al.) [Comp. : συν-επιμαρτυρέω.] *   **1957**

ἐπι-μέλεια, -ας, ἡ, (ἐπιμελής) *care, attention* : Acts xxvii. 3. (Prov. iii. 8 ; 1 Macc. xvi. 14 ; 2 Macc. xi. 23 ; very com. in Grk. prose writ., not used in the poets.)*   **1958**

ἐπι-μέλομαι, -οῦμαι, and ἐπιμέλομαι : fut. ἐπιμελήσομαι ; 1 aor. ἐπεμελήθην ; with gen. of the object, *to take care of* a person or thing (ἐπί denoting direction of the mind toward the object cared for [cf. ἐπί, D. 2]) : Lk. x. 34 sq. ; 1 Tim. iii. 5. (Gen. xliv. 21 ; 1 Macc. xi. 37 ; 1 Esdr. vi. 26 ; used by Grk. writ. esp. of prose fr. Hdt. down.) *   **1959**

ἐπιμελῶς, adv., *diligently, carefully* : Lk. xv. 8.*   **1960**

ἐπι-μένω ; [impf. ἐπέμενον] ; fut. ἐπιμενῶ ; 1 aor. ἐπέμεινα ; *to stay at* or *with* ; *to tarry still* ; *still to abide, to continue, remain* ; **a.** prop. of tarrying in a place : ἐν Ἐφέσῳ, 1 Co. xvi. 8 ; ἐν τῇ σαρκί, to live still longer on earth, Phil. i. 24 (G T WH om. ἐν) ; αὐτοῦ, there, Acts xv. 34 [Rec.]; xxi. 4 [Lchm. αὐτοῖς] ; with dat. of thing: τῇ σαρκί, to abide as it were a captive to life on earth, Phil. i. 24 G T WH ; ἐπί τινι, with one, Acts xxviii. 14 [L T Tr WH παρ']; πρός τινα, with one, 1 Co. xvi. 7 ; Gal. i. 18 ; with specification of time how long : Acts x. 48 ; xxi. 4, 10 ; xxviii. 12, 14 ; 1 Co. xvi. 7. **b.** trop. *to persevere, continue* ; with dat. of the thing continued in [cf. *Win*. De verb. comp. etc. Pt. ii. p.10 sq.] : τῇ ἁμαρτίᾳ, Ro. vi. 1 ; τῇ ἀπιστίᾳ, Ro. xi. 23 ; τῇ πίστει, Col. i. 23 ; in the work of teaching, 1 Tim. iv. 16 (τῷ μὴ ἀδικεῖν, Xen. oec. 14, 7 ; τῇ μνηστείᾳ, Ael. v. h. 10, 15) ; with dat. of the blessing for which one keeps himself fit : τῇ χάριτι, Acts xiii. 43 Rec.; τῇ χρηστότητι, Ro. xi. 22 ; with a ptcp. denoting the action persisted in : Jn. viii. 7 Rec.; Acts xii. 16 ; cf. B. 299 sq. (257), [W. § 54, 4].*   **1961**

1962 ἐπι-νεύω: 1 aor. ἐπένευσα; fr. Hom. down; *to nod to*; trop. (by a nod) *to express approval, to assent*: Acts xviii. 20, as often in Grk. writ.*

1963 ἐπίνοια, -ας, ἡ, (ἐπινοέω to think on, devise), *thought, purpose*: Acts viii. 22. (Jer. xx. 10; Sap. vi. 17, etc.; often in Grk. writ. fr. Soph. and Thuc. down.) *

1964 ἐπιορκέω, -ῶ: fut. ἐπιορκήσω, cf. Krüger § 40 s. v., and § 39, 12, 4; [Veitch s. v.; B. 53 (46)]; (ἐπίορκος, q.v.); *to swear falsely, forswear one's self*: Mt. v. 33. (Sap. xiv. 28; 1 Esdr. i. 46; by Grk. writ. fr. Hom. down.) *

1965 ἐπί-ορκος, -ον, (fr. ἐπί [q. v. D. 7] against, and ὅρκος); [masc. as subst.] *a false swearer, a perjurer*: 1 Tim. i. 10. (From Hom. down.) *

1966; see (1896α) ἐπιοῦσα, see ἔπειμι.

1967 ἐπιούσιος, -ον, a word found only in Mt. vi. 11 and Lk. xi. 3, in the phrase ἄρτος ἐπιούσιος ([Pesh.] Syr. ܟ݁ܣܘܩ ܘܣܢܩܢܢ *the bread of our necessity*, i. e. *necessary for us* [but the Curetonian (earlier) Syriac reads ܐܡܝܢܐ *continual*; cf. Bp. Lghtft. as below, I. 3 p. 214 sqq.; *Taylor*, Sayings of the Jewish Fathers, p. 139 sq.]; Itala [Old Lat.] *panis quotidianus*). Origen testifies [de orat. 27] that the word was not in use in ordinary speech, and accordingly seems to have been coined by the Evangelists themselves. Many commentators, as Beza, Kuinoel, Tholuck, Ewald, Bleek, Keim, Cremer, following Origen, Jerome (who in Mt. only translates by the barbarous phrase *panis supersubstantialis*), Theophylact, Euthymius Zigabenus, explain the word by *bread for sustenance, which serves to sustain life*, deriving the word from οὐσία, after the analogy of ἐξούσιος, ἐνούσιος. But οὐσία very rarely, and only in philosophic language, is equiv. to ὕπαρξις, as in Plato, Theaet. p. 185 c. (opp. to τὸ μὴ εἶναι), Aristot. de part. anim. i. 1 (ἡ γὰρ γένεσις ἕνεκα τῆς οὐσίας ἐστίν, ἀλλ᾽ οὐχ ἡ οὐσία ἕνεκα τῆς γενέσεως; for other exx. see Bonitz's Index to Aristot. p. 544), and generally denotes either *essence, real nature*, or *substance, property, resources*. On this account Leo Meyer (in *Kuhn*, Zeitschr. f. vergleich. Sprachkunde, vii. pp. 401–430), Kamphausen (Gebet des Herrn, pp. 86–102), with whom Keim (ii. 278 sq. [Eng. trans. iii. 340]), Weiss (Mt. l. c.), Delitzsch (Zeitschr. f. d. luth. Theol. 1876 p. 402), agree, prefer to derive the word from ἐπεῖναι (and in particular fr. the ptcp. ἐπών, ἐπούσιος for ἐπόντιος, see below) *to be present*, and to understand it bread *which is ready at hand or suffices*, so that Christ is conjectured to have said in Chald. לַחְמָא דְחָקְנָא (cf. לֶחֶם חֻקִּי my allowance of bread, Prov. xxx. 8) or something of the sort. But this opinion, like the preceding, encounters the great objection (to mention no other) that, although the ι in ἐπί is retained before a vowel in certain words (as ἐπίορκος, ἐπιορκέω, ἐπιόσσομαι, etc. [cf. Bp. Lghtft. as below, I. § 1]), yet in ἐπεῖναι and words derived from it, ἐπουσία, ἐπουσιώδης, it is always elided. Therefore much more correctly do Grotius, Scaliger, Wetstein, Fischer (De vitiis lexx. etc. p. 306 sqq.), Valckenaer, Fritzsche (on Mt. p. 267 sqq.), Winer (97 (92)), Bretschneider, Wahl, Meyer, [Bp. Lghtft. (Revision etc., App.)] and others, compar-

ing the words ἑκούσιος, ἐθελούσιος, γερούσιος, (fr. ἑκών, ἐθέλων, γέρων, for ἑκόντιος, ἐθελόντιος, γερόντιος, cf. Kühner i. § 63, 3 and § 334, 1 Anm. 2), conjecture that the adjective ἐπιούσιος is formed from ἐπιών, ἐπιοῦσα, with reference to the familiar expression ἡ ἐπιοῦσα (see ἔπειμι), and ἄρτος ἐπιούσιος is equiv. to ἄρτος τῆς ἐπιούσης ἡμέρας, *food for the morrow*, i. e. *necessary* or *sufficient food*. Thus ἐπιούσιον and σήμερον admirably answer to each other, and that state of mind is portrayed which, piously contented with *food sufficing from one day to the next*, in praying to God for sustenance does not go beyond the absolute necessity of the nearest future. This explanation is also recommended by the fact that in the Gospel according to the Hebrews, as Jerome testifies, the word ἐπιούσιος was represented by the Aramaic מָחַר, "quod dicitur *crastinus*"; hence it would seem that Christ himself used the Chaldaic expression לַחְמָא דִי לִמְחַר. Nor is the prayer, so understood, at variance with the mind of Christ as expressed in Mt. vi. 34, but on the contrary harmonizes with it finely; for his hearers are bidden to ask of God, in order that they may themselves be relieved of anxiety for the morrow. [See Bp. Lghtft., as above, pp. 195–234; *McClellan*, The New Test. etc. pp. 632–647; *Tholuck*, Bergpredigt, Mt. l. c., for earlier reff.] *

1968 ἐπι-πίπτω; 2 aor. ἐπέπεσον, 3 pers. plur. ἐπέπεσαν, Ro. xv. 3 L T Tr WH [cf. ἀπέρχομαι init.]; pf. ptcp. ἐπιπεπτωκώς; [see πίπτω]; Sept. for נָפַל; *to fall upon*; *to rush or press upon*; **a.** prop.: τινί, upon one, Mk. iii. 10; *to lie upon* one, Acts xx. 10; ἐπὶ τὸν τράχηλόν τινος, to fall into one's embrace, Lk. xv. 20; Acts xx. 37, (Gen. xlvi. 29; Tobit xi. 8, 12; 3 Macc. v. 49); *to fall back upon*, ἐπὶ τὸ στῆθός τινος, Jn. xiii. 25 R G T. **b.** metaph. ἐπί τινα, to fall upon one, i. e. *to seize, take possession of* him: φόβος, Lk. i. 12; Acts xix. 17 [L Tr ἔπεσεν]; Rev. xi. 11 L T Tr WH; ἔκστασις, Acts x. 10 Rec.; ἀχλύς, Acts xiii. 11 [R G]. used also of the Holy Spirit, in its inspiration and impulse: ἐπί τινι, Acts viii. 16; ἐπί τινα, x. 44 [Lchm. ἔπεσε]; xi. 15, (Ezek. xi. 5); of reproaches cast upon one: Ro. xv. 3. [Noteworthy is the absol. use in Acts xxiii. 7 WH mrg. ἐπέπεσεν (al. ἐγένετο) στάσις. (From Hdt. down.)] *

1969 ἐπι-πλήσσω; 1 aor. ἐπέπληξα; **a.** prop. *to strike upon, beat upon*: Hom. Il. 10, 500. **b.** trop. *to chastise with words, to chide, upbraid, rebuke*: 1 Tim. v. 1. (Hom. Il. 12, 211; Xen., Plato, Polyb., al.) *

1971 ἐπι-ποθέω, -ῶ; 1 aor. ἐπεπόθησα; prop. πόθον ἔχω ἐπί τι [i. e. ἐπί is directive, not intensive; cf. ἐπί, D. 2] (cf. Fritzsche on Rom. vol. i. p. 30 sq.); *to long for, desire*: foll. by the inf. 2 Co. v. 2; ἰδεῖν τινα, Ro. i. 11; 1 Th. iii. 6; 2 Tim. i. 4; Phil. ii. 26 L br. WH txt. br.; τί, 1 Pet. ii. 2 (ἐπί τι, Ps. xli. (xlii.) 2); τινά, to be possessed with a desire for, long for, [W. § 30, 10 b.], Phil. ii. 26 R G T Tr WH mrg.; *to pursue with love, to long after*: 2 Co. ix. 14; Phil. i. 8, (τὰς ἐντολὰς θεοῦ, Ps. cxviii. (cxix.) 131); absol. *to lust* [i. e. harbor forbidden desire]: Jas. iv. 5, on which pass. see φθόνος. (Hdt., Plat., Diod., Plut., Lcian.) *

For 1970 see 1909 & 4155.

1972 ἐπι-πόθησις, -εως, ή, longing: 2 Co. vii. 7, 11. (Ezek. xxiii. 11 Aq.; Clem. Alex. strom. 4, 21, 131 p. 527 a.) *

1973 ἐπι-πόθητος, -ον, longed for: Phil. iv. 1. ([Clem. Rom. 1 Cor. 65, 1; Barn. ep. 1, 3]; App. Hisp. 43; Eustath.; [cf. W. § 34, 3].) *

1974 ἐπιποθία [WH -πόθεια, see s. v. ει, ι], -ας, ή, longing: Ro. xv. 23; ἅπαξ λεγόμ. [On the passage cf. B. 294 (252).] *

1975 ἐπι-πορεύομαι; to go or journey to: πρός τινα, Lk. viii. 4; (foll. by ἐπί with the acc. Ep. Jer. 61 (62); Polyb. 4, 9, 2; freq. used by Polyb. with the simple acc. of place: both to go to, traverse regions, cities (so τὴν γῆν, Ezek. xxxix. 14 for עָבַר; τὰς δυνάμεις, 3 Macc. i. 4), and also to make a hostile inroad, overrun, march over). *

1976 ἐπι-ρράπτω (T Tr WH ἐπιράπτω, see P, ρ); (ράπτω to sew); to sew upon, sew to: ἐπί τινι [R G; al. τινα], Mk. ii. 21. *

1977 ἐπι-ρρίπτω (L T Tr WH ἐπιρίπτω, see P, ρ): 1 aor. ἐπέρριψα; (ρίπτω); to throw upon, place upon: τὶ ἐπί τι, Lk. xix. 35; (Vulg. projicere, to throw away, throw off): τὴν μέριμναν ἐπὶ θεόν, i. e. to cast upon, give up to, God, 1 Pet. v. 7, fr. Ps. liv. (lv.) 23. [Occasionally fr. Hom. Od. 5, 310 down.] *

1978 ἐπίσημος, -ον, (σῆμα a sign, mark); **1.** prop. having a mark on it, marked, stamped, coined: ἀργύριον, χρυσός, (Hdt., Thuc., Xen., Polyb., Joseph.). **2.** trop. marked (Lat. insignis), both in a good and bad sense; in a good sense, of note, illustrious: Ro. xvi. 7 (Hdt. et sqq.); in a bad sense, notorious, infamous: Mt. xxvii. 16 (Eur. Or. 249; Joseph. antt. 5, 7, 1; Plut. Fab. Max. 14; al.). *

1979 ἐπισιτισμός, -οῦ, ὁ, (ἐπισιτίζομαι to provision one's self); **1.** a foraging, providing food, (Xen., Plut., al.). **2.** supplies, provisions, food [A. V. victuals]: Lk. ix. 12 (Sept., Xen., Dem., Hdian., al.). *

1980 ἐπι-σκέπτομαι; fut. 3 pers. sing. ἐπισκέψεται, Lk. i. 78 Tr mrg. WH; 1 aor. ἐπεσκεψάμην; fr. Hdt. down; Sept. often for פָּקַד; to look upon or after, to inspect, examine with the eyes; **a.** τινά, in order to see how he is, i. e. to visit, go to see one: Acts vii. 23; xv. 36, (Judg. xv. 1); the poor and afflicted, Jas. i. 27; the sick, Mt. xxv. 36, 43, (Sir. vii. 35; Xen. mem. 3, 11, 10; Plut. mor. p. 129 c. [de sanitate praecept. 15 init.]; Lcian. philops. 6, and in med. writ.). **b.** Hebraistically, to look upon in order to help or to benefit, i. q. to look after, have a care for, provide for, of God: τινά, Lk. vii. 16; Heb. ii. 6, (Gen. xxi. 1; Ex. iv. 31; Ps. viii. 5; lxxix. (lxxx.) 15; Sir. xlvi. 14; Jud. viii. 33, etc.); foll. by a telic inf. Acts xv. 14; absol. (Sir. xxxii. (xxxv.) 21) yet with a statement of the effect and definite blessing added, Lk. i. 68; ἐπεσκέψατο [WH Tr mrg. ἐπισκέψεται] ἡμᾶς ἀνατολὴ ἐξ ὕψους (al. light from on high hath looked [al. shall look] upon us (cf. our the sun looks down on us, etc.), i. e. salvation from God has come to us, Lk. i. 78. (In the O. T. used also in a bad sense of God as punishing, Ps. lxxxviii. (lxxxix.) 33; Jer. ix. 25; xi. 22, etc.) **c.** to look (about) for, look out (one to choose, employ, etc.): Acts vi. 3. *

see 643 ἐπι-σκευάζω: to furnish with things necessary; Mid. to furnish one's self or for one's self: ἐπισκευασάμενοι, hav-

ing gathered and made ready the things necessary for the journey, Acts xxi. 15 L T Tr WH, for R G ἀποσκευ-ασάμενοι (which see in its place). *

1981 ἐπι-σκηνόω, -ῶ: 1 aor. ἐπεσκήνωσα; to fix a tent or habitation on: ἐπὶ τὰς οἰκίας, to take possession of and live in the houses (of the citizens), Polyb. 4, 18, 8; ταῖς οἰκίαις, 4, 72, 1; trop. ἐπί τινα, of the power of Christ descending upon one, working within him and giving him help, [A. V. rest upon], 2 Co. xii. 9. *

1982 ἐπι-σκιάζω; [impf. ἐπεσκίαζον, Lk. ix. 34 L mrg. T Tr txt. WH]; fut. ἐπισκιάσω; 1 aor. ἐπεσκίασα; to throw a shadow upon, to envelop in shadow, to overshadow: τινί, Acts v. 15. From a vaporous cloud that casts a shadow the word is transferred to a shining cloud surrounding and enveloping persons with brightness: τινά, Mt. xvii. 5; Lk. ix. 34; τινί, Mk. ix. 7. Tropically, of the Holy Spirit exerting creative energy upon the womb of the virgin Mary and impregnating it, (a use of the word which seems to have been drawn from the familiar O. T. idea of a cloud as symbolizing the immediate presence and power of God): with the dat. Lk. i. 35. (In prof. auth. generally w. an acc. of the object and in the sense of obscuring: Hdt. 1, 209; Soph., Aristot., Theophr., Philo, Lcian., Hdian., Geop. Sept. for סָכַך to cover, Ps. xc. (xci.) 4; cxxxix. (cxl.) 8; for שָׁכַן, Ex. xl. 29 (35) ἐπεσκίαζεν ἐπὶ τὴν σκηνὴν ἡ νεφέλη; [cf. W. § 52, 4, 7].) *

1983 ἐπι-σκοπέω, -ῶ; to look upon, inspect, oversee, look after, care for: spoken of the care of the church which rested upon the presbyters, 1 Pet. v. 2 [T WH om.] (with τὴν ἐκκλησίαν added, Ignat. ad Rom. 9, 1); foll. by μή [q. v. II. 1 a.] i. q. Lat. caveo, to look carefully, beware: Heb. xii. 15. (Often by Grk. writ. fr. Aeschyl. down.) *

1984 ἐπι-σκοπή, -ῆς, ή, (ἐπισκοπέω), inspection, visitation, (Germ. Besichtigung); **a.** prop.: εἰς ἐπισκ. τοῦ παιδός to visit the boy, Lcian. dial. deor. 20, 6; with this exception no example of the word in prof. writ. has yet been noted. **b.** In biblical Grk., after the Hebr. פְּקֻדָּה, that act by which God looks into and searches out the ways, deeds, character, of men, in order to adjudge them their lot accordingly, whether joyous or sad; inspection, investigation, visitation, (Vulg. usually visitatio): so univ. ἐν ἐπισκοπῇ ψυχῶν, when he shall search the souls of men, i. e. in the time of divine judgment, Sap. iii. 13; also ἐν ὥρᾳ ἐπισκοπῆς, Sir. xviii. 20 (19); so perhaps ἐν ἡμέρᾳ ἐπισκοπῆς, 1 Pet. ii. 12 [see below]; in a good sense, of God's gracious care: τὸν καιρὸν τῆς ἐπισκοπῆς σου, i. e. τὸν καιρὸν ἐν ᾧ ἐπεσκέψατό σε ὁ θεός, in which God showed himself gracious toward thee and offered thee salvation through Christ [see ἐπισκέπτομαι, b.), Lk. xix. 44; ἐν καιρῷ ἐπισκοπῆς, in the time of divine reward, 1 Pet. v. 6 Lchm.; also, in the opinion of many commentators, 1 Pet. ii. 12 [al. associate this pass. with Lk. xix. 44 above; cf. De Wette (ed. Brückner) or Huther ad loc.]; fr. the O. T. cf. Gen. l. 24 sq.; Job xxxiv. 9; Sap. ii. 20; iii. 7, etc. with a bad reference, of divine punishment: Ex. iii. 16; Is. x. 3; Jer. x. 15; Sap. xiv. 11; xix. 14 (15); [etc.; cf. Soph. Lex. s. v.].

c. after the analogy of the Hebr. פְּקֻדָּה (Num. iv. 16; 1 Chr. xxiv. 19 [here Sept. ἐπίσκεψις], etc.), *oversight* i. e. *overseership, office, charge*; Vulg. *episcopatus*: Acts i. 20, fr. Ps. cviii. (cix.) 8; spec. the office of a bishop (the overseer or presiding officer of a Christian church): 1 Tim. iii. 1, and in eccl. writ.*

1985   **ἐπί-σκοπος, -ου, ὁ,** (ἐπισκέπτομαι), *an overseer*, a man charged with the duty of seeing that things to be done by others are done rightly, *any curator, guardian*, or *superintendent*; Sept. for פָּקִיד, Judg. ix. 28; Neh. xi. 9, 14, 22; 2 K. xi. 15, etc.; 1 Macc. i. 51. The word has the same comprehensive sense in Grk. writ. fr. Homer Odys. 8, 163; Il. 22, 255 down; hence in the N. T. ἐπίσκ. τῶν ψυχῶν *guardian of souls*, one who watches over their welfare: 1 Pet. ii. 25 ([τὸν παντὸς πνεύματος κτίστην κ. ἐπίσκοπον, Clem. Rom. 1 Cor. 59, 3]; ἀρχιερεὺς καὶ προστάτης τῶν ψυχῶν ἡμῶν Ἰησοῦς Χρ. ibid. 61, 3; [cf. Sir. i. 6]), cf. Heb. xiii. 17. spec. *the superintendent, head* or *overseer of any Christian church*; Vulg. *episcopus*: Acts xx. 28; Phil. i. 1; 1 Tim. iii. 2; Tit. i. 7; see πρεσβύτερος, 2 b.; [and for the later use of the word, see Dict. of Chris. Antiq. s. v. Bishop].*

see 1986 St.   **ἐπι-σπάω, -ῶ:** fr. Aeschyl. down; *to draw on*: μὴ ἐπισπάσθω, sc. ἀκροβυστίαν, let him not draw on his foreskin (Hesych. μὴ ἐπισπάσθω· μὴ ἑλκυέτω τὸ δέρμα) [A. V. *let him not become uncircumcised*], 1 Co. vii. 18. From the days of Antiochus Epiphanes [B. C. 175–164] down (1 Macc. i. 15; Joseph. antt. 12, 5, 1), there had been Jews who, in order to conceal from heathen persecutors or scoffers the external sign of their nationality, sought artificially to compel nature to reproduce the prepuce, by extending or drawing forward with an iron instrument the remnant of it still left, so as to cover the *glans*. The Rabbins called such persons מְשׁוּכִים, from מָשַׁךְ *to draw out*, see Buxtorf, Lex. Talm. p. 1274 [(ed. Fischer ii. 645 sq.). Cf. BB.DD. s. v. Circumcision, esp. McC. and S. ibid. II. 2.]*

see 4687   **ἐπι-σπείρω:** 1 aor. ἐπέσπειρα; *to sow above* or *besides*: Mt. xiii. 25 L T Tr WH. (Hdt., Theophr., [al.].)*

1987   **ἐπίσταμαι** (seems to be the Ionic form of the Mid. of ἐφίστημι. Isocrates, Aristot., al., also use ἐπιστῆσαι τὴν διάνοιαν, τὸν νοῦν, ἑαυτόν for *to put one's attention on, fix one's thoughts on*; indeed, the simple ἐπιστῆσαι is used in the same sense, by an ellipsis analogous to that of τὸν νοῦν with the verbs προσέχειν, ἐπέχειν, and of τὴν ὄψιν with προσβάλλειν; see Lobeck ad Phryn. p. 281 sq. Hence ἐπίσταμαι is prop. *to turn one's self* or *one's mind to, put one's thought upon* a thing); fr. Hom. down; Sept. chiefly for יָדַע; (cf. Germ. *sich worauf verstehen*); **a.** *to be acquainted with*: τί, Acts xviii. 25; Jas. iv. 14; Jude 10; τινά, Acts xix. 15; with reference to what is said or is to be interpreted, *to understand*: Mk. xiv. 68; 1 Tim. vi. 4. **b.** *to know*: περί τινος, Acts xxvi. 26; foll. by an acc. with a ptcp. Acts xxiv. 10 [W. 346 (324); B. 301 (258)]; foll. by ὅτι, Acts xv. 7; xix. 25; xxii. 19; foll. by ὡς, Acts x. 28; by πῶς, Acts xx. 18; by ποῦ, Heb. xi. 8. [SYN. see γινώσκω.]*

see 1999   **ἐπί-στασις, -εως, ἡ,** (ἐφίστημι, ἐφίσταμαι), *an advanc-*

ing, approach; *incursion, onset, press*: τῆς κακίας (Vulg. *malorum incursio*), 2 Macc. vi. 3, where cf. Grimm; used of the pressure of a multitude asking help, counsel, etc., τινί (on which dat. cf. W. § 31, 3; [B. 180 (156)]; Kühner § 424, 1) to one, 2 Co. xi. 28 L T Tr WH (but others would have us translate it here by *oversight, attention, care*, a com. meaning of the word in Polyb.); used of a tumultuous gathering in Acts xxiv. 12 L T Tr WH. Cf. B. u. s.*

1988   **ἐπι-στάτης, -ου, ὁ,** (ἐφίστημι), *any sort of a superintendent* or *overseer* (often so in prof. writ., and several times in Sept., as Ex. i. 11; v. 14; 1 K. v. 16; 2 K. xxv. 19; Jer. xxxvi. (xxix.) 26; 2 Chr. ii. 2; xxxi. 12); *a master*, used in this sense for רַבִּי by the disciples [cf. Lk. xvii. 13] when addressing Jesus, who called him thus "not from the fact that he was a teacher, but because of his authority" (Bretschneider); found only in Luke: v. 5; viii. 24, 45; ix. 33, 49; xvii. 13.*

1989   **ἐπι-στέλλω;** 1 aor. ἐπέστειλα; prop. *to send to* one a message, command, (Hdt. et sqq.); ἐπιστολάς, to send by letter, write a letter, Plato, epp. p. 363 b., hence simply *to write a letter* [cf. W. § 3, 1 b.]: τινί, Heb. xiii. 22 (Clem. Rom. 1 Cor. 7, 1; 47, 3; 62, 1; and often in Grk. writ.); *to enjoin by letter, to write instructions*: Acts xxi. 25 R G T Tr mrg. WH mrg.; foll. by τοῦ with an inf. expressing purpose [cf. W. 326 (306); B. 270 (232)]: Acts xv. 20.*

1990   **ἐπι-στήμων, -ον,** gen. -ονος, (ἐπίσταμαι), *intelligent, experienced*, [esp. one having the knowledge of an expert; cf. Schmidt ch. 13 §§ 10, 13]: Jas. iii. 13. (From Hom. down; Sept.)*

1991   **ἐπι-στηρίζω;** 1 aor. ἐπεστήριξα; a later word; *to establish besides, strengthen more*; *to render more firm, confirm*: τινά, one's Christian faith, Acts xiv. 22; xv. 32, 41; xviii. 23 R G.*

1992   **ἐπι-στολή, -ῆς, ἡ,** (ἐπιστέλλω), *a letter, epistle*: Acts xv. 30; Ro. xvi. 22; 1 Co. v. 9, etc.; plur., Acts ix. 2; 2 Co. x. 10, etc.; ἐπιστολαὶ συστατικαί, letters of commendation, 2 Co. iii. 1 [W. 176 (165). On the possible use of the plur. of this word interchangeably with the sing. (cf. Thom. Mag. ed. Ritschl p. 113, 8), see Bp. Lghtft. and Meyer on Phil. iii. 1. (Eur., Thuc., al.)].*

1993   **ἐπι-στομίζω;** (στόμα); prop. *to bridle* or *stop up the mouth*; metaph. *to stop the mouth, reduce to silence*: Tit. i. 11. (Plato, Gorg. p. 482 e.; Dem. 85, 4; often in Plut. and Lcian.)*

1994   **ἐπι-στρέφω;** fut. ἐπιστρέψω; 1 aor. ἐπέστρεψα; 2 aor. pass. ἐπεστράφην; fr. Hom. down; Sept. for סָבַב, הָפַךְ, and פָּנָה, הֵקַב, and times without number for שׁוּב and הֵשִׁיב. **1.** transitively, **a.** *to turn to*: ἐπὶ τὸν θεόν, to the worship of the true God, Acts xxvi. 20. **b.** *to cause to return, to bring back*; fig. τινὰ ἐπὶ κύριον τὸν θεόν, to the love and obedience of God, Lk. i. 16; ἐπὶ τέκνα, to love for the children, Lk. i. 17; ἐν φρονήσει δικαίων, that they may be in [R. V. to walk in] the wisdom of the righteous, Lk. i. 17; τινὰ ἐπί τινα, supply from the context ἐπὶ τὴν ἀλήθειαν and ἐπὶ τὴν ὁδόν, Jas. v. 19 sq. **2.** intrans. (W. § 38, 1 [cf. p. 26; B. 144 (126 sq.)]); **a.** *to turn*, to turn one's self : ἐπὶ τὸν κύριον and ἐπὶ τὸν θεόν, of Gentiles passing over to the religion of Christ, Acts ix. 35 ; xi. 21 ; xiv. 15 ; xv. 19 ; xxvi. 20, cf. 1 Pet. ii. 25 ; πρός τι, Acts ix. 40 ; πρὸς τὸν θεόν, 1 Th. i. 9 ; 2 Co. iii. 16 ; ἀπό τινος εἴς τι, Acts xxvi. 18.   b. to turn one's self about, turn back : absol. Acts xvi. 18 ; foll. by an inf. expressing purpose, Rev. i. 12.   c. to return, turn back, come back ;   a. properly : Lk. ii. 20 Rec. ; viii. 55 ; Acts xv. 36 ; with the addition of ὀπίσω (as in Ael. v. h. 1, 6 [var.]), foll. by an inf. of purpose, Mt. xxiv. 18 ; foll. by εἰς with acc. of place, Mt. xii. 44 ; [Lk. ii. 39 T WH Tr mrg.] ; εἰς τὰ ὀπίσω, Mk. xiii. 16 ; Lk. xvii. 31 ; ἐπί τι, to, 2 Pet. ii. 22.   β. metaph. : ἐπί τι, Gal. iv. 9 ; ἐπί τινα, Lk. xvii. 4 Rec., but G om. ἐπί σε ; πρός τινα, ibid. L T Tr WH ; ἐκ τῆς ἐντολῆς, to leave the commandment and turn back to a worse mental and moral condition, 2 Pet. ii. 21 R G ; absol. to turn back morally, to reform : Mt. xiii. 15 ; Mk. iv. 12 ; Lk. xxii. 32 ; Acts iii. 19 ; xxviii. 27. In the mid. and 2 aor. pass.   a. to turn one's self about, to turn around : absol., Mt. ix. 22 R G ; Mk. v. 30 ; viii. 33 ; Jn. xxi. 20.   b. to return : foll. by πρός [WH txt. ἐπί] τινα, Mt. x. 13 (on which pass. see εἰρήνη, 3 fin.) ; ἐπὶ τὸν θεόν, 1 Pet. ii. 25 (see 2 a. above) ; to return to a better mind, repent, Jn. xii. 40 [R G].*

1995   ἐπι-στροφή, -ῆς, ἡ, (ἐπιστρέφω), conversion (of Gentiles fr. idolatry to the true God [cf. W. 26]) : Acts xv. 3. (Cf. Sir. xlix. 2 ; xviii. 21 (20) ; in Grk. writ. in many other senses.) *

1996   ἐπι-συν-άγω ; fut. ἐπισυνάξω ; 1 aor. inf. ἐπισυνάξαι ; 2 aor. inf. ἐπισυναγαγεῖν ; Pass., pf. ptcp. ἐπισυνηγμένος ; 1 aor. ptcp. ἐπισυναχθείς ; [fut. ἐπισυναχθήσομαι, Lk. xvii. 37 T Tr WH] ; Sept. several times for אָסַף, קָבַץ, קָהֵל ; 1. to gather together besides, to bring together to others already assembled, (Polyb.).   2. to gather together against (Mic. iv. 11 ; Zech. xii. 3 ; 1 Macc. iii. 58, etc.). 3. to gather together in one place (ἐπί to) : Mt. xxiii. 37 ; xxiv. 31 ; Mk. xiii. 27 ; Lk. xiii. 34 ; Pass. : Mk. i. 33 ; Lk. xii. 1 ; xvii. 37 T Tr WH, (Ps. ci. (cii.) 23 ; cv. (cvi.) 47 ; 2 Macc. i. 27, etc. ; Aesop 142).*

1997   ἐπι-συν-αγωγή, -ῆς, ἡ, (ἐπισυνάγω, q. v.) ; a. a gathering together in one place, i. q. τὸ ἐπισυνάγεσθαι (2 Macc. ii. 7) : ἐπί τινα, to one, 2 Th. ii. 1.   b. (the religious) assembly (of Christians) : Heb. x. 25. *

1998   ἐπι-συν-τρέχω ; to run together besides (i. e. to others already gathered) : Mk. ix. 25. Not used by prof. writ.*

1999   ἐπι-σύστασις, -εως, ἡ, (ἐπισυνίσταμαι to collect together, conspire against) a gathering together or combining against or at. Hence   1. a hostile banding together or concourse : ποιεῖν ἐπισύστασιν, to excite a riotous gathering of the people, make a mob, Acts xxiv. 12 R G ; 1 Esdr. v. 70 Alex. ; Sext. Empir. adv. eth. p. 127 [p. 571, 20 ed. Bekk. ; cf. Philo in Flac. § 1] ; τινός, against one, Num. xxvi. 9 ; a conspiracy, Joseph. c. Ap. 1, 20.   2. a troublesome throng of persons seeking help, counsel, comfort : τινός, thronging to one, 2 Co. xi. 28 R G (see ἐπίστασις) ; Luther, dass ich werde angelaufen.*

2000   ἐπισφαλής, -ές, (σφάλλω to cause to fall), prone to fall :

πλοῦς, a dangerous voyage, Acts xxvii. 9.   (Plato, Polyb., Plut., al.) *

2001   ἐπι-ισχύω : [impf. ἐπίσχυον] ;   1. trans. to give additional strength ; to make stronger, (Sir. xxix. 1 ; Xen. oec. 11, 13).   2. intrans. to receive greater strength, grow stronger, (1 Macc. vi. 6 ; Theophr., Diod.) : ἐπίσχυον λέγοντες, they were the more urgent saying, i. e. they alleged the more vehemently, Lk. xxiii. 5.*

2002   ἐπι-σωρεύω : fut. ἐπισωρεύσω ; to heap up, accumulate in piles : διδασκάλους, to choose for themselves and run after a great number of teachers, 2 Tim. iv. 3.   (Plut., Athen., Artemid., al.) *

2003   ἐπι-ταγή, -ῆς, ἡ, (ἐπιτάσσω), an injunction, mandate, command : Ro. xvi. 26 ; 1 Co. vii. 25 ; 1 Tim. i. 1 ; Tit. i. 3 ; μετὰ πάσης ἐπιταγῆς, with every possible form of authority, Tit. ii. 15 ; κατ' ἐπιταγήν, by way of command, 1 Co. vii. 6 ; 2 Co. viii. 8.   (Sap. xiv. 16, etc. ; Polyb., Diod.) *

2004   ἐπι-τάσσω ; 1 aor. ἐπέταξα ; (τάσσω) ; to enjoin upon, order, command, charge : absol. Lk. xiv. 22 ; τινί, Mk. i. 27 ; ix. 25 ; Lk. iv. 36 ; viii. 25 ; τινὶ τὸ ἀνῆκον, Philem. 8 ; τινί foll. by the inf., Mk. vi. 39 ; Lk. viii. 31 ; Acts xxiii. 2 ; foll. by acc. and inf. Mk. vi. 27 ; foll. by direct discourse, Mk. ix. 25.   (Several times in Sept. ; Grk. writ. fr. Hdt. down.)   [Syn. see κελεύω, fin.] *

2005   ἐπι-τελέω, -ῶ ; fut. ἐπιτελέσω ; 1 aor. ἐπετέλεσα ; [pres. mid. and pass. ἐπιτελοῦμαι] ;   1. to bring to an end, accomplish, perfect, execute, complete : substantively, τὸ ἐπιτελέσαι, 2 Co. viii. 11 ; τί, Lk. xiii. 32 [R G] ; Ro. xv. 28 ; 2 Co. vii. 1 ; viii. 6, 11 ; Phil. i. 6 ; Heb. viii. 5 ; τὰς λατρείας, to perform religious services, discharge religious rites, Heb. ix. 6 (similarly in prof. writ., as θρησκείας, Hdt. 2, 37 ; ὁρτάς, 4, 186 ; θυσίαν, θυσίας, 2, 63 ; 4, 26 ; Hdian. 1. 5, 4 [2 ed. Bekk.] ; λειτουργίας, Philo de som. i. § 37). Mid. (in Grk. writ. to take upon one's self : τὰ τοῦ γήρως, the burdens of old age, Xen. mem. 4, 8, 8 ; θάνατον, Xen. apol. 33 ; with the force of the act. : τί, Polyb. 1, 40, 16 ; 2, 58, 10) to make an end for one's self, i. e. to leave off (cf. παύω) : τῇ σαρκί, so as to give yourselves up to the flesh, stop with, rest in it, Gal. iii. 3 [others take it passively here : are ye perfected in etc., cf. Meyer].   2. to appoint to, impose upon : τινὶ παθήματα, in pass. 1 Pet. v. 9 (τὴν δίκην, Plat. legg. 10 fin.).*

2006   ἐπιτήδειος, -εία, -ειον, also -ος, -ον, [cf. W. § 11, 1], (ἐπιτηδές, adv., enough ; and this acc. to Buttmann fr. ἐπὶ τάδε [? cf. Vaniček p. 271]) ;   1. fit, suitable, convenient, advantageous.   2. needful ; plur. τὰ ἐπιτήδεια esp. the necessaries of life (Thuc. et sqq.) : with addition of τοῦ σώματος, Jas. ii. 16.*

2007   ἐπι-τίθημι, 3 pers. plur. ἐπιτιθέασι (Mt. xxiii. 4 ; cf. W. § 14, 1 b. ; B. 44 (38) ; Bttm. Ausf. Spr. i. p. 505 ; Kühner i. p. 643 ; [Jelf § 274 ; and on this and foll. forms see Veitch s. vv. τίθημι, τιθέω]), impv. ἐπιτίθει (1 Tim. v. 22 ; see Matthiae § 210, 2 and 6 ; Bttm. Ausf. Spr. i. p. 508 ; Kühner § 209, 5 ; [Jelf § 274 obs. 4]) ; impf. 3 pers. plur. ἐπετίθουν (Acts viii. 17 R G), ἐπετίθεσαν (ib. L T Tr WH ; cf. Bttm. Ausf. Spr. i. p. 509 ; B. 45 (39)) ; fut. ἐπιθήσω ; 1 aor. ἐπέθηκα ; 2 aor. ἐπέθην, impv. ἐπίθες (Mt. ix. 18 ; Gen. xlviii. 18 ; Judg. xviii. 19) ; Mid., [pres. ἐπιτίθεμαι]; fut. ἐπιθήσομαι; 2 aor. ἐπεθέμην; [1 aor. pass. ἐπετέθην (Mk. iv. 21 R G)]; in Sept. chiefly for נָתַן, שׂוּם and שִׂים; 1. Active: a. *to put* or *lay upon*: τὶ ἐπί τι, Mt. xxiii. 4; xxvii. 29 R G L; Mk. iv. 21 R G; Lk. xv. 5; Jn. ix. [6 WH txt. Tr mrg.], 15; [xix. 2 L mrg., see below]; Acts xv. 10 [cf. W. 318 (298); B. 261 (224)]; xxviii. 3; τὶ ἐπί τινος, gen. of thing, Mt. xxvii. 29 T Tr WH; ἐν with dat. of thing, Mt. xxvii. 29 L T Tr WH; τὴν χεῖρα [or τὰς χεῖρας or χεῖρας] ἐπί τινα, Mt. ix. 18; Mk. viii. 25 [(WH Tr txt. ἔθηκεν)]; xvi. 18; Acts viii. 17; [ix. 17]; Rev. i. 17 Rec.; ἐπί τινα πληγάς, calamities, Rev. xxii. 18 [but see b. below]; ἐπάνω τινός, Mt. xxi. 7 R G; xxvii. 37; ἐπί τινος, Lk. viii. 16 R G; τί τινι, Lk. xxiii. 26; Jn. xix. 2 [not L mrg., see above]; Acts xv. 28; τινὶ ὄνομα, Mk. iii. 16 sq.; τινὶ τὰς χεῖρας, Mt. xix. 13 [cf. B. 233 (201); W. 288 (270 sq.)], 15; Mk. v. 23; [viii. 23, here Tr mrg. αὐτοῦ]; Lk. iv. 40; xiii. 13; Acts vi. 6; viii. 19; xiii. 3; xix. 6; xxviii. 8; 1 Tim. v. 22; [τινὶ τὴν χεῖρα, Mk. vii. 32]; χεῖρα [R G, χεῖρας or τὰς χεῖρας L T Tr WH], Acts ix. 12; τινὶ πληγάς, to inflict blows, lay stripes on one, Lk. x. 30; Acts xvi. 23. b. *to add to*: Rev. xxii. 18 (opp. to ἀφαιρεῖν vs. 19). 2. Middle: a. *to have put on, bid to be laid on*; τὶ ἐπί τι (Xen. Cyr. 8, 2, 4): τὰ πρὸς τὴν χρείαν, sc. τινί, to provide one with the things needed [al. *put on board* sc. the ship], Acts xxviii. 10. b. *to lay* or *throw one's self upon*; with dat. of pers. *to attack one, to make an assault on one*: Acts xviii. 10; Ex. xxi. 14; xviii. 11; 2 Chr. xxiii. 13, and often in prof. writ.; cf. Kuinoel ad loc.; [W. 593 (552). Comp.: συν-επιτίθημι.]*

2008 ἐπι-τιμάω, -ῶ; impf. 3 pers. sing. ἐπετίμα, 3 pers. plur. ἐπετίμων; 1 aor. ἐπετίμησα; Sept. for גָּעַר; in Grk. writ. 1. *to show honor to, to honor*: τινά, Hdt. 6, 39. 2. *to raise the price of*: ὁ σῖτος ἐπετιμήθη, Dem. 918, 22; al. 3. *to adjudge, award*, (fr. τιμή in the sense of merited penalty): τὴν δίκην, Hdt. 4, 43. 4. *to tax with fault, rate, chide, rebuke, reprove, censure severely*, (so Thuc., Xen., Plato, Dem., al.): absol. 2 Tim. iv. 2; τινί, charge one with wrong, Lk. [ix. 55]; xvii. 3; xxiii. 40; to rebuke — in order to curb one's ferocity or violence (hence many formerly gave the word the meaning *to restrain*; against whom cf. Fritzsche on Matt. p. 325), Mt. viii. 26; xvi. 18; Mk. iv. 39; Lk. iv. 39, 41; viii. 24; ix. 42; Jude 9 [where Rec.elz strangely ἐπιτιμῆσαι (1 aor. act. inf.) for -μῆσαι (opt. 3 pers. sing.)]; or to keep one away from another, Mt. xix. 13; Lk. xviii. 15; Mk. x. 13; foll. by ἵνα (with a verb expressing the opposite of what is censured): Mt. xx. 31; Mk. x. 48; Lk. xviii. 39; with the addition of λέγων [καὶ λέγει, or the like] and direct discourse: Mk. i. 25 [T om. WH br. λέγων]; viii. 33; ix. 25; Lk. iv. 35; xxiii. 40, (cf. Ps. cv. (cvi.) 9; cxviii. (cxix.) 21; Zech. iii. 2; and the use of גָּעַר in Nah. i. 4; Mal. iii. 11). Elsewhere in a milder sense, *to admonish* or *charge sharply*: τινί, Mt. xvi. 22; Mk. viii. 30; Lk. ix. 21 (ἐπιτιμήσας αὐτοῖς παρήγγειλεν, foll. by the inf.), xix. 39; with ἵνα added, Mt. xvi. 20 L WH txt.; Mk. viii. 30; ἵνα μή, Mt. xii. 16; Mk. iii. 12. [Cf. Trench § iv; Schmidt ch. 4, 11.]*

ἐπιτιμία, -ας, ἡ, (ἐπιτιμάω), *punishment* (in Grk. writ. τὸ ἐπιτίμιον): 2 Co. ii. 6 [B. § 147, 29]. (Sap. iii. 10; [al.].) * **2009**

[ἐπι-το-αυτό, Rec.st in Acts i. 15; ii. 1, etc.; see αὐτός, **see 846** III. 1, and cf. *Lipsius*, Gramm. Unters. p. 125 sq.]

[ἐπι-τρέπω; 1 aor..ἐπέτρεψα; Pass., [pres. ἐπιτρέπομαι]; **2010** 2 aor. ἐπετράπην; pf. 3 pers. sing. ἐπιτέτραπται (1 Co. xiv. 34 R G); fr. Hom. down; 1. *to turn to, transfer, commit, intrust*. 2. *to permit, allow, give leave*: 1 Co. xvi. 7; Heb. vi. 3; τινί, Mk. v. 13; Jn. xix. 38; with an inf. added, Mt. viii. 21; xix. 8; Lk. viii. 32; ix. 59, 61; Acts xxi. 39 sq.; 1 Tim. ii. 12; and without the dat. Mk. x. 4; foll. by acc. with inf. Acts xxvii. 3 (where L T Tr WH πορευθέντι); cf. Xen. an. 7, 7, 8; Plato, legg. 5 p. 730 d. Pass. ἐπιτρέπεταί τινι, with inf.: Acts xxvi. 1; xxviii. 16; 1 Co. xiv. 34.*

[ἐπιτροπεύω; (fr. Hdt. down); *to be ἐπίτροπος* or *proc-* **see 2012** *urator*: of Pontius Pilate in Lk. iii. 1 WH (rejected) mrg.; see their App. ad loc.*]

ἐπι-τροπή, -ῆς, ἡ, (ἐπιτρέπω), *permission, power, commis-* **2011** *sion*: Acts xxvi. 12. (From Thuc. down.) *

ἐπίτροπος, -ου, ὁ, (ἐπιτρέπω), univ. *one to whose care* or **2012** *honor anything has been intrusted; a curator, guardian*, (Pind. Ol. 1, 171, et al.; Philo de mundo § 7 ὁ θεὸς καὶ πατὴρ καὶ τεχνίτης καὶ ἐπίτροπος τῶν ἐν οὐρανῷ τε καὶ ἐν κόσμῳ). Spec. 1. *a steward* or *manager of a household*, or *of lands*; *an overseer*: Mt. xx. 8; Lk. viii. 3; Xen. oec. 12, 2; 21, 9; (Aristot. oec. 1, 5 [p. 1344ª, 26] δούλων δὲ εἴδη δύο, ἐπίτροπος καὶ ἐργάτης). 2. *one who has the care and tutelage of children*, either where the father is dead (*a guardian of minors*: 2 Macc. xi. 1; xiii. 2; ἐπίτροπος ὀρφάνων, Plato, legg. 6 p. 766 c.; Plut. Lyc. 3; Cam. 15), or where the father still lives (Ael. v. h. 3, 26): Gal. iv. 2.*

ἐπι-τυγχάνω: 2 aor. ἐπέτυχον; 1. *to light* or *hit* **2013** *upon any person* or *thing* (Arstph., Thuc., Xen., Plato). 2. *to attain to, obtain*: Jas. iv. 2; with gen. of thing, Heb. vi. 15; xi. 33; with acc. of thing; τοῦτο, Ro. xi. 7 (where Rec. τούτου). Cf. Matthiae § 328; [W. 200 (188)].*

ἐπι-φαίνω; 1 aor. inf. ἐπιφᾶναι (cf. *Lob.* ad Phryn. p. **2014** 24 sqq.; W. 89 (85); B. 41 (35); [Sept. Ps. xxx. (xxxi.) 17; cxvii. (cxviii.) 27, cf. lxvi. (lxvii.) 2]); 2 aor. pass. ἐπεφάνην; fr. Hom. down; 1. trans. *to show to* or *upon*; *to bring to light*. 2. intrans. and in Pass. *to appear, become visible*; a. prop.: of stars, Acts xxvii. 20 (Theocr. 2, 11); τινί, to one, Lk. i. 79. b. fig. i. q. *to become clearly known, to show one's self*: Tit. iii. 4; τινί, Tit. ii. 11.*

ἐπιφάνεια, -ας, ἡ, (ἐπιφανής), *an appearing, appearance*, **2015** (Tertull. *apparentia*); often used by the Greeks of a glorious manifestation of the gods, and esp. of their advent to help; in 2 Macc. of signal deeds and events betokening the presence and power of God as helper; cf. Grimm on Macc. p. 60 sq. 75, [but esp. the thorough exposition by Prof. Abbot (on Titus ii. 13 Note B) in the Journ. Soc. Bibl. Lit. and Exegesis, i. p. 16 sq. (1882)]. In the N. T. the 'advent' of Christ, — not only that which has already taken place and by which his presence and power appear in the saving light he has shed upon mankind, 2 Tim. i. 10 (note the word φωτίσαντος in this pass.); but also that illustrious return from heaven to earth hereafter to occur: 1 Tim. vi. 14; 2 Tim. iv. 1, 8; Tit. ii. 13 [on which see esp. Prof. Abbot u. s.]; ἡ ἐπιφάνεια (i. e. the breaking forth) τῆς παρουσίας αὐτοῦ, 2 Th. ii. 8. [Cf. Trench § xciv.]*

2016 ἐπιφανής, -ές, (ἐπιφαίνω), conspicuous, manifest, illustrious: Acts ii. 20 [Tdf. om.] fr. Joel ii. 31 (iii. 4); the Sept. here and in Judg. xiii. 6 [Alex.]; Hab. i. 7; Mal. i. 14 thus render the word נוֹרָא terrible, deriving it incorrectly from רָאָה and so confounding it with נִרְאָה.*

see 2017 St. ἐπι-φαύσκω (i. q. the ἐπιφώσκω of Grk. writ., cf. W. 90 (85); B. 67 (59)): fut. ἐπιφαύσω; to shine upon: τινί, Eph. v. 14, where the meaning is, Christ will pour upon thee the light of divine truth as the sun gives light to men aroused from sleep. (Job xxv. 5; xxxi. 26; [xli. 9]; Acta Thomae § 34.)*

2018 ἐπι-φέρω; [impf. ἐπέφερον]; 2 aor. inf. ἐπενεγκεῖν; [pres. pass. ἐπιφέρομαι]; **1.** to bring upon, bring forward: of accusers (as in Hdt. 1, 26, and in Attic writ. fr. Thuc. down: Polyb. 5, 41, 3; 40, 5, 2; Joseph. antt. 2, 6, 7; 4, 8, 23; Hdian. 3, 8, 13 (6 ed. Bekk.)), Acts xxv. 18 (where L T Tr WH ἔφερον); κρίσιν, Jude 9. **2.** to lay upon, to inflict: τὴν ὀργήν, Ro. iii. 5 (πληγήν, Joseph. antt. 2, 14, 2). **3.** to bring upon i. e. in addition, to add, increase: θλῖψιν τοῖς δεσμοῖς, Phil. i. 16 (17) Rec., but on this pass. see ἐγείρω, 4 c.; (πῦρ ἐπιφέρειν πυρί, Philo, leg. ad Gaium § 18; [cf. W. § 52, 4, 7]). **4.** to put upon, cast upon, impose, (φάρμακον, Plat. ep. 8 p. 354 b.): τὶ ἐπί τινα, in pass., Acts xix. 12, where L T Tr WH ἀποφέρεσθαι, q. v.*

2019 ἐπι-φωνέω, -ῶ: [impf. ἐπεφώνουν]; to call out to, shout: foll. by direct disc., Lk. xxiii. 21; Acts xii. 22; foll. by the dat. of a pers., Acts xxii. 24; τί, Acts xxi. 34 L T Tr WH. [(Soph. on.)]*

2020 ἐπι-φώσκω; [impf. ἐπέφωσκον]; to grow light, to dawn [cf. B. 68 (60)]: Lk. xxiii. 54; foll. by εἰς, Mt. xxviii. 1, on which see εἰς, A. II. 1.*

2021 ἐπιχειρέω, -ῶ: impf. ἐπεχείρουν; 1 aor. ἐπεχείρησα, (χείρ); **1.** prop. to put the hand to (Hom. Od. 24, 386, 395). **2.** often fr. Hdt. down, to take in hand, undertake, attempt, (anything to be done), foll. by the inf.: Lk. i. 1; Acts ix. 29; xix. 13; (2 Macc. ii. 29; vii. 19). Grimm treats of this word more at length in the Jahrbb. f. deutsche Theol. for 1871, p. 36 sq.*

2022 ἐπι-χέω: fr. Hom. down; to pour upon: τί, Lk. x. 34 (sc. ἐπὶ τὰ τραύματα; Gen. xxviii. 18; Lev. v. 11).*

2023 ἐπι-χορηγέω, -ῶ; 1 aor. impv. ἐπιχορηγήσατε; Pass., [pres. ἐπιχορηγοῦμαι]; 1 fut. ἐπιχορηγηθήσομαι; (see χορηγέω); to supply, furnish, present, (Germ. darreichen): τινί τι, 2 Co. ix. 10; Gal. iii. 5; i. q. to show or afford by deeds: τὴν ἀρετήν, 2 Pet. i. 5; in pass., εἴσοδος, furnished, provided, 2 Pet. i. 11; Pass. to be supplied, ministered unto, assisted, (so the simple χορηγεῖσθαι in Xen. rep. Athen. 1, 13; Polyb. 3, 75, 3; 4, 77, 2; 9, 44, 1; Sir. xliv. 6; 3 Macc. vi. 40): Col. ii. 19, where Vulg. subministratum. (Rare in prof. writ. as Dion. Hal. 1,

42; Phal. ep. 50; Diog. Laërt. 5, 67; [Alex. Aphr. probl. 1, 81].)*

ἐπι-χορηγία, -ας, ἡ, (ἐπιχορηγέω, q. v.), (Vulg. subministratio), a supplying, supply: Eph. iv. 16; Phil. i. 19. (Eccl. writers.)* **2024**

ἐπι-χρίω: 1 aor. ἐπέχρισα; to spread on, anoint: τὶ ἐπί τι, anything upon anything, Jn. ix. 6 [WH txt. Tr mrg. ἐπέθηκεν]; τί, to anoint anything (sc. with anything), ibid. 11. (Hom. Od. 21, 179; Lcian. hist. scrib. 62.)* **2025**

ἐπ-οικοδομέω, -ῶ; 1 aor. ἐπῳκοδόμησα, and without augm. ἐπωκοδόμησα (1 Co. iii. 14 T Tr WH; cf. Tdf.'s note on Acts vii. 47, [see οἰκοδομέω]); Pass., pres. ἐποικοδομοῦμαι; 1 aor. ptcp. ἐποικοδομηθέντες; in the N. T. only in the fig. which likens a company of Christian believers to an edifice or temple; to build upon, build up, (Vulg. superaedifico); absol. [like our Eng. build up] viz. 'to finish the structure of which the foundation has already been laid,' i. e. in plain language, to give constant increase in Christian knowledge and in a life conformed thereto: Acts xx. 32 (where L T Tr WH οἰκοδ. [Vulg. aedifico]); 1 Co. iii. 10; (1 Pet. ii. 5 Tdf.); ἐπὶ τὸν θεμέλιον, 1 Co. iii. 12; τί, ibid. 14; ἐν Χριστῷ, with the pass., in fellowship with Christ to grow in spiritual life, Col. ii. 7; ἐποικοδομηθ. ἐπὶ θεμελίῳ τῶν ἀποστόλων, on the foundation laid by the apostles, i. e. (dropping the fig.) gathered together into a church by the apostles' preaching of the gospel, Eph. ii. 20; ἐποικοδομεῖν ἑαυτὸν τῇ πίστει, Jude 20, where the sense is, 'resting on your most holy faith as a foundation, make progress, rise like an edifice higher and higher.' (Thuc., Xen., Plato, al.)* **2026**

ἐπ-οκέλλω: 1 aor. ἐπώκειλα; to drive upon, strike against: τὴν ναῦν [i. e. to run the ship ashore], Acts xxvii. 41 R G; see ἐπικέλλω. (Hdt. 6, 16; 7, 182; Thuc. 4, 26.)* **2027**

ἐπ-ονομάζω: [pres. pass. ἐπονομάζομαι]; fr. Hdt. down; Sept. for קָרָא; to put a name upon, name; Pass. to be named: Ro. ii. 17; cf. Fritzsche ad loc.* **2028**

ἐπ-οπτεύω [ptcp. 1 Pet. ii. 12 L T Tr WH]; 1 aor. ptcp. ἐποπτεύσαντες; **1.** to be an overseer (Homer, Hesiod). **2.** univ. to look upon, view attentively; to watch (Aeschyl., Dem., al.): τί, 1 Pet. iii. 2; ἔκ τινος, sc. τὴν ἀναστροφήν, 1 Pet. ii. 12.* **2029**

ἐπόπτης, -ου, ὁ, (fr. unused ἐπόπτω) **1.** an overseer, inspector, see ἐπίσκοπος; (Aeschyl., Pind., al.; of God, in 2 Macc. iii. 39; vii. 35; 3 Macc. ii. 21; Add. to Esth. v.; ἀνθρωπίνων ἔργων, Clem. Rom. 1 Cor. 59, 3). **2.** a spectator, eye-witness of anything: so in 2 Pet. i. 16; inasmuch as those were called ἐπόπται by the Grks. who had attained to the third [i. e. the highest] grade of the Eleusinian mysteries (Plut. Alcib. 22, and elsewh.), the word seems to be used here to designate those privileged to be present at the heavenly spectacle of the transfiguration of Christ.* **2030**

ἔπος, -εος (-ους), τό, a word: ὡς ἔπος εἰπεῖν (see εἶπον, 1 a. p. 181*), Heb. vii. 9.* **2031**

[SYN. ἔπος seems primarily to designate a word as an articulate manifestation of a mental state, and so to differ from ῥῆμα (q. v.), the mere vocable; for its relation to λόγος see λόγος I. 1.]

2032   **ἐπ-ουράνιος, -ον,** (οὐρανός), prop. existing *in* or *above heaven, heavenly*; **1.** *existing in heaven*: ὁ πατὴρ ἐπουράνιος, i. e. God, Mt. xviii. 35 Rec. (θεοί, θεός, Hom. Od. 17, 484; Il. 6, 131, etc.; 3 Macc. vi. 28; vii. 6); οἱ ἐπουράνιοι the heavenly beings, the inhabitants of heaven, (Lcian. dial. deor. 4, 3; of the gods, in Theocr. 25, 5): of angels, in opp. to ἐπίγειοι and καταχθόνιοι, Phil. ii. 10; Ignat. ad Trall. 9, [cf. Polyc. ad Philipp. 2]; σώματα, the bodies of the stars (which the apostle, acc. to the universal ancient conception, seems to have regarded as animate [cf. Bp. Lghtft. on Col. p. 376; Gfrörer, Philo etc. 2te Aufl. p. 349 sq.; Siegfried, Philo von Alex. p. 306; yet cf. Mey. ed. Heinrici ad loc.], cf. Job xxxviii. 7; Enoch xviii. 14 sqq.) and of the angels, 1 Co. xv. 40; ἡ βασιλεία ἡ ἐπουρ. (on which see p. 97), 2 Tim. iv. 18; substantially the same as ἡ πατρὶς ἡ ἐπουρ. Heb. xi. 16 and Ἱερουσαλὴμ ἐπουρ. xii. 22; κλῆσις, a calling made (by God) in heaven, Heb. iii. 1 [al. would include a ref. to its end as well as to its origin; cf. Lünem. ad loc.], cf. Phil. iii. 14 [Bp. Lghtft. cites Philo, plant. Noë § 6]. The neut. τὰ ἐπουράνια denotes [cf. W. § 34, 2] **a.** *the things that take place in heaven*, i. e. the purposes of God to grant salvation to men through the death of Christ: Jn. iii. 12 (see ἐπίγειος). **b.** *the heavenly regions*, i. e. heaven itself, the abode of God and angels: Eph. i. 3, 20 (where Lchm. txt. οὐρανοῖς); ii. 6; iii. 10; the lower heavens, or the heaven of the clouds, Eph. vi. 12 [cf. B. D. Am. ed. s. v. Air]. **c.** *the heavenly temple* or *sanctuary*: Heb. viii. 5; ix. 23. **2.** *of heavenly origin and nature*: 1 Co. xv. 48 sq. (opp. to χοϊκός); ἡ δωρεὰ ἡ ἐπουρ. Heb. vi. 4.*

2033   **ἑπτά, οἱ, αἱ, τά,** *seven*: Mt. xii. 45; xv. 34; Mk. viii. 5 sq.; Lk. ii. 36; Acts vi. 3, etc.; often in the Apocalypse; οἱ ἑπτά, sc. διάκονοι, Acts xxi. 8. In Mt. xviii. 22 it is joined (instead of ἑπτάκις) to the numeral adv. ἑβδομηκοντάκις, in imitation of the Hebr. שֶׁבַע, Ps. cxviii. (cxix.) 164; Prov. xxiv. 16; [see ἑβδομηκοντάκις, and cf. Keil, Com. on Mt. l. c.].

2034   **ἑπτάκις,** (ἑπτά), *seven times*: Mt. xviii. 21 sq.; Lk. xvii. 4. [(Pind., Arstph., al.)]*

2035   **ἑπτακις-χίλιοι, -αι, -α,** *seven thousand*: Ro. xi. 4. [(Hdt.)]*
ἔπω, see εἶπον.

2036; **see** **(1512α)**   **Ἔραστος, -ου, ὁ,** *Erastus*, (ἐραστός beloved, [cf. Chandler § 325; Lipsius, Gram. Untersuch. p. 30]), the name of two Christians: **1.** the companion of the apostle Paul, Acts xix. 22; **2.** the city treasurer of Corinth, Ro. xvi. 23. Which of the two is meant in 2 Tim. iv. 20 cannot be determined.*

see 2045   **ἐραυνάω,** a later and esp. Alexandrian [cf. Sturz, Dial. Maced. et Alex. p. 117] form for ἐρευνάω, q. v. Cf. Tdf. ed. 7 min. Proleg. p. xxxvii.; [ed. maj. p. xxxiv.; esp. ed. 8 Proleg. p. 81 sq.]; B. 58 (50).

2038   **ἐργάζομαι;** depon. mid.; impf. εἰργαζόμην (ἠργαζόμην), Acts xviii. 3 L T Tr WH; [so elsewh. at times; this var. in augm. is found in the aor. also]; cf. W. § 12, 8; B. 33 (29 sq.); Steph. Thesaur. iii. 1970 c.; [Curtius, Das Verbum, i. 124; Cramer, Anecd. 4, 412; Veitch s. v.]); 1 aor. εἰργασάμην (ἠργασ. Mt. xxv. 16; [xxvi. 10]; Mk.

xiv. 6, in T WH, [add, 2 Jn. 8 WH and Hebr. xi. 33 T Tr WH; cf. reff. as above]); pf. εἴργασμαι, in a pass. sense [cf. W. § 38, 7 e.], Jn. iii. 21, as often in Grk. writ. [cf. Veitch s. v.]; (ἔργον); Sept. for פָּעַל, עָבַד, sometimes for עָשָׂה; **1.** absol. **a.** *to work, labor, do work*: it is opp. to inactivity or idleness, Lk. xiii. 14; Jn. v. 17; ix. 4; 2 Th. iii. 10; with addition of ταῖς χερσί, 1 Co. iv. 12; 1 Th. iv. 11; with acc. of time: νύκτα καὶ ἡμέραν, 2 Th. iii. 8 [but Ltxt. T Tr WH the gen., as in 1 Th. ii. 9 (see ἡμέρα, 1 a.); cf. W. § 30, 11 and Ellic. on 1 Tim. v. 5]; with the predominant idea of working for pay, Mt. xxi. 28 (ἐν τῷ ἀμπελῶνι); Acts xviii. 3; 1 Co. ix. 6; 2 Th. iii. 12; acc. to the conception characteristic of Paul, ὁ ἐργαζόμενος he that does works conformed to the law (Germ. *der Werkthätige*): Ro. iv. 4 sq. **b.** *to trade, to make gains by trading*, (cf. our "do business"): ἔν τινι, with a thing, Mt. xxv. 16 (often so by Dem.). **2.** trans. **a.** (*to work* i. e.) *to do, work out*: τί, Col. iii. 23; 2 Jn. 8 (with which [acc. to reading of L T Tr txt.] cf. 1 Co. xv. 58 end); μηδέν, 2 Th. iii. 11; ἔργον, Acts xiii. 41 (פָּעַל פֹּעַל, Hab. i. 5); ἔργον καλὸν εἴς τινα, Mt. xxvi. 10; ἔν τινι (dat. of pers. [cf. W. 218 (205)]), Mk. xiv. 6 [Rec. εἰς ἐμέ]; ἔργα, wrought, pass., Jn. iii. 21; τὰ ἔργα τοῦ θεοῦ, what God wishes to be done, Jn. vi. 28; ix. 4; τοῦ κυρίου, to give one's strength to the work which the Lord wishes to have done, 1 Co. xvi. 10; τὸ ἀγαθόν, [Ro. ii. 10]; Eph. iv. 28; πρός τινα, Gal. vi. 10; κακόν τινί τι, Ro. xiii. 10 (τινά τι is more com. in Grk. writ. [Kühner § 411, 5]); τί εἴς τινα, 3 Jn. 5. with acc. of virtues or vices, (*to work* i. e.) *to exercise, perform, commit*: δικαιοσύνην, Acts x. 35; Heb. xi. 33, (Ps. xiv. (xv.) 2; Zeph. ii. 3); τὴν ἀνομίαν, Mt. vii. 23 (Ps. v. 6 and often in Sept.); ἁμαρτίαν, Jas. ii. 9. σημεῖον, bring to pass, effect, Jn. vi. 30; τὰ ἱερά, to be busied with the holy things i. e. to administer those things that pertain to worship, which was the business of priests and among the Jews of the Levites also, 1 Co. ix. 13; τὴν θάλασσαν lit. work the sea (*mare exerceo*, Justin. hist. 43, 3) i. e. to be employed on [cf. "do business on," Ps. cvii. 23] and make one's living from it, Rev. xviii. 17 (so of sailors and fishermen also in native Grk. writ., as Aristot. probl. 38, 2 [p. 966ᵇ, 26]; Dion. Hal. antt. 3, 46; App. Punic. 2; [Lcian. de elect. 5; W. 223 (209)]). *to cause to exist, produce*: τί, so (for R G κατεργάζεται) 2 Co. vii. 10 L T Tr WH; Jas. i. 20 L Tr WH. **b.** *to work for, earn by working, to acquire*, (cf. Germ. *erarbeiten*): τὴν βρῶσιν, Jn. vi. 27 (χρήματα, Hdt. 1, 24; τὰ ἐπιτήδεια, Xen. mem. 2, 8, 2; Dem. 1358, 12; ἀργύριον, Plato, Hipp. maj. p. 282 d.; βίον, Andoc. myst. [18, 42] 144 Bekk.; θησαυρούς, Theodot. Prov. xxi. 6; βρῶμα, Palaeph. 21, 2; al.); acc. to many interpreters also 2 Jn. 8; but see 2 a. above. [Comp.: κατ-, περι-, προσ-εργάζομαι.]

2039   **ἐργασία, -ας, ἡ,** (ἐργάζομαι); **1.** i. q. τὸ ἐργάζεσθαι, *a working, performing*: ἀκαθαρσίας, Eph. iv. 19. **2.** *work, business*: Acts xix. 25 (Xen. oec. 6, 8 et al.). **3.** *gain got by work, profit*: Acts xvi. 19; παρέχειν ἐργασίαν τινί, ib. 16; xix. 24 [yet al. refer this to 2 above];

(Xen. mem. 3, 10, 1; cyneg. 3, 3; Polyb. 4, 50, 3).　**4.** *endeavor, pains*, [A. V. *diligence*]: δίδωμι ἐργασίαν, after the Latinism *operam do*, Lk. xii. 58 (Hermog. de invent. 3, 5, 7).*

2040 **ἐργάτης, -ου, ὁ,** (ἐργάζομαι); **1.** as in Grk. writ. *a workman, a laborer*: usually one who works for hire, Mt. x. 10; Lk. x. 7; 1 Tim. v. 18; esp. an agricultural laborer, Mt. ix. 37 sq.; xx. 1 sq. 8; Lk. x. 2; Jas. v. 4, (Sap. xvii. 16); those whose labor artificers employ [i. e. *workmen* in the restricted sense], Acts xix. 25 (opp. to τοῖς τεχνί-ταις [A. V. *craftsmen*], ib. 24), cf. Bengel ad loc.; those who as teachers labor to propagate and promote Christianity among men: 2 Co. xi. 13; Phil. iii. 2; 2 Tim. ii. 15, cf. Mt. ix. 37 sq.; Lk. x. 2. **2.** *one who does, a worker, perpetrator*: τῆς ἀδικίας, Lk. xiii. 27 (τῆς ἀνομίας, 1 Macc. iii. 6; τῶν καλῶν καὶ σεμνῶν, Xen. mem. 2, 1, 27).*

2041 **ἔργον, -ου, τό,** anciently Ϝέργον, (Germ. *Werk*, [Eng. *work*; cf. Vaníček p. 922]); Sept. for עָבַד פָּעַל and countless times for מְלָאכָה and מַעֲשֶׂה; *work* i. e. **1.** *business, employment, that with which any one is occupied*: Mk. xiii. 34 (διδόναι τινὶ τὸ ἔργον αὐτοῦ); Acts xiv. 26 (πληροῦν); 1 Tim. iii. 1; thus of the work of salvation committed by God to Christ: διδόναι and τελειοῦν, Jn. xvii. 4; of the work to be done by the apostles and other Christian teachers, as well as by the presiding officers of the religious assemblies, Acts xiii. 2; xv. 38; 1 Th. v. 13; Phil. i. 22; τὸ ἔργον τινός, gen. of the subj., the work which one does, service which one either performs or ought to perform, 1 Th. v. 13; ἔργον ποιεῖν τινος to do the work of one (i. e. incumbent upon him), εὐαγγελι-στοῦ, 2 Tim. iv. 5; τὸ ἔργον τινός i. e. assigned by one and to be done for his sake: τὸ ἔργον τοῦ θεοῦ τελειοῦν, used of Christ, Jn. iv. 34; (τοῦ) Χριστοῦ (WH txt. Tr mrg. κυρίου), Phil. ii. 30; τοῦ κυρίου, 1 Co. xv. 58; xvi. 10; with gen. of thing, εἰς ἔργον διακονίας, Eph. iv. 12, which means either to the work in which the ministry consists, the work performed in undertaking the ministry, or to the execution of the ministry. of that which one undertakes to do, *enterprise, undertaking*: Acts v. 38 (Deut. xv. 10; Sap. ii. 12). **2.** *any product whatever, any thing accomplished by hand, art, industry, mind*, (i. q. ποίημα, κτίσμα): 1 Co. iii. 13–15; with the addition of τῶν χειρῶν, things formed by the hand of man, Acts vii. 41; of the works of God visible in the created world, Heb. i. 10, and often in Sept.; τὰ ἐν τῇ γῇ ἔργα, the works of nature and of art (Bengel), 2 Pet. iii. 10; of the arrangements of God for men's salvation: Acts xv. 18 Rec.; τὸ ἔργ. τοῦ θεοῦ what God works in man, i. e. a life dedicated to God and Christ, Ro. xiv. 20; to the same effect, substantially, ἔργον ἀγαθόν, Phil. i. 6 (see ἀγαθός, 2); τὰ ἔργα τοῦ διαβόλου, sins and all the misery that springs from them, 1 Jn. iii. 8. **3.** *an act, deed, thing done*: the idea of working is emphasized in opp. to that which is less than work, Jas. i. 25; Tit. i. 16; τὸ ἔργον is distinguished fr. ὁ λόγος: Lk. xxiv. 19; Ro. xv. 18; 2 Co. x. 11; Col. iii. 17; 2 Th. ii. 17; 1 Jn. iii. 18, (Sir. iii. 8); plur. ἐν λόγοις καὶ ἐν ἔργοις, Acts vii. 22 (4 Macc. v. 38 (37); for the same or similar contrasts, com. in Grk.

writ., see Fritzsche on Rom. iii. p. 268 sq.; Bergler on Alciphr. p. 54; Bornemann and Kühner on Xen. mem. 2, 3, 6; Passow s. v. p. 1159; [L. and S. s. v. I. 4; *Lob.* Paralip. pp. 64 sq., 525 sq.]). ἔργα is used of the acts of God — both as creator, Heb. iv. 10; and as governor, Jn. ix. 3; Acts xiii. 41; Rev. xv. 3; of sundry signal acts of Christ, to rouse men to believe in him and to accomplish their salvation: Mt. xi. 2 [cf. ἔργα τῆς σοφίας ib. 19 T WH Tr txt.], and esp. in the Gosp. of John, as v. 20, 36; vii. 3; x. 38; xiv. 11 sq.; xv. 24, (cf. *Grimm*, Instit. theol. dogmat. p. 63, ed. 2); they are called τὰ ἔργα τοῦ πατρός, i. e. done at the bidding and by the aid of the Father, Jn. x. 37; iii. 3 sq., cf. x. 25, 32; xiv. 10; καλά, as beneficent, Jn. x. 32 sq.; and connected with the verbs δεικνύναι, ποιεῖν, ἐργάζεσθαι, τελειοῦν. ἔργα is applied to the conduct of men, measured by the standard of religion and righteousness, — whether bad, Mt. xxiii. 3; Lk. xi. 48; Jn. iii. 20; Rev. ii. 6; xvi. 11, etc.; or good, Jn. iii. 21; Jas. ii. 14, 17 sq. 20–22, 24–26; iii. 13; Rev. ii. 5, 9 [Rec.], 19; iii. 8; νόμος ἔργων, the law which demands good works, Ro. iii. 27; with a suggestion of toil, or struggle with hindrances, in the phrase καταπαύειν ἀπὸ τῶν ἔργων αὐτοῦ, Heb. iv. 10; to recompense one κατὰ τὰ ἔργα αὐτοῦ, Ro. ii. 6; 2 Tim. iv. 14; Rev. ii. 23 (Ps. lxi. (lxii.) 13), cf. 2 Co. xi. 15; Rev. xviii. 6; xx. 12 sq.; the sing. τὸ ἔργον is taken collectively of an aggregate of actions (Germ. *das Handeln*), Jas. i. 4; τινός, gen. of pers. and subj., his whole way of feeling and acting, his aims and endeavors: Gal. vi. 4; 1 Pet. i. 17; Rev. xxii. 12; τὸ ἔργον τοῦ νόμου, the course of action demanded by the law, Ro. ii. 15. With epithets: ἀγαθὸν ἔργον, i. e. either *a benefaction*, 2 Co. ix. 8; plur. Acts ix. 36; or *every good work* springing from piety, Ro. ii. 7; Col. i. 10; 2 Th. ii. 17; Tit. i. 16; 2 Tim. ii. 21; iii. 17; Heb. xiii. 21 [T WH om. ἔργ.]; plur. Eph. ii. 10; or *what harmonizes with the order of society*, Ro. xiii. 3; Tit. iii. 1; ἔργον καλόν, *a good deed, noble action*, (see καλός, b. and c.): Mt. xxvi. 10; Mk. xiv. 6; plur. (often in Attic writ.), Mt. v. 16; 1 Tim. v. 10, 25; vi. 18; Tit. ii. 7; iii. 8, 14; Heb. x. 24; 1 Pet. ii. 12; τὰ ἔργα τὰ ἐν δικαιοσύνῃ equiv. to τὰ δίκαια, Tit. iii. 5; τὰ ἔργα τοῦ θεοῦ, the works required and approved by God, Jn. vi. 28 (Jer. xxxi. (xlviii.) 10; 1 Esdr. vii. 9, 15), in the same sense ἔργα μου i. e. of Christ, Rev. ii. 26; ἔργον πίστεως, wrought by faith, the course of conduct which springs from faith, 1 Th. i. 3; 2 Th. i. 11; ἔργα ἄξια τῆς μετανοίας, Acts xxvi. 20; ἔργα πεπληρωμένα ἐνώπιον τοῦ θεοῦ, Rev. iii. 2; ἔργα πονηρά, Col. i. 21; 2 Jn. 11, cf. Jn. iii. 19; vii. 7; 1 Jn. iii. 12; ἔργα νεκρά, works devoid of that life which has its source in God, works so to speak *unwrought*, which at the last judgment will fail of the approval of God and of all reward: Heb. vi. 1; ix. 14; ἄκαρπα, Eph. v. 11 (ἄχρηστα, Sap. iii. 11; the wicked man μετὰ τῶν ἔργων αὐτοῦ συναπολεῖται, Barn. ep. 21, 1); ἄνομα, 2 Pet. ii. 8; ἔργα ἀσεβείας, Jude 15; τοῦ σκότους, done in darkness, Ro. xiii. 12; Eph. v. 11; [opp. to ἔργ. τοῦ φωτός, Ro. xiii. 12 L mrg.]; in Paul's writ. ἔργα νόμου, works demanded by and agreeing with the law (cf. *Wieseler,*

Com. üb. d. Br. an d. Gal. p. 194 sqq.): Ro. iii. 20, 28; ix. 32 Rec.; Gal. ii. 16; iii. 2, 5, 10; and simply ἔργα: Ro. iv. 2, 6; ix. 12 (11); ib. 32 G L T Tr WH; xi. 6; Eph. ii. 9; 2 Tim. i. 9, (see δικαιόω, 3 b.). τὰ ἔργα τινὸς ποιεῖν, to do works the same as or like to those of another, to follow in action another's example: Abraham's, Jn. viii. 39; that of the devil, Jn. viii. 41.

2042 ἐρεθίζω; 1 aor. ἠρέθισα; (ἐρέθω to excite); to stir up, excite, stimulate: τινά, in a good sense, 2 Co. ix. 2; as com. in Grk. writ. fr. Hom. down, in a bad sense, to provoke: Col. iii. 21, where Lchm. παροργίζετε.*

2043 ἐρείδω: to fix, prop firmly; intrans., 1 aor. ptcp. ἐρείσασα (ἡ πρῷρα), stuck [R. V. struck], Acts xxvii. 41. (From Hom. down.) *

2044 ἐρεύγομαι: fut. ἐρεύξομαι; **1.** to spit or spue out, (Hom.). **2.** to be emptied, discharge itself, used of streams (App. Mithr. c. 103); with the acc. to empty, discharge, cast forth, of rivers and waters: Lev. xi. 10 Sept. **3.** by a usage foreign to classic Greek [W. 23 (22 sq.)], to pour forth words, to speak out, utter: Mt. xiii. 35 (Ps. lxxvii. (lxxviii.) 2; cf. xviii. (xix.) 3; cxliv. 7 [Alex.]). The word is more fully treated of by Lobeck ad Phryn. p. 63; [cf. Rutherford, New Phryn. p. 138].*

2045 ἐρευνάω, -ῶ; 1 aor. impv. ἐρεύνησον; (ἡ ἔρευνα a search); fr. Hom. down; to search, examine into: absol. Jn. vii. 52; τί, Jn. v. 39; Ro. viii. 27; 1 Co. ii. 10; Rev. ii. 23 with which passage cf. Jer. xi. 20; xvii. 10; xx. 12; foll. by an indir. quest. 1 Pet. i. 11 (2 S. x. 3; Prov. xx. 27). The form ἐραυνάω (q. v. in its place) T Tr WH have received everywhere into the text, but Lchm. only in Rev. ii. 23. [COMP.: ἐξ- ερευνάω.] *

2047 ἐρημία, -ας, ἡ, (ἔρημος), a solitude, an uninhabited region, a waste: Mt. xv. 33; Mk. viii. 4; Heb. xi. 38; opp. to πόλις, 2 Co. xi. 26, as in Joseph. antt. 2, 3, 1.*

2048 ἔρημος, -ον, (in classic Grk. also -ος, -η, -ον, cf. W. § 11, 1; [B. 25 (23); on its accent cf. Chandler §§ 393, 394; W. 52 (51)]); **1.** adj. solitary, lonely, desolate, uninhabited: of places, Mt. xiv. 13, 15; Mk. i. 35; vi. 32; Lk. iv. 42; ix. 10 [R G L], 12; Acts i. 20, etc.; ἡ ὁδός, leading through a desert, Acts viii. 26 (2 S. ii. 24 Sept.), see Γάζα, sub fin. of persons: deserted by others; deprived of the aid and protection of others, esp. of friends, acquaintances, kindred; bereft; (so often by Grk. writ. of every age, as Aeschyl. Ag. 862; Pers. 734; Arstph. pax 112; ἔρημός τε καὶ ὑπὸ πάντων καταλειφθείς, Hdian. 2, 12, 12 [7 ed. Bekk.]; of a flock deserted by the shepherd, Hom. Il. 5, 140): γυνή, a woman neglected by her husband, from whom the husband withholds himself, Gal. iv. 27, fr. Is. liv. 1; of Jerusalem, bereft of Christ's presence, instruction and aid, Mt. xxiii. 38 [L and WH txt. om.]; Lk. xiii. 35 Rec.; cf. Bleek, Erklär. d. drei ersten Evv. ii. p. 206, (cf. Bar. iv. 19; Add. to Esth. viii. 27 (vi. 13); 2 Macc. viii. 35). **2.** subst. ἡ ἔρημος, sc. χώρα; Sept. often for מִדְבָּר; a desert, wilderness, (Hdt. 3, 102): Mt. xxiv. 26; Rev. xii. 6, 14; xvii. 3; αἱ ἔρημοι, desert places, lonely regions: Lk. i. 80; v. 16; viii. 29. an uncultivated region fit for pasturage, Lk. xv. 4. used of the desert of Judæa [cf. W. § 18, 1], Mt. iii. 1; Mk. i. 3 sq.;

Lk. i. 80; iii. 2, 4; Jn. i. 23; of the desert of Arabia, Acts vii. 30, 36, 38, 42, 44; 1 Co. x. 5; Heb. iii. 8, 17. Cf. Win. RWB. s. v. Wüste; Furrer in Schenkel v. 680 sqq.; [B. D. s. vv. Desert and Wilderness (Am. ed.)].

2049 ἐρημόω, -ῶ: Pass., [pres. 3 pers. sing. (cf. B. 38 (33)) ἐρημοῦται]; pf. ptcp. ἠρημωμένος; 1 aor. ἠρημώθην; (ἔρημος); fr. Hdt. down; Sept. usually for חָרַב, הֶחֱרִיב, שָׁמֵם; to make desolate, lay waste; in the N. T. only in the Pass.: πόλιν, Rev. xviii. 19; to ruin, bring to desolation: βασιλείαν, Mt. xii. 25; Lk. xi. 17; to reduce to naught: πλοῦτον, Rev. xviii. 17 (16); ἠρημωμένην καὶ γυμνὴν ποιεῖν τινα, to despoil one, strip her of her treasures, Rev. xvii. 16.*

2050 ἐρήμωσις, -εως, ἡ, ('ἐρημόω), a making desolate, desolation: Mt. xxiv. 15; Mk. xiii. 14; Lk. xxi. 20; see βδέλυγμα, c. (Arr. exp. Alex. 1, 9, 13; Sept. several times for שַׁמָּה, חָרְבָּה, etc.) *

2051 ἐρίζω: [fut. ἐρίσω, cf. B. 37 (32)]; (ἔρις); to wrangle, engage in strife, (Lat. rixari): Mt. xii. 19, where by the phrase οὐκ ἐρίσει the Evangelist seems to describe the calm temper of Jesus in contrast with the vehemence of the Jewish doctors wrangling together about tenets and practices. [(From Hom. down.)] *

2052 ἐριθεία (not ἐρίθεια, cf. W. § 6, 1 g.; [Chandler § 99]) [-θία WH; see I, ι and Tdf. Proleg. p. 88], -είας, ἡ, (ἐριθεύω to spin wool, work in wool, Heliod. 1, 5; Mid. in the same sense, Tob. ii. 11; used of those who electioneer for office, courting popular applause by trickery and low arts, Aristot. polit. 5, 3; the verb is derived from ἔριθος working for hire, a hireling; fr. the Maced. age down, a spinner or weaver, a worker in wool, Is. xxxviii. 12 Sept.; a mean, sordid fellow), electioneering or intriguing for office, Aristot. pol. 5, 2 and 3 [pp. 1302ᵇ, 4 and 1303ᵃ, 14]; hence, apparently, in the N. T. a courting distinction, a desire to put one's self forward, a partisan and factious spirit which does not disdain low arts; partisanship, factiousness: Jas. iii. 14, 16; κατ' ἐριθείαν, Phil. ii. 3; Ignat. ad Philadelph. § 8; οἱ ἐξ ἐριθείας (see ἐκ, II. 7), Phil. i. 16 (17) [yet see ἐκ, II. 12 b.]; i. q. contending against God, Ro. ii. 8 [yet cf. Mey. (ed. Weiss) ad loc.]; in the plur. αἱ ἐριθείαι [W. § 27, 3; B. § 123, 2]: 2 Co. xii. 20; Gal. v. 20. See the very full and learned discussion of the word by Fritzsche in his Com. on Rom. i. p. 143 sq.; [of which a summary is given by Ellic. on Gal. v. 20. See further on its derivation, Lobeck, Path. Proleg. p. 365; cf. W. 94 (89)].*

2053 ἔριον, -ου, τό, (dimin. of τὸ ἔρος or εἶρος), wool: Heb. ix. 19; Rev. i. 14. [From Hom. down.] *

2054 ἔρις, -ιδος, ἡ, acc. ἔριν (Phil. i. 15), pl. ἔριδες (1 Co. i. 11) and ἔρεις (2 Co. xii. 20 [R G Tr txt.]; Gal. v. 20 R G WH mrg.]; Tit. iii. 9 [R G L Tr]; see [WH. App. p. 157]; Lob. ad Phryn. p. 326; Matthiae § 80 note 8; Bttm. Ausf. Spr. p. 191 sq.; [W. 65 (63); B. 24 (22)]); contention, strife, wrangling: Ro. i. 29; xiii. 13; 1 Co. i. 11; iii. 3; 2 Co. xii. 20; Gal. v. 20; Phil. i. 15; 1 Tim. vi. 4; Tit. iii. 9. [From Hom. down.] *

2055 & 2056 ἐρίφιον, -ου, τό, and ἔριφος, -ου, ὁ, a kid, a young goat: Mt. xxv. 32 sq.; Lk. xv. 29. [Ath. 14, p. 661 b.]*

*For 2046 see 4483.

2057   **Ἑρμᾶς**, acc. Ἑρμᾶν [cf. B. 20 (18)], ὁ, (Doric for Ἑρμῆς), *Hermas*, a certain Christian (whom Origen and others thought to be the author of the book entitled " The Shepherd " [cf. *Salmon* in Dict. of Chris. Biog. s. v. Hermas 2]) : Ro. xvi. 14.*

2058   **ἑρμηνεία** [WH -νία; see I, ι], -ας, ἡ, (ἑρμηνεύω), *interpretation* (of what has been spoken more or less obscurely by others) : 1 Co. xii. 10 [L txt. διερμ. q. v.] ; xiv. 26. [From Plato down.]*

see 2059   **ἑρμηνευτής**, -οῦ, ὁ, (ἑρμηνεύω, q. v.), *an interpreter* : 1 Co. xiv. 28 L Tr WH mrg. (Plat. politic. p. 290 c.; for מֵלִיץ in Gen. xlii. 23.) *

2059   **ἑρμηνεύω** : [pres. pass. ἑρμηνεύομαι] ; (fr. Ἑρμῆς, who was held to be the god of speech, writing, eloquence, learning) ;   **1.** *to explain in words, expound* : [Soph., Eur.], Xen., Plato, al.   **2.** *to interpret*, i. e. to translate what has been spoken or written in a foreign tongue into the vernacular (Xen. an. 5, 4, 4) : Jn. i. 38 (39) R G T, 42 (43) ; ix. 7 ; Heb. vii. 2.   (2 Esdr. iv. 7 for תִּרְגַּם.) [COMP. : δι-, μεθ-ερμηνεύω.] *

2060   **Ἑρμῆς**, acc. Ἑρμῆν, ὁ, prop. name, *Hermes* ;   **1.** a Greek deity called by the Romans Mercurius (*Mercury*): Acts xiv. 12.   **2.** a certain Christian : Ro. xvi. 14.*

2061   **Ἑρμογένης**, [i. e. born of Hermes ; Tdf. Ἑρμογ.], -ους, ὁ, *Hermogenes*, a certain Christian : 2 Tim. i. 15.*

2062   **ἑρπετόν**, -οῦ, τό, (fr. ἕρπω to creep, crawl, [Lat. *serpo* ; hence serpent, and fr. same root, reptile ; Vaniček p. 1030 sq.]), *a creeping thing, reptile* ; by prof. writ. used chiefly of serpents ; in Hom. Od. 4, 418 ; Xen. mem. 1, 4, 11 an animal of any sort ; in bibl. Grk. opp. to quadrupeds and birds, Acts x. 12 ; xi. 6 ; Ro. i. 23 ; and to marine animals also, Jas. iii. 7 ; on this last pass. cf. Gen. ix. 3. (Sept. for רֶמֶשׂ and שֶׁרֶץ.) *

2063   **ἐρυθρός**, -ά, -όν, *red* ; fr. Hom. down ; in the N. T. only in the phrase ἡ ἐρυθρὰ θάλασσα *the Red Sea* (fr. Hdt. down [cf. Rawlinson's Herod. vol. i. p. 143]), i. e. the Indian Ocean washing the shores of Arabia and Persia, with its two gulfs, of which the one lying on the east is called the Persian Gulf, the other on the opposite side the Arabian. In the N. T. the phrase denotes the upper part of the Arabian Gulf (the Heroöpolite Gulf, so called [i. e. Gulf of Suez]), through which the Israelites made their passage out of Egypt to the shore of Arabia : Acts vii. 36 ; Heb. xi. 29. (Sept. for יַם-סוּף, *the sea of sedge* or *sea-weed* [cf. B. D. as below]. Cf. *Win.* RWB. s. v. Meer rothes ; *Pressel* in Herzog ix. p. 239 sqq. ; *Furrer* in Schenkel iv. 150 sqq. ; [B. D. s. vv. Red Sea and Red Sea, Passage of ; *Trumbull*, Kadesh-Barnea, p. 352 sqq.].) *

2064   **ἔρχομαι**, impv. ἔρχου, ἔρχεσθε, (for the Attic ἴθι, ἴτε fr. εἶμι) ; impf. ἠρχόμην (for ᾖειν and ᾖα more com. in Attic) ; fut. ἐλεύσομαι ; — (on these forms cf. [esp. *Rutherford*, New Phryn. p. 103 sqq. ; Veitch s. v.] ; Matthiae § 234 ; *Bttm.* Ausf. Spr. ii. 182 sq. ; Krüger § 40 s. v. ; Kühner § 343 ; W. § 15 s. v. ; [B. 58 (50)]) ; pf. ἐλήλυθα ; plpf. ἐληλύθειν ; 2 aor. ἦλθον and (occasionally by L T Tr WH [together or severally]—as Mt. vi. 10 ; [vii. 25, 27 ; x. 13 ; xiv. 34 ; xxv. 36 ; Mk. i. 29 ; vi. 29 ; Lk. i. 59 ; ii. 16 ; v. 7 ; vi. 17 ; viii. 35 ; xi. 2 ; xxiii. 33 ; xxiv 1. 23] ; Jn. [i. 39 (40) ;

iii. 26] ; iv. 27 ; [xii. 9] ; Acts xii. 10 ; [xiv. 24] ; xxviii. 14 sq. etc.) in the Alexandrian form ἦλθα (see ἀπέρχομαι init. for reff.) ; Sept. for בּוֹא, rarely for אָתָה and יָלַךְ ; [fr. Hom. down] ;   **I.** *to come* ;   **1.** prop.   **a.** of persons ;   **a.** univ. *to come from one place into another*, and used both of persons arriving,—as in Mt. viii. 9 ; xxii. 3 ; Lk. vii. 8 ; xiv. 17 [here WH mrg. read the inf., see their Intr. § 404], 20 ; Jn. v. 7 ; Acts x. 29 ; Rev. xxii. 7, and very often ; οἱ ἐρχόμενοι κ. οἱ ὑπάγοντες, Mk. vi. 31 ; —and of those returning, as in Jn. iv. 27 ; ix. 7 ; Ro. ix. 9. Constructions : foll. by ἀπό w. gen. of place, Mk. vii. 1 ; xv. 21 ; Acts xviii. 2 ; 2 Co. xi. 9 ; w. gen. of pers., Mk. v. 35 ; Jn. iii. 2 ; Gal. ii. 12, etc. ; foll. by ἐκ w. gen. of place, Lk. v. 17 [L txt. συνέρχ.] ; Jn. iii. 31, etc. ; foll. by εἰς w. acc. of place, *to come into* : as εἰς τ. οἰκίαν, τὸν οἶκον, Mt. ii. 11 ; viii. 14 ; Mk. i. 29 ; v. 38, etc. ; εἰς τὴν πόλιν, Mt. ix. 1, and many other exx. ; foll. by εἰς *to, towards*, Jn. xx. 3 sq. ; εἰς τὸ πέραν, of persons going in a boat, Mt. viii. 28 ; of persons departing ἐκ ... εἰς, Jn. iv. 54 ; διά w. gen. of place foll. by εἰς (Rec. πρός) *to*, Mk. vii. 31 ; εἰς τ. ἑορτήν, to celebrate the feast, Jn. iv. 45 ; xi. 56 ; ἐν w. dat. of the thing with which one is equipped, Ro. xv. 29 ; 1 Co. iv. 21 ; foll. by ἐπί w. acc. of place, (Germ. *über, over*), Mt. xiv. 28 ; (Germ. *auf*), Mk. vi. 53 ; (Germ. *an*), Lk. xix. 5 ; [xxiii. 33 L Tr] ; Acts xii. 10, 12 ; *to* w. acc. of the thing, Mt. iii. 7 ; xxi. 19 ; Mk. xi. 13 ; xvi. 2 ; Lk. xxiv. 1 ; w. acc. of pers., Jn. xix. 33 ; *to one's tribunal*, Acts xxiv. 8 Rec. ; *against* one, of a military leader, Lk. xiv. 31 ; κατά w. acc., Lk. x. 33 ; Acts xvi. 7 ; παρά w. gen. of pers. Lk. viii. 49 [Lchm. ἀπό] ; w. acc. of place, *to* [the side of], Mt. xv. 29 ; πρός *to*, w. acc. of pers., Mt. iii. 14 ; vii. 15 ; [xiv. 25 L T Tr WH] ; Mk. ix. 14 ; Lk. i. 43 ; Jn. i. 29 ; 2 Co. xiii. 1, and very often, esp. in the Gospels ; ἀπό τινος (gen. of pers.) πρός τινα, 1 Th. iii. 6 ; with simple dat. of pers. (prop. dat. commodi or incommodi [cf. W. § 22, 7 N. 2 ; B. 179 (155)]) : Mt. xxi. 5 ; Rev. ii. 5, 16, (exx. fr. Grk. auth. in Passow s. v. p. 1184ᵃ bot. ; [L and S. s. v. II. 4]). with adverbs of place : πόθεν, Jn. iii. 8 ; viii. 14 ; Rev. vii. 13 ; ἄνωθεν, Jn. iii. 31 ; ὄπισθεν, Mk. v. 27 ; ὧδε, Mt. viii. 29 ; Acts ix. 21 ; ἐνθάδε, Jn. iv. 15 [R G L Tr], 16 ; ἐκεῖ, Jn. xviii. 3 [cf. W. 472 (440)] ; ποῦ, Heb. xi. 8 ; ἕως τινός, Lk. iv. 42 ; ἄχρι τινός, Acts xi. 5. The purpose for which one comes is indicated — either by an inf., Mk. [v. 14 L T Tr WH] ; xv. 36 ; Lk. i. 59 ; iii. 12 ; Jn. iv. 15 [T WH διέρχ.], and very often ; or by a fut. ptcp., Mt. xxvii. 49 ; Acts viii. 27 ; or by a foll. ἵνα, Jn. xii. 9 ; εἰς τοῦτο, ἵνα, Acts ix. 21 ; or by διά τινα, Jn. xii. 9. As one who is about to do something in a place must necessarily come thither, in the popular narrative style the phrases ἔρχεται καί, ἦλθε καί, etc., are usually placed before verbs of action : Mt. xiii. 19, 25 ; Mk. ii. 18 ; iv. 15 ; v. 33 ; vi. 29 ; xii. 9 ; xiv. 37 ; Lk. viii. 12, 47 ; Jn. vi. 15 ; xi. 48 ; xii. 22 ; xix. 38 ; xx. 19, 26 ; xxi. 13 ; 3 Jn. 3 ; Rev. v. 7 ; xvii. 1 ; xxi. 9 ; ἔρχου κ. ἴδε (or βλέπε), Jn. i. 46 (47) ; xi. 34 ; [and Rec. in] Rev. vi. 1, 3, 5, 7, [also Grsb. exc. in vs. 3] ; plur. Jn. i. 39 (40) ([T Tr WH ὄψεσθε], see εἶδω, I. 1 e) ; — or ἐλθών is used, foll. by a finite verb: Mt. ii. 8; viii. 7; ix. 10, 18; xii. 44; xiv. 12, 33 [R G L]; xviii. 31; xxvii. 64; xxviii. 13; Mk. vii. 25 [Tdf. εἰσελθ.]; xii. 14, 42; xiv. 45; xvi. 1; Acts xvi. 37, 39; — or ἐρχόμενος, foll. by a finite verb: Lk. xiii. 14; xvi. 21; xviii. 5. in other places ἐλθών must be rendered *when I* (*thou, he,* etc.) *am come*: Jn. xvi. 8; 2 Co. xii. 20; Phil. i. 27 (opp. to ἀπών). **β.** *to come* i. e. *to appear, make one's appearance, come before the public*: so κατ' ἐξοχήν of the Messiah, Lk. iii. 16; Jn. iv. 25; vii. 27, 31; Heb. x. 37, who is styled pre-eminently ὁ ἐρχόμενος, i. e. he that cometh (i. e. is about to come) acc. to prophetic promise and universal expectation, *the coming one* [W. 341 (320); B. 204 (176 sq.)]: Mt. xi. 3; Lk. vii. 19 sq.; with εἰς τὸν κόσμον added, Jn. vi. 14; xi. 27; ἐν τῷ ὀνόματι τοῦ κυρίου, *he who is* already *coming clothed with divine authority* i. e. *the Messiah,* — the shout of the people joyfully welcoming Jesus as he was entering Jerusalem, — taken fr. Ps. cxvii. (cxviii.) 25 sq.: Mt. xxi. 9; xxiii. 39; Mk. xi. 9; Lk. xiii. 35; xix. 38 [Tdf. om. ἐρχ. (so WH in their first mrg.)]; Jn. xii. 13. ἔρχεσθαι used of Elijah who was to return fr. heaven as the forerunner of the Messiah: Mt. xi. 14; xvii. 10; Mk. ix. 11–13; of John the Baptist, Mt. xi. 18; Lk. vii. 33; Jn. i. 31; with εἰς μαρτυρίαν added, Jn. i. 7; of Antichrist, 1 Jn. ii. 18; of "false Christs" and other deceivers, false teachers, etc.: Mt. xxiv. 5; Mk. xiii. 6; Lk. xxi. 8, (in these pass. with the addition ἐπὶ τῷ ὀνόματί μου, *relying on my name*, i. e. arrogating to themselves and simulating my Messianic dignity); Jn. x. 8; 2 Co. xi. 4; 2 Pet. iii. 3; Rev. xvii. 10; with the addition ἐν τῷ ὀνόματι τῷ ἰδίῳ in his own authority and of his own free-will, Jn. v. 43. of the Holy Spirit, who is represented as a person coming to be the invisible helper of Christ's disciples after his departure from the world: Jn. xv. 26; xvi. 7 sq. 13. of the a p - pearance of Jesus among men, as a religious teacher and the author of salvation: Mt. xi. 19; Lk. vii. 34; Jn. v. 43; vii. 28; viii. 42; with the addition of εἰς τ. κόσμον foll. by ἵνα, Jn. xii. 46; xviii. 37; εἰς κρίμα, ἵνα, Jn. ix. 39; foll. by a telic inf. 1 Tim. i. 15; ἔρχεσθαι ὀπίσω τινός, after one, Mt. iii. 11; Mk. i. 7; Jn. i. 15, 27, 30; ὁ ἐλθὼν δι' ὕδατος καὶ αἵματος, a terse expression for, 'he that publicly appeared and approved himself (to be God's son and ambassador) by accomplishing expiation through the ordinance of baptism and the bloody death which he underwent' [cf. p. 210ᵃ bot.], 1 Jn. v. 6; ἔρχεσθαι foll. by a telic inf., Mt. v. 17; x. 34 sq.; Lk. xix. 10; foll. by ἵνα, Jn. x. 10; ἐληλυθέναι and ἔρχεσθαι ἐν σαρκί are used of the form in which Christ as the divine Logos appeared among men: 1 Jn. iv. 2, 3 [Rec.]; 2 Jn. 7. of the return of Jesus hereafter from heaven in majesty: Mt. x. 23; Acts i. 11; 1 Co. iv. 5; xi. 26; 1 Th. v. 2; 2 Th. i. 10; with ἐν τῇ δόξῃ αὐτοῦ added, Mt. xvi. 27; xxv. 31; Mk. viii. 38; Lk. ix. 26; ἐπὶ τῶν νεφελῶν (borne on the clouds) μετὰ δυνάμεως κ. δόξης, Mt. xxiv. 30; ἐν νεφέλαις, ἐν νεφέλῃ κτλ., Mk. xiii. 26; Lk. xxi. 27; ἐν τῇ βασιλείᾳ αὐτοῦ (see ἐν, I. 5 c p. 210ᵇ top), Mt. xvi. 28; Lk. xxiii. 42 [εἰς τὴν β. L mrg. Tr mrg. WH txt.] **b.** of t i m e, like the Lat. *venio*: with nouns of time, as

ἔρχονται ἡμέραι, in a fut. sense, *will come* [cf. B. 204 (176 sq.); W. § 40, 2 a.], Lk. xxiii. 29; Heb. viii. 8 fr. Jer. xxxviii. (xxxi.) 31; ἐλεύσονται ἡμέραι, Mt. ix. 15; Mk. ii. 20; Lk. v. 35; xvii. 22; xxi. 6; ἦλθεν ἡ ἡμέρα, Lk. xxii. 7; Rev. vi. 17; ἔρχεται ὥρα, ὅτε, Jn. iv. 21, 23; v. 25; xvi. 25; foll. by ἵνα, Jn. xvi. 2, 32; ἦλθεν, is come, i. e. is present, Jn. xvi. 4, 21; Rev. xiv. 7, 15; ἐλήλυθε ἡ ὥρα, ἵνα, Jn. xii. 23; xiii. 1 (L T Tr WH ἦλθεν); xvi. 32; xvii. 1; ἐληλύθει ἡ ὥρα αὐτοῦ, had come (Lat. *aderat*), Jn. vii. 30; viii. 20; ἐρχ. νύξ, Jn. ix. 4; ἡ ἡμέρα τοῦ κυρίου, 1 Th. v. 2; καιροί, Acts iii. 19. with names of events that occur at a definite time: ὁ θερισμός, Jn. iv. 35; ὁ γάμος τοῦ ἀρνίου, Rev. xix. 7; ἦλθεν ἡ κρίσις, Rev. xviii. 10. in imitation of the Hebr. הַבָּא, ὁ, ἡ, τὸ ἐρχόμενος, -ένη, -ενον, is i. q. *to come, future* [cf. B. and W. u. s.]: ὁ αἰών, Mk. x. 30; Lk. xviii. 30; ἡ ἑορτή, Acts xviii. 21 [Rec.]; ἡ ὀργή, 1 Th. i. 10; τὰ ἐρχόμενα, things to come, Jn. xvi. 13 הַבָּאִים the times to come, Is. xxvii. 6); in the periphrasis of the name of Jehovah, ὁ ὢν καὶ ὁ ἦν καὶ ὁ ἐρχόμενος, it is equiv. to ἐσόμενος, Rev. i. 4; iv. 8. **c.** of things and events (so very often in Grk. auth. also); of the advent of natural events: ποταμοί, Mt. vii. 25 [R G]; κατακλυσμός, Lk. xvii. 27; λιμός, Acts vii. 11; of the rain coming down ἐπὶ τῆς γῆς, Heb. vi. 7; of alighting birds, Mt. xiii. 4, 32; Mk. iv. 4; of a voice that is heard (Hom. Il. 10, 139), foll. by ἐκ with gen. of place, Mt. iii. 17 [?]; Mk. ix. 7 [T WH Tr mrg. ἐγένετο]; Jn. xii. 28; of things that are b r o u g h t: ὁ λύχνος, Mk. iv. 21 (ἐπιστολή, Liban. ep. 458; other exx. fr. Grk. writ. are given in Kypke, Kuinoel, al., on Mk. l. c.). **2.** metaph. **a.** of C h r i s t's i n v i s i b l e r e t u r n f r o m h e a v e n, i. e. of the power which through the Holy Spirit he will exert in the souls of his disciples: Jn. xiv. 18, 23; of his invisible advent in the death of believers, by which he takes them to himself into heaven, Jn. xiv. 3. **b.** equiv. to *to come into being, arise, come forth, show itself, find place* or *in-fluence*: τὰ σκάνδαλα, Lk. xvii. 1; τὰ ἀγαθά, Ro. iii. 8 (Jer. xvii. 6); τὸ τέλειον, 1 Co. xiii. 10; ἡ πίστις, Gal. iii. 23, 25; ἡ ἀποστασία, 2 Th. ii. 3; ἡ βασιλεία τοῦ θεοῦ, i. q. *be established*, Mt. vi. 10; Lk. xi. 2; xvii. 20, etc.; ἡ ἐντολή, i. q. *became known*, Ro. vii. 9. **c.** with P r e p o s i t i o n s : ἐκ τῆς [Lchm. ἀπὸ] θλίψεως, suffered tribulation, Rev. vii. 14. foll. by εἰς, *to come* (fall) *into* or *unto*: εἰς τὸ χεῖρον, into a worse condition, Mk. v. 26; εἰς πειρασμόν, Mk. xiv. 38 T WH; εἰς ἀπελεγμόν (see ἀπελεγμός), Acts xix. 27; εἰς τὴν ὥραν ταύτην, Jn. xii. 27; εἰς κρίσιν, to become liable to judgment, Jn. v. 24; εἰς ἐπίγνωσιν, to attain to knowledge, 1 Tim. ii. 4; 2 Tim. iii. 7; εἰς τὸ φανερόν, to come to light, Mk. iv. 22; εἰς προκοπὴν ἐλήλυθε, has turned out for the advancement, Phil. i. 12; ἔρχ. εἴς τι, *to come to a thing*, is used of a writer who after discussing other matters passes on to a new topic, 2 Co. xii. 1; εἰς ἑαυτόν, to come to one's senses, return to a healthy state of mind, Lk. xv. 17 (Epict. diss. 3, 1, 15; Test. xii. Patr., test. Jos. § 3, p. 702 ed. Fabric.). ἔρχ. ἐπί τινα *to come upon one*: in a bad sense, of calamities, Jn. xviii. 4; in a good sense, of the Holy Spirit, Mt. iii. 16; Acts xix. 6; *to devolve* *upon one*, of the guilt and punishment of murder, Mt. xxiii. 35. ἔρχ. πρὸς τὸν Ἰησοῦν, to commit one's self to the instruction of Jesus and enter into fellowship with him, Jn. v. 40; vi. 35, 37, 44, 45, 65; πρὸς τὸ φῶς, to submit one's self to the power of the light, Jn. iii. 20 sq. **II.** *to go*: ὀπίσω τινός (אַחֲרֵי הָלַךְ), to follow one, Mt. xvi. 24; [Mk. viii. 34 R L Tr mrg. WH]; Lk. ix. 23; xiv. 27, (Gen. xxiv. 5, 8; xxxvii. 17, and elsewhere); πρός τινα, Lk. xv. 20; σύν τινι, to accompany one, Jn. xxi. 3 [cf. B. 210 (182)]; ὁδὸν ἔρχεσθαι, Lk. ii. 44 [cf. W. 226 (212)]. [Comp.: ἀν-, ἐπ-αν-, ἀπ-, δι-, εἰσ-, ἐπ-εισ-, παρεισ-, συν-εισ-, ἐξ-, δι-εξ-, κατ-, παρ-, ἀντι-παρ-, περι-, προ-, προσ-, συν-έρχομαι.]

[SYN.: ἔρχεσθαι, (βαίνειν,) πορεύεσθαι, χωρεῖν· with the N.T. use of these verbs and their compounds it may be interesting to compare the distinctions ordinarily recognized in classic Grk., where ἔρχεσθαι denotes motion or progress g e n e r a l l y, and of any sort, hence to *come* and (esp. ἐλθεῖν) arrive at, as well as to *go* (βαίνειν). βαίνειν primarily signifies to *walk, take steps*, picturing the mode of motion; to go *away*. πορεύεσθαι expresses motion in general, — often confined within certain limits, or giving prominence to the b e a r i n g; hence the regular word for the march of an army χωρεῖν always emphasizes the idea of s e p a r a t i o n, change of p l a c e, and does not, like e. g. πορεύεσθαι, note the external and perceptible motion, — (a man may be recognized by his πορεία). Cf. Schmidt ch. xxvii.]

(2064α); see (1512α)

ἐρῶ, see εἶπον.

2065 ——— ἐρωτάω, -ῶ, [(inf. -τᾶν L T Tr, -τᾷν R G WH; see I, ι)]; impf. 3 pers. plur. ἠρώτων and (in Mt. xv. 23 L T Tr WH, Mk. iv. 10 Tdf.) ἠρώτουν, cf. B. 44 (38); [W. 85 (82); *Tdf.* Proleg. p. 122; *Soph.* Lex. p. 41; *WH.* App. p. 166; *Mullach,* Griech. Vulgarspr. p. 252]; fut. ἐρωτήσω; 1 aor. ἠρώτησα; Sept. for שָׁאַל; *to ask*, i. e. **1.** as in Grk. writ. fr. Hom. down *to question*: absol., Lk. xxii. 68; Jn. viii. 7 [R]; τινά, Jn. ix. 21; xvi. 19, 30; [xviii. 21 where Rec. ἐπερ.], etc.; with the addition of λέγων and the words of the questioner: Mt. xvi. 13; Lk. xix. 31 [om. λέγων; xxiii. 3 T Tr WH]; Jn. i. 19, 21; ix. 19; xvi. 5; τινά τι [cf. W. § 32, 4 a.], Mt. xxi. 24; Mk. iv. 10; Lk. xx. 3; Jn. xvi. 23 [al. refer this to 2]; τινὰ περί τινος, Lk. ix. 45 [Lchm. ἐπερ.]; Jn. xviii. 19. **2.** *to ask* i. e. *to request, entreat, beg, beseech*, after the Hebr. שָׁאַל, in a sense very rare in prof. auth. (Joseph. antt. 5, 1, 14 [but here the text is uncertain; substitute antt. 7, 8, 1; cf. Dr. Ezra Abbot in No. Am. Rev. for 1872, p. 173 note]; Babr. fab. [42, 3]; 97, 3; Apoll. synt. p. 289, 20; cf. W. pp. 30 and 32): τινά, Jn. xiv. 16; with the addition of λέγων and the words of the asker, Mt. xv. 23; Jn. xii. 21; foll. by impv. alone [B. 272 sq. (234)], Lk. xiv. 18 sq.; Phil. iv. 3; foll. by ἵνα [cf. W. § 44, 8 a.; B. 237 (204)], Mk. vii. 26; Lk. vii. 36; xvi. 27; Jn. iv. 47; xvii. 15; xix. 31, 38; 2 Jn. 5; 1 Th. iv. 1; by ὅπως, Lk. vii. 3; xi. 37; Acts xxiii. 20; by the inf. [B. 258 (222); cf. W. 335 (315)], Lk. v. 3; viii. 37; Jn. iv. 40; Acts iii. 3; x. 48; xxiii. 18; 1 Th. v. 12; τινὰ περί τινος, Lk. iv. 38; Jn. xvii. 9, 20; 1 Jn. v. 16; ὑπέρ τινος [foll. by εἰς w. inf.; cf. B. 265 (228)], 2 Th. ii. 1 sq.; ἐρωτᾶν τὰ [WH txt. om. τά] πρὸς εἰρήνην (see εἰρήνη, 1), Lk. xiv. 32. [SYN. see αἰτέω, fin. COMP.: δι-, ἐπ-ερωτάω.]

ἐσθής, -ῆτος, ἡ, (fr. ἕννυμι, ἔσθην, hence it would be **2066** more correctly written ἑσθής [so Rec.ᵉˡˢ in Lk.], cf. Kühner i. p. 217, 3), formerly Ϝεσθής (cf. Lat. *vestis*, Germ. *Weste*, Eng. *vest*, etc.), *clothing, raiment, apparel*: Lk. xxiii. 11; xxiv. 4 L T Tr WH; Acts i. 10 R G; x. 30; xii. 21; Jas. ii. 2 sq. [From Hom. down.] *

ἔσθησις [Rec.ᵉˡˢ ἐσθ.], -εως, ἡ, (fr. ἐσθέω, and this fr. **2067** ἐσθής, q. v.), *clothing, apparel*: plur., Lk. xxiv. 4 R G; Acts i. 10 L T Tr WH; [cf. Philo, vit. Moys. iii. § 18; Euseb. h. e. 2, 6, 7 and Heinichen's note]. (Rare in prof. writ. [Aristot. rhet. 2, 8, 14 var.]; cf. W. § 2, 1 c.) *

ἐσθίω and ἔσθω, q. v., (lengthened forms of ἔδω [cf. **2068** *Curtius,* Das Verbum, ii. p. 429]); impf. ἤσθιον; 2 aor. ἔφαγον (fr. ΦΑΓΩ); fut. φάγομαι (2 pers. φάγεσαι, Lk. xvii. 8 [reff. s. v. κατακαυχάομαι, init.]), for the classic ἔδομαι, see *Bttm.* Ausf. Spr. ii. p. 185; Kühner i. p. 824; [W. 89 (85); B. 58 (51); but esp. Veitch s. v.]; Sept. for אָכַל; [fr. Hom. down]; *to eat*: Vulg. *manduco*, [*edo*, etc.]; (of animals, *to devour*); **a.** absol.: Mt. xiv. 20 sq.; v. 37, 38; xxvi. 26; Mk. vi. 31; viii. 8; Jn. iv. 31, and often; ἐν τῷ φαγεῖν, in eating (the supper), 1 Co. xi. 21; διδόναι τινὶ φαγεῖν, to give one (something) to eat, Mt. xiv. 16; xxv. 35, 42; Mk. v. 43; vi. 37; Lk. ix. 13, (and with addition of an acc. of the thing to be eaten, Jn. vi. 31, 52; ἔκ τινος, Rev. ii. 7; [cf. W. 198 (187) sq.]); φέρειν τινὶ φαγεῖν, to bring one (something) to eat, Jn. iv. 33; spec. in opp. to abstinence from certain kinds of food, Ro. xiv. 3, 20; ἐσθίειν κ. πίνειν (and φαγεῖν κ. πιεῖν), to use food and drink to satisfy one's hunger and thirst, 1 Co. xi. 22; contextually, to be supported at the expense of others, 1 Co. ix. 4; not to shun choice food and in a word to be rather a free-liver, opp. to the narrow and scrupulous notions of those who abstain from the use of wine and certain kinds of food, Mt. xi. 19; Lk. vii. 34; opp. to fasting (τὸ νηστεύειν), Lk. v. 33; of those who, careless about greater and esp. graver matters, lead an easy, merry life, Lk. xii. 19; xvii. 27 sq.; 1 Co. xv. 32, (Is. xxii. 13); of the jovial use of a sacrificial feast, 1 Co. x. 7 fr. Ex. xxxii. 6; preceded by a negative, to abstain from all nourishment, Acts xxiii. 12, 21; to use a spare diet, spoken of an ascetic mode of life, Mt. xi. 18; of fasting, Acts ix. 9; ἐσθίειν (κ. πίνειν) μετά τινος, to dine, feast, (in company) with one, Mt. ix. 11; Mk. ii. 16; Lk. v. 30; with one (he providing the entertainment), i. e. *at his house*, Lk. vii. 36; μετὰ τῶν μεθυόντων etc., of luxurious revelling, Mt. xxiv. 49; Lk. xii. 45; ἐπὶ τραπέζης τοῦ Χριστοῦ, the food and drink spread out on Christ's table, i. e. to enjoy the blessings of the salvation procured by Christ (which is likened to a banquet), Lk. xxii. 30; ἐσθίειν τινί, to one's honor, Ro. xiv. 6. **b.** construed w. an acc. of the thing, *to eat (consume) a thing* [W. 198 (187) note]: Mt. vi. 25; Mk. i. 6; Jn. iv. 32; vi. 31; Ro. xiv. 2; 1 Co. viii. 13; x. 25, etc.; ἄρτον, to take food, eat a meal, (after the Hebr. אָכַל לֶחֶם, Gen. xliii. 25; Ex. ii. 20; 1 S. xx. 24; Prov. xxiii. 7), Mt. xv. 2; Mk. iii. 20; Lk. xiv. 1, 15; τὸν ἑαυτοῦ ἄρτον, obtained by his own labor, 2 Th. iii. 12; ἄρτον παρά τινος (gen. of pers.) to be supported by one, 2 Th.

iii. 8; τὰ παρά τινος, the things supplied by one, Lk. x. 7, i. q. τὰ παρατιθέμενα in vs. 8 [cf. W. 366 (343)]; 1 Co. x. 27; μήτε ἄρτον ἐσθ. μήτε οἶνον πίνειν, to live frugally, Lk. vii. 33; τὸ κυριακὸν δεῖπνον φαγεῖν, to celebrate the Lord's supper, 1 Co. xi. 20; τὸ πάσχα, to eat the paschal lamb, celebrate the paschal supper, Mt. xxvi. 17; Mk. xiv. 12, 14; Lk. xxii. 8, 11, 15, 16 L T Tr WH; Jn. xviii. 28; τὰς θυσίας, to celebrate the sacrificial feasts, said of Jews, 1 Co. x. 18; of animals, in Lk. xv. 16 (where ὧν stands by attraction for ἅ, because ἐσθίειν with a simple gen. of thing is nowhere found in the N. T. [W. 198 (187) note]). by a usage hardly to be met with in class. Grk. (W. § 28, 1; [B. 159 (139)]), ἔκ τινος, to (take and) eat of a thing: Lk. xxii. 16 [R G]; Jn. vi. 26, 50 sq.; 1 Co. xi. 28; on the other hand, ἐκ τοῦ καρποῦ (L T Tr WH τὸν καρπόν), ἐκ τοῦ γάλακτος ἐσθίειν, in 1 Co. ix. 7, is to support one's self by the sale of the fruit and the milk [but cf. B. as above, and Meyer ad loc.]. ἐκ with gen. of place: ἐκ τοῦ ἱεροῦ, draw their support from the temple, i. e. from the sacrifices and offerings, 1 Co. ix. 13 [but T Tr WH read τὰ ἐκ τ. ἱ.]; also ἐκ θυσιαστηρίου, i. e. from the things laid on the altar, Heb. xiii. 10 [W. 366 (344)]. by a Hebraism (אָכַל מִן), ἀπό τινος [cf. W. 199 (187)]: Mt. xv. 27; Mk. vii. 28. Metaph. to devour, consume: τινά, Heb. x. 27; τί, Rev. xvii. 16; of rust, Jas. v. 3. [COMP.: κατ-, συν-εσθίω.]

(2068α);   ἔσθω, i. q. ἐσθίω, a poetic form in use fr. Hom. down,
see 2068   very rare in prose writ.; from it are extant in the N. T. the ptcp. ἔσθων in Mk. i. 6 T Tr WH; [Lk. x. 7 L T Tr WH]; Lk. vii. 33 L Tr WH, [also 34 WH]; the pres. subj. 2 pers. plur. ἔσθητε in Lk. xxii. 30 L T Tr WH; [cf. κατεσθίω]. It occurs several times in the Sept., as Lev. xvii. 10; Judg. xiv. 9 [Alex.]; Is. ix. 20; Sir. xx. 16; ἔσθετε, Lev. xix. 26. Cf. [Tdf. Proleg. p. 81]; B. 58 (51).

2069   Ἐσλεί (T Tr WH, [see WH. App. p. 155, and s. v.
*   ει, ι]) or Ἐσλί, ὁ, Esli, one of Christ's ancestors: Lk. iii. 25.*

2072   ἔσ-οπτρον, -ου, τό, (ΟΠΤΩ), a mirror: 1 Co. xiii. 12; Jas. i. 23. (Sap. vii. 26; Sir. xii. 11; Pind. Nem. 7, 20; Anacr. 11, [7 (6)] 3; Plut.; al.) The mirrors of the ancients were made, not of glass [cf. B.D. s. v. Glass, fin.], but of steel; Plin. h. n. 33, (9) 45; 34, (17) 48 [but see the pass. just referred to, and B.D. s. v. mirror].*

2073   ἑσπέρα, -ας, ἡ, (ἕσπερος of or at evening), evening, eventide: Acts iv. 3; xxviii. 23; πρὸς ἑσπ. ἐστίν, it is towards evening, Lk. xxiv. 29. [From Pind. and Hdt. down.]*

see 2073   [ἑσπερινός, -ή, -όν, belonging to the evening, evening: φυλακή, Lk. xii. 38 WH (rejected) mrg. (Sept.; Xen., Dio Cass., Athen., al.)*]

2074   Ἐσρώμ [or Ἐσρών in Lk. Rᵉˡⁱˣ L txt. Tr mrg.; WH
†   Ἐσρ., see their Intr. § 408], ὁ, Esrom or Hezrom or Hesron, one of Christ's ancestors: Mt. i. 3; Lk. iii. 33.*

see 2074 —— [Ἐσρών or Ἐσρ. see the preceding word.]

2078 ———— ἔσχατος, -η, -ον, (fr. ἔχω, ἔσχον adhering, clinging close; [acc. to al. (Curtius § 583 b.) superl. fr. ἐξ, the outermost]), Sept. for אַחֲרִית, אַחֲרוֹן; [fr. Hom. down]; extreme, last in time or in place; **1.** joined to nouns:

τόπος, the last in a series of places [A. V. lowest], Lk. xiv. 9 sq.; in a temporal succession, the last: ἔσχατος ἐχθρός, that remains after the rest have been conquered, 1 Co. xv. 26; κοδράντης, that remains when the rest have one after another been spent, Mt. v. 26; so λεπτόν, Lk. xii. 59; ἡ ἐσχ. σάλπιγξ, the trumpet after which no other will sound, 1 Co. xv. 52, cf. Meyer ad loc.; αἱ ἐσχ. πληγαί, Rev. xv. 1; xxi. 9; ἡ ἐσχάτη ἡμέρα τῆς ἑορτῆς, Jn. vii. 37. When two are contrasted it is i. q. the latter, opp. to ὁ πρῶτος the former (Deut. xxiv. 1–4): thus τὰ ἔργα (opp. to τῶν πρώτων), Rev. ii. 19; ἡ πλάνη, Mt. xxvii. 64 (where the meaning is, 'lest the latter deception, caused by the false story of his resurrection, do more harm than the former, which was about to produce belief in a false Messiah'); ὁ ἔσχατος Ἀδάμ, the latter Adam, i. e. the Messiah (see Ἀδάμ, 1), 1 Co. xv. 45. ἡ ἐσχ. ἡμέρα, the last day (of all days), denotes that with which the present age (הָעוֹלָם הַזֶּה, see αἰών, 3) which precedes the times of the Messiah or the glorious return of Christ from heaven will be closed: Jn. vi. 39 sq. 44, [54]; xi. 24; xii. 48. of the time nearest the return of Christ from heaven and the consummation of the divine kingdom, the foll. phrases are used: ἐσχάτη ὥρα, 1 Jn. ii. 18; ἐν καιρῷ ἐσχ. 1 Pet. i. 5; ἐν ἐσχ. χρόνῳ, Jude 18 Rec., ἐπ' ἐσχάτου χρόνου ibid. Tr WH; ἐν ἐσχάταις ἡμέραις, Acts ii. 17; Jas. v. 3; 2 Tim. iii. 1; for other phrases of the sort see 2 a. below; ἐπ' ἐσχάτων τῶν χρόνων, 1 Pet. i. 20 R G, see below. **2.** ὁ, ἡ, τὸ ἐσχ. absol. or with the genitive, **a.** of time: οἱ ἔσχατοι, who come to work last, Mt. xx. 8, 12, [14]; the meaning of the saying ἔσονται πρῶτοι ἔσχατοι καὶ ἔσχατοι πρῶτοι is not always the same: in Lk. xiii. 30 it signifies, those who were last invited to enter the divine kingdom will be first to enter when the opportunity comes, i. e. they will be admitted forthwith, while others, and those too who were first among the invited, will be shut out then as coming too late; in Mt. xix. 30; xx. 16 it means, the same portion in the future kingdom of God will through his goodness be assigned to those invited last as to those invited first, although the latter may think they deserve something better; cf. Mk. x. 31. ὁ πρῶτος κ. ὁ ἐσχ. i. e. the eternal, Rev. i. 11 Rec., 17; ii. 8; xxii. 13. ἔσχατος as a predicate joined to a verb adverbially [cf. W. 131 (124); § 54, 2]: Mk. xii. 6; ἐσχάτη (R G; but see below) πάντων ἀπέθανε, Mk. xii. 22. ἔσχατον, ἔσχατα, used substantively [cf. B. 94 (82) § 125, 6] in phrases, of the time immediately preceding Christ's return from heaven and the consummation of the divine kingdom: ἐπ' ἐσχάτου or ἐσχάτων τῶν ἡμερῶν, Heb. i. 2 (1); 2 Pet. iii. 3, (Barn. ep. 16, 5); τῶν χρόνων, 1 Pet. i. 20; ἐπ' ἐσχάτου τοῦ χρόνου, Jude 18 L T (see 1 above, and ἐπί, A. II. fin.), cf. Riehm, Lehrbegr. d. Hebräerbriefes, p. 205 sq. τὰ ἔσχατα with gen. of pers. the last state of one: Mt. xii. 45; Lk. xi. 26; 2 Pet. ii. 20 [but without gen. of pers.]. Neut. ἔσχατον, adv., lastly: [w. gen. of pers., Mk. xii. 22 L T Tr WH]; 1 Co. xv. 8. **b.** of space: τὸ ἔσχατον τῆς γῆς, the uttermost part, the end, of the earth, Acts i. 8; xiii. 47. **c.** of rank, grade of worth, *last* i. e. *lowest*: Mk. ix. 35; Jn. viii. 9 Rec.; 1 Co. iv. 9.*

2079 ἐσχάτως, adv., *extremely*, [Xen. an. 2, 6, 1; Aristot., al.]; ἐσχάτως ἔχειν (in extremis esse), *to be in the last gasp, at the point of death*: Mk. v. 23. Diod. excrpt. Vales. p. 242 [i. e. fr. l. 10 § 2, 4 Dind.]; Artem. oneir. 3, 60. The phrase is censured by the Atticists; cf. *Fischer*, De vitiis lexx. etc. p. 704 sq.; *Lob.* ad Phryn. p. 389; Fritzsche on Mk. p. 178 sq.; [Win. 26].*

2080 ἔσω, adv., (fr. ἐς, for εἴσω [fr. Hom. on] fr. εἰς; cf. W. 52; [B. 72 (63); *Rutherford*, New Phryn. p. 432]); **1.** *to within, into*: Mt. xxvi. 58; Mk. xiv. 54; with gen. Mk. xv. 16 [W. § 54, 6]. **2.** *within*: Jn. xx. 26; Acts v. 23; ὁ ἔσω ἄνθρωπος, the internal, inner man, i. e. the soul, conscience, (see ἄνθρωπος, 1 e.), 2 Co. iv. 16 L T Tr WH; Ro. vii. 22; Eph. iii. 16; οἱ ἔσω, those who belong to the Christian brotherhood (opp. to οἱ ἔξω [q. v. in ἔξω, 1 a.]), 1 Co. v. 12.*

2081 ἔσωθεν, (ἔσω), adv. of place, fr. Aeschyl. and Hdt. down; [1. adverbially;] **a.** *from within* (Vulg. *de intus, ab intus, intrinsecus*, [etc.]): Mk. vii. 21, 23; Lk. xi. 7; 2 Co. vii. 5. **b.** *within* (cf. W. § 54, 7): Mt. vii. 15; xxiii. 25, 27, 28; Rev. iv. 8; v. 1 [cf. γράφω, 3]; ὁ ἔσωθεν ἄνθρωπος, 2 Co. iv. 16 R G (see ἔσω, 2); τὸ ἔσωθεν, that which is within, the inside, Lk. xi. 40; with gen. of pers. i. q. *your soul*, ibid. 39. [2. as a prep. with the gen. (W § 54, 6): Rev. xi. 2 Rec.ˢᵗ (see ἔξωθεν, 2).]*

2082 ἐσώτερος, -έρα, -ερον, (compar. of ἔσω, [cf. B. 28 (24 sq.)]), *inner*: Acts xvi. 24; τὸ ἐσώτερον τοῦ καταπετάσματος, the inner space which is behind the veil, i. e. *the shrine, the Holy of holies*, said of heaven by a fig. drawn from the earthly temple, Heb. vi. 19.*

2083 ἑταῖρος, -ου, ὁ, [fr. Hom. down], Sept. רֵעַ; *a comrade, mate, partner*, [A. V. *fellow*]: Mt. xi. 16 (where T Tr WH τοῖς ἑτέροις [q. v. 1 b., and cf. *WH*. Intr. § 404]); voc. in kindly address, *friend* (*my good friend*): Mt. xx. 13; xxii. 12; xxvi. 50.*

2084 ἑτερό-γλωσσος, -ου, ὁ, (ἕτερος and γλῶσσα), *one who speaks* [another i. e.] *a foreign tongue* (opp. to ὁμόγλωσσος): Ps. cxiii. (cxiv.) 1 Aq.; Polyb. 24, 9, 5; Strab. 8 p. 333; [Philo, confus. lingg. § 3; al.]; but differently in 1 Co. xiv. 21, viz. one who speaks what is utterly strange and unintelligible to others unless interpreted; see what is said about 'speaking with tongues' under γλῶσσα, 2.*

2085 ἑτεροδιδασκαλέω, -ῶ; (ἕτερος and διδάσκαλος, cf. κακοδιδασκαλεῖν, Clem. Rom. 2 Cor. 10, 5); *to teach other or different doctrine* i. e. deviating from the truth : 1 Tim. i. 3; vi. 3. (Ignat. ad Polyc. 3, and al. eccl. writ.) *

2086 ἑτερο-ζυγέω, -ῶ; (ἑτερόζυγος yoked with a different yoke; used in Lev. xix. 19 of the union of beasts of different kinds, e. g. an ox and an ass), *to come under an unequal or different yoke* (Beza, *impari jugo copulor*), *to be unequally yoked*: τινί (on the dat. see W. § 31, 10 N. 4; B. § 133, 8), trop. *to have fellowship with one who is not an equal*: 2 Co. vi. 14, where the apostle is forbidding Christians to have intercourse with idolaters.*

2087 ἕτερος, -έρα, -ερον, *the other*; *another, other*; [fr. Hom. on]; Sept. chiefly for אַחֵר. It refers **1.** to **number**, as opp. to some former pers. or thing; **a.** without the article, *other*: joined to a noun (which noun denotes some number or class within which others are distinguished from the one), Mt. xii. 45 and Lk. xi. 26, ἑπτὰ ἕτερα πνεύματα, i. e. from the number of the πνεύματα or demons seven others, to be distinguished from the one already mentioned; add, Mk. xvi. 12; Lk. vi. 6; ix. 56, etc.; Jn. xix. 37; Acts ii. 40; iv. 12, etc.; Ro. vii. 3; viii. 39; xiii. 9; ἕτεραι γενεαί, *other* than the present, i. e. past generations, Eph. iii. 5; as in class. Grk. ἄλλος, so sometimes also ἕτερος is elegantly joined to a noun that is in apposition: twice so in Lk., viz. ἕτεροι δύο κακοῦργοι two others, who were malefactors [Bttm. differently § 150, 3], Lk. xxiii. 32; ἑτέρους ἑβδομήκοντα equiv. to ἑτέρους μαθητάς, οἵτινες ἦσαν ἑβδ. Lk. x. 1; *reliqua privata aedificia* for 'the rest of the buildings, which were private' Caes. b. g. 1, 5; cf. *Bornemann*, Scholia ad Luc. p. 147 sq.; W. 530 (493); [Joseph. c. Ap. 1, 15, 3 and Müller's note]. simply, without a noun, i. q. ἄλλος τις another, Lk. ix. 59; xxii. 58; Acts i. 20; Ro. vii. 4; ἕτεροι πολλοί, Mt. xv. 30; Lk. viii. 3; Acts xv. 35; οὐδὲν ἕτερον, Acts xvii. 21; ἕτερα, other matters, Acts xix. 39 R G T; πολλὰ καὶ ἕτερα, many other things also [hardly "also," see καί, I. 3; cf. remark s. v. πολύς, d. a. fin.], Lk. iii. 18; ἕτερος with gen. of pers. Gal. i. 19; τὰ ἑτέρων (opp. to τὰ ἑαυτοῦ), Phil. ii. 4; ἕτ. with τὶς added, Acts viii. 34; neut. 1 Tim. i. 10; [ἐν ἑτέρῳ, introducing a quotation, Heb. v. 6, cf. Win. 592 (551) — but in Acts xiii. 35 supply ψαλμῷ]. in partitive formulas: ἄλλοι . . . ἕτεροι δέ, Heb. xi. 36 cf. Acts ii. 13; ὁ πρῶτος . . . ἕτερος, Lk. xiv. 19 sq.; xvi. 7; ὁ δεύτερος . . . ἕτερος, Lk. xix. 20 (where L T Tr WH ὁ ἕτερος); τινὲς . . . ἕτεροι δέ, Lk. xi. 16; ᾧ μὲν . . . ἄλλῳ δὲ . . . ἑτέρῳ δὲ . . . ἄλλῳ δέ, 1 Co. xii. 9 sq.; οἱ μὲν . . . ἄλλοι [L οἱ] δὲ . . . ἕτεροι δέ, Mt. xvi. 14. **b.** with the article, *the other* (of two): οἱ ἕτεροι, the others, the other party, Mt. xi. 16 T Tr WH (see ἑταῖρος). distinctively: εἷς or ὁ εἷς . . . ὁ ἕτερος, Mt. vi. 24; Lk. vii. 41; xvi. 13; xvii. 34 sq.; xviii. 10; xxiii. 40; τὸ ἕτερον πλοῖον, Lk. v. 7; τῇ δὲ ἑτέρᾳ sc. ἡμέρᾳ, the next day, the day after, Acts xx. 15; xxvii. 3, (Xen. Cyr. 4, 6, 10, [al.]). ὁ ἕτερος, the other, when the relation of conduct to others is under consideration is often put by way of example for *any other person whatever*, and stands for 'the other affected by the action in question' [and may be trans. *thy neighbor, thy fellow*, etc.]: Ro. ii. 1; xiii. 8; 1 Co. vi. 1; x. 24, 29; xiv. 17; Gal. vi. 4; [Jas. iv. 12 R G]; plur. οἱ, αἱ, τὰ ἕτεροι, -αι, -α, the others i. e. the rest, Lk. iv. 43. It refers **2.** to **quality**; *another* i. e. *one not of the same nature, form, class, kind; different*, (so in Grk. writ. fr. Hom. down): Ro. vii. 23; 1 Co. xiv. 21; xv. 40; 2 Co. xi. 4; Gal. i. 6; Heb. vii. 11, 13, 15; Jas. ii. 25; Jude 7. [Syn. see ἄλλος.]

2088 ἑτέρως, adv., *otherwise, differently*: Phil. iii. 15. [From Hom. (apparently) down.] *

2089 ἔτι, adv., *as yet, yet, still*; **1.** of **time**; **a.** of a thing which went on *formerly*, whereas now a different state of things exists or has begun to exist: added to a ptcp., Mt. xxvii. 63; Lk. xxiv. 6, 44; Acts ix. 1; xviii. 18; 2 Th. ii. 5; with gen. absol.: ἔτι (δὲ) αὐτοῦ λαλοῦντος, Mt. xii. 46; xvii. 5; xxvi. 47; Mk. xiv. 43; Lk. viii. 49; xxii. 47; add, Lk. ix. 42; xxiv. 41; Jn. xx. 1; Acts x. 44; Ro. v. 8; Heb. ix. 8; with a finite verb, Heb. vii. 10; transposed so as to stand at the beginning of a sentence: ἔτι γὰρ Χριστὸς ὄντων ἡμῶν ἀσθ. . . . ἀπέθανε, Ro. v. 6; cf. W. § 61, 5 p. 553 (515); [B. 389 (333)]; with another notation of time, so that it may be trans. *even* (cf. Lat. *jam*): ἔτι ἐκ κοιλίας μητρός, Lk. i. 15 (ἔτι ἐκ βρέφεος, Anthol. 9, 567, 1; ἔτι ἀπ᾽ ἀρχῆς, Plut. consol. ad Apoll. 6 p. 104 d.). **b.** of a thing which continues at present, *even now*: Mk. viii. 17 R G; Lk. xiv. 22; Gal. i. 10; 1 Co. xv. 17; with νῦν added, 1 Co. iii. 2 [L WH br. ἔτι]; *further, longer*, (where it is thought strange that, when one thing has established itself, another has not been altered or abolished, but is still adhered to or continues): Ro. iii. 7; vi. 2; ix. 19; Gal. v. 11. **c.** with negatives: οὐ . . . ἔτι, οὐκ ἔτι, *no longer, no more*, Lk. xvi. 2; xx. 36; xxi. 1, 4; xxii. 3; ἵνα μὴ ἔτι *lest longer, that . . . no more*, Rev. xx. 3; οὐ μὴ ἔτι, Rev. iii. 12; xviii. 21–23; οὐδείς, μηδείς, -δεμία, -δὲν ἔτι, *nobody, nothing more*, Mt. v. 13; Heb. x. 2, (see μηκέτι, οὐκέτι). **2.** of degree and increase; with the comparative, *even, yet*: Phil. i. 9; Heb. vii. 15, (W. 240 (225)). of what remains, [*yet*]: Jn. iv. 35; vii. 33; xii. 35; xiii. 33; Mt. xix. 20; Mk. xii. 6; Lk. xviii. 22; of what is added, *besides, more, further*: ἔτι ἅπαξ, Heb. xii. 26 sq.; ἔτι ἕνα ἢ δύο, Mt. xviii. 16; add, Mt. xxvi. 65; Heb. xi. 32; ἔτι δέ *yea moreover, and further*, (Lat. *praeterea vero*), Heb. xi. 36 (Xen. mem. 1, 2, 1; Diod. 1, 74; cf. Grimm on 2 Macc. vi. 4); ἔτι δὲ καί (*but* or) *yea moreover also* (Lat. *praeterea vero etiam*), Lk. xiv. 26 R G T L mrg.; Acts ii. 26; ἔτι τε καί *and moreover too* (Lat. *insuperque adeo*), Lk. xiv. 26 L txt. Tr WH; Acts xxi. 28, [cf. B. § 149, 8; W. 578 (537) note].

2090   ἐτοιμάζω; fut. ἐτοιμάσω; 1 aor. ἡτοίμασα; pf. ἡτοίμακα (Mt. xxii. 4 L T Tr WH); Pass., pf. ἡτοίμασμαι; 1 aor. ἡτοιμάσθην; (ἔτοιμος); fr. Hom. down; Sept. very often for כּוּן and הֵכִין; *to make ready, prepare*: absol. *to make the necessary preparations, get everything ready*, Lk. xii. 47; of preparing a feast, Lk. xxii. 9, 12, (Gen. xliii. 15; 1 Chr. xii. 39); w. dat. of pers., for one: of preparing a lodging, Lk. ix. 52 [W. 594 (552); B. § 130, 5]; a supper, Mk. xiv. 15; also w. a telic inf. added, Mt. xxvi. 17; foll. by ἵνα [cf. B. 237 (205)], Mk. xiv. 12; w. acc. of the thing: ἃ ἡτοίμασας the things which thou hast prepared (as a store), Lk. xii. 20; [τί δειπνήσω, Lk. xvii. 8]; τὸ ἄριστον, Mt. xxii. 4; τὸ πάσχα, Mt. xxvi. 19; Mk. xiv. 16; Lk. xxii. 8, 13; ἀρώματα, Lk. xxiii. 56; xxiv. 1; τόπον τινί, Jn. xiv. 2 sq.; ξενίαν, Philem. 22; [συμβούλιον, Mk. xv. 1 T WH mrg., cf. συμβ.]; τὴν ὁδὸν κυρίου (by a fig. drawn from the oriental custom of sending on before kings on their journeys persons to level the roads and make them passable), to prepare the minds of men to give the Messiah a fit reception and secure his blessings: Mt. iii. 3; Mk. i. 3; Lk. iii. 4, (fr. Is. xl. 3); i. 76; [ἵνα ἐτοιμασθῇ ἡ ὁδὸς τῶν βασιλέων, Rev. xvi. 12]; w. acc. of pers.,

στρατιώτας, Acts xxiii. 23; τινί τινα, one for one, Lk. i. 17; ἑαυτόν, Rev. xix. 7; foll. by ἵνα [cf. B. 237 (205)], Rev. viii. 6; ἡτοιμασμένη ὡς νύμφη, i. e. beautifully adorned, Rev. xxi. 2; ἡτοιμασμ. εἴς τι, prepared i. e. fit for accomplishing any thing, 2 Tim. ii. 21; Rev. ix. 7; prepared i. e. kept in readiness, εἰς τὴν ὥραν κ. ἡμέραν etc., for the hour and day sc. predetermined, Rev. ix. 15. In a peculiar sense God is said ἐτοιμάσαι τι for men, i. e. to have caused good or ill to befall them, almost i. q. *to have ordained*; of blessings: τί, Lk. ii. 31; Rev. xii. 6; τινί τι, Mt. xx. 23; xxv. 34; Mk. x. 40; [1 Co. ii. 9]; Heb. xi. 16; of punishment: τινί τι, Mt. xxv. 41. [COMP.: προ-ετοιμάζω.] *

2091   ἐτοιμασία, -ας, ἡ, (ἐτοιμάζω, cf. θαυμασία, εἰκασία, ἐργασία); **1.** *the act of preparing*: τῆς τροφῆς, Sap. xiii. 12; τῶν κλιναρίων, Artem. oneir. 2, 57. **2.** i. q. ἐτοιμότης, *the condition of a pers. or thing so far forth as prepared, preparedness, readiness*: Hipp. p. 24 [i. 74 ed. Kühn]; Joseph. antt. 10, 1, 2; readiness of mind (Germ. *Bereitwilligkeit*), τῆς καρδίας, Ps. ix. 38 (x. 17): ἐν ἐτοιμασίᾳ τοῦ εὐαγγελίου, with the promptitude and alacrity which the gospel produces, Eph. vi. 15.*

2092   ἔτοιμος (on the accent cf. [Chandler § 394]; W. 52 (51)), -η (2 Co. ix. 5; 1 Pet. i. 5), -ον and -ος, -ον (Mt. xxv. 10 [cf. *WH.* App. p. 157ᵃ; W. § 11, 1; B. 25 (22)]); fr. Hom. down; *prepared, ready*; **a.** of things: Mt. xxii. 4, 8, [(Lk. xiv. 17)]; Mk. xiv. 15 [L br. ἔτ.]; 2 Co. ix. 5; *ready to hand*: τὰ ἔτοιμα, the things (made) ready (in advance by others), i. e. the Christian churches already founded by them, 2 Co. x. 16; i. q. *opportune, seasonable*, ὁ καιρός, Jn. vii. 6; σωτηρία ἑτοίμη ἀποκαλυφθῆναι, on the point of being revealed, 1 Pet. i. 5. **b.** of persons; *ready, prepared*: to do something, Acts xxiii. 21; to receive one coming, Mt. xxiv. 44; xxv. 10; Lk. xii. 40; πρός τι, for (the doing of) a thing, Tit. iii. 1; 1 Pet. iii. 15; foll. by the inf. [cf. B. 260 (224)], Lk. xxii. 33; by τοῦ with the inf. Acts xxiii. 15 [B. § 140, 15; W. § 44, 4 a.]; ἐν ἐτοίμῳ ἔχω, to be in readiness, foll. by the inf. (Philo, leg. ad Gai. § 34 sub fin.): 2 Co. x. 6 [cf. W. 332 (311)]. (For נָכוֹן, Ex. xix. 11, 15; Josh. viii. 4, etc.) *

2093   ἑτοίμως, adv., [fr. Thuc. on], *readily*; ἑτοίμως ἔχω *to be ready*: foll. by inf., Acts xxi. 13; 2 Co. xii. 14; 1 Pet. iv. 5 [(not WH)]. (Sept. Dan. iii. 15; Diod. 16, 28; Joseph. antt. 12, 4, 2; 13, 1, 1.) *

2094   ἔτος, -ους, [gen. plur. ἐτῶν, cf. B. 14 (13)], τό, [fr. Hom. down], Hebr. שָׁנָה, *a year*: Lk. iii. 1; Acts vii. 30; Heb. i. 12; 2 Pet. iii. 8; Rev. xx. 3, etc.; ἔτη ἔχειν, to have passed years, Jn. viii. 57; with ἐν ἀσθενείᾳ added, Jn. v. 5 [cf. W. § 32, 6]; εἶναι, γίνεσθαι, γεγονέναι ἐτῶν, e. g. δώδεκα, to be twelve years old [cf. Eng. (a boy) *of twelve years*]: Mk. v. 42; Lk. ii. 42; iii. 23 [cf. W. 349 (328)]; viii. 42; Acts iv. 22; γεγονυῖα ἐλάττον ἐτῶν ἑξήκοντα, less than sixty years old, 1 Tim. v. 9 [W. 590 (549)]; dat. plur., of the space of time within which a thing is done [W. § 31, 9 a.; B. § 133, 26], Jn. ii. 20; Acts xiii. 20; acc., in answer to the quest. *how long?*: Mt. ix. 20; Mk. v. 25; Lk. ii. 36; xiii. 7 sq. 11, 16; xv.

29; Acts vii. 6, 36, 42; Heb. iii. 10 (9), 17; Rev. xx. 2, 4, 6. preceded by a prep.: ἀπό, *from . . . on, since*, Lk. viii. 43; Ro. xv. 23; in the same sense ἐκ, Acts ix. 33; xxiv. 10 [A. V. *of many years*]; διά with gen., *. . . years having intervened*, i. e. *after* [see διά, II. 2]: Acts xxiv. 17; Gal. ii. 1; εἰς, *for . . . years*, Lk. xii. 19; ἐπί with acc. (see ἐπί, C. II. 1 p. 235ᵇ bot.), *for* (the space of), Acts xix. 10; μετά with acc., *after*, Gal. i. 18; iii. 17; πρό with gen., *before* [Eng. *ago*; cf. πρό, b.], 2 Co. xii. 2; κατ' ἔτος, *yearly*, Lk. ii. 41. [SYN. cf. ἐνιαυτός.]

2095 εὖ, adv., (prop. ἐΰ, the unused neut. of the adj. ἐΰς in Hom.), *well*: εὖ πράσσω, not as many interp. take it, contrary to ordinary Grk. usage, *to do well* i. e. *act rightly* (which in Greek is expressed by ὀρθῶς or καλῶς πράσσω), but *to be well off, fare well, prosper*, Acts xv. 29 [R. V. *it shall be well with you*] (Xen. mem. 1, 6, 8; 2, 4, 6; 4, 2, 26; oec. 11, 8; Joseph. antt. 12, 4, 1; ὅστις καλῶς πράττει, οὐχὶ καὶ εὖ πράττει; Plat. Alc. i. p. 116 b.; εἰ εὖ πράττουσι ἀδικοῦντες, Prot. p. 333 d.; εἴ τις ἄλλος εὖ μὲν ἐποίησεν ὑμᾶς εὖ πράττων, Dem. 469, 14; and some began their letters with εὖ πράττειν, cf. 2 Macc. ix. 19; Diog. Laërt. 3, 61 and Menagius (Ménage) in loc. In one passage alone, Xen. mem. 3, 9, 14, the drift of the discussion permits Socrates to deviate from common usage by attaching to the phrase the notion of right conduct, *acting well*; [yet this sense occurs in eccles. Grk., see e. g. Justin M. apol. 1, 28 and Otto's note; cf. L. and S. s. v. πράσσω, IV.]); ἵνα εὖ σοι γένηται· that it may be well, things may turn out well, with thee, Eph. vi. 3 (Gen. xii. 13; [Ex. xx. 12]; Deut. iv. 40; [v. 16]; Orat. Az. [i. e. Song of the Three Children] vs. 6); εὖ ποιεῖν τινα, to do one good, Mk. xiv. 7 [here Tom. the acc.; L Tr WH read dat.], (Judith x. 16); Bar. vi. (i. e. Ep. Jer.) 37 (38); Sir. xiv. 11; Xen. Cyr. 1, 6, 30). In commendations, εὖ (δοῦλε ἀγαθέ), *well! well done!* Mt. xxv. 21, 23; Lk. xix. 17 R G; Xen. venat. 6, 20; see εὖγε.*

2096 Εὖα [WH Εὕα (see their Introd. § 408); Rec. Εὔα, so G Tr in 1 Tim. ii. 13, where Rˢᵗ Εὖα], -ας [B. 17 (15)], ἡ, (חַוָּה, explained Gen. iii. 20), *Eve*, the wife of Adam: 2 Co. xi. 3; 1 Tim. ii. 13.*

2097 εὐαγγελίζω: 1 aor. εὐηγγέλισα (Rev. x. 7; xiv. 6; 1 S. xxxi. 9; 2 S. xviii. 19; W. 71 (69); [B. 35 (30)]); Pass., pres. εὐαγγελίζομαι; pf. ptcp. εὐηγγελισμένοι (Heb. iv. 2); 1 aor. εὐηγγελίσθην; Mid., pres. εὐαγγελίζομαι; impf. εὐηγγελιζόμην (Acts viii. 25 L T Tr WH); 1 aor. εὐηγγελισάμην; (εὐάγγελος bringing good news); Sept. for בִּשֵּׂר; *to bring good news, to announce glad tidings*; Vulg. *evangelizo* [etc.]; used in the O. T. of any kind of good news: 1 S. xxxi. 9; 2 S. i. 20; 1 Chr. x. 9; of the joyful tidings of God's kindnesses, Ps. xxxix. (xl.) 10; τὸ σωτήριον θεοῦ, Ps. xcv. (xcvi.) 2; in particular, of the Messianic blessings: Is. xl. 9; lii. 7; lx. 6; lxi. 1, etc.; in the N. T. used esp. of the glad tidings of the coming kingdom of God, and of the salvation to be obtained in it through Christ, and of what relates to this salvation.

I. In the Active (rare in Grk. auth. also, in fact found only in later Grk., as Polyaen. 5, 7; εὐηγγελίκει αὐτῷ,

Dio Cass. 61, 13; cf. Lob. ad Phryn. p. 268; [W. 24]): w. dat. of the pers. to whom the news is brought, Rev. x. 7 Rec.; w. acc. of the pers. to whom the announcement is made, ibid. G L T Tr WH, Rev. xiv. 6 R G; by a construction not found elsewhere, ἐπί τινα (cf. Germ. *die Botschaft an einen bringen*), ibid. G L T Tr WH. **II.** Passive [cf. W. 229 (215); B. 188 (163)]; of persons, *glad tidings are brought to one, one has glad tidings proclaimed to him*: Mt. xi. 5; Lk. vii. 22; Heb. iv. 2, 6; of things, *to be proclaimed*: εὐαγγελίζεται ἡ βασιλεία τοῦ θεοῦ, the glad tidings are published of the kingdom of God close at hand, Lk. xvi. 16; τὸ εὐαγγέλιον, the joyful announcement of man's salvation is delivered, Gal. i. 11 [B. 148 (129 sq.)]; τὸ ῥῆμα τὸ εὐαγγελισθὲν εἰς ὑμᾶς, the word of good tidings brought unto you (see εἰς, A. I. 5 b. [cf. W. 213 (200)]), 1 Pet. i. 25; impers. εὐηγγελίσθη τινί, the good news of salvation was declared, 1 Pet. iv. 6. **III.** as deponent Middle (in Grk. writ. fr. Arstph. eqq. 643 down), *to proclaim glad tidings*; spec. *to instruct* (men) *concerning the things that pertain to Christian salvation*: simply, Lk. ix. 6; xx. 1; Acts xiv. 7; Ro. xv. 20; 1 Co. i. 17; ix. 16, 18; τίνι λόγῳ εὐηγγελισάμην ὑμῖν εἰ κατέχετε, if ye hold fast in your minds with what word (i. e. with what interpretation; for he contrasts his own view of Christian salvation with his opponents' doctrine of the resurrection) I preached to you the glad tidings of salvation, 1 Co. xv. 2. w. dat. of pers. (as com. in Grk. writ.), to any one: Lk. iv. 18 fr. Is. lxi. 1; spec. to bring to one the good tidings concerning Jesus as the Messiah: Gal. i. 8; iv. 13; Ro. i. 15; εὐαγγ. w. acc. of the thing: univ., τὴν πίστιν τινός, to bring good tidings of the faith in which one excels, 1 Th. iii. 6; of Messianic blessings: εἰρήνην, Acts x. 36; Ro. x. 15 [R G Tr mrg. br.] (fr. Is. lii. 7); τὴν βασιλείαν τ. θεοῦ, Lk. viii. 1; τὰ περὶ τῆς βασ. τ. θεοῦ, Acts viii. 12 (where G L T Tr WH om. τά; cf. Joseph. antt. 15, 7, 2 ὁ μὲν . . . τῇ γυναικὶ περὶ τούτων εὐηγγελίζετο); τὴν πίστιν, the necessity of having faith in Christ, Gal. i. 23. τί τινι [B. 150 (131)], Lk. i. 19; ii. 10; Acts xvii. 18 [T Tr WH om. dat.]; Eph. ii. 17; τινί τ. βασ. τοῦ θεοῦ, Lk. iv. 43; εὐαγγ. Ἰησοῦν τὸν Χριστόν or (so L T Tr WH) τὸν Χριστὸν Ἰησοῦν, to proclaim the glad news of Jesus the Christ, Acts v. 42, and (which comes to the same thing) τὸν κύριον Ἰησοῦν, Acts xi. 20; τὸν υἱὸν τοῦ θεοῦ ἐν τοῖς ἔθνεσι, among the Gentiles, Gal. i. 16; τὸν Ἰησοῦν τινι, Acts viii. 35; with καὶ τὴν ἀνάστασίν τινι added, Acts xvii. 18 (where T Tr WH om. αὐτοῖς); τὸν λόγον, to announce the glad tidings of the Messiah, or of the kingdom of God, or of eternal salvation offered through Christ, Acts viii. 4; τὸν λόγον τοῦ κυρίου, Acts xv. 35; τὸ εὐαγγέλιον, 1 Co. xv. 1; w. dat. of the pers. added to whom it is preached, 2 Co. xi. 7; τὸν πλοῦτον [τὸ πλοῦτος] τοῦ Χριστοῦ ἐν τοῖς ἔθνεσι, among the Gentiles [but L Tr WH om. ἐν], Eph. iii. 8. By a constr. unknown to the earlier Grks. (cf. Lob. ad Phryn. p. 268), with acc. of the pers. to whom the announcement is made [W. 223 (209)]: Lk. iii. 18; Acts xvi. 10; Gal. i. 9 (where it is interchanged with εὐαγγ. τινι vs. 8); 1 Pet.

i. 12, (Justin M. apol. 1, 33); τινά τι, acc. of the thing (Alciphr. epp. 3, 12; Heliod. 2, 10; Euseb. h. e. 3, 4; [cf. W. 227 (213); B. 150 (131)]), foll. by ὅτι etc. Acts xiii. 32; τινά foll. by inf. Acts xiv. 15; τὰς κώμας, τὰς πόλεις, Acts viii. 25, 40; xiv. 21; [εἰς τὰ ὑπερέκεινα, 2 Co. x. 16 (cf. W. 213 (200), and II. above). Comp.: προ-ευαγγελίζομαι.] *

2098 εὐαγγέλιον, -ου, τό, (εὐάγγελος [cf. εὐαγγελίζω]), Hebr. בְּשׂוֹרָה and בְּשׂרָה; **1.** a reward for good tidings (cf. τὰ διδασκάλια, the fees given the διδάσκαλος), Hom. Od. 14, 152; Cic. ad Att. 2, 3 and 12; 13, 40; Plut. Demetr. 17; Ages. 33; Sept. 2 S. iv. 10. **2.** good tidings: Lcian. asin. 26; App. b. civ. 4, 20; Plut.; al.; plur. Sept. 2 S. xviii. 22, 25, com. txt.; but in each place εὐαγγελία should apparently be restored, on account of vs. 20 ἀνὴρ εὐαγγελίας. In the N. T. spec. **a.** the glad tidings of the kingdom of God soon to be set up, and subsequently also of Jesus, the Messiah, the founder of this kingdom: Mk. i. 15; viii. 35; x. 29; xiii. 10; xiv. 9; xvi. 15; Mt. xxvi. 13; w. a gen. of the obj. added: τῆς βασιλείας, Mt. iv. 23; ix. 35; xxiv. 14; Mk. i. 14 R L br. After the death of Christ the term τὸ εὐαγγέλιον comprises also the preaching of (concerning) Jesus Christ as having suffered death on the cross to procure eternal salvation for men in the kingdom of God, but as restored to life and exalted to the right hand of God in heaven, thence to return in majesty to consummate the kingdom of God; so that it may be more briefly defined as the glad tidings of salvation through Christ; the proclamation of the grace of God manifested and pledged in Christ; the gospel [A-S. god-spell (see Skeat, Etym. Dict. s. v.)]: Acts xv. 7; Ro. i. 16 G L T Tr WH; x. 16; xi. 28; 1 Co. iv. 15; ix. 14, 18 [G L T Tr WH], 23; xv. 1; 2 Co. viii. 18; Gal. ii. 2; Eph. iii. 6; vi. 19 [L WH br. εὐαγ.]; Phil. i. 5, 7, 12, 17 (16); [ii. 22, cf. εἰς, B. II. 2 d.]; iv. 3, [15, cf. Clem. Rom. 1 Cor. 47, 2]; 1 Th. ii. 4; 2 Tim. i. 8, 10; w. gen. of the obj., the gospel concerning etc.: τοῦ Χριστοῦ [cf. W. 186 (175) sq.], Ro. i. 16 Rec.; xv. 19, 29 Rec.; 1 Co. ix. 12, 18 [Rec.]; 2 Co. ii. 12; ix. 13; x. 14; Gal. i. 7; Phil. i. 27; 1 Th. iii. 2; τοῦ κυρίου ἡμῶν Ἰησ. Χρ. 2 Th. i. 8 [T Tr WH om. L br. Χριστοῦ]; τοῦ υἱοῦ τοῦ θεοῦ, Ro. i. 9 cf. Mk. i. 1; τῆς σωτηρίας ὑμῶν, Eph. i. 13; τῆς εἰρήνης, Eph. vi. 15; τῆς χάριτος τοῦ θεοῦ, Acts xx. 24; τῆς δόξης τοῦ μακαρίου θεοῦ, 1 Tim. i. 11; τῆς δόξης τοῦ Χριστοῦ, 2 Co. iv. 4. ἡ ἀλήθεια τοῦ εὐαγγελίου, the truth contained in the gospel [cf. W. 236 (221 sq.)], Gal. ii. 5, 14; Col. i. 5; ἡ ἐλπὶς τοῦ εὐαγ. the hope which the gospel awakens and strengthens, Col. i. 23; ἡ πίστις τοῦ εὐαγγ. the faith given the gospel, Phil. i. 27; οἱ δεσμοὶ τ. εὐαγγ. (see δεσμός, fin.), Philem. 13; ἕτερον εὐαγγ. of another sort, i. e. different from the true doctrine concerning Christian salvation, Gal. i. 6; 2 Co. xi. 4; αἰώνιον εὐαγγ. the contents of which were decreed by God from eternity, Rev. xiv. 6.   with gen. of the author; and that   **a.** of the author of the subject-matter or facts on which the glad tidings of man's salvation rest, and who wished these glad tidings to be conveyed to men: τὸ εὐαγγ. τοῦ θεοῦ, Ro. xv. 16; 2 Co. xi. 7; 1 Th.

ii. 2, 8 sq.; 1 Pet. iv. 17; more fully τοῦ θεοῦ περὶ τοῦ υἱοῦ αὐτοῦ, Ro. i. 1–3.   **β.** of the author of the particular mode in which the subject-matter of the gospel is understood (conception of the gospel) and taught to others; thus Paul calls his exposition of the gospel (and that of the teachers who agree with him), in opposition to that of those teaching differently, τὸ εὐαγγ. ἡμῶν: 2 Co. iv. 3, [cf. τὸ εὐ. τὸ εὐαγγελισθὲν ὑπ᾽ ἐμοῦ, Gal. i. 11]; κατὰ τὸ εὐαγγ. μου, as I expound it, Ro. ii. 16; xvi. 25; 2 Tim. ii. 8.   **γ.** of him who preaches the gospel: ἡμῶν, 1 Th. i. 5; 2 Th. ii. 14.   with gen. of those to whom it is announced: τῆς περιτομῆς (i. e. τῶν περιτετμημένων), to be preached to the circumcised or Jews; and τὸ εὐ. τῆς ἀκροβυστίας, to be carried to the Gentiles, Gal. ii. 7.   **b.** As the Messianic rank of Jesus was proved by his words, his deeds, and his death, the narrative of the sayings, deeds, and death of Jesus Christ came to be called εὐαγγέλιον: so perhaps in Mk. i. 1; for the passage may also mean, 'glad tidings concerning Jesus Christ began to be proclaimed even as it is written,' viz. by John the Baptist; cf. De Wette ad loc. At length the name was given to a written narrative of the glad tidings; so in the titles of the Gospels, on which see κατά, II. 3 c. a. [On the eccl. senses of the word, see Soph. Lex. s. v.] *

εὐαγγελιστής, -οῦ, ὁ, (εὐαγγελίζω), a bibl. and eccl. word, **2099** a bringer of good tidings, an evangelist (Vulg. evangelista). This name is given in the N. T. to those heralds of salvation through Christ who are not apostles: Acts xxi. 8; Eph. iv. 11; 2 Tim. iv. 5. [B. D. s. v. Evangelist.]*

εὐαρεστέω, -ῶ: 1 aor. inf. εὐαρεστῆσαι; pf. inf. εὐηρε- **2100** στηκέναι, and without augm. εὐαρεστηκ. Heb. xi. 5 L WH [cf. WH. App. p. 162; B. 35 (30)]; to be well-pleasing: τῷ θεῷ (Sept. for הִתְהַלֵּךְ אֶת־הָאֱלֹהִים, Gen. v. 22, 24; vi. 9), Heb. xi. 5 sq. (Sir. xliv. 16; Philo de Abr. § 6; de exsecr. § 9; τινί, Diod. 14, 4). Pass. pres. εὐαρε- στοῦμαι; τινί [B. 188 (163); W. § 39, 1 a.], to be well pleased with a thing: Heb. xiii. 16 (Diod. 3, 55; 20, 79; Diog. Laërt. 10, 137).*

εὐ-άρεστος, -ον, (fr. εὖ and ἀρεστός), well-pleasing, ac- **2101** ceptable: Ro. xii. 2; τινί, to one, Ro. xii. 1; xiv. 18; 2 Co. v. 9; Eph. v. 10; Phil. iv. 18; ἔν τινι, in anything, Tit. ii. 9; ἐν κυρίῳ (see ἐν I. 6 b., p. 211ᵇ mid.), Col. iii. 20 (Rom. ἐν); ἐνώπιον with gen. of pers., in one's judgment: Heb. xiii. 21. (Sap. iv. 10; ix. 10; Clem. Al. [strom. 2, 19 p. 481, 21 etc.; Just. M. apol. 1, 44 sub fin.; Clem. Rom. 1 Cor. 49, 5].) See the foll. word.*

εὐ-αρέστως, adv., in a manner well-pleasing to one, ac- **2102** ceptably: τῷ θεῷ, Heb. xii. 28. (Xen. mem. 3, 5, 5; gladly, willingly, Epict. diss. 1, 12, 21; frag. 11.) *

Εὔβουλος, -ου, ὁ, [lit. of good counsel], Eubulus, a **2103** Christian: 2 Tim. iv. 21.*

εὖ-γε, used in commendation, well done! Lk. xix. 17 L T   **see 2095** Tr WH. (Arstph., Plat., al.; Sept. for הֶאָח.) Cf. εὖ, fin.*

εὐγενής, -ές, (fr. εὖ and γένος); **1.** well-born, of noble **2104** race: Lk. xix. 12 (of a prince); 1 Co. i. 26. **2.** noble-minded: compar. εὐγενέστερος, Acts xvii. 11. (Sept.; often in Grk. writ. fr. Arstph. and Tragg. down.)*

2105   εὐδία, -ας, ἡ, (fr. εὔδιος, -ον, and this fr. εὖ and Ζεύς, gen. Διός, Zeus, the ruler of the air and sky), *a serene sky, fair weather*: Mt. xvi. 2 [T br. WH reject the passage]. (Sir. iii. 15; Pind., Aeschyl., Hippocr., Xen., and sqq.) *

2106   εὐ-δοκέω, -ῶ; impf. 1 pers. plur. εὐδοκοῦμεν (1 Th. ii. 8 [where WH after cod. Vat. ηὐδοκ.; W. and B. as below]); 1 aor. εὐδόκησα and (in Heb. x. 6, 8, L T Tr; 1 Co. x. 5 L Tr WH; Ro. xv. 26, 27 and 1 Th. iii. 1 T Tr WH; Mt. xii. 18 T Tr; Mt. iii. 17 T; Col. i. 19 L mrg.) ηὐδόκησα, cf. Lob. ad Phryn. p. 456 and 140; W. 71 (69); [B. 34 (30); Tdf. Proleg. p. 120; WH. App. p. 162]; (fr. εὖ and δοκέω, cf. Fritzsche on Rom. ii. p. 370, who treats of the word fully and with his usual learning [cf. W. 101 (95)]); Sept. mostly for רָצָה; among Grk. writ. used esp. by Polyb., Diod., and Dion. Hal.;   **1.** as in prof. auth., foll. by an infin., *it seems good to one, is one's good pleasure; to think it good, choose, determine, decide*: Lk. xii. 32; 1 Co. i. 21; Gal. i. 15; once foll. by acc. w. inf., Col. i. 19 [cf. Bp. Lghtft.; W. § 64, 3 b.; B. § 129, 16]; with the included idea of kindness accompanying the decision, Ro. xv. 26 sq.; *to do willingly* what is signified by the inf., *to be ready to*, 1 Th. ii. 8; *to prefer, choose rather*, [A. V. *we thought it good*], 1 Th. iii. 1; Sir. xxv. 16; more fully μᾶλλον εὐδοκῶ, 2 Co. v. 8.   **2.** by a usage peculiar to bibl. writ., foll. by ἔν τινι, *to be well pleased with, take pleasure in*, a pers. or thing [cf. W. 38, 232 (218); B. 185 (160)]: Mt. iii. 17; xii. 18 Tr; xvii. 5; Mk. i. 11; Lk. iii. 22, [on the tense in the preceding pass. cf. W. 278 (261); B. 198 (171)]; 1 Co. x. 5; 2 Co. xii. 10; 2 Th. ii. 12 R G L br.; Heb. x. 38, (חָפֵץ בְּ, 2 S. xxii. 20; Mal. ii. 17; רָצָה בְּ, Ps. cxlix. 4). foll. by εἰς τινα (i. e. when directing the mind, turning the thoughts, *unto*), *to be favorably inclined towards one* [cf. W. § 31, 5; B. § 133, 23]: Mt. xii. 18 R G; 2 Pet. i. 17; w. simple acc. of pers. to be favorable to, take pleasure in [cf. W. 222 (209)]: Mt. xii. 18 L T WH; with acc. of the thing: Heb. x. 6, 8, (Ps. l. (li.) 18, 21; lxxxiv. (lxxxv.) 2; Gen. xxxiii. 10; Lev. xxvi. 34, 41); as in Grk. writ. also, w. the dat. of the pers. or thing with which one is well pleased: 2 Th. ii. 12 T Tr WH (see above); 1 Macc. i. 43; 1 Esdr. iv. 39. [COMP.: συν-ευδοκέω.] *

2107   εὐδοκία, -ας, ἡ, (fr. εὐδοκέω, as εὐλογία fr. εὐλογέω), unknown to prof. auth. [*Boeckh*, Inscrr. 5960], found in the O. T. in some of the Pss. (for רָצוֹן) and often in Sir.; on it cf. Fritzsche on Rom. ii. p. 371 sq.; [esp. Bp. Lghtft. on Phil. i. 15]; prop. *beneplacitum* (Vulg. [ed. Clement.] Eph. i. 9);   **1.** *will, choice*: Mt. xi. 26; Lk. x. 21, (on both pass. see ἔμπροσθεν, 2 b.); Sir. i. 27 (24); xxxvi. 13, etc.; in particular, *good-will, kindly intent, benevolence*: Eph. i. 5, 9; Phil. ii. 13, (Ps. l. (li.) 20; Sir. ii. 16; xi. 17 (15) etc.); δι' εὐδοκίαν, prompted by good will, Phil. i. 15.   **2.** *delight, pleasure, satisfaction*: with gen. of the thing that pleases, Th. i. 11; ἐν ἀνθρώποις εὐδοκία, either *among men pleasure produced by salvation*, or *God's pleasure in men*, Lk. ii. 14 R G Tr mrg. WH mrg.; ἄνθρωποι εὐδοκίας, men in whom God is well pleased [i. e. not a particular class of men (viz. believ-

ers], but the **whole race**, contemplated as blessed in Christ's birth], ibid. L T Tr txt. WH txt. [see WH. App. ad loc.; *Field*, Otium Norv. iii. ad loc.], (Ps. cxliv. (cxlv.) 16; Sir. ix. 12).   **3.** *desire* (for delight in any absent thing easily begets a longing for it): Ro. x. 1; cf. Philippi and Tholuck ad loc.*

2108   εὐεργεσία, -ας, ἡ, (εὐεργέτης); *a good deed, benefit*: 1 Tim. vi. 2 (on which see ἀντιλαμβάνω, 2); with gen. of the pers. on whom the benefit is conferred [W. 185 (174)], Acts iv. 9. (2 Macc. vi. 13; ix. 26; Sap. xvi. 11, 24; in Grk. auth. fr. Hom. down.) *

2109   εὐεργετέω, -ῶ; (εὐεργέτης), *to do good, bestow benefits*: Acts x. 38. (Sept.; often in Attic writ.) *

2110   εὐεργέτης, -ου, ὁ, *a benefactor* (fr. Pind. and Hdt. down); it was also a title of honor, conferred on such as had done their country service, and upon princes; equiv. to *Soter, Pater Patriae*: Lk. xxii. 25. (Cf. Hdt. 8, 85; Thuc. 1, 129; Xen. vect. 3, 11; Hell. 6, 1, 4; Plat. de virt. p. 379 b.; al.; cf. 2 Macc. iv. 2; joined with σωτήρ, Joseph. b. j. 3, 9, 8; Addit. to Esth. vi. 12 [Tdf. viii. l. 25]; Diod. 11, 26.) *

2111   εὔ-θετος, -ον, (fr. εὖ and θετός), Grk. writ. fr. Aeschyl. and Hippocr. down; prop. *well-placed*;   **a.** *fit*: εἴς τι, Lk. ix. 62 R G; xiv. 35 (34), (Diod. 2, 57 et al.); with dat. of the thing *for* which: Lk. ix. 62 L T Tr WH (τῷ πράγματι, Nicol. Stob. fl. 14, 7 [149, 4]).   **b.** *useful*: τινί, Heb. vi. 7 [some would make the dat. here depend on the ptcp.]; (of time, *seasonable*, Ps. xxxi. (xxxii.) 6; Susan. 15).*

2112   εὐθέως, adv., (fr. εὐθύς), *straightway, immediately, forthwith*: Mt. iv. 20, 22; viii. 3, and often in the histor. bks., esp. Mark's Gospel [where, however, T Tr WH have substituted εὐθύς in some 35 out of 41 cases]; elsewhere only in Gal. i. 16; Jas. i. 24; Rev. iv. 2, (for פִּתְאֹם, Job v. 3). *shortly, soon*: 3 Jn. 14. [From Soph. down.]

2113   εὐθυδρομέω, -ῶ: 1 aor. εὐθυδρόμησα [see εὐδοκέω]; (εὐθυδρόμος, i. e. εὐθύς and δρόμος); *to make a straight course, run a straight course*: foll. by εἰς w. acc. of place, Acts xvi. 11; εὐθυδρομήσας ἦλθον εἰς, Acts xxi. 1. (Philo, alleg. legg. iii. § 79; de agricult. § 40.) *

2114   εὐθυμέω, -ῶ; (εὔθυμος);   **1.** trans. *to put in good spirits, gladden, make cheerful*, (Aeschyl. in Plat. de rep. 2, 383 b.). Mid. *to be of good spirits, to be cheerful*, (Xen., Plat.).   **2.** intrans. *to be joyful, be of good cheer, of good courage*: Acts xxvii. 22, 25; Jas. v. 13. (Eur. Cycl. 530; Plut. de tranquill. anim. 2 and 9.) *

2115   εὔ-θυμος, -ον, (εὖ and θυμός);   **1.** *well-disposed, kind*, (Hom. Od. 14, 63).   **2.** *of good cheer, of good courage*: Acts xxvii. 36; [compar. as adv. xxiv. 10 Rec. (see εὐθύμως)], (Grk. writ. fr. Aeschyl. and Pind. down; 2 Macc. xi. 26).*

see 2115   εὐθύμως, adv., [Aeschyl., Xen., al.], *cheerfully*: Acts xxiv. 10 L T Tr WH, for Rec. εὐθυμότερον the more confidently.*

2116   εὐθύνω; 1 aor. impv. 2 pers. plur. εὐθύνατε; (εὐθύς);   **a.** *to make straight, level, plain*: τὴν ὁδόν, Jn. i. 23 (Sir. ii. 6; xxxvii. 15).   **b.** *to lead* or *guide straight, to keep straight, to direct*, (often so in Grk. writ.): ὁ εὐθύνων, the steersman, helmsman of a ship, Jas. iii. 4. (Eur. Cycl.

15; of a charioteer, Num. xxii. 23; Isocr. p. 9; al.)
[COMP.: κατ-ευθύνω.] *

2117   **εὐθύς, -εῖα, -ύ**, Sept. for יָשָׁר, [fr. Pind. down], *straight*;
a. prop. *straight, level*: of a way, [Mt. iii. 3]; Mk. i. 3;
Lk. iii. 4; Acts ix. 11; εἰς εὐθεῖαν (L T Tr WH εἰς εὐθείας),
sc. ὁδόν (an ellipsis com. also in class. Grk. cf. W. § 64,
5), Lk. iii. 5; εὐθεῖα ὁδός *the straight, the right way*, is fig.
used of true religion as a rule of life leading to its goal
i. e. to salvation, 2 Pet. ii. 15; αἱ ὁδοὶ κυρίου, the right
and saving purposes of God, Acts xiii. 10 (Song of the
Three vs. 3). **b.** trop. *straightforward, upright, true,
sincere*, (as often in prof. auth.): καρδία, Acts viii. 21
(εὐθεῖς τῇ καρδίᾳ often in the Pss., as vii. 11; xxxi.
(xxxii.) 11; xxxv. (xxxvi.) 11).*

see 2112   **εὐθύς**, adv., [fr. Pind. down], i. q. εὐθέως, with which it
is often interchanged in the Mss. [see εὐθέως]; *straight-
way, immediately, forthwith*: Mt. iii. 16; xiii. 20; Jn.
xiii. 32, etc. [Cf. Phryn. ed. *Lob.* p. 145.]

2118   **εὐθύτης, -ητος, ἡ**, (fr. the adj. εὐθύς), *rectitude, uprightness*: trop. ῥάβδος εὐθύτητος, an impartial and righteous
government, Heb. i. 8 fr. Ps. xliv. (xlv.) 7.*

2119   **εὐκαιρέω, -ῶ**: impf. εὐκαίρουν [so L T Tr WH in Mk.
vi. 31; R G in Acts xvii. 21] and ηὐκαίρουν [R G in
Mk. l. c.; L T Tr WH in Acts l. c.], (betw. which the
Mss. vary, see εὐδοκέω, init.); 1 aor. subjunc. εὐκαιρήσω;
(εὔκαιρος); a later word, fr. Polyb. onwards (cf. *Lob.*
ad Phryn. p. 125 sq.; [*Rutherford, New Phryn.* p. 205;
Soph. Lex. s. v.]); *to have opportunity*: 1 Co. xvi. 12; *to
have leisure*, foll. by an inf., *to do something*, Mk. vi. 31
[(Plut. ii. p. 223 d. Cleom. Anax. § 9)]; *to give one's
time to a thing*, εἴς τι, Acts xvii. 21.*

2120   **εὐκαιρία, -ας, ἡ**, (εὔκαιρος), *seasonable time, opportunity*:
ζητεῖν εὐκ., foll. by [ἵνα B. 237 (205)], Mt. xxvi. 16;
[Lk. xxii. 6 Lchm. mrg.]; by τοῦ with inf. Lk. xxii. 6.
(Sept.; in Grk. writ. first in Plat. Phaedr. p. 272 a.) *

2121   **εὔ-καιρος, -ον**, (εὖ and καιρός), *seasonable, timely, oppor-
tune*: βοήθεια, Heb. iv. 16; ἡμέρα εὐκ. a convenient day,
Mk. vi. 21. (2 Macc. xiv. 29; [Ps. ciii. (civ.) 27; Soph.
O. C. 32]; Theophr., Polyb., al.) *

2122   **εὐκαίρως**, adv., *seasonably, opportunely*; *when the opportunity occurs*: Mk. xiv. 11; opp. to ἀκαίρως (q. v.),
2 Tim. iv. 2. (Xen. Ages. 8, 3; Plat. and sqq.; Sir.
xviii. 22.) *

see   **εὔ-κοπος, -ον**, (εὖ and κόπος), *that can be done with
2123 St.   easy labor*; *easy*: Polyb. et al.; Sir. xxii. 15; 1 Macc.
iii. 18; in the N. T. only in the phrase εὐκοπώτερόν ἐστι,
—foll. by inf., Mt. ix. 5; Mk. ii. 9; Lk. v. 23; by acc. w.
inf., Mt. xix. 24; Mk. x. 25; Lk. xvi. 17; xviii. 25.*

2124   **εὐλάβεια, -είας, ἡ**, *the character and conduct of one who
is εὐλαβής* (q. v.); **1.** *caution, circumspection, discretion*: Soph., Eur., Plat., Dem., sqq.; Sept. Prov.
xxviii. 14; joined w. πρόνοια, Plut. Marcell. 9; used of
the prudent delay of Fabius Maximus, Polyb. 3, 105, 8;
ἡ εὐλ. σώζει πάντα, Arstph. av. 377; i. q. *avoidance,
πληγῶν*, Plat. legg. 7 p. 815 a. et al. (in which sense Zeno
the Stoic contrasts ἡ εὐλάβ. *caution*, as ἡ εὔλογος ἔκκλισις
a reasonable shunning, with ὁ φόβος, Diog. Laërt. 7, 116,
cf. Cic. Tusc. 4, 6, 13). **2.** *reverence, veneration*: ἡ

πρὸς τὸ θεῖον εὐλ. Diod. 13, 12; Plut. Camill. 21; de ser.
num. vind. c. 4, and elsewh.; πρὸς τοὺς νόμους, Plut. Ages.
15; θεοῦ, objec. gen., Philo, Cherub. § 9; simply *reverence
towards God, godly fear, piety*: Heb. xii. 28 and, in the
opinion of many, also v. 7 [cf. ἀπό, II. 2 b.; see below].
3. *fear, anxiety, dread*: Sap. xvii. 8; for דְּאָגָה, Josh.
xxii. 24; Joseph. antt. 11, 6, 9; Plut. Fab. 1 (the εὐβουλία
of Fabius seemed to be εὐλάβεια); so, most probably, in
Heb. v. 7 (see [above] and ἀπό, I. 3 d.), for by using
this more select word the writer, skilled as he was in the
Greek tongue, speaks more reverently of the Son of
God than if he had used φόβος. [SYN. see δειλία, fin.;
cf. Trench § xlviii.; Delitzsch on Heb. v. 7.] *

2125   **εὐλαβέομαι, -οῦμαι**: 1 aor. ptcp. εὐλαβηθείς; prop. *to
show one's self* εὐλαβής, i. e. **1.** *to act cautiously, circumspectly*, (Tragg., Xen., Plato, and sqq.). **2.** *to beware, fear*: as in 1 Macc. iii. 30; xii. 40 [Alex. etc.] and
often in prof. auth., foll. by μή lest [B. 241 sq. (208)],
Acts xxiii. 10 R G (Deut. ii. 4; 1 S. xviii. 29; Job xiii.
25; Jer. v. 22; Dan. iv. 2; 2 Macc. viii. 16; Sir. xli. 3).
3. *to reverence, stand in awe of*, (τὸν θεόν, Plat. legg. 9
p. 879 e.; Sept. Prov. ii. 8; xxiv. 28 (xxx. 5); Nah. i.
7): God's declaration, Heb. xi. 7.*

2126   **εὐλαβής, -ές**, (εὖ and λαβεῖν), in Grk. writ. fr. Plat.
down; **1.** *taking hold well*, i. e. *carefully and surely*;
cautious. **2.** *reverencing God, pious, religious*, [A. V.
devout]: Acts ii. 5; viii. 2, (Mic. vii. 2 [Alex. etc.]);
joined with δίκαιος (as in Plat. polit. p. 311 b.): Lk. ii.
25; εὐλ. κατὰ τὸν νόμον, Acts xxii. 12 L T Tr WH. [Cf.
reff. s. v. εὐλάβεια, fin.] *

2127   **εὐλογέω, -ῶ**: fut. εὐλογήσω; impf. εὐλόγουν and ηὐλόγουν
(Mk. x. 16, where the Mss. fluctuate betw. the two forms
[cf. WH. App. p. 162)]); 1 aor. εὐλόγησα (ηὐλόγησα, Mt.
xiv. 19 L Tr; Lk. xxiv. 30 L; Heb. xi. 20 and 21 L);
pf. εὐλόγηκα (ηὐλόγηκα, Heb. vii. 6 L; see εὐδοκέω init. [cf.
Veitch s. v.; Tdf. on Lk. l. c.]); Pass., pf. ptcp. εὐλόγη
μένος; 1 fut. εὐλογηθήσομαι; (εὔλογος); Sept. very often
for בֵּרֵךְ and בָּרַךְ; Vulg. *benedico*; mostly w. acc. of the
obj., *to bless one*; **1.** as in Grk. writ., *to praise, celebrate with praises*: τὸν θεόν, Lk. i. 64; ii. 28; xxiv.
51, 53 [Tdf. om.]; Jas. iii. 9; absol. in the giving of
thanks: Mt. xiv. 19; xxvi. 26 [cf. 3 below]; Mk. vi. 41;
viii. 7 R G T [?]; xiv. 22 [cf. 3 below]; Lk. xxiv. 30;
1 Co. xiv. 16. (When used in this sense εὐλογεῖν differs
from εὐχαριστεῖν in referring rather to the f o r m, εὐχ. to
the s u b s t a n c e of the thanksgiving.) By a usage
purely bibl. and eccl. like the Hebr. בֵּרֵךְ, **2.** *to invoke blessings*: τινά, upon one, Mt. v. 44 Rec.; Lk. vi. 28;
Ro. xii. 14; absol. 1 Co. iv. 12; 1 Pet. iii. 9; of one taking leave, Lk. xxiv. 50 sq.; of one at the point of death,
Heb. xi. 20 sq. (Gen. xlviii. 9); in congratulations, Heb.
vii. 1, 6 sq. (Gen. xiv. 19); Mk. x. 16 R G L; Lk. ii. 34;
εὐλογημένος (בָּרוּךְ), praised, blessed, [cf. εὐλογητός]: Mt.
xxi. 9; xxiii. 39; Mk. xi. 9 sq.; Lk. xiii. 35; xix. 38; Jn.
xii. 13, (in all which pass. it is an acclamation borrowed
fr. Ps. cxvii. (cxviii.) 26). **3.** with acc. of a thing, *to
consecrate a thing with solemn prayers; to ask God's blessing on a thing, pray him to bless it to one's use, pronounce*

a consecratory blessing on: ἰχθύδια, Mk. viii. 7 L Tr WH; τοὺς ἄρτους, Lk. ix. 16; τὸ ποτήριον, 1 Co. x. 16; τὴν θυσίαν, 1 S. ix. 13; and perh. τὸν ἄρτον, Mt. xxvi. 26; Mk. xiv. 22, (but see above under 1); cf. Rückert, Das Abendmahl, p. 220 sq. 4. of God, to cause to prosper, to make happy, to bestow blessings on, [cf. W. 32]: τινά, Acts iii. 26; foll. by ἐν with dat. of the blessing, ἐν πάσῃ εὐλογίᾳ, with every kind of blessing, Eph. i. 3 (ἐν ἀγαθοῖς, Test. xii. Patr. [test. Jos. § 18] p. 722 [ἐν εὐλογίαις γῆς, ἐν πρωτογενήμασι καρπῶν, test. Isach. § 5 p. 626 sq.]); εὐλογῶν εὐλογήσω σε (after the Hebr., Gen. xxii. 17; see εἴδω, I. 1 a. [for reff.]), I will bestow on thee the greatest blessings, Heb. vi. 14; Gal. iii. 8 Rec.ᵉˡˢ ᵇᵉˢ (see ἐνευλογέω), 9; εὐλογημένος favored of God, blessed, Lk. i. 42ᵇ (cf. Deut. xxviii. 4); ἐν γυναιξί, blessed among women, i. e. before all other women, Lk. i. 28 R G L Tr txt. br.; 42ᵃ, (cf. W. 246 (231); [B. 83 (73)]); εὐλογημένοι τοῦ πατρός (i. q. ὑπὸ τοῦ πατρός, like εὐλ. ὑπὸ θεοῦ, Is. lxi. 9; lxv. 23; cf. W. 189 (178) and § 30, 4; [cf. B. § 132, 23]), appointed to eternal salvation by my father, Mt. xxv. 34. [Comp.: ἐν-, κατ-ευλογέω.] *

2128 εὐλογητός, -όν, (εὐλογέω), Sept. for בָּרוּךְ, a bibl. and eccl. word; blessed, praised, Vulg. benedictus: applied to God, Lk. i. 68; Ro. i. 25; ix. 5 [on its position here cf. W. 551 (512 sq.); Ps. lxviii. (lxvii.) 20; Gen. xxvii. 29; Pss. of Sol. 8, 40. 41; also 1 K. x. 9; 2 Chr. ix. 8; Job i. 21; Ps. cxii. (cxiii.) 2; Ruth ii. 19; Dan. ii. 20, and esp. the elaborate discussion of Ro. l. c. by Professors Dwight and Abbot in Journ. Soc. Bibl. Lit. etc. i. pp. 22–55, 87–154 (1882)]; 2 Co. i. 3; xi. 31; Eph. i. 3; 1 Pet. i. 3; cf. B. § 129, 22 Rem. [contra, W. 586 (545); Mey. on Gal. i. 5]; absol. ὁ εὐλογητός, of God: Mk. xiv. 61. [The distinction betw. εὐλογητός and εὐλογημένος is thus stated by Philo (de migr. Abr. § 19, i. 453 Mang.): εὐλογητός, οὐ μόνον εὐλογημένος · . . . τὸ μὲν γὰρ τῷ πεφυκέναι, τὸ δὲ τῷ νομίζεσθαι λέγεται μόνον . . . τῷ πεφυκέναι εὐλογίας ἄξιον . . . ὅπερ εὐλογητὸν ἐν τοῖς χρησμοῖς ᾄδεται. Cf. Gen. xiv. 19, 20; 1 S. xxv. 32, 33; Tob. xi. 16 cod. Sin.; contra, Jud. xiii. 18. Εὐλογητός is applied to men in Gen. xxiv. 31; xxvi. 29; Deut. vii. 14; Judg. xvii. 2; 1 S. xv. 13; Ruth ii. 20; Jud. and Tob. u. s. etc. See Prof. Abbot's careful exposition u. s. p. 152 sq.] *

2129 εὐλογία, -ας, ἡ, (εὔλογος); Sept. for בְּרָכָה; Vulg. benedictio; as in class. Grk. 1. praise, laudation, panegyric: of God or Christ, Rev. v. 12, 13; vii. 12. 2. fine discourse, polished language: Plat. rep. 3 p. 400 d.; Luc. Lexiph. 1; in a bad sense, language artfully adapted to captivate the hearer, fair speaking, fine speeches: Ro. xvi. 18 (joined with χρηστολογία, the latter relating to the substance, εὐλογία to the expression); plur. in Aesop, fab. 229 p. 150 ed. Cor. ἐὰν σὺ εὐλογίας εὐπορῇς, ἔγωγέ σου οὐ κήδομαι, [but why not gen. sing.?]. By a usage unknown to native Grks. 3. an invocation of blessings, benediction: Heb. xii. 17; Jas. iii. 10, (Gen. xxvii. 35 sq. 38, al.; Sir. iii. 8; xxxvii. 24; Joseph. antt. 4, 8, 44); see εὐλογέω, 2. 4. consecration: τὸ ποτήριον τῆς εὐλογίας, the consecrated cup (for that this is the meaning is evident from the explanatory adjunct ὁ εὐλο-

γοῦμεν, see εὐλογέω 3 [al. al.; cf. Mey. ed. Heinrici ad loc.; W. 189 (178)]), 1 Co. x. 16. 5. a (concrete) blessing, benefit, (Deut. xi. 26, etc.; Sir. vii. 32; xxxix. 22, etc.); univ. 1 Pet. iii. 9; of the blessings of Christianity, Ro. xv. 29; Eph. i. 3; ἡ εὐλογία τοῦ Ἀβρ. the salvation (by the Messiah) promised to Abraham, Gal. iii. 14; of the continual fertility of the soil granted by God, Heb. vi. 7 (Lev. xxv. 21; ὑετὸς εὐλογίας, Ezek. xxxiv. 26; cf. εὐλογεῖν ἀγρόν, Gen. xxvii. 27); of the blessing of a collection sent from Christians to their brethren, 2 Co. ix. 5 (of the gifts of men, Gen. xxxiii. 11; Judg. i. 15; 1 S. xxv. 27); ἐπ' εὐλογίαις, that blessings may accrue, bountifully (opp. to φειδομένως), 2 Co. ix. 6 (see ἐπί, B. 2 e. p. 234ᵃ top).*

2130 εὐ-μετά-δοτος, -ον, (εὖ and μεταδίδωμι), ready or free to impart; liberal: 1 Tim. vi. 18 [A. V. ready to distribute]. (Antonin. 1, 14; 6, 48.) *

2131 Εὐνίκη [Rˢᵗ -νείκη (see ει, ι); lit. conquering well], -ης, ἡ, Eunice, the mother of Timothy: 2 Tim. i. 5.*

2132 εὐ-νοέω, -ῶ, (εὔνοος); to wish (one) well; to be well-disposed, of a peaceable spirit: τινί, towards any one, Mt. v. 25. (3 Macc. vii. 11; Soph., Arstph., Xen., Polyb., Plut., Hdian.) *

2133 εὔνοια, -ας, ἡ, (εὔνοος), good-will, kindness: 1 Co. vii. 3 Rec.; μετ' εὐνοίας, Eph. vi. 7. [From Aeschyl. down.] *

2134 εὐνουχίζω: 1 aor. εὐνούχισα; 1 aor. pass. εὐνουχίσθην; [on the augm. cf. B. 34 (30); WH. App. p. 162]; to castrate, unman: pass. ὑπό τινος, Mt. xix. 12ᵃ; metaph. εὐνουχ. ἑαυτόν to make one's self a eunuch, viz. by abstaining (like a eunuch) from marriage, Mt. xix. 12ᵇ (Joseph. antt. 10, 2, 2; Lcian., Dio Cass., al.) *

2135 εὐνοῦχος, -ου, ὁ, (fr. εὐνή a bed, and ἔχω), Sept. סָרִים; fr. Hdt. down; prop. a bed-keeper, bed-guard, superintendent of the bedchamber, chamberlain, in the palace of oriental monarchs who support numerous wives; the superintendent of the women's apartment or harem, an office held by eunuchs; hence a. an emasculated man, a eunuch: Mt. xix. 12ᵇ. But eunuchs in oriental courts held other offices of greater or less importance, like the oversight of the treasury, held by the Ethiopian eunuch mentioned in Acts viii. 27, 34, 36, 38 sq.; cf. Gesenius, Thes. ii. p. 973; [B. D. s. v. Eunuch]. b. one naturally incapacitated — either for marriage, Mt. xix. 12ᵃ; or for begetting children, Sap. iii. 14, cf. Grimm, exgt. Hdb. ad loc. c. one who voluntarily abstains from marriage: Mt. xix. 12ᶜ. Fischer, De vitiis lexx. N. T. etc. p. 485 sqq. treats of the word more fully.*

2136 Εὐοδία [(lit. prosperous journey), -ωδία Rˢᵗ (lit. fragrant)], -ας, ἡ, Euodia, a Christian woman [transformed by A. V. into a man, Euodias]: Phil. iv. 2 [see Bp. Lghtf. ad loc.].*

2137 εὐ-οδόω, -ῶ: [Pass., pres. εὐοδοῦμαι; fut. εὐοδωθήσομαι; 1 aor. subj. εὐοδωθῇ, 1 Co. xvi. 2 WH mrg. who regard the εὐοδῶται of the text here as perf. (either ind. or subj.) see their App. p. 172]; (εὔοδος); Sept. principally for צָלַח and הִצְלִיחַ; to grant a prosperous and expeditious journey, to lead by a direct and easy way: Gen. xxiv. 48: much more freq. tropically, to grant a success-

ful issue, to cause to prosper: τί, as τὴν ὁδόν τινος, Gen. xxiv. 21, 40; Is. lv. 11, etc.; τὰ ἔργα τινός, Sap. xi. 1; in the Pass. always trop. *to prosper, be successful*: of persons, Josh. i. 8; Prov. xxviii. 13; 2 Chr. xiii. 12; xviii. 11, etc.; 3 Jn. 2; εἴπως εὐοδωθήσομαι ἐλθεῖν *if haply I shall be so fortunate as to come*, Ro. i. 10; of things: 2 Esdr. v. 8; Tob. iv. 19; 1 Macc. iii. 6, etc.; τῷ Κλεομένει εὐωδώθη τὸ πρῆγμα, Hdt. 6, 73; ὅ, τι ἂν εὐοδῶται [see above, init.] whatever (business) has prospered, i. e. (contextually) its gains, 1 Co. xvi. 2.*

(2137a)
see 2145 εὐ-πάρ-εδρος, -ον, (εὐ, and πάρεδρος [sitting beside]), *sitting constantly by; assiduous*: πρὸς τὸ εὐπάρεδρον τῷ κυρίῳ, that ye may be constantly devoted to the Lord and his cause, 1 Co. vii. 35, for Rec. εὐπρόσεδρον, which does not differ in sense, [A.V. *attend upon*]. (Hesych. εὐπάρεδρον· καλῶς παραμένον.) *

2138 εὐ-πειθής, -ές, (εὐ, and πείθομαι to comply with, obey), *easily obeying, compliant*: [A. V. *easy to be intreated*]: Jas. iii. 17. (Aeschyl., Xen., Plat., and sqq.) *

2139 εὐ-περί-στατος, -ον, (fr. εὐ and περιΐστημι), *skilfully surrounding* i. e. *besetting*, sc. to prevent or retard running: Heb. xii. 1 [some passively (cf. Isocr. 135 e.), *well* or *much admired* (cf. R. V. mrg.)]. (Not found elsewhere.) *

2140 εὐ-ποιΐα [-ποιία WH (cf. I, ι, fin.)], -ας, ἡ, (εὐποιός), *a doing good, beneficence*: Heb. xiii. 16; Arr. exp. Alex. 7, 28, 8; Alciphr. 1, 10; Lcian. imag. 21; a benefit, kindness, Joseph. antt. 2, 11, 2; (plur. ib. 19, 9, 1).*

2141 εὐ-πορέω, and (esp. in later Grk.) mid. εὐπορέομαι, -οῦμαι: impf. 3 pers. sing. ηὐπορεῖτο (R G) and εὐπορ. (L T Tr WH; for reff. see εὐδοκέω, init.); (εὔπορος well off); *to be well off, have means*: Acts xi. 29 [A. V. acc. to his *ability*]. (Lev. xxv. 26, 28, 49; often in the classics.) *

2142 εὐ-πορία, -ας, ἡ, (εὔπορος, see the preced. word), *riches, means, wealth*: Acts xix. 25. (Xen., Plat., al.; in diff. senses in diff. auth.) *

2143 εὐ-πρέπεια, -ας, ἡ, (εὐπρεπής well-looking), *goodly appearance, shapeliness, beauty, comeliness*: τοῦ προσώπου, Jas. i. 11. (Thuc., Plat., Aeschin., Polyb., Plut.; Sept.) *

2144 εὐ-πρόσ-δεκτος, -ον, (εὐ and προσδέχομαι), *well-received, accepted, acceptable*: Ro. xv. 16; 2 Co. vi. 2; viii. 12; τινί, Ro. xv. 31; 1 Pet. ii. 5. (Plut. praecept. rei publ. ger. c. 4, 17 p. 801 c.; eccl. writ.) *

2145;
see
(2137a) εὐ-πρόσ-εδρος, -ον, (εὐ, and πρόσεδρος [sitting near]), see εὐπάρεδρος.

2146 εὐ-προσωπέω, -ῶ: 1 aor. inf. εὐπροσωπῆσαι; (εὐπρόσωπος fair of face, of good appearance); *to make a fair show; to please* [a weak trans. (?); yet Vulg. *placere*]: ἐν σαρκί, in things pertaining to the flesh, Gal. vi. 12. (Elsewh. only in Chrysost. hom. ad Eph. xxii. § 5, Opp. xi. 173 c. ed. Montf. [var.] and several times in Byzant. writ. [cf. *Soph.* Lex. s. v.].) *

see 2148 εὐρ-ακύλων, -ωνος, ὁ, (fr. εὖρος and Lat. *aquilo*, like εὐρόνοτος, and euroauster [B. 16 (15)]), Vulg. *euroaquilo*; the *Euraquilo*, a *N. E. wind*: Acts xxvii. 14 L T Tr WH, for Rec. εὐροκλύδων (Grsb. εὐρυκλ.) q. v. (Not found elsewhere.) [B. D. s. v. Euroclydon.] *

2147 εὑρίσκω; impf. εὕρισκον (Mk. xiv. 55 [R G T]; Lk. xix. 48 [R G T]; Acts vii. 11 [exc. Tr WH]) and more rarely ηὕρισκον (cf. Kühner § 343, i. 825 sq. [esp. Veitch s. v. fin.] and reff. under εὐδοκέω); fut. εὑρήσω; pf. εὕρηκα; 1 aor. εὕρησα (which aor., unknown to the earlier Grks., occurs in Aesop. f. 131 [f. 41 ed. Furia, p. 333 ed. Cor.]; Maneth. 5, 137 and in Byzant. writ.; cf. *Lob.* ad Phryn. p. 721; W. 86 (82); [cf. B. 36 (31)]), Rev. xviii. 14 Rec.; 2 aor. εὗρον, 1 pers. plur. in Alex. form [WH. App. p. 164; B. 39 (34); W. § 13, 1 (see ἀπέρχομαι)] εὕραμεν, Lk. xxiii. 2 T Tr WH, 3 pers. plur. εὕραν, Lk. viii. 35 Tr WH; Acts v. 10 Tr (in Sept. often εὕροσαν); Pass., pres. εὑρίσκομαι; impf. 3 pers. sing. εὑρίσκετο, Heb. xi. 5 R G, ηὑρίσκετο L T Tr WH, (cf. Bleek and Delitzsch ad loc. [Veitch u. s.]); 1 aor. εὑρέθην; fut. εὑρεθήσομαι; 2 aor. mid. εὑρόμην and later εὑράμην (Heb. ix. 12, [cf. reff. above (on 2 aor. act.)]); Sept. numberless times for מָצָא, sometimes for הִשִּׂיג to attain to, and for Chald. שְׁכַח; [fr. Hom. down]; *to find*; i. e.

1. prop. *to come upon, hit upon, to meet with*; **a.** after searching, *to find a thing sought*: absol., opp. to ζητεῖν, Mt. vii. 7 sq.; Lk. xi. 9 sq. (ζήτει καὶ εὑρήσεις, Epict. diss. 4, 1, 51); τινά, Mt. ii. 8; Mk. i. 37; Lk. ii. 45; Acts xi. 26 (25); xii. 22; 2 Co. ii. 13 (12); 2 Tim. i. 17; Rev. xx. 15, etc.; οὐχ εὑρίσκω, he had vanished, Heb. xi. 5; with a specification of place added: πέραν w. gen. Jn. vi. 25; ἐν w. dat. Acts v. 22; εὑρέθη εἰς, Acts viii. 40 (see εἰς, C. 2); w. acc. of the thing, Mt. vii. 14; xiii. 46; xviii. 13; Lk. xxiv. 3; Jn. x. 9; Acts vii. 11; Ro. vii. 18 Rec., etc.; foll. by indir. disc., Lk. v. 19; οὐχ εὑρέθησαν, had disappeared, Rev. xvi. 20, cf. xviii. 21; w. dat. of advantage, Rev. xx. 11; foll. by ἐν w. dat. of place, Mt. xxi. 19; Rev. xii. 8. τινα or τι ζητεῖν κ. οὐχ εὑρίσκειν: Mt. xii. 43; xxvi. 60; Mk. xiv. 55; Lk. xi. 24; xiii. 6 sq.; Jn. vii. 34; Rev. ix. 6, (2 K. ii. 17; Neh. vii. 64; Ps. ix. 36 [x. 15]; Eccl. vii. 29; Ezek. xxii. 30; xxvi. 21 Ald. Comp.; Hos. ii. 7); γῆ καὶ τὰ ἐν αὐτῇ ἔργα εὑρεθήσεται shall be found sc. for destruction, i. e. will be unable to hide themselves from the doom decreed them by God, 2 Pet. iii. 10 Tr WH, after the strange but improbable reading of codd. אB and other authorities; [see WH. Intr. § 365 and App. ad loc.]. **b.** without previous search, *to find* (by chance), *to fall in with*: τινά, Mt. xviii. 28; xxvii. 32; Jn. i. 41 (42), 45 (46); v. 14; ix. 35; Acts xiii. 6; xviii. 2; xix. 1; xxviii. 14; foll. by ἐν w. dat. of place, Jn. ii. 14. τί, Mt. xiii. 44; xvii. 27; Lk. iv. 17; Jn. xii. 14; Acts xvii. 23; foll. by ἐν w. dat. of place, Mt. viii. 10; Lk. vii. 9. **c.** εὑρίσκω τινά or τι with a pred. acc. is used of those who come or return to a place, the predicate ptcp. or adj. describing the state or condition in which the pers. or thing met with is found, or the action which one is found engaged in: w. an adj., Acts v. 10; 2 Co. ix. 4; xii. 20; w. a ptcp. [cf. B. 301 (258)], Mt. xii. 44; xx. 6; xxi. 2; xxiv. 46; xxvi. 40, 43; Mk. xi. 2; xiii. 36; xiv. 37, 40; Lk. ii. 12; vii. 10; viii. 35; xi. 25; xii. 37, 43; xix. 30; xxiii. 2; xxiv. 2, 33; Acts v. 23; ix. 2; x. 27; xxi. 2; xxiv. 12, 18; xxvii. 3; foll. by καθώς, Mk. xiv. 16; Lk.

xix. 32; xxii. 13; foll. by a pred. substantive to which ὄντα must be supplied, Acts xxiv. 5 [cf. W. § 45, 6 b.; B. 304 (261)]. **2.** tropically, *to find by inquiry, thought, examination, scrutiny, observation, hearing ; to find out by practice and experience,* i. e. *to see, learn, discover, understand :* κατηγορίαν, Lk. vi. 7 [T Tr txt. WH κατηγορεῖν]; τινά foll. by ptcp. in the predicate, Acts xxiii. 29 ; by ὅτι, Ro. vii. 21; after an examination (πειράζειν), τινά [τί] w. a pred. adj. [ptcp.], Rev. iii. 2 ; of a judge : αἰτίαν θανάτου, Acts xiii. 28; αἰτίαν, κακόν, ἀδίκημα ἔν τινι, Jn. xviii. 38; xix. 4, 6 ; Acts xxiii. 9 ; xxiv. 20 ; after a computation, w. an acc. of the price or measure, Acts xix. 19 ; xxvii. 28 ; after deliberation, τὸ τί ποιήσωσι, Lk. xix. 48 ; τὸ πῶς κολάσωνται αὐτούς, Acts iv. 21. Pass. εὑρίσκομαι *to be found,* i. e. *to be seen, be present*: Lk. ix. 36 (Gen. xviii. 31); often like the Hebr. נִמְצָא *to be discovered, recognized, detected, to show one's self out,* of one's character or state as found out by others (men, God, or both), (cf. W. § 65, 8) : εὑρέθη ἐν γαστρὶ ἔχουσα, Mt. i. 18 ; ἵνα εὑρεθῶσι καθὼς κ. ἡμεῖς, 2 Co. xi. 12 ; εὑρέθη μοι ἡ ἐντολὴ εἰς θάνατον sc. οὖσα, the commandment, as I found by experience, brought death to me, Ro. vii. 10 ; add, Lk. xvii. 18 (none showed themselves as having returned) ; Acts v. 39 ; 1 Co. iv. 2 ; xv. 15 ; 2 Co. v. 3 ; Gal. ii. 17 ; 1 Pet. i. 7 ; Rev. v. 4 ; τινί, dat. of the pers. taking cognizance and judging [W. § 31, 10 ; B. 187 (162)], 2 Pet. iii. 14, [add 2 Co. xii. 20, yet cf. B. l. c. and § 133, 14 ; W. § 31, 4 a.]; ἵνα εὑρεθῶ ἐν αὐτῷ i. e. ἐν Χριστῷ, sc. ὤν, Phil. iii. 9 ; σχήματι εὑρεθεὶς ὡς ἄνθρωπος, Phil. ii. 7 (8), (Joseph. b. j. 3, 6, 1 ; so the Lat. *invenior,* Cic. de amic. 19, 70; *reperior,* Tuscul. i. 39, 94). εὑρίσκειν θεόν (opp. to ζητεῖν αὐτόν, see ζητέω, 1 c. [cf. ἐκζητέω, a.]), *to get knowledge of, come to know,* God, Acts xvii. 27 ; εὑρίσκεταί (ὁ θεός) τινι, discloses the knowledge of himself to one, Sap. i. 2 ; cf. Grimm, exgt. Hdb. ad loc. [who refers to Philo, monarch. i. § 5 ; Orig. c. Cels. 7, 42]. On the other hand, in the O. T. εὑρίσκεται ὁ θεός is used *of God hearing prayer, granting aid implored,* (1 Chr. xxviii. 9 ; 2 Chr. xv. 2, 4, 15 ; Jer. xxxvi. (xxix.) 13); hence εὑρέθην [L and Tr in br. WH mrg. add ἐν] τοῖς ἐμὲ μὴ ζητοῦσι, Ro. x. 20 fr. Is. lxv. 1, means, acc. to Paul's conception, *I granted the knowledge and deliverance of the gospel.* **3.** Mid., as in Grk. writ., *to find for one's self, to acquire, get, obtain, procure* : λύτρωσιν, Heb. ix. 12 ; contrary to better Grk. usage, the Act. is often used in the Scriptures in the same sense [cf. B. 193 (167); W. 18; 33 (32) n.] : τὴν ψυχήν, Mt. x. 39; xvi. 25 ; ἀνάπαυσιν (Sir. xi. 19) ταῖς ψυχαῖς ὑμῶν, Mt. xi. 29 ; μετανοίας τόπον, place for recalling the decision, changing the mind, (of his father), Heb. xii. 17 [cf. W. 147 (139)] ; σκήνωμα τῷ θεῷ, opportunity of building a house for God, Acts vii. 46 ; εὑρ. χάριν, grace, favor, Heb. iv. 16 ; χάριν παρὰ τῷ θεῷ, Lk. i. 30 ; ἐνώπιον τοῦ θεοῦ, Acts vii. 46 ; ἔλεος παρὰ κυρίου, 2 Tim. i. 18 ; (מָצָא חֵן בְּעֵינַי), Gen. vi. 8; xviii. 3 ; xxx. 27 ; xxxii. 6 ; Ex. xxxiii. 12 ; Deut. xxiv. 1, etc.; 1 Esdr. viii. 4). [COMP. : ἀν-ευρίσκω.]

εὑρο-κλύδων, -ωνος, ὁ, (fr. εὗρος the S. E. wind, and

κλύδων a wave), *a S. E. wind raising mighty waves* : Acts xxvii. 14 Rec. But respectable authorities read εὐρυκλύδων, preferred by Griesbach et al., from εὐρύς broad, and κλύδων, *a wind causing broad waves* (Germ. *der Breitspülende,* the *Wide-washer*); Etym. Magn. p. 772, 30 s. v. τυφῶν · "τυφὼν γάρ ἐστιν ἡ τοῦ ἀνέμου σφοδρὰ πνοή, ὃς καὶ εὐρυκλύδων καλεῖται." Others εὐρακύλων, q. v.*

εὐρύ-χωρος, -ον, (εὐρύς broad, and χώρα), *spacious, broad* : Mt. vii. 13. (Sept.; Aristot. h. anim. 10, 5 [p. 637ᵃ, 32]; Diod. 19, 84 ; Joseph. antt. 1, 18, 2 ; [8, 5, 3 ; c. Ap. 1, 18, 2].) *   **2149**

εὐ-σέβεια, -ας, ἡ, (εὐσεβής), *reverence, respect*; in the Bible everywhere *piety towards God, godliness* : Acts iii. 12 ; 1 Tim. ii. 2 ; iv. 7, 8 ; vi. 5 sq. 11 ; 2 Tim. iii. 5 ; 2 Pet. i. 3, 6 sq. ; ἡ κατ᾽ εὐσέβειαν διδασκαλία, the doctrine that promotes godliness, 1 Tim. vi. 3 [see κατά, II. 3 d.]; ἡ ἀλήθεια ἡ κατ᾽ εὐσέβειαν, the truth that leads to godliness, Tit. i. 1 ; τὸ μυστήριον τῆς εὐσεβείας, the mystery which is held by godliness and nourishes it, 1 Tim. iii. 16 ; in plur., aims and acts of godliness, 2 Pet. iii. 11 ; cf. *Pfleiderer,* Paulinism. p. 477 sq. [Eng. trans. ii. 209 sq.]. (Aeschyl., Soph., Xen., Plat., sqq. ; often in Joseph.; Sept. Prov. i. 7 ; xiii. 11 ; Is. xi. 2 ; Sap. x. 12 ; often in 4 Macc. ; πρὸς τὸν θεόν, Joseph. antt. 18, 5, 2 ; [περὶ τὸ θεῖον] c. Ap. 1, 22, 2 ; εἰς θεοὺς καὶ γονέας, Plat. rep. 10 p. 615 c.) [Cf. Schmidt ch. 181.] *   **2150**

εὐ-σεβέω, -ῶ; (εὐσεβής) ; *to be εὐσεβής (pious), to act piously* or *reverently* (towards God, one's country, magistrates, relations, and all to whom dutiful regard or reverence is due); in prof. auth. foll. by εἰς, περί, πρός τινα ; rarely also trans., as Aeschyl. Ag. 338 (τοὺς θεούς) and in the Bible : τὸν ἴδιον οἶκον, 1 Tim. v. 4 ; θεόν, to worship God, Acts xvii. 23 ; 4 Macc. v. 24 (23) var. ; xi. 5 ; [Joseph. c. Ap. 2, 11, 1].*   **2151**

εὐσεβής, -ές, (εὖ and σέβομαι), *pious, dutiful* (towards God [A.V. *devout, godly*]; εὐσεβέω) : Acts x. 2, 7 ; xxii. 12 R G ; 2 Pet. ii. 9. ([Theogn.], Pind., Tragg., Arstph., Plat., al. ; thrice in Sept. for נָדִיב *noble, generous,* Isa. xxxii. 8 ; for צַדִּיק, Is. xxiv. 16 ; xxvi. 7 ; often in Sir. and 4 Macc.) [Cf. Trench § xlviii.] *   **2152**

εὐσεβῶς, adv., *piously, godly* : ζῆν, 2 Tim. iii. 12 ; Tit. ii. 12. (Pind. [-βέως], Soph., Xen., Plat., al. ; 4 Macc. vii. 21 [Fritzsche om.].) *   **2153**

εὔσημος, -ον, (εὖ and σῆμα a sign), *well-marked, clear and definite, distinct* : λόγος, 1 Co. xiv. 9 [A. V. *easy to be understood*]. (Aeschyl., [Soph.], Theophr., Polyb., Plut.) *   **2154**

εὔσπλαγχνος, -ον, (εὖ and σπλάγχνον, q. v.), prop. *having strong bowels* ; once so in Hippocr. p. 89 c. [ed. Foës., i. 197 ed. Kühn]; in bibl. and eccl. lang. *compassionate, tender-hearted* : Eph. iv. 32 ; 1 Pet. iii. 8 ; prec. Manass. 7 [(see Sept. ed. Tdf. Proleg. § 29)] ; Test. xii. Patr. test. Zab. § 9 ; cf. Harnack's note on Herm. vis. 1, 2].*   **2155**

εὐσχημόνως, adv., (see εὐσχήμων), *in a seemly manner, decently* : 1 Co. xiv. 40 ; περιπατεῖν, Ro. xiii. 13 ; 1 Th. iv. 12. (Arstph. vesp. 1210 ; Xen. mem. 3, 12, 4 ; Cyr. 1, 3, 8 sq. ; al.) *   **2156**

εὐσχημοσύνη, -ης, ἡ, (εὐσχήμων, q. v.), *charm or elegance*   **2157** of figure, external beauty, decorum, modesty, seemliness (Xen., Plat., Polyb., Diod., Plut.); of external charm, comeliness : 1 Co. xii. 23.*

2158   εὐσχήμων, -ον, (εὖ, and σχῆμα the figure, Lat. habitus); **1.** of elegant figure, shapely, graceful, comely, bearing one's self becomingly in speech or behavior, (Eur., Arstph., Xen., Plat.): τὰ εὐσχήμονα ἡμῶν, the comely parts of the body that need no covering (opp. to τὰ ἀσχήμονα ἡμῶν, vs. 23), 1 Co. xii. 24; of morals: πρὸς τὸ εὔσχημον, to promote decorum, 1 Co. vii. 35. **2.** in later usage (cf. Lob. ad Phryn. p. 333), of good standing, honorable, influential, wealthy, respectable, [R. V. of honorable estate]: Mk. xv. 43; Acts xiii. 50; xvii. 12. (Joseph. de vita sua § 9; Plut. parallel. Graec. et Rom. c. 15 p. 309 b.) *

2159   εὐτόνως, adv., (fr. εὔτονος, and this fr. εὖ and τείνω to stretch [cf. at full stretch, well strung, etc.]), vehemently, forcibly : Lk. xxiii. 10; Acts xviii. 28. (Josh. vi. 8; 2 Macc. xii. 23; Xen. Hier. 9, 6; Arstph. Plut. 1095; Diod., al.) *

2160   εὐτραπελία, -ας, ἡ, (fr. εὐτράπελος, fr. εὖ, and τρέπω to turn : easily turning; nimble-witted, witty, sharp), pleasantry, humor, facetiousness, ([Hippocr.], Plat. rep. 8 p. 563 a.; Diod. 15, 6; 20, 63; Joseph. antt. 12, 4, 3; Plut., al.); in a bad sense, scurrility, ribaldry, low jesting (in which there is some acuteness) : Eph. v. 4; in a milder sense, Arist. eth. 2, 7, 13; [ἡ εὐτραπελία πεπαιδευμένη ὕβρις ἐστίν, rhet. 2, 12, 16 (cf. Cope in loc.); cf. Trench § xxxiv.; Matt. Arnold, Irish Essays etc. p. 187 sqq. (Speech at Eton) 1882].*

2161   Εὔτυχος [i. e. fortunate; on accent cf. W. 51; Chandler § 331 sq.], -ου, ὁ, Eutychus, a young man restored to life by Paul : Acts xx. 9.*

2162   εὐφημία, -ας, ἡ, (εὔφημος, q. v.), prop. the utterance of good or auspicious words; hence good report, praise : 2 Co. vi. 8 (opp. to δυσφημία), as in Diod. 1, 2 [4 ed. Dind.]; Ael. v. h. 3, 47. (In diff. senses in other auth. fr. Pind., Soph., and Plat. down.) *

2163   εὔφημος, -ον, (εὖ and φήμη), sounding well; uttering words of good omen, speaking auspiciously : neut. plur. εὔφημα, things spoken in a kindly spirit, with good-will to others, Phil. iv. 8 [A. V. of good report, (R. V. mrg. gracious)]. (In very diverse senses com. in Grk. writ. fr. Aeschyl. down.) *

2164   εὐ-φορέω, -ῶ : 1 aor. εὐφόρησα (Lchm. ηὐφόρησα, see reff. in εὐδοκέω, init.) ; (εὔφορος [bearing well]); to be fertile, bring forth plentifully : Lk. xii. 16. (Joseph. b. j. 2, 21, 2; Hippocr., Geop., al.)*

2165   εὐφραίνω ; Pass., pres. εὐφραίνομαι ; impf. εὐφραινόμην (Acts vii. 41, where a few codd. ηὐφρ. [cf. WH. App. p. 162]) ; 1 aor. εὐφράνθην and L T Tr WH ηὐφρ. (Acts ii. 26 ; see reff. in εὐδοκέω, init.) ; 1 fut. εὐφρανθήσομαι ; (εὖ and φρήν) ; in Sept. very often actively for שָׂמַח to make joyful, and pass. for שָׂמַח to be joyful, sometimes for רָנַן to sing ; in Grk. writ. fr. Hom. down ; to gladden, make joyful : τινά, 2 Co. ii. 2 (opp. to λυπεῖν). Pass. to be glad, to be merry, to rejoice : absol., Lk. xv. 32; Acts ii. 26 (fr. Ps. xv. (xvi.) 9) ; Ro. xv. 10 (fr. Deut. xxxii. 43) ; Gal. iv. 27 (fr. Is. liv. 1) ; Rev. xi. 10; xii.

12; ἔν τινι, to rejoice in, be delighted with, a thing, Acts vii. 41 (Xen. Hier. 1, 16); ἐπί τινι, Rev. xviii. 20 L T Tr WH (for Rec. ἐπ' αὐτήν); of the merriment of a feast, Lk. xii. 19; xv. 23 sq. 29, (Deut. xiv. 25 (26); xxvii. 7); with λαμπρῶς added, to live sumptuously : Lk. xvi. 19 (Hom. Od. 2, 311; Xen. Cyr. 8, 7, 12).*

2166   Εὐφράτης, -ου, ὁ, Euphrates, a large and celebrated river, which rises in the mountains of Armenia Major, flows through Assyria, Syria, Mesopotamia and the city of Babylon, and empties into the Persian Gulf, (Hebr. פְּרָת [i. e. (prob.) 'the great stream' (Gen. i. 18); cf. Fried. Delitzsch, Wo lag d. Par. p. 169]): Rev. ix. 14; xvi. 12. [B. D. s. v. and reff. there.] *

2167   εὐφροσύνη, -ης, ἡ, (εὔφρων [well-minded, cheerful]), fr. Hom. down; good cheer, joy, gladness : Acts ii. 28 (Ps. xv. (xvi.) 11); xiv. 17.*

2168   εὐχαριστέω, -ῶ ; 1 aor. εὐχαρίστησα (Acts xxvii. 35) and ηὐχαρίστησα (Ro. i. 21 G L T Tr WH ; see reff. in εὐδοκέω, init.) ; 1 aor. pass. subj. 3 pers. sing. εὐχαριστηθῇ (2 Co. i. 11) ; (εὐχάριστος, q. v.) ; **1.** to be grateful, feel thankful ; so in the decree of the Byzantines in Dem. pro cor. p. 257, 2. **2.** to give thanks (so Posid. ap. Athen. 5 p. 213 e. ; Polyb., Diod., Philo, Joseph., Plut., Epictet., al. ; cf. Lob. ad Phryn. p. 18 [W. 23 (22)]) : τινί, esp. τῷ θεῷ, Lk. xvii. 16; Acts xxvii. 35; xxviii. 15; Ro. xiv. 6; xvi. 4; 1 Co. xiv. 18 [see below]; Phil. i. 3; Col. i. 3, 12; Philem. 4; (w. the acc. [hence as nom.] in the passive, ἵνα ... ὑπὲρ τῶν ἀγαθῶν ὁ θεὸς εὐχαριστῆται, Philo, quis rer. div. her. § 36). simply, so that τῷ θεῷ must be added mentally : Ro. i. 21; [1 Co. xiv. 17] ; 1 Th. v. 18; esp. where the giving of thanks customary at the beginning of a feast, or in general before eating, is spoken of : Mt. xv. 36; xxvi. 27; Mk. viii. 6; xiv. 23; Lk. xxii. 17, 19; Jn. vi. 11, 23; 1 Co. xi. 24; εὐχαριστεῖν τῷ θεῷ διὰ Ἰησ. Χριστοῦ, through Christ i. e. by Christ's help (because both the favors for which thanks are given and the gratitude which prompts the thanks are due to Christ [cf. W. 378 (354) note]): Ro. i. 8; vii. 25 R WH mrg.; Col. iii. 17; τῷ θεῷ ἐν ὀνόματι Χριστοῦ (see ὄνομα, 2 e.), Eph. v. 20. Of that for or on account of which thanks are given to God, we find—περί τινος, gen. of pers., concerning, with regard to one, [1 Th. i. 2]; 2 Th. i. 3 [cf. Ellic. in loc.]; w. ὅτι added epexegetically, Ro. i. 8 (where R G ὑπέρ); 2 Th. ii. 13; w. addition of ἐπί and dat. of the thing for, on account of, which, 1 Co. i. 4; ὑπέρ τινος, gen. of pers., Eph. i. 16; ὑπέρ w. gen. of the thing, for, on account of, 1 Co. x. 30; Eph. v. 20; the matter or ground of the thanksgiving is expressed by a foll. ὅτι: Lk. xviii. 11; Jn. xi. 41; 1 Co. i. 14; 1 Th. ii. 13; Rev. xi. 17; or is added asyndetically without ὅτι, 1 Co. xiv. 18 (λαλῶ L T Tr WH, for which R G λαλῶν, the ptcp. declaring the cause which prompts to thanksgiving [W. 345 sq. (324); B. 300 (258)]). Once εὐχαρ. τι, for a thing, in the pass. 2 Co. i. 11 [cf. B. 148 (130); W. 222 (209)]; in the Fathers εὐχαριστεῖν τι is to consecrate a thing by giving thanks, to 'bless': ὁ εὐχαριστηθεὶς ἄρτος κ. οἶνος, Justin M. apol. 1, 65 fin.; εὐχαριστηθεῖσα τροφή, ibid. c. 66;

εἰσὶν οἱ εὐχαριστοῦσι ψιλὸν ὕδωρ, Clem. Al. strom. i. p. 317 ed. Sylb.; [cf. *Suicer*, Thesaur. i. 1269. "The words εὐχάριστος, εὐχαριστεῖν, εὐχαριστία, occur in St. Paul's writings alone of the apostolic Epistles" (Bp. Lghtft.; cf. Ellic. on Col. i. 12)].*

2169   **εὐχαριστία**, -ας, ἡ, (εὐχάριστος, q. v.);   **1.** *thankfulness*: decree of the Byzantines in Dem. p. 256, 19; Polyb. 8, 14, 8; Add. to Esth. vi. 4 ed. Fritz.; 2 Macc. ii. 27; Sir. xxxvii. 11; πρός τινα, Diod. 17, 59; Joseph. antt. 3, 3.   **2.** *the giving of thanks*: Acts xxiv. 3; for God's blessings, 1 Co. xiv. 16; 2 Co. iv. 15; Eph. v. 4 (cf. 1 Th. v. 18); Phil. iv. 6; Col. ii. 7; iv. 2; 1 Th. iii. 9; 1 Tim. iv. 3 sq.; Rev. iv. 9; vii. 12; w. dat. of the pers. to whom thanks are given: τῷ θεῷ (cf. W. § 31, 3; [B. 180 (156)]; Kühner § 424, 1), 2 Co. ix. 11 (τοῦ θεοῦ, Sap. xvi. 28); in plur., 2 Co. ix. 12; 1 Tim. ii. 1.*

2170   **εὐχάριστος**, -ον, (εὖ and χαρίζομαι), *mindful of favors, grateful, thankful*: to God, Col. iii. 15 (Xen. Cyr. 8, 3, 49; Plut.; al.); *pleasing, agreeable* [cf. Eng. *grateful* in its secondary sense]: εὐχάριστοι λόγοι, pleasant conversation, Xen. Cyr. 2, 2, 1; *acceptable to others, winning*: γυνὴ εὐχάριστος ἐγείρει ἀνδρὶ δόξαν, Prov. xi. 16; *liberal, beneficent*, Diod. 18, 28.*

2171   **εὐχή**, -ῆς, ἡ, (εὔχομαι), [fr. Hom. down];   **1.** *a prayer to God*: Jas. v. 15.   **2.** *a vow* (often so in Sept. for נֶדֶר and נָזַר, also for נָזִיר *consecration*, see ἁγνίζω): εὐχὴν ἔχειν, to have taken a vow, Acts xviii. 18; with ἐφ' ἑαυτῶν added (see ἐπί, A. I. 1 f. p. 232ᵃ), Acts xxi. 23.*

2172   **εὔχομαι**; impf. ηὐχόμην (Ro. ix. 3) and εὐχόμην (Acts xxvii. 29 T Tr, see εὐδοκέω init. [cf. Veitch s. v.; *Tdf.* Proleg. p. 121]); [1 aor. mid. εὐξάμην Acts xxvi. 29 Tdf., where others read the opt. -αίμην; depon. verb, cf. W. § 38, 7];   **1.** *to pray to God* (Sept. in this sense for הִתְפַּלֵּל and עָתַר): τῷ θεῷ (as very often in class. Grk. fr. Hom. down [cf. W. 212 (199); B. 177 (154)]), foll. by acc. w. inf., Acts xxvi. 29; πρὸς τὸν θεόν (Xen. mem. 1, 3, 2; symp. 4, 55; often in Sept.), foll. by acc. w. inf. 2 Co. xiii. 7; ὑπέρ w. gen. of pers., *for one*, Jas. v. 16 where L WH txt. Tr mrg. προσεύχεσθε (Xen. mem. 2, 2, 10). [SYN. see αἰτέω, fin.]   **2.** *to wish*: τί, 2 Co. xiii. 9; foll. by acc. with inf. 3 Jn. 2, [al. adhere to the religious sense, *to pray, pray for*, in both the preceding pass.]; Acts xxvii. 29; ηὐχόμην (on this use of the impf. cf. W. 283 (266); B. § 139, 15; [Bp. Lghtft. on Philem. 13]) εἶναι, I could wish to be, Ro. ix. 3. [COMP.: προσεύχομαι.] *

2173   **εὔ-χρηστος**, -ον, (εὖ and χράομαι), *easy to make use of, useful*: w. dat. of pers. 2 Tim. ii. 21; opp. to ἄχρηστος, Philem. 11; εἴς τι, for a thing, 2 Tim. iv. 11. (Diod. 5, 40; Sap. xiii. 13; πρός τι, Xen. mem. 3, 8, 5.)*

2174   **εὐψυχέω**, -ῶ; (εὔψυχος); *to be of good courage, to be of a cheerful spirit*: Phil. ii. 19. (Joseph. antt. 11, 6, 9; [Poll. 3, 28 § 135 fin.]; in epitaphs, εὐψύχει! i. q. Lat. *have pia anima!*) *

2175   **εὐωδία**, -ας, ἡ, (fr. εὐώδης; and this fr. εὖ and ὄζω, pf. ὄδωδα),   **a.** *a sweet smell, fragrance*, (Xen., Plat., Plut., Hdian., al.); metaph. Χριστοῦ εὐωδία ἐσμὲν τῷ θεῷ, i. e. (dropping the fig.) our efficiency in which the power of

Christ himself is at work is well-pleasing to God, 2 Co. ii. 15.   **b.** *a fragrant* or *sweet-smelling thing, incense*: Diod. 1, 84; 1 Esdr. i. 11, etc.; hence ὀσμὴ εὐωδίας, an *odor of something sweet-smelling*, in Sept. often for רֵיחַ־נִיחֹחַ, an odor of acquiescence, satisfaction; *a sweet odor*, spoken of the smell of sacrifices and oblations, Ex. xxix. 18; Lev. i. 9, 13, 17, etc., agreeably to the ancient [anthropopathic] notion that God smells as if pleased with the odor of sacrifices, Gen. viii. 21; in the N. T. by a metaphor borrowed from sacrifices, *a thing well-pleasing to God*: Eph. v. 2; Phil. iv. 18, [W. 605 (562) cf. 237 (222)].*

[Εὐωδία, -ας, Phil. iv. 2 Rec.ˢᵗ for Εὐοδία, q. v.]----- see 2136

εὐώνυμος, -ον, (εὖ and ὄνομα);   **1.** *of good name* — **2176** (Hes., Pind.), and *of good omen* (Plat. polit. p. 302 d.; legg. 6 p. 754 e.); in the latter sense used in taking auguries; but those omens were euphemistically called εὐώνυμα which in fact were regarded as unlucky, i. e. which came *from the left, sinister* omens (for which a *good name* was desired); hence   **2.** *left* (so fr. Aeschyl. and Hdt. down): Acts xxi. 3; Rev. x. 2; ἐξ εὐωνύμων [cf. W. § 27, 3; § 19 s. v. δεξιά; B. 89 (78)], on the left hand (to the left): Mt. xx. 21, 23; xxv. 33, 41; xxvii. 38; Mk. x. 37 [R G L], 40; xv. 27.*

ἐφ-άλλομαι; 2 aor. ptcp. ἐφαλόμενος L T Tr WH; (ἐπί — **2177** and ἅλλομαι, q. v.); fr. Hom. down; *to leap upon, spring upon*: ἐπί τινα, Acts xix. 16 [here R G pres. ptcp.]; (1 S. x. 6; xi. 6; xvi. 13).*

ἐφ-άπαξ [Treg. in Heb. ἐφ' ἅπαξ; cf. *Lipsius*, gram. — **2178** Unters. p. 127], adv., (fr. ἐπί and ἅπαξ [cf. W. 422 (393); B. 321 (275)]), *once; at once* i. e.   **a.** *our all at once*: 1 Co. xv. 6.   **b.** *our once for all*: Ro. vi. 10; Heb. vii. 27; ix. 12; x. 10. (Lcian., Dio Cass., al.) *

ἐφεῖδον, see ἐπεῖδον---------------------- see 1896

Ἐφεσῖνος, -η, -ον, *Ephesian*: Rev. ii. 1 Rec.*--------- 2179
Ἐφέσιος, -α, -ον, (an) *Ephesian*, i. e. a native or in----2180 habitant of Ephesus: Acts xix. 28, 34 sq.; xxi. 29.*

Ἔφεσος, -ου, ἡ, *Ephesus*, a maritime city of Asia Minor, — **2181** capital of Ionia and, under the Romans, of proconsular Asia [see Ἀσία], situated on the Icarian Sea between Smyrna and Miletus. Its chief splendor and renown came from the temple of Artemis, which was reckoned one of the wonders of the world. It was burned down B. C. 356 by Herostratus, rebuilt at the common expense of Greece under the supervision of Deinocrates (Pausan. 7, 2, 6 sq.; Liv. 1, 45; Plin. h. n. 5, 29 (31); 36, 14 (21)), and in the middle of the third century after Christ utterly destroyed by the Goths. At Ephesus the apostle Paul founded a very flourishing church, to which great praise is awarded in Rev. ii. 1 sqq. The name of the city occurs in Acts xviii. 19, 21, 24; xix. 1, 17, 26; xx. 16 sq.; 1 Co. xv. 32; xvi. 8; Eph. i. 1 (where ἐν Ἐφέσῳ is omitted by cod. Sin. and other ancient author., [bracketed by T WH Tr mrg.; see *WH.* App. ad loc.; B. D. Am. ed. s. v. Ephesians, The Ep. to the]); 1 Tim. i. 3; 2 Tim. i. 18; iv. 12; Rev. i. 11, and (acc. to G L T Tr WH) ii. 1. Cf. *Zimmermann*, Ephesus im 1. christl. Jahrh., Jena 1874; [*Wood*, Discoveries at Ephesus (1877)].*

2182 ἐφ-ευρετής, -οῦ, ὁ, (ἐφευρίσκω to find out), an inventor, contriver, (Anacr. 41 (36), 3; Schol. ad Arstph. ran. 1499): κακῶν, Ro. i. 30 (κακῶν εὑρεταί, Philo in Flacc. § 4 mid.; ὁ καινῶν ἀδικημάτων εὑρετής, ibid. § 10; πάσης κακίας εὑρετής, 2 Macc. vii. 31; Sejanus facinorum omnium repertor, Tacit. ann. 4, 11).*

2183 ἐφ-ημερία, -ας, ἡ, (ἐφημέριος, -ον, by day, lasting or acting for a day, daily), a word not found in prof. auth.; Sept. in Chron. and Neh.; 1. a service limited to a stated series of days (cf. Germ. Tagdienst, Wochendienst); so used of the service of the priests and Levites: Neh. xiii. 30; 1 Chr. xxv. 8; 2 Chr. xiii. 10, etc. **2.** the class or course itself of priests who for a week at a time performed the duties of the priestly office (Germ. Wöchnerzunft): 1 Chr. xxiii. 6; xxviii. 13, etc.; 1 Esdr. i. 2, 15; so twice in the N. T.: Lk. i. 5, 8. For David divided the priests into twenty-four classes, each of which in its turn discharged the duties of the office for an entire week from sabbath to sabbath, 1 Chr. xxiv. 4; 2 Chr. viii. 14; Neh. xii. 24; these classes Josephus calls πατριαί and ἐφημερίδες, antt. 7, 14, 7; de vita sua 1; Suidas, ἐφημερία· ἡ πατριά. λέγεται δὲ καὶ ἡ τῆς ἡμέρας λειτουργία. Cf. Fritzsche, Com. on 3 Esdr. p. 12. [BB.DD. s. v. Priests; Edersheim, Jesus the Messiah, bk. ii. ch. iii.]*

2184 ἐφ-ήμερος, -ον, (i. q. ὁ ἐπὶ ἡμέραν ὤν); 1. lasting for a day (Pind., Hippocr., Plut., Galen.; al.). 2. daily: ἡ τροφή (Diod. 3, 32; Dion. Hal. 8, 41; Aristid. ii. p. 398 [ed. Jebb; 537 ed. Dind.]), Jas. ii. 15.*

see 1896 ──ἔφιδε, see ἐπεῖδον.

2185 ἐφ-ικνέομαι, -οῦμαι; 2 aor. inf. ἐφικέσθαι; [fr. Hom. down]; to come to: ἄχρι w. gen. of pers. 2 Co. x. 13; to reach: εἴς τινα, ibid. 14.*

2186 ἐφ-ίστημι: 2 aor. ἐπέστην, ptcp. ἐπιστάς, impv. ἐπίστηθι; pf. ptcp. ἐφεστώς; to place at, place upon, place over; in the N. T. only in the mid. [pres. indic. 3 pers. sing. ἐπίσταται (for ἐφίστ.) 1 Th. v. 3 T Tr WH; see reff. s. v. ἀφεῖδον] and the intrans. tenses of the act., viz. pf. and 2 aor. (see ἀνίστημι); to stand by, be present: Lk. ii. 38; Acts xxii. 20; ἐπάνω w. gen. of pers. to stand over one, place one's self above, Lk. iv. 39; used esp. of persons coming upon one suddenly: simply, Lk. x. 40; xx. 1; Acts vi. 12; xxii. 13; xxiii. 27; of an angel, Acts xii. 7; w. dat. of pers., Acts iv. 1; xxiii. 11; of the advent of angels, Lk. ii. 9; xxiv. 4, (of Hephaestus, Lcian. dial. deor. 17, 1; freq. of dreams, as Hom. Il. 10, 496; 23, 106; Hdt. 1, 34; al.); w. dat. of place, Acts xvii. 5; foll. by ἐπί with acc. of place, Acts x. 17; xi. 11; of evils coming upon one: w. dat. of pers., 1 Th. v. 3 [see above]; ἐπί τινα, Lk. xxi. 34 (Sap. vi. 9; al.); Soph. O. R. 777; Thuc. 3, 82). i. q. to be at hand i. e. be ready: 2 Tim. iv. 2, cf. Leo ad loc. (Eur. Andr. 547; Dem. p. 245, 11). to be at hand i. e. impend: of time, 2 Tim. iv. 6. to come on, of rain, Acts xxviii. 2. [COMP.: κατ-, συνν-εφίστημι.]*

see 160 ──[ἐφνίδιος, see αἰφνίδιος.]

2187 ─────Ἐφραίμ or (so R Tr) Ἐφραΐμ [cf. I, ι, fin.], (א L H Ἐφρέμ, Vulg. Ephrem, Efrem), Ephraim, prop. name of a city situated acc. to Eusebius eight [but ed. Larsow

and Parthey, p. 196, 18, t w e n t y], acc. to Jerome twenty miles from Jerusalem; acc. to Joseph. b. j. 4, 9, 9 not far from Bethel; conjectured by Robinson (Palest. i. 444 sq. [cf. Bib. Sacr. for May 1845, p. 398 sq.]), Ewald et al. dissenting, to be the same as the village now called et-Taiyibeh, a short day's journey N. E. of Jerusalem: Jn. xi. 54. Cf. Win. RWB. s. v.; Keim iii. p. 7 sq. [Eng. trans. v. 9].*

2188 ἐφφαθά, ephphatha, Aram. אֶתְפְּתַח (the ethpaal impv. of the verb פְּתַח, Hebr. פָּתַח, to open), be thou opened (i. e. receive the power of hearing; the ears of the deaf and the eyes of the blind being considered as closed): Mk. vii. 34. [See Kautzsch, Gram. d. Bibl.-Aram. p. 10.]*

see 5504 ἐχθές and (Rec., so Grsb. in Acts and Heb.) χθές (on which forms cf. Lob. ad Phryn. p. 323 sq.; [esp. Rutherford. New Phryn. p. 370 sq.]; Bleek, Br. an d. Hebr. ii. 2 p. 1000; [Tdf. Proleg. p. 81; W. pp. 24, 45; B. 72 (63)]), adv., yesterday: Jn. iv. 52; Acts vii. 28; of time just past, Heb. xiii. 8. [From Soph. down.]*

2189 ἔχθρα, -ας, ἡ, (fr. the adj. ἐχθρός), enmity: Lk. xxiii. 12; Eph. ii. 14 (15), 16; plur. Gal. v. 20; ἔχθρα (Lchm. ἐχθρά fem. adj. [Vulg. inimica]) θεοῦ, towards God, Jas. iv. 4 (where Tdf. τῷ θεῷ); εἰς θεόν, Ro. viii. 7; by meton. i. q. cause of enmity, Eph. ii. 14 (15) [but cf. Meyer. (From Pind. down.)]*

2190 ἐχθρός, -ά, -όν, (ἔχθος hatred); Sept. numberless times for אֹיֵב, also for צַר, several times for שׂוֹנֵא and מְשַׂנֵּא, a hater; 1. passively, hated, odious, hateful (in Hom. only in this sense): Ro. xi. 28 (opp. to ἀγαπητός). **2.** actively, hostile, hating and opposing another: 1 Co. xv. 25; 2 Th. iii. 15; w. gen. of the pers. hated or opposed, Jas. iv. 4 Lchm.; Gal. iv. 16, cf. Meyer or Wieseler on the latter pass. used of men as at enmity with God by their sin: Ro. v. 10 (cf. Ro. viii. 7; Col. i. 21; Jas. iv. 4) [but many take ἐχθρ. here (as in xi. 28, see 1 above) passively; cf. Meyer]; τῇ διανοίᾳ, opposing (God) in the mind, Col. i. 21; ἐχθρὸς ἄνθρωπος, a man that is hostile, a certain enemy, Mt. xiii. 28; ὁ ἐχθρός, the hostile one (well known to you), i. e. κατ' ἐξοχήν the devil, the most bitter enemy of the divine government: Lk. x. 19, cf. Mt. xiii. 39 (and eccl. writ.). ὁ ἐχθρός (and ἐχθρός) substantively, enemy [so the word, whether adj. or subst., is trans. in A. V., exc. twice (R. V. once) foe: ἔσχατος ἐχθρός, 1 Co. xv. 26]: w. gen. of the pers. to whom one is hostile, Mt. v. 43 sq.; x. 36; xiii. 25; Lk. i. [71], 74; vi. 27, 35; xix. 27, 43; Ro. xii. 20; Rev. xi. 5, 12; in the words of Ps. cix. (cx.) 1, quoted in Mt. xxii. 44; Mk. xii. 36; Lk. xx. 43; Acts ii. 35; 1 Co. xv. 25 [L br.; al. om. gen. (see above)]; Heb. i. 13; x. 13. w. gen. of the thing: Acts xiii. 10; τοῦ σταυροῦ τοῦ Χριστοῦ, who given up to their evil passions evade the obligations imposed upon them by the death of Christ, Phil. iii. 18.*

2191 ἔχιδνα, -ης, ἡ, a viper: Acts xxviii. 3 (Hes., Hdt., Tragg., Arstph., Plat., al.); γεννήματα ἐχιδνῶν offspring of vipers (anguigenae, Ovid, metam. 3, 531), addressed to cunning, malignant, wicked men: Mt. iii. 7; xii. 34; xxiii. 33; Lk. iii. 7.*

2192 ἔχω; fut. ἕξω; impf. εἶχον, [1 pers. plur. εἴχαμεν, 2 Jn.

5 T Tr WH], 3 pers. plur. εἶχαν (Mk. viii. 7 L T Tr WH; Rev. ix. 8 L T Tr WH; but cf. [*Soph.* Lex., Intr. p. 38; *Tdf.* Proleg. p. 123; *WH.* App. p. 165]; B. 40 (35)) and εἴχοσαν (L T Tr WH in Jn. xv. 22, 24; but cf. *Bttm.* in Theol. Stud. u. Krit. 1858, pp. 485 sqq. 491; see his N. T. Gr. p. 43 (37); [*Soph.* Lex., Intr. p. 39; *Tdf.* Proleg. p. 124; *WH.* App. p. 165; cf. δολιόω]); pres. mid. ptcp. ἐχόμενος; *to have*,—with 2 aor. act. ἔσχον; pf. ἔσχηκα;

I. Transitively. **1.** *to have* i. q. *to hold*; **a.** *to have* (hold) *in the hand*: τὶ ἐν τῇ χειρί, Rev. i. 16; vi. 5; x. 2; xvii. 4; and simply, Rev. v. 8; viii. 3, 6; xiv. 6, etc.; Heb. viii. 3. **b.** in the sense of *wearing* (Lat. *gestare*); of garments, arms and the like: τὸ ἔνδυμα, Mt. iii. 4; xxii. 12; κατὰ κεφαλῆς ἔχων, sc. τί, having a covering hanging down from the head, i. e. having the head covered [B. § 130, 5; W. § 47, k. cf. 594 (552)], 1 Co. xi. 4; θώρακας, Rev. ix. 17; μάχαιραν, Jn. xviii. 10; add, Mt. xxvi. 7; Mk. xiv. 3; of a tree having (bearing) leaves, Mk. xi. 13; ἐν γαστρὶ ἔχειν, sc. ἔμβρυον, to be pregnant [cf. W. 594 (552); B. 144 (126)], (see γαστήρ, 2). Metaph. ἐν ἑαυτῷ ἔχειν τὸ ἀπόκριμα, 2 Co. i. 9; τὴν μαρτυρίαν, 1 Jn. v. 10; ἐν καρδίᾳ ἔχειν τινά, to have (carry) one in one's heart, to love one constantly, Phil. i. 7. **c.** trop. *to have* (hold) *possession of* the mind; said of alarm, agitating emotions, etc.: εἶχεν αὐτὰς τρόμος κ. ἔκστασις, Mk. xvi. 8 (Job xxi. 6; Is. xiii. 8, and often in prof. auth.; cf. Passow s. v. p. 1294 sq.; [L. and S. s. v. A. I. 8]). **d.** *to hold fast, keep*: ἡ μνᾶ σου, ἣν εἶχον ἀποκειμένην ἐν σουδαρίῳ, Lk. xix. 20; trop. τὸν θεὸν ἔχειν ἐν ἐπιγνώσει, Ro. i. 28; to keep in mind, τὰς ἐντολάς, Jn. xiv. 21 (see ἐντολή, sub fin.); τὴν μαρτυρίαν, Rev. vi. 9; xii. 17; xix. 10; τὸ μυστήριον τῆς πίστεως ἐν καθαρᾷ συνειδήσει, 1 Tim. iii. 9; ὑποτύπωσιν ὑγιαινόντων λόγων, 2 Tim. i. 13. **e.** *to have* (in itself or as a consequence), *comprise, involve*: ἔργον, Jas. i. 4; ii. 17; κόλασιν, 1 Jn. iv. 18; μισθαποδοσίαν, Heb. x. 35 (Sap. viii. 16). See exx. fr. Grk. auth. in Passow s. v. p. 1296 sq.; [L. and S. s. v. A. I. 8 and 10]. **f.** by a Latinism i. q. *aestimo, to regard, consider, hold as*, [but this sense is still denied by Meyer, on Lk. as below; Mt. xiv. 5]: τινά w. acc. of the predicate, ἔχε με παρητημένην, have me excused, Lk. xiv. 18; τινὰ ὡς προφήτην, Mt. xiv. 5; xxi. 26, (ἔχειν Ἰαννῆν κ. Ἰαμβρῆν ὡς θεούς, Ev. Nicod. 5); τινὰ ἔντιμον (see ἔντιμος), Phil. ii. 29; τὴν ψυχήν μου [G om. μου] τιμίαν ἐμαυτῷ, Acts xx. 24 R G; τινὰ εἰς προφήτην (a Hebraism [see εἰς, B. II. 3 c. γ. fin.]), for a prophet, Mt. xxi. 46 L T Tr WH, cf. B. § 131, 7; τινά, ὅτι ὄντως [T Tr WH ὄντως, ὅτι etc.] προφήτης ἦν, Mk. xi. 32, cf. B. § 151, 1 a.; [W. § 66, 5 a.]. **2.** *to have* i. q. *to own, possess*; **a.** external things such as pertain to property, riches, furniture, utensils, goods, food, etc.: as τὸν βίον, Lk. xxi. 4; 1 Jn. iii. 17; κτήματα, Mt. xix. 22; Mk. x. 22; θησαυρόν, Mt. xix. 21; Mk. x. 21; ἀγαθά, Lk. xii. 19; πρόβατα, Lk. xv. 4; Jn. x. 16; δραχμάς, Lk. xv. 8; πλοῖα, Rev. xviii. 19; κληρονομίαν, Eph. v. 5; [cf. Mt. xxi. 38 L T Tr WH, where R G *κατασχωμεν*]; μέρος foll. by ἐν w. dat. of the thing, Rev. xx. 6; θυσιαστήριον, Heb. xiii. 10; ὅσα ἔχεις, Mk. x. 21; xii.

44; Mt. xiii. 44, 46; xviii. 25; μηδέν, 2 Co. vi. 10; τί δὲ ἔχεις, ὃ etc. 1 Co. iv. 7; with a pred. acc. added, εἶχον ἅπαντα κοινά, Acts ii. 44; absol. ἔχειν, to have property, to be rich: οὐκ and μὴ ἔχειν [A. V. *to have not*], to be destitute, be poor, Mt. xiii. 12; xxv. 29; Mk. iv. 25; Lk. viii. 18; xix. 26; 1 Co. xi. 22; 2 Co. viii. 12, (Neh. viii. 10; 1 Esdr. ix. 51, 54; Sir. xiii. 5; exx. fr. Grk. auth. in Passow s. v. p. 1295[b]; [L. and S. s. v. A. I. 1; cf. W. 594 (552)]); ἐκ τοῦ ἔχειν, in proportion to your means [see ἐκ, II. 13 fin.], 2 Co. viii. 11. **b.** Under the head of possession belongs the phrase ἔχειν τινά as commonly used of those joined to any one by the bonds of nature, blood, marriage, friendship, duty, law, compact, and the like: πατέρα, Jn. viii. 41; ἀδελφούς, Lk. xvi. 28; ἄνδρα (a husband), Jn. iv. 17 sq.; Gal. iv. 27; γυναῖκα, 1 Co. vii. 2, 12 sq. 29; τέκνα, Mt. xxi. 28; xxii. 24; 1 Tim. iii. 4; Tit. i. 6; υἱούς, Gal. iv. 22; σπέρμα, offspring, Mt. xxii. 25; χήρας, 1 Tim. v. 16; ἀσθενοῦντας, Lk. iv. 40; φίλον, Lk. xi. 5; παιδαγωγούς, 1 Co. iv. 15; ἔχειν κύριον, to have (be subject to) a master, Col. iv. 1; δεσπότην, 1 Tim. v. 2; βασιλέα, Jn. xix. 15; with ἐφ' ἑαυτῶν added, Rev. xi. 11; ἔχει τὸν κρίνοντα αὐτόν, Jn. xii. 48; ἔχειν οἰκονόμον, Lk. xvi. 1; δοῦλον, Lk. xvii. 7; ἀρχιερέα, Heb. iv. 14; viii. 1; ποιμένα, Mt. ix. 36; ἔχων ὑπ' ἐμαυτὸν στρατιώτας, Lk. vii. 8; ἔχειν τὸν υἱὸν κ. τὸν πατέρα, to be in living union with the Son (Christ) and the Father by faith, knowledge, profession, 1 Jn. ii. 23; (v. 12); 2 Jn. 9. With two accusatives, one of which serves as a predicate: πατέρα τὸν Ἀβραάμ, Abraham for our father, Mt. iii. 9; add, Acts xiii. 5; Phil. iii. 17; Heb. xii. 9; ἔχειν τινὰ γυναῖκα, to have (use) a woman (unlawfully) as a wife, Mt. xiv. 4; Mk. vi. 18; 1 Co. v. 1 [where see Meyer], (of lawful marriage, Xen. Cyr. 1, 5, 4). **c.** of attendance or companionship: ἔχειν τινὰ μεθ' ἑαυτοῦ, Mt. xv. 30; xxvi. 11; Mk. ii. 19; xiv. 7; Jn. xii. 8. **d.** ἔχειν τι to have a thing *in readiness, have at hand, have in store*: οὐκ ἔχομεν εἰ μὴ πέντε ἄρτους, Mt. xiv. 17; add, xv. 34; Jn. ii. 3 [not Tdf.]; iv. 11; xii. 35; 1 Co. xi. 22; xiv. 26; οὐκ ἔχω, ὃ παραθήσω αὐτῷ, Lk. xi. 6; ποῦ συνάξω τοὺς καρπούς μου, Lk. xii. 17; τί (cf. B. § 139, 58) φάγωσι, Mk. viii. 1 sq.; ἔχειν τινά, to have one at hand, be able to make use of: Μωϋσέα κ. τ. προφήτας, Lk. xvi. 29; παράκλητον, 1 Jn. ii. 1; μάρτυρας, Heb. xii. 1; οὐδένα ἔχω etc. Phil. ii. 20; ἄνθρωπον, ἵνα etc. Jn. v. 7. **e.** a person or thing is said ἔχειν those things which are its parts or are members of his body: as χεῖρας, πόδας, ὀφθαλμούς, Mt. xviii. 8 sq.; Mk. ix. 43, 45, 47; οὖς, Rev. ii. 7, 11, etc.; ὦτα, Mt. xi. 15; Mk. vii. 16 [T WH om. Tr br. the vs.]; viii. 18; μέλη, Ro. xii. 4; 1 Co. xii. 12; σάρκα κ. ὀστέα, Lk. xxiv. 39; ἀκροβυστίαν, Acts xi. 3; an animal is said ἔχειν head, horns, wings, etc.: Rev. iv. 7 sq.; v. 6; viii. 9; ix. 8 sqq.; xii. 3, etc.; a house, city, or wall, ἔχειν θεμελίους, Heb. xi. 10; Rev. xxi. 14; στάσιν, Heb. ix. 8; [add ἐπιστολὴν ἔχουσαν (R G περιέχ.) τὸν τύπον τοῦτον, Acts xxiii. 25]. **f.** one is said *to have the diseases* or *other ills* with which he is affected or afflicted: μάστιγας, Mk. iii. 10; ἀσθενείας, Acts xxviii. 9; wounds, Rev. xiii. 14; θλῖψιν, Jn. xvi. 33; 1 Co. vii. 28;

Rev. ii. 10. Here belong the expressions δαιμόνιον ἔχειν, to be possessed by a demon, Mt. xi. 18 ; Lk. vii. 33 ; viii. 27 ; Jn. vii. 20 ; viii. 48 sq. 52 ; x. 20 ; Βεελζεβούλ, Mk. iii. 22 ; πνεῦμα ἀκάθαρτον, Mk. iii. 30 ; vii. 25 ; Lk. iv. 33 ; Acts viii. 7 ; πνεῦμα πονηρόν, Acts xix. 13 ; πνεῦμα ἀσθενείας, i. e. a demon causing infirmity, Lk. xiii. 11 ; πνεῦμα ἄλαλον, Mk. ix. 17 ; λεγεῶνα, Mk. v. 15. **g.** one is said *to have* intellectual or spiritual faculties, endowments, virtues, sensations, desires, emotions, affections, faults, defects, etc. : σοφίαν, Rev. xvii. 9 ; γνῶσιν, 1 Co. viii. 1, 10 ; χαρίσματα, Ro. xii. 6 ; προφητείαν, 1 Co. xiii. 2 ; πίστιν, Mt. xvii. 20 ; xxi. 21 ; Mk. xi. 22 ; Lk. xvii. 6 ; Acts xiv. 9 ; Ro. xiv. 22 ; 1 Tim. i. 19 ; Philem. 5 ; πεποίθησιν, 2 Co. iii. 4 ; Phil. iii. 4 ; παρρησίαν, Philem. 8 ; Heb. x. 19 ; 1 Jn. ii. 28 ; iii. 21 ; iv. 17 ; v. 14 ; ἀγάπην, Jn. v. 42 ; xiii. 35 ; xv. 13 ; 1 Jn. iv. 16 ; 1 Co. xiii. 1 sqq. ; 2 Co. ii. 4 ; Phil. ii. 2 ; Philem. 5 ; 1 Pet. iv. 8 ; ἐλπίδα (see ἐλπίς, 2 p. 206ᵃ mid.) ; ζῆλον, zeal, Ro. x. 2 ; envy, jealousy (ἐν τῇ καρδίᾳ), Jas. iii. 14 ; χάριν τινί, to be thankful to one, Lk. xvii. 9 ; 1 Tim. i. 12 ; 2 Tim. i. 3 ; θυμόν, Rev. xii. 12 ; ὑπομονήν, Rev. ii. 3 ; φόβον, 1 Tim. v. 20 ; χαράν, Philem. 7 [Rec.ˢᵗ χάριν] ; 3 Jn. 4 [WH txt. χάριν] ; λύπην, Jn. xvi. 21 ; 2 Co. ii. 3 ; Phil. ii. 27 ; ἐπιθυμίαν, Phil. i. 23 ; ἐπιποθίαν, Ro. xv. 23 ; μνείαν τινος, 1 Th. iii. 6. συνείδησιν καλήν, ἀγαθήν, ἀπρόσκοπον : Acts xxiv. 16 ; 1 Tim. i. 19 ; 1 Pet. iii. 16 ; Heb. xiii. 18 ; συνείδησιν ἁμαρτιῶν, Heb. x. 2 ; ἀγνωσίαν θεοῦ, 1 Co. xv. 34 ; ἀσθένειαν, Heb. vii. 28 ; ἁμαρτίαν, Jn. ix. 41 ; xv. 22, etc. **h.** of age and time : ἡλικίαν, mature years (A. V. *to be of age*), Jn. ix. 21, 23 ; ἔτη, to have (completed) years, be years old, Jn. viii. 57 ; with ἔν τινι added : in a state or condition, Jn. v. 5 [W. 256 (240) note ³ ; B. § 147, 11] ; in a place, τέσσαρας ἡμέρας ἐν τῷ μνημείῳ, Jn. xi. 17 ; beginning or end, or both, Heb. vii. 3 ; Mk. iii. 26 ; Lk. xxii. 37 [see τέλος, 1 a.]. **i.** ἔχειν τι is said of opportunities, benefits, advantages, conveniences, which one enjoys or can make use of : βάθος γῆς, Mt. xiii. 5 ; γῆν πολλήν, Mk. iv. 5 ; ἰκμάδα, Lk. viii. 6 ; καιρόν, Gal. vi. 10 ; Heb. xi. 15 ; Rev. xii. 12 ; ἐξουσίαν, see ἐξουσία, passim ; εἰρήνην διά τινος, Ro. v. 1 (where we must read ἔχομεν, not [with T Tr WH L mrg. (cf. *WH.* Intr. § 404)] ἔχωμεν) ; ἐλευθερίαν, Gal. ii. 4 ; πνεῦμα θεοῦ, 1 Co. vii. 40 ; πνεῦμα Χριστοῦ, Ro. viii. 9 ; νοῦν Χριστοῦ, 1 Co. ii. 16 ; ζωήν, Jn. v. 40 ; x. 10 ; xx. 31 ; τὴν ζωήν, 1 Jn. v. 12 ; ζωὴν αἰώνιον, Mt. xix. 16 ; Jn. iii. 15 sq. 36 [cf. W. 266 (249)] ; v. 24, 39 ; vi. 40, 47, 54 ; 1 Jn. v. 13 ; ἐπαγγελίας, 2 Co. vii. 1 ; Heb. vii. 6 ; μισθόν, Mt. v. 46 ; vi. 1 ; 1 Co. ix. 17 ; τὰ αἰτήματα, the things which we have asked, 1 Jn. v. 15 ; ἔπαινον, Ro. xiii. 3 ; τιμήν, Jn. iv. 44 ; Heb. iii. 3 ; λόγον σοφίας, a reputation for wisdom, Col. ii. 23 [see λόγος, I. 5 fin.] ; καρπόν, Ro. i. 13 ; vi. 21 sq. ; χάριν, benefit, 2 Co. i. 15 [where Tr mrg. WH txt. χαράν] ; χάρισμα, 1 Co. vii. 7 ; προσαγωγήν, Eph. ii. 18 ; iii. 12 ; ἀνάπαυσιν, Rev. iv. 8 ; xiv. 11 ; ἀπόλαυσίν τινος, Heb. xi. 25 ; πρόφασιν, Jn. xv. 22 ; καύχημα, that of which one may glory, Ro. iv. 2 ; Gal. vi. 4 ; καύχησιν, Ro. xv. 17. **k.** ἔχειν τι is used of one on whom something has been laid, on whom it is incumbent as something to be

borne, observed, performed, discharged : ἀνάγκην, 1 Co. vii. 37 ; ἀνάγκην foll. by inf., Lk. xiv. 18 ; xxiii. 17 [R L br. Tr mrg. br.] ; Heb. vii. 27 ; χρείαν τινός (see χρεία, 1) ; εὐχὴν ἐφ' ἑαυτῶν, Acts xxi. 23 ; νόμον, Jn. xix. 7 ; ἐντολήν, 2 Jn. 5 ; Heb. vii. 5 ; ἐπιταγήν, 1 Co. vii. 25 ; διακονίαν, 2 Co. iv. 1 ; πρᾶξιν, Ro. xii. 4 ; ἀγῶνα, Phil. i. 30 ; Col. ii. 1 ; ἔγκλημα, Acts xxiii. 29 ; κρίμα, 1 Tim. v. 12. **l.** ἔχειν τι is used of one to whom something has been intrusted : τὰς κλεῖς, Rev. i. 18 ; iii. 7 ; τὸ γλωσσόκομον, Jn. xii. 6 ; xiii. 29. **m.** in reference to complaints and disputes the foll. phrases are used : ἔχω τι [or without an acc., cf. B. 144 (126)] κατά τινος, *to have something* to bring forward *against one*, to have something to complain of in one, Mt. v. 23 ; Mk. xi. 25 ; foll. by ὅτι, Rev. ii. 4 ; ἔχω κατὰ σοῦ ὀλίγα, ὅτι etc. ib. 14 [here L WH mrg. om. ὅτι], 20 [here G L T Tr WH om. ὀλ.] ; ἔχω τι πρός τινα, *to have some accusation to bring against* one, Acts xxiv. 19 ; συζήτησιν ἐν ἑαυτοῖς, Acts xxviii. 29 [Rec.] ; ζητήματα πρός τινα, Acts xxv. 19 ; λόγον ἔχειν πρός τινα, Acts xix. 38 ; πρᾶγμα πρός τινα, 1 Co. vi. 1 ; μομφὴν πρός τινα, Col. iii. 13 ; κρίματα μετά τινος, 1 Co. vi. 7. **n.** phrases of various kinds : ἔχειν τινὰ κατὰ πρόσωπον, to have one before him, in his presence, [A. V. *face to face* ; see πρόσωπον, 1 a.], Acts xxv. 16 ; κοίτην ἔκ τινος, to conceive by one, Ro. ix. 10 ; τοῦτο ἔχεις, ὅτι etc. thou hast this (which is praiseworthy [cf. W. 595 (553)]) that etc. Rev. ii. 6 ; ἐν ἐμοὶ οὐκ ἔχει οὐδέν, *hath nothing in me* which is his of right, i. q. no power over me (Germ. *er hat mir nichts an*), Jn. xiv. 30 ; ὅ ἐστιν . . . σαββάτου ἔχον ὁδόν, a sabbath-day's journey distant (for the distance is something which the distant place *has*, as it were), Acts i. 12 ; cf. Kypke ad loc. **o.** ἔχω with an inf. [W. 333 (313) ; B. 251 (216)], **a.** like the Lat. *habeo quod* w. the subjunc., i. q. *to be able* : ἔχω ἀποδοῦναι, Mt. xviii. 25 ; Lk. vii. 42 ; xiv. 14 ; τὶ ποιῆσαι, Lk. xii. 4 ; οὐδὲν εἶχον ἀντειπεῖν, they had nothing to oppose (could say nothing against it), Acts iv. 14 ; κατ' οὐδενὸς εἶχε μείζονος ὀμόσαι, Heb. vi. 13 ; add, Jn. viii. 6 (Rec.) ; Acts xxv. 26 [cf. B. as above] ; Eph. iv. 28 ; Tit. ii. 8 ; 2 Pet. i. 15 ; the inf. is om. and to be supplied fr. the context : ὃ ἔσχεν, sc. ποιῆσαι, Mk. xiv. 8 ; see exx. fr. Grk. auth. in Passow s. v. p. 1297ᵃ ; [L. and S. s. v. A. III. 1]. **β.** is used of what there is a certain necessity for doing : βάπτισμα ἔχω βαπτισθῆναι, Lk. xii. 50 ; ἔχω σοί τι εἰπεῖν, vii. 40 ; ἀπαγγεῖλαι, Acts xxiii. 17, 19 ; λαλῆσαι, 18 ; κατηγορῆσαι, Acts xxviii. 19 ; πολλὰ γράφειν, 2 Jn. 12 ; 3 Jn. 13.

II. Intransitively. a. (Lat. *me habeo*) *to hold one's self* or *find one's self* so and so, *to be* in such or such a condition : ἑτοίμως ἔχω, to be ready, foll. by inf., Acts xxi. 13 ; 2 Co. xii. 1 ; 1 Pet. iv. 5 [not WH] ; ἐσχάτως (see ἐσχάτως), Mk. v. 23 ; κακῶς, to be sick, Mt. iv. 24 ; viii. 16 ; ix. 12 ; [xvii. 15 L Tr txt. WH txt.], etc. ; καλῶς, to be well, Mk. xvi. 18 ; κομψότερον, to be better, Jn. iv. 52 ; πῶς, Acts xv. 36 ; ἐν ἑτοίμῳ, foll. by inf., 2 Co. x. 6. **b.** impersonally : ἄλλως ἔχει, it is otherwise, 1 Tim. v. 25 ; οὕτως, Acts viii. 1 ; xii. 15 ; xvii. 11 ; xxiv. 9 ; τὸ νῦν ἔχον, as things now are, for the present, Acts xxiv. 25 (Tob. vii. 11, and exx. fr. later prof. auth. in *Kypke*,

Observv. ii. p. 124; cf. Vig. ed. *Herm.* p. 9; [cf. W. 463 (432)]).

III. Mid. ἔχομαί τινος (in Grk. writ. fr. Hom. down), prop. *to hold one's self to* a thing, *to lay hold of* a thing, *to adhere* or *cling to*; *to be closely joined to* a pers. or thing [cf. W. 202 (190); B. 192 (166 sq.), 161 (140)]: τὰ ἐχόμενα τῆς σωτηρίας, Vulg. *viciniora saluti*, connected with salvation, or which lead to it, Heb. vi. 9, where cf. Bleek; ὁ ἐχόμενος, *near, adjoining, neighboring, bordering, next*: of place, κωμοπόλεις, Mk. i. 38 (νῆσος, Isocr. paneg. § 96; οἱ ἐχόμενοι, neighbors, Hdt. 1, 134); of time, τῇ ἐχομένῃ sc. ἡμέρᾳ, the following day, Lk. xiii. 33; Acts xx. 15, (1 Macc. iv. 28; Polyb. 3, 112, 1; 5, 13, 9); with ἡμέρα added, Acts xxi. 26; σαββάτῳ, Acts xiii. 44 (where R T Tr WH txt. ἐρχομένῳ); ἐνιαυτῷ, 1 Macc. iv. 28 (with var. ἐρχομένῳ ἐν.); τοῦ ἐχομένου ἔτους, Thuc. 6, 3. [COMP.: ἀν-, προσ-αν-, ἀντ-, ἀπ-, ἐν-, ἐπ-, κατ-, μετ-, παρ-, περι-, προ-, προσ-, συν-, ὑπερ-, ὑπ-έχω.]

ἕως, a particle marking a limit, and

I. as a CONJUNCTION signifying **1.** the temporal terminus ad quem, *till, until,* (Lat. *donec, usque dum*); as in the best writ. **a.** with an indic. pret., where something is spoken of which continued up to a certain time: Mt. ii. 9 (ἕως ... ἔστη [ἐστάθη L T Tr WH]); xxiv. 39, (1 Macc. x. 50; Sap. x. 14, etc.). **b.** with ἄν and the aor. subjunc. (equiv. to the Lat. fut. perf.), where it is left doubtful when that will take place till which it is said a thing will continue [cf. W. § 42, 5]: ἴσθι ἐκεῖ, ἕως ἂν εἴπω σοι, Mt. ii. 13; add, v. 18; x. 11; xxiii. 44; Mk. vi. 10; xii. 36; Lk. xvii. 8; xx. 43; Acts ii. 35; Heb. i. 13; after a negative sentence: Mt. v. 18, 26; x. 23 [T WH om. ἄν]; xii. 20; xvi. 28; xxiii. 39; xxiv. 34; Mk. ix. 1; Lk. ix. 27; xxi. 32; 1 Co. iv. 5; with the aor. subj. without the addition of ἄν: Mk. vi. 45 R G; xiv. 32 [here Tr mrg. fut.]; Lk. xv. 4; [xii. 59 T Tr WH]; xxii. 34 L T Tr WH]; 2 Th. ii. 7; Heb. x. 13; Rev. vi. 11 [Rec. ἕως οὗ]; οὐκ ἀνέζησαν ἕως τελεσθῇ τὰ χίλια ἔτη, did not live again till the thousand years had been finished (*elapsi fuerint*), Rev. xx. 5 Rec. Cf. W. § 41 b. 3. **c.** more rarely used with the indic. pres. where the aor. subj. might have been expected [W. u. s.; B. 231 (199)]: so four times ἕως ἔρχομαι, Lk. xix. 13 (where L T Tr WH ἐν ᾧ for ἕως, but cf. Bleek ad loc.); Jn. xxi. 22 sq.; 1 Tim. iv. 13; ἕως ἀπολύει, Mk. vi. 45 L T Tr WH, for R G ἀπολύσῃ (the indic. being due to a blending of dir. and indir. disc.; as in Plut. Lycurg. 29, 3 δεῖν οὖν ἐκείνους ἐμμένειν τοῖς καθεστῶσι νόμοις ... ἕως ἐπάνεισιν). **d.** once with the indic. fut., acc. to an improbable reading in Lk. xiii. 35: ἕως ἥξει Tdf., ἕως ἂν ἥξει Lchm., for R G ἕως ἂν ἥξῃ; [but WH (omitting ἂν ἥξῃ ὅτε) read ἕως εἴπητε; Tr om. ἄν and br. ἥ. ὅ.; cf. B. 231 (199) sq.]. **2.** as in Grk. writ. fr. Hom. down, *as long as, while*, foll. by the indic. in all tenses, — in the N. T. only in the pres.: ἕως ἡμέρα ἐστίν, Jn. ix. 4 [Tr mrg. WH mrg. ὡς]; ἕως (L T Tr WH ὡς) τὸ φῶς ἔχετε, Jn. xii. 35 sq., (ἕως ἔτι φῶς ἐστιν, Plat. Phaedo p. 89 c.); [Mk. vi. 45 (cf. c. above).

II. By a usage chiefly later it gets the force of an ADVERB, Lat. *usque ad*; and **1.** used of a temporal terminus ad quem, *until,* (*unto*); **a.** like a preposition, w. a gen. of time [W. § 54, 6; B. 319 (274)]: ἕως αἰῶνος, Lk. i. 55 Grsb. (Ezek. xxv. 15 Alex.; 1 Chr. xvii. 16; Sir. xvi. 26 Fritz.; xxiv. 9, etc.); τῆς ἡμέρας, Mt. xxvi. 29; xxvii. 64: Lk. i. 80; Acts i. 22 [Tdf. ἄχρι]; Ro. xi. 8, etc.; ὥρας, Mt. xxvii. 45; Mk. xv. 33; Lk. xxiii. 44; τῆς πεντηκοστῆς, 1 Co. xvi. 8; τέλους, 1 Co. i. 8; 2 Co. i. 13; τῆς σήμερον sc. ἡμέρας, Mt. xxvii. 8; τοῦ νῦν, Mt. xxiv. 21; Mk. xiii. 19, (1 Macc. ii. 33); χήρα ἕως ἐτῶν ὀγδοήκ. τεσσάρων a widow (who had attained) even unto eighty-four years, Lk. ii. 37 L T Tr WH; before the names of illustrious men by which a period of time is marked: Mt. i. 17; xi. 13; Lk. xvi. 16 (where T Tr WH μέχρι); Acts xiii. 20; before the names of events: Mt. i. 17 (ἕως μετοικεσίας Βαβυλῶνος); ii. 15; xxiii. 35; xxviii. 20; Lk. xi. 51; Jas. v. 7; ἕως τοῦ ἐλθεῖν, Acts viii. 40 [B. 266 (228); cf. W. § 44, 6; Judith i. 10; xi. 19, etc.]. **b.** with the gen. of the neut. rel. pron. οὗ or ὅτου it gets the force of a conjunction, *until, till* (the time when); **a.** ἕως οὗ (first in Hdt. 2, 143; but after that only in later auth., as Plut. et al. [W. 296 (278) note; B. 230 sq. (199)]): foll. by the indic., Mt. i. 25 [WH br. οὗ]; xiii. 33; Lk. xiii. 21; Acts xxi. 26 [B. l. c.]; foll. by the subj. aor., equiv. to Lat. fut. pf., Mt. xiv. 22; xxvi. 36 (where WH br. οὗ and Lchm. has ἕως οὗ ἄν); Lk. xii. 50 [Rec.; xv. 8 Tr WH]; xxiv. 49; Acts xxv. 21; 2 Pet. i. 19; after a negative sentence, Mt. xvii. 9; Lk. xii. 59 [R G L]; xxii. 18 Tr WH]; Jn. xiii. 38; Acts xxiii. 12, 14, 21. **β.** ἕως ὅτου, **aa.** *until, till* (the time when): foll. by the indic., Jn. ix. 18; foll. by the subj. (without ἄν), Lk. xiii. 8; xv. 8 [R G L T]; after a negation, Lk. xxii. 16, 18 [R G L T]. **ββ.** *as long as, whilst* (Cant. i. 12), foll. by the indic. pres., Mt. v. 25 (see ἄχρι, 1 d. fin.). **c.** before adverbs of time (rarely so in the earlier and more elegant writ., as ἕως ὀψέ, Thuc. 3, 108; [cf. W. § 54, 6 fin.; B. 320 (275)]): ἕως ἄρτι, up to this time, *until now* [Vig. ed. *Herm.* p. 388], Mt. xi. 12; Jn. ii. 10; v. 17; xvi. 24; 1 Jn. ii. 9; 1 Co. iv. 13; viii. 7; xv. 6; ἕως πότε; *how long?* Mt. xvii. 17; Mk. ix. 19; Lk. ix. 41; Jn. x. 24; Rev. vi. 10, (Ps. xii. (xiii.) 2 sq.; 2 S. ii. 26; 1 Macc. vi. 22). **2.** acc. to a usage dating fr. Aristot. down, employed of the local terminus ad quem, *unto, as far as, even to*; **a.** like a prep., with a gen. of place [W. § 54, 6; B. 319 (274)]: ἕως ᾅδου, ἕως τοῦ οὐρανοῦ, Mt. xi. 23; Lk. x. 15; add, Mt. xxiv. 31; xxvi. 58; Mk. xiii. 27; Lk. ii. 15; iv. 29; Acts i. 8; xi. 19, 22; xvii. 15; 2 Co. xii. 2; with gen. of pers., *to the place where one is*: Lk. iv. 42; Acts ix. 38, (ἕως Ὑπερβορέων, Ael. v. h. 3, 18). **b.** with adverbs of place [W. and B. as in c. above]: ἕως ἄνω, Jn. ii. 7; ἕως ἔσω, Mk. xiv. 54; ἕως κάτω, Mt. xxvii. 51; Mk. xv. 38; ἕως ὧδε, Lk. xxiii. 5 [cf. W. § 66, 1 c.]. **c.** with prepositions: ἕως ἔξω τῆς πόλεως, Acts xxi. 5; ἕως εἰς, Lk. xxiv. 50 [R G L mrg., but L txt. T Tr WH ἕως πρός as far as to (Polyb. 3, 82, 6; 12, 17, 4; Gen. xxxviii. 1)]; Polyb. 1, 11, 14; Ael. v. h. 12, 22. **3.** of the limit (terminus) of quantity; with an adv. of number: ἕως ἑπτάκις, Mt. xviii. 21; with numerals: Mt.

xxii. 26 (ἕως τῶν ἑπτά) ; cf. xx. 8 ; Jn. viii. 9 (Rec.) ; Acts viii. 10 ; Heb. viii. 11 ; οὐκ ἔστιν ἕως ἑνός, there is not so much as one, Ro. iii. 12 fr. Ps. xiii. (xiv.) 1.   **4.** of the limit of m e a s u r e m e n t : ἕως ἡμίσους, Mk. vi. 23 ; Esth. v. 3, 6 Alex.   **5.** of the end or limit in a c t i n g

and s u f f e r i n g : ἕως τούτου, Lk. xxii. 51 [see ἐάω, 2] ; ἕως τοῦ θερισμοῦ, Mt. xiii. 30 L Tr WH txt. ; ἕως θανάτου, even to death, so that I almost die, Mk. xiv. 34 ; Mt. xxvi. 38, (Sir. iv. 28 ; xxxi. (xxxiv.) 13 ; xxxvii. 2 ; 4 Macc. xiv. 19).

Z

[Z, ζ, on its substitution for σ see Σ, σ, ς.]

2194   **Zαβουλών,** ὁ, indecl., (זְבֻלוּן [but on the Hebr. form see B. D.] habitation, dwelling, Gen. xxx. 20), Vulg. *Zabulon ; Zebulun,* the tenth son of Jacob ; by meton. *the tribe of Zebulun :* Mt. iv. 13, 15 ; Rev. vii. 8.*

2195   **Zακχαῖος,** -ου, ὁ, (זַךְ pure, innocent ; cf. 2 Esdr. ii. 9 ; Neh. vii. 14), *Zacchæus,* a chief tax-collector : Lk. xix. 2, 5, 8. [B. D. s. v.]*

2196   **Zαρά,** ὁ, (זֶרַח a rising (of light)), indecl., *Zarah* [better *Zerah*], one of the ancestors of Christ : Mt. i. 3 ; cf. Gen. xxxviii. 30.*

2197   **Zαχαρίας,** -ου, ὁ, (זְכַרְיָה and זְכַרְיָהוּ i. e. whom Jehovah remembered), *Zacharias* or *Zachariah* or *Zechariah* ; **1.** a priest, the father of John the Baptist : Lk. i. 5, 12 sq. 18, 21, 40, 59, 67 ; iii. 2.   **2.** a prophet, the son of J e h o i a d a the priest, who was stoned to death in the mid. of the IX. cent. before Christ in the court of the temple : 2 Chr. xxiv. 19 sqq. ; Mt. xxiii. 35 ; Lk. xi. 51. Yet this Zachariah is called in Mt. l. c. the son not of *Jehoiada* but of *Barachiah.* But most interpreters now think (and correctly) that the Evangelist confounded him with that more noted Zachariah the prophet who lived a little after the exile, and was the son of Barachiah (cf. Zech. i. 1), and whose prophecies have a place in the canon. For Christ, to prove that the Israelites throughout their s a c r e d history had been stained with the innocent blood of righteous men, adduced the first and the last example of the murders committed on good men ; for the bks. of the Chron. stand last in the Hebrew canon. But opinions differ about this Zachariah. For according to an ancient tradition, which the Greek church follows (and which has been adopted by *Chr. W. Müller* in the Theol. Stud. u. Krit. for 1841, p. 673 sqq., and formerly by *Hilgenfeld,* krit. Untersuchungen üb. die Evangg. Justins, etc., p. 155 and die Evangg. nach ihrer Entstehung, p. 100), Zachariah the father of John the Baptist is meant (cf. Protev. Jac. c. 23) ; others think (so quite recently Keim, iii. 184 [Eng. trans. v. 218], cf. *Weiss,* das Matthäusevang. p. 499) a certain Zachariah son of *Baruch* (acc. to another reading Βαρισκαίου), who during the war between the Jews and the Romans was slain by the zealots ἐν μέσῳ τῷ ἱερῷ, as Joseph. b. j. 4, 5, 4 relates. Those who hold this opinion believe, either that Jesus divinely predicted this murder and in the

prophetic style said ἐφονεύσατε for φονεύσετε [cf. B. § 137, 4 ; W. 273 (256) n. ; § 40, 5 b.], or that the Evangelist, writing after the destruction of Jerusalem, by an anachronism put this murder into the discourse of Jesus. These inventions are fully refuted by *Fritzsche* on Mt. l. c., and *Bleek,* Erklär. der drei ersten Evangg. ii. p. 177 sqq. ; cf. *Hilgenfeld,* Einl. in d. N. T. p. 487 sq. ; [and Dr. *James Morison,* Com. on Mt., l. c. ; B. D. s. v. Zechariah 6 and s. v. Zacharias 11].*

ζάω, -ῶ, ζῇς, ζῇ, inf. ζῆν [so L T, but R G WH -ῇ-, Tr   **2198** also (exc. 1 Co. ix. 14 ; 2 Co. i. 8) ; cf. W. § 5, 4 c. ; *WH.* Intr. § 410 ; *Lips.* Gram. Unters. p. 5 sq.], ptcp. ζῶν ; impf. ἔζων (Ro. vii. 9, where cod. Vat. has the inferior form ἔζην [found again Col. iii. 7 ἐζῆτε] ; cf. Fritzsche on Rom. ii. p. 38 ; [*WH.* App. p. 169 ; Veitch s. v.]) ; fut. in the earlier form ζήσω (Ro. vi. 2 [not L mrg.] ; Heb. xii. 9 ; L T Tr WH also in Jn. [v. 25] ; vi. [51 T WH], 57, 58 [not L ; xiv. 19 T Tr WH] ; 2 Co. xiii. 4 ; Jas. iv. 15), and much oftener [(?) five times, quotations excepted, viz. Mt. ix. 18 ; Lk. x. 28 ; Jn. xi. 25 ; Ro. viii. 13 ; x. 5 ; cf. Moulton's Winer p. 105] the later form, first used by [Hippocr. 7, 536 (see Veitch s. v.)] Dem., ζήσομαι ; 1 aor. (unused in Attic [Hippocr., Anth. Pal., Plut., al. (see Veitch)]) ἔζησα (Acts xxvi. 5, etc.) ; cf. Bttm. Ausf. Sprachl. ii. 191 sq. ; B. 58 (51) ; Krüger i. p. 172 ; Kühner i. 829 ; W. 86 (83) ; [Veitch s. v.] ; Hebr. חָיָה ; [fr. (Hom.) Theogn., Aeschyl. down] ; *to live ;* **I.** prop.   **1.** *to live, be among the living, be alive* (not *lifeless, not dead*) : Acts xx. 12 ; Ro. vii. 1–3 ; 1 Co. vii. 39 ; 2 Co. i. 8 ; iv. 11 ; 1 Th. iv. 15, 17 ; Rev. xix. 20, etc. ; ψυχὴ ζῶσα, 1 Co. xv. 45 and R Tr mrg. Rev. xvi. 3 ; διὰ παντὸς τοῦ ζῆν, during all their life (on earth), Heb. ii. 15 (διατελεῖν πάντα τὸν τοῦ ζῆν χρόνον, Diod. 1, 74 [cf. B. 262 (225)]) ; ἔτι ζῶν (ptcp. impf. [cf. W. 341 (320)]), while he was yet alive, before his death, Mt. xxvii. 63 ; with ἐν σαρκί added, of the earthly life, Phil. i. 22 ; ὃ δὲ νῦν ζῶ ἐν σαρκί, that life which I live in an earthly body, Gal. ii. 20 [B. 149 (130) ; W. 227 (213)] ; ἐν αὐτῷ ζῶμεν, in God is the cause why we live, Acts xvii. 28 ; ζῶσα τέθνηκε, 1 Tim. v. 6 ; ἐμοὶ τὸ ζῆν Χριστός, my life is devoted to Christ, Christ is the aim, the goal, of my life, Phil. i. 21 ; ζῶντες are opp. to νεκροί, Mt. xxii. 32 ; Mk. xii. 27 ; Lk. xx. 38 ; ζῶντες καὶ νεκροί, Acts x. 42 ; Ro. xiv. 9 ; 2 Tim. iv. 1 ; 1 Pet. iv. 5 ; in the sense of living and thriving, 2 Co. vi. 9; 1 Th. iii. 8; ζῇ ἐν ἐμοὶ Χριστός, Christ is living and operative in me, i. e. the holy mind and energy of Christ pervades and moves me, Gal. ii. 20; ἐκ δυνάμεως θεοῦ ζῆν εἴς τινα, through the power of God to live and be strong toward one (sc. in correcting and judging), 2 Co. xiii. 4; in the absol. sense God is said to be ὁ ζῶν: Mt. xvi. 16; xxvi. 63; Jn. vi. 57; vi. 69 Rec.; Acts xiv. 15; Ro. ix. 26; 2 Co. iii. 3; vi. 16; 1 Th. i. 9; 1 Tim. iii. 15; iv. 10; vi. 17 R G; Heb. iii. 12; ix. 14; x. 31; xii. 22; Rev. vii. 2, (Josh. iii. 10; 2 K. xix. 4, 16; Is. xxxvii. 4, 17; Hos. i. 10; Dan. vi. 20 Theod., 26, etc.); with the addition of εἰς τοὺς αἰῶνας τῶν αἰώνων, Rev. iv. 9; xv. 7; ζῶ ἐγώ (חַי־אָנִי, Num. xiv. 21; Is. xlix. 18, etc.) as I live, (by my life), the formula by which God swears by himself, Ro. xiv. 11. i. q. to continue to live, to be kept alive, (ὅστις ζῆν ἐπιθυμεῖ, πειρᾶσθω νικᾶν, Xen. an. 3, 2, 26 (39)): ἐὰν ὁ κύριος θελήσῃ καὶ ζήσωμεν [-σομεν L T Tr WH], Jas. iv. 15 [B. 210 (181); W. 286 (268 sq.)]; ζῆν ἐπ' ἄρτῳ (Mt. iv. 4, etc.) see ἐπί, B. 2 a. a. (Tob. v. 20); ζῆν ἔκ τινος, to get a living from a thing, 1 Co. ix. 14; also when used of convalescents, Jn. iv. 50 sq. 53; with ἐκ τῆς ἀρρωστίας added, 2 K. i. 2; viii. 8 sq. figuratively, to live and be strong: ἐν τούτοις (for Rec. ἐν αὐτοῖς) in these vices, opp. to the ethical death by which Christians are wholly severed from sin (see ἀποθνήσκω, II. 2 b.), Col. iii. 7; cf. Meyer ad loc. i. q. to be no longer dead, to recover life, be restored to life: Mt. ix. 18; Acts ix. 41; so of Jesus risen from the dead, Mk. xvi. 11; Lk. xxiv. 5, 23; Acts i. 3; xxv. 19; Ro. vi. 10; 2 Co. xiii. 4; opp. to νεκρός, Rev. i. 18; ii. 8; ἔζησεν came to life, lived again, Ro. xiv. 9 G L T Tr WH (opp. to ἀπέθανε); Rev. xiii. 14; xx. 4, 5 [Rec. ἀνέζ.], (Ezek. xxxvii. 9 sq.; on the aorist as marking entrance upon a state see βασιλεύω, fin.); ζῆν ἐκ νεκρῶν, trop. out of moral death to enter upon a new life, dedicated and acceptable to God, Ro. vi. 13; [similarly in Lk. xv. 32 T Tr WH]. i. q. not to be mortal, Heb. vii. 8 (where ἄνθρωποι ἀποθνήσκοντες dying men i. e. whose lot it is to die, are opp. to ὁ ζῶν). **2.** emphatically, and in the Messianic sense, to enjoy real life, i. e. to have true life and worthy of the name,—active, blessed, endless in the kingdom of God (or ζωὴ αἰώνιος; see ζωή, 2 b.): Lk. x. 28; Jn. v. 25; xi. 25; Ro. i. 17; viii. 13; xiv. 9 [(?) see above]; Gal. iii. 12; Heb. xii. 9; with the addition of ἐκ πίστεως, Heb. x. 38; of εἰς τὸν αἰῶνα, Jn. vi. 51, 58; σὺν Χριστῷ, in Christ's society, 1 Th. v. 10; this life in its absolute fulness Christ enjoys, who owes it to God; hence he says ζῶ διὰ τὸν πατέρα, Jn. vi. 57; by the gift and power of Christ it is shared in by the faithful, who accordingly are said ζήσειν δι' αὐτόν, Jn. vi. 57; δι' αὐτοῦ, 1 Jn. iv. 9. with a dat. denoting the respect, πνεύματι, 1 Pet. iv. 6; ὄνομα ἔχεις ὅτι ζῇς καὶ νεκρὸς εἶ, thou art said to have life (i. e. vigorous spiritual life bringing forth good fruit) and (yet) thou art dead (ethically), Rev. iii. 1. In the O. T. ζῆν denotes to live most happily in the enjoyment of the theocratic blessings: Lev. xviii. 5; Deut. iv. 1; viii. 1; xxx. 16. **3.** to live i. e. pass life, of the manner of living and acting; of morals or char-acter: μετὰ ἀνδρός with acc. of time, of a married woman, Lk. ii. 36; χωρὶς νόμου, without recognition of the law, Ro. vii. 9; Φαρισαῖος, Acts xxvi. 5; also ἐν κόσμῳ, Col. ii. 20; with ἐν and a dat. indicating the act or state of the soul: ἐν πίστει, Gal. ii. 20; ἐν τῇ ἁμαρτίᾳ, to devote life to sin, Ro. vi. 2; with adverbs expressing the manner: εὐσεβῶς, 2 Tim. iii. 12; Tit. ii. 12; ἀσώτως, Lk. xv. 13; ἐθνικῶς, Gal. ii. 14; ἀδίκως, Sap. xiv. 28; ζῆν τινι (dat. of pers., a phrase com. in Grk. auth. also, in Lat. vivere alicui; cf. Fritzsche on Rom. vol. iii. p. 176 sqq.), to devote, consecrate, life to one; so to live that life results in benefit to some one or to his cause: τῷ θεῷ, Lk. xx. 38; Ro. vi. 10 sq.; Gal. ii. 19, (4 Macc. xvi. 25); τῷ Χριστῷ, 2 Co. v. 15; that man is said ἑαυτῷ ζῆν who makes his own will his law, is his own master, Ro. xiv. 7; 2 Co. v. 15; w. dat. of the thing to which life is devoted: τῇ δικαιοσύνῃ, 1 Pet. ii. 24; πνεύματι, to be actuated by the Spirit, Gal. v. 25; κατὰ σάρκα, as the flesh dictates, Ro. viii. 12 sq.

II. Metaph. of inanimate things; **a.** ὕδωρ ζῶν, מַיִם חַיִּים (Gen. xxvi. 19; Lev. xiv. 5; etc.), living water, i. e. bubbling up, gushing forth, flowing, with the suggested idea of refreshment and salubrity (opp. to the water of cisterns and pools, [cf. our spring water]), is figuratively used of the spirit and truth of God as satisfying the needs and desires of the soul: Jn. iv. 10 sq.; vii. 38; ἐπὶ ζώσας πηγὰς ὑδάτων, Rev. vii. 17 Rec. **b.** having vital power in itself and exerting the same upon the soul: ἐλπὶς ζῶσα, 1 Pet. i. 3; λόγος θεοῦ, 1 Pet. i. 23; Heb. iv. 12; λόγια sc. τοῦ θεοῦ, Acts vii. 38; cf. Deut. xxxii. 47; ὁδὸς ζῶσα, Heb. x. 20 (this phrase describing that char-acteristic of divine grace, in granting the pardon of sin and fellowship with God, which likens it to a way lead-ing to the heavenly sanctuary). In the same manner the predicate ὁ ζῶν is applied to those things to which persons are compared who possess real life (see I. 2 above), in the expressions λίθοι ζῶντες, 1 Pet. ii. 4; ὁ ἄρτος ὁ ζῶν (see ἄρτος, fin.), Jn. vi. 51; θυσία ζῶσα (tacitly opp. to slain victims), Ro. xii. 1. [Comp.: ἀνα-, συ-ζάω.]

ζβέννυμι, see σβέννυμι and s. v. Σ, σ, ς.   **see 4570**

Ζεβεδαῖος, -ου, ὁ, Zebedee, (זַבְדִּי for זְבַדְיָה [i. e. my gift],   **2199** a form of the prop. name which occurs a few times in the O. T., as 1 Chr. xxvii. 27 (Sept. Ζαβδί), munificent, [others for זְבַדְיָה gift of Jehovah]; fr. זָבַר to give), a Jew, by occupation a fisherman, husband of Salome, fa-ther of the apostles James and John: Mt. iv. 21; x. 2 (3); xx. 20; xxvi. 37; xxvii. 56; Mk. i. 19 sq.; iii. 17; x. 35; Lk. v. 10; Jn. xxi. 2.*

ζεστός, -ή, -όν, (ζέω,) boiling hot, hot, [Strab., App.,   **2200** Diog. Laërt., al.]; metaph. of fervor of mind and zeal: Rev. iii. 15 sq.*

ζεῦγος, -εος (-ους), τό, (ζεύγνυμι to join, yoke,) two   **2201** draught-cattle (horses or oxen or mules) yoked together, a pair or yoke of beasts: Lk. xiv. 19 (צֶמֶד, 1 Kings xix. 19, etc.; often in Grk. writ. fr. Hom. Il. 18, 543 down). **2.** univ. a pair: Lk. ii. 24 (Hdt. 3, 130; Aeschyl. Ag. 44; Xen. oec. 7, 18, and often in Grk. writ.).*

2202   **ζευκτηρία**, -ας, ἡ, (fr. the adj. ζευκτήριος, fit for joining or binding together), *a band, fastening* : Acts xxvii. 40. Found nowhere else.*

2203   **Ζεύς**, [but gen. Διός, (dat. Διΐ), acc. Δία (or Δίαν), (fr. old nom. Δίς), *Zeus*, corresponding to Lat. *Jupiter* (A. V.) : Acts xiv. 12 (see Δίς); ὁ ἱερεὺς τοῦ Διὸς τοῦ ὄντος πρὸ τῆς πόλεως, *the priest of Zeus whose temple was before the city*, ibid. 13 (cf. Meyer ad loc.)]. See Δίς.*

2204   **ζέω**; *to boil with heat, be hot*; often in Grk. writ.; thus of water, Hom. Il. 18, 349; 21, 362 (365); metaph. used of 'boiling' anger, love, zeal for what is good or bad, etc. (Tragg., Plat., Plut., al.); ζέων (on this uncontracted form cf. Bttm. Ausf. Spr. [or his School Gram. (Robinson's trans.)] § 105 N. 2, i. p. 481; Matthiae i. p. 151; [Hadley § 371 b.]) τῷ πνεύματι, *fervent in spirit*, said of zeal for what is good, Acts xviii. 25; Ro. xii. 11; cf. esp. Rückert and Fritzsche on Ro. l. c.*

see 2206   **ζηλεύω**; i. q. ζηλόω, q. v.; **1.** *to envy, be jealous*: Simplicius in Epict. c. 26 p. 131 ed. Salmas. [c. 19, 2 p. 56, 34 Didot] οὐδεὶς τῶν τ᾽ ἀγαθὸν τὸ ἀνθρώπινον ζητούντων φθονεῖ ἢ ζηλεύει ποτέ. **2.** in a good sense, *to imitate emulously, strive after*: ἔργα ἀρετῆς, οὐ λόγους, Democr. ap. Stob. flor. app. 14, 7, iv. 384 ed. Gaisf.; intrans. *to be full of zeal for good, be zealous*: Rev. iii. 19 L T Tr txt. WH, for Rec. ζήλωσον [cf. WH. App. p. 171].*

2205   **ζῆλος**, -ου, ὁ, and (in Phil. iii. 6 L T Tr WH; [2 Co. ix. 2 T Tr WH]) τὸ ζῆλος (Ignat. ad Trall. 4; διὰ ζῆλος, Clem. Rom. 1 Cor. 4, 8 ["in Clem. Rom. §§ 3, 4, 5, 6 the masc. and neut. seem to be interchanged without any law" (Lghtft.). For facts see esp. Clem. Rom. ed. 2 Hilgenfeld (1876) p. 7; cf. WH. App. p. 158; W. § 9, N. 2; B. 23 (20)]; (fr. ζέω [Curtius § 567; Vaniček p. 757]); Sept. for קִנְאָה; *excitement of mind, ardor, fervor of spirit*; **1.** *zeal, ardor in embracing, pursuing, defending anything*: 2 Co. vii. 11; ix. 2; κατὰ ζῆλος, as respects zeal (in maintaining religion), Phil. iii. 6; with gen. of the obj., *zeal in behalf of, for* a pers. or thing, Jn. ii. 17 fr. Ps. lxviii. (lxix.) 10; Ro. x. 2, (1 Macc. ii. 58; Soph. O. C. 943); ὑπέρ τινος, gen. of pers., 2 Co. vii. 7; Col. iv. 13 Rec. with subject. gen. ζῆλῳ θεοῦ, with a jealousy such as God has, hence most pure and solicitous for their salvation, 2 Co. xi. 2; *the fierceness of indignation, punitive zeal*, πυρός (of penal fire, which is personified [see πῦρ, fin.]), Heb. x. 27 (Is. xxvi. 11; Sap. v. 18). **2.** *an envious and contentious rivalry, jealousy*: Ro. xiii. 13; 1 Co. iii. 3; Jas. iii. 14, 16; ἐπλήσθησαν ζήλου, Acts v. 17; xiii. 45; plur. ζῆλοι, now the stirrings or motions of ζῆλος, now its outbursts and manifestations: 2 Co. xii. 20; Gal. v. 20; but in both pass. L T Tr [WH, yet in Gal. l. c. WH only in txt.] have adopted ζῆλος (ζῆλοί τε καὶ φθόνοι, Plat. legg. 3 p. 679 c.). [On the distinction between ζῆλος (which may be used in a good sense) and φθόνος (used only in a bad sense) cf. *Trench*, Syn. § xxvi.; *Cope* on Aristot. rhet. 2, 11, 1 (διὸ καὶ ἐπιεικές ἐστιν ὁ ζῆλος καὶ ἐπιεικῶν, τὸ δὲ φθονεῖν φαῦλον καὶ φαύλων).]*

2206   **ζηλόω**, -ῶ; 1 aor. ἐζήλωσα; pres. pass. inf. ζηλοῦσθαι; (ζῆλος, q. v.); Sept. for קָנָא; *to burn with zeal;* **1.**

---

absol. *to be heated* or *to boil* [A.V. *to be moved*] *with envy, hatred, anger* : Acts vii. 9; xvii. 5 (where Grsb. om. ζηλώσ.); 1 Co. xiii. 4; Jas. iv. 2; in a good sense, *to be zealous in the pursuit of good*, Rev. iii. 19 R G Tr mrg. (the aor. ζήλωσον marks the entrance into the mental state, see βασιλεύω, fin.; ἐζήλωσε, he was seized with indignation, 1 Macc. ii. 24). **2.** trans.; τί, *to desire earnestly, pursue*: 1 Co. xii. 31; xiv. 1, 39, (Sir. li. 18; Thuc. 2, 37; Eur. Hec. 255; Dem. 500, 2; al.); μᾶλλον δέ, sc. ζηλοῦτε, foll. by ἵνα, 1 Co. xiv. 1 [B. 237 (205); cf. W. 577 (537)]. τινά, **a.** *to desire one earnestly, to strive after, busy one's self* about him : to exert one's self for one (that he may not be torn from me), 2 Co. xi. 2; to seek to draw over to one's side, Gal. iv. 17 [cf. ἵνα, II. 1 d.]; to court one's good will and favor, Prov. xxiii. 17; xxiv. 1; Ps. xxxvi. (xxxvii.) 1; so in pass. *to be the object of the zeal of others, to be zealously sought after*: Gal. iv. 18 [here Tr mrg. ζηλοῦσθε, but cf. WH. Intr. § 404]. **b.** *to envy one*: Gen. xxvi. 14; xxx. 1; xxxvii. 11; Hes. opp. 310; Hom. Cer. 168, 223; and in the same sense, acc. to some interpp., in Acts vii. 9; but there is no objection to considering ζηλώσαντες here as used absol. (see 1 above [so A.V. (not R.V.)]) and τὸν Ἰωσήφ as depending on the verb ἀπέδοντο alone. [COMP.: παρα-ζηλόω.]*

2207 & 2208   **ζηλωτής**, -οῦ, ὁ, (ζηλόω), *one burning with zeal; a zealot*; **1.** absol., for the Hebr. קַנָּא, used of God as jealous of any rival and sternly vindicating his control: Ex. xx. 5; Deut. iv. 24, etc. From the time of the Maccabees there existed among the Jews a class of men, called *Zealots*, who rigorously adhered to the Mosaic law and endeavored even by a resort to violence, after the example of Phinehas (Num. xxv. 11, ζηλωτὴς Φινεές 4 Macc. xviii. 12), to prevent religion from being violated by others; but in the latter days of the Jewish commonwealth they used their holy zeal as a pretext for the basest crimes, Joseph. b. j. 4, 3, 9; 4, 5, 1; 4, 6, 3; 7, 8, 1. To this class perhaps Simon the apostle had belonged, and hence got the surname ὁ ζηλωτής: Lk. vi. 15; Acts i. 13; [cf. *Schürer*, Neutest. Zeitgesch., Index s. v. Zeloten; *Edersheim*, Jesus the Messiah, i. 237 sqq.]. **2.** with gen. of the obj.: w. gen. of the thing, *most eagerly desirous of, zealous for, a thing*; **a.** *to acquire a thing*, [zealous of] (see ζηλόω, 2) : 1 Co. xiv. 12; Tit. ii. 14; 1 Pet. iii. 13 L T Tr WH, (ἀρετῆς, Philo, praem. et poen. § 2; τῆς εὐσεβείας, de monarch. l. i. § 3; εὐσεβείας κ. δικαιοσύνης, de poenit. § 1; τῶν πολεμικῶν ἔργων, Diod. 1, 73; περὶ τῶν ἀνηκόντων εἰς σωτηρίαν, Clem. Rom. 1 Cor. 45, 1). **b.** *to defend and uphold a thing*, vehemently contending for a thing, [zealous for] : νόμου, Acts xxi. 20 (2 Macc. iv. 2); τῶν πατρικῶν παραδόσεων, Gal. i. 14 (τῶν αἰγυπτιακῶν πλασμάτων, Philo, vit. Moys. iii. § 19; τῆς ἀρχαίας κ. σώφρονος ἀγωγῆς, Diod. excerpt. p. 611 [fr. l. 37, vol. ii. 564 Didot]); w. gen. of pers. : θεοῦ, intent on protecting the majesty and authority of God by contending for the Mosaic law, Acts xxii. 3. (In prof. auth. also *an emulator, admirer, imitator, follower of any one*.)*

2209   **ζημία**, -ας, ἡ, *damage, loss*, [Soph., Hdt. down]: Acts

xxvii. 10, 21; ἡγεῖσθαι ζημίαν (Xen. mem. 2, 4, 3; τινά, acc. of pers., 2, 3, 2), τί, to regard a thing as a loss: Phil. iii. 7 (opp. to κέρδος), 8.*

2210   ζημιόω, -ῶ: (ζημία), to affect with damage, do damage to: τινά ([Thuc.], Xen., Plat.); in the N. T. only in Pass., fut. ζημιωθήσομαι ([Xen. mem. 3, 9, 12, al.; but "as often"] in prof. auth. [fut. mid.] ζημιώσομαι in pass. sense; cf. Krüger § 39, 11 Anm.; Kühner on Xen. mem. u. s.; [L. and S. s. v.; Veitch s. v.]); 1 aor. ἐζημιώθην; absol. to sustain damage, to receive injury, suffer loss: 1 Co. iii. 15; ἔν τινι ἔκ τινος, in a thing from one, 2 Co. vii. 9; with acc. of the thing: (one from whom another is taken away [as a penalty] by death, is said τὴν ψυχὴν τινος ζημιοῦσθαι, Hdt. 7, 39), τὴν ψυχὴν αὐτοῦ, to forfeit his life, i. e. acc. to the context, eternal life, Mt. xvi. 26; Mk. viii. 36, for which Luke, in ix. 25, ἑαυτόν i. e. himself, by being shut out from the everlasting kingdom of God. πάντα ἐζημιώθην, reflexive [yet see Meyer], I forfeited, gave up all things, I decided to suffer the loss of all these [(?)] things, Phil. iii. 8.*

2211   Ζηνᾶς [cf. Bp. Lghtft. on Col. iv. 15; W. § 16 N. 1], -ᾶν, [B. 20 (18)], ὁ, Zenas, at first a teacher of the Jewish law, afterwards a Christian: Tit. iii. 13. [B.D. s. v.]*

2212   ζητέω, -ῶ; impf. 3 pers. sing. ἐζήτει, plur. ἐζήτουν; fut. ζητήσω; 1 aor. ἐζήτησα; Pass., pres. ζητοῦμαι; impf. 3 pers. sing. ἐζητεῖτο (Heb. viii. 7); 1 fut. ζητηθήσομαι (Lk. xii. 48); [fr. Hom. on]; Sept. for דָּרַשׁ, and much oftener for בָּקַשׁ; to seek, i. e. **1.** to seek in order to find; **a.** univ. and absol.: Mt. vii. 7 sq.; Lk. xi. 9 sq. (see εὑρίσκω, 1 a.); τινά, Mk. i. 37; Lk. ii. [45 R L mrg.], 48; [iv. 42 Rec.]; Jn. vi. 24; xviii. 4, 7; Acts x. 19, and often; foll. by ἐν w. dat. of place, Acts ix. 11; w. acc. of the thing (μαργαρίτας), of buyers, Mt. xiii. 45; something lost, Mt. xviii. 12; Lk. xix. 10; τὶ ἔν τινι, as fruit on a tree, Lk. xiii. 6 sq.; ἀνάπαυσιν, a place of rest, Mt. xii. 43; Lk. xi. 24; after the Hebr. (בַּקֵּשׁ אֶת־נֶפֶשׁ [cf. W. 33 (32); 18]) ψυχήν τινος, to seek, plot against, the life of one, Mt. ii. 20; Ro. xi. 3, (Ex. iv. 19, etc.); univ. τί ζητεῖς; what dost thou seek? what dost thou wish? Jn. i. 38 (39); [iv. 27]. **b.** to seek [i. e. in order to find out] by thinking, meditating, reasoning; to inquire into: περὶ τίνος ζητεῖτε μετ' ἀλλήλων; Jn. xvi. 19; foll. by indirect disc., πῶς, τί, τίνα: Mk. xi. 18; xiv. 1, 11; Lk. xii. 29; xxii. 2; 1 Pet. v. 8; τὸν θεόν, to follow up the traces of divine majesty and power, Acts xvii. 27 (univ. to seek the knowledge of God, Sap. i. 1; xiii. 6; [Philo, monarch. i. § 5]). **c.** to seek after, seek for, aim at, strive after: εὐκαιρίαν, Mt. xxvi. 16; Lk. xxii. 6; ψευδομαρτυρίαν, Mt. xxvi. 59; Mk. xiv. 55; τὸν θάνατον, an opportunity to die, Rev. ix. 6; λύσιν, 1 Co. vii. 27; τὴν βασιλ. τοῦ θεοῦ, Mt. vi. 33; Lk. xii. 31; τὰ ἄνω, Col. iii. 1; εἰρήνην, 1 Pet. iii. 11; ἀφθαρσίαν etc. Ro. ii. 7; δόξαν ἔκ τινος, 1 Th. ii. 6; τὴν δόξαν τὴν παρά τινος, Jn. v. 44; τά τινος, the property of one, 2 Co. xii. 14; τὴν δόξαν θεοῦ, to seek to promote the glory of God, Jn. vii. 18; viii. 50; τὸ θέλημά τινος, to attempt to establish, Jn. v. 30; τὸ σύμφορόν τινος, to seek to further the profit or advantage of one, 1 Co. x. 33, i. q. ζητεῖν τά τινος, ib. x. 24; xiii. 5; Phil. ii. 21; ὑμᾶς, to seek

to win your souls, 2 Co. xii. 14; τὸν θεόν, to seek the favor of God (see ἐκζητέω, a.), Ro. x. 20; [iii. 11 Tr mrg. WH mrg.]. foll. by inf. [B. 258 (222); W. § 44, 3] to seek i. e. desire, endeavor: Mt. xii. 46, [47 (WH in mrg. only)]; xxi. 46; Mk. [vi. 19 L Tr mrg.]; xii. 12; Lk. v. 18; vi. 19; ix. 9; Jn. v. 18; vii. 4 [B. § 142, 4], 19 sq.; Acts xiii. 8; xvi. 10; Ro. x. 3; Gal. i. 10; ii. 17; foll. by ἵνα [B. 237 (205)], 1 Co. xiv. 12. **2.** to seek i. e. require, demand: [σημεῖον, Mk. viii. 12 L T Tr WH; Lk. xi. 29 T Tr WH]; σοφίαν, 1 Co. i. 22; δοκιμήν, 2 Co. xiii. 3; τὶ παρά τινος, to crave, demand something from some one, Mk. viii. 11; Lk. xi. 16; xii. 48; ἔν τινι, dat. of pers., to seek in one i. e. to require of him, foll. by ἵνα, 1 Co. iv. 2. [COMP.: ἀνα-, ἐκ-, ἐπι-, συ-ζητέω.]

2213   ζήτημα, -τος, τό, (ζητέω), a question, debate: Acts xv. 2; xxvi. 3; νόμου, about the law, Acts xxiii. 29; περί τινος, Acts xviii. 15; xxv. 19. [From Soph. down.]

2214   ζήτησις, -εως, ἡ, (ζητέω), **a.** a seeking: [Hdt.], Thuc. 8, 57; al. **b.** inquiry (Germ. die Frage): περί τινος, Acts xxv. 20. **c.** a questioning, debate: Acts xv. 2 (for Rec. συζήτησις); 7 T Tr txt. WH; περί τινος, Jn. iii. 25. **d.** a subject of questioning or debate, matter of controversy: 1 Tim. i. 4 R G L; vi. 4; 2 Tim. ii. 23; Tit. iii. 9.*

2215   ζιζάνιον, -ου, τό, (doubtless a word of Semitic origin; Arab. زوان, Syr. ܙܝܙܢܐ [see Schaaf, Lex. s. v. p. 148], Talmud זוֹנִין or זוּנִין; Suid. ζιζάνιον· ἡ ἐν τῷ σίτῳ αἶρα), zizanium, [A. V. tares], a kind of darnel, bastard wheat [but see reff. below], resembling wheat except that the grains are black: Mt. xiii. 25–27, 29 sq. 36, 38, 40. (Geop. [for reff. see B. D. Am. ed. p. 3177 note]). Cf. Win. RWB. s. v. Lolch; Furrer in Schenkel B. L. iv. 57; [B.D., and Tristram, Nat. Hist. of the Bible, s. v. Tares].*

see 4667   Ζμύρνα, so Tdf. in Rev. i. 11, etc., for Σμύρνα, q. v. --

2216   Ζοροβάβελ, in Joseph. Ζοροβάβηλος, -ου, ὁ, (זְרֻבָּבֶל, i. e. either for זְרוּבָבֶל dispersed in Babylonia, or for זְרֻעַ בְּבֶל begotten in Babylonia), Zerubbabel, Vulg. Zorobabel, a descendant of David, the leader of the first colony of the Jews on their return from the Babylonian exile: Mt. i. 12 sq.; Lk. iii. 27.*

2217   ζόφος, -ου, ὁ, (akin to γνόφος, δνόφος, νέφος, κνέφας, see Bttm. Lexil. ii. p. 266 [Fishlake's trans. p. 378]; cf. Curtius p. 706), darkness, blackness: Heb. xii. 18 L T Tr WH; as in Hom. Il. 15, 191; 21, 56, etc., used of the darkness of the nether world (cf. Grimm on Sap. xvii. 14), 2 Pet. ii. 4; Jude 6; ζόφος τοῦ σκότους (cf. חֹשֶׁךְ־אֲפֵלָה, Ex. x. 22), the blackness of (i. e. the densest) darkness, 2 Pet. ii. 17; Jude 13. [Cf. Trench § c.]*

2218   ζυγός, -οῦ, ὁ, for which in Grk. writ. before Polyb. τὸ ζυγόν was more com., (fr. ζεύγνυμι), **1.** a yoke; **a.** prop. such as is put on draught-cattle. **b.** metaph. used of any burden or bondage: as that of slavery, 1 Tim. vi. 1 (Lev. xxvi. 13), δουλείας, Gal. v. 1 (Soph. Aj. 944; δουλοσύνης, Dem. 322, 12); of troublesome laws imposed on one, esp. of the Mosaic law, Acts xv. 10; Gal. v. 1; hence the name is so transferred to the commands of Christ as to contrast them with the commands of the Pharisees which were a veritable 'yoke'; yet even Christ's commands must be submitted to, though easier to be kept : Mt. xi. 29 sq. (less aptly in Clem. Rom. 1 Cor. 16, 17 Christians are called οἱ ὑπὸ τὸν ζυγὸν τῆς χάριτος ἐλθόντες [cf. Harnack ad loc.]).   **2.** *a balance, pair of scales* : Rev. vi. 5 (as in Is. xl. 12; Lev. xix. 36; Plat. rep. 8, 550 e.; Ael. v. h. 10, 6 ; al.).*

2219   ζύμη, -ης, ἡ, (ζέω [but cf. Curtius p. 626 sq.; Vaniček, p. 760]), *leaven* : Mt. xiii. 33 ; Lk. xiii. 21, (Ex. xii. 15; Lev. ii. 11 ; Deut. xvi. 3, etc.; Aristot. gen. an. 3, 4 ; Joseph. antt. 3, 10, 6 ; Plut. mor. p. 289 sq. [quaest. Rom. 109]) ; τοῦ ἄρτου, Mt. xvi. 12 ; metaph. of inveterate mental and moral corruption, 1 Co. v. [7], 8, (Ignat. ad Magnes. 10) ; viewed in its tendency to infect others, ζύμη τῶν Φαρισαίων: Mt. xvi. 6, 11 ; Mk. viii. 15 ; Lk. xii. 1, which fig. Mt. xvi. 12 explains of the t e a c h i n g of the Phar., Lk. l. c. more correctly [definitely ?] of their h y p o c r i s y. It is applied to that which, though small in quantity, yet by its influence thoroughly pervades a thing : either in a good sense, as in the parable Mt. xiii. 33 ; Lk. xiii. 21, (see ζυμόω) ; or in a bad sense, of a pernicious influence, as in the proverb μικρὰ ζύμη ὅλον τὸ φύραμα ζυμοῖ *a little leaven leaveneth the whole lump,* which is used variously, acc. to the various things to which it is applied, viz. a single sin corrupts a whole church, 1 Co. v. 6 ; a slight inclination to error (respecting the necessity of circumcision) easily perverts the whole conception of faith, Gal. v. 9 ; but many interpp. explain the passage 'even a few false teachers lead the whole church into error.' *

2220   ζυμόω, -ῶ ; 1 aor. pass. ἐζυμώθην ; (ζύμη) ; *to leaven* (to mix leaven with dough so as to make it ferment) : 1 Co. v. 6 ; Gal. v. 9, (on which pass. see ζύμη) ; ἕως ἐζυμώθη ὅλον, sc. τὸ ἄλευρον, words which refer to the saving power of the gospel, which from a small beginning will gradually pervade and transform the whole human race: Mt. xiii. 33 ; Lk. xiii. 21. (Sept., Hipp., Athen., Plut.) *

2221   ζωγρέω, -ῶ ; pf. pass. ptcp. ἐζωγρημένος ; (ζωός alive, and ἀγρέω [poet. form of ἀγρεύω, q. v.]) ;   **1.** *to take alive* (Hom., Hdt., Thuc., Xen., al.; Sept.).   **2.** univ. *to take, catch, capture* : ἐζωγρημένοι ὑπ' αὐτοῦ (i. e. τοῦ διαβόλου) εἰς τὸ ἐκείνου θέλημα, if they are held captive to do his will, 2 Tim. ii. 26 [al. make ἐζ. ὑπ' αὐτ. parenthetic and refer ἐκείνου to G o d ; see ἐκεῖνος, 1 c.; cf. Ellic. in loc.] ; ἀνθρώπους ἔσῃ ζωγρῶν, thou shalt catch men, i. e. by teaching thou shalt win their souls for the kingdom of God, Lk. v. 10.*

2222   ζωή, -ῆς, ἡ, (fr. ζάω, ζῶ), Sept. chiefly for חַיִּים ; *life* ;   **1.** univ. *life*, i. e. *the state of one who is possessed of vitality* or *is animate* : 1 Pet. iii. 10 (on which see ἀγαπάω) ; Heb. vii. 3, 16 ; αὐτὸς (ὁ θεὸς) διδοὺς πᾶσιν ζωὴν κ. πνοήν, Acts xvii. 25 ; πνεῦμα ζωῆς ἐκ τοῦ θεοῦ, the vital spirit, the breath of (i. e. imparting) life, Rev. xi. 11 (Ezek. xxxvii. 5) ; πᾶσα ψυχὴ ζωῆς, gen. of possess., *every living soul,* Rev. xvi. 3 G L T Tr txt. WH ; spoken of earthly life : ἡ ζωή τινος, Lk. xii. 15 ; Acts viii. 33 (see αἴρω, 3 h.); Jas. iv. 14 ; ἐν τῇ ζωῇ σου, whilst thou wast living on earth, Lk. xvi. 25 (ἐν τῇ ζωῇ αὐτοῦ, Sir. xxx. 5 ; l. 1) ; ἐν τῇ ζωῇ ταύτῃ, 1 Co. xv. 19 ; πᾶσαι αἱ ἡμέραι τῆς ζωῆς τινος,

Lk. i. 75 Rec. (Gen. iii. 14 ; Ps. cxxvii. (cxxviii.) 5 ; Sir. xxii. 12 (10)). ἐπαγγελία ζωῆς τῆς νῦν κ. τῆς μελλούσης, a promise looking to the present and the future life, 1 Tim. iv. 8 ; ζωή and θάνατος are contrasted in Ro. viii. 38 ; 1 Co. iii. 22 ; Phil. i. 20 ; of a life preserved in the midst of perils, with a suggestion of vigor, 2 Co. iv. 12 (the life of Paul is meant here, which exerts a saving power on the Corinthians by his discharge of his apostolic duties) ; of the life of persons raised from the dead : ἐν καινότητι ζωῆς, figuratively spoken of a new mode of life, dedicated to God, Ro. vi. 4 ; of the life of Jesus after his resurrection, Acts ii. 28 ; Ro. v. 10 ; of the same, with the added notion of vigor, 2 Co. iv. 10 sq.   **2.** used e m p h a t i c a l l y,   **a.** of *the absolute fulness of life, both essential and ethical, which belongs to God, and through him both to the hypostatic* λ ό γ ο s *and to Christ* in whom the λόγος put on human nature : ὥσπερ ὁ πατὴρ ἔχει ζωὴν ἐν ἑαυτῷ, οὕτως ἔδωκεν καὶ τῷ υἱῷ ζωὴν ἔχειν ἐν ἑαυτῷ, Jn. v. 26 ; ἐν αὐτῷ (sc. τῷ λόγῳ) ζωὴ ἦν καὶ ἡ ζωὴ ἦν τὸ φῶς τῶν ἀνθρώπων, in him life was (comprehended), and the life (transfused from the Logos into created natures) was the light. (i. e. the intelligence) of men (because the life of men is self-conscious, and thus a fountain of intelligence springs up), Jn. i. 4 ; ὁ λόγος τῆς ζωῆς, the Logos having life in itself and communicating it to others, 1 Jn. i. 1 ; ἡ ζωὴ ἐφανερώθη, was manifested in Christ, clothed in flesh, ibid. 2. From this divine fountain of life flows forth that life which is next to be defined : viz.   **b.** *life real and genuine,* "*vita quae sola vita nominanda*" (Cic. de sen. 21, 77), *a life active and vigorous, devoted to God, blessed, the portion even in this world of those who put their trust in Christ, but after the resurrection to be consummated by new accessions (among them a more perfect body), and to last forever* (the writers of the O. T. have anticipated the conception, in their way, by employing חַיִּים to denote a happy life and every kind of blessing : Deut. xxx. 15, 19 ; Mal. ii. 5 ; Ps. xxxiii. (xxxiv.) 13 ; Prov. viii. 35 ; xii. 28, etc.) : Jn. vi. 51, 63 ; xiv. 6 ; Ro. vii. 10 ; viii. 6, 10 ; 2 Co. ii. 16 ; Phil. ii. 16 ; [Col. iii. 4] ; 2 Pet. i. 3 ; 1 Jn. v. 11, 16, 20 ; with the addition of τοῦ θεοῦ, supplied by God [W. 186 (175)], Eph. iv. 18 ; ἡ ἐν Χριστῷ, to be obtained in fellowship with Christ, 2 Tim. i. 1 ; μεταβεβηκέναι ἐκ τοῦ θανάτου εἰς ζωήν, Jn. v. 24 ; 1 Jn. iii. 14 ; ὄψεσθαι τὴν ζωήν, Jn. iii. 36 ; ἔχειν ζωήν, Jn. v. 40 ; x. 10 ; 1 Jn. v. 12 ; with ἐν ἑαυτῷ (or -τοῖς) added, Jn. v. 26 ; [vi. 53] ; διδόναι, Jn. vi. 33 ; χάρις ζωῆς, the grace of God evident in the life obtained, 1 Pet. iii. 7 ; τὸ πνεῦμα τῆς ζωῆς ἐν Χριστῷ Ἰησοῦ, the Spirit, the repository and imparter of life, and which is received by those united to Christ, Ro. viii. 2 ; ὁ ἄρτος τῆς ζωῆς (see ἄρτος, fin.), Jn. vi. 35, 48 ; τὸ φῶς τῆς ζ. the light illumined by which one arrives at life, Jn. viii. 12. more fully ζωὴ αἰώνιος and ἡ ζωὴ ἡ αἰώνιος [cf. B. 90 (79)] ; see below] : Jn. iv. 36 ; [xii. 50] ; xvii. 3 ; 1 Jn. i. 2 ; ii. 25 ; [ῥήματα ζωῆς αἰων. Jn. vi. 68] ; εἰς ζωὴν αἰ. unto the attainment of eternal life [cf. εἰς, B. II. 3 c. δ. p. 185ᵃ], Jn. iv. 14 ; vi. 27 ; διδόναι ζωὴν αἰ., Jn. x. 28 ; xvii. 2 ; 1 Jn. v. 11 ; ἔχειν ζωὴν αἰ., Jn. iii. 15, [and 16], (opp. to ἀπόλλυσθαι), 36 ; v. 24,

39; vi. 40, 47, 54; xx. 31 L br.; 1 Jn. v. 13; οὐκ ἔχειν ζωὴν αἰ. ἐν ἑαυτῷ, 1 Jn. iii. 15; (in Enoch xv. 4, 6 the wicked angels are said before their fall to have been *spiritual* and *partakers of eternal* and *immortal life*). ζωή and ἡ ζωή, without epithet, are used of the blessing of *real life after the resurrection*, in Mt. vii. 14; Jn. xi. 25; Acts iii. 15; v. 20; xi. 18; Ro. v. 17, 18 (on which see δικαίωσις, fin.); 2 Co. v. 4; Col. iii. 3; 2 Tim. i. 10; Tit. i. 2; iii. 7; ζωὴ ἐκ νεκρῶν, life breaking forth from the abode of the dead, Ro. xi. 15; εἰσελθεῖν εἰς τ. ζωήν, Mt. xviii. 8 sq.; xix. 17; Mk. ix. 43, 45; ἀνάστασις ζωῆς i. q. εἰς ζωήν (2 Macc. vii. 14), Jn. v. 29 (on the gen. cf. W. 188 (177)); στέφανος τῆς ζωῆς i. q. ἡ ζωὴ ὡς στέφανος, Jas. i. 12; Rev. ii. 10; ξύλον τῆς ζωῆς, the tree whose fruit gives and maintains eternal life, Rev. ii. 7; xxii. 2, 14, 19 [G L T Tr WH], (cf. Gen. ii. 9; Prov. iii. 18; δένδρον ζωῆς, Prov. xi. 30; xiii. 12); cf. *Bleek*, Vorless. üb. d. Apokalypse, p. 174 sq.; ὕδωρ ζωῆς, water the use of which serves to maintain eternal life, Rev. xxi. 6; xxii. 1, 17; in the same sense ζωῆς πηγαὶ ὑδάτων, Rev. vii. 17 G L T Tr WH; ἡ βίβλος and τὸ βιβλίον τῆς ζωῆς, the book in which the names of those are recorded to whom eternal life has been decreed : Phil. iv. 3; Rev. iii. 5; xiii. 8; xvii. 8; xx. 12, 15; xxi. 27; [xxii. 19 Rec.; cf. Bp. Lghtft. on Phil. l. c.]. more fully ἡ ὄντως [Rec. αἰών.] ζωή, 1 Tim. vi. 19; ζωὴ αἰώνιος [cf. above] (Justin. de resurr. 1 p. 588 c. ὁ λόγος . . . διδοὺς ἡμῖν ἐν ἑαυτῷ τὴν ἐκ νεκρῶν ἀνάστασιν καὶ τὴν μετὰ ταῦτα ζωὴν αἰώνιον), Mt. xxv. 46 (opp. to κόλασις αἰών.); Acts xiii. 46, 48; Ro. ii. 7; vi. 22 sq.; Gal. vi. 8; 1 Tim. vi. 12; after ἐν τῷ αἰῶνι τῷ ἐρχομένῳ, Mk. x. 30; Lk. xviii. 30; ἔχειν ζωὴν αἰ. Mt. xix. 16; κληρονομεῖν, Mt. xix. 29; Mk. x. 17; Lk. x. 25; xviii. 18; εἰς ζωὴν αἰώνιον, unto the attainment of life eternal, Jn. xii. 25; Ro. v. 21; 1 Tim. i. 16; Jude 21, (Dan. xii. 2; 4 Macc. xv. 2; ἀέναος ζωή, 2 Macc. vii. 36; ἀΐδιος ζωή, Ignat. ad Eph. 19). Cf. *Köstlin*, Lehrbegriff des Ev. Johann. etc. pp. 234 sqq. 338 sqq.; *Reuss*, Johann. Theologie (in Beiträge zu d. theol. Wissenschaften, vol. i.) p. 76 sqq. [cf. his Hist. de la Théol. Chrét. bk. vii. ch. xiv.]; *Lipsius*, Paulin. Rechtfertigungslehre, pp. 152 sqq. 185 sq.; *Güder* in Herzog viii. 254 (ed. 2, 509) sqq.; *B. B. Brückner*, De notione vocis ζωή in N. T. Lips. 1858; *Huther*, d. Bedeut. d. Begriffe ζωή u. πιστεύειν im N. T., in the Jahrbb. f. deutsche Theol. 1872, p. 1 sqq. [For the relations of the term to heathen conceptions cf. *G. Teichmüller*, Aristot. Forsch. iii. p. 127 sqq.] Some, as Bretschneider, Wahl, Wilke, esp. Käuffer (in his book De biblica ζωῆς αἰωνίου notione. Dresd. 1838), maintain that ζωὴ αἰώνιος everywhere even in John's writings refers to *life after the resurrection*; but in this way they are compelled not only to assume a p r o p h e t i c use of the perf. in the saying ἐκ τοῦ θανάτου μεταβεβηκέναι εἰς τ. ζωήν (Jn. v. 24; 1 Jn. iii. 14), but also to interpret the common phrase ἔχει ζωὴν αἰ. as meaning *he has eternal life as his certain portion though as yet only in hope*, as well as to explain ζωὴν αἰ. οὐκ ἔχειν ἐν ἑαυτῷ μένουσαν (1 Jn. iii. 15) of *the hope* of eternal life. [SYN. see βίος, fin.]*

ζώνη, -ης, ἡ, ((ζώννυμι), [fr. Hom. down], *a girdle, belt,* serving not only to gird on flowing garments, Mt. iii. 4; Mk. i. 6; Acts xxi. 11; Rev. i. 13; xv. 6; but also, since it was hollow, to carry money in [A. V. *purse*] : Mt. x. 9; Mk. vi. 8; Plut. mor. p. 665 b. quaest. conviv. iv. 2, 3, 2; "argentum in zonis habentes," Liv. 33, 29. [B. D. s. v. Girdle.]*   2223

ζώννυμι and **ζωννύω** : impf. 2 pers. sing. ἐζώννυες; fut. ζώσω; 1 aor. mid. impv. ζῶσαι; *to gird* : τινά, Jn. xxi. 18; Mid. *to gird one's self* : Acts xii. 8 L T Tr WH. (Ex. xxix. 9; Hom. et al.) [COMP. : ἀνα-, δια-, περι-, ὑπο-ζώννυμι.]*   2224

ζωογονέω, -ῶ ; fut. ζωογονήσω; pres. inf. pass. ζωογονεῖσθαι; (fr. ζωογόνος viviparous, and this fr. ζωός and ΓΕΝΩ); **1.** prop. *to bring forth alive* (Theophr., Diod., Lcian., Plut., al.). **2.** *to give life* (Theophr. de caus. pl. 4, 15, 4; Ath. 7 p. 298 c.) : τὰ πάντα, of God, 1 Tim. vi. 13 L T Tr WH, [(1 S. ii. 6)]. **3.** in the Bible *to preserve alive* : τὴν ψυχήν, Lk. xvii. 33; pass. Acts vii. 19. (For חָיָה, Ex. i. 17; Judg. viii. 19; [1 S. xxvii. 9, 11; 1 K. xxi. (xx.) 31].)*   2225

ζῶον [or **ζῷον** (so L WH uniformly, Treg. in Heb. and Rev.; see Etym. Magn. 413, 24, and reff. s. v. I, ι)], -ον, τό, ((ζωός alive); **1.** *a living being.* **2.** *an animal, brute, beast* : Heb. xiii. 11; 2 Pet. ii. 12; Jude 10; Rev. iv. 6–9 [on vs. 8 cf. B. 130 (114)], etc.

[SYN.: ζῷον differs from θηρίον (at least e t y m o l o g i-c a l l y; but cf. Schmidt as below) in giving prominence to the v i t a l element, while θηρίον emphasizes the b e s t i a l element. Hence in Rev. as above ζ. is fitly rendered *living creature* in contradistinction to the θηρίον beast, cf. xi. 7; xiii. 1, etc. See Trench § lxxxi.; Schmidt ii. ch. 70.]   2226

ζωο-ποιέω, -ῶ ; fut. ζωοποιήσω; 1 aor. inf. ζωοποιῆσαι; Pass., pres. ζωοποιοῦμαι; 1 fut. ζωοποιηθήσομαι; 1 aor. ptcp. ζωοποιηθείς; ((ζωοποιός making alive); **1.** *to produce alive, beget* or *bear living young,* (Aristot., Theophr.). **2.** *to cause to live, make alive, give life* : τὰ πάντα, of God, 1 Tim. vi. 13 R G [cf. Neh. ix. 6; 2 K. v. 7; Diogn. ep. 5 fin.]; by spiritual power to arouse and invigorate, 2 Co. iii. 6; Gal. iii. 21; to give ζωὴ αἰώνιος (in the Johannean sense), Jn. vi. 63; of the dead, *to reanimate, restore to life* : 1 Co. xv. 45; τινά, Jn. v. 21; Ro. iv. 17; viii. 11; pass. 1 Co. xv. 22; i. q. *to give increase of life* : thus of physical life, πρῶτον τὸ παιδίον μέλιτι, εἶτα γάλακτι ζωοποιεῖται, Barn. ep. c. 6, 17; of the spirit, ζωοποιηθεὶς πνεύματι, quickened as respects the spirit, endued with new and greater powers of life, 1 Pet. iii. 18, on which cf. *Lechler*, Das apost. u. nachapost. Zeitalter, p. 182 ed. 2; [*Zezschwitz*, De Christi ad inferos descensu (Lips. 1857) p. 20]. metaph. (Geop. 9, 11, 7) of seeds quickening into life, i. e. germinating, springing up, growing : 1 Co. xv. 36. [COMP. : συ-ζωοποιέω.]*   2227

H

2228 & 2229

ἤ, a disjunctive conjunction [cf. W. § 53,6]. Used **1.** to distinguish things or thoughts which either mutually exclude each other, or one of which can take the place of the other: *or* (Lat. *aut, vel*); **a.** to distinguish one thing from another in words of the same construction: Mt. v. 17 (τὸν νόμον ἢ τοὺς προφήτας), 36 (λευκὴν ἢ μέλαιναν); vi. 31; vii. 16; Mk. vi. 56; vii. 11 sq.; Lk. ii. 24; ix. 25; Jn. vii. 48; xiii. 29; Acts i. 7; iii. 12; iv. 7; Ro. i. 21; iii. 1; 1 Co. iv. 3; v. 10 sq.; x. 19; Gal. i. 10, etc. **b.** after an interrogative or a declarative sentence, before a question designed to prove the same thing in another way: Mt. vii. 4, 9; xii. 29; xvi. 26; xxvi. 53; Mk. viii. 37; Lk. xiii. 4; xiv. 31; xv. 8; Ro. ix. 21; xiv. 10; 1 Co. vi. 16. **c.** before a sentence contrary to the one just preceding, to indicate that if one be denied or refuted the other must stand: Mt. xx. 15 (i. e. *or*, if thou wilt not grant this, *is thine eye* etc.); Ro. iii. 29; 1 Co. ix. 6; x. 22; xi. 14 [Rec.]; xiv. 36; 2 Co. xi. 7; ἢ ἀγνοεῖτε etc., Ro. vi. 3; vii. 1 (cf. vi. 14); ἢ οὐκ οἴδατε etc., Ro. xi. 2; 1 Co. vi. 9, 16, 19. **d.** ἤ . . . ἤ, *either* . . . *or*, Mt. vi. 24; xii. 33; Lk. xvi. 13; Acts xxiv. 20 sq.; 1 Co. xiv. 6. **2.** in a disjunctive question it corresponds to the Lat. *an* after *utrum*; **a.** preceded by πότερον, Jn. vii. 17; cf. *Klotz* ad Dev. ii. 2 p. 574 sq.; preceded by the interrog. μή, 1 Co. ix. 8; preceded by μήτι, 2 Co. i. 17. **b.** without an interrog. particle in the first member of the interrogation: τί ἐστι εὐκοπώτερον, εἰπεῖν . . . ἢ εἰπεῖν, Mt. ix. 5; Mk. ii. 9; Lk. v. 23; add, Mt. xxi. 25; xxiii. 17, 19; xxvii. 17; Mk. iii. 4; Lk. vii. 19; Acts viii. 34. **c.** ἤ . . . ἤ . . . ἤ, Mk. xiii. 35. **3.** as a comparative conj., *than*; **a.** after comparatives: Mt. x. 15; xi. 22; Lk. ix. 13; xvi. 17; Jn. iii. 19; iv. 1 [Tr mrg. om. WH br. ἤ]; Acts iv. 19; Ro. xiii. 11, and often. ἤ is wanting after πλείους foll. by a noun of number: Mt. xxvi. 53 T Tr WH; Acts iv. 22; xxiii. 13, 21; xxiv. 11 (where Rec. adds ἤ); cf. Matthiae § 455 note 4; Kühner ii. p. 847; [Jelf § 780 Obs. 1]; W. 595 (554); [B. 168 (146)]; *Lob.* ad Phryn. p. 410 sq. **b.** after ἕτερον: Acts xvii. 21. **c.** πρὶν ἤ, *before that, before,* foll. by acc. with inf. [cf. B. § 139, 35; W. § 44, 6, also p. 297 (279)]: Mt. i. 18; Mk. xiv. 30; Acts ii. 20 R G WH mrg.; vii. 2; foll. by the aor. subjunc., Lk. ii. 26 Tr txt. om. WH br. ἤ; xxii. 34 R G [al. ἕως]; foll. by pres. optat. Acts xxv. 16. **d.** after θέλω i. q. *to prefer*: 1 Co. xiv. 19 (foll. by ἤπερ, 2 Macc. xiv. 42); exx. fr. Grk. auth. are given in *Klotz* ad Devar. ii. 2 p. 589 sq.; W. § 35, 2 c.; [B. § 149, 7]; Kühner ii. p. 841; [Jelf § 779 Obs. 3]. **e.** after οὖ: Jn. xiii. 10 R G, where after οὐ χρείαν ἔχει the sentence goes on as though the writer had said οὐκ ἄλλου τινὸς χρείαν ἔχει, [cf. W. 508 (473)]. **f.** after

positive notions, to which in this way a comparative force is given: after καλόν ἐστι [*it is good* . . . *rather than*] i. q. *it is better*, Mt. xviii. 8 sq.; Mk. ix. 43, 45, 47; cf. Menander's saying καλὸν τὸ μὴ ζῆν, ἢ ζῆν ἀθλίως, and Plaut. rud. 4, 4, 70 tacita mulier est bona semper, quam loquens; similar exx. in the O. T. are Gen. xlix. 12; Ps. cxvii. (cxviii.) 8; Jon. iv. 3, 8; Tob. vi. 13; xii. 8; Sir. xx. 25; xxii. 15; 4 Macc. ix. 1; also after λυσιτελεῖ [*it is gain* . . . *rather than*] i. q. *it is better* (Tob. iii. 6), Lk. xvii. 2; after χαρὰ ἔσται [*there will be joy* . . . *more than*], Lk. xv. 7; see exx. fr. Grk. auth. in *Bttm.* Gram. § 149, 7; [B. p. 360 (309)]; Winer, Kühner, al., as above. **4.** with other particles; **a.** ἀλλ' ἤ, see ἀλλά, I. 10 p. 28ᵃ. **b.** ἢ γάρ, see γάρ, I. fin. **c.** ἢ καί [cf. W. § 53, 6 note], **α.** *or even, or also*, (Lat. *aut etiam, vel etiam*): [Mt. vii. 10 L T Tr WH]; Lk. xi. 11 G L T Tr WH, 12; xviii. 11; Ro. ii. 15; 1 Co. xvi. 6; 2 Co. i. 13. **β.** *or also* (Lat. *an etiam*), (in a disjunctive question): Lk. xii. 41; Ro. iv. 9. **d.** ἤπερ, *than at all* (Lat. *quam forte*; Germ. *als etwa*), after a compar. [cf. Jelf § 779 Obs. 5]: Jn. xii. 43 [L ἤ περ, WH mrg. ὑπέρ], (2 Macc. xiv. 42; Hom., Hes.). **e.** ἤτοι . . . ἤ, *either indeed* [cf. Kühner § 540, 5] . . . *or*: Ro. vi. 16 (Sap. xi. 19; Hdt. and sqq.).

ἦ μήν, *assuredly, most certainly, full surely,* (a particle used in asseverations, promises, oaths [cf. W. § 53, 7 b.; *Paley*, Grk. Particles, p. 38 sq.]): Heb. vi. 14 R G; see εἰ, III. 9. (Sept.; very often in class. Grk. fr. Hom. down.) *   **2252**

ἡγεμονεύω, (ἡγεμών); [fr. Hom. down]; **a.** *to be leader, to lead the way.* **b.** *to rule, command*: with gen. of a province [cf. B. 169 (147)], *to be governor of a province*, said of a proconsul, Lk. ii. 2; of a procurator, Lk. iii. 1.*   **2230**

ἡγεμονία, -ας, ἡ, (ἡγεμών), [Hdt., Thuc., Plat., al.], *chief command, rule, sovereignty*: of the reign of a Roman emperor, Lk. iii. 1; Joseph. antt. 18, 4, 2.*   **2231**

ἡγεμών, -όνος, ὁ, (ἡγέομαι), in class. Grk. a word of very various signification: *a leader of any kind, a guide, ruler, prefect, president, chief, general, commander, sovereign*; in the N. T. spec. **1.** *a 'legatus Caesaris,'* an officer administering a province in the name and with the authority of the Roman emperor; *the governor of a province*: Mt. x. 18; Mk. xiii. 9; Lk. xxi. 12; 1 Pet. ii. 14. **2.** *a procurator* (Vulg. *praeses*; Luth. *Landpfleger*), an officer who was attached to a proconsul or a propraetor and had charge of the imperial revenues; in causes relating to these revenues he administered justice, (called ἐπίτροπος, διοικητής, in prof. auth.). In the smaller provinces also, which were so to speak appendages of the greater, he discharged the functions of governor of the province; and such was the relation of the procu-   **2232** rator of Judæa to the proconsul of Syria (cf. *Krebs*, Observv. p. 61 sqq.; *Fischer*, De vitiis lexx. etc. p. 432 sqq.; *Win.* RWB. s. v. Procuratoren; *Sieffert* in Herzog 2 s. v. Landpfleger; *Krenkel* in Schenkel iv. 7; [BB. DD. s. v. Procurator]); so of Pilate, Felix, Festus: Mt. xxvii. 2, 11, 14 sq. 21, 23 [R G L Tr mrg.], 27; xxviii. 14; Lk. xx. 20; Acts xxiii. 24, 26, 33; xxiv. 1, 10; xxvi. 30; Πιλᾶτος ὁ τῆς Ἰουδαίας ἡγεμών, Joseph. antt. 18, 3, 1; (Tacit. ann. 15, 44 Christus Tiberio imperitante per procuratorem Pontium Pilatum supplicio adfectus erat). **3.** *first, leading, chief*: so of a principal town as *the capital* of the region, Mt. ii. 6, where the meaning is, 'Thou art by no means least among the chief cities of Judah;' others less aptly (Bleek also [(where?)]; in his (posthumous) Synopt. Erklärung etc. i. 119 he repudiates this interp. (ascribed by him to *Hofmann*, Weiss. u. Erfüll. ii. 56)]), 'Thou shalt by no means be regarded as least among i. e. by the princes, the nobles, of the state.' The saying is taken fr. Mic. v. 2 (1), where the Hebr. בְּאַלְפֵי (which the Sept. give correctly, ἐν χιλιάσι) seems to have been read בְּאַלֻּפֵי by the Evangelist [cf. *Edersheim*, Jesus the Messiah, i. 206].*

2233   **ἡγέομαι, -οῦμαι;** pf. ἥγημαι; 1 aor. ἡγησάμην; (fr. ἄγω [cf. *Curtius* p. 688]); dep. mid.; fr. Hom. down; **1.** *to lead*, i. e. **a.** *to go before*; **b.** *to be a leader*; *to rule, command*; *to have authority over*: in the N. T. so only in the pres. ptcp. ἡγούμενος, *a prince*, of regal power (Ezek. xliii. 7 for מֶלֶךְ; Sir. xvii. 17), Mt. ii. 6; a (royal) *governor, viceroy*, Acts vii. 10; *chief*, Lk. xxii. 26 (opp. to ὁ διακονῶν); *leading as respects influence, controlling in counsel*, ἔν τισι, among any, Acts xv. 22; with gen. of the pers. over whom one rules, so of the overseers or leaders of Christian churches: Heb. xiii. 7, 17, 24, (οἴκου, 2 Chr. xxxi. 13; τῶν πατριῶν, 1 Esdr. v. 65 (66), 67 (68); τῆς πόλεως, Judg. ix. 51 Alex.; a military leader, 1 Macc. ix. 30; 2 Macc. xiv. 16; used also in Grk. writ. of any kind of a leader, chief, commander, Soph. Phil. 386; often in Polyb.; Diod. 1, 4 and 72; Lcian. Alex. 44; al.); with gen. of the thing, τοῦ λόγου, the leader in speech, chief speaker, spokesman: Acts xiv. 12 of Mercury, who is called also τοῦ λόγου ἡγεμών in Jamblich. de myster., init. **2.** (like the Lat. *duco*) i. q. *to consider, deem, account, think*: with two acc., one of the obj., the other of the pred., Acts xxvi. 2; Phil. ii. 3, 6 (on which see ἁρπαγμός, 2 [W. § 44, 3 c.]); iii. 7 [cf. B. 59 (51); W. 274 (258)]; 1 Tim. i. 12; vi. 1; Heb. x. 29; xi. 11, 26; 2 Pet. i. 13; ii. 13; iii. 9, 15. τινὰ ὥς τινα, 2 Th. iii. 15 [cf. W. § 65, 1 a.]; τινὰ ὑπερεκπερισσῶς, to esteem one exceedingly, 1 Th. v. 13 (περὶ πολλοῦ, Hdt. 2, 115; περὶ πλείστου, Thuc. 2, 89); w. acc. of the thing foll. by ὅταν, Jas. i. 2; ἀναγκαῖον, foll. by an inf. 2 Co. ix. 5; Phil. ii. 25; δίκαιον, foll. by an inf., 2 Pet. i. 13; foll. by an acc. w. inf., Phil. iii. 8. [COMP.: δι-, ἐκ-δι-, ἐξ-, προ-ηγέομαι.*

SYN.: δοκέω 1, ἡγέομαι 2, νομίζω 2, οἴομαι: ἡγ. and νομ. denote a belief resting not on one's inner feeling or sentiment, but on the due consideration of external grounds, the weighing and comparing of facts; δοκ. and οἴ., on the

---

other hand, describe a subjective judgment growing out of inclination or a view of facts in their relation to us. ἡγ. denotes a more deliberate and careful judgment than νομ.; οἴ. a subjective judgment which has feeling rather than thought (δοκ.) for its ground. Cf. Schmidt ch. 17.]

ἡδέως, adv., (fr. ἡδύς sweet, pleasant), *with pleasure, gladly*: Mk. vi. 20; xii. 37; 2 Co. xi. 19. [From Soph., Plat. down.]*   **2234**

ἤδη, adv., [fr. Hom. down; on deriv. see Vaniček p. 745; Peile p. 395], in the N. T. everywh. of time, *now, already*, (Lat. *jam*): Mt. iii. 10; v. 28; xiv. 15; Mk. iv. 37; xi. 11; Lk. vii. 6; xii. 49; [xxiv. 29 T WH Tr txt., L Tr mrg. br.]; Jn. iv. 35 (36), 51; xix. 28 (that all things were now finished and that nothing further remained for him to do or to suffer); Acts xxvii. 9; Ro. xiii. 11 (that it is already time to wake up and indulge no longer in sleep); 1 Co. iv. 8, and often; νῦν . . . ἤδη, *now already* (Lat. *jam nunc*): 1 Jn. iv. 3; ἤδη ποτέ, *now at last, at length now*: with fut. Ro. i. 10; [with aor. Phil. iv. 10. SYN. see ἄρτι, fin.]   **2235**

ἥδιστα (neut. plur. of the superl. ἥδιστος fr. ἡδύς), adv., *most gladly* (cf. ἡδέως): 2 Co. xii. 9, 15. (Soph., Xen., Plat., al.) *   **2236**

ἡδονή, -ῆς, ἡ, (ἥδομαι), [Simon. 117, Hdt. down], *pleasure*: 2 Pet. ii. 13; plur., Lk. viii. 14 (αἱ ἡδοναὶ τ. βίου); Tit. iii. 3; Jas. iv. 3; by meton. desires for pleasure (Grotius, *cupiditates rerum voluptariarum*), Jas. iv. 1.*   **2237**

ἡδύ-οσμος, -ον, (ἡδύς and ὀσμή), *sweet-smelling* (Plin. *jucunde olens*); neut. τὸ ἡδ. as subst. *garden-mint* (i. q. μίνθη, Strab. 8, 3, 14 p. 344; Theophr. hist. plant. 7, 7; cf. caus. plant. 6, 22 (20)), a kind of small odoriferous herb, with which the Jews used to strew the floors of their houses and synagogues; (it was called by them מִינְתָא, see *Buxtorf*, Lex. talm. s. v. p. 1228 [p. 623 ed. Fischer]): Mt. xxiii. 23; Lk. xi. 42. [BB.DD.]*   **2238**

ἦθος, -εος (-ους), τό, (akin to ἔθος, prob. fr. ΕΩ, whence ἧμαι, ἕζω, [cf. Vaniček p. 379]); **1.** *a customary abode, dwelling-place, haunt, customary state*, (Hom., Hes., Hdt., al.). **2.** *custom, usage*, (cf. Germ. *Sitzen, Sitte*); plur. τὰ ἤθη *morals, character*, (Lat. *mores*): 1 Co. xv. 33 fr. Menander; cf. Menand. fragm. ed. *Meineke* p. 75. (Sir. xx. 26 (25); 4 Macc. i. 29; ii. 7, 21.) *   **2239**

ἥκω; impf. ἧκον (Acts xxviii. 23, where L T Tr WH ἦλθον); fut. ἥξω; 1 aor. ἧξα (Lk. xiii. 35 R G; Rev. ii. 25; iii. 9 Rec.); pf. ἧκα (often in Sept., as Gen. xlii. 7, 9; xlv. 16; [xlvii. 4]; Josh. ix. 12 (7); Job xvi. 22, etc.; in the N. T. once, Mk. viii. 3 R[[*]] L T Tr txt., see WH. App. p. 169; the older and more elegant writ. [Aeschyl., Hdt., Thuc., al.] use only the pres. impf. and fut.; cf. *Lob.* ad Phryn. p. 743 sq.; *Bttm.* Ausf. Spr. ii. 205; [Veitch s. v.]; W. 87 (83); [B. 59 (51)]); Sept. for בּוֹא; *to have come, have arrived, be present*, [W. 274 (258); B. 203 (176)]; hence impf. with force of plupf. (cf. Matthiae ii. p. 1136; Krüger § 53, 1, 4): absol. of persons, Mt. xxiv. 50; Mk. viii. 3; Lk. xii. 46; xv. 27; Jn. viii. 42; Heb. x. 7, 9, 37; 1 Jn. v. 20; Rev. ii. 25; iii. 9; xv. 4; foll. by ἀπό with gen. of place, Mt. viii. 11; Lk. xiii. 29; by ἐκ with gen. of place, Ro. xi. 26; with   **2240**

addition of εἰς w. acc. of place, Jn. iv. 47; μακρόθεν, Mk. viii. 3; πρός τινα, Acts xxviii. 23 Rec.; metaph. *to come to one* i. e. seek an intimacy with one, become his follower: Jn. vi. 37; ἐπί τινα, *to come upon one* (unexpectedly), Rev. iii. 3. of time and events: absol., Mt. xxiv. 14; Jn. ii. 4; 2 Pet. iii. 10; Rev. xviii. 8; ἕως ἂν ἥξῃ [L T WH Tr in br. ἥξει; see above and B. 231 (199)] (sc. ὁ καιρός), ὅτε εἴπητε, Lk. xiii. 35; ἐπί τινα, metaph. *to come upon one*, of things to be endured (as evils, calamitous times): Mt. xxiii. 36; Lk. xix. 43. [Comp.: ἀν-, καθ-ήκω.]*

2241 ἠλί (L ἠλί, T ἠλεί [see *WH*. App. p. 155, and s. v. ει, ι; on the breathing cf. *Tdf*. Proleg. p. 107; *WH*. Intr. § 408; WH ἐλωΐ]), a Hebr. word, אֵלִי, *my God*: Mt. xxvii. 46. [Cf. ἐλωΐ, and the ref. there.]*

2242 Ἡλί (Rⁿ Ἡλί [on the breathing in codd. see *Tdf*. Proleg. p. 107], T Tr WH Ἡλεί [see *WH*. App. p. 155, and s. v. ει, ι]), indecl., *Heli*, the father of Joseph, the husband of Mary: Lk. iii. 23.*

2243 Ἡλίας ([so Rˢᵗ ᵉˡᶻ G; WH Ἡλείας cf. *WH*. App. p. 155; *Tdf*. Proleg. p. 84 and see ει, ι, but] L Tr Ἡλίας, Tdf. Ἡλείας, [on the breathing in codd. see *Tdf*. Proleg. p. 107; *WH*. Intr. § 408; current edd. are not uniform]), -ov [B. 17 (16), 8; but once (viz. Lk. i. 17 T Tr mrg. WH) -α], ὁ, אֵלִיָּהוּ or אֵלִיָּה i. e. either ' strength of Jehovah ' or ' my God is Jehovah '), *Elijah*, a prophet born at Thisbe [but see B. D. s. v., also s. v. Tishbite], the unflinching champion of the theocracy in the reigns of the idolatrous kings Ahab and Ahaziah. He was taken up to heaven without dying, whence the Jews expected he would return just before the advent of the Messiah, whom he would prepare the minds of the Israelites to receive (1 K. xvii.–xix.; 2 K. ii. 6 sqq.; 2 Chr. xxi. 12; Mal. iv. 4 (iii. 22); Sir. xlviii. 1, 4, 12 [cf. *Edersheim*, Jesus the Messiah, App. viii.]): Mt. xi. 14; xvi. 14; xvii. 3 sq. 10–12; xxvii. 47, 49; Mk. vi. 15; viii. 28; ix. 4 sq. 11–13; xv. 35 sq.; Lk. i. 17; iv. 25 sq.; ix. 8, 19, 30, 33, 54 [R G L]; Jn. i. 21, 25; Jas. v. 17; ἐν Ἡλίᾳ, in the narrative concerning Elijah, Ro. xi. 2 [see ἐν, I. 1 d.].*

2244 ἡλικία, -ας, ἡ, (ἧλιξ mature, of full age, Hom. Od. 18, 373 [al. of the same age; cf. *Ebeling*, Lex. Hom. s. v.; *Pape*, Lex. s. v.]); fr. Hom. down; **1.** *age, time of life*; **a.** univ.: Mt. vi. 27; Lk. xii. 25, [in these pass. ' term or length of life '; but others refer them to 2 below; see *Field*, Otium Norv. Pars iii. p. 4; *Jas. Morison*, Com. on Mt. l. c.] cf. πῆχυς, and De Wette, Meyer, Bleek on Mt. l. c.; παρὰ καιρὸν ἡλικίας, beyond the proper stage of life [A. V. past age], Heb. xi. 11 (2 Macc. iv. 40; 4 Macc. v. 4). **b.** *adult age, maturity*: ἔχειν ἡλικίαν [A. V. to be of age], Jn. ix. 21, 23. **c.** *suitable age* for anything; with gen. of the thing for which it is fit: τοῦ γάμου, Dem.; τοῦ ἤδη φρονεῖν, Plat. Eryx. p. 396 b.; metaph. of an attained state of mind fit for a thing: τοῦ πληρώματος τοῦ Χριστοῦ, the age in which we are fitted to receive the fulness (see πλήρωμα, 1) of Christ, Eph. iv. 13 [al. refer this to 2; cf. Ellic. in loc.]. **2.** *stature* (Dem., Plut., al.): τῇ ἡλικίᾳ μικρός, Lk. xix. 3; προκόπτειν ἡλικίᾳ, i. e. in height and comeliness of stature

(Bengel, *justam proceritatem nactus est et decoram*), Lk. ii. 52; cf. Meyer, Bleek, ad loc.*

2245 ἡλίκος, -η, -ον, (ἧλιξ, see ἡλικία), prop. *as old as, as tall as*; univ. (Lat. *quantus*): *how great*, Col. ii. 1; Jas. iii. 5 [cf. B. 253 (217)]; *how small* (Lcian. Hermot. 5), ἡλίκον πῦρ. Jas. iii. 5 L T Tr WH [B. l. c.].*

2246 ἥλιος, -ου, ὁ [often anarthrous, W. 120 (114); B. 89 (78)], (ἕλη [root us to burn, cf. Curtius § 612]); Sept. for שֶׁמֶשׁ; *the sun*: Mt. v. 45; xiii. 43; Mk. xiii. 24; Lk. iv. 40; xxi. 25; Acts xxvi. 13; 1 Co. xv. 41; Rev. i. 16, etc. i. q. *the rays of the sun*, Rev. vii. 16; i. q. *the light of day*: μὴ βλέπων τὸν ἥλιον, of a blind man, Acts xiii. 11. **2247**

2249 ἧλος, -ου, ὁ, *a nail*: Jn. xx. 25. [(From Hom. on.)]*

ἡμεῖς, see ἐγώ. — — — — — — — — — — — see 1473

2250 ἡμέρα, -ας, ἡ, (fr. ἥμερος, -ον, prop. ἡμέρα ὥρα the mild time, cf. *Lob*. Paral. p. 359; [but cf. Curtius p. 594 sq.; Vaniček p. 943]); Hebr. יוֹם; *day*; used **1.** of the *natural day*, or the interval between sunrise and sunset, as distinguished fr. and contrasted with night; **a.** prop. ἡμέρας, by day, in the daytime, [cf. colloq. Eng. *of a day*; W. § 30, 11; B. § 132, 26], Rev. xxi. 25; ἡμέρας κ. νυκτός, day and night [cf. W. 552 (513 sq.); *Lob*. Paralip. p. 62 sq.; Ellic. on 1 Tim. v. 5], Mk. v. 5; Lk. xviii. 7; Acts ix. 24; 1 Th. ii. 9; iii. 10; [2 Th. iii. 8 L txt. T Tr WH]; 1 Tim. v. 5; 2 Tim. i. 3; Rev. iv. 8; vii. 15; xii. 10; xiv. 11; xx. 10; ἡμέρας μέσης, at midday, Acts xxvi. 13; νύκτα καὶ ἡμέραν [W. 230 (216); B. § 131, 11], Mk. iv. 27; Acts xx. 31; 2 Th. iii. 8 R G; hyperbolically i. q. *without intermission*, λατρεύειν, Lk. ii. 37; Acts xxvi. 7; ἡμέρας ὁδός, a day's journey, Lk. ii. 44 (Gen. xxxi. 23 [μιᾶς ἡμέρας ὁδόν, Joseph. c. Ap. 2, 2, 9; cf. W. 188 (177); B. D. Am. ed. s. v. Day's Journey]); τὰς ἡμέρας, acc. of time [W. and B. as above], *during the days*, Lk. xxi. 37; ἐκείνην τ. ἡμέραν, Jn. i. 39 (40); πᾶσαν ἡμέραν, daily, Acts v. 42; ἐκ δηναρίου τὴν ἡμέραν, so sometimes we say, *for a shilling the day*, Mt. xx. 2; δώδεκά εἰσιν ὧραι τῆς ἡμέρας, Jn. xi. 9; to the number of days are added as many nights, Mt. iv. 2; xii. 40; γίνεται ἡμέρα, day dawns, it grows light, Lk. iv. 42; vi. 13; xxii. 66; Acts xii. 18; xvi. 35; xxiii. 12; xxvii. 29, 33, 39, (Xen. an. 2, 2, 13; 7, 2, 34); περιπατεῖν ἐν τ. ἡμέρᾳ, Jn. xi. 9; ἡ ἡμέρα φαίνει, Rev. viii. 12; ἡ ἡμέρα κλίνει, the day declines, it is towards evening, Lk. ix. 12; xxiv. 29. **b.** metaph. the 'day' is regarded as the time for abstaining from indulgence, vice, crime, because acts of the sort are perpetrated at night and in darkness: 1 Th. v. 5, 8; hence ὁ αἰὼν οὗτος (see αἰών, 3) is likened to *the night*, αἰὼν μέλλων to *day*, and Christians are admonished to live decorously as though it were light, i. e. as if ὁ αἰὼν ὁ μέλλων were already come, Ro. xiii. 12 sq. ἕως ἡμέρα ἐστίν while it is day, i. e. while life gives one an opportunity to work, Jn. ix. 4. of the light of knowledge, 2 Pet. i. 19. **2.** of the *civil day*, or the space of twenty-four hours (thus including the night): Mt. vi. 34; Mk. vi. 21; Lk. xiii. 14, etc.; opp. to an hour, Mt. xxv. 13; to hours, months, years, Rev. ix. 15; Gal. iv. 10; ἡ ἐν ἡμέρᾳ τρυφή, the revelling of a day, i. e. ephemeral, very brief, 2 Pet. ii. 13 [al. refer this to 1 b. above];

*For 2248 see 1473.

ἐπτάκις τῆς ἡμ. seven times in the (space of a) day, Lk. xvii. 4; the dat. ἡμέρᾳ of the day *on* (*in*) *which* [cf. W. § 31, 9; B. § 133 (26)]: as τρίτῃ ἡμέρᾳ, Mt. xvi. 21; Mk. ix. 31 [Rec.]; Lk. xvii. 29 sq.; Acts ii. 41, etc.; ἡμέρα κ. ἡμέρᾳ, day by day, every day, 2 Co. iv. 16 (after the Hebr. יוֹם וָיוֹם Esth. iii. 4, where Sept. καθ᾽ ἑκάστην ἡμέραν, and יוֹם יוֹם Ps. lxvii. (lxviii.) 20, where Sept. ἡμέραν καθ᾽ ἡμέραν; [cf. W. 463 (432)]); ἡμέραν ἐξ ἡμέρας (see ἐκ, IV. 2), 2 Pet. ii. 8; as an acc. of time [W. 230 (215 sq.); B. § 131, 11]: ὅλην τ. ἡμέραν, Ro. viii. 36; x. 21; μίαν ἡμέραν, Acts xxi. 7; and in the plur., Jn. ii. 12; iv. 40; xi. 6; Acts ix. 19; x. 48; xvi. 12; xx. 6; xxi. 4, 10; xxv. 6, 14; xxviii. 7, 12 [L dat.], 14; Gal. i. 18; Rev. xi. 3, 9. joined with Prepositions: ἀπό with gen. *from . . . forth, from . . . on*, Mt. xxii. 46; Jn. xi. 53; Acts x. 30; xx. 18; Phil. i. 5; ἄχρι w. gen. *until, up to*, Mt. xxiv. 38; Lk. i. 20; xvii. 27; Acts i. 2; [22 Tdf.]; ii. 29; xxiii. 1; xxvi. 22; ἄχρι πέντε ἡμερῶν, until five days had passed, i. e. after five days, Acts xx. 6; μέχρι w. gen. *until*, Mt. xxviii. 15 [LTr, WH in br.]; ἕως w. gen. *until*, Mt. xxvii. 64; Acts i. 22 [T ἄχρι]; Ro. xi. 8; διά w. gen., see διά, A. II.; πρό w. gen. *before*, Jn. xii. 1 (on which see πρό, b.); ἐν w. dat. sing., Mt. xxiv. 50; Lk. i. 59; Jn. v. 9; 1 Co. x. 8 [L T Tr WH txt. om. ἐν]; Heb. iv. 4, etc.; ἐν w. dat. plur., Mt. xxvii. 40; Mk. xv. 29 [L T Tr om. WH br. ἐν]; Jn. ii. 19 [Tr WH br. ἐν], 20, etc.; εἰς, *unto*, (*against*), Jn. xii. 7; Rev. ix. 15; ἐπί w. acc. *for*, (Germ. *auf . . . hin*), Acts xiii. 31 (for many days successively); xvi. 18; xxvii. 20; Heb. xi. 30; καθ᾽ ἡμέραν, daily [W. 401 (374 sq.)], Mt. xxvi. 55; Mk. xiv. 49; Lk. xvi. 19; xxii. 53; Acts ii. 46 sq.; iii. 2; xvi. 5; xix. 9; 1 Co. xv. 31; 2 Co. xi. 28; Heb. vii. 27; x. 11; also τὸ καθ᾽ ἡμέραν, Lk. xi. 3; xix. 47; Acts xvii. 11 [L T Tr txt. om. WH br. τὸ], (Polyb. 4, 18, 2; cf. Matthiae ii. p. 734; [Jelf § 456]; Bnhdy. p. 329; B. 96 (84)); καθ᾽ ἑκάστην ἡμέραν, every day, Heb. iii. 13 (Xen. mem. 4, 2, 12); also κατὰ πᾶσαν ἡμ. Acts xvii. 17; μετά, *after*, Mt. xvii. 1; xxvi. 2; xxvii. 63; Mk. viii. 31; Lk. i. 24; Jn. iv. 43; xx. 26; Acts i. 5; xv. 36, etc. οὐ πλείους εἰσὶν ἐμοὶ ἡμέραι ἀφ᾽ ἧς, sc. ἡμέρας, Acts xxiv. 11. A specification of the number of days is thrust into the discourse in the nominative, as it were adverbially and without any grammatical connection, (cf. Fritzsche on Mk. p. 310 sq.; W. 516 (481) and § 62, 2; [B. 139 (122)]): ἤδη ἡμέραι (Rec. ἡμέρας, by correction) τρεῖς, Mt. xv. 32; Mk. viii. 2; ὡσεὶ ἡμέραι ὀκτώ, Lk. ix. 28. ἡμερῶν διαγενομένων τινῶν, certain days having intervened, Acts xxv. 13. ἡμέρα and ἡμέραι are used w. the gen. of a noun denoting a festival or some solemnity usually celebrated on a fixed day: τῶν ἀζύμων, Acts xii. 3; τῆς πεντεκοστῆς, Acts ii. 1; xx. 16; τοῦ σαββάτου, Lk. xiii. 14, 16; Jn. xix. 31; ἡ κυριακὴ ἡμέρα, the Lord's day, i. e. the day on which Christ returned to life, Sunday therefore, Rev. i. 10; the foll. phrases also have reference to sacred or festival days: κρίνειν ἡμέραν παρ᾽ ἡμέραν, to exalt one day above another, and κρίνειν πᾶσαν ἡμέραν, to esteem every day sacred, Ro. xiv. 5; φρονεῖν τὴν ἡμέραν, to regard a particular day that is selected for religious services, Ro. xiv. 6; ἡμέρας παρατηρεῖσθαι, to observe days, Gal. iv. 10. After the Hebr. usage, which in reference to a definite period of time now elapsed speaks of a certain number of days as fulfilled or completed (see Gesenius s. v. מָלֵא), we have the phrases ἐπλήσθησαν αἱ ἡμέραι τῆς λειτουργίας, the days spent in priestly service, Lk. i. 23 (when he had been employed in sacred duties for the appointed time); τοῦ περιτεμεῖν αὐτόν, for him to be circumcised, Lk. i. 21; τοῦ καθαρισμοῦ αὐτῶν, ib. 22; συντελεσθεισῶν ἡμερῶν, Lk. iv. 2; τελειωσάντων τὰς ἡμέρας, when they had spent there the time appointed, Lk. ii. 43; ἐν τῷ συμπληροῦσθαι τὰς ἡμ. τῆς ἀναλήψεως αὐτοῦ, when the number of days was now being completed which the reception of Jesus into heaven required, i. e. before which that reception could not occur, Lk. ix. 51; ἡ ἐκπλήρωσις τῶν ἡμερῶν τοῦ ἁγνισμοῦ, the fulfilment of the days required for the purification, Acts xxi. 26; συντελοῦνται αἱ ἡμέραι, ib. 27; ἐν τῷ συμπληροῦσθαι τ. ἡμέραν τῆς πεντεκοστῆς, when the measure of time needed for the day of Pentecost was being completed, i. e. on the very day of Pentecost, Acts ii. 1. As in some of the exx. just adduced ἡμέρα is joined to the gen. of a thing to be done or to happen on a certain day, so also in ἡμ. τοῦ ἐνταφιασμοῦ, Jn. xii. 7; ἀναδείξεως, Lk. i. 80. with gen. of pers., ἐν τῇ ἡμέρᾳ σου [but L T Tr WH om. σου] in the day favorable for thee, the day on which salvation is offered thee and can be obtained, Lk. xix. 42 (Polyb. 18, 5, 8 μὴ παρῇς τὸν καιρόν . . . σὴ νῦν ἐστιν ἡμέρα, σὸς ὁ καιρός; "meus est, tempore accepto utimur" Sen. Med. 1017). **3.** of *the last day of the present age* (see αἰών, 3), the day in which Christ will return from heaven, raise the dead, hold the final judgment, and perfect his kingdom, the foll. expressions are used: ἡ ἡμέρα, simply, Ro. xiii. 12; Heb. x. 25, cf. 1 Th. v. 4; (ἡ) ἡμέρα τοῦ κυρίου, Χριστοῦ, Ἰησοῦ Χριστοῦ, τοῦ υἱοῦ τοῦ ἀνθρώπου, Lk. xvii. 24 R G T Tr WH mrg.; 1 Co. i. 8; v. 5; 2 Co. i. 14; Phil. i. 6, 10; 1 Th. v. 2; 2 Th. ii. 2; 2 Pet. iii. 10; ἡ ἡμέρα κυρίου ἡ μεγάλη, Acts ii. 20 (fr. Joel ii. 31 (iii. 4)); ἡμέρα ᾗ ὁ υἱὸς τοῦ ἀνθρώπου ἀποκαλύπτεται, Lk. xvii. 30; ἡ ἡμέρα τ. θεοῦ, 2 Pet. iii. 12; ἡ ἡμέρα ἐκείνη ἡ μεγάλη τοῦ παντοκράτορος, Rev. xvi. 14, (even in the prophecies of the O.T. *the day of Jehovah* is spoken of, in which Jehovah will execute terrible judgment upon his adversaries, as Joel i. 15; ii. 1, 11; Is. ii. 12; xiii. 6, 9; Am. v. 18, 20; Jer. xxvi. 10 (xlvi. 10); Ezek. xiii. 5; xxx. 2 sqq.; Ob. 15; Zeph. i. 7 sqq.; Mal. iii. 17); ἡ ἡμ. ἐκείνη and ἐκείνη ἡ ἡμ., Mt. vii. 22; Lk. vi. 23; x. 12; xxi. 34; 2 Th. i. 10; 2 Tim. i. 12, 18; iv. 8; ἡ ἐσχάτη ἡμ., Jn. vi. 39 sq. 44, 54; xi. 24; xii. 48; ἡμ. ἀπολυτρώσεως, Eph. iv. 30; ἐπισκοπῆς (see ἐπισκοπή, b.), 1 Pet. ii. 12; κρίσεως, Mt. x. 15; xi. 22, 24; xii. 36; Mk. vi. 11 R L br.; 2 Pet. ii. 9; iii. 7, cf. Acts xvii. 31; τῆς κρίσεως, 1 Jn. iv. 17; ὀργῆς κ. ἀποκαλύψεως δικαιοκρισίας τ. θεοῦ, Ro. ii. 5 (יוֹם־נָקָם, Ezek. xxii. 24; יוֹם אַף־יְהוָה, Zeph. ii. 3 sq.; [יוֹם עֶבְרָה, Prov. xi. 4; Zeph. i. 15, 18, etc.]); ἡ ἡμ. ἡ μεγάλη τῆς ὀργῆς αὐτοῦ, Rev. vi. 17; ἡμ. σφαγῆς, of slaughter (of the wicked), Jas. v. 5 [(Jer. xii. 3, etc.)]. Paul, in allusion to the phrase ἡμέρα κυρίου, uses the expression ἀνθρωπίνη ἡμέρα for a tribunal of assembled judges on the day of trial [A. V. *man's judgment*] (cf. the Germ. *Landtag, Reichstag*), 1 Co. iv. 3. **4.** By a Hebraistic usage (though one not entirely unknown to Grk. writ.; cf. Soph. Aj. 131, 623; Eur. Ion 720) it is used of *time* in general, (as the Lat. *dies* is sometimes): Jn. xiv. 20; xvi. 23, 26; Heb. viii. 9 [cf. B. 316 (271); W. 571 (531)]; τὴν ἐμὴν ἡμέραν, the time when I should appear among men as Messiah, Jn. viii. 56; ἐν τῇ ἡμ. τῇ πονηρᾷ, in the time of troubles and assaults with which demons try Christians, Eph. vi. 13; ἡμ. σωτηρίας, the time when any one is or can be saved, 2 Co. vi. 2; εἰς ἡμέραν αἰῶνος, for all time, forever (see αἰών, 1 a.), 2 Pet. iii. 18; much oftener in the plur.: ἡμέραι πονηραί, Eph. v. 16; ἀφ' ἡμερῶν ἀρχαίων, Acts xv. 7; αἱ πρότερον ἡμ. Heb. x. 32; πάσας τὰς ἡμέρας, through all days, always, Mt. xxviii. 20 (כָּל־הַיָּמִים, Deut. iv. 40; v. 26 (29), and very often; ἤματα πάντα, Hom. Il. 8, 539; 12, 133; 13, 826, etc.); αἱ ἔσχαται ἡμ. (see ἔσχατος, 1 sub fin.), Acts ii. 17; 2 Tim. iii. 1; Jas. v. 3; αἱ ἡμ. αὗται, the present time, Acts iii. 24; the time now spoken of, Lk. i. 39; vi. 12; Acts i. 15, etc.; ἐν ταῖς ἡμ. ἐκείναις (see ἐκεῖνος, 2 b p. 195ᵃ); πρὸ τούτων τῶν ἡμερῶν, Acts v. 36; xxi. 38; πρὸς ὀλίγας ἡμ. for a short time, Heb. xii. 10; ἐλεύσονται ἡμ. ὅταν etc., Mt. ix. 15; Mk. ii. 20; Lk. v. 35; ὅτε etc. Lk. xvii. 22; ἥξουσιν ἡμ. ἐπὶ σέ, καί foll. by a fut. Lk. xix. 43; ἔρχονται ἡμ., καί foll. by fut. Heb. viii. 8; ἐλεύσονται or ἔρχονται ἡμ., ἐν αἷς etc., Lk. xxi. 6; xxiii. 29. with a gen. of the thing done or to happen: τῆς ἀπογραφῆς, Acts v. 37; τῆς φωνῆς, Rev. x. 7; τῆς σαρκὸς αὐτοῦ, of his earthly life, Heb. v. 7. αἱ ἡμ. with the gen. of a pers., *one's time, one's days*, i. e. in which he lived, or held office: Mt. ii. 1; xi. 12; xxiii. 30; xxiv. 37; Lk. i. 5; iv. 25; xvii. 26, 28; Acts vii. 45; xiii. 41; 1 Pet. iii. 20, (Gen. xxvi. 1; 1 S. xvii. 10; 2 S. xxi. 1; 1 K. x. 21; Esth. i. 1; Sir. xliv. 7; xlvi. 7; Tob. i. 2; 1 Macc. xiv. 36, etc.); αἱ ἡμέραι τοῦ υἱοῦ τοῦ ἀνθρ. the time immediately preceding the return of Jesus Christ from heaven, Lk. xvii. 26; μίαν τῶν ἡμ. τοῦ υἱ. τ. ἀνθρ. a single day of that most blessed future time when, all hostile powers subdued, the Messiah will reign, Lk. xvii. 22. Finally, the Hebrews and the Hellenists who imitate them measure the duration and length also of *human life* by the number of days: πάσας τὰς ἡμέρας [L mrg. Tr mrg. WH dat.] τῆς ζωῆς [G L T Tr WH om.] ἡμῶν, during all our life, Lk. i. 75 Rec. (Gen. xlvii. 8 sq.; Judith x. 3; Tob. i. 2 (3); Sir. xxii. 12; xxx. 32 (24); 1 Macc. ix. 71); προβεβηκὼς ἐν ταῖς ἡμέραις αὐτοῦ, far advanced in age, Lk. i. 7, 18; ii. 36 (בָּא בַּיָּמִים, [Sept. προβ. ἡμερῶν or ἡμέραις], Gen. xviii. 11; xxiv. 1; Josh. xiii. 1; [xxiii. 1; 1 K. i. 1; see προβαίνω, fin.]); ἀρχὴ ἡμερῶν, beginning of life, Heb. vii. 3 (αἱ ἔσχαται ἡμέραι τινός, one's last days, his old age, Protev. Jac. c. 1); ἡμέραι ἀγαθαί, 1 Pet. iii. 10.

2251　ἡμέτερος, -έρα, -ερον, (ἡμεῖς), possess. pron. of the 1 pers. plur., [fr. Hom. down], *our*: with a subst., Acts ii. 11; xxiv. 6 [Rec.]; xxvi. 5; Ro. xv. 4; [1 Co. xv. 31 Rec.ᵘᵗ ᵇᵉᵃ]; 2 Tim. iv. 15; 1 Jn. i. 3; ii. 2; οἱ ἡμέτεροι, substantively, 'our people,' (the brethren): Tit. iii. 14.

[Neut. τὸ ἡμέτ. substantively: Lk. xvi. 12 WH txt. Cf. W. § 22, 7 sqq.; B. § 127, 19 sqq.] *see 2252 on p. 275

ἦ μήν, see ἦ. ——————————————————————

ἡμιθανής, -ές, (fr. ἡμι half, and θνήσκω, 2 aor. ἔθανον), *half dead*: Lk. x. 30. ([Dion. Hal. 10, 7]; Diod. 12, 62; Strab. 2 p. 98; Anthol. 11, 392, 4; [4 Macc. iv. 11]; al.) *　**2253**

ἥμισυς, -εια, -υ; gen. ἡμίσους (Mk. vi. 23 [Sept. Ex. **2255** xxv. 9; etc.], for the uncontr. form ἡμίσεος which is more com. in the earlier and more elegant Grk. writ. [fr. Hdt. down]); neut. plur. ἡμίση, Lk. xix. 8 R G, a form in use from Theophr. down, for the earlier ἡμίσεα adopted by Lchm. (cf. Passow [also L. and S.] s. v.; W. § 9, 2 d.; ἡμίσεια in T Tr [ἡμίσια WH] seems due to a corruption of the copyists, see *Steph*. Thes. iv. p. 170; *Bttm*. Ausf. Spr. i. p. 248; *Alex. Bttm*. in Stud. u. Krit. for 1862, p. 194 sq.; [N. T. Gram. 14 (13); *Tdf*. Proleg. p. 118; but esp. *WH*. App. p. 158]); Sept. for מַחֲצִית, much oftener חֵצִי; *half*; it takes the gender and number of the annexed substantive (where τὸ ἥμισυ might have been expected): τὰ ἡμίση τῶν ὑπαρχόντων, Lk. xix. 8 (so Grk. writ. say ὁ ἥμισυς τοῦ βίου, οἱ ἡμίσεις τῶν ἱππέων, see Passow s. v.; [L. and S. s. v. I. 2]; Kühner § 405, 5 c.]; τὰς ἡμίσεις τῶν δυνάμεων, 1 Macc. iii. 34, 37); neut. τὸ ἥμισυ, substantively, *the half*; without the art. *a half*: ἕως ἡμίσους τῆς βασιλείας μου (Esth. v. 3; vii. 2), Mk. vi. 23; ἥμισυ καιροῦ, Rev. xii. 14; as in class. Grk., καὶ ἥμισυ is added to cardinal numbers even where they are connected with masc. and fem. substantives, as τρεῖς ἡμέρας καὶ ἥμισυ, three days and a half, Rev. xi. 9, 11, (ὀψωνεῖν δυοῖν δραχμῶν καὶ ἡμίσους, Ath. 6 p. 274 c.; δύο or ἑνὸς πήχεων καὶ ἡμίσους, Ex. xxv. 16; xxvi. 16; xxxviii. 1 [Alex.]); with καὶ omitted: Rev. xi. 9 Tdf. ed. 7 (μυριάδων ἑπτὰ ἡμίσους, Plut. Mar. 34).*

ἡμιώριον and (L T Tr WH) ἡμιώρον (cf. Kühner § 185, **2256** 6, 2; [Jelf § 165, 6, 1 a.]), -ον, τό, (fr. ἡμι and ὥρα; cf. τὸ * ἡμικοτύλιον, ἡμιμοίριον, ἡμικόσμιον, ἡμιχοινίκιον, ἡμιωβόλιον, etc.), *half an hour*: Rev. viii. 1. (Strab. 2 p. 133; Geop.; † al. [cf. Soph. Lex. s. v.].) *

ἡνίκα, a rel. adv. of time, [fr. Hom. down], *at which* **2259** *time; when*: foll. by the indic. pres., of a thing that actually takes place, 2 Co. iii. 15 R G; foll. by ἄν with subj. pres., *whensoever*: ibid. L T Tr WH; foll. by ἄν and the aor. subj. with the force of the Lat. fut. pf., *at length when (whensoever it shall have etc.)*: 2 Co. iii. 16; Ex. i. 10; Deut. vii. 12; Judith xiv. 2. [On its constr. see W. 296 (278) sq.; 308 (289); B. § 139, 33.] *2260:

ἤπερ, see ἤ, 4 d. ——————————————— see 2229

ἤπιος, -α, -ον, rarely of two terminations, (apparently 2261 derived fr. ἔπος, εἰπεῖν, so that it prop. means *affable* [so Etym. Magn. 434, 20; but cf. Vaniček p. 32]); fr. Hom. down; *mild, gentle*: 1 Th. ii. 7 (where L WH νήπιος, q. v. fin.); πρός τινα, 2 Tim. ii. 24.*

Ἤρ, Lchm. Ἦρ [on the breathing in codd. see *Tdf*. **2262** Proleg. p. 107], (עֵר watchful, fr. עוּר to be awake), *Er*, one of the ancestors of Christ: Lk. iii. 28.*

ἤρεμος, -ον, *quiet, tranquil*: ἤρεμον κ. ἡσύχιον βίον, 1 **2263** Tim. ii. 2. (Lcian. trag. 207; Eustath. Hesych.; com-

*For 2254 & 2257 see 1473.

†For 2258 see 1510.

parat. ἠρεμέστερος, fr. an unused ἠρεμής, Xen. Cyr. 7, 5, 63; more com. in the earlier Grk. writ. is the adv. ἠρέμα. [Cf. W. § 11 fin.; B. 28 (24).])*

2264 'Ηρώδης, -ου, ὁ, (equiv. to 'Ηρωίδης, sprung from a hero; hence the Etym. Magn. pp. 165, 43; 437, 56 directs it to be written 'Ηρώδης [so WH], as it is found also in certain inscriptions [cf. Lipsius, Gram. Unters. p. 9; WH. Intr. § 410; Tdf. Proleg. 109; Pape, Eigennamen, s. v.]), Herod, the name of a royal family that flourished among the Jews in the time of Jesus and the apostles. In the N. T. are mentioned, **1.** the one who gave the family its name, Herod surnamed the Great, a son of Antipater of Idumæa. Appointed king of Judæa B. C. 40 by the Roman senate at the suggestion of Antony and with the consent of Octavian, he at length overcame the great opposition which the country made to him and took possession of the kingdom B. C. 37; and, after the battle of Actium, he was confirmed in it by Octavian, whose favor he ever after enjoyed. He was brave and skilled in war, learned and sagacious; but also extremely suspicious and cruel. Hence he destroyed the entire royal family of the Hasmonæans, put to death many of the Jews that opposed his government, and proceeded to kill even his dearly beloved wife Mariamne of the Hasmonæan line and the two sons she had borne him. By these acts of bloodshed, and especially by his love and imitation of Roman customs and institutions and by the burdensome taxes imposed upon his subjects, he so alienated the Jews that he was unable to regain their favor by his splendid restoration of the temple and other acts of munificence. He died in the 70th year of his age, the 37th of his reign, the 4th before the Dionysian era. Cf. Joseph. antt. 14, 14, 4; 15, 6, 7; 7, 4; 8, 1; 16, 5, 4; 11, 6, etc. In his closing years John the Baptist and Christ were born, Mt. ii. 1; Lk. i. 5; Matthew narrates in ch. ii. (cf. Macrob. sat. 2, 4) that he commanded the male children in Bethlehem from two years old and under to be slain. Cf. especially Keim in Schenkel iii. 27 sqq.; Schürer, Neutest. Zeitgesch. § 15, and the books there mentioned. **2.** Herod surpamed Antipas, son of Herod the Great and Malthace, a Samaritan woman. After the death of his father he was appointed by the Romans tetrarch of Galilee and Peræa. His first wife was a daughter of Aretas, king of Arabia; but he subsequently repudiated her and took to himself Herodias, the wife of his brother Herod (see Φίλιππος, 1); and in consequence Aretas, his father-in-law, made war against him and conquered him. He cast John the Baptist into prison because John had rebuked him for this unlawful connection; and afterwards, at the instigation of Herodias, he ordered him to be beheaded. Induced by her, too, he went to Rome to obtain from the emperor the title of king. But in consequence of accusations brought against him by Herod Agrippa I., Caligula banished him (A.D. 39) to Lugdunum in Gaul, where he seems to have died. [On the statement of Joseph. (b. j. 2, 9, 6) that he died in Spain see the conjecture in B. D. s. v. Herodias.] He was light-minded, sensual,

vicious, (Joseph. antt. 17, 1, 3; 8, 1; 11, 4; 18, 5, 1; 7, 1 sq.; b. j. 2, 9, 6). In the N. T. he is mentioned by the simple name of Herod in Mt. xiv. 1, 3, 6; Mk. vi. 16–18, 20–22; viii. 15; Lk. iii. 1, 19; viii. 3; ix. 7, 9; xiii. 31; xxiii. 7 sq. 11 sq. 15; Acts iv. 27; xiii. 1; once, Mk. vi. 14, he is called βασιλεύς, either improperly, or in the sense of royal lineage (see βασιλεύς). Cf. Keim l. c. p. 42 sqq.; Schürer l. c. p. 232 sqq. **3.** Herod Agrippa I. (who is called by Luke simply Herod, by Josephus everywhere Agrippa), son of Aristobulus and Berenice, and grandson of Herod the Great. After various changes of fortune, he gained the favor of the emperors Caligula and Claudius to such a degree that he gradually obtained the government of all Palestine, with the title of king. He died at Cæsarea, A.D. 44, at the age of 54, in the seventh [or 4th, reckoning from the extension of his dominions by Claudius] year of his reign (Joseph. antt. 17, 1, 2; 18, 6; 19, 4, 5; 6, 1; 7, 3; b. j. 2, 11, 6), just after having ordered James the apostle, son of Zebedee, to be slain, and Peter to be cast into prison: Acts xii. 1, 6, 11, 19–21. Cf. Keim l. c. p. 49 sqq.; Schürer l. c. p. 290 sqq.; [Farrar, St. Paul, vol. ii. Excurs. vi.]. **4.** (Herod) Agrippa II., son of the preceding. When his father died he was a youth of seventeen. In A.D. 48 he received from Claudius Cæsar the government of Chalcis, with the right of appointing the Jewish high-priests, together with the care and oversight of the temple at Jerusalem. Four years later Claudius took from him Chalcis and gave him instead a larger dominion, viz. Batanæa, Trachonitis, and Gaulanitis, with the title of king. To these regions Nero, in A.D. 53, added Tiberias and Tarichaeae and the Peræan Julias, with fourteen neighboring villages. Cf. Joseph. antt. 19, 9, 1 sq.; 20, 1, 3; 5, 2; 7, 1; 8, 4; b. j. 2, 12, 1 and 8. In the N. T. he is mentioned in Acts xxv. 13, 22–26; xxvi. 1 sq. (7), 19, 27 sq. 32. In the Jewish war, although he strove in vain to restrain the fury of the seditious and bellicose populace, he did not desert the Roman side. After the fall of Jerusalem, he was vested with praetorian rank and kept the kingdom entire until his death, which took place in the third year of the emperor Trajan, [the 73d of his life, and 52nd of his reign]. He was the last representative of the Herodian dynasty. Cf. Keim l. c. p. 56 sqq.; Schürer l. c. p. 315 sqq. [Less complete accounts of the family may be found in BB.DD.; Sieffert in Herzog ed. 2 s. v.; an extended narrative in Hausrath, Neutest. Zeitgesch. vol. i. Abschn. v. Cf. also Edersheim, Jesus the Messiah, bk. ii. ch. ii. and App. iv.]

2265 'Ηρωδιανοί [WH 'Ηρῳδ., see 'Ηρώδης and I, ι; cf. W. § 16, 2 γ.], -ῶν, οἱ, Herodians, i. e. Herod's partisans (οἱ τὰ 'Ηρώδου φρονοῦντες, Joseph. antt. 14, 15, 10): Mt. xxii. 16; Mk. iii. 6; xii. 13. Cf. Keim, Jesu von Naz. iii. 130 sqq. [Eng. trans. v. p. 156 sq.], and in Schenkel iii. 65 sqq.; [cf. B. D. s. v.; Edersheim, Index s. v.].*

2266 'Ηρωδιάς [WH 'Ηρῳδιάς, see 'Ηρώδης and I, ι], -άδος, ἡ, Herodias, daughter of Aristobulus and granddaughter of Herod the Great. She was first married to Herod

[Philip (see Φίλιππος, 1)], son of Herod the Great, a man in private life; but she afterwards formed an unlawful union with Herod Antipas, whom she induced not only to slay John the Baptist but also to make the journey to Rome which ruined him; at last she followed him into exile in Gaul (see Ἡρώδης, 2): Mt. xiv. 3, 6; Mk. vi. 17, 19, 22; Lk. iii. 19.*

2267   Ἡρωδίων [WH Ἡρῳδ., see Ἡρώδης and Ι, ι], -ωνος, ὁ, *Herodion*, a certain Christian, [Paul's "kinsman" (see συγγενής)]: Ro. xvi. 11.*

2268   Ἡσαίας (Lchm. Ἡσ. [cf. Tdf. Proleg. p. 107; WH Ἡσαίας, see Ι, ι]), -ου [B. 17 (16), 8], ὁ, (so Sept. for יְשַׁעְיָהוּ, Jehovah's help, fr. יֵשַׁע and יָהּ), *Isaiah* (Vulg. *Isaias*, in the Fathers also *Esaias*), a celebrated Hebrew prophet, who prophesied in the reigns of Uzziah, Jotham, Ahaz, and Hezekiah: Mt. iii. 3; iv. 14; viii. 17; xii. 17; xiii. 14; (xiii. 35 acc. to the reading of cod. Sin. and other authorities, rightly approved of by Bleek [Hort (as below), al.], and received into the text by Tdf. [noted in mrg. by WH, see their App. ad loc.; per contra cf. Meyer or Ellicott (i. e. *Plumptre* in N. T. Com.) ad loc.]); xv. 7; Mk. vii. 6; Lk. iii. 4; iv. 17; Jn. i. 23; xii. 38 sq. 41; Acts xxviii. 25; Ro. ix. 27, 29; x. 16, 20; xv. 12; i. q. the book of the prophecies of Isaiah, Acts viii. 28, 30; ἐν (τῷ) Ἡσαΐᾳ, Mk. i. 2 G L txt. T Tr WH.*

2269   Ἡσαῦ [Ἡσ. Ro. ix. 13 Rˢᵗ Tr; Heb. xii. 16 Rˢᵗ; Heb. xi. 20 Rᵉˡˣ], ὁ, (עֵשָׂו i. e. hairy [Gen. xxv. 25; Joseph. antt. 1, 18, 1]), indecl., *Esau*, the firstborn of Isaac: Ro. ix. 13; Heb. xi. 20; xii. 16.*

see 2274   ἡσσάομαι, see ἡττάω and s. v. Σ, σ, ς.

see 2276   [ἥσσων, see ἥττων.]

2270   ἡσυχάζω; 1 aor. ἡσύχασα; (ἥσυχος [i. q. ἡσύχιος]); as in Grk. writ. fr. Aeschyl. down, *to keep quiet*, i. e. **a.** *to rest, to cease from labor:* Lk. xxiii. 56. **b.** *to lead a quiet life,* said of those who are not running hither and thither, but stay at home and mind their business: 1 Th. iv. 11. **c.** *to be silent,* i. e. *to say nothing, hold one's peace:* Lk. xiv. 4 (3); Acts xi. 18; xxi. 14, (Job xxxii. 7; ἡσύχασαν καὶ οὐχ εὕροσαν λόγον, Neh. v. 8).*

[SYN. ἡσυχάζειν, σιγᾶν, σιωπᾶν: ἡσ. describes a quiet condition in the general, inclusive of silence; σιγ. describes a mental condition and its manifestation, especially in speechlessness (silence from fear, grief, awe, etc.); σιωπ., the more external and physical term, denotes abstinence from speech, esp. as antithetic to loquacity. Schmidt i. ch. 9; iv. ch. 175.]

2271   ἡσυχία, -ας, ἡ, (fr. the adj. ἡσύχιος, q. v.]; the fem. expresses the general notion [W. 95 (90)], cf. αἰτία, ἀρετή,

ἐχθρά, etc.), [fr. Hom. down];   **1.** *quietness:* descriptive of the life of one who stays at home doing his own work, and does not officiously meddle with the affairs of others, 2 Th. iii. 12.   **2.** *silence:* Acts xxii. 2; 1 Tim. ii. 11 sq.*

2272   ἡσύχιος, -α, -ον, [(perh. akin to ἧμαι to sit, Lat. *sedatus;* cf. Curtius § 568; Vaniček p. 77)]; fr. Hom. down; *quiet, tranquil:* 1 Pet. iii. 4; βίος, 1 Tim. ii. 2; Joseph. antt. 13, 16, 1.*

2273:   ἤτοι, see ἤ, 4 e. ------------------   **see 2228 & 5104**

2274   ἡττάω: (ἥττων); *to make less, inferior, to overcome* (the Act. only in Polyb., Diod., Joseph. antt. 12, 7, 1 [other exx. in Veitch s. v.]); Pass. ἡττάομαι, fr. [Soph. and] Hdt. down; pf. ἥττημαι; 1 aor. ἡττήθην (ἡσσώθην, 2 Co. xii. 13 L T Tr WH; in opp. to which form cf. *Fritzsche,* De conform. N. T. crit. quam Lchm. ed. p. 32 [yet see *Kuenen and Cobet,* N. T. ad fid. cod. Vat. p. xc.; WH. App. p. 166; B. 59 (52); Veitch s. v.]); *to be made inferior; to be overcome, worsted:* in war, ὑπό τινος, 2 Macc. x. 24; univ., τινί [cf. B. 168 (147); W. 219 (206)], *to be conquered by one, forced to yield to one,* 2 Pet. ii. 19; absol. ib. 20. τὶ ὑπέρ τινα, i. q. ἧττον ἔχω τι, *to hold a thing inferior, set below,* [on the acc. (ὅ) cf. B. § 131, 10; and on the compar. use of ὑπέρ see ὑπέρ, II. 2 b.], 2 Co. xii. 13.*

2275   ἥττημα [cf. B. 7; WH. App. p. 166], -τος, τό, (ἡττάομαι);   **1.** *a diminution, decrease:* i. e. *defeat,* Is. xxxi. 8; αὐτῶν, brought upon the Jewish people in that so few of them had turned to Christ, Ro. xi. 12 [R. V. *loss*]. **2.** *loss,* sc. as respects salvation, 1 Co. vi. 7 [R. V. txt. *defect*]. Cf. Meyer [but cf. his 6te Aufl.] on each pass. (Elsewhere only in eccl. writ.)*

see 2276 St.   ἥττων or [so L T Tr WH, see Σ, σ, ς] ἥσσων, -ον, *inferior;* neut. adverbially [fr. Hom. down] *less,* 2 Co. xii. 15; εἰς τὸ ἧσσον, *for the worse* (that ye may be made worse; opp. to εἰς τὸ κρεῖττον), 1 Co. xi. 17.*

2278   ἠχέω, -ῶ; (ἦχος, q. v.); [fr. Hesiod down]; *to sound:* 1 Co. xiii. 1; used of the roaring of the sea, Lk. xxi. 25 Rec. [COMP.: ἐξ-, κατ-ηχέω.]*

2279   ἦχος [cf. Lat. *echo, vox,* Germ. *sprechen,* etc.; Vaniček p. 858], -ου, ὁ, and (Lk. xxi. 25 G L T Tr WH) τὸ ἦχος, -ους (cf. W. 65 (64); [B. 23 (20)]; Delitzsch on Heb. xii. 19 p. 638; [or ἦχους may come fr. ἠχώ, -οῦς, see esp. WH. App. p. 158ᵇ; Mey. on Lk. as below]);   **1.** *a sound, noise:* Acts ii. 2; Heb. xii. 19; spoken of the roar of the sea's waves, Lk. xxi. 25 G L T Tr WH.   **2.** *rumor, report:* περί τινος, Lk. iv. 37.*

*For 2277 see 1510.

Θ

2280   Θαδδαῖος, -ου, ὁ, (תַּדַּי), perh. large-*hearted* or *coura-geous*, although it has not been shown that תַּד equiv. to the Hebr. שַׁד can mean *pectus* as well as *mamma*; [some would connect the terms by the fact that the 'child of one's *heart*' may be also described as a '*bosom*-child'; but see B. D. s. v. Jude]), *Thaddæus*, a surname of the apostle Jude; he was also called *Lebbæus* and was the brother of James the less: Mt. x. 3 R G L Tr WH; Mk. iii. 18. [Cf. B. D. s. v.; Keil on Mt. l. c.; *WH*. App. p. 11ᵇ. The latter hold the name Λεββαῖος to be due to an early attempt to bring Levi (Λευείς) the publican (Lk. v. 27) within the Twelve.]*

2281   θάλασσα [cf. B. 7], -ης, ἡ, (akin to ἅλς [better, allied to ταράσσω etc., from its *tossing*; cf. Vaniček, p. 303]; Sept. for יָם), [fr. Hom. down], *the sea*; [on its distinction from πέλαγος see the latter word]; **a.** univ.: Mt. xxiii. 15; Mk. xi. 23; Lk. xvii. 2, 6; xxi. 25; Ro. ix. 27; 2 Co. xi. 26; Heb. xi. 12; Jas. i. 6; Jude 13; Rev. vii. 1–3, etc.; ἐργάζεσθαι τὴν θάλ. (see ἐργάζομαι, 2 a.), Rev. xviii. 17; τὸ πέλαγος τῆς θαλ. (see πέλαγος, a.), Mt. xviii. 6; joined with γῆ and οὐρανός it forms a periphrasis for the whole world, Acts iv. 24; xiv. 15; Rev. v. 13; x. 6 [L WH br.]; xiv. 7, (Hagg. ii. 7; Ps. cxlv. (cxlvi.) 6; Joseph. antt. 4, 3, 2; [c. Ap. 2, 10, 1]); among the visions of the Apocalypse *a glassy sea* or *sea of glass* is spoken of; but what the writer symbolized by this is not quite clear: Rev. iv. 6; xv. 2.   **b.** spec. used [even without the art., cf. W. 121 (115); B. § 124, 8 b.] of the Mediterranean Sea: Acts x. 6, 32; xvii. 14; of the Red Sea (see ἐρυθρός), ἡ ἐρυθρὰ θάλ., Acts vii. 36; 1 Co. x. 1 sq.; Heb. xi. 29.   By a usage foreign to native Grk. writ. [cf. Aristot. meteor. 1, 13 p. 351ᵃ, 8 ἡ ὑπὸ τὸν Καύκασον λίμνη ἣν καλοῦσιν οἱ ἐκεῖ θάλατταν, and Hesych. defines λίμνη: ἡ θάλασσα καὶ ὁ ὠκεανός] employed like the Hebr. יָם [e. g. Num. xxxiv. 11], by Mt. Mk. and Jn. (nowhere by Lk.) of the L a k e of Γεννησαρέτ (q. v.): ἡ θάλ. τῆς Γαλιλαίας, Mt. iv. 18; xv. 29; Mk. i. 16; vii. 31, (similarly Lake Constance, *der Bodensee*, is called *mare Suebicum*, the Suabian Sea); τῆς Τιβεριάδος, Jn. xxi. 1; τῆς Γαλιλ. τῆς Τιβεριάδος (on which twofold gen. cf. W. § 30, 3 N. 3; [B. 400 (343)]), Jn. vi. 1; more frequently simply ἡ θάλασσα: Mt. iv. 15, 18; viii. 24, 26 sq. 32; xiii. 1, etc.; Mk. ii. 13; iii. 7; iv. 1, 39; v. 13, etc.; Jn. vi. 16–19, 22, 25; xxi. 7. Cf. *Furrer* in Schenkel ii. 322 sqq.; [see Γεννησαρέτ].

2282   θάλπω: **1.** prop. *to warm*, *keep warm*, (Lat. *foveo*): Hom. et sqq.   **2.** like the Lat. *foveo*, i. q. *to cherish* with tender love, *to foster* with tender care: Eph. v. 29; 1 Th. ii. 7; ([Theocr. 14, 38]: Alciphr. 2, 4; Antonin. 5, 1).*

Θάμαρ [Treg. Θαμάρ], ἡ, (תָּמָר [i. e. palm-tree]), *Tamar*, prop. name of a woman, the daughter-in-law of Judah, son of the patriarch Jacob (Gen. xxxviii. 6): Mt. i. 3.*   **2283**

θαμβέω, -ῶ; Pass., impf. ἐθαμβούμην; 1 aor. ἐθαμβήθην; (θάμβος, q. v.);   **1.** *to be astonished*: Acts ix. 6 Rec. (Hom., Soph., Eur.)   **2.** *to astonish*, *terrify*: 2 S. xxii. 5; pass. *to be amazed*: Mk. i. 27; x. 32; foll. by ἐπί w. dat. of the thing, Mk. x. 24; *to be frightened*, 1 Macc. vi. 8; Sap. xvii. 3; Plut. Caes. 45; Brut. 20. [Comp.: ἐκ-θαμβέω.]*   **2284**

θάμβος [allied with τάφος amazement, fr. a Sanskrit root signifying *to render immovable*; Curtius § 233; Vaniček p. 1130], -ους, τό; fr. Hom. down; *amazement*: Lk. iv. 36; v. 9; Acts iii. 10.*   **2285**

θανάσιμος, -ον, (θανεῖν, θάνατος), *deadly*: Mk. xvi. 18. ([Aeschyl.], Soph., Eur., Plat., sqq.) *   **2286**

θανατη-φόρος, -ον, (θάνατος and φέρω), *death-bringing*, *deadly*: Jas. iii. 8.   (Num. xviii. 22; Job xxxiii. 23; 4 Macc. viii. 17, 25; xv. 26; Aeschyl., Plat., Arist., Diod., Xen., Plut., al.) *   **2287**

θάνατος, -ου, ὁ, (θανεῖν); Sept. for מָוֶת and מוּת, also for דֶּבֶר pestilence [W. 29 note]; (one of the nouns often anarthrous, cf. W. § 19, 1 s. v.; [B. § 124, 8 c.]; *Grimm*, Com. on Sap. p. 59); *death*;   **1.** prop. *the death of the body*, i. e. *that separation* (whether natural or violent) *of the soul from the body by which the life on earth is ended*: Jn. xi. 4, [13]; Acts ii. 24 [Tr mrg. ᾅδου] (on this see ὠδίν); Phil. ii. 27, 30; Heb. vii. 23; ix. 15 sq.; Rev. ix. 6; xviii. 8; opp. to ζωή, Ro. viii. 38; 1 Co. iii. 22; 2 Co. i. 9; Phil. i. 20; with the implied idea of future misery in the state beyond, 1 Co. xv. 21; 2 Tim. i. 10; Heb. ii. 14 sq.; i. q. the power of death, 2 Co. iv. 12. Since the nether world, the abode of the dead, was conceived of as being very dark, χώρα καὶ σκιὰ θανάτου (צַלְמָוֶת) is equiv. to the region of thickest darkness, i. e. figuratively, a region enveloped in the darkness of ignorance and sin: Mt. iv. 16; Lk. i. 79, (fr. Is. ix. 2); θάνατος is used of the punishment of Christ, Ro. v. 10: vi. 3–5; 1 Co. xi. 26; Phil. iii. 10; Col. i. 22; Heb. ii. [9], 14; σώζειν τινὰ ἐκ θανάτου, to free from the fear of death, to enable one to undergo death fearlessly, Heb. v. 7 [but al. al.]; ῥύεσθαι ἐκ θανάτου, to deliver from the danger of death, 2 Co. i. 10; plur. θάνατοι, *deaths* (i. e. mortal perils) of various kinds, 2 Co. xi. 23; περίλυπος ἕως θανάτου, even unto death, i. e. so that I am almost dying of sorrow, Mt. xxvi. 38; Mk. xiv. 34, (λελύπημαι ἕως θανάτου, Jonah iv. 9; λύπη ἕως θανάτου, Sir. xxxvii. 2, cf. Judg. xvi. 16); μέχρι θανάτου, so as not to refuse to undergo even death, Phil. ii. 8; also ἄχρι θανάτου, Rev. ii.   **2288**

10; xii. 11; ἐσφαγμένος εἰς θάνατον, that has received a deadly wound, Rev. xiii. 3; πληγὴ θανάτου, a deadly wound [death-stroke, cf. W. § 34, 3 b.], Rev. xiii. 3, 12; ἰδεῖν θάνατον, to experience death, Lk. ii. 26; Heb. xi. 5; also γεύεσθαι θανάτου [see γεύω, 2], Mt. xvi. 28; Mk. ix. 1; Lk. ix. 27; διώκειν τινὰ ἄχρι θανάτου, even to destruction, Acts xxii. 4; κατακρίνειν τινὰ θανάτῳ, to condemn one to death (ad mortem damnare, Tacit.), Mt. xx. 18 [here Tdf. εἰς θάν.]; Mk. x. 33, (see κατακρίνω, a.); πορεύεσθαι εἰς θάν. to undergo death, Lk. xxii. 33; παραδιδόναι τινὰ εἰς θάν. that he may be put to death, Mt. x. 21; Mk. xiii. 12; pass. to be given over to the peril of death, 2 Co. iv. 11; παραδ. εἰς κρίμα θανάτου, Lk. xxiv. 20; ἀποκτεῖναί τινα ἐν θανάτῳ (a Hebraism [cf. B. 184 (159 sq.)]), Rev. ii. 23; vi. 8, [cf. W. 29 note]; αἰτία θανάτου (see αἰτία, 2), Acts xiii. 28; xxviii. 18; ἄξιόν τι θανάτου, some crime worthy of the penalty of death, Acts xxiii. 29; xxv. 11, 25; [xxvi. 31]; Lk. xxiii. 15, 22 [here αἴτιον (q. v. 2 b.) θαν.]; ἔνοχος θανάτου, worthy of punishment by death, Mt. xxvi. 66; Mk. xiv. 64; θανάτῳ τελευτάτω, let him surely be put to death, Mt. xv. 4; Mk. vii. 10, after Ex. xxi. 17 Sept. (Hebr. יוּמָת מוֹת); cf. W. § 44 fin. N. 3; [B. u. s.]; θάν. σταυροῦ, Phil. ii. 8; ποίῳ θανάτῳ, by what kind of death, Jn. xii. 33; xviii. 32; xxi. 19. The inevitable necessity of dying, shared alike by all men, takes on in the popular imagination the form of a person, a tyrant, subjugating men to his power and confining them in his dark dominions: Ro. vi. 9; 1 Co. xv. [26], 54, 56; Rev. xxi. 4; Hades is associated with him as his partner: 1 Co. xv. 55 R G; Rev. i. 18 (on which see κλείς); vi. 8; xx. 13, [14ª], (Ps. xvii. (xviii.) 5; cxiv. (cxvi.) 3; Hos. xiii. 14; Sir. xiv. 12). **2.** metaph. *the loss of that life which alone is worthy of the name*, i. e. *the misery of soul arising from sin, which begins on earth but lasts and increases after the death of the body*: 2 Co. iii. 7; Jas. i. 15, (Clem. Rom. 2 Cor. 1, 6 says of life before conversion to Christ, ὁ βίος ἡμῶν ὅλος ἄλλο οὐδὲν ἦν εἰ μὴ θάνατος [cf. Philo, plantat. et poenis § 12, and reff. in 4 below]); opp. to ἡ ζωή, Ro. vii. 10, 13; 2 Co. ii. 16; opp. to σωτηρία, 2 Co. vii. 10; i. q. the cause of death, Ro. vii. 13; σώζειν ψυχὴν ἐκ θανάτου, Jas. v. 20; μεταβεβηκέναι ἐκ τοῦ θανάτου εἰς τ. ζωήν, Jn. v. 24; 1 Jn. iii. 14; μένειν ἐν τῷ θανάτῳ, 1 Jn. iii. 14; θεωρεῖν θάνατον, Jn. viii. 51; γενέσθαι θανάτου, 52 (see 1 above); ἁμαρτία and ἁμαρτάνειν πρὸς θάνατον (see ἁμαρτία, 2 b.), 1 Jn. v. 16 sq. (in the rabbin. writers חַטְא לָמוּת — after Num. xviii. 22, Sept. ἁμαρτία θανατηφόρος — is a *crimen capitale*). **3.** *the miserable state of the wicked dead in hell* is called — now simply θάνατος, Ro. i. 32 (Sap. i. 12 sq.; ii. 24; Tatian or. ad Graec. c. 13; the author of the ep. ad Diognet. c. 10, 7 distinguishes between ὁ δοκῶν ἐνθάδε θάνατος, the death of the body, and ὁ ὄντως θάνατος, ὃς φυλάσσεται τοῖς κατακριθησομένοις εἰς τὸ πῦρ τὸ αἰώνιον); now ὁ δεύτερος θάνατος and ὁ θάν. ὁ δεύτ. (as opp. to the *former death*, i. e. to that by which life on earth is ended), Rev. ii. 11; xx. 6, 14ᵇ; xxi. 8, (as in the Targums on Deut. xxxiii. 6; Ps. xlviii. (xlix.) 11; Is. xxii. 14; lxvi. 15; [for the Grk.

use of the phrase cf. Plut. de facie in orbe lunae 27, 6 p. 942 f.]; θάνατος αἰώνιος, Barn. ep. 20, 1 and in eccl. writ. [ὁ ἀΐδιος θάνατος, Philo, post. Cain. § 11 fin.; see also Wetstein on Rev. ii. 11]). **4.** In the widest sense, *death* comprises *all the miseries arising from sin*, as well *physical death* as *the loss of a life consecrated to God and blessed in him on earth* (Philo, alleg. legg. i. § 33 ὁ ψυχῆς θάνατος ἀρετῆς μὲν φθορά ἐστι, κακίας δὲ ἀνάληψις, [de profug. § 21 θάνατος ψυχῆς ὁ μετὰ κακίας ἐστὶ βίος, esp. §§ 10, 11; quod det. pot. insid. §§ 14, 15; de poster. Cain. § 21, and de praem. et poen. as in 2 above]), *to be followed by wretchedness in the lower world* (opp. to ζωὴ αἰώνιος): θάνατος seems to be so used in Ro. v. 12; vi. 16, 21, [23; yet al. refer these last three exx. to 3 above]; vii. 24; viii. 2, 6; death, in this sense, is personified in Ro. v. 14, 17, 21; vii. 5. Others, in all these pass. as well as those cited under 2, understand physical death; but see Philippi on Ro. v. 12; *Messner*, Lehre der Apostel, p. 210 sqq.*

θανατόω, -ῶ; fut. θανατώσω; 1 aor. inf. θανατῶσαι, [3 pers. plur. subjunc. θανατώσωσι, Mt. xxvi. 59 R G]; Pass., [pres. θανατοῦμαι]; 1 aor. ἐθανατώθην; (fr. θάνατος); fr. Aeschyl. and Hdt. down; Sept. for הֵמִית, הָרַג, etc. **1.** prop. *to put to death*: τινά, Mt. x. 21; xxvi. 59; xxvii. 1; Mk. xiii. 12; xiv. 55; Lk. xxi. 16; 2 Co. vi. 9; 1 Pet. iii. 18; pass., by rhetorical hyperbole, to be in the state of one who is being put to death, Ro. viii. 36. **2.** metaph. **a.** *to make to die* i. e. *destroy, render extinct* (something vigorous), Vulg. *mortifico* [A. V. *mortify*]: τί, Ro. viii. 13. **b.** Pass. with dat. of the thing, *by death to be liberated from the bond of* anything [lit. *to be made dead* in relation *to*; cf. W. 210 (197); B. 178 (155)]: Ro. vii. 4.*

θάπτω; 1 aor. ἔθαψα; 2 aor. pass. ἐτάφην; fr. Hom. down; Sept. for קָבַר; *to bury, inter*, [BB.DD. s. v. Burial; cf. *Becker*, Charicles, sc. ix. Excurs. p. 390 sq.]: τινά, Mt. viii. 21 sq.; xiv. 12; Lk. ix. 59 sq.; xvi. 22; Acts ii. 29; v. 6, 9 sq.; 1 Co. xv. 4. [COMP.: συν-θάπτω.] *

Θάρα [WH Θαρά], ὁ, [תֶּרַח a journey, or a halt on a journey [al. 'loiterer']), indecl. prop. name, *Terah*, the father of Abraham: Lk. iii. 34.*

θαρρέω (a form current fr. Plato on for the Ionic and earlier Attic θαρσέω), -ῶ; 1 aor. inf. θαρρῆσαι; [fr. Hom. on]; *to be of good courage*, *to be hopeful, confident*: 2 Co. v. 6, 8; Heb. xiii. 6; *to be bold*: τῇ πεποιθήσει, with the confidence, 2 Co. x. 2; εἴς τινα, towards (against) one, 2 Co. x. 1; ἔν τινι, the ground of my confidence is in one, I am made of good courage by one, 2 Co. vii. 16. [SYN. see τολμάω.] *

θαρσέω, -ῶ; (see θαρρέω); *to be of good courage, be of good cheer*; in the N. T. only in the impv.: θάρσει, Lk. viii. 48 R G; Mt. ix. 2, 22; Mk. x. 49; Acts xxiii. 11; (Sept. for אַל-תִּירָא, Gen. xxxv. 17, etc.); θαρσεῖτε, Mt. xiv. 27; Mk. vi. 50; Jn. xvi. 33, (Sept. for אַל-תִּירָא, Ex. xiv. 13; Joel ii. 22, etc.). [SYN. see τολμάω.] *

θάρσος, -ους, τό, *courage, confidence*: Acts xxviii. 15.*

θαῦμα, -τος, τό, (ΘΑΟΜΑΙ [to wonder at], to gaze at, cf. *Bttm*. Gram. § 114 s. v.; Ausf. Spr. ii. p. 196; Curtius

Margin numbers: 2289, 2290, 2291, 2292, 2293, 2294, 2295

§ 308);   **1.** *a wonderful thing, a marvel* : 2 Co. xi. 14 L T Tr WH.   **2.** *wonder* : θαυμάζειν θαῦμα μέγα (cf. W. § 32, 2 ; [B. § 131, 5]), to wonder [with great wonder i. e.] exceedingly, Rev. xvii. 6.   (In both senses in Grk. writ. fr. Hom. down ; Sept. Job xvii. 8 ; xviii. 20.) *

2296   **θαυμάζω** ; impf. ἐθαύμαζον ; fut. θαυμάσομαι (Rev. xvii. 8 R G T Tr, a form far more com. in the best Grk. writ. also than θαυμάσω ; cf. Krüger § 40 s. v. ; Kühner § 343 s. v. ; [Veitch s. v.]) ; 1 aor. ἐθαύμασα ; 1 aor. pass. ἐθαυμάσθην in a mid. sense (Rev. xiii. 3 R^a L Tr txt.) ; also 1 fut. pass., in the sense of the mid., θαυμασθήσομαι (Rev. xvii. 8 L WH ; but the very few exx. of the mid. use in prof. auth. are doubtful ; cf. *Stephanus*, Thesaur. iv. p. 259 sq. ; [yet see Veitch s. v.]) ; *to wonder, wonder at, marvel* : absol., Mt. viii. 10, 27 ; ix. 8 Rec., 33 ; xv. 31 ; xxi. 20 ; xxii. 22 ; xxvii. 14 ; Mk. v. 20 ; vi. 51 [Rec. ; L br. Tr mrg. br.] ; xv. 5 ; Lk. i. 21 [see below], 63 ; viii. 25 ; xi. 14 ; xxiv. 41 ; Jn. v. 20 ; vii. 15 ; Acts ii. 7 ; iv. 13 ; xiii. 41 ; Rev. xvii. 7 sq. ; with acc. of the pers. Lk. vii. 9 ; with acc. of the thing, Lk. xxiv. 12 [T om. L Tr br. WH reject the vs. (see πρός, I. 1 a. init. and 2 b.)] ; Jn. v. 28 ; Acts vii. 31 ; θαῦμα μέγα (see θαῦμα, 2), Rev. xvii. 6 ; πρόσωπον, to admire, pay regard to, one's external appearance, **i. e.** to be influenced by partiality, Jude 16 (Sept. for נָשָׂא פָּנִים, Deut. x. 17 ; Job xiii. 10 ; Prov. xviii. 5 ; Is. ix. 14, etc.) ; foll. by διά τι, Mk. vi. 6 ; Jn. vii. 21 where διὰ τοῦτο (omitted by Tdf.) is to be joined to vs. 21 [so G L Tr mrg. ; cf. Meyer (ed. *Weiss*) ad loc. ; W. § 7, 3], (Isocr. p. 52 d. ; Ael. v. h. 12, 6 ; 14, 36) ; [foll. by ἐν w. dat. of object, acc. to the constr. adopted by some in Lk. i. 21 ἐθαύμ. ἐν τῷ χρονίζειν αὐτόν, *at his tarrying* ; cf. W. § 33, b. ; B. 264 (227) ; 185 (160 sq.) ; Sir. xi. 19 (21) ; evang. Thom. 15, 2 ; but see above] ; foll. by ἐπί w. dat. of pers. Mk. xii. 17 [R G L Tr] ; by ἐπί w. dat. of the thing, Lk. ii. 33 ; iv. 22 ; ix. 43 ; xx. 26 ; [Acts iii. 12], (Xen., Plat., Thuc., al. ; Sept.) ; περί τινος, Lk. ii. 18 ; by a pregnant constr. [cf. B. 185 (161)] ἐθαύμασεν ἡ γῆ ὀπίσω τοῦ θηρίου, followed the beast in wonder, Rev. xiii. 3 [cf. B. 59 (52)] ; foll. by ὅτι, to marvel that, etc., Lk. xi. 38 ; Jn. iii. 7 ; iv. 27 ; Gal. i. 6 ; by εἰ (see εἰ, I. 4), Mk. xv. 44 ; 1 Jn. iii. 13.   Pass. *to be wondered at, to be had in admiration*, (Sir. xxxviii. 3 ; Sap. viii. 11 ; 4 Macc. xviii. 3), foll. by ἐν w. dat. of the pers. whose lot and condition gives matter for wondering at another, 2 Th. i. 10 ; ἐν with dat. of the thing, Is. lxi. 6. [Comp. : ἐκ‑θαυμάζω.] *

2297   **θαυμάσιος**, ‑α, ‑ον, rarely of two terminations, (θαῦμα), [fr. Hes., Hom. (h. Merc. 443) down], *wonderful, marvellous* ; neut. plur. θαυμάσια (Sept. often for נִפְלָאוֹת, also for פֶּלֶא), *wonderful deeds, wonders* : Mt. xxi. 15. [Cf. Trench § xci. ; better, Schmidt ch. 168, 6.] *

2298   **θαυμαστός**, ‑ή, ‑όν, (θαυμάζω), in Grk. writ. fr. [Hom. (h. Cer. etc.)], Hdt., Pind. down ; [interchanged in Grk. writ. with θαυμάσιος, cf. *Lob.* Path. Elem. ii. 341] ; *wonderful, marvellous* ; **i. e.** **a.** *worthy of pious admiration, admirable, excellent* : 1 Pet. ii. 9 (Clem. Rom. 1 Cor. 36, 2 ; for אַדִּיר, Ps. viii. 2 ; xcii. (xciii.) 4, (5)).   **b.** *passing human comprehension* : Mt. xxi. 42 and Mk. xii. 11, (fr.

Ps. cxvii. (cxviii.) 22 sq., where for נִפְלָא, as Job xlii. 3 ; Mic. vii. 15, etc.).   **c.** *causing amazement joined with terror* : Rev. xv. 1, 3, (so for נוֹרָא, Ex. xv. 11, etc.).   **d.** *marvellous* i. e. *extraordinary, striking, surprising* : 2 Co. xi. 14 R G (see θαῦμα, 1) ; Jn. ix. 30.*

2299   **θεά**, ‑ᾶς, ἡ, (fem. of θεός), [fr. Hom. down], *a goddess* : Acts xix. 27, and Rec. also in 35, 37.*

2300   **θεάομαι**, ‑ῶμαι : 1 aor. ἐθεασάμην ; pf. τεθέαμαι ; 1 aor. pass. ἐθεάθην in pass. sense (Mt. vi. 1 ; xxiii. 5 ; Mk. xvi. 11 ; Thuc. 3, 38, 3 ; cf. Krüger § 40 s. v. ; [but Krüger himself now reads δρασθεί in Thuc. l. c. ; see Veitch s. v. ; W. § 38, 7 c. ; B. 52 (46)]) ; depon. verb ; (fr. θέα, ΘΑΟΜΑΙ, with which θαῦμα is connected, q. v.) ; *to behold, look upon, view attentively, contemplate*, (in Grk. writ. often used of **public shows** ; cf. θέα, θέαμα, θέατρον, θεατρίζω, etc. [see below]) : τί, Mt. xi. 7 ; Lk. vii. 24 ; Jn. iv. 35 ; xi. 45 ; *of august things and persons that are looked on with admiration* : τί, Jn. i. 14, 32 ; 1 Jn. i. 1 ; Acts xxii. 9, (2 Macc. iii. 36) ; τινά, with a ptcp., Mk. xvi. 14 ; Acts i. 11 ; foll. by ὅτι, 1 Jn. iv. 14 ; θεαθῆναι ὑπό τινος, Mk. xvi. 11 ; πρὸς τὸ θεαθῆναι αὐτοῖς, in order to make a show to them, Mt. vi. 1 ; xxiii. 5 ; *to view, take a view of* : τί, Lk. xxiii. 55 ; τινά, Mt. xxii. 11 ; in the sense of visiting, meeting with a person, Ro. xv. 24 (2 Chr. xxii. 6 ; Joseph. antt. 16, 1, 2) ; *to learn by looking* : foll. by ὅτι, Acts viii. 18 Rec. ; *to see with the eyes*, 1 Jn. iv. 12 ; **i. q.** (Lat. *conspicio*) *to perceive* : τινά, Jn. viii. 10 R G ; Acts xxi. 27 ; foll. by acc. with ptcp., Lk. v. 27 [not L mrg.] ; Jn. i. 38 ; foll. by ὅτι, Jn. vi. 5.*

Cf. *O. F. Fritzsche*, in Fritzschiorum Opusc. p. 295 sqq. [Acc. to *Schmidt*, Syn. i. ch. 11, θεᾶσθαι in its earlier classic use denotes often a **wondering** regard, (cf. even in Strabo 14, 5, τὰ ἑπτὰ θεάματα i. q. θαύματα). This specific shade of meaning, however, gradually faded out, and left the more general signification of such a looking as seeks merely the satisfaction of the sense of sight. Cf. θεωρέω.]

2301   **θεατρίζω** : (θέατρον, q. v.) ; prop. *to bring upon the stage* ; hence *to set forth as a spectacle, expose to contempt* ; Pass., pres. ptcp. θεατριζόμενος [A. V. *being made a gazing-stock*], Heb. x. 33.   (Several times also in eccl. and Byzant. writ. [cf. *Soph.* Lex. s. v.] ; but in the same sense ἐκθεατρίζω in Polyb. 3, 91, 10 ; al. ; [cf. W. 25 (24) note ; also Tdf. ed. 7 Proleg. p. lix. sq.].) *

2302   **θέατρον**, ‑ου, τό, (θεάομαι) ; **1.** *a theatre*, a place in which games and dramatic spectacles are exhibited, and public assemblies held (for the Greeks used the theatre also as a forum) : Acts xix. 29, 31.   **2. i. q.** θέα and θέαμα, *a public show* (Aeschin. dial. socr. 3, 20 ; Achill. Tat. 1, 16 p. 55), and hence, metaph., *a man who is exhibited to be gazed at and made sport of* : 1 Co. iv. 9 [A. V. *a spectacle*].*

2303   **θεῖον**, ‑ου, τό, (apparently the neut. of the adj. θεῖος i. q. divine incense, because burning brimstone was regarded as having power to purify, and to ward off contagion [but Curtius § 320 allies it w. θύω ; cf. Lat. *fumus*, Eng. *dust*]), *brimstone* : Lk. xvii. 29 ; Rev. ix. 17 sq. ; xiv. 10 ; xix. 20 ; [xx. 10] ; xxi. 8. (Gen. xix. 24 ; Ps. x. (xi.) 6 ; Ezek. xxxviii. 22 ; Hom. Il. ¹6, 228 ; Od. 22, 481,

493; (Plat.) Tim. Locr. p. 99 c.; Ael. v. h. 13, 15 [16];
Hdian. 8, 4, 26 [9 ed. Bekk.].)*

2304 θεῖος, -εία, -εῖον, (θεός), [fr. Hom. down], *divine*: ἡ θεία
δύναμις, 2 Pet. i. 3; φύσις (Diod. 5, 31), ibid. 4; neut. τὸ
θεῖον, *divinity*, *deity* (Lat. *numen divinum*), not only
used by the Greeks to denote the divine nature, power,
providence, in the general, without reference to any
individual deity (as Hdt. 3, 108; Thuc. 5, 70; Xen. Cyr.
4, 2, 15; Hell. 7, 5, 13; mem. 1, 4, 18; Plat. Phaedr. p.
242 c.; Polyb. 32, 25, 7; Diod. 1, 6; 13, 3; 12; 16, 60;
Lcian. de sacrif. 1; pro imagg. 13, 17. 28), but also by
Philo (as in mundi opif. § 61; de agric. 17; leg. ad Gai.
1), and by Josephus (antt. 1, 3, 4; 11, 1; 2, 12, 4; 5, 2,
7; 11, 5, 1; 12, 6, 3; 7, 3; 13, 8, 2; 10, 7; 14, 9, 5; 17,
2, 4; 20, 11, 2; b. j. 3, 8, 3; 4, 3, 10), of the one, true
God; hence most appositely employed by Paul, out of
regard for Gentile usage, in Acts xvii. 29.*

2305 θειότης, -ητος, ἡ, *divinity*, *divine nature*: Ro. i. 20.
(Sap. xviii. 9; Philo in opif. § 61 fin.; Plut. symp. 665 a.;
Lcian. calumn. c. 17.) [SYN. see θεότης.]*

2306 θειώδης, -ες, (fr. θεῖον *brimstone* [q. v.]), *of brimstone*,
sulphurous: Rev. ix. 17; a later Grk. word; cf. *Lob.* ad
Phryn. p. 228; [Soph. Lex. s. v.].*

2307 θέλημα, -τος, τό, (θέλω), a word purely bibl. and eccl.
[yet found in Aristot. de plant. 1, 1 p. 815ᵇ, 21];
Sept. for חֵפֶץ and רָצוֹן; *will*, i. e. a. *what one wishes
or has determined shall be done*, [i. e. objectively, *thing
willed*]: Lk. xii. 47; Jn. v. 30; 1 Co. vii. 37; 1 Th. v.
18; 2 Tim. ii. 26; Heb. x. 10; Rev. iv. 11; θέλημα τοῦ
θεοῦ is used — of the purpose of God to bless mankind
through Christ, Acts xxii. 14; Eph. i. 9; Col. i. 9; of what
God wishes to be done by us, Ro. xii. 2; Col. iv. 12 [W.
111 (105)]; 1 Pet. iv. 2; and simply τὸ θέλημα, Ro. ii. 18
[W. 594 (553)] (Sir. xliii. 16 (17) [but here the better
txt. now adds αὐτοῦ, see *Fritzsche*; in patrist. Grk., however, θέλημα is so used even without the art.; cf. Ignat.
ad Rom. 1, 1; ad Eph. 20, 1, etc.]); τοῦ κυρίου, Eph. v.
17; plur. *commands*, *precepts*: [Mk. iii. 35 WH mrg.];
Acts xiii. 22, (Ps. cii. (ciii.) 7; 2 Macc. i. 3); ἐστὶ τὸ θέλημά τινος, foll. by ἵνα, Jn. vi. 39 sq.; 1 Co. xvi. 12, cf.
Mt. xviii. 14; foll. by inf., 1 Pet. ii. 15; by acc. with inf.,
1 Th. iv. 3. [Cf. B. 237 (204); 240 (207); W. § 44, 8.]
b. i. q. τὸ θέλειν, [i. e. the abstract act of *willing*, the
subjective] *will*, *choice*: 1 Pet. iii. 17 [cf. W. 604 (562)];
2 Pet. i. 21; ποιεῖν τ. θέλ. τινος (esp. of God), Mt. vii.
21; xii. 50; xxi. 31; Mk. iii. 35 [here WH mrg. the plur.,
see above]; Jn. iv. 34; vi. 38; vii. 17; ix. 31; Eph. vi.
6; Heb. x. 7, 9, 36; xiii. 21; 1 Jn. ii. 17; τὸ θέλ. (L T Tr
WH βούλημα) τινος κατεργάζεσθαι, 1 Pet. iv. 3; γίνεται τὸ
θέλ. τινος, Mt. vi. 10; xxvi. 42; Lk. xi. 2 L R; xxii. 42;
Acts xxi. 14; ἡ βουλὴ τοῦ θελήματος, Eph. i. 11; ἡ εὐδοκία τοῦ θελ. ib. 5; ἐν τῷ θελ. τοῦ θεοῦ, if God will, Ro. i.
10; διὰ θελήματος θεοῦ, Ro. xv. 32; 1 Co. i. 1; 2 Co. i. 1;
viii. 5; Eph. i. 1; Col. i. 1; 2 Tim. i. 1; κατὰ τὸ θέλ.
τοῦ θεοῦ, Gal. i. 4; [1 Pet. iv. 19]; 1 Jn. v. 14. i. q.
pleasure: Lk. xxiii. 25; i. q. *inclination*, *desire*: σαρκός,
ἀνδρός, Jn. i. 13; plur. Eph. ii. 3. [SYN. see θέλω,
fin.]*

θέλησις, -εως, ἡ, (θέλω), i. q. τὸ θέλειν, *a willing*, *will*: **2308**
Heb. ii. 4. (Ezek. xviii. 23; 2 Chr. xv. 15; Prov. viii. 35;
Sap. xvi. 25; [Tob. xii. 18]; 2 Macc. xii. 16; 3 Macc. ii.
26; [plur. in] Melissa epist. ad Char. p. 62 Orell.; acc. to
Pollux [l. 5 c. 47] a vulgarism (ἰδιωτικόν); [cf. *Lob.*
ad Phryn. p. 353].)*

θέλω (only in this form in the N. T.; in Grk. auth. also **2309**
ἐθέλω [Veitch s. v.; *Lob.* ad Phryn. p. 7; B. 57 (49)]);
impf. ἤθελον; [fut. 3 pers. sing. θελήσει, Rev. xi. 5 WH
mrg.]; 1 aor. ἠθέλησα; (derived apparently fr. ἐλεῖν
with a fuller aspiration, so that it means prop. to seize
with the mind; but Curtius p. 726, ed. 5, regards its
root as uncertain [he inclines, however, to the view of
Pott, Fick, Vaniček and others, which connects it with
a root meaning *to hold to*]); Sept. for אָבָה and חָפֵץ; TO
WILL, (*have in mind*,) *intend*; i. e.   **1.** *to be resolved
or determined*, *to purpose*: absol., ὁ θέλων, Ro. ix. 16;
τοῦ θεοῦ θέλοντος if God will, Acts xviii. 21; ἐὰν ὁ κύριος
θελήσῃ (in Attic ἐὰν θεὸς θέλῃ, ἢν οἱ θεοὶ θέλωσιν [cf. *Lob.*
u. s.]), 1 Co. iv. 19; Jas. iv. 15; καθὼς ἠθέλησε, 1 Co. xii.
18; xv. 38; τί, Ro. vii. 15 sq. 19 sq.; 1 Co. vii. 36; Gal.
v. 17; with the aorist inf., Mt. xx. 14; xxvi. 15; Jn. vi.
21 (where the meaning is, they were willing to receive
him into the ship, but that was unnecessary, because
unexpectedly the ship was nearing the land; cf. Lücke,
B-Crusius, Ewald, [Godet], al. ad loc.; W. § 54, 4; [B.
375 (321)]); Jn. vii. 44; Acts xxv. 9; Col. i. 27; 1 Th.
ii. 18; Rev. xi. 5, etc.; with the present inf., Lk. x. 29
R G; Jn. vi. 67; vii. 17; viii. 44; Acts xxiv. 6 [Rec.];
Ro. vii. 21; Gal. iv. 9 [here T Tr txt. WH txt. 1 aor. inf.];
with an inf. suggested by the context, Jn. v. 21 (οὓς θέλει,
sc. ζωοποιῆσαι); Mt. viii. 2; Mk. iii. 13; vi. 22; Ro. ix.
18; Rev. xi. 6, etc. οὐ θέλω *to be unwilling*: with the
aorist inf., Mt. ii. 18; xv. 32; xxii. 3; Mk. vi. 26; Lk.
xv. 28; Jn. v. 40; Acts vii. 39; 1 Co. xvi. 7; Rev. ii. 21
[not Rec.], etc.; with the present inf., Jn. vii. 1; Acts
xiv. 13; xvii. 18; 2 Th. iii. 10, etc.; with the inf. om-
and to be gathered fr. the context, Mt. xviii. 30; xxi.
29; Lk. xviii. 4, etc.; θέλω and οὐ θέλω foll. by the acc.
with inf., Lk. i. 62; 1 Co. x. 20; on the Pauline phrase οὐ
θέλω ὑμᾶς ἀγνοεῖν, see ἀγνοέω, a.; corresponding to θέλω
ὑμᾶς εἰδέναι, 1 Co. xi. 3; Col. ii. 1.   θέλειν, used of a
purpose or resolution, is contrasted with the carrying out of the purpose into act: opp. to ποιεῖν, πράσσειν, Ro. vii. 15, 19; 2 Co. viii. 10 sq. (on which latter
pass. cf. De Wette and Meyer; W. § 61, 7 b.); to ἐνεργεῖν, Phil. ii. 13, cf. Mk. vi. 19; Jn. vii. 44.   One is said
also θέλειν that which he is on the point of doing: Mk.
vi. 48; Jn. i. 43 (44); and it is used thus also of things
that tend or point to some conclusion [cf. W. § 42, 1 b.;
B. 254 (219)]: Acts ii. 12; xvii. 20.   λανθάνει αὐτοὺς
τοῦτο θέλοντας this (viz. what follows, ὅτι etc.) escapes
them of their own will, i. e. they are purposely, *wilfully*,
ignorant, 2 Pet. iii. 5, where others interpret as follows:
this (viz. what has been said previously) desiring (i. e.
holding as their opinion [for exx. of this sense see *Soph.*
Lex. s. v. 4]), they are ignorant etc.; but cf. De Wette
ad loc. and W. § 54, 4 note; [B. § 150, 8 Rem.].   τὰς

ἐπιθυμίας τοῦ πατρὸς ὑμῶν θέλετε ποιεῖν it is your *purpose* to fulfil the lusts of your father, i. e. ye are actuated by him of your own free knowledge and choice, Jn. viii. 44 [W. u. s.; B. 375 (321)].   **2.** i. q. *to desire, to wish*: τί, Mt. xx. 21; Mk. xiv. 36; Lk. v. 39 [but WH in br.]; Jn. xv. 7; 1 Co. iv. 21; 2 Co. xi. 12; foll. by the aorist inf., Mt. v. 40; xii. 38; xvi. 25; xix. 17; Mk. x. 43 sq.; Lk. viii. 20; xxiii. 8; Jn. v. 6, 35 (ye were desirous of rejoicing); xii. 21; Gal. iii. 2; Jas. ii. 20; 1 Pet. iii. 10; foll. by the present inf., Jn. ix. 27; Gal. iv. 20 (ἤθελον *I could wish*, on which impf. see εὔχομαι, 2); the inf. is wanting and to be supplied fr. the neighboring verb, Mt. xvii. 12; xxvii. 15; Mk. ix. 13; Jn. xxi. 18; foll. by the acc. and inf., Mk. vii. 24; Lk. i. 62; Jn. xxi. 22 sq.; Ro. xvi. 19; 1 Co. vii. 7, 32; xiv. 5; Gal. vi. 13; οὐ θέλω *to be unwilling*, (*desire not*): foll. by the aor. inf., Mt. xxiii. 4; Lk. xix. 14, 27; 1 Co. x. 20; foll. by ἵνα, Mt. vii. 12; Mk. vi. 25; ix. 30; x. 35; Lk. vi. 31; Jn. xvii. 24; cf. W. § 44, 8 b.; [B. § 139, 46]; foll. by the delib. subj. (aor.): θέλεις συλλέξωμεν αὐτά (cf. the Germ. *willst du, sollen wir zusammenlesen*? [Goodwin § 88]), Mt. xiii. 28; add, Mt. xx. 32 [where L br. adds ἵνα]; xxvi. 17; xxvii. 17, 21; Mk. x. 51; xiv. 12; xv. 9, 12 [Tr br. θέλ.]; Lk. ix. 54; xviii. 41; xxii. 9, (cf. W. § 41 a. 4 b.; B. § 139, 2); foll. by εἰ, Lk. xii. 49 (see εἰ, I. 4); foll. by ἤ, *to prefer*, 1 Co. xiv. 19 (see ἤ, 3 d.).   **3.** i. q. *to love*; foll. by an inf., *to like to do a thing, be fond of doing*: Mk. xii. 38; Lk. xx. 46; cf. W. § 54, 4; [B. § 150, 8].   **4.** in imitation of the Hebr. חָפֵץ, *to take delight, have pleasure* [opp. by B. § 150, 8 Rem.; cf. W. § 33, a.; but see exx. below]: ἔν τινι, in a thing, Col. ii. 18 (ἐν καλῷ, to delight in goodness, Test. xii. Patr. p. 688 [test. Ash. 1; (cf. εἰς ζωήν, p. 635, test. Zeb. 3); Ps. cxi. (cxii.) 1; cxlvi. (cxlvii.) 10]; ἔν τινι, dat. of the pers., 1 S. xviii. 22; 2 S. xv. 26; [1 K. x. 9]; 2 Chr. ix. 8; for רָצָה, 1 Chr. xxviii. 4).   τινά, to love one: Mt. xxvii. 43 (Ps. xxi. (xxii.) 9; [xvii. (xviii.) 20]; xl. (xli.) 12]; Ezek. xviii. 32, cf. 23; Tob. xiii. 6; opp. to μισεῖν, Ignat. ad Rom. 8, 3; θεληθῆναι is used of those who find favor, ibid. 8, 1). τί, Mt. ix. 13 and xii. 7, (fr. Hos. vi. 6) Heb. x. 5, 8, (fr. Ps. xxxix. (xl.) 7).   As respects the distinction between βούλομαι and θέλω, the former seems to designate the will which follows d e l i b e r a t i o n, the latter the will which proceeds from i n c l i n a t i o n. This appears not only from Mt. i. 19, but also from the fact that the Sept. express the idea of *pleasure, delight*, by the verb θέλειν (see just above). The reverse of this distinction is laid down by *Bttm.* Lexil. i. p. 26 [Eng. trans. p. 194]; *Delitzsch* on Heb. vi. 17. Acc. to *Tittmann* (Syn. i. p. 124) θέλειν denotes mere *volition*, βούλεσθαι *inclination*; [cf. *Whiston* on Dem. 9, 5; 124, 13].

[Philip Buttmann's statement of the distinction between the two words is quoted with approval by *Schmidt* (Syn. iii. ch. 146), who adduces in confirmation (besides many exx.) the assumed relationship between β. and Fελπίς, ἐλπίς; the use of θ. in the sense of 'resolve' in such passages as Thuc. 5, 9; of θέλων i. q. ἡδέως in the poets; of β. as parallel to ἐπιθυμεῖν in Dem. 29, 45, etc.; and pass. in which the two words occur together and β. is apparently equiv. to 'wish'

while θ. stands for 'will,' as Xen. an. 4, 4, 5; Eur. Alc. 281, etc., etc. At the same time it must be confessed that scholars are far from harmonious on the subject. Many agree with Prof. Grimm that θ. gives prominence to the emotive element, β. to the rational and volitive; that θ. signifies the *choice*, while β. marks the choice as *deliberate* and *intelligent*; yet they acknowledge that the words are sometimes used indiscriminately, and esp. that θ. as the less sharply defined term is put where β. would be proper; see *Ellendt*, Lex. Soph.; *Pape*, Handwörterb.; *Seiler*, Wörterb. d. Hom., s. v. βούλομαι; *Suhle und Schneidewin*, Handwörterb.; *Crosby*, Lex. to Xen. an., s. v. ἐθέλω; (Arnold's) *Pillon*, Grk. Syn. § 129; *Webster*, Synt. and Syn. of the Grk. Test. p. 197; *Wilke*, Clavis N. T., ed. 2, ii. 603; *Schleusner*, N. T. Lex. s. v. βούλ.; *Munthe*, Observv. phil. in N. T. ex Diod. Sic. etc. p. 3; *Valckenaer*, Scholia etc. ii. 23; *Westermann* on Dem. 20, 111; the commentators generally on Mt. as above; Bp. *Lghtft.* on Philem. 13, 14; *Riddle* in Schaff's Lange on Eph. p. 42; this seems to be roughly intended by Ammonius also: βούλεσθαι μὲν ἐπὶ μόνου λεκτέον τοῦ λογικοῦ· τὸ δὲ θέλειν καὶ ἐπὶ ἀλόγου ζῴου· (and Eustath. on Iliad 1, 112, p. 61, 2, says οὐχ' ἁπλῶς θέλω, ἀλλὰ βούλομαι, ὅπερ ἐπίτασις τοῦ θέλειν ἐστίν). On the other hand, *L. and S.* (s. v. ἐθέλω); *Passow* ed. 5; *Rost*, Wörterb. ed. 4; *Schenkl*, Schulwörterb.; *Donaldson*, Crat. § 463 sq.; *Wahl*, Clav. Apocr., s. v. βούλ.; *Cremer* s. vv. βούλομαι and θέλω; esp. *Stallb.* on Plato's de repub. 4, 13 p. 437 b., (cf. too *Cope* on Aristot. rhet. 2, 19, 19); *Franke* on Dem. 1, 1, substantially reverse the distinction, as does *Ellicott* on 1 Tim. v. 14; *Wordsworth* on 1 Th. ii. 18. Although the latter opinion may seem to be favored by that view of the derivation of the words which allies βούλ. with *voluptas* (Curtius § 659, cf. p. 726), and makes θέλ. signify 'to hold to something,' 'form a fixed resolve' (see above, ad init.), yet the predominant u s a g e of the N. T. will be evident to one who looks out the pass. referred to above (Fritzsche's explanation of Mt. i. 19 is hardly natural); to which may be added such as Mt. ii. 18; ix. 13; xii. 38; xv. 28; xvii. 4 (xx. 21, 32); xxvi. 15, 39 (cf. Lk. xxii. 42); Mk. vi. 19; xii. 34; x. 35; xii. 38; xv. 9 (cf. Jn. xviii. 39), 15 (where R. V. *wishing* is questionable; cf. Lk. xxiii. 20); Lk. x. 24; xv. 28; xvi. 26; Jn. v. 6; vi. 11; xii. 21; Acts x. 10; xviii. 15; Ro. vii. 19 (cf. 15, its opp. to μισῶ, and indeed the use of θέλω throughout this chapter); 1 Co. vii. 36, 39; xiv. 35; Eph. i. 11; 2 Th. iii. 10, etc. Such passages as 1 Tim. ii. 4; 2 Pet. iii. 9 will be ranged now on one side, now on the other; cf. 1 Co. xii. 11, 18. θέλω occurs in the N. T. about five times as often as βούλομαι (on the relative use of the words in classic writers see Tycho Mommsen in *Rutherford*, New Phryn. p. 415 sq.). The usage of the Sept. (beyond the particular specified by Prof. Grimm) seems to afford little light; see e. g. Gen. xxiv. 5, 8; Deut. xxv. 7; Ps. xxxix. (xl.) 7, 9, etc. In modern Greek θέλω seems to have nearly driven βούλομαι out of use; on θέλω as an auxiliary cf. *Jebb* in Vincent and Dickson's Handbook, App. §§ 60, 64. For exx. of the associated use of the words in classic Grk., see *Steph.* Thesaur. s. v. βούλομαι p. 366 d.; Bp. Lghtft., Cremer, and esp. Schmidt, as above.]

θεμέλιος, -ον, (θέμα [i. e. thing laid down]), *laid down as a foundation, belonging to a foundation*, (Diod. 5, 66; θεμέλιοι λίθοι, Arstph. av. 1137); generally as a subst., ὁ θεμέλιος [sc. λίθος] (1 Co. iii. 11 sq.; 2 Tim. ii. 19; Rev. xxi. 19), and τὸ θεμέλιον (rarely so in Grk. writ., as [Aristot. phys. auscult. 2, 9 p. 200ᵃ, 4]; Paus. 8, 32, 1; [al.]), *the foundation* (of a building, wall, city): prop., Lk. vi.

49; τιθέναι θεμέλιον, Lk. vi. 48; xiv. 29; plur. οἱ θεμέλιοι (chiefly so in Grk. writ.), Heb. xi. 10; Rev. xxi. 14, 19; neut. τὸ θεμ. Acts xvi. 26 (and often in the Sept.); metaph. the foundations, beginnings, first principles, of an institution or system of truth: 1 Co. iii. 10, 12; the rudiments, first principles, of Christian life and knowledge, Heb. vi. 1 (μετανοίας gen. of apposition [W. 531 (494)]); a course of instruction begun by a teacher, Ro. xv. 20; Christ is called θεμέλ. i. e. faith in him, which is like a foundation laid in the soul on which is built up the fuller and richer knowledge of saving truth, 1 Co. iii. 11; τῶν ἀποστόλων (gen. of appos., on account of what follows: ὄντος . . . Χριστοῦ, [al. say gen. of origin, see ἐποικοδομέω; cf. W. § 30, 1; Meyer or Ellicott ad loc.]), of the apostles as preachers of salvation, upon which foundation the Christian church has been built, Eph. ii. 20; a solid and stable spiritual possession, on which resting as on a foundation they may strive to lay hold on eternal life, 1 Tim. vi. 19; the church is apparently called θεμ. as the foundation of the 'city of God,' 2 Tim. ii. 19, cf. 20 and 1 Tim. iii. 15. (Sept. several times also for אַרְמוֹן, a palace, Is. xxv. 2; Jer. vi. 5; Amos i. 4, etc.) *

θεμελιόω: fut. θεμελιώσω; 1 aor. ἐθεμελίωσα; Pass., pf. ptcp. τεθεμελιωμένος; plupf. 3 pers. sing. τεθεμελίωτο (Mt. vii. 25; Lk. vi. 48 R G; without augm. cf. W. § 12, 9; [B. 33 (29); Tdf. Proleg. p. 121]); Sept. for יסד; [fr. Xen. down]; to lay the foundation, to found: prop., τὴν γῆν, Heb. i. 10 (Ps. ci. (cii.) 26; Prov. iii. 19; Is. xlviii. 13, al.); τὶ ἐπί τι, Mt. vii. 25; Lk. vi. 48. metaph. (Diod. 11, 68; 15, 1) to make stable, establish, [A. V. ground]: of the soul, [1 aor. opt. 3 pers. sing.] 1 Pet. v. 10 [Rec.; but T, Tr mrg. in br., the fut.]; pass., Eph. iii. 17 (18); Col. i. 23.*

θεο-δίδακτος, -ον, (θεός and διδακτός), taught of God: 1 Th. iv. 9. ([Barn. ep. 21, 6 (cf. Harnack's note)]; eccles. writ.)*

θεο-λόγος, -ον, ὁ, (θεός and λέγω), in Grk. writ. [fr. Aristot. on] one who speaks (treats) of the gods and divine things, versed in sacred science; (Grossmann, Quaestiones Philoneae, i. p. 8, shows that the word is used also by Philo, esp. of Moses [cf. de praem. et poen. § 9]). This title is given to John in the inscription of the Apocalypse, acc. to the Rec. text, apparently as the publisher and interpreter of divine oracles, just as Lucian styles the same person θεολόγος in Alex. 19 that he calls προφήτης in c. 22. The common opinion is that John was called θεολόγος in the same sense in which the term was used of Gregory of Nazianzus, viz. because he taught the θεότης of the λόγος. But then the wonder is, why the copyists did not prefer to apply the epithet to him in the title of the Gospel.*

θεομαχέω, -ῶ; (θεομάχος); to fight against God: Acts xxiii. 9 Rec. (Eur., Xen., Diod., al.; 2 Macc. vii. 19.)*

θεομάχος, -ον, ὁ, (θεός and μάχομαι), fighting against God, resisting God: Acts v. 39. (Symm., Job xxvi. 5; Prov. ix. 18; xxi. 16; Heracl. Pont. alleg. Homer. 1; Lcian. Jup. tr. 45.) *

θεόπνευστος, -ον, (θεός and πνέω), inspired by God: γραφή, i. e. the contents of Scripture, 2 Tim. iii. 16 [see πᾶς, I. 1 c.]; σοφίη, [pseudo-] Phocyl. 121; ὄνειροι, Plut. de plac. phil. 5, 2, 3 p. 904 f.; [Orac. Sibyll. 5, 406 (cf. 308); Nonn. paraphr. ev. Ioan. 1, 99]. (ἔμπνευστος also is used passively, but ἄπνευστος, εὔπνευστος, πυρίπνευστος, [δυσδιάπνευστος], actively, [and δυσανάπνευστος appar. either act. or pass.; cf. W. 96 (92) note].)*

θεός, -οῦ, ὁ and ἡ, voc. θεέ, once in the N. T., Mt. xxvii. 46; besides in Deut. iii. 24; Judg. [xvi. 28;] xxi. 3; [2 S. vii. 25; Is. xxxviii. 20]; Sir. xxiii. 4; Sap. ix. 1; 3 Macc. vi. 3; 4 Macc. vi. 27; Act. Thom. 44 sq. 57; Eus. h. e. 2, 23, 16; [5, 20, 7; vit. Const. 2, 55, 1. 59]; cf. W. § 8, 2 c.; [B. 12 (11)]; ([on the eight or more proposed derivations see Vaniček p. 386, who follows Curtius (after Döderlein) p. 513 sqq. in connecting it with a root meaning to supplicate, implore; hence the implored; per contra cf. Max Müller, Chips etc. iv. 227 sq.; L. and S. s. v. fin.]); [fr. Hom. down]; Sept. for אֵל, אֱלֹהִים and יְהוָה; a god, a goddess; **1.** a general appellation of deities or divinities: Acts xxviii. 6; 1 Co. viii. 4; 2 Th. ii. 4; once ἡ θεός, Acts xix. 37 G L T Tr WH; θεοῦ φωνὴ καὶ οὐκ ἀνθρώπου, Acts xii. 22; ἄνθρωπος ὢν ποιεῖς σεαυτὸν θεόν, Jn. x. 33; plur., of the gods of the Gentiles: Acts xiv. 11; xix. 26; λεγόμενοι θεοί, 1 Co. viii. 5ᵃ; οἱ φύσει μὴ ὄντες θεοί, Gal. iv. 8; τοῦ θεοῦ Ῥεφάν [q. v.], Acts vii. 43; of angels: εἰσὶ θεοὶ πολλοί, 1 Co. viii. 5ᵇ (on which cf. Philo de somn. i. § 39 ὁ μὲν ἀληθείᾳ θεὸς εἷς ἐστιν, οἱ δ' ἐν καταχρήσει λεγόμενοι πλείους). [On the use of the sing. θεός (and Lat. deus) as a generic term by (later) heathen writ., see Norton, Genuinen. of the Gosp. 2d ed. iii. addit. note D; cf. Dr. Ezra Abbot in Chris. Exam. for Nov. 1848, p. 389 sqq.; Huidekoper, Judaism at Rome, ch. i. § ii.; see Bib. Sacr. for July 1856, p. 666 sq., and for addit. exx. Nägelsbach, Homer. Theol. p. 129; also his Nachhomerische Theol. p. 139 sq.; Stephanus, Thes. s. v.; and reff. (by Prof. Abbot) in Journ. Soc. Bibl. Lit. and Exeg. i. p. 120 note.] **2.** Whether Christ is called God must be determined from Jn. i. 1; xx. 28; 1 Jn. v. 20; Ro. ix. 5; Tit. ii. 13; Heb. i. 8 sq., etc.; the matter is still in dispute among theologians; cf. Grimm, Institutio theologiae dogmaticae, ed. 2, p. 228 sqq. [and the discussion (on Ro. ix. 5) by Professors Dwight and Abbot in Journ. Soc. Bib. Lit. etc. u. s., esp. pp. 42 sqq. 113 sqq.]. **3.** spoken of the only and true GOD: with the article, Mt. iii. 9; Mk. xiii. 19; Lk. ii. 13; Acts ii. 11, and very often; with prepositions: ἐκ τοῦ θ. Jn. viii. 42, 47 and often in John's writ.; ὑπὸ τοῦ θ. Lk. i. 26 [T Tr WH ἀπό]; Acts xxvi. 6; παρὰ τοῦ θ. Jn. viii. 40; ix. 16 [L T Tr WH here om. art.]; παρὰ τῷ θ. Ro. ii. 13 [Tr txt. om. and L WH Tr mrg. br. the art.]; ix. 14; ἐν τῷ θ. Col. iii. 3; ἐπὶ τῷ θ. Lk. i. 47; εἰς τὸν θ. Acts xxiv. 15 [Tdf. πρός]; ἐπὶ τὸν θ. Acts xv. 19; xxvi. 18, 20; πρὸς τὸν θ. Jn. i. 2; Acts xxiv. [15 Tdf.], 16, and many other exx. without the article: Mt. vi. 24; Lk. i. 2; xx. 38; Ro. viii. 33; 2 Co. i. 9; v. 19; vi. 7; 1 Th. ii. 5, etc.; with prepositions: ἀπὸ θεοῦ, Jn. iii. 2; xvi. 30; Ro. xiii. 1 [L T Tr WH ὑπό]; παρὰ θεοῦ, Jn. i. 6;

ἐκ θεοῦ, Acts v. 39; 2 Co. v. 1; Phil. iii. 9; παρὰ θεῷ, 2 Th. i. 6; 1 Pet. ii. 4; κατὰ θεόν, Ro. viii. 27; 2 Co. vii. 9 sq.; cf. W. § 19 s. v. ὁ θεός τινος (gen. of pers.), the (guardian) God of any one, blessing and protecting him: Mt. xxii. 32; Mk. xii. 26 sq. [29 WH mrg. (see below)]; Lk. xx. 37; Jn. xx. 17; Acts iii. 13; xiii. 17; 2 Co. vi. 16; Heb. xi. 16; Rev. xxi. 3 [without ὁ; but G T Tr WH txt. om. the phrase]; ὁ θεός μου, i. q. οὗ εἰμί, ᾧ καὶ λατρεύω (Acts xxvii. 23): Ro. i. 8; 1 Co. i. 4 [Tr mrg. br. the gen.]; 2 Co. xii. 21; Phil. i. 3; iv. 19; Philem. 4; κύριος ὁ θεός σου, ἡμῶν, ὑμῶν, αὐτῶν (in imit. of Hebr. יְהֹוָה אֱלֹהֶיךָ, אֱלֹהֵינוּ /'', אֱלֹהֵיכֶם /'', אֱלֹהֵיהֶם /''): Mt. iv. 7; xxii. 37; Mk. xii. 29 [see above]; Lk. iv. 8, 12; x. 27; Acts ii. 39; cf. Thilo, Cod. apocr. Nov. Test. p. 169; [and Bp. Lghtft. as quoted s. v. κύριος, c. α. init.]; ὁ θεὸς κ. πατὴρ τοῦ κυρίου ἡμῶν Ἰησοῦ Χριστοῦ: Ro. xv. 6; 2 Co. i. 3; xi. 31 [L T Tr WH om. ἡμ. and Χρ.]; Eph. i. 3; Col. i. 3 [L WH om. καί]; 1 Pet. i. 3; in which combination of words the gen. depends on ὁ θεός as well as on πατήρ, cf. Fritzsche on Rom. iii. p. 232 sq.; [Oltramare on Ro. l. c.; Bp. Lghtft. on Gal. i. 4; but some would restrict it to the latter; cf. e. g. Meyer on Ro. l. c., Eph. l. c.; Ellic. on Gal. l. c., Eph. l. c.]; ὁ θεὸς τοῦ κυρ. ἡμ. Ἰησ. Χρ. Eph. i. 17; ὁ θεὸς κ. πατὴρ ἡμῶν, Gal. i. 4; Phil. iv. 20; 1 Th. i. 3; iii. 11, 13; θεὸς ὁ πατήρ, 1 Co. viii. 6; ὁ θεὸς κ. πατήρ, 1 Co. xv. 24; Eph. v. 20; Jas. i. 27; iii. 9 [Rec.; al. κύριος κ. π.]; ἀπὸ θεοῦ πατρὸς ἡμῶν, Ro. i. 7; 1 Co. i. 3; 2 Co. i. 2; Eph. i. 2; Phil. i. 2; Col. i. 2; 2 Th. i. 2; 1 Tim. i. 2 [Rec., al. om. ἡμ.]; Philem. 3; [ὁ θεὸς πατήρ, Col. iii. 17 L T Tr WH (cf. Bp. Lghtft. ad loc.); elsewhere without the art. as] θεοῦ πατρός (in which phrase the two words have blended as it were into one, equiv. to a prop. name, Germ. Gottvater [A. V. God the Father]): Phil. ii. 11; 1 Pet. i. 2; ἀπὸ θεοῦ πατρός, Gal. i. 3; Eph. vi. 23; 2 Tim. i. 2; Tit. i. 4; παρὰ θεοῦ πατρός, 2 Pet. i. 17; 2 Jn. 3; cf. Wieseler, Com. üb. d. Brief a. d. Galat. p. 10 sqq. ὁ θεός w. gen. of the thing of which God is the author [cf. W. § 30, 1]: τῆς ὑπομονῆς κ. τῆς παρακλήσεως, Ro. xv. 5; τῆς ἐλπίδος, ib. 13; τῆς εἰρήνης, 33; 1 Th. v. 23; τῆς παρακλήσεως, 2 Co. i. 3. τὰ τοῦ θεοῦ, the things of God, i. e. α. his counsels, 1 Co. ii. 11. β. his interests, Mt. xvi. 23; Mk. viii. 33. γ. things due to God, Mt. xxii. 21; Mk. xii. 17; Lk. xx. 25. τὰ πρὸς τὸν θεόν, things respecting, pertaining to, God, — contextually i. q. the sacrificial business of the priest, Ro. xv. 17; Heb. ii. 17; v. 1; cf. Xen. rep. Lac. 13, 11; Fritzsche on Rom. iii. p. 262 sq. Nom. ὁ θεός for the voc.: Mk. xv. 34; Lk. xviii. 11, 13; Jn. xx. 28; Acts iv. 24 [R G; Heb. i. 8?]; x. 7; cf. W. § 29, 2; [B. 140 (123)]. τῷ θεῷ, God being judge [cf. W. § 31, 4 a; 248 (232 sq.); B. § 133, 14]: after δυνατός, 2 Co. x. 4; after ἀστεῖος, Acts vii. 20, (after ἄμεμπτος, Sap. x. 5; after μέγας, Jon. iii. 3; see ἀστεῖος, 2). For the expressions ἄνθρωπος θεοῦ, δύναμις θεοῦ, υἱὸς θεοῦ, etc., θεὸς τῆς ἐλπίδος etc., ὁ ζῶν θεός etc., see under ἄνθρωπος 6, δύναμις a., υἱὸς τοῦ θεοῦ, ἐλπίς 2, ζάω I. 1, etc. 4. θεός is used of whatever can in any respect be likened to God, or resembles him in any way: Hebraistically i. q. God's representative or vicegerent, of magistrates and judges, Jn. x. 34 sq. after Ps. lxxxi. (lxxxii.) 6, (of the wise man, Philo de mut. nom. § 22; quod omn. prob. lib. § 7; [ὁ σοφὸς λέγεται θεὸς τοῦ ἄφρονος . . . θεὸς πρὸς φαντασίαν κ. δόκησιν, quod det. pot. insid. § 44]; πατὴρ κ. μήτηρ ἐμφανεῖς εἰσι θεοί, μιμούμενοι τὸν ἀγέννητον ἐν τῷ ζωοπλαστεῖν, de decal. § 23; ὠνομάσθη (i. e. Moses) ὅλου τοῦ ἔθνους θεὸς κ. βασιλεύς, de vita Moys. i. § 28; [de migr. Abr. § 15; de alleg. leg. i. § 13]); of the devil, ὁ θεὸς τοῦ αἰῶνος τούτου (see αἰών, 3), 2 Co. iv. 4; the pers. or thing to which one is wholly devoted, for which alone he lives, e. g. ἡ κοιλία, Phil. iii. 19.

θεοσέβεια, -ας, ἡ, (θεοσεβής), reverence towards God, godliness: 1 Tim. ii. 10. (Xen. an. 2, 6, 26; Plat. epin. p. 985 d.; Sept. Gen. xx. 11; Job xxviii. 28; Bar. v. 4; Sir. i. 25 (22); 4 Macc. i. 9 (Fritz.); vii. 6, 22 (var.).) *   2317

θεοσεβής, -ές, (θεός and σέβομαι), worshipping God, pious: Jn. ix. 31. (Sept.; Soph., Eur., Arstph., Xen., Plat., al.; [cf. Trench § xlviii.].) *   2318

θεοστυγής, -ές, (θεός and στυγέω; cf. θεομισής, θεομυσής, and the subst. θεοστυγία, omitted in the lexx., Clem. Rom. 1 Cor. 35, 5), hateful to God, exceptionally impious and wicked (Vulg. deo odibilis): Ro. i. 30 (Eur. Troad. 1213 and Cyclop. 396, 602; joined with ἄδικοι in Clem. hom. 1, 12, where just before occurs οἱ θεὸν μισοῦντες). Cf. the full discussion of the word by Fritzsche, Com. on Rom. i. p. 84 sqq.; [and see W. 53 sq. (53)].*   2319

θεότης, -ητος, ἡ, (deitas, Tertull., Augustine [de civ. Dei 7, 1]), deity i. e. the state of being God, Godhead: Col. ii. 9. (Lcian. Icar. 9; Plut. de defect. orac. 10 p. 415 c.) *   2320

[SYN. θεότης, θειότης: θεότ. deity differs from θειότ. divinity, as essence differs from quality or attribute; cf. Trench § ii.; Bp. Lghtft. or Mey. on Col. l. c.; Fritzsche on Ro. i. 20.]

Θεόφιλος, -ου, (θεός and φίλος), Theophilus, a Christian to whom Luke inscribed his Gospel and Acts of the Apostles: Lk. i. 3; Acts i. 1. The conjectures concerning his family, rank, nationality, are reviewed by (among others) Win. RWB. s. v.; Bleek on Lk. i. 3; [B. D. s. v.]; see also under κράτιστος.*   2321

θεραπεία, -ας, ἡ, (θεραπεύω); 1. service, rendered by any one to another. 2. spec. medical service, curing, healing: Lk. ix. 11; Rev. xxii. 2, ([Hippocr.], Plat., Isocr., Polyb.). 3. by meton. household, i. e. body of attendants, servants, domestics: Mt. xxiv. 45 R G; Lk. xii. 42, (and often so in Grk. writ.; cf. Lob. ad Phryn. p. 469; for עֲבָדִים, Gen. xlv. 16).*   2322

θεραπεύω; impf. ἐθεράπευον; fut. θεραπεύσω; 1 aor. ἐθεράπευσα; Pass., pres. θεραπεύομαι; impf. ἐθεραπευόμην; pf. ptcp. τεθεραπευμένος; 1 aor. ἐθεραπεύθην; (θέραψ, i. q. θεράπων); fr. Hom. down; 1. to serve, do service: τινά, to one; pass. θεραπ. ὑπό τινος, Acts xvii. 25. 2. to heal, cure, restore to health: Mt. xii. 10; Mk. vi. 5; Lk. vi. 7; ix. 6; xiii. 14; xiv. 3; τινά, Mt. iv. 24; viii. 7, 16, etc.; Mk. i. 34; iii. 10; Lk. iv. 23; x. 9; pass., Jn. v. 10; Acts iv. 14; v. 16, etc.; τινὰ ἀπό τινος, to cure one of any disease, Lk. vii. 21; pass., Lk. v. 15; viii. 2; θεραπεύειν νόσους, μαλακίαν: Mt. iv. 23; ix. 35; x. 1; Mk. iii. 15   2323

[R G L, Tr mrg. in br.]; Lk. ix. 1; a wound, pass., Rev. xiii. 3, 12.

2324 θεράπων, -οντος, ὁ, [perh. fr. a root *to hold, have about one*; cf. Eng. *retainer*; Vaniček p. 396; fr. Hom. down], Sept. for עֶבֶד, *an attendant, servant*: of God, spoken of Moses discharging the duties committed to him by God, Heb. iii. 5 as in Num. xii. 7 sq.; Josh. i. 2; viii. 31, 33 (ix. 4, 6); Sap. x. 16. [SYN. see διάκονος.]*

2325 θερίζω; fut. θερίσω [B. 37 (32), cf. WH. App. p. 163 sq.]; 1 aor. ἐθέρισα; 1 aor. pass. ἐθερίσθην; (θέρος); Sept. for קָצַר; [fr. Aeschyl., Hdt. down]; *to reap, harvest*; **a.** prop.: Mt. vi. 26; Lk. xii. 24; Jas. v. 4; [fig. Jn. iv. 36 (bis)]. **b.** in proverbial expressions about sowing and reaping: ἄλλος ... ὁ θερίζων, one does the work, another gets the reward, Jn. iv. 37 sq. (where the meaning is 'ye hereafter, in winning over a far greater number of the Samaritans to the kingdom of God, will enjoy the fruits of the work which I have now commenced among them' [al. do not restrict the reference to converted Samaritans]); θερίζων ὅπου οὐκ ἔσπειρας, unjustly appropriating to thyself the fruits of others' labor, Mt. xxv. 24, 26; Lk. xix. 21 sq.; ὁ ἐὰν ... θερίσει, as a man has acted (on earth) so (hereafter by God) will he be requited, either with reward or penalty, (his deeds will determine his doom), Gal. vi. 7 (a proverb: *ut sementem feceris, ita metes*, Cic. de orat. 2, 65; [σὺ δὲ ταῦτα αἰσχρῶς μὲν ἔσπειρας κακῶς δὲ ἐθέρισας, Aristot. rhet. 3, 3, 4; cf. Plato, Phaedr. 260 d.; see Meyer on Gal. l. c.]); τί, to receive a thing by way of reward or punishment: τὰ σαρκικά, 1 Co. ix. 11; φθοράν, ζωὴν αἰώνιον, Gal. vi. 8, (σπείρειν πυρούς, θερίζειν ἀκάνθας, Jer. xii. 13; ὁ σπείρων φαῦλα θερίσει κακά, Prov. xxii. 8; ἐὰν σπείρητε κακά, πᾶσαν ταραχὴν καὶ θλῖψιν θερίσετε, Test. xii. Patr. p. 576 [i. e. test. Levi § 13]); absol.: of the reward of well-doing, Gal. vi. 9; 2 Co. ix. 6. **c.** As the crops are cut down with the sickle, θερίζειν is fig. used for *to destroy, cut off*: Rev. xiv. 15; with the addition of τὴν γῆν, to remove the wicked inhabitants of the earth and deliver them up to destruction, ib. 16 [τὴν Ἀσίαν, Plut. reg. et. imper. apophthegm. (Antig. 1), p. 182 a.].*

2326 θερισμός, -οῦ, ὁ, (θερίζω), *harvest*: i. q. the act of reaping, Jn. iv. 35; fig. of the gathering of men into the kingdom of God, ibid. i. q. the time of reaping, i. e. fig. the time of final judgment, when the righteous are gathered into the kingdom of God and the wicked are delivered up to destruction, Mt. xiii. 30, 39; Mk. iv. 29. i. q. the crop to be reaped, i. e. fig. a multitude of men to be taught how to obtain salvation, Mt. ix. 37 sq.; Lk. x. 2; ἐξηράνθη ὁ θερισμός, the crops are ripe for the harvest, i. e. the time is come to destroy the wicked, Rev. xiv. 15. (Sept. for קָצִיר; rare in Grk. writ., as Xen. oec. 18, 3; Polyb. 5, 95, 5.) *

2327 θεριστής, -οῦ, ὁ, (θερίζω), *a reaper*: Mt. xiii. 30, 39. (Bel and the Dragon 33; Xen., Dem., Aristot., Plut., al.)*

2328 θερμαίνω: Mid., pres. θερμαίνομαι; impf. ἐθερμαινόμην; (θερμός); fr. Hom. down; *to make warm, to heat*; mid. *to warm one's self*: Mk. xiv. 54, 67; Jn. xviii. 18, 25; Jas. ii. 16.*

2329 θέρμη (and θέρμα; cf. Lob. ad Phryn. p. 331, [Rutherford, New Phryn. p. 414]), -ης, ἡ, *heat*: Acts xxviii. 3. (Eccl. iv. 11; Job vi. 17; Ps. xviii. (xix.) 7; Thuc., Plat., Menand., al.) *

2330 θέρος, -ους, τό, (θέρω to heat), *summer*: Mt. xxiv. 32; Mk. xiii. 28; Lk. xxi. 30. (From Hom. down; Hebr. קַיִץ, Prov. vi. 8; Gen. viii. 22.) *

2331 Θεσσαλονικεύς, -έως, ὁ, *a Thessalonian*: Acts xx. 4; xxvii. 2; 1 Th. i. 1; 2 Th. i. 1.*

2332 Θεσσαλονίκη, -ης, ἡ, *Thessalonica* (now *Saloniki*), a celebrated and populous city, situated on the Thermaic Gulf, the capital of the second [(there were four; cf. Liv. xlv. 29)] division of Macedonia and the residence of a Roman governor and quaestor. It was anciently called *Therme*, but was rebuilt by Cassander, the son of Antipater, and called by its new name [which first appears in Polyb. 23, 4, 4] in honor of his wife Thessalonica, the sister of Alexander the Great; cf. Strabo 7, 330. Here Paul the apostle founded a Christian church: Acts xvii. 1, 11, 13; Phil. iv. 16; 2 Tim. iv. 10. [BB. DD. s. v.; Lewin, St. Paul, i. 225 sqq.] *

2333 Θευδᾶς [prob. contr. fr. θεόδωρος, W. 103 (97); esp. Bp. Lghtft. on Col. iv. 15; on its inflection cf. B. 20 (18)], ὁ, *Theudas*, an impostor who instigated a rebellion which came to a wretched end in the time of Augustus: Acts v. 36. Josephus (antt. 20, 5, 1) makes mention of one Theudas, a magician, who came into notice by pretending that he was a prophet and was destroyed when Cuspius Fadus governed Judæa in the time of Claudius. Accordingly many interpreters hold that there were two insurgents by the name of Theudas; while others, with far greater probability, suppose that the mention of Theudas is ascribed to Gamaliel by an anachronism on the part of Luke. On the different opinions of others cf. Meyer on Acts l. c.; Win. RWB. s. v.; Keim in Schenkel v. 510 sq.; [esp. Hackett in B. D. s. v.].*

2334 θεωρέω, -ῶ; impf. ἐθεώρουν; [fut. θεωρήσω, Jn. vii. 3 T Tr WH]; 1 aor. ἐθεώρησα; (θεωρός a spectator, and this fr. θεάομαι, q. v. [cf. Vaniček p. 407; L. and S. s. v.; Allen in the Am. Journ. of Philol. i. p. 131 sq.]); [fr. Aeschyl. and Hdt. down]; Sept. for רָאָה and Chald. חֲזָה; **1.** *to be a spectator, look at, behold*, Germ. *schauen*, (the θεωροί were men who attended the games or the sacrifices as public deputies; cf. Grimm on 2 Macc. iv. 19); absol.: Mt. xxvii. 55; Mk. xv. 40; Lk. xxiii. 35; foll. by indir. disc., Mk. xii. 41; xv. 47; used esp. of persons and things looked upon as in some respect noteworthy: τινά, Jn. vi. 40; xvi. 10, 16 sq. 19; Acts iii. 16; xxv. 24; Rev. xi. 11 sq.; ὁ θεωρῶν τὸν υἱὸν θεωρεῖ τὸν πατέρα, the majesty of the Father resplendent in the Son, Jn. xii. 45; τινά with ptcp. [B. 301 (258): Mk. v. 15]; Lk. x. 18; Jn. vi. 19; [x. 12]; xx. 12, 14; [1 Jn. iii. 17]; τί, Lk. xiv. 29; xxi. 6; xxiii. 48; Acts iv. 13; τὰ σημεῖα, Jn. ii. 23; vi. 2 L Tr WH; Acts viii. 13, (θαυμαστὰ τέρατα, Sap. xix. 8); τὰ ἔργα τοῦ Χριστοῦ, Jn. vii. 3; τί with ptcp., Jn. xx. 6; Acts vii. 56; x. 11; foll. by ὅτι, Acts

xix. 26; *to view attentively, take a view of, survey*: τί, Mt. xxviii. 1; *to view mentally, consider*: foll. by orat. obliq., Heb. vii. 4. **2.** *to see*; i. e. **a.** *to perceive with the eyes*: πνεῦμα, Lk. xxiv. 37; τινά with a ptcp., ibid. 39; τινά, ὅτι, Jn. ix. 8; τὸ πρόσωπόν τινος (after the Hebr.; see πρόσωπον, 1 a.), i. q. to enjoy the presence of one, have intercourse with him, Acts xx. 38; οὐκέτι θεωρεῖν τινα, used of one from whose sight a person has been withdrawn, Jn. xiv. 19; οὐ θεωρεῖ ὁ κόσμος τὸ πνεῦμα, i. e. so to speak, has no eyes with which it can see the Spirit; he cannot render himself visible to it, cannot give it his presence and power, Jn. xiv. 17. **b.** *to discern, descry*: τί, Mk. v. 38; τινά, Mk. iii. 11; Acts ix. 7. **c.** *to ascertain, find out, by seeing*: τινά with a pred. acc., Acts xvii. 22; τί with ptcp., Acts xvii. 16; xxviii. 6; ὅτι, Mk. xvi. 4; Jn. iv. 19; xii. 19; Acts xix. 26; xxvii. 10; foll. by indir. disc., Acts xxi. 20; Hebraistically (see εἴδω, I. 5) i. q. *to get knowledge of*: Jn. vi. 62 (τ. υἱὸν τ. ἀνθρώπου ἀναβαίνοντα the Son of Man by death ascending; cf. Lücke, Meyer [yet cf. Weiss in the 6te Aufl.], Baumg.-Crusius, in loc.); τὸν θάνατον i. e. to die, Jn. viii. 51; and on the other hand, τὴν δόξαν τοῦ Χριστοῦ, to be a partaker of the glory, i. e. the blessed condition in heaven, which Christ enjoys, Jn. xvii. 24, cf. 22. [COMP.: ἀνα-, παρα-θεωρέω.]*

[SYN. θεωρεῖν, θεᾶσθαι, ὁρᾶν, σκοπεῖν: θεωρ. is used primarily not of an indifferent spectator, but of one who looks at a thing with interest and for a purpose; θεωρ. would be used of a general officially reviewing or inspecting an army, θεᾶσθ. of a lay spectator looking at the parade. θεωρ. as denoting the careful observation of details can even be contrasted with ὁρᾶν in so far as the latter denotes only perception in the general; so used θεωρεῖν quite coincides with σκοπ. Schmidt i. ch. 11; see also Green, 'Crit. Note' on Mt. vii. 3. Cf. s. vv. ὁράω, σκοπέω.]

2335 θεωρία, -ας, ἡ, (θεωρός, on which see θεωρέω init.); fr. [Aeschyl.], Hdt. down; **1.** *a viewing, beholding.* **2.** *that which is viewed; a spectacle, sight*: Lk. xxiii. 48 (3 Macc. v. 24).*

2336 θήκη, -ης, ἡ, (τίθημι); fr. [Aeschyl.], Hdt. down; *that in which a thing is put or laid away, a receptacle, repository, chest, box*: used of the *sheath* of a sword, Jn. xviii. 11; Joseph. antt. 7, 11, 7; Poll. 10, (31) 144.*

2337 θηλάζω; 1 aor. ἐθήλασα; (θηλή a breast, [cf. Peile, Etym. p. 124 sq.]); **1.** trans. *to give the breast, give suck, to suckle*: Mt. xxiv. 19; Mk. xiii. 17; Lk. xxi. 23, (Lys., Aristot., al.; Sept. for הֵינִיק; μαστοὶ ἐθήλασαν, Lk. xxiii. 29 R G. **2.** intrans. *to suck*: Mt. xxi. 16 (Aristot., Plat., Lcian., al.; Sept. for יָנַק; μαστούς, Lk. xi. 27; Job iii. 12; Cant. viii. 1; Joel ii. 16; Theocr. iii. 16.*

2338 θῆλυς, -εια, -υ, [cf. θηλάζω, init.], *of the female sex*; ἡ θήλεια, subst. *a woman, a female*: Ro. i. 26 sq.; also τὸ θῆλυ, Mt. xix. 4; Mk. x. 6; Gal. iii. 28. (Gen. i. 27; vii. 2; Ex. i. 16, etc.; in Grk. writ. fr. Hom. down.)*

2339 θήρα [Lat. *fera*; perh. fr. root to run, spring, prey, Vaniček p. 415; cf. Curtius § 314], -ας, ἡ; fr. Hom. down; *a hunting of wild beasts* to destroy them; hence, figuratively, of preparing destruction for men, [A. V. *a trap*], Ro. xi. 9, on which cf. Fritzsche.*

θηρεύω: 1 aor. inf. θηρεῦσαι; (fr. θήρα, as ἀγρεύω fr. **2340** ἄγρα [cf. Schmidt ch. 72, 3]); fr. Hom. down; *to go a hunting, to hunt, to catch in hunting*; metaph. *to lay wait for, strive to ensnare*; *to catch artfully*: τὶ ἐκ στόματός τινος, Lk. xi. 54.*

θηριομαχέω, -ῶ: 1 aor. ἐθηριομάχησα; (θηριομάχος); *to* **2341** *fight with wild beasts* (Diod. 3, 43, 7; Artem. oneir. 2, 54; 5, 49); εἰ ἐθηριομάχησα ἐν Ἐφέσῳ, 1 Co. xv. 32 — these words some take literally, supposing that Paul was condemned to fight with wild beasts; others explain them tropically of a fierce contest with brutal and ferocious men (so θηριομαχεῖν in Ignat. ad Rom. 5, [etc.]; οἶοις θηρίοις μαχόμεθα says Pompey, in App. bell. civ. 2, 61; see θηρίον). The former opinion encounters the objection that Paul would not have omitted this most terrible of all perils from the catalogue in 2 Co. xi. 23 sqq.*

θηρίον, -ου, τό, (dimin. of θήρ; hence *a little beast, little* **2342** *animal*; Plat. Theaet. p. 171 e.; of bees, Theocr. 19, 6; but in usage it had almost always the force of its primitive; the later dimin. is θηρίδιον [cf. Epictet. diss. 2, 9, 6]); [fr. Hom. down]; Sept. for חַיָּה and בְּהֵמָה, *an animal*; *a wild animal, wild beast, beast*: prop., Mk. i. 13; Acts x. 12 Rec.; xi. 6; xxviii. 4 sq.; Heb. xii. 20; [Jas. iii. 7]; Rev. vi. 8; in Rev. xi. 7 and chh. xiii.–xx., under the fig. of a '*beast*' is depicted A n t i c h r i s t, both his person and his kingdom and power, (see ἀντίχριστος); metaph. a brutal, bestial man, savage, ferocious, Tit. i. 12 [colloq. 'ugly dogs'], (so in Arstph. eqq. 273; Plut. 439; nub. 184; [cf. Schmidt ch. 70, 2; apparently never with allusion to the s t u p i d i t y of beasts]; still other exx. are given by *Kypke*, Observv. ii. p. 379; θηρία ἀνθρωπόμορφα, Ignat. Smyrn. 4, cf. ad Ephes. 7). [SYN. see ζῷον.]

θησαυρίζω; 1 aor. ἐθησαύρισα; pf. pass. ptcp. τεθησαυ- **2343** ρισμένος; (θησαυρός); fr. Hdt. down; *to gather and lay up, to heap up, store up*: *to accumulate riches*, Jas. v. 3; τινί, Lk. xii. 21; 2 Co. xii. 14; τί, 1 Co. xvi. 2; θησαυρὸς ἑαυτῷ, Mt. vi. 19 sq.; i. q. *to keep in store, store up, reserve*: pass. 2 Pet. iii. 7; metaph. *so to live from day to day as to increase either the bitterness or the happiness of one's consequent lot*: ὀργὴν ἑαυτῷ, Ro. ii. 5; κακά, Prov. i. 18; ζωήν, Pss. of Sol. 9, 9, (εὐτυχίαν, App. Samn. 4, 3 [i. e. vol. i. p. 23, 31 ed. Bekk.]; τεθησαυρισμένος κατά τινος φθόνος, Diod. 20, 36). [COMP.: ἀπο- θησαυρίζω.]*

θησαυρός, -οῦ, ὁ, (fr. ΘΕΩ [τίθημι] with the paragog. **2344** term. -αυρος); Sept. often for אוֹצָר; Lat. *thesaurus*; i. e. **1.** *the place in which goods and precious things are collected and laid up*; **a.** *a casket, coffer*, or *other receptacle, in which valuables are kept*: Mt. ii. 11. **b.** *a treasury* (Hdt., Eur., Plat., Aristot., Diod., Plut., Hdian.; 1 Macc. iii. 29). **c.** *storehouse, repository, magazine*, (Neh. xiii. 12; Deut. xxviii. 12, etc.; App. Pun. 88, 95): Mt. xiii. 52 [cf. παλαιός, 1]; metaph. of the s o u l, as the repository of thoughts, feelings, purposes, etc.: [Mt. xii. 35ᵃ G L T Tr WH, 35ᵇ]; with epex. gen. τῆς καρδίας, ibid. xii. 35ᵃ Rec.; Lk. vi. 45. **2.** *the things laid up in a treasury*; *collected treasures*: Mt. vi. 19–21; Lk. xii. 33 sq.; Heb. xi. 26. θησαυρὸν ἔχειν ἐν οὐρανῷ, *to have* *treasure* laid up for themselves *in heaven*, is used of those to whom God has appointed eternal salvation : Mt. xix. 21; Mk. x. 21; Lk. xviii. 22; *something precious*, Mt. xiii. 44; used thus of the light of the gospel, 2 Co. iv. 7; with an epex. gen. τῆς σοφίας (Xen. mem. 4, 2, 9; Plat. Phil. p. 15 e.) κ. γνώσεως, i. q. πᾶσα ἡ σοφία κ. γνῶσις ὡς θησαυροί, Col. ii. 3.*

2345 **θιγγάνω** [prob. akin to τεῖχος, *fingo, fiction*, etc.; Curtius § 145]: 2 aor. ἔθιγον; *to touch, handle*: μηδὲ θίγης touch not sc. impure things, Col. ii. 21 [cf. ἅπτω, 2 c.]; τινός, Heb. xii. 20 ([Aeschyl.], Xen., Plat., Tragg., al.); like the Hebr. נֶגַע, *to do violence to, injure*: τινός, Heb. xi. 28 (Eur. Iph. Aul. 1351; ὧν αἱ βλάβαι αὗται θιγγάνουσι, Act. Thom. § 12). [SYN. see ἅπτω, 2 c.] *

2346 **θλίβω**: Pass., pres. θλίβομαι; pf. ptcp. τεθλιμμένος; [allied with *flagrum, affliction*; fr. Hom. down]; *to press* (as grapes), *press hard upon*: prop. τινά [A. V. *throng*], Mk. iii. 9; ὁδὸς τεθλιμμένη a compressed way, i. e. narrow, straitened, contracted, Mt. vii. 14; metaph. *to trouble, afflict, distress,* (Vulg. *tribulo*): τινά, 2 Th. i. 6; pass. (Vulg. *tribulor*, [also *angustior*]; *tribulationem patior*): 2 Co. i. 6; iv. 8; vii. 5; [1 Th. iii. 4; 2 Th. i. 7]; 1 Tim. v. 10; Heb. xi. 37. (οἱ θλίβοντες for צָרִים in Sept.) [COMP.: ἀπο-, συν-θλίβω.] *

2347 **θλίψις**, or **θλῖψις** [so L Tr], (cf. W. § 6, 1 e.; *Lipsius,* Grammat. Untersuch. p. 35), -εως, ἡ, (θλίβω), prop. *a pressing, pressing together, pressure* (Strab. p. 52; Galen) ; in bibl. and eccles. Grk. metaph., *oppression, affliction, tribulation, distress, straits* ; Vulg. *tribulatio*, also *pressura* (2 Co. i. 4ᵇ; Jn. xvi. [21], 33; [Phil. i. 16 (17); and in Col. i. 24 *passio*]); (Sept. for צָרָה, also for צַר, לַחַץ, etc.): Mt. xxiv. 9; Acts vii. 11; xi. 19; Ro. xii. 12; 2 Co. i. 4, 8; iv. 17; vi. 4; viii. 2; 2 Th. i. 6; Rev. i. 9; ii. 9, 22; vii. 14; joined with στενοχωρία [cf. Trench § lv.], Ro. ii. 9; viii. 35, (Deut. xxviii. 53 sq.; Is. [viii. 22]; xxx. 6); with ἀνάγκη, 1 Th. iii. 7; with διωγμός, Mt. xiii. 21; Mk. iv. 17; 2 Th. i. 4; of the afflictions of those hard pressed by siege and the calamities of war, Mt. xxiv. 21, 29; Mk. xiii. 19, 24; of the straits of want, 2 Co. viii. 13; Phil. iv. 14 [here al. give the word a wider reference]; Jas. i. 27; of the distress of a woman in child-birth, Jn. xvi. 21. θλίψιν ἔχω (i. q. θλίβομαι), Jn. xvi. 33; 1 Co. vii. 28; Rev. ii. 10; θλίψις ἐπί τινα ἔρχεται, Acts vii. 11; ἐν θλίψει, 1 Th. i. 6. plur.: Acts vii. 10; xiv. 22; xx. 23; Ro. v. 3; Eph. iii. 13; 1 Th. iii. 3; Heb. x. 33; τοῦ Χριστοῦ, the afflictions which Christ had to undergo (and which, therefore, his followers must not shrink from), Col. i. 24 (see ἀνταναπληρόω); θλίψις τῆς καρδίας (κ. συνοχή), anxiety, burden of heart, 2 Co. ii. 4; θλίψιν ἐπιφέρειν [L T Tr WH ἐγείρειν, see ἐγείρω, 4 c.) τοῖς δεσμοῖς τινος, to increase the misery of my imprisonment by causing me anxiety, Phil. i. 16 (17).*

2348 **θνήσκω**: pf. τέθνηκα, inf. τεθνάναι and L T Tr WH τεθνηκέναι (in Acts xiv. 19), ptcp. τεθνηκώς; plupf. 3 pers. sing. ἐτεθνήκει (Jn. xi. 21 Rec.); [fr. Hom. down]; Sept. for מוּת; *to die*; pf. *to be dead*: Mt. ii. 20; Mk. xv. 44; Lk. vii. 12 [L br.]; viii. 49; Jn. xi. 21, Rec. in 39

and 41, 44; xii. 1 [T WH om. L Tr br.]; xix. 33; Acts xiv. 19; xxv. 19; metaph., of the loss of spiritual life: ζῶσα τέθνηκε, i. e. κἂν δοκῇ ζῆν ταύτην τὴν αἰσθητὴν ζωήν, τέθνηκε κατὰ πνεῦμα (Theoph.): 1 Tim. v. 6 (Philo de prof. § 10 ζῶντες ἔνιοι τεθνήκασι καὶ τεθνηκότες ζῶσι). [COMP.: ἀπο-, συν-απο-θνήσκω.] *

2349 **θνητός**, -ή, -όν, (verbal adj. fr. θνήσκω), [fr. Hom. down], *liable to death, mortal*: Ro. vi. 12; viii. 11; 1 Co. xv. 53 sq.; 2 Co. iv. 11; v. 4. [θνητός *subject to death*, and so still living; νεκρός actually *dead*.] *

see 5182 **θορυβάζω**: (θόρυβος, q. v.); *to trouble, disturb*, (i. e. τυρβάζω, q. v.); Pass. pres. 2 pers. sing. θορυβάζῃ in Lk. x. 41 L T Tr WH after codd. ℵ B C L etc. (Not found elsewh. [Soph. Lex. s. v. quotes Euseb. of Alex. (*Migne,* Patr. Graec. vol. lxxxvi. 1) p. 444 c.].) *

2350 **θορυβέω**, -ῶ: impf. ἐθορύβουν; pres. pass. θορυβοῦμαι; (θόρυβος) ; fr. Hdt. down; **1.** *to make a noise* or *uproar, be turbulent.* **2.** trans. *to disturb, throw into confusion*: τὴν πόλιν, to "set the city on an uproar," Acts xvii. 5; pass. *to be troubled in mind*, Acts xx. 10 [al. here adhere to the outward sense]; *to wail tumultuously,* Mt. ix. 23; Mk. v. 39.*

2351 **θόρυβος**, -ου, ὁ, (akin to θρόος, τύρβη, τυρβάζω, [but τύρβη etc. seem to come from another root; cf. Curtius § 250]), *a noise, tumult, uproar*: of persons wailing, Mk. v. 38; of a clamorous and excited multitude, Mt. xxvii. 24; of riotous persons, Acts xx. 1; xxi. 34; a tumult, as a breach of public order, Mt. xxvi. 5; Mk. xiv. 2; Acts xxiv. 18. (In Grk. writ. fr. Pind. and Hdt. down; several times in Sept.)*

2352 **θραύω**: pf. pass. ptcp. τεθραυσμένος; fr. [Hdt.], Aeschyl. down, *to break, break in pieces, shatter, smite through,* (Ex. xv. 6; Num. xxiv. 17, etc.; 2 Macc. xv. 16): τεθραυσμένοι, broken by calamity [A. V. *bruised*], Lk. iv. 18 (19) fr. Is. lviii. 6 for רְצוּצִים. [SYN. see ῥήγνυμι.] *

2353 **θρέμμα**, -τος, τό, (τρέφω), *whatever is fed* or *nursed*; hence **1.** *a ward, nursling, child,* (Soph., Eur., Plat., al.). **2.** *a flock, cattle,* esp. sheep and goats : Jn. iv. 12. (Xen. oec. 20, 23; Plat., Diod., Joseph., Plut., Lcian., Aelian, al.)*

2354 **θρηνέω**, -ῶ: impf. ἐθρήνουν; fut. θρηνήσω; 1 aor. ἐθρήνησα; (θρῆνος, q. v.); fr. Hom. down; Sept. for הֵילִיל, קוֹנֵן, etc.; **1.** *to lament, to mourn*: Jn. xvi. 20; of the singers of dirges, [*to wail*], Mt. xi. 17; Lk. vii. 32. **2.** *to bewail, deplore*: τινά, Lk. xxiii. 27.*

[On θρηνέω *to lament*, κόπτομαι *to smite the breast in grief,* λυπέομαι *to be pained, saddened,* πενθέω *to mourn,* cf. Trench § lxv. and see κλαίω fin.; yet note that in classic Grk. λυπ. is the most comprehensive word, designating every species of pain of body or soul; and that πενθέω expresses a self-contained grief, never violent in its manifestations; like our Eng. word "mourn" it is associated by usage with the death of kindred, and like it used pregnantly to suggest that event. See Schmidt vol. ii. ch. 83.]

2355 **θρῆνος**, -ου, ὁ, (θρέομαι *to cry aloud, to lament*; cf. Germ. *Thräne* [(?), rather *drönen;* Curtius § 317]), *a lamentation*: Mt. ii. 18 Rec. (Sept. for קִינָה, also נְהִי; O. T. Apocr.; Hom., Pind., Tragg., Xen. Ages. 10, 3; Plat., al.)*

2356   **θρησκεία** Tdf. -ία [see I, ι], (a later word; Ion. θρησκίη in Hdt. [2, 18. 37]), -ας, ἡ, (fr. θρησκεύω, and this fr. θρῆσκος, q. v.; hence apparently primarily *fear of the gods*); *religious worship*, esp. *external, that which consists in ceremonies*: hence in plur. θρησκίας ἐπιτελεῖν μυρίας, Hdt. 2, 37; καθιστὰς ἁγνείας τε καὶ θρησκείας καὶ καθαρμούς, Dion. Hal. 2, 63; univ. *religious worship*, Jas. i. 26 sq.; with gen. of the obj. [W. 187 (176)] τῶν ἀγγέλων, Col. ii. 18 (τῶν εἰδώλων, Sap. xiv. 27; τῶν δαιμόνων, Euseb. h. e. 6, 41, 2; τῶν θεῶν, ib. 9, 9, 14; τοῦ θεοῦ, Hdian. 4, 8, 17 [7 ed. Bekk.]; often in Josephus [cf. Krebs, Observv. etc. p. 339 sq.]; Clem. Rom. 1 Cor. 45, 7); *religious discipline, religion*: ἡμετέρα θρησκεία, of Judaism, Acts xxvi. 5 (τὴν ἐμὴν θρησκείαν καταλιπών, put into the mouth of God by Joseph. antt. 8, 11, 1; with gen. of the subj. τῶν Ἰουδαίων, 4 Macc. v. 6, 13 (12); Joseph. antt. 12, 5, 4; θρ. κοσμική, i. e. worthy to be embraced by all nations, *a world-religion*, b. j. 4, 5, 2; *piety*, περὶ τ. θεόν, antt. 1, 13, 1; κατὰ τὴν ἔμφυτον θρησκείαν τῶν βαρβάρων πρὸς τὸ βασιλικὸν ὄνομα, Charit. 7, 6 p. 165, 18 ed. Reiske; of the reverence of Antiochus the Pious for the Jewish religion, Joseph. antt. 13, 8, 2). Cf. Grimm on 4 Macc. v. 6; [esp. Trench § xlviii.].*

2357   **θρῆσκος** (T WH θρησκός, cf. [Tdf. Proleg. p. 101]; W. § 6, 1 e.; *Lipsius*, Grammat. Untersuch. p. 28), -ου, ὁ, *fearing* or *worshipping God*; *religious*, (apparently fr. τρέω to tremble; hence prop. *trembling, fearful*; cf. *J. G. Müller* in Theol. Stud. u. Krit. for 1835, p. 121; on the different conjectures of others, see Passow s. v. [Curtius § 316 connects with θρα; hence 'to adhere to,' 'be a votary of'; cf. Vaniček p. 395]): Jas. i. 26. [Cf. Trench § xlviii.]*

2358   **θριαμβεύω**; 1 aor. ptcp. θριαμβεύσας; (θρίαμβος, a hymn sung in festal processions in honor of Bacchus; among the Romans, a triumphal procession [Lat. *triumphus*, with which word it is thought to be allied; cf. Vaniček p. 317]);   **1.** *to triumph, to celebrate a triumph*, (Dion. Hal., App., Plut., Hdian., al.); τινά, over one (as Plut. Thes. and Rom. comp. 4): Col. ii. 15 (where it signifies the victory won by God over the demoniacal powers through Christ's death).   **2.** by a usage unknown to prof. auth., with a Hiphil or causative force (cf. W. p. 23 and § 38, 1 [cf. B. 147 (129)]), with the acc. of a pers., *to cause one to triumph*, i. e. metaph. to grant one complete success, 2 Co. ii. 14 [but others reject the causative sense; see Mey. ad loc.; Bp. Lghtft. on Col. l. c.].*

2359   **θρίξ**, τριχός, dat. plur. θριξί, ἡ, [fr. Hom. down], *the hair*;   **a.** *the hair of the head*: Mt. v. 36; Lk. vii. 44; xxi. 18; Jn. xi. 2; xii. 3; Acts xxvii. 34; 1 Pet. iii. 3 [Lchm. om.]; Rev. i. 14; with τῆς κεφαλῆς added (Hom. Od. 13, 399. 431), Mt. x. 30; Lk. vii. 38; xii. 7.   **b.** *the hair of animals*: Rev. ix. 8; ἐνδεδυμ. τρίχας καμήλου, with a garment made of camel's hair, Mk. i. 6, cf. Mt. iii. 4; ἐν ... τριχῶν καμηλείων πλέγμασιν περιεπάτησαν, Clem. Alex. strom. 4 p. 221 ed. Sylb.*

2360   **θροέω**, -ῶ: (θροός clamor, tumult); in Grk. writ. *to cry aloud, make a noise by outcry*; in the N. T. *to trouble,*

frighten; Pass. pres. θροοῦμαι; *to be troubled in mind, to be frightened, alarmed*: Mt. xxiv. 6 [B. 243 (209)]; Mk. xiii. 7; 2 Th. ii. 2; [1 aor. ptcp. θροηθέντες, Lk. xxiv. 37 Tr mrg. WH mrg.]. (Cant. v. 4.)*

2361   **θρόμβος**, -ου, ὁ, [allied with τρέφω in the sense *to thicken*; Vaniček p. 307], *a large thick drop*, esp. *of clotted blood* (Aeschyl. Eum. 184); with αἵματος added (Aeschyl. choeph. 533, 546; Plat. Critias p. 120 a.), Lk. xxii. 44 [L br. WH reject the pass. (see *WH*. App. ad loc.)].*

2362   **θρόνος**, -ου, ὁ, (ΘΡΑΩ to sit; cf. Curtius § 316), [fr. Hom. down], Sept. for כִּסֵּא, *a throne, seat*, i. e. a chair of state having a footstool; assigned in the N. T. to k i n g s, hence by meton. for *kingly power, royalty*: Lk. i. 32, 52; Acts ii. 30. metaph. to G o d, the governor of the world: Mt. v. 34; xxiii. 22; Acts vii. 49 (Is. lxvi. 1); Rev. i. 4; iii. 21; iv. 2–6, 9, 10, etc.; Heb. iv. 16; viii. 1; xii. 2. to the M e s s i a h, the partner and assistant in the divine administration: Mt. xix. 28; xxv. 31; Rev. iii. 21; xx. 11; xxii. 3; hence the divine power belonging to Christ, Heb. i. 8. to j u d g e s, i. q. *tribunal* or *bench* (Plut. mor. p. 807 b.): Mt. xix. 28; Lk. xxii. 30; Rev. xx. 4. to e l d e r s: Rev. iv. 4; xi. 16. to S a t a n: Rev. ii. 13; cf. Bleek ad loc. to the b e a s t (concerning which see θηρίον): Rev. xvi. 10. θρόνος is used by meton. of one who holds dominion or exercises authority; thus in plur. of a n g e l s: Col. i. 16 [see Bp. Lghtft. ad loc.].*

2363   **Θυάτειρα**, -ων, τά, (and once -ας, ἡ, Rev. i. 11 Lchm. Θυάτειραν [cf. Tdf. ad loc.; *WH*.App. p. 156; B. 18 (16)]), *Thyatira*, a city of Lydia, formerly *Pelopia* and *Euhippia* (Plin. h. n. 5, 31), now *Akhissar*, a colony of Macedonian Greeks, situated between Sardis and Pergamum on the river Lycus; its inhabitants gained their living by traffic and the art of dyeing in purple: Acts xvi. 14; Rev. i. 11; ii. 18, 24. [B. D. s. v.]*

2364   **θυγάτηρ**, gen. θυγατρός, dat. θυγατρί, acc. θυγατέρα, voc. θύγατερ, plur. θυγατέρες, acc. -έρας, ἡ, (of the same root as Gothic *dauhtar*, Eng. *daughter*, Germ. *Tochter* [Curtius § 318; Vaniček p. 415]); Hebr. בַּת; [fr. Hom. down]; *a daughter*: prop., Mt. ix. 18; x. 35, 37; xv. 22; Acts vii. 21, etc. improp.   **a.** the vocative [or nom. as voc. cf. W. § 29, 2; B. § 129 a. 5; *WH*.App. p. 158] in kindly address: Mt. ix. 22; Mk. v. 34 [L Tr WH θυγάτηρ]; Lk. viii. 48 [Tr WH θυγάτηρ], (see υἱός 1 a. fin., τέκνον b. a.).   **b.** in phrases modelled after the Hebr.   **a.** *a daughter of God* i. e. acceptable to God, rejoicing in God's peculiar care and protection: 2 Co. vi. 18 (Is. xliii. 6; Sap. ix. 7; see υἱός τ. θεοῦ 4, τέκνον b. γ.).   **β.** with the name of a place, city, or region, it denotes collectively all its inhabitants and citizens (very often so in the O. T., as Is. xxxvii. 22; Jer. xxvi. (xlvi.) 19; Zeph. iii. 14, etc.); in the N. T. twice ἡ θυγ. Σιών, i. e. inhabitants of Jerusalem: Mt. xxi. 5; Jn. xii. 15, (Is. i. 8; x. 32; Zech. ix. 9, etc.; see Σιών, 2).   **γ.** θυγατέρες Ἱερουσαλήμ, women of Jerusalem: Lk. xxiii. 28.   **δ.** *female descendant*: αἱ θυγατέρες Ἀαρών, women of Aaron's posterity, Lk. i. 5; θυγάτηρ Ἀβραάμ daughter of Abraham, i. e. a woman tracing her descent from Abraham, Lk. xiii. 16, (4 Macc

xv. 28 (25); Gen. xxviii. 8; xxxvi. 2; Judg. xi. 40; Is. xvi. 2, etc.).

2365   **θυγάτριον**, -ου, τό, *a little daughter*: Mk. v. 23; vii. 25. [Strattis Incert. 5; Menand., Athen., Plut. reg. et imper. Apophtheg. p. 179 e. (Alex. 6); al.]*

2366   **θύελλα**, -ης, ἡ, (θύω to boil, foam, rage, as ἄελλα fr. ἄω, ἄημι), *a sudden storm, tempest, whirlwind*: Heb. xii. 18. (Deut. iv. 11; v. 22; Hom., Hes., Tragg., al.) [Cf. Schmidt ch. 55, 11; Trench § lxxiii. fin.]*

2367   **θύϊνος** [WH om. the diær. (cf. I, ι, fin.)], -η, -ον, (fr. θυία or θύα, the *citrus*, an odoriferous North-African tree used as incense [and for inlaying; B. D. s. v. Thyine wood; *Tristram*, Nat. Hist. of the Bible, p. 401 sq.]), *thyine* (Lat. *citrinus*): ξύλον, Rev. xviii. 12 as in Diosc. 1, 21; cf. Plin. h. n. 13, 30 (16).*

2368   **θυμίαμα**, -τος, τό, (θυμιάω), Sept. mostly for קְטֹרֶת, *an aromatic substance burnt, incense*: generally in plur., Rev. v. 8; viii. 3 sq.; xviii. 13; ἡ ὥρα τοῦ θ., when the incense is burned, Lk. i. 10; θυσιαστήριον τοῦ θυμ. ib. 11. (Soph., Hdt., Arstph., Plat., Diod., Joseph.; Sept.)*

2369   **θυμιατήριον**, -ου, τό, (θυμιάω), prop. *a utensil for fumigating* or *burning incense* [cf. W. 96 (91)]; hence **1.** *a censer*: 2 Chr. xxvi. 19; Ezek. viii. 11; Hdt. 4, 162; Thuc. 6, 46; Diod. 13, 3; Joseph. antt. 4, 2, 4; 8, 3, 8; Ael. v. h. 12, 51. **2.** *the altar of incense*: Philo, rer. div. haer. § 46; vit. Moys. iii. § 7; Joseph. antt. 3, 6, 8; 3, 8, 3; b. j. 5, 5, 5; Clem. Alex.; Orig.; and so in Heb. ix. 4 [(where Tr mrg. br.), also 2 Tr mrg. in br.], where see Bleek, Lünemann, Delitzsch, Kurtz, in opp. to those [(A. V. included)] who think it means *censer*; [yet cf. *Harnack* in the Stud. u. Krit. for 1876, p. 572 sq.].*

2370   **θυμιάω**, -ῶ: 1 aor. inf. θυμιᾶσαι [RG -άσαι]; (fr. θῦμα, and this fr. θύω, q. v.); in Grk. writ. fr. Pind., Hdt., Plat. down; Sept. for קָטַר and הִקְטִיר; *to burn incense*: Lk. i. 9.*

2371   **θυμομαχέω**, -ῶ; (θυμός and μάχομαι); *to carry on war with great animosity* (Polyb., Diod., Dion. H., Plut.); *to be very angry, be exasperated* [A. V. *highly displeased*]: τινί, with one, Acts xii. 20. Cf. *Kypke*, Observv. ii. p. 62 sq.*

2372   **θυμός**, -οῦ, ὁ, (fr. θύω to rush along or on, be in a heat, breathe violently; hence Plato correctly says, Cratyl. p. 419 e., θυμὸς ἀπὸ τῆς θύσεως κ. ζέσεως τῆς ψυχῆς; accordingly it signifies both *the spirit* panting as it were in the body, and the *rage* with which the man pants and swells), [fr. Hom. down], Sept. often for אַף anger, and חֵמָה excandescentia; also for חָרוֹן aestus. In the N. T. **1.** *passion, angry heat*, (*excandescentia*, Cic. Tusc. 4, 9, 21), *anger forthwith boiling up and soon subsiding again*, (ὀργή, on the other hand, denotes *indignation which has arisen gradually and become more settled*; [cf. (Plato) deff. 415 e. θυμός· ὁρμὴ βίαιος ἄνευ λογισμοῦ· νόσος τάξεως ψυχῆς ἀλογίστου. ὀργή· παράκλησις τοῦ θυμικοῦ εἰς τὸ τιμωρεῖσθαι, Greg. Naz. carm. 34 θυμὸς μέν ἐστιν ἀθρόος ζέσις φρενός, ὀργὴ δὲ θυμὸς ἐμμένων, Herm. mand. 5, 2, 4 ἐκ δὲ τῆς πικρίας θυμός, ἐκ δὲ τοῦ θυμοῦ ὀργή; cf. Aristot. rhet. 2, 2, 1 and Cope's note]; hence we read in Sir. xlviii. 10 κοπάσαι ὀργὴν πρὸ θυμοῦ, before it glows and

bursts forth; [see further, on the distinction betw. the two words, Trench § xxxvii., and esp. Schmidt vol. iii. ch. 142]): Lk. iv. 28; Acts xix. 28; Eph. iv. 31; Col. iii. 8; Heb. xi. 27; ὁ θ. τοῦ θεοῦ, Rev. xiv. 19; xv. 1, 7; xvi. 1; ἔχειν θυμόν, to be in a passion, Rev. xii. 12 (Ael. v. h. 1, 14); ὀργὴ καὶ θυμός (as Sept. Mic. v. 15; Isocr. p. 249 c.; Hdian. 8, 4, 1; al.): Ro. ii. 8 (Rec. in the inverse order; so Deut. ix. 19; xxix. 23, 28, [cf. Trench u. s.]); plur. θυμοί impulses and outbursts of anger [W. 176 (166); B. 77 (67)]: 2 Co. xii. 20; Gal. v. 20, (2 Macc. iv. 25, 38; ix. 7; x. 35; xiv. 45; 4 Macc. xviii. 20; Sap. x. 3; Soph. Aj. 718 [where see *Lob.*]; Plat. Protag. p. 323 e.; [Phileb. p. 40 e.; Aristot. rhet. 2, 13, 13]; Polyb. 3, 10, 5; Diod. 13, 28; Joseph. b. j. 4, 5, 2; Plut. Cor. 1; al.). **2.** *glow, ardor*: ὁ οἶνος τοῦ θυμοῦ [see οἶνος, b.] the wine of passion, inflaming wine, Germ. *Glutwein* (which either drives the drinker mad or kills him with its deadly heat; cf. Is. li. 17, 22; Jer. xxxii. 1 (xxv. 15) sqq.): Rev. xiv. 8; xviii. 3; with τοῦ θεοῦ added, which God gives the drinker, Rev. xiv. 10; with τῆς ὀργῆς τοῦ θεοῦ added [A. V. *fierceness*], Rev. xvi. 19; xix. 15; cf. *Ewald*, Johann. Schriften, Bd. ii. p. 269 note.*

2373   **θυμόω**, -ῶ: 1 aor. pass. ἐθυμώθην; (θυμός); *to cause one to become incensed, to provoke to anger*; pass. (Sept. often for חָרָה) *to be wroth*: Mt. ii. 16. (In Grk. writ. fr. [Aeschyl.], Hdt. down.)*

2374   **θύρα**, -ας, ἡ, (fr. θύω to rush in, prop. that through which a rush is made; hence Germ. *Thür* [Eng. *door*; Curtius § 319]), [fr. Hom. down], Sept. for דֶּלֶת and פֶּתַח, sometimes also for שַׁעַר; *a* (house) *door*; [in plur. i. q. Lat. *fores, folding doors*; cf. W. 176 (166); B. 24 (21); cf. πύλη]: **a.** prop.: κλείειν etc. τὴν θ., Mt. vi. 6; Lk. xiii. 25; pass., Mt. xxv. 10; Lk. xi. 7; Jn. xx. 19, 26; Acts xxi. 30; ἀνοίγειν, Acts v. 19; pass. Acts xvi. 26 sq.; κρούειν, Acts xii. 13; διὰ τῆς θ. Jn. x. 1 sq.; πρὸς τὴν θ., Mk. i. 33; xi. 4 [Tr WH om. τήν; cf. W. 123 (116)]; Acts iii. 2; τὰ πρὸς τὴν θ. the vestibule [so B. § 125, v; al. the space or parts at (near) the door], Mk. ii. 2; πρὸς τῇ θ. Jn. xviii. 16; ἐπὶ τῇ θ. Acts v. 9; πρὸ τῆς θ. Acts xii. 6; ἐπὶ τῶν θυρῶν, Acts v. 23 [R G πρό]. **b.** θύρα is used of any opening like a door, *an entrance, way* or *passage into*: ἡ θ. τοῦ μνημείου, of the tomb, Mt. xxvii. 60; xxviii. 2 R G; Mk. xv. 46; xvi. 3, (Hom. Od. 9, 243; 12, 256; al.). **c.** in parable and metaph. we find a. ἡ θύρα τῶν προβάτων, the door through which the sheep go out and in, the name of him who brings salvation to those who follow his guidance, Jn. x. 7, 9; cf. *Christ. Fr. Fritzsche* in Fritzschiorum opusc. p. 20 sqq.; (in Ignat. ad Philad. 9 Christ is called ἡ θύρα τοῦ πατρός, δι' ἧς εἰσέρχονται Ἀβραὰμ ... καὶ οἱ προφῆται; cf. Harnack on Clem. Rom. 1 Cor. 48, 3 sq.). β. 'an open door' is used of the *opportunity* of doing something: τῆς πίστεως, of getting faith, Acts xiv. 27; open to a teacher, i. e. the opportunity of teaching others, 2 Co. ii. 12; Col. iv. 3; by a bold combination of metaph. and literal language, the phrase θύρα μεγάλη κ. ἐνεργής [A. V. *a great door and effectual*] is used of a large opportunity of teaching a great multitude the way of salvation, and one encouraging the hope of the most successful results: 1 Co. xvi. 9. **γ.** *the door of the kingdom of heaven* (likened to a palace) denotes the c o n d i t i o n s which must be complied with in order to be received into the kingdom of God: Lk. xiii. 24 (for Rec. πύλης); p o w e r of entering, access into, God's eternal kingdom, Rev. iii. 8 cf. 7, [but al. al.; add here Rev. iv. 1]. **δ.** he whose advent is just at hand is said ἐπὶ θύραις εἶναι, Mt. xxiv. 33; Mk. xiii. 29, and πρὸ θυρῶν ἑστηκέναι, Jas. v. 9. **ε.** ἑστηκὼς ἐπὶ τὴν θύραν κ. κρούων is said of Christ seeking entrance into souls, and they who comply with his entreaty are said ἀνοίγειν τ. θύραν, Rev. iii. 20.*

2375 **θυρεός, -οῦ, ὁ,** (fr. θύρα, because shaped like a door [cf. W. 23]), *a shield* (Lat. *scutum*); it was large, oblong, and four-cornered: τὸν θ. τῆς πίστεως, i. q. τὴν πίστιν ὡς θυρεόν, Eph. vi. 16. It differs from ἀσπίς (Lat. *clipeus*), which was smaller and circular. [Polyb., Dion. Hal., Plut., al.]*

2376 **θυρίς, -ίδος, ἡ,** (dimin. of θύρα, prop. *a little door*; Plat., Dio Cass.), *a window*: Acts xx. 9; 2 Co. xi. 33. (Arstph., Theophr., Diod., Joseph., Plut., al.; Sept.)*

2377 **θυρωρός, -οῦ, ὁ, ἡ,** (fr. θύρα, and ὥρα care; cf. ἀρκυωρός, πυλωρός, τιμωρός; cf. Curtius § 501, cf. p. 101; [Vaniček p. 900; *Allen* in Am. Journ. of Philol. i. p. 129]), *a door-keeper, porter*; male or female *janitor*: masc., Mk. xiii. 34; Jn. x. 3; fem. Jn. xviii. 16 sq. ([Sappho], Aeschyl., Hdt., Xen., Plat., Aristot., Joseph., al.; Sept.)*

2378 **θυσία, -ας, ἡ,** (θύω), [fr. Aeschyl. down], Sept. for מִנְחָה an offering, and זֶבַח; *a sacrifice, victim*; **a.** prop.: Mt. ix. 13 and xii. 7, fr. Hos. vi. 6; Mk. ix. 49 ([R G L Tr txt. br.], see ἁλίζω); Eph. v. 2; Heb. x. 5, 26; plur., Mk. xii. 33; Lk. xiii. 1; Heb. ix. 23; [x. 1, 8 (here Rec. sing.)]; ἀνάγειν θυσίαν τινί, Acts vii. 41; ἀναφέρειν, Heb. vii. 27, (see ἀνάγω, and ἀναφέρω 2); [δοῦναι θ. Lk. ii. 24]; προσφέρειν, Acts vii. 42; Heb. v. 1; viii. 3; x. [11], 12; [xi. 4]; pass. Heb. ix. 9; διὰ τῆς θυσίας αὐτοῦ, by his sacrifice, i. e. by the sacrifice which he offered (not, *by offering up himself*; that would have been expressed by διὰ τῆς θυσίας τῆς ἑαυτοῦ, or διὰ τῆς ἑαυτοῦ θυσίας), Heb. ix. 26; ἐσθίειν τὰς θυσίας, to eat the flesh left over from the victims sacrificed (viz. at the sacrificial feasts; cf. [Lev. vii. 15 sqq.; Deut. xii. 7 sq. 17 sq., etc.] *Win.* RWB. s. v. Opfermahlzeiten), 1 Co. x. 18. **b.** in expressions involving a comparison: θυσίαι πνευματικαί (see πνευματικός, 3 a.), 1 Pet. ii. 5; θυσία, a free gift, which is likened to an offered sacrifice, Phil. iv. 18; Heb. xiii. 16 (τοιαύταις θυσίαις, i. e. with such things as substitutes for sacrifices God is well pleased); θυσία ζῶσα (see ζάω, II. b. fin.), Ro. xii. 1; ἀναφέρειν θυσίαν αἰνέσεως, Heb. xiii. 15 (if this meant, as it can mean, αἴνεσιν ὡς θυσίαν, the author would not have

added, as he has, the explanation of the words; he must therefore be supposed to have reproduced the Hebr. phrase זֶבַח־תּוֹדָה, and then defined this more exactly; Lev. vii. 3 (13) [cf. 2 (12)]; Ps. cvi. (cvii.) 22; see αἴνεσις); ἐπὶ τῇ θυσίᾳ . . . τῆς πίστεως ὑμῶν (epex. gen.), in the work of exciting, nourishing, increasing, your faith, as if in providing a sacrifice to be offered to God [cf. ἐπί, p. 233ᵇ bot.], Phil. ii. 17.*

2379 **θυσιαστήριον, -ου, τό,** (neut. of the adj. θυσιαστήριος [cf. W. 96 (91)], and this fr. θυσιάζω to sacrifice), a word found only in Philo [e. g. vita Moys. iii. § 10, cf. § 7; Joseph. antt. 8, 4, 1] and the bibl. and eccl. writ.; Sept. times without number for מִזְבֵּחַ; prop. an *altar for the slaying and burning of victims*; used of **1.** *the altar of whole burnt-offerings* which stood in the court of the priests in the temple at Jerusalem [B. D. s. v. Altar]: Mt. v. 23 sq.; xxiii. 18–20, 35; Lk. xi. 51; 1 Co. ix. 13; x. 18; Heb. vii. 13; Rev. xi. 1. **2.** *the altar of incense*, which stood in the sanctuary or Holy place [B. D. u. s.]: τὸ θυσιαστ. τοῦ θυμιάματος, Lk. i. 11 (Ex. xxx. 1); [symbolically] in H e a v e n: Rev. vi. 9; viii. 3, 5; ix. 13; xiv. 18; xvi. 7. **3.** any other altar, Jas. ii. 21; plur. Ro. xi. 3; metaph., the cross on which Christ suffered an expiatory death: *to eat of this altar* i. e. to appropriate to one's self the fruits of Christ's expiatory death, Heb. xiii. 10.*

2380 **θύω,** impf. ἔθυον; 1 aor. ἔθυσα; Pass., pres. inf. θύεσθαι; pf. ptcp. τεθυμένος; 1 aor. ἐτύθην (1 Co. v. 7, where Rec.ᵇᵉᶻ ᵉˡᵗ ἐθύθην, cf. W. § 5, 1 d. 12); [fr. Hom. down]; Sept. mostly for זָבַח, also for שָׁחַט, to slay; **1.** *to sacrifice, immolate*: absol. Acts xiv. 13; τινί, dat. of pers. (in honor of one), Acts xiv. 18; τινί τι, 1 Co. x. 20. **2.** *to slay, kill*: absol., Acts xi. 7; τί, Lk. xv. 23, 27, 30; pass. Mt. xxii. 4; τὸ πάσχα, the paschal lamb, Mk. xiv. 12; pass., Lk. xxii. 7; 1 Co. v. 7, (Deut. xvi. 2, 6). **3.** *to slaughter*: absol. Jn. x. 10; τινά, Sir. xxxi. (xxxiv.) 24; 1 Macc. vii. 19.*

2381 **Θωμᾶς, -ᾶ, ὁ,** (תְּאוֹם [i. e. twin], see δίδυμος), *Thomas*, one of Christ's apostles: Mt. x. 3; Mk. iii. 18; Lk. vi. 15; Jn. xi. 16; xiv. 5; xx. 24–29 [in 29 Rec. only]; xxi. 2; Acts i. 13. [B. D. s. v.]*

2382 **θώραξ, -ακος, ὁ; 1.** *the breast*, the part of the body from the neck to the navel, where the ribs end, (Aristot. hist. an. 1, 7 [cf. 8, p. 491ᵃ, 28]; Eur., Plat., al.): Rev. ix. 9 [some refer this to the next head]. **2.** *a breast-plate* or *corselet* consisting of two parts and protecting the body on both sides from the neck to the middle, (Hom., Hdt., Xen., Plat., al.): Rev. ix. 9, 17; ἐνδύεσθαι τ. θώρακα τῆς δικαιοσύνης, i. e. δικαιοσύνην ὡς θώρακα, Eph. vi. 14; θώρακα πίστεως, i. e. πίστιν ὡς θώρακα, 1 Th. v. 8, (ἐνδύεσθαι δικαιοσύνην ὡς θώρακα, Is. lix. 17; ἐνδ. θώρακα δικαιοσύνης, Sap. v. 19 (18)).*

I

[**I, ι**: on iota subscript in Mss. and edd. of the N. T. see *Lipsius*, Gram. Untersuch. p. 3 sqq.; *Scrivener*, Introd. etc. p. 42, and Index II. s. v.; *Kuenen and Cobet*, N. T. Vat., praef. p. xi. sq.; *Tdf.* Proleg. p. 109; *WH.* Intr. § 410; W. § 5, 4; B. pp. 11, 44 sq., 69; and s. vv. ἀθῷος, ζῷον, Ἡρῴδης etc., πρῴρα, Τρῳάς, ᾠόν. ι is often substituted for ει, esp. in nouns ending in εια (ια; on their accent see Chandler § 95 sqq.), in proper names, etc.; cf. *WH.* App. p. 153; Intr. § 399; *Tdf.* Proleg. pp. 83, 86 sq.; *Scrivener*, Introd. etc. p. 10 sq.; *Soph.* Lex. s. v. EI; *Meisterhans* p. 23 sq.; (on the usage of the Mss. cf. *Tdf.* Conlatio critica cod. Sin. c. text. Elz. etc. p. xviii.; *Scrivener*, Full Collation of the cod. Sin. etc. 2d ed. p. lii.). Examples of this spelling in recent editions are the following: ἀγνία WH, ἀλαζονία TWH, ἀναιδία T WH, ἀπειθία WH (exc. Heb. iv. 6, 11), ἀρεσκία TWH, δουλία T, ἐθελοθρησκία TWH, εἰδωλολατρία WH, εἰλικρινία T WH, ἐπιεικία WH, ἐριθία WH, ἑρμηνία WH, θρησκία T, ἱερατία WH, κακοηθία WH, κακοπαθία WH, κολακία T WH, κυβία T WH, μαγία TWH, μεθοδία T WH, ὀφθαλμοδουλία T WH, παιδία T (everywhere; see his note on Heb. xii. 5), πραγματία T WH, πραϋπαθία T WH, φαρμακία T WH (exc. Gal. v. 20), ὠφελία WH, Ἀτταλία T WH, Καισαρία T WH, Λαοδικία T WH, Σαμαρία TWH (Σαμαρίτης, Σαμαρῖτις, T), Σελευκία TWH, Φιλαδελφία T WH; occasionally the same substitution occurs in other words: e. g. αἴγιος WH, Ἄριος (πάγος) T, δανίζω T WH, δάνιον WH, δανιστής T WH, εἰδώλιον T WH, ἐξαλιφθῆναι WH, Ἐπικούριος T WH, ἡμίσια WH (see ἥμισυς), καταλελιμμένος WH, λίμμα WH, Νεφθαλίμ WH in Rev. vii. 6, ὁρινός WH, πιθός WH, σκοτινός WH, ὑπόλιμμα WH, φωτινός WH, χρεοφιλέτης (T?) WH; also in augm., as ἱστήκειν WH, ἴδον (see εἴδω I. init.); cf. *WH.* App. p. 162ᵇ. On ι as a demonst. addition to adverbs etc., see νυνί ad init. On the use and the omission of the mark of diæresis with ι in certain words, see *Tdf.* Proleg. p. 108; *Lipsius*, Gram. Untersuch. p. 136 sqq.]

2383 **Ἰάειρος**, *-ου* [cf. B. 18 (16)], ὁ, יָאִיר [i. e. whom Jehovah enlightens], Num. xxxii. 41), *Jairus* [pron. Ja-i′-rus], a ruler of the synagogue, whose daughter Jesus restored to life: Mk. v. 22; Lk. viii. 41. [Cf. B. D. Am. ed. s. v.]*

2384 **Ἰακώβ**, ὁ, (יַעֲקֹב [i. e. heel-catcher, supplanter]), *Jacob*; **1.** the second of Isaac's sons: Mt. i. 2; viii. 11; Jn. iv. 5 sq.; Acts vii. 8; Ro. ix. 13, etc. Hebraistically i. q. *the descendants of Jacob*: Ro. xi. 26, (Num. xxiii. 7; Is. xli. 8; Jer. [Hebr. txt.] xxxii. 26; Sir. xxiii. 12; 1 Macc. iii. 7, and often). **2.** the father of Joseph, the husband of Mary the mother of the Saviour: Mt. i. 15 sq.

2385 **Ἰάκωβος**, *-ου*, ὁ, (see the preceding word [and cf. B. 6, 18 (16)]), *James*; **1.** son of Zebedee, an apostle, and brother of the apostle John, (commonly called *James the greater* or *elder*). He was slain with the sword by the command of king Herod Agrippa I. (c. A. D. 44): Mt. iv. 21; x. 2 (3); xvii. 1; Mk. i. 19, 29; iii. 17; v. 37; ix.

2; x. 35, 41; xiii. 3; xiv. 33; Lk. v. 10; vi. 14; viii. 51; ix. 28, 54; Acts i. 13; xii. 2. **2.** *James* (commonly called *the less*), an apostle, son of Alphæus: Mt. x. 3; Mk. iii. 18; Lk. vi. 15; Acts i. 13; apparently identical with Ἰάκωβος ὁ μικρός *James the little* [A. V. *the less*], the son of Mary, Mk. xv. 40 (Mt. xxvii. 56); xvi. 1, wife of Cleophas [i. e. Clopas q. v.] or Alphæus, Jn. xix. 25; see in Ἀλφαῖος, and in Μαρία, 3. **3.** *James*, the brother of our Lord (see ἀδελφός, 1): Mt. xiii. 55; Mk. vi. 3; Gal. i. 19 (where εἰ μή is employed acc. to a usage illustrated under εἰ, III. 8 c. β.); ii. 9, 12; Acts xii. 17; xv. 13; xxi. 18; 1 Co. xv. 7 (?); Jas. i. 1, the leader of the Jewish Christians, and by them surnamed ὁ δίκαιος *the Just*, the overseer (or bishop) of the church at Jerusalem down to the year 62 or 63 (or acc. to Hegesippus in Euseb. h. e. 2, 23 [trans. in B. D. p. 1206] down to 69, which is hardly probable [see Heinichen's note ad loc.]), in which year he suffered martyrdom, Joseph. antt. 20, 9, 1. In opposition to the orthodox opinion [defended in B. D. s. v. James], which identifies this James with James the son of Alphæus, and understands ὁ ἀδελφὸς τοῦ κυρίου to mean his c o u s i n, cf. esp. *Clemen* in Winer's Zeitschr. f. wissensch. Theol. for 1829, p. 351 sqq.; *Blom*, Diss. de τοῖς ἀδελφοῖς . . . τοῦ κυρίου. Lugd. 1839; *Wilib. Grimm* in Ersch u. Gruber's Encycl., Sect. 2, vol. 23 p. 80 sqq.; *Schaff*, Das Verhältniss des Jacobus, Bruders des Herrn, zu Jacobus Alphäi. Berl. 1842 [also his Church Hist. (1882) i. 272 sq.]; *Hilgenfeld*, Galaterbrief etc. p. 138 sqq.; *Hausrath* in Schenkel iii. p. 175 sqq.; [*Sieffert* in Herzog ed. 2, iv. 464 sqq.; and reff. s. v. ἀδελφός, 1 (esp. Bp. Lghtft.)]. **4.** An unknown *James*, father of the apostle Judas [or Jude]: Lk. vi. 16; Acts i. 13, acc. to the opinion of those interpreters who think that not ἀδελφόν but υἱόν must be supplied in the phrase Ἰούδαν Ἰακώβου; see Ἰούδας, 8.

2386 **ἴαμα**, *-τος*, τό, (ἰάομαι); **1.** *a means of healing, remedy, medicine* (Sap. xi. 4; xvi. 9; Hdt. 3, 130; Thuc. 2, 51; Polyb. 7, 14, 2; Plut., Lcian., al.). **2.** *a healing*: plur., 1 Co. xii. 9, 28, 30; (Jer. xl. (xxxiii.) 6, etc.; Plat. legg. 7 p. 790 d.).*

2387 **Ἰαμβρῆς**, ὁ, and ὁ Ἰαννῆς [cf. B. 20 (18)], *Jambres* (for which the Vulg. seems to have read Μαμβρῆς, as in the Babylonian Talmud tract. Menach. c. 9 in the Gemara; cf. *Buxtorf*, Lex. Talm. p. 945 sq. [p. 481 sq. ed. Fischer]), and *Jannes*, two Egyptian magicians who in the presence of Pharaoh imitated the miracles of Aaron in order to destroy his influence with the king: 2 Tim. iii. 8 (cf. Ex. vii. 11 sq.). The author of the Epistle derived their names from the tradition of the Talmudists and the Rabbins, [cf. B.D. art. *Jannes and Jambres*].

These Magi are mentioned not only in the tract of the Babyl. Talmud just referred to, but also in the Targ. of Jonath. on Ex. vii. 11 ; the book Sohar on Num. xxii. 22 ; Numenius περὶ τἀγαθοῦ in Orig. c. Cels. 4, 51 ; Euseb. praep. evang. 9, 8 ; Evang. Nicod. c. 5, and other writ. enumerated by Thilo in his Cod. apocr. p. 552 sq. ; [and Wetstein on 2 Tim. l. c. ; Holtzmann ibid. p. 140 sq.].*

2388   **'Ιαννά**, (L T Tr WH 'Ιανναί) ; *Jannai*, Vulg. *Janne* [Tdf. txt. (cod. Amiat.) *Iannae*], indecl. prop. name of one of the ancestors of Jesus : Lk. iii. 24.*

2389;   **see 2387**   **'Ιαννῆς**, ὁ, see 'Ιαμβρῆς.

2390   **ἰάομαι, -ῶμαι** : [perh. fr. ἰός, *Lob*. Technol. p. 157 sq. ; cf. Vaniček p. 87] ; a depon. verb, whose pres., impf. ἰώμην, fut. ἰάσομαι, and 1 aor. mid. ἰασάμην have an act. signif., but whose pf. pass. ἴαμαι, 1 aor. pass. ἰάθην, and 1 fut. pass. ἰαθήσομαι have a pass. signif. (cf. Krüger § 40 s. v. ; [Veitch s. v. ; B. 52 (46) ; W. § 38, 7 c.]) ; [fr. Hom. down] ; Sept. for רָפָא ; *to heal, cure* : τινά, Lk. iv. 18 R L br. ; v. 17 ; vi. 19 ; ix. 2 [here T WH om. Tr br. the acc.], 11, 42 ; xiv. 4 ; xxii. 51 ; Jn. iv. 47 ; Acts ix. 34 ; x. 38 ; xxviii. 8 ; pass., Mt. viii. 8, 13 ; xv. 28 ; Lk. vii. 7 ; viii. 47 ; xvii. 15 ; Jn. v. 13 [Tdf. ἀσθενῶν] ; and Acts iii. 11 Rec. ; τινὰ ἀπό τινος, *to cure* (i. e. by curing to free) one of [lit. *from* ; cf. B. 322 (277)] a disease : pass., Mk. v. 29 ; Lk. vi. 18 (17). trop. *to make whole* i. e. to free from errors and sins, *to bring about* (one's) *salvation* : Mt. xiii. 15 ; Jn. xii. 40 ; Acts xxviii. 27, (fr. Is. vi. 10) ; pass., 1 Pet. ii. 24 ; Jas. v. 16 ; in fig. discourse, in pass. : Heb. xii. 13.*

2391   **'Ιαρέδ** (T WH 'Ιάρετ, Lchm. 'Ιάρεθ ; [on the accent in codd. see *Tdf*. Proleg. p. 103]), ὁ, (Heb. יֶרֶד descent), *Jared*, indecl. prop. name ('Ιαράδης ['Ιαρέδες, ed. Bekk.] in Joseph. antt. 1, 2, 2), the father of Enoch (Gen. v. 15, 18 ; 1 Chr. i. 2 [here A. V. *Jered*]) : Lk. iii. 37.*

2392   **ἴασις, -εως, ἡ**, *a healing, cure* : Lk. xiii. 32 ; Acts iv. 22, 30. (Prov. iii. 8 ; iv. 22 ; [Archil.], Hippocr., Soph., Plat., Lcian., al.) *

2393   **ἴασπις, -ιδος, ἡ**, [fr. Plato down], *jasper* ; a precious stone of divers colors (for some are purple, others blue, others green, and others of the color of brass ; Plin. h. n. 37, 37 (8)) : Rev. iv. 3 ; xxi. 11, 18 sq. [But many think (questionably) the *diamond* to be meant here ; others the *precious opal* ; see *Riehm*, HWB. s. v. Edelsteine, 8 and 10 ; B. D. s. v. Jasper ; cf. 'Bible Educator' ii. 352.] *

2394   **'Ιάσων, -ονος, ὁ**, *Jason*, a Thessalonian, Paul's host : Acts xvii. 5–7, 9 ; whether he is the same who is mentioned in Ro. xvi. 21 as a kinsman of Paul is uncertain.*

2395   **ἰατρός, -οῦ, ὁ**, (ἰάομαι), [fr. Hom. down], *a physician* : Mt. ix. 12 ; Mk. ii. 17 ; v. 26 ; Lk. v. 31 ; viii. 43 [here WH om. Tr mrg. br. the cl.] ; Col. iv. 14 ; ἰατρέ, θεράπευσον σεαυτόν, a proverb, applied to Christ in this sense : ' come forth from your lowly and mean condition and create for yourself authority and influence by performing miracles among us also, that we may see that you are what you profess to be,' Lk. iv. 23.*

2396   **ἴδε** [so occasionally Grsb. and Rec.bez els ; e. g. Gal. v. 2 ; Ro. xi. 22] and (later) ἴδε (ἴδε ἀττικῶς ὡς τὸ εἰπέ, λαβέ, εὑρέ · ἴδε ἑλληνικῶς, Moeris [p. 193 ed. Pierson] ;

cf. W. § 6, 1 a. ; [B. 62 (54)]), impv. fr. εἶδον, q. v. ; [fr. Hom. down]. In so far as it retains the force of an imperative it is illustrated under εἴδω, I. 1 e. and 3. But in most places in the N. T. it stands out of construction like an interjection, even when many are addressed, [cf. B. 70 (61) ; and esp. 139 (121 sq.)] ; Lat. *en, ecce* ; *see ! behold ! lo !*   **a.** at the beginning of sentences : as the utterance of one who wishes that something should not be neglected by another, Mt. xxvi. 65 ; Mk. ii. 24 ; xi. 21 ; xiii. 1 ; Jn. v. 14 ; xviii. 21 ; Ro. ii. 17 Rec. ; equiv. to Germ. *sieh' doch* [*see, pray* ; *yet see*], Jn. xi. 36 ; xvi. 29 ; xix. 4 ; Gal. v. 2 ; or of one who brings forward something new and unexpected, Jn. vii. 26 ; xi. 3 ; xii. 19 ; or of one pointing out or showing, Germ. *hier ist, da ist, dieses ist* : ἴδε ὁ τόπος (French, *voici le lieu*), Mk. xvi. 6 ; add, Mk. iii. 34 (L Tr mrg. ἰδού) ; Jn. i. 29, 36, 47 (48) ; xix. 5 [T Tr WH ἰδού], 14, 26 sq. (where some ἰδού) ; where we [might] use simply *here*, Mt. xxv. 25 ; with adverbs of place : ἴδε [R G L ἰδού] ὧδε ὁ Χριστός, ἴδε [R G ἰδού] ἐκεῖ, Mk. xiii. 21.   **b.** inserted into the midst of a sentence, in such a way that the words which precede it serve to render the more evident the strangeness of what follows : Mt. xxv. 20, 22 ; Jn. iii. 26.

2397   **ἰδέα, -ας, ἡ**, (fr. εἶδον, ἰδεῖν), *form, external appearance* ; *aspect, look* : Mt. xxviii. 3 (T Tr WH εἰδέα, q. v.), cf. *Alberti*, Observv. ad loc. ; [*Tdf*. Proleg. p. 81]. (Grk. writ. fr. Pind. and Hdt. down ; 2 Macc. iii. 16 ; for דְּמוּת Gen. v. 3.) [Cf. Schmidt ch. 182, 3.] *

2398   **ἴδιος, -α, -ον**, (in prof. auth. [esp. Attic] also of two term.), [fr. Hom. down] ;   **1.** *pertaining to one's self, one's own* ; used   **a.** univ. of *what is one's own* as opp. to *belonging to another* : τὰ ἴδια πρόβατα, Jn. x. 3 sq. 12 ; τὰ ἱμάτια τὰ ἴδια, Mk. xv. 20 R G Tr (for which T τὰ ἰδ. ἱμ. αὐτοῦ, L WH τὰ ἱμ. αὐτοῦ) ; τὸ ἴδιον (for his own use) κτῆνος, Lk. x. 34 ; διὰ τοῦ ἰδίου αἵματος, Heb. ix. 12 ; xiii. 12, (ἰδίῳ αἵματι, 4 Macc. vii. 8) ; τὸ ἴδιον μίσθωμα, which he had hired for himself (opp. to ἡ ξενία [q. v.], 23), Acts xxviii. 30 ; add, Jn. v. 43 ; vii. 18 ; Acts iii. 12 ; xiii. 36 ; Ro. xi. 24 ; xiv. 4 sq. ; 1 Co. iii. 8 (ἴδιον κόπον) ; vi. 18 ; vii. 4, 37 ; ix. 7 ; xi. 21 ; Gal. vi. 5 ; 1 Tim. iii. 4, 12 ; v. 4 ; 2 Tim. i. 9 ; iv. 3 ; πράσσειν τὰ ἴδια, to do one's own business (and not intermeddle with the affairs of others), 1 Th. iv. 11 ; ἰδία ἐπίλυσις, an interpretation which one thinks out for himself, opp. to that which the Holy Spirit teaches, 2 Pet. i. 20 [see γίνομαι, 5 e. a.] ; τὴν ἰδίαν δικαιοσύνην, which one imagines is his due, opp. to δικαιοσύνη θεοῦ, awarded by God, Ro. x. 3 ; ἰδία ἐπιθυμία, opp. to divine prompting, Jas. i. 14 ; κατὰ τὰς ἰδίας ἐπιθυμίας, opp. to God's requirements, 2 Tim. iv. 3 ; with the possess. pron. αὐτῶν added [B. 118 (103) ; cf. W. 154 (146)], 2 Pet. iii. 3 ; ἴδιος αὐτῶν προφήτης, Tit. i. 12 ; with αὐτοῦ added, Mk. xv. 20 Tdf. (see above) ; τὰ ἴδια [cf. B. § 127, 24], those things in which one differs from others, his nature and personal character,—in the phrase ἐκ τῶν ἰδίων λαλεῖν, Jn. viii. 44 ; cf. the fig. τὰ ἴδια τοῦ σώματος, 2 Co. v. 10 L mrg. (cf. Tr mrg.) ; see διά, A. I. 2] ; ἴδιος, *my own* : ταῖς ἰδίαις χερσί (unassisted by others), 1 Co. iv.

12; *thine own*: ἐν τῷ ἰδίῳ ὀφθαλμῷ, Lk. vi. 41. **b.** of *what pertains to one's property, family, dwelling, country,* etc.; of property, οὐδὲ εἷς τι τῶν ὑπαρχόντων αὐτῷ ἔλεγεν ἴδιον εἶναι, Acts iv. 32; τὰ ἴδια, *res nostrae*, our own things, i. e. house, family, property, Lk. xviii. 28 L T Tr WH [cf. B. § 127, 24; W. 592 (551)]; τῇ ἰδίᾳ γενεᾷ, *in his own generation*, i. e. in the age in which he lived, Acts xiii. 36; ἡ ἰδία πόλις, the city of which one is a citizen or inhabitant, Lk. ii. 3 [R G Tr mrg.]; Mt. ix. 1; τῇ ἰδίᾳ διαλέκτῳ, in their native tongue, Acts i. 19 [WH om. Tr br. ἰδίᾳ]; ii. 6, 8; ἡ ἰδία δεισιδαιμονία, their own (national) religion, Acts xxv. 19; οἱ ἴδιοι, *one's own* people (Germ. *die Angehörigen*), one's fellow-countrymen, associates, Jn. i. 11, cf. 2 Macc. xii. 22; one's household, persons belonging to the house, family, or company, Jn. xiii. 1; Acts iv. 23; xxiv. 23; 1 Tim. v. 8; εἰς τὰ ἴδια (Germ. *in die Heimat*), to one's native land, home, Jn. i. 11 (meaning here, the land of Israel); xvi. 32; xix. 27, (3 Macc. vi. 27; 1 Esdr. v. 46 (47); for אֶל־בֵּיתוֹ, Esth. v. 10; vi. 12); ὁ ἴδιος ἀνήρ, a husband, 1 Co. vii. 2 [B. 117 (102) note; cf. W. 154 (146)]; plur., Eph. v. 22; Tit. ii. 5; 1 Pet. iii. 1, 5; Eph. v. 24 R G; Col. iii. 18 R; οἱ ἴδιοι δεσπόται (of slaves), Tit. ii. 9. of *a person who may be said to belong to one, above all others*: υἱός, Ro. viii. 32; πατήρ, Jn. v. 18; μαθηταί, Mk. iv. 34 T WH Tr mrg. **c.** *harmonizing with,* or *suitable* or *assigned to,* one's nature, character, aims, acts; *appropriate*: τῇ ἰδίᾳ ἐξουσίᾳ, Acts i. 7; τὸν ἴδιον μισθόν, due reward, 1 Co. iii. 8; τὸ ἴδιον σῶμα, 1 Co. xv. 38; κατὰ τὴν ἰδίαν δύναμιν, Mt. xxv. 15; ἐν τῷ ἰδίῳ τάγματι, 1 Co. xv. 23; τὸ ἴδιον οἰκητήριον, Jude 6; εἰς τὸν τόπον τὸν ἴδιον, to the abode after death assigned by God to one acc. to his deeds, Acts i. 25 (Ignat. ad Magnes. 5; *Baal Turim* on Num. xxiv. 25 Balaam ivit *in locum suum,* i. e. in Gehennam; see τόπος, 1 *a.* fin.); καιρῷ ἰδίῳ, at a time suitable to the matter in hand [A. V. *in due season*], Gal. vi. 9; plur., 1 Tim. ii. 6; vi. 15; Tit. i. 3. **d.** By a usage foreign to the earlier Greeks, but found in the church Fathers and the Byzant. writ. (see W. § 22, 7; cf. Fritzsche on Rom. ii. p. 208 sq.; [B. 117 sq. (103)]), it takes the place of the poss. pron. αὐτοῦ: Mt. xxii. 5; xxv. 14; Jn. i. 41 (42), (Sap. x. 1). **2.** *private* (in class. Grk. opp. to δημόσιος, κοινός): ἰδίᾳ [cf. W. 591 (549) note] adv. *severally, separately,* 1 Co. xii. 11 (often in Grk. writ.). κατ' ἰδίαν (sc. χώραν), **a.** *apart*: Mt. xiv. 13; xvii. 19; xx. 17; xxiv. 3; Mk. vi. 31 sq.; vii. 33; ix. 2, 28; xiii. 3; Lk. ix. 10; x. 23; Acts xxiii. 19, (Polyb. 4, 84, 8); with μόνος added, Mk. ix. 2; **β.** *in private, privately*: Mk. iv. 34; Gal. ii. 2, (Diod. 1, 21, opp. to κοινῇ, 2 Macc. iv. 5; Ignat. ad Smyrn. 7, 2). The word is not found in Rev.

ἰδιώτης, -ου, ὁ, (ἴδιος), very com. in Grk. writ. fr. Hdt. down; prop. *a private person,* opp. to a magistrate, ruler, king; but the noun has many other meanings also, each one of which is understood from its antithesis, as e. g. *a common soldier,* as opp. to a military officer; *a writer of prose,* as opp. to a poet. In the N. T. *an unlearned, illiterate, man,* opp. to the learned, the educated: Acts iv. 13; as often in class. Grk., *unskilled in any art*: in

eloquence (Ísocr. p. 43 a.), with dat. of respect, τῷ λόγῳ, 2 Co. xi. 6 [A. V. *rude in speech*]; a Christian who is *not a prophet,* 1 Co. xiv. 24; *destitute of the 'gift of tongues,'* ibid. 16, 23. [Cf. Trench § lxxix.]*

ἰδού, a demonstrative particle, [in Grk. writ. fr. Soph. down], found in the N. T. esp. in the Gospels of Matthew and of Luke, used very often in imitation of the Hebr. הִנֵּה, and giving a peculiar vivacity to the style by bidding the reader or hearer to attend to what is said: *behold! see! lo!* It is inserted in the discourse after a gen. absol., Mt. i. 20; ii. 1, 13; ix. 18; xii. 46; xvii. 5; xxvi. 47; xxviii. 11. καὶ ἰδού is used, when at the close of a narrative something new is introduced, Mt. ii. 9; iii. 16; iv. 11; viii. 2, 24, 29, 32, 34; ix. 2 sq. 20; xii. 10; xv. 22; xvii. 3; xix. 16; xxvi. 51; xxvii. 51; xxviii. 2, 7; Lk. i. 20, 31, 36; ii. 9 [R G L Tr br.], 25; ix. 30, 38 sq.; x. 25; xiv. 2; xxiv. 13; Acts xii. 7; xvi. 1; when a thing is specified which is unexpected yet sure, 2 Co. vi. 9 (καὶ ἰδοὺ ζῶμεν, and nevertheless we live), cf. Mt. vii. 4; when a thing is specified which seems impossible and yet occurs, Lk. xi. 41; Acts xxvii. 24. The simple ἰδού is the exclamation of one pointing out something, Mt. xi. 2, 47 [WH here in mrg. only]; xiii. 3; xxiv. 26; xxviii. 32; Lk. ii. 34; and calling attention, Mk. xv. 35 [T Tr WH ἴδε]; Lk. xxii. 10; Jn. iv. 35; 1 Co. xv. 51; 2 Co. v. 17; Jas. v. 9; Jude 14; Rev. i. 7; ix. 12; xi. 14; xvi. 15; xxii. 7 [Rec.]; in other places it is i. q. *observe* or *consider*: Mt. x. 16; xi. 8; xix. 27; xx. 18; xxii. 4; Mk. x. 28, 33; xiv. 41; Lk. ii. 48; vii. 25; xviii. 28, 31, etc.; also καὶ ἰδού, Mt. xxviii. 20; Lk. xiii. 30; ἰδοὺ γάρ, Lk. i. 44, 48; ii. 10; vi. 23; xvii. 21; Acts ix. 11; 2 Co. vii. 11; ἰδού where examples are adduced: Jas. iii. 4 sq.; v. 4, 7, 11; for the Hebr. הִנְנִי, so that it includes the copula: Lk. i. 38; i. q. *here I am*: Acts ix. 10; Heb. ii. 13. ἰδού is inserted in the midst of a speech, Mt. xxiii. 34 [here WH mrg. ἴδου (see the Comm.)]; Lk. xiii. 16; Acts ii. 7; xiii. 11; xx. 22, 25. The passages of the O. T. containing the particle which are quoted in the New are these: Mt. i. 23; xi. 10; xii. 18; xxi. 5; Mk. i. 2; Lk. vii. 27; Jn. xii. 15; Ro. ix. 33; Heb. ii. 13; viii. 8; x. 7, 9; 1 Pet. ii. 6. Like the Hebr. הִנֵּה, ἰδού and καὶ ἰδού stand before a nominative which is not followed by a finite verb, in such a way as to include the copula or predicate [cf. B. 139 (121 sq.)]: e. g. *was heard,* Mt. iii. 17; *is, is* or *was here, exists,* etc., Mt. xii. 10 L T Tr WH, 41; Mk. xiii. 21 R G L; Lk. v. 12, 18; vii. 37; xi. 31; xiii. 11 [R G add ἦν]; xvii. 21; xix. 2, 20; xxii. 38, 47; xxiii. 50; Jn. xix. 26 [Rec., 27 R G]; Acts viii. 27, 36; 2 Co. vi. 2; Rev. vi. 2, 5, 8; vii. 9 [not L]; xii. 3; xxi. 14; xix. 11; xxi. 5; *is approaching,* Mt. xxv. 6 G L T Tr WH (Rec. adds ἔρχεται); but also in such a way as to have simply a demonstrative force: Mt. xi. 19; Lk. vii. 34.

Ἰδουμαία, -ας, ἡ, *Idumæa,* the name of a region between southern Palestine and Arabia Petræa, inhabited by Esau or Edom (Gen. xxxvi. 30) and his posterity (the Edomites), (Josh. xv. 1, 21; xi. 17; xii. 7). The Edomites were first subjugated by David; but after his death they disputed Solomon's authority and in the reign of Joram recovered their liberty, which they maintained, transmitting from generation to generation their hatred of Israel, until they were conquered again by Hyrcanus and subjected to the government of the Jews: Mk. iii. 8. [For details of boundary and history, see *Bertheau* in Schenkel and *Porter* in B. D. s. v. Edom; also the latter in Kitto's Cycl. s. v. Idumæa.]*

2402 ἱδρώς, -ῶτος, ὁ, [allied w. Lat. sudor, Eng. sweat; Curtius § 283; fr. Hom. down], *sweat*: Lk. xxii. 44 [L br. WH reject the pass.; (Tr accents ἱδρῶς, yet cf. Chandler § 667)].*

2403 Ἰεζάβελ ([so G T WH, L Ἰεζ.; Tr -βελ]; Rec. Ἰεζαβήλ), ἡ, (אִיזֶבֶל ['perh. intact, chaste; cf. Agnes' (Gesenius)]), *Jezebel* [mod. *Isabel*], wife of Ahab ([c.] B. C. 917–897; 1 K. xvi. 29), an impious and cruel queen, who protected idolatry and persecuted the prophets (1 K. xvi. 31–2 K. ix. 30); in Rev. ii. 20 i. q. *a second Jezebel*, the symbolic name of a woman who pretended to be a prophetess, and who, addicted to antinomianism, claimed for Christians the liberty of eating things sacrificed to idols, Rev. ii. 20.*

2404 Ἱεράπολις [WH Ἱερὰ Πόλις; cf. B. 74; Lob. ad Phryn. 604 sq.], -εως, ἡ, *Hierapolis*, a city of Greater Phrygia, near the river Maeander [or rather, near the Lycus a few miles above its junction with the Maeander], not far from Colossæ and Laodicea, now *Pambuck Kulasi*, [for reff. see Bp. Lghtft. on Col. p. 1 sq.; B. D. Am. ed. s. v.]: Col. iv. 13.*

2405 ἱερατεία [WH -τία; cf. I, ι], -ας, ἡ, (ἱερατεύω), *the priesthood*, *the office of priest*: Lk. i. 9; Heb. vii. 5. (Sept. for כְּהֻנָּה; Aristot. pol. 7, 8; Dion. Hal.; *Boeckh*, Inscrr. ii. pp. 127, 23; 363, 27.)*

2406 ἱεράτευμα, -τος, τό, (ἱερατεύω), [*priesthood* i. e.]   **a.** *the office of priest.*   **b.** *the order* or *body of priests* (see ἀδελφότης, αἰχμαλωσία, διασπορά, θεραπεία); so Christians are called, because they have access to God and offer not external but 'spiritual' (πνευματικά) sacrifices: 1 Pet. ii. 5; also ἱεράτ. βασίλειον, ib. 9 (after Ex. xix. 6 Sept.), priests of k i n g l y rank, i. e. exalted to a moral rank and freedom which exempts them from the control of every one but God and Christ. ([Ex. xxiii. 22, etc.; 2 Macc. ii. 17]; not found in prof. auth.)*

2407 ἱερατεύω; (fr. ἱεράομαι and the verbal adj. ἱερατός, though this adj. does not occur); *to be priest*, *discharge the priest's office*, *be busied in sacred duties*: Lk. i. 8. (Joseph. antt. 3, 8, 1; Hdian. 5, 6, 6 [3 ed. Bekk.]; Pausan., Heliod., Inscrr. [see L. and S.]; Sept. for כָּהַן.)*

see 2410 Ἱεριχώ, see Ἱεριχώ.

2408 Ἱερεμίας [WH Ἱερ. (see their Intr. § 408); so Rec.** in Mt. xxvii. 9], -ου [B. 17 (16), 8], ὁ, (יִרְמְיָה or יִרְמְיָהוּ, i. q. יָהּ יִרְמֶה 'Jehovah casts forth' (his enemies?), or 'Jehovah hurls' (his thunderbolts?); cf. *Bleek*, Einl. in das A. T. § 206 p. 469, [cf. B. D. s. v. Jeremiah]), *Jeremiah* [A. V. also *Jeremias*, *Jeremy*], a famous Hebrew prophet, who prophesied from [c] B. C. 627 until the destruction of Jerusalem [B. C. 586]. He afterwards departed into Egypt, where he appears to have died; [cf.

B. D. s. v. Jeremiah, I. 6]: Mt. ii. 17; xvi. 14; xxvii. 9 (in the last pass. his name is given by mistake, for the words quoted are found in Zech. xi. 12 sq.; [cf. Prof. *Brown* in Journ. of Soc. for Bibl. Lit. and Exeg. for Dec. 1882, p. 101 sqq.; *Toy*, Quot. in N. T. p. 68 sqq.; for a history of attempted explanations, see Dr. *Jas. Morison*, Com. on Mt. l. c.]).*

2409 ἱερεύς, -έως, ὁ, (ἱερός), [fr. Hom. down], Hebr. כֹּהֵן, *a priest*; one who offers sacrifices and in general is busied with sacred rites;   **a.** prop., of the priests of the Gentiles, Acts xiv. 13; of the priests of the Jews, Mt. viii. 4; xii. 4 sq.; Mk. i. 44; [ii. 26]; Lk. i. 5; v. 14; Jn. i. 19; Heb. vii. [14 L T Tr WH], 20 (21); viii. 4, etc.; of *the high-priest*, Acts v. 24 R G (Ex. xxxv. 18; 1 K. i. 8; 1 Macc. xv. 1; Joseph. antt. 6, 12, 1); and in the same sense Christ is called ἱερεύς in Heb. v. 6 (fr. Ps. cix. (cx.) 4); Heb. vii. 17; also ἱερεὺς μέγας, Heb. x. 21 (see ἀρχιερεύς, 3) [al. take the adj. here not as blending with ἱερ. into a technical or official appellation, but as descriptive, *great*; cf. iv. 14].   **b.** metaph. of Christians, because, purified by the blood of Christ and brought into close intercourse with God, they devote their life to him alone (and to Christ): Rev. i. 6; v. 10; xx. 6, cf. i. 5; v. 9.

2410 Ἱεριχώ (Tdf. Ἱερειχώ [see his Proleg. p. 85; *WH*. App. p. 155, and s. v. ει, ι; WH Ἱερ. see their Intr. § 408; on its a c c e n t in codd. cf. *Tdf*. Proleg. p. 103]), ἡ, indecl. (on its declens. in other writ. cf. W. § 10, 2; in Strabo Ἱερικούς -οῦντος; Ἱεριχοῦς, -οῦντος in Joseph., cf. W. l. c.; Hebr. יְרִיחוֹ, fr. רִיחַ to smell, so called from its fertility in aromatics), *Jericho*, a noted city, abounding in balsam [i. e. perh. the opobalsamum; cf. *Tristram*, Nat. Hist. etc. p. 337; B. D. s. v. Balm], honey, cyprus [prob. Arab. "el-henna"; cf. *Tristram* u. s., s. v. Camphire], myrobalanus [Arab. "zukkum"], roses, and other fragrant productions. It was situated not far from the northern shore of the Dead Sea, in the tribe of Benjamin, between the city of Jerusalem and the river Jordan, 150 stadia from the former and 60 from the latter. Joseph. b. j. 4, 8, 3 calls its territory θεῖον χωρίον. It is mentioned in the N. T. in Mt. xx. 29; Mk. x. 46; Lk. x. 30; xviii. 35; xix. 1; Heb. xi. 30. As balsam was exported thence to other countries, we read Lk. xix. 2 that τελῶναι were stationed there, with an ἀρχιτελώνης, for the purpose of collecting the revenues. For a fuller account of the city see *Win*. RWB. s. v.; *Arnold* in Herzog vi. p. 494 sq.; *Furrer* in Schenkel iii. 209 sq.; Keim iii. 17 sq. [Eng. trans. v. 21 sq.; BB.DD. s. v.; cf. also *Robinson*, Researches etc. i. 547 sqq.].*

see 1494 ἱερόθυτος, -ον, (fr. ἱερός and θύω, cf. εἰδωλόθυτος), *sacrificed*, *offered in sacrifice*, to the gods; as in Plut. symp. 8, 8, 3 init., used of the *flesh of animals offered in sacrifice*: 1 Co. x. 28 L txt. T Tr WH. On the use of the word in Grk. writ. cf. *Lob*. ad Phryn. p. 159.*

2411 ἱερόν, -οῦ, τό, (neut. of the adj. ἱερός, -ά, -όν; cf. τὸ ἅγιον), [fr. Hdt. on], *a sacred place*, *temple*: of the temple of Artemis at Ephesus, Acts xix. 27; of the temple at Jerusalem twice in the Sept., Ezek. xlv. 19; 1 Chr.

xxix. 4; more freq. in the O. T. Apocr.; in the N. T. often in the Gospels and Acts; once elsewhere, viz. 1 Co. ix. 13. τὸ ἱερόν and ὁ ναός differ, in that the former designates the whole compass of the sacred enclosure, embracing the entire aggregate of buildings, balconies, porticos, courts (viz. that of the men or Israelites, that of the women, that of the priests), belonging to the temple; the latter designates the sacred edifice properly so called, consisting of two parts, the 'sanctuary' or 'Holy place' (which no one except the priests was allowed to enter), and the 'Holy of holies' or 'most holy place' (see ἅγιος, 1 a.) (which was entered only on the great day of atonement by the high priest alone); [cf. Trench, Syn. § iii.]. ἱερόν is employed in the N. T. either explicitly of the whole temple, Mt. xii. 6; xxiv. 1; Mk. xiii. 3; Lk. xxi. 5; xxii. 52; Acts iv. 1; xxiv. 6; xxv. 8; 1 Co. ix. 13, etc.; or so that certain definite parts of it must be thought of, as the courts, esp. where Jesus or the apostles are said to have gone up, or entered, 'into the temple,' to have taught or encountered adversaries, and the like, 'in the temple,' Mt. xxi. 12, 14; xxvi. 55; Mk. xiv. 49; Lk. xix. 47; xxi. 37; xxii. 53; xxiv. 53; Jn. v. 14; vii. 14, 28; viii. 20; xviii. 20; Acts iii. 2; v. 20; xxi. 26, etc.; of the courts and sanctuary, Mt. xii. 5; of the court of the Gentiles, out of which Jesus drove the buyers and sellers and money-changers, Mt. xxi. 12; Mk. xi. 15; Lk. xix. 45; Jn. ii. 14 sq.; of the court of the women, Lk. ii. 37; of any portico or apartment, Lk. ii. 46, cf. Jn. x. 23. On the phrase τὸ πτερύγιον τοῦ ἱεροῦ see πτερύγιον, 2.

2412   ἱεροπρεπής, -ές, (fr. ἱερός, and πρέπει it is becoming), *befitting men, places, actions* or *things sacred to God; reverent*: Tit. ii. 3. (4 Macc. ix. 25; xi. 19; Plat., Philo, Joseph., Lcian., al.) [Cf. Trench § xcii. sub fin.]*

2413   ἱερός, -ά, -όν, [its primary sense is thought to be *mighty*; cf. Curtius § 614; Vaniček p. 88; yet see Schmidt u. i.; fr. Hom. down], *sacred, consecrated to the deity, pertaining to God*: ἱερὰ γράμματα, *sacred Scriptures*, because inspired by God, treating of divine things and therefore to be devoutly revered, 2 Tim. iii. 15 (Joseph. antt. prooem. 3; [10, 10, 4 fin.]; b. j. 6, 5, 4; c. Ap. 1, [10, 3; 18, 6]; 26, 1; ἱεραὶ βίβλοι, antt. 2, 16, 5; [c. Ap. 1, 1; 23, 4], etc.; οὐκ ἐνετράφης οὐδὲ ἐνησκήθης τοῖς ἱεροῖς γράμμασι, Philo, leg. ad Gaium § 29, ed. Mang. ii. p. 574); [κήρυγμα, Mk. xvi. WH in (rejected) 'Shorter Conclusion']; neut. plur. as subst. τὰ ἱερά, *the holy things*, those which pertain to the worship of God in the temple, 1 Co. ix. 13, cf. ἐργάζομαι, 2 a. [See reff. s. v. ἅγιος, fin.; esp. Schmidt ch. 181.]*

2414   Ἱεροσόλυμα [WH Ἱερ., see their Intr. § 408], -ων, τά, (the invariable form in Mk. and Jn., almost everywhere in Mt. and Joseph. [c. Ap. 1, 22, 13, etc.; Philo, leg. ad Gaium § 36; (cf. Polyb. 16, 39, 4); al.]), and Ἱερουσαλήμ [WH Ἱερ. (see ref. u. s.)], ἡ, indecl., (the invariable form in the Sept. [Josh. x. 1, etc.; Philo de somn. ii. 39 init.; so Aristot. in Joseph. c. Ap. 1, 22, 7 (where see Müller)]; in the N. T. where a certain sacred emphasis, so to speak, resides in the very name, as Gal. iv. 25 sq. [see Bp. Lghtft. ad loc.]; Heb. xii. 22; Rev iii. 12; xxi. 2, 10;

thus in direct address: Mt. xxiii. 37; Lk. xiii. 34; both forms are used promiscuously [yet with a marked preference for the indeclinable form] in the O. T. Apocr., and in the writ. of Luke and of Paul; [cf. Tdf. Proleg. p. 119; WH. App. p. 160]. Whether there is also a third and unusual form Ἱεροσόλυμα, -ης, ἡ, in Mt. ii. 3; iii. 5, is extremely doubtful; for in the phrase ἐξεπορεύετο . . . Ἱεροσόλυμα, iii. 5, the noun can be taken as a neut. plur. with a sing. verb, cf. W. § 58, 3 a.; and in the former passage, ii. 3, the unusual coupling of the fem. πᾶσα with the neut. plur. Ἱεροσόλυμα is easily explained by the supposition that the appellative idea, ἡ πόλις, was in the writer's mind; see Fritzsche and Bleek ad loc.; cf. B. 18 (16); [yet see Pape, Eigennamen, s. v.]. Hebr. יְרוּשָׁלַם and יְרוּשָׁלַיִם, Chald. יְרוּשְׁלֶם, Syr. ܐܘܪܫܠܡ. Many suppose that the Hebr. name is composed of יְרוּשׁ possession, and שָׁלֵם, so that it signifies *tranquil possession, habitation of peace*; but the matter is very uncertain and conjectures vary; cf. Gesenius, Thes. ii. p. 628 sq.; [B. D. s. v.]; on the earlier name of the city see below in Σαλήμ; Lat. *Hierosolyma, -orum*, also [Vulg. e. g. codd. Amiat. and Fuld. Mt. xxiii. 37; but esp.] in the ch. Fathers *Hierusalem*, but the form *Hierosolyma, -ae* is uncertain [yet see even Old Lat. codd. in Mt. ii. 1, 3]),—*Jerusalem* [A. V. *Hierusalem* and *Ierusalem*], the capital of Palestine, situated nearly in the centre of the country, on the confines of the tribes of Benjamin and Judah, in a region so elevated that ἀναβαίνειν, עָלָה, *to go up*, fitly describes the approach to it from any quarter. The name is used in the N. T. **1.** to denote, either the city itself, Mt. ii. 1; Mk. iii. 8; Jn. i. 19, etc.; or its inhabitants, Mt. ii. 3; iii. 5; xxiii. 37; Lk. xiii. 34. **2.** ἡ νῦν Ἱερουσ. [*the Jerusalem that now is*], with its present religious institutions, i. e. the Mosaic system, so designated from its primary external location, Gal. iv. 25, with which is contrasted ἡ ἄνω Ἱερ. (after the rabbin. phrase יְרוּשְׁלַיִם שֶׁל מַעֲלָה, *Jerusalem that is above*, i. e. existing in heaven, according to the pattern of which the earthly Jerusalem יְרוּשְׁלַיִם שֶׁל מַטָּה was supposed to be built [cf. Schöttgen, Horae Hebr. i. 1207 sqq.]), i. e. metaph. *the City of God founded by Christ*, now wearing the form of *the church*, but after Christ's return to put on the form of the perfected Messianic kingdom, Gal. iv. 26; Ἱερουσ. ἐπουράνιος, *the heavenly Jerusalem*, i. e. the heavenly abode of God, Christ, the angels, beatified men (as well the saints of the O. T. as Christians), and as citizens of which true Christians are to be regarded while still living on earth, Heb. xii. 22; ἡ καινὴ Ἱερ. in the visions of John 'the Revelator,' *the new Jerusalem*, a splendid visible city to be let down from heaven after the renovation of the world, the future abode of the blessed: Rev. iii. 12; xxi. 2, 10.

Ἱεροσολυμίτης [Tdf. -μείτης, see ει, ι; WH Ἱεροσολυμείτης, see their Intr. § 408], -ου, ὁ, *a citizen or inhabitant of Jerusalem*: Mk. i. 5; Jn. vii. 25. [Joseph. antt. 5, 1, 17, etc.]*   **2415**

ἱερο-συλέω, -ῶ; (ἱερόσυλος, q. v.); *to commit sacrilege,*   **2416** to rob a temple: Ro. ii. 22, where the meaning is, 'thou who abhorrest idols and their contamination, dost yet not hesitate to plunder their shrines'; cf. Fritzsche [and Delitzsch] ad loc. (Arstph., Plat., Dem., al.)*

2417 ἱερόσυλος, -ον, (fr. ἱερόν and συλάω), guilty of sacrilege: Acts xix. 37 [A. V. robbers of temples; cf. Bp. Lghtft. in The Contemp. Rev. for 1878, p. 294 sq.]. (2 Macc. iv. 42; Arstph., Xen., Plat., Polyb., Diod., al.)*

2418 ἱερουργέω, -ῶ; (fr. ἱερουργός, and this fr. ἱερός and ΕΡΓΩ); to be busied with sacred things; to perform sacred rites, (Philo, Hdian.); used esp. of persons sacrificing (Joseph. antt. 7, 13, 4, etc.); trans. to minister in the manner of a priest, minister in priestly service: τὸν νόμον, of those who defend the sanctity of the law by undergoing a violent death, 4 Macc. vii. 8; τὸ εὐαγγέλιον, of the preaching of the gospel, Ro. xv. 16 (where Fritzsche treats of the word fully; [cf. W. 222 sq. (209)]).*

2419 Ἱερουσαλήμ, see Ἱεροσόλυμα.

2420 ἱερωσύνη [on the ω see ἀγαθωσύνη, init.], -ης, ἡ, (ἱερός), priesthood, the priestly office: Heb. vii. 11 sq. 14 R G, 24. (Sir. xlv. 24; 1 Esdr. v. 38; 1 Macc. ii. 54; iii. 49; 4 Macc. v. 34; Hdt., Plat., Dem., Diod., Joseph., Plut., Hdian., al.)*

2421 Ἰεσσαί (Ἰεσσαῖος in Joseph.), ὁ, (יִשַׁי [cf. B. D. Am. ed. s. v.]), Jesse, the father of David the king (1 S. xvi. 1, 10; xvii. 12 Alex.; xx. 27): Mt. i. 5 sq.; Lk. iii. 32; Acts xiii. 22; Ro. xv. 12.*

2422 Ἰεφθάε (Ἰεφθής, -οῦ, in Joseph.), ὁ, (יִפְתָּח [fut. 3 sing. masc.], fr. פָּתַח to open), Jephthah, the son of Gilead [cf. B. D. Am. ed. s. v. Gilead, 4], and a judge of Israel (Judg. xi. sq.): Heb. xi. 32.*

2423 Ἰεχονίας, -ου, ὁ, (יְהוֹיָכִין Jehoiakin, i. e. whom Jehovah appointed; Sept. Ἰωαχίν [(?) see B. D. Am. ed. s. v. Jehoiachin]), Jechoniah, king of Judah, carried off into exile by Nebuchadnezzar [c.] B. C. 600 after a reign of three months, 2 K. xxiv. 8–17; 2 Chr. xxxvi. 9 sq.; Jer. lii. 31. He is mentioned Mt. i. 11 sq. But he was not, as is there stated, the son of Josiah, but of Jehoiakim; nor had he 'brethren,' but his father had. Accordingly in the Evangelist's genealogy the names יְהוֹיָקִים and יְהוֹיָכִין have been confounded; [cf. B. D. u. s., and reff. there].*

2424 Ἰησοῦς, -οῦ, dat. -οῦ, acc. -οῦν, voc. -οῦ, [W. § 10, 1], ὁ, Jesus (יְהוֹשֻׁעַ and acc. to a later form יֵשׁוּעַ, Syr. ܝܶܫܽܘܥ, i. e. whose help is Jehovah; Germ. Gotthilf; but later writ. gave the name the force of יְשׁוּעָה, see Mt. i. 21, cf. Sir. xlvi. 1 Ἰησοῦς ὃς ἐγένετο κατὰ τὸ ὄνομα αὐτοῦ μέγας ἐπὶ σωτηρίᾳ ἐκλεκτῶν αὐτοῦ, of Joshua, the successor of Moses; Philo, nom. mutat. § 21 Ἰησοῦς ἑρμηνεύεται σωτηρία κυρίου), a very com. prop. name among the Israelites; cf. Delitzsch, Der Jesusname, in the Zeitschr. f. d. luth. Theol. for 1876, p. 209 sq. [or Talmud. Stud. xv.]. In the N. T. **1.** Joshua [fully Jehoshua], the famous captain of the Israelites, Moses' successor: Acts vii. 45; Heb. iv. 8. **2.** Jesus, son of Eliezer, one of Christ's ancestors: Lk. iii. 29 L T Tr WH. **3.** Jesus, the Son of God, the Saviour of mankind: Mt. i. 21, 25; Lk. i. 31; ii. 21, and very often; see κύριος and Χριστός. **4.** Jesus Barabbas; see Βαραββᾶς. **5.** Jesus, surnamed Justus, a Jewish Christian, an associate with Paul in preaching the gospel: Col. iv. 11.

2425 ἱκανός, -ή, -όν, (fr. ἵκω, ἱκάνω; prop. 'reaching to', 'attaining to'; hence 'adequate'); as in Grk. writ. fr. Hdt. and Thuc. down, sufficient; **a.** of number and quantity; with nouns, many enough, or enough with a gen.: ὄχλος ἱκανός, a great multitude [A. V. often much people], Mk. x. 46; Lk. vii. 12; Acts xi. 24, 26; xix. 26; λαός, Acts v. 37 R G; κλαυθμός, Acts xx. 37; ἀργύρια ἱκανά, [A. V. large money, cf. the colloq. 'money enough'], Mt. xxviii. 12; λαμπάδες, Acts xx. 8; λόγοι, Lk. xxiii. 9; φῶς ἱκανόν, a considerable light [A. V. a great light], Acts xxii. 6. of time: ἱκανῷ χρόνῳ [cf. W. § 31, 9; B. § 133, 26] for a long time, [Lk. viii. 27 T Tr txt. WH]; Acts viii. 11; also ἱκανὸν χρόνον, Acts xiv. 3; and plur. Lk. xx. 9; ἐξ ἱκανοῦ, of a long time, now for a long time, Lk. xxiii. 8 R G; also ἐκ χρόνων ἱκανῶν, Lk. viii. 27 R G L Tr mrg.; xxiii. 8 L T Tr WH; [ἀπὸ ἱκανῶν ἐτῶν, these many years, Ro. xv. 23 WH Tr txt.]; ἱκανοῦ χρόν. διαγεν. much time having elapsed, Acts xxvii. 9; ἐφ' ἱκανόν, for a long while, Acts xx. 11 (2 Macc. viii. 25; Diod. 13, 100; Palaeph. 28); ἡμέραι [cf. Bp. Lghtft. on Gal. p. 89 n.], Acts ix. 23, 43; xviii. 18; xxvii. 7. absol. ἱκανοί, many, a considerable number: Lk. vii. 11 [R G L br. T Tr mrg. br.]; Acts xii. 12; xiv. 21; xix. 19; 1 Co. xi. 30, (1 Macc. xiii. 49, etc.). ἱκανόν ἐστιν, it is enough, i. q. enough has been said on this subject, Lk. xxii. 38 (for Jesus, saddened at the paltry ideas of the disciples, breaks off in this way the conversation; the Jews, when a companion uttered any thing absurd, were wont to use the phrase רַב לְךֶם [A. V. let it suffice thee, etc.], as in Deut. iii. 26, where Sept. ἱκανούσθω); ἱκανὸν τῷ τοιούτῳ ἡ ἐπιτιμία αὕτη, sc. ἐστί, sufficient . . . is this punishment, 2 Co. ii. 6; after the Lat. idiom satisfacere alicui, τὸ ἱκ. ποιεῖν τινι, to take away from one every ground of complaint [A. V. to content], Mk. xv. 15 (Polyb. 32, 7, 13; App. Pun. p. 68 ed. Toll. [§ 74, i. p. 402 ed. Schweig.]; Diog. Laërt. 4, 50); τὸ ἱκ. λαμβάνω (Lat. satis accipio), to take security (either by accepting sponsors, or by a deposit of money until the case had been decided), Acts xvii. 9. **b.** sufficient in ability, i. e. meet, fit, (Germ. tüchtig [A. V. worthy, able, etc.]) : πρός τι, for something, 2 Co. ii. 16; foll. by an inf. [B. 260 (223 sq.)], Mt. iii. 11; Mk. i. 7; Lk. iii. 16; 1 Co. xv. 9; 2 Co. iii. 5; 2 Tim. ii. 2; foll. by ἵνα with subjunc. [B. 240 (207); cf. W. 335 (314)]: Mt. viii. 8; Lk. vii. 6.*

2426 ἱκανότης, -ητος, ἡ, sufficiency, ability or competency to do a thing: 2 Co. iii. 5. (Plat. Lys. [p. 215, a.] ap. Poll.; [al.].)*

2427 ἱκανόω, -ῶ: 1 aor. ἱκάνωσα; (ἱκανός); to make sufficient, render fit; with two acc., one of the obj. the other of the predicate: to equip one with adequate power to perform the duties of one, 2 Co. iii. 6; τινὰ εἴς τι, Col. i. 12. [Sept.; Dion. Hal., al.]*

2428 ἱκετήριος, -a, -ον, (ἱκέτης a suppliant), *pertaining to a suppliant, fit for a suppliant*; ἡ ἱκετηρία, as subst., sc. ἐλαία or ῥάβδος; **1.** *an olive-branch*; for suppliants approached the one whose aid they would implore holding an olive-branch entwined with white wool and fillets, to signify that they came as suppliants [cf. Trench § li. sub fin.]: λαμβάνειν ἱκετηρίαν, Hdt. 5, 51; ἱκετηρίαν τιθέναι or προβάλλεσθαι παρά τινι, etc. **2.** i. q. ἱκεσία, *supplication* (Isocr. p. 186 d. var.; Polyb. ; 2 Macc. ix. 18): plur. joined with δεήσεις (Polyb. 3, 112, 8; sing. Job xl. 22 Sept.), Heb. v. 7.*

2429 ἱκμάς, -άδος, ἡ, *moisture*: Lk. viii. 6. (Sept. Jer. xvii. 8; Hom. Il. 17, 392; Joseph. antt. 3, 1, 3, and often in other auth.) *

2430 Ἰκόνιον, -ου, τό, *Iconium*, a celebrated city of Asia Minor, which in the time of Xen. (an. 1, 2, 19) was 'the last city of Phrygia,' afterwards the capital of Lycaonia (Strab. 12 p. 568; Cic. ad divers. 15, 4); now *Konia* [or *Konieh*]: Acts xiii. 51; xiv. 1, 19, 21; xvi. 2; 2 Tim. iii. 11. Cf. *Overbeck* in Schenkel iii. 303 sq.; [B. D. (esp. Am. ed.) s. v.; *Lewin*, St. Paul, i. 144 sqq.].*

2431 ἱλαρός, -ά, -όν, (ἵλαος propitious), *cheerful, joyous, prompt to do anything*: 2 Co. ix. 7; Prov. xix. 12; xxii. 8; Sir. xiii. 26 (25); xxvi. 4; 3 Macc. vi. 35; Arstph., Xen., al.*

2432 ἱλαρότης, -ητος, ἡ, *cheerfulness, readiness of mind*: Ro. xii. 8. (Prov. xviii. 22; [Diod., Philo (de plant. Noë § 40), Plut., al.]; Acta Thom. § 14.) *

2433 ἱλάσκομαι, (see below); in class. Grk. the mid. of an act. ἱλάσκω (*to render propitious, appease*) never met with; **1.** *to render propitious to one's self, to appease, conciliate to one's self* (fr. ἵλαος gracious, gentle); fr. Hom. down; mostly w. acc. of a pers., as θεόν, Ἀθήνην, etc. (τὸν θεὸν ἱλάσασθαι, Joseph. antt. 6, 6, 5); very rarely w. acc. of the thing, as τὴν ὀργήν, Plut. Cat. min. 61 (with which cf. ἐξιλάσκεσθαι θυμόν, Prov. xvi. 14 Sept.). In bibl. Grk. used passively, *to become propitious, be placated* or *appeased*; in 1 aor. impv. ἱλάσθητι, *be propitious, be gracious, be merciful*, (in prof. auth. ἵληθι and Dor. ἵλαθι, which the gramm. regard as the pres. of an unused verb ἵλημι, to be propitious; cf. Bttm. Ausf. Sp. ii. p. 206; Kühner § 343, i. p. 839; Passow [or L. and S., or Veitch] s. v. ἵλημι), with dat. of the thing or the pers.: Lk. xviii. 13 (ταῖς ἁμαρτίαις, Ps. lxxviii. (lxxix.) 9; [lxxvii. (lxxviii.) 38]; τῇ ἁμαρτίᾳ, Ps. xxiv. (xxv.) 11; ἱλάσθη ὁ κύριος περὶ τῆς κακίας, Ex. xxxii. 14 Alex.; ἱλασθήσεται κύρ. τῷ δούλῳ σου, 2 K. v. 18). **2.** by an Alexandrian usage, *to expiate, make propitiation for*, (as ἐξιλάσκεσθαι in the O. T.): τὰς ἁμαρτίας, Heb. ii. 17 (ἡμῶν τὰς ψυχάς, Philo, alleg. leg. 3, 61). [Cf. *Kurtz*, Com. on Heb. l. c.; W. 227 (213); *Westcott*, Epp. of S. Jn. p. 83 sq.] *

2434 ἱλασμός, -οῦ, ὁ, (ἱλάσκομαι); **1.** *an appeasing, propitiating*, Vulg. propitiatio, (Plut. de sera num. vind. c. 17; plur. joined with καθαρμοί, Plut. Sol. 12; with gen. of the obj. τῶν θεῶν, Orph. Arg. 39; Plut. Fab. 18; θεῶν μῆνιν ἱλασμοῦ καὶ χαριστηρίων δεομένην, vit. Camill. 7 fin.; ποιεῖσθαι ἱλασμόν, of a priest offering an expia-tory sacrifice, 2 Macc. iii. 33). **2.** in Alex. usage *the means of appeasing, a propitiation*: Philo, alleg. leg. iii. § 61; προσοίσουσιν ἱλασμόν, for חַטָּאת, Ezek. xliv. 27; περὶ τῶν ἁμαρτιῶν, of Christ, 1 Jn. ii. 2; iv. 10, (κριὸς τοῦ ἱλασμοῦ, Num. v. 8; [cf. ἡμέρα τ. ἱλασμοῦ, Lev. xxv. 9]; also for סְלִיחָה, forgiveness, Ps. cxxix. (cxxx.) 4; Dan. ix. 9 Theodot.). [Cf. Trench § lxxvii.]*

2435 ἱλαστήριος, -a, -ον, (ἱλάσκομαι, q. v.), *relating to appeasing* or *expiating, having placating* or *expiating force, expiatory*: μνῆμα ἱλαστήριον, a monument built to propitiate God, Joseph. antt. 16, 7, 1; ἱλαστήριος θάνατος, 4 Macc. xvii. 22; χεῖρας ἱκετηρίους, εἰ βούλει δὲ ἱλαστη-ρίους, ἐκτείνας θεῷ, Niceph. in act. SS. ed. *Mai*, vol. v. p. 335, 17. Neut. τὸ ἱλαστήριον, as subst., *a means of appeasing* or *expiating, a propitiation*, (Germ. *Versöhnungs- oder Sühnmittel*; cf. W. 96 (91); [592 (551)]. So used of **1.** the well-known cover of the ark of the covenant in the Holy of holies, which was sprinkled with the blood of the expiatory victim on the annual day of atonement (this rite signifying that the life of the people, the loss of which they had merited by their sins, was offered to God in the blood as the life of the victim, and that God by this ceremony was appeased and their sins were expiated); hence *the lid of expiation, the propitiatory*, Vulg. propitiatorium; Luth. *Gnadenstuhl*, [A. V. *mercy-seat*]: Heb. ix. 5 (Sept. Ex. xxv. 18 sqq.; Lev. xvi. 2, etc.; more fully ἱλαστήριον ἐπίθεμα, Ex. xxv. 17; xxxviii. (xxxvii.) 7 (6), for the Hebr. כַּפֹּרֶת, fr. כִּפֶּר to cover, sc. sins, i. e. to pardon). Theodoret, Theophyl., Oecum., Luther, Grotius, Tholuck, Wilke, Philippi, Umbreit, [Cremer (4te Aufl.)] and others give this meaning to the word also in Ro. iii. 25, viz. that Christ, besprinkled with his own blood, was **truly** that which the cover or 'mercy-seat' had been **typically**, i. e. the sign and pledge of expiation; but in opp. to this interpretation see Fritzsche, Meyer, Van Hengel, [Godet, Oltramare] and others ad loc. **2.** *an expiatory sacrifice*; *a piacular victim* (Vulg. propitiatio): Ro. iii. 25 (after the analogy of the words χαρι-στήρια sacrifices expressive of gratitude, *thank-offerings*, σωτήρια sacrifices for safety obtained. On the other hand, in Dion Chrys. or. 11, 121, p. 355 ed. Reiske, the reference is not to a sacrifice but to a monument, as the preceding words show: καταλείψειν γὰρ αὐτοὺς ἀνάθημα κάλλιστον καὶ μέγιστον τῇ Ἀθηνᾷ καὶ ἐπιγρά-ψειν, ἱλαστήριον Ἀχαιοὶ τῇ Ἰλιάδι. [See the full discussion of the word in Dr. *Jas. Morison*, Crit. Exposition of the Third Chap. of the Ep. to the Rom. pp. 281–303.] *

2436 ἵλεως, -ων, (Attic for ἵλαος [cf. W. 22], fr. Hom. down), *propitious, merciful*: ἔσομαι ἵλ. ταῖς ἀδικίαις, i. e. I will pardon, Heb. viii. 12; Jer. xxxviii. (xxxi.) 34; xliii. (xxxvi.) 3; also ταῖς ἁμαρτίαις, 1 K. viii. 34; 2 Chr. vi. 25, 27, etc.; ἵλεώς σοι, sc. ἔστω [or εἴη, B. § 129, 22] ὁ θεός, i. e. God avert this from thee, Mt. xvi. 22; Sept. for חָלִילָה foll. by לְ, *be it far from* one, 2 S. xx. 20; xxiii. 17.*

2437 Ἰλλυρικόν, -οῦ, τό, *Illyricum*, a region lying between Italy, Germany, Macedonia and Thrace, having on one side the Adriatic Sea, and on the other the Danube: Ro. xv. 19 [cf. B. D. Am. ed.].*

2438   ἱμάς, -άντος, ὁ, (fr. ἵημι to send; sc. a vessel, which was tied to thongs of leather and let down into a well for the purpose of drawing water; hence ἱμάω also, to draw something made fast to a thong or rope [recent etymol. connect it w. Skt. si to bind; cf. Curtius § 602; Vaniček p. 1041]); fr. Hom. down; *a thong of leather, a strap*; in the N. T. of the thongs with which captives or criminals were either bound or beaten (see προτείνω), Acts xxii. 25 (4 Macc. ix. 11; Sir. xxx. 35); of the thongs or ties by which sandals were fastened to the feet, Mk. i. 7; Lk. iii. 16; Jn. i. 27, (so also in Is. v. 27; Xen. anab. 4, 5, 14; Plut. symp. 4, 2, 3; Suid. ἱμάς · σφαιρωτὴρ σανδαλίου, ζανίχιον, οἷον τὸ λώριον τοῦ ὑποδήματος).*

2439   ἱματίζω: pf. pass. ptcp. ἱματισμένος; (ἱμάτιον); *to clothe*: Mk. v. 15; Lk. viii. 35. (Found neither in Sept. nor in prof. auth. [cf. W. 26 (25)].) *

2440   ἱμάτιον, -ου, τό, (dimin. of ἷμα i. q. εἷμα, an article of clothing, garment; and this fr. ἕννυμι to clothe, cf. Germ. *Hemd*); [fr. Hdt. down]; Sept. mostly for בֶּגֶד, also for שַׂלְמָה, שִׂמְלָה, etc.;   1. *a garment* (of any sort): Mt. ix. 16; xi. 8 [R G L br., al. om.; cf. W. 591 (550); B. 82 (72)]; Mk. ii. 21; xv. 20; Lk. v. 36; vii. 25; Heb. i. 11; plur. *garments*, i. e. the cloak or mantle and the tunic [cf. W. 176 (166); B. 24 (23)]: Mt. xvii. 2; xxiv. 18 [Rec.]; xxvii. 31, 35; Jn. xix. 23; Acts vii. 58; Jas. v. 2, etc.; to rend τὰ ἱμ. (see διαρρήγνυμι), Mt. xxvi. 65; Acts xiv. 14; xxii. 23.   2. the upper garment, *the cloak* or *mantle* (which was thrown over the tunic, ὁ χιτών) [*Rutherford*, New Phryn. p. 22]: Mt. ix. 20; [xxiv. 18 L T Tr WH]; Mk. v. 27; Lk. viii. 44; Jn. xix. 2; Rev. xix. 16; it is distinguished from the χιτών in Mt. v. 40; Lk. vi. 29; [cf. Jn. xix. 23]; Acts ix. 39. [Cf. Trench § l.; BB. DD. s. v. Dress; *Edersheim*, Jewish Social Life, ch. xiii.; esp. 'Jesus the Messiah,' i. 620 sqq.]

2441   ἱματισμός, -οῦ, ὁ, (ἱματίζω), *clothing, apparel*: univ., Lk. vii. 25; Acts xx. 33; 1 Tim. ii. 9; of the tunic, Mt. xxvii. 35 Rec.; Jn. xix. 24; of the cloak or mantle, Lk. ix. 29. (Sept.; Theophr., Polyb., Diod., Plut., Athen.) [Cf. Trench § l.]*

see 2442 St.   ἱμείρω: mid. ἱμείρομαι; (ἵμερος desire, longing, [allied w. ἵλεως; Vaniček p. 88]; cf. οἰκτείρω); *to desire, long for*, esp. of the longing of love: ὑμῶν [W. § 30, 10 b.] i. e. your souls, to win them to Christ, 1 Th. ii. 8 Rec.; see ὁμείρομαι. (Sept. Job iii. 21; in Grk. writ. fr. Hom. down.) *

2443   ἵνα,   I. an adv. of Place, fr. Hom. down, esp. in the poets;   a. *where*; *in what place.*   b. *to what place*; *whither.* Of the former signification C. F. A. Fritzsche (on Mt. p. 836; differently in Fritzschiorum Opusc. p. 186 sqq.) thought he had found two examples in bibl. Greek, and H. A. W. Meyer agrees with him. The first viz. ἵνα μὴ φυσιοῦσθε, 1 Co. iv. 6, they explain thus: *where* (i. e. *in which state of things* viz. when ye have learned from my example to think humbly of yourselves) *the one is not exalted to the other's disadvantage*; the second, ἵνα αὐτοὺς ζηλοῦτε, Gal. iv. 17, thus: *where ye zealously court them*; but see II. 1 d. below.

II. a final Conjunction (for from local direction, indicated by the adverb, the transition was easy to mental direction or intention) denoting **purpose and end**: *to the intent that*; *to the end that, in order that*; ἵνα μή, *that not, lest*; it is used

1. prop. of the **purpose or end**;   a. foll. by the Optative; only twice, and then preceded by the pres. of a verb of **praying or beseeching**, where the **wish** (*optatio*) expressed by the prayer gave occasion for the use of the optat.: Eph. i. 17 but WH mrg. subj.; iii. 16 R G; cf. W. 290 (273); B. 233 (201); and yet in both instances the telic force of the particle is so weakened that it denotes the **substance** rather than the **end** of the prayer; see 2 below.   b. foll. by the **Subjunctive**, not only (according to the rule observed by the best Grk. writ.) after the primary tenses (pres., pf., fut.) or the imperative, but (in accordance with that well-known negligence with which in later times and esp. by Hellenistic writers the distinction between the subjunc. and the optat. was disregarded) after preterites even where the more elegant Grk. writ. were wont to use the optat.; cf. *Hermann* ad Vig. p. 847 sqq.; *Klotz* ad Dev. ii. 2 p. 616 sqq.; W. 287 (270) sqq.; B. 233 (201).   a. after a Present: Mk. iv. 21; vii. 9; Lk. vi. 34; viii. 12; xvi. 28; Jn. iii. 15; v. 34; vi. 30; Acts ii. 25; xvi. 30; Ro. i. 11; iii. 19; xi. 25; 1 Co. vii. 29; ix. 12; 2 Co. i. 17; Gal. vi. 13; Phil. iii. 8; Heb. v. 1; vi. 12; ix. 25; 1 Jn. i. 3; Rev. iii. 18; xi. 6, and often.   β. after a Perfect: Mt. i. 22; xxi. 4; Jn. v. 23; [36 T Tr WH; cf. ε.]; vi. 38; xii. 40, 46; xiv. 29; xvi. 1, 4; xvii. 4; xx. 31; 1 Co. ix. 22; 1 Jn. v. 20 [here T Tr WH pres. indic.; see d.].   γ. after an Imperative (either pres. or aor.): Mt. vii. 1; ix. 6; xiv. 15; xvii. 27; xxiii. 26; Mk. xi. 25; xiii. 18; Jn. iv. 15; v. 14; vii. 3 [R G L]; x. 38; 1 Co. vii. 5; xi. 34; 1 Tim. iv. 15; Tit. iii. 13, etc.; also after a hortative or deliberative subjunc.: Mk. i. 38; Lk. xx. 14; Jn. vi. 5 [R^bez L T Tr WH]; xi. 16; Heb. iv. 16, etc.   δ. after a Future: Lk. xvi. 4; xviii. 5; Jn. v. 20 [here Tdf. indic. pres.; see d.]; xiv. 3, 13, 16; 1 Co. xv. 28; Phil. i. 26.   ε. after Historic tenses: after the impf., Mk. iii. 2 [here L Tr fut. indic.; see c.]; vi. 41; viii. 6; Lk. vi. 7; xviii. 15, etc.; after the plupf., Jn. iv. 8; after the aor., Mt. xix. 13; Mk. iii. 14; xi. 28; xiv. 10 [B. § 139, 37]; Lk. xix. 4, 15; Jn. v. 36 [R G L; cf. β.]; vii. 32; xii. 9; Acts xix. 4 [?]; Ro. vi. 4; 2 Co. viii. 9; Heb. ii. 14; xi. 35; 1 Tim. i. 16; 1 Jn. iii. 5, 8, etc.   c. As prof. auth. join the final particles ὄφρα, μή, and esp. ὅπως, also with the future Indicative (cf. Matthiae § 519, 8 ii. p. 1186 sqq.), as being in nature akin to the subjunc., so the N. T. writ., acc. to a usage extremely doubtful among the better Grk. writ. (cf. Klotz l. c. p. 629 sq.), also join ἵνα with the same [cf. *WH.* App. p. 171^b; *Soph.* Lex. s. v. ἵνα, 17]: ἵνα θήσω, 1 Co. ix. 18; L T Tr WH in the foll. instances: σταυρώσουσιν, Mk. xv. 20 [not WH (see u. s.)], δώσουσιν, Lk. xx. 10; κενώσει, 1 Co. ix. 15 [not Lchm.], [καταδουλώσουσιν, Gal. ii. 4 (but cf. *Hort* in WH u. s. p. 167^a)]; κερδηθήσονται, 1 Pet. iii. 1; σφάξουσιν, Rev. vi. 4; δώσει, Rev. viii. 3;

προσκυνήσουσιν, [Rev. ix. 20]; xiii. 12 [(cf. 2 a. fin. below)]; [ἀναπαήσονται, Rev. xiv. 13 (see ἀναπαύω) cf. 4 b.]; L Tr in the foll.: κατηγορήσουσιν, Mk. iii. 2, (cf. b. ε. above); προσκυνήσουσιν, Jn. xii. 20; T Tr WH in [θεωρήσουσιν, Jn. vii. 3]; ξυρήσονται, Acts xxi. 24; L T WH Tr mrg. in ἀδικήσουσι, Rev. ix. 4 [(cf. 2 b. below)]; [add, ἐρεῖ, Lk. xiv. 10 T WH Tr txt.; ἐξομολογήσεται, Phil. ii. 11 T L mrg. Tr mrg.; κανθήσομαι, 1 Co. xiii. 3 T; δώσει, Jn. xvii. 2 WH Tr mrg.; ἀναπαύσονται, Rev. vi. 11 WH; δώσει, Rev. xiii. 16 WH mrg.], (ἵνα καταργήσει τὸν θάνατον καὶ τὴν ἐκ νεκρῶν ἀνάστασιν δείξει, Barn. ep. 5, 6 [so cod. א, but Hilgenf., Müller, Gebh., al., adopt the subjunc.; yet see Cunningham's note ad loc.]); so that the fut. alternates with the subjunc.: ἵνα ἔσται ... καὶ εἰσέλθωσιν, Rev. xxii. 14; γένηται καὶ ἔση (Vulg. sis), Eph. vi. 3; in other pass. L T Tr WH have restored the indic., as ἵνα ἥξουσι κ. προσκυνήσουσιν ... κ. γνῶσιν, Rev. iii. 9; ἵνα ... πίνητε ... καὶ καθίσεσθε or καθήσεσθε [but WH txt. καθῆσθε] (Vulg. et sedeatis), Lk. xxii. 30; κάμψῃ κ. ἐξομολογήσεται, Phil. ii. 11 [T L mrg. Tr mrg.]; cf. B. § 139, 38; W. § 41 b. 1 b.   **d.** By a solecism freq. in the eccles. and Byzant. writ. ἵνα is joined with the indic. Present: 1 Co. iv. 6 (φυσιοῦσθε); Gal. iv. 17 (ζηλοῦτε); [cf. Test. xii. Patr., test. Gad § 7; Barn. ep. 6, 5; 7, 11; Ignat. ad Eph. 4, 2; ad Trall. 8, 2, and other exx. in Win. and Bttm. as below; but see Hort in WH. App. p. 167ᵃ, cf. pp. 169ᵇ, 171 sq.]; but the indic. is very doubtful in the foll. passages: [Jn. iv. 15 Tr txt.]; v. 20 (Tdf. θαυμάζετε); xvii. 3 T Tr txt.; Gal. vi. 12 T L mrg.; [1 Th. iv. 13 L mrg.]; Tit. ii. 4 T Tr L mrg.; 2 Pet. i. 10 L; [1 Jn. v. 20 T Tr WH (cf. b. β. above)]; Rev. xii. 6 (T Tr τρέφουσιν); [xiii. 17 WH mrg.]; cf. W. § 41 b. 1 c.; B. § 139, 39; Meyer on 1 Co. iv. 6; Wieseler on Gal. iv. 17; [Soph. u. s.].   (In the earlier Grk. writ. ἵνα is joined with the indic. of the past tenses alone, 'to denote something which would have been, if something else had been done, but now has not come to pass' Hermann ad Vig. p. 847, cf. Klotz ad Dev. ii. 2 p. 630 sq.; Kühner § 553, 7 ii. 903; [Jelf § 813; cf. Jebb in App. to Vincent and Dickson's Modern Greek, § 79].)   **e.** the final sentence is preceded by preparatory demonstrative expressions [W. § 23, 5]: εἰς τοῦτο, to this end, Jn. xviii. 37; 1 Jn. iii. 8; Ro. xiv. 9; 2 Co. ii. 9; 1 Pet. ii. 21; iii. 9; iv. 6, (Barn. ep. 5, 1, 11; [14, 5]); εἰς αὐτὸ τοῦτο, Eph. vi. 22; Col. iv. 8; διὰ τοῦτο, i. 31; 2 Co. xiii. 10; Philem. 15; 1 Tim. i. 16; τούτου χάριν, Tit. i. 5.

2. In later Grk., and esp. in Hellenistic writers, the final force of the particle ἵνα is more or less w e a k e n e d, so that it is frequently used where the earlier Greeks employed the I n f i n i t i v e, yet so that the leading and the dependent sentence have each its own subject. The first extant instance of this use occurs in the Amphictyonic decree in [pseudo-] Dem. p. 279, 8 [i. e. de coron. § 155]: πρεσβεῦσαι πρὸς Φίλιππον καὶ ἀξιοῦν ἵνα βοηθήσῃ, [cf. Odyss. 3, 327 λίσσεσθαι ... ἵνα νημερτὲς ἐνίσπῃ (cf. 3, 19)], but it increased greatly in subsequent times; cf. W. § 44, 8; B. 237 (204); [Green 171 sq.; Goodwin § 45 N. 5 b.; Jebb in App. to Vincent and Dickson's Modern

Greek, § 55]. Accordingly ἵνα stands with the subjunc. in such a way that it denotes the p u r p o r t (or o b j e c t) rather than the p u r p o s e of the action expressed by the preceding verb. This occurs   **a.** after verbs of c a r i n g for, d e c i d i n g, d e s i r i n g, s t r i v i n g: βλέπειν, 1 Co. xvi. 10; Col. iv. 17; 2 Jn. 8; ζητῶ, 1 Co. iv. 2; xiv. 12; φυλάσσομαι, ἵνα μή, 2 Pet. iii. 17; μεριμνάω, 1 Co. vii. 34; ζηλόω, 1 Co. xiv. 1; βουλεύομαι, Jn. xi. 53 [R G Tr mrg. συμβου.]; xii. 10; ἀφίημι, Mk. xi. 16; Jn. xii. 7 L T Tr WH; θέλημά ἐστι, Mt. xviii. 14; Jn. vi. 39 sq.; θέλω, Mt. vii. 12; Mk. vi. 25; ix. 30; x. 35; Lk. vi. 31; so that it alternates with the inf., 1 Co. xiv. 5; δίδωμι, to grant, that, Mk. x. 37; Rev. ix. 5, etc.; ποιῶ, Rev. xiii. 12 [here L T Tr WH indic. fut. (cf. 1 c. above)].   **b.** after verbs of s a y i n g (commanding, asking, exhorting; but by no means after κελεύειν [cf. B. 275 (236)]): εἰπεῖν, in the sense of to bid, Mt. iv. 3; Mk. iii. 9; Lk. iv. 3; also λέγειν, Acts xix. 4; 1 Jn. v. 16; ἐρρήθη, Rev. vi. 11 [WH indic. fut.]; ix. 4 [L T Tr mrg. WH indic. fut. (see 1 c. above)]; διαμαρτύρομαι, 1 Tim. v. 21 (otherwise [viz. telic] in Lk. xvi. 28); ἐρωτῶ, to ask, beseech, Mk. vii. 26; Lk. vii. 36; xvi. 27; Jn. iv. 47; xvii. 15, 21; xix. 31; 2 Jn. 5; παρακαλῶ, Mt. xiv. 36; Mk. v. 10, 18; vii. 32; viii. 22; Lk. viii. 32; 1 Co. i. 10; xvi. 12, 15 sq.; 2 Co. viii. 6; ix. 5; xii. 8; 1 Th. iv. 1; 2 Th. iii. 12, (Joseph. antt. 12, 3, 2); προσεύχομαι [q. v.], Mt. xxiv. 20; Mk. [xiii. 18]; xiv. 35; δέομαι, Lk. ix. 40; xxii. 32, (Dion. Hal. antt. 1, 83); ἐπιτιμῶ, Mt. xii. 16; [xvi. 20 L WH txt.]; xx. 31; Mk. iii. 12; viii. 30; x. 48; Lk. xviii. 39; ἐντέλλομαι, Mk. xiii. 34; Jn. xv. 17; ἐντολὴν δίδωμι or λαμβάνω, Jn. xi. 57; xiii. 34; xv. 12; γράφω, with the involved idea of prescribing, Mk. ix. 12 [cf. W. 462 (430) and the txt. of L T]; xii. 19; Lk. xx. 28; διαστέλλομαι, Mt. xvi. 20 [L WH txt. ἐπιτιμῶ (see above)]; Mk. v. 43; vii. 36; ix. 9; παραγγέλλω, Mk. vi. 8 [cf. W. 578 (538)]; συντίθεμαι, Jn. ix. 22; ἀγγαρεύω, Mt. xxvii. 32; Mk. xv. 21; κηρύσσω, Mk. vi. 12; ἀπαγγέλλω, Mt. xxviii. 10; ἐξορκίζω, Mt. xxvi. 63.   [For exx. (of its use with the above verbs and others) drawn from the later Grk. writ. see Sophocles, Glossary etc. § 88, 1.]   **c.** after words by which j u d g m e n t is pronounced concerning that which some one is about to do (or which is going to happen), as to whether it is e x p e d i e n t, befitting, proper, or not; as συμφέρει, Mt. xviii. 6; v. 29 sq.; Jn. xi. 50; xvi. 7; λυσιτελεῖ, Lk. xvii. 2; ἀρκετόν ἐστι, Mt. x. 25; also after ἄξιος, Jn. i. 27; ἱκανός, Mt. viii. 8; Lk. vii. 6; ἐλάχιστόν μοί ἐστιν, ἵνα, 1 Co. iv. 3; ἠγαλλιάσατο, ἵνα ἴδῃ, Jn. viii. 56; χρείαν ἔχω, Jn. ii. 25; xvi. 30; 1 Jn. ii. 27; ἔδει, ἵνα ἐπὶ ξύλου πάθῃ, Barn. ep. 5, 13.   [For other exx. see Soph. as above § 88, 3, 4.]   **d.** after s u b s t a n t i v e s, to which it adds a more exact d e f i n i t i o n of the thing; after subst. of t i m e: χρόνον, ἵνα μετανοήσῃ, Rev. ii. 21; after ὥρα, Jn. xii. 23; xiii. 1; xvi. 2, 32, (elsewhere ὅτε, Jn. iv. 23; v. 25); in these exx. the f i n a l force of the particle is still apparent; we also can say "time that she should repent" [cf. W. 339 (318); B. 240 (207)]; but in other expressions this force has almost disappeared, as in ἔστιν συνήθεια ὑμῖν, ἵνα ... ἀπολύσω, Jn. xviii. 39; after μισθός, 1 Co. ix. 18.　　e. it looks back to a demonstrative pronoun; cf. W. 338 (317); [B. § 139, 45]: πόθεν μοι τοῦτο, ἵνα ἔλθῃ κτλ. for τὸ ἐλθεῖν τὴν etc. Lk. i. 43; esp. in John, cf. vi. 29, 50; xv. 13; xvii. 3 [here T Tr txt. indic.; see 1 d. above]; 1 Jn. iii. 11, 23; v. 3; 2 Jn. 6; Phil. i. 9; ἐν τούτῳ, Jn. xv. 8; 1 Jn. iv. 17, (θεοῦ δὲ τὸ δυνατὸν ἐν τούτῳ δείκνυται, ἵνα ... ἐξ οὐκ ὄντων ποιῇ τὰ γινόμενα, Theophil. ad Autol. 2, 13; after τόδε, Epict. diss. 2, 1, 1; [other exx. in Soph. Lex. s. v. 6]).

3. According to a very ancient tenet of the grammarians, accepted by Kühner, § 553, 2 Anm. 3; [T. S. Green, N. T. Gram. p. 172 sq.], and not utterly rejected by Alex. Bttm. N. T. Gr. p. 238 sq. (206), ἵνα is alleged to be used not only τελικῶς, i. e. of design and end, but also frequently ἐκβατικῶς, i. e. of the result, signifying with the issue, that; with the result, that; so that (equiv. to ὥστε). But C. F. A. Fritzsche on Mt. p. 836 sqq. and Win. 338 (317) and 457 (426) sqq. have clearly shown, that in all the passages adduced from the N. T. to prove this usage the telic (or final) force prevails: thus in ἵνα μὴ λυθῇ ὁ νόμος Μωϋσέως, that the law of Moses may not be broken (which directs a man to be circumcised on the eighth and on no other day), Jn. vii. 23; οὐκ ἐστὲ ἐν σκότει, ἵνα ἡ ἡμέρα ὑμᾶς ... καταλάβῃ, that the day should overtake you (cf. the final force as brought out by turning the sentence into the pass. form in Germ. um vom Tage erfasst zu werden), 1 Th. v. 4; προσευχέσθω, ἵνα διερμηνεύῃ, let him pray (intent on this, or with this aim), that (subsequently) he may interpret, 1 Co. xiv. 13; likewise ἐπενθήσατε, ἵνα etc. 1 Co. v. 2, and μετενόησαν, ἵνα μή, Rev. ix. 20; μετάθεσιν, ... ἵνα etc. that the change may be to this end, that etc. Heb. xii. 27; ἵνα μὴ ... ποιῆτε, that ye may not do, Gal. v. 17 (where ἡ σάρξ and τὸ πνεῦμα are personified antagonistic forces contending for dominion over the will of the Christian; cf. Wieseler ad loc.); the words ἵνα ... φραγῇ κτλ. in Ro. iii. 19 describe the end aimed at by the law. In many passages where ἵνα has seemed to interpreters to be used ἐκβατικῶς, the sacred writers follow the dictate of piety, which bids us trace all events back to God as their author and to refer them to God's purposes (Jo. Damascen. orthod. fid. 4, 19 ἔθος τῇ γραφῇ, τινὰ ἐκβατικῶς ὀφείλοντα λέγεσθαι, αἰτιολογικῶς λέγειν); so that, if we are ever in doubt whether ἵνα is used of design or of result, we can easily settle the question when we can interpret the passage 'that, by God's decree,' or 'that, according to divine purpose' etc.; passages of this sort are the following: Mk. iv. 12; Lk. ix. 45; xi. 50; xiv. 10; Jn. iv. 36; ix. 2; xii. 40; xix. 28; Ro. v. 20; vii. 13; viii. 17; xi. 31 sq.; 1 Co. vii. 29; 2 Co. iv. 7; vii. 9; also the phrase ἵνα πληρωθῇ, wont to be used in reference to the O. T. prophecies: Mt. i. 22; ii. 15; iv. 14; xii. 17 L T Tr WH; xxi. 4; xxvi. 56; xxvii. 35 Rec.; Jn. xiii. 18; xvii. 12; xix. 24, 36; ἵνα πληρωθῇ ὁ λόγος, Jn. xii. 38; xv. 25, cf. xviii. 9, 32. [Cf. Win. 461 (429). Prof. Sophocles although giving (Lex. s. v. ἵνα, 19) a co-

pious collection of exx. of the ecbatic use of the word, defends its telic sense in the phrase ἵνα πληρ., by calling attention not merely to the substitution of ὅπως πληρ. in Mt. viii. 17; xiii. 35, (cf. ii. 23), but esp. to 1 Esdr. i. 54 (εἰς ἀναπλήρωσιν ῥήματος τοῦ κυρίου ἐν στόματι Ἱερεμίου); ii. 1 (εἰς συντέλειαν ῥήματος κυρ. κτλ.); 2 Esdr. i. 1 (τοῦ τελεσθῆναι λόγον κυρίου ἀπὸ στόματος Ἱερεμίου); Joseph. antt. 8, 8, 2 fin. ταῦτα δ' ἐπράττετο κατὰ τὴν τοῦ θεοῦ βούλησιν ἵνα λάβῃ τέλος ἃ προεφήτευσεν Ἀχίας; cf. Bib. Sacr. '61 p. 729 sqq.; Luthardt's Zeitschr. '83 p. 632 sqq.]

4. The elliptical use of the particle; a. the telic ἵνα often depends on a verb not expressed, but to be repeated or educed from the context (cf. Fritzsche on Mt. p. 840 sq.; W. 316 (297); [B. § 139, 47]): ἀλλ' (sc. ἦλθεν, cf. vs. 7) ἵνα μαρτυρήσῃ, Jn. i. 8; ἀλλ' (sc. ἐγένετο ἀπόκρυφον) ἵνα εἰς φανερὸν ἔλθῃ, Mk. iv. 22; ἀλλ' (sc. κρατεῖτέ με) ἵνα etc. Mk. xiv. 49; add, Jn. xv. 25; 1 Jn. ii. 19.　　b. the weakened ἵνα (see 2 above) with the subjunc. (or indic. fut. [cf. 1 c.], Rev. xiv. 13 L T Tr WH) denotes something which one wishes to be done by another, so that before the ἵνα a verb of commanding (exhorting, wishing) must be mentally supplied, (or, as is commonly said, it forms a periphrasis for the imperative): ἵνα ... ἐπιθῆς τὰς χεῖρας αὐτῇ, Mk. v. 23; ἡ γυνὴ ἵνα φόβηται τὸν ἄνδρα, Eph. v. 33; Gal. ii. 10; add 2 Co. viii. 7; ἵνα ἀναπαύσωνται [L T Tr WH -παήσονται (see ἀναπαύω init.)], Germ. sie sollen ruhen [A. V. that they may rest etc.], Rev. xiv. 13; [perh. also Col. iv. 16, cf. Bp. Lghtft. ad loc.], (2 Macc. i. 9; Epict. ench. 23 (17); diss. 4, 1, 41; among the earlier Greeks once so, Soph. O. C. 155; in Latin, Cic. ad divers. 14, 20 'ibi ut sint omnia parata'; in Germ. stern commands: 'dass du gehest!' 'dass du nicht säumest!' cf. W. § 43, 5 a.; [B. 241 (208)]).　　c. ἵνα without a verb following, — which the reader is left to gather from the context; thus we must mentally supply εὐαγγελιζώμεθα, εὐαγγελίζωνται in Gal. ii. 9, cf. W. 587 (546); [B. 394 (338)]; ἵνα κατὰ χάριν, sc. ᾖ, that the promise may be a gift of grace, Ro. iv. 16 [W. 598 (556); B. 392 (336)]; ἵνα ἄλλοις ἄνεσις sc. γένηται, 2 Co. viii. 13 [W. 586 (545); B. § 129, 22]; ἵνα sc. γένηται, 1 Co. i. 31, unless preference be given there to an anacoluthon [W. 599 (557); B. 234 (201)]: ἵνα ... καυχάσθω for καυχᾶται. (ἵνα ὡς ἄνθρωπος, sc. ἐργάζῃ, Epict. diss. 3, 23, 4.)

5. Generally ἵνα stands first in the final sentence; sometimes, however, it is preceded by those words in which the main force of the sentence lies [W. 550 (511); B. § 151, 18]: Acts xix. 4; Ro. xi. 31 (join τῷ ὑμετέρῳ ἐλέει ἵνα); 1 Co. ix. 15 fin. [R G]; 2 Co. ii. 4; xii. 7; Gal. ii. 10; τὸ λοιπὸν ἵνα κτλ. 1 Co. vii. 29 Rec.exc. elz L T. Among N. T. writ. John uses this particle oftener, Luke more rarely, than the rest; [on Jn.'s use see W. 338 (317) sq.; 461 (430); B. 236 (203); 244 (210) note; § 140, 10 and 12; on Luke's cf. B. 235 sq. (203)]. It is not found in the Epistle of Jude. [For Schaeffer's reff. to Grk. usage (and edd.) see the Lond. (Valpy's) ed. of Stephanus s. v., col. 4488.]

2444 ἵνα τί [so L WH uniformly, also Tr exc. (by mistake?) in Mt. xxvii. 46], and written unitedly ἱνατί [so Rec.st.bez G T uniformly; see W. § 5, 2]; Lat. *ut quid?* i. e. *for what purpose? wherefore? why?* an elliptical formula, due to the fact that a questioner begins an answer to his own question with the word ἵνα, but not knowing how to complete it reverts again to the question, as if to ask what will complete the answer: *that (what?) may* or *might happen, (ut (quid?) fiat* or *fieret)*; see *Herm.* ad Vig. p. 847; *Kühner* § 587, 5 ii. p. 1020; W. § 25, 1 fin.; [B. § 149, 2]: Mt. ix. 4; xxvii. 46; Lk. xiii. 7; Acts iv. 25; vii. 26; 1 Co. x. 29. Add, from the Sept., Gen. iv. 6; xxv. 32; xxvii. 46; Num. xiv. 3; xxii. 32 [Ald.]; Judg. vi. 13 [Alex., Ald., Compl.]; 1 S. i. 8; 2 S. iii. 24; xv. 19; Job iii. 12; x. 18; Jer. ii. 29; xiv. 19; xv. 18; Dan. x. 20 [Theodot.]; Is. ii. 1; x. 1 (ix. 22); xxi. (xxii.) 2, etc.; Sir. xiv. 3; 1 Macc. ii. 7. (Arstph., nub. 1192; Plat. apol. c. 14 p. 26 c.; al.) *

2445 Ἰόππη (to which com. spelling the ancient lexicographers prefer Ἰόπη, cf. *Movers*, Phönizier, ii. 2 p. 176 Anm.),-ης, ἡ, (Hebr. יָפוֹ i. e. beauty, fr. יָפָה to shine, be beautiful; [al. make the name mean 'an eminence'; al. al.]), *Joppa*, a city of Palestine on the Mediterranean, lying on the border of the tribes of Dan and Ephraim. It was subject to the Jews from the time of the Maccabees. It had a celebrated but dangerous port and carried on a flourishing trade; now *Yâfa* (not *Jaffa*): Acts ix. 36, 38, 42 sq.; x. 5, 8, 23, 32; xi. 5, 13. Cf. *Win.* RWB. s. v. Joppe; *Rüetschi* in Herzog vii. p. 4 sq.; *Fritzsche* in Schenkel iii. 376 sq.; [BB.DD.]. *

2446 Ἰορδάνης, -ου [B. 17], ὁ [cf. W. § 18, 5 a.], (יַרְדֵּן, fr. יָרַד to descend; for other opinions about the origin of the name see *Gesenius*, Thes. ii. p. 626 [cf. Alex.'s Kitto s. v. Jordan]), *the Jordan*, the largest and most celebrated river of Palestine, which has its origin in numerous torrents and small streams at the foot of Anti-Lebanon, flows at first into Lake Samochonitis (*Merom* so-called; [mod. *el-Hûleh*; see BB.DD. s. v. Merom (Waters of)]), and issuing thence runs into the Lake of Tiberias (the Sea of Galilee). After quitting this lake it is augmented during its course by many smaller streams, and finally empties into the Dead Sea: Mt. iii. 5 sq. 13; iv. 15, 25; xix. 1; Mk. i. 5, 9; iii. 8; x. 1; Lk. iii. 3; iv. 1; Jn. i. 28; iii. 26; x. 40; cf. *Win.* RWB. [and BB.DD.] s. v. Jordan; *Arnold* in Herzog vii. p. 7 sqq.; *Furrer* in Schenkel iii. p. 378 sqq.; [*Robinson*, Phys. Geogr. of the Holy Land, pp. 144–186]. *

2447 ἰός, -οῦ, ὁ, (on its very uncert. deriv. see *Kreussler* in Passow s. v.; Curtius § 591; [Vaniček p. 969]); **1.** *poison* (of animals): ἰὸς ἀσπίδων ὑπὸ τὰ χείλη αὐτῶν, the poison of asps is under their lips, spoken of men given to reviling and calumniating and thereby injuring others, Ro. iii. 13 (fr. Ps. cxxxix. (cxl.) 3 (4)); by the same fig. (γλῶσσα) μεστὴ ἰοῦ θανατηφόρου, Jas. iii. 8; (in Grk. writ. fr. Pind. down). **2.** *rust*: Jas. v. 3; (Ezek. xxiv. 6, 11 sq.; Bar. vi. [Ep. Jer.] 11 (12), 23 (24); Theogn., Theocr., Plat., Theophr., Polyb., Lcian., al.). *

2448 Ἰούδα, (see Ἰούδας, init. and 1), indecl., *Judah,* a prop. name; in Sept. **1.** the fourth son of the patriarch Jacob. **2.** the tribe that sprang from him. **3.** the region which this tribe occupied (cf. W. 114 (108)); so in the N. T. in Mt. ii. 6 (twice); πόλις Ἰούδα (Judg. xvii. 8), a city of the tribe of Judah, Lk. i. 39, where it is a matter of dispute what city is meant; the most probable conjecture seems to be that *Hebron* is referred to, — a city assigned to the priests, situated ' in the hill country' (Χεβρὼν ἐν τῷ ὄρει Ἰούδα, Josh. xxi. 11), the native place of John the Baptist acc. to Jewish tradition. [Cf. B. D. Am. ed. s. v. Juda, a City of.] *

2449 Ἰουδαία, -ας, ἡ [cf. W. § 18, 5 a.], (sc. γῆ, which is added Jn. iii. 22, or χώρα, Mk. i. 5; fr. the adj. Ἰουδαῖος, q. v.), *Judæa* (Hebr. יְהוּדָה); in the O. T. a region of Palestine, named after the tribe of Judah, which inhabited it: Judg. xvii. 7–9; Ruth i. 1 sq.; 2 S. ii. 1, etc. Its boundaries are laid down in Josh. xv. 1 sqq. After the time of David, when the kingdom had been rent asunder, the name was given to *the kingdom of Judah*, to which were reckoned, besides the tribes of Judah and Benjamin, certain cities of the tribes of Dan and Simeon, together with the metropolis of Jerusalem: 1 K. xiv. 21, 29; xv. 7, etc. In the N. T. the name is given **1.** in a narrower sense, to the southern part of Palestine lying on this side of the Jordan and the Dead Sea, to distinguish it from Samaria, Galilee, Peræa, Idumæa (Mk. iii. 8): Mt. ii. 1, 5, 22; iii. 5; iv. 25; xxiv. 16; Mk. iii. 7; xiii. 14; Lk. ii. 4; Jn. iv. 3, 47, 54; Acts i. 8; viii. 1, etc.; it stands for its inhabitants in Mt. iii. 5; Mk. i. 5, (2 Chr. xxxii. 33; xxxv. 24). **2.** in a broader sense, to *all Palestine*: Lk. i. 5; [iv. 44 WH Tr mrg.]; vii. 17; xxiii. 5; Acts ii. 9; x. 37; xi. 1, 29, (and perh. 2 Co. i. 16; Gal. i. 22); πᾶσα ἡ χώρα τῆς Ἰουδαίας, Acts xxvi. 20; εἰς τὰ ὅρια τῆς Ἰουδαίας πέραν τοῦ Ἰορδάνου, *into the borders of Judæa* (in the broader sense) *beyond the Jordan*, i. e. into Peræa, Mt. xix. 1; on the contrary, in the parallel pass. Mk. x. 1 R G, εἰς τὰ ὅρ. τῆς Ἰουδ. διὰ τοῦ πέραν τοῦ Ἰορδ., Jesus is said to have come *into the borders of Judæa* (in the narrower sense) *through Peræa*; but acc. to the reading of L T Tr WH, viz. καὶ πέραν τοῦ Ἰορδ. *and* (in particular that part of Judæa which lay) *beyond the Jordan*, Mark agrees with Matthew; [others regard πέραν τοῦ Ἰορδ. here as parall. with τῆς Ἰουδ. and like it dependent upon ὅρια].

2450 Ἰουδαΐζω; (fr. Ἰουδαῖος, cf. Ἑλληνιστής [W. 92 (87)]), *to adopt Jewish customs and rites, imitate the Jews, Judaize*: of one who observes the ritual law of the Jews, Gal. ii. 14. (Esth. viii. 17; Ignat. ad Magnes. 10, 3; Evang. Nicod. c. 2; Plut. Cic. 7; *to favor the Jews*, Joseph. b. j. 2, 18, 2.) *

2451 Ἰουδαϊκός, -ή, -όν, *Jewish*: Tit. i. 14. (2 Macc. viii. 11; xiii. 21; Joseph. antt. 20, 11, 1; Philo [in Flac. § 8].) *

2452 Ἰουδαϊκῶς, adv., *Jewishly, after the manner of the Jews*: Gal. ii. 14. [(Joseph. b. j. 6, 1, 3.)] *

2453 Ἰουδαῖος, -αία, -αῖον, (Ἰούδα), [Aristot. (in Joseph. c. Ap. 1, 22, 7 where see Müller), Polyb., Diod., Strab., Plut., al.; Sept.; (cf. *Soph.* Lex. s. v.)], *Jewish*; **a.** joined to nouns, *belonging to the Jewish race*: ἀνήρ, Acts x. 28; xxii.

3, (1 Macc. ii. 23); ἄνθρωπος, Acts xxi. 39; ψευδοπροφήτης, Acts xiii. 6; ἀρχιερεύς, Acts xix. 14; γυνή, Acts
xvi. 1; xxiv. 24; γῆ, Jn. iii. 22; χώρα, Mk. i. 5.   **b.**
without a noun, substantively, *Jewish as respects birth,
race, religion*; *a Jew*: Jn. iv. 9; Acts xviii. 2, 24; Ro. ii.
23 sq.; plur., Rev. ii. 9; iii. 9; οἱ 'Ιουδαῖοι (יְהוּדִים), before the exile *citizens of the kingdom of Judah*; after the
exile *all the Israelites* [cf. Wright in B.D. s. v. Jew]), *the
Jews, the Jewish race*: Mt. ii. 2; xxvii. 11, 29; Mk. vii.
3; xv. 2; Jn. ii. 6; iv. 22; v. 1; xviii. 33, etc.; 'Ιουδαῖοί
τε καὶ "Ελληνες, Acts xiv. 1; xviii. 4; xix. 10; 1 Co. i. 24;
'Ιουδαῖοί τε καὶ προσήλυτοι, Acts ii. 11 (10); ἔθνη τε καὶ
'Ιουδαῖοι, Acts xiv. 5; sing., Ro. i. 16; ii. 9; οἱ κατὰ τὰ
ἔθνη 'Ιουδαῖοι, who live in foreign lands, among the Gentiles, Acts xxi. 21; 'Ιουδαῖοι is used of converts from
Judaism, *Jewish Christians* (see ἔθνος, 5) in Gal. ii. 13.
[Syn. Ἑβραῖος, 'Ιουδαῖος, 'Ισραηλίτης: "restricting ourselves to the employment of these three words in the N. T. we
may say that in the first is predominantly noted l a n g u a g e ;
in the second, n a t i o n a l i t y ; in the third (the augustest title
of all), t h e o c r a t i c p r i v i l e g e s and glorious vocation "
(Trench § xxxix.); cf. B.D. s. vv. Hebrew, Israelite, Jew.]
The apostle John, inasmuch as agreeably to the state
of things in his day he looked upon the Jews as a body
of men hostile to Christianity, with whom he had come
to see that both he and all true Christians had nothing
in common as respects religious matters, even in his
record of the life of Jesus not only himself makes a distinction between the Jews and Jesus, but ascribes to
Jesus and his apostles language in which they distinguish themselves from the Jews, as though the latter
sprang from an alien race: Jn. xi. 8; xiii. 33. And
those who (not only at Jerusalem, but also in Galilee, cf.
vi. 41, 52) opposed his divine Master and his Master's
cause, — esp. the rulers, priests, members of the Sanhedrin, Pharisees,—he does not hesitate to style οἱ 'Ιουδαῖοι, since the hatred of these leaders exhibits the
hatred of the whole nation towards Jesus: i. 19; ii. 18,
20; v. 10, 15 sq. 18; vi. 41, 52; vii. 1, 11, 13; ix. 18, 22; x.
24, 31, 33; xviii. 14. [Cf. B.D. s. v. Jew; Franke, Stel-
lung d. Johannes z. Volke d. alt. Bundes. (Halle, 1882).]

2454   **'Ιουδαϊσμός**, -οῦ, ὁ, (ἰουδαΐζω), *the Jewish faith and worship, the religion of the Jews, Judaism*: Gal. i. 13 sq.
(2 Macc. ii. 21, etc.; cf. *Grimm*, Com. on 2 Macc. p. 61.
[B.D. Am. ed. s. v. Judaism].) *

2455   **'Ιούδας**, -α, dat. -ᾳ, acc. -αν, [B. 20 (18)], ὁ, (יְהוּדָה, fr.
the Hoph. of יָדָה, praised, celebrated; see Gen. xxix.
35), *Judah* or *Judas* (see below);   **1.** the fourth son
of the patriarch Jacob: Mt. i. 2 sq.; Lk. iii. 33; Rev. v.
5; vii. 5; by meton., the tribe of Judah, the descendants
of Judah: Heb. vii. 14; ὁ οἶκος 'Ιούδα, citizens of the
kingdom of Judah, Heb. viii. 8.   **2.** *Judah* (or *Judas*)
an unknown ancestor of Christ: Lk. iii. 26 R G L.   **3.**
another of Christ's ancestors, equally unknown: Lk. iii.
30.   **4.** *Judas* surnamed *the Galilæan*, a man who
at the time of the census under Quirinus [better Quiri-
nius], excited a revolt in Galilee: Acts v. 37 (Joseph.
antt. 18, 1, 1, where he is called ὁ Γαυλανίτης because he

came from the city Gamala, near the Lake of Galilee in
lower Gaulanitis; but he is called also ὁ Γαλιλαῖος by
Joseph. antt. 18, 1, 6; 20, 5, 2; b. j. 2, 8, 1).   **5.** [*Judas*] a certain Jew of Damascus: Acts ix. 11.   **6.**
Judas surnamed 'Ισκαριώτης (q. v.), *of Carioth* (from the
city of Kerioth, Josh. xv. 25; Jer. xxxi. (xlviii.) 41; Amos
ii. 2; [but see BB.DD. s. v. Kerioth]; some codd. in Jn.
vi. 71 [cf. Tdf.'s note in loc.]; xii. 4, read ἀπὸ Καριώτου
instead of 'Ισκαριώτης), the son of one Simon (who in
Jn. vi. 71 L T Tr WH; xiii. 26 T Tr WH, is himself surnamed 'Ισκαριώτης), one of the apostles of Jesus, who
betrayed him: Mt. x. 4; xxvi. 14, 25, 47; xxvii. 3; Mk.
iii. 19; xiv. 10, 43; Lk. vi. 16; xxii. 3, 47 sq.; Jn. vi. 71;
xii. 4; xiii. 2, 26, 29; xviii. 2 sq. 5; Acts i. 16, 25. Matthew (xxvii. 5), Luke (Acts i. 18), and Papias [cf. *Wendt*
in Meyer's Apostelgesch. 5te Aufl. p. 23 note] in a frag.
quoted by Oecum. on Acts i. 18 differ in the account of
his death, [see B. D. Am. ed. s. v.]; on his avarice cf.
Jn. xii. 6.   **7.** *Judas*, surnamed *Barsabas* [or *Barsabbas*, see the word], a prophet of the church at Jerusalem: Acts xv. 22, 27, 32.   **8.** *Judas*, an apostle,
Jn. xiv. 22, who is called 'Ιούδας 'Ιακώβου in Lk. vi. 16;
Acts i. 13 (see 'Ιάκωβος, 4), and, as it should seem, was
surnamed *Lebbœus* or *Thaddœus* (see Θαδδαῖος).   According to the opinion of the church he wrote the Epistle
of Jude.   **9.** *Judas*, the brother of our Lord: Mt.
xiii. 55; Mk. vi. 3, and very probably Jude 1; see 'Ιάκωβος, 3.*

'Ιουλία, -ας, ἡ, *Julia*, a Christian woman [cf. Bp. Lghtft.   **2456**
on Philip. p. 177]: Ro. xvi. 15 [L mrg. 'Ιουνίαν].*

'Ιούλιος, -ου, ὁ, *Julius*, a Roman centurion: Acts xxvii.   **2457**
1, 3.*

'Ιουνίας [al. -ιᾶς, as contr. fr. Junianus; cf. W. 102 sq.   **2458**
(97)], -α [but cf. B. 17 sq. (16)], ὁ, *Junias*, a convert from
Judaism, Paul's kinsman and fellow-prisoner: Ro. xvi. 7
[(here A. V. *Junia* (a w o m a n ' s name) which is possible). The name occurs again as the name of a Christian
at Rome in Ro. xvi. 15 Lchm. mrg. (where al. 'Ιουλίαν).]*

'Ιοῦστος, -ου, ὁ, *Justus* [cf. Bp. Lghtft. on Col. iv. 11],   **2459**
the surname   **1.** of *Joseph*, a convert from Judaism,
who was also surnamed Barsabas [better Barsabbas q.
v.]: Acts i. 23.   **2.** of *Titus*, a Corinthian [a Jewish proselyte]: Acts xviii. 7.   **3.** of a certain *Jesus*,
[a Jewish Christian]: Col. iv. 11.*

ἱππεύς, -έως, ὁ, (ἵππος), *a horseman*: Acts xxiii. 23, 32.   **2460**
[From Hom. down.] *

ἱππικός, -ή, -όν, *equestrian*; τὸ ἱππικόν, *the horse* (-men),   **2461**
cavalry: Rev. ix. 16 (as Hdt. 7, 87; Xen., Plat., Polyb.,
al.; more fully τὸ ἱππικὸν στράτευμα, Xen. Cyr. 3, 3, 26;
so τὸ πεζικόν, the foot (-forces), infantry, Xen. Cyr. 5, 3,
38).*

ἵππος, -ου, ὁ, [Curtius § 624; Peile, Grk. and Lat·   **2462**
Etymol., Index s. v.], *a horse*: Jas. iii. 3; Rev. vi. 2, 4 sq.
8; ix. 7, 9, 17, [19 G L T Tr WH]; xiv. 20; xviii. 13; xix.
11–21. [From Hom. down.] *

ἶρις, -ιδος, ἡ, (*Iris*), *a rainbow*: Rev. iv. 3; x. 1. (Hom.,   **2463**
Aristot., Theophr., al.) *

'Ισαάκ, ὁ, indecl. (יִצְחָק, fr. צָחַק to laugh: Gen. xxi. 6;   **2464**

xvii. 17; in Joseph. Ἴσακος, -ου), Isaac, the son of Abraham by Sarah: Mt. i. 2; viii. 11; xxii. 32; Ro. ix. 7, 10; Gal. iv. 28; Heb. xi. 9, 17 sq. 20; Jas. ii. 21, etc.

2465 ἰσάγγελος, -ον, (ἴσος and ἄγγελος, formed like ἰσόθεος [cf. ἰσάδελφος (Eur. Or. 1015), ἰσάστερος (4 Macc. xvii. 5), and other compounds in Koumanoudes, Συναγωγή κτλ. p. 166 sq.]), like the angels: Lk. xx. 36. (Eccl. writ.; [cf. ἴσος ἀγγέλοις γεγονώς, Philo de sacr. Ab. et Cain. § 2; W. § 34, 3 cf. p. 100 (95)].) *

2466 Ἰσαχάρ [Rec.elz] and Ἰσαχάρ [Rst G L] (Ἰσσάχαρ Tdf., Ἰσσαχάρ Tr WH), ὁ, שָּׂשכָר, fr. שׁ there is, and שָׂכָר a reward [(cf. Jer. xxxi. 16) yet cf. Mühlau u. Volck s. v.]; Joseph. Ἰσάσχαρις [Ἰσάχαρις]), Issachar, the son of the patriarch Jacob by Leah (Gen. xxx. 18): Rev. vii. 7.*

2467 ἴσημι, found only in the Doric form ἴσαμι, to know; from which some derive the forms ἴστε and ἴσμεν, contracted from ἴσατε and ἴσαμεν; but these forms are more correctly derived from εἴδω, ἴσμεν i. q. ἴδμεν, etc., (cf. Bttm. Ausf. Spr. i. p. 548); on the phrase ἴστε [R ἐστε] γινώσκοντες, Eph. v. 5, see γινώσκω, I. 2 b.

2469 Ἰσκαριώτης, and (Lchm. in Mt. x. 4; T WH in Mk. xiv. 10; L T Tr WH in Mk. iii. 19; Lk. vi. 16) Ἰσκαριώθ, i. e. קְרִיּוֹת אִישׁ; see Ἰούδας, 6 and Σίμων, 5.

2470 ἴσος (not ἴσος [yet often so Rst elz G Tr], which is Epic; cf. Bornemann, Scholia in Luc. p. 4; Göttling, Lehre vom Accent p. 305; [Chandler § 406]; Lipsius, Grammat. Untersuch. p. 24; [L. and S. s. v. fin.; W. 52]), -η, -ον, equal, in quality or in quantity: ἡ ἴση δωρεά, the same gift, Acts xi. 17; ἴσαι μαρτυρίαι, agreeing testimonies, Mk. xiv. 56, 59; ἴσον ποιεῖν τινά τινι, to make one equal to another, in the payment of wages, Mt. xx. 12; ἑαυτὸν τῷ θεῷ, to claim for one's self the nature, rank, authority, which belong to God, Jn. v. 18; τὰ ἴσα ἀπολαβεῖν, Lk. vi. 34. The neuters ἴσον and ἴσα are often used adverbially fr. Hom. down (cf. Passow s. v. p. 1505*; [L. and S. s. v. IV. 1]; W. § 27, 3 fin.): ἴσα εἶναι (B. § 129, 11), of measurement, Rev. xxi. 16; of state and condition, τῷ θεῷ, Phil. ii. 6 (on which see in μορφή).*

2471 ἰσότης, -ητος, ἡ, (ἴσος); **1.** equality: ἐξ ἰσότητος [cf. ἐκ, V. 3] by equality, 2 Co. viii. 13 (14), i. q. ὅπως γένηται ἰσότης, 14. **2.** equity, fairness, what is equitable, joined with τὸ δίκαιον: Col. iv. 1. (Eur., Plat., Aristot., Polyb., al.; [cf. Bp. Lghtft. on Col. l. c., yet per contra Meyer].) *

2472 ἰσότιμος, -ον, (ἴσος and τιμή), equally precious; equally honored: τινί, to be esteemed equal to, ἰσότιμον ἡμῖν πίστιν [a like precious faith with us], concisely for πίστιν τῇ ἡμῶν πίστει ἰσότιμον [W. § 66, 2 f.; B. § 133, 10]: 2 Pet. i. 1. (Philo, Joseph., Plut., Lcian., Ael., al.) *

2473 ἰσόψυχος, -ον, (ἴσος and ψυχή), equal in soul [A. V. like-minded], (Vulg. unanimus): Phil. ii. 20. (Ps. liv. (lv.) 14; Aeschyl. Ag. 1470.) *

2474 Ἰσραήλ (Joseph. Ἰσράηλος, -ου), ὁ, indecl., יִשְׂרָאֵל, fr. שָׂרָה and אֵל, wrestler with God, Gen. xxxii. 28; Hos. xii. 4, cf. Gen. xxxv. 10), Israel, a name given to the patriarch Jacob (and borne by him in addition to his former name from Gen. xxxii. 28 on): ὁ οἶκος Ἰσραήλ, the family

or descendants of Israel, the race of Israel [A. V. the house of Israel], Mt. x. 6; xv. 24; Acts vii. 42, (Ex. xvi. 31; 1 S. vii. 2, and often); οἱ υἱοὶ Ἰσρ. the [sons i. e. the children, the] posterity of Israel, Lk. i. 16; Acts v. 21; vii. 23, 37; Ro. ix. 27; αἱ φυλαὶ τοῦ Ἰσρ., Mt. xix. 28; Lk. xxii. 30; Rev. vii. 4. By meton. for the posterity of Israel i. e. the Israelites (a name of esp. honor because it made reference to the promises of salvation through the Messiah, which were given to Jacob in preference to Esau, and to be fulfilled to his posterity [see Ἰουδαῖος, b.]): Mt. ii. 6; viii. 10; ix. 33; Lk. i. 54, 68, 80; Acts iv. 8 [R G]; Eph. ii. 12; Ro. xi. 2, 7, 26, etc. (Ex. v. 2; xi. 7, and often); ὁ λαὸς Ἰσρ., Acts iv. 10, 27; γῆ Ἰσρ. i. e. Palestine [(1 S. xiii. 19, etc.)], Mt. ii. 20 sq.; βασιλεὺς Ἰσρ., Mt. xxvii. 42; Jn. i. 49 (50); ἡ ἐλπὶς τοῦ Ἰσρ. Acts xxviii. 20; ὁ Ἰσρ. τοῦ θεοῦ (gen. of possession), i. e. Christians, Gal. vi. 16; ὁ Ἰσρ. κατὰ σάρκα, Israelites by birth, i. e. Jews, 1 Co. x. 18; in an emphat. sense, οὐ γὰρ πάντες οἱ ἐξ Ἰσρ. κτλ. for not all those that draw their bodily descent from Israel are true Israelites, i. e. are those whom God pronounces to be Israelites and has chosen to salvation, Ro. ix. 6.

2475 Ἰσραηλίτης (T WH Ἰσραηλείτης, Tr only in Jn. i. 47 (48); [see Tdf. Proleg. p. 86, and cf. s. v. ει, ι]), -ου, ὁ, (Ἰσραήλ, q. v.), an Israelite (Hebr. יִשְׂרְאֵלִי; Sept. Ἰεζραηλίτης, 2 S. xvii. 25), one of the race of Israel, a name held in honor (see Ἰσραήλ): Jn. i. 47 (48); Ro. ix. 4; xi. 1; 2 Co. xi. 22; ἄνδρες Ἰσραηλῖται [W. § 65, 5 d.; B. 82 (72)], Acts ii. 22; iii. 12; v. 35; xiii. 16; [xxi. 28], (4 Macc. xviii. 1; Joseph. antt. 2, 9, 1). [Cf. B. D. (Am. ed.) s. v. Syn. see Ἰουδαῖος, b.] *

[Ἰσσάχαρ, Ἰσσαχάρ, see Ἰσαχάρ.] ———————— see 2466

2476 ἵστημι, more rarely ἱστάω ([(fr. Hdt. down; cf. Veitch s. v.)] ἱστῶμεν, Ro. iii. 31 R G) and ἱστάνω ([(late; cf. Veitch s. v.)] ἱστάνομεν, Ro. iii. 31 L T Tr WH), [cf. B. 44 (38) sq.; W. § 14, 1 f.; 87 (83); WH. App. p. 168; Veitch p. 337 sq.]; fut. στήσω; 1 aor. ἔστησα; 2 aor. ἔστην, impv. στῆθι, inf. στῆναι, ptcp. στάς; pf. ἔστηκα [with pres. force; W. 274 (257)], inf. ἑστάναι [Relz st bez G Tr -άναι in Acts xii. 14] (nowhere ἑστηκέναι), ptcp. masc. ἑστηκώς with neut. ἑστηκός, and in the shorter form ἑστώς, ἑστῶσα (Jn. viii. 9), with neut. ἑστός and (L T Tr WH in Mt. xxiv. 15 [here Rst also]; Rev. xiv. 1) ἑστός, (cf. Bttm. Ausf. Spr. ii. p. 208; [Rutherford, Babrius p. 39 sq.; W. § 14, 1 i.; B. 48 (41)]); plupf. εἱστήκειν [(but WH uniformly ἱστ.; see I, ι) with force of impf. W. 274 (257)], 3 pers. plur. εἱστήκεισαν (Mt. xii. 46; Jn. xviii. 18; Acts ix. 7 and L Tr WH in Rev. vii. 11) and εἱστήκεσαν (Rev. vii. 11 R G [cf. W. § 14, 1 a.; yet B. 43 (38)]); Pass., 1 aor. ἐστάθην; 1 fut. σταθήσομαι; 1 fut. mid. στήσομαι (Rev. xviii. 15);

I. TRANSITIVELY in the Pres., Impf., Fut., and 1 Aor. act.; likewise in the tenses of the Pass. [cf. B. 47 (41) contra W. 252 (237)], (Sept. for הֶעֱמִיד, הֵקִים, הִצִּיב; [fr. Hom. down]; to cause or make to stand; to place, put, set; **1.** univ. **a.** prop. τινά, to bid to stand by, [set up]: Acts i. 23; vi. 13; in the presence of others: ἐν μέσῳ, in the midst, Jn. viii. 3, and ἐν τῷ μέσῳ,

Acts iv. 7; ἐνώπιόν τινος, Acts vi. 6; before judges: εἰς αὐτούς, before the members of the Sanhedrin, Acts xxii. 30; ἐν τῷ συνεδρίῳ, Acts v. 27; ἐπί with gen. of the judge, pass. σταθήσεσθε, Mk. xiii. 9; τινὰ ἄμωμον κατενώπιόν τινος, to [set one i. e.] cause one to make his appearance faultless before etc. Jude 24; to place (i. e. designate the place for one to occupy): ἐν μέσῳ τινῶν, Mt. xviii. 2; Mk. ix. 36; παρ᾽ ἑαυτῷ, Lk. ix. 47; ἐκ δεξιῶν, Mt. xxv. 33; ἐπί τι (acc. of place), Mt. iv. 5; Lk. iv. 9. Mid. to place one's self, to stand (Germ. sich hinstellen, hintreten): ἀπὸ μακρόθεν, Rev. xviii. 15; likewise in the passive: σταθείς, Lk. xviii. 11, 40; xix. 8; [ἐστάθησαν σκυθρωποί they stood still, looking sad, Lk. xxiv. 17 T WH Tr txt. (cf. II. 1 b. β.)]; Acts ii.14; xi. 13; with ἐν μέσῳ τινός, τινῶν, added, Acts xvii. 22; xxvii. 21; σταθέντες, when they had appeared (before the judge), Acts xxv. 18. β. trop. to make firm, fix, establish: τί, τινά, to cause a pers. or thing to keep his or its place; pass. to stand, be kept intact (of a family, a kingdom): Mt. xii. 25 sq.; Lk. xi. 18; i. q. to escape in safety, Rev. vi. 17; with ἔμπροσθεν τοῦ υἱοῦ τοῦ ἀνθρ. added, Lk. xxi. 36; στῆσαί τινα, to cause one to preserve a right state of mind, Ro. xiv. 4 [see Meyer]; pass. σταθήσεται, shall be made to stand, i. e. shall be kept from falling, ibid. τί, to establish a thing, cause it to stand, i. e. to uphold or sustain the authority or force of any thing: Heb. x. 9 (opp. to ἀναιρεῖν); τὴν παράδοσιν, Mk. vii. 9; τὴν ἰδίαν δικαιοσ. Ro. x. 3; τὸν νόμον (opp. to καταργῶ), Ro. iii. 31, (τὸν ὅρκον, Gen. xxvi. 3; τὴν διαθήκην, Ex. vi. 4; 1 Macc. ii. 27). i. q. to ratify, confirm: σταθῇ, σταθήσεται πᾶν ῥῆμα, Mt. xviii. 16; 2 Co. xiii. 1. to appoint, [cf. colloq. Eng. set]: ἡμέραν, Acts xvii. 31; cf. Grimm on 1 Macc. iv. 59. 2. to set or place in a balance; to weigh: money to one (because in very early times, before the introduction of coinage, the metals used to be weighed) i. e. to pay, Mt. xxvi. 15 (so in Grk. writ. fr. Hom. down; cf. Passow s. v. p. 1508ᵇ; [L. and S. s. v. A. IV.]; Sept. for שָׁקַל, Is. xlvi. 6; Jer. xxxix. (xxxii.) 9 sq.; Zech. xi. 12; 2 Esdr. viii. 25 sq.; etc.); this furnishes the explanation of the phrase μὴ στήσῃς αὐτοῖς τὴν ἁμαρτίαν ταύτην, do not reckon to them, call them to account for, this sin [A. V. lay not this sin to their charge], Acts vii. 60 [(cf. Meyer ad loc.)].

II. INTRANSITIVELY in the Perf. and Plupf. (having the sense of a pres. and an impf. [see above]), also in 2 Aor. act., to stand; Sept. for נָצַב, עָמַד, קוּם; 1. prop. a. foll. by prepositions or adverbs of place: foll. by ἐν w. dat. of place [cf. B. 329 (283)], Mt. vi. 5; xx. 3; xxiv. 15; Lk. xxiv. 36; Jn. viii. 9; xi. 56; Acts v. 25; vii. 33 [L T Tr WH ἐπί w. dat.]; Rev. v. 6; Acts. 17; ἐνώπιόν τινος, Acts x. 30; Rev. vii. 9; viii. 2; xi. 4; xii. 4; πρός w. dat. of place, Jn. xviii. 16; ἐπί w. gen. of place (Germ. auf, upon), Lk. vi. 17; Acts xxi. 40; Rev. v. 8; w. gen. of the judge or tribunal, before [cf. ἐπί, A. I. 2 b.], Acts xxiv. 20; xxv. 10; πέραν with gen. of place, Jn. vi. 22; πρό, Acts v. 23 [R G; but L T Tr WH ἐπὶ τῶν θυρῶν (at, Germ. an; cf. above and see ἐπί, A. I. 2 a.)]; xii. 14; ἔμπροσθέν τινος, before one as judge, Mt. xxvii. 11; κύκλῳ (τινός), around, Rev. vii. 11; μέσος ὑμῶν,

in the midst of you, living among you, Jn. i. 26; ἐκ δεξιῶν τινος, Lk. i. 11; Acts vii. 55 sq.; ἐν μέσῳ, Jn. viii. 9; πρός w. acc. (G L T Tr WH w. dat. [see πρός, II.]) of place, Jn. xx. 11; ἐπί w. acc. of place (see ἐπί, C. I.), Mt. xiii. 2; Rev. iii. 20; vii. 1; xiv. 1; xv. 2; ἐπὶ τοὺς πόδας, to stand upright, Acts xxvi. 16; Rev. xi. 11; παρά w. acc., Lk. v. 2; vii. 38; εἰς, Jn. xxi. 4 (L T Tr mrg. WH mrg. ἐπί [see ἐπί, C. I. 1 d.]); ἐκεῖ, Mt. xxvii. 47; Mk. xi. 5; Jas. ii. 3; ὧδε, Mt. xvi. 28; xx. 6; Mk. ix. 1; Lk. ix. 27 [here T Tr WH αὐτοῦ, q. v.]; ὅπου, Mk. xiii. 14; ἔξω, Mt. xii. 46, 47 [here WH in mrg. only]; Mk. iii. 31; Lk. viii. 20; xiii. 25; μακρόθεν, Lk. xviii. 13; xxiii. 49 [R G Tr txt.]; ἀπὸ μακρόθεν, Rev. xviii. 10, 17; [Lk. xxiii. 49 L T WH Tr mrg. (but ἀπό in br.)]; πόρρωθεν, Lk. xvii. 12. b. absolutely; a. to stand by, stand near, (in a place already mentioned, so that the reader readily understands where): Mt. xxvi. 73; Jn. i. 35; iii. 29; vii. 37; xii. 29; xviii. 18, 25; xx. 14; Acts xvi. 9; xxii. 25; with a ptcp. or adj. (indicating the purpose or act or condition of the one standing): Mt. xx. 6; Lk. xxiii. 10; Acts i. 11; ix. 7; xxvi. 6; opp. to καθίζειν, Heb. x. 11 sq. β. if what is said to stand had been in motion (walking, flowing, etc.), to stop, stand still: Mt. ii. 9 (Rec. ἔστη, L T Tr WH ἐστάθη [cf. I. 1 a.]); Mt. xx. 32; Mk. x. 49; Lk. viii. 44; Acts viii. 38. γ. contextually, to stand immovable, stand firm, of the foundation of a building: 2 Tim. ii. 19. 2. metaph. a. to stand, i. e. continue safe and sound, stand unharmed: Acts xxvi. 22. b. to stand ready or prepared: with a ptcp., Eph. vi. 14. c. to be of a steadfast mind; so in the maxim in 1 Co. x. 12. d. foll. by a ptcp. of quality, Col. iv. 12; ὃς ἕστηκεν ἑδραῖος, who does not hesitate, does not waver, 1 Co. vii. 37; in a fig., of one who vanquishes his adversaries and holds the ground, Eph. vi. 13; also of one who in the midst of the fight holds his position πρός τινα, against the foe, Eph. vi. 11, (cf. Ex. xiv. 13; Ps. xxxvi. (xxxvi.) 13). to persist, continue, persevere: τῇ πίστει, dat. commodi (so as not to fall from thy faith [al. take the dat. instrumentally, by thy faith; cf. W. § 31, 6 c.; B. § 133, 24]), Ro. xi. 20; ἐν τῇ ἀληθείᾳ, Jn. viii. 44 (where the meaning is, his nature abhors, is utterly estranged from, the truth; Vulg. incorrectly, in veritate non stetit; Luther, ist nicht bestanden [A. V. abode not etc.]; but the Zürich version correctly, besteht nicht [WH read ἕστηκεν, impf. of στήκω, q. v.]); ἐν τῇ χάριτι, Ro. v. 2; ἐν τῷ εὐαγγελίῳ, 1 Co. xv. 1; εἰς ἣν (sc. χάριν) ἑστήκατε, into which ye have entered, that ye may stand fast in it, 1 Pet. v. 12 [but L T Tr WH read στῆτε (2 aor. act. impv. 2 pers. plur.) enter and stand fast; B. § 147, 16, cf. p. 329 (283)]. N. B. From ἕστηκα is formed the verb στήκω, which see in its place. [COMP.: ἀν-, ἐπ-αν-, ἐξ-αν-, ἀνθ-, ἀφ-, δι-, ἐν-, ἐξ-, ἐπ- (-μαι), ἐφ-, κατ-εφ-, συν-εφ-, καθ-, ἀντι-καθ-, ἀπο-καθ-, μεθ-, παρ-, περι-, προ-, συν-ίστημι.]

ἱστορέω: 1 aor. inf. ἱστορῆσαι; (ἵστωρ [allied with οἶδα (ἴστω), videre (visus), etc.; Curtius § 282], -ορος, one that has inquired into, knowing, skilled in); fr. Aeschyl. and Hdt. down; 1. to inquire into, examine, investigate. 2. to find out, learn, by inquiry. 3. to gain knowledge of by visiting: something (worthy of being seen), τὴν χώραν, Plut. Thes. 30; Pomp. 40; τινά, some distinguished person, to become personally acquainted with, know face to face: Gal. i. 18; so too in Joseph. antt. 1, 11, 4; b. j. 6, 1, 8 and often in the Clem. homilies; cf. Hilgenfeld, Galaterbrief, p. 122 note; [Ellicott on Gal. l. c.].*

2478 ἰσχυρός, -ά, -όν, (ἰσχύω), [fr. Aeschyl. down], Sept. mostly for אֵל, גִּבּוֹר, חָזָק, עָצוּם, and Chald. תַּקִּיף; strong, mighty; **a.** of living beings: strong either in body or in mind, Mt. xii. 29; Mk. iii. 27; Lk. xi. 21 sq.; Rev. v. 2; x. 1; xviii. 21; ἐν πολέμῳ, mighty i. e. valiant, Heb. xi. 34, cf. Rev. xix. 18; of one who has strength of soul to sustain the assaults of Satan, 1 Jn. ii. 14; univ. strong, and therefore exhibiting many excellences, 1 Co. iv. 10 (opp. to ἀσθενής); compar., Mt. iii. 11; Mk. i. 7; Lk. iii. 16; mighty, — of God, 1 Co. i. 25; Rev. xviii. 8, (Deut. x. 17; 2 Macc. i. 24, etc.); of Christ raised to the right hand of God, 1 Co. x. 22; of those who wield great influence among men by their rank, authority, riches, etc., τὰ ἰσχυρά i. q. τοὺς ἰσχυρούς (on the neut. cf. W. § 27, 5), 1 Co. i. 27 (οἱ ἰσχυροὶ τῆς γῆς, 2 K. xxiv. 15); joined with πλούσιοι, Rev. vi. 15 (Rec. οἱ δυνατοί). **b.** of inanimate things: strong i. q. violent, ἄνεμος, Mt. xiv. 30 [T WH om. ἰσχ.]; forcibly uttered, φωνή, Rev. xviii. 2 [Rec. μεγάλη] (Ex. xix. 19); κραυγή, Heb. v. 7; βρονταί, Rev. xix. 6; λιμός, great, Lk. xv. 14; ἐπιστολαί (stern, [forcible]), 2 Co. x. 10; strong i. q. firm, sure, παράκλησις, Heb. vi. 18; fitted to withstand a forcible assault, πόλις, well fortified, Rev. xviii. 10 (τεῖχος, 1 Macc. i. 33; Xen. Cyr. 7, 5, 7; πύργος, Judg. ix. 51). [Cf. δύναμις, fin.]*

2479 ἰσχύς, -ύος, ἡ, (ἴσχω [allied w. ἔσχον; to hold in check]), [fr. Hes. down], Sept. esp. for כֹּחַ, חַיִל, עֹז, גְּבוּרָה; ability, force, strength, might: 2 Pet. ii. 11 (joined w. δύναμις); Rev. v. 12; vii. 12; τὸ κράτος τῆς ἰσχύος, power (over external things) afforded by strength, Eph. i. 19; vi. 10, (Is. xl. 26); ἡ δόξα τῆς ἰσχ. (see δόξα, III. 3 b. a. fin.), 2 Th. i. 9; κράζειν ἐν ἰσχύϊ, with strength, mightily, Rev. xviii. 2 Rec.; ἐξ ἰσχύος, of one's strength, to the extent of one's ability, 1 Pet. iv. 11; with ὅλης added, Mk. xii. 30, 33; Lk. x. 27 [here L txt. T Tr WH read ἐν ὅλῃ τῇ ἰσχύϊ]. [SYN. see δύναμις, fin.]*

2480 ἰσχύω; impf. ἴσχυον; fut. ἰσχύσω; 1 aor. ἴσχυσα; (ἰσχύς); Sept. for חָזַק, אָמֵץ, עָצַם, etc.; to be strong, i. e. **1.** to be strong in body, to be robust, to be in sound health: οἱ ἰσχύοντες, as subst., Mt. ix. 12; Mk. ii. 17, (Soph. Tr. 234; Xen. Cyr. 6, 1, 24; joined with ὑγιαίνειν, id. mem. 2, 7, 7). **2.** to have power, [fr. Aeschyl. down], i. e. **a.** to have a power evinced in extraordinary deeds, i. e. to exert, wield, power: so of the gospel, Acts xix. 20; Hebraistically, to have strength to overcome: οὐκ ἴσχυσαν, [A. V prevailed not i. e.] succumbed, were conquered, (so לֹא יָכֹל, Gen. xxxii. 26 (25)), Rev. xii. 8; κατά τινος, against one, i. e. to use one's strength against one, to treat one with violence, Acts xix. 16. **b.** i. q. to be of force, avail (Germ. gelten): Heb. ix. 17; τί, Gal. v. 6, and Rec. in vi. 15. **c.** to be serviceable: εἴς τι [A. V. good for], Mt. v. 13. **d.** foll. by inf. to be able, can:

Mt. viii. 28; xxvi. 40; Mk. v. 4; [ix. 18 (inf. to be supplied)]; xiv. 37; Lk. vi. 48; viii. 43; [xiii. 24]; xiv. 6, 29 sq.; xvi. 3; xx. 26; Jn. xxi. 6; Acts vi. 10; xv. 10; xxv. 7; xxvii. 16, (Plut. Pomp. 58). with acc., πάντα, Phil. iv. 13; πολύ, Jas. v. 16. [COMP.: ἐν-, ἐξ-, ἐπ-, κατ-ισχύω.]*

2481 ἴσως, (ἴσος, q. v.), adv., [fr. Soph. down]; **1.** equally, in like manner. **2.** agreeably to expectation, i. e. it may be, probably; freq. an urbane expression of one's reasonable hope (Germ. wohl, hoffentlich): Lk. xx. 13, and often in Attic writ.*

2482 Ἰταλία, -ας, ἡ, Italy: Acts xviii. 2; xxvii. 1, 6; Heb. xiii. 24.*

2483 Ἰταλικός, -ή, -όν, (Ἰταλία), [fr. Plat. down], Italian: σπεῖρα Ἰταλική, the Italian cohort (composed of Italian, not provincial, soldiers), Acts x. 1; cf. Schürer, in the Zeitschrift f. wissensch. Theol. for 1875, p. 422 sqq.; [Hackett, in B.D. Am. ed. s. v. Italian Band].*

2484 Ἰτουραία, -ας, ἡ, Ituræa, a mountainous region, lying northeast of Palestine and west of Damascus (Strabo 16 p. 756 § 18; Plin. h. n. 5, (23) 19). Acc. to Luke (iii. 1) at the time when John the Baptist made his public appearance it was subject to Philip the tetrarch, son of Herod the Great, although it is not mentioned by Joseph. (antt. 17, 8, 1; 11, 4, 18; 4, 6 and b. j. 2, 6, 3) among the regions assigned to this prince after his father's death; (on this point cf. Schürer in the Zeitschr. f. wissensch. Theol. for 1877, p. 577 sq.). It was brought under Jewish control by king Aristobulus c. B.C. 100 (Joseph. antt. 13, 11, 3). Its inhabitants had been noted for robbery and the skilful use of the bow (Verg. geor. 2, 448; Cic. Phil. 13, 8, 18; Strabo 16 p. 755 sq.; Lucan, Phar. 7, 230, 514). Cf. Münter, Progr. de rebus Ituraeorum, Hafn. 1824; Win. RWB. s. v. Ituraea; Kneucker in Schenkel iii. p. 406 sq.; [B.D. Am. ed. s. v.].*

2485 ἰχθύδιον, -ου, τό, (dimin. fr. ἰχθύς), a little fish: Mt. xv. 34; Mk. viii. 7. [From Arstph. on.]*

2486 ἰχθύς, -ύος, ὁ, [fr. Hom. down], a fish: Mt. vii. 10; Mk. vi. 38; Lk. v. 6; Jn. xxi. 11, etc.; 1 Co. xv. 39.

2487 ἴχνος, -εος (-ους), τό, (fr. ἵκω i. q. ἱκνέομαι, to go), [fr. Hom. down], a footprint, track, footstep: in the N. T. metaph., of imitating the example of any one, we find στοιχεῖν τοῖς ἴχνεσί τινος, Ro. iv. 12; περιπατεῖν τοῖς ἴχν. τ. 2 Co. xii. 18; ἐπακολουθεῖν τ. ἴχν. τιν. 1 Pet. ii. 21, (ἐν ἴχνεσί τινος ἐὸν πόδα νέμειν, Pind. Nem. 6, 27); cf. Lat. insistere vestigiis alicuius.*

2488 Ἰωάθαμ, [-θάμ WH], ὁ, (יוֹתָם i. e. Jehovah is perfect), indecl., Jotham [A. V. (1611) Joatham], king of Judah, son of Uzziah, B.C. 758–7 to 741, or 759 to 743: Mt. i. 9.*

2489 Ἰωάννα [Tr WH Ἰωάνα; cf. Tdf. Proleg. p. 79; WH. App. p. 159; s. v. N, ν], -ης, ἡ, (see Ἰωάννης), Joanna, the wife of Chuzas, Herod's steward, and a follower of Jesus: Lk. viii. 3; xxiv. 10.*

2490 Ἰωαννᾶς, -ᾶ, and (acc. to L T Tr WH) Ἰωανάν, indecl., (see Ἰωάννης), ὁ, Joannas [or Joanan], one of the ancestors of Christ: Lk. iii. 27.*

2491 Ἰωάννης and ([so WH uniformly, exc. in Acts iv. 6; xiii. 5; Rev. xxii. 8] Tr in the Gospels of Lk. and Jn., [in the Acts, exc. iv. 6] and the Rev. [exc. xxii. 8]) Ἰωάνη-

[cf. *Tdf.* Proleg. p. 79; *WH.* App. p. 159; *Scrivener*, Intr. p. 562 (cf. s. v. **N**, *ν*)], gen. -ου, dat. -ῃ and (in [Mt. xi. 4 WH]; Rev. i. 1 WH]; Lk. vii. 18 T Tr WH, [22 T Tr WH] -ει [cf. *WH.* App. p. 158; B. 17 (16), 7]), acc. -ην, ὁ, (יוֹחָנָן and יְהוֹחָנָן, to whom Jehovah is gracious, [al. whom Jehovah has graciously given], Germ. *Gotthold*; Sept. 'Ιωαννάν [Tdf. 'Ιωανάν], 1 Chr. iii. 24; 'Ιωνά, 2 K. xxv. 23; 'Ιωάνης, 2 Chr. xxviii. 12, [cf. B.D. Am. ed. s. v. Johanan]), *John*; in the N. T. the men of this name are, **1.** *John the Baptist*, the son of Zacharias the priest and Elisabeth, the forerunner of Christ. By order of Herod Antipas he was cast into prison and afterwards beheaded: Mt. iii. 1; xiv. 3, and often in the histor. bks. of the N. T.; Joseph. antt. 18, 5, 2, [B.D. Am. ed. s. v. Machærus]. **2.** *John the apostle, the writer of the Fourth Gospel*, son of Zebedee and Salome, brother of James the elder: Mt. iv. 21; x. 2 (3); Mk. i. 19; ix. 2, 38; Lk. v. 10; vi. 14; Acts i. 13, and often; Gal. ii. 9. He is that disciple who (without mention by name) is spoken of in the Fourth Gospel as esp. dear to Jesus (Jn. xiii. 23; xix. 26; xxi. 7, 20), and acc. to the traditional opinion is the author of the Apocalypse, Rev. i. 1, 4, 9; xxi. 2 Rec.; xxii. 8. In the latter part of his life he had charge of the churches in Asia Minor, and died there at a very advanced age. That he never came into Asia Minor, but died in Palestine somewhat in years, the following writers among others have attempted to prove, though by considerations far from satisfactory: *Lützelberger*, Die kirchl. Tradition üb. d. Ap. Johannes u. s. Schriften. Lpz. 1840; *Keim*, i. p. 161 sqq. [Eng. trans. i. 218 sqq.]; *Holtzmann* in Schenkel iii. p. 332 sqq.; *Scholten*, Der Ap. Johannes in Kleinasien. Aus. d. Holländ. deutsch v. *Spiegel.* Berl. 1872. On the other side cf., besides others, *Grimm* in Ersch u. Gruber's Encyklop. 2d sect. vol. xxii. p. 6 sqq.; *Steitz*, Die Tradition üb. die Wirksamkeit des Joh. in Ephesus, in the Theol. Stud. u. Krit. for 1868, 3d Heft; *Krenkel*, Der Apost. Johannes. Berl. 1868; *Hilgenfeld* in the Zeitschr. f. wissensch. Theol. for 1872, p. 372 sqq., and for 1877, p. 508 sqq.; [also Einl. in d. N. T. p. 394 sqq.]; *Luthardt*, Der johann. Ursprung des 4ten Evang. (Lpz. 1874) p. 93 sqq. [Eng. trans. p. 115 sqq.; *Godet*, Commentaire etc. 3d ed. vol. i. Intr. l. i. § iv. p. 57 sqq.; *Bleek*, Einl. in d. N. T. (ed. *Mangold*) p. 167 sqq.; *Fisher*, The Beginnings of Christianity, p. 327 sqq.]. **3.** the father of the apostle Peter: Tdf. in Jn. i. 42 (43) and xxi. 15 sqq. (in both pass. R G 'Ιωνᾶ, L Tr WH 'Ιωάνου) [see 'Ιωνᾶς, 2]. **4.** a certain man ἐκ γένους ἀρχιερατικοῦ, a member of the Sanhedrin [cf. ἀρχιερεύς, 2]: Acts iv. 6. **5.** *John* surnamed *Mark*, the companion of Barnabas and Paul: Acts xii. 12, 25; xiii. 5, 13; xv. 37, [Tr everywh. with one *ν*; so WH exc. in xiii. 5]; see Μάρκος. **6.** *John*, acc. to the testimony of Papias in Euseb. h. e. 3, 39 [cf. *Westcott*, Canon, 5th ed. p. 70], a disciple of Christ and afterwards a Christian presbyter in Asia Minor, whom not a few at the present day, following the opinion of Dionysius of Alexandria [in Euseb. h. e. 7, 25] regard as the author of the Apocalypse, and accordingly esteem him as an eminent

prophet of the primitive Christians and as the person referred to in Rev. i. 1, 4, 9; xxi. 2 Rec.; xxii. 8. Full articles respecting him may be found — by *Grimm* in Ersch u. Gruber's Encyklop. 2d sect. vol. xxiv. p. 217 sq.; *Gass* in Herzog vi. p. 763 sqq.; *Holtzmann* in Schenkel iii. p. 352 sq.; [*Salmon* in Dict. of Chris. Biog. iii. 398 sqq.; cf. *C. L. Leimbach*, Das Papiasfragment (Gotha, 1875), esp. p. 114 sqq.].

'Ιώβ, ὁ, indecl., (אִיּוֹב i. e. harassed, afflicted [but questioned; see *Gesenius*, Lex. (8th ed., by Mühlau and Volck) s. v.]), *Job*, the man commended in the didactic poem which bears his name in the canon of the O. T. (cf. Ezek. xiv. 14, 20) for his piety, and his constancy and fortitude in the endurance of trials: Jas. v. 11.*   **2492**

'Ιωβήδ, ὁ, indecl., *Jobed*: Mt. i. 5 and Lk. iii. 32 in L   **see 5601** T Tr [WH; (yet WH in Lk. l. c. -βήλ)] for R G 'Ωβήδ, q. v.*

['Ιωβήλ, see the preceding word.] ------------ **see 5601**
'Ιωδά, ὁ, indecl., *Joda*: Lk. iii. 26 T Tr WH, for R G L-**see 2455** 'Ιούδα, see 'Ιούδας, 2.*

'Ιωήλ, ὁ, indecl., (יוֹאֵל whose *God is Jehovah*, i. q. a ---**2493** worshipper of God, [al. 'Jehovah is God']), *Joel*, the eminent prophet who acc. to the opinion of very many recent writers prophesied in the reign of Uzziah [cf. B. D. s. v. Joel, 3]: Acts ii. 16.*

'Ιωνάν and (so T Tr WH) 'Ιωνάμ, ὁ, indecl., (see 'Ιωάν-   **2494** νης), *Jonan* [or *Jonam*], one of the ancestors of Christ: Lk. iii. 30.*

'Ιωνᾶς, -ᾶ [B. 20 (17 sq.)], ὁ, (יוֹנָה a dove), *Jonah* (or   **2495** *Jonas*): **1.** *Jonah*, the O. T. prophet, a native of Gath-hepher in the tribe of Zebulun. He lived during the reign of Jeroboam II., king of Israel (2 K. xiv. 25). The narrative of his miraculous experiences, constructed for a didactic purpose, is given in the book which bears his name [on the historic character of which cf. B.D. (esp. Am. ed.) or McC. and S. s. v.; also *Ladd*, Doctr. of Sacr. Script. i. 65 sqq.]: Mt. xii. 39–41; xvi. 4; Lk. xi. 29 sq. 32. **2.** *Jonah* (or *Jonas*), a fisherman, father of the apostle Peter: Mt. xvi. 17 [L T WH here Βαριωνᾶ, see Βαριωνᾶς]; Jn. i. 42 (43) [R G L mrg. Tr mrg., and R G in] xxi. 15, [16, 17], (see 'Ιωάννης, 3).*

'Ιωράμ, ὁ, indecl., (יְהוֹרָם i. e. whom Jehovah exalted),   **2496** *Joram*, the son and successor of Jehoshaphat on the throne of Judah, fr. [c.] B. C. 891 to 884 (2 K. viii. 16 sqq.; 2 Chr. xxi. 2 sqq.): Mt. i. 8.*

'Ιωρείμ, ὁ, indecl., *Jorim*, one of the ancestors of Christ: **2497** Lk. iii. 29.*

'Ιωσαφάτ, ὁ, indecl., (יְהוֹשָׁפָט i. e. Jehovah judges),   **2498** *Jehoshaphat*, king of Judah fr. [c.] B. C. 914 to 889 (1 K. xxii. 41 sqq.; 2 Chr. xvii.–xx.): Mt. i. 8.*

['Ιωσή (A. V. *Jose*, incorrectly), see 'Ιωσῆς, init.]   **2499**
'Ιωσῆς, gen. 'Ιωσῆ [R G in Lk. iii. 29 'Ιωσή (which A.   **2500** V. incorrectly takes as nom. *Jose*)] and (L T Tr WH in Mk. vi. 3; xv. 40, 47) 'Ιωσῆτος (cf. *Bttm.* Ausf. Spr. i. p. 199; B. 19 (17) sq.; W. § 10, 1; [*WH.* App. p. 159*]), ὁ, *Joses*: **1.** one of the ancestors of Christ: Lk. iii. 29 ([see above]; L T Tr WH 'Ιησοῦ, q. v. 2). **2.** the own brother of Jesus: Mk. vi. 3, and R G in Mt. xiii.

55 (where L T Tr WH Ἰωσήφ, q. v. 6); see Ἰάκωβος, 3.   **3.** the son of Mary, the sister of the mother of Jesus [see Μαριάμ, 3]: Mt. xxvii. 56 (where T Tr mrg. WH txt. Ἰωσήφ [Ἰωσῆς and Ἰωσήφ seem to have been diff. forms of one and the same name; cf. *Renan* in the Journ. Asiat., 1864, ser. vi. T. iv. p. 536; *Frankel*, Hodeget in Misch. p. 31 note; *Böhl*, Volksbibel u. s. w. p. 15]); Mk. xv. 40, 47.   **4.** a Levite, surnamed Βαρνάβας (q. v.): Acts iv. 36 (where L T Tr WH Ἰωσήφ).*

2501

Ἰωσήφ, indecl., (in Joseph. [e. g. c. Ap. 1, 14, 16; 32, 3; 33, 5] Ἰώσηπος), ὁ, (יוֹסֵף), fr. יָסַף to add, Gen. xxx. 23 sq. [cf. B. D. s. v. Joseph]), *Joseph*;   **1.** the patriarch, the eleventh son of Jacob: Jn. iv. 5; Acts vii. 9, 13 sq. 18; Heb. xi. 21 sq.; φυλὴ Ἰωσήφ, i. e. the tribe of Ephraim, Rev. vii. 8.   **2.** the son of Jonan [or Jonam], one of Christ's ancestors: Lk. iii. 30.   **3.** the son of Judah [or Judas; better Joda] another ancestor of Jesus: Lk. iii. 26 (where L mrg. T Tr WH Ἰωσήχ, q. v.).   **4.** the son of Mattathias, another of the same: Lk. iii. 24.   **5.** the husband of Mary, the

mother of Jesus: Mt. i. 16, 18–20, 24; ii. 13, 19; Lk. i. 27; ii. 4, 16, 33 R L, 43 R G L mrg.; iii. 23; iv. 22; Jn. i. 45 (46); vi. 42.   **6.** an own brother of our Lord: Mt. xiii. 55 L T Tr WH (for R G Ἰωσῆς [q. v. 2]).   **7.** *Joseph of Arimathœa*, a member of the Sanhedrin, who favored Jesus: Mt. xxvii. 57, 59; Mk. xv. 43, 45; Lk. xxiii. 50; Jn. xix. 38.   **8.** *Joseph*, surnamed Βαρνάβας (q. v.): Acts iv. 36 L T Tr WH (for R G Ἰωσῆς [q. v. 4]).   **9.** *Joseph* called *Barsabas* [better *Barsabbas*; see the word], and surnamed *Justus*: Acts i. 23. [See Ἰωσῆς, 3.]

Ἰωσήχ, *Josech*, see Ἰωσήφ, 3.   see 2501

Ἰωσίας (L T Tr WH Ἰωσείας [see *WH*. App. p. 155; s. v. ει, ι]), -ου, ὁ, (יֹאשִׁיָהוּ i. e. whom 'Jehovah heals'), *Josiah*, king of Judah, who restored among the Jews the worship of the true God, and after a reign of thirty-one years was slain in battle c. B. C. 611 (2 K. xxii. sq.; 2 Chr. xxxiv. sq.): Mt. i. 10 sq.*   2502

ἰῶτα, τό, *iota* [A. V. *jot*], the Hebr. letter ', the smallest of them all; hence equiv. to the minutest part: Mt. v. 18.   [Cf. I, ι.]*   2503

K

2504

κἀγώ [so the recent edd. usually, (in opp. to the κᾱγώ etc. of Grsb. et al., cf. *Herm.* Vig. p. 526; W. § 5, 4 a.; *Lipsius*, Gram. Untersuch. p. 4; cf. I, ι)], (by crasis fr. καὶ ἐγώ [retained e. g. in Mt. xxvi. 15 T; Lk. ii. 48 WH; xvi. 9 T Tr WH; Acts x. 26 T Tr WH; xxvi. 29 WH, etc.; cf. B. 10; W. § 5, 3; *WH*. App. p. 145; esp. *Tdf.* Proleg. p. 96 sq.], for the first time in Hom. Il. 21, 108 [var., cf. Od. 20, 296 var. (h. Merc. 17, 3); cf. *Ebeling*, Lex. Hom. p. 619]), dat. κἀμοί [καὶ ἐμοί Acts x. 28 R G], acc. κἀμέ;   **1.** *and I*, the καί simply connecting: Jn. x. 27, etc.; *and I* (together), Lk. ii. 48; distributively, *and I* (in like manner): Jn. vi. 56; xv. 4; xvii. 26; *and I* (on the other hand), Jas. ii. 18 (κἀγὼ ἔργα ἔχω); Lk. xxii. 29; Acts xxii. 19; *and I* (indeed), Jn. vi. 57; Ro. xi. 3. at the beginning of a period, Lat. *et equidem*, *and I* (to speak of myself): Jn. i. 31, 33 sq.; xii. 32; 1 Co. ii. 1; with the καί used consecutively (see under καί, I. 2 d.), cf. our *and so*: Mt. xi. 28; Jn. xx. 15; Acts xxii. 13; 2 Co. vi. 17; κἀγὼ . . . καί, both . . . and: κἀμὲ οἴδατε, καὶ οἴδατε πόθεν εἰμί, both me (my person) and my origin, Jn. vii. 28.   **2.** *I also*; *I as well*; *I likewise*; *in like manner I*: so that one puts himself on a level with others, Mt. ii. 8; x. 32; Lk. xi. 9; xvi. 9; Jn. xv. 9, [10 Tdf.]; xvii. 18; Acts x. 26; 1 Co. vii. 40; 2 Co. xi. 16, 18, 21 sq.; in the second member of a comparison, after ὁποῖος, ὡς, καθώς, Acts xxvi. 29; 1 Co. vii. 8; xi. 1; Rev.

ii. 28 (27); see under καί, II. 1 a. with a suppression of the mention of those with whom the writer compares himself: Eph. i. 15 (as well as others); 1 Th. iii. 5 (as well as my companions at Athens; cf. *Lünemann* ad loc.).   κἀμοί: Lk. i. 3; Acts viii. 19; 1 Co. xv. 8; κἀμέ: 1 Co. xvi. 4.   i. q. *I in turn*: Mt. xvi. 18; xxi. 24; Lk. xx. 3; Gal. vi. 14.   **3.** *even I, this selfsame I*, the καί pointing the statement: Ro. iii. 7; cf. *Herm.* ad Vig. p. 835.

καθά, adv. for καθ' ἅ, *according as, just as*: Mt. xxvii.   2505 10. (Xen., Polyb., Diod., al.; O. T. Apocr.; Sept. for כַּאֲשֶׁר, Gen. vii. 9, 16, etc., and for כְּ, Gen. xix. 8; Ex. xii. 35, etc.)*

καθ-αίρεσις, -εως, ἡ, (καθαιρέω, q. v.), *a pulling down,*   2506 *destruction, demolition*: ὀχυρωμάτων, [A. V. *of strongholds*], 2 Co. x. 4 (τῶν τειχῶν, Xen. Hell. 2, 2, 15; 5, 1, 35; Polyb. 23, 7, 6; Diod. excerpt. leg. 13; *destructio murorum*, Suet. Galba 12); εἰς οἰκοδ. . . . καθαίρεσιν ὑμῶν, for building up (increasing) not for casting down (the extinction of) the godly, upright, blessed life you lead in fellowship with Christ (see οἰκοδομή, 1): 2 Co. x. 8; xiii. 10. [From Thuc. down.]*

καθ-αιρέω, -ῶ; fut. καθελῶ (Lk. xii. 18 [see ἀφαιρέω,   2507 init.]); 2 aor. καθεῖλον, (fr. obsol. ἕλω); pres. pass. καθαιροῦμαι, fr. Hom. down; Sept. for הוֹרִיד, to cause to go down; פָּרַץ, נָתַץ, הָרַס;   **1.** *to take down*: without the notion of violence, τινά, to detach from the cross one crucified, Mk. xv. 36, 46 ; Lk. xxiii. 53, (Polyb. 1, 86, 6 ; Philo in Flacc. § 10) ; τινὰ ἀπὸ τοῦ ξύλου, Acts xiii. 29 (Sept. Josh. viii. 29 ; x. 27) ; with the use of force, to throw down, cast down : τινὰ ἀπὸ θρόνου, Lk. i. 52. **2.** to pull down, demolish : τὰς ἀποθήκας, opp. to οἰκοδομεῖν, Lk. xii. 18 ; λογισμούς, the (subtle) reasonings (of opponents) likened to fortresses, i. q. to refute, 2 Co. x. 4 (5) ; to destroy, ἔθνη, Acts xiii. 19 (Jer. xxiv. 6 ; Thuc. 1, 4 ; Ael. v. h. 2, 25) ; τὴν μεγαλειότητά τινος, Acts xix. 27, where if preference is given (with L T Tr WH) to the reading τῆς μεγαλειότητος αὐτῆς, it must be taken as a partitive gen. somewhat of her magnificence ; cf. B. 158 (138) note [so Meyer ; cf. Xen. Hell. 4, 4, 13. Al. translate that she should even be deposed from her magnificence ; cf. W. § 30, 6 ; B. § 132, 5].*

2508 καθαίρω ; pf. pass. ptcp. κεκαθαρμένος ; (καθαρός) ; to cleanse, prop. from filth, impurity, etc. ; trees and vines (from useless shoots), to prune, Jn. xv. 2 (δένδρα . . . ὑποτεμνόμενα καθαίρεται, Philo de agric. § 2 [cf. de somniis ii. § 9 mid.]) ; metaph. from guilt, to expiate : pass. Heb. x. 2 R G [see καθαρίζω, init.], (Jer. xiii. 27 ; and so in Grk. writ. fr. Hdt. down). [Comp. : δια-, ἐκ-καθαίρω.]*

2509 καθάπερ, (καθ᾽ ἅπερ), according as, just as, even as, [("καθά marking the comparison, πέρ (akin to the prep. περί) the latitude of the application")] : Ro. ix. 13 WH txt. ; x. 15 WH txt. ; also] xi. 8 and 1 Co. x. 10 in T Tr WH ; 2 Co. iii. 13, 18 [here WH mrg. καθώσπερ] ; 1 Th. ii. 11 ; καθάπερ καί, Ro. iv. 6 ; 2 Co. i. 14 ; 1 Th. iii. 6, 12 ; iv. 5 ; Heb. iv. 2, and R G in Heb. v. 4 ; καθάπερ foll. by οὕτω (or οὕτως), Ro. xii. 4 ; 1 Co. xii. 12 ; 2 Co. viii. 11. ([From Arstph. down] ; Sept. for כַּאֲשֶׁר, Ex. vii. 6, 10.)*

2510 καθ-άπτω : 1 aor. καθῆψα ; **1.** to fit or fasten to, bind on. **2.** to lay hold of, fasten on (hostilely) : τῆς χειρὸς αὐτοῦ, Acts xxviii. 3 [cf. W. 257 (241)] ; τοῦ τραχήλου, Epict. diss. 3, 20, 10. [In Mid. fr. Hom. down, (w. gen. fr. Hdt. on).]*

2511 καθαρίζω (Hellenistic for καθαίρω, which classic writ. use) ; Attic fut. [cf. B. 37 (32) ; W. § 13, 1 c. ; WH. App. p. 163] καθαριῶ (Heb. ix. 14) ; 1 aor. ἐκαθάρισα [see below] ; pres. pass. καθαρίζομαι ; 1 aor. pass. ἐκαθαρίσθην ; pf. pass. ptcp. κεκαθαρισμένος (Heb. x. 2 T Tr WH ; on the forms ἐκαθ ερίσθη, T WH in Mt. viii. 3 ; Mk. i. 42, [ἐκαθ έρισεν, Tr in Acts x. 15 ; xi. 9] and κεκαθ ερισμένος Lchm. in Heb. x. 2, cf. [Tdf. Proleg. p. 82 ; WH. App. p. 150] ; Sturz, De dial. Maced. etc. p. 118 ; Delitzsch on Heb. x. 2 ; Krüger Pt. ii. § 2, 2, 6 p. 4 ; [B. 29 (25 sq.) ; W. 43]) ; (καθαρός) ; Sept. mostly for טָהֵר ; **1.** to make clean, to cleanse ; **a.** from physical stains and dirt : e. g. utensils, Mt. xxiii. 25, [fig. 26] ; Lk. xi. 39 ; food, Mk. vii. 19 ; τινά, a leper, to cleanse by curing, Mt. viii. 2 sq. ; x. 8 ; xi. 5 ; Mk. i. 40–42 ; Lk. iv. 27 ; v. 12 sq. ; vii. 22 ; xvii. 14, 17, (Lev. xiv. 8.) ; to remove by cleansing : ἡ λέπρα ἐκαθαρίσθη, Mt. viii. 3 (καθαριεῖς τὸ αἷμα τὸ ἀναίτιον ἐξ Ἰσραήλ, Deut. xix. 13) ; ἐκαθάριζε τὴν περὶ ταῦτα συνήθειαν, the custom of marrying heathen women, Joseph. antt. 11, 5, 4 ; καθαίρειν αἷμα, Hom. Il. 16, 667 ; cf. ἐκκαθαίρω). **b.** in a moral sense ; **a.** to free from the defilement of sin

and from faults ; to purify from wickedness : ἑαυτὸν ἀπὸ μολυσμοῦ σαρκός, 2 Co. vii. 1 ; τῇ πίστει τὰς καρδίας, Acts xv. 9 (καρδίαν ἀπὸ ἁμαρτίας, Sir. xxxviii. 10) ; τὰς χεῖρας, to abstain in future from wrong-doing, Jas. iv. 8. **β.** to free from the guilt of sin, to purify : τινὰ ἀπὸ πάσης ἁμαρτίας, 1 Jn. i. 7 ; [τ. ἀ. π. ἀδικίας, ibid. 9] ; τὴν συνείδησιν ἀπὸ νεκρῶν ἔργων, Heb. ix. 14 ; τὴν ἐκκλησίαν τῷ λουτρῷ τοῦ ὕδατος (instrumental dat.), Eph. v. 26 ; λαὸν ἑαυτῷ, Tit. ii. 14. **γ.** to consecrate by cleansing or purifying : τὶ ἔν τινι, dat. of instr. [W. 388 (363)], Heb. ix. 22 ; i. q. to consecrate, dedicate, τί τινι (dat. of instr.), ibid. 23. **2.** to pronounce clean in a levitical sense : Acts x. 15 ; xi. 9, (Lev. xiii. 13, 17, 23, 28). [Comp. : δια-καθαρίζω.]*

καθαρισμός, -οῦ, ὁ, (καθαρίζω), a cleansing, purification ; **2512** a ritual purgation or washing, (Vulg. purgatio, purificatio, emundatio) : used with a gen. of the subj., τῶν Ἰουδαίων, of the washings of the Jews before and after their meals, Jn. ii. 6 ; without a gen., of baptism (a symbol of moral cleansing), Jn. iii. 25 ; with a gen. of the obj., and that a person, — of the levitical purification of women after childbirth, Lk. ii. 22 ; and of lepers, Mk. i. 44 ; Lk. v. 14 ; with a gen. of the thing, ἁμαρτιῶν or ἁμαρτημάτων, a cleansing from the guilt of sins (see καθαρίζω, 1 b. β.) : wrought now by baptism, 2 Pet. i. 9, now by the expiatory sacrifice of Christ, Heb. i. 3 on which cf. Kurtz, Com. p. 70 ; (Ex. xxx. 10 ; τῆς ἁμαρτίας μου, Job vii. 21 ; of an atonement, Lcian. asin. 22).*

καθαρός, -ά, -όν ; [akin to Lat. castus, in-cestus, Eng. **2513** chaste, chasten ; Curtius § 26 ; Vaniček p. 177] ; fr. Hom. down ; Sept. mostly for טָהוֹר ; clean, pure, (free from the admixture or adhesion of any thing that soils, adulterates, corrupts) ; **a.** physically : Mt. xxiii. 26 ; xxvii. 59 ; Heb. x. 22 (23) ; Rev. xv. 6 ; xix. 8, 14, and Rec. in xxii. 1 ; χρυσίον, purified by fire, Rev. xxi. 18, 21 ; in a similitude, like a vine cleansed by pruning and so fitted to bear fruit, Jn. xv. 3 ; ὁ λελουμ. . . . καθαρὸς ὅλος (where the idea which Christ expresses figuratively is as follows : 'he whose inmost nature has been renovated does not need radical renewal, but only to be cleansed from every several fault into which he may fall through intercourse with the unrenewed world'), Jn. xiii. 10. **b.** in a levitical sense ; clean, i. e. the use of which is not forbidden, imparts no uncleanness : πάντα καθαρά, Ro. xiv. 20 ; Tit. i. 15. **c.** ethically ; free from corrupt desire, from sin and guilt : Tit. i. 15 ; ὑμεῖς καθαροί, Jn. xiii. 10, [11] ; οἱ κ. τῇ καρδίᾳ (as respects heart [W. § 31, 6 a.]), Mt. v. 8 (καθαρὸς χεῖρας, Hdt. 1, 35 ; κατὰ τὸ σῶμα κ. κατὰ τὴν ψυχήν, Plat. Crat. p. 405 b.) ; free from every admixture of what is false, sincere, ἐκ καθαρᾶς καρδίας, 1 Tim. i. 5 ; 2 Tim. ii. 22, and R G in 1 Pet. i. 22 ; ἐν καθαρᾷ συνειδήσει, 1 Tim. iii. 9 ; 2 Tim. i. 3 ; genuine (joined with ἀμίαντος) θρησκεία, Jas. i. 27 ; blameless, innocent, Acts xviii. 6. Hebraistically with the addition of ἀπό τινος, pure from, i. e. unstained with the guilt of, any thing [W. § 30, 6 a. ; B. 157 (137) sq.] : ἀπὸ τ. αἵματος, Acts xx. 26 ; Sus. 46 Alex., cf. Gen. xxiv. 8 ; Tob. iii. 14 ; καθαρὰς ἔχειν τὰς χεῖρας ἀπὸ τοῦ φόνου, Joseph. antt. 4, 8, 16 ; in class. Grk. with a simple gen., as φόνου, Plat. legg. 9 p. 864 e. ; cf.

Passow s. v. p. 1528ᵃ; [L. and S. s. v. 3]; Kühner § 421, 4 ii. p. 344.   d. in a levitical and ethical sense: πάντα καθαρὰ ὑμῖν, Lk. xi. 41, on which see ἔνειμι. [SYN. see ἐλικρινής; cf. Westcott on 1 Jn. iii. 3.]*

2514   **καθαρότης**, -ητος, ἡ, (καθαρός), cleanness, purity; in a levitical sense, τινός, Heb. ix. 13. (Xen. mem. 2, 1, 22; Plato, al.) *

2515   **καθ-έδρα**, -ας, ἡ, (κατά and ἕδρα), a chair, seat: Mt. xxi. 12; Mk. xi. 15, (Sir. xii. 12; Hdian. 2, 3, 17 [7 ed. Bekk.]); of the exalted seat occupied by men of eminent rank or influence, as teachers and judges: ἐπὶ τῆς Μωϋσέως καθέδρας ἐκάθισαν, sit on the seat which Moses formerly occupied, i. e. bear themselves as Moses' successors in explaining and defending his law, Mt. xxiii. 2. (Sept. for מוֹשָׁב and שֶׁבֶת. [Xen., Aristot., al.]) *

2516   **καθ-έζομαι**; impf. ἐκαθεζόμην; [fr. Hom. down]; to sit down, seat one's self, sit: Jn. xx. 12; Lk. ii. 46; Jn. xi. 20; Acts vi. 15; foll. by ἐν with dat. of place, Mt. xxvi. 55; Lk. ii. 46; Jn. xi. 20; Acts vi. 15; foll. by ἐπί with gen., Acts xx. 9 L T Tr WH; by ἐπί with dat., Jn. iv. 6; ἐκεῖ, Jn. vi. 3 Tdf.; [οὗ where, Acts ii. 2 Lchm. Cf. Rutherford, New Phryn. p. 336 sq.; B. 56 (49); 60 (52). COMP.: παρα-καθέζομαι.]*

see 1519 **καθ-εῖς**, more correctly καθ' εἷς, see εἷς, 4 c. p. 187ᵃ.

2517   **καθ-εξῆς**, (κατά and ἑξῆς, q. v.), adv., one after another, successively, in order: Lk. i. 3; Acts xi. 4; xviii. 23; οἱ καθεξ. those that follow after, Acts iii. 24 [cf. W. 633 (588)]; ἐν τῷ καθ. sc. χρόνῳ [R. V. soon afterwards], Lk. viii. 1. (Ael. v. h. 8, 7; Plut. symp. 1, 1, 5; in earlier Grk. ἐξῆς and ἐφεξῆς are more usual.) *

2518   **καθ-εύδω**; impf. 3 pers. plur. ἐκάθευδον; fr. Hom. down; Sept. mostly for שָׁכַב;   1. to fall asleep, to drop off to sleep: Mt. xxv. 5. 2. to sleep; a. prop.: Mt. viii. 24; ix. 24 [on this and its paral. cf. B. D. Am. ed. p. 1198ᵃ]; xiii. 25; xxvi. 40, 43, 45; Mk. iv. 27, 38; v. 39; xiii. 36; xiv. 37, 40 sq.; Lk. viii. 52; xxii. 46; 1 Th. v. 7. b. euphemistically, to be dead: 1 Th. v. 10; (Ps. lxxxviii. (lxxxviii.) 6; Dan. xii. 2). c. metaph. to yield to sloth and sin, and be indifferent to one's salvation: Eph. v. 14; 1 Th. v. 6.*

2519   **καθηγητής**, -οῦ, ὁ, (καθηγέομαι to go before, lead); a. prop. a guide: Numen. ap. Ath. 7, p. 313 d. b. a master, teacher: Mt. xxiii. 8 R G, 10. (Dion. H. jud. de Thuc. 3, 4; several times in Plut. [cf. Wetst. on Mt. l.c.]) *

2520   **καθ-ήκω**; [fr. Aeschyl., Soph. down]; 1. to come down. 2. to come to, reach to; impers. καθήκει, it is becoming, it is fit (cf. Germ. zukommen), Ezek. xxi. 27; οὐ καθῆκεν (Rec. καθῆκον), foll. by the acc. with inf., Acts xxii. 22 [W. 282 (265); B. 217 (187)]; τὰ μὴ καθήκοντα, things not fitting, i. e. forbidden, shameful, Ro. i. 28; 2 Macc. vi. 4. Cf. ἀνήκω.*

2521   **κάθ-ημαι**, 2 pers. sing. κάθη a later form for κάθησαι (Acts xxiii. 3), impv. κάθου for κάθησο [yet cf. Kühner as below] (cf. Lob. ad Phryn. p. 359; Krüger § 38, 6 sq. i. p. 147; Kühner § 301 i. p. 671; W. § 14, 4; [B. 49 (42)]), [subjunc. 2 pers. plur. κάθησθε, Lk. xxii. 30 Tr mrg.; but WH txt. καθῆσθε; see Veitch s. v.; Krüger § 38, 6, 1 (cf. καθίζω), inf. καθῆσθαι, ptcp. καθήμενος]; impf. ἐκαθήμην; and once the rare [cf. Veitch p. 347] fut. καθή-

σομαι, Lk. xxii. 30 T Tr txt. WH mrg. [so WH in Mt. xix. 28 also; cf. καθίζω, fin.]; (ἧμαι); a verb of which only the pres. and impf. are in use in class. Grk. [cf. B. 60 (52)]; Sept. for יָשַׁב;   1. to sit down, seat one's self: foll. by ἐν w. dat. of place [cf. W. § 52, 4, 9], Mk. iv. 1; Lk. xxii. 55 [here T Tr WH μέσος]; εἰς, Mk. xiii. 3 [B. § 147, 16]; μετά w. gen. of pers., Mt. xxvi. 58; κάθου ἐκ δεξιῶν μου, i. e. be a partner of my power, Mt. xxii. 44; Mk. xii. 36 [Tr txt. WH mrg. κάθισον]; Lk. xx. 42; Acts ii. 34; Heb. i. 13 (Ps. cix. (cx.) 1); κάθου ὧδε ὑπό with acc., Jas. ii. 3; παρά w. acc. of place, Mt. xiii. 1; ἐπάνω w. gen. of place, Mt. xxviii. 2; with ἐκεῖ, Mt. xv. 29; Jn. vi. 3 [Tdf. ἐκαθέζετο]; the place to be supplied fr. the context, Mt. xiii. 2. 2. to sit, be seated, of a place occupied: foll. by ἐν with dat. of place [W. as under 1], Mt. xi. 16; xxvi. 69; ἐν τῇ δεξιᾷ τ. θεοῦ, Col. iii. 1; ἐν τοῖς δεξιοῖς, Mk. xvi. 5; ἐπί τινος, Mt. xxiv. 3; xxvii. 19; [Acts xx. 9 R G]; ἐπὶ τοῦ θρόνου [but also, esp. in the crit. edd., with the dat. and the acc. (see below); cf. Alford on the foll. pass.], Rev. iv. 2 etc.; τῆς νεφέλης [or w. the acc.], Rev. xiv. 15, and in other exx.; ἐπί τινι, Acts iii. 10; ἐπί τι [cf. B. 338 (291)], Mt. ix. 9; Mk. ii. 14; Lk. v. 27; Jn. xii. 15; Rev. iv. 4; vi. 2 [R dat. (as in foll.)] 4 sq.; xi. 16; xvii. 3; xix. 11; παρὰ τὴν ὁδόν, Mt. xx. 30; Mk. x. 46; Lk. xviii. 35; πρὸς τὸ φῶς, Lk. xxii. 56; ἐπάνω τινός, Mt. xxiii. 22; Rev. vi. 8; περί τινα, Mk. iii. 32, 34; ἀπέναντί τινος, Mt. xxvii. 61; ἐκ δεξιῶν τινος, Mt. xxvi. 64; Mk. xiv. 62; Lk. xxii. 69; ἐκεῖ, Mk. ii. 6; οὗ, where, Acts ii. 2 [L καθεζόμενοι]; Rev. xvii. 15; without specification of place, Mk. v. 15; Lk. v. 17; viii. 35; Jn. ii. 14; ix. 8; 1 Co. xiv. 30. κάθημαι as descriptive of a certain state or condition is used of those who sit in discharging their office, as judges, κάθη κρίνων, Acts xxiii. 3; of a queen, i. q. to occupy the throne, to reign [A. V. I sit a queen], Rev. xviii. 7; of money-changers, Jn. ii. 14; of mourners and penitents: ἐν σάκκῳ, clothed in sackcloth, ἐν σποδῷ, covered with ashes, Lk. x. 13; of those who, enveloped in darkness, cannot walk about, Mt. iv. 16; Lk. i. 79 (Is. xlii. 7); of a lame man, Acts xiv. 8. i. q. to have a fixed abode, to dwell: ἐπὶ πρόσωπον τῆς γῆς, Lk. xxi. 35; Rev. xiv. 6 (where Rec. κατοικοῦντας); ἐπὶ θρόνων, Rev. xx. 11 G T [WH mrg.; but see above]; ἐν Ἱερουσαλήμ, Neh. xi. 6; [ἐν ὄρει Σαμαρείας, Sir. l. 26. COMP.: συγ-κάθημαι].

καθημέραν, i. q. καθ' ἡμέραν, see ἡμέρα, 2 p. 278ᵃ. see 2250

2522   **καθημερινός**, -ή, -όν, (fr. καθ' ἡμέραν), daily: Acts vi. 1. (Judith xii. 15; Theophr., Athen., Plut., Alciphr. epp. i. 5; Joseph. antt. 3, 10, 1; [11, 7, 1]; Polyaen. 4, 2, 10.) Cf. Lob. ad Phryn. p. 53 [(yet see L. and S.); W. 25 (25 sq.)].*

2523   **καθ-ίζω**; fut. καθίσω [B. 37 (32)]; 1 aor. ἐκάθισα (impv. 2 sing. κάθισον once, Mk. xii. 36 Tr txt. WH mrg.); pf. κεκάθικα (Mk. xi. 2 [not WH Tr mrg.; Heb. xii. 2 L T Tr WH; a late form, see Veitch s. v.]); 1 aor. mid. subjunc. 2 pers. plur. καθίσησθε (Lk. xxii. 30 Rec.); fut. mid. καθίσομαι; fr. Hom. down; [cf. B. 60 (52)]. 1. trans. to make to sit down (κατά; q. v. III. 1), to set, appoint; Sept. for הוֹשִׁיב: τινὰ ἐπὶ θρόνου [L T Tr WH τὸν θρόνον], to confer the kingdom upon one, Acts ii. 30 ; τινὰ ἐν δεξιᾳ αὐτοῦ, Eph. i. 20 ; τινά, to appoint one to act as judge, 1 Co. vi. 4 (δικαστήν, Plat. legg. 9 p. 873 e. ; Polyb. 40, 5, 3 ; συνέδριον κριτῶν, Joseph. antt. 20, 9, 1).   **2.** intrans.; Sept. for יָשַׁב ;   **a.** *to sit down* : univ., Mt. v. 1 ; xiii. 48 ; Mk. ix. 35 ; Lk. iv. 20 ; v. 3 ; xiv. 28, 31 ; xvi. 6 ; Jn. viii. 2 ; Acts xiii. 14 ; xvi. 13 ; with a telic inf. 1 Co. x. 7 ; with specification of the place or seat : ἐν δεξιᾳ τινος, Heb. i. 3 ; viii. 1 ; x. 12 ; xii. 2 ; ἐπί τινι, Mk. xi. 7 [Rec.]; εἰς τὸν ναόν, 2 Th. ii. 4 [B. § 147, 16 ; W. 415 (386)]; ἐπί with acc. [cf. B. 338 (290)], Rev. xx. 4 ; Jn. xii. 14 ; Mk. xi. 2, [7 L T Tr WH]; Lk. xix. 30 ; [add Acts ii. 3, see B. § 129, 17; W. 516 (481)]; ἐπὶ τοῦ βήματος, of a judge, Jn. xix. 13 ; Acts xii. 21 ; xxv. 6, 17 ; κατέναντι [or ἀπέναντι Tr etc.] τινος, Mk. xii. 41 ; with adverbs of place, Mk. xiv. 32 ; Mt. xxvi. 36.   **b.** *to sit* : [absol. (of a dead man restored to life) ἐκάθισεν sat, sat up, Lk. vii. 15 L mrg. WH mrg.]; ἐν τῷ θρόνῳ, Rev. iii. 21 ; ἐπί w. gen. of the seat, Mt. xxiii. 2 ; xxv. 31 ; ἐκ δεξιῶν κ. ἐξ εὐων., Mt. xx. 21, 23 ; Mk. x. 37, 40.   **i. q.** *to have fixed one's abode,* i. e. *to sojourn* [cf. our *settle, settle down*], Acts xviii. 11 ; foll. by ἐν with dat. of place, Lk. xxiv. 49 [here A.V. *tarry*], (Ex. xvi. 29 ; Jer. xxx. 11 (xlix. 33) ; [Neh. xi. 25]).   Mid. [Pass.? cf. *Rutherford*, New Phryn. p. 336 sq.] *to sit* : ἐπὶ θρόνων, Lk. xxii. 30 [R G L : see κάθημαι]; ἐπὶ θρόνους, Mt. xix. 28 [WH καθήσεσθε]; see κάθημαι.   Comp. : ἀνα-, ἐπι-, παρα-, περι-, συγ-καθίζω.]

καθ-ίημι : 1 aor. καθῆκα ; [fr. Hom. on]; *to send down, let down* : εἰς, Lk. v. 19 ; διά w. gen. of place, ibid. and Acts ix. 25 ; pres. pass. ptcp. καθιέμενος *let down,* ἐπὶ τῆς γῆς, Acts x. 11 ; ἐκ τοῦ οὐρανοῦ, Acts xi. 5.*

καθ-ίστημι (also καθιστάω, whence the ptcp. καθιστῶντες Acts xvii. 15 R G ; and καθιστάνω, whence καθιστάνοντες ibid. L T Tr WH ; see ἵστημι, init.) ; fut. καταστήσω ; 1 aor. κατέστησα ; Pass., pres. καθίσταμαι ; 1 aor. κατεστάθην ; 1 fut. κατασταθήσομαι ; Sept. for הִפְקִיד, הֵקִים, נָתַן, הֶעֱמִיד, הִתְיַצֵּב ; (prop. *to set down, put down*), *to set, place, put* :   **a.** τινὰ ἐπί τινος, to set one over a thing (in charge of it), Mt. xxiv. 45 ; xxv. 21, 23 ; Lk. xii. 42 ; Acts vi. 3 ; also ἐπί τινι, Mt. xxiv. 47 ; Lk. xii. 44 ; ἐπί τι, Heb. ii. 7 Rec. fr. Ps. viii. 7.   **b.** τινά, *to appoint one to administer* an office (cf. Germ. *bestellen*) : πρεσβυτέρους, Tit. i. 5 ; τινὰ εἰς τό with inf., to appoint to do something, Heb. viii. 3 ; τὰ πρὸς τ. θεόν to conduct the worship of God, Heb. v. 1 ; foll. by ἵνα, ibid. ; τινά with a pred. acc. indicating the office to be administered [*to make one so and so*; cf. W. § 32, 4 b.; B. § 131, 7], (so very often in Grk. writ. fr. Hdt. down), Lk. xii. 14 ; Acts vii. 10, 27, 35 ; Heb. vii. 28.   **c.** *to set down as, constitute* (Lat. *sisto*), i. q. *to declare, show to be* : pass. with ἁμαρτωλός, δίκαιος, Ro. v. 19 [cf. Prof. *T. Dwight* in New Englander for 1867, p. 590 sqq.; *Dietzsch*, Adam u. Christus (Bonn, 1871) p. 188].   **d.** *to constitute* (Lat. *sisto*) i. q. *to render, make, cause to be* : τινὰ οὐκ ἀργόν, οὐδὲ ἄκαρπον, i. e. (by litotes) laborious and fruitful, 2 Pet. i. 8.   **e.** *to conduct* or *bring to a certain place* : τινά, Acts xvii. 15 (2 Chr. xxviii. 15 for הֵבִיא ; Josh. vi. 23 ; 1 S. v. 3 ; Hom. Od. 13, 274 ; Xen. an. 4, 8, 8 and in

other prof. auth.).   **f.** Mid. *to show* or *exhibit one's self; come forward as* : with a pred. nom., Jas. iv. 4 ; ἡ γλῶσσα . . . ἡ σπιλοῦσα, Jas. iii. 6.   [COMP. : ἀντι-, ἀποκαθίστημι.] *

καθό (i. e. καθ' ὅ), adv., [fr. Lys. and Plat. down], *according to what,* i. e.   **1.** *as* : Ro. viii. 26.   **2.** *according as; in so far as, so far forth as* : 1 Pet. iv. 13 (Rec.elz καθώς) ; 2 Co. viii. 12 [W. 307 (288) ; cf. B. § 139, 30].*   **2526**

καθολικός, -ή, -όν, (καθόλου, q. v.), *general, universal* (occasionally in prof. auth. fr. [Aristot. and] Polyb. down, as καθ. καὶ κοινὴ ἱστορία, Polyb. 8, 4, 11 ; often in eccl. writ.; the title ἡ καθολικὴ ἐκκλησία first in Ignat. ad Smyrn. c. 8 and often in Polyc. martyr. [see ed. (Gebh. Harn.) Zahn, p. 133 note]; cf. καθολικὴ ἀνάστασις, [Justin c. Tryph. 81 sub fin.]; Theoph. ad Autol. [l. i. § 13] p. 40 ed. Otto) ; ἐπιστολαὶ καθολικαί, or simply καθολικαί, in the title of the Epp. of James, Peter, John, and Jude (R G L ; cf. τῶν ἑπτὰ λεγομένων καθολικῶν sc. ἐπιστολῶν, Eus. h. e. 2, 23, 25), most prob. because they seemed to be written not to any one church alone, but to all the churches. [Cf. Dict. of Chris. Antiq. s. v. Catholic.] *   **2526a**

καθόλου (i. e. καθ' ὅλου [" as it is written in auth. before Aristot." (L. and S.)]), adv., *wholly, entirely, at all* : Acts iv. 18. ([Ex. xxii. 11]; Ezek. xiii. 3, 22 ; Am. iii. 3, 4 ; Xen., Plat., Dem., Aristot. and sqq.) *   **2527**

καθ-οπλίζω : pf. pass. ptcp. καθωπλισμένος ; *to arm* [*fully* (cf. κατά, III. 1 fin.)], *furnish with arms* : Lk. xi. 21. (Xen., Plut., al.; Sept.) *   **2528**

καθ-οράω, -ῶ :   **1.** *to look down, see from above, view from on high,* (Hom., Hdt., Xen., Plat., al.).   **2.** *to see thoroughly* [cf. κατά, III. 1 fin.], *perceive clearly, understand* (Germ. *erschauen*) : pres. pass. 3 pers. sing. καθορᾶται, Ro. i. 20 (3 Macc. iii. 11, and often in class. Grk.). Cf. *Fritzsche*, Ep. ad Rom. i. p. 61.*   **2529**

καθότι (i. e. καθ' ὅ τι), *according to what,* i. e.   **1.** *so far as, according as* : Acts ii. 45 ; iv. 35, (Polyb. 18, 19 (36), 5 ; for כַּאֲשֶׁר, Ex. i. 12, 17).   **2.** *because that, because,* [cf. W. § 53, 8] : Lk. i. 7 ; xix. 9 ; Acts ii. 24, and L T Tr WH (for Rec. διότι) in Acts xvii. 31, (Tob. i. 12 ; xiii. 4 ; Polyb. 18, 21 (38), 6).   **3.** *as, just as* : Bar. vi. (Ep. Jer.) 1 ; Judith ii. 13, 15 ; x. 9, and often in Thuc. et al.*   **2530**

καθώς (i. e. καθ' ὥς), a particle found occasionally in prof. auth. fr. Aristot. down for the Attic καθά and καθό, but emphatically censured by Phryn. and the Atticists; cf. *Sturz*, De dial. Maced. etc. p. 74 sqq.; *Lob.* ad Phryn. p. 425 sq.; [W. 26 (25)];   **1.** *according as, just as, even as* : in the first member of a comparison, Lk. vi. 31 ; 1 Jn. ii. 27 ; foll. by οὕτως in the second member [cf. W. § 53, 5], Lk. xi. 30 ; xvii. 26 ; Jn. iii. 14 ; 2 Co. i. 5 ; x. 7 ; (Col. iii. 13 ; 1 Jn. ii. 6) ; foll. by καί *also,* Jn. xv. 9 ; xvii. 18 ; xx. 21 ; 1 Jn. ii. 18 ; iv. 17 ; 1 Co. xv. 49 ; it is annexed to preceding words after the demonstrative οὕτως, Lk. xxiv. 24 ; with οὕτως unexpressed, Mt. xxi. 6 ; xxviii. 6 ; Mk. xvi. 7 ; Lk. i. 2, 55, 70 ; xi. 1 ; Jn. i. 23 ; v. 23 ; Acts x. 47 [here L T Tr WH ὡς]; xv. 8 ; Ro. i. 13 ; xv. 7 ; 1 Co. viii. 2 ; x. 6 ; 2 Co. i. 14 ; ix. 3 ; xi. 12 ; Eph. iv. 17, and   **2531** often; καθὼς διδάσκω, agreeably to my method of teaching, 1 Co. iv. 17; καθὼς γέγραπται, Mt. xxvi. 24; Mk. ix. 13; Acts vii. 42; xv. 15; Ro. i. 17, and often in Paul; the apodosis wanting, and to be gathered fr. the context: καθὼς παρεκάλεσά σε ... ἐν πίστει, sc. οὕτω καὶ νῦν παρακαλῶ, 1 Tim. i. 3, cf. W. 570 (530); [B. 386 (331)]; ἤρξατο αἰτεῖσθαι (sc. οὕτω ποιεῖν αὐτοῖς), καθὼς κτλ. Mk. xv. 8 [B. § 151, 23 b.; cf. W. 584 (543 sq.)]; in comparison by contrary we find the negligent use: ἀγαπῶμεν ἀλλήλους, οὐ καθὼς Κάϊν κτλ. 1 Jn. iii. 11 sq., cf. De Wette ad loc. and W. 623 (579); οὗτός ἐστιν ὁ ἄρτος ... οὐ καθὼς etc., not such as they ate etc., Jn. vi. 58. with the verb εἰμί, equiv. to Lat. qualis, such as, 1 Jn. iii. 2; in a parenthesis, 1 Th. ii. 13 (as it is in truth). **2.** according as i. e. in proportion as, in the degree that: Mk. iv. 33; Acts vii. 17 (cf. Meyer ad loc.); xi. 29; 1 Co. xii. 11, 18; 1 Pet. iv. 10. **3.** since, seeing that, agreeably to the fact that, [cf. W. § 53, 8; 448 (417)]: Jn. xvii. 2; Ro. i. 28 [yet here al. regard καθ. as correspondsive rather than causal or explanatory]; 1 Co. i. 6; v. 7; Eph. i. 4; Phil. i. 7. **4.** it is put for the simple ὡς, **a.** after verbs of speaking, in indir. disc., Acts xv. 14; it serves to add an epexegesis, 3 Jn. 3 (to σου τῇ ἀληθείᾳ). **b.** of time, when, after that, (cf. Lat. ut): 2 Macc. i. 31; [Neh. v. 6]; here many bring in Acts vii. 17; but see 2 above.

(2531α): καθώσ-περ, [Tr καθώς περ], just as, exactly as: Heb. v.
see 2509 4 T Tr WH [also 2 Co. iii. 18 WH mrg.]. (Himer., Psell., Tzetz.) *

2532 καί, a conj., and; the most freq. by far of all the particles in the N. T. [On its uses see W. § 53, 3 sqq.; B. 361 (310) sqq., and cf. Ellicott on Phil. iv. 12; on the difference between it and τέ see s. v. τέ ad init.]

I. It serves as a copulative i. e. to connect (Lat. et, atque, Germ. und); **1.** it connects single words or terms: **a.** univ., as οἱ Φαρισαῖοι καὶ Σαδδουκαῖοι, Mt. xvi. 1; ὁ θεὸς καὶ πατήρ, he who is God and Father (see θεός, 3); ἐν καρδίᾳ καλῇ καὶ ἀγαθῇ, Lk. viii. 15; πολυμερῶς καὶ πολυτρόπως, Heb. i. 1; it is repeated before single terms, to each of which its own force and weight is thus given: ἡ υἱοθεσία καὶ ἡ δόξα καὶ αἱ διαθῆκαι καὶ ἡ νομοθεσία καὶ ἡ λατρεία καὶ αἱ ἐπαγγελίαι, Ro. ix. 4; ἁγία καὶ δικαία καὶ ἀγαθή, Ro. vii. 12; add, Mt. xxiii. 23; Lk. xiv. 21; Jn. xvi. 8; Acts xv. 20, 29; xxi. 25; Heb. ix. 10; Rev. v. 12; xviii. 12 sq.; cf. W. 519 sq. (484). **b.** it connects numerals; and so that (contrary to the more com. usage) the greater number precedes: δέκα κ. ὀκτώ, Lk. xiii. 4, 11, [but in both pass. L and Tr br. WH om. καί; Tdf. δεκαοκτώ], 16; τεσσαράκοντα κ. ἕξ, Jn. ii. 20; add, Jn. v. 5 G T; Acts xiii. 20; cf. W. § 37, 4; [Bp. Lghtft. on Gal. i. 18; noteworthy also is its use in 2 Co. xiii. 1 (cf. Deut. xix. 15 Sept.) ἐπὶ στόματος δύο μαρτύρων καὶ τριῶν (in Mt. xviii. 16 ἢ τρ. cf. W. 440 (410) note) at the mouth of two witnesses and (should there be so many) of three; a similar use of καί, to lend a certain indefiniteness to the expression, occurs occasionally with other than numerical specifications, as Jas. iv. 13 σήμερον καὶ (RᵃG; but L T Tr WH ἢ) αὔριον; cf. Kühner § 521, 2;

Ebeling, Lex. Hom. s. v. p. 614ᵃ]. **c.** it joins to partitive words the general notion; so that is equiv. to and in general, and in a word, in short: ὁ Πέτρος κ. οἱ ἀπόστολοι, Acts v. 29; οἱ ἀρχιερεῖς [καὶ οἱ πρεσβύτεροι Rec.] καὶ τὸ συνέδριον ὅλον, Mt. xxvi. 59; καὶ δικαιώμασι σαρκός, Heb. ix. 10 Rec. Tr br. WH mrg.; καὶ ἐπὶ τὸν Ἰσραὴλ τοῦ θεοῦ, Gal. vi. 16, and often in Grk. writ.; cf. W. 437 sq. (407); 520 sq. (485); [B. 363 (311 sq.); 400 (343)]; with τέ preceding, ἥ τε ... αὐτοῦ δύναμις καὶ θειότης, Ro. i. 20 [see τέ, 2 a.]; and, on the other hand, it joins to a general idea something particular, which is already comprised indeed in that general notion but by this form of expression is brought out more emphatically (which Strabo 8 (1) p. 340 calls συνκαταλέγειν τὸ μέρος τῷ ὅλῳ); so that it is equiv. to and especially [cf. W. u. s.]: τὰ πάντα καὶ τὰ τῶν δαιμονιζομένων, Mt. viii. 33; τοῖς μαθηταῖς αὐτοῦ κ. τῷ Πέτρῳ, Mk. xvi. 7; αἱ φωναὶ αὐτῶν κ. τῶν ἀρχιερέων, Lk. xxiii. 23 [R G]; σὺν γυναιξὶ καὶ Μαριάμ, Acts i. 14; ἐν Ἰούδᾳ κ. Ἰερουσαλήμ, 1 Macc. ii. 6; πᾶς Ἰούδα κ. Ἰερουσαλήμ, 2 Chr. xxxv. 24, cf. xxxii. 33; often so in Grk. writ. also. **2.** It connects clauses and sentences; **a.** univ., as διακαθαριεῖ τὴν ἅλωνα αὐτοῦ κ. συνάξει τὸν σῖτον κτλ. Mt. iii. 12; εἰσῆλθον ... καὶ ἐδίδασκον, Acts v. 21; and in innumerable other exx. **b.** In accordance with the simplicity of the ancient popular speech, and esp. of the Hebr. tongue, it links statement to statement, the logical relations of which the more cultivated language expresses either by more exact particles, or by the use of the participial or the relative construction (cf. W. § 60, 3; B. 288 (248) sqq.; 361 (310) sq.): e. g. that very freq. formula ἐγένετο ... καί (see γίνομαι, 2 b.); καὶ εἶδον καὶ (equiv. to ὅτι) σεισμὸς ἐγένετο, Rev. vi. 12; τέξεται υἱὸν κ. καλέσεις τὸ ὄνομα αὐτοῦ (equiv. to οὗ ὄνομα καλέσεις), Mt. i. 21; καλόν ἐστιν ἡμᾶς ὧδε εἶναι, καὶ (equiv. to ὅθεν) ποιήσωμεν σκηνάς, Mk. ix. 5; clauses are thus connected in clusters; as, Mt. vii. 25, 27 (an example of six clauses linked together by καί; Mt. xiv. 9 sqq.; Mk. i. 12–14; Lk. xviii. 32–34; Jn. ii. 13–16; x. 3; 1 Co. xii. 5–6; Rev. vi. 2, 8, 12–16; ix. 1–4 (where nine sentences are strung together by καί), etc. after a designation of time καί annexes what will be or was done at that time; ἤγγικεν ἡ ὥρα καὶ παραδίδοται κτλ. Mt. xxvi. 45; ἦν δὲ ὥρα τρίτη καὶ ἐσταύρωσαν αὐτόν, Mk. xv. 25; ἐγγὺς ἦν τὸ πάσχα ... κ. ἀνέβη εἰς Ἱεροσ. ὁ Ἰησοῦς, Jn. ii. 13; ἡμέραι ἔρχονται καὶ συντελέσω, Heb. viii. 8; add, Lk. xxiii. 44; Jn. iv. 35; v. 1; xi. 55; Acts v. 7; and not infreq. so in Grk. writ., as ἤδη δὲ ἦν ὀψὲ καὶ οἱ Κορίνθιοι ἐξαπίνης πρύμναν ἐκρούοντο, Thuc. 1, 50; cf. Matthiae § 620, 1 a. p. 1481; W. 436 (405 sq.); [B. 361 (310)]. **c.** it joins affirmative to negative sentences, as μὴ συκοφαντήσατε καὶ ἀρκεῖσθε, Lk. iii. 14; οὔτε ἄντλημα ἔχεις καὶ τὸ φρέαρ ἐστὶ βαθύ, Jn. iv. 11; οὔτε ... ἐπιδέχεται καὶ ... κωλύει, 3 Jn. 10, (rarely so in Grk. writ., as Eur. Iph. Taur. 578; cf. Klotz ad Devar. ii. 2 p. 714); much oftener it annexes a clause depending on the preceding negative: μήποτέ σε παραδῷ ... καὶ ὁ κριτής σε παραδῷ ... καὶ εἰς φυλακὴν βληθήσῃ, Mt. v. 25; add, Mt. vii. 6; x. 38; xiii. 15; xxvii. 64; Lk. xii. 58; xxi. 34; Jn. vi.

53; xii. 40; Acts xxviii. 27; 1 Th. iii. 5; 1 Tim. vi. 1; Heb. xii. 15; Rev. xvi. 15; [see B. 368 (315) d.; cf. W. § 56, 2 a.]. **d.** it annexes what follows from something said before (καί consecutive), so as to be equiv. to *and so*: Mt. v. 15 (καὶ λάμπει); Mt. xxiii. 32 (καὶ πληρώσατε); 2 Co. xi. 9 (καὶ ἐν παντί); Heb. iii. 19; 1 Jn. iii. 19 (καὶ ἔμπροσθεν); 2 Pet. i. 19 (καὶ ἔχομεν); so in statements after imperatives and words having the force of an imperative: δεῦτε ὀπίσω μου, καὶ ποιήσω ὑμᾶς etc. Mt. iv. 19; εἰπὲ λόγῳ, καὶ ἰαθήσεται ὁ παῖς μου, Mt. viii. 8; Lk. vii. 7; ἀντίστητε τῷ διαβόλῳ καὶ φεύξεται ἀφ' ὑμῶν, Jas. iv. 7; add, Mt. vii. 7; Mk. vi. 22; Lk. x. 28; Jn. xiv. 16; Rev. iv. 1; cf. Fritzsche on Mt. pp. 187 (and 416), [cf. Sir. ii. 6; iii. 17]. **e.** with a certain rhetorical emphasis, it annexes something apparently at variance with what has been previously said; so that it is equiv. to *and yet* (cf. Stallbaum on Plat. apol. p. 29 b.); so the Lat. *atque* (cf. Beier on Cic. de off. 3, 11, 48): Mt. iii. 14 (καὶ σὺ ἔρχῃ πρὸς μέ); Mt. vi. 26; x. 29; Mk. xii. 12; Jn. i. 5 (καὶ ἡ σκοτία κτλ.), 10 (καὶ ὁ κόσμος); Jn. iii. 11, 32; v. 40 (καὶ οὐ θέλετε); Jn. vi. 70; vii. 28; viii. 49, 55 (καὶ οὐκ ἐγνώκατε); Jn. ix. 30; 1 Co. v. 2; 2 Co. vi. 9; Heb. iii. 9; Rev. iii. 1 (. . . ζῇς, καὶ νεκρὸς εἶ), etc. when a vain attempt is spoken of: Mt. xii. 43 (ζητεῖ καὶ οὐχ εὑρίσκει); xiii. 17; xxvi. 60; Lk. xiii. 7; 1 Th. ii. 18. **f.** like the Hebr. ן (see *Gesenius*, Thes. i. p. 396ᵃ), it begins an apodosis, which is thus connected with the protasis, cf. the Germ. *da* [or Eng. *then*], (in class. Grk. sometimes δέ; see δέ, 8) [cf. B. 362 (311) d.; W. § 53, 3 f.; Ellic. on Phil. i. 22]: with ὅτε or a temporal ὡς preceding in the protasis [as sometimes in Grk. prose (e. g. Thuc. 2, 93, where see Krüger)], Lk. ii. 21; Acts xiii. 18 sq. [here WH txt. om. καί; see ὡς, I. 7]; ὡς . . . καὶ ἰδού, Lk. vii. 12; Acts i. 10; x. 17 [R G Tr mrg. br.]; ἐὰν . . . καὶ εἰσελεύσ. Rev. iii. 20 T WH mrg., although here καί may be rendered *also* (I also will come in, etc.), declaring that, if the first thing (expressed in the protasis) be done, the second (expressed in the apodosis) will be done also. **g.** as in class. Grk., it begins a question thrown out with a certain impassioned abruptness and containing an urgent rejoinder to another's speech (cf. W. § 53, 3 a.; Matthiae § 620, 1 d.; Kühner § 521, 3 ii. p. 791 sq.): καὶ τίς δύναται σωθῆναι; Mk. x. 26; καὶ τίς ἐστί μου πλησίον; Lk. x. 29; καὶ τίς ἐστιν κτλ. Jn. ix. 36 [G T Tr WH]; add, Jn. xiv. 22 [G T]. Peculiar is 2 Co. ii. 2: εἰ γὰρ ἐγὼ λυπῶ ὑμᾶς, καὶ τίς . . . ἐμοῦ (a swarm of exx. of this form of speech occur in Clem. homil. 2, 43, e. g. εἰ ὁ θεὸς ψεύδεται, καὶ τίς ἀληθεύει;), where the writer after the conditional protasis, interrupting himself as it were, utters the substance of the negative apodosis in a new question, where we render *who then is he that* etc., for *then there is no one who* etc. **h.** it introduces parentheses [cf. W. § 62, 1]: καὶ ἐκωλύθην ἄχρι τοῦ δεῦρο, Ro. i. 13 (Dem. Lept. p. 488, 9; so the Lat. *et*, e. g. praeda — et aliquantum ejus fuit — militi concessa, Liv. 27, 1); cf. *Fritzsche*, Ep. ad Rom. i. p. 35 sq. **3.** It annexes epexegetically both words and sentences (καί epexegetical or 'explicative'). so

that it is equiv. to *and indeed, namely*, [W. § 53, 3 c.; cf. § 66, 7 fin.]: χάριν καὶ ἀποστολήν, Ro. i. 5, where cf. Fritzsche; περὶ ἐλπίδος καὶ ἀναστάσεως νεκρῶν, Acts xxiii. 6; πολλά . . . κ. ἕτερα, Lk. iii. 18; πολλά . . . καὶ ἄλλα σημεῖα, Jn. xx. 30; πολλὰ καὶ βαρέα αἰτιώματα, Acts xxv. 7; πολλοὶ κ. ἀνυπότακτοι, Tit. i. 10 [R G; on the preceding use of καί cf. πολύς, d. α. fin.]; καὶ [L br. κ.] ὅταν ἀπαρθῇ, and indeed [i. e. viz.] when he shall be taken away etc. Lk. v. 35 [others find here an aposiopesis; cf. Meyer ad loc. (ed. *Weiss*)]; καὶ χάριν ἀντὶ χάριτος, Jn. i. 16; καὶ περισσὸν ἔχωσιν, Jn. x. 10, add 33 (where the words καὶ ὅτι κτλ. show what kind of blasphemy is meant); Acts v. 21 (on which see γερουσία); Ro. ii. 15 (where καὶ μεταξὺ κτλ. adds an explanation respecting the testimony of conscience); 1 Co. iii. 5; xv. 38, etc.; cf. *Bornemann*, Scholia, p. 38; *Fritzsche*, Quaest. Lcian. p. 9 sqq.; so the Lat. *et* in Cic. Tusc. 3, 20, 48 laudat, et saepe, virtutem; pro Mil. 25 te enim jam appello et ea voce ut me exaudire possis; cf. *Ramshorn*, Lat. Gram. ii. p. 809; [Harpers' Lat. Dict. s. v. et, II. A.]; **i.** q. *and indeed*, to make a climax, for *and besides*: καὶ ἀκατάκριτον, Acts xxii. 25; καὶ τοῦτον ἐσταυρωμένον, 1 Co. ii. 2; καὶ τοῦτο, Lat. *idque* (Cic. off. 1, 1, 1 te . . . audientem Cratippum idque Athenis), our *and this, and that, and that too*, i. q. *especially*: Ro. xiii. 11; 1 Co. vi. 6, and LT Tr WH in 8, (4 Macc. xiv. 9); also καὶ ταῦτα (com. in Grk. writ.), 1 Co. vi. 8 Rec.; Heb. xi. 12; cf. *Klotz*, Devar. i. p. 108; ii. 2 p. 652 sq.; [cf. W. 162 (153)]. **4.** it connects whole narratives and expositions, and thus forms a transition to new matters: Mt. iv. 23; viii. 14, 23, 28; ix. 1, 9, 27, 35; x. 1; Mk. v. 1, 21; vi. 1, 6; Lk. viii. 26; Jn. i. 19 (cf. 15); 1 Jn. i. 4, etc.; esp. in the very com. καὶ ἐγένετο, Mt. vii. 28; Lk. vii. 11; viii. 1, etc. (see γίνομαι, 2 b.). **5.** καί . . . καί, a repetition which indicates that of two things one takes place no less than the other: *both . . . and, as well . . . as, not only . . . but also*, [W. § 53, 4]: it serves to correlate — not only single terms, as καὶ [L br. κ.] ψυχὴν καὶ σῶμα, Mt. x. 28; add, Mk. iv. 41; Jn. iv. 36 [here Tr WH om. first κ.]; Ro. xi. 33; Phil. ii. 13; iv. 12, etc.; καὶ ἐν ὀλίγῳ καὶ ἐν πολλῷ [L T Tr WH μεγάλῳ] both with little effort and with great [but see μέγας, 1 a. γ. fin.], Acts xxvi. 29; but also clauses and sentences, as Mk. ix. 13; Jn. vii. 28; ix. 37; xii. 28; 1 Co. i. 22; and even things that are contrasted [cf. W. u. s.; B. § 149, 8 b.]: Jn. xv. 24; Acts xxiii. 3; καί . . . καὶ οὐ, Lk. v. 36; Jn. vi. 36; *now . . . now*, Mk. ix. 22; καὶ οὐ . . . καί, Jn. xvii. 25. **6.** τέ . . . καί, see τέ, 2.

II. It marks something added to what has already been said, or that of which something already said holds good; accordingly it takes on the nature of an adverb, *also* (Lat. *etiam, quoque*, Germ. *auch* [cf. W. and B. as ad init. In this use it generally throws an emphasis upon the word which immediately follows it; cf. *Klotz*, Devar. ii. 2 p. 638.]); **1.** used simply, **a.** *also, likewise*: Mt. v. 39 sq.; xii. 45; Mk. ii. 28; Lk. iii. 14; Jn. viii. 19; vii. 17; 1 Co. vii. 29; xi. 6, etc.; very freq. with pronouns: καὶ ὑμεῖς, Mt. xx. 4, 7; Lk. xxi. 31; Jn. vii. 47, etc.; κἀγώ, καὶ ἐγώ, see κἀγώ, 2; καὶ αὐτός, see αὐτός, I. 1 a.　preceded by an adverb of comparison in the former part of the sentence: καθὼς ... καί, Lk. vi. 31 [WH txt. om., L Tr mrg. br., καὶ ὑμεῖς]; Jn. vi. 57; xiii. 15, 33; 1 Jn. ii. 18; iv. 17; 1 Co. xv. 49; ὥσπερ ... οὕτω καί, Ro. xi. 30 sq.; 1 Co. xv. 22; Gal. iv. 29; καθάπερ ... οὕτω καί, 2 Co. viii. 11; ὡς ... καί, Mt. vi. 10; Lk. xi. 2 R L br.; Acts vii. 51 [L καθὼς; 2 Co. xiii. 2 see ὡς, I. 1 fin.]; Gal. i. 9; Phil. i. 20, (Thuc. 8, 1; ὥσπερ ... καί, Xen. mem. [2, 2, 2 (and Kühner ad loc.)]; 3, 1, 4; [4, 4, 7; cf. B. 362 (311) c.]); with εἰ preceding, Gal. iv. 7.　sometimes καί stands in each member of the comparison: 1 Th. ii. 14; Ro. i. 13; Col. iii. 13, (2 Macc. ii. 10; vi. 14; also in Grk. writ., cf. Klotz ad Dev. ii. 2 p. 635; Kühner on Xen. mem. 1, 1, 6 [also in his Grk. Gram. § 524, 2 vol. ii. 799; cf. Ellic. on Eph. v. 23; W. § 53, 5]).　b. i. q. *even* [A. V. sometimes *yea*], (Lat. *vel, adeo*; Germ. *sogar, selbst*): Mt. v. 46 sq.; x. 30; Mk. i. 27; Lk. x. 17; 1 Co. ii. 10; Gal. ii. 17; Eph. v. 12, etc.　c. before a comparative it augments the gradation, *even, still*, (Germ. *noch*): Mt. xi. 9; [Jn. xiv. 12]; Heb. viii. 6 [B. 363 (311) g.; al. regard the καί in this pass. as corresponsive (*also*) rather than ascensive, and connect it with ὅσῳ].　d. with a ptcp. i. q. *although* [cf. Krüger § 56, 13, 2]: Lk. xviii. 7 R G [see μακροθυμέω, 2].　2. joined with pronouns and particles, *also*; a. with comparative adverbs: ὡς καί, Acts xi. 17; 1 Co. vii. 7; ix. 5, etc.; καθὼς καί, Ro. xv. 7; 1 Co. xiii. 12; 2 Co. i. 14; Eph. iv. 17, 32; v. 2, etc.; οὕτω καί, Ro. v. 15 [WH br. καί], 18 sq.; vi. 11; 1 Co. xi. 12, etc.; ὁμοίως καί, Jn. vi. 11; ὡσαύτως καί, Lk. xxii. 20 [R G L Tr mrg., T Tr txt. WH κ. ὡσ. (but WH reject the pass.)]; 1 Co. xi. 25; καθάπερ καί (see καθάπερ).　b. added to words designating the cause, it marks something which follows of necessity from what has been previously said: διὸ καί, Lk. i. 35; Acts x. 29; Ro. i. 24 Rec.; Heb. xiii. 12; [1 Pet. ii. 6 R]; διὰ τοῦτο καί, Lk. xi. 49; Jn. xii. 18 [here Tr txt. om. Tr mrg. br. καί].　c. after the interrog. τί, καί (which belongs not to τί, but to the following word [to the whole sentence, rather; cf. *Bäumlein*, Partikeln, p. 152]) points the significance of the question, and may be rendered *besides, moreover*, (Germ. *noch*) [cf. W. § 53, 3 a. fin.; esp. Krüger § 69, 32, 16]: τί καὶ βαπτίζονται; [A. V. *why then* etc.], 1 Co. xv. 29; τί καὶ ἐλπίζει; (prop. why doth he *also* or *yet* hope for, and not rest in the *sight*?), Ro. viii. 24 [R G T]; ἵνα τί καί, Lk. xiii. 7.　d. ἀλλὰ καί, *but also*: Lk. xxiv. 22; Jn. v. 18; Ro. i. 32; v. 3, 11; viii. 23; ix. 10; 2 Co. vii. 7; viii. 10, 19, 21; ix. 12; 1 Jn. ii. 2, etc.; i. q. Lat. *at etiam* (in an apodosis after εἰ): Ro. vi. 5 [W. 442 (412)].　e. δὲ καί, and δὲ ... καί, *but also*, and *also*: Mt. iii. 10 [R G]; xviii. 17; xxvii. 44; Mk. xiv. 31 [WH br. δέ]; Lk. ii. 4; ix. 61; xiv. 12, 26 [L txt. Tr WH ἔτι τε καί, see ἔτι, 2 fin.]; xviii. 1 [R G], 9 [L br. καί]; Jn. ii. 2; iii. 23; xviii. 2, 5; Acts v. 16; 1 Co. i. 16; iv. 7; xiv. 15; xv. 15; 2 Co. iv. 3, etc.　καὶ ... γάρ, ἐὰν καί, εἰ καί, ἢ καί, καίγε, καὶ ... δέ, see γάρ II. P. 10, ἐάν I. 3, εἰ III. 6 sq., ἤ 4 c., γέ 3 e., δέ 9.　The examples of crasis with καί in the N. T., viz. κἀγώ (κἀμοί, κἀμέ), κἀκεῖ, κἀκεῖθεν, κἀκεῖνος,

κἄν, are noticed each in its place; for references see especially κἀγώ, init.

2533
Καϊάφας [WH Καϊάφας (cf. I, ι fin.); Lchm. in Lk. iii. 2 Καϊφας], -a [B. 20 (18); W. § 8, 1], ὁ, (supposed by many to be the same as כֵּיפָא, a stone, a rock; others more correctly i. q. כָּפָא, depression, Targ. on Prov. xvi. 26 [acc. to Delitzsch (Brief and. Röm. ins Hebr. etc. p. 28) קְיָפָא]), *Caiaphas*; acc. to Joseph. (antt. 18, 2, 2) Ἰώσηπος, ὁ καὶ Καϊάφας (Ἰώσηπον, τὸν καὶ Καϊάφαν ἐπικαλούμενον, antt. 18, 4, 3), high-priest of the Jews. He was appointed to that office by Valerius Gratus, governor of Judæa, after the removal of Simon, son of Camith, A.D. 18 [cf. *Schürer*, N. T. Zeitgesch. § 23 iv.], and was removed A.D. 36 by Vitellius, governor of Syria, who appointed Jonathan, son of the high-priest Ananus [i. e. Annas, father-in-law of Caiaphas, Jn. xviii. 13], his successor (Joseph. antt. 18, 4, 3): Mt. xxvi. 3, 57; Lk. iii. 2; Jn. xi. 49; xviii. 13 sq. 24, 28; Acts iv. 6. Cf. *Hausrath* in Schenkel iii. 463 sq.*

2534; see 2532 & 1065
καίγε, see γέ, 3 e. ————————————

2535
Κάϊν [WH Καΐν (cf. I, ι fin.)], -ό, indecl., (in Joseph. with a Grk. ending, Κάϊς, -ιος; Hebr. קַיִן i. e. a spear, although the author of Genesis, iv. 1, derives it fr. קָנָה to produce, beget, acquire, so that it is i. q. קְנִי, Ps. civ. 24 [cf. B.D. Am. ed. s. v.]), *Cain*, the fratricide, the first-born son of Adam: Heb. xi. 4; 1 Jn. iii. 12; Jude 11.*

2536
Καϊνάν [so R G L both 1 and 2; Tr Καϊνάν in 1 and Tr txt. in 2, but Tr mrg. Καινάμ in 2, WH Καινάμ 1 and 2; T Καϊνάμ both 1 and 2], ὁ, (Hebr. קֵינָן a lance-maker [al. 'possessor' or 'possession']), *Cainan*; 1. son of Enos (Gen. v. 9 sq.): Lk. iii. 37.　2. son of Arphaxad, acc. to the Sept. of Gen. x. 24; xi. 12; [1 Chr. i. 18 Alex.], which Luke follows in iii. 36. [See B. D. s. v.]*

2537
καινός, -ή, -όν [fr. Aeschyl. and Hdt. down]; Sept. for חָדָשׁ; *new*, i. e.　a. as respects form; *recently made, fresh, recent, unused, unworn* (opp. to παλαιός old, antiquated): as ἀσκός, Mt. ix. 17; Mk. ii. 22 [T om. Tr WH br. the cl.]; Lk. v. 38 ἱμάτιον, Lk. v. 36; πλήρωμα, Mk. ii. 21; μνημεῖον, Mt. xxvii. 60; with ἐν ᾧ οὐδέπω οὐδεὶς ἐτέθη added, Jn. xix. 41; καινὰ κ. παλαιά, Mt. xiii. 52; *new, which as recently made is superior to what it succeeds*: διαθήκη, Mt. xxvi. 28 (T WH om. καιν.); Mk. xiv. 24 R L; Lk. xxii. 20 (WH reject the pass.); 1 Co. xi. 25; 2 Co. iii. 6; Heb. viii. 8, 13; ix. 15, (Jer. xxxviii. (xxxi.) 31); καινοὶ οὐρανοί, καινὴ γῆ, 2 Pet. iii. 13; Rev. xxi. 1, (Is. lxv. 17; lxvi. 22); Ἱερουσαλήμ (see Ἱεροσόλυμα, fin.), Rev. iii. 12; xxi. 2; ἄνθρωπος (see the word, 1 f.), Eph. ii. 15; iv. 24, (καρδία, πνεῦμα, Ezek. xviii. 31; xxxvi. 26); καινὰ πάντα ποιῶ, I bring all things into a new and better condition, Rev. xxi. 5; γέννημα τῆς ἀμπέλου, Mt. xxvi. 29; Mk. xiv. 25.　b. as respects substance; *of a new kind; unprecedented, novel, uncommon, unheard of*, (ἕτερα καὶ καινὰ δαιμόνια, Xen. mem. 1, 1, 1): διδαχή, Mk. i. 27; Acts xvii. 19; ἐντολή, given now for the first time, Jn. xiii. 34; 1 Jn. ii. 7 sq.; 2 Jn. 5; ὄνομα, with the added explanation ὃ οὐδεὶς οἶδεν (ἔγνω Rec.), Rev. ii. 17 (Is. lxii. 2; lxv. 15); ᾠδή, Rev. v. 9; xiv. 3, (Ps. cxliii. (cxliv.) 9; ὕμνος,

Is. xlii. 10; ᾆσμα, Ps. xxxii. (xxxiii.) 3; xxxix. (xl.) 4, etc.); λέγειν τι καὶ [ἢ L T Tr WH] ἀκούειν καινότερον, Acts xvii. 21 (*newer* sc. than that which is already; [cf. W. 244 (228 sq.)]); κτίσις, Gal. vi. 15; καινὰ τὰ πάντα, all things are new, previously non-existent, begin to be far different from what they were before, 2 Co. v. 17 [L T Tr WH om. τὰ πάντα]; μηκέτι οὔσης τῆς ἀνομίας, καινῶν δὲ γεγονότων πάντων ὑπὸ κυρίου, Barn. ep. 15, 7. γλῶσσαι (see γλῶσσα, 2): Mk. xvi. 17 [Tr txt. WH txt. om. Tr mrg. br. καιν.]*

[Syn. καινός, νέος: ν. denotes the new primarily in reference to time, the young, recent; κ. denotes the new primarily in reference to quality, the fresh, unworn; 'νέος ad tempus refertur, καινός ad rem;' see Trench § lx.; Tittmann i. p. 59 sq.; *Green*, 'Crit. Note' on Mt. ix. 17 (where the words occur together). The same distinction, in the main, holds in classic usage; cf. Schmidt ii. ch. 47.]

2538 **καινότης, -ητος, ἡ**, (καινός), *newness*: ἐν καινότητι πνεύματος, in the new state (of life) in which the Holy Spirit places us, Ro. vii. 6; ἐν καινότητι ζωῆς in a new condition or state of (moral) life, Ro. vi. 4 (εἰς καινότητα ἀΐδιον ζωῆς, so as to produce a new state which is eternal life, Ignat. ad Eph. 19; among prof. writ. it is used by Thuc. 3, 38; Isocr., Athen., al.; often by Plut., [applied to the 'novelties' of fashion (French *nouveauté*)]).*

2539 **καίπερ** [Treg. καί περ in Heb.; fr. Hom. Od. 7, 224 down], conjunc., [originally *even very much*, cf. Donaldson § 621; Bäumlein p. 200 sq.; Krüger § 56, 13, 2; B. § 144, 23; W. § 45, 2 fin.], *although*; it is joined to a ptcp. (in Grk. writ. sometimes also to an adj., so that ὤν must be supplied): Phil. iii. 4; Heb. v. 8; vii. 5; xii. 17; 2 Pet. i. 12; contrary to ordinary usage [yet so occasionally in Grk. writ.] with a finite verb, καίπερ ἐστίν, Rev. xvii. 8 Rec.; but since Grsb. καὶ πάρεσται [correctly πάρεστι (see in πάρειμι)] has been restored after the best codd.*

2540 **καιρός, -οῦ, ὁ**, (derived by some fr. κάρα or κάρη, τό, the head, summit, [al. al.; cf. Vaniček p. 118]); Sept. for עֵת and מוֹעֵד; in Grk. writ. [fr. Hes. down] **1.** *due measure*; nowhere so in the bibl. writ. **2.** *a measure of time*; a larger or smaller portion of time; hence **a.** univ. *a fixed and definite time*: Ro. xiii. 11; 2 Co. vi. 2; ὕστεροι καιροί, 1 Tim. iv. 1; ἄχρι καιροῦ, up to a certain time, for a season, Lk. iv. 13 [but in ἄχρι, 1 b. referred apparently to b. below; cf. *Fritzsche*, Rom. i. p. 309 sq.]; Acts xiii. 11; πρὸς καιρόν, for a certain time only, for a season, Lk. viii. 13; 1 Co. vii. 5; πρὸς καιρὸν ὥρας, for the season of an hour, i. e. for a short season, 1 Th. ii. 17; κατὰ καιρόν, at certain seasons, (*from time to time*), Jn. v. 4 [R G L]; at the (divinely) appointed time, Ro. v. 6 [al. bring this under b.]; before the time appointed, Mt. viii. 29; 1 Co. iv. 5; ἔσται καιρός, ὅτε etc. 2 Tim. iv. 3; ὀλίγον καιρὸν ἔχει, a short time (in which to exercise his power) has been granted him, Rev. xii. 12; ἐν ἐκείνῳ τῷ καιρῷ, Mt. xi. 25; xii. 1; xiv. 1; Eph. ii. 12; κατ' ἐκείνον τ. κ., Acts xii. 1; xix. 23; κατὰ τ. κ. τοῦτον, Ro. ix. 9; ἐν αὐτῷ τῷ κ. Lk. xiii. 1; ἐν ᾧ κ. Acts vii. 20; ἐν τῷ νῦν κ., Ro. iii. 26; xi. 5; 2 Co. viii. 14 (13); ἐν παντὶ κ. always, at every season, [Aristot. top. 3, 2, 4 p. 117ᵃ, 35], Lk. xxi. 36; Eph. vi. 18; εἰς τίνα καιρόν, 1 Pet. i. 11. with the gen. of a

thing, *the time of* etc. i. e. at which it will occur: τῆς ἐμῆς ἀναλύσεως, 2 Tim. iv. 6; τῆς ἐπισκοπῆς, 1 Pet. v. 6 Lchm.; Lk. xix. 44; πειρασμοῦ, Lk. viii. 13; τοῦ ἄρξασθαι τὸ κρίμα, for judgment to begin, 1 Pet. iv. 17; καιροὶ τῶν λόγων, of the time when they shall be proved by the event, Lk. i. 20; — or when a thing usually comes to pass: τοῦ θερισμοῦ, Mt. xiii. 30; τῶν καρπῶν, when the fruits ripen, Mt. xxi. 34, 41; σύκων, Mk. xi. 13. with the gen. of a pers.: καιροὶ ἐθνῶν, the time granted to the Gentiles, until God shall take vengeance on them, Lk. xxi. 24; ὁ ἑαυτοῦ (T Tr WH αὐτοῦ) κ. the time when antichrist shall show himself openly, 2 Th. ii. 6; ὁ καιρός μου, the time appointed for my death, Mt. xxvi. 18; τῶν νεκρῶν κριθῆναι, the time appointed for the dead to be recalled to life and judged, Rev. xi. 18 [B. 260 (224)]; ὁ ἐμός, ὁ ὑμέτερος, the time for appearing in public, appointed (by God) for me, for you, Jn. vii. 6, 8; καιρῷ ἰδίῳ, the time suited to the thing under consideration, at its proper time, Gal. vi. 9; plur., 1 Tim. ii. 6; vi. 15; Tit. i. 3. ὁ καιρός alone, *the time when things are brought to a crisis, the decisive epoch waited for*: so of the time when the Messiah will visibly return from heaven, Mk. xiii. 33; ὁ καιρὸς ἤγγικεν, Lk. xxi. 8; ἐγγύς ἐστιν, Rev. i. 3; xxii. 10. **b.** *opportune* or *seasonable time*: with verbs suggestive of the idea of advantage, καιρὸν μεταλαμβάνειν, Acts xxiv. 25; ἔχειν, Gal. vi. 10 (Plut. Luc. 16); ἐξαγοράζεσθαι, Eph. v. 16; Col. iv. 5, see ἐξαγοράζω, 2; foll. by an inf., opportunity to do something, Heb. xi. 15; παρὰ καιρὸν ἡλικίας, past the opportunity of life [A. V. *past age*], Heb. xi. 11 (simply παρὰ καιρόν, Pind. Ol. 8, 32; several times in Plato, cf. *Ast*, Lex. Plat. ii. p. 126). **c.** *the right time*: ἐν καιρῷ (often in class. Grk.), in due season, Mt. xxiv. 45; Lk. xii. 42; xx. 10 R G L [(ed. stereotyp. only)]; 1 Pet. v. 6; also καιρῷ, Lk. xx. 10 L T Tr WH; τῷ καιρῷ, Mk. xii. 2. **d.** *a* (limited) *period of time* [1 Co. vii. 29]; plur. the periods prescribed by God to the nations, and bounded by their rise and fall, Acts xvii. 26; καιροὶ καρποφόροι, the seasons of the year in which the fruits grow and ripen, Acts xiv. 17 [cf. Gen. i. 14 Sept.]; καιρὸν καὶ καιροὺς καὶ ἥμισυ καιροῦ, a year and two years and six months [A. V. *a time, and times, and half a time*; cf. W. § 27, 4], Rev. xii. 14 (cf. 6; fr. Dan. vii. 25; xii. 7); stated seasons of the year solemnly kept by the Jews, and comprising several days, as the passover, pentecost, feast of tabernacles, Gal. iv. 10 [2 Chr. viii. 13; cf. Bar. i. 14]. in the divine arrangement of time adjusted to the economy of salvation: ὁ καιρὸς (πεπλήρωται), the preappointed period which acc. to the purpose of God must elapse before the divine kingdom could be founded by Christ, Mk. i. 15; plur., the several parts of this period, Eph. i. 10; ὁ καιρὸς ὁ ἐνεστώς, the present period, i. q. ὁ αἰὼν οὗτος (see αἰών, 3), Heb. ix. 9, opp. to καιρὸς διορθώσεως, the time when the whole order of things will be reformed (i. q. αἰὼν μέλλων), ib. 10; ὁ καιρὸς οὗτος, i. q. ὁ αἰὼν οὗτος (see αἰών, 3), Mk. x. 30; Lk. xviii. 30; ὁ νῦν καιρ. Ro. viii. 18; ἐν καιρῷ ἐσχάτῳ, the last period of the present age, the time just before the return of Christ from heaven (see ἔσχατος,

1 sub fin., etc.), 1 Pet. i. 5 ; καιροὶ ἀναψύξεως ἀπὸ προσώπου τοῦ κυρίου, denotes the time from the return of Christ on, the times of the consummated divine kingdom, Acts iii. 20 (19). e. as often in Grk. writ., and like the Lat. *tempus*, καιρός is equiv. to *what time brings, the state of the times, the things and events of time* : Lk. xii. 56 ; δουλεύειν τῷ καιρῷ, Lat. *tempori servire* (see δουλεύω, 2 a.), Ro. xii. 11 Rec.ʳᵗ ; τὰ σημεῖα τῶν καιρῶν, i. q. ἃ οἱ καιροὶ σημαίνουσι, Mt. xvi. 3 [here T br. WH reject the pass.] ; καιροὶ χαλεποί, 2 Tim. iii. 1 ; χρόνοι ἢ καιροί (*times or seasons*, Germ. *Zeitumstände*), Acts i. 7 ; οἱ χρόν. καὶ οἱ καιρ. 1 Th. v. 1 ; and in the opp. order, Dan. ii. 21 Sept. ; Sap. viii. 8.*

[SYN. κ α ι ρ ό ς, χ ρ ό ν ο ς : χρ. time, in general ; καιρ. a definitely limited portion of time, with the added notion of suitableness. Yet while, on the one hand, its meaning may be so sharply marked as to permit such a combination as χρόνου καιρός 'the nick of time,' on the other, its distinctive sense may so far recede as to allow it to be used as nearly equiv. to χρόνος ; cf. Thom. Mag. ed. *Ritschl* p. 206, 15 sqq. (after Ammonius s. v.) ; p. 215, 10 sqq. καιρός οὐ μόνον ἐπὶ χρόνου ἁπλῶς τίθεται, ἀλλὰ καὶ ἐπὶ τοῦ ἁρμοδίου καὶ πρέποντος, κτλ. ; Schmidt ch. 44 ; Trench § lvii. ; Tittmann i. 41 sqq. ; *Cope* on Aristot. rhet. 1, 7, 32. "In modern Grk. καιρός means *weather*, χρόνος *year*. In both words the kernel of meaning has remained unaltered ; this in the case of καιρ. is changeableness, of χρ. duration." *Curtius*, Etym. p. 110 sq.]

2541   **Καῖσαρ**, -αρος [Bttm. 16 (15)], ὁ, *Caesar* (prop. the surname of Julius Caesar, which being adopted by Octavianus Augustus and his successors afterwards became an appellative, and was appropriated by the Roman emperors as a part of their title [cf. Dict. of Biogr. and Mythol. s. v. Caesar]) : Mt. xxii. 17, 21 ; Mk. xii. 14, 16 sq. ; Lk. ii. 1 ; iii. 1 ; xx. 22 ; xxiii. 2 ; Jn. xix. 12 ; Acts xi. 28 [Rec.] ; xvii. 7, etc. ; Phil. iv. 22.*

2542   **Καισάρεια** [-ία Tdf. (cf. his note on Acts ix. 30), WH ; see I, ι], -ας, ἡ, *Caesarea* ; there were two cities of this name in Palestine : **1.** *Caesarea Philippi* (Καισάρεια ἡ Φιλίππου), situated at the foot of Lebanon near the sources of the Jordan in Gaulanitis, and formerly called *Paneas* (ἣν Πανεάδα Φοίνικες προσαγορεύουσιν, Eus. h. e. 7, 17) ; but after being rebuilt by Philip the tetrarch, it was called by him *Caesarea* in honor of Tiberius Caesar (Joseph. antt. 18, 2, 1 sq.) ; subsequently it was called *Neronias* by Agrippa II., in honor of Nero (Joseph. antt. 20, 9, 4) ; now *Bânias*, a village of about 150 [(?) "about 50" (*Bädeker*), "some forty" (*Murray*)] houses : Mt. xvi. 13 ; Mk. viii. 27. **2.** *Caesarea* (more fully *Caesarea of Palestine* [mod. *Kaisarîyeh*]), built near the Mediterranean by Herod the Great on the site of Strato's Tower, between Joppa and Dora. It was provided with a magnificent harbor and had conferred upon it the name of *Caesarea*, in honor of Augustus. It was the residence of the Roman procurators, and the majority of its inhabitants were Greeks (Joseph. antt. 13, 11, 2 ; 15, 9, 6 ; 19, 8, 2 ; b. j. 2, 9, 1) : Acts viii. 40 ; ix. 30 ; x. 1, 24 ; xi. 11 ; xii. 19 ; xviii. 22 ; xxi. 8, 16 ; xxiii. 23, 33 ; xxv. 1, 4, 6, 13. Cf. *Win*. RWB. [and BB. DD.] s. v. Cæsarea ; *Arnold* in Herzog ii. p. 486 sqq. ;

Overbeck in Schenkel i. p. 499 sq. ; [Schürer § 23, i. 9 ; and for other reff. cf. Mc. and S. s. v.].*

καίτοι, (fr. καί and τοί), conjunction, with a ptcp. [but   **2543**
in class. Grk. with a finite verb also (as in Acts below) ; Krüger § 56, 13, 2 ; cf. reff. s. v. καίπερ], *and yet, although* : Heb. iv. 3 (although the work of creation had been finished long ago, so that the rest spoken of cannot be understood to be that of God himself resting from that work [cf. Kurtz in loc.]) ; [Acts xiv. 17 L T Tr WH (but Tr καί τοι)].*   ── 2544;
see 2543
& 1065
καίτοιγε, see γέ, 3 f. ───────────   see 2533
[**Καϊφας**, see Καϊάφας.] ──────────   ─ 2545
καίω [Vaniček p. 98] ; Pass., pres. καίομαι ; pf. ptcp. κεκαυμένος ; 1 fut. καυθήσομαι (1 Co. xiii. 3 Tdf., where R G L Tr give the solecistic fut. subjunc. καυθήσωμαι, on which cf. *Lob.* ad Phryn. p. 720 sq. ; W. § 13, 1 e. ; B. 35 sq. (31)) ; [*Soph.* Lex., Intr. p. 40 ; *WH.* App. p. 172 ; *Tdf.* Proleg. p. 122. WH txt. Lchm. ed. ster. read καυχήσωμαι (with א A B etc.) ; on this reading see *WH.* App. ad loc. ; *A. W. Tyler* in Bib. Sacr. for July 1873, p. 502 sq. ; cf. *Scrivener*, Introd. etc. p. 629 sq. ; *Tregelles*, Printed Text etc. p. 191 sq. ; Tdf. ad loc.] ; Sept. for בָּעַר, שָׂרַף etc. ; [fr. Hom. down] : **1.** *to set fire to, light* : λύχνον, Mt. v. 15 ; pass. ptcp. καιόμενος, *burning*, Lk. xii. 35 ; Rev. iv. 5 ; viii. 10 ; xix. 20 ; with πυρί added, Heb. xii. 18 ; Rev. viii. 8 ; xxi. 8 ; in fig. disc. λύχνος καιόμενος, *a light showing the right way*, Jn. v. 35 (a comparison pointed at the Jews, to whom John the Baptist had been as a torch lighted for a merry-making) ; metaph. ἡ καρδία ἦν καιομένη *was glowing, burning, i. e. was greatly moved*, Lk. xxiv. 32 [W. § 45, 5 ; B. § 144, 28]. **2.** *to burn, consume with fire* : pass., Jn. xv. 6 ; 1 Co. xiii. 3 [see above] ; with πυρί added (cf. *igni cremare*, Caes. b. g. 1, 4), Mt. xiii. 40 G Tr for R L T WH κατακαίεται. [COMP. : *ἐκ-, κατα-καίω*.] *

κἀκεῖ [Grsb. *κἀκεῖ* ; cf. κἀγώ and reff.], (by crasis fr. καί   **2546**
and ἐκεῖ [cf. W. § 5, 3 ; B. p. 10 ; esp. Tdf. Proleg. p. 96]) ; **1.** *and there* : Mt. v. 23 [Tr mrg. καὶ ἐκεῖ] ; x. 11 ; xxviii. 10 [Tdf. καὶ ἐκεῖ] ; Mk. i. 35 [Lchm. καὶ ἐκεῖ] ; Jn. xi. 54 ; Acts xiv. 7 ; xxii. 10 ; xxv. 20 ; xxvii. 6. **2.** *there also* : Mk. i. 38 (G WH καὶ ἐκεῖ) ; Acts xvii. 13.*

κἀκεῖθεν [Grsb. *κἀκ-* ; see κἀγώ and reff.], (by crasis fr.   **2547**
καί and ἐκεῖθεν [cf. W. § 5, 3 ; B. 10 ; esp. Tdf. Proleg. 96 sq.]) ; Lat. *et inde* ; **a.** of place, *and from thence, and thence* : Mk. ix. 30 (R G καὶ ἐκεῖθεν) ; x. 1 [L T Tr WH καὶ ἐκ.] ; Lk. xi. 53 T Tr txt. WH] ; Acts vii. 4 ; xiv. 26 ; xv. 12 [ἐκεῖθεν τι R G] ; xx. 15 ; xxi. 1 ; xxvii. 4, 12 [L T Tr WH ἐκεῖθεν] ; xxviii. 15. **b.** of time, *and thereafter, and afterward* [cf. Bornem. Scholia in Luc. p. 90 sq.] : Acts xiii. 21.*

κἀκεῖνος [Grsb. *κἀκ-* ; see κἀγώ and reff.], -είνη, -εῖνο,   **2548**
(by crasis fr. καί and ἐκεῖνος [cf. W. § 5, 3 ; esp. *Tdf.* Proleg. p. 97]) ; **1.** ἐκεῖνος referring to the more remote subject : **a.** *and he* (Lat. *et ille*) : Lk. xi. 7 ; xxii. 12 ; Acts xviii. 19 ; ταῦτα . . . κἀκεῖνα [A. V. *the other*], Mt. xxiii. 23 ; Lk. xi. 42. **b.** *he also* : Acts xv. 11 ; Ro. xi. 23 [Rec.ˢᵗ καὶ ἐκ.] ; 1 Co. x. 6. **2.** ἐκεῖνος

referring to the nearer subject [cf. ἐκεῖνος, 1 c.];   **a.** *and he* (Lat. *et is*, Germ. *und selbiger*): Mt. xv. 18; Jn. vii. 29; xix. 35 [L Tr WH καὶ ἐκ.].   **b.** *he also* (Germ. *auch selbiger*): Mt. xx. 4 [T WH καὶ ἐκ.]; Mk. xii. 4 sq.; xvi. 11, 13; Lk. xxii. 12; Jn. xiv. 12; xvii. 24.

2549   **κακία, -ας, ἡ**, (κακός), [fr. Theognis down], Sept. chiefly for רַע, and רָעָה;   **1.** *malignity, malice, ill-will, desire to injure*: Ro. i. 29; Eph. iv. 31; Col. iii. 8; Tit. iii. 3; Jas. i. 21; 1 Pet. ii. 1.   **2.** *wickedness, depravity*: 1 Co. v. 8 [cf. W. 120 (114)]; xiv. 20; Acts viii. 22 (cf. 21); *wickedness that is not ashamed to break the laws,* 1 Pet. ii. 16.   **3.** Hellenistically, *evil, trouble*: Mt. vi. 34 (as Amos iii. 6; [1 S. vi. 9]; Eccl. vii. 15 (14); xii. 1; Sir. xix. 6; 1 Macc. vii. 23, etc.).*

[SYN. κακία, πονηρία: associated Ro. i. 29; 1 Co. v. 8. Acc. to Trench, Syn. § xi., endorsed by Ellic. (on Eph. iv. 31) and Bp. Lghtft. (on Col. iii. 8), κακία denotes rather the vicious disposition, πονηρία the active exercise of the same; cf. Xen. mem. 1, 2, 28 εἰ μὲν αὐτὸς (i. e. Σωκράτης) ἐποίει τι φαῦλον, εἰκότως ἂν ἐδόκει πονηρὸς εἶναι· εἰ δ᾽ αὐτὸς σωφρονῶν διετέλει, πῶς ἂν δικαίως τῆς οὐκ ἐνούσης αὐτῷ κακίας αἰτίαν ἔχοι; But Fritzsche, Meyer (on Ro. l. c.; yet cf. Weiss in ed. 6), al. dissent,—seeming nearly to reverse this distinction; cf. Suidas s. v. κακία· ἔστιν ἡ τοῦ κακῶσαι τὸν πέλας σπουδή, παρὰ τῷ ἀποστόλῳ; see πονηρός, 2 b.]

2550   **κακοήθεια [-θία WH; see I, ι], -ας, ἡ**, (fr. κακοήθης, and this fr. κακός and ἦθος), *bad character, depravity of heart and life*, Xen., Plat., Isocr., al.; 4 Macc. i. 4, where cf. Grimm p. 299; spec. used of *malignant subtlety, malicious craftiness*: Ro. i. 29 (3 Macc. iii. 22; Add. to Esth. viii. l. 12; Clem. Rom. 1 Cor. 35, 5; Joseph. antt. 1, 1, 4; 16, 3, 1; [c. Ap. 1, 24, 4]; Polyb. 5, 50, 5, etc.). On the other hand, Aristot. rhet. 2, 13, [3 p. 81] defines it τὸ ἐπὶ τὸ χεῖρον ὑπολαμβάνειν πάντα, [*taking all things in the evil part*, Genevan N. T. Cf. Trench § xi.].*

2551   **κακολογέω, -ῶ**; 1 aor. inf. κακολογῆσαι; (κακολόγος); i. q. κακῶς λέγω (which the old grammarians prefer, see Lob. ad Phryn. p. 200);   **1.** *to speak ill of, revile, abuse,* one; *to calumniate, traduce*: τινά, Mk. ix. 39; τί, Acts xix. 9; (2 Macc. iv. 1; Lys., Plut., al.).   **2.** Hellenistically, *to imprecate evil on, curse*: τινά, Mt. xv. 4; Mk. vii. 10, (so for קָלַל, Prov. xx. 20; Ezek. xxii. 7; Ex. xxii. 28).*

2552   **κακοπάθεια [-θία WH; see I, ι], -ας, ἡ**, (κακοπαθής suffering evil, afflicted), prop. the suffering of evil, i. e. *trouble, distress, affliction*: Jas. v. 10 (Mal. i. 13; 2 Macc. ii. 26 sq.; [Antipho]; Thuc. 7, 77; Isocr., Polyb., Diod., al.).*

2553   **κακοπαθέω, -ῶ**; 1 aor. impv. 2 sing. κακοπάθησον; (κακοπαθής); *to suffer (endure) evils (hardship, troubles); to be afflicted*: 2 Tim. ii. 9; Jas. v. 13 [W. § 41 a. 3 fin.; cf. § 60, 4 c.; B. § 139, 28], (Sept. Jon. iv. 10; Xen., Plut., al.); used freq. of the hardships of military service (Thuc. 4, 9; Polyb. 3, 72, 5; Joseph. antt. 10, 11, 1; b. j. 1, 7, 4); hence elegantly κακοπάθησον (L T Tr WH συγ-[T WH συν- (q. v. fin.)] κακοπάθησον) ὡς καλὸς στρατιώτης, 2 Tim. ii. 3; ib. iv. 5. [COMP.: συγ-κακοπαθέω.]*

2554   **κακο-ποιέω, -ῶ**; 1 aor. inf. κακοποιῆσαι; (κακοποιός);   **1.** *to do harm*: Mk. iii. 4; Lk. vi. 9.   **2.** *to do evil, do*

wrong: 1 Pet. iii. 17; 3 Jn. 11. ([Aeschyl., Arstph.], Xen., Polyb., Antonin., Plut.; Sept.) *

κακοποιός, -όν, (κακόν and ποιέω), *doing evil*; subst. *an evil-doer, malefactor*: Jn. xviii. 30 [but L mrg. T Tr WH κακὸν ποιῶν]; 1 Pet. ii. 12, 14; iii. 16 [T Tr mrg. WH om. the cl.]; iv. 15. (Prov. xii. 4; Pind., Aristot., Polyb., Plut.) *   2555

κακός, -ή, -όν, Sept. for רַע, [fr. Hom. down], *bad*, [A.V. (almost uniformly) *evil*];   **1.** univ. *of a bad nature; not such as it ought to be*.   **2.** [morally, i. e.] of a mode of thinking, feeling, acting; *base, wrong, wicked*: of persons, Mt. xxi. 41 [cf. W. 637 (592); also B. 143 (126)]; xxiv. 48; Phil. iii. 2; Rev. ii. 2. διαλογισμοί, Mk. vii. 21; ὁμιλίαι, 1 Co. xv. 33; ἐπιθυμία, Col. iii. 5 (Prov. xii. 12); ἔργα [better ἔργον], Ro. xiii. 3. neut. *κακόν, τὸ κακόν, evil* i. e. what is contrary to law, either divine or human, *wrong, crime*: [Jn. xviii. 23]; Acts xxiii. 9; Ro. vii. 21; xiv. 20; xvi. 19; 1 Co. xiii. 5; Heb. v. 14; 1 Pet. iii. 10 sq.; 3 Jn. 11; plur. [*evil things*]: Ro. i. 30; 1 Co. x. 6; 1 Tim. vi. 10 [πάντα τὰ κακά *all kinds of evil*]; Jas. i. 13 [W. § 30, 4; B. § 132, 24]; κακόν ποιεῖν, to do, commit evil: Mt. xxvii. 23; Mk. xv. 14; Lk. xxiii. 22; 2 Co. xiii. 7; 1 Pet. iii. 12; τὸ κακόν, Ro. xiii. 4; τὰ κακά, Ro. i. 30; 1 Co. x. 6; 1 Tim. vi. 10; 8; κακόν, τὸ κακὸν πράσσειν, Ro. vii. 19; ix. 11. [Rec.]; xiii. 4; [2 Co. v. 10 R G L Tr mrg.]; τὸ κακὸν κατεργάζεσθαι, Ro. ii. 9. spec. of *wrongs inflicted*: Ro. xii. 21; κακὸν ἐργάζομαί τινι [*to work ill to one*], Ro. xiii. 10; ἐνδείκνυμι, 2 Tim. iv. 14; ποιῶ, Acts ix. 13; ἀποδίδωμι κακὸν ἀντὶ κακοῦ, Ro. xii. 17; 1 Th. v. 15; 1 Pet. iii. 9.   **3.** *troublesome, injurious, pernicious, destructive, baneful*: neut. *κακόν, an evil*, that which injures, Jas. iii. 8 [W. § 59, 8 b.; B. 79 (69)]; with the suggestion of wildness and ferocity, θηρία, Tit. i. 12; substantially i. q. *bad*, i. e. *distressing,* whether to mind or to body: ἕλκος κακὸν κ. πονηρόν [A.V. *a noisome and grievous sore*], Rev. xvi. 2; κακὸν πράσσω ἐμαυτῷ, Lat. *vim mihi infero,* to do harm to one's self, Acts xvi. 28; κακόν τι πάσχω, to suffer some harm, Acts xxviii. 5; τὰ κακά, evil things, the discomforts which plague one, Lk. xvi. 25 (opp. to τὰ ἀγαθά, the good things, from which pleasure is derived). [SYN. cf. κακία.] *

κακοῦργος, -ον, (contr. from κακόεργος, fr. κακόν and ΕΡΓΩ; cf. πανοῦργος, and on the accent of both see Göttling, Lehre v. Accent, p. 321; [Chandler § 445]), as subst. *a malefactor*: 2 Tim. ii. 9; of a robber, Lk. xxiii. 32 sq. [cf. W. 530 (493); B. § 150, 3], 39. (Prov. xxi. 15; in Grk. writ. fr. [Soph. and] Hdt. down.) *   2557

κακουχέω, -ῶ: (fr. obsol. κακοῦχος, fr. κακόν and ἔχω); *to treat ill, oppress, plague*: τινά; pres. pass. ptcp. κακουχούμενοι, maltreated, tormented, Heb. xi. 37; xiii. 3. (1 K. ii. 26; xi. 39 Alex.; Diod. 3, 23; 19, 11; Dio C. 35 (36), 9 (11); Plut. mor. p. 114 e.) [COMP.: συγ-κακουχέω.] *   2558

κακόω, -ῶ: fut. κακώσω; 1 aor. ἐκάκωσα; (κακός);   **1.** *to oppress, afflict, harm, maltreat*: τινά, Acts vii. 6, 19; xii. 1; xviii. 10; 1 Pet. iii. 13, (Ex. v. 22; xxiii. 9 Alex.; in Grk. writ. fr. Hom. down).   **2.** by a usage foreign to the classics, *to embitter* (Vulg. *ad iracundiam concito*); render evil affected, (Ps. cv. (cvi.) 32; Joseph. antt. 16,   2559

2556

1, 2; 7, 3; 8, 6): τὴν ψυχήν τινος κατά τινος, against one, Acts xiv. 2.*

2560   κακῶς, (κακός), adv., [fr. Hom. down], *badly, ill,* i. e. **a.** [in a physical sense] *miserably* : ἔχειν, *to be ill,* sick [see ἔχω, II. a.], Mt. iv. 24; viii. 16; ix. 12; xiv. 35; [xvii. 15 L Tr txt. WH txt.]; Mk. [i. 32, 34]; ii. 17; [vi. 55]; Lk. v. 31; vii. 2, etc.; πάσχειν, Mt. xvii. 15 [R G T Tr mrg. WH mrg.]; δαιμονίζεσθαι, Mt. xv. 22; κακοὺς κακῶς ἀπολέσει, Mt. xxi. 41, on this combination of words with verbs of destroying, perishing, etc., which is freq. in Grk. writ. also, cf. Kuinoel ad loc.; W. § 68, 1.   **b.** [morally] *improperly, wrongly* : Jn. xviii. 23; κακῶς εἰπεῖν τινα, to speak ill of, revile, one, Acts xxiii. 5; with bad intent, αἰτεῖσθαι, Jas. iv. 3.*

2561   κάκωσις, -εως, ἡ, (κακόω), *ill-treatment, ill-usage,* (Vulg. *afflictio*): Acts vii. 34. (Ps. xvii. (xviii.) 19; Ex. iii. 7, 17; Job xxxi. 29 [Symm.]; Thuc., Xen., Plut., al.) *

2562   καλάμη, -ης, ἡ, *a stalk of grain* or *of a reed, the stalk* (left after the ears are cut off), *stubble*: 1 Co. iii. 12. (Ex. v. 12; xv. 7; Is. xvii. 6; Hom. et sqq.) *

2563   κάλαμος, -ου, ὁ, fr. Pind. down, Lat. *calamus* i. e.   **a.** *a reed* : Mt. xi. 7; xii. 20 (fr. Is. xlii. 3); Lk. vii. 24.   **b.** *a staff made of a reed, a reed-staff,* (as in 2 K. xviii. 21): Mt. xxvii. 29 sq. 48; Mk. xv. 19, 36.   **c.** *a measuring reed* or *rod*: Rev. xi. 1; xxi. 15 sq., (Ezek. xl. 3–6; xlii. 16–19).   **d.** *a writer's reed, a pen*: 3 Jn. 13; [see *Gardthausen*, Griech. Palaeogr. p. 71 sq.].*

2564   καλέω, -ῶ; impf. ἐκάλουν; fut. καλέσω (W. § 13, 3 c.); 1 aor. ἐκάλεσα; pf. κέκληκα; Pass., pres. καλοῦμαι; pf. 3 pers. sing. κέκληται (1 Co. vii. 18 L T Tr WH; [Rev. xix. 13 L Tr WH]), ptcp. κεκλημένος; 1 aor. ἐκλήθην; 1 fut. κληθήσομαι; [fr. Hom. down]; Hebr. קָרָא; Lat. *voco*; i. e. **1.** *to call* (Germ. *rufen* [cf. βοάω, fin.]);   **a.** *to call aloud, utter in a loud voice*: ἄχρις οὖ τὸ σήμερον καλεῖται, as long as the word 'to-day' is called out or proclaimed, Heb. iii. 13; τινά, to call one to approach or stand before one, Mt. xx. 8; xxii. 3 (where εἰς τοὺς γάμους seems to belong to τοὺς κεκλημένους); Mt. xxv. 14; [Mk. iii. 31 L T Tr WH]; Lk. xix. 13; τὰ ἴδια πρόβατα κατ᾽ ὄνομα, his own sheep each by its name, Jn. x. 3 (where L T Tr WH φωνεῖ); used of Christ, calling certain persons to be his disciples and constant companions, Mt. iv. 21 (note what precedes in 19: δεῦτε ὀπίσω μου); Mk. i. 20; to order one to be summoned, Mt. ii. 15 [see just below]; before the judges, Acts iv. 18; xxiv. 2; foll. by ἐκ with gen. of place, i. q. to call out, call forth from: Mt. ii. 15, cf. Heb. xi. 8.   metaph. *to cause to pass from one state into another*: τινὰ ἐκ σκότους εἰς τὸ φῶς, 1 Pet. ii. 9.   **b.** like the Lat. *voco* i. q. *to invite*;   **a.** prop.: εἰς τοὺς γάμους, Mt. xxii. 3, 9; Lk. xiv. 8 sq.; Jn. ii. 2; to a feast, Lk. xiv. 16; 1 Co. x. 27 [cf. W. 593 (552)]; Rev. xix. 9; ὁ καλέσας, Lk. vii. 39; xiv. 9; ὁ κεκληκώς τινα, ibid. 10, 12; οἱ κεκλημένοι, Mt. xxii. 8; Lk. xiv. 7, 17, 24; (2 Sam. xiii. 23; Esth. v. 12; and often so in Grk. writ. fr. Hom. Od. 4, 532; 11, 187 down).   **β.** metaph. : *to invite one,* εἴς τι, to something i. e. to participate in it, enjoy it; used thus in the Epp. of Paul and Peter of God as inviting men by the preaching of the gospel (διὰ τοῦ εὐαγγελίου, 2 Th. ii. 14) to the blessings of the heavenly kingdom: εἰς τὴν βασιλείαν τοῦ θεοῦ, 1 Th. ii. 12; εἰς ζωὴν αἰώνιον, 1 Tim. vi. 12; εἰς δόξαν αἰώνιον, 1 Pet. v. 10; εἰς τὴν κοινωνίαν τοῦ υἱοῦ αὐτοῦ, 1 Co. i. 9; so καλεῖν τινα used alone: Ro. viii. 30; ix. 24 sq.; 1 Co. vii. 17 sq. 20–22, 24; τινὰ καλεῖν κλήσει, 2 Tim. i. 9; ἐν ᾧ ἐκλήθημεν, in whom lies the reason why we were called, who is the ground of our having been invited, Eph. i. 11 Lchm.; ἄξιος τῆς κλήσεως, ἧς (by attraction for ᾖ [or perh. ἥν; cf. W. § 24, 1; B. 287 (247); Ellicott in loc.]) ἐκλήθητε, Eph. iv. 1; God is styled ὁ καλῶν τινα (he that calleth one, *the caller,* cf. W. § 45, 7), Gal. v. 8; 1 Th. v. 24; and ὁ καλέσας τινά, Gal. i. 6; Col. i. 12 Lchm.; 1 Pet. i. 15; 2 Pet. i. 3.   οἱ κεκλημένοι, Heb. ix. 15; καλεῖν and καλεῖσθαι are used with a specification of the mediate end (for the highest or final end of the calling is eternal salvation): ἐπ᾽ ἐλευθερίᾳ, Gal. v. 13; οὐκ ἐπ᾽ ἀκαθαρσίᾳ ἀλλ᾽ ἐν ἁγιασμῷ, 1 Th. iv. 7; ἐν εἰρήνῃ, 1 Co. vii. 15; ἐν ἑνὶ ἐλπίδι, that ye might come into one hope, Eph. iv. 4 (see ἐν, I. 7 [yet cf. W. 417 (389); B. 329 (283); esp. Ellicott in loc.], and ἐπί, B. 2 a. ζ.); εἰς εἰρήνην τοῦ Χριστοῦ ἐν ἑνὶ σώματι, that ye may be in one body i. e. be members of one and the same body, Col. iii. 15; εἰς τοῦτο (which refers to what precedes) foll. by ἵνα, 1 Pet. ii. 21; iii. 9; (but everywhere in the N. T. Epp. only those are spoken of as *called* by God who have listened to his voice addressed to them in the gospel, hence those who have enlisted in the service of Christ— see Ro. viii. 30 and Rückert's Com. in loc. p. 464, cf. 1 Co. i. 24; those who have slighted the invitation are not reckoned among the called); C h r i s t also is said καλεῖν τινα, sc. to embrace the offer of salvation by the Messiah, in Mt. ix. 13 and Mk. ii. 17 (in both which pass. Rec. adds εἰς μετάνοιαν). God is said *to call* those who are not yet born, viz. by promises of salvation which have respect to them, so that καλεῖν is for substance equiv. to *to appoint one to salvation,* Ro. ix. 12 (11); καλοῦντος τὰ μὴ ὄντα ὡς ὄντα, Ro. iv. 17, where cf. Fritzsche, [al. al., cf. Meyer (esp. ed. *Weiss*) ad loc.]. *to call* (i. q. *to select*) *to assume some office,* τινά, of God appointing or committing an office to one, (Germ. *berufen*): Gal. i. 15; Heb. v. 4, (Is. xlii. 6; xlix. 1; li. 2). *to invite* i. q. *to rouse, summon*: to do something, εἰς μετάνοιαν, Lk. v. 32, added in Rec. also in Mt. ix. 13 and Mk. ii. 17.   **2.** *to call* i. e. *to name, call by name*;   **a.** *to give a name to*; with two acc., one of the object the other of the name as a predicate [to call one (by) a name: Mt. x. 25 Rec.; cf. W. § 32, 4 b.; B. 151 (132) note]; pass. w. the nom. of the name, *to receive the name of, receive as a name*: Mt. ii. 23; xxvii. 8; Lk. i. 32, 60, 62; ii. 4, etc.; καλούμενος, *called, whose name or surname is,* Lk. vii. 11; ix. 10; x. 39; Acts vii. 58; xxvii. 8, 16; ὁ καλούμενος [on its position cf. B. § 144, 19]: Lk. vi. 15; viii. 2; [xxii. 3 T Tr WH]; xxiii. 33; Acts i. 23; x. 1; xiii. 1; [xv. 22 L T Tr WH]; xxvii. 14; Rev. xii. 9; xvi. 16; with ὀνόματι added, Lk. xix. 2; καλεῖσθαι ὀνόματί τινι, to be called by a name, Lk. i. 61; καλεῖν τινα ἐπὶ τῷ ὀνόματι τινος, Lk. i. 59 (see ἐπί, B. 2 a. η. p. 233ᵇ); after the Hebr. קָרָא

אֶת־שְׁמוֹ, καλεῖν τὸ ὄνομά τινος, with the name in the acc., to give some name to one, call his name: Mt. i. 21, 23, 25; Lk. i. 13, 31; pass., Lk. ii. 21; Rev. xix. 13; Gen. xvii. 19; 1 S. i. 20, etc. (similarly sometimes in Grk. writ., cf. Fritzsche on Mt. p. 45 [B. 151 (132)]). **b.** Pass. καλοῦμαι with predicate nom. to be called i. e. to bear a name or title (among men) [cf. W. § 65, 8]: Lk. i. 35; xxii. 25; Acts viii. 10 [Rec. om. καλ.]; 1 Co. xv. 9; to be said to be (i. q. to be acknowledged, pass as, the nominative expressing the judgment passed on one): Mt. v. 9, 19; Lk. i. 32, 35, 76; ii. 23; xv. 19; Ro. ix. 26; Jas. ii. 23; opp. to εἶναι, 1 Jn. iii. 1 LT Tr WH; Hebraistically (Gen. xxi. 12) ἐν Ἰσαὰκ κληθήσεταί σοι σπέρμα, through [better in, cf. ἐν, I. 6 c. and Meyer (ed. Weiss) ad Ro. l. c.] Isaac shall a seed be called for thee, i. e. Isaac (not Ishmael) is the one whose posterity shall obtain the name and honor of thy descendants, Ro. ix. 7 and Heb. xi. 18.　　**c.** καλῶ τινα, with an acc. of the predicate or a title of honor, to salute one by a name: Mt. xxiii. 9; Pass., ib. 7 sq. 10; Rev. xix. 11 [but Tr mrg. WH br. κ.]; to give a name to one and mention him at the same time, Mt. xxii. 43, 45; Lk. xx. 44. [COMP.: ἀντι-, ἐν-, εἰσ-(-μαι), ἐπι-, μετα-, παρα-, συν-παρα-, προ-, προσ-, συγ-καλέω.]

2565 ---- καλλι-έλαιος, -ου, ἡ, (fr. κάλλος and ἐλαία), the garden olive, [A. V. good olive tree], (opp. to ἀγριέλαιος the wild olive): Ro. xi. 24.　Aristot. de plant. 1, 6 p. 820ᵇ, 40.*

see 2566 St. & 2570 ----καλλίων, see καλός, fin.

2567 ----καλο-διδάσκαλος, -ου, ὁ, ἡ, (διδάσκαλος and καλόν, cf. ἱεροδιδάσκαλος, νομοδιδάσκαλος, χοροδιδάσκαλος), teaching that which is good, a teacher of goodness: Tit. ii. 3. Nowhere else.*

2568　　καλοὶ λιμένες (καλός and λιμήν), Fair Havens (Germ. Schönhafen; Luth. Gutfurt), a bay of Crete, near the city Lasæa; so called because offering good anchorage; now Limenes kali [BB.DD.]: Acts xxvii. 8.*

2569　　καλο-ποιέω, -ῶ; (i. q. καλῶς ποιῶ, cf. Lob. ad Phryn. p. 199 sq. [W. 25]); to do well, act uprightly: 2 Th. iii. 13. (Etym. Magn. 189, 24; [Lev. v. 4 Ald. (as quoted in) Philo de somn. l. ii. § 44].) *

2570　　καλός, -ή, -όν, [prob. primarily 'sound,' 'hale,' 'whole;' cf. Vaniček p. 140 sq.; Curtius § 31], Sept. for יָפֶה beautiful, but much oftener for טוֹב good; beautiful, applied by the Greeks to everything so distinguished in form, excellence, goodness, usefulness, as to be pleasing; hence (acc. to the context) i. q. beautiful, handsome, excellent, eminent, choice, surpassing, precious, useful, suitable, commendable, admirable;　**a.** beautiful to look at, shapely, magnificent: λίθοις καλοῖς κεκόσμηται [A. V. goodly], Lk. xxi. 5.　　**b.** good, excellent in its nature and characteristics, and therefore well-adapted to its ends: joined to the names of material objects, univ. 1 Tim. iv. 4 (i. q. pure); esp. of things so constituted as to answer the purpose for which that class of things was created; good of its kind: τὰ καλά, of fish, opp. to such as are thrown away (τὰ σαπρά), Mt. xiii. 48; σπέρμα, Mt. xiii. 24, 27, 37 sq.; καρπός, Mt. iii. 10; vii. 17–19; xii. 33; Lk. iii. 9 [L WH br. καλ.]; vi. 43; δένδρον, opp. to σαπρόν, Mt. xii. 33; Lk. vi. 43; γῆ, Mt. xiii. 8, 23; Mk. iv. 8, 20; Lk. viii. 15;

καλὸν τὸ ἅλας (is an excellent thing), Mk. ix. 50; Lk. xiv. 34; so too ὁ νόμος, good in its substance and nature, and fitted to beget good, Ro. vii. 16; 1 Tim. i. 8; διδασκαλία, true and approved teaching, 1 Tim. iv. 6; καρδία καλὴ κ. ἀγαθή, Lk. viii. 15; παραθήκη [q. v.] (containing [rather, consisting of] καλά), 2 Tim. i. 14; μέτρον, ample measure (rabbin. מִדָּה טוֹבָה; Eng. good measure), Lk. vi. 38; βαθμός (firm [but see βαθμός]), 1 Tim. iii. 13; also θεμέλιος, 1 Tim. vi. 19; i. q. genuine, approved, πάντα δοκιμάζετε, τὸ καλὸν κατέχετε, 1 Th. v. 21; i. q. precious [A.V. goodly], μαργαρίται, Mt. xiii. 45; i. q. superior to other kinds, οἶνος, Jn. ii. 10;　joined to names of men designated by their office, competent, able, such as one ought to be: ποιμήν, Jn. x. 11, 14; διάκονος, 1 Tim. iv. 6; οἰκονόμος, 1 Pet. iv. 10; στρατιώτης, 2 Tim. ii. 3;　joined to nouns denoting an effect estimated by the power it involves, or by its constancy, or by the end aimed at by its author, i. q. praiseworthy, noble: στρατεία, 1 Tim. i. 18; ἀγών, 1 Tim. vi. 12; 2 Tim. iv. 7; ὁμολογία, 1 Tim. vi. 12 sq.; ἔργον, Mt. xxvi. 10; Mk. xiv. 6; Jn. x. 33; 1 Tim. iii. 1; plur. Jn. x. 32.　καλόν ἐστιν, it is expedient, profitable, wholesome: foll. by an inf. as subject, 1 Co. vii. 1; w. τινί added [so in 1 Co. l. c. also], Mt. xviii. 8 sq. [cf. W. 241 (226); B. § 149, 7]; Mk. ix. 43, 45, 47, R G [also L Tr mrg. in 47]; 1 Co. vii. 26; ix. 15; κ. ἐστιν foll. by the acc. and inf., Mk. ix. 43, 45, 47, L (but see above) T Tr (but not mrg., see above) WH; Heb. xiii. 9; foll. by εἰ [cf. B. 217 (187 sq.); W. 282 (265)], Mt. xxvi. 24; Mk. ix. 42; xiv. 21; foll. by ἐάν [B. and W. u. s.], 1 Co. vii. 8; it is pleasant, delightful, foll. by acc. with inf.: Mt. xvii. 4; Mk. ix. 5; Lk. ix. 33.　**c.** beautiful by reason of purity of heart and life, and hence praiseworthy; morally good, noble, (Lat. honestus; [cf. Aristot. τὸ καθ᾽ αὑτὸ καλόν]): διάκρισις καλοῦ τε καὶ κακοῦ, Heb. v. 14; ἔργα, Mt. v. 16; 1 Tim. v. 10, 25; vi. 18; Tit. ii. 7, 14; iii. 8, 14; Heb. x. 24; 1 Pet. ii. 12, and Lchm. in 2 Pet. i. 10; ἀναστροφή, Jas. iii. 13; 1 Pet. ii. 12; καλὴ συνείδησις, consciousness of good deeds, [A.V. a good conscience], Heb. xiii. 18; καλά, καλὸν ἐνώπιόν τινος, in one's judgment, Ro. xii. 17; 2 Co. viii. 21; 1 Tim. ii. 3 and Rec. in v. 4; ζηλοῦσθαι ἐν καλῷ, Gal. iv. 18; τὸ καλὸν κατεργάζεσθαι, Ro. vii. 18; ποιεῖν, ib. 21; 2 Co. xiii. 7; Gal. vi. 9; Jas. iv. 17; καλόν ἐστιν, it is right, proper, becoming, foll. by an inf.: Mt. xv. 26 [L Tr ἔξεστιν]; [Mk. vii. 27]; Gal. iv. 18 [here Tr mrg. impv.]; Ro. xiv. 21.　**d.** honorable, conferring honor: μαρτυρία, 1 Tim. iii. 7; ὄνομα, Jas. ii. 7; οὐ καλὸν τὸ καύχημα ὑμῶν, 1 Co. v. 6.　**e.** affecting the mind agreeably, comforting and confirming: θεοῦ ῥῆμα (Sept. for דָּבָר טוֹב, which is spoken of the divine promises, Josh. xxi. 45; Zech. i. 13), the gospel and its promises full of consolation, Heb. vi. 5.　Compar. καλλίων, -ον, better: neut. adverbially, σὺ κάλλιον ἐπιγινώσκεις, i. e. better than by thy question thou seemest to know, Acts xxv. 10 [W. 242 (227)].　The word is not found in the Apocalypse. [Cf. Trench § cvi. fin.; Zezschwitz, Profangräcität u. s. w. p. 60 sq. (cf. ἀγαθός, fin.).　Westcott on Jn. x. 11.]*

2571　　κάλυμμα, -τος, τό, (καλύπτω), a veil, a covering: 2 Co. iii. 13 (Ex. xxxiv. 33); [κάλυμμα, or its equiv., is suggested to the reader by the context in 1 Co. xi. 4 κατὰ κεφαλῆς ἔχων; see ἔχω, I. 1 b.]; metaph., 2 Co. iii. 14–16, of that which prevents a thing from being understood. (Hom., Tragg., Arstph., al.; Sept.)*

2572 καλύπτω; fut. καλύψω; 1 aor. ἐκάλυψα; Pass., pres. inf. καλύπτεσθαι; pf. ptcp. κεκαλυμμένος; [allied with κρύπτω; Vaniček p. 1091; Curtius, Das Verbum, i. 242;] Sept. for כָּסָה; often in Hom., Tragg. and other poets, more rarely in prose; to cover, cover up; prop.: τινά, Lk. xxiii. 30; τί τινι, a thing with anything, Lk. viii. 16; pass. Mt. viii. 24; trop. to hide, veil, i. e. to hinder the knowledge of a thing: pf. pass., Mt. x. 26; 2 Co. iv. 3; πλῆθος ἁμαρτιῶν, not to regard or impute them, i. e. to pardon them, 1 Pet. iv. 8; to procure pardon of them from God, Jas. v. 20; cf. Ps. lxxxiv. (lxxxv.) 3 (2); xxxi. (xxxii.) 1 sq. [Comp.: ἀνα-, ἀπο-, ἐπι-, κατα-, παρα-, περι-, συγ-καλύπτω.]*

2573 καλῶς, (καλός), adv., [fr. Hom. down], beautifully, finely, excellently, well: [univ. διὰ τὸ καλῶς οἰκοδομῆσθαι (Tr -μεῖσθαι, q. v.), Lk. vi. 48 T Tr WH]; spec. **a.** rightly, so that there shall be no room for blame: joined to verbs of speaking (ἀποκρίνεσθαι, λαλεῖν, λέγειν, προφητεύειν, etc.), well, truly, Mt. xv. 7; Mk. vii. 6; Lk. xx. 39; Jn. iv. 17; viii. 48; xiii. 13; [xviii. 23]; Acts xxviii. 25; fitly, i. e. agreeably to the facts and words of the case, Mk. xii. 28; καλῶς right! well! an expression of approval: Mk. xii. 32; Ro. xi. 20; of deeds: κ. ποιεῖν, to do well, act uprightly, Jas. ii. 19; 1 Co. vii. 37 sq. (where the teaching is, that one can do καλῶς, but another κρεῖσσον); καλῶς ποιεῖν with ptcp. to do well that, etc. [B. § 144, 15 a.; W. 345 (323)], Acts x. 33; Phil. iv. 14; 2 Pet. i. 19; 3 Jn. 6, (1 Macc. xii. 18, 22; 2 Macc. ii. 16, etc.); with verbs denoting a duty or office which one fulfils well: 1 Tim. iii. 4, 12 sq.; v. 17; spec. honestly, uprightly: Gal. iv. 17; ἀναστρέφεσθαι, Heb. xiii. 18; ποιεῖν, Jas. ii. 8. **b.** excellently, nobly, commendably: 1 Co. xiv. 17; Gal. v. 7; καλῶς πάντα πεποίηκε, Mk. vii. 37; with bitter irony, Mk. vii. 9 (where cf. Fritzsche p. 271 sq.); 2 Co. xi. 4. **c.** honorably, in honor: Jas. ii. 3 [al. give it here an outward reference, i. q. in a good place, comfortably]. **d.** καλῶς εἰπεῖν τινα, to speak well of one, Lk. vi. 26; κ. ποιεῖν τινα, to do good to, benefit one, Mt. v. 44 Rec.; τινί [W. § 32, 1 β.; B. 146 (128)], Lk. vi. 27; καλῶς ποιεῖν, simply, to do good: Mt. xii. 12. **e.** καλῶς ἔχειν, to be well (of those recovering health): Mk. xvi. 18.*

2574 [καμέ, see κἀγώ.]
κάμηλος, -ου, ὁ, ἡ, Hebr. גָּמָל, [fr. Hdt. down], a camel [BB.DD. s. v.; Tristram, Nat. Hist. etc. p. 58 sqq.]: Mt. iii. 4; Mk. i. 6; in proverbs, Mt. xix. 24; Mk. x. 25; Lk. xviii. 25, (meaning, 'something almost or altogether impossible' [cf. Farrar in The Expositor for 1876 i. p. 369 sqq.; esp. Wetzstein in the Sitzungsberichte d. Akad. d. Wissensch. zu München, 1873, pp. 581–596]); Mt. xxiii. 24 (of one who is careful not to sin in trivial matters, but pays no heed to the more important matters).*

κάμιλος, -ου, ὁ, a cable; the reading of certain Mss. in Mt. xix. 24 and Lk. xviii. 25, [see Tdf.'s notes]. The word is found only in Suidas [1967 c.] and the Schol. on Arstph. vesp. [1030]: "κάμιλος τὸ παχὺ σχοινίον διὰ τοῦ

i." Cf. Passow [or L. and S.] s. v.; [WH. App. p. 151ᵇ].*

2575 κάμινος, -ου, ὁ, ἡ, [Hom. ep. 14, 2 etc., Hdt. on], a furnace (either for smelting, Xen. vectig. 4, 49, or for burning earthen ware, or baking bread, Gen. xix. 28; Ex. xix. 18; Jer. xi. 4; Dan. iii. 6): Mt. xiii. 42, 50; Rev. i. 15; ix. 2.*

2576 καμμύω, a form which passed over from the Epic (cf. Hom. batrach. 191) and com. language [Apoll. Dysc. synt. 323, 22; 326, 9] into the Alexandrian and decaying Greek; condemned by Phryn. [as below]; derived by syncope and assimilation from καταμύω (which the earlier and more elegant Greeks use), (cf. καμμέν, καμμονή, κάμμορος, fr. κατὰ μέν, καταμονή, κατάμορος, cf. Bttm. Gram. § 117, 2 Anm. 2; Ausf. Gram. ii. p. 373; Fischer, De vitiis lexx. N. T. p. 678 sq.; Sturz, De dial. Maced. etc. p. 173 sq.; Lob. ad Phryn. p. 339|sq.; Schäfer ad Lamb. Bos p. 368; [cf. B. 62 (55); W. 24, 46]): 1 aor. ἐκάμμυσα; to shut the eyes, close the eyes: often w. τοὺς ὀφθαλμούς added; so Mt. xiii. 15 and Acts xxviii. 27, (fr. Sept. Is. vi. 10, for יָשַׁע, i. e. to besmear), in both which pass. the phrase designates the inflexible pertinacity and obstinacy of the Jews in their opposition to the gospel. (Is. xxix. 10; Lam. iii. 43; καμμύειν τὸ τῆς ψυχῆς ὄμμα, Philo de somn. i. § 26.)*

2577 κάμνω; 2 aor. ἔκαμον; pf. κέκμηκα; **1.** to grow weary, be weary, (so fr. Hom. down): Rev. ii. 3 Rec.; Heb. xii. 3. **2.** to be sick: Jas. v. 15 (Soph., [Hdt.], Arstph., Eur., Xen., Plat., Aristot., Diod., Lcian. al.).*

see 2504 [κάμοί, see κἀγώ.]
2578 κάμπτω; fut. κάμψω; 1 aor. ἔκαμψα; **a.** to bend, bow: τὸ γόνυ (and τὰ γούνατα), the knee (the knees), used by Hom. of those taking a seat or sitting down to rest (Il. 7, 118; 19, 72); in bibl. Grk. with dat. of pers. to one i. e. in honor of one, in religious veneration; used of worshippers: Ro. xi. 4 and 1 K. xix. 18 (where for כָּרַע foll. by לְ); πρός τινα, towards (unto) one, Eph. iii. 14. **b.** reflexively, to bow one's self: κάμψει πᾶν γόνυ ἐμοί, shall bow to me (in honor), i. e. every one shall worship me, Ro. xiv. 11 (fr. Is. xlv. 23); ἐν τῷ ὀνόματι Ἰησοῦ, in devout recognition of the name (of κύριος) which Jesus received from God, Phil. ii. 10 [cf. W. 390 (365); Bp. Lghtft., Meyer, in loc.; also ὄνομα, esp. sub fin. Comp.: ἀνα-, συγ-κάμπτω.]*

2579 κἄν [Grsb. κἄν; so κἀγώ, init.], by crasis for καὶ ἐάν [cf. W. § 5, 3; B. p. 10; Tdf. Proleg. p. 97; WH. App. p. 145ᵇ]; hence joined with the subjunctive; **1.** and if: Mt. x. 23 G L; Mk. xvi. 18; [Lk. xii. 38 (bis) T Tr txt. WH; Jn. viii. 55 L T Tr WH; 1 Co. xiii. 2ᵃ L WH, 2ᵇ Tr txt. WH, 3ᵃ L Tr WH, 3ᵇ L WH]; Jas. v. 15; by aposiopesis with the suppression of the apodosis, κἂν μὲν ποιήσῃ καρπόν, sc. εὖ ἔχει it is well (or some such phrase), Lk. xiii. 9; cf. W. 600 (558); [B. § 151, 26]. **2.** also or even if; **a.** if only, at least, in abridged discourse: κἂν τῶν ἱματίων αὐτοῦ, sc. ἅψωμαι, Mk. v. 28; also ἵνα (sc. ἅψωνται αὐτοῦ) κἂν τοῦ κρασπέδου . . . ἅψωνται, Mk. vi. 56; ἵνα ἐρχομένου Πέτρου (sc. τι αὐτοῦ ἐπισκιάσῃ αὐτῶν) κἂν ἡ σκιά etc. Acts v. 15; κἂν ὡς ἄφρονα sc. δέξησθέ με, 2 Co. xi. 16 ; (Sap. xiv. 4 ; xv. 2). Cf. B. § 149, 6 ; [W. 584 (543); *Green*, Gram. of the N. T. p. 230; *Klotz* ad Devar. ii. 1 p. 139 sq.; L. and S. s. v.; *Soph.* Lex. s. v.].   **b.** *even if*: Mt. xxi. 21 ; xxvi. 35 ; Jn. viii. 14 ; x. 38 ; [xi. 25]; Heb. xii. 20.*

2580   **Kανâ** [-*νά* WH ; cf. *Tdf.* Proleg. p. 103; W. § 6, 1 m.], ἡ [B. 21 (19)], *Cana*, indecl. [W. 61 (60); but dat. -*νᾷ* Rec.ˢᵗ in Jn. ii. 1, 11], prop. name of a village of Galilee about three hours distant from Nazareth towards the northwest, surviving at present in a place (partly uninhabited and partly ruinous) called *Kana el-Jelil*; cf. *Robinson*, Bibl. Researches, ii. 346 sq. ; also his Later Bibl. Researches, p. 108 ; cf. *Ewald*, Gesch. Christus u. s. w. p. 147 (ed. 1); *Rüetschi* in Herzog vii. 234 ; [*Porter* in Alex.'s Kitto s. v.   Several recent writers are inclined to reopen the question of the identification of Cana ; see e. g. B. D. Am. ed. s. v.; *Zeller*, in Quart. Statem. of Palest. Expl. Fund, No. iii. p. 71 sq.; *Arnaud*, Palestine p. 412 sq.; *Conder*, Tent Work etc. i. 150 sq.]: Jn. ii. 1, 11 ; iv. 46 ; xxi. 2.*

see 2581   **Kανανᾱῖος** L T Tr WH in Mt. x. 4 and Mk. iii. 18 (for R G *Kανανίτης*, q. v.); acc. to the interp. of Bleek (Erklär. d. drei ersten Evv. i. p. 417) et al. *a native of Cana* (see **Kανᾶ**) ; but then it ought to be written **Kανᾶῖος**. The reading **Kανανᾱῖος** seems to be a clerical error occasioned by the preceding Θαδδαῖος [or Λεββαῖος]; cf. Fritzsche on Mt. x. 4. [But -*αῖος* is a common ending of the Grecized form of names of sects (cf. Ἀσσιδαῖος, Φαρισαῖος, Σαδδουκαῖος, Ἐσσαῖος). Hence the word is prob. derived fr. the Aramaic קַנְאָן (see next word) and corresponds to ζηλωτής, q. v. (cf. Lk. vi. 15; Acts i. 13). See Bp. *Lghtft*. Fresh Revision etc. p. 138 sq.]*

2581   **Kανανίτης**, -ου, ὁ, (fr. Chald. קַנְאָן, Hebr. קַנָּא), i. q. ὁ ζηλωτής (acc. to the interpr. of Luke in vi. 15 ; Acts i. 13), q. v., *the Zealot*, a surname of the apostle Simon : R G (the latter with small κ) in Mt. x. 4 and Mk. iii. 18.*

2582   **Kανδάκη**, -ης, ἡ, *Can'dace*, a name common to the queens of a region of Ethiopia whose capital was Napata ; just as the proper name *Ptolemy* was common to the Egyptian kings, and *Henry* to the Reuss princes (Strabo 17, 1, 54 p. 820; Plin. h. n. 6, 35 ; Dio Cass. 54, 5): Acts viii. 27 ; cf. *Laurent*, Die Königin Kandake, in der Zeitschr. f. d. luth. Theol. for 1862, p. 632 sq. [reprinted in his N. T. Studien p. 140 sq.; cf. esp. B. D. Am. ed. s. v.].*

2583   **κανών**, -όνος, ὁ, (κάννα, Hebr. קָנֶה a cane, reed; Arab. ﻗﻨﺎة a reed, and a spear, and a straight stick or staff [cf. *Vaniček*, Fremdwörter etc. p. 21]), prop. a rod or straight piece of rounded wood to which any thing is fastened to keep it straight; used for various purposes (see Passow [or L. and S.] s. v.); a measuring rod, rule; a carpenter's line or measuring tape, Schol. on Eur. Hippol. 468 ; hence i. q. τὸ μέτρον τοῦ πηδήματος (Pollux, Onom. 3, 30, 151), the measure of a leap, as in the Olympic games; accordingly in the N. T.   **1.** *a definitely bounded* or *fixed space within the limits of which one's power* or *influence is confined*; *the province assigned one*; *one's sphere of activity*: 2 Co. x. 13, 15 sq.   **2.**

Metaph. *any rule* or *standard, a principle* or *law* of investigating, judging, living, acting, (often so in class. Grk., as τοῦ καλοῦ, Eur. Hec. 602 ; ὅροι τῶν ἀγαθῶν κ. κανόνες, Dem. pro cor. p. 324, 27) : Gal. vi. 16 ; Phil. iii. 16 Rec.   Cf. *Credner*, Zur Gesch. des Kanons (Hal. 1847), p. 6 sqq. ; [esp. *Westcott*, The Canon of the N. T., App. A ; briefly in B. D. s. v. Canon of Scripture; for exx. of later usage see *Soph*. Lex. s. v.].*

2584   **Kαπερναούμ** or more correctly (with L T Tr WH [cf. *WH*. App. p. 160 ; *Scrivener*, Introd. p. 561]) Kαφαρναούμ, (כְּפַר a village, and נחוּם consolation; hence 'the village of consolation,' [al. 'village of Nachum' (a prop. name)]; *Kαπαρναούμ*, Ptol. 5, 16, 4), ἡ, *Capernaum* or *Capharnaum*, a flourishing city of Galilee (Mt. xi. 23 ; Lk. x. 15), situated on the western shore of the Sea of Galilee or Lake of Gennesaret (Jn. vi. 17, 24 ; hence ἡ παραθαλασσία, Mt. iv. 13), near the place where the Jordan flows into the lake. Being nowhere mentioned in the O. T. it seems to have been built after the exile [cf. also B. D. s. v. Caphar]. Josephus mentions (b. j. 3, 10, 8) a fountain in Galilee called by the neighboring residents Kαφαρναούμ, and (vita 72) 'κώμην Kεφαρνώμην', and it is quite probable that he meant the town we are speaking of. It is mentioned in the N. T. (besides the pass. already cited) in Mt. viii. 5 ; xvii. 24 ; Mk. i. 21 ; ii. 1 ; ix. 33 ; Lk. iv. 23, 31 ; vii. 1 ; Jn. ii. 12 ; iv. 46 ; vi. 59. Cf. *Win*. RWB. s. v.; *Vaihinger* in Herzog vii. 369 ; *Furrer* in Schenkel iii. 493 sq.; [the last named writ. gives at length (see also Zeitschr. d. Deutsch. Palaest.-Vereins for 1879, p. 63 sqq.) his reasons for preferring (contra Robinson, Sepp, etc.) to identify C. with Tell Hum; so (after earlier writ.; cf. Arnaud p. 414), Winer u. s., Dr. Wilson, Lynch, Ritter, Delitzsch, Tristram (Land of Israel, ed. 3, p. 428 sqq.) and more recently Capt. Wilson ('Our Work in Palestine' p. 186 sq. and 'Recovery of Jerusalem' p. 266 sq. (292 sqq.)). But *Conder* (Tent Work in Palestine ii. 182 sqq.) argues fr. Jewish author. in favor of Khan Minyeh ; see B. D. Am. ed. s. v.].*

2585   **καπηλεύω**; (κάπηλος, i. e. **a.** an inn-keeper, esp. a vintner; **b.** a petty retailer, a huckster, pedler; cf. Sir. xxvi. 29 οὐ δικαιωθήσεται κάπηλος ἀπὸ ἁμαρτίας);   **a.** *to be a retailer, to peddle* ;   **b.** with acc. of the thing, *to make money by selling anything* ; *to get sordid gain by dealing in anything, to do a thing for base gain* (οἱ τὰ μαθήματα περιάγοντες κατὰ πόλεις καὶ πωλοῦντες κ. καπηλεύοντες, Plat. Prot. p. 313 d.; μάχην, Aeschyl. Sept. 551 (545) ; Lat. *cauponari bellum*, i. e. to fight for gain, trade in war, Enn. ap. Cic. offic. 1, 12, 38 ; ἑταίραν τὸ τῆς ὥρας ἄνθος καπηλεύουσαν, Philo de caritat. § 14, cf. leg. ad Gaium § 30, and many other exx. in other auth.). Hence some suppose that καπηλεύειν τ. λόγον τοῦ θεοῦ in 2 Co. ii. 17 is equiv. to *to trade in the word of God*, i. e. to try to get base gain by teaching divine truth. But as pedlers were in the habit of adulterating their commodities for the sake of gain (οἱ κάπηλοί σου μίγουσι τὸν οἶνον ὕδατι, Is. i. 22 Sept.; κάπηλοι, οἱ τὸν οἶνον κεραννύντες, Pollux, onomast. 7, 193 ; οἱ φιλόσοφοι ἀποδίδονται τὰ μαθήματα, ὥσπερ οἱ κάπηλοι, κερασάμενοί γε οἱ πολλοὶ καὶ δολώσαντες καὶ κακομετροῦντες, Lucian. Hermot. 59), καπηλεύειν τι was also used as synonymous with to corrupt, to adulterate (Themist. or. 21 p. 247 ed. Hard. says that the false philosophers τὸ θειότατον τῶν ἀνθρωπίνων ἀγαθῶν κιβδηλεύειν τε καὶ αἰσχύνειν κ. καπηλεύειν); and most interp. rightly decide in favor of this meaning (on account of the context) in 2 Co. ii. 17, cf. δολοῦν τὸν λόγον τοῦ θεοῦ, ib. iv. 2. [Cf. Trench § lxii.]*

2586 **καπνός**, -οῦ, ὁ, [fr Hom. down], smoke: Rev. viii. 4; ix. 2 sq. 17, 18; xiv. 11; xv. 8; xviii. 9, 18; xix. 3; ἀτμὶς καπνοῦ, A. V. vapor of smoke, Acts ii. 19 after Joel ii. 30 (iii. 3).*

2587 **Καππαδοκία**, -ας, ἡ, Cappadocia, a region of Asia Minor, bounded under the Roman empire on the N. by Pontus, on the E. by Armenia Minor, on the S. by Cilicia and Commagene, and on the W. by Lycaonia and Galatia [BB. DD. s. v.]: Acts ii. 9; 1 Pet. i. 1.*

2588 **καρδία**, -ας, ἡ, poetic κραδία and καρδίη (in the latter form almost always in Hom. [only at the beginning of a line in three places; everywhere else by metathesis κραδίη; Ebeling, Lex. Hom. s. v.]), [fr. a root signifying to quiver or palpitate; cf. Curtius § 39; Vaniček p. 1097 (Etym. Magn. 491, 56 παρὰ τὸ κραδαίνω, τὸ σείω· ἀεικίνητος γὰρ ἡ καρδία); allied with Lat. cor; Eng. heart]; Sept. for לֵב and לֵבָב; the heart; **1.** prop. that organ in the animal body which is the centre of the circulation of the blood, and hence was regarded as the seat of physical life: 2 S. xviii. 14; 2 K. ix. 24; Tob. vi. 5 (4), 7 (6) sq., 17 (16). Hence **2.** univ. καρδία denotes the seat and centre of all physical and spiritual life; and **a.** the vigor and sense of physical life (Ps. ci. (cii.) 5; στήρισον τὴν καρδίαν σου ψωμῷ ἄρτου, Judg. xix. 5; to which add Ps. ciii. (civ.) 15): τρέφειν τὰς καρδίας, Jas. v. 5; ἐμπιπλῶν τὰς καρδίας τροφῆς, Acts xiv. 17; βαρεῖν τ. καρδίας κραιπάλῃ καὶ μέθῃ, Lk. xxi. 34; [but see b. δ. below]; **b.** the centre and seat of spiritual life, the soul or mind, as it is the fountain and seat of the thoughts, passions, desires, appetites, affections, purposes, endeavors [so in Eng. heart, inner man, etc.]; **α.** univ.: Mt. v. 8; vi. 21; Mk. vii. 19; Lk. i. 51; ii. 51; viii. 12, 15; Acts v. 3; Ro. x. 9 sq.; 1 Co. ii. 9; 2 Co. vi. 11; Eph. vi. 5; Col. iii. 22; 1 Pet. iii. 4, etc.; Plur.: Mt. ix. 4; Mk. ii. 6, 8; iv. 15 [R L txt. Tr mrg.]; Lk. i. 17; ii. 35; v. 22; [xxiv. 38 R G L mrg.; Acts vii. 51 L T Tr WH txt.]; Ro. ii. 15; xvi. 18; 2 Co. iii. 2; Gal. iv. 6; Phil. iv. 7; Eph. v. 19 Lchm.; Heb. viii. 10 [T WH mrg. sing.]; x. 16, etc. ἡ καρδία is distinguished fr. τὸ στόμα or fr. τὰ χείλεα: Mt. xv. 8, 18 sq.; Mk. vii. 6; 2 Co. vi. 11; Ro. x. 8 sq.; fr. τὸ πρόσωπον: 2 Co. v. 12; 1 Th. ii. 17; περιτομὴ καρδίας, Ro. ii. 29; ἀπερίτμητοι τῇ καρδίᾳ, Acts vii. 51 [L T Tr WH txt. -δίας, WH mrg. gen. -δίας, cf. B. 170 (148)]. of things done from the heart i. e. cordially or sincerely, truly (without simulation or pretence) the foll. phrases are used: ἐκ καρδίας (Arstph. nub. 86), Ro. vi. 17; and L T Tr WH in 1 Pet. i. 22, where R G ἐκ καθαρᾶς καρδίας, as in 1 Tim. i. 5; 2 Tim. ii. 22· ἀπὸ τῶν καρδιῶν, Mt. xviii. 35 (ἀπὸ καρδίας εὐχάριστος τοῖς θεοῖς, Antonin. 2,

3); ἐν ὅλῃ τ. κ. and ἐξ ὅλης τ. κ., Mt. xxii. 37; Mk. xii. 30, 33; Lk. x. 27, and Rec. in Acts viii. 37, (Deut. vi. 5; xxvi. 16; Ps. cxviii. (cxix.) 34); μετ᾿ ἀληθινῆς καρδίας, Heb. x. 22. ἐρευνᾶν τὰς καρδίας, Ro. viii. 27; Rev. ii. 23; δοκιμάζειν, 1 Th. ii. 4; γινώσκειν, Lk. xvi. 15, (ἐτάζειν, Jer. xvii. 10; Ps. vii. 10); διανοίγειν τὴν κ. (see διανοίγω, 2), Acts xvi. 14; ἦν ἡ καρδία κ. ἡ ψυχὴ μία, there was perfect unanimity, agreement of heart and soul, Acts iv. 32; τιθέναι τι ἐν τῇ κ. (שׂוּם עַל לֵב and בְּלֵב), 1 S. xxi. 12; Mal. ii. 2; Dan. i. 8; τιθέναι ἐν στήθεσσιν, ἐν φρεσίν, etc., in Hom.), to lay a thing up in the heart to be considered more carefully and pondered, Lk. i. 66; to fix in the heart i. e. to purpose, plan, to do something, Acts v. 4 [A. V. conceived in thy heart]; also εἰς τ. καρδίαν [L T Tr WH ἐν τ. κ.] foll. by the inf., Lk. xxi. 14; βάλλειν εἰς τὴν κ. τινός, foll. by ἵνα, to put into one's mind the design of doing a thing, Jn. xiii. 2; also διδόναι foll. by an inf., Rev. xvii. 17; ἀναβαίνει ἐπὶ τὴν κ. τινός, foll. by an inf., the purpose to do a thing comes into the mind, Acts vii. 23; ἐν τῇ καρδίᾳ joined to verbs of thinking, reflecting upon, doubting, etc.: ἐνθυμεῖσθαι, διαλογίζεσθαι, Mt. ix. 4; Mk. ii. 6, 8; Lk. iii. 15; v. 22; λέγειν, εἰπεῖν (אָמַר בְּלֵב), to think, consider with one's self, Mt. xxiv. 48; Lk. xii. 45; Ro. x. 6; Rev. xviii. 7, (Deut. viii. 17; ix. 4); συμβάλλειν, to revolve in mind, Lk. ii. 19; διακρίνεσθαι, to doubt, Mk. xi. 23; διαλογισμοὶ ἀναβαίνουσι, of persons in doubt, Lk. xxiv. 38 [R G L mrg. plur.]; ἀναβαίνει τι ἐπὶ καρδίαν, the thought of a thing enters the mind, 1 Co. ii. 9. **β.** spec. of the understanding, the faculty and seat of intelligence (often so in Hom. also [cf. Nägelsbach, Homer. Theol. p. 319 sq.; Zezschwitz, Profangräcität u. s. w. pp. 25 sq. 50]; "cor domicilium sapientiae," Lact. de opif. dei c. 10, cf. Cic. Tusc. 1, 9; לֵב, 1 K. x. 2; Job xii. 3; xvii. 4, etc.; [cf. Meyer on Eph. i. 18 and reff.]): Ro. i. 21; 2 Co. iv. 6; Eph. i. 18 [Rec. διανοίας]; 2 Pet. i. 19; ἐν τῇ καρδίᾳ, Mt. xiii. 15; Acts xxviii. 27; νοεῖν τῇ κ. Jn. xii. 40. of the dulness of a mind incapable of perceiving and understanding divine things the foll. expressions occur: ἐπαχύνθη ἡ κ. Mt. xiii. 15; Acts xxviii. 27, (fr. Is. vi. 10); πωροῦν τὴν καρδίαν, Jn. xii. 40; πεπωρωμένη καρδία, Mk. vi. 52; viii. 17; ἡ πώρωσις τῆς κ. Mk. iii. 5; Eph. iv. 18; βραδὺς τῇ κ. slow of heart, Lk. xxiv. 25; κάλυμμα ἐπὶ τὴν κ. κεῖται, 2 Co. iii. 15. **γ.** of the will and character: ἁγνίζειν καρδίας, Jas. iv. 8; καθαρίζειν τὰς κ. Acts xv. 9· ῥεῤραντισμένοι τὰς κ. Heb. x. 22; καρδία εὐθεῖα [cf. W. 32], Acts viii. 21; πονηρά, Heb. iii. 12 [cf. B. § 132, 24; W. 194 (183)]; ἀμετανόητος, Ro. ii. 5; γεγυμνασμένη πλεονεξίας, 2 Pet. ii. 14; στηρίζειν τὰς κ. 1 Th. iii. 13; βεβαιοῦν, in pass., Heb. xiii. 9; σκληρύνειν, Heb. iii. 8; ἡ ἐπίνοια τῆς κ. Acts viii. 22; αἱ βουλαὶ τῶν κ. 1 Co. iv. 5; προαιρεῖσθαι τῇ κ. 2 Co. ix. 7; κρίνειν (to determine) and ἑδραῖος ἐν τῇ κ. 1 Co. vii. 37. **δ.** of the soul so far forth as it is affected and stirred in a bad way or good, or of the soul as the seat of the sensibilities, affections, emotions, desires, appetites, passions; ἡ καρδία καιομένη ἦν, of the soul as greatly and peculiarly moved, Lk. xxiv. 32; αἱ ἐπιθυμίαι τῶν καρδιῶν, Ro. i. 24; στηρίζειν τὰς κ. of the cultivation of constancy and endurance, Jas. v. 8. in ref. to good-will and love: ἔχειν τινὰ ἐν τῇ κ. *to have one in one's heart*, of constant remembrance and steadfast affection, Phil. i. 7 ('te tamen in toto pectore semper habet' Ovid. trist. 5, 4, 24); εἶναι ἐν τῇ κ. τινός, to be cherished in one's heart, to be loved by one perpetually and unalterably, 2 Co. vii. 3; εὐδοκία τῆς κ. Ro. x. 1. in ref. to joy and pleasure: ηὐφράνθη ἡ κ. Acts ii. 26 (fr. Ps. xv. (xvi.) 9); χαρήσεται ἡ κ. Jn. xvi. 22; ἀνὴρ κατὰ τὴν κ. τοῦ θεοῦ, i. e. in whom God delights, Acts xiii. 22; of the pleasure given by food, Acts xiv. 17 ([W. 156 (148) note] see 2 a. above). in ref. to grief, pain, anguish, etc.: ἡ λύπη πεπλήρωκε τὴν κ. Jn. xvi. 6; ὀδύνη τῇ καρδίᾳ μου, Ro. ix. 2; ἡ κ. ταράσσεται, Jn. xiv. 1, 27; συνοχὴ καρδίας, 2 Co. ii. 4; βαρεῖν τ. καρδίας μεριμναῖς βιωτικαῖς, Lk. xxi. 34 [cf. 2 a. above]; διαπρίομαι τῇ κ. Acts vii. 54; συντετριμμένος τὴν κ. Lk. iv. 18 R L br.; κατενύγησαν τῇ κ. Acts ii. 37 [L T Tr WH τὴν κ.]; συνθρύπτειν τὴν κ. Acts xxi. 13. **e.** *of a soul conscious of good* or *bad deeds* (our *conscience*): 1 Jn. iii. 20 sq. (Eccl. vii. 22; so לֵב, Job xxvii. 6; ἡ καρδία πατάσσει τινά, 1 S. xxiv. 6; 2 S. xxiv. 10). **3.** used *of the middle* or *central* or *inmost part of any thing, even though inanimate*: τῆς γῆς (which some understand of Hades, others of the sepulchre), Mt. xii. 40 (τῆς θαλάσσης, Jon. ii. 4 for לֵב; and for the same ἐν μέσῳ θαλάσσης, Ex. xv. 8, 19; add Bar. vi. [Ep. Jer.] 19; τῆς κλεψύδρας, Aristot. probl. 16, 8 [al. κωδία]). Cf. *Beck*, Bibl. Seelenlehre, ch. iii. § 20 sqq. p. 64 sqq.; *Delitzsch*, Bibl. Psychologie (Leipz. 1861) iv. § 12 p. 248 sqq. [also in Herzog 2, vi. 57 sqq.]; *Oehler* in Herzog vi. p. 15 sqq. [also in his O. T. Theol. (ed. *Day*) § 71]; *Wittichen* in Schenkel iii. 71 sq.

2589 **καρδιο-γνώστης**, -ου, ὁ, (καρδία, γνώστης), *knower of hearts*: Acts i. 24; xv. 8. (Eccl. writ. [W. 100 (94)].)*

2591 **Κάρπος** [cf. W. p. 51], -ου, ὁ, *Carpus*, the name of an unknown man: 2 Tim. iv. 13.*

2590 **καρπός**, -οῦ, ὁ, [cf. Lat. *carpo*; A-S. *hearf-est* (*harvest* i. e. the ingathering of crops); Curtius § 42]; Hebr. פְּרִי; fr. Hom. down; *fruit*; **1.** prop.: the fruit of trees, Mt. xii. 33; xxi. 19; Mk. xi. 14; Lk. vi. 44; xiii. 6 sq.; of vines, Mt. xxi. 34; Mk. xii. 2; Lk. xx. 10; 1 Co. ix. 7; of the fields, Lk. xii. 17; Mk. iv. 29; 2 Tim. ii. 6; [Jas. v. 7]; βλαστάνειν, Jas. v. 18; ποιεῖν, to bear fruit (after the Hebr. עָשָׂה פְּרִי [see ποιέω, I. 1 e.]), Mt. iii. 10; vii. 17–19; xiii. 26; Lk. iii. 9; vi. 43; viii. 8; xiii. 9; Rev. xxii. 2; διδόναι, Mt. xiii. 8; Mk. iv. 7 sq.; φέρειν, Mt. vii. 18 T WH; Jn. xii. 24; xv. 2, 4 sq.; (trop. xv. 8, 16); ἀποδιδόναι, to yield fruit, Rev. xxii. 2; to render (pay) the fruit, Mt. xxi. 41; by a Hebraism, ὁ καρπὸς τῆς κοιλίας, i. e. the unborn child, Lk. i. 42 (פְּרִי בֶּטֶן, Deut. xxviii. 4, where Sept. τὰ ἔκγονα τῆς κοιλίας); τῆς ὀσφύος *the fruit of one's loins*, i. e. *his progeny, his posterity*, Acts ii. 30 (Gen. xxx. 2; Ps. cxxvi. (cxxvii.) 3; cxxxi. (cxxxii.) 11; Mic. vi. 7); cf. W. 33 (32). **2.** Metaph. *that which originates* or *comes from something*; *an effect*, *result*; **a.** i. q. ἔργον, *work, act, deed*: with gen. of the author, τοῦ πνεύματος, Gal. v. 22; τοῦ φωτός, Eph. v. 9 (Rec. τ. πνεύματος); τῆς δικαιοσύνης, Phil. i. 11 [cf. b. below]; of Christian charity, i. e. benefit, Ro. xv. 28;

καρπὸν πολὺν φέρειν, to accomplish much (for the propagation of Christianity and its furtherance in the souls of men), Jn. xv. 8, 16; used of men's deeds as exponents of their hearts [cf. W. 372 (348)], Mt. vii. 16, 20; ἀγαθοί, Jas. iii. 17; καρποὶ τῆς βασ. τοῦ θεοῦ, deeds required for the attainment of salvation in the kingdom of God, Mt. xxi. 43; ποιεῖν καρποὺς ἀξίους τῆς μετανοίας, to exhibit deeds agreeing with a change of heart, Mt. iii. 8; Lk. iii. 8, (cf. ἄξια τῆς μετανοίας ἔργα πράσσειν, Acts xxvi. 20). **b.** *advantage, profit, utility*: Phil. i. 22; iv. 17; ἔχειν καρπόν, to get fruit, Ro. i. 13; vi. 21 sq.; τῆς δικαιοσύνης, benefit arising from righteousness [al. make it gen. of apposition, W. § 59, 8 a.], Jas. iii. 18 [cf. Phil. i. 11 in a. above, and Meyer ad loc.; Prov. xi. 30; Amos vi. 12]. **c.** by a Hebraism οἱ καρποὶ τῶν χειλέων, praises, which are presented to God as a thank-offering: Heb. xiii. 15 (Hos. xiv. 2; Prov. xii. 14; xxix. 49 (xxxi. 31)). Cf. W. 33 (32) note 1. **d.** συνάγειν καρπὸν εἰς ζωὴν αἰώνιον, to gather fruit (i. e. a reaped harvest) into life eternal (as into a granary), is used in fig. discourse of those who by their labors have fitted souls to obtain eternal life, Jn. iv. 36.*

2592 **καρπο-φορέω**, -ῶ; 1 aor. ἐκαρποφόρησα; pres. pass. ptcp. καρποφορούμενος; (καρποφόρος, q. v.); *to bear fruit*; (Vulg. *fructifico*; Colum., Tertull.) **a.** prop. ([Xen., Aristot.], Theophr. de hist. plant. 3, 3, 7; Diod. 2, 49): χόρτον, Mk. iv. 28 (φυτά, Sap. x. 7). **b.** metaph. *to bear, bring forth, deeds*: thus of men who show their knowledge of religion by their conduct, Mt. xiii. 23; Mk. iv. 20; Lk. viii. 15; ἐν (for R G L Tr mrg. WH mrg. ἔν [cf. B. 103 (90), see εἷς, 4 a.]) τριάκοντα etc. sc. καρποῖς, Mk. iv. 20 T Tr txt. WH txt. [see ἐν, I. 5 f.]; ἐν παντὶ ἔργῳ ἀγαθῷ, Col. i. 10; τινί (dat. commodi) to one who reaps the fruit, i. e. fruit acceptable to him, τῷ θεῷ, Ro. vii. 4; τῷ θανάτῳ, i. e. (without the fig.) to produce works rewarded with death, Ro. vii. 5; in mid. *to bear fruit of one's self*, Col. i. 6 [cf. Bp. Lghtft. ad loc.].*

2593 **καρπο-φόρος**, -ον, (καρπός and φέρω), *fruit-bearing, fruitful, productive*: Acts xiv. 17. (Pind., Xen., Theophr., Diod., Sept.)*

2594 **καρτερέω**, -ῶ; 1 aor. ἐκαρτέρησα; (καρτερός [fr. κάρτος i. e. κράτος, 'strong']); *to be steadfast*: Heb. xi. 27 [A.V. *endured*]. (Job ii. 9; Sir. ii. 2; xii. 15; often in Grk. writ. fr. Soph. and Thuc. down.) [COMP.: προσ-καρτερέω.]*

2595 **κάρφος**, -εος (-ους), τό, (fr. κάρφω to contract, dry up, wither), *a dry stalk* or *twig, a straw; chaff*, [A.V. *mote*]: Mt. vii. 3–5; Lk. vi. 41 sq., where it figuratively denotes a smaller fault. (Gen. viii. 11; in Grk. writ. fr. Aeschyl. and Hdt. down.)*

2596 **κατά**, [on its neglect of elision before a vowel see *Tdf.* Proleg. p. 95; cf. W. § 5, 1 a.; B. 10; *WH.* App. p. 146*], a preposition denoting motion or diffusion or direction from the higher to the lower; as in class. Grk., joined with the gen. and the acc.

 I. With the GENITIVE (W. § 47, k. p. 381 (357); [B. § 147, 20]); **1.** prop. **a.** *down from, down*: κατὰ τοῦ κρημνοῦ, Mt. viii. 32; Mk. v. 13; Lk. viii. 33; κατέχεεν κατὰ τῆς κεφαλῆς (so that it flowed down from his head [cf. W. 381 (357) note]; but it is more correct here to omit κατά with L T Tr WH; see καταχέω), Mk. xiv. 3; hence κατὰ κεφαλῆς (a veil hanging down from his head) ἔχων, 1 Co. xi. 4 ([A. V. *having his head covered*] cf. καταπέτασμα [or rather κάλυμμα (q. v.), but see ἔχω, I. 1 b.]). **b.** *down upon* (*down into*) anything: Acts xxvii. 14 [W. 381 (357) note[1]; cf. B.D. Am. ed. s. v. Crete]; trop. ἡ κατὰ βάθους πτωχεία reaching down into the depth, i. e. deep or extreme poverty, 2 Co. viii. 2 (cf. Strabo 9, 5 p. 419 ἐστὶ τὸ μαντεῖον ἄντρον κοῖλον κατὰ βάθους). **c.** used of motion or extension through a space from top to bottom; hence *through, throughout*: in the N. T. [and in Luke's writ.; B. § 147, 20] everywh. with the adj. ὅλος, as καθ᾽ ὅλης τῆς περιχώρου τῆς Ἰουδαίας, τῆς Ἰόππης, Lk. iv. 14; xxiii. 5; Acts ix. 31; x. 37, (διεσπάρησαν κατὰ τῆς νήσου, Polyb. 3, 19, 7; ἐσκεδασμένοι κατὰ τῆς χώρας, 1, 17, 10; 3, 76, 10; μὴ παραβαίνειν τὰς ἁρματοτροχίας, ἀλλὰ κατ᾽ αὐτῶν ἰέναι, Ael. v. h. 2, 27). **2.** metaph. **a.** after verbs of s w e a r i n g, a d j u r i n g, (the hand being, as it were, placed down upon the thing sworn by [cf. Bnhdy. p. 238; Kühner § 433 fin.]), *by*: Mt. xxvi. 63; Heb. vi. 13, 16, (Is. xlv. 23; 2 Chr. xxxvi. 13; Judith i. 12; Dem. 553, 17; 554, 23). **b.** *against* (prop. *down upon* [W. 382 (358)]; Hebr. עַל): opp. to ὑπέρ, Mk. ix. 40; 2 Co. xiii. 8; Ro. viii. 31; opp. to μετά, Mt. xii. 30; Lk. xi. 23; after ἐπιθυμεῖν, Gal. v. 17; εἰπεῖν πονηρὸν (ῥῆμα), Mt. v. 11; λαλεῖν, Acts vi. 13; Jude 15; μαρτυρία, Mk. xiv. 55; Mt. xxvi. 59; μαρτυρεῖν, 1 Co. xv. 15 [here many take κ. i. q. *with regard to, of*; cf. De Wette ad loc.; Lob. ad Phryn. p. 272]; ψευδομαρτυρεῖν, Mk. xiv. 56 sq.; γογγύζειν, Mt. xx. 11 (Ex. xv. 24 Alex.); διδάσκειν, Acts xxi. 28; ψεύδεσθαι, Jas. iii. 14 (Xen. apol. 13); συμβούλιον λαβεῖν or ποιεῖν, Mt. xxvii. 1; Mk. iii. 6; αἰτεῖσθαί τι, Acts xxv. 3, 15; after verbs of a c c u s i n g, etc.: ἔχειν τι, Mt. v. 23; Mk. xi. 25; Rev. ii. 4, 14, 20; κατηγορεῖν, Lk. xxiii. 14; κατηγορία, Jn. xviii. 29 [Tdf. om. κατά]; ἐγκαλεῖν, Ro. viii. 33; ἐντυγχάνειν τινί, Ro. xi. 2; add, Acts xxiv. 1; xxv. 2; Jas. v. 9; τὸ χειρόγραφον, Col. ii. 14; κρίσιν ποιεῖν, Jude 15; after verbs of r e b e l l i n g, f i g h t i n g, p r e v a i l i n g: Mt. x. 35; xii. 25; Acts xiv. 2; 1 Co. iv. 6; 2 Co. x. 5; 1 Pet. ii. 11; [Rev. xii. 7 Rec.]; ἰσχύειν, Acts xix. 16; ἐξουσίαν ἔχειν, Jn. xix. 11.

II. With the Accusative; cf. W. § 49 d.; Bnhdy. p. 239 sqq. **1.** of P l a c e: **a.** of the place through which anything is done or is extended (prop. *down through*; opp. to ἀνά, *up through*): καθ᾽ ὅλην τὴν πόλιν κηρύσσειν, Lk. viii. 39; ἐκφέρειν κατὰ τὰς πλατείας, Acts v. 15 [R G]; add, Lk. ix. 6; xiii. 22; xv. 14; Acts viii. 1; xi. 1; xv. 23; xxi. 21; xxiv. 5, 12; xxvii. 2; τοὺς κατὰ τὰ ἔθνη (throughout Gentile lands) πάντας Ἰουδαίους, Acts xxi. 21, cf. Grimm on 2 Macc. i. 1; κατὰ τὴν ὁδόν, along the way i. e. on the journey [W. 400 (374) note[1]], Lk. x. 4; Acts viii. 36; xxv. 3; xxvi. 13; *along* (Lat. *secundum* or *praeter* [R. V. *off*]), πέλαγος τὸ κατὰ τὴν Κιλικίαν, Acts xxvii. 5. **b.** of the place *to* which one is brought (*down*): γενόμενος [Tr WH om. γ.] κατὰ τὸν τόπον [ἐλ-

θών etc.], Lk. x. 32 [cf. *Field*, Otium Norv. Pars iii. ad loc.]; ἐλθόντες κατὰ τὴν Μυσίαν, Acts xvi. 7; κατὰ τὴν Κνίδον, Acts xxvii. 7; κατ᾽ αὐτόν, (came) to him, i. e. to the place where he was lying, Lk. x. 33. **c.** of direction; *towards*: Λιβύη ἡ κατὰ Κυρήνην, that Libya which lay towards Cyrene, i. e. Libya of Cyrene (i. e. the chief city of which was Cyrene), Acts ii. 10; βλέπειν, to look, lie towards (see βλέπω, 3), Acts xxvii. 12; πορεύεσθαι κατὰ μεσημβρίαν, Acts viii. 26; κατὰ σκοπόν, *towards the goal*, my eye on the goal, Phil. iii. 14. *against* (Lat. *adversus* w. the acc.); *over against, opposite*: κατὰ πρόσωπον, *to the face*, Gal. ii. 11 (see πρόσωπον, 1 a.); i. q. *present*, Acts xxv. 16 [A. V. *face to face*]; 2 Co. x. 1; w. gen. of pers. added, *before the face of, in the presence of, one*: Lk. ii. 31; Acts iii. 13; τὰ κατὰ πρόσωπον, the things that are open to view, known to all, 2 Co. x. 7; κατ᾽ ὀφθαλμούς, before the eyes, Gal. iii. 1; here, too, acc. to some [cf. W. 400 (374) note[3]] belongs κατὰ θεόν, Ro. viii. 27, but it is more correctly referred to 3 c. a. below. **d.** of the place w h e r e: κατ᾽ οἶκον (opp. to ἐν τῷ ἱερῷ), *at home*, privately [W. 400 (374) note[1]], Acts ii. 46; v. 42. **e.** of that which so joins itself to one thing as to separate itself from another; one *for, by*: κατ᾽ ἰδίαν, *apart*, see ἴδιος, 2; καθ᾽ ἑαυτόν, alone (*by himself*), Acts xxviii. 16; Jas. ii. 17 [R. V. *in itself*], (2 Macc. xiii. 13; οἱ καθ᾽ αὑτοὺς Ἕλληνες, Thuc. 1, 138; οἱ Βοιωτοὶ καθ᾽ αὑτούς, Diod. 13, 72; other exx. are given by *Alberti*, Observv. etc. p. 293; *Loesner*, Observv. e Philone p. 460 sq.); ἔχειν τι καθ᾽ ἑαυτόν, to have a thing by and to one's self, i. e. to keep it hidden in one's mind, Ro. xiv. 22 (Joseph. antt. 2, 11, 1; Heliod. 7, 16; [cf. W. 401 (375) note[1]]); hence, of that which b e l o n g s to some pers. or thing: κατὰ τὴν οὖσαν ἐκκλησίαν, belonging to [A. V. *in*] the church that was there, Acts xiii. 1; ἡ ἐκκλησία κατ᾽ οἶκόν τινος, belonging to one's household (see ἐκκλησία, 4 b. aa.); hence it forms a periphrasis now for the gen., as τὰ κατὰ Ἰουδαίους ἔθη (i. q. τῶν Ἰουδαίων), Acts xxvi. 3; now for the possessive pron., οἱ καθ᾽ ὑμᾶς ποιηταί, your own poets, Acts xvii. 28 [here WH mrg. καθ᾽ ἡμᾶς, see their Intr. § 404]; νόμου τοῦ καθ᾽ ὑμᾶς, [a law of your own], Acts xviii. 15; τὸ κατ᾽ ἐμὲ πρόθυμον, my inclination, Ro. i. 15 [see πρόθυμος]; ἡ καθ᾽ ὑμᾶς πίστις, Eph. i. 15, (ἡ κατὰ τὸν τύραννον ὠμότης τε καὶ δύναμις, Diod. 14, 12; μέχρι τῶν καθ᾽ ἡμᾶς χρόνων, Dion. Hal. antt. 2, 1; cf. Grimm on 2 Macc. iv. 21 p. 88; a throng of exx. fr. Polyb. may be seen in *Schweighaeuser*, Lex. Polyb. p. 323 sq.; [cf. W. 154 (146); 400 (374) note[2]; esp. B. § 132, 2]). **2.** of T i m e [cf. W. 401 (374)]; *during, about*; Lat. *tempore*: κατ᾽ ἐκεῖνον or τοῦτον τὸν καιρόν, Acts xii. 1; xix. 23; Ro. ix. 9; Heb. ix. 9 [R G]; κατὰ τὸ αὐτό, at the same time, together, Acts xiv. 1 (see αὐτός, III. 1); κατὰ τὸ μεσονύκτιον, Acts xvi. 25; κατὰ μέσον τῆς νυκτός, Acts xxvii. 27; [possibly also κατὰ μεσημβρίαν, at noon, Acts viii. 26 (see μεσημβρία, b.)]; κατὰ καιρόν, see καιρός, 2 a.; κατ᾽ ἀρχάς (Hdt. 3, 153), in the beginning (of things), Heb. i. 10; κατὰ τὴν ἡμέραν τοῦ πειρασμοῦ, Heb. iii. 8 [as the Sept. in this pass. have rendered the prep. בְּ in the context by ὡς (ἐν τῷ παραπικρασμῷ, Ps. xciv. (xcv.) 8), some would take it and κατά here i. q. *like as* in the day etc.; Vulg. *secundum*]; κατὰ πᾶν σάββατον, Acts xiii. 27; xv. 21; xviii. 4; καθ᾽ ἑκάστην ἡμέραν, Heb. iii. 13; κατὰ μῆνα (ἕνα) ἕκαστον, Rev. xxii. 2; κατ᾽ ὄναρ, during a dream, see ὄναρ. **3.** it denotes r e f-e r e n c e, r e l a t i o n, p r o p o r t i o n, of various sorts; **a.** d i s t r i b u t i v e l y, indicating a succession of things following one another [W. 401 (374); B. § 147, 20]; **α.** in ref. to p l a c e: κατὰ πόλιν, in every city, (*city by city, from city to city*), Lk. viii. 1, 4; Acts xv. 21; xx. 23; Tit. i. 5, (Thuc. 1, 122); κατ᾽ ἐκκλησίαν, in every church, Acts xiv. 23; w. the plur., κατὰ πόλεις, Lk. xiii. 22; κατὰ τὰς κώμας, Lk. ix. 6 (Hdt. 1, 96); κατὰ τόπους, Mt. xxiv. 7; Mk. xiii. 8; Lk. xxi. 11; κατὰ τὰς συναγωγάς, in every synagogue, Acts xxii. 19; [cf. κατὰ τ. οἴκους εἰσπορευόμενος, Acts viii. 3]. **β.** in ref. to t i m e: κατ᾽ ἔτος, yearly, year by year, Lk. ii. 41; also κατ᾽ ἐνιαυτόν (see ἐνιαυτός); καθ᾽ ἡμέραν etc., see ἡμέρα, 2 p. 278ᵃ; κατὰ μίαν σαββάτου [R G -των], on the first day of every week, 1 Co. xvi. 2; κατὰ ἑορτήν, at any and every feast, Mt. xxvii. 15; Mk. xv. 6; Lk. xxiii. 17 [Rec.; cf. B. § 133, 26. Others understand the phrase in these pass. (contextually) *at* or *during* (see 2 above) t h e feast, viz. the Passover; cf. W. 401 (374)]. **γ.** univ.: καθ᾽ ἕνα πάντες, all one by one, successively, 1 Co. xiv. 31, see more fully in εἷς, 4 c.; κατὰ δύο, by two, 1 Co. xiv. 27; κατὰ ἑκατὸν κ. κατὰ πεντήκοντα, by hundreds and by fifties, Mk. vi. 40 L T Tr WH; κατὰ μέρος, *severally*, singly, part by part, Heb. ix. 5 (Hdt. 9, 25; Xen. anab. 3, 4, 22); κατ᾽ ὄνομα, by name i. e. each by its own name (Vulg. *nominatim* [or *per nomen*]): Jn. x. 3; 3 Jn. 15 (14); cf. *Herm. ad Vig.* p. 858 sq. **b.** equiv. to the Lat. *ratione habita alicuius rei vel personae; as respects; with regard to; in reference to; so far as relates to; as concerning;* [W. 401 (375)]: κατὰ σάρκα or κατὰ τὴν σ., as to the flesh (see σάρξ [esp. 2 b.]), Ro. i. 3; ix. 3, 5; 1 Co. i. 26; x. 18; 2 Co. xi. 18; οἱ κύριοι κατὰ σ. (Luther well, *die leiblichen Herren*), in earthly relations, acc. to the arrangements of society, Eph. vi. 5; κατὰ τὸ εὐαγγ., κατὰ τὴν ἐκλογήν, Ro. xi. 28; add, Ro. i. 4; vii. 22; Phil. iii. 5 sq.; Heb. ix. 9; τὰ κατά τινα, one's affairs, one's case, Acts xxiv. 22; xxv. 14; Eph. vi. 21; Phil. i. 12; Col. iv. 7, (and very often in class. Grk.); κατὰ πάντα τρόπον, in every way, in every respect, Ro. iii. 2; the opp. κατὰ μηδένα τρόπον, *in no wise*, 2 Th. ii. 3; κατὰ πάντα, in all respects, in all things, Acts xvii. 22; Col. iii. 20, 22; Heb. ii. 17; iv. 15, (Thuc. 4, 81). **c.** *according to, agreeably to;* in reference to agreement or conformity to a standard, in various ways [W. 401 (375)]; **a.** *according to anything as a standard, agreeably to*: περιπατεῖν κατά τι, Mk. vii. 5; Ro. viii. 1 [Rec.], 4; xiv. 15; 2 Th. iii. 6; Eph. ii. 2; ζῆν κατά, Acts xxvi. 5; Ro. viii. 12 sq.; πορεύεσθαι, 2 Pet. iii. 3; ἀποδιδόναι τινί, Mt. xvi. 27, etc. (see ἀποδίδωμι, [esp. 4]); λαμβάνειν, 1 Co. iii. 8; so with many other verbs a thing is said *to be done* or *to occur* κατά, as in Lk. ii. 27, 29; Jn. vii. 24; Col. ii. 8; iii. 10; 1 Tim. i. 18; Heb. vii. 15; viii. 5, 9; 1 Jn. v. 14, etc.; (on the phrase κατ᾽ ἄνθρωπον, see ἄνθρωπος, esp. 1 c.; [cf. ε. below; W. 402 (376)]);

κατὰ τὴν γραφήν, τὰς γραφάς, Jas. ii. 8; 1 Co. xv. 3 sq.; κατὰ τὸ γεγραμμένον, 2 Co. iv. 13; κατὰ τὸ εἰρημένον, Ro. iv. 18; κατὰ τὸν νόμον, Lk. ii. 39; Jn. xviii. 31; xix. 7; Heb. ix. 22; κατὰ τὸ εὐαγγ. μου, Ro. ii. 16; xvi. 25; 2 Tim. ii. 8, cf. 1 Tim. i. 11; κατὰ τὸ ὡρισμένον, Lk. xxii. 22; καθ᾽ ὁμοίωσιν θεοῦ, Jas. iii. 9; κατὰ λόγον rightly, justly, [A. V. *reason would* etc.], Acts xviii. 14; κατά τινα, agreeably to the will of any one, as pleases him, [W. 401 sq. (375)]: so κατὰ θεόν, Ro. viii. 27 [cf. 1 c. above]; 2 Co. vii. 9, 11; κατὰ Χριστὸν Ἰησοῦν, Ro. xv. 5; κατὰ κύριον, 2 Co. xi. 17; κατὰ τὸν καθαρισμόν, after the manner of purifying, as the rite of purification prescribed, Jn. ii. 6; οἱ κατὰ σάρκα ὄντες, who bear, reflect, the nature of the flesh, i. q. οἱ σαρκικοί, and οἱ κατὰ πνεῦμα ὄντες i. q. οἱ πνευματικοί, Ro. viii. 5; κατὰ τί γνώσομαι; in accordance with what criterion i. e. by what sign shall I know? Lk. i. 18. Here belongs the use of the preposition in the titles of the records of the life of Christ: εὐαγγ. (which word codd. Sin. and Vat. omit) κατὰ Ματθαῖον, Μάρκον, etc., *as* Matthew etc. *composed* or *wrote* (it). This use of the prep. was not primarily a mere periphrasis for the gen. (Ματθαίου, etc., see II. 1 e. above), but indicated that the same subject had been otherwise handled by others, cf. ἡ παλαιὰ διαθήκη κατὰ τοὺς ἑβδομήκοντα (in tacit contrast not only to the Hebrew text, but also to the Greek translations made by others); οἱ ὑπομνηματισμοὶ οἱ κατὰ Νεεμίαν, 2 Macc. ii. 13 [see Grimm ad loc.]. Subsequently κατά with an acc. of the writer came to take the place of the gen., as ἡ κατὰ Μωϋσέα πεντάτευχος in Epiphanius [haer. 8, 4. Cf. W. 402 (375); B. 3; 157 (137); and see, further, *Soph. Lex.* s. v. εὐαγγέλιον, *Jas. Morison,* Com. on Mt., Intr. § 4]. **β.** *in proportion to, according to the measure of:* χαρίσματα κατὰ τὴν χάριν τὴν δοθεῖσαν ἡμῖν διάφορα, Ro. xii. 6; κατὰ τὸ μέτρον, 2 Co. x. 13; Eph. iv. 7; κατὰ τὴν σκληρότητά σου, Ro. ii. 5; κατὰ τὸν χρόνον, Mt. ii. 16; ἑκάστῳ κατὰ τὴν ἰδίαν δύναμιν, Mt. xxv. 15; without the art. κατὰ δύναμιν, 2 Co. viii. 3 (opp. to ὑπὲρ δύναμιν, as Hom. Il. 3, 59 κατ᾽ αἶσαν, οὐδ᾽ ὑπὲρ αἶσαν); καθ᾽ ὅσον, by so much as, inasmuch as, Heb. iii. 3; vii. 20; ix. 27; κατὰ τοσοῦτο, by so much, Heb. vii. 22. **γ.** used of the c a u s e; *through, on account of, from, owing to,* (in accordance with i. e. *in consequence of, by virtue of*) [W. 402 (376)]: κατὰ πᾶσαν αἰτίαν, [*for every cause*], Mt. xix. 3; κατὰ τὴν χάριν τοῦ θεοῦ, 1 Co. iii. 10; 2 Tim. i. 9, (κατὰ τὴν τοῦ θεοῦ πρόνοιαν, Joseph. antt. 20, 8, 6); κατὰ χάριν, Ro. iv. 16; also opp. to κατὰ ὀφείλημα [R. V. *as of ... as of*], Ro. iv. 4; οἱ κατὰ φύσιν κλάδοι, the natural branches, Ro. xi. 21 [cf. B. 162 (141)]; ἡ κατὰ φύσιν ἀγριέλαιος, the natural wild olive tree, ib. 24; ἡ κατὰ πίστιν δικαιοσύνη, righteousness proceeding from faith, Heb. xi. 7; add, Ro. viii. 28; ix. 11; xi. 5; xvi. 25 sq.; 1 Co. xii. 8; Gal. ii. 2; iii. 29; Eph. i. 5, 7, 9, 11, 19; iii. 7, 11, 16, 20; Col. i. 11, 29; Phil. i. 20; iii. 21; iv. 11, 19; 2 Th. i. 12; ii. 9; 2 Tim. i. 8 sq.; Heb. ii. 4; vii. 16; Tit. i. 3; 1 Pet. i. 3; 2 Pet. iii. 15. adverbial phrases [W. § 51, 2 g.]: κατ᾽ ἐξουσίαν [*with* authority], Mk. i. 27; κατ᾽ ἀνάγκην, κατὰ ἑκούσιον (q. v), [*of* necessity, *of* free will], Philem. 14; κατὰ γνῶσιν, 1 Pet. iii. 7; κατ' ἐπίγνωσιν, Ro. x. 2 [cf. W. 403 (376)]; κατὰ ἄγνοιαν, [in ignorance], Acts iii. 17. **δ.** of likeness; *as, like as*: συντελέσω ... διαθήκην καινήν, οὐ κατὰ τὴν διαθήκην κτλ. Heb. viii. 8 sq. (1 K. xi. 10); so with the acc. of a pers. [cf. under *a.* above], Gal. iv. 28; 1 Pet. i. 15; κατὰ θεόν, after the image of God, Eph. iv. 24; κρίνεσθαι κατὰ ἀνθρώπους, ζῆν κατὰ θεόν, to be judged as it is fit men should be judged, to live as God lives, 1 Pet. iv. 6. Hence it is used **ε.** of the mode in which a thing is done; of the quality: ἄνδρες οἱ κατ' ἐξοχὴν τῆς πόλεως, the principal men of the city, Acts xxv. 23; καθ' ὑπομενήν ἔργου ἀγαθοῦ, i. q. ὑπομένοντες ἐν ἔργῳ ἀγαθῷ, [by constancy in well-doing], Ro. ii. 7; esp. in adverbial phrases: κατὰ ταῦτα in [or after] the same [or this] manner, Lk. vi. 23 (L txt. T Tr WH κ. τὰ αὐτά, L. mrg. κ. ταυτά), [26 edd. as before]; Lk. xvii. 30 (T Tr WH κ. τὰ αὐτά, G L κ. ταυτά); καθ' ὑπερβολήν, Ro. vii. 13; 1 Co. xii. 31, etc., [cf. W. 466 (434); B. 96 (84)]; κατὰ πίστιν i. q. πιστεύοντες [A. V. in faith; W. 403 (376)], Heb. xi. 13; κατὰ συγγνώμην, οὐ κατ' ἐπιταγήν, by way of concession, not by way of commandment, 1 Co. vii. 6, cf. 2 Co. viii. 8; κατὰ κράτος, Acts xix. 20; καθ' ὁμοιότητα, Heb. iv. 15; on the phrase κατὰ ἄνθρωπον see ἄνθρωπος, 1 c. [cf. *a.* above]. **d.** of the end aimed at; the goal to which anything tends; (Lat. *ad* [W. 402 sq. (376)]): κατ' ἐπαγγελίαν ζωῆς, to proclaim life, 2 Tim. i. 1 [but see ἐπαγγελία, 1]; κατ' εὐσέβειαν, tending to godliness, [1 Tim. vi. 3; Tit. i. 1] (see εὐσέβεια; yet al. refer these exx., and that which follows, to the use set forth above, in c.]); κατὰ πίστιν, to awaken, produce faith, Tit. i. 1, (exx. of this use of κατά fr. Hom., Hdt., Thuc., Xen., may be seen in Passow s. v. II. 3 p. 1598ᵇ; [L. and S. s. v. B. III. 1]; cf. *Herm.* ad Vig. p. 632; Kühner ii. p. 412); many refer to this head also κατ' ἀτιμίαν (to my dishonor [W. 402 sq. (376)]) λέγω, 2 Co. xi. 21 (κατὰ τὴν τιμὴν τοῦ θεοῦ τοῦτο ποιῶν, to the honor of God, Joseph. antt. 3, 11, 4); but see ἀτιμία.

III. In Composition κατά denotes, **1.** *from, down from, from a higher to a lower place*: with special ref. to the terminus from which, as καταβαίνω, καταβιβάζω, etc. [cf. W. 431 (401 sq.)]; with more prominent ref. to the lower terminus (*down*), as καταβάλλω, καταπατέω, etc. [cf. W. u. s.]; also of the situation or local position, as κατάκειμαι, καθεύδω, κατατίθημι, καθίζω, etc. *from top to bottom*, metaph. of things done with care, *thoroughly*, as καταμανθάνω, καθοράω, etc. **2.** *in succession, in course*: καθεξῆς; one part after another, καταρτίζω, κατευθύνω, etc. **3.** *under, underneath*: καταχθόνιος; the idea of *putting under* resides in verbs denoting victory, rule, etc., over others, as καταδυναστεύω, κατακυριεύω, κατεξουσιάζω, καταδουλόω; likewise in verbs naming that with which anything is covered, concealed, overwhelmed, etc., as κατακαλύπτω, καταλιθάζω, κατασφραγίζω, κατασκιάζω, καταισχύνω, (where the Germ. uses the prefix *über* [Eng. *over*], as *überschatten, überdecken*, or the syllable *be*, as *beschatten, besiegeln*); also in adjj. denoting an abundance of that with which a thing is filled up or as it were covered up; see below in κατείδωλος. **4.**

like the Germ. *ver-, zer-*, it denotes separation, dissolution, in verbs of wasting, dissolving, etc., as κατακόπτω, κατάγνυμι, κατακαίω, κατακλάω, καταλύω, κατακλύζω, καταναλίσκω, καταφθείρω, etc. **5.** i. q. *after, behind*: καταδιώκω, καταλείπω, κατακολουθέω, etc. **6.** used of proportion and distribution, as κατακληροδοτέω, κατακληρονομέω, etc. **7.** of hostility, *against* etc.: καταδικάζω, κατακρίνω, καταλαλέω, καταγινώσκω, etc. Cf. *Herm.* ad Vig. p. 637 sqq. [On the constr. of verbs compounded w. κατά, see W. u. s.; cf. B. 165 (143 sq.).]

κατα-βαίνω; impf. 3 pers. plur. κατέβαινον; fut. καταβήσομαι; 2 aor. κατέβην, impv. κατάβηθι (Mt. xxvii. 40; Lk. xix. 5; Jn. iv. 49; Acts x. 20) and κατάβα (Mk. xv. 30 [R G (where L T Tr WH ptcp. καταβάς)], see ἀναβαίνω]; pf. καταβέβηκα; [fr. Hom. on]; Sept. for יָרַד; *to go down, come down, descend*; **1.** of persons; **a.** prop.: absol., the place from which one has come down being evident from the context, καταβὰς ἔστη, Lk. vi. 17 (cf. 12); xvii. 31 [foll. here by inf.], so Mt. xxiv. 17]; Lk. xix. 5 sq.; Jn. v. 7; Acts xx. 10; Eph. iv. 10; foll. by ἀπό w. gen. of the place, Mt. viii. 1; xiv. 29; xvii. 9 Rec.; xxvii. 40, 42; Mk. ix. 9 [L Tr mrg. WH txt. ἐκ]; xv. 30, 32; by ἐκ w. gen. of place, Mt. xvii. 9 G L T Tr WH [see ἐκ, I. 3]; by εἰς w. acc. of place, Mk. xiii. 15 [R G L br. Tr; al. om. εἰς etc.]; Acts viii. 38; [Ro. x. 7]; Eph. iv. 9. **b.** *to come down*, as fr. the temple at Jerusalem, fr. the city of Jerusalem; also of celestial beings coming down to earth: absol., Mt. iii. 16; Lk. ii. 51; x. 31; Jn. iv. 47, 49, 51; Acts [vii. 34]; viii. 15; x. 20; [xxiii. 10]; xxiv. 1, 22; foll. by ἀπό w. gen. of the place, Mk. iii. 22; Lk. x. 30; Acts xxv. 7; 1 Th. iv. 16; ἐκ τοῦ οὐρανοῦ, Mt. xxviii. 2; Jn. i. 32; iii. 13, 38 [R G; al. ἀπό], 41 sq. 50 sq. 58, [on these pass. cf. B. 297 (255)]; Rev. x. 1; xviii. 1; xx. 1. foll. by εἰς w. acc. of place, Lk. x. 30; xviii. 14; Jn. ii. 12; Acts vii. 15; xiv. 25; xvi. 8; xviii. 22; xxv. 6; by ἐπί w. acc. of place, Jn. vi. 16; w. acc. of the pers., Mk. i. 10 [R G L mrg.]; Lk. iii. 22; Jn. i. 33, 51 (52); by ἐν w. dat. of place, Jn. v. 4 [R L] (see ἐν, I. 7); by πρός w. acc. of pers., Acts x. 21; xi. 11; contextually i. q. *to be cast down*, of the devil, Rev. xii. 12. **2.** of things, *to come* (i. e. *be sent*) *down*: Acts x. 11 (Rec. adds ἐπ' αὐτόν); xi. 5; foll. by ἀπό w. a gen. of pers., Jas. i. 17; ἐκ τοῦ οὐρανοῦ ἀπὸ τοῦ θεοῦ, Rev. iii. 12; xxi. 2, 10; *to come* (i. e. *fall*) *down*: fr. the upper regions of the air; as βροχή, Mt. vii. 25, 27; λαῖλαψ, Lk. viii. 23; πῦρ ἀπὸ [Lchm. ἐκ] τοῦ οὐρ. Lk. ix. 54; ἐκ τοῦ οὐρ. εἰς τ. γῆν, Rev. xiii. 13; ἐκ τοῦ οὐρ. ἀπὸ τ. θεοῦ, Rev. xx. 9 [R G Tr]; χάλαζα ἐκ τοῦ οὐρ. ἐπί τινα, Rev. xvi. 21; θρόμβοι ἐπὶ τὴν γῆν, Lk. xxii. 44 [L br. WH reject the pass.]; of a way leading downwards, Acts viii. 26. **3.** figuratively, καταβ. ἕως ᾅδου, to (go i. e.) be cast down to the lowest state of wretchedness and shame: Mt. xi. 23 L T Tr WH; [Lk. x. 15 WH txt. Tr mrg. COMP.: συγκαταβαίνω.]*

κατα-βάλλω: Pass. and Mid. pres. ptcp. καταβαλλόμενος; 1 aor. pass. κατεβλήθην; [fr. Hom. down]; Sept. for הִפִּיל; **1.** *to cast down*: τινά, pass., Rev. xii. 10 Rec.; *to throw to the ground, prostrate*: pass., 2 Co. iv. 9

(where the metaph. is taken from an athlete or combatant).   2. *to put in a lower place*: in the phrase θεμέλιον καταβάλλομαι, *to lay (down) a foundation* (Joseph. antt. 11, 4, 4; 15, 11, 3; Dion. II. antt. 3, 69; al.), Heb. vi. 1.*

2599 **κατα-βαρέω, -ῶ**: 1 aor. κατεβάρησα; prop. *to press down by an imposed weight; to weigh down*; metaph. *to burden*: τινά, any one, 2 Co. xii. 16.   (Polyb., Diod., App., Lcian.) *

see 916 **κατα-βαρύνω**: i. q. καταβαρέω (q. v.); pres. pass. ptcp. καταβαρυνόμενος, Mk. xiv. 40 L T Tr WH; see βαρέω. (Sept.; Theophr. et al.) *

2600 **κατά-βασις, -εως, ἡ**, (καταβαίνω), [fr. Hdt. down], *descent*;   a. *the act of descending*.   b. *the place of descent*: τοῦ ὄρους, i. e. that part of the mountain where the descent is made, Lk. xix. 37; so Josh. x. 11 Sept.; Diod. 4, 21; opp. to ἀνάβασις, the place of ascent, way up, 1 Macc. iii. 16, 24; Xen. Cyr. 7, 2, 3. So Lat. *descensus*; cf. Herzog on Sall. Cat. 57, 3.*

2601 **κατα-βιβάζω**: 1 fut. pass. καταβιβασθήσομαι; *to cause to go down* (Hdt. 1, 87; Xen. Cyr. 7, 5, 18; Sept. several times for הוֹרִיד; *to bring down*, Bar. iii. 29); *to cast down, thrust down*: pass., ἕως ᾅδου (see ᾅδης, 2), Mt. xi. 23 R G T; Lk. x. 15 [Tr mrg. WH txt. καταβήσῃ (q. v. 3)]; εἰς ᾅδου, Ezek. xxxi. 16.*

2602 **κατα-βολή, -ῆς, ἡ**, (καταβάλλω, q. v.);   **1.** *a throwing* or *laying down*: τοῦ σπέρματος (sc. εἰς τὴν μήτραν), the injection or depositing of the virile semen in the womb, Lcian. amor. 19; Galen, aphorism. iv. § 1; of the seed of animals and plants, Philo de opif. mund. §§ 22, 45; σπέρματα τὰ εἰς γῆν ἢ μήτραν καταβαλλόμενα, Antonin. 4, 36; accordingly many interpret the words Σάρρα δύναμιν εἰς καταβολὴν σπέρματος ἔλαβε in Heb. xi. 11, she received power to conceive seed. But since it belongs to the male καταβάλλειν τὸ σπέρμα, not to the female, this interpretation cannot stand [(acc. to the reading of WH mrg. αὐτῆ Σάρρᾳ, Abr. remains the subj. of ἔλαβεν; but see 2 below)]; cf. Bleek [and, on the other side, Kurtz] ad loc.   **2.** *a founding* (*laying down a foundation*): εἰς καταβ. σπέρματος, to found a posterity, Heb. xi. 11 [but cf. above] (τυραννίδος, Polyb. 13, 6, 2; ἅμα τῇ πρώτῃ καταβολῇ τῶν ἀνθρώπων, Plut. aquae et ignis comp. c. 2). ἀπὸ καταβολῆς κόσμον, from the foundation of the world: Mt. xiii. 35 [L T Tr WH om. κόσμον]; xxv. 34; Lk. xi. 50; Heb. iv. 3; ix. 26; Rev. xiii. 8; xvii. 8; πρὸ καταβολῆς κόσμον, Jn. xvii. 24; Eph. i. 4; 1 Pet. i. 20.*

2603 **κατα-βραβεύω**, impv. 3 pers. sing. καταβραβευέτω; (prop. βραβεύω to be an umpire in a contest, κατά sc. τινός, against one); *to decide as umpire against* one, *to declare him unworthy of the prize; to defraud of the prize of victory*: τινά, metaph., *to deprive of salvation*, Col. ii. 18, where cf. Meyer, [Bp. Lghtft., esp. *Field, Otium Norv.* Pars iii.]. (Eustath. ad Il. 1, 93, 33 (vss. 402 sq.) καταβραβεύει αὐτόν, ὥς φασιν οἱ παλαιοί; but in the earlier Grk. writ. that have come down to us, it is found only in [pseudo-] Dem. adv. Mid. p. 544 end, where it is used of one who by bribing the judges causes another to be condemned.) *

2604 **καταγγελεύς, -έως, ὁ**, (καταγγέλλω, q. v.), *announcer* (Vulg. *annuntiator*), *proclaimer*: with gen. of the obj., Acts xvii. 18. (Eccles. writ.) *

2605 **κατ-αγγέλλω**; impf. κατήγγελλον; 1 aor. κατήγγειλα; Pass., pres. καταγγέλλομαι; 2 aor. κατηγγέλην; *to announce, declare, promulgate, make known; to proclaim publicly, publish*: τὸν λόγον τοῦ θεοῦ, Acts xiii. 5; xv. 36; pass. Acts xvii. 13; ἔθη, Acts xvi. 21; τὸ εὐαγγέλιον, 1 Co. ix. 14; τὴν ἀνάστασιν τὴν ἐκ νεκρῶν, Acts iv. 2; τὰς ἡμέρας ταύτας, Acts iii. 24 G L T Tr WH; θεόν [al. ὅ], Acts xvii. 23; Ἰησοῦν, ib. 3; Christ, Phil. i. 16 (17), 18; Col. i. 28; τινί τι, Acts xiii. 38; xvi. 17; 1 Co. ii. 1; with the included idea of celebrating, commending, openly praising (Lat. *praedicare*): τί, Ro. i. 8 [A.V. *is spoken of*]; 1 Co. xi. 26. (Occasionally in Grk. writ. fr. Xen. an. 2, 5, 38 where it means *to denounce, report, betray*; twice in the O. T. viz. 2 Macc. viii. 36; ix. 17. [Cf. Westcott on 1 Jn. i. 5.]) [COMP.: προ-καταγγέλλω.] *

2606 **κατα-γελάω, -ῶ**: impf. 3 pers. plur. κατεγέλων; *to deride*, [A. V. *laugh to scorn*]: τινός, any one [cf. B. § 132, 15], Mt. ix. 24; Mk. v. 40; Lk. viii. 53. (From [Aeschyl. and] Hdt. down; Sept.) *

2607 **κατα-γινώσκω**: pf. pass. ptcp. κατεγνωσμένος; *to find fault with, blame*: κατεγνωσμένος ἦν, he had incurred the censure of the Gentile Christians; Luther rightly, *es war Klage über ihn kommen* [i. e. *a charge had been laid against him*; but al. *he stood condemned*, see Meyer or Ellic. in loc.; cf. Bttm. § 134, 4. 8], Gal. ii. 11; *to accuse, condemn*: τινός, any one, 1 Jn. iii. 20 sq., with which cf. Sir. xiv. 2 μακάριος, οὗ οὐ κατέγνω ἡ ψυχὴ αὐτοῦ. (In these and other signif. in Grk. writ. fr. [Aeschyl. and] Hdt. down; [see Ellicott u. s.].) *

2608 **κατ-άγνυμι**: fut. κατεάξω; 1 aor. κατέαξα (impv. κάταξον, Deut. xxxiii. 11); Pass., 2 aor. κατεάγην, whence subjunc. 3 pers. plur. κατεαγῶσιν; 1 aor. κατεάχθην in Sept. Jer. xxxi. (xlviii.) 25; (on the syllabic augment of these forms cf. Bttm. Ausf. Spr. ii. p. 97 sq., cf. i. p. 323 sq.; Matthiae i. p. 520 sq.; W. § 12, 2; [Curtius, Das Verbum, i. p. 118; Veitch s. v.; Kuenen and Cobet, N. T., Praef. p. lxxix.]); fr. Hom. down; *to break*: τί, Mt. xii. 20; Jn. xix. 31–33. [SYN. see Schmidt ch. 115, 5 and cf. ῥήγνυμι.] *

see 1125 **κατα-γράφω**: impf. 3 pers. sing. κατέγραφεν; *to draw* (forms or figures), *to delineate*: Jn. viii. 6 cod. D etc. which T Tr WH (txt.) would substitute for R G ἔγραφεν. (Pausan. 1, 28, 2. Differently in other Grk. writ.) [Perh. it may be taken in Jn. l. c. in a more general sense: *to mark* (cf. Pollux 9, 7, 104, etc.).] *

2609 **κατ-άγω**: 2 aor. κατήγαγον; 1 aor. pass. κατήχθην; Sept. for הוֹרִיד, to make to descend; *to lead down, bring down*: τινά, Acts xxii. 30; Ro. x. 6; τινά foll. by εἰς w. acc. of place, Acts ix. 30; xxiii. [15 L T Tr WH], 20, 28; τινά foll. by πρός w. acc. of pers., Acts xxiii. 15 [R G]; τὸ πλοῖον ἐπὶ τὴν γῆν to bring the vessel (down from deep water) *to the land*, Lk. v. 11; κατάγεσθαι, to be brought (down) in a ship, to land, touch at: foll. by εἰς w. acc. of place, Acts xxi. 3 [L T Tr WH κατήλθομεν]; xxvii. 3; xxviii. 12; often so in Grk. writ.*

2610 **κατ-αγωνίζομαι**: deponent mid.; 1 aor. κατηγωνισάμην; **1.** *to struggle against* (Polyb. 2, 42, 3, etc.). **2.** *to overcome* (cf. Germ. *niederkämpfen*): Heb. xi. 33. (Polyb., Joseph., Lcian., Plut., Aelian.) *

2611 κατα-δέω, -ῶ: 1 aor. κατέδησα; fr. Hom. down; *to bind up*: τὰ τραύματα, Lk. x. 34. (Sir. xxvii. 21 acc. to the true reading τραύμα.) *

2612 κατά-δηλος, -ον, (δῆλος), *thoroughly clear, plain, evident*: Heb. vii. 15. ([Soph.], Hdt., Xen., Plat., al.) [Cf. δῆλος, fin.] *

2613 κατα-δικάζω; 1 aor. κατεδίκασα; 1 aor. pass. κατεδικάσθην; 1 fut. pass. καταδικασθήσομαι; *to give judgment against* (one), *to pronounce guilty*; *to condemn*; in class. Grk. [where it differs fr. κρίνειν in giving prominence to the f o r m a l and o f f i c i a l as distinguished from the i n w a r d and l o g i c a l judging (cf. *Schmidt*, Syn. ch. 18, 6)] it is foll. by the gen. of the pers., in the N. T. by the acc. [B. § 132, 16]: Mt. xii. 7; Lk. vi. 37 [here Tr mrg. the simple verb]; Jas. v. 6; pass., Mt. xii. 37; [Lk. vi. 37ᵇ (not Tr mrg.)]. (Sept. Lam. iii. 35; Joseph. antt. 7, 11, 3.) *

see 1349; κατα-δίκη, -ης, ἡ; **1.** *damnatory sentence, condemnation*: Acts xxv. 15 L T Tr WH; ([Epicharm. in Ath. **2613** 2, 3 p. 36 d.], Polyb., Plut., Iren. 1, 16, 3). **2.** *penalty*, esp. *a fine*; (Thuc., Dem., Lcian.).*

2614 κατα-διώκω: 1 aor. κατεδίωξα; Sept. often for רָדַף; *to follow after, follow up*, (esp. of enemies [Thuc. et al.]); in a good sense, of those in search of any one: τινά, Mk. i. 36. (τὸ ἔλεός σου καταδιώξεται με, Ps. xxii. (xxiii.) 6; οὐ κατεδίωξαν μεθ' ἡμῶν, 1 S. xxx. 22; ὀπίσω τινός, to follow after one in order to gain his favor, Sir. xxvii. 17.) *

2615 κατα-δουλόω, -ῶ; fut. καταδουλώσω; 1 aor. mid. κατεδουλωσάμην; (κατά under [see κατά, III. 3]); [fr. Hdt. down]; *to bring into bondage, enslave*: τινά, Gal. ii. 4 L T Tr WH; 2 Co. xi. 20 [cf. W. 255 sq. (240)]; mid. *to enslave to one's self, bring into bondage to one's self*: Gal. ii. 4 R G.*

2616 κατα-δυναστεύω; pres. pass. ptcp. καταδυναστευόμενος; Sept. for הוֹנָה, עָשַׁק, etc.; with gen. of pers. [W. 206 (193); B. 169 (147)], *to exercise harsh control over one, to use one's power against one*: Jas. ii. 6 [not Tdf. (see below)] (Diod. 13, 73); τινά, *to oppress one* (Xen. conv. 5, 8; often in Sept.): Jas. ii. 6 Tdf.; pass. Acts x. 38.*

(2616a); κατά-θεμα, -τος, τό, i. q. καταράθεμα (q. v.), of which it seems to be a vulgar corruption by syncope [cf. *Koumanoudes*, Συναγωγὴ λέξεων ἀθησαύρ. κτλ. s. v. κατάς]; *a curse*; by meton. *worthy of execration, an accursed thing*: Rev. xxii. 3 [Rec. καταανάθεμα; cf. Just. M. quaest. et resp. 121 fin.; 'Teaching' 16, 5]. Not found in prof. auth.*

see 2653 κατα-θεματίζω; (κατάθεμα, q. v.); *to call down direst evils on, to curse vehemently*: Mt. xxvi. 74 (Rec. καταναθεματί-**2617** ζειν). (Iren. adv. haer. 1, 13, 4 and 16, 3.) *

2617 κατ-αισχύνω; Pass., impf. κατῃσχυνόμην; 1 aor. κατῃσχύνθην; fut. Sept. chiefly for בּוֹשׁ and הֹבִישׁ; as in Grk. writ. fr. Hom. down; **1.** *to dishonor, disgrace*: τὴν κεφαλήν, 1 Co. xi. 4 sq. (σποδῷ τὴν κεφαλήν, Joseph. antt. 20, 4, 2). **2.** *to put to shame, make ashamed*: τινά, 1 Co. i. 27; xi. 22; pass. *to be ashamed, blush with shame*: Lk. xiii. 17; 2 Co. vii. 14; ix. 4: 1 Pet.

iii. 16; by a Hebr. usage one is said *to be put to shame* who *suffers a repulse*, or *whom some hope has deceived*; hence ἐλπὶς οὐ καταισχύνει, *does not disappoint*: Ro. v. 5 (cf. Ps. xxi. (xxii.) 6; xxiv. (xxv.) 2 sq.; cxviii. (cxix.) 116); pass., Ro. ix. 33; x. 11; 1 Pet. ii. 6, (Is. xxviii. 16; Sir. ii. 10).*

2618 κατα-καίω: impf. 3 pers. plur. κατέκαιον; fut. κατακαύσω; 1 aor. inf. κατακαῦσαι; Pass., pres. κατακαίομαι; 2 aor. κατεκάην; 2 fut. κατακαήσομαι [cf. *Tdf.* Proleg. p. 123; *WH.* App. p. 170ᵃ]; 1 fut. κατακαυθήσομαι (Kühner i. 841; [Veitch s. v. καίω; B. 60 (53); W. 87 (83)]); Sept. chiefly for שָׂרַף; fr. Hom. down; *to burn up* [see κατά, III. 4], *consume by fire*: τί, Mt. xiii. 30; Acts xix. 19; pass., 1 Co. iii. 15; Heb. xiii. 11; 2 Pet. iii. 10 [Tr WH εὑρεθήσεται, see εὑρίσκω, 1 a. fin.]; Rev. viii. 7; with πυρί added, Mt. iii. 12; xiii. 40 R L T WH, but G Tr καίω; Lk. iii. 17, (Ex. xxix. 14; xxxii. 20 Alex., etc.; see καίω); ἐν πυρί (often so in Sept.), Rev. xvii. 16; xviii. 8. (καίω and κατακαίω are distinguished in Ex. iii. 2.) *

2619 κατα-καλύπτω: Sept. for כָּסָה; fr. Hom. down; *to cover up* [see κατά, III. 3]; Mid. pres. κατακαλύπτομαι, *to veil* or *cover one's self*: 1 Co. xi. 6; τὴν κεφαλήν, one's head, ib. 7.*

2620 κατα-καυχάομαι, -ῶμαι, 2 pers. sing. κατακαυχᾶσαι (contr. fr. κατακαυχάεσαι) for the Attic κατακαυχᾷ (Ro. xi. 18; cf. W. § 13, 2 b.; [B. 42 (37); *Soph.* Lex., Introd. p. 40 sq.; *Tdf.* Proleg. p. 123 sq.]; *Lob.* ad Phryn. p. 360), impv. 2 pers. sing. κατακαυχῶ (Ro. xi. 18); (κατά against [cf. κατά, III. 7]); prop. *to glory against, to exult over, to boast one's self to the injury of* (a person or a thing): τινός, Ro. xi. 18; Tdf. in Jas. iii. 14; κατά τινος, ibid. R G L Tr WH [B. 185 (160); W. § 30, 9 b. (cf. 432 (402))]; ἔλεος (i. q. ὁ ἐλεῶν) κατακαυχᾶται κρίσεως, mercy boasts itself superior to judgment, i. e. full of glad confidence has no fear of judgment, Jas. ii. 13. (Zech. x. 12; Jer. xxvii. (l.) 10, 38; not found in prof. auth.)*

2621 κατά-κειμαι; impf. 3 pers. sing. κατέκειτο; (κεῖμαι, to lie [see κατά, III. 1]); *to have lain down* i. e. *to lie prostrate*; **a.** of the sick [cf. colloq. 'down sick'] (Hdt. 7, 229; Lcian. Icarom. 31; [Plut. vit. Cic. 43, 3]): Mk. i. 30; Jn. v. 6; Acts xxviii. 8; foll. by ἐπί w. dat. of the couch or pallet, Mk. ii. 4 R G Lmrg. [Acts ix. 33 R G]; Lk. v. 25 R L; ἐπί τινος, Acts ix. 33 [L T Tr WH]; ἐπί τι, Lk. v. 25 Tr WH [B. § 147, 24 note; W. 408 (381) note]; ἐν w. dat. of place, Jn. v. 3. **b.** of those at meals, *to recline* (Athen. 1, 42 p. 23 c.; Xen. an. 6, 1, 4; conv. 1, 14; Plat. conv. p. 177 d.; rep. p. 372 d., etc.; Diog. Laërt. 7, 1, 19; see ἀνάκειμαι): absol., Mk. xiv. 3; Lk. v. 29; foll. by ἐν w. dat. of place, Mk. ii. 15; 1 Co. viii. 10; Lk. vii. 37 L T Tr WH.*

2622 κατα-κλάω, -ῶ: 1 aor. κατέκλασα; fr. Hom. down; *to break in pieces* (cf. Germ. *zerbrechen* [see κατά, III. 4]): τοὺς ἄρτους, Mk. vi. 41; Lk. ix. 16.*

2623 κατα-κλείω: 1 aor. κατέκλεισα; fr. [Hdt.], Thuc. and Xen. down; *to shut up, confine*: τινὰ ἐν τῇ φυλακῇ, Lk. iii. 20; ἐν (which Rec. om.) φυλακαῖς, Acts xxvi. 10 (Jer. xxxix. (xxxii.) 3).*

2624 κατα-κληροδοτέω, -ῶ (see κατά, III. 6): 1 aor. κατεκληροδότησα; to distribute by lot; to distribute as an inheritance: τινί τι, Acts xiii. 19 Rec.; see the foll. word. (Deut. i. 38; xxi. 16; Josh. xix. 51 Ald., Compl.; 1 Macc. iii. 36, — in all with the var. κατακληρονομεῖν. Not found in prof. auth.) *

(2624α); **κατα-κληρονομέω, -ῶ** [see κατά, III. 6]: 1 aor. κατεκληρο-
see 2624 νόμησα; to distribute by lot, to distribute as an inheritance: τινί τι, Acts xiii. 19 G L T Tr WH. (Num. xxxiv. 18; Deut. iii. 28; Josh. xiv. 1; Judg. xi. 24 Alex.; 1 S. ii. 8; 1 Esr. viii. 82. Also often intrans. to receive, obtain, acquire as an inheritance; as, Deut. i. 8 var., 38; ii. 21. Not found in prof. auth.) *

2625 **κατα-κλίνω**: 1 aor. κατέκλινα; 1 aor. pass. κατεκλίθην; fr. Hom. down; in the N. T. in ref. to eating, to make to recline: τινά, Lk. ix. 14, [also 15 T Tr WH], (ἐπὶ τὸ δεῖπνον, Xen. Cyr. 2, 3, 21); mid., with 1 aor. pass., to recline (at table): Lk. vii. 36 L T Tr WH; xxiv. 30; εἰς τὴν πρωτοκλισίαν, Lk. xiv. 8, (εἰς τὸ ἐσθίειν, Judith xii. 15; εἰς τὸ δεῖπνον, Joseph. antt. 6, 8, 1 [var.]).*

2626 **κατα-κλύζω**: 1 aor. pass. ptcp. κατακλυσθείς; fr. [Pind., Hdt.], Aeschyl. down; to overwhelm with water, to submerge, deluge, [cf. κατά, III. 4]: 2 Pet. iii. 6. (Sept. several times for שָׁטַף.)*

2627 **κατα-κλυσμός, -οῦ, ὁ**, (κατακλύζω), inundation, deluge: of Noah's deluge, Mt. xxiv. 38 sq.; Lk. xvii. 27; 2 Pet. ii. 5. (Sept. for מַבּוּל; Plato, Diod., Philo, Joseph., Plut.)*

2628 **κατ-ακολουθέω, -ῶ**; 1 aor. ptcp. κατακολουθήσας; to follow after [see κατά, III. 5]: Lk. xxiii. 55; τινί, Acts xvi. 17. [Sept., Polyb., Plut., Joseph., al.]*

2629 **κατα-κόπτω**: **1.** to cut up, cut to pieces, [see κατά, III. 4]; to slay: Is. xxvii. 9; 2 Chr. xxxiv. 7, etc.; Hdt. et sqq. **2.** to beat, bruise: ἑαυτὸν λίθοις, Mk. v. 5; [al. retain here the primary meaning, to cut, gash, mangle].*

2630 **κατα-κρημνίζω**: 1 aor. inf. κατακρημνίσαι; to cast down a precipice; to throw down headlong: Lk. iv. 29. (2 Chr. xxv. 12; 2 Macc. xiv. 43; 4 Macc. iv. 25; Xen. Cyr. 1, 4, 7; 8, 3, 41; Dem. 446, 11; Diod. 4, 31; [Philo de agric. Noë § 15]; Joseph. antt. 6, 6, 2; 9, 9, 1.) *

2631 **κατά-κριμα, -τος, τό**, (κατακρίνω), damnatory sentence, condemnation: Ro. v. 16 (on which see κρίμα, 2), ib. 18; viii. 1. (κατακριμάτων ἀφέσεις, Dion. Hal. 6, 61.) *

2632 **κατα-κρίνω**: fut. κατακρινῶ; 1 aor. κατέκρινα; Pass., pf. κατακέκριμαι; 1 aor. κατεκρίθην; 1 fut. κατακριθήσομαι; to give judgment against (one [see κατά, III. 7]), to judge worthy of punishment, to condemn; **a.** prop.: Ro. viii. 34; τινά, Jn. viii. 10 sq.; Ro. ii. 1, where it is disting. fr. κρίνειν, as in 1 Co. xi. 32; pass., Mt. xxvii. 3; Ro. xiv. 23; τινὰ θανάτῳ, to adjudge one to death, condemn to death, Mt. xx. 18 [Tdf. εἰς θάνατον]; Mk. x. 33, (κεκριμμένοι θανάτῳ, to eternal death, Barn. ep. 10, 5); τῇ καταστροφῇ, 2 Pet. ii. 6 [WH om. Tr mrg. br. καταστροφῇ], (the Greeks say κατακρ. τινὰ θανάτου or θάνατον; cf. W. 210 (197 sq.); B. § 132, 16; Grimm on Sap. ii. 20); w. the acc. and inf., τινὰ ἔνοχον εἶναι θανάτου, Mk. xiv. 64; simply, of God condemning one to eternal misery: pass., Mk. xvi. 16; 1 Co. xi. 32; Jas. v. 9 Rec. **b.** improp. i. e. by one's good example to render another's

wickedness the more evident and censurable: Mt. xii. 41 sq.; Lk. xi. 31 sq.; Heb. xi. 7. In a peculiar use of the word, occasioned by the employment of the term κατάκριμα (in vs. 1), Paul says, Ro. viii. 3, ὁ θεὸς κατέκρινε τὴν ἁμαρτίαν ἐν τῇ σαρκί, i. e. through his Son, who partook of human nature but was without sin, God deprived sin (which is the ground of the κατάκριμα) of its power in human nature (looked at in the general), broke its deadly sway, (just as the condemnation and punishment of wicked men puts an end to their power to injure or do harm). [(From Pind. and Hdt. down.)]*

2633 **κατά-κρισις, -εως, ἡ**, (κατακρίνω), condemnation: 2 Co. iii. 9 (see διακονία, 2 a.); πρὸς κατάκρισιν, in order to condemn, 2 Co. vii. 3. (Not found in prof. auth.)*

2634 **κατά-κυριεύω**; 1 aor. ptcp. κατακυριεύσας; (κατά [q. v. III. 3] under); **a.** to bring under one's power, to subject to one's self, to subdue, master: τινός, Acts xix. 16 (Diod. 14, 64; for כָּבַשׁ Gen. i. 28; Sir. xvii. 4). **b.** to hold in subjection, to be master of, exercise lordship over: τινός, Mt. xx. 25; Mk. x. 42; 1 Pet. v. 3; (of the benign government of God, Jer. iii. 14). *

2635 **κατα-λαλέω, -ῶ**; to speak against one, to criminate, traduce: τινός (in class. Grk. mostly w. the acc.; in the Sept. chiefly foll. by κατά τινος), Jas. iv. 11; 1 Pet. ii. 12; iii. 16 [here T Tr mrg. WH ἐν ᾧ καταλαλεῖσθε, wherein ye are spoken against].*

2636 **κατα-λαλιά, -ᾶς, ἡ**, (κατάλαλος, q. v.), defamation, evil-speaking: 2 Co. xii. 20; 1 Pet. ii. 1, [on the plur. cf. W. 176 (166); B. 77 (67)]. (Sap. i. 11; Clem. Rom. 1 Cor. 30, 1; 35, 5, and eccl. writ.; not found in class. Grk.) *

2637 **κατά-λαλος, -ον, ὁ**, a defamer, evil speaker, [A. V. backbiters]: Ro. i. 30. (Found nowhere else [Herm. sim. 6, 5, 5; also as adj. 8, 7, 2; 9, 26, 7].)*

2638 **κατα-λαμβάνω**: 2 aor. κατέλαβον; pf. inf. κατειληφέναι; Pass., pf. 3 pers. sing. κατείληπται (Jn. viii. 4 as given in L T Tr WH txt.), pf. ptcp. κατειλημμένος; 1 aor. κατειλήφθην (Jn. viii. 4 R^st bez els G) [on the augm. cf. W. § 12, 6], and κατελήφθην (Phil. iii. 12 R G), and κατελήμφθην (ibid. L T Tr WH; on the μ see s. v. M, μ); Mid., pres. καταλαμβάνομαι; 2 aor. κατελαβόμην; cf. Kühner i. p. 856; [Veitch, s. v. λαμβάνω]; Sept. for לְכַד, also for מָצָא, etc.; [fr. Hom. down]; to lay hold of; i. e. **1.** to lay hold of so as to make one's own, to obtain, attain to: w. the acc. of the thing; the prize of victory, 1 Co. ix. 24; Phil. iii. 12 sq.; τὴν δικαιοσύνην, Ro. ix. 30; i. q. to make one's own, to take into one's self, appropriate: ἡ σκοτία αὐτό (i. e. τὸ φῶς) οὐ κατέλαβεν, Jn. i. 5. **2.** to seize upon, take possession of, (Lat. occupare); **a.** of evils overtaking one (so in Grk. writ. fr. Hom. down): τινά, σκοτία, Jn. xii. 35; [so physically, Jn. vi. 17 Tdf.]; of the last day overtaking the wicked with destruction, 1 Th. v. 4; of a demon about to torment one, Mk. ix. 18. **b.** in a good sense, of Christ by his holy power and influence laying hold of the human mind and will, in order to prompt and govern it, Phil. iii. 12. **3.** to detect, catch: τινὰ ἔν τινι, in pass. Jn. viii. 3 [WH ἐπί τ.]; with a ptcp. indicating the crime, ib. 4. **4.** to lay hold of with the mind;

to understand, perceive, learn, comprehend, (Plat. Phaedr. p. 250 d.; Axioch. p. 370 a.; Polyb. 8, 4, 6; Philo, vita contempl. § 10; Dion. Hal. antt. 5, 46); Mid. (Dion. Hal. antt. 2, 66; [cf. W. 253 (238)]), foll. by ὅτι, Acts iv. 13; x. 34; foll. by the acc. w. inf., Acts xxv. 25; foll. by indir. disc., Eph. iii. 18.*

2639 κατα-λέγω: pres. pass. impv. καταλεγέσθω; **1.** prop. to lay down; mid. to lie down (Hom.). **2.** to narrate at length, recount, set forth, [fr. Hom. on]. **3.** to set down in a list or register, to enroll, (esp. soldiers; see Passow s. v. 5; [L. and S. s. v. II. 2 (yet the latter connect this use with the signif. to choose)]) : of those widows who held a prominent place in the church and exercised a certain superintendence over the rest of the women, and had charge of the widows and orphans supported at public expense, 1 Tim. v. 9 [W. 590 (549)]; cf. De Wette [or Ellicott] ad loc.*

2640 κατά-λειμμα, -τος, τό, (καταλείπω), a remnant, remains: Ro. ix. 27 R G, where it is equiv. to a few, a small part; see ὑπόλειμμα. (Sept., Galen.) *

2641 κατα-λείπω; fut. καταλείψω; 1 aor. κατέλειψα (in later auth.; cf. Lob. ad Phryn. p. 713 sqq.; [Veitch s. v. λείπω; WH. App. p. 169 sq.]); 2 aor. κατέλιπον; Pass., pres. καταλείπομαι; pf. ptcp. καταλελειμμένος [WH -λιμμένος, see (their App. p. 154ᵇ, and) s. v. Ι, ι]; 1 aor. κατελείφθην; (see κατά, III. 5); Sept. for הוֹתִיר, הִשְׁאִיר, עָזַב; [fr. Hom. down]; to leave behind; with acc. of place or pers.; **a.** i. q. to depart from, leave, a pers. or thing: Mt. iv. 13; xvi. 4; xxi. 17; Heb. xi. 27; metaph. εὐθεῖαν ὁδόν, to forsake true religion, 2 Pet. ii. 15. pass. to be left: Jn. viii. 9; i. q. to remain, foll. by ἐν with dat. of place, 1 Th. iii. 1. **b.** i. q. to bid (one) to remain: τινά in a place, Acts xviii. 19; Tit. i. 5 [R G; al. ἀπολείπω]. **c.** to forsake, leave to one's self a pers. or thing, by ceasing to care for it, to abandon, leave in the lurch: τὸν πατέρα κ. τὴν μητέρα, Mt. xix. 5; Mk. x. 7; Eph. v. 31, fr. Gen. ii. 24; pass. to be abandoned, forsaken: εἰς ᾅδου [or ᾅδην (q. v. 2)], Acts ii. 31 Rec. (see ἐγκαταλείπω, 1); w. acc. of the thing, Mk. xiv. 52; Lk. [v. 28]; xv. 4; τὸν λόγον, to neglect the office of instruction, Acts vi. 2. **d.** to cause to be left over, to reserve, to leave remaining: ἐμαυτῷ, Ro. xi. 4 (1 K. xix. 18); καταλείπεται, there still remains, ἐπαγγελία, a promise (to be made good by the event), Heb. iv. 1 (μάχη, Xen. Cyr. 2, 3, 11; σωτηρίας ἐλπίς, Joseph. b. j. 4, 5, 4); τινά with inf. (to leave any business to be done by one alone), Lk. x. 40. **e.** like our leave behind, it is used of one who on being called away cannot take another with him: Acts xxiv. 27; xxv. 14; spec. of the dying (to leave behind), Mk. xii. 19, [21 L mrg. T Tr WH]; Lk. xx. 31, [Deut. xxviii. 54]; Prov. xx. 7; and often in Grk. writ. fr. Hom. Il. 24, 726; Od. 21, 33 on). **f.** like our leave i. q. leave alone, disregard: of those who sail past a place without stopping, Acts xxi. 3. [Comp.: ἐγ-κατα-λείπω.] *

2642 κατα-λιθάζω: fut. καταλιθάσω; (see κατά, III. 3 [cf. W. 102 (97)]); to overwhelm with stones, to stone: Lk. xx. 6. (Eccles. writ.) *

2643 κατ-αλλαγή, -ῆς, ἡ, (καταλλάσσω, q. v.); **1.** ex-

change; of the business of money-changers, exchanging equiv. values [(Aristot., al.)]. Hence **2.** adjustment of a difference, reconciliation, restoration to favor, [fr. Aeschyl. on]; in the N. T., of the restoration of the favor of God to sinners that repent and put their trust in the expiatory death of Christ: 2 Co. v. 18 sq.; w. the gen. of the one received into favor, τοῦ κόσμου (opp. to ἀποβολή), Ro. xi. 15; καταλλαγὴν ἐλάβομεν, we received the blessing of the recovered favor of God, Ro. v. 11; w. the gen. of him whose favor is recovered, 2 Macc. v. 20. [Cf. Trench § lxxvii.] *

2644 κατ-αλλάσσω; 1 aor. ptcp. καταλλάξας; 2 aor. pass. κατηλλάγην; prop. to change, exchange, as coins for others of equal value; hence to reconcile (those who are at variance): τινάς, as τοὺς Θηβαίους καὶ τοὺς Πλαταιέας, Hdt. 6, 108; κατήλλαξάν σφεας οἱ Πάριοι, 5, 29; Aristot. oecon. 2, 15, 9 [p. 1348ᵇ, 9] κατήλλαξεν αὐτοὺς πρὸς ἀλλήλους; pass. τινί, to return into favor with, be reconciled to, one, Eur. Iph. Aul. 1157; Plat. rep. 8 p. 566 e.; πρὸς ἀλλήλους, Thuc. 4, 59; but the Pass. is used also where only one ceases to be angry with another and receives him into favor; thus καταλλαγείς, received by Cyrus into favor, Xen. an. 1, 6, 1; καταλλάττεται πρὸς αὐτήν, regained her favor, Joseph. antt. 5, 2, 8; and, on the other hand, God is said καταλλαγῆναί τινι, with whom he ceases to be offended, to whom he grants his favor anew, whose sins he pardons, 2 Macc. i. 5; vii. 33; viii. 29; Joseph. antt. 6, 7, 4 cf. 7, 8, 4, (so ἐπικαταλλάττεσθαί τινι, Clem. Rom. 1 Cor. 48, 1). In the N. T. God is said καταλλάσσειν ἑαυτῷ τινα, to receive one into his favor, [A. V. reconcile one to himself], 2 Co. v. 18 sq. (where in the added ptcps. two arguments are adduced which prove that God has done this: first, that he does not impute to men their trespasses; second, that he has deposited the doctrine of reconciliation in the souls of the preachers of the gospel); καταλλαγῆναι τῷ θεῷ, to be restored to the favor of God, to recover God's favor, Ro. v. 10 [but see ἐχθρός, 2]; καταλλάγητε τῷ θεῷ, allow yourselves to be reconciled to God; do not oppose your return into his favor, but lay hold of that favor now offered you, 2 Co. v. 20. of a woman: καταλλαγήτω τῷ ἀνδρί, let her return into harmony with [A. V. be reconciled to] her husband, 1 Co. vii. 11. Cf. Fritzsche on Rom. vol. i. p. 276 sqq. [who shows (in opp. to Tittmann, N. T. Syn. i. 102, et al.) that καταλλάσσω and διαλλάσσω are used promiscuously; the prepp. merely intensify (in slightly different modes) the meaning of the simple verb, and there is no evidence that one compound is stronger than the other; διαλλ. and its derivatives are more common in Attic, καταλλ. and its derivatives in later writers. Comp.: ἀπο-κατ-αλλάσσω.] *

2645 κατά-λοιπος, -ον, (λοιπός), left remaining: [οἱ κατάλοιποι τ. ἀνθρώπων A. V. the residue of men], Acts xv. 17. (Plat., Aristot., Polyb.; Sept.) *

2646 κατά-λυμα, -τος, τό, (fr. καταλύω, c.; q. v.), an inn, lodging-place: Lk. ii. 7 (for מָלוֹן, Ex. iv. 24); an eating-room, dining-room, [A.V. guest-chamber]: Mk. xiv. 14; Lk. xxii. 11; in the same sense for לִשְׁכָּה, 1 S. ix. 22. (Polyb. 2,

36, 1 [plur.]; 32, 19, 2; Diod. 14, 93, 5; [al.; cf. W. 25, 93 (89)].)*

2647   **κατα-λύω**; fut. καταλύσω; 1 aor. κατέλυσα; 1 aor. pass. κατελύθην; 1 fut. pass. 3 pers. sing. καταλυθήσεται; *to dissolve, disunite,* [see κατά, III. 4];   **a.** (what has been joined together) i. q. *to destroy, demolish:* λίθους [A. V. *throw down*], Mt. xxiv. 2; Mk. xiii. 2; Lk. xxi. 6; τὸν ναόν, Mt. xxvi. 61; xxvii. 40; Mk. xiv. 58; xv. 29; Acts vi. 14; οἰκίαν, 2 Co. v. 1; univ. opp. to οἰκοδομεῖν, Gal. ii. 18 (2 Esdr. v. 12; Hom. Il. 9, 24 sq.; 2, 117; τεύχη, Eur. Tro. 819; γέφυραν, Hdian. 8, 4, 4 [2 ed. Bekk.]).   **b.** metaph. *to overthrow* i. e. *render vain, deprive of success, bring to naught:* τὴν βουλὴν ἢ τὸ ἔργον, Acts v. 38 (τὰς ἀπειλάς, 4 Macc. iv. 16); τινά, to render fruitless one's desires, endeavors, etc. ibid. 39 G L T Tr WH (Plat. legg. 4 p. 714 c.); *to subvert, overthrow:* τὸ ἔργον τοῦ θεοῦ (see ἀγαθός, 2), Ro. xiv. 20. As in class. Grk. fr. Hdt. down, of institutions, forms of government, laws, etc., *to deprive of force, annul, abrogate, discard:* τὸν νόμον, Mt. v. 17 (2 Macc. ii. 22; Xen. mem. 4, 4, 14; Isocr. paneg. § 55; Philost. v. Apoll. 4, 40).   **c.** of travellers, *to halt on a journey, to put up, lodge,* (the fig. expression originating in the circumstance that, to put up for the night, the straps and packs of the beasts of burden are unbound and taken off; or, perh. more correctly, fr. the fact that the traveller's garments, tied up when he is on the journey, are unloosed at its end; cf. ἀναλύω, 2): Lk. ix. 12; xix. 7; so in Grk. writ. fr. Thuc., Xen., Plat. down; Sept. for לוּן, Gen. xix. 2; xxiv. 23, 25, etc.; Sir. xiv. 25, 27; xxxvi. 31; [cf. B. 145 (127)].*

2648   **κατα-μανθάνω**; 2 aor. κατέμαθον; met with fr. Hdt. down; esp. freq. in Xen. and Plat.; *to learn thoroughly* [see κατά, III. 1], *examine carefully; to consider well:* τί foll. by πῶς, Mt. vi. 28. (Gen. xxiv. 21; Job xxxv. 5, etc.; παρθένον, Sir. ix. 5; κάλλος ἀλλότριον, ibid. 8.)*

2649   **κατα-μαρτυρέω, -ῶ**; *to bear witness against:* τί τινος, testify a thing against one [B. 165 (144), cf. 178 (154)], Mt. xxvi. 62; xxvii. 13; Mk. xiv. 60, and R G in xv. 4. (1 K. xx. (xxi.) 10, 13; Job xv. 6; among Grk. writ. esp. by the Attic orators.)*

2650   **κατα-μένω**; *to remain* permanently, *to abide:* Acts i. 13. (Num. xxii. 8; Judith xvi. 20; Arstph., Xen., Philo de gigant. § 5.)*

2651   **καταμόνας**, and (as it is now usually written [so L T Tr WH]) separately, κατὰ μόνας (sc. χώρας), *apart, alone:* Mk. iv. 10; Lk. ix. 18. (Thuc. 1, 32. 37; Xen. mem. 3, 7, 4; Joseph. antt. 18, 3, 4; Sept. for בָּדָד and לְבָדָד, Ps. iv. 9; Jer. xv. 17, etc.)*

2652; see――**κατ-ανά-θεμα**, -τος, τό, once in Rev. xxii. 3 Rec.; see
(2616α)   ἀνάθεμα and κατάθεμα. Not found in prof. auth.*

2653; see――**κατ-ανα-θεματίζω**, (κατανάθεμα, q. v.); i. q. καταθεμα-
(2616b)   τίζω (q. v.)· Mt. xxvi. 74 Rec. (Just. M. dial. c. Tr. c. 47, and other eccl. writ.)*

2654   **κατ-αν-αλίσκω**, (see ἀναλίσκω, and κατά, III. 4); *to consume:* of fire, Heb. xii. 29 after Deut. iv. 24; ix. 3. (In Grk. writ. fr. Xen. and Plat. down; Sept. several times for אָכַל.)*

2655   **κατα-ναρκάω, -ῶ**: fut. καταναρκήσω; 1 aor. κατενάρκησα;

(ναρκάω to become numb, torpid; in Sept. trans. to affect with numbness, make torpid, Gen. xxxii. 25, 32; Job xxxiii. 19; fr. νάρκη torpor); prop. *to cause to grow numb or torpid;* intrans. *to be torpid, inactive,* to the detriment of one; *to weigh heavily upon, be burdensome to:* τινός (gen. of pers.), 2 Co. xi. 9 (8); xii. 13 sq. (Hesych. κατενάρκησα· κατεβάρησα [al. ἐβάρυνα]); Jerome, ad Algas. 10 [(iv. 204 ed. Benedict.)], discovers a Cilicism in this use of the word [cf. W. 27]. Among prof. auth. used by Hippocr. alone, and in a pass. sense, *to be quite numb or stiff.*

κατα-νεύω; 1 aor. κατένευσα; fr. Hom. down; *to nod*   **2656** *to, make a sign to:* τινί, foll. by τοῦ w. aor. inf., to indicate to another by a nod or sign what one wishes him to do [A. V. *beckoned to . . . that they should come,* etc.], Lk. v. 7.*

κατα-νοέω, -ῶ; impf. κατενόουν; 1 aor. κατενόησα; fr.   **2657** Hdt. down; Sept. here and there for הִבִּיט, הִתְבּוֹנֵן, רָאָה;   **1.** *to perceive, remark, observe, understand:* τί, Mt. vii. 3; Lk. vi. 41; xx. 23; Acts xxvii. 39.   **2.** *to consider attentively, fix one's eyes* or *mind upon:* τί, Lk. xii. 24, 27; Acts xi. 6; Ro. iv. 19; w. the acc. of the thing omitted, as being understood fr. the context, Acts vii. 31 sq.; τινά, Heb. iii. 1; x. 24; Jas. i. 23 sq.*

κατ-αντάω, -ῶ: 1 aor. κατήντησα; pf. κατήντηκα (1 Co.   **2658** x. 11 L T Tr WH); *to come to, arrive at;*   **a.** prop.: foll. by εἰς w. acc. of place, Acts xvi. 1; xviii. 19, 24; xxi. 7; xxv. 13; xxvii. 12; xxviii. 13, (2 Macc. iv. 44); ἀντικρύ τινος, to a place over against, opposite another, Acts xx. 15; εἴς τινα τὰ τέλη τῶν αἰώνων κατήντηκεν, i. e. whose lifetime occurs at the ends of the ages, 1 Co. x. 11.   **b.** metaph. εἴς τι, like the Lat. *ad aliquid pervenio,* i. e. *to attain to* a thing: Acts xxvi. 7; Eph. iv. 13; Phil. iii. 11; καταντᾷ τι εἴς τινα, to one, that he may become partaker of it, 1 Co. xiv. 36. (Polyb., Diod.; eccl. writ.)*

κατά-νυξις, -εως, ἡ, (κατανύσσω, q. v.);   **1.** *a prick-*   **2659** *ing, piercing,* (Vulg. *compunctio*)   **2.** *severe sorrow, extreme grief.*   **3.** *insensibility* or *torpor of mind,* such as extreme grief easily produces; hence πνεῦμα κατανύξεως, *a spirit of stupor,* which renders their souls torpid, i. e. so insensible that they are not affected by all the offer made them of salvation through the Messiah, Ro. xi. 8 fr. Is. xxix. 10 Sept. (where the Hebr. רוּחַ תַּרְדֵּמָה, a spirit of *deep sleep,* is somewhat loosely so rendered; οἶνος κατανύξεως for יַיִן תַּרְעֵלָה, wine which produces dizziness, reeling, Germ. *Taumelwein,* Ps. lix. (lx.) 5). Not found in prof. auth. Cf. Fritzsche's full discussion of the word in his Com. on Rom. vol. ii. p. 558 sqq.; [cf. W. 94 (90); Bp. *Lghtft.* 'Fresh Revision' etc. p. 139 note].*

κατα-νύσσω: 2 aor. pass. κατενύγην [B. 63 (55)]; *to*   **2660** *prick, pierce;* metaph. *to pain the mind sharply, agitate it vehemently:* used esp. of the emotion of sorrow; κατενύγησαν τῇ καρδίᾳ (τὴν καρδίαν L T Tr WH), they were smitten in heart with poignant sorrow [A. V. lit. *pricked*], Acts ii. 37 (κατενενυγμένον τῇ καρδίᾳ, Ps. cviii. (cix.) 16; add, Gen. xxxiv. 7; Sir. xii. 12; xiv. 1, etc.; of lust, Sus.

10; of violent pity, Joann. Malal. chronogr. 1, 18, ed. Bonn. p. 460). Cf. Fritzsche on Rom. ii. p. 558 sqq.*

2661 κατ-αξιόω, -ῶ: 1 aor. pass. κατηξιώθην; *to account worthy, judge worthy*: τινά τινος, one of a thing, 2 Th. i. 5 (Polyb. 1, 23, 3, etc.; Diod. 2, 60; Joseph. antt. 15, 3, 8); foll. by an inf., Lk. xx. 35; xxi. 36 [T Tr txt. WH κατισχύσητε]; Acts v. 41, (Dem. 1383, 11 [cf. Plat. Tim. 30 c.]).*

2662 κατα-πατέω, -ῶ; fut. καταπατήσω (Mt. vii. 6 L T Tr WH); 1 aor. κατεπάτησα; Pass., pres. καταπατοῦμαι; 1 aor. κατεπατήθην; *to tread down* [see κατά, III. 1], *trample under foot*: τί and τινά, Mt. v. 13; vii. 6; Lk. viii. 5; xii. 1, (Hdt. et sqq.; Sept.); metaph., like the Lat. *conculco, to trample on* i. q. *to treat with rudeness and insult,* 2 Macc. viii. 2, etc.; cf. Grimm on 1 Macc. p. 61 [where its use to denote desecration is illustrated]; *to spurn, treat with insulting neglect*: τὸν υἱὸν τοῦ θεοῦ, Heb. x. 29; ὅρκια, Hom. Il. 4, 157; τοὺς νόμους, Plat. legg. 4, 714 a.; τὰ γράμματα, Gorg. p. 484 a.; τοὺς λόγους, Epict. 1, 8, 10; τὰ ῥήματά μου, Job vi. 3 Aq.*

2663 κατά-παυσις, -εως, ἡ, (καταπαύω, q. v.); **1.** actively, *a putting to rest*: τῶν πνευμάτων, a calming of the winds, Theophr. de ventis 18; τυράννων, removal from office, Hdt. 5, 38. **2.** In the Grk. Scriptures (Sept. several times for מְנוּחָה) intrans. *a resting, rest*: ἡμέρα τῆς καταπ. the day of rest, the sabbath, 2 Macc. xv. 1; τόπος τῆς καταπ. μου, where I may rest, Acts vii. 49. Metaph. ἡ κατάπ. τοῦ θεοῦ, the heavenly blessedness in which God dwells, and of which he has promised to make persevering believers in Christ partakers after the toils and trials of life on earth are ended: Heb. iii. 11, 18; iv. 1, 3, 5, 10 sq., (after Ps. xciv. (xcv.) 11, where the expression denotes the fixed and tranquil abode promised to the Israelites in the land of Palestine).*

2664 κατα-παύω: 1 aor. κατέπαυσα; (κατά, like the Germ. *nieder*, down); **1.** trans. (Sept. for הֵנִיחַ, הִשְׁבִּית) *to make quiet, to cause to be at rest, to grant rest*; i. e. **a.** *to lead to a quiet abode*: τινά, Heb. iv. 8 (Ex. xxxiii. 14; Deut. iii. 20; v. 33; xii. 10; Josh. i. 13, 15; 2 Chr. xiv. 7; xxxii. 22; Sir. xxiv. 11). **b.** *to still, restrain, to cause* (one striving to do something) *to desist*: foll. by τοῦ μή and an inf., Acts xiv. 18 [cf. B. § 140, 16 β.; W. 325 (305)]. **2.** intrans. *to rest, take rest* (Hebr. נוּחַ, שָׁבַת): ἀπό τινος, Heb. iv. 4, 10, (Gen. ii. 2). In the same and other senses in Grk. writ. fr. Hom. down.*

2665 κατα-πέτασμα, -τος, τό, (καταπετάννυμι *to spread out over, to cover*), an Alex. Grk. word for παραπέτασμα, which the other Greeks use fr. Hdt. down; *a veil spread out, a curtain,* — the name given in the Grk. Scriptures, as well as in the writings of Philo and Josephus, to the two curtains in the temple at Jerusalem (τὰ καταπετάσματα, 1 Macc. iv. 51; [yet cf. *Edersheim*, Jesus the Messiah, ii. 611]): one of them (Hebr. מָסָךְ) at the entrance of the temple separated the Holy place from the outer court (Ex. xxvi. 37; xxxviii. 18; Num. iii. 26; Joseph. b. j. 5, 5, 4; it is called also τὸ κάλυμμα by the Sept. and Philo, Ex. xxvii. 16; Num. iii. 25; Philo, vit. Moys. iii. §§ 5 and 9), the other veiled the Holy of holies from the Holy place (in Hebr. the פָּרֹכֶת; ἐνδότερον κα-

ταπέτασμα, Joseph. antt. 8, 3, 3; τὸ ἐσώτατον καταπέτασμα Philo de gig. § 12; by the Sept. and Philo this is called pre-eminently τὸ καταπέτασμα, Ex. xxvi. 31 sqq.; Lev. xxi. 23; xxiv. 3; Philo, vit. Moys. u. s.). This latter καταπέτασμα is the only one mentioned in the N. T.: τὸ καταπέτασμα τοῦ ναοῦ, Mt. xxvii. 51; Mk. xv. 38; Lk. xxiii. 45; τὸ δεύτερον καταπέτασμα, Heb. ix. 3; τὸ ἐσώτερον τοῦ καταπετάσματος (cf. Lev. xvi. 2, 12, 15; Ex. xxvi. 33) *the space more inward than the veil*, equiv. to 'the space within the veil,' i. e. the Holy of holies, figuratively used of heaven, as the true abode of God, Heb. vi. 19; in a similar figurative way the body of Christ is called καταπέτασμα, in (Heb.) x. 20, because, as the veil had to be removed in order that the high-priest might enter the most holy part of the earthly temple, so the body of Christ had to be removed by his death on the cross, that an entrance might be opened into the fellowship of God in heaven.*

2666 κατα-πίνω; 2 aor. κατέπιον; 1 aor. pass. κατεπόθην; [fr. Hes. and Hdt. down]; prop. *to drink down, swallow down*: Mt. xxiii. 24; Rev. xii. 16; *to devour*, 1 Pet. v. 8 [here Tr -πίειν by mistake; (see πίνω, init.)]; *to swallow up, destroy*, pass., 1 Co. xv. 54; 2 Co. v. 4; Heb. xi. 29; trop. λύπῃ καταποθῆναι, to be consumed with grief, 2 Co. ii. 7.*

2667 κατα-πίπτω; 2 aor. κατέπεσον; [fr. Hom. down]; *to fall down*: Acts xxviii. 6; εἰς τὴν γῆν, Acts xxvi. 14; ἐπὶ τὴν πέτραν, Lk. viii. 6 T Tr WH.*

2668 κατα-πλέω; 1 aor. κατέπλευσα; [fr. Hom. on]; *to sail down* from the deep sea to land; *to put in*: εἰς τὴν χώραν, Lk. viii. 26.*

2669 κατα-πονέω, -ῶ: pres. pass. ptcp. καταπονούμενος; prop. *to tire down with toil, exhaust with labor*; hence *to afflict* or *oppress with evils*; *to make trouble for*; *to treat roughly*: τινά, in pass., Acts vii. 24; 2 Pet. ii. 7 [R. V. *sore distressed*]. (3 Macc. ii. 2, 13; Hippocr., Theophr., Polyb., Diod., Joseph., Aelian., al.) *

2670 κατα-ποντίζω: Pass., pres. καταποντίζομαι; 1 aor. κατεποντίσθην; *to plunge* or *sink in the sea*; Pass. in the intrans. sense, *to sink, to go down*: Mt. xiv. 30; a grievous offender for the purpose of killing him, *to drown*: pass. Mt. xviii. 6. (Lys., Dem., Polyb., Diod., Plut., [Joseph. antt. 10, 7, 5; 14, 15, 10; c. Apion. 2, 34, 3], al.; Sept.; [cf. W. 24; *Lob.* Phryn. p. 361 note].) *

2671 κατ-άρα, -ας, ἡ, (κατά and ἀρά, cf. Germ. *Verfluchung, Verwünschung*, [cf. κατά, III. 4]); Sept. chiefly for קְלָלָה; *an execration, imprecation, curse*: opp. to εὐλογία (q. v.), Jas. iii. 10; γῆ κατάρας ἐγγύς, near to being cursed by God i. e. to being given up to barrenness (the allusion is to Gen. iii. 17 sq.), Heb. vi. 8; ὑπὸ κατάραν εἶναι, to be under a curse i. e. liable to the appointed penalty of being cursed, Gal. iii. 10; ἐξαγοράζειν τινὰ ἐκ τῆς κ. to redeem one exposed to the threatened penalty of a curse, ib. 13; τέκνα κατάρας, men worthy of execration, 2 Pet. ii. 14; abstract for the concrete, one in whom the curse is exhibited, i. e. undergoing the appointed penalty of cursing, Gal. iii. 13; ἐγὼ κατάρα ἐγενήθην, Protev. Jac. c. 3. (Aeschyl., Eur., Plat., al.) *

2672 κατ-αράομαι, -ῶμαι; (dep. mid. fr. κατάρα); 1 aor. 2 pers. sing. κατηράσω; [pf. pass. ptcp. κατηραμένος (see below)]; fr. Hom. down; Sept. mostly for קלל and אָרַר; *to curse, doom, imprecate evil on*: (opp. to εὐλογεῖν) absol. Ro. xii. 14; w. dat. of the obj. (as in the earlier Grk. writ.), Lk. vi. 28 Rec. (Bar. vi. [Ep. Jer. 65] 66; [Joseph. c. Ap. 1, 22, 16]); w. acc. of the obj. (as often in the later Grk. writ., as Plut. Cat. min. 32, 1 var. [B. § 133, 9; W. 222 (208)]), Mt. v. 44 Rec.; Lk. vi. 28 G Ltxt. T Tr WH; Jas. iii. 9; *a tree*, i. e. to wither it by cursing, Mk. xi. 21 (see Heb. vi. 8 in κατάρα). pf. pass. ptcp. κατηραμένος in a pass. sense, *accursed* (Sap. xii. 11; [2 K. ix. 34]; Plut. Luc. 18; and κεκατηραμ. Deut. xxi. 23; [Sir. iii. 16]): Mt. xxv. 41 (also occasionally κεκατάρανται, Num. xxii. 6; xxiv. 9; [but Tdf. etc. -ήρ-; see Veitch s. v. ἀράομαι]).*

2673 κατ-αργέω, -ῶ; fut. καταργήσω; 1 aor. κατήργησα; pf. κατήργηκα; Pass., pres. καταργοῦμαι; pf. κατήργημαι; 1 aor. κατηργήθην; 1 fut. καταργηθήσομαι; causative of the verb ἀργέω, equiv. to ἀργὸν (i. e. ἄεργον [on the accent cf. Chandler § 444]) ποιῶ; freq. with Paul, who uses it 25 times [elsewhere in N. T. only twice (Lk., Heb.), in Sept. 4 times (2 Esdr., see below)]; **1.** *to render idle, unemployed, inactive, inoperative*: τὴν γῆν, to deprive of its strength, make barren [A. V. *cumber*], Lk. xiii. 7; to cause a pers. or a thing to have no further efficiency; to deprive of force, influence, power, [A. V. *bring to nought, make of none effect*]: τί, Ro. iii. 3; 1 Co. i. 28; τινά, 1 Co. ii. 6 [but in pass.]; diabolic powers, 1 Co. xv. 24 (Justin, apol. 2, 6); Antichrist, 2 Th. ii. 8; τὸν θάνατον, 2 Tim. i. 10 (Barnab. ep. 5, 6); τὸν διάβολον, Heb. ii. 14; pass. 1 Co. xv. 26; to make void, τὴν ἐπαγγελίαν, Gal. iii. 17; pass. Ro. iv. 14. **2.** *to cause to cease, put an end to, do away with, annul, abolish*: τί, 1 Co. vi. 13; xiii. 11; τὸν νόμον, Ro. iii. 31; Eph. ii. 15; τὸν καιρὸν τοῦ ἀνόμου, Barnab. ep. 15, 5; pass. πόλεμος καταργεῖται ἐπουρανίων καὶ ἐπιγείων, Ignat. ad Eph. 13, 2; ἵνα καταργηθῇ τὸ σῶμα τῆς ἁμαρτίας, that the body of sin might be done away, i. e. not the material of the body, but the body so far forth as it is an instrument of sin; accordingly, that the body may cease to be an instrument of sin, Ro. vi. 6. Pass. *to cease, pass away, be done away*: of things, Gal. v. 11; 1 Co. xiii. 8, 10; 2 Co. iii. 7, 11, 13 sq.; of persons, foll. by ἀπό τινος, *to be severed from, separated from, discharged from, loosed from*, any one; *to terminate all intercourse with* one [a pregn. constr., cf. W. 621 (577); B. 322 (277)]: ἀπὸ τοῦ Χριστοῦ, Gal. v. 4 [on the aor. cf. W. § 40, 5 b.]; ἀπὸ τοῦ νόμου, Ro. vii. [2 (Rᵉˡˢ om. τ. ν.)], 6. The word is rarely met with in prof. auth., as Eur. Phoen. 753 καταργῶ. χέρα, to make idle, i. e. to leave the hand unemployed; Polyb. ap. Suid. [s. v. κατηργηκέναι] τοὺς καιρούς, in the sense of *to let slip, leave unused*; in Sept. four times for Chald. בְּטַל, to make to cease, i. e. restrain, check, hinder, 2 Esdr. iv. 21, 23; v. 5; vi. 8.*

2674 κατ-αριθμέω, -ῶ: *to number with*: pf. pass. ptcp. κατηριθμημένος ἐν (for Rec. σὺν) ἡμῖν, *was numbered among us*, Acts i. 17; cf. 2 Chr. xxxi. 19; [Plat. politicus 266 a. etc.].*

2675 κατ-αρτίζω; fut. καταρτίσω (1 Pet. v. 10 L T Tr WH [B. 37 (32); but Rec. καταρτίσαι, 1 aor. optat. 3 pers. sing.]); 1 aor. inf. καταρτίσαι; Pass., pres. καταρτίζομαι; pf. κατήρτισμαι; 1 aor. mid. 2 pers. sing. κατηρτίσω; prop. *to render ἄρτιος* i. e. *fit, sound, complete*, [see κατά, III. 2]; hence **a.** *to mend* (what has been broken or rent), *to repair*: τὰ δίκτυα, Mt. iv. 21; Mk. i. 19, [al. ref. these exx. to next head]; i. q. *to complete*, τὰ ὑστερήματα, 1 Th. iii. 10. **b.** *to fit out, equip, put in order, arrange, adjust*: τοὺς αἰῶνας, the worlds, pass. Heb. xi. 3 (so, for הֵכִין, ἥλιον, Ps. lxxiii. (lxxiv.) 16; σελήνην, lxxxviii. (lxxxix.) 38); σκεύη κατηρτισμένα εἰς ἀπώλειαν, of men whose souls God has so constituted that they cannot escape destruction [but see Mey. (ed. Weiss) in loc.], Ro. ix. 22 (πλοῖα, Polyb. 5, 46, 10, and the like); of the mind: κατηρτισμένοι ὡς etc. so instructed, equipped, as etc. [cf. B. 311 (267); but al. take κατηρτ. as a circumstantial ptcp. *when perfected* shall be as (not 'above') his master (see Mey. in loc.); on this view the passage may be referred to the next head], Lk. vi. 40; mid. *to fit* or *frame for one's self, prepare*: αἶνον, Mt. xxi. 16 (fr. Ps. viii. 3; Sept. for יָסַד); σῶμα, Heb. x. 5. **c.** ethically, *to strengthen, perfect, complete, make one what he ought to be*: τινά, [1 Pet. v. 10 (see above)]; Gal. vi. 1 (of one who by correction may be brought back into the right way); pass. 2 Co. xiii. 11; τινὰ ἐν παντὶ ἔργῳ [(T WH om.)] ἀγαθῷ, Heb. xiii. 21; κατηρτισμένοι ἐν τῷ αὐτῷ νοΐ κτλ. of those who have been restored to harmony (so πάντα εἰς τωὐτό, Hdt. 5, 106; ἵνα καταρτισθῇ ἡ στασιάζουσα πόλις, Dion. Hal. antt. 3, 10), 1 Co. i. 10. [Comp.: προ-καταρτίζω.] *

2676 κατ-άρτισις, -εως, ἡ, (καταρτίζω, q. v.), *a strengthening, perfecting*, of the soul, (Vulg. *consummatio*): 2 Co. xiii. 9. (*a training, disciplining, instructing*, Plut. Them. 2, 7 [var.]; Alex. 7, 1.)*

see 2677 St. καταρτισμός, -οῦ, ὁ, i. q. κατάρτισις, q. v.: τινὸς εἴς τι, Eph. iv. 12. [(Galen, al.)]*

2678 κατα-σείω; 1 aor. κατέσεισα; **1.** *to shake down, throw down*, [cf. κατά, III. 1; (fr. Thuc. on)]. **2.** *to shake*: τὴν χεῖρα, to make a sign by shaking (i. e. rapidly waving) the hand (Philo, leg. ad Gaium § 28; τὰς χεῖρας, ib. de Josepho § 36); of one about to speak who signals for silence, Acts xix. 33; hence simply κατασείειν τινί, to make a sign, to signal with the hand *to one*, Xen. Cyr. 5, 4, 4; Joseph. antt. 8, 11, 2; then, with a disregard of the origin of the phrase, the instrument. dat. τῇ χειρί was added, Polyb. 1, 78, 3; Joseph. antt. 4, 8, 48; so of one about to make an address: Acts xii. 17; xiii. 16; xxi. 40; Joseph. antt. 8, 11, 2.*

2679 κατα-σκάπτω; 1 aor. κατέσκαψα; pf. pass. ptcp. κατεσκαμμένος; *to dig under, dig down, demolish, destroy*: τί, Ro. xi. 3, fr. 1 K. xix. 10; pass. Acts xv. 16 [R G L], fr. Amos ix. 11 [(but see καταστρέφω)]. (Tragg., Thuc., Xen., sqq.).*

2680 κατα-σκευάζω: fut. κατασκευάσω; 1 aor. κατεσκεύασα; Pass., pres. κατασκευάζομαι; pf. ptcp. κατεσκευασμένος; 1 aor. κατεσκευάσθην; *to furnish, equip, prepare, make ready*; **a.** of one who makes any thing ready for a pers. or thing: τὴν ὁδόν, Mt. xi. 10; Mk. i. 2; Lk. vii. 27; pf. pass. ptcp. prepared *in spirit*, Lk. i. 17 (Xen. Cyr. 5, 5, 10). **b.** of builders, *to construct, erect*, with the included idea *of adorning and equipping with all things necessary*, (often so in Grk. auth.; cf. *Bleek*, Brief a. d. Hebr. ii. 1 p. 398 sq.): οἶκον, Heb. iii. 3 sq.; κιβωτόν, Heb. xi. 7; 1 Pet. iii. 20; σκηνήν, Heb. ix. 2, 6; Sept. for בָּרָא, Is. xl. 28; xliii. 7.*

2681 **κατα-σκηνόω**, -ῶ, inf. -σκηνοῖν (Mt. xiii. 32 L T Tr WH, Mk. iv. 32 WH, see ἀποδεκατόω; [but also -σκηνοῦν, Mt. l. c. RG; Mk. l. c. RG L T Tr; cf. *Tdf.* Proleg. p. 123]); fut. κατασκηνώσω; 1 aor. κατεσκήνωσα; prop. *to pitch one's tent, to fix one's abode, to dwell*: ἐφ' ἐλπίδι, Acts ii. 26 fr. Ps. xv. (xvi.) 9; foll. by ἐν w. dat. of place, Mt. xiii. 32; Lk. xiii. 19; ὑπό w. acc. of place, Mk. iv. 32. (Xen., Polyb., Diod., al.; κατεσκήνωσεν ὁ θεὸς τῷ ναῷ τούτῳ, Joseph. antt. 3, 8, 5; add, Sir. xxiv. 4, 8; Sept. mostly for שָׁכַן.) *

2682 **κατα-σκήνωσις**, -εως, ἡ, (κατασκηνόω, q. v.), prop. *the pitching of tents, encamping; place of tarrying, encampment, abode*: of the haunts of birds, Mt. viii. 20; Lk. ix. 58; (for מִשְׁכָּן, Ezek. xxxvii. 27; cf. Sap. ix. 8; Tob. i. 4; Polyb. 11, 26, 5; Diod. 17, 95).*

2683 **κατα-σκιάζω**; *to overshadow, cover with shade*, [see κατά, III. 3]: τί, Heb. ix. 5. (Hes., Eur., Plato, al.; κατασκιάω, Hom. Od. 12, 436.) *

2684 **κατα-σκοπέω**, -ῶ; 1 aor. inf. κατασκοπῆσαι; *to inspect, view closely, in order to spy out and plot against*: τί, Gal. ii. 4; (of a reconnoitre or treacherous examination, 2 S. x. 3; Josh. ii. 2 sq.; 1 Chr. xix. 3; Eur. Hel. 1607 (1623); so used, esp. in mid., in the other Grk. writ. fr. Xen. down).*

2685 **κατά-σκοπος**, -ου, ὁ, (κατασκέπτομαι [i. q. κατασκοπέω]), *an inspector, a spy*: Heb. xi. 31. (Gen. xlii. 9, 11; 1 S. xxvi. 4; 1 Macc. xii. 26; in prof. auth. fr. Hdt. down.) *

2686 **κατα-σοφίζομαι**: 1 aor. ptcp. κατασοφισάμενος; (σοφίζω); dep. mid., in prof. auth. sometimes also pass.; *to circumvent by artifice or fraud, conquer by subtle devices; to outwit, overreach; to deal craftily with*: τινά, Acts vii. 19 fr. Ex. i. 10. (Judith v. 11; x. 19; Diod., Philo, Joseph., Lcian., al.) *

2687 **κατα-στέλλω**: 1 aor. ptcp. καταστείλας; pf. pass. ptcp. κατεσταλμένος; **a.** prop. *to send or put down, to lower.* **b.** *to put or keep down* one who is roused or incensed, *to repress, restrain, appease, quiet*: τινά, Acts xix. 35 sq.; 3 Macc. vi. 1; Joseph. antt. 20, 8, 7; b. j. 4, 4, 4; Plut. mor. p. 207 e.*

2688 **κατά-στημα**, -τος, τό, (καθίστημι), (Lat. *status, habitus*), [*demeanor, deportment, bearing*]: Tit. ii. 3. (3 Macc. v. 45; Joseph. b. j. 1, 1, 4 [of a city; cf. ἀτρεμαίῳ τῷ καταστήματι πρὸς τ. θάνατον ἀπῄει, Joseph. antt. 15, 7, 5; Plut. Marcell. 23, 6; cf. Tib. Gracch. 2, 2. See Wetst. on Tit. l. c.; cf. Ignat. ad Trall. 3, 2 (and Jacobson or Zahn in loc.)].) *

2689 **κατα-στολή**, -ῆς, ἡ, (καταστέλλω, q. v.); **1.** prop. *a lowering, letting down*; hence **2.** in bibl. Grk. twice, *a garment let down, dress, attire*: 1 Tim. ii. 9, Vulg. *habitus*, which the translator, acc. to later Lat.

usage, seems to understand of clothing (cf. the French *l'habit*); [cf. Joseph. b. j. 2, 8, 4]; for מַעֲטֶה, Is. lxi. 3, with which in mind Hesych. says καταστολήν· περιβολήν [cf. W. 23, but esp. Ellicott on 1 Tim. l. c.].*

2690 **κατα-στρέφω**: 1 aor. κατέστρεψα; pf. pass. ptcp. κατεστραμμένος (Acts xv. 16 T [WH, but Tr -στρεμμένος; cf. *WH.* App. p. 170 sq.]); **1.** *to turn over, turn under*: the soil with a plow, Xen. oec. 17, 10. **2.** *to overturn, overthrow, throw down*: τί, Mt. xxi. 12; Mk. xi. 15; [τὰ κατεστρ. *ruins*], Acts xv. 16 T Tr WH [(cf. κατασκάπτω)]; so Hag. ii. 22; Job ix. 5; Joseph. antt. 8, 7, 6; Anthol. 11, 163, 6; Diog. L. 5, 82.*

2691 **κατα-στρηνιάω**: 1 aor. subjunc. καταστρηνιάσω [(fut. 1 Tim. v. 11 Lchm. mrg.)]; (see στρηνιάω); *to feel the impulses of sexual desire*, [A. V. *to grow wanton*]; (Vulg. *luxurior*): τινός, to one's loss [A. V. *against*], 1 Tim. v. 11; Ignat. ad Antioch. c. 11.*

2692 **κατα-στροφή**, -ῆς, ἡ, (καταστρέφω), (Vulg. *subversio*, [*eversio*]), *overthrow, destruction*: of cities, 2 Pet. ii. 6 [WH om. Tr mrg. br. καταστρ.] (Gen. xix. 29); metaph. of the extinction of a spirit of consecration to Christ, [A. V. *the subverting*]: 2 Tim. ii. 14. (Aeschyl. Eum. 490.) *

2693 **κατα-στρώννυμι**: 1 aor. pass. κατεστρώθην; *to strew over* (the ground); *to prostrate, slay*, [cf. our *to lay low*]: 1 Co. x. 5 [A. V. *overthrown*]. ⟨Num. xiv. 16; Judith vii. 14; xiv. 4; 2 Macc. v. 26, etc.; Hdt. 8, 53; 9, 76; Xen. Cyr. 3, 3, 64.) *

2694 **κατα-σύρω**; [fr. Hdt. down]; **1.** prop. *to draw down, pull down*, [see κατά, III. 1]. **2.** *to draw along, drag forcibly*, (τινὰ διὰ μέσης ἀγορᾶς, Philo in Flacc. § 20; leg. ad Gaium § 19): τινὰ πρὸς τὸν κριτήν, Lk. xii. 58. (Cic. pro Mil. c. 14, 38 quom in judicium detrahi non posset.) *

see 2695 St. **κατα-σφάζω** [or -σφάττω]: 1 aor. κατέσφαξα; *to kill off* [cf. κατά, III. 1], *to slaughter*: Lk. xix. 27. (Sept.; Hdt., Tragg., Xen., Joseph. antt. 6, 6, 4; Ael. v. h. 13, 2; Hdian. 5, 5, 16 [8 ed. Bekk.].) *

2696 **κατα-σφραγίζω**: pf. pass. ptcp. κατεσφραγισμένος; *to cover with a seal* [see κατά, III. 3], *to seal up, close with a seal*: βιβλίον σφραγῖσιν, Rev. v. 1. (Job ix. 7; Sap. ii. 5; Aeschyl., Eur., Plat., Plut., Lcian., al.) *

2697 **κατά-σχεσις**, -εως, ἡ, (κατέχω), Sept. often for אֲחֻזָּה, *possession*; **1.** *a holding back, hindering*: anonym. in *Walz*, Rhetor. i. p. 616, 20. **2.** *a holding fast, possession*: γῆν δοῦναι εἰς κατάσχ. to give in possession the land, Acts vii. 5, as in Gen. xvii. 8; Deut. xxxii. 49 Alex.; Ezek. xxxiii. 24; xxxvi. 2 sq. 5; Joseph. antt. 9, 1, 2; [Test. xii. Patr., test. Benj. § 10]; w. gen. of the subj. τῶν ἐθνῶν, of the territory possessed by [*the possession of*] the nations, Acts vii. 45; (a portion given to keep, Philo, rer. div. haer. § 40 [cf. Ps. ii. 8]).*

2698 **κατα-τίθημι**: 1 aor. κατέθηκα; 2 aor. mid. inf. καταθέσθαι; [fr. Hom. down]; *to lay down* [see κατά, III. 1], *deposit, lay up*: act. prop. τινὰ ἐν μνημείῳ, Mk. xv. 46 [L Tr WH ἔθηκεν]; mid. *to lay by* or *lay up for one's self*, for future use: τινί, with any one; χάριν [better -τα; see χάρις, init.] and χάριτας κατατ. τινι, *to lay up favor*

for one's self with any one, to gain favor with (to do something for one which may win favor), Acts xxiv. 27; xxv. 9; so Hdt. 6, 41; Thuc. 1, 33; Xen. Cyr. 8, 3, 26; Dem. 193, 22 (20); φιλίαν τινί, 1 Macc. x. 23; εὐεργεσίαν τινί, Joseph. antt. 11, 6, 5; [cf. Dem. u. s.]. [COMP.: συγκατατίθημι.]*

2699 κατα-τομή, -ῆς, ἡ, (fr. κατατέμνω [cf. κατά, III. 4] to cut up, mutilate), mutilation (Lat. concisio): Phil. iii. 2, where Paul sarcastically alludes to the word περιτομή which follows in vs. 3; as though he would say, Keep your eye on that boasted circumcision, or to call it by its true name 'concision' or 'mutilation.' Cf. the similar passage, Gal. v. 12; see ἀποκόπτω.*

2700 κατα-τοξεύω: 1 fut. pass. κατατοξευθήσομαι; to shoot down or thrust through-with an arrow: τινὰ βολίδι, Heb. xii. 20 Rec. fr. Ex. xix. 13. (Num. xxiv. 8; Ps. x. (xi.) 2; Hdt., Thuc., Xen., al.)*

2701 κατα-τρέχω: 2 aor. κατέδραμον; to run down, hasten down: ἐπί τινας, to quell a tumult, Acts xxi. 32.[Hdt. on.]*

see 826 [κατ-αυγάζω: 1 aor. inf. καταυγάσαι; to beam down upon; to shine forth, shine brightly: 2 Co. iv. 4 L mrg. Tr mrg., where al. αὐγάσαι q. v.; cf. φωτισμός, b.; (trans. Sap. xvii. 5, etc.; intrans. 1 Macc. vi. 39; Heliod. 5, 31).*]

see 2719 καταφάγω, see κατεσθίω.

2702 κατα-φέρω; 1 aor. κατήνεγκα; Pass., pres. καταφέρομαι; 1 aor. κατηνέχθην; [fr. Hom. down]; to bear down, bring down, cast down: ψῆφον, prop. to cast a pebble or calculus sc. into the urn, i. e. to give one's vote, to approve, Acts xxvi. 10; αἰτιώματα κατά τινος (see κατά, I. 2 b. [but the crit. edd. reject κατὰ κτλ.]), Acts xxv. 7 L T Tr WH. Pass. to be borne down, to sink, (from the window to the pavement), ἀπὸ τοῦ ὕπνου, from sleep (from the effect of his deep sleep [cf. B. 322 (277); W. 371 (348)]), Acts xx. 9ᵇ; metaph. to be weighed down by, overcome, carried away, καταφερόμενος ὕπνῳ βαθεῖ, sunk in a deep sleep, Acts xx. 9ᵃ; of a different sort [contra W. 431 (401)] is the expression in prof. auth. καταφέρομαι εἰς ὕπνον, to sink into sleep, drop asleep, Joseph. antt. 2, 5, 5; Hdian. 2, 1, 3 [2]; 9, 6 [5]; τοῖσιν ὕπνοισιν, Hipp. p. 1137 c. [(Kühn iii. p. 539)], and in the same sense simply καταφέρομαι; cf. [L and S. s. v. I. 2 d.]; Steph. Thes. iv. col. 1286 [where the pass. fr. Acts is fully discussed].*

2703 κατα-φεύγω: 2 aor. κατέφυγον; [fr. Hdt. down]; to flee away, flee for refuge: foll. by εἰς w. acc. of place, Acts xiv. 6; οἱ καταφυγόντες, we who [cf. B. § 144, 9 c.] have fled from sc. the irreligious mass of mankind, foll. by an infin. of purpose, Heb. vi. 18; cf. Delitzsch ad loc.*

2704 κατα-φθείρω: pf. pass. ptcp. κατεφθαρμένος; 2 fut. pass. καταφθαρήσομαι; [see κατά, III. 4]. **1.** to corrupt, deprave: κατεφθαρμένοι τὸν νοῦν, corrupted in mind, 2 Tim. iii. 8. **2.** to destroy; pass. to be destroyed, to perish: foll. by ἐν w. dat. indicating the state, 2 Pet. ii. 12 RG. [From Aeschyl. down.]*

2705 κατα-φιλέω, -ῶ; impf. κατεφίλουν; 1 aor. κατεφίλησα; to kiss much, kiss again and again, kiss tenderly, (Lat. d e-osculor, etc.): τινά, Mt. xxvi. 49; Mk. xiv. 45; Lk. vii. 38, 45; xv. 20; Acts xx. 37. (Tob. vii. 6; 3 Macc. v. 49; Xen. Cyr. 6, 4, 10; 7, 5, 32; Polyb. 15, 1, 7; Joseph. antt.

7, 11, 7; Ael. v. h. 13, 4; Plut. Brut. 16; Lcian. dial. deor. 4, 5; 5, 3; φιλεῖν and καταφιλεῖν are distinguished in Xen. mem. 2, 6, 33; Plut. Alex. c. 67. Sept. for פָּשַׁק, prop. to join mouth to mouth.) Cf. Fritzsche on Mt. p. 780; Win. De verb. comp. etc. Pt. ii. p. 18, note ²¹.*

2706 κατα-φρονέω, -ῶ; fut. καταφρονήσω; 1 aor. κατεφρόνησα; [fr. Hdt. down]; to contemn, despise, disdain, think little or nothing of: w. gen. of the obj. [B. § 132, 15], Mt. vi. 24; xviii. 10; Lk. xvi. 13; Ro. ii. 4; 1 Co. xi. 22; 1 Tim. iv. 12; vi. 2; 2 Pet. ii. 10; Heb. xii. 2.*

2707 καταφρονητής, -οῦ, ὁ, (καταφρονέω), a despiser: Acts. xiii. 41. (Hab. i. 5; ii. 5; Zeph. iii. 4; Philo, leg. ad Gaium § 41; Joseph. antt. 6, 14, 4; b. j. 2, 8, 3; Plut. Brut. 12, and in eccl. writ.)*

2708 κατα-χέω: 1 aor. 3 pers. sing. κατέχεεν (see ἐκχέω); to pour down upon; pour over, pour upon: ἐπὶ τὴν κεφαλήν (L T Tr WH ἐπὶ τῆς κεφαλῆς), Mt. xxvi. 7; κατὰ τῆς κεφαλῆς (Plat. rep. 3 p. 398 a.; Epict. diss. 2, 20, 29), Mk. xiv. 3 (where L T Tr WH om. κατά [cf. W. 381 (357) sq.; Hdt. 4, 62; Plat. legg. 7 p. 814 b.; Joseph. c. Ap. 2, 36, 2. Cf. Rutherford, New Phryn. p. 66 sq.]).*

2709 κατα-χθόνιος, -ον, (κατά [see κατά, III. 3], χθών [the earth]), subterranean, Vulg. infernus: plur., of those who dwell in the world below, i. e. departed souls [cf. W. § 34, 2; but al. make the adj. a neut. used indefinitely; see Bp. Lghtft. in loc.], Phil. ii. 10. (Hom., Dion. H., Anthol., etc., Inscrr.)*

2710 κατα-χράομαι, -ῶμαι; 1 aor. mid. inf. καταχρήσασθαι; in class. Grk. **1.** to use much or excessively or ill. **2.** to use up, consume by use, (Germ. v e r brauchen). **3.** to use fully, the κατά intensifying the force of the simple verb (Germ. g e brauchen), (Plato, Dem., Diod., Joseph., al.): 1 Co. vii. 31 [cf. B. § 133, 18; W. 209 sq. (197)]; τινί, ib. ix. 18.*

2711 κατα-ψύχω: 1 aor. κατέψυξα; to cool off, (make) cool: Lk. xvi. 24. (Gen. xviii. 4; Hippocr., Aristot., Theophr., Plut., al.)*

2712 κατείδωλος, -ον, (κατά and εἴδωλον; after the analogy of κατάμπελος, κατάγομος, κατάχρυσος, κατάδενδρος, etc., [see κατά, III. 3, and cf. Herm. ad Vig. p. 638]), full of idols: Acts xvii. 16. (Not found in prof. auth. [cf. W. § 34, 3].)*

2713 κατ-έναντι, adv.; not found in prof. auth. [W. 102 (97)]; in Sept. mostly for נֶגֶד, לְנֶגֶד, לִפְנֵי, (see ἔναντι and ἀπέναντι); prop. over against, opposite, before: foll. by the gen. [B. 319 (273); cf. W. § 54, 6], Mk. xi. 2; xii. 41 [Tr txt. WH mrg. ἀπέναντι]; xiii. 3, and L T Tr WH in Mt. xxi. 2; L Tr WH txt. also in xxvii. 24; ἡ κατέναντι κώμη, the village opposite, Lk. xix. 30. Metaph., w. gen. of pers., before one i. e. he being judge (see ἐνώπιον [esp. 2 e. and 1 c.]): τοῦ θεοῦ, Ro. iv. 17 (which, by a kind of attraction rather rare, is to be resolved κατέναντι θεοῦ, ᾧ ἐπίστευσε, who is the father of us all acc. to the judgment and appointment of God, whom he believed, — the words καθὼς ... τέθεικα forming a parenthesis; cf. Fritzsche ad loc. [B. 287 (247); but al. resolve it, κατέναντι τ. θεοῦ κατέν. οὗ ἐπίστ., cf. Meyer (per contra ed. Weiss) ad loc. W. 164 (155)]); or, he being witness [in the sight of]: τοῦ θεοῦ, L T Tr WH in 2 Co. ii. 17 and xii. 19.*

2714   κατ-ενώπιον, adv., not met with in prof. auth. ([W. 102 (97)] see ἐνώπιον), over against, opposite, before the face of, before the presence of, in the sight of, before: foll. by the gen. [B. 319 (273 sq.); cf. W. § 54, 6];   a. prop. of place, Jude 24 (Lev. iv. 17; Josh. i. 5; iii. 7; xxiii. 9).   b. metaph. having one as it were before the eyes, before one as witness: τοῦ θεοῦ, Rec. in 2 Co. ii. 17; xii. 19, (see κατέναντι); before God as judge, Eph. i. 4; Col. i. 22 [cf. Bp. Lghtft. in loc.; also B. 173, 180, 188].*

2715   κατ-εξουσιάζω; not found in prof. auth.; to exercise authority, wield power, [see κατά, III. 3]: τινός, over one, Mt. xx. 25; Mk. x 42.*

2716   κατ-εργάζομαι; pf. inf. κατειργάσθαι (1 Pet. iv. 3 L T Tr WH); 1 aor. mid. κατειργασάμην, and κατηργασάμην (Ro. vii. 8 T Tr.; [2 Co. vii. 11 T]); 1 aor. pass. κατειργάσθην, and κατηργάσθην (2 Co. xii. 12 Tdf.); see ἐργάζομαι, init.; a depon. mid. verb; [acc. to Fritzsche, Rom. i. p. 107 the κατά is either intensive (Lat. perficere) or descensive (Lat. perpetrare)];   a. to perform, accomplish, achieve, [R. V. often work]: Ro. vii. 15, 17 sq. 20; τὶ διά τινος (gen. of pers.), Ro. xv. 18; ἅπαντα κατεργασάμενοι having gone through every struggle of the fight, Eph. vi. 13 [cf. Meyer in loc.]; σημεῖα, pass. 2 Co. xii. 12; of disgraceful actions, i. q. to perpetrate, Ro. i. 27; ii. 9; 1 Co. v. 3; 1 Pet. iv. 3.   b. to work out (Lat. efficere), i. e. to do that from which something results; of man: τὴν σωτηρίαν, make every effort to obtain salvation, Phil. ii. 12; of things: bring about, result in, Ro. iv. 15; v. 3; vii. 8; 2 Co. vii. 10 (where L T Tr WH ἐργάζ.); Jas. i. 3, and R G in 20; τί τινι, Ro. vii. 13; 2 Co. iv. 17; vii. 11; ix. 11.   c. κατεργ. τινα εἴς τι, to fashion, i. e. render one fit for a thing: 2 Co. v. 5. (Often in Grk. writ. fr. Soph. and Hdt. down; several times in Sept.)*

2718   κατ-έρχομαι; 2 aor. κατῆλθον, 1 pers. plur. κατήλθαμεν (Acts xxvii. 5 T Tr WH; on which form see ἀπέρχομαι, init.); [fr. Hom. down]; to come down, go down; prop. of one who goes from a higher to a lower locality: foll. by εἰς w. acc. of place, Lk. iv. 31; Acts viii. 5; xiii. 4; [xix. 1 T Tr mrg.]; and L T Tr WH in xv. 30; foll. by ἀπό w. gen. of place, Lk. ix. 37; Acts xv. 1; xxi. 10; foll. by ἀπό and εἰς, Acts xi. 27; xii. 19; of those who come to a place by ship [Eustath. (ad Hom.) 1408, 29 (Od. 1, 183) κατελθεῖν, οὐ μόνον τὸ ἁπλῶς κάτω που ἐλθεῖν, ἀλλὰ καὶ τὸ ἐς λιμένα ἐλθεῖν, ὥσπερ καὶ καταβῆναι κ. καταπλεῦσαι κ. καταχθῆναι κ. κατᾶραι, τὸ ἐλλιμενίσαι λέγεται; also 1956, 35 (Od. 24, 115) κατῆλθον ἢ ἀντὶ τοῦ ἐνελιμενίσθην, ὡς πολλαχοῦ ἐρρέθη, ἢ ἀντὶ τοῦ ἁπλῶς ἦλθον; cf. Ebeling, Lex. Homer. s. v.]: foll. by εἰς, Acts xviii. 22; xxi. 3 L T Tr WH; xxvii. 5; πρός τινα, Acts ix. 32. Metaph. of things sent down from heaven by God: Jas. iii. 15.*

2719   κατ-εσθίω, ptcp. plur. κατέσθοντες (Mk. xii. 40 Tr WH; see ἐσθίω and ἔσθω; cf. Fritzsche, Hdbch. z. d. Apokryphen, i. p. 150 [who says, 'The shorter form occurs freq. in the Sept., Lev. xix. 26; Sir. xx. 15, (16), elsewh. almost

exclusively poetic; see Bttm. Ausf. Sprachl. ii. p. 185' (cf. Veitch s. v. ἐσθίω)]); fut. καταφάγομαι (Jn. ii. 17 G L T Tr WH; see ἐσθίω); 2 aor. κατέφαγον; Sept. for אָכַל;   1. prop. to consume by eating, to eat up, devour: τί, of birds, Mt. xiii. 4; Mk. iv. 4; Lk. viii. 5; of a dragon, Rev. xii. 4; of a man, eating up the little book, i. e. eagerly taking its entire contents into his inmost soul, and, as we say, digesting it (borrowed fr. the fig. in Ezek. ii. 10; iii. 1–3, cf. Jer. xv. 16): Rev. x. 9 sq.   2. Metaph. in various uses;   a. to devour i. e. squander, waste, substance: Lk. xv. 30 (often so in Grk. writ. fr. Hom. Od. 3, 315; 15, 12 down; devorare patrimonium, Catull. 29, 23).   b. to devour i. e. forcibly appropriate: τὰς οἰκίας τῶν χηρῶν, widows' property, Mt. xxiii. 14 (13) Rec.; Mk. xii. 40 [cf. B. 79 (69); W. § 29, 2]; Lk. xx. 47.   c. with an acc. of the pers.   a. to strip one of his goods: 2 Co. xi. 20.   β. to ruin (by the infliction of injuries): Gal. v. 15.   d. of fire, to devour i. e. utterly consume, destroy: τινά, Rev. xi. 5; xx. 9.   e. of the consumption of the strength of body and mind by strong emotions: τινά, Jn. ii. 17 (Ps. lxviii. (lxix.) 10; Joseph. antt. 7, 8, 1).*

2720   κατ-ευθύνω: 1 aor. inf. κατευθῦναι; 3 pers. sing. opt. κατευθύναι; (see κατά, III. 2); Sept. mostly for יָשַׁר and הֵכִין, כּוּן; to make straight, guide, direct: τοὺς πόδας εἰς ὁδὸν εἰρ. Lk. i. 79; τὴν ὁδὸν πρός τινα, of the removal of the hindrances to coming to one, 1 Th. iii. 11; τὰς καρδίας (1 Chr. xxix. 18; 2 Chr. xix. 3) εἰς τὴν ἀγάπην τοῦ θεοῦ, 2 Th. iii. 5. (Plat., Aristot., Plut., al.)*

see 2127   κατ-ευλογέω: impf. 3 pers. sing. κατευλόγει (T WH) and κατηυλόγει (Tr), [cf. εὐδοκέω, init.]; to call down blessings on: τινά, Mk. x. 16 T Tr WH. (Tob. [x. 13]; xi. 16; Plut. amator. 4.)*

2721   κατ-εφ-ίστημι: to set up against; [2 aor. act. 3 pers. plur.] κατεπέστησαν τῷ Παύλῳ, they rose up against Paul, i. e. with hostile intent, Acts xviii. 12. Found nowhere else.*

2722   κατ-έχω; impf. κατεῖχον; 2 aor. subjunc. κατάσχω; impf. pass. κατειχόμην;   1. to hold back, detain, retain;   a. τινά, from going away, foll. by τοῦ μή w. inf., Lk. iv. 42 [B. § 140, 16 β.; cf. W. 604 (561)]; τινὰ πρὸς ἐμαυτόν, Philem. 13.   Pass. (as often in Grk. writ. fr. Hom. down; cf. Passow s. v. p. 1677ᵃ; [L. and S. s. v. II. 6]), of some troublesome condition or circumstance by which one is held as it were bound: νοσήματι, Jn. v. 4 [G T Tr WH om. the passage]; ἔν τινι, Ro. vii. 6.   b. to restrain, hinder (the course or progress of): τ. ἀλήθειαν ἐν ἀδικίᾳ, Ro. i. 18; absol. τὸ κατέχον, that which hinders, sc. Antichrist from making his appearance (see ἀντίχριστος); the power of the Roman empire is meant; ὁ κατέχων he that hinders, checks, sc. the advent of Antichrist, denotes the one in whom that power is lodged, the Roman emperor: 2 Th. ii. 6 sq. (cf., besides De Wette and Lünemann ad loc., [Bp. Lghtft. in B.D. s. v. Thess. Second Ep. to the], esp. Schneckenburger in the Jahrbücher f. deutsche Theol. for 1859 p. 421 sq.). κατέχω (sc. τὴν ναῦν) εἰς τὴν αἰγιαλόν, to check the ship's headway [better (cf. the preceding context) to hold or head

---

*2717 was omitted from use by Strong.

the ship, cf. Hdt. 7, 59. 188 etc.; Bos, Ellips. (ed. Schaefer) p. 318; see, too, Od. 11, 455 sq. (cf. Eustath. 1629, 18; Thom. Mag. ed. Ritschl p. 310, 7 sqq.); but Passow (as below) et al. take the verb as intrans. in such a connection, viz. *to make for*; cf. *Kypke*, Observv. ii. 144] in order to land, Acts xxvii. 40 (Xen. Hell. 2, 1, 29 κατα-σχὼν ἐπὶ τὴν Ἀβερνίδα; many other exx. are given in Passow s. v. II. 3; [L. and S. s. v. B. 2]).   **c.** *to hold fast, keep secure, keep firm possession of*: with acc. of the thing, τὸν λόγον, Lk. viii. 15; foll. by the orat. obliq., 1 Co. xv. 2 [B. §§ 139, 58; 150, 20; W. 561 (522)]; τὰς παραδόσεις, 1 Co. xi. 2; τὸ καλόν, 1 Th. v. 21; τὴν παρρησίαν [τ. ἀρχήν etc.] μέχρι τέλους βεβαίαν κατασχεῖν, Heb. iii. 6, 14; τὴν ὁμολογίαν τῆς ἐλπίδος ἀκλινῆ, Heb. x. 23.   **2.** equiv. to Lat. *obtinere*, i. e.   **a.** *to get possession of, take*: Mt. xxi. 38 R G; Lk. xiv. 9.   **b.** *to possess*: 1 Co. vii. 30; 2 Co. vi. 10.*

2723   **κατηγορέω, -ῶ**; impf. κατηγόρουν; fut. κατηγορήσω; 1 aor. κατηγόρησα; pres. pass. κατηγοροῦμαι; (κατά and ἀγορεύω, prop. to speak against [cf. κατά, III. 7] in court, in the assembly of the people), *to accuse*;   **a.** before a judge: absol. [*to make accusation*], Acts xxiv. 2, 19; τινός, to accuse one, Mt. xii. 10; Mk. iii. 2; Lk. vi. 7 T Tr txt. WH; xi. 54 R L Tr br.; xxiii. 2, 10; Jn. viii. 6; Acts xxv. 5; xxviii. 19; with the addition of a gen. of the thing of which one is accused (as Dem. 515 fin.): Acts xxiv. 8; xxv. 11, (unless it be thought preferable to regard the relative in these instances as in the gen. by attraction [so B. § 132, 16 fin.], since the com. constr. in Grk. authors is κατηγ. τί τινος, cf. Matthiae § 370 Anm. 2 p. 849 sq., and § 378 p. 859; cf. W. § 30, 9 a.); τινὸς περί τινος, Acts xxiv. 13 (Thuc. 8, 85; Xen. Hell. 1, 7, 2); w. gen. of pers. and acc. of the thing, Mk. xv. 3 (unless πολλά should be taken adverbially: *much, vehemently*); πόσα, ib. 4 L T Tr WH (Eur. Or. 28); foll. by κατά w. gen. of pers., Lk. xxiii. 14 (Xen. Hell. 1, 7, 9 [cf. W. § 28, 1; p. 431 (402); B. § 132, 16]); pass. *to be accused* (as 2 Macc. x. 13; Xen. Hell. 3, 5, 25; cf. B. § 134, 4): ὑπό τινος, Mt. xxvii. 12; Acts xxii. 30 L T Tr WH for Rec. παρά (τὸ τί κτλ. *why* [A. V. *wherefore*] he was accused; unless it is to be explained, *what accusation was brought forward* etc.); ὁ κατηγορούμενος, Acts xxv. 16.   **b.** of an extra-judicial accusation (Xen. mem. 1, 3, 4): absol. Ro. ii. 15; τινός, Jn. v. 45 [cf. B. 295 (254)]; Rev. xii. 10 R G Tr; solecistically τινά, Rev. xii. 10 L T WH [cf. B. § 132, 16].*

[SYN. αἰτιᾶσθαι, διαβάλλειν, ἐγκαλεῖν, ἐπικαλεῖν, κατηγορεῖν: αἰτιᾶσθαι to accuse with primary reference to the ground of accusation (αἰτία), the crime; κατηγορεῖν to accuse formally and before a tribunal, bring a charge against (κατά suggestive of animosity) publicly; ἐγκαλεῖν to accuse with publicity (καλεῖν) but not necessarily formally or before a tribunal; ἐπικαλεῖν 'to cry out upon', suggestive of publicity and hostility; διαβάλλειν prop. to make a verbal assault which reaches its goal (διά); in distinction from the words which allude to authorship (αἰτιάομαι), to judicial procedure (κατηγορέω), or to open averment (ἐγκαλέω, ἐπικαλέω), διαβάλλω expresses the giving currency to a damaging insinuation. διάβολος a secret and calumnious, in distinction from κατήγορος an open and formal, accuser. Schmidt ch. 5.]

κατηγορία, -ας, ἡ, (κατήγορος), [fr. Hdt. down], *accusation, charge*: w. gen. of the pers. accused, Lk. vi. 7 R G L Tr mrg.; [Jn. xviii. 29 T WH]; κατά τινος, Jn. xviii. 29 [R G L Tr]; 1 Tim. v. 19; w. gen. of the crime, Tit. i. 6.*   **2724**

κατήγορος, -ου, ὁ, (κατηγορέω [q. v. ad fin.]), *an accuser*: Jn. viii. 10; Acts xxiii. 30, 35; xxiv. 8 [R]; xxv. 16, 18; Rev. xii. 10 R Tr. [(Fr. Soph. and Hdt. down.)]*   **2725**

κατήγωρ, ὁ, *an accuser*: Rev. xii. 10 G L T WH. It is a form unknown to Grk. writ., a literal transcription of the Hebr. קטיגור, a name given to the devil by the Rabbins; cf. *Buxtorf*, Lex. Chald. talm. et rabb. p. 2009 (p. 997 ed. Fischer); [*Schöttgen*, Horae Hebr. i. p. 1121 sq.; cf. B. 25 (22)].*   **see 2725**

κατήφεια, -ας, ἡ, (fr. κατηφής, of a downcast look; and this fr. κατά, and τὰ φάη the eyes; Etym. Magn. [496, 53] κατήφεια· ἀπὸ τοῦ κάτω τὰ φάη βάλλειν τοὺς ὀνειδιζομένους ἢ λυπουμένους; because, as Plut. de dysopia [al. de vitioso pudore (528 e.)] c. 1 says, it is λύπη κάτω βλέπειν ποιοῦσα), prop. *a downcast look expressive of sorrow*; hence *shame, dejection, gloom*, [A. V. *heaviness*]: Jas. iv. 9. (Hom. Il. 3, 51; 16, 498 etc.; Thuc. 7, 75; Joseph. antt. 13, 16, 1; Plut. Cor. 20; [Pelop. 33, 3, and often; Dion. Hal., Char., etc.]; often in Philo.)*   **2726**

κατηχέω, -ῶ: 1 aor. κατήχησα; Pass., pres. κατηχοῦμαι; pf. κατήχημαι; 1 aor. κατηχήθην; nowhere met with in the O. T.; very rare in prof. auth.;   **1.** prop. *to sound towards, sound down upon, resound*: ἁρμονία κατηχεῖ τῆς θαλάττης, Philostr. p. 791 [icon. 1, 19]; to charm with resounding sound, to fascinate, τινὰ μύθοις, Lcian. Jup. trag. 39.   **2.** *to teach orally, to instruct*: Lcian. asin. § 48; Philopatr. 17. In the N. T. only used by Luke and Paul: τινά, 1 Co. xiv. 19; pass. ἐκ τοῦ νόμου, by hearing the law, wont to be publicly read in the synagogues, Ro. ii. 18; w. acc. of the thing, αὐτός σε πολλὰ κατηχήσω τῶν ἀγνοουμένων, Joseph. de vita sua § 65 fin.; w. acc. of a thing and of a pers., τοῦ ἀληθοῦς λόγου βραχέα κατηχήσας με, Clem. hom. 1, 6; pass. w. acc. of the thing: τὴν ὁδὸν τοῦ κυρίου, Acts xviii. 25; τὸν λόγον, Gal. vi. 6; hence some [(see Meyer in loc.)] resolve Lk. i. 4 thus: περὶ τῶν λόγων, οὓς κατηχήθης (see below).   **3.** *to inform by word of mouth*; pass. *to be orally informed*: foll. by ὅτι, Philo de leg. ad Gaium § 30; περί τινος (gen. of pers.), foll. by ὅτι, Acts xxi. 21; w. acc. of the thing, ὧν κατήχηνται περὶ σοῦ i. e. τούτων, ἃ κτλ. ibid. 24 (κατηχηθεὶς περὶ τῶν συμβεβηκότων, [pseudo-] Plut. de fluviis [7, 2]; 8, 1; 7, 1). To this construction the majority refer Lk. i. 4, construing it thus: τὴν ἀσφάλ. τῶν λόγων, περὶ ὧν κατηχήθης [W. 165 (156); B. § 143, 7; (see above)]. Cf. *Gilbert*, Dissertatio de christianae catecheseos historia (Lips. 1836) Pt. i. p. 1 sqq.; *Zezschwitz*, System der christl. Katechetik (Leipz. 1863) i. p. 17 sqq.; [and for eccl. usage, *Suicer*, Thes. ii. 69 sqq.; *Soph*. Lex. s. v.].*   **2727**

κατ' ἰδίαν, see ἴδιος, 2.   **see 2398**

κατ-ιόω, -ῶ: pf. pass. κατίωμαι; (see ἰός, 2); *to rust over* [cf. κατά, III. 3], *cover with rust*: Jas. v. 3. (Epictet. diss. 4, 6, 14; [Sir. xii. 11].) *   **2728**

κατ-ισχύω: impf. κατίσχυον; fut. κατισχύσω; 1 aor.   **2729**

subjunc. 2 pers. plur. κατισχύσητε (Lk. xxi. 36 T Tr txt. WH) ; Sept. mostly for חזק ; among Grk. writ. esp. by Polyb., Diod., Dion. H. ; prop. *to be strong to another's detriment, to prevail against* ; *to be superior in strength* ; *to overpower* : foll. by an inf., Lk. xxi. 36 T Tr txt. WH [*prevail* (i. e. have full strength) *to escape* etc.] ; *to overcome*, τινός (Jer. xv. 18), Mt. xvi. 18 (meaning, 'not even the gates of Hades — than which nothing was supposed to be stronger — shall surpass the church in strength') ; absol. *to prevail* (i. e. succeed, accomplish one's desire) : Lk. xxiii. 23.*

2730   **κατ-οικέω, -ῶ** ; 1 aor. κατῴκησα ; [fr. Soph. and Hdt. down] ; Sept. times uncounted for יָשַׁב, more rarely for שָׁכַן ;   **1.** intrans. *to dwell, settle* ;   a. prop. : foll. by ἐν w. dat. of place, Lk. xiii. 4 [Tr WH Hom. ἐν] ; Acts i. 20 ; 5 [T WH mrg. εἰς (see below)] ; vii. 2, 4, 48 ; ix. 22 ; xi. 29 ; xiii. 27 ; xvii. 24 ; Heb. xi. 9 ; Rev. xiii. 12 ; foll. by εἰς (a pregnant construction ; see εἰς, C. 2 p. 186ᵃ), Mt. ii. 23 ; iv. 13 ; Acts vii. 4 ; ἐπὶ τῆς γῆς, Rev. iii. 10 ; vi. 10 ; viii. 13 ; xi. 10 ; xiii. 8, 14 ; xiv. 6 Rec. ; xvii. 8, (Num. xiii. 33 ; xiv. 14 ; xxxv. 32, 34) ; ἐπὶ πᾶν τὸ πρόσωπον [παντὸς προσώπου L T Tr WH (cf. ἐπί, C. I. 1 a.)] τῆς γῆς, Acts xvii. 26 ; ὅπου, Rev. ii. 13 ; so that ἐκεῖ must be added mentally, Acts xxii. 12 ; demons taking possession of the bodies of men are said κατοικεῖν ἐκεῖ, Mt. xii. 45 ; Lk. xi. 26.   b. metaph., divine powers, influences, etc., are said κατοικεῖν ἔν τινι (dat. of pers.), or ἐν τῇ καρδίᾳ τινός, to dwell in his soul, to pervade, prompt, govern it : ὁ θεὸς ἐν ἡμῖν, Barn. ep. 16, 8 ; ὁ Χριστός, Eph. iii. 17 ; the Holy Spirit, Jas. iv. 5 R G (Herm. past., mand. 5, 2 ; [sim. 5, 5 etc. ; cf. Harnack's reff. on mand. 3, 1]) ; τὸ πλήρωμα τῆς θεότητος in Christ, Col. ii. 9, cf. i. 19 ; ἡ σοφία ἐν σώματι, Sap. i. 4 ; δικαιοσύνη is said to dwell where righteousness prevails, is practised, 2 Pet. iii. 13.   **2.** trans. *to dwell in, inhabit* : with acc. of place, Acts i. 19 ; ii. 9, 14 ; iv. 16 ; ix. 32, 35 ; xix. 10, 17 ; Rev. xii. 12 Rec. ; xvii. 2 ; God is said *to dwell in the temple*, i. e. to be always present for worshippers : Mt. xxiii. 21. [Comp. : ἐγκατοικέω.] *

[Syn. κατοικεῖν, in the Sept. the ordinary rendering of יָשַׁב, *to settle, dwell*, differs from παροικεῖν, the common representative of גּוּר *to sojourn*, as the permanent differs from the transitory ; e. g. Gen. xxxvii. 1 κατῴκει δὲ Ἰακὼβ ἐν τῇ γῇ οὗ παρῴκησεν ὁ πατὴρ αὐτοῦ, ἐν γῇ Χαναάν ; Philo de sacrif. Ab. et Cain. § 10 ὁ γὰρ τοῖς ἐγκυκλίοις μόνοις ἐπανέχων, παροικεῖ σοφίᾳ, οὐ κατοικεῖ. Cf. Bp. Lghtft. on Col. i. 19 and on Clem. Rom. 1 Cor. 1.]

2731   **κατ-οίκησις, -εως, ἡ**, (κατοικέω), *dwelling, abode* : Mk. v. 3. (Gen. x. 30 ; Num. xv. 2, etc. ; Thuc., Plat., Plut.) *

2732   **κατ-οικητήριον, -ου, τό**, (κατοικέω), *an abode, a habitation* : Eph. ii. 22 ; Rev. xviii. 2. (Sept. ; Barn. ep. [6, 15] ; 16, 7. 8, and other eccl. writ.) *

2733   **κατ-οικία, -ας, ἡ**, (κατοικέω), *dwelling, habitation* : Acts xvii. 26. (Sept. ; Polyb. 2, 32, 4 ; Strab., Plut., al.) *

see 2730   **κατ-οικίζω** ; 1 aor. κατῴκισα ; fr. Hdt. down ; Sept. for הוֹשִׁיב ; *to cause to dwell, to send* or *bring into an abode* ; *to give a dwelling to* : metaph. τὸ πνεῦμα, ὃ κατῴκισεν ἐν ἡμῖν, i. e. the Spirit which he placed within us, to pervade and prompt us (see κατοικέω, 1 b.), Jas. iv. 5 L T Tr WH.*

κατοπτρίζω : (κάτοπτρον a mirror), *to show in a mirror, to make to reflect, to mirror* : κατοπτρίζων ὁ ἥλιος τὴν ἶριν, Plut. mor. p. 894 f. [i. e. de plac. philos. 3, 5, 11]. Mid. pres. κατοπτρίζομαι ; *to look at one's self in a mirror* (Artem. oneir. 2, 7 ; Athen. 15 p. 687 c. ; Diog. Laërt. 2, 33 ; [7, 17]) ; *to behold for one's self as in a mirror* [W. 254 (238) ; B. 193 sq. (167)] : τὴν δόξαν τοῦ κυρίου, the glory of Christ (which we behold in the gospel as in a mirror from which it is reflected), 2 Co. iii. 18. Plainly so in Philo, alleg. leg. iii. § 33 μηδὲ κατοπτρισαίμην ἐν ἄλλῳ τινὶ τὴν σὴν ἰδέαν ἢ ἐν σοὶ τῷ θεῷ.*   **see 2734 St.**

κατόρθωμα, -τος, τό, (κατορθόω to make upright, erect), *a right action, a successful achievement* : plur. of wholesome public measures or institutions, Acts xxiv. 2 (3) [R G ; see διόρθωμα] ; (3 Macc. iii. 23 ; Polyb., Diod., Strab., Joseph., Plut., Lcian.). Cf. Lob. ad Phryn. p. 251 ; [Win. 25].*   **2735**

κάτω (fr. κατά), adv., [fr. Hom. down], compar. κατωτέρω ; [cf. W. 472 (440)] ;   **1.** *down, downwards* : Mt. iv. 6 ; Lk. iv. 9 ; Jn. viii. 6, 8 ; Acts xx. 9.   **2.** *below, beneath*, [cf. W. u. s.] ;   a. of place : Mk. xiv. 66 ; Acts ii. 19 ; ἕως κάτω [A. V. *to the bottom*], Mt. xxvii. 51 ; Mk. xv. 38, (Ezek. i. 27 ; viii. 2) ; τὰ κάτω, the parts or regions that lie beneath (opp. to τὰ ἄνω, heaven), i. e. the earth, Jn. viii. 23.   b. of temporal succession : ἀπὸ διετοῦς καὶ κατωτέρω, from a child of two years and those that were of a lower age [cf. W. 370 (347)], Mt. ii. 16 ; ἀπὸ εἰκοσαετοῦς καὶ κάτω, 1 Chr. xxvii. 23.*   **2736**

κατώτερος, -έρα, -ερον, (compar. of κάτω, see ἀνώτερος), [Hippocr., Theophr., Athen., al.], *lower* : (ὁ Χριστὸς) κατέβη εἰς τὰ κατώτερα μέρη τῆς γῆς, Eph. iv. 9, which many understand of Christ's descent into Hades (τὸν τόπον τὸν κάτω καλούμενον, Plat. Phaedo p.112c.), taking τῆς γῆς as a partit. gen. (see ᾅδης, 2). But the mention of this fact is at variance with the connection. Paul is endeavoring to show that the passage he has just before quoted, Ps. lxvii. (lxviii.) 19, must be understood of Christ, not of God, because *'an ascent into heaven'* necessarily presupposes a descent to earth (which was made by Christ in the incarnation), whereas God does not leave his abode in heaven. Accordingly τὰ κατώτ. τῆς γῆς denotes the *lower parts of the universe*, which the earth constitutes, τῆς γῆς being a gen. of apposition ; cf. W. § 59, 8 a. ; Grimm, Institutio theol. dogmat. ed. 2, p. 355 sqq.*   **2737**

κατωτέρω, see κάτω, esp. 2 b. —————————— **see 2736**

Καῦδα, see Κλαύδη. ——————————— **see 2802**

καῦμα, -τος, τό, (καίω), *heat* : of painful and burning heat, Rev. vii. 16 ; xvi. 9. (Sept. ; in Grk. writ. fr. Hom. down.)*   **2738**

καυματίζω ; 1 aor. inf. καυματίσαι ; 1 aor. pass. ἐκαυματίσθην ; (καῦμα) ; *to burn with heat, to scorch* : τινά, with ἐν πυρί added, Rev. xvi. 8 ; pass., Mt. xiii. 6 ; Mk. iv. 6 ; w. addition of καῦμα μέγα (see ἀγαπάω sub fin. for exx. and reff.), to be tortured with intense heat, Rev. xvi. 9. (Antonin. 7, 64 ; Epict. diss. 1, 6, 26 ; 3, 22, 52 ; of the heat of fever, Plut. mor. p. 100 d. [de virt. et vit. 1], 691 e. [quaest. conviv. vi. 2, 6].)*   **2739**

καῦσις, -εως, ἡ, (καίω), *burning, burning up* : ἧς τὸ τέλος   **2740**

εἰς καῦσιν, the fate of which land (appointed it by God) is, to be burned up (by fire and brimstone from heaven; cf. Deut. xxix. 23), Heb. vi. 8; cf. Bleek ad loc. (Hdt., Plat., Isocr., Plut., al.; Sept.)*

2741　　καυσόω, -ῶ: (καῦσος); to burn up, set fire to; pres. ptcp. pass. καυσούμενος, 2 Pet. iii. 10, 12, [A. V. with fervent heat]. (Elsewhere only [chiefly; see Soph. Lex. s. v.] in Diosc. and Galen: to suffer from feverish burning, be parched with fever.)*

see 2743　　καυστηριάζω: pf. pass. ptcp. κεκαυστηριασμένος, to burn in with a branding iron (τὰς ἵππους λύκον, a figure of a wolf, Strab. 5, 1, 9 p. 215): 1 Tim. iv. 2 L ed. ster. T Tr WH, on which pass. see καυτηριάζω. (Not found elsewhere.)*

2742　　καύσων, -ωνος, ὁ; 1. burning heat of the sun: Mt. xx. 12; Lk. xii. 55; Jas. i. 11, [al. refer all these pass. to the next head]; (Is. xlix. 10; [Gen. xxxi. 40 Alex.; cf. Judith viii. 3]; Sir. xviii. 16; Athen. 3 p. 73 b.). 2. Eurus, a very dry, hot, east wind, scorching and drying up everything; for קָדִים, Job xxvii. 21; Hos. xii. 1; ἄνεμος καύσων, Jer. xviii. 17; Ezek. xvii. 10; Hos. xiii. 15: πνεῦμα καύσων, Jon. iv. 8, [cf. Hos. xii. 1]; (on this wind cf. Schleusner, Thes. ad Sept. iii. p. 297; Win. RWB. [also BB. DD.] s. v. Wind). Many suppose it to be referred to in Jas. i. 11; yet the evils there mentioned are ascribed not to the καύσων, but to the ἥλιος.*

2743　　καυτηριάζω: (καυτήριον [(cf. καίω)] a branding-iron); to mark by branding, to brand: [pf. pass. ptcp.] κεκαυτηριασμένοι τὴν ἰδίαν συνείδησιν, i. e. κεκαυτηριασμένην ἔχοντες τὴν ἰδ. συν. [cf. W. 230 (216)] (cf. καταφθείρω), [branded in their own conscience i. e.] whose souls are branded with the marks of sin, i. e. who carry about with them the perpetual consciousness of sin, 1 Tim. iv. 2 R G L ed. maj., see καυστηριάζω; [some (cf. R. V. mrg.) would give it here the sense of seared, cf. Eph. iv. 19]. (In Hippocr. in a medical sense, to cauterize, remove by cautery.)*

2744　　καυχάομαι, -ῶμαι, 2 pers. sing. καυχᾶσαι (Ro. ii. 17, 23; 1 Co. iv. 7; see κατακαυχάομαι); fut. καυχήσομαι, 1 aor. ἐκαυχησάμην; pf. κεκαύχημαι; (καύχη a boast); [fr. Pind. and Hdt. down]; Sept. mostly for הִתְהַלֵּל; in the N. T. often used by Paul [some 35 times; by Jas. twice]; to glory (whether with reason or without): absol., 1 Co. i. 31ᵃ; iv. 7; xiii. 3 L [ed. ster. WH (see καίω)]; 2 Co. x. [13], 17ᵃ; xi. 16, 18; xii. 1, 6, 11 Rec.; Eph. ii. 9; Jas. iv. 16; τί (acc. of the thing) [cf. W. 222 (209)]), to glory (on account) of a thing: 2 Co. ix. 2 (ἣν καυχῶμαι ὑπὲρ ὑμῶν Μακεδόσιν, which I boast of on your behalf unto the Macedonians [B. § 133, 1]; cf. vii. 14, [and see below]); 2 Co. xi. 30, (Prov. xxvii. 1; Lcian. ocyp. 120); foll. by ἐν w. dat. of the obj. [W. § 33 d.; B. § 133, 23], to glory in a thing, (by a usage foreign to class. Grk.; but the Lat. says glorior in aliquo): Ro. ii. 23; 1 Co. iii. 21; 2 Co. v. 12; x. 15; xi. 12 [cf. B. 105 (92)]; xii. 5, 9; Gal. vi. 13 sq.; 2 Th. i. 4 R G; Jas. i. 9, (Jer. ix. 23 sq.; 1 Chr. xvi. 35); ἐν θεῷ, ἐν τῷ θεῷ, in God, i. e. the knowledge of God, intimacy with him, his favors, etc. Ro. ii. 17; v. 11, (ἐν τοῖς θεοῖς, Theoph. ad Autol. 1, 1, 1); ἐν κυρίῳ, 1 Co. i. 31ᵇ; 2 Co. x. 17ᵇ; ἐν Χριστῷ Ἰησοῦ, Phil. iii. 3; foll. by ἐπί w. dat. of the obj. [cf. W. § 33 d.;

B. § 133, 23], Ro. v. 2 (Prov. xxv. 14; Sir. xxx. 2: Diod. xvi. 70); περί τινος, 2 Co. x. 8; εἴς τι, in regard of, in reference to, 2 Co. x. 16 (Aristot. pol. 5, 10 p. 1311, 4). ὑπέρ w. gen. of pers., to one's advantage, to the praise of one, [on one's behalf]: 2 Co. vii. 14; xii. 5. ἐνώπιον τοῦ θεοῦ, as though standing in his presence, 1 Co. i. 29 [cf. B. 173 (150). COMP.: ἐν-, κατα-καυχάομαι.]*

καύχημα, -τος, τό, (καυχάομαι), very rare in prof. auth.; 　　2745
Sept. for תְּהִלָּה praise, and תִּפְאֶרֶת ornament, beauty; several times in Sir. 1. that of which one glories or can glory, matter or ground of glorying: Ro. iv. 2; 1 Co. ix. 15 sq.; 2 Co. i. 14; Phil. ii. 16; τὸ καύχημα ἔχειν εἰς ἑαυτὸν μόνον, his glorying confined to himself [R. V. in regard of himself alone], Gal. vi. 4; τὸ κ. τῆς ἐλπίδος, the matter for glorying which hope gives, i. e. the hope, of which we glory, Heb. iii. 6. 2. As γέννημα, δίωγμα, θέλημα, ἴαμα, κήρυγμα (2 Tim. iv. 17), κλαύμα, πλήρωμα, φρόνημα, etc., are used for γέννησις, δίωξις, θέλησις, κτλ. [cf. Ellicott on Phil. iv. 6], so also (which H. A. W. Meyer persists in denying [as respects the New Testament (see his note on Ro. iv. 2); so Ellicott and Bp. Lghtft. on Gal. vi. 4; Lünem. on Heb. u. s.]) is καύχημα used for καύχησις (Pind. Isthm. 5, 65 [cf. Meyer on Phil. i. 26 note; on the apparent use of nouns in μα in an active sense see Bp. Lghtft. on Col. p. 257 sq.]), a glorying, boasting: 1 Co. v. 6; Phil. i. 26; ὑπέρ τινος (see καυχάομαι, sub fin.), 2 Co. v. 12; ix. 3.*

καύχησις, -εως, ἡ, (καυχάομαι), the act of glorying: Ro. 　　2746
iii. 27; 2 Co. ix. 4 Rec.; 2 Co. xi. 10, 17; Jas. iv. 16; στέφανος καυχήσεως, crown of which we can boast, 1 Th. ii. 19; Ezek. xvi. 12; Prov. xvi. 31; ὑπέρ τινος, (on behalf) of one [cf. καυχάομαι, sub fin.], 2 Co. vii. 4; viii. 24; ἐπί τινος, before one, 2 Co. vii. 14; ἔχω [τὴν crit. edd.] καύχησιν ἐν Χριστῷ Ἰησοῦ, the glorying which I have I ascribe to Christ, or I owe it to Christ that I am permitted to glory [see ἐν, I. 6 b. p. 211ᵇ), Ro. xv. 17; 1 Co. xv. 31; that of which one glories, cause of glorying, 2 Co. i. 12. (Sept. several times for תִּפְאֶרֶת; [Diog. Laërt. 10, 7 fin.]; Philod. in Vol. Hercul. Oxfort. i. p. 16.)*

Καφαρναούμ, see Καπερναούμ.　　　　　　　　see 2584

Κεγχρεαί [T WH Κενχρ. (cf. WH. App. p. 150)], -ῶν, 　　2747
αἱ, Cenchreæ or Kenchreæ, a port of Corinth, about 60 [70; Strabo (as below)] stadia from the city, on the eastern side of the isthmus, the emporium of its trade with Asia (Strabo 8 p. 380): Acts xviii. 18; Ro. xvi. 1. [It still retains the ancient name; cf. B. D. Am. ed. s. v.; Lewin, St. Paul, i. 299 sq.]*

κέδρος, -ου, ἡ, [fr. Hom. down], a cedar, a well-known 　　see 2748
tree, the wood of which is fragrant: χείμαρρος τῶν κέδρων, Jn. xviii. 1 R Tr txt. WH (so also 2 S. xv. 23; 1 K. xv. 13, [cf. ii. 37]); τοῦ (sic!) κέδρου, ibid. Tdf.; but see the foll. word.*

Κεδρών, ὁ [B. 21 (19)], indecl. (in Joseph. Κεδρών, 　　2748
-ῶνος [see below]), Cedron [or Kidron], (Hebr. קִדְרוֹן i. e. dark, turbid), the name of a [winter-] torrent, rising near Jerusalem and flowing down through a valley of the same name (having the Mt. of Olives on the E.) into the Dead Sea: χείμαρρος τοῦ Κεδρών, Jn. xviii. 1 G L Tr

mrg., acc. to the more correct reading [but see WH. App. ad loc.]; (χείμαρρος Κεδρῶνος, Joseph. antt. 8, 1, 5; φάραγξ Κεδρῶνος, ib. 9, 7, 3; b. j. 5, 6, 1; φάραγγι βαθείᾳ . . . ἡ Κεδρὼν ὠνόμασται, ib. 5, 2, 3). [B. D. s. v. Kidron, cf. Cedron, 2; Robinson, Phys. Geogr. of the Holy Land, p. 96 sq.]*

2749 κεῖμαι; impf. 3 pers. sing. ἔκειτο; to lie; **1.** prop.: of an infant, foll. by ἐν w. dat. of place, Lk. ii. 12 [Tdf. om. κείμ.], 16; of one buried: ὅπου or οὖ, Mt. xxviii. 6; Lk. xxiii. 53; Jn. xi. 41 Rec.; xx. 12; of things that quietly cover some spot, Lk. xxiv. 12 [R G L br.]; Jn. xx. 5–7; xxi. 9; with ἐπί τι added, 2 Co. iii. 15; ἐπάνω τινός (of a city situated on a hill), Mt. v. 14; also of things put or set in any place, in ref. to which we often use to stand: thus of vessels, Jn. ii. 6; xix. 29, (χύτρας κειμένας, Xen. oec. 8, 19); of a throne, Rev. iv. 2 (Jer. xxiv. 1; Hom. Il. 2, 777; Od. 17, 331); κεῖσθαι πρός τι, to be brought near to a thing [see πρός, I. 2 a.], Mt. iii. 10; Lk. iii. 9; absol., of the site of a city, τετράγωνος κεῖται, Rev. xxi. 16; of grain and other things laid up, gathered together, Lk. xii. 19; of a foundation, 1 Co. iii. 11. **2.** metaph. **a.** to be (by God's intent) set, i. e. destined, appointed: foll. by εἰς w. acc. indicating the purpose, Lk. ii. 34; Phil. i. 17 (16); 1 Th. iii. 3. **b.** as very often in prof. auth. (cf. Passow s. v. p. 1694^b; [L. and S. s. v. IV. 2]), of laws, to be made, laid down: τινί, 1 Tim. i. 9. **c.** ὁ κόσμος ὅλος ἐν τῷ πονηρῷ κεῖται, lies in the power of the evil one, i. e. is held in subjection by the devil, 1 Jn. v. 19. [Comp.: ἀνά-, συν-ανά-, ἀντί-, ἀπό-, ἐπί-, κατά-, παρά-, περί-, πρό-κειμαι.]*

2750 κειρία, -ας, ἡ, a band, either for a bed-girth (Schol. ad Arstph. av. 817 κειρία· εἶδος ζώνης ἐκ σχοινίων, παρεοικὸς ἱμάντι, ᾗ δεσμοῦσι τὰς κλίνας, cf. Prov. vii. 16; [Plut. Alcib. 16, 1]), or for tying up a corpse after it has been swathed in linen: in the latter sense in Jn. xi. 44; [al. take it here of the swathings themselves].*

2751 κείρω; [1 aor. ἔκειρα (Acts viii. 32 T WH mrg.)]; 1 aor. mid. ἐκειράμην; fr. Hom. down; to shear: a sheep, Acts viii. 32 ([cf. above] fr. Is. liii. 7). Mid. to get or let be shorn [W. § 38, 2 b.; B. § 135, 4]: τὴν κεφαλήν, Acts xviii. 18; absol. of shearing or cutting short the hair of the head, 1 Co. xi. 6 [cf. W. § 43, 1].*

see 2797 Κείς, see Κίς.

see 2752 St. κέλευσμα, -τος, τό, (κελεύω), fr. Aeschyl. and Hdt. down, an order, command, spec. a stimulating cry, either that by which animals are roused and urged on by man, as horses by charioteers, hounds by hunters, etc., or that by which a signal is given to men, e. g. to rowers by the master of a ship (Lcian. tyr. or catapl. c. 19), to soldiers by a commander (Thuc. 2, 92; Prov. xxiv. 62 (xxx. 27)): ἐν κελεύσματι, with a loud summons, a trumpet-call, 1 Th. iv. 16.*

2753 κελεύω; impf. ἐκέλευον; 1 aor. ἐκέλευσα; to command, order: τινά, foll. by an aor. inf., Mt. xiv. 19, 28; Acts iv. 15; by the acc. with aor. inf., Mt. xviii. 25; xxvii. 58 [R G L], 64; Lk. xviii. 40; Acts v. 34; viii. 38; xxii. 30; xxiii. 10; xxv. 6, 17; the acc. is wanting because evident fr. the context, Mt. viii. 18; xiv. 9; [xxvii. 58 T WH

(Tr in br.)]; Acts xii. 19; xxi. 33; foll. by acc. with pres. inf., Acts xxi. 34; xxii. 24; xxiii. 3, 35; xxiv. 8 R G; xxv. 21; xxvii. 43; the acc. is wanting because easily discernible fr. the context, Acts xvi. 22 [cf. B. 201 (174); W. § 40, 3 d.]; by a use not infreq. in Hom., but somewhat rare in prose writ., with the dat. of a pers. (Plat. rep. 3 p. 396 a.; Thuc. 1, 44; Diod. 19, 17; Joseph. antt. 20, 6, 2; Tob. viii. 18; cf. Poppo on Xen. Cyr. 1, 3, 9 var.), foll. by an inf., Mt. xv. 35 R G; cf. B. 275 (236). κελεύσαντός τινος, at one's command, Acts xxv. 23. [On the constr. of κελ., esp. with the pass. inf. and acc., see B. § 141, 5 cf. p. 237 (204) note; also W. 336 (315), 332 (311).]*

[Syn.: κελεύειν, παραγγέλλειν, ἐντέλλεσθαι, τάσσειν (and its comp.): κελ. to command, designates verbal orders, emanating (usually) from a superior; παραγγέλλω to charge, etc., is used esp. of the order of a military commander which is passed along the line by his subordinates, (Xen. Cyr. 2, 4, 2); ἐντέλλεσθαι to enjoin, is employed esp. of those whose office or position invests them with claims, and points rather to the contents of the command, cf. our "instructions"; τάσσω lit. assign a post to, with a suggestion of duties as connected therewith; often used of a military appointment (cf. τάξις); its compounds ἐπιτάσσειν and προστάσσειν differ from ἐντ. in denoting fixed and abiding obligations rather than specific or occasional instructions, duties arising from the office rather than emanating from the personal will of a superior. Schmidt ch. 8.]

2754 κενοδοξία, -ας, ἡ, (κενόδοξος, q. v.), vain-glory, groundless self-esteem, empty pride: Phil. ii. 3. (4 Macc. ii. 15; viii. 18; Polyb., Plut., Lcian.; [Philo de mut. nom. § 15]; leg. ad Gaium § 16; etc.]; eccl. writ.; univ. a vain opinion, error, Sap. xiv. 14.) *

2755 κενόδοξος, -ον, (κενός, δόξα), glorying without reason, conceited, vain-glorious, eager for empty glory: Gal. v. 26. (Polyb., Diod.; Antonin. 5, 1; [cf. Philo de trib. virt. § 2 fin.]; eccl. writ.) *

2756 κενός, -ή, -όν, [fr. Hom. down], Sept. for ריק, רק, ריקם, etc., empty, **1.** prop. of places, vessels, etc., which contain nothing (Judg. vii. 16; Gen. xxxvii. 24); metaph. empty, vain; devoid of truth: λόγοι, Eph. v. 6 (Ex. v. 9); ἀπάτη, Col. ii. 8; κήρυγμα, πίστις, 1 Co. xv. 14. **2.** of men, empty-handed; without a gift: ἀποστέλλειν and ἐξαποστέλλειν τινὰ κενόν (Gen. xxxi. 42; Deut. xv. 13; xvi. 16), Mk. xii. 3; Lk. i. 53; xx. 10 sq.; metaph. destitute of spiritual wealth, of one who boasts of his faith as a transcendent possession, yet is without the fruits of faith, Jas. ii. 20. **3.** metaph. of endeavors, labors, acts, which result in nothing, vain, fruitless, without effect: ἡ χάρις, 1 Co. xv. 10; κόπος, ib. 58; ἡ εἴσοδος, 1 Th. ii. 1; neut. plur. κενά, things that will not succeed, Acts iv. 25 (fr. Ps. ii. 1); εἰς κενόν, in vain, to no purpose, [cf. W. 592 (551)]: 2 Co. vi. 1; Gal. ii. 2; Phil. ii. 16; 1 Th. iii. 5, (Is. lxv. 23; Jer. vi. 29, etc.; Diod. 19, 9; Heliod. 10, 30). [Cf. Trench, Syn. § xlix.]*

2757 κενοφωνία, -ας, ἡ, (κενόφωνος uttering emptiness), (vaniloquium, Vulg. [ed. Clem. (in 2 Tim. ii. 16)]), empty discussion, discussion of vain and useless matters, [A. V. babbling]: 1 Tim. vi. 20; 2 Tim. ii. 16. ([Dioscor. 1 prooem. p. 3, 1]; eccles. writ.) *

2758 κενόω, -ῶ: [fut. κενώσω, 1 Co. ix. 15 L txt. T Tr WH]; 1 aor. ἐκένωσα; Pass., pf. κεκένωμαι; 1 aor. ἐκενώθην; (κενός); **1.** *to empty, make empty*: ἑαυτὸν ἐκένωσε, sc. τοῦ εἶναι ἴσα θεῷ or τῆς μορφῆς τοῦ θεοῦ, i. e. he laid aside equality with or the form of God (said of Christ), Phil. ii. 7 (see a fuller exposition of this passage in μορφή). **2.** *to make void* i. e. *deprive of force, render vain, useless, of no effect*: pass., Ro. iv. 14; 1 Co. i. 17. **3.** *to make void* i. e. *cause a thing to be seen to be empty, hollow, false*: τὸ καύχημα, 1 Co. ix. 15; pass. 2 Co. ix. 3. (Twice in Sept. viz. Jer. xiv. 2; xv. 9; often in Attic writ.) *

2759 κέντρον, -ου, τό, (κεντέω to prick); **1.** *a sting*, as that of bees (4 Macc. xiv. 19), scorpions, locusts, Rev. ix. 10. Since animals wound by their sting and even cause death, Paul in 1 Co. xv. 55 (after Hos. xiii. 14 Sept.) attributes to death, personified, a κέντρον, i. e. a deadly weapon, and that κέντρον is said to be ἡ ἁμαρτία [56], because sin is death's cause and punishment [?] (Ro. v. 12). **2.** as in the Grk. writ. *an iron goad*, for urging on oxen, horses and other beasts of burden; hence the proverb πρὸς κέντρα λακτίζειν, *to kick against the goad*, i. e. *to offer vain and perilous or ruinous resistance*: Acts ix. 5 Rec.; xxvi. 14; cf. Pind. Pyth. 2, 173; Aeschyl. [Ag. 1624, cf.] Prom. 323; Eurip. Bacch. 795; Terent. Phorm. 1, 2, 28; Ammian. 18, 5.*

2760 κεντυρίων, -ωνος, ὁ, a Lat. word, *a centurion*: Mk. xv. 39, 44 sq. [Polyb. 6, 24, 5.]*

see 2747 [Κεγχρεαί, see Κεγχρεαί.]

2761 κενῶς, adv., *vainly, in vain*, [W. 463 (431); Aristot. on]: Jas. iv. 5.*

2762 κεραία [WH κεραία (see their App. p. 151)], -ας, ἡ, (κέρας), *a little horn*; *extremity, apex, point*; used by the Grk. grammarians of the accents and diacritical points. In Mt. v. 18 [(where see Wetstein; cf. also *Edersheim, Jesus the Messiah*, i. 537 sq.)]; Lk. xvi. 17 of the little lines, or projections, by which the Hebr. letters in other respects similar differ from each other, as ה and ח, ד and ר, ב and כ, [A.V. *tittle*]; the meaning is, 'not even the minutest part of the law shall perish.' [(Aeschyl.,Thuc.,al.)]*

2763 κεραμεύς, -έως, ὁ, (κεράννυμι), *a potter*: Mt. xxvii. 7, 10; Ro. ix. 21. (Hom., Hes., Arstph., Plat., Plut., al.; Sept. several times for יֹצֵר.) *

2764 κεραμικός, -ή, -όν, (κέραμος); **1.** in class. Grk. *of or belonging to a potter*: hence κ. γῆ, such as a potter uses, Hippocr.; τέχνη, Plat. polit. p. 288 a. **2.** in the Bible *made of clay, earthen*: Rev. ii. 27 (Dan. ii. 41), for which the Greeks use κεραμεοῦς, -ᾶ, -οῦν, and κεράμιος [al. -μειος; cf. Lob. ad Phryn. p. 147; [W. 99 (94)].*

2765 κεράμιον, -ου, τό, (neut. of the adj. κεράμιος, see the preceding word [al. make it a dimin. fr. κέραμος]), *an earthen vessel, a pot*; *a jug* or *pitcher*: with ὕδατος added, a water-pitcher, Mk. xiv. 13; Lk. xxii. 10. (Theophr. caus. plant. 3, 4, 3; οἴνου, Jer. xlii. (xxxv.) 5; Xen. anab. 6, 1, 15; Dem. p. 934, 26; Polyb. 4, 56, 3; ἐλαίου, Joseph. antt. 8, 13, 2.) *

2766 κέραμος, -ου, ὁ, (κεράννυμι); **1.** *clay, potter's earth.* **2.** *anything made of clay, earthen ware.* **3.** spec. *a*

(roofing) *tile* (Thuc., Athen., Hdian , al.); *the roof* itself (Arstph. fr. 129 d.): so διὰ τῶν κεράμων, through the roof, i. e. through the door in the roof to which a ladder or stairway led up from the street (accordingly the Rabbins distinguish two ways of entering a house, 'the way through the door' and 'the way through the roof' [*Lghtft.* Horae Hebr. p. 601]; cf. *Win.* RWB. s. v. Dach; Keim ii. p. 176 sq. [Eng. trans. iii. 215; *Edersheim*, Jesus the Messiah, i. 501 sq.; Jewish Social Life, p. 93 sqq.]), Lk. v. 19. Mark (ii. 4) describes the occurrence differently (see ἀποστεγάζω), evidently led into error by misapprehending the words of Luke. [But, to say nothing of the improbability of assuming Mark's narrative to be dependent on Luke's, the alleged discrepance disappears if Luke's language is taken literally, "through the tiles" (see διά, A. I. 1); he says nothing of "the door in the roof." On the various views that have been taken of the details of the occurrence, see B. D. (esp. Am. ed.) s. v. House; Dr. *Jas. Morison*, Com. on Mk. l. c.]*

2767 κεράννυμι (κεράννύω): 1 aor. ἐκέρασα; pf. pass. κεκέρασμαι (for the more com. κέκραμαι, cf. *Lob.* ad Phryn. p. 582; *Bttm.* Ausf. Sprchl. ii. p. 214; Krüger § 40 s. v. i. p. 175; [Veitch s. v.]); [fr. Hom. down]: **1.** *to mix, mingle*. **2.** *to mix wine and water*. **3.** *to pour out for drinking*: τινί τι, Rev. xviii. 6 [R.V. *mingle*]; pass., Rev. xiv. 10; (so Bel and the Dragon 11; Anthol. 11, 137, 12). [COMP.: συγ-κεράννυμι.]*

[SYN. κεράννυμι, μίγνυμι: in strict usage κερ. denotes such a mixing as combines the ingredients into a new compound, chemical mixture; μίγν. such a mixing as merely blends or intermingles them promiscuously, mechanical mixture.]

2768 κέρας, -ατος, plur. κέρατα, gen. -άτων (W. 65 (63); B. 15 (13)), τό, [fr. Hom. down], Hebr. קֶרֶן, *a horn*; **a.** prop.: of animals, Rev. v. 6; xii. 3; xiii. 1, 11; xvii. 3, 7, 12, 16. **b.** Since animals (esp. bulls) defend themselves with their horns, the horn with the Hebrews (and other nations) is a symbol of strength and courage, and is used as such in a variety of phrases (Ps. lxxxviii. (lxxxix.) 18; cxxxi. (cxxxii.) 17; cxlviii. 14; 1 S. ii. 10; Sir. xlvii. 5, 7, 11; 1 Macc. ii. 48, etc.; cf. *Gesenius*, Thes. iii. p. 1238; [B. D. s. v. Horn]); hence κέρας σωτηρίας (of God, Ps. xvii. (xviii.) 3; 2 S. xxii. 3), i. q. *a mighty and valiant helper, the author of deliverance*, of the Messiah, Lk. i. 69. **c.** trop. *a projecting extremity in shape like a horn, a point, apex*: as, of an altar, Rev. ix. 13; (Ex. xxix. 12; Lev. iv. 7, 18; xvi. 18; Am. iii. 14; Ps. cxvii. (cxviii.) 27).*

2769 κεράτιον, -ου, τό, (dimin. of κέρας); **1.** *a little horn*. **2.** the name of the fruit of the κερατέα or κερατεία [or -τία], the Ceratonia siliqua (Linn.) or *carob-tree* (called also St. John's Bread, [from the notion that its pods, which resemble those of the 'locust', constituted the food of the Baptist]). This fruit is shaped like a horn and has a sweet taste; it was [and is] used not only in fattening swine, but as an article of food by the lower classes: Lk. xv. 16 [A. V. *husks*]; cf. *Win.* RWB. s. v. Johannisbrodbaum; [B. D. (esp. Am. ed.) s. v. Husks].*

2770　κερδαίνω: [fut. κερδήσω, Jas. iv. 13 Rec.ᵇᵉˢ ᵉˡᶻ L T Tr WH; see also below]; 1 aor. ἐκέρδησα (an Ionic form fr. κερδάω, which later writ. use for the earlier ἐκέρδανα, see *Lob.* ad Phryn. p. 740; *Bttm.* Ausf. Sprchl. ii. p. 215; W. 87 (83); [*Veitch* s. v.]), once 1 aor. subj. κερδάνω (1 Co. ix. 21 L T Tr [but WH (cf. also Grsb. note) read the fut. κερδανῶ, cf. B. 60 (53); § 139, 38]); 1 fut. pass. κερδηθήσομαι (the subjunc. κερδηθήσωνται, 1 Pet. iii. 1 R G is a clerical error [cf. reff. s. v. καίω, init.], for which L T Tr WH have restored κερδηθήσονται [cf. B. § 139, 38]); [fr. Hes. down]; (fr. κέρδος) *to gain, acquire*; (Vulg. passim *lucrifacio* [also *lucro*, etc.]); **a.** prop.: τὸν κόσμον, Mt. xvi. 26; Mk. viii. 36; Lk. ix. 25; money, Mt. xxv. 16 [L T WH], 17, 20, 22; absol. *to get gain*, Jas. iv. 13. **b.** metaph. **α.** with nouns signifying loss, damage, injury, it is used of the gain arising from s h u n n i n g or e s c a p i n g f r o m the evil (where we say *to spare one's self, be spared*): τὴν ὕβριν ταύτην κ. ζημίαν, Acts xxvii. 21; τό γε μιανθῆναι τὰς χεῖρας κερδαίνειν, to avoid the crime of fratricide, Joseph. antt. 2, 3, 2; ζημίαν, to escape a loss, Eur. Cycl. 312; other exx. in *Kypke*, Observv. ii. p. 139 sq. **β.** τινά, *to gain any one* i. e. to win him over to the kingdom of God, which none but the placable enter, Mt. xviii. 15; to gain one to faith in Christ, 1 Pet. iii. 1; 1 Co. ix. 19–22; Χριστόν, to gain Christ's favor and fellowship, Phil. iii. 8. Not found in the O. T.*

2771　κέρδος, -εος (-ους), τό, *gain, advantage*: Phil. i. 21 (with which cf. Ael. v. h. 4, 7 τοῖς κακοῖς οὐδὲ τὸ ἀποθανεῖν κέρδος); Tit. i. 11; plur. Phil. iii. 7. [From Hom. down.]*

see 2762　[κερέα, see κεραία.]

2772　κέρμα, -τος, τό, (κείρω to cut into bits), *small pieces of money, small coin, change*; generally and collectively, τὸ κέρμα *money*: Jn. ii. 15, where L mrg. Tr WH τὰ κέρματα; (Arstph., Dem., Joseph., al.). Cf. the full exhibition of the use of the word given by *Fischer*, De vitiis lexicorum N. T. etc. p. 264 sqq.*

2773　κερματιστής, -οῦ ὁ, (κερματίζω [to cut into small pieces, to make small change]), *a money-changer, money-broker*: Jn. ii. 14. In the court of the Gentiles [(see ἱερόν, and *Edersheim*, Jesus the Messiah, i. 244 sq.)] in the temple at Jerusalem were the seats of those who sold such animals for sacrifice as had been selected, examined, and approved, together with incense, oil, and other things needed in making offerings and in worship; and the magnitude of this traffic had introduced the banker's or broker's business; [cf. BB.DD. s. v. Money-changers; esp. Edersheim u. s. p. 367 sqq.]. (Nicet. annal. 7, 2 p. 266 ed. Bekk.; Max. Tyr. diss. 2 p. 15 ed. Markland.)*

2774　κεφάλαιον, -ου, τό, (neut. of the adj. κεφάλαιος, belonging to the head); **1.** *the chief* or *main point, the principal thing*, (Vulg. *capitulum*): Heb. viii. 1 [cf. B. 154 (134)]; (freq. so in Grk. writ. fr. Pind., Thuc. and Plat. down). **2.** *the pecuniary sum total* of a reckoning, *amount*, (Plut. Fab. 4); *the principal, capital*, as distinguished fr. the interest (Plut. legg. 5, 742 c.); univ. *a sum of money, sum*, (Vulg. *summa*): Acts xxii. 28; so Lev. vi. 5; Num. v. 7; xxxi. 26; Joseph. antt. 12, 2, 3;

Artem. oneir. 1, 17; see other exx. in *Kypke*, Observv. ii. p. 116; [L. and S. s. v. 5 b.].*

2775　κεφαλαιόω, -ῶ: 1 aor. ἐκεφαλαίωσα [T WH ἐκεφαλίωσα (see below)]; (κεφάλαιον); **1.** *to bring under heads, to sum up, to summarize*, (Thuc., Aristot., al.). **2.** in an unusual sense, *to smite* or *wound in the head*: Mk. xii. 4. It is of no use to appeal to the analogy of the verb γναθόω, which means εἰς γνάθους τύπτω to smite on the cheek, since κεφάλαιον is nowhere used of the head of the body. Tdf. [WH] (after codd. א B L) have adopted ἐκεφαλίωσαν (fr. κεφάλιον, i. q. κεφαλίς, q. v.). But neither κεφαλιόω nor κεφαλίζω has yet been noted in any Greek author. Cf. *Lob.* ad Phryn. p. 95. [COMP.: ἀνα-κεφαλαιόω.] *

2776　κεφαλή, -ῆς, ἡ, Sept. for ראֹשׁ; *the head*, both of men: Mt. v. 36; Mk. vi. 24; Lk. vii. 38, 44 [Rec.], 46; Jn. xiii. 9; Acts xviii. 18; 1 Co. xi. 4; Rev. i. 14; iv. 4, and often; and of animals: Rev. ix. 7, 17, 19, etc.; on the phrases κλίνειν τὴν κ., ἐπαίρειν τὴν κ., see κλίνω, 1 and ἐπαίρω; on the saying in Ro. xii. 20, see under ἄνθραξ. Since the loss of the head destroys the life, κεφαλή is used in phrases relating to capital and extreme punishments: so in τὸ αἷμα ὑμῶν ἐπὶ τὴν κ. ὑμῶν (see αἷμα, 2 a. p. 15ᵇ), Acts xviii. 6, and similar phrases in class. Grk.; see Passow s. v. p. 1717ᵃ; Pape s. v. 3; [L. and S. s. v. I. 3 and 4]. Metaph. anything *supreme, chief, prominent*; of persons, *master, lord*: τινός, of a husband in relation to his wife, 1 Co. xi. 3; Eph. v. 23; of Christ, the lord of the husband, 1 Co. xi. 3 [cf. B. 124 sq. (109)]; of the church, Eph. iv. 15; v. 23; Col. ii. 19 [cf. B. 143, 4 c.]; τοῦ σώματος τῆς ἐκκλ. Col. i. 18; πάσης ἀρχῆς καὶ ἐξουσίας, Col. ii. 10; so Judg. xi. 11; 2 S. xxii. 44, and in Byzant. writ. of things: κεφ. γωνίας, *the corner-stone*, see γωνία, a. [(From Hom. down.)]*

see 2775　κεφαλιόω: Mk. xii. 4 T WH (approved also by Weiss, Volkmar, al.), for κεφαλαιόω, q. v.

2777　κεφαλίς, -ίδος, ἡ, (dimin. of κεφαλή, formed after the analogy of ἁμαξίς, πινακίς, etc.; cf. *Bttm.* Ausf. Spr. ii. p. 443; Kühner § 330 Anm. 5, i. p. 708); **1.** *a little head* (Lat. *capitellum, capitulum*). **2.** *the highest part, extremity* or *end* of anything; as the capital of a column, 1 K. vii. 9, 31 etc.; Geop. 14, 6, 6; hence the tips or knobs (the *umbilici* of the Romans [or rather the *cornua*; see *Gardthausen*, Griech. Palaeogr. p. 52 sq.; *Rich*, Dict. s. v. umbilicus]) of the wooden rod around which parchments were rolled seem to have been called κεφαλίδες, because they resembled little heads; so that **3.** the Alexand. writ. transferred the name κεφαλίς to the roll or volume itself; so ἐν κεφαλίδι βιβλίου, Heb. x. 7 (fr. Sept. of Ps. xxxix. (xl.) 8 for בִּמְגִלַּת־סֵפֶר, as in Ezek. ii. 9, and without βιβλίου, iii. 1–3; 2 Esdr. vi. 2 [cf. *Birt*, Antikes Buchwesen, (Berl. 1882), p. 116]), Itala: *in volumine libri*, in the roll of the book [cf. W. 23 (22)]. The different opinions are noticed by Bleek ad loc.*

see 5392　κημόω, -ῶ: fut. κημώσω; (κημός a muzzle); *to stop the mouth by a muzzle, to muzzle*: βοῦν, 1 Co. ix. 9 T Tr WHmrg. (Xen. r. eq. 5, 3); see φιμόω.*

2778　κῆνσος, -ου, ὁ, the Lat. word *census* (among the Romans, denoting a register and valuation of property in accordance with which taxes were paid), in the N. T. (as in Cod. Just. 4, 47) *the tax* or *tribute levied on individuals and to be paid yearly* (Hesych. κῆνσος· εἶδος νομίσματος, ἐπικεφάλαιον, our *capitation* or *poll tax*): Mt. xvii. 25; xxii. 17; Mk. xii. 14; τὸ νόμισμα τοῦ κήνσου, the coin with which the tax is paid, *tribute money*, Mt. xxii. 19.*

2779 κῆπος, -ου, ὁ, [thought to be allied with σκάπτω, Lat. *campus*, etc.], fr. Hom. down, Sept. for נַּנָּה, גָּנָּה; גַּן; a *garden*: Lk. xiii. 19; Jn. xviii. 1, 26; xix. 41. [BB. DD. s. v. Garden.]*

2780 κηπ-ουρός, -οῦ, ὁ, (κῆπος and οὖρος), a *keeper of a garden*, a *gardener*: Jn. xx. 15 [BB. DD. s. v. Garden]. (Plat., Theophr., Polyb., Diod., Epictet., al.)*

2781 κηρίον, -ου, τό, (κηρός wax), fr. Hes. and Hdt. down, *honeycomb*: κηρίον μελίσσιον, a honeycomb (still containing the honey), Lk. xxiv. 42 R G Tr br. (1 S. xiv. 27; Prov. xvi. 24; xxiv. 13).*

2782 κήρυγμα, -τος, τό, (κηρύσσω), in Grk. writ. esp. Attic, *that which is promulgated by a herald* or *public crier*, a *proclamation by herald*; in the N. T. *the message* or *proclamation by the heralds of God or Christ*: thus the proclamation of the necessity of repentance and reformation made by the prophet Jonah [A.V. *preaching*], τὸ κήρυγμα Ἰωνᾶ, Mt. xii. 41; Lk. xi. 32, (Jon. iii. 4); the announcement of salvation procured by Christ and to be had through him: absol., 1 Co. i. 21; Tit. i. 3; w. gen. of the subj., *made by one*, 1 Co. ii. 4; xv. 14; w. gen. of the obj. Ἰησοῦ Χριστοῦ, *concerning Jesus Christ*, Ro. xvi. 25, cf. Philippi ad loc.; [τῆς αἰωνίου σωτηρίας, Mk. xvi. WH in (rejected) 'Shorter Conclusion']; the act of publishing, absol. 2 Tim. iv. 17 [but R. V. *that the message might be fully proclaimed*; see πληροφορέω, a.].*

2783 κήρυξ, less correctly [yet so L WH] κῆρυξ (on the accent see W. § 6, 1 c.; [B. 13 (12)]; *Lipsius*, Gramm. Untersuch. p. 36; [Chandler § 622; Göttling p. 254 sq.; *Lob*. Paralip. p. 411; W. Dindorf in *Steph*. Thes. s. v.; *Tdf*. Proleg. p. 101]), -υκος, ὁ, (akin to γῆρυς a voice, a sound, γηρύω to utter a sound, to speak; [yet cf. Vaniček p. 140]); com. in Grk. writ. fr. Hom. down; a *herald*, a *messenger* vested with public authority, who conveyed the official messages of kings, magistrates, princes, military commanders, or who gave a public summons or demand, and performed various other duties. In the O. T., Gen. xli. 43; Dan. iii. 4; Sir. xx. 15. In the N. T. *God's ambassador, and the herald* or *proclaimer of the divine word*: δικαιοσύνης, one who summoned to righteousness, of Noah, 2 Pet. ii. 5; used of the apostles, as the divine messengers of the salvation procured by Christ and to be embraced through him, 1 Tim. ii. 7; 2 Tim. i. 11.*

2784 κηρύσσω; impf. ἐκήρυσσον; fut. κηρύξω; 1 aor. ἐκήρυξα, [inf. κηρύξαι R G Tr WH, κῆρυξαι L T; cf. *Lipsius*, Gramm. Untersuch. p. 32 sqq.; *Tdf*. Proleg. p. 101; W. § 6, 1 f. (see reff. s. v. κῆρυξ)]; Pass., pres. κηρύσσομαι; 1 aor. ἐκηρύχθην; 1 fut. κηρυχθήσομαι; (κῆρυξ, q. v.); fr. Hom. down; Sept. for קָרָא; *to be a herald*; *to officiate as herald*; *to proclaim after the manner of a herald*; always with a suggestion of formality, gravity, and an authority

which must be listened to and obeyed; **a.** univ. *to publish, proclaim openly*: something which has been done, Mk. vii. 36; τὸν λόγον, Mk. i. 45 (here joined with διαφημίζειν); foll. by indir. disc., Mk. v. 20; Lk. viii. 39; something which ought to be done, foll. by the inf. (cf. W. 322 (302); [B. § 141, 2]), Ro. ii. 21; Μωϋσῆν, the authority and precepts of Moses, Acts xv. 21; περιτομήν, the necessity of circumcision, Gal. v. 11. **b.** spec. used *of the public proclamation of the gospel and matters pertaining to it*, made by John the Baptist, by Jesus, by the apostles and other Christian teachers: absol., Mt. xi. 1; Mk. i. 38; iii. 14; xvi. 20; Ro. x. 15; w. dat. of the pers. to whom the proclamation is made, 1 Co. ix. 27; 1 Pet. iii. 19; εἰς [R ἐν w. dat.] τὰς συναγωγάς (see εἰς, A. I. 5 b.; cf. W. 213 (200)), Mk. i. 39; [Lk. iv. 44 T Tr txt. WH]; (ὁ) κηρύσσων, Ro. x. 14; κηρύσσειν w. acc. of the thing, Mt. x. 27; Lk. [iv. 19]; xii. 3; τινί τι, Lk. iv. 18 (19); τὸ εὐαγγέλιον τῆς βασιλ., Mt. iv. 23; ix. 35; Mk. i. 14 (where G L br. T Tr WH τὸ εὐ. τοῦ θεοῦ); τὸ εὐαγγ. simply, Mk. xvi. 15; Gal. ii. 2; τὸ εὐαγγ. τοῦ θεοῦ εἴς τινας (see above), 1 Th. ii. 9; pass., Mt. xxiv. 14; xxvi. 13; Col. i. 23; with εἰς πάντα τὰ ἔθνη or εἰς ὅλον τ. κόσμον added, Mk. xiii. 10; xiv. 9; τὸν λόγον, 2 Tim. iv. 2; τὸ ῥῆμα τῆς πίστεως, Ro. x. 8; τὴν βασιλ. τοῦ θεοῦ, Lk. viii. 1; ix. 2; Acts xx. 25 [here G L T Tr WH om. τοῦ θεοῦ]; xxviii. 31; βάπτισμα, the necessity of baptism, Mk. i. 4; Lk. iii. 3; Acts x. 37; μετάνοιαν καὶ ἄφεσιν ἁμαρτιῶν, by public proclamation to exhort to repentance and promise the pardon of sins, Lk. xxiv. 47; ἵνα μετανοῶσιν [R G μετανοήσωσι] (see ἵνα, II. 2 b.; [B. 237 (204)]), Mk. vi. 12. τινά τισι, to proclaim to persons one whom they are to become acquainted with in order to learn what they ought to do: Χριστόν, or τὸν Ἰησοῦν, Acts viii. 5; xix. 13; Phil. i. 15; 1 Co. i. 23; 2 Co. iv. 5 (where it is opp. to ἑαυτὸν κηρ. to proclaim one's own excellence and authority); 2 Co. xi. 4; pass., ὁ κηρυχθείς, 1 Tim. iii. 16; with διά and gen. of pers. added, 2 Co. i. 19; with the epexegetic addition, ὅτι οὗτός ἐστιν ὁ υἱὸς τ. θεοῦ, Acts ix. 20; ὅτι ἐκ νεκρῶν ἐγήγερται, 1 Co. xv. 12; τινί foll. by ὅτι, Acts x. 42; κηρ. foll. by λέγων with direct disc., Mt. [iii. 1 L T WH]; x. 7; Mk. i. 7; κηρύσσειν κ. λέγειν foll. by direct disc., Mt. iii. 1 [R G Tr br.]; iv. 17; κηρ. ἐν (omitted in Rec.) φωνῇ μεγάλῃ, foll. by direct disc. (of an angel as God's herald), Rev. v. 2; κηρ. with οὕτως added, 1 Co. xv. 11. On this word see *Zezschwitz*, Petri apost. de Christi ad inferos descensu sententia. (Lips. 1857) p. 31 sqq.; [*Campbell*, Dissert. on the Gospels, diss. vi. pt. v. Comp.: προκηρύσσω.]*

2785 κῆτος, -εος (-ους), τό, a *sea-monster, whale, huge fish*, (Hom., Aristot., al.): Mt. xii. 40, fr. Jon. ii. 1 where Sept. κήτει μεγάλῳ for דָּג גָּדוֹל.*

2786 Κηφᾶς, -ᾶ [B. 20 (18)], ὁ, (Chald. כֵּיפָא a rock), *Cephas* (i. q. Πέτρος [cf. B.D. (Am. ed.) p. 2459]), the surname of Simon the apostle: Jn. i. 42 (43); 1 Co. i. 12; iii. 22; ix. 5; xv. 5; Gal. ii. 9; and L T Tr WH also in Gal. i. 18; ii. 11, 14.*

2787 κιβωτός, -οῦ, ἡ, (κίβος [cf. Suidas 2094 c.]), a *wooden chest, box*, ([Hecatae. 368 (Müller's Frag. i. p. 30), Simon.], Arstph., Lysias, Athen., Ael., al.) : in the N. T., the ark of the covenant, in the temple at Jerusalem, Heb. ix. 4 (Philo, Joseph.; Sept. very often for אֲרוֹן) ; in the heavenly temple, Rev. xi. 19 ; of Noah's vessel, built in the form of an ark, Mt. xxiv. 38 ; Lk. xvii. 27 ; Heb. xi. 7 ; 1 Pet. iii. 20, (4 Macc. xv. 31 ; Sept. for תֵּבָה).*

2788 κιθάρα, -ας, ή, a harp [cf. Stainer, Music of the Bible, ch. iv. ; B.D. s. v. Harp] : 1 Co. xiv. 7 ; Rev. v. 8 ; xiv. 2 ; τοῦ θεοῦ, to which the praises of God are sung in heaven, Rev. xv. 2 ; cf. W. § 36, 3 b. [From Hom. h. Merc., Hdt. on.]*

2789 κιθαρίζω ; pres. pass. ptcp. κιθαριζόμενος ; to play upon the harp [(see the preceding word)] : with ἐν ταῖς κιθάραις added, [A.V. harping with their harps], Rev. xiv. 2 ; τὸ κιθαριζόμενον, what is harped, 1 Co. xiv. 7. (Is. xxiii. 16 ; in the Grk. writ. fr. Hom. Il. 18, 570 down.) *

2790 κιθαρ-ῳδός, -οῦ, ὁ, (κιθάρα [q. v.], and ᾠδός, contr. fr. ἀοιδός, a singer), a harper, one who plays on the harp and accompanies it with his voice : Rev. xiv. 2 ; xviii. 22. ([Hdt., Plat., al.], Diphil. in Athen. 6 p. 247 d.; Plut. mor. 166 a.; Ael. v. h. 4, 2 ; superl. (extended form) κιθαραοιδότατος, Arstph. vesp. 1278. Varro de r. r. 2, 1, 3 "non omnes, qui habent citharam, sunt citharoedi.")*

2791 Κιλικία, -ας, ή, Cilicia, a province of Asia Minor, bounded on the N. by Cappadocia, Lycaonia and Isauria, on the S. by the Mediterranean, on the E. by Syria, and on the W. by Pamphylia. Its capital, Tarsus, was the birthplace of Paul : Acts vi. 9 ; xv. 23, 41 ; xxi. 39 ; xxii. 3 ; xxiii. 34 ; xxvii. 5 ; Gal. i. 21. [Cf. Conybeare and Howson, St. Paul, i. 19 sqq.; Lewin, St. Paul, i. 78 sq.]*

2792 κινάμωμον, more correctly [so L T Tr WH] κιννάμωμον, -ον, τό, Hebr. קִנָּמוֹן, [(see L. and S. s. v.)], cinnamon : Rev. xviii. 13. (Hdt., Theophr., Strab., Diod., Joseph., al.; Sept.) Cf. Win. RWB. s. v. Zimmt ; [B.D. s. v. Cinnamon ; Alex.'s Kitto s. v. Kinnamon].*

2793 κινδυνεύω ; impf. ἐκινδύνευον ; (κίνδυνος) ; to be in jeopardy, to be in danger, to be put in peril : Lk. viii. 23 ; 1 Co. xv. 30 ; τοῦτο τὸ μέρος κινδυνεύει εἰς ἀπελεγμὸν ἐλθεῖν, this trade is in danger of coming into disrepute, Acts xix. 27 ; κινδ. ἐγκαλεῖσθαι, we are in danger of being accused, ib. 40. (From [Pind.] and Hdt. down ; Sept.) *

2794 κίνδυνος, -ου, ὁ, danger, peril : Ro. viii. 35 ; ἔκ τινος, prepared by one, [from one], 2 Co. xi. 26 ; ibid. with a gen. of the source from which the peril comes, [of, cf. W. § 30, 2 a.] ; so τῆς θαλάσσης, Plat. Euthyd. p. 279 e. ; de rep. i. p. 332 e. ; θαλασσῶν, Heliod. 2, 4, 65.*

2795 κινέω, -ῶ ; fut. κινήσω ; 1 aor. inf. κινῆσαι ; Pass., pres. κινοῦμαι ; 1 aor. ἐκινήθην ; (fr. κίω, poetic for ΙΩ, εἶμι, Curtius § 57 ; hence) **1.** prop. to cause to go, i. e. to move, set in motion, [fr. Hom. down] ; **a.** prop. in pass. [cf. W. 252 (237)] to be moved, move : of that motion which is evidence of life, Acts xvii. 28 (Gen. vii. 21) ; κινεῖν δακτύλῳ φορτία, to move burdens with a finger, Mt. xxiii. 4 ; τὴν κεφαλήν, to move to and fro [A.V. wag], (expressive of derision), Mt. xxvii. 39 ; Mk. xv. 29, (Sept. for רֹאשׁ הֵנִיעַ, Ps. xxi. (xxii.) 8 ; Job xvi. 4 ; Sir. xiii. 18, etc.) ; **b.** to move from a place, to remove : τὶ ἐκ τοῦ τόπου, Rev. ii. 5 ; ἐκ τῶν τόπων, pass., Rev. vi. 14. **2.**

Metaph. to move i. e. excite : στάσιν, a riot, disturbance, Acts xxiv. 5 ([see στάσις, 2] ; ταραχήν, Joseph. b. j. 2, 9, 4) ; τὴν πόλιν, to throw into commotion, pass., Acts xxi. 30. [Comp. : μετα-, συγ-κινέω.] *

2796 κίνησις, -εως, ή, (κινέω), [fr. Plato on], a moving, agitation : τοῦ ὕδατος, Jn. v. 3 [R L].*

2797 Κίς (L T Tr WH Κείς [cf. WH. App. p. 155; Tdf. Proleg. p. 84 ; B. 6 note[1], and see ει, ι]), ὁ, indecl., (קִישׁ [perh. 'a bow' (Gesen.)] fr. קוֹשׁ to lay snares), Kish, the father of Saul, the first king of Israel : Acts xiii. 21.*

(2797a); **see 5531** κίχρημι : 1 aor. act. impv. χρῆσον ; to lend : τινί τι, Lk. xi. 5. (From Hdt. down.) [Syn. see δανείζω, fin.] *

2798 κλάδος, -ου, ὁ, (κλάω) ; **a.** prop. a young, tender shoot, broken off for grafting. **b.** univ. a branch : Mt. xiii. 32 ; xxi. 8 ; xxiv. 32 ; Mk. iv. 32 ; xiii. 28 ; Lk. xiii. 19 ; as the Jewish patriarchs are likened to a root, so their posterity are likened to branches, Ro. xi. 16–19, 21 ; cf. Sir. xxiii. 25 ; xl. 15 ; Menand. frag. ed. Meineke p. 247 [frag. 182, vol. iv. 274 (Ber. 1841)]. (Tragg., Arstph., Theophr., Geop., al.) *

2799 κλαίω ; impf. ἔκλαιον ; fut. κλαύσω (Lk. vi. 25 ; Jn. xvi. 20 ; and Tr WHtxt. in Rev. xviii. 9, for κλαύσομαι, more com. in Grk. writ., esp. the earlier, and found in Lev. x. 6 ; Joel ii. 17, and acc. to most edd. in Rev. xviii. 19 ; cf. Krüger § 40 s. v., i. p. 175 sq.; Kühner § 343 s. v., i. p. 847 ; [Veitch s. v.] ; B. 60 (53) ; [W. 87 (83)]) ; 1 aor. ἔκλαυσα ; Sept. freq. for בָּכָה ; [from Hom. down] ; to mourn, weep, lament ; **a.** intrans.: Mk. xiv. 72 ; xvi. 10 ; Lk. vii. 13, 38 ; Jn. xi. 31, 33 ; xx. 11, 13, 15 ; Acts ix. 39 ; xxi. 13 ; Rev. [v. 5] ; xviii. 15, 19 ; πολλά, for which L T Tr WH πολύ, Rev. v. 4 ; πικρῶς, Mt. xxvi. 75 ; Lk. xxii. 62 ; weeping as the sign of pain and grief for the thing signified (i. e. for pain and grief), Lk. vi. 21, 25, (opp. to γελᾶν) ; Jn. xvi. 20 ; Ro. xii. 15, (opp. to χαίρειν) ; Phil. iii. 18 ; 1 Co. vii. 30 ; Jas. iv. 9 ; v. 1 ; of those who mourn the dead : Mk. v. 38 sq. ; Lk. vii. 32 ; viii. 52 ; ἐπί τινι, over any one, Lk. xix. 41 RG (Sir. xxii. 11) ; also joined with πενθεῖν, Rev. xviii. 11 R G L ; κλ. ἐπί τινα, Lk. xix. 41 L T Tr WH ; xxiii. 28 ; joined with κόπτεσθαι foll. by ἐπί τινα, Rev. xviii. 9 T Tr WH. **b.** trans. τινά, to weep for, mourn for, bewail, one [cf. B. § 131, 4 ; W. 32, 1 γ.] : Mt. ii. 18, and Rec. in Rev. xviii. 9.*

[Syn. δακρύω, κλαίω, ὀδύρομαι, θρηνέω, ἀλαλάζω (ὀλολύζω), στενάζω : strictly, δ. denotes to shed tears, weep silently ; κλ. to weep audibly, to cry as a child ; ὀδ. to give verbal expression to grief, to lament ; θρ. to give formal expression to grief, to sing a dirge ; ἀλ. to wail in oriental style, to howl in a consecrated, semi-liturgical fashion ; στεν. to express grief by inarticulate or semi-articulate sounds, to groan. Cf. Schmidt chh. 26, 126.]

2800 κλάσις, -εως, ή, (κλάω, q. v.), a breaking : τοῦ ἄρτου, Lk. xxiv. 35 ; Acts ii. 42. (Plat., Theophr., al.) *

2801 κλάσμα, -τος, τό, (κλάω), a fragment, broken piece : plur., of remnants of food, Mt. xiv. 20 ; xv. 37 ; Mk. vi. 43 ; viii. 8, 19 sq. ; Lk. ix. 17 ; Jn. vi. 12 sq. (Xen. cyn. 10, 5 ; Diod. 17, 13 ; Plut. Tib. Gr. 19 ; Anthol. ; Sept.) *

2802 Κλαύδη (L Tr WH Καῦδα [see WH. App. p. 160], T Κλαῦδα), -ης, ή, Clauda or Cauda the name of a small island lying near Crete on the south, called by Ptolem.

3, 17, 11 Κλαῦδος, by Pomp. Mela 2, 7 and Plin. h. n. 4, 20 (12), 61 *Gaudos*, [(now *Gaudo-nesi* or *Clauda-nesa*)]: Acts xxvii. 16.*

2803 **Κλαυδία**, -ας, ἡ, *Claudia*, a Christian woman: 2 Tim. iv. 21. [Cf. B. D. (esp. Am. ed.) s. v., also reff. s. v. Πούδης.]*

2804 **Κλαύδιος**, -ου, ὁ, *Claudius*.   **1.** *Tiberius Claudius Drusus Nero Germanicus*, the Roman emperor, who came into power A. D. 41, and was poisoned by his wife Agrippina in the year 54: Acts xi. 28; xviii. 2.   **2.** *Claudius Lysias*, a Roman military tribune: Acts xxiii. 26 [see B. D. Am. ed. s. v. Lysias].*

2805 **κλαυθμός**, -οῦ, ὁ, (κλαίω); fr. Hom. down; Sept. for בְּכִי; *weeping, lamentation*: Mt. ii. 18; [viii. 12]; xiii. 42, 50; xxii. 13; xxiv. 51; xxv. 30; Lk. xiii. 28; Acts xx. 37.*

2806 **κλάω**; 1 aor. ἔκλασα; Pass., [pres. ptcp. κλώμενος, 1 Co. xi. 24 R G (see below)]; 1 aor. ἐκλάσθην (Ro. xi. 20 L Tr); [fr. Hom. down]; *to break*: used in the N. T. of the breaking of bread (see ἄρτος, 1), Mt. xiv. 19; xv. 36; xxvi. 26; Mk. viii. 6; xiv. 22; Lk. xxii. 19; [xxiv. 30]; Acts ii. 46; xx. 7, 11; xxvii. 35; 1 Co. x. 16; xi. 24; with εἴς τινας added, a pregnant constr., equiv. to ‘to break and distribute among’ etc. (see εἰς, C. 1), Mk. viii. 19; metaph. τὸ σῶμα, shattered, as it were, by a violent death, 1 Co. xi. 24 R G. [COMP.: ἐκ-, κατα-κλάω.]*

2807 **κλείς**, -δός, acc. κλεῖδα and κλεῖν (Lk. xi. 52; Rev. iii. 7), acc. plur. κλεῖδας and κλεῖς (Mt. xvi. 19; Rev. i. 18; cf. Kühner § 130, i. p. 357; W. 65 (63), cf. B. 24 (22); [WH. App. p. 157]), ἡ, [fr. Hom. down]; *a key*. Since the keeper of the keys has the power to open and to shut, the word κλείς is fig. used in the N. T. to denote power and authority of various kinds [cf. B. D. s. v. Key], viz. τοῦ φρέατος, to open or unlock the pit, Rev. ix. 1, cf. 2; τῆς ἀβύσσου, to shut, Rev. xx. 1, cf. 3; τοῦ θανάτου καὶ τοῦ ᾅδου, the power to bring back into life from Hades and to leave there, Rev. i. 18; τῆς γνώσεως, the ability and opportunity to obtain knowledge, Lk. xi. 52; τῆς βασιλείας τῶν οὐρανῶν (see βασιλεία, 3 e. p. 97ᵇ sub fin.), Mt. xvi. 19; τοῦ Δαυίδ, the power of David (who is a type of the Messiah, the second David), i. e. of receiving into the Messiah's kingdom and of excluding from it, Rev. iii. 7 (apparently after Is. xxii. 22, where ἡ κλ. οἴκου Δαυίδ is given to the steward of the royal palace).*

2808 **κλείω**; fut. κλείσω, Rev. iii. 7 L T Tr WH; 1 aor. ἔκλεισα; Pass., pf. κέκλεισμαι, ptcp. κεκλεισμένος; 1 aor. ἐκλείσθην; Hebr. סָגַר; [fr. Hom. down]; *to shut, shut up*; prop.: τὴν θύραν, Mt. vi. 6; pass., Mt. xxv. 10; Lk. xi. 7; plur., Jn. xx. 19, 26; Acts xxi. 30; a prison, pass. Acts v. 23; πυλῶνας, pass. Rev. xxi. 25; τὴν ἄβυσσον, Rev. xx. 3 G L T Tr WH. metaph.: τὸν οὐρανόν, i. e. to cause the heavens to withhold rain, Lk. iv. 25; Rev. xi. 6; τὰ σπλάγχνα αὐτοῦ ἀπό τινος, to shut up compassion so that it is like a thing inaccessible to one, to be devoid of pity towards one [W. § 66, 2 d., cf. B. 322 (277)], 1 Jn. iii. 17; τὴν βασιλ. τῶν οὐρανῶν, to obstruct the entrance into the kingdom of heaven, Mt. xxiii. 13 (14); so used that τὴν βασ. τοῦ θεοῦ must be understood, Rev. iii. 7; τ.

θύραν, sc. τῆς βασ. τ. θεοῦ, ibid. 8; cf. Bleek ad loc. [COMP.: ἀπο-, ἐκ-, κατα-, συγ-κλείω.]*

2809 **κλέμμα**, -τος, τό, (κλέπτω)   **a.** *thing stolen* [Aristot.].   **b.** i. q. κλοπή *theft*, i. e. *the act committed* [Eur.. Arstph., al.]: plur. Rev. ix. 21.*

2810 **Κλεόπας** [on the decl. cf. B. 20 (18)], (apparently contr. fr. Κλεόπατρος, see Ἀντίπας [cf. Letronne in the Revue Archéologique, 1844–45, i. p. 485 sqq.]), ὁ, *Cleopas*, one of Christ's disciples: Lk. xxiv. 18. [Cf. Bp. Lghtft. Com. on Gal. p. 267; B. D. s. v.]*

2811 **κλέος**, -ους, τό, (κλέω equiv. to καλέω);   **1.** *rumor, report*.   **2.** *glory, praise*: 1 Pet. ii. 20. (In both senses com. in Grk. writ. fr. Hom. down; for שֶׁמַע, Job xxviii. 22.) *

2812 **κλέπτης**, -ου, ὁ, (κλέπτω), [fr. Hom. down], Sept. for גַּנָּב, *a thief*: Mt. vi. 19 sq.; xxiv. 43; Lk. xii. 33, 39; Jn. x. 1, 10; 1 Co. vi. 10; 1 Pet. iv. 15; an embezzler, pilferer, Jn. xii. 6; ἔρχεσθαι or ἥκειν ὡς κλ. ἐν νυκτί, i. q. to come unexpectedly, 1 Th. v. 2, 4; 2 Pet. iii. 10; Rev. iii. 3; xvi. 15; the name is transferred to false teachers, who do not care to instruct men, but abuse their confidence for their own gain, Jn. x. 8. [SYN. see λῃστής, fin.]*

2813 **κλέπτω**; fut. κλέψω (Sept. also in Ex. xx. 14; Lev. xix. 11; Deut. v. 19, for κλέψομαι more com. [(?) cf. Veitch s. v.; Kühner § 343 s. v., i. 848] in prof. auth.); 1 aor. ἔκλεψα; [fr. Hom. down]; Sept. for גָּנַב;   **a.** *to steal*; absol. *to commit a theft*: Mt. vi. 19 sq.; xix. 18; Mk. x. 19; Lk. xviii. 20; Jn. x. 10; Ro. ii. 21; xiii. 9; Eph. iv. 28.   **b.** trans. *to steal* i. e. *take away by stealth*: τινά, the dead body of one, Mt. xxvii. 64; xxviii. 13.*

2814 **κλῆμα**, -ατος, τό, (fr. κλάω, q. v.), i. q. κλάδος, *a tender and flexible branch*; spec. *the shoot* or *branch of a vine, a vine-sprout*: Jn. xv. 2–6 (so Arstph. eccles. 1031; Aeschin. in Ctes. p. 77, 27; Theophr. h. pl. 4, 13, 5; ἀμπέλου κλῆμα, Plat. rep. i. p. 353 a.; Sept., Ezek. xv. 2; xvii. 6 sq.; Joel i. 7).*

2815 **Κλήμης** [cf. B. 16 sq. (15)], -εντος, ὁ, *Clement*, a companion of Paul and apparently a member of the church at Philippi: Phil. iv. 3. Acc. to the rather improbable tradition of the catholic church, he is identical with that Clement who was bishop of Rome towards the close of the first century; [but see Bp. Lghtft. Com. on Phil. l. c. ‘Detached Note’; Salmon in Dict. of Chris. Biogr. i. 555 sq.].*

2816 **κληρονομέω**, -ῶ; fut. κληρονομήσω; 1 aor. ἐκληρονόμησα; pf. κεκληρονόμηκα; (κληρονόμος, q. v.; cf. οἰκονόμος); Sept. for נָחַל and much oftener for יָרַשׁ;   **1.** *to receive a lot, receive by lot*; esp. *to receive a part of an inheritance, receive as an inheritance, obtain by right of inheritance*; so, particularly in the Attic orators, w. a gen. of the thing; in later writ. not infreq. w. an acc. of the thing (cf. Lob. ad Phryn. p. 129; Sturz, De dial. Maced. etc. p. 140; W. 200 (188); [B. § 132, 8]); absol. *to be an heir, to inherit*: Gal. iv. 30 fr. Gen. xxi. 10.   **2.** univ. *to receive the portion assigned to one, receive an allotted portion, receive as one's own* or *as a possession*; *to become partaker of, to obtain* [cf. Eng. "inherit"], (as φήμην, Polyb. 18, 38

(55), 8 ; τὴν ἐπ' εὐσεβείᾳ δόξαν, 15, 22, 3) ; in bibl. Grk. everywh. w. the acc. of the thing ; so very freq. in the O. T. in the phrase κληρ. γῆν and τὴν γῆν, of the occupation of the land of Canaan by the Israelites, as Lev. xx. 24 ; Deut. iv. 22, 26 ; vi. 1, etc. But as the Israelites after taking possession of the land were harassed almost perpetually by their hostile neighbors, and even driven out of the country for a considerable period, it came to pass that the phrase was transferred to denote the tranquil and stable possession of the holy land crowned with all divine blessings, an experience which p i o u s Israelites were to expect under the M e s s i a h : Ps. xxiv. (xxv.) 13 ; xxxvi. (xxxvii.) 9, 11, 22, 29, 34 Alex. ; Is. lx. 21 ; Tob. iv. 12 ; ἐκ δευτέρας κληρονομήσουσι τὴν γῆν, Is. lxi. 7 ; hence it became a formula denoting *to partake of eternal salvation in the Messiah's kingdom* : Mt. v. 5 (4) (fr. Ps. xxxvi. (xxxvii.) 11), where see Bleek. ζωὴν αἰώνιον, Mt. xix. 29 ; Mk. x. 17 ; Lk. x. 25 ; xviii. 18 ; τὴν βασιλείαν, Mt. xxv. 34 ; βασιλείαν θεοῦ, 1 Co. vi. 9 sq. ; xv. 50 ; Gal. v. 21 ; σωτηρίαν, Heb. i. 14 ; τὰς ἐπαγγελίας, Heb. vi. 12 ; ἀφθαρσίαν, 1 Co. xv. 50 ; ταῦτα [Rec. πάντα], Rev. xxi. 7 ; ὄνομα, Heb. i. 4 ; τὴν εὐλογίαν, Heb. xii. 17 ; 1 Pet. iii. 9. [COMP. : κατα-κληρονομέω.] *

2817 κληρονομία, -ας, ἡ, (κληρονόμος), Sept. time and again for נַחֲלָה, several times for מוֹרָשָׁה‎ יְרֻשָּׁה, etc. ; **1.** *an inheritance, property received* (or *to be received*) *by inheritance*, (Isocr., Dem., Aristot.) : Mt. xxi. 38 ; Mk. xii. 7 ; Lk. xii. 13 ; xx. 14. **2.** *what is given to one as a possession* ([cf. Eng. "inheritance"] ; see κληρονομέω, 2) : διδόναι τί τινι κληρονομίαν, Acts vii. 5 ; λαμβάνειν τι εἰς κληρ. Heb. xi. 8 [(cf. Aristot. eth. Nic. 7, 14 p. 1153ᵇ, 33)]. Agreeably to the O. T. usage, which employs נַחֲלָה now of the portion of the holy land allotted to each of the several tribes (Josh. xiii. 23, 28, etc.), now of the whole territory given to Israel for a possession (Deut. iv. 38 ; xv. 4, etc. — and nothing appeared to the Israelites more desirable than the quiet, prosperous, permanent possession of this land, see κληρονομέω, 2), the noun κληρονομία, lifted to a loftier sense in the N. T., is used to denote **a.** *the eternal blessedness in the consummated kingdom of God which is to be expected after the visible return of Christ* : Gal. iii. 18 ; Col. iii. 24 (τῆς κληρ. gen. of appos. [W. § 59, 8 a.]) ; Heb. xv. 15 ; 1 Pet. i. 4 ; ἡμῶν, destined for us, Eph. i. 14 ; τοῦ θεοῦ, given by God, 18. **b.** *the share which an individual will have in that eternal blessedness* : Acts xx. 32 ; Eph. v. 5.*

2818 κληρο-νόμος, -ου, ὁ, (κλῆρος, and νέμομαι to possess), prop. *one who receives by lot* ; hence **1.** *an heir* (in Grk. writ. fr. Plat. down) ; **a.** prop. : Mt. xxi. 38 ; Mk. xii. 7 ; Lk. xx. 14 ; Gal. iv. 1. **b.** in Messianic usage, *one who receives his allotted possession by right of sonship* : so of Christ, as κληρονόμος πάντων, all things being subjected to his sway, Heb. i. 2 ; of Christians, as exalted by faith to the dignity of sons of Abraham and so of sons of God, and hence to receive the blessings of God's kingdom promised to Abraham : absol., Ro. viii. 17 ; Gal. iii. 29 ; with τοῦ θεοῦ added, i. e. of God's possessions, equiv. to τῆς δόξης (see δόξα, III. 4 b.), Ro. viii. 17 ; θεοῦ

διὰ Χριστοῦ, by the favor of Christ (inasmuch as through him we have obtained ἡ υἱοθεσία), Gal. iv. 7 Rec., for which L T Tr WH read διὰ θεοῦ [see διά, A. III. 1] (cf. *C. F. A. Fritzsche* in Fritzschiorum opuscc. p. 148 [who advocates the Rec. as that reading in which the others prob. originated (but cf. Meyer in loc.; WH in loc.)]) ; τοῦ κόσμου, of government over the world, Ro. iv. 13 sq.; ζωῆς αἰωνίου, Tit. iii. 7 ; τῆς βασιλείας, Jas. ii. 5. **2.** the idea of inheritance having disappeared, *one who has acquired* or *obtained the portion allotted him* : w. gen. of the thing, Heb. vi. 17 ; xi. 7 ; τοῦ σκότους, used of the devil, Ev. Nicod. c. 20 [or Descens. Chr. ad Inferos 4, 1]. (Sept. four times for יוֹרֵשׁ : Judg. xviii. 7 ; 2 S. xiv. 7 ; Jer. viii. 10 ; Mic. i. 15.) *

2819 κλῆρος, -ου, ὁ, fr. Hom. down ; Sept. mostly for גּוֹרָל and נַחֲלָה ; *a lot* ; i. e. **1.** *an object used in casting or drawing lots*, which was either a pebble, or a potsherd, or a bit of wood, (hence κλῆρος is to be derived fr. κλάω [cf. Ellicott on Col. i. 12]) : Acts i. 26 (see below) ; βάλλειν κλῆρ., Mt. xxvii. 35 ; Mk. xv. 24 ; Lk. xxiii. 34 ; Jn. xix. 24, (Ps. xxi. (xxii.) 19 ; Jon. i. 7, etc.) ; the lots of the several persons concerned, inscribed with their names, were thrown together into a vase, which was then shaken, and he whose lot first fell out upon the ground was the one chosen (Hom. Il. 3, 316, 325 ; 7, 175, etc. ; Liv. 23, 3 [but cf. B. D. Am. ed. s. v. Lot]) ; hence ὁ κλῆρος πίπτει ἐπί τινα, Acts i. 26 (Ezek. xxiv. 6 ; Jon. i. 7). **2.** *what is obtained by lot, allotted portion* : λαγχάνειν and λαμβάνειν τὸν κλῆρον τῆς διακονίας, a portion in the ministry common to the apostles, Acts i. 17, 25 R G ; ἔστι μοι κλῆρος ἔν τινι, dat. of the thing, Acts viii. 21 ; like κληρονομία (q. v.) it is used of the part which one will have in eternal salvation, λαβεῖν τὸν κλ. ἐν τοῖς ἡγιασμένοις, among the sanctified, Acts xxvi. 18 (Sap. v. 5) ; of eternal salvation itself, κλῆρος τῶν ἁγίων, i. e. the eternal salvation which God has assigned to the saints, Col. i. 12 [where cf. Bp. Lghtft.]. of persons, οἱ κλῆροι, those whose care and oversight has been assigned to one [allotted charge], used of Christian churches, the administration of which falls to the lot of the presbyters : 1 Pet. v. 3, cf. Acts xvii. 4 ; [for patristic usage see Soph. Lex. s. v.; cf. Bp. Lghtft. on Phil. p. 246 sq.].*

2820 κληρόω, -ῶ : 1 aor. pass. ἐκληρώθην ; (κλῆρος) ; in class. Grk. **1.** *to cast lots, determine by lot.* **2.** *to choose by lot* : τινά [Hdt. 1, 94 ; al.]. **3.** *to allot, assign by lot* : τινά τινι, one to another as a possession, Pind. Ol. 8, 19. **4.** once in the N. T., *to make a κλῆρος i. e. a heritage, private possession* : τινά, pass. ἐν ᾧ ἐκληρώθημεν [but Lchm. ἐκλήθημεν] in whom lies the reason why we were made the κλῆρος τοῦ θεοῦ (a designation transferred from the Jews in the O. T. to Christians, cf. Add. to Esth. iii. 10 [iv. line 12 sq. (Tdf.)] and Fritzsche in loc.; [cf. Deut. iv. 20 ; ix. 29]), the heritage of God Eph. i. 11 [see Ellicott in loc.]. (In eccles. writ. it signifies *to become a clergyman* [see reff. s. v. κλῆρος, fin.].) [COMP. : προσ-κληρόω.] *

2821 κλῆσις, -εως, ἡ, (καλέω) ; **1.** *a calling, calling to,* [(Xen., Plat., al.)]. **2.** *a call, invitation* : to a feast

(3 Macc. v. 14; Xen. symp. 1, 7); in the N. T. everywhere in a technical sense, *the divine invitation to embrace salvation in the kingdom of God*, which is made esp. through the preaching of the gospel: with gen. of the author, τοῦ θεοῦ, Eph. i. 18; ἀμεταμέλ. . . . ἡ κλ. τοῦ θεοῦ, God does not repent of the invitation to salvation, which he decided of old to give to the people of Israel, and which he promised their fathers (i. e. the patriarchs), Ro. xi. 29; ἡ ἄνω [q. v. (a.)] κλῆσις τοῦ θεοῦ ἐν Χριστῷ, which was made in heaven by God on the ground of Christ, Phil. iii. 14; also ἡ ἐπουράνιος κλῆσις, Heb. iii. 1; καλεῖν τινα κλήσει, 2 Tim. i. 9; pass. Eph. iv. 1; ἀξιοῦν τινα κλήσεως is used of one whom God declares worthy of the calling which he has commanded to be given him, and therefore fit to obtain the blessings promised in the call, 2 Th. i. 11; w. gen. of the obj., ὑμῶν, which ye have shared in, Eph. iv. 4; 2 Pet. i. 10; what its characteristics have been in your case, as having no regard to learning, riches, station, etc. 1 Co. i. 26; used somewhat peculiarly, of the condition in which the calling finds one, whether circumcised or uncircumcised, slave or freeman, 1 Co. vii. 20.*

2822 κλητός, -ή, -όν (καλέω), [fr. Hom. down], *called, invited,* (to a banquet, [1 K. i. 41, 49]; 3 Macc. v. 14; Aeschin. 50, 1); in the N. T.   **a.** *invited (by God in the proclamation of the gospel) to obtain eternal salvation in the kingdom of God through Christ* (see καλέω, 1 b. β. [cf. W. 35 (34)]): Ro. viii. 28; 1 Co. i. 24; Jude 1; κλητοὶ κ. ἐκλεκτοὶ κ. πιστοί, Rev. xvii. 14; κλητοί and ἐκλεκτοί are distinguished (see ἐκλεκτός, 1 a.) in Mt. xx. 16 [T WH om. Tr br. the cl.]; xxii. 14, a distinction which does not agree with Paul's view (see καλέω, u. s.; [Weiss, Bibl. Theol. § 88; Bp. Lghtft. Com. on Col. iii. 12]); κλητοὶ Ἰησοῦ Χριστοῦ, gen. of possessor [W. 195 (183); B. § 132, 23], devoted to Christ and united to him, Ro. i. 6; κλητοὶ ἅγιοι, *holy* (or 'saints') *by the calling of God,* Ro. i. 7; 1 Co. i. 2.   **b.** *called to* (the discharge of) *some office:* κλητὸς ἀπόστολος, i. e. divinely selected and appointed (see καλέω, u. s.), Ro. i. 1; 1 Co. i. 1 [L br. κλ.]; cf. Gal. i. 15.*

2823 κλίβανος, -ου, ὁ, (for κρίβανος, more com. in earlier [yet κλίβ. in Hdt. 2, 92 (cf. Athen. 3 p. 110 c.)] and Attic Grk.; see Lob. ad Phryn. p. 179; Passow s. v. κρίβανος; [W. 22]);   **1.** *a clibanus,* an earthen vessel for baking bread (Hebr. תַּנּוּר, Ex. viii. 3 (vii. 29 Hebr.); Lev. ii. 4; xxvi. 26; Hos. vii. 4). It was broader at the bottom than above at the orifice, and when sufficiently heated by a fire kindled within, the dough was baked by being spread upon the outside [but acc. to others, the dough was placed inside and the fire or coals outside, the vessel being often perforated with small holes that the heat might the better penetrate; cf. Rich, Dict. of Grk. and Rom. Antiq. s. v. clibanus; see Schol. on Arstph. Acharn. 86 (iv. 2 p. 339, 20 sq. Dind.)].   **2.** i. q. ἰπνός, *a furnace, an oven:* so Mt. vi. 30; Lk. xii. 28.*

2824 κλίμα or κλῖμα (on the accent cf. reff. s. v. κρίμα), -τος, τό, (κλίνω);   **1.** *an inclination, slope, declivity:* τῶν ὁρῶν, Polyb. 2, 16, 3; [al.]. spec.   **2.** *the* [supposed]

sloping of the earth fr. the equator towards the poles, a zone: Aristot., Dion. H., Plut., al.; Joseph. b. j. 5, 12, 2.   **3.** *a tract of land, a region:* Ro. xv. 23; 2 Co. xi. 10; Gal. i. 21; (Polyb. 5, 44, 6; 7, 6, 1; Hdian. 2, 11, 8 [4 ed. Bekk.]; al.).*

κλινάριον, -ου, τό, (dimin. of κλίνη; see γυναικάριον), *a small bed, a couch:* Acts v. 15 L T Tr WH. (Arstph. frag. 33 d.; Epict. diss. 3, 5, 13; Artem. oneir. 2, 57; [cf. κλινίδιον, and Pollux as there referred to].)*   **see 2825**

κλίνη, -ης, ἡ, (κλίνω); fr. Hdt. down; Sept. for מִטָּה, also for עֶרֶשׂ; *a bed:* univ., Mk. vii. 30; Lk. xvii. 34; *a couch to recline on at meals,* Mk. iv. 21; vii. 4 [T WH om.]; Lk. viii. 16; *a couch on which a sick man is carried,* Mt. ix. 2, 6; Lk. v. 18; plur. Acts v. 15 R G; βάλλειν εἰς κλίνην, to cast into a bed, i. e. to afflict with disease, Rev. ii. 22.*   **2825**

κλινίδιον, -ου, τό, (κλίνη), *a small bed, a couch:* Lk. v. 19, 24. (Dion. H. antt. 7, 68; Artem. oneir. 1, 2; Antonin. 10, 28; several times in Plut.; [cf. Pollux 10, 7].) *   **2826**

κλίνω; 1 aor. ἔκλινα; pf. κέκλικα;   **1.** trans.   **a.** *to incline, bow:* τὴν κεφαλήν, of one dying, Jn. xix. 30; τὸ πρόσωπον εἰς τ. γῆν, of the terrified, Lk. xxiv. 5.   **b.** i. q. *to cause to fall back:* παρεμβολάς, Lat. *inclinare acies,* i. e. to turn to flight, Heb. xi. 34 (μάχην, Hom. Il. 14, 510; Τρῶας, 5, 37; Ἀχαιούς, Od. 9, 59).   **c.** *to recline:* τὴν κεφαλήν, in a place for repose [A. V. lay one's head], Mt. viii. 20; Lk. ix. 58.   **2.** intrans. *to incline one's self* [cf. B. 145 (127); W. § 38, 1]: of the declining day [A. V. wear away, be far spent], Lk. ix. 12; xxiv. 29; Jer. vi. 4; ἅμα τῷ κλῖναι τὸ τρίτον μέρος τῆς νυκτός, Polyb. 3, 93, 7; ἐγκλίναντος τοῦ ἡλίου ἐς ἑσπέραν, Arr. anab. 3, 4, 2. [COMP.: ἀνα-, ἐκ-, κατα-, προσ-κλίνω.]*   **2827**

κλισία, -ας, ἡ, (κλίνω); fr. Hom. down; prop. a place for lying down or reclining; hence   **1.** *a hut,* erected to pass the night in.   **2.** *a tent.*   **3.** any thing to recline on; a chair in which to lean back the head, *reclining-chair.*   **4.** *a company reclining; a row* or *party of persons reclining at meal:* so in plur., Lk. ix. 14, on which cf. W. 229 (214); likewise in Joseph. antt. 12, 2, 12; Plut. Sert. 26.*   **2828**

κλοπή, -ῆς, ἡ, (κλέπτω), *theft:* plur. [cf. B. 77 (67); W. 176 (166)], Mt. xv. 19; Mk. vii. 21 (22). [From Aeschyl. down.] *   **2829**

κλύδων, -ωνος, ὁ, (κλύζω, to wash against); fr. Hom. down; *a dashing or surging wave, a surge, a violent agitation of the sea:* τοῦ ὕδατος, Lk. viii. 24; τῆς θαλάσσης, Jas. i. 6 (Jon. i. 4, 12; Sap. xiv. 5).*   **2830**

[SYN. κλύδων, κῦμα: κῦμα *a wave,* suggesting uninterrupted succession; κλύδων *a billow, surge,* suggesting size and extension. So too in the fig. application of the words. Schmidt ch. 56.]

κλυδωνίζομαι, ptcp. κλυδωνιζόμενος; (κλύδων); *to be tossed by the waves;* metaph. *to be agitated* (like the waves) *mentally* [A. V. tossed to and fro]: with dat. of instrum. παντὶ ἀνέμῳ τῆς διδασκαλίας, Eph. iv. 14 (cf. Jas. i. 6; οἱ ἄδικοι κλυδωνισθήσονται καὶ ἀναπαύσασθαι οὐ δυνήσονται, Is. lvii. 20; ὁ δῆμος ταρασσόμενος καὶ κλυδωνιζόμενος οἰχήσεται φεύγων, Joseph. antt. 9 11, 3; κλυδωνιζόμενος   **2831** ἐκ τοῦ πόθου, Aristaenet. epp. 1, 26, p. 121 ed. Boissonade [ep. 27, 14 ed. Abresch]).*

2832   **Κλωπᾶς**, -ᾶ [B 20 (18); W. § 8, 1], ὁ, (חַלְפָּא); appar. identical with Alphæus, see Ἀλφαῖος, 2 [cf. Heinichen's note on Euseb. h. e. 3, 11, 2]), *Clopas* (Vulg. [*Cleopas* and] *Cleophas*), the father of the apostle James the less, and husband of Mary the sister of the mother of Jesus: Jn. xix. 25 (ἡ τοῦ Κλωπᾶ sc. γυνή [cf. W. 131 (125) note]).*

2833   **κνήθω**: pres. pass. κνήθομαι; (fr. κνάω, inf. κνᾶν and Attic κνῆν); *to scratch, tickle, make to itch*; pass. *to itch*: κνηθόμενοι τὴν ἀκοήν (on the acc. cf. W. § 32, 5), i. e. desirous of hearing something pleasant (Hesych. κνήθ. τ. ἀκοήν· ζητοῦντές τι ἀκοῦσαι καθ᾽ ἡδονήν), 2 Tim. iv. 3. (Mid. τὸν ὄνον κνήθεσθαι εἰς τὰς ἀκάνθας τὰ ἕλκη, its sores, Aristot. h. a. 9, 1 p. 609ᵃ, 32; κνῆν Ἀττικοί, κνήθειν Ἕλληνες, Moeris p. 234; cf. Veitch s. v. κνάω].)*

2834   **Κνίδος**, -ου, ἡ, *Cnidus* or *Gnidus*, a peninsula [now *Cape Crio*] and a city of the same name, on the coast of Caria: Acts xxvii. 7 (1 Macc. xv. 23). [B. D. s. v. Cnidus; Lewin, St. Paul, ii. 190.] *

2835   **κοδράντης**, -ου [B. 17 (16)], ὁ; a Lat. word, *quadrans* (i. e. the fourth part of an *as*); in the N. T. a coin equal to one half the Attic chalcus or to two λεπτά (see λεπτόν): Mk. xii. 42; Mt. v. 26. The word is fully discussed by Fischer, De vitiis lexx. N. T. p. 447 sqq. [A. V. *farthing*; see BB. DD. s. v.] *

2836   **κοιλία**, -ας, ἡ, (κοῖλος hollow); Sept. for בֶּטֶן the belly, מֵעִים the bowels, קֶרֶב the interior, the midst of a thing, רֶחֶם the womb; *the belly*: and   **1.** *the whole belly*, the entire cavity; hence ἡ ἄνω and ἡ κάτω κοιλία, *the upper* [i. e. *the stomach*] *and the lower belly* are distinguished; very often so in Grk. writ. fr. Hdt. down.   **2.** *the lower belly*, the alvine region, the receptacle of the excrement (Plut. symp. 7, 1, 3 sub fin. εἴπερ εἰς κοιλίαν ἐχώρει διὰ στομάχου πᾶν τὸ πινόμενον): Mt. xv. 17; Mk. vii. 19.   **3.** *the gullet* (Lat. *stomachus*): Mt. xii. 40; Lk. xv. 16 [WH Tr mrg. χορτασθῆναι ἐκ etc.]; 1 Co. vi. 13; Rev. x. 9 sq.; δουλεύειν τῇ κοιλίᾳ, to be given up to the pleasures of the palate, to gluttony, (see δουλεύω, 2 b.), Ro. xvi. 18; also ὧν ὁ θεὸς ἡ κοιλία, Phil. iii. 19; κοιλίας ὄρεξις, Sir. xxiii. 6.   **4.** *the womb*, the place where the fœtus is conceived and nourished till birth: Lk. i. 41 sq. 44; ii. 21; xi. 27; xxiii. 29; Jn. iii. 4, (very often so in Sept.; very rarely in prof. auth.; Epict. diss. 3, 22, 74; of the uterus of animals, ibid. 2, 16, 43); ἐκ (beginning from [see ἐκ, IV. 1]) κοιλίας μητρός, Mt. xix. 12; Lk. i. 15; Acts iii. 2; xiv. 8; Gal. i. 15, (for מִבֶּטֶן אֵם, Ps. xxi. (xxii.) 11; lxx. (lxxi.) 6; Job i. 21; Is. xlix. 1; Judg. xvi. 17 [Vat. ἀπὸ κ. μ.; cf. W. 33 (32)]).   **5.** in imitation of the Hebr. בֶּטֶן, tropically, *the innermost part of a man, the soul, heart*, as the seat of thought, feeling, choice, (Job xv. 35; xxxii. 18 [Sept. γαστήρ]; Prov. xviii. 8 [Sept. ψυχή]; xx. 27, 30; xxvi. 22 [Sept. σπλάγχνα]; Hab. iii. 16; Sir. xix. 12; li. 21): Jn. vii. 38.*

2837   **κοιμάω**, -ῶ: Pass., pres. κοιμάομαι, κοιμῶμαι; pf. κεκοίμημαι [cf. W. 274 (257)]; 1 aor. ἐκοιμήθην; 1 fut. κοιμηθήσομαι; (akin to κεῖμαι; Curtius § 45); *to cause to sleep, put to sleep*, (Hom. et al.); metaph. *to still, calm, quiet*, (Hom., Aeschyl., Plat.); Pass. *to sleep, fall asleep*: prop., Mt. xxviii. 13; Lk. xxii. 45; Jn. xi. 12; Acts xii. 6; Sept. for שָׁכַב. metaph. and euphemistically i. q. *to die* [cf. Eng. *to fall asleep*]: Jn. xi. 11; Acts vii. 60; xiii. 36; 1 Co. vii. 39; xi. 30; xv. 6, 51 [cf. W. 555 (517); B. 121 (106) note]; 2 Pet. iii. 4; οἱ κοιμώμενοι, κεκοιμημένοι, κοιμηθέντες, i. q. *the dead*: Mt. xxvii. 52; 1 Co. xv. 20; 1 Th. iv. 13-15; with ἐν Χριστῷ added (see ἐν, I. 6 b. p. 211ᵇ), 1 Co. xv. 18; in the same sense Is. xiv. 8; xliii. 17; 1 K. xi. 43; 2 Macc. xii. 45; Hom. Il. 11, 241; Soph. Electr. 509.*

2838   **κοίμησις**, -εως, ἡ, *a reposing, taking rest*: Jn. xi. 13 [cf. W. § 59, 8 a.]; of death, Sir. xlvi. 19; xlviii. 13; *a lying, reclining*, Plat. conv. p. 183 a.*

2839   **κοινός**, -ή, -όν, (fr. ξύν, σύν, with; hence esp. in Epic ξυνός for κοινός, whence the Lat. *cena* [(?); see Vaniček p. 1065]);   **1.** as in Grk. writ. fr. Hesiod (opp. 721) down (opp. to ἴδιος) *common* (i. e. belonging to several, Lat. *communis*): Acts ii. 44; iv. 32; κοινὴ πίστις, Tit. i. 4; σωτηρία, Jude 3.   **2.** by a usage foreign to class. Grk., *common* i. e. ordinary, belonging to the generality (Lat. *vulgaris*); by the Jews opp. to ἅγιος, ἡγιασμένος, καθαρός; hence *unhallowed*, Lat. *profanus*, levitically *unclean*, (in class. Grk. βέβηλος, q. v. 2): Mk. vii. 2, 5 (where R L mrg. ἀνίπτοις); Ro. xiv. 14; Heb. x. 29; Rev. xxi. 27 [Rec. κοινοῦν], (1 Macc. i. 47; φαγεῖν κοινά, ib. 62; κοινοὶ ἄνθρωποι, common people, *profanum vulgus*, Joseph. antt. 12, 2, 14; οἱ τὸν κοινὸν βίον προῃρημένοι, i. e. a life repugnant to the holy law, ibid. 13, 1, 1; οὐ γὰρ ὡς κοινὸν ἄρτον οὐδὲ ὡς κοινὸν πόμα ταῦτα (i. e. the bread and wine of the sacred supper) λαμβάνομεν, Justin Mart. apol. 1, 66; (οἱ Χριστιανοὶ) τράπεζαν κοινὴν παρατίθενται, ἀλλ᾽ οὐ κοινήν, a table *communis* but not *profanus*, Ep. ad Diogn. 5, on which cf. Otto's note); κοινὸν καὶ [R G ἢ] ἀκάθαρτον, Acts x. 14; κοιν. ἢ ἀκάθ., ib. x. 28; xi. 8, (κοινὰ ἢ ἀκάθαρτα οὐκ ἐσθίομεν, Justin Mart. dial. c. Tr. c. 20). [Cf. Trench § ci.]*

2840   **κοινόω**, -ῶ; 1 aor. inf. κοινῶσαι [cf. W. 91 (86)]; pf. κεκοίνωκα; pf. pass. ptcp. κεκοινωμένος; (κοινός);   **1.** in class. Grk. *to make common*.   **2.** in bibl. use (see κοινός, 2),   **a.** *to make* (levitically) *unclean, render unhallowed, defile, profane* (which the Grks. express by βεβηλόω, cf. Win. De verb. comp. etc. Pt. ii. p. 24 note 33 [where he calls attention to Luke's accuracy in putting κοινοῦν into the mouth of Jews speaking to Jews (Acts xxi. 28) and βεβηλοῦν when they address Felix (xxiv. 6)]): Rev. xxi. 27 Rec.; Mt. xv. 11, 18, 20; Mk. vii. 15, 18, 20, 23; pass. Heb. ix. 13; τί, Acts xxi. 28; γαστέρα μιαροφαγίᾳ, 4 Macc. vii. 6.   **b.** *to declare* or *count unclean*: Acts x. 15 (cf. 28); xi. 9; see δικαιόω, 3.*

2841   **κοινωνέω**, -ῶ; 1 aor. ἐκοινώνησα; pf. κεκοινώνηκα; (κοινωνός);   **a.** *to come into communion* or *fellowship, to become a sharer, be made a partner*: as in Grk. writ. w. gen. of the thing, Heb. ii. 14 [(so Prov. i. 11; 2 Macc. xiv. 25)]; w. dat. of the thing (rarely so in Grk. writ.), Ro. xv. 27; [1 Pet. iv. 13].   **b.** *to enter into fellowship, join one's self as an associate, make one's self a sharer*

or *partner*: as in Grk. writ., w. dat. of the thing, 1 Tim.
v. 22; 2 Jn. 11; ταῖς χρείαις τινός, so to make another's
necessities one's own as to relieve them [A. V. *communicating to the necessities* etc.], Ro. xii. 13; w. dat. of pers.
foll. by εἴς τι (as in Plat. rep. 5 p. 453 a.), Phil. iv. 15;
foll. by ἐν w. dat. of the thing which one shares with
another, Gal. vi. 6 (κοινωνήσεις ἐν πᾶσι τῷ πλησίον σου
καὶ οὐκ ἐρεῖς ἴδια εἶναι, Barnab. ep. 19, 8); cf. W. § 30,
8 a.; [B. § 132, 8; Bp. Lghtft. or Ellicott on Gal. l. c.
COMP.: συγ-κοινωνέω.]*

2842 κοινωνία, -ας, ἡ, (κοινωνός), *fellowship, association, community, communion, joint participation, intercourse*; in
the N. T. as in class. Grk.   **1.** *the share which one
has in anything, participation*; w. gen. of the thing in
which he shares: πνεύματος, Phil. ii. 1; τοῦ ἁγίου πνεύματος, 2 Co. xiii. 13 (14); τῶν παθημάτων τοῦ Χριστοῦ, Phil.
iii. 10; τῆς πίστεως, Philem. 6 [cf. Bp. Lghtft.]; τοῦ
αἵματος τοῦ Χριστοῦ, i. e. in the benefits of Christ's death,
1 Co. x. 16 [cf. Meyer ad loc.]; τοῦ σώματος τοῦ Χρ. in the
(mystical) body of Christ or the church, ibid.; τῆς διακονίας, 2 Co. viii. 4; τοῦ μυστηρίου, Eph. iii. 9 Rec. εἰς
κοινωνίαν τοῦ υἱοῦ τοῦ θεοῦ, to obtain fellowship in the
dignity and blessings of the Son of God, 1 Co. i. 9, where
cf. Meyer.   **2.** *intercourse, fellowship, intimacy*:
δεξιὰ κοινωνίας, the right hand as the sign and pledge
of fellowship (in fulfilling the apostolic office), Gal. ii. 9
[where see Bp. Lghtft.]; τίς κοιν. φωτὶ πρὸς σκότος; what
in common has light with darkness? 2 Co vi. 14 (τίς οὖν
κοινωνία πρὸς Ἀπόλλωνα τῷ μηδὲν οἰκεῖον ἐπιτετηδευκότι,
Philo, leg. ad Gaium § 14 fin.; εἰ δέ τις ἐστι κοινωνία πρὸς
θεοὺς ἡμῖν, Stob. serm. 28 [i. p. 87 ed. Gaisf.]); used of
the intimate bond of fellowship which unites Christians:
absol. Acts ii. 42; with εἰς τὸ εὐαγγέλιον added, Phil. i.
5; κοινωνίαν ἔχειν μεθ᾽ ἡμῶν, μετ᾽ ἀλλήλων, 1 Jn. i. 3, 7;
of the fellowship of Christians with God and Christ, μετὰ
τοῦ πατρὸς κ. μετὰ τοῦ υἱοῦ αὐτοῦ, 1 Jn i. 3, 6, (which fellowship, acc. to John's teaching, consists in the fact that
Christians are partakers in common of the same mind as
God and Christ, and of the blessings arising therefrom).
By a use unknown to prof. auth. κοινωνία in the N. T.
denotes   **3.** *a benefaction jointly contributed, a collection, a contribution*, as exhibiting an embodiment and
proof of fellowship (cf. *Grimm*, Exeget. Hdbch. on Wisd.
viii. 18, p. 176): 2 Co. viii. 4; εἴς τινα, for the benefit of
one, 2 Co. ix. 13; ποιεῖσθαι κοιν. (to make a contribution) εἴς τινα, Ro. xv. 26; joined with εὐποιΐα, Heb. xiii.
16.   [Cf. B. § 132, 8.]*

2843 κοινωνικός, -ή, -όν, (κοινωνία);   **1.** *social, sociable,
ready and apt to form and maintain communion and fellowship*: Plat. deff. p. 411 e.; Aristot. pol. 3, 13 [p. 1283ᵃ,
38; eth. Eudem. 8, 10 p. 1242ᵃ, 26 κοινωνικὸν ἄνθρωπος
ζῷον]; Polyb. 2, 44, 1; Antonin. 7, 52. 55; often in Plut.;
πράξεις κοιν. actions having reference to human society,
Antonin. 4, 33; 5, 1.   **2.** *inclined to make others
sharers in one's possessions, inclined to impart, free in giving, liberal*, (Aristot. rhet. 2, 24, 2 [where, however, see
Cope]; Lcian. Tim. 56): 1 Tim. vi. 18.*

2844 κοινωνός, -ή, -όν, (κοινός), [as adj. Eur. Iph. Taur. 1173;

commonly as subst.];   **a.** *a partner, associate, comrade, companion*: 2 Co. viii. 23; ἔχειν τινὰ κοινωνόν,
Philem. 17; εἰμὶ κοινωνός τινι, to be one's partner, Lk. v.
10; τινός (gen. of pers.), to be the partner of one doing
something, Heb. x. 33; τινὸς ἐν τῷ αἵματι, to be one's
partner in shedding the blood etc. Mt. xxiii. 30.   **b.**
a partaker, sharer, in any thing; w. gen. of the thing:
τῶν παθημάτων, 2 Co. i. 7; τῆς δόξης, 1 Pet. v. 1; θείας
φύσεως, 2 Pet. i. 4; τοῦ θυσιαστηρίου, of the altar (at
Jerusalem) on which sacrifices are offered, i. e. sharing
in the worship of the Jews, 1 Co. x. 18; τῶν δαιμονίων,
partakers of (or with) demons, i. e. brought into fellowship with them, because they are the authors of the
heathen worship, ibid. 20; (ἐν τῷ ἀφθάρτῳ κοινωνοὶ ...
ἐν τοῖς φθαρτοῖς, joint partakers in that which is imperishable ... in the blessings which perish, Barnab. ep.
19, 8; see κοινωνέω, fin.).*

κοίτη, -ης, ἡ, (ΚΕΩ, ΚΕΙΩ, κεῖμαι, akin to κοιμάω); fr.   2845
Hom. Od. 19, 341 down; Sept. chiefly for מִשְׁכָּב, also
for שְׁכָבָה etc.;   **a.** *a place for lying down, resting,
sleeping in*; *a bed, couch*: εἰς τὴν κοίτην (see εἰμί, V. 2 a.)
εἰσίν, Lk. xi. 7.   **b.** spec. *the marriage-bed*, as in the
Tragg.: τ. κοίτην μιαίνειν, of adultery (Joseph. antt. 2,
4, 5; Plut. de fluv. 8, 3), Heb. xiii. 4.   **c.** *cohabitation*, whether lawful or unlawful (Lev. xv. 4 sq. 21–25,
etc.; Sap. iii. 13, 16; Eur. Med. 152; Alc. 249): plur.
sexual intercourse (see περιπατέω, b. a.), Ro. xiii. 13 [A.V.
chambering]; by meton. of the cause for the effect we
have the peculiar expression κοίτην ἔχειν ἔκ τινος, *to have
conceived by a man*, Ro. ix. 10; κοίτη σπέρματος, Lev. xv.
16; xxii. 4; xviii. 20, 23 [here κ. εἰς σπερματισμόν]; on
these phrases cf. *Fritzsche*, Com. on Rom. ii. p. 291 sq.*

κοιτών, -ῶνος, ὁ, (fr. κοίτη; cf. νυμφών etc.), *a sleeping-   2846
room, bed-chamber*: ὁ ἐπὶ τοῦ κοιτ. the officer who is over
the bed-chamber, the chamberlain, Acts xii. 20 (2 S. iv. 7;
Ex. viii. 3; 1 Esdr. iii. 3; the Atticists censure the word,
for which Attic writ. generally used δωμάτιον; cf. *Lob.*
ad Phryn. p. 252 sq.).*

κόκκινος, -η, -ον, (fr. κόκκος a kernel, the grain or berry   2847
of the *ilex coccifera*; these berries are the clusters of
eggs of a female insect, the kermes [(cf. Eng. *carmine,
crimson*)], was collected and pulverized produce a
red which was used in dyeing, Plin. h. n. 9, 41, 65; 16,
8, 12; 24, 4), *crimson, scarlet-colored*: Mt. xxvii. 28;
Heb. ix. 19; Rev. xvii. 3. neut. as a subst. i. q. *scarlet
cloth* or *clothing*: Rev. xvii. 4; xviii. 12, 16, (Gen. xxxviii.
28; Ex. xxv. 4; Lev. xiv. 4, 6; Josh. ii. 18; 2 S. i. 24;
2 Chr. ii. 7, 14; Plut. Fab. 15; φορεῖν κόκκινα, scarlet
robes, Epict. diss. 4, 11, 34; ἐν κοκκίνοις περιπατεῖν, 3, 22,
10). Cf. *Win.* RWB. s. v. Carmesin; *Roskoff* in Schenkel
i. p. 501 sq.; *Kamphausen* in Riehm p. 220; [B. D. s. v.
Colors, II. 3].*

κόκκος, -ου, ὁ, [cf. *Vaniček*, Fremdwörter etc. p. 26],   2848
a grain: Mt. xiii. 31; xvii. 20; Mk. iv. 31; Lk. xiii.
19; xvii. 6; Jn. xii. 24; 1 Co. xv. 37. [Hom. h. Cer.,
Hdt., down.]*

κολάζω: pres. pass. ptcp. κολαζόμενος; 1 aor. mid. sub-   2849
junc. 3 pers. plur. κολάσωνται; (κόλος lopped); in Grk

writ. **1.** prop. *to lop, prune,* as trees, wings. **2.** *to check; curb, restrain.* **3.** *to chastise, correct, punish*: so in the N. T.; pass. 2 Pet. ii. 9, and Lchm. in 4; mid. *to cause to be punished* (3 Macc. vii. 3): Acts iv. 21.*

2850 **κολακεία** (T WH -κία [see I, ι]), -ας, ἡ, (κολακεύω), *flattery*: λόγος κολακείας, flattering discourse, 1 Th. ii. 5. (Plat., Dem., Theophr., Joseph., Hdian., al.) *

2851 **κόλασις**, -εως, ἡ, (κολάζω), *correction, punishment, penalty*: Mt. xxv. 46; κόλασιν ἔχει, brings with it or has connected with it the thought of punishment, 1 Jn. iv. 18. (Ezek. xiv. 3 sq., etc.; 2 Macc. iv. 38; 4 Macc. viii. 8; Sap. xi. 14; xvi. 24, etc.; Plat., Aristot., Diod. 1, 77, (9); 4, 44, (3); Ael. v. h. 7, 15; al.) *

[SYN. κόλασις, τιμωρία: the noted definition of Aristotle which distinguishes κόλασις from τιμωρία as that which (is disciplinary and) has reference to him who suffers, while the latter (is penal and) has reference to the satisfaction of him who inflicts, may be found in his rhet. 1, 10, 17; cf. *Cope*, Intr. to Arist. Rhet. p. 232. To much the same effect, Plato, Protag. 324 a. sq., also deff. 416. But, as in other cases, usage (esp. the later) does not always recognize the distinction; see e. g. Philo de legat. ad Gaium § 1 fin.; frag. ex Euseb. prep. evang. 8, 13 (Mang. ii. 641); de vita Moys. i. 16 fin.; Plut. de sera num. vind. §§ 9, 11, etc. Plutarch (ibid. § 25 sub fin.) uses κολάζομαι of those undergoing the penalties of the other world (cf. Just. Mart. 1 apol. 8; Clem. Rom. 2 Cor. 6, 7; Just. Mart. 1 apol. 43; 2 apol. 8; Test. xii. Patr., test. Reub. 5; test. Levi 4, etc.; Mart. Polyc. 2, 3; 11, 2; Ign. ad Rom. 5, 3; Mart. Ign. vat. 5 etc.). See *Trench*, Syn. § vii.; *McClellan*, New Test. vol. i. marg. reff. on Mt. u. s.; *Bartlett*, Life and Death Eternal. Note G.; *C. F. Hudson*, Debt and Grace, p. 188 sqq.; Schmidt ch. 167, 2 sq.]

see 2858 **Κολασσαεύς**, see Κολοσσαεύς.

see 2857 **Κολασσαί**, see Κολοσσαί.

2852 **κολαφίζω** 1 aor. ἐκολάφισα; pres. pass. κολαφίζομαι; (κόλαφος a fist, and this fr. κολάπτω to peck, strike); *to strike with the fist, give* one *a blow with the fist* (Terence, *colaphum infringo*, Quintil. *col. duco*), [A. V. *to buffet*]: τινά, Mt. xxvi. 67; Mk. xiv. 65; as a specific term for a general, i. q. *to maltreat, treat with violence and contumely*, 2 Co. xii. 7; pres. pass., 1 Co. iv. 11; 1 Pet. ii. 20. (Elsewhere only in eccl. writ.) The word is fully discussed by *Fischer*, De vitiis lexx. N. T. etc. p. 67 sqq.; cf. *Lob.* ad Phryn. p. 175 sq.*

2853 **κολλάω**, -ῶ: Pass., pres. κολλῶμαι; 1 aor. ἐκολλήθην; 1 fut. κολληθήσομαι (Mt. xix. 5 L T Tr WH); (κόλλα gluten, glue); prop. *to glue, glue to, glue together, cement, fasten together*; hence univ. *to join or fasten firmly together*; in the N. T. only the pass. is found, with reflexive force, *to join one's self to, cleave to*; Sept. for דָּבַק; ὁ κονιορτὸς ὁ κολληθεὶς ἡμῖν, Lk. x. 11; ἐκολλήθησαν αὐτῆς αἱ ἁμαρτίαι ἄχρι τοῦ οὐρανοῦ, her sins were such a heap as to reach even unto heaven (that is, came to the knowledge of heaven), Rev. xviii. 5 G L T Tr WH (ἐκολλ. ἡ ψυχή μου ὀπίσω σου, Ps. lxii. (lxiii.) 9; αἱ ἅγιαι ἡμῶν ὑπερήνεγκαν ἕως τοῦ οὐρανοῦ, 1 Esdr. viii. 72 (74); ὕβρις τε βίη τε οὐρανὸν ἵκει, Hom. Od. 15, 329; 17, 565). of persons, w. dat. of the thing, κολλήθητι τῷ ἅρματι join thyself to etc. Acts viii. 29; w. dat. of pers., to form an intimate connection with, enter into the closest relations

with, unite one's self to, (so Barn. ep. c. 10, 3 sq. 5. 8; also with μετά and gen. of pers., ibid. 10, 11; 19, 2. 6; Clem. Rom. 1 Cor. 15, 1; 30, 3; 46, 2 [cf. Bp. Lghtft.'s note], 4): τῇ γυναικί, Mt. xix. 5 L T Tr WH; τῇ πόρνῃ, 1 Co. vi. 16 (Sir. xix. 2); τῷ κυρίῳ, 1 Co. vi. 17 (2 K. xviii. 6; Sir. ii. 3); *to join one's self to one as an associate, keep company with*, Acts v. 13; ix. 26; x. 28; *to follow one, be on his side*, Acts xvii. 34 (2 S. xx. 2; 1 Macc. iii. 2; vi. 21); *to join or attach one's self to a master or patron*, Lk. xv. 15; w. dat. of the thing, *to give one's self steadfastly to, labor for*, [A.V. *cleave to*]: τῷ ἀγαθῷ, Ro. xii. 9, ἀγαθῷ, κρίσει δικαίᾳ, Barn. ep. 20, 2; τῇ εὐλογίᾳ, so cleave to as to share, Clem. Rom. 1 Cor. 31, 1. (Aeschyl. Ag. 1566; Plat., Diod., Plut., al.) [COMP.: προσ-κολλάω.] *

2854 **κολλούριον** (T Tr κολλύριον, the more common form in prof. auth. [cf. *Lob.* Pathol. proleg. p. 461; *WH.* App. p. 152]), -ου, τό, (dimin. of κολλύρα coarse bread of a cylindrical shape, like that known in Westphalia as *Pumpernickel*), Lat. *collyrium* [A.V. *eye-salve*], a preparation shaped like a κολλύρα, composed of various materials and used as a remedy for tender eyelids (Hor. sat. 1, 5, 30; Epict. diss. 2, 21, 20; 3, 21, 21; Cels. 6, 6, 7): Rev. iii. 18.*

2855 **κολλυβιστής**, -οῦ, ὁ, (fr. κόλλυβος i. q. a. a small coin, cf. κολοβός clipped; b. rate of exchange, premium), *a money-changer, banker*: Mt. xxi. 12; Mk. xi. 15; Jn. ii. 15. Menand., Lys. in Poll. 7, 33, 170; ὁ μὲν κόλλυβος δόκιμον, τὸ δὲ κολλυβιστὴς ἀδόκιμον, Phryn. ed. *Lob.* p. 440. Cf. what was said under κερματιστής.*

see 2854 **κολλύριον**, see κολλούριον.

2856 **κολοβόω**, -ῶ: 1 aor. ἐκολόβωσα; Pass., 1 aor. ἐκολοβώθην; 1 fut. κολοβωθήσομαι; (fr. κολοβός lopped, mutilated); *to cut off* (τὰς χείρας, 2 S iv. 12; τοὺς πόδας, Aristot. h. a. 1, 1 [p. 487, 24]; τὴν ῥίνα, Diod. 1, 78); *to mutilate* (Polyb. 1, 80, 13); hence in the N. T. of time, (Vulg. *brevio*) *to shorten, abridge, curtail*: Mt. xxiv. 22; Mk. xiii. 20.*

2858 **Κολοσσαεύς**, and (so L Tr WH) Κολασσαεύς (see the foll. word; in Strabo and in Inscrr. Κολοσσηνός), -έως, ὁ, Vulg. *Colossensis*, Pliny *Colossinus*; *Colossian, a Colossian*; in the heading [and the subscription (R Tr)] of the Ep. to the Col.*

2857 **Κολοσσαί** (R T WH, the classical form), and Κολασσαί (R[n] L Tr, apparently the later popular form; [see *WH*. Intr. §423, and esp. Bp. *Lghtft.* Com. on Col. p. 16 sq.]; cf. W. p. 44; and on the plur. W. § 27, 3), -ῶν, αἱ, *Colossæ*, anciently a large and flourishing city, but in Strabo's time a πόλισμα [i. e. "*small town*" (Bp. Lghtft.)] of Phrygia Major situated on the Lycus, not far from its junction with the Mæander, and in the neighborhood of Laodicea and Hierapolis (Hdt. 7, 30; Xen. an. 1, 2, 6; Strab. 12, 8, 13 p. 576; Plin. h. n. 5, 41), together with which cities it was destroyed by an earthquake [about] A. D. 66 ([Euseb. chron. Ol. 210]; Oros. 7, 7 [see esp. Bp. Lghtft. u. s. p. 38]): Col. i. 2. [See the full description, with copious reff., by Bp. Lghtft. u. s. pp. 1–72.] *

2859 **κόλπος**, -ου, ὁ, (apparently akin to κοῖλος hollow, [yet cf. Vaniček p. 179 ; L. and S. s. v.]), Hebr. חֵיק ; *the bosom* (Lat. *sinus*), i. e. as in the Grk. writ. fr. Hom. down   **1.** *the front of the body between the arms* : hence ἀνακεῖσθαι ἐν τῷ κόλπῳ τινός, of the one who so reclines at table that his head covers the bosom as it were, the chest, of the one next him [cf. B. D. s. v. Meals], Jn. xiii. 23. Hence the figurative expressions, ἐν τοῖς κόλποις (on the plur., which occurs as early as Hom. Il. 9, 570, cf. W. § 27, 3 ; [B. 24 (21)]) τοῦ Ἀβραὰμ εἶναι, to obtain the seat next to Abraham, i. e. to be partaker of the same blessedness as Abraham in paradise, Lk. xvi. 23 ; ἀποφέρεσθαι εἰς τὸν κ. Ἀβρ. to be borne away to the enjoyment of the same felicity with Abraham, ibid. 22 (οὕτω γὰρ παθόντας — acc. to another reading θανόντας — Ἀβραὰμ καὶ Ἰσαὰκ καὶ Ἰακὼβ ὑποδέξονται εἰς τοὺς κόλπους αὐτῶν, 4 Macc. xiii. 16 ; [see B. D. s. v. Abraham's bosom, and] on the rabbin. phrase בחיקו של אברהם, in *Abraham's bosom*, to designate bliss in paradise, cf. *Lightfoot*, Hor. Hebr. et Talmud. p. 851 sqq.) ; ὁ ὢν εἰς τὸν κ. τοῦ πατρός, lying (turned) unto the bosom of his father (God), i. e. in the closest and most intimate relation to the Father, Jn. i. 18 [W. 415 (387)] ; cf. Cic. ad div. 14, 4 iste vero sit in sinu semper et complexu meo.   **2.** *the bosom of a garment*, i. e. the hollow formed by the upper forepart of a rather loose garment bound by a girdle, used for keeping and carrying things [*the fold* or *pocket* ; cf. B. D. s. v. Dress], (Ex. iv. 6 sq. ; Prov. vi. 27) ; so, figuratively, μέτρον καλὸν διδόναι εἰς τ. κ. τινός, to repay one liberally, Lk. vi. 38 (ἀποδιδόναι εἰς τ. κ. Is. lxv. 6 ; Jer. xxxix. (xxxii.) 18).   **3.** *a bay of the sea* (cf. Ital. golfo [Eng. *gulf*, — which may be only the mod. representatives of the Grk. word]) : Acts xxvii. 39.*

2860   κολυμβάω, -ῶ ; *to dive, to swim* : Acts xxvii. 43. (Plat. Prot. p. 350 a. ; Lach. p. 193 c., and in later writ.) [Comp. : ἐκ-κολυμβάω.] *

2861   κολυμβήθρα, -ας, ἡ, (κολυμβάω), *a place for diving, a swimming-pool* [A. V. simply *pool*] : Jn. ix. 7, and Rec. in 11 ; *a reservoir* or *pool* used for bathing, Jn. v. 2, 4 [(acc. to txt. of R L), 7]. (Plat. rep. 5 p. 453 d. ; Diod., Joseph., al. ; Sept., 2 K. xviii. 17 ; Neh. ii. 14 ; Nah. ii. 8.) *

2862   κολωνία (R G Tr), κολωνία (L T WH KC [cf. Chandler § 95]), [Tdf. edd. 2, 7 -νεια ; see his note on Acts as below, and cf. ει, ι], -ας, ἡ, (a Lat. word), *a colony* : in Acts xvi. 12 the city of Philippi is so called, where Octavianus had planted a Roman colony (cf. Dio Cass. 51, 4 ; Digest. 50, tit. 15, 8). The exegetical difficulties of this pass. are best removed, as Meyer shows, by connecting κολωνία closely with πρώτη πόλις, the chief city, a [Roman] colony (a colonial city) ; [but cf. Bp. Lghtft. Com. on Philip. p. 50 sq.].*

2863   κομάω, -ῶ ; (κόμη) ; *to let the hair grow, have long hair*, [cf. κόμη fin.] : 1 Co. xi. 14 sq. (In Grk. writ. fr. Hom. down.) *

2864   κόμη, -ης, ἡ, [fr. Hom. down], *hair, head of hair* : 1 Co. xi. 15. [Acc. to Schmidt (21, 2) it differs fr. θρίξ (the anatomical or physical term) by designating the hair as an **o r n a m e n t** (the notion of **l e n g t h** being only secondary and suggested). Cf. B.D. s. v. Hair.] *

2865   κομίζω : 1 aor. ptcp. fem. κομίσασα ; Mid., pres. ptcp. κομιζόμενος ; 1 fut. κομίσομαι (Eph. vi. 8 L T Tr WH ; Col. iii. 25 L txt. WH) and Attic κομιοῦμαι (Col. iii. 25 R G L mrg. T Tr ; [Eph. vi. 8 R G] ; 1 Pet. v. 4 ; cf. [WH. App. p. 163 sq.] ; B. 37 (33) ; [W. § 13, 1 c. ; Veitch s. v.]), ptcp. κομιούμενος (2 Pet. ii. 13 [here WH Tr mrg. ἀδικούμενοι ; see ἀδικέω, 2 b.]) ; 1 aor. ἐκομισάμην [B. § 135, 1] ; rare in Sept., but in Grk. writ. fr. Hom. down freq. in various senses ;   **1.** *to care for, take care of, provide for*.   **2.** *to take up* or *carry away in order to care for and preserve*.   **3.** univ. *to carry away, bear off*.   **4.** *to carry, bear, bring to* : once so in the N. T., viz. ἀλάβαστρον, Lk. vii. 37. Mid. (as often in prof. auth.) *to carry away for one's self* ; *to carry off what is one's own, to bring back* ; i. e.   **a.** *to receive, obtain* : τὴν ἐπαγγελίαν, the promised blessing, Heb. x. 36 ; xi. 39 [τὰς ἐπαγγ. L ; so T Tr WH in xi. 13] ; σωτηρίαν ψυχῶν, 1 Pet. i. 9 ; τῆς δόξης στέφανον, 1 Pet. v. 4 ; μισθὸν ἀδικίας, 2 Pet. ii. 13 [see above], (τὸν ἄξιον τῆς δυσσεβείας μισθόν, 2 Macc. viii. 33 ; δόξαν ἐσθλήν [al. καρπίζεται], Eur. Hipp. 432 ; τὴν ἀξίαν παρὰ θεῶν, Plat. legg. 4 p. 718 a., and other exx. elsewh.).   **b.** *to receive what was previously one's own, to get back, receive back, recover* : τὸ ἐμὸν σὺν τόκῳ, Mt. xxv. 27 ; His son (of Abraham after he had consented to sacrifice Isaac), Heb. xi. 19 (2 Macc. vii. 29 ; τὸν ἀδελφὸν ἀνύβριστον, Philo de Josepho § 35 ; οἱ δὲ παρ' ἐλπίδας ἑαυτοὺς κεκομισμένοι, having received each other back, been restored to each other, contrary to their expectations, of Abraham and Isaac after the sacrifice of the latter had been prevented by God, Joseph. antt. 1, 13, 4 ; τὴν ἀδελφήν, Eur. Iph. T. 1362 ; used of the recovery of hostages, captives, etc., Thuc. 1, 113 ; Polyb. 1, 83, 8 ; 3, 51, 12 ; 3, 40, 10 ; the city and temple, 2 Macc. x. 1 ; a citadel, a city, often in Polyb. ; τὴν βασιλείαν, Arstph. av. 549 ; τὴν πατρῴαν ἀρχήν, Joseph. antt. 13, 4, 1). Since in the rewards and punishments of deeds, the deeds themselves are as it were requited and so given back to their authors, the meaning is obvious when one is said κομίζεσθαι that which he has done, i. e. either the reward or the punishment of the deed [W. 620 sq. (576)] : 2 Co. v. 10 ; Col. iii. 25 ; with παρὰ κυρίου added, Eph. vi. 8 ; ([ἁμαρτίαν, Lev. xx. 17]) ; ἕκαστος, καθὼς ἐποίησε, κομιεῖται, Barn. ep. 4, 12). [Comp. : ἐκ-, συγ-κομίζω.] *

2866   κομψότερον, neut. compar. of the adj. κομψός (fr. κομέω to take care of, tend) neat, elegant, nice, fine ; used adverbially, *more finely, better* : κομψότ. ἔχω to be better, of a convalescent, Jn. iv. 52 (ὅταν ὁ ἰατρὸς εἴπῃ · κόμψως ἔχεις, Epict. diss. 3, 10, 13 ; so in Latin *belle habere*, Cic. epp. ad div. 16, 15 ; [cf. Eng. 'he's doing *nicely*,' 'he's getting on *finely*' ; and] Germ. er befindet sich h ü b s c h ; es geht h ü b s c h mit ihm). The gloss. of Hesych. refers to this pass. : κομψότερον · βελτιώτερον, ἐλαφρότερον.*

2867   κονιάω, -ῶ : pf. ptcp. pass. κεκονιαμένος ; (fr. κονία, which signifies not only 'dust' but also 'lime') ; *to cover with lime, plaster over, whitewash* : τάφοι κεκονιαμένοι (the Jews were accustomed to whitewash the entrances to their sepulchres, as a warning against defilement by touching them [B. D. s. v. Burial, 1 fin.; cf. *Edersheim, Jesus the Messiah*, ii. 316 sqq.]), Mt. xxiii. 27; τοῖχος κεκον. is applied to a hypocrite who conceals his malice under an outward assumption of piety, Acts xxiii. 3. (Dem., Aristot., Plut., al.; for שִׂיד, Deut. xxvii. 2, 4.) *

2868 κονιορτός, -οῦ, ὁ, (fr. κονία, and ὄρνυμι to stir up); **1.** prop. *raised dust, flying dust*, (Hdt., Plat., Polyb., al.). **2.** univ. *dust*: Mt. x. 14; Lk. ix. 5; x. 11; Acts xiii. 51; xxii. 23. (For אָבָק, Ex. ix. 9; Nah. i. 3; for עָפָר, Deut. ix. 21.) *

2869 κοπάζω: 1 aor. ἐκόπασα; (κόπος); prop. *to grow weary or tired*; hence *to cease from violence, cease* raging: ὁ ἄνεμος (Hdt. 7, 191), Mt. xiv. 32; Mk. iv. 39; vi. 51. (Gen. viii. 1; Jon. i. 11 sq.; [cf. esp. Philo, somn. ii. 35].)*

2870 κοπετός, -οῦ, ὁ, (fr. κόπτομαι, see κόπτω), Sept. for מִסְפֵּד; Lat. *planctus*, i. e. *lamentation with beating of the breast* as a sign of grief: κοπετὸν ποιεῖσθαι ἐπί τινι, Acts viii. 2; ἐπί τινα, Zech. xii. 10. (Eupolis in Bekker's annott. ad Etym. Magn. p. 776; Dion. H. antt. 11, 31; Plut. Fab. 17.) *

2871 κοπή, -ῆς, ἡ, (κόπτω); **1.** prop. several times in Grk. writ. *the act of cutting, a cut*. **2.** in bibl. Grk. *a cutting in pieces, slaughter*: Heb. vii. 1; Gen. xiv. 17; Deut. xxviii. 25; Josh. x. 20; Judith xv. 7.*

2872 κοπιάω, -ῶ, [3 pers. plur. κοπιοῦσιν (for -ῶσιν), Mt. vi. 28 Tr; cf. ἐρωτάω, init.]; 1 aor. ἐκοπίασα; pf. κεκοπίακα (2 pers. sing. κεκοπίακες, Rev. ii. 3 L T Tr WH, cf. [W. § 13, 2 c.]; B. 43 (38) [and his trans. of Apollon. Dysk. p. 54 n.; *Tdf*. Proleg. p. 123; *WH*. App. p. 166; Soph. Lex. p. 39]); (κόπος, q. v.); **1.** as in Arstph., Joseph., Plut., al., *to grow weary, tired, exhausted*, (with toil or burdens or grief): Mt. xi. 28; Rev. ii. 3; κεκοπιακὼς ἐκ τῆς ὁδοιπορίας, Jn. iv. 6 (ὑπὸ τῆς ὁδοιπορίας, Joseph. antt. 2, 15, 3; δραμοῦνται καὶ οὐ κοπιάσουσι, Is. xl. 31). **2.** in bibl. Grk. alone, *to labor with wearisome effort, to toil* (Sept. for יָגַע); of bodily labor: absol., Mt. vi. 28; Lk. v. 5; xii. 27 [not *Tdf*.]; Jn. iv. 38; Acts xx. 35; 1 Co. iv. 12; Eph. iv. 28; 2 Tim. ii. 6 [cf. W. 556 (517); B. 390 (334)]; τί, upon a thing, Jn. iv. 38. of the toilsome efforts of teachers in proclaiming and promoting the kingdom of God and Christ: 1 Co. xv. 10; xvi. 16, (cf. Jn. iv. 38); foll. by ἐν w. dat. of the thing in which one labors, ἐν λόγῳ κ. διδασκαλίᾳ, 1 Tim. v. 17; ἐν ὑμῖν, among you, 1 Th. v. 12; ἐν κυρίῳ (see ἐν, I. 6 b. p. 211ᵇ mid. [L br. the cl.]), Ro. xvi. 12; εἴς τινα, for one, for his benefit, Ro. xvi. 6; Gal. iv. 11 [cf. B. 242 (209); W. 503 (469)]; εἰς τοῦτο, looking to this (viz. that piety has the promise of life), 1 Tim. iv. 10; εἰς ὅ, to which end, Col. i. 29; εἰς κενόν, in vain, Phil. ii. 16 (κενῶς ἐκοπίασα, of the frustrated labor of the prophets, Is. xlix. 4).*

2873 κόπος, -ου, ὁ, (κόπτω); **1.** i. q. τὸ κόπτειν, *a beating*. **2.** i. q. κοπετός, *a beating of the breast in grief, sorrow*, (Jer. li. 33 (xlv. 3)). **3.** *labor* (so Sept. often for עָמָל), i. e. **a.** *trouble* (Aeschyl., Soph.): κόπους παρέχειν τινί, to cause one trouble, make work for him, Mt. xxvi. 10; Mk. xiv. 6; Lk. xi. 7; Gal. vi. 17; κόπον παρέχ. τινί, Lk. xviii. 5. **b.** *intense labor united with trouble, toil* (Eur., Arstph., al.): univ., plur., 2 Co. vi. 5;

xi. 23; of manual labor, joined with μόχθος [(see below)], 1 Th. ii. 9; ἐν κόπῳ κ. μόχθῳ, [*toil and travail*], 2 Co. xi. 27 (where L Tr WH om. ἐν); 2 Th. iii. 8; of the laborious efforts of Christian virtue, 1 Co. xv. 58; Rev. ii. 2; plur. Rev. xiv. 13; ὁ κόπος τῆς ἀγάπης, the labor to which love prompts, and which voluntarily assumes and endures trouble and pains for the salvation of others, 1 Th. i. 3; Heb. vi. 10 Rec.; of toil in teaching, Jn. iv. 38 (on which see εἰς, B. I. 3); 1 Th. iii. 5; of that which such toil in teaching accomplishes, 1 Co. iii. 8; plur. 2 Co. x. 15 (cf. Sir. xiv. 15).*

[Syn. κόπος, μόχθος, πόνος: primarily and in general classic usage, πόνος gives prominence to the effort (work as requiring force), κόπος to the fatigue, μόχθος (chiefly poetic) to the hardship. But in the N. T. πόνος has passed over (in three instances out of four) to the meaning *pain* (hence it has no place in the 'new Jerusalem', Rev. xxi. 4); cf. the deterioration in the case of the allied πονηρός, πένης. Schmidt, ch. 85; cf. Trench § cii. (who would trans. π. 'toil', κ. 'weariness', μ. 'labor').]

2874 κοπρία [Chandler § 96], -ας, ἡ, i. q. ἡ κόπρος, *dung*: Lk. xiii. 8 Rec.ˢᵗ; xiv. 35 (34). (Job ii. 8; 1 S. ii. 8; Neh. ii. 13; 1 Macc. ii. 62; [Strab., Poll., al.].) *

see 2874 κόπριον, -ου, τό, i. q. ἡ κόπρος, *dung, manure*: plur. Lk. xiii. 8 [Rec.ˢᵗ κοπρίαν]. (Heraclit. in Plut. mor. p. 669 [quaest. conviv. lib. iv. quaest. iv. § 3, 6]; Strab. 16, § 26 p. 784; Epict. diss. 2, 4, 5; Plut. Pomp. c. 48; [Is. v. 25; Jer. xxxii. 19 (xxv. 33); Sir. xxii. 2], and other later writ.)

2875 κόπτω: impf. 3 pers. plur. ἔκοπτον; 1 aor. ptcp. κόψας (Mk. xi. 8 T Tr txt. WH); Mid., impf. ἐκοπτόμην; fut. κόψομαι; 1 aor. ἐκοψάμην; [fr. Hom. down]; *to cut, strike, smite*, (Sept. for הִכָּה, כָּרַת, etc.): τὶ ἀπό or ἔκ τινος, *to cut from, cut off*, Mt. xxi. 8; Mk. xi. 8. Mid. to beat one's breast for grief, Lat. *plango* [R. V. *mourn*]: Mt. xi. 17; xxiv. 30, (Aeschyl. Pers. 683; Plat., al.; Sept. often so for סָפַד); τινά, *to mourn or bewail one* [cf. W. § 32, 1 γ.]: Lk. viii. 52; xxiii. 27, (Gen. xxiii. 2; 1 S. xxv. 1, etc.; Arstph. Lys. 396; Anthol. 11, 135, 1); ἐπί τινα, Rev. i. 7; [xviii. 9 T Tr WH], (2 S. xi. 26); ἐπί τινι, Rev. xviii. 9 [R G L], cf. Zech. xii. 10. [Comp.: ἀνα-, ἀπο-, ἐκ-, ἐν-, κατα-, προ-, προσκόπτω. Syn. cf. θρηνέω.] *

2876 κόραξ, -ακος, ὁ, *a raven*: Lk. xii. 24. [Fr. Hom. down.] *

2877 κοράσιον, -ου, τό, (dimin. of κόρη), prop. a colloq. word used disparagingly (like the Germ. *Mädel*), *a little girl* (in the epigr. attributed to Plato in Diog. Laërt. 3, 33; Lcian. as. 6); used by later writ. without disparagement [W. 24 (23)], *a girl, damsel, maiden*: Mt. ix. 24 sq.; xiv. 11; Mk. v. 41 sq.; vi. 22, 28; (occasionally, as in Epictet. diss. 2, 1, 28; 3, 2, 8; 4, 10, 33; Sept. for נַעֲרָה; twice also for יַלְדָּה, Joel iii. 3 (iv. 3); Zech. viii. 5; [Tob. vi. 12; Judith xvi. 12; Esth. ii. 2]). The form and use of the word are fully discussed in *Lobeck* ad Phryn. p. 73 sq., cf. *Sturz*, De dial. Maced. etc. p. 42 sq.*

2878 κορβᾶν [-βάν WH; but see *Tdf*. Proleg. p. 102], indecl., and κορβανᾶς, acc. -ᾶν [B. 20 (18)], ὁ, (Hebr. קָרְבָּן i. e. *an offering*, Sept. everywh. δῶρον, a term which comprehends all kinds of sacrifices, the bloody as well as the bloodless); **1.** κορβᾶν, *a gift offered* (or to be offered) to God: Mk. vii. 11 (Joseph. antt. 4, 4, 4, of the Nazirites, οἱ κορβᾶν αὐτοὺς ὀνομάσαντες τῷ θεῷ, δῶρον δὲ τοῦτο σημαίνει κατὰ Ἑλλήνων γλῶτταν; cf. contr. Apion. 1, 22, 4; [BB.DD. s. v. Corban; *Ginsburg* in the Bible Educator, i. 155]).   **2.** κορβανᾶς, -ᾶ [see B. u. s.], *the sacred treasury:* Mt. xxvii. 6 [L mrg. Tr mrg. κορβᾶν] (τὸν ἱερὸν θησαυρόν, καλεῖται δὲ κορβανᾶς, Joseph. b. j. 2, 9, 4).*

2879   **Κορέ** (in Joseph. antt. 4, 2, 2 sqq. with the Grk. terminations -έου, ῆ-, -ῆν), ὁ, (Hebr. קֹרַח i. e. ice, hail), *Korah* (Vulg. *Core*), a man who, with others, rebelled against Moses (Num. xvi.): Jude 11.*

2880   **κορέννυμι**; (κόρος satiety); *to satiate, sate, satisfy :* 1 aor. pass. ptcp. κορεσθέντες, as in Grk. writ. fr. Hom. down, w. gen. of the thing with which one is filled [B. § 132, 19], τροφῆς, Acts xxvii. 38; trop. (pf.) κεκορεσμένοι ἐστέ, every wish is satisfied in the enjoyment of the consummate Messianic blessedness, 1 Co. iv. 8.*

2881   **Κορίνθιος**, -ου, ὁ, *a Corinthian, an inhabitant of Corinth:* Acts xviii. 8; 2 Co. vi. 11. [(Hdt., Xen., al.)]*

2882   **Κόρινθος**, -ου, ἡ, *Corinth*, the metropolis of Achaia proper, situated on the isthmus of the Peloponnesus between the Ægean and Ionian Seas (hence called *bimaris*, Hor. car. 1, 7, 2; Ovid. metam. 5, 407), and having two harbors, one of which called Cenchreæ (see Κεγχρεαί) was the roadstead for ships from Asia, the other, called Lechæon or Lechæum, for ships from Italy. It was utterly destroyed by L. Mummius, the Roman consul, in the Achæan war, B. C. 146; but after the lapse of a century it was rebuilt by Julius Caesar [B. C. 44]. It was eminent in commerce and wealth, in literature and the arts, especially the study of rhetoric and philosophy; but it was notorious also for luxury and moral corruption, particularly the foul worship of Venus. Paul came to the city in his second missionary journey, [c.] A. D. 53 or 54, and founded there a Christian church: Acts xviii. 1; xix. 1; 1 Co. i. 2; 2 Co. i. 1, 23; 2 Tim. iv. 20. [BB. DD. s. v.; Dict. of Geogr. s. v.; *Lewin*, St. Paul, i. 269 sqq.] *

2883   **Κορνήλιος**, -ου, ὁ, a Lat. name, *Cornelius*, a Roman centurion living at Cæsarea, converted to Christianity by Peter : Acts x. 1 sqq.*

2884   **κόρος**, -ου, ὁ, (Hebr. כֹּר), a *corus* or *cor* [cf. Ezek. xlv. 14], the largest Hebrew dry measure (i. e. for wheat, meal, etc.); acc. to Josephus (antt. 15, 9, 2) equal to ten Attic medimni, [but cf. B.D. s. v. Weights and Measures sub fin.; *F. R. Conder* in the Bible Educator, iii. 10 sq.]: Lk. xvi. 7 [A. V. *measure*]. (Sept. [Lev. xxvii. 16; Num. xi. 32]; 1 K. iv. 22; v. 11; 2 Chr. ii. 10; [xxvii. 5].) *

2885   **κοσμέω**, -ῶ; 3 pers. plur. impf. ἐκόσμουν; 1 aor. ἐκόσμησα; pf. pass. κεκόσμημαι; (κόσμος);   **1.** *to put in order, arrange, make ready, prepare:* τὰς λαμπάδας, put in order [A. V. *trim*], Mt. xxv. 7 (δόρπον, Hom. Od. 7, 13; τράπεζαν, Xen. Cyr. 8, 2, 6; 6, 11; Sept. Ezek. xxiii. 41 for עָרַךְ; Sir. xxix. 26; προσφοράν, Sir. l. 14, and other exx. elsewhere).   **2.** *to ornament, adorn*, (so in Grk. writ. fr. Hesiod down; Sept. several times for

עָדָה); prop.: οἶκον, in pass., Mt. xii. 44; Lk. xi. 25; τὰ μνημεῖα, to decorate [A.V. *garnish*], Mt. xxiii. 29 (τάφους, Xen. mem. 2, 2, 13); τὸ ἱερὸν λίθοις καὶ ἀναθέμασι, in pass. Lk. xxi. 5; τοὺς θεμελίους τοῦ τείχους λίθῳ τιμίῳ, Rev. xxi. 19; τινά (with garments), νύμφην, pass. Rev. xxi. 2; ἑαυτὰς ἔν τινι, 1 Tim. ii. 9 (on this pass. see καταστολή, 2). metaph. i. q. *to embellish with honor, gain honor*, (Pind. nem. 6, 78; Thuc. 2, 42; κεκοσμ. τῇ ἀρετῇ, Xen. Cyr. 8, 1, 21): ἑαυτάς, foll. by a ptcp. designating the act by which the honor is gained, 1 Pet. iii. 5; τὴν διδασκαλίαν ἐν πᾶσιν, in all things, Tit. ii. 10.*

2886   **κοσμικός**, -ή, -όν, (κόσμος), *of* or *belonging to the world* (Vulg. *saecularis*); i. e.   **1.** *relating to the universe :* τοὐρανοῦ τοῦδε καὶ τῶν κοσμικῶν πάντων, Aristot. phys. 2, 4 p.196ᵃ, 25; opp. to ἀνθρώπινος, Lcian. paras. 11; κοσμικὴ διάταξις, Plut. consol. ad Apoll. c. 34 p. 119 e.   **2.** *earthly:* τὸ ἅγιον κοσμικόν, [its] earthly sanctuary [R.V. *of this world*], Heb. ix. 1.   **3.** *worldly*, i. e. *having the character of this* (present) *corrupt age*: αἱ κοσμικαὶ ἐπιθυμίαι, Tit. ii. 12; (so also in eccles. writ.).*

2887   **κόσμιος**, -ον, of three term. in class. Grk., cf. *WH*. App. p. 157; W. § 11, 1; [B. 25 (22 sq.)], (κόσμος), *well-arranged, seemly, modest :* 1 Tim. ii. 9 [WH mrg. -μίως]; of a man living with decorum, a well-ordered life, 1 Tim. iii. 2. (Arstph., Xen., Plat., Isocr., Lys., al.) [Cf. Trench § xcii.] *

see 2887   [κοσμίως, adv. (*decently*), fr. κόσμιος, q. v.: 1 Tim. ii. 9 WH mrg. (Arstph., Isocr., al.)*]

2888   **κοσμοκράτωρ**, -ορος, ὁ, (κόσμος and κρατέω), *lord of the world, prince of this age :* the devil and demons are called in plur. οἱ κοσμοκράτορες τοῦ σκότους τοῦ αἰῶνος [but crit. edd. om. τ. αἰῶν.] τούτου [R. V. *the world-rulers of this darkness*], Eph. vi. 12; cf. 11; Jn. xii. 31; 2 Co. iv. 4; see ἄρχων. (The word occurs in Orph. 8, 11; 11, 11; in eccl. writ. of Satan; in rabbin. writ. קוֹזְמוֹקְרָטוֹר is used both of human rulers and of the angel of death; cf. *Buxtorf*, Lex. talm. et rabb. p. 2006 [p. 996 ed. Fischer].)*

2889   **κόσμος**, -ου, ὁ;   **1.** in Grk. writ. fr. Hom. down, *an apt and harmonious arrangement* or *constitution, or der*.   **2.** as in Grk. writ. fr. Hom. down, *ornament, decoration, adornment:* ἐνδύσεως ἱματίων, 1 Pet. iii. 3 (Sir. vi. 30; xxi. 21; 2 Macc. ii. 2; Sept. for צָבָא of the arrangement of the stars, 'the heavenly hosts,' as the ornament of the heavens, Gen. ii. 1; Deut. iv. 19; xvii. 3; Is. xxiv. 21; xl. 26; besides occasionally for עֲדִי; twice for תִּפְאֶרֶת, Prov. xx. 29; Is. iii. 19).   **3.** *the world*, i. e. *the universe* (quem κόσμον Graeci nomine ornamenti appellarunt, eum nos a perfecta absolutaque elegantia *mundum*, Plin. h. n. 2, 3; in which sense Pythagoras is said to have been the first to use the word, Plut. de plac. philos. 2, 1, 1 p. 886 c.; but acc. to other accounts he used it of the *heavens*, Diog. L. 8, 48, of which it is used several times also by other Grk. writ. [see *Menag.* on Diog. Laërt.l. c.; *Bentley*, Epp. of Phalar. vol. i. 391 (Lond. 1836); M. Anton. 4, 27 and Gataker's notes; cf. L. and S. s. v. IV.]): Acts xvii. 24; Ro. iv. 13 (where cf. Meyer, Tholuck, Philippi); 1 Co. iii. 22; viii. 4; Phil. ii. 15; with a predominant notion of space, in hyperbole, Jn. xxi. 25 (Sap. vii. 17 ; ix. 3 ; 2 Macc. viii. 18 ; κτίζειν τ. κόσμον, Sap. xi. 18 ; ὁ τοῦ κόσμου κτίστης, 2 Macc. vii. 23 ; 4 Macc. v. 25 (24) ; — a sense in which it does not occur in the other O. T. books, although there is something akin to it in Prov. xvii. 6, on which see 8 below) ; in the phrases πρὸ τοῦ τὸν κόσμον εἶναι, Jn. xvii. 5 ; ἀπὸ καταβολῆς κόσμου [Mt. xiii. 35 R G ; xxv. 34 ; Lk. xi. 50 ; Heb. iv. 3 ; .ix. 26 ; Rev. xiii. 8 ; xvii. 8] and πρὸ κατ. κόσμου [Jn. xvii. 24 ; Eph. i. 4 ; 1 Pet. i. 20], (on which see καταβολή, 2) ; ἀπὸ κτίσεως κόσμου, Ro. i. 20 ; ἀπ᾽ ἀρχῆς κ. Mt. xxiv. 21 ; (on the om. of the art. cf. W. p. 123 (117) ; B. § 124, 8 b.; [cf. Ellicott on Gal. vi. 14]). **4.** _the circle of the earth, the earth,_ (very rarely so in Grk. writ. until after the age of the Ptolemies ; so in _Boeckh,_ Corp. inscrr. i. pp. 413 and 643, nos. 334 and 1306): Mk. xvi. 15 ; [Jn. xii. 25] ; 1 Tim. vi. 7 ; βασιλεία τοῦ κόσμου, Rev. xi. 15 ; βασιλεῖαι (plur.) τ. κόσμου, Mt. iv. 8 (for which Lk. iv. 5 τῆς οἰκουμένης) ; τὸ φῶς τοῦ κόσμου τούτου, of the sun, Jn. xi. 9 ; ἐν ὅλῳ τῷ κ., properly, Mt. xxvi. 13 ; hyperbolically, i. q. far and wide, in widely separated places, Ro. i. 8 ; [so ἐν παντὶ τῷ κόσμῳ, Col. i. 6] ; ὁ τότε κόσμος, 2 Pet. iii. 6 ; the earth with its inhabitants : ζῆν ἐν κόσμῳ, opp. to the dead, Col. ii. 20 (λῃστὴς ἦν καὶ κλέπτης ἐν τῷ κόσμῳ, i. e. among those living on earth, Ev. Nicod. 26). By a usage foreign to prof. auth. **5.** _the inhabitants of the world_ : θέατρον ἐγενήθημεν τῷ κόσμῳ καὶ ἀγγέλοις κ. ἀνθρώποις, 1 Co. iv. 9 [W. 127 (121)] ; particularly _the inhabitants of the earth, men, the human race_ (first so in Sap. [e. g. x. 1]) : Mt. xiii. 38 ; xviii. 7 ; Mk. xiv. 9 ; Jn. i. 10, 29, [36 L in br.] ; iii. 16 sq. ; vi. 33, 51 ; viii. 26 ; xii. 47 ; xiii. 1 ; xiv. 31 ; xvi. 28 ; xvii. 6, 21, 23 ; Ro. iii. 6, 19 ; 1 Co. i. 27 sq. [cf. W. 189 (178)] ; iv. 13 ; v. 10 ; xiv. 10 ; 2 Co. v. 19 ; Jas. ii. 5 [cf. W. u. s.] ; 1 Jn. ii. 2 [cf. W. 577 (536)] ; ἀρχαῖος κόσμος, of the antediluvians, 2 Pet. ii. 5 ; γεννᾶσθαι εἰς τ. κ. Jn. xvi. 21 ; ἔρχεσθαι εἰς τὸν κόσμον (Jn. ix. 39) and εἰς τ. κ. τοῦτον, to make its appearance or come into existence among men, spoken of the light which in Christ shone upon men, Jn. i. 9 ; iii. 19, cf. xii. 46 ; of the Messiah, Jn. vi. 14 ; xi. 27 ; of Jesus as the Messiah, Jn. ix. 39 ; xvi. 28 ; xviii. 37 ; 1 Tim. i. 15 ; also εἰσέρχεσθαι εἰς τ. κ. Heb. x. 5 ; of false teachers, 2 Jn. 7 (yet here L T Tr WH ἐξέρχ. εἰς τ. κ. ; [so all texts in 1 Jn. iv. 1]) ; _to invade,_ of evils coming into existence among men and beginning to exert their power : of sin and death, Ro. v. 12 (of death, Sap. ii. 24 ; Clem. Rom. 1 Cor. 3, 4 ; of idolatry, Sap. xiv. 14). ἀποστέλλειν τινὰ εἰς τ. κ., Jn. iii. 17 ; x. 36 ; xvii. 18 ; 1 Jn. iv. 9 ; φῶς τ. κ., Mt. v. 14 ; Jn. viii. 12 ; ix. 5 ; σωτὴρ τ. κ., Jn. iv. 42 ; 1 Jn. iv. 14, (σωτηρία τοῦ κ. Sap. vi. 26 (25) ; ἐλπὶς τ. κ. Sap. xiv. 6 ; πρωτόπλαστος πατὴρ τοῦ κ., of Adam, Sap. x. 1) ; στοιχεῖα τοῦ κ. (see στοιχεῖον, 3 and 4) ; ἐν τῷ κόσμῳ, among men, Jn. xvi. 33 ; xvii. 13 ; Eph. ii. 12 ; ἐν κόσμῳ (see W. 123 (117)), 1 Tim. iii. 16 ; εἶναι ἐν τῷ κ., to dwell among men, Jn. i. 10 ; ix. 5 ; xvii. 11, 12 R G ; 1 Jn. iv. 3 ; εἶναι ἐν κόσμῳ, to be present, Ro. v. 13 ; ἐξελθεῖν ἐκ τοῦ κόσμου, to withdraw from human society and seek an abode outside of it, 1 Co. v. 10 ; ἀναστρέφεσθαι ἐν τῷ κ., to behave one's self, 2 Co. i. 12 ; likewise εἶναι ἐν τῷ

κ. τούτῳ, 1 Jn. iv. 17. used spec. of _the Gentiles collectively,_ Ro. xi. 12 (where it alternates with τὰ ἔθνη), 15 ; [the two in combination : τὰ ἔθνη τοῦ κόσμου, Lk. xii. 30]. hyperbolically or loosely i. q. _the majority_ of men in a place, _the multitude_ or _mass_ (as we say _the public_) : Jn. vii. 4 ; xii. 19 [here Tr mrg. adds ὅλος in br.] ; xiv. 19, 22 ; xviii. 20. i. q. _the entire number,_ ἀσεβῶν, 2 Pet. ii. 5. **6.** _the ungodly multitude ; the whole mass of men alienated from God, and therefore hostile to the cause of Christ_ [cf. W. 26] : Jn. vii. 7 ; xiv. [17], 27 ; xv. 18 sq. ; xvi. 8, 20, 33 ; xvii. 9, 14 sq. 25 ; 1 Co. i. 21 ; vi. 2 ; xi. 32 ; 2 Co. vii. 10 ; Jas. i. 27 ; 1 Pet. v. 9 ; 2 Pet. i. 4 ; ii. 20 ; 1 Jn. iii. 1, 13 ; iv. 5 ; v. 19 ; of the aggregate of ungodly and wicked men in O. T. times, Heb. xi. 38 ; in Noah's time, ibid. 7 ; with οὗτος added, Eph. ii. 2 (on which see αἰών, 3) ; εἶναι ἐκ τοῦ κ. and ἐκ τοῦ κ. τούτου (see εἰμί, V. 3 d.), Jn. viii. 23 ; xv. 19 ; xvii. 14, 16 ; 1 Jn. iv. 5 ; λαλεῖν ἐκ τοῦ κόσμου, to speak in accordance with the world's character and mode of thinking, 1 Jn. iv. 5 ; ὁ ἄρχων τοῦ κ. τούτου, i. e. the devil, Jn. xii. 31 ; xiv. 30 ; xvi. 11 ; ὁ ἐν τῷ κ. he that is operative in the world (also of the devil), 1 Jn. iv. 4 ; τὸ πνεῦμα τοῦ κ. 1 Co. ii. 12 ; ἡ σοφία τοῦ κ. τούτου, ibid. i. 20 [here G L T Tr WH om. τούτ.] ; iii. 19. [τὰ στοιχεῖα τοῦ κόσμου, Gal. iv. 3 ; Col. ii. 8, 20, (see 5 above, and στοιχεῖον, 3 and 4).] **7.** _worldly affairs ; the aggregate of things earthly ; the whole circle of earthly goods, endowments, riches, advantages, pleasures,_ etc., _which, although hollow and frail and fleeting, stir desire, seduce from God and are obstacles to the cause of Christ_ : Gal. vi. 14 ; 1 Jn. ii. 16 sq. ; iii. 17 ; εἶναι ἐκ τοῦ κ., to be of earthly origin and nature, Jn. xviii. 36 ; somewhat differently in 1 Jn. ii. 16 (on which see εἰμί, V. 3 d.) ; κερδαίνειν τὸν κ. ὅλον, Mt. xvi. 26 ; Mk. viii. 36 ; Lk. ix. 25 ; οἱ χρώμενοι τῷ κ. τούτῳ [crit. txt. τὸν κόσμον ; see χράομαι, 2], 1 Co. vii. 31* ; μεριμνᾶν τὰ τοῦ κ. 33 sq. ; φίλος and φιλία τοῦ κ. Jas. iv. 4 ; ἀγαπᾶν τὸν κ. 1 Jn. ii. 15 ; νικᾶν τὸν κ., the incentives to sin proceeding from the world, 1 Jn. v. 4 sq. ; the obstacles to God's cause, Jn. xvi. 33 ; [cf. ἐλθέτω χάρις κ. παρελθέτω ὁ κόσμος οὗτος, Teaching of the Twelve Apostles, c. 10]. **8.** _any aggregate_ or _general collection of particulars of any sort_ [cf. Eng. "a world of curses " (Shakspere), etc.] : ὁ κόσμος τῆς ἀδικίας, the sum of all iniquities, Jas. iii. 6 ; τοῦ πιστοῦ ὅλος ὁ κόσμος τῶν χρημάτων, τοῦ δὲ ἀπίστου οὐδὲ ὀβολός (a statement due to the Alex. translator), Prov. xvii. 6. Among the N. T. writers no one uses κόσμος oftener than John ; it occurs in Mark three times, in Luke's writings four times, and in the Apocalypse three times. Cf. _Kreiss,_ Sur le sens du mot κόσμος dans le N. T. (Strasb. 1837) ; _Düsterdieck_ on 1 Jn. ii. 15, pp. 247–259 ; _Zezschwitz,_ Profangräcität u. bibl. Sprachgeist, p. 21 sqq. ; _Diestel_ in Herzog xvii. p. 676 sqq. ; [_Trench,_ Syn. § lix.] ; on John's use of the word cf. _Reuss,_ Histoire de la théologie chrétienne au siècle apostolique, ii. p. 463 sqq. [i. e. livre vii. ch. viii.] ; cf. his Johanneische Theologie, in the Beiträge zu den theol. Wissenschaften, Fasc. i. p. 29 sqq. ; [Westcott on Jn. i. 10, 'Additional Note'].*

2890   **Κούαρτος**, -ου, ὁ, (a Lat. name), *Quartus*, an unknown Christian: Ro. xvi. 23.*

2891   **κούμι**, Tr txt. κούμ, T WH κούμ, (the Hebr. קוּמִי [impv. fem.; the other (masc.) form must be regarded as having become an interjection]), *arise*: Mk. v. 41.*

2892   **κουστωδία**, -ας [B. 17 (16)], ἡ, (a Lat. word), *guard*: used of the Roman soldiers guarding the sepulchre of Christ, Mt. xxvii. 65 sq.; xxviii. 11. (Ev. Nic. c. 13.) *

2893   **κουφίζω**: impf. 3 pers. plur. ἐκούφιζον; (κοῦφος light); **1.** intrans. *to be light* (Hes., Eur., Dio C.). **2.** fr. Hippocr. down generally trans. *to lighten*: a ship, by throwing the cargo overboard, Acts xxvii. 38. (Sept. Jonah i. 5, and often in Polyb.) *

2894   **κόφινος**, -ου, ὁ, *a basket, wicker basket*, [cf. B. D. s. v. Basket]: Mt. xiv. 20; [xvi. 9]; Mk. vi. 43; [viii. 19]; Lk. ix. 17; Jn. vi. 13. (Judg. vi. 19; Ps. lxxx. (lxxxi.) 7; Arstph. av. 1310; Xen. mem. 3, 8, 6; al.) *

2895   **κράββατος** (L T Tr WH κράβαττος; cod. Sin. κράβακτος [exc. in Acts v. 15; cf. *KC.* Nov. Test. ad fid. cod. Vat. praef. p. lxxxi. sq.; *Tdf.* Proleg. p. 80]), -ου, ὁ, (Lat. *grabatus*), *a pallet, camp bed*, (a rather mean bed, holding only one person, called by the Greeks σκίμπους, σκιμπόδιον): Mk. ii. 4, 9, 11 sq.; vi. 55; Jn. v. 8–12 [in 12 T WH om. Tr br. the cl.]; Acts v. 15; ix. 33. Cf. *Sturz*, De dial. Maced. etc. p. 175 sq.; *Lob.* ad Phryn. p. 62; *Volkmar*, Marcus u d. Synopse u.s.w. p. 131; [*McClellan*, New Testament etc. p. 106; W. 25].*

2896   **κράζω** (with a long; hence ptcp. κρᾶζον, Gal. iv. 6 L T Tr WH [(where RG κράζον; cf. B. 61 (53)]); impf. ἔκραζον; fut. κεκράξομαι (Lk. xix. 40 R G L Tr mrg.), and κράξω (ibid. T WH Tr txt.), the former being more com. in Grk. writ. and used by the Sept. (cf. Mic. iii. 4; Job xxxv. 12, etc. [but ἀνα-κράξομαι, Joel iii. 16 Alex.; cf. W. 279 (262); esp. B. as below]); 1 aor. ἔκραξα (once viz. Acts xxiv. 21 T Tr WH ἐκέκραξα, a reduplicated form freq. in Sept. [e. g. Ps. xxi. (xxii.) 6; Judg. iii. 15; 1 Macc. xi. 49, etc.; see Veitch s. v.]; more com. in native Grk. writ. is 2 aor. ἔκραγον [" the simple ἔκραγον seems not to occur in good Attic" (Veitch s. v.)]); pf. κέκραγα, with pres. force [W. 274 (258)] (Jn. i. 15); cf. *Bttm.* Ausf. Spr. ii. p. 223; B. 61 (53); Kühner i. p. 851; [esp. Veitch s. v.]; Sept. for עוּק, צָעַק, קָרָא, שָׁוַע [fr. Aeschyl. down]; **1.** prop. [onomatopoetic] *to croak* (Germ. *krächzen*), of the cry of the raven (Theophr.); hence univ. *to cry out, cry aloud, vociferate*: particularly of inarticulate cries, Mk. v. 5; ix. 26; xv. 39 [here T WH om. Tr br. κρ.]; Lk. ix. 39; Rev. xii. 2; ἀπὸ τοῦ φόβου, Mt. xiv. 26; with φωνῇ μεγάλῃ added, Mt. xxvii. 50; Mk. i. 26 [here T Tr WH φωνῆσαν]; Acts vii. 57; Rev. x. 3; ὄπισθέν τινος, to cry after one, follow him up with outcries, Mt. xv. 23; like זָעַק and צָעַק (Gen. iv. 10; xviii. 20), i. q. *to cry* or *pray for vengeance*, Jas. v. 4. **2.** *to cry* i. e. *call out aloud, speak with a loud voice*, [Germ. *laut rufen*]: τί, Acts xix. 32; xxiv. 21; foll. by direct discourse, Mk. x. 48; xv. 14; Lk. xviii. 39; Jn. xii. 13 R G; Acts xix. 34; xxi. 28, 36; xxiii. 6; with the addition φωνῇ μεγάλῃ foll. by direct disc., Mk. v. 7; Acts vii. 60; ἐν φωνῇ μεγ. Rev. xiv. 15, κράζω λέγων, to

cry out saying, etc., Mt. viii. 29; xiv. 30; [xv. 22 (where RG ἐκραύγασεν)]; xx. 30 sq.; xxi. 9; xxvii. 23; Mk. iii. 11; xi. 9 [T Tr WH om. L br. λέγ.]; Jn. xix. 12 [here L T Tr WH ἐκραύγ.]; Acts xvi. 17; xix. 28; Rev. xviii. 18; κράζω φωνῇ μεγάλῃ λέγων, Rev. vi. 10; vii. 10; xix. 17 [here T WH br. add ἐν]; κράξας ἔλεγε, Mk. ix. 24; κράζειν κ. λέγειν, Mt. ix. 27; xxi. 15; Mk. x. 47; Lk. iv. 41 R G Tr txt. WH; Acts xiv. 14; of those who utter or teach a thing publicly and solemnly, Ro. ix. 27; κέκραγε and ἔκραξε λέγων, foll. by direct disc., Jn. i. 15; vii. 37; ἔκραξε διδάσκων κ. λέγων, Jn. vii. 28; ἔκραξε κ. λέγων, Jn. xii. 44; of those who offer earnest, importunate, prayers to God, foll. by direct disc., Ro. viii. 15; Gal. iv. 6, (often so in O. T., as Job xxxv. 12; Ps. xxxiii. (xxxiv.) 7; commonly with πρὸς κύριον, πρὸς τὸν θεόν added, Judg. x. 12 [Alex.]; Ps. iii. 5; cvi. (cvii.) 13, etc.). τινί, *to cry* or *call to*: Rev. vii. 2; xiv. 15, (cf. Ps. cxviii. (cxix.) 145; ἕτερος πρὸς ἕτερον, Is. vi. 3). [COMP.: ἀνα-κράζω. SYN. see βοάω, fin.] *

2897   **κραιπάλη** [WH κρεπάλη, see their App. p. 151], -ης, ἡ, (fr. ΚΡΑΣ the head, and πάλλω to toss about; so explained by Galen and Clem. Alex. Paedag. 2, 2, 26 and Phryn. in *Bekker*, Anecd. p. 45, 13 [cf. *Vaniček* p. 148]), Lat. *crapula* (i. e. the giddiness and headache caused by drinking wine to excess): Lk. xxi. 34 [A. V. *surfeiting*; cf. Trench § lxi.]. (Arstph. Acharn. 277; Alciphr. 3, 24; Plut. mor. p. 127 f. [de sanitate 11]; Lcian., Hdian. 2, 5, 1.) *

2898   **κρανίον**, -ου, τό, (dimin. of the noun κρανον [i. e. κάρα, Curtius § 38]), *a skull* (Vulg. *calvaria*): Mt. xxvii. 33; Mk. xv. 22; Lk. xxiii. 33; Jn. xix. 17; see Γολγοθά. (Judg. ix. 53; 2 K. ix. 35; Hom. Il. 8, 84; Pind., Eur., Plat., Lcian., Hdian.) *

2899   **κράσπεδον**, -ου, τό, in class. Grk. *the extremity* or *prominent part of a thing, edge, skirt, margin*; *the fringe of a garment*; in the N. T. for Hebr. צִיצִת, i. e. *a little appendage hanging down from the edge of the mantle or cloak*, made cf twisted wool; *a tassel, tuft*: Mt. ix. 20; xiv. 36; xxiii. 5; Mk. vi. 56; Lk. viii. 44. The Jews had such appendages attached to their mantles to remind them of the law, acc. to Num. xv. 37 sq. Cf. *Win.* RWB. s. v. *Saum*; [B. D. s. v. Hem of Garment; *Edersheim*, Jesus the Messiah, i. 624; esp. *Ginsburg* in Alex.'s Kitto s. v. Fringes].*

2900   **κραταιός**, -ά, -όν, (κράτος), Sept. mostly for חָזָק, *mighty*: ἡ κρ. χεὶρ τοῦ θεοῦ, i. e. the power of God, 1 Pet. v. 6; τοῦ κυρίου, Bar. ii. 11; 1 Esdr. viii. 46 (47), 60 (61), and often in Sept. (In earlier Grk. only poetic [Hom., al.] for the more com. κρατερός; but later, used in prose also [Plut., al.].) *

2901   **κραταιόω**, -ῶ: Pass., pres. impv. 2 pers. plur. κραταιοῦσθε impf. 3 pers. sing. ἐκραταιοῦτο; 1 aor. inf. κραταιωθῆναι; (κράτος); only bibl. and eccles., for the classic κρατύνω; Sept. mostly for חָזַק; in pass. several times for אָמַץ; *to strengthen, make strong*, (Vulg. *conforto* [and in Eph. iii. 16 *conroboro*]); Pass. *to be made strong, to increase in strength, to grow strong*: pass. with dat. of respect, πνεύματι, Lk. i. 80; ii. 40 [here G L T T^r WH om. πνεύματι]; δυνάμει, Eph. iii. 16, (cf. ἰσχύειν τοῖς σώμασι, Xen. mem. 2, 7, 7); ἀνδρίζεσθε, κραταιοῦσθε, i. e. show yourselves brave [A. V. *be strong*], 1 Co. xvi. 13 (ἀνδρίζεσθε κ. κραταιούσθω ἡ καρδία ὑμῶν, Ps. xxx. (xxxi.) 25; κραταιοῦσθε κ. γίνεσθε εἰς ἄνδρας, 1 S. iv. 9; ἀνδρίζου κ. κραταιωθῶμεν, 2 S. x. 12).*

2902 **κρατέω**; impf. 2 pers. plur. ἐκρατεῖτε, Mk. xiv. 49 Tr mrg. WH mrg.; fut. κρατήσω; 1 aor. ἐκράτησα; pf. inf. κεκρατηκέναι; Pass., pres. κρατοῦμαι; impf. ἐκρατούμην; pf. 3 pers. plur. κεκράτηνται; (κράτος [q. v.]); Sept. chiefly for חָזַק, also for אָחַז (to seize), etc.; fr. Hom. down; **1.** *to have power, be powerful; to be chief, be master of, to rule* : absol. for מָלַךְ, Esth. i. 1; 1 Esdr. iv. 38; ὁ κρατῶν, Sap. xiv. 19; οἱ κρατοῦντες, 2 Macc. iv. 50; τινός, to be ruler of one, Prov. xvi. 32; xvii. 2, (for מָשַׁל); Sap. iii. 8; never so in the N. T. **2.** *to get possession of*; i. e. **a.** *to become master of, to obtain* : τῆς προθέσεως, Acts xxvii. 13 [(Diod. Sic. 16, 20; al.) cf. B. 161 (140); on the tense, W. 334 (313)]. **b.** *to take hold of* : τῆς χειρός τινος [cf. W. § 30, 8 d.; B. u. s.], Mt. ix. 25; Mk. i. 31; v. 41; ix. 27 L T Tr WH; Lk. viii. 54; τινὰ τῆς χειρός, to take one by the hand, Mk. ix. 27 R G, cf. Matthiae § 331; τινά, to hold one fast in order not to be sent away, Acts iii. 11, cf. Meyer ad loc.; τοὺς πόδας τινός, to embrace one's knees, Mt. xxviii. 9; trop. τὸν λόγον, to lay hold of mentally [cf. our 'catch at'; but al. refer this ex. to 3 b. below], Mk. ix. 10 (join πρὸς ἑαυτούς with συζητοῦντες). **c.** *to lay hold of, take, seize* : τινά, to lay hands on one in order to get him into one's power, Mt. xiv. 3; xviii. 28; xxi. 46; xxii. 6; xxvi. 4, 48, 50, 55, 57; Mk. iii. 21; vi. 17; xii. 12; xiv. 1, 44, 46, 49, 51; Acts xxiv. 6; Rev. xx. 2, (2 S. vi. 6; Ps. cxxxvi. (cxxxvii.) 9); τί, Mt. xii. 11. **3.** *to hold*; i. e. **a.** *to hold in the hand* : τὶ ἐν τῇ δεξιᾷ, Rev. ii. 1 (τῇ ἀριστερᾷ τὸν ἄρτον, Plut. mor. p. 99 d.). **b.** *to hold fast*, i. e. trop. *not to discard or let go*; *to keep carefully and faithfully*: ὃ ἔχετε, ἔχεις, Rev. ii. 25; iii. 11; τὸ ὄνομά μου, Rev. ii. 13; one's authority, τὴν κεφαλήν, i. e. ἐκεῖνον ὅς ἐστιν ἡ κεφαλή, Christ, Col. ii. 19; τὴν παράδοσιν, Mk. vii. 3 sq. 8; τὰς παραδόσεις, 2 Th. ii. 15; τὴν διδαχήν, Rev. ii. 14 sq.; also with a gen. of the thing, of blessings in which different individuals are participants: τῆς ὁμολογίας, Heb. iv. 14; τῆς ἐλπίδος, Heb. vi. 18 [al. refer this ex. to 2 above], (cf. 2 S. iii. 6). **c.** *to continue to hold, to retain*: of death continuing to hold one, pass. Acts ii. 24; τὰς ἁμαρτίας (opp. to ἀφίημι), to retain sins, i. e. not to remit, Jn. xx. 23; *to hold in check, restrain*: foll. by ἵνα μή, Rev. vii. 1; by τοῦ μή [W. 325 (305); B. § 140, 16 β.], Lk. xxiv. 16. On the constr. of this verb with gen. and acc. cf. Matthiae § 359 sq.; W. § 30, 8 d.; B. 161 (140).*

2903 **κράτιστος**, -η, -ον, superl. of the adj. κρατύς, (κράτος), [fr. (Hom.) Pind. down], *mightiest, strongest, noblest, most illustrious, best, most excellent* : voc. κράτιστε used in addressing men of conspicuous rank or office, Acts xxiii. 26; xxiv. 3; xxvi. 25, (Otto, De ep. ad Diognetum etc. Jena 1845, p. 79 sqq., and in his Epist. ad Diognet. Leips. ed. p. 53 sq., has brought together exx. fr. later

writ.). Perhaps also it served simply to express friendship in Lk. i. 3 (as in Theophr. char. 5; Dion. Hal. de oratt. 1; Joseph. antt. 4, 6, 8), because in Acts i. 1 it is omitted in addressing the same person. Cf. *Grimm* in Jahrbb. f. deutsche Theol. for 1871, p. 50 sq.*

2904 **κράτος**, -εος (-ους), [fr. a root meaning 'to perfect, complete' (Curtius § 72); fr. Hom. down], τό, Hebr. עֹז; **1.** *force, strength.* **2.** *power, might* : τὸ κράτος τῆς ἰσχύος αὐτοῦ, the might of his strength, Eph. i. 19; vi. 10; τῆς δόξης αὐτοῦ, Col. i. 11; κατὰ κράτος, *mightily, with great power*, ηὔξανε, Acts xix. 20; meton. *a mighty deed, a work of power* : ποιεῖν κρ. (cf. ποιεῖν δυνάμεις), Lk. i. 51. **3.** *dominion* : in the doxologies, 1 Tim. vi. 16; 1 Pet. iv. 11; v. 11; Jude 25; Rev. i. 6; v. 13; τινός (gen. of obj.), Heb. ii. 14 (τὸ Περσέων κράτος ἔχοντα, Hdt. 3, 69). [Syn. see δύναμις, fin.]*

2905 **κραυγάζω**; impf. 3 pers. plur. ἐκραύγαζον; fut. κραυγάσω; 1 aor. ἐκραύγασα; (κραυγή); *to cry out, cry aloud*, (i. q. κράζω [see βοάω, fin., and below]): Mt. xii. 19; Acts xxii. 23; *to shout*, foll. by direct disc., Jn. xix. 15 and L T Tr WH in xii. 13; with λέγων added, to cry out in these words, foll. by direct disc. : Jn. xviii. 40; xix. 6 (where T om. λέγοντες), and L T Tr WH also in 12; κραυγάζειν κ. λέγειν, Lk. iv. 41 L T Tr mrg.; κραυγάζ. φωνῇ μεγάλῃ, foll. by direct disc., Jn. xi. 43. τινί, *to cry out to, call to, one* (see κράζω, 2 and fin.), foll. by direct disc. Mt. xv. 22 R G. The word is rare in Grk. writ.: Dem. p. 1258, 26; of the shouts in the theatres, Epict. diss. 3, 4, 4; of a raven, ib. 3, 1, 37; Galen, al.; first in a poetic fragm. in Plat. rep. 10 p. 607 b.; once in the O. T. viz. 2 Esdr. iii. 13. Cf. *Lob.* ad Phryn. p. 337.*

2906 **κραυγή**, -ῆς, ἡ, [cf. κράζω; on its class. use see *Schmidt*, Syn. i. ch. 3 § 4; fr. Eur. down], Sept. for צְעָקָה, זְעָקָה, תְּרוּעָה, שַׁוְעָה, etc.; *a crying, outcry, clamor* : Mt. xxv. 6; Lk. i. 42 T WH Tr txt.; Acts xxiii. 9; Eph. iv. 31, and R G in Rev. xiv. 18; of the wailing of those in distress, Heb. v. 7; Rev. xxi. 4.*

2907 **κρέας**, τό, [cf. Lat. *caro, cruor*; Curtius § 74], plur. κρέα (cf. W. 65 (63); [B. 15 (13)]); [fr. Hom. down]; Sept. very often for בָּשָׂר; (the) *flesh* (of a sacrificed animal) : Ro. xiv. 21; 1 Co. viii. 13.*

2908 & **2909** **κρείττων** and (1 Co. vii. 38; Phil. i. 23; in other places the reading varies between the two forms, esp. in 1 Co. vii. 9 [here T Tr WH L txt. -ττ-]; xi. 17; Heb. vi. 9 [here and in the preced. pass. L T Tr WH -σσ-; see *WH.* App. p. 148 sq.; cf. Σ, σ, ς]) κρείσσων, -ονος, neut. -ον, (compar. of κρατύς, see κράτιστος, cf. Kühner i. p. 436; [B. 27 (24)]), [fr. Hom. down], *better*; i. e. **a.** *more useful, more serviceable* 1 Co. xi. 17; xii. 31 R G; Heb. xi. 40; xii. 24; with πολλῷ μᾶλλον added, Phil. i. 23 [cf. μᾶλλον, 1 b.]; κρεῖσσον (adv.) ποιεῖν, 1 Co. vii. 38; κρεῖττόν ἐστιν, *it is more advantageous*, foll. by an inf., 1 Co. vii. 9; 2 Pet. ii. 21, [cf. B. 217 (188); W. § 41 a. 2 a]. **b.** *more excellent* : Heb. i. 4; vi. 9; vii. 7, 19, 22; viii. 6; ix. 23; x. 34; xi. 16, 35; κρ. ἐστι, foll. by an inf., 1 Pet. iii. 17.*

see 2910 **κρέμαμαι**, see the foll. word.

2910 **κρεμάννυμι**, also κρεμαννύω ["scarcely classic" (Veitch

s. v.)], κρεμάω -ῶ ["still later" (ibid.)], and (Sept. Job xxvi. 7 and Byzant. writ.) κρεμάζω, (in the N. T. the pres. does not occur): 1 aor. ἐκρέμασα; 1 aor. pass. ἐκρεμάσθην; fr. Hom. down; Sept. for תלה; to hang up, suspend: τὶ ἐπί τι (Rec.), περί τι (L T Tr WH), [εἴς τι, Tdf. edd. 2, 7], Mt. xviii. 6; τινὰ ἐπὶ ξύλου, Acts v. 30; x. 39, (Gen. xl. 19, 22; Deut. xxi. 22; Esth. vi. 4, etc.); simply κρεμασθείς, of one crucified, Lk. xxiii. 39. Mid. κρέμαμαι (for κρεμάννυμαι, cf. Bttm. Ausf. Spr. ii. p. 224); intrans. to be suspended, to hang: foll. by ἐκ with gen. of the thing, Acts xxviii. 4 (see ἐκ, I. 3); ἐπὶ ξύλου, of one hanging on a cross, Gal. iii. 13; trop. ἔν τινι, Mt. xxii. 40, where the meaning is, all the Law and the Prophets (i. e. the teaching of the O. T. on morality) is summed up in these two precepts. [COMP.: ἐκ-κρέμαμαι.]*

(2910a)
see 2897 —— κρεπάλη, see κραιπάλη.]

2911 —— κρημνός, -οῦ, ὁ, (fr. κρεμάννυμι), a steep (place), a precipice: Mt. viii. 32; Mk. v. 13; Lk. viii. 33. (2 Chr. xxv. 12; Grk. writ. fr. Hom. down.)*

2912 Κρής, ὁ, plur. Κρῆτες, a Cretan, an inhabitant of the island of Crete: Acts ii. 11; Tit. i. 12 [cf. Farrar, St. Paul, ii. 534].*

2913 Κρήσκης [cf. B. 17 (15)], ὁ, Lat. Crescens, an unknown man: 2 Tim. iv. 10.*

2914 Κρήτη, -ης, ἡ, Crete, the largest and most fertile island of the Mediterranean archipelago or Ægean Sea, now called Candia: Acts xxvii. 7, 12 sq. 21; Tit. i. 5. [Dict. of Geog. or McC. and S. s. v.]*

2915 κριθή, -ῆς, ἡ, (in Grk. writ. [fr. Hom. down] only in plur. αἱ κριθαί), Sept. for שְׂעֹרָה, barley: Rev. vi. 6 κριθῆς R G, κριθῶν L T Tr WH.*

2916 κρίθινος, -η, -ον, (κριθή), of barley, made of barley: ἄρτοι (2 K. iv. 42, cf. Judg. vii. 13), Jn. vi. 9, 13. [(Hippon., al.)]*

2917 κρίμα [G T WH] or κρίμα [L Tr (more commonly)] (on the accent cf. W. p. 50; Lipsius, Grammat. Untersuch. p. 40 sq. [who gives the preference to κρίμα, as do Bttm. 73 (64); Cobet (N. T. ad fid. etc. p. 49 sq.); Fritzsche(Rom. vol. i. 96, 107); al.; "videtur ἰ antiquitati Graecae, ἰ Alexandrinae aetati placuisse," Tdf. Proleg. to Sept. ed. 4 p. xxx.; on the accent in extant codd. see Tdf. Proleg. p. 101; cf. esp. Lobeck, Paralip. p. 418]),-τος, ró, (fr. κρίνω, q. v.; as κλίμα fr. κλίνω), [Aeschyl. down], Sept. very often for מִשְׁפָּט; 1. a decree: plur., τοῦ θεοῦ, Ro. xi. 33 [al. here (with A. V.) judgments; cf. Weiss in Meyer ad loc.] (Ps. cxviii. (cxix.) 75). 2. judgment; i. e. condemnation of wrong, the decision (whether severe or mild) which one passes on the faults of others: κρίματί τινι κρίνειν, Mt. vii. 2. In a forensic sense, the sentence of a judge: with a gen. of the punishment to which one is sentenced, θανάτου, Lk. xxiv. 20; esp. the sentence of God as judge: τὸ κρίμα ... εἰς κατάκριμα, the judgment (in which God declared sin to be punishable with death) issued in condemnation, i. e. was condemnation to all who sinned and therefore paid the penalty of death Ro. v. 16; esp. where the justice of God in punishing is to be shown, κρίμα denotes condemnatory sentence, penal judgment, sentence, 2 Pet. ii. 3; Jude 4; with gen. of the one who pronounces

judgment, τοῦ θεοῦ, Ro. ii. 2 sq.; λαμβάνεσθαι κρίμα, Mt. xxiii. 13 (14) Rec.; Mk. xii. 40; Lk. xx. 47; Ro. xiii. 2; Jas. iii. 1; the one on whom God passes judgment is said ἔχειν κρίμα, 1 Tim. v. 12; βαστάζειν τὸ κρίμα, to bear the force of the condemnatory judgment in suffering punishment (see βαστάζω, 2), Gal. v. 10; κρίμα ἐσθίειν ἑαυτῷ, so to eat as to incur the judgment or punishment of God, 1 Co. xi. 29; εἰς κρίμα συνέρχεσθαι, to incur the condemnation of God, 34; εἶναι ἐν τῷ αὐτῷ κρίματι, to lie under the same condemnation, pay the same penalty, Lk. xxiii. 40; with gen. of the one on whom condemnation is passed, Ro. iii. 8; 1 Tim. iii. 6; Rev. xvii. 1. the judgment which is formed or passed: by God, through what Christ accomplished on earth, εἰς κρίμα ἐγὼ εἰς τ. κόσμον τοῦτον ἦλθον, where by way of explanation is added ἵνα κτλ. to this end, that etc. Jn. ix. 39; τὸ κρίμα ἄρχεται, the execution of judgment as displayed in the infliction of punishment, 1 Pet. iv. 17; the last or final judgment is called τὸ κρ. τὸ μέλλον, Acts xxiv. 25; κρ. αἰώνιον, eternally in force, Heb. vi. 2; the vindication of one's right, κρίνειν τὸ κρίμα τινὸς ἔκ τινος, to vindicate one's right by taking vengeance or inflicting punishment on another, Rev. xviii. 20 ([R. V. God hath judged your judgment on her], see ἐκ, I. 7); i. q. the power and business of judging: κρ. διδόναι τινί, Rev. xx. 4. 3. a matter to be judicially decided, a lawsuit, a case in court: κρίματα ἔχειν μετά τινος, 1 Co. vi. 7.*

κρίνον, -ου, τό, a lily: Mt. vi. 28; Lk. xii. 27. [From Hdt. down.]* 2918

κρίνω; fut. κρινῶ; 1 aor. ἔκρινα; pf. κέκρικα; 3 pers. sing. plupf., without augm. (W. § 12, 9; [B. 33 (29)]), κεκρίκει (Acts xx. 16 G L T Tr WH); Pass., pres. κρίνομαι; impf. ἐκρινόμην; pf. κέκριμαι; 1 aor. ἐκρίθην [cf. B. 52 (45)]; 1 fut. κριθήσομαι; Sept. for שָׁפַט, and also for דּוּן and רִיב; Lat. cerno, i. e. 1. to separate, put asunder; to pick out, select, choose, (Hom., Hdt., Aeschyl., Soph., Xen., Plat., al.; μετὰ νεανίσκων ἀρίστων κεκριμένων [chosen, picked], 2 Macc. xiii. 15; κεκριμένοι ἄρχοντες, Joseph. antt. 11, 3, 10); hence 2. to approve, esteem: ἡμέραν παρ' ἡμέραν, one day above another, i. e. to prefer [see παρά, III. 2 b.], Ro. xiv. 5 (so τὶ πρό τινος, Plat. Phil. p. 57 e.); τὸν Ἀπόλλω πρὸ Μαρσύου, rep. 3 p. 399 e.); πᾶσαν ἡμ. to esteem every day, i. e. hold it sacred, ibid. 3. to be of opinion, deem, think: ὀρθῶς ἔκρινας, thou hast decided (judged) correctly, Lk. vii. 43; foll. by an inf. Acts xv. 19; foll. by a direct quest. 1 Co. xi. 13; τοῦτο, ὅτι etc. to be of opinion that 2 Co. v. 14; foll. by the acc. with inf. Acts xvi. 15; τινά or τί foll. by a predicate acc., κρίνειν τινὰ ἄξιόν τινος, to judge one (to be) worthy of a thing, Acts xiii. 46; ἄπιστον κρίνεται, Acts xxvi. 8. 4. to determine, resolve, decree: τί, 1 Co. vii. 37 (κρῖναί τι καὶ προθέσθαι, Polyb. 3, 6, 7; τὸ κριθέν, which one has determined on, one's resolve, 5, 52, 6; 9, 13, 7; τοῖς κριθεῖσι ἐμμένειν δεῖ, Epict. diss. 2, 15, 7 sqq.); δόγματα, pass. [the decrees that had been ordained (cf. A. V.)], Acts xvi. 4; τοῦτο κρίνατε, foll. by an inf. preceded by the art. τό, Ro. xiv. 13; also with ἐμαυτῷ added, for myself i. e. for my own benefit

2919

(lest I should prepare grief for myself by being compelled to grieve you), 2 Co. ii. 1; foll. by an inf., Acts xx. 16; xxv. 25; 1 Co. ii. 2 G L T Tr WH [(see below)]; v. 3; Tit. iii. 12, (1 Macc. xi. 33; 3 Macc. i. 6; vi. 30; Judith xi. 13; Sap. viii. 9; Diod. 17, 95; Joseph. antt. 7, 1, 5; 12, 10, 4; 13, 6, 1); with τοῦ prefixed, 1 Co. ii. 2 Rec. [(see above)]; foll. by the acc. with inf. Acts xxi. 25 (2 Macc. xi. 36); with τοῦ prefixed, Acts xxvii. 1 [cf. B. § 140, 16 δ.]; (κρίνεταί τινι, it is one's pleasure, *it seems good to one*, 1 Esdr. vi. 20 (21) sq.; viii. 90 (92)). **5.** *to judge*; **a.** *to pronounce an opinion concerning right and wrong*; **α.** in a forensic sense [(differing from δικάζειν, the o f f i c i a l term, in giving prominence to the i n t e l l e c t u a l process, the sifting and weighing of evidence)], of a human judge: τινά, to give a decision respecting one, Jn. vii. 51; κατὰ τὸν νόμον, Jn. xviii. 31; Acts xxiii. 3; xxiv. 6 Rec.; the substance of the decision is added in an inf., Acts iii. 13; pass. *to be judged*, i. e. *summoned to trial that one's case may be examined and judgment passed upon it*, Acts xxv. 10; xxvi. 6; Ro. iii. 4 (fr. Ps. l. (li.) 6 (4)); περί w. gen. of the thing, Acts xxiii. 6; xxiv. 21; [xxv. 20]; with addition of ἐπί and the gen. of the judge, *before one*, Acts xxv. 9. Where the context requires, used of a condemnatory judgment, i. q. *to condemn*: simply, Acts xiii. 27. **β.** of the judgment of God or of Jesus the Messiah, deciding between the righteousness and the unrighteousness of men: absol., Jn. v. 30; viii. 50; δικαίως, 1 Pet. ii. 23; ἐν δικαιοσύνῃ, Rev. xix. 11; τινά, 1 Co. v. 13; pass. Jas. ii. 12; ζῶντας κ. νεκρούς, 2 Tim. iv. 1; 1 Pet. iv. 5; νεκρούς, pass., Rev. xi. 18 [B. 260 (224)]; τὴν οἰκουμένην, the inhabitants of the world, Acts xvii. 31 [cf. W. 389 (364)]; τὸν κόσμον, Ro. iii. 6; τὰ κρυπτὰ τῶν ἀνθρώπων, Ro. ii. 16; κρίνειν τὸ κρίμα τινὸς ἔκ τινος (see κρίμα, 2 sub fin.), Rev. xviii. 20, cf. vi. 10; κρίνειν κατὰ τὸ ἑκάστου ἔργον, 1 Pet. i. 17; τοὺς νεκροὺς ἐκ τῶν γεγραμμένων ἐν τοῖς βιβλίοις κατὰ τὰ ἔργα αὐτῶν, pass., Rev. xx. 12 sq.; with acc. of the substance of the judgment, *thou didst pronounce this judgment*, ταῦτα ἔκρινας, Rev. xvi. 5; contextually, used specifically of the act of *condemning* and *decreeing* (or inflicting) *penalty on one*: τινά, Jn. iii. 18; v. 22; xii. 47 sq.; Acts vii. 7; Ro. ii. 12; 1 Co. xi. 31 sq.; 2 Th. ii. 12; Heb. x. 30; xiii. 4; 1 Pet. iv. 6 [cf. W. 630 (585)]; Jas. v. 9 (where Rec. κατακρ.); Rev. xviii. 8; xix. 2, (Sap. xii. 10, 22); τὸν κόσμον, opp. to σώζειν, Jn. iii. 17; xii. 47; of the devil it is said ὁ ἄρχων τοῦ κόσμου τούτου κέκριται, because the victorious cause of Christ has rendered the supreme wickedness of Satan evident to all, and put an end to his power to dominate and destroy, Jn. xvi. 11. **γ.** of Christians as hereafter to sit with Christ at the judgment: τὸν κόσμον, 1 Co. vi. 2; ἀγγέλους, ib. 3 [cf. ἄγγελος, 2 sub fin.; yet see Meyer ed. *Heinrici* ad ll. cc.]. **b.** *to pronounce judgment*; *to subject to censure*; of those who act the part of judges or arbiters in the matters of common life, or pass judgment on the deeds and words of others: univ. and without case, Jn. viii. 16, 26; κατά τι, Jn. viii. 15; κατ' ὄψιν, Jn. vii. 24; ἐν κρίματί τινι κρίνειν, Mt. vii. 2; τινά, pass. [with nom.

of pers.], Rom. iii. 7; ἐκ τοῦ στόματός σου κρινῶ σε, out of thine own mouth (i. e. from what thou hast just said) will I take the judgment that must be passed on thee, Lk. xix. 22; τί, 1 Co. x. 15; pass. ib. 29; τὸ δίκαιον, Lk. xii. 57; foll. by εἰ, *whether*, Acts iv. 19; with acc. of the substance of the judgment: τί i. e. κρίσιν τινά, 1 Co. iv. 5; κρίσιν κρίνειν (Plat. rep. 2 p. 360 d.) δικαίαν [cf. B. § 131, 5], Jn. vii. 24 (ἀληθινὴν κ. δικαίαν, Tob. iii. 2; κρίσεις ἀδίκους, Sus. 53); of the disciplinary judgment to which Christians subject the conduct of their fellows, passing censure upon them as the facts require, 1 Co. v. 12; of those who judge severely (unfairly), finding fault with this or that in others, Mt. vii. 1; Lk. vi. 37; Ro. ii. 1; τινά, Ro. ii. 1, 3; xiv. 3 sq. 10, 13; foll. by ἐν with dat. of the thing, Col. ii. 16; Ro. xiv. 22; hence i. q. *to condemn*: Ro. ii. 27; Jas. iv. 11 sq. **6.** Hebraistically i. q. *to rule, govern*; *to preside over with the power of giving judicial decisions*, because it was the prerogative of kings and rulers to pass judgment: Mt. xix. 28; Lk. xxii. 30, (τὸν λαόν, 2 K. xv. 5; 1 Macc. ix. 73; Joseph. antt. 5, 3, 3; οἱ κρίνοντες τ. γῆν, Ps. ii. 10; Sap. i. 1; cf. *Gesenius*, Thes. iii. p. 1463 sq.). **7.** Pass. and mid. *to contend together*, of warriors and combatants (Hom., Diod., al.); *to dispute* (Hdt. 3, 120; Arstph. nub. 66); in a forensic sense, *to go to law, have a suit at law*: with dat. of the pers. with whom [W. § 31, 1 g.], Mt. v. 40 (Job ix. 3; xiii. 19; Eur. Med. 609); foll. by μετά with gen. of the pers. with whom one goes to law, and ἐπί with gen. of the judge, 1 Co. vi. (1), 6. [Comp.: ἀνα-, ἀπο-, ἀντ-απο- (-μαι), δια-, ἐν-, ἐπι-, κατα-, συν-, ὑπο- (-μαι), συν- ὑπο-(-μαι).] *

κρίσις, -εως, ἡ, Sept. for רִיב, רִיב (a suit), but chiefly for מִשְׁפָּט; in Grk. writ. [(fr. Aeschyl. and Hdt. down)] **1.** *a separating, sundering, separation*; *a trial, contest*. **2.** *selection*. **3.** *judgment*; i. e. *opinion* or *decision given concerning anything*, esp. concerning justice and injustice, right and wrong; **a.** univ.: Jn. viii. 16; 1 Tim. v. 24 (on which see ἐπακολουθέω); Jude 9; 2 Pet. ii. 11; κρίσιν κρίνειν (see κρίνω, 5 b.), Jn. vii. 24. **b.** in a forensic sense, of the judgment of God or of Jesus the Messiah: univ., Jas. ii. 13; 2 Th. i. 5; Heb. x. 27; plur., Rev. xvi. 7; xix. 2; of *the last judgment*: Heb. ix. 27; ἡ ἡμέρα κρίσεως [Mt. x. 15; xi. 22, 24; xii. 36; Mk. vi. 11 R L in br.; 2 Pet. ii. 9; iii. 7] or τῆς κρίσεως [1 Jn. iv. 17], the day appointed for the judgment, see ἡμέρα, 3; εἰς κρίσιν μεγάλης ἡμέρας, Jude 6; ἡ ὥρα τῆς κρίσεως αὐτοῦ, i. e. τοῦ θεοῦ, Rev. xiv. 7; ἐν τῇ κρίσει, at the time of the judgment, when the judgment shall take place, Mt. xii. 41 sq.; Lk. x. 14; xi. 31 sq.; κρίσιν ποιεῖν κατὰ πάντων, to execute judgment against (i. e. to the destruction of) all, Jude 15. spec. *sentence of condemnation, damnatory judgment, condemnation and punishment*: Heb. x. 27; 2 Pet. ii. 4; with gen. of the pers. condemned and punished, Rev. xviii. 10; ἡ κρίσις αὐτοῦ ἤρθη, the punishment appointed him was taken away, i. e. was ended, Acts viii. 33 fr. Is. liii. 8 Sept.; πίπτειν εἰς κρίσιν [Rˢᵗ εἰς ὑπόκρισιν], to become liable to condemnation, Jas. v. 12; αἰώνιος κρίσις, eternal damnation, Mk. iii. 29 [Rec.]; ἡ κρίσις τῆς γεέννης, the judgment condemning one to Gehenna, the penalty of Gehenna, i. e. to be suffered in hell, Mt. xxiii. 33. In John's usage κρίσις denotes **a.** that judgment which Christ occasioned, in that wicked men rejected the salvation he offered, and so of their own accord brought upon themselves misery and punishment: αὕτη ἐστὶν ἡ κρίσις, ὅτι etc. judgment takes place by the entrance of the light into the world and the hatred which men have for this light, iii. 19; κρίσιν ποιεῖν, to execute judgment, v. 27; ἔρχεσθαι εἰς κρ. to come into the state of one condemned, ib. 24; κρ. τοῦ κόσμου τούτου, the condemnatory sentence passed upon this world, in that it is convicted of wickedness and its power broken, xii. 31; περὶ κρίσεως, of judgment passed (see κρίνω, 5 a. β. fin.), xvi. 8, 11. **β.** the last judgment, the damnation of the wicked: ἀνάστασις κρίσεως, followed by condemnation, v. 29 [cf. W. § 30, 2 β.]. **γ.** both the preceding notions are combined in v. 30; ἡ κρίσις πᾶσα, the whole business of judging [cf. W. 548 (510)], ib. 22. Cf. *Groos*, Der Begriff der κρίσις bei Johannes (in the Stud. u. Krit. for 1868, pp. 244–273). **4.** Like the Chald. דִּינָא (Dan. vii. 10, 26; cf. Germ. *Gericht*) i. q. *the college of judges* (a tribunal of seven men in the several cities of Palestine; as distinguished from the S a n-h e d r i n, which had its seat at Jerusalem [cf. *Schürer*, Neutest. Zeitgesch. § 23, ii.; *Edersheim*, Jesus the Messiah, ii. 287]): Mt. v. 21 sq. (cf. Deut. xvi. 18; 2 Chr. xix. 6; Joseph. antt. 4, 8, 14; b. j. 2, 20, 5). **5.** Like the Hebr. מִשְׁפָּט (cf. *Gesenius*, Thes. iii. p. 1464[b] [also Sept. in Gen. xviii. 19, 25; Is. v. 7; lvi. 1; lix. 8; Jer. xvii. 11; 1 Macc. vii. 18; and other pass. referred to in Gesenius l. c.]), *right, justice*: Mt. xxiii. 23; Lk. xi. 42; what shall have the force of right, ἀπαγγέλλειν τινί, Mt. xii. 18; *a just cause*, Mt. xii. 20 (on which see ἐκβάλλω, 1 g.).*

2921 Κρίσπος, -ου, ὁ, *Crispus*, the ruler of a synagogue at Corinth, Acts xviii. 8; baptized by Paul, 1 Co. i. 14.*

2922 κριτήριον, -ου, τό, (fr. κριτήρ, i. q. κριτής); **1.** prop. *the instrument* or *means of trying* or *judging anything*; *the rule by which one judges*, (Plat., Plut., al.). **2.** *the place where judgment is given*; *the tribunal of a judge*; *a bench of judges*: plur., 1 Co. vi. 2; Jas. ii. 6, (Sept.; Plat., Polyb., Plut., al.). **3.** in an exceptional usage, *the matter judged, thing to be decided, suit, case*: plur. 1 Co. vi. 4 [this sense is denied by many; cf. e. g. Meyer on vs. 2].*

2923 κριτής, -οῦ, ὁ, (κρίνω), [fr. Aeschyl. and Hdt. down], Sept. chiefly for שָׁפַט; *a judge*; **1.** univ. one who passes, or arrogates to himself, judgment on anything: w. gen. of the object, Jas. iv. 11; w. gen. of quality (see διαλογισμός, 1), Jas. ii. 4; in a forensic sense, of the one who tries and decides a case [cf. δικαστής, fin.]: Mt. v. 25; Lk. xii. 14 L T Tr WH, 58; [xviii. 2]; w. gen. of quality [cf. B. § 132, 10; W. § 34, 3 b.], τῆς ἀδικίας, Lk. xviii. 6; w. gen. of the object (a thing), an arbiter, Acts xviii. 15; of a Roman procurator administering justice, Acts xxiv. 10; of God passing judgment on the charac-

ter and deeds of men, and rewarding accordingly, Heb. xii. 23; Jas. iv. 12; also of Christ returning to sit in judgment, Acts x. 42; 2 Tim. iv. 8; Jas. v. 9; in a peculiar sense, of a person whose conduct is made the standard for judging another and convicting him of wrong: w. gen. of the object (a pers.), Mt. xii. 27; Lk. xi. 19. **2.** like the Hebr. שֹׁפֵט, *of the leaders* or *rulers of the Israelites*: Acts xiii. 20 (Judg. ii. 16, 18 sq.; Ruth i. 1; Sir. x. 1 sq. 24, etc.).*

2924 κριτικός, -ή, -όν, (κρίνω), *relating to judging, fit for judging, skilled in judging*, (Plat., Plut., Lcian., al.): with gen. of the obj., ἐνθυμήσεων κ. ἐννοιῶν καρδίας, tracing out and passing judgment on the thoughts of the mind, Heb. iv. 12.*

2925 κρούω; 1 aor. ptcp. κρούσας; *to knock*: τὴν θύραν, to knock at the door, Lk. xiii. 25; Acts xii. 13, (Arstph. eccles. 317, 990; Xen. symp. 1, 11; Plat. Prot. p. 310 a.; 314 d.; symp. 212 c.; but κόπτειν τὴν θύραν is better, acc. to Phryn. with whom Lobeck agrees, p. 177 [cf. Schmidt (ch. 113, 9), who makes κόπτειν to knock with a heavy blow, κρούειν to knock with the knuckles]); without τὴν θύραν [cf. W. 593 (552)], Mt. vii. 7 sq.; Lk. xi. 9, 10; xii. 36; Acts xii. 16; Rev. iii. 20 (on which see θύρα, c. ε.).*

2926 κρυπτή [so R[els] G L T Tr KC], (but some prefer to write it κρύπτη [so WH, Meyer, Bleek, etc., Chandler § 183; cf. Tdf. on Lk. as below]), -ῆς, ἡ, *a crypt, covered way, vault, cellar*: εἰς κρυπτήν, Lk. xi. 33 (Athen. 5 (4), 205 a. equiv. to κρυπτὸς περίπατος p. 206; [Joseph. b. j. 5, 7, 4 fin.; Strab. 17, 1, 37]; Sueton. Calig. 58; Juvenal 5, 106; Vitruv. 6, 8 (5); al.). Cf. Meyer ad l. c.; W. 238 (223).*

2927 κρυπτός, -ή, -όν, (κρύπτω), [fr. Hom. down], *hidden, concealed, secret*: Mt. x. 26; Mk. iv. 22; Lk. viii. 17; xii. 2 [cf. W. 441 (410)]; ὁ κρυπτὸς τῆς καρδίας ἄνθρωπος, the inner part of man, the soul, 1 Pet. iii. 4; neut., ἐν τῷ κρυπτῷ, in secret, Mt. vi. 4, 6, 18 Rec.; ἐν κρυπτῷ, privately, in secret, Jn. vii. 4, 10; xviii. 20; ὁ ἐν κρυπτῷ Ἰουδαῖος, he who is a Jew inwardly, in soul and not in circumcision alone, Ro. ii. 29; τὰ κρυπτὰ τοῦ σκότους, [the hidden things of darkness i. e.] things covered by darkness, 1 Co. iv. 5; τὰ κρ. τῶν ἀνθρ. the things which men conceal, Ro. ii. 16; τὰ κρ. τῆς καρδίας, his secret thoughts, feelings, desires, 1 Co. xiv. 25; τὰ κρ. τῆς αἰσχύνης (see αἰσχύνη, 1), 2 Co. iv. 2; εἰς κρυπτόν into a secret place, Lk. xi. 33 in some edd. of Rec., but see κρυπτή.*

2928 κρύπτω; 1 aor. ἔκρυψα; Pass., pf. 3 pers. sing. κέκρυπται, ptcp. κεκρυμμένος; 2 aor. ἐκρύβην (so also in Sept., for the earlier ἐκρύφην, cf. *Bttm.* Ausf. Spr. i. p. 377; *Fritzsche* on Mt. p. 212; [Veitch s. v.]); [cf. καλύπτω]; fr. Hom. down; Sept. for כָּפָה, כָּחַד, טָמַן, צָפַן, הִסְתִּיר, הֶחְבִּיא; *to hide, conceal*: **a.** prop. τί, Mt. xiii. 44 and L T Tr WH in xxv. 18; pass., Heb. xi. 23; Rev. ii. 17; κρυβῆναι i. q. *to be hid*, escape notice, Mt. v. 14; 1 Tim. v. 25; ἐκρύβη (quietly withdrew [cf. W. § 38, 2 a.]) κ. ἐξῆλθεν, i. e. departed secretly, Jn. viii. 59 [cf. W. 469 (437)]; κρύπτω τι ἐν with dat. of place, Mt. xxv. 25; pass. xiii. 44; κεκρ. ἐν τῷ θεῷ, is kept laid up with God in heaven,

Col. iii. 3 ; τὶ εἴς τι, Lk. xiii. 21 [R G L ἐνέκρυψεν] ; ἑαυτὸν εἰς with acc. of place, Rev. vi. 15 ; τινὰ ἀπὸ προσώπου τινός to cover (and remove [cf. W. § 30, 6 b. ; 66, 2 d.]) from the view of any one, i. e. to take away, rescue, from the sight, Rev. vi. 16 ; ἐκρύβη ἀπ᾿ αὐτῶν, withdrew from them, Jn. xii. 36 (in Grk. auth. generally κρ. τινά τι ; cf. ἀποκρύπτω, b.).   b. metaph. to conceal (that it may not become known) : κεκρυμμένος, clandestine, Jn. xix. 38 ; τὶ ἀπό τινος (gen. of pers.), Mt. xi. 25 L T Tr WH ; [Lk. xviii. 34] ; κεκρυμμένα things hidden i. e. unknown, used of God's saving counsels, Mt. xiii. 35 ; ἀπ᾿ ὀφθαλμῶν τινος, Lk. xix. 42 [cf. B. § 146, 1 fin. COMP.: ἀπο-, ἐν-, περι-κρύπτω.] *

2929 κρυσταλλίζω ; (κρύσταλλος, q. v.) ; to be of crystalline brightness and transparency ; to shine like crystal : Rev. xxi. 11. (Not found elsewhere.) *

2930 κρύσταλλος, -ου, ὁ, (fr. κρύος ice ; hence prop. anything congealed (cf. Lat. crusta) and transparent), [fr. Hom. down], crystal : a kind of precious stone, Rev. iv. 6 ; xxii. 1 ; [cf. B. D. s. v. Crystal. On its gend. cf. L. and S. s. v. II.] *

see 2927 κρυφαῖος, -αία, -αῖον, (κρύφα), hidden, secret : twice in Mt. vi. 18 L T Tr WH. (Jer. xxiii. 24 ; Sap. xvii. 3 ; in Grk. writ. fr. Aeschyl. and Pind. down.) *

2931 κρυφῆ [L WH -φῇ; cf. εἰκῆ, init.], adv., (κρύπτω), secretly, in secret : Eph. v. 12. (Pind., Soph., Xen. ; Sept.) *

2932 κτάομαι, -ῶμαι ; fut. κτήσομαι (Lk. xxi. 19 L Tr WH) ; 1 aor. ἐκτησάμην ; [fr. Hom. down]. Sept. for קָנָה ; to acquire, get or procure a thing for one's self [cf. W. 260 (244)] ; (pf. κέκτημαι, to possess [cf. W. 274 (257) note] ; not found in the N. T.) : τί, Mt. x. 9 ; Acts viii. 20 ; ὅσα κτῶμαι, all my income, Lk. xviii. 12 ; with gen. of price added [W. 206 (194)], πολλοῦ, Acts xxii. 28 ; with ἐκ and gen. of price (see ἐκ, II. 4), Acts i. 18 ; τὸ ἑαυτοῦ σκεῦος ἐν ἁγιασμῷ κ. τιμῇ, to procure for himself his own vessel (i. e. for the satisfaction of the sexual passion ; see σκεῦος, 1) in sanctification and honor, i. e. to marry a wife (opp. to the use of a harlot ; the words ἐν ἁγ. κ. τιμῇ are added to express completely the idea of marrying in contrast with the baseness of procuring a harlot as his 'vessel' ; cf. κτᾶσθαι γυναῖκα, of marrying a wife, Ruth iv. 10 ; Sir. xxxvi. 29 (xxxiii. 26) ; Xen. symp. 2, 10), 1 Th. iv. 4 ; τὰς ψυχὰς ὑμῶν, the true life of your souls, your true lives, i. e. eternal life (cf. the opp. ζημιοῦσθαι τὴν ψ. αὐτοῦ under ζημιόω), Lk. xxi. 19 ; cf. Meyer ad loc. and W. p. 274 (257).*

2933 κτῆμα, -τος, τό, (fr. κτάομαι, as χρῆμα fr. χράομαι), a possession : as in Grk. writers, of property, lands, estates, etc., Mt. xix. 22 ; Mk. x. 22 ; Acts ii. 45 ; v. 1.*

2934 κτῆνος, -ους, τό, (fr. κτάομαι ; hence prop. a possession, property, esp. in cattle) ; a beast, esp. a beast of burden : Lk. x. 34 ; plur., Acts xxiii. 24 ; Rev. xviii. 13 ; it seems to be used for quadrupeds as opp. to fishes and birds in 1 Co. xv. 39 ; so for בְּהֵמָה, Gen. i. 25 sq. ; ii. 20. [Cf. Hom. hymn. 30, 10 ; of swine in Polyb. 12, 4, 14.]*

2935 κτήτωρ, -ορος, ὁ, (κτάομαι), a possessor : Acts iv. 34. (Diod. excpt. p. 599, 17 ; Clem. Alex. ; Byzant. writ.) *

2936 κτίζω : 1 aor. ἔκτισα ; pf. pass. ἔκτισμαι ; 1 aor. pass. ἐκτίσθην ; Sept. chiefly for בָּרָא ; prop. to make habitable,

to people, a place, region, island, (Hom., Hdt., Thuc. Diod., al.) ; hence to found, a city, colony, state, etc (Pind. et sqq. ; 1 Esdr. iv. 53). In the Bible, to create : of God creating the world, man, etc., Mk. xiii. 19 ; 1 Co. xi. 9 ; Col. i. 16 [cf. W. 272 (255)] ; iii. 10 ; Eph. iii. 9 ; 1 Tim. iv. 3 ; Rev. iv. 11 ; x. 6, (Deut. iv. 32 ; Eccl. xii. 1 ; often in O. T. Apocr., as Judith xiii. 18 ; Sap. ii. 23 ; xi. 18 (17) ; 3 Macc. ii. 9 ; [Joseph. antt. 1, 1, 1 ; Philo de decal. § 20]) ; absol. ὁ κτίσας, the creator, Ro. i. 25 ; [Mt. xix. 4 Tr WH] ; i. q. to form, shape, i. e. (for substance) completely to change, to transform (of the moral or new creation of the soul, as it is called), κτισθέντες ἐν Χριστῷ Ἰησοῦ ἐπὶ ἔργοις ἀγαθοῖς, in intimate fellowship with Christ constituted to do good works [see ἐπί, B. 2 a. ζ.], Eph. ii. 10 ; τοὺς δύο εἰς ἕνα καινὸν ἄνθρωπον, ibid. 15 ; τὸν κτισθέντα κατὰ θεόν, formed after God's likeness [see κατά, II. 3 c. δ.], Eph. iv. 24, (καρδίαν καθαρὰν κτίσον ἐν ἐμοί, Ps. l. (li.) 12).*

2937 κτίσις, -εως, ἡ, (κτίζω), in Grk. writ. the act of founding, establishing, building, etc. ; in the N. T. (Vulg. everywhere creatura [yet Heb. ix. 11 creatio])   1. the act of creating, creation : τοῦ κόσμου, Ro. i. 20.   2. i. q. κτίσμα, creation i. e. thing created, [cf. W. 32] ; used   a. of individual things and beings, a creature, a creation : Ro. i. 25 ; Heb. iv. 13 ; any created thing, Ro. viii. 39 ; after a rabbin. usage (by which a man converted from idolatry to Judaism was called בְּרִיָּה חֲדָשָׁה [cf. Schöttgen, Horae Hebr. i. 328, 704 sq.]), καινὴ κτίσις is used of a man regenerated through Christ, Gal. vi. 15 ; 2 Co. v. 17.   b. collectively, the sum or aggregate of created things : Rev. iii. 14 (on which see ἀρχή, 3 ; [ἡ κτίσις τ. ἀνθρώπων, Teaching of the Twelve etc. c. 16]) ; ὅλη ἡ κτίσις, Sap. xix. 6 ; πᾶσα ἡ κτίσις, Judith xvi. 14 ; and without the art. (cf. Grimm on 3 Macc. [ii.] p. 235 ; [Bp. Lghtft. on Col. as below]), πᾶσα κτίσις, Col. i. 15 ; 3 Macc. ii. 2 ; Judith ix. 12 ; σωτὴρ πάσης κτίσεως, Acta Thomae p. 19 ed. Thilo [§ 10 p. 198 ed. Tdf.], (see πᾶς, I. 1 c.) ; ἀπ᾿ ἀρχῆς κτίσεως, Mk. x. 6 ; xiii. 19 ; 2 Pet. iii. 4 ; οὐ ταύτης τῆς κτίσεως, not of this order of created things, Heb. ix. 11 ; acc. to the demands of the context, of some particular kind or class of created things or beings : thus of the human race, πάσῃ τῇ κτ. Mk. xvi. 15 ; ἐν πάσῃ [Rec. adds τῇ] κτίσει τῇ ὑπὸ τὸν οὐρ., among men of every race, Col. i. 23 ; the aggregate of irrational creatures, both animate and inanimate, (what we call nature), Ro. viii. 19-2. (Sap. v. 17 (18) ; xvi. 24) ; πᾶσα ἡ κτ. ibid. 22 ; where cf. Reiche, Philippi, Meyer, Rückert, al., [Arnold in Bapt. Quart. for Apr. 1867, pp. 143-153].   3. an institution, ordinance : 1 Pet. ii. 13 ; cf. Huther ad loc. [(Pind., al.)]*

2938 κτίσμα, -τος, τό, (κτίζω) ; thing founded ; created thing ; (Vulg. creatura) [A. V. creature] : 1 Tim. iv. 4 ; Rev. v. 13 ; viii. 9, (Sap. ix. 2 ; xiii. 5) ; contextually and metaph. κτ. θεοῦ, transformed by divine power to a moral newness of soul, spoken of true Christians as created anew by regeneration [al. take it here unrestrictedly], Jas. i. 18 (see ἀπαρχή, metaph. a. ; also κτίζω sub fin., κτίσις, 2 a.) ; τὰ ἐν ἀρχῇ κτίσματα θεοῦ, of the Israelites, Sir. xxxvi. 20 (15). [(Strab., Dion. II.)] *

2939 κτίστης (on the accent cf. W. § 6, 1 h. [cf. 94 (89); esp. Chandler §§ 35, 36]), -ου, ὁ, (κτίζω), a founder; a creator [Aristot., Plut., al.]: of God, 1 Pet. iv. 19 [cf. W. 122 (116)]; (Judith ix. 12; Sir. xxiv. 8; 2 Macc. i. 24, etc.).*

2940 κυβεία [-βία TWH; see I, ι], -ας, ἡ, (fr. κυβεύω, and this fr. κύβος a cube, a die), dice-playing (Xen., Plat., Aristot., al.); trop. ἡ κ. τῶν ἀνθρ. the deception [A. V. sleight] of men, Eph. iv. 14, because dice-players sometimes cheated and defrauded their fellow-players.*

2941 κυβέρνησις, -εως, ἡ, (κυβερνάω [Lat. gubernare, to govern]), a governing, government: 1 Co. xii. 28 [al. would take it tropically here, and render it wise counsels (R. V. mrg.); so Hesych.: κυβερνήσεις· προνοητικαὶ ἐπιστῆμαι καὶ φρονήσεις; cf. Schleusner, Thesaur. in Sept. s. v., and to the reff. below add Prov. xi. 14; Job xxxvii. 12 Symm.]; (Prov. i. 5; xxiv. 6; Pind., Plat., Plut., al.).*

2942 κυβερνήτης, -ου, ὁ, (κυβερνάω ['to steer'; see the preceding word]); fr. Hom. down; steersman, helmsman, sailing-master; [A. V. master, ship-master]: Acts xxvii. 11; Rev. xviii. 17. (Ezek. xxvii. 8, 27 sq.)*

see 2944 κυκλεύω: 1 aor. ἐκύκλευσα; to go round (Strabo and other later writ.); to encircle, encompass, surround: τὴν παρεμβολήν, Rev. xx. 9 (where R G Tr ἐκύκλωσαν); [τινά, Jn. x. 24 Tr mrg. WH mrg.]; (see WH. App. p. 171)].*

2943 κυκλόθεν, (κύκλος [see κύκλῳ]), adv. round about, from all sides, all round: Rev. iv. 8; κυκλ. τινός, Rev. iv. 3 sq., and Rec. in v. 11. (Lys. p. 110, 40 [olea sacr. 28]; Qu. Smyrn. 5, 16; Nonn. Dion. 36, 325; Sept. often for סָבִיב, סְבִיב, and simply סָבִיב; many exx. fr. the Apocr. are given in Wahl, Clavis Apocryphorum etc. s. v.)*

2944 κυκλόω, -ῶ: 1 aor. ἐκύκλωσα; Pass., pres. ptcp. κυκλούμενος; 1 aor. ptcp. κυκλωθείς; (κύκλος); Sept. chiefly for סָבַב;   **1.** to go round, lead round, (Pind., Eur., Polyb., al.).   **2.** to surround, encircle, encompass: of persons standing round, τινά, Jn. x. 24 [Tr mrg. WH mrg. ἐκύκλευσαν (q. v.)]; Acts xiv. 20; of besiegers (often so in prof. auth. and in Sept.), Lk. xxi. 20; Heb. xi. 30, and R G Tr in Rev. xx. 9. [Comp.: περι-κυκλόω.] *

2945 κύκλῳ (dat. of the subst. κύκλος, a ring, circle [cf. Eng. cycle]); fr. Hom. down; Sept. times without number for סָבִיב, also for מִסָּבִיב and סָבִיב סָבִיב; in a circle, around, round about, on all sides: Mk. iii. 34; vi. 6; οἱ κύκλῳ ἀγροί, the circumjacent country [see ἀγρός, c.], Mk. vi. 36 [here WH (rejected) mrg. gives ἔγγιστα]; Lk. ix. 12; ἀπὸ Ἱερουσ. καὶ κύκλῳ, and in the region around, Ro. xv. 19; τινός, around anything (Xen. Cyr. 4, 5, 5; Polyb. 4, 21, 9, al.; Gen. xxxv. 5; Ex. vii. 24, etc.) : Rev. iv. 6; v. 11 [here R κυκλόθεν]; vii. 11.*

2946 κύλισμα, -τος, τό, (κυλίω, q. v.), thing rolled: with epexeget. gen. βορβόρου, rolled (wallowed) mud or mire, 2 Pet. ii. 22 [R G L Tr mrg.]. The great majority take the word to mean 'wallowing-place', as if it were the same as κυλίστρα, (Vulg. in volutabro luti). But just as τὸ ἐξέραμα signifies the vomit, thing vomited, and not the place of vomiting; so τὸ κύλισμα denotes nothing else than the thing rolled or wallowed. But see [the foll. word, and] βόρβορος.*

2946 (right col.) κυλισμός, -οῦ, ὁ, i. q. κύλισις, a rolling, wallowing, (Hippiatr. p. 204, 4; [cf. Prov. ii. 18 Theod.]) : εἰς κυλισμ. βορβόρου, to a rolling of itself in mud, [to wallowing in the mire], 2 Pet. ii. 22 T Tr txt. WH. See the preceding word.*   **see 2946**

2947 St. κυλίω: (for κυλίνδω more com. in earlier writ.), to roll; Pass. impf. 3 pers. sing. ἐκυλίετο; to be rolled, to wallow: Mk. ix. 20. ([Aristot. h. a. 5, 19, 18, etc.; Dion. Hal.; Sept.]; Polyb. 26, 10, 16; Ael. n. a. 7, 33; Epict. diss. 4, 11, 29.) [Comp.: ἀνα-, ἀπο-, προσκυλίω.]*   **see**

2948 κυλλός, -ή, -όν, [akin to κύκλος, κυλίω, Lat. circus, curvus, etc.; Curtius § 81];   **1.** crooked; of the members of the body (Hippocr., Arstph. av. 1379): as distinguished fr. χωλός, it seems to be injured or disabled in the hands [but doubted by many], Mt. xv. 30, 31 [but here Tr mrg. br. κυλ. and WH read it in mrg. only].   **2.** maimed, mutilated, (οὖς, Hippocr. p. 805 [iii. p. 186 ed. Kühn]): Mt. xviii. 8; Mk. ix. 43.*

2949 κῦμα, -τος, τό, [fr. κυέω to swell; Curtius § 79; fr. Hom. down], a wave [cf. Eng. swell], esp. of the sea or of a lake: Mt. viii. 24; xiv. 24; Mk. iv. 37; Acts xxvii. 41 [R G Tr txt. br.]; κύματα ἄγρια, prop., Sap. xiv. 1; with θαλάσσης added, of impulsive and restless men, tossed to and fro by their raging passions, Jude 13. [Syn. cf. κλύδων.]*

2950 κύμβαλον, -ου, τό, (fr. κύμβος, ὁ, a hollow [cf. cup, cupola, etc.; Vaniček p. 164]), a cymbal, i. e. a hollow basin of brass, producing (when two are struck together) a musical sound [see B. D. s. v. Cymbal; Stainer, Music of the Bible, ch. ix.] : 1 Co. xiii. 1. (1 Chr. xiii. 8; xv. 16, 19, 28; Ps. cl. 5. Pind., Xen., Diod., Joseph., al.]*

2951 κύμινον, -ου, τό, cumin (or cummin), Germ. Kümmel, (for כַּמֹּן, Is. xxviii. 25, 27): Mt. xxiii. 23. (Theophr., Diosc., Plut., al.) [Tristram, Nat. Hist. etc. p. 443.]*

2952 κυνάριον, -ου, τό, (dimin. of κύων, i. q. κυνίδιον, which Phryn. prefers; see Lob. ad Phryn. p. 180; cf. γυναικάριον), a little dog [see Mt. xv. 26 sq.; Mk. vii. 27 sq. (Xen., Plat., Theophr., Plut., al.)*

2953 Κύπριος, -ου, ὁ, a Cyprian or Cypriote, i. e. a native or an inhabitant of Cyprus: Acts iv. 36; xi. 20; xxi. 16, (2 Macc. iv. 29). [(Hdt., al.)]*

2954 Κύπρος, -ου, ἡ, Cyprus, a very fertile and delightful island of the Mediterranean, lying between Cilicia and Syria: Acts xi. 19; xiii. 4; xv. 39; xxi. 3; xxvii. 4, (1 Macc. xv. 23; 2 Macc. x. 13). [BB. DD. s. v.; Lewin, St. Paul, i. 120 sqq.]*

2955 κύπτω: 1 aor. ptcp. κύψας; (fr. κύβη the head [cf. Vaniček p. 164; esp. Curtius, index s. v.]); fr. Hom. down; Sept. chiefly for קדד; to bow the head, bend forward, stoop down: Mk. i. 7; with κάτω added (Arstph. vesp. 279), Jn. viii. 6, 8. [Comp.: ἀνα-, παρα-, συγκύπτω.]*

2956 Κυρηναῖος, -ου, ὁ, (Κυρήνη, q. v.), a Cyrenæan [A. V. (R. V. Acts vi. 9) Cyrenian], a native of Cyrene: Mt. xxvii. 32; Mk. xv. 21; Lk. xxiii. 26; Acts vi. 9; xi. 20; xiii. 1. [(Hdt., al.)]*

2957 Κυρήνη, -ης, ἡ, Cyrene, a large and very flourishing city of Libya Cyrenaica or Pentapolitana, about 11 Roman miles from the sea. Among its inhabitants were great numbers of Jews, whom Ptolemy I. had brought thither, and invested with the rights of citizens : Acts ii. 10. [BB. DD. s. v.] *

2958   **Κυρήνιος** (Lchm. Κυρῖνος [-ρείνος Tr mrg. WH mrg. (see ει, ι)]), -ον, ὁ, Quirin[-i-]us (in full, Publius Sulpicius Quirinus [correctly Quirinius ; see Woolsey in Bib. Sacr. for 1878, pp. 499–513]), a Roman consul A. U. C. 742 ; afterwards (not before the year 759) governor of Syria (where perhaps he may previously have been in command, 751–752). While filling that office after Archelaus had been banished and Judæa had been reduced to a province of Syria, he made the enrolment mentioned in Acts v. 37 (cf. Joseph. antt. 18, 1, 1). Therefore Luke in his Gospel ii. 2 has made a mistake [yet see added reff. below] in defining the time of this enrolment. For in the last years of Herod the Great, not Quirinius but Sentius Saturninus was governor of Syria. His successor, A. U. C. 750, was Quintilius Varus ; and Quirinius (who died in the year 774) succeeded Varus. Cf. Win. RWB. s. vv. Quirinius and Schatzung ; Strauss, Die Halben u. die Ganzen (Berl. 1865) p. 70 sqq. ; Hilgenfeld in the Zeitschr. f. wissensch. Theologie for 1865, p. 480 sqq. ; Keim i. 399 sq. [Eng. trans. ii. 115] ; Schürer, Neutest. Zeitgeschichte, p. 161 sq. ; Weizsäcker in Schenkel v. p. 23 sqq. ; [Keil, Com. üb. Mark. u. Luk. p. 213 sqq. ; McClellan, New Testament etc., i. p. 392 sqq. ; and Woolsey in B. D. Am. ed. s. v. Cyrenius, and at length in Bib. Sacr. for Apr. 1870, p. 291 sqq.].*

2959   **Κυρία**, -ας, ἡ, Cyria, a Christian woman to whom the second Ep. of John is addressed : 2 Jn. 1, 5, [G L T K C (and WH mrg. in vs. 1)]. This prop. name is not uncommon in other writers also ; cf. Lücke, Comm. üb. die Brr. des Joh. 3d ed. p. 444. [But R Tr al. κυρία, regarding the word as an appellative, lady ; (αἱ γυναῖκες εὐθὺς ἀπὸ τεσσαρεσκαίδεκα ἐτῶν ὑπὸ τῶν ἀνδρῶν κ υ ρ ί α ι καλοῦνται, Epictet. enchir. 40). Cf. Westcott on 2 Jn. u. s.] *

2960   **κυριακός**, -ή, -όν, a bibl. and eccles. word [cf. W. § 34, 3 and Soph. Lex. s. v.], of or belonging to the Lord ;   **1.** i. q. the gen. of the author τοῦ κυρίου, thus κυριακὸν δεῖπνον, the supper instituted by the Lord, 1 Co. xi. 20 ; λόγια κυριακά, the Lord's sayings, Papias ap. Eus. h. e. 3, 39, 1.   **2.** relating to the Lord, ἡ κυριακὴ ἡμέρα, the day devoted to the Lord, sacred to the memory of Christ's resurrection, Rev. i. 10 [cf. ' κυριακὴ κυρίου ', Teaching 14, 1 (where see Harnack) ; cf. B. D. s. v. Lord's Day ; Bp. Lghtft. Ign. ad Magn. p. 129 ; Müller on Barn. ep. 15, 9] ; γραφαὶ κυρ. the writings concerning the Lord, i. e. the Gospels, Clem. Alex., al. [Cf. Soph. Lex. s. v.] *

2961   **κυριεύω** ; fut. κυριεύσω ; 1 aor. subjunc. 3 pers. sing. κυριεύσῃ ; (κύριος) ; to be lord of, to rule over, have dominion over : with gen. of the obj. [cf. B. 169 (147)], Lk. xxii. 25 ; Ro. xiv. 9 ; 2 Co. i. 24 ; absol. οἱ κυριεύοντες, supreme rulers, kings, 1 Tim. vi. 15 ; of things and forces i. q. to exercise influence upon, to have power over : with gen. of the obj., ὁ θάνατος, Ro. vi. 9 ; ἡ ἁμαρτία, 14 ; ὁ νόμος, Ro. vii. 1. (Xen., Aristot., Polyb., sqq. ; Sept. for כָּשַׁל [etc.].) [COMP.: κατα-κυριεύω.] *

2962   **κύριος**, -ον, ὁ, (prop. an adj. κύριος, -α, -ον, also of two

term. ; prop. i. q. ὁ ἔχων κῦρος, having power or authority), [fr. Pind. down], he to whom a person or thing belongs, about which he has the power of deciding ; master, lord ; used   **a.** univ. of the possessor and disposer of a thing, the owner, (Sept. for בַּעַל אָדוֹן,): with gen. of the thing, as τοῦ ἀμπελῶνος, Mt. xx. 8 ; xxi. 40 ; Mk. xii. 9 ; Lk. xx. 15 ; τοῦ θερισμοῦ, Mt. ix. 38 ; Lk. x. 2 ; τῆς οἰκίας, the master, Mk. xiii. 35 (Judg. xix. 12) ; τοῦ πώλου, Lk. xix. 33 ; τοῦ σαββάτου, possessed of the power to determine what is suitable to the sabbath, and of releasing himself and others from its obligations, Mt. xii. 8 ; Mk. ii. 28 ; Lk. vi. 5. with gen. of a pers., one who has control of the person, the master [A. V. lord] ; in the household : δούλου, παιδίσκης, οἰκονόμου, Mt. x. 24 ; Lk. xii. 46 sq. ; xiv. 21 ; xvi. 3, 5 ; Acts xvi. 16, 19, etc. ; absol., opp. to οἱ δοῦλοι, Eph. vi. 5, 9 ; Col. iv. 1, etc. ; in the state, the sovereign, prince, chief : the Roman emperor [(on this use of κύριος see at length Woolsey in Bib. Sacr. for July 1861, pp. 595–608)], Acts xxv. 26 ; once angels are called κύριοι, as those to whom, in the administration of the universe, departments are intrusted by God (see ἄγγελος, 2) : 1 Co. viii. 5.   **b.** κύριος is a title of honor, expressive of respect and reverence, with which servants salute their master, Mt. xiii. 27 ; xxv. 20, 22 ; Lk. xiii. 8 ; xiv. 22, etc. ; the disciples salute Jesus their teacher and master, Mt. viii. 25 ; xvi. 22 ; Lk. ix. 54 ; x. 17, 40 ; xi. 1 ; xxii. 33, 38 ; Jn. xi. 12 ; xiii. 6, 9, 13 ; xxi. 15–17, 20 sq., etc., cf. xx. 13 ; Lk. xxiv. 34 ; his followers salute Jesus as the Messiah, whose authority they acknowledge (by its repetition showing their earnestness [cf. W. § 65, 5 a.]), κύριε, κύριε, Mt. vii. 21 ; and R G in Lk. xiii. 25 ; employed, too, by a son in addressing his father, Mt. xxi. 30 ; by citizens towards magistrates, Mt. xxvii. 63 ; by any one who wishes to honor a man of distinction, Mt. viii. 2, 6, 8 ; xv. 27 ; Mk. vii. 28 ; Lk. v. 12 ; xiii. 25 ; Jn. iv. 11, 15, 19 ; v. 7 ; xii. 21 ; xx. 15 ; Acts ix. 5 ; xvi. 30 ; xxii. 8.   **c.** this title is given   **α.** to GOD, the ruler of the universe (so the Sept. for יָהּ יְהֹוָה, אֱלֹהִים, אֱלוֹהַּ, אֲדֹנָי and ; [the term κύριος is used of the gods from Pind. and Soph. down, but "the address κύριε, used in prayer to God, though freq. in Epict. does not occur (so far as I am aware) in any heathen writing before the apostolic times ; sometimes we find κύριε ὁ θεός, and once (2, 7, 12) he writes κύριε ἐλέησον" (Bp. Lghtft. on Philip. p. 314 note ³))],—both with the art., ὁ κύριος : Mt. i. 22 [R G] ; v. 33 ; Mk. v. 19 ; Lk. i. 6, 9, 28, 46 ; Acts vii. 33 ; viii. 24 ; xi. 21 ; 2 Tim. i. 16, 18, [but see ἔλεος, 3] ; Heb. viii. 2 ; Jas. iv. 15 ; v. 15 ; Jude 5 [R G], etc. ; and without the art. (cf. W. 124 (118) ; B. 88 (77) sq.) : Mt. xxi. 9 ; xxvii. 10 ; Mk. xiii. 20 ; Lk. i. 17, 38, 58, 66 ; ii. 9, 23, 26, 39 ; Acts vii. 49 ; Heb. vii. 21 ; xii. 6 ; 1 Pet. i. 25 ; 2 Pet. ii. 9 ; Jude [5 T Tr txt. WH txt.], 9 ; κύριος τοῦ οὐρανοῦ κ. τῆς γῆς, Mt. xi. 25 ; Lk. x. 21 ; Acts xvii. 24 ; κύριος τῶν κυριευόντων, 1 Tim. vi. 15 ; κύριος ὁ θεός, see θεός, 3 p. 288ᵃ [and below] ; κύριος ὁ θεὸς ὁ παντοκράτωρ, Rev. iv. 8 ; κύριος σαβαώθ, Ro. ix. 29 ; ἄγγελος and ὁ ἄγγελος κυρίου, Mt. i. 20 ; ii. 13, 19 ; xxviii. 2 ; Lk. i. 11 ; ii. 9 ;

Acts v. 19; viii. 26; xii. 7; πνεῦμα κυρίου, Lk. iv. 18;
Acts viii. 39; with prepositions: ὑπό (R G add the art.)
κυρίου, Mt. i. 22; ii. 15; παρὰ κυρίου, Mt. xxi. 42 and
Mk. xii. 11, fr. Ps. cxvii. (cxviii.) 23; παρὰ κυρίῳ, 2 Pet.
iii. 8.   β. to the MESSIAH; and that   aa. to
the Messiah regarded univ.: Lk. i. 43; ii. 11; Mt. xxi.
3; xxii. 45; Mk. xi. 3; xii. 36; Lk. xix. 34; xx. 44.   ββ.
to JESUS as the Messiah, since by his death he acquired
a special ownership in mankind, and after his resurrection was exalted to a partnership in the divine administration (this force of the word when applied to Jesus
appears esp. in Acts x. 36; Ro. xiv. 8; 1 Co. vii. 22; viii.
6; Phil. ii. 9–11): Eph. iv. 5; with the art. ὁ κύρ., Mk.
xvi. 19 sq.; Acts ix. 1; Ro. xiv. 8; 1 Co. iv. 5; vi. 13 sq.;
vii. 10, 12, 34 sq.; ix. 5, 14; x. 22; xi. 26; [xvi. 22 G L
T Tr WH]; Phil. iv. 5; [2 Tim. iv. 22 T Tr WH]; Heb.
ii. 3 (cf. 7 sqq.); Jas. v. 7, etc.   after his resurrection
Jesus is addressed by the title ὁ κύριός μου καὶ ὁ θεός μου,
Jn. xx. 28.   ἀπὸ τοῦ κυρ., 1 Co. xi. 23; 2 Co. v. 6; πρὸς
τὸν κ. 2 Co. v. 8; ὁ κύριος Ἰησοῦς, Acts i. 21; iv. 33; xvi.
31; xx. 35; 1 Co. xi. 23; [xvi. 23 T Tr WH]; 2 Co. i.
14; [2 Tim. iv. 22 Lchm.]; Rev. xxii. 20; ὁ κύρ. Ἰησ.
Χριστός, 1 Co. xvi. 22 [R; 23 R G L]; 2 Co. xiii. 13 (14)
[WH br. Χρ.]; Eph. i. 2; 2 Tim. iv. 22 [R G], etc.; ὁ
κύριος ἡμῶν, 1 Tim. i. 14; 2 Tim. i. 8; Heb. vii. 14; 2 Pet.
iii. 15; Rev. xi. 15, etc.; with Ἰησοῦς added, [L T Tr
WH in 1 Th. iii. 11 and 13]; Heb. xiii. 20; Rev. xxii. 21
[L T Tr (yet without ἡμ.)]; so with Χριστός, Ro. xvi. 18
[G L T Tr WH]; and Ἰησοῦς Χριστός, 1 Th. i. 3 [cf. B.
155 (136)]; xii. 11 [R G], 13 [Rec.]; v. 23; 2 Th. ii. 1,
14, 16; iii. 6 [(ἡμῶν)]; 1 Co. i. 2; 2 Co. i. 3; Gal. vi. 18
[WH br. ἡμῶν]; Eph. i. 3; vi. 24; Ro. xvi. 24 [R G];
1 Tim. vi. 3, 14; Philem. 25 [T WH om. ἡμῶν]; Phil. iv.
23 [G L T Tr WH om. ἡμ.], etc.; Ἰησοῦς Χριστὸς ὁ κύριος
ἡμῶν, Ro. i. 4; and Χρ. Ἰησ. ὁ κύρ. (ἡμῶν), Col. ii. 6; Eph.
iii. 11; 1 Tim. i. 2; 2 Tim. i. 2; ὁ κύρ. καὶ ὁ σωτήρ, 2 Pet.
iii. 2 [cf. B. 155 (136)]; with Ἰησοῦς Χριστός added, 2 Pet.
iii. 18; without the art., simply κύριος : 1 Co. vii. 22, 25;
x. 21; xvi. 10; 2 Co. iii. 17; xii. 1; 2 Tim. ii. 24; Jas. v.
11; 2 Pet. iii. 10; κύριος κυρίων i. e. Supreme Lord (cf. W.
§ 36, 2; [B. § 123, 12]): Rev. xix. 16 (cf. in a. above;
of God, Deut. x. 17); with prepositions: ἀπὸ κυρίου, Col.
iii. 24; κατὰ κύριον, 2 Co. xi. 17; πρὸς κύριον, 2 Co. iii. 16;
σὺν κυρ. 1 Th. iv. 17; ὑπὸ κυρ. 2 Th. ii. 13; on the phrase
ἐν κυρίῳ, freq. in Paul, and except in his writings found
only in Rev. xiv. 13, see ἐν, I. 6 b. p. 211ᵇ. The appellation ὁ κύριος, applied to Christ, passed over in Luke
and John even into historic narrative, where the words
and works of Jesus prior to his resurrection are related:
Lk. vii. 13; x. 1; xi. 39; xii. 42; xiii. 15; xvii. 5 sq.;
xxii. 31 [R G L Tr br.]; Jn. iv. 1 [here T Tr mrg. Ἰη-
σοῦς]; vi. 23; xi. 2. There is nothing strange in the
appearance of the term in the narrative of occurrences
after his resurrection: Lk. xxiv. 34; Jn. xx. 2, 18, 20,
25; xxi. 7, 12.   d. There are some who hold that
Paul (except in his quotations from the O. T. viz. Ro.
iv. 8; ix. 28 sq.; x. 34; 1 Co. i. 31; ii. 16; iii. 20; x. 26;
2 Co. vi. 17 sq.; x. 17; 2 Tim. ii. 19) uses the title κύριος

everywhere not of God, but of Christ. But, to omit
instances where the interpretation is doubtful, as 1 Co.
vii. 25; 2 Co. viii. 21; 1 Th. iv. 6; 2 Th. iii. 16 (ὁ κύριος
τῆς εἰρήνης, cf. ὁ θεὸς τῆς εἰρήνης, 1 Th. v. 23; but most
of the blessings of Christianity are derived alike from
God and from Christ), it is better at least in the words
ἑκάστῳ ὡς ὁ κύριος ἔδωκεν, 1 Co. iii. 5, to understand God
as referred to on account of what follows, esp. on account of the words κατὰ τὴν χάριν τοῦ θεοῦ τὴν δοθεῖσάν
μοι in vs. 10. On the other hand, κρινόμενοι ὑπὸ τοῦ κυρ.
in 1 Co. xi. 32 must certainly, I think, be taken of
Christ, on account of x. 22, cf. 21. Cf. Gabler, Kleinere theol. Schriften, Bd. i. p. 186 sqq.; Winer, De sensu
vocum κύριος et ὁ κύριος in actis et epistolis apostolorum.
Erlang. 1828; Wesselus Scheffer, diss. theol. exhibens
disquisitionem de vocis κύριος absolute positae in N. T.
usu. Lugd. 1846 (a monograph I have not seen); [Stuart
in the Bib. Repos. for Oct. 1831 pp. 733–776; cf. Weiss,
Bibl. Theol. d. N. T. § 76; Cremer, Bibl.-theol. Lex. s. v.;
Abbot in the Journ. Soc. Bib. Lit. and Exeg. for June
and Dec. 1881 p. 126 sqq., June and Dec. 1883 p. 101 sq.
On the use of a capital initial, see WH. Intr. § 414].
The word does not occur in the [Ep. to Tit. (crit. edd.),
the] 1 Ep. of John, [nor in the Second or the Third; for
in 2 Jn. 3 κυρίου is dropped by the critical editors. SYN.
see δεσπότης, fin.].

κυριότης, -ητος, ἡ, (ὁ κύριος), dominion, power, lordship;   **2963**
in the N. T. one who possesses dominion (see ἐξουσία, 4 c.
β.; cf. Germ. Herrschaft, [or Milton's "dominations"];
in Tac. ann. 13, 1 dominationes is equiv. to dominantes),
so used of angels (κύριοι, 1 Co. viii. 5; see κύριος, a. fin.):
Eph. i. 21; 2 Pet. ii. 10; Jude 8; plur. Col. i. 16. (Eccles.
[e. g. 'Teaching' c. 4] and Byzant. writ.) *

κυρόω, -ῶ: 1 aor. inf. κυρῶσαι; pf. pass. ptcp. κεκυρω-   **2964**
μένος; (κῦρος the head, that which is supreme, power,
influence, authority); fr. Aeschyl. and Hdt. down; to
make valid; to confirm publicly or solemnly, to ratify:
διαθήκην, pass. Gal. iii. 15; ἀγάπην εἴς τινα, to make a
public decision that love be shown to a transgressor by
granting him pardon, 2 Co. ii. 8. [COMP. : προ-κυρόω.] *

κύων, κυνός; in prof. auth. of the com. gend., in the   **2965**
N. T. masc.; Hebr. כֶּלֶב; a dog; prop.: Lk. xvi. 21;
2 Pet. ii. 22; metaph. (in various [but always reproach-
ful] senses; often so even in Hom.) a man of impure
mind, an impudent man, [cf. Bp. Lghtft. on Phil. l. s.]:
Mt. vii. 6; Phil. iii. 2; Rev. xxii. 15, in which last pass.
others less probably understand sodomites (like כְּלָבִים in
Deut. xxiii. 18 (19)) [cf. B. D. s. v. Dog].*

κῶλον, -ου, τό; in Grk. writ. fr. Aeschyl. down a mem-   **2966**
ber of the body, particularly the more external and prominent members, esp. the feet; in Sept. (Lev. xxvi. 30;
Num. xiv. 29, 32 sq.; 1 S. xvii. 46; Is. lxvi. 24) for פֶּגֶר
and פְּגָרִים, a dead body, carcase, inasmuch as the members of a corpse are loose and fall apart: so the plur. in
Heb. iii. 17 fr. Num. xiv. 29, 32, [A. V. carcases].*

κωλύω; impf. 1 pers. plur. ἐκωλύομεν (Mk. ix. 38 T Tr   **2967**
txt. WH); 1 aor. ἐκώλυσα; Pass., pres. κωλύομαι; 1 aor.
ἐκωλύθην; (fr. κόλος, lopped, clipped; prop. to cut off, cut

short, hence) to hinder, prevent, forbid; [fr. Pind. down];
Sept. for כָּלָא, twice (viz. 1 S. xxv. 26; 2 S. xiii. 13) for
מָנַע: τινά foll. by an inf. [W. § 65, 2 β.; cf. B. § 148, 13],
Mt. xix. 14; Lk. xxiii. 2; Acts xvi. 6; xxiv. 23; 1 Th.
ii. 16; Heb. vii. 23; τί κωλύει με βαπτισθῆναι; what doth
hinder me from being (to be) baptized? Acts viii. 36;
the inf. is omitted, as being evident from what has gone
before, Mk. ix. 38 sq.; x. 14; Lk. ix. 49; xi. 52; xviii.
16; Acts xi. 17; Ro. i. 13; 3 Jn. 10; αὐτόν is wanting,
because it has preceded, Lk. ix. 50; the acc. is wanting,
because easily supplied from the context, 1 Tim. iv. 3;
as often in Grk. writ., constr. w. τινά τινος, to keep one
from a thing, Acts xxvii. 43; with acc. of the thing, τὴν
παραφρονίαν, to restrain, check, 2 Pet. ii. 16; τὸ λαλεῖν
γλώσσαις, 1 Co. xiv. 39; τί, foll. by τοῦ μή, can any one
hinder the water (which offers itself), that these should
not be baptized? Acts x. 47; in imitation of the Hebr.
כָּלָא foll. by מִן of the pers. and the acc. of the thing, to
withhold a thing from any one, i. e. to deny or refuse one
a thing: Lk. vi. 29 [B. § 132, 5] (τὸ μνημεῖον ἀπὸ σοῦ,
Gen. xxiii. 6). [COMP.: διακωλύω.]*

2968 κώμη, -ης, ἡ, (akin to κεῖμαι, κοιμάω, prop. the common
sleeping-place to which laborers in the fields return;
Curtius § 45 [related is Eng. home]), [fr. Hes., Hdt.
down], a village: Mt. ix. 35; x. 11; Mk. xi. 2; Lk. v.
17; ix. 52 [here Tdf. πόλιν], and often in the Synopt.
Gospels; Jn. xi. 1, 30; with the name of the city near
which the villages lie and to whose municipality they
belong: Καισαρείας, Mk. viii. 27 (often so in Sept. for
בְּנוֹת with the name of a city; cf. Gesenius, Thes. i. p.
220ᵃ [B. D. s. v. Daughter, 7]; also for חֲצֵרִי and חַצְרוֹת
with the name of a city); by meton. the inhabitants of
villages, Acts viii. 25; used also of a small town, as Bethsaida, Mk. viii. 23, 26, cf. 22; Jn. i. 45; of Bethlehem,
Jn. vii. 42; for עִיר, Josh. x. 39; xv. 9 [Compl.]; Is. xlii.
11. [B. D. s. v. Villages.]

2969 κωμό-πολις, -εως, ἡ, a village approximating in size and
number of inhabitants to a city, a village-city, a town
(Germ. Marktflecken): Mk. i. 38. (Strabo, [Josh.
xviii. 28 Aq., Theod. (Field)]; often in the Byzant. writ.
of the middle ages.) *

κῶμος, -ου, ὁ, (fr. κεῖμαι; accordingly i. q. Germ. Ge-
lag; cf. Curtius § 45); fr. [Hom. h. Merc., Theogn.]
Hdt. down; a revel, carousal, i. e. in the Grk. writ. prop.
a nocturnal and riotous procession of half-drunken and
frolicsome fellows who after supper parade through the
streets with torches and music in honor of Bacchus or
some other deity, and sing and play before the houses
of their male and female friends; hence used generally,
of feasts and drinking-parties that are protracted till late
at night and indulge in revelry; plur. [revellings]: Ro.
xiii. 13; Gal. v. 21; 1 Pet. iv. 3. (Sap. xiv. 23; 2 Macc.
vi. 4.) [Trench § lxi.]*   **2970**

κώνωψ, -ωπος, ὁ, a gnat ([Aeschyl.], Hdt., Hippocr.,
al.); of the wine-gnat or midge that is bred in (ferment-
ing and) evaporating wine (Aristot. h. an. 5, 19 [p. 552ᵇ,
5; cf. Bochart, Hierozoicon, iii. 444; Buxtorf, Lex. talm.
etc. 927 (474ᵃ ed. Fischer)]): Mt. xxiii. 24.*   **2971**

Κώς, gen. Κῶ, ἡ, Cos [A. V. Coos] (now Stanco or
Stanchio [which has arisen from a slurred pronunciation of ἐς τὰν Κῶ (mod. Grk.) like Stambul fr. ἐς τὰν
πόλιν. (Hackett)]), a small island of the Ægean Sea,
over against the cities of Cnidus and Halicarnassus,
celebrated for its fertility and esp. for its abundance of
wine and corn: Acts xxi. 1, where for the Rec. Κῶν
Grsb. [foll. by subsequent editors] has restored Κῶ, as
in 1 Macc. xv. 23; see Matthiae § 70 note 3; W. § 8,
2 a.; [B. 21 (19); WH. App. p. 157]. Cf. Kuester,
De Co insula, Hal. 1833; ["but the best description is
in Ross, Reisen nach Kos u. s. w. (Halle 1852)" (Howson); cf. Lewin, St. Paul, ii. 96].*   **2972**

Κωσάμ, ὁ, (fr. קָסַם to divine, [but cf. B. D.]), Cosam,
one of Christ's ancestors: Lk. iii. 28.*   **2973**

κωφός, -ή, -όν, (κόπτω to beat, pound), blunted, dull;
prop. βέλος, Hom. Il. 11, 390; hence **a.** blunted
(or lamed) in tongue; dumb: Mt. ix. 32 sq.; xii. 22;
xv. 30 sq.; Lk. i. 22; xi. 14, (Hdt. et sqq.; Sept. for אִלֵּם
Hab. ii. 18). **b.** blunted, dull, in hearing; deaf:
Mt. xi. 5; Mk. vii. 32, 37; ix. 25; Lk. vii. 22, (Hom.
h. Merc. 92; Aeschyl., Xen., Plat., sqq.; Sept. for
חֵרֵשׁ, Ex. iv. 11; Is. xliii. 8; Ps. xxxvii. (xxxviii.) 14,
etc.).*   **2974**

Λ

2975 λαγχάνω: 2 aor. ἔλαχον; **1.** to obtain by lot (fr.
Hom. down): with gen. of the thing, Lk. i. 9 [cf. B. 269
(231); W. 319 (299)]; to receive by divine allotment,
obtain: τί, Acts i. 17; 2 Pet. i. 1; on the constr. of this
verb w. gen. and acc. of the thing, see Matthiae § 328;
W. 200 (188); [cf. B. § 132, 8]. **2.** to cast lots,
determine by lot, (Isocr. p. 144 b.; Diod. 4, 63, [cf. ps.-
Dem. in Mid. p. 510, 26]): περί τινος, Jn. xix. 24.*

Λάζαρος, -ου, ὁ, (rabb. לַעֲזָר, apparently the same as
אֶלְעָזָר, whom God helps [cf. Philo, quis haeres § 12];
acc. to others, i. q. עֶזֶר לֹא without help), Lazarus; **1.**
an inhabitant of Bethany, beloved by Christ and raised
from the dead by him: Jn. xi. 1 sqq. 43; xii. 1 sq. 9 sq.
17. **2.** an imaginary person, extremely poor and
wretched: Lk. xvi. 20, 23–25.*   **2976**

λάθρα [so R G T Tr] (in Hom. λάθρη, fr. λανθάνω,   **2977** λαθεῖν), and L [WH KC (see the latter's Praef. p. xii. and s. v. εἰκῇ)] λάθρᾳ (fr. λάθρος, -a, -ον, cf. Passow [esp. L. and S.] s. v.; W. 47; B. 69 (61)), adv. *secretly*: Mt. i. 19; ii. 7; Jn. xi. 28; Acts xvi. 37. (From Hom. down; Sept.) *

2978 λαῖλαψ ([L T Tr WH] not λαίλαψ [Grsb.], cf. W. § 6, 1 e.; *Lipsius*, Grammat. Untersuch. p. 37 sq.; [Chandler § 620; *Tdf.* Proleg. p. 101]), -απος, ἡ [masc. in א* Mk. iv. 37; cf. Thom. Mag. ed. Ritschl p. 226, 4], *a whirlwind, tempestuous wind*: 2 Pet. ii. 17; λαῖλαψ ἀνέμου (cf. Germ. *Sturmwind*; ἄνεμος σὺν λαίλαπι πολλῇ, Hom. Il. 17, 57), a violent attack of wind [A. V. *a storm of wind*], a squall [(see below)], Mk. iv. 37; Lk. viii. 23. (Sept. Job xxi. 18; xxxviii. 1; Sap. v. 15, 24; Sir. xlviii. 9.) [Acc. to Schmidt (ch. 55 § 13), λ. is never a single gust, nor a steadily blowing wind, however violent; but a storm breaking forth from black thunder-clouds in furious gusts, with floods of rain, and throwing everything topsy-turvy; acc. to Aristot. de mund. 4 p. 395 ᵃ, 7 it is 'a whirlwind revolving from below upwards.'] *

see 2997 ΛΑΚΩ and λακέω, see λάσκω.

2979 λακτίζω; (fr. adv. λάξ, with the heel); [fr. Hom. down]; *to kick, strike with the heel*: Acts xxvi. 14, and Rec. in ix. 5; see κέντρον, 2.*

2980 λαλέω, -ῶ; impf. 3 pers. sing. ἐλάλει, plur. ἐλάλουν; fut. λαλήσω; 1 aor. ἐλάλησα; pf. λελάληκα; Pass., pres. λαλοῦμαι; pf. λελάλημαι; 1 aor. ἐλαλήθην; 1 fut. λαληθήσομαι: [fr. Soph. down]; found in bibl. Grk. much more freq. than in prof. auth., in Sept. times without number for דָבַר or דִבֶּר, more rarely for אָמַר; prop. *to utter a sound* (cf. [onomatop. *la-la*, etc.] Germ. *lallen*), *to emit a voice, make one's self heard*; hence *to utter* or *form words with the mouth, to speak*, having reference to the sound and pronunciation of the words and in general the form of what is uttered. while λέγω refers to the meaning and substance of what is spoken; hence λαλεῖν is employed not only of men, esp. when *chatting and prattling*, but also of animals (of birds, Mosch. 3, 47; of locusts, Theocr. 5, 34; λαλοῦσι μέν, οὐ φράζουσι δέ, of dogs and apes, Plut. mor. ii. p. 909 a.), and so of inanimate things (as trees, Theocr. 27, 56 (57); of an echo, Dio C. 74, 21, 14). Accordingly, everything λεγόμενον is also λαλούμενον, but not everything λαλούμενον is also λεγόμενον (Eupolis in Plut. Alc. 13 λαλεῖν ἄριστος, ἀδυνατώτατος λέγειν); [the difference between the words is evident where they occur in proximity, e. g. Ro. iii. 19 ὅσα ὁ νόμος λέγει, τοῖς ἐν τῷ νόμῳ λαλεῖ, and the very com. ἐλάλησεν ... λέγων, Mt. xiii. 3, etc.]. Moreover, the primary meaning of λαλεῖν, *to utter one's self*, enables us easily to understand its very frequent use in the sacred writers to denote the utterances by which God indicates or gives proof of his mind and will, whether immediately or through the instrumentality of his messengers and heralds. [Perhaps this use may account in part for the fact that, though in classic Grk. λαλ. is the term for light and familiar speech, and so assumes readily a disparaging notion. in bibl. Grk. it is nearly if not quite free from any such suggestion.] Cf. *Dav. Schulz* die Geis-

tesgaben der ersten Christen, p. 94 sqq.; *Tittmann* de Synonymis N. T. p. 79 sq.; *Trench*, Syn. § lxxvi.; [and on class. usage *Schmidt*, Syn. i. ch. 1]. But let us look at the N. T. usage in detail:

1. *to utter a voice, emit a sound*: of things inanimate, as βρονταί, Rev. x. 4; with τὰς ἑαυτῶν φωνάς added, each thunder uttered its particular voice (the force and meaning of which the prophet understood, cf. Jn. xii. 28 sq.), ib. 3; σάλπιγγος λαλούσης μετ' ἐμοῦ, λέγων (Rec. λέγουσα) foll. by direct disc. Rev. iv. 1; of the expiatory blood of Christ, metaph. *to crave the pardon of sins*, Heb. xii. 24; of the murdered Abel, long since dead, i. q. *to call for vengeance* (see Gen. iv. 10, and cf. κράζω, 1 fin.), Heb. xi. 4 acc. to the true reading λαλεῖ [G L T Tr WH; the Rec. λαλεῖται must be taken as pass., in the exceptional sense *to be talked of, lauded*; see below, 5 fin. (πρᾶγμα κατ' ἀγορὰν λαλούμενον, Arstph. Thesm. 578, cf. πάντες αὐτὴν λαλοῦσιν, Alciphro frag. 5, ii. p. 222, 10 ed. Wagner)]. **2.** *to speak*, i. e. *to use the tongue* or *the faculty of speech*; *to utter articulate sounds*: absol. 1 Co. xiv. 11; of the dumb, receiving the power of speech, Mt. ix. 33; xii. 22; xv. 31; Lk. xi. 14; Rev. xiii. 15; (τοὺς [T Tr WH om.]) ἀλάλους λαλεῖν, Mk. vii. 37; ἐλάλει ὀρθῶς, ib. 35; of a dumb man, μὴ δυνάμενος λαλῆσαι, Lk. i. 20 (of idols, στόμα ἔχουσι κ. οὐ λαλήσουσι, Ps. cxiii. 13 (cxv. 5); cxxxiv. 16; cf. 3 Macc. iv. 16); *to speak*, i. e. *not to be silent*, opp. to holding one's peace, λαλεῖ κ. μὴ σιωπήσῃς, Acts xviii. 9; opp. to hearing, Jas. i. 19; opp. to the soul's inner experiences, 2 Co. iv. 13 fr. Ps. cxv. 1 (cxvi. 10); opp. to ποιεῖν (as λόγος to ἔργον q. v. 3), Jas. ii. 12. **3.** *to talk*, of the outward form of speech: τῇ ἰδίᾳ διαλέκτῳ, Acts ii. 6; ἑτέραις καιναῖς γλώσσαις, ib. 4; Mk. xvi. 17 [here Tr txt. WH txt. om. καιν.], from which the simple γλώσσαις λαλεῖν, and the like, are to be distinguished, see γλῶσσα, 2. **4.** *to utter, tell*: with acc. of the thing, 2 Co. xii. 4. **5.** *to use words in order to declare one's mind and disclose one's thoughts*; *to speak*: absol., ἔτι αὐτοῦ λαλοῦντος, Mt. xii. 46; xvii 5; xxvi. 47; Mk. v. 35; xiv. 43; Lk. viii. 49; xxii. 47, 60; with the advs. κακῶς, καλῶς, Jn. xviii. 23; ὡς νήπιος ἐλάλουν, 1 Co. xiii. 11; ὡς δράκων, Rev. xiii. 11; στόμα πρὸς στόμα, face to face (Germ. *mündlich*), 2 Jn. 12 (after the Hebr. of Num. xii. 8); εἰς ἀέρα λαλεῖν, 1 Co. xiv. 9; ἐκ τοῦ περισσεύματος τῆς καρδίας τὸ στόμα λαλεῖ, of the abundance of the heart the mouth speaketh, sc. so that it expresses the soul's thoughts, Mt. xii. 34; Lk. vi. 45; ἐκ τῶν ἰδίων λαλεῖν, to utter words in accordance with one's inner character, Jn. viii. 44. with acc. of the thing: τί λαλήσω, λαλήσητε, etc., what I shall utter in speech, etc., Jn. xii. 50; Mt. x. 19; Mk. ix. 6 [here T Tr WH ἀποκριθῇ]; xiii. 11; τί, anything, Mk. xi. 23 L T Tr txt. WH; Ro. xv. 18; 1 Th. i. 8; οὐκ οἴδαμεν τί λαλεῖ, what he says, i. e. what the words uttered by him mean [WH br. τί λαλ.], Jn. xvi. 18; ταῦτα, these words, Lk. xxiv. 36; Jn. viii. 30; xvii. 1, 13; 1 Co. ix. 8; τὸ λαλούμενον, 1 Co. xiv. 9; plur. Acts xvi. 14 (of the words of a teacher); τὸν λόγον λαλούμενον, Mk. v. 36 [see B. 302 (259) note]; λόγους, 1 Co. xiv. 19; ῥήματα, Jn. viii. 20; Acts x. 44;

παραβολήν, Mt. xiii. 33; βλασφημίας, Mk. ii. 7 [L T Tr WH βλασφημεῖ]; Lk. v. 21; ῥήματα βλάσφημα εἴς τινα, Acts vi. 11; ῥήματα (Rec. adds βλάσφημα) κατά τινος, Acts vi. 13; σκληρὰ κατά τινος, Jude 15; ὑπέρογκα, ib. 16 (Dan. [Theodot.] xi. 36); τὰ μὴ δέοντα, 1 Tim. v. 13 (ἃ μὴ θέμις, 2 Macc. xii. 14; εἴς τινα τὰ μὴ καθήκοντα, 3 Macc. iv. 16; [cf. W. 480 (448)]); διεστραμμένα, Acts xx. 30; τὸ ψεῦδος, Jn. viii. 44; δόλον, 1 Pet. iii. 10 fr. Ps. xxxiii. (xxxiv.) 14; ἀγαθά, Mt. xii. 34; σοφίαν, 1 Co. ii. 6 sq.; μυστήρια, ib. xiv. 2; foll. by ὅτι (equiv. to περὶ τούτου, ὅτι etc. to speak of this, viz. that they knew him [see ὅτι, I. 2 sub fin.]), Mk. i. 34; Lk. iv. 41; contrary to classic usage, foll. by direct disc., Mk. xiv. 31 Ltxt. T Tr WH; Heb. v. 5; xi. 18, (but in these last two pass. of the utterances of God); more correctly elsewhere ἐλάλησε λέγων (in imitation of Hebr. יְדַבֵּר לֵאמֹר [cf. above (init.)]), foll. by direct disc.: Mt. xiv. 27; xxiii. 1; xxviii. 18; Jn. viii. 12; Acts viii. 26; xxvi. 31; xxviii. 25; Rev. xvii. 1; xxi. 9; λαλοῦσα κ. λέγουσα, Rev. x. 8. λαλῶ with dat. of pers. to speak to one, address him (esp. of teachers): Mt. xii. 46; xxiii. 1; Lk. xxiv. 6; Jn. ix. 29; xv. 22; Acts vii. 38, 44; ix. 27; xvi. 13; xxii. 9; xxiii. 9; Ro. vii. 1; 1 Co. iii. 1; xiv. 21, 28; 1 Th. ii. 16; Heb. i. 2 (1); of one commanding, Mt. xxviii. 18; Mk. xvi. 19; to speak to, i. e. converse with, one [cf. B. § 133, 1]: Mt. xii. 46, [47 but WH mrg. only]; Lk. i. 22; xxiv. 32; Jn. iv. 26; xii. 29; ἑαυτοῖς (dat. of pers.) ψαλμοῖς κ. ὕμνοις (dat. of instrument), Eph. v. 19; οὐ λαλεῖν τινι is used of one who does not answer, Jn. xix. 10; to accost one, Mt. xiv. 27; λαλῶ τί τινι, to speak anything to any one, to speak to one about a thing (of teaching): Mt. ix. 18; Jn. viii. 25 (on which see ἀρχή, 1 b.); x. 6; xiv. 25; xv. 11; xviii. 20 sq.; 2 Co. vii. 14; ῥήματα, Jn. vi. 63; xiv. 10; Acts xiii. 42; οἰκοδομὴν κ. παράκλησιν, things which tend to edify and comfort the soul, 1 Co. xiv. 3; of one promulgating a thing to one, τὸν νόμον, pass. Heb. ix. 19; λαλῶ πρός τινα, to speak unto one: Lk. i. 19; [ii. 15 L mrg. T WH]; Acts iv. 1; viii. 26; ix. 29; xxi. 39; xxvi. 14 [R G], 26, 31; Heb. v. 5, (דִּבֶּר אֶל, Gen. xxvii. 6; Ex. xxx. 11, 17, 22); λόγους πρός τινα, Lk. xxiv. 44; ἐλάλησαν πρὸς αὐτοὺς εὐαγγελιζόμενοι . . . Ἰησοῦν, Acts xi. 20; ὅσα ἂν λαλήσῃ πρὸς ὑμᾶς, Acts iii. 22; σοφίαν ἔν τισιν, wisdom among etc. 1 Co. ii. 6; λαλ. μετά τινος, to speak, converse, with one [cf. B. § 133, 3]: Mk. vi. 50; Jn. iv. 27; ix. 37; xiv. 30; Rev. i. 12; x. 8; xvii. 1; xxi. 9, 15; λαλεῖν ἀλήθειαν μετὰ etc. to show one's self a lover of truth in conversation with others, Eph. iv. 25 [cf. Ellicott]; λαλεῖν περί τινος, concerning a person or thing: Lk. ii. 33; ix. 11; Jn. vii. 13; viii. 26; xii. 41; Acts ii. 31; Heb. ii. 5; iv. 8; with τινί, dat. of pers., added, Lk. ii. 38; Acts xxii. 10; τὶ περί τινος, Acts xxviii. 21; Lk. ii. 17; εἴς τινα περί τινος (gen. of the thing), to speak something as respects a person concerning a thing, Heb. vii. 14 R G; εἴς τινα περί w. gen. of pers., ibid. L T Tr WH. Many of the exx. already cited show that λαλεῖν is freq. used in the N. T. of teachers, — of Jesus, the apostles, and others. To those pass. may be added, Lk. v. 4; Jn.

i. 37; vii. 46; viii. 30, 38; xii. 50; Acts vi. 10; xi. 15; xiv. 1, 9; xvi. 14; 1 Co. xiv. 34 sq.; 2 Co. ii. 17; Col. iv. 3; 1 Th. ii. 4; 1 Pet. iv. 11; with παρρησίᾳ added, Jn. vii. 26; xvi. 29; ἐπὶ ὀνόματι Ἰησοῦ, Acts v. 40, cf. iv. 17, see ἐπί, B. 2 a. β.; τῷ ὀνόματι κυρίου [where L T Tr WH prefix ἐν], of the prophets, Jas. v. 10 (see ὄνομα, 2 f.); τινὶ (to one) ἐν παραβολαῖς, Mt. xiii. 3, 10, 13, 34; ἐν παροιμίαις, Jn. xvi. 25; ἐξ ἐμαυτοῦ, to speak from myself (i. e. utter what I myself have thought out), Jn. xii. 49; ἀπ' ἐμαυτοῦ (see ἀπό, II. 2 d. aa. p. 59ᵃ), Jn. vii. 17 sq.; xiv. 10; xvi. 13; ἐκ τῆς γῆς (see ἐκ, II. 2 sub fin.), Jn. iii. 31; ἐκ τοῦ κόσμου, 1 Jn. iv. 5 (see κόσμος, 6); ἐκ θεοῦ, prompted by divine influence, 2 Co. ii. 17; λαλεῖν τὸν λόγον, to announce or preach the word of God or the doctrine of salvation: Mk. viii. 32; Acts xiv. 25 [here in T WH mrg. foll. by εἰς τὴν Πέργην; see εἰς, A. I. 5 b.]; xvi. 6; Phil. i. 14, etc.; τὸν λόγ. τοῦ θεοῦ, Acts iv. 29, 31; τινὶ τ. λόγον, Mk. ii. 2; with παραβολαῖς added, Mk. iv. 33; τινὶ τὸν λόγ. τοῦ κυρίου [WH txt. θεοῦ], Acts xvi. 32 (Barn. ep. 19, 9); τινὶ τ. λόγ. τοῦ θεοῦ, Acts xiii. 46; Heb. xiii. 7; τὰ ῥήματα τοῦ θεοῦ, Jn. iii. 34; τὰ ῥήμ. τῆς ζωῆς, Acts v. 20; πρός τινα τὸ εὐαγγ. τοῦ θεοῦ, 1 Th. ii. 2; λαλεῖν κ. διδάσκειν τὰ περὶ τοῦ Ἰησοῦ [R G κυρίου], Acts xviii. 25; τὸ μυστήριον τοῦ Χριστοῦ, Col. iv. 3. λαλεῖν is used of the O. T. prophets uttering their predictions: Lk. xxiv. 25; Acts iii. 24; xxvi. 22 [cf. B. § 144, 20, and p. 301 (258)]; 2 Pet. i. 21; Jas. v. 10; of the declarations and prophetic announcements of God: Lk. i. 45, 55; Jn. ix. 29; Acts vii. 6; esp. in the Ep. to the Heb.: i. 1, 2 (1); iii. 5; iv. 8; xi. 18; xii. 25; God, the Holy Spirit, Christ, are said λαλεῖν ἔν τινι: Heb. i. 1, 2 (1); Mt. x. 20; 2 Co. xiii. 3; διὰ στόματός τινος, Lk. i. 70; Acts iii. 21; διὰ Ἡσαΐου, Acts xxviii. 25; of the sayings of angels: Lk. ii. 17, 20; Jn. xii. 29; Acts x. 7; xxiii. 9; xxvii. 25; the Holy Spirit is said λαλήσειν what it will teach the apostles, Jn. xvi. 13; ὁ νόμος as a manifestation of God is said λαλεῖν τινι what it commands, Ro. iii. 19; finally, even voices are said λαλεῖν, Acts xxvi. 14 [R G]; Rev. i. 12; x. 8. i. q. to make known by speaking, to speak of, relate, with the implied idea of extolling: Mt. xxvi. 13; Mk. xiv. 9; Lk. xxiv. 36; Acts iv. 20; [cf. Heb. xi. 4 Rec. (see 1 fin. above)]. 6. Since λαλεῖν strictly denotes the act of one who utters words with the living voice, when writers speak of themselves or are spoken of by others as λαλοῦντες, they are conceived of as present and addressing their readers with the living voice, Ro. vii. 1; 1 Co. ix. 8; 2 Co. xi. 17, 23; xii. 19; Heb. ii. 5; vi. 9; 2 Pet. iii. 16, or λαλεῖν is used in the sense of commanding, Heb. vii. 14. The verb λαλεῖν is not found in the Epp. to Gal. and 2 Thess. [Comp.: δια-, ἐκ-, κατα-, προσ-, συλ-λαλέω; cf. the catalogue of comp. in Schmidt, Syn. ch. 1 § 60.]

λαλιά, -ᾶς, ἡ, (λάλος, cf. Bttm. Ausf. Sprchl. § 119 Anm. 21), in prof. auth. [fr. Arstph. down] loquacity, talkativeness, talk (Germ. Gerede) [see λαλέω, init.]; in a good sense conversation; in the N. T. 1. speech, i. q. story: Jn. iv. 42. 2. dialect, mode of speech, pronunciation, [W. 23]: Mk. xiv. 70 Rec.; Mt. xxvi. 73; speech which discloses the speaker's native country : hence of the speech by which Christ may be recognized as having come from heaven, Jn. viii. 43 [where cf. Meyer].*

2982 λαμά [R G (on the accent see *Tdf.* Proleg. 102)] in Mt. xxvii. 46 and λαμμᾶ [R G] Mk. xv. 34, (the Hebr. word לָמָה fr. Ps. xxi. (xxii.) 1), *why*; in the former pass. Lchm. reads λημά, in the latter λεμά, Tdf. λεμά in both, Tr WH λεμά in Mt. but λαμά in Mk.; the form in η or ε reproduces the Chald. לְכָא or לְמָה; on the remarkable diversity of spelling in the codd. cf. Tdf. on each pass., [WH on Mt. l. c.], and Fritzsche on Mk. p. 693.*

2983 λαμβάνω; impf. ἐλάμβανον; fut. λήψομαι, (L T Tr WH λήμψομαι, an Alexandrian form; see s. v. M, μ); 2 aor. ἔλαβον (2 pers. plur. once [in Tdf. 7 after B*] ἐλάβατε, 1 Jn. ii. 27; see reff. s. v. ἀπέρχομαι, init.), impv. λάβε (Rev. x. 8 sq.), not λαβέ (W. § 6, 1 a.; B. 62 (54)); pf. εἴληφα, 2 pers. εἴληφας [and εἴληφες (Rev. xi. 17 WH; see κοπιάω); on the use of the pf. interchangeably with an aor. (Rev. v. 7; viii. 5, etc.) cf. B. 197 (170); W. 272 (255); Jebb in Vincent and Dickson's Mod. Grk. 2d ed. App. §§ 67, 68], ptcp. εἰληφώς; [Pass., pres. ptcp. λαμβανόμενος; pf. 3 pers. sing. εἴληπται, Jn. viii. 4 WH mrg. (rejected section)]; Sept. hundreds of times for לקח, very often for נשׂא, also for לכד and several times for אחז; [fr. Hom. down];

I. *to take*, i. e. **1.** *to take with the hand, lay hold of*, any pers. or thing in order to u s e it: absol., where the context shows what is taken, Mt. xxvi. 26; Mk. xiv. 22; (τόν) ἄρτον, Mt. xxvi. 26; Acts xxvii. 35; τὸ βιβλίον, Rev. v. 7–9, [see B. and W. u. s.]; μάχαιραν (grasp, lay hand to), Mt. xxvi. 52, and in many other exx. After a circumstantial style of description (see ἀνίστημι, II. 1 c.) in use from Hom. down (cf. Passow s. v. C.; [L. and S. s. v. I. 11]; Matthiae § 558, Anm. 2; [W. § 65, 4 c.]), the ptcp. λαβών with acc. of the object is placed before an act. verb where it does not always seem to us necessary to mention the act of taking (as λαβὼν κύσε χεῖρα [cf. our 'he took and kissed'], Hom. Od. 24, 398): Mt. xiii. 31, 33; xvii. 27; Mk. ix. 36; Lk. xiii. 19, 21; Jn. xii. 3; Acts ii. 23 Rec.; ix. 25; xvi. 3; λαβὼν τὸ αἷμα ... τὸν λαὸν ἐρράντισε (equiv. to τῷ αἵματι ... τὸν λ. ἐρρ.), Heb. ix. 19; or the verb λαβεῖν in a finite form foll. by καί precedes, as ἔλαβε τὸν Ἰησοῦν καὶ ἐμαστίγωσεν, Jn. xix. 1; add, ib. 40; xxi. 13; Rev. viii. 5; also λαβεῖν τὸν ἄρτον ... καὶ βαλεῖν etc., Mt. xv. 26; Mk. vii. 27; ἔλαβον ... καὶ ἐποίησαν, Jn. xix. 23. metaph., ἀφορμήν (see the word, 2), Ro. vii. 8, 11; ὑπόδειγμά τινός (gen. of the thing) τινα, to take one as an example of a thing, for imitation, Jas. v. 10; *to take in order to wear*, τὰ ἱμάτια, i. e. *to put on*: Jn. xiii. 12 (ἐσθῆτα, ὑποδήματα, Hdt. 2, 37; 4, 78); μορφὴν δούλου, Phil. ii. 7. *to take in the mouth*: something to eat, Jn. xiii. 30; Acts ix. 19; 1 Tim. iv. 4, (cf. Lat. *cibum capio, to take food*); *to take anything to drink*, i. e. drink, swallow, ὕδωρ, Rev. xxii. 17; to drink, τὸ ὄξος, Jn. xix. 30; οὐκ ἔλαβε, he did not take it, i. e. refused to drink it, Mk. xv. 23. *to take*

up a thing *to be carried*; *to take upon one's self*: τὸν σταυρὸν αὐτοῦ, Mt. x. 38 [L mrg. ἄρῃ]; *to take with one for future use*: ἄρτους, Mt. xvi. 5, 7; λαμπάδας, Mt. xxv. 1; ἔλαιον μεθ' ἑαυτῶν, ibid. 3. **2.** *to take in order to carry away*: without the notion of violence, τὰς ἀσθενείας, i. e. to remove, take away, Mt. viii. 17; with the notion of violence, *to seize, take away forcibly*: Mt. v. 40; Rev. iii. 11; τὴν εἰρήνην ἐκ [Rec. ἀπὸ, (WH br. ἐκ)] τῆς γῆς, Rev. vi. 4. **3.** *to take what is one's own, to take to one's self, to make one's own*; **a.** *to claim, procure, for one's self*: τί, Jn. iii. 27 (opp. to what is g i v e n); ἑαυτῷ βασιλείαν, Lk. xix. 12; with acc. of the pers. *to associate with one's self as companion, attendant*, etc.: λαβὼν τ. σπεῖραν ἔρχεται, taking with him the band of soldiers (whose aid he might use) he comes, Jn. xviii. 3 (στρατὸν λαβὼν ἔρχεται, Soph. Trach. 259); λαμβ. γυναῖκα, to take i. e. marry a wife, Mk. xii. 19–22; Lk. xx. 28–31, (Gen. iv. 19, etc.; Xen. Cyr. 8, 4, 16; Eur. Alc. 324; with ἑαυτῷ added, Gen. iv. 19; vi. 2, and often). **b.** of that which when taken is not let go, like the Lat. *capio*, i. q. *to seize, lay hold of, apprehend*: τινά, Mt. xxi. 35, 39; Mk. xii. 3, 8, and very often in Grk. writ. fr. Hom. down; trop. τί, i. e. *to get possession of, obtain*, a thing, Phil. iii. 12 [cf. W. 276 (259)]; metaph., of affections or evils seizing on a man (Lat. *capio, occupo*): τινὰ ἔλαβεν ἔκστασις, Lk. v. 26; φόβος, Lk. vii. 16 (very often so even in Hom., as τρόμος ἔλαβε γυῖα, Il. 3, 34; μὲ ἵμερος αἱρεῖ, 3, 446; χόλος, 4, 23; Sept. Ex. xv. 15; Sap. xi. 13 (12)); πνεῦμα (i. e. a demon), Lk. ix. 39; πειρασμός, 1 Co. x. 13. **c.** *to take by craft* (our *catch*, used of hunters, fishermen, etc.): οὐδένα, Lk. v. 5; trop. τινά, *to circumvent one by fraud*, 2 Co. xi. 20; with δόλῳ added, ib. xii. 16. **d.** *to take to one's self, lay hold upon, take possession of*, i. e. *to appropriate to one's self*: ἑαυτῷ τὴν τιμήν, Heb. v. 4. **e.** Lat. *capto, catch at, reach after, strive to obtain*: τὶ παρά τινος (gen. of pers.), Jn. v. 34, 41; alternating with ζητεῖν, ib. 44. **f.** *to take a thing due* acc. to agreement or law, *to collect, gather* (tribute): τὰ δίδραχμα, Mt. xvii. 24; τέλη ἀπό τινος, ib. 25; δεκάτας, Heb. vii. 8 sq.; καρπούς, Mt. xxi. 34; παρὰ τῶν γεωργῶν ἀπὸ τοῦ καρποῦ, Mk. xii. 2. **4.** *to take* i. e. *to admit, receive*: τινὰ ῥαπίσμασιν, Mk. xiv. 65 L T Tr WH [cf. Lat. *verberibus aliquem accipere*], but see βάλλω, 1; τινὰ εἰς τὰ ἴδια, unto his own home [see ἴδιος, 1 b.], Jn. xix. 27; εἰς οἰκίαν, 2 Jn. 10; εἰς τὸ πλοῖον, Jn. vi. 21. *to receive what is offered; not to refuse or reject*: τινά, one, in order to obey him, Jn. i. 12; v. 43; xiii. 20; τί, prop., *to receive*, Mt. xxvii. 6; trop.: τὸν λόγον, to admit or receive into the mind, Mt. xiii. 20; Mk. iv. 16, (for which in Lk. viii. 13 δέχονται); τὴν μαρτυρίαν, to believe the testimony, Jn. iii. 11, 32 sq.; τὰ ῥήματά τινος, Jn. xii. 48; xvii. 8. In imitation of the Hebr. נשׂא פָנִים (on the various senses of which in the O. T. cf. *Gesenius*, Thes. ii. p. 915 sq.), πρόσωπον λαμβάνω, to receive a person, give him access to one's self, i. e. *to regard any one's power, rank, external circumstances*, and on that account to do some injustice or neglect something: used of p a r t i a l i t y [A. V. *to accept the person*], Lk. xx. 21; with ἀνθρώπου added, Gal.

ii. 6, (Lev. xix. 15; Mal. ii. 9, etc.; θαυμάζειν τὸ πρόσωπ., Deut. x. 17; Job xxxii. 22); [cf. Bp. Lghtft. on Gal. l. c.]. **5.** *to take*, i. q. *to choose, select*: τινὰ ἔκ τινων, pass. Heb. v. 1. **6.** To the signification *to take* may be referred that use, freq. in Grk. auth. also (cf. Passow s. v. B. d. fin.; [L. and S. II. 3]), by which λαμβάνειν joined to a subst. forms a periphrasis of the verb whose idea is expressed by the subst.: λαμβ. ἀρχήν *to take beginning*, i. q. ἄρχομαι *to begin*, Heb. ii. 3 (Polyb. 1, 12, 9, and often; Ael. v. h. 2, 28; 12, 53, and in other auth.); λήθην τινός, *to forget*, 2 Pet. i. 9 (Joseph. antt. 2, 6, 10; 9, 1; 4, 8, 44; Ael. v. h. 3, 18 sub fin.; h. anim. 4, 35); ὑπόμνησίν τινος, *to be reminded of a thing*, 2 Tim. i. 5; πεῖράν τινος, *to prove anything*, i. e. either *to make trial of*: ἧς sc. θαλάσσης, which they attempted to pass through, Heb. xi. 29; or *to have trial of, to experience*: also with gen. of the thing, ib. 36, (in both senses often also in class. Grk.; see πεῖρα, and *Bleek*, Br. a. d. Heb. ii. 2 p. 811); συμβούλιον λαμβ. *to take counsel*, i. q. συμβουλεύεσθαι, *to deliberate* (a combination in imitation apparently of the Lat. phrase *consilium capere*, although that signifies *to form a plan, to resolve*): Mt. xii. 14; xxii. 15; xxvii. 1, 7; xxviii. 12; θάρσος, to take, receive, courage, Acts xxviii. 15; τὸ χάραγμά τινος, i. q. χαράσσομαί τι, to receive the mark of, i. e. let one's self be marked or stamped with: Rev. xiv. 9, 11; xix. 20; xx. 4.

II. *to receive* (what is given); *to gain, get, obtain*: absol., opp. to αἰτεῖν, Mt. vii. 8; Lk. xi. 10; Jn. xvi. 24; opp. to διδόναι, Acts xx. 35; Mt. x. 8; with acc. of the thing, Mt. xx. 9 sq.; Mk. x. 30; [Lk. xviii. 30 L txt. WH txt. Tr mrg.]; Jn. vii. 39; Acts ii. 38; x. 43; Ro. i. 5; v. 11; 1 Co. ii. 12; ix. 24 sq.; 2 Co. xi. 4; Gal. iii. 14; Heb. ix. 15; [xi. 13 R G, see ἐπαγγελία, 2 b.; cf. W. 237 (222)]; Jas. i. 12; v. 7; 1 Pet. iv. 10; Rev. iv. 11; v. 12, and many other exx.; μισθόν, Mt. x. 41; Jn. iv. 36; 1 Co. iii. 8, 14; ἐλεημοσύνην, Acts iii. 3; ἔλεος, Heb. iv. 16; τόπον ἀπολογίας, Acts xxv. 16; τὴν ἐπισκοπήν, Acts i. 20; διάδοχον, Acts xxiv. 27 (*successorem accipio*, Plin. ep. 9, 13); τὸ ἱκανὸν παρά τινος (gen. of pers.), Acts xvii. 9 (see ἱκανός, a. fin.); of punishments: κρίμα, Mt. xxiii. 14 (13) Rec.; Mk. xii. 40 [cf. W. 183 (172)]; Lk. xx. 47 Jas. iii. 1; with dat. incommodi added, ἑαυτῷ, Ro. xiii. 2 (δίκην, Hdt. 1, 115; Eur. Bacch. 1312; ποινάς, Eur. Tro. 360). οἰκοδομήν, to receive edifying, i. q. οἰκοδομοῦμαι, 1 Co. xiv. 5; περιτομήν, i. q. περιτέμνομαι, Jn. vii. 23; τὶ ἔκ τινος, Jn. i. 16; ἐξ ἀναστάσεως τοὺς νεκρούς, substantially i. q. *to receive, get back*, Heb. xi. 35 [see ἔκ, II. 6]; ἔκ, a part of a thing [see ἔκ, II. 9], Rev. xviii. 4; τὶ παρά τινος (gen. of pers.), [Lk. vi. 34 T Tr txt. WH]; Jn. x. 18; Acts ii. 33; iii. 5; xx. 24; xxvi. 10; Jas. i. 7; 1 Jn. iii. 22 R G; 2 Jn. 4; Rev. ii. 28 (27); ἀπό τινος (gen. of pers.), 1 Jn. ii. 27; [iii. 22 L̇ T Tr WH]; on the difference betw. παρά and ἀπό τινος λαμβ. cf. W. 370 (347) note; [B. § 147, 5; yet see Bp. Lghtft. on Gal. i. 12]; ὑπό τινος, 2 Co. xi. 24; πῶς εἴληφας, how thou hast received by instruction in the gospel, i. e. hast learned, Rev. iii. 3. The verb λαμβάνω does not occur in the Epp. to the Thess., Philem., Titus, nor in the Ep. of Jude.

[COMP.: ἀνα-, ἀντι-, συν-αντι- (-μαι), ἀπο-, ἐπι-, κατα-, μετα-, παρα-, συν-παρα-, προ-, προσ-, συν-, συν-περι-, ὑπο-λαμβάνω. SYN. see δέχομαι, fin.]

Λάμεχ, ὁ, (Hebr. לֶמֶךְ), *Lamech*, the father of Noah (Gen. v. 25 sqq.): Lk. iii. 36.*   **2984**

λαμμᾶ, see λαμά.   **see 2982**

λαμπάς, -άδος, ἡ, (λάμπω, cf. our *lamp*), [fr. Aeschyl. and Thuc. down], Sept. for לַפִּיד; **1.** *a torch*: Rev. iv. 5 [where A. V. *lamps*]; viii. 10. **2.** *a lamp*, the flame of which is fed with oil: Mt. xxv. 1, 3 sq. 7 sq.; Jn. xviii. 3; Acts xx. 8. [Cf. Trench, Syn. § xlvi.; Edersheim, Jesus the Messiah, ii. 455 sqq.; Becker, Charicles, Sc. ix. (Eng. trans. p. 153).]*   **2985**

λαμπρός, -ά, -όν, (λάμπω); **a.** *shining*; *brilliant*: ἀστήρ, Rev. xxii. 16 (Hom. Il. 4, 77, etc.); *clear, transparent*, Rev. xxii. 1. **b.** *splendid, magnificent*, [A. V. *gorgeous, bright* (see below)]: ἐσθής, Lk. xxiii. 11; Acts x. 30; Jas. ii. 2 sq.; λίνον [L Tr WH λίθον], Rev. xv. 6; βύσσινος, xix. 8; neut. plur. *splendid* [(R. V. *sumptuous*)] *things*, i. e. elegancies or luxuries in dress and style, Rev. xviii. 14. The word is sometimes used of brilliant and glistening whiteness (hence λαμπρὰ τήβεννα, *toga candida*, Polyb. 10, 4, 8; 10, 5, 1); accordingly the Vulg. in Acts x. 30; Jas. ii. 2; Rev. xv. 6 renders it by *candidus*; and some interpreters, following the Vulg. ("indutum veste *alba*"), understand '*white* apparel' to be spoken of in Lk. xxiii. 11 [A. V. *gorgeous*; (see above)]; cf. Keim iii. p. 380 note [Eng. trans. vi. 104].*   **2986**

λαμπρότης, -ητος, ἡ, *brightness, brilliancy*: τοῦ ἡλίου, Acts xxvi. 13. [From Hdt. (metaph.) down.]*   **2987**

λαμπρῶς, adv., *splendidly, magnificently* (of sumptuous living, Lk. xvi. 19. [From Aeschyl. down.]*   **2988**

λάμπω; fut. λάμψω (2 Co. iv. 6 L txt. T Tr WH); 1 aor. ἔλαμψα; [fr. Hom. down]; *to shine*: Mt. v. 15 sq.; xvii. 2; Lk. xvii. 24; Acts xii. 7; 2 Co. iv. 6. [COMP.: ἐκ-, περι-λάμπω.]*   **2989**

λανθάνω (lengthened form of λήθω); 2 aor. ἔλαθον, (whence Lat. *latere*); Sept. several times for נֶעְלַם, etc.; [fr. Hom. down]; *to be hidden*: Mk. vii. 24; Lk. viii. 47; τινά, *to be hidden from one*, Acts xxvi. 26; 2 Pet. iii. 5 (on which see θέλω, 1 sub fin.), 8; acc. to the well-known classic usage, joined in a finite form to a ptcp. i. q. *secretly, unawares, without knowing*, (cf. Matthiae § 552 β.; Passow s. v. ii. p. 18ᵇ; [L. and S. s. v. A. 2]; W. § 54, 4; [B. § 144, 14]): ἔλαθον ξενίσαντες, have unawares entertained, Heb. xiii. 2. [COMP.: ἐκ-, ἐπι- (-μαι).]*   **2990**

λαξευτός, -ή, -όν, (fr. λαξεύω, and this fr. λᾶς a stone, and ξέω to polish, hew), *cut out of stone*: μνῆμα, Lk. xxiii. 53, and thence in Evang. Nicod. c. 11 fin.; (once in Sept., Deut. iv. 49; Aquila in Num. xxi. 20; xxiii. 14; Deut. xxxiv. 1; [Josh. xiii. 20]; nowhere in Grk. auth.).*   **2991**   *

Λαοδικεία [-κία T WH (see I, ι); R G L Tr accent -δίκεια, cf. Chandler § 104], -ας, ἡ, *Laodicea*, a city of Phrygia, situated on the river Lycus not far from Colossæ. After having been successively called Diospolis and Rhoas, it was named Laodicea in honor of Laodice, the wife of Antiochus II. [B. C. 261–246]. It was de-   **2993**

stroyed by an earthquake, A. D. 66 [or earlier, see Bp. Lghtft. Com. on Col. and Philem. p. 38 sq.], together with Colossæ and Hierapolis (see Κολοσσαί); and afterwards rebuilt by Marcus Aurelius. It was the seat of a Christian church: Col. ii. 1; iv. 13, 15 sq. [(on the 'Ep. to (or 'from') the Laodiceans' see Bp. Lghtft. Com. u. s. pp. 274–300)]; Rev. i. 11; iii. 14, and in the [Rec.] subscription of the 1 Ep. to Tim. [See Bp. Lghtft. Com. on Col. and Philem. Intr. § 1; Forbiger, Hndbch. d. alten Geogr. 2te Ausg. ii. 347 sq.]*

2994 Λαοδικεύς, -έως, ὁ, a Laodicean, inhabitant of Laodicea: Col. iv. 16, and Rec. in Rev. iii. 14.*

2992 λαός, -οῦ, ὁ, [(cf. Curtius § 535)]; Sept. more than fifteen hundred times for עַם; rarely for גּוֹי and לְאֹם; [fr. Hom. down]; people; **1.** a people, tribe, nation, all those who are of the same stock and language: univ. of any people; joined with γλῶσσα, φυλή, ἔθνος, Rev. v. 9; vii. 9; x. 11; xi. 9; xiii. 7 [Rec. om.]; xiv. 6; xvii. 15, (see γλῶσσα, 2); πάντες οἱ λαοί, Lk. ii. 31; Ro. xv. 11; esp. of the people of Israel: Mt. iv. 23; xiii. 15; Mk. vii. 6; Lk. ii. 10; Jn. xi. 50 (where it alternates with ἔθνος); xviii. 14; Acts iii. 23; Heb. ii. 17; vii. 11, etc.; with Ἰσραήλ added, Acts iv. 10; distinguished fr. τοῖς ἔθνεσιν, Acts xxvi. 17, 23; Ro. xv. 10; the plur. λαοὶ Ἰσραήλ [R.V. the peoples of Is.] seems to be used of the tribes of the people (like עַמִּים, Gen. xlix. 10; Deut. xxxii. 8; Is. iii. 13, etc.) in Acts iv. 27 (where the plur. was apparently occasioned by Ps. ii. 1 in its reference to Christ, cf. 25); οἱ πρεσβύτεροι τοῦ λαοῦ, Mt. xxi. 23; xxvi. 3, 47; xxvii. 1; οἱ γραμματεῖς τοῦ λαοῦ, Mt. ii. 4; οἱ πρῶτοι τοῦ λαοῦ, Lk. xix. 47; τὸ πρεσβυτέριον τοῦ λαοῦ, Lk. xxii. 66; ἄρχοντες τοῦ λαοῦ, Acts iv. 8. with a gen. of the possessor, τοῦ θεοῦ, αὐτοῦ, μοῦ (i. e. τοῦ θεοῦ, Hebr. עַם יְהוָה, עַם הָאֱלֹהִים), the people whom God has chosen for himself, selected as peculiarly his own: Heb. xi. 25; Mt. ii. 6; Lk. i. 68; vii. 16; without the art. Jude 5 (Sir. xlvi. 7; Sap. xviii. 13); cf. W. § 19, 1; the name is transferred to the community of Christians, as that which by the blessing of Christ has come to take the place of the theocratic people of Israel, Heb. iv. 9; Rev. xviii. 4; particularly to a church of Christians gathered from among the Gentiles, Acts xv. 14; Ro. ix. 25 sq.; 1 Pet. ii. 10; with εἰς περιποίησιν added, 1 Pet. ii. 9; περιούσιος, Tit. ii. 14, cf. Acts xviii. 10; Lk. i. 17. ὁ λαός the people (of Israel) is distinguished from its princes and rulers [(1 Esdr. i. 10; v. 45; Judith viii. 9, 11; etc.)], Mt. xxvi. 5; Mk. xi. 32 [here WH Tr mrg. read ὄχλος]; xiv. 2; Lk. xx. 19; xxii. 2; xxiii. 5; Acts v. 26, etc.; from the priests, Heb. v. 3; vii. 5, 27. **2.** indefinitely, of a great part of the population gathered together anywhere: Mt. xxvii. 25; Lk. i. 21; iii. 15; vii. 1, 29; viii. 47; ix. 13; xviii. 43, etc.; τὸ πλῆθος τοῦ λαοῦ, Lk. i. 10. [The Gospels of Mk. and Jn. use the word but three times each. SYN. see δῆμος, fin.]

2995 λάρυγξ, -γγος, ὁ, the throat (Etym. Magn. [557, 16]: λάρυγξ μὲν δι' οὗ λαλοῦμεν ... φάρυγξ δὲ δι' οὗ ἐσθίομεν κ. πίνομεν): of the instrument or organ of speech (as Ps. v. 10; Prov. viii. 7; Sir. vi. 5 (4)), Ro. iii. 13, where

the meaning is, their speech threatens and imprecates destruction to others. (Arstph., Eur., Aristot., Galen, al.; Sept. several times for גָּרוֹן; oftener for חֵךְ, the palate.)*

2996 Λασαία, -ας, ἡ, (Lchm. Ἄλασσα, Tr WH Λασέα [see WH. App. p. 160], Vulg. Thalassa), Lasœa, Acts xxvii. 8, a city of Crete not mentioned by any ancient geographical or other writer. But this need not excite surprise, since probably it was one of the smaller and less important among the ninety or a hundred cities of the island; cf. Kuinoel ad loc. [Its site was discovered in 1856, some five miles to the E. of Fair Havens and close to Cape Leonda; see Smith, Voyage and Shipwr. of St. Paul, (3d ed. p. 259 sq.) 4th ed. p. 262 sq.; Alford, Grk. Test. vol. ii. Proleg. p. 27 sq.]*

2997 λάσκω: 1 aor. ἐλάκησα; (cf. Bttm. Ausf. Sprchl. ii. p. 233; Krüger ii. 1, p. 134; Kühner § 343, i. p. 858; [Veitch s. v.]; W. 88 (84)); **1.** to crack, crackle, crash: Hom., Hes., Tragg., Arstph. **2.** to burst asunder with a crack, crack open: Acts i. 18; ὁ δράκων φυσηθεὶς (after having sucked up the poison) ἐλάκησε καὶ ἀπέθανε καὶ ἐξεχύθη ὁ ἰὸς αὐτοῦ καὶ ἡ χολή, Act. Thomae § 33, p. 219 ed. Tdf.*

2998 λατομέω, -ῶ: 1 aor. ἐλατόμησα; pf. pass. ptcp. λελατομημένος; (fr. λατόμος a stone-cutter, and this fr. λᾶς a stone, and τέμνω); to cut stones, to hew out stones: Mt. xxvii. 60; Mk. xv. 46. (Sept. several times for חָצֵב; once for כָּרָה, Ex. xxi. 33 sqq.; Diod., [Dion. H., Strab., al. (cf. Soph. Lex. s. v.)], Justin Mart.)*

2999 λατρεία, -ας, ἡ, (λατρεύω, q. v.); **1.** in Grk. auth. service rendered for hire; then any service or ministration (Tragg., Plut., Lcian.); the service of God: τοῦ θεοῦ, Plat. apol. 23 b; καταφυγεῖν πρὸς θεῶν εὐχάς τε καὶ λατρείας, ibid. Phaedr. p. 244 e.; servitus religionis, quam λατρείαν Graeci vocant, August. civ. dei 5, 15. **2.** in the Grk. Bible, the service or worship of God acc. to the requirements of the levitical law (Hebr. עֲבֹדָה, Ex. xii. 25 sq., etc.): Ro. ix. 4; Heb. ix. 1, (1 Macc. ii. 19, 22); λατρείαν προσφέρειν τῷ θεῷ [to offer service to God] i. q. θυσίαν προσφέρειν εἰς λατρείαν [to offer a sacrifice in service], Jn. xvi. 2; ἐπιτελεῖν τὰς λατρείας, to perform the sacred services (see ἐπιτελέω, 1), spoken of the priests, Heb. ix. 6; univ. of any worship of God, ἡ λογικὴ λ. Ro. xii. 1 [cf. W. § 59, 9 a.]; (of the worship of idols, 1 Macc. i. 43).*

3000 λατρεύω, fut. λατρεύσω; 1 aor. ἐλάτρευσα; (λάτρις a hireling, Lat. latro in Enn. and Plaut.; λάτρον hire); in Grk. writ. **a.** to serve for hire; **b.** univ. to serve, minister to, either gods or men, and used alike of slaves and of freemen; in the N. T. to render religious service or homage, to worship, (Hebr. עָבַד, Deut. vi. 13; x. 12; Josh. xxiv. 15); in a broad sense, λατρ. θεῷ: Mt. iv. 10 and Lk. iv. 8, (after Deut. vi. 13); Acts vii. 7; xxiv. 14; xxvii. 23; Heb. ix. 14; Rev. vii. 15; xxii. 3; of the worship of idols, Acts vii. 42; Ro. i. 25, (Ex. xx. 5; xxiii. 24; Ezek. xx. 32). Phrases relating to the manner of worshipping are these: θεῷ [so R G] λατρεύειν πνεύματι (dat. of instr.), with the spirit or soul, Phil. iii. 3, but L T Tr WH have correctly restored πνεύματι θεοῦ, i. e. prompted by, filled with, the Spirit of God, so that the dat. of the pers. (τῷ θεῷ) is suppressed; ἐν τῷ πνεύματί μου ἐν τῷ εὐαγγ., in my spirit in delivering the glad tidings, Ro. i. 9; τῷ θεῷ ἐν καθαρᾷ συνειδήσει, 2 Tim. i. 3; μετὰ αἰδοῦς καὶ εὐλαβείας or [so L T Tr WH] μετ᾽ εὐλαβ. κ. δέους, Heb. xii. 28; ἐν ὁσιότητι κ. δικαιοσύνῃ, Lk. i. 74; (without the dat. θεῷ) νηστείαις κ. δεήσεσι, Lk. ii. 37; λατρεύειν, absol., to worship God [cf. W. 593 (552)], Acts xxvi. 7. in the strict sense; to perform sacred services, to offer gifts, to worship God in the observance of the rites instituted for his worship: absol., Heb. ix. 9; x. 2; spec. of the priests, to officiate, to discharge the sacred office: with a dat. of the sacred thing to which the service is rendered, Heb. viii. 5; xiii. 10. [(Eur., al.)]*

3001 λάχανον, -ου, τό, (fr. λαχαίνω to dig; hence herbs grown on land cultivated by digging; garden-herbs, as opp. to wild plants); any potherb, vegetables: Mt. xiii. 32; Mk. iv. 32; Lk. xi. 42; Ro. xiv. 2. (1 K. xx. (xxi.) 2; Gen. ix. 3; Ps. xxxvi. (xxxvii.) 2, etc.; Arstph., Plat., Plut., al.)*

3002; **see 2280** Λεββαῖος, see Θαδδαῖος.

3003 λεγεών and (so T, Tr [but not in Mt. xxvi. 53], WH [see fin.], also Lchm. in Mk. v. 9, 15) λεγιών (cf. Tdf. ed. 7 Proleg. p. l.; [esp. ed. 8 p. 83; B. 16 (15)]; so, too, in inscrr. in Boeckh; [Diod., Plut., al.]), -ῶνος, ἡ, (a Lat. word), a legion (a body of soldiers whose number differed at different times, and in the time of Augustus seems to have consisted of 6826 men [i. e. 6100 foot, and 726 horse]): Mt. xxvi. 53; Mk. v. 9, 15; Lk. viii. 30 [here WH (ex errore?) λεγίων (cf. Chandler § 593)].*

3004 λέγω (in the N. T. only the pres. and impf. act. and pres. pass. are in use; 3 pers. plur. impf. ἔλεγαν, Jn. xi. 56 Tdf. [cf. ἔχω, init.]); **I.** in its earliest use in Hom. to lay (like Lat. lego, Germ. legen; cf. J. G. Müller in Theol. Stud. u. Krit. for 1835, p. 127 sqq.; Curtius § 538); to cause to lie down, put to sleep; **1.** to collect, gather; to pick out. **2.** to lay with, count with; to enumerate, recount, narrate, describe; [cf. Eng. tale, Germ. zählen]. **II.** to put word to word in speaking, join words together, i. e. to say (how it differs fr. λαλεῖν, see under that word ad init.); once so by Hom. in Il. 2, 222 [yet cf. Schmidt, Syn. i. ch. 1, §§ 20; 48, 2; L. and S. s. v. B. II. 2]; often in Pind., and by far the most com. use in Attic; Sept. more than thirteen hundred times for אָמַר; often also for נְאֻם (saying, dictum); very rarely for דָּבַר; and so in N. T. **1.** univ. **a.** absol. to speak: Acts xiii. 15; xxiv. 10; to say, foll. by direct disc., Mt. ix. 34; xii. 44; xvi. 2 [here T br. WH reject the pass.]; Mk. iii. 30; Lk. v. 39 [WH br. the cl.]; Jn. i. 29, 38; [1 Co. xii. 3 L T Tr WH]; Jas. iv. 13, and very often; the direct discourse is preceded by ὅτι recitative, Mt. ix. 18 [T om. ὅτι]; Mk. i. 15 [T om. WH br. λέγ.]; ii. 12 [L and WH br. λέγ.]; iii. 21 sq.; v. 28; vi. 14 sq. 35; vii. 20; Lk. i. 24; iv. 41; xvi. 10; Jn. vi. 14; vii. 12; viii. 33; ix. 9, 41; xvi. 17; Acts iii. 13; xi. 3; Heb. x. 8; Rev. iii. 17, etc.; foll. by acc. with inf., Lk. xi. 18; xxiv. 23; Jn. xii. 29; Acts iv. 32; xxviii. 6, etc.; foll. by ὅτι, Lk. xxii. 70;

Jn. viii. 48; xviii. 37; 1 Tim. iv. 1, (for other exx. see 2 a. below); foll. by an indir. question, Mt. xxi. 27; Mk. xi. 33; Lk. xx. 8. **b.** The N. T. writers, particularly the historical, are accustomed to add the verb λέγειν foll. by direct disc. to another verb which already contains the idea of speaking, or which states an opinion concerning some person or thing; as τὸ ῥηθὲν . . . προφήτου λέγοντος, Mt. ii. 17; viii. 17; xii. 17; xiii. 35; κηρύσσων κ. [L T WH om. Tr br. καὶ] λέγων, Mt. iii. 2; κράζειν καὶ λέγειν, Mt. ix. 27; xxi. 15; Mk. x. 47; Lk. iv. 41 [here L T Tr mrg. κραυγάζειν]; Acts xiv. 15; προσφωνεῖν κ. λέγειν, Mt. xi. 17; Lk. vii. 32; ἀπεκρίθη καὶ λέγει, Mk. vii. 28; αἰνεῖν τ. θεὸν κ. λέγειν, Lk. ii. 13; γογγύζειν κ. λέγειν, Jn. vi. 42. to verbs of speaking, judging, etc., and those which denote in general the nature or the substance of the discourse reported, the ptcp. λέγων is added (often so in Sept. for לֵאמֹר [W. 535 sq. (499), cf. 602 (560)]) foll. by direct disc.: ἀπεκρίθη λέγων, Mt. xxv. 9, 44 sq.; Mk. ix. 38 [T WH om. λέγων]; Acts xv. 13; Rev. vii. 13, etc. (see ἀποκρίνομαι, 1 c.); εἶπε λ., Mk. [viii. 28 T WH Tr mrg.]; xii. 26; Lk. xx. 2, (in Grk. writ. ἔφη λέγων); ἐλάλησε λέγων (see λαλῶ, 5); ἐμαρτύρησεν, Jn. i. 32; κέκραγε λ. ib. 15; ἐδίδασκε λ. Mt. v. 2; [ἐβόησε or] ἀνεβόησε λ. Mt. xxvii. 46; Lk. ix. 38; ἀνέκραξε λ., Mk. i. 24; Lk. iv. 34 [T WH om. Tr br. λέγ.]; also after ᾄδειν, Rev. v. 9; xv. 3; αἴρειν [or ἐπαίρ.] φωνήν, Lk. xvii. 13; Acts xiv. 11; θαυμάζειν, Mt. viii. 27; ix. 33; xxi. 20; after προφητεύειν, Mt. xv. 7; γογγύζειν, Mt. xx. 12; εἶπεν ἐν παραβολαῖς, Mt. xxii. 1; παρέθηκε παραβολὴν, Mt. xiii. 24; διεμαρτύρατο, Heb. ii. 6; ἐπήγγελται, Heb. xii. 26, and a great many other exx. It is likewise added to verbs of every kind which denote an act conjoined with speech; as ἐφάνη, φαίνεται λέγων, Mt. i. 20; ii. 13; προσεκύνει λέγων, Mt. viii. 2; ix. 18; xiv. 33; xv. 25; add, Mt. viii. 3; ix. 29; xiv. 15; Mk. v. 35; Lk. i. 66; v. 8; viii. 38; x. 17; xv. 9; xviii. 3; xix. 18; Acts viii. 10, 18 sq.; xiii. 7; xxvii. 23 sq.; 1 Co. xi. 25, etc. On the other hand, the verb λέγω in its finite forms is added to the participles of other verbs: Mt. xxvii. 41; Mk. viii. 12; xiv. 45, 63, 67; xv. 35; Lk. vi. 20; Jn. i. 36; ix. 8; Acts ii. 13; Heb. viii. 8; ἀποκριθεὶς λέγει, Mk. viii. 29; ix. 5, 19; x. 24, 51; xi. 22, 33 [L Tr mrg. br. T Tr WH om. ἀπ.]; Lk. iii. 11; xi. 45; xiii. 8, (nowhere so in Acts, nor in Mt. nor in Jn.); κράξας λέγει, Mk. v. 7 [Rec. εἶπε]; ix. 24. ἔγραψε λέγων (וַיִּכְתֹּב לֵאמֹר), 2 K. x. 6; 2 S. xi. 15, etc.), he wrote in these words, or he wrote these words [A. V. retains the idiom, he wrote saying (cf. e. below)]: Lk. i. 63; 1 Macc. viii. 31; xi. 57; Joseph. antt. 11, 2, 2; 13, 4, 1; exx. fr. the Syriac are given by Gesenius in Rosenmüller's Repertor. i. p. 135. ἔπεμψε or ἀπέστειλε λέγων, i. e. he ordered it to be said by a messenger: Mt. xxii. 16; xxvii. 19; Lk. vii. 19 sq.; xix. 14; Jn. xi. 8; Acts xiii. 15; xvi. 35, (see in εἶπον, 3 b.); otherwise in Mt. xxi. 37; Mk. xii. 6. **c.** ἡ φωνὴ λέγουσα: Mt. iii. 17; xvii. 5; Lk. iii. 22 [G L Tr WH om. λέγ.]; Rev. vi. 6; x. 4, 8; xii. 10; xiv. 13, etc. λέγειν φωνῇ μεγάλῃ, Rev. v. 12; viii. 13; ἐν φωνῇ μ., ib. xiv. 7, 9. **d.** In accordance with the Hebr. conception which regards thought as internal speech (see εἶπον, 5), we find λέγειν ἐν ἑαυτῷ, *to say within one's self,* i. e. *to think with one's self*: Mt. iii. 9; ix. 21; Lk. iii. 8; ἐν τῇ καρδίᾳ αὐτοῦ, Rev. xviii. 7. **e.** One is said *to speak,* λέγειν, not only when he uses language or ally, but also when he expresses himself in writing [(cf. b. sub fin.)]: 2 Co. vii. 3; viii. 8; ix. 3, 4; xi. 16, 21; Phil. iv. 11, and often in Paul; so of the writers of the O. T.: Ro. x. 16, 20; xi. 9; xv. 12; λέγει ἡ γραφή, Ro. iv. 3; x. 11; xi. 2; Jas. ii. 23, etc.; and simply λέγει, sc. ἡ λέγουσα, i. e. ἡ γραφή (our *it is said*): Ro. xv. 10, [11 L Tr mrg.]; Gal. iii. 16; Eph. iv. 8; v. 14; cf. W. 522 (486 sq.) and 588 (547); B. § 129, 16; λέγει, sc. ὁ θεός, 2 Co. vi. 2; λέγει Δαυὶδ ἐν ψαλμῷ, Acts xiii. 35; λέγει ὁ θεός, Heb. v. 6; ἐν τῷ Ὡσηέ, Ro. ix. 25; ἐν Ἠλίᾳ, Ro. xi. 2; ἐν Δαυίδ, Heb. iv. 7; λέγει τὸ πνεῦμα τὸ ἅγιον, Heb. iii. 7; ὁ νόμος λέγει, 1 Co. xiv. 34; τί, 1 Co. ix. 8; Ro. iii. 19. **f.** λέγειν is used of every variety of speaking: as of inquiry, Mt. ix. 14; xv. 1; xvii. 25; xviii. 1; Mk. ii. 18; v. 30 sq.; Lk. iv. 22; vii. 20; Jn. vii. 11; ix. 10; xix. 10; Ro. x. 18 sq.; xi. 1, 11, etc.; foll. by εἰ interrog. [see εἰ, II. 2], Acts xxi. 37; λέγει τις, i. q. one bids the question be asked, Mk. xiv. 14; Lk. xxii. 11; of reply, Mt. xvii. 25; xx. 7; Mk. viii. 24 [L mrg. εἶπεν]; Jn. i. 21; xviii. 17; of acclaim, Rev. iv. 8, 10; of exclamation, Rev. xviii. 10, 16; of entreaty, Mt. xxv. 11; Lk. xiii. 25; i. q. *to set forth in language, make plain,* Heb. v. 11. **g.** λέγω w. acc. of the thing. *to say a thing:* ὅ, Lk. ix. 33 (i. e. not knowing whether what he said was appropriate or not); Lk. xxii. 60; to express in words, Philem. 21; τοῦτο, Jn. viii. 6; xii. 33; τοιαῦτα, Heb. xi. 14; ταῦτα, Lk. viii. 8; xi. 27, 45; xiii. 17; Jn. v. 34; Acts xiv. 18; 1 Co. ix. 8; τάδε (referring to what follows), Acts xxi. 11; Rev. ii. 1, 8, 12, 18; iii. 1, 7, 14; τί, *what ?* Ro. x. 8; xi. 4; Gal. iv. 30; 1 Co. xiv. 16; πολλά, Jn. xvi. 12; τὰ λεγόμενα, Lk. xviii. 34; Acts xxviii. 24; Heb. viii. 1; ὑπό τινος, Acts viii. 6; xiii. 45 [L T Tr WH λαλουμένοις]; xxvii. 11; λέγω ἀλήθειαν, Jn. viii. 45 sq.; Ro. ix. 1; 1 Tim. ii. 7; ἀληθῆ, Jn. xix. 35; ἀνθρώπινον, Ro. vi. 19; σὺ λέγεις, sc. αὐτό, prop. *thou sayest,* i. e. thou grantest *what thou askest,* equiv. to *it is just as thou sayest; to be sure, certainly,* [see εἶπον, 1 c.]: Mt. xxvii. 11; Mk. xv. 2; Lk. xxiii. 3, cf. xxii. 70; Jn. xviii. 37, [(all these pass. WH mrg. punctuate interrogatively)]; παραβολήν, to put forth, Lk. xiv. 7; τὸ αὐτό, to profess one and the same thing, 1 Co. i. 10 cf. 12. **h.** with dat. of the pers. to whom anything is said: foll. by direct discourse, Mt. viii. 20; xix. 4; xviii. 32; xix. 10; Mk. ii. 17, 27; vii. 9; viii. 1; Jn. i. 43 (44); ii. 10, and scores of other exx.; λέγειν τινί· κύριε, κύριε, to salute any one as lord, Mt. vii. 21; impv. λέγε μοι, Acts xxii. 27 (generally εἰπέ μοι, ἡμῖν); plur. Lk. x. 9; ἀμὴν λέγω ὑμῖν, I solemnly declare to you, (in the Gospels of Mt. Mk. and Lk.); for which the Greek said ἐπ' ἀληθείας λέγω ὑμῖν, Lk. iv. 25, and λέγω ὑμῖν ἀληθῶς, ib. ix. 27; in Jn. everywhere [twenty-five times, and always uttered by Christ] ἀμὴν ἀμὴν λέγω σοι (ὑμῖν), I most solemnly declare to thee

(you), i. 51 (52); iii. 11, etc.; with the force of an asseveration λέγω τινί, without ἀμήν: Mt. xi. 22; xii. 36; xxiii. 39; Lk. vii. 9, 28; x. 12; xii. 8; xvii. 34; xviii. 8, 14; ναὶ λέγω ὑμῖν, Mt. xi. 9; Lk. vii. 26; xi. 51; xii. 5; λέγω σοι, Lk. xii. 59. with a dat. of the thing, in the sense of commanding (see 2 c. below), Mt. xxi. 19; Lk. xvii. 6; in the sense of asking, imploring, Lk. xxiii. 30; Rev. vi. 16. λέγω τινί τι, *to tell a thing to one*: Mt. x. 27; 2 Th. ii. 5; τὴν ἀλήθειαν, Jn. xvi. 7; μυστήριον, 1 Co. xv. 51; παραβολήν, Lk. xviii. 1; of a promise, Rev. ii. 7, 11, 17, 29; iii. 6; i. q. *to unfold, explain,* Mk. x. 32; foll. by indirect disc., Mt. xxi. 27; Mk. xi. 33; Lk. xx. 8; τινί τινα, to speak to one about one, Jn. viii. 27; Phil. iii. 18. **i.** λέγω foll. by prepositions: πρός τινα, which denotes — either *to one* (equiv. to the dat.): foll. by direct disc., Mk. iv. 41; x. 26; Lk. viii. 25; ix. 23; xvi. 1; Jn. ii. 3; iii. 4; iv. 15; vi. 5; viii. 31; Acts iii. 7 [R G], 12; xxviii. 4, 17; foll. by ὅτι recitative, Lk. iv. 21; πρός τινά τι, Lk. xi. 53 R G L Tr mrg.; xxiv 10; — or *as respects one, in reference to one* [cf. B. § 133, 3; W. § 31, 5; 405 (378); Krüger § 48, 7, 13; Bleek on Heb. i. 7; Meyer on Ro. x. 21]: Lk. xii. 41; Heb. i. 7, [al. add 8, 13; vii. 21]; μετά τινος, to speak with one, Jn. xi. 56; περί τινος, of, concerning, one [cf. W. § 47, 4], Mt. xxi. 45; Jn. i. 47 (48); ii. 21; xi. 13; xiii. 18, 22; Heb. ix. 5; περί τινος, ὅτι, Lk. xxi. 5; τὶ περί τινος, Jn. i. 22; ix. 17; Acts viii. 34; Tit. ii. 8; τινὶ περί τινος, Mt. xi. 7; Mk. i. 30; viii. 30 [Lchm. εἴπωσιν]; πρός τινα περί τινος, Lk. vii. 24; ὑπέρ τινος, to speak for, on behalf of, one, to defend one, Acts xxvi. 1 [L T Tr WH mrg. περί]; ἐπί τινα, to speak in reference to, *of* [see ἐπί, C. I. 2 g. γγ.; B. § 147, 23], one, Heb. vii. 13; εἰς τινα (τὶ βλασφημῶν), against one, Lk. xxii. 65; in speaking to have reference to one, speak with respect to one, Acts ii. 25 [cf. W. 397 (371)]; in speaking to refer (a thing) to one, with regard to, Eph. v. 32; εἰς τὸν κόσμον, to the world (see εἰς, A. I. 5 b.), Jn. viii. 26 [L T Tr WH λαλῶ]. **k.** with adverbs, or with phrases having adverbial force: καλῶς, *rightly,* Jn. viii. 48; xiii. 13; ὡσαύτως, Mk. xiv. 31; τὶ κατὰ συγγνώμην, ἐπιταγήν, by way of advice [concession (see συγγνώμη)], by way of command, 1 Co. vii. 6; 2 Co. viii. 8; κατὰ ἄνθρωπον [see ἄνθρωπος, 1 c.], Ro. iii. 5; Gal. iii. 15; 1 Co. ix. 8; Λυκαονιστί, Acts xiv. 11. In conformity with the several contexts where it is used, λέγω, like the Lat. *dico,* is **2.** specifically **a.** i. q. *to asseverate, affirm, aver, maintain*: foll. by an acc. with inf., Mt. xxii. 23; Mk. xii. 18; Lk. xx. 41; xxiii. 2; xxiv. 23; Acts v. 36; viii. 9; xvii. 7; xxviii. 6; Ro. xv. 8; 2 Tim. ii. 18; Rev. ii. 9; iii. 9; with the included idea of *insisting on,* περιτέμνεσθαι (*that you must be* [cf. W. § 44, 3 b.; B. § 141, 2]), Acts xv. 24 Rec.; with the simple inf. without a subject-acc., Lk. xxiv. 23; Jas. ii. 14; 1 Jn. ii. 6, 9; foll. by ὅτι (where the acc. with inf. might have been used), Mt. xvii. 10; Mk. ix. 11; xii. 35; Lk. ix. 7; Jn. iv. 20; xii. 34; 1 Co. xv. 12; λέγω τινὶ ὅτι etc. to declare to one that etc. [cf. B. § 141, 1]: Mt. iii. 9; v. 20, 22; xii. 36; xiii. 17; xvii. 12; xxi. 43 [WH mrg. om. ὅτι]; xxvi. 21]; Mk. ix. 13; xiv. 18,

25, 30; Lk. iii. 8; x. 12; xiii. 35 [Tr WH om. L br. ὅτι];
xiv. 24; xviii. 8; xix. 26, 40 [WH txt. om. Tr br. ὅτι];
xxi. 3; xxii. 16, 37, etc.; Jn. iii. 11; v. 24 sq.; viii. 34;
x. 7 [Tr WH om. L br. ὅτι]; xvi. 20; Gal. v. 2; λέγω
τινά, ὅτι, by familiar attraction [cf. W. § 66, 5 a.; B.
§ 151, 1] for λέγω, ὅτι τις: Jn. viii. 54; ix. 19; x. 36
(where for ὑμεῖς λέγετε, ὅτι οὗτος, ὃν ... ἀπέστειλε, βλασφημεῖ; the indirect discourse passes into the direct, and
βλασφημεῖς is put for βλασφημεῖ [B. § 141, 1]).   b.
i. q. to teach: with dat. of pers. foll. by direct disc., 1 Co.
vii. 8, 12; τί τινι, Jn. xvi. 12; Acts i. 3; τοῦτο foll. by
ὅτι, 1 Th. iv. 15.   c. to exhort, advise; to command,
direct: with an acc. of the thing, Lk. vi. 46; λέγουσι (sc.
αὐτά) κ. οὐ ποιοῦσιν, Mt. xxiii. 3; τί τινι, Mk. xiii. 37;
Jn. ii. 5; τινί foll. by an imperative, Mt. v. 44; Mk. ii.
11; Lk. vii. 14; xi. 9; xii. 4; xvi. 9; Jn. ii. 8; xiii. 29;
1 Co. vii. 12; λέγω with an inf. of the thing to be done
or to be avoided [cf. W. § 44, 3 b.; B. § 141, 2]: Mt.
v. 34, 39; Acts xxi. 4, 21; Ro. ii. 22; xii. 3; foll. by
ἵνα, Acts xix. 4; περί τινος (gen. of the thing) foll. by
ἵνα, 1 Jn. v. 16, (see ἵνα, II. 2 b.); foll. by μή with subjunc.
2 Co. xi. 16.   in the sense of asking, seeking, entreating:
with dat. of pers. foll. by an impv., 1 Co. x. 15; 2 Co.
vi. 13; foll. by an inf. [W. 316 (296 sq.); B. u. s.], Rev.
x. 9 [Rec. impv.]. χαίρειν τινὶ λέγω, to give one a greeting, bid him welcome, salute him, 2 Jn. 10 sq. (see χαίρω,
fin.).   d. to point out with words, intend, mean, mean
to say, (often so in Grk. writ.; cf. Passow s. v. p. 30ᵃ;
[L. and S. s. v. C. 10]): τινά, Mk. xiv. 71; Jn. vi. 71;
τί, 1 Co. x. 29; τοῦτο foll. by direct disc., Gal. iii. 17;
τοῦτο foll. by ὅτι, 1 Co. i. 12.   e. to call by a name, to
call, name; i. q. καλῶ τινα with acc. of pred.: τί με λέγεις
ἀγαθόν; Mk. x. 18; Lk. xviii. 19; add, Mk. xii. 37; Jn. v.
18; xv. 15; Acts x. 28; [1 Co. xii. 3 RG]; Rev. ii. 20;
pass. with predicate nom.: Mt. xiii. 55; 1 Co. viii. 5;
Eph. ii. 11; 2 Th. ii. 4; Heb. xi. 24; ὁ λεγόμενος, with
pred. nom. he that is surnamed, Mt. i. 16 (so xxvii. 17);
x. 2; Jn. xx. 24; Col. iv. 11; he that is named: Mt. ix.
9; xxvi. 3, 14; xxvii. 16; Mk. xv. 7; Lk. xxii. 47; Jn.
ix. 11; cf. Fritzsche on Mt. p. 31 sq.; of things, places,
cities, etc.: τὸ ὄνομα λέγεται, Rev. viii. 11; ptcp. called,
Mt. ii. 23; xxvi. 36; xxvii. 33; Jn. iv. 5; xi. 54; xix.
13; Acts iii. 2; vi. 9; Heb. ix. 3; with Ἑβραϊστί added,
Jn. xix. 13, 17; [cf. v. 2 Tdf.]; applied to foreign words
translated into Greek, in the sense that is: Mt. xxvii.
33; Jn. iv. 25; xi. 16; xxi. 2; also ὃ λέγεται, Jn. xx. 16;
ὃ λέγεται ἑρμηνευόμενον [L TrWH μεθερμ.], Jn. i. 38 (39);
διερμην. λέγεται, Acts ix. 36.   f. to speak out, speak
of, mention: τί, Eph. v. 12 (with which cf. ὀκνῶ καὶ λέγειν,
Plat. rep. 5 p. 465 c.); [Mk. vii. 36 T Tr txt. WH.   On
the apparent ellipsis of λέγω in 2 Co. ix. 6, cf. W. 596
sq. (555); B. 394 (338).   COMP.: ἀντι-, δια- (-μαι), ἐκ-,
ἐπι-, κατα-, παρα- (-μαι), προ-, συλ-λέγω; cf. the catalogue
of comp. in Schmidt, Syn. ch. 1, 60.]

3005   λεῖμμα [WH λίμμα, see their App. p. 154 and cf. I, ι],
-τος, τό, (λείπω), a remnant: Ro. xi. 5. (Hdt. 1, 119;
Plut. de profect. in virtut. c. 5; for שְׁאֵרִית, 2 K. xix. 4.)*

3006   λεῖος, -εία, -εῖον, [(cf. Lat. levis)], smooth, level: opp.

to τραχύς, of ways, Lk. iii. 5. (Is. xl. 4 Alex.; Prov. ii.
20; 1 S. xvii. 40; in Grk. writ. fr. Hom. down.)*

3007   λείπω; [2 aor. subj. 3 pers. sing. λίπῃ, Tit. iii. 13 TWH
mrg.; pres. pass. λείπομαι; fr. Hom. down];   1.
trans. to leave, leave behind, forsake; pass. to be left behind (prop. by one's rival in a race, hence),   a. to
lag, be inferior: ἐν μηδενί, Jas. i. 4 (Hdt. 7, 8, 1); [al.
associate this ex. with the two under b.].   b. to be
destitute of, to lack: with gen. of the thing, Jas. i. 5; ii.
15, (Soph., Plat., al.).   2. intrans. to be wanting or
absent, to fail: λείπει τί τινι, Lk. xviii. 22; Tit. iii. 13,
(Polyb. 10, 18, 8; al.); τὰ λείποντα, the things that remain [so Justin Mart. apol. 1, 52, cf. 32; but al. are
wanting], Tit. i. 5. [COMP.: ἀπο-, δια-, ἐκ-, ἐπι-, κατα-,
ἐν-κατα-, περι-, ὑπο-λείπω.]*

3008   λειτουργέω, ptcp. λειτουργῶν; 1 aor. inf. λειτουργῆσαι;
(fr. λειτουργός, q. v.);   1. in Attic, esp. the orators,
to serve the state at one's own cost; to assume an office
which must be administered at one's own expense; to discharge a public office at one's own cost; to render public
service to the state, (cf. Melanchthon in Apol. Confes.
August. p. 270 sq. [Corpus Reformat. ed. Bindseil [post
Bretschn.] vol. xxvii. p. 623, and F. Francke, Conf. Luth.,
Pt. i. p. 271 note (Lips. 1846)]; Wolf, Dem. Lept. p.
lxxxv. sqq.; Böckh, Athen. Staatshaush. i. p. 480 sqq.;
Lübker, Reallex. des class. Alterth. [or Smith, Dict. of
Grk. and Rom. Antiq.] s. v. λειτουργία).   2. univ.
to do a service, perform a work; Vulg. ministro, [A. V.
to minister];   a. of the priests and Levites who were
busied with the sacred rites in the tabernacle or the
temple (so Sept. often for שֵׁרֵת; as Num. xviii. 2; Ex.
xxviii. 31, 39; xxix. 30; Joel i. 9, etc.; several times for
עָבַד, Num. iv. 37, 39; xvi. 9; xviii. 6 sq.; add, Sir. iv. 14
[xlv. 15; l. 14; Judith iv. 14]; 1 Macc. x. 42; [Philo,
vit. Moys. iii. 18; cf. ὑμῖν λειτουργοῦσι κ. αὐτοὶ τὴν λει-
τουργίαν τῶν προφητῶν κ. διδασκάλων (of bishops and
deacons), Teaching of the Twelve Apost. c. 15 (cf. Clem.
Rom. 1 Cor. 44, 2 etc.)]): Heb. x. 11.   b. λ. τῷ κυρίῳ,
of Christians serving Christ, whether by prayer, or by
instructing others concerning the way of salvation, or in
some other way: Acts xiii. 2; cf. De Wette ad loc.   c.
of those who aid others with their resources, and relieve their poverty: τινὶ ἔν τινι, Ro. xv. 27, cf. Sir. x. 25.*

3009   λειτουργία, -ας, ἡ, (fr. λειτουργέω, q. v.);   1. prop.
a public office which a citizen undertakes to administer at
his own expense: Plat. legg. 12 p. 949 c.; Lys. p. 163, 22;
Isocr. p. 391 d.; Theophr. Char. 20 (23), 5; 23 (29), 4,
and others.   2. univ. any service: of military service, Polyb.; Diod. 1, 63. 73; of the service of workmen, c. 21; of that done to nature in the cohabitation
of man and wife, Aristot. oec. 1, 3 p. 1343ᵇ, 20.   3. in
biblical Greek   a. the service or ministry of the priests
relative to the prayers and sacrifices offered to God: Lk. i.
23; Heb. viii. 6; ix. 21, (for עֲבֹדָה, Num. viii. 22; xvi. 9;
xviii. 4; 2 Chr. xxxi. 2; Diod. 1, 21; Joseph.; [Philo de
caritat. § 1 sub fin.; al.; see Soph. Lex. s. v.]); hence
the phrase in Phil. ii. 17, explained s. v. θυσία, b. fin.
[(cf. Bp. Lghtft. on Clem. Rom. 1 Cor. 44)].   b. a

3010 *gift* or *benefaction*, for the relief of the needy (see λειτουργέω, 2 c.) : 2 Co. ix. 12; Phil. ii. 30.*

λειτουργικός, -ή, -όν, (λειτουργία), *relating to the performance of service, employed in ministering*: σκεύη, Num. iv. [12], 26, etc.; στολαί, Ex. xxxi. 10, etc.; πνεύματα, of angels executing God's behests, Heb. i. 14; also αἱ λειτ. τοῦ θεοῦ δυνάμεις, Ignat. ad Philad. 9 (longer recension); τὸ πᾶν πλῆθος τῶν ἀγγέλων αὐτοῦ, πῶς τῷ θελήματι αὐτοῦ λειτουργοῦσι παρεστῶτες, Clem. Rom. 1 Cor. 34, 5, cf. Dan. (Theodot.) vii. 10. (Not found in prof. auth.)*

3011 **λειτουργός, -οῦ, ὁ,** (fr. ΕΡΓΩ i. e. ἐργάζομαι, and unused λεῖτος i. q. λήϊτος equiv. to δημόσιος public, belonging to the state (Hesych.), and this from λεώς Attic for λαός), Sept. for מְשָׁרֵת (Piel ptcp. of שָׁרַת); **1.** *a public minister; a servant of the state:* τῆς πόλεως, Inscrr.; of the lictors, Plut. Rom. 26; (it has not yet been found in its primary and proper sense, of one who at Athens assumes a public office to be administered at his own expense [cf. L. and S. s. v. I.]; see λειτουργέω). **2.** univ. *a minister, servant:* so of military laborers, often in Polyb.; of the servants of a king, 1 K. x. 5; Sir. x. 2; [of Joshua, Josh. i. 1 Alex.; univ. 2 S. xiii. 18 (cf. 17)]; of the servants of the priests, joined with ὑπηρέται, Dion. Hal. antt. 2, 73; τῶν ἁγίων, of the temple, i. e. *one busied with holy things,* of a priest, Heb. viii. 2, cf. [Philo, alleg. leg. iii. § 46]; Neh. x. 39; Sir. vii. 30; τῶν θεῶν, of heathen priests, Dion. H. 2, 22 cf. 73; Plut. mor. p.417 a.; Ἰησοῦ Χριστοῦ, of Paul likening himself to a priest, Ro. xv. 16; plur. τοῦ θεοῦ, those by whom God administers his affairs and executes his decrees: so of magistrates, Ro. xiii. 6; of angels, Heb. i. 7 fr. Ps. ciii. (civ.) 4 [cf. Philo de caritat. § 3]; τῆς χάριτος τοῦ θεοῦ, those whose ministry the grace of God made use of for proclaiming to men the necessity of repentance, as Noah, Jonah: Clem. Rom. 1 Cor. 8, 1 cf. c. 7; τὸν ἀπόστολον καὶ λειτουργὸν ὑμῶν τῆς χρείας μου, by whom ye have sent to me those things which may minister to my needs, Phil. ii. 25.*

see 2982 [λεμά, see λαμά.]

3012 **λέντιον, -ου, τό,** (a Lat. word, *linteum*), *a linen cloth, towel* (Arr. peripl. mar. rubr. 4): of the *towel* or *apron,* which servants put on when about to work (Suet. Calig. 26), Jn. xiii. 4 sq.; with which it was supposed the nakedness of persons undergoing crucifixion was covered, Ev. Nicod. c. 10; cf. *Thilo, Cod. Apocr.* p. 582 sq.*

3013 **λεπίς, -ίδος, ἡ,** (λέπω to strip off the rind or husk, to peel, to scale), *a scale:* Acts ix. 18. (Sept.; Aristot. al. [cf. Hdt. 7, 61].)*

3014 **λέπρα, -ας, ἡ,** (fr. the adj. λεπρός, q. v.), Hebr. צָרַעַת, *leprosy* [lit. morbid *scaliness*], a most offensive, annoying, dangerous, cutaneous disease, the virus of which generally pervades the whole body; common in Egypt and the East (Lev. xiii. sq.): Mt. viii. 3; Mk. i. 42; Lk. v. 12 sq. (Hdt., Theophr., Joseph., Plut., al.) [Cf. *Orelli* in Herzog 2 s. v. Aussatz; *Greenhill* in Bible Educator iv. 76 sq. 174 sq.; *Ginsburg* in Alex.'s Kitto s. v.; *Edersheim,* Jesus the Messiah, i. 492 sqq.; McCl. and S. s. v.]*

3015 **λεπρός, -οῦ, ὁ,** (as if for λεπερός, fr. λεπίς. λέπος -εος,

τό, a scale, husk, bark); **1.** in Grk. writ. *scaly, rough.* **2.** specifically, *leprous, affected with leprosy,* (Sept. several times for מְצֹרָע and צָרוּעַ; [Theophr. c. p. 2, 6, 4] see λέπρα): Mt. viii. 2; x. 8; xi. 5; Mk. i. 40; Lk. iv. 27; vii. 22; xvii. 12; of one [(Simon)] who had formerly been a leper, Mt. xxvi. 6; Mk. xiv. 3.*

3016 **λεπτός, -ή, -όν,** (λέπω to strip off the bark, to peel), *thin; small;* τὸ λεπτόν, *a very small brass coin,* equiv. to the eighth part of an as, [A. V. *a mite*; cf. Alex.'s Kitto and B.D. s. v.; cf. *F. R. Conder* in the Bible Educator, iii. 179]: Mk. xii. 42; Lk. xii. 59; xxi. 2; (Alciphr. epp. 1, 9 adds κέρμα; Pollux, onom. 9, 6, sect. 92, supplies νόμισμα).*

3017 & 3018 **Λευΐ and Λευΐς** (T Tr (yet see below) WH Λευείς [but Lchm. -ῑς; see ει, ι]), gen. Λευΐ (T Tr WH Λευεί), acc. Λευΐν (T WH Λευείν, so Tr exc. in Mk. ii. 14), [B. 21 (19); W. § 10, 1], ὁ, (Hebr. לֵוִי a joining, fr. לָוָה, cf. Gen. xxix. 34), *Levi*; **1.** the third son of the patriarch Jacob by his wife Leah, the founder of the tribe of Israelites which bears his name: Heb. vii. 5, 9; [Rev. vii. 7]. **2.** the son of Melchi, one of Christ's ancestors: Lk. iii. 24. **3.** the son of Simeon, also an ancestor of Christ: Lk. iii. 29. **4.** the son of Alphæus, a collector of customs [(A. V. *publican*)]: Mk. ii. 14 [here WH (rejected) mrg. Ἰάκωβον (see their note ad loc., cf. *Weiss* in Mey. on Mt. 7te Aufl. p. 2)]; Lk. v. 27, 29; acc. to com. opinion he is the same as *Matthew* the apostle (Mt. ix. 9); but cf. *Grimm* in the Theol. Stud. u. Krit. for 1870 p. 727 sqq.; [their identity is denied also by Nicholson on Matt. ix. 9; yet see *Patritius,* De Evangeliis, l. i. c. i. quaest. 1; *Venables* in Alex.'s Kitto, s. v. Matthew; *Meyer,* Com. on Matt., Intr. § 1].*

3019 **Λευΐτης** (T WH Λευείτης [so Tr exc. in Acts iv. 36; see ει, ι]), -ου, ὁ, *a Levite;* **a.** one of Levi's posterity. **b.** in a narrower sense those were called Levites (Hebr. לְוִיִּם, בְּנֵי לֵוִי) who, not being of the race of Aaron, for whom alone the priesthood was reserved, served as assistants of the priests. It was their duty to keep the sacred utensils and the temple clean, to provide the sacred loaves, to open and shut the gates of the temple, to sing sacred hymns in the temple, and do many other things; so Lk. x. 32; Jn. i. 19; Acts iv. 36; [(Plut. quaest. conv. l. iv. quaest. 6, 5; Philo de vit. Moys. i. § 58). See BB.DD. s. v. Levites; *Edersheim,* The Temple, 2d ed. p. 63 sqq.] *

3020 **Λευϊτικός** [T WH Λευειτ.; see ει, ι], -ή, -όν, *Levitical, pertaining to the Levites*: Heb. vii. 11. [Philo de vit. Moys. iii. § 20.] *

3021 **λευκαίνω**: 1 aor. ἐλεύκανα [cf. W. § 13, 1 d.; B. 41 (35)]; (λευκός); fr. Hom. down; Sept. for הִלְבִּין; *to whiten, make white:* τί, Mk. ix. 3; Rev. vii. 14.*

see 1039 [λευκοβύσσινον: Rev. xix. 14 WH mrg., al. βύσσινον λευκ. see in βύσσινος.]

3022 **λευκός, -ή, -όν,** (λεύσσω to see, behold, look at; akin to Lat. *luceo,* Germ. *leuchten;* cf. Curtius p. 113 and § 87; [Vaniček p. 817]), Sept. for לָבָן; **1.** *light, bright, brilliant:* τὰ ἱμάτια ... λευκὰ ὡς τὸ φῶς, Mt. xvii. 2; esp. *bright* or *brilliant from* whiteness, (dazzling) *white:*

spoken of the garments of angels, and of those exalted to the splendor of the heavenly state, Mk. xvi. 5; Lk. ix. 29; Acts i. 10; Rev. iii. 5; iv. 4; vi. 11; vii. 9, 13; xix. 14, (shining or white garments were worn on festive and state occasions, Eccles. ix. 8; cf. Heindorf on Hor. sat. 2, 2, 61); with ὡσεὶ or ὡς ὁ χιών added: Mk. ix. 3 R L; Mt. xxviii. 3, (ἵπποι λευκότεροι χιόνος, Hom. Il. 10, 437); ἐν λευκοῖς sc. ἱματίοις (added in Rev. iii. 5; iv. 4), Jn. xx. 12; Rev. iii. 4; cf. W. 591 (550); [B. 82 (72)]; used of white garments as the sign of innocence and purity of soul, Rev. iii. 18; of the heavenly throne, Rev. xx. 11.   **2.** (dead) *white*: Mt. v. 36 (opp. to μέλας); Rev. i. 14; ii. 17; iv. 4; vi. 2; xiv. 14; xix. 11; spoken of the whitening color of ripening grain, Jn. iv. 35.*

3023   **λέων**, -οντος, ὁ, [fr. Hom. down], Sept. for אֲרִי, אַרְיֵה, אַרְיֵה, כְּפִיר (a young lion), etc.; *a lion*: **a.** prop.: Heb. xi. 33; 1 Pet. v. 8; Rev. iv. 7; ix. 8, 17; x. 3; xiii. 2.   **b.** metaph. ἐρρύσθην ἐκ στόματος λέοντος, I was rescued out of the most imminent peril of death, 2 Tim. iv. 17 (the fig. does not lie in the word lion alone, but in the whole phrase); equiv. to *a brave and mighty hero*: Rev. v. 5, where there is allusion to Gen. xlix. 9; cf. Nah. ii. 13.*

3024   **λήθη**, -ης, ἡ, (λήθω to escape notice, λήθομαι to forget), [fr. Hom. down], *forgetfulness*: λήθην τινὸς λαβεῖν (see λαμβάνω, I. 6), 2 Pet. i. 9.*

see 2982   [λημά, see λαμά.]

3025   **ληνός**, -οῦ, ἡ, (also ὁ, Gen. xxx. 38, 41 [cf. below]), [Theocr., Diod., al.]; **1.** *a tub- or trough-shaped receptacle, vat, in which grapes are trodden* [A. V. *wine-press*] (Hebr. גַּת): Rev. xiv. 20; xix. 15; τὴν ληνὸν ... τὸν μέγαν (for R Tr mrg. τὴν μεγάλην), Rev. xiv. 19 — a variation in gender which (though not rare in Hebrew, see *Gesenius*, Lehrgeb. p. 717) can hardly be matched in Grk. writ.; cf. W. 526 (490) and his Exeget. Studd. i. p. 153 sq.; B. 81 (71).   **2.** i. q. ὑπολήνιον (Is. xvi. 10; Mk. xii. 1) or προλήνιον (Is. v. 2), Hebr. יֶקֶב, *the lower vat*, dug in the ground, into which the must or new wine flowed from the press: Mt. xxi. 33. Cf. *Win.* RWB. s. v. Kelter; *Roskoff* in Schenkel iii. 513; [BB.DD. s. v. Wine-press].*

3026   **λῆρος**, -ου, ὁ, *idle talk, nonsense*: Lk. xxiv. 11. (4 Macc. v. 10; Xen. an. 7, 7, 41; Arstph., al.; plur. joined with παιδιαί, Plat. Protag. p. 347 d.; with φλυαρίαι, ib. Hipp. maj. p. 304 b.)*

3027   **λῃστής**, -οῦ, ὁ, (for λῃϊστής fr. λῄϊζομαι, to plunder, and this fr. Ion. and Epic λῃΐς, for which the Attics use λεία, booty), [fr. Soph. and Hdt. down], *a robber; a plunderer, freebooter, brigand*: Mt. xxvi. 55; Mk. xiv. 48; Lk. xiii. 52; Jn. x. 1; xviii. 40; plur., Mt. xxi. 13; xxvii. 38, 44; Mk. xi. 17; xv. 27; Lk. x. 30, 36; xix. 46; Jn. x. 8; 2 Co. xi. 26. [Not to be confounded with κλέπτης *thief*, one who takes property by stealth, (although the distinction is obscured in A. V.); cf. Trench § xliv.]*

3028   **λῆψις** (L T Tr WH λήμψις, see M, μ), -εως, ἡ, (λαμβάνω, λήψομαι), [fr. Soph. and Thuc. down], *a receiving*: Phil. iv. 15, on which pass. see δόσις, 1.*

3029   **λίαν** (in Hom. and Ion. λίην), [for λι-λαν, λάω to desire; cf. Curtius § 532], adv., *greatly, exceedingly*: Mt. ii. 16;

iv. 8; viii. 28; xxvii. 14; Mk. i. 35; ix. 3; xvi. 2; Lk. xxiii. 8; 2 Tim. iv. 15; 2 Jn. 4; 3 Jn. 3; (2 Macc. xi. 1; 4 Macc. viii. 16; Tob. ix. 4, etc.; for מְאֹד, Gen. i. 31; iv. 5; 1 S. xi. 15); λίαν ἐκ περισσοῦ, *exceedingly beyond measure*, Mk. vi. 51 [WH om. Tr br. ἐκπερισ.]. See ὑπερλίαν.*

λίβανος, -ου, ὁ, (more rarely ἡ [cf. Lob. u. i.]);   **1.** *the frankincense-tree* (Pind., Hdt., Soph., Eur., Theophr., al.).   **2.** *frankincense* (Hebr. לְבֹנָה; Lev. ii. 1 sq.; 16; Is. lx. 6, etc.): Mt. ii. 11; Rev. xviii. 13; (Soph., Theophr., al.). Cf. *Lob.* ad Phryn. p. 187; [*Vaniček*, Fremdwörter, s. v. On frankincense see esp. *Birdwood* in the Bible Educator, i. 328 sqq. 374 sqq.]*   **3030**

λιβανωτός, -οῦ, ὁ, (λίβανος);   **1.** in prof. auth. *frankincense*, the gum exuding ἐκ τοῦ λιβάνου, (1 Chr. ix. 29; Hdt., Menand., Eur., Plat., Diod., Hdian., al.).   **2.** *a censer* (which in prof. auth. is ἡ λιβανωτίς [or rather -τρίς, cf. *Lob.* ad Phryn. p. 255]): Rev. viii. 3, 5.*   **3031**

λιβερτῖνος, -ου, ὁ, a Lat. word, *libertinus*, i. e. either *one who has been liberated from slavery, a freedman*, or *the son of a freedman* (as distinguished fr. *ingenuus*, i. e. the son of a free man): ἡ συναγωγὴ ἡ λεγομένη (or τῶν λεγομένων Tdf.) λιβερτίνων, Acts vi. 9. Some suppose these libertini [A.V. *Libertines*] to have been manumitted R o m a n slaves, who having embraced Judaism had their synagogue at Jerusalem; and they gather as much from Tac. Ann. 2, 85, where it is related that four thousand libertini, infected with the Jewish superstition, were sent into Sardinia. Others, owing to the names Κυρηναίων καὶ Ἀλεξανδρέων that follow, think that a geographical meaning is demanded for λιβερτ., and suppose that Jews are spoken of, the dwellers in L i b e r t u m, a city or region of proconsular Africa. But the existence of a city or region called L i b e r t u m is a conjecture which has nothing to rest on but the mention of a bishop with the prefix "libertinensis" at the synod of Carthage A. D. 411. Others with far greater probability appeal to Philo, leg. ad Gaium § 23, and understand the word as denoting Jews who had been made captives by the Romans under Pompey but were afterwards set free; and who, although they had fixed their abode at Rome, had built at their own expense a synagogue at Jerusalem which they frequented when in that city. The name *Libertines* adhered to them to distinguish them from the f r e e - b o r n Jews who had subsequently taken up their residence at Rome. Cf. *Win.* RWB. s. v. Libertiner; *Hausrath* in Schenkel iv. 38 sq.; [B. D. s. v. Libertines. Evidence seems to have been discovered of the existence of a "synagogue of the libertines" at Pompeii; cf. *De Rossi*, Bullet. di Arch. Christ. for 1864, pp. 70, 92 sq.]*   **3032**

Λιβύη, -ης, ἡ, *Libya*, a large region of northern Africa, bordering on Egypt. In that portion of it which had Cyrene for its capital and was thence called Libya Cyrenaica (ἡ πρὸς Κυρήνην Λιβύη, Joseph. antt. 16, 6, 1; ἡ Λ. ἡ κατὰ Κυρήνην [q. v.], Acts ii. 10) dwelt many Jews (Joseph. antt. 14, 7, 2; 16, 6, 1; b. j. 7, 11; c. Apion. 2, 4 [where cf. Müller's notes]): Acts ii. 10.*   **3033**

λιθάζω; 1 aor. ἐλίθασα; 1 aor. pass. ἐλιθάσθην; (λίθος);   **3034**

to stone; i. e.   **a.** *to overwhelm* or *bury with stones*, (*lapidibus cooperio*, Cic.) : τινά, of stoning, which was a Jewish mode of punishment, (cf. *Win.* RWB. s. v. Steinigung; [B. D. s. v. Punishment, III. a. 1]) : Jn. x. 31–33 (where λιθάζετε and λιθάζομεν are used of the act of beginning; [cf. W. § 40, 2 a.; B. 205 (178)]); Jn. xi. 8; Heb. xi. 37.   **b.** *to pelt one with stones, in order either to wound* or *to kill him*: Acts xiv. 19; pass., Acts v. 26 [cf. W. 505 (471); B. 242 (208)]; 2 Co. xi. 25. (Aristot., Polyb., Strab.; λιθάζειν ἐν λίθοις, 2 S. xvi. 6.)   [COMP.: κατα-λιθάζω.] *

3035   **λίθινος, -η, -ον**, (λίθος); fr. Pind. down; *of stone*: Jn. ii. 6; 2 Co. iii. 3; Rev. ix. 20.*

3036   **λιθο-βολέω, -ῶ**; impf. 3 pers. plur. ἐλιθοβόλουν; 1 aor. ἐλιθοβόλησα; Pass., pres. λιθοβολοῦμαι; 1 fut. λιθοβοληθήσομαι; (λιθοβόλος, and this fr. λίθος and βάλλω [cf. W. 102 (96); 25, 26]); Sept. for סָקַל and רָגַם; i. q. λιθάζω (q. v.), *to stone*; i. e.   **a.** *to kill by stoning, to stone* (of a species of punishment, see λιθάζω): τινά, Mt. xxi. 35; xxiii. 37; Lk. xiii. 34; Acts vii. 58 sq.; pass., Jn. viii. 5; Heb. xii. 20.   **b.** *to pelt with stones*: τινά, Mk. xii. 4 [Rec.]; Acts xiv. 5. ([Diod. 17, 41, 8]; Plut. mor. p. 1011 e.)*

3037   **λίθος, -ου, ὁ**, Sept. for אֶבֶן, [fr. Hom. down]; *a stone*: of small stones, Mt. iv. 6; vii. 9; Lk. iii. 8; iv. [3], 11; xi. 11; xxii. 41; Jn. viii. 7; plur., Mt. iii. 9; iv. 3; Mk. v. 5; Lk. iii. 8; xix. 40; Jn. viii. 59; x. 31; of a large stone, Mt. xxvii. 60, 66; xxviii. 2; Mk. xv. 46; xvi. 3 sq.; Lk. xxiv. 2; Jn. xi. 38 sq. 41; xx. 1; of building stones, Mt. xxi. 42, 44 [T om. L WH Tr mrg. br. the vs.]; xxiv. 2; Mk. xii. 10; xiii. 1 sq.; Lk. xix. 44; xx. 17 sq.; xxi. 5 sq.; Acts iv. 11; 1 Pet. ii. 7; metaph. of Christ: λίθος ἀκρογωνιαῖος (q. v.), ἐκλεκτός (cf. 2 Esdr. v. 8), ἔντιμος, 1 Pet. ii. 6 (Is. xxviii. 16); ζῶν (see ζάω, II. b.), 1 Pet. ii. 4; λίθος προσκόμματος, one whose words, acts, end, men (so stumble at) take such offence at, that they reject him and thus bring upon themselves ruin, ibid. 8 (7); Ro. ix. 33; of Christians: λίθοι ζῶντες, living stones (see ζάω, u. s.), of which the temple of God is built, 1 Pet. ii. 5; of the truths with which, as with building materials, a teacher builds Christians up in wisdom, λίθοι τίμιοι, costly stones, 1 Co. iii. 12. λίθος μυλικός, Mk. ix. 42 R G; Lk. xvii. 2 L T Tr WH, cf. Rev. xviii. 21. of precious stones, gems: λίθ. τίμιος, Rev. xvii. 4; xviii. 12, 16; xxi. 11, 19, (2 S. xii. 30; 1 K. x. 2, 11); ἴασπις, Rev. iv. 3; ἐνδεδυμένοι λίθον (for R G T λίνον) καθαρόν, Rev. xv. 6 L Tr txt. WH (Ezek. xxviii. 13 πάντα [or πᾶν] λίθον χρηστὸν ἐνδέδεσαι; [see WH. Intr. ad l. c.]); but (against the reading λίθον) [cf. Scrivener, Plain Introduction etc. p. 658]. spec. stones cut in a certain form: stone tablets (engraved with letters), 2 Co. iii. 7; statues of idols, Acts xvii. 29 (Deut. iv. 28; Ezek. xx. 32).*

3038   **λιθό-στρωτος, -ον**, (fr. λίθος and the verbal adj. στρωτός fr. στρώννυμι), *spread* (*paved*) *with stones* (νυμφεῖον, Soph. Antig. 1204–5); τὸ λιθ., substantively, *a mosaic* or *tessellated pavement*: so of a place near the praetorium or palace at Jerusalem, Jn. xix. 13 (see Γαββαθᾶ); of places in the outer courts of the temple, 2 Chr. vii. 3; Joseph.

---

b. j. 6, 1, 8 and 3, 2; of an apartment whose pavement consists of tessellated work, Epict. diss. 4, 7, 37, cf. Esth. i. 6; Suet. Jul. Caes. 46; Plin. h. n. 36, 60 cf. 64.*

3039   **λικμάω, -ῶ**: fut. λικμήσω; (λικμός a winnowing-van); **1.** *to winnow, cleanse away the chaff from grain by winnowing*, (Hom., Xen., Plut., al.; Sept.).   **2.** in a sense unknown to prof. auth., *to scatter* (opp. to συνάγω, Jer. xxxi. (or xxxviii.) 10; add, Is. xvii. 13; Am. ix. 9).   **3.** *to crush to pieces, grind to powder*: τινά, Mt. xxi. 44 [R G L br. WH br.]; Lk. xx. 18; cf. Dan. ii. 44 [Theodot.]; Sap. xi. 19 (18). [But in Dan. l. c. it represents the Aphel of סוֹף *finem facere*, and on Sap. l. c. see Grimm. Many decline to follow the rendering of the Vulg. (*conterere, comminuere*), but refer the exx. under this head to the preceding.] *

3040   **λιμά**, so Tdf. ed. 7, for λαμά, q. v.   see 2982

3040   **λιμήν, -ένος, ὁ**, [allied with λίμνη, q. v.; fr. Hom. down], *a harbor, haven*: Acts xxvii. 8, 12; see καλοὶ λιμένες, p. 322ª.*

3041   **λίμνη, -ης, ἡ**, (fr. λείβω to pour, pour out [cf. Curtius § 541]), [fr. Hom. down], *a lake*: λ. Γεννησαρέτ [q. v.], Lk. v. 1; absol., of the same, Lk. v. 2; viii. 22 sq. 33; τοῦ πυρός, Rev. xix. 20; xx. 10, 14 sq.; καιομένη πυρί, Rev. xxi. 8.*

3042   **λιμός, -οῦ, ὁ**, (and ἡ in Doric and later writ.; so L T Tr WH in Lk. xv. 14; Acts xi. 28; so, too, in Is. viii. 21; 1 K. xviii. 2; cf. Lob. ad Phryn. p. 188; [L. and S. s. v. init.; WH. App. p. 157ª]; B. 12 (11); W. 63 (62) [cf. 36], and 526 (490)); Sept. very often for רָעָב; *hunger*: Lk. xv. 17; Ro. viii. 35; ἐν λιμῷ κ. δίψει, 2 Co. xi. 27; Xen. mem. 1, 4, 13; i. q. *scarcity of harvest, famine*: Lk. iv. 25; xv. 14; Acts vii. 11; xi. 28 [cf. B. 81 (71)]; Rev. vi. 8; xviii. 8; λιμοί, *famines* in divers lands, Mk. xiii. 8; λιμοὶ κ. λοιμοί, Mt. xxiv. 7 [L T Tr txt. WH om. κ. λοιμ.]; Lk. xxi. 11; Theoph. ad Autol. 2, 9; the two are joined in the sing. in Hes. opp. 226; Hdt. 7, 171; Philo, vit. Moys. i. § 19; Plut. de Is. et Osir. 47.*

3043   **λίνον** (Treg. λῖνον [so R G in Mt. as below], incorrectly, for ι is short; [cf. Lipsius, Gramm. Untersuch. p. 42]), -ου, τό, Sept. several times for פִּשְׁתָּה, in Grk. writ. fr. Hom. down, *flax*: Ex. ix. 31; *linen*, as clothing, Rev. xv. 6 R G T Tr mrg.; the wick of a lamp, Mt. xii. 20, after Is. xlii. 3.*

3044   **Λίνος** (not Λῖνος [with R G Tr]); see Passow [or L. and S.] s. v.; cf. Lipsius, Gramm. Untersuch. p. 42), -ου, ὁ, *Linus*, one of Paul's Christian associates; acc. to eccl. tradition bishop of the church at Rome (cf. Hase, Polemik, ed. 3 p. 131; Lipsius, Chronologie d. röm. Bischöfe, p. 146; [Dict. of Chris. Biog. s. v.]): 2 Tim. iv. 21.*

3045   **λιπαρός, -ά, -όν**, (λίπα [or rather, λίπος grease, akin to ἀλείφω]); fr. Hom. down; *fat*: τὰ λιπαρά (joined with τὰ λαμπρά, q. v.) things which pertain to a sumptuous and delicate style of living [A. V. *dainty*], Rev. xviii. 14.*

3046   **λίτρα, -ας, ἡ**, *a pound*, a weight of twelve ounces: Jn. xii. 3; xix. 39. [Polyb. 22, 26, 19; Diod. 14, 116, 7; Plut. Tib. et G. Grac. 2, 3; Joseph. antt. 14, 7, 1; al.] *

3047   **λίψ, λιβός, ὁ**, (fr. λείβω [to pour forth], because it brings moisture); **1.** *the SW. wind* : Hdt. 2, 25 ; Polyb. 10, 10, 3 ; al. **2.** *the quarter of the heavens* whence the SW. wind blows: Acts xxvii. 12 [on which see βλέπω, 3 and κατά, II. 1 c.] (Gen. xiii. 14 ; xx. 1 ; Num. ii. 10 ; Deut. xxxiii. 23).*

3048 **λογία, -ας, ἡ**, (fr. λέγω to collect), (Vulg. *collecta*), *a collection* : of money gathered for the relief of the poor, 1 Co. xvi. 1 sq. (Not found in prof. auth. [cf. W. 25].)*

3049 **λογίζομαι**; impf. ἐλογιζόμην ; 1 aor. ἐλογισάμην ; a depon. verb with 1 aor. pass. ἐλογίσθην and 1 fut. pass. λογισθήσομαι ; in bibl. Grk. also the pres. is used passively (in prof. auth. the pres. ptcp. is once used so, in Hdt. 3, 95 ; [cf. Veitch s. v. ; W. 259 (243) ; B. 52 (46)]) ; (λόγος) ; Sept. for חָשַׁב ; [a favorite word with the apostle Paul, being used (exclusive of quotations) some 27 times in his Epp., and only four times in the rest of the N. T.] ; **1.** (rationes conferre) *to reckon, count, compute, calculate, count over* ; hence **a.** *to take into account, to make account of* : τί τινι, Ro. iv. 3, [4] ; metaph. *to pass to one's account, to impute*, [A. V. *reckon*] : τί, 1 Co. xiii. 5 ; τινί τι, 2 Tim. iv. 16 [A. V. *lay to one's charge*] ; τινὶ δικαιοσύνην, ἁμαρτίαν, Ro. iv. 6, [8 (yet here L mrg. T Tr WH txt. read οὗ)] ; τὰ παραπτώματα, 2 Co. v. 19 ; in imitation of the Hebr. לְ חָשַׁב, λογίζεταί τι (or τις) εἴς τι (equiv. to εἰς τὸ or ὥστε εἶναί τι), *a thing is reckoned as or to be something*, i. e. *as availing for or equivalent to something, as having the like force and weight*, (cf. Fritzsche on Rom. vol. i. p. 137 ; [cf. W. § 29, 3 Note a. ; 228 (214) ; B. § 131, 7 Rem.]) : Ro. ii. 26 ; ix. 8 ; εἰς οὐδέν, Acts xix. 27 ; Is. xl. 17 ; Dan. [(Theodot. ὡς)] iv. 32 ; Sap. iii. 17 ; ix. 6 ; ἡ πίστις εἰς δικαιοσύνην, Ro. iv. 3, 5, 9–11, 22 sq. 24 ; Gal. iii. 6 ; Jas. ii. 23 ; Gen. xv. 6 ; Ps. cv. (cvi.) 31 ; 1 Macc. ii. 52. **b.** i. q. *to number among, reckon with* : τινὰ μετά τινων, Mk. xv. 28 [yet G TWH om. Tr br. the vs.] and Lk. xxii. 37, after Is. liii. 12, where Sept. ἐν τοῖς ἀνόμοις. **c.** *to reckon or account, and treat accordingly* : τινὰ ὥς τι, Ro. viii. 36 fr. Ps. xliii. (xliv.) 23 ; cf. B. 151 (132) ; [W. 602 (560)] ; [Ro. vi. 11 foll. by acc. w. inf., but G L om. Tr br. the inf. ; cf. W. 321 (302)]. **2.** (in animo rationes conferre) *to reckon inwardly, count up or weigh the reasons, to deliberate*, [A. V. *reason*] : πρὸς ἑαυτούς, one addressing himself to another, Mk. xi. 31 R G (πρὸς ἐμαυτόν, with myself, in my mind, Plat. apol. p. 21 d.). **3.** *by reckoning up all the reasons to gather or infer* ; i. e. **a.** *to consider, take account, weigh, meditate on* : τί, a thing, with a view to obtaining it, Phil. iv. 8 ; foll. by ὅτι, Heb. xi. 19 ; [Jn. xi. 50 (Rec. διαλογ.)] ; τοῦτο foll. by ὅτι, 2 Co. x. 11. **b.** *to suppose, deem, judge* : absol. 1 Co. xiii. 11 ; ὡς λογίζομαι, 1 Pet. v. 12 ; τί, anything relative to the promotion of the gospel, 2 Co. iii. 5 ; τὶ εἴς τινα (as respects one) ὑπὲρ (τοῦτο) ὅ etc. to think better of one than agrees with what etc. [' account of one above that which' etc.], 2 Co. xii. 6 ; foll. by ὅτι, Ro. viii. 18 ; τοῦτο foll. by ὅτι, Ro. ii. 3 ; 2 Co. x. 7 ; foll. by an inf. belonging to the subject, 2 Co. xi. 5 ; foll. by an acc. with inf., Ro. iii. 28 ; xiv. 14 ; Phil. iii. 13 [cf. W. 321 (302)] ; τινὰ ὥς τινα, to hold [A. V. ' count'] one as, 2 Co. x. 2 [cf. W. 602 (560)] ;

with a preparatory οὗτως preceding, 1 Co. iv. 1. **c.** *to determine, purpose, decide*, [cf. American ' calculate '], foll. by an inf. (Eur. Or. 555) : 2 Co. x. 2. [COMP. : ἀνα-, δια-, παρα-, συλ-λογίζομαι.] *

3050 **λογικός, -ή, -όν**, (fr. λόγος reason), [Tim. Locr., Dem., al.], *rational* (Vulg. *rationabilis*) ; *agreeable to reason, following reason, reasonable* : λατρεία λογική, the worship which is rendered by the reason or soul, [' spiritual '], Ro. xii. 1 (λογικὴ καὶ ἀναίμακτος προσφορά, of the offering which angels present to God, Test. xii. Patr. [test. Levi § 3] p. 547 ed. Fabric. ; [cf. Athenag. suppl. pro Christ. § 13 fin.]) ; τὸ λογικὸν γάλα, the milk which nourishes the soul (see γάλα), 1 Pet. ii. 2 (λογικὴ τροφή, Eus. h. e. 4, 23 fin.).*

3051 **λόγιον, -ου, τό**, (dimin. of λόγος [so Bleek (on Heb. v. 12) et al. ; al. neut. of λόγιος (Mey. on Ro. iii. 2)]), prop. *a little word* (so Schol. ad Arstph. ran. 969 (973)), *a brief utterance*, in prof. auth. a divine *oracle* (doubtless because oracles were generally brief) ; Hdt., Thuc., Arstph., Eur. ; Polyb. 3, 112, 8 ; 8, 30, 6 ; Diod. 2, 14 ; Ael. v. h. 2, 41 ; of the Sibylline oracles, Diod. p. 602 [fr. l. 34] ; Plut. Fab. 4 ; in Sept. for חֹשֶׁן *the breast-plate* of the high priest, which he wore when he consulted Jehovah, Ex. xxviii. 15 ; xxix. 5, etc. ; [once for אָמַר, of the words of a man, Ps. xviii. (xix.) 15] ; but chiefly for אִמְרָה of any utterance of God, whether precept or promise ; [cf. Philo de congr. erud. grat. § 24 ; de profug. § 11 sub fin.] ; of the prophecies of God in the O. T., Joseph. b. j. 6, 5, 4 ; νόμους καὶ λόγια θεσπισθέντα διὰ προφητῶν καὶ ὕμνους, Philo vit. contempl. § 3 ; τὸ λόγιον τοῦ προφήτου (Moses), vit. Moys. iii. 35, cf. [23, and] de praem. et poen. § 1 init. ; τὰ δέκα λόγια, the ten commandments of God or the decalogue, in Philo, who wrote a special treatise concerning them (Opp. ed. Mang. ii. p. 180 sqq. [ed. Richter iv. p. 246 sqq.]) ; [Constit. Apost. 2, 36 (p. 63, 7 ed. Lagarde)] ; Euseb. h. e. 2, 18. In the N. T. spoken of the words or utterances of God : of the contents of the Mosaic law, Acts vii. 38 ; with τοῦ θεοῦ or θεοῦ added, of his commands in the Mosaic law and his Messianic promises, Ro. iii. 2, cf. Philippi and Umbreit ad loc. ; of the substance of the Christian religion, Heb. v. 12 ; of the utterances of God through Christian teachers, 1 Pet. iv. 11. (In eccl. writ. λόγια τοῦ κυρίου is used of Christ's precepts, by Polyc. ad Philipp. 7, 1 ; κυριακὰ λόγια of the sayings and discourses of Christ which are recorded in the Gospels, by Papias in Euseb. h. e. 3, 39 ; Phot. c. 228 p. 248 [18 ed. Bekk.] ; [τὰ λόγια τ. θεοῦ] of the words and admonitions of God in the sacred Scriptures, Clem. Rom. 1 Cor. 53, 1 [where parallel with αἱ ἱεραὶ γραφαί], cf. 62, 3 ; [and τὰ λόγ. simply, like αἱ γραφαί, of the N e w T. in the interpol. ep. of Ign. ad Smyrn. 3]. Cf. Schwegler [(also Heinichen)], Index iv. ad Euseb. h. e. s. v. λόγιον ; [esp. Soph. Lex. s. v. and Lghtft. in the Contemp. Rev. for Aug. 1875, p. 399 sqq. On the general use of the word cf. Bleek, Br. a. d. Hebr. iii. pp. 114–117].) *

3052 **λόγιος, -ον**, (λόγος), in class. Grk. **1.** *learned*, a man of letters, *skilled in literature and the arts* ; esp. *versed* *in history and antiquities.*　　**2.** *skilled in speech, eloquent*: so Acts xviii. 24 [which, however, al. refer to 1 (finding its explanation in the foll. δυνατὸς κτλ.)]. The use of the word is fully exhibited by *Lobeck* ad Phryn. p. 198. [(Hdt., Eur., al.)]*

3053　**λογισμός, -οῦ, ὁ,** (λογίζομαι);　　**1.** *a reckoning, computation.*　　**2.** *a reasoning*: such as is hostile to the Christian faith, 2 Co. x. 4 (5) [A. V. *imaginations*].　　**3.** *a judgment, decision*: such as conscience passes, Ro. ii. 15 [A. V. *thoughts*]. (Thuc., Xen., Plat., Dem., al.; Sept. for מַחֲשָׁבָה, as Prov. vi. 18; Jer. xi. 19; Ps. xxxii. (xxxiii.) 10.)*

3054　**λογομαχέω, -ῶ;** (fr. λογομάχος, and this fr. λόγος and μάχομαι); *to contend about words*; contextually, *to wrangle about empty and trifling matters*: 2 Tim. ii. 14. (Not found in prof. auth.) *

3055　**λογομαχία, -ας, ἡ,** (λογομαχέω), *dispute about words, war of words, or about trivial and empty things*: plur. 1 Tim. vi. 4. (Not found in prof. auth.) *

3056　**λόγος, -ου, ὁ,** (λέγω), [fr. Hom. down], Sept. esp. for דָּבָר, also for אֹמֶר and מִלָּה; prop. *a collecting, collection*, (see λέγω), — and that, as well of those things which are put together in t h o u g h t, as of those which, having been thought i. e. gathered together in the mind, are expressed in w o r d s. Accordingly, a twofold use of the term is to be distinguished: one which relates to s p e a k i n g, and one which relates to t h i n k i n g.

I. As respects SPEECH:　　**1.** *a word,* yet not in the grammatical sense (i. q. *vocabulum,* the mere name of an object), but language, *vox,* i. e. a word which, uttered by the living v o i c e, embodies a conception or idea; (hence it differs from ῥῆμα and ἔπος [q. v.; cf. also λαλέω, ad init.]): Heb. xii. 19; ἀποκριθῆναι λόγον, Mt. xxii. 46; εἰπεῖν λόγῳ, Mt. viii. 8 [Rec. λόγον (cf. εἶπον, 3 a. fin.)]; Lk. vii. 7; λαλῆσαι πέντε, μυρίους, λόγους, 1 Co. xiv. 19; διδόναι λόγον εὔσημον, to utter a distinct word, intelligible speech, 1 Co. xiv. 9; εἰπεῖν λόγον κατά τινος, to speak a word against, to the injury of, one, Mt. xii. 32; also εἴς τινα, Lk. xii. 10; to drive out demons λόγῳ, Mt. viii. 16; ἐπερωτᾶν τινα ἐν λόγοις ἱκανοῖς, Lk. xxiii. 9; of the words of a conversation, ἀντιβάλλειν λόγους, Lk. xxiv. 17.　　**2.** *what some one has said*; *a saying*;　　**a.** univ.: Mt. xix. 22 [T om.]; Mk. v. 36 [cf. B. 302 (259) note]; vii. 29; Lk. i. 29; xx. 20; xxii. 61 [Tr mrg. WH ῥήματος]; Jn. ii. 22; iv. 39, 50; vi. 60; vii. 36; xv. 20; xviii. 9; xix. 8; Acts vii. 29; ὁ λόγος οὗτος, this (twofold) saying (of the people), Lk. vii. 17, cf. 16; τὸν αὐτὸν λόγον εἰπών, Mt. xxvi. 44; [Mk. xiv. 39]; παγιδεύειν τινὰ ἐν λόγῳ, in a word or saying which they might elicit from him and turn into an accusation, Mt. xxii. 15; ἀγρεύειν τινὰ λόγῳ, i. e. by propounding a question, Mk. xii. 13; plur., Lk. i. 20; Acts v. 5, 24; with gen. of the contents: ὁ λ. ἐπαγγελίας, Ro. ix. 9; ὁ λ. τῆς ὁρκωμοσίας, Heb. vii. 28; λ. παρακλήσεως, Acts xiii. 15; ὁ λ. τῆς μαρτυρίας, Rev. xii. 11; οἱ λ. τῆς προφητείας, Rev. i. 3 [Tdf. τὸν λ.]; xxii. 6 sq. 10, 18; ὁ προφητικὸς λόγος, the prophetic promise, collectively of the sum of the O. T. prophecies, particularly the Messianic,

2 Pet. i. 19; of the sayings and statements of t e a c h e r s: οἱ λόγοι οὗτοι, the sayings previously related, Mt. vii. 24 [here L Tr WH br. τούτ.], 26; Lk. ix. 28; οἱ λόγοι τινός, the words, commands, counsels, promises, etc., of any teacher, Mt. x. 14; xxiv. 35; Mk. viii. 38; Lk. ix. 44; Jn. xiv. 24; Acts xx. 35; λόγοι ἀληθινοί, Rev. xix. 9; xxi. 5; πιστοί, Rev. xxii. 6; κενοί, Eph. v. 6; πλαστοί, 2 Pet. ii. 3 [cf. W. 217 (204)];　　**b.** of *the sayings of G o d*;　　**a.** i. q. *decree, mandate, order*: Ro. ix. 28; with τοῦ θεοῦ added, 2 Pet. iii. 5, 7 [Rˢᵗ G Tr txt.]; ὁ λ. τοῦ θεοῦ ἐγένετο πρός τινα (a phrase freq. in the O. T.), Jn. x. 35.　　**β.** of the moral precepts given by God in the O. T.: Mk. vii. 13; [Mt. xv. 6 L Tr WH txt.]; Ro. xiii. 9; Gal. v. 14, (cf. οἱ δέκα λόγοι, [Ex. xxxiv. 28]; Deut. x. 4 (cf. ῥήματα, iv. 13); Philo, quis rer. div. her. § 35; de decalog. § 9]; Joseph. antt. 3, 6, 5 [cf. 5, 5]).　　**γ.** i. q. *promise*: ὁ λ. τῆς ἀκοῆς (equiv. to ὁ ἀκουσθείς), Heb. iv. 2; ὁ λ. τοῦ θεοῦ, Ro. ix. 6; plur. Ro. iii. 4; univ. *a divine declaration recorded in the O. T.*, Jn. xii. 38; xv. 25; 1 Co. xv. 54.　　**δ.** διὰ λόγου θεοῦ etc. *through prayer in which the language of the O. T. is employed*: 1 Tim. iv. 5; cf. De Wette and Huther ad loc.　　**ε.** ὁ λόγος τοῦ θεοῦ, as דְּבַר יְהֹוָה often in the O. T. prophets, *an oracle or utterance by which God discloses, to the prophets or through the prophets, future events*: used collectively of the sum of such utterances, Rev. i. 2, 9; cf. Düsterdieck and Bleek ad ll. cc.　　**c.** *what is declared, a thought, declaration, aphorism*, (Lat. *sententia*): τὸν λόγον τοῦτον (reference is made to what follows, so that γάρ in vs. 12 is explicative), Mt. xix. 11; *a dictum, maxim or weighty saying*: 1 Tim. i. 15; iii. 1; 2 Tim. ii. 11; Tit. iii. 8; i. q. *proverb,* Jn. iv. 37 (as sometimes in class. Grk., e. g. [Aeschyl. Sept. adv. Theb. 218]; ὁ παλαιὸς λόγος, Plat. Phaedr. p. 240 c.; conviv. p. 195 b.; legg. 6 p 757 a.; Gorg. p. 499 c.; *verum est verbum quod memoratur, ubi amici, ibi opes*, Plaut. Truc. 4, 4, 32; add, Ter. Andr. 2, 5, 15; al.).　　**3.** *discourse* (Lat. *oratio*);　　**a.** *the act of speaking, speech*: Acts xiv. 12; 2 Co. x. 10; Jas. iii. 2; διὰ λόγου, by word of mouth, Acts xv. 27; opp. to δι' ἐπιστολῶν, 2 Th. ii. 15; διὰ λόγου πολλοῦ, Acts xv. 32; λόγῳ πολλῷ, Acts xx. 2; περὶ οὗ πολὺς ἡμῖν ὁ λόγος, of whom we have many things to say, Heb. v. 11; ὁ λόγος ὑμῶν, Mt. v. 37; Col. iv. 6; λ. κολακείας, 1 Th. ii. 5. λόγος is distinguished from σοφία in 1 Co. ii. 1; fr. ἀναστροφή, 1 Tim. iv. 12; fr. δύναμις, 1 Co. iv. 19 sq.; 1 Th. i. 5; fr. ἔργον, Ro. xv. 18; 2 Co. x. 11; Col. iii. 17; fr. ἔργον κ. ἀλήθεια, 1 Jn. iii. 18 (see ἔργον, 3 p. 248ᵃ bot.); οὐδενὸς λόγου τίμιον, not worth mentioning (λόγου ἄξιον, Hdt. 4, 28; cf. Germ. *der Rede werth*), i. e. a thing of no value, Acts xx. 24 T Tr WH (see II. 2 below).　　**b.** i. q. *the faculty of speech*: Eph. vi. 19; *skill and practice in speaking*: ἰδιώτης τῷ λόγῳ ἀλλ' οὐ τῇ γνώσει, 2 Co. xi. 6; δυνατὸς ἐν ἔργῳ κ. λόγῳ, Lk. xxiv. 19 (ἄνδρας λόγῳ δυνατούς, Diod. 13, 101); λόγος σοφίας or γνώσεως, the art of speaking to the purpose about things pertaining to wisdom or knowledge, 1 Co. xii. 8.　　**c.** *a kind* (or *style*) *of speaking*: ἐν παντὶ λόγῳ, 1 Co. i. 5 [A. V. *utterance*].　　**d.** c o n t i n u o u s s p e a k-

ing, discourse, such as in the N. T. is characteristic of teachers: Lk. iv. 32, 36; Jn. iv. 41; Acts iv. 4 (cf. iii. 12–26); xx. 7; 1 Co. i. 17; ii. 1; plur., Mt. vii. 28; xix. 1; xxvi. 1; Lk. ix. 26; Acts ii. 40; δυνατὸς ἐν λόγοις κ. ἔργοις αὐτοῦ, Acts vii. 22. Hence, the thought of the subject being uppermost, **e.** *instruction*: Col. iv. 3; Tit. ii. 8; 1 Pet. iii. 1; joined with διδασκαλία, 1 Tim. v. 17; with a gen. of the teacher, Jn. v. 24; viii. 52; xv. 20; xvii. 20; Acts ii. 41; 1 Co. ii. 4; 2 Co. i. 18 (cf. 19); ὁ λόγος ὁ ἐμός, Jn. viii. 31, 37, 43, 51; xiv. 23; τίνι λόγῳ, with what instruction, 1 Co. xv. 2 (where construe, εἰ κατέχετε, τίνι λόγῳ etc.; cf. B. §§ 139, 58; 151, 20); i. q. κήρυγμα, *preaching,* with gen. of the obj.: λ. ἀληθείας, 2 Co. vi. 7; Jas. i. 18; ὁ λ. τῆς ἀληθείας, Col. i. 5; Eph. i. 13; 2 Tim. ii. 15; τῆς καταλλαγῆς, 2 Co. v. 19; ὁ λ. τῆς σωτηρίας ταύτης, concerning this salvation (i. e. the salvation obtained through Christ) [cf. W. 237 (223); B. 162 (141)], Acts xiii. 26; ὁ λόγος τῆς βασιλείας (τοῦ θεοῦ), Mt. xiii. 19; τοῦ σταυροῦ, 1 Co. i. 18; ὁ τῆς ἀρχῆς τοῦ Χριστοῦ λόγος, the first instruction concerning Christ [cf. B. 155 (136); W. 188 (177)], Heb. vi. 1. Hence **4.** in an objective sense, what is communicated by instruction, *doctrine*: univ. Acts xviii. 15; ὁ λόγ. αὐτῶν, 2 Tim. ii. 17; plur. ἡμέτεροι λόγοι, 2 Tim. iv. 15; ὑγιαίνοντες λόγοι, 2 Tim. i. 13; with a gen. of obj. added: τοῦ κυρίου, 1 Tim. vi. 3; τῆς πίστεως, the doctrines of faith [see πίστις, 1 c. β.], 1 Tim. iv. 6. specifically, *the doctrine concerning the attainment through Christ of salvation in the kingdom of God*: simply, Mt. xiii. 20–23; Mk. iv. 14–20; viii. 32; xvi. 20; Lk. i. 2; viii. 12; Acts viii. 4; x. 44; xi. 19; xiv. 25; xvii. 11; Gal. vi. 6; Phil. i. 14; 1 Th. i. 6; 2 Tim. iv. 2; 1 Pet. ii. 8; τὸν λόγον, ὃν ἀπέστειλε τοῖς etc. the doctrine which he commanded to be delivered to etc. Acts x. 36 [but L WH txt. om. Tr br. ὅν; cf. W. § 62, 3 fin.; B. § 131, 13]; τὸν λόγον ἀκούειν, Lk. viii. 15; Jn. xiv. 24; Acts iv. 4; 1 Jn. ii. 7; λαλεῖν, Jn. xv. 3 (see other exx. s. v. λαλέω, 5 sub fin.); ἀπειθὴς τῷ λ., 1 Pet. ii. 8; iii. 1; διδαχὴ πιστοῦ λόγου, Tit. i. 9; with gen. of the teacher: ὁ λ. αὐτῶν, Acts ii. 41; with gen. of the author: τοῦ θεοῦ, Lk. v. 1; viii. 11, 21; xi. 28; Jn. xvii. 6, 14; 1 Co. xiv. 36; 2 Co. iv. 2; Col. i. 25; 2 Tim. ii. 9; Tit. i. 3; ii. 5; Heb. xiii. 7; 1 Jn. i. 10; ii. 5, 14; Rev. vi. 9; xx. 4; very often in the Acts: iv. 29, 31; vi. 2, 7; viii. 14; xi. 1, 19; xii. 24; xiii. 5, 44, 46; xvii. 13; xviii. 11; opp. to λ. ἀνθρώπων [B. § 151, 14], 1 Th. ii. 13; λόγος ζῶν θεοῦ, 1 Pet. i. 23; ὁ λ. τοῦ κυρίου, Acts viii. 25; xiii. 48 [(WH txt. Tr mrg. θεοῦ)] sq.; xv. 35 sq.; xix. 10, 20; 1 Th. i. 8; 2 Th. iii. 1; τοῦ Χριστοῦ, Col. iii. 16; Rev. iii. 8; with gen. of apposition, τοῦ εὐαγγελίου, Acts xv. 7; with gen. of the obj., τῆς χάριτος τοῦ θεοῦ, Acts xiv. 3; xx. 32; δικαιοσύνης (see δικαιοσύνη, 1 a.), Heb. v. 13; with gen. of quality, τῆς ζωῆς, containing in itself the true life and imparting it to men, Phil. ii. 16. **5.** *anything reported in speech; a narration, narrative*: of a written narrative, a continuous account of things done, Acts i. 1 (often so in Grk. writ. fr. Hdt. down [cf. L. and S. s. v. A. IV.]); *a fictitious narrative, a story,* Mt. xxviii. 15, cf. 13. *report* (in a good sense): ὁ λόγ.

the news concerning the success of the Christian cause, Acts xi. 22; περί τινος, Lk. v. 15; *rumor,* i. e. current story, Jn. xxi. 23; λόγον ἔχειν τινός, *to have the* (unmerited) *reputation of* any excellence, Col. ii. 23 (so λόγον ἔχει τις foll. by an inf., Hdt. 5, 66; Plat. epin. p. 987 b.; [see esp. Bp. Lghtft. on Col. l. c. (cf. L. and S. s. v. A. III. 3)]). **6.** *matter under discussion, thing spoken of, affair*: Mt. xxi. 24; Mk. xi. 29; Lk. xx. 3; Acts viii. 21; xv. 6, and often in Grk. writ. [L. and S. s. v. A. VIII.]; *a matter in dispute, case, suit at law,* (as דָּבָר in Exod. xviii. 16; xxii. 8): ἔχειν λόγον πρός τινα, to have a ground of action against any one, Acts xix. 38, cf. Kypke ad loc.; παρεκτὸς λόγου πορνείας ([cf. II. 6 below] בִּלְתִּי עַל־דְּבַר or מִלְּבַד דְּבַר וְנַת, *Delitzsch*), Mt. v. 32; [xix. 9 L WH mrg.]. **7.** *thing spoken of* or *talked about; event; deed,* (often so in Grk. writ. fr. Hdt. down): διαφημίζειν τὸν λόγον, to blaze abroad the occurrence, Mk. i. 45; plur. Lk. i. 4 (as often in the O. T.; μετὰ τοὺς λόγους τούτους, 1 Macc. vii. 33).

II. Its use as respects the MIND alone, Lat. *ratio*; i. e. **1.** *reason,* the mental faculty of thinking, meditating, reasoning, calculating, etc.: once so in the phrase ὁ λόγος τοῦ θεοῦ, of the divine mind, pervading and noting all things by its proper force, Heb. iv. 12. **2.** *account,* i. e. *regard, consideration*: λόγον ποιεῖσθαί τινος, to have regard for, make account of a thing, care for a thing, Acts xx. 24 R G (Job xxii. 4; Hdt. 1, 4. 13 etc.; Aeschyl. Prom. 231; Theocr. 3, 33; Dem., Joseph., Dion. H., Plut., al. [cf. L. and S. s. v. B. II. 1]); also λόγον ἔχειν τινός, Acts l. c. Lchm. (Tob. vi. 16 (15)) [cf. I. 3 a. above]. **3.** *account,* i. e. *reckoning, score*: δόσεως κ. λήψεως (see δόσις, 1), Phil. iv. 15 [where cf. Bp. Lghtft.]; εἰς λόγον ὑμῶν, to your account, i. e. trop. to your advantage, ib. 17; συναίρειν λόγον (an expression not found in Grk. auth.), to make a reckoning, settle accounts, Mt. xviii. 23; xxv. 19. **4.** *account,* i. e. *answer* or *explanation* in reference to judgment: λόγον διδόναι (as often in Grk. auth.), to give or render an account, Ro. xiv. 12 R G T WH L mrg. Tr mrg.; also ἀποδιδόναι, Heb. xiii. 17; 1 Pet. iv. 5; with gen. of the thing, Lk. xvi. 2; Acts xix. 40 [R G]; περί τινος, Mt. xii. 36; [Acts xix. 40 L T Tr WH]; τινὶ περὶ ἑαυτοῦ, Ro. xiv. 12 L txt. br. Tr txt.; αἰτεῖν τινα λόγον περί τινος, 1 Pet. iii. 15 (Plat. polit. p. 285 e.). **5.** *relation*: πρὸς ὃν ἡμῖν ὁ λόγος, with whom as judge we stand in relation [A. V. *have to do*], Heb. iv. 13; κατὰ λόγον, as is right, justly, Acts xviii. 14 [A. V. *reason would* (cf. Polyb. 1, 62, 4. 5; 5, 110, 10)], (παρὰ λόγον, unjustly, 2 Macc. iv. 36; 3 Macc. vii. 8). **6.** *reason, cause, ground*: τίνι λόγῳ, for what reason? why? Acts x. 29 (ἐκ τίνος λόγου; Aeschyl. Choeph. 515; ἐξ οὐδενὸς λόγου, Soph. Phil. 730; τίνι δικαίῳ λόγῳ κτλ.; Plat. Gorg. p. 512 c.); παρεκτὸς λόγου πορνείας (Vulg. *exceptâ fornicationis causâ*) is generally referred to this head, Mt. v. 32; [xix. 9 L WH mrg.]; but since where λόγος is used in this sense the gen. is not added, it has seemed best to include this passage among those mentioned in I. 6 above.

III. In several passages in the writings of John ὁ λόγος denotes the essential WORD *of God*, i. e. the personal (hypostatic) wisdom and power in union with God, his minister in the creation and government of the universe, the cause of all the world's life both physical and ethical, which for the procurement of man's salvation put on human nature in the person of Jesus the Messiah and shone forth conspicuously from his words and deeds: Jn. i. 1, 14; (1 Jn. v. 7 Rec.); with τῆς ζωῆς added (see ζωή, 2 a.), 1 Jn. i. 1; τοῦ θεοῦ, Rev. xix. 13 (although the interpretation which refers this passage to the hypostatic λόγος is disputed by some, as by *Baur*, Neutest. Theologie p. 216 sq.). Respecting the combined Hebrew and Greek elements out of which this conception originated among the Alexandrian Jews, see esp. *Lücke*, Com. üb. d. Evang. des Johan. ed. 3, i. pp. 249–294; [cf. esp. B. D. Am. ed. s. v. Word (and for works which have appeared subsequently, see *Weiss* in Meyer on Jn. ed. 6; *Schürer*, Neutest. Zeitgesch. § 34 II.); Bp. Lghtft. on Col. i 15 p. 143 sq.; and for reff. to the use of the term in heathen, Jewish, and Christian writ., see *Soph.* Lex. s. v. 10].

3057 λόγχη, -ης, ἡ;   **1.** the iron point or head of a spear: Hdt. 1, 52; Xen. an. 4, 7, 16, etc.   **2.** *a lance, spear*, (shaft armed with iron): Jn. xix. 34. (Sept.; Pind., Tragg., sqq.) *

3058 λοιδορέω, -ῶ; 1 aor. ἐλοιδόρησα; pres. pass. ptcp. λοιδορούμενος; (λοίδορος); *to reproach, rail at, revile, heap abuse upon*: τινά, Jn. ix. 28; Acts xxiii. 4; pass., 1 Co. iv. 12; 1 Pet. ii. 23. (From Pind. and Aeschyl. down; Sept. several times for רִיב.) [COMP.: ἀντι-λοιδορέω.] *

3059 λοιδορία, -ας, ἡ, (λοιδορέω), *railing, reviling*: 1 Tim. v. 14; 1 Pet. iii. 9. (Sept.; Arstph., Thuc., Xen., sqq.) *

3060 λοίδορος, -ου, ὁ, *a railer, reviler*: 1 Co. v. 11; vi. 10. (Prov. xxv. 24; Sir. xxiii. 8; Eur. [as adj.], Plut., al.) *

3061 λοιμός, -οῦ, ὁ, [fr. Hom. down], *pestilence*; plur. a pestilence in divers regions (see λιμός), Mt. xxiv. 7 [R G Tr mrg. br.]; Lk. xxi. 11; metaph., like the Lat. *pestis* (Ter. Adelph. 2, 1, 35; Cic. Cat. 2, 1), *a pestilent fellow, pest, plague*: Acts xxiv. 5 (so Dem. p. 794, 5; Ael. v. h. 14, 11; Prov. xxi. 24; plur., Ps. i. 1; 1 Macc. xv. 21; ἄνδρες λοιμοί, 1 Macc. x. 61, cf. 1 S. x. 27; xxv. 17, etc.).*

3062, 3063, &3064 λοιπός, -ή, -όν, (λείπω, λέλοιπα), [fr. Pind. and Hdt. down], Sept. for יֶתֶר, נוֹתָר, שְׁאָר, *left*; plur. *the remaining, the rest*: with substantives, as οἱ λοιποὶ ἀπόστολοι, Acts ii. 37; 1 Co. ix. 5; add, Mt. xxv. 11; Ro. i. 13; 2 Co. xii. 13; Gal. ii. 13; Phil. iv. 3; 2 Pet. iii. 16; Rev. viii. 13; absol. *the rest of any number* or *class* under consideration: simply, Mt. xxii. 6; xxvii. 49; Mk. xvi. 13; Lk. xxiv. 10; Acts xvii. 9; xxvii. 44; with a description added: οἱ λοιποὶ οἱ etc., Acts xxviii. 9; 1 Th. iv. 13; Rev. ii. 24; οἱ λοιποὶ πάντες, 2 Co. xiii. 2; Phil. i. 13; πᾶσι τοῖς λ. Lk. xxiv. 9; with a gen. - οἱ λοιποὶ τῶν ἀνθρώπων, Rev. ix. 20; τοῦ σπέρματος, ib. xii. 17; τῶν νεκρῶν, ib. xx. 5; with a certain distinction and contrast, *the rest, who are not of the specified class* or *number*: Lk. viii. 10; xviii. 9; Acts v. 13; Ro. xi. 7; 1 Co. vii. 12; 1 Th. v. 6; 1 Tim. v. 20; Rev. xi. 13; xix. 21; τὰ λοιπά, *the rest, the things that remain*: Mk. iv. 19; Lk. xii. 26; 1 Co. xi. 34; Rev. iii. 2. Neut. sing. adverbially, τὸ

λοιπόν *what remains* (Lat. *quod superest*), i. e.   **a.** *hereafter, for the future, henceforth*, (often so in Grk. writ. fr. Pind. down): Mk. xiv. 41 R T WH (but τό in br.); Mt. xxvi. 45 [WH om. Tr br. τό]; 1 Co. vii. 29; Heb. x. 13; and without the article, Mk. xiv. 41 G L Tr [WH (but see above)]; 2 Tim. iv. 8; cf. *Herm.* ad Vig. p. 706. τοῦ λοιποῦ, *henceforth, in the future*, Eph. vi. 10 L T Tr WH; Gal. vi. 17; Hdt. 2, 109; Arstph. pax 1084; Xen. Cyr. 4, 4, 10; oec. 10, 9; al; cf. *Herm.* ad Vig. p. 706; often also in full τοῦ λ. χρόνου. [Strictly, τὸ λ. is 'for the fut.' τοῦ λ. 'in (the) fut.'; τὸ λ. may be used for τοῦ λ., but not τοῦ λ. for τὸ λ.; cf. Meyer and Ellicott on Gal. u. s.; B. §§ 128, 2; 132, 26; W. 463 (432).]   **b.** *at last; already*: Acts xxvii. 20 (so in later usage, see Passow or L. and S. s. v.).   **c.** τὸ λοιπόν, dropping the notion of time, signifies *for the rest, besides, moreover*, [A. V. often *finally*], forming a transition to other things, to which the attention of the hearer or reader is directed: Eph. vi. 10 R G; Phil. iii. 1; iv. 8; 1 Th. iv. 1 Rec.; 2 Th. iii. 1; ὁ δὲ λοιπόν has the same force in 1 Co. iv. 2 R G; λοιπόν in 1 Co. i. 16; iv. 2 L T Tr WH; 1 Th. iv. 1 G L T Tr WH.

3065 Δουκᾶς, -ᾶ, ὁ, (contr. fr. Λουκανός; [cf. Bp. Lghtft. on Col. iv. 14], W. 103 (97) [cf. B. 20 (18); on the diverse origin of contr. or abbrev. prop. names in ᾶς cf. *Lobeck*, Patholog. Proleg. p. 506; Bp. Lghtft. on Col. iv. 15]), *Luke*, a Christian of Gentile origin, the companion of the apostle Paul in preaching the gospel and on many of his journeys (Acts xvi. 10–17; xx. 5–15; xxi. 1–18; xxviii. 10–16); he was a physician, and acc. to the tradition of the church from Irenæus [3, 14, 1 sq.] down, which has been recently assailed with little success, the author of the third canonical Gospel and of the Acts of the Apostles: Col. iv. 14; 2 Tim. iv. 11; Philem. 24.*

3066 Δούκιος, -ου, ὁ, (a Lat. name), *Lucius*, of Cyrene, a prophet and teacher of the church at Antioch: Acts xiii. 1; perhaps the same Lucius that is mentioned in Ro. xvi. 21.*

3067 λουτρόν, -οῦ, τό, (λούω), fr. Hom. down (who uses λοετρόν fr. the uncontr. form λοέω), *a bathing, bath*, i. e. as well the **act** of bathing [a sense disputed by some (cf. Ellicott on Eph. v. 26)], as the **place**; used in the N. T. and in eccles. writ. of *baptism* [for exx. see *Soph.* Lex. s. v.]: with τοῦ ὕδατος added, Eph. v. 26; τῆς παλιγγενεσίας, Tit. iii. 5.*

3068 λούω: 1 aor. ἔλουσα; pf. pass. ptcp. λελουμένος and (in Heb. x. 23 T WH) λελουσμένος, a later Greek form (cf. Lobeck on Soph. Aj. p. 324; *Steph.* Thesaur. v. 397 c.; cf. Kühner § 343 s. v.; [Veitch s. v., who cites Cant. v. 12 Vat.]); 1 aor. mid. ptcp. λουσάμενος; fr. Hom. down; Sept. for רָחַץ; *to bathe, wash*: prop. τινά, a dead person, Acts ix. 37; τινὰ ἀπὸ τῶν πληγῶν, by washing to cleanse from the blood of the wounds, Acts xvi. 33 [W. 372 (348), cf. § 30, 6 a.; B. 322 (277)]; ὁ λελουμένος, absol., he that has bathed, Jn. xiii. 10 (on the meaning of the passage see καθαρός, a. [and cf. Syn. below]); λελ. τὸ σῶμα, with dat. of the instr., ὕδατι, Heb. x. 22 (23); mid. *to wash one's self* [cf. W. § 38, 2 a.]: 2 Pet. ii. 22; trop.

Christ is described as ὁ λούσας ἡμᾶς ἀπὸ τῶν ἁμαρτιῶν ἡμῶν, i. e. who by suffering the bloody death of a vicarious sacrifice cleansed us from the guilt of our sins, Rev. i. 5 R G [al. λύσας (q. v. 2 fin.). Comp.: ἀπο-λούω.]*

[Syn. λ ο ύ ω, ν ί π τ ω, π λ ύ ν ω: πλ. is used of things, esp. garments; λ. and ν. of p e r s o n s,—ν. of a p a r t of the body (hands, feet, face, eyes), λ. of the w h o l e. All three words occur in Lev. xv. 11. Cf. Trench, N. T. Syn. § xlv.]

3069   **Λύδδα**, -ης [Acts ix. 38 R G L, but -as T Tr WH; see WH. App. p. 156], ἡ, and Λύδδα, -ων, τά ([L T Tr WH in] Acts ix. 32, 35; cf. Tdf. Proleg. p. 116; B. 18 (16) sq. [cf. W. 61 (60)]); Hebr. לֹד (1 Chr. viii. 12; Ezra ii. 33; Neh. xi. 35); Lydda, a large Benjamite [cf. 1 Chr. l. c.] town (Λύδδα κώμη, πόλεως τοῦ μεγέθους οὐκ ἀποδέουσα, Joseph. antt. 20, 6, 2), called also Diospolis under the Roman empire, about nine ['eleven' (Ordnance Survey p. 21)] miles distant from the Mediterranean; now Ludd: Acts ix. 32, 35, 38. Cf. Robinson, Palestine ii. pp. 244–248; Arnold in Herzog viii. p. 627 sq.; [BB. DD. s. v.].*

3070   **Λυδία**, -as, ἡ, Lydia, a woman of Thyatira, a seller of purple, converted by Paul to the Christian faith: Acts xvi. 14, 40. The name was borne by other women also, Horat. carm. 1, 8; 3, 9.*

3071   **Λυκαονία**, -as, ἡ, Lycaonia, a region of Asia Minor, situated between Pisidia, Cilicia, Cappadocia, Galatia and Phrygia, whose chief cities were Lystra, Derbe and Iconium [cf. reff. in Bp. Lghtft. on Col. p. 1]. Its inhabitants spoke a peculiar and strange tongue the character of which cannot be determined: Acts xiv. 6. Cf. Win. RWB. s. v.; Lassen, Zeitschr. d. deutsch. morgenl. Gesellsch. x. ('56) p. 378; [Wright, Hittites ('84) p. 56].*

3072   **Λυκαονιστί**, (Λυκαονίζω, to use the language of Lycaonia), adv., in the speech of Lycaonia: Acts xiv. 11 (see Λυκαονία).*

3073   **Λυκία**, -as, ἡ, Lycia, a mountainous region of Asia Minor, bounded by Pamphylia, Phrygia, Caria and the Mediterranean: Acts xxvii. 5 (1 Macc. xv. 23). [B. D. s. v.; Dict. of Geogr. s. v.; reff. in Bp. Lghtft. on Col. p. 1.]*

3074   **λύκος**, -ου, ὁ, Hebr. זְאֵב, a wolf: Mt. x. 16; Lk. x. 3; Jn. x. 12; applied figuratively to cruel, greedy, rapacious, destructive men: Mt. vii. 15; Acts xx. 29; (used trop. even in Hom. Il. 4, 471; 16, 156; in the O. T., Ezek. xxii. 27; Zeph. iii. 3; Jer. v. 6).*

3075   **λυμαίνομαι**: impf. ἐλυμαινόμην; dep. mid.; (λύμη injury, ruin, contumely); fr. Aeschyl. and Hdt. down; **1.** to affix a stigma to, to dishonor, spot, defile, (Ezek. xvi. 25; Prov. xxiii. 8; 4 Macc. xviii. 8). **2.** to treat shamefully or with injury, to ravage, devastate, ruin: ἐλυμαίνετο τὴν ἐκκλησίαν, said of Saul as the cruel and violent persecutor, [A. V. made havock of], Acts viii. 3.*

3076   **λυπέω**, -ῶ; 1 aor. ἐλύπησα; pf. λελύπηκα; Pass., pres. λιπούμαι; 1 aor. ἐλυπήθην; fut. λυπηθήσομαι; (λύπη); [fr. Hes. down]; to make sorrowful; to affect with sadness, cause grief; to throw into sorrow: τινά, 2 Co. ii. 2, 5; vii. 8; pass., Mt. xiv. 9; xvii. 23; xviii. 31; xix. 22; xxvi. 22; Mk. x. 22; xiv. 19; Jn. xvi. 20; xxi. 17; 2 Co.

ii. 4; 1 Th. iv. 13; 1 Pet. i. 6; joined with ἀδημονεῖν, Mt. xxvi. 37; opp. to χαίρειν, 2 Co. vi. 10; κατὰ θεόν, in a manner acceptable to God [cf. W. 402 (375)], 2 Co. vii. 9, 11; in a wider sense, to grieve, offend: τὸ πνεῦμα τὸ ἅγιον, Eph. iv. 30 (see πνεῦμα, 4 a. fin.); to make one uneasy, cause him a scruple, Ro. xiv. 15. [Comp.: συλλυπέω. Syn. see θρηνέω, fin.]*

3077   **λύπη**, -ης, ἡ, [fr. Aeschyl. and Hdt. down], sorrow, pain, grief: of persons mourning, Jn. xvi. 6; 2 Co. ii. 7; opp. to χαρά, Jn. xvi. 20; Heb. xii. 11; λύπην ἔχω (see ἔχω, I. 2 g. p. 267ᵃ), Jn. xvi. 21 sq.; Phil. ii. 27; with addition of ἀπό and gen. of pers., 2 Co. ii. 3; λ. μοί ἐστι, Ro. ix. 2; ἐν λύπῃ ἔρχεσθαι, of one who on coming both saddens and is made sad, 2 Co. ii. 1 (cf. λυπῶ ὑμᾶς, vs. 2; and λύπην ἔχω, vs. 3); ἀπὸ τῆς λύπης, for sorrow, Lk. xxii. 45; ἐκ λύπης, with a sour, reluctant mind [A. V. grudgingly], (opp. to ἱλαρός), 2 Co. ix. 7; ἡ κατὰ θεὸν λύπη, sorrow acceptable to God, 2 Co. vii. 10 (see λυπέω), and ἡ τοῦ κόσμου λύπη, the usual sorrow of men at the loss of their earthly possessions, ibid.; objectively, annoyance, affliction, (Hdt. 7, 152): λύπας ὑποφέρειν [R. V. griefs], 1 Pet. ii. 19.*

3078   **Λυσανίας**, -ου, ὁ, Lysanias; **1.** the son of Ptolemy, who from B. C. 40 on was governor of Chalcis at the foot of Mount Lebanon, and was put to death B. C. 34 at the instance of Cleopatra: Joseph. antt. 14, 7, 4 and 13, 3; 15, 4, 1; b. j. 1, 13, 1, cf. b. j. 1, 9, 2. **2.** a tetrarch of Abilene (see Ἀβιληνή), in the days of John the Baptist and Jesus: Lk. iii. 1. Among the regions assigned by the emperors Caligula and Claudius to Herod Agrippa I. and Herod Agrippa II., Josephus mentions ἡ Λυσανίου τετραρχία (antt. 18, 6, 10, cf. 20, 7, 1), βασιλεία ἡ τοῦ Λυσανίου καλουμένη (b. j. 2, 11, 5), Ἄβιλα ἡ Λυσανίου (antt. 19, 5, 1); accordingly, some have supposed that in these passages Lysanias the son of Ptolemy must be meant, and that the region which he governed continued to bear his name even after his death. Others (as Credner, Strauss, Gfrörer, Weisse), denying that there ever was a second Lysanias, contend that Luke was led into error by that designation of Abilene (derived from Lysanias and retained for a long time afterwards), so that he imagined that Lysanias was tetrarch in the time of Christ. This opinion, however, is directly opposed by the fact that Josephus, in antt. 20, 7, 1 and b. j. 2, 12, 8, expressly distinguishes Chalcis from the tetrarchy of Lysanias; nor is it probable that the region which Lysanias the son of Ptolemy governed for only six years took its name from him ever after. Therefore it is more correct to conclude that in the passages of Josephus where the tetrarchy of Lysanias is mentioned a s e c o n d Lysanias, perhaps the grandson of the former, must be meant; and that he is identical with the one spoken of by Luke. Cf. Winer, RWB. s. v. Abilene; Wieseler in Herzog i. p. 64 sqq., [esp. in Beiträge zur richtig. Würdigung d. Evang. sm. pp. 196–204]; Bleek, Synopt. Erklär. u. s. w. i. p. 154 sq.; Kneucker in Schenkel i. p. 26 sq.; Schürer, Neutest. Zeitgesch. § 19 Anh. 1 p. 313 [also in Riehm s. v.; Robinson in Bib. Sacra for 1848, pp. 79 sqq.;

Renan, La Dynastie des Lysanias d'Abilène (in the Mémoires de l'Acad. des inscrip. et belles-lettres for 1870, Tom. xxvi. P. 2, pp. 49–84); BB.DD. s. v.].*

3079   **Λυσίας**, -ου, ὁ, (Claudius) Lysias, a Roman chiliarch [A. V. 'chief captain']: Acts xxiii. 26; xxiv. 7 [Rec.], 22. [B. D. Am. ed. s. v.]*

3080   **λύσις**, -εως, ἡ, (λύω), [fr. Hom. down], a loosing of any bond, as that of marriage; hence once in the N. T. of divorce, 1 Co. vii. 27.*

see 3081 St.   **λυσιτελέω**, -ῶ; (fr. λυσιτελής, and this fr. λύω to pay, and τὰ τέλη [cf. τέλος, 2]); [fr. Hdt. down]; prop. to pay the taxes; to return expenses, hence to be useful, advantageous; impers. λυσιτελεῖ, it profits; foll. by ἤ (see ἤ, 3 f.), it is better: τινί foll. by εἰ, Lk. xvii. 2.*

3082   **Λύστρα**, -ας, ἡ, and [in Acts xiv. 8; xvi. 2; 2 Tim. iii. 11] -ων, τά, (see Λύδδα), Lystra, a city of Lycaonia: Acts xiv. 6, 8, 21; xvi. 1 sq.; 2 Tim. iii. 11. [Cf. reff. in Bp. Lghtft. on Col. p. 1.]*

3083   **λύτρον**, -ου, τό, (λύω), Sept. passim for פִּדְיוֹן, גְּאֻלָּה, כֹּפֶר, etc.; the price for redeeming, ransom (paid for slaves, Lev. xix. 20; for captives, Is. xlv. 13; for the ransom of a life, Ex. xxi. 30; Num. xxxv. 31 sq.): ἀντὶ πολλῶν, to liberate many from the misery and penalty of their sins, Mt. xx. 28; Mk. x. 45. (Pind., Aeschyl., Xen., Plat., al.)*

3084   **λυτρόω**, -ῶ: Pass., 1 aor. ἐλυτρώθην; Mid., pres. inf. λυτροῦσθαι; 1 aor. subj. 3 pers. sing. λυτρώσηται; (λύτρον, q. v.); Sept. often for גָּאַל and פָּדָה;   **1.** to release on receipt of ransom: Plat. Theaet. p. 165 e.; Diod. 19, 73; Sept., Num. xviii. 15, 17.   **2.** to redeem, liberate by payment of ransom, [(Dem., al.)], generally expressed by the mid.; univ. to liberate: τινὰ ἀργυρίῳ, and likewise ἐκ with the gen. of the thing; pass. ἐκ τῆς ματαίας ἀναστροφῆς, 1 Pet. i. 18; Mid. to cause to be released to one's self [cf. W. 254 (238)] by payment of the ransom, i. e. to redeem; univ. to deliver: in the Jewish theocratic sense, τὸν Ἰσραήλ, viz. from evils of every kind, external and internal, Lk. xxiv. 21; ἀπὸ πάσης ἀνομίας, Tit. ii. 14 [cf. W. § 30, 6 a.]; τινὰ ἐκ, spoken of God, Deut. xiii. 5; 2 S. vii. 23; Hos. xiii. 14.*

3085   **λύτρωσις**, -εως, ἡ, (λυτρόω), a ransoming, redemption: prop. αἰχμαλώτων, Plut. Arat. 11; for גְּאֻלָּה, Lev. xxv. [29], 48; univ. deliverance, redemption, in the theocratic sense (see λυτρόω, 2 [cf. Graec. Ven. Lev. xxv. 10, etc.]; Ps. xlviii. (xlix.) 9]): Lk. i. 68; ii. 38; specifically, redemption from the penalty of sin: Heb. ix. 12. [(Clem. Rom. 1 Cor. 12, 7; 'Teaching' 4, 6; etc.)]*

3086   **λυτρωτής**, -οῦ, ὁ, (λυτρόω), redeemer; deliverer, liberator: Acts vii. 35; [Sept. Lev. xxv. 31, 32; Philo de sacrif. Ab. et Cain. § 37 sub fin.]; for גֹּאֵל, of God, Ps. xviii. (xix.) 15; lxxvii. (lxxviii.) 35. Not found in prof. auth.*

3087   **λυχνία**, -ας, ἡ, a later Grk. word for the earlier λυχνίον, see Lob. ad Phryn. p. 313 sq.; [Wetst. on Mt. v. 15; W. 24]; Sept. for מְנוֹרָה; a (candlestick) lampstand, candelabrum: Mt. v. 15; Mk. iv. 21; Lk. viii. 16; [xi. 33]; Heb. ix. 2; the two eminent prophets who will precede Christ's return from heaven in glory are likened to 'candlesticks,'

Rev. xi. 4 [B. 81 (70); W. 536 (499)]; to the seven 'candlesticks' (Ex. xxv. 37 [A. V. lamps; cf. B. D. (esp. Am. ed.) s. v. Candlestick]) also the seven more conspicuous churches of Asia are compared in Rev. i. 12 sq. 20; ii. 1; κινεῖν τὴν λυχνίαν τινὸς (ἐκκλησίας) ἐκ τοῦ τόπου αὐτῆς, to move a church out of the place which it has hitherto held among the churches; to take it out of the number of churches, remove it altogether, Rev. ii. 5.*

λύχνος, -ου, ὁ, Sept. for נֵר, [fr. Hom. down]; a lamp, candle [?], that is placed on a stand or candlestick (Lat. candelabrum), [cf. Trench, N. T. Syn. § xlvi.; Becker, Charicles, Sc. ix. (Eng. trans. p. 156 n. 5)]: Mt. v. 15; Mk. iv. 21; [Lk. xi. 36]; xii. 35; Rev. xxii. 5; φῶς λύχνου, Rev. xviii. 23; opp. to φῶς ἡλίου, xxii. 5 L T Tr WH; ἅπτειν λύχνον ([Lk. viii. 16; xi. 33; xv. 8], see ἅπτω, 1). To a "lamp" are likened—the eye, ὁ λύχνος τοῦ σώματος, i. e. which shows the body which way to move and turn, Mt. vi. 22; Lk. xi. 34; the prophecies of the O. T., inasmuch as they afforded at least some knowledge relative to the glorious return of Jesus from heaven down even to the time when by the Holy Spirit that same light, like the day and the day-star, shone upon the hearts of men, the light by which the prophets themselves had been enlightened and which was necessary to the full perception of the true meaning of their prophecies, 2 Pet. i. 19; to the brightness of a lamp that cheers the beholders a teacher is compared, whom even those rejoiced in who were unwilling to comply with his demands, Jn. v. 35; Christ, who will hereafter illumine his followers, the citizens of the heavenly kingdom, with his own glory, Rev. xxi. 23.*   3088

λύω; impf. ἔλυον; 1 aor. ἔλυσα; Pass., pres. λύομαι; impf. ἐλυόμην; pf. 2 pers. sing. λέλυσαι, ptcp. λελυμένος; 1 aor. ἐλύθην; 1 fut. λυθήσομαι; fr. Hom. down; Sept. several times for פָּתַח to open, הִתִּיר and Chald. שְׁרָא (Dan. iii. 25; v. 12); to loose; i. e.   **1.** to loose any person (or thing) tied or fastened: prop. the bandages of the feet, the shoes, Mk. i. 7; Lk. iii. 16; Jn. i. 27; Acts [xiii. 25]; vii. 33, (so for נָשַׁל to take off, Ex. iii. 5; Josh. v. 15); πῶλον (δεδεμένον), Mt. xxi. 2; Mk. xi. 2, [3 L mrg.], 4 sq.; Lk. xix. 30 sq. 33; bad angels, Rev. ix. 14 sq.; τὸν βοῦν ἀπὸ τῆς φάτνης, Lk. xiii. 15; trop. of husband and wife joined together by the bond of matrimony, λέλυσαι ἀπὸ γυναικός (opp. to δέδεσαι γυναικί), spoken of a single man, whether he has already had a wife or has not yet married, 1 Co. vii. 27.   **2.** to loose one bound, i. e. to unbind, release from bonds, set free: one bound up (swathed in bandages), Jn. xi. 44; bound with chains (a prisoner), Acts xxii. 30 (where Rec. adds ἀπὸ τῶν δεσμῶν); hence i. q. to discharge from prison, let go, Acts xxiv. 26 Rec. (so as far back as Hom.); in Apocalyptic vision of the devil (κεκλεισμένον), Rev. xx. 3; ἐκ τῆς φυλακῆς αὐτοῦ, 7; metaph. to free (ἀπὸ δεσμοῦ) from the bondage of disease (one held by Satan) by restoration to health, Lk. xiii. 16; to release one bound by the chains of sin, ἐκ τῶν ἁμαρτιῶν, Rev. i. 5 L T Tr WH (see λούω fin. [cf. W. § 30, 6 a.]).   **3.** to loosen, undo, dissolve, anything bound, tied, or compacted to-   3089 gether: the seal of a book, Rev. v. 2, [5 Rec.]; trop., τὸν δεσμὸν τῆς γλώσσης τινός, to remove an impediment of speech, restore speech to a dumb man, Mk. vii. 35 (Justin, hist. 13, 7, 1 cui nomen Battos propter linguae obligationem fuit; 6 linguae nodis solutis loqui primum coepit); an assembly, i. e. to dismiss, break up: τὴν συναγωγήν, pass., Acts xiii. 43 (ἀγορήν, Hom. Il. 1, 305; Od. 2, 257, etc.; Apoll. Rh. 1, 708; τὴν στρατιάν, Xen. Cyr. 6, 1, 2); of the bonds of death, λύειν τὰς ὠδῖνας τοῦ θανάτου, Acts ii. 24 (see ὠδίν). Laws, as having binding force, are likened to bonds; hence λύειν is i. q. to annul, subvert; to do away with; to deprive of authority, whether by precept or by act: ἐντολήν, Mt. v. 19; τὸν νόμον, Jn. vii. 23; τὸ σάββατον, the commandment concerning the sabbath, Jn. v. 18; τὴν γραφήν, Jn. x. 35; cf. Kuinoel on Mt. v. 17; [on the singular reading λύει τὸν Ἰησοῦν, 1 Jn. iv. 3 WH mrg. see Westcott, Com. ad loc.]; by a Chald. and Talmud. usage (equiv. to אֲתַר שְׁרָא [cf.

W. 32]), opp. to δέω (q. v. 2 c.), to declare lawful: Mt. xvi. 19; xviii. 18, [but cf. Weiss in Meyer 7te Aufl. ad ll. cc.]. to loose what is compacted or built together, to break up, demolish, destroy: prop. in pass. ἐλύετο ἡ πρύμνα, was breaking to pieces, Acts xxvii. 41; τὸν ναόν, Jn. ii. 19; τὸ μεσότοιχον τοῦ φραγμοῦ, Eph. ii. 14 (τὰ τείχη, 1 Esdr. i. 52; γέφυραν, Xen. an. 2, 4, 17 sq.); to dissolve something coherent into parts, to destroy: pass., [τούτων πάντων λυομένων, 2 Pet. iii. 11]; τὰ στοιχεῖα (καυσούμενα), 2 Pet. iii. 10; οὐρανοί (πυρούμενοι), ib. 12; metaph. to overthrow, do away with: τὰ ἔργα τοῦ διαβόλου, 1 Jn. iii. 8. [COMP.: ἀνα-, ἀπο-, δια-, ἐκ-, ἐπι-, κατα-, παρα-λύω.] *

Λωΐς [WH Λωΐς], -ίδος, ἡ, Lois, a Christian matron, the grandmother of Timothy: 2 Tim. i. 5.* **3090**

Λώτ, ὁ, (לוֹט a covering, veil), [indecl.; cf. B.D.], Lot, **3091** the son of Haran the brother of Abraham (Gen. xi. 27, 31; xii. 4 sqq.; xiii. 1 sqq.; xiv. 12 sqq.; xix. 1 sqq.): Lk. xvii. 28 sq. 32: 2 Pet. ii. 7.*

M

|M, μ: on its (Alexandrian, cf. Sturz, De dial. Maced. et Alex. p. 130 sq.) retention in such forms as λήμψομαι, ἀνελήμφθη, προσωπολήμπτης, ἀνάλημψις, and the like, see (the several words in their places, and) W. 48; B. 62 (54); esp. Tdf. Proleg. p. 72; Kuenen and Cobet, Praef. p. lxx.; Scrivener, Collation etc. p. lv. sq., and Introd. p. 14; Fritzsche, Rom. vol. i. p. 110; on -μ- or -μμ- in pf. pass. ptcps. (e. g. διεστραμμένος, περιρεραμμένος, etc., see each word in its place, and) cf. WH. App. p. 170 sq.; on the dropping of μ in ἐμπίπλημι, ἐμπιπράω, see the words.]

3092 **Μαάθ, ὁ,** (מַעַט to be small), Maath, one of Christ's ancestors: Lk. iii. 26.*

see 3093 –**Μαγαδάν,** see the foll. word.

3093 ––––**Μαγδαλά,** a place on the western shore of the Lake of Galilee, about three miles distant from Tiberias towards the north; according to the not improbable conjecture of Gesenius (Thesaur. i. p. 267) identical with מִגְדַּל־אֵל (i. e. tower of God), a fortified city of the tribe of Naphtali (Josh. xix. 38); in the Jerus. Talmud מִגְדָּל (Magdal or Migdal); now Medschel or Medjdel, a wretched Mohammedan village with the ruins of an ancient tower (see Win. RWB. s. v.; Robinson, Palest. ii. p. 396 sq.; Arnold in Herzog viii. p. 661; Kneucker in Schenkel iv. p. 84; [Hackett in B.D. s. v.; Edersheim, Jesus the Messiah, i. 571 sq.]): Mt. xv. 39 RG, with the var. reading (adopted by L T Tr WH [cf. WH. App. p. 160]) Μαγαδάν, Vulg. Magedan, (Syr. ܡܓܕܘ); if either of these forms was the one used by the Evangelist it could very easily have been changed by the copyists into the more familiar name Μαγδαλά.*

Μαγδαληνή, -ῆς, ἡ, (Μαγδαλά, q. v.), Magdalene, a **3094** woman of Magdala: Mt. xxvii. 56, 61; xxviii. 1; Mk. xv. 40, 47; xvi. 1, 9; Lk. viii. 2; xxiv. 10; Jn. xix. 25; xx. 1, 18.*

[**Μαγεδών** (Rev. xvi. 16 WH), see Ἁρμαγεδών.] –––– **see 717**

μαγεία (T WH μαγία, see I, ι), -ας, ἡ, (μάγος, q. v.), –––– **3095** magic; plur. magic arts, sorceries: Acts viii. 11. (Theophr., Joseph., Plut., al.) *

μαγεύω; (μάγος;) to be a magician; to practise magical **3096** arts: Acts viii. 9. (Eur. Iph. 1338; Plut. Artax. 3, 6, and in other auth.) *

μαγία, see μαγεία. –––––––––––––––––––– **see 3095**

μάγος, -ου, ὁ, (Hebr. מַג, plur. מָגִים; a word of Indo- –––**3097** Germanic origin; cf. Gesenius, Thes. ii. p. 766; J. G. Müller in Herzog viii. p. 678; [Vaniček, Fremdwörter, s. v.; but the word is now regarded by many as of Babylonian origin; see Schrader, Keilinschriften u.s.w. 2te Aufl. p. 417 sqq.]); fr. Soph. and Hdt. down; Sept. Dan. ii. 2 and several times in Theodot. ad Dan. for אַשָּׁף; a magus; the name given by the Babylonians (Chaldæans) Medes, Persians, and others, to the wise men, teachers, priests, physicians, astrologers, seers, interpreters of dreams, augurs, soothsayers, sorcerers etc.; cf. Win. RWB. s. v.; J. G. Müller in Herzog l. c. pp. 675–685; Holtzmann in Schenkel iv. p. 84 sq.; [BB.DD. s. v. Magi]. In the N. T. the name is given **1.** to the oriental wise men (astrologers) who, having discovered by the rising of a remarkable star [see ἀστήρ, and cf. Edersheim, Jesus the Messiah, i. 209 sqq.] that the Messiah had just been born, came to Jerusalem to worship him: Mt. ii. 1, 7, 16. **2.** to false prophets and sorcerers: Acts xiii. 6, 8, cf. viii. 9, 11.*

3098;~. see 1136 ‒‒Μαγώγ, ὁ, see Γώγ.

see 3099 St. Μαδιάμ, ἡ, (Hebr. מִדְיָן [i. e. ‘strife’]), Midian [in A. V. (ed. 1611) N. T. Madian], prop. name of the territory of the Midianites in Arabia; it took its name from Midian, son of Abraham and Keturah (Gen. xxv. 1 sq.): Acts vii. 29.*

see 3149 μαζός, -οῦ, ὁ, the breast: of a man, Rev. i. 13 Lchm. [(see μαστός). From Hom. down.]*

3100 μαθητεύω: 1 aor. ἐμαθήτευσα; 1 aor. pass. ἐμαθητεύθην; (μαθητής); **1.** intrans. τινί, to be the disciple of one; to follow his precepts and instruction: Mt. xxvii. 57 R G WH mrg., cf. Jn. xix. 38 (so Plut. mor. pp. 832 b. (vit. Antiph. 1), 837 c. (vit. Isocr. 10); Jamblichus, vit. Pythag. c. 23). **2.** trans. (cf. W. p. 23 and § 38, 1; [B. § 131, 4]) to make a disciple; to teach, instruct: τινά, Mt. xxviii. 19; Acts xiv. 21; pass. with a dat. of the pers. whose disciple one is made, Mt. xxvii. 57 L T Tr WH txt.; μαθητευθεὶς εἰς τὴν βασιλείαν τῶν οὐρ. (see γραμματεύς, 3), Mt. xiii. 52 Rec., where long since the more correct reading τῇ βασ. τῶν οὐρ. was adopted, but without changing the sense; [yet Lchm. inserts ἐν].*

3101 μαθητής, -οῦ, ὁ, (μανθάνω), a learner, pupil, disciple: univ., opp. to διδάσκαλος, Mt. x. 24; Lk. vi. 40; τινός, one who follows one's teaching: Ἰωάννου, Mt. ix. 14; Lk. vii. 18 (19); Jn. iii. 25; τῶν Φαρισ., Mt. xxii. 16; Mk. ii. 18; Lk. v. 33; Μωϋσέως, Jn. ix. 28; of Jesus,—in a wide sense, in the Gospels, those among the Jews who favored him, joined his party, became his adherents: Jn. vi. 66; vii. 3; xix. 38; ὄχλος μαθητῶν αὐτοῦ, Lk. vi. 17; οἱ μ. αὐτοῦ ἱκανοί, Lk. vii. 11; ἅπαν τὸ πλῆθος τῶν μαθ. Lk. xix. 37; but especially the twelve apostles: Mt. x. 1; xi. 1; xii. 1; Mk. viii. 27; Lk. viii. 9; Jn. ii. 2; iii. 22, and very often; also simply οἱ μαθηταί, Mt. xiii. 10; xiv. 19; Mk. x. 24; Lk. ix. 16; Jn. vi. 11 [Rec.], etc.; in the Acts οἱ μαθηταί are all those who confess Jesus as the Messiah, Christians: Acts vi. 1 sq. 7; ix. 19; xi. 26, and often; with τοῦ κυρίου added, Acts ix. 1. The word is not found in the O. T., nor in the Epp. of the N. T., nor in the Apocalypse; in Grk. writ. fr. [Hdt.], Arstph., Xen., Plato, down.

3102 μαθήτρια, -ας, ἡ, (a fem. form of μαθητής; cf. ψάλτης, ψάλτρια, etc., in Bttm. Ausf. Spr. ii. p. 425), a female disciple; i. q. a Christian woman: Acts ix. 36. (Diod. 2, 52; Diog. Laërt. 4, 2; 8, 42.)*

see 3161 ~. see 3156 ~. [Μαθθαθίας, see Ματταθίας.]
& 3157 Μαθθαῖος, Μαθθάν, see Ματθαῖος, Ματθάν.
see 3158 ‒‒Μαθθάτ, see Ματθάτ.

3103 ‒‒‒‒Μαθουσάλα, T WH Μαθουσαλά [cf. Tdf. Proleg. p. 103], ὁ, (מְתוּשֶׁלַח) man of a dart, fr. מְתוּ, construct form of the unused מַת a man, and שֶׁלַח a dart [cf. B. D. s. v.]), Methuselah, the son of Enoch and grandfather of Noah (Gen. v. 21): Lk. iii. 37.*

3104 Μαϊνάν (T Tr WH Μεννά), indecl., (Lchm. Μέννας, gen. Μεννᾶ), ὁ, Menna or Menan, [A. V. (1611) Menam], the name of one of Christ's ancestors: Lk. iii. 31 [Lchm. br. τοῦ Μ.].*

μαίνομαι; [fr. Hom. down]; to be mad, to rave: said of 3105 one who so speaks that he seems not to be in his right mind, Acts xii. 15; xxvi. 24; 1 Co. xiv. 23; opp. to σωφροσύνης ῥήματα ἀποφθέγγεσθαι, Acts xxvi. 25; joined with δαιμόνιον ἔχειν, Jn. x. 20. [Comp.: ἐμ-μαίνομαι.]*

μακαρίζω; Attic fut. μακαριῶ [cf. B. 37 (32)]; (μακά- 3106 ριος); fr. Hom. down; Sept. for אִשֵּׁר; to pronounce blessed: τινά, Lk. i. 48; Jas. v. 11 (here Vulg. beatifico).*

μακάριος, -α, -ον, (poetic μάκαρ), [fr. Pind., Plat. down], 3107 blessed, happy: joined to names of God, 1 Tim. i. 11; vi. 15 (cf. μάκαρες θεοί in Hom. and Hes.); ἐλπίς, Tit. ii. 13; as a predicate, Acts xx. 35; 1 Pet. iii. 14; iv. 14; ἡγοῦμαί τινα μακ. Acts xxvi. 2; μακάρ. ἔν τινι, Jas. i. 25. In congratulations, the reason why one is to be pronounced blessed is expressed by a noun or a ptcp. taking the place of the subject, μακάριος ὁ etc. (Hebr. אַשְׁרֵי פּ״, Ps. i. 1; Deut. xxxiii. 29, etc.) blessed the man, who etc. [W. 551 (512 sq.)]: Mt. v. 3–11; Lk. vi. 20–22; Jn. xx. 29; Rev. i. 3; xvi. 15; xix. 9; xx. 6; xxii. 14; by the addition to the noun of a ptcp. which takes the place of a predicate, Lk. i. 45; x. 23; xi. 27 sq.; Rev. xiv. 13; foll. by ὅς with a finite verb, Mt. xi. 6; Lk. vii. 23; xiv. 15; Ro. iv. 7 sq.; the subject noun intervening, Lk. xii. 37, 43; xxiii. 29; Jas. i. 12; μακ. . . . ὅτι, Mt. xiii. 16; xvi. 17; Lk. xiv. 14; foll. by ἐάν, Jn. xiii. 17; 1 Co. vii. 40. [See Schmidt ch. 187, 7.]

μακαρισμός, -οῦ, ὁ, (μακαρίζω), declaration of blessed- 3108 ness: Ro. iv. 9; Gal. iv. 15; λέγειν τὸν μακ. τινος, to utter a declaration of blessedness upon one, a fuller way of saying μακαρίζειν τινά, to pronounce one blessed, Ro. iv. 6. (Plat. rep. 9 p. 591 d.; [Aristot. rhet. 1, 9, 34]; Plut. mor. p. 471 c.; eccles. writ.) *

Μακεδονία, -ας, ἡ [on use of art. with cf. W. § 18, 5 a. 3109 c.], Macedonia, a country bounded on the S. by Thessaly and Epirus, on the E. by Thrace and the Ægean Sea, on the W. by Illyria, and on the N. by Dardania and Moesia [cf. B. D. (esp. Am. ed.)]: Acts xvi. 9 sq. 12; xviii. 5; xix. 21 sq.; xx. 1, 3; Ro. xv. 26; 1 Co. xvi. 5; 2 Co. i. 16; ii. 13; vii. 5; viii. 1; xi. 9; Phil. iv. 15; 1 Th. i. 7 sq.; iv. 10; 1 Tim. i. 3.*

Μακεδών, -όνος, ὁ, a Macedonian: Acts xvi. 9 [cf. B. 3110 § 123, 8 Rem.]; xix. 29; xxvii. 2; 2 Co. ix. 2, 4.*

μάκελλον, -ου, τό, a Lat. word, macellum [prob. akin to 3111 μάχ-η; Vaniček p. 687 (cf. Plut. as below)], a place where meat and other articles of food are sold, meat-market, provision-market, [A. V. shambles]: 1 Co. x. 25. (Dio Cass. 61, 18 τὴν ἀγορὰν τῶν ὄψων, τὸ μάκελλον; [Plut. ii. p. 277 d. (quaest. Rom. 54)].)*

μακράν (prop. fem. acc. of the adj. μακρός, sc. ὁδόν, a 3112 long way [W. 230 (216); B. § 131, 12]), adv., Sept. for רָחוֹק, [fr. Aeschyl. down]; far, a great way: absol., ἀπέχειν, Lk. xv. 20; of the terminus to which, far hence, ἐξαποστελῶ σε, Acts xxii. 21; with ἀπό τινος added, Mt. viii. 30; Lk. vii. 6 [T om. ἀπό]; Jn. xxi. 8; τὸν θεὸν . . . οὐ μακρὰν ἀπὸ ἑνὸς ἑκάστου ἡμῶν ὑπάρχοντα, i. e. who is near every one of us by his power and influence (so that we have no need to seek the knowledge of him from without), Acts xvii. 27; οἱ εἰς μακράν [cf. W. 415 (387)] those that are afar off, the inhabitants of remote regions, i. e. the Gentiles, Acts ii. 39, cf. Is. ii. 2 sqq.; Zech. vi. 15. metaph. οὐ μακρὰν εἶ ἀπὸ τῆς βασ. τοῦ θεοῦ, but little is wanting for thy reception into the kingdom of God, or thou art almost fit to be a citizen in the divine kingdom, Mk. xii. 34; οἱ ποτὲ ὄντες μακράν (opp. to οἱ ἐγγύς), of heathen (on the sense, see ἐγγύς, 1 b.), Eph. ii. 13; also οἱ μακράν, ib. 17.*

3113   **μακρόθεν**, (μακρός), adv., esp. of later Grk. [Polyb., al.; cf. Lob. ad Phryn. p. 93]; Sept. for רָחוֹק, מֵרָחוֹק, etc.; *from afar, afar*: Mk. viii. 3; xi. 13; Lk. xviii. 13; xxii. 54; xxiii. 49; with the prep. ἀπό prefixed (cf. W. 422 (393); § 65, 2; B. 70 (62)): Mt. xxvi. 58 [here T om. WH br. ἀπό]; xxvii. 55; Mk. v. 6; xiv. 54; xv. 40, Lk. xvi. 23; Rev. xviii. 10, 15, 17; also L T Tr WH in Mk. xi. 13; L T Tr mrg. WH in Lk. xxiii. 49; T Tr WH in Mk. viii. 3, (Ps. cxxxvii. (cxxxviii.) 6; 2 K. xix. 25 cod. Alex.; 2 Esdr. iii. 13).*

3114   **μακροθυμέω**, -ῶ; 1 aor., impv. μακροθύμησον, ptcp. μακροθυμήσας; (fr. μακρόθυμος, and this fr. μακρός and θυμός); *to be of a long spirit, not to lose heart*; hence   **1.** *to persevere patiently and bravely* (i. q. καρτερῶ, so Plut. de gen. Socr. c. 24 p. 593 f.; Artem. oneir. 4, 11) *in enduring misfortunes and troubles*: absol., Heb. vi. 15; Jas. v. 8; with the addition of ἕως and a gen. of the desired event, ib. 7; with ἐπί and a dat. of the thing hoped for, ibid.; add, Sir. ii. 4.   **2.** *to be patient in bearing the offences and injuries of others; to be mild and slow in avenging; to be long-suffering, slow to anger, slow to punish*, (for הֶאֱרִיךְ אַף, to defer anger, Prov. xix. 11): absol. 1 Co. xiii. 4; πρός τινα, 1 Th. v. 14; ἐπί with dat. of pers. (see ἐπί, B. 2 a. δ.), Mt. xviii. 26, 29 [here L Tr with the acc., so Tr in 26; see ἐπί, C. I. 2 g. β.]; Sir. xviii. 11; xxix. 8; hence spoken of God deferring the punishment of sin: εἴς τινα, towards one, 2 Pet. iii. 9 [here L T Tr mrg. διά (q. v. B. II. 2 b. sub fin.)]; ἐπί with dat. of pers., Lk. xviii. 7; in this difficult passage we shall neither preserve the constant usage of μακροθυμεῖν (see just before) nor get a reasonable sense, unless we regard the words ἐπ' αὐτοῖς as negligently (see αὐτός, II. 6) referring to the enemies of the ἐκλεκτῶν, and translate καὶ μακροθυμῶν ἐπ' αὐτοῖς *even though he is long-suffering, indulgent, to them*; — this negligence being occasioned by the circumstance that Luke seems to represent Jesus as speaking with Sir. xxxii. (xxxv.) 22 (18) in mind, where ἐπ' αὐτοῖς must be referred to ἀνελεημόνων. The reading [of L T Tr WH] καὶ μακροθυμεῖ ἐπ' αὐτοῖς; by which τὸ μακροθυμεῖν is denied to God [cf. W. § 55, 7] cannot be accepted, because the preceding parable certainly demands the notion of slowness on God's part in avenging the right; cf. De Wette ad loc.; [but to this it is replied, that the denial of actual delay is not inconsistent with the assumption of apparent delay; cf. Meyer (ed. Weiss) ad loc.].*

3115   **μακροθυμία**, -ας, ἡ, (μακρόθυμος [cf. μακροθυμέω]), (Vulg. longanimitas, etc.), i. e.   **1.** *patience, endurance, constancy, steadfastness, perseverance*; esp. as shown in bearing troubles and ills, (Plut. Luc. 32 sq.; ἄνθρωπος ὢν μηδέποτε τὴν ἀλυπίαν αἰτοῦ παρὰ θεῶν, ἀλλὰ μακροθυμίαν, Menand. frag. 19, p. 203 ed. Meineke [vol. iv. p. 238 Frag. comic. Graec. (Berl. 1841)]): Col. i. 11; 2 Tim. iii. 10; Heb. vi. 12; Jas. v. 10; Clem. Rom. 1 Cor. 64; Barn. ep. 2, 2; [Is. lvii. 15; Joseph. b. j. 6, 1, 5; cf. 1 Macc. viii. 4].   **2.** *patience, forbearance, long-suffering, slowness in avenging wrongs*, (for אֶרֶךְ אַפַּיִם, Jer. xv. 15): Ro. ii. 4; ix. 22; 2 Co. vi. 6; Gal. v. 22; Eph. iv. 2; Col. iii. 12; 1 Tim. i. 16 [cf. B. 120 (105)]; 2 Tim. iv. 2; 1 Pet. iii. 20; 2 Pet. iii. 15; (Clem. Rom. 1 Cor. 13, 1; Ignat. ad Eph. 3, 1).*

[Syn. μακροθυμία, ὑπομονή (occur together or in the same context in Col. i. 11; 2 Cor. vi. 4, 6; 2 Tim. iii. 10; Jas. v. 10, 11; cf. Clem. Rom. 1 Cor. 64; Ignat. ad Eph. 3, 1): Bp. Lghtft. remarks (on Col. l. c.), "The difference of meaning is best seen in their opposites. While ὑπο. is the temper which does not easily succumb under suffering, μακ. is the self-restraint which does not hastily retaliate a wrong. The one is opposed to cowardice or despondency, the other to wrath or revenge (Prov. xv. 18; xvi. 32) ... This distinction, though it applies generally, is not true without exception"... ; cf. also his note on Col. iii. 12, and see (more at length) Trench, N. T. Syn. § liii.]

μακροθύμως, adv., *with longanimity* (Vulg. longanimiter, Heb. vi. 15), i. e. *patiently*: Acts xxvi. 3.*   **3116**

μακρός, -ά, -όν, [fr. Hom. down], *long*; of place, *remote, distant, far off*: χώρα, Lk. xv. 13; xix. 12. of time, *long, lasting long*: μακρὰ προσεύχομαι, to pray long, make long prayers, Mt. xxiii. 14 (13) Rec.; Mk. xii. 40; Lk. xx. 47.*   **3117**

μακρο-χρόνιος, -ον, (μακρός and χρόνος), lit. 'long-timed' (Lat. longaevus), *long-lived*: Eph. vi. 3. (Ex. xx. 12; Deut. v. 16; very rare in prof. auth.) *   **3118**

μαλακία, -ας, ἡ, (μαλακός);   **1.** prop. *softness* [fr. Hdt. down].   **2.** in the N. T. (like ἀσθένεια, ἀρρωστία) *infirmity, debility, bodily weakness, sickness*, (Sept. for חֳלִי, disease, Deut. vii. 15; xxviii. 61; Is. xxxviii. 9, etc.); joined with νόσος, Mt. iv. 23; ix. 35; x. 1.*   **3119**

μαλακός, -ή, -όν, *soft*; *soft to the touch*: ἱμάτια, Mt. xi. 8 R G L br.; Lk. vii. 25, (ἱματίων πολυτελῶν κ. μαλακῶν, Artem. oneir. 1, 78; ἐσθής, Hom. Od. 23, 290; Artem. oneir. 2, 3; χιτών, Hom. Il. 2, 42); and simply τὰ μαλακά, soft raiment (see λευκός, 1): Mt. xi. 8 T Tr WH. Like the Lat. mollis, metaph. and in a bad sense: *effeminate*, of a catamite, a male who submits his body to unnatural lewdness, 1 Co. vi. 9 (Dion. Hal. antt. 7, 2 sub fin.; [Diog. Laërt. 7, 173 fin.]).*   **3120**

Μαλελεήλ (Μελελεήλ, Tdf.), ὁ, (מַהֲלַלְאֵל praising God, fr. מָהֲלַל and אֵל), *Mahalaleel* [A. V. *Maleleel*], son of Cainan: Lk. iii. 37.*   **3121**

μάλιστα (superlative of the adv. μάλα), [fr. Hom. down], adv., *especially, chiefly, most of all, above all*: Acts xx. 38; xxv. 26; Gal. vi. 10; Phil. iv. 22; 1 Tim. iv. 10; v. 8, 17; 2 Tim. iv. 13; Tit. i. 10; Philem. 16; 2 Pet. ii. 10; μάλιστα γνώστης, especially expert, thoroughly well-informed, Acts xxvi. 3.*   **3122**

μᾶλλον (compar. of μάλα, very, very much), [fr. Hom. down], adv., *more, to a greater degree; rather;*   **1.** added to verbs and adjectives, it denotes increase, a   **3123**

greater quantity, a larger measure, a higher degree, *more, more fully*, (Germ. *in höherem Grade, Maasse*); **a.** words defining the measure or size are joined to it in the ablative (dat.): πολλῷ *much, by far*, Mk. x. 48; Lk. xviii. 39; Ro. v. 15, 17, (in both these verses the underlying thought is, the measure of salvation for which we are indebted to Christ is far greater than that of the ruin which came from Adam; for the difference between the consequences traceable to Adam and to Christ is not only one of quality, but of quantity also; cf. *Rückert*, Com. on Rom. vol. i. 281 sq. [al. (fr. Chrys. to Meyer and Godet) content themselves here with a logical increase, *far more certainly*]); 2 Co. iii. 9, 11; Phil. ii. 12; πόσῳ *how much*, Lk. xii. 24; Ro. xi. 12; Philem. 16; Heb. ix. 14; τοσούτῳ *by so much*, ὅσῳ *by as much*, (sc. μᾶλλον), Heb. x. 25. **b.** in comparison it often so stands that *than* before must be mentally added, [A. V. *the more, so much the more*], as Mt. xxvii. 24 (μᾶλλον θόρυβος γίνεται [but al. refer this to 2 b. *a.* below]); Lk. v. 15 (διήρχετο μᾶλλον); Jn. v. 18 (μᾶλλον ἐζήτουν); xix. 8; Acts v. 14; ix. 22; xxii. 2; 2 Co. vii. 7; 1 Th. iv. 1, 10; 2 Pet. i. 10; ἔτι μᾶλλον καὶ μᾶλλον, Phil. i. 9; or the person or thing with which the comparison is made is evident from what precedes, as Phil. iii. 4; it is added to comparatives, Mk. vii. 36; 2 Co. vii. 13; πολλῷ μᾶλλον κρεῖσσον, Phil. i. 23; see [Wetstein on Phil. l. c.]; W. § 35, 1 cf. 603 (561); [B. § 123, 11]; to verbs that have a comparative force, μᾶλλον διαφέρειν τινός, to be of much more value than one, Mt. vi. 26. μᾶλλον ἤ, *more than*, Mt. xviii. 13; μᾶλλον with gen., πάντων ὑμῶν, 1 Co. xiv. 18 (Xen. mem. 3, 12, 1). joined to positive terms it forms a periphrasis for a comparative [cf. W. § 35, 2 a.], foll. by ἤ, as μακάριον μ. for μακαριώτερον, Acts xx. 35; add, 1 Co. ix. 15; Gal. iv. 27; πολλῷ μᾶλλον ἀναγκαία, 1 Co. xii. 22; sometimes μᾶλλον seems to be omitted before ἤ; see under ἤ, 3 f. **c.** μᾶλλον δέ, *what moreover is of greater moment*, [A. V. *yea rather*]: Ro. viii. 34 (2 Macc. vi. 23). **2.** it marks the preference of one thing above another, and is to be rendered *rather, sooner*, (Germ. *eher, vielmehr, lieber*); **a.** it denotes that which occurs *more easily* than something else, and may be rendered *sooner*, (Germ. *eher*): thus πολλῷ μᾶλλον in arguing from the less to the greater, Mt. vi. 30; Ro. v. 9 sq.; Heb. xii. 9 [here L T Tr WH πολὺ μ.]; also πολὺ [R G πολλῷ] μᾶλλον sc. οὐκ ἐκφευξόμεθα, i. e. much more shall we not escape (cf. W. p. 633 (588) note [B. § 148, 3 b.]), or even ἔνδικον μισθαποδοσίαν ληψόμεθα (Heb. ii. 2), or something similar (cf. Matthiae § 634, 3), Heb. xii. 25. πόσῳ μᾶλλον, Mt. vii. 11; x. 25; Lk. xii. 28; Ro. xi. 12, 24; Philem. 16. in a question, οὐ μᾶλλον; (Lat. *nonne potius?*) [*do not . . . more*], 1 Co. ix. 12. **b.** it is opposed to something else and does away with it; accordingly it may be rendered *the rather* (Germ. *vielmehr*); **a.** after a preceding negative or prohibitive sentence: Mt. x. 6, 28; xxv. 9; Mk. v. 26; Ro. xiv. 13; 1 Tim. vi. 2; Heb. xii. 13; μᾶλλον δέ, Eph. iv. 28; v. 11. οὐχὶ μᾶλλον; (*nonne potius?*) *not rather* etc.? 1 Co. v. 2; vi. 7. **β.** so that μᾶλλον belongs to the thing which is preferred, consequently to a noun, not to a

verb: Jn. iii. 19 (ἠγάπησαν μᾶλλον τὸ σκότος ἢ τὸ φῶς, i. e. when they ought to have loved the light they (hated it, and) loved the darkness, vs. 20); xii. 43; Acts iv. 19; v. 29; 2 Tim. iii. 4 that which it opposes and sets aside must be learned from the context [cf. W. § 35, 4]: Mk. xv. 11 (sc. ἢ τὸν Ἰησοῦν); Phil. i. 12 (where the meaning is, ʻso far is the gospel from suffering any loss or disadvantage from my imprisonment, that the number of disciples is increased in consequence of it ʼ). **γ.** by way of correction, μᾶλλον δέ, *nay rather*; *to speak more correctly*: Gal. iv. 9 (Joseph. antt. 15, 11, 3; Ael. v. h. 2, 13 and often in prof. auth.; cf. *Grimm*, Exeg. Hdbch. on Sap. p. 176 sq.). **c.** it does not do away with that with which it is in opposition, but marks what has the preference: *more willingly, more readily, sooner* (Germ. *lieber*), θέλω μᾶλλον and εὐδοκῶ μᾶλλον, *to prefer*, 1 Co. xiv. 5; 2 Co. v. 8, (βούλομαι μᾶλλον, Xen. Cyr. 1, 1, 1); ζηλοῦν, 1 Co. xiv. 1 (μᾶλλον sc. ζηλοῦτε); χρῶμαι, 1 Co. vii. 21.

Μάλχος (מֶלֶךְ) Grecized; cf. *Delitzsch* in the Zeitschr. f. Luth. Theol., 1876, p. 605), -ου, ὁ, *Malchus*, a servant of the high-priest: Jn. xviii. 10. [Cf. *Hackett* in B. D. s. v.]*   **3124**

μάμμη, -ης, ἡ, **1.** in the earlier Grk. writ. *mother* (the name infants use in addressing their mother). **2.** in the later writ. ([Philo], Joseph., Plut., App., Hdian., Artem.) i. q. τήθη, *grandmother* (see *Lob.* ad Phryn. pp. 133–135 [cf. W. 25]): 2 Tim. i. 5; 4 Macc. xvi. 9.*   **3125**

μαμωνᾶς (G L T Tr WH), incorrectly μαμμωνᾶς (Rec. [in Mt.]), -ᾶ [B. 20 (18); W. § 8, 1], ὁ, *mammon* (Chald. מָאמוֹנָא, to be derived, apparently, fr. אָמַן; hence *what is trusted* [cf. *Buxtorf*, Lex. chald. talmud. et rabbin. col. 1217 sq. (esp. ed. Fischer p. 613 sq.); acc. to *Gesenius* (Thesaur. i. 552) contr. fr. מַטְמוֹן *treasure* (Gen. xliii. 23); cf. B. D. s. v.; *Edersheim*, Jesus the Messiah, ii. 269]), *riches*: Mt. vi. 24 and Lk. xvi. 13, (where it is personified and opposed to God; cf. Phil. iii. 19); Lk. xvi. 9, 11. (ʻʻ*lucrum* punice *mammon* dicitur,ʼʼ Augustine [de serm. Dom. in monte, l. ii. c. xiv. (§ 47)]; the Sept. trans. the Hebr. אֱמוּנָה in Is. xxxiii. 6 θησαυροί, and in Ps. xxxvi. (xxxvii.) 3 πλοῦτος.)*   **3126**

Μαναήν, ὁ, (מְנַחֵם consoler), *Manaen*, a certain prophet in the church at Antioch: Acts xiii. 1. [See *Hackett* in B. D. s. v.]*   **3127**

Μανασσῆς [Treg. Μανν. in Rev.], gen. and acc. -ῆ [B. 19 (17); W. § 10, 1; but see *WH.* App. p. 159ᵃ], ὁ, (מְנַשֶּׁה causing to forget, fr. נָשָׁה to forget), *Manasseh*; **1.** the firstborn son of Joseph (Gen. xli. 51): Rev. vii. 6. **2.** the son of Hezekiah, king of Judah (2 K. xxi. 1–18): Mt. i. 10.*   **3128**

μανθάνω; 2 aor. ἔμαθον; pf. ptcp. μεμαθηκώς; Sept. for לָמַד; [fr. Hom. down]; *to learn, be apprised*; **a.** univ.: absol. *to increase* one's *knowledge*, 1 Tim. ii. 11; 2 Tim. iii. 7; *to be increased in knowledge*, 1 Co. xiv. 31; τί, Ro. xvi. 17; 1 Co. xiv. 35; Phil. iv. 9; 2 Tim. iii. 14; Rev. xiv. 3; in Jn. vii. 15 supply αὐτά; foll. by an indir. quest., Mt. ix. 13; Χριστόν, to be imbued with the knowledge of Christ, Eph. iv. 20; τί foll. by ἀπό w.   **3129**

gen. of the thing furnishing the instruction, Mt. xxiv. 32; Mk. xiii. 28; ἀπό w. gen. of the pers. teaching, Mt. xi. 29; Col. i. 7; as in class. Grk. (cf. Krüger § 68, 34, 1; B. § 147, 5 [cf. 167 (146) and ἀπό, II. 1 d.]); foll. by παρά w. gen. of pers. teaching, 2 Tim. iii. 14 cf. Jn. vi. 45; foll. by ἐν w. dat. of pers., *in one* i. e. by his example [see ἐν, I. 3 b.], 1 Co. iv. 6 [cf. W. 590 (548 sq.); B. 394 sq. (338)]. **b.** i. q. *to hear, be informed*: foll. by ὅτι, Acts xxiii. 27; τὶ ἀπό τινος (gen. of pers.), Gal. iii. 2 [see ἀπό, u. s.]. **c.** *to learn by use and practice*; [in the Pret.] *to be in the habit of, accustomed to*: foll. by an inf., 1 Tim. v. ; Tit. iii. 14; Phil. iv. 11, (Aeschyl. Prom. 1068; Xen. an. 3, 2, 25); ἔμαθεν ἀφ' ὧν ἔπαθε τὴν ὑπακοήν, Heb. v. 8 [cf. W. § 68, 1 and ἀπό, u. s.]. In the difficult passage 1 Tim. v. 13, neither ἀργαί depends upon the verb μανθάνουσι (which would mean "they learn to be idle", or "learn idleness"; so Bretschneider [Lex. s. v. 2 b.], and W. 347 (325 sq.); [cf. Stallbaum's note and reff. on Plato's Euthydemus p. 276 b.]), nor περιερχόμενοι ("they learn to go about from house to house," — so the majority of interpreters; for, acc. to uniform Grk. usage, a ptcp. joined to the verb μανθάνειν and belonging to the subject denotes *what sort of a person one learns or perceives himself to be*, as ἔμαθεν ἔγκυος οὖσα, "she perceived herself to be with child," Hdt. 1, 5); but μανθάνειν must be taken absolutely (see a. above) and emphatically, of what they learn by going about from house to house and what it is unseemly for them to know; cf. Bengel ad loc., and B. § 144, 17; [so Wordsworth in loc.]. [Comp.: κατα-μανθάνω.]*

3130 **μανία, -ας, ἡ,** (μαίνομαι), *madness, frenzy*: Acts xxvi. 24. [From Theognis, Hdt., down.]*

3131 **μάννα, τό,** indecl.; [also] ἡ μάννα in Joseph. (antt. 3, 13, 1 [etc.; ἡ μάννη, Orac. Sibyll. 7, 149]); Sept. τὸ μάν [also τὸ μάννα, Num. xi. 7] for Hebr. מָן (fr. the unused מָנַן, Arab. مَنَّ, to be kind, beneficent, to bestow liberally; whence the subst. مَنٌّ, prop. a gift [al. prefer the deriv. given Ex. xvi. 15, 31; Joseph. antt. 3, 1, 6. The word *mannu* is said to be found also in old Egyptian; *Ebers*, Durch Gosen u.s.w. p. 226; cf. "Speaker's Commentary" Exod. xvi. note]); *manna* (Vulg. in N. T. *manna* indecl.; in O. T. *man*; yet *manna*, gen. *-ae*, is used by Pliny [12, 14, 32, etc.] and Vegetius [Vet. 2, 39] of the grains of certain plants); according to the accounts of travellers a very sweet dew-like juice, which in Arabia and other oriental countries exudes from the leaves [acc. to others only from the t w i g s and b r a n c h e s; cf. *Robinson*, Pal. i. 115] of certain trees and shrubs, particularly in the summer of rainy years. It hardens into little white pellucid grains, and is collected before sunrise by the inhabitants of those countries and used as an article of food, very sweet like honey. The Israelites in their journey through the wilderness met with a great quantity of food of this kind; and tradition, which the biblical writers follow, regarded it as bread sent down in profusion from heaven, and in various ways gave the occurrence the dig-

nity of an illustrious miracle (Ex. xvi. 12 sqq.; Ps. lxxvii. (lxxviii.) 24; civ. (cv.) 40; Sap. xvi. 20); cf. *Win.* RWB. s. v. Manna; Knobel on Exod. p. 171 sqq.; *Furrer* in Schenkel iv. 109 sq.; [*Robinson* as above, and p. 590; *Tischendorf*, Aus dem heil. Lande, p. 54 sqq. (where on p. vi. an analysis of diff. species of natural manna is given after Berthelot (Comptes rendus hebdom. d. séances de l'acad. des sciences. Paris 1861, 2de sémestre (30 Sept.) p. 583 sqq.); esp. *Ritter*, Erdkunde Pt. xiv. pp. 665-695 (Gage's trans. vol. i. pp. 271-292, where a full list of reff. is given); esp. *E. Renaud and E. Lacour*, De la manne du désert etc. (1881). Against the identification of the natural manna with the miraculous, see BB.DD. s. v.; esp. *Riehm* in his HWB.; *Carruthers* in the Bible Educator ii. 174 sqq.]. In the N. T. mention is made of **a.** that manna with which the Israelites of old were nourished: Jn. vi. 31, 49, and R L in 58; **b.** that which was kept in the ark of the covenant: Heb. ix. 4 (Ex. xvi. 33); **c.** that which in the symbolic language of Rev. ii. 17 is spoken of as kept in the heavenly temple for the food of angels and the blessed; [see δίδωμι, B. Γ΄. p. 146ᵃ].*

μαντεύομαι; (μάντις [a seer; allied to μανία, μαίνομαι; cf. Curtius § 429]); fr. Hom. down; *to act as seer; deliver an oracle, prophesy, divine*: Acts xvi. 16 μαντευομένη, of a false prophetess [A. V. *by soothsaying*]. Sept. for קָסַם, to practise divination; said of false prophets. [On the h e a t h e n character of the suggestions and associations of the word, as distinguished fr. προφητεύω, see *Trench*, N. T. Syn. § vi.]* **3132**

μαραίνω: 1 fut. pass. μαρανθήσομαι; fr. Hom. Il. 9, 212; 23, 228 on; *to extinguish* (a flame, fire, light, etc.); *to render arid, make to waste away, cause to wither*; pass. *to wither, wilt, dry up* (Sap. ii. 8 of roses; Job xv. 30). Trop. *to waste away, consume away, perish*, (νόσῳ, Eur. Alc. 203; τῷ λιμῷ, Joseph. b. j. 6, 5, 1); i. q. *to have a miserable end*: Jas. i. 11, where the writer uses a fig. suggested by what he had just said (10); [B. 52 (46)].* **3133**

μαραναθά [so Lchm., but μαρὰν ἀθά R G T Tr WH], the Chald. words מָרַנָא אֲתָה, i. e. *our Lord cometh* or *will come*: 1 Co. xvi. 22. [BB.DD.; cf. *Klostermann*, Probleme etc. (1883) p. 220 sqq.; *Kautzsch*, Gr. pp. 12, 174; *Nestle* in Theol. Stud. aus Würtem. 1884 p. 186 sqq.]* **3134**

μαργαρίτης, -ου, ὁ, *a pearl*: Mt. xiii. 45 sq.; 1 Tim. ii. 9; Rev. xvii. 4; xviii. [12], 16; xxi. 21 [here L T WH accent -ρῖται, R G Tr -ρίται (cf. *Tdf.* Proleg. p. 101)]; τοὺς μαργαρίτας βάλλειν ἔμπροσθεν χοίρων, a proverb, i. e. to thrust the most sacred and precious teachings of the gospel upon the most wicked and abandoned men (incompetent as they are, through their hostility to the gospel, to receive them), and thus to profane them, Mt. vii. 6 (cf. Prov. iii. 15 sq.; Job xxviii. 18 sq.).* **3135**

Μάρθα, -ας (Jn. xi. 1 [cf. B. 17 (15); *WH*. App. p. 156]), **ἡ,** (Chald. מַרְתָא mistress, Lat. *domina*), *Martha*, the sister of Lazarus of Bethany: Lk. x. 38, 40 sq.; Jn. xi. 1, 5, 19-39; xii. 2. [On the accent cf. Kautzsch p. 8.]* **3136**

Μαριάμ indecl., and **Μαρία, -ας, ἡ,** (מִרְיָם 'obstinacy,' 'rebelliousness'; the well-known prop. name of the sister **3137**

of Moses; in the Targums מִרְיָם; cf. *Delitzsch*, Zeitschr. f. luth. Theol. for 1877 p. 2 [Maria is a good L a t i n name also]), *Mary*. The women of this name mentioned in the N. T. are the foll.   **1.** the mother of Jesus Christ, the wife of Joseph; her name is written Μαρία [in an o b l i q u e case] in Mt. i. 16, 18; ii. 11; Mk. vi. 3; Lk. i. 41; Acts i. 14 [R G L]; Μαριάμ in Mt. xiii. 55; Lk. i. 27, 30-56 [(in 38 L mrg. Μαρία)]; ii. 5, 16, 34; [Acts i. 14 T Tr WH]; the reading varies between the two forms in Mt. i. 20 [WH txt. -ρίαν]; Lk. ii. 19 [L T Tr WH txt. -ρία]; so where the other women of this name are mentioned, [see *Tdf*. Proleg. p. 116, where it appears that in h i s t e x t the gen. is always (seven times) -ρίας; the nom. in Mk. always (seven times) -ρία; that in Jn. -ριάμ occurs eleven times, -ρία (or -αν) only three times, etc.; for the facts respecting the Mss., see (Tdf. u. s. and) *WH.* App. p. 156]; cf. B. 17 (15).   **2.** *Mary Magdalene* (a native of Magdala): Mt. xxvii. 56, 61; xxviii. 1; Mk. xv. 40, 47; xvi. 1, 9; Lk. viii. 2; xxiv. 10; Jn. xix. 25; xx. 1, 11, 16, 18.   **3.** the mother of James the less and Joses, the wife of Clopas (or Alphæus) and sister of the mother of Jesus: Mt. xxvii. 56, 61; xxviii. 1; Mk. xv. 40, 47; xvi. 1; Lk. xxiv. 10; Jn. xix. 25 (see Ἰάκωβος, 2). There are some, indeed, who, thinking it improbable that there were t w o living sisters of the name of Mary (the common opinion), suppose that not three but four women are enumerated in Jn. xix. 25, and that these are distributed into two pairs so that ἡ ἀδελφὴ τῆς μητρὸς Ἰησοῦ designates Salome, the wife of Zebedee; so esp. *Wieseler* in the Theol. Stud. u. Krit. for 1840, p. 648 sqq., [cf. Bp. Lghtft. com. on Gal., Dissert. ii. esp. pp. 255 sq. 264] with whom Lücke, Meyer, Ewald and others agree; in opp. to them cf. *Grimm* in Ersch and Gruber's Encykl. sect. 2 vol. xxii. p. 1 sq. In fact, instances are not wanting among the Jews of two living brothers of the same name, e. g. *Onias*, in Joseph. antt. 12, 5, 1; *Herod*, sons of Herod the Great, one by Mariamne, the other by Cleopatra of Jerusalem, Joseph. antt. 17, 1, 3; b. j. 1, 28, 4; [cf. B. D. s. v. Mary of Cleophas; Bp. Lghtft. u. s. p. 264].   **4.** the sister of Lazarus and Martha: Lk. x. 39, 42; Jn. xi. 1-45; xii. 3.   **5.** the mother of John Mark: Acts xii. 12.   **6.** a certain Christian woman mentioned in Ro. xvi. 6.*

3138   **Μάρκος**, -ου, ὁ, *Mark*; acc. to the tradition of the church the author of the second canonical Gospel and identical with the *John Mark* mentioned in the Acts (see Ἰωάννης, 5). He was the son of a certain Mary who dwelt at Jerusalem, was perhaps converted to Christianity by Peter (Acts xii. 11 sq.), and for this reason called (1 Pet. v. 13) Peter's s o n. He was the cousin of Barnabas and the companion of Paul in some of his apostolic travels; and lastly was the associate of Peter also: Acts xii. 12, 25; xv. 37, 39; Col. iv. 10; 2 Tim. iv. 11; Philem. 24 (23); 1 Pet v. 13, cf. Euseb. h. e. 2, 15 sq.; 3, 39. Some, as Grotius, [*Tillemont*, Hist. Eccl. ii. 89 sq. 503 sq.; *Patritius*, De Evangeliis l. 1, c. 2, quaest. 1 (cf. *Cotelerius*, Patr. Apost. i. 262 sq.)], Kienlen (in the Stud. u. Krit. for 1843, p. 423), contend that there were two Marks, one the

disciple and companion of Paul mentioned in the Acts and Pauline Epp., the other the associate of Peter and mentioned in 1 Pet. v. 13; [cf. *Jas. Morison*, Com. on Mk. Introd. § 4; Bp. Lghtft. on Col. iv. 10].*

μάρμαρος, -ου, ὁ, ἡ, (μαρμαίρω to sparkle, glisten);   **1.**   **3139** *a stone, rock*, (Hom., Eur.).   **2.** *marble* ([cf. Ep. Jer. 71], Theophr., Strabo, al.): Rev. xviii. 12.*

μάρτυρ, -υρος, ὁ, see μάρτυς. — — — — — — — — — — — see 3144

μαρτυρέω, -ῶ; impf. 3 pers. plur. ἐμαρτύρουν; fut. μαρ- — — — 3140 τυρήσω; 1 aor. ἐμαρτύρησα; pf. μεμαρτύρηκα; Pass., pres. μαρτυροῦμαι; impf. ἐμαρτυρούμην; pf. μεμαρτύρημαι; 1 aor. ἐμαρτυρήθην; fr. [Simon., Pind.], Aeschyl., Hdt. down; *to be a witness, to bear witness, testify*, i. e. *to affirm that one has seen* or *heard* or *experienced something*, or *that* (so in the N. T.) *he knows it because taught by divine revelation* or *inspiration*, (sometimes in the N. T. the apostles are said μαρτυρεῖν, as those who had been eye- and ear- witnesses of the extraordinary sayings, deeds and sufferings of Jesus, which proved his Messiahship; so too Paul, as one to whom the risen Christ had visibly appeared; cf. Jn. xv. 27; xix. 35; xxi. 24; Acts xxiii. 11; 1 Co. xv. 15; 1 Jn. i. 2, cf. Acts i. 22 sq.; ii. 32; iii. 15; iv. 33; v. 32; x. 39, 41; xiii. 31; xxvi. 16; [cf. *Westcott*, ("Speaker's") Com. on Jn., Introd. p. xlv. sq.]);   **a.** in general; absol. *to give* (*not to keep back*) *testimony*: Jn. xv. 27; Acts xxvi. 5; foll. by ὅτι recitative and the orat. direct., Jn. iv. 39; also preceded by λέγων, Jn. i. 32; μαρτυρεῖν εἰς with an acc. of the place into (unto) which the testimony (concerning Christ) is borne, Acts xxiii. 11 [see εἰς, A. I. 5 b.]; μαρτυρῶ, inserted parenthetically (W. § 62, 2), 2 Co. viii. 3; i. q. *to prove* or *confirm by testimony*, 1 Jn. v. 6 sq.; used of Jesus, predicting what actually befell him, Jn. xiii. 21; of God, who himself testifies in the Scriptures that a thing is so (viz. as the author declares), foll. by the recitative ὅτι, Heb. vii. 17 R. μαρτ. foll. by περί w. gen. of a pers., *to bear witness concerning one*: Jn. i. 7 sq.; περὶ τοῦ ἀνθρώπου, concerning man, i. e. to tell what one has himself learned about the nature, character, conduct, of men, Jn. ii. 25 [see ἄνθρωπος, 1 a.]; περί τινος, foll. by direct disc., Jn. i. 15; the Scriptures are said to testify περὶ Ἰησοῦ, i. e. to declare things which make it evident that he was truly sent by God, Jn. v. 39; God is said to do the same,—through the Scriptures, ib. 37 cf. viii. 18; through the expiation wrought by the baptism and death of Christ, and the Holy Spirit giving souls assurance of this expiation, 1 Jn. v. 6-9; so John the Baptist, as being a 'prophet', Jn. v. 32; so the works which he himself did, ib. 36 (there foll. by ὅτι); x. 25; so the Holy Spirit, Jn. xv. 26; the apostles, 27; so Christ himself περὶ ἑαυτοῦ, Jn. v. 31; viii. 13 sq. 18. περὶ w. gen. of the thing, Jn. xxi. 24; περὶ τοῦ κακοῦ, to bring forward evidence to prove τὸ κακόν, Jn. xviii. 23. with the acc. of a cognate noun, μαρτυρίαν μαρτυρεῖν περί w. a gen. of the pers., Jn. v. 32; 1 Jn. v. 9 Rec.; 10, (τὴν αὐτὴν μαρτυρίαν μαρτυρεῖν, Plat. Eryx. p. 399 b.; τὴν μαρτυρίαν αὐτοῦ ἣν τῇ ἀρετῇ μαρτυρεῖ, Epict. diss. 4, 8, 32 [cf. W. 225 (211); B. 148 (129)]); w. an acc. of the thing, *to* *testify a thing, bear witness to (of) anything*: Jn. iii. 11, 32; supply αὐτό in Jn. xix. 35; τινί τι, 1 Jn. i. 2; ὃς ἐμαρτύρησε ... Χριστοῦ, who has borne witness of (viz. in this book, i. e. the Apocalypse) what God has spoken and Jesus Christ testified (sc. concerning future events; see λόγος, I. 2 b. ε.), Rev. i. 2; ὁ μαρτυρῶν ταῦτα he that *testifieth these things* i. e. has caused them to be testified by the prophet, his messenger, Rev. xxii. 20; μαρτυρῆσαι ὑμῖν ταῦτα ἐπί [L Tr mrg. WH mrg. ἐν] ταῖς ἐκκλησίαις, to cause these things to be testified to you *in* the churches or *for, on account of,* the churches, Rev. xxii. 16, — unless ἐπί be dropped from the text and the passage translated, *to you,* viz. *the* (seven) *churches* (of Asia Minor), the prophet reverting again to i. 4; cf. De Wette, Bleek, Düsterdieck, ad loc.; [al., retaining ἐπί, render it *over, concerning,* cf. x. 11; W. 393 (368) c.; see ἐπί, B. 2 f. β. fin.]. of testimony borne not in word but by deed, in the phrase used of Christ μαρτυρεῖν τὴν καλὴν ὁμολογίαν, to witness the good confession, to attest the truth of the (Christian) profession by his sufferings and death, 1 Tim. vi. 13, where cf. Hofmann. Pass.: Ro. iii. 21 (a righteousness such as the Scriptures testify that God ascribes to believers, cf. iv. 3). μαρτ. foll. by ὅτι *that,* Jn. i. 34 [cf. W. 273 (256)]; [iv. 44]; xii. 17 [here Rˢᵗ Tr txt. WH ὅτε]; 1 Jn. iv. 14; περί w. gen. of a pers. foll. by ὅτι, Jn. v. 36; vii. 7; κατά τινος, against [so W. 382 (357), Mey., al.; yet see κατά, I. 2 b.] one, foll. by ὅτι, 1 Co. xv. 15. w. a dat. of the thing i. e. for the benefit of, in the interests of, a thing [cf. B. § 133, 11]: τῇ ἀληθείᾳ, Jn. v. 33; xviii. 37; σοῦ τῇ ἀληθείᾳ (see ἀλήθεια, II.), to bear witness unto thy truth, how great it is, 3 Jn. 3, 6; used of the testimony which is given in deeds to promote some object: τῷ λόγῳ, Acts xiv. 3 [T prefixes ἐπί]; with a dat. (of a thing) incommodi: μαρτυρεῖτε (T Tr WH μάρτυρές ἐστε) τοῖς ἔργοις τῶν πατέρων, by what ye are doing ye add to the deeds of your fathers a testimony which proves that those things were done by them, Lk. xi. 48. w. a dat. of the person: *to declare to one by testimony* (by suggestion, instruction), Heb. x. 15; foll. by direct discourse, Rev. xxii. 18 G L T Tr WH; *to testify to one what he wishes one to testify concerning him*: Acts xxii. 5; foll. by ὅτι, Mt. xxiii. 31; Jn. iii. 28; Ro. x. 2; Gal. iv. 15; Col. iv. 13; foll. by an acc. w. inf. Acts x. 43; to give testimony in one's favor, to commend [W. § 31, 4 b.; B. as above]: Jn. iii. 26; Acts xiii. 22; xv. 8; pass. μαρτυροῦμαι *witness is borne to me, it is witnessed of me* (W. § 39, 1; B. § 134, 4): foll. by ὅτι, Heb. vii. 8; foll. by ὅτι recitative and direct disc., Heb. vii. 17 L T Tr WH; foll. by an inf. belonging to the subject, Heb. xi. 4 sq. **b.** emphatically; *to utter honorable testimony, give a good report:* w. a dat. of the pers., Lk. iv. 22; ἐπί τινι, on account of, for a thing, Heb. xi. 4 [here L Tr read μαρ. ἐπὶ κτλ. τῷ θεῷ (but see the Comm.)]; μεμαρτύρηταί τινι ὑπό τινος, 3 Jn. 12; pass. μαρτυροῦμαι *to be borne (good) witness to, to be well reported of, to have (good) testimony borne to one, accredited, attested, of good report, approved:* Acts vi. 3 (Clem. Rom. 1 Cor. 17, 1 sq.; 18,

1; 19, 1; 47, 4); foll. by ἐν w. a dat. of the thing in which the commended excellence appears, 1 Tim. v. 10; Heb. xi. 2, (ἐπί τινι, for a thing, Athen. 1 p. 25 f.; [yet cf. W. 387 (362) note]); διά τινος, to have (honorable) testimony borne to one through (by) a thing, Heb. xi. 39; ὑπό w. gen. of the pers. giving honorable testimony, Acts x. 22; xvi. 2; xxii. 12, (Clem. Rom. 1 Cor. 38, 2; 44, 3; Ignat. ad Philad. c. 5, 2 cf. 11, 1 and ad Eph. 12, 2; Antonin. 7, 62); w. dat. of the pers. testifying (i. q. ὑπό τινος), Acts xxvi. 22 R G; c. Mid., acc. to a false reading, *to conjure, implore*: 1 Th. ii. 12 (11), where T Tr WH have rightly restored μαρτυρόμενοι. [COMP.: ἐπι-, συν-επι-, κατα-, συμ-μαρτυρέω.] *

μαρτυρία, -ας, ἡ, (μαρτυρέω, q. v.), [fr. Hom. down]; **1.** *a testifying:* the office committed to the prophets of testifying concerning future events, Rev. xi. 7. **2.** what one testifies, *testimony:* univ. Jn. v. 34; in a legal sense, of testimony before a judge: Lk. xxii. 71; Mk. xiv. 56; w. gen. of the subj., Mk. xiv. 59; Jn. viii. 17; 1 Jn. v. 9; κατά τινος, against one, Mk. xiv. 55; in an historical sense, of the testimony of an historian: Jn. xix. 35; xxi. 24; in an ethical sense, of testimony concerning one's character: 3 Jn. 12; 1 Tim. iii. 7; Tit. i. 13; in a predominantly dogmatic sense respecting matters relating to the truth of Christianity: of the testimony establishing the Messiahship and the divinity of Jesus (see μαρτυρέω, a.), given by — John the Baptist: Jn. i. 7; v. 32; ἡ μαρτ. τοῦ Ἰωάννου, i. 19; Jesus himself, w. a gen. of the subj., Jn. v. 31; viii. 13 sq.; God, in the prophecies of Scripture concerning Jesus the Messiah, in the endowments conferred upon him, in the works done by him, Jn. v. 36; through the Holy Spirit, in the Christian's blessed consciousness of eternal life and of reconciliation with God, obtained by baptism [(cf. reff. s. v. βάπτισμα, 3)] and the expiatory death of Christ, w. a subject. gen. τοῦ θεοῦ, Jn. v. 9–11, cf. 6–8; the apostles, σοῦ τὴν μαρτ. περὶ ἐμοῦ, Acts xxii. 18 [W. 137 (130)]; the other followers of Christ: Rev. vi. 9; w. a gen. of the subj. αὐτῶν, Rev. xii. 11; w. a gen. of the obj. Ἰησοῦ, ib. 17; xix. 10; xx. 4 (ἔχειν this μαρτ. is to *hold the testimony,* to persevere steadfastly in bearing it, Rev. vi. 9; xii. 17; xix. 10, [see ἔχω, I. 1 d.]; others, however, explain it *to have the duty of testifying laid upon one's self*); elsewhere the "testimony" of Christ is that which he gives concerning divine things, of which he alone has thorough knowledge, Jn. iii. 11, 32 sq.; ἡ μαρτ. Ἰησοῦ, that testimony which he gave concerning future events relating to the consummation of the kingdom of God, Rev. i. 2 (cf. xxii. 16, 20); διὰ τὴν μ. Ἰησοῦ Χριστοῦ, to receive this testimony, ib. 9.*

μαρτύριον, -ου, τό, (μάρτυρ [cf. μάρτυς]), [fr. Pind., Hdt. down], Sept. for יֵעֵר, יְעָדָה, oftener for עֵדוּת (an ordinance, precept); most freq. for מוֹעֵד (an assembly), as though that came fr. יָעַד to testify, whereas it is fr. יָעַד to appoint; *testimony;* **a.** w. a gen. of the subj.: τῆς συνειδήσεως, 2 Co. i. 12; w. gen. of obj.: ἀποδιδόναι τὸ μ. τῆς ἀναστάσεως Ἰησοῦ, Acts iv. 33. **b.** τοῦ Χριστοῦ, concerning Christ the Saviour [cf. W. § 30,

3141

3142

1 a.] : the proclamation of salvation by the apostles is so called (for reasons given under μαρτυρέω, init.), 1 Co. i. 6 ; also τοῦ κυρίου ἡμῶν, 2 Tim. i. 8 ; τοῦ θεοῦ, concerning God [W. u. s.], i. e. concerning what God has done through Christ for the salvation of men, 1 Co. ii. 1 [here WH txt. μυστήριον] ; w. the subject. gen. ἡμῶν, given by us, 2 Th. i. 10. εἰς μαρτ. τῶν λαληθησομένων, to give testimony concerning those things which were to be spoken (in the Messiah's time) i. e. concerning the Christian revelation, Heb. iii. 5 ; cf. Delitzsch ad loc. [al. refer it to the Mosaic law (Num. xii. 7, esp. 8) ; cf. Riehm, Lehrbegriff d. Heb. i. 312]. c. εἰς μαρτύριον αὐτοῖς for a testimony unto them, that they may have testimony, i. e. evidence, in proof of this or that : e. g. that a leper has been cured, Mt. viii. 4 ; Mk. i. 44 ; Lk. v. 14 ; that persons may get knowledge of something the knowledge of which will be for their benefit, Mt. x. 18 ; xxiv. 14 ; Mk. xiii. 9 ; that they may have evidence of their impurity, Mk. vi. 11 ; in the same case we find εἰς μαρτ. ἐπ' αὐτούς, for a testimony against them [cf. ἐπί, C. I. 2 g. γ. ββ.], Lk. ix. 5 ; ἀποβήσεται ὑμῖν εἰς μαρτ. it will turn out to you as an opportunity of bearing testimony concerning me and my cause, Lk. xxi. 13 ; εἰς μ. ὑμῖν ἔσται, it will serve as a proof of your wickedness, Jas. v. 3 ; by apposition to the whole preceding clause (W. § 59, 9 a.), τὸ μαρτ. καιροῖς ἰδίοις, that which (to wit, that Christ gave himself as a ransom) would be (the substance of) the testimony i. q. was to be testified (by the apostles and the preachers of the gospel) in the times fitted for it, 1 Tim. ii. 6 [where Lchm. om. τὸ μαρτ.] ; cf. the full exposition of this pass. in Fritzsche, Ep. ad Rom. iii. p. 12 sqq. ἡ σκηνὴ τοῦ μαρτυρίου, Acts vii. 44 ; Rev. xv. 5 ; in Sept. very often for אֹהֶל־מוֹעֵד (see above), and occasionally for אֹהֶל הָעֵדֻת, as Ex. xxxviii. 26 ; Lev. xxiv. 3, etc.*

3143 μαρτύρομαι (fr. μάρτυρ [cf. μάρτυς]) ; **1.** to cite a witness, bring forward a witness, call to witness, (Tragg., Thuc., Plato, sqq.) ; to affirm by appeal to God, to declare solemnly, protest : ταῦτα, Plat. Phil. p. 47 c. ; ὅτι, Acts xx. 26 ; Gal. v. 3. **2.** to conjure, beseech as in God's name, exhort solemnly : τινί, Acts xxvi. 22 L T Tr WH ; foll. by the acc. w. inf., Eph. iv. 17 ; εἰς τό foll. by acc. w. inf. [cf. B. § 140, 10, 3], 1 Th. ii. 12 (11) T Tr WH. [COMP. : δια-, προ-μαρτύρομαι.] *

3144 μάρτυς (Aeolic μάρτυρ, a form not found in the N. T. ; [etymologically one who is mindful, heeds ; prob. allied with Lat. memor, cf. Vaniček p. 1201 ; Curtius § 466]), -υρος, acc. -υρα, ὁ ; plur. μάρτυρες, dat. plur. μάρτυσι ; Sept. for עֵד ; [Hes., Simon., Theogn., al.] ; a witness (one who avers, or can aver, what he himself has seen or heard or knows by any other means) : **a.** in a legal sense : Mt. xviii. 16 ; xxvi. 65 ; Mk. xiv. 63 ; Acts vi. 13 ; vii. 58 ; 2 Co. xiii. 1 ; 1 Tim. v. 19 ; Heb. x. 28. **b.** in an historical sense : Acts x. 41 ; 1 Tim. vi. 12 ; [2 Tim. ii. 2] ; one who is a spectator of anything, e. g. of a contest, Heb. xii. 1 ; w. a gen. of the obj., Lk. xxiv. 48 ; Acts i. 22 ; ii. 32 ; iii. 15 ; v. 32 G L T Tr WH ; x. 39 ; xxvi. 16 ; 1 Pet. v. 1 ; w. a gen. of the possessor ' one

who testifies for one ', Acts i. 8 L T Tr WH ; xiii. 31 ; w. a gen. of the possessor of and of the obj., Acts v. 32 Rec. ; μάρτυρα εἶναί τινι, to be a witness for one, serve him by testimony, Acts i. 8 R G ; xxii. 15 ; [Lk. xi. 48 T Tr WH]. He is said to be a witness, to whose attestation appeal is made ; hence the formulas μάρτυς μού ἐστιν ὁ θεός, Ro. i. 9 ; Phil. i. 8 ; θεὸς μάρτυς, 1 Th. ii. 5 ; μάρτυρα τὸν θεὸν ἐπικαλοῦμαι, 2 Co. i. 23 ; ὑμεῖς μάρτυρες κ. ὁ θεός, 1 Th. ii. 10 ; the faithful interpreters of God's counsels are called God's witnesses : Rev. xi. 3 ; Christ is reckoned among them, Rev. i. 5 ; iii. 14. **c.** in an ethical sense those are called μάρτυρες Ἰησοῦ, who after his example have proved the strength and genuineness of their faith in Christ by undergoing a violent death [cf B. D. Am. ed. and Dict. of Chris. Antiq. s. v. Martyr] : Acts xxii. 20 ; Rev. ii. 13 ; xvii. 6.*

μασθός, Doric for μασός (q. v.) : Rev. i. 13 Tdf. [" this form seems to be Western " (Hort, App. p. 149)]. **see 3149**

μασσάομαι (R G) more correctly μασάομαι (L T Tr WH) : impf. 3 pers. plur. ἐμασῶντο ; (ΜΑΩ, μάσσω, to knead) ; to chew, consume, eat, devour, (κρέας, Arstph. Plut. 321 ; τὰ δέρματα τῶν θυρεῶν, Joseph. b. j. 6, 3, 3 ; ῥίζας ξύλων, Sept. Job xxx. 4, and other exx. in other auth.) : ἐμασῶντο τὰς γλώσσας αὐτῶν, they gnawed their tongues (for pain), Rev. xvi. 10.* **3145**

μαστιγόω, -ῶ, 3 pers. sing. μαστιγοῖ ; fut. μαστιγώσω ; 1 aor. ἐμαστίγωσα ; (μάστιξ) ; fr. Hdt. down ; Sept. chiefly for הִכָּה ; to scourge ; prop. : τινά, Mt. x. 17 ; xx. 19 ; xxiii. 34 ; Mk. x. 34 ; Lk. xviii. 33 ; Jn. xix. 1 ; [cf. B. D. s. v. Scourging ; Farrar, St. Paul, vol. i. excurs. xi.]. metaph. of God as a father chastising and training men as children by afflictions : Heb. xii. 6 ; cf. Jer. v. 3 ; Prov. iii. 12 ; Judith viii. 27.* **3146**

μαστίζω ; i. q. μαστιγόω, q. v. ; τινά, Acts xxii. 25. (Num. xxii. 25 ; Sap. v. 11, and often in Hom.) * **3147; see 3146**

μάστιξ, -ιγος, ἡ, a whip, scourge, (for שׁוֹט, 1 K. xii. 11, 14 ; Prov. xxvi. 3) : Acts xxii. 24 ; Heb. xi. 36 ; metaph. a scourge, plague, i. e. a calamity, misfortune, esp. as sent by God to discipline or punish (Ps. lxxxviii. (lxxxix.) 33) ; with Διός added, Hom. Il. 12, 37 ; 13, 812 ; θεοῦ, Aeschyl. sept. 607) : of distressing bodily diseases, Mk. iii. 10 ; v. 29, 34 ; Lk. vii. 21 ; 2 Macc. ix. 11.* **3148**

μασός, -οῦ, ὁ, (μάσσω to knead [more prob. akin to μαδάω, Lat. madidus, etc. ; cf. Vaniček p. 693 ; Curtius § 456]), fr. Soph., Hdt. down ; the breast (for שַׁד, Job iii. 12 ; Cant. i. 13, etc.) ; plur., the breasts (nipples) of a man, Rev. i. 13 R G Tr WH [here Tdf. μασθοῖς (cf. WH. App. p. 149ª), Lchm. μαζοῖς] ; breasts of a woman, Lk. xi. 27 ; xxiii. 29.* **3149**

[**Ματαθίας,** see Ματταθίας.] **see 3161**

ματαιολογία, -ας, ἡ, (ματαιολόγος), vain talking, empty talk, (Vulg. vaniloquium) : 1 Tim. i. 6. (Plut. mor. p. 6 f. ; Porphyr. de abstin. 4, 16.) * **3150**

ματαιολόγος, -ου, ὁ, (μάταιος and λέγω), an idle talker, one who utters empty, senseless things : Tit. i. 10.* **3151**

μάταιος, -αία (1 Co. xv. 17 ; [1 Pet. i. 18]), -αιον, also -ος, -ον, (Jas. i. 26 ; Tit. iii. 9), [cf. WH. App. p. 157 ; W. § 11, 1], (fr. μάτην), Sept. for הֶבֶל שָׁוְא כָּזָב (a lie), etc. ; **3152**

as in prof. auth. (Lat. *vanus*) *devoid of force, truth, success, result*, [A.V. uniformly *vain*]: univ.: ἡ θρησκεία, Jas. i. 26; *useless, to no purpose*, ἡ πίστις, 1 Co. xv. 17; foolish, διαλογισμοί, 1 Co. iii. 20; ζητήσεις, Tit. iii. 9; given to vain things and leading away from salvation, ἀναστροφή, 1 Pet. i. 18. τὰ μάταια, *vain things, vanities*, of heathen deities and their worship (הֶבֶל, Jer. ii. 5; x. 3; יֵלֵךְ אַחֲרֵי הַהֶבֶל, πορεύεσθαι ὀπίσω τῶν ματ. 2 K. xvii. 15; הֲבָלִים, μάταια, Jer. viii. 19; εἴδωλα, Deut. xxxii. 21; Jer. xiv. 22): Acts xiv. 15. [Cf. Trench, Syn. § xlix.]*

3153   ματαιότης, -ητος, ἡ, (μάταιος, q. v.), a purely bibl. and eccles. word [(Pollux l. 6 c. 32 § 134)]; Sept. for הֶבֶל (often in Eccles.), also for שָׁוְא, etc.; *vanity*;   **a.** *what is devoid of truth and appropriateness*: ὑπέρογκα ματαιότητος (gen. of quality), 2 Pet. ii. 18.   **b.** *perverseness, depravation*: τοῦ νοός, Eph. iv. 17.   **c.** *frailty, want of vigor*: Ro. viii. 20.*

3154   ματαιόω: (μάταιος); 1 aor. pass. ἐματαιώθην; *to make empty, vain, foolish*: ἐματαιώθησαν ἐν τοῖς διαλογισμοῖς αὐτῶν, were brought to folly in their thoughts, i. e. fell into error, Ro. i. 21. (2 K. xvii. 15; Jer. ii. 5; 1 Chr. xxi. 8; [etc.]; nowhere in Grk. auth.) *

3155   μάτην (accus. [cf. W. 230 (216); B. § 131, 12] of μάτη, i. q. ματία, a futile attempt, folly, fault), adv., fr. Pind., Aeschyl. down, *in vain, fruitlessly*: Mt. xv. 9 and Mk. vii. 7, after Isa. xxix. 13 Sept.*

3156   Ματθαῖος (L T Tr WH Μαθθαῖος, cf. B. 8 (7); [WH. App. 159ᵇ; Scrivener, Introd. ch. viii. § 5 p. 562]), -ou [B. 18 (16)], ὁ, (commonly regarded as Hebr. מַתִּיָה gift of God, fr. מַתָּן and יָהּ; but מַתִּיָה is in Greek Ματθίας, and the analogy of the names חַגַּי (fr. חָג a festival) in Greek Ἀγγαῖος, זַכַּי Ζακχαῖος, and others, as well as the Syriac form of the name before us ܡܰܬܰܝ, [and its form in the Talmud, viz. מַתִּי or מַתָּאִי; Sanhedrin 43ᵃ; Meuschen, N. T. ex Talm. illustr. p. 8] certainly lead us to adopt the Aramaic form מַתַּי, and to derive that from the unused sing. מַת, a man, plur. מְתִים; hence i. q. manly, cf. Grimm in the Stud. u. Krit. for 1870, p. 723 sqq.), *Matthew*, at first a collector of imposts, afterwards an apostle of Jesus: Mt. ix. 9 sqq. (cf. Mk. ii. 14; Lk. v. 27 sqq.; see Λευί, 4); Mt. x. 3; Mk. iii. 18; Lk. vi. 15; Acts i. 13. Acc. to Papias (in Euseb. h. e. 3, 39) he wrote down ἑβραΐδι διαλέκτῳ τὰ (κυριακὰ) λόγια, i. e. *the sayings of our Lord*; this collection of discourses, perhaps already retouched by some one else and translated into Greek, the author of our first canonical Gospel combined with accounts of the acts and sufferings of Christ, and so it came to pass that this Gospel was ascribed by the church to Matthew as its author. [But this theory seems to be rendered unnecessary by the fact that λόγια had already come to denote "sacred oracles" i. q. ἱερὰ γράμματα, Joseph. b. j. 6, 5, 4, or ἱεραὶ γραφαί, Clem. Rom. 1 Cor. 53, 1; see the added reff. s. v. λόγιον. Cf. Fisher, Supernat. Origin of Christianity, pp. 160–167; and reff. in Schaff, Hist. of the Christ. Church, i. 622 sq.; Bleek, Einl. ins N. T. (ed. Mangold) p. 115 sq.]*

3157   Ματθάν (L T Tr WH Μαθθάν [see reff. s. v. Ματθαῖος]),

ὁ, (מַתָּן a gift), *Matthan*, one of Christ's ancestors: Mt. i. 15.*

3158   Ματθάτ (Tdf. Μαθθάθ, [see reff. s. v. Ματθαῖος]), ὁ, (כַּתָּת, fr. נָתַן), *Matthat*;   **1.** one of Christ's ancestors, the son of Levi: Lk. iii. 24.   **2.** one of the ancestors of the man just spoken of: Lk. iii. 29 [here Tr WH Μαθθάτ (see as above)].*

3159   Ματθίας (T Tr WH Μαθθίας [see reff. s. v. Ματθαῖος]), -α [yet cf. B. 18 (16)], ὁ, (see Ματθαῖος), *Matthias*, the apostle who took the place of Judas Iscariot: Acts i. 23, 26.*

3160   Ματταθά, ὁ, (see the preceding names), *Mattatha*, the son of Nathan and grandson of David: Lk. iii. 31.*

3161   Ματταθίας, -ου [B. 18 (16)], ὁ, *Mattathias*;   **1.** one of Christ's ancestors: Lk. iii. 25 [here Treg. Μαθθαθίου (cf. reff. s. v. Ματθαῖος, init.)].   **2.** one of the ancestors of the man just mentioned: Lk. iii. 26 [Tr mrg. Ματαθίου].*

3162   μάχαιρα, gen. -ας [so (with R G) Lchm. in Lk. xxi. 24] and -ης, dat. -ᾳ [so (with R G) Lchm. in Lk. xxii. 49]; Acts xii. 2] and -ῃ (betw. which forms the codd. vary, cf. [Scrivener, Collation, etc. p. lvi.; Tdf. Proleg. p. 117; WH. App. p. 156ᵃ]; W. 62 (61); B. 11; Delitzsch on Heb. xi. 34 p. 584 note), ἡ, (akin to μάχη and Lat. *mactare*);   **1.** *a large knife*, used for killing animals and cutting up flesh: Hom., Pind., Hdt., al.; hence Gen. xxii. 6, 10; Judg. xix. 29 Alex., for מַאֲכֶלֶת.   **2.** *a small sword*, distinguished fr. the large sword (the ῥομφαία Joseph. antt. 6, 9, 5 ἀποτέμνει τὴν κεφαλὴν τῇ ῥομφαίᾳ τῇ ἐκείνου (Goliath's), μάχαιραν οὐκ ἔχων αὐτός), and curved, *for a cutting stroke*; distinct also fr. ξίφος, *a straight sword, for thrusting*, Xen. r. eq. 12, 11, cf. Hell. 3, 3, 7; but the words are freq. used interchangeably. In the N. T. univ. *a sword* (Sept. often for חֶרֶב): as a weapon for making or repelling an attack, Mt. xxvi. 47, 51, 52, [55]; Mk. xiv. 43, 47 sq.; Lk. xxii. 36, 38, 49, 52; Jn. xviii. 10 sq.; Acts xvi. 27; Heb. xi. 37; Rev. vi. 4; xiii. 10, [14]; by a Hebraism, στόμα μαχαίρας, *the edge of the sword* (פִּי חֶרֶב, Gen. xxxiv. 26; Josh. viii. 24; 1 S. xiii. 22; Judg. iii. 16, etc. [but in the Sept. the rendering στ. ξίφους or στ. ῥομφαίας is more com.]): Lk. xxi. 24; Heb. xi. 34; μάχαιρα δίστομος (see δίστομος), Heb. iv. 12.   of the sword as the instrument of a magistrate or judge: death by the sword, Ro. viii. 35; ἀναιρεῖν τινα μαχαίρᾳ, Acts xii. 2; τὴν μ. φορεῖν, *to bear the sword*, is used of him to whom the sword has been committed, viz. to use when a malefactor is to be punished; hence i. q. *to have the power of life and death*, Ro. xiii. 4 (so ξίφος, ξίφη ἔχειν, Philostr. vit. Apoll. 7, 16; vit. sophist. 1, 25, 2 (3), cf. Dion Cass. 42, 27; and in the Talmud *the king who bears the sword*, of the Hebrew king). Metaph. μάχ., a weapon of war, is used for *war*, or for quarrels and dissensions that destroy peace; so in the phrase βαλεῖν μάχαιραν ἐπὶ τὴν γῆν, to send war on earth, Mt. x. 34 (for which Lk. xii. 51 says διαμερισμόν); ἡ μάχ. τοῦ πνεύματος, the sword with which the Spirit subdues the impulses to sin and proves its own power and efficacy (which sword is said to be ῥῆμα θεοῦ [cf. B. 128 (112)]), Eph. vi. 17 [on the gen. in this pass. cf. Ellicott or Meyer].*

3163   **μάχη, -ης, ἡ,** [μάχομαι; fr. Hom. down], Sept. several times for רִיב, מָדוֹן, etc.; *a fight, combat*; **1.** of those in arms, *a battle*. **2.** of persons at variance, disputants, etc., *strife, contention; a quarrel*: 2 Co. vii. 5; 2 Tim. ii. 23; Jas. iv. 1; μάχαι νομικαί, contentions about the law, Tit. iii. 9.*

3164   **μάχομαι**; impf. 3 pers. plur. ἐμάχοντο; [allied with μάχαιρα; Curtius § 459; Vaniček p. 687; fr. Hom. down]; *to fight*: prop. of armed combatants, or those who engage in a hand-to-hand struggle, Acts vii. 26; trop. of those who engage in a war of words, *to quarrel, wrangle, dispute*: 2 Tim. ii. 24; πρὸς ἀλλήλους, Jn. vi. 52 [cf. W. § 31, 5; B. § 133, 8]; of those who contend at law for property and privileges, Jas. iv. 2. [COMP.: διαμάχομαι. SYN. see πόλεμος, b.]*

3166   **μεγαλ-αυχέω, -ῶ;** (μεγάλαυχος, and this fr. μεγάλα and αὐχέω); *to be grandiloquent; to boast great things, to bear one's self loftily in speech* or *action*: ἡ γλῶσσα μεγαλαυχεῖ (L T Tr WH μεγάλα αὐχεῖ), Jas. iii. 5, where it seems to denote any kind of haughty language which wounds and provokes others, and stirs up strife. (Aeschyl. Ag. 1528; Polyb. 12, 13, 10; 8, 23, 11; Diod. 15, 16, al.; mid. γυναῖκα πρὸς θεοὺς ἐρίζουσαν καὶ μεγαλαυχουμένην, Plat. rep. 3 p. 395 d.; for נבה, to exalt one's self, carry one's self haughtily, Ezek. xvi. 50; Zeph. iii. 11; add, 2 Macc. xv. 32; Sir. xlviii. 18.)*

3167   **μεγαλεῖος, -εία, -εῖον,** (μέγας), *magnificent, excellent, splendid, wonderful*, (Xen., Joseph., Artem., al.); absol. μεγαλεῖα (ποιεῖν τινι) to do great things for one (show him conspicuous favors), Lk. i. 49 R G; τὰ μεγαλεῖα τοῦ θεοῦ (Vulg. *magnalia dei* [A. V. *the mighty works of God*]), i. e. the glorious perfections of God and his marvellous doings (נְדֹלוֹת, Ps. lxx. (lxxi.) 19; Sir. xxxiii. (xxxvi.) 10; xlii. 21), Acts ii. 11.*

3168   **μεγαλειότης, -ητος, ἡ,** (fr. the preceding word), *greatness, magnificence,* (Athen. 4, 6 p. 130 fin.; for תִּפְאֶרֶת Jer. xl. (xxxiii.) 9); *the majesty* of God, Lk. ix. 43; τῆς Ἀρτέμιδος, Acts xix. 27; of the visible splendor of the divine majesty as it appeared in the transfiguration of Christ, 2 Pet. i. 16.*

3169   **μεγαλοπρεπής, -ές,** gen. -οῦς, (μέγας, and πρέπει it is becoming [see πρέπω]), *befitting a great man, magnificent, splendid; full of majesty, majestic*: 2 Pet. i. 17. (2 Macc. viii. 15; xv. 13; 3 Macc. ii. 9; Hdt., Xen., Plat., al.)*

3170   **μεγαλύνω;** impf. ἐμεγάλυνον; Pass., [impf. 3 pers. sing. ἐμεγαλύνετο]; 1 aor. inf. μεγαλυνθῆναι; 1 fut. μεγαλυνθήσομαι; (μέγας); fr. [Aeschyl. and] Thuc. down; Sept. mostly for הִגְדִּיל; **1.** *to make great, magnify,* (Vulg. *magnifico*) τινά or τί, prop. of dimension, Mt. xxiii. 5 [here A.V. *enlarge*]; pass. *to increase*: of bodily stature, ἐμεγαλύνθη τὸ παιδάριον, 1 S. ii. 21; so in a figure, 2 Co. x. 15, of Paul, that his apostolic efficiency among the Corinthians may increase more and more and have more abundant results [al. refer this to 2; see Meyer (ed. Heinrici) in loc.]. metaph. *to make conspicuous*: Lk. i. 58 (on which see ἔλεος, 2 a.). **2.** *to deem* or *declare great,* i. e. *to esteem highly, to extol, laud, celebrate*: Lk. i. 46; Acts v. 13; x. 46; xix. 17. (often so in class. Grk.)

*For 3165 see 1691.

---

also); pass. i. q. to get glory and praise: ἔν τινι, in a thing, Phil. i. 20.*

3171   **μεγάλως, adv.,** *greatly*: Phil. iv. 10. [Fr. Hom. down.]*

3172   **μεγαλωσύνη, -ης, ἡ,** only in bibl. and eccl. writ. [cf. W. 26, 95 (90); B. 73, and see ἀγαθωσύνη], (μέγας), Sept. for גְּדֻלָּה and גְּדוּלָּה; *majesty*: of the majesty of God, Heb. i. 3; viii. 1; Jude 25, (so 2 S. vii. 23; Ps. cxliv. (cxlv.) 3, 6; Sap. xviii. 24; Sir. ii. 18, and often).*

3173   **μέγας, μεγάλη, μέγα,** [(related to Lat. *magnus, magister*, Goth. *maist* (cf. τὸ πλεῖστον), etc.; Vaniček p. 682; Curtius § 462)], acc. μέγαν, μεγάλην, μέγα; plur. μεγάλοι, -αι, -α; comp. μείζων, -ον, (acc. masc. and fem. μείζονα, once contr. μείζω, Jn. v. 36 [R G T WH, but L Tr μείζων (cf. Tdf. Proleg. p. 119)]; neut. plur. μείζονα, once contr. μείζω, Jn. i. 50 (51)) and μειζότερος, 3 Jn. 4 (fr. the compar. μείζων), a poet. compar., on which see the remark quoted under ἐλαχιστότερος, cf. Matthiae § 136; superl. μέγιστος (found only in 2 Pet. i. 4); [fr. Hom. down]; Sept. for נָדֹל; also for רַב; *great*; **1.** predicated **a.** of the external form or sensible appearance of things (or of persons); in particular, of space and its dimensions, — as respects **a.** m a s s a n d w e i g h t: λίθος, Mt. xxvii. 60; Mk. xvi. 4; Rev. xviii. 21; ὄρος, Rev. viii. 8; ἀστήρ, ibid. 10; δράκων Rev. xii. 3, 9; ἀετός, ibid. 14; δένδρον, Lk. xiii. 19 [T WH om. L Tr br. μέγ.]; κλάδοι, Mk. iv. 32; ἰχθύες, Jn. xxi. 11; **β.** c o m p a s s and e x t e n t; *large, spacious:* σκηνή (μείζων), Heb. ix. 11; ἀνάγαιον [R ἀνώγεον, q. v.], Mk. xiv. 15; ἀποθήκη, Lk. xii. 18; κάμινος, Rev. ix. 2; πόλις, Rev. xi. 8; xvi. 19; xvii. 18; xviii. 2, 16, 18, 19; προαυλίς, Rev. xiv. 14; xvi. 12; θύρα, 1 Co. xvi. 9; ληνός, Rev. xiv. 19; ὀθόνη, Acts x. 11; xi. 5; χάσμα, Lk. xvi. 26 (2 S. xviii. 17). **γ.** m e a s u r e and h e i g h t: οἰκοδομαί, Mk. xiii. 2; θρόνος, Rev. xx. 11; *long,* μάχαιρα, Rev. vi. 4; as respects stature and age, μικροὶ καὶ μεγάλοι, small and great, young and old, Acts viii. 10; xxvi. 22; Heb. viii. 11; Rev. xi. 18; xiii. 16; xix. 5, 18; xx. 12, (Gen. xix. 11; 2 K. xxiii. 2; 2 Chr. xxxiv. 30). [neut. sing. used adverbially: ἐν μεγάλῳ, Acts xxvi. 29 L T Tr WH (for R G ἐν πολλῷ, q. v. in πολύς, d.) in *great* sc. degree. The apostle plays upon Agrippa's words ἐν ὀλίγῳ (q. v.) *in a little* (time) thou wouldst fain etc. . . . I would to God that both in little and in *great* i. e. in all respects etc.; cf. the use of ὀλίγον κ. μέγα or σμικρόν κ. μέγα (yet in n e g a t i v e sentences) to express totality; e. g. Plat. Phileb. 21 e.; Apol. 19 c.; 21 b.; 26 b.; but see d. below.] **b.** of n u m b e r and q u a n t i t y, i. q. *numerous, large:* ἀγέλη, Mk. v. 11; *abundant,* πορισμός, 1 Tim. vi. 6; μισθαποδοσία, Heb. x. 35. **c.** of a g e: ὁ μείζων, *the elder,* Ro. ix. 12 after Gen. xxv. 23, (Σκιπίων ὁ μέγας, Polyb. 18, 18 (35), 9; 32, 12, 1). **d.** used of in-t e n s i t y and its degrees: δύναμις, Acts iv. 33; viii. 10; neut. ἐν μεγάλῳ, with great effort, Acts xxvi. 29 L T Tr WH [but see γ. above]; of the affections and emotions of the mind: χαρά, Mt. ii. 10; xxviii. 8; Lk. ii. 10; xxiv. 52; Acts xv. 3; φόβος, Mk. iv. 41; Lk. ii. 9; viii. 37; Acts v. 5, 11; Rev. xi. 11; θυμός, Rev. xii. 12; λύπη, Ro. ix. 2; ἔκστασις, Mk. v. 42 (Gen. xxvii. 33); πίστις, Mt. xv. 28; χάρις, Acts iv. 33; ἀγάπη, Jn. xv. 13. of natural events powerfully affecting the senses, i. q. *violent, mighty, strong*: ἄνεμος, Jn. vi. 18; Rev. vi. 13; βροντή, Rev. xiv. 2; χάλαζα, Rev. xi. 19; xvi. 21; σεισμός, Mt. viii. 24; xxviii. 2; Lk. xxi. 11; Acts xvi. 26; Rev. vi. 12; xi. 13; xvi. 18; λαῖλαψ, Mk. iv. 37; πτῶσις, Mt. vii. 27. of other external things, such as are perceived by h e a r i n g: κραυγή, Acts xxiii. 9; Rev. xiv. 18 [R G]; μεῖζον κράζειν, to cry out the louder, Mt. xx. 31; φωνή, Mt. xxiv. 31 [T om. φ., WH only in mrg.]; xxvii. 46, 50; Lk. xxiii. 23; Jn. xi. 43; Acts viii. 7; Rev. i. 10; v. 2, 12; vi. 10; vii. 2, 10; viii. 13; x. 3; xi. 12, 15; [xiv. 18 L T Tr WH; xviii. 2 Rec.], and elsewhere; γαλήνη, Mt. viii. 26; Mk. iv. 39. of objects of s i g h t which excite admiration and wonder: φῶς, Mt. iv. 16; σημεῖον, Mt. xxiv. 24; Lk. xxi. 11; Acts vi. 8; viii. 13; Rev. xiii. 13; ἔργα, Rev. xv. 3; μείζω, μείζονα τούτων, greater things than these, i.e. more extraordinary, more wonderful, Jn. i. 50 (51); v. 20; xiv. 12. of things that are f e l t: καῦμα, Rev. xvi. 9; πυρετός, Lk. iv. 38; of other things that distress: ἀνάγκη, Lk. xxi. 23; θλίψις, Mt. xxiv. 21; Acts vii. 11; Rev. ii. 22; vii. 14; διωγμός, Acts viii. 1; λιμός, Lk. iv. 25; Acts xi. 28; πληγή, Rev. xvi. 21. **2.** predicated of r a n k, as belonging to **a.** p e r s o n s, eminent for ability, virtue, authority, power; as God, and sacred personages: θεός, Tit. ii. 13 [(on which see Prof. Abbot, Note C. in Journ. Soc. Bibl. Lit. etc. i. p. 19, and cf. ἐπιφάνεια)]; Ἄρτεμις, Acts xix. 27 sq. 34 sq.; ἀρχιερεύς, Heb. iv. 14; ποιμήν, Heb. xiii. 20; προφήτης, Lk. vii. 16; absol. οἱ μεγάλοι, great men, leaders, rulers, Mt. xx. 25; Mk. x. 42; univ. *eminent, distinguished*: Mt. v. 19; xx. 26; Lk. i. 15, 32; Acts viii. 9. μείζων is used of those who surpass others — either in n a t u r e and p o w e r, as God: Jn. x. 29 [here T Tr WH txt. give the neut. (see below)]; xiv. 28; Heb. vi. 13; 1 Jn. iv. 4; add, Jn. iv. 12; viii. 53; or in e x c e l l e n c e, w o r t h, a u t h o r i t y, etc.: Mt. xi. 11; xviii. 1; xxiii. 11; Mk. ix. 34; Lk. vii. 28; ix. 46; xxii. 26 sq.; Jn. xiii. 16; xv. 20; 1 Co. xiv. 5; δυνάμει μείζονες, 2 Pet. ii. 11; neut. μεῖζον, *something higher, more exalted, more majestic* than the temple, to wit the august person of Jesus the Messiah and his preëminent influence, Mt. xii. 6 L T Tr WH; [cf. Jn. x. 29 above]; contextually i. q. *strict in condemning*, of God, 1 Jn. iii. 20. **b.** t h i n g s to be esteemed highly for their i m p o r t a n c e, i. q. Lat. *gravis*; *of great moment, of great weight, important*: ἐπαγγέλματα, 2 Pet. i. 4; ἐντολή, Mt. xxii. 36, 38; μυστήριον, Eph. v. 32; 1 Tim. iii. 16; ἁμαρτία, Jn. xix. 11; μείζων μαρτυρία, of greater proving power, Jn. v. 36 [see above ad init.]; 1 Jn. v. 9, (μαρτυρίαν μείζω κ. σαφεστέραν, Isocr. Archid. § 32). μέγας i. q. *solemn, sacred*, of festival days [cf. Is. i. 13 Sept.]: ἡμέρα, Jn. vii. 37; xix. 31; *notable, august*, ἡμέρα, of the day of the final judgment, Acts ii. 20; Jude 6; Rev. vi. 17; xvi. 14. neut. μέγα, a great matter, thing of great moment: 1 Co. ix. 11 (Gen xlv. 28; Is. xlix. 6); οὐ μέγα, 2 Co. xi. 3. **c.** a t h i n g to be highly esteemed for its e x c e l l e n c e, i. q. *excellent*: 1 Co. xiii. 13 [cf. W. § 35, 1; B. § 123, 13]; τὰ χαρίσματα τὰ μείζονα (R G κρείττονα), 1 Co. xii. 31 L T Tr WH. **3.** *splendid, prepared on a grand scale*.

stately: δοχή, Lk. v. 29 (Gen. xxi. 8); δεῖπνον, Lk. xiv. 16; Rev. xix. 17 [G L T Tr WH], (Dan. v. 1 [Theodot.]); οἰκία, 2 Tim. ii. 20 (Jer. lii. 13; [οἶκος], 2 Chr. ii. 5, 9). **4.** neut. plur. μεγάλα, *great things*: of God's preëminent blessings, Lk. i. 49 L T Tr WH (see μεγαλεῖος); of things which overstep the province of a c r e a t e d being, *proud* (presumptuous) *things, full of arrogance*, derogatory to the majesty of God: λαλεῖν μεγ. joined with βλασφημίας, Rev. xiii. 5; Dan. vii. 8, 11, 20; like μέγα εἰπεῖν, Hom. Od. 3, 227; 16, 243; 22, 288.

μέγεθος, -ους, τό, (μέγας), [fr. Hom. down], *greatness*: Eph. i. 19.* — 3174

μεγιστάν, -ᾶνος, ὁ, (fr. μέγιστος, as νεάν fr. νέος, ξυνάν fr. ξυνός), a later Grk. word (see Lob. ad Phryn. p. 196), once in sing. Sir. iv. 7; commonly in plur. οἱ μεγιστᾶνες, *the grandees, magnates, nobles, chief men of a city or a people, the associates or courtiers of a king*, (Vulg. *principes*): Rev. vi. 15; τῆς γῆς, xviii. 23; τοῦ Ἡρώδου, Mk. vi. 21. (Sept. for אַדִּירִים, Jer. xiv. 3; Nah. ii. 6; Zech. xi. 2; גְּדוֹלִים, Jon. iii. 7; Nah. iii. 10; רַבְרְבִין, Dan. Theodot. iv. 33, etc.; שָׂרִים, Is. xxxiv. 12; Jer. xxiv. 8, etc.; 1 Macc. ix. 37; often in Sir. Manetho 4, 41; Joseph., Artem. In Lat. *megistanes*, Tac. ann. 15, 27; Suet. Calig. 5.)* — see 3175 St.

μέγιστος, see μέγας, init. — 3176; see 3173

μεθ-ερμηνεύω: Pass., 3 pers. sing. μεθερμηνεύεται, ptcp. μεθερμηνευόμενον; *to translate into the language of one with whom I wish to communicate, to interpret*: Mt. i. 23; Mk. v. 41; xv. 22, 34; Jn. i. 38 (39) L Tr WH, 41 (42); Acts iv. 36; xiii. 8. (Polyb., Diod., Plut., [Sir. prol. l. 19; al.].)* — 3177

μέθη, -ης, ἡ, (akin to μέθυ, wine; perh. any intoxicating drink, Lat. *temetum*; cf. Germ. *Meth* [*mead*]), *intoxication; drunkenness*: Lk. xxi. 34; plur., Ro. xiii. 13; Gal. v. 21. (Hebr. שֵׁכָר, intoxicating drink, Prov. xx. 1; Is. xxviii. 7; and שִׁכָּרוֹן, intoxication, Ezek. xxiii. 32; xxxix. 19; [Antipho], Xen., Plat., al.) [Cf. Trench § lxi.] * — 3178

μεθ-ίστημι and (in 1 Co. xiii. 2 R G WH [cf. ἵστημι]) **μεθιστάνω**; 1 aor. μετέστησα; 1 aor. pass. subj. μετασταθῶ; fr. Hom. down; prop. *to transpose, transfer, remove from one place to another*: prop. of change of situation or place, ὄρη, 1 Co. xiii. 2 (Isa. liv. 10); τινὰ εἴς τι, Col. i. 13; τινὰ [T Tr WH ind ἐκ, so L in br.] .ῆς οἰκονομίας, to remove from the office of steward, pass. Lk. xvi. 4 (τῆς χρείας, 1 Macc. xi. 63); τινὰ ἐκ τοῦ ζῆν, to remove from life, Diod. 2, 57, 5; 4, 55, 1; with ἐκ τοῦ ζῆν omitted, Acts xiii. 22 (in Grk. writ. also in the mid. and in the intrans. tenses of the act. *to depart from life, to die*, Eur. Alc. 21; Polyb. 32, 21, 3; Heliod. 4, 14). metaph. τινά, without adjunct (cf. Germ. *verrücken*, [Eng. *pervert*]), i. e. *to lead aside* [A. V. *turn away*] to other tenets: Acts xix. 26 (τὴν καρδίαν τοῦ λαοῦ, Josh. xiv. 8).* — 3179

μεθ-οδεία (T WH μεθοδία, see I, ι,), -ας, ἡ, (fr. μεθοδεύω, i. e. 1. to follow up or investigate by method and settled plan; 2. to follow craftily, frame devices, deceive; Diod. 7, 16; 2 S. xix. 27; [Ex. xxi. 13 Aq.; (mid.) Charit. 7, 6 p. 166, 21 ed. Reiske (1783); Polyb. 38, 4, 10]), a noun occurring neither in the O. T. nor in prof. auth., — 3180 cunning arts, deceit, craft, trickery : ἡ μεθ. τῆς πλάνης, which ἡ πλάνη uses, Eph. iv. 14 ; τοῦ διαβόλου, plur. ib. vi. 11 [A.V. wiles. Cf. Bp. Lghtft. Polyc. ad Phil. 7 p. 918.] *

see 3181 St.

μεθ-όριον, -ου, τό, (neut. of adj. μεθόριος, -α, -ον ; fr. μετά with, and ὅρος a boundary), a border, frontier : τὰ μεθόριά τινος, the confines (of any land or city), i. e. the places adjacent to any region, the vicinity, Mk. vii. 24 R G. (Thuc., Xen., Plat., al.) *

3182

μεθύσκω : Pass., pres. μεθύσκομαι ; 1 aor. ἐμεθύσθην ; (fr. μέθυ, see μέθη) ; fr. Hdt. down ; Sept. for רָוָה ,הִרְוָה , (Kal רָוָה), and שָׁכַר, to intoxicate, make drunk ; pass. [cf. W. 252 (237)] to get drunk, become intoxicated : Lk. xii. 45 ; Jn. ii. 10 ; 1 Th. v. 7 [B. 62 (54)] ; οἴνῳ [W. 217 (203)], Eph. v. 18 ; ἐκ τοῦ οἴνου, Rev. xvii. 2 (see ἐκ, II. 5) ; τοῦ νέκταρος, Plat. symp. p. 203 b. ; Lcian. dial. deor. 6, 3 ; ἀπό τινος, Sir. i. 16 ; xxxv. 13.*

3183

μέθυσος, -ύση, -υσον, in later Grk. also of two terminations, (μέθυ, see μέθη), drunken, intoxicated : 1 Co. v. 11 ; vi. 10. (Phryn. : μέθυσος ἀνήρ, οὐκ ἐρεῖς, ἀλλὰ μεθυστικός · γυναῖκα δὲ ἐρεῖς μέθυσον καὶ μεθύσην [Arstph.] ; but Menand., Plut., Lcian., Sext. Empir., a!., [Sept. Prov. xxiii. 21, etc. ; Sir. xix. 1, etc.] use it also of men ; cf. Lob. ad Phryn. p. 151.) *

3184

μεθύω (fr. μέθυ, see μέθη) ; fr. Hom. down ; Sept. for רָוָה and שָׁכַר ; to be drunken : Mt. xxiv. 49 ; Acts ii. 15 ; 1 Co. xi. 21 ; 1 Th. v. 7 [cf. B. 62 (54)] ; ἐκ τοῦ αἵματος [see ἐκ, II. 5 ; Tr mrg. τῷ αἵματι], of one who has shed blood profusely, Rev. xvii. 6 (Plin. h. n. 14, 28 (22) ebrius jam sanguine civium et tanto magis eum sitiens).*

*

3186 ; —
see 3173   μειζότερος, -α, -ον, see μέγας, init.
3187 ; — —   μείζων, see μέγας, init.
see 3173   μέλαν, -ανος, τό, see the foll. word.
3188 ; —   μέλας, -αινα, -αν, gen. -ανος, -αίνης, -ανος, [fr. Hom. down],
see 3189   Sept. several times for שָׁחֹר, black : Rev. vi. 5, 12 ; opp.
3189 — —   to λευκός, Mt. v. 36. Neut. τὸ μέλαν, subst. black ink (Plat. Phaedr. p. 276 c. ; Dem. p. 313, 11 ; Plut. mor. p. 841 e. ; al.) : 2 Co. iii. 3 ; 2 Jn. 12 ; 3 Jn. 13 ; [cf. Gardthausen, Palaeographie, Buch i. Kap. 4 ; Edersheim, Jesus the Messiah, ii. 270 sq. ; B. D. s. v. Writing, sub fin.] *

3190

Μελεᾶς, gen. -ᾶ [B. 20 (17) sq.], (T Tr WH Μελεά, indecl., [on the accent in codd. cf. Tdf. Proleg. p. 103]), ὁ, (כִּלְאָה abundance), Melea, one of king David's descendants : Lk. iii. 31.*

see 3199 St.

μέλει, 3 pers. sing. pres. of μέλω used impers. ; impf. ἔμελεν ; it is a care ; τινί, to one ; as in Grk. writ. with nom. of the thing, οὐδὲν τούτων, Acts xviii. 17 ; with gen. of the thing (as often in Attic), μὴ τῶν βοῶν μέλει τῷ θεῷ ; 1 Co. ix. 9 [B. § 132, 15 ; cf. W. 595 (554)] ; the thing which is a care to one, or about which he is solicitous, is evident from the context, 1 Co. vii. 21 ; περί τινος, gen. of obj., to care about, have regard for, a pers. or a thing : Mt. xxii. 16 ; Mk. xii. 14 ; Jn. x. 13 ; xii. 6 ; 1 Pet. v. 7, (Hdt. 6, 101 ; Xen. mem. 3, 6, 10 ; Cyr. 4, 5, 17 ; Hier. 9, 10 ; 1 Macc. xiv. 43 ; Sap. xii. 13 ; Barnab. ep. 1, 5 ; cf. W. § 30, 10 d.) ; foll. by ὅτι, Mk. iv. 58 ; Lk. x. 40.*

see 3121   [Μελελήλ : Lk. iii. 37 Tdf., see Μαλ.]
3191   μελετάω, -ῶ ; 1 aor. ἐμελέτησα ; (fr. μελέτη care, prac-

tice) ; esp. freq. in Grk. writ. fr. Soph. and Thuc. down ; Sept. chiefly for הָגָה ; to care for, attend to carefully, practise : τί, 1 Tim. iv. 15 [R. V. be diligent in] ; to meditate i. q. to devise, contrive : Acts iv. 25 fr. Ps. ii. 1 ; used by the Greeks of the meditative pondering and the practice of orators and rhetoricians, as μ. τὴν ἀπολογίαν ὑπὲρ ἑαυτῶν, Dem. p. 1129, 9 (cf. Passow s. v. d. [L. and S. s. v. II. 2 and III. 4 b.]), which usage seems to have been in the writer's mind in Mk. xiii. 11 [R L br. Comp. : προ-μελετάω].*

μέλι, -τος, τό, Sept. for דְּבַשׁ, [fr. Hom. down], honey : Rev. x. 9 sq. ; ἄγριον (q. v.), Mt. iii. 4 ; Mk. i. 6.*   3192

μελίσσιος, -α, -ον, (fr. μέλισσα a bee, as θαλάσσιος fr. θάλασσα ; μέλισσα is fr. μέλι), of bees, made by bees : Lk. xxiv. 42 [R G Tr in br.]. (Not found elsewh. [cf. W. 24] ; μελισσαῖος, -α, -ον is found in Nic. th. 611, in Eust. μελίσσειος.) *   3193

Μελίτη, -ης, ἡ, Melita, the name of an island in the Mediterranean, lying between Africa and Sicily, now called Malta ; (this Sicula Melita must not be confounded with Melita Illyrica in the Adriatic, now called Meleda [see B. D. s. v. Melita ; Smith, Voyage and Shipwr. of St. Paul, Diss. ii.]) : Acts xxviii. 1 [where WH Μελι-ήνη ; see their App. p. 160].*   3194

[Μελιτήνη, see the preceding word.]   see 3194

μέλλω ; fut. μελλήσω (Mt. xxiv. 6 ; and L T Tr WH in 2 Pet. i. 12) ; impf. ἔμελλον [so all edd. in Lk. ix. 31 (exc. T WH) ; Jn. vi. 6, 71 (exc. RG) ; vii. 39 (exc. T) ; xi. 51 (exc. L Tr) ; Acts xxi. 27 ; Rev. iii. 2 (where R pres.) ; x. 4 (exc. L Tr)] and ἤμελλον [so all edd. in Lk. vii. 2 ; x. 1 (exc. R G) ; xix. 4 ; Jn. iv. 47 ; xii. 33 ; xviii. 32 ; Acts xii. 6 (exc. R G L) ; xvi. 27 (exc. R G) ; xxvii. 33 (exc. R G T) ; Heb. xi. 8 (exc. L) ; cf. reff. s. v. βούλομαι, init. and Rutherford's note on Babrius 7, 15], to be about to do anything ; so   1. the ptcp., ὁ μέλλων, absol. : τὰ μέλλοντα and τὰ ἐνεστῶτα are contrasted, Ro. viii. 38 ; 1 Co. iii. 22 ; εἰς τὸ μέλλον, for the future, hereafter, Lk. xiii. 9 [but see εἰς, A. II. 2 (where Grimm supplies ἔτος)] ; 1 Tim. vi. 19 ; τὰ μέλλοντα, things future, things to come, i. e., acc. to the context, the more perfect state of things which will exist in the αἰὼν μέλλων, Col. ii. 17 ; with nouns, ὁ αἰὼν ὁ μέλλων, Mt. xii. 32 ; Eph. i. 21 ; ἡ μέλλ. ζωή, 1 Tim. iv. 8 ; ἡ οἰκουμένη ἡ μέλλ. Heb. ii. 5 ; ἡ μ. ὀργή, Mt. iii. 7 ; τὸ κρίμα τὸ μέλλον, Acts xxiv. 25 ; πόλις, Heb. xiii. 14 ; τὰ μέλλοντα ἀγαθά, Heb. ix. 11 [but L Tr mrg. WH txt. γενομένων] ; x. 1 ; τοῦ μέλλοντος sc. Ἀδάμ, i. e. the Messiah, Ro. v. 14.   2. joined to an infin. [cf. W. 333 sq. (313) ; B. § 140, 2], to be on the point of doing or suffering something : w. inf. present, ἤμελλεν ἑαυτὸν ἀναιρεῖν, Acts xvi. 27 ; τελευτᾶν, Lk. vii. 2 ; ἀποθνήσκειν, Jn. iv. 47 ; add, Lk. xxi. 7 ; Acts iii. 3 ; xviii. 14 ; xx. 3 ; xxii. 26 ; xxiii. 27 ; w. inf. passive, Acts xxi. 27 ; xxvii. 33, etc.   b. to intend, have in mind, think to : w. inf. present, Mt. ii. ; Lk. x. 1 ; xix. 4 ; Jn. vi. 6, 15 ; vii. 35 ; xii. 4 ; xiv. 22 , Acts v. 35 ; xvii. 31 ; xx. 7, 13 ; xxii. 26 ; xxvi. 2 ; xxvii. 30 ; Heb. viii. 5 ; [2 Pet. i. 12 L T Tr WH] ; Rev. x. 4 ; w. inf. aorist (a constr. censured by Phryn. p. 336, but authenticated more recently   3195 by many exx. fr. the best writ. fr. Hom. down; cf. W. 333 (313) sq.; *Lob.* ad Phryn. p. 745 sqq.; [but see *Rutherford*, New Phryn. p. 420 sqq.]): Acts xii. 6 L T WH; Rev. ii. 10 (βαλεῖν R G); iii. 16; xii. 4; w. fut. inf. ἔσεσθαι, Acts xxiii. 30 R G.   **c.** as in Grk. writ. fr. Hom. down, of those things which will come to pass (or which one will do or suffer) by fixed **necessity** or **divine appointment** (Germ. *sollen* [are to be, *destined* to be, etc.]); w. pres. inf. active: Mt. xvi. 27; xvii. 12; xx. 22; Lk. ix. 31; Jn. vi. 71; vii. 39; xi. 51; xii. 33; xviii. 32; Acts xx. 38; xxvi. 22, 23; Heb. i. 14; xi. 8; Rev. ii. 10*; iii. 10; viii. 13, etc.; Ἡλίας ὁ μέλλων ἔρχεσθαι, Mt. xi. 14; ὁ μέλλων λυτροῦσθαι, Lk. xxiv. 12; κρίνειν, 2 Tim. iv. 1 [WH mrg. κρῖναι]; w. pres. inf. passive: Mt. xvii. 22; Mk. xiii. 4; Lk. ix. 44; xix. 11; xxi. 36; Acts xxvi. 22; Ro. iv. 24; 1 Th. iii. 4; Jas. ii. 12; Rev. i. 19 [Tdf. γενέσθαι]; vi. 11; τῆς μελλούσης ἀποκαλύπτεσθαι δόξης, 1 Pet. v. 1; w. aor. inf.: τὴν μέλλουσαν δόξαν ἀποκαλυφθῆναι, Ro. viii. 18; τὴν μέλλουσαν πίστιν ἀποκαλυφθῆναι, Gal. iii. 23; used also of those things which we infer from certain preceding events will of necessity follow: w. inf. pres., Acts xxviii. 6; Ro. viii. 13; w. inf. fut., Acts xxvii. 10.   **d.** in general, of what is *sure* to happen: w. inf. pres., Mt. xxiv. 6; Jn. vi. 71; 1 Tim. i. 16; Rev. xii. 5; xvii. 8; w. inf. fut. ἔσεσθαι, Acts xi. 28; xxiv. 15.   **e.** to be always on the point of doing without ever doing, i. e. *to delay*: τί μέλλεις; Acts xxii. 16 (Aeschyl. Prom. 36; τί μέλλετε; Eur. Hec. 1094; Lcian. dial. mort. 10, 13, and often in prof. auth.; 4 Macc. vi. 23; ix. 1).

3196   μέλος, -ους, τό, [fr. Hom. down], *a member, limb*: prop. a member of the human body, Ro. xii. 4; 1 Co. xii. 12, 14, 18–20, 25 sq.; Jas. iii. 5; τὰ μ. τοῦ σώματος, 1 Co. xii. 12, 22; μοῦ, σοῦ, ἡμῶν, ὑμῶν, Mt. v. 29 sq.; Ro. vi. 13, 19; vii. 5, 23; Col. iii. 5; Jas. iii. 6; iv. 1; πόρνης μέλη is said of bodies given up to criminal intercourse, because they are as it were members belonging to the harlot's body, 1 Co. vi. 15. Since Christians are closely united by the bond of one and the same spirit both among themselves and with Christ as the head, their fellowship is likened to the **body**, and individual Christians are metaph. styled μέλη — now one of another, ἀλλήλων: Ro. xii. 5; Eph. iv. 25; Clem. Rom. 1 Cor. 46, 7, (cf. *Fritzsche*, Com. on Rom. iii. p. 45), — now of the mystical body, i. e. the church: 1 Co. xii. 27; Eph. v. 30, [cf. iv. 16 WH mrg.]; τὰ σώματα of Christians are called μέλη of Christ, because the body is the abode of the spirit of Christ and is consecrated to Christ's service, 1 Co. vi. 15.*

3197   Μελχί (T Tr WH Μελχεί; see ει, ι), ὁ, (מַלְכִּי my king), *Melchi*; **1.** one of Christ's ancestors: Lk. iii. 24.   **2.** another of the same: ib. iii. 28.*

3198   Μελχισεδέκ (in Joseph. antt. 1, 10, 2 Μελχισεδέκης, -ου), ὁ, (מַלְכִּי־צֶדֶק king of righteousness), *Melchizedek*, king of Salem (see under Σαλήμ) and priest of the most high God, who lived in the days of Abraham: Heb. v. 6, 10; vi. 20; vii. 1, 10 sq. 15, 17, 21 [R G L]; cf. Gen. xiv. 18 sqq.; Ps. cix. (cx.) 4. [Cf. B. D. s. v.] *

*For 3199 see p. 396 & 3199 St.

3200   μεμβράνα [*Soph.* Lex. -άνα; cf. Chandler § 136], -ας [B. 17 (15)], ἡ, Lat. *membrana*, i. e. *parchment*, first made of dressed skins at Pergamum, whence its name: 2 Tim. iv. 13 [Act. Barn. 6 fin. Cf. *Birt*, Antikes Buchwesen, ch. ii.; *Gardthausen*, Palaeographie, p. 39 sq.].*

3201   μέμφομαι; 1 aor. ἐμεμψάμην; in class. Grk. fr. Hesiod (opp. 184) down; *to blame, find fault*: absol. Ro. ix. 19; the thing found fault with being evident from what precedes, Mk. vii. 2 Rec.; αὐτούς, Heb. viii. 8 L T Tr mrg. WH txt., where R G T rst. WH mrg. αὐτοῖς, which may join with μεμφόμενος (for the person or thing blamed is added by Grk. writ. now in the dat., now in the acc.; see Passow [or L. and S.] s. v., cf. Krüger § 46, 7, 3); but it is more correct to supply αὐτήν, i. e. διαθήκην, which the writer wishes to prove was not "faultless" (cf. 7), and to join αὐτοῖς with λέγει; [B. § 133, 9].*

3202   μεμψίμοιρος, -ον, (μέμφομαι, and μοῖρα fate, lot), *complaining of one's lot, querulous, discontented*: Jude 16. (Isocr. p. 234 c. [p. 387 ed. Lange]; Aristot. h. a. 9, 1 [p. 608b, 10]; Theophr. char. 17, 1; Lcian. dial. deor. 20, 4; Plut. de ira cohib. c. 13.) *

3303   μέν, a weakened form of μήν, and hence properly a particle of affirmation: *truly, certainly, surely, indeed*, — its affirmative force being weakened, yet it retained most in Ionic, Epic, and Herodotus, and not wholly lost in Attic and Hellenistic writers (μέν 'confirmative'; cf. 4 Macc. xviii. 18). Owing to this its original meaning it adds a certain force to the terms and phrases with which it is connected, and thus contrasts them with or distinguishes them from others. Accordingly it takes on the character of a **concessive** and very often of a merely **distinctive** particle, which stands related to a following δέ or other adversative conjunction, either expressed or understood, and in a sentence composed of several members is so placed as to point out the first member, to which a second, marked by an adversative particle, is added or opposed. It corresponds to the Lat. *quidem, indeed*, Germ. *zwar* (i. e. prop. *zu Wahre*, i. e. *in Wahrheit* [*in truth*]); but often its force cannot be reproduced. Its use in classic Greek is exhibited by Devarius i. p. 122 sqq., and Klotz on the same ii. 2 p. 656 sqq.; Viger i. p. 531 sqq., and Hermann on the same p. 824 sq.; al.; Matthiae § 622; Kühner ii. p. 806 sqq. §§ 527 sqq.; p. 691 sqq.; § 503; [Jelf § 729, 1, 2; §§ 764 sqq.]; Passow, and Pape, [and L. and S.] s. v.

I. Examples in which the particle μέν is followed in another member by an adversative particle expressed. Of these examples there are two kinds: **1.** those in which μέν has a concessive force, and δέ (or ἀλλά) introduces a restriction, correction, or amplification of what has been said in the former member, *indeed . . . but, yet, on the other hand*. Persons or things, or predications about either, are thus correlated: Mt. iii. 11, cf. Mk. i. 8 (where T Tr WH om. L br. μέν); Lk. iii. 16 (where the meaning is, 'I indeed baptize as well as he who is to come after me, but his baptism is of greater efficacy'; cf. Acts i. 5); Mt. ix. 37 and Lk. x. 2 (although the harvest is great, yet the laborers are few);

Mt. xvii. 11 sq. (rightly indeed is it said that Elijah will come and work the ἀποκατάστασις, but he has already come to bring about this very thing); Mt. xx. 23; xxii. 8; xxiii. 28; Jn. xvi. 22; xix. 32 sq.; Acts xxi. 39 (although I am a Jew, and not that Egyptian, yet etc.); Acts xxii. 3 [R]; Ro. ii. 25; vi. 11; 1 Co. i. 18; ix. 24; xi. 14 sq.; xii. 20 [R G L br. Tr br. WH mrg.]; xv. 51 [R G L br.]; 2 Co. x. 10; Heb. iii. 5 sq.; 1 Pet. i. 20, and often. μέν and δέ are added to articles and pronouns: οἱ μὲν ... οἱ δέ, the one indeed ... but the other (although the latter, yet the former), Phil. i. 16 sq. [acc. to crit. txt.]; ὃς μὲν ... ὃς δέ, the one indeed, but (yet) the other etc. Jude 22 sq.; τινὲς μὲν ... τινὲς δὲ καί, Phil. i. 15; with conjunctions: εἰ μὲν οὖν, if indeed then, if therefore ... εἰ δέ, but if, Acts xviii. 14 sq. R G; xix. 38 sq.; xxv. 11 L T Tr WH [εἰ μὲν οὖν ... νυνὶ δέ, Heb. viii. 4 sq. (here R G εἰ μὲν γάρ)]; εἰ μὲν ... νῦν δέ, if indeed (conceding or supposing this or that to be the case) ... but now, Heb. xi. 15; κἂν μὲν ... εἰ δὲ μήγε, Lk. xiii. 9; μὲν γὰρ ... δέ, 1 Co. xi. 7; Ro. ii. 25; μὲν οὖν ... δέ, Lk. iii. 18; εἰς μὲν ... εἰς δέ, Heb. ix. 6 sq.; μὲν ... ἀλλά, indeed ... but, although ... yet, Ro. xiv. 20; 1 Co. xiv. 17; μὲν ... πλήν, Lk. xxii. 22. [Cf. W. 443 (413); B. § 149, 12 a.] **2.** those in which μέν loses its concessive force and serves only to distinguish, but δέ retains its adversative power: Lk. xi. 48; Acts xiii. 36 sq.; xxiii. 8 [here WH txt. om. Tr br. μέν]; 1 Co. i. 12, 23; Phil. iii. 1; Heb. vii. 8; ἀπὸ μὲν ... ἐπὶ δέ, 2 Tim. iv. 4; ὁ μὲν οὖν (Germ. er nun [he, then,]) ... οἱ δέ, Acts xxviii. 5 sq.; ὃς μὲν ... ὃς δέ, and one ... and another, 1 Co. xi. 21; οἱ μὲν ... ὁ δέ (he, on the contrary), Heb. vii. 20 sq. 23 sq.; ἐκεῖνοι μὲν οὖν ... ἡμεῖς δέ, 1 Co. ix. 25; εἰ μὲν οὖν ... εἰ δέ, Acts xviii. 14 sq. [R G]; xix. 38; xxv. 11 [L T Tr WH]; and this happens chiefly when what has already been included in the words immediately preceding is separated into parts, so that the adversative particle contrasts that which the writer especially desires to contrast: ἑκάστῳ ... τοῖς μὲν ζητοῦσιν ... τοῖς δὲ ἐξ ἐριθείας etc. Ro. ii. 6–8; πᾶς ... ἐκεῖνοι μὲν ... ἡμεῖς δέ etc. 1 Co. ix. 25; add, Mt. xxv. 14 sq. 33; Ro. v. 16; xi. 22. **3.** μὲν ... δέ serve only to distribute a sentence into clauses: both ... and; not only ... but also; as well ... as: Jn. xvi. 9–11; Ro. viii. 17; Jude 8; πρῶτον μὲν ... ἔπειτα, Heb. vii. 2; ὁ μὲν ... ὁ δὲ ... ὁ δέ, some ... some ... some, Mt. xiii. 8; [ἕκαστος ... ὁ μὲν ... ὁ δέ, each ... one ... another, 1 Co. vii. 7 L T Tr WH]; ὃς μὲν ... ὃς δέ, one ... another, Mt. xxi. 35; Acts xvii. 32; 1 Co. vii. 7 [R G]; οἱ μὲν ... ἄλλοι [L οἱ] δέ ... ἕτεροι δέ, Mt. xvi. 14; ᾧ μὲν γὰρ ... ἄλλῳ δέ ... ἑτέρῳ δέ [here T Tr WH om. L br. δέ], 1 Co. xii. 8–10; ἃ μὲν ... foll. by ἄλλα δέ three times, Mt. xiii. 4 sq. 7 sq.; ἄλλος μέν, ἄλλος δέ, 1 Co. xv. 39; τοῦτο μὲν ... τοῦτο δέ, on the one hand ... on the other; partly ... partly, Heb. x. 33, also found in prof. auth. cf. W. 142 (135). μέν is followed by another particle: ἔπειτα, Jn. xi. 6; 1 Co. xii. 28; Jas. iii. 17; καὶ νῦν, Acts xxvi. 4, 6; τὰ νῦν, Acts xvii. 30; πολὺ [R G πολλῷ] μᾶλλον, Heb. xii. 9.

II. Examples in which μέν is followed neither by δέ nor by any other adversative particle (μέν 'solitarium'); cf. W. 575 (534) sq.; B. 365 (313) sq. These exx. are of various kinds; either **1.** the antithesis is evident from the context; as, Col. ii. 23 ('have indeed a show of wisdom', but are folly [cf. Bp. Lghtft. in loc.]); ἡ μὲν ... σωτηρίαν, sc. but they themselves prevent their own salvation, Ro. x. 1; τὰ μὲν ... δυνάμεσιν, sc. but ye do not hold to my apostolic authority, 2 Co. xii. 12; ἄνθρωποι μὲν [L T Tr WH om. μέν] ... ὀμνύουσιν, sc. ὁ δὲ θεὸς καθ' ἑαυτοῦ ὀμνύει, Heb. vi. 16. Or **2.** the antithetic idea is brought out by a different turn of the sentence: Acts xix. 4 [Rec.], where the expected second member, Ἰησοῦς δέ ἐστιν ὁ ἐρχόμενος, is wrapped up in τοῦτ' ἔστιν εἰς τὸν Ἰησοῦν; Ro. xi. 13 ἐφ' ὅσον μὲν κτλ., where the antithesis παραζηλῶ δὲ κτλ. is contained in εἴπως παραζηλώσω; Ro. vii. 12 ὁ μὲν νόμος κτλ., where the thought of the second member, 'but sin misuses the law,' is expressed in another form in 13 sqq. by an anacoluthon, consisting of a change from the disjunctive to a conjunctive construction (cf. Herm. ad Vig. p. 839), we find μὲν ... τέ, Acts xxvii. 21; μὲν ... καί, 1 Th. ii. 18; in distributions or partitions, Mk. iv. 4–8 [here R G μὲν ... δὲ ... καὶ ... καί]; Lk. viii. 5–8; or, finally, that member in which δέ would regularly follow immediately precedes (Herm. ad Vig. p. 839), Acts xxviii. 22 [yet see Meyer ad loc.; cf. B. § 149, 12 d.]. Or **3.** the writer, in using μέν, perhaps had in mind a second member to be introduced by δέ, but was drawn away from his intention by explanatory additions relating to the first member: thus Acts iii. 13 (ὃν ὑμεῖς μέν — Rec. om. this μέν — etc., where ὁ θεὸς δὲ ἤγειρεν ἐκ νεκρῶν, cf. 15, should have followed); esp. (as occasionally in class. Grk. also) after πρῶτον μέν: Ro. i. 8; iii. 2; 1 Co. xi. 18; τὸν μὲν πρῶτον λόγον κτλ. where the antithesis τὸν δὲ δεύτερον λόγον κτλ. ought to have followed, Acts i. 1. **4.** μὲν οὖν [in Lk. xi. 28 T Tr WH μενοῦν], Lat. quidem igitur, [Eng. so then, now therefore, verily, etc.], (where μέν is confirmatory of the matter in hand, and οὖν marks an inference or transition, cf. Klotz ad Devar. ii. 2 p. 662 sq.; [Herm. Vig. pp. 540 sq. 842; B. § 149, 16]): Acts i. 18; v. 41; xiii. 4; xvii. 30; xxiii. 22; xxvi. 9; 1 Co. vi. 4, 7 [here T om. Tr br. οὖν]; ἀλλὰ μὲν οὖν, Phil. iii. 8 G L Tr; εἰ μὲν οὖν, Heb. vii. 11. **5.** μέν solitarium has a concessive and restrictive force, indeed, verily, (Germ. freilich), [cf. Klotz, Devar. ii. 2 p. 522; Hartung, Partikeln, ii. 404]: εἰ μέν, 2 Co. xi. 4; μὲν οὖν now then, (Germ. nun freilich), Heb. ix. 1 [cf. B. u. s. On the use of μὲν οὖν in the classics cf. Cope's note on Aristot. rhet. 2, 9, 11.] **6.** μενοῦνγε, q. v. in its place.

III. As respects the Position of the particle: it never stands at the beginning of a sentence, but yet as near the beginning as possible; generally in the second or third place, by preference between the article and noun, [exx. in which it occupies the fourth place are Acts iii. 21; 2 Co. x. 1; Col. ii. 23; Acts xiv. 12 Rec.; the fifth place, Eph. iv. 11; Ro. xvi. 19 R WH br.; 1 Co. ii. 15 R G; (Jn. xvi. 22, see below)]; moreover, in the midst of a clause also it attaches itself to a word the force of which is to be strengthened, as καὶ ὑμεῖς οὖν λύπην μὲν νῦν ἔχετε [but L T Tr WH ... οὖν νῦν μὲν λύπ.], Jn. xvi. 22; cf. W. § 61, 6. The word is not found in the Rev. or in the Epp. of John.

(3303a)﹥

see 3104 ━━━Μεννά or Μέννας, see Μαϊνάν.

see 3303 ━━μεν-οὖν i. q. μὲν οὖν, see μέν, II. 4 sq.

3304; ━━━━μεν-οῦν-γε [μενοῦν γε L Tr], (μέν, οὖν, γέ), nay surely,
see 3303, nay rather; three times in answers by which what was
3767 & previously said is corrected (and standing at the begin-
1065 ning of the clause, contrary to Attic usage where μὲν οὖν is never so placed; cf. Sturz, De dial. Mac. et Alex. p. 203 sq.; Lob. ad Phryn. p. 342; [B. 370 sq. (318); W. § 61, 6]): Lk. xi. 28 [where T Tr WH μενοῦν]; Ro. ix. 20; x. 18; also Phil. iii. 8 [where L G Tr μὲν οὖν, WH μὲν οὖν γε], and Nicet. ann. 21, 11. 415 [p. 851 ed. Bekk.].*

3305　μέν-τοι, (μέν, τοί), [Tr μέν τοι in 2 Tim. ii. 19], a par-ticle of affirmation, and hence also often of opposition (on its various use in class. Grk. cf. Devar. p. 124 sq. and Klotz's comments, vol. ii. 2 pp. 60 and 663 sqq.; Herm. ad Vig. p. 840 sq.), but yet, nevertheless, howbeit: Jn. iv. 27; vii. 13; xx. 5; xxi. 4; 2 Tim. ii. 19; Jude 8 (the connection of which vs. with what precedes is as follows: 'although these examples were set forth as warnings, nevertheless' etc.); ὅμως μέντοι, yet nevertheless, Jn. xii. 42; μέντοι, i. q. rather, Jas. ii. 8 (if ye do not have re-spect of persons, but rather observe the law of love, with which προσωποληψία is incompatible; [if however, howbeit if]).*

3306　μένω; impf. ἔμενον; fut. μενῶ; 1 aor. ἔμεινα; plupf. μεμενήκειν without augm. (1 Jn. ii. 19; cf. ἐκβάλλω, [and see Tdf. Proleg. p. 120 sq.]); [fr. Hom. down]; Sept. chiefly for עָמַד and קוּם, also for יָשַׁב, חָכָה, etc.; to re-main, abide;　　I. intransitively; in reference　　1. to PLACE;　　a. prop. i. q. Lat. commoror, to sojourn, tarry: ἐν w. dat. of place, Lk. viii. 27; x. 7; Jn. vii. 9; xi. 6; Acts xx. 15; xxvii. 31; xxviii. 30 [R G L]; 2 Tim. iv. 20; with adverbs of place: ἐκεῖ, Mt. x. 11; Jn. ii. 12; x. 40; [xi. 54 WH Tr txt.]; ὧδε, Mt. xxvi. 38; Mk. xiv. 34; παρά τινι, with one, Jn. i. 39 (40); xiv. 25; Acts xviii. 20 [R G]; xxi. 7; σύν τινι, Lk. i. 56; καθ' ἑαυτόν, dwell at his own house, Acts xxviii. 16, cf. 30. i. q. tarry as a guest, lodge: ποῦ, Jn. i. 38 (39); ἐν w. dat. of place, Lk. xix. 5; Acts ix. 43; παρά τινι, in one's house, Acts ix. 43; xviii. 3; xxi. 8; of tarrying for a night, μετά τινος, σύν τινι, Lk. xxiv. 29. i. q. to be kept, to remain: dead bodies ἐπὶ τοῦ σταυροῦ, Jn. xix. 31; τὸ κλῆμα ἐν τῇ ἀμπέλῳ, Jn. xv. 4.　　b. tropically;　　a. i. q. not to depart, not to leave, to continue to be present: μετά τινος (gen. of pers.), to maintain unbroken fellowship with one, adhere to his party, 1 Jn. ii. 19; to be constantly present to help one, of the Holy Spirit, Jn. xiv. 16 R G; also παρά w. dat. of pers., Jn. xiv. 17; ἐπί τινα, to put forth constant influence upon one, of the Holy Spirit, Jn. i. 32 sq.; also of the wrath of God, ib. iii. 36; τὸ κάλυμμα ἐπὶ τῇ ἀναγνώσει, of that which continually pre-vents the right understanding of what is read, 2 Co. iii.

14. In the mystic phraseology of John, God is said μένειν in Christ, i. e. to dwell as it were within him, to be con-tinually operative in him by his divine influence and en-ergy, Jn. xiv. 10; Christians are said μένειν ἐν τῷ θεῷ, to be rooted as it were in him, knit to him by the spirit they have received from him, 1 Jn. ii. 6, 24, 27; iii. 6; hence one is said μένειν in Christ or in God, and conversely Christ or God is said μένειν in one: Jn. vi. 56; xv. 4 sq.; 1 Jn. iii. 24; iv. 13, 16; ὁ θεὸς μένει ἐν αὐτῷ κ. αὐτὸς ἐν τῷ θεῷ, 1 Jn. iv. 15; cf. Rückert, Abendmahl, p. 268 sq. μένει τι ἐν ἐμοί, something has established itself perma-nently within my soul, and always exerts its power in me: τὰ ῥήματά μου, Jn. xv. 7; ὁ λόγος τοῦ θεοῦ, 1 Jn. ii. 14; ἡ χαρὰ ἡ ἐμή (not joy in me i. e. of which I am the object, but the joy with which I am filled), Jn. xv. 11 Rec.; ὃ ἠκούσατε, 1 Jn. ii. 24; the Holy Spirit, Jn. ii. 17; iii. 9; ἡ ἀλήθεια, 2 Jn. 2; love towards God, 1 Jn. iii. 17; in the same sense one is said ἔχειν τι μένον ἐν ἑαυτῷ, as τὸν λόγον τοῦ θεοῦ, Jn. v. 38; ζωὴν αἰώνιον, 1 Jn. iii. 15. i. q. to persevere; ἔν τινι, of him who cleaves, holds fast, to a thing: ἐν τῷ λόγῳ, Jn. viii. 31; ἐν τῇ ἀγάπῃ, 1 Jn. iv. 16; ἐν πίστει, 1 Tim. ii. 15; ἐν οἷς (ἐν τούτοις, ἃ) ἔμαθες, 2 Tim. iii. 14; ἐν τῇ διδαχῇ, 2 Jn. 9, (ἐν τῷ Ἰουδαϊσμῷ, 2 Macc. viii. 1); differently ἐν τῇ ἀγάπῃ τινός, i. e. to keep one's self always worthy of his love, Jn. xv. 9 sq.　　β. to be held, or kept, continually: ἐν τῷ θανάτῳ, in the state of death, 1 Jn. iii. 14; ἐν τῇ σκοτίᾳ, Jn. xii. 46; ἐν τῷ φωτί, 1 Jn. ii. 10.　　2. to TIME; to continue to be, i. e. not to perish, to last, to endure: of persons, to survive, live, (exx. fr. prof. auth. are given in Kypke, Observv. i. p. 415 sq.): Phil. i. 25 [so ἐμμένειν, Sir. xxxix. 11]; with εἰς τὸν αἰῶνα added, Jn. xii. 34; Heb. vii. 24; also of him who becomes partaker of the true and everlasting life, opp. to παράγεσθαι, 1 Jn. ii. 17; ἕως ἄρτι, opp. to οἱ κοιμηθέντες, 1 Co. xv. 6; ὀλίγον, Rev. xvii. 10; ἕως ἔρχομαι, Jn. xxi. 22 sq.; of things, not to perish, to last, stand : of cities, Mt. xi. 23; Heb. xiii. 14; of works, opp. to κατακαίεσθαι, 1 Co. iii. 14; of purposes, moral excellences, Ro. ix. 11; 1 Co. xiii. 13; Heb. xiii. 1; λόγος θεοῦ, 1 Pet. i. 23; (where Rec. adds εἰς τ. αἰῶνα); of institutions, Heb. xii. 27. ὁ καρπός, Jn. xv. 16; ὕπαρξις, Heb. x. 34; ἁμαρτία, Jn. ix. 41; βρῶσις, opp. to ἡ ἀπολλυμένη, Jn. vi. 27; one's δικαιοσύνη with εἰς τὸν αἰῶνα added, 2 Co. ix. 9; τὸ ῥῆμα κυρίου, 1 Pet. i. 25. things which one does not part with are said μένειν to him, i. e. to remain to him, be still in (his) possession: Acts v. 4 (1 Macc. xv. 7).　　3. to STATE or CONDITION; to remain as one is, not to become another or different; with a predicate nom. μόνος, Jn. xii. 24; ἀσάλευτος, Acts xxvii. 41; ἄγαμος, 1 Co. vii. 11; πιστός, 2 Tim. ii. 13; ἱερεύς, Heb. vii. 3; with adverbs, οὕτως, 1 Co. vii. 40; ὡς κἀγώ, ibid. 8; ἐν w. dat. of the state, ibid. 20, 24.　　II. transitively; τινά, to wait for, await one [cf. B. § 131, 4]: Acts xx. 23; with ἐν and dat. of place added, ibid. 5. [COMP.: ἀνα-, δια-, ἐν-, ἐπι-, κατα-, παρα-, συν-παρα-, περι-, προσ-, ὑπο-μένω.]*

3307　μερίζω: 1 aor. ἐμέρισα; pf. μεμέρικα (1 Co. vii. 17 T Tr txt. WH txt.); Pass., pf. μεμέρισμαι; 1 aor. ἐμερί-σθην; Mid., 1 aor. inf. μερίσασθαι; (fr. μέρος, as μελίζω fr. μέλος); fr. Xen. down; Sept. for חָלַק; to divide; i. e. **a.** to separate into parts, cut into pieces: pass. μεμέρισται ὁ Χριστός; i. e. has Christ himself, whom ye claim as yours, been like yourselves divided into parts, so that one has one part and another another part? 1 Co. i. 13 [L WH txt. punctuate so as to take it as an exclamatory declaration; see Meyer in loc.]; trop. μεμέρισται ἡ γυνὴ καὶ ἡ παρθένος, differ in their aims, follow different interests, [A. V. there is a difference between; but L Tr WH connect μεμ. with what precedes], 1 Co. vii. 33 (34); to divide into parties, i. e. be split into factions (Polyb. 8, 23, 9): καθ' ἐμαυτοῦ to be at variance with one's self, to rebel [A. V. divided] against one's self, Mt. xii. 25; also ἐπ' ἐμαυτόν, ib. 26; Mk. iii. 24–26. **b.** to distribute: τί τισι, a thing among persons, Mk. vi. 41; to bestow, impart: τινί, 1 Co. vii. 17; τί τινι, Ro. xii. 3; 2 Co. x. 13; Heb. vii. 2, (Sir. xlv. 20; Polyb. 11, 28, 9); mid. μερίζομαί τι μετά τινος, to divide (for one's self) a thing with one, Lk. xii. 13 (Dem. p. 913, 1). [COMP.: δια-, συμ-μερίζω.]*

3308   **μέριμνα, -ας, ἡ,** (fr. μερίζω, μερίζομαι, to be drawn in different directions, cf. [Eng. 'distraction' and 'curae quae meum animum divorse trahunt'] Ter. Andr. 1, 5, 25; Verg. Aen. 4, 285 sq.; [but acc. to al. derived fr. a root meaning to be thoughtful, and akin to μάρτυς, memor, etc.; cf. Vaniček p. 1201; Curtius § 466; Fick iv. 283; see μάρτυς]), care, anxiety: 1 Pet. v. 7 (fr. Ps. liv. (lv.) 23); Lk. viii. 14; xxi. 34; w. gen. of the obj., care to be taken of, care for a thing, 2 Co. xi. 28; τοῦ αἰῶνος (τούτου), anxiety about things pertaining to this earthly life, Mt. xiii. 22; Mk. iv. 19. [(Hom. h. Merc.), Hes., Pind., al.]*

3309   **μεριμνάω, -ῶ** fut. μεριμνήσω; 1 aor. subj. 2 pers. plur. μεριμνήσητε; (μέριμνα); **a.** to be anxious; to be troubled with cares: absol., Mt. vi. 27, 31; Lk. xii. 25; μηδὲν μερ. be anxious about nothing, Phil. iv. 6; with dat. of the thing for the interests of which one is solicitous [cf. W. § 31, 1 b.]: τῇ ψυχῇ, about sustaining life, τῷ σώματι, Mt. vi. 25; Lk. xii. 22; περί τινος, about a thing, Mt. vi. 28; Lk. xii. 26; εἰς τὴν αὔριον, for the morrow, i. e. about what may be on the morrow, Mt. vi. 34; foll. by an indir. quest. πῶς ἢ τί, Mt. x. 19; Lk. xii. 11 [here Tr txt. WH br. ἢ τί]; joined with τυρβάζεσθαι (θορυβάζ.) foll. by περὶ πολλά, Lk. x. 41 [WH mrg. om.] **b.** to care for, look out for, (a thing); to seek to promote one's interests: τὰ ἑαυτῆς, Mt. vi. 34 Rec.; τὰ τοῦ κυρίου, 1 Co. vii. 32–34; τὰ τοῦ κόσμου, 1 Co. vii. 34; ἑαυτῆς, Mt. vi. 34 L T Tr WH (a usage unknown to Grk. writ., although they put a gen. after other verbs of caring or providing for, as ἐπιμελεῖσθαι, φροντίζειν, προνοεῖν, cf. Krüger § 47, 11; W. 205 (193); B. § 133, 25); τὰ περί τινος, Phil. ii. 20; ἵνα τὸ αὐτὸ ὑπὲρ ἀλλήλων μεριμνῶσι τὰ μέλη, that the members may have the same care one for another, 1 Co. xii. 25. (Sept. for דָּאַג, to be anxious, Ps. xxxvii. (xxxviii.) 19; רָגַן to be disturbed, annoyed in spirit, 2 S. vii. 10; 1 Chr. xvii. 9; in Grk. writ. fr. Xen. and Soph. down.) [COMP.: προ-μεριμνάω.]*

3310   **μερίς, -ίδος, ἡ,** (see μέρος), Sept. chiefly for חֶלְקָה, חֵלֶק,

; [fr. Antipho and Thuc. down]; a part, i. q. **1.** a part as distinct from the whole: (τῆς) Μακεδονίας, Acts xvi. 12 [on which see Hort in WH. App. ad loc.]. **2.** an assigned part, a portion, share: Lk. x. 42 (see ἀγαθός, 2); ἔστι μοι μερὶς μετά τινος, I have a portion, i. e. fellowship, with one, 2 Co. vi. 15. οὐκ ἔστι μοι μερὶς ἢ κλῆρος ἐν τινι, I have neither part nor lot, take no share, in a thing, Acts viii. 21; ἱκανοῦν τινα εἰς τὴν μερίδα τινός, to make one fit to obtain a share in a thing [i. e. partit. gen.; al. gen. of apposition], Col. i. 12.*

3311   **μερισμός, -οῦ, ὁ,** (μερίζω), a division, partition, (Plat., Polyb., Strab., [al.]); **1.** a distribution; plur. distributions of various kinds: πνεύματος ἁγίου, gen. of the obj., Heb. ii. 4. **2.** a separation: ἄχρι μερισμοῦ ψυχῆς κ. πνεύματος, which many take actively: 'up to the dividing' i. e. so far as to cleave asunder or separate; but it is not easy to understand what the dividing of the 'soul' is. Hence it is more correct, I think, and more in accordance with the context, to take the word passively (just as other verbal subst. ending in μός are used, e. g. ἁγιασμός, πειρασμός), and translate even to the division, etc., i. e. to that most hidden spot, the dividing line between soul and spirit, where the one passes into the other, Heb. iv. 12; [cf. Siegfried, Philo von Alex. u. s. w. p. 325 sq.].*

3312   **μεριστής, -οῦ, ὁ,** (μερίζω), a divider: of an inheritance, Lk. xii. 14. (Pollux [4, 176].) *

3313   **μέρος, -ους, τό,** (μείρομαι to share, receive one's due portion), [fr. Pind., Aeschyl., Hdt. down], a part; i. e. **1.** a part due or assigned to one, (Germ. Antheil): ἀφαιρεῖν τὸ μέρος τινός (gen. of pers.) ἀπό or ἔκ τινος (gen. of the thing), Rev. xxii. 19; ἔχειν μέρος ἐν with dat. of the thing, Rev. xx. 6; μέρος ἔχειν μετά τινος, (participation in the same thing, i. e.) to have part (fellowship) with one, Jn. xiii. 8; hence, as sometimes in class. Grk. (Eur. Alc. 477 [474]), lot, destiny, assigned to one, Rev. xxi. 8; τιθέναι τὸ μέρος τινὸς μετά τινων, to appoint one his lot with certain persons, Mt. xxiv. 51; Lk. xii. 46. **2.** one of the constituent parts of a whole; **a.** univ.: in a context where the whole and its parts are distinguished, Lk. xi. 36; Jn. xix. 23; Rev. xvi. 19; w. a gen. of the whole, Lk. xv. 12; xxiv. 42; where it is evident from the context of what whole it is a part, Acts v. 2; Eph. iv. 16; τὸ ἓν μέρος, sc. τοῦ συνεδρίου, Acts xxiii. 6; μέρος τῶν Φαρισαίων, of that part of the Sanhedrin which consisted of Pharisees, Acts xxiii. 9 [not Lchm.]; τὰ μέρη, w. gen. of a province or country, the divisions or regions which make up the land or province, Mt. ii. 22; Acts ii. 10; w. gen. of a city, the region belonging to a city, country around it, Mt. xv. 21; xvi. 13; Mk. viii. 10; τὰ ἀνωτερικὰ μέρη, the upper districts (in tacit contrast with τὰ κατώτερα, and with them forming one whole), Acts xix. 1; τὰ μέρη ἐκεῖνα, those regions (which are parts of the country just mentioned, i. e. Macedonia), Acts xx. 2; τὰ κατώτερα μέρη w. gen. of apposition, τῆς γῆς, Eph. iv. 9 (on which see κατώτερος); εἰς τὰ δεξιὰ μέρη τοῦ πλοίου, i. e. into the parts (i. e. spots sc. of the lake) on the right side of the ship, Jn. xxi. 6. Adverbial phrases:

ἀνὰ μέρος (see ἀνά, 1), 1 Co. xiv. 27 ; κατὰ μέρος, sever-ally, part by part, in detail, Heb. ix. 5 [see κατά, II. 3 a. γ.] ; μέρος τι (acc. absol.) in part, partly, 1 Co. xi. 18 (Thuc. 2, 64 ; 4, 30 ; Isocr. p. 426 d.) ; ἀπὸ μέρους, in part, i. e. somewhat, 2 Co. i. 14 ; in a measure, to some de-gree, ib. ii. 5 ; [Ro. xv. 24] ; as respects a part, Ro. xi. 25 : here and there, Ro. xv. 15 ; ἐκ μέρους as respects indi-vidual persons and things, severally, individually, 1 Co. xii. 27 ; in part, partially, i. e. imperfectly, 1 Co. xiii. 9, 12 ; τὸ ἐκ μέρους (opp. to τὸ τέλειον) [A. V. that which is in part] imperfect (Luth. well, das Stückwerk), ibid. 10. [Green (Crit. Note on 2 Co. i. 14) says "ἀπὸ μ. differs in Paul's usage from ἐκ μ. in that the latter is a contrasted term in express opposition to the idea of a complete whole, the other being used simply without such aim" ; cf. Bnhdy. Syntax, p. 230 ; Meyer on 1 Co. xii. 27.]   b. any particular, Germ. Stück, (where the writer means to intimate that there are other matters, to be separated from that which he has specified) : ἐν τῷ μέρει τούτῳ, in this particular i. e. in regard to this, in this respect, 1 Pet. iv. 16 R ; 2 Co. iii. 10 ; ix. 3 ; w. a gen. of the thing, Col. ii. 16 [where see Bp. Lghtft.] ; τοῦτο τὸ μέρος, sc. τῆς ἐργασίας ἡμῶν (branch of business), Acts xix. 27, cf. 25.*

3314   μεσημβρία, -ας, ἡ, (μέσος and ἡμέρα), fr. Hdt. down, mid-day [on the omission of the art. cf. W. 121 (115)] ;   a. (as respects time) noon : Acts xxii. 6.   b. (as re-spects locality) the south : Acts viii 26 [al. refer this also to a. ; see κατά, II. 2].*

3315   μεσιτεύω : 1 aor. ἐμεσίτευσα ; (μεσίτης [cf. W. p. 25 e.]) ;   1. to act as mediator, between litigating or covenanting parties ; trans. to accomplish something by interposing between two parties, to mediate, (with acc. of the result) : τὴν διάλυσιν, Polyb. 11, 34, 3 ; τὰς συνθήκας, Diod. 19, 71 ; Dion. Hal. 9, 59 ; [cf. Philo de plant. Noë, ii. 2 fin.].   2. as a μεσίτης is a sponsor or surety (Jo-seph. antt. 4, 6, 7 ταῦτα ὀμνύντες ἔλεγον καὶ τὸν θεὸν μεσί-την ὧν ὑπισχνοῦντο ποιούμενοι [cf. Philo de spec. legg. iii. 7 ἀοράτῳ δὲ πράγματι πάντως ἀόρατος μεσιτεύει θεός etc.]), so μεσιτεύω comes to signify to pledge one's self, give surety : ὅρκῳ, Heb. vi. 17.*

3316   μεσίτης, -ου, ὁ, (μέσος), one who intervenes between two, either in order to make or restore peace and friend-ship, or to form a compact, or for ratifying a covenant ; a medium of communication, arbitrator, (Vulg. [and A. V.] mediator) : ὁ μεσίτης [generic art. cf. W. § 18, 1 sub fin.], i. e. every mediator, whoever acts as mediator, ἑνὸς οὐκ ἔστι, does not belong to one party but to two or more, Gal. iii. 20.   Used of Moses, as one who brought the commands of God to the people of Israel and acted as mediator with God on behalf of the people, ib. 19 (cf. Deut. v. 5 ; hence he is called μεσίτης καὶ διαλλάκτης by Philo also, vit. Moys. iii. § 19).   Christ is called μεσ. θεοῦ κ. ἀνθρώπων, since he interposed by his death and restored the harmony between God and man which human sin had broken, 1 Tim. ii. 5 ; also μεσ. διαθήκης, Heb. viii. 6 ; ix. 15 ; xii. 24.   (Polyb. 28, 15, 8 ; Diod. 4, 54 ; Philo de somn. i. § 22 ; Joseph. antt. 16, 2, 2 ; Plut.

de Is. et Os. 46 ; once in Sept., Job ix. 33.)   Cf. Fischer, De vitiis lexx. N. T. p. 351 sqq.*

3317   μεσο-νύκτιον, -ου, τό, (neut. of the adj. μεσονύκτιος in Pind. et al., fr. μέσος and νύξ, νυκτός), midnight : μεσο-νυκτίου, at midnight [W. § 30, 11 ; B. § 132, 26], Mk. xiii. 35 [here T Tr WH acc. ; cf. W. 230 (215 sq.) ; B. § 131, 11] ; Lk. xi. 5 ; κατὰ τὸ μ. about midnight, Acts xvi. 25 ; μέχρι μ. until midnight, Acts xx. 7.   (Sept. ; Hippocr., Aristot., Diod., Strabo, Lcian., Plut. ; cf. Lob. ad Phryn. p. 53, [W. p. 23 c.].)*

3318   Μεσοποταμία, -ας, ἡ, (fem. of μεσοποτάμιος, -α, -ον, sc. χώρα ; fr. μέσος and ποταμός), Mesopotamia, the name, not so much political as geographical (scarcely in use before the time of Alexander the Great), of a region in Asia, lying between the rivers Euphrates and Tigris (whence it took its name ; cf. Arrian. anab. Alex. 7, 7 ; Tac. ann. 6, 37 ; אֲרַם נַהֲרַיִם, Aram of the two rivers, Gen. xxiv. 10), bounded on the N. by the range of Taurus and on the S. by the Persian Gulf ; many Jews had settled in it (Joseph. antt. 12, 3, 4) : Acts ii. 9 ; vii. 2. [Cf. Socin in Encycl. Brit. ed. 9 s. v. ; Rawlinson, He-rodotus, vol. i. Essay ix.]*

3319   μέσος, -η, -ον, [fr. Hom. down], middle, (Lat. medius, -a, -um) ;   1. as an adjective : μέσης νυκτός, at mid-night, Mt. xxv. 6 ; μέσης ἡμέρας, Acts xxvi. 13 (acc. to Lob. ad Phryn. pp. 53, 54, 465, the better writ. said μέ-σον ἡμέρας, μεσοῦσα ἡμέρα, μεσημβρία) ; w. gen. : [ἑκά-θητο ὁ Πέτρος μέσος αὐτῶν, Lk. xxii. 55 (R G L ἐν μέσῳ)] ; μέσος ὑμῶν ἕστηκε [al. στήκει], stands in the midst of you, Jn. i. 26, (Plat. de rep. 1 p. 330 b. ; polit. p. 303 a.) ; ἐσχίσθη μέσον, (the veil) was rent in the midst, Lk. xxiii. 45 [W. 131 (124) note] ; ἐλάκησε μέσος, Acts i. 18 ; (ἐσταύρωσαν) μέσον τὸν Ἰησοῦν, Jn. xix. 18.   2. the neut. τὸ μέσον or (without the art. in adverb. phrases, διὰ μέσου, ἐν μέσῳ, cf. W. 123 (117) ; [cf. B. § 125, 6]) μέσον is used as a substantive ; Sept. for תָּוֶךְ (constr. state תּוֹךְ), and קֶרֶב ; the midst : ἀνὰ μέσον (see ἀνά, 1 [and added note below]) ; διὰ μέσου (τινός), through the midst (Am. v. 17 ; Jer. xliv. (xxxvii.) 4) : αὐτῶν, through the midst of them, Lk. iv. 30 ; Jn. viii. 59 [Rec.] ; Σαμα-ρείας, Lk. xvii. 11 [R G, but L T Tr WH διὰ μέσον (see διά, B. I.) ; others take the phrase here in the sense of between (Xen. an. 1, 4, 4 ; Aristot. de anim. 2, 11 vol. i. p. 423ᵇ, 12 ; see L. and S. s. v. III. 1 d.) ; cf. Meyer ed. Weiss in loc. and added note below] ; εἰς τὸ μέσον, into the midst, i. e., acc. to the context, either the mid-dle of a room or the midst of those assembled in it : Mk. iii. 3 ; xiv. 60 Rec. ; Lk. iv. 35 ; v. 19 ; vi. 8 ; Jn. xx. 19, 26 ; εἰς μέσον (cf. Germ. mittenhin), Mk. xiv. 60 G L T Tr WH ; ἐν τῷ μέσῳ, in the middle of the apart-ment or before the guests, Mt. xiv. 6 ; ἐν μέσῳ, in the midst of the place spoken of, Jn. viii. 3, 9 ; in the middle of the room, before all, Acts iv. 7 ; w. gen. of place, Rev. ii. 7 Rec. ; Lk. xxi. 21 ; (i. q. Germ. mittenauf) τῆς πλατείας, Rev. xxii. 2 [but see below] ; add, Lk. 55ᵃ; Acts xvii. 22 ; τῆς θαλάσσης, in the midst (of the surface of) the sea, Mk. vi. 47 ; w. gen. plur. in the midst of, amongst : w. gen of things, Mt. x. 16 ; Lk. viii. 7 ; x. 3 ;

Rev. i. 13; ii. 1; w. gen. of pers., Mt. xviii. 2; Mk. ix. 36; Lk. ii. 46; xxii. 55ᵇ [here T Tr WH μέσος; see 1 above]; xxiv. 36; Acts i. 15; ii. 22; xxvii. 21; Rev. v. 6 [ᵇ? (see below); vi. 6]; trop. *ἐν μέσῳ αὐτῶν εἰμι*, I am present with them by my divine power, Mt. xviii. 20; w. gen. of a collective noun, Phil. ii. 15 R [see 3 below]; Heb. ii. 12; where association or intercourse is the topic, equiv. to *among, in intercourse with*: Lk. xxii. 27; 1 Th. ii. 7. *in the midst of*, i. e. *in the space within, τοῦ θρόνου* (which must be conceived of as having a semicircular shape): Rev. iv. 6; v. 6 [ᵃ?] where cf. De Wette and Bleek; [but De Wette's note on v. 6 runs "*And I saw between the throne and the four living creatures and the elders* (i. e. in the vacant space between the throne and the living creatures [on one side] and elders [on the other side], accordingly nearest the throne" etc.); *ἀνὰ μέσον* in vii. 17 also he interprets in the same way; further see xxii. 2; cf. *Kliefoth*, Com. vol. ii. p. 40. For *ἐν μέσῳ* in this sense see Xen. an. 2, 2, 3; 2, 4, 17. 21; 5, 2, 27, etc.; Hab. iii. 2; *ἀνὰ μέσον* Polyb. 5, 55, 7; often in Aristot. (see Bonitz's index s. v. *μέσος*); Num. xvi. 48; Deut. v. 5; Josh. xxii. 25; Judg. xv. 4; 1 K. v. 12; Ezek. xlvii. 18; xlviii. 22; cf. Gen. i. 4; see Meyer on 1 Co. vi. 5; cf. *ἀνά*, 1]. *κατὰ μέσον τῆς νυκτός*, about midnight, Acts xxvii. 27 [see *κατά*, II. 2]. *ἐκ τοῦ μέσου*, like the Lat. *e medio*, i. e. *out of the way, out of sight*: *αἴρω τι*, to take out of the way, to abolish, Col. ii. 14 [Plut. de curiositate 9; Is. lvii. 2]; *γίνομαι ἐκ μέσου*, to be taken out of the way, to disappear, 2 Th. ii. 7; w. gen. of pers., *ἐκ μέσου τινῶν*, from the society or company of, *out from among*: Mt. xiii. 49; Acts xvii. 33; xxiii. 10; 1 Co. v. 2; 2 Co. vi. 17, (Ex. xxxi. 14; Num. xiv. 44 Alex.). **3.** the neut. *μέσον* is used adverbially with a gen., *in the midst of* anything: *ἦν μέσον τῆς θαλάσσης*, Mt. xiv. 24 [otherwise Tr txt. WH txt.; yet cf. W. § 54, 6] ([so Exod. xiv. 27]; *Τέων γὰρ μέσον εἶναι τῆς Ἰωνίης*, Hdt. 7, 170); *γενεᾶς σκολιᾶς*, Phil. ii. 15 L T Tr WH (*τῆς ἡμέρας*, the middle of the day, Sus. 7 Theodot.); cf. B. 123 (107 sq.), [cf. 319 (274); W. as above]. *

3320   **μεσότοιχον**, -ου, τό, (*μέσος*, and *τοῖχος* the wall of a house), *a partition-wall*: *τὸ μ. τοῦ φραγμοῦ* (i. e. *τὸν φραγμὸν τὸν μεσότοιχον ὄντα* [A. V. *the middle wall of partition*; W. § 59, 8 a.]), Eph. ii. 14. (Only once besides, and that too in the masc.: *τὸν τῆς ἡδονῆς κ. ἀρετῆς μεσότοιχον*, Eratosth. ap. Athen. 7 p. 281 d.) *

3321   **μεσουράνημα**, -τος, τό, (fr. *μεσουρανέω*; the sun is said *μεσουρανεῖν to be in mid-heaven*, when it has reached the meridian), *mid-heaven, the highest point in the heavens*, which the sun occupies at noon, where what is done can be seen and heard by all: Rev. viii. 13 (cf. Düsterdieck ad loc.); xiv. 6; xix. 17. (Manetho, Plut., Sext. Emp.) *

3322   **μεσόω**; (*μέσος*); *to be in the middle, be midway*: *τῆς ἑορτῆς μεσούσης* [where a few codd. *μεσαζούσης* (*νύκτος μεσαζ*. Sap. xviii. 14)], when it was the midst of the feast, the feast half-spent, Jn. vii. 14 (*μεσούσης τῆς νυκτός*, Ex. xii. 29; Judith xii. 5; *τῆς ἡμέρας*, Neh. viii. 3 [Ald., Compl.]; in Grk. writ. fr. Aeschyl. and Hdt. down; *θέρους μεσοῦντος*, Thuc. 6, 30). *

Μεσσίας, -ου [cf. B. 18 (16)], ὁ, *Messiah*; Chald. מְשִׁיחָא, Hebr. מָשִׁיחַ, i. q. Grk. χριστός, q. v.: Jn. i. 41 (42); iv. 25. Cf. *Delitzsch* in the Zeitschr. f. d. luth. Theol., 1876, p. 603; [*Lagarde*, Psalt. vers. Memphit., 1875, p. vii. On the general subject see esp. Abbot's supplement to art. Messiah in B. D. Am. ed. and reff. added by *Orelli* (cf. Schaff-Herzog) in Herzog 2 s. v. to Oehler's art.] *   **3323**

μεστός, -ή, -όν, fr. Hom. [i. e. Epigr.] down, Sept. for מָלֵא, *full*; w. gen. of the thing: prop., Jn. xix. 29; xxi. 11; Jas. iii. 8; trop. in reference to persons, whose minds are as it were filled with thoughts and emotions, either good or bad, Mt. xxiii. 28; Ro. i. 29; xv. 14; 2 Pet. ii. 14; Jas. iii. 17, (Prov. vi. 34).*   **3324**

μεστόω, -ῶ; (*μεστός*); *to fill, fill full*: *γλεύκους μεμεστω- μένος*, Acts ii. 13. (Soph., Plat., Aristot., al.; 3 Macc. v. 1, 10.) *   **3325**

μετά, [on its neglect of elision before proper names beginning with a vowel, and before sundry other words (at least in Tdf.'s text) see *Tdf.* Proleg. p. 95; cf. *WH*. Intr. p. 146ᵇ; W. § 5, 1 a.; B. p. 10], a preposition, akin to *μέσος* (as Germ. *mit* to *Mitte, mitten*) and hence prop. *in the midst of, amid*, denoting association, union, accompaniment; [but some recent etymologists doubt its kinship to *μέσος*; some connect it rather with *ἅμα*, Germ. *sammt*, cf. Curtius § 212; Vaniček p. 972]. It takes the gen. and acc. (in the Grk. poets also the dat.). [On the distinction between μετά and σύν, see σύν, init.]   **3326**

I. with the GENITIVE (Sept. for אֵת, עִם, אַחַר, etc.), *among, with*, [cf. W. 376 (352) sq.];   **1.** *amid, among*;   **a.** prop.: *μετὰ τῶν νεκρῶν*, among the dead, Lk. xxiv. 5 (*μετὰ νεκρῶν κείσομαι*, Eur. Hec. 209); *θάψετέ με μετὰ τῶν πατέρων μου*, Gen. xlix. 29 Sept.; *μετὰ ζώντων εἶναι*, to be among the living, Soph. Phil. 1312); *λογί- ζεσθαι μετὰ ἀνόμων*, to be reckoned, numbered, among transgressors, Mk. xv. 28 [G T WH om. Tr br. the vs.] and Lk. xxii. 37, fr. Is. liii. 12 (where Sept. *ἐν ἀνόμοις*); *μετὰ τῶν θηρίων εἶναι*, Mk. i. 13; *γογγύζειν μετ' ἀλλήλων*, Jn. vi. 43; *σκηνὴ τοῦ θεοῦ μετὰ τ. ἀνθρώπων*, Rev. xxi. 3; add, Mt. xxiv. 51; xxvi. 58; Mk. xiv. 54; Lk. xii. 46; Jn. xviii. 5, 18; Acts i. 26, etc.   **b.** trop.: *μετὰ διωγμῶν*, amid persecutions, Mk. x. 30 (*μετὰ κινδύνων*, amid perils, Thuc. 1, 18); *ἡ ἀγάπη μεθ' ἡμῶν*, love among us, mutual love, 1 Jn. iv. 17 [al. understand *μεθ' ἡμῶν* here of the sphere or abode, and connect it with the verb; cf. De Wette, or Huther, or Westcott, in loc.]. Hence used   **2.** of association and companionship, *with* (Lat. *cum*; Germ. *mit*, often also *bei*);   **a.** after verbs of going, coming, departing, remaining, etc., w. the gen. of the associate or companion: Mt. xx. 20; xxvi. 36; Mk. i. 29; iii. 7; xi. 11; xiv. 17; Lk. vi. 17; xiv. 31; Jn. iii. 22; xi. 54; Gal. ii. 1; Jesus the Messiah is said will come hereafter *μετὰ τ. ἀγγέλων*, Mt. xvi. 27; Mk. viii. 38; 1 Th. iii. 13; 2 Th. i. 7; on the other hand, w. the gen. of the pers. to whom one joins himself as a companion: Mt. v. 41; Mk. v. 24; Lk. ii. 51; Rev. xxii. 12; *ἄγγελοι μετ' αὐτοῦ*, Mt. xxv. 31; *μετά τινος*, contextually i. q. *with one as leader*, Mt. xxv. 10;

xxvi. 47; Mk. xiv. 43; Acts vii. 45. περιπατεῖν μετά τινος, to associate with one as his follower and adherent, Jn. vi. 66; γίνομαι μ. τινος, to come into fellowship and intercourse with, become associated with, one : Mk. xvi. 10; Acts vii. 38; ix. 19; xx. 18. παραλαμβάνειν τινὰ μεθ' ἑαυτοῦ, to take with or to one's self as an attendant or companion: Mt. xii. 45; xviii. 16; Mk. xiv. 33; ἄγειν, 2 Tim. iv. 11; ἔχειν μεθ' ἑαυτοῦ, to have with one's self: τινά, Mt. xv. 30; xxvi. 11; Mk. ii. 19; xiv. 7; Jn. xii. 8; τί, Mk. viii. 14; λαμβάνειν, Mt. xxv. 3; ἀκολουθεῖν μετά τινος, see ἀκολουθέω, 1 and 2, [cf. W. 233 sq. (219)]. **b.** εἶναι μετά τινος is used in various senses, **a.** prop. of those who associate with one and accompany him wherever he goes: in which sense the disciples of Jesus are said *to be* (or to have been) *with* him, Mk. iii. 14; Mt. xxvi. 69, 71; Lk. xxii. 59, cf. Mk. v. 18; with ἀπ' ἀρχῆς added, Jn. xv. 27; of those who at a particular time associate with one or accompany him anywhere, Mt. v. 25; Jn. iii. 26; ix. 40; xii. 17; xx. 24, 26; 2 Tim. iv. 11; sometimes the ptcp. ὤν, ὄντα, etc., must be added mentally: Mt. xxvi. 51; Mk. ix. 8; Jn. xviii. 26; οἱ (ὄντες) μετά τινος, his attendants or companions, Mt. xii. 4; Mk. ii. 25; Lk. vi. 3; Acts xx. 34; sc. ὄντες, Tit. iii. 15. Jesus says that he is or has been with his disciples, Jn. xiii. 33; xiv. 9; and that, to advise and help them, Jn. xvi. 4; Mt. xvii. 17, (Mk. ix. 19 and Lk. ix. 41 πρὸς ὑμᾶς), even as one whom they could be said to have with them, Mt. ix. 15; Lk. v. 34; just as he in turn desires that his disciples may hereafter be with himself, Jn. xvii. 24. s h i p s also are said *to be with* one who is travelling by vessel, i. e. to attend him, Mk. iv. 36. **β.** trop. the phrase [*to be with*, see b.] is used of God, if he is present to guide and help one : Jn. iii. 2; viii. 29; xvi. 32; Acts vii. 9; x. 38; 2 Co. xiii. 11; Phil. iv. 9; with εἶναι omitted, Mt. i. 23; Lk. i. 28; Ro. xv. 33; here belongs ὅσα ἐποίησεν ὁ θεὸς μετ' αὐτῶν sc. ὤν, by being present with them by his divine assistance [cf. W. 376 (353); Green p. 218], Acts xiv. 27; xv. 4, [cf. h. below]; and conversely, πληρώσεις με εὐφροσύνης μετὰ τοῦ προσώπου σου sc. ὄντα, i. e. being in thy presence [yet cf. W. 376 (352) note], Acts ii. 28 fr. Ps. xv. (xvi.) 11; ἡ χεὶρ κυρίου is used as a substitute for God himself (by a Hebraism [see χεὶρ, sub fin.]) in Lk. i. 66; Acts xi. 21; of Christ, who is to be present with his followers by his divine power and aid: Mt. xxviii. 20; Acts xviii. 10, (μένειν μετά is used of the Holy Spirit as a perpetual helper, Jn. xiv. 16 R G); at the close of the Epistles, the writers pray that there may be with the readers (i. e. always present to help them) — ὁ θεός, 2 Co. xiii. 11; — ὁ κύριος, 2 Th. iii. 16; 2 Tim. iv. 22; — ἡ χάρις τοῦ κ. Ἰησοῦ Χρ. (where ἔστω must be supplied [cf. W. § 64, 2 b.; B. § 129, 22]), Ro. xvi. 20, 24 [R G]; 1 Co. xvi. 23; 2 Co. xiii. 13 (14); Gal. vi. 18; Phil. iv. 23; 1 Th. v. 28; 2 Th. iii. 18; Philem. 25; Rev. xxii. 21; — ἡ χάρις simply, Eph. vi. 24; Col. iv. 18; 1 Tim. vi. 21 (22); Tit. iii. 15; Heb. xiii. 25; 2 Jn. 3; — ἡ ἀγάπη μου, 1 Co. xvi. 24; the same phrase is used also of truth, compared to a guide, 2 Jn. 2. **γ.** opp. to εἶναι κ α τ ά τινος, *to be with* one i. e. on one's side :

Mt. xii. 30; Lk. xi. 23, (and often in class. Grk.); similarly μένειν μετά τινος, to side with one steadfastly, 1 Jn. ii. 19. **c.** with the gen. of the person who is another's associate either in acting or in his experiences; so after verbs of eating, drinking, supping, etc.: Mt. viii. 11; ix. 11; xxiv. 49; xxvi. 18, 23, 29; Mk. xiv. 18, 20; Lk. v. 30; vii. 36; xxii. 11, 15; xxiv. 30; Jn. xiii. 18; Gal. ii. 12; Rev. iii. 20, etc.; γρηγορεῖν, Mt. xxvi. 38, 40; χαίρειν, κλαίειν, Ro. xii. 15; εὐφραίνεσθαι, Ro. xv. 10; παροικεῖν, Heb. xi. 9; δουλεύειν, Gal. iv. 25; βασιλεύειν, Rev. xx. 4, 6; ζῆν, Lk. ii. 36; ἀποθνήσκειν, Jn. xi. 16; βάλλεσθαι εἰς τὴν γῆν, Rev. xii. 9; κληρονομεῖν, Gal. iv. 30; συνάγειν, Mt. xii. 30; Lk. xi. 23, and other exx. **d.** with a gen. of the pers. with whom one (of two) does anything m u t u a l l y or by turns: so after συναίρειν λόγον, to make a reckoning, settle accounts, Mt. xviii. 23; xxv. 19; συνάγεσθαι, Mt. xxviii. 12; Jn. xviii. 2; συμβούλιον ποιεῖν, Mk. iii. 6; λαλεῖν (see λαλέω, 5); συλλαλεῖν, Mt. xvii. 3; Acts xxv. 12; μοιχεύειν, Rev. ii. 22; μολύνεσθαι, Rev. xiv. 4; πορνεύειν, Rev. xvii. 2; xviii. 3, 9; μερίζομαι, Lk. xii. 13; after verbs of disputing, waging war, contending at law: πολεμεῖν, Rev. ii. 16; xii. 7 (where Rec. κατά); xiii. 4; xvii. 14, (so for "כ עם נלחם, 1 S. xvii. 33; 1 K. xii. 24, a usage foreign to the native Greeks, who say πολεμεῖν τινι, also πρός τινα, ἐπί τινα, to wage war against one; but πολεμεῖν μετά τινος, to wage war with one as an ally, in conjunction with, Thuc. 1, 18; Xen. Hell. 7, 1, 27; [cf. B. § 133, 8; W. § 28, 1; 214 (201); 406 (379) note]); πόλεμον ποιεῖν, Rev. xi. 7; xii. 17; xiii. 7; xix. 19, (so in Lat. bellare cum etc. Cic. Verr. 2, 4, 33; bellum gerere, Cic. de divinat. 1, 46); ζήτησις ἐγένετο, Jn. iii. 25; ζητεῖν, Jn. xvi. 19; κρίνεσθαι, κρίματα ἔχειν, 1 Co. vi. 6 sq.; after verbs and phrases which indicate mutual inclinations and pursuits, the entering into agreement or relations with, etc.; as εἰρηνεύειν, εἰρήνην διώκειν, Ro. xii. 18; 2 Tim. ii. 22; Heb. xii. 14; φίλος, Lk. xxiii. 12; συμφωνεῖν, Mt. xx. 2; μερὶς μετὰ τινος, 2 Co. vi. 15; ἔχειν μέρος, Jn. xiii. 8; συγκατάθεσις, 2 Co. vi. 16; κοινωνίαν ἔχειν, 1 Jn. i. 3, 6 sq.; αἰτία (see the word, 3), Mt. xix. 10. **e.** of divers other associations of persons or things; — where the action or condition expressed by the verb refers to persons or things besides those specified by the dat. or acc. (somewhat rare in Grk. auth., as ἰσχύν τε καὶ κάλλος μετὰ ὑγιείας λαμβάνειν, Plat. rep. 9, p. 591 b. [cf. W. § 47, h.]): εἶδον (Rec. εὗρον) τὸ παιδίον μετὰ Μαρίας, Mt. ii. 11; ἀνταποδοῦναι . . . ὑμῖν . . . μεθ' ἡμῶν, 2 Th. i. 6 sq.; after ἐκδέχεσθαι, 1 Co. xvi. 11; after verbs of sending, Mt. xxii. 16; 2 Co. viii. 18. ἀγάπη μετὰ πίστεως, Eph. vi. 23; ἐν πίστει . . . μετὰ σωφροσύνης, 1 Tim. ii. 15; ἡ εὐσέβεια μετὰ αὐταρκείας, 1 Tim. vi. 6; in this way the term which follows is associated as secondary with its predecessor as primary; but when καί stands between them they are co-ordinated. Col. i. 11; 1 Tim. i. 14. of mingling one thing with another, μίγνυμί τι μετὰ τινος (in class. auth. τί τινι [cf. B. § 133, 8]): Lk. xiii. 1; pass. Mt. xxvii. 34. **f.** with the gen. of mental feelings desires and emotions, of bodily movements, and of other acts which are so to speak the attendants of what is done or occurs; so that in this way the c h a r a c t e r i s t i c of the action or occurrence is described, — which in most cases can be expressed by a cognate adverb or participle [cf. W. u. s.] : μετὰ αἰδοῦς, 1 Tim. ii. 9; Heb. xii. 28 [Rec.]; αἰσχύνης, Lk. xiv. 9; ἡσυχίας, 2 Th. iii. 12; χαρᾶς, Mt. xiii. 20; Mk. iv. 16; Lk. viii. 13; x. 17; xxiv. 52; Phil. ii. 29; 1 Th. i. 6; Heb. x. 34; προθυμίας, Acts xvii. 11; φόβου κ. τρόμου, 2 Co. vii. 15; Eph. vi. 5; Phil. ii. 12; φόβου κ. χαρᾶς, Mt. xxviii. 8; πραΰτητος κ. φόβου, 1 Pet. iii. 16 (15); παρρησίας, Acts ii. 29; iv. 29, 31; xxviii. 31; Heb. xi. 31; εὐχαριστίας, Acts xxiv. 3; Phil. iv. 6; 1 Tim. iv. 3 sq.; ἀληθινῆς καρδίας, Heb. x. 22; ταπεινοφροσύνης κτλ., Eph. iv. 2; Acts xx. 19; ὀργῆς, Mk. iii. 5; εὐνοίας, Eph. vi. 7; βίας, Acts v. 26; xxiv. 7 Rec.; μετὰ δακρύων, with tears, Mk. ix. 24 [R G WH (rejected) mrg.]; Heb. v. 7; xii. 17, (Plat. apol. p. 34 c.); εἰρήνης, Acts xv. 33; Heb. xi. 31; ἐπιθέσεως τῶν χειρῶν, 1 Tim. iv. 14 [W. u. s.]; φωνῆς μεγάλης, Lk. xvii. 15; νηστειῶν, Acts xiv. 23; ὅρκου or ὁρκωμοσίας, Mt. xiv. 7; xxvi. 72; Heb. vii. 21; θορύβου, Acts xxiv. 18; παρακλήσεως, 2 Co. viii. 4; παρατηρήσεως, Lk. xvii. 20; σπουδῆς, Mk. vi. 25; Lk. i. 39; ὕβρεως κ. ζημίας, Acts xxvii. 10; φαντασίας, xxv. 23; ἀφροῦ, Lk. ix. 39; to this head may be referred μετὰ κουστωδίας, posting the guard, Mt. xxvii. 66 [so W. (l. c.) et al. (cf. Meyer ad loc.); others ' in company with the guard'; cf. Jas. Morison ad loc.; Green p. 218].   **g.** after verbs of coming, departing, sending, with gen. of the thing with which one is furnished or equipped: μετὰ δόξης κ. δυνάμεως, Mt. xxiv. 30; Mk. xiii. 26; Lk. xxi. 27; ἐξουσίας κ. ἐπιτροπῆς, Acts xxvi. 12; μαχαιρῶν κ. ξύλων, Mt. xxvi. 47, 55; Mk. xiv. 43, 48; Lk. xxii. 52; φανῶν κ. ὅπλων, Jn. xviii. 3; μετὰ σάλπιγγος, Mt. xxiv. 31 [cf. B. § 132, 10]. where an instrumental dat. might have been used [cf. W. § 31, 8 d.], μετὰ βραχίονος ὑψηλοῦ ἐξάγειν τινά, Acts xiii. 17.   **h.** in imitation of the Hebr.: ἔλεος ποιεῖν μετά τινος, to show mercy toward one, and μεγαλύνειν ἔλ. μ. τ. to magnify, show great, mercy toward one; see τὸ ἔλεος, 1. To this head many refer ὅσα ἐποίησεν ὁ θεὸς μετ' αὐτῶν, Acts xiv. 27; xv. 4, but see above, 2 b. β.

II. with the ACCUSATIVE [W. § 49, f.];   **1.** prop. into the middle of, into the midst of, among, after verbs of coming, bringing, moving; so esp. in Hom.   **2.** it denotes (following accompaniment), sequence, i. e. the order in which one thing follows another;   **a.** in order of P l a c e; after, behind, (so fr. Hom. down); once in the N. T. [W. u. s.]: Heb. ix. 3 (Judith ii. 4).   **b.** in order of T i m e; after (Sept. for אַחַר, אַחֲרֵי, מִקֵּץ, etc.): μεθ' ἡμέρας ἕξ, after six days (had passed), Mt. xvii. 1; Mk. ix. 2; add, Mt. xxvi. 2; Mk. xiv. 1; Lk. i. 24; ii. 46, etc., cf. Fritzsche, Com. on Mt. p. 22 sq.; μετ' οὐ πολλὰς ἡμέρας, Lk. xv. 13; μετά τινας ἡμ., Acts xv. 36; xxiv. 21; οὐ μετὰ πολλὰς ταύτας ἡμέρας, not long after these days [A. V. not many days hence], Acts i. 5, cf. De Wette ad loc. and W. 161 (152); [B. § 127, 4]; μ. τρεῖς μῆνας, Acts xxviii. 11; μ. ἔτη τρία, Gal. i. 18, etc.; μ. χρόνον πολύν, Mt. xxv. 19; μ. τοσοῦτον χρ. Heb. iv. 7.   added to the names of events or achievements, and of festivals : μ.

τὴν μετοικεσίαν Βαβ. Mt. i. 12; μ. τὴν θλίψιν, Mt. xxiv. 29; Mk. xiii. 24; add, Mt. xxvii. 53; Acts x. 37; xx. 29; 2 Pet. i. 15; μ. τὴν ἀνάγνωσιν, Acts xiii. 15; μ. μίαν κ. δευτέραν νουθεσίαν, Tit. iii. 10; μ. τὸ πάσχα, Acts xii. 4 cf. xx. 6; with the names of persons or things having the notion of time associated with them: μετὰ τοῦτον, αὐτόν, etc., Acts v. 37; vii. 5; xiii. 25; xix. 4; μ. τὸν νόμον, Heb. vii. 28; μετὰ τὸ ψωμίον, after the morsel was taken, Jn. xiii. 27 [cf. B. § 147, 26]; foll. by the neut. demonstr. pron. [cf. W. 540 (503)]: μετὰ τοῦτο, Jn. ii. 12; xi. 7, 11; xix. 28; Heb. ix. 27; [Rev. vii. 1 L T Tr WH], μετὰ ταῦτα [cf. W. 162 (153)], Mk. xvi. 12; Lk. v. 27; x. 1; xii. 4 [W. u. s.]; xvii. 8; xviii. 4; Acts vii. 7; xiii. 20; xv. 16; xviii. 1; Jn. iii. 22; v. 1, 14; vi. 1; vii. 1; xiii. 7; xix. 38; xxi. 1; Heb. iv. 8; 1 Pet. i. 11; Rev. i. 19; iv. 1; vii. 1 [Rec.], 9; ix. 12; xv. 5; xviii. 1; xix. 1; xx. 3, and very often in Grk. writ. it stands before the neut. of adjectives of quantity, measure, and time: μετ' οὐ πολύ, not long after [R. V. after no long time], Acts xxvii. 14; μετὰ μικρόν, shortly after [A. V. after a little while], Mt. xxvi. 73; Mk. xiv. 70; μετὰ βραχύ, Lk. xxii. 58; also before infinitives with the neut. art. (Lat. postquam with a finite verb, [cf. B. § 140, 11; W. § 44, 6]) ;—the aorist inf.: Mt. xxvi. 32; Mk. i. 14; xiv. 28; xvi. 19; Lk. xii. 5; xxii. 20 [WH reject the pass.]; Acts i. 3; vii. 4; x. 41; xv. 13; xx. 1; 1 Co. xi. 25; Heb. x. 26.

III. In COMPOSITION, μετά denotes   **1.** association, fellowship, participation, with: as in μεταδιδόναι, μεταλαμβάνειν, μετέχειν, μετοχή.   **2.** exchange, transfer, transmutation; (Lat. trans, Germ. um): μεταλλάσσω, μεταμέλομαι [Prof. Grimm prob. means here μετανοέω; see 3 and in μεταμέλομαι], μετοικίζω, μεταμορφόω, etc.   **3.** after: μεταμέλομαι.   Cf. Viger. ed. Herm. p. 639.

μετα-βαίνω; fut. μεταβήσομαι; 2 aor. μετέβην, impv. μετάβηθι and (in Mt. xvii. 20 L T Tr WH) μετάβα (see ἀναβαίνω, init.); pf. μεταβέβηκα; fr. Hom. down; to pass over from one place to another, to remove, depart: foll. by ἀπό w. a gen. of the place, Mt. viii. 34; ἐξ οἰκίας εἰς οἰκίαν [cf. W. § 52, 4. 10], Lk. x. 7; ἐκ τοῦ κόσμου πρὸς τὸν πατέρα, Jn. xiii. 1; ἐντεῦθεν, Jn. vii. 3; ἐκεῖθεν, Mt. xi. 1; xii. 9; xv. 29; Acts xviii. 7; ἐντεῦθεν [L T Tr WH ἔνθεν] ἐκεῖ (for ἐκεῖσε [cf. W. § 54, 7; B. 71 (62)]), of a thing, i. q. to be removed, Mt. xvii. 20; metaph. ἐκ τοῦ θανάτου εἰς τὴν ζωήν, Jn. v. 24; 1 Jn. iii. 14.*   **3327**

μετα-βάλλω: prop. to turn round; to turn about; pass. and mid. to turn one's self about, change or transform one's self; trop. to change one's opinion; [Mid., pres. ptcp.] μεταβαλλόμενοι [(2 aor. ptcp. βαλόμενοι Tr WH)] ἔλεγον, they changed their minds and said, Acts xxviii. 6 (μεταβαλόμενος λέγεις, having changed your mind you say, Plat. Gorg. 481 e.; in the same sense, Thuc., Xen., Dem.).*   **3328**

μετ-άγω; pres. pass. μετάγομαι; to transfer, lead over, (Polyb., Diod., al.), hence univ. to direct [A. V. to turn about]: Jas. iii. 3 sq.*   **3329**

μετα-δίδωμι; 2 aor. subj. μεταδῶ, impv. 3 pers. sing. μεταδότω, inf. μεταδοῦναι; [fr. Theogn., Hdt. down]; to share a thing with any one [see μετά, III. 1], to impart: absol. ὁ μεταδιδούς, he that imparteth of his substance, Ro.   **3330**

xii. 8, cf. Fritzsche ad loc.; τινί, Eph. iv. 28; τινί τι (a constr. somewhat rare in Grk. auth. [Hdt. 9, 34 etc.], with whom μεταδ. τινί τινος is more common; cf. Matthiae ii. p. 798; [W. § 30, 7 b.; B. § 132, 8]), Ro. i. 11; 1 Th. ii. 8; the acc. evident from the preceding context, Lk. iii. 11.*

3331 μετά-θεσις, -εως, ἡ, (μετατίθημι);   **1.** *a transfer*: from one place to another (Diod. 1, 23); τινός (gen. of obj.), the translation of a person to heaven, Heb. xi. 5.   **2.** *change* (of things instituted or established, as ἱερωσύνης, νόμου): Heb. vii. 12; τῶν σαλευομένων, Heb. xii. 27. (Thuc. 5, 29; Aristot., Plut.) *

3332 μετ-αίρω: 1 aor. μετῆρα;   **1.** trans. *to lift up and remove from one place to another, to transfer*, (Eur., Theophr., al.).   **2.** in the N. T. intrans. (cf. W. § 38, 1; [B. § 130, 4]) *to go away, depart*, (Germ. *aufbrechen*): ἐκεῖθεν, Mt. xiii. 53 (Gen. xii. 9 Aq.); foll. by ἀπό w. gen. of place, Mt. xix. 1.*

3333 μετα-καλέω, -ῶ: Mid., 1 aor. μετεκαλεσάμην; 1 fut. μετακαλέσομαι; *to call from one place to another, to summon,* (Hos. xi. 1 sq.; Plat. Ax. fin.); mid. *to call to one's self, to send for*: τινά, Acts viii. 14; x. 32; xx. 17; xxiv. 25.*

3334 μετα-κινέω, -ῶ: *to move from a place, to move away*: Deut. xxxii. 30; in Grk. writ. fr. Hdt. down; Pass. pres. ptcp. μετακινούμενος; trop. ἀπὸ τῆς ἐλπίδος, from the hope which one holds, on which one rests, Col. i. 23.*

3335 μετα-λαμβάνω; impf. μετελάμβανον; 2 aor. inf. μεταλαβεῖν, ptcp. μεταλαβών; [see μετά, III. 1; fr. Pind. and Hdt. down] *to be or to be made a partaker*: gen. of the thing, 2 Tim. ii. 6; Heb. vi. 7; xii. 10; τροφῆς, *to partake of, take* [some] *food*, Acts ii. 46; xxvii. 33 sq. [in 34 Rec. προσλαβεῖν]; w. acc. of the thing, *to get, find* (a whole): καιρόν, Acts xxiv. 25; on the constr. w. gen. and acc. see Krüger § 47, 15; cf. W. § 30, 8.*

3336 μετά-ληψις (L T Tr WH -λημψις [see M, μ]), -εως, ἡ, (μεταλαμβάνω), *a taking, participation*, (Plat., Plut., al.): of the use of food, εἰς μετάλ. to be taken or received, 1 Tim. iv. 3.*

3337 μετ-αλλάσσω: 1 aor. μετήλλαξα; fr. Hdt. down; [not in Sept., yet nine times in 2 Macc.; also 1 Esdr. i. 31]; *to exchange, change*, [cf. μετά, III. 2]: τὶ ἔν τινι, one thing with (for) another (on this constr. see ἀλλάσσω), Ro. i. 25; τὶ εἴς τι, one thing into another, Ro. i. 26.*

3338 μετα-μέλομαι; impf. μετεμελόμην; Pass., 1 aor. μετεμελήθην; 1 fut. μεταμεληθήσομαι; (fr. μέλομαι, mid. of μέλω); fr. Thuc. down; Sept. for נחם; a depon. pass.; prop. *it is a care to one afterwards* [see μετά, III. 2], i. e. *it repents one*; *to repent one's self* [in R. V. uniformly with this reflexive rendering (exc. 2 Co. vii. 8, where *regret*)]: Mt. xxi. 29, 32; xxvii. 3; 2 Co. vii. 8; Heb. vii. 21 fr. Ps. cix. (cx.) 4.*

[Syn. μεταμέλομαι, μετανοέω: The distinctions so often laid down between these words, to the effect that the former expresses a merely e m o t i o n a l change the latter a change of c h o i c e, the former has reference to p a r t i c u l a r s the latter to the e n t i r e l i f e, the former signifies nothing but r e g r e t even though amounting to remorse, the latter that reversal of moral purpose known as r e p e n t a n c e — seem hardly to be sustained by usage. But that

μετανοέω is the fuller and nobler term, expressive of moral action and issues, is indicated not only by its derivation, but by the greater frequency of its use, by the fact that it is often employed in the impv. (μεταμέλομαι never), and by its construction with ἀπό, ἐκ, (cf. ἡ εἰς θεὸν μετάνοια, Acts xx. 21). Cf. Trench, N. T. Syn. § lxix.; esp. *Gataker*, Adv. Post. xxix.]

3339 μετα-μορφόω, -ῶ: Pass., pres. μεταμορφοῦμαι; 1 aor. μετεμορφώθην; *to change into another form* [cf. μετά, III. 2], *to transfigure, transform*: μετεμορφώθη, of Christ, *his appearance was changed* [A. V. *he was transfigured*], i. e. was resplendent with a divine brightness, Mt. xvii. 2; Mk. ix. 2 (for which Lk. ix. 29 gives ἐγένετο τὸ εἶδος τοῦ προσώπου αὐτοῦ ἕτερον); of Christians: τὴν αὐτὴν εἰκόνα μεταμορφούμεθα, we are transformed into the same image (of consummate excellence that shines in Christ), reproduce the same image, 2 Co. iii. 18; on the simple acc. after verbs of motion, change, division, cf. *Bos*, Ellips. (ed. Schaefer), p. 679 sqq.; Matthiae § 409; [Jelf § 636 obs. 2; cf. B. 190 (164); 396 (339); W. § 32, 5]; used of the change of moral character for the better, Ro. xii. 2; with which compare Sen. epp. 6 init., intelligo non emendari me tantum, sed *transfigurari*. ([Diod. 4, 81; Plut. de adulat. et amic. 7; al.]; Philo, vit. Moys. i. § 10 sub fin.; leg. ad Gaium § 13; Athen. 8 p. 334 c.; Ael. v. h. 1, 1; Lcian. as. 11.) [Syn. cf. μετασχηματίζω.] *

3340 μετα-νοέω, -ῶ: fut. μετανοήσω; 1 aor. μετενόησα; fr. [Antipho], Xen. down; Sept. several times for נחם; *to change one's mind*, i. e. *to repent* (to feel sorry that one has done this or that, Jon. iii. 9), of having offended some one, Lk. xvii. 3 sq.; with ἐπί τινι added (dat. of the wrong, Hebr., Am. vii. 3; Joel ii. 13; Jon. iii. 10; iv. 2), *of (on account of) something* (so Lat. *me paenitet alicujus rei*), 2 Co. xii. 21; used esp. of those who, conscious of their sins and with manifest tokens of sorrow, are intent on obtaining God's pardon; *to repent* (Lat. *paenitentiam agere*): μετανοῶ ἐν σάκκῳ καὶ σποδῷ, clothed in sackcloth and besprinkled with ashes, Mt. xi. 21; Lk. x. 13. *to change one's mind for the better, heartily to amend with abhorrence of one's past sins*: Mt. iii. 2; iv. 17; Mk. i. 15, (cf. Mt. iii. 6 ἐξομολογούμενοι τὰς ἁμαρτίας αὐτῶν; ib. 8 and Lk. iii. 8 καρποὺς ἀξίους τῆς μετανοίας, i. e. conduct worthy of a heart changed and abhorring sin); [Mt. xi. 20; Mk. vi. 12]; Lk. xiii. 3, 5; xv. 7, 10; xvi. 30; Acts ii. 38; iii. 19; xvii. 30; Rev. ii. 5, 16; iii. 3, 19; on the phrase μετανοεῖν εἰς τὸ κήρυγμά τινος, Mt. xii. 41 and Lk. xi. 32, see εἰς, B. II. 2 d.; [W. 397 (371)]. Since τὸ μετανοεῖν expresses mental direction, the t e r m i n i from which and to which may be specified: ἀπὸ τῆς κακίας, to withdraw or turn one's soul from, etc. [cf. W. 622 (577); esp. B. 322 (277)]; ἔκ τινος, Rev. ii. 21 sq.; ix. 20 sq.; xvi. 11 (see ἐκ, I. 6; [cf. B. 327 (281), and W. u. s.]); μετανοεῖν κ. ἐπιστρέφειν ἐπὶ τὸν θεόν, Acts xxvi. 20; foll. by an inf. indicating purpose [W. 318 (298)], Rev. xvi. 9. [Syn. see μεταμέλομαι.] *

3341 μετάνοια, -οίας, ἡ, (μετανοέω), *a change of mind*: as it appears in one who repents of a purpose he has formed or of something he has done, Heb. xii. 17 on which see εὑρίσκω, 3 ([Thuc. 3, 36, 3]; Polyb. 4, 66, 7; Plut. Peric.

c. 10; mor. p. 26 a.; τῆς ἀδελφοκτονίας μετάνοια, Joseph. antt. 13, 11, 3); esp. the change of mind of those who have begun to abhor their errors and misdeeds, and have determined to enter upon a better course of life, so that it embraces both a recognition of sin and sorrow for it and hearty amendment, the tokens and effects of which are good deeds (Lact. 6, 24, 6 would have it rendered in Lat. by *resipiscentia*), [A. V. *repentance*]: Mt. iii. 8, 11; Lk. iii. 8, [16 Lchm.]; xv. 7; xxiv. 47; Acts xxvi. 20; βάπτισμα μετανοίας, a baptism binding its subjects to repentance [W. § 30, 2 β.], Mk. i. 4; Lk. iii. 3; Acts xiii. 24; xix. 4; [ἡ εἰς (τὸν) θεὸν μετ. Acts xx. 21, see μετανοέω, fin.]; διδόναι τινὶ μετάνοιαν, to give one the ability to repent, or to cause him to repent, Acts v. 31; xi. 18; 2 Tim. ii. 25; τινὰ εἰς μετάνοιαν καλεῖν, Lk. v. 32, and Rec. in Mt. ix. 13; Mk. ii. 17; ἄγειν, Ro. ii. 4 (Joseph. antt. 4, 6, 10 fin.); ἀνακαινίζειν, Heb. vi. 6; χωρῆσαι εἰς μετάν. to come to the point of repenting, or be brought to repentance, 2 Pet. iii. 9 [but see χωρέω, 1 fin.]; μετ. ἀπὸ νεκρῶν ἔργων, that change of mind by which we turn from, desist from, etc. Heb. vi. 1 [B. 322 (277)]; used merely of the improved spiritual state resulting from deep sorrow for sin, 2 Co. vii. 9 sq. (Sir. xliv. 16; Sap. xi. 24 (23); xii. 10, 19; Or. Man. 7 sq. [cf. Sept. ed. Tdf. Proleg. p. lxii. sq.)]; Philo, quod det. pot. insid. § 26 init.; Antonin. 8, 10; [Cebes, tab. 10 fin.].)*

3342 μεταξύ, (fr. μετά and ξύν, i. q. σύν), adv.; **1.** *between* (*in the midst*, Hom. Il. 1, 156; Sap. xviii. 23), **a.** adverbially of time, ἐν τῷ μεταξύ, *meanwhile, in the mean time*, cf. ἐν τῷ καθεξῆς (see καθεξῆς): Jn. iv. 31 (Xen. symp. 1, 14; with χρόνῳ added, Plat. rep. 5 p. 450 c.; Joseph. antt. 2, 7, 1; ὁ μεταξὺ χρόνος, Hdian. 3, 8, 20 [10 ed. Bekk. cf. W. 592 sq. (551)]). **b.** like a prep. w. a gen. [cf. W. 54, 6]: of place [fr. Hdt. 1, 6 down], Mt. xxiii. 35; Lk. xi. 51; xvi. 26; Acts xii. 6; of parties, Mt. xviii. 15; Acts xv. 9; Ro. ii. 15. **2.** acc. to a somewhat rare usage of later Grk. (Joseph. c. Ap. 1, 21, 2 [(yet see Müller ad loc.)]; b. j. 5, 4, 2; Plut. inst. Lac. 42; de discr. amici et adul. c. 22; Theoph. ad Autol. 1, 8 and Otto in loc.; [Clem. Rom. 1 Cor. 44, 2. 3; Barn. ep. 13, 5]), *after, afterwards*: τὸ μεταξὺ σάββ. the next (following) sabbath, Acts xiii. 42 [(where see Meyer)].*

3343 μετα-πέμπω: 1 aor. pass. ptcp. μεταπεμφθείς; Mid., pres. ptcp. μεταπεμπόμενος; 1 aor. μετεπεμψάμην; **1.** *to send* one *after* another [see μετά, III. 3; cf. Herm. ad Vig. p. 639]. **2.** like our *to send after* i. q. *to send for*: μεταπεμφθείς, sent for, Acts x. 29ᵇ. Mid. *to send after for one's self, cause to be sent for*: Acts x. 5, 29ᵇ; xi. 13; [xx. 1 T Tr WH]; xxiv. 24, 26; foll. by εἰς, w. an acc. of place, Acts x. 22; xxv. 3. (Gen. xxvii. 45; Num. xxiii. 7; 2 Macc. xv. 31; 4 Macc. xii. 3, 6; in prof. auth. fr. Hdt. down.)*

3344 μετα-στρέφω: 1 aor. inf. μεταστρέψαι; Pass., 2 aor. impv. 3 pers. sing. μεταστραφήτω; 2 fut. μεταστραφήσομαι; fr. Hom. down; Sept. for הָפַךְ; *to turn about, turn around*, [cf. μετά, III. 2]: τὶ εἰς τι [to turn one thing into another], pass., Acts ii. 20 (fr. Joel ii. 31); Jas.

iv. 9 [cf. B. 52 (46); (WH txt. μετατρέπω, q. v.)]; i. q. *to pervert, corrupt*, τί (Sir. xi. 31; Aristot. rhet. 1, 15, 24 [cf. 30 and 3, 11, 6]): Gal. i. 7.*

3345 μετα-σχηματίζω: fut. μετασχηματίσω [cf. B. 37 (32)]; 1 aor. μετεσχημάτισα; Mid. pres. μετασχηματίζομαι; to change the figure of, to transform, [see μετά, III. 2]: τί, Phil. iii. 21 [see below]; mid. foll. by εἰς τινα, to transform one's self into some one, to assume his appearance, 2 Co. xi. 13 sq.; foll. by ὡς τις, so as to have the appearance of some one, 2 Co. xi. 15; μετασχηματίζω τι εἰς τινα, to shape one's discourse so as to transfer to one's self what holds true of the whole class to which one belongs, i. e. so as to illustrate by what one says of himself what holds true of all: 1 Co. iv. 6, where the meaning is, 'by what I have said of myself and Apollos, I have shown what holds true of all Christian teachers.' (4 Macc. ix. 22; Plat. legg. 10 p. 903 e.; [Aristot. de caelo 3, 1 p. 298ᵇ, 31, etc.]; Joseph. antt. 7, 10, 5; 8, 11, 1; Plut. Ages. 14; def. orac. c. 30; [Philo, leg. ad Gaium § 11]; Sext. Empir. 10, p. 688 ed. Fabric. [p. 542, 23 ed. Bekk.].)*

[Syn. μεταμορφόω, μετασχηματίζω. (cf. Phil. iii. 21) "μετασχημ. would here refer to the transient condition *from* which, μεταμορφ. to the permanent state *to* which, the change takes place. Abp. Trench [N. T. Syn. § lxx.], however, supposes that μετασχημ. is here preferred to μεταμορφ. as expressing 'transition but no absolute solution of continuity', 'he spiritual body being developed from the natural, as the butterfly from the caterpillar" (Bp. Lghtft. on Phil. 'Detached Note' p. 131). See μορφή, fin.]

3346 μετα-τίθημι; 1 aor. μετέθηκα; pres. mid. μετατίθεμαι; 1 aor. pass. μετετέθην; *to transpose* (two things, one of which is put in place of the other, [see μετά, III. 2]); i. e. **1.** *to transfer*: τινά foll. by εἰς w. acc. of place, pass., Acts vii. 16; without mention of the place, it being well known to the readers, Heb. xi. 5 (Gen. v. 24; Sir. xliv. 16, cf. Sap. iv. 10). **2.** *to change* (Hdt. 5, 68); pass. of an office the mode of conferring which is changed, Heb. vii. 12; τὶ εἰς τι, to turn one thing into another (τινὰ εἰς πτηνὴν φύσιν, Anth. 11, 367, 2); figuratively, τὴν . . . χάριν εἰς ἀσέλγειαν, to pervert the grace of God to license, i. e. to seek from the grace of God an argument in defence of licentiousness, Jude 4 [cf. Huther in loc.]. **3.** pass. or [more commonly] mid., *to transfer one's self* or *suffer one's self to be transferred*, i. e. *to go* or *pass over*: ἀπό τινος εἰς τι, to fall away or desert from one person or thing to another, Gal. i. 6 (cf. 2 Macc. vii. 24; Polyb. 5, 111, 8; 26, 2, 6; Diod. 11, 4; [ὁ μεταθέμενος, turncoat, Diog. Laërt. 7, 166 cf. 37; Athen. 7, 281 d.]).*

see 3344 [μετα-τρέπω: 2 aor. pass. impv. 3 pers. sing. μετατραπήτω; *to turn about*, fig. *to transmute*: Jas. iv. 9 WH txt. From Hom. down; but "seems not to have been used in Attic" (L. and S.).*]

3347 μετ-έπειτα, adv., fr. Hom. down, *afterwards, after that*: Heb. xii. 17. (Judith ix. 5; 3 Macc. iii. 24.)*

3348 μετ-έχω; pf. μετέσχηκα; *to be or become partaker*; *to partake*: τῆς ἐλπίδος αὐτοῦ, of the thing hoped for, ? Co. ix. 10 Rec.. but G L T Tr WH have rightly restored ἐπ᾽ ἐλπίδι τοῦ μετέχειν, in hope of partaking (of the harvest); with a gen. of the thing added, 1 Co. ix. 12; x. 21; Heb. ii. 14; φυλῆς ἑτέρας, to belong to another tribe, be of another tribe, Heb. vii. 13; sc. τῆς τροφῆς, to partake of, eat, 1 Co. x. 30; γάλακτος, to partake of, feed on, milk, Heb. v. 13; ἐκ τοῦ ἑνὸς ἄρτου sc. τί or τινός (see ἐκ, I. 2 b.), 1 Co. x. 17; cf. B. § 132, 8; [W. §§ 28, 1; 30, 8 a.].*

3349　μετ-εωρίζω: [pres. impv. pass. 2 pers. plur. μετεωρίζεσθε; (see below); (fr. μετέωρος in mid-air, high; raised on high; metaph.　**a.** elated with hope, Diod. 13, 46; lofty, proud, Polyb. 3, 82, 2; 16, 21, 2; Sept. Is. v. 15.　**b.** wavering in mind, unsteady, doubtful, in suspense: Polyb. 24, 10, 11; Joseph. antt. 8, 8, 2; b. j. 4, 2, 5; Cic. ad Att. 5, 11, 5; 15, 14; hence μετεωρίζω);　**1.** prop. to raise on high (as ναῦν εἰς τὸ πέλαγος, to put a ship [out to sea] up upon the deep, Lat. propellere in altum, Philostr. v. Ap. 6, 12, 3 [cf. Thuc. 8, 16, 2]; τὸ ἔρυμα, to raise fortifications, Thuc. 4, 90): ἑαυτόν, of birds, Ael. h. a. 11, 33; pass. μετεωρίζεσθαι ἢ καπνὸν ἢ κονιορτόν, Xen. Cyr. 6, 3, 5; of the wind, ἄνεμος ξηρὸς μετεωρισθείς, Arstph. nub. 404; and many other exx. also in prof. auth.; in Sept. cf. Mic. iv. 1; Ezek. x. 16; Obad. 4.　**2.** metaph.　**a.** to lift up one's soul, raise his spirits; to buoy up with hope; to inflate with pride: Polyb. 26, 5, 4; 24, 3, 6 etc.; joined with φυσᾶν, Dem. p. 169, 23; Philo, vit. Moys. i. § 35; [quis rer. div. her. §§ 14, 51; cong. erud. grat. § 23]; pass. to be elated; to take on airs, be puffed up with pride: Arstph. av. 1447; often in Polyb.; Diod. 11, 32, 41; 16, 18 etc.; Ps. cxxx. (cxxxi.) 1; 2 Macc. vii. 34; with the addition of τὴν διάνοιαν, v. 17. Hence μὴ μετεωρίζεσθε, Lk. xii. 29, some (following the Vulg. nolite in sublime tolli) think should be interpreted, do not exalt yourselves, do not seek great things, (Luth. fahret nicht hoch her); but this explanation does not suit the preceding context.　**b.** by a metaphor taken from ships that are tossed about on the deep by winds and waves, to cause one to waver or fluctuate in mind, Polyb. 5, 70, 10; to agitate or harass with cares; to render anxious: Philo de monarch. § 6; Schol. ad Soph. Oed. Tyr. 914; ad Eur. Or. 1537; hence Lk. xii. 29 agreeably to its connection is best explained, neither be ye anxious, or and waver not between hope and fear [A. V. neither be ye of doubtful mind (with mrg. Or, live not in careful suspense)]. Kuinoel on Lk. l. c. discusses the word at length; and numerous exx. from Philo are given in Loesner, Observv. p. 115 sqq.*

3350　μετοικεσία, -ας, ἡ, (for the better form μετοίκησις, fr. μετοικέω [cf. W. 24 (23)]), a removal from one abode to another, esp. a forced removal: with the addition Βαβυλῶνος (on this gen. cf. W. § 30, 2 a.) said of the Babylonian exile, Mt. i. 11 sq. 17. (Sept. for גָּלָה i. e. migration, esp. into captivity; of the Babylonian exile, 2 K. xxiv. 16; 1 Chr. v. 22; Ezek. xii. 11; for גָּלוּת, Obad. 20; Nah. iii. 10. Elsewh. only in Anthol. 7, 731, 6.) *

3351　μετ-οικίζω: fut. (Attic) μετοικιῶ [cf. B. 37 (32); W. § 13, 1 c.]; 1 aor. μετῴκισα; to transfer settlers; to cause to remove into another land [see μετά, III. 2]: τινά foll. by

εἰς w. acc. of place, Acts vii. 4; ἐπέκεινα w. gen. of place (Amos v. 27), Acts vii. 43. (Thuc. 1, 12; Arstph., Aristot., Philo, [Joseph. c. Ap. 1, 19, 3], Plut., Ael.; Sept. several times for הִגְלָה.) *

μετοχή, -ῆς, ἡ, (μετέχω), (Vulg. participatio); a sharing,　**3352** communion, fellowship: 2 Co. vi. 14. (Ps. cxxi. (cxxii.) 3; Hdt., Anthol., Plut., al.) *

μέτοχος, -ον, (μετέχω);　**1.** sharing in, partaking　**3353** of, w. gen. of the thing [W. § 30, 8 a.]: Heb. iii. 1; vi. 4; xii. 3; τοῦ Χριστοῦ, of his mind, and of the salvation procured by him, Heb. iii. 14; cf. Bleek ad loc.　**2.** a partner (in a work, office, dignity): Heb. i. 9 (fr. Ps. xliv. (xlv.) 8); Lk. v. 7. (Hdt., Eur., Plat., Dem., al.) *

μετρέω, -ῶ; 1 aor. ἐμέτρησα; 1 fut. pass. μετρηθήσομαι;　**3354** (μέτρον); fr. Hom. Od. 3, 179 down; Sept. several times for מָדַד; to measure; i. e.　**1.** to measure out or off,　**a.** prop. any space or distance with a measurer's reed or rule: τὸν ναόν, τὴν αὐλήν, etc., Rev. xi. 2; xxi. 15, 17; with τῷ καλάμῳ added, Rev. xxi. 16; ἐν αὐτῷ, i. e. τῷ καλάμῳ, Rev. xi. 1.　**b.** metaph. to judge according to any rule or standard, to estimate: ἐν ᾧ μέτρῳ μετρεῖτε, by what standard ye measure (others) [but the instrumental ἐν seems to point to a measure of capacity; cf. W. 388 (363); B. § 133, 19. On the proverb see further below], Mt. vii. 2; Mk. iv. 24; pass. to be judged, estimated, ibid.; μετρεῖν ἑαυτὸν ἐν ἑαυτῷ, to measure one's self by one's self, to derive from one's self the standard by which one estimates one's self, 2 Co. x. 12 [cf. W. § 31, 8 fin.].　**2.** to measure to, mete out to, i. e. to give by measure: in the proverb τῷ αὐτῷ μέτρῳ ᾧ μετρεῖτε [or (so L T Tr WH) ᾧ μέτρῳ μετρ.], i. e., dropping the fig., 'in proportion to your own beneficence,' Lk. vi. 38. [Comp.: ἀντι-μετρέω.] *

μετρητής [on the accent see Chandler § 51 sq.], -οῦ, ὁ,　**3355** (μετρέω), prop. a measurer, the name of a utensil known as an amphora, which is a species of measure used for liquids and containing 72 sextarii or ξέστοι [i. e. somewhat less than nine Eng. gallons; see B. D. s. v. Weights and Measures, sub fin. (p. 3507 Am. ed.)] (Hebr. בַּת, 2 Chr. iv. 5): Jn. ii. 6. (Polyb. 2, 15, 1; Dem. p. 1045, 7; Aristot. h. a. 8, 9.) *

μετριοπαθέω, -ῶ, ([cf. W. 101 (95)]; fr. μετριοπαθής,　**3356** adhering to the true measure in one's passions or emotions; ἔφη (viz. Aristotle) τὸν σοφὸν μὴ εἶναι μὲν ἀπαθῆ, μετριοπαθῆ δέ, Diog. Laërt. 5, 31; μετριοπάθεια, moderation in passions or emotions, esp. anger and grief, is opp. to the ἀπάθεια of the Stoics; fr. μέτριος and πάθος); i. q. μετρίως or κατὰ τὸ μέτρον πάσχω, to be affected moderately or in due measure; to preserve moderation in the passions, esp. in anger or grief, (Philo de Abrah. § 44; de Josepho § 5; [Joseph. antt. 12, 3, 2; al.]); hence of one who is not unduly disturbed by the errors, faults, sins, of others, but bears with them gently; like other verbs of emotion (cf. Krüger § 48, 8), with a dat. of the pers. toward whom the feeling is exercised: Heb. v. 2; cf. the full discussion by Bleek ad loc.*

μετρίως, (μέτριος), adv., [fr. Hdt. down];　**a.** in　**3357** due measure.　**b.** moderately: οὐ μετρίως, [A. V.

not a little], exceedingly, (Plut. Flam. 9, et al.), Acts xx. 12.*

3358 **μέτρον, -ου, τό**, Sept. chiefly for מִדָּה, [cf. μήτηρ], *measure*; **1.** *an instrument for measuring*; **a.** *a vessel for receiving and determining the quantity of things, whether dry or liquid*: in proverb. disc., μετρεῖν μέτρῳ, of the measure of the benefits which one confers on others, Lk. vi. 38; μέτρον πεπιεσμένον καὶ σεσαλευμένον, fig. equiv. to most abundant requital, ibid.; πληροῦν τὸ μέτρον τῶν πατέρων, to add what is wanting in order to fill up their ancestors' prescribed number of crimes, Mt. xxiii. 32 [see πληρόω, 2 a.]; ἐκ μέτρου [A. V. *by measure*; see ἐκ, V. 3] i. e. *sparingly*, Jn. iii. 34 (also ἐν μέτρῳ, Ezek. iv. 11). **b.** *a graduated staff for measuring, measuring-rod*: Rev. xxi. 15; with ἀνθρώπου added [*man's measure*], such as men use, Rev. xxi. 17; hence in proverb. disc. *the rule or standard of judgment*: Mt. vii. 2; Mk. iv. 24. **2.** *determined extent, portion measured off, measure or limit*: with a gen. of the thing received, Ro. xii. 3; 2 Co. x. 13; [Eph. iv. 7]; ἐν μέτρῳ, in proportion to the measure [cf. W. § 48, a. 3 b. and see ἐνέργεια; al. *in due measure*], Eph. iv. 16; *the required measure, the due, fit, measure*: τῆς ἡλικίας, the proper i. e. ripe, full age [see ἡλικία, 1 c.] (of a man), Eph. iv. 13 (ἥβης, Hom. Il. 11, 225; Od. 11, 317; Solon 5, 52 [Poet. Min. Gr. (ed. Gaisford) iii. 135]).*

3359 **μέτωπον, -ου, τό**, (μετά, ὤψ 'eye'), fr. Hom. down; Sept. for מֵצַח, [lit. the space *between the eyes*] *the forehead*: Rev. vii. 3; ix. 4; xiii. 16; xiv. 1, 9; xvii. 5; xx. 4; xxii. 4.*

3360 **μέχρι and μέχρις** (the latter never stands in the N. T. before a consonant, but μέχρι stands also before a vowel in Lk. xvi. 16 T Tr WH; see ἄχρι, init.; and on the distinction betw. ἄχρι and μέχρι see ἄχρι, fin.), a particle indicating the terminus ad quem: *as far as, unto, until*; **1.** it has the force of a preposition with the gen. [(so even in Hom.) W. § 54, 6], and is used **a.** of time: Mt. xiii. 30 R G T WH mrg.; Lk. xvi. 16 T Tr WH; Acts xx. 7; 1 Tim. vi. 14; Heb. ix. 10; μ. θανάτου, Phil. ii. 30; μέχρι τῆς σήμερον sc. ἡμέρας, Mt. xi. 23; xxviii. 15; μέχρι τέλους, Heb. iii. 6 [here WH Tr mrg. br. the clause], 14; ἀπὸ . . . μέχρι, Acts x. 30; Ro. v. 14; μέχρις οὗ (see ἄχρι, 1 d.; [B. 230 (198) sq.; W. 296 (278 sq.)]) foll. by an aor. subjunc. having the force of a fut. pf. in Lat.: Mk. xiii. 30; Gal. iv. 19 T Tr WH. **b.** of place: ἀπὸ . . . μέχρι, Ro. xv. 19. **c.** of measure and degree: μέχρι θανάτου, so that he did not shrink even from death, Phil. ii. 8 (2 Macc. xiii. 14; Plat. de rep. p. 361 c. fin., μ. φόνου, Clem. hom. 1, 11); κακοπαθεῖν μ. δεσμῶν, 2 Tim. ii. 9; μέχρις αἵματος ἀντικατέστητε, Heb. xii. 4. **2.** with the force of a conjunction: *till*, foll. by the subj., Eph. iv. 13.*

3361 **μή**, Sept. for אַל, אִין, אֵין, a particle of negation, which differs from οὐ (which is always an adverb) in that οὐ denies the thing itself (or to speak technically, denies simply, absolutely, categorically, directly, objectively), but μή denies the thought of the thing, or the thing according to the judgment, opinion, will, purpose, preference, of some one (hence, as we say technically, in-directly, hypothetically, subjectively). This distinction holds also of the compounds οὐδείς, μηδείς, οὐκέτι, μηκέτι, etc. But μή is either an adverb of negation, *not* (Lat. *non, ne*); or a conjunction, *that . . . not, lest*, (Lat. *ne*); or an interrogative particle, (Lat. *num*) [i. e. (generally) implying a neg. ans.; in indir. quest. *whether not* (suggesting apprehension)]. Cf. *Herm.* ad Vig. § 267 p. 802 sqq.; *Matthiae* § 608; *Bttm. Gram.* § 148 (cf. *Alex. Bttm.* N. T. Gr. p. 344 (296) sqq.); *Kühner* ii. §§ 512 sq. p. 739 sqq.; [*Jelf* §§ 738 sqq.]; *Rost* § 135; *Win.* §§ 55, 56; *F. Franke*, De particulis negantibus. (two Comm.) Rintel. 1832 sq.; *G. F. Gayler*, Particularum Graeci sermonis negativarum accurata disputatio, etc. Tub. 1836; *E. Prüfer*, De μή et οὐ particulis epitome. Vratisl. 1836; [*Gildersleeve* in Am. Jour. of Philol. vol. i. no. i. p. 45 sqq.; *Jebb* in Vincent and Dickson's Hdbk. to Mod. Grk. ed. 2, App. §§ 82 sqq.].

I. As a negative ADVERB; **1.** univ.: ᾧ μὴ πάρεστι ταῦτα, where μή is used because reference is made merely to the thought that there are those who lack these things, 2 Pet. i. 9; ἃ μὴ ἑώρακεν, which (in my opinion) he hath not seen (because they are not visible), Col. ii. 18 [but here G T Tr WH om. L br. μή; cf. Bp. Lghtft. ad loc.; W. 480 sq. (448)]; ἤδη κέκριται, ὅτι μὴ πεπίστευκεν, *because he hath not believed*, represented by the writer as the thought τοῦ κρίναντος, Jn. iii. 18 (differently in 1 Jn. v. 10, where the faith denied is considered as something positive and actual); ἃ μὴ δεῖ, in the judgment of the writer, Tit. i. 11. **2.** in deliberative questions with the subjunctive: δῶμεν ἢ μὴ δῶμεν, Mk. xii. 14 (πότερον βίαν φῶμεν ἢ μὴ φῶμεν εἶναι, Xen. mem. 1, 2, 45); μὴ ποιήσωμεν τὰ κακά (for so it would have run had there been no anacoluthon; but Paul by the statement which he interposes is drawn away from the construction with which he began, and proceeds ὅτι ποιήσωμεν κτλ., so that these words depend on λέγειν in the intervening statement [W. 628 (583); B. § 141, 3]), Ro. iii. 8. **3.** in conditional and final sentences (cf. W. § 55, 2; [B. 344 (296) sqq.]): ἐὰν μή, *unless, if not*, see exx. in ἐάν, I 3 c. ἐὰν etc. καὶ μή, Mk. xii. 19; ἐὰν etc. δὲ μή, Jas. ii. 14; ἐὰν τις ἴδῃ . . . μὴ πρὸς θάνατον, 1 Jn. v. 16; εἰ μή, εἰ δὲ μή, εἰ δὲ μήγε, etc., see εἰ, III. p. 171 sq. To this head belong the formulae that have ἄν or ἐάν as a modifier (W. § 55, 3 e.; [B. § 148, 4]), ὅς, ὅστις, ὅσοι ἄν or ἐὰν μή: Mt. x. 14; xi. 6; Mk. vi. 11; x. 15; Lk. vii. 23; ix. 5; xviii. 17; Rev. xiii. 15; ὃς ἂν etc. καὶ μή, Mk. xi. 23; Lk. x. 10; ὃς ἂν . . . μὴ ἐπὶ πορνείᾳ, Mt. xix. 9 G T Tr WH txt.; of the same sort is πᾶν πνεῦμα, ὃ μὴ ὁμολογεῖ, 1 Jn. iv. 3. ἵνα μή, Mt. vii. 1; xvii. 27; Mk. iii. 9; Ro. xi. 25; Gal. v. 17; vi. 12, etc.; ἵνα . . . καὶ μή, Mt. v. 29 sq.; Mk. iv. 12; Jn. vi. 50; xi. 50; 2 Co. iv. 7, etc.; ἵνα . . . μή, 2 Co. xiii. 10; ἵνα ὁ . . . μή, Jn. iii. 16; παρακαλῶ, ἵνα . . . καὶ μή, 1 Co. i. 10; ὅπως μή, Mt. vi. 18; Acts xx. 16; 1 Co. i. 29; ὅπως οἱ . . . μή, Lk. xvi. 26. **4.** joined with the Infinitive (W. § 55, 4 f.; [B. §§ 140, 16; 148, 6; cf. Prof. Gildersleeve

3362

3363: **see 2443**

u. s. p. 48 sq.]);   **a.** after verbs of s a y i n g, d e c l a r i n g, d e n y i n g, c o m m a n d i n g, etc.: ἀποκριθῆναι, Lk. xx. 7; ἦν αὐτῷ κεχρηματισμένον μὴ ἰδεῖν, *that he should not see*, Lk. ii. 26; χρηματισθέντες μὴ ἀνακάμψαι, Mt. ii. 12; ὤμοσε (αὐτοῖς) μὴ εἰσελεύσεσθαι, Heb. iii. 18; after λέγω, Mt. v. 34, 39; xxii. 23; Mk xii. 18; Acts xxi. 4; xxiii. 8; Ro. ii. 22; xii. 3; κηρύσσω, Ro. ii. 21; γράφω, 1 Co. v. 9, 11 ; παραγγέλλω, Acts i. 4; iv. 18; v. 28, 40; 1 Co. vii. 10 sq.; 1 Tim. i. 3; vi. 17; παρακαλῶ, Acts ix. 38 R G; xix. 31; 2 Co. vi. 1; αἰτοῦμαι, Eph. iii. 13; διαμαρτύρομαι, 2 Tim. ii. 14; εὔχομαι, 2 Co. xiii. 7; παραιτοῦμαι, Heb. xii. 19 [here WH txt. om. μή; cf. W. and B. as below]; ἀξιῶ, Acts xv. 38; ἐπιβοῶ [L T Tr WH βοῶ], Acts xxv. 24; ἀντιλέγω (cf. W. §65, 2 β.; [B. § 148, 13]), Lk. xx. 27 [Tr WH L mrg. λέγω]; ἀπαρνοῦμαι (q. v.), Lk. xxii. 34; also after verbs of d e c i d i n g: Lk. xxi. 14; κρίνω, Acts xv. 19; κρίνω τοῦτο, τὸ μή, Ro. xiv. 13 ; 2 Co. ii. 1; θέλω, Ro. xiii. 3; after verbs of h i n d e r i n g, a v o i d i n g, etc.: ἐγκόπτω (Rec. ἀνακόπτω) τινὰ μή, Gal. v. 7 (cf. W. [and B. u. s.; also § 140, 16]); τοῦ μή, *that . . . not*, (Lat. *ne*), after κατέχω, Lk. iv. 42; κρατοῦμαι, Lk. xxiv. 16; κωλύω, Acts x. 47; καταπαύω, Acts xiv. 18; παύω, 1 Pet. iii. 10; ὑποστέλλομαι, Acts xx. 20, 27; προσέχω μή, Mt. vi. 1 ; but τοῦ μή is added also to other expressions in the sense of Lat. *ut ne, that . . . not*: Ro. vii. 3; ὀφθαλμοὶ τοῦ μὴ βλέπειν, ὦτα τοῦ μὴ ἀκούειν, Ro. xi. 8, 10.   After clauses denoting n e c e s s i t y, a d v a n t a g e, p o w e r, f i t n e s s, μή is used with an inf. specifying the thing [B. § 148, 6], καλόν ἐστι μή, 1 Co. vii. 1; Gal. iv. 18; foll. by τὸ μή, Ro. xiv. 21 ; ἄλογον μή, Acts xxv. 27; κρεῖττον ἦν, 2 Pet. ii. 21; ἐξουσία τοῦ [L T Tr WH om. τοῦ] μὴ ἐργάζεσθαι, a right to forbear working, 1 Co. ix. 6 ; δεῖ, Acts xxvii. 21; οὐ δύναμαι μή, *I cannot but*, Acts iv. 20; ἀνένδεκτόν ἐστι τοῦ μή, Lk. xvii. 1 [cf. ἀνένδεκτος].   **b.** μή with an inf. which has the article follows a preposition, to indicate the purpose or end : as, πρὸς τὸ μή, *that . . . not*, 2 Co. iii. 13 ; 1 Th. ii. 9; 2 Th. iii. 8 ; εἰς τὸ μή (Lat. *in id . . ne*), *to the end* (or *intent*) *that . . . not*, Acts vii. 19; 1 Co. x. 6 ; 2 Co. iv. 4; foll. by an acc. and inf., 2 Th. ii. 2; 1 Pet. iii. 7; διὰ τὸ μή, *because . . . not*, Mt. xiii. 5 sq.; Mk. iv. 5 sq.; Lk. viii. 6 ; Jas. iv. 2 [cf. W. 482 (449)], (2 Macc. iv. 19).   **c.** in other expressions where an infin. with the art. is used substantively : τῷ μή (dat. of the cause or reason [cf. W. § 44, 5; B. 264 (227)]), 2 Co. ii. 13 (12); in the accus., τὸ μή : Ro. xiv. 13; 1 Co. iv. 6 [R G]; 2 Co. ii. 1; x. 2; 1 Th. iv. 6, cf. 3.   **d.** in sentences expressing c o n s e q u e n c e or r e s u l t : ὥστε μή, *so that . . . not*, Mt. viii. 28; Mk. iii. 20; 1 Co. i. 7; 2 Co. iii. 7; 1 Th. i. 8.   **5.** μή is joined with a P a r t i c i p l e (W. § 55, 5 g.; [B. § 148, 7 ; see C. J. Vaughan's Com. on Ro. ii. 14]),   **a.** in sentences expressing a command, exhortation, purpose, etc. : Lk. iii. 11 ; Jn. ix. 39; Acts xv. 38; xx. 29; Ro. viii. 4; xiv. 3; 2 Co. xii. 21; Eph. v. 27; Phil. i. 28; ii. 4 [here Rec. impv.]; 1 Th. iv. 5; 2 Th. i. 8; 1 Pet. ii. 16; Heb. vi. 1; xiii. 17, etc.   **b.** in general sentences, in which no definite person is meant but it is merely assumed that there is some one of the character denoted by the participle : as ὁ μὴ ὢν μετ᾽ ἐμοῦ, *he that is not on my side*, whoever he is,

or if there is any such person, Mt. xii. 30 ; Lk. xi. 23 ; ὁ δὲ μὴ πιστεύων, whoever believeth not, Jn. iii. 18 ; οἱ μὴ ὁμολογοῦντες Ἰησοῦν Χρ. if any do not confess, or belong to the class that do not confess, 2 Jn. 7 ; add, Mt. x. 28; Lk. vi. 49; xii. 21, 47 sq.; xxii. 36 ; Jn. v. 23 ; x. 1 ; xii. 48; xiv. 24; Ro. iv. 5; v. 14; x. 20; 1 Co. vii. 38; xi. 22; 2 Th. i. 8; Jas. ii. 13 ; 1 Jn. ii. 4, etc.; πᾶς ὁ μή, Mt. vii. 26; (πᾶν δένδρον μή, Mt. iii. 10; vii. 19); 1 Jn. iii. 10 ; 2 Jn. 9 ; 2 Th. ii. 12 [here L mrg. T Tr WH mrg. ἅπαντες οἱ μή etc.]; μακάριος ὁ μή, Jn. xx. 29; Ro. xiv. 22.   **c.** where, indeed, a definite person or thing is referred to, but in such a way that his (its) quality or action (indicated by the participle) is denied in the thought or judgment either of the writer or of some other person [cf. esp. W. 484 (451)]: τὰ μὴ ὄντα, that are deemed as nothing, 1 Co. i. 28; ὡς μὴ λαβών, as if thou hadst not received, 1 Co. iv. 7; ὡς μὴ ἐρχομένου μου, as though I were not coming, 1 Co. iv. 18; ὡς μὴ ἐφικνούμενοι εἰς ὑμᾶς, 2 Co. x. 14 ; add, 1 Co. vii. 29. ᾔδει . . . τίνες εἰσὶν οἱ μὴ πιστεύοντες (acc. to the opinion of ὁ εἰδώς), Jn. vi. 64; the same holds true of Acts xx. 29; τὰ μὴ βλεπόμενα (in the opinion of οἱ μὴ σκοποῦντες), 2 Co. iv. 18 (on the other hand, in Heb. xi. 1, οὐ βλεπόμ. actually invisible); τὸν μὴ γνόντα ἁμαρτίαν ὑπὲρ ἡμῶν ἁμαρτίαν ἐποίησεν (μὴ γνόντα is said agreeably to the judgment of ὁ ποιήσας), 2 Co. v. 21 (τὸν οὐ γνόντα would be equiv. to ἀγνοοῦντα). in predictions, where it expresses the opinion of those who predict: ἔση σιωπῶν καὶ μὴ δυνάμενος λαλῆσαι, Lk. i. 20; ἔση τυφλὸς μὴ βλέπων, Acts xiii. 11. where the writer or speaker does not regard the thing itself so much as the thought of the thing, which he wishes to remove from the mind of the reader or hearer (Klotz ad Devar. ii. 2 p. 666), — to be rendered without etc. (Germ. ohne zu with inf.) [cf. B. § 148, 7 b.]: ἐξῆλθε μὴ ἐπιστάμενος, ποῦ ἔρχεται, Heb. xi. 8; add, Mt. xxii. 12; Lk. xiii. 11 [(but cf. B. § 148, 7 c.)]; Acts v. 7; xx. 22; Heb. ix. 9. where the participles have a c o n d i t i o n a l, c a u s a l, or c o n c e s s i v e force, and may be resolved into clauses introduced by *if, on condition that*, etc. : θερίσομεν μὴ ἐκλυόμενοι, Gal. vi. 9 ; μὴ ὄντος νόμου, Ro. v. 13; *although*: νόμον μὴ ἔχοντες, Ro. ii. 14; μὴ ὢν αὐτὸς ὑπὸ νόμον, 1 Co. ix. 20 [Rec. om.]; we have both the negative particles in ὃν οὐκ εἰδότες [or (with L T Tr WH) ἰδόντες] . . . μὴ ὁρῶντες, whom being ignorant of (in person) [or (acc. to crit. txt.) not having seen] . . . although now not seeing, 1 Pet. i. 8; also with the article : τὰ μὴ νόμον ἔχοντα (Germ. die doch nicht haben, they that have not, etc.), Ro. ii. 14; ὁ δὲ μὴ γενεαλογούμενος, but he, although not etc. Heb. vii. 6; — or since, because, inasmuch as: μὴ ἀσθενήσας τῇ πίστει οὐ [but G L T Tr WH om. οὐ; cf. B. § 148, 14] κατενόησε τὸ ἑαυτοῦ σῶμα νενεκρωμ. (οὐκ ἀσθενήσας would be equiv. to δυνατός, strong), Ro. iv. 19; πῶς οὗτος γράμματα οἶδε μὴ μεμαθηκώς ; since he has not learned [W. 483 (450)], Jn. vii. 15; add, Mt. xviii. 25 ; xxii. 25, 29; Lk. ii. 45; vii. 30; xi. 24; xii. 47; xxiv. 23; Acts ix. 26; xvii. 6; xxi. 34; xxvii. 7; 2 Co. v. 19; also with the article: ὁ μὴ γινώσκων τὸν νόμον, since it knoweth not the law, Jn. vii. 49; add, Jude 5.   **d.** where (with the ptcp.) it can be resolved by (being) *such* (a person) *as not, of such a sort as not* : μὴ ζητῶν τὸ ἐμαυτοῦ σύμφορον, 1 Co. x. 33 ; add, Acts ix. 9 ; Gal. iv. 8. neut. plur. as subst. : τὰ μὴ ὄντα, Ro. iv. 17 ; τὰ μὴ σαλευόμενα, Heb. xii. 27 ; τὰ μὴ δέοντα, 1 Tim. v. 13 ; τὰ μὴ καθήκοντα, Ro. i. 28 ; 2 Macc. vi. 4, (on the other hand, in τὰ οὐκ ἀνήκοντα, Eph. v. 4 [where L T Tr WH ἃ οὐκ ἀνῆκεν], the οὐκ coalesces with ἀνήκοντα and forms a single idea, *unseemly, unlawful*). **6.** in independent sentences of forbidding, dehorting, admonishing, desiring, etc., μή is Prohibitive (cf. W. § 56, 1), Lat. *ne, not* ; **a.** with the 1 pers. plur. of the subjunc. present : μὴ γινώμεθα κενόδοξοι, Gal. v. 26 ; add, Gal. vi. 9 ; 1 Th. v. 6 ; 1 Jn. iii. 18 ; aorist : Jn. xix. 24 ; before the word depending on the exhortation, 1 Co. v. 8. **b.** with a present imperative, generally where one is bidden to cease from something already begun, or repeated, or continued : Mt. vi. 16, 19 ; vii. 1 ; xix. 6 ; Mk. ix. 39 ; xiii. 11 ; Lk. vi. 30 ; vii. 6, 13 ; viii. 49, 52 ; x. 4, 7, 20 ; Jn. ii. 16 ; v. 28, 45 ; vi. 43 ; vii. 24 ; xiv. 1, 27 ; xix. 21 ; Acts x. 15 ; xi. 9 ; xx. 10 ; Ro. vi. 12 ; xi. 18, 20 ; xii. 2 [here L Tr mrg. WH mrg. give the inf.], 14 ; 1 Co. vi. 9 ; vii. 5 ; 2 Co. vi. 14, 17 ; Gal. v. 1 ; vi. 7 ; Eph. iv. 30 ; Col. iii. 9, 19, 21 ; 1 Th. v. 19 ; 2 Th. iii. 15 ; 1 Tim. iv. 14 ; v. 16, 19 ; Heb. xii. 5 ; xiii. 2 ; Jas. i. 7, 16 ; 1 Pet. iv. 12, 15 sq. ; 1 Jn. ii. 15 ; iii. 13 ; Rev. v. 5, and very often. **c.** with the third person (nowhere in the N. T. with the second) of the aorist impv. where the prohibition relates to something not to be begun, and where things about to be done are forbidden : μὴ ἐπιστρεψάτω, Mt. xxiv. 18 ; Lk. xvii. 31 ; μὴ καταβάτω, Mk. xiii. 15, and L T Tr WH in Mt. xxiv. 17 (where R G badly καταβαινέτω) ; μὴ γνώτω, Mt. vi. 3 ; γενέσθω [but T Tr WH γινέσθω], Lk. xxii. 42 ; cf. Xen. Cyr. 7, 5, 73 ; Aeschyl. Sept. c. Theb. 1036. **d.** as in the more elegant Grk. writ. where future things are forbidden (cf. *Herm.* ad Vig. p. 807), with the 2 pers. of the aorist subjunctive : μὴ δόξητε, Mt. iii. 9 ; v. 17 ; μὴ φοβηθῇς, Mt. i. 20 ; x. 26, 31 [here L T Tr WH pres. impv. φοβεῖσθε], (alternating with the impv. pres. φοβεῖσθε in Mt. x. 28 [G L T Tr]) ; μὴ ἅψῃ, Col. ii. 21 ; μὴ ἀποστραφῇς, Mt. v. 42 ; μὴ κτήσησθε, Mt. x. 9 ; add, Mt. vi. 2, 7, 13, 31 ; Mk. v. 7 ; x. 19 ; Lk. vi. 29 ; viii. 28 ; xiv. 8 ; Jn. iii. 7 ; Acts vii. 60 ; Ro. x. 6 ; 1 Co. xvi. 11 ; 2 Co. xi. 16 ; 2 Th. ii. 3, —[in the last three exx. with the third pers., contrary to W. 502 (467)] ; 1 Tim. v. 1 ; 2 Tim. i. 8 ; Rev. vi. 6 ; **x.** 4 (μὴ γράψῃς, for ἔμελλον γράφειν precedes ; but in Jn. xix. 21 μὴ γράφε is used, because that Pilate had already written) ; Rev. xi. 2 ; xxii. 10, and very often. We have the impv. pres. and the aor. subj. together in Lk. x. 4 ; Acts xviii. 9. **e.** with the 2 pers. of the present subjunc. : μὴ σκληρύνητε, Heb. iii. 8, 15, (a rare constr. though not wholly unknown to Grk. writ. [" more than doubtful " (L. and S. s. v. A. I. 2)] ; see Delitzsch on the latter passage, and *Schaefer* ad Greg. Corinth. p. 1005 sq. ; [*Soph.* Lex. s. v. μή. Others regard the above exx. as subjunc. aorist ; cf. 2 K. ii. 10 ; Is. lxiii. 17 ; Jer. xvii. 23 ; xix. 15, etc.]). **f.** with the optative, in wishes : in that freq. formula μὴ γένοιτο, *far be it* ! see γίνομαι, 2 a. ; μὴ αὐτοῖς λογισθείη, 2 Tim. iv. 16 (Job xxvii. 5).

II. As a Conjunction, Lat. *ne* with the subjunctive ; **1.** our *that, that not* or *lest*, (cf. W. § 56, 2 ; [B. § 139, 48 sq. ; Goodwin § 46]) ; after verbs of f e a r ing, c a u t i o n, etc. **a.** with the subjunc. present, where one fears lest something now exists and at the same time indicates that he is ignorant whether it is so or not (*Hermann* on Soph. Aj. 272) : ἐπισκοποῦντες, μὴ . . . ἐνοχλῇ, Heb. xii. 15. **b.** with the subjunc. aorist, of things which may occur immediately or very soon : preceded by an aor., εὐλαβηθείς (L T Tr WH φοβηθείς) μὴ διασπασθῇ, Acts xxiii. 10 ; by a pres. : φοβοῦμαι, Acts xxvii. 17 ; βλέπω, Mt. xxiv. 4 ; Mk. xiii. 5 ; Lk. xxi. 8 ; Acts xiii. 40 ; 1 Co. x. 12 ; Gal. v. 15 ; Heb. xii. 25 ; σκοπέω ἐμαυτόν, Gal. vi. 1 [B. 243 (209) would refer this to 2 b. below ; cf. Goodwin p. 66] ; ὁράω, Mt. xviii. 10 ; 1 Th. v. 15 ; elliptically, ὅρα μή (sc. τοῦτο ποιήσῃς [cf. W. § 64, 7 a. ; B. 395 (338)]) : Rev. xix. 10 ; xxii. 9. **c.** with the indicative fut. (as being akin to the subjunc. [cf. gram. reff. at the beginning]) : φοβοῦμαι, μὴ ταπεινώσει με ὁ θεός μου, 2 Co. xii. 20 sq. [L txt. T Tr] ; add, Col. ii. 8. **2.** *in order that not* (Lat. *eo consilio ne*) ; **a.** with the optative : τῶν στρατιωτῶν βουλὴ ἐγένετο, ἵνα τοὺς δεσμώτας ἀποκτείνωσι, μή τις . . . διαφύγοι, Acts xxvii. 42 Rec. (the more elegant Greek to express the thought and purpose of the soldiers ; but the best codd. read διαφύγῃ, which G L T Tr WH have adopted). **b.** with the subjunctive aor. : preceded by the pres., Mk. xiii. 36 ; 2 Co. viii. 20 [cf. Goodwin § 43 Rem.] ; xii. 6 ; Col. ii. 4 (where L T Tr WH ἵνα μηδείς for R G μή τις [— an oversight ; in R G as well as in the recent crit. edd. the purpose is expressed by an inserted ἵνα]).

III. As an Interrogative particle it is used when   **see 2443** a negative answer is expected, Lat. *num* ; (W. § 57, 3 b. ; [B. 248 (213)]) ; **1.** in a d i r e c t question : Mt. vii. 9 sq. ; ix. 15 ; Mk. ii. 19 ; Lk. xvii. 9 ; Jn. iii. 4 ; iv. 12, 33 ; vi. 67 ; vii. 35, 51 sq. ; Acts vii. 28 ; Ro. iii. 3 ; ix. 20 ; 1 Co. i. 13 ; ix. 8 sq. ; x. 22 ; Jas. ii. [1 WH], 14 ; iii. 12, etc. ; μὴ γάρ (see γάρ, I.), Jn. vii. 41 ; μὴ οὐκ (where οὐκ belongs to the verb, and μή is interrogative), Ro. x. 18 sq. ; 1 Co. ix. 4 sq. ; μὴ γὰρ . . . οὐ, 1 Co. xi. 22. **2.** in an i n d i r e c t question with the indicative (Germ. *ob etwa, ob wohl, whether possibly, whether perchance*), where in admonishing another we intimate that possibly the case is as we fear [cf. B. § 139, 57 ; W. § 41 b. 4 a.] : Lk. xi. 35, cf. B. 243 (209) ; *Ast*, Lex. Plat. ii. p. 334 sq. ; [*Riddell*, Plato's Apol. Digest of Idioms §§ 137, 138].

IV. The particles οὐ μή in combination augment the   **3364** force of the negation, and signify *not at all, in no wise, by no means* ; (this formula arose from the fuller expressions οὐ δεινόν or δέος or φόβος, μή, which are still found sometimes in Grk. auth., cf. Kühner ii. § 516, 9 p. 773 sq. ; but so far was this origin of the phrase lost sight of that οὐ μή is used even of things not at all to be feared, but rather to be desired ; so in the N. T. in Mt. v. 18, 26 ; xviii. 3 ; Lk. xviii. 17 ; xxii. 16 ; Jn. iv. 48 ; xx. 25 ; 1 Th. v. 3) ; cf. Matthiae § 517 ; Kühner ii. p. 775 ; Bnhdy. p. 402 sqq. ; [Gildersleeve in the Amer. Jour. of Philol. for 1882, p. 202 sq. ; Goodwin § 89] ; W. § 56, 3 ;

[B. 211 (183) sq.].   **1.** with the fut. indicative: οὐ μὴ ἔσται σοι τοῦτο, this shall never be unto thee, Mt. xvi. 22; add, Mt. xxvi. 35; Lk. xxii. 34 R G L; x. 19 (where Rˢᵗ G WH mrg. ἀδικήσῃ); Jn. vi. 35 [here L Tr mrg. πεινάσει, and L T Tr WH διψήσει]; xiii. 38 R G; Mk. xiii. 31 T Tr WH; Heb. x. 17 L T Tr WH; in many passages enumerated by W. 506 (472); [cf. B. 212 (183)], the manuscripts vary between the indic. fut. and the subjunc. aor. In a question, οὐ μὴ ποιήσει τὴν ἐκδίκησιν; Lk. xviii. 7 R G.   **2.** with the aor. subjunctive (the use of which in the N. T. scarcely differs from that of the fut.; cf. W. § 56, 3; [B. § 139, 7]), in confident assertions: — subjunc. of the 1 aor., Mt. xxiv. 2; Mk. xiii. 2; Lk. vi. 37; Jn. xiii. 8; Heb. viii. 12; 1 Pet. ii. 6; Rev. ii. 11; vii. 16; xviii. 21, 22, 23; xxi. 27, etc.; 1 aor. mid. subj., Jn. viii. 52 (where Rec. γεύσεται); thus these N. T. exx. prove that Dawes made a great mistake in denying (in his Miscellanea Critica, p. 221 sqq. [ed. (Th. Kidd) 2, p. 408 sq.]) that the first aor. subjunc. is used after οὐ μή; [cf. Goodwin in Transactions of Am. Philol. Assoc. for 1869–70, pp. 46–55; L. and S. s. v. οὐ μή, I. 1 b.; B. § 139, 8]; — subjunc. of 2 aor., Mt. v. 18, 20, 26; Mk. x. 15; Lk. i. 15; xii. 59; Jn. x. 28; xi. 26; 1 Co. viii. 13; Heb. xiii. 5; Rev. iii. 3 [R G L Tr mrg. WH txt.], and often. in questions: with 1 aor., Lk. xviii. 7 L T Tr WII; Rev. xv. 4 (in L T Tr WII with the subj. aor. and the fut.); with 2 aor., Jn. xviii. 11. in declarations introduced by ὅτι: with 1 aor., 1 Th. iv. 15; with 2 aor., Mt. xxiv. 34 [here R G T om. ὅτι]; xxvi. 29 [L T Tr WH om. ὅτι]; Lk. xiii. 35 [T WII om. L br. ὅτι]; xxii. 16; Jn. xi. 56; in relative clauses: with 1 aor., Mt. xvi. 28; Mk. ix. 1; Acts xiii. 41; Ro. iv. 8; with 2 aor., Lk. xviii. 30.   **3.** with the present subjunc. (as sometimes in Grk. auth., cf. W. 507 (473)): οὐδὲ οὐ μή σε ἐγκαταλείπω, Heb. xiii. 5 Tdf. (for ἐγκαταλίπω Rec. et al.), [cf. B. 213 (184)].

(3364α)
see 1065 μήγε, εἰ δὲ μήγε, see γέ, 3 d.

3365 —— μηδαμῶς, (adv. fr. μηδαμός, and this fr. μηδέ, and ἀμός some one [perh. allied w. ἅμα, q. v.]), [fr. Aeschyl., Hdt. down], by no means, not at all: sc. τοῦτο γένοιτο, in replies after an impv. [A. V. Not so], Acts x. 14; xi. 8. (Sept. for חָלִילָה.) *

3366 μηδέ, (μή, q. v., and δέ), [fr. Hom. down], a negative disjunctive conjunction; [cf. W. § 55, 6; B. § 149, 13];   **1.** used in continuing a negation or prohibition, but not, and not, neither; preceded by μή, — either so that the two negatives have one verb in common: preceded by μή with a participle, Mt. xxii. 29; Mk. xii. 24; by μή w. a pres. subjunc., 1 Co. v. 8 [here L mrg. pres. indic.]; 1 Jn. iii. 18; by μή w. impv., Mt. vi. 25; Lk. x. 4; xii. 22; xiv. 12; 1 Jn. iii. 15; by μή w. an aor. subj. 2 pers. plur., Mt. x. 9 sq.; by εἰς τὸ μή, 2 Th. ii. 2 L T Tr WH; — or so that μηδέ has its own verb: preceded by ὃς ἐὰν (ἂν) μή, Mt. x. 14; Mk. vi. 11; by ἵνα μή, Jn. iv. 15; by ὅπως μή, Lk. xvi. 26; w. a ptcp. after μή w. a ptcp., Lk. xii. 47; 2 Co. iv. 2; w. an impv. after μή w. impv., Jn. xiv. 27; Ro. vi. 12 sq.; Heb. xii. 5; μηδενὶ ἐπιτίθει, foll. by μηδέ w. impv. 1 Tim. v. 22; w.

2 pers. of the aor. subj. after μή w. 2 pers. of the aor. subj., Mt. vii. 6; xxiii. 9 sq.; Lk. xvii. 23; Col. ii. 21; 1 Pet. iii. 14; after μηδέ w. an aor. subj. Mk. viii. 26 [T reads μή for the first μηδέ, T WH Tr mrg. om. the second clause]; after μηδένα w. an aor. subj. Lk. iii. 14 [Tdf. repeats μηδένα]; μηδὲ . . . μηδέ w. 1 pers. plur. pres. subj. 1 Co. x. 8 sq. [see below]; παραγγέλλω foll. by μή w. inf. . . . μηδέ w. inf., Acts iv. 18; 1 Tim. i. 4; vi. 17; καλὸν τὸ μή . . . μηδέ with inf. Ro. xiv. 21; w. gen. absol. after μήπω w. gen. absol. Ro. ix. 11; w. impv. after εἰς τὸ μή, 1 Co. x. 7; μηδέ is repeated several times in a negative exhortation after εἰς τὸ μή in 1 Co. x. 7–10.   **2.** not even (Lat. ne . . . quidem): w. an inf. after ἔγραψα, 1 Co. v. 11; after ὥστε, Mk. ii. 2; iii. 20 (where R G T badly μήτε [cf. W. 489 sq. (456); B. pp. 367, 369]); w. a pres. impv., Eph. v. 3; 2 Th. iii. 10.

μηδείς, μηδεμία, μηδέν (and μηθέν, Acts xxvii. 33 L T Tr WH, — a form not infreq. fr. Aristot. on [found as early as B. c. 378, cf. Meisterhans, Gr. d. Att. Inschr. p. 73]; cf. Lob. ad Phryn. p. 181 sq.; W. § 5, 1 d. 11; [B. 28 (25)]; Kühner § 187, 1 vol. i. 487 sq.), (fr. μηδέ and εἷς), [fr. Hom. down]; it is used either in connection with a noun, no, none, or absolutely, no one, not one, no man, neut. nothing, and in the same constructions as μή: accordingly   **a.** with an imperative: μηδείς being the person to whom something is forbidden, 1 Co. iii. 18, 21; x. 24; Gal. vi. 17; Eph. v. 6; Col. ii. 18; 1 Tim. iv. 12; Tit. ii. 15; Jas. i. 13; 1 Jn. iii. 7; neut. μηδέν, sc. ἔστω [A. V. have thou nothing to do with etc.], Mt. xxvii. 19; μηδείς with the dat. or the acc. depending on the impv., Ro. xiii. 8; 1 Tim. v. 22; μηδέν (accusative), Lk. iii. 13; ix. 3; μ. φοβοῦ, Rev. ii. 10 [here L Tr WH txt. μή].   **b.** μηδείς with the optative: once in the N. T., Mk. xi. 14 (where Rec. οὐδείς) [cf. W. 476 (443)].   **c.** with the 2 pers. of the aor. subjunc., the μηδείς depending on the verb; as, μηδενὶ εἴπῃς, Mt. viii. 4; xvii. 9; accus., Lk. iii. 14; x. 4; μηδέν (acc.), Acts xvi. 28; κατὰ μηδένα τρόπον, 2 Th. ii. 3.   **d.** with the particles ἵνα and ὅπως (see μή, I. 3): with ἵνα, Mt. xvi. 20; Mk. v. 43; vi. 8; vii. 36; ix. 9; Tit. iii. 13; Rev. iii. 11; with ὅπως, Acts viii. 24.   **e.** with an infinitive;   **α.** with one that depends on another verb: — as on παραγγέλλω, Lk. viii. 56; ix. 21; Acts xxiii. 22; δείκνυμι, Acts x. 28; διατάσσομαι, Acts xxiv. 23; ἀναθεματίζω ἐμαυτόν, Acts xxiii. 14; κρίνω (acc. w. inf.), Acts xxi. 25 Rec.; εὔχομαι, 2 Co. xiii. 7; βούλομαι (acc. w. inf.), 1 Tim. v. 14; ὑπομιμνήσκω τινά, Tit. iii. 2, etc.; παρακαλῶ τινα foll. by τὸ μή w. acc. and inf., 1 Th. iii. 3 L (ed. ster.) T Tr WH.   **β.** with an inf. depending on διὰ τό: Acts xxviii. 18; Heb. x. 2.   **f.** with a participle (see μή, I. 5); in dat., Acts xi. 19; Ro. xii. 17; accus. μηδένα, Jn. viii. 10; Acts ix. 7; μηδέν, Acts iv. 21; xxvii. 33; 1 Co. x. 25, 27; 2 Co. vi. 10; 2 Th. iii. 11; 1 Tim. vi. 4; Tit. ii. 8; Jas. i. 6; 3 Jn. 7; μηδεμίαν προσκοπήν, 2 Co. vi. 3; μηδεμίαν πτόησιν, 1 Pet. iii. 6; μηδεμίαν αἰτίαν, Acts xxviii. 18; ἀναβολὴν μηδ. xxv. 17.   **g.** noteworthy are — μηδείς with a gen., Acts iv. 17; xxiv. 23; μηδείς sc. τούτων, Rev. ii. 10 [R G T WH mrg.]; ἐν

3367

μηδενί, *in nothing,* 1 Co. i. 7 [but χαρίσματι is expressed here] ; 2 Co. [vi. 3 (see h. below)] ; vii. 9 ; Phil. i. 28 ; Jas. i. 4. μηδὲν εἶναι, to be nothing i. e. of no account, opp. to εἶναί τι, Gal. vi. 3 (Soph. Aj. 754 ; other exx. fr. Grk. auth. see in Passow ii. p. 231ᵇ ; [L. and S. s. v. II. ; cf. B. § 129, 5]) ; μηδέν (acc.), *nothing* i. e. *not at all, in no respect* : Acts x. 20 ; xi. 12, (Lcian. dial. deor. 2, 4 ; Tim. 43) ; as accus. of the obj. after verbs of harm, loss, damage, advantage, care, [cf. W. 227 (213) ; B. § 131, 10] : as, βλάπτειν, Lk. iv. 35 [cf. W. 483 (450)] ; ὠφελεῖσθαι, Mk. v. 26 ; ὑστερεῖν, 2 Co. xi. 5 ; μεριμνᾶν, Phil. iv. 6. **h.** examples of a d o u b l e negation, by which the denial is strengthened, where in Lat. *quisquam* follows a negation (cf. W. § 55, 9 b.) : μηκέτι μηδείς, Mk. xi. 14 ; Acts iv. 17 ; μηδενὶ μηδέν, Mk. i. 44 [L om. Tr br. μηδέν] ; Ro. xiii. 8 ; μηδεμίαν ἐν μηδενί, 2 Co. vi. 3 ; μὴ . . . ἐν μηδενί, Phil. i. 28 ; μὴ . . . μηδέν, 2 Co. xiii. 7 ; μὴ . . . μηδεμίαν, 1 Pet. iii. 6 ; μή τις . . . κατὰ μηδένα τρόπον, 2 Th. ii. 3.

3368   **μηδέποτε,** (μηδέ and ποτέ), adv., *never* : 2 Tim. iii. 7.*
3369   **μηδέπω,** (μηδέ and πώ), adv., *not yet* : Heb. xi. 7.*
3370   **Μῆδος,** -ου, ὁ, *a Mede,* a native or an inhabitant of Media, a well-known region of Asia whose chief city was Ecbatana [see B. D. s. v.] : Acts ii. 9. [Cf. B. D. and Schaff-Herzog s. v. Media.]*

see 3367 —— **μηθέν,** see μηδείς.

3371 ———— **μηκέτι,** (fr. μή and ἔτι), adv., employed in the same constructions as μή ; *no longer* ; *no more* ; *not hereafter* :   **a.** with 3 pers. sing. 2 aor. subj. Mt. xxi. 19 R G Tr txt. ; with 2 pers. sing. Mk. ix. 25.   **b.** with 1 pers. plur. pres. subj. Ro. xiv. 13.   **c.** with a pres. imperative : [Lk. viii. 49 L T Tr txt. WH] ; Jn. v. 14 ; viii. 11 ; Eph. iv. 28 ; 1 Tim. v. 23.   **d.** with the optative : Mk. xi. 14.   **e.** ἵνα μηκέτι : 2 Co. v. 15 ; Eph. iv. 14.   **f.** with an infin. depending — on another verb : on βοῶ (ἐπιβοῶ), Acts xxv. 24 ; on ἀπειλῶ, Acts iv. 17 ; on λέγω κ. μαρτύρομαι, Eph. iv. 17 ; on εἰς τό, 1 Pet. iv. 2 ; on ὥστε, Mk. i. 45 ; ii. 2 ; τοῦ μηκέτι δουλεύειν, Ro. vi. 6.   **g.** with a ptcp. : Acts xiii. 34 [cf. W. § 65, 10] ; Ro. xv. 23 ; 1 Th. iii. 1.   **h.** οὐ μηκέτι (see μή, IV. 2) : with 2 aor. subj. Mt. xxi. 19 L T Tr mrg. WH.*

3372   **μῆκος,** -εος (-ους), τό, fr. Hom. down ; Sept. very often for אֹרֶךְ ; *length* : Rev. xxi. 16 ; τὸ πλάτος καὶ μῆκος καὶ βάθος καὶ ὕψος, language used in shadowing forth the greatness, extent, and number of the blessings received from Christ, Eph. iii. 18.*

3373   **μηκύνω :** (μῆκος) ; fr. Hdt. and Pind. down ; *to make long, to lengthen* ; in the Bible twice of plants, i. q. *to cause to grow, increase* : ὃ ἐφύτευσε κύριος καὶ ὑετὸς ἐμήκυνεν (גָּדַל), Is. xliv. 14 ; hence Pass. [al. Mid.] pres. μηκύνομαι ; *to grow up* : Mk. iv. 27 [μηκύνηται (Tr mrg. -εται)].*

3374   **μηλωτή,** -ῆς, ἡ, (fr. μῆλον a sheep, also a goat ; as καμηλωτή ['camlet'] fr. κάμηλος [cf. *Lob.* Paralip. p. 332]), *a sheepskin* : Heb. xi. 37, and thence in Clem. Rom. 1 Cor. 17, 1. For אַדֶּרֶת an outer robe, mantle, Sept. in 1 K. xix. 13, 19 ; 2 K. ii. 8, 13 sq., doubtless because these mantles were made of skins ; hence more closely אַדֶּרֶת שֵׂעָר, a mantle of hair, Zech. xiii. 4 (where Sept.

δέρρις τριχίνη). In the Byzant. writ. [Apoll. Dysk. 191, 9] μηλωτή denotes a monk's garment.*

3375   **μήν,** [(fr. Hom. down)], a particle of affirmation, *verily, certainly, truly,* (Sap. vi. 25) ; ἦ μήν, see under ἦ fin.

3376   **μήν,** gen. μηνός, ὁ, (w. Alex. acc. μῆναν, Rev. xxii. 2 Lchm. ; on which form see reff. under ἄρσην, fin.) ; [fr. Hom. down] ;   **1.** *a month* : Lk. i. 24, 26, 36, 56 ; iv. 25 ; Acts vii. 20 ; xviii. 11 ; xix. 8 ; xx. 3 ; xxviii. 11 ; Jas. v. 17 ; Rev. ix. 5, 10, 15 ; xi. 2 ; xiii. 5 ; xxii. 2.   **2.** *the time of new moon, new moon,* (barbarous Lat. *novilunium* : after the use of the Hebr. חֹדֶשׁ, which denotes both a 'month' and a 'new moon,' as in Num. xxviii. 11 ; xxix. 1) : Gal. iv. 10 [Bp. Lghtft. compares Is. lxvi. 23] (the first day of each month, when the new moon appeared, was a festival among the Hebrews ; cf. Lev. xxiii. 24 ; Num. xxviii. 11 ; Ps. lxxx. (lxxxi.) 4) ; [al. refer the passage to 1 (see Mey. ad loc.)].*

3377   **μηνύω** [cf. Curtius § 429] : 1 aor. ἐμήνυσα ; 1 aor. pass. ptcp. fem. μηνυθεῖσα ; as in Grk. writ. fr. Hdt. and Pind. down ;   **1.** *to disclose* or *make known something secret* ; in a forensic sense, *to inform, report* : foll. by ποῦ ἐστίν, Jn. xi. 57 ; τινί τι, pass., Acts xxiii. 30.   **2.** univ. *to declare, tell, make known* : 1 Co. x. 28.   **3.** *to indicate, intimate* : of a teacher ; foll. by ὅτι, Lk. xx. 37. [A. V. uniformly *show.*]*

— — 3378;
/ see 3361
μὴ οὐκ, see μή, III. 1. — — — — — — — — — — — — -3363

3379   **μήποτε,** (fr. μή and ποτέ), [μή ποτε (separately) L WH (exc. Mt. xxv. 9, see below) Tr (exc. 2 Tim. ii. 25)], differing from οὔποτε as μή does from οὐ ; [fr. Hom. down]. Accordingly it is   **1.** a particle of N e g a t i o n ; *not ever, never* : ἐπεὶ μήποτε ἰσχύει, since *it is never of force,* because the writer thinks that the very i d e a of its having force is to be denied, Heb. ix. 17 [where WH txt. μὴ τότε], on which see W. 480 (447), cf. B. 353 (304) ; but others refer this passage to 3 a. below.   **2.** a p r o h i b i t o r y C o n j u n c t i o n ; *lest ever, lest at any time, lest haply,* (also written separately μή ποτε [(see init.), esp. when the component parts retain each its distinctive force ; cf. *Lipsius,* Gram. Untersuch. p. 129 sq. ; *Ellendt,* Lex. Soph. ii. 107. In the N. T. use of this particle the notion of time usual to ποτέ seems to recede before that of contingency, *lest perchance*]), so that it refers to the preceding verb and indicates the purpose of the designated action [W. § 56, 2] : w. a subj. pres. Lk. xii. 58 ; w. a subj. aor., Mt. iv. 6 and Lk. iv. 11, fr. Ps. xc. (xci.) 12 (where Sept. for פֶּן) ; Mt. v. 25 [(cf. below)] ; vii. 6 [R G] ; xiii. 15 and Acts xxviii. 27 (both from Is. vi. 10, where Sept. for פֶּן) ; Mt. xiii. 29 (οὐ sc. θέλω) ; xv. 32 ; xxvii. 64 ; Mk. iv. 12 ; Lk. xiv. 12 ; with ἵνα prefixed, ibid. 29 ; w. a fut. indic. [see B. § 139, 7, cf. also p. 368 (315) d.] : [Mt. vii. 6 L T Tr WH ; (cf. v. 25)] ; Mk. xiv. 2 ; [Lk. xii. 58 L T Tr WH]. after verbs of f e a r i n g, t a k i n g c a r e, [W. u. s. ; B. § 139, 48] : w. subj. aor., — so after προσέχω, to take heed, lest etc., Lk. xxi. 34 ; Heb. ii. 1, (Sir. xi. 33) ; so that an antecedent φοβούμενοι or προσέχοντες must be mentally supplied, Acts v. 39 ; μήποτε οὐκ ἀρκέσῃ, *lest perchance there be not enough* (so that οὐκ ἀρκέσῃ forms one idea, and φοβούμεθα must be supplied before μήποτε), Mt. xxv. 9 R T WH mrg. ; but L Tr WH txt., together with Meyer et al., have correctly restored μήποτε (sc. τοῦτο γενέσθω [W. § 64, 7 a.])· οὐ μὴ ἀρκέσῃ, i. e. *not so! there will in no wise be enough* (see μή, IV. 2) ; cf. *Bornemann* in the Stud. u. Krit. for 1843, p. 143 sq. ; [but all the e d i t o r s above named remove the punctuation mark after μήποτε ; in which case it may be connected directly with the words which follow it and translated (with R. V.) '*peradventure there will not be enough*'; cf. B. § 148, 10, esp. p. 354 (304) note. For additional exx. of μήποτε in this sense (cf. Aristot. eth. Nic. 10, 10 p. 1179ᵃ, 24 ; with indic., ibid. pp. 1172ᵃ, 33 ; 1173ᵃ 22, etc.), see *Soph.* Lex. s. v. ; *B.tm.* in his trans. of Apoll. Dysk., index s. v. ; (cf. L. and S. s. v. μή, B. 9)]. after φοβοῦμαι, w. pres. subjunc. Heb. iv. 1 ; so that φοβούμενος must be supplied before it, Lk. xiv. 8. after βλέπειν w. a fut. indic. [cf. W. § 56, 2 b. *a.* ; B. 243 (209)], Heb. iii. 12. **3.** a particle of I n t e r r o g a t i o n accompanied with doubt (see **μή, III.**), *whether ever, whether at any time* ; *whether perchance, whether haply*, (Germ. *doch nicht etwa* ; *ob nicht etwa*) ; **a.** in a direct question introduced by ἐπεί, *for, else*, (see ἐπεί, 2 sub fin.) : so acc. to the not improbable interpretation of some [e. g. L WII mrg., Delitzsch] in Heb. ix. 17, see in 1 above. In the remaining N. T. passages so used that the inquirer, though he doubts and expects a negative answer, yet is inclined to believe what he doubtfully asks about ; thus, in a direct question, in Jn. vii. 26. **b.** in indirect questions ; **α.** w. the optative (where the words are regarded as the thought of some one [W. § 41 b. 4 c. ; B. § 139, 60]) : Lk. iii. 15. [See *β.*] **β.** w. the subjunctive : 2 Tim. ii. 25 [R G L (cf. B. 46 (40))] ; but T Tr WH txt. give the o p t a t i v e], where μήποτε κτλ. depend on the suppressed idea διαλογιζόμενος [cf. B. § 139, 62 fin. ; W. u. s.].*

(3379a) **μήπου** [T Tr] or **μή που** [WH], *that nowhere, lest anywhere*, [*lest haply*] : Acts xxvii. 29 T Tr WH. (Hom. et al.) *

3380 **μήπω** [or **μή πω**, L Tr in Ro. ix. 11], (μή and πώ). [fr. Hom. down], adv. ; **1.** *not yet* : in construction with the acc. and inf., Heb. ix. 8 ; w. a ptcp., μήπω γὰρ γεννηθέντων, though they were not yet born, Ro. ix. 11, where cf. Fritzsche. **2.** *lest in any way* [?] : Acts xxvii. 29 Lchm.*

3381 **μήπως** [G T, or **μή πως** L Tr WH], (μή and πώς), [fr. Hom. down] ; **1.** a conjunction, *lest in any way, lest perchance* ; **a.** in final sentences, w. an aor. subj., preceded by a pres. 1 Co. ix. 27 ; preceded by an aor., 2 Co. ii. 7 ; ix. 4. **b.** after verbs of f e a r i n g, t a k i n g h e e d : w. an aor. subj., — after βλέπειν, 1 Co. viii. 9 ; after φοβεῖσθαι, Acts xxvii. 29 R ; 2 Co. xi. 3 ; xii. 20 ; w. a perf. indic., to indicate that what is feared has actually taken place [W. § 56, 2 b. *a.* ; B. 242 (209)], Gal. iv. 11 ; w. an aor. subj., the idea of fearing being suppressed, Ro. xi. 21 Rec. [B. § 148, 10 ; cf. W. 474 (442)]. **2.** an interrogative particle, *whether in any way, whether by any means* : in an indirect question, with an indic. present (of a thing still continuing) and

aorist (of a thing already done), Gal. ii. 2 (*I laid before them the gospel* etc., sc. inquiring, *whether haply* etc. ; Paul expects a negative answer, by which he wished his teaching concerning Christ to be approved by the apostles at Jerusalem, yet by no means because he himself had any doubt about its soundness, but that his adversaries might not misuse the authority of those apostles in assailing this teaching, and thereby frustrate his past and present endeavors ; cf. Hofmann ad loc. [B. 353 (303). Others, however, take τρέχω as a s u b j u n c t i v e, and render *lest haply I should be running* etc. ; see W. 504 sq. (470), cf. Ellicott ad loc.]). w. the indicative (of a thing perhaps already done, but which the writer wishes had not been done) and the aor. subjunctive (of a thing future and uncertain, which he desires God to avert) in one and the same sentence, 1 Th. iii. 5 (where μήπως depends on γνῶναι ; cf. Schott, Lünemann, [Ellicott], ad loc. ; [B. 353 (304) ; W. 505 (470)].*

3382 **μηρός, -οῦ, ὁ,** *the thigh* : Rev. xix. 16. (From Hom. down ; Sept. for יָרֵךְ.)*

3383 **μήτε,** (μή and the enclitic τέ), [fr. Hom. down], a copulative conjunction of negation, *neither, nor,* (differing fr. οὔτε as μή does fr. οὐ). It differs fr. μηδέ in that μηδέ separates different things, but μήτε those which are of the same kind or which are parts of one whole ; cf. W. § 55, 6 ; [B. § 149, 13 b.]) : μήτε . . . μήτε, *neither . . . nor*, Lk. vii. 33 [T μὴ . . . μηδέ] ; ix. 3 (five times) ; Acts xxiii. 12, 21 ; xxvii. 20 ; Heb. vii. 3 ; (but in Eph. iv. 27 for μὴ . . . μήτε we must with L T Tr WH substitute μὴ . . . μηδέ). μὴ . . . μήτε . . . μήτε, Mt. v. 34–36 (four times) ; 1 Tim. i. 7 ; Jas. v. 12 ; Rev. vii. 3 ; ἵνα μὴ . . . μήτε . . . μήτε, Rev. vii. 1 ; μηδὲ . . . μήτε, 2 Th. ii. 2 L T Tr WH ; μὴ εἶναι ἀνάστασιν, μηδὲ ἄγγελον (for that is something other than ἀνάστασις), μήτε πνεῦμα (because angels belong to the genus πνεύματα), Acts xxiii. 8 R G ; cf. W. 493 (459) ; [B. 367 (314) sq.].*

3384 **μήτηρ,** gen. μητρός, dat. μητρί, acc. μητέρα, ἡ, [fr. Hom. down ; fr. Skr. ma 'to measure' ; but whether denoting the 'moulder,' or the 'manager' is debated ; cf. Vaniček p. 657 ; Curtius § 472 ; (cf. μέτρον)], Hebr. אֵם, *a mother* ; prop. : Mt. i. 18 ; ii. 11, and often ; trop. of that which is like a mother : Mt. xii. 49 sq. ; Mk. iii. 35 ; Jn. xix. 27 ; Ro. xvi. 13, cf. 1 Tim. v. 2 ; a city is called ἡ μήτηρ τῶν πορνῶν, that produces and harbors the harlots, Rev. xvii. 5 ; of a city where races of men [i. e. Christians] originated, Gal. iv. 26 [here G T Tr WH om. L br. πάντων (on the origin of which cf. Bp. Lghtft. ad loc.)].

3385 **μήτι** [so G T WH R (commonly), but μή τι L (exc. 1 Co. vi. 3) Tr (exc. Mt. xxvi. 22, 25 ; Mk. iv. 21)], (μή and τί), *whether at all, whether perchance*, an interrogative expecting a negative answer ; in a direct question (Germ. *doch nicht etwa?* [in Eng. generally untranslated ; cf. W. § 57, 3 b. ; B. 248 (213)]) : Mt. vii. 16 ; xxvi. 22, 25 ; Mk. iv. 21 ; xiv. 19 ; Lk. vi. 39 ; Jn. vii. 31 [R G] ; viii. 22 ; xviii. 35 ; xxi. 5 [here all texts μή τι (properly)] ; Acts x. 47 ; 2 Co. xii. 18 ; Jas. iii. 11 ; μήτι ἄρα, 2 Co. i. 17 ; used by one asking doubtfully yet inclining to believe what he asks about (see μήποτε, 3 a.) : Mt. xii. 23 ; Jn

iv. 29. **εἰ μήτι**, see εἰ, III. 10. **μήτιγε** (or **μήτι γε**) see in its place.*

3386   **μήτιγε** [so G T WH; but μήτι γε R L, μή τι γε Tr], (fr. μή, τί, γέ), to say nothing of, not to mention, which acc. to the context is either   a. much less; or   b. much more, much rather; so once in the N. T., 1 Co. vi. 3. Cf. Herm. ad Vig. p. 801 sq.*

3387   **μήτις** [so R G Jn. iv. 33], more correctly μή τις;   1. prohibitive, let no one [cf. B. 31 (28)]: [w. 1 aor. subj. 1 Co. xvi. 11]; w. 2 aor. subj. 2 Th. ii. 3.   2. interrogative, (Lat: num quis?) hath any one etc.: Jn. vii. 48; [2 Co. xii. 17, cf. B. § 151, 7; W. 574 (534)]; where one would gladly believe what he asks about doubtfully (see μήτι, sub fin.): Jn. iv. 33.*

3388   **μήτρα**, -ας, ἡ, (μήτηρ), the womb: Lk. ii. 23 (on which see διανοίγω, 1); Ro. iv. 19. (Hdt., Plat., al.; Sept. for רֶחֶם.) *

3389   **μητραλῴας** (also μητραλοίας), L T Tr WH [see WH. App. p. 152] μητρολῴας, -ου, ὁ, (μήτηρ, and ἀλοιάω to thresh, smite), a matricide: 1 Tim. i. 9. (Aeschyl., Plat., Lcian., al.) *

3390   **μητρό-πολις**, -εως, ἡ, (μήτηρ and πόλις), a metropolis, chief city; in the spurious subscription 1 Tim. vi. (22) fin.; [in this sense fr. Xen. down].*

3391; — **-μία**, see under εἷς.
see 1520

3392   **μιαίνω**; Pass., 1 aor. subj. 3 pers. plur. μιανθῶσιν; pf. 3 pers. sing. μεμίανται (unless it be better to take this form as a plur.; cf. Krüger § 33, 3 Anm. 9; Bttm. Gram. § 101 Anm. 7; Ausf. Spr. § 101 Anm. 13; B. 41 (36); [W. § 58, 6 b. β.]), ptcp. μεμιασμένος (Tit. i. 15 R G) and μεμιαμμένος (ibid. L T Tr WH; also Sap. vii. 25; Tob. ii. 9; Joseph. b. j. 4, 5, 2 ed. Bekk.; cf. Matthiae i. p. 415; Krüger § 40 s. v.; Lob. ad Phryn. p. 35; Otto on Theophil. ad Autol. 1, 1 p. 2 sq.; [Veitch s. v.]); fr. Hom. down;   1. to dye with another color, to stain: ἐλέφαντα φοίνικι, Hom. Il. 4, 141.   2. to defile, pollute, sully, contaminate, soil, (Sept. often for טמא): in a physical and a moral sense, σάρκα (of licentiousness), Jude 8; in a moral sense, τὴν συνείδησιν, τὸν νοῦν, pass. Tit. i. 15; absol. to defile with sin, pass. ibid. and in Heb. xii. 15; for הֶחֱטִיא, Deut. xxiv. 6 (4); in a ritual sense, of men, pass. Jn. xviii. 28 (Lev. xxii. 5, 8; Num. xix. 13, 20; Tob. ii. 9).*

[SYN. μιαίνω, μολύνω: acc. to Trench (N. T. Syn. § xxxi.) μιαίνω to stain differs from μολύνω to smear not only in its primary and outward sense, but in the circumstance that (like Eng. stain) it may be used in good part, while μολ. admits of no worthy reference.]

3393   **μίασμα**, -τος, τό, (μιαίνω), that which defiles [cf. καύχημα, 2]; defilement (Vulg. coinquinatio): trop. μιάσματα τοῦ κόσμου, vices the foulness of which contaminates one in his intercourse with the ungodly mass of mankind, 2 Pet. ii. 20. (Tragg., Antiph., Dem., Polyb., Joseph., Plut.; Sept., Lev. vii. 8 (18); Jer. xxxix. (xxxii.) 34; Judith ix. 2; 1 Macc. xiii. 50.) *

3394   **μιασμός**, -οῦ, ὁ, (μιαίνω), the act of defiling, defilement, pollution: ἐπιθυμία μιασμοῦ, defiling lust [W. § 34, 3 b.], 2 Pet. ii. 10. (Sap. xiv. 26; 1 Macc. iv. 43; Plut. mor.

---

p. 393 c.; Test. xii. Patr. [test. Lev. 17; test. Benj. 8; Graec. Ven. (passim); Herm. Past. sim. 5, 7, 2].) *

3395   **μίγμα** or (so L T) μῖγμα, (on the accent cf. Lipsius, Gramm. Untersuch. pp. 32 and 34, [cf. W. § 6, 1 e.; κρίμα, init.]), -τος, τό, (μίγνυμι), that which is produced by mixing, a mixture: Jn. xix. 39 [WH txt. ἕλιγμα, q. v.]. (Sir. xxxviii. 8; Aristot., Plut., al.) *

3396   **μίγνυμι** and μίσγω: 1 aor. ἔμιξα; pf. pass. ptcp. μεμιγμένος; fr. Hom. down; to mix, mingle: τί τινι, one thing with another, Rev. viii. 7 Rec.; xv. 2; also τὶ ἔν τινι [cf. B. § 133, 8], Rev. viii. 7 G L T Tr WH; μετά τινος, with a thing, Mt. xxvii. 34; Lk. xiii. 1 (on which see αἷμα, 2 a.). [SYN. see κεράννυμι, fin. COMP.: συν-ανα-μίγνυμι.] *

3397 &
3398   **μικρός**, -ά, -όν, compar. μικρότερος, -έρα, -ερον, [fr. Hom. down], Sept. for קָטֹן, קָטָן, מְעַט, small, little; used   a. of size: Mt. xiii. 32; Mk. iv. 31; hence of stature, τῇ ἡλικίᾳ, Lk. xix. 3; of length, Jas. iii. 5.   b. of space: neut. προελθὼν [προσελθ. T Tr WH mrg. in Mt., Tr WH mrg. in Mk. (see προσέρχομαι, a.)] μικρόν, having gone forward a little, Mt. xxvi. 39; Mk. xiv. 35, [cf. W. § 32, 6; B. § 131, 11 sq.].   c. of age: less by birth, younger, Mk. xv. 40 [al. take this of stature]; οἱ μικροί, the little ones, young children, Mt. xviii. 6, 10, 14; Mk. ix. 42; ἀπὸ μικροῦ ἕως μεγάλου [A. V. from the least to the greatest], Acts viii. 10; Heb. viii. 11, (Jer. vi. 13; xxxviii. (xxxi.) 34); μικρός τε καὶ μέγας, [both small and great] i. e. all, Acts xxvi. 22; plur., Rev. xi. 18; xiii. 16; xix. 5, 18; xx. 12.   d. of time, short, brief: neuter — nom., ἔτι [or ἔτι om.] μικρὸν (sc. ἔσται) καί, (yet) a little while and etc. i. e. shortly (this shall come to pass), Jn. xiv. 19; xvi. 16 sq. 19, [(cf. Ex. xvii. 4)]; ἔτι μικρὸν ὅσον ὅσον (see ὅσος, a.); without καί, Heb. x. 37 (Is. xxvi. 20); τὸ μικρόν [Tr WH om. τό], Jn. xvi. 18; — μικρόν acc. (of duration), Jn. xiii. 33 (Job xxxvi. 2); μικρὸν χρόνον, Jn. vii. 33; xii. 35; Rev. vi. 11; xx. 3; μετὰ μικρόν, after a little while, Mt. xxvi. 73; Mk. xiv. 70, (πρὸ μικροῦ, Sap. xv. 8).   e. of quantity, i. e. number or amount: μικρὰ ζύμη, 1 Co. v. 6; Gal. v. 9; of number, μικρὸν ποίμνιον, Lk. xii. 32; of quantity, μικρὰ δύναμις, Rev. iii. 8; neut. μικρόν (τι), a little, 2 Co. xi. 1, 16.   f. of rank or influence: Mt. x. 42; Lk. ix. 48; xvii. 2; ὁ μικρότερος ἐν τῇ βασιλείᾳ τῶν οὐρ. he that is inferior to the other citizens of the kingdom of heaven in knowledge of the gospel [R. V. but little in etc.; cf. W. 244 (229); B. § 123, 13], Mt. xi. 11; Lk. vii. 28.*

3399   **Μίλητος**, -ου, ἡ, Miletus, a maritime city [now nearly ten miles fr. the coast (cf. Acts xx. 38)] of Caria or Ionia, near the mouths of the Mæander and not far [c. 35 m. S.] from Ephesus. It was the mother of many [some eighty] colonies, and the birth-place of Thales, Anaximander, and other celebrated men: Acts xx. 15, 17; 2 Tim. iv. 20. [Lewin, St. Paul, ii. 90 sq.] *

3400   **μίλιον**, -ου, τό, (a word of Lat. origin [cf. B. 18 (16)]), a mile, among the Romans the distance of a thousand paces or eight stadia, [somewhat less than our mile]: Mt. v. 41. (Polyb., Strab., Plut.) *

3401   **μιμέομαι**, -οῦμαι; (μῖμος [an actor, mimic]); to imitate:

τινά, any one, 2 Th. iii. 7, 9; τί, Heb. xiii. 7; 3 Jn. 11. [Pind., Aeschyl., Hdt., al.]*

3402 μιμητής, -οῦ, ὁ, *an imitator*: γίνομαί τινος (gen. of pers.), 1 Co. iv. 16; xi. 1; Eph. v. 1; 1 Th. i. 6; ii. 14; Heb. vi. 12; w. gen. of the thing, 1 Pet. iii. 13 Rec. (where L T Tr WH ζηλωταί). [Plat., Isocr., al.]*

3403 μιμνήσκω: (ΜΝΑΩ [allied w. μένω, μανθάνω; cf. Lat. *maneo, moneo, mentio*, etc.; cf. Curtius § 429]); *to remind*: Hom., Pind., Theogn., Eur., al.; Pass. and Mid., pres. μιμνήσκομαι (Heb. ii. 6; xiii. 3; rare in Attic); 1 aor. ἐμνήσθην; pf. μέμνημαι; 1 fut. pass. in a mid. sense, μνησθήσομαι (Heb. x. 17 L T Tr WH); Sept. for זָכַר; *to be recalled* or *to return to one's mind, to remind one's self of, to remember*; ἐμνήσθην, with a pass. signif. [cf. B. 52 (46)], *to be recalled to mind, to be remembered, had in remembrance*: ἐνώπιόν τινος, before i. e. in the mind of one (see ἐνώπιον, 1 c.), Acts x. 31; Rev. xvi. 19, (passively also in Ezek. xviii. 22; [Sir. xvi. 17 Rec.]; and ἀναμνησθῆναι, Num. x. 9; Ps. cviii. (cix.) 16); — with a mid. signif., foll. by a gen. of the thing [W. § 30, 10 c.], *to remember a thing*: Mt. xxvi. 75; Lk. xxiv. 8; Acts xi. 16; 2 Pet. iii. 2; Jude 17; μνησθῆναι ἐλέους, to call to remembrance former love, Lk. i. 54 (cf. Ps. xxiv. (xxv.) 6); τῆς διαθήκης, Lk. i. 72 (Gen. ix. 15; Ex. ii. 24; 1 Macc. iv. 10; 2 Macc. i. 2); μὴ μνησθῆναι τῶν ἁμαρτιῶν τινος, [A. V. *to remember no more*] i. e. to forgive, Heb. viii. 12; x. 17, (after the Hebr.; see Ps. xxiv. (xxv.) 7; lxxviii. (lxxix.) 8; Is. xliii. 25; and on the other hand, *to remember the sins of any one* is said of one about to punish them, Jer. xiv. 10; 1 Macc. v. 4; vi. 12); w. gen. of a pers., *to remember a pers., remember and care for*: Lk. xxiii. 42; foll. by ὅτι, Mt. v. 23; xxvii. 63; Lk. xvi. 25; Jn. ii. 17, 22; xii. 16; by ὡς, Lk. xxiv. 6. pf. μέμνημαι, in the sense of a present [cf. W. 274 (257)], *to be mindful of*: w. gen. of the thing, 2 Tim. i. 4; πάντα μου μέμνησθε, in all things ye are mindful of me, 1 Co. xi. 2; pres. μιμνήσκομαι, w. gen. of the pers., to remember in order to care for him, Heb. ii. 2 (fr. Ps. viii. 5); xiii. 3. [COMP.: ἀνα-, ἐπ-ανα-, ὑπο-μιμνήσκω.]*

3404 μισέω, -ῶ; impf. ἐμίσουν; fut. μισήσω; 1 aor. ἐμίσησα; pf. μεμίσηκα; Pass., pres. ptcp. μισούμενος; pf. ptcp. μεμισημένος (Rev. xviii. 2); Sept. for שָׂנֵא; [fr. Hom. down]; *to hate, pursue with hatred, detest*; pass. *to be hated, detested*: τινά, Mt. v. 43 and Rec. in 44; xxiv. 10; Lk. i. 71; vi. 22, 27; xix. 14; Jn. vii. 7; xv. 18 sq. 23-25; xvii. 14; Tit. iii. 3; 1 Jn. ii. 9, [11]; iii. 13, 15; iv. 20; Rev. xvii. 16; pass., Mt. x. 22; xxiv. 9; [Mk. xiii. 13]; Lk. xxi. 17; τί: Jn. iii. 20; Ro. vii. 15; Eph. v. 29; Heb. i. 9; Jude 23; Rev. ii. 6 and Rec. in 15; pass. ib. xviii. 2. — Not a few interpreters have attributed to μισεῖν in Gen. xxix. 31 (cf. 30); Deut. xxi. 15 sq.; Mt. vi. 24; Lk. xiv. 26; xvi. 13; [Jn. xii. 25]; Ro. ix. 13, the signification *to love less, to postpone in love* or *esteem, to slight*, through oversight of the circumstance that 'the Orientals, in accordance with their greater excitability, are wont both to feel and to profess *love* and *hate* where we Occidentals, with our cooler temperament, feel and express nothing more than *interest* in, or *disregard and*

indifference *to a thing*'; *Fritzsche*, Com. on Rom. ii. p. 304; cf. *Rückert*, Magazin f. Exegese u. Theologie des N. T. p. 27 sqq.*

3405 μισθαποδοσία, -ας, ἡ, (μισθός and ἀποδίδωμι; cf. the μισθοδοσία of the Grk. writ. [W. 24]), *payment of wages due, recompense*: of reward, Heb. x. 35; xi. 26; of punishment, Heb. ii. 2. (Several times in eccles. writ.) *

3406 μισθ-απο-δότης, -ου, ὁ, (μισθός and ἀποδίδωμι; cf. the μισθοδότης of the Grk. writ.), (Vulg. *remunerator*); *one who pays wages, a rewarder*: Heb. xi. 6. (Several times in eccles. writ.) *

3407 μίσθιος, -α, -ον, also of two terminations [cf. W. § 11, 1], (μισθός), *employed for hire, hired*: as subst. [A. V. *hired servant*], Lk. xv. 17, 19, [21 WH in br.], (Sept. for שָׂכִיר, Lev. xxv. 50; Job vii. 1. Tob. v. 12; Sir. vii. 20; xxxi. 27; xxxvii. 11. Anth. 6, 283, 3 Plut.).*

3408 μισθός, -οῦ, ὁ, [fr. Hom. down], Sept. for שָׂכָר, also for מַשְׂכֹּרֶת, etc.; **1.** *dues paid for work*; *wages, hire*: Ro. iv. 4 (κατὰ ὀφείλημα); in a prov., Lk. x. 7 and 1 Tim. v. 18; Mt. xx. 8; Jas. v. 4; Jude 11 (on which see ἐκχέω, fin.); μισθὸς ἀδικίας, wages obtained by iniquity, Acts i. 18; 2 Pet. ii. 15, [cf. W. § 30, 1 a.]. **2.** *reward*: used — of the fruit naturally resulting from toils and endeavors, Jn. iv. 36; 1 Co. ix. 18; — of *divine recompense*: **a.** in both senses, rewards and punishments: Rev. xxii. 12. **b.** of the rewards which God bestows, or will bestow, upon good deeds and endeavors (on the correct theory about which cf. *Weiss*, Die Lehre Christi vom Lohn, in the Deutsche Zeitschr. für christl. Wissenschaft, 1853, p. 319 sqq.; *Mehlhorn*, d. Lohnbegr. Jesu, in the Jahrbb. f. protest. Theol., 1876, p. 721 sqq.; [cf. *Beyer* in Herzog xx. pp. 4–14]): Mt. v. 12; vi. 2, 5, 16; x. 41 sq.; Mk. ix. 41; Lk. vi. 23, 35; 1 Co. iii. 8, 14; 2 Jn. 8; Rev. xi. 18; ἔχειν μισθόν, to have a reward, is used of those for whom a reward is reserved by God, whom a divine reward awaits, Mt. v. 46; 1 Co. ix. 17; with παρὰ τῷ πατρὶ ὑμῶν τῷ ἐν τ. οὐρ. added, Mt. vi. 1. **c.** of punishments: μισθὸς ἀδικίας, 2 Pet. ii. 13; τῆς δυσσεβείας, 2 Macc. viii. 33.*

3409 μισθόω, -ῶ: (μισθός); 1 aor. mid. ἐμισθωσάμην; *to let out for hire*; *to hire* [cf. W. § 38, 3]: τινά, Mt. xx. 1, 7. (Hdt., Arstph., Xen., Plat., al.; Sept. for שָׂכַר, Deut. xxiii. 4; 2 Chr. xxiv. 12.) *

3410 μίσθωμα, -τος, τό, (μισθόω); **1.** *the price for which anything is either let or hired* (Hdt., Isocr., Dem., Ael., al.; of a harlot's hire, Hos. ii. 12; Deut. xxiii. 18; Mic. i. 7; Prov. xix. 13; Ezek. xvi. 31–34, and in class. Grk. [cf. Philo in Flac. § 16 fin.]). **2.** *that which is either let or hired for a price*, as a house, dwelling, lodging [(cf. Bp. *Lghtft.* Com. on Philip. p. 9 note [3])]: Acts xxviii. 30.*

3411 μισθωτός, -οῦ, ὁ, (μισθόω), *one hired, a hireling*: Mk. i. 20; Jn. x. 12 sq. (Arstph., Plat., Dem., al.; Sept. for שָׂכִיר.) *

3412 Μιτυλήνη, -ης, ἡ, *Mitylene*, the chief maritime town of the island of Lesbos in the Ægean: Acts xx. 14. [*Lewin*, St. Paul, ii. 84 sq.]*

3413 Μιχαήλ, ὁ, (מִיכָאֵל, i. e. 'who like God?'), *Michael*, the name of an archangel, who was supposed to be the guardian angel of the Israelites (Dan. xii. 1; x. 13, 21): Jude 9; Rev. xii. 7. [BB.DD. s. v.] *

3414 μνᾶ, -ᾶς, ἡ, a word of Eastern origin [cf. *Schrader*, Keilinschriften u. s. w. p. 143], Arab. مَنَا, Syr. ܡܢܐ, Hebr. מָנֶה (fr. מָנָה to appoint, mark out, count, etc.), Lat. *mina*; **1.** in the O. T. a weight, and an imaginary coin or money of account, equal to one hundred shekels: 1 K. x. 17, cf. 2 Chr. ix. 16; 2 Esdr. ii. 69, (otherwise in Ezek. xlv. 12 [cf. Bible Educator, index s. v. Maneh; *Schrader* in Riehm s. v. Mine p. 1000 sq.]). **2.** In Attic a weight and a sum of money equal to one hundred drachmae (see δραχμή [and B. D. s. v. Pound; esp. *Schrader* in Riehm u. s.]): Lk. xix. 13, 16, 18, 20, 24 sq.*

3415; see 3403 -μνάομαι, see μιμνήσκω.

3416 Μνάσων, -ωνος, ὁ, (ΜΝΑΩ), Mnason, a Christian of Cyprus: Acts xxi. 16. (The name was com. also among the Grks.; [cf. Benseler's Pape's Eigennamen, s. v.].) *

3417 μνεία, -ας, ἡ, (μιμνήσκω), *remembrance, memory, mention*: ἐπὶ πάσῃ τῇ μνείᾳ ὑμῶν, as often as I remember you [lit. 'on all my remembrance' etc. cf. W. § 18, 4], Phil. i. 3; ποιεῖσθαι μνείαν τινός, to make mention of one, Ro. i. 9; Eph. i. 16; 1 Th. i. 2; Philem. 4, (Plat. Phaedr. p. 254 a.; Diog. Laërt. 8, 2, 66; Sept. Ps. cx. (cxi.) 4); μν. ἔχειν τινός, to be mindful of one, 1 Th. iii. 6 (Soph., Arstph., Eur., al.); ἀδιάλειπτον ἔχειν τὴν περί τινος μνείαν, 2 Tim. i. 3.*

3418 μνῆμα, -τος, τό, (μνάομαι, pf. pass. μέμνημαι); **1.** *a monument* or *memorial* to perpetuate the memory of any person or thing (Hom., Pind., Soph., al.). **2.** *a sepulchral monument* (Hom., Eur., Xen., Plat., al.). **3.** *a sepulchre* or *tomb* (receptacle where a dead body is deposited [cf. *Edersheim*, Jesus the Messiah, ii. 316 sq.]): Mk. v. 3 G L T Tr WH; v. 5; [xv. 46 T WH]; Lk. viii. 27; xxiii. 53; xxiv. 1; Acts ii. 29; vii. 16; Rev. xi. 9, (Joseph. antt. 7, 1, 3; Sept. for קֶבֶר).*

3419 μνημεῖον, -ου, τό; **1.** *any visible object for preserving* or *recalling the memory of any person* or *thing*; *a memorial, monument,* (Aeschyl., Pind., Soph., sqq.); in bibl. Grk. so in Sap. x. 7; specifically, *a sepulchral monument*: οἰκοδομεῖν μνημεῖα, Lk. xi. 47; Joseph. antt. 13, 6, 5. **2.** in the Scriptures *a sepulchre, tomb*: Mt. xxiii. 29; xxvii. 52, 60; xxviii. 8; Mk. v. 2; vi. 29; Lk. xi. 44; Jn. v. 28; xi. 17, 31, and often in the Gospels; Acts xiii. 29; Sept. for קֶבֶר, Gen. xxiii. 6, 9; l. 5; Is. xxii. 16, etc.

3420 μνήμη, -ης, ἡ, (μνάομαι); **a.** *memory, remembrance*; **b.** *mention*: μνήμην ποιεῖσθαί τινος, to remember a thing, call it to remembrance, 2 Pet. i. 15; the same expression occurs in Grk. writ. fr. Hdt. down, but in the sense of Lat. *mentionem facere, to make mention of a thing*.*

3421 μνημονεύω; impf. 3 pers. plur. ἐμνημόνευον; 1 aor. ἐμνημόνευσα; (μνήμων mindful); fr. Hdt. down; Sept. for זָכַר; **1.** *to be mindful of, to remember, to call to mind*: absol. Mk. viii. 18; τινός, Lk. xvii. 32; Jn. xv. 20; xvi. 4, 21; Acts xx. 35; 1 Th. i. 3; [Heb. xiii. 7]; contextually i. q. *to think of and feel for a person* or *thing*: w. gen. of the thing, Col. iv. 18; τῶν πτωχῶν, Gal. ii. 10

(see μιμνήσκω, fin.); w. an acc. of the obj. *to hold in memory, keep in mind*: τινά, 2 Tim. ii. 8; τί, Mt. xvi. 9; 1 Th. ii. 9; τὰ ἀδικήματα, of God as punishing them, Rev. xviii. 5 (see μιμνήσκω). Cf. Matthiae § 347 Anm. 2; W. p. 205 (193); [B. § 132, 14]. foll. by ὅτι, Acts xx. 31; Eph. ii. 11; 2 Th. ii. 5; foll. by an indir. question, Rev. ii. 5; iii. 3. **2.** *to make mention of*: τινός, Heb. xi. 15 [but al. refer this to 1 above] (Plut. Them. 32; τί, Plat. de rep. 4 p. 441 d.; legg. 4 p. 723 c.); περί τινος (as μνᾶσθαι in classic Grk., Matthiae § 347 Anm. 1), Heb. xi. 22; so in Lat. *memini de aliquo*; cf. *Ramshorn*, Lat. Gr. § 111 note 1; [Harpers' Lat. Dict. s. v. memini, I. 3; cf. Eng. *remember about*, etc.]. *

3422 μνημόσυνον, -ου, τό, (μνήμων), *a memorial* (*that by which the memory of any person* or *thing is preserved*), *a remembrance*: εἰς μνημόσυνόν τινος, to perpetuate one's memory, Mt. xxvi. 13; Mk. xiv. 9; αἱ προσευχαί σου ... ἀνέβησαν εἰς μνημ. ἐνώπιον τ. θεοῦ, (without the fig.) have become known to God, so that he heeds and is about to help thee, Acts x. 4. (Hdt., Arstph., Thuc., Plut., al.; Sept. for זִכָּרוֹן, זֵכֶר; also for אַזְכָּרָה, i. e. that part of a sacrifice which was burned on the altar together with the frankincense, that its fragrance might ascend to heaven and commend the offerer to God's remembrance, Lev. ii. 9, 16; v. 12; Num. v. 26; hence εὐωδία εἰς μνημόσυνον, Sir. xlv. 16; and often in Siracid., 1 Macc., etc.) *

3423 μνηστεύω: Pass., pf. ptcp. μεμνηστευμένος (R G) and ἐμνηστευμένος (L T Tr WH) [cf. W. § 12, 10; Veitch s. v.; *Tdf.* Proleg. p. 121]; 1 aor. ptcp. μνηστευθείς; (μνηστός betrothed, espoused); fr. Hom. down; Sept. for אָרַשׂ; τινά (γυναῖκα), *to woo her and ask her in marriage*; pass. *to be promised in marriage, be betrothed*: τινί, Mt. i. 18; Lk. i. 27; ii. 5.*

see 3424 μογγι-λάλος, (fr. μόγγος [al. μογγός, cf. Chandler § 366] one who has a hoarse, hollow voice, and λάλος), *speaking with a harsh* or *thick voice*: Mk. vii. 32 Tdf. ed. 2, Tr txt.; but the common reading μογιλάλος deserves the preference; cf. Fritzsche ad loc. p. 302 sq. (Etym. Magn. [s. v. βατταρίζειν].) *

3424 μογι-λάλος [on its accent cf. *Tdf.* Proleg. p. 101], -ον, (μόγις and λάλος), *speaking with difficulty*, [A. V. *having an impediment in his speech*]: Mk. vii. 32 [not Tr txt.]. (Aët. 8, 38; Schol. ad Lcian. Jov. trag. c. 27; Bekker, Anecd. p. 100, 22; Sept. for אִלֵּם, dumb, Is. xxxv. 6.) *

3425 μόγις, (μόγος toil), fr. Hom. down, *hardly, with difficulty*: Lk. ix. 39 [yet WH Tr mrg. μόλις, q. v.]. (3 Macc. vii. 6.) *

3426 μόδιος, -ου, ὁ, the Lat. *modius*, a dry measure holding 16 sextarii (or one sixth of the Attic medimnus; Corn. Nep. Att. 2 [i. e. about a peck, A. V. *bushel*; cf. BB. DD. s. v. Weights and Measures]): Mt. v. 15; Mk. iv. 21; Lk. xi. 33.*

3428 μοιχαλίς, -ίδος, ἡ, (μοιχός), a word unknown to the earlier writ. but found in Plut., Heliod., al.; see *Lob.* ad Phryn. p. 452; [W. 24]; Sept. for נֹאֶפֶת (Ezek. xvi. 38; xxiii. 45) and מְנָאֶפֶת (Hos. iii. 1; Prov. xxiv. 55 (xxx. 20)); *an adulteress*; **a.** prop.: Ro. vii. 3; ὀφθαλμοὶ μεστοὶ μοιχαλίδος, eyes always on the watch for an adul-

*For 3427 see 1698 St.

teress, or from which adulterous desire beams forth, 2 Pet. ii. 14.   **b.** As the intimate alliance of God with the people of Israel was likened to a marriage, those who relapse into idolatry are said *to commit adultery* or *play the harlot* (Ezek. xvi. 15 sqq.; xxiii. 43 sqq., etc.); hence μοιχαλίς is fig. equiv. to *faithless to God, unclean, apostate*: Jas. iv. 4 [where cf. Alford]; as an adj. (cf. Matthiae § 429, 4), γενεὰ μοιχ.: Mt. xii. 39; xvi. 4; Mk. viii. 38. [Cf. Clem. Alex. strom. vi. c. 16 § 146 p. 292, 5 ed. Sylb.]*

3429   **μοιχάω, -ῶ**: *to have unlawful intercourse with another's wife, to commit adultery with*: τινά. in bibl. Grk. mid. μοιχῶμαι, to commit adultery: of the man, Mt. v. 32ᵇ [yet WH br.]; xix. 9 [yet not WH mrg.], 9ᵇ [R G L Tr br. WH mrg.]; ἐπ' αὐτήν, commits the sin of adultery *against her* (i. e. that has been put away), Mk. x. 11; of the woman, Mt. v. 32ᵃ (where L T Tr WH μοιχευθῆναι for μοιχᾶσθαι); Mk. x. 12. (Sept. for נָאַף, Jer. iii. 8; v. 7; ix. 2, etc.; in Grk. writ. fig. in the active, with τὴν θάλασσαν, to usurp unlawful control over the sea, Xen. Hell. 1, 6, 15; τὸ λεχθέν, to falsify, corrupt, Ael. n. a. 7, 39.) *

3430   **μοιχεία, -ας, ἡ, (μοιχεύω)**, *adultery*: Jn. viii. 3; Gal. v. 19 Rec.; plur. [W. § 27, 3; B. § 123, 2]: Mt. xv. 19; Mk. vii. 21. (Jer. xiii. 27; Hos. ii. 2; iv. 2; [Andoc., Lys.], Plat., Aeschin., Lcian., al.) *

3431   **μοιχεύω**; fut. μοιχεύσω; 1 aor. ἐμοίχευσα; Pass., pres. ptcp. μοιχευομένη; 1 aor. inf. μοιχευθῆναι; (μοιχός); fr. Arstph. and Xen. down; Sept. for נָאַף; *to commit adultery*;   **a.** absol. (*to be an adulterer*): Mt. v. 27; xix. 18; Mk. x. 19; Lk. xvi. 18; xviii. 20; Ro. ii. 22; xiii. 9; Jas. ii. 11.   **b.** τινά (γυναῖκα), *to commit adultery with*, have unlawful intercourse with another's wife: Mt. v. 28 (Deut. v. 18; Lev. xx. 10; Arstph. av. 558; Plat. rep. 2 p. 360 b.; Lcian. dial. deor. 6, 3; Aristaenet. epp. 1, 20; Aeschin. dial. Socr. 2, 14); pass. of the wife, *to suffer adultery, be debauched*: Mt. v. 32ᵃ L T Tr WH; [xix. 9 WH mrg.]; Jn. viii. 4. By a Hebraism (see μοιχαλίς, b.) trop. μετά τινος (γυναικός) μοιχεύειν is used of those who at a woman's solicitation are drawn away to idolatry, i. e. to the eating of things sacrificed to idols, Rev. ii. 22; cf. Jer. iii. 9, etc.*

3432   **μοιχός, -οῦ, ὁ**, *an adulterer*: Lk. xviii. 11; 1 Co. vi. 9; Heb. xiii. 4. Hebraistically (see μοιχαλίς, b.) and fig. *faithless toward God, ungodly*: Jas. iv. 4 R G. (Soph., Arstph., Xen., Plut., sqq.; Sept.) *

3433   **μόλις, (μόλος toil)**; an adv. used by post-Hom. writ. indiscriminately with μόγις;   **a.** *with difficulty, hardly*, (cf. Sap. ix. 16, where μετὰ πόνου corresponds to it in the parallel member): [Lk. ix. 39 Tr mrg. WH (al. μόγις, q. v.)]; Acts xiv. 18; xxvii. 7 sq. 16; 1 Pet. iv. 18.   **b.** *not easily*, i. e. *scarcely, very rarely*: Ro. v. 7.*

3434   **Μολόχ, ὁ**, (Hebr. מֹלֶךְ, מַלְכָּם, also מַלְכָּם; cf. *Gesenius*, Thes. ii. p. 794 sq.), indecl., *Moloch*, name of the idol-god of the Ammonites, to which human victims, particularly young children, were offered in sacrifice. According to the description in the Jalkut ([Rashi (vulg. Jarchi)] on Jer. vii. [31]), its image was a hollow brazen figure, with the head of an ox, and outstretched human

arms. It was heated red-hot by fire from within, and the little ones placed in its arms to be slowly burned, while to prevent their parents from hearing their dying cries the sacrificing-priests beat drums (see γέεννα): Acts vii. 43 fr. Am. v. 26 Sept., where Hebr. מַלְכְּכֶם, which ought to have been translated βασιλέως ὑμῶν, i. e. of your idol. Cf. *Win.* RWB. s. v. Moloch; *J. G. Müller* in Herzog ix. 714 sq.; *Merx* in Schenkel v. 194 sq.; [BB.DD. s. v. Molech, Moloch; *W. Robertson Smith* in Encyc. Brit. ed. 9, s. v.; *Baudissin*, Jahve et Moloch etc. and esp. in Herzog 2 vol. x. 168–178].*

3435   **μολύνω**: 1 aor. act. ἐμόλυνα; Pass. pres. μολύνομαι; 1 aor. ἐμολύνθην; fr. Arstph. down; *to pollute, stain, contaminate, defile*; in the N. T. used only in symbolic and fig. discourse: οὐκ ἐμόλυναν τὰ ἱμάτια αὐτῶν, of those who have kept themselves pure from the defilement of sin, Rev. iii. 4 (cf. Zech. iii. 3 sq.); μετὰ γυναικῶν οὐκ ἐμολύνθησαν, who have not soiled themselves by fornication and adultery, Rev. xiv. 4; ἡ συνείδησις μολύνεται, of a conscience reproached (defiled) by sin, 1 Co. viii. 7 (inexplebili quodam laedendi proposito conscientiam polluebat, Amm. Marcell. 15, 2; opp. to καθαρὰ συνείδησις, 1 Tim. iii. 9; 2 Tim. i. 3; μολύνειν τὴν ψυχήν, Sir. xxi. 28; but see μιαίνω, 2). [Syn. see μιαίνω, fin.] *

3436   **μολυσμός, -οῦ, ὁ, (μολύνω)**, *defilement* (Vulg. *inquinamentum*); an action by which anything is defiled: with gen. of the thing defiled, σαρκὸς καὶ πνεύματος, 2 Co. vii. 1. (Jer. xxiii. 15; 1 Esdr. viii. 80; 2 Macc. v. 27; Plut. mor. p. 779 c.; [Joseph. c. Ap. 1, 32, 2; 2, 24, 5; etc.]; often in eccl. writ.) *

3437   **μομφή, -ῆς, ἡ, (μέμφομαι)**, *blame*: ἔχειν μομφὴν πρός τινα, to have matter of complaint against any one, Col. iii. 13. (Pind., Tragg., al.) *

3438   **μονή, -ῆς, ἡ, (μένω)**, [fr. Hdt. down], *a staying, abiding, dwelling, abode*: Jn. xiv. 2; μονὴν ποιεῖν (L T Tr WH ποιεῖσθαι, as in Thuc. 1, 131; Joseph. antt. 8, 13, 7; 13, 2, 1), *to make an (one's) abode*, παρά τινι metaph. of God and Christ by their power and spirit exerting a most blessed influence on the souls of believers, Jn. xiv. 23; see ποιῶ, 1 c.*

3439   **μονογενής, -ές, (μόνος and γένος)**, (Cic. *unigena*; Vulg. [in Lk. *unicus*, elsewh.] and in eccl. writ. *unigenitus*), *single of its kind, only*, [A.V. *only-begotten*]; used of only sons or daughters (viewed in relation to their parents), Hes. theog. 426, 448; Hdt. 7, 221; Plat. Critias 113 d.; Joseph. antt. 1, 13, 1; 2, 7, 4; μονογενὲς τέκνον πατρί, Aeschyl. Ag. 898. So in the Scriptures: Heb. xi. 17; μονογενῆ εἶναί τινι (to be one's only son or daughter), Judg. xi. 34; Tob. iii. 15; Lk. vii. 12; viii. 42; ix. 38; [cf. Westcott on Epp. of Jn. p. 162 sqq.]. Hence the expression ὁ μονογ. υἱὸς τοῦ θεοῦ and υἱὸς τοῦ θεοῦ ὁ μονογ., Jn. iii. 16, 18; i. 18 [see below]; 1 Jn. iv. 9; μονογενὴς παρὰ πατρός, Jn. i. 14 [some take this generally, owing to the omission of the art. (cf. Green p. 48 sq.)], used of Christ, denotes *the only son of God* or one who in the sense in which he himself is the son of God has no brethren. He is so spoken of by John not because ὁ λόγος which was ἐνσαρκωθείς in him was eternally generated by God the Father (the orthodox interpretation), or came forth from the being of God just before the beginning of the world (Subordinationism), but because by the incarnation (ἐνσάρκωσις) of the λόγος in him he is of nature or essentially Son of God, and so in a very different sense from that in which men are made by him τέκνα τοῦ θεοῦ (Jn. i. 13). For since in the writings of John the title ὁ υἱὸς τοῦ θεοῦ is given only to the historic Christ so called, neither the Logos alone, nor Jesus alone, but ὁ λόγος ὁ ἐνσαρκωθείς or Jesus through the λόγος united with God, is ὁ μονογ. υἱὸς τοῦ θεοῦ. The reading μονογενὴς θεός (without the article before μονογ.) in Jn. i. 18,—which is supported by no inconsiderable weight of ancient testimony, received into the text by Tregelles, and Westcott and Hort, defended with much learning by Dr. Hort (" On μονογενὴς θεός in Scripture and Tradition " in his "Two Dissertations " Camb. and Lond. 1876), and seems not improbable to Harnack (in the Theol. Lit.-Zeit. for 1876, p. 541 sqq.) [and Weiss (in Meyer 6te Aufl. ad loc.)], but is foreign to John's mode of thought and speech (iii. 16, 18; 1 Jn. iv. 9), dissonant and harsh,—appears to owe its origin to a dogmatic zeal which broke out soon after the early days of the church; [see articles on the reading by Prof. Abbot in the Bib. Sacr. for Oct. 1861 and in the Unitarian Rev. for June 1875, (in the latter copious reff. to other discussions of the same passage are given); see also Prof. Drummond in the Theol. Rev. for Oct. 1871]. Further, see Grimm, Exgt. Hdbch. on Sap. p. 152 sq.; [Westcott u. s.].*

3440 & 3441   μόνος, -η, -ον, Sept. chiefly for לְבַד, [fr. Hom. down]; 1. an adjective, alone (without a companion); a. with verbs: εἶναι, εὑρίσκεσθαι, καταλείπεσθαι, etc., Mt. xiv. 23 ; Mk. vi. 47 ; Lk. ix. 36 ; Jn. viii. 9 ; 1 Th. iii. 1 ; added to the pronouns ἐγώ, αὐτός, οὑ, etc.: Mt. xviii. 15 ; Mk. ix. 2 ; Lk. xxiv. 18 ; Ro. xi. 3 ; xvi. 4, etc.   b. it is joined with its noun to other verbs also, so that what is predicated may be declared to apply to some one person alone [cf. W. 131 (124) note]: Mt. iv. 10; Lk. iv. 8; xxiv. 12 [T om. L Tr br. WH reject the vs.]; Jn. vi. 22 ; Heb. ix. 7 ; 2 Tim. iv. 11 ; with a neg. foll. by ἀλλά, Mt. iv. 4. ὁ μόνος θεός, he who alone is God: Jn. v. 44 ; xvii. 3 ; Ro. xvi. 27 ; ὁ μόνος δεσπότης, Jude 4. οὐκ . . . εἰ μὴ μόνος: Mt. xii. 4 ; xvii. 8 ; xxiv. 36 ; Lk. vi. 4 ; οὐδεὶς . . . εἰ μὴ μόνος, Phil. iv. 15. i. q. forsaken, destitute of help, Lk. x. 40 ; Jn. viii. 16 ; xvi. 32, (Sap. x. 1). 2. Neut. μόνον as adv., alone, only, merely : added to the obj., Mt. v. 47 ; x. 42 ; Acts xviii. 25 ; Gal. iii. 2 ; to the gen. Ro. iii. 29 [here WH mrg. μόνων] ; referring to an action expressed by a verb, Mt. ix. 21 ; xiv. 36 ; Mk. v. 36 ; Lk. viii. 50 ; Acts viii. 16 ; 1 Co. xv. 19 ; Gal. i. 23 ; ii. 10. μόνον μή, Gal. v. 13 ; οὐ (μὴ) μόνον, Gal. iv. 18 ; Jas. i. 22 ; ii. 24 ; foll. by ἀλλά, Acts xix. 26 [L ἀλλὰ καί ; cf. W. 498 (464) ; B. 370 (317)] ; by ἀλλὰ πολλῷ μᾶλλον, Phil. ii. 12 ; by ἀλλὰ καί, Mt. xxi. 21 ; Jn. v. 18 ; xi. 52 ; xii. 9 ; xiii. 9 ; xvii. 20 ; Acts xix. 26 [Lchm. (see as above, esp. B.)] ; xxi. 13 ; xxvi. 29 ; xxvii. 10 ; Ro. i. 32 ; iv. 12, 16, 23 ; 2 Co. vii. 7, etc. ; οὐ μόνον δέ, ἀλλὰ καί: Acts xix. 27 ; and often by Paul [cf. W. 583 (543)], Ro. v. 3, 11 ; viii.

---

23 ; ix. 10 ; 2 Co. vii. 7 ; viii. 19 ; Phil. ii. 27 [here οὐ δὲ μόνον etc.] ; 1 Tim. v. 13 ; [2 Tim. iv. 8. κατὰ μόνας (sc. χώρας), see καταμόνας].

μον-όφθαλμος, -ον, (μόνος, ὀφθαλμός), (Vulg. luscus, Mk. ix. 47), deprived of one eye, having one eye : Mt. xviii. 9 ; Mk. ix. 47. (Hdt., Apollod., Strab., Diog. Laërt., al. ; [Lob. ad Phryn. p. 136 ; Bekk. Anecd. i. 280 ; Rutherford, New Phryn. p. 209 ; W. 24].) *   3442

μονόω, -ῶ; (μόνος); fr. Hom. down; to make single or solitary; to leave alone, forsake : pf. pass. ptcp. χήρα μεμονωμένη, i. e. without children, 1 Tim. v. 5, cf. 4.*   3443

μορφή, -ῆς, ἡ, [fr. root signifying 'to lay hold of', 'seize' (cf. Germ. Fassung); Fick, Pt. i. p. 174; Vaniček p. 719], fr. Hom. down, the form by which a person or thing strikes the vision ; the external appearance : children are said to reflect ψυχῆς τε καὶ μορφῆς ὁμοιότητα (of their parents), 4 Macc. xv. 3 (4) ; ἐφανερώθη ἐν ἑτέρᾳ μορφῇ, Mk. xvi. 12 ; ἐν μορφῇ θεοῦ ὑπάρχων, Phil. ii. 6 ; μορφὴν δούλου λαβών, ibid. 7 ; — this whole passage (as I have shown more fully in the Zeitschr. f. wissensch. Theol. for 1873, p. 33 sqq., with which compare the different view given by Holsten in the Jahrbb. f. protest. Theol. for 1875, p. 449 sqq.) is to be explained as follows : who, although (formerly when he was λόγος ἄσαρκος) he bore the form (in which he appeared to the inhabitants of heaven) of God (the sovereign, opp. to μορφ. δούλου), yet did not think that this equality with God was to be eagerly clung to or retained (see ἁρπαγμός, 2), but emptied himself of it (see κενόω, 1) so as to assume the form of a servant, in that he became like unto men (for angels also are δοῦλοι τοῦ θεοῦ, Rev. xix. 10 ; xxii. 8 sq.) and was found in fashion as a man. (God μένει ἀεὶ ἁπλῶς ἐν τῇ αὑτοῦ μορφῇ, Plat. de rep. 2 p. 381 c., and it is denied that God φαντάζεσθαι ἄλλοτε ἐν ἄλλαις ἰδέαις . . . καὶ ἀλλάττοντα τὸ αὑτοῦ εἶδος εἰς πολλὰς μορφὰς . . . καὶ τῆς ἑαυτοῦ ἰδέας ἐκβαίνειν, p. 380 d. ; ἥκιστ᾽ ἂν πολλὰς μορφὰς ἴσχοι ὁ θεός, p. 381 b. ; ἑνὸς σώματος οὐσίαν μετασχηματίζειν καὶ μεταχαράττειν εἰς πολυτρόπους μορφάς, Philo leg. ad Gaium § 11 ; οὐ γὰρ ὥσπερ τὸ νόμισμα παράκομμα καὶ θεοῦ μορφὴ γίνεται, ibid. § 14 fin.; God ἔργοις μὲν καὶ χάρισιν ἐναργὴς καὶ παντὸς οὑτινοσοῦν φανερώτερος, μορφὴν δὲ καὶ μέγεθος ἡμῖν ἀφανέστατος, Joseph. c. Ap. 2, 22, 2.) *

[SYN. μορφή, σχῆμα : acc. to Bp. Lghtft. (see the thorough discussion in his 'Detached Note' on Phil. ii.) and Trench (N. T. Syn. § lxx.), μορφή form differs from σχῆμα figure, shape, fashion, as that which is intrinsic and essential, from that which is outward and accidental. So in the main Bengel, Philippi, al., on Ro. xii. 2 ; but the distinction is rejected by many; see Meyer and esp. Fritzsche in loc. Yet the last-named commentator makes μορφὴ δούλου in Phil. l. c. relate to the complete form, or nature, of a servant; and σχῆμα to the external form, or human body.

μορφόω, -ῶ : 1 aor. pass. subj. 3 pers. sing. μορφωθῇ ; [cf. μορφή, init.] ; to form : in fig. discourse ἄχρις [T Tr WH μέχρις, q. v. 1 a.] οὗ μορφωθῇ Χριστὸς ἐν ὑμῖν, i. e. literally, until a mind and life in complete harmony with the mind and life of Christ shall have been formed in you, Gal. iv. 19. (Arat. phaen. 375 ; Anth. 1, 33, 1 ; Sept. Is. xliv. 13.) [COMP.: μετα-, συμ-μορφόω.] *   3445

3446 μόρφωσις, -εως, ή, (μορφόω); 1. *a forming, shaping*: τῶν δένδρων, Theophr. c. pl. 3, 7, 4. 2. *form*; i. e. a. *the mere form, semblance*: εὐσεβείας, 2 Tim. iii. 5. b. *the form befitting the thing* or *truly expressing the fact, the very form*: τῆς γνώσεως κ. τῆς ἀληθείας, Ro. ii. 20.*

3447 μοσχο-ποιέω, -ῶ: 1 aor. ἐμοσχοποίησα; (μόσχος and ποιέω, [cf. W. 26]); *to make* (an image of) *a calf*: Acts vii. 41, for which Ex. xxxii. 4 ἐποίησε μόσχον. (Eccles. writ.) *

3448 μόσχος, -ου, ό, [cf. Schmidt ch. 76, 12; Curtius p. 593]; 1. *a tender, juicy, shoot; a sprout,* of a plant or tree. 2. ό, ή, μ. *offspring*; a. of men [(cf. fig. Eng. *scion*)], *a boy, a girl,* esp. if fresh and delicate. b. of animals, *a young one.* 3. *a calf, a bullock, a heifer;* so everywhere in the Bible, and always masc.: Lk. xv. 23, 27, 30; Heb. ix. 12, 19; Rev. iv. 7; (Sept. chiefly for פַּר a bull, esp. a young bull; then for בָּקָר cattle; for שׁוֹר an ox or a cow; also for עֵגֶל a calf). [(Eur. on.)]*

3451 μουσικός, -ή, -όν, (μοῦσα [music, eloquence, etc.]); freq. in Grk. writ.; prop. *devoted to and skilled in the arts sacred to the muses; accomplished in the liberal arts;* specifically, *skilled in music; playing on musical instruments;* so Rev. xviii. 22 [R. V. *minstrels*].*

3449 μόχθος, -ου, ό, *hard and difficult labor, toil, travail; hardship, distress:* 2 Co. xi. 27; 1 Th. ii. 9; 2 Th. iii. 8; see κόπος, 3 b. (Hes. scut. 306; Pind., Tragg., Xen., al.; Sept. chiefly for עָמָל.) [SYN. see κόπος, fin.]*

3452 μυελός, -οῦ, ό, (enclosed within, fr. μύω to close, shut), *marrow*: Heb. iv. 12. (From Hom. down; Sept. Job xxi. 24.) *

3453 μυέω, -ῶ: pf. pass. μεμύημαι; (fr. μύω to close, shut [(cf. Lat. *mutus*); Curtius § 478]); a. *to initiate into the mysteries* (Hdt., Arstph., Plat., Plut., al.; 3 Macc. ii. 30). b. univ. *to teach fully, instruct; to accustom one to a thing; to give one an intimate acquaintance with a thing:* ἐν παντὶ κ. ἐν πᾶσι μεμύημαι, to every condition and to all the several circumstances of life have I become wonted; I have been so disciplined by experience that whatsoever be my lot I can endure, Phil. iv. 12; [but others, instead of connecting ἐν παντί etc. here (as object) with μεμ. (a constr. apparently without precedent; yet cf. Lünemann in W. § 28, 1) and taking the infinitives that follow as explanatory of the ἐν παντί etc., regard the latter phrase as stating the sphere (see πᾶς, II. 2 a.) and the infinitives as epexegetic (W. § 44, 1): *in everything and in all things have I learned the secret both to be filled* etc.].*

3454 μῦθος, -ου, ό, fr. Hom. down; 1. *a speech, word, saying.* 2. *a narrative, story*; a. *a true narrative.* b. *a fiction, a fable*; univ. *an invention, falsehood*: 2 Pet. i. 16; the fictions of the Jewish theosophists and Gnostics, esp. concerning the emanations and orders of the æons, are called μῦθοι [A. V. *fables*] in 1 Tim. i. 4; iv. 7; 2 Tim. iv. 4; Tit. i. 14. [Cf. Trench § xc., and reff. s. v. γενεαλογία.] *

3455 μυκάομαι, -ῶμαι; (fr. μύ or μῦ, the sound which a cow utters [Lat. *mugio*]), *to low, bellow,* prop. of horned cattle (Hom., Aeschyl., Eur., Plat., al.); *to roar,* of a lion, Rev. x. 3.*

3456 μυκτηρίζω: (μυκτήρ the nose); pres. pass. 3 pers. sing. μυκτηρίζεται; prop. *to turn up the nose* or *sneer at; to mock, deride*: τινά, pass. οὐ μυκτηρίζεται, does not suffer himself to be mocked, Gal. vi. 7. (For לָעַג, Job xxii. 19; Ps. lxxix. (lxxx.) 7; Jer. xx. 7; גָּאַץ, Prov. i. 30; בּוּז, Prov. xv. 20; [cf. Clem. Rom. 1 Cor. 39, 1 (and Harnack's note)]. 1 Macc. vii. 34; [1 Esdr. i. 49]; Sext. Emp. adv. math. i. 217 [p. 648, 11 ed. Bekk.].) [COMP.: ἐκμυκτηρίζω.] *

3457 μυλικός, -ή, -όν, (μύλη a mill), *belonging to a mill*: Mk. ix. 42 R G; Lk. xvii. 2 L T Tr WH.*

see 3457 & 3458 μύλινος, -η, -ον; 1. *made of mill-stones*: Boeckh, Inscrr. ii. p. 784, no. 3371, 4. 2. i. q. μυλικός (see the preceding word): Rev. xviii. 21 L WH.*

3458 μύλος, -ου, ό, [(Lat. *mola*; Eng. *mill, meal*)]; 1. *a mill-stone* [(Anthol. etc.)]: Rev. xviii. 21 [L WH μύλινος, q. v.]; μύλος ὀνικός, Mt. xviii. 6; Mk. ix. 42 L T Tr WH; Lk. xvii. 2 Rec.; a large mill consisted of two stones, an upper and an under one; the "nether" stone was stationary, but the upper one was turned by an ass, whence the name μ. ὀνικός. 2. equiv. to μύλη, *a mill* [(Diod., Strab., Plut.)]: Mt. xxiv. 41 L T Tr WH; φωνὴ μύλου, the noise made by a mill, Rev. xviii. 22.*

3459 μυλών [not paroxytone; see Chandler § 596 cf. § 584], -ῶνος, ό, *place where a mill runs; mill-house*: Mt. xxiv. 41 R G. (Eur., Thuc., Dem., Aristot., al.) *

3460 Μύρα (L T Tr WH Μύρρα (Tr -ρρ- see P, ρ) [cf. Tdf. on Acts as below and *WH*. App. p. 160]), -ων, τά, *Myra*, a city on the coast [or rather, some two miles and a half (20 stadia) distant from it] of Lycia, a maritime region of Asia Minor between Caria and Pamphylia [B. D. s. v. Myra; Lewin, St. Paul, ii. 186 sq.]: Acts xxvii. 5. *

3461 μυριάς, -άδος, ή, (μυρίος), [fr. Hdt. down], Sept. for רְבָבָה and רִבּוֹ; a. *ten thousand*: Acts xix. 19 (on which pass. see ἀργύριον, 3 fin.). b. plur. with gen. i. q. *an innumerable multitude, an unlimited number,* ([like our *myriads*], the Lat. *sexcenti*, Germ. *Tausend*): Lk. xii. 1; Acts xxi. 20; Rev. v. 11 [not Rec.]; ix. 16 [here L T δισμυριάδες, q. v.]; used simply, of *innumerable hosts of angels*: Heb. xii. 22 [here G L Tr put a comma after μυριάσιν]; Jude 14; Deut. xxxiii. 2; Dan. vii. 10.*

3462 μυρίζω: 1 aor. inf. μυρίσαι; (μύρον); fr. Hdt. down; *to anoint*: Mk. xiv. 8.*

see 3463 St. μυρίος, -α, -ον, [fr. Hom. down]; 1. *innumerable, countless,* [A. V. *ten thousand*]: 1 Co. iv. 15; xiv. 19. 2. with the accent drawn back (cf. *Bttm.* Ausf. Sprchl. § 70 Anm. 15, vol. i. 278; Passow s. v. fin.; [L. and S. s. v. III.]), μύριοι, -αι, -α, *ten thousand*: Mt. xviii. 24.*

3464 μύρον, -ου, τό, (the grammarians derive it fr. μύρω to flow, accordingly a flowing juice, trickling sap: but prob. more correct to regard it as an oriental word akin to μύρρα, Hebr. מֹר, מוֹר; [Fick (i. 836) connects it with r. smar 'to smear', with which Vaniček 1198 sq. associates σμύρνα, μύρτος, etc.; cf. Curtius p. 714]), *ointment*: Mt. xxvi. 7, 9 Rec., 12; Mk. xiv. 3–5; Lk. vii. 37 sq.; xxiii.

*For 3450 see 1473 St.

56 ; Jn. xi. 2 ; xii. 3, 5 ; Rev. xviii. 13 ; distinguished fr. ἔλαιον [q. v. and see *Trench*, Syn. § xxxviii.], Lk. vii. 46. ([From Aeschyl., Hdt. down] ; Sept. for שֶׁמֶן fat, oil, Prov. xxvii. 9 ; for טוּב שֶׁמֶן, Ps. cxxxii. (cxxxiii.) 2.) *

3465 **Μυσία**, -ας, ἡ, *Mysia*, a province of Asia Minor on the shore of the Ægean Sea, between Lydia and the Propontis ; it had among its cities Pergamum, Troas, and Assos : Acts xvi. 7 sq.*

3466 **μυστήριον**, -ου, τό, (μύστης [one initiated ; fr. μυέω, q. v.]), in class. Grk. *a hidden thing, secret, mystery*: μυστήριόν σου μὴ κατείπῃς τῷ φίλῳ, Menand. ; plur. generally *mysteries, religious secrets*, confided only to the initiated and not to be communicated by them to ordinary mortals ; [cf. *K. F. Hermann*, Gottesdienstl. Alterthümer der Griechen, § 32]. In the Scriptures **1.** *a hidden* or *secret thing, not obvious to the understanding* : 1 Co. xiii. 2 ; xiv. 2 ; (of the secret rites of the Gentiles, Sap. xiv. 15, 23). **2.** *a hidden purpose* or *counsel*; *secret will* : of men, τοῦ βασιλέως, Tob. xii. 7, 11 ; τῆς βουλῆς αὐτοῦ, Judith ii. 2 ; of God : μυστήρια θεοῦ, the secret counsels which govern God in dealing with the righteous, which are hidden from ungodly and wicked men but plain to the godly, Sap. ii. 22. In the N. T., God's plan of providing salvation for men through Christ, which was once hidden but now is revealed : Ro. xvi. 25 ; 1 Co. ii. 7 (on this see ἐν, I. 5 f.) ; Eph. iii. 9 ; Col. i. 26 sq. ; with τοῦ θελήματος αὐτοῦ added, Eph. i. 9 ; τοῦ θεοῦ, which God formed, Col. ii. 2 ; [1 Co. ii. 1 WH txt.] ; τοῦ Χριστοῦ, respecting Christ, Col. iv. 3 ; τοῦ εὐαγγελίου, which is contained and announced in the gospel, Eph. vi. 19 ; ἐτελέσθη τὸ μυστ. τοῦ θεοῦ, said of the consummation of this purpose, to be looked for when Christ returns, Rev. x. 7 ; τὰ μ. τῆς βασιλείας τῶν οὐρ. or τοῦ θεοῦ, the secret purposes relative to the kingdom of God, Mt. xiii. 11 ; Mk. iv. 11 ; Lk. viii. 10 ; used of certain single events decreed by God having reference to his kingdom or the salvation of men, Ro. xi. 25 ; 1 Co. xv. 51 ; of God's purpose to bless the Gentiles also with salvation through Christ [cf. Bp. Lghtft. on Col. i. 26], Eph. iii. 3 cf. 5 ; with τοῦ Χριστοῦ added, ibid. vs. 4 ; οἰκονόμοι μυστηρίων θεοῦ, the stewards of God's mysteries, i. e. those intrusted with the announcement of God's secret purposes to men, 1 Co. iv. 1 ; used generally, of Christian truth as hidden from ungodly men : with the addition of τῆς πίστεως, τῆς εὐσεβείας, which faith and godliness embrace and keep, 1 Tim. iii. 9, 16 ; τὸ μυστ. τῆς ἀνομίας *the mystery of lawlessness*, the secret purpose formed by lawlessness, seems to be a tacit antithesis to God's saving purpose, 2 Th. ii. 7. **3.** Like רָזָא and סוֹד in rabbinic writers, it denotes *the mystic* or *hidden sense* : of an O. T. saying, Eph. v. 32 ; of a name, Rev. xvii. 5 ; of an image or form seen in a vision, Rev. i. 20 ; xvii. 5 ; of a dream, Dan. (Theodot.) ii. 18 sq. 27–30, where the Sept. so render רָז. (The Vulg. translates the word *sacramentum* in Dan. ii. 18 ; iv. 6 ; Tob. xii. 7 ; Sap. ii. 22 ; Eph. i. 9 ; iii. 3, 9 ; v. 32 ; 1 Tim. iii. 16 ; Rev. i. 20). [On the distinctive N. T. use of the word cf. *Campbell*, Dissertations on the Gospels. diss. ix.

pt. i. ; *Kendrick* in B. D. Am. ed. s. v. Mystery ; Bp. Lghtft. on Col. i. 26.] *

3467 **μυ-ωπάζω** ; (μύωψ, and this fr. μύειν τοὺς ὦπας to shut the eyes) ; *to see dimly, see only what is near* : 2 Pet. i. 9 [some (cf. R. V. mrg.) would make it mean here *closing the eyes*; cf. our Eng. *blink*]. (Aristot. problem. 31, 16, 25.) *

3468 **μώλωψ**, -ωπος, ὁ, (Hesych. τραῦμα καὶ ὁ ἐκ πληγῆς αἱματώδης τόπος ἢ καὶ τὰ ἐξερχόμενα τῶν πληγῶν ὕδατα, a bruise, wale, wound that trickles with blood* : 1 Pet. ii. 24 fr. Is. liii. 5 [where A. V. *stripes*]. (Gen. iv. 23 ; Ex. xxi. 25 ; Is. i. 6. Aristot., Plut., Anthol., al.) *

3469 **μωμάομαι**, -ῶμαι : 1 aor. mid. ἐμωμησάμην ; 1 aor. pass. ἐμωμήθην ; (μῶμος, q. v.) ; fr. Hom. down ; *to blame, find fault with, mock at* : 2 Co. vi. 3 ; viii. 20. (Prov. ix. 7 ; Sap. x. 14.) *

3470 **μῶμος**, -ου, ὁ, [perh. akin to μύω, Curtius § 478 ; cf. Vaniček p. 732], *blemish, blot, disgrace* ; **1.** *censure.* **2.** *insult* : of men who are a disgrace to a society, 2 Pet. ii. 13 [A. V. *blemishes*]. (From Hom. down ; Sept. for מוּם, of bodily defects and blemishes, Lev. xxi. 16 sqq. ; Deut. xv. 21 ; Cant. iv. 7 ; Dan. i. 4 ; of a mental defect, fault, Sir. xx. 24 (23).) *

3471 **μωραίνω** : 1 aor. ἐμώρανα ; 1 aor. pass. ἐμωράνθην ; (μωρός) ; **1.** in class. Grk. *to be foolish, to act foolishly.* **2.** in bibl. Grk. **a.** *to make foolish* : pass. Ro. i. 22 (Is. xix. 11) ; Jer. x. 14 ; 2 S. xxiv. 10) ; i. q. *to prove a person or thing to be foolish* : τὴν σοφίαν τοῦ κόσμου, 1 Co. i. 20 (τὴν βουλὴν αὐτῶν, Is. xliv. 25). **b.** *to make flat and tasteless* : pass. of salt that has lost its strength and flavor, Mt. v. 13 ; Lk. xiv. 34.*

3472 **μωρία**, -ας, ἡ, (μωρός), first in Hdt. 1, 146 [Soph., al.], *foolishness* : 1 Co. i. 18, 21, 23 ; ii. 14 ; iii. 19, (Sir. xx. 31).*

3473 **μωρολογία**, -ας, ἡ, (μωρολόγος), (*stultiloquium*, Plaut., Vulg.), *foolish talking* : Eph. v. 4. (Aristot. h. a. 1, 11 ; Plut. mor. p. 504 b.) [Cf. *Trench*, N. T. Syn. § xxxiv.] *

3474 **μωρός**, -ά, -όν, [on the accent cf. W. 52 (51) ; Chandler §§ 404, 405], *foolish* : with τυφλός, Mt. xxiii. 17, 19 [here T Tr WH txt. om. L br. μωρ.] ; τὸ μωρὸν τοῦ θεοῦ, an act or appointment of God deemed foolish by men, 1 Co. i. 25 ; i. q. *without learning* or *erudition*, 1 Co. i. 27 ; iii. 18 ; iv. 10 ; *imprudent, without forethought* or *wisdom*, Mt. vii. 26 ; xxiii. 17, 19 [see above] ; xxv. 2 sq. 8 ; i. q. *empty, useless*, ζητήσεις, 2 Tim. ii. 23 ; Tit. iii. 9 ; in imitation of the Hebr. נָבָל (cf. Ps. xiii. (xiv.) 1 ; Job ii. 10) i. q. *impious, godless*, (because such a man neglects and despises what relates to salvation), Mt. v. 22 ; [some take the word here as a Hebr. term (מוֹרֶה *rebel*) expressive of condemnation ; cf. Num. xx. 10 ; Ps. lxviii. 8 ; but see the Syriac ; *Field*, Otium Norv. pars iii. ad loc. ; *Levy*, Neuhebräisch. u. Chald. Wörterbuch s. v. מוֹרוּם]. (Sept. for נָבָל, Deut. xxxii. 6 ; Is. xxxii. 5 sq. ; for כְּסִיל, Ps. xciii. (xciv.) 8. [Aeschyl., Soph., al.]) *

3475 **Μωσῆς** (constantly so in the text. Rec. [in Strabo (16, 2, 35 ed. Meineke) ; Dan. ix. 10, 11, Sept.], and in Philo [cf. his "Buch v. d. Weltschöpf." ed. Müller p. 117 (but Richter in his ed. has adopted Μωϋσῆς)], after the

Hebr. form מֹשֶׁה, which in Ex. ii. 10 is derived fr. מָשָׁה to draw out), and **Μωϋσῆς** (so in the Sept. [see Tdf.'s 4th ed. Proleg. p. xlii.], Josephus ["in Josephus the readings vary; in the Antiquities he still adheres to the classic form (**Μωσῆς**), which moreover is the common form in his writings," Müller's note on Joseph. c. Ap. 1, 31, 4. (Here, again, recent editors, as Bekker, adopt **Μωϋσῆς** uniformly.) On the fluctuation of Mss. cf. Otto's note on Justin Mart. apol. i. § 32 init.], and in the N. T. ed. Tdf.; — a word which signifies in Egyptian *water-saved*, i. e. 'saved from water'; cf. *Fritzsche*, Rom. vol. ii. p. 313; and esp. *Gesenius*, Thesaur. ii. p. 824; Knobel on Ex. ii. 10; [but its etymol. is still in dispute; many recent Egyptologists connect it with *mesu* i. e. 'child'; on the various interpretations of the name cf. *Müller* on Joseph. c. Ap. l. c.; *Stanley* in B. D. s. v. Moses; *Schenkel* in his BL. iv. 240 sq.]. From the remarks of Fritzsche, Gesenius, etc., it is evident also that the word is a trisyllable, and hence should not be written **Μωσῆς** as it is by L Tr WH, for ωυ is a diphthong, as is plain from ἑωυτοῦ, τωὐτό, Ionic for ἑαυτοῦ, ταὐτό; [cf. *Lipsius*,

Gramm. Untersuch. p. 140]; add, W. p. 44; [B. 19 (17)]; *Ewald*, Gesch. des Volkes Israel ed. 3 p. 119 note), -έως, ὁ, *Moses*, (Itala and Vulg. *Moyses*), the famous leader and legislator of the Israelites in their migration from Egypt to Palestine. As respects its declension, everywhere in the N. T. the gen. ends in -έως (as if from the nominative **Μωϋσεύς**), in Sept. -ῆ, as Num. iv. 41, 45, 49, etc. dat. -ῆ (as in Sept., cf. Ex. v. 20; xii. 28; xxiv. 1; Lev. viii. 21, etc.) and -εῖ (for the Mss. and accordingly the editors vary between the two [but T WH -ῆ only in Acts vii. 44 (influenced by the Sept. ?), Tr in Acts l. c. and Mk. ix. 4, 5,; L in Acts l. c. and Ro. ix. 15 txt.; see *Tdf.* Proleg. p. 119; *WH.* App. p. 158]), Mt. xvii. 4; Mk. ix. 4; Jn. v. 46; ix. 29; Acts vii. 44; Ro. ix. 15; 2 Tim. iii. 8. acc. -ῆν (as in Sept.), Acts vi. 11; vii. 35; 1 Co. x. 2; Heb. iii. 3; once -έα, Lk. xvi. 29; cf. [Tdf. and WH. u. s.]; W. § 10, 1; B. u. s.; [Etym. Magn. 597, 8]. By meton. i. q. *the books of Moses*: Lk. xvi. 29; xxiv. 27; Acts xv. 21; 2 Co. iii. 15.

N

[**N, ν**: ν (ἐφελκυστικόν), cf. W. § 5, 1 b.; B. 9 (8); *Tdf.* Proleg. p. 97 sq.; *WH.* App. p. 146 sq.; *Thiersch*, De Pentat. vers. Alex. p. 84 sq.; *Scrivener*, Plain Introd. etc. ch. viii. § 4; Collation of Cod. Sin. p. liv.; see s. vv. δύο, εἴκοσι, πᾶς. Its omission by the recent editors in the case of verbs (esp. in 3 pers. sing.) is rare. In WH, for instance, (where "the omissions are all deliberate and founded on evidence") it is wanting in the case of ἐστι five times only (Mt. vi. 25; Jn. vi. 55 *bis*; Acts xviii. 10; Gal. iv. 2, — apparently without principle); in Tdf. never; see esp. Tdf. u. s. In the dat. plur. of the 3d decl. the Mss. vary; see esp. *Tdf.* Proleg. p. 98 and *WH.* App. p. 146 sq. On ν appended to accus. sing. in α or η (ῆ) see ἄρσην. On the neglect of assimilation, particularly in compounds with σύν and ἐν, see those prepp. and *Tdf.* Proleg. p. 73 sq.; *WH.* App. p. 149; cf. B. 8; W.48. On the interchange of ν and νν in such words as ἀποκτέννω (ἀποκτένω), ἐκχύννω (ἐκχύνω), ἔνατος (ἔννατος), ἐνενήκοντα (ἐννενήκοντα), ἐνεός (ἐννεός), Ἰωάννης (Ἰωάνης), and the like, see the several words.]

3476   **Ναασσών**, (נַחְשׁוֹן [i. e. 'diviner', 'enchanter']), ὁ, indecl., *Naasson* [or *Naashon*, or (best) *Nahshon*], a man mentioned in (Ex. vi. 23; Num. i. 7; Ruth iv. 20) Mt. i. 4 and Lk. iii. 32.*

3477   **Ναγγαί**, (fr. נָגַהּ to shine), ὁ, indecl., (Vulg. [*Naggae*, and (so A. V.)] *Nagge*), *Naggai*, one of Christ's ancestors: Lk. iii. 25.*

3478   **Ναζαρέτ** [(so Rec.ˢᵗ everywhere; Lchm. also in Mk. i. 9; Lk. ii. 39, 51; iv. 16; Jn. i. 45 (46) sq.; Tdf. in Mk.

i. 9; Jn. i. 45 (46) sq.; Tr txt. in Lk. i. 26; ii. 4; iv. 16; Jn. i. 45 (46) sq.; Tr mrg. in Mk. i. 9; Lk. ii. 39, 51; and WH everywhere except in four pass. soon to be mentioned), **Ναζαρέθ** (so Rec.ᵉˡᶻ ten times, Rec.ᵇᵉᶻ six times, T and Tr except in the pass. already given or about to be given; L in Mt. ii. 23; xxi. 11 (so WH here); Lk. i. 26; Acts x. 38 (so WH here)), **Ναζαράθ** (L in Mt. iv. 13 and Lk. ii. 4, after cod. Δ but with "little other attestation" (Hort)), **Ναζαρά** (Mt. iv. 13 T Tr WH; Lk. iv. 16 T WH)], ἡ, indecl., (and τὰ Νάζαρα, Orig. and Jul. African. in Euseb. h. e. 1, 7, 14; cf. *Keim*, Jesu von Naz. i. p. 319 sq. [Eng. trans. ii. p. 16] and ii. p. 421 sq. [Eng. trans. iv. p. 108], who thinks *Nazara* preferable to the other forms [but see *WH.* App. p. 160ᵃ; *Tdf.* Proleg. p. 120; *Scrivener*, Introd. ch. viii. § 5; *Alford*, Greek Test. vol. i. Proleg. p. 97]), *Nazareth*, a town of lower Galilee, mentioned neither in the O. T., nor by Josephus, nor in the Talmud (unless it is to be recognized in the appellation נֵצֶר **בֶּ**, נֵצֶר, given there to Jesus Christ). It was built upon a hill, in a very lovely region (cf. *Renan*, Vie de Jésus, 14ᵐᵉ éd. p. 27 sq. [Wilbour's trans. (N. Y. 1865) p. 69 sq.; see also *Robinson*, Researches, etc. ii. 336 sq.]), and was distant from Jerusalem a three days' journey, from Tiberias eight hours [or less]; it was the home of Jesus (Mt. xiii. 54; Mk. vi. 1); its present name is *en Nazirah*, a town of from five to six thousand inhabitants (cf.

Baedeker, Palestine and Syria, p. 359) : Mt. ii. 23 ; iv. 13 ; xxi. 11 ; Mk. i. 9 ; Lk. i. 26 ; ii. 4, 39, 51 ; iv. 16 ; Jn. i. 45 (46) sq.; Acts x. 39. As respects the Hebrew form of the name, it is disputed whether it was נֵצֶר 'a sprout', 'shoot', (so, besides others, *Hengstenberg,* Christol. des A. T. ii. 124 sq. [Eng. trans. ii. 106 sq.]; but cf. *Gieseler* in the Stud. u. Krit. for 1831, p. 588 sq.), or נְצֻרָה 'protectress', 'guard', (cf. 2 K. xvii. 9 ; so Keim u. s.), or נְצֶרֶת 'sentinel' (so *Delitzsch* in the Zeitschr. f. Luth. Theol. for 1876, p. 401), or נָצְרַת 'watch-tower' (so *Ewald* in the Götting. gelehrt. Anzeigen for 1867, p. 1602 sq.). For a further account of the town cf. *Robinson,* as above, pp. 333–343 ; *Tobler,* Nazareth in Palästina. Berl. 1868 ; [*Hackett* in B. D. s. v. Nazareth].*

3479 **Ναζαρηνός, -οῦ, ὁ,** *a Nazarene, of Nazareth, sprung from Nazareth,* a patrial name applied by the Jews to Jesus, because he had lived at Nazareth with his parents from his birth until he made his public appearance : Mk. i. 24 ; xiv. 67 ; xvi. 6 ; Lk. iv. 34 ; [xxiv. 19 L mrg. T Tr txt. WH]; and L T Tr WH in Mk. x. 47.*

3480 **Ναζωραῖος, -ου, ὁ,** i. q. Ναζαρηνός. q. v.; Jesus is so called in Mt. ii. 23 [cf. B. D. s. v. Nazarene ; *Bleek,* Synopt. Evang. ad loc.]; xxvi. 71 ; Mk. x. 47 R G; Lk. xviii. 37 ; xxiv. 19 R G Ltxt. Tr mrg.; Jn. xviii. 5, 7 ; xix. 19 ; Acts ii. 22 ; iii. 6 ; iv. 10 ; vi. 14 ; [ix. 5 L br.]; xxii. 8 ; xxvi. 9. οἱ Ναζωραῖοι [A.V. *the Nazarenes*], followers of Ἰησοῦς ὁ Ναζωραῖος, was a name given to the Christians by the Jews, Acts xxiv. 5.*

3481 **Ναθάν** (or so L mrg. T WH) Ναθάμ, ὁ, (נָתָן ['given' sc. of God]), *Nathan:* a son of David the king (2 S. v. 14), Lk. iii. 31.*

3482 **Ναθαναήλ, ὁ,** (נְתַנְאֵל gift of God), *Nathanael,* an intimate disciple of Jesus : Jn. i. 45–49 (46–50) ; xxi. 2. He is commonly thought to be identical with *Bartholomew,* because as in Jn. i. 45 (46) he is associated with Philip, so in Mt. x. 3 ; Mk. iii. 18 ; Lk. vi. 14 Bartholomew is ; *Nathanael,* on this supposition, was his personal name, and *Bartholomew* a title derived from his father (see Βαρθολομαῖος). But in Acts i. 13 Thomas is placed between Philip and Bartholomew ; [see B. D. s. v. Nathaniel]. *Späth* in the Zeitschr. f. wissensch. Theologie, 1868, pp. 168 sqq. [again 1880, p. 78 sqq.] acutely but vainly tries to prove that the name was formed by the Fourth Evangelist symbolically to designate 'the disciple whom Jesus loved' (see Ἰωάννης, 2).*

3483 **ναί,** a particle of assertion or confirmation [akin to νή ; cf. *Donaldson,* Cratylus § 189], fr. Hom. down, *yea, verily, truly, assuredly, even so:* Mt. xi. 26 ; Lk. x. 21 ; Philem. 20 ; Rev. i. 7 ; xvi. 7 ; xxii. 20 ; ναί, λέγω ὑμῖν κτλ., Mt. xi. 9 ; Lk. vii. 26 ; xi. 51 ; xii. 5 ; ναί, λέγει τὸ πνεῦμα, Rev. xiv. 13 ; it is responsive and confirmatory of the substance of some question or statement : Mt. ix. 28 ; xiii. 51 ; xv. 27 ; xvii. 25 ; xxi. 16 ; Mk. vii. 28 ; Jn. xi. 27 ; xxi. 15 sq.; Acts v. 8 (9) ; xxii. 27 ; Ro. iii. 29 ; a repeated ναί, *most assuredly,* [A. V. yea, yea], expresses emphatic assertion, Mt. v. 37 ; ἤτω ὑμῶν τὸ ναὶ ναί, let your ναί be ναί, i. e. let your allegation be true, Jas. v. 12 [B. 163 (142) ; W. 59 (58)]; εἶναι or γίνεσθαι ναὶ καὶ οὔ, to

be or show one's self double-tongued, i. e. faithless, wavering, false, 2 Co. i. 18 sq.; ἵνα παρ᾽ ἐμοὶ τὸ ναὶ ναὶ καὶ τὸ οὐ οὔ, that with me should be found both a solemn affirmation and a most emphatic denial, i. e. that I so form my resolves as, at the dictate of pleasure or profit, not to carry them out, ibid. 17 [cf. W. 460 (429)]; ναὶ ἐν αὐτῷ γέγονεν, in him what was promised has come to pass, ibid. 19 ; ἐπαγγελίαι ἐν αὐτῷ τὸ ναί sc. γεγόνασιν, have been fulfilled, have been confirmed by the event, ibid. 20 [cf. *Meyer* ad loc.]. It is a particle of appeal or entreaty, like the [Eng. *yea*] (Germ. *ja*) : with an imperative, ναί . . . συλλαμβάνου αὐταῖς, Phil. iv. 3 (where Rec. has καί for ναί); ναὶ ἔρχου, Rev. xxii. 20 Rec.; so ναὶ ναί, Judith ix. 12. [A classification of the uses of ναί in the N. T. is given by Ellicott on Phil. iv. 3 ; cf. *Green,* 'Crit. Note' on Mt. xi. 26.] *

Ναιμάν, see Νεεμάν.   see 3497

Ναΐν [WH Ναίν, (cf. I, ι)], (נָאִין a pasture ; cf. *Simonis,* 3484 Onomast. N. T. p. 115), ἡ, *Nain,* a town of Galilee, situated at the northern base of Little Hermon ; modern *Nein,* a petty village inhabited by a very few families, and not to be confounded with a village of the same name beyond the Jordan (Joseph. b. j. 4, 9, 4) : Lk. vii. 11. [Cf. *Edersheim,* Jesus the Messiah, i. 552 sq.] *

ναός, -οῦ, ὁ, (ναίω to dwell), Sept. for הֵיכָל, used of the 3485 temple at Jerusalem, but only of the s a c r e d e d i f i c e (or sanctuary) i t s e l f, consisting of the Holy place and the Holy of holies (in class. Grk. used of the sanctuary or cell of a temple, where the image of the god was placed, called also δόμος, σηκός, which is to be distinguished from τὸ ἱερόν, the w h o l e temple, the entire consecrated enclosure ; this distinction is observed also in the Bible ; see ἱερόν, p. 299ª) : Mt. xxiii. 16 sq. 35 xxvii. 40 ; Mk. xiv. 58 ; xv. 29 ; Jn. ii. 19 sq.; Rev. xi. 2 ; nor need Mt. xxvii. be regarded as an exception, provided we suppose that Judas in his desperation entered the Holy place, which no one but the priests was allowed to enter [(note the εἰς (al. ἐν) of T Tr WH)]. with θεοῦ, τοῦ θεοῦ, added : Mt. xxvi. 61 ; 1 Co. iii. 17 ; 2 Co. vi. 16 ; 2 Th. ii. 4 ; Rev. xi. 1 ; used specifically of the Holy place, where the priests officiated : Lk. i. 9, 21 sq.; of the Holy of holies (see καταπέτασμα), Mt. xxvii. 51 ; Mk. xv. 38 ; Lk. xxiii. 45. in the visions of the Revelation used of the temple of the 'New Jerusalem' : Rev. iii. 12 ; vii. 15 ; xi. 19 ; xiv. 15, 17 ; xv. 5 sq. 8 ; xvi. 1, 17 ; of any temple whatever prepared for the true God, Acts vii. 48 Rec.; xvii. 24. of miniature silver temples modelled after the temple of Diana [i. e. Artemis (q. v.)] of Ephesus, Acts xix. 24. ὁ θεὸς ναὸς αὐτῆς ἐστιν, takes the place of a temple in it, Rev. xxi. 22. metaph. of a company of Christians, a Christian church, as dwelt in by the Spirit of God : 1 Co. iii. 16 ; 2 Co. vi. 16 ; Eph. ii. 21; for the same reason, of the bodies of Christians, 1 Co. vi. 19. of the body of Christ, ὁ ναὸς τοῦ σώματος αὐτοῦ (epexeget. gen. [W. 531 (494)]), Jn. ii. 21, and acc. to the Evangelist's interpretation in 19 also. [(From Hom. on.)] *

Ναούμ, (נַחוּם consolation), ὁ, *Nahum,* a certain Is- 3486 raelite, one of the ancestors of Christ : Lk. iii. 25.*

3487 νάρδος, -ου, ἡ, (a Sanskrit word [cf. Fick as in Löw below]; Hebr. נֵרְדְּ, Cant. i. 12; iv. 13 sq.); **a.** *nard*, the head or spike of a fragrant East Indian plant belonging to the genus V a l e r i a n a, which yields a juice of delicious odor which the ancients used (either pure or mixed) in the preparation of a most precious ointment; hence **b.** *nard oil* or *ointment*; so Mk. xiv. 3; Jn. xii. 3. Cf. *Winer*, RWB. s. v. Narde; *Rüetschi* in Herzog x. p. 203; *Furrer* in Schenkel p. 286 sq.; [*Löw*, Aramäische Pflanzennamen (Leip. 1881), § 316 p. 368 sq.; *Royle* in Alex.'s Kitto s. v. Nerd; *Birdwood* in the 'Bible Educator' ii. 152].*

3488 Νάρκισσος, -ου, ὁ, *Narcissus* [i. e. 'daffodil'], a Roman mentioned in Ro. xvi. 11, whom many interpreters without good reason suppose to be the noted freedman of the emperor Claudius (Suet. Claud. 28; Tac. ann. 11, 29 sq.; 12, 57 etc.) [cf. Bp. Lghtft. on Philip. p. 175]; in opposition to this opinion cf. *Win.* RWB. s. v.; *Rüetschi* in Herzog x. 202 sq.; [B. D. s. v.].*

3489 ναυαγέω, -ῶ: 1 aor. ἐναυάγησα; (fr. ναυαγός shipwrecked; and this fr. ναῦς, and ἄγνυμι to break); freq. in Grk. writ. from Aeschyl. and Hdt. down, *to suffer shipwreck*: prop. 2 Co. xi. 25; metaph. περὶ τὴν πίστιν (as respects [A. V. *concerning*, see περί, II. b.] the faith), 1 Tim. i. 19.*

3490 ναύ-κληρος, -ου, ὁ, (ναῦς and κλῆρος), fr. Hdt. [and Soph.] down, *a ship-owner, ship-master*, i. e. one who hires out his vessel, or a portion of it, for purposes of transportation: Acts xxvii. 11.*

3491 ναῦς, acc. ναῦν, ἡ, (fr. νάω or νέω, to flow, float, swim), *a ship, vessel* of considerable size: Acts xxvii. 41. (From Hom. down; Sept. several times for אֳנִי and אֳנִיָּה.) *

3492 ναύτης, -ου, ὁ, *a sailor, seaman, mariner*: Acts xxvii. 27, 30; Rev. xviii. 17. (From Hom. down.)*

3493 Ναχώρ, ὁ, (נָחוֹר fr. חָרַר to burn; [Philo de cong. erud. grat. § 9 N. ἑρμηνεύεται φωτὸς ἀνάπαυσις; al. al.; see B.D. Am. ed. s. v.]), the indecl. prop. name, *Nachor* [or (more com. but less accurately) *Nahor*] (Gen. xi. 22), of one of the ancestors of Christ: Lk. iii. 34.*

3494 νεανίας, -ου, ὁ, (fr. νεάν, and this fr. νέος; cf. μεγιστάν [q. v.], ξυνάν), fr. Hom. down; Hebr. נַעַר and בָּחוּר; a *young man*: Acts xx. 9; xxiii. 17, and R G in 18 [so here WH txt.], 22; it is used as in Grk. writ., like the Lat. *adulescens* and the Hebr. נַעַר (Gen. xli. 12), of men between twenty-four and forty years of age [cf. *Lob.* ad Phryn. p. 213; *Diog.* Laërt. 8, 10; other reff. in *Steph.* Thesaur. s. vv. νεᾶνις, νεανίσκος]: Acts vii. 58.*

3495 νεανίσκος, -ου, ὁ, (fr. νεάν, see νεανίας; on the ending -ίσκος, -ίσκη, which has dimin. force, as ἀνθρωπίσκος, βασιλίσκος, παιδίσκη, etc., cf. *Bttm.* Ausf. Spr. ii. p. 443), fr. Hdt. down; Sept. chiefly for בָּחוּר and נַעַר; *a young man, youth*: Mt. xix. 20, 22; Mk. xiv. 51ᵃ; xvi. 5; Lk. vii. 14; Acts ii. 17; [and L T Tr WH in xxiii. 18 (here WH mrg. only), 22]; 1 Jn. ii. 13 sq.; like נַעַר (2 S. ii. 14; Gen. xiv. 24, etc.; cf. Germ. *Bursche, Knappe* i. q. *Knabe*, [cf. our colloquial "boys", "lads"]) used of *a young attendant* or *servant*: so the plur. in Mk. xiv. 51 Rec.; Acts v. 10.*

3496 Νεάπολις, -εως, ἡ, *Neapolis*, a maritime city of Macedonia, on the gulf of Strymon, having a port [cf. *Lewin*, St. Paul, i. 203 n.] and colonized by Chalcidians [see B. D. s. v. Neapolis; cf. Bp. Lghtft. on Philip., Introd. § iii.]: Acts xvi. 11 [here Tdf. Νέαν πόλιν, WH Νέαν Πόλιν, Tr Νεάν πόλιν; cf. B. 74; *Lob.*ad Phryn. p. 604 sq.]. (Strab. 7 p. 330; Plin. 4, (11) 18.) *

3497 Νεεμάν and (so L T Tr WH after the Sept. [see *WH.* App. p. 159 sq.]) Ναιμάν, ὁ, (נַעֲמָן pleasantness), *Naaman* (so Vulg. [also *Neman*]), a commander of the Syrian armies (2 K. v. 1): Lk. iv. 27.*

3498 νεκρός, -ά, -όν, (akin to the Lat. *neco, nex* [fr. a r. signifying 'to disappear' etc.; cf. Curtius § 93; Fick i. p. 123; Vaniček p. 422 sq.]), Sept. chiefly for מֵת; *dead*, i. e. **1.** prop. **a.** *one that has breathed his last, lifeless*: Mt. xxviii. 4; Mk. ix. 26; Lk. vii. 15; Acts v. 10; xx. 9; xxviii. 6; Heb. xi. 35; Rev. i. 17; ἐπὶ νεκροῖς, if men are dead (where death has occurred [see ἐπί, B. 2 a. ε. p. 233ᵃ fin.]), Heb. ix. 17; ἐγείρειν νεκρούς, Mt. x. 8; xi. 5; Lk. vii. 22; hyperbolically and proleptically i. q. *as if already dead, sure to die, destined inevitably to die*: τὸ σῶμα, Ro. viii. 10 (τὸ σῶμα and τὸ σωμάτιον φύσει νεκρόν, Epict. diss. 3, 10, 15 and 3, 22, 41; in which sense Luther called the human body, although alive, *einen alten Madensack* [cf. Shakspere's *thou worms-meat !*]); said of the body of a dead man (so in Hom. often; for נְבֵלָה, *a corpse*, Deut. xxviii. 26; Is. xxvi. 19; Jer. vii. 33; ix. 22; xix. 7): μετὰ τῶν νεκρῶν, among the dead, i. e. the buried, Lk. xxiv. 5; θάψαι τοὺς νεκρούς, Mt. viii. 22; Lk. ix. 60; ὀστέα νεκρῶν, Mt. xxiii. 27; of the corpse of a murdered man, αἷμα ὡς νεκροῦ, Rev. xvi. 3 (for הָרוּג, Ezek. xxxvii. 9; for חָלָל, thrust through, slain, Ezek. ix. 7; xi. 6). **b.** *deceased, departed, one whose soul is in Hades*: Rev. i. 18; ii. 8; νεκρὸς ἦν, was like one dead, as good as dead, Lk. xv. 24, 32; plur., 1 Co. xv. 29; Rev. xiv. 13; ἐν Χριστῷ, dead Christians (see ἐν, I. 6 b. p. 211ᵇ), 1 Th. iv. 16; very often οἱ νεκροί and νεκροί (without the art.; see W. p. 123 (117) and cf. B. 89 (78) note) are used of the assembly of the dead (see ἀνάστασις, 2 and ἐγείρω, 2): 1 Pet. iv. 6; Rev. xx. 5, 12 sq.; τὶς ἀπὸ τῶν νεκρῶν, one (returning) from the dead, the world of spirits, Lk. xvi. 30; ἐκ νεκρῶν, from the dead, occurs times too many to count (see ἀνάστασις, ἀνίστημι, ἐγείρω): ἀνάγειν τινὰ ἐκ ν., Ro. x. 7; Heb. xiii. 20; ζωὴ ἐκ νεκρῶν, life springing forth from death, i. e. the return of the dead to life [see ἐκ, I. 5], Ro. xi. 15; πρωτότοκος ἐκ τῶν νεκρ. who was the first that returned to life from among the dead, Col. i. 18; also πρωτότ. τῶν νεκρ. Rev. i. 5; ζωοποιεῖν τοὺς ν. Ro. iv. 17; ἐγείρειν τινὰ ἀπὸ τῶν ν. to rouse one to quit (the assembly of) the dead, Mt. xiv. 2; xxvii. 64; xxviii. 7; κρίνειν ζῶντας κ. νεκρούς, 2 Tim. iv. 1; 1 Pet. iv. 5; κριτὴς ζώντων κ. νεκρῶν, Acts x. 42; νεκρῶν κ. ζώντων κυριεύειν, Ro. xiv. 9. **c.** *destitute of life, without life, inanimate* (i. q. ἄψυχος): τὸ σῶμα χωρὶς πνεύματος νεκρόν ἐστιν, Jas. ii. 26; οὐκ ἔστιν (ὁ) θεὸς νεκρῶν ἀλλὰ ζώντων, God is the guardian God not of the dead but of the living, Mt. xxii. 32; Mk. xii. 27; Lk. xx. 38. **2.** trop. **a.** [spiritually dead i. e.] *destitute of a life that recognizes and is devoted to God, because given* up to trespasses and sins; inactive as respects doing right: Jn. v. 25; Ro. vi. 13; Eph. v. 14; Rev. iii. 1; with τοῖς παραπτώμασιν (dat. of cause [cf. W. 412 (384 sq.)]) added, Eph. ii. 1, 5; ἐν [but T Tr WH om. ἐν] τοῖς παραπτ. Col. ii. 13; in the pointed saying ἄφες τοὺς νεκροὺς θάψαι τοὺς ἑαυτῶν νεκρούς, leave those who are indifferent to the salvation offered them in the gospel, to bury the bodies of their own dead, Mt. viii. 22; Lk. ix. 60. **b.** univ. *destitute of force* or *power, inactive, inoperative*: τῇ ἁμαρτίᾳ, unaffected by the desire to sin [cf. W. 210 (199); B. § 133, 12], Ro. vi. 11; of things: ἁμαρτία, Ro. vii. 8; πίστις, Jas. ii. 17, 20 [R G], 26; ἔργα, powerless and fruitless (see ἔργον, 3 p. 248ᵇ bot.), Heb. vi. 1; ix. 14. [Cf. θνητός, fin.]

3499 **νεκρόω, -ῶ**: 1 aor. impv. νεκρώσατε; pf. pass. ptcp. νενεκρωμένος; *to make dead* (Vulgate and Lat. Fathers *mortifico*), *to put to death, slay*: τινά, prop., Anthol. app. 313, 5; pass. νενεκρωμένος, hyperbolically, *worn out*, of an impotent old man, Heb. xi. 12; also σῶμα νενεκρ. Ro. iv. 19; equiv. to *to deprive of power, destroy the strength of*: τὰ μέλη, i. e. the evil desire lurking in the members (of the body), Col. iii. 5. (τὰ δόγματα, Antonin. 7, 2; τὴν ἕξιν, Plut. de primo frig. 21; [ἄνθρωπος, of obduracy, Epictet. diss. 1, 5, 7].)*

3500 **νέκρωσις, -εως, ἡ,** (νεκρόω); **1.** prop. *a putting to death* (Vulg. *mortificatio* in 2 Co. iv. 10), *killing.* **2.** i. q. τὸ νεκροῦσθαι, [the being put to death], with τοῦ Ἰησοῦ added, i. e. the (protracted) death [A. V. *the dying*] which Jesus underwent in God's service [on the gen. cf. W. 189 (178) note], Paul so styles the marks of perpetual trials, misfortunes, hardships attended with peril of death, evident in his body [cf. Meyer], 2 Co. iv. 10. **3.** i. q. τὸ νενεκρωμένον εἶναι, the dead state [A. V. *deadness*], utter sluggishness, (of bodily members and organs, Galen): Ro. iv. 19.*

see 3561 **νεο-μηνία,** see νουμηνία.

3501 **νέος, -α, -ον,** [allied with Lat. *novus*, Germ. *neu*, Eng. *new*; Curtius § 433], as in Grk. auth. fr. Hom. down, **1.** *recently born, young, youthful*: Tit. ii. 4 (for נַעַר, Gen. xxxvii. 2; Ex. xxxiii. 11); οἶνος νέος, recently made, Mt. ix. 17; Mk. ii. 22; Lk. v. 37–39 [but 39 WH in br.], (Sir. ix. 10). **2.** *new*: 1 Co. v. 7; Heb. xii. 24; i. q. born again, ἄνθρωπος (q. v. 1 f.), Col. iii. 10. [SYN. see καινός, fin.]*

3502 **νεοσσός** and (so T WH, see νοσσιά) νοσσός, -οῦ, ὁ, (νέος), *a young* (creature), *young bird*: Lk. ii. 24. The form νοσσός appears in the Vat. txt. of the Sept.; but in cod. Alex. everywhere νεοσσός; cf. Sturz, De dial. Maced. p. 185 sq.; Lob. ad Phryn. p. 206 sq.; [cf. W. 24]. (In Grk. writ. fr. Hom. down; Sept. often for בֵּן, of the young of animals, as Lev. xii. 6, 8; Job xxxviii. 41.)*

3503 **νεότης, -ητος, ἡ,** (νέος), fr. Hom. down; Sept. chiefly for נְעוּרִים; *youth, youthful age*: 1 Tim. iv. 12; ἐκ νεότητός μου, from my boyhood, from my youth, Mt. xix. 20 [R G]; Mk. x. 20; Lk. xviii. 21; Acts xxvi. 4; Gen. viii. 21; Job xxxi. 18, etc.*

3504 **νεό-φυτος, -ον,** (νέος and φύω), *newly-planted* (Job xiv.

9; Is. v. 7, etc.); trop. *a new convert, neophyte*, [A. V. *novice*, i. e.] (one who has recently become a Christian): 1 Tim. iii. 6. (Eccles. writ.)*

3505 **Νέρων** [by etymol. 'brave', 'bold'], -ωνος, ὁ, *Nero*, the well-known Roman emperor: 2 Tim. iv. 23 Rec. [i. e. in the subscription].*

3506 **νεύω**; 1 aor. ptcp. νεύσας; *to give a nod; to signify by a nod*, [A. V. *to beckon*]: τινί, foll. by an inf. of what one wishes to be done, Jn. xiii. 24; Acts xxiv. 10. (From Hom. down; Sept. Prov. iv. 25.) [COMP.: δια-, ἐκ-, ἐν-, ἐπι-, κατα-νεύω.]*

3507 **νεφέλη, -ης, ἡ,** (νέφος), [fr. Hom. down], Sept. esp. for עָנָן, but also for עָב and שַׁחַק; *a cloud*: [ν. φωτεινή, Mt. xvii. 5]; Mt. xxiv. 30; xxvi. 64; Mk. ix. 7; xiii. 26; xiv. 62; Lk. ix. 34 sq.; xii. 54; xxi. 27; Acts i. 9; 1 Th. iv. 17; 2 Pet. ii. 17 [Rec.]; Jude 12; Rev. i. 7; x. 1; xi. 12; xiv. 14 sqq.; of that cloud in which Jehovah is said (Ex. xiii. 21 sq., etc.) to have gone before the Israelites on their march through the wilderness, and which Paul represents as spread over them (ὑπὸ τὴν νεφέλην ἦσαν, cf. Ps. civ. (cv.) 39; Sap. x. 17): 1 Co. x. 1 sq. [SYN. see νέφος.]*

3508 **Νεφθαλείμ** [and (so T edd. 2, 7, WH in Rev. vii. 6) Νεφθαλίμ; see WH. App. p. 155, and s. v. I, ι], ὁ, (נַפְתָּלִי, i. e. 'my wrestling' [cf. Gen. xxx. 8], or acc. to what seems to be a more correct interpretation 'my craftiness' [cf. Joseph. antt. 1, 19, 8; Test. xii. Patr. test. Neph. § 1], fr. פָּתַל unused in Kal; cf. Rüetschi in Herzog x. p. 200 sq.), *Naphtali*, the sixth son of the patriarch Jacob, by Bilhah, Rachel's maid: Rev. vii. 6; by meton. his posterity, the tribe of Naphtali, Mt. iv. 13, 15.*

3509 **νέφος, -ους,** [allied with Lat. *nubes*, *nebula*, etc.], τό, Sept. for עָב and עָנָן, *a cloud*; in the N. T. once trop. *a large, dense multitude, a throng*: μαρτύρων, Heb. xii. 1; often so in prof. auth., as νέφ. Τρώων, πεζῶν, ψαρῶν, κολοιῶν, Hom. Il. 4, 274; 16, 66; 17, 755; 23, 133; ἀνθρώπων, Hdt. 8, 109; στρουθῶν, Arstph. av. 578; ἀκρίδων, Diod. 3, 29; peditum equitumque nubes, Liv. 35, 49.*

[SYN. νέφος, νεφέλη: νέφος is general, νεφέλη specific; the former denotes the great, shapeless collection of vapor obscuring the heavens; the latter designates particular and definite masses of the same, suggesting form and limit. Cf. Schmidt vol. i. ch. 36.]

3510 **νεφρός, -οῦ, ὁ,** *a kidney* (Plat., Arstph.); plur. *the kidneys, the loins*, as Sept. for כְּלָיוֹת, used of the inmost thoughts, feelings, purposes, of the soul: with the addition of καρδίας, Rev. ii. 23, with which cf. Ps. vii. 10; Jer. xi. 20; xvii. 10; Sap. i. 6.*

3511 **νεω-κόρος, -ου, ὁ, ἡ,** (νεώς or ναός, and κορέω to sweep; [questioned by some; a hint of this deriv. is found in Philo de sacerd. honor. § 6 (cf. νεωκορία, de somniis 2, 42), and Hesych. s. v. defines the word ὁ τὸν ναὸν κοσμῶν· κορεῖν γὰρ τὸ σαίρειν ἔλεγον (cf. s. v. σηκοκόρος; so Etym. Magn. 407, 27, cf. s. v. νεωκόρος); yet Suidas s. v. κόρη p. 2157 c. says ν. οὐχ ὁ σαρῶν τ. ν. ἀλλ' ὁ ἐπιμελούμενος αὐτοῦ (cf. s. vv. νεωκόρος, σηκοκόρος); hence some connect the last half with root κορ, κολ, cf. Lat. *curo, colo*]); **1.** prop. *one who sweeps and cleans a temple.* **2.** *one* who has charge of a temple, to keep and adorn it, a sacristan : Xen. an. 5, 3, 6 ; Plat. legg. 6 p. 759 a.   **3.** the worshipper of a deity (οὓς i. e. the Israelites ὁ θεὸς ἑαυτῷ νεωκόρους ἦγεν through the wilderness, Joseph. b. j. 5, 9, 4) ; as appears from coins still extant, it was an honorary title [temple-keeper or temple-warden (cf. 2 above)] of certain cities, esp. of Asia Minor, in which the special worship of some deity or even of some deified human ruler had been established (cf. Stephanus, Thes. v. p. 1472 sq. ; [cf. B. D. s. v. worshipper]) ; so ν. τῆς Ἀρτέμιδος, of Ephesus, Acts xix. 35 ; [see Bp. Lghtft. in Contemp. Rev. for 1878, p. 294 sq. ; Wood, Discoveries at Ephesus (Lond. 1877), App. passim].*

3512   **νεωτερικός, -ή, -όν,** (νεώτερος, q. v.), peculiar to the age of youth, youthful : ἐπιθυμίαι, 2 Tim. ii. 22. (3 Macc. iv. 8 ; Polyb. 10, 24, 7 ; Joseph. antt. 16, 11, 8.) *

see 3501   **νεώτερος, -α, -ον,** (compar. of νέος, q. v.), [fr. Hom. down], younger ; i. e.   **a.** younger (than now), Jn. xxi. 18.   **b.** young, youthful, [A. V. younger (relatively)] : 1 Tim. v. 11, 14 ; Tit. ii. 6 ; opp. to πρεσβύτεροι, 1 Tim. v. 1 sq. ; 1 Pet. v. 5.   **c.** [strictly] younger by birth : Lk. xv. 12 sq. (4 Macc. xii. 1).   **d.** an attendant, servant, (see νεανίσκος, fin.) : Acts v. 6 ; inferior in rank, opp. to ὁ μείζων, Lk. xxii. 26.*

3513   **νή,** a particle employed in affirmations and oaths, (common in Attic), and joined to an acc. of the pers. (for the most part, a divinity) or of the thing affirmed or sworn by [B. § 149, 17] ; by (Lat. per, Germ. bei) : 1 Co. xv. 31 (Gen. xlii. 15 sq.).*

3514   **νήθω** ; to spin : Mt. vi. 28 ; Lk. xii. 27. (Plat. polit. p. 289 c. ; Anthol. ; for טָוָה, Ex. xxxv. 25 sq.) *

3515   **νηπιάζω** [cf. W. 92 (87)] ; (νήπιος, q. v.) ; to be a babe (infant) : 1 Co. xiv. 20. (Hippocr. ; eccles. writ.) *

3516   **νήπιος, -α, -ον,** (fr. νη, an insep. neg. prefix [Lat. nefas, ne-quam, ni-si, etc. cf. Curtius § 437], and ἔπος) ; as in Grk. writers fr. Hom. down,   **a.** an infant, little child : Mt. xxi. 16 (fr. Ps. viii. 3) ; 1 Co. xiii. 11 ; Sept. esp. for עוֹלֵל and עוֹלָל.   **b.** a minor, not of age : Gal. iv. 1 [cf. Bp. Lghtft. ad loc.].   **c.** metaph. childish, untaught, unskilled, (Sept. for פֶּתִי, Ps. xviii. (xix.) 8 ; cxviii. (cxix.) 130 ; Prov. i. 32) : Mt. xi. 25 ; Lk. x. 21 ; Ro. ii. 20 ; Gal. iv. 3 ; Eph. iv. 14 ; opp. to τέλειοι, the more advanced in understanding and knowledge, Heb. v. 13 sq. (Philo de agric. § 2) ; νήπ. ἐν Χριστῷ, in things pertaining to Christ, 1 Co. iii. 1.   In 1 Th. ii. 7 L WH [cf. the latter's note ad loc.] have hastily received νήπιοι for the common reading ἤπιοι.*

3517   **Νηρεύς** [(cf. Vaniček p. 1158)], -έως, ὁ, Nereus, a Christian who lived at Rome : Ro. xvi. 15 [where L mrg. Νηρέαν].*

3518   **Νηρί** and (so T Tr WH) Νηρεί [see ει, ι], ὁ, (fr. נֵר a lamp), Neri, the grandfather of Zerubbabel : Lk. iii. 27.*

3519   **νησίον, -ου, τό,** (dimin. of νῆσος), a small island : Acts xxvii. 16 [(Strabo)].*

3520   **νῆσος, -ου, ἡ,** (νέω to swim, prop. ʻfloating land'), an island : Acts xiii. 6 ; xxvii. 26 ; xxviii. 1, 7, 9, 11 ; Rev. i. 9 ; vi. 14 ; xvi. 20. (Sept. for אִי ; [fr. Hom. down].) *

3521   **νηστεία, -ας, ἡ,** (νηστεύω, q. v.), a fasting, fast, i. e. abstinence from food, and   **a.** voluntary, as a religious exercise : of private fasting, Mt. xvii. 21 [T WH om. Tr br. the vs.] ; Mk. ix. 29 [T WH om. Tr mrg. br.] ; Lk. ii. 37 ; Acts xiv. 23 ; 1 Co. vii. 5 Rec. of the public fast prescribed by the Mosaic Law (Lev. xvi. 29 sqq. ; xxiii. 27 sqq. [BB.DD. s. v. Fasts, and for reff. to Strab., Philo, Joseph., Plut., see Soph. Lex. s. v. 1]) and kept yearly on the great day of atonement, the tenth of the month Tisri : Acts xxvii. 9 (the month Tisri comprises a part of our September and October [cf. B.D. s. v. month (at end)] ; the fast, accordingly, occurred in the autumn, ἡ χειμέριος ὥρα, when navigation was usually dangerous on account of storms, as was the case with the voyage referred to).   **b.** a fasting to which one is driven by want : 2 Co. vi. 5 ; xi. 27 ; (Hippocr., Aristot., Philo, Joseph., Plut., Ael., Athen., al. ; Sept. for צוֹם).*

3522   **νηστεύω** ; fut. νηστεύσω ; 1 aor. [inf. νηστεῦσαι (Lk. v. 34 T WH Tr txt.)], ptcp. νηστεύσας ; (fr. νῆστις, q. v.) ; to fast (Vulg. and eccles. writ. jejuno), i. e. to abstain as a religious exercise from food and drink : either entirely, if the fast lasted but a single day, Mt. vi. 16–18 ; ix. 14 sq. ; Mk. ii. 18–20 ; Lk. v. 33, [34, 35] ; xviii. 12 ; Acts x. 30 R G ; xiii. 2, [3] ; or from customary and choice nourishment, if it continued several days, Mt. iv. 2, cf. xi. 18 ; νηστεύει συνεχῶς καὶ ἄρτον ἐσθίει μόνον μετὰ ἅλατος καὶ τὸ ποτὸν αὐτοῦ ὕδωρ, Acta Thom. § 20. (Arstph., Plut. mor. p. 626 sq. ; Ael. v. h. 5, 20 ; [Joseph. c. Ap. 1, 34, 5 (where see Müller)] ; Sept. for צום.) *

3523   **νῆστις,** acc. plur. νήστεις and (so Tdf. [cf. Proleg. p. 118]) νήστις (see Lob. ad Phryn. p. 326 ; Fritzsche, Com. on Mk. p. 796 sq. ; cf. [WH. App. p. 157ᵇ] ; B. 26 (23)), ὁ, ἡ, (fr. νη and ἐσθίω, see νήπιος), fasting, not having eaten : Mt. xv. 32 ; Mk. viii. 3. (Hom., Aeschyl., Hippocr., Arstph., al.) *

3524   **νηφάλεος** (so Rec.ˢᵗ in 1 Tim. iii. 2, 11, [where Rec.ᵇᵉˢ -λαιος], after a later form) and νηφάλιος [" alone well attested " (Hort)], -ον, (in Grk. auth. generally of three term. ; fr. νήφω), sober, temperate ; abstaining from wine, either entirely (Joseph. antt. 3, 12, 2) or at least from its immoderate use : 1 Tim. iii. 2, 11 ; Tit. ii. 2.   (In prof. auth., esp. Aeschyl. and Plut., of things free from all infusion or addition of wine, as vessels, offerings, etc.) *

3525   **νήφω** ; 1 aor. impv. 2 pers. plur. νήψατε ; fr. Theogn., Soph., Xen. down ; to be sober ; in the N. T. everywh. trop. to be calm and collected in spirit ; to be temperate, dispassionate, circumspect : 1 Th. v. 6, 8 ; 2 Tim. iv. 5 ; 1 Pet. i. 13 ; v. 8 ; εἰς τὰς προσευχάς, unto (the offering of) prayer, 1 Pet. iv. 7. [Syn. see ἀγρυπνέω ; and on the word see Ellic. on Tim. l. c. Comp. : ἀνα-, ἐκ-νήφω.]*

3526   **Νίγερ, ὁ,** (a Lat. name [ʻ black ']), Niger, surname of the prophet Symeon : Acts xiii. 1.*

3527   **Νικάνωρ,** [(i. e. ʻ conqueror ')], -ορος, ὁ, Nicanor, of Antioch [?], one of the seven deacons of the church at Jerusalem : Acts vi. 5.*

3528   **νικάω, -ῶ** ; pres. ptcp. dat. νικοῦντι, Rev. ii. 7 Lchm. 17 L T Tr, [yet all νικῶντας in xv. 2] (cf. ἐρωτάω, init.) ; fut. νικήσω ; 1 aor. ἐνίκησα ; pf. νενίκηκα ; (νίκη) ; [fr. Hom. down] ; to conquer [A. V. overcome] ;   **a.** absol. to carry off the victory, come off victorious: of Christ, victorious over all his foes, Rev. iii. 21; vi. 2; ἐνίκησεν … ἀνοῖξαι κτλ. hath so conquered that he now has the right and power to open etc. Rev. v. 5; of Christians, that hold fast their faith even unto death against the power of their foes, and their temptations and persecutions, Rev. ii. 7, 11, 17, 26; iii. 5, 12, 21; xxi. 7; w. ἐκ τοῦ θηρίου added, to conquer and thereby free themselves from the power of the beast [R. V. to come victorious from; cf. W. 367 (344 sq.); B. 147 (128)], Rev. xv. 2. when one is arraigned or goes to law, to win the case, maintain one's cause, (so in the Attic orators; also νικᾶν δίκην, Eur. El. 955): Ro. iii. 4 (from Sept. of Ps. l. (li.) 6).   b. with acc. of the obj.: τινά, by force, Lk. xi. 22; Rev. xi. 7; xiii. 7 [L om. WH Tr mrg. br. the cl.]; of Christ the conqueror of his foes, Rev. xvii. 14; τὸν κόσμον, to deprive it of power to harm, to subvert its influence, Jn. xvi. 33; νικᾶν τινα or τι is used of one who by Christian constancy and courage keeps himself unharmed and spotless from his adversary's devices, solicitations, assaults: the devil, 1 Jn. ii. 13 sq.; Rev. xii. 11; false teachers, 1 Jn. iv. 4; τὸν κόσμον, ibid. v. 4 sq. νικᾶν τὸ πονηρὸν ἐν τῷ ἀγαθῷ, by the force which resides in goodness, i. e. in kindness, to cause an enemy to repent of the wrong he has done one, Ro. xii. 21; νικᾶσθαι ὑπὸ τοῦ κακοῦ, to be disturbed by an injury and driven to avenge it, ibid. [COMP.: ὑπερ-νικάω.] *

3529   νίκη, -ης, ἡ, [fr. Hom. down], victory: 1 Jn. v. 4 [cf. νῖκος].*

3530   Νικόδημος, (νίκη and δῆμος [i. e. 'conqueror of the people']), -ου, ὁ, Nicodemus, (rabbin. נקְדִּימוֹן), a member of the Sanhedrin who took the part of Jesus: Jn. iii. 1, 4, 9; vii. 50; xix. 39.*

3531   Νικολαΐτης, -ου, ὁ, a follower of Nicolaus, a Nicola'itan: plur., Rev. ii. 6, 15, — a name which, it can scarcely be doubted, refers symbolically to the same persons who in vs. 14 are charged with holding τὴν διδαχὴν Βαλαάμ, i. e. after the example of Balaam, casting a stumbling-block before the church of God (Num. xxiv. 1–3) by upholding the liberty of eating things sacrificed unto idols as well as of committing fornication; for the Grk. name Νικόλαος coincides with the Hebr. בִּלְעָם acc. to the interpretation of the latter which regards it as signifying destruction of the people. See in Βαλαάμ; [cf. BB.DD. s. vv. Nicolaitans, Nicolas; also Comm. on Rev. ll. cc.].*

3532   Νικόλαος, -ου, ὁ, (νίκη and λαός), Nicolaus [A. V. Nicolas], a proselyte of Antioch and one of the seven deacons of the church at Jerusalem: Acts vi. 5.*

3533   Νικόπολις, -εως, ἡ, (city of victory), Nicopolis: Tit. iii. 12. There were many cities of this name — in Armenia, Pontus, Cilicia, Epirus, Thrace — which were generally built, or had their name changed, by some conqueror to commemorate a victory. The one mentioned above seems to be that which Augustus founded on the promontory of Epirus, in grateful commemoration of the victory he won at Actium over Antony. The author of the spurious subscription of the Epistle seems to have had in mind the Thracian Nicopolis, founded by Trajan [(?) cf. Pape, Eigennamen, s. v.] on the river Nestus (or

Nessus), since he calls it a city 'of Macedonia.' [B. D. s. v.] *

3534   νῖκος, -ους, τό, a later form i. q. νίκη (cf. Lob. ad Phryn. p. 647; [B. 23 (20); W. 24]), victory: 1 Co. xv. 55, 57, (2 Macc. x. 38; [1 Esdr. iii. 9]); εἰς νῖκος, until he have gained the victory, Mt. xii. 20; κατεπόθη ὁ θάνατος εἰς νῖκος, [A. V. death is swallowed up in victory] i. e. utterly vanquished, 1 Co. xv. 54. (The Sept. sometimes translate the Hebr. לָנֶצַח i. e. to everlasting, forever, by εἰς νῖκος, 2 S. ii. 26; Job xxxvi. 7; Lam. v. 20; Am. i. 11; viii. 7, because נֶצַח denotes also splendor, 1 Chr. xxix. 11, and in Syriac victory.) *

3535   Νινευΐ, ἡ, Hebr. נִינְוֵה (supposed to be compounded of נִין and נֶוֶה, the abode of Ninus; [cf. Fried. Delitzsch as below; Schrader as below, pp. 102, 572]), in the Grk. and Rom. writ. ἡ Νῖνος [on the accent cf. Pape, Eigennamen, s. v.], Nineveh (Vulg. Ninive [so A. V. in Lk. as below]), a great city, the capital of Assyria, built apparently about B. C. 2000, on the eastern bank of the Tigris opposite the modern city of Mosul. It was destroyed [about] B. C. 606, and its ruins, containing invaluable monuments of art and archaeology, began to be excavated in recent times (from 1840 on), especially by the labors of the Frenchman Botta and the Englishman Layard; cf. Layard, Nineveh and its Remains, Lond. 1849, 2 vols.; and his Discoveries in the Ruins of Nineveh and Babylon, Lond. 1853; [also his art. in Smith's Dict. of the Bible]; H. J. C. Weissenborn, Ninive u. s. Gebiet etc. 2 Pts. Erf. 1851–56; Tuch, De Nino urbe, Lips. 1844; Spiegel in Herzog x. pp. 361–381; [esp. Fried. Delitzsch in Herzog 2 (cf. Schaff-Herzog) x. pp. 587–603; Schrader, Keilinschriften u. s. w. index s. v.; and in Riehm s. v.; W. Robertson Smith in Encyc. Brit. s. v.]; Hitzig in Schenkel iv. 334 sqq.; [Rawlinson, Five Great Monarchies etc.; Geo. Smith, Assyrian Discoveries, (Lond. 1875)]. In the N. T. once, viz. Lk. xi. 32 R G.*

3536   [Νινευΐτης R G (so Tr in Lk. xi. 32), or] Νινευΐτης [L (so Tr in Lk. xi. 30)] or Νινευ είτης T WH (so Tr in Mt. xii. 41) [see ει, ι and Tdf. Proleg. p. 86; WH. App. p. 154ᵇ], -ου, ὁ, (Νινευΐ, q. v.), i. q. Νίνιος in Hdt. and Strabo; a Ninevite, an inhabitant of Nineveh: Mt. xii. 41; Lk. xi. 30, and L T Tr WH in 32.*

3537   νιπτήρ, -ῆρος, ὁ, (νίπτω), a vessel for washing the hands and feet, a basin: Jn. xiii. 5. (Eccles. writ.) *

3538   νίπτω; (a later form for νίζω; cf. Lob. ad Phryn. p. 241 [Veitch s. v. νίζω; B. 63 (55); W. 88 (84)]); 1 aor. ἔνιψα; Mid., pres. νίπτομαι; 1 aor. ἐνιψάμην; Sept. for רָחַץ; to wash: τινά, Jn. xiii. 8; τοὺς πόδας τινός, ibid. 5 sq. 8, 12, 14; 1 Tim. v. 10; mid. to wash one's self [cf. B. § 135, 5; W. § 38, 2 b.]: Jn. ix. 7, 11, 15; τὰς χεῖρας, to wash one's (own) hands, Mk. vii. 3; τοὺς πόδας, Jn. xiii. 10 [T om. WH br. τοὺς π.]; νίψαι τὸ πρόσωπόν σου, Mt. vi. 17; νίπτονται τὰς χεῖρας αὐτῶν, Mt. xv. 2. [COMP.: ἀπο-νίπτω. SYN. see λούω, fin.] *

see 3539 St.   νοέω, -ῶ; 1 aor. ἐνόησα; [pres. pass. ptcp. (neut. plur.) νοούμενα]; (νοῦς); fr. Hom. down; Sept. for הֵבִין and הָבִין, and for הִשְׂכִּיל; **1.** to perceive with the mind, to understand: absol., with the addition τῇ καρδίᾳ, Jn. xii.

40 (Is. xliv. 18); w. an acc. of the thing, Eph. iii. 4, 20; 1 Tim. i. 7; pass.: Ro. i. 20; foll. by ὅτι, Mt. xv. 17; xvi. 11; Mk. vii. 18; foll. by acc. w. inf., Heb. xi. 3; absol. i. q. *to have understanding*: Mt. xvi. 9; Mk. viii. 17. **2.** *to think upon, heed, ponder, consider*: νοείτω, sc. let him attend to the events that occur, which will show the time to flee, Mt. xxiv. 15; Mk. xiii. 14; [similarly νόει ὃ (R G ἅ) λέγω, 2 Tim. ii. 7]. [COMP.: εὐ-, κατα-, μετα-, προ-, ὑπο-νοέω.]*

3540   **νόημα**, -τος, τό, fr. Hom. down; **1.** *a mental perception, thought.* **2.** spec. (an evil) *purpose*: αἰχμαλωτίζειν πᾶν νόημα εἰς τὴν ὑπακοὴν τοῦ Χριστοῦ, to cause whoever is devising evil against Christ to desist from his purpose and submit himself to Christ (as Paul sets him forth), 2 Co. x. 5; plur.: 2 Co. ii. 11 (τοῦ διαβόλου, Ignat. ad Eph. [interpol.] 14; τῆς καρδίας αὐτῶν πονηρᾶς, Bar. ii. 8). **3.** that which thinks, *the mind*: plur. (where the minds of many are referred to), 2 Co. iii. 14; iv. 4, and perh. [xi. 3]; Phil. iv. 7, for here the word may mean thoughts and purposes; [others would so take it also in all the exx. cited under this head (cf. καύχημα, 2)].*

3541   **νόθος**, -η, -ον, *illegitimate, bastard*, i. e. born, not in lawful wedlock, but of a concubine or female slave: Heb. xii. 8; cf. Bleek ad loc. (Sap. iv. 3; from Hom. down.)*

3542   **νομή**, -ῆς, ἡ, (νέμω to pasture), fr. Hom. [i. e. batrach.] down; **1.** *pasturage, fodder, food*: in fig. discourse εὑρήσει νομήν, i. e. he shall not want the needful supplies for the true life, Jn. x. 9; (Sept. for מִרְעִית, מִרְעֶה, נָוֶה). **2.** trop. *growth, increase*, (Germ. *Umsichfressen, Umsichgreifen*): of evils spreading like a gangrene, 2 Tim. ii. 17 (of ulcers, νομὴν ποιεῖται ἕλκος, Polyb. 1, 81, 6; of a conflagration, τὸ πῦρ λαμβάνει νομήν, 11, 4 (5), 4 cf. 1, 48, 5; Joseph. b. j. 6, 2, 9).*

3543   **νομίζω**, impf. ἐνόμιζον; 1 aor. ἐνόμισα; impf. pass. ἐνομιζόμην; (νόμος); as in Grk. auth. fr. Aeschyl. and Hdt. down; **1.** *to hold by custom or usage, own as a custom or usage; to follow custom or usage*; pass. νομίζεται *it is the custom, it is the received usage*: οὗ ἐνομίζετο προσευχὴ εἶναι, where acc. to custom was a place of prayer, Acts xvi. 13 [but L T Tr WH read οὗ ἐνομίζομεν προσευχὴν εἶν. *where we supposed there was*, etc.; cf. 2 below], (2 Macc. xiv. 4). **2.** *to deem, think, suppose*: foll. by an inf., Acts viii. 20; 1 Co. 36; foll. by an acc. w. inf., Lk. ii. 44; Acts vii. 25; xiv. 19; xvi. [13 (see 1 above)], 27; xvii. 29; 1 Co. vii. 26; 1 Tim. vi. 5; foll. by ὅτι, Mt. v. 17; x. 34 [W. § 56, 1 b.]; xx. 10; Acts xxi. 29; ὡς ἐνομίζετο, as was wont to be supposed, Lk. iii. 23. [SYN. see ἡγέομαι, fin.]*

3544   **νομικός**, -ή, -όν, (νόμος), *pertaining to* (the) *law* (Plat., Aristot., al.): μάχαι, Tit. iii. 9; ὁ νομικός, one learned in the law, in the N. T. an interpreter and teacher of the Mosaic law [A. V. *a lawyer*; cf. γραμματεύς, 2]: Mt. xxii. 35; Lk. x. 25; Tit. iii. 13; plur., Lk. vii. 30; xi. 45 sq. 52; xiv. 3.*

3545   **νομίμως**, adv., (νόμιμος), *lawfully, agreeably to the law, properly*: 1 Tim. i. 8; 2 Tim. ii. 5. (Thuc., Xen., Plat., al.)*

3546   **νόμισμα**, -τος, τό, (νομίζω, q. v.); **1.** *anything received and sanctioned by usage or law* (Tragg., Arstph.). **2.** *money*, (current) *coin*, [cf. our *lawful* money]: Mt. xxii. 19 (and in Grk. writ. fr. Eur. and Arstph. down).*

νομο-διδάσκαλος, -ου, ὁ, (νόμος and διδάσκαλος, cf. ἑτεροδιδάσκαλος, ἱεροδιδάσκαλος, χοροδιδάσκαλος), *a teacher and interpreter of the law*: among the Jews [cf. γραμματεύς, 2], Lk. v. 17; Acts v. 34; of those who among Christians also went about as champions and interpreters of the Mosaic law, 1 Tim. i. 7. (Not found elsewh. [exc. in eccl. writ.])*   **3547**

νομοθεσία, -ας, ἡ, (νόμος, τίθημι), *law-giving, legislation*: Ro. ix. 4. (Plat., Aristot., Polyb., Diod., Philo, al.)*   **3548**

νομοθετέω, -ῶ: Pass., pf. 3 pers. sing. νενομοθέτηται; plupf. 3 pers. sing. νενομοθέτητο (on the om. of the augm. see W. 72 (70); B. 33 (29)); (νομοθέτης); fr. [Lys.], Xen. and Plat. down; Sept. several times for הוֹרָה; **1.** *to enact laws*; pass. *laws are enacted or prescribed for one, to be legislated for, furnished with laws* (often so in Plato; cf. *Ast*, Lex. Plat. ii. p. 391 [for exx.]); ὁ λαὸς ἐπ᾽ αὐτῆς (R G ἐπ᾽ αὐτῇ) νενομοθέτηται (R G νενομοθέτητο) the people received the Mosaic law established upon the foundation of the priesthood, Heb. vii. 11 [W. § 39, 1 b.; cf. B. 337 (290); many refer this ex. (with the gen.) to time (A. V. *under it*); see ἐπί, A. II., cf. B. 2 a. γ.]. **2.** *to sanction by law, enact*: τί, pass. Heb. viii. 6 [cf. W. and B. u. s.].*   **3549**

νομο-θέτης, -ου, ὁ, (νόμος and τίθημι), *a lawgiver*: Jas. iv. 12. ([Antipho, Thuc.], Xen., Plat., Dem., Joseph., al.; Sept. Ps. ix. 21.)*   **3550**

νόμος, -ου, ὁ, (νέμω to divide, distribute, apportion), in prof. auth. fr. Hes. down, *anything established, anything received by usage, a custom, usage, law*; in Sept. very often for תּוֹרָה, also for חֻקָּה, דָּת, etc. In the N. T. *a command, law*; and **1.** of *any law whatsoever*: διὰ ποίου νόμου; Ro. iii. 27; νόμος δικαιοσύνης, a law or rule producing a state approved of God, i. e. by the observance of which we are approved of God, Ro. ix. 31, cf. Meyer [see ed. *Weiss*], Fritzsche, Philippi ad loc.; *a precept or injunction*: κατὰ νόμον ἐντολῆς σαρκ. Heb. vii. 16; plur. of the things prescribed by the divine will, Heb. viii. 10; x. 16; νόμος τοῦ νοός, the rule of action prescribed by reason, Ro. vii. 23; the mention of the divine law causes those things even which in opposition to this law impel to action, and therefore seem to have the force of a law, to be designated by the term νόμος, as ἕτερος νόμος ἐν τοῖς μέλεσί μου, a different law from that which God has given, i. e. the impulse to sin inherent in human nature, and ὁ νόμος τῆς ἁμαρτίας (gen. of author), Ro. vii. 23, 25; viii. 2, also ὁ ν. τοῦ θανάτου, emanating from the power of death, Ro. viii. 2; with which is contrasted ὁ νόμος τοῦ πνεύματος, the impulse to (right) action emanating from the Spirit, ibid. **2.** of *the Mosaic law*, and referring, acc. to the context, either to the volume of the law or to its contents: w. the article, Mt. v. 18; xii. 5; xxii. 36; Lk. ii. 27; x. 26; xvi. 17, 45 (46); vii. 51; viii. 17; x. 34; xv. 25; Acts vi. 13; vii. 53; xviii. 13, 15; xxi. 20; xxiii. 3; Ro. ii. 13 [(bis) here L T Tr WH om. art. (also G in 13b)], 15, 18, 20, 23b, 26; iv. 15a; vii. 1b, 5, 14,   **3551**

21 (on the right interpretation of this difficult passage cf. *Knapp*, Scripta varii Argumenti, ii. p. 385 sqq. and *Fritzsche*, Com. ad Rom. ii. p. 57; [others take νόμ. here generally, i. q. controlling principle; see 1 above sub fin. and cf. W. 557 (578); B. § 151, 15]); Ro. viii. 3 sq.; 1 Co. ix. 8; xv. 56; Gal. iii. 13, 24; Eph. ii. 15 (on which pass. see δόγμα, 2); 1 Tim. i. 8; Heb. vii. 19, 28; x. 1, etc.; with the addition of Μωϋσέως, Lk. ii. 22; Jn. vii. 23; viii. 5; Acts xiii. 38 (39) [here L T Tr WH om. art.]; xv. 5; xxviii. 23; 1 Co. ix. 9; of κυρίου, Lk. ii. 39; of τοῦ θεοῦ, [Mt. xv. 6 T WH mrg.]; Ro. vii. 22; viii. 7. **κατὰ τὸν νόμον**, acc. to the (standard or requirement of the) law, Acts xxii. 12; Heb. vii. 5; ix. 22. νόμος without the art. (in the Epp. of Paul and James and the Ep. to the Heb.; cf. W. p. 123 (117); B. 89 (78); [some interpreters contend that νόμος without the art. denotes not the law of Moses but law viewed as 'a principle', 'abstract and universal'; cf. Bp. Lghtft. on Gal. ii. 19; also "Fresh Revision," etc. p. 99; Vaughan on Ro. ii. 23; esp. Van Hengel on Ro. ii. 12; *Gifford* in the Speaker's Com. on Rom. p. 41 sqq. (cf. Cremer s. v.). This distinction is contrary to usage (as exhibited e. g. in Sap. xviii. 4; Sir. xix. 17; xxi. 11; xxxi. 8; xxxii. 1; xxxv. (xxxii.) 15, 24; xxxvi. (xxxiii.) 2, 3; 1 Macc. ii. 21; 4 Macc. vii. 7, and many other exx. in the Apocr.; see *Wahl*, Clavis Apocrr. s. v. p. 343), and to the context in such Pauline pass. as the foll.: Ro. ii. 17, 25, 27; vii. 1 (7); xiii. 8, 10; Gal. iii. 17, 18, 23, 24, (cf. Ro. ii. 12 and iii. 19; v. 13 and 14); etc. It should be added, perhaps, that neither the list of pass. with the art. nor of those without it, as given by Prof. Grimm, claims to be complete]): Ro. ii. 23ᵃ, 25; iii. 31; iv. 15ᵇ, v. 13; vii. 1ᵃ, 2ᵃ; x. 4; xiii. 10; Gal. iii. 21ᶜ; v. 23; 1 Tim. i. 9; Heb. vii. 12, etc.; with the addition of κυρίου, Lk. ii. 23 [here L has the art.], 24 [L T Tr WH add the art.]; of θεοῦ, Ro. vii. 25; of Μωϋσέως, Heb. x. 28; esp. after prepositions, as διὰ νόμου, Ro. ii. 12; iii. 20; Gal. ii. 21; χωρὶς νόμου, without the co-operation of the law, Ro. iii. 21; destitute or ignorant of the law, Ro. vii. 9; where no law has been promulged, Ro. vii. 8; οἱ ἐκ νόμου, those who rule their life by the law, Jews, Ro. iv. 14, 16 [here all edd. have the art.]; οἱ ἐν νόμῳ, who are in the power of the law, i. e. bound to it, Ro. iii. 19 [but all texts here ἐν τῷ ν.]; ὑπὸ νόμον, under dominion of the law, Ro. vi. 14 sq.; Gal. iii. 23; iv. 4, 21; v. 18; οἱ ὑπὸ νόμον, 1 Co. ix. 20; δικαιοῦσθαι ἐν νόμῳ, Gal. v. 4; ἔργα νόμου (see ἔργον, sub fin.); ἐν νόμῳ ἁμαρτάνειν, *under law* i. e. with knowledge of the law, Ro. ii. 12 (equiv. to ἔχοντες νόμου, cf. vs. 14); they to whom the Mosaic law has not been made known are said νόμον μὴ ἔχειν, ibid. 14; ἑαυτοῖς εἰσι νόμος, their natural knowledge of right takes the place of the Mosaic law, ibid.; νόμος ἔργων, the law demanding works, Ro. iii. 27; διὰ νόμου νόμῳ ἀπέθανον, by the law itself (when I became convinced that by keeping it I could not attain to salvation, cf. Ro. vii. 9–24) I became utterly estranged from the law, Gal. ii. 19 [cf. W. 210 (197); B. § 133, 12]. **κατὰ νόμον**, as respects the interpretation and observance of the law, Phil. iii. 5. The o b s e r v a n c e of the law is

designated by the foll. phrases: πληροῦν νόμον, Ro. xiii. 8; τὸν ν. Gal. v. 14; πληροῦν τὸ δικαίωμα τοῦ νόμου, Ro. viii. 4; φυλάσσειν (τὸν) ν., Acts xxi. 24; Gal. vi. 13; τὰ δικαιώμ. τοῦ ν. Ro. ii. 26; πράσσειν νόμον, Ro. ii. 25; ποιεῖν τὸν ν., Jn. vii. 19; Gal. v. 3; τηρεῖν, Acts xv. 5, 24 [Rec.]; Jas. ii. 10; τελεῖν, Ro. ii. 27 (cf. Jas. ii. 8) [on the other hand, ἀκυροῦν τὸν νόμ. Mt. xv. 6 T WH mrg.]. ὁ νόμος is used of some particular ordinance of the Mosaic law in Jn. xix. 7; Jas. ii. 8; with a gen. of the obj. added, τοῦ ἀνδρός, the law enacted respecting the husband, i. e. binding the wife to her husband, Ro. vii. 2 where Rec.ᵉˡᶻ om. τοῦ νόμ. (so ὁ νόμος τοῦ πάσχα, Num. ix. 12; τοῦ λεπροῦ, Lev. xiv. 2; other exx. are given in *Fritzsche*, Ep. ad Rom. ii. p. 9; cf. W. § 30, 2 β.). Although the Jews did not make a distinction as we do between the m o r a l, the c e r e m o n i a l, the c i v i l, precepts of the law, but thought that all should be honored and kept with the same conscientious and pious regard, yet in the N. T. not infrequently the law is so referred to as to show that the speaker or writer has his eye on the e t h i c a l part of it alone, as of primary importance and among Christians also of perpetual validity, but does not care for the ceremonial and civil portions, as being written for Jews alone: thus in Gal. v. 14; Ro. xiii. 8, 10; ii. 26 sq.; vii. 21, 25; Mt. v. 18, and often; τὰ τοῦ νόμου, the precepts, moral requirements, of the law, Ro. ii. 14. In the Ep. of James νόμος (without the article) designates only the ethical portion of the Mosaic law, confirmed by the authority of the Christian religion: ii. 9–11; iv. 11; in the Ep. to the Heb., on the other hand, the c e r e m o n i a l part of the law is the prominent idea. **3.** of *the C h r i s t i a n religion*: νόμος πίστεως, the law demanding faith, Ro. iii. 27; τοῦ Χριστοῦ, the moral instruction given by Christ, esp. the precept concerning love, Gal. vi. 2; τῆς ἐλευθερίας (see ἐλευθερία, a.), Jas. i. 25; ii. 12; cf. ὁ καινὸς νόμος τοῦ κυρίου ἡμῶν Ἰησοῦ Χριστοῦ, ἄνευ ζυγοῦ ἀνάγκης ὤν, Barn. ep. 2, 6 [see Harnack's note in loc.]. **4.** by metonymy ὁ νόμος, the name of the more important part (i. e. the Pentateuch), is put for *the entire collection of the sacred books of the O. T.*: Jn. vii. 49; x. 34 (Ps. lxxxi. (lxxxii.) 6); Jn. xii. 34 (Ps. cix. (cx.) 4; Dan. (Theodot.) ii. 44; vii. 14); Jn. xv. 25 (Ps. xxxiv. (xxxv.) 19; lxviii. (lxix.) 15); Ro. iii. 19; 1 Co. xiv. 21 (Is. xxviii. 11 sq.; so 2 Macc. ii. 18, where cf. Grimm); ὁ νόμος καὶ οἱ προφῆται, Mt. xi. 13; Jn. i. 46; Acts xiii. 15; xxiv. 14; xxviii. 23; Ro. iii. 21, (2 Macc. xv. 9); i. q. the system of morals taught in the O. T., Mt. v. 17; vii. 12; xxii. 40; ὁ νόμ. (οἱ) προφ. καὶ ψαλμοί, the religious dispensation contained in the O. T., Lk. xxiv. 44 (ὁ νόμος, οἱ προφ. κ. τὰ ἄλλα πάτρια βιβλία, prol. to Sir.). Paul's doctrine concerning ὁ νόμος is exhibited by (besides others) *Weiss*, Bibl. Theol. §§ 71, 72; *Pfleiderer*, Paulinismus, p. 69 sq. [Eng. trans. i. p. 68 sq.; *A. Zahn*, Das Gesetz Gottes nach d. Lehre u. Erfahrung d. Apostel Paulus, Halle 1876; *R. Tiling*, Die Paulinische Lehre vom νόμος nach d. vier Hauptbriefen, u.s.w. Dorpat, 1878]. νόμος does not occur in the foll. N. T. books: 2 Co., Col., Thess., 2 Tim., Pet., Jude, Jn., Rev.

νόος, see νοῦς.

(3551a); see 3563

3552 **νοσέω, -ῶ**; (νόσος); fr. [Aeschyl.], Hdt. down; *to be sick*; metaph. of any ailment of the **mind** (ἀνηκέστῳ πονηρίᾳ νοσεῖν Ἀθηναίους, Xen. mem. 3, 5, 18 and many c ther exx. in Grk. auth.): περί τι, to be taken with such **an** interest in a thing as amounts to a disease, to have a morbid fondness for, 1 Tim. vi. 4 (περὶ δόξαν, Plat. mor. p. 546 d.).*

3553 **νόσημα, -τος, τό**, *disease, sickness*: Jn. v. 4 Rec. Lchm. (Tragg., Arstph., Thuc., Xen., Plat., sqq.)*

3554 **νόσος, -ου, ἡ**, *disease, sickness*: Mt. iv. 23 sq.; viii. 17; ix. 35; x. 1; Mk. i. 34; iii. 15 [R G L]; Lk. iv. 40; vi. 18 (17); vii. 21; ix. 1; Acts xix. 12. (Deut. vii. 15; xxviii. 59; Ex. xv. 26, etc. [Hom., Hdt., al.]) *

3555 **νοσσιά, -ᾶς, ἡ**, (for νεοσσιά, the earlier and more common form [cf. WH. App. p. 145], fr. νεοσσός, q. v.), Sept. for קֵן; **1.** *a nest of birds*. **2.** *a brood of birds*: Lk. xiii. 34 [but L txt. νοσσία, see the foll. word]. (Deut. xxxii. 11 [Gen. vi. 14; Num. xxiv. 22; Prov. xvi. 16, etc.].) *

3556 **νοσσίον, -ου, τό**, (see νοσσιά), *a brood of birds*: Mt. xxiii. 37 and Lchm. txt. in Lk. xiii. 34 [where al. νοσσιά, see the preced. word]. (Arstph., Aristot., Ael.; for אֶפְרֹחִים Ps. lxxxiii. (lxxxiv.) 4.) *

see 3502 — **νοσσός**, see νεοσσός.

see 3557 St. **νοσφίζω**: Mid., pres. ptcp. νοσφιζόμενος; 1 aor. ἐνοσφισάμην; (νόσφι afar, apart); *to set apart, separate, divide*; mid. *to set apart* or *separate for one's self*, i. e. *to purloin, embezzle, withdraw covertly and appropriate to one's own use*: χρήματα, Xen. Cyr. 4, 2, 42; Plut. Lucull. 37; Aristid. 4; μηδὲν τῶν ἐκ τῆς διαρπαγῆς, Polyb. 10, 16, 6; χρυσώματα, 2 Macc. iv. 32; ἀλλότρια, Joseph. antt. 4, 8, 29; absol. Tit. ii. 10; (τὶ) ἀπό τινος, Acts v. 2, 3 [here A. V. keep back]; Sept. Josh. vii. 1; ἔκ τινος, Athen. 6 p. 234 a.*

3558 **νότος, -ου, ὁ**, *the south wind*; **a.** prop.: Lk. xii. 55; Acts xxvii. 13; xxviii. 13. **b.** *the South* (cf. βορρᾶς): Mt. xii. 42; Lk. xi. 31; xiii. 29; Rev. xxi. 13. (From Hom. down; Sept. chiefly for נֶגֶב, the southern quarter, the South; and for דָּרוֹם, the southern (both) wind and quarter; תֵּימָן, the same; קָדִים, the eastern (both) quarter and wind.) *

3559 **νουθεσία, -ας, ἡ**, (νουθετέω, q. v.); *admonition, exhortation*: Sap. xvi. 6; 1 Co. x. 11; Tit. iii. 10; κυρίου, such as belongs to the Lord (Christ) or proceeds from him, Eph. vi. 4 [cf. W. 189 (178)]. (Arstph. ran. 1009; Diod. 15, 7; besides in Philo, Joseph. and other recent writ. for νουθέτησις and νουθετία, forms more com. in the earlier writ. cf. Lob. ad Phryn. p. 512; [W. 24].) [Cf. Trench § xxxii.] *

3560 **νουθετέω, -ῶ**; (νουθέτης, and this fr. νοῦς and τίθημι; hence prop. i. q. ἐν τῷ νῷ τίθημι, lit. 'put in mind', Germ. 'an das Herz legen'); *to admonish, warn, exhort*: τινά, Acts xx. 31; Ro. xv. 14; 1 Co. iv. 14; Col. i. 28; iii. 16; 1 Th. v. 12, 14; 2 Th. iii. 15. ([1 S. iii. 13]; Job iv. 3; Sap. xi. 11; xii. 2; Tragg., Arstph., Xen., Plat., al.) *

3561 **νουμηνία**, and acc. to a rarer uncontr. form (cf. Lob. ad Phryn. p. 148 [Bp. Lghtft. on Col. as below; WH. App. p. 145]) **νεομηνία** (so L txt. Tr WH), **-ας, ἡ**, (νέος, μήν a month), *new-moon* (Vulg. neomenia; barbarous Lat. novilunium): of the Jewish festival of the new moon [BB.DD. s. v. New Moon], Col. ii. 16. (Sept. chiefly for חֹדֶשׁ; also for רֹאשׁ חֹדֶשׁ, Ex. xl. 2; and שׁ חֹדֶשׁ, Num. x. 10; xxviii. 11; see μήν, 2. Pind., Arstph., Thuc., Xen., al.) *

3562 **νουνεχῶς**, (νοῦς and ἔχω [cf. Lob. ad Phryn. p. 599]), adv. *wisely, prudently, discreetly*: Mk. xii. 34. ([Aristot. rhet. Alex. 30 p. 1436ᵇ, 33 νουνεχῶς κ. δικαίως]; Polyb. 1, 83, 3 νουνεχῶς κ. φρονίμως; [2, 13, 1]; 5, 88, 2 νουνεχῶς κ. πραγματικῶς; [al.].) *

3563 **νοῦς**, (contr. fr. νόος), ὁ, gen. νοός, dat. νοΐ, (so in later Grk. for the earlier forms νοῦ, νῷ, contr. fr. νόου, νόῳ; cf. Lob. ad Phryn. p. 453; W. § 8, 2 b; [B. 12 sq. (12)]), acc. νοῦν (contr. fr. νόον), Sept. for לֵב and לֵבָב, [fr. Hom. down]; *mind* (Germ. Sinn), i. e. **1.** *the mind*, comprising alike *the faculties of perceiving and understanding* and those of *feeling, judging, determining*; hence spec. **a.** *the intellective faculty, the understanding*: Lk. xxiv. 45 (on which see διανοίγω, 2); Phil. iv. 7; Rev. xiii. 18; xvii. 9; opp. to τὸ πνεῦμα, the spirit intensely roused and completely absorbed with divine things, but destitute of clear ideas of them, 1 Co. xiv. 14 sq. 19; ἔχειν τὸν νοῦν κυρίου [L txt., al. Χριστοῦ], to be furnished with the understanding of Christ, 1 Co. ii. 16ᵇ. **b.** *reason* (Germ. die Vernunft) in the narrower sense, as the capacity for spiritual truth, the higher powers of the soul, *the faculty of perceiving divine things, of recognizing goodness and of hating evil*: Ro. i. 28; vii. 23; Eph. iv. 17; 1 Tim. vi. 5; 2 Tim. iii. 8 [cf. W. 229 (215); B. § 134, 7]; Tit. i. 15; opp. to ἡ σάρξ, Ro. vii. 25; ἀνανεοῦσθαι τῷ πνεύματι τοῦ νοός, to be so changed that the spirit which governs the mind is renewed, Eph. iv. 23; [cf. ἡ ἀνακαίνωσις τοῦ νοός, Ro. xii. 2]. **c.** *the power of considering and judging soberly, calmly and impartially*: 2 Th. ii. 2. **2.** *a particular mode of thinking and judging*: Ro. xiv. 5; 1 Co. i. 10; i. q. *thoughts, feelings, purposes*: τοῦ κυρίου (fr. Is. xl. 13), Ro. xi. 34; 1 Co. ii. 16ᵃ; i. q. *desires, τῆς σαρκός*, Col. ii. 18 [cf. Meyer ad loc.].*

3564 **Νυμφᾶς, -ᾶ, ὁ**, [perh. contr. fr. Νυμφόδωρος; cf. W. 102 sq. (97); on accent cf. Chandler § 32], *Nymphas*, a Christian inhabitant of Laodicea: Col. iv. 15 [L WH Tr mrg. read Νύμφαν i. e. Nympha, the name of a woman; see esp. Bp. Lghtft. ad loc., and p. 256].*

3565 **νύμφη, -ης, ἡ**, (appar. allied w. Lat. nubo; Vaniček p. 429 sq.), Sept. for כַּלָּה; **1.** *a betrothed woman, a bride*: Jn. iii. 29; Rev. xviii. 23; xxi. 2, 9; xxii. 17. **2.** in the Grk. writ. fr. Hom. down, *a recently married woman, young wife*; *a young woman*; hence in bibl. and eccl. Grk., like the Hebr. כַּלָּה (which signifies both a bride and a daughter-in-law [cf. W. 32]), *a daughter-in-law*: Mt. x. 35; Lk. xii. 53. (Mic. vii. 6; Gen. xi. 31; [xxxviii. 11]; Ruth i. 6, [etc.]; also Joseph. antt. 5, 9, 1.) *

3566 **νυμφίος, -ου, ὁ**, (νύμφη), *a bridegroom*: Mt. ix. 15; xxv. 1, 5 sq. 10; Mk. ii. 19 sq.; Lk. v. 34 sq.; Jn. ii. 9; iii. 29; Rev. xviii. 23. (From Hom. down; Sept for חָתָן.) *

3567   **νυμφών, -ῶνος, ὁ,** (νύμφη), *the chamber containing the bridal bed, the bride-chamber*: οἱ υἱοὶ τοῦ νυμφῶνος (see υἱός, 2), of the friends of the bridegroom whose duty it was to provide and care for whatever pertained to the bridal chamber, i. e. whatever was needed for the due celebration of the nuptials: Mt. ix. 15; Mk. ii. 19; Lk. v. 34, ([W. 33 (32)]; Tob. vi. 13 (14), 16 (17)); eccles. writ.; Heliod. 7, 8); *the room in which the marriage cere-monies are held*: Mt. xxii. 10 T WH Tr mrg.*

3568   **νῦν, and νυνί** (which see in its place), adv. *now*, Lat. *nunc*, (Sept. for עַתָּה; [fr. Hom. down]); **1.** adv. of Time, *now*, i. e. *at the present time*; **a.** so used that by the thing which is now said to be or to be done the present time is opposed to past time: Jn. iv. 18; ix. 21; Acts xvi. 37; xxiii. 21; Ro. xiii. 11; 2 Th. ii. 6; 2 Co. vii. 9; xiii. 2; Phil. i. 30; ii. 12; iii. 18; Col. i. 24, etc.; freq. it denotes a somewhat extended portion of present time as opp. to a former state of things: Lk. xvi. 25; Acts vii. 4; Gal. i. 23; iii. 3; spec. the time since certain persons received the Christian religion, Ro. v. 9, 11; vi. 19, 21; viii. 1; Gal. ii. 20; iv. 29; 1 Pet. ii. 10, 25; or the time since man has had the blessing of the gospel, as opp. to past times, i. q. *in our times, our age*: Acts vii. 52; Ro. xvi. 26; 2 Co. vi. 2; Eph. iii. 5, 10; 2 Tim. i. 10; 1 Pet. i. 12; iii. 21, [cf. ep. ad Diogn. 1]. **b.** opp. to future time: Jn. xii. 27; xiii. 36 (opp. to ὕστερον); xvi. 22; Ro. xi. 31; 1 Co. xvi. 12; νῦν κ. εἰς πάντας τοὺς αἰῶνας, Jude 25; used to distinguish this present age, preceding Christ's return, from the age which follows that return: Lk. vi. 21, 25; Eph. ii. 2; Heb. ii. 8; 2 Pet. iii. 18; 1 Jn. ii. 28; with ἐν τῷ καιρῷ τούτῳ added, Mk. x. 30. **c.** Sometimes νῦν with the present is used of what will occur *forthwith* or *soon*, Lk. ii. 29; Jn. xii. 31; xvi. 5; xvii. 13; Acts xxvi. 17. with a preterite, of what has *just* been done, Mt. xxvi. 65; Jn. xxi. 10; or *very lately* (*but now, just now*, hyperbolically i. q. *a short time ago*), νῦν ἐζήτουν σε λιθάσαι οἱ Ἰουδαῖοι, Jn. xi. 8; cf. Kypke ad loc.; Vig. ed. *Herm.* p. 425 sq. with a future, of those future things which are thought of as already begun to be done, Jn. xii. 31; or of those which will be done *instantly*, Acts xiii. 11 [here al. supply ἐστί; W. § 64, 2 a.]; or *soon*, Acts xx. 22 [here πορ. merely has inherent fut. force; cf. B. § 137, 10 a.]. **d.** with the imperative it often marks the proper or fit time for doing a thing: Mt. xxvii. 42 sq.; Mk. xv. 32; Jn. ii. 8. Hence it serves to point an exhortation in ἄγε νῦν, *come now*: Jas. iv. 13; v. 1, (where it is more correctly written ἄγε νυν, cf. Passow ii. p. 372). **e.** with other particles, by which the contrast in time is marked more precisely: καὶ νῦν, *even now* (*now also*), Jn. xi. 22; Phil. i. 20; *and now*, Jn. xvii. 5; Acts vii. 34 [cf. 2 below]; x. 5 [W. § 43, 3 a.]; xx. 25; xxii. 16; ἀλλὰ νῦν, Lk. xxii. 36; ἀλλὰ καὶ νῦν, *but even now*, Jn. xi. 22 [T Tr txt. WH om. L Tr mrg. br. ἀλλά]; ἔτι νῦν, 1 Co. iii. 2 (3) [L WH br. ἔτι]; νῦν δέ (see νυνί below) *but now*, Jn. xvi. 5; xvii. 13; Heb. ii. 8; τότε ... νῦν δέ, Gal. iv. 9; Ro. vi. 21 sq. [here νυνὶ δέ]; Heb. xii. 26; ποτὲ ... νῦν δέ, Ro. xi. 30 [WH mrg. νυνί]; Eph. v. 8; 1 Pet. ii. 10; νῦν ἤδη, *now already*, 1 Jn. iv. 3.

νῦν οὖν, *now therefore*, Acts x. 33; xv. 10; xvi. 36; xxiii. 15, (Gen. xxvii. 8, 43; xxxi. 13, 30; xlv. 8; 1 Macc. x. 71). τὸ νῦν ἔχον, see ἔχω, II. b. **f.** with the article; **a.** w. neut. acc. absol. of the article, τὰ νῦν, *as respects the present*; *at present, now* (in which sense it is written also τανῦν [so Grsb. always, Rec. twice; classic edd. often τανύν; cf. Tdf. Proleg. p. 111; *Chandler*, Accent, § 826]): Acts iv. 29; xvii. 30; xx. 32; xxvii. 22, (2 Macc. xv. 8; often in class. Grk.; also τὸ νῦν, 1 Macc. vii. 35; ix. 9; cf. Krüger § 50, 5, 13; Bnhdy. p. 328; *Bttm.* Gram. § 125, 8 Anm. 8 (5)); *the things that now are, the present things*, Judith ix. 5; acc. absol. *as respects the things now taking place*, equiv. to *as respects the case in hand*, Acts v. 38. **β.** ὁ, ἡ, τὸ νῦν, *the present*, joined to substantives: as ὁ νῦν αἰών, 1 Tim. vi. 17; 2 Tim. iv. 10; Tit. ii. 12; καιρός, Ro. iii. 26; viii. 18; xi. 5; [2 Co. viii. 14 (13)]; ἡ νῦν Ἰερουσαλήμ, Gal. iv. 25; οἱ νῦν οὐρανοί, 2 Pet. iii. 7; μου τῆς πρὸς ὑμᾶς νῦν (or νυνί) ἀπολογίας, Acts xxii. 1. **γ.** τὸ νῦν with prepositions: ἀπὸ τοῦ νῦν (Sept. for מֵעַתָּה), *from this time onward*, [A. V. *from henceforth*], Lk. i. 48; v. 10; xii. 52; xxii. 69; Acts xviii. 6; 2 Co. v. 16; ἄχρι τοῦ νῦν, Ro. viii. 22; Phil. i. 5; ἕως τοῦ νῦν (Sept. for עַד עַתָּה), Mt. xxiv. 21; Mk. xiii. 19. **2.** Like our *now* and the Lat. *nunc*, it stands in a c o n c l u s i o n or s e q u e n c e; *as things now are, the matter now stands; under these circumstances; in the present state of affairs; since these things are so; as it is*: Lk. xi. 39 (νῦν i. e. since ye are intent on observing the requirements of tradition; [but al. take νῦν here of t i m e — a covert allusion to a former and better state of things]); Col. i. 24 [al. of time; cf. Mey., Bp. Lghtft., Ellic. ad loc.]; καὶ νῦν, 1 Jn. ii. 28; 2 Jn. 5; καὶ νῦν δεῦρο, Acts vii. 34. νῦν δέ (and νυνὶ δέ see νυνί), *but now; now however; but as it is*; (often in class. Grk.; cf. Vig. ed. *Herm.* p. 426; Matthiae ii. p. 1434 sq.; Kühner § 498, 2 [or Jelf § 719, 2]): 1 Co. vii. 14; Jas. iv. 16, and R G in Heb. ix. 26; esp. after a conditional statement with εἰ and the indic. preterite, Lk. xix. 42; Jn. viii. 40; ix. 41; xv. 22, 24; xviii. 36; 1 Co. xii. 20; [cf. B. § 151, 26]. In Rev. νῦν does not occur. [Syn. see ἄρτι.]

3570   **νυνί** (νῦν with iota demonstr. [Krüger § 25, 6, 4 sq.; Kühner § 180, e. (Jelf § 160, e.); *Bttm.* Gram. § 80, 2]), in Attic *now, at this very moment* (precisely now, neither before nor after; Lat. *nunc ipsum*), and only of T i m e, almost always with the pres., very rarely with the fut. (cf. *Lob.* ad Phryn. p. 19). Not found in the N. T. exc. in the writ. of Paul and in a few places in Acts and the Ep. to the Heb.; and it differs here in no respect from the simple νῦν; cf. *Fritzsche*, Rom. i. p. 182; [W. 23]; **1.** of T i m e: with a pres. (Job xxx. 9), Acts xxiv. 13 L T Tr WH; Ro. xv. 23, 25; 1 Co. xiii. 13 (ἄρτι ... τότε δέ ... νυνὶ δέ); 2 Co. viii. 11, 22; Philem. 9, 11 (sc. ὄντα); with a perf. indicating continuance, Ro. iii. 21 [al. refer this to 2]; with a preterite (Ps. xvi. (xvii.) 11), Ro. vi. 22 (opp. to τότε); vii. 6; Eph. ii. 13 (opp. to ἐν τῷ καιρῷ ἐκείνῳ); Col. i. 22 (21) [and iii. 8; also Ro. xi. 30 WH mrg.], (opp. to πότε); Col. i. 26 [R G L mrg.; cf. W. § 63 I. 2 b.; B. 382 (328)] (opp. to ἀπὸ τῶν αἰώνων);

*For 3569 see 3588 & 3568.

with a fut., Job vii. 21; Bar. vi. 4 (Ep. Jer. 3); 2 Macc. x. 10; τῆς πρὸς ὑμᾶς νυνὶ ἀπολογίας, Acts xxii. 1.   **2.** contrary to Grk. usage, in stating a c o n c l u s i o n (see νῦν, 2), *but since the case stands thus*, [*as it is*]: 1 Co. [v. 11 R G T L mrg.]; xiv. 6 R G (i. e. since ὁ γλώσσῃ λαλῶν without an interpretation cannot edify the church); *but now* (Germ. *so aber*), Heb. ix. 26 L T Tr WH; after a conditional statement with εἰ (see νῦν, fin.), Ro. vii. 17; 1 Co. xii. 18 [R G T WH mrg.]; xv. 20; Heb. viii. 6 [here L Tr mrg. WH txt. νῦν], cf. 4; xi. 16 Rec., cf. 15; [B. § 151, 26].*

3571   **νύξ**, gen. νυκτός, ἡ, [fr. a root meaning 'to disappear'; cf. Lat. *nox*, Germ. *nacht*, Eng. *night*; Curtius § 94], (Sept. for לַיְל and לַיְלָה), [fr. Hom. down], *night*: Mk. vi. 48; Acts xvi. 33; xxiii. 23; Jn. xiii. 30; Rev. xxi. 25; xxii. 5; ἵνα ἡ νὺξ μὴ φαίνῃ τὸ τρίτον αὐτῆς, i. e. that the night should want a third part of the light which the moon and the stars give it, Rev. viii. 12 [al. understand this of the want of the light etc. for a third part of the night's d u r a t i o n]; gen. νυκτός, *by night* [W. § 30, 11; B. § 132, 26], Mt. ii. 14; xxviii. 13; Lk. ii. 8 [but note here the a r t i c l e; some make τῆς νυκτός depend on φυλακάς; Jn. iii. 2; Acts ix. 25; 1 Th. v. 7; νυκτὸς καὶ ἡμέρας, Mk. v. 5; 1 Th. iii. 9; iii. 10; 1 Tim. v. 5, [where see Ellicott on the o r d e r]; ἡμέρας κ. νυκτός, Lk. xviii. 7; Acts ix. 24; Rev. iv. 8; vii. 15; xii. 10, etc.; μέσης νυκτός, *at midnight*, Mt. xxv. 6; in answer to the question w h e n: ταύτῃ τῇ νυκτί, *this night*, Lk. xii. 20; xvii. 34; Acts xxvii. 23; τῇ νυκτὶ ἐκείνῃ, Acts xii. 6; τῇ ἐπιούσῃ ν. Acts xxiii. 11; in answer to the question h o w l o n g: νύκτα καὶ ἡμέραν, Lk. ii. 37; Acts xx. 31; xxvi. 7; differently in Mk. iv. 27 (night and day, sc. applying himself to what he is here said to be doing); τὰς νύκτας, *during the nights, every night*, Lk. xxi. 37; νύκτας τεσσαράκ. Mt. iv. 2; τρεῖς, ib. xii. 40; διὰ τῆς νυκτός, see διά, A. II. 1 b.; δι' ὅλης (τῆς) νυκτός, *the whole night through, all night*, Lk. v. 5; ἐν νυκτί, *when he was asleep*, Acts xviii. 11; 1 Th. v. 2, and Rec. in 2 Pet. iii. 10; ἐν τῇ νυκτί, in (the course of) the night, Jn. xi. 10; ἐν τῇ νυκτὶ ταύτῃ, Mt. xxvi. 31, 34; Mk. xiv. 30; ἐν τῇ νυκτὶ ᾗ κτλ. 1 Co. xi. 23; κατὰ μέσον τῆς νυκτός, *about midnight*, Acts xxvii. 27. Metaph. the time when work ceases, i. e. the time of death, Jn. ix. 4; the time for deeds of sin and shame, the time of moral stupidity and darkness, Ro. xiii. 12; the time

when the weary and also the drunken give themselves up to slumber, put for torpor and sluggishness, 1 Th. v. 5.

νύσσω (-ττω): 1 aor. ἔνυξα; *to strike* [?], *pierce*; *to*   **3572** *pierce through, transfix*; often in Hom. of severe or even deadly wounds given one; as, τὸν μὲν ἔγχεϊ νύξ ... στυγερὸς δ' ἄρα μιν σκότος εἷλε, Il. 5, 45. 47; φθάσας αὐτὸν ἐκεῖνος νύττει κάτωθεν ὑπὸ τὸν βουβῶνα δόρατι καὶ παραχρῆμα διεργάζεται, Joseph. b. j. 3, 7, 35; so τὴν πλευρὰν λόγχῃ, Jn. xix. 34, cf. xx. 25, 27. On the further use of the word cf. *Fritzsche*, Rom. ii. p. 559. [Comp.: κατα-νύσσω.] *

νυστάζω; 1 aor. ἐνύσταξα; (ΝΥΩ, cf. νεύω, νευστάζω);   **3573** Sept. for נוּם.   **1.** prop. *to nod in sleep, to sleep*, (Hippocr., Arstph., Xen., Plato, al.); *to be overcome* or *oppressed with sleep*; *to fall asleep, drop off to sleep*, [(cf. Wiclif) *to nap it*]: Mt. xxv. 5; Sept. for נִרְדַּם, Ps. lxxv. (lxxvi.) 7.   **2.** like the Lat. *dormito* [cf. our *to be napping*], trop. i. q. *to be negligent, careless*, (Plat., Plut., al.): of a thing i. q. *to linger, delay*, 2 Pet. ii. 3.*

νυχθήμερον, -ου, τό, (νύξ and ἡμέρα), *a night and a day*,   **3574** the space of twenty-four hours: 2 Co. xi. 25. (Alex. Aphr.; Geopon.) Cf. *Sturz*, De dial. Mac. etc. p. 186; [*Soph.* Lex. s. v.; cf. W. 25].*

Νῶε (Νώεος, -ου, in Joseph. [antt. 1, 3, 1 sqq.]), ὁ, (נֹחַ   **3575** rest), *Noah*, the second father of the human race: Mt. xxiv. 37 sq.; Lk. iii. 36; xvii. 26 sq.; Heb. xi. 7; 1 Pet. iii. 20; 2 Pet. ii. 5.*

νωθρός, -ά, -όν, (i. q. νωθής, fr. νη [cf. νήπιος] and ὠθέω   **3576** [to push; al. ὄθομαι to care about (cf. Vaniček p. 879)], cf. νώδυνος, νώνυμος, fr. νη and ὀδύνη, ὄνομα), *slow, sluggish, indolent, dull, languid*: Heb. vi. 12; with a dat. of reference [W. § 31, 6 a.; B. § 133, 21], ταῖς ἀκοαῖς, of one who apprehends with difficulty, Heb. v. 11; νωθρὸς καὶ παρειμένος ἐν τοῖς ἔργοις, Sir. iv. 29; νωθρὸς κ. παρειμένος ἐργάτης, Clem. Rom. 1 Cor. 34, 1. (Plat., Aristot., Polyb., Dion. Hal., Anthol., al.) [Syn. see ἀργός, fin.] *

νῶτος, -ου, ὁ, [fr. root 'to bend,' 'curve,' akin to Lat.   **3577** *natis*; Fick i. 128; Vaniček p. 420], *the back*: Ro. xi. 10 fr. Ps. lxviii. (lxix.) 24. (In Hom. ὁ νῶτος ["the gend. of the sing. is undetermined in Hom. and Hes." (L. and S.)], plur. τὰ νῶτα; in Attic generally τὸ νῶτον, very rarely ὁ νῶτος; plur. always τὰ νῶτα; Sept. ὁ νῶτος, plur. οἱ νῶτοι; cf. *Lob.* ad Phryn. p. 290; [*Rutherford*, New Phryn. p. 351]; Passow [L. and S.] s. v.) *

Ξ

3578   [ξ, on its occasional substitution for σ see Σ, σ, ς.]   **ξενία**, -ας, ἡ, (ξένιος, -α, -ον, and this fr. ξένος), fr. Hom. down, *hospitality, hospitable reception*; i. q. *a lodging-place, lodgings*: Acts xxviii. 23 (i. q. τὸ μίσθωμα in vs. 30 [but this is doubtful; the more prob. opinion receives the preference s. v. ἴδιος, 1 a.]); Philem. 22. [See esp. Bp. Lghtft. on Phil. p. 9, and on Philem. l. c.] *

ξενίζω; 1 aor. ἐξένισα; Pass., pres. ξενίζομαι; 1 aor.   **3579** ἐξενίσθην; fr. Hom. down;   **1.** *to receive as a guest, to entertain hospitably*: τινά, Acts x. 23; xxviii. 7; Heb. xiii. 2; pass. *to be received hospitably*; *to stay as a guest, to lodge* (be lodged): ἐνθάδε, Acts x. 18; ἐν οἰκίᾳ τινός, Acts x. 32; παρά τινι, Acts x. 6; xxi. 16 [cf. B. 284 (244); W. 214 (201)], and sundry codd. in 1 Co. xvi. 19; (Diod.

14, 30). **2.** *to surprise* or *astonish by the strangeness and novelty of a thing* (cf. Germ. *befremden*): ξενίζοντά τινα, Acts xvii. 20 (ξενίζουσα πρόσοψις καὶ καταπληκτική, Polyb. 3, 114, 4 ; τὸν θεὸν ἐξένιζε τὸ πραττόμενον, Joseph. antt. 1, 1, 4 ; ξενίζουσαι συμφοραί, 2 Macc. ix. 6) ; pass. *to be surprised, astonished at the novelty* or *strangeness of a thing* ; *to think strange, be shocked* : w. dat. of the thing [W. § 31, 1 f.], 1 Pet. iv. 12 (Polyb. 1, 23, 5 ; 3, 68, 9) ; ἐν w. dat. of the thing [cf. B. § 133, 23], 1 Pet. iv. 4.*

3580   **ξενοδοχέω** (for the earlier form ξενοδοκέω in use fr. Hdt. down; cf. *Lob.* ad Phryn. p. 307), -ῶ : 1 aor. ἐξενοδόχησα ; (ξενοδόχος, i. e. ξένους δεχόμενος) ; *to receive and entertain hospitably, to be hospitable* : 1 Tim. v. 10. (Dio Cass. 78, 3 ; [Graec. Ven. Gen. xxvi. 17 ; eccl. writ.].) *

3581   **ξένος**, -η, -ον, fr. Hom. down, masc. *a guest-friend* (Lat. *hospes*, [of parties bound by ties of hospitality]), i. e. **1.** *a foreigner, stranger*, (opp. to ἐπιχώριος, Plat. Phaedo c. 2 p. 59 b. ; Joseph. b. j. 5, 1, 3) ; **a.** prop. : Mt. xxv. 35, 38, 43 sq. ; xxvii. 7 ; 3 Jn. 5 ; ξένοι κ. παρεπίδημοι ἐπὶ τῆς γῆς, Heb. xi. 13 ; οἱ ἐπιδημοῦντες ξένοι, Acts xvii. 21 ; opp. to συμπολίτης, Eph. ii. 19 ; (Sept. for אָרַח *a travel-ler*, 2 S. xii. 4 cod. Alex.; for גֵּר, Job xxxi. 32 ; sev-eral times for נָכְרִי. [as adj. with] δαιμόνια, Acts xvii. 18. **b.** trop. *alien* (from a person or thing) ; *without knowledge of, without a share in* : with a gen. of the thing, τῶν διαθηκῶν τῆς ἐπαγγελίας, Eph. ii. 12 [cf. W. § 30, 4, 6] (τοῦ λόγου, Soph. O. T. 219). **β.** *new, un-heard of* : διδαχαί, Heb. xiii. 9 ; ξένον τι, *a strange, won-derful thing*, 1 Pet. iv. 12 (Aeschyl. Prom. 688 ; Diod. 3, 15 and 52 ; al.). **2.** *one who receives and enter-tains another hospitably* ; *with whom he stays* or *lodges, a host* : ὁ ξένος μου, Ro. xvi. 23, where καὶ τῆς ἐκκλησίας ὅλης is added, i. e. either 'who receives hospitably all the members of the church who cross his threshold,' or 'who kindly permits the church to worship in his house' (*Fritzsche*).*

3582   **ξέστης**, -ου, ὁ, (a corruption of the Lat. sextarius); **1.** *a sextarius*, i. e. a vessel for measuring liquids, holding about a pint (Joseph. antt. 8, 2, 9 — see βάτος ; Epict. diss. 1, 9, 33 ; 2, 16, 22 ; [Dioscor.], Galen and med. writ.). **2.** *a wooden pitcher* or *ewer* (Vulg. *urceus* [A. V. *pot*]) from which water or wine is poured, whether holding a sextarius or not : Mk. vii. 4, 8 [here T WH om. Tr br. the cl.].*

3583   **ξηραίνω** : 1 aor. ἐξήρανα (Jas. i. 11) ; Pass., pres. ξηραί-νομαι ; pf. 3 pers. sing. ἐξήρανται (Mk. xi. 21), ptcp. ἐξη-ραμμένος ; 1 aor. ἐξηράνθην ; cf. B. 41 (36) ; (fr. ξηρός, q. v.) ; fr. Hom. down ; Sept. chiefly for יָבֵשׁ and הוֹבִישׁ ; *to make dry, dry up, wither*: act., τὸν χόρτον, Jas. i. 11 ; pass. *to become dry, to be dry, be withered* [cf. B. 52 (45)] (Sept. for יָבֵשׁ) : of plants, Mt. xiii. 6 ; xxi. 19 sq. ; Mk. iv. 6 ; xi. 20 sq. ; Lk. viii. 6 ; Jn. xv. 6 ; [1 Pet. i. 24] ; of the ripening of crops, Rev. xiv. 15 ; of fluids : ἡ πηγή, Mk. v. 29 ; τὸ ὕδωρ, Rev. xvi. 12, (Gen. viii. 7 ; Is. xix. 5) ; of

members of the body, *to waste away, pine away* : Mk. ix. 18 ; ἐξηραμμένη χείρ, a withered hand, Mk. iii. 1, and R G in 3.*

ξηρός, -ά, -όν, fr. Hdt. down, *dry* : τὸ ξύλον, Lk. xxiii.   3584 31 (in a proverb. saying, 'if a good man is treated so, what will be done to the wicked ?' cf. Ps. i. 3 ; Ezek. xx. 47. Is. lvi. 3 ; Ezek. xvii. 24) ; of members of the body deprived of their natural juices, *shrunk, wasted, withered* : as χείρ, Mt. xii. 10 ; Mk. iii. 3 L T Tr WH ; Lk. vi. 6, 8 ; men are spoken of as ξηροί, withered, Jn. v. 3. of the land in distinction from water, ἡ ξηρά sc. γῆ (Sept. for יַבָּשָׁה, Gen. i. 9 sq. ; Jon. i. 9 ; ii. 11, and often [W. 18 ; 592 (550)]) : Mt. xxiii. 15 ; Heb. xi. 29 where L T Tr WH add γῆς.*

ξύλινος, -ίνη, -ινον, (ξύλον), fr. Pind. and Hdt. down,   3585 *wooden, made of wood* : σκεύη, 2 Tim. ii. 20 ; neut. plur. εἴδωλα, Rev. ix. 20 (θεοί, Bar. vi. 30 [Ep. Jer. 29]).*

ξύλον, -ου, τό, (fr. ξύω to scrape, plane), fr. Hom. down ;   3586 Sept. for עֵץ ; **1.** *wood* : univ. 1 Co. iii. 12 ; ξ. θύϊνον, Rev. xviii. 12 ; *that which is made of wood*, as a beam from which any one is suspended, *a gibbet, a cross*, [A. V. *tree*, q. v. in B. D. Am. ed.], Acts v. 30 ; x. 39 ; xiii. 29 ; Gal. iii. 13 ; 1 Pet. ii. 24, (עֵץ, Gen. xl. 19 ; Deut. xxi. 23 ; Josh. x. 26 ; Esth. v. 14), — a use not found in the classics [cf. L. and S. s. v. II. 4]. A log or timber with holes in which the feet, hands, neck, of prisoners were inserted and fastened with thongs (Gr. κᾶλον, ξυλοπέδη, ποδοκάκη, ποδοστράβη, Lat. *nervus*, by which the Lat. renders the Hebr. סַד, a fetter, or shackle for the feet, Job [xiii. 27] ; xxxiii. 11 ; cf. *Fischer*, De vitiis lexx. N. T. p. 458 sqq. ; [B. D. s. v. Stocks]) : Acts xvi. 24 (Hdt. 6, 75 ; 9, 37 ; Arstph. eq. 367, 394, 705) ; *a cudgel, stick, staff* : plur., Mt. xxvi. 47, 55 ; Mk. xiv. 43, 48 ; Lk. xxii. 52, (Hdt. 2, 63 ; 4, 180 ; Dem. p. 645, 15 ; Polyb. 6, 37, 3 ; Joseph. b. j. 2, 9, 4 ; Hdian. 7, 7, 4). **2.** *a tree* : Lk. xxiii. 31 (Gen. i. 29 ; iii. 9 ; iii. 1 ; Is. xiv. 8, etc.) ; ξ. τῆς ζωῆς, see ζωή, 2 b. p. 274ᵃ.

[**ξύν**, older form of σύν, retained occasionally in com-   see 4819 pounds, as ξυμβαίνω, 1 Pet. iv. 12 ed. Bezae ; see Meister-   & 4862 hans § 49, 11 ; L. and S. s. v. σύν, init. ; and cf. Σ, σ, ς.]

ξυράω (a later form, fr. Diod. [1, 84] down, for ξυρέω,   3587 which the earlier writ. used fr. Hdt. down ; [W. 24 ; B. 63 (55)] ; esp. *Bttm.* Ausf. Spr. ii. p. 53]), -ῶ : pf. pass. ptcp. ἐξυρημένος ; Mid., pres. inf. ξυρᾶσθαι [for which some would read (1 Co. xi. 6) ξύρασθαι (1 aor. mid. inf. fr. ξύρω) ; see WH. App. p. 166] ; 1 aor. subjunc. 3 pers. plur. ξυρήσωνται [but T Tr WH read the fut. -σονται] ; (fr. ξυρόν a razor, and this fr. ξύω) ; Sept. for גָּלַח ; *to shear, shave* : pass. 1 Co. xi. 5 ; mid. *to get one's self shaved*, ibid. vs. 6 ; 1 Co. xi. 4 ; with an acc. specifying the obj. more precisely [cf. B. § 134, 7 ; W. § 32, 5] : τὴν κεφαλήν, Acts xxi. 24 (Sept. Num. vi. 9, 19 ; Lev. xxi. 5 ; τὰς ὀφρύας, Hdt. 2, 66 ; τὸ σῶμα, 2, 37).*

Ο

ὁ, ἡ, τό, originally τός, τή, τό, (as is evident from the forms τοί, ταί for οἱ, αἱ in Hom. and the Ionic writ.), corresponds to our definite article *the* (Germ. *der, die, das*), which is properly a demonstrative pronoun, which we see in its full force in Homer, and of which we find certain indubitable traces also in all kinds of Greek prose, and hence also in the N. T.

I. As a DEMONSTRATIVE PRONOUN; Lat. *hic, haec, hoc*; Germ. *der, die, das*, emphatic; cf. W. § 17, 1; B. 101 (89) sq.; **1.** in the words of the poet Aratus, τοῦ γὰρ καὶ γένος ἐσμέν, quoted by Paul in Acts xvii. 28. **2.** in prose, where it makes a partition or distributes into parts: ὁ μὲν ... ὁ δέ, *that ... this, the one ... the other*: Mt. xiii. 23 R G Tr [here the division is threefold]; Gal. iv. 23 [here L WH Tr mrg. br. μέν]; οἱ μὲν ... οἱ δέ, Acts xxviii. 24; Phil. i. 16 sq.; οἱ μὲν ... ὁ δέ, Heb. vii. 5 sq. 20 (21), 23 sq.; τοὺς μὲν ... τοὺς δέ, Mk. xii. 5 R G; Eph. iv. 11; οἱ μὲν ... ἄλλοι δὲ (Lchm. οἱ δὲ) ... ἕτεροι δέ, Mt. xvi. 14 cf. Jn. vii. 12; τινές foll. by οἱ δέ, Acts xvii. 18; ὅς (see ὅς I.) μέν foll. by ὁ δέ, Ro. xiv. 2; οἱ δέ stands as though οἱ μέν had preceded, Mt. xxvi. 67; xxviii. 17. **3.** in narration, when either two persons or two parties are alternately placed in opposition to each other and the discourse turns from one to the other; ὁ δέ, *but he, and he*, (Germ. *er aber*): Mt. ii. 14; iv. 4; xxi. 29 sq.; Mk. i. 45; xii. 15; Lk. viii. 21, 30, 48; xxii. 10, 34; Jn. ix. 38, and very often; plur., Mt. ii. 5, 9; iv. 20; Mk. xii. 14 [R G L mrg.], 16 [L br. οἱ δέ]; Lk. vii. 4; xx. 5, 12; xxii. 9, 38, 71; Acts iv. 21; xii. 15, and often; οἱ μὲν οὖν, in the Acts alone: i. 6; v. 41; xv. 3, 30; ὁ μὲν οὖν, xxiii. 18; xxviii. 5.

II. As the DEFINITE or PREPOSITIVE ARTICLE (to be distinguished from the postpositive article, — as it is called when it has the force of a relative pronoun, like the Germ. *der, die, das*, exx. of which use are not found in the N. T.), whose use in the N. T. is explained at length by W. §§ 18–20; B. 85 (74) sqq.; [Green p. 5 sqq.]. As in all languages the article serves to distinguish things, persons, notions, more exactly, it is prefixed **1.** to substantives that have no modifier; and **a.** those that designate a person or a thing that is the only one of its kind; the art. thus distinguishes the same from all other persons or things, as ὁ ἥλιος, ὁ οὐρανός, ἡ γῆ, ἡ θάλασσα, ὁ θεός, ὁ λόγος (Jn. i. 1 sq.), ὁ διάβολος, τὸ φῶς, ἡ σκοτία, ἡ ζωή, ὁ θάνατος, etc. **b.** appellative names of persons and things definite enough in themselves, or made so by the context, or sufficiently well-known from history; thus, to the names of virtues and vices, as ἡ δικαιοσύνη, ἡ σοφία, ἡ δύναμις, ἡ ἀλήθεια, etc. ὁ ἐρχόμενος, the well-known personage who is to come, i. e. the Messiah, Mt. xi. 3; Lk. vii. 19; ὁ προφήτης, the (promised and expected) prophet, Jn. i. 21; vii. 40; ἡ σωτηρία, the salvation which all good men hope for, i. e. the Messianic salvation; ἡ γραφή, etc.; ἡ νεφέλη, the cloud (well known from the O. T.), 1 Co. x. 1 sq.; τοὺς ἀγγέλους, Jas. ii. 25; τῷ ἐκτρώματι, 1 Co. xv. 8. to designations of eminent personages: ὁ υἱὸς τοῦ θεοῦ, ὁ υἱὸς τοῦ ἀνθρώπου, (see υἱός); ὁ διδάσκαλος τοῦ Ἰσραήλ, Jn. iii. 10; cf. Fritzsche on Mk. p. 613. The article is applied to the repeated name of a person or thing already mentioned or indicated, and to which the reader is referred, as τοὺς μάγους, Mt. ii. 7 cf. 1; οἱ ἀσκοί, Mt. ix. 17; οἱ δαίμονες, Mt. viii. 31 cf. 28; τὴν ὄνον καὶ τὸν πῶλον, Mt. xxi. 7 cf. 2, and countless other exx. The article is used with names of things not yet spoken of, in order to show that definite things are referred to, to be distinguished from others of the same kind and easily to be known from the context; as τὰ βρέφη, the babes belonging to the people of that place, Lk. xviii. 15; ἀπὸ τῶν δένδρων, sc. which were there, Mt. xxi. 8; τῷ ἱερεῖ, to the priest whose duty it will be to examine thee, when thou comest, Mt. viii. 4; Mk. i. 44; Lk. v. 14; τὸ πλοῖον, the ship which stood ready to carry them over, Mt. viii. 23 [R G T, cf. 18]; ix. 1 [R G]; xiii. 2 [R G]; τὸ ὄρος, the mountain near the place in question (*der an Ort u. Stelle befindliche Berg*) [but some commentators still regard τὸ ὄρος as used here generically or Hebraistically like ἡ ὀρεινή, the mountain region or the highlands, in contrast with the low country, (cf. Sept. Josh. xvii. 16; xx. 7; Gen. xix. 17, 19, etc.); cf. Bp. *Lghtft.* 'Fresh Revision' etc. p. 111 sq.; *Weiss*, Matthäusevangelium, p. 129 note; and in Meyer's Mt. 7te Aufl.], Mt. v. 1; Mk. iii. 13; Lk. ix. 28; Jn. vi. 3, 15, (1 Macc. ix. 38, 40); ἡ οἰκία, the house in which (Jesus) was wont to lodge, Mt. ix. 10, 28; xiii. 36; xvii. 25; ὑπὸ τὸν μόδιον, sc. that is in the house, Mt. v. 15; also ἐπὶ τὴν λυχνίαν, ibid.; ἐν τῇ φάτνῃ, in the manger of the stable of the house where they were lodging, Lk. ii. 7 R G; ὁ ἔπαινος, the praise of which he is worthy, 1 Co. iv. 5; so everywhere in the doxologies: ἡ δόξα, τὸ κράτος, 1 Pet. iv. 11; Rev. v. 13, etc. **c.** The article prefixed to the Plural often either includes all and every one of those who by the given name are distinguished from other things having a different name, — as οἱ ἀστέρες, Mt. xxiv. 29; Mk. xiii. 25; αἱ ἀλώπεκες, Mt. viii. 20; Lk. ix. 58, etc.; — or defines the class alone, and thus indicates that the whole class is represented by the individuals mentioned, however many and whosoever they may be; as in οἱ Φαρισαῖοι, οἱ γραμματεῖς, οἱ τελῶναι, οἱ ἄνθρωποι, people, the multitude, (Germ. *die Leute*); οἱ ἀετοί, Mt. xxiv. 28; τοῖς κυσίν, Mt. vii. 6. **d.** The article prefixed to the Singular sometimes so defines only the class, that all and every one of those who bear the name are brought to mind; thus, ὁ ἄνθρωπος, Mt. xv. 11; ὁ ἐθνικὸς κ. τελώνης, Mt. xviii. 17; ὁ ἐργάτης, Lk. x. 7; 1 Tim. v. 18; ὁ μεσίτης, Gal. iii. 20; ὁ κληρονόμος, Gal. iv. 1; ὁ δίκαιος, Ro. i. 17; Heb. x. 38; τὰ σημεῖα τοῦ ἀποστόλου, the signs required of any one who claims to be an apostle, 2 Co. xii. 12, and other exx. **e.** The article is prefixed to the nominative often put for the vocative in addresses [cf. W. § 29, 2; B. § 129 a. 5]: χαῖρε ὁ βασιλεὺς τῶν Ἰουδ. (prop. σὺ ὁ βασ., thou who art the king), Jn. xix. 3; ναί, ὁ πατήρ, Mt. xi. 26; ἄγε νῦν οἱ πλούσιοι, κλαύσατε, Jas. v. 1; οὐρανὲ καὶ οἱ ἅγιοι, Rev. xviii. 20; add, Mk. v. 41; x. 47; Lk. xii. 32; xviii. 11, 13; Jn. viii. 10; xx. 28; Acts xiii. 41; Ro. viii. 15; Eph. v. 14, 22, 25; vi. 1, 4 sq.; Rev. xii. 12. **f.** The Greeks employ the article, where we abstain from its use, before nouns denoting things that pertain to him who is the subject of discourse: εἶπε or φησὶ μεγάλῃ τῇ φωνῇ, Acts xiv. 10 [R G]; xxvi. 24, (Prov. xxvi. 25); γυνὴ προσευχομένη ... ἀκατακαλύπτῳ τῇ κεφαλῇ, 1 Co. xi. 5; esp. in the expression ἔχειν τι, when the object and its adjective, or what is equivalent to an adjective, denotes a part of the body or something else which naturally belongs to any one (as in French, *il a les épaules larges*); so, ἔχειν τὴν χεῖρα ξηράν, Mt. xii. 10 R G; Mk. iii. 1; τὸ πρόσωπον ὡς ἀνθρώπου [(Rec. ἄνθρωπος)], Rev. iv. 7; τὰ αἰσθητήρια γεγυμνασμένα, Heb. v. 14; ἀπαράβατον τὴν ἱερωσύνην, Heb. vii. 24; τὴν κατοίκησιν κτλ. Mk. v. 3; τὴν εἰς ἑαυτοὺς ἀγάπην ἐκτενῆ, 1 Pet. iv. 8. Cf. Grimm on 2 Macc. iii. 25. the gen. of a pers. pron. αὐτοῦ, ὑμῶν, is added to the substantive: Mt. iii. 4; Mk. viii. 17; Rev. ii. 18; 1 Pet. ii. 12, cf. Eph. i. 18; cf. W. § 18, 2; [B. § 125, 5]. **g.** Proper Names sometimes have the article and sometimes are anarthrous; cf. W. § 18, 5 and 6; B. § 124, 3 and 4; [Green p. 28 sq.]; **α.** as respects names of Persons, the person without the article is simply named, but with the article is marked as either well known or as already mentioned; thus we find Ἰησοῦς and ὁ Ἰης., Παῦλος and ὁ Παῦλ., etc. Πιλᾶτος has the article everywhere in John's Gospel and also in Mark's, if xv. 43 (in R G L) be excepted (but T Tr WH insert the article there also); Τίτος is everywhere anarthrous. Indeclinable names of persons in the oblique cases almost always have the article, unless the case is made evident by a preposition: τῷ Ἰωσήφ, Mk. xv. 45; τὸν Ἰακὼβ καὶ τὸν Ἠσαῦ, Heb. xi. 20, and many other exx., esp. in the genealogies, Mt. i. 1 sqq.; Lk. iii. 23; but where perspicuity does not require the article, it is omitted also in the oblique cases, as τῶν υἱῶν Ἰωσήφ, Heb. xi. 21; τῶν υἱῶν Ἐμμώρ, Acts vii. 16; ὁ θεὸς Ἰσαάκ, Mt. xxii. 32; Acts vii. 32; ὅταν ὄψησθε Ἀβραὰμ κ. Ἰσαὰκ ... καὶ πάντας τοὺς προφήτας, Lk. xiii. 28. The article is commonly omitted with personal proper names to which is added an apposition indicating the race, country, office, rank, surname, or something else, (cf. Matthiae § 274): let the foll. suffice as exx.:

Ἀβραὰμ ὁ πατὴρ ἡμῶν, Jn. viii. 56; Ro. iv. 1; Ἰάκωβον τὸν τοῦ Ζεβεδαίου καὶ Ἰωάννην τὸν ἀδελφὸν αὐτοῦ, Mt. iv. 21; Μαρία ἡ Μαγδαληνή, Mt. xxvii. 56, etc.; Ἰωάννης ὁ βαπτιστής, Mt. iii. 1; Ἡρώδης ὁ τετράρχης, Lk. ix. 7; Ἰησοῦς ὁ λεγόμενος Χριστός, Mt. i. 16; Σαῦλος δὲ ὁ καὶ Παῦλος sc. καλούμενος, Acts xiii. 9; Σίμωνος τοῦ λεπροῦ, Mk. xiv. 3; Βαρτίμαιος ὁ τυφλός, Mk. x. 46 [R G]; Ζαχαρίου τοῦ ἀπολομένου, Lk. xi. 51. But there are exceptions also to this usage · ὁ δὲ Ἡρώδης ὁ τετράρχης, Lk. iii. 19; ὁν Σαούλ, υἱὸν Κίς, Acts xiii. 21; in the opening of the Epistles: Παῦλος ἀπόστολος, Ro. i. 1; 1 Co. i. 1, etc. **β.** Proper names of countries and regions have the article far more frequently than those of cities and towns, for the reason that most names of countries, being derived from adjectives, get the force of substantives only by the addition of the article, as ἡ Ἀχαΐα (but cf. 2 Co. ix. 2), ἡ Γαλατία, ἡ Γαλιλαία, ἡ Ἰταλία, ἡ Ἰουδαία, ἡ Μακεδονία (but cf. Ro. xv. 26; 1 Co. xvi. 5), etc. Only Αἴγυπτος, if Acts vii. 11 L T Tr WH be excepted, is everywhere anarthrous. The names of cities, esp. when joined to prepositions, particularly ἐν, εἰς and ἐκ, are without the article; but we find ἀπὸ (R G ἐκ) τῆς Ῥώμης in Acts xviii. 2. **γ.** Names of rivers and streams have the article in Mt. iii. 13; Mk. i. 5; Lk. iv. 1; xiii. 4; Jn. i. 28; τοῦ Κεδρών, Jn. xviii. 1 G L Tr mrg. **2.** The article is prefixed to substantives expanded and more precisely defined by modifiers; **a.** to nouns accompanied by a gen. of the pronouns μοῦ, σοῦ, ἡμῶν, ὑμῶν, αὐτοῦ, ἑαυτῶν, αὐτῶν: Mt. i. 21, 25; v. 45; vi. 10-12; xii. 49; Mk. ix. 17; Lk. vi. 27; x. 7; xvi. 6; Acts xix. 25 [L T Tr WH ἡμῖν]; Ro. iv. 19; vi. 6, and in numberless other places; it is rarely omitted, as in Mt. xix. 28; Lk. i. 72; ii. 32; 2 Co. viii. 23; Jas. v. 20, etc.; cf. B. § 127, 27. **b.** The possessive pronouns ἐμός, σός, ἡμέτερος, ὑμέτερος, joined to substantives (if Jn. iv. 34 be excepted) always take the article, and John generally puts them after the substantive (ἡ κρίσις ἡ ἐμή, Jn. v. 30; ὁ λόγος ὁ σός, xvii. 17; ἡ κοινωνία ἡ ἡμετέρα, 1 Jn. i. 3; ὁ καιρὸς ὁ ὑμέτερος, Jn. vii. 6), very rarely between the article and the substantive (τοῖς ἐμοῖς ῥήμασιν, Jn. v. 47; ἡ ἐμὴ διδαχή, vii. 16; τὴν σὴν λαλιάν, iv. 42), yet this is always done by the other N. T. writ., Mt. xviii. 20; Mk. viii. 38; Lk. ix. 26; Acts xxiv. 6 [Rec.]; xxvi. 5; Ro. iii. 7, etc. **c.** When adjectives are added to substantives, either the adjective is placed between the article and the substantive, — as τὸ ἴδιον φορτίον, Gal. vi. 5; ὁ ἀγαθὸς ἄνθρωπος, Mt. xii. 35; τὴν δικαίαν κρίσιν, Jn. vii. 24; ἡ ἀγαθὴ μερίς, Lk. x. 42; τὸ ἅγιον πνεῦμα, Lk. xii. 10; Acts i. 8; ἡ αἰώνιος ζωή, Jn. xvii. 3, and many other exx.; — or the adjective preceded by an article is placed after the substantive with its article, as τὸ πνεῦμα τὸ ἅγιον, Mk. iii. 29; Jn. xiv. 26; Acts i. 16; Heb. iii. 7; ix. 8; x. 15; ἡ ζωὴ ἡ αἰώνιος, 1 Jn. i. 2; ii. 25; ὁ ποιμὴν ὁ καλός, Jn. x. 11; τὴν πύλην τὴν σιδηρᾶν, Acts xii. 10, and other exx.; — very rarely the adjective stands before a substantive which has the article, as in Acts [xiv. 10 R G]; xxvi. 24; 1 Co. xi. 5, [cf. B. § 125, 5; W. § 20, 1 c.]. As to the adjectives of quantity, ὅλος, πᾶς, πολύς, see each in its own place. **d.** What has been said concerning adjectives holds true also of all other limitations added to substantives, as ἡ κατ᾽ ἐκλογὴν πρόθεσις, Ro. ix. 11; ἡ παρ᾽ ἐμοῦ διαθήκη, Ro. xi. 27; ὁ λόγος ὁ τοῦ σταυροῦ, 1 Co. i. 18; ἡ εἰς Χριστὸν πίστις, Col. ii. 5; on the other hand, ἡ πίστις ὑμῶν ἡ πρὸς τὸν θεόν, 1 Th. i. 8; τῆς διακονίας τῆς εἰς τοὺς ἁγίους, 2 Co. viii. 4; see many other exx. of each usage in W. 131 (124) sqq.; [B. 91 (80) sqq.]. **e.** The noun has the article before it when a demonstrative pronoun (οὗτος, ἐκεῖνος) belonging to it either precedes or follows [W. § 18, 4; B. § 127, 29–31]; as, ὁ ἄνθρωπος οὗτος, Jn. ix. 24 [οὗτος ὁ ἄνθρ. L Tr mrg. WH]; Acts vi. 13; xxii. 26; ὁ λαὸς οὗτος, Mt. xv. 8; ὁ υἱός σου οὗτος, Lk. xv. 30; plur. Lk. xxiv. 17, and numberless other exx.; οὗτος ὁ ἄνθρωπος, Lk. xiv. 30; οὗτος ὁ λαός, Mk. vii. 6 [ὁ λ. οὗτ. L WH mrg.]; οὗτος ὁ υἱός μου, Lk. xv. 24; οὗτος ὁ τελώνης, Lk. xviii. 11 [ὁ τελ. οὗτ. L mrg.]; οὗτος ὁ λόγος, Jn. vii. 36 [ὁ λόγ. οὗτ. L T Tr WH], and many other exx. on ἐκεῖνος, see ἐκεῖνος, 2; on αὐτὸς ὁ etc., see αὐτός (I. 1 b. etc.); on ὁ αὐτός etc., see αὐτός, III. **3.** The neuter article prefixed to adjectives changes them into substantives [cf. W. § 34, 2; B. § 128, 1]; as, τὸ ἀγαθόν, τὸ καλόν (which see each in its place) ; with a gen. added, τὸ ἔλαττον, Heb. vii. 7; τὸ γνωστὸν τοῦ θεοῦ, Ro. i. 19; τὸ ἀδύνατον τοῦ νόμου, Ro. viii. 3; τὸ ἀσθενὲς τοῦ θεοῦ, 1 Co. i. 25; αὐτῆς, Heb. vii. 18; τὰ ἀόρατα τ. θεοῦ, Ro. i. 20; τὰ κρυπτὰ τῆς αἰσχύνης, 2 Co. iv. 2, etc. **4.** The article with cardinal numerals: εἷς one; ὁ εἷς the one (of two), see εἷς, 4 a.; but differently ὁ εἷς in Ro. v. 15, 17, the (that) one. So also οἱ δύο (our the twain), Mt. xix. 5; οἱ δέκα the (those) ten, and οἱ ἐννέα, Lk. xvii. 17; ἐκεῖνοι οἱ δέκα (καὶ) ὀκτώ, Lk. xiii. 4. **5.** The article prefixed to participles **a.** gives them the force of substantives [W. §§ 18, 3; 45, 7; B. §§ 129, 1 b.; 144, 9]; as, ὁ πειράζων, Mt. iv. 3; 1 Th. iii. 5; ὁ βαπτίζων, Mk. vi. 14 (for which Mt. xiv. 2 ὁ βαπτιστής); ὁ σπείρων, Mt. xiii. 3; Lk. viii. 5; ὁ ὀλοθρεύων, Heb. xi. 28; οἱ βαστάζοντες, Lk. vii. 14; οἱ βόσκοντες, Mt. viii. 33; Mk. v. 14; οἱ ἐσθίοντες, the eaters (convivae), Mt. xiv. 21; τὸ ὀφειλόμενον, Mt. xviii. 30, 34; τὰ ὑπάρχοντα (see ὑπάρχω, 2). **b.** the ptcp. with the article must be resolved into he who [and a fin. verb; cf. B. § 144, 9]: Mt. x. 40; Lk. vi. 29; xi. 23; Jn. xv. 23; 2 Co. i. 21; Phil. ii. 13, and very often. πᾶς ὁ foll. by a ptcp. [W. 111 (106)], Mt. v. 22; vii. 26; Lk. vi. 30 [T WH om. L Tr mrg. br. art.]; xi. 10; Ro. ii. 1; 1 Co. xvi. 16; Gal. iii. 13, etc.; μακάριος ὁ w. a ptcp., Mt. v. 4 (5), 6, 10, etc.; οὐαὶ ὑμῖν οἱ w. a ptcp., Lk. vi. 25; the neut. τό w. a ptcp. must be resolved into that which [with a fin. verb], τὸ γεννώμενον, Lk. i. 35; τὸ γεγεννημένον, Jn. iii. 6. **c.** the article with ptcp. is placed in apposition: Mk. iii. 22; Acts xvii. 24; Eph. iii. 20; iv. 22, 24; 2 Tim. i. 14; 1 Pet. i. 21, etc. **6.** The neut. τό before infinitives **a.** gives them the force of substantives (cf. B. 261 (225) sqq. [cf. W. § 44, 2 a.; 3 c.]); as, τὸ καθίσαι, Mt. xx. 23; Mk. x. 40; τὸ θέλειν, Ro. vii. 18; 2 Co. viii. 10; τὸ ποιῆσαι, τὸ ἐπιτελέσαι, 2 Co. viii. 11,

and other exx.; τοῦτο κρίνατε· τὸ μὴ τιθέναι κτλ. Ro. xiv. 13. On the infin. w. the art. depending on a preposition (ἀντὶ τοῦ, ἐν τῷ, εἰς τό, etc.), see under each prep. in its place. **b.** Much more frequent in the N. T. than in the earlier and more elegant Grk. writ., esp. in the writings of Luke and Paul (nowhere in John's Gospel and Epistles), is the use of the gen. τοῦ w. an inf. (and in the Sept. far more freq. than in the N. T.), which is treated of at length by Fritzsche in an excursus at the end of his Com. on Mt. p. 843 sqq. ; W. § 44, 4 ; B. 266 (228) sqq. The examples fall under the foll. classes: τοῦ with an inf. is put **a.** after words which naturally require a genitive (of a noun also) after them; thus after ἄξιον, 1 Co. xvi. 4; ἔλαχε, Lk. i. 9 (1 S. xiv. 47); ἐξαπορούμαι, 2 Co. i. 8. **β.** for the simple expletive [i. e. 'complementary'] or (as it is commonly called) epexegetical infin., which serves to fill out an incomplete idea expressed by a noun or a verb or a phrase, (where in Germ. zu is commonly used); thus after προθυμία, 2 Co. viii. 11; βραδεῖς, Lk. xxiv. 25; ἐλπίς, Acts xxvii. 20; 1 Co. ix. 10 [not Rec.]; ἐζήτει εὐκαιρίαν, Lk. xxii. 6 [not L mrg.]; ὁ καιρὸς (sc. ἐστί) τοῦ ἄρξασθαι, to begin, 1 Pet. iv. 17 (καιρὸν ἔχειν w. the simple inf. Heb. xi. 15); διδόναι τὴν ἐξουσίαν, Lk. x. 19 (ἐξουσίαν ἔχειν with simple inf., Jn. xix. 10; 1 Co. ix. 4); ὀφειλέται ἐσμέν (equiv. to ὀφείλομεν), Ro. viii. 12 (with inf. alone, Gal. v. 3); ἕτοιμον εἶναι, Acts xxiii. 15 (1 Macc. iii. 58; v. 39; xiii. 37; with inf. alone, Lk. xxii. 33); χρείαν ἔχειν, Heb. v. 12; ἔδωκεν ὀφθαλμοὺς τοῦ μὴ βλέπειν καὶ ὦτα τοῦ μὴ ἀκούειν, that they should not see . . . that they should not hear [cf. B. 267 (230)], Ro. xi. 8 (ἔχειν ὦτα elsewh. always with a simple inf.; see οὖς, 2); ἐπλήσθη ὁ χρόνος τοῦ τεκεῖν αὐτήν, at which she should be delivered [cf. B. l. c.], Lk. i. 57; ἐπλήσθ. ἡμέραι . . . τοῦ περιτεμεῖν αὐτόν, that they should circumcise him [cf. B. l. c.], Lk. ii. 21; after ἀνένδεκτόν ἐστιν, Lk. xvii. 1 [so B. § 140, 15; (W. 328 (308) otherwise)]; quite unusually after ἐγένετο [cf. B. § 140, 16 δ.; W. l. c.], Acts x. 25 [Rec. om. art.]. **γ.** after verbs of deciding, entreating, exhorting, commanding, etc.: after κρίνειν (see κρίνω, 4); ἐγένετο γνώμη [-μης T Tr WH (see γίνομαι, 5 e. a.)], Acts xx. 3; τὸ πρόσωπον ἐστήριξεν, Lk. ix. 51; συντίθεσθαι, Acts xxiii. 20 (with inf. alone, Lk. xxiii. 5); προσεύχεσθαι, Jas. v. 17; παρακαλεῖν, Acts xxi. 12; τέλλεσθαι, Lk. iv. 10; ἐπιστέλλειν, Acts xv. 20 (with inf. alone, xxi. 25 [R G T, but L Tr txt. WH here ἀποστελ.; B. 270 (232)]); κατανεύειν, Lk. v. 7. **δ.** after verbs of hindering, restraining, removing, (which naturally require the genitive), and according to the well-known pleonasm with μή before the inf. [see μή, I. 4 a.; B. § 148, 13; W. 325 (305)]; thus, after κατέχω τινά, Lk. iv. 42; κρατοῦμαι, Lk. xxiv. 16; κωλύω, Acts x. 47; ὑποστέλλομαι, Acts xx. 20, 27; παύω, 1 Pet. iii. 10; καταπαύω, Acts xiv. 18; without μή before the inf. after ἐγκόπτομαι, Ro. xv. 22. **ε.** τοῦ with an inf. is added as a somewhat loose epexegesis: Lk. xxi. 22; Acts ix. 15; xiii. 47; Phil. iii. 21; εἰς ἀκαθαρσίαν τοῦ ἀτιμάζεσθαι τὰ σώματα αὐτῶν, to the uncleanness of their bodies being dishonored, Ro. i. 24 [cf. B. § 140, 14]; W. 325 (305) sq.   ζ. it takes the place of an entire final clause, *in order that* [W. § 44, 4 b.; B. § 140, 17]; esp. after verbs implying motion: Mt. ii. 13; iii. 13; xiii. 3; xxiv. 45; Mk. iv. 3 (where L T WH om. Tr br. τοῦ); Lk. i. 77, 79; ii. 24, 27; v. 1 [R G L txt. Tr mrg.]; viii. 5; xii. 42 (here L om. Tr br. τοῦ); xxii. 31; xxiv. 29; Acts iii. 2; xx. 30; xxvi. 18; Ro. vi. 6; xi. 10; Gal. iii. 10; Phil. iii. 10; Heb. x. 7, 9; xi. 5.   η. used of result, *so that*: Acts vii. 19; Ro. vii. 3; after ποιῶ, *to cause that, make to*, Acts iii. 12; [cf. W. 326 (306); B. § 140, 16 δ.].   **7.** The article with adverbs [B. § 125, 10 sq.; W. § 18, 3],   a. gives them the force of substantives; as, τὸ πέραν, the region beyond; τὰ ἄνω, τὰ κάτω, τὸ νῦν, τὰ ἔμπροσθεν, τὰ ὀπίσω, etc.; see these words in their proper places.   b. is used when they stand adjectively, as ἡ ἄνω Ἰερουσαλήμ, ὁ τότε κόσμος, ὁ ἔσω ἄνθρωπος, ὁ νῦν αἰών, etc., on which see these several words.   c. the neut. τό is used in the acc. absol., esp. in specifications of time: both with adverbs of time, τὸ πάλιν, 2 Co. xiii. 2; τὰ νῦν or τανῦν, and with neuter adjectives used adverbially, as τὸ λοιπόν, τὸ πρότερον (Jn. vi. 62; Gal. iv. 13); τὸ πρῶτον (Jn. x. 40; xii. 16; xix. 39); τὸ πλεῖστον (1 Co. xiv. 27); see these words themselves.   **8.** The article before prepositions with their cases is very often so used that ὤν, ὄντες, ὄντα, must be supplied in thought [cf. B. § 125, 9; W. § 18, 3]; thus, οἱ ἀπὸ Ἰταλίας, ἀπὸ Θεσσαλονίκης, Acts xvii. 13; Heb. xiii. 24 [cf. W. § 66, 6]; ὁ ἐν τινι, Mt. vi. 9; Ro. viii. 1; see τὰ πρός, Mk. ii. 2; οἱ ἔκ τινος, Ro. ii. 8; iv. 14, 16; Phil. iv. 22 etc.; οἱ παρά τινος, Mk. iii. 21 (see παρά, I. e.). τὰ περὶ τινος, Lk. xxiv. 19; Acts xxiv. 10; Phil. i. 27; [add, τὰ (T Tr WH τὸ) περὶ ἐμοῦ, Lk. xxii. 37], etc. (see περί, I. b. β.); τὰ περί τινα, Phil. ii. 23 [see περί, II. b.]; οἱ μετά τινος, those with one, his companions, Mt. xii. 3; οἱ περί τινα, and many other exx. which are given under the several prepositions.   the neut. τό in the acc. absol. in adverbial expressions [cf. W. 230 (216); B. §§ 125, 12; 131, 9]: τὸ καθ᾽ ἡμέραν, *daily, day by day*, Lk. xi. 3; xix. 47; Acts xvii. 11 [R G WH br.]; τὸ καθόλου, *at all*, Acts iv. 18 [L T WH om. τό]; besides, in τὸ κατὰ σάρκα, as respects human origin, Ro. ix. 5 [on the force of the art. here see *Abbot* in Journ. Soc. Bibl. Lit. etc. for 1883, p. 108]; τὰ κατ᾽ ἐμέ, as respects what relates to me, my state, my affairs, Col. iv. 7; Eph. vi. 21; τὸ ἐξ ὑμῶν, as far as depends on you, Ro. xii. 18; τὸ ἐφ᾽ ὑμῖν, as far as respects you, if I regard you, Ro. xvi. 19 R G; τὰ πρὸς (τὸν) θεόν, acc. absol., as respects the things pertaining to God, i. e. in things pertaining to God, Ro. xv. 17; Heb. ii. 17; v. 1, (ἱερεῖ τὰ πρὸς τοὺς θεούς, στρατηγῷ δὲ τὰ πρὸς τοὺς ἀνθρώπους, Xen. resp. Laced. 13, 11; cf. *Fritzsche*, Ep. ad Rom. iii. p. 262 sq.); τὸ ἐκ μέρους sc. ὄν, that which has been granted us in part, that which is imperfect, 1 Co. xiii. 10.   **9.** The article, in all genders, when placed before the genitive of substantives indicates *kinship, affinity*, or *some kind of connection, association* or *fellowship*, or in general *that which in some way pertains to a person* or *thing*

[cf. W. § 30, 3; B. § 125, 7];   a. the masc. and the fem. article: Ἰάκωβος ὁ τοῦ Ζεβεδαίου, ὁ τοῦ Ἀλφαίου, the son, Mt. x. 2 (3), 3; Μαρία ἡ τοῦ Ἰακώβου, the mother, Mk. xvi. 1 [T om. Tr br. τοῦ]; Lk. xxiv. 10 [L T Tr WH]; Ἐμμὸρ τοῦ Συχέμ, of Hamor, the father of Shechem, Acts vii. 16 R G; ἡ τοῦ Οὐρίου, the wife, Mt. i. 6; οἱ Χλόης, either the kinsfolk, or friends, or domestics, or work-people, or slaves, of Chloe, 1 Co. i. 11; also οἱ Ἀριστοβούλου, οἱ Ναρκίσσου, Ro. xvi. 10 sq.; οἱ τοῦ Χριστοῦ, the followers of Christ [A. V. *they that are Christ's*], 1 Co. xv. 23 G L T Tr WH; Gal. v. 24; οἱ τῶν Φαρισαίων, the disciples of the Pharisees, Mk. ii. 18ᵃ Rec., 18ᵇ R G L; Καισαρεία ἡ Φιλίππου, the city of Philip, Mk. viii. 27.   b. τό and τά τινος: as τὰ τοῦ θεοῦ, the cause or interests, the purposes, of God, opp. to τὰ τῶν ἀνθρώπων, Mt. xvi. 23; Mk. viii. 33; in the same sense τὰ τοῦ κυρίου, opp. to τὰ τοῦ κόσμου, 1 Co. vii. 32–34; τὰ τῆς σαρκός, τὰ τοῦ πνεύματος, Ro. viii. 5; τὰ ὑμῶν, your possessions, 2 Co. xii. 14; ζητεῖν τό or τά τινος, 1 Co. x. 24; xiii. 5; Phil. ii. 21; τὰ τῆς εἰρήνης, τῆς οἰκοδομῆς, which make for, Ro. xiv. 19; τὰ τῆς ἀσθενείας μου, which pertain to my weakness, 2 Co. xi. 30; τὰ Καίσαρος, τὰ τοῦ θεοῦ, due to Cæsar, due to God, Mt. xxii. 21; Mk. xii. 17; Lk. xx. 25; τὰ τοῦ νηπίου, the things wont to be thought, said, done, by a child, 1 Co. xiii. 11; τά τινος, the house of one (τὰ Λύκωνος, Theocr. 2, 76; [εἰς τὰ τοῦ ἀδελφοῦ, Lysias c. Eratosth. § 12 p. 195]; cf. ἐν τοῖς πατρικοῖς, in her father's house, Sir. xlii. 10; [Chrysost. hom. lii. (on Gen. xxvi. 16), vol. iv. pt. ii. col. 458 ed. Migne; Gen. xli. 51; Esth. vii. 9, (Hebr. בֵּ֫ת); Job xviii. 19 (Hebr. מִגּוּר)]); with the name of a deity, *the temple* (τὰ τοῦ Διός, Joseph. c. Ap. 1, 18, 2; also τὸ τοῦ Διός, Lycurg. adv. Leocr. p. 231 [(orat. Att. p. 167, 15)]), Lk. ii. 49 (see other exx. in *Lob.* ad Phryn. p. 100). τὰ τοῦ νόμου, the precepts of the (Mosaic) law, Ro. ii. 14; τὸ τῆς παροιμίας, the (saying) of (that which is said in) the proverb, 2 Pet. ii. 22; τὰ τῶν δαιμονιζομένων, what the possessed had done and experienced, Mt. viii. 33; τὸ τῆς συκῆς, what has been done to the fig-tree, Mt. xxi. 21.   **10.** The neuter τό is put   a. before entire sentences, and sums them up into one conception [B. § 125, 13; W. 109 (103 sq.)]: εἶπεν αὐτῷ τό Εἰ δύνασαι πιστεῦσαι, said to him this: 'If thou canst believe', Mk. ix. 23 [but L T Tr WH τό Εἰ δύνῃ 'If thou canst!']; cf. *Bleek* ad loc.; [*Riddell*, The Apology etc. Digest of Idioms § 19 γ.].   before the sayings and precepts of the O. T. quoted in the New: τό Οὐ φονεύσεις, the precept, 'Thou shalt not kill', Mt. xix. 18; add, Lk. xxii. 37 (where Lchm. ὅτι for τό); Ro. xiii. 9; [1 Co. iv. 6 L T Tr WH]; Gal. v. 14. before indir. questions: τὸ τίς etc., τὸ τί etc., τὸ πῶς etc., Lk. i. 62; ix. 46; xix. 48; xxii. 2, 4, 23 sq.; Acts iv. 21; xxii. 30; Ro. viii. 26; 1 Th. iv. 1; cf. Matthiae § 280; Krüger § 50, 6, 10; Passow ii. p. 395ᵇ; [L. and S. s. v. B. I. 3 sq.].   b. before single words which are explained as parts of some discourse or statement [reff. as above]: τὸ Ἄγαρ, the name Ἄγαρ, Gal. iv. 25 [T L txt. WH mrg. om. Tr br. Ἄγαρ]; τὸ 'ἀνέβη', this word ἀνέβη, Eph. iv. 9, [cf. Bp. Lghtft. on

Gal. l. c.]; τὸ 'ἔτι ἅπαξ', Heb. xii. 27; cf. Matthiae ii. p. 731 sq.　　**11.** We find the unusual expression ἡ οὐαί (apparently because the interjection was to the writer a substitute for the term ἡ πληγή or ἡ θλίψις [W. 179 (169)]), misery, calamity, [A. V. *the Woe*], in Rev. ix. 12; xi. 14.

III. Since it is the business, not of the lexicographer, but of the grammarian, to exhibit the instances in which the article is omitted in the N. T. where according to the laws of our language it would have been expected, we refer those interested in this matter to the Grammars of Winer (§ 19) and Alex. Buttmann (§ 124, 8) [cf. also Green ch. ii. § iii.; *Middleton*, The Doctrine of the Greek Article (ed. Rose) pp. 41 sqq., 94 sq.; and, particularly with reference to Granville Sharp's doctrine (Remarks on the uses of the Def. Art. in the Grk. Text of the N. T., 3d ed. 1803), a tract by *C. Winstanley* (A Vindication etc.) republished at Cambr. 1819], and only add the foll. remarks: **1.** More or less frequently the art. is wanting before appellatives of persons or things of which only one of the kind exists, so that the art. is not needed to distinguish the individual from others of the same kind, as ἥλιος, γῆ, θεός, Χριστός, πνεῦμα ἅγιον, ζωὴ αἰώνιος, θάνατος, νεκροί (of the whole assembly of the dead [see νεκρός, 1 b. p. 423ᵇ]); and also of those persons and things which the connection of discourse clearly shows to be well-defined, as νόμος (the Mosaic law [see νόμος, 2 p. 428ᵃ]), κύριος, πατήρ, υἱός, ἀνήρ (husband), γυνή (wife), etc. **2.** Prepositions which with their cases designate a state and condition, or a place, or a mode of acting, usually have an anarthrous noun after them; as, εἰς φυλακήν, ἐν φυλακῇ, εἰς ἀέρα, ἐκ πίστεως, κατὰ σάρκα, ἐπ' ἐλπίδι, παρ' ἐλπίδα, ἀπ' ἀγορᾶς, ἀπ' ἀγροῦ, ἐν ἀγρῷ, εἰς ὁδόν, ἐν ἡμέραις Ἡρώδου, εἰς ἡμέραν ἀπολυτρώσεως, and numberless other examples.

3589　**3590** ὀγδοήκοντα, *eighty*: Lk. ii. 37; xvi. 7. [(Thuc., al.)]*

3590 ὄγδοος, -η, -ον, [fr. Hom. down], *the eighth*: Lk. i. 59; Acts vii. 8; Rev. xvii. 11; xxi. 20; *one who has seven other companions, who with others is the eighth*, 2 Pet. ii. 5; so δέκατος, *with nine others*, 2 Macc. v. 27; cf. Matthiae § 469, 9; Viger. ed. *Herm.* p. 72 sq. and 720 sq.; W. § 37, 2; [B. 30 (26)].*

3591 ὄγκος, -ου, ὁ, (apparently fr. ΕΓΚΩ, ἐνεγκεῖν, i. q. φόρτος, see *Buttmann*, Lexil. i. 288 sqq. [Fishlake's trans. p. 151 sq.], *whatever is prominent, protuberance, bulk, mass*, hence), *a burden, weight, encumbrance*: Heb. xii. 1. (In many other uses in Grk. writ. of all ages.) *

[Syn. ὄγκος, βάρος, φορτίον: β. refers to *weight*, ο. to *bulk*, and either may be oppressive (contra *Tittmann*); β. *a load* in so far as it is heavy, φορτίον *a burden* in so far as it is borne; hence the φορτ. may be either 'heavy' (Mt. xxiii. 4; Sir. xxi. 16), or 'light' (Mt. xi. 30).]

3592 ὅδε, ἥδε, τόδε, (fr. the old demonstr. pron. ὁ, ἡ, τό, and the enclit. δέ), [fr. Hom. down], *this one here*, Lat. *hicce*, *haecce*, *hocce*; **a.** it refers to what precedes: Lk. x. 39 and Rec. in xvi. 25; τάδε πάντα, 2 Co. xii. 19 Grsb.; to what follows: neut. plur. τάδε, *these* (viz. *the following*) *things, as follows, thus*, introducing words spoken, Acts

xv. 23 R G; τάδε λέγει etc., Acts xxi. 11; Rev. ii. 1, 8, 12, 18; iii. 1, 7, 14.　**b.** εἰς τήνδε τὴν πόλιν, [where we say *into this or that city*] (the writer not knowing what particular city the speakers he introduces would name), Jas. iv. 13 (cf. W. 162 (153), who adduces as similar τήνδε τὴν ἡμέραν, Plut. symp. 1, 6, 1; [but see *Lünemann's* addition to Win. and esp. B. § 127, 2]).*

3593 ὁδεύω; (ὁδός); *to travel, journey*: Lk. x. 33. (Hom. Il. 11, 569; Xen. an. 7, 8, 8; Joseph. antt. 19, 4, 2; b. j. 3, 6, 3; Hdian. 7, 3, 9 [4 ed. Bekk.]; Plut., al.; Tob. vi. 6.) [Comp.: δι-, συν-οδεύω.]*

3594 ὁδηγέω, -ῶ; fut. ὁδηγήσω; 1 aor. subj. 3 pers. sing. ὁδηγήσῃ; (ὁδηγός, q. v.); Sept. chiefly for נָחָה, also for הוֹלִיךְ, הִדְרִיךְ, etc.; **a.** prop. *to be a guide, lead on one's way, to guide*: τινά, Mt. xv. 14; Lk. vi. 39; τινὰ ἐπί τι, Rev. vii. 17; (Aeschyl., Eur., Diod., Alciphr., Babr., al.). **b.** trop. *to be a guide* or *teacher; to give guidance to*: τινά, Acts viii. 31 (Plut. mor. 954 b.); εἰς τὴν ἀλήθειαν, Jn. xvi. 13 [R G L Tr WH txt. (see below)] (ὁδήγησόν με ἐπὶ τὴν ἀλήθειάν σου καὶ δίδαξόν με, Ps. xxiv. (xxv.) 5 [foll. by εἰς and πρός in "Teaching of the Apostles" ch. 3]); foll. by ἐν w. dat. of the thing in which one gives guidance, instruction or assistance to another, ἐν τῇ ἀληθείᾳ, Jn. xvi. 13 T WH mrg. [see above] (ὁδήγησόν με ἐν τῇ ὁδῷ σου κ. πορεύσομαι ἐν τῇ ἀληθείᾳ σου, Ps. lxxxv. (lxxxvi.) 11; cf. Ps. cxviii. (cxix.) 35; Sap. ix. 11; x. 17).*

3595 ὁδηγός, -οῦ, ὁ, (ὁδός and ἡγέομαι; cf. χορηγός), *a leader of the way, a guide*; **a.** prop.: Acts i. 16 (Polyb. 5, 5, 15; Plut. Alex. 27; 1 Macc. iv. 2; 2 Macc. v. 15). **b.** in fig. and sententious discourse ὁδ. τυφλῶν, i. e. like one who is literally so called, namely *a teacher of the ignorant and inexperienced*, Ro. ii. 19; plur. ὁδ. τυφλοὶ τυφλῶν, i. e. like blind guides in the literal sense, in that, while themselves destitute of a knowledge of the truth, they offer themselves to others as teachers, Mt. xv. 14; xxiii. 16, 24.'

3596 ὁδοιπορέω, -ῶ; (ὁδοιπόρος a wayfarer, traveller); *to travel, journey*: Acts x. 9. (Hdt., Soph., Xen., Ael. v. h. 10, 4; Hdian. 7, 9, 1, al.) *

3597 ὁδοιπορία, -ας, ἡ, (ὁδοιπόρος), *a journey, journeying*: Jn. iv. 6; 2 Co. xi. 26. (Sap. xiii. 18; xviii. 3; 1 Macc. vi. 41; Hdt., Xen., Diod. 5, 29; Hdian. al.) *

see 3598 ὁδο-ποιέω, -ῶ; in Grk. writ. fr. Xen. down, *to make a road; to level, make passable, smooth, open, a way*; and so also in the Sept.: ὡδοποίησε τρίβον τῇ ὀργῇ αὐτοῦ, for פֶּלֶס, Ps. lxxvii. (lxxviii.) 50; for סָלַל, to construct a level way by casting up an embankment, Job xxx. 12; Ps. lxvii. (lxviii.) 5; for פָּנָה, Ps. lxxix. (lxxx.) 10; for בִּנָּה דֶרֶךְ Is. lxii. 10; — and so, at least apparently, in Mk. ii. 23 L Tr mrg. WH mrg. [see ποιέω, I. 1 a. and c.] (with ὁδόν added, Xen. anab. 4, 8, 8).*

3598 ὁδός, -οῦ, ἡ, [appar. fr. r. ΕΔ to go (Lat. *adire, accedere*), allied w. Lat. *solum*; Curtius § 281]; Sept. numberless times for דֶּרֶךְ, less frequently for אֹרַח; [fr. Hom. down]; *a way*; **1.** prop. **a.** *a travelled way, road*: Mt. ii. 12; vii. 13 sq.; xiii. 4, 19; Mk. iv. 4, 15; x. 46; Lk. viii. 5, 12; x. 31; xviii. 35; xix. 36; Acts viii. 26; ix. 17; Jas. ii. 25, etc.; κατὰ τὴν ὁδόν (as ye pass along

the way [see κατά, II. 1 a.]) *by the way, on the way,* Lk.
x. 4; Acts viii. 36; xxv. 3; xxvi. 13; σαββάτου ὁδός,
[A. V. *a sabbath-day's journey*] the distance that one is
allowed to travel on the sabbath, Acts i. 12 (see σάββατον,
1 a.). ἡ ὁδός with a gen. of the object, the way leading
to a place (the Hebr. דֶּרֶךְ also is construed with a gen.,
cf. *Gesenius*, Lehrgeb. p. 676 [Gr. § 112, 2; cf. W. § 30,
2]): ἐθνῶν, Mt. x. 5; τῶν ἁγίων into the holy place, Heb.
ix. 8, cf. x. 20, where the grace of God is symbolized by
a way, cf. ζάω, II. b., (τοῦ ξύλου, Gen. iii. 24; Αἰγύπτου
. . . Ἀσσυρίων, Jer. ii. 18; γῆς Φιλιστιείμ, Ex. xiii. 17;
τοῦ Σινᾶ, Judith v. 14; Lat. *via mortis,* Tibull. 1, 10, 4; cf.
Kühner ii. p. 286, 4). in imitation of the Hebr. דֶּרֶךְ, the
acc. of which takes on almost the nature of a preposition,
in the way to, towards, (cf. *Gesenius,* Thes. i. p. 352ᵃ), we
find ὁδὸν θαλάσσης in Mt. iv. 15 fr. Is. viii. 23 (ix. 1), (so
ὁδὸν [τῆς θαλάσσης, 1 K. xviii. 43]; γῆς αὐτῶν, 1 K. viii.
48; 2 Chr. vi. 38; ὁδὸν δυσμῶν ἡλίου, Deut. xi. 30; moreover, once with the acc., ὁδὸν θάλασσαν ἐρυθράν, Num.
xiv. 25; [Deut. ii. 1]; cf. *Thiersch,* De Alex. Pentateuchi
versione, p. 145 sq.; [B. § 131, 12]). with a gen. of the
subject, *the way in which one walks:* ἐν ταῖς ὁδοῖς αὐτῶν,
Ro. iii. 16; ἑτοιμάζειν τὴν ὁδὸν τῶν βασιλέων, Rev. xvi.
12; in metaph. phrases, κατευθύνειν τὴν ὁδόν τινος, to remove the hindrances to the journey, 1 Th. iii. 11; ἑτοιμάζειν (and εὐθύνειν, Jn. i. 23; κατασκευάζειν, Mt. xi. 10;
Mk. i. 2; Lk. vii. 27) τὴν ὁδὸν τοῦ κυρίου, see ἑτοιμάζω.
b. *a traveller's way, journey, travelling:* ἐν τῇ ὁδῷ, on the
journey, on the road, Mt. v. 25; xv. 32; xx. 17; Mk. viii.
27; ix. 33; x. 32, 52; Lk. xii. 58; xxiv. 32, 35; Acts ix.
27; ἐξ ὁδοῦ, from a journey, Lk. xi. 6; αἴρειν or κτᾶσθαί
τι εἰς ὁδόν, Mt. x. 10; Mk. vi. 8, and εἰς τὴν ὁδόν, Lk. ix.
3; πορεύομαι τὴν ὁδόν, to make a journey (Xen. Cyr. 5, 2,
22), w. αὐτοῦ added [A. V. *to go on one's way*], to continue the journey undertaken, Acts viii. 39; ὁδὸς ἡμέρας,
a journey requiring a (single) day for its completion,
used also, like our *a day's journey,* as a *measure of distance,* Lk. ii. 44 (Gen. xxx. 36; xxxi. 23; Ex. iii. 18;
Judith ii. 21; 1 Macc. v. 24; vii. 45; ἀπέχειν παμπόλλων
ἡμερῶν ὁδόν, Xen. Cyr. 1, 1, 3, cf. Hdt. 4, 101 [W. 188
(177)]); on the phrase ὁδὸν ποιεῖν, Mk. ii. 23 see ποιέω,
I. 1 a. and b. **2.** Metaph. **a.** according to the
familiar fig. of speech, esp. freq. in Hebr. [cf. W. § 32] and
not unknown to the Greeks, by which an **action** is
spoken of as a *proceeding* (cf. the Germ. *Wandel*), ὁδός
denotes *a course* of conduct, *a way* (i. e. manner) *of thinking, feeling, deciding:* a person is said ὁδὸν δεικνύναι τινί,
who shows him how to obtain a thing, what helps he
must use, 1 Co. xii. 31; with a gen. of the obj., i. e. of
the thing to be obtained, εἰρήνης, Ro. iii. 17; ζωῆς, Acts
ii. 28; σωτηρίας, Acts xvi. 17; with a gen. of the subj., τῆς
δικαιοσύνης, the way which ἡ δικαιοσ. points out and which
is wont to characterize ἡ δικ., so in Mt. xxi. 32 (on which
see δικαιοσύνη, 1 b. p. 149ᵃ bot.); used of the Christian
religion, 2 Pet. ii. 21; likewise τῆς ἀληθείας, ibid. 2; with
gen. of the person deciding and acting, Jas. v. 20; τοῦ
Κάϊν, Jude 11; τοῦ Βαλαάμ, 2 Pet. ii. 15; ἐν πάσαις ταῖς
ὁδοῖς αὐτοῦ, in all his purposes and actions, Jas. i. 8; τὰς

ὁδούς μου ἐν Χριστῷ, the methods which I as Christ's minister and apostle follow in the discharge of my office, 1 Co.
iv. 17; those are said πορεύεσθαι ταῖς ὁδοῖς αὐτῶν [*to walk
in their own ways*] who take the course which pleases them,
even though it be a perverse one, Acts xiv. 16 [on the dat.
see πορεύω, sub fin.]; αἱ ὁδοὶ τοῦ θεοῦ or κυρίου, the purposes
and ordinances of God, his ways of dealing with men,
Acts xiii. 10; Ro. xi. 33; Rev. xv. 3, (Hos. xiv. 9; Ps.
xciv. (xcv.) 10; cxliv. (cxlv.) 17; Sir. xxxix. 24; Tob.
iii. 2, etc.). ἡ ὁδὸς τοῦ θεοῦ, the course of thought, feeling, action, prescribed and approved by God: Mt. xxii.
16; Mk. xii. 14; Lk. xx. 21; used of the Christian religion, Acts xviii. 26; also ἡ ὁ. τοῦ κυρίου, ibid. 25; ὁδός
used generally of a method of knowing and worshipping
God, Acts xxii. 4; xxiv. 14; ἡ ὁδός simply, of the Christian religion [cf. B. 163 (142)], Acts ix. 2; xix. 9, 23;
xxiv. 22. **b.** in the saying of Christ, ἐγώ εἰμι ἡ ὁδός *I
am the way* by which one passes, i. e. with whom all who
seek approach to God must enter into closest fellowship,
Jn. xiv. 6. [On the omission of ὁδός in certain formulas
and phrases (Lk. v. 19; xix. 4), see W. 590 (549) sq.; B.
§ 123, 8; *Bos,* Ellipses etc. (ed. Schaefer) p. 331 sq.]

ὀδούς, [acc. to Etym. Magn. 615, 21 (Pollux 6, 38) fr. | **3599**
ἔδω, Lat. *edere,* etc., cf. Curtius § 289; al. fr. root da to
divide, cf. δαίω, δάκνω; (Lat. *dens*); Fick i. p. 100],
-όντος, ὁ, fr. Hom. down; Sept. for שֵׁן; *a tooth:* Mt. v.
38; Mk. ix. 18; Acts vii. 54; plur. Rev. ix. 8; ὁ βρυγμὸς
τῶν ὀδόντων, see βρυγμός.*

ὀδυνάω, -ῶ: pres. indic. pass. ὀδυνῶμαι; pres. ind. mid. | **3600**
2 pers. sing. ὀδυνᾶσαι (see κατακαυχάομαι), ptcp. ὀδυνώμε-
νος; (ὀδύνη); *to cause intense pain;* pass. *to be in anguish,
be tormented:* Lk. xvi. 24 sq.; mid. *to torment* or *distress
one's self,* [A. V. *to sorrow*], Lk. ii. 48; ἐπί τινι, Acts xx.
38. (Arstph., Soph., Eur., Plat., al.; Sept.) *

ὀδύνη, [perh. allied w. ἔδω; *consuming* grief; cf. Lat. | **3601**
curae edaces], -ης, ἡ, *pain, sorrow:* Ro. ix. 2; 1 Tim. vi. 10.
(From Hom. down; Sept.) *

ὀδυρμός, -οῦ, ὁ, (ὀδύρομαι to wail, lament, [see κλαίω, | **3602**
fin.]), *a wailing, lamentation, mourning:* Mt. ii. 18 (fr.
Jer. xxxviii. (xxxi.) 15 for תַּמְרוּרִים); 2 Co. vii. 7. (2 | *
Macc. xi. 6; Aeschyl., Eur., Plat., Joseph., Plut., Ael.
v. h. 14, 22.) *

Ὀζίας (L T Tr WH Ὀζείας [cf. *Tdf.* Proleg. p. 84; | **3604**
WH. App. p. 155, and see ει, ι]), -ου [but cf. B. 18 (16)],
ὁ, (עֻזִּיָּה and עֲזַרְיָהוּ strength of Jehovah, or my strength
is Jehovah), *Ozias* or *Uzziah,* son of Amaziah, king of
Judah, [c.] B. C. 811–759 (2 K. xv. 30 sqq.): Mt. i. 8 sq.,
where the Evangelist ought to have preserved this order:
Ἰωράμ, Ὀχοζίας, Ἰωάς, Ἀμαζίας, Ὀζίας. He seems
therefore to have confounded Ὀχοζίας and Ὀζίας; see
another example of [apparent] confusion under Ἰεχονίας.
[But Matthew has simply omitted three links; such
omissions were not uncommon, cf. e. g. 1 Chr. vi. 3 sqq.
and Ezra vii. 1 sqq. See the commentators.] *

ὅζω; [fr. root ὀδ, cf. Lat. and Eng. *odor* etc.; Curtius | **3605**
§ 288]; fr. Hom. down; *to give out an odor* (either good
or bad), *to smell, emit a smell:* of a decaying corpse, Jn.
xi. 39; cf. Ex. viii. 14.*

*For 3603 see 1510.

3606   ὅθεν, (fr. the rel. pron. ὅ and the enclitic θεν which denotes motion from a place), [fr. Hom. down], adv., *from
which*; *whence*; it is used   a. of the place from which:
Mt. xii. 44; Lk. xi. 24; Acts xiv. 26; xxviii. 13; by attraction for ἐκεῖθεν ὅπου etc., Mt. xxv. 24, 26; cf. B. § 143,
12; [W. 159 (150)].   b. of the source from which a
thing is known, *from which, whereby*: 1 Jn. ii. 18.   c.
of the cause from which, *for which reason, wherefore, on
which account,* [A. V. *whereupon* (in the first two instances)]: Mt. xiv. 7; Acts xxvi. 19; Heb. ii. 17; iii.
1; vii. 25; viii. 3; ix. 18; xi. 19; often in the last three
books of Macc.*

3607   ὀθόνη, -ης, ἡ, [fr. Hom. down];   a. *linen* [i. e. fine
white linen for women's clothing; cf. *Vaniček*, Fremdwörter, s. v.].   b. *linen cloth* (sheet or sail); so Acts
x. 11; xi. 5.*

3608   ὀθόνιον, -ου, τό, (dimin. of ὀθόνη, q. v.), *a piece of linen,
small linen cloth*: plur. strips of linen cloth for swathing
the dead, Lk. xxiv. 12 [T om. L Tr br. WH reject the
vs.]; Jn. xix. 40; xx. 5–7. (In Grk. writ. of ships' sails
made of linen, bandages for wounds, and other articles;
Sept. for כָּרִין, Judg. xiv. 13; for בֶּשֶׁת or פִּשְׁתָּה, Hos. ii.
5 (7), 9 (11).) *

see 1492—οἶδα, see εἴδω, II. p. 174.

see 3615—οἰκειακός, -ή, -όν, see οἰκιακός.

3609   οἰκεῖος, -α, -ον, (οἶκος), fr. Hes. down, *belonging to a
house or family, domestic, intimate*: belonging to one's
household, *related by blood, kindred*, 1 Tim. v. 8; οἰκεῖοι
τοῦ θεοῦ, belonging to God's household, i. e. to the theocracy, Eph. ii. 19; in a wider sense, with a gen. of the
thing, *belonging to, devoted to, adherents of* a thing, οἱ οἰκεῖοι
τῆς πίστεως, professors of the (Christian) faith, Gal. vi.
10 [but al. associate this pass. with that fr. Eph. as above;
see Bp. Lghtft. ad loc.]; so οἰκ. φιλοσοφίας, Strab. 1 p.
13 b. [1, 17 ed. Sieben.]; γεωγραφίας, p. 25 a. [1, 34 ed.
Sieben.]; ὀλιγαρχίας, Diod. 13, 91; τυραννίδος, 19, 70.
(Sept. for שְׁאֵר related by blood; דּוֹד, 1 S. x. 14 sqq.;
שַׁאֲרָה, consanguinity, Lev. xviii. 17; οἰκ. τοῦ σπέρματος
for בְּשָׂר, Is. lviii. 7.) *

see 3610   οἰκέτεια [al. -εία, cf. Chandler § 99 sqq.], -ας, ἡ, (οἰκέτης,
q. v.), *household* i. e. *body of servants* (Macrob., Appul.
famulitium, Germ. *Dienerschaft*): Mt. xxiv. 45 L T Tr
WH. (Strab., Lcian., Inscrr.; plur. Joseph. antt. 12, 2,
3.) *

3610   οἰκέτης, -ου, ὁ, (οἰκέω), fr. [Aeschyl. and] Hdt. down,
Lat. *domesticus*, i. e. one who lives in the same house with
another, spoken of all who are under the authority of
one and the same householder, Sir. iv. 30; vi. 11, esp.
a servant, domestic; so in Lk. xvi. 13; Acts x. 7; Ro. xiv.
4; 1 Pet. ii. 18; Sept. for עֶבֶד. See more fully on the
word, Meyer on Rom. l. c. [where he remarks that οἰκ.
is a more restricted term than δοῦλος, designating a
house-servant, one holding closer relations to the family
than other slaves; cf. διάκονος fin., Schmidt ch. 162.]*

3611   οἰκέω, -ῶ; (οἶκος); fr. Hom. down; Sept. for יָשַׁב, a few
times for שָׁכַן; Lat. *habito*, [trans.] *to dwell in*: τί (Hdt.
and often in Attic), 1 Tim. vi. 16; [intrans. *to dwell*],
μετά τινος, with one (of the husband and wife), 1 Co. vii.

12 sq.; trop. ἔν τινι, to be fixed and operative in one's
soul: of sin, Ro. vii. 17 sq. 20; of the Holy Spirit, Ro.
viii. [9], 11; 1 Co. iii. 16. [COMP.: ἐν-, κατ-, ἐν-κατ-,
παρ-, περι-, συν-οικέω.] *

3612   οἴκημα, -τος, τό, fr. [Pind. and] Hdt. down, *a dwelling-
place, habitation*; euphemistically *a prison*, [R. V. *cell*],
Acts xii. 7, as in Thuc. 4, 47 sq.; Dem., Lcian. Tox. 29;
Plut. Agis 19; Ael. v. h. 6, 1.*

3613   οἰκητήριον, -ου, τό, (οἰκητήρ), *a dwelling-place, habitation*: Jude 6; of the body as the dwelling-place of the
spirit, 2 Co. v. 2 (2 Macc. xi. 2; 3 Macc. ii. 15; [Joseph.
c. Ap. 1, 20, 7]; Eur., Plut., Ceb. tab. 17).*

3614   οἰκία, -ας, ἡ, (οἶκος), Sept. for בַּיִת, [fr. Hdt. down], *a
house*;   a. prop. an inhabited edifice, a dwelling: Mt.
ii. 11; vii. 24–27; Mk. i. 29; Lk. xv. 8; Jn. xii. 3; Acts
iv. 34; 1 Co. xi. 22; 2 Tim. ii. 20, and often; οἱ ἐν τῇ οἰκίᾳ
sc. ὄντες, Mt. v. 15; οἱ ἐκ τῆς οἰκίας with gen. of pers.,
Phil. iv. 22; ἡ οἰκία τοῦ (πατρός μου) θεοῦ, i. e. heaven,
Jn. xiv. 2; of the body as the habitation of the soul, 2
Co. v. 1.   b. *the inmates of a house, the family*: Mt. xii.
25; ἡ οἰκία τινός, the household, the family of any one,
Jn. iv. 53; 1 Co. xvi. 15 [cf. W. § 58, 4; B. § 129, 8 a.];
univ. for persons dwelling in the house, Mt. x. 13.   c.
property, wealth, goods, [cf. Lat. *res familiaris*]: τινός, Mt.
xxiii. 14 (13) Rec. [cf. Wetst. ad loc.]; Mk. xii. 40; Lk.
xx. 47; so οἶκος in Hom. (as Od. 2, 237 κατέδουσι βιαίως
οἶκον Ὀδυσσῆος, cf. 4, 318), in Hdt. 3, 53 and in Attic;
Hebr. בַּיִת, Gen. xlv. 18 (Sept. τὰ ὑπάρχοντα); Esth. viii.
1 (Sept. ὅσα ὑπῆρχεν). Not found in Rev. [SYN. see
οἶκος, fin.]

3615   οἰκιακός (in prof. auth. and in some N. T. codd. also
οἰκειακός [cf. ει, ι] fr. οἶκος), -οῦ, ὁ, (οἰκία), *one belonging to
the house* (Lat. *domesticus*), *one under the control of the
master of a house*, whether a son, or a servant: Mt. x.
36; opp. to ὁ οἰκοδεσπότης, ib. 25. (Plut. Cic. 20.) *

3616   οἰκο-δεσποτέω, -ῶ; (οἰκοδεσπότης); *to be master* (or *head*)
of a house; *to rule a household, manage family affairs*: 1
Tim. v. 14. (A later Grk. word; see *Lob.* ad Phryn.
p. 373.) *

3617   οἰκο-δεσπότης, -ου, ὁ, (οἶκος, δεσπότης), *master of a house,
householder*: Mt. x. 25; xiii. 27; xx. 11; xxiv. 43; Mk.
xiv. 14; Lk. xiii. 39; xiii. 25; xiv. 21; ἄνθρωπος οἰκοδ. (see
ἄνθρωπος, 4 a.), Mt. xiii. 52; xx. 1; xxi. 33; οἰκοδεσπ. τῆς
οἰκίας, Lk. xxii. 11, on this pleonasm cf. *Bornemann*, Schol.
ad loc.; W. § 65, 2. (Alexis, a comic poet of the IV. cent.
B. C. ap. Poll. 10, 4, 21; Joseph. c. Ap. 2, 11, 3; Plut.
quaest. Rom. 30; Ignat. ad Eph. 6. *Lob.* ad Phryn. p.
373 shows that the earlier Greeks said οἴκου or οἰκίας
δεσπότης.) *

3618   οἰκοδομέω, -ῶ; impf. ᾠκοδόμουν; fut. οἰκοδομήσω; 1 aor.
ᾠκοδόμησα [οἰκ. Tr WH in Acts vii. 47; see Tdf. ad loc.;
Proleg. p. 120; *WH*. App. p. 161; *Lob.* ad Phryn. p. 153;
W. § 12, 4; B. 34 (30)]; Pass., [pres. οἰκοδομοῦμαι (inf.
-μεῖσθαι, Lk. vi. 48 Treg.); pf. inf. οἰκοδομῆσθαι (Lk. vi.
48 T WH)]; plupf. 3 pers. sing. ᾠκοδόμητο [οἰκ. T WH in Jn. ii. 20]; 1 fut. οἰκοδομηθήσομαι;
(οἰκοδόμος, q. v.); fr. Hdt. down; Sept. for בָּנָה; *to build
a house, erect a building*;   a. prop.   a. *to build* (up

from the foundation): absol., Lk. xi. 48 G T WH Tr txt.; xiv. 30; xvii. 28; οἱ οἰκοδομοῦντες, subst., *the builders* [cf. W. § 45, 7; B. § 144, 11], Mt. xxi. 42; Mk. xii. 10; Lk. xx. 17; Acts iv. 11 Rec.; 1 Pet. ii. 7, fr. Ps. cxvii. (cxviii) 22; ἐπ᾽ ἀλλότριον θεμέλιον, to build upon a foundation laid by others, i. e. (without a fig.) to carry on instruction begun by others, Ro. xv. 20; οἰκοδομεῖν τι, Gal. ii. 18; πύργον, Mt. xxi. 33; Mk. xii. 1; Lk. xiv. 28; ἀποθήκας, Lk. xii. 18; ναόν, Mk. xiv. 58; pass. Jn. ii. 20 [on the aor. cf. 2 Esdr. v. 16]; οἶκον, pass., 1 Pet. ii. 5 ([here T ἐποικ.], cf. W. 603 (561), and add οἰκουργεῖν τὰ κατὰ τὸν οἶκον, Clem. Rom. 1 Cor. 1, 3); [οἰκίαν, Lk. vi. 48 (cf. W. l. c.)]; συναγωγήν or οἶκόν τινι, for the use of or in honor of one, Lk. vii. 5; Acts vii. 47, 49, (Gen. viii. 20; Ezek. xvi. 24); οἰκίαν ἐπί τι, Mt. vii. 24, 26; Lk. vi. 49; πόλιν ἐπ᾽ ὄρους, Lk. iv. 29. β. contextually i. q. *to restore by building, to rebuild, repair*: τί, Mt. xxiii. 29; xxvi. 61; xxvii. 40; Mk. xv. 29; Lk. xi. 47 and R [L br. Tr mrg.] in 48. b. metaph. a. i. q. *to found*: ἐπὶ ταύτῃ τῇ πέτρᾳ οἰκοδομήσω μου τὴν ἐκκλησίαν, i. e. by reason of the strength of thy faith thou shalt be my principal support in the establishment of my church, Mt. xvi. 18. β. Since both a Christian church and individual Christians are likened to a building or temple in which God or the Holy Spirit dwells (1 Co. iii. 9, 16 sqq.; 2 Co. vi. 16; Eph. ii. 21), the erection of which temple will not be completely finished till the return of Christ from heaven, those who, by action, instruction, exhortation, comfort, promote the Christian wisdom of others and help them to live a correspondent life are regarded as taking part in the erection of that building, and hence are said οἰκοδομεῖν, i. e. (dropping the fig.) *to promote growth in Christian wisdom, affection, grace, virtue, holiness, blessedness*: absol., Acts xx. 32 LTTr WH ; 1 Co. viii. 1; x. 23; τινά, xiv. 4; 1 Th. v. 11; pass. *to grow in wisdom, piety,* etc., Acts ix. 31; 1 Co. xiv. 17; univ. *to give one strength and courage, dispose to*: εἰς τὴν πίστιν, Polyc. ad Philip. 3, 2 [yet here *to be built up into* (in) etc.]; even to do what is wrong [A. V. *embolden*], εἰς τὸ τὰ εἰδωλόθυτα ἐσθίειν, 1 Co. viii. 10 [cf. W. § 39, 3 N. 3]. This metaphorical use of the verb Paul, in the opinion of *Fritzsche* (Ep. ad Rom. iii. p. 205 sq.), did not derive from the fig. of building a temple, but from the O. T., where "בָּנָה and הָרַס with an acc. of the pers. (*to build one up* and *to pull one down*) denote *to bless* and *to ruin*, to prosper and to injure, any one"; cf. Ps. xxvii. (xxviii.) 5; Jer. xxiv. 6; xl. (xxxiii.) 7. [COMP.: ἀν-, ἐπ-, συν-οικοδομέω.]*

3619　οἰκο-δομή, -ῆς, ἡ, (οἶκος, and δέμω to build), a later Grk. word, condemned by Phryn., yet used by Aristot., Theophr., [(but both these thought to be doubtful)], Diod. (1, 46), Philo (vit. Moys. i. § 40; de monarch. ii. § 2), Joseph., Plut., Sept., and many others, for οἰκοδόμημα and οἰκοδόμησις; cf. *Lob.* ad Phryn. p. 487 sqq. cf. p. 421; [W. 24]. 1. (*the act of*) *building, building up*, i. q. τὸ οἰκοδομεῖν; as, τῶν τειχέων, 1 Macc. xvi. 23; τοῦ οἴκου τοῦ θεοῦ, 1 Chr. xxvi. 27; in the N. T. metaph., *edifying, edification*, i. e. *the act of one who promotes another's growth in Christian wisdom, piety,*

holiness, happiness, (see οἰκοδομέω, b. β. [cf. W. 35 (34)]): Ro. xiv. 19; xv. 2; [1 Co. xiv. 26]; 2 Co. x. 8 [see below]; xiii. 10; Eph. iv. 29; with a gen. of the person whose growth is furthered, ὑμῶν, 2 Co. xii. 19, [cf. x. 8]; ἑαυτοῦ [Tdf. αὐτοῦ], Eph. iv. 16; τοῦ σώματος τοῦ Χριστοῦ, ibid. 12; τῆς ἐκκλησίας, 1 Co. xiv. 12; i. q. τὸ οἰκοδομοῦν, what contributes to edification, or augments wisdom, etc. λαλεῖν, λαβεῖν, οἰκοδομή; 1 Co. xiv. 3, 5. 2. i. q. οἰκοδόμημα, *a building* (i. e. thing built, edifice): Mk. xiii. 1 sq.; τοῦ ἱεροῦ, Mt. xxiv. 1; used of the heavenly body, the abode of the soul after death, 2 Co. v. 1; trop. of *a body of Christians, a Christian church,* (see οἰκοδομέω, b. β.), Eph. ii. 21 [cf. πᾶς, I. 1 c.]; with a gen. of the owner or occupant, θεοῦ, 1 Co. iii. 9.*

3620　οἰκοδομία, -ας, ἡ, (οἰκοδομέω), (*the act of*) *building, erection,* (Thuc., Plat., Polyb., Plut., Lcian., etc.; but never in the Sept.); metaph. οἰκοδομίαν θεοῦ τὴν ἐν πίστει, the increase which God desires in faith (see οἰκοδομή), 1 Tim. i. 4 Rec. bez els; but see οἰκονομία. Not infreq. οἰκον. and οἰκοδ. are confounded in the Mss.; see Grimm on 4 Macc. p. 365, cf. *Hilgenfeld*, Barn. epist. p. 28; [*D'Orville*, Chariton 8, 1 p. 599].*

see 3618　οἰκο-δόμος, -ου, ὁ, (οἶκος, δέμω to build; cf. οἰκονόμος), *a builder, an architect*: Acts iv. 11 L T Tr WH. (Hdt., Xen., Plat., Plut., al.; Sept.) *

3621　οἰκονομέω, -ῶ; (οἰκονόμος); *to be a steward; to manage the affairs of a household*: absol. Lk. xvi. 2. (Univ. *to manage, dispense, order, regulate*: Soph., Xen., Plat., Polyb., Joseph., Plut., al.; 2 Macc. iii. 14.) *

3622　οἰκονομία, -ας, ἡ, (οἰκονομέω), fr. Xen. and Plat. down, *the management of a household* or *of household affairs*; specifically, *the management, oversight, administration, of others' property; the office of a manager* or *overseer, stewardship*: Lk. xvi. 2–4; hence the word is transferred by Paul in a theocratic sense to the office (duty) intrusted to him by God (the lord and master) of proclaiming to men the blessings of the gospel, 1 Co. ix. 17; ἡ οἰκονομία τοῦ θεοῦ, *the office of administrator (stewardship) intrusted by God,* Col. i. 25. univ. *administration, dispensation,* which in a theocratic sense is ascribed to God himself as providing for man's salvation: αἵτινες ... ἡ οἰκονομίαν θεοῦ τὴν ἐν πίστει, which furnish matter for disputes rather than the (knowledge of the) dispensation of the things by which God has provided for and prepared salvation, which salvation must be embraced by faith, 1 Tim. i. 4 L T Tr WH; ἥν προέθετο ... καιρῶν, which good-will he purposed to show with a view to (that) dispensation (of his) by which the times (sc. of infancy and immaturity cf. Gal. iv. 1–4) were to be fulfilled, Eph. i. 9 sq.; ἡ οἰκ. τῆς χάριτος τοῦ θεοῦ τῆς δοθείσης μοι, that dispensation (or arrangement) by which the grace of God was granted me, Eph. iii. 2; ἡ οἰκ. τοῦ μυστηρίου, the dispensation by which he carried out his secret purpose, Eph. iii. 9 G L T Tr WH.*

3623　οἰκονόμος, -ου, ὁ, (οἶκος, νέμω ['to dispense, manage'] Hesych. ὁ τὸν οἶκον νεμόμενος), *the manager of a household* or *of household affairs*; esp. *a steward, manager, superintendent,* (whether free-born, or, as was usually the case, a freed-man or slave) to whom the head of the house or proprietor has intrusted the management of his affairs, the care of receipts and expenditures, and the duty of dealing out the proper portion to every servant and even to the children not yet of age : Lk. xii. 42; 1 Co. iv. 2; Gal. iv. 2; *the manager of a farm or landed estate, an overseer,* [A. V. *steward*]: Lk. xvi. 1, 3, 8; ὁ οἰκ. τῆς πόλεως, *the superintendent of the city's finances, the treasurer of the city* (Vulg. *arcarius civitatis*): Ro. xvi. 23 (of the treasurers or quaestors of kings, Esth. viii. 9; 1 Esdr. iv. 49; Joseph. antt. 12, 4, 7; 11, 6, 12; 8, 6, 4). Metaph. the apostles and other Christian teachers (see οἰκονομία) are called οἰκ. μυστηρίων τοῦ θεοῦ, as those to whom the counsels of God have been committed to be made known to men : 1 Co. iv. 1; a bishop (or overseer) is called οἰκονόμος θεοῦ, of God as the head and master of the Christian theocracy [see οἶκος, 2], Tit. i. 7; and any and every Christian who rightly uses the gifts intrusted to him by God for the good of his brethren, belongs to the class called καλοὶ οἰκονόμοι ποικίλης χάριτος θεοῦ, 1 Pet. iv. 10. (Aeschyl., Xen., Plat., Aristot., al.; for עַל־בַּיִת Sept. 1 K. iv. 6; xvi. 9, etc.) *

3624 οἶκος, -ου, ὁ, [cf. Lat. *vicus*, Eng. ending -*wich*; Curtius § 95], fr. Hom. down; Sept. in numberless places for בַּיִת, also for הֵיכָל a palace, אֹהֶל a tent, etc.; **1.** *a house*; **a.** strictly, *an inhabited house* [differing thus fr. δόμος the building]: Acts ii. 2; xix. 16; τινός, Mt. ix. 6 sq.; Mk. ii. 11; v. 38; Lk. i. 23, 40, 56; viii. 39, 41, etc.; ἔρχεσθαι εἰς οἶκον, to come into a house (*domum venire*), Mk. iii. 20 (19); εἰς τὸν οἶκον, into the (i. e. *his* or *their*) house, *home*, Lk. vii. 10; xv. 6; ἐν τῷ οἴκῳ, in the (her) house, Jn. xi. 20; ἐν οἴκῳ, at home, 1 Co. xi. 34; xiv. 35; οἱ εἰς τὸν οἶκον (see εἰς, C. 2), Lk. ix. 61; κατ' οἶκον, opp. to ἐν τῷ ἱερῷ, in a household assembly, *in private*, [R. V. *at home*; see κατά, II. 1 d.], Acts iii. 46; v. 42; κατ' οἴκους, opp. to δημοσίᾳ, in private houses, [A. V. *from house to house*; see κατά, II. 3 a.], Acts xx. 20; κατὰ τοὺς οἴκους εἰσπορευόμενος, entering house after house, Acts viii. 3; ἡ κατ' οἶκόν τινος ἐκκλησία, see ἐκκλησία, 4 b. aa. **b.** *any building whatever*: ἐμπορίου, Jn. ii. 16; προσευχῆς, Mt. xxi. 13; Mk. xi. 17; Lk. xix. 46; τοῦ βασιλέως, τοῦ ἀρχιερέως, *the palace of* etc., Mt. xi. 8; Lk. xxii. 54 [here T Tr WH οἰκία]; τοῦ θεοῦ, the house where God was regarded as present,—of the tabernacle, Mt. xii. 4; Mk. ii. 26; Lk. vi. 4; of the temple at Jerusalem, Mt. xxi. 13; Mk. xi. 17; Lk. xix. 46; Jn. ii. 16 sq., (Is. lvi. 5, 7); cf. Lk. xi. 51; Acts vii. 47, 49; of the heavenly sanctuary, Heb. x. 21 (οἶκος ἅγιος θεοῦ, of heaven, Deut. xxvi. 15; Bar. ii. 16); a body of Christians (a church), as pervaded by the Spirit and power of God, is called οἶκος πνευματικός, 1 Pet. ii. 5. **c.** *any dwelling-place*: of the human body as the abode of demons that possess it, Mt. xii. 44; Lk. xi. 24; (used in Grk. auth. also of tents and huts, and later, of the nests, stalls, lairs, of animals). univ. *the place where one has fixed his residence*, one's *settled abode, domicile*: οἶκος ὑμῶν, of the city of Jerusalem, Mt. xxiii. 38; Lk. xiii. 35. **2.** *by me-*

ton. *the inmates of a house, all the persons forming one family, a household*: Lk. x. 5; xi. 17 [al. refer this to 1, and take ἐπί either locally (see ἐπί, C. I. 1), or of succession (see ἐπί, C. I. 2 c.)]; xix. 9; Acts vii. 10; x. 2; xi. 14; xvi. 31; xviii. 8; 1 Co. i. 16; 1 Tim. iii. 4 sq.; v. 4; 2 Tim. i. 16; iv. 19; Heb. xi. 7; plur., 1 Tim. iii. 12; Tit. i. 11, (so also Gen. vii. 1; xlvii. 12, and often in Grk. auth.); metaph. and in a theocratic sense ὁ οἶκος τοῦ θεοῦ, *the family of God*, of the Christian church, 1 Tim. iii. 15; 1 Pet. iv. 17; of the church of the Old and New Testament, Heb. iii. 2, 5 sq. (Num. xii. 7). **3.** *stock, race, descendants* of one, [A. V. *house*]: ὁ οἶκος Δαυίδ, Lk. i. 27, 69; ii. 4, (1 K. xii. 16); οἶκ. Ἰσραήλ, Mt. x. 6; xv. 24; Lk. i. 33; Acts ii. 36; vii. 42; [(ὁ οἶκ. Ἰακώβ), 46 L T Tr mrg.]; Heb. viii. 8, 10, (Jer. xxxviii. (xxxi.) 31; Ex. vi. 14; xii. 3; xix. 3; 1 S. ii. 30; [cf. ὁ σεβαστὸς οἶκος, Philo in Flac. § 4]). The word is not found in the Apocalypse.

[SYN. οἶκος, οἰκία: in Attic (and esp. legal) usage, οἶκος denotes one's *household establishment*, one's *entire property*, οἰκία, the *dwelling itself*; and in prose οἶκος is not used in the sense of οἰκία. In the sense of *family* οἶκος and οἰκία are alike employed; Schmidt vol. ii. ch. 80. In relation to distinctions (real or supposed) betw. οἶκος and οἰκία the foll. pass. are of interest (cf. Valckenaer on Hdt. 7, 224): Xen. oecon. 1, 5 οἶκος δὲ δὴ τί δοκεῖ ἡμῖν εἶναι; ἆρα ὅπερ οἰκία, ἦ καὶ ὅσα τις ἔξω τῆς οἰκίας κέκτηται, πάντα τοῦ οἴκου ταῦτά ἐστιν ... πάντα τοῦ οἴκου εἶναι ὅσα τις κέκτηται. Aristot. polit. 1, 2 p. 1252ᵇ, 9 sqq. ἐκ μὲν οὖν τούτων τῶν δύο κοινωνιῶν (viz. of a man with wife and servant) πρώτη, καὶ ὀρθῶς Ἡσίοδος εἶπε ποιήσας "οἶκον μὲν πρώτιστα γυναῖκά τε βοῦν τ' ἀροτῆρα·" ... ἡ μὲν οὖν εἰς πᾶσαν ἡμέραν συνεστηκυῖα κοινωνία κατὰ φύσιν οἶκός ἐστιν. ibid. 3 p. 1253ᵇ, 2 sqq. πᾶσα πόλις ἐξ οἰκιῶν σύγκειται· οἰκίας δὲ μέρη, ἐξ ὧν αὖθις οἰκία συνίσταται· οἰκία δὲ τέλειος ἐκ δούλων κ. ἐλευθέρων. ... πρῶτα δὲ καὶ ἐλάχιστα μέρη οἰκίας δεσπότης κ. δοῦλος κ. πόσις κ. ἄλοχος . πατὴρ κ. τέκνα etc. Plut. de audiend. poetis § 6 καὶ γὰρ Οἶκόν ποτε μὲν τὴν οἰκίαν καλοῦσιν, "οἶκον ἐς ὑψόροφον" · ποτὲ δὲ τὴν οὐσίαν, "ἐσθίεταί μοι οἶκος"· (see οἰκία, c.) Hesych. Lex. s. v. οἰκία· οἶκοι. s. v. οἶκος· ὀλίγη οἰκία ... καὶ μέρος τι τῆς οἰκίας ... καὶ τὰ ἐν τῇ οἰκίᾳ. In the N. T. although the words appear at times to be used with some discrimination (e. g. Lk. x. 5, 6, 7; Acts xvi. 31, 32, 34; cf. Jn. xiv. 2), yet other pass. seem to show that no distinction can be insisted upon: e. g. Mt. ix. 23; Mk. v. 38; Lk. vii. 36, 37; Acts x. 17, (22, 32); xvii. 5; xix. 16; xxi. 8; xi. 11, 12, 13; xvi. 15; (1 Co. i. 16; xvi. 15).]

3625 οἰκουμένη, -ης, ἡ, (fem. of the pres. pass. ptcp. fr. οἰκέω, [sc. γῆ; cf. W. § 64, 5; B. § 123, 8]); **1.** *the inhabited earth*; **a.** in Grk. writ. often *the portion of the earth inhabited by the Greeks*, in distinction from the lands of the barbarians, cf. Passow ii. p. 415ᵃ; [L. and S. s. v. I.]. **b.** in the Grk. auth. who wrote about Roman affairs, (like the Lat. *orbis terrarum*) i. q. *the Roman empire*: so πᾶσα ἡ οἰκ. contextually i. q. all the subjects of this empire, Lk. ii. 1. **c.** *the whole inhabited earth, the world*, (so in [Hyperid. Eux. 42 ("probably" L. and S.)] Sept. for תֵּבֵל and אֶרֶץ): Lk. iv. 5; xxi. 26; Acts xxiv. 5; Ro. x. 18; Rev. xvi. 14; Heb. i. 6, (πᾶσα ἡ οἰκ. Joseph. b. j. 7, 3, 3); ὅλη ἡ οἰκ., Mt. xxiv. 14; Acts xi. 28, (in the same sense Joseph. antt. 8, 13, 4 πᾶσα ἡ οἰκ.:

cf. *Bleek*, Erklär. d. drei ersten Evv. i. p. 68); by meton. *the inhabitants of the earth, men* : Acts xvii. 6, 31 (Ps. ix. 9) ; xix. 27 ; ἡ οἰκ. ὅλη, all mankind, Rev. iii. 10 ; xii. 9.   **2.** *the universe, the world* : Sap. i. 7 (alternating there with τὰ πάντα) ; ἡ οἰκ. ἡ μέλλουσα, that consummate state of all things which will exist after Christ's return from heaven, Heb. ii. 5 (where the word alternates with πάντα and τὰ πάντα, vs. 8, which there is taken in an absolute sense).*

(3625α);
see 3626

οἰκουργός, -όν, (οἶκος, ΕΡΓΩ [cf. ἔργον], cf. ἀμπελουργός, γεωργός, etc.), *caring for the house, working at home* : Tit. ii. 5 L T Tr WH ; see the foll. word. Not found elsewhere.*

3626

οἰκ-ουρός, -οῦ, ὁ, ἡ, (οἶκος, and οὖρος a keeper ; see θυρωρός and κηπουρός) ;   **a.** prop. *the (watch* or) *keeper of a house* (Soph., Eur., Arstph., Paus., Plut., al.).   **b.** trop. *keeping at home and taking care of household affairs, domestic* : Tit. ii. 5 R G ; cf. Fritzsche, De conformatione N. T. critica etc. p. 29 ; [W. 100 sq. (95)] ; (Aeschyl. Ag. 1626 ; Eur. Hec. 1277 ; σώφρονας, οἰκουροὺς καὶ φιλάνδρους, Philo de exsecr. § 4).*

3627

οἰκτείρω ; fut. (as if fr. οἰκτειρέω, a form which does not exist) as in the Sept. οἰκτειρήσω, for the earlier οἰκτειρῶ, see *Lob.* ad Phryn. p. 741 ; [Veitch s. v. ; W. 88 (84) ; B. 64 (56)] ; (fr. οἶκτος pity, and this fr. the interjection οἴ, *oh !*) ; *to pity, have compassion on* : τινά, Ro. ix. 15 (fr. Ex. xxxiii. 19. Hom., Tragg., Arstph., Xen., Plat., Dem., Lcian., Plut., Ael. ; Sept. for חָנַן and רָחַם). [Syn. see ἐλεέω, fin.]*

3628

οἰκτιρμός, -οῦ, ὁ, (οἰκτείρω), Sept. for רַחֲמִים (the viscera, which were thought to be the seat of compassion [see σπλάγχνον, b.]), *compassion, pity, mercy* : σπλάγχνα οἰκτιρμοῦ (Rec. οἰκτιρμῶν), bowels in which compassion resides, *a heart of compassion*, Col. iii. 12 ; in the Scriptures mostly plural (conformably to the Hebr. רַחֲמִים), *emotions, longings, manifestations of pity*, [Eng. *compassions*] (cf. Fritzsche, Ep. ad Rom. iii. p. 5 sqq. ; [W. 176 (166) ; B. 77 (67)]), τοῦ θεοῦ, Ro. xii. 1 ; Heb. x. 28 ; ὁ πατὴρ τῶν οἰκτ. (gen. of quality [cf. B. § 132, 10 ; W. 237 (222)]), the father of mercies i. e. most merciful, 2 Co. i. 3 ; joined with σπλάγχνα, Phil. ii. 1. (Pind. Pyth. 1, 164.) [Syn. see ἐλεέω, fin.]*

3629

οἰκτίρμων, -ον, gen. -ονος, (οἰκτείρω), *merciful* : Lk. vi. 36 ; Jas. v. 11. (Theocr. 15, 75 ; Anth. 7, 359, 1 [Epigr. Anth. Pal. Append. 223, 5] ; Sept. for רַחוּם)   ["In classic Grk. only a poetic term for the more common ἐλεήμων." Schmidt iii. p. 580.]*

see 3633   οἶμαι, see οἴομαι.
3630

οἰνο-πότης, -ον, ὁ, (οἶνος, and πότης a drinker), *a wine-bibber, given to wine* : Mt. xi. 19 ; Lk. vii. 34.   (Prov. xxiii. 20 ; Polyb. 20, 8, 2 ; Anacr. frag. 98 ; Anthol. 7, 28, 2.)*

3631

οἶνος, -ου, ὁ, [fr. Hom. down], Sept. for יַיִן, also for תִּירוֹשׁ (must, new wine), חֶמֶר, etc. ; *wine* :   **a.** prop. : Mt. ix. 17 ; [xxvii. 34 L txt. T Tr WH] ; Mk. xv. 23 ; Lk. i. 15 ; Jn. ii. 3 ; Ro. xiv. 21 ; Eph. v. 18 ; 1 Tim. v. 23 ; Rev. xvii. 2, etc. ; οἴνῳ προσέχειν, 1 Tim. iii. 8 ; δουλεύειν, Tit. ii. 3.   **b.** metaph. : οἶνος τοῦ θυμοῦ (see

θυμός, 2), fiery wine, which God in his wrath is represented as mixing and giving to those whom he is about to punish by their own folly and madness, Rev. xiv. 10 ; xvi. 19 ; xix. 15 ; with τῆς πορνείας added [cf. W. § 30, 3 N. 1 ; B. 155 (136)], *a love-potion* as it were, wine exciting to fornication, which he is said to give who entices others to idolatry, Rev. xiv. 8 ; xviii. 3 [here L om. Tr WH br. οἴν.], and he is said to be drunk with who suffers himself to be enticed, Rev. xvii. 2.   **c.** by meton. i. q. *a vine* : Rev. vi. 6.

οἰνοφλυγία, -ας, ἡ, (οἰνοφλυγέω, and this fr. οἰνόφλυξ, which is compounded of οἶνος and φλύω, to bubble up, overflow), *drunkenness*, [A. V. *wine-bibbing*] : 1 Pet. iv. 3. (Xen. oec. 1, 22 ; Aristot. eth. Nic. 3, 5, 15 ; Polyb. 2, 19, 4 ; Philo, vita Moys. iii. § 22 [for other exx. see *Siegfried*, Philo etc. p. 102] ; Ael. v. h. 3, 14.)   [Cf. Trench § lxi.]*   **3632**

οἴομαι, contr. οἶμαι ; [fr. Hom. down] ; *to suppose, think* : foll. by an acc. w. inf. Jn. xxi. 25 [T om. vs.] ; by the inf. alone, where the subj. and the obj. are the same, Phil. i. 16 (17) ; by ὅτι, Jas. i. 7.   [Syn. see ἡγέομαι, fin.]*   **3633**

οἶος, -α, -ον, [fr. Hom. down], relat. pron. (correlative to the demonstr. τοῖος and τοιοῦτος), *what sort of, what manner of, such as* (Lat. *qualis*) : οἶος . . . τοιοῦτος, 1 Co. xv. 48 ; 2 Co. x. 11 ; τὸν αὐτὸν . . . οἶον, Phil. i. 30 ; with the pron. τοιοῦτος suppressed, Mt. xxiv. 21 ; Mk. ix. 3 ; xiii. 19 [here however the antecedent demonstr. is merely attracted into the relat. clause or perhaps repeated for rhetorical emphasis, cf. B. § 143, 8 ; W. 148 (140) ; see τοιοῦτος, b.] ; 2 Co. xii. 20 ; 2 Tim. iii. 11 ; Rev. xvi. 18 ; οἱῳδηποτοῦν νοσήματι, of what kind of disease soever, Jn. v. 4 Lchm. [cf. *Lob.* ad Phryn. p. 373 sq.] ; in indir. quest., Lk. ix. 55 [Rec.] ; 1 Th. i. 5.   οὐχ οἶον δὲ ὅτι ἐκπέπτωκεν, concisely for οὐ τοῖόν ἐστιν οἶον ὅτι ἐκπ. but the thing (state of the case) *is not such as this, that the word of God hath fallen to the ground*, i. e. *the word of God hath by no means come to nought* [A. V. *but not as though the word of God hath* etc.], Ro. ix. 6 ; cf. W. § 64 I. 6 ; B. § 150, 1 Rem.*   **3634**

οἱοσδηποτοῦν, Jn. v. 4 Lchm., see οἶος.   **see 3634**
οἴσω, see φέρω.   **see 5342**

ὀκνέω, -ῶ : 1 aor. ὤκνησα ; (ὄκνος [perh. allied w. the frequent. *cunc-tari* (cf. Curtius p. 708)] delay) ; fr. Hom. down ; *to feel loath, to be slow ; to delay, hesitate* : foll. by an inf. Acts ix. 38. (Num. xxii. 16 ; Judg. xviii. 9, etc.)*   **3635**

ὀκνηρός, -ά, -όν, (ὀκνέω), *sluggish, slothful, backward* : Mt. xxv. 26 ; with a dat. of respect [cf. W. § 31, 6 a. ; B. § 133, 21], Ro. xii. 11 ; οὐκ ὀκνηρόν μοί ἐστι, foll. by an inf., *is not irksome to me, I am not reluctant*, Phil. iii. 1 [cf. Bp. Lghtft. ad loc.]. (Pind., Soph., Thuc., Dem., Theocr., etc. ; Sept. for עָצֵל.)*   **3636**

ὀκταήμερος, -ον, (ὀκτώ, ἡμέρα), *eight days old ; passing the eighth day* : περιτομῇ [cf. W. § 31, 6 a. ; B. § 133, 21] ; but Rec. -μῇ ὀκταήμερος, *circumcised on the eighth day*, Phil. iii. 5 ; see τεταρταῖος ; ['the word denotes prop. not interval but duration' (see Bp. Lghtft. on Phil. l. c.). Graec. Ven. Gen. xvii. 12 ; eccl. writ.].*   **3637**

3638   ὀκτώ, *eight*: Lk. ii. 21; Jn. xx. 26; Acts ix. 33, etc. [(From Hom. on.)]

see 3645   ὀλεθρεύω (Lchm. in Heb. xi. 28), see ὀλοθρεύω.

see 3639   ὀλέθριος, -ον, (in prof. auth. also of three term., as in Sap. xviii. 15), (ὄλεθρος), fr. [Hom.], Hdt. down, *destructive, deadly*: δίκην, 2 Th. i. 9 Lchm. txt.*

3639   ὄλεθρος, -ον, (ὄλλυμι to destroy [perh. (ὄλνυμι) allied to Lat. *vulnus*]), fr. Hom. down, *ruin, destruction, death*: 1 Th. v. 3; 1 Tim. vi. 9; εἰς ὄλεθρον τῆς σαρκός, *for the destruction of the flesh*, said of the external ills and troubles by which the lusts of the flesh are subdued and destroyed, 1 Co. v. 5 [see παραδίδωμι, 2]; i. q. the loss of a life of blessedness after death, future misery, αἰώνιος (as 4 Macc. x. 15): 2 Th. i. 9 [where L txt. ὀλέθριον, q. v.], cf. Sap. i. 12.*

see 570 & 3640   ὀλιγοπιστία, -ας, ἡ, *littleness of faith, little faith*: Mt. xvii. 20 L T Tr WH, for R G ἀπιστία. (Several times in eccles. and Byzant. writ.) *

3640   ὀλιγό-πιστος, -ου, ὁ, ἡ, (ὀλίγος and πίστις), *of little faith, trusting too little*: Mt. vi. 30; viii. 26; xiv. 31; xvi. 8; Lk. xii. 28. (Not found in prof. auth.) *

3641   ὀλίγος, -η, -ον, [on its occasional aspiration (ὀλ.)` see WH. App. p. 143; Tdf. Proleg. pp. 91, 106; Scrivener, Introd. p. 565, and reff. s. v. οὐ init.], Sept. for מְעַט, [fr. Hom. down], *little, small, few*, of number, multitude, quantity, or size: joined to nouns [cf. W. § 20, 1 b. note; B. § 125, 6], Mt. ix. 37; xv. 34; Mk. vi. 5; viii. 7; Lk. x. 2; xii. 48 (ὀλίγας sc. πληγάς [cf. B. § 134, 6; W. § 32, 5, esp. § 64, 4], opp. to πολλαί, 47); Acts xix. 24; 1 Tim. v. 23; Heb. xii. 10; Jas. iii. 5 R G; 1 Pet. iii. 20 R G; Rev. iii. 4; of time, *short*: χρόνος, Acts xiv. 28; καιρός, Rev. xii. 12; of degree or intensity, *light, slight*: τάραχος, Acts xii. 18; xix. 23; στάσις, xv. 2; χειμών, xxvii. 20. plur. w. a partitive gen.: γυναικῶν, Acts xvii. 4; ἀνδρῶν, ib. 12. ὀλίγοι, absol.: Mt. vii. 14; xx. 16; [T WH m. Tr br. the cl.]; xxii. 14; Lk. xiii. 23; 1 Pet. iii. 20 L T Tr WH; neut. sing.: Lk. vii. 47; τὸ ὀλίγον, 2 Co. viii. 15; πρὸς ὀλίγον ὠφέλιμος, *profitable for little* (Lat. *parum utilis*); [cf. W. 213 (200); *some, for a little* (sc. time); see below], 1 Tim. iv. 8; ἐν ὀλίγῳ, *in few words* [cf. Shakspere's *in a few*], i. e. *in brief, briefly* (γράφειν), Eph. iii. 3; *easily*, without much effort, Acts xxvi. 28 sq. on other but incorrect interpretations of this phrase cf. Meyer ad loc. [see μέγας, 1 a. γ.]; πρὸς ὀλίγον, for a little time, Jas. iv. 14; simply ὀλίγον, adverbially: of time, *a short time, a (little) while*, Mk. vi. 31; 1 Pet. i. 6; v. 10; Rev. xvii. 10; of space, *a little (further)*, Mk. i. 19; Lk. v. 3. plur. ὀλίγα, *a few things*: [Lk. x. 41 WH]; Rev. ii. 14, 20 [Rec.]; ἐπ᾽ ὀλίγα [see init. and] ἐπί, C. I. 2 e.], Mt. xxv. 21, 23; δι᾽ ὀλίγων, briefly, in few words, γράφειν, 1 Pet. v. 12 [see διά, A. III. 3] (ῥηθῆναι, Plat. Phil. p. 31 d.; legg. 6 p. 778 c.).*

3642   ὀλιγόψυχος, -ον, (ὀλίγος, ψυχή), *faint-hearted*: 1 Th. v. 14. (Prov. xiv. 29; xviii. 14; Is. lvii. 15, etc.; Artem. oneir. 3, 5.) *

3643   ὀλιγωρέω, -ῶ; (ὀλίγωρος, and this fr. ὀλίγος and ὥρα care); *to care little for, regard lightly, make small account of*: τινός (see Matthiae § 348; [W. § 30, 10 d.]), Heb.

xii. 5 fr. Prov. iii. 11. (Thuc., Xen., Plat., Dem., Aristot., Philo, Joseph., al.) *

see 3689 & 3641   ὀλίγως, (ὀλίγος), adv., *a little, scarcely*, [R. V. *just* (escaping)]: 2 Pet. ii. 18 G L T Tr WH [for Rec. ὄντως]. (Anthol. 12, 205, 1; [Is. x. 7 Aq.].) *

3644   ὀλοθρευτής [Rec. ὀλ.], -οῦ, ὁ, (ὀλοθρεύω, q. v.), *a destroyer*; found only in 1 Co. x. 10.*

3645   ὀλοθρεύω and, acc. to a preferable form, ὀλεθρεύω (Lchm.; see *Bleek*, Hebr.-Br. ii. 2 p. 809; cf. *Delitzsch*, Com. on Heb. as below; [*Tdf.* Proleg. p. 81; WH. App. p. 152]); (ὄλεθρος); an Alex. word [W. 92 (88)]; *to destroy*: τινά, Heb. xi. 28. (Ex. xii. 23; Josh. iii. 10; vii. 25; Jer. ii. 30; Hag. ii. 22, etc.; [Philo, alleg. ii. 9].) [COMP.: ἐξ-ολοθρεύω.] *

3646   ὁλοκαύτωμα, -τος, τό, (ὁλοκαυτόω to burn whole, Xen. Cyr. 8, 3, 24; Joseph. antt. 1, 13, 1; and this fr. ὅλος and καυτός, for καυστός, verbal adj. fr. καίω, cf. *Lob.* ad Phryn. p. 524; [W. 33]), *a whole burnt offering* (Lat. *holocaustum*), i. e. a victim the whole (and not like other victims only a part) of which is burned: Mk. xii. 33; Heb. x. 6, 8. (Sept. esp. for עֹלָה; also for אִשֶּׁה, Ex. xxx. 20; Lev. v. 12; xxiii. 8, 25, 27; 1 Macc. i. 45; 2 Macc. ii. 10; not found in prof. auth. [exc. Philo de sacr. Ab. et Cain. § 33]; Joseph. antt. 3, 9, 1 and 9, 7, 4 says ὁλοκαύτωσις.) *

3647   ὁλοκληρία, -ας, ἡ, (ὁλόκληρος, q. v.), Lat. *integritas*; used of an unimpaired condition of body, in which all its members are healthy and fit for use; Vulg. *integra sanitas* [A. V. *perfect soundness*]: Acts iii. 16 [joined with ὑγίεια, Plut. mor. p. 1063 f.; with τοῦ σώματος added, ibid. p. 1047 e.; cf. Diog. Laërt. 7, 107; *corporis integritas*, i. q. health, in Cic. de fin. 5, 14, 40; Sept. for מְתֹם, Is. i. 6).*

3648   ὁλό-κληρος, -ον, (ὅλος and κλῆρος, prop. all that has fallen by lot), *complete in all its parts, in no part wanting or unsound, complete, entire, whole*: λίθοι, untouched by a tool, Deut. xxvii. 6; Josh. ix. 4 (viii. 31); 1 Macc. iv. 47; of a body without blemish or defect, whether of a priest or of a victim, Philo de vict. § 12; Joseph. antt. 3, 12, 2 [(cf. Havercamp's Joseph. ii. p. 321)]. Ethically, *free from sin, faultless*, [R. V. *entire*]: 1 Th. v. 23; plur., connected with τέλειοι and with the addition of ἐν μηδενὶ λειπόμενοι, Jas. i. 4; *complete in all respects, consummate*, δικαιοσύνη, Sap. xv. 3; εὐσέβεια, 4 Macc. xv. 17. (Plat., Polyb., Lcian., Epict., al.; Sept. for שָׁלֵם, Deut. xxvii. 6; תָּמִים, Lev. xxiii. 15; Ezek. xv. 5.) *

[SYN. ὁλόκληρος, τέλειος (cf. Trench § xxii.): 'in the ὁλόκληρος no grace which ought to be in a Christian man is deficient; in the τέλειος no grace is merely in its weak imperfect beginnings, but all have reached a certain ripeness and maturity.']

3649   ὀλολύζω; an onomatopoetic verb (cf. the similar οἰμώζειν, αἰάζειν, ἀλαλάζειν, πιπίζειν, κοκκύζειν, τίζειν. Compare the Germ. term.-*zen*, as in *grunzen, krächzen, ächzen*), *to howl, wail, lament*: Jas. v. 1. (In Grk. writ. fr. Hom. down of a loud cry, whether of joy or of grief; Sept. for הֵילִיל.) [SYN. cf. κλαίω, fin.] *

3650   ὅλος, -η, -ον, Sept. for כֹּל, [fr. Pind. (Hom.) down], *whole, (all)*: with an anarthrous subst. five [six] times in the N. T., viz. ὅλον ἄνθρωπον, Jn. vii. 23; ἐνιαυτὸν ὅλον, Acts xi. 26; ὅλη Ἱερουσαλήμ, xxi. 31; διετίαν ὅλην, xxviii. 30; ὅλους οἴκους, Tit. i. 11; [to which add, δι' ὅλης νυκτός, Lk. v. 5 L T Tr WH]. usually placed before a substantive which has the article: ὅλη ἡ Γαλιλαία, Mt. iv. 23; ὅλη ἡ Συρία, 24; καθ' ὅλην τὴν πόλιν, Lk. viii. 39; ὅλον τὸ σῶμα, Mt. v. 29 sq.; vi. 22. sq.; Lk. xi. 34; 1 Co. xii. 17; Jas. iii. 2, etc.; [ὅλη ἡ ἐκκλησία, Ro. xvi. 23 L T Tr WH]; ὅλην τ. ἡμέραν, Mt. xx. 6; Ro. viii. 36; ὅλος ὁ νόμος, Mt. xxii. 40; Gal. v. 3; Jas. ii. 10; ἐν ὅλῃ τῇ καρδίᾳ σου, Mt. xxii. 37; ἐξ ὅλης τ. καρδίας σου, Mk. xii. 30, and many other exx. it is placed after a substantive which has the article [W. 131 (124) note; B. § 125, 6]: ἡ πόλις ὅλη, Mk. i. 33; Acts xix. 29 [Rec.]; xxi. 30 — (the distinction which Krüger § 50, 11, 7 makes, viz. that ἡ ὅλη πόλις denotes the whole city as opp. to its parts, but that ὅλη ἡ πόλις and ἡ πόλις ἡ ὅλη denotes the whole city in opp. to other ideas, as the country, the fields, etc., does not hold good at least for the N. T., where even in ἡ πόλις ὅλη the city is opposed only to its parts); add the foll. exx.: Mt. xvi. 26; xxvi. 59; Lk. ix. 25; xi. 36ᵃ; Jn. iv. 53; Ro. xvi. 23 [R G]; 1 Jn. v. 19; Rev. iii. 10; vi. 12 G L T Tr WH; xii. 9; xvi. 14. It is subjoined to an adjective or a verb to show that the idea expressed by the adj. or verb belongs to the whole person or thing under consideration: Mt. xiii. 33; Lk. xi. 36ᵇ; xiii. 21; Jn. ix. 34; xiii. 10, (Xen. mem. 2, 6, 28). Neut. τοῦτο δὲ ὅλον, Mt. i. 22; xxi. 4 (where G L T Tr WH om. ὅλον); xxvi. 56; δι' ὅλου, throughout, Jn. xix. 23.

3651   **ὁλοτελής, -ές**, (ὅλος, τέλος), *perfect, complete in all respects*: 1 Th. v. 23. (Plut. plac. philos. 5, 21; [*Field, Hexapla, Lev. vi. 23*; Ps. l. 21]); eccles. writ.) *

3652   **Ὀλυμπᾶς** [perh. contr. fr. Ὀλυμπιόδωρος, W. 103 (97); cf. *Fick*, Gr. Personennamen, pp. 63 sq. 201], -ᾶ, [B. 20 (18)], ὁ, *Olympas*, a certain Christian: Ro. xvi. 15.*

3653   **ὄλυνθος, -ου, ὁ**, *an unripe fig* (Lat. *grossus*), which grows during the winter, yet does not come to maturity but falls off in the spring [cf. B. D. s. v. Fig]: Rev. vi. 13. (Hes. fr. 14; Hdt. 1, 193; Dioscorid. 1, 185; Theophr. caus. plant. 5, 9, 12; Sept. cant. ii. 13.) *

3654   **ὅλως**, (ὅλος), adv., *wholly, altogether*, (Lat. *omnino*), [with a neg. *at all*]: Mt. v. 34 (with which compare Xen. mem. 1, 2, 35); 1 Co. v. 1 [R. V. *actually*]; vi. 7; xv. 29. [(Plat., Isocr., al.)] *

3655   **ὄμβρος, -ου, ὁ**, (Lat. *imber*) *a shower*, i. e. a violent rain, accompanied by high wind with thunder and lightning: Lk. xii. 54. (Deut. xxxii. 2; Sap. xvi. 16; in Grk. writ. fr. Hom. down.) *

see 2442   **ὁμείρομαι** [or ὀμ., see below] i. q. ἱμείρομαι; *to desire, long for, yearn after*, [A. V. *to be affectionately desirous*]: τινός, 1 Th. ii. 8 G L T Tr WH [but the last read ὀμ., cf. their App. p. 144 and *Lob.* Pathol. Element. i. 72], on the authority of all the uncial and many cursive Mss., for Rec. ἱμειρόμενοι. The word is unknown to the Grk. writ., but the commentators ad loc. recognize it, as do Hesychius, Phavorinus, and Photius, and interpret it by ἐπιθυμεῖν. It

is found in Ps. lxii. 2 Symm., and acc. to some Mss. in Job iii. 21. Acc. to the conjecture of *Fritzsche*, Com. on Mk. p. 792, it is composed of ὁμοῦ and εἴρειν, just as Photius [p. 331, 8 ed. Porson] explains it ὁμοῦ ἡρμόσθαι [so Theophylact (cf. Tdf.'s note)]. But there is this objection, that all the verbs compounded with ὁμοῦ govern the dative, not the genitive. Since Nicander, ther. vs. 402, uses μείρομαι for ἱμείρομαι, some suppose that the original form is μείρομαι, to which, after the analogy of κέλλω and ὀκέλλω, either ἱ or ὁ is for euphony prefixed in ἱμείρ. and ὁμείρ. But as ἱμείρομαι is derived from ἵμερος, we must suppose that Nicander dropped the syllable ἱ to suit the metre. Accordingly ὁμείρεσθαι seems not to differ at all from ἱμείρεσθαι, and its form must be attributed to a vulgar pronunciation. Cf. [*WH.* App. p. 152]; W. 101 (95); [B. 64 (56); Ellic. on 1 Th. l. c.; (*Kuenen and Cobet*, N. T. Vat. p. ciii.)].*

3656   **ὁμιλέω, -ῶ**; impf. ὡμίλουν; 1 aor. ptcp. ὁμιλήσας; (ὅμιλος, q. v.); freq. in Grk. writ. fr. Hom. down; *to be in company with; to associate with; to stay with*; hence *to converse with, talk with*: τινί, *with one* (Dan. i. 19), Acts xxiv. 26; sc. αὐτοῖς, Acts xx. 11 [so A. V. *talked*], unless one prefer to render it *when he had stayed in their company*; πρός τινα, Lk. xxiv. 14 (Xen. mem. 4, 3, 2; Joseph. antt. 11, 6, 11; [cf. W. 212 sq. (200); B. § 133, 8]); ἐν τῷ ὁμιλεῖν αὐτούς sc. ἀλλήλοις, ibid. 15. [COMP.: συν-ομιλέω.]*

3657   **ὁμιλία, -ας, ἡ**, (ὅμιλος), *companionship, intercourse, communion*: 1 Co. xv. 33, on which see ἦθος. (Tragg., Arstph., Xen., Plat., and sqq.) *

3658   **ὅμιλος, -ου, ὁ**, (ὁμός, ὁμοῦ, and ἴλη a crowd, band, [Curtius § 660; Vaniček p. 897; but Fick iii. 723 fr. root *mil* 'to be associated,' 'to love']), fr. Hom. down, *a multitude of men gathered together, a crowd, throng*: Rev. xviii. 17 Rec.*

see 3509   **ὀμίχλη, -ης, ἡ**, (in Hom. ὀμίχλη, fr. ὀμιχέω to make water), *a mist, fog*: 2 Pet. ii. 17 G L T Tr WH. (Am. iv. 13; Joel ii. 2; Sir. xxiv. 3; Sap. ii. 4.) *

3659   **ὄμμα, -τος, τό**, (fr. ὄπτομαι [see ὁράω], pf. ὦμμαι), fr. Hom. down, *an eye*: plur. Mt. xx. 34 L T Tr WH; Mk. viii. 23. (Sept. for עַיִן, Prov. vi. 4; vii. 2; x. 26.) *

3660   **ὀμνύω** (Mt. xxiii. 20 sq.; xxvi. 74; Heb. vi. 16; Jas. v. 12; [W. 24]) and **ὄμνυμι** (ὀμνύναι, Mk. xiv. 71 G L T Tr WH [cf. B. 45 (39)]) form their tenses fr. ΟΜΟΩ; hence 1 aor. ὤμοσα; Sept. for שָׁבַע; *to swear; to affirm, promise, threaten, with an oath*: absol., foll. by direct discourse, Mt. xxvi. 74; Mk. xiv. 71; Heb. vii. 21; foll. by εἰ, Heb. iii. 11; iv. 3; see εἰ, I. 5. ὀμν. ὅρκον (often so in Grk. writ. fr. Hom. down [W. 226 (212)]) πρός τινα, to one (Hom. Od. 14, 331; 19, 288), Lk. i. 73; ὀμνύειν with dat. of the person to whom one promises or threatens something with an oath: foll. by direct disc. Mk. vi. 23; by an inf. [W. 331 (311)], Heb. iii. 18; with ὅρκῳ added, Acts ii. 30 [W. 603 (561)]; τινί τι, Acts vii. 17 [Rec. i. e. gen. by attraction; cf. B. § 143, 8; W. § 24, 1]. that by which one swears is indicated by an acc., τινά or τί (so in class. Grk. fr. Hom. down [cf. W. § 32, 1 b. γ.; B. 147 (128)]), *in swearing to call a person* or *thing as witness, to invoke, swear by*, (Is. lxv. 16; Joseph. antt. 5, 1, 2; 7, 14, 5); τὸν οὐρανόν, τὴν γῆν, Jas. v. 12; with prepositions [cf. B. u. s.]: κατά τινος (see κατά, I. 2 a.), Heb. vi. 13, 16, (Gen. xxii. 16; xxxi. 54; 1 S. xxviii. 10 [Comp.]; Is. xlv. 23; lxii. 8; Am. iv. 2; Dem. p. 553, 17; 553, 26 [al. ἀπομ.], etc.; κατὰ πάντων ὤμνυε θεῶν, Long. past. 4, 16); in imitation of the Hebr. עַל foll. by בְּ, ἕν τινι is used [W. 389 (364); B. l. c.; see ἐν, I. 8 b.]: Mt. v. 34, 36; xxiii. 16, 18, 20–22; Rev. x. 6; εἴς τι, with the mind directed unto [W. 397 (371); B. as above; see εἰς, B. II. 2 a.], Mt. v. 35.*

3661   ὁμοθυμαδόν (fr. ὁμόθυμος, and this fr. ὁμός and θυμός; on advs. in -δόν [chiefly derived fr. nouns, and designating form or structure] as γνωμηδόν, ῥοιζηδόν, etc., cf. Bttm. Ausf. Spr. ii. p. 452), with one mind, of one accord, (Vulg. unanimiter [etc.]): Ro. xv. 6; Acts i. 14; ii. 46; iv. 24; vii. 57; viii. 6; xii. 20; xv. 25; xviii. 12; xix. 29, and R G in ii. 1, (Arstph., Xen., Dem., Philo, Joseph., Hdian., Sept. Lam. ii. 8; Job xvii. 16; Num. xxiv. 24, etc.); with ἅπαντες [L T WH πάντες] (Arstph. pax 484, and often in class. Grk.), Acts v. 12 [cf. ii. 1 above].*

3662   ὁμοιάζω; (ὅμοιος, [cf. W. 25]); to be like: Mt. xxiii. 27 L Tr txt. WH mrg.; Mk. xiv. 70 Rec. where see Fritzsche p. 658 sq.; [on the dat. cf. W. § 31, 1 h.]. Not found elsewhere. [Comp.: παρ-ομοιάζω.]*

3663   ὁμοιοπαθής, -ές, (ὅμοιος, πάσχω), suffering the like with another, of like feelings or affections: τινί, Acts xiv. 15; Jas. v. 17. (Plat. rep. 3, 409 b., Tim. 45 c.; Theophr. h. pl. 5, 8 (7, 2); Philo, conf. ling. § 3; 4 Macc. xii. 13; γῇ, i. e. trodden alike by all, Sap. vii. 3; see exx. fr. eccles. writ. [viz. Ignat. (interpol.) ad Trall. 10; Euseb. h. e. 1, 2, 1, (both of the incarnate Logos)] in Grimm on 4 Macc. p. 344.) *

3664   ὅμοιος (on the accent cf. [Chandler §§ 384, 385]; W. 52 (51); Bttm. Ausf. Spr. § 11 Anm. 9), -οία, -οιον, also of two term. (once in the N. T., Rev. iv. 3 Rˢᵗ G L T Tr WH; cf. W. § 11, 1; [B. 26 (23)]), (fr. ὁμός [akin to ἅμα (q. v.), Lat. similis, Eng. same, etc.]), [fr. Hom. down], like, similar, resembling: a. like i. e. resembling: τινί, in form or look, Jn. ix. 9; Rev. i. 13, 15; ii. 18; iv. 6 sq.; ix. 7, 10 [but here Tr txt. WH mrg. ὁμοίοις], 19; xi. 1; xiii. 2, 11; xiv. 14 [but here T WH w. the accus. (for dat.)]; xvi. 13 Rec.; ὁράσει, in appearance, Rev. iv. 3; in nature, Acts xvii. 29; Gal. v. 21; Rev. xxi. 11, 18; in nature and condition, 1 Jn. iii. 2; in mode of thinking, feeling, acting, Mt. xi. 16; xiii. 52; Lk. vi. 47–49; vii. 31 sq.; xii. 36, and L WH Tr txt. (see below) in Jn. viii. 55; i. q. may be compared to a thing, so in parables: Mt. xiii. 31, 33, 44 sq. 47; xx. 1; Lk. xiii. 18 sq. 21.   b. like i. e. corresponding or equiv. to, the same as: ὅμοιον τούτοις τρόπον, Jude 7; equal in strength, Rev. xiii. 4; in power and attractions, Rev. xviii. 18; in authority, Mt. xxii. 39; Mk. xii. 31 [here T WH om. Tr mrg. br. ὅμ.]; in mind and character, τινός (cf. W. 195 (183), [cf. § 28, 2]; B. § 132, 24), Jn. viii. 55 R G T Tr mrg. (see above).*

3665   ὁμοιότης, -ητος, ἡ, (ὅμοιος), likeness: καθ᾽ ὁμοιότητα, in like manner, Heb. iv. 15 [cf. W. 143 (136)]; κατὰ τὴν ὁμοιότητα (Μελχισεδέκ), after the likeness, Heb. vii. 15. (Gen. i. 11; 4 Macc. xv. 4 (3); Plat., Aristot., Isocr., Polyb., Philo, Plut.) *

ὁμοιόω, -ῶ: fut. ὁμοιώσω; Pass., 1 aor. ὡμοιώθην, and   3666 without augm. ὁμοιώθην (once Ro. ix. 29 L mrg. T edd. 2, 7, [but see WH. App. p. 161]; cf. B. 34 (30); Sturz, De dial. Maced. etc. p. 124; [cf.] Lob. ad Phryn. p. 153); 1 fut. ὁμοιωθήσομαι; (ὅμοιος); fr. [Hom. and] Hdt. down; Sept. esp. for דָּמָה;   a. to make like: τινά τινι; pass. to be or to become like to one: Mt. vi. 8; Acts xiv. 11; Heb. ii. 17; ὡμοιώθη ἡ βασιλ. τῶν οὐρ., was made like, took the likeness of, (aor. of the time when the Messiah appeared), Mt. xiii. 24; xviii. 23; xxii. 2; ὁμοιωθήσεται (fut. of the time of the last judgment), Mt. xxv. 1; ὥς τι, to be made like and thus to become as a thing [i. e. a blending of two thoughts; cf. Fritzsche on Mk. iv. 31; B. § 133, 10; W. § 65, 1 a.], Ro. ix. 29 (כְּ נִדְמָה Ezek. xxxii. 2).   b. to liken, compare: τινά τινι, or τί τινι, Mt. vii. 24 [R G (see below)]; xi. 16; Mk. iv. 30 R L txt. Tr mrg.; Lk. vii. 31; xiii. 18, 20; pass. Mt. vii. [24 L T WH Tr txt.], 26; to illustrate by comparison, πῶς ὁμοιώσωμεν τὴν βασ. τοῦ θεοῦ, Mk. iv. 30 T WH Tr txt. L mrg. [Comp.: ἀφ-ομοιόω.] *

ὁμοίωμα, -τος, τό, (ὁμοιόω), Sept. for צֶלֶם, דְּמוּת, תְּמוּנָה,   3667 תַּבְנִית; prop. that which has been made after the likeness of something, hence   a. a figure, image, likeness, representation: Ps. cv. (cvi.) 20; 1 Macc. iii. 48; of the image or shape of things seen in a vision, Rev. ix. 7 [cf. W. 604 (562)] (Ezek. i. 5, 26, 28, etc. Plato, in Parmen. p. 132 d., calls finite things ὁμοιώματα, likenesses as it were, in which τὰ παραδείγματα, i. e. αἱ ἰδέαι or τὰ εἴδη, are expressed).   b. likeness i. e. resemblance (inasmuch as that appears in an image or figure), freq. so much as amounts well-nigh to equality or identity: τινός, Ro. vi. 5; viii. 3 (on which see σάρξ, 3 fin. [cf. Weiss, Bibl. Theol. etc. §§ 69 c. note, 78 c. note]); Phil. ii. 7 (see μορφή); εἰκόνος, a likeness expressed by an image, i. e. an image like, Ro. i. 23; ἐπὶ τῷ ὁμοιώματι τῆς παραβάσεως Ἀδάμ, in the same manner in which Adam transgressed a command of God [see ἐπί, B. 2 a. η.], Ro. v. 14. Cf. the different views of this word set forth by Holsten, Zum Evangel. des Paulus u. Petrus, p. 437 sqq. and [esp. for exx.] in the Jahrbüch. f. protest. Theol. for 1875, p. 451 sqq., and by Zeller, Zeitschr. f. wissensch. Theol. for 1870, p. 301 sqq. [Syn. cf. εἰκών, fin.; Schmidt ch. 191.]*

ὁμοίως, (ὅμοιος), adv., [fr. Pind., Hdt. down], likewise,   3668 equally, in the same way: Mk. iv. 16 (Tr mrg. br. ὁμ.); Lk. iii. 11; x. 37; xiii. 3 L T Tr WH; 5 R G L Tr mrg.; xvi. 25; xvii. 31; Jn. v. 19; xxi. 13; 1 Pet. iii. 1, 7; v. 5; Heb. ix. 21; Rev. ii. 15 (for Rec. ὃ μισῶ); viii. 12; ὁμοίως καί, Mt. xxii. 26; xxvi. 35; Mk. xv. 31 [here Rec. ὁμ. δὲ καί]; Lk. v. 33; xvii. 28 R G L; xxii. 36; Jn. vi. 11; 1 Co. vii. 22 R G; ὁμοίως μέντοι καί, Jude 8; ὁμοίως δὲ καί, Mt. xxvii. 41 R G (where T om. L br. δὲ καί, Tr br. δέ, WH om. δέ and br. καί); Lk. v. 10; x. 32; 1 Co. vii. 3 (where L br. δέ), 4; Jas. ii. 25; and correctly restored by L Tr mrg. in Ro. i. 27, for R T Tr txt. WH ὁμοίως τε καί; cf. Fritzsche, Rom. i. p. 77; [W. 571 (531); B. § 149, 8]; ὁμοίως preceded by καθώς, Lk. vi. 31.*

ὁμοίωσις, -εως, ἡ, (ὁμοιόω);   1. a making like: 3669 opp. to ἀλλοίωσις, Plat. rep. 5, 454 c.   2. likeness,

(Plat., Aristot., Theophr.) : καθ᾽ ὁμοίωσιν θεοῦ, after the likeness of God, Jas. iii. 9 fr. Gen. i. 26. [Cf. Trench § xv.]*

3670   ὁμολογέω, -ῶ; impf. ὡμολόγουν; fut. ὁμολογήσω; 1 aor. ὡμολόγησα; pres. pass. 3 pers. sing. ὁμολογεῖται; (fr. ὁμόλογος, and this fr. ὁμόν and λέγω) ; fr. [Soph. and] Hdt. down ;   1. prop. to say the same thing as another, i. e. to agree with, assent, both absol. and w. a dat. of the pers.; often so in Grk. writ. fr. Hdt. down; hence   2. univ. to concede; i. e.   a. not to refuse, i. e. to promise: τινὶ τὴν ἐπαγγελίαν, Acts vii. 17 L T Tr WH [here R. V. vouchsafe]; foll. by an object. inf., Mt. xiv. 7 (Plat., Dem., Plut., al.).   b. not to deny, i. e. to confess; declare: joined w. οὐκ ἀρνεῖσθαι, foll. by direct disc. with recitative ὅτι, Jn. i. 20; foll. by ὅτι, Heb. xi. 13 ; τινί τι, ὅτι, Acts xxiv. 14 ; to confess, i. e. to admit or declare one's self guilty of what one is accused of : τὰς ἁμαρτίας, 1 Jn. i. 9 (Sir. iv. 26).   3. to profess (the diff. betw. the Lat. profiteor [' to declare openly and voluntarily'] and confiteor [' to declare fully,' implying the yielding or change of one's conviction; cf. professio fidei, confessio peccatorum] is exhibited in Cic. pro Sest. 51, 109), i. e. to declare openly, speak out freely, [A. V. confess]; on its constr. see B. § 133, 7]: [foll. by an inf., εἰδέναι θεόν, Tit. i. 16]; τινί [cf. B. u. s.; W. § 31, 1 f.] foll. by direct disc. with ὅτι recitative, Mt. vii. 23 ; one is said ὁμολογεῖν that of which he is convinced and which he holds to be true (hence ὁμ. is disting. fr. πιστεύειν in Jn. xii. 42; Ro. x. 9 sq.) : pass. absol., with στόματι (dat. of instrum.) added, Ro. x. 10 ; τί, Acts xxiii. 8 ; τινά with a predicate acc. [B. u. s.], αὐτὸν Χριστόν, Jn. ix. 22; κύριον (pred. acc.) Ἰησοῦν, Ro. x. 9 [here WH τὸ ῥῆμα . . . ὅτι κύριος etc., L mrg. Tr mrg. simply ὅτι etc.; again with ὅτι in 1 Jn. iv. 15]; Ἰησοῦν Χρ. ἐν σαρκὶ ἐληλυθότα [Tr mrg. WH mrg. ἐληλυθέναι], 1 Jn. iv. 2 and Rec. also in 3 [see below] ; ἐρχόμενον ἐν σαρκί, 2 Jn. 7, [cf. B. u. s.; W. 346 (324)]; τινά, to profess one's self the worshipper of one, 1 Jn. iv. 3 [here WH mrg. λύει, cf. Westcott, Epp. of Jn. p. 156 sqq.] and G L T Tr WH in ii. 23 ; ἐν with a dat. of the pers. (see ἐν, I. 8 c.), Mt. x. 32 ; Lk. xii. 8 ; with cognate acc. giving the substance of the profession [cf. B. § 131, 5; W. § 32, 2], ὁμολογίαν, 1 Tim. vi. 12 (also foll. by περί τινος, Philo de mut. nom. § 8) ; τὸ ὄνομά τινος, to declare the name (written in the book of life) to be the name of a follower of me, Rev. iii. 5 G L T Tr WH.   4. Acc. to a usage unknown to Grk. writ. to praise, celebrate, (see ἐξομολογέω, 2 ; [B. § 133, 7]) : τινί, Heb. xiii. 15. [COMP.: ἀνθ-(-μαι), ἐξ-ομολογέω.] *

3671   ὁμολογία, -ας, ἡ, (ὁμολογέω, q. v. [cf. W. 35 (34)]), in the N. T. profession [R. V. uniformly confession] ;   a. subjectively: ἀρχιερέα τῆς ὁμολ. ἡμῶν, i. e. whom we profess (to be ours), Heb. iii. 1 [but al. refer this to b.].   b. objectively, profession [confession] i. e. what one professes [confesses] : Heb. iv. 14; 1 Tim. vi. 12 (see ὁμολογέω, 3) 13 (see μαρτυρέω, a. p. 391ᵃ); τῆς ἐλπίδος, the substance of our profession, which we embrace with hope, Heb. x. 23 ; εἰς τὸ εὐαγγέλιον τοῦ Χριστοῦ, relative to the gospel, 2 Co. ix. 13 (translate, for the obedience ye render to what

ye profess concerning the gospel; cf. ἡ εἰς τὸν τοῦ θεοῦ Χριστὸν ὁμολογία, Justin M. dial. c. Tryph. c. 47, — a constr. occasioned perhaps by ἡ εἰς τὸν Χριστὸν πίστις, Col. ii. 5 ; [cf. W. 381 (357)]). [(Hdt., Plat., al.)]*

ὁμολογουμένως, (ὁμολογέω), adv., by consent of all, confessedly, without controversy: 1 Tim. iii. 16. (4 Macc. vi. 31; vii. 16 ; xvi. 1 ; in prof. auth. fr. Thuc., Xen., Plat. down ; with ὑπὸ πάντων added, Isocr. paneg. § 33, where see Baiter's note.)*   **3672**

ὁμότεχνος, -ον, (ὁμός and τέχνη), practising the same trade or craft, of the same trade: Acts xviii. 3. (Hdt. 2, 89 ; Plat., Dem., Joseph., Lcian., al.) *   **3673**

ὁμοῦ, (ὁμός), [fr. Hom. down], adv., together : Jn. iv. 36 ; xx. 4 ; εἶναι ὁμοῦ, of persons assembled together, Acts ii. 1 L T Tr WH; xx. 18 Lchm.; Jn. xxi. 2. [SYN. see ἅμα, fin.]*   **3674**

ὁμόω, see ὄμνύω.   see **3660**

ὁμόφρων, -ον, (ὁμός, φρήν), of one mind, [A. V. likeminded], concordant : 1 Pet. iii. 8. (Hom., Hes., Pind., Arstph., Anthol., Plut., al.) *   **3675**

ὅμως, (ὁμός), fr. Hom. down, yet; it occurs twice in the N. T. out of its usual position [cf. W. § 61, 5 f.; B. § 144, 23], viz. in 1 Co. xiv. 7, where resolve thus : τὰ ἄψυχα, καίπερ φωνὴν διδόντα, ὅμως, ἐὰν διαστολὴν . . . πῶς κτλ. instruments without life, although giving forth a sound, yet, unless they give a distinction in the sounds, how shall it be known etc., Fritzsche, Conject. spec. i. p. 52 ; cf. Meyer ad loc.; [W. 344 (323)]; again, ὅμως ἀνθρώπου . . . οὐδεὶς ἀθετεῖ for ἀνθρώπου κεκυρ. διαθήκην, καίπερ ἀνθρώπου οὖσαν, ὅμως οὐδεὶς κτλ. a man's established covenant, though it be but a man's, yet no one etc. Gal. iii. 15; ὅμως μέντοι, but yet, nevertheless, [cf. W. 444 (413)], Jn. xii. 42.*   **3676**

ὄναρ, τό, (an indecl. noun, used only in the nom. and acc. sing.; the other cases are taken from ὄνειρος), [fr. Hom. down], a dream : κατ᾽ ὄναρ, in a dream, Mt. i. 20; ii. 12 sq. 19, 22 ; xxvii. 19, — a later Greek phrase, for which Attic writ. used ὄναρ without κατά [q. v. II. 2⁻; see Lob. ad Phryn. p. 422 sqq.; [Photius, Lex. p. 14?, 25 sq.].*   **3677**

ὀνάριον, -ου, τό, (dimin. of ὄνος; cf. [W. 24 and] γυναικάριον), a little ass : Jn. xii. 14. (Machon ap. Athen. 13 p. 582 c.; [Epictet. diss. 2, 24, 18].) *   **3678**

ὀνειδίζω; impf. ὠνείδιζον; 1 aor. ὠνείδισα; pres. pass. ὀνειδίζομαι; (ὄνειδος, q. v.); fr. Hom. down ; Sept. esp. for חָרַף ; to reproach, upbraid, revile ; [on its constr. cf. W. § 32, 1 b. β.; B. § 133, 9] : of deserved reproach, τινά, foll. by ὅτι, Mt. xi. 20 ; τί (the fault) τινος, foll. by ὅτι, Mk. xvi. 14. of unjust reproach, to revile: τινά, Mt. v. 11; Mk. xv. 32; Lk. vi. 22; Ro. xv. 3 fr. Ps. lxviii. (lxix.) 10 ; pass. 1 Pet. iv. 14 ; foll. by ὅτι, 1 Tim. iv. 10 R G Tr mrg. WH mrg.; τὸ αὐτὸ ὠνείδιζον αὐτόν (Rec. αὐτῷ), Mt. xxvii. 44 (see αὐτός, III. 1). to upbraid, cast (favors received) in one's teeth: absol. Jas. i. 5 ; μετὰ τὸ δοῦναι μὴ ὀνείδιζε, Sir. xli. 22, cf. xx. 14 ; τινὶ σωτηρίαν, deliverance obtained by us for one, Polyb. 9, 31, 4.*   **3679**

ὀνειδισμός, -οῦ, ὁ, (ὀνειδίζω), [cf. W. 24], a reproach : Ro. xv. 3 ; 1 Tim. iii. 7; Heb. x. 33 ; ὁ ὀνειδισμὸς τοῦ Χρι-   **3680** στοῦ i. e. such as Christ suffered (for the cause of God, from its enemies), Heb. xi. 26; xiii. 13; cf. W. 189 (178). (Plut. Artax. 22; [Dion. Hal.]; Sept. chiefly for חֶרְפָּה.) *

3681 ὄνειδος, -ους, τό, (fr. ὄνομαι to blame, to revile), fr. Hom. down, *reproach*; i. q. *shame*: Lk. i. 25. (Sept. chiefly for חֶרְפָּה; three times for כְּלִמָּה disgrace, Is. xxx. 3; Mich. ii. 6; Prov. xviii. 13.) *

3682 Ὀνήσιμος, -ου, ὁ, (i. e. profitable, helpful; fr. ὄνησις profit), *Onesimus*, a Christian, the slave of Philemon: Philem. 10; Col. iv. 9. [Cf. Bp. *Lghtft.* Com. Intr. § 4; Hackett in B. D.]*

3683 Ὀνησίφορος, -ου, ὁ, [i. e. ʻ profit-bringer ʼ], *Onesiphorus*, the name of a certain Christian: 2 Tim. i. 16; iv. 19.*

3684 ὀνικός, -ή, -όν, (ὄνος), *of* or *for an ass*: μύλος ὀνικός i. e. turned by an ass (see μύλος, 1), Mk. ix. 42 L T Tr WH; Lk. xvii. 2 Rec.; Mt. xviii. 6. Not found elsewhere.*

3685 ὀνίνημι: fr. Hom. down; *to be useful, to profit, help*, (Lat. *juvo*); Mid., pres. ὀνίναμαι; 2 aor. ὠνήμην (and later ὠνάμην, see *Lob.* ad Phryn. p. 12 sq.; Kühner § 343 s. v., i. p. 880; [Veitch s. v.]), optat. ὀναίμην; *to receive profit* or *advantage, be helped* [or *have joy*, (Lat. *juvor*)]: τινός, of one, Philem. 20 [see Bp. Lghtft. ad loc.]. (Elsewh. in the Scriptures only in Sir. xxx. 2.) *

3686 ὄνομα, -τος, τό, (NOM [others ΓΝΟ; see Vaniček p. 1239], cf. Lat. *nomen* [Eng. *name*], with prefixed o [but see Curtius § 446]), Sept. for שֵׁם, [fr. Hom. down], the *name* by which a person or a thing is called, and distinguished from others; **1.** univ.: of prop. names, Mk. iii. 16; vi. 14; Acts xiii. 8, etc.; τῶν ἀποστόλων τὰ ὀνόματα, Mt. x. 2; Rev. xxi. 14; ἄνθρωπος or ἀνὴρ ᾧ ὄνομα, πόλις ᾗ ὄν. sc. ἦν, *named*, foll. by the name in the nom. [cf. B. § 129, 20, 3]: Lk. i. 26 sq.; ii. 25; viii. 41; xxiv. 13, 18; Acts xiii. 6, (Xen. mem. 3, 11, 1); οὗ [L ᾧ] τὸ ὄνομα, Mk. xiv. 32; καὶ τὸ ὄν. αὐτοῦ, αὐτῆς, etc., Lk. i. 5, 27; ὄνομα αὐτῷ sc. ἦν or ἐστίν [B. u. s.], Jn. i. 6; iii. 1; xviii. 10; Rev. vi. 8; ὀνόματι, foll. by the name cf. B. § 129 a. 3; W. 182 (171)], Mt. xxvii. 32; Mk. v. 22; Lk. v. 38; xvi. 20; xxiii. 50; Acts v. 1, 34; viii. 9; ix. 10–12, 33, 36; x. 1; xi. 28; xii. 13; xvi. 1, 14; xvii. 34; xviii. 2, 7, 24; xix. 24; xx. 9; xxi. 10; xxvii. 1; xxviii. 7; Rev. ix. 11, (Xen. anab. 1, 4, 11); τοὔνομα (i. e. τὸ ὄνομα), acc. absol. [B. § 131, 12; cf. W. 230 (216)], i. e. by name, Mt. xxvii. 57; ὄνομά μοι sc. ἐστίν, my name is, Mk. v. 9; Lk. viii. 30, (Οὖτίς ἐμοί γ ὄνομα, Hom. Od. 9, 366); ἔχειν ὄνομα, foll. by the name in the nom., Rev. ix. 11; καλεῖν τὸ ὄνομά τινος, foll. by the acc. of the name, see καλέω, 2 a.; καλεῖν τινα ὀνόματί τινι, Lk. i. 61; ὀνόματι καλούμενος, Lk. xix. 2; καλεῖν τινα ἐπὶ τῷ ὀν. Lk. i. 59 (see ἐπί, B. 2 a. η. p. 233ᵇ); κατ᾽ ὄνομα (see κατά, II. 3 a. γ. p. 328ᵃ); τὰ ὀνόματα ὑμῶν ἐγράφη [ἐνγέγραπται T WH Tr] ἐν τοῖς οὐρανοῖς, your names have been enrolled by God in the register of the citizens of the kingdom of heaven, Lk. x. 20; τὸ ὄνομά τινος (ἐγράφη) ἐν βίβλῳ (τῷ βιβλίῳ) ζωῆς, Phil. iv. 3; Rev. xiii. 8; ἐπὶ τὸ βιβλίον τῆς ζ. Rev. xvii. 8; ἐκβάλλειν (q. v. 1 h.) τὸ ὄνομά τινος ὡς πονηρόν, since the wickedness of the man is called to mind by his name, Lk. vi. 22; ἐπικαλεῖσθαι τὸ ὄνομα τοῦ κυρίου, see ἐπικαλέω, 5; ἐπικέκληται τὸ ὄνομά τινος ἐπί τινα, see ἐπικ. 2; ὀνόματα (ὄνομα)

βλασφημίας i. q. βλάσφημα (-μον) [cf. W. § 34, 3 b.; B. § 132, 10], names by which God is blasphemed, his majesty assailed, Rev. xiii. 1; xvii. 3 [R G Tr, see γέμω]. so used that the name is opp. to the reality: ὄνομα ἔχεις, ὅτι ζῇς, καὶ νεκρὸς εἶ, thou art said [A. V. *hast a name*] to live, Rev. iii. 1 (ὄνομα εἶχεν, ὡς ἐπ᾽ Ἀθήνας ἐλαύνει, Hdt. 7, 138). i. q. *title*: περὶ ὀνομάτων, about titles (as of the Messiah), Acts xviii. 15; κληρονομεῖν ὄνομα, Heb. i. 4; χαρίζεσθαί τινι ὄνομά τι, Phil. ii. 9 (here the title ὁ κύριος is meant [but crit. txts. read τὸ ὄνομα etc., which many either strictly or absolutely; cf. Meyer and Bp. Lghtft. ad loc. (see below just before 3)]); spec. a title of honor and authority, Eph. i. 21 [but see Meyer]; ἐν τῷ ὀνόματι Ἰησοῦ, in devout recognition of the title conferred on him by God (i. e. the title ὁ κύριος), Phil. ii. 10 [but the interp. of ὄνομα here follows that of ὄνομα in vs. 9 above; see Meyer and Bp. Lghtft., and cf. W. 390 (365)]. **2.** By a usage chiefly Hebraistic the *name* is used for everything which the name covers, everything the thought or feeling of which is roused in the mind by mentioning, hearing, remembering, the name, i. e. for *one's rank, authority, interests, pleasure, command, excellences, deeds*, etc.; thus, εἰς ὄνομα προφήτου, out of regard for [see εἰς, B. II. 2 d.] the name of prophet which he bears, i. q. because he is a prophet, Mt. x. 41; βαπτίζειν τινὰ εἰς ὄνομά τινος, by baptism to bind any one to recognize and publicly acknowledge the dignity and authority of one [cf. βαπτίζω, II. b. (aa.)], Mt. xxviii. 19; Acts viii. 16; xix. 5; 1 Co. i. 13, 15. *to do a thing ἐν ὀνόματί τινος*, i. e. *by one's command and authority, acting on his behalf, promoting his cause*, [cf. W. 390 (365); B. § 147, 10]; as, ὁ ἐρχόμενος ἐν ὀνόματι κυρίου (fr. Ps. cxvii. (cxviii.) 26), of the Messiah, Mt. xxi. 9; xxiii. 39; Mk. xi. 9; Lk. xiii. 35; xix. 38; Jn. xii. 13; ἐν τῷ ὀνόματι τοῦ πατρός μου, Jn. v. 43; x. 25; ἐν τῷ ὀνόματι τῷ ἰδίῳ, of his own free-will and authority, Jn. v. 43; to do a thing ἐν τῷ ὀν. of Jesus, Acts v. 48; 1 Co. v. 4; 2 Th. iii. 6; and L T Tr WH in Jas. v. 10 [but surely κ. here denotes *God*; cf. 2 f. below]. Acc. to a very freq. usage in the O. T. (cf. יְהֹוָה שֵׁם), the *name of God* in the N. T. is used for all those qualities which to his worshippers are summed up in that name, and by which God makes himself known to men; it is therefore equiv. to his *divinity*, Lat. *numen*, (not his nature or essence as it is in itself), *the divine majesty and perfections, so far forth as these are apprehended, named, magnified*, (cf. *Winer*, Lex. Hebr. et Chald. p. 993; *Oehler* in Herzog x. p. 196 sqq.; *Wittichen* in Schenkel iv. p. 282 sqq.); so in the phrases ἅγιον τὸ ὄνομα αὐτοῦ sc. ἐστίν, Lk. i. 49; ἁγιάζειν τὸ ὄν. τοῦ θεοῦ, Mt. vi. 9; Lk. xi. 2; ὁμολογεῖν τῷ ὀν. αὐτοῦ, Heb. xiii. 15; ψάλλειν, Ro. xv. 9; δοξάζειν, Jn. xii. 28; [Rev. xv. 4]; φανεροῦν, γνωρίζειν, Jn. xvii. 6, 26; φοβεῖσθαι τὸ ὄν. τοῦ θεοῦ, Rev. xi. 18; xv. 4 [G L T Tr WH]; διαγγέλλειν, Ro. ix. 17; ἀπαγγέλλειν, Heb. ii. 12; βλασφημεῖν, Ro. ii. 24; 1 Tim. vi. 1; Rev. xiii. 6; xvi. 9; ἀγάπην ἐνδείκνυσθαι εἰς τὸ ὄν. τοῦ θεοῦ, Heb. vi. 10; τήρησον αὐτοὺς ἐν τῷ ὀνόματί σου, ᾧ (by attraction for ὅ [cf. B. § 143, 8 p. 286; W. § 24, 1; Rec. incorrectly οὓς]) δέδωκάς μοι, keep them consecrated and united to thy name (character), which thou didst commit to me to declare and manifest (cf. vs. 6), Jn. xvii. 11; [cf. ὑπὲρ τοῦ ἁγίου ὀνόματός σου, οὗ κατεσκήνωσας ἐν ταῖς καρδίαις ἡμῶν, 'Teaching' etc. ch. 10, 2]. After the analogy of the preceding expression, the name of Christ ('Ιησοῦ, 'Ιησοῦ Χριστοῦ, τοῦ κυρίου 'Ιησ., τοῦ κυρίου ἡμῶν, etc.) is used in the N.T. of all those things which, in hearing or recalling that name, we are bidden to recognize in Jesus and to profess; accordingly, his Messianic dignity, divine authority, memorable sufferings, in a word the peculiar services and blessings conferred by him on men, so far forth as these are believed, confessed, commemorated, [cf. Westcott on the Epp. of Jn. p. 232]: hence the phrases εὐαγγελίζεσθαι τὰ περὶ τοῦ ὀν. Ἰ. Χρ. Acts viii. 12; μεγαλύνειν τὸ ὀν. Acts xix. 17; τῷ ὀνομ. [Rec. ἐν τ. ὀν.] αὐτοῦ ἐλπίζειν, Mt. xii. 21 [B. 176 (153)]; πιστεύειν, 1 Jn. iii. 23; πιστ. εἰς τὸ ὀν., Jn. i. 12; ii. 23; iii. 18; 1 Jn. v. 13ᵃ [Rec., 13ᵇ]; πίστις τοῦ ὀν. Acts iii. 16; ὁ ὀνομάζων τὸ ὄνομα κυρίου, whoever nameth the name of the Lord sc. as his Lord (see ὀνομάζω, a.), 2 Tim. ii. 19; κρατεῖν, to hold fast i. e. persevere in professing, Rev. ii. 13; οὐκ ἀρνεῖσθαι, Rev. iii. 8; τὸ ὀν. 'Ιησοῦ ἐνδοξάζεται ἐν ὑμῖν, 2 Th. i. 12; βαστάζειν τὸ ὀν. ἐνώπιον ἐθνῶν (see βαστάζω, 3), Acts ix. 15; to do or to suffer anything ἐπὶ τῷ ὀνόματι Χρ. see ἐπί, B. 2 a. β. p. 232ᵇ. The phrase ἐν τῷ ὀνόματι Χρ. is used in various senses: **a.** by the command and authority of Christ: see exx. just above. **b.** in the use of the name of Christ i. e. the power of his name being invoked for assistance, Mk. ix. 38 Rᵉˡᶻ L T Tr WH (see f. below); Lk. x. 17; Acts iii. 6; iv. 10; xvi. 18; Jas. v. 14; univ. ἐν ποίῳ ὀνόματι ἐποιήσατε τοῦτο; Acts iv. 7. **c.** through the power of Christ's name, pervading and governing their souls, Mk. xvi. 17. **d.** in acknowledging, embracing, professing, the name of Christ: σωθῆναι, Acts iv. 12; δικαιωθῆναι, 1 Co. vi. 11; [ζωὴν ἔχειν, Jn. xx. 31]; in professing and proclaiming the name of Christ, παρρησιάζεσθαι, Acts ix. 27, 28 (29). **e.** relying or resting on the name of Christ, rooted (so to speak) in his name, i. e. mindful of Christ: ποιεῖν τι, Col. iii. 17; εὐχαριστεῖν, Eph. v. 20; αἰτεῖν τι, i. e. (for substance) to ask a thing, as prompted by the mind of Christ and in reliance on the bond which unites us to him, Jn. xiv. 13 sq.; xv. 16; xvi. 24, [26], and R G L in 23; cf. Ebrard, Gebet im Namen Jesu, in Herzog iv. 692 sqq. G o d is said to do a thing ἐν ὀν. Χρ. regardful of the name of Christ, i. e. moved by the name of Christ, for Christ's sake, διδόναι the thing asked, Jn. xvi. 23 T Tr WH; πέμπειν τὸ πνεῦμα τὸ ἅγ. Jn. xiv. 26. **f.** ἐν ὀνόματι Χριστοῦ, [A. V. for the name of Christ] (Germ. auf Grund Namens Christi), i. e. because one calls himself or is called by the name of Christ: ὀνειδίζεσθαι, 1 Pet. iv. 14 (equiv. to ὡς Χριστιανός, 16). The simple dat. τῷ ὀν. Χρ. signifies by the power of Christ's name, pervading and prompting souls, Mt. vii. 22; so also τῷ ὀνόματι τοῦ κυρίου (i. e. of God) λαλεῖν, of the prophets, Jas. v. 10 R G; τῷ ὀν. σου, by uttering thy name as a spell, Mk. ix. 38 Rˢᵗ ᵇᵉᶻ G (see b. above). εἰς τὸ ὄνομα τοῦ Χριστοῦ συνάγεσθαι is used of those who come together to deliberate concerning any matter relating to Christ's cause, (Germ. auf den Na-

men), with the mind directed unto, having regard unto, his name, Mt. xviii. 20. ἔνεκεν τοῦ ὀν. [A. V. for my name's sake], i. e. on account of professing my name, Mt. xix. 29; also διὰ τὸ ὀν. μου, αὐτοῦ, etc.: Mt. x. 22; xxiv. 9; Mk. xiii. 13; Lk. xxi. 17; Jn. xv. 21; 1 Jn. ii. 12; Rev. ii. 3. διὰ τοῦ ὀν. τοῦ κυρ. παρακαλεῖν τινα, to beseech one by employing Christ's name as a motive or incentive [cf. W. 381 (357)], 1 Co. i. 10; by embracing and avowing his name, ἄφεσιν ἁμαρτιῶν λαβεῖν, Acts x. 43; ὑπὲρ τοῦ ὀν. αὐτοῦ, i. q. for defending, spreading, strengthening, the authority of Christ, Acts v. 41 (see below); ix. 16; xv. 26; xxi. 13; Ro. i. 5; 3 Jn. 7; — [but acc. to the better txts. in Acts v. 41; 3 Jn. 7, τὸ ὄνομα is used absolutely, the Name, sc. κυρίου, of the Lord Jesus; so cod. Vat. Jas. v. 14; cf. Lev. xxiv. 11, 16; Bp. Lghtft. on Ignat. ad Eph. 3, 1; B. 163 (142) note; W. 594 (553). So Bp. Lghtft. in Phil. ii. 9; (see 1 above)]. πρὸς τὸ ὄνομα 'Ιησοῦ τοῦ Ναζ. ἐναντία πρᾶξαι, Acts xxvi. 9. **3.** In imitation of the Hebr. שֵׁמוֹת (Num. i. 2, 18, 20; iii. 40, 43; xxvi. 53), the plur. ὀνόματα is used i.q. persons reckoned up by name: Acts i. 15; Rev. iii. 4; xi. 13. **4.** Like the Lat. nomen, i. q. the cause or reason named: ἐν τῷ ὀνόματι τούτῳ, in this cause, i. e. on this account, sc. because he suffers as a Christian, 1 Pet. iv. 16 L T Tr WH [al. more simply take ὀν. here as referring to Χριστιανός preceding]; ἐν ὀνόματι, ὅτι (as in Syriac ، ܒܫܡ) Χριστοῦ ἐστε, in this name, i. e. for this reason, because ye are Christ's (disciples), Mk. ix. 41.

ὀνομάζω; 1 aor. ὠνόμασα; Pass., pres. ὀνομάζομαι; 1 aor. ὠνομάσθην; (ὄνομα); fr. Hom. down; to name [cf. W. 615 (572)]; **a.** τὸ ὄνομα, to name i. e. to utter: pass. Eph. i. 21; τοῦ κυρίου [Rec. Χριστοῦ], the name of the Lord (Christ) sc. as his Lord, 2 Tim. ii. 19 (Sept. for יַזְכִּיר שֵׁם יְהוָה, to make mention of the name of Jehovah in praise, said of his worshippers, Is. xxvi. 13; Am. vi. 10); τὸ ὄνομα 'Ιησοῦ ἐπί τινα, Acts xix. 13, see ἐπί, C. I. 1 c. p. 234ᵇ mid. **b.** τινά, with a proper or an appellative name as pred. acc., to name, i. e. give name to, one: Lk. vi. 13 sq.; pass. to be named, i. e. bear the name of, 1 Co. v. 11; ἐκ w. gen. of the one from whom the received name is derived, Eph. iii. 15 (Hom. Il. 10, 68; Xen. mem. 4, 5, 12). **c.** τινά or τί, to utter the name of a person or thing: ὅπου ὠνομάσθη Χριστός, of the lands into which the knowledge of Christ has been carried, Ro. xv. 20 (1 Macc. iii. 9); ὀνομάζεσθαι of things which are called by their own name because they are present or exist (as opp. to those which are unheard of), 1 Co. v. 1 Rec.; Eph. v. 3. [COMP.: ἐπ-ονομάζω.]*

3687

ὄνος, -ου, ὁ, ἡ, [fr. Hom. down], Sept. for חֲמוֹר and אָתוֹן, an ass: Lk. xiv. 5 Rec.; Mt. xxi. 5; Jn. xii. 15; — ὁ, Lk. xiii. 15; ἡ, Mt. xxi. 2, 7.*

3688

ὄντως (fr. ὤν; on advs. formed fr. ptcps. cf. Bttm. Ausf. Spr. § 115 a. Anm. 3; Kühner § 335 Anm. 2), adv., truly, in reality, in point of fact, as opp. to what is pretended, fictitious, false, conjectural: Mk. xi. 32 [see ἔχω, I. 1 f.]; Lk. xxiii. 47; xxiv. 34; Jn. viii. 36; 1 Co. xiv. 25; Gal. iii. 21 and Rec. in 2 Pet. ii. 18; ὁ, ἡ, τὸ

3689

ὄντως foll. by a noun, *that which is truly* etc., *that which is indeed*, (τὰ ὄντως ἀγαθὰ ἢ καλά, Plat. Phaedr. p. 260 a.; τὴν ὄντως καὶ ἀληθῶς φιλίαν, Plat. Clit. p. 409 e.; οἱ ὄντως βασιλεῖς, Joseph. antt. 15, 3, 5) : as ἡ ὄντως (Rec. αἰώνιος) ζωή, 1 Tim. vi. 19 ; ἡ ὄντως χήρα, a widow that is a widow indeed, not improperly called a widow (as παρθένος ἡ λεγομένη χήρα, i. e. a virgin that has taken a vow of celibacy, in Ign. ad Smyrn. 13 [cf. Bp. Lghtft. in loc.]; cf. Baur, Die sogen. Pastoralbriefe, p. 46 sqq.), 1 Tim. v. 3, 5, 16. (Eur., Arstph., Xen., Plat., sqq.; Sept. for אָמְנָה, Num. xxii. 37 ; for אַךְ, Jer. iii. 23 ; for אַךְ, Jer. x. 19.) *

3690   ὄξος, -εος (-ους), τό, (ὀξύς), *vinegar* (Aeschyl., Hippocr., Arstph., Xen., sqq.; for חֹמֶץ, Ruth ii. 14 ; Num. vi. 3, etc.); used in the N. T. for Lat. *posca*, i. e. the mixture of sour wine or vinegar and water which the Roman soldiers were accustomed to drink: Mt. xxvii. 34 R L mrg., 48 ; Mk. xv. 36 ; Lk. xxiii. 36 ; Jn. xix. 29 sq.*

3691   ὀξύς, -εῖα, -ύ, [allied w. Lat. *acer, acus*, etc.; cf. Curtius § 2]; **1.** *sharp* (fr. Hom. down) : ῥομφαία, δρέπανον, Rev. i. 16 ; ii. 12 ; xiv. 14, 17 sq.; xix. 15, (Is. v. 28 ; Ps. lvi. (lvii.) 5). **2.** *swift, quick*, (so fr. Hdt. 5, 9 down ; cf. ὠκύς fleet) : Ro. iii. 15 (Am. ii. 15 ; Prov. xxii. 29).*

3692   ὀπή, -ῆς, ἡ, (perh. fr. ὄψ [root ὀπ (see ὁράω); cf. Curtius § 627]), prop. *through which one can see* (Pollux [2, 53 p. 179] ὀπή, δι' ἧς ἔστιν ἰδεῖν, cf. Germ. *Luke, Loch* [?]), *an opening, aperture*, (used of a window, Cant. v. 4) : of fissures in the earth, Jas. iii. 11 (Ex. xxxiii. 22); of caves in rocks or mountains, Heb. xi. 38 [here R. V. *holes*]; Obad. 3. (Of various other kinds of holes and openings, in Arstph., Aristot., al.) *

3693   ὄπισθεν, (see ὀπίσω), adv. of place, *from behind, on the back, behind, after* : Mt. ix. 20 ; Mk. v. 27 ; Lk. viii. 44 ; Rev. iv. 6 ; v. 1 (on which see γράφω, 3). As a preposition it is joined with the gen. (like ἔμπροσθεν, ἔξωθεν, etc. [W. § 54, 6 ; B. § 146, 1]) : Mt. xv. 23 ; Lk. xxiii. 26 ; [Rev. i. 10 WH mrg.]. (From Hom. down ; Sept. for אַחֲרֵי, sometimes for אָחוֹר.) *

3694   ὀπίσω, ([perh.] fr. ἡ ὄπις ; and this fr. ἔπω, ἕπομαι, to follow [but cf. Vaniček p. 530]), adv. of place and time, fr. Hom. down ; Sept. for אַחַר, אָחוֹר and esp. for אַחֲרֵי ; (at the) *back, behind, after* ; **1.** adverbially of place : ἑστάναι, Lk. vii. 38 ; ἐπιστρέψαι ὀπίσω, *back*, Mt. xxiv. 18 (ὑποστρέφειν ὀπίσω, Joseph. antt. 6, 1, 3) ; τὰ ὀπίσω, *the things that are behind*, Phil. iii. 13 (14) ; εἰς τὰ ὀπίσω ἀπέρχεσθαι, *to go backward*, Vulg. *abire retrorsum*, Jn. xviii. 6 ; *to return home*, of those who grow recreant to Christ's teaching and cease to follow him, Jn. vi. 66 ; στρέφεσθαι, to turn one's self back, Jn. xx. 14 ; ἐπιστρέφειν, to return back to places left, Mk. xiii. 16 ; Lk. xvii. 31 ; ὑποστρέψαι εἰς τὰ ὀπίσω, trop., of those who return to the manner of thinking and living already abandoned, 2 Pet. ii. 21 Lchm.; βλέπειν (Vulg. [*aspicere* or] *respicere retro* [A. V. *to look back*]), Lk. ix. 62. **2.** By a usage unknown to Grk. auth., as a prep. with the gen. [W. § 54, 6 ; B. § 146, 1]; **a.** of place : Rev. i. 10 [WH mrg. ὄπισθεν] ; xii. 15, (Num. xxv. 8 ; Cant. ii. 9) ; in phrases resembling the Hebr. [cf. W. 30 ; B. u. s. and 172 (150)] : ὀπίσω τινὸς ἔρχεσθαι to follow any one as a guide, to be his disciple or follower, Mt. xvi. 24 ; Lk. ix. 23 ; Mk. viii. 34 R L Tr mrg. WH ; [cf. Lk. xiv. 27]; also ἀκολουθεῖν, Mk. viii. 34 G T Tr txt.; Mt. x. 38, (see ἀκολουθέω, 2 fin.) ; πορεύεσθαι, to join one's self to one as an attendant and follower, Lk. xxi. 8 (Sir. xlvi. 10) ; to seek something one lusts after, 2 Pet. ii. 10 [cf. W. 594 (553) ; B. 184 (160)] ; ἀπέρχομαι ὀπίσω τινός, to go off in order to follow one, to join one's party, Mk. i. 20 ; Jn. xii. 19 ; to run after a thing which one lusts for [cf. B. u. s.], ἑτέρας σαρκός, Jude 7 ; δεῦτε ὀπίσω μου (see δεῦτε, 1), Mt. iv. 19 ; Mk. i. 17 ; ἀποστέλλειν τινὰ ὀπίσω τινός, Lk. xix. 14 ; ἀφιστάναι, ἀποσπᾶν τινα ὀπίσω αὑτοῦ, to draw one away to (join) his party, Acts v. 37; xx. 30 ; ἐκτρέπεσθαι, to turn out of the right path, turn aside from rectitude, 1 Tim. v. 15 ; by a pregnant construction, after θαυμάζειν, *to wonder after* i. e. to be drawn away by admiration to follow one [B. 185 (160 sq.)], Rev. xiii. 3 (πᾶς ὁ λαὸς ἐξέστη ὀπίσω αὐτοῦ, 1 S. xiii. 7) ; ὕπαγε ὀπίσω μου, [A. V. *get thee behind me*], out of my sight : Lk. iv. 8 R L br.; Mt. iv. 10 [G L br.]; xvi. 23 ; Mk. viii. 33. **b.** of time, *after* : ἔρχεσθαι ὀπίσω τινός, to make his public appearance after (subsequently to) one, Mt. iii. 11 ; Mk. i. 7 ; Jn. i. 15, 27, 30, (ὀπίσω τοῦ σαββάτου, Neh. xiii. 19).*

3695   ὁπλίζω : [1 aor. mid. impv. 2 pers. plur. ὁπλίσασθε] ; (ὅπλον) ; fr. Hom. down ; *to arm, furnish with arms* ; univ. *to provide* ; mid. τί, *to furnish one's self with a thing* (as with arms) ; metaph. τὴν αὐτὴν ἔννοιαν ὁπλίσασθε, [A. V. *arm yourselves with* i. e.] take on the same mind, 1 Pet. iv. 1 (θράσος, Soph. Electr. 995). [COMP. : καθ-οπλίζω.] *

3696   ὅπλον, [allied to ἕπω, Lat. *sequor, socius*, etc.; Curtius § 621], -ου, τό, as in class. Grk. fr. Hom. down, *any tool* or *implement* for preparing a thing, (like the Lat. *arma*) ; hence **1.** plur. *arms* used in warfare, *weapons* : Jn. xviii. 3 ; 2 Co. x. 4 ; metaph. τῆς δικαιοσύνης, which ἡ δικ. furnishes, 2 Co. vi. 7 ; τοῦ φωτός, adapted to the light, such as light demands, Ro. xiii. 12 [here L mrg. ἔργα]. **2.** *an instrument* : ὅπλα ἀδικίας, for committing unrighteousness, opp. to ὅπλα δικαιοσύνης, for practising righteousness, Ro. vi. 13.*

3697   ὁποῖος, -οία, -οῖον, (ποῖος w. the rel. ὅ), [fr. Hom. down], *of what sort* or *quality, what manner of* : 1 Co. iii. 13 ; Gal. ii. 6 ; 1 Th. i. 9 ; Jas. i. 24 ; preceded by τοιοῦτος, [*such as*], Acts xxvi. 29.*

3698   ὁπότε, (πότε w. the rel. ὅ), [fr. Hom. down], *when* [cf. B. § 139, 34 ; W. § 41 b. 3] : Lk. vi. 3 R G T (where L Tr WH ὅτε).*

3699   ὅπου, (from ποῦ and the rel. ὅ), [from Hom. down], *where* ; **1.** adv. of place, **a.** *in which place, where* ; **a.** in relative sentences with the Indicative it is used to refer to a preceding noun of place ; as, ἐπὶ τῆς γῆς, ὅπου etc. Mt. vi. 19 ; add, ib. 20 ; xiii. 5 ; xxviii. 6 ; Mk. vi. 55 ; ix. 44, 46, [which verses T WH om. Tr br.], 48 ; Lk. xii. 33 ; Jn. i. 28 ; iv. 20, 46 ; vi. 23 ;

vii. 42; x. 40; xi. 30; xii. 1; xviii. 1, 20; xix. 18, 20, 41;
xx. 12; Acts xvii. 1; Rev. xi. 8; xx. 10. it refers to
ἐκεῖ or ἐκεῖσε to be mentally supplied in what precedes
or follows: Mt. xxv. 24, 26; Mk. ii. 4; iv. 15; v. 40;
xiii. 14; Jn. iii. 8; vi. 62; vii. 34; xi. 32; xiv. 3; xvii.
24; xx. 19; Ro. xv. 20; Heb. ix. 16; x. 18; Rev. ii. 13.
it refers to ἐκεῖ expressed in what follows: Mt. vi. 21;
Lk. xii. 34; xvii. 37; Jn. xii. 26; Jas. iii. 16. in imitation of the Hebr. אֲשֶׁר־שָׁם (Gen. xiii. 3; Eccl. ix. 10,
etc.): ὅπου ἐκεῖ, Rev. xii. 6 [G T Tr WH], 14, (see ἐκεῖ,
a.); ὅπου . . . ἐπʼ αὐτῶν, Rev. xvii. 9. ὅπου also refers
to men, so that it is equiv. to *with (among) whom, in
whose house*: Mt. xxvi. 57; [add, Rev. ii. 13; cf. W. § 54,
7 fin.]; *in which state* (viz. of the renewed man), Col. iii.
11. it is loosely connected with the thought to which
it refers, so that it is equiv. to *wherein* [A. V. *whereas*],
2 Pet. ii. 11 (in the same sense in indir. quest., Xen.
mem. 3, 5, 1). ὅπου ἄν, *wherever,* — with impf. indic.
(see ἄν, II. 1), Mk. vi. 56 [Tdf. ἐάν]; with aor. subjunc. (Lat. fut. pf.), Mk. ix. 18 (where L T Tr WH ὅπου
ἐάν); Mk. xiv. 9 [here too T WH ὅπ. ἐάν]; also ὅπου ἐάν
(see ἐάν, II.), Mt. xxvi. 13; Mk. vi. 10; xiv. 14ᵃ, (in
both which last pass. L Tr ὅπου ἄν); with subj. pres.
Mt. xxiv. 28.   β. in indir. questions [yet cf. W. § 57,
2 fin.], with subjunc. aor.: Mk. xiv. 14ᵇ; Lk. xxii.
11.   b. joined to verbs signifying motion into a
place instead of ὅποι, *into which place, whither*, (see
ἐκεῖ, b.): foll. by the indic., Jn. viii. 21 sq.; xiii. 33, 36;
xiv. 4; xxi. 18; [Jas. iii. 4 T Tr WH (see below)]; ὅπου
ἄν, *where(whither)soever*, w. indic. pres., Rev. xiv. 4 L
Tr WH [cf. below], cf. B. § 139, 30; with subjunc. pres.,
Lk. ix. 57 R G T WH [al. ὅπ. ἐάν, see below]; Jas. iii. 4
[R G L]; Rev. xiv. 4 R G T (see above); ὅπου ἐάν, w.
subjunc. pres., Mt. viii. 19, and L Tr in Lk. ix. 57.   2.
It gets the force of a conditional particle *if* (*in case
that, in so far as,* [A. V. *whereas* (cf. 2 Pet. ii. 11 above)]):
1 Co. iii. 3 (Clem. Rom. 1 Cor. 43, 1, and often in Grk.
writ.; cf. Grimm on 4 Macc. ii. 14; Meyer on 1 Co. iii.
3; [Müller on Barn. ep. 16, 6]).*

see
3700 St.   ὀπτάνω (ΟΠΤΩ): *to look at, behold*; mid. pres. ptcp.
ὀπτανόμενος; *to allow one's self to be seen, to appear*: τινί,
Acts i. 3. (1 K. viii. 8; Tob. xii. 19; [Graec. Ven. Ex.
xxxiv. 24].)*

3701   ὀπτασία, -ας, ἡ, (ὀπτάζω);   1. *the act of exhibiting
one's self to view*: ὀπτασίαι κυρίου, 2 Co. xii. 1 [A. V.
visions; cf. Meyer ad loc.] (ἐν ἡμέραις ὀπτασίας μου, Add.
to Esth. iv. l. 44 (13); [cf. Mal. iii. 2]; ἥλιος ἐν ὀπτασίᾳ,
coming into view, Sir. xliii. 2).   2. *a sight, a vision*,
an appearance presented to one whether asleep or
awake: οὐράνιος ὀπτ. Acts xxvi. 19; ἑωρακέναι ὀπτασίαν,
Lk. i. 22; w. gen. of appos. ἀγγέλων, Lk. xxiv. 23. A
later form for ὄψις [cf. W. 24], Anthol. 6, 210, 6; for
מַרְאֶה, Dan. [Theodot.] ix. 23; x. 1, 7 sq.*

3702   ὀπτός, -ή, -όν, (ὀπτάω [to roast, cook]), *cooked, broiled*:
Lk. xxiv. 42.   (Ex. xii. 8, 9; in class. Grk. fr. Hom.
down.)*

see 3708   ὄπτω, see ὁράω.

3703   ὀπώρα, -ας, ἡ, (derived by some fr. ὄπις [cf. ὀπίσω],

ἕπομαι, and ὥρα; hence, the time that follows the ὥρα
[Curtius § 522]; by others fr. ὀπός [cf. our *sap*] juice,
and ὥρα, i. e. the time of juicy fruits, the time when
fruits become ripe), fr. Hom. down;   1. *the season
which succeeds θέρος, from the rising of Sirius to that of
Arcturus*, i. e. late summer, early autumn, our dog-days
(the year being divided into seven seasons as follows:
ἔαρ, θέρος, ὀπώρα, φθινόπωρον, σπορητός, χειμών, φυτα-
λιά).   2. *ripe fruits* (of trees): σοῦ τῆς ἐπιθυμίας
τῆς ψυχῆς for ὧν ἡ ψυχή σου ἐπιθυμεῖ, Rev. xviii. 14.
(Jer. xlvii. (xl.) 10, and often in Grk. writ.) *

ὅπως, (fr. πῶς and the relat. ὅ), with the indicative, a
relat. adverb but, like the Lat. *ut*, assuming also the
nature of a conjunction [cf. W. 449 (418 sq.)].   I.
As an Adverb; *as, in what manner, how*; once so in
the N. T. in an indir. question, with the indic.: οὐκ
ἔγνως, ὅπως κτλ. Lk. xxiv. 20, where cf. Bornemann,
Scholia etc.   II. A Conjunction, Lat. *ut*, answering to the Germ. *dass, that*; in class. Grk. with the
optat., and subjunc., and fut. indic.; cf. esp. *Klotz* ad
Devar. ii. 2 p. 681 sqq. But the distinction observed
between these constructions by the more elegant Grk.
writ. is quite neglected in the N. T., and if we except
Mt. xxvi. 59 L T Tr (ὅπως θανατώσουσιν), [1 Co. i. 29
Rec.ᵉˡᶻ], only the subjunctive follows this particle (for
in Mk. v. 23, for ὅπως . . . ζήσεται, L txt. T Tr WH have
correctly restored ἵνα . . . ζήσῃ); cf. W. 289 (271); B.
233 (201) sq.; [214 (185)].   1. It denotes the purpose or end, *in order that; with the design or to the
end that; that*;   a. without ἄν, — after the present,
Mt. vi. 2, 16; Philem. 6; Heb. ix. 15; after ἐστέ to be
supplied, 1 Pet. ii. 9; after the perfect, Acts ix. 17;
Heb. ii. 9; ὅπως μή, Lk. xvi. 26; after the imperfect, Mt. xxvi. 59 [R G (see above)]; Acts ix. 24;
after the aorist, Acts ix. 2, 12; xxv. 26; Ro. ix. 17;
Gal. i. 4; ὅπως μή, Acts xx. 16; 1 Co. i. 29; after the
pluperfect, Jn. xi. 57; after the future, Mt. xxiii.
35; and Rec. in Acts xxiv. 26; after an aor. subjunc. by which something is asked for, Mk. v. 23 Rec.;
after imperatives, Mt. ii. 8; v. 16, 45; vi. 4; Acts
xxiii. 15, 23; 2 Co. viii. 11; ὅπως μή, Mt. vi. 18; after
clauses with ἵνα an the aor. subjunc., Lk. xvi. 28; 2 Co.
viii. 14; 2 Th. i. 12. Noteworthy is the phrase ὅπως
πληρωθῇ, i. e. *that acc. to God's purpose it might be
brought to pass* or *might be proved by the event*, of O. T.
prophecies and types (see ἵνα, II. 3 fin.): Mt. ii. 23;
viii. 17; xii. 17 (where L T Tr WH ἵνα); xiii. 35.   b.
ὅπως ἄν; *that, if it be possible*, Mt. vi. 5 R G; *that, if what
I have just said shall come to pass*, Lk. ii. 35; Acts iii.
20 (19) [R. V. *that so*]; xv. 17; Ro. iii. 4 [B. 234 (201)];
exx. fr. the Sept. are given in W. § 42, 6.   2. As
in the Grk. writ. also (cf. W. 338 (317); [B. § 139, 41]),
ὅπως with the subjunctive is used after verbs of praying, entreating, asking, exhorting, to denote
what one wishes to be done: Mt. viii. 34 [here L ἵνα];
ix. 38; Lk. vii. 3; x. 2; xi. 37; Acts viii. 15, 24; ix. 2;
xxiii. 20; xxv. 3; Jas. v. 16; after a verb of deliberating: Mt. xii. 14; xxii. 15; Mk. iii. 6, (fr. which exx.

it is easy to see how the use noted in II. arises from the original adverbial force of the particle; for συμβούλ. ἔλαβον, ὅπως ἀπολέσωσιν αὐτόν, *they took counsel to destroy him* is equiv. to *how they might destroy him*, and also to *to this end that they might destroy him*; cf. Kühner § 552 Anm. 3, ii. p. 892).*

3705   ὅραμα, -τος, τό, (ὁράω), *that which is seen, a sight, spectacle*: Acts vii. 31; Mt. xvii. 9; *a sight divinely granted in an ecstasy* or *in sleep, a vision*, Acts x. 17, 19; δι' ὁράματος, Acts xviii. 9; ἐν ὁράματι, Acts ix. 10, 12 [R G]; x. 3; ὅραμα βλέπειν, Acts xii. 9; ἰδεῖν, Acts xi. 5; xvi. 10. (Xen., Aristot., Plut., Ael. v. h. 2, 3 [al. εἰκών]; Sept. several times for מַרְאֶה, חָזוֹן, Chald. חֵזוּ etc.; see ὀπτασία.)*

3706   ὅρασις, -εως, ἡ, (ὁράω);   1. *the act of seeing*: ὀμμάτων χρῆσις εἰς ὅρασιν, Sap. xv. 15; *the sense of sight*, Aristot. de anima 3, 2; Diod. 1, 59; Plut. mor. p. 440 sq.; plur. *the eyes*, ἐκκόπτειν τὰς ὁράσεις, Diod. 2, 6.   2. *appearance, visible form*: Rev. iv. 3 (Num. xxiv. 4; Ezek. i. 5, 26, 28; Sir. xli. 20, etc.).   3. *a vision*, i. e. an appearance divinely granted in an ecstasy: Rev. ix. 17; ὁράσεις ὄψονται, Acts ii. 17 fr. Joel ii. 28. (Sept. chiefly for מַרְאֶה and חָזוֹן.) *

3707   ὁρατός, -ή, -όν, (ὁράω), *visible, open to view*: neut. plur. substantively, Col. i. 16. (Xen., Plat., Theocr., Philo; Sept.) *

3708   ὁράω, -ῶ; impf. 3 pers. plur. ἑώρων (Jn. vi. 2, where L Tr WH ἐθεώρουν); pf. ἑώρακα and (T WH in Col. ii. 1, 18; [1 Co. ix. 1]; Tdf. ed. 7 also in Jn. ix. 37; xv. 24; xx. 25; 1 Jn. iii. 6; iv. 20; 3 Jn. 11) ἑόρακα (on which form cf. [WH. App. p. 161]; Tdf. Proleg. p. 122; Steph. Thesaur. s. v. 2139 d.]; Bttm. Ausf. Spr. i. p. 325; [B. 64 (56); Veitch s. v.]), [2 pers. sing. -κες (Jn. viii. 57 Tr mrg.) see κοπιάω, init.], 3 pers. plur. ἑωράκασιν (and -καν in Col. ii. 1 L Tr WH; Lk. ix. 36 T Tr WH; see γίνομαι, init.); plupf. 3 pers. sing. ἑωράκει (Acts vii. 44); fut. ὄψομαι (fr. ΟΠΤΩ), 2 pers. sing. ὄψει (cf. Bttm. Ausf. Spr. i. p. 347 sq.; Kühner § 211, 3, i. p. 536), Mt. xxvii. 4; Jn. i. 50 (51); xi. 40; but L T Tr WH [G also in Jn. i. 50 (51)] have restored ὄψῃ (cf. W. § 13, 2; B. 42 sq. (37)), 2 pers. plur. ὄψεσθε, Jn. i. 39 (40) T Tr WH, etc.; Pass., 1 aor. ὤφθην; fut. ὀφθήσομαι; 1 aor. mid. subjunc. 2 pers. plur. ὄψησθε (Lk. xiii. 28 [R G L WH txt. Tr mrg.]) fr. a Byzant. form ὠψάμην (see Lob. ad Phryn. p. 734, cf. Bttm. Ausf. Spr. ii. 258 sq.; [Veitch s. v.]); Sept. for רָאָה and חָזָה; [fr. Hom. down]; TO SEE, i. e.   1. *to see with the eyes*: τινὰ ὁρᾶν, ἑωρακέναι, Lk. xvi. 23; Jn. viii. 57; xiv. 7, 9; xx. 18, 25, 29; 1 Co. ix. 1, etc.; fut. ὄψομαι, Mt. xxviii. 7, 10; Mk. xvi. 7; Rev. i. 7, etc.; τὸν θεόν, 1 Jn. iv. 20; ἀόρατον ὡς ὁρῶν, Heb. xi. 27; with a ptcp. added as a predicate [B. 301 (258); W. § 45, 4], Mt. xxiv. 30; Mk. xiii. 26; xiv. 62; Lk. xxi. 27; Jn. i. 51 (52); ἑωρακέναι or ὄψεσθαι τὸ πρόσωπόν τινος, Col. ii. 1; Acts xx. 25; ὃ (which divine majesty, i. e. τοῦ θείου λόγου) ἑωράκαμεν τοῖς ὀφθαλμοῖς ἡμῶν (on this addition cf. W. 607 (564); [B. 398 (341)]), 1 Jn. i. 1; ὄψεσθαί τινα i. e. come to see, visit, one, Heb. xiii. 23; ἑωρακέναι Christ, i. e. to have seen him exhibiting proofs of his divinity

and Messiahship, Jn. vi. 36; ix. 37; xv. 24; ὁρᾶν and ὄψεσθαι with an acc. of the thing, Lk. xxiii. 49; Jn. i. 50 (51); iv. 45; vi. 2 [L Tr WH ἐθεώρουν]; xix. 35; Acts ii. 17; vii. 44; Rev. xviii. 18 [Rec.], etc.; [ἔρχ. κ. ὄψεσθε (sc. ποῦ μένω), Jn. i. 40 (39) T TrWH; cf. B. 290 (250)]; ὄψῃ τὴν δόξαν τοῦ θεοῦ, the glory of God displayed in a miracle, Jn. xi. 40. metaph. ὄψεσθαι τὸν θεόν, τὸν κύριον, to be admitted into intimate and blessed fellowship with God in his future kingdom, Mt. v. 8; Heb. xii. 14; also τὸ πρόσωπον τοῦ θεοῦ, Rev. xxii. 4—(a fig. borrowed from those privileged to see and associate with kings; see βλέπω, 1 b. β.); οὐκ εἶδος θεοῦ ἑωράκατε, trop. i. q. his divine majesty as he discloses it in the Scriptures ye have not recognized, Jn. v. 37; cf. Meyer ad loc.   2. *to see with the mind, to perceive, know*: absol. Ro. xv. 21; τινά foll. by a ptcp. in the acc. [B. § 144, 15 b.; W. § 45, 4], Acts viii. 23; τί, Col. ii. 18; with a ptcp. added, Heb. ii. 8; foll. by ὅτι, Jas. ii. 24; *to look at* or *upon, observe, give attention to*: εἴς τινα, Jn. xix. 37 (Soph. El. 925; Xen. Cyr. 4, 1, 20; εἴς τι, Solon in Diog. Laërt. 1, 52); ἑωρακέναι παρὰ τῷ πατρί, to have learned from [see παρά, II. b.] the father (a metaphorical expression borrowed fr. sons, who learn what they see their fathers doing), Jn. viii. 38 (twice in Rec.; once in L T Tr WH); Christ is said to deliver to men ἃ ἑώρακεν, the things which he has seen, i. e. which he learned in his heavenly state with God before the incarnation, i. e. things divine, the counsels of God, Jn. iii. 11, 32; ἑωρακέναι θεόν, to know God's will, 3 Jn. 11; from the intercourse and influence of Christ to have come to see (know) God's majesty, saving purposes, and will [cf. W. 273 (257)], Jn. xiv. 7, 9; in an emphatic sense, of Christ, who has an immediate and perfect knowledge of God without being taught by another, Jn. i. 18; vi. 46; ὄψεσθαι θεὸν καθὼς ἐστιν, of the knowledge of God that may be looked for in his future kingdom, 1 Jn. iii. 2; ὄψεσθαι Christ, used in reference to the apostles, about to perceive his invisible presence among them by his influence upon their souls through the Holy Spirit, Jn. xvi. 16 sq. 19; Christ is said ὄψεσθαι the apostles, i. e. will have knowledge of them, ibid. 22.   3. *to see* i. e. *to become acquainted with by experience, to experience*: ζωήν, i. q. to become a partaker of, Jn. iii. 36; ἡμέραν, (cf. Germ. *erleben*) see εἴδω, I. 5), Lk. xvii. 22 (Soph. O. R. 831).   4. *to see to, look to*; i. e.   a. i. q. *to take heed, beware*, [see esp. B. § 139, 49; cf. W. 503 (469)]: ὅρα μή, with aor. subjunc., *see that . . . not, take heed lest*, Mt. viii. 4; xviii. 10; Mk. i. 44; 1 Th. v. 15; supply τοῦτο ποιήσῃς in Rev. xix. 10; xxii. 9, [W. 601 (558); B. 395 (338)], (Xen. Cyr. 3, 1, 27, where see *Poppo*; Soph. Philoct. 30, 519; El. 1003); foll. by an impv., Mt. ix. 30; xxiv. 6; ὁρᾶτε καὶ προσέχετε ἀπό, Mt. xvi. 6; ὁρᾶτε, βλέπετε ἀπό, Mk. viii. 15; ὁρᾶτε, καὶ φυλάσσεσθε ἀπό, Lk. xii. 15; ὅρα, τί μέλλεις ποιεῖν, i. q. *weigh well*, Acts xxii. 26 Rec. (ὅρα τί ποιεῖς, Soph. Philoct. 589).   b. i. q. *to care for, pay heed to*: σὺ ὄψῃ [R G ὄψει (see above)], *see thou to it, that will be thy concern*, [cf. W. § 40, 6], Mt. xxvii. 4; plur., 24; Acts xviii. 15, (Epict. diss. 2, 5, 30; 4, 6, 11 sq.; [Antonin. 5, 25 (and Gataker ad loc.)]).   **5.** Pass. 1 aor. ὤφθην, *I was seen, showed myself, appeared* [cf. B. 52 (45)]: Lk. ix. 31; with dat. of pers. (cf. B. u. s., [also § 134, 2; cf. W. § 31, 10]): of angels, Lk. i. 11; xxii. 43 [L br. WH reject the pass.]; Acts vii. 30, 35, (Ex. iii. 2); of God, Acts vii. 2 (Gen. xii. 7; xvii. 1); of the dead, Mt. xvii. 3; Mk. ix. 4, cf. Lk. ix. 31; of Jesus after his resurrection, Lk. xxiv. 34; Acts ix. 17; xiii. 31; xxvi. 16; 1 Co. xv. 5–8; 1 Tim. iii. 16; of Jesus hereafter to return, Heb. ix. 28; of visions during sleep or ecstasy, Acts xvi. 9; Rev. xi. 19; xii. 1, 3; in the sense of *coming upon unexpectedly*, Acts ii. 3; vii. 26. fut. pass. ὧν ὀφθήσομαί σοι, on account of which I will appear unto thee, Acts xxvi. 16; on this pass. see W. § 39, 3 N. 1; cf. B. 287 (247). [Comp.: ἀφ-, καθ-, προ-οράω.]

[Syn. ὁρᾶν, βλέπειν, both denote the physical act: ὁρ. in general, βλ. the single look; ὁρ. gives prominence to the discerning mind, βλ. to the particular mood or point. When the physical side recedes, ὁρ. denotes perception in general (as resulting principally from vision), the prominence in the word of the mental element being indicated by the constr. of the acc. w. inf. (in contrast with that of the ptcp. required w. βλέπειν), and by the absol. ὁρᾷς; βλέπ. on the other hand, when its physical side recedes, gets a purely outward sense, *look* (i. e. open, incline) *towards*, Lat. *spectare, vergere*. Schmidt ch. xi. Cf. θεωρέω, σκοπέω, εἴδω, I. fin.]

3709   ὀργή, -ῆς, ἡ, (fr. ὀργάω to teem, denoting an internal motion, esp. that of plants and fruits swelling with juice [Curtius § 152]; cf. Lat. *turgere alicui* for *irasci alicui* in Plaut. Cas. 2, 5, 17; Most. 3, 2, 10; cf. Germ. *arg, Aerger*), in Grk. writ. fr. Hesiod down *the natural disposition, temper, character; movement* or *agitation of soul, impulse, desire, any violent emotion*, but esp. (and chiefly in Attic) *anger*. In bibl. Grk. *anger, wrath, indignation*, (on the distinction between it and θυμός, see θυμός, 1): Eph. iv. 31; Col. iii. 8; Jas. i. 19 sq.; μετ᾽ ὀργῆς, *indignant*, [A. V. *with anger*], Mk. iii. 5; χωρὶς ὀργῆς, 1 Tim. ii. 8; *anger exhibited in punishing*, hence used for the *punishment* itself (Dem. or. in Mid. § 43): of the punishments inflicted by magistrates, Ro. xiii. 4; διὰ τὴν ὀργήν, i. e. because disobedience is visited with punishment, ib. 5. The ὀργή attributed to God in the N. T. is *that in God which stands opposed to man's disobedience, obduracy (esp. in resisting the gospel) and sin, and manifests itself in punishing the same*: Jn. iii. 36; Ro. i. 18; iv. 15; ix. 22ᵃ; Heb. iii. 11; iv. 3; Rev. xiv. 10; xvi. 19; xix. 15; absol. ἡ ὀργή, Ro. xii. 19 [cf. W. 594 (553)]; σκεύη ὀργῆς, *vessels into which wrath will be poured* (at the last day), explained by the addition κατηρτισμένα εἰς ἀπώλειαν, Ro. ix. 22ᵇ; ἡ μέλλουσα ὀργή, which at the last day will be exhibited in penalties, Mt. iii. 7; Lk. iii. 7, [al. understand in these two pass. the (national) judgments immediately impending to be referred to—at least primarily]; also ἡ ὀργὴ ἡ ἐρχομένη, 1 Th. i. 10; ἡμέρα ὀργῆς, the day on which the wrath of God will be made manifest in the punishment of the wicked [cf. W. § 30, 2 a.], Ro. ii. 5; and ἡ ἡμέρα ἡ μεγάλη τῆς ὀργῆς αὐτοῦ (Rev. vi. 17; see ἡμέρα, 3 ad fin.); ἔρχεται ἡ ὀργὴ τοῦ θεοῦ ἐπί τινα, the wrath of God cometh upon

one in the infliction of penalty [cf. W. § 40, 2 a.], Eph. v. 6; Col. iii. 6 [T Tr WH om. L br. ἐπί etc.]; ἔφθασε [-κεν L txt. WH mrg.] ἐπ᾽ αὐτοὺς ἡ ὀργή, 1 Th. ii. 16; so ἡ ὀργή passes over into the notion of *retribution and punishment*, Lk. xxi. 23; Ro. [ii. 8]; iii. 5; v. 9; Rev. xi. 18; τέκνα ὀργῆς, men exposed to divine punishment, Eph. ii. 3; εἰς ὀργήν, *unto wrath*, i. e. to undergo punishment in misery, 1 Th. v. 9. ὀργή is attributed to Christ also when he comes as Messianic judge, Rev. vi. 16. (Sept. for עֶבְרָה, *wrath, outburst of anger*, חֵמָה, זַעַם, חָרוֹן, קֶצֶף, etc.; but chiefly for אַף.) Cf. *Ferd. Weber*, Vom Zorne Gottes. Erlang. 1862; *Ritschl*, Die christl. Lehre v. d. Rechtfertigung u. Versöhnung, ii. p. 118 sqq.*

ὀργίζω : Pass., pres. ὀργίζομαι; 1 aor. ὠργίσθην; (ὀργή); **3710** fr. Soph., Eur., and Thuc. down; *to provoke, arouse to anger*; pass. *to be provoked to anger, be angry, be wroth*, (Sept. for חָרָה, קָצַף, also חָרָה אַף etc.): absol., Mt. xviii. 34; xxii. 7; Lk. xiv. 21; xv. 28; Eph. iv. 26 [B. 290 (250); cf. W. §§ 43, 2; 55, 7]; Rev. xi. 18; τινί, Mt. v. 22; ἐπί τινι, Rev. xii. 17 [L om. ἐπί] as in 1 K. xi. 9; [Andoc. 5, 10]; Isocr. p. 230 c.; [cf. W. 232 (218)]. [Comp.: παρ-οργίζω.]*

ὀργίλος, -η, -ον, (ὀργή), *prone to anger, irascible*, [A. V. **3711** *soon angry*]: Tit. i. 7. (Prov. xxii. 24; xxix. 22; Xen. de re equ. 9, 7; Plat. [e. g. de rep. 411 b.]; Aristot. [e. g. eth. Nic. 2, 7, 10]; al.)*

ὀργυιά, -ᾶς, ἡ, (ὀρέγω to stretch out), *the distance* **3712** *across the breast from the tip of one middle finger to the tip of the other when the arms are outstretched; five or six feet, a fathom*: Acts xxvii. 28. (Hom., Hdt., Xen., al.)*

ὀρέγω : (cf. Lat. *rego*, Germ. *recken, strecken, reichen*, **see** [Eng. *reach*; Curtius § 153]); fr. Hom. down; *to stretch* **3713 St.** *forth*, as χεῖρα, Hom. Il. 15, 371, etc.; pres. mid. [cf. W. p. 252 (237) note], *to stretch one's self out in order to touch* or *to grasp something, to reach after* or *desire something*: with a gen. of the thing, 1 Tim. iii. 1; Heb. xi. 16; φιλαργυρίας, to give one's self up to the love of money (not quite accurately since φιλαργ. is itself the ὄρεξις; [cf. Ellicott ad loc.]), 1 Tim. vi. 10.*

ὀρεινός, -ή, -όν, (ὄρος), *mountainous, hilly*; ἡ ὀρεινή [WH **3714** ὀρινή, see I, ι] sc. χώρα [cf. W. 591 (550)] (which is added in Hdt. 1, 110; Xen. Cyr. 1, 3, 3), *the mountain-district, hill-country*: Lk. i. 39, 65, (Aristot. h. a. 5, 28, 4; Sept. for הַר, Gen. xiv. 10; Deut. xi. 11; Josh. ii. 16, etc.).*

ὄρεξις, -εως, ἡ, (ὀρέγομαι, q. v.), *desire, longing, craving,* **3715** *for; eager desire, lust, appetite*: of lust, Ro. i. 27. It is used both in a good and a bad sense, as well of natural and lawful and even of proper cravings (of the appetite for food, Sap. xvi. 2 sq.; Plut. mor. p. 635 c.; al.; ἐπιστήμης, Plat. de fin. p. 414 b.), as also of corrupt and unlawful desires, Sir. xviii. 30; xxiii. 6; ἄλογοι and λογιστικαὶ ὀρέξεις are contrasted in Aristot. rhet. 1, 10, 7. [Cf. Trench § lxxxvii.]*

ὀρθοποδέω, -ῶ; (ὀρθόπους with straight feet, going **3716** straight; and this fr. ὀρθός and πούς); *to walk in a straight course*; metaph. *to act uprightly*, Gal. ii. 14 [cf.

πρός, I. 3 f.]. Not found elsewhere; [cf. W. 26; 102 (96)].*

3717 ὀρθός, -ή, -όν, (ΟΡΩ, ὄρνυμι [to stir up, set in motion; acc. to al. fr. r. to lift up; cf. Fick iii. p. 775; Vaniček p. 928; Curtius p. 348]), straight, erect; i. e. **a.** upright: ἀνάστηθι, Acts xiv. 10; so with στῆναι in 1 Esdr. ix. 46, and in Grk. writ., esp. Hom. **b.** opp. to σκολιός, straight i. e. not crooked: τροχιαί, Heb. xii. 13 (for יָשָׁר, Prov. xii. 15 etc.; [Pind., Theogn., al.]).*

3718 ὀρθοτομέω, -ῶ; (ὀρθοτόμος cutting straight, and this fr. ὀρθός and τέμνω) ; **1.** to cut straight: τὰς ὁδούς, to cut straight ways, i. e. to proceed by straight paths, hold a straight course, equiv. to to do right (for יִשֵּׁר), Prov. iii. 6; xi. 5, (viam secare, Verg. Aen. 6, 899). **2.** dropping the idea of cutting, to make straight and smooth; Vulg. recte tracto, to handle aright: τὸν λόγον τῆς ἀληθείας, i. e. to teach the truth correctly and directly, 2 Tim. ii. 15; τὸν ἀληθῆ λόγον, Eustath. opusc. p. 115, 41. (Not found elsewhere [exc. in eccles. writ. (W. 26); e. g. constt. apost. 7, 31 ἐν τ. τοῦ κυρίου δόγμασιν; cf. Suicer ii. 508 sq.]. Cf. καινοτομέω, to cut new veins in mining; dropping the notion of cutting, to make something new, introduce new things, make innovations or changes, etc.)*

3719 ὀρθρίζω : 3 pers. sing. impf. ὤρθριζεν; (ὄρθρος); not found in prof. auth. ([cf. W. 26; 33; 91 (87)]; Moeris [p. 272 ed. Pierson] ὀρθρεύει ἀττικῶς, ὀρθρίζει ἑλληνικῶς); Sept. often for הִשְׁכִּים; (cf. Grimm on 1 Macc. iv. 52 and on Sap. vi. 14); to rise early in the morning: πρός τινα, to rise early in the morning in order to betake one's self to one, to resort to one early in the morning, (Vulg. manico ad aliquem), Lk. xxi. 38, where see Meyer.*

3720 ὀρθρινός, -ή, -όν, (fr. ὄρθρος; cf. ἡμερινός, ἑσπερινός, ὀπωρινός, πρωϊνός), a poetic [Anth.] and later form for ὄρθριος (see Lob. ad Phryn. p. 51; Sturz, De dial. Maced. et Alex. p. 186; [W. 25]), early: Rev. xxii. 16 Rec., Lk. xxiv. 22 L T Tr WH. (Hos. vi. 4; Sap. xi. 23 (22).) *

3721 ὄρθριος, -α, -όν, (fr. ὄρθρος, q. v.; cf. ὄψιος, πρωΐος), early; rising at the first dawn or very early in the morning: Lk. xxiv. 22 R G (Job xxix. 7; 3 Macc. v. 10, 23). Cf. the preced. word. [Hom. (h. Merc. 143), Theogn., al.] *

3722 ὄρθρος, -ου, ὁ, (fr. ΟΡΩ, ὄρνυμι to stir up, rouse; cf. Lat. orior, ortus), fr. Hes. down; Sept. for שַׁחַר dawn, and several times for בֹּקֶר; daybreak, dawn: ὄρθρου βαθέος or βαθέως (see βαθέως and βαθύς [on the gen. cf. W. § 30, 11; B. § 132, 26]), at early dawn, Lk. xxiv. 1; ὄρθρου, at daybreak, at dawn, early in the morning, Jn. viii. 2 (Hes. opp. 575; Sept. Jer. xxv. 4; xxxiii. (xxvi.) 5, etc.); ὑπὸ τὸν ὄρθρον, Acts v. 21 (Dio Cass. 76, 17).*

3723 ὀρθῶς, (ὀρθός), adv., rightly: Mk. vii. 35; Lk. vii. 43; x. 28; xx. 21. [Aeschyl. and Hdt. down.]*

3724 ὁρίζω; 1 aor. ὥρισα; Pass., pf. ptcp. ὡρισμένος; 1 aor. ptcp. ὁρισθείς; (fr. ὅρος a boundary, limit); fr. [Aeschyl. and] Hdt. down; to define; i. e. **1.** to mark out the boundaries or limits (of any place or thing): Hdt., Xen., Thuc., al.; Num. xxxiv. 6; Josh. xiii. 27. **2.** to determine, appoint: with an acc. of the thing, ἡμέραν, Heb.

iv. 7; καιρούς, Acts xvii. 26, (numerous exx. fr. Grk. auth. are given in Bleek, Hebr.-Br. ii. 1 p. 538 sq.); pass. ὡρισμένος, 'determinate,' settled, Acts ii. 23; τὸ ὡρισμ. that which hath been determined, acc. to appointment, decree, Lk. xxii. 22; with an acc. of pers. Acts xvii. 31 (ᾧ by attraction for ὅν [W. § 24, 1; B. § 143, 8]); pass. with a pred. nom. Ro. i. 4 (for although Christ was the Son of God before his resurrection, yet he was openly appointed [A.V. declared] such among men by this transcendent and crowning event); ὁρίζω, to ordain, determine, appoint, Acts x. 42; foll. by an inf. Acts xi. 29 (Soph. fr. 19 d. [i. e. Aegeus (539), viii. p. 8 ed. Brunck]). [COMP.: ἀφ-, ἀπο-δι-, προ-ορίζω.]*

[ὀρινός, see ὀρεινός.]　　　see 3714

3725 ὅριον, -ου, τό, (fr. ὅρος [boundary]), [fr. Soph. down], a bound, limit, in the N. T. always in plur. (like Lat. fines) boundaries, [R. V. borders], i. q. region, district, land, territory: Mt. ii. 16; iv. 13; viii. 34; xv. 22, 39; xix. 1; Mk. v. 17; vii. 24 L T Tr WH, 31; x. 1; Acts xiii. 50. (Sept. very often for גְּבוּל; several times for גְּבוּלָה.) *

3726 ὁρκίζω; (ὅρκος); **1.** to force to take an oath, to administer an oath to: Xen. conviv. 4, 10; Dem., Polyb.; cf. Lob. ad Phryn. p. 361. **2.** to adjure, (solemnly implore), with two acc. of pers., viz. of the one who is adjured and of the one by whom he is adjured (cf. Matthiae § 413, 10; [B. 147 (128)]): 1 Th. v. 27 R G (see ἐνορκίζω); Mk. v. 7; Acts xix. 13. (Sept. for הִשְׁבִּיעַ, τινά foll. by κατά w. gen., 1 K. ii. (iii.) 42; 2 Chr. xxxvi. 13; ἐν, Neh. xiii. 25.) [COMP.: ἐν-, ἐξ-ορκίζω.] *

3727 ὅρκος, -ου, ὁ, (fr. ἔργω, εἴργω; i. q. ἕρκος an enclosure, confinement; hence Lat. orcus), [fr. Hom. down], for שְׁבֻעָה, an oath: Mt. xiv. 7, 9; xxvi. 72; Mk. vi. 26; Lk. i. 73 [W. 628 (583); B. § 144, 13]; Acts ii. 30 [W. 226 (212); 603 (561)]; Heb. vi. 16 sq.; Jas. v. 12; by meton. that which has been pledged or promised with an oath; plur. vows, Mt. v. 33 [(cf. Wünsche ad loc.)].*

3728 ὁρκωμοσία, -ας, ἡ, (ὁρκωμοτέω [ὅρκος and ὄμνυμι]; cf. ἀπωμοσία, ἀντωμοσία), affirmation made on oath, the taking of an oath, an oath: Heb. vii. 20 (21), 21, 28. (Ezek. xvii. 18; 1 Esdr. viii. 90 (92); Joseph. antt. 16, 6, 2. Cf. Delitzsch, Com. on Heb. l. c.)*

3729 ὁρμάω, -ῶ: 1 aor. ὥρμησα; (fr. ὁρμή); **1.** trans. to set in rapid motion, stir up, incite, urge on; so fr. Hom. down. **2.** intrans. to start forward impetuously, to rush, (so fr. Hom. down): εἴς τι, Mt. viii. 32; Mk. v. 13; Lk. viii. 33; Acts xix. 29; ἐπί τινα, Acts vii. 57.*

3730 ὁρμή, -ῆς, ἡ, [fr. r. sar to go, flow; Fick i. p. 227; Curtius § 502], fr. Hom. down, a violent motion, impulse: Jas. iii. 4; a hostile movement, onset, assault, Acts xiv. 5 [cf. Trench § lxxxvii.].*

3731 ὅρμημα, -τος, τό, (ὁρμάω), a rush, impulse: Rev. xviii. 21 [here A. V. violence]. (For זַעֲרָה outburst of wrath, Am. i. 11; Hab. iii. 8, cf. Schleusner, Thesaur. iv. p. 123; an enterprise, venture, Hom. Il. 2, 356, 590, although interpreters differ about its meaning there [cf. Ebeling, Lex. Hom. or L. and S. s. v.]; that to which one is impelled or hurried away by impulse, [rather, incitement, stimulus], Plut. mor. [de virt. mor. § 12] p. 452 c.) *

3732   **ὄρνεον, -ου, τό,** *a bird* : Rev. xviii. 2; xix. 17, 21. (Sept.; Hom., Thuc., Xen., Plat., Joseph. antt. 3, 1, 5.) *

see 3733   **ὄρνιξ** [so codd. א D], i. q. ὄρνις (q. v.) : Lk. xiii. 34 Tdf. The nom. is not found in prof. writ., but the trisyllabic forms ὄρνιχος, ὄρνιχι for ὄρνιθος, etc., are used in Doric [Photius (ed. Porson, p. 348, 22) Ἴωνες ὄρνιξ . . . καὶ Δωριεῖς ὄρνιξ. Cf. Curtius p. 495].*

3733   **ὄρνις, -ιθος, ὁ, ἡ,** (ΟΡΩ, ὄρνυμι [see ὄρθρος]);   **1.** *a bird* ; so fr. Hom. down.   **2.** spec. *a cock, a hen* : Mt. xxiii. 37; Lk. xiii. 34 [Tdf. ὄρνιξ, q. v.]; (so Aeschyl. Eum. 866; Xen. an. 4, 5, 25 ; Theocr., Polyb. 12, 26, 1 ; [al.]).*

3734   **ὁροθεσία, -ας, ἡ,** (fr. ὁροθέτης ; and this fr. ὅρος [a boundary ; see ὅριον], and τίθημι) ;   **a.** prop. *a setting of boundaries, laying down limits.*   **b.** *a definite limit* ; plur. *bounds,* Acts xvii. 26.   (Eccl. writ. ; [W. 25].) *

3735   **ὅρος, -ους, τό,** (ΟΡΩ, ὄρνυμι [i. e. a rising ; see ὄρθρος]), [fr. Hom. down], Sept. for הַר, *a mountain* : Mt. v. 14; Lk. iii. 5; Rev. vi. 14, and often; τὸ ὄρος, the mountain nearest the place spoken of, the mountain near by [but see ὁ, II. 1 b.], Mt. v. 1 ; Mk. iii. 13 ; Lk. ix. 28 ; Jn. vi. 3, 15; plur. ὄρη, Mt. xviii. 12; xxiv. 16 ; Mk. v. 5 ; Rev. vi. 16, etc.; gen. plur. ὀρέων (on this uncontracted form, used also in Attic, cf. Bttm. Gram. § 49 note 3 ; W. § 9, 2 c.; [B. 14 (13); *Dindorf* in Fleckeisen's Jahrb. for 1869 p. 83]), Rev. vi. 15; ὄρη μεθιστάνειν a proverb. phrase, used also by rabbin. writ., *to remove mountains,* i. e. *to accomplish most difficult, stupendous, incredible things* : 1 Co. xiii. 2, cf. Mt. xvii. 20 ; xxi. 21; Mk. xi. 23.

3736   **ὀρύσσω :** 1 aor. ὤρυξα ; fr. Hom. down ; Sept. for חָפַר, כָּרָה, etc. ; *to dig* : to make τί by digging, Mk. xii. 1 ; τὶ ἔν τινι, Mt. xxi. 33; i. q. to make a pit, ἐν τῇ γῇ, Mt. xxv. 18 [here T Tr WH ὀρ. γῆν]. [COMP.: δι-, ἐξ-ορύσσω.] *

3737   **ὀρφανός, -ή, -όν,** (ΟΡΦΟΣ, Lat. *orbus* ; [Curtius § 404]), fr. Hom. Od. 20, 68 down, Sept. for יָתוֹם ; *bereft* (of a father, of parents), Jas. i. 27 [A. V. *fatherless*] ; of those bereft of a teacher, guide, guardian, Jn. xiv. 18 (Lam. v. 3).*

3738   **ὀρχέομαι, -οῦμαι :** 1 aor. ὠρχησάμην ; (fr. χορός, by transposition ὀρχός; cf. ἅρπω, ἁρπάζω, and Lat. *rapio,* μορφή and Lat. *forma* ; [but these supposed transpositions are extremely doubtful, cf. Curtius § 189; Fick iv. 207, 167. Some connect ὀρχέομαι with r. argh 'to put in rapid motion'; cf. Vaniček p. 59]); *to dance* : Mt. xi. 17 ; xiv. 6; Mk. vi. 22; Lk. vii. 32. (From Hom. down; Sept. for רָקַד, 1 Chr. xv. 29 ; Ecclus. iii. 4 ; 2 S. vi. 21.)*

3739   **ὅς, ἥ, ὅ,** the postpositive article, which has the force of **I.** a **demonstrative** pronoun, *this, that,* (Lat. *hic, haec, hoc* ; Germ. emphat. *der, die, das*) ; in the N. T. only in the foll. instances : ὃς δέ, *but he* (Germ. *er aber*), Jn. v. 11 L Tr WH ; [Mk. xv. 23 T Tr txt. WH ; cf. B. § 126, 2] ; in distributions and distinctions : ὃς μὲν ... ὃς δέ, *this ... that, one ... another, the one ... the other,* Mt. xxi. 35 ; xxii. 5 L T Tr WH ; xxv. 15 ; Lk. xxiii. 33 ; Acts xxvii. 44 ; Ro. xiv. 5 ; 1 Co. vii. 7 R G ; xi. 21 ; 2 Co. ii. 16 ; Jude 22 ; ὁ μὲν ... ὁ δέ, *the one ... the other,* Ro. ix. 21 ; [ὁ μὲν ... ὁ δὲ ... ὁ δέ, *some ... some ... some,* Mt. xiii. 23 L T WH] ; ὃ δὲ ... ὃ δὲ ... ὃ δέ, *some ... some ... some,*

Mt. xiii. 8 ; ᾧ (masc.) μὲν ... ἄλλῳ (δὲ) ... ἑτέρῳ δέ [but L T Tr WH om. this δέ] κτλ. 1 Co. xii. 8–10 ; ὁ μὲν ... ἄλλο δέ [L txt. T Tr WH καὶ ἄλλο], Mk. iv. 4 ; with a variation of the construction also in the foll. pass. : ὁ μὲν ... καὶ ἕτερον, Lk. viii. 5 ; οὓς μέν with the omission of οὓς δέ by anacoluthon, 1 Co. xii. 28 ; ὃς μὲν ... ὁ δὲ ἀσθενῶν etc. *one man ... but he that is weak* etc. Ro. xiv. 2. On this use of the pronoun, chiefly by later writers from Demosth. down, cf. Matthiae § 289 Anm. 7 ; Kühner § 518, 4 b. ii. p. 780; [Jelf § 816, 3 b.]; *Bttm.* Gram. § 126, 3 ; B. 101 (89) ; W. 105 (100); Fritzsche on Mk. p. 507.

II. a **relative** pronoun *who, which, what* ;   **1.** in the common constr., acc. to which the relative agrees as respects its **gender** with the noun or pron. which is its antecedent, but as respects **case** is governed by its own verb, or by a substantive, or by a preposition : ὁ ἀστὴρ ὃν εἶδον, Mt. ii. 9 ; ὁ .. Ἰουδαῖος, οὗ ὁ ἔπαινος κτλ. Ro. ii. 29 ; οὗτος περὶ οὗ ἐγὼ ἀκούω τοιαῦτα, Lk. ix. 9 ; ἀπὸ τῆς ἡμέρας, ἀφ᾽ ἧς, Acts xx. 18; θεὸς δι᾽ οὗ, ἐξ οὗ, 1 Co. viii. 6, and numberless other exx. it refers to a more remote noun in 1 Co. i. 8, where the antecedent of ὅς is not the nearest noun Ἰησοῦ Χριστοῦ, but τῷ θεῷ in 4 ; yet cf. W. 157 (149) ; as in this passage, so very often elsewhere the relative is the subject of its own clause : ἀνὴρ ὅς etc. Jas. i. 12 ; πᾶς ὅς, Lk. xiv. 33 ; οὐδεὶς ὅς, Mk. x. 29 ; Lk. xviii. 29, and many other exx.   **2.** in constructions peculiar in some respect ;   **a.** the gender of the relative is sometimes made to conform to that of the following noun : τῆς αὐλῆς, ὅ ἐστι πραιτώριον, Mk. xv. 16 ; λαμπάδες, ἅ εἰσι (L ἐστιν) τὰ πνεύματα, Rev. iv. 5 [L T WH] ; σπέρματι, ὅς ἐστι Χριστός, Gal. iii. 16 ; add, Eph. i. 14 [L WH txt. Tr mrg. ὅ] ; vi. 17 ; 1 Tim. iii. 15 ; Rev. v. 8 [T WH mrg. ἅ] ; cf. *Herm.* ad Vig. p. 708 ; Matthiae § 440 p. 989 sq. ; W. § 24, 3 ; B. § 143, 3.   **b.** in constructions ad sensum [cf. B. § 143, 4] ;   **α.** the **plural** of the relative is used after collective nouns in the sing. [cf. W. § 21, 3 ; B. u. s.] : πλῆθος πολύ, οἳ ἦλθον, Lk. vi. 17; πᾶν τὸ πρεσβυτέριον, παρ᾽ ὧν, Acts xxii. 5 ; γενεᾶς, ἐν οἷς, Phil. ii. 15.   **β.** κατὰ πᾶσαν πόλιν, ἐν αἷς, Acts xv. 36 ; ταύτην δευτέραν ὑμῖν γράφω ἐπιστολήν, ἐν αἷς (because the preceding context conveys the idea of two Epistles), 2 Pet. iii. 1.   **γ.** the gender of the relative is conformed not to the grammatical but to the natural gender of its antecedent [cf. W. § 21, 2 ; B. u. s.] : παιδάριον ὅς, Jn. vi. 9 L T Tr WH ; θηρίον ὅς, of Nero, as antichrist, Rev. xiii. 14 L T Tr WH ; κεφαλὴ ὅς, of Christ, Col. ii. 19 ; [add μυστήριον ὅς etc. 1 Tim. iii. 16 G L T Tr WH ; cf. B. u. s.; W. 588 sq. (547)] ; σκεύη (of men) οὕς, Ro. ix. 24 ; ἔθνη οἵ, Acts xv. 17 ; xxvi. 17 ; τέκνα, τεκνία οἵ, Jn. i. 13 ; Gal. iv. 19 ; 2 Jn. 1, (Eur. suppl. 12) ; τέκνον ὅς, Philem. 10.   **c.** In attractions [B. § 143, 8 ; W. §§ 24, 1 ; 66, 4 sqq.] ;   **a.** the accusative of the rel. pron. depending on a transverb is changed by attraction into the oblique case of its antecedent : κτίσεως ἧς ἔκτισεν ὁ θεός, Mk. xiii. 19 [R G] ; τοῦ ῥήματος οὗ εἶπεν, Mk. xiv. 72 [Rec.] ; add, Jn. iv. 14 ; vii. 31, 39 [but Tr mrg. WH mrg. ὅ] ; xv. 20 ; xxi. 10 ; Acts iii. 21, 25 ; vii. 17, 45 ; ix. 36 ; x. 39 ; xxii. 10 ; Ro. xv. 18 ; 1 Co. vi. 19 ; 2 Co. i. 6 ; x. 8, 13 ; Eph. i. 8 ; Tit.

iii. 5 [R G], 6; Heb. vi. 10; ix. 20; Jas. ii. 5; 1 Jn. iii. 24; Jude 15; for other exx. see below; ἐν ἄρᾳ ᾗ οὐ γινώσκει, Mt. xxiv. 50; τῇ παραδόσει ᾗ παρεδώκατε, Mk. vii. 13; add, Lk. ii. 20; v. 9; ix. 43; xii. 46; xxiv. 25; Jn. xvii. 5; Acts ii. 22; xvii. 31; xx. 38; 2 Co. xii. 21; 2 Th. i. 4; Rev. xviii. 6; cf. W. § 24, 1; [B. as above]. Rarely attraction occurs where the verb governs the d a t i v e [but see below]: thus, κατέναντι οὗ ἐπίστευσε θεοῦ for κατέναντι θεοῦ, ᾧ ἐπίστευσε (see κατέναντι), Ro. iv. 17; φωνῆς, ἧς ἔκραξα (for ᾗ [al. ἥν, cf. W. 164 (154 sq.) B. 287 (247)]), Acts xxiv. 21, cf. Is. vi. 4; (ἤγετο δὲ καὶ τῶν ἑαυτοῦ τε πιστῶν, οἷς ἥδετο καὶ ὧν ἠπίστει πολλούς, for καὶ πολλοὺς τούτων, οἷς ἠπίστει, Xen. Cyr. 5, 4, 39; ὧν ἐγὼ ἐντετύχηκα οὐδείς, for οὐδεὶς τούτων, οἷς ἐντετ. Plato, Gorg. p. 509 a.; Protag. p. 361 e.; de rep. 7 p. 531 e.; παρ' ὧν βοηθεὶς, οὐδεμίαν λήψει χάριν, for παρὰ τούτων, οἷς κτλ. Aeschin. f. leg. p. 43 (117); cf. Fritzsche, Ep. ad Rom. i. p. 237; [B. § 143, 11; W. 163 (154) sq.; but others refuse to recognize this rare species of attraction in the N. T.; cf. Meyer on Eph. i. 8]). The foll. expressions, however, can hardly be brought under this construction: τῆς χάριτος ἧς ἐχαρίτωσεν (as if for ᾗ), Eph. i. 6 L T Tr WH; τῆς κλήσεως, ἧς ἐκλήθητε, Eph. iv. 1; διὰ τῆς παρακλήσεως ἧς παρακαλούμεθα, 2 Co. i. 4, but must be explained agreeably to such phrases as χάριν χαριτοῦν, κλῆσιν καλεῖν, etc., [(i. e. accus. of kindred abstract subst.; cf. W. § 32, 2; B. § 131, 5)]; cf. W. [and B. u. s.]. β. The noun to which the relative refers is so conformed to the case of the relative clause that either   αα. it is itself incorporated into the relative construction, but without the article [B. § 143, 7; W. § 24, 2 b.]: ὃν ἐγὼ ἀπεκεφάλισα Ἰωάννην, οὗτος ἠγέρθη, for Ἰωάννης, ὃν κτλ. Mk. vi. 16; add, Lk. xxiv. 1; Philem. 10; Ro. vi. 17; εἰς ἣν οἰκίαν, ἐκεῖ, i. q. ἐν τῇ οἰκίᾳ, εἰς ἥν, Lk. ix. 4; or   ββ. it is placed before the relative clause, either with or without the article [W. § 24, 2 a.; B. § 144, 13]: τὸν ἄρτον ὃν κλῶμεν, οὐχὶ κοινωνία τοῦ σώματος, 1 Co. x. 16; λίθον ὃν ἀπεδοκίμασαν οἱ οἰκοδομοῦντες, οὗτος ἐγενήθη (for ὁ λίθος, ὃς κτλ.), Mt. xxi. 42; Mk. xii. 10; Lk. xx. 17; 1 Pet. ii. 7.   γ. Attraction in the phrases ἄχρι ἧς ἡμέρας for ἄχρι τῆς ἡμέρας, ᾗ [W. § 24, 1 fin.]: Mt. xxiv. 38; Lk. i. 20; xvii. 27; Acts i. 2; ἀφ' ἧς ἡμέρας for ἀπὸ τῆς ἡμέρας, ᾗ, Col. i. 6, 9; ὃν τρόπον, as, just as, for τοῦτον τὸν τρόπον ὅν or ᾧ Mt. xxiii. 37; Lk. xiii. 34; Acts vii. 28; [preceded or] foll. by οὕτως, Acts i. 11; 2 Tim. iii. 8.   δ. A noun common to both the principal clause and the relative is placed in the relative clause after the relative pron. [W. 165 (156)]: ἐν ᾧ κρίματι κρίνετε, κριθήσεσθε, for κριθ. ἐν τῷ κρίματι, ἐν ᾧ κρίνετε, Mt. vii. 2; xxiv. 44; Mk. iv. 24; Lk. xii. 40, etc.   3. The N e u t e r ὅ a. refers to nouns of the masculine and the feminine gender, and to plurals, when that which is denoted by these nouns is regarded as a t h i n g [cf. B. § 129, 6]: λεπτὰ δύο, ὅ ἐστι κοδράντης, Mk. xii. 42; ἀγάπην, ὅ ἐστι σύνδεσμος, Col. iii. 14 L T Tr WH; ἄρτους, ὅ etc. Mt. xii. 4 L txt. T Tr WH.   b. is used in the phrases [B. u. s.] — ὅ ἐστιν, which (term) signifies: Βοανεργές ὅ ἐστιν υἱοὶ βρ. Mk. iii. 17; add, v. 41; vii. 11, 34; Heb. vii. 2; ὅ ἐστι μεθερμηνευόμενον, and the like: Mt.

i. 23; Mk. xv. 34; Jn. i. 38 (39), 41 (42) sq.; ix. 7; xx. 16.   c. refers to a whole sentence [B. u. s.]: τοῦτον ἀνέστησεν ὁ θεός, οὗ ... ἐσμὲν μάρτυρες, Acts ii. 32; iii. 15; περὶ οὗ ... ὁ λόγος, Heb. v. 11; ὃ καὶ ἐποίησαν (and the like), Acts xi. 30; Gal. ii. 10; Col. i. 29; ὅ (which thing viz. that I write a new commandment [cf. B. § 143, 3]) ἐστιν ἀληθές, 1 Jn. ii. 8; ὅ (sc. to have one's lot assigned in the lake of fire) ἐστιν ὁ θάνατος ὁ δεύτερος, Rev. xxi. 8.   4. By an idiom to be met with from Hom. down, in the second of two coördinate clauses a pronoun of the third person takes the place of the relative (cf. Passow ii. p. 552b; [L. and S. s. v. B. IV. 1]; B. § 143, 6; [W. 149 (141)]): ὃς ἔσται ἐπὶ τοῦ δώματος καὶ τὰ σκεύη αὐτοῦ ἐν τῇ οἰκίᾳ μὴ καταβάτω, Lk. xvii. 31; ἐξ οὗ τὰ πάντα καὶ ἡμεῖς εἰς αὐτόν, 1 Co. viii. 6.   5. Sometimes, by a usage esp. Hebraistic, an oblique case of the pronoun αὐτός is introduced into the relative clause redundantly; as, ἧς τὸ θυγάτριον αὐτῆς, Mk. vii. 25; see αὐτός, II. 5.   6. The relative pron. very often so includes the demonstrative οὗτος or ἐκεῖνος that for the sake of perspicuity a demons. pron. must be in thought supplied, either in the clause preceding the relative clause or in that which follows it [W. § 23, 2; B. § 127, 5]. The foll. examples may suffice: a. a demons. pron. must be added in thought in the p r e c e d i n g clause: οἷς ἡτοίμασται, for τούτοις δοθήσεται, οἷς ἡτ. Mt. xx. 23; δεῖξαι (sc. ταῦτα), ἃ δεῖ γενέσθαι, Rev. i. 1; xxii. 6; ᾧ for ἐκεῖνος ᾧ, Lk. vii. 43, 47; οὗ for τούτῳ οὗ, Ro. v. 14; with the attraction of ὧν for τούτων ἅ, Lk. ix. 36; Ro. xv. 18; ὧν for ταῦτα ὧν, Mt. vi. 8; with a prep. intervening, ἔμαθεν ἀφ' ὧν (for ἀπὸ τούτων ἃ) ἔπαθεν, Heb. v. 8. b. a demons. pron. must be supplied in the s u b s e q u e n t clause: Mt. x. 38; Mk. ix. 40; Lk. iv. 6; ix. 50; Jn. xix. 22; Ro. ii. 1, and often.   7. Sometimes the p u r p o s e and e n d is expressed in the form of a relative clause (cf. the Lat. qui for ut is): ἀποστέλλω ἄγγελον, ὃς (for which Lchm. in Mt. has καί) κατασκευάσει, who shall etc. i. q. that he may etc., Mt. xi. 10; Mk. i. 2; Lk. vii. 27; [1 Co. ii. 16]; so also in Grk. auth., cf. Passow s. v. VIII. vol. ii. p. 553; [L. and S. s. v. B. IV. 4]; Matthiae § 481, d.; [Kühner § 563, 3 b.; Jelf § 836, 4; B. § 139, 32]; — or the c a u s e: ὃν παραδέχεται, because he acknowledges him as his own, Heb. xii. 6; — or the relative stands where ὥστε might be used (cf. Matthiae § 479 a.; Krüger § 51, 13, 10; [Kühner § 563, 3 e.]; Passow s. v. VIII. 2, ii. p. 553b; [L. and S. u. s.]): Lk. v. 21; vii. 49.   8. For the interrog. τίς, τί, in indirect questions (cf. Ellendt, Lex. Soph. ii. 372; [cf. B. § 139, 58]): οὐκ ἔχω ὃ παραθήσω, Lk. xi. 6; by a later Grk. usage, in a d i r e c t quest. (cf. W. § 24, 4; B. § 139, 59): ἐφ' ὅ (or Rec. ἐφ' ᾧ) πάρει, Mt. xxvi. 50 (on which [and the more than doubtful use of ὅς in direct quest.] see ἐπί, B. 2 a. ζ. p. 233b and C. I. 2 g. γ. αα. p. 235b).   9. Joined to a preposition it forms a periphrasis for a conjunction [B. 105 (92)]: ἀνθ' ὧν, for ἀντὶ τούτων ὅτι, — because, Lk. i. 20; xix. 44; Acts xii. 23; 2 Th. ii. 10; for which reason, wherefore, Lk. xii. 3 (see ἀντί, 2 d.); ἐφ' ᾧ, for that, since (see ἐπί, B. 2 a. δ. p. 233b); ἀφ' οὗ, (from the time that), when, since, Lk. xiii. 25;

xxiv. 21, [see ἀπό, I. 4 b. p. 58ᵇ]; ἄχρις οὗ, see ἄχρι, 1 d.; ἐξ οὗ, whence, Phil. iii. 20 cf. W. § 21, 3; [B. § 143, 4 a.]; ἕως οὗ, until (see ἕως, II. 1 b. a. p. 268ᵇ); also μέχρις οὗ, Mk. xiii. 30; ἐν ᾧ, while, Mk. ii. 19; Lk. v. 34; Jn. v. 7; ἐν οἷς, meanwhile, Lk. xii. 1; [cf. ἐν, I. 8 e.]. **10.** With particles: ὅς ἄν and ὅς ἐάν, whosoever, if any one ever, see ἄν, II. 2 and ἐάν, II. p. 163ᵃ; οὗ ἐάν, whereso-ever (whithersoever) with subjunc., 1 Co. xvi. 6 [cf. B. 105 (92)]. ὅς γε, see γέ, 2. ὅς καί, who also, he who, (cf. Klotz ad Devar. ii. 2 p. 636): Mk. iii. 19; Lk. vi. 13 sq.; x. 39 [here WH br. ἥ]; Jn. xxi. 20; Acts i. 11; vii. 45; x. 39 [Rec. om. καί]; xii. 4; xiii. 22; xxiv. 6; Ro. v. 2; 1 Co. xi. 23; 2 Co. iii. 6; Gal. ii. 10; Heb. i. 2, etc.; ὅς καί αὐτός, who also himself, who as well as others: Mt. xxvii. 57. ὅς δήποτε, whosoever, Jn. v. 4 Rec.; ὅσπερ [or ὅς περ L Tr txt.], who especially, the very one who (cf. Klotz ad Devar. ii. 2 p. 724): Mk. xv. 6 [but here T WH Tr mrg. now read ὅν παρητοῦντο, q. v.]. **11.** The genitive οὗ, used absolutely [cf. W. 590 (549) note; Jelf § 522, Obs. 1], becomes an adverb (first so in Attic writ., cf. Passow II. p. 546ᵃ; [Meisterhans § 50, 1]);   a. where (Lat. ubi): Mt. ii. 9; xviii. 20; Lk. iv. 16 sq.; xxiii. 53; Acts i. 13; xii. 12; xvi. 13; xx. 6 [T Tr mrg. ὅπου]; xxv. 10; xxviii. 14; Ro. iv. 15; ix. 26; 2 Co. iii. 17; Col. iii. 1; Heb. iii. 9; Rev. xvii. 15; after verbs denoting motion (see ἐκεῖ, b.; ὅπου, 1 b.) it can be rendered whither [cf. W. § 54, 7; B. 71 (62)], Mt. xxviii. 16; Lk. x. 1; xxiv. 28; 1 Co. xvi. 6.   b. when (like Lat. ubi i. q. eo tempore quo, quom): Ro. v. 20 (Eur. Iph. Taur. 320), [but al. take οὗ in Ro. l. c. locally).

3740   ὁσάκις, (ὅσος), relative adv., as often as; with the ad-dition of ἄν, as often soever as, 1 Co. xi. 25 sq. [RG; cf. W. § 42, 5 a.; B. § 139, 34]; also of ἐάν, [L T Tr WH in 1 Co. l. c.]; Rev. xi. 6.   [(Lys., Plat., al.)]*

see 1065   ὅσγε, for ὅς γε, see γέ, 2.
3741   ὅσιος, -α, -ον, and once (1 Tim. ii. 8) of two termina-tions (as in Plato, legg. 8 p. 831 d.; Dion. Hal. antt. 5, 71 fin.; cf. W. § 11, 1; B. 26 (23); the fem. occurs in the N. T. only in the passage cited); fr. Aeschyl. and Hdt. down; Sept. chiefly for חָסִיד (cf. Grimm, Exgt. Hdbch. on Sap. p. 81 [and reff. s. v. ἅγιος, fin.]); un-defiled by sin, free from wickedness, religiously observing every moral obligation, pure, holy, pious, (Plato, Gorg. p. 507 b. περὶ μὲν ἀνθρώπους τὰ προσήκοντα πράττων δίκαι’ ἄν πράττοι, περὶ δὲ θεοὺς ὅσια. The distinction between δίκαιος and ὅσιος is given in the same way by Polyb. 23, 10, 8; Schol. ad Eurip. Hec. 788; Charit. 1, 10; [for other exx. see Trench § lxxxviii.; Wetstein on Eph. iv. 24; but on its applicability to N. T. usage see Trench u. s.; indeed Plato elsewh. (Euthyphro p. 12 e.) makes δίκαιος the generic and ὅσιος the specific term]); of men: Tit. i. 8; Heb. vii. 26; οἱ ὅσιοι τοῦ θεοῦ, the pious towards God, God's pious worshippers, (Sap. iv. 15 and often in the Psalms); so in a peculiar and pre-eminent sense of the Messiah [A. V. thy Holy One]: Acts ii. 27; xiii. 35, after Ps. xv. (xvi.) 10; χεῖρες (Aes-chyl. cho. 378; Soph. O. C. 470), 1 Tim. ii. 8. of God, holy: Rev. xv. 4; xvi. 5, (also in prof. auth. occasion-

ally of the gods; Orph. Arg. 27; hymn. 77, 2; of God in Deut. xxxii. 4 for שַׂר; Ps. cxliv. (cxlv.) 17 for חָסִיד, cf. Sap. v. 19); τὰ ὅσια Δαυΐδ, the holy things (of God) promised to David, i. e. the Messianic blessings, Acts xiii. 34 fr. Is. lv. 3.*

3742   ὁσιότης, -ητος, ἡ, (ὅσιος), piety towards God, fidelity in observing the obligations of piety, holiness: joined with δικαιοσύνη (see ὅσιος [and δικαιοσύνη, 1 b.]): Lk. i. 75; Eph. iv. 24; Sap. ix. 3; Clem. Rom. 1 Cor. 48, 4. (Xen., Plat., Isocr., al.; Sept. for שָׁר, Deut. ix. 5; for חָסָד, 1 K. ix. 4.) [Meinke in St. u. Krit. '84 p. 743; Schmidt ch. 181.] *

3743   ὁσίως, (ὅσιος), [fr. Eur. down], adv., piously, holily: joined with δικαίως, 1 Th. ii. 10 (ἀγνῶς καὶ ὁσίως κ. δι-καίως, Theoph. ad Autol. 1, 7).*

3744   ὀσμή, -ῆς, ἡ, (ὄζω [q. v.]), a smell, odor: Jn. xii. 3; 2 Co. ii. 14; θανάτου (L T Tr WH ἐκ θαν.), such an odor as is emitted by death (i. e. by a deadly, pestiferous thing, a dead body), and itself causes death, 2 Co. ii. 16; ζωῆς (or ἐκ ζωῆς) such as is diffused (or emitted) by life, and itself imparts life, ibid. [A. V. both times savor]; ὀσμὴ εὐωδίας, Eph. v. 2; Phil. iv. 18; see εὐω-δία, b. (Tragg., Thuc., Xen., Plat., al.; in Hom. ὀδμή; Sept. for רֵיחַ.) *

3745   ὅσος, -η, -ον, [fr. Hom. down], a relative adj. corre-sponding to the demon. τοσοῦτος either expressed or un-derstood, Lat. quantus, -a, -um; used   a. of space [as great as]: τὸ μῆκος αὐτῆς (Rec. adds τοσοῦτόν ἐστιν) ὅσον καί [G T Tr WH om. καί] τὸ πλάτος, Rev. xxi. 16; of time [as long as]: ἐφ’ ὅσον χρόνον, for so long time as, so long as, Ro. vii. 1; 1 Co. vii. 39; Gal. iv. 1; also without a prep., ὅσον χρόνον, Mk. ii. 19; neut. ἐφ’ ὅσον, as long as, Mt. ix. 15; 2 Pet. i. 13, (Xen. Cyr. 5, 3, 25); ἔτι μικρὸν ὅσον ὅσον, yet a little how very, how very, (Vulg. modicum [ali]quantulum), i. e. yet a very little while, Heb. x. 37 (Is. xxvi. 20; of a very little thing, Arstph. vesp. 213; cf. Herm. ad Vig. p. 726 no. 93; W. 247 (231) note; B. § 150, 2).   b. of abundance and mul-titude; how many, as many as; how much, as much as: neut. ὅσον, Jn. vi. 11; plur. ὅσοι, as many (men) as, all who, Mt. xiv. 36; Mk. iii. 10; Acts iv. 6, 34; xiii. 48; Ro. ii. 12; vi. 3; Gal. iii. 10, 27; Phil. iii. 15; 1 Tim. vi. 1; Rev. ii. 24; ὅσαι ἐπαγγελίαι, 2 Co. i. 20; ὅσα ἱμάτια, Acts ix. 39; neut. plur., absol. [A. V. often whatsoever], Mt. xvii. 12; Mk. x. 21; Lk. xi. 8; xii. 3; Ro. iii. 19; xv. 4; Jude 10; Rev. i. 2. πάντες ὅσοι, [all as many as], Mt. xxii. 10 [here T WH π. οὕς]; Lk. iv. 40; Jn. x. 8; Acts v. 36 sq.; neut. πάντα ὅσα [all things whatsoever, all that], Mt. xiii. 46; xviii. 25; xxviii. 20; Mk. xii. 44; Lk. xviii. 22; Jn. iv. 29 [T WH Tr mrg. π. ἅ], 39 [T WH Tr txt. π. ἅ]; πολλὰ ὅσα, Jn. xxi. 25 R G, (Hom. Il. 22, 380; Xen. Hell. 3, 4, 3). ὅσοι... οὗτοι, Ro. viii. 14; ὅσα ... ταῦτα, Phil. iv. 8; ὅσα ... ἐν τούτοις, Jude 10; ὅσοι ... αὐτοί, Jn. i. 12; Gal. vi. 16. ὅσοι ἄν or ἐάν, how many soever, as many soever as [cf. W. § 42, 3]; foll. by an indic. pret. (see ἄν, II. 1), Mk. vi. 56; by an indic. pres. Rev. iii. 19; by a subjunc. aor., Mt. xxii. 9; Mk. iii. 28; vi. 11; Lk. ix. 5 [Rec.]; Acts iii. 39 [here Lchm. οὓς ἄν]; Rev. xiii. 15; ὅσα ἄν, Mt. xviii. 18; Jn. xi. 22; xvi. 13

[R G]; πάντα ὅσα ἄν, all things whatsoever: foll. by subjunc. pres. Mt. vii. 12; by subjunc. aor., Mt. xxi. 22; xxiii. 3; Acts iii. 22. ὅσα in indirect disc.; how many things: Lk. ix. 10; Acts ix. 16; xv. 12; 2 Tim. i. 18.   c. of importance: ὅσα, how great things, i. e. how extraordinary, in indir. disc., Mk. iii. 8 [L mrg. ἅ]; v. 19 sq.; Lk. viii. 39; Acts xiv. 27; xv. 4, [al. take it of number in these last two exx. how many; cf. b. above]; how great (i. e. bitter), κακά, Acts ix. 13.   d. of measure and degree, in comparative sentences, acc. neut. ὅσον ... μᾶλλον περισσότερον, the more ... so much the more a great deal (A. V.), Mk. vii. 36; καθ᾽ ὅσον with a compar., by so much as with the compar. Heb. iii. 3; καθ᾽ ὅσον ... κατὰ τοσοῦτον [τοσοῦτο L T Tr WH], Heb. vii. 20, 22; καθ᾽ ὅσον (inasmuch) as foll. by οὕτως, Heb. ix. 27; τοσούτῳ with a compar. foll. by ὅσῳ with a compar., by so much ... as, Heb. i. 4 (Xen. mem. 1, 4, 40; Cyr. 7, 5, 5 sq.); without τοσούτῳ, Heb. viii. 6 [A. V. by how much]; τοσούτῳ μᾶλλον, ὅσῳ (without μᾶλλον), Heb. x. 25; ὅσα ... τοσοῦτον, how much ... so much, Rev. xviii. 7; ἐφ᾽ ὅσον, for as much as, in so far as, without ἐπὶ τοσοῦτον, Mt. xxv. 40, 45; Ro. xi. 13.

3746; see 3739 ὅσπερ, ἥπερ, ὅπερ, see ὅς, ἥ, ὅ, 10.

3747 ὀστέον, contr. ὀστοῦν, gen. -οῦ, τό, [akin to Lat. os, ossis; Curtius § 213, cf. p. 41], a bone: Jn. xix. 36; plur. ὀστέα, Lk. xxiv. 39; gen. ὀστέων, (on these uncontr. forms cf. [WH. App. p. 157]; W. § 8, 2 d.; [B. p. 13 (12)]), Mt. xxiii. 27; Eph. v. 30 [R G Tr mrg. br.]; Heb. xi. 22. (From Hom. down; Sept. very often for עֶצֶם.) *

3748 ὅστις, ἥτις, ὅ,τι (separated by a hypodiastole [comma], to distinguish it from ὅτι; but L T Tr write ὅ τι, without a hypodiastole [cf. Tdf. Proleg. p. 111], leaving a little space between ὅ and τι; [WH ὅτι]; W. 46 (45 sq.); [Lipsius, Gramm. Untersuch. p. 118 sq.; WH. Intr. § 411]), gen. οὗτινος (but of the oblique cases only the acc. neut. ὅ,τι and the gen. ὅτου, in the phrase ἕως ὅτου, are found in the N. T.), [fr. Hom. down], comp. of ὅς and τὶς, hence prop. any one who; i. e.   1. whoever, every one who: ὅστις simply, in the sing. chiefly at the beginning of a sentence in general propositions, esp. in Matt.; w. an indic. pres., Mt. xiii. 12 (twice); Mk. viii. 34 (where L Tr WH εἴ τις); Lk. xiv. 27; neut. Mt. xviii. 28 Rec.; w. a fut., Mt. v. 39 [R G Tr mrg.], 41; xxiii. 12, etc.; Jas. ii. 10 R G; plur. οἵτινες, whosoever (all those who): w. indic. pres., Mk. iv. 20; Lk. viii. 15; Gal. v. 4; w. indic. aor., Rev. i. 7; ii. 24; xx. 4; πᾶς ὅστις, w. indic. pres. Mt. vii. 24; w. fut. Mt. x. 32; with w. subjunc. (where ἄν is wanting very rarely [cf. W. § 42, 3 esp. fin.]; B. § 139, 31]) aor. (having the force of the fut. pf. in Lat.), Mt. xviii. 4 Rec.; Jas. ii. 10 L T Tr WH. ὅστις ἄν w. subjunc. aor. (Lat. fut. pf.), Mt. x. 33 [R G T]; xii. 50; w. subjunc. pres. Gal. v. 10 [ἐάν T Tr WH]; neut. w. subjunc. aor., Lk. x. 35; Jn. xiv. 13 [Tr mrg. WH mrg. pres. subjunc.]; xv. 16 [Tr mrg. WH mrg. pres. subjunc.]; with subjunc. pres., Jn. ii. 5; 1 Co. xvi. 2 [Tr WH ἐάν; WH mrg. aor. subjunc.]; ὃ ἐάν τι for ὅ,τι ἄν w. subjunc. aor. Eph. vi. 8 [R G]; πᾶν ὅ,τι ἄν or ἐάν w. subjunc. pres., Col. iii. 17, 23 [Rec.]; cf. B. § 139, 19;

W. § 42, 3].   2. it refers to a single person or thing, but so that regard is had to a general notion or class to which this individual person or thing belongs, and thus it indicates quality: one who, such a one as, of such a nature that, (cf. Kühner § 554 Anm. 1, ii. p. 905; [Jelf § 816, 5]; Lücke on 1 Jn. i. 2, p. 210 sq.): ἡγούμενος, ὅστις ποιμανεῖ, Mt. ii. 6; add, Mt. vii. 26; xiii. 52; xvi. 28; xx. 1; xxv. 1; Mk. xv. 7; Lk. ii. 10; vii. 37; viii. 3; Jn. viii. 25; xxi. 25 [Tdf. om. the vs.]; Acts xi. 28; xvi. 12; xxiv. 1; Ro. xi. 4; 1 Co. v. 1; vii. 13 [Tdf. εἴ τις]; Gal. iv. 24, 26; v. 19; Phil. ii. 20; Col. ii. 23; 2 Tim. i. 5; Heb. ii. 3; viii. 5; x. 11; xii. 5; Jas. iv. 14; 1 Jn. i. 2; Rev. i. 12; ix. 4; xvii. 12; ὁ ναὸς τοῦ θεοῦ ἅγιός ἐστιν, οἵτινές ἐστε ὑμεῖς (where οἵτινες makes reference to ἅγιος) and such are ye, 1 Co. iii. 17 [some refer it to ναός].   3. Akin to the last usage is that whereby it serves to give a reason, such as equiv. to seeing that he, inasmuch as he: Ro. xvi. 12 [here Lchm. br. the cl.]; Eph. iii. 13; [Col. iii. 5]; Heb. viii. 6; plur., Mt. vii. 15; Acts x. 47; xvii. 11; Ro. i. 25, 32; ii. 15; vi. 2; ix. 4; xvi. 7; 2 Co. viii. 10; [Phil. iv. 3 (where see Bp. Lghtft.)]; 1 Tim. i. 4; Tit. i. 11; 1 Pet. ii. 11.   4. Acc. to a later Greek usage it is put for the interrogative τίς in direct questions (cf. Lob. ad Phryn. p. 57; Lachmann, larger ed., vol. i. p. xliii; B. 253 (218); cf. W. 167 (158)); thus in the N. T. the neut. ὅ, τι stands for τί i. q. διὰ τί in Mk. ii. 16 T Tr WH [cf. 7 WH mrg.]; ix. 11, 28, (Jer. ii. 36; 1 Chr. xvii. 6—for which in the parallel, 2 S. vii. 7, ἵνα τί appears; Barnab. ep. 7, 9 [(where see Müller); cf. Tdf. Proleg. p. 125]; Evang. Nicod. pars i. A. xiv. 3 p. 245 and note; cf. also Soph. Lex. s. v. 4]); many interpreters bring in Jn. viii. 25 here; but respecting it see ἀρχή, 1 b.   5. It differs scarcely at all from the simple relative ὅς (cf. Matthiae p. 1073; B. § 127, 18; [Krüger § 51, 8; Ellicott on Gal. iv. 24; cf. Jebb in Vincent and Dickson's Hdbk. to Modern Greek, App. § 24]; but cf. C. F. A. Fritzsche in Fritzschiorum opusc. p. 182 sq., who stoutly denies it): Lk. ii. 4; ix. 30; Acts xvii. 10; xxiii. 14; xxviii. 18; Eph. i. 23.   6. ἕως ὅτου, on which see ἕως, II. 1 b. β. p. 268ᵇ mid.

3749 ὀστράκινος, -η, -ον, (ὄστρακον baked clay), made of clay, earthen: σκεύη ὀστράκινα, 2 Tim. ii. 20; with the added suggestion of frailty, 2 Co. iv. 7. (Jer. xix. 1, 11; xxxix. (xxxii.) 14; Is. xxx. 14, etc.; Hippocr., Anthol., [al.].) *

3750 ὄσφρησις, -εως, ἡ, (ὀσφραίνομαι [to smell]), the sense of smell, smelling: 1 Co. xii. 17. (Plat. Phaedo p. 111 b. [(yet cf. Stallbaum ad loc.)]; Aristot., Theophr.) *

3751 ὀσφύς [or -φῦς, so R Tr in Eph. vi. 14; G in Mt. iii. 4; cf. Chandler §§ 658, 659; Tdf. Proleg. p. 101], -ύος, ἡ, fr. Aeschyl. and Hdt. down;   1. the hip (loin), as that part of the body where the ζώνη was worn (Sept. for כְּתָנִים; Mt. iii. 4; Mk. i. 6; hence περιζώννυσθαι τὰς ὀσφύας, to gird, gird about, the loins, Lk. xii. 35; Eph. vi. 14; and ἀναζώνν. τὰς ὀσφ. [to gird up the loins], 1 Pet. i. 13; on the meaning of these metaph. phrases see ἀναζώννυμι.   2. a loin, Sept. several times for חֲלָצַיִם,

the (two) *loins*, where the Hebrews thought the generative power (*semen*) resided [?]; hence καρπὸς τῆς ὀσφύος, fruit of the loins, offspring, Acts ii. 30 (see καρπός, 1 fin.); ἐξέρχεσθαι ἐκ τῆς ὀσφύος τινός, to come forth out of one's loins i. e. derive one's origin or descent from one, Heb. vii. 5 (see ἐξέρχομαι, 2 b.); ἔτι ἐν τῇ ὀσφύϊ τινός, to be yet in the loins of some one (an ancestor), Heb. vii. 10.*

3752   ὅταν, a particle of time, comp. of ὅτε and ἄν, *at the time that, whenever,* (Germ. *dann wann; wann irgend*); used of things which one assumes will really occur, but the time of whose occurrence he does not definitely fix (in prof. auth. often also of things which one assumes can occur, but whether they really will or not he does not know; hence like our *in case that,* as in Plato, Prot. p. 360 b.; Phaedr. p. 256 e.; Phaedo p. 68 d.); [cf. W. § 42, 5; B. § 139, 33];   **a.** with the **subjunctive present:** Mt. vi. 2, 5; x. 23; Mk. xiii. 11 [here Rec. aor.]; xiv. 7; Lk. xi. 36; xii. 11; xiv. 12 sq.; xxi. 7; Jn. vii. 27; xvi. 21; Acts xxiii. 35; 1 Co. iii. 4; 2 Co. xiii. 9; 1 Jn. v. 2; Rev. x. 7; xviii. 9; preceded by a specification of time: ἕως τῆς ἡμέρας ἐκείνης, ὅταν etc., Mt. xxvi. 29; Mk. xiv. 25; foll. by τότε, 1 Th. v. 3; 1 Co. xv. 28; i. q. *as often as,* of customary action, Mt. xv. 2; Jn. viii. 44; Ro. ii. 14; *at the time when* i. q. *as long as,* Lk. xi. 34; Jn. ix. 5.   **b.** with the **subjunctive aorist:** i. q. the Lat. *quando acciderit, ut* w. subjunc. pres., Mt. v. 11; xii. 43; xiii. 32; xxiii. 15; xxiv. 32; Mk. iv. 15 sq. 29 [R G]; 31 sq.; xiii. 28; Lk. vi. 22, 26; viii. 13; xi. 24; xii. 54 sq.; xxi. 30; Jn. ii. 10; x. 4; xvi. 21; 1 Tim. v. 11 [here L mrg. fut.]; Rev. ix. 5. **i. q.** *quando* w. fut. pf., Mt. xix. 28; xxi. 40; Mk. viii. 38; ix. 9; xii. 23 [G Tr WH om. L br. the cl.], 25; Lk. ix. 26; xvi. 4, 9; xvii. 10; Jn. iv. 25; vii. 31; xiii. 19; xiv. 29; xv. 26; xvi. 4, 13, 21; xxi. 18; Acts xxiii. 35; xxiv. 22; Ro. xi. 27; 1 Co. xv. 24 [here L Tr WH pres.], 27 (where the meaning is, 'when he shall have said that the ὑπόταξις predicted in the Psalm is now accomplished'; cf. Meyer ad loc.); xvi. 2 sq. 5, 12; 2 Co. x. 6; Col. iv. 16; 1 Jn. ii. 28 [L T Tr WH ἐάν]; 2 Th. i. 10; Heb. i. 6 (on which see εἰσάγω, 1); Rev. xi. 7; xii. 4; xvii. 10; xx. 7. foll. by τότε, Mt. ix. 15; xxiv. 15; xxv. 31; Mk. ii. 20; xiii. 14; Lk. v. 35; xxi. 20; Jn. viii. 28; 1 Co. xiii. 10 [G L T Tr WH om. τότε]; xv. 28, 54; Col. iii. 4.   **c.** Acc. to the usage of later authors, a usage, however, not altogether unknown to the more elegant writers (W. 309 (289 sq.); B. 222 (192) sq.; [Tdf. Proleg. p. 124 sq.; WH. App. p. 171; for exx. additional to these given by W. and B. u. s. see Soph. Lex. s. v.; cf. Jebb in Vincent and Dickson's Hdbk. to Mod. Grk., App. § 78]), with the **indicative**;   **α.** future: *when*, [Mt. v. 11 Tdf.]; Lk. xiii. 28 T Tr txt. WH mrg.; [1 Tim. v. 11 L mrg.]; *as often as,* Rev. iv. 9 (cf. Bleek ad loc.). **β.** present: Mk. xi. 25 L T Tr WH; xiii. 7 Tr txt.; [Lk. xi. 2 Tr mrg.]. **γ.** very rarely indeed, with the **imperfect**: *as often as,* [*whensoever*], ὅταν ἐθεώρουν, Mk. iii. 11 (Gen. xxxviii. 9; Ex. xvii. 11; 1 S. xvii. 34; see ἄν, II. 1).   **δ.** As in Byz-

antine auth. i. q. ὅτε, *when,* with the indic. **aorist**: ὅταν ἤνοιξεν, Rev. viii. 1 L T Tr WH; [add ὅταν ὀψὲ ἐγένετο, Mk. xi. 19 T Tr txt. WH, cf. B. 223 (193); but al. take this of **customary** action, *whenever* evening came (i. e. *every* evening, R. V.)]. ὅταν does not occur in the Epp. of Peter and Jude.

ὅτε, a particle of time, [fr. Hom. down], *when*;   **1.**   **3753** with the **Indicative** [W. 296 (278) sq.]; indic. **present** (of something certain and customary, see *Herm.* ad Vig. p. 913 sq.), *while*: Jn. ix. 4; Heb. ix. 17; w. an historical pres. Mk. xi. 1. w. the **imperfect** (of a thing done on occasion or customary): Mk. xiv. 12; xv. 41; Mk. vi. 21 R G; Jn. xxi. 18; Acts xii. 6; xxii. 20; Ro. vi. 20; vii. 5; 1 Co. xiii. 11; Gal. iv. 3; Col. iii. 7; 1 Th. iii. 4; 2 Th. iii. 10; 1 Pet. iii. 20. w. an indic. **aorist**, Lat. *quom* w. plupf. (W. § 40, 5; [B. § 137, 6]): Mt. ix. 25; xiii. 26, 48; xvii. 25 [R G]; xxi. 34; Mk. i. 32; iv. 10; viii. 19; xv. 20; Lk. ii. 21 sq. 42; iv. 25; vi. [3 L T WH], 13; xxii. 14; xxiii. 33; Jn. i. 19; ii. 22; iv. 45 [where Tdf. ὡς], etc.; Acts i. 13; viii. 12, 39; xi. 2; xxi. 5, 35; xxvii. 39; xxviii. 16; Ro. xiii. 11 ("than when we gave in our allegiance to Christ;" Lat. *quom Christo nomen dedissemus,* [R. V. *than when we first believed*]); Gal. i. 15; ii. 11, 12, 14; iv. 4; Phil. iv. 15; Heb. vii. 10; Rev. i. 17; vi. 3, 5, 7, 9, 12; viii. 1, etc.; so also Mt. xii. 3; Mk. ii. 25; (Jn. xii. 41 R Tr mrg. ὅτε εἶδεν, when it had presented itself to his sight [but best texts ὅτι: *because* he saw etc.]). ἐγένετο, ὅτε ἐτέλεσεν, a common phrase in Mt., viz. vii. 28; xi. 1; xiii. 53; xix. 1; xxvi. 1. ὅτε ... τότε, Mt. xxi. 1; Jn. xii. 16. w. the indic. **perfect**, *since* [R. V. *now that* I am become], 1 Co. xiii. 11; w. the indic. **future**: Lk. xvii. 22; Jn. iv. 21, 23; v. 25; xvi. 25; Ro. ii. 16 [R G T Tr txt. WH mrg.] (where Lchm. ᾗ [al. al.]); 2 Tim. iv. 3.   **2.** with the aor. **Subjunctive**: ἕως ἂν ἥξῃ, ὅτε εἴπητε (where ὅταν might have been expected), until the time have come, when ye have said, Lk. xiii. 35 [R G (cf. Tr br.)]; cf. Matthiae ii. p. 1196 sq.; Bornemann, Scholia in Lucae evang. p. 92; W. 298 (279); [Bnhdy. p. 400; cf. B. 231 sq. (199)].

ὅ, τε, ἥ, τε, τό, τε, see τέ 2 a.   **see 5037**

ὅτι [properly neut. of ὅστις], a conjunction [fr. Hom. **3754** down], (Lat. *quod* [cf. W. § 53, 8 b.; B. § 139, 51; § 149, 3]), marking

  I. the **substance** or **contents** (of a statement), *that*;   **1.** joined to verbs of **saying** and **declaring** (where the acc. and infin. is used in Lat.): ἀναγγέλλειν, Acts xiv. 27; διηγεῖσθαι, Acts xi. 27; εἰπεῖν, Mt. xvi. 20; xxviii. 7, 13; Jn. vii. 42; xvi. 15; 1 Co. i. 15; λέγειν, Mt. iii. 9; viii. 11; Mk. iii. 28; Lk. xv. 7; Jn. xvi. 20; Ro. iv. 9 [T Tr WH om. L br. ὅτι]; ix. 2, and very often; προειρηκέναι, 2 Co. vii. 3; before the ὅτι in Acts xiv. 22 supply λέγοντες, contained in the preceding παρακαλοῦντες [cf. B. § 151, 11]; ὅτι after γράφειν, 1 Co. ix. 10; 1 Jn. ii. 12–14; μαρτυρεῖν, Mt. xxiii. 31; Jn. i. 34; iii. 28; iv. 44; ὁμολογεῖν, Heb. xi. 13; δεικνύειν, Mt. xvi. 21; δηλοῦν, 1 Co. i. 11; διδάσκειν, 1 Co. xi. 14. after ἐμφανίζειν, Heb. xi. 14; δῆλον (ἐστίν), 1 Co. xv. 27; Gal. iii. 11; 1 Tim. vi.

7 (where L T Tr WH om. δῆλον [and then ὅτι simply introduces the reason, *because* (B. 358 (308) to the contrary)]); φανερούμαι (for φανερὸν γίνεται περὶ ἐμοῦ), 2 Co. iii. 3; 1 Jn. ii. 19. It is added — to verbs of s w e a r i n g, and to forms of o a t h and a f f i r m a t o n: ὄμνυμι, Rev. x. 6; ζῶ ἐγώ (see ζάω, I. 1 p. 270ᵃ), Ro. xiv. 11; μάρτυρα τὸν θεὸν ἐπικαλοῦμαι, 2 Co. i. 23; πιστὸς ὁ θεός, 2 Co. i. 18; ἔστιν ἀλήθεια Χριστοῦ ἐν ἐμοί, 2 Co. xi. 10; ἰδοὺ ἐνώπιον τοῦ θεοῦ, Gal. i. 20; cf. *Fritzsche*, Ep. ad Rom. ii. p. 242 sq.; [W. § 53, 9; B. 394 (338)]; — to verbs of p e r c e i v i n g, k n o w i n g, r e m e m b e r i n g, etc.: ἀκούειν, Jn. xiv. 28; βλέπειν, 2 Co. vii. 8; Heb. iii. 19; Jas. ii. 22; θεᾶσθαι, Jn. vi. 5; γινώσκειν, Mt. xxi. 45; Lk. x. 11; Jn. iv. 53; 2 Co. xiii. 6; 1 Jn. ii. 5, etc.; after τοῦτο, Ro. vi. 6; εἰδέναι, Mt. vi. 32; xxii. 16; Mk. ii. 10; Lk. ii. 49; Jn. iv. 42; ix. 20, 24 sq.; Ro. ii. 2; vi. 9; Phil. iv. 15 sq., and very often; γνωστόν ἐστιν, Acts xxviii. 28; ἐπιγινώσκειν, Mk. ii. 8; Lk. i. 22; Acts iv. 13; ἐπίστασθαι, Acts xv. 7; νοεῖν, Mt. xv. 17; ὁρᾶν, Jas. ii. 24; καταλαμβάνειν, Acts iv. 13; x. 34; συνιέναι, Mt. xvi. 12; ἀγνοεῖν, Ro. i. 13; ii. 4; vi. 3, etc.; ἀναγινώσκειν, Mt. xii. 5; xix. 4; μνημονεύειν, Jn. xvi. 4; μνησθῆναι, Mt. v. 23; Jn. ii. 22; ὑπομιμνῄσκειν, Jude 5; — to verbs of t h i n k i n g, b e l i e v i n g, j u d g i n g, h o p i n g: λογίζεσθαι, Jn. xi. 50 L T Tr WH; after τοῦτο, Ro. ii. 3; 2 Co. x. 11; νομίζειν, Mt. v. 17; οἶμαι, Jas. i. 7; πέπεισμαι, Ro. viii. 38; xiv. 14; xv. 14; 2 Tim. i. 5, 12; πεποιθέναι, Lk. xviii. 9; 2 Co. ii. 3; Phil. ii. 24; Gal. v. 10; 2 Th. iii. 4; Heb. xiii. 18; πιστεύειν, Mt. ix. 28; Mk. xi. 23; Ro. x. 9; ὑπολαμβάνειν, Lk. vii. 43; δοκεῖν, Mt. vi. 7; xxvi. 53; Jn. xx. 15; ἐλπίζειν, Lk. xxiv. 21; 2 Co. xiii. 6; κρίνειν τοῦτο ὅτι, 2 Co. v. 14 (15); — to verbs of e m o t i o n (where in Lat. now the acc. and inf. is used, now *quod*): θαυμάζειν, Lk. xi. 38; χαίρειν, Jn. xiv. 28; 2 Co. vii. 9, 16; Phil. iv. 10; 2 Jn. 4; ἐν τούτῳ, ὅτι, Lk. x. 20; συγχαίρειν, Lk. xv. 6, 9; μέλει μοι (σοι, αὐτῷ), Mk. iv. 38; Lk. x. 40; — to verbs of p r a i s i n g, t h a n k i n g, b l a m i n g, (where the Lat. uses *quod*): ἐπαινεῖν, Lk. xvi. 8; 1 Co. xi. 2, 17; ἐξομολογεῖσθαι, Mt. xi. 25; Lk. x. 21; εὐχαριστεῖν, Lk. xviii. 11; χάρις τῷ θεῷ, Ro. vi. 17; χάριν ἔχω τινί, 1 Tim. i. 12; ἔχω κατά τινος, ὅτι etc. Rev. ii. 4; ἔχω τοῦτο ὅτι, I have this (which is praiseworthy) that, Rev. ii. 6; add, Jn. vii. 23 [but here ὅτι is c a u s a l; cf. W. § 53, 8 b.]; 1 Co. vi. 7; — to the verb εἶναι, when that precedes with a demons. pron., in order to define more exactly what a thing is or wherein it may be seen: αὕτη ἐστὶν ὅτι (Lat. *quod*), Jn. iii. 19; ἐν τούτῳ ὅτι, 1 Jn. iii. 16; iv. 9 sq. 13, etc.; περὶ τούτου ὅτι, Jn. xvi. 19; οὐχ οἷον ὅτι (see οἷος), Ro. ix. 6; — to the verbs γίνεσθαι and εἶναι with an interrog. pron., as τί γέγονεν ὅτι etc., *what has come to pass that?* our *how comes it that?* Jn. xiv. 22; τί [L mrg. τίς] ἐστιν ἄνθρωπος, ὅτι, Heb. ii. 6 fr. Ps. viii. 5. τίς ὁ λόγος οὗτος (sc. ἐστίν), ὅτι, Lk. iv. 36; ποταπός ἐστιν οὗτος, ὅτι, Mt. viii. 27; τίς ἡ διδαχὴ αὕτη, ὅτι, Mk. i. 27 Rec.; add Mk. iv. 41.   **2.** in elliptical formulas (B. 358 (307); [W. 585 (544) note]): τί ὅτι etc., i. q. τί ἐστιν ὅτι, [A. V. *how is it that*], *wherefore?* Mk. ii. 16 R G L [al. om. τί; cf. 5 below, and see ὅστις, 4]; Lk. ii. 49; Acts v. 4, 9.   οὐχ ὅτι for οὐ λέγω ὅτι, our *not that*, not as though, cf.

B. § 150, 1; [W. 597 (555)]; thus, Jn. vi. 46; vii. 22; 2 Co. i. 24; iii. 5; Phil. iii. 12; iv. 11.   ὅτι is used for εἰς ἐκεῖνο ὅτι (*in reference to the fact that* [Eng. *seeing that, in that*]) : thus in Jn. ii. 18; [Meyer (see his note on 1 Co. i. 26) would add many other exx., among them Jn. ix. 17 (see below)]; for ἐν τούτῳ ὅτι, Ro. v. 8; for περὶ τούτου ὅτι, *concerning this, that*: so after λαλεῖν, Mk. i. 34; Lk. iv. 41 [al. take ὅτι in these exx. and those after διαλογ. which follow in a c a u s a l sense; cf. W. as below (Ellicott on 2 Thess. iii. 7)]; after λέγειν, Jn. ix. 17 [see above]; after διαλογίζεσθαι, Mt. xvi. 8; Mk. viii. 17, (after ἀποστέλλειν ἐπιστολάς, 1 Macc. xii. 7). See exx. fr. classic authors in Fritzsche on Mt. p. 248 sq.; [Meyer, u. s.; cf. W. § 53, 8 b.].   **3.** Noteworthy is the a t t r a c t i o n, not uncommon, by which the noun that would naturally be the subject of the subjoined clause, is attracted by the verb of the principal clause and becomes its object [cf. W. § 66, 5; B § 151, 1 a.]; as, οἴδατε τὴν οἰκίαν Στεφανᾶ, ὅτι ἐστὶν ἀπαρχή. for οἴδατε, ὅτι ἡ οἰκία Στ. κτλ., 1 Co. xvi. 15; also after εἰδέναι and ἰδεῖν, Mk. xii. 34; 1 Th. ii. 1; so after other verbs of k n o w i n g, d e c l a r i n g, etc.: Mt. xxv. 24; Jn. ix. 8; Acts iii. 10; ix. 20; 1 Co. iii. 20; 2 Th. ii. 4; Rev. xvii. 8, etc.; ὃν ὑμεῖς λέγετε ὅτι θεὸς ὑμῶν ἐστι, for περὶ οὗ (cf. Lk. xxi. 5) ὑμεῖς λέγετε ὅτι, Jn. viii. 54.   **4.** As respects c o n s t r u c t i o n, ὅτι is joined in the N. T.   **a.** to the i n d i c a t i v e even where the opinion of another is introduced, and therefore according to class. usage the optative should have been used; as, διεστείλατο . . . ἵνα μηδενὶ εἴπωσιν, ὅτι αὐτός ἐστιν ὁ Χριστός, Mt. xvi. 20; add, 21; iv. 12; xx. 30, etc.   **b.** to that s u b j u n c t i v e after οὐ μή which differs scarcely at all from the future (see μή, IV. 2 p. 411ᵃ; [cf. W. 508 (473)]): Mt. v. 20; xxvi. 29 [R G; al. om. ὅτι]; Mk. xiv. 25; Lk. xxi. 32; Jn. xi. 56 (where before ὅτι supply δοκεῖτε, borrowed from the preceding δοκεῖ); but in Ro. iii. 8 ὅτι before ποιήσωμεν (hortatory subjunc. [cf. W. § 41 a. 4 a.; B. 245 (211)]) is recitative [see 5 below], depending on λέγουσι [W. 628 (583); B. § 141, 3].   **c.** to the i n f i n i t i v e, by a mingling of two constructions, common even in classic Grk., according to which the writer beginning the construction with ὅτι falls into the construction of the acc. with inf.: Acts xxvii. 10; cf. W. 339 (318) N. 2; [§ 63, 2 c.; B. 383 (328)].   On the anacoluthon found in 1 Co. xii. 2, acc. to the reading ὅτι ὅτε (which appears in cod. Sin. also [and is adopted by L br. T Tr WH (yet cf. their note)]), cf. B. 383 (328) sq.   **5.** ὅτι is placed before direct discourse ('r e c i t a t i v e' ὅτι [B. § 139, 51; W. § 65, 3 c.; § 60, 9 (and Moulton's note]): Matt. ii. 23[?]; vii. 23; xvi. 7; xxi. 16; xxvi. 72, 74; xxvii. 43; Mk. [ii. 16 T Tr WH (see 2 above); but see ὅστις, 4]; vi. 23; xii. 19 [cf. B. 237 (204)]; Lk. i. 61; ii. 23; iv. 43; xv. 27; Jn. i. 20; iv. 17; xv. 25; xvi. 17; Acts xv. 1; Heb. xi. 18; 1 Jn. iv. 20; Rev. iii. 17, etc.; most frequently after λέγω, q. v. II. 1 a., p. 373ᵃ bot. [Noteworthy is 2 Thess. iii. 10, cf. B. § 139, 53.]

II. the r e a s o n why anything is said to be or to be done, *because, since, for that, for*, (a causal conjunc.; Lat.

quod, quia, quom, nam); [on the diff. betw. it and γάρ cf. *Westcott*, Epp. of Jn. p. 70]; **a.** it is added to a speaker's words to show what ground he gives for his opinion; as, μακάριος etc. ὅτι, Mt. v. 4–12; xiii. 16; Lk. vi. 20 sq.; xiv. 14; after οὐαί, Mt. xi. 21; xxiii. 13–15, 23, 25, 27, 29; Lk. vi. 24 sq.; x. 13; xi. 42–44, 46, 52; Jude 11; cf. further, Mt. vii. 13; xvii. 15; xxv. 8; Mk. v. 9; ix. 38 [G Tr mrg. om. Tr txt. br. the cl.]; Lk. vii. 47; xxiii. 40; Jn. i. 30; v. 27; ix. 16; xvi. 9–11, 14, 16 [T Tr WH om. L br. cl.]; Acts i. 5, and often;—or is added by the narrator, to give the reason for his own opinion: Mt. ii. 18; ix. 36; Mk. iii. 30; vi. 34; Jn. ii. 25; Acts i. 17;—or, in general, by a teacher, and often in such a way that it relates to his entire statement or views: Mt. v. 45; 1 Jn. iv. 18; 2 Jn. 7; Rev. iii. 10.　**b.** ὅτι makes reference to some word or words that precede or immediately follow it [cf. W. § 23, 5; § 53, 8 b.; B. § 127, 6]; as, διὰ τοῦτο, Jn. viii. 47; x. 17; xii. 39; 1 Jn. iii. 1, etc.　διὰ τί; Ro. ix. 32; 2 Co. xi. 11.　χάριν τίνος; 1 Jn. iii. 12.　οὕτως, Rev. iii. 16.　ἐν τούτῳ, 1 Jn. iii. 20. ὅτι in the protasis, Jn. i. 50 (51); xx. 29. It is followed by διὰ τοῦτο, Jn. xv. 19.　οὐχ ὅτι . . . ἀλλ' ὅτι, *not because . . . but because*, Jn. vi. 26; xii. 6.

III. On the combination ὡς ὅτι see ὡς, I. 3.

see 3748 —— [ὅτι interrog., i. e. ὅ, τι or ὅ τι, see ὅστις, 4 (and ad init.).]
3755:
see 3748 — ὅτου, see ὅστις ad init.
3757: ———— οὗ, see ὅς, ἥ, ὅ, II. 11.
see 3739
3756 οὐ before a consonant, οὐκ before a vowel with a smooth breathing, and οὐχ before an aspirated vowel; but sometimes in the best codd. οὐχ occurs even before a smooth breathing; accordingly L T WH mrg. have adopted οὐχ ἰδού, Acts ii. 7; L T οὐχ Ἰουδαϊκῶς, Gal. ii. 14 (see *WH*. Introd. § 409); L οὐχ ὀλίγος, Acts xix. 23; οὐχ ἠγάπησαν, Rev. xii. 11; and contrariwise οὐκ before an aspirate, as οὐκ ἕστηκεν, Jn. viii. 44 T; [οὐκ ἕνεκεν, 2 Co. vii. 12 T]; (οὐκ εὖρον, Lk. xxiv. 3; [οὐκ ὑπάρχει, Acts iii. 6] in cod. ℵ [also C *; cf. cod. Alex. in 1 Esdr. iv. 2, 12; Job xix. 16; xxxviii. 11, 26]); cf. W. § 5, 1 d. 14; B. 7; [*A. v. Schütz*, Hist. Alphab. Att., Berol. 1875, pp. 54–58; *Sophocles*, Hist. of Grk. Alphab., 1st ed. 1848, p. 64 sq. (on the breathing); *Tdf.* Sept., ed. 4, Proleg. pp. xxxiii. xxxiv.; *Scrivener*, Collation etc., 2d ed., p. lv no. 9; *id.* cod. Bezae p. xlvii. no. 11 (cf. p. xlii. no. 5); *Kuenen and Cobet*, N. T. etc. p. lxxxvii. sq.; *Tdf.* Proleg. p. 90 sq.; *WH*. Intr. §§ 405 sqq., and App. p. 143 sq.]; Sept. for לֹא, אַיִן, אֵין; a particle of negation, *not* (how it differs fr. μή has been explained in μή, ad init.); it is used　**1.** absol. and accented, οὔ, *nay, no*, [W. 476 (444)]: in answers, ὁ δέ φησιν· οὔ, Mt. xiii. 29; ἀπεκρίθη· οὔ, Jn. i. 21; [xxi. 5], cf. vii. 12; repeated, οὐ οὔ, it strengthens the negation, *nay, nay, by no means*, Mt. v. 37; ἤτω ὑμῶν τὸ οὐ οὔ, let your denial be truthful, Jas. v. 12; on 2 Co. i. 17–19, see ναί.　**2.** It is joined to other words,—to a finite verb, simply to deny that what is declared in the verb applies to the subject of the sentence: Mt. i. 25 (οὐκ ἐγίνωσκεν αὐτήν); Mk. iii. 25; Lk. vi. 43; Jn. x. 28; Acts vii. 5; Ro. i. 16, and

times without number. It has the same force when conjoined to **participles**: ὡς οὐκ ἀέρα δέρων, 1 Co. ix. 26; οὐκ ὄντος αὐτῷ τέκνου, at the time when he had no child, Acts vii. 5 (μὴ ὄντος would be, *although he had no child*); add, Ro. viii. 20; 1 Co. iv. 14; 2 Co. iv. 8; Gal. iv. 8, 27; Col. ii. 19; Phil. iii. 3; Heb. xi. 35; 1 Pet. i. 8; ὁ . . . οὐκ ὢν ποιμήν, Jn. x. 12 (where acc. to class. usage μή must have been employed, because such a person is imagined as is not a shepherd; [cf. B. 351 (301) and μή, I. 5 b.]).　in relative sentences: εἰσὶν . . . τινὲς οἳ οὐ πιστεύουσιν, Jn. vi. 64; add, Mt. x. 38; xii. 2; Lk. vi. 2; Ro. xv. 21; Gal. iii. 10, etc.; οὐκ ἕστιν ὅς and οὐδέν ἕστιν ὅ foll. by a fut.: Mt. x. 26; Lk. viii. 17; xii. 2; τίς ἐστιν, ὃς οὐ foll. by a pres. indic.: Acts xix. 35; Heb. xii. 7; cf. W. 481 (448); B. 355 (305); in statements introduced by ὅτι after verbs of understanding, perceiving, saying, etc.: Jn. v. 42; viii. 55, etc.; ὅτι οὐκ (where οὐκ is pleonastic) after ἀρνεῖσθαι, 1 Jn. ii. 22; cf. B. § 148, 13; [W. § 65, 2 β.];—to an infin., where μή might have been expected: τίς ἔτι χρεία κατὰ τὴν τάξιν Μελχισ. ἕτερον ἀνίστασθαι ἱερέα καὶ οὐ κατὰ τὴν τάξιν Ἀαρὼν λέγεσθαι, Heb. vii. 11 (where the difficulty is hardly removed by saying [e. g. with W. 482 (449)] that οὐ belongs only to κατὰ τὴν τάξιν Ἀαρ., not to the infin.).　it serves to deny other parts of statements: οὐκ ἐν σοφίᾳ λόγου, 1 Co. i. 17; οὐ μέλανι, οὐκ ἐν πλαξὶ λιθίναις, 2 Co. iii. 3, and many other exx.;—to deny the object, ἕλεος (R G ἕλεον) θέλω, οὐ θυσίαν, Mt. ix. 13; xii. 7; οὐκ ἐμὲ δέχεται, Mk. ix. 37. It blends with the term to which it is prefixed into a single and that an affirmative idea [W. 476 (444); cf. B. 347 (298)]; as, οὐκ ἐάω, to prevent, hinder, Acts xvi. 7; xix. 30, (cf., on this phrase, *Herm.* ad Vig. p. 887 sq.); οὐκ ἔχω, to be poor, Mt. xiii. 12; Mk. iv. 25, (see ἔχω, I. 2 a. p. 266ᵇ); τὰ οὐκ ἀνήκοντα [or ἃ οὐκ ἀνήκεν, L T Tr WH], unseemly, dishonorable, Eph. v. 4 (see μή, I. 5 d. fin. p. 410ᵃ; [cf. B. § 148, 7 a.; W. 486 (452)]); often so as to form a litotes; as, οὐκ ἀγνοέω, to know well, 2 Co. ii. 11 (Sap. xii. 10); οὐκ ὀλίγοι, not a few, i. e. very many, Acts xvii. 4, 12; xix. 23 sq.; xv. 2; xiv. 28; xxvii. 20; οὐ πολλαὶ ἡμέραι, a few days, Lk. xv. 13; Jn. ii. 12; Acts i. 5; οὐ πολύ, Acts xxvii. 14; οὐ μετρίως, Acts xx. 12; οὐκ ἄσημος, not undistinguished [A. V. no mean etc.], Acts xxi. 39; οὐκ ἐκ μέτρου, Jn. iii. 34.　it serves to limit the term to which it is joined: οὐ πάντως, not altogether, not entirely (see πάντως, c. β.); οὐ πᾶς, not any and every one, Mt. vii. 21; plur. οὐ πάντες, not all, Mt. xix. 11; Ro. ix. 6; x. 16; οὐ πᾶσα σάρξ, not every kind of flesh, 1 Co. xv. 39; οὐ παντὶ τῷ λαῷ, not to all the people, Acts x. 41; on the other hand, when οὐ is joined to the verb, πᾶς . . . οὐ must be rendered no one, no, (as in Hebrew, now כֹּל . . . לֹא, now לֹא . . . כָּל; cf. *Winer*, Lex. Hebr. et Chald. p. 513 sq.): Lk. i. 37; Eph. v. 5; 1 Jn. ii. 21; Rev. xxii. 3; πᾶσα σάρξ . . . οὐ w. a verb, no flesh, no mortal, Mt. xxiv. 22; Mk. xiii. 20; Ro. iii. 20; Gal. ii. 16; cf. W. § 26, 1; [B. 121 (106)].　Joined to a noun it denies and annuls the idea of the noun; as, τὸν οὐ λαόν, a people that is not a people (Germ. *ein Nichtvolk, a no-people*), Ro. ix. 25, cf. 1 Pet. ii. 10; ἐπ' οὐκ ἔθνει,

[R. V. *with that which is no nation*], Ro. x. 19 (so לֹא עָם; לֹא אֵל, a no-god, Deut. xxxii. 21; לֹא עֵץ, a *not-wood*, Is. x. 15; οὐκ ἀρχιερεύς, 2 Macc. iv. 13; ἡ οὐ διάλυσις, Thuc. 1, 137, 4; ἡ οὐ περιτείχισις 3, 95, 2; ἡ οὐκ ἐξουσία 5, 50, 3; δι’ ἀπειροσύναν . . . κοὐκ ἀπόδειξιν, Eur. Hippol. 196, and other exx. in Grk. writ.; *non sutor*, Hor. sat. 2, 3, 106; *non corpus*, Cic. acad. 1, 39 fin.); cf. W. 476 (444); [B. § 148, 9]; ἡ οὐκ ἠγαπημένη, Ro. ix. 25; οἱ οὐκ ἠλεημένοι, 1 Pet. ii. 10. **3.** followed by another negative, **a.** it strengthens the negation: οὐ κρίνω οὐδένα, Jn. viii. 15; add, Mk. v. 37; 2 Co. xi. 9 (8); οὐ οὐκ ἦν οὐδέπω οὐδεὶς κείμενος, Lk. xxiii. 53 [see οὐδέπω]; οὐκ . . . οὐδέν, nothing at all, Lk. iv. 2; Jn. vi. 63; xi. 49; xii. 19; xv. 5; οὐ μέλει σοι περὶ οὐδενός, Mt. xxii. 16; οὐκ . . . οὐκέτι, Acts viii. 39; cf. Matthiae § 609, 3; Kühner ii. § 516; W. § 55, 9 b.; [B. § 148, 11]. **b.** as in Latin, it changes a negation into an affirmation (cf. Matthiae § 609, 2; *Klotz* ad Devar. ii. 2 p. 695 sq.; W. § 55, 9 a.; B. § 148, 12); οὐ παρὰ τοῦτο οὐκ ἔστιν ἐκ τοῦ σώματος, *not on this account is it not of the body*, i. e. it belongs to the body, does not cease to be of the body, 1 Co. xii. 15; οὐ δυνάμεθα ἃ εἴδομεν καὶ ἠκούσαμεν μὴ λαλεῖν, *we are unable not to speak* [A.V. *we cannot but speak*], Acts iv. 20. **4.** It is used in disjunctive statements where one thing is denied that another may be established [W. § 55, 8; cf. B. 356 (306)]: οὐκ . . . ἀλλά, Lk. viii. 52; xxiv. 6 [WH reject the cl.]; Jn. i. 33; vii. 10, 12, 16; viii. 49; Acts x. 41; Ro. viii. 20; 1 Co. xv. 10; 2 Co. iii. 3; viii. 5; Heb. ii. 16, etc.; see ἀλλά, II. 1; οὐχ ἵνα . . . ἀλλ’ ἵνα, Jn. iii. 17; οὐχ ἵνα . . . ἀλλὰ καί, Jn. xi. 30; οὐ μόνον . . . ἀλλὰ καί, see ἀλλά, II. 1 and μόνος, 2; οὐκ . . . εἰ μή, see εἰ, III. 8 c. p. 171ᵇ; οὐ μή w. subjunc. aor. foll. by εἰ μή, Rev. xxi. 27 [see εἰ as above, β.]. **5.** It is joined to other particles: οὐ μή, *not at all, by no means, surely not, in no wise*, see μή, IV.; οὐ μηκέτι w. aor. subjunc. Mt. xxi. 19 L T Tr mrg. WH. μὴ οὐ, where μή is interrog. (Lat. *num*) and οὐ negative [cf. B. 248 (214), 354 (304); W. 511 (476)]: Ro. x. 18 sq.; 1 Co. ix. 4 sq.; xi. 22. εἰ οὐ, see εἰ, III. 11 p. 172ᵃ. οὐ γάρ (see γάρ, I. p. 109ᵇ), Acts xvi. 37. **6.** As in Hebr. לֹא w. impf., so in bibl. Grk. οὐ w. 2 pers. fut. is used in emphatic prohibition (in prof. auth. it is milder; cf. W. § 43, 5 c.; also 501 sq. (467); [B. § 139, 64]; Fritzsche on Mt. p. 259 sq. [cf. p. 252 sq.] thinks otherwise, but not correctly): Mt. vi. 5; and besides in the moral precepts of the O. T., Mt. iv. 7; xix. 18; Lk. iv. 12; Acts xxiii. 5; Ro. vii. 7; xiii. 9. **7.** οὐ is used interrogatively — when an affirmative answer is expected (Lat. *nonne*; [W. § 57, 3 a.; B. 247 (213)]): Mt. vi. 26, 30; xvii. 24; Mk. iv. 21; xii. 24; Lk. xi. 40; Jn. iv. 35; xi. 25; Acts ix. 21; Ro. ix. 21; 1 Co. ix. 1, 6 sq. 12; Jas. ii. 4, and often; οὐκ οἴδατε κτλ.; and the like, see εἴδω, II. 1 p. 174ᵃ; ἀλλ’ οὐ, Heb. iii. 16 (see ἀλλά, I. 10 p. 28ᵃ); οὐκ ἀποκρίνῃ οὐδέν; answerest thou nothing at all? Mk. xiv. 60; xv. 4; — where an exclamation of reproach or wonder, which denies directly, may take the place of a negative question: Mk. iv. 13, 38; Lk. xvii. 18; Acts xiii. 10 [cf. B. § 139, 65]; xxi. 38 (on which see ἄρα, 1);

cf. W. u. s.; οὐ μὴ πίω αὐτό; shall I not drink it? Jn. xviii. 11; cf. W. p. 512 (477); [cf. B. § 139, 2].

οὐά, Tdf. οὐᾶ [see Proleg. p. 101; cf. Chandler § 892],   **3758**
ah! ha! an interjection of wonder and amazement: Epict. diss. 3, 22, 34; 3, 23, 24; Dio Cass. 63, 20; called out by the overthrow of a boastful adversary, Mk. xv. 29.*

οὐαί, an interjection of grief or of denunciation; Sept.   **3759**
chiefly for הוֹי and אוֹי; *alas! woe!* with a dat of pers. added, Mt. xi. 21; xviii. 7; xxiii. 13–16, 23, 25, 27, 29; xxiv. 19; xxvi. 24; Mk. xiii. 17; xiv. 21; Lk. vi. 24–26; x. 13; xi. 42–44, 46 sq. 52; xxi. 23; xxii. 22; Jude 11; Rev. xii. 12 R G L ed. min. [see below], (Num. xxi. 29; Is. iii. 9, and often in Sept.); thrice repeated, and foll. by a dat., Rev. viii. 13 R G L WH mrg. [see below]; the dat. is omitted in Lk. xvii. 1; twice repeated and foll. by a nom. in place of a voc., Rev. xviii. 10, 16, 19, (Is. i. 24; v. 8–22; Hab. ii. 6, 12, etc.); exceptionally, with an acc. of the pers., in Rev. viii. 13 T Tr WH txt., and xii. 12 L T Tr WH; this accus., I think, must be regarded either as an acc. of exclamation (cf. Matthiae § 410), or as an imitation of the constr. of the acc. after verbs of injuring, (B. § 131, 14 judges otherwise); with the addition of ἀπό and a gen. of the evil the infliction of which is deplored [cf. B. 322 (277); W. 371 (348)], Mt. xviii. 7; also of ἐκ, Rev. viii. 13. As a substantive, ἡ οὐαί (the writer seems to have been led to use the fem. by the similarity of ἡ θλίψις or ἡ ταλαιπωρία; cf. W. 179 (169)) *woe, calamity*: Rev. ix. 12; xi. 14; δύο οὐαί, Rev. ix. 12, (οὐαὶ ἐπὶ οὐαὶ ἔσται, Ezek. vii. 26; οὐαὶ ἡμᾶς λήψεται, Evang. Nicod. c. 21 [Pars ii. v. 1 (ed. Tdf.)]); so also in the phrase οὐαί μοί ἐστιν woe is unto me, i. e. divine penalty threatens me, 1 Co. ix. 16, cf. Hos. ix. 12; [Jer. vi. 4]; Epict. diss. 3, 19, 1, (frequent in eccles. writ.).*

οὐδαμῶς (fr. οὐδαμός, not even one; and this fr. οὐδέ and   **3760**
ἀμός [allied perh. w. ἅμα; cf. Vaniček p. 972; Curtius § 600]), adv., fr. Hdt. [and Aeschyl.] down, *by no means, in no wise*: Mt. ii. 6.*

οὐδέ, [fr. Hom. down], a neg. disjunctive conjunction,   **3761**
compounded of οὐ and δέ, and therefore prop. i. q. *but not*; generally, however, its oppositive force being lost, it serves to continue a negation. [On the elision of ε when the next word begins with a vowel (observed by Tdf. in eight instances, neglected in fifty-eight), see *Tdf.* Proleg. p. 96; cf. *WH.* App. p. 146; W. § 5, 1 a.; B. p. 10 sq.] It signifies   **1.** *and not*, continuing a negation, yet differently from οὔτε; for the latter connects parts or members of the same thing, since τέ is adjunctive like the Lat. *que*; but οὐδέ places side by side things that are equal and mutually exclude each other [(?). There appears to be some mistake here in what is said about ‘mutual exclusion’ (cf. W. § 55, 6): οὐδέ, like δέ, always makes reference to something preceding; οὔτε to what follows also; the connection of clauses negatived by οὔτε is close and internal, so that they are mutually complementary and combine into a unity, whereas clauses negatived by οὐδέ follow one another much more loosely, often almost by accident as it were; see W. l. c., and esp. the quotations there given from Benfey and

Klotz.] It differs from μηδέ as οὐ does from μή [q. v. ad init.]; after οὐ, where each has its own verb: Mt. v. 15; vi. 28; Mk. iv. 22; Lk. vi. 44; Acts ii. 27; ix. 9; xvii. 24 sq.; Gal. i. 17; iv. 14; οὐκ οἶδα οὐδὲ ἐπίσταμαι, Mk. xiv. 68 R G L mrg. [al. οὔτε ... οὔτε] (Cic. pro Rosc. Am. 43 "non novi neque scio"); cf. W. 490 (456) c.; [B. 367 (315) note]; οὐ ... οὐδὲ ... οὐδέ, not ... nor ... nor, Mt. vi. 26; οὐδεὶς ... οὐδὲ ... οὐδὲ ... οὐδέ, Rev. v. 3 [R G; cf. B. 367 (315); W. 491 (457)]; οὐ ... οὐδὲ foll. by a fut. ... οὐδὲ μή foll. by subjunc. aor. ... οὐδέ, Rev. vii. 16. οὐ ... οὐδέ, the same verb being common to both: Mt. x. 24; xxv. 13; Lk. vi. 43; viii. 17 [cf. W. 300 (281); B. 355 (305) cf. § 139, 7]; Jn. vi. 24; xiii. 16; Acts viii. 21; xvi. 21; xxiv. 18; Ro. ii. 28; ix. 16; Gal. i. 1; iii. 28; 1 Th. v. 5; 1 Tim. ii. 12; Rev. xxi. 23. preceded by οὔπω, Mk. viii. 17; — by οὐδείς, Mt. ix. 17; — by ἵνα μή, which is foll. by οὐδὲ ... οὐδέ, where μηδὲ ... μηδέ might have been expected (cf. B. § 148, 8; [W. 474 (442)]): Rev. ix. 4. οὐδὲ γάρ, for neither, Jn. viii. 42; Ro. viii. 7. **2.** also not [A. V. generally neither]: Mt. vi. 15; xxi. 27; xxv. 45; Mk. xi. 26 [R L]; Lk. xvi. 31; Jn. xv. 4; Ro. iv. 15; xi. 21; 1 Co. xv. 13, 16; Gal. i. 12 (οὐδὲ γὰρ ἐγώ [cf. B. 367 (315) note; 492 (458)]); Heb. viii. 4, etc.; ἀλλ' οὐδέ, Lk. xxiii. 15; ἢ οὐδέ, in a question, or doth not even etc.? 1 Co. xi. 14 Rec.; the simple οὐδέ, num ne quidem (have ye not even etc.) in a question where a negative answer is assumed (see οὐ, 7): Mk. xii. 10; Lk. vi. 3; xxiii. 40; and G L T Tr WH in 1 Co. xi. 14. **3.** not even [B. 369 (316)]: Mt. vi. 29; viii. 10; Mk. vi. 31; Lk. vii. 9; xii. 27; Jn. xxi. 25 [Tdf. om. the vs.]; 1 Co. v. 1; xiv. 21; οὐδὲ εἷς [W. 173 (163); B. § 127, 32], Acts iv. 32; Ro. iii. 10; 1 Co. vi. 5 [L T Tr WH οὐδείς]; οὐδὲ ἕν, Jn. i. 3; ἀλλ' οὐδέ, Acts xix. 2; 1 Co. iii. 2 (Rec. ἀλλ' οὔτε); iv. 3; Gal. ii. 3. in a double negative for the sake of emphasis, οὐκ ... οὐδέ [B. 369 (316); W. 500 (465)]: Mt. xxvii. 14; Lk. xviii. 13; Acts vii. 5.

3762   **οὐδείς, οὐδεμία** (the fem. only in these pass.: Mk. vi. 5; Lk. iv. 26; Jn. xvi. 29; xviii. 38; xix. 4; Acts xxv. 18; xxvii. 22; Phil. iv. 15; 1 Jn. i. 5, and Rec. in Jas. iii. 12), **οὐδέν** (and, acc. to a pronunciation not infreq. fr. Aristot. and Theophr. down, οὐθείς, οὐθέν: 1 Co. xiii. 2 Rᵗ L T Tr WH; Acts xix. 27 L T Tr WH; 2 Co. xi. 8 (9)L T Tr WH; Lk. xxii. 35 T Tr WH; xxiii. 14 T Tr WH; Acts xv. 9 T Tr WH txt.; Acts xxvi. 26 T WH Tr br.; 1 Co. xiii. 3 Tdf.; see μηδείς init. and Göttling on Aristot. pol. p. 278; [Meisterhans, Grammatik d. Attisch. Inschriften, § 20, 5; see L. and S. s. v. οὐθείς; cf. Lob. Pathol. Elem. ii. 344]; Bttm. Ausf. Spr. § 70 Anm. 7), (fr. οὐδέ and εἷς), [fr. Hom. down], and not one, no one, none, no; it differs from μηδείς as οὐ does from μή [q. v. ad init.]; **1.** with nouns: masc., Lk. iv. 24; xvi. 13; 1 Co. viii. 4; οὐδεὶς ἄλλος, Jn. xv. 24; οὐδεμία in the passages given above; neut., Lk. xxiii. 4; Jn. x. 41; Acts xvii. 21; xxiii. 9; xxviii. 5; Ro. viii. 1; xiv. 14; Gal. v. 10, etc. **2.** absolutely: masc., Mt. vi. 24; ix. 16; Mk. iii. 27; v. 4; vii. 24; Lk. i. 61; v. 39 [WH in br.]; vii. 28; Jn. i. 18; iv. 27; Acts xviii. 10; xxv. 11;

Ro. xiv. 7, and very often. with a partitive gen.: Lk. iv. 26; xiv. 24; Jn. xiii. 28; Acts v. 13; 1 Co. i. 14; ii. 8; 1 Tim. vi. 16. οὐδεὶς εἰ μή, Mt. xix. 17 Rec.; xvii. 8; Mk. x. 18; Lk. xviii. 19; Jn. iii. 13; 1 Co. xii. 3; Rev. xix. 12, etc.; ἐὰν μή, Jn. iii. 2; vi. 44, 65. οὐκ ... οὐδείς (see οὐ, 3 a.), Mt. xxii. 16; Mk. v. 37; vi. 5; xii. 14; Lk. viii. 43; Jn. viii. 15; xviii. 9, 31; Acts iv. 12; 2 Co. xi. 9 (8); οὐκέτι ... οὐδείς, Mk. ix. 8; οὐδέν ... οὐδέ, Rev. xxiii. 53 [Tdf. οὐδεὶς ... οὐδέπω; L Tr WH οὐδεὶς οὔπω]; Jn. xix. 41; Acts viii. 16 [L Tr WH]; οὐδεὶς ... οὐκέτι, Mk. xii. 34; Rev. xviii. 11. neut. οὐδέν, nothing, Mt. x. 26 [cf. W. 300 (281); B. 355 (305)]; xvii. 20; xxvi. 62; xxvii. 12, and very often; with a partitive gen., Lk. ix. 36; xviii. 34; Acts xviii. 17; 1 Co. ix. 15; xiv. 10 [R G]; οὐδὲν εἰ μή, Mt. v. 13; xxi. 19; Mk. ix. 29; xi. 13; μή τινος; with the answer οὐδενός, Lk. xxii. 35; οὐδὲν ἐκτός w. gen., Acts xxvi. 22; οὐδέν μοι διαφέρει, Gal. ii. 6; it follows another negative, thereby strengthening the negation (see οὐ, 3 a.): Mk. xv. 4 sq.; xvi. 8; Lk. iv. 2; ix. 36; xx. 40; Jn. iii. 27; v. 19, 30; ix. 33; xi. 49; xiv. 30; Acts xxvi. 26 [Lchm. om.]; 1 Co. viii. 2 [R G]; ix. 15 [G L T Tr WH]; οὐδέν οὐ μή w. aor. subjunc. Lk. x. 19 [Rᵗ G WH mrg.; see μή, IV. 2]. οὐδέν, absol., nothing whatever, not at all, in no wise, [cf. B. § 131, 10]: ἀδικεῖν (see ἀδικέω, 2 b.), Acts xxv. 10; Gal. iv. 12; οὐδὲν διαφέρειν τινός, Gal. iv. 1; ὑστερεῖν, 2 Co. xii. 11; ὠφελεῖν, Jn. vi. 63; 1 Co. xiii. 3. οὐδέν ἐστιν, it is nothing, of no importance, etc. [cf. B. § 129, 5]: Mt. xxiii. 16, 18; Jn. viii. 54; 1 Co. vii. 19; with a gen., none of these things is true, Acts xxi. 24; xxv. 11; οὐδέν εἰμι, I am nothing, of no account: 1 Co. xiii. 2; 2 Co. xii. 11, (see exx. fr. Grk. auth. in Passow s. v. 2; [L. and S. s. v. II. 2; Meyer on 1 Co. l. c.]); εἰς οὐδὲν λογισθῆναι (see λογίζομαι, 1 a.), Acts xix. 27; εἰς οὐδὲν γίνεσθαι, to come to nought, Acts v. 36 [W. § 29, 3 a.; ἐν οὐδενί, in no respect, in nothing, Phil. i. 20 (cf. μηδείς, g.].

3763   **οὐδέποτε**, adv., denying absolutely and objectively, (fr. οὐδέ and ποτέ, prop. not ever), [fr. Hom. down], never: Mt. vii. 23; ix. 33; xxvi. 33; Mk. ii. 12; [Lk. xv. 29 (bis)]; Jn. vii. 46; Acts x. 14; xi. 8; xiv. 8; 1 Co. xiii. 8; Heb. x. 1, 11. interrogatively, did ye never, etc.: Mt. xxi. 16, 42; Mk. ii. 25.*

3764   **οὐδέπω**, adv., simply negative, (fr. οὐδέ and the enclitic πώ), [fr. Aeschyl. down], not yet, not as yet: Jn. vii. 39 (where L Tr WH οὔπω); xx. 9. οὐδέπω οὐδείς, never any one [A. V. never man yet], Jn. xix. 41; [οὐδέπω ... ἐπ' οὐδενί, as yet ... upon none, Acts viii. 16 L T Tr WH]; οὐκ ... οὐδέπω οὐδεὶς οὔπω (see οὐ, 3 a.), Lk. xxiii. 53 [L Tr WH οὐκ ... οὐδεὶς οὐδέπω; Tdf. οὐκ ... οὐδεὶς οὐδέπω]; οὐδέπω οὐδέν (L T Tr WH simply οὔπω) not yet (anything), 1 Co. viii. 2.*

see 3762   **οὐθείς, οὐθέν**, see οὐδείς, init.

3765   **οὐκέτι** [also written separately by Recᵗ (generally), Tr (nine times in Jn.), Tdf. (in Philem. 16)], (οὐκ, ἔτι), an adv. which denies simply, and thus differs from μηκέτι (q. v.), no longer, no more, no further: Mt. xix. 6; Mk. x. 8; Lk. xv. 19, 21; Jn. iv. 42; vi. 66; Acts xx. 25, 38; Ro. vi. 9; xiv. 15; 2 Co. v. 16; Gal. iii. 25; iv. 7; Eph.

ii. 19; Philem. 16; Heb. x. 18, 26, etc.; οὐκέτι ἦλθον, I came not again [R. V. *I forebore to come*], 2 Co. i. 23. with another neg. particle in order to strengthen the negation: οὐδὲ ... οὐκέτι, Mt. xxii. 46; οὐκ ... οὐκέτι, Acts viii. 39; οὐδείς ... οὐκέτι, Mk. xii. 34; Rev. xviii. 11; οὐκέτι ... οὐδέν, Mk. vii. 12; xv. 5; Lk. xx. 40; οὐκέτι ... οὐδένα, Mk. ix. 8; οὐκέτι οὐ μή, Mk. xiv. 25; Lk. xxii. 16 [WH om. L Tr br. οὐκέτι]; Rev. xviii. 14 [Tr om.]; οὐδὲ ... οὐκέτι οὐδείς, Mk. v. 3 L T WH Tr txt. οὐκέτι is used logically [cf. W. § 65, 10]; as, οὐκέτι ἐγώ for *it cannot now be said* ὅτι ἐγώ etc., Ro. vii. 17, 20; Gal. ii. 20; add, Ro. xi. 6; Gal. iii. 18. [(Hom., Hes., Hdt., al.)]

3766   **οὐκοῦν**, (fr. οὐκ and οὖν), adv., *not therefore*; and since a speaker often introduces in this way his own opinion [see Krüger as below], the particle is used affirmatively, *therefore, then*, the force of the negative disappearing. Hence the saying of Pilate οὐκοῦν βασιλεὺς εἶ σύ must be taken affirmatively: *then* (since thou speakest of thy βασιλεία) thou art a king! (Germ. *also bist du doch ein König!*), Jn. xviii. 37 [cf. B. 249 (214)]; but it is better to write οὔκουν, so that Pilate, arguing from the words of Christ, asks, not without irony, *art thou not a king then?* or *in any case, thou art a king, art thou not?* cf. W. 512 (477). The difference between οὐκοῦν and οὔκουν is differently stated by different writers; cf. *Herm.* ad Vig. p. 792 sqq.; Krüger § 69, 51, 1 and 2; Kühner § 508, 5 ii. p. 715 sqq., also the 3d excurs. appended to his ed. of Xen. memor.; [Bäumlein, Partikeln, pp. 191–198].*

see 3364 — οὐ μή, see μή, IV.

3767 οὖν a conj. indicating that something follows from another necessarily; [al. regard the primary force of the particle as confirmatory or continuative, rather than illative; cf. Passow, or L. and S. s. v.; Kühner § 508, 1 ii. p. 707 sqq.; Bäumlein p. 173 sqq.; Krüger § 69, 52; Donaldson p. 571; Rost in a program "Ueber Ableitung" u. s. w. p. 2; Klotz p. 717; Hartung ii. 4]. Hence it is used in drawing a conclusion and in connecting sentences together logically, *then, therefore, accordingly, consequently, these things being so*, [(Klotz, Rost, al., have wished to derive the word fr. the neut. ptcp. ὄν (cf. ὄντως); but see Bäumlein or Kühner u. s.); cf. W. § 53, 8]: Mt. iii. 10; x. 32 (since persecutions are not to be dreaded, and consequently furnish no excuse for denying me [cf. W. 455 (424)]); Mt. xviii. 4; Lk. iii. 9; xvi. 27; Jn. viii. 38 (καὶ ὑμεῖς οὖν, and ye accordingly, i. e. 'since, as is plain from my case, sons follow the example of their fathers'; Jesus says this in sorrowful irony [W. 455 (424)]); Acts i. 21 (since the office of the traitor Judas must be conferred on another); Ro. v. 9; vi. 4; xiii. 10; 1 Co. iv. 16 (since I hold a father's place among you); 2 Co. v. 20; Jas. iv. 17, and many other exx. As respects details, notice that it stands   **a.** in exhortations (to show what ought now to be done by reason of what has been said), i. q. *wherefore*, [our transitional *therefore*]: Mt. iii. 8; v. 48; ix. 38; Lk. xi. 35; xxi. 14, 36 [R G L mrg. Tr mrg.]; Acts iii. 19; xiii. 40; Ro. vi. 12; xiv. 13; 1 Co. xvi. 11; 2 Co. viii. 24; Eph. v. 1; vi. 14; Phil. ii. 29; Col. ii. 16; 2 Tim. i. 8; Heb. iv. 1, 11; x.

35; Jas. iv. 7; v. 7; 1 Pet. iv. 7; v. 6; Rev. i. 19 [G L T Tr WH]; iii. 3, 19, and often; νῦν οὖν, *now therefore*, Acts xvi. 36.   **b.** in questions, *then, therefore*, (Lat. *igitur*);   **α.** when the question is, what follows or seems to follow from what has been said: Mt. xxii. 28; xxvii. 22 [W. 455 (424)]; Mk. xv. 12; Lk. iii. 10; xx. 15, 33; Jn. viii. 5; τί οὖν ἐροῦμεν; Ro. vi. 1; vii. 7; ix. 14; τί οὖν φημί; 1 Co. x. 19; τί οὖν; *what then?* i. e. how then does the matter stand? [cf. W. § 64, 2 a.], Jn. i. 21 [here WH mrg. punct. τί οὖν σύ;] Ro. iii. 9; v. 15; xi. 7; also τί οὖν ἐστίν; [*what is it then?*] Acts xxi. 22; 1 Co. xiv. 15, 26.   **β.** when it is asked, whether this or that follows from what has just been said: Mt. xiii. 28; Lk. xxii. 70; Jn. xviii. 39; Ro. iii. 31; Gal. iii. 21.   **γ.** when it is asked, how something which is true or regarded as true, or what some one does, can be reconciled with what has been previously said or done: Mt. xii. 26; xiii. 27; xvii. 10 (where the thought is, 'thou commandest us to tell no one about this vision we have had of Elijah; what relation then to this vision has the doctrine of the scribes concerning the coming of Elijah? Is not this doctrine confirmed by the vision?'); Mt. xix. 7; xxvi. 54; Lk. xx. 17; Jn. iv. 11 [Tdf. om. οὖν]; Acts xv. 10 (νῦν οὖν, *now therefore*, i. e. at this time, therefore, when God makes known his will so plainly); Acts xix. 3; Ro. iv. 1 (where the meaning is, 'If everything depends on *faith*, what shall we say that Abraham gained by outward things, i. e. by works?' [but note the crit. texts]); 1 Co. vi. 15; Gal. iii. 5.   **δ.** in general, it serves simply to subjoin questions suggested by what has just been said: Ro. iii. 27; iv. 9 sq.; vi. 21; xi. 11; 1 Co. iii. 5, etc.   **c.** in epanalepsis, i. e. it serves to resume a thought or narrative interrupted by intervening matter (Matthiae ii. p. 1497; [W. 444 (414)]), like Lat. *igitur, inquam*, our *as was said, say I, to proceed*, etc.: Mk. iii. 31 [R G] (cf. 21); Lk. iii. 7 (cf. 3); Jn. iv. 45 (cf. 43); vi. 24 (cf. 22); 1 Co. viii. 4; xi. 20 (cf. 18); add, Mk. xvi. 19 [Tr mrg. br. οὖν]; Acts viii. 25; xii. 5; xiii. 4; xv. 3, 30; xxiii. 31; xxv. 1; xxviii. 5. It is used also when one passes at length to a subject about which he had previously intimated an intention to speak: Acts xxvi. 4, 9.   **d.** it serves to gather up summarily what has already been said, or even what cannot be narrated at length: Mt. i. 17; vii. 24 (where no reference is made to what has just before been said [?], but all the moral precepts of the Serm. on the Mount are summed up in a single rule common to all); Lk. iii. 18; Jn. xx. 30; Acts xxvi. 22.   **e.** it serves to adapt examples and comparisons to the case in hand: Jn. iii. 29; xvi. 22; — or to add examples to illustrate the subject under consideration: Ro. xii. 20 Rec.   **f.** In historical discourse it serves to make the transition from one thing to another, and to connect the several parts and portions of the narrative, since the new occurrences spring from or are occasioned by what precedes [cf. W. § 60, 3]: Lk. vi. 9 R G; numberless times so in John, as i. 22 [Lchm. om.]; ii. 18; iv. 9 [Tdf. om.]; vi. 60, 67; vii. 6 [G T om.], 25, 28, 33, 35, 40; viii. 13, 19, 22, 25,

31, 57; ix. 7 sq. 10, 16; xi. 12, 16, 21, 32, 36; xii. 1–4; xiii. 12; xvi. 17, 22; xviii. 7, 11 sq. 16, 27–29; xix. 20–24, 32, 38, 40; xxi. 5–7, etc.   **g.** with other conjunctions: ἄρα οὖν, *so then*, Lat. *hinc igitur*, in Paul; see ἄρα, 5. εἰ οὖν, *if then* (where what has just been said and proved is carried over to prove something else), see εἰ, III. 12; [εἰ μὲν οὖν, see μέν, II. 4 p. 398ᵇ]. εἴτε οὖν . . . εἴτε, *whether then* . . . *or*: 1 Co. x. 31; xv. 11. ἐπεὶ οὖν, *since then*: Heb. ii. 14; iv. 6; for which also a participle is put with οὖν, as Acts ii. 30; xv. 2 [T Tr WH δέ]; xvii. 29; xix. 36; xxv. 17; xxvi. 22; Ro. v. 1; xv. 28; 2 Co. iii. 12; v. 11; vii. 1; Heb. iv. 14; x. 19; 1 Pet. iv. 1; 2 Pet. iii. 11 [WH Tr mrg. οὕτως]. ἐὰν οὖν, *if then ever, in case then*, or rather, *therefore if, therefore in case*, (for in this formula, οὖν, although placed in the protasis, yet belongs more to the apodosis, since it shows what will necessarily follow from what precedes if the condition introduced by ἐάν shall ever take place): Mt. v. 23 [cf. W. 455 (424)]; vi. 22 [here Tdf. om. οὖν]; xxiv. 26; Lk. iv. 7; Jn. vi. 62; viii. 36; Ro. ii. 26; 1 Co. xiv. 11, 23; 2 Tim. ii. 21; ἐὰν οὖν μή, Rev. iii. 3; so also ὅταν οὖν, *when therefore*: Mt. vi. 2; xxi. 40; xxiv. 15, and R G in Lk. xi. 34. ὅτε οὖν, *when* (or *after*) *therefore*, *so when*: Jn. xiii. 12, 31 [(30) Rec.ᵇᵉᶻ ᵉˡᶻ L T Tr WH]; xix. 30; xxi. 15; i. q. *hence it came to pass that, when* etc., Jn. ii. 22; xix. 6, 8. ὡς οὖν, *when* (or *after*) *therefore*: Jn. iv. 1, 40; xi. 6; xviii. 6; xx. 11; xxi. 9; ὡς οὖν, *as therefore*, Col. ii. 6. ὥσπερ οὖν, Mt. xiii. 40. μὲν οὖν, foll. by δέ [cf. B. § 149, 16], Mk. xvi. 19 [Tr mrg. br. οὖν]; Jn. xix. 25; Acts i. 6; viii. 4, 25; 1 Co. ix. 25, etc.; without an adversative conjunc. following, see μέν, II. 4. νῦν οὖν, see above under a., and b. γ.   **h.** As to position, it is never the first word in the sentence, but generally the second, sometimes the third, [sometimes even the fourth, W. § 61, 6]; as, [περὶ τῆς βρώσεως οὖν etc. 1 Co. viii. 4]; οἱ μὲν οὖν, Acts ii. 41, and often; πολλὰ μὲν οὖν, Jn. xx. 30.   **i.** John uses this particle in his Gospel far more frequently [(more than two hundred times in all)] than the other N. T. writers; in his Epistles only in the foll. passages: 1 Jn. ii. 24 (where G L T Tr WH have expunged it); iv. 19 Lchm.; 3 Jn. 8. [(From Hom. down.)]

3768   **οὔπω**, (fr. οὐ and the enclitic πώ), adv., [fr. Hom. down], (differing fr. μήπω, as οὐ does fr. μή [q. v. ad init.]), *not yet*;   **a.** in a negation: Mt. xxiv. 6; Mk. xiii. 7; Jn. ii. 4; iii. 24; vi. 17 L txt. T Tr WH; vii. 6, 8ᵃ R L WH txt., 8ᵇ, 30, 39; viii. 20, 57; xi. 30; xx. 17; 1 Co. iii. 2; Heb. ii. 8; xii. 4; 1 Jn. iii. 2; Rev. xvii. 10, 12 (where Lchm. οὐκ); οὐδεὶς οὔπω, *no one ever yet* (see οὐδείς, 2, and cf. οὐ, 3 a.), Mk. xi. 2 L T Tr WH; Lk. xxiii. 53 L Tr WH; Acts viii. 16 Rec.   **b.** in questions, *nondumne? do ye not yet* etc.: Mt. xv. 17 R G; xvi. 9; Mk. iv. 40 L Tr WH; viii. 17, [21 L txt. T Tr WH].*

3769   **οὐρά**, -ᾶς, ἡ, *a tail*: Rev. ix. 10, 19; xii. 4. (From Hom. down. Sept. several times for זָנָב.) *

3770   **οὐράνιος**, -ον, in class. Grk. generally of three term. [W. § 11, 1; B. 25 (23)], (οὐρανός), *heavenly*, i. e.   **a.** *dwelling in heaven*: ὁ πατὴρ ὁ οὐρ., Mt. vi. 14, 26, 32; xv.

13; besides L T Tr WH in v. 48; xviii. 35; xxiii. 9; στρατιὰ οὐρ. Lk. ii. 13 (where Tr txt. WH mrg. οὐρανοῦ).   **b.** *coming from heaven*: ὀπτασία οὐρ. Acts xxvi. 19. (Hom. in Cer. 55; Pind., Tragg., Arstph., al.) *

3771   **οὐρανόθεν**, (οὐρανός), adv., *from heaven*: Acts xiv. 17; xxvi. 13. (Hom., Hes., Orph., 4 Macc. iv. 10.) Cf. *Lob.* ad Phryn. p. 93 sq.*

3772   **οὐρανός**, -οῦ, ὁ, [fr. a root meaning 'to cover,' 'encompass'; cf. *Vaniček* p. 895; *Curtius* § 509], *heaven*; and, in imitation of the Hebr. שָׁמַיִם (i. e. prop. *the heights above, the upper regions*), οὐρανοί, -ῶν, οἱ, *the heavens* [W. § 27, 3; B. 24 (21)], (on the use and the omission of the art. cf. W. 121 (115)), i. e.   **1.** *the vaulted expanse of the sky with all the things visible in it*;   **a.** generally: as opp. to the earth, Heb. i. 10; 2 Pet. iii. 5, 10, 12; ὁ οὐρ. κ. ἡ γῆ, [*heaven and earth*] i. q. *the universe, the world*, (acc. to the primitive Hebrew manner of speaking, inasmuch as they had neither the conception nor the name of *the universe*, Gen. i. 1; xiv. 19; Tob. vii. 17 (18); 1 Macc. ii. 37, etc.): Mt. v. 18; xi. 25; xxiv. 35; Mk. xiii. 31; Lk. x. 21; xvi. 17; xxi. 33; Acts iv. 24; xiv. 15; xvii. 24; Rev. x. 6; xiv. 7; xx. 11. The ancients conceived of the expanded sky as an arch or vault the outmost edge of which touched the extreme limits of the earth [see B. D. s. v. Firmament, cf. Heaven]; hence such expressions as ἀπ᾽ ἄκρων οὐρανῶν ἕως ἄκρων αὐτῶν, Mt. xxiv. 31; ἀπ᾽ ἄκρου γῆς ἕως ἄκρου οὐρανοῦ, Mk. xiii. 27; ὑπὸ τὸν οὐρανόν (תַּחַת הַשָּׁמַיִם, Eccl. i. 13; ii. 3, etc.), *under heaven*, i. e. *on earth*, Acts ii. 5; iv. 12; Col. i. 23; ἐκ τῆς (sc. χώρας, cf. W. 591 (550); [B. 82 (71 sq.)]) ὑπ᾽ [here L T Tr WH ὑπὸ τὸν οὐρ.] οὐρανὸν εἰς τὴν ὑπ᾽ οὐρανόν, *out of the one part under the heaven unto the other part under heaven* i. e. *from one quarter of the earth to the other*, Lk. xvii. 24; as by this form of expression the greatest longitudinal distance is described, so to one looking up from the earth heaven stands as the extreme measure of altitude; hence, κολλᾶσθαι ἄχρι τοῦ οὐρανοῦ, Rev. xviii. 5 [L T Tr WH] (on which see κολλάω); ὑψωθῆναι ἕως τοῦ οὐρανοῦ, metaph. of a city that has reached the acme, zenith, of glory and prosperity, Mt. xi. 23; Lk. x. 15, (κλέος οὐρανὸν ἵκει, Hom. Il. 8, 192; Od. 19, 108; πρὸς οὐρανὸν βιβάζειν τινά, Soph. O. C. 382 (381); exx. of similar expressions fr. other writ. are given in *Kypke*, Observv. i. p. 62); καινοὶ οὐρανοί (καὶ γῆ καινή), *better heavens which will take the place of the present after the renovation of all things*, 2 Pet. iii. 13; Rev. xxi. 1; οἱ νῦν οὐρανοί, *the heavens which now are, and which will one day be burnt up*, 2 Pet. iii. 7; also ὁ πρῶτος οὐρανός, Rev. xxi. 1, cf. Heb. xii. 26. But the heavens are also likened in poetic speech to an expanded curtain or canopy (Ps. ciii. (civ.) 2; Is. xl. 22), and to an unrolled scroll; hence, ἑλίσσειν [T Tr mrg. ἀλλάσσειν] τοὺς οὐρ. ὡς περιβόλαιον, Heb. i. 12 (fr. Sept. of Ps. ci. (cii.) 26 cod. Alex.); καὶ ὁ οὐρ. ἀπεχωρίσθη ὡς βιβλίον ἑλισσόμενον [or εἱλισσ.], Rev. vi. 14.   **b.** *the aerial heavens* or *sky*, the region where the clouds and tempests gather, and where thunder and lightning are produced: ὁ οὐρ. πυρράζει, Mt. xvi. 2 [T br. WH reject the pass.] ;

στυγνάζων, ib. 3 [see last ref.]; ὑετὸν ἔδωκε, Jas. v. 18; add Lk. ix. 54; xvii. 29; Acts ix. 3; xxii. 6; Rev. xiii. 13; xvi. 21; xx. 9; σημεῖον ἐκ or ἀπὸ τοῦ οὐρ., Mt. xvi. 1; Mk. viii. 11; Lk. xi. 16; xxi. 11; τέρατα ἐν τῷ οὐρ. Acts ii. 19; κλείειν τὸν οὐρανόν, to keep the rain in the sky, hinder it from falling on the earth, Lk. iv. 25; Rev. xi. 6, (συνέχειν τὸν οὐρ. for יַעֲצֹר הַשָּׁמַיִם, Deut. xi. 17; 2 Chr. vi. 26; vii. 13; ἀνέχειν τὸν οὐρ. Sir. xlviii. 3); αἱ νεφέλαι τοῦ οὐρ., Mt. xxiv. 30; xxvi. 64; Mk. xiv. 62; τὸ πρόσωπον τοῦ οὐρ., Mt. xvi. 3 [T br. WH reject the pass.]; Lk. xii. 56; τὰ πετεινὰ τ. οὐρ. (gen. of place), that fly in the air (Gen. i. 26; Ps. viii. 9; Bar. iii. 17; Judith xi. 7), Mt. vi. 26; viii. 20; xiii. 32; Mk. iv. 32; Lk. viii. 5; ix. 58; xiii. 19; Acts x. 12. These heavens are opened by being cleft asunder, and from the u p p e r heavens, or abode of heavenly beings, come down upon earth — now the Holy Spirit, Mt. iii. 16; Mk. i. 10; Lk. iii. 21 sq.; Jn. i. 32; now angels, Jn. i. 51 (52); and now in vision appear to human sight some of the things within the highest heaven, Acts vii. 55; x. 11, 16; through the aerial heavens sound voices, which are uttered in the heavenly abode: Mt. iii. 17; Mk. i. 11; Lk. iii. 22; Jn. xii. 28; 2 Pet. i. 18.   c. *the sidereal or starry heavens*: τὰ ἄστρα τοῦ οὐρ. Heb. xi. 12 (Deut. i. 10; x. 22; Eur. Phoen. 1); οἱ ἀστέρες τ. οὐρ., Mk. xiii. 25; Rev. vi. 13; xii. 4, (Is. xiii. 10; xiv. 13); αἱ δυνάμεις τῶν οὐρ. *the heavenly forces* (hosts), i. e. *the stars* [al. take δυν. in this phrase in a general sense (see δύναμις, f.) of the powers which uphold and regulate the heavens]: Mt. xxiv. 29; Lk. xxi. 26; αἱ ἐν τοῖς οὐρ. Mk. xiii. 25, (Hebr. צְבָא הַשָּׁמַיִם, Deut. xvii. 3; Jer. xxxiii. 22; Zeph. i. 5); so ἡ στρατιὰ τοῦ οὐρανοῦ, Acts vii. 42.   2. *the region above the sidereal heavens, the seat of an order of things eternal and consummately perfect, where God dwells and the other heavenly beings*: this heaven Paul, in 2 Co. xii. 2, seems to designate by the name of ὁ τρίτος οὐρ., but certainly not the third of the seven distinct heavens described by the author of the Test. xii. Patr., Levi § 3, and by the Rabbins [(cf. Wetstein ad loc.; *Hahn*, Theol. d. N. T. i. 247 sq.; *Drummond*, Jewish Messiah, ch. xv.)]; cf. De Wette ad loc. Several distinct heavens are spoken of also in Eph. iv. 10 (ὑπεράνω πάντων τῶν οὐρ.); cf. Heb. vii. 26, if it be not preferable here to understand the numerous regions or parts of the one and the same heaven where God dwells as referred to. The highest heaven is *the dwelling-place of God*: Mt. v. 34; xxiii. 22; Acts vii. 49; Rev. iv. 1 sqq., (Ps. x. (xi.) 4; cxiii. 24 (cxv. 16 sq.)); hence θεὸς τοῦ οὐρ., Rev. xi. 13; xvi. 11, (Gen. xxiv. 3); ὁ ἐν (τοῖς) οὐρ., Mt. v. 16, 45; vi. 1, 9; vii. 21; x. 33; xii. 50; xvi. 17; xviii. 10 [here LWH mrg. ἐν τῷ οὐρανῷ in br.], 14, 19; Mk. xi. 25 sq., etc. From this heaven the πνεῦμα ἅγ. is sent down, 1 Pet. i. 12 and the pass. already cited [cf. 1 b. sub fin.]; and Christ is said to have come, Jn. iii. 13, 31; vi. 38, 41 sq.; 1 Co. xv. 47; it is the abode of the angels, Mt. xxiv. 36; xxii. 30; xviii. 10; xxviii. 2; Mk. xii. 25; xiii. 32; Lk. ii. 15; xxii. 43 [L br. WH reject the pass.]; Gal. i. 8; 1 Co. viii. 5; Eph. iii. 15; Heb. xii. 22; Rev. x. 1 : xii. 7; xviii. 1; xix. 14,

(Gen. xxi. 17; xxii. 11); τὰ ἐν τοῖς οὐρανοῖς καὶ τὰ ἐπὶ τῆς γῆς, the things and beings in the heavens (i. e. angels) and on the earth, Eph. i. 10; Col. i. 16, 20; γίνεται τὸ θέλημα τοῦ θεοῦ ἐν οὐρανῷ, i. e. by the inhabitants of heaven, Mt. vi. 10; χαρὰ ἔσται ἐν τῷ οὐρ., God and the angels will rejoice, Lk. xv. 7. this heaven is the abode to which Christ ascended after his resurrection, Mk. xvi. 19; Lk. xxiv. 51 [T om. WH reject the cl.]; Acts i. 10 sq.; ii. 34; iii. 21; Ro. x. 6; [Eph. i. 20 Lchm. txt.]; 1 Pet. iii. 22; Heb. i. 4 (ἐν ὑψηλοῖς); viii. 1; ix. 24; Rev. iv. 2, and from which he will hereafter return, 1 Th. i. 10; iv. 16; 2 Th. i. 7; into heaven have already been received the souls (πνεύματα) both of the O. T. saints and of departed Christians, Heb. xii. 23 (see ἀπογράφω, b. fin.), and heaven is appointed as the future abode of those who, raised from the dead and clothed with superior bodies, shall become partakers of the heavenly kingdom, 2 Co. v. 1, and enjoy the reward of proved virtue, Mt. v. 12; Lk. vi. 23; hence eternal blessings are called θησαυρὸς ἐν οὐρανῷ, Mt. vi. 20; Lk. xii. 33, and those on whom God has conferred eternal salvation are said ἔχειν θησαυρὸν ἐν οὐρανῷ (-νοῖς), Mt. xix. 21; Mk. x. 21; Lk. xviii. 22, cf. Heb. x. 34 [RG]; or the salvation awaiting them is said *to be laid up for them in heaven*, Col. i. 5; 1 Pet. i. 4; or their names are said to have been written in heaven, Lk. x. 20; moreover, Christ, appointed by God the leader and lord of the citizens of the divine kingdom, is said to have all power in heaven and on earth, Mt. xxviii. 18; finally, the seer of the Apocalypse expects a new Jerusalem to come down out of heaven as the metropolis of the perfectly established Messianic kingdom, Rev. iii. 12; xxi. 2, 10. By meton. ὁ οὐρανός is put for the inhabitants of heaven: εὐφραίνου οὐρανέ, Rev. xviii. 20, cf. xii. 12, (Ps. xcv. (xcvi.) 11; Is. xliv. 23; Job xv. 15); in particular for *God* (Dan. iv. 23, and often by the Rabbins, influenced by an over-scrupulous reverence for the names of God himself; cf. *Schürer* in the Jahrbb. f. protest. Theol., 1876, p. 178 sq.; [Keil, as below]: ἁμαρτάνειν εἰς τὸν οὐρ., Lk. xv. 18, 21; ἐκ τοῦ οὐρ., i. q. by God, Jn. iii. 27; ἐξ οὐρ., of divine authority, Mt. xxi. 25; Mk. xi. 30; Lk. xx. 4; ἐναντίον τοῦ οὐρανοῦ, 1 Macc. iii. 18 (where the τοῦ θεοῦ before τοῦ οὐρ. seems questionable); ἐκ τοῦ οὐρ. ἡ ἰσχύς, ib. 19; ἡ ἐξ οὐρ. βοήθεια, xii. 15; xvi. 3, cf. iii. 50–53, 59; iv. 10, 24, 30, 40, 55; v. 31; vii. 37, 41; ix. 46; cf. *Keil*, Comm. üb. d. Büch. d. Macc. p. 20. On the phrase ἡ βασιλεία τῶν οὐρ. and its meaning, see βασιλεία, 3; [Cremer s. v. βασ.; Edersheim i. 265].

Οὐρβανός, -οῦ, ὁ, [a Lat. name; cf. Bp. Lghtft. on Philip. p. 174], *Urbanus*, a certain Christian: Ro. xvi. 9.*   3773

Οὐρίας, -ου [B. 17 sq. (16) no. 8], ὁ, (אוּרִיָּה light of Jehovah [or, my light is Jehovah]), *Uriah*, the husband of Bathsheba the mother of Solomon by David: Mt. i. 6.*   3774

οὖς, gen. ὠτός, plur. ὦτα, dat. ὠσίν, τό, [cf. Lat. *auris, ausculto, audio*, etc.; akin to ἀΐω, αἰσθάνομαι; cf. Curtius § 619; Vaniček p. 67]; fr. Hom. down; Hebr. אֹזֶן; *the ear*:   1. prop.: Mt. xiii. 16; Mk. viii. 33; Lk. xxii. 50; 1 Co. ii. 9; xii. 16; ὠτά τινος εἰς δέησιν, to hear supplication, 1 Pet. iii. 12; ἡ γραφὴ πληροῦται ἐν τοῖς ὠσὶ   3775 τινος, while present and hearing, Lk. iv. 21 (Bar. i. 3 sq.); those unwilling to hear a thing are said συνέχειν [q. v. 2 a.] τὰ ὦτα, *to stop their ears*, Acts vii. 57; ἠκούσθη τι εἰς τὰ ὦτά τινος, something was heard by, came to the knowledge of [A. V. *came to the ears of*] one, Acts xi. 22; likewise εἰσέρχεσθαι, Jas. v. 4; γίνεσθαι, to come unto the ears of one, Lk. i. 44; ἀκούειν εἰς τὸ οὖς, to hear [A. V. *in the ear* i. e.] in familiar converse, privately, Mt. x. 27 (εἰς οὖς often so in class. Grk.; cf. Passow [L. and S.] s. v. 1); also πρὸς τὸ οὖς λαλεῖν, Lk. xii. 3.   **2.** metaph. i. q. *the faculty of perceiving with the mind, the faculty of understanding and knowing*: Mt. xiii. 16; ὁ ἔχων (or εἴ τις ἔχει) ὦτα (or οὖς, in Rev.) [sometimes (esp. in Mk. and Lk.) with ἀκούειν added; cf. B. § 140, 3] ἀκουέτω, whoever has the faculty of attending and understanding, let him use it, Mt. xi. 15; xiii. 9, 43; Mk. iv. 9, 23; vii. 16 [T WH om. Tr br. the vs.]; Lk. viii. 8; xiv. 35 (34); Rev. ii. 7, 11, 17, 29; iii. 6, 13, 22; xiii. 9; τοῖς ὠσὶ βαρέως ἀκούειν, to be slow to understand or obey [A. V. *their ears are dull of hearing*], Mt. xiii. 15; Acts xxviii. 27, (fr. Is. vi. 10); ὦτα ἔχοντες οὐκ ἀκούετε, Mk. viii. 18; ὦτα τοῦ μὴ ἀκούειν, [ears that they should not hear; cf. B. 267 (230)], Ro. xi. 8; θέσθε τ. λόγους τούτους εἰς τὰ ὦτα, [A. V. *let these words sink into your ears* i. e.] take them into your memory and hold them there, Lk. ix. 44; ἀπερίτμητος τοῖς ὠσίν (see ἀπερίτμητος), Acts vii. 51.*

3776   **οὐσία, -ας, ἡ**, (fr. ὤν, οὖσα, ὄν, the ptcp. of εἰμί), *what one has*, i. e. *property, possessions, estate*, [A.V. *substance*]: Lk. xv. 12 sq. (Tob. xiv. 13; Hdt. 1, 92; Xen., Plat., Attic oratt., al.) *

3777   **οὔτε**, (οὐ and τέ), an adjunctive negative conj., [fr. Hom. down], (differing fr. μήτε as οὐ does fr. μή [q. v. ad init.], and fr. οὐδέ as μήτε does fr. μηδέ; see μήτε and οὐδέ), *neither*; *and not*.   **1.** Examples in which οὔτε stands singly: **a.** οὐ . . . οὔτε, Rev. xii. 8 Rec. (where G L T Tr WH οὐδέ); xx. 4 R G (where L T Tr WH οὐδέ); οὐδεὶς ἄξιος εὑρέθη ἀνοῖξαι τὸ βιβλίον οὔτε βλέπειν αὐτό, Rev. v. 4; cf. W. 491 (457); B. 367 (315); οὐ . . . οὐδέ . . . οὔτε, 1 Th. ii. 3 R G (where L T Tr WH more correctly οὐδέ) [W. 493 (459); B. 368 (315)]; οὐδὲ . . . οὔτε (so that οὔτε answers only to the οὐ in οὐδέ), Gal. i. 12 R G T WH txt. [W. 492 (458); B. 366 (314)].   **b.** οὔτε . . . καί, like Lat. *neque . . . et, neither . . . and*: Jn. iv. 11; 3 Jn. 10, (Eur. Iph. T. 591; but the more common Grk. usage was οὐ . . . τέ, cf. Klotz ad Devar. ii. 2 p. 714; Passow s. v. B. 2; [L. and S. s. v. II. 4]; W. § 55, 7; [B. § 149, 13 c.]).   **c.** By a solecism οὔτε is put for οὐδέ, *not . . . even*: 1 Co. iii. 2 Rec. (where G L T Tr WH οὐδέ) [W. 493 (459); B. 367 (315); § 149, 13 f.]; Mk. v. 3 R G (where L T Tr WH have restored οὐδέ [W. 490 (456); B. u. s.]); Lk. xii. 26 R G (where L T Tr WH οὐδέ [W. u. s. and 478 (445); B. 347 (298)]); οὔτε μετενόησαν, Rev. ix. 20 R L Tr (where G WH txt. οὐ, T οὐδέ *not . . . even*; WH mrg. οὔτε or οὐδέ [cf. B. 367 (315)]); after the question μὴ δύναται . . . σῦκα; follows οὔτε ἁλυκὸν γλυκὺ ποιῆσαι ὕδωρ, Jas. iii. 12 G L T Tr WH (as though οὔτε δύναται . . . σῦκα had previously been in the writer's mind [cf. W. 493 (459); B. u. s.]).   **2.**

used twice or more, *neither . . . nor*, (Lat. *nec . . . nec*; *neque . . . neque*): Mt. vi. 20; xxii. 30; Mk. xii. 25; [xiv. 68 L txt. T Tr WH]; Lk. xiv. 35 (34); Jn. iv. 21; v. 37; viii. 19; ix. 3; Acts xv. 10; xix. 37; xxv. 8; xxviii. 21; Ro. viii. 38 sq. (where οὔτε occurs ten times); 1 Co. iii. 7; vi. 9 sq. (οὔτε eight times [yet T WH Tr mrg. the eighth time οὐ]); xi. 11; Gal. v. 6; vi. 15; 1 Th. ii. 6; Rev. iii. 15 sq.; ix. 20; xxi. 4; οὔτε . . . οὔτε . . . οὐδέ (Germ. *auch nicht, also not*), L Tr WH in Lk. xx. 35 sq., and L T Tr mrg. WH in Acts xxiv. 12 sq.; cf. W. 491 (457 sq.); B. 368 (315) note.

οὗτος, αὕτη, τοῦτο, demonstrative pron. [cf. Curtius p. 543], Hebr. זֶה, זֹאת, *this*; used   **I.** absolutely.   **1.**   **a.** *this one*, visibly present here: Mt. iii. 17; xvii. 5; Mk. ix. 7; Lk. vii. 44 sq.; ix. 35; 2 Pet. i. 17. Mt. ix. 3; xxi. 38; Mk. xiv. 69; Lk. ii. 34; xxiii. 2; Jn. i. 15, 30; vii. 25; ix. 8 sq. 19; xviii. 21, 30; xxi. 21; Acts iii. 15; iv. 10; ix. 21; according to the nature and character of the person or thing mentioned, it is used with a suggestion — either of contempt, as Mt. xiii. 55 sq.; Mk. vi. 2 sq.; Lk. v. 21; vii. 39, 49; Jn. vi. 42, 52; vii. 15; or of admiration, Mt. xxi. 11; Acts ix. 21; cf. Wahl, Clavis apocryphor. V. T. p. 370ᵇ.   **b.** it refers to a subject immediately preceding, *the one just named*: Lk. i. 32; ii. 37 [R G L]; Jn. i. 2; vi. 71; 2 Tim. iii. 6, 8, etc.; at the beginning of a narrative about one already mentioned, Mt. iii. 3; Lk. xvi. 1; Jn. i. 41 (42); iii. 2; xii. 21; xxi. 21; Acts vii. 19; xxi. 24. *this one just mentioned and no other*: Jn. ix. 9; Acts iv. 10 (ἐν τούτῳ); ix. 20; 1 Jn. v. 6; *such as I have just described*, 2 Tim. iii. 5; 2 Pet. ii. 17. καὶ οὗτος, *this one just mentioned also*, i. e. as well as the rest, Lk. xx. 30 R G L; Heb. viii. 3. καὶ τοῦτον, *and him too*, *and him indeed*, 1 Co. ii. 2.   **c.** it refers to the leading subject of a sentence although in position more remote (W. § 23, 1; [B. § 127, 3]): Acts iv. 11; vii. 19; viii. 26 (on which see Γάζα sub fin.); 1 Jn. v. 20 (where οὗτος is referred by [many] orthodox interpreters incorrectly [(see Alford ad loc.; W. and B. ll. cc.)] to the immediately preceding subject, *Christ*); 2 Jn. 7.   **d.** it refers to what follows; οὗτος, αὕτη ἐστί, *in this appears . . . that* etc.; *on this depends . . . that* etc.: foll. by ὅτι, as αὕτη ἐστὶν ἡ ἐπαγγελία, ὅτι, 1 Jn. i. 5; add, v. 11, 14; — by ἵνα, Jn. xv. 12; 1 Jn. iii. 11, 23; v. 3; 2 Jn. 6; τοῦτό ἐστι τὸ ἔργον, τὸ θέλημα τοῦ θεοῦ, ἵνα, Jn. vi. 29, 39 sq.   **e.** it serves to repeat the subject with emphasis: οὐ πάντες οἱ ἐξ Ἰσραήλ, οὗτοι Ἰσραήλ, Ro. ix. 6; add, ib. 8; ii. 14 [L mrg. οἱ τοιοῦτοι]; vii. 10; Gal. iii. 7; it refers, not without special force, to a description given by a participle or by the relative ὅς, ὅστις; which description either follows, as Mk. iv. 16, 18; Lk. viii. 15, 21; ix. 9; Jn. xi. 37; foll. by a relative sentence, Jn. i. 15; 1 Pet. v. 12; — or precedes: in the form of a participle, Mt. x. 22; xiii. 20, 22 sq.; xxiv. 13; xxvi. 23; Mk. xii. 40; Lk. ix. 48 (ὁ . . . ὑπάρχων, οὗτος); Jn. vi. 46; vii. 18; xv. 5; 2 Jn. 9; Acts xvii. 7; (and R G in Rev. iii. 5); or of the relative ὅς, Mt. v. 19; Mk. iii. 35; Lk. ix. 24, 26; Jn. i. 33 [here L mrg. αὐτός]; iii. 26; v. 38;

3778

Ro. viii. 30; 1 Co. vii. 20; Heb. xiii. 11; 1 Jn. ii. 5; 2 Pet. ii. 19; in the neut., Jn. viii. 26; Ro. vii. 16; 1 Co. vii. 24; Phil. iv. 9; 2 Tim. ii. 2; or of a preceding ὅστις, Mt. xviii. 4; in the neut. Phil. iii. 7. ὅσοι . . . οὗτοι, Ro. viii. 14; Gal. vi. 12; also preceded by εἴ τις, 1 Co. iii. 17 [here Lchm. αὐτός]; viii. 3; Jas. i. 23; iii. 2; by ἐάν τις, Jn. ix. 31; cf. W. § 23, 4. **f.** with αὐτός annexed, *this* man *himself*, Acts xxv. 25; plur. *these themselves*, Acts xxiv. 15, 20; on the neut. see below, 2 a. b. etc. **g.** As the relat. and interrog. pron. so also the demonstrative, when it is the subject, conforms in gender and number to the noun in the predicate : οὗτοί εἰσιν οἱ υἱοὶ τῆς βασ. Mt. xiii. 38; add, Mk. iv. 15 sq. 18; αὕτη ἐστὶν ἡ μεγάλη ἐντολή, Mt. xxii. 38; οὗτός ἐστιν ὁ πλάνος (Germ. *diese sind*), 2 Jn. 7. **2.** The n e u t e r τοῦτο **a.** refers to what precedes: Lk. v. 6; Jn. vi. 61; Acts xix. 17; τοῦτο εἰπών and the like, Lk. xxiv. 40 [T om. Tr br. WH reject the vs.]; Jn. iv. 18; viii. 6; xii. 33; xviii. 38; διὰ τοῦτο, see διά, B. II. 2 a.; εἰς τοῦτο, see εἰς, B. II. 3 c. β.; αὐτὸ τοῦτο, *for this very cause*, 2 Pet. i. 5 [Lchm. αὐτοί]; cf. Matthiae § 470, 7; Passow s. v. C. 1 a. fin. [L. and S. s. v. C. IX. 1 fin.; W. § 21, 3 note 2; Kühner § 410 Anm. 6]; μετὰ τοῦτο, see μετά, II. 2 b. ἐκ τούτου, *for this reason* [see ἐκ, II. 8], Jn. vi. 66; xix. 12; *from this*, i. e. *hereby, by this* note, 1 Jn. iv. 6 [cf. Westcott ad loc.]. ἐν τούτῳ, for this cause, Jn. xvi. 30; Acts xxiv. 16; *hereby, by this* token, 1 Jn. iii. 19. ἐπὶ τούτῳ, *in the meanwhile*, while this was going on [but see ἐπί, B. 2 e. fin. p. 234ᵃ], Jn. iv. 27. τούτου χάριν, Eph. iii. 14. plur. ταῦτα, Jn. vii. 4 (*these* so great, so wonderful, *things*); μετὰ ταῦτα, see μετά, II. 2 b. κατὰ ταῦτα, *in this* same *manner*, Rec. in Lk. vi. 23, and xvii. 30, [al. τὰ αὐτά or ταυτά]. it refers to the substance of the preceding discourse: Lk. viii. 8; xi. 27; xxiv. 26; Jn. v. 34; xv. 11; xxi. 24, and very often. καθὼς . . . ταῦτα, Jn. viii. 28. **b.** it prepares the reader or hearer and renders him attentive to what follows, which thus gets special weight (W. § 23, 5) : 1 Jn. iv. 2; αὐτὸ τοῦτο ὅτι, Phil. i. 6; τοῦτο λέγω foll. by direct discourse, Gal. iii. 17 [see λέγω, II. 2 d.]. it is prefixed to sentences introduced by the particles ὅτι, ἵνα, etc.: τοῦτο λέγω or φημί foll. by ὅτι, 1 Co. i. 12 [(see λέγω u. s.); 1 Co. vii. 29]; xv. 50; γινώσκεις τοῦτο foll. by ὅτι, Ro. vi. 6; 2 Tim. iii. 1; 2 Pet. i. 20; λογίζεσθαι τοῦτο ὅτι, Ro. ii. 3; after ὁμολογεῖν, Acts xxiv. 14; after εἰδώς, 1 Tim. i. 9; ἐν τούτῳ ὅτι, 1 Jn. iii. 16, 24; iv. 9 sq.; τοῦτο, ἵνα, Lk. i. 43; εἰς τοῦτο, ἵνα, Acts ix. 21; Ro. xiv. 9; 2 Co. ii. 9; 1 Pet. iii. 9; iv. 6; 1 Jn. iii. 8; διὰ τοῦτο, ἵνα, 2 Co. xiii. 10; 1 Tim. i. 16; Philem. 15; τούτων (on this neut. plur. referring to a single object see W. 162 (153); [cf. *Riddell*, Platonic Idioms, § 41]), ἵνα, 3 Jn. 4; ἐν τούτῳ, ἐάν, 1 Jn. ii. 3; ὅταν, 1 Jn. v. 2; τοῦτο αὐτὸ, ἵνα, *on this very account, that* (see a. above [but others take it here as acc. of obj.; see Meyer ad loc. (for instances of αὐτὸ τοῦτο see B. § 127, 12)]), 2 Co. ii. 3; εἰς αὐτὸ τοῦτο, ἵνα, Eph. vi. 22; Col. iv. 8; ὅπως, Ro. ix. 17. In the same manner τοῦτο is put before an infin. with τό for the sake of emphasis [W. § 23, 5; B. § 140, 7, 9, etc.]: 2 Co. ii. 1; before a simple infin. 1 Co. vii. 37

[here R G prefix τοῦ to the inf.]; before an acc. and inf. Eph. iv. 17; before nouns, as τοῦτο εὔχομαι, τὴν ὑμῶν κατάρτισιν, 2 Co. xiii. 9, cf. 1 Jn. iii. 24; v. 4. **c.** καὶ τοῦτο, *and this, and that too, and indeed, especially* : Ro. xiii. 11; 1 Co. vi. 6, L T Tr WH also in 8; Eph. ii. 8; καὶ ταῦτα, *and that too*, 1 Co. vi. 8 Rec.; Heb. xi. 12; (so καὶ ταῦτα also in class. Grk.; cf. Devar. ed. *Klotz* i. p. 108; *Viger.* ed. *Herm.* p. 176 sq.; Matthiae § 470, 6). **d.** ταῦτα, *of this sort, such*, spoken contemptuously of men, 1 Co. vi. 11 (cf. Soph. O. R. 1329; Thuc. 6, 77; Liv. 30, 30; cf. Bnhdy. p. 281; [W. 162 (153)]). **e.** τοῦτο μὲν . . . τοῦτο δέ, *partly . . . partly*, Heb. x. 33 (for exx. fr. Grk. auth. see W. 142 (135); Matthiae ii. § 288 Anm. 2; [Kühner § 527 Anm. 2]). **f.** τοῦτ᾽ ἔστιν, see εἰμί, II. 3 p. 176ᵇ.

II. Joined to nouns it is used like an adjective ; **a.** so that the article stands between the demonstrative and the noun, οὗτος ὁ, αὕτη ἡ, τοῦτο τό, [cf. W. § 23 fin.; B. § 127, 29] : Mt. xii. 32; xvi. 18; xvii. 21 [T WH om. Tr br. the vs.]; xx. 12; xxvi. 29; Mk. ix. 29; Lk. vii. 44; x. 36; xiv. 30; xv. 24; Jn. iv. 15; vii. 46 [L WH om. Tr br. the cl.]; viii. 20; x. 6; xi. 47; xii. 5; Acts i. 11; Ro. xi. 24; 1 Tim. i. 18; Heb. vii. 1; viii. 10; [1 Jn. iv. 21]; Rev. xix. 9; xx. 14; xxi. 5; xxii. 6. etc.; τοῦτο τὸ παιδίον, *such a little child as* ye see here, Lk. ix. 48; cf. Bornemann ad loc. [who takes τοῦτο thus as representing the class, 'this and the like;' but cf. Meyer (ed. *Weiss*) ad loc.]. **b.** so that the noun stands between the article and the demonstrative [cf. W. 548 (510)] ; as, οἱ λίθοι οὗτοι, the stones which ye see lying near, Mt. iii. 9; iv. 3; add, Mt. v. 19; vii. 24 [L Tr WH br. τούτους], 26, 28 ; ix. 26 [Tr mrg. WH mrg. αὐτῆς]; x. 23, etc.; Mk. xii. 16; xiii. 30; Lk. xi. 31; xxiii. 47; Jn. iv. 13, 21; vii. 49; xi. 9; xviii. 29; Acts vi. 13; xix. 26; Ro. xv. 28; 1 Co. i. 20; ii. 6; xi. 26; 2 Co. iv. 1, 7; viii. 6; xi. 10; xii. 13; Eph. iii. 8; v. 32; 2 Tim. ii. 19; Rev. ii. 24, and very often — (which constr. is far more freq. with Paul than the other [see W. u. s.]); it is added to a noun which has another adjective, ἡ χήρα ἡ πτωχὴ αὕτη, Lk. xxi. 3; πάντα τὰ ῥήματα ταῦτα, Lk. ii. 19, 51 [(T WH L mrg. om. L txt. Tr mrg. br. ταῦτα) ; ἀπὸ τῆς γενεᾶς τῆς σκολιᾶς ταύτης, Acts ii. 40]. **c.** Passages in which the reading varies between οὗτος ὁ and ὁ . . . οὗτος : viz. οὗτος ὁ, Mk. xiv. 30 L txt. T Tr WH; Jn. vi. 60 R L mrg.; Jn. vi. 60 R G; Jn. vii. 36 R G; Jn. ix. 24 L WH Tr mrg.; Jn. xxi. 23 L T Tr WH. ὁ . . . οὗτος, Mk. xiv. 30 R G L mrg.; Jn. iv. 20 G L txt. T Tr WH; Jn. vi. 60 L T Tr WH; Jn. vii 36 L T Tr WH; Jn. ix. 24 G T Tr txt.; Jn. xxi. 23 R G; etc. **d.** with anarthrous nouns, esp. numerical specifications [W. § 37, 5 N. 1] : τρίτον τοῦτο, *this third time*, 2 Co. xiii. 1; τοῦτο τρίτον, Jn. xxi. 14, (Judg. xvi. 15; δεύτερον τοῦτο, Gen. xxvii. 36; τοῦτο δέκατον, Num. xiv. 22; τέταρτον τοῦτο, Hdt. 5, 76). [The passages which follow, although introduced here by Prof. Grimm, are (with the exception of Acts i. 5) clearly instances of the p r e d i c a t i v e use of οὗτος; cf. W. 110 (105) note; B. § 127, 31; Rost § 98, 3 A. c. a. sq.] : τοῦτο πάλιν δεύτερον σημεῖον ἐποίησεν, Jn. iv. 54; τρίτην ταύτην ἡμέραν ἄγει,

3779

this is the third day that Israel is passing [but see ἄγω, 3], Lk. xxiv. 21 (κεῖμαι τριακοστὴν ταύτην ἡμέραν, this is now the thirtieth day that I lie (unburied), Lcian. dial. mort. 13, 3); οὐ μετὰ πολλὰς ταύτας ἡμέρας (see μετά, II. 2 b. [W. 161 (152); B. § 127, 4]), Acts i. 5; οὗτος μὴν ἕκτος ἐστὶν αὐτῇ, this is the sixth month with her etc. Lk. i. 36; αὕτη ἀπογραφὴ πρώτη ἐγένετο, Lk. ii. 2 L (T) Tr WH; ταύτην ἐποίησεν ἀρχὴν τῶν σημείων, Jn. ii. 11 L T Tr WH.

οὕτω and οὕτως (formerly in printed editions οὕτω appeared before a consonant, οὕτως before a vowel; but [recent critical editors, following the best Mss. ("cod. Sin. has -τω but fourteen times in the N. T." Scrivener, Collation etc. p. liv.; cf. his Introduction etc. p. 561), have restored οὕτως; viz. Treg. uniformly, 205 times; Tdf. 203 times, 4 times -τω; Lchm. 196 times, 7 times -τω (all before a consonant); WH 196 times, 10 times -τω (all before a consonant); cf. Tdf. Proleg. p. 97; WH. App. p. 146 sq.]; cf. W. § 5, 1 b.; B. 9; [Lob. Pathol. Elementa ii. 213 sqq.]; cf. Krüger § 11, 12, 1; Kühner § 72, 3 a.), adv., (fr. οὗτος), [fr. Hom. down], Sept. for כֵּן, in this manner, thus, so; 1. by virtue of its native demonstrative force it refers to what precedes; in the manner spoken of; in the way described; in the way it was done; in this manner; in such a manner; thus, so: Mt. vi. 30; xi. 26; xvii. 12; xix. 8; Mk. xiv. 59; Lk. i. 25; ii. 48; xii. 28; Ro. xi. 5; 1 Co. viii. 12; xv. 11; Heb. vi. 9; [2 Pet. iii. 11 WH Tr mrg.]; οὐχ οὕτως ἔσται [L Tr WH ἐστὶν (so also T in Mk.)] ἐν ὑμῖν, it will not be so among you (I hope), Mt. xx. 26; Mk. x. 43; ὑμεῖς οὐχ οὕτως sc. ἔσεσθε, Lk. xxii. 26; ἐὰν ἀφῶμεν αὐτὸν οὕτως sc. ποιοῦντα, thus as he has done hitherto [see ἀφίημι, 2 b.], Jn. xi. 48; it refers to similitudes and comparisons, and serves to adapt them to the case in hand, Mt. v. 16 (even so, i. e. as the lamp on the lamp-stand); Mt. xii. 45; xiii. 49; xviii. 14; xx. 16; Lk. xii. 21 [WH br. the vs.]; xv. 7, 10; Jn. iii. 8; 1 Co. ix. 24; likewise οὕτως καί, Mt. xvii. 12; xviii. 35; xxiv. 33; Mk. xiii. 29; Lk. xvii. 10. οὕτως ἔχειν, to be so (Lat. sic or ita se habere): Acts vii. 1; xii. 15; xvii. 11; xxiv. 9. it serves to resume participles (Joseph. antt. 8, 11, 1; b. j. 2, 8, 5; see exx. fr. Grk. auth. in Passow s. v. 1 h.; [L. and S. s. v. I. 7]): Acts xx. 11; xxvii. 17; but Jn. iv. 6 must not [with W. § 65, 9 fin.; B. § 144, 21] be referred to this head, see Meyer [and 5 d. below]; on Rev. iii. 5, see 5 c. below. it takes the place of an explanatory participial clause, i. q. matters being thus arranged, under these circumstances, in such a condition of things, [B. § 149, 1; cf. W. § 60, 5]: Ro. v. 12 (this connection between sin and death being established [but this explanation of the οὕτως appears to be too general (cf. Meyer ad loc.)]); Heb. vi. 15 (i. e. since God had pledged the promise by an oath); i. q. things having been thus settled, this having been done, then: Mt. xi. 26; Acts vii. 8; xxviii. 14; 1 Co. xiv. 25; 1 Th. iv. 17; 2 Pet. i. 11; cf. Fritzsche, Com. ad Rom. i. p. 298. Closely related to this use is that of οὕτως (like Lat. ita for itaque, igitur) in the sense of consequently [cf. Eng. so at the beginning of a sentence]: Mt. vii. 17; Ro. i. 15; vi. 11;

Rev. iii. 16, ([cf. Fritzsche on Mt. p. 220]; Passow s. v. 2; [L. and S. s. v. II.]). 2. it prepares the way for what follows: Mt. vi. 9; Lk. xix. 31; Jn. xxi. 1; οὕτως ἦν, was arranged thus, was on this wise, [W. 465 (434); B. § 129, 11], Mt. i. 18; οὕτως ἐστὶ τὸ θέλημα τοῦ θεοῦ foll. by an infin., so is the will of God, that, 1 Pet. ii. 15. before language quoted from the O. T.: Mt. ii. 5; Acts vii. 6; xiii. 34, 47; 1 Co. xv. 45; Heb. iv. 4. 3. with adjectives, so [Lat. tam, marking degree of intensity]: Heb. xii. 21; Rev. xvi. 18; postpositive, τί δειλοί ἐστε οὕτως; Mk. iv. 40 [L Tr WH om.]; in the same sense with adverbs, Gal. i. 6; or with verbs, so greatly, 1 Jn. iv. 11; οὕτως ... ὥστε, Jn. iii. 16. οὐδέποτε ἐφάνη οὕτως, it was never seen in such fashion, i. e. such an extraordinary sight, Mt. ix. 33 (ἐφάνη must be taken impersonally; cf. Bleek, Synopt. Erklär. i. p. 406 [or Meyer ad loc.]); οὐδέποτε οὕτως εἴδομεν, we never saw it so, i. e. with such astonishment, Mk. ii. 12. 4. οὕτως or οὕτως καί in comparison stands antithetic to an adverb or a relative pron. [W. § 53, 5; cf. B. 362 (311) c.]: καθάπερ ... οὕτως, Ro. xii. 4 sq.; 1 Co. xii. 12; 2 Co. viii. 11; καθὼς ... οὕτως, Lk. xi. 30; xvii. 26; Jn. iii. 14; xii. 50; xiv. 31; xv. 4; 2 Co. i. 5; x. 7; 1 Th. ii. 4; Heb. v. 3; οὕτως ... καθώς, Lk. xxiv. 24; Ro. xi. 26; Phil. iii. 17; ὡς ... οὕτως, Acts viii. 32; xxiii. 11; Ro. v. 15, 18; 1 Co. vii. 17; 2 Co. vii. 14; 1 Th. ii. 8; v. 2; οὕτως ... ὡς, Mk. iv. 26; Jn. vii. 46 [L WH om. Tr br. the cl.]; 1 Co. iii. 15; iv. 1; ix. 26; Eph. v. 28; Jas. ii. 12; οὕτως ὡς ... μὴ ὡς, 2 Co. v. 3 [GL T Tr WH]; ὥσπερ ... οὕτως, Mt. xii. 40; xiii. 40; xxiv. 27, 37, 39; Lk. xvii. 24; Jn. v. 21, 26; Ro. v. 12, 19, 21; vi. 4; xi. 31; 1 Co. xi. 12; xv. 22; xvi. 1; 2 Co. i. 7 R G; Gal. iv. 29; Eph. v. 24 R G; after καθ᾽ ὅσον, Heb. ix. 27 sq.; οὕτως ... ὃν τρόπον, Acts i. 11; xxvii. 25; ὃν τρόπον ... οὕτως, 2 Tim. iii. 8 (Is. lii. 14); κατὰ τὴν ὁδὸν ἣν λέγουσιν αἵρεσιν οὕτω κτλ. after the Way (i. e. as it requires [cf. ὁδός, 2 a. fin.]) so etc. Acts xxiv. 14. 5. Further, the foll. special uses deserve notice: a. (ἔχει) ὃς [better ὁ] μὲν οὕτως ὃς [better ὁ] δὲ οὕτως, one after this manner, another after that, i. e. different men in different ways, 1 Co. vii. 7 (ποτὲ μὲν οὕτως καὶ ποτὲ οὕτως φάγεται ἡ μάχαιρα, 2 S. xi. 25). b. οὕτως, in the manner known to all, i. e. acc. to the context, so shamefully, 1 Co. v. 3. c. in that state in which one finds one's self, such as one is, [cf. W. 465 (434)]: τί με ἐποίησας οὕτως, Ro. ix. 20; οὕτως εἶναι, μένειν, of those who remain unmarried, 1 Co. vii. 26, 40; ὁ νικῶν οὕτως περιβαλεῖται viz. as (i. e. because he is) victor [al. in the manner described in vs. 4], Rev. iii. 5 L T Tr WH. d. thus forthwith, i. e. without hesitation [cf. Eng. off-hand, without ceremony, and the colloquial right, just]: Jn. iv. 6; cf. Passow s. v. 4; [L. and S. s. v. IV.; see 1 above; add Jn. xiii. 25 T WH Tr br. (cf. Green, Crit. Notes ad loc.)] e. in questions (Lat. sicine?) [Eng. exclamatory so then, what]: Mk. vii. 18 (Germ. sonach) [al. take οὕτως here as expressive of degree. In Mt. xxvi. 40, however, many give it the sense spoken of; cf. too 1 Co. vi. 5]; οὕτως ἀποκρίνῃ; i. e. so impudently, Jn. xviii. 22; with an adjective, so (very), Gal. iii. 3. [But these exx., although classed together by Fritzsche also (Com. on Mark p. 150 sq.), seem to be capable of discrimination. The passage from Gal., for instance, does not seem to differ essentially from examples under 3 above.]   **f.** In class. Grk. οὕτως often, after a conditional, concessive, or temporal protasis, introduces the apodosis (cf. Passow s. v. 1 h.; [L. and S. s. v. I. 7]). 1 Th. iv. 14 and Rev. xi. 5 have been referred to this head; B. 357 (307); [cf. W. § 60, 5 (esp. a.)]. But questionably; for in the first passage οὕτως may also be taken as equiv. to *under these circumstances*, i. e. if we believe what I have said [better cf. W. u. s.]; in the second passage οὕτως denotes *in the manner spoken of*, i. e. by fire proceeding out of their mouth.

(3779a);
see 3756   **οὐχ**, see οὐ.

3780 ———— **οὐχί**, i. q. οὐ, not, but stronger [cf. νυνί ad init.];   **a.** in simple negative sentences, *by no means, not at all*, [A. V. *not*]: Jn. xiii. 10 sq.; xiv. 22; 1 Co. v. 2; vi. 1; foll. by ἀλλά, 1 Co. x. 29; 2 Co. x. 13 (L T Tr WH οὐκ); in denials or contradictions [A. V. *nay*; *not so*], Lk. i. 60; xii. 51; xiii. 3, 5; xvi. 30; Ro. iii. 27.   **b.** in a question, Lat. *nonne?* (asking what no one denies to be true): Mt. v. 46 sq.; x. 29; xiii. 27; xx. 13; Lk. vi. 39; xvii. 17 [L Tr WH οὐχ]; xxiv. 26; Jn. xi. 9; Acts ii. 7 Tr WH txt.; Ro. ii. 26 (L T Tr WH οὐχ); 1 Co. i. 20; Heb. i. 14, etc.; (Sept. for הֲלֹא, Gen. xl. 8; Judg. iv. 6); ἀλλ' οὐχί, will he *not rather*, Lk. xvii. 8.

3781   **ὀφειλέτης**, -ου, ὁ, (ὀφείλω), one who owes another, a *debtor*: prop. of one who owes another money (Plat. legg. 5, 736 d.; Plut.; al.); with a gen. of the sum due, Mt. xviii. 24. Metaph.   **a.** one held by some obligation, bound to some duty: ὀφειλέτης εἰμί, i. q. ὀφείλω, foll. by an inf., Gal. v. 3 (Soph. Aj. 590); ὀφειλ. εἰμί τινος, to be one's debtor i. e. under obligations of gratitude to him for favors received, Ro. xv. 27; τινί (dat. commodi), to be under obligation to do something for some one, Ro. i. 14; viii. 12.   **b.** one who has not yet made amends to one whom he has injured: Mt. vi. 12; in imitation of the Chald. חַיָּב, one who owes God penalty or of whom God can demand punishment as something due, i. e. a sinner, Lk. xiii. 4.*

3782   **ὀφειλή**, -ῆς, ἡ, (ὀφείλω), that which is owed; prop. a *debt*: Mt. xviii. 32; metaph. plur. dues: Ro. xiii. 7; spec. of conjugal duty [R. V. her due], 1 Co. vii. 3 G L T Tr WH.   Found neither in the Grk. O. T. nor in prof. auth.; cf. Lob. ad Phryn. p. 90.*

3783   **ὀφείλημα**, -τος, τό, (ὀφείλω), that which is owed;   **a.** prop. that which is justly or legally due, a debt; so for מַשָּׁאָה, Deut. xxiv. 12 (10); ἀφιέναι, 1 Macc. xv. 8; ἀποτίνειν, Plat. legg. 4 p. 717 b.; ἀποδιδόναι, Aristot. eth. Nic. 9, 2, 5 [p. 1165ᵃ, 3]. κατὰ ὀφείλημα, as of debt, Ro. iv. 4.   **b.** in imitation of the Chald. חוֹב or חוֹבָא (which denotes both *debt* and *sin*), metaph. *offence, sin*, (see ὀφειλέτης, b.); hence, ἀφιέναι τινὶ τὰ ὀφειλ. αὐτοῦ, to remit the penalty of one's sins, to forgive them, (Chald. שְׁבַק חוֹבִין), Mt. vi. 12. [Cf. W. 30, 32, 33.] *

3784   **ὀφείλω**; impf. ὤφειλον; pres. pass. ptcp. ὀφειλόμενος; fr. Hom. down; *to owe*;   **a.** prop. *to owe money*, be

in debt for: τινί τι, Mt. xviii. 28; Lk. xvi. 5; without a dat., Mt. xviii. 28; Lk. vii. 41; xvi. 7; Philem. 18; τὸ ὀφειλόμενον, that which is due, *the debt*, Mt. xviii. 30; αὐτῷ (which L Tr WH om.), that due to him, ib. 34.   **b.** metaph.: τί, pass. τὴν εὔνοιαν ὀφειλομένην, the good-will due [A. (not R.) V. *due benevolence*], 1 Co. vii. 3 Rec.; μηδενὶ μηδὲν ὀφείλετε (here ὀφείλετε, on account of what precedes and what follows, must be taken in its broadest sense, both literal and tropical), εἰ μὴ τὸ ἀλλήλους ἀγαπᾶν, owe no one anything except to love one another, because we must never cease loving and the debt of love can never be paid, Ro. xiii. 8.   absol. *to be a debtor, be bound*: Mt. xxiii. 16, 18; foll. by an inf. *to be under obligation, bound by duty* or *necessity, to do something; it behoves* one; one *ought*; used thus of a necessity imposed either by law and duty, or by reason, or by the times, or by the nature of the matter under consideration [acc. to Westcott (Epp. of Jn. p. 5), Cremer, al., denoting obligation in its special and personal aspects]: Lk. xvii. 10; Jn. xiii. 14; xix. 7 (ὀφείλει ἀποθανεῖν, he ought to die); Acts xvii. 29; Ro. xv. 1, 27; 1 Co. v. 10; [vii. 36 (A. V. *need so requireth*)]; ix. 10; xi. 7, 10; 2 Co. xii. 14; Eph. v. 28; 2 Th. i. 3; ii. 13; Heb. ii. 17; v. 3, 12; 1 Jn. ii. 6; iii. 16; iv. 11; 3 Jn. 8; ὤφειλον συνίστασθαι, I ought to have been commended, i. e. I can demand commendation, 2 Co. xii. 11.   **c.** after the Chaldee (see ὀφειλέτης, b., ὀφείλημα, b.), ὀφείλω τινί, to have wronged one and not yet made amends to him [A. V. *indebted*], Lk. xi. 4.   [Comp.: προσ-οφείλω.] *

ὄφελον (for ὤφελον, without the augm., 2 aor. of ὀφείλω;   3785
in earlier Grk. with an inf., as ὤφελον θανεῖν, I ought to have died, expressive of a wish, i. q. *would that I were dead*; in later Grk. it assumes the nature of an interjection, to be rendered) *would that*, where one wishes that a thing had happened which has not happened, or that a thing be done which probably will not be done [cf. W. 301 sq. (283); B. § 150, 5]: with an optative pres. Rev. iii. 15 Rec.; with an indicative impf., Rev. ibid. G L T Tr WH; 2 Co. xi. 1, (Epict. diss. 2, 18, 15; Ignat. ad Smyrn. c. 12); with an indic. aorist, 1 Co. iv. 8 (Ps. cxviii. (cxix.) 5; ὄφελον ἀπεθάνομεν, Ex. xvi. 3; Num. xiv. 2; xx. 3); with the future, Gal. v. 12 (Lcian. soloec. [or Pseudosoph.] 1, where this construction is classed as a solecism). Cf. Passow ii. p. 603ᵃ; [L. and S. s. v. ὀφείλω, II. 3].*

ὄφελος, -ους, τό, (ὀφέλλω to increase), advantage, profit: 3786
1 Co. xv. 32; Jas. ii. 14, 16. (From Hom. down; Sept. Job xv. 3.) *

ὀφθαλμο-δουλεία [T WH -λία; see I, ι], -ας, ἡ, (ὀφθαλ-   3787
μόδουλος, Constit. apost. [4, 12, Coteler. Patr. Apost.] i. p. 299ᵃ; and this fr. ὀφθαλμός and δοῦλος), [A. V. eyeservice i. e.] service performed [only] under the master's eye (μὴ κατ' ὀφθαλμοδ., τουτέστι μὴ μόνον παρόντων τῶν δεσποτῶν καὶ ὁρώντων, ἀλλὰ καὶ ἀπόντων, Theophyl. on Eph. vi. 6; "for the master's eye usually stimulates to greater diligence; his absence, on the other hand, renders sluggish." H. Stephanus): Eph. vi. 6; Col. iii. 22. Not found elsewhere; [cf. W. 100 (94)].*

3788 ὀφθαλμός, -οῦ, ὁ, [fr. r. ὀπ to see; allied to ὄψις, ὄψομαι, etc.; Curtius § 627], Sept. for יַעִן, [fr. Hom. down], *the eye*: Mt. v. 38; vi. 22; Mk. ix. 47; Lk. xi. 34; Jn. ix. 6; 1 Co. xii. 16; Rev. vii. 17; xxi. 4, and often; ῥιπῇ ὀφθαλμοῦ, 1 Co. xv. 52; οἱ ὀφθαλμοί μου εἶδον (see the remark in γλῶσσα, 1), Lk. ii. 30; cf. iv. 20; x. 23; Mt. xiii. 16; 1 Co. ii. 9; Rev. i. 7; [ἀνέβλεψαν οἱ ὀφθαλμοί Mt. xx. 34 RG]; ἰδεῖν τοῖς ὀφθ., Mt. xiii. 15; Jn. xii. 40; Acts xxviii. 27; ὁρᾶν τοῖς ὀφθ. (see ὁράω, 1), 1 Jn. i. 1; ἡ ἐπιθυμία τῶν ὀφθ. desire excited by seeing, 1 Jn. ii. 16. Since the eye is the index of the mind, the foll. phrases have arisen: ὀφθ. σου πονηρός ἐστιν, i. e. *thou art envious*, Mt. xx. 15; ὀφθ. πονηρός, envy, Mk. vii. 22 (רַע עַיִן, an envious man, Prov. xxiii. 6; xxviii. 22; cf. Sir. xxxiv. 13; רָעָה עֵינְךָ בְּאָחִיךָ, thine eye is evil toward thy brother, i. e. thou enviest [grudgest] thy brother, Deut. xv. 9; ὀφθ. πονηρὸς φθονερὸς ἐπ' ἄρτῳ, Sir. xiv. 10; μὴ φθονεσάτω σου ὁ ὀφθ. Tob. iv. 7; the opposite, ἀγαθὸς ὀφθαλμός, is used of a willing mind, Sir. xxxii. (xxxv.) 10, 12); on the other hand, ὀφθαλμὸς πονηρός in Mt. vi. 23 is a *diseased, disordered eye*, just as we say *a bad eye*, *a bad finger* [see πονηρός, 2 a. (where Lk. xi. 34)]. κρατεῖν τοὺς ὀφθ. τοῦ μή κτλ. [A. V. *to hold the eyes* i. e.] to prevent one from recognizing another, Lk. xxiv. 16; ὑπολαμβάνω τινὰ ἀπὸ τῶν ὀφθ. τινος, by receiving one to withdraw him from another's sight [A. V. *received him out of their sight*], Acts i. 9. Metaph. of *the eyes of the mind*, the faculty of knowing: ἐκρύβη ἀπὸ τῶν ὀφθ. σου, *hid from thine eyes*, i. e. concealed from thee [cf. B. 320 (274)], Lk. xix. 42; διδόναι τινὶ ὀφθαλμοὺς τοῦ μὴ βλέπειν, to cause one to be slow to understand, Ro. xi. 8 [cf. B. 267 (230)]; τυφλοῦν τοὺς ὀφθ. τινος, Jn. xii. 40; 1 Jn. ii. 11; σκοτίζονται οἱ ὀφθ. Ro. xi. 10; πεφωτισμένοι ὀφθαλμοὶ τῆς διανοίας [cf. B. § 145, 6], Eph. i. 18 Rec.; τῆς καρδίας (as in Clem. Rom. 1 Cor. 36, 2), ibid. G L T Tr WH; ἐν ὀφθαλμοῖς τινος (עֵינֵי בְ) [cf. B. § 146, 1 fin.]), in the judgment [cf. our *view*] of one, Mt. xxi. 42; Mk. xii. 11; οὐκ ἔστι τι ἀπέναντι τῶν ὀφθ. τινος, to neglect a thing (cf. our leave, put, out of sight), Ro. iii. 18; γυμνόν ἐστί τι τοῖς ὀφθ. τινος (see γυμνός, 2 a.), Heb. iv. 13; οἱ ὀφθ. τοῦ κυρίου ἐπὶ δικαίους (sc. ἐπι- [or ἀπο-] βλέπουσιν, which is added in Ps. x. (xi.) 4), are (fixed) upon the righteous, i. e. the Lord looks after, provides for them, 1 Pet. iii. 12. Other phrases in which ὀφθαλμός occurs may be found under ἀνοίγω p. 48ᵇ, ἁπλοῦς, διανοίγω 1, ἐξορύσσω 1, ἐπαίρω p. 228ᵃ, καμμύω, μοιχαλίς a., προγράφω 2.

3789 ὄφις, -εως, ὁ, [perh. named fr. its sight; cf. δράκων, init., and see Curtius s. v. ὀφθαλμός; fr. Hom. Il. 12, 208 down; Sept. mostly for נָחָשׁ; *a snake, serpent*: Mt. vii. 10; Mk. xvi. 18; Lk. x. 19; xi. 11; Jn. iii. 14; 1 Co. x. 9; Rev. ix. 19; with the ancients the serpent was an emblem of cunning and wisdom, 2 Co. xi. 3, cf. Gen. iii. 1; hence, φρόνιμοι ὡς οἱ ὄφεις, Mt. x. 16 [here WH mrg. ὁ ὄφις]; hence, crafty hypocrites are called ὄφεις, Mt. xxiii. 33. The serpent narrated to have deceived Eve (see Gen. u. s.) was regarded by the later Jews as the devil (Sap. ii. 23 sq. cf. 4 Macc. xviii. 8); hence he is called ὁ ὄφις ὁ ἀρχαῖος, ὁ ὄφις: Rev. xii. 9, 14 sq.; xx. 2; see [Grimm on Sap. u. s.; *Fr. Lenormant*, Beginnings of History etc. ch. ii. p. 109 sq., and] δράκων.*

3790 ὀφρύς, -ύος, ἡ, **1.** *the eyebrow*, so fr. Hom. down. **2.** *any prominence* or *projection*; as [Eng. *the brow*] of a mountain (so the Lat. *supercilium*, Verg. georg. 1, 108; Hirt. bell. afr. 58; Liv. 27, 18; 34, 29): Lk. iv. 29 (Hom. Il. 20, 151; often in Polyb., Plut., al.).*

see 856 [ὀχετός, -οῦ, ὁ, **1.** *a water-pipe, duct*. **2.** *the intestinal canal*: Mk. vii. 19 WH (rejected) mrg. (al. ἀφεδρών).*]

3791 ὀχλέω, -ῶ: pres. pass. ptcp. ὀχλούμενος; (ὄχλος); prop. *to excite a mob against one*; [in Hom. (Il. 21, 261) *to disturb, roll away*]; univ. *to trouble, molest*, (τινά, Hdt. 5, 41; Aeschyl., al.); absol. *to be in confusion, in an uproar*, (3 Macc. v. 41); pass. *to be vexed, molested, troubled*: by demons, Lk. vi. 18 RGL (where T Tr WH ἐνοχλ., — the like variation of text in Hdian. 6, 3, 4); Acts v. 16; Tob. vi. 8 (7); Acta Thomae § 12. [Comp.: ἐν-, παρεν-οχλέω.]*

3792 ὀχλο-ποιέω, -ῶ: 1 aor. ptcp. ὀχλοποιήσας; (ὄχλος, ποιέω); *to collect a crowd, gather the people together*: Acts xvii. 5. Not found elsewhere.*

3793 ὄχλος, -ου, ὁ, in the N. T. only in the historical bks. and five times in the Rev.; as in Grk. writ. fr. Pind. and Aeschyl. down, *a crowd*, i. e. **1.** *a casual collection of people*; *a multitude of men who have flocked together in some place, a throng*: Mt. ix. 23, 25; xv. 10, etc.; Mk. ii. 4; iii. 9, and often; Lk. v. 1, 19; vii. 9, etc.; Jn. v. 13; vi. 22, 24; vii. 20, 32, 49, etc.; Acts xiv. 14; xvii. 8; xxi. 34; τὶς ἐκ τοῦ ὄχλου, Lk. xi. 27; xii. 13; or ἀπὸ τοῦ ὄχλου, xix. 39; ix. 38; ἀπὸ (for i. e. *on account of* [cf. ἀπό, II. 2 b.]) τ. ὄχλου, Lk. xix. 3; ἡ βία τ. ὄχλου, Acts xxi. 35; πολὺς ὄχλος and much oftener ὄχλος πολύς, Mt. xiv. 14; xx. 29; xxvi. 47; Mk. v. 21, 24; vi. 34; xii. 14; xiv. 43 [here T Tr WH om. L Tr mrg. br. πολ.]; Lk. vii. 11; viii. 4; ix. 37; Jn. vi. 2, 5; xii. 12 [but here Tr mrg. br. WH prefix ὁ; cf. B. 91 (80)]; Rev. xix. 1, 6; with the art. ὁ πολὺς ὄχλος, *the great multitude* present, Mk. xii. 37; [ὁ ὄχλος πολύς (the noun forming with the adj. a single composite term, like our) *the common people*, Jn. xii. 9 T WH Tr mrg.; cf. B. u. s.; some would give the phrase the same sense in Mk. l. c.]; πάμπολυς, Mk. viii. 1 [Rec.]; ἱκανός, Mk. x. 46; Lk. vii. 12; Acts xi. 24, 26; xix. 26; ὁ πλεῖστος ὄχλ. [the most part of the multitude], Mt. xxi. 8; πᾶς ὁ ὄχλ., Mt. xiii. 2; Mk. ii. 13; iv. 1; vii. 14 [Rec.]; ix. 15; xi. 18; Lk. xiii. 17; Acts xxi. 27; ὄχλ. τοσοῦτος, Mt. xv. 33; αἱ μυριάδες τοῦ ὄχλ. Lk. xii. 1; οὐ μετὰ ὄχλου, not having a crowd with me, Acts xxiv. 18; ἄτερ ὄχλου, in the absence of the multitude [(see ἄτερ)], Lk. xxii. 6. plur. οἱ ὄχλοι, very often in Mt. and Lk., as Mt. v. 1; vii. 28; ix. 8, 33, 36; xi. 7; xii. 46; xiii. 34, 36, etc.; Lk. iii. 7, 10; iv. 42; v. 3; viii. 42, 45; ix. 11; xi. 14, etc.; Acts viii. 6; xiii. 45; xiv. 11, 13, 18 sq.; xvii. 8; once in Jn. vii. 12 [where Tdf. the sing.]; in Mk. only vi. 33 Rec.; and without the art. Mk. x. 1; ὄχλοι πολλοί, Mt. iv. 25; viii. 1; xii. 15 [RG]; xiii. 2; xv. 30; xix. 2; Lk. v. 15; xiv. 25; πάντες οἱ ὄχλοι, Mt. xii. 23. **2.** *the multi-*

tude i. e. *the common people*, opp. to the rulers and leading men : Mt. xiv. 5 ; xxi. 26 ; Mk. xii. 12 ; [Jn. vii. 12ᵇ (provided the plur. is retained in the first part of the vs.)] ; with contempt, *the ignorant multitude, the populace*, Jn. vii. 49 ; ἐπισύστασις ὄχλου, a riot, a mob, Acts xxiv. 12 [L T Tr WH ἐπίστασις (q. v.) ὄχ.]. **3.** univ. *a multitude* : with a gen. of the class, as τελωνῶν, Lk. v. 29 ; μαθητῶν, Lk. vi. 17 ; ὀνομάτων (see ὄνομα, 3), Acts i. 15 ; τῶν ἱερέων, Acts vi. 7 ; the plur. ὄχλοι, joined with λαοί and ἔθνη, in Rev. xvii. 15 seems to designate troops of men assembled together without order. (Sept. chiefly for הָמוֹן.)

3794 ὀχύρωμα, -τος, τό, (ὀχυρόω [to make strong, to fortify]) ; **1.** prop. *a castle, stronghold, fortress, fastness*, Sept. for מִבְצָר, etc. ; very often in 1 and 2 Macc. ; Xen. Hellen. 3, 2, 3. **2.** trop. *anything on which one relies* : καθεῖλε τὸ ὀχύρωμα, ἐφ᾽ ᾧ ἐπεποίθεισαν, Prov. xxi. 22 ; ὀχύρωμα ὁσίου φόβος κυρίου, Prov. x. 29 ; in 2 Co. x. 4 of the arguments and reasonings by which a disputant endeavors to fortify his opinion and defend it against his opponent.*

3795 ὀψάριον, -ου, τό, (dimin. fr. ὄψον [cf. Curtius § 630] i. e. whatever is eaten with bread, esp. food boiled or roasted ; hence specifically), *fish* : Jn. vi. 9, 11 ; xxi. 9 sq. 13. (Comic. ap. Athen. 9, c. 35 p. 385 e. ; Lcian., Geop. [cf. Wetstein on Jn. vi. 9] ; see γυναικάριον, fin. [W. 23 (22)].) *

3796 ὀψέ, (apparently fr. ὄπις ; see ὀπίσω, init.), adv. of time, *after a long time, long after, late* ; **a.** esp. *late in the day* (sc. τῆς ἡμέρας, which is often added, as Thuc. 4, 93 ; Xen. Hellen. 2, 1, 23), i. e. *at evening* (Hom., Thuc., Plat., al. ; for ἔρεβ יַעֵת, Gen. xxiv. 11) : Mk. xi. [11 T Tr mrg. WH txt. (cf. Plut. Alex. 16, 1)], 19 ; xiii. 35. **b.** with a gen. [W. § 54, 6], ὀψέ σαββάτων, *the sabbath having just passed, after the sabbath*, i. e: at the early dawn of the first day of the week — (an interpretation absolutely demanded by the added specification τῇ ἐπιφωσκ. κτλ.), Mt. xxviii. 1 cf. Mk. xvi. 1 (ὀψέ τῶν βασιλέως χρόνων, long after the times of the king, Plut. Num. 1 ; ὀψέ μυστηρίων, the mysteries being over, Philostr. vit. Apoll. 4, 18) ; [but an examination of the instances just cited (and others) will show that they fail to sustain the rendering *after* (although it is recognized by Passow, Pape, Schenkl, and other lexicographers) ; ὀψέ seems always to be p a r t i t i v e, denoting *late in* the period specified by the gen. (and consequently still belonging to it), cf. B. § 132, 7 Rem. ; Kühner § 414, 5 c. β. Hence in Mt. l. c. 'late on the sabbath'. Keim iii. p. 552 sq. [Eng. trans. vi. 303 sq.] endeavors to relieve the passage differently [by adopting the Vulg. *vespere*

sabbati, on the evening of the sabbath], but without success. [(Cf. *Keil*, Com. über Matth. ad loc.)] *

ὄψιμος, -ον, (ὀψέ), *late, latter*, (Hom. Il. 2, 325 ; ὀψιμώτατος σπόρος, Xen. oec. 17, 4 sq. ; ἐν τοῖς ὀψίμοις τῶν ὑδάτων, of the time of subsidence of the waters of the Nile, Diod. 1, 10 ; [cf. *Lob.* ad Phryn. p. 51 sq.]) : ὄψ. ὑετός, the *latter* or vernal rain, which falls chiefly in the months of March and April just before the harvest (opp. to the *autumnal* or πρώϊμος [cf. B. D. s. v. Rain]), Jas. v. 7 [but L T Tr WH om. ὑετόν, cod. Sin. and a few other authorities substitute καρπόν] ; Sept. for מַלְקוֹשׁ, Deut. xi. 14 ; Jer. v. 24 ; Hos. vi. 3 ; Joel ii. 23 ; Zech. x. 1.* **3797**

ὄψιος, -α, -ον, (ὀψέ), *late* ; **1.** as an adjective ([Pind.,] Thuc., Dem., Aristot., Theophr., al. ; [*Lob.* ad Phryn. p. 51 sq.]) : ἡ ὥρα, Mk. xi. 11 [but T Tr mrg. WH txt. ὀψέ, q. v.] (ὀψίᾳ ἐν νυκτί, Pind. Isthm. 4, 59). **2.** contrary to the usage of prof. auth. ἡ ὀψία as a subst. (sc. ὥρα [cf. W. 591 sq. (550) ; B. 82 (71)]), *evening* : i. e. either from our three to six o'clock P. M., Mt. viii. 16 ; xiv. 15 ; xxvii. 57 ; Mk. iv. 35 ; or from our six o'clock P. M. to the beginning of night, Mt. xiv. 23 ; xvi. 2 [here T br. WH reject the pass.] ; xx. 8 ; xxvi. 20 ; Mk. i. 32 ; vi. 47 ; xiv. 17 ; xv. 42 ; Jn. vi. 16 ; xx. 19, (hence בֵּין הָעַרְבַּיִם, between the two evenings, Ex. xii. 6 ; xvi. 12 ; xxix. 39 [cf. *Gesenius*, Thesaur. p. 1064 sq. (and addit. et emend. p. 106) ; B. D. s. v. Day]). Besides only in Judith xiii. 1.* **3798**

ὄψις, -εως, ἡ, (ΟΠΤΩ, ὄψομαι [cf. ὀφθαλμός]), fr. Hom. down ; Sept. chiefly for מַרְאֶה ; **1.** *seeing, sight*. **2.** *face, countenance* : Jn. xi. 44 ; Rev. i. 16. **3.** *the outward appearance, look*, [many lexicographers give this neuter and objective sense precedence : κρίνειν κατ᾽ ὄψιν, Jn. vii. 24.* **3799**

ὀψώνιον, -ου, τό, (fr. ὄψον — on which see ὀψάριον, init. — and ὠνέομαι to buy), a later Grk. word (cf. *Sturz*, De dial. Maced. et Alex. p. 187 ; Phryn. ed. *Lob.* p. 418), prop. whatever is bought to be eaten with bread, as fish, flesh, and the like (see ὀψάριον). And as corn, meat, fruits, salt, were given to soldiers instead of pay (Caes. b. g. 1, 23, 1 ; Polyb. 1, 66 sq. ; 3, 13, 8), ὀψώνιον began to signify **1.** univ. *a soldier's pay, allowance*, (Polyb. 6, 39, 12 ; Dion. Hal. antt. 9, 36), more commonly in the plur. [W. 176 (166) ; B. 24 (21)] ὀψώνια, prop. that part of a soldier's support given in place of pay [i. e. rations] and the money in which he is paid (Polyb. 1, 67, 1 ; 6, 39, 15 ; 1 Macc. iii. 28 ; xiv. 32 ; 1 Esdr. iv. 56 ; Joseph. antt. 12, 2, 3) : Lk. iii. 14 ; 1 Co. ix. 7 [cf. W. § 31, 7 d.]. **2.** metaph. *wages* : sing. 2 Co. xi. 8 ; τῆς ἁμαρτίας, the hire that sin pays, Ro. vi. 23.* **3800**

*For 3801 see 3801 St.

Π

3802   **παγιδεύω** : 1 aor. subj. 3d pers. plur. παγιδεύσωσιν; (παγίς, q. v.) ; a word unknown to the Greeks; *to ensnare, entrap* : birds, Eccl. ix. 12 ; metaph., τινὰ ἐν λόγῳ, of the attempt to elicit from one some remark which can be turned into an accusation against him, Mt. xxii. 15. ([τοῖς λόγοις, Prov. vi. 2 Graec. Venet.; cf. also Deut. vii. 25 ; xii. 30 in the same] ; 1 S. xxviii. 9.) *

3803   **παγίς**, -ίδος, ἡ, (fr. πήγνυμι to make fast, 2 aor. ἔπαγον; prop. that which holds fast [cf. Anth. Pal. 6, 5]), Sept. for פַּח, רֶשֶׁת, מוֹקֵשׁ, etc.; *a snare, trap, noose*; **a.** prop. of snares in which birds are entangled and caught, Prov. vi. 5; vii. 23; Ps. xc. (xci.) 3 ; cxxiii. (cxxiv.) 7 ; παγίδας ἱστάναι, Arstph. av. 527; hence ὡς παγίς, as a snare, i. e. *unexpectedly, suddenly*, because birds and beasts are caught unawares, Lk. xxi. 35. **b.** trop. *a snare, i. e. whatever brings peril, loss, destruction* : of a sudden and unexpected deadly peril, Ro. xi. 9 fr. Ps. lxviii. (lxix.) 23; of the allurements and seductions of sin, ἐμπίπτειν εἰς πειρασμὸν κ. παγίδα, 1 Tim. vi. 9 (ἐμπίπτει εἰς παγίδα ἁμαρτωλός, Prov. xii. 13, cf. xxix. 6 ; joined with σκάνδαλον, Sap. xiv. 11) ; τοῦ διαβόλου, the allurements to sin by which the devil holds one bound, 2 Tim. ii. 26 ; 1 Tim. iii. 7. (In Grk. writ. also of the snares of love.) *

3804   **πάθημα**, -τος, τό, (fr. παθεῖν, πάσχω, as μάθημα fr. μαθεῖν), fr. [Soph.,] Hdt. down; **1.** *that which one suffers* or *has suffered*; **a.** externally, *a suffering, misfortune, calamity, evil, affliction* : plur., Ro. viii. 18; 2 Co. i. 6 sq.; Col. i. 24; 2 Tim. iii. 11; Heb. ii. 10; x. 32; 1 Pet. v. 9 ; τὰ εἰς Χριστόν, that should subsequently come unto Christ [W. 193 (182)], 1 Pet. i. 11 ; τοῦ Χριστοῦ, which Christ endured, 1 Pet. v. 1 ; also the afflictions which Christians must undergo in behalf of the same cause for which Christ patiently endured, are called παθήματα τοῦ Χριστοῦ [W. 189 (178) note], 2 Co. i. 5; Phil. iii. 10; 1 Pet. iv. 13. **b.** of an inward state, *an affection, passion*: Gal. v. 24; τῶν ἁμαρτιῶν, that lead to sins, Ro. vii. 5. **2.** i. q. τὸ πάσχειν (see καύχημα, 2), *an enduring, undergoing, suffering*, (so the plur. in Arstph. thesm. 199)ˑ θανάτου, gen. of the obj., Heb. ii. 9. [Syn. cf. πάθος, init.] *

3805   **παθητός**, -ή, -όν, (πάσχω, παθεῖν); **1.** *passible* (Lat. *patibilis*, Cic. de nat. deor. 3, 12, 29), *endued with the capacity of suffering, capable of feeling*; often in Plut., as παθητὸν σῶμα. **2.** *subject to the necessity of suffering, destined to suffer*, (Vulg. *passibilis*) : Acts xxvi. 23 (with the thought here respecting Christ as παθητός compare the similar language of Justin Mart. dial. c. Tr. cc. 36, 39, 52, 68, 76, 89) ; cf. W. 97 (92) ; [B. 42 (37)]; (so in eccl. writ. also, cf. Otto's Justin, Grk. index s. v.;

Christ is said to be παθητός and ἀπαθής in Ignat. ad Eph. 7, 2 ; ad Polyc. 3, 2).*

3806   **πάθος**, -ους, τό, (παθεῖν, πάσχω), fr. Aeschyl. and Hdt. down; i. q. πάθημα (q. v.; [the latter differs fr. πάθος (if at all) only in being the more individualizing and concrete term; cf. *Schmidt*, Syn. ch. 24 § 11]) ; **1.** *whatever befalls one, whether it be sad* or *joyous*; spec. *a calamity, mishap, evil, affliction*. **2.** *a feeling which the mind suffers, an affection of the mind, emotion, passion; passionate desire*; used by the Greeks in either a good or a bad sense (cf. Aristot. eth. Nic. 2, 4 [cf. *Cope*, Introd. to Aristotle's Rhet. p. 133 sqq.; and his note on rhet. 2, 22, 16]). In the N. T. in a bad sense, *depraved passion* : Col. iii. 5 ; πάθη ἀτιμίας, *vile passions*, Ro. i. 26 (see ἀτιμία) ; ἐν πάθει ἐπιθυμίας, [in the passion of lust], gen. of apposit. [W. § 59, 8 a.], 1 Th. iv. 5.*

[Syn. π ά θ ο ς, ἐ π ι θ υ μ ί α : π. presents the passive, ἐπ. the active side of a vice ; ἐπ. is more comprehensive in meaning than π.; ἐπ. is (evil) desire, π. ungovernable desire. Cf. Trench § lxxxvii.; Bp. Lghtft. on Col. iii. 5.]

3807   **παιδαγωγός**, -οῦ, ὁ, (fr. παῖς, and ἀγωγός a leader, escort), fr. Hdt. 8, 75 down ; *a tutor* (Lat. *paedagogus*) i. e. a guide and guardian of boys. Among the Greeks and Romans the name was applied to trustworthy slaves who were charged with the duty of supervising the life and morals of boys belonging to the better class. The boys were not allowed so much as to step out of the house without them before arriving at the age of manhood; cf. *Fischer* s. v. in index i. to Aeschin. dial. Socr.; *Hermann*, Griech. Privatalterthümer, § 34, 15 sqq.; [*Smith*, Dict. of Grk. and Rom. Antiq. s. v.; also *Becker*, Charicles (Eng. trans. 4th ed.), p. 226 sq.]. They are distinguished from οἱ διδάσκαλοι: Xen. de rep. Lac. 3, 2 ; Plat. Lys. p. 208 c.; Diog. Laërt. 3, 92. The name carries with it an idea of severity (as of a stern censor and enforcer of morals) in 1 Co. iv. 15, where the f a t h e r is distinguished from the tutor as one whose discipline is usually milder, and in Gal. iii. 24 sq. where the Mosaic law is likened to a tutor because it arouses the consciousness of sin, and is called παιδαγωγὸς εἰς Χριστόν, i. e. preparing the soul for Christ, because those who have learned by experience with the law that they are not and cannot be commended to God by their w o r k s, welcome the more eagerly the hope of salvation offered them through the death and resurrection of Christ, the Son of God.*

3808   **παιδάριον**, -ου, τό, (dimin. of παῖς, see γυναικάριον), *a little boy, a lad* : Mt. xi. 16 Rec.; Jn. vi. 9. (Arstph., Xen., Plat., sqq.; Sept. very often for נַעַר, also for יֶלֶד;

[παιδάριον of an adult youth, Tob. vi. 2, etc. (cf. 11 sq.)].) [SYN. see παῖς, fin.]*

3809 **παιδεία** (Tdf. -ία; [see I, ι]), -ας, ἡ, (παιδεύω), Sept. for מוּסָר; 1. *the whole training and education of children* (which relates to the cultivation of mind and morals, and employs for this purpose now commands and admonitions, now reproof and punishment): Eph. vi. 4 [cf. W. 388 (363) note]; (in Grk. writ. fr. Aeschyl. on, it includes also the care and training of the body.) [See esp. *Trench*, Syn. § xxxii.; cf. Jowett's Plato, index s. v. Education]. 2. *whatever in adults also cultivates the soul, esp. by correcting mistakes and curbing the passions*; hence **a.** *instruction which aims at the increase of virtue:* 2 Tim. iii. 16. **b.** acc. to bibl. usage *chastisement, chastening,* (of the evils with which God visits men for their amendment): Heb. xii. 5 (Prov. iii. 11), 7 sq. [see ὑπομένω, 2 b.], 11; (Prov. xv. 5, and often in the O. T.; cf. *Grimm*, Exgt. Hdbch. on Sap. p. 51; [cf. (Plat.) defin. παιδεία· δύναμις θεραπευτικὴ ψυχῆς]).*

3810 **παιδευτής**, -οῦ, ὁ, (παιδεύω); 1. *an instructor, preceptor, teacher:* Ro. ii. 20 (Sir. xxxvii. 19; 4 Macc. v. 34; Plat. legg. 7 p. 811 d., etc.; Plut. Lycurg. c. 12, etc.; Diog. Laërt. 7, 7). 2. *a chastiser:* Heb. xii. 9 (Hos. v. 2; Psalt. Sal. 8, 35).*

3811 **παιδεύω**; impf. ἐπαίδευον; 1 aor. ptcp. παιδεύσας; Pass., pres. παιδεύομαι; 1 aor. ἐπαιδεύθην; pf. ptcp. πεπαιδευμένος; (παῖς) Sept for יָסַר; 1. as in class. Grk. prop. *to train children:* τινά with a dat. of the thing in which one is instructed, in pass., σοφίᾳ [W. 227 (213) n.], Acts vii. 22 R G L WH [cf. B. § 134, 6] (γράμμασιν, Joseph. c. Ap. 1, 4 fin.); ἐν σοφίᾳ, ibid. T Tr; τινὰ κατὰ ἀκρίβειαν, in pass., Acts xxii. 3. Pass. *to be instructed* or *taught, to learn:* foll. by an inf., 1 Tim. i. 20; *to cause one to learn:* foll. by ἵνα, Tit. ii. 12. 2. *to chastise*; **a.** *to chastise* or *castigate with words, to correct:* of those who are moulding the character of others by reproof and admonition, 2 Tim. ii. 25 (τινὰ παιδεύειν καὶ ῥυθμίζειν λόγῳ, Ael. v. h. 1, 34). **b.** in bibl. and eccl. use employed of God, *to chasten by the infliction of evils and calamities* [cf. W. § 2, 1 b.]: 1 Co. xi. 32; 2 Co. vi. 9; Heb. xii. 6; Rev. iii. 19, (Prov. xix. 18; xxix. 17; Sap. iii. 5; xi. 10 (9); 2 Macc. vi. 16; x. 4). **c.** *to chastise with blows, to scourge:* of a father punishing a son, Heb. xii. 7, [10]; of a judge ordering one to be scourged, Lk. xxiii. 16, 22, [(Deut. xxii. 18)].*

3812 **παιδιόθεν**, (παιδίον), adv., *from childhood, from a child,* (a later word, for which the earlier writ. used ἐκ παιδός, Xen. Cyr. 5, 1, 2; or ἐκ παιδίου, mem. 2, 2, 8; or ἐκ παιδίων, oec. 3, 10; [cf. W. 26 (25); 463 (431)]): Mk. ix. 21, where L T Tr WH ἐκ παιδιόθεν [cf. Win. § 65,2]. (Synes. de provid. p. 91 b.; Joann. Zonar. 4, 184 a.).*

3813 **παιδίον**, -ου, τό, (dimin. of παῖς), [fr. Hdt. down], Sept. for טַף, בֵּן, נַעַר, etc.; *a young child, a little boy, a little girl*; plur. τὰ παιδία, *infants; children; little ones.* In sing.: univ., of *an infant* just born, Jn. xvi. 21; of *a* (male) *child* recently born, Mt. ii. 8 sq. 11, 13, 14, 20 sq.; Lk. i. 59, 66, 76, 80; ii. 17, 21 [Rec.], 27, 40; Heb. xi. 23;

of a more advanced child, Mt. xviii. 2, 4 sq.; Mk. ix. 36 sq.; [x. 15]; Lk. ix. 47 sq.; [Lk. xviii. 17]; of a mature child, Mk. ix. 24; τινός, the son of some one, Jn. iv. 49; of a girl, Mk. v. 39–41; [vii. 30 L txt. T Tr WH]. In plur. of (partly grown) children: Mt. xi. 16 G L T Tr WH; xiv. 21; xv. 38; xviii. 3; xix. 13 sq.; Mk. vii. 28; x. 13 sqq.; Lk. vii. 32; xviii. 16; [Heb. ii. 14]; τινός, of some one, Lk. xi. 7, cf. Heb. ii. 13. Metaph. παιδία ταῖς φρεσί, *children* (i. e. like children) where the use of the mind is required, 1 Co. xiv. 20; in affectionate address, i. q. Lat. *carissimi* [A.V. *children*], Jn. xxi. 5; 1 Jn. ii. 14 (13), 18; [iii. 7 WH mrg. SYN. see παῖς, fin.]*

3814 **παιδίσκη**, -ης, ἡ, (fem. of παιδίσκος, a young boy or slave; a dimin. of παῖς, see νεανίσκος); 1. *a young girl, damsel,* (Xen., Menand., Polyb., Plut., Lcian.; Sept. Ruth iv. 12). 2. *a maid-servant, a young female slave;* cf. Germ. *Mädchen* [our *maid*] for a young female-servant (Hdt. 1, 93; Lys., Dem., al.): Lk. xii. 45; Acts xvi. 16; opp. to ἡ ἐλευθέρα, Gal. iv. 22 sq. 30 sq.; spec. of the maid-servant who had charge of the door: Mt. xxvi. 69; Mk. xiv. 66, 69; Lk. xxii. 56; Acts xii. 13; ἡ π. ἡ θυρωρός, Jn. xviii. 17; (also in the Sept. of a female *slave,* often for שִׁפְחָה, אָמָה). Cf. *Lob.* ad Phryn. p. 239. [SYN. see παῖς, fin.]*

3815 **παίζω**; fr. Hom. down; prop. *to play like a child*; then univ. *to play, sport, jest; to give way to hilarity,* esp. by joking, singing, dancing; so in 1 Co. x. 7, after Ex. xxxii. 6 where it stands for צָחַק, as in Gen. xxi. 9; xxvi. 8; Judg. xvi. 25; also in the Sept. for שָׂחַק. [COMP.: ἐμ-παίζω.]*

3816 **παῖς**, gen. παιδός, ὁ, ἡ, fr. Hom. down; in the N. T. only in the Gospels and Acts; 1. *a child, boy* or *girl*; Sept. for נַעַר and נַעֲרָה (Gen. xxiv. 28; Deut. xxii. 15, etc.): ὁ παῖς, Mt. xvii. 18; Lk. ii. 43; ix. 42; Acts xx. 12; ἡ παῖς, Lk. viii. 51, 54; plur. *infants, children,* Mt. ii. 16; xxi. 15; ὁ παῖς τινος, the son of one, Jn. iv. 51. 2. (Like the Lat. *puer,* i. q.) *servant, slave,* (Aeschyl. choëph. 652; Arstph. nub. 18, 132; Xen. mem. 3, 13, 6; symp. 1, 11; 2, 23; Plat. Charm. p. 155 a.; Protag. p. 310 c. and often; Diod. 17, 76; al.; so Sept. times without number for עֶבֶד [cf. W. p. 30, no. 3]; cf. the similar use of Germ. *Bursch,* [French *garçon,* Eng. *boy*]): Mt. viii. 6, 8, 13; Lk. vii. 7 cf. 10; xii. 45; xv. 26. *an attendant, servant,* spec. *a king's attendant, minister:* Mt. xiv. 2 (Diod. xvii. 36; hardly so in the earlier Grk. writ.; Gen. xli. 37 sq.; 1 S. xvi. 15–17; xviii. 22, 26; Dan. ii. 7; 1 Macc. i. 6, 8; 1 Esdr. ii. 16; v. 33, 35); hence, in imitation of the Hebr. יְהוָֹה עֶבֶד, παῖς τοῦ θεοῦ is used of a devout worshipper of God, one who fulfils God's will, (Ps. lxviii. (lxix.) 18; cxii. (cxiii.) 1; Sap. ii. 13, etc.); thus, the people of Israel, Lk. i. 54 (Is. xli. 8; xlii. 19; xliv. 1 sq. 21, etc.); David, Lk. i. 69; Acts iv. 25, (Ps. xvii. (xviii.) 1; xxxv. (xxxvi.) 1 [Ald., Compl.], etc.); likewise any upright and godly man whose agency God employs in executing his purposes; thus in the N. T. *Jesus the Messiah:* Mt. xii. 18 (fr. Is. xlii. 1); Acts iii. 13, 26; iv. 27, 30, [cf. Harnack on Barn. ep. 6, 1 and Clem. Rom. 1 Cor. 59, 2]; in the O. T. also Moses, Neh. i. 7 sq.;

the prophets, 1 Esdr. viii. 79 (81); Bar. ii. 20, 24; and others.*

[Syn. παῖς, παιδάριον, παιδίον, παιδίσκη, τέκνον: The grammarian Aristophanes is quoted by Ammonius (s. v. γέρων) as defining thus: παιδίον, τὸ τρεφόμενον ὑπὸ τιθηνοῦ· παιδάριον δέ, τὸ ἤδη περιπατοῦν καὶ τῆς λέξεως ἀντεχόμενον· παιδίσκος δ', ὁ ἐν τῇ ἐχομένῃ ἡλικίᾳ· παῖς δ' ὁ διὰ τῶν ἐγκυκλίων μαθημάτων δυνάμενος ἰέναι. Philo (de mund. opif. § 36) quotes the physician Hippocrates as follows: ἐν ἀνθρώπου φύσει ἑπτά εἰσιν ὧραι κ.τ.λ.· παιδίον μέν ἐστιν ἄχρις ἑπτὰ ἐτῶν, ὀδόντων ἐκβολῆς· παῖς δὲ ἄχρι γονῆς ἐκφύσεως, εἰς τὰ δὶς ἑπτά· μειράκιον δὲ ἄχρι γενείου λαχνώσεως, ἐς τὰ τρὶς ἑπτά, etc. According to Schmidt, παιδίον denotes exclusively a little child; παιδάριον a child up to its first school years; παῖς a child of any age; (παιδίσκος and) παιδίσκη, in which reference to descent quite disappears, cover the years of late childhood and early youth. But usage is untrammelled: from a child is expressed either by ἐκ παιδός (most frequently), or ἐκ παιδίον, or ἐκ (ἀπὸ) παιδαρίου. παῖς and τέκνον denote a child alike as respects descent and age, reference to the latter being more prominent in the former word, to descent in τέκνον; but the period παῖς covers is not sharply defined; and, in classic usage as in modern, youthful designations cleave to the female sex longer than to the male. See Schmidt ch. 69; Höhne in Luthardt's Zeitschrift u. s. w. for 1882, p. 57 sqq.]

3817 **παίω**: 1 aor. ἔπαισα; from Aeschyl. and Hdt. down; Sept. mostly for הִכָּה; *to strike, smite*: with the fists, Mt. xxvi. 68 [cf. ῥαπίζω, 2]; Lk. xxii. 64; with a sword, Mk. xiv. 47; Jn. xviii. 10; *to sting* (to strike or wound with a sting), Rev. ix. 5.*

3818 **Πακατιανή, -ῆς, ἡ,** *Pacatiana* (Phrygia). In the fourth century after Christ, Phrygia was divided into Phrygia Salutaris and Phrygia Pacatiana [later, Capatiana]; Laodicea was the metropolis of the latter: 1 Tim. vi. 22 (in the spurious subscription). [Cf. *Forbiger*, Hndbch. d. alt. Geogr. 2te Ausg. ii. 338, 347 sq.; Bp. Lghtft. on Col., Introd. (esp. pp. 19, 69 sq.).]*

3819 **πάλαι**, adv. of time, fr. Hom. down; **1.** *of old*: Heb. i. 1; (as adj.) *former*, 2 Pet. i. 9. [πάλαι properly designates the past not like πρίν and πρότερον r e l a t i v e l y, i. e. with a reference, more or less explicit, to some other time (whether past, pres., or fut.), but s i m p l y and a b s o l u t e l y.] **2.** *long ago*: Mt. xi. 21; Lk. x. 13; Jude 4; so also of time just past, Mk. xv. 44 [A. V. *any while*] (where L Tr txt. WH txt. ἤδη); 2 Co. xii. 19 L T Tr WH [R. V. *all this time*], (so in Hom. Od. 20, 293; Joseph. antt. 14, 15, 4).*

3820 **παλαιός, -ά, -όν,** (πάλαι, q. v.), fr. Hom. down; **1.** *old, ancient*, (Sept. several times for יָשָׁן and עַתִּיק): οἶνος παλαιός (opp. to νέος), Lk. v. 39 [but WH in br.] (Hom. Od. 2, 340; Sir. ix. 10); διαθήκη, 2 Co. iii. 14; ἐντολή (opp. to καινή), given long since, 1 Jn. ii. 7; ζύμη (opp. to νέον φύρ.), 1 Co. v. 7 sq.; neut. plur. παλαιά (opp. to καινά), old things, Mt. xiii. 52 (which seems to allude to such articles of food as are fit for use only after having been kept some time [al. consider clothing, jewels, etc., as referred to; cf. θησαυρός, 1 c.]; dropping the fig., old and new commandments; cf. Sir. xxiv. 23; Heb. v. 12 sqq.); ὁ παλαιὸς ἡμῶν ἄνθρωπος (opp. to ὁ νέος). *our old*

man, i. e. we, as we were before our mode of thought, feeling, action, had been changed, Ro. vi. 6; Eph. iv. 22; [Col. iii. 9]. **2.** *no longer new, worn by use, the worse for wear, old*, (for בָּלֶה, Josh. ix. 10 (4) sq.): ἱμάτιον, ἀσκός, Mt. ix. 16 sq.; Mk. ii. 21 sq.; Lk. v. 39 sq. [Syn. see ἀρχαῖος, fin.]*

3821 **παλαιότης, -ητος, ἡ,** (παλαιός), *oldness*: γράμματος, the old state of life controlled by 'the letter' of the law, Ro. vii. 6; see καινότης, and γράμμα, 2 c. ([Eur.], Plat., Aeschin., Dio Cass. 72, 8.)*

3822 **παλαιόω, -ῶ**: pf. πεπαλαίωκα; Pass., pres. ptcp. παλαιούμενος; fut. παλαιωθήσομαι; (παλαιός); **a.** *to make ancient* or *old*, Sept. for בָּלָה; pass. *to become old, to be worn out*, Sept. for בָּלָה, עָתַק: of things worn out by time and use, as βαλάντιον, Lk. xii. 33; ἱμάτιον, Heb. i. 11 (Ps. ci. (cii.) 27; Deut. xxix. 5; Josh. ix. 19 (13); Neh. ix. 21; Is. l. 9; li. 6; Sir. xiv. 17). pass. τὸ παλαιούμενον, that which is becoming old, Heb. viii. 13 (Plat. symp. p. 208 b.; Tim. p. 59 c.). **b.** *to declare a thing to be old and so about to be abrogated*: Heb. viii. 13 [see γηράσκω, fin.].*

3823 **πάλη, -ης, ἡ,** (fr. πάλλω to vibrate, shake), fr. Hom. down, *wrestling* (a contest between two in which each endeavors to throw the other, and which is decided when the victor is able θλίβειν καὶ κατέχειν his prostrate antagonist, i. e. hold him down with his hand upon his neck; cf. Plat. legg. 7 p. 796; Aristot. rhet. 1, 5, 14 p. 1361b, 24; Heliod. aethiop. 10, 31; [cf. *Krause*, Gymn. u. Agon. d. Griech. i. 1 p. 400 sqq.; Guhl and Koner p. 219 sq.; Dict. of Antiq. s. v. *lucta*]); the term is transferred to the struggle of Christians with the powers of evil: Eph. vi. 12.*

3824 **παλιγγενεσία** (T WH παλινγεν. [cf. *Tdf.* Proleg. p. 77 bot.]), **-ας, ἡ,** (πάλιν and γένεσις), prop. *new birth, reproduction, renewal, re-creation*, (see Halm on Cic. pro Sest. § 140), Vulg. and Augustine *regeneratio*; hence, *moral renovation, regeneration, the production of a new life consecrated to God, a radical change of mind for the better*, (effected in baptism [cf. reff. s. v. βάπτισμα, 3]): Tit. iii. 5 [cf. the Comm. ad loc. (esp. Holtzmann, where see p. 172 sq. for reff.); *Weiss*, Bibl. Theol. esp. §§ 84, 108; cf. *Suicer*, Thes. s. v.]. Commonly, however, the word denotes *the restoration of a thing to its pristine state, its renovation*, as the renewal or restoration of life after death, Philo leg. ad Gaium § 41; de cherub. § 32; [de poster. Cain. § 36]; Long. past. 3, 4 (2) (παλιγγ. ἐκ θανάτου); Lcian. encom. muscae 7; Schol. ad Soph. Elec. 62 (Πυθαγόρας περὶ παλιγγενεσίας ἐτερατεύετο; Plut. mor. p. 998 c. [i. e. de esu carn. ii. 4, 4] (ὅτι χρῶνται κοινοῖς αἱ ψυχαὶ σώμασιν ἐν ταῖς παλιγγενεσίαις [cf. ibid. i. 7, 5; also de Is. et Osir. 72; de Ei ap. Delph. 9; etc.]); the renovation of the earth after the deluge, Philo de vita Moys. ii. § 12; Clem. Rom. 1 Cor. 9, 4; the renewal of the world to take place after its destruction by fire, as the Stoics taught, Philo [de incorrupt. mundi §§ 3, 14, 17]; de mund. § 15; Antonin. 11, 1 [(cf. Gataker ad loc.)]; *Zeller*, Philos. d. Griech. iii. p. 138]; *that signal and glorious change of all things* (in heaven and earth) for the better, that restoration of the primal and perfect condition of things which existed before the fall of our first parents, which the Jews looked for in connection with the advent of the Messiah, and which the primitive Christians expected in connection with the visible return of Jesus from heaven: Mt. xix. 28 (where the Syriac correctly ܚ݁ܕ݂ܬ݂ܳܐ ܥܳܠܡܳܐ, in the new age or world); cf. Bertholdt, Christologia Judaeorum, p. 214 sq.; Gfrörer, Jahrhundert des Heils, ii. p. 272 sqq.; [Schürer, Neutest. Zeitgesch. § 29, 9; Weber, Altsynagog. Paläst. Theol. § 89]. (Further, the word is used of Cicero's restoration to rank and fortune on his recall from exile, Cic. ad Att. 6, 6; of the restoration of the Jewish nation after the exile, παλ. πατρίδος, Joseph. antt. 11, 3, 9; of the recovery of knowledge by recollection, παλιγγ. τῆς γνώσεώς ἐστιν ἡ ἀνάμνησις, Olympiodor. quoted by Cousin in the Journal des Savans for 1834, p. 488.) [Cf. Trench § xviii.; Cremer 3te Aufl. s. v.]*

3825 πάλιν, adv., fr. Hom. down; **1.** anew, again, [but the primary meaning seems to be back; cf. (among others) Ellendt, Lex. Soph. s. v. ii. p. 485]; **a.** joined to verbs of all sorts, it denotes renewal or repetition of the action: Mt. iv. 8; xx. 5; xxi. 36; xxii. 1, 4; Mk. ii. 13; iii. 20; Lk. xxiii. 20; Jn. i. 35; iv. 13; viii. 2, 8, 12, 21; ix. 15, 17; x. 19; Acts xvii. 32; xxvii. 28; Ro. xi. 23; 1 Co. vii. 5; 2 Co. xi. 16; Gal. i. 9; ii. 18; iv. 19; 2 Pet. ii. 20; Phil. ii. 28; iv. 4; Heb. i. 6 (where πάλιν is tacitly opposed to the time when God first brought his Son into the world, i. e. to the time of Jesus' former life on earth); Heb. v. 12; vi. 1, 6; Jas. v. 18; Rev. x. 8, 11; πάλιν μικρόν sc. ἔσται, Jn. xvi. 16 sq. 19; εἰς τὸ πάλιν, again (cf. Germ. zum wiederholten Male; [see εἰς, A. II. 2 fin.]), 2 Co. xiii. 2; with verbs of going, coming, departing, returning, where again combines with the notion of back; thus with ἄγωμεν, Jn. xi. 7; ἀναχωρεῖν, Jn. vi. 15 [where Tdf. φεύγει and Grsb. om. πάλιν], (cf. ib. 3); ἀπέρχεσθαι, Jn. iv. 3; x. 40; xx. 10; εἰσέρχεσθαι, Mk. ii. 1; iii. 1; Jn. xviii. 33; xix. 9; ἐξέρχεσθαι, Mk. vii. 31; ἔρχεσθαι, Jn. iv. 46; xiv. 3; 2 Co. i. 16; xii. 21 [cf. W. 554 (515) n.; B. § 145, 2 a.]; ὑπάγειν, Jn. xi. 8; ἀνακάμπτειν, Acts xviii. 21; διαπερᾶν, Mk. v. 21; ὑποστρέφειν, Gal. i. 17; ἡ ἐμὴ παρουσία πάλιν πρὸς ὑμᾶς, my presence with you again, i. e. my return to you, Phil. i. 26 [cf. B. § 125, 2]; also with verbs of taking, Jn. x. 17 sq.; Acts x. 16 Rec.; xi. 10. **b.** with other parts of the sentence: πάλιν εἰς φόβον, Ro. viii. 15; πάλιν ἐν λύπῃ, 2 Co. ii. 1. **c.** πάλιν is explained by the addition of more precise specifications of time [cf. W. 604 (562)]: πάλιν ἐκ τρίτου, Mt. xxvi. 44 [L Tr mrg. br. ἐκ τρ.]; ἐκ δευτέρου, Mt. xxvi. 42; Acts x. 15; πάλιν δεύτερον, Jn. iv. 54; xxi. 16; πάλιν ἄνωθεν, again, anew, [R. V. back again (yet cf. Mey. ad loc.)], Gal. iv. 9 (Sap. xix. 6; πάλιν ἐξ ἀρχῆς, Arstph. Plut. 866; Plat. Eut. p. 11 b. and 15 c.; Isoc. areiop. 6 p. 338 [p. 220 ed. Lange]; cf. W. u. s.). **2.** again, i. e. further, moreover, (where the subject remains the same and a repetition of the action or condition is indicated): Mt. v. 33 (πάλιν ἠκούσατε); xiii. 44 (where T Tr WH om. L br. πάλιν), 45, 47; xix.

24; Lk. xiii. 20; Jn. x. 7 [not Tdf.]; esp. where to O. T. passages already quoted others are added: Mt. iv. 7; Jn. xii. 39; xix. 37; Ro. xv. 10–12; 1 Co. iii. 20; Heb. i. 5; ii. 13; iv. 5; x. 30; Clem. Rom. 1 Cor. 15, 3 sq. and often in Philo; cf. Bleek, Br. a. d. Hebr. ii. 1 p. 108. **3.** in turn, on the other hand: Lk. vi. 43 T WH L br. Tr br.; 1 Co. xii. 21; 2 Co. x. 7; 1 Jn. ii. 8, (Sap. xiii. 8; xvi. 23; 2 Macc. xv. 39; see exx. fr. prof. auth. in Pape s. v. 2; Passow s. v. 3; [Ellendt u. s. (ad init.); L. and S. s. v. III.; but many (e. g. Fritzsche and Meyer on Mt. iii. 7) refuse to recognize this sense in the N. T.]). John uses πάλιν in his Gospel far more freq. than the other N. T. writ., in his Epp. but once; Luke two or three times; the author of the Rev. twice.

παλινγενεσία, see παλιγγενεσία.   see 3824

παμπληθεί (T WH πανπλ. [cf. WH. App. p. 150]), adv., (fr. the adj. παμπληθής, which is fr. πᾶς and πλῆθος), with the whole multitude, all together, one and all: Lk. xxiii. 18 (Dio Cass. 75, 9, 1). [Cf. W. § 16, 4 B. a.]*   3826

πάμπολυς, παμπόλλη, πάμπολυ, (πᾶς and πολύς), very great: Mk. viii. 1 Rec. [where L T Tr WH πάλιν πολλοῦ]. (Arstph., Plat., Plut., [al.].) *   3827

Παμφυλία, -ας, ἡ, Pamphylia, a province of Asia Minor, bounded on the E. by Cilicia, on the W. by Lycia and Phrygia Minor, on the N. by Galatia and Cappadocia, and on the S. by the Mediterranean Sea (there called the Sea [or Gulf] of Pamphylia [now of Adalia]): Acts ii. 10; xiii. 13; xiv. 24; xv. 38; xxvii. 5. [Conybeare and Howson, St. Paul, ch. viii.; Lewin, St. Paul, index s. v.; Dict. of Geogr. s. v.] *   3828

παν-δοκίον, see πανδοχεῖον.   see 3829
πανδοκεύς, see πανδοχεύς.   see 3830
παν-δοχεῖον (-δοκίον, Tdf. [cf. his note on Lk. x. 34, and Hesych. s. v.]), -ου, τό, (fr. πανδοχεύς, q. v.), an inn, a public house for the reception of strangers (modern caravansary, khan, manzil): Lk. x. 34. (Polyb. 2, 15, 5; Plut. de sanit. tuenda c. 14; Epict. enchirid. c. 11; but the Attic form πανδοκεῖον is used by Arstph. ran. 550; Theophr. char. 11 (20), 2; Plut. Crass. 22; Palaeph. fab. 46; Ael. v. h. 14, 14; Polyaen. 4, 2, 3; Epict. diss. 2, 23, 36 sqq.; 4, 5, 15; cf. Lob. ad Phryn. p. 307.) *   3829

παν-δοχεύς, -έως, ὁ, (πᾶς and δέχομαι [hence lit. 'one who receives all comers']), for the earlier and more elegant πανδοκεύς (so Tdf.; [cf. W. 25 note]), an inn-keeper, host: Lk. x. 35. (Polyb. 2, 15, 6; Plut. de sanit. tuenda c. 14.) *   3830

πανήγυρις, -εως, ἡ, (fr. πᾶς and ἄγυρις fr. ἀγείρω), fr. Hdt. and Pind. down; **a.** a festal gathering of the whole people to celebrate public games or other solemnities. **b.** univ. a public festal assembly; so in Heb. xii. 22 (23) where the word is to be connected with ἀγγέλων [so G L Tr (Tdf.); yet see the Comm.]. (Sept. for מוֹעֵד, Ezek. xlvi. 11; Hos. ii. 11 (13); ix. 5; עֲצָרָה, Am. v. 21.) [Cf. Trench § i.]*   3831

πανοικί [so R G L Tr] and **πανοικεί** (T [WH; see WH. App. p. 154 and cf. εἰ, ι]), on this difference in writing cf. W. 43 sq.; B. 73 (64), (πᾶς and οἶκος; a form rejected by the Atticists for πανοικία, πανοικεσία, πανοικησία, [cf. W.   3832

26 (25) ; Lob. ad Phryn. p. 514 sq.]), with all (his) house, with (his) whole family : Acts xvi. 34. (Plat. Eryx. p. 392 c.; Aeschin. dial. 2, 1 ; Philo de Joseph. § 42; de vita Moys. i. 2 ; Joseph. antt. 4, 8, 42 ; 5, 1, 2 ; 3 Macc. iii. 27 where Fritzsche -κία.) *

3833   πανοπλία, -ας, ἡ, (fr. πάνοπλος wholly armed, in full armor ; and this fr. πᾶς and ὅπλον), full armor, complete armor, (i. e. a shield, sword, lance, helmet, greaves, and breastplate, [cf. Polyb. 6, 23, 2 sqq.]) : Lk. xi. 22 ; θεοῦ, which God supplies [W. 189 (178)], Eph. vi. 11, 13, where the spiritual helps needed for overcoming the temptations of the devil are so called. (Hdt., Plat., Isocr., Polyb., Joseph., Sept. ; trop. of the various appliances at God's command for punishing, Sap. v. 18.) *

3834   πανουργία, -ας, ἡ, (πανοῦργος, q. v.), craftiness, cunning : Lk. xx. 23 ; 2 Co. iv. 2 ; xi. 3 ; Eph. iv. 14; contextually i. q. a specious or false wisdom, 1 Co. iii. 19. (Aeschyl., Soph., Arstph., Xen., Plat., Lcian., Ael., al. ; πᾶσά τε ἐπιστήμη χωριζομένη δικαιοσύνης καὶ τῆς ἄλλης ἀρετῆς πανουργία οὐ σοφία φαίνεται, Plat. Menex. p. 247 a. for עָרְמָה in a good sense, prudence, skill, in undertaking and carrying on affairs, Prov. i. 4 ; viii. 5 ; Sir. xxxi. (xxxiv. 11) 10.) *

3835   πανοῦργος, -ον, (πᾶς and ΕΡΓΩ i. q. ἐργάζομαι ; on the accent, see κακοῦργος), Sept. for עָרוּם ; skilful, clever, i. e.   **1.** in a good sense, fit to undertake and accomplish anything, dexterous ; wise, sagacious, skilful, (Aristot., Polyb., Plut., al. ; Sept. Prov. xiii. 1 ; xxviii. 2). But far more freq.   **2.** in a bad sense, crafty, cunning, knavish, treacherous, deceitful, (Tragg., Arstph., Plat., Plut., al.; Sept.; Sir. vi. 32 (31) [but here in a good sense] ; xxi. 12, etc.) : 2 Co. xii. 16.*

see 3826 —— πανπληθεί, see παμπληθεί.

see 3837 —— πανταχῆ or πανταχῇ (L Tr WH ; see εἰκῆ), adv., everywhere : Acts xxi. 28 L T Tr WH, for πανταχοῦ, — a variation often met with also in the Mss. of prof. auth. [From Hdt. down ; cf. Meisterhans, Gr. d. Att. Inschr. p. 64.] *

3836   πανταχόθεν, adv., from all sides, from every quarter : Mk. i. 45 Rec. [Hdt., Thuc., Plat., al.] *

3837   πανταχοῦ, adv., everywhere : Mk. i. 28 T WH Tr br. ; xvi. 20 ; Lk. ix. 6 ; Acts xvii. 30 ; xxi. 28 Rec. ; xxiv. 3 ; xxviii. 22 ; 1 Co. iv. 17. [Soph., Thuc., Plat., al.] *

3838   παντελής, -ές, (πᾶς and τέλος), all-complete, perfect, (Aeschyl., Soph., Plat., Diod., Plut., al. ; 3 Macc. vii. 16) ; εἰς τὸ παντελές (prop. unto completeness [W. § 51, 1 c.]) completely, perfectly, utterly : Lk. xiii. 11 ; Heb. vii. 25, (Philo leg. ad Gaium 21 ; Joseph. antt. 1, 18, 5 ; 3, 11, 3 and 12, 1 ; 6, 2, 3 ; 7, 13, 3 ; Ael. v. h. 7, 2 ; n. a. 17, 27).*

3839   πάντη (R G L Tr WH πάντῃ, see reff. s. v. εἰκῆ), (πᾶς), adv., fr. Hom. down, everywhere ; wholly, in all respects, in every way : Acts xxiv. 3.*

3840   πάντοθεν, (πᾶς), adv., fr. Hom. down, from all sides, from every quarter : Mk. i. 45 L T WH Tr [but the last named here παντόθεν ; cf. Chandler § 842] ; Lk. xix. 43 ; Jn. xviii. 20 Rec.bez elz ; Heb. ix. 4.*

3841   παντοκράτωρ, -ορος, ὁ, (πᾶς and κρατέω), he who holds sway over all things ; the ruler of all ; almighty : of God,

2 Co. vi. 18 (fr. Jer. xxxviii. (xxxi.) 35) ; Rev. i. 8 ; iv. 8 ; xi. 17 ; xv. 3 ; xvi. 7, 14 ; xix. 6, 15 ; xxi. 22. (Sept. for צְבָאוֹת in the phrase יְהֹוָה צְבָאוֹת or אֱלֹהֵי צְבָאוֹת Jehovah or God of hosts ; also for שַׁדַּי ; Sap. vii. 25 ; Sir. xlii. 17 ; l. 14 ; often in Judith and 2 and 3 Macc. ; Anthol. Gr. iv. p. 151 ed. Jacobs ; Inscrr. ; eccles. writ. [e. g. Teaching etc. 10, 3 ; cf. Harnack's notes on Clem. Rom. 1 Cor. init. and the Symb. Rom. (Patr. apost. opp. i. 2 p. 134)].) *

3842   πάντοτε, (πᾶς), adv., (for which the Atticists tell us that the better Grk. writ. used ἑκάστοτε ; cf. Sturz, De dial. Maced. et Alex. p. 187 sq. ; [W. 26 (25)]), at all times, always, ever : Mt. xxvi. 11 ; Mk. xiv. 7 ; Lk. xv. 31 ; xviii. 1 ; Jn. vi. 34 ; vii. 6 ; viii. 29 ; xi. 42 ; xii. 8 ; xviii. 20a [20b Rec.n] ; Ro. i. 10 (9) ; 1 Co. i. 4 ; xv. 58 ; 2 Co. ii. 14 ; iv. 10 ; v. 6 ; [vii. 14 L mrg.] ; ix. 8 ; Gal. iv. 18 ; Eph. v. 20; Phil. i. 4, 20; [iv. 4]; Col. i. 3 ; iv. 6, [12] ; 1 Th. i. 2 ; ii. 16 ; [iii. 6] ; iv. 17 ; [v. 15, 16] ; 2 Th. i. 3, 11 ; ii. 13 ; 2 Tim. iii. 7 ; Philem. 4 ; Heb. vii. 25. (Sap. xi. 22 (21) ; xix. 17 (18) ; Joseph., Dion. Hal., Plut., Hdian. 3, 9, 13 [(7 ed. Bekk.)] ; Artem. oneir. 4, 20 ; Athen., Diog. Laërt.) *

3843   πάντως, (from πᾶς), adv., altogether (Latin omnino), i. e.   **a.** in any and every way, by all means : 1 Co. ix. 22 (so fr. Hdt. down).   **b.** doubtless, surely, certainly : Lk. iv. 23 ; Acts xviii. 21 [Rec.] ; xxi. 22 ; xxviii. 4 ; 1 Co. ix. 10, (Tob. xiv. 8 ; Ael. v. h. 1, 32 ; by Plato in answers [cf. our colloquial by all means]).   **c.** with the negative οὐ,   **α.** where οὐ is postpositive, in no wise, not at all : 1 Co. xvi. 12 (often so as far back as Hom.).   **β.** when the negative precedes, the force of the adverb is restricted : οὐ πάντως, not entirely, not altogether, 1 Co. v. 10 ; not in all things, not in all respects, Ro. iii. 9 ; (rarely i. q. πάντως οὐ, as in Ep. ad Diogn. 9 ' God οὐ πάντως ἐφηδόμενος τοῖς ἁμαρτήμασιν ἡμῶν.' Likewise οὐδὲν πάντως in Hdt. 5, 34. But in Theogn. 305 ed. Bekk. οἱ κακοὶ οὐ πάντως κακοὶ ἐκ γαστρὸς γεγόνασι κτλ. is best translated not wholly, not entirely. Cf. W. 554 (515) sq. ; B. 389 (334) sq. [on whose interpretation of Ro. l. c., although it is that now generally adopted, see Weiss in Meyer 6te Aufl.]).*

3844   παρά, [it neglects elision before prop. names beginning with a vowel, and (at least in Tdf.'s text) before some other words ; see Tdf. Proleg. p. 95, cf. W. § 5, 1 a.; B. 10], a preposition indicating close proximity, with various modifications corresponding to the various cases with which it is joined ; cf. Viger. ed. Herm. p. 643 sqq. ; Matthiae § 588; Bnhdy. p. 255 sqq.; Kühner § 440; Krüger § 68, 34–36. It is joined

I. with the GENITIVE ; and as in Grk. prose writ. always with the gen. of a person, to denote that a thing proceeds from the side or the vicinity of one, or from one's sphere of power, or from one's wealth or store, Lat. a, ab ; Germ. von . . . her, von neben ; French de chez ; [Eng. from beside, from] ; Sept. for מִלִּפְנֵי, מִיַּד, מֵאֵצֶל (1 S. xvii. 30) ; cf. W. 364 (342) sq.   **a.** properly, with a suggestion of union of place or of residence, after verbs of coming, departing, setting out, etc. (cf. French *venir, partir de chez quelqu'un*) : Mk. xiv. 43 ; Lk. viii. 49 [here Lchm. ἀπό] ; Jn. xv. 26 ; xvi. 27 ; xvii. 8 ; [παρ' ἧς ἐκβεβλήκει ἑπτὰ δαιμόνια, Mk. xvi. 9 L Tr txt. WH] ; εἶναι παρὰ θεοῦ, of Christ, *to be* sent *from God*, Jn. ix. 16, 33 ; *to be* sprung *from God* (by the nature of the λόγος), vi. 46 ; vii. 29 (where for the sake of the context κἀκεῖνός με ἀπέστειλεν [Tdf. ἀπέσταλκεν] is added) ; μονογενοῦς παρὰ πατρός sc. ὄντος, Jn. i. 14 ; ἐστί τι παρά τινος, *is* given *by one*, Jn. xvii. 7 [cf. d. below]. **b.** joined to passive verbs, παρά makes one the author, the giver, etc. [W. 365 (343) ; B. § 134, 1] ; so after ἀποστέλλεσθαι, Jn. i. 6 (the expression originates in the fact that one who is sent is conceived of as having been at the time with the sender, so that he could be selected or commissioned from among a number and then sent off) ; γίνεσθαι, Mt. xxi. 42 ; Mk. xii. 11 (παρὰ κυρίου, from the Lord, by divine agency or by the power at God's command) ; akin to which is οὐκ ἀδυνατήσει παρὰ τοῦ θεοῦ πᾶν ῥῆμα, Lk. i. 37 L mrg. T Tr WH [see ἀδυνατέω, b.] ; λαλεῖσθαι, Lk. i. 45 (not ὑπό, because God had not spoken in person, but by an angel) ; κατηγορεῖσθαι, Acts xxii. 30 Rec. (not ὑπό [yet so L T Tr WH] because Paul had not yet been formally accused by the Jews, but the tribune inferred from the tumult that the Jews accused him of some crime). **c.** after verbs of seeking, asking, taking, receiving, buying, [cf. W. 370 (347) n. ; B. § 147, 5 ; yet see Bp. Lghtft. on Gal. i. 12] ; as, αἰτῶ, αἰτοῦμαι, Mt. xx. 20 (where L Tr txt. WH txt. ἀπ' αὐτοῦ) ; Jn. iv. 9 ; Acts iii. 2 ; ix. 2 ; Jas. i. 5 ; 1 Jn. v. 15 (where L T Tr WH ἀπ' αὐτοῦ) ; ζητῶ, Mk. viii. 11 ; Lk. xi. 16 ; xii. 48 ; λαμβάνω, Mk. xii. 2 ; Jn. v. 34, 41, 44 ; x. 18 ; Acts ii. 33 ; iii. 5 ; xvii. 9 ; xx. 24 ; xxvi. 10 ; Jas. i. 7 ; 2 Pet. i. 17 ; 1 Jn. iii. 22 (L T Tr WH ἀπ' αὐτοῦ) ; 2 Jn. 4 ; Rev. ii. 28 (27) ; παραλαμβάνω, Gal. i. 12 ; 1 Th. ii. 13 ; iv. 1 ; ἀπολαμβάνω, Lk. vi. 34 R G L Tr mrg. ; κομίζομαι, Eph. vi. 8 ; γίνεταί μοί τι, Mt. xviii. 19 ; δέχομαι, Acts xxii. 5 ; Phil. iv. 18 ; ἔχω, Acts ix. 14 ; ὠνέομαι, Rev. iii. 18 ; ἀγοράζομαι, Rev. iii. 18 ; also after ἄρτον φαγεῖν (sc. δοθέντα), 2 Th. iii. 8 ; εὑρεῖν ἔλεος, 2 Tim. i. 18 ; ἔσται χάρις, 2 Jn. 3. after verbs of hearing, ascertaining, learning, making inquiry ; as, ἀκούω τι, Jn. i. 40 (41) ; vi. 45 sq. ; vii. 51 ; viii. 26, 40 ; xv. 15 ; Acts x. 22 ; xxviii. 22 ; 2 Tim. i. 13 ; ii. 2 ; πυνθάνομαι, Mt. ii. 4 ; Jn. iv. 52 ; ἀκριβῶ, Mt. ii. 16 ; ἐπιγινώσκω, Acts xxiv. 8 ; μανθάνω, 2 Tim. iii. 14. **d.** in phrases in which things are said εἶναι or ἐξέρχεσθαι *from one* : Lk. ii. 1 ; vi. 19 ; Jn. xvii. 7 [see a. above]. **e.** ὁ, ἡ, τὸ παρά τινος [see ὁ, II. 8 ; cf. B. § 125, 9 ; W. § 18, 3] ; **a.** absol. : οἱ παρ' αὐτοῦ, those of one's family, i. e. *his kinsmen, relations*, Mk. iii. 21 (Sus. 33 ; *one's* descendants [yet here Vulg. *qui cum eo erant*], 1 Macc. xiii. 52 ; [Joseph. antt. 1, 10, 5]) ; cf. Fritzsche ad loc. p. 101 ; [*Field*, Otium Norv. pars iii. ad loc.] ; τὰ παρά τινος, what one has *beside* him, and so at his service, i. e. *one's means, resources*, Mk. v. 26 ; τὰ παρά τινων, sc. ὄντα, i. e. δοθέντα, Lk. x. 7 ; Phil. iv. 18 ; [cf. W. 366 (343) ; Joseph. antt. 8, 6, 6 ; b. j. 2, 8, 4 ; etc.]. **β.** where it refers to a preceding noun : ἡ ἐξουσία ἡ παρά τινος, sc. received,

Acts xxvi. 12 [R G] ; ἐπικουρίας τῆς παρὰ (L T Tr WH ἀπὸ) τοῦ θεοῦ, Acts xxvi. 22 (ἡ παρά τινος εὔνοια, Xen. mem. 2, 2, 12) ; ἡ παρ' ἐμοῦ διαθήκη, of which I am the author, Ro. xi. 27 [cf. W. 193 (182)].

II. with the Dative, παρά indicates that something is or is done either in the immediate vicinity of some one, or (metaph.) in his mind, *near by, beside, in the power of, in the presence of, with*, Sept. for אֵצֶל (1 K. xx. (xxi.) 1 ; Prov. viii. 30), יָד (Gen. xliv. 16 sq. ; Num. xxxi. 49), בְּעֵינֵי (see b. below) ; cf. W. § 48, d. p. 394 sq. (369) ; [B. 339 (291 sq.)]. **a.** *near, by* : εἱστήκεισαν παρὰ τῷ σταυρῷ, Jn. xix. 25 (this is the only pass. in the N. T. where παρά is joined with a dat. of the thing, in all others with a dat. of the person). after a verb of motion, to indicate the rest which follows the motion [cf. B. 339 (292)], ἔστησεν αὐτὸ παρ' ἑαυτῷ, Lk. ix. 47. **b.** *with*, i. e. *in one's house* ; *in one's town* ; *in one's society* : ξενίζεσθαι [q. v.], Acts x. 6 ; xxi. 16 ; μένειν, of guests or lodgers, Jn. i. 39 (40) ; iv. 40 ; xiv. 17, 25 ; Acts ix. 43 ; xviii. 3, 20 [R G] ; xxi. 7 sq. ; ἐπιμένειν, Acts xxviii. 14 L T Tr WH ; καταλύειν, Lk. xix. 7 (Dem. de corona § 82 [cf. B. 339 (292)]) ; ἀριστᾶν, Lk. xi. 37 ; ἀπολείπειν τι, 2 Tim. iv. 13 ; παρὰ τῷ θεῷ, dwelling with God, Jn. viii. 38 ; i. q. in heaven, Jn. xvii. 5 ; μισθὸν ἔχειν, to have a reward laid up with God in heaven, Mt. vi. 1 ; εὑρεῖν χάριν (there where God is, i. e. God's favor [cf. W. 365 (343)]), Lk. i. 30 ; a pers. is also said to have χάρις παρά one with whom he is acceptable, Lk. ii. 52 ; τοῦτο χάρις παρὰ θεῷ, this is acceptable with God, pleasing to him, 1 Pet. ii. 20 (for בְּעֵינֵי, Ex. xxxiii. 12, 16 ; Num. xi. 15) ; παρὰ θεῷ, in fellowship with God (of those who have embraced the Christian religion and turned to God from whom they had before been estranged), 1 Co. vii. 24 ; παρὰ κυρίῳ (in heaven), before the Lord as judge, 2 Pet. ii. 11 [G L om. and Tr WH br. the phrase] ; παρ' ὑμῖν, in your city, in your church, Col. iv. 16 ; w. a dat. plur. i. q. *among*, Mt. xxii. 25 ; xxviii. 15 ; Rev. ii. 13 ; παρ' ἑαυτῷ, *at his home*, 1 Co. xvi. 2. **c.** παρ' (L Tr WH txt. ἐν) ἑαυτῷ, *with one's self* i. e. *in one's own mind*, διαλογίζεσθαι, Mt. xxi. 25. **d.** a thing is said to be or not to be παρά τινι, *with one*, **a.** which belongs to his nature and character, or is in accordance with his practice or the reverse ; as, μὴ ἀδικία παρὰ τῷ θεῷ ; Ro. ix. 14 ; add, Ro. ii. 11 ; 2 Co. i. 17 ; Eph. vi. 9 ; Jas. i. 17. **β.** which is or is not within one's power : Mt. xix. 26 ; Mk. x. 27 ; Lk. xviii. 27, cf. i. 37 R G L txt. **e.** παρά τινι, *with one* i. e. *in his judgment, he being judge*, (so in Hdt. and the Attic writ. ; cf. Passow s. v. II. 2, vol. ii. p. 667 ; [L. and S. s. v. B. II. 3]) : παρὰ τῷ θεῷ, Ro. ii. 13 ; 1 Co. iii. 19 ; Gal. iii. 11 ; 2 Th. i. 6 ; Jas. i. 27 ; 1 Pet. ii. 4 ; 2 Pet. iii. 8 [π. κυρίῳ] ; φρόνιμον εἶναι παρ' ἑαυτῷ, [A. V. in one's own conceit], Ro. xi. 25 (where Tr txt. WH txt. ἐν) ; xii. 16.

III. with an Accusative ; Sept. for עַל יַד, אֵצֶל, בְּעֵבֶר (Josh. vii. 7 ; xxii. 7) ; cf. W. § 49 g. p. 403 (377) sq. ; [B. 339 (292)] ; **1.** prop. of place, *at, by, near, by the side of, beside, along* ; so with verbs of motion : περιπατεῖν παρὰ τὴν θάλασσαν (Plat. Gorg. p. 511 e.), Mt.

iv. 18; Mk. i. 16 [here L T Tr WH παράγω]; πίπτειν, Mt. xiii. 4; Mk. iv. 4; Lk. viii. 5, 41; xvii. 16; Acts v. 10 (where L T Tr WH πρός); σπαρῆναι, Mt. xiii. 19; ῥίπτειν, Mt. xv. 30; τιθέναι, Acts iv. 35, 37 [here Tdf. πρός]; v. 2; ἀποτιθέναι, Acts vii. 58; ἔρχεσθαι, ἐξέρχεσθαι, Mt. xv. 29; Mk. ii. 13 [here Tdf. εἰς]; Acts xvi. 13; οἱ παρὰ τὴν ὁδόν, sc. πεσόντες, Mk. iv. 15, cf. 4; Lk. viii. 12, cf. 5. with verbs of r e s t: καθῆσθαι, Mt. xiii. 1; xx. 30; Lk. viii. 35; with εἶναι, Mk. v. 21; Acts x. 6. with verbs denoting the business in which one is engaged, as παιδεύειν in pass., Acts xxii. 3 [so G L T Tr WH punctuate]; διδάσκειν, Mk. iv. 1. without a verb, in specifications of place, Acts x. 32; Heb. xi. 12. **2.** beside, beyond, i. e. metaph. **a.** i. q. contrary to: παρὰ τὴν διδαχήν, Ro. xvi. 17; παρ᾽ ἐλπίδα, lit. beyond hope, i. e. where the laws and course of nature left no room for hope, hence i. q. without [A. V. against] hope, Ro. iv. 18 (in prof. auth., of things which happen against hope, beyond one's expectation, cf. Passow s. v. III. 3, vol. ii. p. 669ᵇ; Dion. Hal. antt. 6, 25); παρὰ τὸν νόμον, contrary to the law, Acts xviii. 13 (παρὰ τοὺς νόμους, opp. to κατὰ τοὺς νόμους, Xen. mem. 1, 1, 18); παρ᾽ ὅ, contrary to that which, i. e. at variance with that which, Gal. i. 8 sq.; παρὰ φύσιν, Ro. i. 26; xi. 24, (Thuc. 6, 17; Plat. rep. 5 p. 466 d.); after ἄλλος, other than, different from, 1 Co. iii. 11 (see exx. fr. prof. auth. in Passow s. v. III. 3 fin. vol. ii. p. 670ᵃ); παρὰ τὸν κτίσαντα, omitting or passing by the Creator, Ro. 1. 25, where others explain it before (above) the Creator, rather than the Creator, agreeably indeed to the use of the prep. in Grk. writ. (cf. Ast, Lex. Plat. iii. p. 28 [cf. Riddell, Platonic Idioms, § 165 β.; L. and S. s. v. C. I. 5 d.]), but not to the thought of the passage. except, save, i. q. if you subtract from a given sum, less: τεσσαράκοντα παρὰ μίαν, one (stripe) excepted, 2 Co. xi. 24 (τεσσαράκοντα ἐτῶν παρὰ τριάκοντα ἡμέρας, Joseph. antt. 4, 8, 1; παρὰ πέντε ναῦς, five ships being deducted, Thuc. 8, 29; [παρ᾽ ὀλίγας ψήφους, Joseph. c. Ap. 2, 37, 3]; see other exx. fr. Grk. auth. in Bnhdy. p. 258; [W. u. s.; esp. Soph. Lex. s. v. 3]). **b.** above, beyond: παρὰ καιρὸν ἡλικίας, Heb. xi. 11; παρ᾽ ὅ δεῖ (Plut. mor. p. 83 f. [de profect. in virt. § 13]), Ro. xii. 3; i. q. more than: ἁμαρτωλοὶ παρὰ πάντας, Lk. xiii. 2; ἔχρισέ σε ἔλαιον παρὰ τοὺς μετ. more copiously than [A. V. above] thy fellows, Heb. i. 9 (fr. Ps. xliv. (xlv.) 8; ὑψοῦν τινα παρά τινα, Sir. xv. 5); κρίνειν ἡμέραν παρ᾽ ἡμέραν, to prefer one day to another (see κρίνω, 2), Ro. xiv. 5. Hence it is joined to comparatives: πλέον παρά τ. Lk. iii. 13; διαφορώτερον παρ᾽ αὐτοὺς ὄνομα, Heb. i. 4; add, iii. 3; ix. 23; xi. 4; xii. 24; see exx. fr. Grk. auth. in W. § 35, 2 b. [and as above]. ἐλαττοῦν τινα παρά τ., to make one inferior to another, Heb. ii. 7, 9. **3.** on account of (cf. Lat. propter i. q. ob): παρὰ τοῦτο, for this reason, therefore, 1 Co. xii. 15 sq.; cf. W. § 49 g. c.

IV. In Composition παρά denotes **1.** situation or motion either from the side of, or to the side of; near, beside, by, to: παραβαλάσσιος, παράλιος, παροικέω, παρακολουθέω, παραλαμβάνω, παραλέγομαι, παραπλέω, παράγω; of what is done secretly or by stealth, as παρεισέρχομαι,

παρεισάγω, παρεισδύω; cf. [the several words and] Fritzsche, Com. on Rom. vol. i. p. 346. by the side of i. e. ready, present, at hand, (παρά τινι): πάρειμι, παρουσία, παρέχω, etc. **2.** violation, neglect, aberration, [cf. our beyond or aside i. q. amiss]: παραβαίνω, παραβάτης, παρανομέω, παρακούω, παρίημι, πάρεσις, παραλογίζομαι, παράδοξος, παραφρονία, etc. **3.** like the Germ. an (in anreizen, antreiben, etc.): παραζηλόω, παραπικραίνω, παροξύνω, παροργίζω. [Cf. Vig. ed. Herm. p. 650 sq.]

παρα-βαίνω; 2 aor. παρέβην; prop. to go by the side of (in Hom. twice παρβεβαώς of one who stands by another's side in a war-chariot, Il. 11, 522; 13, 708 [but here of men on foot]); to go past or to pass over without touching a thing; trop. to overstep, neglect, violate, transgress, w. an acc. of the thing (often so in prof. auth. fr. Aeschyl. down [cf. παρά, IV. 1 and 2]): τὴν παράδοσιν, Mt. xv. 2; τὴν ἐντολὴν τοῦ θεοῦ, ibid. 3; ὁ παραβαίνων, he that transgresseth, oversteppeth, i. e. who does not hold to the true doctrine, opp. to μένειν ἐν τῇ διδαχῇ, 2 Jn. 9 R G [where L T Tr WH ὁ προάγων (q. v.)] (so οἱ παραβαίνοντες, transgressors of the law, Sir. xl. 14 [cf. Joseph. c. Ap. 2, 18, 2; 29, 4; 30, 1]); (τὴν διαθήκην, Josh. vii. 11, 15; Ezek. xvi. 59, and often; τὸ ῥῆμα κυρίου, Num. xiv. 41; 1 S. xv. 24, etc.; τὰς συνθήκας, Polyb. 7, 5, 1; Joseph. antt. 4, 6, 5; Ael. v. h. 10, 2; besides, παραβ. δίκην, τὸν νόμον, τοὺς ὅρκους, πίστιν, etc., in Grk. writ.). in imitation of the Hebr. כּוּר foll. by מִן, we find παραβ. ἔκ τινος and ἀπό τινος, so to go past as to turn aside from, i. e. to depart, leave, be turned from: ἐκ τῆς ὁδοῦ, Ex. xxxii. 8; Deut. ix. 12; ἀπὸ τῶν ἐντολῶν, Deut. xvii. 20; ἀπὸ τῶν λόγων, Deut. xxviii. 14 cod. Alex.; once so in the N. T.: ἐκ (L T Tr WH ἀπὸ) τῆς ἀποστολῆς, of one who abandons his trust, [R. V. fell away], Acts i. 25. (In the Sept. also for עָבַר הֵפִיר to break, שָׂטָה to deviate, turn aside.) [Syn.: παραβαίνειν to overstep, παραπορεύεσθαι to proceed by the side of, παρέρχεσθαι to go past.]*

παρα-βάλλω; 2 aor. παρέβαλον; **1.** to throw before, cast to, [cf. παρά, IV. 1], (Hom., Plat., Polyb., Dio Cass., al.; as fodder to horses, Hom. Il. 8, 504). **2.** to put one thing by the side of another for the sake of comparison, to compare, liken, (Hdt., Xen., Plat., Polyb., Joseph., Hdian.): τὴν βασιλείαν τοῦ θεοῦ ἐν παραβολῇ, to portray the kingdom of God (in), by the use of, a similitude, Mk. iv. 30 R G L mrg. Tr mrg. [cf. B. § 133, 22]. **3.** reflexively, to put one's self, betake one's self, into a place or to a person (Plat., Polyb., Plut., Diog. Laërt.); of seamen (Hdt. 7, 179; Dem. p. 163, 4; εἰς Ποτιόλους, Joseph. antt. 18, 6, 4), εἰς Σάμον, Acts xx. 15 [put in at (R. V. touched at)]. For another use of this verb in Grk. writ. see παραβολεύομαι.*

παρά-βασις, -εως, ἡ, (παραβαίνω, q. v.), prop. a going over; metaph. a disregarding, violating; Vulg. praevaricatio, and once (Gal. iii. 19) transgressio; [A. V. transgression]: w. a gen. of the object, τῶν ὅρκων, 2 Macc. xv. 10; τῶν δικαίων, Plut. compar. Ages. and Pomp. 1; τοῦ νόμου, of the Mosaic law, Ro. ii. 23 (Joseph. antt. 18, 8, 2); absolutely, the breach of a definite, promulgated, ratified law: Ro. v. 14; 1 Tim. ii. 14, (but ἁμαρτία is wrong-doing which even a man ignorant of the law may be guilty of [cf. *Trench*, N. T. Syn. § lxvi.]) ; τῶν παραβ. χάριν, *to create transgressions*, i. e. that sins might take on the character of transgressions, and thereby the conscious-ness of sin be intensified and the desire for redemption be aroused, Gal. iii. 19 ; used of the transgression of the Mosaic law, Ro. iv. 15 ; Heb. ii. 2 ; ix. 15 ; Ps. c. (ci.) 3 ; w. a gen. of the subj., τῶν ἀδίκων, Sap. xiv. 31.*

3848 **παρα-βάτης**, -ου, ὁ, (παραβαίνω [cf. W. 26]), *a trans-gressor* (Vulg. *praevaricator*, *transgressor*) : νόμου, *a law-breaker* (Plaut. *legirupa*), Ro. ii. 25, 27 ; Jas. ii. 11 ; absol., Gal. ii. 18 ; Jas. ii. 9. [Aeschyl. (παρβάτης) ; Graec. Ven. Deut. xxi. 18, 20.]*

3849 **παρα-βιάζομαι** : 1 aor. παρεβιασάμην ; depon. verb, *to employ force contrary to nature and right* [cf. παρά, IV. 2], *to compel by employing force* (Polyb. 26, 1, 3) : τινά, *to constrain one by entreaties*, Lk. xxiv. 29 ; Acts xvi. 15 ; so Sept. in Gen. xix. 9 ; 1 S. xxviii. 23, etc.*

(3849α); see 3851 **παραβολεύομαι** : 1 aor. mid. ptcp. παραβολευσάμενος ; *to be* παράβολος i. e. *one who rashly exposes himself to dan-gers, to be venturesome, reckless*, (cf. W. 93 (88) ; *Lob.* ad Phryn. p. 67) ; *recklessly to expose one's self to dan-ger* : with a dat. of respect, τῇ ψυχῇ, *as respects life* ; hence, *to expose one's life boldly, jeopard life, hazard life*, Phil. ii. 30 G L T Tr WH for the παραβουλευσάμ. of Rec. ; on the difference between these readings cf. *Gabler*, Kleinere theol. Schriften, i. p. 176 sqq. This verb is not found in the Grk. writ., who say παραβάλλεσθαι, now absol. *to expose one's self to danger* (see Passow s. v. παραβάλλω, 2 ; L. and S. ib. II.), now with an acc. of the thing [*to risk, stake*, as ψυχήν, Hom. Il. 9, 322 ; σῶμα καὶ ψυχήν, 2 Macc. xiv. 38 (see other exx. in Passow [and L. and S.] l. c.) ; now w. a dat. of reference, ταῖς ψυχαῖς, Diod. 3, 35 ; τῇ ἐμαυτοῦ κεφαλῇ, ἀργυρίῳ, Phryn. ed. *Lob.* p. 238 ; [cf. Bp. Lghtft. on Philip. l. c.].*

3850 **παραβολή**, -ῆς, ἡ, (παραβάλλω, q. v.), Sept. for מָשָׁל ; **1.** *a placing* of one thing *by the side of* another, *juxta-position*, as of ships in battle, Polyb. 15, 2, 13 ; Diod. 14, 60. **2.** metaph. *a comparing, comparison of one thing with another, likeness, similitude*, (Plat., Isocr., Polyb., Plut.) : univ., Mt. xxiv. 32 ; Mk. xiii. 28 ; an example by which a doctrine or precept is illustrated, Mk. iii. 23 ; Lk. xiv. 7 ; a thing serving as a figure of something else, Heb. ix. 9 ; this meaning also very many interpreters give the word in Heb. xi. 19, but see 5 be-low ; spec. *a narrative, fictitious but agreeable to the laws and usages of human life, by which either the duties of men* or *the things of God, particularly the nature and history of God's kingdom, are figuratively portrayed* [cf. B. D. s. vv. Fable, Parable, (and reff. there ; add Aristot. rhet. 2, 20, 2 sqq. and Cope's notes)] : Mt. xiii. 3, 10, 13, 24, 31, 33–35, 53 ; xxi. 33, 45 ; [xxii. 1] ; Mk. iv. 2, 10, [11], 13, 30, 33 sq. ; [vii. 17] ; xii. 1, [12] ; Lk. viii. 4, 9–11 ; xii. 16, 41 ; xiii. 6 ; xiv. 7 ; xv. 3 ; xviii. 1, 9 ; xix. 11 ; xx. 9, 19 ; xxi. 29 ; with a gen. of the pers. or thing to which the contents of the parable refer [W. § 30, 1 a.] : τοῦ σπείροντος, Mt. xiii. 18 ; τῶν ζιζανίων, ib. 36 ; τὴν βασιλείαν τοῦ θεοῦ ἐν παραβολῇ τιθέναι (lit. *to set forth*

the kingdom of God in a parable), to illustrate (the na-ture and history of) the kingdom of God by the use of a parable, Mk. iv. 30 L txt. T Trtxt. WH. **3.** *a pithy and instructive saying, involving some likeness* or *compar-ison and having preceptive* or *admonitory force; an aphorism, a maxim*: Lk. v. 36 ; vi. 39 ; Mt. xv. 15, (Prov. i. 6 ; Eccl. i. 17 ; Sir. iii. 29 (27) ; xiii. 26 (25), etc.). Since sayings of this kind often pass into proverbs, παραβολή is **4.** *a proverb* : Lk. iv. 23 (1 S. x. 12 ; Ezek. xii. 22 sq. ; xviii. 2 sq.). **5.** *an act by which one exposes himself* or *his possessions to danger, a ven-ture, risk*, (in which sense the plur. seems to be used by Plut. Arat. 22 : διὰ πολλῶν ἑλιγμῶν καὶ παραβολῶν περαί-νοντες πρὸς τὸ τεῖχος [cf. Diod. Sic. frag. lib. xxx. 9, 2 ; also var. in Thuc. 1, 131, 2 (and Poppo ad loc.)]) ; ἐν παραβολῇ, in risking him, i. e. at the very moment when he exposed his son to mortal peril (see παραβολεύομαι), Heb. xi. 19 (Hesych. ἐκ παραβολῆς · ἐκ παρακινδυνεύμα-τος) ; others with less probability explain it, *in a figure*, i. e. as a figure, either of the future general resurrection of all men, or of Christ offered up to God and raised again from the dead ; others otherwise.*

3851: see (3849α) **παρα-βουλεύομαι** : 1 aor. ptcp. παραβουλευσάμενος ; *to consult amiss* [see παρά, IV. 2] : w. a dat. of the thing, Phil. ii. 30 Rec. Not found in prof. auth. See παρα-βολεύομαι.*

3852 **παρ-αγγελία**, -ας, ἡ, (παραγγέλλω), prop. *announcement, a proclaiming* or *giving a message to*; hence *a charge, command* : Acts xvi. 24 ; a prohibition, Acts v. 28 ; used of the Christian doctrine relative to right living, 1 Tim. i. 5 ; of particular directions relative to the same, 18 ; plur. in 1 Th. iv. 2. (Of a military order in Xen., Polyb. ; of instruction, Aristot. eth. Nic. 2, 2 p. 1104ᵃ, 7 ; Diod. exc. p. 512, 19 [i. e. frag. lib. xxvi. 1, 1].) *

3853 **παρ-αγγέλλω** ; impf. παρήγγελλον ; 1 aor. παρήγγειλα ; (παρά and ἀγγέλλω) ; fr. Aeschyl. and Hdt. down ; **1.** prop. *to transmit a message along from one to another* [(cf. παρά, IV. 1)], *to declare, announce*. **2.** *to com-mand, order, charge* : w. dat. of the pers. 1 Th. iv. 11 [cf. Mk. xvi. WH (rejected) 'Shorter Conclusion '] ; foll. by λέγων and direct disc. Mt. x. 5 ; foll. by an inf. aor., Mt. xv. 35 L T Tr WH ; Mk. viii. 6 ; Lk. viii. 29 ; Acts x. 42 ; xvi. 18 ; with μή inserted, Lk. v. 14 ; viii. 56 ; Acts xxiii. 22 ; 1 Co. vii. 10 [here Lchm. inf. pres.] ; foll. by an inf. pres., Acts xvi. 23 ; xvii. 30 [here T Tr mrg. WH have ἀπαγγ.] ; 2 Th. iii. 6 ; with μή inserted, Lk. ix. 21 [G L T Tr WH] ; Acts i. 4 ; iv. 18 ; v. 28 (παραγγελίᾳ παραγ-γέλλειν, to charge strictly, W. §54,3 ; B. 184 (159 sq.)), 40 ; 1 Tim. i. 3 ; vi. 17 ; τινί τι, 2 Th. iii. 4 [but T Tr WH om. L br. the dat.] ; τοῦτο foll. by ὅτι, 2 Th. iii. 10 ; τινί foll. by acc. and inf., [Acts xxiii. 30 L T Tr mrg.] ; 2 Th. iii. 6 ; 1 Tim. vi. 13 [here Tdf. om. dat.] ; foll. by an inf. alone, Acts xv. 5 ; by ἵνα (see ἵνα, II. 2 b.), Mk. vi. 8 ; 2 Th. iii. 12 ; with an acc. of the thing alone, 1 Co. xi. 17 ; 1 Tim. iv. 11 ; v. 7. [Syn. see κελεύω, fin.]*

3854 **παρα-γίνομαι** ; impf. 3 pers. plur. παρεγίνοντο (Jn. iii. 23) ; 2 aor. παρεγενόμην ; fr. Hom. down ; Sept. for בּוֹא ; (prop. *to become near, to place one's self by the side of*, hence) *to be present, to come near, approach* : absol., Mt. iii. 1 [but in ed. 1 Prof. Grimm (more appropriately) associates this with Heb. ix. 11 ; Lk. xii. 51 below] ; Lk. [xiv. 21] ; xix. 16 ; Jn. iii. 23 ; Acts v. 21 sq. 25 ; ix. 39 ; x. 32 [R G Tr mrg. br.], 33 ; xi. 23 ; xiv. 27 ; xvii. 10 ; xviii. 27 ; xxi. 18 ; xxiii. 16, 35 ; xxiv. 17, 24 ; xxv. 7 ; xxviii. 21 ; 1 Co. xvi. 3 ; foll. by ἀπό w. gen. of place and εἰς w. acc. of place, Mt. ii. 1 ; Acts xiii. 14 ; by ἀπό with gen. of place and ἐπί w. acc. of place and πρός w. acc. of pers. Mt. iii. 13 ; by παρά w. gen. of pers. (i. e. sent by one [cf. W. 365 (342)]), Mk. xiv. 43 ; by πρός τινα, Lk. vii. 4, 20 ; viii. 19 ; Acts xx. 18 ; πρός τινα ἐκ w. gen. of place, Lk. xi. 6 ; by εἰς w. acc. of place, Jn. viii. 2 ; Acts ix. 26 (here Lchm. ἐν) ; xv. 4 ; by ἐπί τινα (*against*, see ἐπί, C. I. 2 g. γ. ββ.), Lk. xxii. 52 [Tdf. πρός]. i. q. *to come forth, make one's public appearance*, of teachers : of the Messiah, absol. Heb. ix. 11 ; foll. by an inf. denoting the purpose, Lk. xii. 51 ; [of John the Baptist, Mt. iii. 1 (see above)]. i. q. *to be present with help* [R. V. *to take one's part*], w. a dat. of the pers. 2 Tim. iv. 16 L T Tr WH. [COMP. : συμ-παραγίνομαι.] *

3855   **παρ-άγω** ; impf. παρῆγον (Jn. viii. 59 Rec.) ; pres. pass. 3 pers. sing. παράγεται ; fr. [Archil., Theogn.], Pind. and Hdt. down ; Sept. several times for עָבַר in Kal and Hiphil ; **1.** trans. [(cf. παρά, IV.)] ; **a.** *to lead past, lead by.* **b.** *to lead aside, mislead* ; *to lead away.* **c.** *to lead to* ; *to lead forth, bring forward.* **2.** intrans. (see ἄγω, 4) ; **a.** *to pass by, go past* : Mt. xx. 30 ; Mk. ii. 14 ; xv. 21 ; [Lk. xviii. 39 L mrg.] ; foll. by παρά w. an acc. of place, Mk. i. 16 L T Tr WH (by κατά w. acc. of place, 3 Macc. vi. 16 ; θεωροῦντες παράγουσαν τὴν δύναμιν, Polyb. 5, 18, 4). **b.** *to depart, go away* : Jn. viii. 59 Rec. ; ix. 1 ; ἐκεῖθεν, Mt. ix. 9, 27. [Al. adhere to the meaning *pass by* in all these pass.] Metaph. *to pass away, disappear* : 1 Co. vii. 31 (Ps. cxliii. (cxliv.) 5) ; in the passive in the same sense, 1 Jn. ii. 8, 17.*

3856   **παρα-δειγματίζω** ; 1 aor. inf. παραδειγματίσαι ; (παράδειγμα [(fr. δείκνυμι)] an example ; also an example in the sense of a warning [cf. Schmidt ch. 128]) ; *to set forth as an example, make an example of* ; in a bad sense, *to hold up to infamy* ; *to expose to public disgrace* : τινά, Mt. i. 19 R G ; Heb. vi. 6 [A. V. *put to open shame*]. (Num. xxv. 4 ; Jer. xiii. 22 ; Ezek. xxviii. 17 ; [Dan. ii. 5 Sept.] ; Add. to Esth. iv. 8 [36] ; Evang. Jac. c. 20 ; often in Polyb. ; Plut. de curios. 10 ; Euseb. quaest. ad Steph. 1, 3 (iv. 884 d. ed. Migne).) [Cf. Schmidt ch. 128.] *

3857   **παράδεισος**, -ου, ὁ, (thought by most to be of Persian origin, by others of Armenian, cf. *Gesenius*, Thes. ii. p. 1124 ; [B. D. s. v. ; esp. *Fried. Delitzsch*, Wo lag das Paradies? Leipzig 1881, pp. 95–97 ; cf. *Max Müller*, Selected Essays, i. 129 sq.]), **1.** among the Persians *a grand enclosure* or *preserve, hunting-ground, park*, shady and well-watered, in which wild animals were kept for the hunt ; it was enclosed by walls and furnished with towers for the hunters : Xen. Cyr. 1, 3, 14 ; [1, 4, 5] ; 8, 1, 38 ; oec. 4, 13 and 14 ; anab. 1, 2, 7. 9 ; Theophr. h. pl. 5, 8, 1 ; Diod. 16, 41 ; 14, 80 ; Plut. Artax.

25, cf. Curt; 8, 1, 11.   **2.** univ. *a garden, pleasure-ground* ; *grove, park* : Lcian. v. h. 2, 23 ; Ael. v. h. 1, 33 ; Joseph. antt. 7, 14, 4 ; 8, 7, 3 ; 9, 10, 4 ; 10, 3, 2 and 11, 1 ; b. j. 6, 1, 1 ; [c. Apion. 1, 19, 9 (where cf. *Müller*)] ; Sus. 4, 7, 15, etc. ; Sir. xxiv. 30 ; and so it passed into the Hebr. language, פַּרְדֵּס, Neh. ii. 8 ; Eccl. ii. 5 ; Cant. iv. 13 ; besides in Sept. mostly for גַּן : thus for that delightful region, 'the garden of Eden,' in which our first parents dwelt before the fall : Gen. ii. 8 sqq. ; iii. 1 sqq.   **3.** *that part of Hades which was thought* by the later Jews *to be the abode of the souls of the pious until the resurrection* : Lk. xxiii. 43, cf. xvi. 23 sqq. But some [e. g. Dillmann (as below p. 379)] understand that passage of the **heavenly** paradise.   **4.** *an upper region in the heavens* : 2 Co. xii. 4 (where some maintain, others deny, that the term is equiv. to ὁ τρίτος οὐρανός in vs. 2) ; with the addition of τοῦ θεοῦ, gen. of possessor, the abode of God and heavenly beings, to which true Christians will be taken after death, Rev. ii. 7 (cf. Gen. xiii. 10 ; Ezek. xxviii. 13 ; xxxi. 8). According to the opinion of many of the church Fathers, the paradise in which our first parents dwelt before the fall still exists, neither on earth nor in the heavens, but above and beyond the world ; cf. *Thilo*, Cod. apocr. Nov. Test., on Evang. Nicod. c. xxv. p. 748 sqq. ; and Bleek thinks that the word ought to be taken in this sense in Rev. ii. 7. Cf. *Dillmann* s. v. Paradies in Schenkel iv. 377 sqq. ; also *Hilgenfeld*, Die Clement. Recogn. und Hom. p. 87 sq. ; *Klöpper* on 2 Co. xii. 2–4, p. 507 sqq. [(Göttingen, 1869). See also B. D. s. v. ; McC. and S. s. v. ; *Hamburger*, Real-Encyclopädie, Abtheil. ii. s. v.] *

3858   **παρα-δέχομαι** ; fut. 3 pers. plur. παραδέξονται ; depon. mid., but in bibl. and eccles. Grk. w. 1 aor. pass. παρεδέχθην (Acts xv. 4 L T Tr WH ; 2 Macc. iv. 22 ; [cf. B. 51 (44)]) ; **1.** in class. Grk. fr. Hom. down, prop. *to receive, take up, take upon one's self.* Hence **2.** *to admit* i. e. not to reject, *to accept, receive* : τὸν λόγον, Mk. iv. 20 ; ἔθη, Acts xvi. 21 ; τὴν μαρτυρίαν, Acts xxii. 18 ; κατηγορίαν, 1 Tim. v. 19, (τὰς δοκίμους δράχμας, Epict. diss. 1, 7, 6) ; τινά, of a son, *to acknowledge* as one's own [A. V. *receiveth*], Heb. xii. 6 (after Prov. iii. 12, where for רָצָה) ; of a delegate or messenger, to give due reception to, Acts xv. 4 L T Tr WH. [Cf. δέχομαι, fin.] *

3859 ; see (1275a)   **παρα-δια-τριβή**, -ῆς, ἡ, *useless occupation, empty business, misemployment* (see παρά, IV. 2) : 1 Tim. vi. 5 Rec. [cf. W. 102 (96)], see διαπαρατριβή. Not found elsewhere ; [cf. παραδιατυπόω in Justinian (in *Koumanoudes*, Λέξεις ἀθησαύρ. s. v.)].*

3860   **παρα-δίδωμι**, subjunc. 3 pers. sing. παραδιδῷ (1 Co. xv. 24 [L mrg. Tr mrg. WH, cod. Sin., etc.]) and παραδιδοῖ (ibid. L txt. T Tr txt. ; cf. B. 46 (40) [and δίδωμι, init.]) ; impf. 3 pers. sing. παρεδίδου (Acts viii. 3 ; 1 Pet. ii. 23), plur. παρεδίδουν (Acts xvi. 4 R G ; xxvii. 1) and παρεδίδοσαν (Acts xvi. 4 L T Tr WH ; cf. W. § 14, 1 c. ; B. 45 (39)) ; fut. παραδώσω ; 1 aor. παρέδωκα ; 2 aor. παρέδων, subjunc. 3 pers. sing. παραδῷ and several times παραδοῖ (so L T Tr WH in Mk. iv. 29 ; xiv. 10, 11 ; Jn. xiii. 2 ; see δίδωμι, init.) ; pf. ptcp. παραδεδωκώς (Acts xv. 26) ;

plupf. 3 pers. plur. without augm. παραδεδώκεισαν (Mk. xv. 10; W. § 12, 9; [B. 33 (29); Tdf. Proleg. p. 120 sq.]); Pass., pres. παραδίδομαι; impf. 3 pers. sing. παρεδίδετο (1 Co. xi. 23 L T Tr WH for R G παρεδίδοτο, see ἀποδίδωμι); pf. 3 pers. sing. παραδέδοται (Lk. iv. 6), ptcp. παραδεδομένος, Acts xiv. 26; 1 aor. παρεδόθην; 1 fut. παραδοθήσομαι; fr. Pind. and Hdt. down; Sept. mostly for נָתַן; *to give over*; **1.** prop. *to give into the hands* (of another). **2.** *to give over into* (one's) *power* or *use*: τινί τι, *to deliver to one something* to keep, use, take care of, manage, Mt. xi. 27; Lk. iv. 6 [cf. W. 271 (254)]; x. 22; τὰ ὑπάρχοντα, τάλαντα, Mt. xxv. 14, 20, 22; τὴν βασιλείαν, 1 Co. xv. 24; τὸ πνεῦμα sc. τῷ θεῷ, Jn. xix. 30; τὸ σῶμα, ἵνα etc., to be burned, 1 Co. xiii. 3; τινά, *to deliver one up* to custody, to be judged, condemned, punished, scourged, tormented, put to death, (often thus in prof. auth.): τινά, absol., so that *to be put in prison* must be supplied, Mt. iv. 12; Mk. i. 14; τηρουμένους, who are kept, 2 Pet. ii. 4 [G T Tr WH; but R τετηρημένους, L κολαζομένους τηρεῖν]; to be put to death (cf. Germ. *dahingeben*), Ro. iv. 25; with the addition of ὑπέρ τινος, for one's salvation, Ro. viii. 32; τινά τινι, Mt. v. 25; xviii. 34; xx. 18; xxvii. 2; Mk. xv. 1; Lk. xii. 58; xx. 20; Jn. xviii. 30, 35 sq.; xix. 11 etc.; Acts xxvii. 1; xxviii. 16 Rec.; τῷ θελήματι αὐτῶν, to do their pleasure with, Lk. xxiii. 25; τινά τινι, foll. by ἵνα, Jn. xix. 16; with an inf. of purpose, φυλάσσειν αὐτόν, to guard him, Acts xii. 4; without the dat., Mt. x. 19; xxiv. 10; xxvii. 18; Mk. xiii. 11; xv. 10; Acts iii. 13; foll. by ἵνα, Mt. xxvii. 26; Mk. xv. 15; τινὰ εἰς τὸ σταυρωθῆναι, Mt. xxvi. 2 (σταυροῦ θανάτῳ, Ev. Nicod. c. 26); εἰς χεῖράς τινος, i. e. into one's power, Mt. xvii. 22; xxvi. 45; Mk. ix. 31; xiv. 41; Lk. ix. 44; xxiv. 7; Acts xxi. 11; xxviii. 17, (Jer. xxxiii. (xxvi.) 24; xxxix. (xxxii.) 4); εἰς συνέδρια, to councils [see συνέδριον, 2 b.] (παραδιδόναι involving also the idea of conducting), Mt. x. 17; Mk. xiii. 9; εἰς συναγωγάς, Lk. xxi. 12; εἰς θλῖψιν, Mt. xxiv. 9; εἰς φυλακήν, Acts viii. 3; εἰς φυλακάς, Acts xxii. 4; εἰς θάνατον, Mt. x. 21; Mk. xiii. 12; 2 Co. iv. 11; εἰς κρίμα θανάτου, Lk. xxiv. 20; τὴν σάρκα εἰς καταφθοράν, of Christ undergoing death, Barn. ep. 5, 1; παραδιδόναι ἑαυτὸν ὑπέρ τινος, to give one's self up for, give one's self to death for, to undergo death for (the salvation of) one, Gal. ii. 20; Eph. v. 25; with the addition of τῷ θεῷ and a pred. acc., Eph. v. 2; τὴν ψυχὴν ἑαυτοῦ ὑπὲρ τοῦ ὀνόματος Ἰησοῦ Χριστοῦ, to jeopard life to magnify and make known the name of Jesus Christ, Acts xv. 26. Metaph. expressions: τινὰ τῷ Σατανᾷ, to deliver one into the power of Satan to be harassed and tormented with evils, 1 Tim. i. 20; with the addition of εἰς ὄλεθρον σαρκός (see ὄλεθρος), 1 Co. v. 5 (the phrase seems to have originated from the Jewish formulas of excommunication [yet see Meyer (ed. *Heinrici*) ad loc. (cf. B. D. s. vv. Hymenæus II., Excommunication II.)], because a person banished from the theocratic assembly was regarded as deprived of the protection of God and delivered up to the power of the devil). τινὰ εἰς ἀκαθαρσίαν, to cause one to become unclean, Ro. i. 24; cf. Fritzsche, Rückert, and

others ad loc. [in this ex. and several that follow A. V. renders *to give up*]; εἰς πάθη ἀτιμίας, to make one a slave of vile passions, ib. 26; εἰς ἀδόκιμον νοῦν, to cause one to follow his own corrupt mind, — foll. by an inf. of purpose [or epexegetic inf. (Meyer)], ib. 28; ἑαυτὸν τῇ ἀσελγείᾳ, to make one's self the slave of lasciviousness, Eph. iv. 19; τινὰ λατρεύειν, to cause one to worship, Acts vii. 42. *to deliver up treacherously*, i. e. by betrayal to cause one to be taken: τινά τινι, of Judas betraying Jesus, Mt. xxvi. 15; Mk. xiv. 10; Lk. xxii. 4, 6; without the dat., Mt. xxvi. 16, 21, 23, 25; Mk. xiv. 11, 18; Lk. xxii. 21, 48; Jn. vi. 64, 71; xii. 4; in the pass., Mk. xiv. 21; Lk. xxii. 22; 1 Co. xi. 23; pres. ptcp. ὁ παραδιδοὺς αὐτόν, of him as plotting the betrayal (cf. B. § 144, 11, 3): Mt. xxvi. 25, 46, 48; Mk. xiv. 42, 44; Jn. xiii. 11; xviii. 2, 5. *to deliver one to be taught, moulded*, etc.: εἴς τι, in pass., Ro. vi. 17 (to be resolved thus, ὑπηκ. τῷ τύπῳ etc· εἰς ὃν παρεδόθητε [W. § 24, 2 b.]). **3.** i. q. *to commit, to commend*: τινά τῇ χάριτι τ. θεοῦ, in pass., Acts xiv. 26; xv. 40; παρεδίδου τῷ κρίνοντι δικαίως, sc. τὰ ἑαυτοῦ, his cause (B. 145 (127) note[2] [cf. W. 590 (549)]), 1 Pet. ii. 23. **4.** *to deliver verbally*: commands, rites, Mk. vii. 13; Acts vi. 14; 1 Co. xi. 2; 2 Pet. ii. 21 (here in pass.); πίστιν, the tenets [see πίστις, 1 c. β.], in pass., Jude 3; φυλάσσειν τὰ δόγματα, the decrees to keep, Acts xvi. 4; *to deliver by narrating, to report*, i. e. to perpetuate the knowledge of events by narrating them, Lk. i. 2; 1 Co. xi. 23; xv. 3, (see exx. fr. Grk. auth. in Passow [or L. and S.] s. v. 4). **5.** *to permit, allow*: absol. ὅταν παραδῷ or παραδοῖ ὁ καρπός, when the fruit will allow, i. e. when its ripeness permits, Mk. iv. 29 (so τῆς ὥρας παραδιδούσης, Polyb. 22, 24, 9; for other exx. see Passow s. v. 3 [L. and S. s. v. II.]; others take the word in Mk. l. c. intransitively, in a quasi-reflexive sense, *gives itself up, presents itself*, cf. W. 251 (236); B. 145 (127)]).

παράδοξος, -ον, (παρά contrary to [see παρά, IV. 2], and δόξα opinion; hence i. q. ὁ παρὰ τὴν δόξαν ὤν), *unexpected, uncommon, incredible, wonderful*: neut. plur. Lk. v. 26 [A. V. *strange things*, cf. Trench § xci. fin.]. (Judith xiii. 13; Sap. v. 2 etc.; Sir. xliii. 25; 2 Macc. ix. 24; 4 Macc. ii. 14; Xen., Plat., Polyb., Ael. v. h. 4, 25; Lcian. dial. deor. 20, 7; 9, 2; Joseph. c. Ap. 1, 10, 2; Hdian. 1, 1, 5 [(4 Bekk.)].) *   **3861**

παράδοσις, -εως, ἡ, (παραδίδωμι), *a giving over, giving up*; i. e. **1.** *the act of giving up, the surrender*: of cities, Polyb. 9, 25, 5; Joseph. b. j. 1, 8, 6; χρημάτων, Aristot. pol. 5, 7, 11 p. 1309ᵃ, 10. **2.** *a giving over which is done by word of mouth or in writing*, i. e. tradition by instruction, narrative, precept, etc. (see παραδίδωμι, 4); hence i. q. *instruction*, Epict. diss. 2, 23, 40; joined with διδασκαλία, Plat. legg. 7 p. 803 a. objectively, *what is delivered, the substance of the teaching*: so of Paul's teaching, 2 Th. iii. 6; in plur. of the particular injunctions of Paul's instruction, 1 Co. xi. 2; 2 Th. ii. 15. used in the sing. of a written narrative, Joseph. c. Ap. 1, 9, 2; 10, 2; again, of the body of precepts, esp. ritual, which in the opinion of the later Jews were orally delivered by Moses and orally transmitted in unbroken   **3862**

succession to subsequent generations, which precepts, both illustrating and expanding the written law, as they did, were to be obeyed with equal reverence (Joseph. antt. 13, 10, 6 distinguishes between τὰ ἐκ παραδόσεως τῶν πατέρων and τὰ γεγραμμένα, i. e. τὰ ἐν τοῖς Μωϋσέως νόμοις γεγραμμένα νόμμα) : Mt. xv. 2 sq. 6 ; Mk. vii. 3, 5, 9, 13 ; with τῶν ἀνθρώπων added, as opp. to the divine teachings, Mk. vii. 8 ; Col. ii. 8 [where see Bp. Lghtft.] ; πατρικαὶ παραδόσεις, precepts received from the fathers, whether handed down in the O. T. books or orally, Gal. i. 14 [(al. restrict the word here to the extra-biblical traditions ; cf. Meyer or Bp. Lghtft. ad loc.). Cf. B. D. Am. ed. s. v. Tradition.] *

3863 **παρα-ζηλόω, -ῶ** ; fut. παραζηλώσω ; 1 aor. παρεζήλωσα ; *to provoke to ζῆλος* [see παρά, IV. 3] ; **a.** *to provoke to jealousy* or *rivalry* : τινά, Ro. xi. 11, 14, (1 K. xiv. 22 ; Sir. xxx. 3) ; ἐπί τινι (see ἐπί, B. 2 a. δ. fin.), Ro. x. 19 (Deut. xxxii. 21). **b.** *to provoke to anger* : 1 Co. x. 22 [on this see Prof. Hort in *WH.* App. p. 167] (Ps. xxxvi. (xxxvii.) 1, 7 sq.).*

3864 **παρα-θαλάσσιος, -α, -ον,** (παρά and θάλασσα), *beside the sea, by the sea* : Mt. iv. 13. (Sept. ; Hdt., Xen., Thuc., Polyb., Diod., al.) *

3865 **παρα-θεωρέω, -ῶ** : impf. pass. 3 pers. plur. παρεθεωροῦντο ; **1.** (παρά i. q. *by the side of* [see παρά, IV. 1]) *to examine things placed beside each other, to compare,* (Xen., Plut., Lcian.). **2.** (παρά i. q. *over, beyond,* [Lat. *praeter* ; see παρά, IV. 2]) *to overlook, neglect* : Acts vi. 1 (Dem. p. 1414, 22 ; Diod., Dion. Hal., al.).*

3866 **παρα-θήκη, -ης, ἡ,** (παρατίθημι, q. v.), *a deposit, a trust* or *thing consigned to one's faithful keeping,* (Vulg. *depositum*) : used of the correct knowledge and pure doctrine of the gospel, to be held firmly and faithfully, and to be conscientiously delivered unto others : 2 Tim. i. 12 (μοῦ possess. gen. [*the trust committed unto me* ; Rec.^elz 1633 reads here παρακαταθήκην, q. v.]) ; G L T Tr WH in 1 Tim. vi. 20 and 2 Tim. i. 14, (Lev. vi. 2, 4 ; 2 Macc. iii. 10, 15 ; Hdt. 9, 45 ; [al.]). In the Grk. writ. παρακαταθήκη (q. v.) is more common ; cf. *Lob.* ad Phryn. p. 312 ; W. 102 (96).*

3867 **παρ-αινέω, -ῶ** ; impf. 3 pers. sing. παρῄνει ; *to exhort, admonish* : with the addition of λέγων foll. by direct discourse, Acts xxvii. 9 ; τινά (in class. Grk. more commonly τινί [W. 223 (209) ; B. § 133, 9]), foll. by an inf. Acts xxvii. 22 [B. §§ 140, 1 ; 141, 2]. (From Hdt. and Pind. down ; 2 Macc. vii. 25 sq. ; 3 Macc. v. 17.) *

3868 **παρ-αιτέομαι, -οῦμαι,** impv. pres. παραιτοῦ ; [impf. 3 pers. plur. παρῃτοῦντο, Mk. xv. 6 T WH Tr mrg., where al. ὅνπερ ᾐτοῦντο (q. v.)] ; 1 aor. παρῃτησάμην ; pf. pass. ptcp. παρῃτημένος with a pass. signif. ; fr. Aeschyl. and Pind. down ; **1.** prop. *to ask alongside* (παρά [IV. 1]), *beg to have near one* ; *to obtain by entreaty* ; *to beg from, to ask for, supplicate* : [Mk. xv. 6 (see above)]. **2.** *to avert* (παρά *aside* [see παρά, IV. 1]) *by entreaty* or *seek to avert, to deprecate* ; **a.** prop. foll. by μή and acc. w. inf. [*to intreat that . . . not*], Heb. xii. 19 (Thuc. 5, 63) ; cf. W. 604 (561) ; [B. § 148, 13]. **b.** i. q. *to refuse, decline* : τὸ ἀποθανεῖν, Acts xxv. 11 (θανεῖν οὐ παραι-

τοῦμαι, Joseph. de vita sua 29). **c.** i. q. *to shun, avoid* : τί, 1 Tim. iv. 7 ; 2 Tim. ii. 23 ; τινά, 1 Tim. v. 11 ; Tit. iii. 10 ; i. q. *to refuse, reject,* Heb. xii. 25. **d.** *to avert displeasure by entreaty,* i. e. *to beg pardon, crave indulgence, to excuse* : ἔχε με παρῃτημένον (see ἔχω, I. 1 f.), Lk. xiv. 18 sq. (of one excusing himself for not accepting an invitation to a feast, Joseph. antt. 7, 8, 2).*

παρα-καθέζομαι : *to sit down beside* [παρά, IV. 1], *seat one's self,* (Xen., Plat., al.) ; 1 aor. pass. ptcp. παρακαθεσθείς (Joseph. antt. 6, 11, 9) ; πρός τι, Lk. x. 39 T Tr WH [cf. *Lob.* ad Phryn. p. 269].*

3869 **παρα-καθίζω** : 1 aor. ptcp. fem. παρακαθίσασα, *to make to sit down beside* [(παρά, IV. 1)] ; *to set beside, place near* ; intrans. *to sit down beside* : παρά τι, Lk. x. 39 R G L [but L mrg. πρός] (Sept. Job ii. 13 ; Plut. Marius 17 ; Cleom. 37 ; in this sense the mid. is more com. in the Grk. writ.).*

3870 **παρα-καλέω, -ῶ** ; impf. 3 pers. sing. παρεκάλει, 1 and 3 pers. plur. παρεκάλουν ; 1 aor. παρεκάλεσα ; Pass., pres. παρακαλοῦμαι ; pf. παρακέκλημαι ; 1 aor. παρεκλήθην ; 1 fut. παρακληθήσομαι ; fr. Aeschyl. and Hdt. down ; **I.** as in Grk. writ. *to call to one's side, call for, summon* : τινά, w. an inf. indicating the purpose, Acts xxviii. 20 [al. (less naturally) refer this to II. 2, making the acc. the subj. of the inf.]. **II.** *to address, speak to,* (*call to, call on*), which may be done in the way of exhortation, entreaty, comfort, instruction, etc. ; hence result a variety of senses, on which see *Knapp,* Scripta varii arg. ed. 2 p. 117 sqq. ; cf. *Fritzsche,* Ep. ad Rom. i. p. 32 sq. **1.** as in Grk. auth., *to admonish, exhort* : absol., Lk. iii. 18 ; [Acts xx. 1 (R G om.)] ; Ro. xii. 8 ; 2 Tim. iv. 2 ; Heb. x. 25 ; 1 Pet. v. 12 ; foll. by direct disc. 2 Co. v. 20 ; foll. by λέγων w. direct disc. Acts ii. 40 ; foll. by an inf. where in Lat. *ut,* 1 Tim. ii. 1 ; τινά, Acts xv. 32 ; xvi. 40 ; 2 Co. x. 1 ; 1 Th. ii. 12 (11) ; v. 11 ; 1 Tim. v. 1 ; Heb. iii. 13 ; τινὰ λόγῳ πολλῷ, Acts xx. 2 ; τινά foll. by direct disc., 1 Co. iv. 16 ; 1 Th. v. 14 ; Heb. xiii. 22 [here L WH mrg. inf.] ; 1 Pet. v. 1 sq. ; τινά foll. by an inf. where in Lat. *ut* [cf. B. §§ 140, 1 ; 141, 2 ; W. 332 (311) ; 335 (315) n.] : inf. pres., Acts xi. 23 ; xiv. 22 ; Phil. iv. 2 ; 1 Th. iv. 10 ; Tit. ii. 6 ; 1 Pet. ii. 11 (here Lchm. adds ὑμᾶς to the inf., and WH mrg. with codd. A C L etc. read ἀπέχεσθε) ; Jude 3 ; inf. aor., Acts xxvii. 33 sq. ; Ro. xii. 1 ; xv. 30 ; 2 Co. ii. 8 ; vi. 1 ; Eph. iv. 1 ; 1 Tim. i. 3 ; Heb. xiii. 19 ; τινά foll. by ἵνα w. subjunc. [cf. B. § 139, 42 ; W. 335 u. s.], 1 Co. i. 10 ; xvi. 15 sq. ; 2 Co. viii. 6 ; 1 Th. iv. 1 ; 2 Th. iii. 12 ; to enjoin a thing by exhortation [cf. B. § 141, 2], 1 Tim. vi. 2 ; Tit. ii. 15. **2.** *to beg, entreat, beseech,* (Joseph. antt. 6, 7, 4 ; [11, 8, 5]) ; often in Epict. cf. *Schweighäuser,* Index graecit. Epict. p. 411 ; Plut. apophth. regum, Mor. ii. p. 30 ed. Tauchn. [vi. 695 ed. Reiske ; exx. fr. Polyb., Diod., Philo, al., in *Soph.* Lex. s. v.] ; not thus in the earlier Grk. auth. exc. where the gods are called on for aid, in the expressions, παρακαλεῖν θεούς, so θεόν in Joseph. antt. 6, 2, 2 and 7, 4 ; [cf. W. 22]) : [absol., Philem. 9 (yet see the Comm. ad loc.)] ; τινά, Mt. viii. 5 ; xviii. 32 ; xxvi. 53 ; Mk. i. 40 ; Acts xvi. 9 ; 2 Co. xii. 18 ; πολλά, *much,* Mk. v. 23 ; τινὰ περί τινος,

Philem. 10; foll. by direct disc. Acts ix. 38 L T Tr WH; with λέγων added and direct disc., Mt. xviii. 29; Mk. v. 12; [Lk. vii. 4 (Tdf. ἠρώτων)]; without the acc. Acts xvi. 15; τινά foll. by an inf. [W. and B. u. s.], Mk. v. 17; Lk. viii. 41; Acts viii. 31; xix. 31; xxviii. 14, (1 Macc. ix. 35); τινά foll. by ὅπως, Mt. viii. 34 [here Lchm. ἵνα (see above)]; Acts xxv. 2, (4 Macc. iv. 11; Plut. Demetr. c. 38); τινά foll. by ἵνα [W. § 44, 8 a.; B. § 139, 42], Mt. xiv. 36; Mk. v. 18; vi. 56; vii. 32; viii. 22; Lk. viii. 31 sq., [2 Co. ix. 5]; τινὰ ὑπέρ τινος, ἵνα, 2 Co. xii. 8; πολλά (much) τινα, ἵνα, Mk. v. 10; 1 Co. xvi. 12; foll. by τοῦ μή w. inf. [B. § 140, 16 δ.; W. 325 (305)], Acts xxi. 12; by an inf. Acts ix. 38 RG; by an acc. w. inf., Acts xiii. 42; xxiv. 4; [Ro. xvi. 17]. to strive to appease by entreaty: absol. 1 Co. iv. 13; τινά, Lk. xv. 28; Acts xvi. 39, (2 Macc. xiii. 23). **3.** to console, to encourage and strengthen by consolation, to comfort, (Sept. for נחם; very rarely so in Grk. auth., as Plut. Oth. 16): absol. 2 Co. ii. 7; τινά, 2 Co. i. 6; vii. 6 sq.; ἐν w. a dat. of the thing with which one comforts another, 1 Th. iv. 18; τινὰ διὰ παρακλήσεως, 2 Co. i. 4; w. an acc. of the contents, διὰ τῆς παρακλ. ἧς (for ἥν, see ὅς, ἥ, ὅ, II. 2 c. a.) παρακαλούμεθα, ibid.; in pass. to receive consolation, be comforted, Mt. ii. 18; 2 Co. xiii. 11; ἐπί τινι over (in) a thing [see ἐπί, B. 2 a. δ.], 2 Co. i. 4; of the consolation (comfort) given not in words but by the experience of a happier lot or by a happy issue, i. q. to refresh, cheer: pass., Mt. v. 4 (5); Lk. xvi. 25; Acts xx. 12; 2 Co. vii. 13 (where a full stop must be put after παρακεκλήμ.); ἔν τινι, by the help of a thing, 2 Co. vii. 13; 6 sq.; ἐπί τινι, 1 Th. iii. 7; with (ἐν) παρακλήσει added, 2 Co. vii. 7. **4.** to encourage, strengthen, [i. e. in the language of A. V. comfort (see Wright, Bible Word-Book, 2d ed., s. v.)], (in faith, piety, hope): τὰς καρδίας, your hearts, Eph. vi. 22; Col. ii. 2; iv. 8; 2 Th. ii. 17, (also χεῖρας ἀσθενεῖς, Job iv. 3 for חזק; γόνατα παραλελυμένα, Is. xxxv. 3 sq. [see the Hebr.] for אמץ). **5.** it combines the ideas of exhorting and comforting and encouraging in Ro. xii. 8; 1 Co. xiv. 31; 1 Th. iii. 2. **6.** to instruct, teach: ἐν τῇ διδασκαλίᾳ, Tit. i. 9. [COMP.: συμ-παρακαλέω.] *

3871 παρα-καλύπτω : to cover over, cover up, hide, conceal: trop. ἦν παρακεκαλυμμένον ἀπ' αὐτῶν [it was concealed from them], a Hebraism, on which see in ἀποκρύπτω, b.), Lk. ix. 45 (Ezek. xxii. 26; Plat., Plut., al.).*

3872 παρα-κατα-θήκη, -ης, ἡ, (παρακατατίθημι), a deposit, a trust: so Rec. in 1 Tim. vi. 20; 2 Tim. i. 14; [Rec.elz 1633 in 2 Tim. i. 12 also]. (Hdt., Thuc., Xen., Aristot. eth. Nic. 5, 8, 5 p. 1135,b 4; Polyb., Diod. 15, 76; Joseph. antt. 4, 8, 38; Ael. v. h. 4, 1); see παραθήκη above.*

3873 παρά-κειμαι; (παρά and κεῖμαι); to lie beside [παρά, IV. 1], to be near (fr. Hom. down); to be present, at hand: Ro. vii. 18 (where see Meyer), 21.*

3874 παρά-κλησις, -εως, ἡ, (παρακαλέω, q. v.); **1.** prop. a calling near, summons, (esp. for help, Thuc. 4, 61; Dem. p. 275, 20). **2.** imploration, supplication, entreaty: 2 Co. viii. 4 (Strab. 13 p. 581; Joseph. antt. 3, 1, 5; [c. Ap. 2, 23, 3 π. πρὸς τὸν θεὸν ἔστω]; λόγοι παρακλήσεως, words of appeal, containing entreaties, 1 Macc.

x. 24). **3.** exhortation, admonition, encouragement: Acts xv. 31 [al. refer this to 4]; 1 Co. xiv. 3; 2 Co. viii. 17; Phil. ii. 1; 1 Tim. iv. 13; Heb. xii. 5; λόγος τῆς παρακλήσεως, Heb. xiii. 22, (2 Macc. xii. 24; xv. 9 (11); Plat. def. 415 e.; Thuc. 8, 92; Aeschin., Polyb., al.). **4.** consolation, comfort, solace: 2 Co. i. 4-7; Heb. vi. 18; [add, Acts ix. 31; 2 Thess. ii. 16], (Jer. xvi. 7; Hos. xiii. 14; [Job xxi. 2; Nah. iii. 7]; Phalar. ep. 97 init.); τῶν γραφῶν, afforded by the contents of the Scriptures, Ro. xv. 4 [W. 189 (178)]; θεὸς τῆς παρακλ., God the author and bestower of comfort, Ro. xv. 5; 2 Co. i. 3; solace or cheer which comes from a happy lot or a prosperous state of things, Lk. vi. 24; 2 Co. vii. 4, 7, 13 [cf. W. 393 (368)]; Philem. 7; by meton. that which affords comfort or refreshment; thus of the Messianic salvation, Lk. ii. 25 (so the Rabbins call the Messiah the consoler, the comforter, κατ' ἐξοχήν, מְנַחֵם [cf. Wünsche, Neue Beiträge u. s. w. ad loc.; Schöttgen, Horae Hebr. etc. ii. 18]). **5.** univ. persuasive discourse, stirring address, — instructive, admonitory, consolatory; powerful hortatory discourse: Ro. xii. 8; λόγος παρακλήσεως [A. V. word of exhortation], Acts xiii. 15; υἱὸς παρ. [a son of exhortation], a man gifted in teaching, admonishing, consoling, Acts iv. 36; used of the apostles' instruction or preaching, 1 Th. ii. 3.*

3875 παρά-κλητος, -ον, ὁ, (παρακαλέω), prop. summoned, called to one's side, esp. called to one's aid; hence **1.** one who pleads another's cause before a judge, a pleader, counsel for defence, legal assistant; an advocate: Dem. p. 341, 11; Diog. Laërt. 4, 50, cf. Dio Cass. 46, 20. **2.** univ. one who pleads another's cause with one, an intercessor: Philo, de mund. opif. § 59; de Josepho § 40; in Flaccum §§ 3 and 4; so of Christ, in his exaltation at God's right hand, pleading with God the Father for the pardon of our sins, 1 Jn. ii. 1 (in the same sense, of the divine Logos in Philo, vita Moys. iii. § 14). **3.** in the widest sense, a helper, succorer, aider, assistant; so of the Holy Spirit destined to take the place of Christ with the apostles (after his ascension to the Father), to lead them to a deeper knowledge of gospel truth, and to give them the divine strength needed to enable them to undergo trials and persecutions on behalf of the divine kingdom: Jn. xiv. 16, 26; xv. 26; xvi. 7, cf. Mt. x. 19 sq.; Mk. xiii. 11; Lk. xii. 11 sq. (Philo de mund. opif. § 6 init. says that God in creating the world had no need of a παράκλητος, an adviser, counsellor, helper. The Targums and Talmud borrow the Greek words פְּרַקְלִיט and פְּרַקְלִיטָא and use them of any intercessor, defender, or advocate; cf. Buxtorf, Lex. Talm. p. 1843 [(ed. Fischer p. 916)]; so Targ. on Job xxxiii. 23 for מֵלִיץ, i. e. an angel that pleads man's cause with God; [cf. πλουσίων παράκλητοι in 'Teaching' etc. 5 sub fin.; Barn. ep. 20, 2; Constitt. apost. 7, 18]). Cf. Knapp, Scripta varii Argumenti, p. 124 sqq.; Düsterdieck on 1 Jn. ii. 1, p. 147 sqq.; [Watkins, Excursus G, in Ellicott's N. T. Com. for Eng. Readers; Westcott in the "Speaker's Com." Additional Note on Jn. xiv. 16; Schaff in Lange ibid.].*

3876 παρ-ακοή, -ῆς, ἡ, (παρά Lat. praeter [see παρά, IV.

2]);　　**1.** prop. *a hearing amiss* (Plat. epp. 7 p. 341 b.).　　**2.** [*unwillingness to hear* i. e.] *disobedience*: Ro. v. 19; 2 Co. x. 6; Heb. ii. 2.　[Cf. Trench § lxvi.]*

3877　παρ-ακολουθέω, -ῶ: fut. παρακολουθήσω; 1 aor. παρηκολούθησα (1 Tim. iv. 6 L mrg. WH mrg.; 2 Tim. iii. 10 L T Tr WH txt.); pf. παρηκολούθηκα;　　**1.** *to follow after*; *so to follow one as to be always at his side* [see παρά, IV. 1]; *to follow close, accompany*, (so fr. Arstph. and Xen. down).　　**2.** metaph.　　**a.** *to be always present, to attend one wherever he goes*: τινί, Mk. xvi. 17 [where Tr WH txt. ἀκολουθ., q. v.].　　**b.** *to follow up a thing in mind so as to attain to the knowledge of it*, i. e. *to understand*, [cf. our *follow a matter up, trace its course*, etc.]; *to examine thoroughly, investigate*: πᾶσιν (i. e. πράγμασιν), all things that have taken place, Lk. i. 3 (very often so in Grk. auth., as Dem. pro cor. c. 53 [p. 285, 23]).　　**c.** *to follow faithfully* sc. *a standard* or *rule*, *to conform one's self to*: with a dat. of the thing, 1 Tim. iv. 6; 2 Tim. iii. 10, (2 Macc. ix. 27). Cf. the full discussion of this word by *Grimm* in the Jahrbb. f. deutsche Theol. for 1871, p. 46 sq.*

3878　παρ-ακούω: 1 aor. παρήκουσα;　　**1.** *to hear aside* i. e. *casually* or *carelessly* or *amiss* [see παρά, IV. 2] (often so in class. Grk.; on the freq. use of this verb by Philo see *Siegfried*, Philo von Alex. u. s. w. (1875) p. 106).　　**2.** *to be unwilling to hear*, i. e. *on hearing to neglect, to pay no heed to*, (w. a gen. of the pers., Polyb. 2, 8, 3; 3, 15, 2); contrary to Grk. usage [but cf. Plut. Philop. § 16, 1 καὶ παριδεῖν τι κ. παρακοῦσαι τῶν ἁμαρτανομένων, de curios. § 14 πειρῶ καὶ τῶν ἰδίων ἔνια παρακοῦσαί ποτε κ. παριδεῖν], w. an accus., τὸν λόγον, Mk. v. 36 T WH Tr txt. [al. 'overhearing the word as it was being spoken'; cf. B. 302 (259)]; *to refuse to hear, pay no regard to, disobey*: τινός, what one says, Mt. xviii. 17 (Tob. iii. 4; τὰ ὑπὸ τοῦ βασιλέως λεγόμενα, Esth. iii. 3).*

3879　παρα-κύπτω: 1 aor. παρέκυψα; *to stoop to* [cf. παρά, IV. 1] *a thing in order to look at it*; *to look at with head bowed forwards*; *to look into with the body bent*; *to stoop and look into*: Lk. xxiv. 12 [T om. L Tr br. WH reject the vs.]; Jn. xx. 5; εἰς τὸ μνημεῖον, Jn. xx. 11; metaph. *to look carefully into, inspect curiously*, εἴς τι, of one who would become acquainted with something, Jas. i. 25; 1 Pet. i. 12. (Arstph., Theocr., Philo, Dio Cass., Plut., al.; Sept.) *

3880　παρα-λαμβάνω; fut. παραλήψομαι, in L T Tr WH -λήμψομαι (Jn. xiv. 3; see M, μ); 2 aor. παρέλαβον, 3 pers. plur. παρελάβοσαν (2 Th. iii. 6 G T L mrg. Tr mrg. WH mrg.; cf. δολιόω [yet see *WH*. App. p. 165]); Pass., pres. παραλαμβάνομαι; 1 fut. παραληφθήσομαι, in L T Tr WH -λημφθήσομαι (see M, μ; Lk. xvii. 34–36); fr. Hdt. down; Sept. for לָקַח;　　**1.** *to take to* [cf. παρά, IV. 1], *to take with one's self, to join to one's self*: τινά, an associate, a companion, Mt. xvii. 1; xxvi. 37; Mk. iv. 36; v. 40; ix. 2; x. 32; Lk. ix. 10, 28; xi. 26; xviii. 31; Acts xv. 39; in pass., Mt. xxiv. 40, 41; Lk. xvii. 34–36; one to be led off as a prisoner, Jn. xix. 16; Acts xxiii. 18; to take with one in order to carry away, Mt. ii. 13 sq. 20 sq.; τινὰ μεθ' ἑαυτοῦ, Mt. xii. 45; xviii. 16; Mk. xiv. 33;

παραλαμβάνειν γυναῖκα, to take one's betrothed to his home, Mt. i. 20, 24; τινά foll. by εἰς w. an acc. of place, to take [and bring, cf. W. § 66, 2 d.] one with one into a place, Mt. iv. 5, 8; xxvii. 27; τινὰ κατ' ἰδίαν, Mt. xx. 17; mid. with πρὸς ἐμαυτόν, to my companionship, where I myself dwell, Jn. xiv. 3. The ptcp. is prefixed to other act. verbs to describe the action more in detail, Acts xvi. 33; xxi. 24, 26, 32 [here L WH mrg. λαβών]. Metaph. i. q. *to accept* or *acknowledge one to be such as he professes to be; not to reject, not to withhold obedience*: τινά, Jn. i. 11.　　**2.** *to receive something transmitted*;　　**a.** prop.: παραλ. διακονίαν, an office to be discharged, Col. iv. 17; βασιλείαν, Heb. xii. 28, (so for the Chald. קַבֵּל in Dan. v. 31; vii. 18, Theodot.; Hdt. 2, 120; [Joseph. c. Ap. 1, 20, 5 (where see Müller)]; τὴν ἀρχήν, Plat., Polyb., Plut.).　　**b.** *to receive with the mind*; *by oral transmission*: τί foll. by ἀπό w. a gen. of the author from whom the tradition proceeds, 1 Co. xi. 23 (on which cf. *Paret* in the Jahrbb. f. deutsche Theol. for 1858, Bd. iii. p. 48 sqq.; [see reff. in ἀπό, II. 2 d. aa.]); *by the narration of others, by the instruction of teachers* (used of disciples): [τὸν Χρ. Ἰ. τὸν κύριον, Col. ii. 6]; τί, 1 Co. xv. 1, 3; Gal. i. 9; Phil. iv. 9; [τί foll. by an infin., Mk. vii. 4]; τὶ παρά τινος [see reff. s. v. παρά, I. c.], Gal. i. 12; 1 Th. ii. 13; 2 Th. iii. 6; παρά τινος, καθὼς . . . τὸ πῶς δεῖ etc. 1 Th. iv. 1, (σοφίαν παρά τινος, Plat. Lach. p. 197 d.; Euthyd. p. 304 c.). [COMP.: συμ-παραλαμβάνω.]*

3881　παρα-λέγομαι; [παρελεγόμην]; (παρά beside, and λέγω to lay); Vulg. in Acts xxvii. 8 lego, i. e. *to sail past, coast along*: τὴν Κρήτην, Acts xxvii. 8 [here some, referring αὐτήν to Σαλμώνην, render *work past, weather*], 13, (τὴν Ἰταλίαν, Diod. 13, 3; γῆν, 14, 55; [Strabo]; Lat. *legere oram*).*

3882　παρ-άλιος, -ον, also of three term. [cf. W. § 11, 1], (παρά and ἅλς), *by the sea, maritime*: ἡ παράλιος, sc. χώρα, the sea-coast, Lk. vi. 17 (Polyb. 3, 39, 3; Diod. 3, 15, 41; Joseph. c. Ap. 1, 12; Sept. Deut. xxxiii. 19; and the fem. form ἡ παραλία in Deut. i. 7; Josh. ix. 1; Judith i. 7; iii. 6; v. 2, 23; vii. 8; 1 Macc. xi. 8; xv. 38; Hdt. 7, 185; often in Polyb.; Joseph. antt. 12, 7, 1).*

3883　παρ-αλλαγή, -ῆς, ἡ, (παραλλάσσω), *variation, change*: Jas. i. 17. (Aeschyl., Plat., Polyb., al.)*

3884　παρα-λογίζομαι; (see παρά, IV. 2);　　**a.** *to reckon wrong, miscount*: Dem. p. 822, 25; 1037, 15.　　**b.** *to cheat by false reckoning* (Aeschin., Aristot.); *to deceive by false reasoning* (joined to ἐξαπατᾶν, Epict. diss. 2, 20, 7); hence　　**c.** univ. *to deceive, delude, circumvent*: τινά, Col. ii. 4; Jas. i. 22, (Sept. several times for רָמָה).*

3885　παρα-λυτικός, -ή, -όν, (fr. παραλύω, q. v.), *paralytic*, i. e. suffering from the relaxing of the nerves of one side; univ. *disabled, weak of limb*, [A. V. *palsied, sick of the palsy*]: Mt. iv. 24; viii. 6; ix. 2, 6; Mk. ii. 3–5, 9; and L WH mrg. in Lk. v. 24.　[Cf. *Riehm*, HWB. s. v. Krankheiten, 5; B. D. Am. ed. p. 1866ᵇ.] *

3886　παρα-λύω; [pf. pass. ptcp. παραλελυμένος]; prop. *to loose on one side* or *from the side* [cf. παρά, IV. 1]; *to loose* or *part things placed side by side*; *to loosen, dissolve*, hence, *to weaken, enfeeble*: παραλελυμένος, *suffering from the relaxing of the nerves, unstrung, weak of limb*, [*palsied*], Lk. v. 18, 24 ([not L WH mrg.] see παραλυτικός); Acts viii. 7; ix. 33; παραλελ. γόνατα, i. e. *tottering, weakened, feeble knees*, Heb. xii. 12; Is. xxxv. 3; Sir. xxv. 23; χεῖρες παραλελ. Ezek. vii. 27; Jer. vi. 24; [xxvii. (l.) 15, 43]; παρελύοντο αἱ δεξιαί, *of combatants*, Joseph. b. j. 3, 8, 6; παρελύθη κ. οὐκ ἐδύνατο ἔτι λαλῆσαι λόγον, 1 Macc. ix. 55, where cf. Grimm; σωματικῇ δυνάμει παραλελ. Polyb. 32, 23, 1; τοῖς σώμασι καὶ ταῖς ψυχαῖς, id. 20, 10, 9.*

3887   **παρα-μένω**; fut. παραμενῶ; 1 aor. ptcp. παραμείνας; fr. Hom. down; *to remain beside, continue always near*, [cf. παρά, IV. 1]: Heb. vii. 23; opp. to ἀπεληλυθέναι, Jas. i. 25 (*and continues to do so*, not departing till all stains are washed away, cf. vs. 24); *with one*, πρός τινα, 1 Co. xvi. 6; τινί (as often in Grk. auth.), *to survive, remain alive* (Hdt. 1, 30), Phil. i. 25 L T Tr WH [where Bp. Lghtft.: "παραμενῶ is relative, while μενῶ is absolute." Comp.: συμ-παραμένω.] *

3888   **παρα-μυθέομαι**, -οῦμαι; 1 aor. παρεμυθησάμην; fr. Hom. down; *to speak to, address* one, whether *by way of admonition and incentive*, or *to calm and console*; hence i. q. *to encourage, console*: τινά, Jn. xi. 31; 1 Th. ii. 12 (11); v. 14; τινὰ περί τινος, Jn. xi. 19.*

3889   **παραμυθία**, -ας, ἡ, (παραμυθέομαι), in class. Grk. *any address*, whether made *for the purpose of persuading*, or *of arousing and stimulating*, or *of calming and consoling*; once in the N. T., like the Lat. *allocutio* (Sen. ad Marc. 1; ad Helv. 1), i. q. *consolation, comfort*: 1 Co. xiv. 3. (So Plat. Ax. p. 365 a.; Aeschin. dial. Socr. 3, 3; Joseph. b. j. 3, 7, 15; Lcian. dial. mort. 15, 3; Ael. v. h. 12, 1 fin.) *

3890   **παραμύθιον**, -ου, τό, (παραμυθέομαι), *persuasive address*: Phil. ii. 1. (*consolation*, Sap. iii. 18 and often in Grk. writ. [fr. Soph., Thuc., Plat. on].) *

3891   **παρανομέω**, -ῶ; *to be* a παράνομος, *to act contrary to law, to break the law*: Acts xxiii. 3. (Sept.; Thuc., Xen., Plat., sqq.) *

3892   **παρανομία**, -ας, ἡ, (παράνομος [fr. παρά (q. v. IV. 2) and νόμος]), *breach of law, transgression, wickedness*: 2 Pet. ii. 16. (Thuc., Plat., Dem., al.; Sept.) *

3893   **παρα-πικραίνω**: 1 aor. παρεπίκρανα; (see παρά, IV. 3); Sept. chiefly for מָרָה‎, הִמְרָה‎, *to be rebellious, contumacious, refractory*; also for סָרַר‎, הִכְעִיס‎, etc.; *to provoke, exasperate*; *to rouse to indignation*: absol. (yet so that God is thought of as the one provoked), Heb. iii. 16, as in Ps. cv. (cvi.) 7; lxv. (lxvi.) 7; lxvii. (lxviii.) 7; Ezek. ii. 5–8; with τὸν θεόν added, Jer. xxxix. (xxxii.) 29; li. (xliv.) 3, 8; Ps. v. 11; Ezek. xx. 21, and often; in pass., Lam. i. 20; joined with ὀργίζεσθαι, Philo de alleg. legg. iii. § 38; w. πληροῦσθαι ὀργῆς δικαίας, vita Moys. i. § 55 [al. πάνυ πικρ.]; παραπικραίνειν κ. παροργίζειν, de somn. ii. § 26.*

3894   **παρα-πικρασμός**, -οῦ, ὁ, (παραπικραίνω), *provocation*: ἐν τῷ παραπικρασμῷ, *when they provoked* (*angered*) me by rebelliousness, Heb. iii. 8, 15, fr. Ps. xciv. (xcv.) 8 (where Sept. for מְרִיבָה‎); cf. Num. xvi.*

3895   **παρα-πίπτω**: 2 aor. ptcp. παραπεσών; prop. *to fall beside* a pers. or thing; *to slip aside*; hence *to deviate from the right path, turn aside, wander*: τῆς ὁδοῦ, Polyb. 3, 54, 5; metaph. τῆς ἀληθείας, Polyb. 12, 12 (7), 2 [(here ed. Didot ἀντέχηται); τοῦ καθήκοντος, 8, 13, 8]; i. q. *to err*, Polyb. 18, 19, 6; ἔν τινι, Xen. Hell. 1, 6, 4. In the Scriptures, *to fall away* (from the true faith): from the worship of Jehovah, Ezek. xiv. 13; xv. 8 (for מָעַל‎); from Christianity, Heb. vi. 6.*

3896   **παρα-πλέω**: 1 aor. inf. παραπλεῦσαι; *to sail by, sail past*, [παρά, IV. 1]: w. an acc. of place, Acts xx. 16. (Thuc. 2, 25; Xen. anab. 6, 2, 1; Hell. 1, 3, 3; Plat. Phaedr. p. 259 a.) *

3897   **παρα-πλήσιον**, (neut. of the adj. παραπλήσιος), adv., *near to, almost to*: ἠσθένησε παραπλ. θανάτῳ [cf. W. § 54, 6], Phil. ii. 27. (Thuc. 7, 19; *in like manner*, Polyb.) *

3898   **παρα-πλησίως**, adv., (παραπλήσιος, see παραπλήσιον), *similarly, in like manner, in the same way*: Heb. ii. 14 (where it is equiv. to κατὰ πάντα vs. 17, and hence is used of a similarity which amounts to equality, as in the phrase ἀγωνίζεσθαι παραπλ. *to fight with equal advantage, aequo Marte*, Hdt. 1, 77; so too the adj., σὺ δὲ ἄνθρωπος ὢν παραπλήσιος τοῖς ἄλλοις, πλὴν γε δὴ ὅτι πολυπράγμων καὶ ἀτάσθαλος κτλ. the words in which an oriental sage endeavors to tame the pride of Alexander the Great, Arr. exp. Alex. 7, 1, 9 (6)).*

3899   **παρα-πορεύομαι**; impf. παρεπορευόμην; fr. Aristot. and Polyb. down; Sept. for עָבַר‎; *to proceed at the side, go past, pass by*: Mt. xxvii. 39; Mk. xi. 20; xv. 29; διὰ τῶν σπορίμων, to go along through the grain-fields so that he had the grain on either side of him as he walked [see ποιέω, I. 1 a. and c.], Mk. ii. 23 R G T WH mrg.; διὰ τῆς Γαλιλαίας, Vulg. *praetergredi Galilaeam*, i. e. "*obiter proficisci per Galilaeam*," i. e. 'they passed right along through, intent on finishing the journey, and not stopping to receive hospitality or to instruct the people' (Fritzsche), Mk. ix. 30 [but L txt. Tr txt. WH txt. ἐπορεύοντο]; διὰ τῶν ὁρίων, Deut. ii. 4. [Syn. cf. παραβαίνω, fin.] *

3900   **παρά-πτωμα**, -τος, τό, (παραπίπτω, q. v.); **1.** prop.. *a fall beside* or *near* something; but nowhere found in this sense. **2.** trop. *a lapse* or *deviation from truth and uprightness*; *a sin, misdeed*, [R. V. *trespass*, 'differing from ἁμάρτημα (q. v.) in figure not in force' (Fritzsche); cf. Trench § lxvi.]: Mt. vi. 14, [15ᵃ G T om. WH br.], 15ᵇ; xviii. 35 Rec.; Mk. xi. 25, 26 R G L; Ro. iv. 25; v. 15–18, 20; xi. 11 sq.; 2 Co. v. 19; Gal. vi. 1; Eph. i. 7; ii. 1, 5; Col. ii. 13; Jas. v. 16 (where L T Tr WH ἁμαρτίας). (Polyb. 9, 10, 6; Sap. iii. 13; x. 1; Sept. several times for מַעַל‎, עָוֶל‎, פֶּשַׁע‎, etc.; of literary faults, Longin. 36, 2.) *

see 3901 St.   **παρα-ρρέω**; (παρά and ῥέω); fr. Soph., Xen., and Plat. down; *to flow past* (παραρρέον ὕδωρ, Is. xliv. 4), *to glide by*: μήποτε παραρρυῶμεν (2 aor. pass. subjunc.; cf. *Bttm.* Ausf. Spr. ii. p. 287; [Veitch s. v. ῥέω; WH. App. p. 170]; but L T Tr WH παραρυῶμεν; see P, ρ), *lest we be carried past, pass by*, [R. V. *drift away* from them] (missing the thing), i. e. lest the salvation which the things heard show us how to obtain slip away from us, Heb. ii. 1. In

Grk. auth. παρραρεῖ μοί τι, *a thing escapes me*, Soph. Philoct. 653; trop. *slips from my mind*, Plat. legg. 6 p. 781 a.; in the sense of *neglect*, μὴ παρραρυῇς, τήρησον δὲ ἐμὴν βουλήν, Prov. iii. 21.*

3902　παράσημος, -ον, (παρά [q. v. IV. 2], and σῆμα [a mark]); 1. *marked falsely, spurious, counterfeit*; as coin. 2. *marked beside* or *on the margin*; so of noteworthy words, which the reader of a book marks on the margin; hence 3. univ. *noted, marked, conspicuous, remarkable*, (of persons, in a bad sense, *notorious*); *marked with a sign*: ἐν πλοίῳ παρασήμῳ Διοσκούροις, in a ship marked with the image or figure of the Dioscuri, Acts xxviii. 11 [cf. B. D. s. v. Castor and Pollux].*

3903　παρα-σκευάζω; pf. pass. παρεσκεύασμαι; fut. mid. παρασκευάσομαι; fr. Hdt. down; *to make ready, prepare*: sc. τὸ δεῖπνον (added in Hdt. 9, 82; Athen. 4, 15 p. 138), Acts x. 10 (συμπόσιον, Hdt. 9, 15; 2 Macc. ii. 27). Mid. *to make one's self ready, to prepare one's self*, [cf. W. § 38, 2 a.]: εἰς πόλεμον, 1 Co. xiv. 8 (Jer. xxvii. (l.) 42; εἰς μάχην, εἰς ναυμαχίαν, etc., in Xen.). Pf. pass. in mid. sense, *to have prepared one's self, to be prepared* or *ready*, 2 Co. ix. 2 sq. (see Matthiae § 493).*

3904　παρα-σκευή, -ῆς, ἡ, fr. Hdt. down; 1. *a making ready, preparation, equipping*. 2. *that which is prepared, equipment*. 3. in the N. T. in a Jewish sense, *the day of preparation*, i. e. the day on which the Jews made the necessary preparation to celebrate a sabbath or a feast: Mt. xxvii. 62; Mk. xv. 42; Lk. xxiii. 54; Jn. xix.-31, (Joseph. antt. 16, 6, 2); with a gen. of the obj., τοῦ πάσχα [acc. to W. 189 (177 sq.) a possess. gen.], Jn. xix. 14 (cf. *Rückert*, Abendmahl, p. 31 sq.); w. a gen. of the subj., τῶν Ἰουδαίων, ibid. 42. Cf. *Bleek*, Beiträge zur Evangelienkritik, p. 114 sqq.; [on later usage cf. 'Teaching' 8, 1 (and Harnack's note); Mart. Polyc. 7, 1 (and Zahn's note); *Soph.* Lex. s. v. 3].*

3905　παρα-τείνω: 1 aor. παρέτεινα; fr. Hdt. down; *to extend beside, to stretch out lengthwise, to extend*; *to prolong*: τὸν λόγον, his discourse, Acts xx. 7 (λόγους, Aristot. poet. 17, 5 p. 1455ᵇ, 2; μῦθον, 9, 4 p. 1451ᵇ, 38).*

3906　παρα-τηρέω, -ῶ: impf. 3 pers. plur. παρετήρουν; 1 aor. παρετήρησα; Mid., pres. παρατηροῦμαι; impf. 3 pers. plur. παρετηροῦντο; prop. *to stand beside and watch* [cf. παρά, IV. 1]; *to watch assiduously, observe carefully*; a. *to watch, attend to*, with the eyes: τὰ ἐκ τοῦ οὐρανοῦ γιγνόμενα, of auguries, Dio Cass. 38, 13; τινά, one, to see what he is going to do (Xen. mem. 3, 14, 4); contextually in a bad sense, *to watch insidiously*, Lk. xx. 20 [Tr mrg. ἀποχωρήσαντες] (joined with ἐνεδρεύειν, Polyb. 17, 3, 2); τινά (Polyb. 11, 9, 9; Sept. Ps. xxxvi. (xxxvii.) 12; Sus. 16) foll. by the interrog. εἰ, Mk. iii. 2 R G T WH Tr txt.; Lk. vi. 7 Rec.; mid. *to watch for one's self*: Mk. iii. 2 L Tr mrg.; Lk. vi. 7 L T Tr WH, [(in both pass. foll. by interrog. εἰ)]; Lk. xiv. 1; active w. an acc. of place (Polyb. 1, 29, 4): τὰς πύλας [foll. by ὅπως, cf. B. 237 (205)], Acts ix. 24 R G, where L T Tr WH give mid. παρετηροῦντο. b. *to observe* i. q. *to keep scrupulously*; *to neglect nothing requisite to the religious observance of*: ἑβδομάδας, Joseph. antt. 3, 5, 5; [τὴν τῶν σαββ. ἡμέραν,

id. 14, 10, 25]; mid. (*for one's self*, i. e. *for one's salvation*), ἡμέρας, μῆνας, καιρούς, Gal. iv. 10 (ὅσα προστάττουσιν οἱ νόμοι, Dio Cass. 53, 10; [τὰ εἰς βρῶσιν οὐ νενομισμένα, Joseph. c. Ap. 2, 39, 2]).*

3907　παρα-τήρησις, -εως, ἡ, (παρατηρέω), *observation* ([Polyb. 16, 22, 8], Diod., Joseph., Antonin., Plut., al.): μετὰ παρατηρήσεως, in such a manner that it can be watched with the eyes, i. e. in a visible manner, Lk. xvii. 20.*

3908　παρα-τίθημι; fut. παραθήσω; 1 aor. παρέθηκα; 2 aor. subjunc. 3 pers. plur. παραθῶσιν, infin. παραθεῖναι (Mk. viii. 7 R G); Pass., pres. ptcp. παρατιθέμενος; 1 aor. infin. παρατεθῆναι (Mk. viii. 7 Lchm.); Mid., pres. παρατίθεμαι; fut. παραθήσομαι; 2 aor. 3 pers. plur. παρέθεντο, impv. παράθου (2 Tim. ii. 2); fr. Hom. down; Sept. chiefly for שׂים, 1. *to place beside, place near* [cf. παρά, IV. 1] or *set before*: τινί τι, as a. food: Mk. vi. 41; viii. 6 sq.; Lk. ix. 16; xi. 6; τράπεζαν *a table*, i. e. food placed on a table, Acts xvi. 34 (Ep. ad Diogn. 5, 7); τὰ παρατιθέμενα ὑμῖν, [A. V. *such things as are set before you*], of food, Lk. x. 8 (Xen. Cyr. 2, 1, 30); sing. 1 Co. x. 27. b. *to set before* (one) *in teaching* (Xen. Cyr. 1, 6, 14; Sept. Ex. xix. 7): τινὶ παραβολήν, Mt. xiii. 24, 31. Mid. *to set forth* (*from one's self*), *to explain*: foll. by ὅτι, Acts xvii. 3. 2. Mid. *to place down* (*from one's self* or *for one's self*) *with any one, to deposit*; *to intrust, commit to one's charge*, (Xen. respub. Athen. 2, 16; Polyb. 33, 12, 3; Plut. Num. 9; Tob. iv. 1): τί τινι, a thing to one to be cared for, Lk. xii. 48; a thing to be religiously kept and taught to others, 1 Tim. i. 18; 2 Tim. ii. 2; τινά τινι, to commend one to another for protection, safety, etc., Acts xiv. 23; xx. 32, (Diod. 17, 23); τὰς ψυχάς to God, 1 Pet. iv. 19; τὸ πνεῦμά μου εἰς χεῖρας θεοῦ, Lk. xxiii. 46; Ps. xxx. (xxxi.) 6.*

3909　παρα-τυγχάνω; fr. Hom. (Il. 11, 74) down; *to chance to be by* [cf. παρά, IV. 1], *to happen to be present, to meet by chance*: Acts xvii. 17.*

3910　παρ-αυτίκα [cf. B. § 146, 4], adv., *for the moment*: 2 Co. iv. 17. (Tragg., Xen., Plat., sqq.) *

3911　παρα-φέρω: [1 aor. inf. παρενέγκαι (Lk. xxii. 42 Tdf., cf. Veitch p. 669)]; 2 aor. inf. παρενεγκεῖν (Lk. xxii. 42 R G), impv. παρένεγκε [(ibid. L Tr WH)]; pres. pass. παραφέρομαι; see reff. s. v. φέρω]; 1. *to bear to* [cf. παρά, IV. 1], *bring to, put before*: of food (Hdt., Xen., al.). 2. *to lead aside* [cf. παρά, IV. 2] *from the right course* or *path, to carry away*: Jude 12 [R. V. *carried along*] (where Rec. περιφέρ.); from the truth, Heb. xiii. 9 where Rec. περιφέρ., (Plat. Phaedr. p. 265 b.; Plut. Timol. 6; Antonin. 4, 43; Hdian. 8, 4, 7 [4 ed. Bekk.]). 3. *to carry past, lead past*, i. e. *to cause to pass by, to remove*: τὶ ἀπό τινος, Mk. xiv. 36; Lk. xxii. 42.*

3912　παρα-φρονέω, -ῶ; (παράφρων [fr. παρά (q. v. IV. 2) and φρήν, 'beside one's wits']); *to be beside one's self, out of one's senses, void of understanding, insane*: 2 Co. xi. 23. (From Aeschyl. and Hdt. down; once in Sept., Zech. vii. 11.) *

3913　παρα-φρονία, -ας, ἡ, (παράφρων [see the preceding word]), *madness, insanity*: 2 Pet. ii. 16. The Grk. writ use not this word but παραφροσύνη [cf. W. 24; 95 (90)].*

3914   **παρα-χειμάζω**: fut. παραχειμάσω; 1 aor. inf. παραχειμάσαι; pf. ptcp. παρακεχειμακώς; *to winter, pass the winter, with one* or *at a place*: Acts xxvii. 12; 1 Co. xvi. 6; ἐν τῇ νήσῳ, Acts xxviii. 11; ἐκεῖ, Tit. iii. 12. (Dem. p. 909, 15; Polyb. 2, 64, 1; Diod. 19, 34; Plut. Sertor. 3; Dio Cass. 40, 4.)*

3915   **παρα-χειμασία, -ας, ἡ,** (παραχειμάζω), *a passing the winter, wintering*: Acts xxvii. 12. (Polyb. 3, 34, 6; [3, 35, 1]; Diod. 19, 68.) *

3916   **παρα-χρῆμα,** (prop. i. q. παρὰ τὸ χρῆμα; cf. our *on the spot*), fr. Hdt. down; *immediately, forthwith, instantly*: Mt. xxi. 19 sq.; Lk. i. 64; iv. 39; v. 25; viii. 44, 47, 55; xiii. 13; xviii. 43; xix. 11; xxii. 60; Acts iii. 7; v. 10; ix. 18 Rec.; xii. 23; xiii. 11; xvi. 26 [WH br. παραχρ.], 33. (Sap. xviii. 17; 2 Macc. iv. 34, 38, etc.; Sept. for פִּתְאֹם, Num. vi. 9; xii. 4; Is. xxix. 5; xxx. 13.) *

3917   **πάρδαλις, -εως, ἡ,** fr. Hom. down; Sept. for נָמֵר; *a pard, panther, leopard*; a very fierce Asiatic and African animal, having a tawny skin marked with large black spots [cf. *Tristram,* Nat. Hist. etc. p. 111 sqq.; BB. DD. s. v.]: Rev. xiii. 2.*

see 4332   **παρ-εδρεύω**; (fr. πάρ-εδρος, sitting beside [cf. παρά, IV. 1]); *to sit beside, attend constantly,* (Lat. *assidere*), (Eur., Polyb., Diod., al.): τῷ θυσιαστηρίῳ, *to perform the duties pertaining to the offering of sacrifices and incense,* [*to wait upon*], 1 Co. ix. 13 L T Tr WH (for Rec. προσεδρ.).*

3918   **πάρ-ειμι;** impf. 3 pers. pl. παρῆσαν; fut. 3 pers. sing. παρέσται (Rev. xvii. 8 L T [not as G Tr WH Alf., al.] πάρεσται; see *Bttm.* Ausf. Spr. §108, Anm. 20; Chandler §803]); (παρά near, by, [see παρά, IV. 1 fin.] and εἰμί); Sept. chiefly for בּוֹא; as in Grk. auth. fr. Hom. down **a.** *to be by, be at hand, have arrived, to be present*: of persons, Lk. xiii. 1; Jn. xi. 28; Acts x. 21; Rev. xvii. 8; παρών, *present* (opp. to ἀπών), 1 Co. v. 3; 2 Co. x. 2, 11; xiii. 2, 10; ἐπί τινος, before one (a judge), Acts xxiv. 19; ἐπί τινι, for (to do) something, Mt. xxvi. 50 Rec.; ἐπί τι, ibid. G L T Tr WH (on which see ἐπί, B. 2 a. ζ.); ἐνώπιον θεοῦ, in the sight of God, Acts x. 33 [not Tr mrg.]; ἐνθάδε, ib. xvii. 6; πρός τινα, with one, Acts xii. 20; 2 Co. xi. 9 (8); Gal. iv. 18, 20. of time: ὁ καιρὸς πάρεστιν, Jn. vii. 6; τὸ παρόν, the present, Heb. xii. 11 (3 Macc. v. 17; see exx. fr. Grk. auth. in Passow s. v. 2 b.; [L. and S. s. v. II.; *Soph.* Lex. s. v. b.]). of other things: τοῦ εὐαγγελίου τοῦ παρόντος εἰς ὑμᾶς, which is come unto (and so is present among) you, Col. i. 6 (foll. by εἰς w. an acc. of place, 1 Macc. xi. 63, and often in prof. auth. fr. Hdt. down; see εἰς, C. 2). **b.** *to be ready, in store, at command*: ἡ παροῦσα ἀλήθεια, the truth which ye now hold, so that there is no need of words to call it to your remembrance, 2 Pet. i. 12; (μὴ) πάρεστίν τινί τι, ibid. 9 [A. V. *lacketh*], and Lchm. in 8 also [where al. ὑπάρχοντα], (Sap. xi. 22 (21), and often in class. Grk. fr. Hom. down; cf. Passow u. s.; [L. and S. u. s.]); τὰ παρόντα, *possessions, property,* [A. V. *such things as ye have* (cf. our 'what one *has* by him')], Heb. xiii. 5 (οἷς τὰ παρόντα

ἀρκεῖ, ἥκιστα τῶν ἀλλοτρίων ὀρέγονται, Xen. symp. 4, 42). [COMP. : συμ-πάρειμι.]*

3919   **παρ-εισ-άγω**: fut. παρεισάξω; (see παρά, IV. 1); *to introduce* or *bring in secretly* or *craftily*: αἱρέσεις ἀπωλείας, 2 Pet. ii. 1. In the same sense of heretics: ἕκαστος ἰδίως καὶ ἑτέρως ἰδίαν δόξαν παρεισηγάγοσαν, Hegesipp. ap. Euseb. h. e. 4, 22, 5; δοκοῦσι παρεισάγειν τὰ ἄρρητα αὐτῶν ... μυστήρια, Orig. philos. [i. q. Hippol. refut. omn. haeres.] 5, 17 fin.; of Marcion, νομίζων καινόν τι παρεισάγειν, ibid. 7, 29 init.; — passages noted by *Hilgenfeld,* Zeitschr. f. wissensch. Theol. 1860, p. 125 sq. (οἱ προδόται τοὺς στρατιώτας παρεισαγαγόντες ἐντὸς τῶν τειχῶν κυρίους τῆς πόλεως ἐποίησαν, Diod. 12, 41 [cf. Polyb. 1, 18, 3; 2, 7, 8]. In other senses in other prof. auth.) *

3920   **παρ-είσ-ακτος, -ον,** (παρεισάγω), *secretly* or *surreptitiously brought in*; [A. V. *privily brought in*]; *one who has stolen in* (Vulg. *subintroductus*): Gal. ii. 4; cf. *C. F. A. Fritzsche* in Fritzschiorum opusc. p. 181 sq.*

3921   **παρ-εισ-δύω** or παρεισδύνω: 1 aor. παρεισέδυσα [acc. to class. usage trans., cf. δύνω; (see below)]; *to enter secretly, slip in stealthily; to steal in;* [A. V. *creep in unawares*]: Jude 4 [here WH παρεισεδύησαν, 3 pers. plur. 2 aor. pass. (with mid. or intrans. force); see their App. p. 170, and cf. B. 56 (49); Veitch s. v. δύω, fin.]; cf. the expressions παρείσδυσιν πλάνης ποιεῖν, Barn. ep. 2, 10; ἔχειν, ibid. 4, 9. (Hippocr., Hdian. 1, 6, 2; 7, 9, 18 [8 ed. Bekk.]; Philo de spec. legg. §15]; Plut., Galen, al.) *

3922   **παρ-εισ-έρχομαι:** 2 aor. παρεισῆλθον; **1.** *to come in secretly* or *by stealth* [cf. παρά, IV. 1], *to creep* or *steal in,* (Vulg. *subintroeo*): Gal. ii. 4 (Polyb. 1, 7, 3; 1, 8, 4; [esp.] 2, 55, 3; Philo de opif. mund. §52; de Abrah. §19, etc.; Plut. Poplic. 17; Clem. homil. 2, 23). **2.** *to enter in addition, come in besides,* (Vulg. *subintro*): Ro. v. 20, cf. 12.*

3923   **παρ-εισ-φέρω:** 1 aor. παρεισήνεγκα; **a.** *to bring in besides* (Dem., al.). **b.** *to contribute besides* to something: σπουδήν, 2 Pet. i. 5 [R. V. *adding on your part*].*

3924   **παρ-εκτός** (for which the Grk. writ. fr. Hom. down use παρέκ, παρέξ); **1.** prep. w. gen. [cf. W. § 54, 6], *except; with the exception of* (a thing, expressed by the gen.): Mt. v. 32; xix. 9 L WH mrg.; Acts xxvi. 29, (Deut. i. 36 Aq.; Test. xii. Patr. p. 631; ['Teaching' 6, §1]; Geop. 13, 15, 7). **2.** adv. *besides*: τὰ παρεκτός sc. γινόμενα, the things that occur besides or in addition, 2 Co. xi. 28 [cf. our 'extra matters'; al. *the things that I omit*; but see Meyer].*

see 4016   **παρ-εμ-βάλλω:** fut. παρεμβαλῶ; fr. Arstph. and Dem. down; **1.** *to cast in by the side of* or *besides* [cf. παρά, IV. 1], *to insert, interpose; to bring back into line.* **2.** from Polyb. on, in military usage, *to assign* to soldiers *a place, whether in camp* or *in line of battle, to draw up in line, to encamp* (often in 1 Macc., and in Sept. where for חָנָה): τινὶ χάρακα, *to cast up a bank about a city,* Lk. xix. 43 L mrg. T WH txt.*

3925   **παρ-εμ-βολή, -ῆς, ἡ,** (παρεμβάλλω, q. v.); **1.** *interpolation, insertion* (into a discourse of matters foreign to the subject in hand, Aeschin.). **2.** In the Maced. dialect (cf. *Sturz,* De dial. Maced. et Alex. p. 30; *Lob.*

ad Phryn. p. 377; [W. 22]) *an encampment* (Polyb., Diod., Joseph., Plut.); **a.** *the camp of the Israelites in the desert* (an enclosure within which their tents were pitched), Ex. xxix. 14; xix. 17; xxxii. 17; hence in Heb. xiii. 11 used for *the city of Jerusalem*, inasmuch as that was to the Israelites what formerly the encampment had been in the desert; of *the sacred congregation* or *assembly of Israel*, as that had been gathered formerly in camps in the wilderness, ib. 13. **b.** *the barracks of the Roman soldiers*, which at Jerusalem were in the castle Antonia: Acts xxi. 34, 37; xxii. 24; xxiii. 10, 16, 32. **3.** *an army in line of battle*: Heb. xi. 34; Rev. xx. 9 [here A. V. *camp*], (Ex. xiv. 19, 20; Judg. iv. 16; viii. 11; 1 S. xiv. 16; very often in Polyb.; Ael. v. h. 14, 46). Often in Sept. for מַחֲנֶה, which signifies both *camp* and *army*; freq. in both senses in 1 Macc.; cf. Grimm on 1 Macc. iii. 3.*

3926 **παρ-εν-οχλέω, -ῶ;** (see ἐνοχλέω); *to cause trouble in a matter* (παρά equiv. to παρά τινι πράγματι), *to trouble, annoy*: τινί, Acts xv. 19. (Sept.; Polyb., Diod., Plut., Epict., Lcian., al.)*

3927 **παρ-επί-δημος, -ον,** (see ἐπιδημέω), prop. *one who comes from a foreign country into a city* or *land to reside there by the side of the natives*; hence *stranger*; *sojourning in a strange place, a foreigner*, (Polyb. 32, 22, 4; Athen. 5 p. 196 a.); in the N. T. metaph. in ref. to heaven as the native country, *one who sojourns on earth*: so of Christians, 1 Pet. i. 1; joined with πάροικοι, 1 Pet. ii. 11, cf. i. 17, (Christians πατρίδας οἰκοῦσιν ἰδίας, ἀλλ' ὡς πάροικοι· μετέχουσι πάντων ὡς πολῖται, καὶ πάνθ' ὑπομένουσιν ὡς ξένοι· πᾶσα ξένη πατρίς ἐστιν αὐτῶν, καὶ πᾶσα πατρὶς ξένη, Ep. ad Diogn. c. 5); of the patriarchs, ξένοι κ. παρεπίδημοι ἐπὶ τῆς γῆς, Heb. xi. 13 (Gen. xxiii. 4; Ps. xxxviii. (xxxix.) 13; παρεπιδημία τίς ἐστιν ὁ βίος, Aeschin. dial. Socr. 3, 3, where see Fischer.)*

3928 **παρ-έρχομαι;** fut. παρελεύσομαι; pf. παρελήλυθα; 2 aor. παρῆλθον, 3 pers. impv. παρελθάτω (Mt. xxvi. 39 L T Tr WH; see ἀπέρχομαι, init.); fr. Hom. down; Sept. mostly for עָבַר; **1.** (παρά past [cf. παρά, IV. 1]) *to go past, pass by*; **a.** prop. **α.** of persons moving forward: *to pass by*, absol. Lk. xviii. 37; τινά, *to go past one*, Mk. vi. 48; w. an acc. of place, Acts xvi. 8 (Hom. Il. 8, 239; Xen. an. 4, 2, 12; Plat. Alc. 1 p. 123 b.); διὰ τῆς ὁδοῦ ἐκείνης, Mt. viii. 28. **β.** of time: Mt. xiv. 15; ὁ παρεληλυθὼς χρόνος [A. V. *the time past*], 1 Pet. iv. 3, (Soph., Isocr., Xen., Plat., Dem., al.); of an act continuing for a time [viz. the Fast], Acts xxvii. 9. (τὰ παρελθόντα and τὰ ἐπιόντα are distinguished in Ael. v. h. 14, 6.) **b.** metaph. **a.** *to pass away, perish*: ὡς ἄνθος, Jas. i. 10 ὁ οὐρανός, Mt. v. 18; xxiv. 35; Mk. xiii. 31; Lk. xvi. 17; xxi. 33; 2 Pet. iii. 10; Rev. xxi. 1 Rec.; ἡ γενεὰ αὕτη, Mt. xxiv. 34; Mk. xiii. 30 sq.; Lk. xxi. 32; οἱ λόγοι μου, Mt. xxiv. 35; Mk. xiii. 31; Lk. xxi. 33; τὰ ἀρχαῖα παρῆλθεν, 2 Co. v. 17, (Ps. xxxvi. (xxxvii.) 36; Dan. vii. 14 Theodot.; Sap. ii. 4; v. 9; Dem. p. 291, 12; Theocr. 27, 8). Here belongs also Mt. v. 18 ('not even the smallest part shall pass away from the law,' i. e. so as no longer to belong to it). **β.** *to pass by* (*pass over*), i. e. *to neg-*lect, omit, (transgress): w. an acc. of the thing, Lk. xi. 42; xv. 29, (Deut. xvii. 2; Jer. xli. (xxxiv.) 18; Judith xi. 10; 1 Macc. ii. 22; Διὸς νόον, Hes. theog. 613; νόμον, Lys. p. 107, 52; Dem. p. 977, 14). **γ.** *to be led by, to be carried past, be averted*: ἀπό τινος, *from one* i. e. so as not to hit, not to appear to, (2 Chr. ix. 2); παρελθάτω ἀπ' ἐμοῦ τὸ ποτήριον, Mt. xxvi. 39; παρελθεῖν, 42 [here G T Tr WH om. L br. ἀπ' ἐμοῦ]; ἀπ' αὐτοῦ ἡ ὥρα, Mk. xiv. 35. **2.** (παρά to [cf. παρά, IV. 1]) *to come near, come forward, arrive*: Lk. xii. 37; xvii. 7; Acts xxiv. 7 Rec. (and in Grk. auth. fr. Aeschyl. and Hdt. down). [SYN. see παραβαίνω, fin. COMP. ἀντι-παρέρχομαι.] *

3929 **πάρεσις, -εως, ἡ,** (παρίημι, q. v.), *pretermission, passing over, letting pass, neglecting, disregarding*: διὰ τὴν πάρεσιν ... ἀνοχῇ τοῦ θεοῦ, because God had patiently let pass the sins committed previously (to the expiatory death of Christ), i. e. had tolerated, had not punished (and so man's conception of his holiness was in danger of becoming dim, if not extinct), Ro. iii. 25, where cf. Fritzsche; [Trench § xxxiii. (Hippocr., Dion. Hal., al.)].*

3930 **παρ-έχω;** impf. παρεῖχον, 3 pers. plur. παρεῖχαν (Acts xxviii. 2 L T Tr WH; see ἔχω, init., and ἀπέρχομαι, init.); fut. 3 pers. sing. παρέξει (Lk. vii. 4 R G; see below); 2 aor. 3 pers. plur. παρέσχον, ptcp. παρασχών; Mid., [pres. παρέχομαι]; impf. παρειχόμην; fut. 2 pers. sing. παρέξῃ (Lk. vii. 4 L T Tr WH); fr. Hom. down; Plautus's *praehibeo* i. e. *praebeo* (Lat. *prae* fr. the Grk. παραί [but see Curtius §§ 346, 380 (cf. παρά, IV. 1 fin.)]); i. e. **a.** *to reach forth, offer*: τί τινι, Lk. vi. 29. **b.** *to show, afford, supply*: τινὶ ἡσυχίαν, Acts xxii. 2; φιλανθρωπίαν, Acts xxviii. 2; πάντα, 1 Tim. vi. 17. **c.** *to be the author of*, or *to cause one to have*; *to give, bring, cause*, one something — either unfavorable: κόπους, Mt. xxvi. 10; Mk. xiv. 6; Lk. xi. 7; xviii. 5; Gal. vi. 17 (παρ. πόνον, Sir. xxix. 4; ἀγῶνα, Is. vii. 13; πράγματα, very often fr. Hdt. down; also ὄχλον, see Passow s. v. ὄχλος, 3; [L. and S. s. v. II.]); — or favorable: ἐργασίαν, Acts xvi. 16, and Lchm. in xix. 24; πίστιν, [A. V. *to give assurance*], Acts xvii. 31, on which phrase cf. Fischer, De vitiis lexic. N. T. pp. 37–39; i. q. *to occasion* (ζητήσεις, see οἰκονομία), 1 Tim. i. 4. Mid. **1.** *to offer, show*, or *present one's self*: with ἑαυτόν added (W. § 38, 6; [B. § 135, 6]), w. an acc. of the predicate, τύπον, a pattern, Tit. ii. 7; παράδειγμα ... τοιόνδε ἑαυτὸν παρείχετο, Xen. Cyr. 8, 1, 39; [Joseph. c. Ap. 2, 15, 4]; in the act., Plut. puer. educ. c. 20 init. **2.** *to exhibit* or *offer on one's own part*: τὸ δίκαιον τοῖς δούλοις, Col. iv. 1; *to render* or *afford from one's own resources* or *by one's own power*: τινί τι, Lk. vii. 4 (where if we read, with Rec., παρέξει, it must be taken as the 3d pers. sing. of the fut. act. [in opp. to W. § 13, 2 a.], the elders being introduced as talking among themselves; but undoubtedly the reading παρέξῃ should be restored [see above ad init.], and the elders are addressing Jesus; cf. Meyer ad loc.; [and on the construction, cf. B. § 139, 32]). On the mid. of this verb, cf. Krüger § 52, 8, 2; W. § 38, 5 end; [Ellic. and Lghtft. on Col. u. s.].*

3931 **παρηγορία, -ας, ἡ,** (παρηγορέω [to address]), prop. *an* *addressing, address*; i. e.   **a.** *exhortation* (4 Macc. v. 11; vi. 1; Apoll. Rh. 2, 1281).   **b.** *comfort, solace, relief, alleviation, consolation* : Col. iv. 11 [where see Bp. Lghtft.]. (Aeschyl. Ag. 95; Philo, q. deus immort. § 14; de somn. i. § 18; Joseph. antt. 4, 8, 3; often in Plut.; Hierocl.) *

3932   παρθενία, -ας, ἡ, (παρθένος), *virginity* : Lk. ii. 36. (Jer. iii. 4; Pind., Aeschyl., Eur., Diod., Plut., Hdian., al. [cf. *Field, Otium Norv.* pars iii. ad loc.].) *

3933   παρθένος, -ου, ἡ,   **1.** *a virgin* : Mt. i. 23 (fr. Is. vii. 14); xxv. 1, 7, 11; Lk. i. 27; Acts xxi. 9; 1 Co. vii. 25, 28, 33(34), (fr. Hom. down; Sept. chiefly for בְּתוּלָה, several times for נַעֲרָה; twice for עַלְמָה; i. e. either *a marriageable maiden,* or *a young (married) woman*, Gen. xxiv. 43; Is. vii. 14, on which (last) word cf., besides *Gesenius, Thes.* p. 1037, *Credner, Beiträge* u.s.w. ii. p. 197 sqq.; παρθένος of a young bride, newly married woman, Hom. Il. 2, 514); ἡ παρθ. τινός, one's marriageable daughter, 1 Co. vii. 36 sqq.; παρθ. ἀγνή, a pure virgin, 2 Co. xi. 2.   **2.** *a man who has abstained from all uncleanness and whoredom attendant on idolatry, and so has kept his chastity* : Rev. xiv. 4, where see De Wette. In eccl. writ. *one who has never had commerce with women* ; so of Joseph, in *Fabricius,* Cod. pseudepigr. Vet. Test. ii. pp. 92, 98; of Abel and Melchizedek, in Suidas [10 a. and 2450 b.]; esp. of the apostle John, as in Nonnus, metaph. ev. Joann. 19, 140 (Jn. xix. 26), ἠνίδε παρθένον υἷα.*

3934   Πάρθος, -ου, ὁ, *a Parthian,* an inhabitant of Parthia, a district of Asia, bounded on the N. by Hyrcania, on the E. by Ariana, on the S. by Carmania Deserta, on the W. by Media; plur. in Acts ii. 9 of the Jewish residents of Parthia. [B. D. s. v. Parthians; *Geo. Rawlinson,* Sixth Great Oriental Monarchy, etc. (Lond. 1873).]*

3935   παρ-ίημι : 2 aor. inf. παρεῖναι (Lk. xi. 42 L T Tr WH); pf. pass. ptcp. παρειμένος; fr. Hom. down;   **1.** *to let pass; to pass by, neglect,* (very often in Grk. writ. fr. Pind., Aeschyl., Hdt. down), *to disregard, omit* : τί, Lk. xi. 42 [R G ἀφιέναι] (ἁμαρτήματα, *to pass over,* let go unpunished, Sir. xxiii. 2; [τιμωρίαν, Lycurg. 148, 41]).   **2.** *to relax, loosen, let go,* [see παρά, IV. 2], (e. g. a bow); pf. pass. ptcp. παρειμένος, *relaxed, unstrung, weakened, exhausted,* (Eur., Plat., Diod., Plut., al.) : χεῖρες, Heb. xii. 12; Sir. ii. 13; xxv. 23, cf. Zeph. iii. 16; Jer. iv. 31; ἀργοὶ καὶ παρειμένοι ἐπὶ ἔργον ἀγαθόν, Clem. Rom. 1 Cor. 34, 4 cf. 1. Cf. παραλύω.*

παραιστάνω, see παρίστημι.

3936   παρ-ίστημι and (in later writ., and in the N. T. in Ro. vi. 13, 16) παριστάνω; fut. παραστήσω; 1 aor. παρέστησα; 2 aor. παρέστην; pf. παρέστηκα, ptcp. παρεστηκώς and παρεστώς; plupf. 3 pers. plur. παρειστήκεισαν (Acts i. 10 [WH παριστ.; see ἵστημι, init.]); 1 fut. mid. παραστήσομαι; fr. Hom. down.   **1.** The pres., impf., fut. and 1 aor. act. have a transitive sense (Sept. chiefly for הֶעֱמִיד),   **a.** *to place beside* or *near* [παρά, IV. 1]; *to set at hand; to present; to proffer; to provide* : κτήνη, Acts xxiii. 24 (σκάφη, 2 Macc. xii. 3); τινά or τί τινι, *to place a person or thing at one's disposal,* Mt. xxvi.

53; *to present a person for another to see and question,* Acts xxiii. 33; *to present* or *show,* τινά or τί with an acc. of the quality which the person or thing exhibits : οἷς παρέστησεν ἑαυτὸν ζῶντα, Acts i. 3; add, Ro. vi. 13, 16, 19; 2 Co. xi. 2; Eph. v. 27; 2 Tim. ii. 15, ("te vegetum nobis in Graecia siste," Cic. ad Att. 10, 16, 6); τινά with a pred. acc. foll. by κατενώπιόν τινος, Col. i. 22; ἑαυτὸν ὥς [ὡσεί] τινά τινι, Ro. vi. 13; *to bring, lead to,* in the sense of *presenting,* without a dat. : Acts ix. 41; Col. i. 28. of sacrifices or of things consecrated to God: τὰ σώματα ὑμῶν θυσίαν . . . τῷ θεῷ, Ro. xii. 1 (so also in prof. auth. : Polyb. 16, 25, 7; Joseph. antt. 4, 6, 4; Lcian. deor. concil. 13; Lat. *admoveo,* Verg. Aen. 12, 171; *sisto,* Stat. Theb. 4, 445); τινά (a first-born) τῷ κυρίῳ, Lk. ii. 22; *to bring to, bring near,* metaphorically, i. e. *to bring into one's fellowship* or *intimacy* : τινὰ τῷ θεῷ, 1 Co. viii. 8; sc. τῷ θεῷ, 2 Co. iv. 14.   **b.** *to present (show) by argument, to prove* : τί, Acts xxiv. 13 (Epict. diss. 2, 23, 47; foll. by πῶς, id. 2, 26, 4; τινί τι, Xen. oec. 13, 1; τινί, ὅτι, Joseph. antt. 4, 3, 2; de vita sua § 6).   **2.** Mid. and pf., plupf., 2 aor. act., in an intransitive sense (Sept. chiefly for עָמַד, also for נִצָּב), *to stand beside, stand by* or *near, to be at hand, be present;*   **a.** univ. *to stand by* : τινί, *to stand beside one,* Acts i. 10; ix. 39; xxiii. 2; xxvii. 23; ὁ παρεστηκώς, *a by-stander,* Mk. xiv. 47, 69 [here T Tr WH παρεστώσιν]; xv. 35 [here Tdf. παρεστώτων, WH mrg. ἑστηκότων], 39; Jn. xviii. 22 [L mrg. Tr mrg. παρεστώτων]; ὁ παρεστώς, Mk. xiv. 70; Jn. xix. 26 [here anarthrous].   **b.** *to appear* : w. a pred. nom. foll. by ἐνώπιόν τινος, Acts iv. 10 [A. V. *stand here*]; before a judge, Καίσαρι, Acts xxvii. 24; mid. τῷ βήματι τοῦ θεοῦ [R G Χριστοῦ], Ro. xiv. 10.   **c.** *to be at hand, stand ready* : of assailants, absol. Acts iv. 26 [A. V. *stood up*] (fr. Ps. ii. 2); *to be at hand for service,* of servants in attendance on their master (Lat. *appareo*), τινί, Esth. iv. 5; ἐνώπιόν τινος, 1 K. x. 8; ἐνώπιον τοῦ θεοῦ, of a presence-angel [A. V. *that stand in the presence of God*], Lk. i. 19, cf. Rev. viii. 2; absol. οἱ παρεστῶτες, *them that stood by,* Lk. xix. 24; with αὐτῷ added (viz. the high-priest), Acts xxiii. 2, 4.   **d.** *to stand by to help, to succor,* (Germ. *beistehen*) : τινί, Ro. xvi. 2; 2 Tim. iv. 17, (Hom. Il. 10, 290; Hes. th. 439; Arstph. vesp. 1388; Xen.; Dem. p. 366, 20; 1120, 26, and in other authors).   **e.** *to be present; to have come* : of time, Mk. iv. 29.*

3937   Παρμενᾶς [prob. contr. fr. Παρμενίδης 'steadfast'; cf. W. 103 (97)], acc. -ᾶν [cf. B. 20 (18)], ὁ, *Parmenas,* one of the seven "deacons" of the primitive church at Jerusalem : Acts vi. 5.*

3938   πάρ-οδος, -ου, ἡ, (παρά, near by; ὁδός), *a passing by* or *passage* : ἐν παρόδῳ, *in passing,* [A. V. *by the way*], 1 Co. xvi. 7. (Thuc. 1, 126; v. 4; Polyb. 5, 68, 8; Cic. ad Att. 5, 20, 2; Lcian. dial. deor. 24, 2.) *

3939   παρ-οικέω, -ῶ; 1 aor. παρῴκησα;   **1.** prop. *to dwell beside (one)* or *in one's neighborhood* [παρά, IV. 1]; *to live near;* (Xen., Thuc., Isocr., al.).   **2.** in the Scriptures *to be* or *dwell in a place as a stranger, to sojourn,* (Sept. for גּוּר, several times also for יָשַׁב and שָׁכֵן) : foll.

by ἐν w. a dat. of place, Lk. xxiv. 18 R L (Gen. xx. 1 ; xxi. 34 ; xxvi. 3 ; Ex. xii. 40 cod. Alex. ; Lev. xviii. 3 [Ald.], etc.) ; w. an acc. of place, ibid. G T Tr WH (Gen. xvii. 8 ; Ex. vi. 4) ; εἰς w. acc. of place (in pregn. constr. ; see εἰς, C. 2), Heb. xi. 9. (Metaph. and absol. *to dwell on the earth*, Philo de cherub. § 34 [cf. Clem. Rom. 1 Cor. 1, 1 and Lghtft. and Harnack ad loc. ; *Holtzmann*, Einl. ins N. T. p. 484 sq. Syn. see κατοικέω.].) *

3940   **παρ-οικία, -ας, ἡ,** (παροικέω, q. v.), a bibl. and eccl. word, *a dwelling near* or *with one* ; hence *a sojourning, dwelling in a strange land* : prop. Acts xiii. 17 (2 Esdr. viii. 35 ; Ps. cxix. (cxx.) 5 ; Sap. xix. 10 ; Prol. of Sir. 21 ; cf. Fritzsche on Judith v. 9). Metaph. the life of man here on earth, likened to a sojourning : 1 Pet. i. 17 (Gen. xlvii. 9) ; see παρεπίδημος [and reff. under παροικέω].*

3941   **πάρ-οικος, -ον,** (παρά and οἶκος) ;   **1.** in class. Grk. *dwelling near, neighboring.*   **2.** in the Scriptures *a stranger, foreigner, one who lives in a place without the right of citizenship* ; [R. V. *sojourner*] ; Sept. for גֵּר and תּוֹשָׁב (see παροικέω 2, and παροικία, [and cf. *Schmidt*, Syn. 43, 5 ; L. and S. s. v.]) : foll. by ἐν w. dat. of place, Acts vii. 6, 29 ; metaph. *without citizenship in God's kingdom* : joined with ξένος and opp. to συμπολίτης, Eph. ii. 19 (μόνος κύριος ὁ θεὸς πολίτης ἐστί, πάροικον δὲ καὶ ἐπήλυτον τὸ γεννητὸν ἅπαν, Philo de cherub. § 34 [cf. Mangey i. 161 note]) ; *one who lives on earth as a stranger, a sojourner on the earth* : joined with παρεπίδημος (q. v.), of Christians, whose fatherland is heaven, 1 Pet. ii. 11. [Cf. Ep. ad Diognet. § 5, 5.]*

3942   **παροιμία, -ας, ἡ,** (παρά by, aside from [cf. παρά, IV. 2], and οἶμος way), prop. *a saying out of the usual course* or *deviating from the usual manner of speaking* [cf. Suidas 654, 15 ; but Hesych. s. v. et al. 'a saying heard *by the wayside*' (παρά, IV. 1), i. e. a *current* or *trite saying, proverb* ; cf. Curtius § 611 ; *Steph.* Thes. s. v.], hence   **1.** *a clever and sententious saying, a proverb*, (Aeschyl. Ag. 264 ; Soph., Plat., Aristot., Plut., al. ; exx. fr. Philo are given by *Hilgenfeld*, Die Evangelien, p. 292 sq. [as de ebriet. § 20 ; de Abr. § 40 ; de vit. Moys. i. § 28 ; ii. § 5 ; de exsecrat. § 6] ; for מָשָׁל in Prov. i. 1 ; xxv. 1 cod. Alex. ; Sir. vi. 35, etc.) : τὸ τῆς παροιμίας, what is in the *proverb* (Lcian. dial. mort. 6, 2 ; 8, 1), 2 Pet. ii. 22.   **2.** *any dark saying which shadows forth some didactic truth*, esp. *a symbolic* or *figurative saying* : παροιμίαν λέγειν, Jn. xvi. 29 ; ἐν παροιμίαις λαλεῖν, ibid. 25 ; *speech* or *discourse in which a thing is illustrated by the use of similes and comparisons* ; *an allegory,* i. e. *extended and elaborate metaphor* : Jn. x. 6.*

3943   **πάρ-οινος, -ον,** a later Grk. word for the earlier παροίνιος, (παρά [q. v. IV. 1] and οἶνος, one who sits long at his wine), *given to wine, drunken* : 1 Tim. iii. 3 ; Tit. i. 7 ; [al. give it the secondary sense, 'quarrelsome over wine' ; hence, *brawling, abusive*].*

3944   **παρ-οίχομαι** : pf. ptcp. παρῳχημένος ; *to go by, pass by* : as in Grk. writ. fr. Hom. Il. 10, 252 down, of time, Acts xiv. 16.*

3945   **παρ-ομοιάζω** ; (fr. παρόμοιος, and this fr. παρά [q. v. IV. 1 (?)] and ὅμοιος) ; *to be like* ; *to be not unlike* : Mt. xxiii.

27 R G T Tr mrg. WH txt. (Several times also in eccl. writ.) *

παρ-όμοιος, -ον, (also of three term. [see ὅμοιος, init.]),   **3946** *like* : Mk. vii. 8 [T WH om. Tr br. the cl.], 13. (Hdt., Thuc., Xen., Dem., Polyb., Diod., al.) *

παρ-οξύνω : prop. *to make sharp, to sharpen,* [παρά, IV.   **3947** 3] : τὴν μάχαιραν, Deut. xxxii. 41. Metaph. (so always in prof. auth. fr. Eur., Thuc., Xen., down),   **a.** *to stimulate, spur on, urge,* (πρός τι, ἐπί τι).   **b.** *to irritate, provoke, rouse to anger* ; Pass., pres. παροξύνομαι ; impf. παρωξυνόμην : Acts xvii. 16 ; 1 Co. xiii. 5. Sept. chiefly for נָאַץ *to scorn, despise* ; besides for הִכְעִיס *to provoke, make angry,* Deut. ix. 18 ; Ps. cv. (cvi.) 29 ; Is. lxv. 3 ; for הִקְצִיף *to exasperate,* Deut. ix. 7, 22, etc.; pass. for חָרָה *to burn with anger,* Hos. viii. 5 ; Zech. x. 3, and for other verbs.*

παροξυσμός, -οῦ, ὁ, (παροξύνω, q. v.) ;   **1.** *an inciting, incitement* : εἰς παρ. ἀγάπης [A. V. *to provoke unto*   **3948** *love*], Heb. x. 24.   **2.** *irritation,* [R. V. *contention*] : Acts xv. 39 ; Sept. twice for קֶצֶף, violent anger, passion, Deut. xxix. 28 ; Jer. xxxix. (xxxii.) 37 ; Dem. p. 1105, 24.*

παρ-οργίζω ; Attic fut. [cf. B. 37 (32) ; *WH.* App. 163]   **3949** παροργιῶ ; *to rouse to wrath, to provoke, exasperate, anger,* [cf. παρά, IV. 3] : Ro. x. 19 ; Eph. vi. 4 ; and Lchm. in Col. iii. 21. (Dem. p. 805, 19 ; Philo de somn. ii. § 26 ; Sept. chiefly for הִכְעִיס.) *

παρ-οργισμός, -οῦ, ὁ, (παροργίζω), *indignation, exasper-*   **3950** *ation, wrath* : Eph. iv. 26. (1 K. xv. 30 ; 2 K. xxiii. 26 ; Neh. ix. 18 ; [Jer. xxi. 5 Alex.] ; not found in prof. auth.) [Syn. cf. Trench § xxxvii.]*

παρ-οτρύνω : 1 aor. παρώτρυνα ; [ὀτρύνω to stir up (cf.   **3951** παρά, IV. 3)] ; *to incite, stir up* : τινά, Acts xiii. 50. (Pind. Ol. 3, 68 ; Joseph. antt. 7, 6, 1 ; Lcian. deor. concil. 4.) *

παρ-ουσία, -ας, ἡ, (παρών, -οῦσα, -όν, fr. πάρειμι q. v.),   **3952** in Grk. auth. fr. the Tragg., Thuc., Plat., down ; not found in Sept. ;   **1.** *presence* : 1 Co. xvi. 17 ; 2 Co. x. 10 ; opp. to ἀπουσία, Phil. ii. 12 (2 Macc. xv. 21 ; [Aristot. phys. 2, 3 p. 195ᵃ, 14 ; metaphys. 4, 2 p. 1013ᵇ, 14 ; meteor. 4, 5 p. 382ᵃ, 33 etc.]).   **2.** *the presence of one coming, the coming, arrival, advent,* ([Polyb. 3, 41, 1. 8] ; Judith x. 18 ; 2 Macc. viii. 12 ; [Herm. sim. 5, 5, 3]) : 2 Co. vii. 6 sq. ; 2 Th. ii. 9 (cf. 8 ἀποκαλυφθήσεται) ; ἡ ... πάλιν πρός τινα, of a return, Phil. i. 26. In the N. T. esp. of *the advent,* i. e. the future, visible, *return from heaven* of Jesus, the Messiah, to raise the dead, hold the last judgment, and set up formally and gloriously the kingdom of God : Mt. xxiv. 3 ; ἡ παρ. τοῦ υἱοῦ τοῦ ἀνθρώπου, [27], 37, 39 ; τοῦ κυρίου, 1 Th. iii. 13 ; iv. 15 ; v. 23 ; 2 Th. ii. 1 ; Jas. v. 7 sq. ; 2 Pet. iii. 4 ; Χριστοῦ, 2 Pet. i. 16 ; αὐτοῦ, 1 Co. xv. 23 ; [1 Th. ii. 19] ; 2 Th. ii. 8 ; 2 Pet. iii. 4 ; [1 Jn. ii. 28] ; τῆς τοῦ θεοῦ ἡμέρας, 2 Pet. iii. 12. It is called in eccles. ἡ δευτέρα παρουσία, Ev. Nicod. c. 22 fin. ; Justin. apol. 1, 52 [where see Otto's note] ; dial. c. Tr. cc. 40, 110, 121 ; and is opp. to ἡ πρώτη παρ. which took place in the incarnation, birth, and earthly career of Christ, Justin. dial. c. Tr. cc. 52, 121, cf. 14, 32, 49, etc. ; [cf. Ignat. ad Phil. 9 (and Lghtft.)] ; see ἔλευσις.*

3953   παρ-οψίς, -ίδος, ἡ, (παρά [q. v. IV. 1], and ὄψον, on which see ὀψάριον);   **1.** *a side-dish, a dish of dainties* or *choice food suited not so much to satisfy as to gratify the appetite*; *a side-accompaniment of the more solid food*; hence i. q. παρόψημα; so in Xen. Cyr. 1, 3, 4 and many Attic writ. in Athen. 9 p. 367 d. sq.   **2.** *the dish itself in which the delicacies are served up*: Mt. xxiii. 25, 26 [here T om. WH br. παροψ.]; Artem. oneir. 1, 74; Alciphr. 3, 20; Plut. de vitand. aere alien. § 2. This latter use of the word is condemned by the Atticists; cf. *Sturz*, Lex. Xen. iii. 463 sq.; *Lob.* ad Phryn. p. 176; [*Rutherford*, New Phryn. p. 265 sq.]; Poppo on Xen. Cyr. 1, 3, 4.*

3954   παρρησία, -ας, ἡ, (πᾶν and ῥῆσις; cf. ἀρρησία silence, κατάρρησις accusation, πρόρρησις prediction);   **1.** *freedom in speaking, unreservedness in speech*, (Eur., Plat., Dem., al.): ἡ π. τινός, Acts iv. 13; χρῆσθαι παρρησίᾳ, 2 Co. iii. 12; παρρησίᾳ adverbially,— *freely*: λαλεῖν, Jn. vii. 13, 26; xviii. 20; — *openly, frankly*, i. e. without concealment: Mk. viii. 32; Jn. xi. 14; — without ambiguity or circumlocution: εἰπὲ ἡμῖν παρρησίᾳ (Philem. ed. *Meineke* p. 405), Jn. x. 24; — without the use of figures and comparisons, opp. to ἐν παροιμίαις: Jn. xvi. 25, and R G in 29 (where L T Tr WH ἐν παρρησίᾳ); ἐν παρρησίᾳ, *freely*, Eph. vi. 19; μετὰ παρρησίας, Acts xxviii. 31; εἰπεῖν, Acts ii. 29; λαλεῖν, Acts iv. 29, 31.   **2.** *free and fearless confidence, cheerful courage*, boldness, assurance, (1 Macc. iv. 18; Sap. v. 1; Joseph. antt. 9, 10, 4; 15, 2, 7; [cf. W. 23]): Phil. i. 20 (opp. to αἰσχύνεσθαι, cf. Wiesinger ad loc.); ἐν πίστει, resting on, 1 Tim. iii. 13, cf. Huther ad loc.; ἔχειν παρρησίαν εἴς τι, Heb. x. 19; πολλή μοι (ἐστί) παρρ. πρὸς ὑμᾶς, 2 Co. vii. 4; of the confidence impelling one to do something, ἔχειν παρρ. with an infin. of the thing to be done, Philem. 8 [Test. xii. Patr., test. Rub. 4]; of the undoubting confidence of Christians relative to their fellowship with God, Eph. iii. 12; Heb. iii. 6; x. 35; μετὰ παρρησίας, Heb. iv. 16; ἔχειν παρρησίαν, opp. to αἰσχύνεσθαι to be covered with shame, 1 Jn. ii. 28; before the judge, 1 Jn. iv. 17; with πρὸς τὸν θεόν added, 1 Jn. iii. 21; v. 14.   **3.** *the deportment by which one becomes conspicuous* or *secures publicity* (Philo de victim. offer. § 12): ἐν παρρησίᾳ, before the public, in view of all, Jn. vii. 4 (opp. to ἐν τῷ κρυπτῷ); xi. 54 [without ἐν]; Col. ii. 15 [where cf. Bp. Lghtft.].*

3955   παρρησιάζομαι; impf. ἐπαρρησιαζόμην; 1 aor. ἐπαρρησιασάμην; (παρρησία, q. v.); a depon. verb; Vulg. chiefly *fiducialiter ago*; *to bear one's self boldly* or *confidently*;   **1.** *to use freedom in speaking, be free-spoken*; *to speak freely* ([A. V. *boldly*]): Acts xviii. 26; xix. 8; ἐν τῷ ὀνόματι τοῦ Ἰησοῦ, relying on the name of Jesus, Acts ix. 27, 28 (29); also ἐπὶ τῷ κυρίῳ, Acts xiv. 3.   **2.** *to grow confident, have boldness, show assurance, assume a bold bearing*: εἰπεῖν, Acts xiii. 46 [R. V. *spake out boldly*]; λαλεῖν, Acts xxv. 26; παρρησ. ἔν τινι, in reliance on one to take courage, foll. by an inf. of the thing to be done: λαλῆσαι, Eph. vi. 20; 1 Th. ii. 2. (Xen., Dem., Aeschin., Polyb., Philo, Plut., al.; Sept.; Sir. vi. 11.)*

3956   πᾶς, πᾶσα, πᾶν, gen. παντός, πάσης, παντός, [dat. plur. Lchm. πᾶσι ten times, -σιν seventy-two times; Tdf. -σι

---

five times (see Proleg. p. 98 sq.), -σιν seventy-seven times; Treg. -σιν eighty-two times; WH -σι fourteen times, -σιν sixty-eight times; see N, ν (ἐφελκυστικόν)], Hebr. לֹכ, [fr. Hom. down], *all, every*; it is used
   I. adjectively, and   **1. with anarthrous nouns**;   **a.** *any, every* one (sc. of the class denoted by the noun annexed to πᾶς); with the Singular: as πᾶν δένδρον, Mt. iii. 10; πᾶσα θυσία, Mk. ix. 49 [T WH Tr mrg. om. Tr txt. br. the cl.]; add, Mt. v. 11; xv. 13; Lk. iv. 37; Jn. ii. 10; xv. 2; Acts ii. 43; v. 42; Ro. xiv. 11; 1 Co. iv. 17; Rev. xviii. 17, and very often; πᾶσα ψυχὴ ἀνθρώπου, Ro. ii. 9 (πᾶσα ἀνθρ. ψυχή, Plat. Phaedr. p. 249 e.); πᾶσα συνείδησις ἀνθρώπων, 2 Co. iv. 2; πᾶς λεγόμενος θεός, 2 Th. ii. 4; πᾶς ἅγιος ἐν Χριστῷ, Phil. iv. 21 sqq. with the Plural, *all* or *any* that are of the class indicated by the noun: as πάντες ἄνθρωποι, Acts xxii. 15; Ro. v. 12, 18; xii. 17 sq.; 1 Co. vii. 7; xv. 19; πάντες ἅγιοι, Ro. xvi. 15; πάντες ἄγγελοι θεοῦ, Heb. i. 6; πάντα [L T Tr WH τὰ] ἔθνη, Rev. xiv. 8; on the phrase πᾶσα σάρξ, see σάρξ, 3.   **b.** *any and every, of every kind*, [A. V. often *all manner of*]: πᾶσα νόσος καὶ μαλακία, Mt. iv. 23; ix. 35; x. 1; εὐλογία, blessings of every kind, Eph. i. 3; so esp. with nouns designating virtues or vices, emotions, character, condition, to indicate every mode in which such virtue, vice or emotion manifests itself, or any object whatever to which the idea expressed by the noun belongs: — thus, πᾶσα ἐλπίς, Acts xxvii. 20; σοφία, Acts vii. 22; Col. i. 28; γνῶσις, Ro. xv. 14; ἀδικία, ἀσέβεια, etc., Ro. i. 18, 29; 2 Co. x. 6; Eph. iv. 19, 31; v. 3; σπουδή, 2 Co. viii. 7; 2 Pet. i. 5; ἐπιθυμία, Ro. vii. 8; χαρά, Ro. xv. 13; αὐτάρκεια, 2 Co. ix. 8; ἐν παντὶ λόγῳ κ. γνώσει, 1 Co. i. 5; σοφίᾳ κ. φρονήσει etc. Eph. i. 8; ἐν π. ἀγαθωσύνῃ κ. δικαιοσύνῃ, κ. ἀληθείᾳ, Eph. v. 9; αἰσθήσει, Phil. i. 9; ὑπομονῇ, θλίψις, etc., 2 Co. i. 4; xii. 12; add, Col. i. 9–11; iii. 16; 2 Th. i. 11; ii. 9; 1 Tim. i. 15; v. 1; 2 Tim. iv. 2; Tit. ii. 15 (on which see ἐπιταγή); iii. 2; Jas. i. 21; 1 Pet. ii. 1; v. 10; πᾶσα δικαιοσύνη, i. e. ὃ ἂν ᾖ δίκαιον, Mt. iii. 15; πᾶν θέλημα τοῦ θεοῦ, everything God wills, Col. iv. 12; πᾶσα ὑποταγή, obedience in all things, 1 Tim. ii. 11; πάσῃ συνειδήσει ἀγαθῇ, consciousness of rectitude in all things, Acts xxiii. 1; — or it signifies *the highest degree, the maximum*, of the thing which the noun denotes [cf. W. 110 (105 sq.); Ellicott on Eph. i. 8; Meyer on Phil. i. 20; Krüger § 50, 11, 9 and 10]: as μετὰ πάσης παρρησίας, Acts iv. 29; xxviii. 31; μετὰ πάσ. ταπεινοφροσύνης, Acts xx. 19; προθυμίας, Acts xvii. 11; χαρᾶς, Phil. ii. 29, cf. Jas. i. 2; ἐν πάσῃ ἀσφαλείᾳ, Acts v. 23; ἐν παντὶ φόβῳ, 1 Pet. ii. 18; πᾶσα ἐξουσία, Mt. xxviii. 18, (πᾶν κράτος, Soph. Phil. 142).   **c.** *the whole* (*all*, Lat. *totus*): so before proper names of countries, cities, nations; as, πᾶσα Ἱεροσόλυμα, Mt. ii. 3; πᾶς Ἰσραήλ, Ro. xi. 26; before collective terms, as πᾶς οἶκος Ἰσραήλ, Acts ii. 36; πᾶσα κτίσις (see κτίσις, 2 b.); πᾶσα γραφή (nearly equiv. to the ὅσα προεγράφη in Ro. xv. 4), 2 Tim. iii. 16 (cf. *Rothe*, Zur Dogmatik, p. 181); πᾶσα γερουσία υἱῶν Ἰσραήλ, Ex. xii. 21; πᾶς ἵππος Φαραώ, Ex. xiv. 23; πᾶν δίκαιον ἔθνος, Add. to Esth. i. 9; by a somewhat rare usage before other substantives also, as [πᾶν

πρόσωπον τῆς γῆς, Acts xvii. 26 L T Tr WH]; πᾶσα οἰκοδομή, Eph. ii. 21 G L T Tr WH, cf. Harless ad loc. p. 262 [al. find no necessity here for resorting to this exceptional use, but render (with R. V.) *each several building* (cf. Meyer)]; πᾶν τέμενος, 3 Macc. i. 13 (where see Grimm); Παύλου . . . ὃς ἐν πάσῃ ἐπιστολῇ μνημονεύει ὑμῶν, Ignat. ad Eph. 12 [(yet cf. Bp. Lghtft.)]; cf. Passow s. v. πᾶς, 2; [L. and S. s. v. A. II.]; W. § 18, 4; [B. § 127, 29]; Krüger § 50, 11, 8 to 11; Kühner ii. 545 sq.   **2.** with nouns which have the article, *all the, the whole,* (see c. just above) : — with the Singular; as, πᾶσα ἡ ἀγέλη, *the whole herd,* Mt. viii. 32; πᾶς ὁ ὄχλος, Mt. xiii. 2; πᾶς ὁ κόσμος, Ro. iii. 19; Col. i. 6; πᾶσα ἡ πόλις (i. e. all its inhabitants), Mt. viii. 34; xxi. 10, etc.; πᾶσα ἡ Ἰουδαία, Mt. iii. 5; add, Mt. xxvii. 25; Mk. v. 33; Lk. i. 10; Acts vii. 14; x. 2; xx. 28; xxii. 5; Ro. iv. 16; ix. 17; 1 Co. xiii. 2 (πίστιν καὶ γνῶσιν in their whole compass and extent); Eph. iv. 16; Col. i. 19; ii. 9, 19; Phil. i. 3; Heb. ii. 15; Rev. v. 6, etc.; the difference between πᾶσα ἡ θλίψις [*all*] and πᾶσα θλίψις [*any*] appears in 2 Co. i. 4. πᾶς ὁ λαὸς οὗτος, Lk. ix. 13; πᾶσαν τὴν ὀφειλὴν ἐκείνην, Mt. xviii. 32; πᾶς placed after the noun has the force of a predicate: τὴν κρίσιν πᾶσαν δέδωκε, *the judgment he hath given wholly* [cf. W. 548 (510)], Jn. v. 22; τὴν ἐξουσίαν . . . πᾶσαν ποιεῖ, Rev. xiii. 12; it is placed between the article and noun [B. § 127, 29; W. 549 (510)], as τὸν πάντα χρόνον, i. e. *always,* Acts xx. 18; add, Gal. v. 14; 1 Tim. i. 16 [here L T Tr WH ἅπας]; — with a Plural, *all* (*the totality of the persons or things designated by the noun*): πάντας τοὺς ἀρχιερεῖς, Mt. ii. 4; add, Mt. iv. 8; xi. 13; Mk. iv. 13; vi. 33; Lk. i. 6, 48; Acts x. 12, 43; Ro. i. 5; xv. 11; 1 Co. xii. 26; xv. 25; 2 Co. viii. 18, and very often; with a demonstr. pron. added, Mt. xxv. 7; Lk. ii. 19, 51 [here T WH om. L Tr mrg. br. the pron.]; πάντες is placed after the noun: τὰς πόλεις πάσας, *the cities all* (of them) [cf. W. u. s.], Mt. ix. 35; Acts viii. 40; add, Mt. x. 30; Lk. vii. 35 [here L Tr WH txt. πάντων τῶν etc.]; xii. 7; Acts viii. 40; xvi. 26; Ro. xii. 4; 1 Co. vii. 17; x. 1; xiii. 2; xv. 7; xvi. 20; 2 Co. xiii. 2, 12 (13); Phil. i. 13; 1 Th. v. 26; 2 Tim. iv. 21 [WH br. π.]; Rev. viii. 3; οἱ πάντες foll. by a noun, Acts xix. 7; xxvii. 37; τοὺς κατὰ τὰ ἔθνη πάντας Ἰουδαίους, Acts xxi. 21 [here L om. Tr br. π.].

II. without a substantive;   **1.** masc. and fem. *every* one, *any* one : in the singular, without any addition, Mk. ix. 49; Lk. xvi. 16; Heb. ii. 9; foll. by a rel. pron., πᾶς ὅστις, Mt. vii. 24; x. 32; Mk. xix. 29 [L T Tr WH ὅστις]; Gal. iii. 10; πᾶς ὃς ἂν (ἐάν Tr WH), *whosoever,* Acts ii. 21; πᾶς ἐξ ὑμῶν ὅς, Lk. xiv. 33; with a ptcp. which has not the article [W. 111 (106)]: παντὸς ἀκούοντος (*if any one heareth,* whoever he is), Mt. xiii. 19; παντὶ ὀφείλοντι ἡμῖν, *every one owing* (if he owe) *us* anything, unless ὀφείλοντι is to be taken substantively, *every debtor of ours,* Lk. xi. 4; with a ptcp. which has the article and takes the place of a relative clause [W. u. s.]: πᾶς ὁ ὀργιζόμενος, *every one that is angry,* Mt. v. 22; add, Mt. vii. 8; Lk. vi. 47; Jn. iii. 8, 20; vi. 45; Acts x. 43 sq.; xiii. 39; Ro. i. 16; ii. 10; xii. 3; 1 Co. ix. 25; xvi. 16;

Gal. iii. 13; 1 Jn. ii. 23; iii. 3 sq. 6, etc. Plural πάντες, without any addition, *all men* : Mt. x. 22; Mk. xiii. 13; Lk. xx. 38; xxi. 17; Jn. i. 7; iii. 31ᵇ [in 31ᵇ G T WH mrg. om. the cl.]; v. 23; vi. 45; xii. 32; Acts xvii. 25; Ro. x. 12; 1 Co. ix. 19; 2 Co. v. 14 (15); Eph. iii. 9 [here T WH txt. om. L br. π.]; of a certain definite whole : *all* (the people), Mt. xxi. 26; *all* (we who hold more liberal views), 1 Co. viii. 1; *all* (the members of the church), ibid. 7; by hyperbole i. q. the great majority, the multitude, Jn. iii. 26; *all* (just before mentioned), Mt. xiv. 20; xxii. 27 sq.; xxvii. 22; Mk. i. 27 [here T Tr WH ἅπαντες], 37; vi. 39, 42; [xi. 32 Lchm.]; Lk. i. 63; iv. 15; Jn. ii. 15, 24, and very often; [*all* (about to be mentioned), διὰ πάντων sc. τῶν ἁγίων (as is shown by the foll. καὶ κτλ.), Acts ix. 32]. οἱ πάντες, *all* taken together, *all* collectively, [cf. W. 116 (110)]: of all men, Ro. xi. 32; of a certain definite whole, Phil. ii. 21; with the 1 pers. plur. of the verb, 1 Co. x. 17; Eph. iv. 13; with a definite number, *in all* [cf. B. § 127, 29]: ἦσαν δὲ οἱ πάντες ἄνδρες ὡσεὶ δεκαδύο (or δώδεκα), Acts xix. 7; ἤμεθα αἱ πᾶσαι ψυχαὶ διακόσιαι ἑβδομήκοντα ἕξ, Acts xxvii. 37, (ἐπ᾽ ἄνδρας τοὺς πάντας δύο, Judith iv. 7; ἐγένοντο οἱ πάντες ὡς τετρακόσιοι, Joseph. antt. 6, 12, 3; τοὺς πάντας εἰς δισχιλίους, id. 4, 7, 1; ὡς εἶναι τὰς πάσας δέκα, Ael. v. h. 12, 35; see other exx. fr. Grk. auth. in Passow s. v. πᾶς, 5 b.; [L. and S. s. v. C.]; "relinquitur ergo, ut *omnia tria* genera sint causarum," Cic. de invent. 1, 9); οἱ πάντες, *all* those I have spoken of, 1 Co. ix. 22; 2 Co. v. 14 (15). πάντες ὅσοι, *all as many as,* Mt. xxii. 10; Lk. iv. 40 [here Tr mrg. WH txt. ἅπ.]; Jn. x. 8; Acts v. 36 sq.; πάντες οἱ w. a ptcp., *all* (they) *that* : Mt. iv. 24; Mk. i. 32; Lk. ii. 18, 38; Acts ii. 44; iv. 16; Ro. i. 7; x. 12; 1 Co. i. 2; 2 Co. i. 1; Eph. vi. 24; 1 Th. i. 7; 2 Th. i. 10; Heb. iii. 16; 2 Jn. 1; Rev. xiii. 8; xviii. 19, 24, and often. πάντες οἱ sc. ὄντες : Mt. v. 15; Lk. v. 9; Jn. v. 28; Acts iii. 39; v. 17; xvi. 32; Ro. ix. 6; 2 Tim. i. 15; 1 Pet. v. 14, etc. πάντες with personal and demonst. pronouns [compare W. 548 (510)]: ἡμεῖς πάντες, Jn. i. 16; Ro. viii. 32; 2 Co. iii. 18; Eph. ii. 3; πάντες ἡμεῖς, Acts ii. 32; x. 33; xxvi. 14; xxviii. 2; Ro. iv. 16; οἱ πάντες ἡμεῖς, 2 Co. v. 10; ὑμεῖς πάντες, Acts xx. 25; πάντες ὑμεῖς, Mt. xxiii. 8; xxvi. 31; Lk. ix. 48; Acts xxii. 3; Ro. xv. 33; 2 Co. vii. 15; [Gal. iii. 28 R G L WH]; Phil. i. 4, 7 sq.; 1 Th. i. 2; 2 Th. iii. 16, 18; Tit. iii. 15; Heb. xiii. 25, etc.; αὐτοὶ πάντες, 1 Co. xv. 10; πάντες αὐτοί, Acts iv. 33; xix. 17; xx. 36; οὗτοι πάντες, Acts i. 14; xvii. 7; Heb. xi. 13, 39; πάντες [L T ἅπ.] οὗτοι, Acts ii. 7; οἱ δὲ πάντες, *and they all,* Mk. xiv. 64.   **2.** Neuter πᾶν, *everything,* (*anything*) *whatsoever :*   **a.** in the Sing.: πᾶν τό, foll. by a ptcp. [on the neut. in a concrete and collective sense cf. B. § 128, 1], 1 Co. x. 25, 27; Eph. v. 13; 1 Jn. v. 4; πᾶν τό sc. ὄν, 1 Jn. ii. 16; πᾶν ὅ, Ro. xiv. 23; Jn. vi. 37, 39, [R. V. *all that*]; Jn. xvii. 2; πᾶν ὅ, τι ἂν or ἐάν, *whatsoever,* Col. iii. 17, and Rec. in 23. Joined to prepositions it forms adverbial phrases: διὰ παντός or διαπαντός, *always, perpetually,* see διά, A. II. 1 a.; ἐν παντί, either *in every condition,* or *in every matter,* Phil. iv. 6; 1 Th. v. 18; *in everything, in every way, on every side, in every particular* or *relation,* 2 Co. iv. 8; vii.

5, 11, 16; xi. 6, 9; Eph. v. 24; πλουτίζεσθαι, 1 Co. i. 5; [περισσεύειν], 2 Co. viii. 7; ἐν παντὶ καὶ ἐν πᾶσιν (see μυέω, b.), Phil. iv. 12.   b. Plural πάντα (without the article [cf.W. 116 (110); Matthiae § 438]) *all things*;   a. of a certain definite t o t a l i t y or sum of things, the context shewing w h a t things are meant: Mk. iv. 34; vi. 30; Lk. i. 3; [v. 28 L T Tr WH]; Jn. iv. 25 [here T Tr WH ἅπ.]; Ro. viii. 28; 2 Co. vi. 10; Gal. iv. 1; Phil. ii. 14; 1 Th. v. 21; 2 Tim. ii. 10; Tit. i. 15; 1 Jn. ii. 27; πάντα ὑμῶν, all ye do with one another, 1 Co. xvi. 14; πάντα γίνεσθαι πᾶσιν, [A. V. *to become all things to all men*], i. e. to adapt one's self in all ways to the needs of all, 1 Co. ix. 22 L T Tr WH (Rec. τὰ πάντα i. e. in all the ways possible or necessary); cf. Kypke, Obs. ii. p. 215 sq.   β. accusative πάντα [adverbially], *wholly, altogether, in all ways, in all things, in all respects*: Acts xx. 35; 1 Co. ix. 25; x. 33; xi. 2; cf. Matthiae § 425, 5; Passow ii. p. 764ᵃ; [L. and S. s. v. D. II. 4].   γ. πάντα, in an absolute sense, *all things* that exist, all created things: Jn. i. 3; 1 Co. ii. 10; xv. 27; Heb. ii. 8 (and L T Tr WH in iii. 4); Eph. i. 22; Col. i. 17; 1 Pet. iv. 7; Rev. xxi. 5; (in Ro. ix. 5 πάντων is more fitly taken as gen. masc. [but see the Comm. ad loc.]). ποία ἐστὶν ἐντολὴ πρώτη πάντων (gen. neut.; Rec. πασῶν), what commandment is first of all (things), Mk. xii. 28 (ἔφασκε λέγων κορυδὸν π ά ν τ ω ν πρώτην ὄρνιθα γενέσθαι, προτέραν τῆς γῆς, Arstph. av. 472; τὰς πόλεις . . . ἐλευθεροῦν καὶ π ά ν τ ω ν μάλιστα Ἄντανδρον, Thuc. 4, 52; cf. W. § 27, 6; [B. § 150, 6; Green p. 109]; Fritzsche on Mk. p. 538).   δ. with the article [cf. reff. in b. above], τὰ πάντα;   aa. in an absolute sense, *all things* collectively, the totality of created things, the universe of things: Ro. xi. 36; 1 Co. viii. 6; Eph. iii. 9; iv. 10; Phil. iii. 21; Col. i. 16 sq.; Heb. i. 3; ii. 10; Rev. iv. 11; τὰ πάντα ἐν πᾶσι πληροῦσθαι, to fill the universe of things in all places, Eph. i. 23 [Rec. om. τά; but al. take ἐν π. here m o d a l l y (see θ. below), al. i n s t r u m e n - t a l l y (see Meyer ad loc.)].   ββ. in a relative sense: Mk. iv. 11 [Tdf. om. τά] (the whole substance of saving teaching); Acts xvii. 25 [not Rec.ˢᵗ] (all the necessities of life); Ro. viii. 32 (all the things that he can give for our benefit); all intelligent beings [al. include things material also], Eph. i. 10; Col. i. 20; it serves by its universality to designate every class of men, all mankind, [cf. W. § 27, 5; B. § 128, 1], Gal. iii. 22 (cf. Ro. xi. 32); 1 Tim. vi. 13; εἶναι τὰ [T WH om. τὰ] πάντα, to avail for, be a substitute for, to possess supreme authority, καὶ ἐν πᾶσιν (i. e. either *with all men* or *in the minds of all* [al. take πᾶσιν as neut., cf. Bp. Lghtft. ad loc.]), Col. iii. 11; ἵνα ᾖ ὁ θεὸς τὰ [L Tr WH om. τὰ] πάντα ἐν πᾶσιν [neut. acc. to Grimm (as below)], i. e. that God may rule supreme by his spiritual power working within all, 'may be the immanent and controlling principle of life,' 1 Co. xv. 28, (so in prof. auth. πάντα or ἅπαντα without the article: πάντα ἦν ἐν τοῖσι Βαβυλωνίοισι Ζώπυρος, Hdt. 3, 157; cf. Herm. ad Vig. p. 727; other exx. fr. prof. auth. are given in Kypke, Observv. ii. p. 230 sq.; Palairet, Observv. p. 407; cf. Grimm in the Zeitschr. f. wissensch. Theol. for 1873, p. 394 sqq.); accus. [adverbially, cf. β. above] τὰ

πάντα, in all the parts [in which we grow (Meyer)], in all respects, Eph. iv. 15.   The Article in τὰ πάντα refers— in 1 Co. xi. 12 to the things before mentioned (husband and wife, and their mutual dependence); in 2 Co. iv. 15 to 'all the things that befall me'; in 1 Co. xv. 27 sq.; Phil. iii. 8, to the preceding πάντα; in Col. iii. 8 τὰ πάντα serves to sum up what follows [W. 107 (102)].   ε. πάντα τά foll. by a ptcp. (see πᾶς, πάντες, II. 1 above): Mt. xviii. 31; Lk. xii. 44; xvii. 10; xviii. 31; xxi. 22; xxiv. 44; Jn. xviii. 4; Acts x. 33; xxiv. 14; Gal. iii. 10; τὰ πάντα w. ptcp., Lk. ix. 7; Eph. v. 13; πάντα τά sc. ὄντα (see πᾶς, [πᾶν], πάντες, II. 1 and 2 above), Mt. xxiii. 20; Acts iv. 24; xiv. 15; xvii. 24; πάντα τὰ ὧδε, sc. ὄντα, Col. iv. 9; τὰ κατ' ἐμέ, ibid. 7 [see κατά, II. 3 b.].   ζ. πάντα and τὰ πάντα with pronouns: τὰ ἐμὰ πάντα, Jn. xvii. 10; πάντα τὰ ἐμά, Lk. xv. 31; ταῦτα πάντα, *these things all taken together* [W. 548 (510); Fritzsche on Mt. xxiv. 33, 34; cf. Bornemann on Lk. xxi. 36; Lobeck, Paralip. p. 65]: Mt. iv. 9; vi. 33; xiii. 34, 51; Lk. xii. 30; xvi. 14; xxi. 36 [π. τ. L mrg.]; xxiv. 9 [Tdf. π. τ.]; Acts vii. 50; Ro. viii. 37; 2 Pet. iii. 11; πάντα ταῦτα, *all these things* [reff. as above]: Mt. vi. 32; xxiv. 8, 33 [T Tr txt. τ.π.], 34 [Tr mrg. τ. π.]; Lk. vii. 18; Acts xxiv. 8; 1 Co. xii. 11; Col. iii. 14; 1 Th. iv. 6; the reading varies also between π. τ. and τ. π. in Mt. xix. 20; xxiii. 36; xxiv. 2; πάντα τὰ συμβεβηκότα ταῦτα, Lk. xxiv. 14; πάντα ἅ, Jn. iv. [29 T WH Tr mrg. (see next head)]; iv. 45 [here L Tr WH ὅσα (see next head)]; v. 20; Acts x. 39; xiii. 39.   η. πάντα ὅσα: Mt. vii. 12; xiii. 46; xviii. 25; xxviii. 20; Mk. xii. 44; Jn. iv. 29 [see ζ. above], 45 L Tr WH; x. 41; xvi. 15; xvii. 7; Acts iii. 22; π. ὅσα ἄν (or ἐάν), Mt. xxi. 22; xxiii. 3; Mk. xi. 24 [G L T Tr WH om. ἄν]; Acts iii. 22.   θ. πάντα with prepositions forms adverbial phrases: πρὸ πάντων, *before* or *above all things* [see πρό, c.], Jas. v. 12; 1 Pet. iv. 8. (But περὶ πάντων, 3 Jn. 2, must not be referred to this head, as though it signified *above all things*; it is rather *as respects all things*, and depends on εὔχομαι [apparently a mistake for εὐοδοῦσθαι; yet see περί, I. c. a.], cf. Lücke ad loc., 2d ed. p. 370 [3d ed. p. 462 sq.]; Westcott ad loc.]; W. 373 (350)). [on διὰ πάντων, Acts ix. 32, see 1 above.] ἐν πᾶσιν, *in all things, in all ways, altogether*: 1 Tim. iii. 11; iv. 15 [Rec.]; 2 Tim. ii. 7; iv. 5; Tit. ii. 9; Heb. xiii. 4, 18; 1 Pet. iv. 11, [see also 2 a. fin. above]; ἐπὶ πᾶσιν, see ἐπί, B. 2 d. p. 233ᵇ. κατὰ πάντα, *in all respects*: Acts xvii. 22; Col. iii. 20, 22; Heb. ii. 17; iv. 15.

III. with n e g a t i v e s;   1. οὐ πᾶς, *not every one*.   2. πᾶς οὐ (where οὐ belongs to the verb), *no one, none*, see οὐ, 2 p. 460ᵇ; πᾶς μή (so that μή must be joined to the verb), *no one, none*, in final sentences, Jn. iii. 15 sq.; vi. 39; xii. 46; 1 Co. i. 29; w. an impv. Eph. iv. 29 (1 Macc. v. 42); πᾶς . . . οὐ μή w. the aor. subjunc. (see μή, IV. 2), Rev. xviii. 22.

πάσχα, τό, (Chald. פַּסְחָא, Heb. פֶּסַח, fr. פָּסַח to pass over, to pass over by sparing; the Sept. also constantly use the Chald. form πάσχα, except in 2 Chron. [and Jer. xxxviii. (xxxi.) 8] where it is φασέκ; Josephus has φάσκα, antt. 5, 1, 4; 14, 2, 1; 17, 9, 3; b. j. 2, 1, 3), an indeclinable noun [W. § 10, 2]; prop. *a passing over*;   1.

3957

the paschal sacrifice (which was accustomed to be offered for the people's deliverance of old from Egypt), or   **2.** *the paschal lamb*, i. e. the lamb which the Israelites were accustomed to slay and eat on the fourteenth day of the month Nisan (the first month of their year) in memory of that day on which their fathers, preparing to depart from Egypt, were bidden by God to slay and eat a lamb, and to sprinkle their door-posts with its blood, that the destroying angel, seeing the blood, might pass over their dwellings (Ex. xii. sq.; Num. ix.; Deut. xvi.): θύειν τὸ π. (שָׁחַט הַפֶּסַח), Mk. xiv. 12; Lk. xxii. 7, (Ex. xii. 21); Christ crucified is likened to the slain paschal lamb, 1 Co. v. 7; φαγεῖν τὸ π., Mt. xxvi. 17; Mk. xiv. 12, 14; Lk. xxii. 11, 15; Jn. xviii. 28; אָכַל הַפֶּסַח, 2 Chr. xxx. 17 sq. **3.** *the paschal supper*: ἑτοιμάζειν τὸ π., Mt. xxvi. 19; Mk. xiv. 16; Lk. xxii. 8, 13; ποιεῖν τὸ π. to celebrate the paschal meal, Mt. xxvi. 18. **4.** *the paschal festival, the feast of Passover*, extending from the fourteenth to the twentieth day of the month Nisan: Mt. xxvi. 2; Mk. xiv. 1; Lk. ii. 41; xxii. 1; Jn. ii. 13, 23; vi. 4; xi. 55; xii. 1; xiii. 1; xviii. 39; xix. 14; Acts xii. 4; πεποίηκε τὸ π. *he instituted the Passover* (of Moses), Heb. xi. 28 [cf. W. 272 (256); B. 197 (170)]; γίνεται τὸ π. the Passover is celebrated [R. V. *cometh*], Mt. xxvi. 2. [See BB.DD. s. v. Passover; *Dillmann* in Schenkel iv. p. 392 sqq.; and on the question of the relation of the "Last Supper" to the Jewish Passover, see (in addition to reff. in BB.DD. u. s.) *Kirchner*, die Jüdische Passahfeier u. Jesu letztes Mahl. Gotha, 1870; *Keil*, Com. über Matth. pp. 513–528; *J. B. McClellan*, The N. T. etc. i. pp. 473–494; but esp. *Schürer*, Ueber φαγεῖν τὸ πάσχα, akademische Festschrift (Giessen, 1883).]*

3958   **πάσχω**; 2 aor. ἔπαθον; pf. πέπονθα (Lk. xiii. 2; Heb. ii. 18); fr. Hom. down; *to be affected* or have been affected, *to feel, have a sensible experience, to undergo*; it is a vox media — used in either a good or a bad sense; as, ὅσα πεπόνθασι καὶ ὅσα αὐτοῖς ἐγένετο, of perils and deliverance from them, Esth. ix. 26 (for רָאָה); hence κακῶς πάσχειν, *to suffer sadly, be in bad plight*, of a sick person, Mt. xvii. 15 where L Tr txt. WH txt. κ. ἔχειν (on the other hand, εὖ πάσχειν, *to be well off, in good case*, often in Grk. writ. fr. Pind. down). **1.** *in a bad sense, of misfortunes, to suffer, to undergo evils, to be afflicted*, (so everywhere in Hom. and Hes.; also in the other Grk. writ. where it is used absol.): absol., Lk. xxii. 15; xxiv. 46; Acts i. 3; iii. 18; xvii. 3; 1 Co. xii. 26; Heb. ii. 18; ix. 26; 1 Pet. ii. 19 sq. 23; iii. 17; iv. 15, 19; Heb. xiii. 12; ὀλίγον, a little while, 1 Pet. v. 10; πάσχειν τι, Mt. xxvii. 19; Mk. ix. 12; Lk. xiii. 2; [xxiv. 26]; Acts xxviii. 5; 2 Tim. i. 12; [Heb. v. 8 cf. W. 166 (156) a.; B. § 143, 10]; Rev. ii. 10; παθήματα πάσχειν, 2 Co. i. 6; τὶ ἀπό w. gen. of pers., Mt. xvi. 21; Lk. ix. 22; xvii. 25; πάσχ. ὑπό w. gen. of pers. Mt. xvii. 12; τὶ ὑπό τινος, Mk. v. 26; 1 Th. ii. 14; πάσχ. ὑπέρ τινος, in behalf of a pers. or thing, Acts ix. 16; Phil. i. 29; 2 Th. i. 5; with the addition of a dat. of reference or respect [cf. W. § 31, 6], σαρκί, 1 Pet. iv. 1ᵃ; ἐν σαρκί, ibid.ᵇ [yet G L T Tr WH om. ἐν; cf. W. 412 (384)]; πάσχ. περί w.

gen. of the thing and ὑπέρ w. gen. of pers. 1 Pet. iii. 18 [R G WH mrg.; cf. W. 373 (349); 383 (358) note]; πάσχ. διὰ δικαιοσύνην, 1 Pet. iii. 14. **2.** *in a good sense, of pleasant experiences*; but nowhere so unless either the adv. εὖ or an acc. of the thing be added (ὑπομνῆσαι, ὅσα παθόντες ἐξ αὐτοῦ (i. e. θεοῦ) καὶ πηλίκων εὐεργεσιῶν μεταλαβόντες ἀχάριστοι πρὸς αὐτὸν γένοιντο, Joseph. antt. 3, 15, 1; exx. fr. Grk. auth. are given in Passow s. v. II. 5; [L. and S. s. v. II. 2]): Gal. iii. 4, on which see γέ, 3 c. [COMP.: προ-, συμ-πάσχω.] *

Πάταρα, -άρων, τά, [cf. W. 176 (166)], *Patara*, a maritime city of Lycia, celebrated for an oracle of Apollo: Acts xxi. 1. [B. D. s. v. Patara; *Lewin*, St. Paul, ii. 99 sq.]*   **3959**

πατάσσω; fut. πατάξω; 1 aor. ἐπάταξα; Sept. times without number for הִכָּה (Hiphil of נָכָה, unused in Kal), also for נָגַן, etc.; (in Hom. intrans. *to beat*, of the heart; fr. Arstph., Soph., Plat., al. on used transitively). **1.** *to strike gently*: τί (as a part or a member of the body), Acts xii. 7. **2.** *to strike, smite*: absol., ἐν μαχαίρᾳ, with the sword, Lk. xxii. 49; τινά, Mt. xxvi. 51; Lk. xxii. 50. by a use solely biblical, *to afflict; to visit with evils*, etc.: as with a deadly disease, τινά, Acts xii. 23; τινὰ ἐν w. dat. of the thing, Rev. xi. 6 G L T Tr WH; xix. 15, (Gen. viii. 21; Num. xiv. 12; Ex. xii. 23, etc.). **3.** by a use solely biblical, *to smite down, cut down, to kill, slay*: τινά, Mt. xxvi. 31 and Mk. xiv. 27, (after Zech. xiii. 7); Acts vii. 24.*   **3960**

πατέω, -ῶ; fut. πατήσω; Pass., pres. ptcp. πατούμενος; 1 aor. ἐπατήθην; fr. Pind., Aeschyl., Soph., Plat. down; Sept. for דָּרַךְ, etc.; *to tread*, i. e. **a.** *to trample, crush with the feet*: τὴν ληνόν, Rev. xiv. 20; xix. 15, (Judg. ix. 27; Neh. xiii. 15; Jer. xxxi. (xlviii.) 33; Lam. i. 15). **b.** *to advance by setting foot upon, tread upon*: ἐπάνω ὄφεων καὶ σκορπίων καὶ ἐπὶ πᾶσαν τὴν δύναμιν τοῦ ἐχθροῦ, to encounter successfully the greatest perils from the machinations and persecutions with which Satan would fain thwart the preaching of the gospel, Lk. x. 19 (cf. Ps. xc. (xci.) 13). **c.** *to tread under foot, trample on*, i. e. *treat with insult and contempt*: to desecrate the holy city by devastation and outrage, Lk. xxi. 24; Rev. xi. 2, (fr. Dan. viii. 13); see καταπατέω. [COMP.: κατα-, περι-, ἐμ-περι-πατέω.] *   **3961**

πατήρ [fr. r. pâ; lit. nourisher, protector, upholder; (Curtius § 348)], πατρός, -τρί, -τέρα, voc. πάτερ [for which the nom. ὁ πατήρ is five times used, and (anarthrous) πατήρ in Jn. xvii. 21 T Tr WH, 24 and 25 L T Tr WH; cf. B. § 129, 5; W. § 29, 2; *WH*. App. p. 158], plur. πατέρες, πατέρων, πατράσι (Heb. i. 1), πατέρας, ὁ, [fr. Hom. down], Sept. for אָב, *a father*; **1.** prop., i. q. *'generator* or *male ancestor*, and either **a.** *the nearest ancestor*: Mt. ii. 22; iv. 21 sq.; viii. 21; Lk. i. 17; Jn. iv. 53; Acts vii. 14; 1 Co. v. 1, etc.; οἱ πατέρες τῆς σαρκός, fathers of the corporeal nature, natural fathers, (opp. to ὁ πατὴρ τῶν πνευμάτων), Heb. xii. 9; plur. of both parents, Heb. xi. 23 (not infreq. in prof. auth., cf. Delitzsch ad loc.); or **b.** *a more remote ancestor, the founder of a race* or *tribe, progenitor of a people, forefather*: so Abraham is called, Mt. iii. 9; Lk. i. 73; xvi. 24; Jn. viii.   **3962**

39, 53; Acts vii. 2; Ro. iv. 1 Rec., 17 sq., etc.; Isaac, Ro. ix. 10; Jacob, Jn. iv. 12; David, Mk. xi. 10; Lk. i. 32; plur. *fathers* i. e. *ancestors, forefathers,* Mt. xxiii. 30, 32; Lk. vi. 23, 26; xi. 47 sq.; Jn. iv. 20; vi. 31; Acts iii. 13, 25; 1 Co. x. 1, etc., and often in Grk. writ. fr. Hom. down; so too אָבוֹת, 1 K. viii. 21; Ps. xxi. (xxii.) 5 etc.; in the stricter sense of *the founders of a race,* Jn. vii. 22; Ro. ix. 5; xi. 28.   c. i. q. *one advanced in years, a senior:* 1 Jn. ii. 13 sq.   2. metaph.;   a. the originator and transmitter of anything: πατὴρ περιτομῆς, Ro. iv. 12; the author of a family or society of persons animated by the same spirit as himself: so π. πάντων τῶν πιστευόντων, Ro. iv. 11, cf. 12, 16, (1 Macc. ii. 54); one who has infused his own spirit into others, who actuates and governs their minds, Jn. viii. 38, 41 sq. 44; the phrase ἐκ πατρός τινος εἶναι is used of one who shows himself as like another in spirit and purpose as though he had inherited his nature from him, ibid. 44.   b. one who stands in a father's place, and looks after another in a paternal way: 1 Co. iv. 15.   c. a title of honor [cf. *Sophocles,* Lex. s. v.], applied to   a. *teachers,* as those to whom pupils trace back the knowledge and training they have received: Mt. xxiii. 9 (of prophets, 2 K. ii. 12; vi. 21).   β. *the members of the Sanhedrin,* whose prerogative it was, by virtue of the wisdom and experience in which they excelled, to take charge of the interests of others: Acts vii. 2; xxii. 1; cf. *Gesenius,* Thesaur. i. p. 7ᵃ.   3. *God* is called *the Father,*   a. τῶν φώτων, [A. V. *of lights* i. e.] of the stars, the heavenly luminaries, because he is their creator, upholder, ruler, Jas. i. 17.   b. *of all rational and intelligent beings, whether angels* or *men,* because he is their creator, preserver, guardian and protector: Eph. iii. 14 sq. G L T Tr WH; τῶν πνευμάτων, of spiritual beings, Heb. xii. 9; and, for the same reason, *of all men* (πατὴρ τοῦ παντὸς ἀνθρώπων γένους, Joseph. antt. 4, 8, 24): so in the Synoptic Gospels, esp. Matthew, Mt. vi. 4, 8, 15; xxiv. 36; Lk. vi. 36; xi. 2; xii. 30, 32; Jn. iv. 21, 23; Jas. iii. 9; ὁ πατὴρ ὁ ἐν (τοῖς) οὐρανοῖς, the Father in heaven, Mt. v. 16, 45, 48; vi. 1, 9; vii. 11, 21; xviii. 14; Mk. xi. 25, 26 R G L; Lk. xi. 13 [ἐξ οὐρανοῦ; cf. B. § 151, 2 a.; W. § 66, 6]; ὁ πατ. ὁ οὐράνιος, the heavenly Father, Mt. vi. 14, 26, 32; xv. 13.   c. *of Christians,* as those who through Christ have been exalted to a specially close and intimate relationship with God, and who no longer dread him as the stern judge of sinners, but revere him as their reconciled and loving Father. This conception, common in the N. T. Epistles, shines forth with especial brightness in Ro. viii. 15; Gal. iv. 6; in John's use of the term it seems to include the additional idea of one who by the power of his Spirit, operative in the gospel, has begotten them anew to a life of holiness (see γεννάω, 2 d.): absol., 2 Co. vi. 18; Eph. ii. 18; 1 Jn. ii. 1, 14 (13), 16; iii. 1; θεὸς κ. πατὴρ πάντων, of all *Christians,* Eph. iv. 6; with the addition of a gen. of quality [W. § 34, 3 b.; B. § 132, 10], ὁ πατ. τῶν οἰκτιρμῶν, 2 Co. i. 3; τῆς δόξης, Eph. i. 17; on the phrases ὁ θεὸς κ. πατὴρ ἡμῶν, θεὸς πατήρ, etc., see θεός, 3 p. 288ᵃ.   d. *the Father of Jesus Christ,*

as one whom God has united to himself in the closest bond of love and intimacy, made acquainted with his purposes, appointed to explain and carry out among men the plan of salvation, and (as appears from the teaching of John) made to share also in his own divine nature; he is so called,   a. by Jesus himself: simply ὁ πατήρ (opp. to ὁ υἱός), Mt. xi. 25–27; Lk. x. 21 sq.; Jn. v. 20– 23, 26, 36 sq.; x. 15, 30, etc.; ὁ πατήρ μου, Mt. xi. 27; xxv. 34; xxvi. 53; Lk. x. 22; Jn. v. 17; viii. 19, 49; x. 18, 32, and often in John's Gospel; Rev. ii. 28 (27); iii. 5, 21; with ὁ ἐν τοῖς οὐρανοῖς added, Mt. vii. 11, 21; x. 32 sq.; xii. 50; xvi. 17; xviii. 10, 19; ὁ οὐράνιος, Mt. xv. 13; ὁ ἐπουράνιος, Mt. xviii. 35 Rec.   β. by the apostles: Ro. xv. 6; 2 Co. i. 3; xi. 31; Eph. i. 3; iii. 14 Rec.; Col. i. 3; Heb. i. 5; 1 Pet. i. 3; Rev. i. 6. See [*Tholuck* (Bergrede Christi) on Mt. vi. 9; *Weiss,* Bibl. Theol. d. N. T., Index s. v. Vater; *C. Wittichen,* Die Idee Gottes als d. Vaters, (Göttingen, 1865); *Westcott,* Epp. of St. John, pp. 27–34, and] below in υἱός and τέκνον.

Πάτμος, -ου, ἡ, *Patmos,* a small and rocky island in the Ægean Sea, reckoned as one of the Sporades (Thuc. 3, 33; Strab. 10 p. 488; Plin. h. n. 4, 23); now called *Patino* or [chiefly "in the middle ages" (Howson)] *Palmosa* and having from four to five thousand Christian inhabitants (cf. *Schubert,* Reise in das Morgenland, Th. iii. pp. 425– 443; *Bleek,* Vorless. üb. die Apokalypse, p. 157; *Kneucker* in Schenkel iv. p. 403 sq.; [BB. DD. s. v.]). In it John, the author of the Apocalypse, says the revelations were made to him of the approaching consummation of God's kingdom: Rev. i. 9. It has been held by the church, ever since the time of [Just. Mart. (dial. c. Tryph. § 81 p. 308 a. cf. Euseb. h. e. 4, 18, 8; see *Charteris,* Canonicity, ch. xxxiv. and note) and] Iren. adv. haer. 5, 30, that this John is the Apostle; see Ἰωάννης, 2 and 6.*   **3963**

πατραλῴας (Attic πατραλοίας, Arstph., Plat., Dem. p. 732, 14; Aristot., Lcian.), L T Tr WH πατρολῴας (see μητραλῴας), -ου, ὁ, *a parricide*: 1 Tim. i. 9.*   **3964**

πατριά, -ᾶς, ἡ, (fr. πατήρ);   1. *lineage running back to some progenitor, ancestry*: Hdt. 2, 143; 3, 75.   2. *a race or tribe,* i. e. *a group of families, all those who in a given people lay claim to a common origin*: εἰσὶ αὐτέων (Βαβυλωνίων) πατριαὶ τρεῖς, Hdt. 1, 200. The Israelites were distributed into (twelve) מַטּוֹת, φυλαί, *tribes,* descended from the twelve sons of Jacob; these were divided into מִשְׁפָּחוֹת, πατριαί, deriving their descent from the several sons of Jacob's sons; and these in turn were divided into בֵּית הָאָבוֹת, οἶκοι, *houses* (or *families*); cf. *Gesenius,* Thes. i. p. 193; iii. p. 1463; *Win.* RWB. s. v. Stämme; [*Keil,* Archaeol. § 140]; hence ἐξ οἴκου καὶ πατριᾶς Δαυΐδ, i. e. belonging not only to the same 'house' (πατριά) as David, but to the very 'family' of David, descended from David himself, Lk. ii. 4 (αὗται αἱ πατριαὶ τῶν υἱῶν Συμεών, Ex. vi. 15; ὁ ἀνὴρ αὐτῆς Μανασσῆς τῆς φυλῆς αὐτῆς καὶ τῆς πατριᾶς αὐτῆς, Judith viii. 2; τῶν φυλῶν κατὰ πατριὰς αὐτῶν, Num. i. 16; οἶκοι πατριῶν, Ex. xii. 3; Num. i. 2, and often; add, Joseph. antt. 6, 4, 1; 7, 14, 7; 11, 3, 10).   3. *family* in a wider sense, i. q. *nation, people*: Acts iii. 25 (1 Chr. xvi. 28; Ps. xxi.   **3965**

(xxii.) 28) ; πᾶσα πατριὰ ἐν οὐρανοῖς (i. e. every order of angels) καὶ ἐπὶ γῆς, Eph. iii. 15.*

3966   **πατριάρχης**, -ου, ὁ, (πατριά and ἄρχω ; see ἑκατοντάρχης), a Hellenistic word [W. 26], *a patriarch, founder of a tribe, progenitor*: used of David, Acts ii. 29 ; of the twelve sons of Jacob, founders of the several tribes of Israel, Acts vii. 8 sq. ; of Abraham, Heb. vii. 4 ; of the same and Isaac and Jacob, 4 Macc. vii. 19 ; xvi. 25 ; used for רֹאשׁ הָאָבוֹת, 1 Chr. xxiv. 31 [but the text here is uncertain] ; שַׂר שְׁבָטִים, 1 Chr. xxvii. 22 ; for שַׂר הַבֵּאָוֹת, 2 Chr. xxiii. 20.*

3967   **πατρικός**, -ή, -όν, (πατήρ), *paternal, ancestral*, i. q. handed down by or received from one's fathers : Gal. i. 14. (Thuc., Xen., Plat., sqq.; Sept.) [Syn. see πατρῷος, fin.]*

3968   **πατρίς**, -ίδος, ἡ, (πατήρ), *one's native country*;   **a.** as in class. Grk. fr. Hom. down, *one's father-land, one's* (own) *country* : Jn. iv. 44 [cf. γάρ, II. 1] ; i. q. a fixed abode (*home* [R. V. *a country of their own*], opp. to the land where one παρεπιδημεῖ), Heb. xi. 14.   **b.** *one's native* (own) *place* i. e. *city* : Mt. xiii. 54, 57 ; Mk. vi. 1, 4 ; Lk. iv. 23, [24] ; so Philo, leg. ad Gaium § 36 (ἔστι δέ μοι Ἱεροσόλυμα πατρίς); Joseph. antt. 10, 7, 3 ; 6, 4, 6 ; ᾧ πατρὶς ἡ Ἀκυληΐα ἦν, Hdian. 8, 3, 2 (1 ed. Bekk.).*

3969   **Πατρόβας** [al. -βᾶς, as contr. fr. πατρόβιος; cf. B. D. s. v.; Bp. Lghtft. on Philip. p. 176 sq.; Chandler § 32], acc. -αν [cf. B. 19 (17) sq. ; W. § 8, 1], *Patrobas*, a certain Christian : Ro. xvi. 14.*

see 3964   **πατρολῴας**, see πατραλῴας.

3970   **πατρο-παρά-δοτος**, -ον, (πατήρ and παραδίδωμι), *handed down from one's fathers* or *ancestors* : 1 Pet. i. 18 [B. 91 (79)]. (Diod. 4, 8 ; 15, 74 ; 17, 4 ; Dion. Hal. antt. 5, 48 ; Theophil. ad Autol. 2, 34 ; Euseb. h. e. 4, 23, 10 ; 10, 4, 16.) *

3971   **πατρῷος** (poetic and Ionic πατρώϊος), -α, -ον, (πατήρ), fr. Hom. down, *descending from father to son* or *from ancestors to their posterity as it were by right of inheritance; received from the fathers* : νόμος, Acts xxii. 3 (2 Macc. vi. 1 ; Ael. v. h. 6, 10) ; θεός, Acts xxiv. 14 (4 Macc. xii. 19 ; and often in Grk. writ. θεοὶ πατρ., Ζεὺς πατρ. etc.) ; τὰ ἔθη τὰ π. Acts xxviii. 17 (Justin dial. c. Tr. c. 63 ; πατρ. ἔθος, Ael. v. h. 7, 19 var.).*

[Syn. π α τ ρ ῷ ο ς, π α τ ρ ι κ ό ς : on the distinction of the grammarians (see Photius, Suidas, Ammonius, etc. s. vv.) acc. to which πατρῷος is used of p r o p e r t y descending from father to son, πατρικός of p e r s o n s in friendship or feud, etc., see *Ellendt*, Lex. Soph. ii. p. 530 sq. ; L. and S. s. v. πατρῷος ; Schmidt ch. 154.]

3972   **Παῦλος**, -ου, ὁ, (a Lat. prop. name, *Paulus*), *Paul*. Two persons of this name are mentioned in the N. T., viz.   **1.** *Sergius Paulus*, a Roman propraetor [proconsul ; cf. Σέργιος, and B. D. s. v. Sergius Paulus], converted to Christ by the agency of the apostle Paul : Acts xiii. 7.   **2.** *the apostle Paul*, whose Hebrew name was *Saul* (see Σαούλ, Σαῦλος). He was born at Tarsus in Cilicia (Acts ix. 11 ; xxi. 39 ; xxii. 3) of Jewish parents (Phil. iii. 5). His father was a Pharisee (Acts xxiii. 6) and a Roman citizen ; hence he himself

was a Roman citizen by birth (Acts xxii. 28 ; xvi. 37). He was endowed with remarkable gifts, both moral and intellectual. He learned the trade of a σκηνοποιός (q. v.). Brought to Jerusalem in early youth, he was thoroughly indoctrinated in the Jewish theology by the Pharisee Gamaliel (Acts xxii. 3 ; v. 34). At first he attacked and persecuted the Christians most fiercely ; at length, on his way to Damascus, he was suddenly converted to Christ by a miracle, and became an indefatigable and undaunted preacher of Christ and the founder of many Christian churches. And not only by his unwearied labors did he establish a claim to the undying esteem of the friends of Christianity, but also by the fact, which appears from his immortal Epistles, that he caught perfectly the mind of his heavenly Master and taught most unequivocally that salvation was designed by God for all men who repose a l i v i n g f a i t h in Jesus Christ, and that bondage to the Mosaic law is wholly incompatible with the spiritual liberty of which Christ is the author. By his zeal and doctrine he drew upon himself the deadly hatred of the Jews, who at Jerusalem in the year 57 [or 58 acc. to the more common opinion ; yet see the chronological table in Meyer (or Lange) on Acts; *Farrar*, St. Paul, ii. excurs. x.] brought about his imprisonment ; and as a captive he was carried first to Cæsarea in Palestine, and two years later to Rome, where he suffered martyrdom (in the year 64). For the number of those daily grows smaller who venture to defend the ecclesiastical tradition for which Eusebius is responsible (h. e. 2, 22, 2) [but of which traces seem to be found in Clem. Rom. 1 Cor. 5, 7 ; can. Murator. (cf. *Westcott*, Canon, 5th ed. p. 521 sq.)], according to which Paul, released from this imprisonment, is said to have preached in Spain and Asia Minor ; and subsequently, imprisoned a second time, to have been at length put to death at Rome in the year 67 or 68, while Nero was still emperor. [On this point cf. Meyer on Ro., Introd. § 1 ; Harnack on Clem. Rom. l. c.; Lghtft. ibid. p. 49 sq.; *Holtzmann*, Die Pastoralbriefe, Einl. ch. iv. p. 37 sqq.; reff. in *Heinichen's* note on Euseb. h. e. as above; v. *Hofmann*, Die heilige Schrift Neuen Testaments. 5ter Theil p. 4 sqq.; *Farrar*, St. Paul, vol. ii. excurs. viii.; *Schaff*, Hist. of Apostolic Christ. (1882) p. 331 sq.] Paul is mentioned in the N. T. not only in the Acts and in the Epp. from his pen, but also in 2 Pet. iii. 15. [For bibliog. reff. respecting his life and its debatable points see the art. Paulus by Woldemar Schmidt in Herzog ed. 2 vol. xi. pp. 356-389.]

πανω : 1 aor. impv. 3 pers. sing. παυσάτω (1 Pet. iii. 10) ; Mid., pres. παύομαι ; impf. ἐπαυόμην ; fut. παύσομαι (see ἀναπαύω and ἐπαναπαύω [and on the forms παῆναι etc. cf. further *Hilgenfeld*, Hermae Pastor, ed. alt. proleg. p. xviii. note, also his ed. of the 'Teaching' 4, 2 note (p. 97)]); pf. πέπαυμαι ; 1 aor. ἐπαυσάμην ; fr. Hom. down ; *to make to cease* or *desist* : τὶ or τινὰ ἀπό τινος, *to restrain* [A. V. *refrain*] *a thing* or *a person from something*, 1 Pet. iii. 10, fr. Ps. xxxiii. (xxxiv.) 14 ; cf. W. § 30, 6 ; [(cf. 326 (305)) ; B. § 132, 5]. Mid. Sept. for חָדַל כָּלָה, שָׁבַת,

                                                               3973

etc. *to cease, leave off*, [cf. W. 253 (238)] : Lk. viii. 24 ; Acts xx. 1 ; 1 Co. xiii. 8 ; the action or state desisted from is indicated by the addition of a pres. ptcp. (cf. Matthiae § 551 d. ; Passow s. v. II. 3 ; [L. and S. I. 4] ; W. § 45, 4 ; [B. § 144, 15]) : ἐπαύσατο λαλῶν, Lk. v. 4 (Gen. xviii. 33 ; Num. xvi. 31 ; Deut. xx. 9) ; add, Acts v. 42 ; vi. 13 ; xiii. 10 ; xx. 31 ; xxi. 32 ; Eph. i. 16 ; Col. i. 9 ; Heb. x. 2 ; the ptcp. is wanting, as being evident fr. the context, Lk. xi. 1. Pass. [cf. W. § 39, 3 and N. 3] πέπαυται ἁμαρτίας, *hath got release* [A. V. *hath ceased*] *from sin*, i. e. is no longer stirred by its incitements and seductions, 1 Pet. iv. 1 ; cf. *Kypke*, Observv. ad loc., and W. u. s.; [B. § 132, 5 ; but WH txt. ἁμαρτίαις, dat., *unto sins*. COMP. : ἀνα-, ἐπ-ανα-, συν-ανα- (-μαι), κατα- παύω].*

3974 Πάφος [perh. fr. r. meaning 'to cozen' ; cf. *Pape*, Eigennamen, s. v.], -ον, ἡ, *Paphos* [now *Baffa*], a maritime city on the island of Cyprus, with a harbor. It was the residence of the Roman proconsul. "Old Paphos" [now *Kuklia*], formerly noted for the worship and shrine of Venus [Aphrodite], lay some 7 miles or more S. E. of it (Mela 2, 7 ; Plin. h. n. 5, 31. 35 ; Tac. hist. 2, 2) : Acts xiii. 6, 13. [*Lewin*, St. Paul, i. 120 sqq.] *

3975 παχύνω : 1 aor. pass. ἐπαχύνθην ; (fr. παχύς [thick, stout] ; cf. βραδύνω ; ταχύνω) ; *to make thick* ; *to make fat, fatten* : τὰ σώματα, Plat. Gorg. p. 518 c. ; βοῦν, de rep. p. 343 b.; ἵππον, Xen. oec. 12, 20. Metaph. *to make stupid* (*to render the soul dull* or *callous*): τὰς ψυχάς, Plut. mor. p. 995 d. [i. e. de esu carn. 1, 6, 3] ; νοῦν, Philostr. vit. Apoll. 1, 8 ; παχεῖς τὰς διανοίας, Hdian. 2, 9, 15 [11 ed. Bekk.]; τὴν διάνοιαν, Ael. v. h. 13, 15 (Lat. *pingue* ingenium) [cf. W. 18].; ἐπαχύνθη ἡ καρδία (Vulg. incrassatum est cor [A. V. *their heart is waxed gross*]): Mt. xiii. 15 ; Acts xxviii. 27, after Is. vi. 10 (for הַשְׁמֵן לֵב). *

3976 πέδη, -ης, ἡ, (fr. πέζα the foot, instep), *a fetter, shackle for the feet* : Mk. v. 4 ; Lk. viii. 29. (From Hom. down ; Sept.) *

3977 πεδινός, -ή, -όν, (πεδίον [a plain], πέδον [the ground]), *level, plain* : Lk. vi. 17. (Xen., Polyb., Plut., Dio Cass., al. ; Sept.) *

3978 πεζεύω ; (πεζός, q. v.) ; *to travel on foot* (not on horseback or in a carriage), or (if opp. to going by sea) *by land* : Acts xx. 13. (Xen., Isocr., Polyb., Strab., al.) *

3979 πεζῇ (dat. fem. fr. πεζός, q. v. ; cf. Matthiae § 400), *on foot* or (if opp. to going by sea) *by land* : Mt. xiv. 13 R G Tr L txt. WH txt.; Mk. vi. 33. (Hdt., Thuc., Xen., Dem., al.) *

see 3979 πεζός, -ή -όν, [πέζα ; see πέδη], fr. Hom. down ; 1. *on foot* (as opp. to riding). 2. *by land* (as opp. to going by sea) : ἠκολούθησαν πεζοί, Mt. xiv. 13 T L mrg. WH mrg. (so cod. Sin. also) for R G πεζῇ, [cf. W. § 54, 2 ; B. § 123, 9]. (Sept. for רַגְלִי and בְּרֶגֶל.) *

3980 πειθαρχέω, -ῶ ; 1 aor. ptcp. πειθαρχήσας ; and this fr. πείθομαι and ἀρχή) ; *to obey* (a ruler or a superior) : θεῷ, Acts v. 29, 32 ; magistrates, Tit. iii. 1 [al. take it here absol. *to be obedient*] ; τῷ λόγῳ τῆς δικαιοσύνης, Polyc. ad Philipp. 9, 1 ; [A. V. *to hearken to*] one advising something, Acts xxvii. 21. (Soph., Xen., Polyb., Diod., Joseph., Plut., al. ; on the very freq. use

of the verb by Philo see *Siegfried*, Philo von Alex. u. s. w. p. 43 [esp. p. 108].) *

3981 πειθός [WH πιθός ; see I, ι], -ή, -όν, (fr. πείθω, like φειδός fr. φείδομαι [cf.W. 96 (91)]), *persuasive* : ἐν πειθοῖς λόγοις, 1 Co. ii. 4 [cf. B. 73]. Not found elsewhere [W. 24]. The Grks. say πιθανός ; as πιθανοὶ λόγοι, Joseph. antt. 8, 9, and often in Grk. auth. See Passow s. v. πιθανός, 1 e. ; [L. and S. ibid. I. 2 ; *WH*. App. p. 153].*

see 3982 Πειθώ, -οῦς, ἡ, 1. *Peitho*, prop. name of a goddess, lit. *Persuasion* ; Lat. *Suada* or *Suadela*. 2. *persuasive power, persuasion* : 1 Co. ii. 4 ἐν πειθοῖ — acc. to certain inferior authorities. [On the word, see Müller's note on Joseph. c. Ap. 2, 21, 3. (Hes., Hdt., al.)] *

3982 πείθω [(fr. r. meaning 'to bind' ; allied w. πίστις, fides, foedus, etc.; Curtius § 327 ; Vaniček p. 592)] ; impf. ἔπειθον ; fut. πείσω ; 1 aor. ἔπεισα ; 2 pf. πέποιθα ; plupf. ἐπεποίθειν (Lk. xi. 22) ; Pass. [or Mid., pres. πείθομαι ; impf. ἐπειθόμην] ; pf. πέπεισμαι ; 1 aor. ἐπείσθην ; 1 fut. πεισθήσομαι (Lk. xvi. 31) ; fr. Hom. down ; 1. Active ; a. *to persuade*, i. e. *to induce one by words to believe* : absol. πείσας μετέστησεν ἱκανὸν ὄχλον, Acts xix. 26 ; τί, *to cause belief in a thing* (which one sets forth), Acts xix. 8 R G T [cf. B. 150 (131) n.] (Soph. O. C. 1442) ; περί w. gen. of the thing, ibid. L Tr WH ; τινά, one, Acts xviii. 4 ; τινά τι, one of a thing, Acts xxviii. 23 Rec. (Hdt. 1, 163 ; Plat. apol. p. 37 a., and elsewhere ; [cf. B. u. s.]) ; τινὰ περί τινος, concerning a thing, ibid. G L T Tr WH. b. as in class. Grk. fr. Hom. down, w. an acc. of a pers., *to make friends of, win one's favor, gain one's good-will*, Acts xii. 20 ; or *to seek to win one, strive to please one*, 2 Co. v. 11 ; Gal. i. 10 ; *to conciliate* by persuasion, Mt. xxviii. 14 [here T WH om. Tr br. αὐτόν] ; Acts xiv. 19 ; i. q. *to tranquillize* [A. V. *assure*], τὰς καρδίας ἡμῶν, 1 Jn. iii. 19. c. *to persuade unto* i. e. *move* or *induce one by persuasion to do something* : τινά foll. by an inf. [B. § 139, 46], Acts xiii. 43 ; xxvi. 28, (Xen. an. 1, 3, 19 ; Polyb. 4, 64, 2 ; Diod. 11, 15 ; 12, 39 ; Joseph. antt. 8, 10, 3) ; τινά foll. by ἵνα [cf. W. 338 (317) ; B. § 139, 46], Mt. xxvii. 20 [Plut. apoph. Alex. 21]. 2. Passive and Middle [cf. W. 253 (238)] ; a. *to be persuaded, to suffer one's self to be persuaded* ; *to be induced to believe* : absol., Lk. xvi. 31 ; Acts xvii. 4 ; *to have faith*, Heb. xi. 13 Rec. ; τινί, *in a thing*, Acts xxviii. 24 ; *to believe*, sc. ὅτι, Heb. xiii. 18 L T Tr WH. πέπεισμαί τι [on the neut. acc. cf. B. § 131, 10] *περί τινος* (gen. of pers.), *to be persuaded* (of) *a thing concerning a person*, Heb. vi. 9 [A. V. *we are persuaded better things of you*, etc.] ; πεπεισμένος εἰμί, *to have persuaded one's self*, and πείθομαι, *to believe*, [cf. Eng. *to be persuaded*], foll. by acc. w. inf., Lk. xx. 6 ; Acts xxvi. 26 ; πέπεισμαι ὅτι, Ro. viii. 38 ; 2 Tim. i. 5, 12 ; with ἐν κυρίῳ added (see ἐν, I. 6 b.), Ro. xiv. 14 ; περί τινος ὅτι, Ro. xv. 14. b. *to listen to, obey, yield to, comply with* : τινί, one, Acts v. 36 sq. 39 (40) ; xxiii. 21 ; xxvii. 11 ; Ro. ii. 8 ; Gal. iii. 1 Rec. ; v. 7 ; Heb. xiii. 17 ; Jas. iii. 3. 3. 2 pf. πέποιθα (Sept. mostly for בָּטַח, also for חָסָה נִשְׁעַן Niphal of the unused שָׁעַן), intrans. *to trust, have confidence, be confident* : foll. by acc. w. inf., Ro. ii. 19 ; by ὅτι, Heb.

xiii. 18 Rec.; by ὅτι with a preparatory αὐτὸ τοῦτο [W. § 23, 5], Phil. i. 6; τοῦτο πεποιθὼς οἶδα ὅτι, ibid. 25; πέποιθα w. a dat. of the pers. or the thing in which the confidence reposes (so in class. Grk. [on its constr. in the N. T. see B. § 133, 5; W. 214 (201); § 33, d.]): Phil. i. 14; Philem. 21, (2 K. xviii. 20; Prov. xiv. 16; xxviii. 26; Is. xxviii. 17; Sir. xxxv. (xxxii.) 24; Sap. xiv. 29); ἑαυτῷ foll. by an inf. 2 Co. x. 7; ἔν τινι, to trust in, put confidence in a pers. or thing [cf. B. u. s.], Phil. iii. 3, 4; ἐν κυρίῳ foll. by ὅτι, Phil. ii. 24; ἐπί τινι, Mt. xxvii. 43 L txt. WH mrg.; Mk. x. 24 [where T WH om. Tr mrg. br. the cl.]; Lk. xi. 22; xviii. 9; 2 Co. i. 9; Heb. ii. 13, (and very often in Sept., as Deut. xxviii. 52; 2 Chr. xiv. 11; Ps. ii. 13; Prov. iii. 5; Is. viii. 17; xxxi. 1); ἐπί τινα, Mt. xxvii. 43 where L txt. WH mrg. ἐπί w. dat. (Is. xxxvi. 5; Hab. ii. 18; 2 Chr. xvi. 7 sq., etc.); ἐπί τινα foll. by ὅτι, 2 Co. ii. 3; 2 Th. iii. 4; εἴς τινα foll. by ὅτι, Gal. v. 10. [Comp.: ἀνα-πείθω.]*

(3982a); see 4091 Πειλᾶτος, see Πιλάτος [and cf. ει, ι].

3983 πεινάω, -ῶ, inf. πεινᾶν (Phil. iv. 12); fut. πεινάσω (Lk. vi. 25; Rev. vii. 16); 1 aor. ἐπείνασα, — for the earlier forms πεινῆν, πεινήσω, ἐπείνησα; cf. *Lob.* ad Phryn. pp. 61 and 204; W. § 13, 3 b.; [B. 37 (32); 44 (38)]; see also διψάω; (fr. πεῖνα hunger; [see πένης]); fr. Hom. down; Sept. for רָעֵב; *to hunger, be hungry*; a. prop.: Mt. iv. 2; xii. 1, 3; xxi. 18; xxv. 35, 37, 42, 44; Mk. ii. 25; xi. 12; Lk. iv. 2; vi. 3, 25; i. q. *to suffer want*, Ro. xii. 20; 1 Co. xi. 21, 34; *to be needy*, Lk. i. 53; vi. 21; Phil. iv. 12; in this same sense it is joined with διψᾶν, 1 Co. iv. 11; in figurative disc. οὐ πεινᾶν κ. οὐ διψᾶν is used to describe the condition of one who is in need of nothing requisite for his real (spiritual) life and salvation, Jn. vi. 35; Rev. vii. 16. b. metaph. *to crave ardently, to seek with eager desire*: w. acc. of the thing, τὴν δικαιοσύνην, Mt. v. 6 (in the better Grk. auth. w. a gen., as χρημάτων, Xen. Cyr. 8, 3, 39; συμμάχων, 7, 5, 50; ἐπαίνου, oec. 13, 9; cf. W. § 30, 10, b. fin.; [B. § 131, 4]; Kuinoel on Mt. v. 6, and see διψάω, 2).*

3984 πεῖρα, -ας, ἡ, (πειράω), fr. Aeschyl. down, *a trial, experiment, attempt*: πεῖραν λαμβάνειν τινός, i. q. *to attempt a thing, to make trial of a thing* or *a person*, (a phrase common in prof. auth.; cf. Xen. mem. 1, 4, 18; Cyr. 3, 3, 38; see other exx. in *Sturz*, Lex. Xenoph. iii. p. 488; Plat. Protag. p. 342 a.; Gorg. p. 448 a.; Joseph. antt. 8, 6, 5; Ael. v. h. 12, 22; often in Polyb., cf. *Schweighäuser*, Lex. Polyb. p. 460; Sept. Deut. xxviii. 56; [other exx. in Bleek on Heb. l. c.; *Field*, Otium Norv. pars iii. p. 146]), θαλάσσης, to try whether the sea can be crossed dry-shod like the land, Heb. xi. 29; *to have trial of a thing*, i. e. *to experience, learn to know by experience*, μαστίγων, Heb. xi. 36 (often in Polyb.; τῆς προνοίας, Joseph. antt. 2, 5, 1).*

3985 πειράζω (a form found several times in Hom. and Apoll. Rhod. and later prose, for πειράω [which see in Veitch] more com. in the other Grk. writ.); impf. ἐπείραζον; 1 aor. ἐπείρασα; Pass., pres. πειράζομαι; 1 aor. ἐπειράσθην; pf. ptcp. πεπειρασμένος (Heb. iv. 15; see πειράω, 1); 1 aor. mid. 2 pers. sing. ἐπειράσω (Rev. ii. 2 Rec.); Sept. for נִסָּה; *to try*, i. e. 1. *to try whether a thing can be done; to attempt, endeavor*: with an inf., Acts ix. 26 L T Tr WH; xvi. 7; xxiv. 6. 2. *to try, make trial of, test*: τινά, for the purpose of ascertaining his quality, or what he thinks, or how he will behave himself; a. in a good sense: Mt. xxii. 35 [al. refer this to b.]; Jn. vi. 6; [2 Co. xiii. 5]; Rev. ii. 2. b. in a bad sense: to test one maliciously, craftily to put to the proof his feelings or judgment, Mt. xvi. 1; xix. 3; xxii. 18, 35; Mk. viii. 11; x. 2; xii. 15; Lk. xi. 16; xx. 23 (where G T WH Tr txt. om. Tr mrg. br. the words τί με πειράζετε); Jn. viii. 6. c. to try or test one's faith, virtue, character, by enticement to sin; hence acc. to the context i. q. *to solicit to sin, to tempt*: Jas. i. 13 sq.; Gal. vi. 1; Rev. ii. 10; of the temptations of the devil, Mt. iv. 1, 3; Mk. i. 13; Lk. iv. 2; 1 Co. vii. 5; 1 Th. iii. 5; hence, ὁ πειράζων, subst., Vulg. *tentator*, etc., *the tempter*: Mt. iv. 3; 1 Th. iii. 5. d. After the O. T. usage α. of God; *to inflict evils upon one in order to prove his character and the steadfastness of his faith*: 1 Co. x. 13; Heb. ii. 18; iv. 15 [see πειράω]; xi. 17, 37 [where see *WH*. App.]; Rev. iii. 10, (Gen. xxii. 1; Ex. xx. 20; Deut. viii. 2; Sap. iii. 5; xi. 10 (9); Judith viii. 25 sq.). β. Men are said πειράζειν τὸν θεόν, — by exhibitions of distrust, as though they wished to try whether he is not justly distrusted; by impious or wicked conduct to test God's justice and patience, and to challenge him, as it were, to give proof of his perfections: Acts xv. 10; Heb. iii. 9 R G, (Ex. xvii. 2, 7; Num. xiv. 22; Ps. lxxvii. (lxxviii.) 41, 56; cv. (cvi.) 14, etc.; cf. *Grimm*, Exgt. Hdb. on Sap. p. 49); sc. τὸν Χριστόν [L T Tr txt. WH τ. κύριον], 1 Co. x. 9 [but L mrg. T WH mrg. ἐξεπείρασαν]; τὸ πνεῦμα κυρίου, Acts v. 9; absol. πειράζειν ἐν δοκιμασίᾳ (see δοκιμασία), Heb. iii. 9 L T Tr WH. [On πειράζω (as compared with δοκιμάζω), see Trench § lxxiv.; cf. Cremer s. v. Comp.: ἐκ-πειράζω.]*

πειρασμός, -οῦ, ὁ, (πειράζω, q. v.), Sept. for מַסָּה, *an experiment, attempt, trial, proving*; (Vulg. *tentatio*); 3986
a. univ. *trial, proving*: Sir. xxvii. 5, 7; τὸν πειρασμὸν ὑμῶν ἐν τῇ σαρκί μου, the trial made of you by my bodily condition, since this condition served to test the love of the Galatians towards Paul, Gal. iv. 14 L T Tr WH [cf. b. below, and Bp. Lghtft. ad loc.]. b. spec. *the trial of man's fidelity, integrity, virtue, constancy*, etc.: 1 Pet. iv. 12; also *an enticement to sin, temptation*, whether arising from the desires or from outward circumstances, Lk. viii. 13; 1 Co. x. 13; ὑπομένειν πειρασμόν, Jas. i. 12; an internal temptation to sin, 1 Tim. vi. 9; of the temptation by which the devil sought to divert Jesus the Messiah from his divine errand, Lk. iv. 13; of a condition of things, or a mental state, by which we are enticed to sin, or to a lapse from faith and holiness: in the phrases εἰσφέρειν τινὰ εἰς πειρ., Mt. vi. 13; Lk. xi. 4; εἰσέρχεσθαι εἰς π., Mt. xxvi. 41; Mk. xiv. 38 [here T WH ἔρχ.]; Lk. xxii. 40, 46; *adversity, affliction, trouble*, [cf. our *trial*], sent by God and serving to test or prove one's faith, holiness, character: plur., Lk. xxii. 28; Acts xx. 19; Jas. i. 2; 1 Pet. i. 6; τὸν πειρ. μου τὸν ἐν τῇ σαρκί μου,

my temptation arising from my bodily infirmity, Gal. iv.
14 Rec. [but see a. above]; ὥρα τοῦ πειρασμοῦ, Rev. iii.
10; ἐκ π. ῥύεσθαι, 2 Pet. ii. 9, (Deut. vii. 19; xxix. 3;
Sir. ii. 1; vi. 7; xxxvi. (xxxiii.) 1; 1 Macc. ii. 52).　　c.
'*temptation*' (i. e. *trial*) *of God by men*, i. e. rebellion
against God, by which his power and justice are, as it
were, put to the proof and challenged to show themselves: Heb. iii. 8 (Deut. vi. 16; ix. 22; Ps. xciv. (xcv.)
8). Cf. *Fried. B. Koester*, Die bibl. Lehre von der Ver-
suchung. Gotha, 1859. (The word has not yet been
found in prof. auth. exc. Diosc. praef. 1: τοὺς ἐπὶ παθῶν
π. experiments made on diseases.)*

3987   **πειράω**: impf. mid. 3 pers. (sing. and plur), ἐπειρᾶτο,
ἐπειρῶντο; pf. pass. ptcp. πεπειραμένος (see below); com.
in Grk. writ. fr. Hom. down; *to try*; i. e.   **1.** *to make
a trial, to attempt*, [A. V. *to assay*], foll. by an infin.;
often so fr. Hom. down; also so in the mid. in Acts ix. 26
R G; xxvi. 21, (Xen. symp. 4, 7; Cyr. 1, 4, 5, etc.; often
in Polyb.; Ael. v. h. 1, 34; 2 Macc. ii. 23; 3 Macc. i. 25;
4 Macc. xii. 2, etc.); hence πεπειραμένος *taught by trial, experienced*, Heb. iv. 15 in certain codd. and edd. ([Rec.ˢᵗ],
Tdf. formerly) [see below, and cf. πειράζω, d. a.].   **2.**
In post-Hom. usage with the acc. of a pers. *to test, make
trial of* one, *put* him *to the proof*: his mind, sentiments,
temper, Plut. Brut. 10; in particular, to attempt to induce one to commit some (esp. a c a r n a l) crime; cf.
Passow s. v. 3 a.; [L. and S. s. v. A. IV. 2]. Hence
πεπειραμένος in Heb. iv. 15 (see 1 above) is explained
by some [cf. W. § 15 Note ad fin.] *tempted* to sin; but
the Pass. in this sense is not found in Grk. writ.; see
Delitzsch ad loc.*

3988   **πεισμονή**, -ῆς, ἡ, (πείθω, q. v.; like πλησμονή), *persuasion*: in an active sense [yet cf. Bp. Lghtft. on Gal. as
below] and contextually, *treacherous* or *deceptive persuasion*, Gal. v. 8 [cf. W. § 68, 1 fin.]. (Found besides in
Ignat. ad Rom. 3, 3 longer recens.; Justin apol. 1, 53
init.; (Irenæus 4, 33, 7]; Epiph. 30, 21; Chrysost. on
1 Th. i. 3; Apollon. Dys. syntax p. 195, 10 [299, 17];
Eustath. on Hom. Il. α'. p. 21, 46 vs. 22; 99, 45 vs. 442;
ι'. p. 637, 5 vs. 131; and Od. χ'. p. 785, 22 vs. 285.)*

3989   **πέλαγος**, -ους, τό, [by some (e. g. *Lob.* Pathol. Proleg.
p. 305) connected with πλάξ, i. e. the 'flat' expanse (cf.
Lat. *aequor*); but by Curtius § 367 et al. (cf. Vaniček
p. 515) with πλήσσω, i. e. the 'beating' waves (cf. our
' plash ')], fr. Hom. down;   **a.** prop. *the sea* i. e. *the
high sea, the deep*, (where ships sail; accordingly but a
p a r t of the sea, θάλασσα, Aristot. Probl. sect. 23 quaest.
3 [p. 931ᵇ, 14 sq.] ἐν τῷ λιμένι ὀλίγη ἐστὶν ἡ θάλασσα, ἐν
δὲ τῷ πελάγει βαθεῖα. Hence) τὸ πέλαγος τῆς θαλάσσης,
aequor maris, [A. V. *the depth of the sea*; cf. Trench
§ xiii.], Mt. xviii. 6 (so too Apollon. Rhod. 2, 608; πέλαγος αἰγαίας ἁλός, Eur. Tro. 88; Hesych. πέλαγος·...
βυθός, πλάτος θαλάσσης. Cf. W. 611 (568); [Trench
u. s.]).   **b.** univ. *the sea*: τὸ πέλ. τὸ κατὰ τὴν Κιλικίαν,
Acts xxvii. 5 (see exx. fr. Grk. auth. in Passow s. v. πέλαγος, 1; [L. and S. s. v. I.]).*

3990   **πελεκίζω**: pf. pass. ptcp. πεπελεκισμένος; (πέλεκυς, an
axe or two-edged hatchet); *to cut off with an axe, to

behead: τινά, Rev. xx. 4. (Polyb., Diod., Strab., Joseph.
antt. 20, 5, 4; Plut. Ant. 36; [cf. W. 26 (25)].)*

3991   **πέμπτος**, -η, -ον, [fr. Hom. down], *fifth*: Rev. vi. 9; ix.
1; xvi. 10; xxi. 20.*

3992   **πέμπω**; fut. πέμψω; 1 aor. ἔπεμψα [on its epistolary
use (for the pres. or the pf.) see W. 278 (261); B. 198
(172); Bp. Lghtft. on Phil. ii. (25), 28; Philem. 11];
Pass., pres. πέμπομαι; 1 aor. ἐπέμφθην (Lk. vii. 10); fr.
Hom. down; Sept. for שָׁלַח; *to send*: τινά, absol., one
to do something, Mt. xxii. 7; Lk. vii. 19; xvi. 24; Jn. i.
22; vii. 18; xiii. 16, 20; xx. 21 [Treg. mrg. ἀποστελλ.];
2 Co. ix. 3; Phil. ii. 23, 28, etc.; τινά or τινάς is omitted
where the ptcp. is joined to another finite verb, as πέμψας
ἀπεκεφάλισε τὸν Ἰωάννην, he sent (a deputy) and beheaded John, Mt. xiv. 10; add, Acts xix. 31; xxiii. 30,
(for other exx. see ἀποστέλλω, 1 d.); in imitation of the
Hebr. ´´פ בְּיַד שָׁלַח (1 S. xvi. 20; 2 S. xi. 14; xii. 25; 1 K.
ii. 25) we find πέμψας διὰ τῶν μαθητῶν αὐτοῦ, he sent by
his disciples (unless with Fritzsche, and *Bornemann*,
Schol. in Luc. p. lxv., one prefer to take πέμψας absol.
and to connect διὰ τ. μαθ. with the foll. εἶπεν [so *Mey.*,
but see (7te Aufl. ed. Weiss), Keil, De Wette, al.]), Mt.
xi. 2 L T Tr WH, (so ἀποστείλας διὰ τοῦ ἀγγέλου, Rev.
i. 1). Teachers who come forward by God's command
and with his authority are said to be (or to have been)
sent by God: as, John the Baptist, Jn. i. 33; Jesus, Jn.
iv. 34; v. 23 sq. 30, 37; vi. 38–40, 44; vii. 16, 28, etc.;
Ro. viii. 3; the Holy Spirit, rhetorically personified, Jn.
xiv. 26; xv. 26; xvi. 7. τινά, w. dat. of the pers. to whom
one is sent: 1 Co. iv. 17; Phil. ii. 19; τινά τινι παρά τινος
(prop. to send one to one from one's abode [see παρά, I.
a.]), Jn. xv. 26; πρός τινα, Lk. iv. 26; Jn. xvi. 7; Acts x.
33; xv. 25; xxiii. 30; [xxv. 21 R G]; Eph. vi. 22; Phil.
ii. 25; Col. iv. 8; Tit. iii. 12; with the ptcp. λέγων added
(Hebr. לֵאמֹר שָׁלַח, Gen. xxxviii. 25; 2 S. xiv. 32, etc.),
said by messenger (Germ. *liess sagen*), Lk. vii. 6, 19;
τινὰ εἴς τι w. an acc. of place, Mt. ii. 8; Lk. xv. 15; xvi. 27;
Acts x. 5; *the end*, for which one is sent is indicated —
by the prep. εἰς, Eph. vi. 22; Col. iv. 8; 1 Pet. ii. 14;
by an infin., Jn. i. 33; 1 Co. xvi. 3; Rev. xxii. 16. Of
t h i n g s, τί τινι,   **a.** to bid a thing to be carried to
one: Rev. xi. 10; with εἰς and an acc. of place added,
Rev. i. 11; εἰς w. an acc. indicating the purpose, Acts xi.
29; Phil. iv. 16 [here Lchm.br. εἰς; cf. B. 329 (283)].   **b.**
to send (thrust or insert) *a thing into another*: Rev. xiv.
15, 18, (Ael. hist. an. 12, 5); τινί τι εἰς τό w. an inf., 2 Th.
ii. 11. [COMP.: ἀνα-, ἐκ-, μετα-, προ-, συμ-πέμπω.]
[SYN. π έ μ π ω, ἀ π ο σ τ έ λ λ ω: πέμπω is the general term
(differing from ἵημι in directing attention not to the e x i t
but to the a d v e n t); it may even imply accompaniment
(as when the sender is G o d). ἀποστέλλω includes a reference to equipment, and suggests official or authoritative sending. Cf. Schmidt ch. 104; Westcott on Jn. xx. 21, 'Additional Note '; also ' Additional Note ' on 1 Jn. iii. 5.]

3993   **πένης**, -ητος, ὁ, (πένομαι to work for one's living; the
Lat. *penuria* and Grk. πεινάω are akin to it [cf. Vaniček
p. 1164]; hence πένης i. q. ἐκ πόνου καὶ ἐνεργείας τὸ ζῆν
ἔχων, Etym. Magn.), *poor*: 2 Co. ix. 9. (From Soph. and
Hdt. down; Sept. for אֶבְיוֹן, עָנִי, דַּל, רָשׁ, etc.)*

[SYN. πένης, πτωχός: "πένης occurs but once in the N.T., and then in a quotation fr. the Old, while πτωχός occurs between thirty and forty times. . . . The πένης may be so poor that he earns his bread by daily labor; the πτωχός that he only obtains his living by begging." Trench § xxxvi.; cf. Schmidt ch. 85, 4; ch. 186.]

3994   πενθερά, -ᾶς, ἡ, (fem. of πενθερός, q. v.), a mother-in-law, a wife's mother: Mt. viii. 14; x. 35; Mk. i. 30; Lk. iv. 38; xii. 53. (Dem., Plut., Lcian., al.; Sept. for חֲמוֹת.) *

3995   πενθερός, -οῦ, ὁ, a father-in-law, a wife's father: Jn. xviii. 13. (Hom., Soph., Eurip., Plut., al.; Sept. [for חָם, חֹתֵן].) *

3996   πενθέω, -ῶ; fut. πενθήσω; 1 aor. ἐπένθησα; (πένθος); fr. Hom. down; Sept. chiefly for אָבַל; to mourn;   **a.** intrans.: Mt. v. 4 (5); ix. 15; 1 Co. v. 2; πενθεῖν κ. κλαίειν, Mk. xvi. 10; Lk. vi. 25; Jas. iv. 9; Rev. xviii. 15, 19; ἐπί τινι, over one, Rev. xviii. 11 R G L (Is. lxvi. 10); ἐπί τινα, ibid. T Tr WH (2 S. xiii. 37; 2 Chr. xxxv. 24, etc.).   **b.** trans. to mourn for, lament, one: 2 Co. xii. 21 [cf. W. 635 sq. (590); B. § 131, 4. SYN. see θρηνέω, fin.] *

3997   πένθος, -ους, τό, (πένθω [(?); akin, rather, to πάθος, πένομαι (cf. πένης); see Curtius p. 53; Vaniček p. 1165]), fr. Hom. down, Sept. for אָבַל, mourning: Jas. iv. 9; Rev. xviii. 7 sq.; xxi. 4. *

3998   πενιχρός, -ά, -όν, (fr. πένομαι, see πένης), needy, poor: Lk. xxi. 2. (Occasionally in Grk. auth. fr. Hom. Od. 3, 348 down; for יָגֵן in Ex. xxii. 25; for דַּל in Prov. xxix. 7.) *

3999   πεντάκις, adv., five times: 2 Co. xi. 24. [From Pind., Aeschyl., down.] *

4000   πεντακισ-χίλιοι, -αι, -α, five times a thousand, five thousand: Mt. xiv. 21; xvi. 9; Mk. vi. 44; viii. 19; Lk. ix. 14; Jn. vi. 10. [Hdt., Plat., al.] *

4001   πεντακόσιοι, -αι, -α, five hundred: Lk. vii. 41; 1 Co. xv. 6. [From Hom. (-ηκ-) down.] *

4002   πέντε, οἱ, αἱ, τά, five: Mt. xiv. 17, and often. [From Hom. down.]

4003   πεντε-και-δέκατος, -η, -ον, the fifteenth: Lk. iii. 1. [Diod., Plut., al.] *

4004   πεντήκοντα, οἱ, αἱ, τά, fifty: Lk. vii. 41; xvi. 6; Jn. viii. 57; xxi. 11 [R G πεντηκοντατριῶν (as one word)]; Acts xiii. 20; ἀνὰ πεντήκ. by fifties [see ἀνά, 2], Mk. vi. 40 [here L T Tr WH κατὰ π.; see κατά, II. 3 a. γ.]; Lk. ix. 14. [From Hom. down.] *

4005   πεντηκοστή, -ῆς, ἡ, (sc. ἡμέρα) fem. of πεντηκοστός fiftieth), [fr. Plat. down.], Pentecost (prop. the fiftieth day after the Passover, Tob. ii. 1; 2 Macc. xii. 32; [Philo de septen. § 21; de decal. § 30; cf. W. 26]), the second of the three great Jewish festivals; celebrated at Jerusalem yearly, the seventh week after the Passover, in grateful recognition of the completed harvest (Ex. xxiii. 16; Lev. xxiii. 15 sq.; Deut. xvi. 9): Acts ii. 1; xx. 16; 1 Co. xvi. 8, (Joseph. antt. 3, 10, 6; [14, 13, 4; etc.]). [BB. DD. (esp. Ginsburg in Alex.'s Kitto) s. v. Pentecost; Hamburger, Real-Encycl. i. s. v. Wochenfest; Edersheim, The Temple, ch. xiii.] *

4006   πεποίθησις, -εως, ἡ, (πείθω, 2 pf. πέποιθα), trust, confi-

dence [R. V.], reliance: 2 Co. i. 15; iii. 4; x. 2; Eph. iii. 12; εἴς τινα, 2 Co. viii. 22; ἔν τινι, Phil. iii. 4. (Philo de nobilit. § 7; Joseph. antt. 1, 3, 1; 3, 2, 2; 10, 1, 4; [11, 7, 1; Clem. Rom. 1 Cor. 2, 3]; Zosim., Sext. Emp., al.; Sept. once for בְּטָחוֹן, 2 K. xviii. 19.) The word is condemned by the Atticists; cf. Lob. ad Phryn. p. 295.*

4007   πέρ, an enclitic particle, akin to the prep. περί [Herm. de part. ἄν, p. 6; Curtius § 359; cf. Lob. Pathol. Elementa, i. 290; al. (connect it directly with πέραν, etc., and) give 'throughly' as its fundamental meaning; cf. Bäumlein, Partikeln, p. 198], showing that the idea of the word to which it is annexed must be taken in its fullest extent; it corresponds to the Lat. circiter, cunque, Germ. noch so sehr, immerhin, wenigstens, ja; [Eng. however much, very much, altogether, indeed]; cf. Hermann ad Vig. p. 791; Klotz ad Devar. ii. 2 p. 722 sqq.; [Donaldson, New Crat. § 178 fin.]. In the N. T. it is affixed to the pron. ὅς and to sundry particles, see διόπερ, ἐάνπερ, εἴπερ, ἐπείπερ, ἐπειδήπερ, ἤπερ, καθάπερ, καίπερ, ὅσπερ, ὥσπερ. [(From Hom. down.)]

see 4012 & 2087   περαιτέρω, (fr. περαίτερος, compar. of πέρα), adv., fr. Aeschyl. down, further, beyond, besides: Acts xix. 39 L Tr WH, for R G περὶ ἑτέρων. With this compare οὐδὲν ζητήσετε περαιτέρω, Plat. Phaedo c. 56 fin. p. 107 b.*

4008   πέραν, Ionic and Epic πέρην, adv., fr. Hom. down; Sept. for עֵבֶר; beyond, on the other side;   **a.** τὸ πέραν, the region beyond, the opposite shore: Mt. viii. 18, 28; xiv. 22; xvi. 5; Mk. iv. 35; v. 21; vi. 45; viii. 13.   **b.** joined (like a prep.) with a gen. [W. § 54, 6]: πέραν τῆς θαλ. Jn. vi. 22, 25; πέραν τοῦ Ἰορδάνου, Mt. iv. 15; xix. 1; [Mk. x. 1 L T Tr WH]; Jn. i. 28; iii. 26]; with verbs of going it marks direction towards a place [over, beyond], Jn. vi. 1, 17; x. 40; xviii. 1; of the place whence, [Mt. iv. 25]; Mk. iii. 8. τὸ πέραν τῆς θαλάσσης, Mk. v. 1; [τοῦ Ἰορδάνου, Mk. x. 1 R G]; τῆς λίμνης, Lk. viii. 22, (τοῦ ποταμοῦ, Xen. an. 3, 5, 2). [See Sophocles, Lex. s. v.]

4009   πέρας, -ατος, τό, (πέρα beyond), fr. Aeschyl. down, extremity, bound, end, [see τέλος, 1 a. init.];   **a.** of a portion of space (boundary, frontier): πέρατα τῆς γῆς, [the ends of the earth], i. q. the remotest lands, Mt. xii. 42; Lk. xi. 31, (Hom. Il. 8, 478 [πεῖραρ]; Thuc. 1, 69; Xen. Ages. 9, 4; Sept. for אֶרֶץ אַפְסֵי [W. 30]); also τῆς οἰκουμένης, Ro. x. 18 (Ps. lxxi. (lxxii.) 8).   **b.** of a thing extending through a period of time (termination): ἀντιλογίας, Heb. vi. 16 (τῶν κακῶν, Aeschyl. Pers. 632; Joseph. b. j. 7, 5, 6, and other exx. in other writ.).*

4010   Πέργαμος [perh. -μον, τό, (the gend. in the N. T. is indeterminate; cf. Lob. ad Phryn. p. 421 sq.; Pape, Eigennamen, s. vv.)], -ον, ἡ, Pergamus [or Pergamum, (cf. Curtius § 413]), a city of Mysia Major in Asia Minor, the seat of the dynasties of Attalus and Eumenes, celebrated for the temple of Aesculapius, and the invention [(?) cf. Gardthausen, Griech. Palaeogr. p. 39 sq.; Birt, Antikes Buchwesen, ch. ii.] and manufacture of parchment. The river Selinus flowed through it and the Cetius ran past it (Strab. 13 p. 623; Plin. 5, 30 (33); 13, 11 (21); Tac. ann. 3, 63). It was the birthplace of the physician Galen, and had a great royal library. Modern *Berghama*. There was a Christian church there: Rev. i. 11; ii. 12.*

4011   **Πέργη**, -ης, ἡ, [cf. the preceding word], *Perge* or *Perga*, a town of Pamphylia, on the river Cestrus about seven miles (sixty stadia) from the sea. On a hill near the town was the temple of Diana [i. e. Artemis] (Strab. 14 p. 667; Mel. 1, 14; Liv. 38, 37) : Acts xiii. 13 sq.; xiv. 25. [BB. DD.; *Lewin*, St. Paul, i. 134 sq.] *

4012   **περί**, (akin to πέρα, πέραν; [Curtius § 359]), prep., joined in the N. T. with the gen. and the acc. (in class. Grk. also with the dat.), and indicating that the person or thing relative to which an act or state is predicated is as it were encompassed by this act or state; Lat. *circum*, *circa*; *around*, *about*.

I. with the GENITIVE it denotes that *around* which an act or state revolves; *about, concerning, as touching,* etc., (Lat. *de, quod attinet ad, causa* w. a gen., *propter*) [cf. W. 372 sq. (349)].   **a.** *about, concerning,* (Lat. *de*; in later Lat. also *circa*): after verbs of s p e a k i n g, t e a c h i n g, w r i t i n g, etc., see under ἀναγγέλλω, ἀπαγγέλλω, ἀπολογοῦμαι, γογγύζω, γράφω, δηλόω, διαβεβαιοῦμαι, διαγνωρίζω, διαλέγομαι, διδάσκω, διηγοῦμαι (Heb. xi. 32), διήγησις, εἶπον and προεῖπον, ἐπερωτάω and ἐρωτάω, κατηχέω, λαλέω, λέγω, λόγον αἰτέω, λόγον ἀποδίδωμι, λόγον δίδωμι, μαρτυρέω, μνεία, μνημονεύω, προκαταγγέλλω, προφητεύω, ὑπομιμνήσκω, χρηματίζομαι, ἦχος, φήμη, etc.; after verbs of h e a r i n g, k n o w i n g, a s c e r t a i n i n g, i n q u i r i n g, see under ἀκούω, γινώσκω, ἐπίσταμαι, εἶδον, ἐξετάζω, ζητέω, ἐκζητέω, ἐπιζητέω, ζήτημα, πυνθάνομαι, etc.; after verbs of t h i n k i n g, d e c i d i n g, s u p p o s i n g, d o u b t i n g, etc.; see under διαλογίζομαι, ἐνθυμέομαι, πέπεισμαι, πιστεύω, διαπορέω, ἐλέγχω, etc.   **b.** *as respects* [A. V. often (*as*) *touching*],   **a.** with verbs, to indicate that what is expressed by the verb (or verbal noun) holds so far forth as some person or thing is concerned; *with regard to, in reference to*: Acts xxviii. 21; Heb. xi. 20; ἡ περὶ σοῦ μνεία, 2 Tim. i. 3; ἐξουσίαν ἔχειν, 1 Co. vii. 37; ἐπιταγὴν ἔχειν, ibid. 25; see ἐντέλλομαι, ἐντολή, παρακαλέω, παραμυθέομαι, πρόφασις, ἔκδικος, λαγχάνω to cast lots.   **β.** with the neut. plur. [and sing.] of the article, τὰ περί τινος *the things concerning a person* or *thing*, i. e. *what relates to, can be said about,* etc.: τὰ περὶ τῆς βασιλείας τοῦ θεοῦ, Acts i. 3; viii. 12 [Rec.]; xix. 8 [here L Tr WH om. τά]; τὰ περὶ τῆς ὁδοῦ, Acts xxiv. 22; with the gen. of a pers. *one's affairs, his condition* or *state*: Acts xxviii. 15; Eph. vi. 22; Phil. i. 27; ii. 19 sq.; Col. iv. 8; in a forensic sense, *one's cause* or *case*, Acts xxiv. 10; τὰ περὶ Ἰησοῦ (or τοῦ κυρίου), [*the* (rumors) *about Jesus* (as a worker of miracles), Mk. v. 27 T Tr mrg. br. WH]; *the things* (necessary to be known and believed) *concerning Jesus*, Acts xviii. 25; xxiii. 11; xxviii. 23 Rec., 31; the things that befell Jesus, his death, Lk. xxiv. 19; the things in the O. T. relative to him, the prophecies concerning him, ibid. 27; the career, death, appointed him by God, Lk. xxii. 37 [here T Tr WH τὸ etc.].   **γ.** περί τινος, absol., at the beginning of sentences, *concerning, as to*: 1 Co. vii. 1; viii. 1; xvi. 1, 12;

but in other places it is more properly taken with the foll. verb, Mt. xxii. 31; xxiv. 36; Mk. xii. 26; 1 Co. vii. 25; viii. 1, 4; xii. 1; 1 Th. iv. 9; v. 1; cf. W. 373 (350).   **c.** *on account of*;   **a.** of the s u b j e c t- m a t t e r, which at the same time occasions the action expressed by the verb: so after verbs of a c c u s i n g, see ἐγκαλέω, κατηγορέω, κρίνω τινὰ περί τινος, etc.; after verbs expressing e m o t i o n, see θαυμάζω, ἀγανακτέω, καυχάομαι, σπλαγχνίζομαι, εὐχαριστέω, εὐχαριστία, αἰνέω, μέλει μοι, μεριμνάω; also after εὔχομαι, 3 Jn. 2, see πᾶς, II. 2 b. θ.   **β.** of the c a u s e for (on account of) which a thing is done, or of that which gave occasion for the action or occurrence: Mk. i. 44; Lk. v. 14; Jn. x. 33, (περὶ τῆς βλασφημίας λάβετε αὐτόν, Ev. Nic. c. 4, p. 546 ed. Thilo [p. 221 ed. Tdf.]); Acts xv. 2; xix. 23; xxv. 15, 18, 24; Col. ii. 1 [R G].   **γ.** *on account of,* i. e. *for, for the benefit* or *advantage of*: Mt. xxvi. 28; Mk. xiv. 24 R G; Lk. iv. 38; Jn. xvi. 26; xvii. 9, 20; Heb. v. 3; xi. 40; περί and ὑπέρ alternate in Eph. vi. 18 sq. [cf. W. 383 (358) n. also § 50, 3; B. § 147, 21. 22; Wieseler, Meyer, Bp. Lghtft., Ellic. on Gal. i. 4].   **δ.** περί is used of the design or purpose for removing something or taking it away: περὶ ἁμαρτίας, to destroy sin, Ro. viii. 3; διδόναι ἑαυτὸν περὶ τῶν ἁμαρτιῶν, to expiate, atone for, sins, Gal. i. 4 (where R WH txt. ὑπέρ [see as in γ. above, and cf. ὑπέρ, I. 6]); also *to offer sacrifices,* and simply *sacrifices,* περὶ ἁμαρτιῶν, Heb. v. 3 [R G ὑπέρ; see u. s.]; x. 18, 26; περὶ ἁμαρτιῶν ἔπαθε [ἀπέθανεν], 1 Pet. iii. 18; περὶ ἁμαρτίας αε. θυσίαι, sacrifices *for sin,* expiatory sacrifices, Heb. x. 6 (fr. Ps. xxxix. (xl.) 7; cf. Num. viii. 8; see ἁμαρτία, 3; τὰ περὶ τῆς ἁμ. Lev. vi. 25; τὸ περὶ τ. ἁ. Lev. xiv. 19); ἱλασμὸς περὶ τ. ἁμαρτιῶν, 1 Jn. ii. 2; iv. 10.

II. with the ACCUSATIVE (W. 406 (379));   **a.** of P l a c e; *about, around*: as, *about parts of the body,* Mt. iii. 4; [xviii. 6 L T Tr WH]; Mk. i. 6; ix. 42; Lk. xvii. 2; Rev. xv. 6. about places: Lk. xiii. 8; Acts xxii. 6; Jude 7; τὰ περὶ τὸν τόπον ἐκεῖνον, the neighborhood of that place, Acts xxviii. 7; οἱ περί w. an acc. of place, those dwelling about a place or in its vicinity, Mk. iii. 8 [T Tr WH om. L br. οἱ]. οἱ περί τινα, those about one i. e. with him, his companions, associates, friends, etc., Mk. iv. 10; Lk. xxii. 49; [add, Mk. xvi. WH (rejected) "Shorter Conclusion"]; acc. to Grk. idiom οἱ περὶ τὸν Παῦλον, Paul and his companions (Germ. *die Paulusgesellschaft*) [cf. W. 406 (379); B. § 125, 8], Acts xiii. 13; acc. to a later Grk. usage αἱ περὶ Μάρθαν denotes Martha herself, Jn. xi. 19 (although others [e. g. Meyer, Weiss, Keil, Godet, al.] understand by it Martha and her attendants or domestics; but L Tr WH read πρὸς τὴν (for τὰς περὶ) Μάρθαν); cf. Matthiae § 583, 2; Bnhdy. p. 263; Kühner ii. p. 230 sq.; [W. and B. u. s.]. in phrases the underlying notion of which is that of r e v o l v i n g a b o u t something : of persons engaged in any occupation, οἱ περὶ τὰ τοιαῦτα ἐργάται [A. V. *the workmen of like occupation*], Acts xix. 25; περιπασπᾶσθαι, τυρβάζεσθαι περί τι, Lk. x. 40, 41 [but here L T Tr WH txt. θορυβάζῃ q. v. (and WH mrg. om. περὶ πολλά)], (περὶ τὴν γεωργίαν γίνεσθαι, 2 Macc. xii. 1).   **b.** *as to, in reference to, concerning*: so after ἀδόκιμος, 2 Tim. iii. 8; ἀστοχεῖν, 1 Tim. vi. 21; 2 Tim. ii. 18; ναυαγεῖν, 1 Tim. i. 19; νοσεῖν, 1 Tim. vi. 4; περὶ πάντα ἑαυτὸν παρέχεσθαι τύπον, Tit. ii. 7; τὰ περὶ ἐμέ, the state of my affairs, Phil. ii. 23; αἱ περὶ τὰ λοιπὰ ἐπιθυμίαι, Mk. iv. 19 (αἱ περὶ τὸ σῶμα ἐπιθυμίαι, Aristot. rhet. 2, 12, 3; τὰ περὶ ψυχὴν κ. σῶμα ἀγαθά, eth. Nic. 1, 8); cf. W. § 30, 3 N. 5; [B. § 125, 9].   **c.** of Time; in a somewhat indefinite specification of time, *about, near*: περὶ τρίτην ὥραν, Mt. xx. 3; add, 5 sq. 9; xxvii. 46; Mk. vi. 48; Acts x. [3 L T Tr WH], 9; xxii. 6.

   III. in COMPOSITION περί in the N. T. signifies   **1.** *in a circuit, round about, all around*, as περιάγω, περιβάλλω, περιαστράπτω, περίκειμαι, περιοικέω, etc., etc.   **2.** *beyond* (because that which surrounds a thing does not belong to the thing itself but is beyond it): περίεργος, περιεργάζομαι, περιλείπω, περιμένω, περιούσιος, περισσός, περισσεύω.   **3.** *through* [(?) — intensive, rather (cf. περιάπτω, 2)]: περιπείρω.

4013   περι-άγω; impf. περιῆγον; fr. Hdt. down; **1.** trans.   **a.** *to lead around* [cf. περί, III. 1].   **b.** i. q. *to lead about with one's self*: τινά (Xen. Cyr. 2, 2, 28; τρεῖς παῖδας ἀκολούθους, Dem. p. 958, 16), 1 Co. ix. 5.   **2.** intrans. *to go about, walk about*, (Ceb. tab. c. 6): absol. Acts xiii. 11; with an acc. of place (depending on the prep. in compos., cf. Matthiae § 426; [B. 144, (126); W. § 52, 2 c.; 432 (402)]), Mt. iv. 23 [R G; (al. read the dat. with or without ἐν)]; ix. 35; xxiii. 15; Mk. vi. 6.*

4014   περι-αιρέω, -ῶ: 2 aor. inf. περιελεῖν, [ptcp. plur. περιελόντες]; Pass., pres. 3 pers. sing. περιαιρεῖται; impf. 3 pers. sing. περιῃρεῖτο; fr. Hom. down; Sept. chiefly for הֵסִיר;   **a.** *to take away that which surrounds* or *envelops a thing* [cf. περί, III. 1]: τὸ κάλυμμα, pass., 2 Co. iii. 16 (πορφύραν, 2 Macc. iv. 38; τὸν δακτύλιον, Gen. xli. 42; Joseph. antt. 19, 2, 3); ἀγκύρας, the anchors from both sides of the ship, [R. V. *casting off*], Acts xxvii. 40; [2 aor. ptcp., absol., in a nautical sense, *to cast loose*, Acts xxviii. 13 WH (al. περιελθόντες)].   **b.** metaph. *to take away altogether* or *entirely*: τὰς ἁμαρτίας (with which one is, as it were, enveloped), the guilt of sin, i. e. to expiate perfectly, Heb. x. 11; τὴν ἐλπίδα, pass., Acts xxvii. 20.*

see 681   περι-άπτω: 1 aor. ptcp. περιάψας; [fr. Pind. down]; **1.** *to bind* or *tie around, to put around*, [περί, III. 1]; *to hang upon, attach to.*   **2.** *to kindle a fire around* [or *thoroughly*; see περικρύπτω, περικαλύπτω, περικρατής, περίλυπος, etc.] (Phalar. ep. 5, p. 28): Lk. xxii. 55 T WH Tr txt.*

4015   περι-αστράπτω: 1 aor. περιήστραψα [Rᵉˡˢ L περιέστρ. (see B. 34 sq. (30) and Tdf.'s note)], *to flash around, shine about*, [περί, III. 1]: τινά, Acts ix. 3; περί τινα, Acts xxii. 6. ([4 Macc. iv. 10]; eccl. and Byzant. writ.) *

4016   περι-βάλλω: fut. περιβαλῶ; 2 aor. περιέβαλον; pf. pass. ptcp. περιβεβλημένος; 2 aor. mid. περιεβαλόμην; 2 fut. mid. περιβαλοῦμαι; fr. Hom. down; Sept. chiefly for כָּסָה to cover, cover up; also for לָבַשׁ to clothe, and עָטָה to veil; *to throw around, to put round*;   **a.** πόλει

χάρακα, *to surround a city with a bank* (palisade), Lk. xix. 43 ([R G Tr L txt. WH mrg.]; see παρεμβάλλω, 2).   **b.** of garments, τινά, *to clothe one*: Mt. xxv. 36, 38, 43; τινά τι, *to put a thing on one, to clothe one with* a thing [B. 149 (130); W. § 32, 4 a.]: Lk. xxiii. 11 [here T WH om. L Tr br. acc. of pers.]; Jn. xix. 2; pass., Mk. xiv. 51; xvi. 5; Rev. vii. 9, 13; x. 1; xi. 3; xii. 1; xvii. 4 (where Rec. has dat. of the thing; [so iv. 4 L WH txt., but al. ἐν w. dat. of thing]); xviii. 16; xix. 13; Mid. *to put on* or *clothe one's self*: absol. Rev. iii. 18; w. acc. of the thing [cf. B. § 135, 2], Mt. vi. 31; Acts xii. 8; passively, — in 2 aor., Mt. vi. 29; Lk. xii. 27; in 2 aor. w. acc. of the thing, Rev. iii. 18; xix. 8; in 2 fut. with ἔν τινι [B. u. s.; see ἐν, I. 5 b. p. 210ᵃ], Rev. iii. 5.*

4017   περι-βλέπω: impf. mid. 3 pers. sing. περιεβλέπετο; 1 aor. ptcp. περιβλεψάμενος; *to look around*. In the N. T. only in the mid. (*to look round about one's self*): absol., Mk. ix. 8; x. 23; foll. by an inf. of purpose, Mk. v. 32; τινά, *to look round on one* (i. e. to look for one's self at one near by), Mk. iii. 5, 34; Lk. vi. 10; εἴς τινας, Ev. Nic. c. 4; πάντα, Mk. xi. 11. (Arstph., Xen., Plat., al.; Sept.) *

4018   περι-βόλαιον, -ου, τό, (περιβάλλω), prop. *a covering thrown around, a wrapper*; in the N. T.   **1.** *a mantle*: Heb. i. 12 (Ps. ci. (cii.) 27; Ezek. xvi. 13; xxvii. 7; Is. lix. 17; περιβ. βασιλικόν and περιβ. ἐκ πορφύρας, Palaeph. 52, 4).   **2.** *a veil* [A.V. *a covering*]: 1 Co. xi. 15. [(From Eur. down)] *

4019   περι-δέω: plupf. pass. 3 pers. sing. περιεδέδετο; [fr. Hdt. down] *to bind around, tie over*, [cf. περί, III. 1]: τινά τινι, Jn. xi. 44. (Sept. Job xii. 18; Plut. mor. p. 825 e. [i. e. praecepta ger. reipub. 32, 21; Aristot. h. a. 9, 39 p. 623ᵃ, 14].) *

see 4063   περι-δρέμω, see περιτρέχω.

4020   περι-εργάζομαι; (see περί, III. 2); *to bustle about uselessly, to busy one's self about trifling, needless, useless matters*, (Sir. iii. 23; Hdt. 3, 46; Plat. apol. p. 19 b.; al.): used apparently of a person officiously inquisitive about others' affairs [A. V. *to be a busybody*], 2 Th. iii. 11, as in Dem. p. 150, 24 [cf. p. 805, 4 etc.].*

4021   περίεργος, -ον, (περί and ἔργον; see περί, III. 2), *busy about trifles and neglectful of important matters, esp. busy about other folks' affairs, a busybody*: 1 Tim. v. 13 (often so in prof. auth. fr. Xen. mem. 1, 3, 1; περ. καὶ πολυπράγμων, Epict. diss. 3, 1, 21); of things: τὰ περίεργα, *impertinent and superfluous*, of magic [A. V. *curious*] arts, Acts xix. 19 (so περίεργος practising magic, Aristaen. epp. 2, 18, 2 [cf. Plut. Alex. 2, 5]); cf. Kypke, Observv. and Kuinoel, Com. ad loc.*

4022   περι-έρχομαι; 2 aor. περιῆλθον; fr. Hdt. down; *to go about*: of strollers, Acts xix. 13; of wanderers, Heb. xi. 37; of navigators (making a circuit), Acts xxviii. 13 [here WH περιελόντες, see περιαιρέω, a.]; τὰς οἰκίας, *to go about from house to house*, 1 Tim. v. 13.*

4023   περι-έχω; 2 aor. περιέσχον; fr. Hom. down; in the N. T. *to surround, encompass*; i. e.   **a.** *to contain*: of the subject-matter, contents, of a writing (ἡ βίβλος περιέχει τὰς πράξεις, Diod. 2, 1; [Joseph. c. Ap. (1, 1);

1, 8, 2 ; 2, 4, 1 ; 2, 38, 1]), ἐπιστολὴν περιέχουσαν τὸν τύπον τοῦτον, a letter of which this is a sample, or a letter written after this form [cf. τύπος, 3], Acts xxiii. 25 [L T Tr WH ἔχουσαν (cf. Grimm on 1 Macc. as below)] (τὸν τρόπον τοῦτον, 1 Macc. xv. 2 ; 2 Macc. xi. 16) ; intrans. [B. § 129, 17 n. ; 144 (126) n.]: περιέχει ἐν (τῇ) γραφῇ, it is contained in (holy) scripture, 1 Pet. ii. 6 R G T Tr WH ; absol., περιέχει ἡ γραφή (our runs), foll. by direct disc., ibid. Lchm. ; likewise ὁ νόμος ὑμῶν περιέχει, Ev. Nicod. c. 4 ; with adverbs : περιέχειν οὕτως, 2 Macc. ix. 18 ; xi. 22 ; καθὼς περιέχει βίβλος Ἐνώχ, Test. xii. Patr., test. Levi 10 ; ὡς ἡ παράδοσις περιέχει, Euseb. h. e. 3, 1 ; see Grimm on 1 Macc. xi. 29.　　b. i. q. to take possession of, to seize : τινά, Lk. v. 9 (2 Macc. iv. 16 ; Joseph. b. j. 4, 10, 1).*

see 4024 St.
περι-ζωννύω, or -ζώννυμι : Mid., 1 fut. περιζώσομαι ; 1 aor. impv. περίζωσαι, ptcp. περιζωσάμενος ; pf. pass. ptcp. περιεζωσμένος ; to gird around [περί, III. 1] ; to fasten garments with a girdle : τὴν ὀσφύν, to fasten one's clothing about the loins with a girdle (Jer. i. 17), pass., Lk. xii. 35. Mid. to gird one's self : absol., Lk. xii. 37 ; xvii. 8 ; Acts xii. 8 Rec. ; τὴν ὀσφὺν ἐν ἀληθείᾳ, with truth as a girdle, figuratively i. q. to equip one's self with knowledge of the truth, Eph. vi. 14 ; with an acc. of the thing with which one girds himself (often so in Sept., as σάκκον, Jer. iv. 8 ; vi. 26 ; Lam. ii. 10 ; στολὴν δόξης, Sir. xlv. 7 ; and in trop. expressions, δύναμιν, εὐφροσύνην, 1 S. ii. 4 ; Ps. xvii. (xviii.) 33 ; [B. § 135, 2]) : πρὸς τοῖς μαστοῖς ζώνην, Rev. i. 13 ; ζώνας περὶ τὰ στήθη, Rev. xv. 6. (Arstph., Polyb., Paus., Plut., al. ; Sept. for חָגַר and אָזַר.) Cf. ἀναζώννυμι.*

4025
περί-θεσις, -εως, ἡ, (περιτίθημι), the act of putting around [περί, III. 1], (Vulg. circumdatio, [A.V. wearing]) : περιθέσεως χρυσίων κόσμος, the adornment consisting of the golden ornaments wont to be placed around the head or the body, 1 Pet. iii. 3. ([Arr. 7, 22], Galen, Sext. Empir., al.) *

4026
περι-ίστημι : 2 aor. περιέστην ; pf. ptcp. περιεστώς ; pres. mid. impv. 2 pers. sing. περιίστασο (on which form see W. § 14, 1 e. ; [B. 47 (40), who both call it passive (but see Veitch p. 340)]) ;　　1. in the pres., impf., fut., 1 aor., active, to place around (one).　　2. in the perf., plupf., 2 aor. act., and the tenses of the mid., to stand around : Jn. xi. 42 ; Acts xxv. 7 [in L T Tr WH w. an acc. ; cf. W. § 52, 4, 12]. Mid. to turn one's self about sc. for the purpose of avoiding something, hence to avoid, shun, (Joseph. antt. 4, 6, 12 ; 10, 10, 4 ; b. j. 2, 8, 6 ; Antonin. 3, 4 ; Artem. oneir. 4, 59 ; Athen. 15 p. 675 e. ; Diog. Laërt. 9, 14 ; Jambl. vit. Pyth. 31 [p. 392 ed. Kiessl.] ; Sext. Empir. ; joined with φεύγειν, Joseph. antt. 1, 1, 4 ; with ἐκτρέπεσθαι, Lcian. Hermot. § 86 ; Hesych. περιΐστασο · ἀπόφευγε, ἀνάτρεπε ; [cf. further, D'Orville's Chariton, ed. Reiske, p. 282] ; this use of the verb is censured by Lcian. soloec. 5) : in the N. T. so with an acc. of the thing [cf. W. l. c.], 2 Tim. ii. 16 ; Tit. iii. 9.*

4027
περι-κάθαρμα, -τος, τό, (περικαθαίρω, to cleanse on all sides [περί, III. 1]), off-scouring, refuse : plur. τὰ περικ. τοῦ κόσμου [A. V. the filth of the world], metaph. the most abject and despicable men, 1 Co. iv. 13. (Epict. diss. 3,

22, 78 ; purgamenta urbis, Curt. 8, 5, 8 ; 10, 2, 7 ; [sce Wetstein on 1 Co. l. c.] ; Sept. once for כֹּפֶר, the price of expiation or redemption, Prov. xxi. 18, because the Grks. used to apply the term καθάρματα to victims sacrificed to make expiation for the people, and even to criminals who were maintained at the public expense, that on the outbreak of a pestilence or other calamity they might be offered as sacrifices to make expiation for the state.) *

περι-καθ-ίζω : 1 aor. ptcp. περικαθίσας ;　　1. in class. see 4776
Grk. trans. to bid or make to sit around, to invest, besiege, a city, a fortress.　　2. intrans. to sit around, be seated around ; so in Lk. xxii. 55 Lchm. txt.*

περι-καλύπτω ; 1 aor. ptcp. περικαλύψας ; pf. pass. ptcp.　　4028
περικεκαλυμμένος ; fr. Hom. down ; to cover all around [περί, III. 1], to cover up, cover over : τὸ πρόσωπον, Mk. xiv. 65 ; Lk. xxii. 64 [A. V. blindfold] ; τὶ χρυσίῳ, Heb. ix. 4 (Ex. xxviii. 20).*

περί-κειμαι ; (περί and κεῖμαι) ; fr. Hom. down ;　　1.　　4029
to lie around [cf. περί, III. 1] : περί [cf. W. § 52, 4, 12] τι, [A. V. were hanged, Mk. ix. 42] ; Lk. xvii. 2 ; ἔχοντες περικείμενον ἡμῖν νέφος, [A. V. are compassed about with a cloud etc.], Heb. xii. 1.　　2. passively [cf. B. 50 (44)], to be compassed with, have round one, [with acc. ; cf. W. § 32, 5 ; B. § 134, 7] : ἅλυσιν, Acts xxviii. 20 (δεσμά, 4 Macc. xii. 3) ; ἀσθένειαν, infirmity cleaves to me, Heb. v. 2 (ὕβριν, Theocr. 23, 14 ; ἀμαύρωσιν, νέφος, Clem. Rom. 2 Cor. 1, 6).*

περι-κεφαλαία, -ας, ἡ, (περί and κεφαλή), a helmet : 1 Th.　　4030
v. 8 ; τοῦ σωτηρίου (fr. Is. lix. 17), i. e. dropping the fig., the protection of soul which consists in (the hope of) salvation, Eph. vi. 17.　　(Polyb. ; Sept. for כּוֹבַע.) *

περι-κρατής, -ές, (κράτος), τινός, having full power over a　　4031
thing : [περικ. γενέσθαι τῆς σκάφης, to secure], Acts xxvii. 16. (Sus. 39 cod. Alex. ; eccl. writ.) *

περι-κρύπτω : 2 aor. περιέκρυβον (on this form cf. Bttm.　　4032
Ausf. Spr. i. p. 400 sq. ; ii. p. 226 ; [WH. App. p. 170 ; al. make it (in Lk. as below) a late imperfect ; cf. B. 40 (35) ; Soph. Lex. s. v. κρύβω ; Veitch s. v. κρύπτω]) ; to conceal on all sides or entirely, to hide : ἑαυτόν, to keep one's self at home, Lk. i. 24. (Lcian., Diog. Laërt., al.) *

περι-κυκλόω, -ῶ : fut. περικυκλώσω ; to encircle, compass　　4033
about : of a city (besieged), Lk. xix. 43. (Arstph. av. 346 ; Xen. an. 6, 1 (3), 11 ; Aristot. h. a. 4, 8 [p. 533ᵇ, 11] ; Lcian., al. ; Sept. for סָבַב.) *

περι-λάμπω : 1 aor. περιέλαμψα ; to shine around : τινά,　　4034
Lk. ii. 9 ; Acts xxvi. 13. (Diod., Joseph., Plut., al.) *

περι-λείπω : pres. pass. ptcp. περιλειπόμενος (cf. περί,　　4035
III. 2) ; to leave over ; pass. to remain over, to survive : 1 Th. iv. 15, 17. (Arstph., Plat., Eur., Polyb., Hdian. ; 2 Macc. i. 31.) *

περί-λυπος, -ον, (περί and λύπη, and so prop. 'encom-　　4036
passed with grief' [cf. περί, III. 3]), very sad, exceedingly sorrowful : Mt. xxvi. 38 : Mk. vi. 26 ; xiv. 34 ; Lk. xviii. 23, 24 [where T WH om. Tr br. the cl.]. (Ps. xli. (xlii.) 6, 12 ; 1 Esdr. viii. 69 ; Isocr., Aristot., al.) *

περι-μένω ; (περί further [cf. περί, III. 2]) ; to wait for :　　4037 τί, Acts i. 4. (Gen. xlix. 18; Sap. viii. 12; Arstph., Thuc., Xen., Plat., Dem., Joseph., Plut., al.) *

4038 πέριξ [on the formative or strengthening ξ cf. *Lob.* Paralip. p. 131], adv., fr. Aeschyl. down, *round about*: αἱ πέριξ πόλεις, *the cities round about*, the circumjacent cities, Acts v. 16.*

4039 περι-οικέω, -ῶ; *to dwell round about*: τινά [cf. W. § 52, 4, 12], to be one's neighbor, Lk. i. 65. (Hdt., Arstph., Xen., Lys., Plut.) *

4040 περί-οικος, -ον, (περί and οἶκος), *dwelling around, a neighbor*: Lk. i. 58. (Gen. xix. 29; Deut. i. 7; Jer. xxx. (xlix.) 5; Hdt., Thuc., Xen., Isocr., al.) *

4041 περιούσιος, -ον, (fr. περιών, περιοῦσα, ptcp. of the verb περίειμι, to be over and above — see ἐπιούσιος; hence περιουσία, abundance, plenty; riches, wealth, property), *that which is one's own, belongs to one's possessions*: λαὸς περιούσιος, *a people* selected by God from the other nations *for his own possession*, Tit. ii. 14; Clem. Rom. 1 Cor. 64; in Sept. for עַם סְגֻלָּה, (Ex. xix. 5); Deut. vii. 6; xiv. 2; xxvi. 18. [Cf. Bp. *Lghtft.* 'Fresh Revision' etc. App. ii.] *

4042 περιοχή, -ῆς, ἡ, (περιέχω, q. v.);   **1.** *an encompassing, compass, circuit*, (Theophr., Diod., Plut., al.).   **2.** *that which is contained*; spec. *the contents* of any writing, Acts viii. 32 (Cic. ad Attic. 13, 25; Stob. eclog. ethic. p. 164 [ii. p. 541 ed. Gaisford]) [but A. V. *place* i. e. passage; cf. Soph. Lex. s. v.].*

4043 περι-πατέω, -ῶ; impf. 2 pers. sing. περιεπάτεις, 3 pers. περιεπάτει, plur. περιεπάτουν; fut. περιπατήσω; 1 aor. περιεπάτησα; plupf. 3 pers. sing. περιεπεπατήκει (Acts xiv. 8 Rec.ᶜˡˣ), and without the augm. (cf. W. § 12, 9; [B. 33 (29)]) περιπεπατήκει (ibid. Rec.ˢᵗ Grsb.); Sept. for הָלַךְ; *to walk*; [*walk about* A. V. 1 Pet. v. 8]; **a.** prop. (as in Arstph., Xen., Plat., Isocr., Joseph., Ael., al.): absol., Mt. ix. 5; xi. 5; xv. 31; Mk. ii. 9 [Tdf. ὕπαγε]; v. 42; viii. 24; xvi. 12; Lk. v. 23; vii. 22; xxiv. 17; Jn. i. 36; v. 8 sq. 11 sq.; xi. 9 sq.; Acts iii. 6, 8 sq. 12; xiv. 8, 10; 1 Pet. v. 8; Rev. ix. 20; i. q. *to make one's way, make progress*, in fig. disc. equiv. to *to make a due use of opportunities*, Jn. xii. 35ᵃ. with additions: περιπ. γυμνός, Rev. xvi. 15; ἐπάνω (τινός), Lk. xi. 44; διά w. gen. of the thing, Rev. xxi. 24 [G L T Tr WH]; ἐν w. dat. of place, i. q. *to frequent, stay in*, a place, Mk. xi. 27; Jn. vii. 1; x. 23; Rev. ii. 1; ἐν τισι, among persons, Jn. xi. 54; [π. ὅπου ἤθελες, of personal liberty, Jn. xxi. 18]; metaph. ἐν τῇ σκοτίᾳ, to be subject to error and sin, Jn. viii. 12; xii. 35ᵇ; 1 Jn. i. 6 sq.; ii. 11; ἐν with dat. of the garment one is clothed in, Mk. xii. 38; Lk. xx. 46; Rev. iii. 4, (ἐν κοκκίνοις, Epict. diss. 3, 22, 10); ἐπὶ τῆς θαλάσσης, [Mt. xiv. 25 R G; 26 L T Tr WH; Mk. vi. 48, 49], see ἐπί, A. I. 1 a. and 2 a.; ἐπὶ τὴν θάλ., ἐπὶ τὰ ὕδατα, [Mt. xiv. 25 L T Tr WH, 26 R G, 29], see ἐπί, C. I. 1 a.; [παρὰ τὴν θάλασσαν, Mk. i. 16 Rec., see παρά, III. 1]; μετά τινος, to associate with one, to be one's companion, used of one's followers and votaries, Jn. vi. 66; Rev. iii. 4.   **b.** Hebraistically, *to live* [cf. W. 32; com. in Paul and John, but not found in James or in Peter (cf. ἀναστρέφω 3 b., ἀναστροφή)], i. e.   **a.** *to regulate one's*

life, to conduct one's self (cf. ὁδός, 2 a., πορεύω, b. γ.): ἀξίως τινός, Eph. iv. 1; Col. i. 10; 1 Th. ii. 12; εὐσχημόνως, Ro. xiii. 13; 1 Th. iv. 12; ἀκριβῶς, Eph. v. 15; ἀτάκτως, 2 Th. iii. 6, 11; ὡς or καθώς τις, Eph. iv. 17; v. 8, 15; οὕτω π. καθώς, Phil. iii. 17; [καθὼς π. οὕτω π. 1 Jn. ii. 6 (L Tr txt. WH om. οὕτω)]; πῶς, καθώς, 1 Th. iv. 1; οὕτως, ὡς, 1 Co. vii. 17; so that a nom. of quality must be sought from what follows, ἐχθροὶ τοῦ σταυροῦ τοῦ Χριστοῦ, Phil. iii. 18. with a dat. of the thing to which the life is given or consecrated: κώμοις, μέθαις, etc., Ro. xiii. 13, cf. Fritzsche on Rom. vol. iii. p. 140 sq.; w. a dat. of the standard acc. to which one governs his life [cf. Fritzsche u. s. p. 142; also B. § 133, 22 b.; W. 219 (205)]: Acts xxi. 21; Gal. v. 16; 2 Co. xii. 18; foll. by ἐν w. a dat. denoting either the state in which one is living, or the virtue or vice to which he is given [cf. ἐν, I. 5 e. p. 210ᵇ bot.]: Ro. vi. 4; 2 Co. iv. 2; Eph. ii. 2, 10; iv. 17; v. 2; Col. iii. 7; iv. 5; 2 Jn. 4, 6; 3 Jn. 3 sq.; ἐν βρώμασι, of those who have fellowship in the sacrificial feasts, Heb. xiii. 9; ἐν Χριστῷ [see ἐν, I. 6 b.], to live a life conformed to the union entered into with Christ, Col. ii. 6; κατά w. an acc. of the pers. or thing furnishing the standard of living, [Mk. vii. 5]; 2 Jn. 6; κατὰ ἄνθρωπον, 1 Co. iii. 3; κατὰ σάρκα, Ro. viii. 1 Rec., 4; xiv. 15; 2 Co. x. 2.   **β.** i. q. *to pass (one's) life*: ἐν σαρκί, in the body, 2 Co. x. 3; διὰ πίστεως (see διά, A. I. 2), 2 Co. v. 7. [COMP.: ἐμπεριπατέω.]*

4044 περι-πείρω: 1 aor. περιέπειρα; *to pierce through* [see περί, III. 3]: τινὰ ξίφεσι, δόρατι, etc., Diod., Joseph., Plut., Lcian., al.; metaph. ἑαυτὸν . . . ὀδύναις, to torture one's soul with sorrows, 1 Tim. vi. 10 (ἀνηκέστοις κακοῖς, Philo in Flacc. § 1).*

4045 περι-πίπτω: 2 aor. περιέπεσον; fr. Hdt. down; *so to fall into as to be encompassed by* [cf. περί, III. 1]: λῃσταῖς, among robbers, Lk. x. 30; τοῖς πειρασμοῖς, Jas. i. 2, (αἰκίαις, Clem. Rom. 1 Cor. 51, 2; θανάτῳ, Dan. ii. 9; Diod. 1, 77; νόσῳ, Joseph. antt. 15, 7, 7; συμφορᾷ, ibid. 1, 1, 4; τοῖς δεινοῖς, Aesop 79 (110 ed. Halm); ψευδέσι κ. ἀσεβέσι δόγμασιν, Orig. in Joann. t. ii. § 2; numerous other exx. in Passow s. v. 1. c. [L. and S. s. v. II. 3]; to which add, 2 Macc. vi. 13; x. 4; Polyb. 1, 37, 1 and 9); εἰς τόπον τινά, upon a certain place, Acts xxvii. 41.*

see 4046 St. περι-ποιέω, -ῶ: Mid., pres. περιποιοῦμαι; 1 aor. περιεποιησάμην; (see περί, III. 2); fr. Hdt. down; *to make to remain over*; *to reserve, to leave* or *keep safe, lay by*; mid. *to make to remain for one's self*, i. e.   **1.** *to preserve for one's self* (Sept. for הֶחֱיָה): τὴν ψυχήν, life, Lk. xvii. 33 T Tr WH (τὰς ψυχάς, Xen. Cyr. 4, 4, 10).   **2.** *to get for one's self, purchase*: τί, Acts xxv. 28 (Is. xliii. 21; δύναμιν, Thuc. 1, 9; Xen. mem. 2, 7, 3); τὶ ἐμαυτῷ, gain for myself (W. § 38, 6), 1 Tim. iii. 13 (1 Macc. vi. 44; Xen. an. 5, 6, 17).*

4047 περι-ποίησις, -εως, ἡ, (περιποιέω);   **1.** *a preserving, preservation*: εἰς περιποίησιν ψυχῆς, to the preserving of the soul, sc. that it may be made partaker of eternal salvation [A. V. *unto the saving of the soul*], Heb. x. 39 (Plat. deff. p. 415 c.).   **2.** *possession. one's own property*: 1 Pet. ii. 9 (Is. xliii. 20 sq.); Eph. i. 14 (on this pass. see ἀπολύτρωσις, 2). **3.** *an obtaining*: with a gen. of the thing to be obtained, 1 Th. v. 9; 2 Th. ii. 14.*

(4047a); see 911

περι-ρραίνω (Tdf. περιρ., with one ρ; see P, ρ): pf. pass. ptcp. περιρεραμμένος (cf. M, μ); (περί and ῥαίνω to sprinkle); *to sprinkle around, besprinkle*: ἱμάτιον, pass., Rev. xix. 13 Tdf. [al. βεβαμμένον (exc. WH ῥεραντισμένον, see ῥαντίζω, and their App. ad loc.)]. (Arstph., Menand., Philo, Plut., al.; Sept.)*

4048   **περι-ρρήγνυμι** (L T Tr WH περιρ., with one ρ; see the preceding word): 1 aor. ptcp. plur. περιρρήξαντες; (περί and ῥήγνυμι); *to break off on all sides, break off all round*, [cf. περί, III. 1]: τὸ ἱμάτιον, to rend or tear off all around, Acts xvi. 22. So of garments also in 2 Macc. iv. 38 and often in prof. auth.; Aeschyl. sept. 329; Dem. p. 403, 3; Polyb. 15, 33, 4; Diod. 17, 35.*

4049   **περι-σπάω, -ῶ**: impf. pass. 3 pers. sing. περιεσπᾶτο; fr. Xen. down; *to draw around* [περί, III. 1], *to draw away, distract*; pass. metaph., *to be driven about mentally, to be distracted*: περί τι, i. e. *to be over-occupied, too busy, about a thing*, Lk. x. 40 [A. V. cumbered]; in the same sense with τῇ διανοίᾳ added, Polyb. 3, 105, 1; 4, 10, 3; Diod. 1, 74; περισπᾶν τὸν ἀργὸν δῆμον περὶ τὰς ἔξω στρατείας, Dion. Hal. antt. 9, 43; pass. *to be distracted with cares, to be troubled, distressed*, [cf. W. 23], for עָנָה, Eccl. i. 13; iii. 10.*

4050   **περισσεία, -ας, ἡ**, (περισσεύω, q. v.); **1.** *abundance*: τῆς χάριτος, Ro. v. 17; τῆς χαρᾶς, 2 Co. viii. 2; εἰς περισσείαν, adverbially, *superabundantly, superfluously*, [A. V. out of measure], 2 Co. x. 15, (Boeckh, Corp. inscrr. i. p. 668, no. 1378, 6; Byzant. writ.). **2.** *superiority; preference, pre-eminence*: יֹתֵר, Eccl. vi. 8; for יִתְרוֹן, Eccl. ii. 13; x. 10. **3.** *gain, profit*: for יִתְרוֹן, Eccl. i. 3; ii. 11; iii. 9, etc. **4.** *residue, remains*: κακίας, the wickedness remaining over in the Christian from his state prior to conversion, Jas. i. 21, see περίσσευμα, 2; [al. adhere in this pass. to the meaning which the word bears elsewhere in the N. T. viz. 'excess', 'superabundance,' (A. V. superfluity)].*

4051   **περίσσευμα, -τος, τό**, (περισσεύω); **1.** *abundance, in which one delights*; opp. to ὑστέρημα, 2 Co. viii. 14 (13), 14; trop. of that which fills the heart, Mt. xii. 34; Lk. vi. 45, (Eratosth., Plut.). **2.** *what is left over, residue, remains*: plur. Mk. viii. 8.*

4052   **περισσεύω**; impf. ἐπερίσσευον (Acts xvi. 5); fut. inf. περισσεύσειν (Phil. iv. 12 Rec.bez); 1 aor. ἐπερίσσευσα; Pass., pres. περισσεύομαι (Lk. xv. 17, see below); 1 fut. 3 pers. sing. περισσευθήσεται; (περισσός, q. v.); **1.** intrans. and prop. *to exceed a fixed number or measure; to be over and above a certain number or measure*: μύριοι εἰσὶν ἀριθμὸν ... εἰς δὲ περισσεύει, Hes. fr. 14, 4 [clxix. (187), ed. Göttling]; hence **a.** *to be over, to remain*: Jn. vi. 12; τὸ περισσεῦον τῶν κλασμάτων, i. q. τὰ περισσεύοντα κλάσματα, Mt. xiv. 20; xv. 37; περισσεύει μοί τι, Jn. vi. 13 (Tob. iv. 16); τὸ περισσεῦσάν τινι, what remained over to one, Lk. ix. 17. **b.** *to exist or be at hand in abundance*: τινί, Lk. xii. 15; τὸ περισσεῦόν τινι, one's abundance, wealth, [(R. V. superfluity); opp. to ὑστέρησις], Mk. xii. 44; opp. to ὑστέρημα, Lk. xxi. 4: *to be*

great (abundant), 2 Co. i. 5ᵇ; ix. 12; Phil. i. 26; περισσεύει τι εἰς τινα, *a thing comes in abundance*, or *overflows, unto one; something falls to the lot of one in large measure*: Ro. v. 15; 2 Co. i. 5ᵃ; περισσεύω εἰς τι, *to redound unto, turn out abundantly for, a thing*, 2 Co. viii. 2; ἡ ἀλήθεια τοῦ θεοῦ ἐν τῷ ἐμῷ ψεύσματι ἐπερίσσευσεν εἰς τὴν δόξαν αὐτοῦ, i. e. by my lie it came to pass that God's veracity became the more conspicuous, and becoming thus more thoroughly known increased his glory, Ro. iii. 7; *to be increased*, τῷ ἀριθμῷ, Acts xvi. 5. **c.** *to abound, overflow*, i. e. **a.** *to be abundantly furnished with, to have in abundance, abound in* (a thing): absol. [A. V. to abound], *to be in affluence*, Phil. iv. 18; opp. to ὑστερεῖσθαι, ib. 12; in spiritual gifts, 1 Co. xiv. 12; with a gen. of the thing in which one abounds (W. § 30, 8 b.; [cf. B. § 132, 12]): ἄρτων, Lk. xv. 17 R G L T Tr mrg. **β.** *to be pre-eminent, to excel*, [cf. B. § 132, 22]: absol. 1 Co. viii. 8; foll. by ἐν w. a dat. of the virtues or the actions in which one excels [B. § 132, 12], Ro. xv. 13; 1 Co. xv. 58; 2 Co. iii. 9 [here L T Tr WH om. ἐν]; viii. 7; Col. ii. 7; περισσ. μᾶλλον, to excel still more, to increase in excellence, 1 Th. iv. 1, 10; μᾶλλον κ. μᾶλλον περισσ. Phil. i. 9; περισσ. πλεῖον, to excel more than [A. V. exceed; cf. B. § 132, 20 and 22], Mt. v. 20, (περισσ. ὑπέρ τινα, 1 Macc. iii. 30; τί ἐπερίσσευσεν ὁ ἄνθρωπος παρὰ τὸ κτῆνος; Eccl. iii. 19). **2.** by later Greek usage transitively [cf. W. p. 23; § 38,1], *to make to abound*, i. e. **a.** *to furnish one richly so that he has abundance*: pass., Mt. xiii. 12; xxv. 29; w. gen. of the thing with which one is furnished, pass. Lk. xv. 17 WH Trtxt.; τι εἴς τινα, to make a thing to abound unto one, to confer a thing abundantly upon one, 2 Co. ix. 8; Eph. i. 8. **b.** *to make abundant or excellent*: τί, 2 Co. iv. 15; *to cause one to excel*: τινά, w. a dat. of the thing, 1 Th. iii. 12. (τὰς ὥρας, to extend the hours beyond the prescribed time, Athen. 2 p. 42 b.) [Comp.: ὑπερ-περισσεύω.]*

4053   **περισσός, -ή, -όν**, (fr. περί, q. v. III. 2), fr. Hes. down, Sept. for יֹתֵר, יֶתֶר, etc.; *exceeding some number or measure or rank or need*; **1.** *over and above, more than is necessary, superadded*: τὸ π. τούτων, what is added to [A. V. more than; cf. B. § 132, 21 Rem.] these, Mt. v. 37; ἐκ περισσοῦ, *exceedingly, beyond measure*, Mk. vi. 51 [WH om. Tr br. ἐκ π.]; xiv. 31 Rec.; ὑπὲρ ἐκ περισσοῦ (written as one word ὑπερεκπερισσοῦ [q. v.]), *exceeding abundantly, supremely*, Eph. iii. 20 [cf. B. u. s.]; 1 Th. iii. 10; v. 13 [R G WH txt.]; περισσόν μοί ἐστιν, it is superfluous for me, 2 Co. ix. 1; περισσὸν ἔχειν, to have abundance, Jn. x. 10 (οἱ μὲν ... περισσὰ ἔχουσιν, οἱ δὲ οὐδὲ τὰ ἀναγκαῖα δύνανται πορίζεσθαι, Xen. oec. 20, 1); neut. compar. περισσότερόν τι, *something further, more*, Lk. xii. 4 (L Tr mrg. περισσότ.; περισσότ. the more, ibid. 48; [περισσότερον πάντων etc. much more than all etc. Mk. xii. 33 T Tr txt. WH]; adverbially, *somewhat more* [R. V. somewhat abundantly], 2 Co. x. 8; (Vulg. abundantius [A.V. more abundantly]) i. e. *more plainly*, Heb. vi. 17; μᾶλλον περισσότερον, much more, Mk. vii. 36; περισσότερον πάντων, more [abundantly] than all, 1 Co. xv. 10; with an adj. it forms a periphrasis for the compar. περισσότερον κατάδηλον, more [abundantly] evident, Heb. vii. 15 [cf. W. § 35, 1]. **2.** superior, extraordinary, surpassing, uncommon : Mt. v. 47 [A. V. more than others] ; τὸ περισσόν, as subst., pre-eminence, superiority, advantage, Ro. iii. 1 ; compar. περισσότερος, more eminent, more remarkable, (οὐκ ἔση περισσότερος, Gen. xlix. 3 Symm.; περιττότερος φρονήσει, Plut. mor. p. 57 f. de adulatore etc. 14) : Mt. xi. 9 ; Lk. vii. 26, although in each pass. περισσότερον can also be taken as neut. (something) more excellent (Vulg. plus [R. V. much more than etc.]) ; with substantives : περισσότερον κρίμα, i. e. a severer, heavier judgment, Mt. xxiii. 14 (13) Rec. ; Mk. xii. 40 ; Lk. xx. 47 ; τιμή, greater honor, more [abundant] honor, 1 Co. xii. 23ª, [24 ; εὐσχημοσύνη, ibid. 23ᵇ] ; λύπη, 2 Co. ii. 7.*

περισσοτέρως, adv., (fr. περισσῶς, q. v.), [cf. W. § 11, 2 c.; B. 69 (61)]. **1.** prop. more abundantly (so in Diod. 13, 108 ; Athen. 5 p. 192 f.) ; in the N. T. more, in a greater degree; more earnestly, more exceedingly, [cf. W. 243 (228)]: Mk. xv. 14 Rec. ; 2 Co. vii. 15 ; xi. 23 ; Gal. i. 14 ; Phil. i. 14 ; 1 Th. ii. 17 ; Heb. ii. 1 ; xiii. 19 ; opp. to ἧττον, 2 Co. xii. 15 ; περισσοτέρως μᾶλλον, much more, [R.V. the more exceedingly], 2 Co. vii. 13. **2.** especially, above others, [A. V. more abundantly] : 2 Co. i. 12 ; ii. 4.*

4057   **περισσῶς**, (περισσός, q. v.), adv., beyond measure, extraordinarily (Eur.) ; i. q. magnificently, Polyb., Athen.) ; i. q. greatly, exceedingly : ἐκπλήσσεσθαι, Mk. x. 26 ; κράζειν, Mt. xxvii. 23 and G L T Tr WH in Mk. xv. 14 ; ἐμμαίνεσθαι, Acts xxvi. 11.*

4058   **περιστερά**, -ᾶς, ἡ, Hebr. יוֹנָה, a dove : Mt. iii. 16 ; x. 16 ; xxi. 12 ; Mk. i. 10 ; xi. 15 ; Lk. ii. 24 ; iii. 22 ; Jn. i. 32 ; ii. 14, 16. [From Hdt. down.]*

4059   **περι-τέμνω** (Ion. περιτάμνω) ; 2 aor. περιέτεμον ; Pass., pres. περιτέμνομαι ; pf. ptcp. περιτετμημένος ; 1 aor. περιετμήθην ; [fr. Hes. down] ; Sept. chiefly for מוּל ; to cut around [cf. περί, III. 1] : τινά, to circumcise, cut off one's prepuce (used of that well-known rite by which not only the male children of the Israelites, on the eighth day after birth, but subsequently also 'proselytes of righteousness' were consecrated to Jehovah and introduced into the number of his people ; [cf. BB. DD. s. v. Circumcision ; Oehler's O. T. Theol. (ed. Day) §§ 87, 88 ; Müller, Barnabasbrief, p. 227 sq.]), Lk. i. 59 ; ii. 21 ; Jn. vii. 22 ; Acts vii. 8 ; xv. 5 ; xvi. 3 ; xxi. 21 ; of the same rite, Diod. 1, 28 ; pass. and mid. to get one's self circumcised, present one's self to be circumcised, receive circumcision [cf. W. § 38, 3] : Acts xv. 1, 24 Rec. ; 1 Co. vii. 18 ; Gal. ii. 3 ; v. 2 sq.; vi. 12 sq.; with τὰ αἰδοῖα added, Hdt. 2, 36 and 104 ; Joseph. antt. 1, 10, 5 ; c. Ap. 1, 22. Since by the rite of circumcision a man was separated from the unclean world and dedicated to God, the verb is transferred to denote the extinguishing of lusts and the removal of sins, Col. ii. 11, cf. Jer. iv. 4 ; Deut. x. 16, and eccl. writ. [see Bp. Lghtft. on Phil. iii. 3].*

4060   **περι-τίθημι**, 3 pers. plur. περιτιθέασιν (Mk. xv. 17 ; see reff. in ἐπιτίθημι) ; 1 aor. περιέθηκα ; 2 aor. ptcp. περιθείς, περιθέντες ; fr. Hom. down ;   **a.** prop. to place

*For 4055 & 4056 see 4053.

around, set about, [cf. περί, III. 1] : τινί τι, as φραγμὸν τῷ ἀμπελῶνι, Mt. xxi. 33 ; Mk. xii. 1 ; to put a garment on one, Mt. xxvii. 28 ; στέφανον, put on (encircle one's head with) a crown, Mk. xv. 17 (Sir. vi. 31 ; Plat. Alcib. 2 p. 151 a.) ; τί τινι, to put or bind one thing around another, Mt. xxvii. 48 ; Mk. xv. 36 ; Jn. xix. 29.   **b.** trop. τινί τι, to present, bestow, confer, a thing upon one (so in class. Grk. fr. Hdt. down, as ἐλευθερίαν, Hdt. 3, 142 ; δόξαν, Dem. p. 1417, 3 ; see Passow ii. p. 881 sq.; [L. and S. s. v. II.]; τὸ ὄνομα, Sap. xiv. 21 ; Thuc. 4, 87) : τιμήν, 1 Co. xii. 23 ; Esth. i. 20.*

4061   **περι-τομή**, -ῆς, ἡ, (περιτέμνω), circumcision (on which see περιτέμνω) ;   **a.** prop.   **α.** the act or rite of circumcision : Jn. vii. 22 sq.; Acts vii. 8 ; Ro. iv. 11 ; Gal. v. 11 ; Phil. iii. 5 ; οἱ ἐκ τῆς περιτ. (see ἐκ, II. 7), the circumcised, they of the circumcision, used of Jews, Ro. iv. 12 ; of Christians gathered from among the Jews, Acts xi. 2 ; Gal. ii. 12 ; Tit. i. 10 ; οἱ ὄντες ἐκ περιτ. Col. iv. 11.   **β.** the state of circumcision, the being circumcised : Ro. ii. 25–28 ; iii. 1 ; 1 Co. vii. 19 ; Gal. v. 6 ; vi. 15 ; Col. iii. 11 ; ἐν περιτομῇ ὤν, circumcised, Ro. iv. 10.   **γ.** by meton. 'the circumcision' for οἱ περιτμηθέντες the circumcised, i. e. Jews : Ro. iii. 30 ; iv. 9, 12 ; xv. 8 ; Gal. ii. 7–9 ; Eph. ii. 11 ; οἱ ἐκ περιτομῆς πιστοί, Christian converts from among the Jews, Jewish Christians, Acts x. 45.   **b.** metaph.   **α.** of Christians : (ἡμεῖς ἐσμεν) ἡ περιτομή, separated from the unclean multitude and truly consecrated to God, Phil. iii. 3 [(where see Bp. Lghtft.)].   **β.** ἡ περιτομὴ ἀχειροποίητος, the extinction of the passions and the removal of spiritual impurity (see περιτέμνω, fin.), Col. ii. 11ª ; ἡ περιτομὴ καρδίας in Ro. ii. 29 denotes the same thing ; περιτ. Χριστοῦ, of which Christ is the author, Col. ii. 11ᵇ. (The noun περιτομή occurs three times in the O. T., viz. Gen. xvii. 13 ; Jer. xi. 16 ; for מוּלָה, Ex. iv. 26 ; besides in Philo, whose tract περὶ περιτομῆς is found in Mangey's ed. ii. pp. 210–212 [Richter's ed. iv. pp. 282–284] ; Joseph. antt. 1, 10, 5 ; [13, 11 fin.; c. Ap. 2, 13, 1. 6] ; plur., antt. 1, 12, 2.) *

4062   **περι-τρέπω** ; to turn about [περί, III. 1], to turn ; to transfer or change by turning : τὶ or τινὰ εἴς τι, a pers. or thing into some new state ; once so in N. T. viz. σὲ εἰς μανίαν περιτρέπει, is turning thee mad, Acts xxvi. 24 ; τοὺς παρόντας εἰς χαρὰν περιέστρεψε, Joseph. antt. 9, 4, 4 ; τὸ θεῖον εἰς ὀργὴν περιτραπέν, 2, 14, 1. In various other uses in Grk. auth. [fr. Lys. and Plat. on].*

4063   **περι-τρέχω** ; 2 aor. [περιέδραμον T Tr WH], ptcp. περιδραμόντες [R G L] ; fr. [Hom.], Theogn., Xen., Plat. down ; to run around, run round about : with an acc. of place, Mk. vi. 55. (Sept. twice for שׁוּט, Jer. v. 1 ; Am. viii. 12.) *

4064   **περι-φέρω** ; pres. pass. περιφέρομαι ; fr. Hdt. down ; to carry round : to bear about everywhere with one, τί, 2 Co. iv. 10 ; to carry hither and thither, τοὺς κακῶς ἔχοντας, Mk. vi. 55 (where the Evangelist wishes us to conceive of the sick as brought to Jesus while he is travelling about and visiting different places); pass. to be driven [A. V. carried] about : παντὶ ἀνέμῳ τῆς διδασκαλίας, i. e. in doubt and hesitation to be led away now to this opinion, now to that, Eph. iv. 14. In Heb. xiii. 9 and Jude 12 for περιφέρ. editors from Griesbach on have restored παραφέρ.*

4065   περι-φρονέω, -ῶ;   **1.** *to consider* or *examine on all sides* [περί, III. 1], i. e. *carefully, thoroughly*, (Arstph. nub. 741).   **2.** (fr. περί, beyond, III. 2), *to set one's self in thought beyond (exalt one's self in thought above)* a pers. or thing; *to contemn, despise*: τινός (cf. Kühner § 419, 1 b. vol. ii. p. 325), Tit. ii. 15 (4 Macc. vi. 9 ; vii. 16 ; xiv. 1 ; Plut., al. ; τοῦ ζῆν, Plat. Ax. p. 372 ; Aeschin. dial. Socr. 3, 22).*

4066   περί-χωρος, -ον, (περί and χῶρος), *lying round about, neighboring*, (Plut., Aelian., Dio Cass.) ; in the Scriptures ἡ περίχωρος, sc. γῆ, *the region round about* [q. v. in B. D.] : Mt. xiv. 35 ; Mk. i. 28 ; vi. 55 [R G L txt.] ; Lk. iii. 3 ; iv. 14, 37 ; vii. 17 ; viii. 37 ; Acts xiv. 6, (Gen. xix. 17 ; Deut. iii. 13, etc. ; τῆς γῆς τῆς περιχώρου, Gen. xix. 28 cod. Alex.) ; ἡ περίχ. τοῦ Ἰορδάνου, Lk. iii. 3 (Gen. xiii. 10 sq. ; for כִּכַּר הַיַּרְדֵּן, *the region* of the Jordan [cf. B. D. u. s.]) ; by meton. for its inhabitants : Mt. iii. 5. (τὸ περίχωρον and τὰ περίχωρα, Deut. iii. 4 ; 1 Chr. v. 16 ; 2 Chr. iv. 17, etc.) *

4067   περί-ψημα, -τος, τό, (fr. περιψάω 'to wipe off all round'; and this fr. περί [q. v. III. 1], and ψάω ' to wipe,' ' rub '), prop. *what is wiped off ; dirt rubbed off ; offscouring, scrapings* : 1 Co. iv. 13, used in the same sense as περικάθαρμα, q. v. Suidas and other Greek lexicographers s. v. relate that the Athenians, in order to avert public calamities, yearly threw a criminal into the sea as an offering to Poseidon ; hence ἀργύριον . . . περίψημα τοῦ παιδίου ἡμῶν γένοιτο, (as if to say) let it become an expiatory offering, a ransom, for our child, i. e. in comparison with the saving of our son's life let it be to us a despicable and worthless thing, Tob. v. 18 (where see Fritzsche ; [cf. also Müller on Barn. ep. 4, 9]). It is used of a man who in behalf of religion undergoes dire trials for the salvation of others, Ignat. ad Eph. 8, 1 ; 18, 1 ; [see Bp. Lghtft.'s note on the former passage].*

4068   περπερεύομαι ; (to be πέρπερος, i. e. vain-glorious, braggart, Polyb. 32, 6, 5 ; 40, 6, 2 ; Epict. diss. 3, 2, 14) ; *to boast one's self* [A. V. *vaunt one's self*] : 1 Co. xiii. 4 (Antonin. 5, 5 ; the compound ἐμπερπερεύεσθαι is used of adulation, employing rhetorical embellishments in extolling another excessively, in Cic. ad Attic. 1, 14. Hesych. περπερεύεται· κατεπαίρεται) ; cf. Osiander [or Wetstein] on 1 Co. l. c. [Gataker on Marc. Antonin. 5, 5 p. 143].*

4069   Περσίς [lit. ' a Persian woman '], ή, acc. -ίδα, *Persis*, a Christian woman : Ro. xvi. 12.*

4070   πέρυσι, (fr. πέρας), adv., *last year ; the year just past* : ἀπὸ πέρυσι, *for a year past, a year ago*, [W. 422 (393)], 2 Co. viii. 10 ; ix. 2. ([Simon.], Arstph., Plat., Plut., Lcian.) *

see 4072   πετάομαι, -ῶμαι ; a doubtful later Grk. form for the earlier πέτομαι (see Lob. ad Phryn. p. 581 ; Bttm. Ausf. Spr. ii. p. 271 sq. ; cf. W. 88 (84) ; [B. 65 (58) ; Veitch s. v.]) ; *to fly* : in the N. T. found only in pres. ptcp. πε-

τόμενος, Rec. in Rev. iv. 7 ; viii. 13 ; xiv. 6 ; xix. 17, where since Griesbach πετόμενος has been restored.*

4071   πετεινός, -ή, -όν, (Attic for πετηνός, fr. πέτομαι), *flying, winged* ; in the N. T. found only in neut. plur. πετεινά and τὰ πετεινά, as subst., *flying* or *winged animals, birds* : Mt. xiii. 4 ; Mk. iv. 4 [G L T Tr WH] ; Lk. xii. 24 ; Ro. i. 23 ; Jas. iii. 7 ; τὰ πετ. τοῦ οὐρανοῦ (Sept. for עוֹף הַשָּׁמַיִם ; see οὐρανός, 1 b.), the birds of heaven, i. e. flying in the heavens (air), Mt. vi. 26 ; viii. 20 ; xiii. 32 ; Mk. iv. 4 [Rec], 32 ; Lk. viii. 5 ; ix. 58 ; xiii. 19 ; Acts x. 12 [here L T Tr WH om. τά] ; xi. 6. [(Theogn., Hdt., al.)]*

4072   πέτομαι ; [fr. Hom. down] ; Sept. for עוּף ; *to fly* : Rev. iv. 7 ; viii. 13 ; xii. 14 ; xiv. 6 ; xix. 17 ; see πετάομαι.*

4073   πέτρα, -ας, ή, fr. Hom. down ; Sept. for סֶלַע and צוּר ; *a rock, ledge, cliff* ;   **a.** prop. : Mt. vii. 24 sq. ; xxvii. 51, 60 ; Mk. xv. 46 ; Lk. vi. 48 ; 1 Co. x. 4 (on which see πνευματικός, 3 a.) ; a projecting rock, crag, Rev. vi. 15 sq. ; rocky ground, Lk. viii. 6, 13.   **b.** *a rock, large stone* : Ro. ix. 33 ; 1 Pet. ii. 8 (7).   **c.** metaph. *a man like a rock, by reason of his firmness and strength of soul* : Mt. xvi. 18 [some interpp. regard the distinction (generally observed in classic Greek ; see the Comm. and cf. Schmidt, Syn. ch. 51, §§ 4–6) between πέτρα, the massive living rock, and πέτρος, a detached but large fragment, as important for the correct understanding of this passage ; others explain the different genders here as due first to the personal then to the material reference. Cf. Meyer, Keil, al. ; *Green, Crit. Note on Jn. i. 43*].*

4074   Πέτρος, -ου, ὁ, (an appellative prop. name, signifying ' a stone,' ' a rock,' ' a ledge' or 'cliff' ; used metaph. of a s o u l hard and unyielding, and so resembling a rock, Soph. O. R. 334 ; Eur. Med. 28 ; Herc. fur. 1397 ; answering to the Chald. Κηφᾶς, q. v., Jn. i. 42 (43)), *Peter*, the surname of the apostle *Simon*. He was a native of Bethsaida, a town of Galilee, the son of a fisherman (see Ἰωάννης, 3, and Ἰωνᾶς, 2), and dwelt with his wife at Capernaum, Mt. viii. 14 ; Mk. i. 30 ; Lk. iv. 38, cf. 1 Co. ix. 5. He had a brother Andrew, with whom he followed the occupation of a fisherman, Mt. iv. 18 ; Mk. i. 16 ; Lk. v. 3. Both were received by Jesus as his companions, Mt. iv. 19 ; Mk. i. 17 ; Lk. v. 10 ; Jn. i. 40–42 (41–43) ; and Simon, whose pre-eminent courage and firmness he discerned and especially relied on for the future establishment of the kingdom of God, he honored with the name of *Peter*, Jn. i. 42 (43) ; Mt. xvi. 18 ; Mk. iii. 16. Excelling in vigor of mind, eagerness to learn, and love for Jesus, he enjoyed, together with James and John the sons of Zebedee, the special favor and intimacy of his divine Master. After having for some time presided, in connection with John and James the brother of our Lord [see Ἰάκωβος, 3], over the affairs of the Christians at Jerusalem, he seems to have gone abroad to preach the gospel especially to Jews (Gal. ii. 9 ; 1 Co. ix. 5 ; 1 Pet. v. 13 ; Papias in Euseb. 3, 39, 15 ; for Papias states that Peter employed Mark as 'interpreter' (ἑρμηνευτής), an aid of which he had no need except beyond the borders of Palestine, especially among those who spoke Latin [but on the disputed meaning of the word 'interpreter' here, see *Morison*, Com. on Mk., ed. 2, Introd. p. xxix. sqq.]). But just as, on the night of the betrayal, Peter proved so far faithless to himself as thrice to deny that he was a follower of Jesus, so also some time afterwards at Antioch he made greater concessions to the rigorous Jewish Christians than Christian liberty permitted; accordingly he was rebuked by Paul for his weakness and 'dissimulation' (ὑπόκρισις), Gal. ii. 11 sqq. Nevertheless, in the patristic age Jewish Christians did not hesitate to claim the authority of Peter and of James the brother of the Lord in defence of their narrow views and practices. This is not the place to relate and refute the ecclesiastical traditions concerning Peter's being the founder of the church at Rome and bishop of it for twenty-five years and more; the discussion of them may be found in *Hase*, Protestant. Polemik gegen die röm.-kathol. Kirche, ed. 4, p. 123 sqq.; [cf. *Schaff*, Church History, 1882, vol. i. §§ 25, 26; *Sieffert* in Herzog ed. 2, vol. xi. p. 524 sqq., and (for reff.) p. 537 sq.]. This one thing seems to be evident from Jn. xxi. 18 sqq., that Peter suffered death by crucifixion [cf. Keil ad loc.; others doubt whether Christ's words contain anything more than a general prediction of martyrdom]. If he was crucified at Rome, it must have been several years after the death of Paul. [Cf. BB. DD. and reff. u. s.] He is called in the N. T., at one time, simply Σίμων (once Συμεών, Acts xv. 14), and (and that, too, most frequently [see B. D. s. v. Peter, sub fin. (p. 2459 Am. ed.)]), Πέτρος and Κηφᾶς (q. v.), then again Σίμων Πέτρος, Mt. xvi. 16; Lk. v. 8; Jn. [i. 42 (43)]; vi. [8], 68; xiii. 6, 9, 24, [36]; xviii. 10, 15, 25; xx. 2, 6; xxi. 2 sq. 7, 11, 15; once Συμεὼν Πέτρος (2 Pet. i. 1 where L WH txt. Σίμων); Σίμων ὁ λεγόμενος Πέτρος, Mt. iv. 18; x. 2; Σίμων ὁ ἐπικαλούμενος Πέτρος, Acts x. 18; xi. 13; Σίμων ὃς ἐπικαλεῖται Πέτρος, Acts x. 5, 32.

4075 πετρώδης, -ες, (fr. πέτρα and εἶδος; hence prop. 'rock-like,' 'having the appearance of rock'), *rocky*, *stony*: τὸ πετρῶδες and τὰ πετρώδη, of ground full of rocks, Mt. xiii. 5, 20; Mk. iv. 5, 16. (Soph., Plat., Aristot., Diod. 3, 45 (44), Plut., al.) *

4076 πήγανον, -ου, τό, [thought to be fr. πήγνυμι to make solid, on account of its thick, fleshy leaves; cf. Vaniček p. 457], *rue*: Lk. xi. 42. (Theophr. hist. plant. 1, 3, 4; Dioscorid. 3, 45 (52); Plut., al.) [B. D. s. v.; *Tristram*, Nat. Hist. etc. p. 478; Carruthers in the "Bible Educator," iii. 216 sq.] *

4077 πηγή, -ῆς, ἡ, fr. Hom. down, Sept. chiefly for עַיִן, מַעְיָן, מָקוֹר; *a fountain*, *spring*: Jas. iii. 11, and Rec. in 12; 2 Pet. ii. 17; ὕδατος ἁλλομένου, Jn. iv. 14; τῶν ὑδάτων, Rev. viii. 10; xiv. 7; xvi. 4; of a well fed by a spring, Jn. iv. 6. ζωῆς πηγαὶ ὑδάτων, Rev. vii. 17; ἡ π. τ. ὕδατος τῆς ζωῆς, Rev. xxi. 6, (on both pass. see in ζωή, p. 274ᵃ); ἡ π. τοῦ αἵματος, a flow of blood, Mk. v. 29.*

4078 πήγνυμι: 1 aor. ἔπηξα; fr. Hom. down; *to make fast*, *to fix*; *to fasten together*, *to build by fastening together*: σκηνήν, Heb. viii. 2 [A. V. *pitched*. COMP.: προσ-πήγνυμι.] *

4079 πηδάλιον, -ου, τό, (fr. πηδόν the blade of an oar, an oar), fr. Hom. down, a ship's *rudder*: Acts xxvii. 40 [on the plur. see *Smith*, Voy. and Shipwreck of St. Paul, 4th ed., p. 183 sqq.; B. D. s. v. Ship (2); cf. *Graser*, Das Seewesen des Alterthums, in the Philologus for 1865, p. 266 sq.]; Jas. iii. 4.*

4080 πηλίκος, -η, -ον, (fr. ἡλιξ [?]), interrog., *how great, how large*: in a material reference (denoting geometrical magnitude as disting. fr. arithmetical, πόσος) (Plat. Men. p. 82 d.; p. 83 e.; Ptol. 1, 3, 3; Zech. ii. 2, [6]), Gal. vi. 11, where cf. Winer, Rückert, Hilgenfeld, [Hackett in B. D. Am. ed. s. v. Epistle; but see Bp. Lghtft. or Meyer]. in an ethical reference, i. q. *how distinguished*, Heb. vii. 4.*

4081 πηλός, -οῦ, ὁ, fr. Aeschyl. and Hdt. down; **a.** *clay*, which the potter uses (Is. xxix. 16; xli. 25; Nah. iii. 14): Ro. ix. 21. **b.** i. q. *mud* [wet 'clay']: Jn. ix. 6, 11, 14 sq.*

4082 πήρα, -ας, ἡ, *a wallet* (a leathern sack, in which travellers and shepherds carried their provisions) [A. V. *scrip* (q. v. in B.D.)]: Mt. x. 10; Mk. vi. 8; Lk. ix. 3; x. 4; xxii. 35 sq. (Hom., Arstph., Joseph., Plut., Hdian., Lcian., al.; with τῶν βρωμάτων added, Judith xiii. 10.) *

4083 πῆχυς: gen. πήχεως (not found in the N. T.), gen. plur. πηχῶν contr. fr. Ionic πηχέων (Jn. xxi. 8; Rev. xxi. 17; 1 K. vii. 3 (15), 39 (2); Esth. vii. 9; Ezek. xl. 5) acc. to later usage, for the earlier and Attic πήχεων, which is common in the Sept. (cf. *Lob.* ad Phryn. p. 245 sq.; [*WH* App. p. 157]; W. § 9, 2 e.), ὁ, *the fore-arm* i. e. that part of the arm between the hand and the elbow-joint (Hom. Od. 17, 38; Il. 21, 166, etc.); hence *a cubit*, (*ell*, Lat. *ulna*), a measure of length equal to the distance from the joint of the elbow to the tip of the middle finger [i. e. about one foot and a half, but its precise length varied and is disputed; see B. D. s. v. Weights and Measures, II. 1]: Mt. vi. 27; Lk. xii. 25, [on these pass. cf. ἡλικία, 1 a.]; Jn. xxi. 8; Rev. xxi. 17. (Sept. very often for אַמָּה.) *

4084 πιάζω (Doric for πιέζω, cf. B. 66 (58)): 1 aor. ἐπίασα; 1 aor. pass. ἐπιάσθην; **1.** *to lay hold of*: τινὰ τῆς χειρός, Acts iii. 7 [Theocr. 4, 35]. **2.** *to take, capture*: fishes, Jn. xxi. 3, 10; θηρίον, pass., Rev. xix. 20, (Cant. ii. 15). *to take* i. e. *apprehend*: a man, in order to imprison him, Jn. vii. 30, 32, 44; viii. 20; x. 39; xi. 57; Acts xii. 4; 2 Co. xi. 32. [COMP.: ὑπο-πιάζω.] *

4085 πιέζω: pf. pass. ptcp. πεπιεσμένος; fr. Hom. down; *to press, press together*: Lk. vi. 38. Sept. once for דָּרַךְ, Mic. vi. 15.*

4086 πιθανολογία, -ας, ἡ, (fr. πιθανολόγος; and this fr. πιθανός, on which see πειθός, and λόγος), *speech adapted to persuade*, discourse in which probable arguments are adduced; once so in class. Grk., viz. Plat. Theaet. p. 162 e.; in a bad sense, *persuasiveness of speech*, *specious discourse leading others into error*: Col. ii. 4, and several times in eccl. writers.*

[πιθός, see πειθός and cf. I, ι.] see 3981

4087 πικραίνω: fut. πικρανῶ; Pass., pres. πικραίνομαι; 1 aor. ἐπικράνθην; (πικρός, q. v.); **1.** prop. *to make bitter*: τὰ ὕδατα, pass., Rev. viii. 11; τὴν κοιλίαν, to produce a bitter taste in the stomach (Vulg. *amarico*), Rev. x.

9 sq.   **2.** trop. *to embitter, exasperate,* i. e. render angry, indignant ; pass. *to be embittered, irritated,* (Plat., Dem., al.) : πρός τινα, Col. iii. 19 (Athen. 6 p. 242 c. ; ἐπί τινα, Ex. xvi. 20 ; Jer. xliv. (xxxvii.) 15 ; 1 Esdr. iv. 31 ; [ἔν τινι, Ruth i. 20]) ; contextually i. q. *to visit with bitterness, to grieve,* (deal bitterly with), Job xxvii. 2 ; 1 Macc. iii. 7. [COMP. : παρα-πικραίνω.]*

4088   **πικρία,** -ας, ἡ, (πικρός), *bitterness :* χολὴ πικρίας, i. q. χολὴ πικρά [W. 34, 3 b. ; B. § 132, 10], *bitter gall,* i. q. extreme wickedness, Acts viii. 23 ; ῥίζα πικρίας [reff. as above], *a bitter root,* and so producing bitter fruit, Heb. xii. 15 (fr. Deut. xxix. 18 cod. Alex.), cf. Bleek ad loc.; metaph. *bitterness,* i. e. bitter hatred, Eph. iv. 31 ; of speech, Ro. iii. 14 after Ps. ix. 28 (x. 7). (In various uses in Sept., [Dem., Aristot.], Theophr., Polyb., Plut., al.) *

4089   **πικρός,** -ά, -όν, [fr. r. meaning 'to cut,' 'prick'; Vaniček 534; Curtius § 100; Fick i. 145], fr. Hom. down, Sept. for מַר ; *bitter:* prop. Jas. iii. 11 (opp. to τὸ γλυκύ) ; metaph. *harsh, virulent,* Jas. iii. 14.*

4090   **πικρῶς,** adv., [fr. Aeschyl. down], *bitterly :* metaph. ἔκλαυσε, i. e. with poignant grief, Mt. xxvi. 75 ; Lk. xxii. 62 [here WH br. the cl.]; cf. πικρὸν δάκρυον, Hom. Od. 4, 153.*

4091   **Πιλᾶτος,** [L] Tr better Πιλᾶτος ([on the accent in codd. see *Tdf.* Proleg. p. 103 ; . cf. Chandler § 326 ; B. p. 6 n.]; W. § 6, 1 m.), T WH incorrectly Πειλᾶτος [but see *Tdf.* Proleg. p. 84 sq.; *WH.* App. p. 155; and cf. ει, ι], (a Lat. name, i. q. 'armed with a pilum or javelin,' like *Torquatus* i. q. 'adorned with the collar or neck-chain'; [so generally ; but some would contract it from *pileatus* i. e. ' wearing the felt cap' (pileus), the badge of a manumitted slave ; cf. *Leyrer* in Herzog as below ; *Plumptre* in B. D. s. v. Pilate (note)]), -ου, ὁ [on the use of the art. with the name cf. W. 113 (107) n.], *Pontius Pilate,* the fifth procurator of the Roman emperor in Judæa and Samaria (having had as predecessors Coponius, Marcus Ambivius, Annius Rufus, and Valerius Gratus; [Some writ. (e. g. BB. DD. s. v.) call Pilate the s i x t h procurator, reckoning Sabinus as the first, he having had charge for a time, during the absence of Archelaus at Rome, shortly after the death of Herod ; cf. Joseph. antt. 17, 9, 3.] He was sent into Judæa in the year 26 A. D., and remained in office ten years ; (cf. *Keim,* Jesus von Naz. iii. p. 485 sq. [Eng. trans. vi. 226 sq.]). Although he saw that Jesus was innocent, yet, fearing that the Jews would bring an accusation against him before Caesar for the wrongs he had done them, and dreading the emperor's displeasure, he delivered up Jesus to their blood-thirsty demands and ordered him to be crucified. At length, in consequence of his having ordered the slaughter of the Samaritans assembled at Mt. Gerizim, Vitellius, the governor of Syria and father of the Vitellius who was afterwards emperor, removed him from office and ordered him to go to Rome and answer their accusations; but before his arrival Tiberius died. Cf. Joseph. antt. 18, 2–4 and ch. 6, 5 ; b. j. 2, 9, 2 and 4 ; Philo, leg. ad Gaium § 38 ; Tac. ann. 15, 44. Eusebius (h. e. 2,

7, and Chron. ad ann. I. Gaii) reports that he died by his own hand. Various stories about his death are related in the Evangelia apocr. ed. Tischendorf p. 426 sqq. [Eng. trans. p. 231 sqq.]. He is mentioned in the N. T. in Mt. xxvii. 2 sqq. ; Mk. xv. 1 sqq. ; Lk. iii. 1 ; xiii. 1 ; xxiii. 1 sqq. ; Jn. xviii. 29 sqq. ; xix. 1 sqq. ; Acts iii. 13 ; iv. 27 ; xiii. 28 ; 1 Tim. vi. 13. A full account of him is given in *Win.* RWB. s. v. Pilatus ; [BB. DD. ibid.]; *Ewald,* Geschichte Christus' u. seiner Zeit, ed. 3 p. 82 sqq. ; *Leyrer* in Herzog xi. p. 663 sqq. [ed. 2 p. 685 sqq.]; *Renan,* Vie de Jésus, 14me éd. p. 413 sqq. [Eng. trans. (N. Y. 1865) p. 333 sqq.]; *Klöpper* in Schenkel iv. p. 581 sq. ; *Schürer,* Neutest. Zeitgesch. § 17 c. p. 252 sqq. ; [*Warneck,* Pont. Pilatus u.s.w. (pp. 210. Gotha, 1867)].*

πίμπλημι (a lengthened form of the theme ΠΛΕΩ, whence πλέος, πλήρης [cf. Curtius § 366]) : 1 aor. ἔπλησα ; Pass., 1 fut. πλησθήσομαι ; 1 aor. ἐπλήσθην ; fr. Hom. on ; Sept. for מָלֵא, also for שָׂבַע (to satiate) and pass. שָׂבַע (to be full) ; *to fill:* τί, Lk. v. 7 ; τί τινος [W. § 30, 8 b.], a thing with something, Mt. xxvii. 48 ; [Jn. xix. 29 R G]; in pass., Mt. xxii. 10 ; Acts xix. 29 ; [ἐκ τῆς ὀσμῆς, Jn. xii. 3 Tr mrg ; cf. W. u. s. note ; B. § 132, 12]. what wholly *takes possession* of the m i n d is said *to fill* it : pass. φόβου, Lk. v. 26 ; θάμβους, Acts iii. 10 ; ἀνοίας, Lk. vi. 11 ; ζήλου, Acts v. 17 ; xiii. 45 ; θυμοῦ, Lk. iv. 28 ; Acts iii. 10 ; πνεύματος ἁγίου, Lk. i. 15, 41, 67 ; Acts ii. 4 ; iv. 8, 31 ; ix. 17 ; xiii. 9. p r o p h e c i e s are said πλησθῆναι, i. e. *to come to pass, to be confirmed by the event,* Lk. xxi. 22 G L T Tr WH (for Rec. πληρωθῆναι). time is said πλησθῆναι, *to be fulfilled* or *completed,* i. e. *finished, elapsed,* Lk. i. 23, 57 [W. 324 (304) ; B. 267 (230)]; ii. 6, 21 sq. ; so מָלֵא, Job xv. 32 ; and מָלֵא to (ful-) fill the time, i. e. *to complete, fill up,* Gen. xxix. 27 ; Job xxxix. 2. [COMP. : ἐμ-πίπλημι.]*

πιμπράω (for the more common πίμπρημι [cf. Curtius § 378, Vaniček p. 510 sq.]) : [pres. inf. pass. πιμπρᾶσθαι ; but R G L Tr WH πίμπρασθαι fr. the form πίμπρημι (Tdf. ἐμπιπρᾶσθαι, q. v.)]; in Grk. writ. fr. Hom. [(yet only the aor. fr. πρήθω)] down; *to blow, to burn,* [on the connection betw. these meanings cf. *Ebeling,* Lex. Hom. s. v. πρήθω]; in the Scriptures four times *to cause to swell, to render tumid,* [cf. *Soph.* Lex. s. v.]: γαστέρα, Num. v. 22 ; pass. *to swell, become swollen,* of parts of the body, Num. v. 21, 27 : Acts xxviii. 6 (see above and in ἐμπιπράω). [COMP. ἐμπιπράω.]*

πινακίδιον, -ου, τό, (dimin. of πινακίς, -ίδος), [Aristot., al.];   **a.** *a small tablet.*   **b.** spec. *a writing-tablet :* Lk. i. 63 [Tr mrg. πινακίδα; see the foll. word] ; Epict. diss. 3, 22, 74.*

[**πινακίς,** -ίδος, ἡ, i. q. πινακίδιον (q. v.) : Lk. i. 63 Tr mrg. (Epict., Plut., Artem., al.) *]

πίναξ, -ακος, ὁ, (com. thought to be fr. ΠΙΝΟΣ a pine, and so prop. ' a pine-board'; acc. to the conjecture of *Buttmann,* Ausf. Spr. i. 74 n., fr. πνάξ for π λ ά ξ [i. e. anything broad and *flat* (cf. Eng. *plank*)] with ι inserted, as in πινυτός for πνυτός [acc. to Fick i. 146 fr. Skr. pinaka, a stick, staff]), fr. Hom. down ;   **1.** *a board, a tablet.*   **2.** *a dish, plate, platter :* Mt. xiv. 8,

see
4130 St.

see
4092 St.

4093

see 4093

4094

4095   **4098**

11; Mk. vi. 25, [27 Lchm. br.], 28; Lk. xi. 39; Hom. Od. 1, 141; 16, 49; al.*

πίνω; impf. ἔπινον; fut. πίομαι [cf. W. 90 sq. (86)], 2 pers. sing. πίεσαι (Lk. xvii. 8 [(see reff. in κατακαυχάομαι)]); pf. 3 pers. sing. (Rev. xviii. 3) πέπωκε R G, but L T WH mrg. plur. -καν, for which L ed. ster. Tr txt. WH txt. read πέπτωκαν (see γίνομαι); 2 aor. ἔπιον, impv. πίε (Lk. xii. 19), inf. πιεῖν ([Mt. xx. 22; xxvii. 34 (not Tdf.); Mk. x. 38]; Acts xxiii. 12 [not WH], 21; Ro. xiv. 21 [not WH], etc.), and in colloquial form πῖν (Lchm. in Jn. iv. 9; Rev. xvi. 6), and πεῖν (T Tr WH in Jn. iv. 7, 9 sq.; T WH in 1 Co. ix. 4; x. 7; Rev. xvi. 6; T in Mt. xxvii. 34 (bis); WH in Acts xxiii. 12, 21; Ro. xiv. 21, and often among the var. of the codd.) — on these forms see [esp. WH. App. p. 170]; Fritzsche, De conformatione N. T. critica etc. p. 27 sq.; B. 66 (58) sq.; [Curtius, Das Verbum, ii. 103]; Sept. for שָׁתָה; [fr. Hom. down]; to drink: absol., Lk. xii. 19; Jn. iv. 7, 10; 1 Co. xi. 25; figuratively, to receive into the soul what serves to refresh, strengthen, nourish it unto life eternal, Jn. vii. 37; on the various uses of the phrase ἐσθίειν κ. πίνειν see in ἐσθίω, a.; τρώγειν κ. πίνειν, of those living in fancied security, Mt. xxiv. 38; πίνω with an acc. of the thing, to drink a thing [cf. W. 198 (187) n.], Mt. vi. 25 [G T om. WH br. the cl.], 31; xxvi. 29; Mk. xiv. 25; xvi. 18; Rev. xvi. 6; to use a thing for drink, Lk. i. 15; xii. 29; Ro. xiv. 21; 1 Co. x. 4 [cf. W. § 40, 3 b.]; τὸ αἷμα of Christ, see αἷμα, fin.; τὸ ποτήριον i. e. what is in the cup, 1 Co. x. 21; xi. 27, etc. (see ποτήριον, a.). ἡ γῆ is said πίνειν τὸν ὑετόν, to suck in, absorb, imbibe, Heb. vi. 7 (Deut. xi. 11; Hdt. 3, 117; 4, 198; Verg. ecl. 3, 111 sat prata biberunt). πίνω ἐκ w. a gen. of the vessel out of which one drinks, ἐκ τοῦ ποτηρίου, Mt. xxvi. 27; Mk. xiv. 23; 1 Co. x. 4 [cf. above]; xi. 28, (Arstph. eqq. 1289); ἐκ w. a gen. denoting the drink of which as a supply one drinks, Mt. xxvi. 29; Mk. xiv. 25; ἐκ τοῦ ὕδατος, Jn. iv. 13 sq.; ἐκ τοῦ οἴνου (or θυμοῦ), Rev. xiv. 10; xviii. 3 [L om. Tr WH br. τοῦ οἴνου]; ἀπό w. a gen. of the drink, Lk. xxii. 18. [Cf. B. § 132, 7; W. 199 (187). COMP.: κατα-, συμ-πίνω.]

4096   **πιότης**, -ητος, ἡ, (πίων fat), fatness: Ro. xi. 17. (Aristot., Theophr., al.; Sept. for דֶּשֶׁן.)*

4097   **πιπράσκω**: impf. ἐπίπρασκον; pf. πέπρακα; Pass., pres. ptcp. πιπρασκόμενος; pf. ptcp. πεπραμένος; 1 aor. ἐπράθην; (fr. περάω to cross, to transport to a distant land); fr. Aeschyl. and Hdt. down; Sept. for מָכַר; to sell: τί, Mt. xiii. 46 [on the use of the pf., cf. Soph. Glossary etc. Introd. § 82, 4]; Acts ii. 45; iv. 34; v. 4; w. gen. of price, Mt. xxvi. 9; Mk. xiv. 5; Jn. xii. 5, (Deut. xxi. 14); τινά, one into slavery, Mt. xviii. 25; hence metaph. πεπραμένος ὑπὸ τὴν ἁμαρτίαν, [A. V. sold under sin] i. e. entirely under the control of the love of sinning, Ro. vii. 14 (ἐπράθησαν τοῦ ποιῆσαι τὸ πονηρόν, 2 K. xvii. 17; 1 Macc. i. 15, cf. 1 K. xx. (xxi.) 25; w. a dat. of the master to whom one is sold as a slave, Lev. xxv. 39; Deut. xv. 12; xxviii. 68; Bar. iv. 6; Soph. Trach. 252; ἑαυτόν τινι, of one bribed to give himself up wholly to another's will, τῷ Φιλίππῳ, Dem. p. 148, 8).*

πίπτω; [impf. ἔπιπτον (Mk. xiv. 35 T Tr mrg. WH)]; fut. πεσοῦμαι; 2 aor. ἔπεσον and acc. to the Alex. form (received everywhere by Lchm. [exc. Lk. xxiii. 30], Tdf. [exc. Rev. vi. 16], Tr [exc. ibid.], WH; and also used by R G in Rev. i. 17; v. 14; vi. 13; xi. 16; xvii. 10) ἔπεσα (cf. [WH. App. p. 164; Tdf. Proleg. p. 123]; Lob. ad Phryn. p. 724 sq.; Bttm. Ausf. Spr. ii. p. 277 sq., and see ἀπέρχομαι init.); pf. πέπτωκα, 2 pers. sing. -κες (Rev. ii. 5 T WH; see κοπιάω), 3 pers. plur. -καν (Rev. xviii. 3, L ed. ster. Tr txt. WH txt.; see γίνομαι); (fr. ΠΕΤΩ, as τίκτω fr. ΤΕΚΩ [cf. Curtius, Etymol. § 214; Verbum, ii. p. 398]); fr. Hom. down; Sept. chiefly for נָפַל; to fall; used   **1.** of descent from a higher place to a lower;   **a.** prop. to fall (either from or upon, i. q. Lat. incido, decido): ἐπί w. acc. of place, Mt. x. 29; xiii. 5, [7], 8; xxi. 44 [T om. L WH Tr mrg. br. the vs.]; Mk. iv. 5; Lk. viii. 6 [here T Tr WH καταπ.], 8 Rec.; Rev. viii. 10; εἰς τι (of the thing that is entered; into), Mt. xv. 14; xvii. 15; Mk. iv. 7 [L mrg. ἐπί] sq.; Lk. vi. 39 R G L mrg. (but L txt. T Tr WH ἐμπίπτ.); viii. 8 G L T Tr WH, [14; xiv. 5 L T Tr WH]; Jn. xii. 24; εἰς (upon) τὴν γῆν, Rev. vi. 13; ix. 1; ἐν μέσῳ, w. gen. of the thing, Lk. viii. 7; παρὰ τὴν ὁδόν, Mt. xiii. 4; Mk. iv. 4; Lk. viii. 5; to fall from or down: foll. by ἀπό w. gen. of place, Mt. xv. 27; xxiv. 29 [here Tdf. ἐκ; Lk. xxi. 21]; Acts xx. 9; foll. by ἐκ w. gen. of place, [Mk. xiii. 25 L T Tr WH]; Rev. viii. 10; ix. 1; i. q. to be thrust down, Lk. x. 18.   **b.** metaph.: οὐ πίπτει ἐπί τινα ὁ ἥλιος, i. e. the heat of the sun does not strike upon them or incommode them, Rev. vii. 16; [ἀχλὺς κ. σκότος, Acts xiii. 11 L T Tr WH]; ὁ κλῆρος πίπτει ἐπί τινα, the lot falls upon one, Acts i. 26; φόβος πίπτει ἐπί τινα, falls upon or seizes one, [Acts xix. 17 L Tr]; Rev. xi. 11 Rec.; [τὸ πνεῦμα τὸ ἅγιον, Acts x. 44 Lchm.]; πίπτω ὑπὸ κρίσιν, to fall under judgment, come under condemnation, James v. 12 [where Rec.st εἰς ὑπόκρισιν].   **2.** of descent from an erect to a prostrate position (Lat. labor, ruo; prolabor, procido; collabor, etc.);   **a.** properly;   **α.** to fall down: ἐπὶ λίθον, Lk. xx. 18; λίθος πίπτει ἐπί τινα, Mt. xxi. 44 [T om. L WH Tr mrg. br. the vs.]; Lk. xx. 18; τὸ ὄρος ἐπί τινα, Lk. xxiii. 30; Rev. vi. 16.   **β.** to be prostrated, fall prostrate; of those overcome by terror or astonishment or grief: χαμαί, Jn. xviii. 6; εἰς τὸ ἔδαφος, Acts xxii. 7; ἐπὶ τὴν γῆν, Acts ix. 4; [ἐπὶ πρόσωπον, Mt. xvii. 6]; or under the attack of an evil spirit: ἐπὶ τῆς γῆς, Mk. ix. 20; or falling dead suddenly: πρὸς τοὺς πόδας τινὸς ὡς νεκρός, Rev. i. 17; πεσὼν ἐξέψυξε, Acts v. 5; πίπτ. παρὰ (L T Tr WH πρὸς) τοὺς πόδας τινός, ibid. 10; absol. 1 Co. x. 8; στόματι μαχαίρας, Lk. xxi. 24; absol. of the dismemberment of corpses by decay, Heb. iii. 17 (Num. xiv. 29, 32).   **γ.** to prostrate one's self; used now of suppliants, now of persons rendering homage or worship to one: ἐπὶ τῆς γῆς, Mk. xiv. 35; ptcp. with προσκυνεῖν, as finite verb, Mt. ii. 11; iv. 9; xviii. 26; πίπτειν κ. προσκυνεῖν, Rev. v. 14; xix. 4; ἔπεσα προσκυνῆσαι, Rev. xxii. 8; πίπτ. εἰς τοὺς πόδας (αὐτοῦ), Mt. xviii. 29 Rec.; εἰς [T Tr WH πρὸς] τ. πόδας τινός, Jn. xi. 32; πρὸς τ. πόδας τινός, Mk. v. 22; [παρὰ τοὺς πόδας τινός, Lk. viii. 41]; ἔμπροσθεν τῶν ποδῶν τινος, Rev. xix. 10; ἐνώπιόν τινος, Rev. iv. 10; v. 8; ἐπὶ πρόσωπον, Mt. xxvi. 39; Lk. v. 12; ἐπὶ πρόσωπον παρὰ τοὺς πόδας τινός, Lk. xvii. 16; πεσὼν ἐπὶ τοὺς πόδας προσεκύνησε, Acts x. 25; πεσὼν ἐπὶ πρόσωπον προσκυνήσει, 1 Co. xiv. 25; ἐπὶ τὰ πρόσωπα καὶ προσκυνεῖν, Rev. vii. 11 [ἐπὶ πρόσωπον Rec.]; xi. 16.   **δ.** to fall out, fall from: θρὶξ ἐκ τῆς κεφαλῆς πεσεῖται, i. q. shall perish, be lost, Acts xxvii. 34 Rec.   **ε.** to fall down, fall in ruin: of buildings, walls, etc., Mt. vii. 25, [27]; Lk. vi. 49 (where T Tr WH συνέπεσε); Heb. xi. 30; οἶκος ἐπ' οἶκον πίπτει, Lk. xi. 17 [see ἐπί, C. I. 2 c.]; πύργος ἐπί τινα, Lk. xiii. 4; σκηνὴ ἡ πεπτωκυῖα, the tabernacle that has fallen down, a fig. description of the family of David and the theocracy as reduced to extreme decay [cf. σκηνή, fin.], Acts xv. 16. of a city: ἔπεσε, i. e. has been overthrown, destroyed, Rev. xi. 13; xiv. 8; xvi. 19; xviii. 2, (Jer. xxviii. (li.) 8).   **b.** metaph.   **a.** to be cast down from a state of prosperity: πόθεν πέπτωκας, from what a height of Christian knowledge and attainment thou hast declined, Rev. ii. 5 G L T Tr WH (see above ad init.).   **β.** to fall from a state of uprightness, i. e. to sin: opp. to ἑστάναι, 1 Co. x. 12; opp. to στήκειν, w. a dat. of the pers. whose interests suffer by the sinning [cf. W. § 31, 1 k.], Ro. xiv. 4; to fall into a state of wickedness, Rev. xviii. 3 L ed. ster. Tr WH txt. [see πίνω].   **γ.** to perish, i. e. to come to an end, disappear, cease: of virtues, 1 Co. xiii. 8 L T Tr WH [R. V. fail]; to lose authority, no longer have force, of sayings, precepts, etc., Lk. xvi. 17 (ὥστε οὐ χαμαὶ πεσεῖται ὅ τι ἂν εἴπῃς, Plat. Euthyphr. § 17; irrita cadunt promissa, Liv. 2, 31). i. q. to be removed from power by death, Rev. xvii. 10; to fail of participating in, miss a share in, the Messianic salvation, Ro. xi. 11, [22]; Heb. iv. 11 [(yet see ἐν, I. 5 f.).   COMP.: ἀνα-, ἀντι-, ἀπο-, ἐκ-, ἐν-, ἐπι-, κατα-, παρα-, περι-, προσ-, συμ- πίπτω.]*

4099 Πισιδία, -ας, ἡ, Pisidia, a region of Asia Minor, bounded by Pamphylia and the Pamphylian Sea, Phrygia, and Lycaonia: Acts xiii. 14 R G; xiv. 24. [B. D. s. v. Pisidia.]*

see 4099 Πισίδιος, -α, -ον, i. q. Πισιδικός, belonging to Pisidia: Ἀντιόχεια ἡ Πισιδία, i. e. taking its name from Pisidia (see Ἀντιόχεια, 2): Acts xiii. 14 L T Tr WH.*

4100 πιστεύω; impf. ἐπίστευον; fut. πιστεύσω; 1 aor. ἐπίστευσα; pf. πεπίστευκα; plupf. (without augm., cf. W. § 12, 9; [B. 33 (29)]) πεπιστεύκειν (Acts xiv. 23); Pass., pf. πεπίστευμαι; 1 aor. ἐπιστεύθην; (πιστός); Sept. for הֶאֱמִין; in class. Grk. fr. Aeschyl., Soph., Eur., Thuc. down;   **I.** intrans. to think to be true; to be persuaded of; to credit, place confidence in;   **a.** univ.: the thing believed being evident from the preceding context, Mt. xxiv. 23, [26]; Mk. xiii. 21; 1 Co. xi. 18; w. an acc. of the thing, Acts xiii. 41 (L T Tr WH ὅ for Rec. ᾧ); to credit, have confidence, foll. by ὅτι, Acts ix. 26; τινί, to believe one's words, Mk. xvi. 13 sq.; 1 Jn. iv. 1; τινὶ ὅτι, Jn. iv. 21; τῷ ψεύδει, 2 Th. ii. 11; περί τινος, ὅτι, Jn. ix. 18.   **b.** spec., in a moral and religious reference, πιστεύειν is used in the N. T. of the conviction and trust to which a man is impelled by a

certain inner and higher prerogative and law of his soul; thus it stands   **a.** absol. to trust in Jesus or in God as able to aid either in obtaining or in doing something: Mt. viii. 13; xxi. 22; Mk. v. 36; ix. 23 sq.; Lk. viii. 50; Jn. xi. 40; foll. by ὅτι, Mt. ix. 28; Mk. xi. 23; [Heb. xi. 6]; τῷ λόγῳ, ᾧ (ὃν) εἶπεν ὁ Ἰησοῦς, Jn. iv. 50.   **β.** of the credence given to God's messengers and their words, w. a dat. of the person or thing: Μωϋσεῖ, Jn. v. 46. to the prophets, Jn. xii. 38; Acts xxiv. 14; xxvi. 27; Ro. x. 16; ἐπὶ πᾶσιν οἷς ἐλάλησαν οἱ προφῆται, to place reliance on etc. Lk. xxiv. 25. to an angel, Lk. i. 20; foll. by ὅτι, ibid. 45. to John the Baptist, Mt. xxi. 25 (26), 32; Mk. xi. 31; Lk. xx. 5. to Christ's words, Jn. iii. 12; v. 38, 46 sq.; vi. 30; viii. 45 sq.; x. [37], 38ᵃ; τοῖς ἔργοις of Christ, ibid. 38ᵇ. to the teachings of evangelists and apostles, Acts viii. 12; τῇ ἀληθείᾳ, 2 Th. ii. 12; ἐπιστεύθη τὸ μαρτύριον, the testimony was believed, 2 Th. i. 10 [cf. W. § 39, 1 a.; B. 175 (152)]; τῇ γραφῇ, Jn. ii. 22. ἐν τῷ εὐαγγελίῳ, to put faith in the gospel, Mk. i. 15 [B. 174 (151 sq.); cf. W. 213 (200 sq.)] (Ignat. ad Philad. 8, 2 [(but see Zahn's note); cf. Jn. iii. 15 in γ. below]).   **γ.** used especially of the faith by which a man embraces Jesus, i. e. a conviction, full of joyful trust, that Jesus is the Messiah—the divinely appointed author of eternal salvation in the kingdom of God, conjoined with obedience to Christ: πιστ. τὸν υἱὸν τοῦ θεοῦ εἶναι Ἰησοῦν Χριστόν, Acts viii. 37 Rec.; ἐπιστεύθη (was believed in [cf. W. § 39, 1 a.; B. 175 (152)]) ἐν κόσμῳ, 1 Tim. iii. 16. the phrase πιστεύειν εἰς τὸν Ἰησοῦν, εἰς τ. υἱὸν τοῦ θεοῦ, etc., is very common; prop. to have a faith directed unto, believing or in faith to give one's self up to, Jesus, etc. (cf. W. 213 (200 sq.); [B. 174 (151)]): Mt. xviii. 6; Mk. ix. 42 [R G L Tr txt.]; Jn. ii. 11; iii. 15 R G, 16, 18, 36; vi. 29, 35, 40, 47 [R G L]; vii. 5, [38], 39, 48; viii. 30; ix. 35 sq.; x. 42; xi. 25 sq. 45, 48; xii. 11, 37, 42, 44, [46]; xiv. 1, 12; xvi. 9; xvii. 20; Acts x. 43; xix. 4; Ro. x. 14; Gal. ii. 16; Phil. i. 29; 1 Jn. v. 10; 1 Pet. i. 8; εἰς τὸ φῶς, Jn. xii. 36; εἰς τὸ ὄνομα αὐτοῦ, Jn. i. 12; ii. 23; iii. 18; 1 Jn. v. 13; τῷ ὀνόμ. αὐτοῦ, to commit one's self trustfully to the name (see ὄνομα, 2 p. 448ᵃ), 1 Jn. iii. 23; ἐπ' αὐτόν, ἐπὶ τὸν κύριον, to have a faith directed towards, etc. (see ἐπί, C. I. 2 g. a. p. 235ᵇ [cf. W. and B. u. s., also B. § 147, 25]): Mt. xxvii. 42 T Tr txt. WH; Jn. iii. 15 L txt.; Acts ix. 42; xi. 17; xvi. 31; xxii. 19, [(cf. Sap. xii. 2)]; ἐπ' αὐτῷ, to build one's faith on, to place one's faith upon, [see ἐπί, B. 2 a. γ. p. 233ᵃ; B. u. s.]: Ro. ix. 33; x. 11; 1 Tim. i. 16; 1 Pet. ii. 6; ἐν αὐτῷ, to put faith in him, Jn. iii. 15 [L mrg.; cf. T Tr WH also (who prob. connect ἐν αὐτῷ with the foll. ἔχῃ; cf. Westcott, Com. ad loc., Meyer, al.)] (cf. Jer. xii. 6; Ps. lxxvii. (lxxviii.) 22, where πιστ. ἔν τινι means to put confidence in one, to trust one; [cf. Mk. i. 15 above, β. fin.]); ἐν τούτῳ πιστεύομεν, on this rests our faith [A. V. by this we believe], Jn. xvi. 30; with the simple dative, τῷ κυρίῳ, to (yield faith to) believe [cf. B. 173 (151)]: Mt. xxvii. 42 R G L Tr mrg.; Acts v. 14; xviii. 8; supply τούτῳ before οὗ in Ro. x. 14; to trust in Christ [God], 2 Tim. i. 12; διά τινος, through one's agency to be brought to faith, Jn. i. 7; 1 Co. iii. 5; διὰ Ἰησοῦ εἰς θεόν, 1 Pet. i. 21 R G Tr mrg.; διὰ τῆς χάριτος, Acts xviii. 27; διὰ τοῦ λόγου αὐτῶν εἰς ἐμέ, Jn. xvii. 20; διά τι, Jn. iv. 39, [41], 42; xiv. 11. πιστεύω foll. by ὅτι with a sentence in which either the nature and dignity of Christ or his blessings are set forth: Jn. vi. 69; viii. 24; x. 38ᶜ R G; xi. 27, [42]; xiii. 19; [xiv. 10]; xvi. 27, 30; xvii. 8, 21; 1 Jn. v. 1, 5; Ro. vi. 8; 1 Th. iv. 14; μοὶ ὅτι, Jn. xiv. 11; τί, Jn. xi. 26; πιστεύω σωθῆναι, Acts xv. 11; the simple πιστεύειν is used emphatically, of those who acknowledge Jesus as the saviour and devote themselves to him: Mk. xv. 32 [here L adds αὐτῷ]; Lk. viii. 12 sq.; xxii. 67; Jn. i. 50 (51); iii. 18; iv. 42, 48, 53; v. 44; vi. 36, 64; ix. 38; x. 25 sq.; xii. 39, 47 Rec.; xvi. 30; xx. 31; Acts v. 14; [xiii. 39]; xv. 5; xviii. 8; [xxi. 25]; Ro. i. 16; iii. 22; iv. 11; x. 4; xv. 13; 2 Co. iv. 13; Eph. i. 13, [19]; 2 Th. i. 10; Heb. iv. 3; with ἐξ ὅλης καρδίας added, Acts viii. 37 Rec.; w. a dat. of instr. καρδίᾳ, Ro. x. 10; ptcp. pres. οἱ πιστεύοντες, as subst.: Acts ii. 44; Ro. iii. 22; 1 Co. i. 21; Gal. iii. 22; [Eph. i. 19]; 1 Th. i. 7; ii. 10, 13; 2 Th. i. 10 Rec.; 1 Pet. ii. 7; i. q. who are on the point of believing, 1 Co. xiv. 22, cf. 24 sq.; aor. ἐπίστευσα (marking entrance into a state; see βασιλεύω, fin.), I became a believer, a Christian, [A. V. believed]: Acts iv. 4; viii. 13; xiii. 12, 48; xiv. 1; xv. 7; xvii. 12, 34; Ro. xiii. 11; 1 Co. iii. 5; xv. 2, 11; with the addition of ἐπὶ τὸν κύριον (see above), Acts ix. 42; ptcp. πιστεύσας, Acts xi. 21; xix. 2; ὁ πιστεύσας, Mk. xvi. 16; plur., ibid. 17; Acts iv. 32; οἱ πεπιστευκότες, they that have believed (have become believers): Acts xix. 18; xxi. 20; [on (John's use of) the tenses of πιστεύω see Westcott on 1 Jn. iii. 23]. It must be borne in mind, that in Paul's conception of τὸ πιστεύειν.εἰς Χριστόν, the prominent element is the grace of God towards sinners as manifested and pledged (and to be laid hold of by faith) in Jesus, particularly in his death and resurrection, as appears esp. in Ro. iii. 25; iv. 24; x. 9; 1 Th. iv. 14; but in John's conception, it is the metaphysical relationship of Christ with God and close ethical intimacy with him, as well as the true 'life' to be derived from Christ as its source; cf. Rückert, Das Abendmahl, p. 251. Moreover, πιστεύειν is used by John of various degrees of faith, from its first beginnings, its incipient stirring within the soul, up to the fullest assurance, Jn. ii. 23 (cf. 24); viii. 31; of a faith which does not yet recognize Jesus as the Messiah, but as a prophet very like the Messiah, Jn. vii. 31; and to signify that one's faith is preserved, strengthened, increased, raised to the level which it ought to reach, xi. 15; xiii. 19; xiv. 29; xix. 35; xx. 31; 1 Jn. v. 13ᵇ Rec.; [cf. reff. s. v. πίστις, fin.]. πιστεύειν is applied also to the faith by which one is persuaded that Jesus was raised from the dead, inasmuch as by that fact God declared him to be his Son and the Messiah: Jn. xx. 8, 25, 29; ἐν τῇ καρδίᾳ πιστ. ὅτι ὁ θεὸς αὐτὸν ἤγειρεν ἐκ νεκρῶν, Ro. x. 9 [cf. B. § 133, 19]. Since acc. to the conception of Christian faith Christ alone is the author of salvation, ὁ πιστεύων repudiates all the various things which aside from Christ are commended as means

of salvation (such e. g. as abstinence from flesh and wine), and understands that all things are lawful to him which do not lead him away from Christ; hence πιστεύει (τις) φαγεῖν πάντα, hath faith to eat all things or so that he eats all things, Ro. xiv. 2; cf. Rückert ad loc. [W. § 44, 3 b.; per contra B. 273 sq. (235)]. **δ.** πιστεύειν used in ref. to God has various senses: **aa.** it denotes the mere acknowledgment of his existence: ὅτι ὁ θεὸς εἷς ἐστιν, Jas. ii. 19; acknowledgment joined to appropriate trust, absol. Jude 5; εἰς θεόν, Jn. xii. 44; xiv. 1; i. q. to believe and embrace what God has made known either through Christ or concerning Christ: τῷ θεῷ, Jn. v. 24; Acts xvi. 34; Tit. iii. 8; 1 Jn. v. 10; ἐπὶ τὸν θεόν, Ro. iv. 5; τὴν ἀγάπην, ἣν ἔχει ὁ θεός, 1 Jn. iv. 16; εἰς τὴν μαρτυρίαν, ἣν κτλ., 1 Jn. v. 10. **ββ.** to trust: τῷ θεῷ, God promising a thing, Ro. iv. 3, 17 (on which see κατέναντι); Gal. iii. 6; [Jas. ii. 23]; absol. Ro. iv. 18; foll. by ὅτι, Acts xxvii. 25. **ε.** πιστ. is used in an ethical sense, of confidence in the goodness of men: ἡ ἀγάπη πιστεύει πάντα, 1 Co. xiii. 7. τὸ πιστεύειν is opp. to ἰδεῖν, Jn. xx. 29; to ὁρᾶν, ibid. and 1 Pet. i. 8, (Theoph. ad Autol. 1, 7 fin.), cf. 2 Co. v. 7; to διακρίνεσθαι, Ro. iv. 19 sq.; xiv. 1, 23, cf. Jas. i. 6; to ὁμολογεῖν, Ro. x. 9. **2.** transitively, τινί τι, to intrust a thing to one, i. e. to his fidelity: Lk. xvi. 11; ἑαυτόν τινι, Jn. ii. 24; pass. πιστεύομαί τι, to be intrusted with a thing: Ro. iii. 2; 1 Co. ix. 17; Gal. ii. 7; 1 Th. ii. 4; 1 Tim. i. 11; Tit. i. 3, (Ignat. ad Philad. 9; exx. fr. prof. auth. are given in W. § 39, 1 a.). On the grammat. constr. of the word cf. B. § 133, 4 [and the summaries in Ellicott on 1 Tim. i. 16; Vaughan on Ro. iv. 5; Cremer s. v.]. It does not occur in the Rev., nor in Philem., 2 Pet., 2 and 3 Jn. [Cf. the reff. s. v. πίστις, fin.]*

πιστικός, -ή, -όν, (πιστός), pertaining to belief; **a.** having the power of persuading, skilful in producing belief: Plat. Gorg. p. 455 a. **b.** trusty, faithful, that can be relied on: γυνὴ πιστ. καὶ οἰκουρὸς καὶ πειθομένη τῷ ἀνδρί, Artem. oneir. 2, 32; often so in Cedrenus [also (of persons) in Epiph., Jn. Mosch., Sophron.; cf. Soph. Lex. s. v.]; of commodities i. q. δόκιμος, genuine, pure, unadulterated: so νάρδος πιστική [but A. V. spike- (i. e. spiked) nard, after the nardi spicati of the Vulg. (in Mk.)], Mk. xiv. 3; Jn. xii. 3, (for nard was often adulterated; see Plin. h. n. 12, 26; Diosc. de mater. med. 1, 6 and 7); hence metaph. τὸ πιστικὸν τῆς καινῆς διαθήκης κρᾶμα, Euseb. demonstr. evang. 9, 8 [p. 439 d.]. Cf. the full discussion of this word in Fritzsche on Mk. p. 596 sqq.; Lücke on Jn. xii. 3 p. 494 sqq.; W. 97 (92) sq.; [esp. Dr. Jas. Morison on Mk. l. c.].*   4101

πίστις, -εως, ἡ, (πείθω [q. v.]), fr. [Hes., Theogn., Pind.], Aeschyl., Hdt. down; Sept. for אֱמוּנָה, several times for אֱמֶת and אֲמָנָה; faith; i. e. **1.** conviction of the truth of anything, belief, (Plat., Polyb., Joseph., Plut.; θαυμάσια καὶ μείζω πίστεως, Diod. 1, 86); in the N. T. of a conviction or belief respecting man's relationship to God and divine things, generally with the included idea of trust and holy fervor born of faith and conjoined with it: Heb. xi. 1 (where πίστις is called ἐλπιζομένων ὑπόστασις,   4102 πραγμάτων ἔλεγχος οὐ βλεπομένων); opp. to εἶδος, 2 Co. v. 7; joined with ἀγάπη and ἐλπίς, 1 Co. xiii. 13.   **a.** when it relates to God, πίστις is *the conviction that God exists and is the creator and ruler of all things, the provider and bestower of eternal salvation through Christ*: Heb. xi. 6; xii. 2; xiii. 7; πίστις ἐπὶ θεόν, Heb. vi. 1; ἡ πίστις ὑμῶν ἡ πρὸς τὸν θεόν, by which ye turned to God, 1 Th. i. 8; τὴν π. ὑμῶν κ. ἐλπίδα εἰς θεόν, directed unto God, 1 Pet. i. 21; with a gen. of the object [faith *in*] (τῶν θεῶν, Eur. Med. 414; τοῦ θεοῦ, Joseph. c. Ap. 2, 16, 5; cf. *Grimm*, Exgt. Hdbch. on Sap. vi. 17 sq. p. 132; [cf. Meyer on Ro. iii. 22; also Mey., Ellic., Bp. Lghtft. on Col. as below; W. 186 (175)]): ἡ π. τῆς ἐνεργείας τοῦ θεοῦ τοῦ ἐγείραντος αὐτὸν (Christ) ἐκ τῶν νεκρῶν, Col. ii. 12; διὰ πίστεως, by the help of faith, Heb. xi. 33, 39; κατὰ πίστιν, i. q. πιστεύοντες, Heb. xi. 13; πίστει, dat. of means or of mode *by faith* or *by believing, prompted, actuated, by faith*, Heb. xi. 3 sq. 7-9, 17, 20-24, 27-29, 31; dat. of cause, *because of faith*, Heb. xi. 5, 11, 30.   **b.** in reference to Christ, it denotes *a strong and welcome conviction* or *belief that Jesus is the Messiah, through whom we obtain eternal salvation in the kingdom of God* (on this see more at length in πιστεύω, 1 b. γ.);   **a.** univ.: w. gen. of the object (see above, in a.), Ἰησοῦ Χριστοῦ, Ro. iii. 22; Gal. ii. 16; iii. 22; Eph. iii. 12; Ἰησοῦ, Rev. xiv. 12; Χριστοῦ, Phil. iii. 9; τοῦ υἱοῦ τοῦ θεοῦ, Gal. ii. 20; τοῦ κυρίου ἡμῶν Ἰησοῦ Χριστοῦ, Jas. ii. 1; μοῦ (i. e. in Christ), Rev. ii. 13, (certainly we must reject the interpretation, *faith in God of which Jesus Christ is the author*, advocated by *Van Hengel*, Ep. ad Rom. i. p. 314 sqq., and *H. P. Berlage*, Disquisitio de formulae Paulinae πίστις Ἰησοῦ Χριστοῦ significatione. Lugd. Bat. 1856); τοῦ εὐαγγελίου, Phil. i. 27; ἀληθείας, 2 Th. ii. 13. with Prepositions: εἰς (toward [cf. εἰς, B. II. 2 a.]) τὸν κύριον ἡμῶν Ἰησοῦν, Acts xx. 21; εἰς Χριστόν, Acts xxiv. 24; xxvi. 18; ἡ εἰς Χριστὸν πίστιν ὑμῶν, Col. ii. 5; [πίστιν ἔχειν εἰς ἐμέ, Mk. ix. 42 Tr mrg.]; πρὸς τὸν κύρ. Philem. 5 [L Tr WH εἰς] ([see πρός, I. 1 c.; cf. Bp. Lghtft. ad loc.]; unless here we prefer to render πίστιν *fidelity* [see 2, below]; cf. Meyer ad loc. and W. § 50, 2); π. ἐν Χρ. Ἰησοῦ, reposed in Christ Jesus, 1 Tim. iii. 13; 2 Tim. iii. 15; ἡ π. ὑμῶν ἐν Χρ. Ἰησ. Col. i. 4; ἡ κατά τινα (see κατά, II. 1 e.) πίστις ἐν τῷ κυρίῳ, Eph. i. 15; ἐν τῷ αἵματι αὐτοῦ, Ro. iii. 25 [yet cf. Meyer].   πίστις [cf. W. 120 (114)] and ἡ πίστις simply: Lk. xviii. 8; Acts xiii. 8; xiv. 22, 27; xv. 9; xvii. 31; Ro. [iii. 27 (on which see νόμος, 3)], 31; iv. 14; v. 2 [L Tr WH br. τῇ πίστει]; ix. 32; x. 8, 17; xii. 3, 6; 1 Co. [xii. 9 (here of a charism.)]; xvi. 13; 2 Co. iv. 13; [viii. 7]; x. 15; Gal. iii. 14, 23, 25 sq.; v. 5; vi. 10; Eph. ii. 8; iii. 17; iv. 5; vi. 16; 2 Th. i. 4; 1 Tim. i. 2, 4 (on the latter pass. see οἰκονομία, 19; ii. 7 (on which see ἀλήθεια, I. 2 c.); iii. 9; iv. 1, 6; v. 8; vi. 10, 12, 21; 2 Tim. i. 5; ii. 18; iii. 8, 10; iv. 7; Tit. i. 1, 4, 13; ii. 2; iii. 15; Jas. ii. 5; 1 Pet. i. 5; 2 Pet. i. 1, 5. with a gen. of the subject: Lk. xxii. 32; Ro. i. 8, 12; 1 Co. ii. 5; xv. 14, 17; 2 Co. i. 24; Phil. i. 25; ii. 17; 1 Th. iii. 2, 5-7, 10; 2 Th. i. 3; iii. 2; Philem. 6; Jas. i. 3; 1 Pet. i. 7, 9 [here WH om. gen.]; 1 Jn. v. 4;

Rev. xiii. 10; πλήρης πίστεως κ. πνεύματος, Acts vi. 5; πνεύματος κ. πίστεως, Acts xi. 24; πίστεως κ. δυνάμεως, Acts vi. 8 Rec.; τῇ πίστει ἑστηκέναι, Ro. xi. 20; 2 Co. i. 24; ἐν τῇ πίστει στήκειν, 1 Co. xvi. 13; εἶναι, 2 Co. xiii. 5; μένειν, 1 Tim. ii. 15; ἐμμένειν τῇ π. Acts xiv. 22; ἐπιμένειν, Col. i. 23; στερεὸς τῇ π. 1 Pet. v. 9; στερεοῦμαι τῇ π. Acts xvi. 5; βεβαιοῦμαι ἐν [L T Tr WH om. ἐν] τῇ π. Col. ii. 7.   Since faith is a power that seizes upon the soul, one who yields himself to it is said ὑπακούειν τῇ πίστει, Acts vi. 7; hence ὑπακοὴ τῆς πίστεως, obedience rendered to faith [W. 186 (175)], Ro. i. 5; xvi. 26; ὁ ἐκ πίστεως sc. ὤν, depending on faith, i. q. ὁ πιστεύων [see ἐκ, II. 7], Ro. iii. 26; plur., Gal. iii. 7, 9; ὁ ἐκ πίστεως Ἀβραάμ, he who has the same faith as Abraham, Ro. iv. 16; ἐκ πίστεως εἶναι, to be related, akin to, faith [cf. ἐκ, u. s.], Gal. iii. 12.   δίκαιος ἐκ πίστεως, Ro. i. 17; Gal. iii. 11; δικαιοσύνη ἡ ἐκ πίστ. Ro. ix. 30; ἡ ἐκ πίστ. δικ. Ro. x. 6; δικαιοσ. ἐκ πίστεως εἰς πίστιν, springing *from faith* (and availing) *to* (arouse) *faith* (in those who as yet have it not), Ro. i. 17; δικαιοσύνη ἡ διὰ πίστεως Χριστοῦ, . . . ἡ ἐκ θεοῦ δικ. ἐπὶ τῇ πίστει, Phil. iii. 9; pass. δικαιοῦσθαι πίστει, Ro. iii. 28; δικαιοῦν τινα διὰ πίστεως Χριστοῦ, Gal. ii. 16; διὰ τ. πίστεως, Ro. iii. 30; δικ. τινα ἐκ πίστεως, ibid.; Gal. iii. 8; pass., Ro. v. 1; Gal. iii. 24; εὐαγγελίζομαι τὴν πίστιν, to proclaim the glad tidings of faith in Christ, Gal. i. 23; ἀκοὴ πίστεως, instruction concerning the necessity of faith [see ἀκοή, 3 a.], Gal. iii. 2, 5; ἡ πίστις is joined with ἡ ἀγάπη: 1 Th. iii. 6; v. 8; 1 Tim. i. 14; ii. 15; iv. 12; vi. 11; 2 Tim. ii. 22; with a subj. gen. Rev. ii. 19; πίστις δι᾽ ἀγάπης ἐνεργουμένη, Gal. v. 6; ἀγάπη μετὰ πίστεως, Eph. vi. 23; ἀγάπη ἐκ πίστεως ἀνυποκρίτου, 1 Tim. i. 5; πίστις καὶ ἀγάπη ἡ ἐν Χριστῷ Ἰησοῦ, 2 Tim. i. 13; φιλεῖν τινα ἐν πίστει, Tit. iii. 15 (where see De Wette); ἔργον πίστεως (cf. ἔργον, 3 p. 248ᵇ near bot.), 1 Th. i. 3; 2 Th. i. 11.   **β.** in an ethical sense, *persuasion* or *conviction* (which springs from faith in Christ as the sole author of salvation; cf. πιστεύω, 1 b. γ. fin.) *concerning things lawful for a Christian*: Ro. xiv. 1, 23; πίστιν ἔχειν, ibid. 22.   **c.** univ. *the religious belief of Christians*:   **a.** subjectively: Eph. iv. 13, where cf. Meyer; in the sense of a mere acknowledgment of divine things and of the claims of Christianity, Jas. ii. 14, 17 sq. 20, 22, 24, 26.   **β.** objectively, *the substance of Christian faith* or *what is believed* by Christians: ἡ παραδοθεῖσα π. Jude 3; ἡ ἁγιωτάτη ὑμῶν πίστις, ib. 20.   There are some who think this meaning of the word is to be recognized also in 1 Tim. i. 4, 19; ii. 7; iii. 9; iv. 1, 6; v. 8; vi. 10, 21, (cf. *Pfleiderer*, Paulinismus p. 468 [Eng. trans. ii. p. 200]); but Weiss (Bibl. Theol. d. N. T. § 107 a. note) correctly objects, "πίστις is rather the form in which the truth (as the substance of right doctrine) is subjectively appropriated"; [cf. Meyer on Ro. i. 5 (and Prof. Dwight's additional note); Ellicott on Gal. i. 23; Bp. Lghtft. on Gal. p. 157].   **d.** with the predominant idea of *trust* (or confidence) whether *in God* or *in Christ, springing from faith in the same*: Mt. viii. 10; xv. 28; Lk. vii. 9, 50; xvii. 5; Heb. ix. 28 Lchm. ed. ster.; x. 22; Jas.

i. 6; with a gen. of the subject: Mt. ix. 2, 22, 29; xv. 28; Mk. ii. 5; v. 34; x. 52; [Lk. v. 20]; viii. 25, 48; xvii. 19; xviii. 42; w. a gen. of the object in which trust is placed: τοῦ ὀνόματος αὐτοῦ, Acts iii. 16; πίστιν ἔχειν, [Mt. xvii. 20]; xxi. 21; Mk. iv. 40; Lk. xvii. 6; πᾶσαν τὴν πίστιν, ('all the faith' that can be thought of), 1 Co. xiii. 2; ἔχειν πίστιν θεοῦ, to trust in God, Mk. xi. 22; ἔχειν πίστιν τοῦ σωθῆναι, to be healed (see Fritzsche on Mt. p. 843 sq.; [cf. W. § 44, 4 a.; B. 268 (230)]), Acts xiv. 9; ἡ δι' αὐτοῦ π., awakened through him, Acts iii. 16; εὐχὴ τῆς πίστεως, that proceeds from faith, Jas. v. 15; of trust in the promises of God, Ro. iv. 9, 16, 19 sq.; Heb. iv. 2; vi. 12; x. 38 sq.; w. a gen. of the subject, Ro. iv. 5, 12; πίστις ἐπὶ θεόν, faith which relies on God who grants the forgiveness of sins to the penitent [see ἐπί, C. I. 2 g. a.], Heb. vi. 1; δικαιοσύνη τῆς πίστεως [cf. W. 186 (175)], Ro. iv. 11, 13; ἡ κατὰ πίστιν δικαιοσύνη, Heb. xi. 7. **2.** *fidelity, faithfulness*, i. e. *the character of one who can be relied on*: Mt. xxiii. 23; Gal. v. 22; Pʰilem. 5 (? see above in b. a.); Tit. ii. 10. of one who keeps his promises: ἡ πίστις τοῦ θεοῦ, subj. gen., Ro. iii. 3. objectively, *plighted faith* (often so in Attic writ. fr. Aeschyl. down): ἀθετεῖν (see ἀθετέω, a.) τὴν πίστιν, 1 Tim. v. 12. Cf. especially *Koolhaas*, Diss. philol. I. et II. de vario usu et constructione vocum πίστις, πιστός et πιστεύειν in N. T. (Traj. ad Rhen. 1733, 4to.); *Dav. Schulz*, Was heisst Glauben, etc. (Leipz. 1830), p. 62 sqq.; *Rückert*, Com. üb. d. Röm., 2d ed., i. p. 51 sqq.; *Lutz*, Bibl. Dogmatik, p. 312 sqq.; *Huther*, Ueber ζωή u. πιστεύειν im N. T., in the Jahrbb. f. deutsch. Theol. for 1872, pp. 1–33; [Bp. *Lghtft.* Com. on Gal. p. 154 sqq.]. On P a u l's conception of πίστις, cf. *Lipsius*, Paulin. Rechtfertigungslehre, p. 94 sqq.; *Weiss*, Bibl. Theol. d. N. T., § 82 c. d. (cf. the index s. v. Glaube); *Pfleiderer*, Paulinismus, p. 162 sqq. [Eng. trans. i. p. 161 sqq.; *Schnedermann*, De fidei notione ethica Paulina. (Lips. 1880)]. On the idea of faith in the Ep. to the H e b r e w s see *Riehm*, Lehrbegr. des Hebr.-Br. p. 700 sqq.; *Weiss*, as above § 125 b. c. On J o h n's conception, see *Reuss*, die Johann. Theol. § 10 in the Beiträge zu d. theol. Wissensch. i. p. 56 sqq. [cf. his Histoire de la Théol. Chrétienne, etc., 3me éd., ii. p. 508 sqq. (Eng. trans. ii. 455 sqq.)]; *Weiss*, as above § 149, and the same author's Johann. Lehrbegriff, p. 18 sqq.*

4103 πιστός, -ή, -όν, (πείθω [q. v.]), [fr. Hom. down], Sept. mostly for נֶאֱמָן; **1.** *trusty, faithful*; of p e r s o n s who show themselves faithful in the transaction of business, the execution of commands, or the discharge of official duties: δοῦλος, Mt. xxiv. 45; xxv. 21, 23; οἰκονόμος, Lk. xii. 42; 1 Co. iv. 2; διάκονος, Eph. vi. 21; Col. i. 7; iv. 7; ἀρχιερεύς, Heb. ii. 17; iii. 2; of G o d, abiding by his promises, 1 Co. i. 9; x. 13; 2 Co. i. 18; 1 Th. v. 24; 2 Th. iii. 3; Heb. x. 23; xi. 11; 2 Tim. ii. 13; 1 Jn. i. 9; 1 Pet. iv. 19; add, 1 Co. iv. 17; Col. iv. 9; 1 Tim. i. 12; Heb. iii. 5; 1 Pet. v. 12; πιστὸς ἔν τινι, in a thing, Lk. xvi. 10–12; xix. 17; 1 Tim. iii. 11; ἐπί τι, Mt. xxv. 23; ἄχρι θανάτου, Rev. ii. 10. *one who kept his plighted faith*, Rev. ii. 13; *worthy of trust; that can be relied on*: 1 Co. vii. 25; 2 Tim. ii. 2; Christ is called

μάρτυς ὁ πιστός, Rev. i. 5; with καὶ ἀληθινός added, Rev. iii. 14; [cf. xix. 11]. of t h i n g s, *that can be relied on*: ὁ λόγος, 1 Tim. iii. 1; 2 Tim. ii. 11; Tit. i. 9; [iii. 8; οὗτοι οἱ λόγοι, Rev. xxi. 5; xxii. 6]; with πάσης ἀποδοχῆς ἄξιος added, 1 Tim. i. 15; iv. 9; τὰ ὅσια Δαυίδ τὰ πιστά (see ὅσιος, fin.), Acts xiii. 34. **2.** *easily persuaded*; *believing, confiding, trusting*, (Theogn., Aeschyl., Soph., Plat., al.); in the N. T. one who trusts in God's promises, Gal. iii. 9; is convinced that Jesus has been raised from the dead, opp. to ἄπιστος, Jn. xx. 27; *one who has become convinced that Jesus is the Messiah and the author of salvation* (opp. to ἄπιστος, see πιστεύω, 1 b. γ. and πίστις, 1 b.), [*a believer*]: Acts xvi. 1; 2 Co. vi. 15; 1 Tim. v. 16; with the addition of τῷ κυρίῳ, dat. of the pers. in whom faith or trust is reposed, Acts xvi. 15; plur. in Col. i. 2 [where cf. Bp. Lghtft.]; 1 Tim. iv. 10; vi. 2; Tit. i. 6; Rev. xvii. 14; οἱ πιστοί, substantively [see Bp. Lghtft. on Gal. p. 157], Acts x. 45; 1 Tim. iv. 3, 12; with ἐν Χριστῷ Ἰησοῦ added [cf. B. 174 (152)], Eph. i. 1; εἰς θεὸν κτλ. 1 Pet. i. 21 L T Tr txt. WH; πιστὸν ποιεῖν τι, to do something harmonizing with (Christian) faith, [R. V. *a faithful work*], 3 Jn. 5.*

πιστόω, -ῶ· 1 aor. pass. ἐπιστώθην; (πιστός); **1.** **4104** *to make faithful, render trustworthy*: τὸ ῥῆμα, 1 K. i. 36; τινὰ ὅρκοις, Thuc. 4, 88; univ. *to make firm, establish*, 1 Chr. xvii. 14. **2.** Pass. (Sept. in various senses for נֶאֱמָן) and mid. *to be firmly persuaded*; *to be assured of*: τί (Opp. cyn. 3, 355. 417; Lcian. philops. 5), 2 Tim. iii. 14; Hesych. ἐπιστώθη· ἐπείσθη, ἐπληροφορήθη. (In various other senses in prof. auth. fr. Hom. down.)*

πλανάω, -ῶ; fut. πλανήσω; 1 aor. ἐπλάνησα; Pass., pres. **4105** πλανῶμαι; pf. πεπλάνημαι; 1 aor. ἐπλανήθην; (πλάνη); fr. Aeschyl. and Hdt. down; Sept. for הִתְעָה; **1.** *to cause to stray, to lead astray, lead aside from the right way;* **a.** prop.; in pass., Sept. chiefly for תָּעָה, *to go astray, wander, roam about*, (first so in Hom. Il. 23, 321): Mt. xviii. 12 sq.; 1 Pet. ii. 25 (fr. Is. liii. 6, cf. Ex. xxiii. 4; Ps. cxviii. (cxix.) 176); Heb. xi. 38. **b.** metaph. to lead away from the truth, *to lead into error, to deceive*: τινά, Mt. xxiv. 4, 5, 11, 24; Mk. xiii. 5, 6; Jn. vii. 12; 1 Jn. ii. 26; iii. 7; 2 Tim. iii. 13ᵃ; Rev. ii. 20 G L T Tr WH; xii. 9; xiii. 14; xix. 20; xx. 3, 8, 10; ἑαυτόν, 1 Jn. i. 8; pass. *to be led into error*, [R.V. *be led astray*]: Lk. xxi. 8; Jn. vii. 47; Rev. ii. 20 Rec.; *to err*, Mt. xxii. 29; Mk. xii. 24, 27; μὴ πλανᾶσθε, 1 Co. vi. 9; xv. 33; Gal. vi. 7; Jas. i. 16; esp. through ignorance *to be led aside from the path of virtue, to go astray, sin*: Tit. iii. 3; Heb. v. 2; τῇ καρδίᾳ, Heb. iii. 10; ἀπὸ τῆς ἀληθείας, Jas. v. 19; *to wander or fall away from the true faith*, of heretics, 2 Tim. iii. 13ᵇ; 2 Pet. ii. 15; *to be led away into error and sin*, Rev. xviii. 23. [COMP.: ἀπο-πλανάω.]*

πλάνη, -ης, ἡ, *a wandering, a straying about*, whereby **4106** one, led astray from the right way, roams hither and thither (Aeschyl., [Hdt.], Eur., Plat., Dem., al.). In the N. T. metaph. mental straying, i. e. *error, wrong opinion* relative to morals or religion: Eph. iv. 14; 1 Th. ii. 3; 2 Th. ii. 11; 2 Pet. ii. 18; iii. 17; 1 Jn. iv. 6; Jude 11 (on which [cf. W. 189 (177) and] see ἐκχέω, b. fin.); *er-*

ror which shows itself in action, a wrong mode of acting:
Ro. i. 27; πλάνη ὁδοῦ τινος, [R. V. error of one's way
i. e.] the wrong manner of life which one follows, Jas. v.
20 (πλάνη ζωῆς, Sap. i. 12); as sometimes the Lat. error,
i. q. that which leads into error, deceit, fraud: Mt. xxvii.
64.*

(4106α); ∿64.*

see 4107 [πλάνης, -ητος, ὁ, see πλανήτης.]

4107 ————πλανήτης, -ου, ὁ, (πλανάω), a wanderer: ἀστέρες πλανῆται, wandering stars (Aristot., Plut., al.), Jude 13 [where
WH mrg. ἀστ. πλάνητες (Xen. mem. 4, 7, 5)]; see ἀστήρ,
fin.*

4108 πλάνος, -ον, wandering, roving; trans. and trop. misleading, leading into error: πνεύματα πλάνα, 1 Tim. iv. 1
(πλάνοι ἄνθρωποι, Joseph. b. j. 2, 13, 4). ὁ πλάνος
substantively (Cic. al. planus), as we say, a vagabond,
'tramp,' impostor, (Diod., Athen., al.); hence univ. a
corrupter, deceiver, (Vulg. seductor): Mt. xxvii. 63; 2 Co.
vi. 8; 2 Jn. 7. [Cf. ὁ κοσμοπλάνος, 'Teaching' etc. 16,
4.]*

4109 πλάξ, -ακός, ἡ, [(akin to πλάτος, etc.; Fick iv. 161)], a
flat thing, broad tablet, plane, level surface (as of the sea),
(cf. our plate), (Pind., Tragg., al.; Sept. for לוּחַ): αἱ
πλάκες τῆς διαθήκης (see διαθήκη, 2 p. 136ᵇ), Heb. ix. 4;
οὐκ ἐν πλαξὶ λιθίναις (tables of stone, such as those on
which the law of Moses was written), ἀλλ' ἐν πλαξὶ καρδίας σαρκίναις, 2 Co. iii. 3.*

4110 πλάσμα, -τος, τό, (πλάσσω), what has been moulded or
formed, as from wax (Plat. Theaet. p. 197 d. and p. 200 b.);
the thing formed by a potter, earthen vessel, (Vulg. figmen-
tum): Ro. ix. 20 (with πηλοῦ added, Arstph. av. 686).*

4111 πλάσσω: 1 aor. ptcp. πλάσας; 1 aor. pass. ἐπλάσθην;
[(perh. akin to πλατύς; Curtius § 367 b)]; fr. Hes. down;
Sept. chiefly for יָצַר; to form, mould, (prop. something
from clay, wax, etc.): used of a potter, Ro. ix. 20; of
God as Creator (Gen. ii. 7 sq. 19 etc.), pass. 1 Tim. ii. 13.*

4112 πλαστός, -ή, -όν, (πλάσσω) 1. prop. moulded,
formed, as from clay, wax, stone, (Hes., Plat., Aristot.,
Plut., al.). 2. trop. feigned: 2 Pet. ii. 3 ([Hdt. 1,
68], Eur., Xen., Lcian., al.).*

4113 πλατεῖα, -ας, ἡ, (fem. of the adj. πλατύς, sc. ὁδός [cf.
W. 590 (549)]), a broad way, a street: Mt. vi. 5; xii.
19; Lk. x. 10; xiii. 26; xiv. 21; Acts v. 15; Rev. xi.
8; xxi. 21; xxii. 2. (Eur., Plat., al.; in Sept. chiefly for
רְחֹב.) *

4114 πλάτος, -ους, τό, [(cf. πλάξ), fr. Hdt. down], breadth:
Eph. iii. 18 (on which see μῆκος); Rev. xxi. 16; carrying with it the suggestion of great extent, τῆς γῆς, opp.
to the ends or corners of the earth, Rev. xx. 9; (for
מֶרְחָב, Hab. i. 6).*

4115 πλατύνω; Pass., pf. 3 pers. sing. πεπλάτυνται (see μιαίνω); 1 aor. ἐπλατύνθην; (πλατύς); to make broad, to
enlarge: τί, Mt. xxiii. 5; ἡ καρδία ἡμῶν πεπλάτυνται, our
heart expands itself sc. to receive you into it, i. e. to
welcome and embrace you in love, 2 Co. vi. 11 (πλατύνειν
τὴν καρδίαν for הִרְחִיב לֵב, to open the heart sc. to instruction, Ps. cxviii. (cxix.) 32 [cf. W. 30]); πλατύνθητε
καὶ ὑμεῖς, be ye also enlarged in heart, viz. to receive me
therein, ibid. 13. (Xen., Plut., Anthol., al.) *

πλατύς, -εῖα, -ύ, [cf. Lat. planus, latus; Curtius § 367 b;   4116
Vaniček p. 552], fr. Hom. down, Sept. several times for
רָחָב, broad: Mt. vii. 13.*

πλέγμα, -τος, τό, (πλέκω), what is woven, plaited, or twisted   4117
together; a web, plait, braid: used thus of a net, Xen.
Cyr. 1, 6, 28; of a basket, Eur., Plat.; πλέγμα βύβλινον,
in which the infant Moses was laid, Joseph. antt. 2, 9, 4;
by other writ. in other senses. braided hair (Vulg. crines
torti, ringlets, curls): 1 Tim. ii. 9 (cf. 1 Pet. iii. 3).*

πλεῖστος, -η, -ον, (superl. of πολύς), most: plur. Mt. xi.   4118
20; [ὄχλος πλεῖστος, a very great multitude, Mk. iv. 1 T
Tr WH]; ὁ πλεῖστος ὄχλος, the most part of the multitude, Mt. xxi. 8 (Thuc. 7, 78; Plat. rep. 3 p. 397 d.;
λαός, Hom. Il. 16, 377); τὸ πλεῖστον, adverbially, at the
most, 1 Co. xiv. 27.*

πλείων, -ονος, ὁ, ἡ, neut. πλεῖον [eighteen times] and (in   4119
Lk. iii. 13; [Jn. xxi. 15 L T Tr WH]; Acts xv. 28) πλέον
(cf. [WH. App. p. 151]; Matthiae i. p. 333; Krüger § 23,
7, 4; Kühner § 156, 3; Passow s. v. πολύς, B. 1; [L. and
ί. s. v. B.]), plur. πλείονες and contr. πλείους, acc. πλείονας and contr. πλείους (which forms are used indiscriminately in the N. T.), neut. πλείονα and (L T Tr WH in
Mt. xxvi. 53; L T in Lk. xxi. 3) contr. πλείω; (compar.
of πολύς); more, i. e.   1. greater in quantity: the
object with which the comparison is made being added
in the genitive, as πλείονας τῶν πρώτων, more in number
than the first, Mt. xxi. 36; πλεῖον (or πλείω) πάντων,
more than all, Mk. xii. 43; Lk. xxi. 3; πλείονα . . . τούτων,
more than these, Jn. vii. 31 [here L T Tr WH om. the
gen. (see below)]; πλείονα τῶν πρώτων, more than the
first, Rev. ii. 19; πλεῖον τούτων, more than these, Jn. xxi.
15; [πλείονα τιμὴν ἔχειν τοῦ οἴκου, Heb. iii. 3ᵇ (cf. W. 190
(178), 240 (225))]; περισσεύειν πλεῖον, more than, foll. by
a gen. [A. V. exceed], Mt. v. 20. more than (πλεῖον) ἤ,
Mt. xxvi. 53 R G [L πλείω (br. ἤ)]; Jn. iv. 1 [Tr mrg. om.
WH br. ἤ]   πλεῖον ἤ, more than, Lk. ix. 13; πλέον πλὴν
w. a gen. Acts xv. 28; πλεῖον παρά [τι or τινα (see παρά,
III. 2 b.)], Lk, iii. 13; [Heb. iii. 3ᵃ];   ἤ is omitted before
numerals without change of construction: ἐτῶν ἦν πλειόνων τεσσαράκοντα ὁ ἄνθρωπος, Acts iv. 22; οὐ πλείους εἰσὶν
μοι ἡμέραι δεκαδύο, Acts xxiv. 11 (here Rec. inserts ἤ);
ἡμέρας οὐ πλείους ὀκτὼ ἢ δέκα (Rec. πλείους ἢ δέκα), Acts
xxv. 6; add, Acts xxiii. 13, 21; as in Grk. writ. after
a neuter: πλείω [Lchm. ἤ in br.] δώδεκα λεγεῶνας, Mt. xxvi.
53 [T Tr WH (but T λεγιώνων)], (πλεῖν — Attic for πλεῖον
—ἑξακοσίους, Arstph. av. 1251; ἔτη γεγονὼς πλείω ἑβδομήκοντα, Plat. apol. Socr. p. 17 d.; see ἤ, 3 a.; on the omission of quam in Latin after plus and amplius, cf. Ramshorn, Lat. Gram. p. 491; [Roby, Lat. Gram. § 1273]).
the objects with which the comparison is made are not
added because easily supplied from the context: Jn.
iv. 41; [vii. 31 (see above)]; xv. 2; Heb. vii. 23; τὸ
πλεῖον, the more (viz. the greater debt mentioned), Lk.
vii. 43; πλεῖον, adverbially, more, i. e. more earnestly,
Lk. vii. 42; ἐπὶ πλεῖον, more widely, further, διανέμεσθαι,
Acts iv. 17; [cf. xx. 9 WH mrg. (see below)]; προκόπτειν,
2 Tim. iii. 9; ἐπὶ πλεῖον ἀσεβείας, 2 Tim. ii. 16; ἐπὶ πλεῖον,
longer (than proper), Acts xx. 9 [not WH mrg. (see

above)]; xxiv. 4; plural πλείονα, *more*, i. e. a larger reward, Mt. xx. 10 [but L Tr WH πλεῖον]; without comparison, used of an indefinite number, with a subst.: Acts ii. 40; xiii. 31; xviii. 20; xxi. 10; xxiv. 17; xxv. 14; xxvii. 20; xxviii. 23; neut. περὶ πλειόνων [A. V. *of many things*], Lk. xi. 53; with the article οἱ πλείονες (πλείους), *the more part, very many*: Acts xix. 32; xxvii. 12; 1 Co. ix. 19; x. 5; xv. 6; 2 Co. ii. 6; iv. 15; ix. 2; Phil. i. 14.   2. *greater in quality, superior, more excellent*: foll. by the gen. of comparison, Mt. vi. 25; xii. 41, 42; Mk. xii. 33 [here T WH Tr txt. περισσότερον]; Lk. xi. 31, 32; xii. 23; [πλείονα θυσίαν ... παρὰ Κάϊν, Heb. xi. 4 (see παρά, u. s.). From Hom. down.]*

4120   **πλέκω**: 1 aor. ptcp. πλέξαντες; [(cf. Curtius § 103; Vanicek p. 519)]; fr. Hom. down; *to plait, braid, weave together*: πλέξαντες στέφανον, Mt. xxvii. 29; Mk. xv. 17; Jn. xix. 2. [COMP.: ἐμ-πλέκω.]*

see 4119   **πλέον**, see πλείων.

4121   **πλεονάζω**; 1 aor. ἐπλεόνασα; (πλέον); Sept. for יָעַדְף and רָבָה;   1. intrans.: used of one possessing, *to superabound* [A. V. *to have over*], 2 Co. viii. 15. of things, *to exist in abundance* [R. V. *be multiplied*], 2 Co. iv. 15; *to increase, be augmented*, Ro. v. 20; vi. 1; 2 Th. i. 3; Phil. iv. 17; 2 Pet. i. 8.   2. trans. *to make to increase*: τινά τινι, one in a thing, 1 Th. iii. 12; for הִרְבָּה, Num. xxvi. 54; Ps. lxx. (lxxi.) 21; add 1 Macc. iv. 35. By prof. writ. [(fr. Hippocr. on)] in various other senses. [COMP.: ὑπερ-πλεονάζω.]*

4122   **πλεονεκτέω**, -ῶ; 1 aor. ἐπλεονέκτησα; 1 aor. pass. subj. 1 pers. plur. πλεονεκτηθῶμεν; (πλεονέκτης);   1. intrans. *to have more*, or *a greater part* or *share*: Thuc., Xen., Plut., al.; *to be superior, excel, surpass, have an advantage over*, τινός (gen. of pers.) τινι (dat. of thing): Xen., Plat., Isocr., Dem., al.   2. trans. *to gain* or *take advantage of another, to overreach*: [Hdt. 8, 112], Plat., Diod., Dion. Hal., Dio Cass., al.; and so in the N. T. in 2 Co. vii. 2; xii. 17, 18; 1 Th. iv. 6 (see πρᾶγμα, b.); pass. [cf. B. § 132, 22] ὑπό τινος, 2 Co. ii. 11 (10).*

4123   **πλεονέκτης**, -ου, ὁ, (πλέον and ἔχω);   1. *one eager to have more*, esp. *what belongs to others* ([Thuc. 1, 40, 1 (cf. Hdt. 7, 158)]; Xen. mem. 1, 5, 3);   2. *greedy of gain, covetous*: 1 Co. v. 10, 11; vi. 10; Eph. v. 5; Sir. xiv. 9.*

4124   **πλεονεξία**, -ας, ἡ, (πλεονέκτης, q. v.), *greedy desire to have more, covetousness, avarice*: Lk. xii. 15; Ro. i. 29; Eph. iv. 19; v. 3; Col. iii. 5; 1 Th. ii. 5; 2 Pet. ii. 3, [on the cᵐ. of the art. in the last two pass. cf. W. 120 (114)], 14; ὡς Rec. ὥσπερ] πλεονεξίαν, [*as a matter of covetousness*], i. e. a gift which betrays the giver's covetousness, 2 Co. ix. 5 [here R. V. txt. *extortion*]; plur. various modes in which covetousness shows itself, *covetings* [cf. W. § 27, 3; B. 77 (67)], Mk. vii. 22. (In the same and various other senses by prof. writ. fr. Hdt. and Thuc. down.) [*Trench*, N. T. Syn. § xxiv., and (in partial correction) Bp. *Lghtft.* Com. on Col. iii. 5.]*

4125   **πλευρά**, -ᾶς, ἡ, fr. Hom. (who always uses the plur.) down; *the side* of the body: Jn. xix. 34; xx. 20, 25, 27; Acts xii. 7.*

ΠΛΕΩ, see πίμπλημι. ------------------------------see 4130, p. 509

πλέω; impf. 1 pers. plur. ἐπλέομεν; [allied w. πλύνω, Lat. *pluo, fluo*, our *float, flow*, etc.; Curtius § 369]; fr. Hom. down; *to sail, navigate, travel by ship*: Lk. viii. 23; Acts xxvii. 24; foll. by εἰς with an acc. of place, Acts xxi. 3; xxvii. 6; ἐπὶ τόπον, Rev. xviii. 17 G L T Tr WH; by a use common only to the poets (cf. Matthiae § 409, 4 a.; Kühner ii. § 409, 6; [Jelf § 559; W. 224 (210)]), with a simple acc. indicating the direction: Acts xxvii. 2 (Eur. Med. vs. 7), where L T Tr WH add εἰς. [COMP.: ἀπο-, δια-, ἐκ-, κατα-, παρα-, ὑπο-πλέω.]* ------4126

4127   **πληγή**, -ῆς, ἡ, (πλήσσω), fr. Hom. down; Sept. chiefly for מַכָּה, also for מַגֵּפָה;   1. *a blow, stripe*: plur., Lk. x. 30; xii. 48; Acts xvi. 23, 33; 2 Co. vi. 5; xi. 23; *a wound*: ἡ πληγὴ τοῦ θανάτου, deadly wound [R. V. *death-stroke*], Rev. xiii. 3, 12; τῆς μαχαίρας, wound made by a sword [sword-stroke], Rev. xiii. 14. [On its idiomatic omission (Lk. xii. 47, etc.) cf. B. 82 (72); W. § 64, 4.]   2. *a public calamity, heavy affliction*, [cf. Eng. *plague*], (now tormenting now destroying the bodies of men, and sent by God as a punishment): Rev. ix. 18 [Rec. om.], 20; xi. 6; xv. 1, 6, 8; xvi. 9, [21]; xviii. 4, 8; xxi. 9; xxii. 18. [Cf. πλ. Διός, Soph. Aj. 137 (cf. 279); al.]*

4128   **πλῆθος**, -ους, τό, (ΠΛΕΩ), fr. Hom. down; Sept. chiefly for רֹב, often for הָמוֹן; *a multitude*;   a. *a great number*, sc. of men or things: Acts xxi. 22 [not Tr WH]; Heb. xi. 12 [cf. W. 120 (114) n.]; with πολύ added, Mk. iii. 7, 8; πλῆθος with a gen., Lk. ii. 13; Jn. xxi. 6; Acts v. 14; xxviii. 3 [A. V. *bundle* (L T Tr WH add τί)]; Jas. v. 20; 1 Pet. iv. 8; πολὺ πλῆθος and πλῆθος πολύ [cf. W. § 59, 2] with a gen., Lk. v. 6; vi. 17; xxiii. 27; Jn. v. 3 [here L br. G T Tr WH om. πολύ]; Acts xiv. 1; xvii. 4.   b. with the article, *the whole number, the whole multitude*; *the assemblage*: Acts xv. 30; xxiii. 7; τοῦ λαοῦ, Acts xxi. 36; πᾶν τὸ πλῆθος, Acts xv. 12; with a gen., Lk. i. 10; [viii. 37 (τῆς περιχώρου); xix. 37]; xxiii. 1; Acts [iv. 32]; v. 16; [vi. 2, 5]; xxv. 24; *the multitude of people*, Acts ii. 6; xix. 9; with τῆς πόλεως added, Acts xiv. 4.*

4129   **πληθύνω**; fut. πληθυνῶ; 1 aor. opt. 3 pers. sing. πληθύναι (2 Co. ix. 10 Rec.); Pass., impf. ἐπληθυνόμην; 1 aor. ἐπληθύνθην; (fr. πληθύς fulness); Aeschyl., Aristot., Hdian., Geop.; Sept. very often for הָרְבָּה, רִבָּה, רָבָה, sometimes for רָבַב;   1. trans. *to increase, to multiply*: 2 Co. ix. 10; Heb. vi. 14 (fr. Gen. xxii. 17); pass. *to be increased*, (be multiplied) *multiply*: Mt. xxiv. 12; Acts vi. 7; vii. 17; ix. 31; xii. 24; τινί, [A. V. *be multiplied* to one i. e.] be richly allotted to, 1 Pet. i. 2; 2 Pet. i. 2; Jude 2, (Dan. iii. 31 (98); Dan. vi. 25 Theodot.; Clem. Rom. 1 Cor. 1 inscr. [also Mart. Polyc. inscr., Constt. Apost. inscr.]).   2. intrans. *to be increased, to multiply*: Acts vi. 1.* ----see 4130, p. 509

πλήθω, see πίμπλημι. ------------------

4131   **πλήκτης**, -ου, ὁ, (πλήσσω), (Vulgate *percussor*), [A. V. *striker*], *bruiser, ready with a blow*; *a pugnacious, contentious, quarrelsome person*: 1 Tim. iii. 3; Tit. i. 7. (Plut. Marcell. 1; Pyrrh. 30; Crass. 9; Fab. 19; Diog. Laërt. 6, 38; al.) *

4132   **πλημμύρα** [so all edd.] (or πλημύρα [cf. Bttm. Ausf. Spr. § 7 Anm. 17 note; Lob. Rhemat. p. 264]) [better accented as pro paroxytone; Chandler § 160], -ας and (so G T Tr WH) -ης (see μάχαιρα), ή, (fr. πλήμμη or πλήμη i. e. πλήσμη [fr. πλήθω, πίμπλημι, q. v.]), a flood, whether of the sea or of a river: Lk. vi. 48. (Job xl. 18; [Dion. Hal. antt. 1, 71]; Joseph. antt. 2, 10, 2; Plut., Sext. Emp.; with ποταμῶν added, Philo de opif. mund. § 19; [cf. de vita Moys. i. § 36; iii. § 24; de Abrah. § 19; de leg. alleg. i. § 13].) *

4133   **πλήν**, adv., (fr. πλέον 'more' [Curtius § 375; Lob. Path. Element. i. 143; ii. 93 (cf. Bp. Lghtft. on Phil. iii. 16)]; hence prop. beyond, besides, further); it stands **1.** adverbially, at the beginning of a sentence, serving either to restrict, or to unfold and expand what has preceded: moreover, besides, so that, according to the requirements of the context, it may also be rendered but, nevertheless; [howbeit; cf. B. § 146, 2]: Mt. xi. 22, 24; xviii. 7; xxvi. 39, 64; Lk. vi. 24, 35; x. 11, 14, 20; xi. 41; xii. 31; xiii. 33; xvii. 1 L Tr txt. WH; xviii. 8; xix. 27; xxii. 21, 22, 42; xxiii. 28; 1 Co. xi. 11; Eph. v. 33; Phil. i. 18 [R G (see Ellicott)]; iii. 16; iv. 14; Rev. ii. 25; πλὴν ὅτι, except that, save that, (exx. fr. class. Grk. are given by Passow s. v. II. 1 e.; [L. and S. s. v. B. II. 4]): Acts xx. 23 [(W. 508 (473); Phil. i. 18 L T Tr WH (R. V. only that)]. **2.** as a preposition, with the gen. (first so by Hom. Od. 8, 207; [cf. W. § 54, 6]), besides, except, but: Mk. xii. 32; Jn. viii. 10; Acts viii. 1; xv. 28; xxvii. 22. Cf. Klotz ad Devar. II. 2 p. 724 sq.*

4134   **πλήρης**, -ες, (ΠΛΕΩ) fr. Aeschyl. and Hdt. down, Sept. chiefly for מָלֵא;   **a.** full, i. e. filled up (as opp. to empty): of hollow vessels, Mt. xiv. 20; xv. 37; Mk. vi. 43 [R G L]; with a gen. of the thing, Mk. viii. 19; of a surface, covered in every part: λέπρας, Lk. v. 12; of the soul, thoroughly permeated with: πνεύματος ἁγίου, Lk. iv. 1; Acts vi. 3; vii. 55; xi. 24; πίστεως, Acts vi. 5; χάριτος, Acts vi. 8 [Rec. πίστεως]; χάριτος καὶ ἀληθείας, Jn. i. 14; δόλου, Acts xiii. 10 (Jer. v. 27); θυμοῦ, Acts xix. 28; abounding in, ἔργων ἀγαθῶν, Acts ix. 36. **b.** full i. e. complete; lacking nothing, perfect, (so the Sept. sometimes for שָׁלֵם; σελήνη πλήρης, Sir. l. 6, cf. Hdt. 6, 106): μισθός, 2 Jn. 8 (Ruth ii. 12); σῖτος, a full grain of corn (one completely filling the follicle or hull containing it), Mk. iv. 28.*

4135   **πληρο-φορέω, -ῶ:** [1 aor. impv. πληροφόρησον, inf. πληροφορῆσαι (Ro. xv. 13 L mrg.); Pass., pres. impv. πληροφορείσθω; pf. ptcp. πεπληροφορημένος; 1 aor. ptcp. πληροφορηθείς]; (fr. the unused adj. πληροφόρος, and this fr. πλήρης and φέρω); to bear or bring full, to make full; **a.** to cause a thing to be shown to the full: τὴν διακονίαν, i. e. to fulfil the ministry in every respect, 2 Tim. iv. 5 (cf. πληροῦν τὴν διακονίαν, Acts xii. 25); also τὸ κήρυγμα, ibid. 17. **b.** to carry through to the end, accomplish: πράγματα πεπληροφορημένα, things that have been accomplished, (Itala and Vulg. completae), Lk. i. 1 (cf. ὡς ἐπληρώθη ταῦτα, Acts xix. 21) [cf. Meyer ed. Weiss ad loc.]. **c.** τινά, to fill one with any thought, conviction, or inclination: [Ro. xv. 13 L mrg. (foll. by ἐν w. dat. of thing); al. πληρόω,

q. v. 1]; hence to make one certain, to persuade, convince, one (πολλοῖς οὖν λόγοις καὶ ὅρκοις πληροφορήσαντες Μεγάβυζον, extr. fr. Ctes. in Phot. p. 41, 29 [(ed. Bekk.); but on this pass. see Bp. Lghtft. as below]); pass. to be persuaded, Ro. xiv. 5; πληροφορηθείς, persuaded, fully convinced or assured, Ro. iv. 21; also πεπληροφορημένοι, Col. iv. 12 L T Tr WH; οἱ ἀπόστολοι . . . πληροφορηθέντες διὰ τῆς ἀναστάσεως τοῦ κυρίου Ἰ. Χρ. καὶ πιστωθέντες ἐν τῷ λόγῳ τοῦ θεοῦ, Clem. Rom. 1 Cor. 42, 3; freq. so in eccl. writ.; to render inclined or bent on, ἐπληροφορήθη ἡ καρδία . . . τοῦ ποιῆσαι τὸ πονηρόν, Eccl. viii. 11, [cf. Test. xii. Patr., test. Gad 2]. The word is treated of fully by Bleek, Brief an d. Heb. ii. 2 p. 233 sqq.; Grimm in the Jahrbb. f. Deutsche Theol. for 1871, p. 38 sqq.; [Bp. Lghtft. Com. on Col. iv. 12. Cf. also Soph. Lex. s. v.] *

4136   **πληροφορία**, -ας, ή, (πληροφορέω, q. v.), fulness, abundance: πίστεως, Heb. x. 22; τῆς ἐλπίδος, Heb. vi. 11; τῆς συνέσεως, Col. ii. 2; full assurance, most certain confidence, (see πληροφορέω, c. [al. give it the same meaning in one or other of the preceding pass. also; cf. Bp. Lghtft. on Col. l. c.]), 1 Th. i. 5. (Not found elsewh. exc. in eccl. writ. [cf. W. 25].) *

4137   **πληρόω -ῶ,** (inf. -ροῦν Lk. ix. 31, see WH. App. p. 166); impf. 3 pers. sing. ἐπλήρου; fut. πληρώσω; 1 aor. ἐπλήρωσα; pf. πεπλήρωκα; Pass., pres. πληροῦμαι; impf. ἐπληρούμην; pf. πεπλήρωμαι; 1 aor. ἐπληρώθην; 1 fut. πληρωθήσομαι; fut. mid. πληρώσομαι (once, Rev. vi. 11 Rec.); (fr. ΠΛΗΡΟΣ equiv. to πλήρης); fr. Aeschyl. and Hdt. down; Sept. for מָלֵא; **1.** to make full, to fill, to fill up: τὴν σαγήνην, pass. Mt. xiii. 48; i. q. to fill to the full, πᾶσαν χρείαν, Phil. iv. 19; to cause to abound, to furnish or supply liberally: πεπλήρωμαι, I abound, I am liberally supplied, sc. with what is necessary for subsistence, Phil. iv. 18; Hebraistically, with the accus. of the thing in which one abounds [cf. B. § 134, 7; W. § 32, 5]: of spiritual possessions, Phil. i. 11 (where Rec. has καρπῶν); Col. i. 9, (ἐνέπλησα αὐτὸν πνεῦμα σοφίας, Ex. xxxi. 3; xxxv. 31); i. q. to flood, ή οἰκία ἐπληρώθη [Tr mrg. ἐπλήσθη] ἐκ τῆς ὀσμῆς, Jn. xii. 3 (see ἐκ, II. 5); ἦχος ἐπλήρωσε τὸν οἶκον, Acts ii. 2; with a gen. of the thing, τὴν Ἱερουσαλὴμ τῆς διδαχῆς, Acts v. 28 (Liban. epp. 721 πάσας — i. e. πόλεις — ἐνέπλησας τῶν ὑπὲρ ἡμῶν λόγων; Justin. hist. 11, 7 Phrygiam religionibus implevit); τινά, i. q. to fill, diffuse throughout one's soul: with a gen. of the thing, Lk. ii. 40 R G L txt. T Tr mrg. (see below); Acts ii. 28; pass., Acts xiii. 52; Ro. xv. 13 [where L mrg. πληροφορέω, q. v. in c.], 14; 2 Tim. i. 4; w. a dat. of the thing (cf. W. § 31, 7), pass., [Lk. ii. 40 L mrg. Tr txt. WH]; Ro. i. 29; 2 Co. vii. 4; foll. by ἐν w. a dat. of the instrument: ἐν πνεύματι, Eph. v. 18; ἐν παντὶ θελήματι θεοῦ, with everything which God wills (used of those who will nothing but what God wills), Col. iv. 12 R G [but see πληροφορέω, c.]; πληροῦν τὴν καρδίαν τινός, to pervade, take possession of, one's heart, Jn. xvi. 6; Acts v. 3; Christians are said πληροῦσθαι, simply, as those who are pervaded (i. e. richly furnished) with the power and gifts of the Holy Spirit: ἐν αὐτῷ, rooted as it were in Christ, i. e. by virtue of the intimate relationship entered into with him, Col. ii. 10 [cf. ἐν, I. 6 b.]; εἰς πᾶν τὸ πλήρωμα τοῦ θεοῦ (see πλήρωμα, 1), Eph. iii. 19 [not WH mrg.]; Christ, exalted to share in the divine administration, is said πληροῦν τὰ πάντα, to fill (pervade) the universe with his presence, power, activity, Eph. iv. 10; also πληροῦσθαι (mid. *for himself*, i. e. to execute his counsels [cf. W. 258 (242); B. § 134, 7]) τὰ πάντα ἐν πᾶσιν, all things in all places, Eph. i. 23 (μὴ οὐχὶ τὸν οὐρανὸν καὶ τὴν γῆν ἐγὼ πληρῶ, λέγει κύριος, Jer. xxiii. 24; *Grimm*, Exeget. Hdbch. on Sap. i. 7 p. 55, cites exx. fr. Philo and others; [(but ἐν πᾶσιν here is variously understood; see πᾶς, II. 2 b. δ. aa. and the Comm.)]). **2.** *to render full*, i. e. *to complete*; **a.** prop. *to fill up* to the top: πᾶσαν φάραγγα, Lk. iii. 5; so that nothing shall be wanting to full measure, fill to the brim, τὸ μέτρον (q. v. 1 a.), Mt. xxiii. 32. **b.** *to perfect, consummate*; **a.** a number: ἕως πληρωθῶσι καὶ οἱ σύνδουλοι, until the number of their comrades also shall have been made complete, Rev. vi. 11 L WH txt., cf. Düsterdieck ad loc. [see γ. below]. by a Hebraism (see πίμπλημι, fin.) time is said πληροῦσθαι, πεπληρωμένος, either when a period of time that was to elapse has passed, or when a definite time is at hand: Mk. i. 15; Lk. xxi. 24; Jn. vii. 8; Acts vii. 23, 30; ix. 23; xxiv. 27, (Gen. xxv. 24; xxix. 21; Lev. viii. 33; xii. 4; xxv. 30; Num. vi. 5; Joseph. antt. 4, 4, 6; 6, 4, 1; πληροῦν τὸν τέλεον ἐνιαυτόν, Plat. Tim. p. 39 d.; τοὺς χρόνους, legg. 9 p. 866 a.). **β.** *to make complete in every particular; to render perfect:* πᾶσαν εὐδοκίαν κτλ. 2 Th. i. 11; τὴν χαράν, Phil. ii. 2; pass. Jn. iii. 29; xv. 11; xvi. 24; xvii. 13; 1 Jn. i. 4; 2 Jn. 12; τὰ ἔργα, pass. Rev. iii. 2; τὴν ὑπακοήν, to cause *all* to obey, pass. 2 Co. x. 6; τὸ πάσχα, Lk. xxii. 16 (Jesus speaks here allegorically: until perfect deliverance and blessedness be celebrated in the heavenly state). **γ.** *to carry through to the end, to accomplish, carry out*, (some undertaking): πάντα τὰ ῥήματα, Lk. vii. 1; τὴν διακονίαν, Acts xii. 25; Col. iv. 17; τὸ ἔργον, Acts xiv. 26; τὸν δρόμον, Acts xiii. 25; sc. τὸν δρόμον, Rev. vi. 11 acc. to the reading πληρώσωσι (G T Tr WH mrg.) or πληρώσονται (Rec.) [see a. above]; ὡς ἐπληρώθη ταῦτα, when these things were ended, Acts xix. 21. Here belongs also πληροῦν τὸ εὐαγγέλιον, to cause to be everywhere known, acknowledged, embraced, [A. V. *I have fully preached*], Ro. xv. 19; in the same sense τὸν λόγον τοῦ θεοῦ, Col. i. 25. **c.** *to carry into effect, bring to realization, realize;* **a.** of matters of duty, *to perform, execute:* τὸν νόμον, Ro. xiii. 8; Gal. v. 14; τὸ δικαίωμα τοῦ νόμου, pass., ἐν ἡμῖν, among us, Ro. viii. 4; πᾶσαν δικαιοσύνην, Mt. iii. 15 (εὐσέβειαν, 4 Macc. xii. 15); τὴν ἔξοδον (as something appointed and prescribed by God), Lk. ix. 31. **β.** of sayings, promises, prophecies, *to bring to pass, ratify, accomplish*; so in the phrases ἵνα or ὅπως πληρωθῇ ἡ γραφή, τὸ ῥηθέν, etc. (cf. *Knapp*, Scripta var. Arg. p. 533 sq.): Mt. i. 22; ii. 15, 17, 23; iv. 14; viii. 17; xii. 17; xiii. 35; xxi. 4; xxvi. 54, 56; xxvii. 9, 35 Rec.; Mk. xiv. 49; xv. 28 (which vs. G T WH om. Tr br.); Lk. i. 20; iv. 21; xxi. 22 Rec.; xxiv. 44; Jn. xii. 38; xiii. 18; xv. 25; xvii. 12; xviii. 9, 32; xix. 24, 36; Acts i. 16;

iii. 18; xiii. 27; Jas. ii. 23, (1 K. ii. 27; 2 Chr. xxxvi. 22). **γ.** universally and absolutely, *to fulfil*, i. e. *to cause God's will* (as made known in the law) *to be obeyed as it should be, and God's promises* (given through the prophets) *to receive fulfilment:* Mt. v. 17; cf. *Weiss*, Das Matthäusevang. u.s.w. p. 146 sq. [COMP.: ἀνα-, ἀντ-ανα-, προσ-ανα-, ἐκ-, συμ-πληρόω.] *

πλήρωμα, -τος, τό, (πληρόω), Sept. for מְלֹא; **1.** etymologically it has a passive sense, *that which is* (or *has been*) *filled*; very rarely so in class. Grk.: *a ship*, inasmuch as it is filled (i. e. manned) with sailors, rowers, and soldiers; ἀπὸ δύο πληρωμάτων ἐμάχοντο, Lcian. ver. hist. 2, 37; πέντε εἶχον πληρώματα, ibid. 38. In the N. T. the body of believers, as that which is filled with the presence, power, agency, riches of God and of Christ: τοῦ Χριστοῦ, Eph. iv. 13 (see ἡλικία, 1 c. [cf. W. § 30, 3 N. 1; B. 155 (136)]); i. 23; εἰς πᾶν τὸ πλήρωμα τοῦ θεοῦ, that ye may become a body wholly filled and flooded by God, Eph. iii. 19 [but WH mrg. reads πληρωθῇ πᾶν τὸ πλ.]. **2.** *that which fills* or *with which a thing is filled:* so very frequently in class. Grk. fr. Hdt. down; esp. of those things with which ships are filled, freight and merchandise, sailors, oarsmen, soldiers, [cf. our 'complement' (yet cf. Bp. Lghtft. as below p. 258 sq.)], (of the animals filling Noah's ark, Philo de vit. Moys. ii. §12); πλήρωμα πόλεως, the inhabitants or population filling a city, Plat. de rep. 2 p. 371 e.; Aristot. polit. 3, 13 p. 1284ᵃ, 5; 4, 4 p. 1291ᵃ, 17; al. So in the N. T. ἡ γῆ καὶ τὸ πλήρωμα αὐτῆς, whatever fills the earth or is contained in it, 1 Co. x. 26, 28 Rec. (Ps. xxiii. (xxiv.) 1; xlix. (l.) 12; Jer. viii. 16; Ezek. xii. 19, etc.; τὸ πλήρωμα τῆς θαλάσσης, Ps. xcv. (xcvi.) 11; 1 Chr. xvi. 32); κοφίνων πληρώματα, those things with which the baskets were filled, [basketfuls], Mk. vi. 43 T Tr WH [on this pass. cf. Bp. Lghtft. as below p. 260]; also σπυρίδων πληρώματα, Mk. viii. 20; *the filling* (Lat. *complementum*) by which a gap is filled up, Mt. ix. 16; Mk. ii. 21; *that by which a loss is repaired*, spoken of the reception of all the Jews into the kingdom of God (see ἥττημα, 1), Ro. xi. 12. Of time (see πληρόω, 2 b. a.), that portion of time by which a longer antecedent period is completed; hence *completeness, fulness*, of time: τοῦ χρόνου, Gal. iv. 4; τῶν καιρῶν, Eph. i. 10 (on which see οἰκονομία). **3.** *fulness, abundance:* Jn. i. 16; Col. i. 19; ii. 9; *full number*, Ro. xi. 25. **4.** i. q. πλήρωσις (see καύχημα, 2), i. e. *a fulfilling, keeping:* τοῦ νόμου (see πληρόω, 2 c. a.), Ro. xiii. 10. For a full discussion of this word see *Fritzsche*, Ep. ad Rom. ii. p. 469 sqq.; [esp. Bp. *Lghtft*. Com. on Col. p. 257 sqq.]. *

πλησίον, (neut. of the adj. πλησίος, -α, -ον), adv., fr. Hom. down, *near*: with a gen. of place [cf. W. § 54, 6], Jn. iv. 5; with the article, ὁ πλησίον sc. ὤν [cf. B. § 125, 10; W. 24] (Sept. very often for רֵעַ; sometimes for עָמִית), prop. Lat. *proximus* (so Vulg. in the N. T.), *a neighbor;* i. e. **a.** *friend:* Mt. v. 43. **b.** *any other person*, and where two are concerned *the other* (thy fellow-man, thy neighbor) i. e., acc. to the O. T. and Jewish conception, a member of the Hebrew race and commonwealth : Acts vii. 27 ; and Rec. in Heb. viii. 11 ; acc. to the teaching of Christ, any other man irrespective of race or religion with whom we live or whom we chance to meet (which idea is clearly brought out in the parable Lk. x. 25–37) : Mt. xix. 19 ; xxii. 39 ; Mk. xii. 31, 33 ; Lk. x. 27 ; Ro. xiii. 9, 10 ; [xv. 2] ; Gal. v. 14 ; Eph. iv. 25 ; Jas. ii. 8 and L T Tr WH in iv. 12 ; πλησίον εἶναί τινος, to be near one [one's neighbor], i. e. in a pass. sense, worthy to be regarded as a friend and companion, Lk. x. 29 ; actively, to perform the offices of a friend and companion, ibid. 36 ; [on the om. of the art. in the last two exx. see B. § 129, 11 ; W. § 19 fin.].*

4140 πλησμονή, -ῆς, ἡ, (πίμπλημι [cf. W. 94 (89)]), repletion, satiety, (Vulg. saturitas) : πρὸς πλησμονὴν σαρκός, for the satisfying of the flesh, to satiate the desires of the flesh (see σάρξ, 4), Col. ii. 23, cf. Meyer ad loc. ; [others (including R. V.) render the phrase against (i. e. for the remedy of) the indulgence of the flesh ; see Bp. Lghtft. ad loc., and πρός, I. 1 c.]. (Arstph., Eur., Xen., Plato, Plut., al. ; Sept.) *

4141 πλήσσω [cf. πληγή, (πέλαγος), Lat. plango, plaga ; Curtius § 367] : 2 aor. pass. ἐπλήγην ; fr. Hom. down ; Sept. for הָכָה (see πατάσσω, init.) ; to strike, to smite : pass. (of the heavenly bodies smitten by God that they may be deprived of light and shrouded in darkness), Rev. viii. 12. [Comp. : ἐκ-, ἐπι- πλήσσω.] *

4142 πλοιάριον, -ου, τό, (dimin. of πλοῖον ; see γυναικάριον, fin.), a small vessel, a boat : Mk. iii. 9 ; iv. 36 Rec. ; Lk. v. 2 L mrg. T Tr mrg. WH mrg. ; Jn. vi. [22ᵃ], 22ᵇ Rec., 23 [where L Tr mrg. WH πλοῖα], 24 L T Tr WH ; xxi. 8. [Cf. B. D. s. v. Ship (13).] (Arstph., Xen., Diod., al.) *

4143 πλοῖον, -ου, τό, (πλέω), fr. Hdt. down, Sept. chiefly for אֳנִיָּה, a ship : Mt. iv. 21, 22 ; Mk. i. 19 ; Lk. v. 2 [R G L txt. Tr txt. WH txt.] ; Jn. vi. 17 ; Acts xx. 13, and often in the historical bks. of the N. T. ; Jas. iii. 4 ; Rev. viii. 9 ; xviii. 19. [BB. DD. s. v. Ship.]

4144 πλόος-οῦς, gen. -όου -οῦ, and in later writ. πλοῦς (Acts xxvii. 9 ; Arr. peripl. erythr. p. 176 § 61 ; see νοῦς [and cf. Lob. Paralip. p. 173 sq.]), (πλέω), fr. Hom. Od. 3, 169 down ; voyage : Acts xxi. 7 ; xxvii. 9, 10, (Sap. xiv. 1).*

4145 πλούσιος, -α, -ον, (πλοῦτος), fr. Hes. opp. 22 down, Sept. for עָשִׁיר, rich ; **a.** prop. wealthy, abounding in material resources : Mt. xxvii. 57 ; Lk. xii. 16 ; xiv. 12 ; xvi. 1, 19 ; xviii. 23 ; xix. 2 ; ὁ πλούσιος, substantively, Lk. xvi. 21, 22 ; Jas. i. 10, 11 ; οἱ πλούσιοι, Lk. vi. 24 ; xxi. 1 ; 1 Tim. vi. 17 ; Jas. ii. 6 ; v. 1 ; Rev. vi. 15 ; xiii. 16 ; πλούσιος, without the art., a rich man, Mt. xix. 23, 24 ; Mk. x. 25 ; xii. 41 ; Lk. xviii. 25. **b.** metaph. and univ. abounding, abundantly supplied : foll. by ἐν w. a dat. of the thing in which one abounds (cf. W. § 30, 8 b. note), ἐν ἐλέει, Eph. ii. 4 ; ἐν πίστει, Jas. ii. 5 ; absol. abounding (rich) in Christian virtues and eternal possessions, Rev. ii. 9 ; iii. 17, on which see Düsterdieck. ἐπτώχευσε πλούσιος ὤν, of Christ, 'although as the ἄσαρκος λόγος he formerly abounded in the riches of a heavenly condition, by assuming human nature he entered into a state of (earthly) poverty,' 2 Co. viii. 9.*

πλουσίως, adv., [fr. Hdt. down], abundantly, richly :   **4146** Col. iii. 16 ; 1 Tim. vi. 17 ; Tit. iii. 6 ; 2 Pet. i. 11.*

πλουτέω, -ῶ ; 1 aor. ἐπλούτησα ; pf. πεπλούτηκα ; (πλοῦ-   **4147** τος) ; fr. Hes. down ; Sept. sometimes for עָשַׁר ;   **a.** to be rich, to have abundance : prop. of outward possessions, absol., Lk. i. 53 ; 1 Tim. vi. 9 ; 1 aor. I have been made rich, have become rich, have gotten riches (on this use of the aorist see βασιλεύω, fin.), ἀπό τινος, Rev. xviii. 15 (Sir. xi. 18 ; [cf. ἀπό, II. 2 a.]) ; also ἐκ τινος (see ἐκ, II. 5), Rev. xviii. 3, 19 ; ἔν τινι (cf. W. § 30, 8 b. note ; the Greeks say πλουτεῖν τινος, or τινι, or τι), 1 Tim. vi. 18.   **b.** metaph. to be richly supplied : πλουτεῖν εἰς πάντας, is affluent in resources so that he can give the blessings of salvation unto all, Ro. x. 12 ; πλουτεῖν εἰς θεόν (see εἰς, B. II. 2 b. a.), Lk. xii. 21 ; aor. ἐπλούτησα, absolutely, I became rich, i. e. obtained the eternal spiritual possessions : 1 Co. iv. 8 ; 2 Co. viii. 9 ; Rev. iii. 18 ; πεπλού-τηκα, I have gotten riches, Rev. iii. 17.*

πλουτίζω ; Pass., pres. ptcp. πλουτιζόμενος ; 1 aor. ἐπλου-   **4148** τίσθην ; (πλοῦτος) ; to make rich, to enrich : τινά, pass. 2 Co. ix. 11 ; used of spiritual riches : τινά, 2 Co. vi. 10 ; ἐν with a dat. of the thing (see πλουτέω, a.), pass., to be richly furnished, 1 Co. i. 5. (Aeschyl., Soph., Xen., Plut. ; Sept. for הֶעֱשִׁיר.) *

πλοῦτος, -ου, ὁ, and (acc. to L T Tr WH in 2 Co. viii. 2 ;   **4149** Eph. i. 7 ; ii. 7 ; iii. 8, 16 ; Phil. iv. 19 ; Col. i. 27 ; ii. 2, but only in the nom. and acc. ; cf. [Tdf. Proleg. p. 118 ; WH. App. p. 158] ; W. 65 (64) ; B. 22 sq. (20)) τὸ πλοῦτος, (apparently i. q. πλέοτος, fr. πλέος full [cf. πίμπλημι]), fr. Hom. down, Sept. for עֹשֶׁר, and also for הָמוֹן a multitude, הַיִל, הוֹן ; riches, wealth ;   **a.** prop. and absol. abundance of external possessions : Mt. xiii. 22 ; Mk. iv. 19 ; Lk. viii. 14 ; 1 Tim. vi. 17 ; Jas. v. 2 ; Rev. xviii. 17 (16).   **b.** univ. fulness, abundance, plenitude : with a gen. of the excellence in which one abounds, as τῆς χρηστότητος, Ro. ii. 4 ; ix. 23 ; 2 Co. viii. 2 ; Eph. i. 7, 18 ; ii. 7 ; iii. 16 ; Col. i. 27 ; ii. 2. the πλοῦτος of God is extolled, i. e. the fulness of his perfections, — of which two are mentioned, viz. σοφία and γνῶσις, Ro. xi. 33 (for σοφίας καὶ γνώσεως here depend on βάθος, not on πλούτου [cf. B. 155 (135) ; W. § 30, 3 N. 1]) ; the fulness of all things in store for God's uses, Phil. iv. 19 ; in the same sense πλοῦτος is attributed to Christ, exalted at the right hand of God, Rev. v. 12 ; in a more restricted sense, πλοῦτος τοῦ Χριστοῦ is used of the fulness of the things pertaining to salvation with which Christ is able to enrich others, Eph. iii. 8.   **c.** univ. i. q. a good [(to point an antithesis)] : Heb. xi. 26 ; i. q. that with which one is enriched, with a gen. of the person enriched, used of Christian salvation, Ro. xi. 12.*

πλύνω ; impf. ἔπλυνον ; 1 aor. ἔπλυνα ; [(cf. πλέω)] ; fr.   **4150** Hom. down ; Sept. for כָּבַס and רָחַץ ; to wash : τὰ δίκτυα, Lk. v. 2 L T Tr WH [(T WH mrg. -αν ; see ἀποπλύνω)] ; used fr. Hom. down esp. in ref. to c l o t h i n g (Gen. xlix. 11 ; Ex. xix. 10, 14 ; Lev. xiii. 6, 34, etc.) ; hence figuratively πλύνειν τὰς στολὰς αὐτῶν ἐν τῷ αἵματι τοῦ ἀρνίου is used of those who by faith so appropriate the results of Christ's expiation as to be regarded by God as pure and sinless, Rev. vii. 14, and L T Tr WH in xxii. 14; cf. Ps. l. (li.) 4, 9. [COMP.: ἀπο-πλύνω. SYN. see λούω, fin.]*

4151   **πνεῦμα**, -τος, τό, (πνέω), Grk. writ. fr. Aeschyl. and Hdt. down; Hebr. רוּחַ, Lat. *spiritus*; i. e.

1. *a movement of air*, (gentle) *blast*;   **a.** of the wind: ἀνέμων πνεύματα, Hdt. 7, 16, 1; Paus. 5, 25; hence the *wind* itself, Jn. iii. 8; plur. Heb. i. 7, (1 K. xviii. 45; xix. 11; Job i. 19; Ps. ciii. (civ.) 4, etc.; often in Grk. writ.).   **b.** *breath* of the nostrils or mouth, often in Grk. writ. fr. Aeschyl. down: πνεῦμα τοῦ στόματος, 2 Th. ii. 8 (Ps. xxxii. (xxxiii.) 6, cf. Is. xi. 4); πν. ζωῆς, the *breath of life*, Rev. xi. 11 (Gen. vi. 17, cf. πνοὴ ζωῆς, ii. 7). [πνεῦμα and πνοή seem to have been in the main coincident terms; but πνοή became the more poetical. Both retain a suggestion of their evident etymology. Even in class. Grk. πνεῦμα became as freq. and as wide in its application as ἄνεμος. (Schmidt ch. 55, 7; Trench § lxxiii.)]

2. *the spirit*, i. e. *the vital principle by which the body is* animated [(Aristot., Polyb., Plut., al.; see below)]: Lk. viii. 55; xxiii. 46; Jn. xix. 30; Acts vii. 59; Rev. xiii. 15 [here R.V. *breath*]; ἀφιέναι τὸ πνεῦμα, to breathe out the spirit, to expire, Mt. xxvii. 50 cf. Sir. xxxviii. 23; Sap. xvi. 14 (Grk. writ. said ἀφιέναι τὴν ψυχήν, as Gen. xxxv. 18, see ἀφίημι, 1 b. and *Kypke*, Observv. i. p. 140; but we also find ἀφιέναι πνεῦμα θανασίμῳ σφαγῇ, Eur. Hec. 571); σῶμα χωρὶς πνεύματος νεκρόν ἐστιν, Jas. ii. 26; τὸ πνεῦμά ἐστι τὸ ζωοποιοῦν, ἡ σὰρξ οὐκ ὠφελεῖ οὐδέν, the spirit is that which animates and gives life, the body is of no profit (for the spirit imparts life to it, not the body in turn to the spirit; cf. *Chr. Frid. Fritzsche*, Nova opusc. p. 239), Jn. vi. 63. *the* r a t i o n a l *spirit, the power by which a human being feels, thinks, wills, decides*; *the soul*: τὸ πνεῦμα τοῦ ἀνθρώπου τὸ ἐν αὐτῷ, 1 Co. ii. 11; opp. to σάρξ (q. v. [esp. 2 a.]), Mt. xxvi. 41; Mk. xiv. 38; 1 Co. v. 5; 2 Co. vii. 1; Col. ii. 5; opp. to τὸ σῶμα, Ro. viii. 10; 1 Co. vi. 17, 20 Rec.; vii. 34; 1 Pet. iv. 6. Although for the most part the words πνεῦμα and ψυχή are used indiscriminately and so σῶμα and ψυχή put in contrast (but never by Paul; see ψυχή, esp. 2), there is also recognized a threefold distinction, τὸ πνεῦμα καὶ ἡ ψυχὴ καὶ τὸ σῶμα, 1 Th. v. 23, acc. to which τὸ πνεῦμα is the r a t i o n a l part of man, the power of perceiving and grasping divine and eternal things, and upon which the Spirit of God exerts its influence; (πνεῦμα, says Luther, "is the highest and noblest part of man, which qualifies him to lay hold of incomprehensible, invisible, eternal things; in short, it is the house where Faith and God's word are at home" [see reff. at end]): ἄχρι μερισμοῦ ψυχῆς καὶ πνεύματος (see μερισμός, 2), Heb. iv. 12; ἐν ἑνὶ πνεύματι, μιᾷ ψυχῇ, Phil. i. 27 (where instead of μιᾷ ψυχῇ Paul acc. to his mode of speaking elsewhere would have said more appropriately μιᾷ καρδίᾳ), Mk. ii. 8; viii. 12; Lk. i. 47; Acts xvii. 16; Ro. i. 9; viii. 16; 1 Co. v. 4; xvi. 18; 2 Co. ii. 13; vii. 13; Gal. vi. 18; [Phil. iv. 23 L T Tr WH]; Philem. 25; 2 Tim. iv. 22; ὁ θεὸς τῶν πνευμάτων (for which Rec. has ἁγίων) τῶν προφητῶν,

who incites and directs the souls of the prophets, Rev. xxii. 6, where cf. Düsterdieck. the dative τῷ πνεύματι is used to denote the seat (locality) where one does or suffers something, like our *in spirit*: ἐπιγινώσκειν, Mk. ii. 8; ἀναστενάζειν, Mk. viii. 12; ἐμβριμᾶσθαι, Jn. xi. 33; ταράσσεσθαι, Jn. xiii. 21; ζέειν, Acts xviii. 25; Ro. xii. 11; ἀγαλλιᾶσθαι, Lk. x. 21 (but L T Tr WH here add ἁγίῳ); dat. of respect: 1 Co. v. 3; Col. ii. 5; 1 Pet. iv. 6; κραταιοῦσθαι, Lk. i. 80; ii. 40 Rec.; ἅγιον εἶναι, 1 Co. vii. 34; ζωοποιηθείς, 1 Pet. iii. 18; ζῆν, 1 Pet. iv. 6; πτωχοί, Mt. v. 3; dat. of instrument: δεδεμένος, Acts xx. 22; συνέχεσθαι, xviii. 5 Rec.; θεῷ λατρεύειν, Phil. iii. 3 R G; dat. of advantage: ἄνεσιν τῷ πνεύματί μου, 2 Co. ii. 13 (12); ἐν τῷ πνεύματι, is used of the instrument, 1 Co. vi. 20 Rec. [it is surely better to take ἐν τ. π. here l o c a l l y, of the 'sphere' (W. 386 (362), cf. vs. 19)]; also ἐν πνεύματι, nearly i. q. πνευματικῶς [but see W. § 51, 1 e. note], Jn. iv. 23; of the seat of an action, ἐν τῷ πνεύματί μου, Ro. i. 9; τιθέναι ἐν τῷ πν., to propose to one's self, purpose foll. by the infin. Acts xix. 21. πνεύματα προφητῶν, acc. to the context the souls (spirits) of the prophets moved by the Spirit of God, 1 Co. xiv. 32; in a peculiar sense πνεῦμα is used of a soul thoroughly roused by the Holy Spirit and wholly intent on divine things, yet destitute of distinct self-consciousness and clear understanding; thus in the phrases τὸ πνεῦμά μου προσεύχεται, opp. to ὁ νοῦς μου, 1 Co. xiv. 14; πνεύματι λαλεῖν μυστήρια, ibid. 2; προσεύχεσθαι, ψάλλειν, εὐλογεῖν, τῷ πν., as opp. to τῷ νοΐ, ibid. 15, 16.

3. *a spirit*, i. e. *a simple essence, devoid of all or at least all grosser matter, and possessed of the power of knowing, desiring, deciding, and acting*;   **a.** generically: Lk. xxiv. 37; Acts xxiii. 8 (on which see μήτε, fin.); ibid. 9; πνεῦμα σάρκα καὶ ὀστέα οὐκ ἔχει, Lk. xxiv. 39; πνεῦμα ζωοποιοῦν, [*a life-giving spirit*], spoken of Christ as raised from the dead, 1 Co. xv. 45; πνεῦμα ὁ θεός (*God is spirit* essentially), Jn. iv. 24; πατὴρ τῶν πνευμάτων, of God, Heb. xii. 9, where the term comprises both the spirits of men and of angels.   **b.** *a human soul that has left the body* [(Babr. 122, 8)]: plur. (Lat. *manes*), Heb. xii. 23; 1 Pet. iii. 19.   **c.** *a spirit higher than man but lower than God*, i. e. *an angel*: plur. Heb. i. 14; used of demons, or evil spirits, who were conceived of as inhabiting the bodies of men: [Mk. ix. 20]; Lk. ix. 39; Acts xvi. 18; plur., Mt. viii. 16; xii. 45; Lk. x. 20; xi. 26; πνεῦμα πύθωνος or πύθωνα, Acts xvi. 16; πνεύματα δαιμονίων, Rev. xvi. 14; πνεῦμα δαιμονίου ἀκαθάρτου, Lk. iv. 33 (see δαιμόνιον, 2); πνεῦμα ἀσθενείας, causing infirmity, Lk. xiii. 11; πνεῦμα ἀκάθαρτον, Mt. x. 1; xii. 43; Mk. i. 23, 26, 27; iii. 11, 30; v. 2, 8, 13; vi. 7; vii. 25; ix. 25; Lk. iv. 36; vi. 18; viii. 29; ix. 42; xi. 24, 26; Acts v. 16; viii. 7; Rev. xvi. 13; xviii. 2; ἄλαλον, κωφόν (for the Jews held that the same evils with which the men were afflicted afflicted the demons also that had taken possession of them [cf. *Wetstein*, N. T. i. 279 sqq.; *Edersheim*, Jesus the Messiah, App. xvi.; see δαιμονίζομαι etc. and reff.]), Mk. ix. 17, 25; πονηρόν, Lk. vii. 21; viii. 2; Acts xix. 12, 13, 15, 16, [(cf. Judg. ix. 23; 1 S. xvi. 14; xix. 9, etc.)].   **d.**

the spiritual nature of Christ, higher than the highest angels, close to God and most intimately united to him (in doctrinal phraseology the divine nature of Christ): 1 Tim. iii. 16; with the addition of ἁγιωσύνης (on which see ἁγιωσύνη, 1 [yet cf. 4 a. below]), Ro. i. 4 [but see Meyer ad loc., Ellicott on 1 Tim. l. c.]; it is called πνεῦμα αἰώνιον, in tacit contrast with the perishable ψυχαί of sacrificial animals, in Heb. ix. 14, where cf. Delitzsch [and esp. Kurtz].

4. The Scriptures also ascribe a πνεῦμα to GOD, i. e. God's power and agency,—distinguishable in thought (or modalistice, as they say in technical speech) from God's essence in itself considered, — manifest in the course of affairs, and by its influence upon souls productive in the theocratic body (the church) of all the higher spiritual gifts and blessings; [cf. the resemblances and differences in Philo's use of τὸ θεῖον πνεῦμα, e. g. de gigant. § 12 (cf. § 5 sq.); quis rer. div. § 53; de mund. opif. § 46, etc.].   a. This πνεῦμα is called in the O. T. רוּחַ יְהֹוָה, רוּחַ אֱלֹהִים; in the N. T. πνεῦμα ἅγιον, τὸ ἅγιον πνεῦμα, τὸ πνεῦμα τὸ ἅγιον (first so in Sap. i. 5; ix. 17; for רוּחַ קָדְשׁ, in Ps. l. (li.) 13, Is. lxiii. 10, 11, the Sept. renders by πνεῦμα ἁγιωσύνης), i. e. the Holy Spirit (august, full of majesty, adorable, utterly opposed to all impurity): Mt. i. 18, 20; iii. 11; xii. 32; xxviii. 19; Mk. i. 8; iii. 29; xii. 36; xiii. 11; Lk. i. 15, 35; ii. 25, 26; iii. 16, 22; iv. 1; xi. 13; xii. 10, 12; Jn. i. 33; vii. 39 [L T WH om. Tr br. ἅγ.]; xiv. 26; xx. 22; Acts i. 2, 5, 8, 16; ii. 33, 38; iv. 25 L T Tr WH; v. 3, 32; viii. 18 [L T WH om. Tr br. τὸ ἅγ.], 19; ix. 31; x. 38, 44, 45, 47; xi. 15, 16, 24; xiii. 2, 4, 9, 52; xv. 8, 28; xvi. 6; xix. 6; xx. 28; Ro. ix. 1; xiv. 17; xv. 13, 16, 19 [L Tr WH in br.]; 1 Co. vi. 19; xii. 3; 2 Co. vi. 6; xiii. 13 (14); Eph. i. 13; 1 Th. i. 5, 6; 2 Tim. i. 14; Tit. iii. 5; Heb. ii. 4; vi. 4; ix. 8; 1 Jn. v. 7 Rec.; Jude 20; other exx. will be given below in the phrases; (on the use and the omission of the art., see Fritzsche, Ep. ad Rom. ii. p. 105 [in opposition to Harless (on Eph. ii. 22) et al.; cf. also Meyer on Gal. v. 16; Ellicott on Gal. v. 5; W. 122 (116); B. 89 (78)]); τὸ πν. τὸ ἅγιον τοῦ θεοῦ, Eph. iv. 30; 1 Th. iv. 8; πνεῦμα θεοῦ, Ro. viii. 9, 14; τὸ τοῦ θεοῦ πνεῦμα, 1 Pet. iv. 14; (τὸ) πνεῦμα (τοῦ) θεοῦ, Mt. iii. 16; xii. 18, 28; 1 Co. iii. 14; iii. 16; Eph. iii. 16; 1 Jn. iv. 2; τὸ πν. τοῦ θεοῦ ἡμῶν, 1 Co. vi. 11; τὸ πν. τοῦ πατρός, Mt. x. 20; πν. θεοῦ ζῶντος, 2 Co. iii. 3; τὸ πν. τοῦ ἐγείραντος Ἰησοῦν, Ro. viii. 11; τὸ πν. τὸ ἐκ θεοῦ (emanating from God and imparted unto men), 1 Co. ii. 12; πνεῦμα τοῦ κυρίου, i. e. of God, Lk. iv. 18; Acts v. 9 (cf. vs. 4); viii. 39; κυρίου, i. e. of Christ, 2 Co. iii. 17, 18 [cf. B. 343 (295)]; τὸ πνεῦμα Ἰησοῦ, since the same Spirit in a peculiar manner dwelt in Jesus, Acts xvi. 7 (where Rec. om. Ἰησοῦ); Χριστοῦ, Ro. viii. 9; Ἰησοῦ Χριστοῦ, Phil. i. 19; τὸ ἕν τινι (in one's soul [not WH mrg.]) πνεῦμα Χριστοῦ, 1 Pet. i. 11; τὸ πν. τοῦ υἱοῦ τοῦ θεοῦ, Gal. iv. 6; simply τὸ πνεῦμα or πνεῦμα: Mt. iv. 1; xii. 31, 32; xxii. 43; Mk. i. 10, 12; Lk. iv. 1, 14; Jn. i. 32, 33; iii. 6, 8, 34; vii. 39; Acts ii. 4; viii. 29; x. 19; xi. 12, 28; xxi. 4; Ro. viii. 6, 16, 23, 26, 27; xv. 30; 1 Co. ii. 4, 10, 13 (where Rec. adds ἁγίου); xii. 4, 7, 8; 2 Co.

i. 22; iii. 6, 8; v. 5; Gal. iii. 3, 5, 14; iv. 29; v. 5, 17, 22, 25; Eph. iv. 3; v. 9 Rec.; vi. 17; Phil. ii. 1; 2 Th. ii. 13; 1 Tim. iv. 1; Jas. iv. 5; 1 Pet. i. 22 Rec.; 1 Jn. iii. 24; v. 6, 8; Rev. xxii. 17.   Among the beneficent and very varied operations and effects ascribed to this Spirit in the N. T., the foll. are prominent: by it the man Jesus was begotten in the womb of the virgin Mary (Mt. i. 18, 20; Lk. i. 35), and at his baptism by John it is said to have descended upon Jesus (Mt. iii. 16; Mk. i. 10; Lk. iii. 22), so that he was perpetually (μένον ἐπ' αὐτόν) filled with it (Jn. i. 32, 33, cf. iii. 34; Mt. xii. 28; Acts x. 38); hence to its prompting and aid the acts and words of Christ are traced, Mt. iv. 1; xii. 28; Mk. i. 12; Lk. iv. 1, 14. After Christ's resurrection it was imparted also to the apostles, Jn. xx. 22; Acts ii. Subsequently other followers of Christ are related to have received it through faith (Gal. iii. 2), or by the instrumentality of baptism (Acts ii. 38; 1 Co. xii. 13) and the laying on of hands (Acts xix. 5, 6), although its reception was in no wise connected with baptism by any magical bond, Acts viii. 12, 15; x. 44 sqq. To its agency are referred all the blessings of the Christian religion, such as regeneration wrought in baptism (Jn. iii. 5, 6, 8; Tit. iii. 5, [but see the commentators on the passages, and reff. s. v. βάπτισμα, 3]); all sanctification (1 Co. vi. 11; hence ἁγιασμὸς πνεύματος, 2 Th. ii. 13; 1 Pet. i. 2); the power of suppressing evil desires and practising holiness (Ro. viii. 2 sqq.; Gal. v. 16 sqq. 22; 1 Pet. i. 22 [Rec.], etc.); fortitude to undergo with patience all persecutions, losses, trials, for Christ's sake (Mt. x. 20; Lk. xii. 11, 12; Ro. viii. 26); the knowledge of evangelical truth (Jn. xiv. 17, 26; xv. 26; xvi. 12, 13; 1 Co. ii. 6–16; Eph. iii. 5),—hence it is called πνεῦμα τῆς ἀληθείας (Jn. ll. cc.; 1 Jn. iv. 6), πνεῦμα σοφίας καὶ ἀποκαλύψεως (Eph. i. 17); the sure and joyful hope of a future resurrection, and of eternal blessedness (Ro. v. 5; viii. 11; 2 Co. i. 22; v. 5; Eph. i. 13 sq.); for the Holy Spirit is the seal and pledge of citizenship in the kingdom of God, 2 Co. i. 22; Eph. i. 13. He is present to teach, guide, prompt, restrain, those Christians whose agency God employs in carrying out his counsels: Acts viii. 29, 39; xi. 12; xiii. 2, 4; xv. 28; xvi. 6, 7; xx. 28. He is the author of charisms or special "gifts" (1 Co. xii. 7 sqq.; see χάρισμα), prominent among which is the power of prophesying: τὰ ἐρχόμενα ἀναγγελεῖ, Jn. xvi. 13; hence τὸ πνεῦμα τῆς προφητείας (Rev. xix. 10); and his efficiency in the prophets is called τὸ πνεῦμα simply (1 Th. v. 19), and their utterances are introduced with these formulas: τάδε λέγει τὸ πνεῦμα τὸ ἅγιον, Acts xxi. 11; τὸ πνεῦμα λέγει, 1 Tim. iv. 1; Rev. xiv. 13; with ταῖς ἐκκλησίαις added, Rev. ii. 7, 11, 17, 29; iii. 6, 13, 22. Since the Holy Spirit by his inspiration was the author also of the O. T. Scriptures (2 Pet. i. 21; 2 Tim. iii. 16), his utterances are cited in the foll. terms: λέγει or μαρτυρεῖ τὸ πνεῦμα τὸ ἅγιον, Heb. iii. 7; x. 15; τὸ πν. τὸ ἅγ. ἐλάλησε διὰ Ἡσαΐου, Acts xxviii. 25, cf. i. 16. From among the great number of other phrases referring to the Holy Spirit the following seem to be noteworthy here: God is said διδόναι τινὶ τὸ πν. τὸ ἅγ., Lk. xi. 13; Acts xv. 8; pass. Ro. v. 5; more precisely, ἐκ τοῦ πνεύματος αὐτοῦ, i. e. a portion from his Spirit's fulness [B. § 132, 7; W. 366 (343)], 1 Jn. iv. 13; or ἐκχεῖν ἀπὸ τοῦ πνεύματος αὐτοῦ, Acts ii. 17, 18, (for its entire fulness Christ alone receives, Jn. iii. 34); men are said, λαμβάνειν πν. ἅγ., Jn. xx. 22; Acts viii. 15, 17, 19; xix. 2; or τὸ πν. τὸ ἅγ. Acts x. 47; or τὸ πν. τὸ ἐκ θεοῦ, 1 Co. ii. 12; or τὸ πνεῦμα, Gal. iii. 2, cf. Ro. viii. 15; πν. θεοῦ ἔχειν, 1 Co. vii. 40; πνεῦμα μὴ ἔχειν, Jude 19; πληροῦσθαι πνεύματος ἁγίου, Acts xiii. 52; ἐν πνεύματι, Eph. v. 18; πλησθῆναι, πλησθήσεσθαι, πνεύματος ἁγίου, Lk. i. 15, 41, 67; Acts ii. 4; iv. 8, 31; ix. 17; xiii. 9; πνεύματος ἁγίου πλήρης, Acts vi. 5; vii. 55; xi. 24; πλήρεις πνεύματος (Rec. adds ἁγίου) καὶ σοφίας, Acts vi. 3; πνεύματι and πνεύματι θεοῦ ἄγεσθαι, to be led by the Holy Spirit, Ro. viii. 14; Gal. v. 18; φέρεσθαι ὑπὸ πν. ἁγ. 2 Pet. i. 21; the Spirit is said to dwell in the minds of Christians, Ro. viii. 9, 11; 1 Co. iii. 16; vi. 19; 2 Tim. i. 14; Jas. iv. 5, (other expressions may be found under βαπτίζω, II. b. bb.; γεννάω, 1 fin. and 2 d.; ἐκχέω b.; χρίω, a.); γίνεσθαι ἐν πνεύματι, to come to be in the Spirit, under the power of the Spirit, i. e. in a state of inspiration or ecstasy, Rev. i. 10; iv. 2. Dative πνεύματι, by the power and aid of the Spirit, the Spirit prompting, Ro. viii. 13; Gal. v. 5; τῷ πν. τῷ ἁγίῳ, Lk. x. 21 L Tr WH; πνεύματι ἁγίῳ, 1 Pet. i. 12 (where R G T have ἐν πν. ἁγ.); πνεύματι θεοῦ, Phil. iii. 3 L T Tr WH; also ἐν πνεύματι, Eph. ii. 22; iii. 5 (where ἐν πνεύματι must be joined to ἀπεκαλύφθη); ἐν πνεύματι, in the power of the Spirit, possessed and moved by the Spirit, Mt. xxii. 43; Rev. xvii. 3; xxi. 10; also ἐν τῷ πνεύματι, Lk. ii. 27; iv. 1; ἐν τῷ πν. τῷ ἁγ. Lk. x. 21 Tdf.; ἐν τῇ δυνάμει τοῦ πν. Lk. iv. 14; ἐν τῷ πνεύματι τῷ ἁγ. εἰπεῖν, Mk. xii. 36; ἐν πνεύματι (ἁγ.) προσεύχεσθαι, Eph. vi. 18; Jude 20; ἐν πν. θεοῦ λαλεῖν, 1 Co. xii. 3; ἀγάπη ἐν πνεύματι, love which the Spirit begets, Col. i. 8; περιτομὴ ἐν πν., effected by the Holy Spirit, opp. to γράμματι, the prescription of the written law, Ro. ii. 29; τύπος γίνου τῶν πιστῶν ἐν πν., in the way in which you are governed by the Spirit, 1 Tim. iv. 12 Rec.; [ἐν ἑνὶ πνεύματι, Eph. ii. 18]; ἡ ἑνότης τοῦ πνεύματος, effected by the Spirit, Eph. iv. 3; καινότης τοῦ πν. Ro. vii. 6. τὸ πνεῦμα is opp. to ἡ σάρξ i. e. human nature left to itself and without the controlling influence of God's Spirit, subject to error and sin, Gal. v. 17, 19, 22; [vi. 8]; Ro. viii. 6; so in the phrases περιπατεῖν κατὰ πνεῦμα (opp. to κατὰ σάρκα), Ro. viii. 1 Rec., 4; οἱ κατὰ πνεῦμα sc. ὄντες (opp. to οἱ κατὰ σάρκα ὄντες), those who bear the nature of the Spirit (i. e. οἱ πνευματικοί), ib. 5; ἐν πνεύματι εἶναι (opp. to ἐν σαρκί), to be under the power of the Spirit, to be guided by the Spirit, ib. 9; πνεύματι (dat. of 'norm'; [cf. B. § 133, 22 b.; W. 219 (205)]) περιπατεῖν (opp. to ἐπιθυμίαν σαρκὸς τελεῖν), Gal. v. 16. The Holy Spirit is a δύναμις, and is expressly so called in Lk. xxiv. 49, and δύναμις ὑψίστου, Lk. i. 35; but we find also πνεῦμα (or πν. ἅγ.) καὶ δύναμις, Acts x. 38; 1 Co. ii. 4; and ἡ δύναμις τοῦ πνεύματος, Lk. iv. 14, where πνεῦμα is regarded as the essence, and δύναμις its efficacy; but in 1 Th. i. 5 ἐν πνεύματι ἁγίῳ is epexegetical

of ἐν δυνάμει. In some pass. the Holy Spirit is rhetorically represented as a Person [(cf. reff. below)]: Mt. xxviii.19; Jn. xiv. 16 sq. 26; xv. 26; xvi. 13–15 (in which pass. fr. Jn. the personification was suggested by the fact that the Holy Spirit was about to assume with the apostles the place of a person, namely of Christ); τὸ πν., καθὼς βούλεται, 1 Co. xii. 11; what any one through the help of the Holy Spirit has come to understand or decide upon is said to have been spoken to him by the Holy Spirit: εἶπε τὸ πνεῦμά τινι, Acts viii. 29; x. 19; xi. 12; xiii. 4; τὸ πν. τὸ ἅγ. διαμαρτύρεταί μοι, Acts xx. 23. τὸ πν. τὸ ἅγ. ἔθετο ἐπισκόπους, i. e. not only rendered them fit to discharge the office of bishop, but also exercised such an influence in their election (xiv. 23) that none except fit persons were chosen to the office, Acts xx. 28; τὸ πνεῦμα ὑπερεντυγχάνει στεναγμοῖς ἀλαλήτοις in Ro. viii. 26 means, as the whole context shows, nothing other than this: 'although we have no very definite conception of what we desire (τί προσευξώμεθα), and cannot state it in fit language (καθὸ δεῖ) in our prayer but only disclose it by inarticulate groanings, yet God receives these groanings as acceptable prayers inasmuch as they come from a soul full of the Holy Spirit.' Those who strive against the sanctifying impulses of the Holy Spirit are said ἀντιπίπτειν τῷ πν. τῷ ἁγ. Acts vii. 51; ἐνυβρίζειν τὸ πν. τῆς χάριτος, Heb. x. 29. πειράζειν τὸ πν. τοῦ κυρίου is applied to those who by falsehood would discover whether men full of the Holy Spirit can be deceived, Acts v. 9; by anthropopathism those who disregard decency in their speech are said λυπεῖν τὸ πν. τὸ ἅγ., since by that they are taught how they ought to talk, Eph. iv. 30 (παροξύνειν τὸ πν. Is. lxiii. 10; παραπικραίνειν, Ps. cv. (cvi.) 33). Cf. Grimm, Institutio theologiae dogmaticae, § 131; [Weiss, Bibl. Theol. § 155 (and Index s. v. 'Geist Gottes,' 'Spirit of God'); Kahnis, Lehre vom Heil. Geiste; Fritzsche, Nova opuscc. acad. p. 278 sqq.; B. D. s. v. Spirit the Holy; Swete in Dict. of Christ. Biog. s. v. Holy Ghost]. **b.** τὰ ἑπτὰ πνεύματα τοῦ θεοῦ, Rev. [iii. 1 (where Rec.st om. ἑπτά)]; iv. 5; v. 6 [here L om. WH br. ἑπτά], which are said to be ἐνώπιον τοῦ θρόνου τοῦ θεοῦ (i. 4) are not seven angels, but one and the same divine Spirit manifesting itself in seven energies or operations (which are rhetorically personified, Zech. iii. 9; iv. 6, 10); cf. Düsterdieck on Rev. i. 4; [Trench, Epp. to the Seven Churches, ed. 3 p. 7 sq.]. **c.** by meton. πνεῦμα is used of **α.** one in whom a spirit (πνεῦμα) is manifest or embodied; hence i. q. actuated by a spirit, whether divine or demoniacal; one who either is truly moved by God's Spirit or falsely boasts that he is: 2 Th. ii. 2; 1 Jn. iv. 2, 3; hence διακρίσεις πνευμάτων, 1 Co. xii. 10; μὴ παντὶ πνεύματι πιστεύετε, 1 Jn. iv. 1; δοκιμάζετε τὰ πνεύματα, εἰ ἐκ τοῦ θεοῦ ἐστίν, ibid.; πνεύματα πλάνα joined with διδασκαλίαι δαιμονίων, 1 Tim. iv. 1. But in the truest and highest sense it is said ὁ κύριος τὸ πνεῦμά ἐστιν, he in whom the entire fulness of the Spirit dwells, and from whom that fulness is diffused through the body of Christian believers, 2 Co. iii. 17. **β.** the plur. πνεύματα denotes the various modes and gifts by which the Holy Spirit shows itself operative in those in whom it dwells (such as τὸ πνεῦμα τῆς προφητείας, τῆς σοφίας, etc.), 1 Co. xiv. 12.

5. univ. *the disposition* or *influence which fills and governs the soul of any one*; *the efficient source of any power, affection, emotion, desire*, etc.: τῷ αὐτῷ πνεύματι περιεπατήσαμεν, 2 Co. xii. 18 ; ἐν πνεύματι 'Ηλίου, in the same spirit with which Elijah was filled of old, Lk. i. 17 ; τὰ ῥήματα ... πνευμά ἐστιν, exhale a spirit (and fill believers with it), Jn. vi. 63 ; οἵου πνεύματός ἐστε ὑμεῖς, [*what manner of spirit ye are of*] viz. a divine spirit, that I have imparted unto you, Lk. ix. 55 [Rec.; (cf. B. § 132, 11 I.; W. § 30, 5)] ; τῷ πνεύματι, ᾧ ἐλάλει, Acts vi. 10, where see Meyer; πραὺ καὶ ἡσύχιον πνεῦμα, 1 Pet. iii. 4 ; πνεῦμα πραότητος, such as belongs to the meek, 1 Co. iv. 21 ; Gal. vi. 1 ; τὸ πν. τῆς προφητείας, such as characterizes prophecy and by which the prophets are governed, Rev. xix. 10 ; τῆς ἀληθείας, σοφίας καὶ ἀποκαλύψεως, see above p. 521ᵇ mid. (Is. xi. 2 ; Deut. xxxiv. 9 ; Sap. vii. 7) ; τῆς πίστεως, 2 Co. iv. 13 ; τῆς υἱοθεσίας, such as belongs to sons, Ro. viii. 15 ; τῆς ζωῆς ἐν Χριστῷ, of the life which one gets in fellowship with Christ, ibid. 2 ; δυνάμεως καὶ ἀγάπης καὶ σωφρονισμοῦ, 2 Tim. i. 7 ; ἐν πνεῦμα εἶναι with Christ, i. q. to be filled with the same spirit as Christ and by the bond of that spirit to be intimately united to Christ, 1 Co. vi. 17 ; ἐν ἑνὶ πνεύματι, by the reception of one Spirit's efficiency, 1 Co. xii. 13 ; εἰς ἓν πνεῦμα, so as to be united into one body filled with one Spirit, ibid. R G ; ἐν πνεῦμα ποτίζεσθαι, [*made to drink of* i. e.] imbued with one Spirit, ibid. L T Tr WH [see ποτίζω] ; ἐν σῶμα καὶ ἐν πνεῦμα, one (social) body filled and animated by one spirit, Eph. iv. 4 ; — in all these pass. although the language is general, yet it is clear from the context that the writer means a spirit begotten of the Holy Spirit or even identical with that Spirit [(cf. Clem. Rom. 1 Cor. 46, 6 ; Herm. sim. 9, 13. 18 ; Ignat. ad Magn. 7)]. In opposition to the divine Spirit stand, τὸ πνεῦμα τὸ ἐνεργοῦν ἐν τοῖς υἱοῖς τῆς ἀπειθείας (a spirit that comes from the devil), Eph. ii. 2 ; also τὸ πνεῦμα τοῦ κόσμου, the spirit that actuates the unholy multitude, 1 Co. ii. 12 ; δουλείας, such as characterizes and governs slaves, Ro. viii. 15 ; κατανύξεως, Ro. xi. 8 ; δειλίας, 2 Tim. i. 7 ; τῆς πλάνης, 1 Jn. iv. 6 (πλανήσεως, Is. xix. 14 ; πορνείας, Hos. iv. 12 ; v. 4) ; τὸ τοῦ ἀντιχρίστου sc. πνεῦμα, 1 Jn. iv. 3 ; ἕτερον πνεῦμα λαμβάνειν, i. e. different from the Holy Spirit, 2 Co. xi. 4 ; τὸ πν. τοῦ νοός, the governing spirit of the mind, Eph. iv. 23.   Cf. *Ackermann*, Beiträge zur theol. Würdigung u. Abwägung der Begriffe πνεῦμα, νοῦς, u. Geist, in the Theol. Stud. u. Krit. for 1839, p. 873 sqq. ; *Büchsenschütz*, La doctrine de l'Esprit de Dieu selon l'ancien et nouveau testament. Strasb. 1840 ; *Chr. Fr. Fritzsche*, De Spiritu Sancto commentatio exegetica et dogmatica, 4 Pts. Hal. 1840 sq., included in his Nova opuscula academica (Turici, 1846) p. 233 sqq.; *Kahnis*, Die Lehre v. heil. Geist. Pt. i. (Halle, 1847) ; an anonymous publication [by Prince *Ludwig Solms Lich*, entitled] Die biblische Bedeutung des Wortes Geist. (Giessen, 1862) ; *H. H. Wendt*, Die Begriffe Fleisch u. Geist im bibl. Sprachgebrauch. (Gotha, 1878) ; [*Cremer*

in Herzog ed. 2, s. v. Geist des Menschen ; *G. L. Hahn*, Theol. d. N. Test. i. § 149 sqq.; *J. Laidlaw*, The Bible Doctrine of Man. (Cunningham Lects., 7th Series, 1880); *Dickson*, St. Paul's use of the terms Flesh and Spirit. (Glasgow, 1883) ; and reff. in B. D. (esp. Am. ed.) and Dict. of Christ. Biog., as above, 4 a. fin.]*

πνευματικός, -ή, -όν, (πνεῦμα), *spiritual* (Vulg. *spiritalis*);   **4152** in the N. T.   **1.** *relating to the human spirit*, or *rational soul, as the part of man which is akin to God and serves as his instrument or organ*, opp. to ἡ ψυχή (see πνεῦμα, 2) : hence τὸ πνευματικόν, that which possesses the nature of the rational soul, opp. to τὸ ψυχικόν, 1 Co. xv. 46 [cf. W. 592 (551)] ; σῶμα πνευματικόν, the body which is animated and controlled only by the rational soul and by means of which the rational life, or life of the πνεῦμα, is lived ; opp. to σῶμα ψυχικόν, verse 44.   **2.** *belonging to a spirit*, or *a being higher than man but inferior to God* (see πνεῦμα, 3 c.) : τὰ πνευματικά (i. e. spiritual beings or powers, [R. V. *spiritual hosts*], cf. W. 239 (224)) τῆς πονηρίας (gen. of quality), i. e. *wicked spirits*, Eph. vi. 12.   **3.** *belonging to the Divine Spirit*;   **a.** *in reference to things*; *emanating from the Divine Spirit*, or *exhibiting its effects and so its character* : χάρισμα, Ro. i. 11 ; εὐλογία, Eph. i. 3 ; σοφία καὶ σύνεσις πνευματική (opp. to σοφία σαρκική, 2 Co. i. 12 ; ψυχική, Jas. iii. 15), Col. i. 9 ; ᾠδαί, divinely inspired, and so redolent of the Holy Spirit, Col. iii. 16 ; [Eph. v. 19 Lchm. br.] ; ὁ νόμος (opp. to a σάρκινος man), Ro. vii. 14 ; θυσίαι, tropically, the acts of a life dedicated to God and approved by him, due to the influence of the Holy Spirit (tacitly opp. to the sacrifices of an external worship), 1 Pet. ii. 5 ; i. q. *produced by the sole power of God himself without natural instrumentality, supernatural*, βρῶμα, πόμα, πέτρα, 1 Co. x. 3, 4, [(cf. 'Teaching' etc. 10, 3)] ; πνευματικά, thoughts, opinions, precepts, maxims, ascribable to the Holy Spirit working in the soul, 1 Co. ii. 13 (on which see συγκρίνω, 1) ; τὰ πνευματικά, spiritual gifts, — of the endowments called χαρίσματα (see χάρισμα), 1 Co. xii. 1 ; xiv. 1 ; univ. the spiritual or heavenly blessings of the gospel, opp. to τὰ σαρκικά, Ro. xv. 27 ; [1 Co. ix. 11].   **b.** *in reference to persons*; *one who is filled with and governed by the Spirit of God* : 1 Co. ii. 15 (cf. 10–13, 16) ; [iii. 1] ; xiv. 37 ; Gal. vi. 1 ; οἶκος πνευματικός, of a body of Christians (see οἶκος, 1 b. fin.), 1 Pet. ii. 5.   (The word is not found in the O. T. [cf. W. § 34, 3]. In prof. writ. fr. Aristot. down it means *pertaining to the wind* or *breath*; *windy, exposed to the wind*; *blowing*; [but *Soph.* Lex. s. v. cites πν. οὐσία, Cleomed. i, 8 p. 46 ; τὸ πν. τὸ πάντων τούτων αἴτιον, Strab. **1,** 3, 5 p. 78, 10 ed. Kramer ; and we find it opp. to σωματικόν in Plut. mor. p. 129 c. (de sanitate praecepta 14) ; cf. Anthol. Pal. 8, 76. 175].)*

πνευματικῶς, adv., *spiritually*, (Vulg. *spiritaliter*) : i. e.   **4153** by the aid of the Holy Spirit, 1 Co. ii. [13 WH mrg.], 14 ; in a sense apprehended only by the aid of the Divine Spirit, i. e. in a hidden or mystical sense, Rev. xi. 8. Its opposite σαρκικῶς in the sense of *literally* is used by Justin Mart. dial. c. Tryph. c. 14 p. 231 d.*

4154 πνέω; 1 aor. ἔπνευσα; fr. Hom. down; *to breathe, to blow*: of the wind, Mt. vii. 25, 27; Lk. xii. 55; Jn. iii. 8; vi. 18; Rev. vii. 1; τῇ πνεούσῃ sc. αὔρᾳ (cf. W. 591 (550); [B. 82 (72)]), Acts xxvii. 40. [COMP.: ἐκ-, ἐν-, ὑπο- πνέω.]*

4155 πνίγω: impf. ἔπνιγον; 1 aor. ἔπνιξα; impf. pass. 3 pers. plur. ἐπνίγοντο; **a.** *to choke, strangle*: used of thorns crowding down the seed sown in a field and hindering its growth, Mt. xiii. 7 T WH mrg.; in the pass. of perishing by drowning (Xen. anab. 5, 7, 25; cf. Joseph. antt. 10, 7, 5), Mk. v. 13. **b.** *to wring one's neck, throttle,* [A. V. *to take one by the throat*]: Mt. xviii. 28. [COMP.: ἀπο-, ἐπι-, συμ- πνίγω.]*

4156 πνικτός, -ή, -όν, (πνίγω), *suffocated, strangled*: τὸ πνικτόν, [*what is strangled*, i. e.] an animal deprived of life without shedding its blood, Acts xv. 20, 29; xxi. 25. [(Several times in Athen. and other later writ., chiefly of cookery; cf. our "smothered" as a culinary term.)]*

4157 πνοή, -ῆς, ἡ, (πνέω), fr. Hom. down, Sept. for נְשָׁמָה; **1.** *breath, the breath of life*: Acts xvii. 25 (Gen. ii. 7; Prov. xxiv. 12; Sir. xxx. 29 (21); 2 Macc. iii. 31; vii. 9). **2.** *wind*: Acts ii. 2 (Job xxxvii. 9). [Cf. πνεῦμα, 1 b.]*

4158 ποδήρης, -ες, acc. -ρην, Lchm. ed. ster. Tdf. ed. 7 in Rev. i. 13; see ἄρσην, (πούς, and ἄρω 'to join together,' 'fasten'), *reaching to the feet* (Aeschyl., Eur., Xen., Plut., al.): ὁ ποδήρης (sc. χιτών, Ex. xxv. 6; xxviii. 4; xxxv. 8; Ezek. ix. 3) or ἡ ποδήρης (sc. ἐσθής), *a garment reaching to the ankles, coming down to the feet*, Rev. i. 13 (Sir. xxvii. 8; xlv. 8; χιτὼν ποδήρης, Xen. Cyr. 6, 4, 2; Paus. 5, 19, 6; ὑποδύτης ποδ. Ex. xxviii. 27; ἔνδυμα ποδ. Sap. xviii. 24; [Joseph. b. j. 5, 5, 7]). [Cf. Trench § l. sub fin.]*

4159 πόθεν, adv., [fr. Hom. down], *whence*; **a.** of place, *from what place*: Mt. xv. 33; Lk. xiii. 25, 27; Jn. iii. 8; vi. 5; viii. 14; ix. 29, 30; xix. 9; Rev. vii. 13; *from what condition*, Rev. ii. 5. **b.** of origin or source, i. q. *from what author* or *giver*: Mt. xiii. [27], 54, 56; xxi. 25; Mk. vi. 2; Lk. xx. 7; Jn. ii. 9; Jas. iv. 1; *from what parentage*, Jn. vii. 27 sq. (cf. vi. 42), see Meyer ad loc. **c.** of cause, *how is it that? how can it be that?* Mk. viii. 4; xii. 37; Lk. i. 43; Jn. i. 48 (49); iv. 11.*

see 4169 ποία, -ας, ἡ, [cf. Curtius § 387], *herbage, grass*: acc. to some interpreters found in Jas. iv. 14; but ποία there is more correctly taken as the fem. of the adj. ποῖος (q. v.), *of what sort.* (Jer. ii. 22; Mal. iii. 2; in Grk. writ. fr. Hom. down.)*

4160 ποιέω, -ῶ; impf. 3 pers. sing. ἐποίει, plur. 2 pers. ἐποιεῖτε, 3 pers. ἐποίουν; fut. ποιήσω; 1 aor. ἐποίησα, 3 pers. plur. optat. ποιήσειαν (Lk. vi. 11 R G; cf. W. § 13, 2 d.; [B. 42 (37)]) and ποιήσαιεν (ibid. L T Tr WH [see WH. App. p. 167]); pf. πεποίηκα; plpf. πεποιήκειν without augm. (Mk. xv. 7; see W. § 12, 9; B. 33 (29)); Mid., pres. ποιοῦμαι; impf. ἐποιούμην; fut. ποιήσομαι; 1 aor. ἐποιησάμην; pf. pass. ptcp. πεποιημένος (Heb. xii. 27); fr. Hom. down; Hebr. עָשָׂה; Lat. *facio*, i. e.

I. *to make* (Lat. *efficio*), **1.** τί; **a.** with the names of the things made, *to produce, construct, form, fashion*, etc.: ἀνθρακιάν, Jn. xviii. 18; εἰκόνα, Rev. xiii.

14; ἱμάτια, Acts ix. 39; ναούς, Acts xix. 24; σκηνάς, Mt. xvii. 4; Mk. ix. 5; Lk. ix. 33; τύπους, Acts vii. 43; πηλόν, Jn. ix. 11, 14; πλάσμα, Ro. ix. 20; acc. to some interpreters (also W. 256 n.¹ (240 n.²)) ὁδὸν ποιεῖν, *to make a path*, Mk. ii. 23 R G T Tr txt. WH txt. (so that the meaning is, that the disciples of Christ made a path for themselves through the standing grain by plucking the heads; see ὁδοποιέω, fin. If we adopt this interpretation, we must take the ground that Mark does not give us the true account of the matter, but has sadly corrupted the narrative received from others; [those who do accept it, however, not only lay stress on the almost unvarying lexical usage, but call attention to the fact that the other interpretation (see below) finds the leading idea expressed in the participle—an idiom apparently foreign to the N. T. (see W. 353 (331)), and to the additional circumstance that Mk. introduces the phrase after having already expressed the idea of 'going', and expressed it by substantially the same word (παραπορεύεσθαι) which Matthew (xii. 1) and Luke (vi. 1) employ and regard as of itself sufficient. On the interpretation of the pass., the alleged 'sad corruption,' etc., see *Jas. Morison*, Com. on Mk. 2d ed. p. 57 sq.; on the other side, *Weiss*, Marcusevangelium, p. 100]. But see just below, under c.). *to create, to produce*: of God, as the author of all things, τί or τινά, Mt. xix. 4; Mk. x. 6; Lk. xi. 40; Heb. i. 2; Acts iv. 24; vii. 50; xvii. 24; Rev. xiv. 7; pass. Heb. xii. 27, (Sap. i. 13; ix. 9; 2 Macc. vii. 28, and often in the O. T. Apocrypha; for עָשָׂה in Gen. i. 7, 16, 25, etc.; for בָּרָא in Gen. i. 21, 27; v. 1, etc.; also in Grk. writ.: γένος ἀνθρώπων, Hes. op. 109, etc.; absol. ὁ ποιῶν, the creator, Plat. Tim. p. 76 c.); here belongs also Heb. iii. 2, on which see Bleek and Lünemann [(cf. below, 2 c. β.)]. In imitation of the Hebr. עָשָׂה (cf. Winer ['s Simonis (4th ed. 1828)], Lex. Hebr. et Chald. p. 754; *Gesenius*, Thes. ii. p. 1074 sq.) absol. of men, *to labor, to do work*, Mt. xx. 12 (Ruth ii. 19); i. q. *to be operative, exercise activity*, Rev. xiii. 5 R not elz. L T Tr WH [cf. Dan. xi. 28; but al. render ποιεῖν in both these exx. *spend, continue*, in ref. to time; see II. d. below]. **b.** joined to nouns denoting a state or condition, it signifies *to be the author of, to cause*: σκάνδαλα, Ro. xvi. 17; εἰρήνην (to be the author of harmony), Eph. ii. 15; Jas. iii. 18; ἐπισύστασιν [L T Tr WH ἐπίστασιν], Acts xxiv. 12; συστροφήν, Acts xxiii. 12; ποιῶ τινί τι, to bring, afford, a thing to one, Lk. i. 68; Acts xv. 3, (so also Grk. writ., as Xen. mem. 3, 10, 8 [cf. L. and S. s. v. A. II. 1 a.]). **c.** joined to nouns involving the idea of action (or of something which is accomplished by action), so as to form a periphrasis for the verb cognate to the substantive, and thus to express the idea of the verb more forcibly,—in which species of periphrasis the Grks. more commonly use the middle (see 3 below, and W. 256 (240); [B. § 135, 5]): μονὴν ποιῶ παρά τινι, Jn. xiv. 23 (where L T Tr WH ποιησόμεθα; cf. Thuc. 1, 131); ὁδὸν ποιεῖν, to make one's way, go, Mk. ii. 23 (where render as follows: *they began, as they went, to pluck the ears*; cf. ποιῆσαι ὁδὸν αὐτοῦ, Judg. xvii. 8; the Greeks say ὁδὸν ποιεῖσθαι, Hdt. 7, 42; see above, under a.); πόλεμον, Rev. xiii. 5 Rec.ᵉˡˢ; with the addition of μετά τινος (i. q. πολεμεῖν), Rev. xi. 7; xii. 17; xiii. 7 [here L om. WH Tr mrg. br. the cl.]; xix. 19, (see μετά, I. 2 d. p. 403ᵇ); ἐκδίκησιν, Lk. xviii. 7, 8; τινί, Acts vii. 24, (Mic. v. 15); ἐνέδραν, i. q. ἐνεδρεύω, to make an ambush, lay wait, Acts xxv. 3; συμβούλιον, i. q. συμβουλεύομαι, to hold a consultation, deliberate, Mk. iii. 6 [R G T Tr mrg. WH mrg. συμβ. ἐποίησαν]; xv. 1 [here T WH mrg. συμβ. ἐτοιμάσαντες]; συνωμοσίαν, i. q. συνόμνυμι, Acts xxiii. 13 (where L T Tr WH ποιησάμενοι for Rec. πεποιηκότες; see in 3 below); κρίσιν, to execute judgment, Jn. v. 27; Jude 15. To this head may be referred nouns by which the mode or kind of action is more precisely defined; as δυνάμεις, δύναμιν, ποιεῖν, Mt. vii. 22; xiii. 58; Mk. vi. 5; Acts xix. 11; τὴν ἐξουσίαν τινός, Rev. xiii. 12; ἔργον (a notable work), ἔργα, of Jesus, Jn. v. 36, vii. 3, 21; x. 25; xiv. 10, 12; xv. 24; κράτος, Lk. i. 51; σημεῖα, τέρατα καὶ σημεῖα, [Mk. xiii. 22 Tdf.]; Jn. ii. 23; iii. 2; iv. 54; vi. 2, 14, 30; vii. 31; ix. 16; x. 41; xi. 47; xii. 18, 37; xx. 30; Acts ii. 22; vi. 8; vii. 36; viii. 6; xv. 12; Rev. xiii. 13, 14; xvi. 14; xix. 20; θαυμάσια, Mt. xxi. 15; ὅσα ἐποίει, ἐποίησαν, etc., Mk. iii. 8; vi. 30; Lk. ix. 10; in other phrases it is used of marvellous works, Mt. ix. 28; Lk. iv. 23; Jn. iv. 45; vii. 4; xi. 45, 46; xxi. 25 [not Tdf.]; Acts x. 39; xiv. 11; xxi. 19; etc. **d.** i. q. *to make ready, to prepare*: ἄριστον, Lk. xiv. 12; δεῖπνον, Mk. vi. 21; Lk. xiv. 16; Jn. xii. 2, (δεῖπνον ποιεῖσθαι, Xen. Cyr. 3, 3, 25); δοχήν, Lk. v. 29; xiv. 13, (Gen. xxi. 8); γάμους, Mt. xxii. 2 (γάμον, Tob. viii. 19). **e.** of things effected by generative force, *to produce, bear, shoot forth*: of trees, vines, grass, etc., κλάδον, Mk. iv. 32; καρπούς, Mt. iii. 8, etc., see καρπός, 1 and 2 a. (Gen. i. 11, 12; Aristot. de plant. [1, 4 p. 819ᵇ, 31]; 2, 10 [829ᵃ, 41]; Theophr. de caus. plant. 4, 11 [(?)]); ἐλαίας, Jas. iii. 12 (τὸν οἶνον, of the vine, Joseph. antt. 11, 3, 5); of a fountain yielding water, ibid. **f.** ποιῶ ἐμαυτῷ τι, *to acquire, to provide a thing for one's self* (i. e. for one's use): βαλάντια, Lk. xii. 33; φίλους, Lk. xvi. 9; without a dative, *to gain*: of tradesmen (like our colloq. *to make* something), Mt. xxv. 16 [L Tr WH ἐκέρδησεν]; Lk. xix. 18, (Polyb. 2, 62, 12; *pecuniam maximam facere*, Cic. Verr. 2, 2, 6). **2.** With additions to the accusative which define or limit the idea of making: **a.** τὶ ἔκ τινος (gen. of material), *to make* a thing *out of* something, Jn. ii. 15; ix. 6; Ro. ix. 21; κατά τι, according to the pattern of a thing [see κατά, II. 3 c. a.], Acts vii. 44. with the addition, to the acc. of the thing, of an adjective with which the verb so blends that, taken with the adj., it may be changed into the verb cognate to the adj.: εὐθείας ποιεῖν (τὰς τρίβους), i. q. εὐθύνειν, Mt. iii. 3; Mk. i. 3; Lk. iii. 4; τρίχα λευκὴν ἢ μέλαιναν, i. q. λευκαίνειν, μελαίνειν, Mt. v. 36; add, Acts vii. 19; Heb. xii. 13; Rev. xxi. 5. **b.** τὸ ἱκανόν τινι; see ἱκανός, a. **c.** ποιεῖν τινα with an accus. of the predicate, **a.** *to (make* i. e.) *render one anything*: τινὰ ἴσον τινί, Mt. xx. 12; τινὰ δῆλον, Mt. xxvi. 73; add, Mt. xii. 16; xxviii. 14; Mk. iii. 12; Jn. v. 11, 15; vii. 23; xvi. 2; Ro. ix. 28 [R G, Tr mrg. in br.]; Heb. i. 7; Rev. xii. 15; τινὰς ἁλιεῖς, to make

them fit (qualify them) for fishing, Mt. iv. 19; [ποιῶν ταῦτα γνωστὰ ἀπ᾽ αἰῶνος, Acts xv. 17 sq. G T Tr WH (see γνωστός, and cf. II. a. below)]; τὰ ἀμφότερα ἕν, to make the two different things one, Eph. ii. 14; to change one thing into another, Mt. xxi. 13; Mk. xi. 17; Lk. xix. 46; Jn. ii. 16; iv. 46; 1 Co. vi. 15. **β.** *to (make* i. e.) *constitute or appoint one anything*: τινὰ κύριον, Acts ii. 36; Rev. v. 10; to this sense some interpreters would refer Heb. iii. 2 also, where after τῷ ποιήσαντι αὐτὸν they supply from the preceding context τὸν ἀπόστολον καὶ ἀρχιερέα κτλ.; but it is more correct to take ποιεῖν here in the sense of *create* (see 1 a. above); τινά, ἵνα with the subjunc. *to appoint or ordain one that* etc. Mk. iii. 14. **γ.** *to (make* i. e.) *declare one anything*: Jn. v. 18; viii. 53; x. 33; xix. 7, 12; 1 Jn. i. 10; v. 10; τί with an acc. of the pred. Mt. xii. 33 (on which see Meyer). **d.** with adverbs: καλῶς ποιῶ τι, Mk. vii. 37 [A. V. *do*]; τινὰ ἔξω, *to put one forth, to lead him out* (Germ. *hinausthun*), Acts v. 34 (Xen. Cyr. 4, 1, 3). **e.** ποιῶ τινα with an infin. *to make one do a thing*, Mk. viii. 25 [R G L Tr mrg.]; Lk. v. 34; Jn. vi. 10; Acts xvii. 26; or *become something*, Mk. i. 17; τινά foll. by τοῦ with an infin. *to cause one to* etc. Acts iii. 12 [W. 326 (306); B. § 140, 16 δ.]; also foll. by ἵνα [B. § 139, 43; W. § 44, 8 b. fin.], Jn. xi. 37; Col. iv. 16; Rev. xiii. 15 (here T om. WH br. ἵνα); iii. 9; xiii. 12, 16; [other exx. in Soph. Lex. s. v. 8]. **3.** As the active ποιεῖν (see 1 c. above), so also the middle ποιεῖσθαι, joined to accusatives of abstract nouns forms a periphrasis for the verb cognate to the substantive; and then, while ποιεῖν signifies *to be the author of a thing* (*to cause, bring about*, as ποιεῖν πόλεμον, εἰρήνην), ποιεῖσθαι denotes an action which pertains in some way to the actor (*for one's self, among themselves*, etc., as σπονδάς, εἰρήνην ποιεῖσθαι), or which is done by one with his own resources ([the 'dynamic' or 'subjective' mid.], as πόλεμον ποιεῖσθαι [*to make, carry on*, war]; cf. Passow s. v. I. 2 a. ii. p. 974 sq.; [L. and S. s. v. A. II. 4]; Krüger § 52, 8, 1; *Blume* ad Lycurg. p. 55; [W. § 38, 5 n.; B. § 135, 5]; although this distinction is not always observed even by the Greeks): ποιεῖσθαι μονήν, [make *our* abode], Jn. xiv. 23 L T Tr WH, (see 1 c. above); συνωμοσίαν (Hdian. 7, 4, 7 [3 ed. Bekk.]; Polyb. 1, 70, 6; 6, 13, 4; in the second instance Polyb. might more fitly have said ποιεῖν), Acts xxiii. 13 L T Tr WH, see 1 c. above; λόγον, to compose a narrative, Acts i. 1; to make account of, regard, (see λόγος, II. 2 [and cf. I. 3 a.]), Acts xx. 24 [T Tr WH, λόγου]; ἀναβολήν (see ἀναβολή), Acts xxv. 17; ἐκβολήν (see ἐκβολή, b.), Acts xxvii. 18; κοπετόν (i. q. κόπτομαι), Acts viii. 2 [here L T Tr WH give the active, cf. B. § 135, 5 n.]; πορείαν (i. q. πορεύομαι), Lk. xiii. 22 (Xen. Cyr. 5, 2, 31; anab. 5, 6, 11; Joseph. vit. §§ 11 and 52; Plut. de solert. anim. p. 971 e.; 2 Macc. iii. 8; xii. 10); κοινωνίαν, to make a contribution among themselves and from their own means, Ro. xv. 26; σπουδήν, Jude 3 (Hdt. 1, 4; 9, 8; Plat. legg. 1 p. 628 e.; Polyb. 1, 46, 2 and often; Diod. 1, 75; Plut. puer. educ. 7, 13; al.); αὔξησιν (i. q. αὐξάνομαι), to make increase, Eph. iv. 16; δέησιν, δεήσεις, i. q. δέομαι, to make supplication, Lk. v. 33; Phil. i. 4;

1 Tim. ii. 1; μνείαν (q. v.); μνήμην (q. v. in b.), 2 Pet. i. 15; πρόνοιαν (i. q. προνοοῦμαι), to have regard for, care for, make provision for, τινός, Ro. xiii. 14 (Isocr. paneg. §§ 2 and 136 [pp. 52 and 93 ed. Lange]; Dem. p. 1163, 19; 1429, 8; Polyb. 4, 6, 11; Dion. Hal. antt. 5, 46; Joseph. b. j. 4, 5, 2; antt. 5, 7, 9; c. Ap. 1, 2, 3; Ael. v. h. 12, 56; al.; cf. *Kypke*, Observv. ii. p. 187); καθαρισμόν, Heb. i. 3 (Job vii. 21); βέβαιον ποιεῖσθαί τι, i. q. βεβαιοῦν, 2 Pet. i. 10.

II. *to do* (Lat. *ago*), i. e. to follow some method in expressing by deeds the feelings and thoughts of the mind;   **a.** univ., with adverbs describing the mode of action: καλῶς, to act rightly, do well, Mt. xii. 12; 1 Co. vii. 37, 38; Jas. ii. 19; καλῶς ποιεῖν foll. by a participle [cf. B. § 144, 15 a.; W. § 45, 4 a.], Acts x. 33; Phil. iv. 14; 2 Pet. i. 19; 3 Jn. 6, (exx. fr. Grk. writ. are given by Passow s. v. II. 1 b. vol. ii. p. 977ᵃ; [L. and S. s. v. B. I. 3]); κρεῖσσον, 1 Co. vii. 38; φρονίμως, Lk. xvi. 8; οὕτω (οὕτως), Mt. v. 47 [R G]; xxiv. 46; Lk. ix. 15; xii. 43; Jn. xiv. 31; Acts xii. 8; 1 Co. xvi. 1; Jas. ii. 12; ὡς, καθώς, Mt. i. 24; xxi. 6; xxvi. 19; xxviii. 15; Lk. vi. 54 [T Tr txt. WH om. Tr mrg. br. the cl.]; 1 Th. v. 11; ὥσπερ, Mt. vi. 2; ὁμοίως, Lk. iii. 11; x. 37; ὡσαύτως, Mt. xx. 5. κατά τι, Mt. xxiii. 3; Lk. ii. 27; πρός τι, to do according to a thing [see πρός, I. 3 f.], Lk. xii. 47. with a ptcp. indicating the mode of acting, ἀγνοῶν ἐποίησα, I acted [A. V. *did it*] ignorantly, 1 Tim. i. 13. with the accus. of a thing, and that the accus. of a pronoun: with τί indef. 1 Co. x. 31; with τί interrog., Mt. xii. 12; Mk. ii. 25; xi. 3 [not Lchm. mrg.]; Lk. iii. 12, 14; vi. 2; x. 25; xvi. 3, 4; xviii. 18; Jn. vii. 51; xi. 47, etc.; with a ptcp. added, τί ποιεῖτε λύοντες; i. q. διὰ τί λύετε; Mk. xi. 5; τί ποιεῖτε κλαίοντες; Acts xxi. 13; but differently τί ποιήσουσι κτλ.; i. e. what must be thought of the conduct of those who receive baptism? Will they not seem to act foolishly? 1 Co. xv. 29. τί περισσόν, Mt. v. 47; with the relative ὅ, Mt. xxvi. 13; Mk. xiv. 9; Lk. vi. 3; Jn. xiii. 7; 2 Co. xi. 12, etc.; τοῦτο, i. e. what has just been said, Mt. xiii. 28; Mk. v. 32; Lk. v. 6; xxii. 19 [(WH reject the pass.)]; Ro. vii. 20; 1 Co. xi. 25; 1 Tim. iv. 16; Heb. vi. 3; vii. 27, etc.; τοῦτο to be supplied, Lk. vi. 10; αὐτὸ τοῦτο, Gal. ii. 10; ταῦτα, Mt. xxiii. 23; Gal. v. 17; 2 Pet. i. 10; [ταῦτα foll. by a pred. adj. Acts xv. 17 sq. G T Tr WH (acc. to one construction; cf. R. V. mrg., see I. 2 c. a. above, and cf. γνωστός)]; αὐτά, Ro. ii. 3; Gal. iii. 10. With nouns which denote a command, or some rule of action, ποιῶ signifies to carry out, to execute; as, τὸν νόμον, in class. Grk. to make a law, Lat. *legem ferre*, of legislators; but in bibl. Grk. to do the law, meet its demands, *legi satisfacere*, Jn. vii. 19; Gal. v. 3, (Josh. xxii. 5; 1 Chron. xxii. 12; עָשָׂה הַתּוֹרָה, 2 Chron. xiv. 3 (4)); τὰ τοῦ νόμου, the things which the law commands, Ro. ii. 14; τὰς ἐντολάς, Mt. v. 19; 1 Jn. v. 2 L T Tr WH; Rev. xxii. 14 R G; τὸ θέλημα τοῦ θεοῦ, Mt. vii. 21; xii. 50; Mk. iii. 35; Jn. iv. 34; vi. 38; vii. 17; ix. 31; Eph. vi. 6; Heb. xiii. 21; τὰ θελήματα τῆς σαρκός, Eph. ii. 3; τὰς ἐπιθυμίας τινός, Jn. viii. 44; τὴν γνώμην τινός, Rev. xvii. 17; μίαν γνώμην, to follow one and the same mind

(purpose) in acting, ibid. R G T Tr WH; τὸν λόγον τοῦ θεοῦ, Lk. viii. 21; τοὺς λόγους τινός, Mt. vii. 24, 26; Lk. vi. 47, 49; ἅ or ὅ or ὅ, τι etc. λέγει τις, Mt. xxiii. 3; Lk. vi. 46; Jn. ii. 5; Acts xxi. 23; ἃ παραγγέλλει τις, 2 Th. iii. 4; τὴν πρόθεσιν, Eph. iii. 11; τὰ διαταχθέντα, Lk. xvii. 10 (τὸ προσταχθέν, Soph. Phil. 1010); ὃ αἰτεῖ τις, Jn. xiv. 13 sq.; Eph. iii. 20; ὃ ἐντέλλεταί τις, Jn. xv. 14; τὰ ἔθη, Acts xvi. 21. With nouns describing a plan or course of action, *to perform, accomplish*: ἔργα, Tit. iii. 5; ποιεῖν τὰ ἔργα τινός, to do the same works as another, Jn. viii. 39, 41; τὰ πρῶτα ἔργα, Rev. ii. 5; τὰ ἔργα τοῦ θεοῦ, delivered by God to be performed, Jn. x. 37 sq.; τὸ ἔργον, work committed to me by God, Jn. xvii. 4; τὸ ἔργον εὐαγγελιστοῦ, to perform what the relations and duties of an evangelist demand, 2 Tim. iv. 5; ἔργον τι, to commit an evil deed, 1 Co. v. 2 [T WH Tr mrg. πρᾶξας]; plur. 3 Jn. 10; ἀγαθόν, to do good, Mt. xix. 16; [Mk. iii. 4 Tdf.]; 1 Pet. iii. 11; τὸ ἀγαθόν, Ro. xiii. 3; ὃ ἐάν τι ἀγαθόν, Eph. vi. 8; τὰ ἀγαθά, Jn. v. 29; τὸ καλόν, Ro. vii. 21; 2 Co. xiii. 7; Gal. vi. 9; Jas. iv. 17; τὰ ἀρεστὰ τῷ θεῷ, Jn. viii. 29; τὸ ἀρεστὸν ἐνώπιον τοῦ θεοῦ, Heb. xiii. 21; 1 Jn. iii. 22; τὶ πιστόν, to perform something worthy of a Christian [see πιστός, fin.], 3 Jn. 5; τὴν δικαιοσύνην, Mt. vi. 1 (for Rec. ἐλεημοσύνην); 1 Jn. ii. 29; iii. 7, 10 [not Lchm.; Rev. xxii. 11 G L T Tr WH]; τὴν ἀλήθειαν (to act uprightly; see ἀλήθεια, I. 2 c.), Jn. iii. 21; 1 Jn. i. 6; χρηστότητα, Ro. iii. 12; ἔλεος, to show one's self merciful, Jas. ii. 13; with μετά τινος added (see ἔλεος, -ους, 1 and 2 b.), Lk. i. 72; x. 37; ἐλεημοσύνην, Mt. vi. 2 sq.; plur., Acts ix. 36; x. 2 (see ἐλεημοσύνη, 1 and 2). *to commit*: τὴν ἁμαρτίαν, Jn. viii. 34; 1 Jn. iii. 4, 8; ἁμαρτίαν, 2 Co. xi. 7; Jas. v. 15; 1 Pet. ii. 22; 1 Jn. iii. 9; τὴν ἀνομίαν, Mt. xiii. 41; ἁμάρτημα, 1 Co. vi. 18; τὰ μὴ καθήκοντα, Ro. i. 28; ὃ οὐκ ἔξεστιν, Mt. xii. 2; Mk. ii. 24; ἄξια πληγῶν, Lk. xii. 48; βδέλυγμα, Rev. xxi. 27; φόνον, Mk. xv. 7; ψεῦδος, Rev. xxi. 27; xxii. 15; κακόν, Mt. xxvii. 23; Mk. xv. 14; Lk. xxiii. 22; 2 Co. xiii. 7; τὸ κακόν, Ro. xiii. 4; plur. κακά, 1 Pet. iii. 12; τὰ κακά, Ro. iii. 8.   **b.** ποιεῖν τι with the case of a person added;   **a.** w. an accus. of the person: τί ποιήσω Ἰησοῦν; what shall I do unto Jesus? Mt. xxvii. 22; Mk. xv. 12; cf. W. 222 (208); [B. § 131, 6; Kühner § 411, 5]; Matthiae § 415, 1 a. β.; also with an adverb, εὖ ποιῶ τινα, to do well i. e. show one's self good (kind) to one [see εὖ, sub fin.], Mk. xiv. 7 R G; also καλῶς ποιῶ, Mt. v. 44 Rec.   **β.** w. a dative of the person, *to do* (a thing) *unto* one (to his advantage or disadvantage), rarely so in Grk. writ. [cf. W. and B u. s.; Kühner u. s. Anm. 6]: Mt. vii. 12; xviii. 35; xx. 32; xxi. 40; xxv. 40, 45; Mk. v. 19, 20; x. 51; Lk. i. 49; vi. 11; viii. 39; xviii. 41; xx. 15; Jn. ix. 26; xii. 16; xiii. 12; Acts iv. 16; also with an adverb: καθώς, Mk. xv. 8; Lk. vi. 31; Jn. xiii. 15; ὁμοίως, Lk. vi. 31; οὕτως, Lk. i. 25; ii. 48; ὡσαύτως, Mt. xxi. 36; καλῶς ποιεῖν τινι, Lk. vi. 27; εὖ, Mk. xiv. 7 L Tr WH; κακά τινι, to do evil to one, Acts ix. 13; τί, *what* (sc. κακόν), Heb. xiii. 6 [acc. to punctuation of G L T Tr WH]; ταῦτα πάντα, all these evils, Jn. xv. 21 R G L mrg.; ποιεῖν τινι κατὰ τὰ αὐτά [L T Tr WH (Rec. ταῦτα)], *in the same manner*, Lk.

vi. 23, 26. **γ.** ποιεῖν τι with the more remote object added by means of a preposition: ἔν τινι (Germ. *an einem*), *to do to one*, Mt. xvii. 12; Lk. xxiii. 31 [here A.V. '*in* the green tree,' etc.]; also εἴς τινα, unto one, Jn. xv. 21 L txt. T Tr WH. **c.** God is said ποιῆσαί τι μετά τινος, when present with and aiding [see μετά, I. 2 b. β.], Acts xiv. 27; xv. 4. **d.** with designations of time [B. § 131, 1], *to pass, spend*: χρόνον, Acts xv. 33; xviii. 23; μῆνας τρεῖς, Acts xx. 3; νυχθήμερον, 2 Co. xi. 25; ἐνιαυτόν or ἐνιαυτὸν ἔνα, Jas. iv. 13, (Tob. x. 7; Joseph. antt. 6, 1, 4 fin.; Stallbaum on Plato, Phileb. p. 50 c., gives exx. fr. Grk. writ. [and reff.; cf. also *Soph.* Lex. s. v. 9]; in the same sense עָשָׂה in Eccl. vi. 12 (vii. 1); and the Lat. *facere*: Cic. ad Att. 5, 20 Apameae quinque dies *morati*, ... Iconii decem *fecimus*; Seneca, epp. 66 [l. 7, ep. 4, ed. Haase], quamvis autem paucissimos una *fecerimus* dies); some interpreters bring in here also Mt. xx. 12 and Rev. xiii. 5 Rec.[not elz.] L T Tr WH; but on these pass. see I. 1 a. above. **e.** like the Lat. *ago* i. q. *to celebrate, keep*, with the accus. of a noun designating a feast: τὸ πάσχα, Mt. xxvi. 18 (Josh. v. 10; but in Heb. xi. 28 the language denotes *to make ready*, and so at the same time *to institute*, the celebration of the passover; Germ. *veranstalten*); τὴν ἑορτήν, Acts xviii. 21 Rec. **f.** i. q. (Lat. *perficio*) *to perform*: as opposed to λέγειν, Mt. xxiii. 3; to θέλειν, 2 Co. viii. 10 sq.; to a promise, 1 Th. v. 24. [COMP.: περι-, προσ- ποιέω.]

[SYN. ποιεῖν, πράσσειν: roughly speaking, π. may be said to answer to the Lat. *facere* or the English *do*, πρ. to *agere* or Eng. *practise*; π. to designate performance, πρ. intended, earnest, habitual, performance; π. to denote merely productive action, πρ. definitely directed action; π. to point to an actual result, πρ. to the scope and character of the result. "In Attic in certain connections the difference between them is great, in others hardly perceptible" (*Schmidt*); see his Syn. ch. 23, esp. § 11; cf. *Trench*, N. T. Syn. § xcvi.; *Green*, 'Crit. Note' on Jn. v. 29; (cf. πράσσω, init. and 2). The words are associated in Jn. iii. 20, 21; v. 29; Acts xxvi. 9, 10; Ro. i. 32; ii. 3; vii. 15 sqq.; xiii. 4, etc.]

4161 ποίημα, -τος, τό, (ποιέω), *that which has been made*: *a work*: of the works of God as creator, Ro. i. 20; those κτισθέντες by God ἐπὶ ἔργοις ἀγαθοῖς are spoken of as ποίημα τοῦ θεοῦ [A. V. his *workmanship*], Eph. ii. 10. (Hdt., Plat., al.; Sept. chiefly for מַעֲשֶׂה.)*

4162 ποίησις, -εως, ἡ, (ποιέω); **1.** *a making* (Hdt. 3, 22; Thuc. 3, 2; Plat., Dem., al.; Sept. several times for מַעֲשֶׂה. **2.** *a doing* or *performing*: ἐν τῇ ποιήσει αὐτοῦ [*in his doing*, i. e.] in the obedience he renders to the law, Jas. i. 25; add Sir. xix. 20 (18).*

4163 ποιητής, -οῦ, ὁ, (ποιέω); **1.** *a maker, producer, author*, (Xen., Plat., al.). **2.** *a doer, performer*, (Vulg. *factor*): τοῦ νόμου, one who obeys or fulfils the law, Ro. ii. 13; Jas. iv. 11; 1 Macc. ii. 67, (see ποιέω, II. a.); ἔργου, Jas. i. 25; λόγου, Jas. i. 22, 23. **3.** *a poet*: Acts xvii. 28 ([Hdt. 2, 53, etc.], Aristoph., Xen., Plat., Plut., al.).*

4164 ποικίλος, -η, -ον, fr. Hom. down, *various* i. e. **a.** *of divers colors, variegated*: Sept. **b.** i. q. *of divers sorts*: Mt. iv. 24; Mk. i. 34; Lk. iv. 40; 2 Tim. iii. 6; Tit.

iii. 3; Heb. ii. 4; xiii. 9; Jas. i. 2; 1 Pet. i. 6; iv. 10, [(A. V. in the last two exx. *manifold*)].*

4165 ποιμαίνω; fut. ποιμανῶ; 1 aor. impv. 2 pers. plur. ποιμάνατε (1 Pet. v. 2); (ποιμήν, q. v.); fr. Hom. down; Sept. for רָעָה; *to feed, to tend a flock, keep sheep*; **a.** prop.: Lk. xvii. 7; ποίμνην, 1 Co. ix. 7. **b.** trop. **α.** *to rule, govern*: of rulers, τινά, Mt. ii. 6; Rev. ii. 27; xii. 5; xix. 15, (2 S. v. 2; Mic. v. 6 (5); vii. 14, etc.; [cf. W. 17]), (see ποιμήν, b. fin.); of the overseers (pastors) of the church, Jn. xxi. 16; Acts xx. 28; 1 Pet. v. 2. **β.** *to furnish pasturage* or *food*; *to nourish*: ἑαυτόν, to cherish one's body, to serve the body, Jude 12; to supply the requisites for the soul's needs [R. V. *shall be their shepherd*], Rev. vii. 17. [SYN. see βόσκω, fin.]*

4166 ποιμήν, -ένος, ὁ, (akin to the noun ποία, q. v.; [or fr. r. meaning 'to protect'; cf. Curtius § 372; Fick i. 132]), fr. Hom. down; Sept. for רָעָה, *a herdsman*, esp. *a shepherd*; **a.** prop.: Mt. ix. 36; xxv. 32; xxvi. 31; Mk. vi. 34; xiv. 27; Lk. ii. 8, 15, 18, 20; Jn. x. 2, 12; in the parable, he to whose care and control others have committed themselves, and whose precepts they follow, Jn. x. 11, 14. **b.** metaph. *the presiding officer, manager, director, of any assembly*: so of Christ the Head of the church, Jn. x. 16; 1 Pet. ii. 25; Heb. xiii. 20, (of the Jewish Messiah, Ezek. xxxiv. 23); of the overseers of the Christian assemblies [A. V. *pastors*], Eph. iv. 11; cf. *Ritschl*, Entstehung der altkathol. Kirche, ed. 2, p. 350 sq.; [*Hatch*, Bampton Lects. for 1880, p. 123 sq.]. (Of kings and princes we find ποιμένες λαῶν in Hom. and Hes.)*

4167 ποίμνη, -ης, ἡ, (contr. fr. ποιμένη; see ποιμήν), [fr. Hom. (Od. 9, 122) on], *a flock* (esp.) *of sheep*: Mt. xxvi. 31; Lk. ii. 8; 1 Co. ix. 7; trop. [of Christ's flock i. e.] the body of those who follow Jesus as their guide and keeper, Jn. x. 16.*

4168 ποίμνιον, -ου, τό, (contr. fr. ποιμένιον, i. q. ποίμνη, see ποιμήν; [on the accent cf. W. 52; Chandler § 343 b.]), *a flock* (esp.) *of sheep*: so of a group of Christ's disciples, Lk. xii. 32; of bodies of Christians (churches) presided over by elders [cf. reff. s. v. ποιμήν, b.], Acts xx. 28, 29; 1 Pet. v. 3; with a possessive gen. added, τοῦ θεοῦ, 1 Pet. v. 2, as in Jer. xiii. 17; τοῦ Χριστοῦ, Clem. Rom. 1 Cor. 16, 1; 44, 3; 54, 2; 57, 2. (Hdt., Soph., Eur., Plat., Lcian., al.; Sept. chiefly for עֵדֶר and צֹאן.)*

4169 ποῖος, -α, -ον, (interrog. pron., corresponding to the rel. οἷος and the demonstr. τοῖος), [fr. Hom. down], *of what sort or nature* (Lat. *qualis*): absol. neutr. plur. in a direct question, Lk. xxiv. 19; with substantives, in direct questions: Mt. xix. 18; xxi. 23; xxii. 36; Mk. xi. 28; Lk. vi. 32–34; Jn. x. 32; Acts iv. 7; vii. 49; Ro. iii. 27; 1 Co. xv. 35; Jas. iv. 14; 1 Pet. ii. 20; in indirect discourse: Mt. xxi. 24, 27; xxiv. 43; Mk. xi. 29, 33; Lk. xii. 39; Jn. xii. 33; xviii. 32; xxi. 19; Acts xxiii. 34; Rev. iii. 3; εἰς τίνα ἢ ποῖον καιρόν, 1 Pet. i. 11; ποίας (Rec. διὰ ποίας) sc. ὁδοῦ, Lk. v. 19; cf. W. § 30, 11; [(also § 64, 5); B. §§ 123, 8; 132, 26; cf. Tob. x. 7].

4170 πολεμέω, -ῶ; fut. πολεμήσω; 1 aor. ἐπολέμησα; (πόλεμος); [fr. Soph. and Hdt. down]; Sept. chiefly for נִלְחַם;

to war, carry on war; to fight: Rev. xix. 11; μετά τινος (on which constr. see μετά, I. 2 d. p. 403ᵇ), Rev. ii. 16; xii. 7 (where Rec. κατά; [cf. on this vs. B. § 140, 14 and s. v. μετά as above]); xiii. 4; xvii. 14; i. q. to wrangle, quarrel, Jas. iv. 2.*

4171 πόλεμος, -ου, ὁ, (fr. ΠΕΛΩ, πολέω, to turn, to range about, whence Lat. pello, bellum; [but cf. Fick i. 671; Vaniček 513]), [fr. Hom. down], Sept. for כִּלְחָכָה; **1.** prop. **a.** war: Mt. xxiv. 6; Mk. xiii. 7; Lk. xiv. 31; xxi. 9; Heb. xi. 34; in imitation of the Hebr. עָשָׂה כִּלְחָכָה foll. by אֶת or עָם (Gen. xiv. 2; Deut. xx. 12, 20), πόλ. ποιεῖν μετά τινος, Rev. xi. 7; xii. 17; xiii. 7 [here Lom. WH Tr mrg. br. the cl.]; xix. 19, [cf. μετά, I. 2 d.]. **b.** a fight, a battle, [more precisely μάχη; "in Hom. (where Il. 7, 174 it is used even of single combat) and Hes. the sense of battle prevails; in Attic that of war" (L. and S. s. v.); cf. Trench §lxxxvi. and (in partial modification) Schmidt ch. 138, 5 and 6]: 1 Co. xiv. 8; Heb. xi. 34; Rev. ix. 7, 9; xii. 7; xvi. 14; xx. 8. **2.** a dispute, strife, quarrel: πόλεμοι καὶ μάχαι, Jas. iv. 1 (Soph. El. 219; Plat. Phaedo p. 66 c.).*

4172 πόλις, -εως, ἡ, (πέλομαι, to dwell [or rather denoting originally ‘ fulness,’ ‘ throng’; allied with Lat. pleo, plebs, etc.; cf. Curtius p. 79 and § 374; Vaniček p. 499; (otherwise Fick i. 138)]), [fr. Hom. down], Sept. chiefly for עִיר, besides for קִרְיָה, שַׁעַר (gate), etc., a city; **a.** univ.: Mt. ii. 23; Mk. i. 45; Lk. iv. 29; Jn. xi. 54; Acts v. 16, and very often in the historical bks. of the N. T.; κατὰ τὴν πόλιν, through the city [A. V. in; see κατά, II. 1 a.], Acts xxiv. 12; κατὰ πόλιν, κατὰ πόλεις, see κατά, II. 3 a. a. p. 328ᵃ; opp. to κώμαι, Mt. ix. 35; x. 11; Lk. viii. 1; xiii. 22; to κώμαι καὶ ἀγροί, Mk. vi. 56; ἡ ἰδία πόλις, see ἴδιος, 1 b. p. 297ᵃ; πόλις with the gen. of a pers. one's native city, Lk. ii. 4, 11; Jn. i. 44 (45); or the city in which one lives, Mt. xxii. 7; Lk. iv. 29; x. 11; Acts xvi. 20; Rev. xvi. 19; Jerusalem is called, on account of the temple erected there, πόλις τοῦ μεγάλου βασιλέως, i. e. in which the great King of Israel, Jehovah, has his abode, Mt. v. 35; Ps. xlvii. (xlviii.) 2; cf. Tob. xiii. 15; also ἁγία πόλις (see ἅγιος, 1 a. p. 7ᵃ) and ἡ ἠγαπημένη, the beloved of God, Rev. xx. 9. with the gen. of a gentile noun: Δαμασκηνῶν, 2 Co. xi. 32; Ἐφεσίων, Acts xix. 35; τῶν Ἰουδαίων, Lk. xxiii. 51; τοῦ Ἰσραήλ, Mt. x. 23; Σαμαρειτῶν, Mt. x. 5; with the gen. of a region: τῆς Γαλιλαίας, Lk. i. 26; iv. 31; Ἰούδα, of the tribe of Judah, Lk. i. 39; Λυκαονίας, Acts xiv. 6; Κιλικίας, Acts xxi. 39; τῆς Σαμαρείας, Jn. iv. 5; Acts viii. 5. As in class. Grk. the proper name of the city is added, — either in the nom. case, as πόλις Ἰόππη, Acts xi. 5; or in the gen., as πόλις Σοδόμων, Γομόρρας, 2 Pet. ii. 6; Θυατείρων, Acts xvi. 14. **b.** used of the heavenly Jerusalem (see Ἱεροσόλυμα, 2), i. e. **a.** the abode of the blessed, in heaven: Heb. xi. 10, 16; with θεοῦ ζῶντος added, Heb. xii. 22; ἡ μέλλουσα πόλις, Heb. xiii. 14. **β.** in the visions of the Apocalypse it is used of the visible capital of the heavenly kingdom, to come down to earth after the renovation of the world: Rev. iii. 12; xxi. 14 sqq.; xxii. 14; ἡ πόλις ἡ ἁγία, Rev. xxii. 19; with Ἱερουσαλὴμ

καινή added, Rev. xxi. 2. **c.** πόλις by meton. for the inhabitants: Mt. viii. 34; Acts xiv. 21; πᾶσα ἡ πόλις, Mt. xxi. 10; Acts xiii. 44; ἡ πόλις ὅλη, Mk. i. 33; Acts xxi. 30; πόλις μερισθεῖσα καθ᾽ ἑαυτῆς, Mt. xii. 25.

4173 πολιτάρχης, -ου, ὁ, (i. e. ὁ ἄρχων τῶν πολιτῶν; see ἑκατοντάρχης), a ruler of a city or citizens: Acts xvii. 6, 8. (Boeckh, Corp. inscrr. Graec. ii. p. 52 sq. no. 1967 [cf. Boeckh's note, and Tdf. Proleg. p. 86 note²]; in Grk. writ. πολίαρχος was more common.) *

4174 πολιτεία, -ας, ἡ, (πολιτεύω); **1.** the administration of civil affairs (Xen. mem. 3, 9, 15; Arstph., Aeschin., Dem., [al.]). **2.** a state, commonwealth, (2 Macc. iv. 11; xiii. 17; xiii. 14; Xen., Plat., Thuc., [al.]): with a gen. of the possessor, τοῦ Ἰσραήλ, spoken of the theocratic or divine commonwealth, Eph. ii. 12. **3.** citizenship, the rights of a citizen, [some make this sense the primary one]: Acts xxii. 28 (3 Macc. iii. 21, 23; Hdt. 9, 34; Xen. Hell. 1, 1, 26; 1, 2, 10; [4, 4, 6, etc.]; Dem., Polyb., Diod., Joseph., al.).*

4175 πολίτευμα, -τος, τό, (πολιτεύω), in Grk. writ. fr. Plat. down; **1.** the administration of civil affairs or of a commonwealth [R. V. txt. (Phil. as below) citizenship]. **2.** the constitution of a commonwealth, form of government and the laws by which it is administered. **3.** a state, commonwealth [so R. V. mrg.]: ἡμῶν, the commonwealth whose citizens we are (see πόλις, b.), Phil. iii. 20, cf. Meyer and Wiesinger ad loc.; of Christians it is said ἐπὶ γῆς διατρίβουσιν, ἀλλ᾽ ἐν οὐρανῷ πολιτεύονται, Epist. ad Diogn. c. 5; (τῶν σοφῶν ψυχαὶ) πατρίδα μὲν τὸν οὐράνιον χῶρον, ἐν ᾧ πολιτεύονται, ξένον δὲ τὸν περίγειον ἐν ᾧ παρῴκησαν νομίζουσαι, Philo de confus. ling. § 17; [γυναῖκες . . . τῷ τῆς ἀρετῆς ἐγγεγραμμέναι πολιτεύματι, de agricult. § 17 fin. Cf. esp. Bp. Lghtft. on Phil. l. c.].*

see 4176 St. πολιτεύω: Mid. [cf. W. 260 (244)], pres. impv. 2 pers. plur. πολιτεύεσθε; pf. πεπολίτευμαι; (πολίτης); **1.** to be a citizen (Thuc., Xen., Lys., Polyb., al.). **2.** to administer civil affairs, manage the state, (Thuc., Xen.). **3.** to make or create a citizen (Diod. 11, 72); Middle **a.** to be a citizen; so in the passages fr. Philo and the Ep. ad Diogn. cited in πολίτευμα, 3. **b.** to behave as a citizen; to avail one's self of or recognize the laws; so fr. Thuc. down; in Hellenist. writ. to conduct one's self as pledged to some law of life: ἀξίως τοῦ εὐαγγελίου, Phil. i. 27 [R. V. txt. let your manner of life be worthy of etc.]; ἀξ. τοῦ Χριστοῦ, Polyc. ad Philip. 5, 2; ἀξ. τοῦ θεοῦ, Clem. Rom. 1 Cor. 21, 1; ὁσίως, ibid. 6, 1; κατὰ τὸ καθῆκον τῷ Χριστῷ, ibid. 3, 4; μετὰ φόβου κ. ἀγάπης, ibid. 51, 2; ἐννόμως, Justin. dial. c. Tr. c. 67; ἠρξάμην πολιτεύεσθαι τῇ Φαρισαίων αἱρέσει κατακολουθῶν, Joseph. vit. 2; other phrases are cited by Grimm on 2 Macc. vi. 1; τῷ θεῷ, to live in accordance with the laws of God, Acts xxiii. 1 [A. V. I have lived etc.].*

4177 πολίτης, -ου, ὁ, (πόλις), fr. Hom. down, a citizen; i. e. **a.** the inhabitant of any city or country: πόλεως, Acts xxi. 39; τῆς χώρας ἐκείνης, Lk. xv. 15. **b.** the associate of another in citizenship, i. e. a fellow-citizen, fellow-countryman, (Plat. apol. p. 37 c.; al.): with the gen. of a person, Lk. xix. 14; Heb. viii. 11 (where Rec.

has τὸν πλησίον) fr. Jer. xxxviii. (xxxi.) 34, where it is used for יָד, as in Prov. xi. 9, 12; xxiv. 43 (28).*

4178 πολλάκις, (fr. πολύς, πολλά), adv., [fr. Hom. down], *often, frequently*: Mt. xvii. 15; Mk. v. 4; ix. 22; Jn. xviii. 2; Acts xxvi. 11; Ro. i. 13; xv. 22 L Tr mrg.; 2 Co. viii. 22; xi. 23, 26 sq.; Phil. iii. 18; 2 Tim. i. 16; Heb. vi. 7; ix. 25 sq.; x. 11.*

4179 πολλαπλασίων, -ον, gen. -ονος, (πολύς), *manifold, much more*: Mt. xix. 29 L T Tr WH; Lk. xviii. 30. (Polyb., Plut., al.; [cf. B. 30 (27)].)*

4180 πολυ-εύσπλαγχνος, -ον, (πολύ and εὔσπλαγχνος), *very tender-hearted, extremely full of pity*: so a few minusc. Mss. in Jas. v. 11, where al. πολύσπλαγχνος, q. v. (Eccles. and Byzant. writ.) *

4181 πολυλογία, -ας, ἡ, (πολυλόγος), *much speaking*, (Plaut., Vulg., *multiloquium*): Mt. vi. 7. (Prov. x. 19; Xen. Cyr. 1, 4, 3; Plat. legg. 1 p. 641 e.; Aristot. polit. 4, 10 [p. 1295ᵃ, 2]; Plut. educ. poer. 8, 10.)*

4182 πολυμερῶς, (πολυμερής), *by many portions*: joined with πολυτρόπως, at many times (Vulg. *multifariam* [or *-rie*]), and in many ways, Heb. i. 1. (Joseph. antt. 8, 3, 9 [var.; Plut. mor. p. 537 d., i. e. de invid. et od. 5]; οὐδὲν δεῖ τῆς πολυμεροῦς ταύτης καὶ πολυτρόπου μούσης τε καὶ ἁρμονίας, Max. Tyr. diss. 37 p. 363; [cf. W. 463 (431)].) *

4183 πολυ-ποίκιλος, -ον, (πολύς and ποίκιλος); 1. *much-variegated*; marked with a great variety of colors: of cloth or a painting; φάρεα, Eur. Iph. T. 1149; στέφανον πολυποίκιλον ἀνθέων, Eubul. ap Athen. 15 p. 679 d. 2. *much varied, manifold*: σοφία τοῦ θεοῦ, manifesting itself in a great variety of forms, Eph. iii. 10; Theophil. ad Autol. 1, 6; ὀργή, Orac. Sibyll. 8, 120; λόγος, Orph. hymn. 61, 4, and by other writ. with other nouns.*

πολύς, πολλή (fr. an older form πολλός, found in Hom., Hes., Pind.), πολύ; [(cf. Curtius § 375)]; Sept. chiefly for רַב; *much*; used a. of multitude, number, etc., *many, numerous, great*: ἀριθμός, Acts xi. 21; λαός, Acts xviii. 10; ὄχλος, Mk. v. 24; vi. 34; [viii. 1 L T Tr WH]; Lk. vii. 11; viii. 4; Jn. vi. 2, 5; Rev. vii. 9; xix. 6, etc.; πλῆθος, Mk. iii. 7 sq.; Lk. v. 6; Acts xiv. 1, etc.; i. q. *abundant, plenteous* [A. V. often *much*], καρπός, Jn. xii. 24; xv. 5, 8; θερισμός, (the harvest to be gathered), Mt. ix. 37; Lk. x. 2; γῆ, Mt. xiii. 5; Mk. iv. 5; χόρτος, Jn. vi. 10; οἶνος, 1 Tim. iii. 8; plur. πολλοὶ τελῶναι, Mt. ix. 10; Mk. ii. 15; πολλοὶ προφῆται, Mt. xiii. 17; Lk. x. 24; σοφοί, Co. i. 26; πατέρες, 1 Co. iv. 15; δυνάμεις, Mt. vii. 22; xiii. 58, etc.; ὄχλοι, Mt. iv. 25; viii. 1; xii. 15 [but here L T WH om. Tr br. ὄχ.]; Lk. v. 15, etc.; δαιμόνια, Mk. i. 34; and in many other exx.; with participles used substantively, Mt. viii. 16; 1 Co. xvi. 9, etc.; with the article prefixed: αἱ ἁμαρτίαι αὐτῆς αἱ πολλαί, her sins which are many, Lk. vii. 47; τὰ πολλὰ γράμματα, the great learning with which I see that you are furnished, Acts xxvi. 24; ὁ πολὺς ὄχλος, the great multitude of common people present, Mk. xii. 37 [cf. ὁ ὄχλ. πολύς, Jn. xii. 9 T Tr mrg. WH; see ὄχλος, 1]. Plur. masc. πολλοί, absol. and without the art., *many, a large part of mankind*: πολλοί simply, Mt. vii. 13, 22; xx. 28; xxvi. 28; Mk. ii. 2; iii. 10; x. 45; xiv. 24; Lk. i. 1, 14; Heb. ix. 28, and very

often; opp. to ὀλίγοι, Mt. xx. 16 [T WH om. Tr br. the cl.]; ἕτεροι πολλοί, Acts xv. 35; ἄλλαι πολλαί, Mk. xv. 41; ἕτεραι πολλαί, Lk. viii. 3; πολλοί foll. by a partit. gen., as τῶν Φαρισαίων, Mt. iii. 7; add, Lk. i. 16; Jn. xii. 11; Acts iv. 4; xiii. 43; 2 Co. xii. 21; Rev. viii. 11, etc.; foll. by ἐκ with a gen. of class, as πολλοὶ ἐκ τῶν μαθητῶν αὐτοῦ, Jn. vi. 60; add, vii. 31, 40; x. 20; xi. 19, 45; Acts xvii. 12; πολλοὶ ἐκ τῆς πόλεως, Jn. iv. 39. with the article prefixed, οἱ πολλοί, *the many* [cf. W. 110 (105)]: those contrasted with ὁ εἷς (i. e. both with Adam and with Christ), acc. to the context equiv. to the rest of mankind, Ro. v. 15, 19, cf. 12, 18; we the (i. e. who are) many, Ro. xii. 5; 1 Co. x. 17; the many whom ye know, 2 Co. ii. 17; *the many* i. e. the most part, the majority, Mt. xxiv. 12; 1 Co. x. 33. b. with nouns denoting an action, an emotion, a state, which can be said to have as it were measure, weight, force, intensity, size, continuance, or repetition, *much* i. q. *great, strong, intense, large*: ἀγάπη, Eph. ii. 4; ὀδύνη, 1 Tim. vi. 10; θρῆνος, κλαυθμός, ὀδυρμός, Mt. ii. 18; χαρά [Rec.ˢᵗ χάρις], Philem. 7; ἐπιθυμία, 1 Th. ii. 17; μακροθυμία, Ro. ix. 22; ἔλεος, 1 Pet. i. 3; γογγυσμός, Jn. vii. 12; τρόμος, 1 Co. ii. 3; πόνος [Rec. ζῆλος], Col. iv. 13; ἀγών, 1 Th. ii. 2; ἄθλησις, Heb. x. 32; θλίψις, 2 Co. ii. 4; 1 Th. i. 6; καύχησις, 2 Co. vii. 4; πεποίθησις, 2 Co. viii. 22; πληροφορία, 1 Th. i. 5; παρρησία, 2 Co. iii. 12; vii. 4; 1 Tim. iii. 13; Philem. 8; παράκλησις, 2 Co. viii. 4; συζήτησις [T WH Tr txt. ζήτησις], Acts xv. 7; xxviii. 29 [Rec.]; στάσις, Acts xxiii. 10; ἀσιτία, Acts xxvii. 21; βία, Acts xxiv. 7 [Rec.]; διακονία, Lk. x. 40; σιγή, deep silence, Acts xxi. 40 (Xen. Cyr. 7, 1, 25); φαντασία, Acts xxv. 23; δύναμις καὶ δόξα, Mt. xxiv. 30; Lk. xxi. 27; μισθός, Mt. v. 12; Lk. vi. 23, 35; εἰρήνη, Acts xxiv. 2 (3); περὶ οὗ πολὺς ἡμῖν ὁ λόγος, about which [but see λόγος, I. 3 a.] we have much (in readiness) to say, Heb. v. 11 (πολὺν λόγον ποιεῖσθαι περί τινος, Plat. Phaedo p. 115 d.; cf. Ast, Lex. Plat. iii. p. 148). c. of time, *much, long*: πολὺν χρόνον, Jn. v. 6; μετὰ χρόνον πολύν, Mt. xxv. 19; ὥρα πολλή, much time (i. e. a large part of the day) is spent [see ὥρα, 2], Mk. vi. 35; ὥρας πολλῆς γενομένης [Tdf. γινομ.], of a late hour of the day, ibid. (so πολλῆς ὥρας, Polyb. 5, 8, 3; ἐπὶ πολλὴν ὥραν, Joseph. antt. 8, 4, 4; ἐμάχοντο . . . ἄχρι πολλῆς ὥρας, Dion. Hal. 2, 54); πολλοῖς χρόνοις, for a long time, Lk. viii. 29 (οὐ πολλῷ χρόνῳ, Hdian. 1, 6, 24 [8 ed. Bekk.]; χρόνοις πολλοῖς ὕστερον, Plut. Thes. 6 [see χρόνος, sub fin.]); εἰς ἔτη πολλά, Lk. xii. 19; (ἐκ or ἀπὸ πολλῶν ἐτῶν, 17; Ro. xv. 23 [here WH Tr txt. ἀπὸ ἱκανῶν ἐτ.]; ἐπὶ πολύ, (for) a long time, Acts xxviii. 6; μετ' οὐ πολύ, not long after [see μετά, II. 2 b.], Acts xxvii. 14. d. Neut. sing. πολύ, *much*, substantively, i. q. *many things*: Lk. xii. 48; *much*, adverbially, of the mode and degree of an action: ἡγάπησε, Lk. vii. 47; πλανᾶσθε, Mk. xii. 27; so ὠφελεῖ, Ro. iii. 2. πολλοῦ as a gen. of price (fr. Hom. down; cf. Passow s. v. IV. b. vol. ii. p. 1013ᵃ; [cf. W. 206 (194)]): πραθῆναι, for much, Mt. xxvi. 9. ἐν πολλῷ, in (administering) *much* (i. e. many things), Lk. xvi. 10; with great labor, great effort, Acts xxvi. 29 (where L T Tr WH ἐν μεγάλῳ [see μέγας, 1 a. γ.]). with a compar. [cf. W.

§ 35, 1] : πολὺ σπουδαιότερον, 2 Co. viii. 22 (in Grk. writ. fr. Hom. down) ; πολλῷ πλείους, many more, Jn. iv. 41 ; πολλῷ [or πολύ] μᾶλλον, see μᾶλλον, 1 a. sq. with the article, τὸ πολύ, Germ. *das Viele* (opp. to τὸ ὀλίγον), 2 Co. viii. 15 [cf. B. 395 (338) ; W. 589 (548)]. Plural πολλά   a. *many things* ; as, διδάσκειν, λαλεῖν, Mt. xiii. 3 ; Mk. iv. 2 ; vi. 34 ; Jn. viii. 26 ; xiv. 30 ; παθεῖν, Mt. xvi. 21 ; Mk. v. 26 ; ix. 12 ; Lk. ix. 22, etc., and often in Grk. writ. fr. Pind. Ol. 13, 90 down ; ποιεῖν, Mk. vi. 20 [T Tr mrg. WH ἀπορεῖν] ; πρᾶξαι, Acts xxvi. 9 ; add as other exx., Mt. xxv. 21, 23 ; Mk. xii. 41 ; xv. 3 ; Jn. xvi. 12 ; 2 Co. viii. 22 ; 2 Jn. 12 ; 3 Jn. 13 ; πολλὰ καὶ ἄλλα, Jn. xx. 30. [On the Grk. (and Lat.) usage which treats the notion of multitude not as something external to a thing and consisting merely in a comparison of it with other things, but as an attribute inhering in the thing itself, and hence capable of being co-ordinated with another attributive word by means of καί (q. v. I. 3), see Kühner § 523, 1 (or on Xen. mem. 1, 2, 24) ; *Bäumlein*, Partikeln, p. 146 ; Krüger § 69, 32, 3 ; *Lob.* Paral. p. 60 ; *Herm.* ad Vig. p. 835 ; W. § 59, 3 fin. ; B. 362 sq. (311). Cf. Passow s. v. I. 3 a. ; L. and S. s. v. II. 2.]   β. adverbially [cf. W. 463 (432) ; B. § 128, 2], *much* : Mk. [vi. 20 T Tr mrg. (?) WH (see ἀπορέω)] ; iv. 6, 12 [L br. the cl.] ; *in many ways*, Jas. iii. 2 ; *with many words*, [R. V. *much*], with verbs of saying ; as, κηρύσσειν, παρακαλεῖν, etc., Mk. i. 45 ; iii. 12 ; v. 10, 23, 43 ; 1 Co. xvi. 12 ; *many times, often, repeatedly* : Mt. ix. 14 [R G Tr WH mrg.] (and often in Grk. writ. fr. Hom. down ; cf. Passow s. v. V. 1 a. vol. ii. p. 1013ᵇ ; [L. and S. III. a.] ; Stallbaum on Plat. Phaedo p. 61 c.) ; with the art. τὰ πολλά, *for the most part*, [R. V. *these many times*] (Vulg. *plurimum*), Ro. xv. 22 [L Tr mrg. πολλάκις] (exx. fr. Grk. writ. are given by Passow l. c., [L. and S. l. c.], and by *Fritzsche*, Ep. ad Rom. iii. p. 281).

4184   **πολύσπλαγχνος, -ον**, (πολύς, and σπλάγχνον q. v.), *full of pity, very kind* : Jas. v. 11 ; Hebr. רַב חֶסֶד, in the Sept. πολυέλεος. (Theod. Stud. p. 615.) *

4185   **πολυτελής, -ές**, (πολύς, and τέλος cost), [from Hdt. down], *precious* ;   a. *requiring great outlay, very costly* : Mk. xiv. 3 ; 1 Tim. ii. 9. (Thuc. et sqq. ; Sept.)   b. *excellent, of surpassing value*, [A. V. *of great price*] : 1 Pet. iii. 4. [(Plat., al.)] *

4186   **πολύτιμος, -ον**, (πολύς, τιμή), *very valuable, of great price* : Mt. xiii. 46 ; xxvi. 7 L T Tr mrg. ; Jn. xii. 3 ; compar. πολυτιμότερον, 1 Pet. i. 7, where Rec. πολὺ τιμώτερον. (Plut. Pomp. 5 ; Hdian. 1, 17, 5 [3 ed. Bekk.] ; Anthol., al.) *

4187   **πολυτρόπως**, (fr. πολύτροπος, in use in various senses fr. Hom. down), adv., *in many manners* : Heb. i. 1 [(Philo de incor. mund. § 24)] ; see πολυμερῶς.*

4188   **πόμα** (Attic πῶμα ; [cf. *Lob.* Paralip. p. 425]), -τος, τό, (πίνω, πέπομαι), *drink* : 1 Co. x. 4 ; Heb. ix. 10.*

4189   **πονηρία, -ας, ἡ**, (πονηρός), [fr. Soph. down], Sept. for רֹעַ and רָעָה, *depravity, iniquity, wickedness* [(so A. V. almost uniformly)], *malice* : Mt. xxii. 18 ; Lk. xi. 39 ; Ro. i. 29 ; 1 Co. v. 8 ; Eph. vi. 12 ; plur. αἱ πονηρίαι [cf. W. § 27, 3 ; B. § 123, 2 ; R. V. *wickednesses*], evil purposes

and desires, Mk. vii. 22 ; wicked ways [A. V. *iniquities*], Acts iii. 26. [SYN. see κακία, fin.] *

4190 & 4191   **πονηρός** (on the accent cf. *Lob.* ad Phryn. p. ? *Göttling*, Lehre v. Accent, p. 304 sq. ; [Chandler §§ 404, 405] ; *Lipsius*, Grammat. Untersuch. p. 26), -ά, -όν ; compar. πονηρότερος (Mt. xii. 45 ; Lk. xi. 26) ; (πονέω, πόνος) ; fr. Hes., [Hom. (ep. 15, 20), Theog.] down ; Sept. often for רַע ;   1. *full of labors, annoyances, hardships* ;   a. *pressed and harassed by labors* ; thus Hercules is called πονηρότατος καὶ ἄριστος, Hes. frag. 43, 5.   b. *bringing toils, annoyances, perils* : (καιρός, Sir. li. 12) ; ἡμέρα πονηρά, of a time full of peril to Christian faith and steadfastness, Eph. v. 16 ; vi. 13, (so in the plur. ἡμέραι πον. Barn. ep. 2, 1) ; *causing pain and trouble* [A. V. *grievous*], ἕλκος, Rev. xvi. 2.   2. *bad, of a bad nature or condition* :   a. in a physical sense : ὀφθαλμός, diseased or blind, Mt. vi. 23 ; Lk. xi. 34, (πονηρία ὀφθαλμῶν, Plat. Hipp. min. p. 374 d. ; the Greeks use πονηρῶς ἔχειν or διακεῖσθαι of the sick ; ἐκ γενετῆς πονηροὺς ὑγιεῖς πεποιηκέναι, Justin apol. 1, 22 [(cf. Otto's note) ; al. take πον. in Mt. and Lk. u. s. ethically ; cf. b. and Meyer on Mt.]) ; καρπός, Mt. vii. 17 sq.   b. in an ethical sense, *evil, wicked, bad*, etc. ["this use of the word is due to its association with the working (largely the servile) class ; not that contempt for labor is thereby expressed, for such words as ἐργάτης, δραστήρ, and the like, do not take on this evil sense, which connected itself only with a word expressive of unintermitted toil and carrying no suggestion of results" (cf. Schmidt ch. 85, § 1) ; see κακία, fin.] ; of persons : Mt. vii. 11 ; xii. 34 sq. ; xviii. 32 ; xxv. 26 ; Lk. vi. 45 ; xi. 13 ; xix. 22 ; Acts xvii. 5 ; 2 Th. iii. 2 ; 2 Tim. iii. 13 ; γενεὰ πον., Mt. xii. 39, 45 ; xvi. 4 ; Lk. xi. 29 ; πνεῦμα πονηρόν, an evil spirit (see πνεῦμα, 3 c.), Mt. xii. 45 ; Lk. vii. 21 ; viii. 2 ; xi. 26 ; Acts xix. 12 sq. 15 sq. ; substantively οἱ πονηροί, *the wicked*, bad men, opp. to οἱ δίκαιοι, Mt. xiii. 49 ; πονηροὶ καὶ ἀγαθοί, Mt. v. 45 ; xxii. 10 ; ἀχάριστοι κ. πονηροί, Lk. vi. 35 ; τὸν πονηρόν, *the wicked man*, i. e. the evil-doer spoken of, 1 Co. v. 13 ; τῷ πονηρῷ, *the evil* man, who injures you, Mt. v. 39.   ὁ πονηρός is used pre-eminently of *the devil, the evil one* : Mt. v. 37 ; vi. 13 ; xiii. 19, 38 ; Lk. xi. 4 R L ; Jn. xvii. 15 ; 1 Jn. ii. 13 sq. ; iii. 12 ; v. 18 sq. (on which see κεῖμαι, 2 c.) ; Eph. vi. 16.   of things : αἰών, Gal. i. 4 ; ὄνομα (q. v. 1 p. 447ᵃ bot.), Lk. vi. 22 ; ῥαδιούργημα, Acts xviii. 14 ; the heart as a storehouse out of which a man brings forth πονηρά words is called θησαυρὸς πονηρός, Mt. xii. 35 ; Lk. vi. 45 ; συνείδησις πονηρά, a soul conscious of wickedness, [conscious wickedness ; see συνείδησις, b. sub fin.], Heb. x. 22 ; καρδία πονηρὰ ἀπιστίας, an evil heart such as is revealed in distrusting [cf. B. § 132, 24 ; W. § 30, 4], Heb. iii. 12 ; ὀφθαλμός (q. v.), Mt. xx. 15 ; Mk. vii. 22 ; διαλογισμοί, Mt. xv. 19 ; Jas. ii. 4 ; ὑπόνοιαι, 1 Tim. vi. 4 ; καύχησις, Jas. iv. 16 ; ῥῆμα, a reproach, Mt. v. 11 [R G ; al. om. ῥ.] ; λόγοι, 3 Jn. 10 ; ἔργα, Jn. iii. 19 ; vii. 7 ; 1 Jn. iii. 12 ; 2 Jn. 11 ; Col. i. 21 ; ἔργον, (acc. to the context) wrong committed against me, 2 Tim. iv. 18 ; αἰτία, charge of crime, Acts xxv. 18 L T Tr mrg. WH mrg. The neuter πονηρόν, and τὸ πονηρόν, substantively, *evil, that which is* *wicked*: εἶδος πονηροῦ (see εἶδος, 2; [al. take πον. here as an adj., and bring the ex. under εἶδος, 1 (R. V. mrg. *appearance of evil*)]), 1 Th. v. 22; 2 Th. iii. 3 (where τοῦ πονηροῦ is held by many to be the gen. of the masc. ὁ πονηρός, but cf. Lünemann ad loc.); [τὶ πονηρόν, Acts xxviii. 21]; opp. to τὸ ἀγαθόν, Lk. vi. 45; Ro. xii. 9; plur. [W. § 34, 2], Mt. ix. 4; Lk. iii. 19; wicked deeds, Acts xxv. 18 Tr txt. WH txt.; ταῦτα τὰ πονηρά, *these evil things* i. e. the vices just enumerated, Mk. vii. 23.*

4192   πόνος, -ου, ὁ, (πένομαι [see πένης]), fr. Hom. down, Sept. for יָגִיעַ, עָמָל, etc., *labor, toil*;   **1.** i. q. *great trouble, intense desire*: ὑπέρ τινος (gen. of pers.), Col. iv. 13 (where Rec. has ζῆλον [cf. Bp. Lghtft. ad loc.]).   **2.** *pain*: Rev. xvi. 10 sq.; xxi. 4. [Syn. see κόπος, fin.]*

4193   Ποντικός, -ή, -όν, (Πόντος, q. v.), *belonging to Pontus, born in Pontus*: Acts xviii. 2. [(Hdt., al.)]*

4194   Πόντιος, -ου, ὁ, *Pontius* (a Roman name), the praenomen of Pilate, procurator of Judæa (see Πιλάτος): Mt. xxvii. 2 [R G L]; Lk. iii. 1; Acts iv. 27; 1 Tim. vi. 13.*

4195   Πόντος, -ου, ὁ, *Pontus*, a region of eastern Asia Minor, bounded by the Euxine Sea [fr. which circumstance it took its name], Armenia, Cappadocia, Galatia, Paphlagonia, [BB. DD. s. v.; *Ed. Meyer*, Gesch. d. Königreiches Pontos (Leip. 1879)]: Acts ii. 9; 1 Pet. i. 1.*

4196   Πόπλιος, -ου, ὁ, *Publius* (a Roman name), the name of a chief magistrate [(Grk. ὁ πρῶτος) but see Dr. Woolsey's addition to the art. 'Publius' in B. D. (Am. ed.)] of the island of Melita; nothing more is known of him: Acts xxviii. 7, 8.*

4197   πορεία, -ας, ἡ, (πορεύω), fr. Aeschyl. down; Sept. for הֲלִיכָה; *a journey*: Lk. xiii. 22 (see ποιέω, I. 3); Hebraistically (see ὁδός, 2 a.), *a going* i. e. *purpose, pursuit, undertaking*: Jas. i. 11.*

see 4198 St.   πορεύω: *to lead over, carry over, transfer*, (Pind., Soph., Thuc., Plat., al.); Mid. (fr. Hdt. down), pres. πορεύομαι; impf. ἐπορευόμην; fut. πορεύσομαι; pf. ptcp. πεπορευμένος; 1 aor. subjunc. 1 pers. plur. πορευσώμεθα (Jas. iv. 13 Rec.ˢᵗ Grsb.); 1 aor. pass. ἐπορεύθην; (πόρος a ford, [cf. Eng. *pore* i. e. passage through; Curtius § 356; Vaniček p. 479]); Sept. often for הָלַךְ, הִתְהַלֵּךְ, יָלַךְ; prop. *to lead one's self across*; i. e. *to take one's way, betake one's self, set out, depart*;   **a.** prop.: τὴν ὁδόν μου, to pursue the journey on which one has entered, continue one's journey, [A. V. *go on one's way*], Acts viii. 39; πορ. foll. by ἀπό w. a gen. of place, *to depart from*, Mt. xxiv. 1 [R G]; ἀπό w. a gen. of the pers., Mt. xxv. 41; Lk. iv. 42; ἐκεῖθεν, Mt. xix. 15; ἐντεῦθεν, Lk. xiii. 31; foll. by εἰς w. an acc. of place, *to go, depart, to some place*: Mt. ii. 20; xvii. 27; Mk. xvi. 12; Lk. i. 39; ii. 41; xxii. 39; xxiv. 13; Jn. vii. 35; viii. 1; Acts i. 11, 25; xx. 1; Ro. xv. 24 sq.; Jas. iv. 13, etc.; w. an acc. denoting the state: εἰς εἰρήνην, Lk. vii. 50; viii. 48, (also ἐν εἰρήνῃ, Acts xvi. 36; see εἰρήνη, 3); εἰς θάνατον, Lk. xxii. 33; foll. by ἐπί w. an acc. of place, Mt. xxii. 9; Acts viii. 26; ix. 11; ἐπί w. the acc. of a pers. Acts xxv. 12; ἕως with a gen. of place, Acts xxiii. 23; ποῦ [q. v.] for ποῖ, Jn. vii. 35; οὗ [see ὅς, II. 11 a.] for ὅποι, Lk. xxiv. 28; 1 Co.

xvi. 6; πρός w. the acc. of a pers., Mt. xxv. 9; xxvi. 14; Lk. xi. 5; xv. 18; xvi. 30; Jn. xiv. 12, 28; xvi. 28; xx. 17; Acts xxvii. 3; xxviii. 26; κατὰ τὴν ὁδόν, Acts viii. 36; διά w. a gen. of place, Mt. xii. 1; [Mk. ix. 30 L txt. Tr txt. WH txt.]; the purpose of the journey is indicated by an infinitive: Mt. xxviii. 8 (9) Rec.; Lk. ii. 3; xiv. 19, 31; Jn. xiv. 2; by the prep. ἐπί with an acc. [cf. ἐπί, C. I. 1 f.], Lk. xv. 4; foll. by ἵνα, Jn. xi. 11; by σύν w. a dat. of the attendance, Lk. vii. 6; Acts x. 20; xxvi. 13; 1 Co. xvi. 4; ἔμπροσθέν τινος, to go before one, Jn. x. 4. absol. i. q. *to depart, go one's way*: Mt. ii. 9; viii. 9; xi. 7; xxviii. 11; Lk. vii. 8; xvii. 19; Jn. iv. 50; viii. 11; xiv. 3; Acts v. 20; viii. 27; xxi. 5; xxii. 21, etc.; i. q. *to be on one's way, to journey*: [Lk. viii. 42 L Tr mrg.]; ix. 57; x. 38; xiii. 33; Acts ix. 3; xxii. 6. *to enter upon a journey; to go to do something*: 1 Co. x. 27; Lk. x. 37. In accordance with the oriental fashion of describing an action circumstantially, the ptcp. πορευόμενος or πορευθείς is placed before a finite verb which designates some other action (cf. ἀνίστημι, II. 1 c. and ἔρχομαι, I. 1 a. a. p. 250ᵇ bot.): Mt. ii. 8; ix. 13 (on which cf. the rabbin. phrase וּלְכֹד אַל [cf. Schoettgen or Wettstein ad loc.]); xi. 4; xxvii. 66; xxviii. 7; Lk. vii. 22; ix. 13, 52; xiii. 32; xiv. 10; xv. 15; xvii. 14; xxii. 8; 1 Pet. iii. 19.   **b.** By a Hebraism, metaphorically,   **a.** *to depart from life*: Lk. xxii. 22; so הָלַךְ, Gen. xv. 2; Ps. xxxix. 14.   **β.** ὀπίσω τινός, *to follow one*, i. e. *become his adherent* [cf. B. 184 (160)]: Lk. xxi. 8 (Judg. ii. 12; 1 K. xi. 10; Sir. xlvi. 10); *to seek* [cf. Eng. *run after*] *any thing*, 2 Pet. ii. 10.   **γ.** *to lead or order one's life* (see περιπατέω, b. a. and ὁδός, 2 a.); foll. by ἐν with a dat. of the thing to which one's life is given up: ἐν ἀσελγείαις, 1 Pet. iv. 3; ἐν ταῖς ἐντολαῖς τοῦ κυρίου, Lk. i. 6; κατὰ τὰς ἐπιθυμίας, 2 Pet. iii. 3; Jude 16, 18; ταῖς ὁδοῖς μου, dat. of place, [to walk in one's own ways], to follow one's moral preferences, Acts xiv. 16; τῇ ὁδῷ τινος, to imitate one, to follow his ways, Jude 11; τῷ φόβῳ τοῦ κυρίου, Acts ix. 31; see W. § 31, 9; B. § 133, 22 b.; ὑπὸ μεριμνῶν, to lead a life subject to cares, Lk. viii. 14, cf. Bornemann ad loc.; [Meyer ed. Weiss ad loc.; yet see ὑπό, I. 2 a.; W. 869 (346) note; B. § 147, 29; R. V. *as they go on their way they are choked with cares*, etc. Comp.: δια-, εἰσ- (-μαι), ἐκ- (-μαι), ἐν- (-μαι), ἐπι- (-μαι), παρα- (-μαι), προ-, προσ- (-μαι), συν- (-μαι). Syn. see ἔρχομαι, fin.]

4199   πορθέω: impf. ἐπόρθουν; 1 aor. ptcp. πορθήσας; (πέρθω, πέπορθα, to lay waste); fr. Hom. down; *to destroy, to overthrow*, [R. V. uniformly *to make havock*]: τινά, Acts ix. 21; τὴν ἐκκλησίαν, Gal. i. 13; τὴν πίστιν, ibid. 23.*

4200   πορισμός, -οῦ, ὁ, (πορίζω to cause a thing to get on well, to carry forward, to convey, to acquire; mid. to bring about or procure for one's self, to gain; fr. πόρος [cf. πορεύω]);   **a.** *acquisition, gain*, (Sap. xiii. 19; xiv. 2; Polyb., Joseph., Plut.).   **b.** *a source of gain*: 1 Tim. vi. 5 sq. (Plut. Cat. Maj. 25; [Test. xii. Patr., test. Is. § 4]).*

4201; see 5347   Πόρκιος, see Φῆστος.

4202   πορνεία, -ας, ἡ, (πορνεύω), Sept. for זְנוּנִים, זְנוּת, תַּזְנוּת,

fornication (Vulg. *fornicatio* [and (Rev. xix. 2) *prostitutio*]); used   a. prop. of illicit sexual intercourse in general (Dem. 403, 27; 433, 25): Acts xv. 20, 29; xxi. 25, (that this meaning must be adopted in these passages will surprise no one who has learned from 1 Co. vi. 12 sqq. how leniently converts from among the heathen regarded this vice and how lightly they indulged in it; accordingly, all other interpretations of the term, such as of marriages within the prohibited degrees and the like, are to be rejected); Ro. i. 29 Rec.; 1 Co. v. 1; vi. 13, 18; vii. 2; 2 Co. xii. 21; Eph. v. 3; Col. iii. 5; 1 Th. iv. 3; Rev. ix. 21; it is distinguished from μοιχεία in Mt. xv. 19; Mk. vii. 21; and Gal. v. 19 Rec.; used of adultery [(cf. Hos. ii. 2 (4), etc.)], Mt. v. 32; xix. 9.   b. In accordance with a form of speech common in the O. T. and among the Jews which represents the close relationship existing between Jehovah and his people under the figure of a marriage (cf. *Gesenius*, Thes. i. p. 422ª sq.), πορνεία is used metaphorically of the worship of idols: Rev. xiv. 8; xvii. 2, 4; xviii. 3; xix. 2; ἡμεῖς ἐκ πορνείας οὐ γεγεννήμεθα (we are not of a people given to idolatry), ἕνα πατέρα ἔχομεν τὸν θεόν, Jn. viii. 41 (ἄθεος μὲν ὁ ἄγονος, πολύθεος δὲ ὁ ἐκ πόρνης, τυφλώττων περὶ τὸν ἀληθῆ πατέρα καὶ διὰ τοῦτο πολλοὺς ἀνθ' ἑνὸς γονεῖς αἰνιττόμενος, Philo de mig. Abr. § 12; τέκνα πορνείας, of idolaters, Hos. i. 2; [but in Jn. l. c. others understand physical descent to be spoken of (cf. Meyer)]); of the defilement of idolatry, as incurred by eating the sacrifices offered to idols, Rev. ii. 21.*

4203   πορνεύω; 1 aor. ἐπόρνευσα; (πόρνος, πόρνη q. v.); Sept. for זנה in Grk. writ. ([Hdt.], Dem., Aeschin., Dio Cass., Lcian., al.)   1. *to prostitute one's body to the lust of another.* In the Scriptures   2. *to give one's self to unlawful sexual intercourse; to commit fornication* (Vulg. *fornicor*): 1 Co. vi. 18; x. 8; Rev. ii. 14, 20; [Mk. x. 19 WH (rejected) mrg.].   3. by a Hebraism (see πορνεία, b.) metaph. *to be given to idolatry, to worship idols*: 1 Chr. v. 25; Ps. lxxiii. (lxxiii.) 27; Jer. iii. 6; Ezek. xxiii. 19; Hos. ix. 1, etc.; μετά τινος, *to permit one's self to be drawn away by another into idolatry*, Rev. xvii. 2; xviii. 3, 9. [Comp.: ἐκ-πορνεύω.]*

4204 πόρνη, -ης, ἡ, (fr. περάω, πέρνημι, to sell; Curtius § 358), properly *a woman who sells her body for sexual uses* [cf. Xen. mem. 1, 6, 13], Sept. for זונה;   1. prop. *a prostitute, a harlot*, one who yields herself to defilement for the sake of gain, (Arstph., Dem., al.); in the N. T. univ. *any woman indulging in unlawful sexual intercourse, whether for gain or for lust*: Mt. xxi. 31 sq.; Lk. xv. 30; 1 Co. vi. 15 sq.; Heb. xi. 31; Jas. ii. 25.   2. Hebraistically (see πορνεία, b. and πορνεύω, 3), metaph. *an idolatress*; so of 'Babylon' i. e. Rome, the chief seat of idolatry: Rev. xvii. 1, 5, 15 sq.; xix. 2.*

4205 πόρνος, -ου, ὁ, (for the etym. see πόρνη), *a man who prostitutes his body to another's lust for hire, a male prostitute*, ([Arstph.], Xen., Dem., Aeschin., Lcian.); univ. *a man who indulges in unlawful sexual intercourse, a fornicator*, (Vulg. *fornicator, fornicarius*, [Rev. xxii. 15 *impudicus*]): 1 Co. v. 9-11; vi. 9; Eph. v. 5; 1 Tim. i. 10;

Heb. xii. 16; xiii. 4; Rev. xxi. 8; xxii. 15.   (Sir. xxiii. 16 sq.)*

4206 &   πόρρω, [(allied w. πρό, Curtius § 380)], adv., [fr. Plat.,
4208   Xen. down], *far, at a distance, a great way off*: Mt. xv. 8; Mk. vii. 6; Lk. xiv. 32 [cf. W. § 54, 2 a.; B. § 129, 11]; compar. πορρωτέρω, in L Tr WH πορρώτερον [(Polyb., al.)], *further*: Lk. xxiv. 28.*

4207   πόρρωθεν, (πόρρω), adv., [fr. Plat. on], *from afar, afar off*: Lk. xvii. 12; Heb. xi. 13; Sept. chiefly for מֵרָחוֹק.*

4209   πορφύρα, -ας, ἡ, Sept. for אַרְגָּמָן;   1. *the purple-fish*, a species of shell-fish or mussel: [Aeschyl., Soph.], Isocr., Aristot., al.; add 1 Macc. iv. 23, on which see Grimm; [cf. B. D. s. v. Colors 1].   2. *a fabric colored with the purple dye, a garment made from purple cloth*, (so fr. Aeschyl. down): Mk. xv. 17, 20; Lk. xvi. 19; Rev. xvii. 4 Rec.; xviii. 12.*

see   πορφύρεος, -α, -ον, in Attic and in the N. T. contr. -οῦς,
4210 St.   -ᾶ, -οῦν, (πορφύρα), fr. Hom. down, *purple, dyed in purple, made of a purple fabric*: Jn. xix. 2, 5; πορφυροῦν sc. ἔνδυμα ([B. 82 (72)]; cf. W. p. 591 (550)), Rev. xvii. 4 [G L T Tr WH]; xviii. 16.*

4211   πορφυρόπωλις, -ιδος, ἡ, (πορφύρα and πωλέω), *a female seller of purple or of fabrics dyed in purple* (Vulg. *purpuraria*): Acts xvi. 14.   (Phot., Suid., al.)*

4212   ποσάκις, (πόσος), adv., *how often*: Mt. xviii. 21; xxiii. 37; Lk. xiii. 34.   [(Plat. ep., Aristot., al.)]*

4213   πόσις, -εως, ἡ, (πίνω), fr. Hom. down, *a drinking, drink*: Jn. vi. 55; Ro. xiv. 17; Col. ii. 16, (see βρῶσις).*

4214   πόσος, -η, -ον, [(cf. Curtius § 631), fr. Aeschyl. down, Lat. *quantus*], *how great*: Mt. vi. 23; 2 Co. vii. 11; πόσος χρόνος, how great (a space) i. e. how long time, Mk. ix. 21; neut. *how much*, Lk. xvi. 5, 7; πόσῳ, (by) how much, Mt. xii. 12; πόσῳ μᾶλλον, Mt. vii. 11; x. 25; Lk. xi. 13; xii. 24, 28; Ro. xi. 12, 24; Philem. 16; Heb. ix. 14; πόσῳ χείρονος τιμωρίας, Heb. x. 29; plur. *how many*: with nouns, Mt. xv. 34; xvi. 9 sq.; Mk. vi. 38; viii. 4, 19 sq.; Lk. xv. 17; Acts xxi. 20; πόσα, how grave, Mt. xxvii. 13; Mk. xv. 4.*

4215   ποταμός, -οῦ, ὁ, fr. Hom. down, Sept. for נָהָר and יְאֹר, *a stream, a river*: Mt. iii. 6 L T Tr WH; Mk. i. 5; Acts xvi. 13; 2 Co. xi. 26 [W. § 30, 2 a.]; Rev. viii. 10; ix. 14; xii. 15; xvi. 4, 12; xxii. 1 sq.; i. q. *a torrent*, Mt. vii. 25, 27; Lk. vi. 48 sq.; Rev. xii. 15 sq.; plur. figuratively i. q. the greatest abundance [cf. colloq. Eng. "streams," "floods"], Jn. vii. 38.*

4216   ποταμο-φόρητος, -ου, ὁ, (ποταμός and φορέω; like ἀνεμοφόρητος [cf. W. 100 (94)]), *carried away by a stream* (i. e. whelmed, drowned in the waters): Rev. xii. 15. Besides only in Hesych. s. v. ἀπόερσε.*

4217   ποταπός ([in Dion. Hal., Joseph., Philo, al.] for the older ποδαπός [cf. *Lob.* Phryn. p. 56 sq.; *Rutherford,* New Phryn. p. 129; W. 24; Curtius p. 537, 5th ed.]; acc. to the Grk. grammarians i. q. ἐκ ποίου δαπέδου, *from what region*; acc. to the conjecture of others i. q. ποῦ ἀπό [(*Buttmann*, Lexil. i. 126, compares the Germ. *wovon*)], the δ being inserted for the sake of euphony, as in the Lat. *prodire, prodesse*; cf. Fritzsche on Mark p. 554 sq. [still others regard -δαπός merely as an ending; cf.

Apollon. Dysk., ed. *Buttmann*, index s. v.]), -ή, -όν ;   **1.** *from what country, race, or tribe ?* so fr. Aeschyl. down. **2.** from Demosth. down also i. q. *ποῖος, of what sort or quality ? [what manner of ?]* : absol. of persons, Mt. viii. 27 ; 2 Pet. iii. 11 ; with a pers. noun, Lk. vii. 39 ; w. names of things, Mk. xiii. 1 ; Lk. i. 29 ; 1 Jn. iii. 1.*

4219   **πότε**, [Curtius § 631], direct interrog. adv., fr. Hom. down, *when ? at what time ?* Mt. xxv. 37–39, 44 ; Lk. xxi. 7 ; Jn. vi. 25 ; loosely used (as sometimes even by Attic writ.) for the relative *ὁπότε* in indirect questions (W. 510 (475)) : Mt. xxiv. 3 ; Mk. xiii. 4, 33, 35 ; Lk. xii. 36 ; xvii. 20. *ἕως πότε, how long ?* in direct questions [cf. W. § 54, 6 fin. ; B. § 146, 4] : Mt. xvii. 17 ; Mk. ix. 19 ; Lk. ix. 41 ; Jn. x. 24 ; Rev. vi. 10.*

4218   **ποτέ**, an enclitic particle, fr. Hom. down ;   **1.** *once*, i. e. *at some time or other, formerly, aforetime* ;   **a.** of the Past : Jn. ix. 13 ; Ro. vii. 9 ; xi. 30 ; Gal. i. 13, 23 [cf. W. § 45, 7] ; Eph. ii. 2 sq. 11, 13 ; v. 8 ; Col. i. 21 ; iii. 7 ; 1 Th. ii. 5 ; Tit. iii. 3 ; Philem. 11 ; 1 Pet. ii. 10 ; iii. 5, 20 ; *ἤδη ποτέ, now at length*, Phil. iv. 10.   **b.** of the Future : Lk. xxii. 32 ; *ἤδη ποτέ, now at length*, Ro. i. 10.   **2.** *ever* : after a negative, *οὐδείς ποτε*, Eph. v. 29 [B. 202 (175)] ; *οὐ . . . ποτέ*, 2 Pet. i. 21 ; *μή ποτε* (see *μήποτε*) ; after *οὐ μή* with the aor. subjunc. 2 Pet. i. 10 ; in a question, *τίς ποτε*, 1 Co. ix. 7 ; Heb. i. 5, 13 ; *ὁποῖοί ποτε, whatsoever*, Gal. ii. 6 [but some would render *ποτέ* here *formerly, once* ; cf. Bp. Lghtft. ad loc.].*

4220   **πότερος**, -α, -ον, [fr. Hom. down], *which of two* ; *πότερον . . . ἤ, utrum . . . an, whether . . . or*, [W. § 57, 1 b. ; B. 250 (215)] : Jn. vii. 17.*

4221   **ποτήριον**, -ου, τό, (dimin. of *ποτήρ*), *a cup, a drinking vessel* ;   **a.** prop. : Mt. xxiii. 25 sq. ; xxvi. 27 ; Mk. vii. 4, 8 [T WH om. Tr br. the vs.] ; xiv. 23 ; Lk. xi. 39 ; xxii. 17, 20 ; 1 Co. xi. 25 ; Rev. xvii. 4 ; *πίνειν ἐκ τοῦ ποτηρίου*, 1 Co. xi. 28 ; *τὸ ποτήριον τῆς εὐλογίας* (see *εὐλογία*, 4), 1 Co. x. 16 ; with a gen. of the thing with which the cup is filled : *ψυχροῦ*, Mt. x. 42 ; *ὕδατος*, Mk. ix. 41 ; by meton. of the container for the contained, the contents of the cup, what is offered to be drunk, Lk. xxii. 20ᵇ [(WH reject the pass.) cf. Win. 635 (589) sq.] ; 1 Co. xi. 25 sq. ; *τὸ ποτήριόν τινος*, gen. of the pers. giving the entertainment (cf. *Rückert*, Abendmahl, p. 217 sq.) : *πίνειν*, 1 Co. x. 21 [cf. W. 189 (178)] ; xi. 27 [cf. W. 441 (410)].   **b.** By a figure common to Hebrew, Arabic, Syriac, and not unknown to Latin writers, one's **l o t** or **e x p e r i e n c e**, whether joyous or adverse, **d i v i n e a p p o i n t m e n t s**, whether favorable or unfavorable, are likened to a cup which God presents one to drink [cf. W. 32] : so of prosperity, Ps. xv. (xvi.) 5 ; xxii. (xxiii.) 5 ; cxv. (cxvi.) 13 ; of adversity, Ps. x. (xi.) 6 ; lxxiv. (lxxv.) 9 ; Is. li. 17, 22. In the N. T. of the bitter lot (the sufferings) of Christ : Mt. xxvi. 39, 42 Rec. ; Mk. xiv. 36 ; Lk. xxii. 42 ; Jn. xviii. 11 ; *πίνειν τὸ ποτ. μου* or *ὁ ἐγὼ πίνω*, to undergo the same calamities which I undergo, Mt. xx. 22, 23 ; Mk. x. 38, 39, (Plaut. Cas. 5, 2, 53 (50) ut senex hoc eodem poculo quod ego bibi biberet, i. e. that he might be treated as harshly as I was) ; used of the divine penalties : Rev. xiv. 10 ; xvi.

---

19 ; xviii. 6. ([Alcaeus, Sappho], Hdt., Ctes., Arstph., Lcian., al. ; Sept. for כּוֹס.) *

4222   **ποτίζω** ; impf. *ἐπότιζον* ; 1 aor. *ἐπότισα* ; pf. *πεπότικα* (Rev. xiv. 8) ; 1 aor. pass. *ἐποτίσθην* ; (*πότος*) ; fr. [Hippocr.], Xen., Plat. down ; Sept. for הִשְׁקָה ; *to give to drink, to furnish drink*, (Vulg. in 1 Co. xii. 13 and Rev. xiv. 8 *poto* [but in Rev. l. c. Tdf. gives *potiono* ; A. V. *to make to drink*]) : *τινά*, Mt. xxv. 35, 37, 42 ; xxvii. 48 ; Mk. xv. 36 ; Lk. xiii. 15 ; Ro. xii. 20 ; *τινά τι*, to offer one anything to drink (W. § 32, 4 a. ; [B. § 131, 6]) : Mt. x. 42 ; Mk. ix. 41, and often in the Sept. ; in fig. discourse *π. τινὰ γάλα*, to give one teaching easy to be apprehended, 1 Co. iii. 2 (where by zeugma *οὐ βρῶμα* is added ; [cf. W. § 66, 2 e. ; B. § 151, 30 ; A. V. *I have fed you with milk*, etc.]) ; *τινὰ ἐκ τοῦ οἴνου*, Rev. xiv. 8 (see *οἶνος*, b. and *θυμός*, 2) ; i. q. *to water, irrigate*, (plants, fields, etc.) : 1 Co. iii. 6–8 (Xen. symp. 2, 25 ; Lcian., Athen., Geop., [Strab., Philo] ; Sept. [Gen. xiii. 10] ; Ezek. xvii. 7) ; metaph. *to imbue, saturate, τινά*, one's mind, w. the addition of an accus. of the thing, *ἐν πνεῦμα*, in pass., 1 Co. xii. 13 L T Tr WH [W. § 32, 5 ; B. § 134, 5] ; *εἰς ἓν πνεῦμα*, that we might be united into one body which is imbued with one spirit, ibid. R G, (*τινὰ πνεύματι κατανύξεως*, Is. xxix. 10 [cf. Sir. xv. 3]).*

4223   **Ποτίολοι**, -ων, οἱ, *Puteoli*, a city of Campania in Italy, situated on the Bay of Naples, now called Pozzuoli : Acts xxviii. 13. [Cf. *Lewin*, St. Paul, ii. 218 sqq. ; *Smith*, Dict. of Geog. s. v.] *

4224   **πότος**, -ου, ὁ, (ΠΟΩ [cf. *πίνω*]), *a drinking, carousing* : 1 Pet. iv. 3. (Xen., Plat., Dem., Joseph., Plut., Ael., al. ; Sept. for מִשְׁתֶּה.) *

4226   **ποῦ**, [cf. Curtius § 631], an interrog. adv., fr. Hom. down, Sept. for אַיֵּה, אָנָה, אֵי, *where ? in what place ?*   **a.** in direct questions : Mt. ii. 2 ; xxvi. 17 ; Mk. xiv. 12, 14 ; Lk. xvii. 17, 37 ; xxii. 9, 11 ; Jn. i. 38 (39) ; vii. 11 ; viii. 10, 19 ; ix. 12 ; xi. 34 ; *ποῦ ἐστιν* [(*ἐστ.* sometimes unexpressed)], in questions indicating that a person or thing is gone, or cannot be found, is equiv. to *it is nowhere, does not exist* : Lk. viii. 25 ; Ro. iii. 27 ; 1 Co. i. 20 ; xii. 17, 19 ; xv. 55 ; Gal. iv. 15 L T Tr WH ; 2 Pet. iii. 4 ; *ποῦ φανεῖται*, [A. V. *where shall . . . appear*] i. q. there will be no place for him, 1 Pet. iv. 18.   **b.** in indirect questions, for the relative *ὅπου* [cf. W. § 57, 2 fin.] : foll. by the indic., Mt. ii. 4 ; Mk. xv. 47 ; Jn. i. 39 (40) ; xi. 57 ; xx. 2, 13, 15 ; Rev. ii. 13 [cf. W. 612 (569)] ; foll. by the subjunc., Mt. viii. 20 ; Lk. ix. 58 ; xii. 17.   **c.** joined to verbs of going or coming, for *ποῖ* in direct quest. [cf. our colloq. *where* for *whither* ; see W. § 54, 7 ; B. 71 (62)] : Jn. vii. 35 [cf. W. 300 (281) ; B. 358 (307)] ; xiii. 36 ; xvi. 5 ; in indir. question, foll. by the indic. : Jn. iii. 8 ; viii. 14 ; xii. 35 ; xiv. 5 ; Heb. xi. 8 ; 1 Jn. ii. 11.*

4225   **πού**, an enclitic particle, fr. Hom. down ;   **1.** *somewhere* : Heb. ii. 6 ; iv. 4.   **2.** it has a limiting force, *nearly* ; with numerals *somewhere about, about*, (Hdt. 1, 119 ; 7, 22 ; Paus. 8, 11, 2 ; Hdian. 7, 5, 3 [2 ed. Bekk.] ; Ael. v. h. 13, 4 ; al.) : Ro. iv. 19.*

4227   **Πούδης**, [B. 17 (15)], *Pudens*, proper name of a Christian mentioned in 2 Tim. iv. 21. Cf. *Lipsius*, Chronologie d. römisch. Bischöfe (1869) p. 146; [B. D. s. v., also (Am. ed.) s. v. Claudia; Bib. Sacr. for 1875, p. 174 sqq.; *Plumptre* in the 'Bible Educator' iii. 245 and in Ellicott's 'New Test. Com.' ii. p. 186 sq.].*

4228 πούς (not πούς, see *Lob.* ad Phryn. p. 765; *Göttling,* Accentl. p. 244; [*Chandler,* Grk. Accentuation, § 566]; W. § 6, 1 d.; *Lipsius,* Gram. Untersuch. p. 48), ποδός, ὁ, [allied w. πέδον, πέζα, Lat. *pes,* etc.; Curtius § 291; Vaniček p. 473], dat. plur. ποσίν, fr. Hom. down, Hebr. רֶגֶל; *a foot,* both of men and of beasts: Mt. iv. 6; vii. 6; xxii. 13; Mk. ix. 45; Lk. i. 79; Jn. xi. 44; Acts vii. 5; 1 Co. xii. 15; Rev. x. 2, and often. From the oriental practice of placing the foot upon the vanquished (Josh. x. 24), come the foll. expressions: ὑπὸ τοὺς πόδας συντρίβειν (q. v.) τινά, Ro. xvi. 20; ὑποτάσσειν τινά, 1 Co. xv. 27; Eph. i. 22; Heb. ii. 8; τιθέναι, 1 Co. xv. 25; τιθέναι τινὰ ὑποκάτω τῶν ποδῶν, Mt. xxii. 44 L T Tr WH; ὑποπόδιον τῶν ποδῶν, Mt. xxii. 44 R G; Mk. xii. 36 [here WH ὑποκάτω τ. π.]; Lk. xx. 43; Acts ii. 35; Heb. i. 13; x. 13; disciples listening to their teacher's instruction are said παρὰ (or πρὸς) τοὺς πόδας τινὸς καθῆσθαι or παρακαθίσαι, Lk. x. 39; Acts xxii. 3, cf. Lk. viii. 35; to lay a thing παρὰ (or πρὸς) τοὺς πόδας τινός is used of those who consign it to his power and care, Mt. xv. 30; Acts iv. 35, 37; v. 2; vii. 58. In saluting, paying homage, supplicating, etc., persons are said πρὸς τοὺς πόδας τινὸς πίπτειν or προσπίπτειν: Mk. v. 22; vii. 25; Lk. viii. 41; xvii. 16 παρά; Rev. i. 17; εἰς τοὺς π. τινός, Mt. xviii. 29 [Rec.]; Jn. xi. 32 [here T Tr WH πρός]; πίπτειν ἔμπροσθεν τ. ποδῶν τινος, Rev. xix. 10; προσκυνεῖν ἔμπροσθεν (or ἐνώπιον) τῶν ποδῶν τινος, Rev. iii. 9; xxii. 8; πίπτ. ἐπὶ τοὺς π. Acts x. 25. By a poetic usage that member of the body which is the chief organ or instrument in any given action is put for the man himself (see γλῶσσα, 1); thus οἱ πόδες τινός is used for the man in motion: Lk. i. 79 (Ps. cxviii. (cxix.) 101); Acts v. 9; Ro. iii. 15; x. 15; Heb. xii. 13.

4229 πρᾶγμα, -τος, τό, (πράσσω), fr. [Pind.], Aeschyl., Hdt. down, Sept. chiefly for דָּבָר a. *that which has been done, a deed, an accomplished fact:* Lk. i. 1; Acts v. 4; 2 Co. vii. 11; Heb. vi. 18. b. *what is doing* or *being accomplished:* Jas. iii. 16; spec. *business* (commercial transaction), 1 Th. iv. 6 [so W. 115 (109); al. refer this example to c. and render *in the matter* (spoken of, or conventionally understood; cf. *Green,* Gram. p. 26 sq.)]. c. *a matter* (in question), *affair:* Mt. xviii. 19; Ro. xvi. 2; spec. in a forensic sense, *a matter at law, case, suit,* (Xen. mem. 2, 9, 1; Dem. 1120, 26; Joseph. antt. 14, 10, 17): πρᾶγμα ἔχειν πρός τινα, [A. V. *having a matter against,* etc.], 1 Co. vi. 1. d. *that which is* or *exists, a thing:* Heb. x. 1; πράγματα οὐ βλεπόμενα, Heb. xi. 1 [see ἐλπίζω].*,

4230 πραγματεία [T WH -τία; see I, ι], -ας, ἡ, (πραγματεύομαι), prosecution of any affair; *business, occupation:* plur. with the addition of τοῦ βίου, pursuits and occupations pertaining to civil life, opp. to warfare [A. V. *the affairs of this life*], 2 Tim. ii. 4. (In the same and other senses in Grk. writ. fr. [Hippocr.], Xen., Plato down.)*

4231 πραγματεύομαι: 1 aor. mid. impv. 2 pers. plur. πραγ-

ματεύσασθε; (πρᾶγμα); in Grk. prose writ. fr. Hdt. down; *to be occupied in anything; to carry on a business;* spec. *to carry on the business of a banker* or *trader* (Plut. Sull. 17; Cat. min. 59): Lk. xix. 13 [here WH txt. reads the infinitive (see their Intr. § 404); R. V. *trade.* COMP.: δια- πραγματεύομαι.]*

4232 πραιτώριον, -ου, τό, a Lat. word, *praetorium* (neut. of the adj. *praetorius* used substantively); the word denotes 1. 'head-quarters' in a Roman camp, *the tent of the commander-in-chief.* 2. *the palace in which the governor* or *procurator of a province resided,* to which use the Romans were accustomed to appropriate the palaces already existing, and formerly dwelt in by the kings or princes (at Syracuse "illa domus praetoria, quae regis Hieronis fuit," Cic. Verr. ii. 5, 12, 30); at Jerusalem it was that magnificent palace which Herod the Great had built for himself, and which the Roman procurators seem to have occupied whenever they came from Caesarea to Jerusalem to transact public business: Mt. xxvii. 27; Mk. xv. 16; Jn. xviii. 28, 33; xix. 9; cf. Philo, leg. ad Gaium, § 38; Joseph. b. j. 2, 14, 8; also the one at Caesarea, Acts xxiii. 35. Cf. Keim iii. p. 359 sq. [Eng. trans. vi. p. 79; B. D. s. v. Praetorium]. 3. *the camp of praetorian soldiers* established by Tiberius (Suet. 37): Phil. i. 13. Cf. *Win.* RWB. s. v. Richthaus; [Bp. Lghtft. (Com. on Philip. p. 99 sqq.) rejects, as destitute of evidence, the various attempts to give a l o c a l sense to the word in Phil. l. c., and vindicates the meaning *praetorian guard* (so R.V.)].*

4233 πράκτωρ, -ορος, ὁ, (πράσσω); 1. *one who does anything, a doer,* (Soph.). 2. *one who does the work of inflicting punishment* or *taking vengeance;* esp. *the avenger of a murder* (Aeschyl., Soph.); *the exactor of a pecuniary fine* ([Antipho], Dem., al.); *an officer of justice of the lower order whose business it is to inflict punishment:* Lk. xii. 58.*

4234 πρᾶξις, -εως, ἡ, (πράσσω), fr. Hom. down; a. *a doing, a mode of acting; a deed, act, transaction:* univ. πράξεις τῶν ἀποστόλων (Grsb.; Rec. inserts ἁγίων, L Tr WH om. τῶν, Tdf. has simply πράξεις), *the doings of* (i. e. things done by) *the apostles,* in the inscription of the Acts; sing. in an ethical sense: both good and bad, Mt. xvi. 27; in a bad sense, i. q. *wicked deed, crime,* Lk. xxiii. 51; plur. *wicked doings* (cf. our *practices* i. e. *trickery;* often so by Polyb.): Acts xix. 18; Ro. viii. 13; Col. iii. 9; (with κακή added, as Ev. Nicod. 1 Ἰησοῦς ἐθεράπευσε δαιμονιζομένους ἀπὸ πράξεων κακῶν). b. *a thing to be done, business,* [A. V. *office*], (Xen. mem. 2, 1, 6): Ro. xii. 4.*

4235 πρᾶος (so R G in Mt. xi. 29; on the iota subscr. cf. *Lob.* ad Phryn. p. 403 sq.; *Bttm.* Ausf. Spr. § 64, 2 i. p. 255; [*Lipsius,* Gramm. Untersuch. p. 7 sq.; cf. W. § 5, 4 d. and p. 45 (44)]) or πρᾶος, -α, -ον, and πραύς (L T Tr WH, so R G in Mt. xxi. 5 (4); [cf. *Tdf.* Proleg. p. 82]), -εῖα, -ύ, gen. πραέως T Tr WH for the common form πραέος (so Lchm.; πραέος R G), see βαθέως [cf. B. 26 (23)], plur. πραεῖς L T Tr WH, πρᾳεῖς R G; fr. Hom. down; *gentle, mild, meek:* Mt. v. 5 (4); xi. 29; xxi. 5; 1 Pet. iii. 4; Sept. several times for יָגֵעַ and יָנֵעַ. [Cf. Schmidt ch. 98, 2; Trench § xlii.; Clem. Alex. strom. 4, 6, 36.]*

4236   **πραότης** (Rec. and Grsb. [exc. in Jas. i. 21; iii. 13; 1 Pet. iii. 15]; see the preceding word), πραότης (so Lchm.), and acc. to a later form πραΰτης (so R and G, but with ι subscr. under the α, in Jas. i. 21; iii. 13; 1 Pet. iii. 15; Lchm. everywhere exc. in Gal. vi. 1; Eph. iv. 2; Treg. everywhere [exc. in 2 Co. x. 1; Gal. v. 23 (22); vi.1; Eph. iv. 2], TWH everywhere; cf. B. 26 (23) sq.),-ητος, ἡ, gentleness, mildness, meekness: 1 Co. iv. 21; 2 Co. x. 1; Gal. v. 23 (22); vi. 1; Col. iii. 12; Eph. iv. 2; 1 Tim. vi. 11 R; 2 Tim. ii. 25; Tit. iii. 2; Jas. i. 21; iii. 13; 1 Pet. iii. 16 (15). (Xen., Plato, Isocr., Aristot., Diod., Joseph., al.; for עֲנָוָה, Ps. xlv. (xlv.) 4.) [SYN. see ἐπιείκεια, fin.; Trench (as there referred to, but esp.) § xlii.; Bp. Lghtft. on Col. iii. 13.]*

4237   **πρασιά**, -ᾶς, ἡ, a plot of ground, a garden-bed, Hom. Od. 7, 127; 24, 247; Theophr. hist. plant. 4, 4, 3; Nicand., Diosc., al.; Sir. xxiv. 31; ἀνέπεσον πρασιαὶ πρασιαί (a Hebraism), i. e. they reclined in ranks or divisions, so that the several ranks formed, as it were, separate plots, Mk. vi. 40; cf. Gesenius, Lehrgeb. p. 669; [Hebr. Gram. § 106, 4; B. 30 (27); W. 464 (432) also] § 37, 3; (where add fr. the O. T. συνήγαγον αὐτοὺς θημωνίας θημωνίας, Ex. viii. 14).*

4238   **πράσσω** and (once viz. Acts xvii. 7 RG) **πράττω**; fut. πράξω; 1 aor. ἔπραξα; pf. πέπραχα; pf. pass. ptcp. πεπραγμένος; fr. Hom. down; Sept. several times for עָשָׂה and בָּצַע; to do, practise, effect, Lat. agere, (but ποιεῖν to make, Lat. facere; [see ποιέω, fin.]); i.e. **1.** to exercise, practise, be busy with, carry on: τὰ περίεργα, Acts xix. 19; τὰ ἴδια, to mind one's own affairs, 1 Th. iv. 11 (τὰ ἑαυτοῦ, [Soph. Electr. 678]; Xen. mem. 2, 9, 1; Plat. Phaedr. p. 247 a.; Dem. p. 150, 21; al.); used of performing the duties of an office, 1 Co. ix. 17. to undertake to do, μηδὲν προπετές, Acts xix. 36. **2.** to accomplish, to perform: πεπραγμένον ἐστίν, has been accomplished, has taken place, Acts xxvi. 26; εἴτε ἀγαθόν, εἴτε κακόν, 2 Co. v. 10; ἀγαθὸν ἢ φαῦλον (κακόν), Ro. ix. 11 (δίκαια ἢ ἄδικα, Plat. apol. p. 28 b.); ἄξια τῆς μετανοίας ἔργα, Acts xxvi. 20; add, Ro. vii. 15, 19; Phil. iv. 9; νόμον, to do i. e. keep the law, Ro. ii. 25; of unworthy acts, to commit, perpetrate, (less freq. so in Grk. writ., as πολλὰ καὶ ἀνόσια, Xen. symp. 8, 22; with them ποιεῖν [(see Schmidt, Syn. ch. 23, 11, 3; L. and S. s. v. B.)] is more com. in reference to bad conduct; hence τοὺς ἐπισταμένους μὲν ἃ δεῖ πράττειν, ποιοῦντας δὲ τἀναντία, Xen. mem. 3, 9, 4), Acts xxvi. 9; 2 Co. xii. 21; τὸ ἔργον τοῦτο, this (criminal) deed, 1 Co. v. 2 TWH Tr mrg.; add, Lk. xxii. 23; Acts iii. 17; v. 35; Ro. vii. 19; τὰ τοιαῦτα, such nameless iniquities, Ro. i. 32 (where ποιεῖν and πράσσειν are used indiscriminately [but cf. Meyer]); ii. 1–3; Gal. v. 21; φαῦλα, Jn. iii. 20; v. 29; τι ἄξιον θανάτου, Lk. xxiii. 15; Acts xxv. 11, 25; xxvi. 31; τὸ κακόν, Ro. vii. 19; xiii. 4; ἄτοπον, Lk. xxiii. 41; τί τινι κακόν, to bring evil upon one, Acts xvi. 28. **3.** to manage public affairs, transact public business, (Xen., Dem., Plut.); fr. this use has come a sense met with fr. Pind., Aeschyl., Hdt. down, viz. to exact tribute, revenue,

debts: Lk. iii. 13 [here R. V. extort]; τὸ ἀργύριον, Lk. xix. 23, (so agere in Lat., cf. the commentators on Suet. Vesp. 1; [cf. W. § 42, 1 a.]). **4.** intrans. to act (see εὖ p. 256*): ἀπέναντί τινος, contrary to a thing, Acts xvii. 7. **5.** fr. Aeschyl. and Hdt. down reflexively, me habere: τί πράσσω, how I do, the state of my affairs, Eph. vi. 21; εὖ πράξετε (see εὖ), Acts xv. 29 [cf. B. 300 (258)].

πραϋπάθεια (-θία TWH; see I, ι), -ας, ἡ, (πραϋπαθής [(πάσχω)]), mildness of disposition, gentleness of spirit, meekness, (i. q. πραΰτης): 1 Tim. vi. 11 L T Tr WH. (Philo de Abrah. § 37; Ignat. ad Trall. 8, 1.)*   **see 4236**
   4239;
   see 4235

πραΰς, see πρᾶος.

πραΰτης, see πραότης.   **4240;**

πρέπω; impf. 3 pers. sing. ἔπρεπε;   **1.** to stand out,   **see 4236** to be conspicuous, to be eminent; so fr. Hom. Il. 12, 104 down. **2.** to be becoming, seemly, fit, (fr. Pind.,   **4241** Aeschyl., Hdt. down): πρέπει τινί with a subject nom. Heb. vii. 26 (Ps. xxxii. (xxxiii.) 1); ὃ or ἃ πρέπει, which becometh, befitteth, 1 Tim. ii. 10; Tit. ii. 1; impers. καθὼς πρέπει τινί, Eph. v. 3; πρέπον ἐστίν foll. by the inf., Mt. iii. 15; Heb. ii. 10; foll. by an acc. with the inf. 1 Co xi. 13. On its constr. cf. Bttm. § 142, 2.*

πρεσβεία, -ας, ἡ, (πρεσβεύω);   **1.** age, dignity, right   **4242** of the first born: Aeschyl. Pers. 4; Plat. de rep. 6 p. 509 b.; Paus. 3, 1, 4; 3, 3, 8. **2.** the business wont to be intrusted to elders, spec. the office of an ambassador, an embassy, (Arstph., Xen., Plat.); abstr. for the concrete, an ambassage i. e. ambassadors, Lk. xiv. 32; xix. 14.*

πρεσβεύω; (πρέσβυς an old man, an elder, [Curtius p.   **4243** 479; Vaniček p. 186]);   **1.** to be older, prior by birth or in age, ([Soph.], Hdt. and sqq.). **2.** to be an ambassador, act as an ambassador: 2 Co. v. 20; Eph. vi. 20, ([Hdt. 5, 93 init.], Arstph., Xen., Plat., sqq.).*

πρεσβυτέριον, -ον, τό, (πρεσβύτερος, q. v.), body of elders,   **4244** presbytery, senate, council: of the Jewish elders (see συνέδριον, 2), Lk. xxii. 66; Acts xxii. 5; [cf. Dan. Theod. init. 50]; of the elders of any body (church) of Christians, 1 Tim. iv. 14 (eccl. writ. [cf. reff. s. v. πρεσβύτερος, 2 b.]).*

πρεσβύτερος, -α, -ον, (compar. of πρέσβυς), [fr. Hom.   **4245** down], elder; used **1.** of age; **a.** where two persons are spoken of, the elder: ὁ υἱὸς ὁ πρεσβ. (Ael. v. h. 9, 42), Lk. xv. 25. **b.** univ. advanced in life, an elder, a senior: opp. to νεανίσκοι, Acts iii. 17; opp. to νεώτερος, 1 Tim. v. 1 sq., (Gen. xviii. 11 sq.; Sap. viii. 10; Sir. vi. 34 (33); vii. 14; 2 Macc. viii. 30). οἱ πρεσβύτεροι, [A.V. the elders], forefathers, Heb. xi. 2; παράδοσις (q. v.) τῶν πρεσβ., received from the fathers, Mt. xv. 2; Mk. vii. 3, 5. **2.** a term of rank or office; as such borne by, **a.** among the Jews, **a.** members of the great council or Sanhedrin (because in early times the rulers of the people, judges, etc., were selected from the elderly men): Mt. xvi. 21; xxvi. 47, 57, 59 Rec.; xxvii. 3, 12, 20, 41; xxviii. 12; Mk. viii. 31; xi. 27; xiv. 43, 53; xv. 1; Lk. ix. 22; xx. 1; xxii. 52; Jn. viii. 9; Acts iv. 5, 23; vi. 12; xxiii. 14; xxiv. 1; with the addition of τοῦ Ἰσραήλ, Acts iv. 8 R G; of τῶν Ἰουδαίων, Acts xxv. 15; of τοῦ λαοῦ, Mt. xxi. 23; xxvi. 3; xxvii. 1. **β.** those who in the separate cities managed public affairs and administered justice: Lk. vii. 3. [Cf. BB. DD. s. v. Elder.] **b.** among Christians, *those who presided over the assemblies* (or *churches*): Acts xi. 30; xiv. 23; xv. 2, 4, 6, 22 sq.; xvi. 4; xxi. 18; 1 Tim. v. 17, 19; Tit. i. 5; 2 Jn. 1; 3 Jn. 1; 1 Pet. v. 1, 5; with τῆς ἐκκλησίας added, Acts xx. 17; Jas. v. 14. That they did not differ at all from the (ἐπίσκοποι) bishops or overseers (as is acknowledged also by Jerome on Tit. i. 5 [cf. Bp. *Lghtft.* Com. on Phil. pp. 98 sq. 229 sq.]) is evident from the fact that the two words are used indiscriminately, Acts xx. 17, 28; Tit. i. 5, 7, and that the duty of presbyters is described by the terms ἐπισκοπεῖν, 1 Pet. v. 1 sq., and ἐπισκοπή, Clem. Rom. 1 Cor. 44, 1; accordingly only two ecclesiastical officers, οἱ ἐπίσκοποι and οἱ διάκονοι, are distinguished in Phil. i. 1; 1 Tim. iii. 1, 8. The title ἐπίσκοπος denotes the function, πρεσβύτερος the dignity; the former was borrowed from Greek institutions, the latter from the Jewish; cf. [Bp. *Lghtft.*, as above, pp. 95 sqq. 191 sqq.]; *Ritschl*, Die Entstehung der altkathol. Kirche, ed. 2 p. 350 sqq.; *Hase*, Protest. Polemik, ed. 4 p. 98 sqq.; [*Hatch*, Bampton Lects. for 1880, Lect. iii. and Harnack's Analecten appended to the Germ. trans. of the same (p. 229 sqq.); also Harnack's note on Clem. Rom. 1 Cor. 1, 3 (cf. reff. at 44 init.), and *Hatch* in Dict. of Christ. Antiq. s. v. Priest. Cf. ἐπίσκοπος.]. **c.** *the twenty-four members of the heavenly Sanhedrin* or *court*, seated on thrones around the throne of God: Rev. iv. 4, 10; v. 5, 6, 8, 11, 14; vii. 11, 13; xi. 16; xiv. 3; xix. 4.*

4246 **πρεσβύτης, -ου, ὁ,** (πρέσβυς [see πρεσβεύω]), *an old man, an aged man*: Lk. i. 18; Tit. ii. 2; Philem. 9 [here many (cf. R. V. mrg.) regard the word as a substitute for πρεσβευτής, *ambassador*; see Bp. *Lghtft.* Com. ad loc.; *WH.* App. ad loc.; and add to the exx. of the interchange πρεσβεντέρος in *Wood*, Discoveries at Ephesus, App., Inscr. fr. the Great Theatre p. 24 (col. 5, l. 72)]. (Aeschyl., Eur., Xen., Plat., al.; Sept. for זָקֵן.) *

4247 **πρεσβῦτις, -ιδος, ἡ,** (fem. of πρεσβύτης), *an aged woman*: Tit. ii. 3. (Aeschyl., Eur., Plat., Diod., Plut., Hdian. 5, 3, 6 (3 ed. Bekk.).) *

4248 **πρηνής, -ές,** [allied w. πρό; Vaniček p. 484], Lat. *pronus, headlong*: Acts i. 18. (Sap. iv. 19; 3 Macc. v. 43; in Grk. writ. fr. Hom. down, but in Attic more com. πρανής, see *Lob.* ad Phryn. p. 431; [W. 22].) *

4249 **πρίζω** (or πρίω, q. v.): 1 aor. pass. ἐπρίσθην; *to saw, to cut in two with a saw*: Heb. xi. 37. To be 'sawn asunder' was a kind of punishment among the Hebrews (2 S. xii. 31; 1 Chr. xx. 3), which according to ancient tradition was inflicted on the prophet Isaiah; cf. *Win.* RWB. s. v. Säge; *Roskoff* in Schenkel v. 135; [B. D. s. v. Saw]. (Am. i. 3; Sus. 59; Plat. Theag. p. 124 b. and freq. in later writ.) *

4250 **πρίν,** [(acc. to Curtius § 380 compar. προ- ιον, προ -ιν, πριν)], as in Grk. writ. fr. Hom. down **1.** an adv. *previously, formerly,* [cf. πάλαι, 1]: 3 Macc. v. 28; vi. 4, 31; but never so in the N. T. **2.** with the force of a

conjunction, *before, before that*: with an acc. and aor. infin. of things past [cf. W. § 44, 6 fin.; B. § 142, 3]; πρὶν Ἀβραὰμ γενέσθαι, before Abraham existed, came into being, Jn. viii. 58; also πρὶν ἤ (cf. Meyer on Mt. i. 18), Mt. i. 18; [Acts vii. 2]; with an aor. inf. having the force of the Lat. fut. perf., of things future [cf. W. 332 (311)]: πρὶν ἀλέκτορα φωνῆσαι, before the cock shall have crowed, Mt. xxvi. 34, 75; Mk. xiv. 72; Lk. xxii. 61; add, Jn. iv. 49; xiv. 29; also πρὶν ἤ, Mk. xiv. 30; Acts ii. 20 (where L T Tr WH txt. om. ἤ); πρὶν ἤ, preceded by a negative sentence [B. § 139, 35], with the aor. subjunc. having the force of a fut. pf. in Lat. [B. 231 (199)], Lk. ii. 26 [R G L T Tr mrg., but WH br. ἤ], and R G in Lk. xxii. 34; πρὶν ἤ, foll. by the optat. of a thing as entertained in thought, Acts xxv. 16 [W. 297 (279); B. 230 (198)]. Cf. Matthiae § 522, 2 p. 1201 sq.; *Bttm.* Gram. § 139, 41; *Klotz* ad Devar. ii. 2 p. 726 sqq.; W. [and B.] as above.*

4251 **Πρίσκα, ἡ,** [acc. -αν], Prisca (a Lat. name [lit. 'ancient']), a Christian woman, wife of Aquila (concerning whom see Ἀκύλας): Ro. xvi. 3 G L T Tr WH; 1 Co. xvi. 19 L ed. ster. T Tr WH; 2 Tim. iv. 19. She is also called by the dimin. name Πρισκίλλα [better (with all edd.) Πρίσκιλλα; see Chandler § 122; Etymol. Magn. 19, 50 sq.] (cf. Livia, Livilla; Drusa, Drusilla; Quinta, Quintilla; Secunda, Secundilla): Acts xviii. 2, 18, 26; besides, Ro. xvi. 3 Rec.; 1 Co. xvi. 19 R G L.*

4252 **Πρίσκιλλα,** see the preceding word.

4249 πρίω, see πρίζω. [COMP.: δια- πρίω.] ---------- see

4253 **πρό,** a prep. foll. by the Genitive, (Lat. *pro*), [fr. Hom. down], Sept. chiefly for לִפְנֵי, *before*; used **a.** of Place: πρὸ τῶν θυρῶν, τῆς θύρας, etc., Acts v. 23 R G; xii. 6, 14; xiv. 13; Jas. v. 9; by a Hebraism, πρὸ προσώπου with the gen. of a pers. *before* (the face of) *one* (who is following) [B. 319 (274)]: Mt. xi. 10; Mk. i. 2; Lk. i. 76; vii. 27; ix. 52; x. 1, (Mal. iii. 1; Zech. xiv. 20; Deut. iii. 18). **b.** of Time: πρὸ τούτων τῶν ἡμερῶν, Acts v. 36; xxi. 38; [πρὸ τοῦ πάσχα, Jn. xi. 55]; acc. to a later Greek idiom, πρὸ ἓξ ἡμερῶν τοῦ πάσχα, prop. before six days reckoning from the Passover, which is equiv. to ἓξ ἡμέρας πρὸ τοῦ πάσχα, on the sixth day before the Passover, Jn. xii. 1 (πρὸ δύο ἐτῶν τοῦ σεισμοῦ, Am. i. 1; πρὸ μιᾶς ἡμέρας τῆς Μαρδοχαϊκῆς ἡμέρας, 2 Macc. xv. 36; exx. fr. prof. writ. are cited by W. 557 (518); [cf. B. § 131, 11]; fr. eccles. writ. by *Hilgenfeld*, Die Evangelien etc. pp. 298, 302; also his Paschastreit der alten Kirche, p. 221 sq.; [cf. *Soph.* Lex. s. v. πρό, 1 and 2]); [πρὸ τῆς ἑορτῆς, Jn. xiii. 1]; πρὸ καιροῦ, Mt. viii. 29; 1 Co. iv. 5; τῶν αἰώνων, 1 Co. ii. 7; παντὸς τοῦ αἰῶνος, Jude 25 L T Tr WH; ἐτῶν δεκατεσσ. [*fourteen years ago*], 2 Co. xii. 2; add, 2 Tim. i. 9; iv. 21; Tit. i. 2; τοῦ ἀρίστου, Lk. xi. 38; κατακλυσμοῦ, Mt. xxiv. 38; πρὸ τῆς μεταθέσεως, Heb. xi. 5; πρὸ καταβολῆς κόσμου, Jn. xvii. 24; Eph. i. 4; 1 Pet. i. 20; πρὸ πάντων, prior to all created things, Col. i. 17; [πρὸ τούτων πάντων (Rec. ἁπάντ.), Lk. xxi. 12]; by a Hebraism, πρὸ προσώπου with the gen. of a thing is used of time for the simple πρό (W. § 65, 4 b.; [B. 319 (274)]), Acts xiii. 24 [(lit. *before the face of his entering in*)]. πρό with the gen. of a pers.: Jn. v. 7; x. 8 [not Tdf.];

Ro. xvi. 7; οἱ πρό τινος, those that existed before one, Mt. v. 12; with a pred. nom. added, Gal. i. 17. πρό with the gen. of an infin. that has the art., Lat. *ante quam* (*before, before that*) foll. by a fin. verb [B. § 140, 11; W. 329 (309)] : Mt. vi. 8; Lk. ii. 21; xxii. 15; Jn. i. 48 (49); xiii. 19; xvii. 5; Acts xxiii. 15; Gal. ii. 12; iii. 23.   **c.** of superiority or pre-eminence [W. 372 (349)]: πρὸ πάντων, *above all things*, Jas. v. 12; 1 Pet. iv. 8.   **d.** In Composition, πρό marks   **a.** place : προαύλιον; motion forward (Lat. *porro*), προβαίνω, προβάλλω, etc.; *before another who follows, in advance*, προάγω, πρόδρομος, προπέμπω, προτρέχω, etc.; *in public view, openly*, πρόδηλος, πρόκειμαι.   **β.** time: *before this, previously*, προαμαρτάνω; in reference to the time of an occurrence, *beforehand, in advance*, προβλέπω, προγινώσκω, προθέσμιος, προορίζω, etc.   **γ.** superiority or preference: προαιρέομαι. [Cf. *Herm.* ad Vig. p. 658.] *

4254   **προ-άγω** : impf. προῆγον; fut. προάξω; 2 aor. προήγαγον; fr. Hdt. down;   **1.** trans. *to lead forward, lead forth* : τινά, one from a place in which he has lain hidden from view, — as from prison, ἔξω, Acts xvi. 30; [from Jason's house, Acts xvii. 5 L T Tr WH]; in a forensic sense, to bring one forth to trial, Acts xii. 6 [WH txt. προσαγαγεῖν] ; with addition of ἐπί and the gen. of the pers. about to examine into the case, before whom the hearing is to be had, Acts xxv. 26 (εἰς τὴν δίκην, Joseph. b. j. 1, 27, 2; εἰς ἐκκλησίαν τοὺς ἐν αἰτίᾳ γενομένους, antt. 16, 11, 7).   **2.** intrans. (see ἄγω, 4 [and cf. πρό, d. a.]),   **a.** *to go before* : Lk. xviii. 39 [L mrg. παράγ.]; opp. to ἀκολουθέω, Mt. xxi. 9 R G; Mk. xi. 9; foll. by εἰς with an acc. of place, Mt. xiv. 22; Mk. vi. 45; εἰς κρίσιν, 1 Tim. v. 24 (on which pass. see ἐπακολουθέω); ptcp. προάγων, *preceding* i. e. *prior in point of time, previous*, 1 Tim. i. 18 [see προφητεία fin., and s. v. ἐπί, C. I. 2 g. γ. γγ. (but R. V. mrg. led the way to, etc.)]; Heb. vii. 18. τινά, to precede one, Mt. ii. 9; Mk. x. 32; and L T Tr WH in Mt. xxi. 9, [cf. Joseph. b. j. 6, 1, 6; B. § 130, 4]; foll. by εἰς with an acc. of place, Mt. xxvi. 32; xxviii. 7; Mk. xiv. 28; xvi. 7; τινὰ εἰς τὴν βασιλείαν τοῦ θεοῦ, to take precedence of one in entering into the kingdom of God, Mt. xxi. 31 [cf. B. 204 (177)].   **b.** *to proceed, go forward* : in a bad sense, *to go further than is right or proper*, i. q. μὴ μένειν ἐν τῇ διδαχῇ, to transgress the limits of true doctrine [cf. our colloq. 'advanced' (views, etc.) in a disparaging sense], 2 Jn. 9 L T Tr WH [but R. V. mrg. *taketh the lead*].*

see 4255 St.   **προ-αιρέω, -ῶ** : by prose writ. fr. Hdt. [rather, fr. Thuc. 8, 90 fin. (in poetry, fr. Arstph. Thesm. 419)] down, *to bring forward, bring forth from one's stores*; Mid. *to bring forth for one's self, to choose for one's self before another* i. e. *to prefer*; to purpose : καθὼς προαιρεῖται (L T Tr WH the pf. προῄρηται) τῇ καρδίᾳ, 2 Co. ix. 7.*

4256   **προ-αιτιάομαι, -ῶμαι** : 1 aor. 1 pers. plur. προῃτιασάμεθα; *to bring a charge against previously* (i. e. in what has previously been said) : τινά foll. by an infin. indicating the charge, Ro. iii. 9; where the prefix προ- makes reference to i. 18–31; ii. 1–5, 17–29. Not found elsewhere.*

4257   **προ-ακούω** : 1 aor. 2 pers. plur. προηκούσατε : *to hear*

---

before : τὴν ἐλπίδα, the hoped for salvation, before its realization, Col. i. 5 [where cf. Bp. Lghtft.]. (Hdt., Xen., Plat., Dem., al.) *

προ-αμαρτάνω : pf. ptcp. προημαρτηκώς; *to sin before* : οἱ προημαρτηκότες, of those who before receiving baptism had been guilty of the vices especially common among the Gentiles, 2 Co. xii. 21; xiii. 2; in this same sense also in Justin Martyr, apol. i. c. 61; Clem. Al. strom. 4, 12; cf. *Lücke*, Conjectanea Exeget. I. (Götting. 1837) p. 14 sqq. [but on the ref. of the προ- see Meyer on 2 Co. ll. cc. (R. V. *heretofore*)]. (Hdian. 3, 14, 18 [14 ed. Bekk.]; eccl. writ.) *   **4258**

προ-αύλιον, -ου, τό, (πρό and αὐλή), *fore-court, porch* :   **4259** Mk. xiv. 68 [(cf. Pollux 1, 8, 77 and see αὐλή, 2)].*

προ-βαίνω : pf. ptcp. προβεβηκώς; 2 aor. ptcp. προβάς;   **4260** fr. Hom. down; *to go forwards, go on*, [cf. πρό, d. a.] : prop. on foot, Mt. iv. 21; Mk. i. 19; trop. ἐν ταῖς ἡμέραις προβεβηκώς, advanced in age, Lk. i. 7, 18; ii. 36, (see ἡμέρα, fin.); τὴν ἡλικίαν, 2 Macc. iv. 40; vi. 18; Hdian. 2, 7, 7 [5 ed. Bekk.]; τῇ ἡλικίᾳ, Lys. p. 169, 37; [Diod. 12, 18]; ταῖς ἡλικίαις, Diod. 13, 89; [cf. L. and S. s. v. I. 2]).*

προ-βάλλω : 2 aor. προέβαλον; fr. Hom. down; *to throw*   **4261** *forward* [cf. πρό, d. a.]; of trees, to shoot forth, put out, sc. leaves; *to germinate*, [cf. B. § 130, 4; W. 593 (552)] (with καρπόν added, Joseph. antt. 4, 8, 19; Epict. 1, 15, 7) : Lk. xxi. 30; *to push forward, thrust forward, put forward* : τινά, Acts xix. 33.*

προβατικός, -ή, -όν, (πρόβατον), *pertaining to sheep* : ἡ   **4262** προβατική, sc. πύλη (which is added in Neh. iii. 1, 32; xii. 39, for שַׁעַר הַצֹּאן), *the sheep-gate*, Jn. v. 2 [(W. 592 (551); B. § 123, 8) ; but some (as Meyer, Weiss, Milligan and Moulton, cf. Treg. mrg. and see Tdf.'s note ad loc.) would connect προβ. with the immediately following κολυμβήθρα (pointed as a dat.); see Tdf. u. s.; WH. App. ad loc. On the supposed locality see B. D. s. v. Sheep Gate (Sheep-Market)].*

προβάτιον, -ου, τό, (dimin. of the foll. word), *a little* *sheep* : Jn. xxi. [16 T Tr mrg. WH txt.], 17 T Tr WH txt. (Hippocr., Arstph., Plat.) *

πρό-βατον, -ου, τό, (fr. προβαίνω, prop. 'that which walks   **4263** forward'), fr. Hom. down, Sept. chiefly for צֹאן, then for שֶׂה, sometimes for כֶּבֶשׂ and כֶּשֶׂב (a lamb), prop. *any four-footed, tame animal accustomed to graze, small cattle* (opp. to large cattle, horses, etc.), most com. *a sheep* or *a goat*; but esp. *a sheep*, and so always in the N. T. : Mt. vii. 15; x. 16; xii. 11 sq.; Mk. vi. 34; Lk. xv. 4, 6; Jn. ii. 14 sq.; x. 1–4, 11 sq.; Acts viii. 32 (fr. Is. liii. 7); 1 Pet. ii. 25; Rev. xviii. 13; πρόβατα σφαγῆς, sheep destined for the slaughter, Ro. viii. 36. metaph. πρόβατα, *sheep*, is used of the followers of any master : Mt. xxvi. 31 and Mk. xiv. 27, (fr. Zech. xiii. 7); of mankind, as needing salvation obey the injunctions of him who provides it and leads them to it; so of the followers of Christ : Jn. x. 7 sq. 15 sq. 26 sq.; xxi. 16 [R G L Tr txt. WH mrg.], 17 [R G L WH mrg.]; Heb. xiii. 20; τὰ πρόβατα ἀπολωλότα (see ἀπόλλυμι, fin.), Mt. x. 6; xv. 24; τὰ πρόβ. in distinction from τὰ ἐρίφια, are good men as distinguished fr. bad, Mt. xxv. 33.

4264 **προ-βιβάζω** 1 aor. 3 pers. plur. προεβίβασαν; 1 aor. pass. ptcp. fem. προβιβασθεῖσα; **1.** prop. *to cause to go forward, to lead forward, to bring forward, drag forward* : Acts xix. 33 R G [(fr. Soph. down)]. **2.** metaph. i. q. προτρέπω, *to incite, instigate, urge forward, set on; to induce by persuasion*: Mt. xiv. 8 (εἴς τι, Xen. mem. 1, 5, 1; Plat. Prot. p. 328 b.; [in Deut. vi. 7 Sept. with an accus. of the thing (and of the pers.) i. q. *to teach*]).*

4265 **προ-βλέπω** : *to foresee* (Ps. xxxvi. (xxxvii.) 13; Dion. Hal. antt. 11, 20); 1 aor. mid. ptcp. προβλεψάμενος; *to provide*: τὶ περί τινος, Heb. xi. 40 [W. § 38, 6; B. 194 (167)].*

4266 **προ-γίνομαι**: pf. ptcp. προγεγονώς; *to become or arise before, happen before,* (so fr. Hdt. down [in Hom. (Il. 18, 525) *to come forward* into view]): προγεγονότα ἁμαρτήματα, sins previously committed, Ro. iii. 25.*

4267 **προ-γινώσκω**; 2 aor. 3 pers. sing. προέγνω; pf. pass. ptcp. προεγνωσμένος; *to have knowledge of beforehand; to foreknow*: sc. ταῦτα, 2 Pet. iii. 17, cf. 14, 16; τινά, Acts xxvi. 5; οὓς προέγνω, whom he (God) foreknew, sc. that they would love him, or (with reference to what follows) whom he foreknew to be fit to be conformed to the likeness of his Son, Ro. viii. 29 (τῶν εἰς αὐτὸν [Χριστὸν] πιστεύειν προεγνωσμένων, Justin M. dial. c. Tr. c. 42; προγινώσκει [ὁ θεός] τινας ἐκ μετανοίας σωθήσεσθαι μέλλοντας, id. apol. i. 28]); ὃν προέγνω, whose character he clearly saw beforehand, Ro. xi. [1 Lchm. in br.], 2, (against those who in the preceding passages fr. Ro. explain προγινώσκειν as meaning *to predestinate*, cf. Meyer, Philippi, Van Hengel); προεγνωσμένου, sc. ὑπὸ τοῦ θεοῦ (foreknown by God, although not yet 'made manifest' to men), 1 Pet. i. 20. (Sap. vi. 14; viii. 8; xviii. 6; Eur., Xen., Plat., Hdian., Philostr., al.) *

4268 **πρό-γνωσις, -εως, ἡ,** (προγινώσκω); **1.** *foreknowledge*: Judith ix. 6; xi. 19, (Plut., Lcian., Hdian.). **2.** *forethought, pre-arrangement,* (see προβλέπω): 1 Pet. i. 2; Acts ii. 23, [but cf. προγινώσκω, and see Mey. on Acts l. c.].*

4269 **πρό-γονος, -ου, ὁ,** (προγίνομαι), *born before, older*: Hom. Od. 9, 221; plur. *ancestors,* Lat. *majores,* (often so by Grk. writ. fr. Pind. down): ἀπὸ προγόνων, in the spirit and after the manner received from (my) forefathers [cf. ἀπό, II. 2 d. aa. p. 59ᵃ bot.], 2 Tim. i. 3; used of a mother, grandparents, and (if such survive) great-grandparents, 1 Tim. v. 4 [A. V. *parents*] (of surviving ancestors also in Plato, legg. 11 p. 932 init.).*

4270 **προ-γράφω**: 1 aor. προέγραψα; 2 aor. pass. προεγράφην; pf. pass. ptcp. προγεγραμμένος; **1.** *to write before* (of time): Ro. xv. 4ᵃ R G L txt. T Tr WH, 4ᵇ Rec.; Eph. iii. 3; οἱ πάλαι προγεγραμμ. εἰς τοῦτο τὸ κρίμα, of old set forth or designated beforehand (in the Scriptures of the O. T. and the prophecies of Enoch) unto this condemnation, Jude 4. **2.** *to depict* or *portray openly* [cf. πρό, d. a.]: οἷς κατ᾽ ὀφθαλμοὺς Ἰησοῦς Χριστὸς προεγράφη ἐν ὑμῖν [but ἐν ὑμ. is dropped by G L T Tr WH] ἐσταυρωμένος, before whose eyes was portrayed the picture of Jesus Christ crucified (the attentive contemplation of which picture ought to have been a preventive against that

bewitchment), i. e. who were taught most definitely and plainly concerning the meritorious efficacy of the death of Christ, Gal. iii. 1. Since the simple γράφειν is often used of painters, and προγράφειν certainly signifies also *to write before the eyes of all* who can read (Plut. Demetr. 46 fin. προγράφει τις αὐτοῦ πρὸ τῆς σκηνῆς τὴν τοῦ Οἰδίποδος ἀρχήν), I see no reason why προγράφειν may not mean *to depict* (*paint, portray*) *before the eyes*; [R. V. *openly set forth*]. Cf. Hofmann ad loc. [*Farrar, St. Paul,* ch. xxiv., vol. i. 470 note; al. adhere to the meaning *to placard, write up publicly,* see Bp. Lghtft. ad loc.; al. al.; see Meyer].*

4271 **πρό-δηλος, -ον,** (πρό [d. a. and] δῆλος), *openly evident, known to all, manifest*: 1 Tim. v. 24 sq.; neut. foll. by ὅτι, Heb. vii. 14. [(From Soph. and Hdt. down)] *

4272 **προ-δίδωμι**: 1 aor. 3 pers. sing. προέδωκεν; **1.** *to give before, give first*: Ro. xi. 35 (Xen., Polyb., Aristot.). **2.** *to betray*: Aeschyl., Hdt., Eur., Plat., al.; τὴν πατρίδα, 4 Macc. iv. 1.*

4273 **προ-δότης, -ου, ὁ,** (προδίδωμι, 2), *a betrayer, traitor*: Lk. vi. 16; Acts vii. 52; 2 Tim. iii. 4. (From [Aeschyl.], Hdt. down; 2 Macc. v. 15; 3 Macc. iii. 24.) *

4274 **πρό-δρομος, -ου, ὁ, ἡ,** (προτρέχω, προδραμεῖν), *a forerunner* (esp. one who is sent before to take observations or act as spy, a scout, a light-armed soldier; Aeschyl., Hdt., Thuc., Polyb., Diod., Plut., al.; cf. Sap. xii. 8); *one who comes in advance to a place whither the rest are to follow*: Heb. vi. 20.*

4275 St. **προ-εῖδον,** [fr. Hom. down] 2 aor. of the verb προοράω, *to foresee*: Acts ii. 31 [(here WH προιδών without diaeresis; cf. I, ι fin.)]; Gal. iii. 8.*

4257α; **προ-εῖπον** [2 aor. act. fr. an unused pres. (see εἴπον,
see init.)], 1 pers. plur. προείπομεν (1 Th. iv. 6 Grsb.), προ-
(1512α) είπαμεν (ibid. R L T Tr WH [see *WH.* App. p. 164]);
on p. 180 pf. προείρηκα; pf. pass. προείρημαι (see εἴπον, p. 181ᵃ top); fr. Hom. [(by tmesis); Hdt. and Plat.] down; *to say before; i. e.* **a.** *to say in what precedes, to say above*: foll. by ὅτι, 2 Co. vii. 3; foll. by direct disc., [Heb. iv. 7 L T Tr WH txt.]; x. 15 [Rec.]. **b.** *to say before i. e. heretofore, formerly*: foll. by ὅτι, 2 Co. xiii. 2; Gal. v. 21; foll. by direct disc., Gal. i. 9; [Heb. iv. 7 WH mrg.]; καθὼς προείπαμεν ὑμῖν, 1 Th. iv. 6; [in the passages under this head (exc. Gal. i. 9) some would give προ- the sense of *openly, plainly,* (cf. R. V. mrg.)]. **c.** *to say beforehand i. e. before the event;* so used in ref. to prophecies: τί, Acts i. 16; τὰ ῥήματα τὰ προειρημένα ὑπὸ τινος, Jude 17; 2 Pet. iii. 2; προείρηκα ὑμῖν πάντα, Mk. xiii. 23; sc. αὐτό, Mt. xxiv. 25; foll. by direct discourse, Ro. ix. 29.*

see 4275α **προ-είρηκα,** see προεῖπον.

4276 **προ-ελπίζω**: pf. ptcp. acc. plur. προηλπικότας; *to hope before*: ἔν τινι, to repose hope in a person or thing before the event confirms it, Eph. i. 12. (Posidipp. ap. Athen. 9 p. 377 c., Dexipp., Greg. Nyss.) *

4278 **προ-εν-άρχομαι**: 1 aor. προενηρξάμην; *to make a beginning before*: 2 Co. viii. 6; τί, ib. 10 [here al. render 'to make a beginning *before others,*' 'to be the first to make a beginning,' (cf. Meyer ad loc.)]. Not found elsewhere.*

*For 4277 see Strong.

see
4279 St.

προ-επ-αγγέλλω: 1 aor. mid. προεπηγγειλάμην; pf. ptcp. προεπηγγελμένος; *to announce before* (Dio Cass.); mid. *to promise before*: τί, Ro. i. 2, and L T Tr WH in 2 Co. ix. 5, ([Arr. 6, 27, 1]; Dio Cass. 42, 32; 46, 40).*

4281 **προ-έρχομαι**: impf. προηρχόμην; fut. προελεύσομαι; 2 aor. προῆλθον; fr. Hdt. down; **1.** *to go forward, go on*: μικρόν, a little, Mt. xxvi. 39 [here T Tr WH mrg. προσελθών (q. v. in a.)]; Mk. xiv. 35 [Tr WH mrg. προσελθ.]; w. an acc. of the way, Acts xii. 10 (Xen. Cyr. 2, 4, 18; Plato, rep. 1 p. 328 e.; 10 p. 616 b.). **2.** *to go before*; i. e. **a.** *to go before, precede*, (locally; Germ. *vorangehen*): ἐνώπιόν τινος, Lk. i. 17 [(ἔμπροσθέν τινος, Gen. xxxiii. 3), WH mrg. προσέρχ. q. v. in a.]; τινός, *to precede one*, Lk. xxii. 47 Rec. [(Judith ii. 19)]; τινά, ibid. G L T Tr WH (not so construed in prof. writ.; cf. B. 144 (126); *Fritzsche*, Ep. ad Rom. iii. p. 70; [W. § 52, 4, 13]; but in Lat. we find *antecedere, anteire, praeire, aliquem*, and in Grk. writ. προθεῖν τινα; see προηγέομαι); *to outgo, outstrip*, (Lat. *praecurrere, antevertere aliquem*; for which the Greeks say φθάνειν τινά), Mk. vi. 33. **b.** *to go before*, i. e. (set out) *in advance of another* (Germ. *vorausgehen*): Acts xx. 5 [Tr WH txt. προσελθ.]; εἰς [L Tr πρὸς] ὑμᾶς, *unto* (as far as to) *you*, 2 Co. ix. 5; ἐπὶ τὸ πλοῖον, *to the ship*, Acts xx. 13 [Tr WH mrg. προσελθόντες].*

4282 **προ-ετοιμάζω**: 1 aor. προητοίμασα; *to prepare before, to make ready beforehand*: ἃ προητοίμασεν εἰς δόξαν, i. e. for whom he appointed glory beforehand (i. e. from eternity), and accordingly rendered them fit to receive it, Ro. ix. 23; to prepare beforehand in mind and purpose, i. e. to decree, Eph. ii. 10, where οἷς stands by attraction for ἅ [cf. W. 149 (141); B. § 143, 8]. (Is. xxviii. 24; Sap. ix. 8; Hdt., Philo, Joseph., Plut., Geop., al.) *

4283 **προ-ευαγγελίζομαι**: 1 aor. 3 pers. sing. προευηγγελίσατο; *to announce* or *promise glad tidings beforehand* (viz. before the event by which the promise is made good): Gal. iii. 8. (Philo de opif. mund. § 9; mutat. nom. § 29; Byzant. writ.) *

see
4284 St.

προ-έχω [(fr. Hom. down)]: pres. mid. 1 pers. plur. προεχόμεθα; *to have before* or *in advance of another, to have pre-eminence over another, to excel, to surpass*; often so in prof. auth. fr. [Soph. and] Hdt. down; mid. *to excel to one's advantage* (cf. Kühner § 375, 1); *to surpass in excellences which can be passed to one's credit*: Ro. iii. 9; it does not make against this force of the middle in the present passage that the use is nowhere else met with, nor is there any objection to an interpretation which has commended itself to a great many and which the context plainly demands. [But on this difficult word see esp. *Jas. Morison*, Crit. Expos. of the Third Chap. of Rom. p. 93 sqq.; *Gifford* in the 'Speaker's Com.' p. 96; W. § 38, 6; § 39 fin., cf. p. 554 (516).] *

4285 **προ-ηγέομαι**, -οῦμαι; *to go before and show the way, to go before and lead, to go before as leader*, (Hdt. 2, 48; often in Xen.; besides in Arstph., Polyb., Plut., Sept., al.): τῇ τιμῇ ἀλλήλους προηγούμενοι, one going before another as an example of deference [A. V. *in honor preferring one another* (on the dat. cf. W. § 31, 6 a.)], Ro.

xii. 10. The Grk. writ. connect this verb now with the dat. (Arstph. Plut. 1195; Polyb. 6, 53, 8; etc.), now with the gen. (Diod. 1, 87); see προέρχομαι, 2 a.*

4286 **πρό-θεσις, -εως, ἡ**, (προτίθημι); **1.** *the setting forth* of a thing, placing of it in view, (Plat., Dem., Plut.); οἱ ἄρτοι τῆς προθέσεως (Vulg. *panes propositionis*), *the showbread*, Sept. for לֶחֶם הַפָּנִים (Ex. xxxv. 13; xxxix. 18 (xxxviii. 36); 1 K. vii. 48 (34)), and לֶחֶם הַמַּעֲרֶכֶת (1 Chr. ix. 32; xxiii. 29); twelve loaves of wheaten bread, corresponding to the number of the tribes of Israel, which loaves were offered to God every Sabbath, and separated into two rows, lay for seven days upon a table placed in the sanctuary or anterior portion of the tabernacle, and afterwards of the temple (cf. *Winer*, RWB. s. v. Schaubrode; *Roskoff* in Schenkel v. p. 213 sq.; [*Edersheim*, The Temple, ch. ix. p. 152 sqq.; BB. DD.]): Mt. xii. 4; Mk. ii. 26; Lk. vi. 4, (οἱ ἄρτοι τοῦ προσώπου, sc. θεοῦ, Neh. x. 33; ἄρτοι ἐνώπιοι, Ex. xxv. 29); ἡ πρόθεσις τῶν ἄρτων, (the rite of) the setting forth of the loaves, Heb. ix. 2. **2.** *a purpose* (2 Macc. iii. 8; [Aristot.], Polyb., Diod., Plut.): Acts xxvii. 13; Ro. viii. 28; ix. 11; Eph. i. 11; iii. 11; 2 Tim. i. 9; iii. 10; τῇ προθέσει τῆς καρδίας, with purpose of heart, Acts xi. 23.*

4287 **προ-θέσμιος, -α, -ον**, (πρό [q. v. in d. β.] and θεσμός fixed, appointed), *set beforehand, appointed* or *determined beforehand, pre-arranged*, (Lcian. Nigr. 27); ἡ προθεσμία, sc. ἡμέρα, *the day previously appointed*; univ. *the pre-appointed time*: Gal. iv. 2. (Lys., Plat., Dem., Aeschin., Diod., Philo — cf. *Siegfried*, Philo p. 113, Joseph., Plut., al.; eccles. writ.; cf. *Kypke* and *Hilgenfeld* on Gal. l. c.) *

4288 **προθυμία, -ας, ἡ**, (πρόθυμος), fr. Hom. down; **1.** *zeal, spirit, eagerness*; **2.** *inclination; readiness* of mind: so Acts xvii. 11; 2 Co. viii. 11 sq. 19; ix. 2.*

4289 **πρόθυμος, -ον**, (πρό and θυμός), fr. [Soph. and] Hdt. down, *ready, willing*: Mt. xxvi. 41; Mk. xiv. 38; neut. τὸ πρόθυμον, i. q. ἡ προθυμία: Ro. i. 15, as in Thuc. 3, 82; Plat. legg. 9 p. 859 b.; Eur. Med. vs. 178; Joseph. antt. 4, 8, 13; Hdian. 8, 3, 15 [6 ed. Bekk.] (on which cf. Irmisch); 3 Macc. v. 26.*

4290 **προθύμως**, adv., fr. Hdt. and Aeschyl. down, *willingly, with alacrity*: 1 Pet. v. 2.*

see 4406 **πρόϊμος**, see πρώϊμος.

4291 **προ-ΐστημι**: 2 aor. inf. προστῆναι; pf. ptcp. προεστώς; pres. mid. προΐσταμαι; fr. Hom. Il. 4, 156 down; **1.** in the trans. tenses *to set* or *place before; to set over*. **2.** in the pf. plpf. and 2 aor. act. and in the pres. and impf. mid. **a.** *to be over, to superintend, preside over*, [A.V. *rule*], (so fr. Hdt. down): 1 Tim. v. 17; with a gen. of the pers. or thing over which one presides, 1 Th. v. 12; 1 Tim. iii. 4 sq. 12. **b.** *to be a protector* or *guardian; to give aid*, (Eur., Dem., Aeschin., Polyb.): Ro. xii. 8 [(al. with A.V. *to rule*; cf. Fritzsche ad loc.; *Stuart*, Com. excurs. xii.)]. **c.** *to care for, give attention to*: w. a gen. of the thing, καλῶν ἔργων, Tit. iii. 8, 14; for exx. fr. prof. writ. see Kypke and Lösner; [some (cf. R.V. mrg.) would render these two exx. *profess honest occu-*

pations (see ἔργον, 1); but cf. ἔργον, 3 p. 248ᵇ mid. and *Field*, Otium Norv. pars iii. ad l. c.].*

4292 προ-καλέω, -ῶ: pres. mid. ptcp. προκαλούμενος; *to call forth* [cf. πρό, d. *a*.]; Mid. *to call forth to one's self*, esp. *to challenge* to a combat or contest with one; often so fr. Hom. down; hence *to provoke, to irritate*: Gal. v. 26 [(εἰς ὠμότητα κ. ὀργήν, Hdian. 7, 1, 11, 4 ed. Bekk.)].*

4293 προ-κατ-αγγέλλω: 1 aor. προκατήγγειλα; pf. pass. ptcp. προκατηγγελμένος; *to announce beforehand* (that a thing will be): of prophecies, — foll. by an acc. with inf. Acts iii. 18; τί, Acts iii. 24 Rec.; περί τινος, Acts vii. 52. To *pre-announce* in the sense of *to promise*: τί, pass. 2 Co. ix. 5 Rec. (Joseph. antt. 1, 12, 3; 2, 9, 4; eccles. writ.) *

4294 προ-κατ-αρτίζω: 1 aor. subjunc. 3 pers. plur. προκαταρτίσωσι; *to prepare* [A. V. *make up*] *beforehand*: τί, 2 Co. ix. 5. (Hippocr.; eccles. writ.) *

4295 πρό-κειμαι; (πρό [q. v. d. *a*.] and κεῖμαι): fr. Hom. down; **1.** prop. *to lie* or *be placed before* (a person or thing), or *in front* (often so in Grk. writ.). **2.** *to be set before*, i. e. **a.** *to be placed before the eyes, to lie in sight; to stand forth*: with a pred. nom., δεῖγμα, as an example, Jude 7 (καλὸν ὑπόδειγμά σοι πρόκειται, Joseph. b. j. 6, 2, 1). **b.** i. q. *to be appointed, destined*: προκειμένη ἐλπίς, the hope open to us, offered, given, Heb. vi. 18; used of those things which by any appointment are destined to be done, borne, or attained by any one; so προκείμενος ἀγών, Heb. xii. 1; προκειμ. χαρά, the destined joy (see ἀντί, 2 b.), ibid. 2 (the phrase τὰ ἆθλα προκεῖσθαι occurs often in prof. writ. fr. Hdt. down; cf. *Bleek*, Br. an die Heb. ii. 2 p. 268 sqq.). **c.** *to be there, be present, be at hand*, (so that it can become actual or available): 2 Co. viii. 12.*

4296 προ-κηρύσσω: 1 aor. ptcp. προκηρύξας; pf. pass. ptcp. προκεκηρυγμένος; **1.** *to announce* or *proclaim by herald beforehand* (Xen. resp. Lac. 11, 2; Isae. p. 60, 2; Polyb., Joseph., Plut., al.). **2.** univ. *to announce beforehand* (of the herald himself, Soph. El. 684): 'Ιησοῦν Χριστόν, i. e. his advent, works, and sufferings, pass. Acts iii. 20 Rec.; τί, Acts xiii. 24 ('Ιερεμίας τὰ μέλλοντα τῇ πόλει δεινὰ προεκήρυξεν, Joseph. antt. 10, 5, 1).*

4297 προ-κοπή, -ῆς, ἡ, (προκόπτω, q. v.), *progress, advancement*: Phil. i. 12, 25; 1 Tim. iv. 15. (Polyb., Diod., Joseph., Philo, al.; rejected by the Atticists, cf. Phrynich. ed. *Lob.* p. 85; [Sir. li. 17; 2 Macc. viii. 8].) *

4298 προ-κόπτω; impf. προέκοπτον; fut. προκόψω; 1 aor. προέκοψα; *to beat forward*: **1.** *to lengthen out by hammering* (as a smith forges metals); metaph. *to promote, forward, further*: Hdt., Eur., Thuc., Xen., al. **2.** fr. Polyb. on intransitively [cf. B. 145 (127); W. 251 (236)], *to go forward, advance, proceed*; of time: ἡ νὺξ προέκοψεν, the night is advanced [A. V. *is far spent*], (day is at hand), Ro. xiii. 12 (Joseph. b. j. 4, 4, 6; [προκοπτούσης τῆς ὥρας] Charit. 2, 3, 3 [p. 38, 1 ed. Reiske; τὰ τῆς νυκτός, ib. 2, 3, 4]; ἡ ἡμέρα προκόπτει, Just. Mart. dial. c. Tryph. p. 277 d.; Lat. *procedere* is used in the same way, Livy 28, 15; Sallust. Jug. 21, 52, 109). metaph. *to increase, make progress*: with a dat. of the thing in which one grows, Lk. ii. 52 [not Tdf.] (Diod. 11 87);

ἐν with a dat. of the thing, ibid. Tdf.; Gal. i. 14, (Diod. [excerpt. de virt. et vitiis] p. 554, 69; Antonin. 1, 17); ἐπὶ πλεῖον, further, 2 Tim. iii. 9 (Diod. 14, 98); ἐπὶ πλεῖον ἀσεβείας, 2 Tim. ii. 16; ἐπὶ τὸ χεῖρον, will grow worse, i. e. will make progress in wickedness, 2 Tim. iii. 13 (τῶν 'Ιεροσολύμων πάθη προύκοπτε καθ' ἡμέραν ἐπὶ τὸ χεῖρον, Joseph. b. j. 6, 1, 1).*

4299 πρό-κριμα, -τος, τό, (πρό and κρίμα), *an opinion formed before the facts are known, a pre-judgment, a prejudice*, (Vulg. *praejudicium*): 1 Tim. v. 21 (anonym. in Suidas s. v.; [Athan. apol. c. Arian. 25 (i. 288 a. ed. Migne); Justinian cod. 10, 11, 8, § ε]).*

4300 προ-κυρόω, -ῶ: pf. pass. ptcp. προκεκυρωμένος; *to sanction, ratify*, or *establish beforehand*: Gal. iii. 17. ([Euseb. praep. evang. 10, 4 (ii. p. 70, 3 ed. Heinichen)]; Byzant. writ.) *

4301 προ-λαμβάνω; 2 aor. προέλαβον; 1 aor. pass. subjunc. 3 pers. sing. προληφθῇ [-λημφθῇ L T Tr WH; see s. v. M, μ]; fr. Hdt. down; **1.** *to take before*: τί, 1 Co. xi. 21. **2.** *to anticipate, to forestall*: προέλαβε μυρίσαι, she has anticipated the anointing, [*hath anointed beforehand*], Mk. xiv. 8; cf. Meyer ad loc.; W. § 54, 4. **3.** *to take* one *by forestalling* (him i. e. before he can flee or conceal his crime), i. e. *surprise, detect*, (Sap. xvii. 16): τινὰ ἐν παραπτώματι, pass. Gal. vi. 1; cf. *Winer*, Ep. ad Gal. l. c.*

4302 προ-λέγω; impf. προέλεγον; *to say beforehand, to predict*, (so fr. Aeschyl. and Hdt. down): 2 Co. xiii. 2; Gal. v. 21; 1 Th. iii. 4; [some (see R. V. mrg.) would give προ- the sense of *plainly* in all these exx.; cf. L. and S. s. v. II. 2, and see πρό, d. *a*. fin.].*

4303 προ-μαρτύρομαι; **1.** *antetestor* (in the old lexicons). **2.** *to testify beforehand*, i. e. *to make known by prediction*: 1 Pet. i. 11; so also [Basil. Seleuc. 32 a. (Migne vol. lxxxv.) and] by Theodorus Metochita (c. 75, misc. p. 504) — a writ. of the fourteenth century.*

4304 προ-μελετάω, -ῶ; *to meditate beforehand*: Lk. xxi. 14 (Arstph., Xen., Plato).*

4305 προ-μεριμνάω; *to be anxious beforehand*: Mk. xiii. 11 (Clem. Alex. strom. 4, 9, 72; [Hippol. ref. haer. 6, 52 p. 330, 69; 8, 15 p. 432, 3]).*

4306 προ-νοέω, -ῶ; pres. mid. προνοοῦμαι; fr. Hom. down; **1.** *to perceive before, foresee*. **2.** *to provide, think of beforehand*: τινός (see Matthiae § 348, vol. ii. p. 821 [but cf. § 379 p. 862]; Kühner § 419, 1 b. ii. p. 325; [Jelf § 496]; W. § 30, 10 c.), *to provide for one*, 1 Tim. v. 8 (where T Tr txt. WH mrg. προνοεῖται); περί τινος, Sap. vi. 8. Mid. with an acc. of the thing, i. q. *to take thought for, care for* a thing: Ro. xii. 17; 2 Co. viii. 21 (where L T Tr WH have adopted προνοούμεν).*

4307 πρό-νοια, -ας, ἡ, (πρόνοος), fr. [Aeschyl., Soph.], Hdt. down, *forethought, provident care*: Acts xxiv. 2 (3) [A.V. *providence*]; ποιοῦμαι πρόνοιάν τινος, *to make provision for* a thing (see ποιέω, I. 3 p. 526ᵃ top), Ro. xiii. 14.*

4308 προ-οράω, -ῶ; pf. ptcp. προεωρακώς; impf. mid. (Acts ii. 25) προωρώμην, and without augm. (see ὁμοιόω, init.) προορώμην L T Tr WH; fr. Hdt. down; **1.** *to see before* (whether as respects p l a c e or time): τινά, Acts

xxi. 29.   **2.** Mid. (rare use) *to keep before one's eyes*: metaph. τινά, with ἐνώπιόν μου added, *to be mindful of one always*, Acts ii. 25 fr. Ps. xv. (xvi.) 8.*

4309   προ-ορίζω: 1 aor. προώρισα; 1 aor. pass. ptcp. προορισθέντες; *to predetermine, decide beforehand*, Vulg. [exc. in Acts] praedestino, [R. V. *to foreordain*]: in the N. T. of God decreeing from eternity, foll. by an acc. with the inf. Acts iv. 28; τί, with the addition of πρὸ τῶν αἰώνων, 1 Co. ii. 7; τινά, with a pred. acc., *to foreordain, appoint beforehand*, Ro. viii. 29 sq.; τινὰ εἴς τι, one to obtain a thing. Eph. i. 5; προορισθέντες sc. κληρωθῆναι, Eph. i. 11. (Heliod. and eccl. writ. [Ignat. ad Eph. tit.]) *

4310   προ-πάσχω: 2 aor. ptcp. προπαθόντες; *to suffer before*: 1 Th. ii. 2. (Hdt., Soph., Thuc., Plat., al.) *

see 3962   προ-πάτωρ, -ορος, ὁ, (πατήρ), *a forefather, founder of a family or nation*: Ro. iv. 1 L T Tr WH. (Pind., Hdt., Soph., Eur., Plat., Dio Cass. 44, 37; Lcian., al.; Plut. consol. ad Apoll. c. 10; Joseph. antt. 4, 2, 4; b. j. 5, 9, 4; Ev. Nicod. 21. 24. 25 sq.; eccl. writ.) *

4311   προ-πέμπω: impf. προέπεμπον; 1 aor. act. προέπεμψα; 1 aor. pass. προεπέμφθην; fr. Hom. down; **1.** *to send before*. **2.** *to send forward, bring on the way, accompany* or *escort*: τινά, 1 Co. xvi. 6, 11, [al. associate these exx. with the group at the close]; with ἐκεῖ (for ἐκεῖσε) added, Ro. xv. 24; εἰς with an acc. of place, Acts xx. 38; 2 Co. i. 16 [here R. V. *set forward* (see below)]; ἕως ἔξω τῆς πόλεως, Acts xxi. 5. to set one forward, fit him out with the requisites for his journey: Acts xv. 3 [al. associate this ex. with the preceding]; Tit. iii. 13; 3 Jn. 6; 1 Macc. xii. 4, cf. 1 Esdr. iv. 47.*

4312   προπετής, -ές, (πρό and πέτω i. e. πίπτω); **1.** *falling forwards, headlong, sloping, precipitous*: Pind. Nem. 6, 107; Xen. r. eq. 1, 8; al.   **2.** *precipitate, rash, reckless*: Acts xix. 36; 2 Tim. iii. 4, (Prov. x. 14; xiii. 3; Sir. ix. 18; Clem. Rom. 1 Cor. 1, 1; and often in Grk. writ.).*

4313   προ-πορεύω: 1 fut. mid. προπορεύσομαι; *to send before, to make to precede*, (Ael. nat. an. 10, 22 [var.]); mid. *to go before, to precede*, [see πρό, d. a.]: τινός (on which gen. see W. § 52, 2 c.), *to go before one*, of a leader, Acts vii. 40; πρὸ προσώπου τινός (after the Hebr., Ex. xxxii. 34; Deut. iii. 18; ix. 3), of a messenger or a herald, Lk. i. 76; (of the van of an army, 1 Macc. ix. 11; Xen. Cyr. 4, 2, 23; Polyb.). [Cf. ἔρχομαι, fin.] *

4314   πρός, a preposition, i. q. Epic προτί, from πρό and the adverbial suffix τι, (cf. the German vor ... hin [Curtius § 381]); it is joined

I. with the ACCUSATIVE, *to, towards*, Lat. *ad*, denoting direction towards a thing, or position and state looking towards a thing (W. § 49 h. p. 404 (378)); it is used   **1.** of the goal or limit towards which a movement is directed: πρός τινα or τι,   a. prop. after verbs of going, departing, running, coming, etc.: ἄγω, Jn. xi. 15; ἀναβαίνω, Mk. vi. 51; Jn. xx. 17; Acts xv. 2; ἀνακάμπτω, Mt. ii. 12; Acts xviii. 21; ἀνέρχομαι, Gal. i. 17 [L Tr mrg. ἀπέρχ.]; ἀπέρχομαι, Mt. xiv. 25 [Rec.]; Mk. iii. 13, etc.; πρὸς ἑαυτόν, to his house, Lk. xxiv. 12 [T om. L Tr br. WH reject the vs.; Tr reads

πρ. αὐτόν; some connect the phrase w. .θαυμάζων (see 2 b. below)]; Jn. xx. 10 [T Tr αὑτούς, WH αὐτ. (cf. s. v. αὐτοῦ sub fin.)]; γίνεσθαι πρός τινα, to come to one, 1 Co. ii. 3; xvi. 10; διαπεράω, Lk. xvi. 26; ἐγγίζω, Mk. xi. 1; Lk. xix. 29; εἰσέρχομαι, Mk. vi. 25; Lk. i. 28; Acts x. 3; [πρὸς τ. Λυδίαν, *into* the house of L. Acts xvi. 40 (Rec. εἰς)]; etc.; Rev. iii. 20; εἰσπορεύομαι, Acts xxviii. 30; ἐκπορεύομαι, Mt. iii. 5; Mk. i. 5; ἐξέρχομαι, Jn. xviii. 29, 38; 2 Co. viii. 17; Heb. xiii. 13; ἐπιστρέφω, to turn (one's self), Acts ix. 40; 2 Co. iii. 16; 1 Th. i. 9; ἐπισυνάγεσθαι, Mk. i. 33; ἔρχομαι, Mt. iii. 14; vii. 15, and often; ἥκω, Jn. vi. 37; Acts xxviii. 23 [Rec.]; καταβαίνω, Acts x. 21; xiv. 11; Rev. xii. 12; μεταβαίνω, Jn. xiii. 1; ὀρθρίζω, Lk. xxi. 38; παραγίνομαι, Mt. iii. 13; Lk. vii. 4, 20; viii. 19; xi. 6; [xxii. 52 Tdf.]; πορεύομαι, Mt. x. 6; Lk. xi. 5; Jn. xiv. 12, etc.; συνάγεσθαι, Mt. xiii. 2; xxvii. 62; Mk. iv. 1; vi. 30; vii. 1; συντρέχειν, Acts iii. 11; ὑπάγω, Mt. xxvi. 18; Mk. v. 19; Jn. vii. 33; xiii. 3; xvi. 5, 10, 16 [T Tr WH om. L br. the cl.], 17; κατευθύνειν τὴν ὁδόν, 1 Th. iii. 11; also after [kindred] nouns: εἴσοδος, 1 Th. i. 9; ii. 1; προσαγωγή, Eph. ii. 18.   after verbs of moving, leading, sending, drawing, bringing, directing: ἄγω, Mk. xi. 7 [R L]; Lk. xviii. 40; Jn. i. 42 (43); [xviii. 13 L T Tr WH]; Acts ix. 27, etc.; ἀπάγω, Mt. xxvi. 57 [R. V. *to the house of C.* (cf. Acts xvi. 40 above)]; Mk. xiv. 53; Jn. xviii. 13 [RG]; Acts xxiii. 17; 1 Co. xii. 2; [ἐξάγω ἕως πρός (see ἕως, II. 2 c.), Lk. xxiv. 50 L txt. T Tr WH]; κατασύρω, Lk. xii. 58; ἁρπάζω, Rev. xii. 5; ἑλκύω, Jn. xii. 32; παραλαμβάνω, Jn. xiv. 3; φέρω, Mk. i. 32; ix. 17, 19, 20; [xi. 7 T Tr WH]; πέμπω, Lk. vii. 6 [not T WH], 19; Acts xxv. 21 [L T Tr WH ἀναπ.], etc. (see πέμπω); ἀναπέμπω, Lk. xxiii. 7, 15; ἀποστέλλω, Mt. xxiii. 34, etc. (see ἀποστέλλω, 1 b. and d.); στρέφομαι, Lk. vii. 44; xxiii. 28.   after verbs of falling: πίπτειν πρὸς τοὺς πόδας τινός, Mk. v. 22; vii. 25; [Acts v. 10 L T Tr WH]; Rev. i. 17.   after other verbs and substantives with which the idea of direction is connected: as ἐπιστολὴ πρός τινα, 2 Co. iii. 1; xxii. 5; 2 Co. iii. 1; ἐντολή, Acts xvii. 15; ἀνάδειξις, Lk. i. 80; κάμπτω τὰ γόνατα, Eph. iii. 14; ἐκπετάννυμι τὰς χεῖρας, Ro. x. 21 (fr. Is. lxv. 2); πρόσωπον πρὸς πρόσωπον, face (turned) to face, i. e. in immediate presence, 1 Co. xiii. 12 (after the Hebr., Gen. xxxii. 30; Judges vi. 22); στόμα πρὸς στόμα, mouth (turned) to mouth, i. e. in each other's presence, 2 Jn. 12; 3 Jn. 14, (see στόμα, 1); λαλεῖν πρὸς τὸ οὖς, the mouth being put to the ear, Lk. iii. 3.   after verbs of adding, joining to: προστιθέναι τινὰ πρὸς τοὺς πατέρας, to lay one unto, i. e. bury him by the side of, his *fathers*, Acts xiii. 36 (after the Hebr., 2 K. xxii. 20; Judg. ii. 10); θάπτειν τινὰ πρός τινα, Acts v. 10.   after verbs of saying (because speech is directed towards some one), invoking, swearing, testifying, making known: w. an acc. of the pers., ἀνοίγω τὸ στόμα, 2 Co. vi. 11; εἶπον, Lk. i. 13, and very often by Luke; Jn. iv. 48; vii. 3, etc.; Heb. i. 13; λαλέω, Lk. i. 19, 55; ii. 18, etc.; 1 Th. ii. 2; Heb. v. 5; xi. 18; λέγω, Lk. v. 36, etc.; Jn. ii. 3; iv. 15, etc.; Heb. vii. 21; φημί, Lk. xxii. 70; Acts ii. 38 [R G]; x. 28, etc.; διαλέγομαι, Acts xxiv. 12; ἀποκρίνομαι, Lk.

iv. 4; Acts iii. 12; δέομαι, Acts viii. 24; βοάω, Lk. xviii. 7 [R G L]; αἴρειν φωνήν, Acts iv. 24; εὔχομαι, 2 Co. xiii. 7; ὄμνυμι, Lk. i. 73; μαρτύς εἰμι, Acts xiii. 31; xxii. 15; δημηγορέω, Acts xii. 21; κατηγορέω, to accuse to, bring, as it were, to the judge by accusation, Jn. v. 45; ἐμφανίζω, Acts xxiii. 22; γνωρίζεται, be made known unto, Phil. iv. 6. also after [kindred] substantives [and phrases]: ἀπολογία, addressed unto one, Acts xxii. 1; λόγος, 2 Co. i. 18; λόγος παρακλήσεως, Acts xiii. 15; ὁ λόγος γίνεται πρός τινα, Jn. x. 35 (Gen. xv. 1, 4; Jer. i. 2, 11; xiii. 8; Ezek. vi. 1; Hos. i. 1); γίνεται φωνή, Acts vii. 31 Rec.; x. 13, 15; γίνεται ἐπαγγελία, Acts xiii. 32 and Rec. in xxvi. 6 [where L T Tr WH εἰς]; προσευχή, Ro. xv. 30; δέησις, Rb. x. 1; προσφέρειν δεήσεις, Heb. v. 7. πρὸς ἀλλήλους after ἀντιβάλλειν λόγους, Lk. xxiv. 17; διαλαλεῖν, Lk. vi. 11; διαλέγεσθαι, Mk. ix. 34; διαλογίζεσθαι, Mk. viii. 16; εἰπεῖν, Lk. ii. 15 [(L mrg. T WH λαλεῖν)]; xxiv. 32; Jn. xvi. 17; xix. 24; λέγειν, Mk. iv. 41; Lk. viii. 25; Jn. iv. 33; Acts xxviii. 4; ὁμιλεῖν, Lk. xxiv. 14; συλλαλεῖν, Lk. iv. 36. πρὸς ἑαυτούς i. q. πρὸς ἀλλήλους: after συζητεῖν, Mk. i. 27 [T WH txt. read simply αὐτούς (as subj.)]; cf. x. 16; Lk. xxii. 23; εἰπεῖν, Mk. xii. 7; Jn. xii. 19; λέγειν, Mk. xvi. 3; ἀγανακτεῖν, [R. V. had indignation among themselves, saying], Mk. xiv. 4 T WH (cf. Tr); see 2 b. below. b. of a time drawing towards a given time [cf. f. below]: πρὸς ἑσπέραν ἐστίν, towards evening, Lk. xxiv. 29 (Gen. viii. 11; Zech. xiv. 7; Plato de rep. 1 p. 328 a.; Joseph. antt. 5, 4, 3; πρὸς ἡμέραν, Xen. anab. 4, 5, 21; Plato, conviv. p. 223 c.); [πρὸς σάββατον, Mk. xv. 42 L Tr txt.]. c. metaph. of mental direction, with words denoting desires and emotions of the mind, to, towards: ἐνδεικνύειν πραΰτητα, Tit. iii. 2; μακροθυμεῖν, 1 Th. v. 14; ἤπιος, 2 Tim. ii. 24; ἔχθρα, Lk. xxiii. 12; πεποίθησιν ἔχειν, 2 Co. iii. 4; [ἐλπίδα ἔχ. Acts xxiv. 15 Tdf.]; πίστις, 1 Th. i. 8; παρρησία, 2 Co. vii. 4; 1 Jn. iii. 21; v. 14; with verbs signifying the mode of bearing one's self towards a pers., ἐργάζεσθαι τὸ ἀγαθόν, Gal. vi. 10; ποιεῖν τὰ αὐτά, Eph. vi. 9 (Xen. mem. 1, 1, 6). of a hostile direction, against; so after ἀνταγωνίζεσθαι, Heb. xii. 4; στῆναι, Eph. vi. 11; λακτίζειν, Acts ix. 5 Rec.; xxvi. 14, (see κέντρον, 2); πάλη, Eph. vi. 12; μάχεσθαι, Jn. vi. 52; διακρίνομαι, Acts xi. 2; γογγυσμός, Acts vi. 1; βλασφημία, Rev. xiii. 6; πικραίνεσθαι, Col. iii. 19; ἔχειν τι, Acts xxiv. 19; ἔχειν ζήτημα, xxv. 19; μομφήν, Col. iii. 13; πρᾶγμα, 1 Co. vi. 1; λόγον (see λόγος, I. 6), Acts xix. 38; ἔχειν πρός τινα, to have something to bring against one [R. V. wherewith to answer], 2 Co. v. 12; τὰ [which Tr txt. WH om.] πρός τινα, the things to be said against one, Acts xxiii. 30 [R G Tr WH; here may be added πρὸς πλησμονὴν σαρκός, against (i. e. to check) the indulgence of the flesh, Col. ii. 23 (see πλησμονή)]. d. of the issue or end to which anything tends or leads: ἡ ἀσθένεια οὐκ ἔστι πρὸς θάνατον, Jn. xi. 4; ἁμαρτάνειν, ἁμαρτία πρὸς θάνατον, 1 Jn. v. 16 sq.; ἃ στρεβλοῦσι πρὸς τὴν ἰδίαν αὐτῶν ἀπώλειαν, 2 Pet. iii. 16; τὰ πρὸς τὴν εἰρήνην sc. ὄντα, — now, the things which tend to the restoration of peace [A. V. conditions of peace], Lk. xiv. 32; now, which tend to the attainment of safety [A. V. which belong unto

peace], Lk. xix. 42; τὰ πρὸς ζωὴν καὶ εὐσέβειαν, [A. V. that pertain unto], 2 Pet. i. 3; πρὸς δόξαν τῷ θεῷ, 2 Co. i. 20; τοῦ κυρίου, 2 Co. viii. 19. e. of an intended end or purpose: πρὸς νουθεσίαν τινός, 1 Co. x. 11; as other exx. add, Mt. xxvi. 12; Ro. iii. 26; xv. 2; 1 Co. vi. 5; vii. 35; xii. 7; xiv. 12, 26; xv. 34; 2 Co. iv. 6; vii. 3; xi. 8; Eph. iv. 12; 1 Tim. i. 16; Heb. vi. 11; ix. 13; πρὸς τί, to what end, for what intent, Jn. xiii. 28; πρὸς τὴν ἐλεημοσύνην, for the purpose of asking alms, Acts iii. 10; πρὸς τό with an inf. in order to, etc.: Mt. v. 28; vi. 1; xiii. 30; xxiii. 5; xxvi. 12; Mk. xiii. 22; 2 Co. iii. 13; Eph. vi. 11; 1 Th. ii. 9; 2 Th. iii. 8, also R G in Jas. iii. 3. f. of the time for which a thing has been, as it were, appointed, i. e. during which it will last; where we use our for (Germ. für or auf) [cf. b. above]: πρὸς καιρόν (Lat. ad tempus, Cic. de off. 1, 8, 27; de amicitia 15, 53; Liv. 21, 25, 14), i. e. for a season, for a while, Lk. viii. 13; 1 Co. vii. 5; πρὸς καιρὸν ὥρας, [R. V. for a short season], 1 Th. ii. 17; πρὸς ὥραν, for a short time, for an hour, Jn. v. 35; 2 Co. vii. 8; Gal. ii. 5; Philem. 15; πρὸς ὀλίγας ἡμέρας, Heb. xii. 10; πρὸς τὸ παρόν, for the present, ibid. 11 (Thuc. 2, 22; Plato legg. 5 p. 736 a.; Joseph. antt. 6, 5, 1; Hdian. 1, 3, 13 [5 ed. Bekk.]; Dio Cass. 41, 15); πρὸς ὀλίγον, for a little time, Jas. iv. 4 (Lcian. dial. deor. 18, 1; Aelian v. h. 12, 63). 2. it is used of close proximity — the idea of direction, though not entirely lost, being more or less weakened; a. answering to our at or by (Germ. an); after verbs of fastening, adhering, moving (to): δεδέσθαι πρὸς τὴν θύραν, Mk. xi. 4; προσκολλᾶσθαι, Mk. x. 7 R G Tr (in mrg. br.); Eph. v. 31 R G WH txt.; προσκόπτειν, Mt. iv. 6; Lk. iv. 11; κεῖσθαι, i. q. to be brought near to, Mt. iii. 10; Lk. iii. 9, [(cf. 2 Macc. iv. 33)]; τιθέναι, Acts iii. 2; [iv. 37 Tdf. (al. παρά)]; add, βεβλῆσθαι, Lk. xvi. 20; τὰ πρὸς τὴν θύραν, the fore-court [see θύρα, a.], Mk. ii. 2; εἶναι πρὸς τὴν θάλασσαν (prop. towards the sea [A. V. by the sea]), Mk. iv. 1; θερμαίνεσθαι πρὸς τὸ φῶς, turned to the light [R. V. in the light], Mk. xiv. 54; καθῆσθαι πρὸς τὸ φῶς, Lk. xxii. 56; εἱστήκει πρὸς τὸ μνημεῖον, Jn. xx. 11 Rec.; cf. Fritzsche on Mk. p. 201 sq. b. i. q. (Lat. apud) with, with the acc. of a person, after verbs of remaining, dwelling, tarrying, etc. (which require one to be conceived of as always turned towards one), cf. Fritzsche u. s.: after εἶναι, Mt. xiii. 56; Mk. vi. 3; ix. 19; xiv. 49; Lk. ix. 41; Jn. i. 1 sq.; 1 Jn. i. 2; 1 Th. iii. 4; 2 Th. ii. 5; iii. 10; παρεῖναι, Acts xii. 20; 2 Co. xi. 9 (8); Gal. iv. 18, 20; παρουσία, Phil. i. 26; διαμένειν, Gal. ii. 5; παραμένειν, 1 Co. xvi. 6; ἐπιμένειν, ibid. 7; Gal. i. 18; καθέζεσθαι, Mt. xxvi. 55 [R G L Tr br.]; ἐνδημεῖν, 2 Co. v. 8; κατέχειν τινὰ πρὸς ἑαυτόν, Philem. 13. πρὸς ἐμαυτόν, etc., (apud animum meum), with myself, etc., (2 Macc. xi. 13; exc. Fr. Grk. writ. are given in Passow s. v. I. 2 p. 1157ᵃ; [L. and S. s. v. C. I. 5]), συλλογίζομαι, Lk. xx. 5; προσεύχομαι, Lk. xviii. 11 [Tdf. om. πρὸς ἑ., Grsb. connects it with σταθείς]; ἀγανακτεῖν, Mk. xiv. 4 [(cf. 1 a. fin.); θαυμάζειν, Lk. xxiv. 12 (acc. to some; see above, 1 a. ad init.)]. Further, ποιεῖν τι πρός τινα, Mt. xxvi. 18; ἔχω χάριν πρός τινα, Acts ii. 47; καύχῆμα ἔχ. πρ. τ. to have whereof to glory with one (prop. turned '*toward*' one), Ro. iv. 2; παράκλητον πρός τινα, 1 Jn. ii. 1.   **3.** of relation or reference to any person or thing; thus   **a.** of fitness: joined to adjectives, ἀγαθός, Eph. iv. 29; ἕτοιμος, Tit. iii. 1; 1 Pet. iii. 15; ἱκανός, 2 Co. ii. 16; δυνατός, 2 Co. x. 4; ἐξηρτισμένος, 2 Tim. iii. 17; ὠφέλιμος, 1 Tim. iv. 8; 2 Tim. iii. 16; ἀδόκιμος, Tit. i. 16; ἀνεύθετος, Acts xxvii. 12; λευκός, *white* and so ready *for*, Jn. iv. 35; τὰ πρὸς τὴν χρείαν sc. ἀνάγκαια, [R. V. *such things as we needed*], Acts xxviii. 10.   **b.** of the relation or close connection entered (or to be entered) into by one person with another: περιπατεῖν πρός (Germ. *im Verkehr mit*, [*in intercourse with* (A. V. *toward*)]; cf. Bnhdy. p. 265; Passow s. v. I. 2 p. 1157ᵃ; [L. and S. s. v. C. I. 5]) τινα, Col. iv. 5; 1 Th. iv. 12; ἀναστρέφεσθαι, 2 Co. i. 12; of ethical relationship (where we use *with*), ἀσύμφωνος πρὸς ἀλλήλους, Acts xxviii. 25; κοινωνία, συμφώνησις πρός τινα or τι, 2 Co. vi. 15 sq.; εἰρήνην ἔχειν [see εἰρήνη, 5], Ro. v. 1; συνείδησιν ἔχειν πρὸς τὸν θεόν, Acts xxiv. 16; διαθήκην ἐντέλλομαι πρός τινα, Heb. ix. 20 [see ἐντέλλω, fin.]; διαθήκην διατίθημι, Acts iii. 25, (in Grk. writ. συνθήκας, σπονδὰς, συμμαχίαν ποιεῖσθαι πρός τινα, and similar expressions; cf. Passow [or L. and S.] u. s.); μὴ ταπεινώσῃ ... πρὸς ὑμᾶς, in my relation to you [R. V. *before*], 2 Co. xii. 21; πρὸς ὃν ἡμῖν ὁ λόγος (see λόγος, II. 5), Heb. iv. 13. Here belongs also 2 Co. iv. 2 [A. V. *to every man's conscience*].   **c.** *with regard to* (any person or thing), *with respect to, as to*; after verbs of saying: πρός τινα, Mk. xii. 12; Lk. xii. 41; xviii. 9; xix. 9; xx. 19; Ro. x. 21; Heb. i. 7 sq.; πρὸς τὸ δεῖν προσεύχεσθαι, Lk. xviii. 1; ἐπιτρέπειν, γράφειν τι πρός τι, Mt. xix. 8; Mk. x. 5; ἀποκριθῆναί τι πρός τι, Mt. xxvii. 14; ἀνταποκριθῆναι, Lk. xiv. 6; τί ἐρούμεν πρὸς ταῦτα, Ro. viii. 31, (Xen. mem. 3, 9, 12; anab. 2, 1, 20).   **d.** *pertaining to*: τὰ πρὸς τὸν θεόν (see θεός, 3 γ.), Ro. xv. 17; Heb. ii. 17; v. 1; τί πρὸς ἡμᾶς; sc. ἐστίν, *what is that to us?* i. e. it is none of our business to care for that, Mt. xxvii. 4; also τί πρὸς σέ; Jn. xxi. 22, 23 [here Tdf. om.].   **e.** in comparison (like Lat. *ad*) i. q. *in comparison with*: so after ἄξιος (q. v. in a.), Ro. viii. 18 (οὐ λογισθήσεται ἕτερος πρὸς αὐτόν, Bar. iii. 36 (35); cf. Viger. ed. *Herm.* p. 666; [B. § 147, 28]).   **f.** *agreeably to, according to*: πρὸς ἅ (i. e. πρὸς ταῦτα ἅ) ἔπραξε, 2 Co. v. 10; ποιεῖν πρὸς τὸ θέλημά τινος, Lk. xii. 47; ὀρθοποδεῖν πρὸς τὴν ἀλήθειαν, Gal. ii. 14. Here belong Eph. iii. 4; iv. 14.   **g.** akin to this is the use of πρός joined to nouns denoting desires, emotions, virtues, etc., to form a periphrasis of the adverbs [cf. W. § 51, 2 h.]: πρὸς φθόνον, enviously, Jas. iv. 5 ([on this pass. see φθόνος]; πρὸς ὀργήν i. q. ὀργίλως, Soph. El. 369; πρὸς βίαν i. q. βιαίως, Aeschyl. [Prom. 208, 353, etc.] Eum. 5; al.; πρὸς ἡδονὴν καὶ πρὸς χάριν, pleasantly and graciously, Joseph. antt. 12, 10, 3; [other exx. in L. and S. s. v. C. III. 7]).

II. with the DATIVE, *at, near, hard by*, denoting close local proximity (W. 395 (369 sq.)); so six times in the N. T. (much more freq. in the Sept. and in the O. T. Apocr.): Mk. v. 11 G L T Tr WH [R. V. *on the moun-

tain side*]; Lk. xix. 37; Jn. xviii. 16; xx. 11 (where Rec. has πρὸς τὸ μν.), 12; Rev. i. 13.

III. with the GENITIVE,   **a.** prop. used of that from which something proceeds;   **b.** (Lat. *a parte* i. e.) *on the side of*; hence tropically πρός τινος εἶναι or ὑπάρχειν, to pertain to one, lie in one's interests, be to one's advantage: so once in the N. T. τοῦτο πρὸς τῆς ὑμετέρας σωτηρίας ὑπάρχει, conduces to [A. V. *is for*] your safety, Acts xxvii. 34. (Κροῖσος ἐλπίσας πρὸς ἑωυτοῦ τὸν χρησμὸν εἶναι, Hdt. 1, 75; οὐ πρὸς τῆς ὑμετέρας δόξης, it will not redound to your credit, Thuc. 3, 59; add, Plat. Gorg. p. 459 c.; Lcian. dial. deor. 20, 3; Dion. Hal. antt. 10, 30; Arr. exp. Alex. 1, 19, 6; cf. Viger. ed. *Herm.* p. 659 sq.; Matthiae p. 1385 sq.; [L. and S. s. v. A. IV.]; W. 374 (350).)

IV. in COMPOSITION πρός signifies   **1.** direction or motion to a goal: προσάγω, προσεγγίζω, προσέρχομαι, προστρέχω.   **2.** addition, accession, *besides*: προσανατίθημι, προσαπειλέω, προσοφείλω.   **3.** vicinity: προσεδρεύω, προσμένω.   **4.** our *on, at*, as in προσκόπτω; and then of things which adhere *to* or are fastened *to* others, as προσηλόω, προσπήγνυμι.   **5.** *to* or *for*, of a thing adjusted to some standard: πρόσκαιρος. Cf. *Zeune* ad Viger. ed. *Herm.* p. 666.

προ-σάββατον, -ου, τό, *the day before the sabbath*: Mk. xv. 42 R G T WH [L Tr txt. πρὸς σάβ. (cf. πρός, I. 1 b.)]. (Judith viii. 6; [Ps. xcii. (xciii.) heading; Nonn. paraph. Ioan. 19, 66; Euseb. de mart. Pal. 6, 1].)*   **4315**

προσ-αγορεύω: 1 aor. pass. ptep. προσαγορευθείς; *to speak to, to address, accost, salute*, (Aeschyl., Hdt., Aristph., Xen., Plat., al.); esp. *to address* or *accost by some name, call by name*: τινά with a pred. acc., and in the pass. with a pred. nom. (1 Macc. xiv. 40; 2 Macc. xiv. 37), Heb. v. 10. (*to give a name to publicly, to style*, τινά or τί with a pred. acc., Xen. mem. 3, 2, 1; Γάϊος Ἰούλιος Καῖσαρ ὁ διὰ τὰς πράξεις προσαγορευθεὶς θεός, Diod. 1, 4; add [Sap. xiv. 22]; 2 Macc. iv. 7; x. 9; xiv. 37; φρούριον ... Καισάρειαν ὑπ᾽ αὐτοῦ προσαγορευθέν, Joseph. antt. 15, 8, 5.) Cf. *Bleek*, Brief an d. Hebr. ii. 2 p. 97 sq.*   **4316**

προσ-άγω; 2 aor. προσήγαγον; 1 aor. pass. προσήχθην (Mt. xviii. 24 L Tr WH); fr. Hom. down; Sept. for הִגִּישׁ, הִקְרִיב, sometimes for הֵבִיא;   **1.** transitively, *to lead to, bring*, [see πρός, IV. 1]: τινὰ ὧδε, Lk. ix. 41; τινά τινι, one to one [cf. W. § 52, 4, 14], Mt. xviii. 24 L Tr WH; Acts xvi. 20; *to open a way of access*, τινὰ τῷ θεῷ, for [A. V. *to bring*] one to God, i. e. to render one acceptable to God and assured of his grace (a fig. borrowed from those who secure for one the privilege of an interview with the sovereign), 1 Pet. iii. 18 [noteworthy is the use, without specification of the goal, in a forensic sense, *to summon* (to trial or punishment), Acts xii. 6 WH txt. (where al. προάγω, q. v. 1)].   **2.** intransitively (see ἄγω, 4), *to draw near to, approach*, (Josh. iii. 9; Jer. xxvi. (xlvi.) 3, etc.): τινί, Acts xxvii. 27 [(not WH mrg.)], where Luke speaks in nautical style phenomenally, the land which the sailor is approaching seeming to approach him; cf. Kuinoel [or Wetstein] ad loc.; [see προσανέχω 2, and προσαχέω].*   **4317**

4318　προσ-αγωγή, -ῆς, ἡ;　1. the act of bringing to, a moving to, (Thuc., Aristot., Polyb., al.).　2. access, approach, (Hdt. 2, 58; Xen. Cyr. 7, 5, 45) [al., as Meyer on Ro. as below (yet see Weiss in the 6th ed.), Ellic. on Eph., insist on the transitive sense, introduction]: εἰς τὴν χάριν, Ro. v. 2; to God, i. e. (dropping the figure) that friendly relation with God whereby we are acceptable to him and have assurance that he is favorably disposed towards us, Eph. ii. 18; iii. 12.*

4319　προσ-αιτέω, -ῶ;　1. to ask for in addition [(see πρός, IV. 2); Pind., Aeschyl., al.].　2. to approach one with supplications, (Germ. anbetteln [to importune; cf. πρός, IV. 4]), to ask alms, ([Hdt.], Xen., Arstph., Eur., Plut., al.): Mk. x. 46 R G L; Lk. xviii. 35 (where L T Tr WH have ἐπαιτῶν); Jn. ix. 8.*

see 5185 & 4319　προσαίτης, -ου, ὁ, a beggar: Mk. x. 46 T Tr WH; Jn. ix. 8 (where for the Rec. τυφλός). (Plut., Lcian., Diog. Laërt. 6, 56.)*

4320　προσ-ανα-βαίνω: 2 aor. impv. 2 pers. sing. προσανάβηθι; to go up farther: with ἀνώτερον added, Lk. xiv. 10 [A. V. go up higher; al. regard the προσ- as adding the suggestion of 'motion to' the place where the host stands: 'come up higher' (cf. Prov. xxv. 7). Xen., Aristot., al.]*

4321　προσ-αναλίσκω: 1 aor. ptcp. fem. προσαναλώσασα; to expend besides [πρός, IV. 2]: ἰατροῖς (i. e. upon physicians, B. § 133, 1; Rec. εἰς ἰατρούς [cf. W. 213 (200)]) τὸν βίον, Lk. viii. 43 [WH om. Tr mrg. br. the cl.]. (Xen., Plat., Dem., Plut., al.)*

4322　προσ-ανα-πληρόω, -ῶ; 1 aor. προσανεπλήρωσα; to fill up by adding to [cf. πρός, IV. 2]; to supply: τί, 2 Co. ix. 12; xi. 9. (Sap. xix. 4; Aristot., Diod., Philo, al.)*

4323　προσ-ανα-τίθημι: 2 aor. mid. προσανεθέμην;　1. to lay upon in addition [cf. πρός, IV. 2].　2. Middle,　a. to lay upon one's self in addition: φόρτον, Poll. 1, 9, 99; to undertake besides: τί, Xen. mem. 2, 1, 8.　b. with a dat. of the pers. to put one's self upon another by going to him (πρός), i. e. to commit or betake one's self to another sc. for the purpose of consulting him, hence to consult, to take one into counsel, [A. V. confer with], (Diod. 17, 116 τοῖς μάντεσι προσαναθέμενος περὶ τοῦ σημείου; Lcian. Jup. trag. § 1 ἐμοὶ προσανάθου, λάβε με σύμβουλον πόνων), Gal. i. 16.　c. to add from one's store (this is the force of the middle), to communicate, impart: τί τινι, Gal. ii. 6.*

see 4317　προσ-αν-έχω;　1. to hold up besides.　2. intrans. to rise up so as to approach, rise up towards: Acts xxvii. 27 Lchm. ed. ster. (see προσάγω 2, and προσαχέω),　— a sense found nowhere else.*

4324　προσ-απειλέω, -ῶ: 1 aor. mid. ptcp. προσαπειλησάμενος; to add threats, threaten further, [cf. πρός, IV. 2]: Acts iv. 21. (Dem. p. 544, 26.)*

see 4317　[προσ-αχέω, -ῶ, Doric for προσηχέω, to resound: Acts xxvii. 27 WH mrg. (see their App. p. 151; al. προσάγειν, q. v.), of the roar of the surf as indicating nearness to land to sailors at night.*]

4325　προσ-δαπανάω, -ῶ: 1 aor. subjunc. 2 pers. sing. προσδαπανήσῃς, to spend besides [cf. πρός, IV. 2], Vulg. supererogo: τί, Lk. x. 35. (Lcian., Themist.)*

προσ-δέομαι; depon. pass. to want besides, need in addition, [cf. πρός, IV. 2]: προσδεόμενός τινος, "quom nullius boni desideret accessionem" (Erasmus), [A. V. as though he needed anything], Acts xvii. 25. (Xen., Plat., sqq.; Sept.; [in the sense to ask of, several times n Hdt.].)*　**4326**

προσ-δέχομαι; depon. mid.; impf. προσεδεχόμην; 1 aor. προσεδεξάμην;　1. as in Grk. writ. fr. Aeschyl. and Hdt. down, to receive to one's self, to admit, to give access to one's self: τινά, to admit one, receive into intercourse and companionship, τοὺς ἁμαρτωλούς, Lk. xv. 2; to receive one (coming from some place), Ro. xvi. 2; Phil. ii. 29, (1 Chr. xii. 18); τί, to accept (not to reject) a thing offered: οὐ προσδ. to reject, Heb. xi. 35; προσδέχονται ἐλπίδα, to admit (accept) hope, i. e. not to repudiate but to entertain, embrace, its substance, Acts xxiv. 15 [al. refer this to the next head (R. V. txt. look for)]; not to shun, to bear, an impending evil [A. V. took the spoiling etc.], Heb. x. 34.　2. as fr. Hom. down, to expect [A. V. look for, wait for]: τινά, Lk. xii. 36; τί, Mk. xv. 43; Lk. ii. 25, 38; xxiii. 51; [Acts xxiii. 21]; Tit. ii. 13; Jude 21; τὰς ἐπαγγελίας, the fulfilment of the promises, Heb. xi. 13 Lchm. [Cf. δέχομαι, fin.]*　**4327**

προσ-δοκάω, -ῶ; impf. 3 pers. plur. προσεδόκων (Acts xxviii. 6); (the simple verb is found only in the form δοκεύω; πρός [q. v. IV. 1] denotes mental direction); fr. Aeschyl. and Hdt. down; to expect (whether in thought, in hope, or in fear); to look for, wait for: when the preceding context shews who or what is expected, Mt. xxiv. 50; Lk. iii. 15; xii. 46; Acts xxvii. 33; xxviii. 6; τινά, one's coming or return, Mt. xi. 3; Lk. i. 21; vii. 19 sq.; viii. 40; Acts x. 24; τί, 2 Pet. iii. 12-14; foll. by an acc. with infin. Acts xxviii. 6; foll. by an infin. belonging to the subject, Acts iii. 5.*　**4328**

προσ-δοκία, -ας, ἡ, (προσδοκάω), fr. Thuc. and Xen. down, expectation (whether of good or of evil): joined to φόβος (Plut. Ant. 75; Demetr. 15) with a gen. of the object added [W. § 50, 7 b.], Lk. xxi. 26; τοῦ λαοῦ (gen. of subject), the expectation of the people respecting Peter's execution, Acts xii. 11.*　**4329**

προσδρέμω, see προστρέχω.　**see 4370**

προσ-εάω, -ῶ; to permit one to approach or arrive: Acts xxvii. 7 [R. V. txt. to suffer further; cf. πρός, IV. 2; Smith, Voyage and Shipwreck of St. Paul, 3d ed., p. 78; Hackett ad loc.)]. Not found elsewhere.*　**4330**

προσ-εγγίζω: 1 aor. inf. προσεγγίσαι; to approach unto [πρός, IV. 1]: with the dat. of a pers. [cf. W. § 52, 4, 14], Mk. ii. 4 [where T Tr mrg. WH προσενέγκαι]. (Sept.; Polyb., Diod., Lcian.)*　**4331**

προσεδρεύω; (πρόσεδρος sitting near, [cf. πρός, IV. 3]);　1. prop. to sit near [(Eur., al.)].　2. to attend assiduously: τῷ θυσιαστηρίῳ (see παρεδρεύω), 1 Co. ix. 13 Rec.; Protev. Jac. 23, 1 (where we also find the var. παρεδρεύω); τῇ θεραπείᾳ τοῦ θεοῦ, Joseph. c. Ap. 1, 7, 1; ταῖς φιλοπονίαις, Aristot. pol. 8, 4, 4 p. 1338b, 25; τοῖς πράγμασι, Dem. p. 14, 15 [i. e. Olynth. 1, 18]; with dat. of pers. to be in attendance upon, not to quit one's side, Joseph. c. Ap. 1, 9, 1; [cf. Dem. 914, 28].*　**4332**

προσ-εργάζομαι: 1 aor. 3 pers. sing. προσειργάσατο　**4333**

(R G Tr), προσηργάσ. (L T WH; see ἐργάζομαι, init.);
1. *to work besides* (Eur., Plut.).   2. *by working or
trading to make* or *gain besides*: Lk. xix. 16 (Xen. Hell.
3, 1, 28).*

4334 προσ-έρχομαι; impf. 3 pers. plur. προσήρχοντο (Acts
xxviii. 9); [fut. 3 pers. sing. προσελεύσεται, Lk. i. 17 WH
mrg.]; 2 aor. 3 pers. plur. προσῆλθον and [so L Tr WH
in Mt. ix. 28; xiii. 36; xiv. 15; T Tr WH in Mt. v. 1;
Lk. xiii. 31; WH in Mt. xix. 3; xxi. 23; Jn. xii. 21] in
the Alex. form προσῆλθαν (see ἀπέρχομαι, and ἔρχομαι);
pf. προσελήλυθα (Heb. xii. 18, 22); fr. Aeschyl. and Hdt.
down; Sept. for קָרַב and נָגַשׁ; *to come to, to approach,*
[πρός, IV. 1]; a. prop. absol., Mt. iv. 11; Lk.
[i. 17 WH mrg.]; ix. 42; xxiii. 36; Acts viii. 29; xxviii.
9; προσῆλθον λέγοντες, Lk. xiii. 31; with rhetorical fulness of description (see ἀνίστημι, II. 1 c. [also ἔρχομαι, p.
250ᵇ bot.]) the ptcp. προσελθών is joined to a finite verb
which denotes a different action: Mt. viii. 2 L T Tr WH,
19, 25; ix. 20; xiii. 10, 27; xiv. 12; xv. 12, 23; xvi. 1;
xvii. 7 [R G]; xix. 16; xxv. 20, 22, 24; xxvi. 39 T Tr
WH mrg. (acc. to a reading no doubt corrupt [cf. *Scrivener*, Introd. p. 16]), 50, 60, 73; xxviii. 2, 9, 18; Mk. i.
31; x. 2; xii. 28; [xiv. 35 Tr WH mrg.]; Lk. vii. 14; viii.
24, 44; ix. 12, 42; x. 34; xx. 27; xxiii. 36; Acts xxii. 26
sq.; προσέρχομαι foll. by an infin. indicating the reason
why one has drawn near, Mt. xxiv. 1; Acts vii. 31; xii.
13 [here WH mrg. προῆλθε]; with a dat. of the place
(exx. fr. Grk. auth. are given in Passow s. v. 1 a. p. 1190ᵃ;
[L. and S. s. v. I. 1]), Heb. xii. 18, 22; with the dat. of
a pers. (see Lexx. u. s.), Mt. v. 1; viii. 5; ix. 14, 28; xiii.
36; xiv. 15; xv. 1, 30; xvii. 14, 24; xviii. 1; xix. 3; xx.
20; xxi. 14, 23; xxii. 23; xxiv. 3; xxvi. 7, 17, 69; Jn.
xii. 21; Acts x. 28; xviii. 2; xxiv. 23 Rec.; [with ἐπί and
the acc. Acts xx. 13 Tr WH mrg.]. The ptcp. προσ-
ελθὼν αὐτῷ with a finite verb (see above) occurs in Mt.
iv. 3; xviii. 21; xxi. 28, 30; xxvi. 49; xxvii. 58; Mk. vi.
35; xiv. 45; Lk. xx. 27; xxiii. 52; Acts ix. 1; xxiii.
14. b. trop. a. προσέρχ. τῷ θεῷ, *to draw near to
God* in order to seek his grace and favor, Heb. vii. 25;
xi. 6; τῷ θρόνῳ τῆς χάριτος, Heb. iv. 16; without τῷ
θεῷ, Heb. x. 1, 22, (in the O. T. προσέρχ., simply, is used
of the priests about to offer sacrifices, Lev. xxi. 17, 21;
Deut. xxi. 5; with the addition of πρὸς θεόν, of one about
to ask counsel of God, 1 S. xiv. 36; with τοῖς θεοῖς, of
suppliants about to implore the gods, Dio Cass. 56, 9);
πρὸς Χριστόν, to attach one's self to Christ, to come to a
participation in the benefits procured by him, 1 Pet. ii.
4 [cf. W. § 52, 3]. β. i. q. *to assent to* (cf. Germ.
beitreten [Lat. *accedere*; Eng. *come* (over) *to*, used fig.]):
ὑγιαίνουσι λόγοις, 1 Tim. vi. 3 [Tdf. προσέχεται, q. v. 3].

4335 προσ-ευχή, -ῆς, ἡ, (προσεύχομαι), Sept. for תְּפִלָּה, i. q.
εὐχὴ πρὸς τὸν θεόν [cf. πρός, IV. 1]; 1. *prayer addressed to God*: Mt. xvii. 21 [T WH om. Tr br. the vs.];
xxi. 22; Mk. ix. 29; Lk. xxii. 45; Acts iii. 1; vi. 4; x.
31; Ro. xii. 12; 1 Co. vii. 5; Col. iv. 2; Phil., Acts ii.
42; x. 4; Ro. i. 10 (9); Eph. i. 16; Col. iv. 12; 1 Th. i.
2; Philem. 4, 22; 1 Pet. iii. 7; iv. 7; Rev. v. 8; viii. 3, 4
(where ταῖς προσευχαῖς is a dat. commodi, *for*, in aid of,

the prayers [W. § 31, 6 c.; cf. Green p. 101 sq.]); οἶκος
προσευχῆς, a house devoted to the offering of prayer to
God, Mt. xxi. 13; Mk. xi. 17; Lk. xix. 46, (Is. lvi. 7; 1
Macc. vii. 37); προσευχὴ καὶ δέησις, Acts i. 14 Rec.;
Eph. vi. 18; Phil. iv. 6, (1 K. viii. 38; 2 Chr. vi. 29; 1
Macc. vii. 37; on the distinction between the two words
see δέησις); plur., 1 Tim. ii. 1; v. 5; ἡ πρ. τοῦ θεοῦ,
prayer to God, Lk. vi. 12 (εὐχαριστία θεοῦ, Sap. xvi. 28;
cf. reff. in πίστις, 1 a.); πρὸς τὸν θεὸν ὑπέρ [L T Tr WH
περί] τινος, Acts xii. 5; plur. Ro. xv. 30; προσευχῇ προσεύχεσθαι, a Hebraistic expression (cf. W. § 54, 3; [B.
§ 133, 22 a.]), to pray fervently, Jas. v. 17. 2. *a
place set apart* or *suited for the offering of prayer*; i. e. a.
a synagogue (see συναγωγή, 2 b.): 3 Macc. vii. 20 [acc. to
the reading προσευχήν; see *Grimm*, Com. in loc.]; Philo
in Flaccum § 6 [also § 14]; leg. ad Gaium §§ 20, 43, 46; Juvenal, sat. 1, 3, 296; συνάγονται πάντες εἰς τὴν προσευχήν,
μέγιστον οἴκημα πολὺν ὄχλον ἐπιδέξασθαι δυνάμενον, Joseph. vita § 54. b. a place in the open air where the
Jews were wont to pray, outside of those cities where they
had no synagogue; such places were situated upon the
bank of a stream or the shore of the sea, where there
was a supply of water for washing the hands before
prayer: Acts xvi. 13, 16; Joseph. antt. 14, 10, 23, cf.
Epiph. haer. 80, 1. Tertullian in his ad nationes 1, 13
makes mention of the "orationes litorales" of the Jews,
and in his de jejuniis c. 16 says "Judaicum certe jeju-
nium ubique celebratur, cum omissis templis *per omne
litus quocunque in aperto* aliquando jam preces ad caelum
mittunt." [Josephus (c. Apion. 2, 2, 2) quotes Apion as
representing Moses as offering αἴθριοι προσευχαί.] Cf.
De Wette, Archäologie, § 242; [*Schürer*, Zeitgesch. § 27
vol. ii. p. 369 sqq.]. Not used by prof. auth. except in
the passages cited above from Philo, Josephus, and Juvenal [to which add Cleomedes 71, 16; cf. *Boeckh*, Corp.
inscrr. ii. 1004 no. 2114 b. and 1005 no. 2114 bb. (A. D.
81), see Index s. v.].*

4336 προσ-εύχομαι; depon. mid.; impf. προσηυχόμην; fut.
προσεύξομαι; 1 aor. προσηυξάμην; [on the augm. see *WH*.
App. p. 162; cf. *Tdf*. Proleg. p. 121]; fr. Aeschyl. and
Hdt. down; Sept. for הִתְפַּלֵּל; *to offer prayers, to pray,*
(everywhere of prayers to the gods, or to God [cf. δέησις,
fin.]): absol., Mt. vi. 5–7, 9; xiv. 23; xxvi. 36, 39, 44; Mk.
i. 35; vi. 46; xi. 24 sq.; xiii. 33 [L T WH om. Tr br. the
cl.]; xiv. [32], 39; Lk. i. 10; iii. 21; v. 16; vi. 12; ix. 18,
28 sq.; xi. 1 sq.; xviii. 1, 10; xxii. 44 [L br. WH reject
the pass.]; Acts i. 24; vi. 6; ix. 11, 40; x. 9, 30; xi. 5;
xii. 12; xiii. 3; xiv. 23; xvi. 25; xx. 36; xxi. 5; xxii. 17;
xxviii. 8; 1 Co. xi. 4 sq.; xiv. 14; 1 Th. v. 17; 1 Tim. ii.
8; Jas. v. 13, 18; foll. by λέγων and direct disc. containing the words of the prayer, Mt. xxvi. 39, 42; Lk.
xxii. 41; προσεύχ. with a dat. indicating the manner or
instrument, 1 Co. xi. 5 [W. § 31, 7 d.]; xiv. 14 sq. [cf. W.
279 (262) sq.]; μακρά, to make long prayers, Mt. xxiii.
14 (13) Rec.; Mk. xii. 40; Lk. xx. 47; ἐν πνεύματι (see
πνεῦμα, 4 a. p. 522ᵃ mid.), Eph. vi. 18; ἐν πν. ἁγίῳ, Jude
20; προσευχῇ (see προσευχή, 1 fin.), Jas. v. 17; προσεύχ.
with the acc. of a thing, Lk. xviii. 11; Ro. viii. 26 [cf. W.

§ 41 b. 4 b.; B. § 139, 61 c.]; *ἐπί τινα*, over one, i. e. with hands extended over him, Jas. v. 14 [cf. W. 408 (381) n.]; sc. *ἐπί τινα*, Mt. xix. 13. as commonly in Grk. writ. with the dat. of the pers. to whom the prayers are offered [cf. W. § 52, 4, 14]: Mt. vi. 6; 1 Co. xi. 13, (Is. xliv. 17); *περί* with the gen. of a pers., Col. i. 3 [R G T WH txt.]; 1 Th. v. 25; Heb. xiii. 18; *ὑπέρ* with the gen. of a pers., Mt. v. 44; Lk. vi. 28 [where T WH Tr mrg. *περί* (see *περί*, I. c. γ., also *ὑπέρ*, I. 6); Col. i. 3 L Tr WH mrg. (see reff. as above), 9]; *προσεύχ.* foll. by *ἵνα*, *with the design of,* 1 Co. xiv. 13, cf. Meyer in loc. [W. 460 (428)]; the thing prayed for is indicated by a following *ἵνα* (see *ἵνα*, II. 2 b.): Mt. xxiv. 20; xxvi. 41; Mk. xiii. 18; xiv. 35, 38; Lk. xxii. 46, [but in Mt. xxvi. 41; Mk. xiv. 38; (Lk. xxii. 46?), *ἵνα* is more com. regarded as giving the aim of the twofold command preceding]; *τοῦτο ἵνα*, Phil. i. 9; *περί τινος ἵνα*, Col. iv. 3; 2 Th. i. 11; iii. 1; *ὑπέρ τινος ἵνα*, Col. i. 9; *ὑπέρ τινος ὅπως*, Jas. v. 16 L WH txt. Tr mrg.; *περί τινος ὅπως*, Acts viii. 15, (ὅπως [q. v. II. 2] seems to indicate not so much the contents of the prayer as its end and aim); foll. by an inf. belonging to the subject, Lk. xxii. 40; foll. by *τοῦ* with the inf., Jas. v. 17.*

4337 **προσ-έχω**; impf. *προσεῖχον*; pf. *προσέσχηκα*; [pres. mid. 3 pers. sing. *προσέχεται* (1 Tim. vi. 3 Tdf.)]; *to turn to* [cf. *πρός*, IV. 1], i. e. **1.** *to bring to, bring near*; thus very freq. in Grk. writ. fr. Hdt. down with *ναῦν* (quite as often omitting the *ναῦν*) and a dat. of place, or foll. by *πρός* with an acc. of place, *to bring a ship to land,* and simply *to touch at, put in.* **2. a.** *τὸν νοῦν, to turn the mind to, attend to, be attentive*: *τινί*, to a person or thing, Arstph. eqq. 503; Plat., Dem., Polyb., Joseph., Lcian., Plut., al.; once so in the Bible, viz. Job vii. 17. The simple *προσέχειν τινί* (Sept. for הִקְשִׁיב, also for הֶאֱזִין), with *τὸν νοῦν* omitted, is often used in the same sense from Xen. down; so in the N. T. [cf. W. 593 (552); B. 144 (126)]: Acts viii. 6; xvi. 14; Heb. ii. 1; 2 Pet. i. 19, (1 Macc. vii. 11; 4 Macc. i. 1; Sap. viii. 12); in the sense of *caring for, providing for,* Acts xx. 28. **b.** *προσέχω ἐμαυτῷ, to attend to one's self,* i. e. *to give heed to one's self* (Sept. for נִשְׁמַר, *to guard one's self,* i. e. *to beware,* Gen. xxiv. 6; Ex. x. 28; Deut. iv. 9; vi. 12, etc.): Lk. xvii. 3; Acts v. 35 [cf. B. 337 (290); W. 557 (518); yet see *ἐπί*, B. 2 f. a.]; with the addition of *ἀπό τινος, to be on one's guard against, beware of,* a thing [cf. B. § 147, 3 (*ἀπό*, I. 3 b.)]: Lk. xii. 1 (Tob. iv. 12; [Test. xii. Patr., test. Dan 6]); also without the dat. *προσέχ. ἀπό τινος*: Mt. vii. 15; x. 17; xvi. 6, 11 sq.; Lk. xx. 46, (Sir. vi. 13; xi. 33; xvii. 14; xviii. 27; ['Teaching' etc. 6, 3; 12, 5]); foll. by *μή* with an inf., *to take heed lest one do a thing,* Mt. vi. 1; *ἐμαυτῷ, μήποτε* with the subjunc. Lk. xxi. 34; absol. *to give attention, take heed*: Sir. xiii. 13; Barn. ep. 4, 9; 7, 4. 6. [9]; foll. by *πῶς*, Barn. ep. 7, 7; by the interrog. *τί*, ib. 15, 4; *ἵνα*, ib. 16, 8; *ἵνα μήποτε*, Barn. ep. 4, 13 [var.; *ἵνα μή*, 2 Chr. xxv. 16]; [*μήποτε*, Barn. ep. 4, 14]. **3.** sc. *ἐμαυτόν, to apply one's self to, attach one's self to, hold or cleave to* a person or a thing, [R.V. mostly *give heed*]: with the dat. of a pers. *to one*, Acts viii. 10 sq.; 1 Tim. iv. 1; *τῷ ἐπισκόπῳ πρ. καὶ τῷ πρεσβυτερίῳ καὶ δια-*

κόνοις, Ignat. ad Philad. 7, 1; ad Polyc. 6, 1; with the dat. of a thing, *μύθοις,* 1 Tim. i. 4; Tit. i. 14; [mid. *ὑγιαίνουσι λόγοις,* 1 Tim. vi. 3 Tdf. (al. *προσέρχεται,* q. v. b. β.)]; *to be given* or *addicted to*: *οἴνῳ,* 1 Tim. iii. 8 (τρυφῇ, Julian. Caes. 22 [p. 326 ed. Spanh.]; *τρυφῇ καὶ μέθῃ,* Polyaen. strateg. 8, 56); *to devote thought and effort to*: *τῇ ἀναγνώσει κτλ.* 1 Tim. iv. 13; *τῷ θυσιαστηρίῳ,* [A.V. *give attendance*], Heb. vii. 13, (ναυτικοῖς, Thuc. 1, 15; for other exx. fr. Grk. writ. see Passow s. v. 3 c.; [L. and S. s. v. 4 b.]).*

προσ-ηλόω, -ῶ: 1 aor. ptcp. *προσηλώσας*; *to fasten with nails to, nail to,* [cf. *πρός*, IV. 4]: *τὶ τῷ σταυρῷ,* Col. ii. 14. (3 Macc. iv. 9; Plat., Dem., Polyb., Diod., Philo, Joseph., Plut., Lcian., al.) * **4338**

προσήλυτος, -ον, ὁ, (fr. *προσέρχομαι,* pf. *προσελήλυθα,* cf. B. 74 (64); [W. 24. 26. 97 (92)]); **1.** *a newcomer* [Lat. *advena*; cf. *πρός*, IV. 1]; *a stranger, alien,* (Schol. ad Apoll. Rhod. 1, 834; Sept. often for גֵּר [cf. Philo de monarch. 1, 7 ad init.]). **2.** *a proselyte,* i. e. one who has come over from a Gentile religion to Judaism (Luther, *Judengenosse*): Mt. xxiii. 15; Acts ii. 11 (10); vi. 5; xiii. 43. The Rabbins distinguish two classes of proselytes, viz. גֵּרֵי הַצֶּדֶק *proselytes of righteousness,* who received circumcision and bound themselves to keep the whole Mosaic law and to comply with all the requirements of Judaism, and גֵּרֵי הַשַּׁעַר *proselytes of the gate* (a name derived apparently from Ex. xx. 10; Deut. xiv. 14; [xiv. 21]; xxiv. 16 (14), 21 (19)), who dwelt among the Jews, and although uncircumcised observed certain specified laws, esp. the seven precepts of Noah (as the Rabbins called them), i. e. against the seven chief sins, idolatry, blasphemy against God, homicide, unchastity, theft or plundering, rebellion against rulers, and the use of "flesh with the blood thereof." [Many hold that this distinction of proselytes into classes is purely theoretical, and was of no practical moment in Christ's day; cf. *Lardner*, Works, xi. 306–324; cf. vi. 522–533; *Schürer* in Riehm as below.] Cf. *Leyrer* in Herzog xii. p. 237 sqq. [rewritten in ed. 2 by Delitzsch (xii. 293 sqq.)]; *Steiner* in Schenkel iv. 629 sq.; [BB. DD.]; *Schürer,* Neutest. Zeitgesch. p. 644 [(whose views are somewhat modified, esp. as respects c l a s s e s of proselytes, in his 2te Aufl. § 31 V. p. 567, and his art. ' Proselyten' in Riehm p. 1240 sq.)] and the bks. he refers to.* **4339**

πρόσ-καιρος, -ον, (i. q. ὁ πρὸς καιρὸν ὤν), *for a season* [cf. *πρός*, IV. 5], enduring only *for a while, temporary*: Mt. xiii. 21; Mk. iv. 17; 2 Co. iv. 18; Heb. xi. 25. (4 Macc. xv. 2; Joseph. antt. 2, 4, 4; Dio Cass., Dion. Hal., [Strabo 7, 3, 11], Plut., Hdian.; ὁ παρὼν καὶ πρόσκαιρος κόσμος, Clem. homil. 20, 2.) * **4340**

προσ-καλέω, -ῶ: Mid., pres. *προσκαλοῦμαι*; 1 aor. *προσεκαλεσάμην*; pf. *προσκέκλημαι*; from [Antipho, Arstph., Thuc.], Xen., Plat. down; *to call to*; in the N. T. found only in the mid. [cf. B. § 135, 4], *to call to one's self*; *to bid to come to one's self*: *τινά,* **a.** prop.: Mt. x. 1; xv. 10, 32; xviii. 2, 32; xx. 25; Mk. iii. 13, 23; vi. 7; vii. 14; viii. 1, 34; x. 42; xii. 43; xv. 44; Lk. vii. 18 (19); xv. 26; xvi. 5; xviii. 16; Acts v. 40; vi. 2; xiii. 7; xx. 1 [RG **see 4341 St.**

L]; xxiii. 17, 18, 23; Jas. v. 14.   **b.** metaph. God is said προσκαλεῖσθαι the Gentiles, aliens as they are from him, by inviting and drawing them, through the preaching of the gospel, unto fellowship with himself in the Messiah's kingdom, Acts ii. 39; the Holy Spirit and Christ are said *to call unto themselves* [cf. W. § 39, 3] those preachers of the gospel to whom they have decided to intrust a service having reference to the extension of the gospel: foll. by an inf. indicating the purpose, Acts xvi. 10; foll. by εἴς τι, Acts xiii. 2 (where ὅ is for εἰς ὅ, acc. to that familiar Grk. usage by which a prep. prefixed to the antecedent is not repeated before the relative; cf. W. 421 sq. (393); [B. 342 (294)]).*

4342   προσ-καρτερέω, -ῶ; fut. προσκαρτερήσω; (καρτερέω, fr. καρτερός ['strong,' 'steadfast'], of which the root is (τὸ) κάρτος for κράτος ['strength']; cf. Curtius § 72]); *to persevere* [*'continue steadfastly'*] in any thing [cf. πρός, IV. 4]: of persons, with the dat. of a thing, *to give constant attention to a thing,* Acts ii. 42 [here Lchm. adds ἐν (once) in br.]; τῇ προσευχῇ, Acts i. 14; vi. 4; Ro. xii. 12; Col. iv. 2, (ταῖς θήραις, Diod. 3, 17; τῇ πολιορκίᾳ, Polyb. 1, 55, 4; Diod. 14, 87; τῇ καθέδρᾳ, persist in the siege, Joseph. antt. 5, 2, 6); with the dat. of a person, *to adhere to one, be his adherent; to be devoted* or *constant to one* : Acts viii. 13; x. 7, (Dem. p. 1386, 6; Polyb. 24, 5, 3; Diog. Laërt. 8, 1, 14); εἴς τι, *to be steadfastly attentive unto, to give unremitting care to* a thing, Ro. xiii. 6 [cf. Meyer ad loc.]; ἐν with a dat. of place, *to continue* all the time *in* a place, Acts ii. 46 (Sus. 6); absol. *to persevere, not to faint* (in a thing), Xen. Hell. 7, 5, 14; *to show one's self courageous,* for הִתְחַזַּק, Num. xiii. 21 (20). of a thing, with the dat. of a pers., *to be in constant readiness for one, wait on continually* : Mk. iii. 9.*

4343   προσ-καρτέρησις, -εως, ἡ, (προσκαρτερέω), *perseverance* : Eph. vi. 18. Nowhere else; [*Koumanoudes, Λέξ. ἀθησ.* s. v.].*

4344   προσ-κεφάλαιον, -ου, τό, (fr. πρός [q. v. IV. 3] and the adj. κεφάλαιος [cf. κεφάλαιον]), *a pillow, a cushion* : Mk. iv. 38. (Ezek. xiii. 18, 20; Arstph., Plat., Plut., al.) *

4345   προσ-κληρόω, -ῶ : 1 aor. pass. 3 pers. plur. προσεκληρώθησαν; *to add* or *assign to by lot, to allot* : προσεκληρώθησαν τῷ Παύλῳ, *were allotted* by God *to Paul,* viz. as disciples, followers, Acts xvii. 4 [W. § 39, 2 fin.]; al. give it a middle force, *joined their lot to,* attached themselves to, (A. V. *consorted with*); cf. leg. ad Gaium § 10 and other exx. fr. Philo as below]. (Plut. mor. p. 738 d.; Lcian. am. 3; freq. in Philo, cf. *Loesner,* Observv. p. 209 sqq.) *

see 4346   πρόσ-κλησις, -εως, ἡ,   **1.** *a judicial summons* : Arstph., Plat., Dem.   **2.** *an invitation* : μηδὲν ποιῶν κατὰ πρόσκλησιν, 1 Tim. v. 21 L Tr mrg.; this reading, unless (as can hardly be doubted) it be due to itacism, must be translated *by invitation,* i. e. the invitation or summons of those who seek to draw you over to their side [see quotations in Tdf. ad loc. Cf. *πρόσκλισις.*] *

see 4347   προσ-κλίνω : 1 aor. pass. 3 pers. sing. προσεκλίθη;   **1.** trans. (to cause) *to lean against* [cf. πρός, IV. 4] (Hom., Pind.).   **2.** intrans. τινί, *to incline towards one, lean*

to his side or *party* : Polyb. 4, 51, 5, etc.; 1 aor. pass. προσεκλίθην with a mid. signif. *to join one's self to one* : Acts v. 36 L T Tr WH [(cf. W. § 52, 4, 14)]; 2 Macc. xiv. 24; τοῖς δικαίοις προσεκλίθη, Schol. ad Arstph. Plut. 1027; προσεκλίθητε τοῖς ἀποστόλοις, Clem. Rom. 1 Cor. 47, 4 and in other later writ.*

4346   πρόσ-κλισις, -εως, ἡ, *an inclination* or *proclivity of mind, a joining the party of one,* (Polyb., [Diod.]); *partiality* : κατὰ πρόσκλισιν, led by partiality (Vulg. *in* [*aliam* or] *alteram partem declinando*), 1 Tim. v. 21 [RGTWH Tr txt.]; κατὰ προσκλίσεις, Clem. Rom. 1 Cor. 21, 7; δίχα προσκλίσεως ἀνθρωπίνης, ib. 50, 2, cf. 47, 3 sq. (Cf. *πρόσκλησις.*) *

4347   προσ-κολλάω, -ῶ : 1 aor. pass. προσεκολλήθην; 1 fut. pass. προσκολληθήσομαι; Sept. for דָּבַק; *to glue upon, glue to,* [cf. πρός, IV. 4]; prop. Joseph. antt. 7, 12, 4; trop. in the pass. with a reflexive force, *to join one's self to closely, cleave to, stick to,* (Plato) : w. dat. of a pers. (Sir. vi. 34; xiii. 16), Acts v. 36 Rec. (see προσκλίνω, 2); τῇ γυναικί, Mt. xix. 5 Rec. [al. κολληθήσεται, q. v.] : Mk. x. 7 Lchm.; Eph. v. 31 L T Tr WH mrg.; πρὸς τὴ, γυν. (fr. Gen. ii. 24), Mk. x. 7 R G Tr txt.; Eph. v. 31 R G WH txt. [Cf. W. § 52, 4, 14.] *

4348   πρόσ-κομμα, -ατος, τό, (προσκόπτω), *a stumbling-block,* i. e. an obstacle in the way which if one strike his foot against he necessarily stumbles or falls; trop. that over which the soul stumbles, i. e. by which it is impelled to sin : 1 Co. viii. 9 (Sir. xvii. 25 (20)); xxxi. (xxxiv.) 19 (16); xxxix. 24); τιθέναι πρόσκ. τινι, to put a stumbling-block in one's way, i. e. trop. to furnish one an occasion for sinning, Ro. xiv. 13 [WH mrg. om.]; ὁ διὰ προσκόμματος ἐσθίων, [A.V.] *who eateth with offence* (see διά, A. I. 2), by making no discrimination as to what he eats occasions another to act against his conscience, ibid. 20; λίθος προσκόμματος (fr. Is. viii. 14 for אֶבֶן נֶגֶף), prop. a stone against which the foot strikes [A. V. *stone of stumbling*], used figuratively of Christ Jesus, with regard to whom it especially annoyed and offended the Jews that his words, deeds, career, and particularly his ignominious death on the cross, quite failed to correspond to their preconceptions respecting the Messiah; hence they despised and rejected him, and by that crime brought upon themselves woe and punishment : Ro. ix. 32, 33; 1 Pet. ii. 8 (7). (In the Sept. for מִכְשׁוֹל, Ex. xxiii. 33; xxxiv. 12; [cf. Judith viii. 22]. *a sore* or *bruise caused by striking the foot* against any object, Athen. 3 p. 97 f.; *a hindrance* [?], Plut. mor. p. 1048 c. [i. e. de Stoic. repugn. 30, 8 fin.].) *

4349   προσ-κοπή, -ῆς, ἡ, (προσκόπτω), *an occasion of stumbling* [so R.V. (but A.V. *offence*) : διδόναι προσκοπήν (sc. ἄλλοις), to do something which causes others to stumble, i. e. leads them into error or sin, 2 Co. vi. 3 [cf. W. 484 (451)]. (Polyb.; [for כִּשָּׁלוֹן *fall,* Prov. xvi. 18 Graecus Ven.].) *

4350   προσ-κόπτω; 1 aor. προσέκοψα; *to strike against* [cf. πρός, IV. 4]: absol. of those who strike against a stone or other obstacle in the path, *to stumble,* Jn. xi. 9, 10; πρὸς λίθον τὸν πόδα, to strike the foot against a stone, i. e.

(dropping the fig.) to meet with some harm, Mt. iv. 6 ; Lk. iv. 11, (fr. Ps. xc. (xci.) 12) ; *to rush upon, beat against*, οἱ ἄνεμοι τῇ οἰκίᾳ, Mt. vii. 27 [L mrg. προσέρρηξαν, see προσρήγνυμι]. ἔν τινι, to be made to stumble by a thing, i. e. metaph. to be induced to sin, Ro. xiv. 21 [cf. W. 583 (542) ; B. § 151, 23 d.]. Since we are angry with an obstacle in our path which we have struck and hurt our foot against, one is trop. said προσκόπτειν, *to stumble at*, a person or thing which highly displeases him ; thus the Jews are said προσκόψαι τῷ λίθῳ τοῦ προσκ. i. e. to have recoiled from Jesus as one who failed to meet their ideas of the Messiah (see πρόσκομμα), Ro. ix. 32 ; the enemies of Christianity are said πρ. τῷ λόγῳ, 1 Pet. ii. 8 [some (cf. R. V. mrg.) take πρ. here absolutely, and make τῷ λ. depend on ἀπειθέω, q. v. in a.]. (Exx. of this and other fig. uses of the word by Polyb., Diod., M. Antonin. are cited by Passow [L. and S.] s. v. and *Fritzsche*, Ep. ad Rom. ii. p. 362 sq.) *

4351   προσ-κυλίω : 1 aor. προσεκύλισα ; *to roll to* : τί τινι, Mt. xxvii. 60 [where Lchm. inserts ἐπί] ; τὶ ἐπί τι, Mk. xv. 46. (Arstph. vesp. 202.) *

4352   προσ-κυνέω, -ῶ ; impf. προσεκύνουν ; fut. προσκυνήσω ; 1 aor. προσεκύνησα ; fr. Aeschyl. and Hdt. down ; Sept. very often for הִשְׁתַּחֲוָה (to prostrate one's self) ; prop. *to kiss the hand to* (towards) one, in token of reverence : Hdt. 1, 134 ; [cf. *K. F. Hermann*, Gottesdienstl. Alterthümer d. Griech. § 21 ; esp. *Hoelemann*, Die bibl. Gestalt. d. Anbetung in his 'Bibelstudien' i. 106 sqq.] ; hence among the Orientals, esp. the Persians, *to fall upon the knees and touch the ground with the forehead* as an expression of profound reverence, [*to make a 'salam'*] ; Lat. *veneror* (Nep. Conon. 3, 3), *adoro* (Plin. h. n. 28, 5, 25 ; Suet. Vitell. 2) ; hence in the N. T. *by kneeling or prostration to do homage* (to one) or *make obeisance*, whether in order to express respect or to make supplication. It is used   **a.** of homage shown to men of superior rank : absol., Mt. xx. 20 (the Jewish high-priests are spoken of in Joseph. b. j. 4, 5, 2 as προσκυνούμενοι) ; πεσὼν ἐπὶ τοὺς πόδας προσεκύνησεν, Acts x. 25 ; τινί (acc. to the usage of later writ. ; cf. W. 36, 210 (197) ; [B. § 131, 4] ; *Lob.* ad Phryn. p. 463), Mt. ii. 2, 8 ; viii. 2 ; ix. 18 ; xiv. 33 ; xv. 25 ; [xviii. 26] ; xxviii. 9, 17 [RG] ; Mk. v. 6 [here WH Tr mrg. have the acc.] ; xv. 19 ; Jn. ix. 38 ; with πεσών preceding, Mt. ii. 11 ; iv. 9 ; ἐνώπιον τῶν ποδῶν τινος, Rev. iii. 9 ; [it may perh. be mentioned that some would bring in here Heb. xi. 21 προσεκύνησεν ἐπὶ τὸ ἄκρον τῆς ῥάβδου αὐτοῦ, explaining it by the (Egyptian) custom of bowing upon the magistrate's staff of office in taking an oath ; cf. *Chabas*, Mélanges Égypt. III. i. p. 80 cf p. 91 sq. ; but see below].   **b.** of homage rendered to God and the ascended Christ, to heavenly beings, and to demons : absol. (our *to worship*) [cf. W. 593 (552)], Jn. iv. 20 ; xii. 20 ; Acts viii. 27 ; xxiv. 11 ; Heb. xi. 21 [cf. above] ; Rev. xi. 1 ; πίπτειν καὶ προσκυνεῖν, Rev. v. 14 ; τινί, Jn. iv. 21, 23 ; Acts vii. 43 ; Heb. i. 6 ; Rev. iv. 10 ; vii. 11 ; xi. 16 ; xiv. 7 ; xvi. 2 ; xix. 4, 20 ; xxii. 8 sq. ; Rev. xiii. 4 G L T Tr WH (twice [the 2d time WH txt. only]) ; xiii. 15 G T Tr WH txt. ; xx. 4 Rec. ;   πεσὼν ἐπὶ

πρόσωπον προσκυνήσει τῷ θεῷ, 1 Co. xiv. 25 ; πίπτειν ἐπὶ τὰ πρόσωπα καὶ προσκυνεῖν τῷ θεῷ, Rev. xi. 16 ; preceded by πίπτειν ἔμπροσθεν τῶν ποδῶν τινος, Rev. xix. 10. in accordance with the usage of the older and better writ. with τινά or τί (cf. Matthiae § 412) : Mt. iv. 10 ; Lk. iv. 8 ; Rev. ix. 20 ; xiii. 12 ; xiv. 9, 11 ; also xiii. 4 (Rec. twice ; [WH mrg. once]), 8 [where Rec. dat.], 15 R L WH mrg. ; xx. 4ᵃ (where Rec. dat.), 4ᵇ (where Rᵉˡˢ dat.) ; Lk. xxiv. 52 R G L Tr br. WH reject ; (the Sept. also connects the word far more freq. with the dat. than with the acc. [cf. Hoelemann u. s. p. 116 sqq.]) ; ἐνώπιόν τινος, Lk. iv. 7 ; Rev. xv. 4.*

προσ-κυνητής, -οῦ, ὁ, (προσκυνέω), *a worshipper* : Jn. iv. 23. (Inscrr. ; [eccl. and] Byzant. writ.) *   **4353**

προσ-λαλέω, -ῶ ; 1 aor. inf. προσλαλῆσαι ; w. τινί, *to speak to* : Acts xiii. 43 ; sc. ὑμῖν [some say μοί (see παρακαλέω, I.)], Acts xxviii. 20. (Sap. xiii. 17 ; Theophr., Plut., Lcian.) *   **4354**

προσ-λαμβάνω : 2 aor. inf. προσλαβεῖν (Acts xxvii. 34 Rec. see below) ; Mid., pres. προσλαμβάνομαι ; 2 aor. προσελαβόμην ; fr. Aeschyl. and Hdt. down ; *to take to, take in addition*, [cf. πρός, IV. 2] ; in the N. T. found only in the Middle, *to take to one's self* [cf. B. § 135, 4] : τινά [cf. B. 160 sq. (140)] ;   **a.** *to take as one's companion* [A. V. *take one unto one*] : Acts xvii. 5 ; xviii. 26.   **b.** *to take by the hand* in order to lead aside [A. V. (simply) *take*] : Mt. xvi. 22 ; Mk. viii. 32.   **c.** to take or [so A. V.] *receive* into one's home, with the collateral idea of kindness : Philem. 12 R G, 17 ; into shelter, Acts xxviii. 2.   **d.** *to receive*, i. e. grant one access to one's heart ; to take into friendship and intercourse : Ro. xiv. 1 ; xv. 7 ; God and Christ are said προσλαβέσθαι (*to have received*) those whom, formerly estranged from them, they have reunited to themselves by the blessings of the gospel, Ro. xiv. 3 ; xv. 7 ; Clem. Rom. 1 Cor. 49, 6, (cf. Ps. xxvi. (xxvii.) 10 ; lxiv. (lxv.) 5 ; lxxii. (lxxiii.) 24).   **e.** *to take to one's self, to take* : μηδέν, [A. V. *having taken nothing*] i. e. no food, Acts xxvii. 33 ; τροφῆς, (a portion of [A.V. (not R.V.) 'some']) food, cf. B. 160 sq. (140), ibid. 36 (in vs. 34 G L T Tr WH have restored μεταλαβεῖν [so R. V. ('to take some food')] for προσλαβεῖν).*   **4355**

πρόσ-ληψις [L T Tr WH -λημψις, see M, μ], -εως, ἡ, (προσλαμβάνω), Vulg. *assumptio, a receiving* : τινός, into the kingdom of God, Ro. xi. 15. [(Plat., al.)]*   **4356**

προσ-μένω ; 1 aor. ptcp. προσμείνας, inf. προσμεῖναι ; fr. Aeschyl. and Hdt. down ;   **a.** *to remain with* [see πρός, IV. 3] : with a dat. of the pers. *to continue with* one, Mt. xv. 32 ; Mk. viii. 2 [here L WH mrg. om. Tr br. the dat.] ; τῷ κυρίῳ, to be steadfastly devoted to [A. V. *cleave unto*] the Lord, Acts xi. 23 (Sap. iii. 9 ; Joseph. antt. 14, 2, 1) ; τῇ χάριτι τοῦ θεοῦ, to hold fast to [A. V. *continue in*] the grace of God received in the gospel, Acts xiii. 43 G L T Tr WH ; δεήσεσι κ. προσευχαῖς, [A.V. *to continue in* supplications and prayers], 1 Tim. v. 5.   **b.** *to remain still* [cf. πρός, IV. 2], *stay, tarry* : Acts xviii. 18 ; foll. by ἐν with a dat. of place, 1 Tim. i. 3.*   **4357**

προσ-ορμίζω : 1 aor. pass. 3 pers. plur. προσωρμίσθησαν ;   **4358**

(ὅρμος a roadstead, anchorage) ; *to bring a ship to moorings* (Lcian. am. 11) ; esp. so in the mid., prop. *to take one's station near the shore* ; *to moor, come to anchor*, (Hdt., Dem., Plut., al.) ; the 1 aor. pass. is used in the same sense (Arr. exp. Alex. 6, 4 and 20 ; Ael. v. h. 8, 5 ; Dio Cass. 41, 48 ; 64, 1), Mk. vi. 53.*

4359 προσ-οφείλω ; *to owe besides* [see πρός, IV. 2] : σεαυτόν, i. e. *besides* what I have just asked of thee *thou owest to me even thine own self*, since it was by my agency that thou wast brought to faith in Christ, Philem. 19. (Thuc., Xen., Dem., Polyb., Plut.) *

4360 προσ-οχθίζω : 1 aor. προσώχθισα ; *to be wroth* or *displeased with* : τινί, Heb. iii. 10, 17, (fr. Ps. xciv. (xcv.) 10) ; not found besides exc. in the Sept. for גָּעַל, to loathe ; קִיא, to spue out ; קוּץ, to be disgusted with, etc. ; add, Sir. vi. 25 ; xxv. 2 ; xxxviii. 4 ; [l. 25 ; Test. xii Patr., test. Jud. § 18 ; Orac. Sibyll. 3, 272]. Profane writ. use ὀχθέω, more rarely ὀχθίζω. πρός denotes direction towards that with which we are displeased [πρός, IV. 1]. Cf. *Bleek*, Br. an d. Hebr. ii. 1 p. 441 sq.*

see 4363 προσ-παίω (for the more com. προσπταίω) : 1 aor. προσέπαισα ; *to beat against, strike upon* : intrans. προσέπαισαν τῇ οἰκίᾳ, Mt. vii. 25 Lchm. ; but cf. B. 40 (34) n. (Schol. ad Aeschyl. Prom. 885 ; [Soph. frag. 310 var.] ; Byzant. writ.) *

4361 πρόσ-πεινος, -ον, (πεῖνα hunger [cf. πεινάω]), *very* (lit. *besides*, in accession, [cf. πρός, IV. 2 ; al. (cf. R. V.) do not recognize any i n t e n s i v e force in πρός here]) *hungry* : Acts x. 10. Not found elsewhere.*

4362 προσ-πήγνυμι : 1 aor. ptcp. προσπήξας ; *to fasten to* [see πρός, IV. 4] : Acts ii. 23 [here absol., of crucifixion]. (Dio Cass., al.) *

4363 προσ-πίπτω : impf. προσέπιπτον ; 2 aor., 3 pers. sing. προσέπεσε, 3 pers. plur. (Mt. vii. 25) προσέπεσον R G. -σαν T Tr WH [see πίπτω, init.], ptcp. fem. προσπεσοῦσα ; fr. Hom. down ; prop. *to fall towards, fall upon*, [πρός, IV. 1] i. e. **1.** *to fall forward, to fall down, prostrate one's self before*, in homage or supplication : with the dat. of a pers., at one's feet, Mk. iii. 11 ; v. 33 ; Lk. viii. 28, 47 ; Acts xvi. 29, (Ps. xciv. (xcv.) 6 ; Polyb., Plut., al.) ; τοῖς γόνασί τινος, Lk. v. 8 (Eur. Or. 1332 ; Plut.) ; πρὸς τοὺς πόδας τινός, Mk. vii. 25. **2.** *to rush upon, beat against* : τῇ οἰκίᾳ (of winds beating against a house), Mt. vii. 25 [not Lchm. ; cf. προσπαίω].*

see 4364 St. προσ-ποιέω ; Mid., pres. ptcp. προσποιούμενος (see below) ; impf. 3 pers. sing. προσεποιεῖτο (Lk. xxiv. 28, for which L txt. T Tr WH give the 1 aor. προσεποιήσατο) ; in prose writ. fr. Hdt. down ; *to add to* [cf. Germ. hinzumachen] ; mid. **1.** *to take* or *claim* (a thing) *to one's self.* **2.** *to conform one's self to a thing*, or rather *to affect to one's self* ; therefore *to pretend*, foll. by an inf. [A. V. *made as though he would* etc.], Lk. xxiv. 28 ; κατέγραφεν εἰς τὴν γῆν μὴ προσποιούμενος, Jn. viii, 6 acc. to codd. E G H K etc. [cf. Matthaei (ed. 1803) ad loc.]. (So in Thuc., Xen., Plat., Dem., al. ; Diod. 15, 46 ; Philo in Flacc. § 6 ; [in § 12 foll. by ptcp. ; Joseph. c. Ap. 1, 1] ; Ael. v. h. 8, 5 ; Plut. Timol. 5 ; [Test. xii. Patr., test. Jos. § 3].) *

προσ-πορεύομαι ; *to draw near, approach* : with a dat. of **4365** the person approached, Mk. x. 35. (Sept. ; Aristot., Polyb.) *

προσ-ρήγνυμι, and in later writ. [W. 22] προσρήσσω ; **4366** 1 aor. προσέρρηξα R G L, προσέρηξα T Tr WH (see P, ρ) ; *to break against, break by dashing against* : παιδία ἀπολεῖς προσρηγνὺς πέτραις, Joseph. antt. 9, 4, 6 ; λέοντα προσρήξας τῇ γῇ, 6, 9, 3 ; intraus. (cf. W. § 38, 1 ; [B. § 130, 4]) : ὁ ποταμὸς τῇ οἰκίᾳ, Lk. vi. 48, [49 ; Mt. vii. 27 L mrg.] ; in pass. τῇ ἄκρᾳ ᾗ τὰ κύματα προσρήσσεται, Antonin. 4, 49.*

προσ-τάσσω : 1 aor. προσέταξα ; pf. pass. ptcp. προστε- **4367** ταγμένος ; fr. [Aeschyl. and] Hdt. down ; **1.** *to assign* or *ascribe to, join to.* **2.** *to enjoin, order, prescribe, command* : Sept. for צִוָּה ; absol. καθὼς προσέταξε, Lk. v. 14 ; with the dat. of a pers., Mt. i. 24 ; xxi. 6 R G T ; τί, Mt. viii. 4 ; Mk. i. 44 ; τινί τι, pass. Acts x. 33 ; foll. by an acc. w. inf. Acts x. 48 ; *to appoint, to define*, pass. προστεταγμένοι καιροί, Acts xvii. 26 G L (ed. ster. [larger ed. πρὸς τεταγ.]) T Tr WH, for the Rec. προτεταγμένοι. [SYN. : see κελεύω, fin.] *

προστάτις, -ιδος, ἡ, (fem. of the noun προστάτης, fr. **4368** προΐστημι) : **a.** prop. *a woman set over others.* **b.** *a female guardian, protectress, patroness*, caring for the affairs of others and aiding them with her resources [A. V. *succourer*] : Ro. xvi. 2 ; cf. Passow on the word and under προστάτης fin. ; [*Schürer*, Die Gemeindeverfassung der Juden in Rom, u.s.w. (Leip. 1879) p. 31 ; *Heinrici*, Die Christengemeinde Korinths, in Hilgenfeld's Zeitschr. for 1876, p. 517 sq.].*

προσ-τίθημι : impf. 3 pers. sing. προσετίθει (Acts ii. 47) ; **4369** 1 aor. προσέθηκα ; 2 aor. προσέθην, impv. πρόσθες (Lk. xvii. 5), inf. προσθεῖναι, ptcp. προσθείς ; Pass., impf. 3 pers. plur. προσετίθεντο ; 1 fut. προστεθήσομαι ; 2 aor. mid. προσεθέμην ; fr. Hom. Od. 9, 305 down ; Sept. very often for יָסַף, also for אָסַף, etc. ; **1.** prop. *to put to.* **2.** *to add*, i. e. *join to, gather with any company*, the number of one's followers or companions : τινὰ τῇ ἐκκλησίᾳ, Acts ii. 47 [R G] ; τῷ κυρίῳ, Acts v. 14 ; xi. 24 ; sc. τῷ κυρίῳ, or τοῖς πιστεύουσιν, Acts ii. 41 ; Hebraistically, προσετέθη πρὸς τοὺς πατέρας αὐτοῦ (Judg. ii. 10 ; 1 Macc. ii. 69), *he was gathered to his fathers* assembled in Sheol (which is בֵּית מוֹעֵד לְכָל־חָי, the house of assembly for all the living, Job xxx. 23), Acts xiii. 36 (others explain it, *he was added to the bodies of his ancestors, buried with them in a common tomb* ; but cf. Knobel on Gen. xxv. 8 ; [*Böttcher*, De inferis, p. 54 sqq.]) ; i. q. *to add* viz. to what one already possesses : τί, Lk. xvii. 5 [A.V. here *increase*] ; pass., Mt. vi. 33 ; Lk. xii. 31 ; Mk. iv. 24 ; Heb. xii. 19 (μὴ προστεθῆναι αὐτοῖς λόγον, R. V. *that no word more should be spoken to them*)] ; — to what already exists : ὁ νόμος προσετέθη, was added to (supervened upon) sc. the ἐπαγγελία, Gal. iii. 19 R L T Tr WH ; τὶ ἐπί τινι, some thing to (upon) a thing (which has preceded [cf. ἐπί, B. 2 d.]), Lk. iii. 20 ; τὶ ἐπί τι, to a thing that it may thereby be increased, Mt. vi. 27 ; Lk. xii. 25. In imitation of the Hebr. (יָסַף) the mid. (in the Sept. the active also) foll. by an inf. signifies (*to add* i. e.) *to go on to do a thing*, for *to do further, do again*, (as

Gen. iv. 2 ; viii. 12 ; xviii. 29): προσέθετο πέμψαι (וַיֹּסֶף לִשְׁלֹחַ), he continued to send (as he had already sent), Lk. xx. 11, 12, (i. q. πάλιν ἀπέστειλεν, Mk. xii. 4) ; προσέθετο συλλαβεῖν καὶ Πέτρον, he besides apprehended Peter also [A.V. he proceeded etc.], Acts xii. 3 ; in the same way also the ptcp. is used with a finite verb : προσθεὶς εἶπεν, i. e. he further spake [A. V. he added and spake], Lk. xix. 11 (προσθεῖσα ἔτεκεν, Gen. xxxviii. 5 ; προσθέμενος ἔλαβε γυναῖκα, Gen. xxv. 1) ; cf. W. § 54, 5 ; B. § 144, 14.*

4370 προσ-τρέχω ; 2 aor. act. ptcp. προσδραμών; to run to : Mk. ix. 15 ; x. 17 ; Acts viii. 30. (From Arstph. and Xen. down ; for רוּץ in Gen. xviii. 2, etc.) *

4371 προσφάγιον, -ου, τό, (προσφαγεῖν [cf. πρός, IV. 2]), i. q. ὄψον (on which see ὀψάριον), any thing eaten with bread (Moeris [ed. Piers. p. 274, 1]: ὄψον ἀττικῶς, προσφάγιον ἑλληνικῶς) : spoken of fish boiled or broiled, Jn. xxi. 5 (Schol., Lexx., [Moschion 55 p. 26 ; Roehl, Inscrr. graec. 395 a. 12]). Cf. Fischer, De vitiis lexx. etc. p. 697 sq. ; Sturz, Dial. Maced. et Alex. p. 191.*

4372 πρόσφατος, -ον, (fr. πρό and σφάω or σφάζω ; cf. Delitzsch, Com. on Hebr. [as below] p. 478 ; [cf. Lob. Technol. p. 106]) ; 1. prop. lately slaughtered, freshly killed : Hom. Il. 24, 757. 2. univ. recently or very lately made, new : ὁδός, Heb. x. 20 (so fr. Aeschyl. down ; φίλος πρόσφατος, Sir. ix. 10 ; οὐκ ἔστι πᾶν πρόσφατον ὑπὸ τὸν ἥλιον, Eccl. i. 9). Cf. Lob. ad Phryn. p. 374 sq.*

4373 προσφάτως, adv., (see the preceding word), lately : Acts xviii. 2. (Deut. xxiv. 7 (5) ; Ezek. xi. 3 ; Judith iv. 3, 5 ; 2 Macc. xiv. 36 ; Polyb., Alciphr., al.) *

4374 προσ-φέρω ; impf. προσέφερον ; 1 aor. προσήνεγκα ; 2 aor. προσήνεγκον ; pf. προσενήνοχα (Heb. xi. 17) ; Pass., pres. προσφέρομαι ; 1 aor. προσηνέχθην ; [see reff. s. v. φέρω] ; fr. [Pind.], Aeschyl., and Hdt. down ; Sept. often for הִקְרִיב, also for הֵבִיא, הִגִּישׁ, etc., sometimes also for הֶעֱלָה where offering sacrifices is spoken of (as 1 K. xviii. 36 Compl. ; 2 Chr. xxix. 7 ; Jer. xiv. 12) ; 1. to bring to, lead to : τινά τινι, one to a person who can heal him or is ready to show him some other kindness, Mt. iv. 24 ; viii. 16 ; ix. 2, 32 ; xiv. 35 ; xvii. 16 ; Mk. ii. 4 (sc. τινά) T WH Tr mrg. ; x. 13 ; Lk. xviii. 15 ; pass. in Mt. xii. 22 [where L WH txt. act.] ; xviii. 24 R G T ; xix. 13 ; — one to a person who is to judge him : Lk. xxiii. 14 ; τινὰ ἐπὶ τὰς συναγωγὰς καὶ τὰς ἀρχάς, Lk. xii. 11 [W. § 52, 3] (where T Tr txt. WH εἰσφέρωσιν). προσφέρω τι, to bring or present a thing, Mt. xxv. 20 ; τί τινι, to reach or hand a thing to one, Mt. xxii. 19 ; Lk. xxiii. 36 [here A.V. offering]; τὶ τῷ στόματί τινος, to put to, Jn. xix. 29 ; a thing to one that he may accept it, to offer : χρήματα, Acts viii. 18 ; δῶρα, Mt. ii. 11 ; used, as often in the Sept., of persons offering sacrifices, gifts, prayers to God (cf. Kurtz, Brief a. d. Hebr. p. 154 sqq.) : τῷ θεῷ σφάγια καὶ θυσίας, Acts vii. 42 ; θυσίαν, Heb. xi. 4 ; λατρείαν, Jn. xvi. 2 ; προσφέρειν δῶρον or δῶρα sc. τῷ θεῷ, Mt. v. 23, 24 ; viii. 4 ; Heb. viii. 3, 4 ; ix. 9 ; θυσίαν, Heb. x. 12 ; plur., Heb. x. 1, 11 ; [pass. ibid. 2 ; θυσίας (R G -αν) καὶ προσφοράς (R G -ρὰν) καὶ ὁλοκαυτώματα καὶ περὶ ἁμαρτίας, ibid. 8] ; δῶρά τε καὶ θυσίας ὑπὲρ ἁμαρτιῶν, to expiate [see ὑπέρ, I. 4] sins, Heb. v. 1 ; αἷμα ὑπὲρ ἑαυτοῦ καὶ τῶν τοῦ

λαοῦ ἀγνοημάτων, Heb. ix. 7 ; τὴν προσφορὰν ὑπὲρ ἑνὸς ἑκάστου, pass. Acts xxi. 26 ; προσφέρειν used absol. [cf. W. 593 (552)] : περί τινος, on account of [see περί, I. c. β.], Mk. i. 44 ; Lk. v. 14 ; περὶ τοῦ λαοῦ περὶ [R G ὑπὲρ (see περί, I. c. δ.)] ἁμαρτιῶν, to offer expiatory sacrifices for the people, Heb. v. 3 ; τινά, sc. τῷ θεῷ, to offer up, i. e. immolate, one, Heb. xi. 17 ; ἑαυτόν, of Christ, Heb. vii. 27 T Tr mrg. WH mrg. ; ix. [14], 25 ; προσενεχθείς (the passive pointing to the fact that what he suffered was due to God's will) ibid. 28, (it is hardly to be found in native Grk. writ. used of offering sacrifices ; but in Joseph. antt. 3, 9, 3, we have ἄρνα καὶ ἔριφον) ; πρός τινα (God) δεήσεις τε καὶ ἱκετηρίας, Heb. v. 7 (προσφέρειν δέησιν, Achill. Tat. 7, 1 ; τῷ θεῷ εὐχήν, Joseph. b. j. 3, 8, 3). 2. The pass. with the dat. signifies to be borne towards one, to attack, assail ; then figuratively, to behave one's self towards one, deal with one : ὡς υἱοῖς ὑμῖν προσφέρεται ὁ θεός, Heb. xii. 7 (very often so in Attic writ. fr. Thuc. and Xen. down ; Philo de Josepho § 10 ; de ebrietate § 16 ; Joseph. b. j. 7, 8, 1 ; Ael. v. h. 12, 27 ; Hdian. 1, 13, 14 [7 ed. Bekk.]).*

4375 προσφιλής, -ές, (πρός and φιλέω), acceptable, pleasing, [A. V. lovely] : Phil. iv. 8. (From [Aeschyl. and] Hdt. down ; Sir. iv. 7 ; xx. 13.) *

4376 προσ-φορά, -ᾶς, ἡ, (προσφέρω), offering ; i. e. 1. the act of offering, a bringing to, (Plat., Aristot., Polyb.). 2. that which is offered, a gift, a present, (Soph. O. C. 1270 ; Theophr. char. 30 sub fin.). In the N. T. a sacrifice [A.V. offering], whether bloody or not : Acts xxi. 26 ; xxiv. 17 ; Eph. v. 2 ; Heb. x. 5, 8, 14, (Sir. xiv. 11 ; xxxi. (xxxiv.) 21 (19) ; xxxii. (xxxv.) 1, 6 (8) ; once for מִנְחָה, Ps. xxxix. (xl.) 7) ; περὶ ἁμαρτίας, offering for sin, expiatory sacrifice, Heb. x. 18 ; with the gen. of the object, τοῦ σώματος Ἰησοῦ Χρ. Heb. x. 10 ; τῶν ἐθνῶν, the sacrifice which I offer in turning the Gentiles to God, Ro. xv. 16.*

4377 προσ-φωνέω, -ῶ ; impf. 3 pers. sing. προσεφώνει ; 1 aor. προσεφώνησα ; 1. to call to ; to address by calling : absol., Lk. xiii. 12 ; xxiii. 20 (where L WH add αὐτοῖς) ; Acts xxi. 40, (Hom. Od. 5, 159 etc.) ; with the dat. of a pers. [cf. W. 36], Mt. xi. 16 ; Lk. vii. 32 ; Acts xxii. 2, (Diog. Laërt. 7, 7). 2. to call to one's self, summon : τινά (so the better Grk. writ. ; see Matthiae § 402 b. ; [W. § 52, 4, 14]), Lk. vi. 13.*

4378 πρόσ-χυσις, -εως, ἡ, (προσχέω to pour on), a pouring or sprinkling upon, affusion : τοῦ αἵματος, Heb. xi. 28. (Eccles. writ. [e. g. Just. M. apol. 2, 12 p. 50 d.].) *

4379 προσ-ψαύω, to touch : τινί [cf. W. § 52, 4, 14], a thing, Lk. xi. 46. (Pind., Soph., Byzant. writ.)*

4380 προσωπολημπτέω (L T Tr WH -λημπτέω [see M, μ]), -ῶ ; a Hellenistic verb (derived fr. the foll. word [cf. Win. 33, 101 (96)]), to respect the person (i. e. the external condition of a man), to have respect of persons : Jas. ii. 9.*

4381 προσωπο-λήπτης (L T Tr WH -λήμπτης [see M, μ]), -ου, ὁ, (a Hellenistic formation fr. πρόσωπον and λαμβάνω ; see λαμβάνω, I. 4 p. 370b bot.), an accepter [A. V. respecter] of persons (Vulg. personarum acceptor) : Acts x. 34. Not found elsewhere [exc. in Chrysost.].*

4382   προσωποληψία (L T Tr WH -λημψία [see M, μ]), -as, ή, (a Hellenistic formation; [see προσωπολήπτης]), *respect of persons* (Vulg. *personarum acceptio*), *partiality*, the fault of one who when called on to require or to give judgment has respect to the outward circumstances of men and not to their intrinsic merits, and so prefers, as the more worthy, one who is rich, high-born, or powerful, to another who is destitute of such gifts: Ro. ii. 11; Eph. vi. 9; Col. iii. 25; plur. (which relates to the various occasions and instances in which this fault shows itself [cf. W. 176 (166); B. § 123, 2, 2]), Jas. ii. 1. (Eccles. writ.)*

4383   πρόσωπον, -ου, τό, (fr. πρός and ὤψ, cf. μέτωπον), fr. Hom. down; Sept. hundreds of times for פָּנִים, also for אַפַּיִם, etc.;   **1. a.** *the face*, i. e. the anterior part of the human head: Mt. vi. 16, 17; xvii. 2; xxvi. 67; Mk. xiv. 65; Lk. [ix. 29]; xxii. 64 [T Tr WH om. Lchm. br. the cl.]; Acts vi. 15; 2 Co. iii. 7, 13, 18; [xi. 20]; Rev. iv. 7; ix. 7; x. 1; τὸ πρόσωπον τῆς γενέσεως, the face with which one is born [A. V. *his natural face*], Jas. i. 23; πίπτειν ἐπὶ πρόσ. [cf. W. § 27, 1 n.; 122 (116)] and ἐπὶ τὸ πρόσ., Mt. xvii. 6; xxvi. 39; Lk. v. 12; xvii. 16; 1 Co. xiv. 25; [Rev. vii. 11 Rec.; πίπτ. ἐπὶ τὰ πρόσ., Rev. xi. 16; vii. 11 G L T Tr WH], unknown to one by face, i. e. *personally unknown*, Gal. i. 22; bereaved of one προσώπῳ, οὐ καρδία [A. V. *in presence, not in heart*], 1 Th. ii. 17; κατὰ πρόσωπον, *in* or *towards* (i. e. so as to look into) *the face*, i. e. *before, in the presence of*, [see κατά, II. 1 c.]: opp. to ἀπών, 2 Co. x. 1; with τινός added, *before* (the face of) *one*, Lk. ii. 31; Acts iii. 13; ἔχω τινὰ κατὰ πρόσωπον, i. e. to have one present in person [A. V. *face to face*], Acts xxv. 16; ἀντέστην κατὰ πρόσωπον, I resisted him to the face (with a suggestion of fearlessness), Gal. ii. 11, (κατὰ πρόσωπον λέγειν τοὺς λόγους, Polyb. 25, 5, 2; add Job xvi. 8; but in Deut. vii. 24; ix. 2; Judg. ii. 14; 2 Chr. xiii. 7, ἀντιστῆναι κατὰ πρόσ. simply denotes to *stand against, resist, withstand*); τὰ κατὰ πρόσ. the things before the face, i. e. open, known to all, 2 Co. x. 7. Expressions modelled after the Hebrew: ὁρᾶν τὸ πρόσωπόν τινος, *to see one's face*, see him personally, Acts xx. 25; Col. ii. 1; ἰδεῖν, 1 Th. ii. 17; iii. 10; θεωρεῖν, Acts xx. 38 [cf. θεωρέω, 2 a.]; particularly, βλέπειν τὸ πρόσ. τοῦ θεοῦ (see βλέπω, 1 b. β.), Mt. xviii. 10; ὁρᾶν τ. πρ. τ. θεοῦ (see ὁράω, 1), Rev. xxii. 4; ἐμφανισθῆναι τῷ προσ. τοῦ θεοῦ, *to appear before the face of God*, spoken of Christ, the eternal priest, who has entered into the heavenly sanctuary, Heb. ix. 24; in imitation of the Hebr. פָּנִים אֶל־פָּנִים we have the phrase πρόσωπον πρὸς πρόσωπον, face (turned [see πρός, I. 1 a. p. 541ᵇ]) *to face* (εἶδόν τινα, Gen. xxxii. 30; Judg. vi. 22): trop. βλέπω sc. τὸν θεόν, see God *face to face*, i. e. discern perfectly his nature, will, purposes, 1 Co. xiii. 12; a person is said to be sent or to go πρὸ προσώπου τινός ("לִפְנֵי פ") [cf. W. § 65, 4 b. fin.; B. 319 (274)], i. e. *before one*, to announce his coming and remove the obstacles from his way, Mt. xi. 10; Mk. i. 2; Lk. i. 76; vii. 27, (Mal. iii. 1); ix. 52; x. 1; πρὸ προσ. τινός, (of time) *before a thing*, Acts xiii. 24 (so לִפְנֵי in

Am. i. 1; Zech. viii. 10; where the Sept. simply πρό [cf. πρό, b. p. 536ᵇ bot.]). πρὸς φωτισμὸν τῆς γνώσεως τῆς δόξης τοῦ θεοῦ ἐν προσώπῳ Ἰησοῦ Χριστοῦ, that we may bring forth into the light the knowledge of the glory of God as it shines in the face of Jesus Christ, 2 Co. iv. 6 (Paul really means, the majesty of God manifest in the person of Christ; but the signification of πρόσωπον is '*face*,' and Paul is led to use the word by what he had said in iii. 13 of the brightness visible in the *face* of Moses). **b.** *countenance, look* (Lat. *vultus*), i. e. the face so far forth as it is the organ of sight, and (by its various movements and changes) the index of the inward thoughts and feelings: κλίνειν τὸ πρόσ. εἰς τὴν γῆν, to bow the face to the earth (a characteristic of fear and anxiety), Lk. xxiv. 5; Hebraistic phrases relating to the direction of the countenance, the look: τὸ πρόσωπον τοῦ κυρίου ἐπί τινα, sc. ἐστίν, the face of the Lord is (turned) upon one, i. e. he looks upon and watches him, 1 Pet. iii. 12 (fr. Ps. xxxiii. (xxxiv.) 17); στηρίζειν τὸ πρόσ. (Hebr. שׂוּם or נָתַן פָּנִים; cf. *Gesenius, Thes.* ii. p. 1109 on the same form of expression in Syriac, Arabic, Persian, Turkish) τοῦ πορεύεσθαι εἰς with an acc. of the place [A.V. *steadfastly to set one's face to go* etc. (see στηρίζω, a.)], Lk. ix. 51; moreover, even τὸ πρόσ. τινός ἐστι πορευόμενον εἰς with acc. of place, ib. 53 (τὸ πρόσωπόν σου πορευόμενον ἐν μέσῳ αὐτῶν, 2 S. xvii. 11); ἀπὸ προσώπου τινός φεύγειν, *to flee* in terror *from the face* (Germ. *Anblick*) *of* one enraged, Rev. xx. 11; κρύπτειν τινά etc. (see κρύπτω, a.), Rev. vi. 16; ἀνάψυξις ἀπὸ προσώπου θεοῦ, the refreshing which comes from the bright and smiling countenance of God to one seeking comfort, Acts iii. 20 (19); on 2 Th. i. 9 see ἀπό, p. 59ᵃ mid.; μετὰ τοῦ προσώπου σου, sc. ὄντα, in the presence of thy joyous countenance [see μετά, I. 2 b. β.], Acts ii. 28 (fr. Ps. xv. (xvi.) 11); εἰς πρόσωπον τῶν ἐκκλησιῶν, turned unto [i. e. *in* (R.V.)] the face of the churches as the witnesses of your zeal, 2 Co. viii. 24; ἵνα ἐκ πολλῶν προσώπων ... διὰ πολλῶν εὐχαριστηθῇ, that from many faces (turned toward God and expressing the devout and grateful feelings of the soul) thanks may be rendered by many (accordingly, both ἐκ πολλ. προσ. and διὰ πολλῶν belong to εὐχαριστηθῇ [cf. Meyer ad loc.; see below]), 2 Co. i. 11. ἀπὸ προσώπου τινός ("מִפְּנֵי פ), *from the sight* or *presence of one*, Acts v. 41; vii. 45 [here A.V. *before the face*; Rev. xii. 14]; ἐν προσώπῳ Χριστοῦ, in the presence of Christ, i. e. Christ looking on (and approving), 2 Co. ii. 10 (Prov. viii. 30); [some would render πρόσωπον here and in i. 11 above *person* (cf. R.V.):— here nearly i. q. *on the part of* (Vulg. *in persona Christi*); there i. q. 'an individual' (Plut. de garrul. 13 p. 509 b.; Epict. diss. 1, 2, 7; Polyb. 8, 13, 5; 12, 27, 10; 27, 6, 4; Clem. Rom. 1 Cor. 1, 1; 47,6; Phryn. p. 379, and Lobeck's note p. 380)]. **c.** Hebraistically, *the appearance one presents* by his wealth or poverty, his rank or low condition; *outward circumstances, external condition*; so used in expressions which denote *to regard the person* in one's judgment and treatment of men: βλέπειν εἰς πρόσωπον ἀνθρώπων, Mt. xxii. 16; Mk. xii. 14; θαυμάζειν πρόσωπα, Jude 16; λαμβάνειν πρόσωπον (τινός), Lk. xx. 21; Gal. ii. 6, (on which see βλέπω, 2 c., θαυμάζω, λαμβάνω, I. 4). καυχᾶσθαι ἐν προσώπῳ καὶ οὐ καρδίᾳ, to glory in those things which they simulate in *look*, viz. piety, love, righteousness, although their *heart* is devoid of these virtues, 2 Co. v. 12, cf. 1 S. xvi. 7. **2.** *the outward appearance* of inanimate things [A. V. *face* (exc. in Jas. as below)]: τοῦ ἄνθους, Jas. i. 11; τοῦ οὐρανοῦ, τῆς γῆς, Mt. xvi. 3 [here Tbr. WH reject the pass.]; Lk. xii. 56 (Ps. ciii. (civ.) 30); (so in Lat., *naturae vultus*, Ovid. metam. 1, 6; *maris facies*, Verg. Aen. 5, 768; on this use of the noun *facies* see Gell. noctes atticae 13, 29); *surface*: τῆς γῆς, Lk. xxi. 35; Acts xvii. 26 [on the omitted art. here cf. πᾶς, I. 1 c.], (Gen. ii. 6; xi. 8).*

4384   **προ-τάσσω**: pf. pass. ptcp. προτεταγμένος; **1.** *to place before*. **2.** *to appoint before, define beforehand*: χρόνον, Soph. Trach. 164; καιρούς, pass. Acts xvii. 26 Rec. (see προστάσσω, 2); νόμους, pass. 2 Macc. viii. 36.*

4385   **προ-τείνω**: 1 aor. προέτεινα; [fr. Hdt. down]; *to stretch forth, stretch out*: ὡς προέτειναν [Rec. -νεν] αὐτὸν τοῖς ἱμᾶσιν, when they had stretched him out for the thongs i. e. to receive the blows of the thongs, (by tying him up to a beam or a pillar; for it appears from vs. 29 that Paul had already been bound), Acts xxii. 25 [W. § 31 init.; al. (cf. R. V. txt.) 'with the thongs' (cf. ἱμάς)].*

4386 &   **πρότερος**, -α, -ον, (compar. of πρό), [fr. Hom. down], *be-*
4387   *fore, prior*; of time, *former*: ἡ προτέρα ἀναστροφή, Eph. iv. 22. Neut. adverbially, *before* (something else is or was done): Jn. vii. 51 R G; 2 Co. i. 15; opp. to ἔπειτα, Heb. vii. 27; *before* i. e. *aforetime, in time past*: Jn. vii. 50 [L Tr WH]; Heb. iv. 6; and R G in 1 Tim. i. 13; also τὸ πρότερον (contrasting the past with the present [cf. πάλαι, 1 fin.]), Jn. vi. 62; ix. 8, and L T Tr WH in 1 Tim. i. 13, (1 Macc. iii. 46; v. 1; xi. 34, 39; Deut. ii. 12; Josh. xi. 10; Hdt. 7, 75; Xen., Plat.); i. q. our *the first time*, Gal. iv. 13 (on which cf. Meyer); it is placed between the art. and the noun, as αἱ πρότερον ἡμέραι, the former days, Heb. x. 32; αἱ πρότ. ἐπιθυμίαι, the lusts which you formerly indulged, 1 Pet. i. 14.*

see   **προ-τίθημι**: 2 aor. mid. προεθέμην; [fr. Hom. down];
4388 St.   **1.** *to place before, to set forth*, [cf. πρό, d. a.]; spec. *to set forth to be looked at, expose to view*: Ex. xl. 4; 4 Macc. viii. 11; Ael. v.h. 14, 8; and often in the mid. in this sense: ποτήρια ἀργύρεά τε καὶ χρύσεα, his own cups, Hdt. 3, 148; *to expose to public view*, in which sense it is the technical term with profane authors in speaking of the bodies of the dead, [*to let lie in state*], (cf. Passow s. v. I. 2; [L. and S. s. v. II. 1]; Stallbaum on Plat. Phaedo p.115 e.; [Krüger on Thuc. 2, 34, 1]); the mid. points to the owner of the thing exposed: so with τινά and a pred. acc. Ro. iii. 25 (the mid. seems to denote that it was his own Son whom he thus "set forth"; cf. viii. 32). **2.** Mid. *to set before one's self, propose to one's self*; *to purpose, determine*, (Plato, Polyb., al.): foll. by the inf. Ro. i. 13; with an acc. of the thing and ἐν αὐτῷ [(sic); see αὐτοῦ] added, *in himself* (W. § 38, 6; [cf. p. 152 (144)]), Eph. i. 9; [al. (reading ἐν αὐτῷ with L T Tr WH) render '*in him*,' i. e. (probably) Christ].*

προ-τρέπω: 1 aor. mid. ptcp. προτρεψάμενος; *to urge*   **4389**
forwards, exhort, encourage, (often so by Attic writ., both in the act. and the mid.): Acts xviii. 27. (Sap. xiv. 18; 2 Macc. xi. 7. [From Hom. down.]) *

προ-τρέχω: 2 aor. προέδραμον; *to run before, to outrun*:   **4390**
Jn. xx. 4; with ἔμπροσθεν added, i. e. ahead, in advance, [R. V. 'to run *on* before'], cf. W. 603 (561); [B. § 151, 27], Lk. xix. 4; ἔμπρ. with the gen. of a pers. Tob. xi. 2. (1 S. viii. 11; Xen., Isocr., Theophr., al.) *

προ-ϋπ-άρχω: impf. προϋπῆρχον; fr. Thuc. and Plato   **4391**
down; *to be before, exist previously*: with a ptcp. Acts viii. 9; προϋπῆρχον ὄντες, Lk. xxiii. 12; cf. *Bornemann*, Schol. ad h. l.; W. 350 (328); [B. § 144, 14].*

πρό-φασις, -εως, ἡ, (προφαίνω, i. e. prop. 'to cause to   **4392**
shine before' [or 'forth'; but many derive πρόφασις directly fr. πρό-φημι]), fr. Hom. down;   **a.** *a pretext* (alleged reason, pretended cause): τῆς πλεονεξίας, such as covetousness is wont to use, 1 Th. ii. 5 ([A. V. *cloak of covetousness*] the meaning being, that he had never misused his apostolic office in order to disguise or to hide avaricious designs); πρόφασιν ἔχειν (a phrase freq. in Grk. auth., cf. Passow s. v. πρ. 1 b. vol. ii. p. 1251ᵇ; [L. and S. s. v. I. 3 e.]) περὶ τῆς ἁμαρτίας, Jn. xv. 22 [A. V. mrg. R.V. *excuse*].   **b.** *show*: προφάσει ὡς κτλ. [A. V.] *under color as though they would* etc. Acts xxvii. 30; προφάσει, [A. V. *for a pretence*], in pretence, ostensibly: Mt. xxiii. 14 (13) Rec.; Mk. xii. 40; Lk. xx. 47; Phil. i. 18.*

προ-φέρω; [fr. Hom. down]; *to bring forth*: τὶ ἔκ τινος,   **4393**
Lk. vi. 45.*

προφητεία, -ας, ἡ, (προφητεύω, q. v.), Hebr. נְבוּאָה,   **4394**
prophecy, i. e. discourse emanating from divine inspiration and declaring the purposes of God, whether by reproving and admonishing the wicked, or comforting the afflicted, or revealing things hidden; esp. by foretelling future events. Used in the N. T. — of. the utterances of the O. T. prophets: Mt. xiii. 14; 2 Pet. i. 20, 21 (on this pass. see γίνομαι, 5 e. a.); — of the prediction of events relating to Christ's kingdom and its speedy triumph, together with the consolations and admonitions pertaining thereto: Rev. xi. 6; xxii. 19; τὸ πνεῦμα τῆς προφητείας, the spirit of prophecy, the divine mind, to which the prophetic faculty is due, Rev. xix. 10; οἱ λόγοι τῆς προφητείας, Rev. i. 3; xxii. 7, 10, 18; — of the endowment and speech of the Christian teachers called προφῆται (see προφήτης, II. 1 f.): Ro. xii. 6; 1 Co. xii. 10; xiii. 2; xiv. 6, 22; plur. the gifts and utterances of these prophets, 1 Co. xiii. 8; 1 Th. v. 20; — spec. of the prognostication of those achievements which one set apart to teach the gospel will accomplish for the kingdom of Christ, 1 Tim. iv. 14; plur. i. 18 [see προάγω, 2 a. and cf. the Comm.]. ([Sept., Joseph.]; among native Grk. writ. used only by Lcian. Alex. 40, 60; [to which add inscrr. (see L. and S. s. v. I.)].)*

προφητεύω; fut. προφητεύσω; impf. προεφήτευον (Acts   **4395**
xix. 6 R G) and ἐπροφήτευον (ibid. L T Tr WH; [1 K. xxii. 12]; Jer. [ii. 8]; xxiii. 21; xxv. 13); 1 aor. προεφήτευσα (R G in Mt. vii. 22; xi. 13; xv. 7; Mk. vii. 6; Lk. i. 67; [Jn. xi. 51; Jude 14]) and ἐπροφήτευσα (which form

cod. Sin. gives everywh., and T Tr WH have everywh. restored, and Lchm. also with the single exception of Jude 14; add, Sir. xlviii. 13; 1 Esdr. vi. 1; Jer. xxxiii. (xxvi.) 9, 11, 20; xxxv. (xxviii.) 8; xxxvi. (xxix.) 31; the Alexandrian translators more com. use the forms προεφήτευον, προεφήτευσα, pf. ptcp. προπεφητευκώς, Eus. h. e. 5, 17; pf. pass. inf. προπεφητεῦσθαι, Clem. Alex. strom. p. 603; on the forms used by Justin M. see Otto's prolegg. to his works, I. i. p. lxxv. ed. 3; cf. [WH. App. p. 162; Veitch s. v.]; W. § 12, 5; [B. 35 (30 sq.)]; cf. Fritzsche on Mk. p. 268; [Soph. Lex. s. v.]); (προφήτης, q. v.); Sept. for נבא and התנבא; Vulg. propheto [three times prophetizo]; to prophesy, i. e. to be a prophet, speak forth by divine inspiration; to predict (Hdt., Pind., Eur., Plat., Plut., al.); **a.** univ.: Mt. vii. 22. **b.** with the idea of foretelling future events pertaining esp. to the kingdom of God: Mt. xi. 13; Acts ii. 17, 18; xxi. 9; περί τινος, Mt. xv. 7; Mk. vii. 6; 1 Pet. i. 10; ἐπί τινι, over i. e. concerning one (see ἐπί, B. 2 f. β. p. 234ᵃ), Rev. x. 11; εἴς τινα (i. e. Christ), Barn. ep. 5, 6; προφ. foll. by λέγων with the words uttered by the prophet, Jude 14; foll. by ὅτι, Jn. xi. 51. **c.** to utter forth, declare, a thing which can only be known by divine revelation: Mt. xxvi. 68; Mk. xiv. 65; Lk. xxii. 64, cf. vii. 39; Jn. iv. 19. **d.** to break forth under sudden impulse in lofty discourse or in praise of the divine counsels: Lk. i. 67; Acts xix. 6, (1 S. x. 10, 11; xix. 20, 21, etc.); — or, under the like prompting, to teach, refute, reprove, admonish, comfort others (see προφήτης, II. 1 f.), 1 Co. xi. 4, 5; xiii. 9; xiv. 1, 3, 4, 5, 24, 31, 39. **e.** to act as a prophet, discharge the prophetic office: Rev. xi. 3. [On the word see Trench, N. T. Syn. § vi.] *

προφήτης, -ου, ὁ, (πρόφημι, to speak forth, speak out; hence prop. 'one who speaks forth'; see πρό, d. α.), Sept. for נָבִיא (which comes fr. the same root as نبأ, 'to divulge,' 'make known,' 'announce' [cf. Fleischer in Delitzsch, Com. ü. d. Gen., 4te Aufl. p. 551 sq.], therefore prop. i. q. interpreter, Ex. vii. 1, cf. iv. 16; hence an interpreter or spokesman for God; one through whom God speaks; cf. esp. Bleek, Einl. in d. A. T. 4te Aufl. p. 309 [B. D. s. v. Prophet and reff. there; esp. also Day's note on Oehler's O. T. Theol. § 161, and W. Robertson Smith, Prophets of Israel, p. 389 (note on Lect. ii.)]), one who speaks forth by divine inspiration; **I.** In Grk. writ. fr. Aeschyl., Hdt., and Pind. down **1.** an interpreter of oracles (whether uttered by the gods or the μάντεις), or of other hidden things. **2.** a foreteller, soothsayer, seer. **II.** In the N. T. **1.** one who, moved by the Spirit of God and hence his organ or spokesman, solemnly declares to men what he has received by inspiration, esp. future events, and in particular such as relate to the cause and kingdom of God and to human salvation. The title is applied to **a.** the O. T. prophets, — and with allusion to their age, life, death, deeds: Mt. v. 12; xii. 39; xiii. 17; xxiii. 29–31; Mk. vi. 15; Lk. iv. 27; x. 24; xi. 47; xiii. 28; Jn. viii. 52, 53; Acts iii. 25; vii. 52; xiii. 20; Ro. xi. 3; 1 Th. ii. 15; Heb.

xi. 32; Jas. v. 10; appeal is made to their utterances as having foretold the kingdom, deeds, death, of Jesus the Messiah: Mt. i. 22; ii. 5, 15, 17, 23; iii. 3; iv. 14; viii. 17; xi. 13; xii. 17; xiii. 35; xxi. 4; xxiv. 15; xxvi. 56; xxvii. 9; Mk. xiii. 14 Rec.; Lk. i. 70; iii. 4; iv. 17; xviii. 31; xxiv. 25; Jn. i. 23, 45 (46); xii. 38; Acts ii. 16; iii. 18, 21, 24; vii. 37, 48; x. 43; xiii. 27; xv. 15; xxvi. 22 sq.; Ro. i. 2; Heb. i. 1; 1 Pet. i. 10; 2 Pet. iii. 2; Rev. x. 7; in the number of prophets David also is reckoned, as one who predicted the resurrection of Christ, Acts ii. 30 sq.; so too is Balaam, 2 Pet. ii. 16 (see Βαλαάμ). by meton. προφῆται is put for the books of the prophets: Lk. xxiv. 27, 44; Acts viii. 28; xiii. 15; xxiv. 14; xxviii. 23; ἐν τοῖς προφήταις, i. q. ἐν βίβλῳ τῶν προφ. (Acts vii. 42), in the volume of the prophets (which in Hebr. has the title נביאים), Jn. vi. 45; Acts xiii. 40; — or for the teaching set forth in their books: Mt. v. 17; vii. 12; xxii. 40; Lk. xvi. 29, 31; Acts xxvi. 27. See νόμος, 4. **b.** John the Baptist, the herald of Jesus the Messiah: Mt. xxi. 26; Mk. vi. 15; xi. 32; Lk. i. 76; xx. 6, whom Jesus declares to be greater than the O. T. prophets, because in him the hope of the Jews respecting Elijah as the forerunner of the Messiah was fulfilled: Mt. xi. 9–11, 14, (cf. xvii. 11, 12; Mk. ix. 12 sq.); Lk. vii. 28 [R G T Tr br.]. **c.** That illustrious prophet whom the Jews (apparently on the ground of Deut. xviii. 15) expected to arise just before the Messiah's advent: Jn. i. 21, 25; vii. 40. those two illustrious prophets, the one Elijah, the other Enoch or Moses [but cf. the Comm.; e. g. Stuart, Com. vol. ii. p. 219 sq.], who according to the writer of the Apocalypse will publicly appear shortly before the visible return of Christ from heaven: Rev. xi. 10 (cf. 3). **d.** the Messiah: Acts iii. 22, 23; vii. 37, after Deut. xviii. 15; Jesus the Messiah, inasmuch as he is about to fulfil the expectation respecting this Messiah, Mt. xxi. 11; Jn. vi. 14. **e.** univ. a man filled with the Spirit of God, who by God's authority and command in words of weight pleads the cause of God and urges the salvation of men: Mt. xxi. 46; Lk. xiii. 33; xxiv. 19; Jn. viii. 52; in the proverb that a prophet is without honor in his own country, Mt. xiii. 57; Mk. vi. 4; Lk. iv. 24; Jn. iv. 44. he may be known — now by his supernatural knowledge of hidden things (even though past), Lk. vii. 39; Jn. iv. 19, (προφήτης ἀληθείας ἐστὶν ὁ πάντοτε πάντα εἰδώς, τὰ μὲν γεγονότα ὡς ἐγένετο, τὰ δὲ γινόμενα ὡς γίνεται, τὰ δὲ ἐσόμενα ὡς ἔσται, Clem. hom. 2, 6), — now by his power of working miracles, Lk. vii. 16; xxiv. 19; Jn. ix. 17; such a prophet Jesus is shown to have been by the passages cited, nor is it denied except by his enemies, Lk. vii. 39; Jn. vii. 52. **f.** The prophets that appeared in the apostolic age among the Christians: Mt. x. 41; xxiii. 34; Acts xv. 32; 1 Co. xiv. 29, 37; Rev. xxii. 6, 9; they are associated with apostles in Lk. xi. 49; 1 Co. xii. 28, 29; Eph. ii. 20; iii. 5; iv. 11; Rev. xviii. 20; they discerned and did what was best for the Christian cause, Acts xiii. 1 sq.; foretold certain future events, Acts xi. 27 sq.; xxi. 10 sqq.; and in the religious assemblies of the Christians, being suddenly seized by the Spirit (whose promptings, however, do not impair their self-government, 1 Co. xiv. 32), give utterance in glowing and exalted but intelligible language to those things which the Holy Spirit teaches them, and which have power to instruct, comfort, encourage, rebuke, convict, stimulate, their hearers, 1 Co. xiv. 3, 24. [Cf. *Harnack*, Lehre der Zwölf Apostel, Proleg. § 5 i. 2 p. 93 sqq. 119 sqq.; *Bonwetsch* in (Luthardt's) Zeitschr. f. kirchl. Wissen. u. s. w. 1884, pp. 408 sqq. 460 sqq.] g. Prophets both of the Old Test. and of the New are grouped together under the name προφῆται in Rev. xi. 18; xvi. 6; xviii. 24. 2. *a poet* (because poets were believed to sing under divine inspiration): so of Epimenides, Tit. i. 12.

4397 προφητικός, -ή, -όν, (προφήτης), *proceeding from a prophet*; prophetic: Ro. xvi. 26; 2 Pet. i. 19. [Philo de migr. Abr. § 15, etc.; Lcian. Alex. 60; eccles. writ.] *

4398 προφῆτις, -ιδος, ή, (προφήτης), Sept. for נְבִיאָה, a *prophetess* (Vulg., Tertull. *prophetissa, prophetis*), a woman to whom future events or things hidden from others are at times revealed, either by inspiration or by dreams and visions: Lk. ii. 36; Rev. ii. 20. In Grk. usage, *a female who declares* or *interprets oracles* (Eur., Plat., Plut.): ἡ προφῆτις τῆς ἀληθείας ἱστορία, Diod. 1, 2.*

4399 προ-φθάνω: 1 aor. προέφθασα; *to come before, to anticipate*: αὐτὸν προέφθασε λέγων, he spoke before him [R.V. *spake first to him*], or anticipated his remark, Mt. xvii. 25. (Aeschyl., Eur., Arstph., Plut.; Sept.) *

4400 προ-χειρίζω (πρόχειρος at hand [cf. πρό, d. a.] or ready): 1 aor. mid. προεχειρισάμην; pf. pass. ptcp. προκεχειρισμένος; *to put into the hand, to deliver into the hands*: far more freq. in the mid. *to take into one's hands*; trop. *to set before one's self, to propose, to determine*; with an acc. of the pers. *to choose, to appoint*, (Isocr., Polyb., Dion. Hal., Plut., al.; 2 Macc. iii. 7; viii. 9; Ex. iv. 13): foll. by an inf. of purpose, Acts xxii. 14; τινά with a pred. acc. Acts xxvi. 16; τινά with a dat. of the pers. *for one's use*, Josh. iii. 12; *for one's salvation*, pass. Acts iii. 20 for Rec. προκεκηρυγμένον (cf. προκηρύσσω, 2).*

4401 προ-χειρο-τονέω, -ῶ: pf. pass. ptcp. προκεχειροτονημένος; (see χειροτονέω); *to choose* or *designate beforehand*: Acts x. 41. (Plat. legg. 6 p. 765 b. c., [Aeschin., Dem.], Dio Cass. 50, 4.) *

4402 Πρόχορος, [-ου, ὁ, (lit. 'leader of the dance')], *Proch'orus*, one of the seven 'deacons' of the church at Jerusalem: Acts vi. 5.*

4403 πρύμνα, -ης, ή, (fem. of the adj. πρυμνός, -ή, -όν, last, hindmost; used substantively with recessive accent; [cf. W. 22]), fr. Hom. down, *the stern* or hinder part of a ship: Mk. iv. 38; Acts xxvii. 29; opp. to πρῷρα, ib. 41.*

4404 πρωΐ [WH πρωΐ (cf. I, ι, init.)] (Attic πρῴ [cf. W. § 5, 4 d.]), adv., (fr. πρό), fr. Hom. down, Sept. often for בֹּקֶר, *in the morning, early*, (opp. to ὀψέ): Jn. xviii. 28 G L T Tr WH; Mt. xvi. 3 (opp. here to ὀψίας γενομένης [but T br. WH reject the pass.]); [xxi. 18 T Tr txt. WH]; Mk. i. 35; xi. 20; xvi. 9; [πρωΐ, σκοτίας ἔτι οὔσης, Jn. xx. 1]; λίαν πρωΐ, foll. [in R G] by a gen. of the day (cf. Kühner § 414, 5 c. β. ii. p. 292), Mk. xvi. 2; ἅμα πρωΐ, Mt. xx. 1; ἐπὶ τὸ πρωΐ, Mk. xv. 1 [R G]; ἀπὸ πρωΐ ἕως

ἑσπέρας, Acts xxviii. 23. Used spec. of the fourth watch of the night, i. e. the time fr. 3 o'clock in the morning till 6, acc. to our reckoning [(cf. B. D. s. v. Watches of the Night)], Mk. xiii. 35.* **4405;** **see 4404 & (4407α)**

πρωΐα, see πρώϊος. ------------------------

πρώϊμος (for the more com. πρώϊος; cf. *Lob.* ad Phryn. p. 52), T Tr WH πρόϊμος (so also cod. Sin.; [see *WH.* App. p. 152]), -η, -ον, (πρωΐ), *early*: ὑετός, the early rain (Hebr. יוֹרֶה, Deut. xi. 14; Jer. v. 24), which fell fr. October on [(cf. B.D. s. v. Rain)], Jas. v. 7 [L T Tr WH om. ὑετ.; cf. W. 592 (550); B. 82 (72)]. (Xen. oec. 17, 4; Geop., al.) * --- **4406**

πρωϊνός [WH πρωινός (see their App. p. 152), Tdf. ed. 7 πρωϊνός (cf. I, ι)], (for the older πρώϊος, see ὀρθρινός; the same term. in the Lat. *serotinus, diutinus*), -ή, -όν, (πρωΐ), pertaining to the *morning*: ὁ ἀστὴρ ὁ πρ. Rev. ii. 28 (on which see ἀστήρ); xxii. 16 (where Rec. ὀρθρινός). [Sept.; Babr., Plut., Ath., al.] * **4407**

πρώϊος [WH πρώϊος], -α, -ον, (πρωΐ), *early*, pertaining to the *morning*, (fr. Hom. down); as a subst. ἡ πρωΐα (in full ἡ ὥρα ἡ πρωΐα, 3 Macc. v. 24; [Diod., Joseph., al.]; see ὄψιος, 2), Sept. several times for בֹּקֶר, *morning*: Mt. xxvii. 1; Jn. xviii. 28 Rec.; xxi. 4 [πρωΐας ἤδη γινομένης (T WH Tr txt.), *when day was now breaking* (R.V.)]; πρωΐας, in the morning, Mt. xxi. 18 [R G L Tr mrg.].* **(4407α): see 4404**

πρῷρα [so R G, πρῶρα Tr], more correctly πρῷρα (see *Göttling*, Lehre v. Accent, p. 142 sq.; [Chandler § 164; Etym. Magn. p. 692, 34 sq.; cf. 318, 57 sq.; cf. I, ι]), -ας (L T WH -ης, cf. μάχαιρα, init.), ή, [contr. fr. πρόειρα fr. πρό; *Lob.* Pathol. Element. ii. 136, cf. Paralip. p. 215], fr. Hom. down; *the prow* or forward part of a ship [R.V. *foreship*]: Acts xxvii. 30; in vs. 41 distinguished fr. ἡ πρύμνα.* **4408**

πρωτεύω; (πρῶτος); *to be first, hold the first place*, [A. V. *have the pre-eminence*]: Col. i. 18. (From Xen. and Plat. down.) * **4409**

πρωτοκαθεδρία, -ας, ή, (πρῶτος and καθέδρα q. v.), a *sitting in the first seat, the first* or *chief seat*: Mt. xxiii. 6; Mk. xii. 39; Lk. xi. 43; xx. 46. (Eccles. writ.) * **4410**

πρωτο-κλισία, -ας, ή, (πρῶτος and κλισία), the *first reclining-place, the chief place*, at table [cf. *Rich*, Dict. of Rom. and Grk. Antiq. s. v. *lectus tricliniaris*; the relative rank of the several places at table varied among Persians, Greeks, and Romans; and what arrangement was currently followed by the Jews in Christ's day can hardly, perhaps, be determined; (yet see *Edersheim*, Jesus the Messiah, ii. pp. 207 sq. 494)]: Mt. xxiii. 6; Mk. xii. 39; Lk. xi. 43 Lchm. in br.; xiv. 7, 8; xx. 46. (Eccles. writ.).* **4411**

πρῶτος, -η, -ον, (superl. of πρό, contr. fr. πρόατος, whence the Doric πρᾶτος; the compar. πρότερος see in its place), [fr. Hom. down], Sept. for רִאשׁוֹן and often for אֶחָד and אִישׁ, *first*; **1.** either in time or place, in any succession of things or of persons; **a.** absolutely (i. e. without a noun) and substantively; **a.** with the article: ὁ πρῶτος καὶ ὁ ἔσχατος, i. e. the eternal One, Rev. i. 17; ii. 8; xxii. 13; ὁ πρῶτος, sc. τῶν κεκλημένων, Lk. xiv. 18; the first of two (cf. W. § 35, 4 N. 1; [B. 32 **4412 & 4413**

(28)]), Jn. xix. 32; 1 Co. xiv. 30; plur. opp. to οἱ ἔσχατοι, Mt. xx. 16, on which see ἔσχατος, 2 a.   Neut. τὸ πρῶτον, opp. to τὸ δεύτερον, Heb. x. 9 ; τὰ πρῶτα, opp. to τὰ ἔσχατα, one's first state, Mt. xii. 45 ; Lk. xi. 26 ; 2 Pet. ii. 20 ; the first order of things, Rev. xxi. 4.   β. without the article : Mt. x. 2 (πρῶτος, sc. of the apostles to be mentioned) ; plur., Mt. xix. 30 ; Mk. x. 31 ; Lk. xiii. 30, (on the meaning of which three pass. see ἔσχατος, 2 a.) ; neut. ἐν πρώτοις, [A. V. *first of all*], among the first things delivered to you by me, 1 Co. xv. 3.   b. where it agrees with some substantive :   a. anarthrous, and in place of an adjective : πρώτῃ (sc. ἡμέρᾳ) σαββάτου, on the first day of the week, Mk. xvi. 9 ; φυλακή, opp. to δευτέρα, Acts xii. 10 ; as a pred. Lk. ii. 2 (on which cf. W. § 35, 4 N. 1 ; [B. § 127, 31]). where it is added to the subject or the object of the verb (and we often use an adv.; W. § 54, 2 ; [B. § 123, 9]) : εὑρίσκει οὗτος πρῶτος, Jn. i. 41 (42) (where L Tr WH πρῶτον) ; add, Jn. viii. 7 ; xx. 4, 8 ; Acts xxvii. 43 ; Ro. x. 19 ; 1 Tim. i. 16 ; 1 Jn. iv. 19 ; opp. to εἶτα, 1 Tim. ii. 13 ; ὁ πρῶτος ἐμβάς, Jn. v. 4 (the art. belongs to ἐμβάς [G T Tr WH om. the pass.]) ; but Acts xxvi. 23 πρῶτος ἐξ ἀναστάσεως νεκρῶν is to be translated *as the first.* By a later Grk. usage it is put where πρότερος might have been expected with the gen. (cf. *Herm.* ad Vig. p. 717 ; Passow s. v. πρότερος, B. I. 2 c. ii. p. 1243ᵃ ; [L. and S. ibid. B. I. 4 e.] ; *Fritzsche*, Ep. ad Rom. ii. 420 sq. ; W. § 35, 4 N. 1 ; B. § 123, 14) : πρῶτός μου ἦν, Jn. i. 15, 30, (οἱ πρῶτοί μου ταῦτα ἀνιχνεύσαντες, Ael. nat. anim. 8, 12).   β. with the article : ὁ (ἡ, τό,) πρῶτος (-η, -ον,), in a series which is so complete, either in fact or in thought, that other members are conceived of as following the first in regular order ; as, τὸν πρῶτον λόγον, Acts i. 1 ; add, Mk. xiv. 12 ; 2 Tim. iv. 16 ; Rev. iv. 1, 7 ; xiii. 12, etc.; (opp. to ὁ ἔσχατος), ἡ πρ. πλάνη, Mt. xxvii. 64 ; add, Mt. xx. 8, 10, 16 ; 1 Co. xv. 45, etc.; also 'the first' of two, where Lat. usage requires and the Vulg. ordinarily employs *prior* (cf. W. [and B.] u. s.) : Mt. xxi. 28, 31 [L Tr WH ὕστερος] ; ἄλλους δούλους πλείονας τῶν πρώτων, Mt. xxi. 36 ; ἡ πρώτη διαθήκη, Heb. viii. 7, 13 ; ix. 15, 18 ; ἡ πρώτη, sc. διαθήκη, Heb. ix. 1 G L T Tr WH ; σκηνή, Heb. ix. 1 Rec., 2, 6, 8 ; ἡ πρ. γῆ, ὁ πρ. οὐρανός, Rev. xxi. 1 ; ἀνάστασις, Rev. xx. 5, 6 ; ὁ πρῶτος, 1 Co. xv. 47 ; foll. by ὁ δεύτερος, τρίτος, etc.: Mt. xxii. 25 ; Mk. xii. 20 ; Lk. xix. 16 ; xx. 29 ; Rev. viii. 7 ; xvi. 2 ; xxi. 19 ; foll. by ἕτερος, Lk. xvi. 5 ; ὁ πρῶτος, i. q. *the former, previous, pristine* : τὴν πρώτην πίστιν, the faith which they formerly plighted, 1 Tim. v. 12 ; ἡ πρώτη ἀγάπη, Rev. ii. 4 ; τὰ πρ. ἔργα, ibid. 5.   **2.** *first in rank, influence, honor* ; *chief* ; *principal* : without the art., and absol., πρῶτος *chief*, (opp. to δοῦλος), Mt. xx. 27 ; Mk. x. 44 ; opp. to ἔσχατος and διάκονος, Mk. ix. 35 ; added to a noun, *principal*, ἐντολή, Mt. xxii. 38 ; Mk. xii. 30 [T WH om. Tr mrg. br. the cl.] ; Eph. vi. 2 ; with a partitive gen., Mk. xii. 28, 29, [see πᾶς, II. 2 b. γ.] ; 1 Tim. i. 15 with the art., Lk. xv. 22 ; Acts xvii. 4 ; οἱ πρῶτοι τῆς Γαλιλαίας, the chief men of Galilee, Mk. vi. 21 ; τοῦ λαοῦ, Lk. xix. 47 ; τῆς πόλεως, Acts xiii. 50 ;

τῶν Ἰουδαίων, Acts xxv. 2 ; xxviii. 17 ; τῆς νήσου, Acts xxviii. 7 [cf. *Lewin*, St. Paul, ii. p. 208 sq., but see Πόπλιος].   **3.** neut. πρῶτον as adv., *first, at the first* ;   a. in order of time : Lk. x. 5 ; Jn. xviii. 13 ; Acts xi. 26 [here T Tr WH πρώτως, q. v.] ; foll. by εἶτα, ἔπειτα, or δεύτερον, Mk. iv. 28 ; 1 Co. xv. 46 ; 1 Th. iv. 16 ; 1 Tim. iii. 10 ; foll. by μετὰ ταῦτα, Mk. xvi. 9 cf. 12 ; *the first time*, opp. to ἐν τῷ δευτέρῳ (the second time), Acts vii. 12, 13 ; τὲ πρῶτον καί, first and also (or afterwards), i. e. as well as, Ro. i. 16 [but here L Tr mrg. WH br. πρ.] ; ii. 9, 10 ; without τέ, 2 Co. viii. 5 ; 2 Tim. i. 5. *first* i. e. before anything else is done ; *first of all* : Mt. vi. 33 ; Lk. xii. 1 ; Jn. vii. 51 L T Tr WH ; Ro. i. 8 ; 1 Tim. v. 4 ; 2 Pet. i. 20 ; iii. 3 ; πρῶτον πάντων, 1 Tim. ii. 1. *first* i. e. before something else : Mt. viii. 21 ; Mk. vii. 27 ; ix. 11, 12 ; Lk. xi. 38 ; xiv. 28 ; Ro. xv. 24 ; 2 Th. ii. 3 ; 1 Pet. iv. 17, etc.; before other nations, Acts iii. 26 ; xiii. 46 ; before others [R. V. *the first to partake* etc.], 2 Tim. ii. 6 ; foll. by τότε or καὶ τότε, Mt. v. 24 ; vii. 5 ; xii. 29 ; Mk. iii. 27 ; Lk. vi. 42 ; Jn. ii. 10 [T WH om. L Tr br. τότε] ; ἐμὲ πρῶτον ὑμῶν [Tdf. om. ὑμ.] *me before* it hated *you*, Jn. xv. 18 (see 1 b. a.).   τὸ πρῶτον, *at the first* i. e. at the time when one did a thing for the first time : Jn. x. 40 ; xii. 16 ; xix. 39.   b. in enumerating several particulars ; *first, then*, etc.: Ro. iii. 2 ; 1 Co. xi. 18 ; xii. 28 ; Heb. vii. 2 ; Jas. iii. 17.

πρωτο-στάτης, -ου, ὁ, (πρῶτος and ἵστημι), prop. *one who stands in the front rank, a front-rank man,* (Thuc., Xen., Polyb., Diod., Dion. Hal., al.; ὥσπερ στρατηγὸς πρωτοστάτης, Job xv. 24) ; hence, *a leader, chief, champion*: trop. [A. V. *a ringleader*] τῆς αἱρέσεως, Acts xxiv. 5.*   **4414**

πρωτο-τόκια, -ων, τά, (πρωτότοκος), in the Sept. also πρωτοτοκεία [al. -κεῖα (cf. Chandler § 99), -κία, cod. Venet., Aq.], for בְּכֹרָה, *primogeniture, the right of the first-born,* (in class. Grk. ἡ πρεσβεία, and τὸ πρεσβεῖον) : Heb. xii. 16. (Philo repeats the word after the Sept. in his alleg. legg. 3, 69 ; sacrif. Abel. § 5. Occasionally also in Byzant. writ.) *   **4415**

πρωτό-τοκος, -ον, (πρῶτος, τίκτω), Sept. for בְּכוֹר, *first-born* ;   a. prop. : τὸν υἱὸν αὐτῆς τὸν πρωτ. Mt. i. 25 (where τὸν πρωτότ. is omitted by L T Tr WH but found in cod. Sin. [see Tdf., WH., ad loc.]) ; Lk. ii. 7 ; τὰ πρωτότοκα αὐτῶν (gen. of the possessor [(?) ; αὐτῶν is more naturally taken w. θίγῃ (W. § 30, 8 c.), as by Prof. Grimm himself s. v. θιγγάνω]), the first-born whether of man or of beast, Heb. xi. 28 (πᾶν πρωτότοκον . . . ἀπὸ ἀνθρώπου ἕως κτήνους, Ex. xii. 29 ; Ps. civ. (cv.) 36 ; [Philo de cherub. § 16 ; Poll. 4, 208]).   b. trop. Christ is called πρωτότοκος πάσης κτίσεως (partit. gen. [see below], as in τὰ πρωτότοκα τῶν προβάτων, Gen. iv. 4 ; τῶν βοῶν, Deut. xii. 17 ; τῶν υἱῶν σου, Ex. xxii. 29), who came into being through God prior to the entire universe of created things [R. V. *the firstborn of all creation*] (see κτίσις, 2 b.), Col. i. 15 ;—this passage does not with c e r t a i n t y prove that Paul reckoned the λόγος in the number of c r e a t e d beings (as, among others, *Usteri*, Paulin. Lehrbegriff. p. 315, and *Baur*, Das Christenthum der drei   **4416**

ersten Jahrhh. 1st ed. p. 295, hold); since even Origen, who is acknowledged to have maintained the eternal generation of the Son by the Father, did not hesitate to call him (cf. *Gieseler*, Kirch.- Gesch. i. p. 261 sq. ed. 3; [i. 216 Eng. trans. of ed. 4, edited by Smith]) τὸν ἀγένητον καὶ πάσης γενετῆς φύσεως πρωτότοκον (c. Cels. 6, 17), and even κτίσμα (a term which Clement of Alexandria also uses of the λόγος); cf. Joan. Damascen. orthod. fid. 4, 8 καὶ αὐτὸς ἐκ τοῦ θεοῦ καὶ ἡ κτίσις ἐκ τοῦ θεοῦ; [al. would make the gen. in Col. l. c. depend upon the compar. force in (the first half of) πρωτότ. (cf. πρωτότοκος ἐγὼ ἦ σύ, 2 S. xix. 43); but see Bp. Lghtft. ad loc. (esp. for the patristic interpretation)]. In the same sense, apparently, he is called simply ὁ πρωτότοκος, Heb. i. 6; πρ. ἐκ τῶν νεκρῶν, the first of the dead who was raised to life, Col. i. 18; also τῶν νεκρῶν (partit. gen.), Rev. i. 5 [Rec. inserts ἐκ]; πρωτότοκος ἐν πολλοῖς ἀδελφοῖς, who was the Son of God long before those who by his agency and merits are exalted to the nature and dignity of sons of God, with the added suggestion of the supreme rank by which he excels these other sons (cf. Ps. lxxxviii. (lxxxix.) 28; Ex. iv. 22; Jer. xxxviii. (xxxi.) 9), Ro. viii. 29; ἐκκλησία πρωτοτόκων, the congregation of the pious Christian dead already exalted to the enjoyment of the blessedness of heaven (tacitly opp. to those subsequently to follow them thither), Heb. xii. 23; cf. De Wette ad loc. (Anthol. 8, 34; 9, 213.) *

(4416α); see 4413

πρώτως, adv., *first*: Acts xi. 26 T Tr WH. Cf. Passow s. v. πρότερος fin.; [L. and S. ib. B. IV.; Phryn. ed. *Lob.* p. 311 sq.; *Rutherford*, New Phryn. p. 366].*

4417 πταίω; fut. πταίσω; 1 aor. ἔπταισα; (akin to ΠΕΤΩ and πίπτω [cf. Vaniček p. 466]); fr. [Pind.], Aeschyl., and Hdt. down; **1.** trans. τινά, *to cause one to stumble* or *fall*. **2.** intrans. *to stumble*: δὶς πρὸς τὸν αὐτὸν λίθον, Polyb. 31, 19, 5. trop. [cf. Eng. *trip, stumble*] **a.** *to err, to make a mistake*, (Plat. Theaet. c. 15 p. 160 d.); *to sin*: absol. Ro. xi. 11 (ἴδιον ἀνθρώπου φιλεῖν καὶ τοὺς πταίοντας, Antonin. 7, 22); πολλά, in many ways, Jas. iii. 2; ἐν ἑνί (sc. νόμῳ), to stumble in, i. e. sin against, one law, Jas. ii. 10 [but see ch. 2. a. fin.]; ἐν λόγῳ (for the [more com.] simple dat.), to sin in word or speech, Jas. iii. 2. **b.** *to fall into misery, become wretched*, (often so in Grk. writ.): of the loss of salvation, 2 Pet. i. 10. [Cf. προσ-παίω.]*

4418 πτέρνα, -ης, ἡ, *the heel* (of the foot): ἐπαίρειν τὴν πτέρναν ἐπί τινα, to lift up the heel against one, i. e. dropping the fig. (which is borrowed either from kicking, or from a wrestler tripping up his antagonist), *to injure one by trickery*, Jn. xiii. 18 after Ps. xl. (xli.) 10. (Often in Grk. writ. fr. Hom. down; Sept. for עָקֵב.) *

4419 πτερύγιον, -ου, τό, (dimin. of πτέρυξ, q. v.), Sept. for כָּנָף; **1.** *a wing, little wing.* **2.** *any pointed extremity* (of the fins of fishes, סְנַפִּיר, Lev. xi. 9–12; Deut. xiv. 9, 10; Aristot., Theophr.; of a part of the dress hanging down in the form of a wing, Ruth iii. 9; 1 S. xxiv. 5; [Num. xv. 38]; Poll. 7, 14, 62): τὸ πτερύγιον τοῦ ναοῦ and τοῦ ἱεροῦ, the top of the temple at Jerusalem, Hegesipp. ap. Euseb. h. e. 2, 23, 11; τοῦ ἱεροῦ, Mt.

iv. 5; Lk. iv. 9; some understand this of the top or apex of the sanctuary (τοῦ ναοῦ), others of the top of Solomon's porch, and others of the top of the Royal Portico; this last Josephus (antt. 15, 11, 5) says was of such great height ὡς εἴ τις ἀπ' ἄκρου τοῦ ταύτης τέγους ἄμφω συντιθεὶς τὰ βάθη διοπτεύοι σκοτοδινιᾶν, οὐκ ἐξικνουμένης τῆς ὄψεως εἰς ἀμέτρητον τὸν βυθόν; [cf. "Recovery of Jerusalem," esp. ch. v.].*

4420 πτέρυξ, -υγος, ἡ, (πτερόν a wing), fr. Hom. down, Sept. often for כָּנָף; *a wing*: of birds, Mt. xxiii. 37; Lk. xiii. 34; Rev. xii. 14; of imaginary creatures, Rev. iv. 8; ix. 9.*

4421 πτηνός, -ή, -όν, (πέτομαι, πτῆναι), *furnished with wings*; *winged, flying*: τὰ πτηνά, *birds* (often so in Grk. writ. fr. Aeschyl. down), 1 Co. xv. 39.*

4422 πτοέω, -ῶ: 1 aor. pass. ἐπτοήθην; (πτόα terror); from Hom. down; *to terrify*; pass. *to be terrified* (Sept. chiefly for חָתַת): Lk. xxi. 9; xxiv. 37 [Tr mrg. WH mrg. θροηθέντες. SYN. see φοβέω, fin.]*

4423 πτόησις, -εως, ἡ, (πτοέω), *terror*: φοβεῖσθαι πτόησιν, i. q. φόβον φοβεῖσθαι *to be afraid with terror* [al. take πτ. objectively: R. V. txt. *to be put in fear by* any *terror*], 1 Pet. iii. 6 (Prov. iii. 25); see φοβέω, 2; [W. § 32, 2; B. § 131, 5. (1 Macc. iii. 25; Philo, quis rer. div. her. § 51)].*

4424 Πτολεμαΐς, -ΐδος, ἡ, *Ptolemais*, a maritime city of Phoenicia, which got its name, apparently, from Ptolemy Lathyrus (who captured it B. C. 103, and rebuilt it more beautifully [cf. Joseph. antt. 13, 12, 2 sq.]); it is called in Judg. i. 31 and in the Talmud עַכּוֹ, in the Sept. Ἀκχώ, by the Greeks Ἄκη [on the varying accent cf. *Pape*, Eigennam. s. v. Πτολεμαΐς], and Romans *Ace*, and by modern Europeans [*Acre* or] *St. Jean d' Acre* (from a church erected there in the middle ages to St. John); it is now under Turkish rule and contains about 8000 inhabitants (cf. *Baedeker*, Pal. and Syria, Eng. ed. p. 356): Acts xxi. 7. (Often mentioned in the books of the Maccabees and by Josephus under the name of Πτολεμαΐς, cf. esp. b. j. 2, 10, 2 sq.; [see *Reland*, Palaest. p. 534 sqq.; *Ritter*, Palestine, Eng. trans. iv. p. 361 sqq.].) *

4425 πτύον, -ου, τό, freq. in class. Grk. fr. Hom. down, Attic πτέον W. 24, [(perh. fr. r. pu 'to cleanse'; cf. Curtius p. 498 sq.)], *a winnowing-shovel* [A. V. *fan*; cf. B. D. s. v. Agriculture, sub fin.; *Rich*, Dict. of Antiq. s. vv. ventilabrum, pala 2, vannus]: Mt. iii. 12; Lk. iii. 17.*

4426 πτύρω: [(cf. Curtius p. 706)]; *to frighten, affright*: pres. pass. ptcp. πτυρόμενος, Phil. i. 28. (Hippocr., Plat., Diod., Plut., al.) *

4427 πτύσμα, -τος, τό, (πτύω, q. v.), *spittle*: Jn. ix. 6 ([Hippocr.], Polyb. 8, 14, 5; Or. Sibyll. 1, 365).*

4428 πτύσσω: 1 aor. ptcp. πτύξας; in class. Grk. fr. Hom. down; *to fold together, roll up*: τὸ βιβλίον, Lk. iv. 20 [A. V. *closed*]; see ἀναπτύσσω, [and cf. Schlottmann in Riehm s. v. Schrift; *Strack* in Herzog ed. 2 s. v. Schreibkunst, etc. COMP.: ἀνα-πτύσσω.]*

4429 πτύω: [(Lat. *spuo*, our *spue*; Curtius § 382)]; 1 aor. ἔπτυσα; fr. Hom. down; *to spit*: Mk. vii. 33; viii. 23; Jn. ix. 6. [COMP.: ἐκ-, ἐμ-πτύω.]*

4430 πτῶμα, -τος, τό, (πίπτω, pf. πέπτωκα); **1.** in Grk. writ. fr. Aeschyl. down, *a fall, downfall*; metaph. *a failure, defeat, calamity; an error, lapse, sin.* **2.** *that which is fallen*; hence with the gen. of a pers. or with νεκροῦ added, *the* (fallen) *body of one dead* or *slain, a corpse, carcase*; later also with νεκροῦ omitted (Polyb., Sept., Philo, Joseph., Plut., Hdian.), cf. Thom. Mag. p. 765 [ed. Ritschl p. 290, 14]; Phryn. ed. *Lob.* p. 375; [W. 23], and so in the N. T.: Mt. xiv. 12 L T Tr WH; Mk. xv. 45 L T Tr WH; Mt. xxiv. 28; τινός, Mk. vi. 29; Rev. xi. 8, 9.*

4431 πτῶσις, -εως, ἡ, (πίπτω, pf. πέπτωκα), *a falling, downfall*: prop. τῆς οἰκίας, Mt. vii. 27 (πτώσεις οἴκων, Maneth. 4, 617); trop. εἰς πτῶσιν πολλῶν (opp. to εἰς ἀνάστασιν), *that many may fall and bring upon themselves ruin,* i. e. the loss of salvation, utter misery, Lk. ii. 34, cf. Ro. xi. 11. (Sept. chiefly for מַגֵּפָה, plague, defeat.) *

4432 πτωχεία, -ας, ἡ, (πτωχεύω); **1.** *beggary* (Hdt. 3, 14; Arstph. Plut. 549; Plat. legg. 1 p. 936 b.; Lysias p. 898, 9; Aristot. poet. c. 23 p. 1459ᵇ, 6). **2.** in the N. T. *poverty*, the condition of one destitute of riches and abundance: opp. to πλουτεῖν, 2 Co. viii. 9; opp. to πλούσιος, Rev. ii. 9; ἡ κατὰ βάθους πτωχεία (opp. to πλοῦτος), *deep* i. e. extreme *poverty* [see κατά, I. 1 b.], 2 Co. viii. 2. (Sept. chiefly for עֳנִי, affliction, misery.) *

4433 πτωχεύω: 1 aor. ἐπτώχευσα; (πτωχός, q. v.); prop. *to be a beggar, to beg*; so in class. Grk. fr. Hom. down; in the N. T. once, *to be poor*: 2 Co. viii. 9, on which see πλούσιος, b. fin. (Tob. iv. 21; Sept. for דָּלַל to be weak, afflicted, Judg. vi. 6; Ps. lxxviii. (lxxix.) 8; for נוֹרָשׁ to be reduced to want, Prov. xxiii. 21; רוּשׁ to be needy, Ps. xxxiii. (xxxiv.) 11.) *

4434 πτωχός, -ή, -όν, (πτώσσω, to be thoroughly frightened, to cower down or hide one's self for fear; hence πτωχός prop. one who slinks and crouches), often involving the idea of roving about in wretchedness [see πένης, fin.; "but it always had a bad sense till it was ennobled in the Gospels; see Mt. v. 3; Lk. vi. 20, cf. 2 Co. viii. 9 " (L. and S. s. v. I.)]; hence **1.** in class. Grk. from Hom. down, *reduced to beggary, begging, mendicant, asking alms*: Lk. xiv. 13, 21; xvi. 20, 22. **2.** *poor, needy,* (opp. to πλούσιος): Mt. xix. 21; xxvi. 9, 11; Mk. x. 21; xii. 42, 43; xiv. 5, 7; Lk. xviii. 22; xix. 8; xxi. 3; Jn. xii. 5, 6, 8; xiii. 29; Ro. xv. 26; 2 Co. vi. 10; Gal. ii. 10; Jas. ii. 2, 3, 6; Rev. xiii. 16; in a broader sense, *destitute of wealth, influence, position, honors; lowly, afflicted*: Mt. xi. 5; Lk. iv. 18, (fr. Is. lxi. 1); vi. 20; vii. 22; οἱ πτωχοὶ τοῦ κόσμου (partit. gen.), the poor of the human race, Jas. ii. 5; but the more correct reading is that of L T Tr WH viz. τῷ κόσμῳ [*unto the world*], i. e. the ungodly world being judge, cf. W. § 31, 4 a.; B. § 133, 14; [R. V. *as to the world* (see next head, and cf. κόσμος, 7)]. trop. *destitute of the Christian virtues and the eternal riches,* Rev. iii. 17; like the Lat. *inops,* i. q. *helpless, powerless to accomplish an end*: στοιχεῖα, Gal. iv. 9 ['bringing no rich endowment of spiritual treasure' (Bp. Lghtft.)]. **3.** univ. *lacking in anything,* with a dat. of the respect: τῷ πνεύματι, as respects their spirit, i. e. destitute of the wealth of learning and intellectual culture which the schools afford (men of this class most readily gave themselves up to Christ's teaching and proved themselves fitted to lay hold of the heavenly treasure, Mt. xi. 25; Jn. ix. 39; 1 Co. i. 26, 27; [al. make the idea more inward and ethical: 'conscious of their spiritual need']), Mt. v. 3; compare with this the Ep. of Barn. 19, 2: ἔσῃ ἁπλοῦς τῇ καρδίᾳ καὶ πλούσιος τῷ πνεύματι, abounding in Christian graces and the riches of the divine kingdom. (Sept. for עָנִי, דַּל, רָשׁ, אֶבְיוֹן, etc.) *

4435 πυγμή, -ῆς, ἡ, (πύξ, fr. ΠΥΚΩ, Lat. pungo, pupugi, [pugnus]; O. H. G. 'fûst', Eng. 'fist'; cf. Curtius § 384]), fr. Hom. down, Sept. for אֶגְרוֹף (Ex. xxi. 18; Is. lviii. 4), *the fist*: πυγμῇ νίπτεσθαι τὰς χεῖρας, to wash the hands with the fist, i. e. so that one hand is rubbed with the clenched fist of the other [R. V. mrg. (after Theoph., al.) *up ,o the elbow*; but cf. *Edersheim*, Jesus the Messiah, ii. 11], Mk. vii. 3 (where Tdf. πυκνά, see πυκνός). [Cf. *Jas. Morison,* Com. ad loc.] *

4436 Πύθων, -ωνος, ὁ, *Python*; **1.** in Grk. mythology the name of the Pythian serpent or dragon that dwelt in the region of Pytho at the foot of Parnassus in Phocis, and was said to have guarded the oracle of Delphi and been slain by Apollo. **2.** i. q. δαιμόνιον μαντικόν (Hesych. s. v.), *a spirit of divination*: πνεῦμα πύθωνος or more correctly (with L T Tr WH) πνεῦμα πύθωνα (on the union of two substantives one of which has the force of an adj. see Matthiae p. 962, 4; [Kühner § 405, 1; *Lob.* Paralip. 344 sq.]), Acts xvi. 16; some interpreters think that the young woman here mentioned was *a ventriloquist,* appealing to Plutarch, who tells us (mor. p. 414 e. de def. orac. 9) that in his time ἐγγαστρίμυθοι were called πύθωνες; [cf. Meyer].*

4437 πυκνός, -ή, -όν, (ΠΥΚΩ, see πυγμή), fr. Hom. down, *thick, dense, compact*; in ref. to time, *frequent, often recurring,* (so in Grk. writ. fr. Aeschyl. down), 1 Tim. v. 23; neut. plur. πυκνά, as adv. [W. 463 (432); B. § 128, 2], *vigorously, diligently,* (? [cf. Morison as in πυγμή]), Mk. vii. 3 Tdf.; *often,* Lk. v. 33; πυκνότερον, *more frequently, the oftener,* Acts xxiv. 26.*

4438 πυκτεύω; (πύκτης a pugilist [see πυγμή, init.]); *to be a boxer, to box,* [A. V. *fight*]: 1 Co. ix. 26. (Eur., Xen., Plat., Plut., al.) *

see 4438 St.

4439 πύλη, -ης, ἡ, [perh. fem. of πόλος (cf. Eng. *pole* i. e. axis) fr. r. πελ-ω to turn (Curtius p. 715)], fr. Hom. down; Sept. very often for שַׁעַר, occasionally for דֶּלֶת, sometimes for פֶּתַח; *a gate* (of the larger sort, in the wall either of a city or a palace; Thom. Mag. [p. 292, 4] πύλαι ἐπὶ τείχους· θύραι ἐπὶ οἰκίας): of a town, Lk. vii. 12; Acts ix. 24; xvi. 13 L T Tr WH; Heb. xiii. 12; of the temple, Acts iii. 10; in the wall of a prison, Acts xii. 10; πύλαι ᾅδου, the gates of Hades (likened to a vast prison; hence the 'keys' of Hades, Rev. i. 18), Mt. xvi. 18 (on which see κατισχύω); Sap. xvi. 13; 3 Macc. v. 51, and often by prof. writ.; see Grimm on 3 Macc. v. 51. in fig. disc. i. q. *access* or *entrance* into any state: Mt. vii. 13ᵃ, 13ᵇ R G T br. Tr WH mrg., 14 R G

L br. T br. Tr WH; Lk. xiii. 24 R L mrg. [On its omission see προβατικός.] *

4440 πυλών, -ῶνος, ὁ, (πύλη), [Aristot., Polyb., al.], Sept. often for פֶּתַח, sometimes for שַׁעַר; **1.** *a large gate*: of a palace, Lk. xvi. 20; of a house, Acts x. 17; plur. (of the gates of a city), Acts xiv. 13; Rev. xxi. 12, 13, 15, 21, 25; xxii. 14. **2.** *the anterior part of a house*, into which one enters through the gate, *porch*: Mt. xxvi. 71 (cf. 69 and 75); Acts xii. 14; hence ἡ θύρα τοῦ πυλῶνος, ib. 13.*

4441 πυνθάνομαι; impf. ἐπυνθανόμην; 2 aor. ἐπυθόμην; [cf. Curtius § 328]; a depon. verb; as in class. Grk. fr. Hom. down **1.** *to inquire, ask*: foll. by an indir. quest. — w. the indic. Acts x. 18; with the opt., Jn. xiii. 24 R G; Lk. xv. 26; xviii. 36; Acts xxi. 33; foll. by a dir. quest., Acts iv. 7; x. 29; xxiii. 19; παρά τινός τι [B. 167 (146)], Jn. iv. 52; παρά τινος foll. by an indir. quest. w. the indic. Mt. ii. 4; τὶ περί τινος, Acts xxiii. 20. **2.** *to ascertain by inquiry*: foll. by ὅτι, Acts xxiii. 34 [A. V. *understood*].*

4442 πῦρ, gen. πυρός, τό, [prob. fr. Skr. pu 'to purify' (cf. Germ. *feuer*); Vaniček p. 541; Curtius § 385], fr. Hom. down; *fire*: Mt. iii. 10, 12; vii. 19; xvii. 15; Mk. ix. 22; Lk. iii. 9, 17; ix. 54; Jn. xv. 6; Acts ii. 19; xxviii. 5; 1 Co. iii. 13; Heb. xi. 34; Jas. iii. 5; v. 3; Rev. viii. 5, 7; ix. 17, 18; xi. 5; xiii. 13; xiv. 18; xv. 2; xvi. 8; xx. 9; ἅπτειν πῦρ, to kindle a fire, Lk. xxii. 55 [T Tr txt. WH περιάπτ.]; ἔβρεξε πῦρ καὶ θεῖον, Lk. xvii. 29; κατακαίειν τι ἐν [T om. WH br. ἐν] πυρί, Rev. xviii. 8; καίομαι πυρί, Mt. xiii. 40 [R L T WH κατακ.]; Heb. xii. 18 [W. § 31, 7 d.]; Rev. viii. 8; xxi. 8; φλὸξ πυρός, a fiery flame or flame of fire, Acts vii. 30; 2 Th. i. 8 L txt. Tr txt.; Heb. i. 7; Rev. i. 14; ii. 18; xix. 12, (Ex. iii. 2 cod. Alex.; Is. xxix. 6); πῦρ φλογός, a flaming fire or fire of flame, 2 Th. i. 8 R G L mrg. T Tr mrg. WH (Ex. iii. 2 cod. Vat.; Sir. xlv. 19); λαμπάδες πυρός, lamps of fire, Rev. iv. 5; στῦλοι πυρός, Rev. x. 1; ἄνθρακες π. coals of fire, Ro. xii. 20 (see ἄνθραξ); γλῶσσαι ὡσεὶ πυρός, which had the shape of little flames, Acts ii. 3; δοκιμάζειν διὰ πυρός, 1 Pet. i. 7; πυροῦσθαι (see πυρόω, b.) ἐκ π. Rev. iii. 18; ὡς διὰ πυρός, as one who in a conflagration has escaped through the fire not uninjured, i. e. dropping the fig. *not without damage*, 1 Co. iii. 15; מֻצָּל מֵאֵשׁ, Zech. iii. 2, cf. Am. iv. 11. of the fire of hell we find the foll. expressions, — which are to be taken either tropically (of the extreme penal torments which the wicked are to undergo after their life on earth; so in the discourses of Jesus), or literally (so apparently in the Apocalypse): τὸ πῦρ, Mk. ix. 44, 46, [T WH om. Tr br. both verses], 48; τὸ πῦρ τὸ αἰώνιον, Mt. xviii. 8; xxv. 41, cf. 4 Macc. xii. 12; ἄσβεστον, Mk. ix. 43, 45 [G T Tr WH om. L br. the cl.]; πυρὸς αἰωνίου δίκην ὑπέχειν, Jude 7; γέεννα τοῦ πυρός, Mt. v. 22; xviii. 9; Mk. ix. 47 [R G Tr br.]; κάμινος τ. πυρός, Mt. xiii. 42, 50, (Dan. iii. 6); ἡ λίμνη τοῦ πυρός, Rev. xix. 20; xx. 10, 14, 15; πυρὶ τηρεῖσθαι, 2 Pet. iii. 7; βασανισθῆναι ἐν πυρί, Rev. xiv. 10 (cf. Lk. xvi. 24); βαπτίζειν τινὰ πυρί (see βαπτίζω, II. b. bb.), Mt. iii. 11; Lk. iii. 16. the tongue

is called πῦρ, as though both itself on fire and setting other things on fire, partly by reason of the fiery spirit which governs it, partly by reason of the destructive power it exercises, Jas. iii. 6; since fire disorganizes and sunders things joined together and compact, it is used to symbolize *dissension*, Lk. xii. 49. Metaphorical expressions: ἐκ πυρὸς ἁρπάζειν, to snatch from danger of destruction, Jude 23; πυρὶ ἁλίζεσθαι (see ἁλίζω), Mk. ix. 49; ζῆλος πυρός, fiery, burning anger [see ζῆλος, 1], Heb. x. 27 (πῦρ ζῆλου, Zeph. i. 18; iii. 8); God is called πῦρ καταναλίσκον, as one who when angry visits the obdurate with penal destruction, Heb. xii. 29.*

4443 πυρά, -ᾶς, ἡ, (πῦρ), fr. Hom. down, *a fire*, a pile of burning fuel: Acts xxviii. 2 sq.*

4444 πύργος, -ου, ὁ, (akin to Germ. *Burg*, anciently *Purg*; [yet cf. Curtius § 413]), as in Grk. writ. fr. Hom. down, *a tower; a fortified structure rising to a considerable height*, to repel a hostile attack or to enable a watchman to see in every direction. The πύργος ἐν τῷ Σιλωάμ [(q. v.)] seems to designate a tower in the walls of Jerusalem near the fountain of Siloam, Lk. xiii. 4; the tower occupied by the keepers of a vineyard is spoken of in Mt. xxi. 33; Mk. xii. 1, (after Is. v. 2); a tower-shaped building as a safe and convenient dwelling, Lk. xiv. 28.*

4445 πυρέσσω; (πῦρ); (Vulg., Cels., Senec., al. *febricito*); *to be sick with a fever*: Mt. viii. 14; Mk. i. 30. (Eur., Arstph., Plut., Lcian., Galen, al.) *

4446 πυρετός, -οῦ, ὁ, (πῦρ); **1.** *fiery heat* (Hom. Il. 22, 31 [but interpreters now give it the sense of 'fever' in this pass.; cf. Ebeling, Lex. Hom. s. v.; *Schmidt*, Syn. ch. 60 § 14]). **2.** *fever*: Mt. viii. 15; Mk. i. 31; Lk. iv. 39; Jn. iv. 52; Acts xxviii. 8, (Hippocr., Arstph., Plat., sqq.; Deut. xxviii. 22); πυρ. μέγας, Lk. iv. 38 (as Galen de different. feb. 1, 1 says σύνηθες τοῖς ἰατροῖς ὀνομάζειν . . . τὸν μέγαν τε καὶ μικρὸν πυρετόν; [cf. Wetstein on Lk. l. c.]).*

4447 πύρινος, -η, -ον, (πῦρ), *fiery*: θώρακες πύρ. i. e. shining like fire, Rev. ix. 17. (Ezek. xxviii. 14, 16; Aristot., Polyb., Plut., al.) *

4448 πυρόω: Pass., pres. πυροῦμαι; pf. ptcp. πεπυρωμένος; (πῦρ); fr. Aeschyl. and Pind. down; *to burn with fire, to set on fire, to kindle*; in the N. T. it is used only in the pass. **a.** *to be on fire, to burn*: prop. 2 Pet. iii. 12; trop. of the heat of the passions: of g r i e f, 2 Co. xi. 29 [Eng. Versions *burn* (often understood of i n d i g n a t i o n, but cf. Meyer); W. 153 (145)]; of a n g e r, with τοῖς θυμοῖς added, i. q. *to be incensed, indignant*, 2 Macc. iv. 38; x. 35; xiv. 45; to be inflamed with s e x u a l desire, 1 Co. vii. 9. * **b.** pf. ptcp. πεπυρωμένος, *made to glow* [R. V. *refined*]: Rev. i. 15 [(cf. B. 80 (69) n.)]; *full of fire; fiery, ignited*: τὰ βέλη τὰ πεπ. darts filled with inflammable substances and set on fire, Eph. vi. 16 (Apollod. bibl. 2, 5, 2 § 3); *melted by fire and purged of dross*: χρυσίον πεπυρ. ἐκ πυρός, [*refined by fire*], Rev. iii. 18 (so πυρόω in the Sept. for צָרַף; as τὸ ἀργύριον, Job xxii. 25; Zech. xiii. 9; Ps. xi. (xii.) 7; lxv. (lxvi.) 10].*

4449 πυρράζω; i. q. πυρρὸς γίνομαι, *to become glowing, grow* red, be red: Mt. xvi. 2 sq. [but Tbr. WH reject the pass.] (Byzant. writ.; πυρρίζω in Sept. and Philo.)*

4450   πυρρός, -ά, -όν, (fr. πῦρ), fr. Aeschyl. and Hdt. down, *having the color of fire, red*: Rev. vi. 4; xii. 3. Sept. several times for אָדֹם.*

see 4450   Πύρρος [('fiery-red'; *Fick*, Griech. Personennamen, p. 75)], -ου, ὁ, *Pyrrhus*, the proper name of a man: Acts xx. 4 G L T Tr WH.*

4451   πύρωσις, -εως, ἡ, (πυρόω), *a burning*: Rev. xviii. 9, 18; the burning by which metals are roasted or reduced; by a fig. drawn fr. the refiner's fire (on which cf. Prov. xxvii. 21), calamities or trials that test character: 1 Pet. iv. 12 (Tertullian adv. Gnost. 12 ne expavescatis ustionem, quae agitur in vobis in tentationem), cf. i. 7 [(ἡ πύρωσις τῆς δοκιμασίας, 'Teaching' etc. 16, 5)]. (In the

see 4452 Si. & 3380   same and other senses by Aristot., Theophr., Plut., al.)* [πώ, an enclitic particle, see μήπω etc.]

4453 ———— πωλέω, -ῶ; impf. ἐπώλουν; 1 aor. ἐπώλησα; pres. pass. πωλοῦμαι; (πέλω, πέλομαι, to turn, turn about, [Curtius § 633 p. 470], fr. which [through the noun πωλή; *Lob.* in Bttm. Ausf. Spr. ii. 57 bot.] πωλοῦμαι, Lat. *versor*, foll. by εἰς with acc. of place, to frequent a place; cf. the Lat. *venio* and *veneo*); fr. Hdt. down; Sept. for מָכַר; prop. *to barter*, i. e. *to sell*: absol. (opp. to ἀγοράζειν), Lk. xvii. 28; Rev. xiii. 17; οἱ πωλοῦντες (opp. to οἱ ἀγοράζοντες, buyers), *sellers*, Mt. xxi. 12; xxv. 9; Mk. xi. 15; Lk. xix. 45; with acc. of a thing, Mt. xiii. 44; xix. 21; xxi. 12; Mk. x. 21; xi. 15; Lk. [xii. 33]; xviii. 22; xxii. 36; Jn. ii. 14, 16; Acts v. 1; supply αὐτόν, Acts iv. 37; αὐτά, ib. 34; pass. 1 Co. x. 25; with a gen. of price added, Mt. x. 29; Lk. xii. 6.*

4454   πῶλος, -ου, ὁ (in class. Grk. ἡ also), [Lat. *pullus*, O. H. G. *folo*, Eng. *foal*; perh. allied with παῖς; cf. Curtius § 387]; **1.** *a colt, the young of the horse*: so very often fr. Hom. down. **2.** univ. *a young creature*: Ael. v. h. 4, 9; spec. of the young of various animals; in the N. T. of *a young ass, an ass's colt*: Mt. xxi. 2, 5, 7; Mk. xi. 2, [3 Lmrg.], 4, 5, 7; Lk. xix. 30, 33, 35; Jn. xii. 15, (also in Geopon.); Sept. several times for עַיִר; for עֶיְרָה a female ibex, Prov. v. 19.*

4455   πώποτε, adv., *ever, at any time*: Lk. xix. 30; Jn. i. 18; v. 37; vi. 35; viii. 33; 1 Jn. iv. 12. [(From Hom. down.)]*

4456   πωρόω, -ῶ: 1 aor. ἐπώρωσα (Jn. xii. 40 T Tr WH); pf. πεπώρωκα; pf. pass. ptcp. πεπωρωμένος; 1 aor. pass. ἐπωρώθην; (πῶρος, hard skin, a hardening, induration); *to cover with a thick skin, to harden by covering with a callus*, [R. V. everywhere simply *to harden*]: metaph., καρδίαν, to make the heart dull, Jn. xii. 40; Pass. *to grow hard* or *callous, become dull, lose the power of understanding*: Ro. xi. 7; τὰ νοήματα, 2 Co. iii. 14; ἡ καρδία, Mk. vi. 52; viii. 17. Cf. *Fritzsche*, Com. on Mk. p. 78 sq.; on Rom. ii. p. 451 sq. [(Hippocr., Aristot., al.)]*

4457   πώρωσις, -εως, ἡ, (πωρόω, q. v.), prop. *the covering with a callus*; trop. *obtuseness of mental discernment, dulled perception*: γέγονέ τινι, the mind of one has been blunted [R. V. *a hardening hath befallen*], Ro. xi. 25; τῆς καρδίας [*hardening of heart*], of stubbornness, obduracy, Mk. iii. 5; Eph. iv. 18. [(Hippocr.)]*

*For 4458 see p. 560.

4459   πῶς, (fr. obsol. ΠΟΣ, whence πού, ποῖ, etc. [cf. Curtius § 631]), adv., [fr. Hom. down]; **I.** in interrogation; *how? in what way?*—in a direct question, foll. by **a.** the indicative, it is the expression **a.** of one seeking information and desiring to be taught: Lk. i. 34; x. 26; Jn. iii. 9; ix. 26; 1 Co. xv. 35 [cf. W. 266 (250)]; πῶς οὖν, Jn. ix. 10 Tdf. (but L WH br. οὖν), 19; Ro. iv. 10. **β.** of one about to controvert another, and emphatically deny that the thing inquired has happened or been done: Mt. xii. 29; Mk. iii. 23; Lk. xi. 18; Jn. iii. 4, 12; v. 44, 47; vi. 52; ix. 16; 1 Jn. iii. 17; iv. 20; Ro. iii. 6; vi. 2; 1 Co. xiv. 7, 9, 16; 1 Tim. iii. 5; Heb. ii. 3; καὶ πῶς, Mk. iv. 13; Jn. xiv. 5 [here Ltxt. Tr WH om. καί]; πῶς οὖν, Mt. xii. 26; Ro. x. 14 R G; πῶς δέ, Ro. x. 14ᵃ R G Lmrg., 14ᵇ R G T, 15 R G, (on this see in b. below). where something is asserted and an affirmative answer is expected, πῶς οὐχί is used: Ro. viii. 32; 2 Co. iii. 8. **γ.** of surprise, intimating that what has been done or is said could not have been done or said, or not rightly done or said,—being equiv. to *how is it*, or *how has it come to pass, that* etc.: Gal. ii. 14 G L T Tr WH; Mt. xxii. 12; Jn. iv. 9; vi. 52; vii. 15; πῶς λέγεις, λέγουσι, κτλ., Mk. xii. 35; Lk. xx. 41; Jn. viii. 33; καὶ πῶς, Lk. xx. 44; Acts ii. 8; καὶ πῶς σὺ λέγεις, Jn. xii. 34; xiv. 9 [here L T WH om. Tr br. καί]; πῶς οὖν, Jn. vi. 42 [here T WH Tr txt. πῶς νῦν]; Mt. xxii. 43; πῶς οὐ, *how is it that . . . not, why not?* Mt. xvi. 11; Mk. viii. 21 R G Lmrg.; iv. 40 [R G T]; Lk. xii. 56. **b.** the delib. subjunctive (where the question is, how that can be done which ought to be done): πῶς πληρωθῶσιν αἱ γραφαί, *how are the Scriptures* (which ought to be fulfilled) *to be fulfilled?* Mt. xxvi. 54; πῶς φύγητε, *how shall ye* (who wish to escape) *escape* etc. Mt. xxiii. 33; add, πῶς οὖν, Ro. x. 14 L T Tr WH; πῶς δέ, x. 14ᵃ Ltxt. T Tr WH; 14ᵇ L T Tr WH; 15 L T Tr WH, (Sir. xlix. 11); cf. Fritzsche on Rom. vol. ii. 405 sq. **c.** foll. by ἄν with the optative: πῶς γὰρ ἂν δυναίμην; Acts viii. 31 (on which see ἄν, III. p. 34ᵇ). **II.** By a somewhat negligent use, occasionally met with even in Attic writ. but more freq. in later authors, πῶς is found in indirect discourse, where regularly ὅπως ought to have stood; cf. W. § 57, 2 fin.; [L. and S. s. v. IV.]. **a.** with the indicative—pres.: Mt. vi. 28; Mk. xii. 41; Lk. xii. 27; Acts xv. 36; 1 Co. iii. 10; Eph. v. 15; Col. iv. 6; 1 Tim. iii. 15; τὸ πῶς (on the art. see ὁ, II. 10 a.); with the impf. Lk. xiv. 7; with the perf. Rev. iii. 3; with the aor., Mt. xii. 4; Mk. ii. 26 [here Tr WH br. πῶς]; Lk. viii. 36; Acts ix. 27, etc.; after ἀναγινώσκειν, Mk. xii. 26 T Tr WH; *how* it came to pass that, etc. Jn. ix. 15; with the fut.: μεριμνᾷ, πῶς ἀρέσει (because the direct quest. would be πῶς ἀρέσω;), 1 Co. vii. 32–34 [but L T Tr WH -σῃ]; ἐζήτουν πῶς αὐτὸν ἀπολέσουσιν, how they shall destroy him (so that they were in no uncertainty respecting his destruction, but were only deliberating about the way in which they will accomplish it), Mk. xi. 18 R G (but the more correct reading here, acc. to the best Mss., including cod. Sin., is ἀπολέσωσιν 'how they should destroy him' [cf. W. § 41 b. 4 b.; B. § 139,

61; see next head]).   **b.** with the subjunctive, of the aor. and in deliberation: Mk. xi. 18 L T Tr WH; xiv. 1, 11 [R G]; Mt. x. 19; Lk. xii. 11; τὸ πῶς, Lk. xxii. 2, 4; Acts iv. 21.   **III.** in exclamation, *how*: πῶς δύσκολόν ἐστιν, Mk. x. 24; πῶς παραχρῆμα, Mt. xxi.

20; πῶς δυσκόλως, Mk. x. 23; Lk. xviii. 24; with a verb, *how* (greatly): πῶς συνέχομαι, Lk. xii. 50; πῶς ἐφίλει αὐτόν, Jn. xi. 36.

πῶς, an enclitic particle, on which see under εἴπως [i. e. εἰ, III. 14] and μήπως.   4458; see 1513 &3381

P

[P, ρ: the practice of doubling ρ (after a prep. or an augm.) is sometimes disregarded by the Mss., and accordingly by the critical editors; so, too, in the middle of a word; see ἀναντίρη-τος, ἀπορίπτω, ἀραβών, ἄραφος, διαρήγνυμι, ἐπιράπτω, ἐπιρί-πτω, παραρέω, ῥαβδίζω, ῥαντίζω, ῥαπίζω, ῥίπτω, ῥύομαι, etc.; cf. W. § 13, 1 b.; B. 32 (28 sq.); *WH*. App. p. 163; *Tdf.* Proleg. p. 80. Recent editors, L T (cf. the Proleg. to his 7th ed. p. cclxxvi.), Kuenen and Cobet (cf. their Praef. p. xcvi.), WH (but not Treg.), also follow the older Mss. in omitting the breathings from ρρ in the middle of a word; cf. *Lipsius*, Grammat. Untersuch. p. 18 sq.; *Greg.* Corinth. ed. *Bast* p. 732 sq.; in opposition see *Donaldson*, Greek Gram. p. 16; W. 48 (47). On the smooth breathing over the initial ρ when ρ begins two successive syllables, see Lipsius u. s.; WH. u. s. pp. 163, 170; Kühner § 67 Anm. 4; *Goettling*, Accent, p. 205 note; and on the general subject of the breathings cf. the Proleg. to Tdf. ed. 8 p. 105 sq. and reff. there. On the usage of modern edd. of the classics cf. Veitch s. vv. ῥάπτω, ῥέζω, etc.]

4460   **'Ραάβ** (and 'Ραχάβ, Mt. **i.** 5; 'Ραχάβη, -ης, in Joseph. [antt. 5, 1, 2 etc.]), ἡ, (רָחָב 'broad', 'ample'), *Rahab*, a harlot of Jericho: Heb. xi. 31; Jas. ii. 25. [Cf. B.D. s. v.; Bp. *Lghtft*. Clement of Rome, App. (Lond. 1877) p. 413.]*

4461   **ῥαββί**, T WH ῥαββεί [cf. B. p. 6; *WH*. App. p. 155; see ει, ι], (Hebr. רַבִּי, fr. רַב much, great), prop. *my great one*, *my honorable sir* ; (others incorrectly regard the ־ִ as the yodh paragogic); *Rabbi*, a title with which the Jews were wont to address their teachers (and also to honor them when not addressing them; cf. the French *monsieur*, *monseigneur*): Mt. xxiii. 7; translated into Greek by διδάσκαλος, Mt. xxiii. 8 G L T Tr WH; John the Baptist is addressed by this title, Jn. iii. 26; Jesus: both by his disciples, Mt. xxvi. 25, 49; Mk. ix. 5; xi. 21; Jn. i. 38 (39), 49 (50); iv. 31; ix. 2; xi. 8; and by others, Jn. iii. 2; vi. 25; repeated to indicate earnest-ness [cf. W. § 65, 5 a.] ῥαββί, ῥαββί, R G in Mt. xxiii. 7 and Mk. xiv. 45; (so רַבִּי רַבִּי for אַבִּי אַבִּי in the Targ. on 2 K. ii. 12). Cf. *Lghtft*. Horae Hebr. et Talmud. on Mt. xxiii. 7; *Pressel* in Herzog ed. 1 xii. p. 471 sq.; [*Gins-burg* in Alex.'s Kitto s. v. Rabbi; *Hamburger*, Real-En-cyclopädie, s. v. Rabban, vol. ii. p. 943 sq.].*

4462   **ῥαββονί** (so Rec. in Mk. x. 51) and ῥαββουνί [WH -νεί, see reff. under ῥαββί, init.], (Chald. רַבּוֹן lord; רַבָּן

master, chief, prince; cf. *Levy*, Chald. WB. üb. d. Tar-gumim, ii. p. 401), *Rabboni*, *Rabbuni* (apparently [yet cf. reff. below] the Galilæan pronunciation of רִבּוֹנִי), a title of honor and reverence by which Jesus is ad-dressed; as interpreted by John, equiv. to διδάσκαλος: Jn. xx. 16; Mk. x. 51, (see ῥαββί). Cf. Keim iii. p. 560 [Eng. trans. vi. p. 311 sq.]; *Delitzsch* in the Zeitschr. f. d. luth. Theol. for 1876, pp. 409 and 606; also for 1878, p. 7; [Ginsburg and Hamburger, as in the preced-ing word; *Kautzsch*, Gram. d. Bibl.-Aram. p. 10].*

4463   **ῥαβδίζω**; 1 aor. pass. ἐρραβδίσθην and (so L T Tr WH) ἐραβδίσθην (see P, ρ); (ῥάβδος); *to beat with rods*: Acts xvi. 22; 2 Co. xi. 25. (Judg. vi. 11; Ruth ii. 17; Arstph., Diod., al.)*

4464   **ῥάβδος**, -ου, ἡ, [prob. akin to ῥαπίς, Lat. *verber*; cf. Curtius § 513], in various senses fr. Hom. down; Sept. for מַטֶּה, שֵׁבֶט, מַקֵּל, מִשְׁעֶנֶת, etc., *a staff*, *walking-stick*: i. q. *a twig*, *rod*, *branch*, Heb. ix. 4 (Num. xvii. 2 sqq. Hebr. text xvii. 16 sqq.); Rev. xi. 1; *a rod*, with which one is beaten, 1 Co. iv. 21 (Plato, legg. 3 p. 700 c.; Plut., al.; πατάσσειν τινὰ ἐν ῥάβδῳ, Ex. xxi. 20; Is. x. 24); *a staff*: as used on a journey, Mt. x. 10; Mk. vi. 8; Lk. ix. 3; or to lean upon, Heb. xi. 21 (after the Sept. of Gen. xlvii. 31, where the translators read מַטֶּה, for מִטָּה *a bed*; [cf. προσκυνέω, a.]); or by shepherds, Rev. ii. 27; xii. 5; xix. 15, in which passages as ἐν ῥάβδῳ ποιμαίνειν is fig. applied to a king, so ῥάβδῳ σιδηρᾷ, *with a rod of iron*, indicates the severest, most rigorous, rule; hence ῥάβδος is equiv. to a royal *sceptre* (like שֵׁבֶט, Ps. ii. 9; xlv. 8; for שַׁרְבִיט, Esth. iv. 11; v. 2): Heb. i. 8 (fr. Ps. xlv. 8).*

4465   **ῥαβδοῦχος**, -ου, ὁ, (ῥάβδος and ἔχω; cf. εὐνοῦχος), *one who carries the rods* i. e. *the fasces*, *a lictor* (a public offi-cer who bore the fasces or staff and other insignia of office before the magistrates), [A. V. *serjeants*]: Acts xvi. 35, 38. (Polyb.; Diod. 5, 40; Dion. Hal.; Hdian. 7, 8, 10 [5 ed. Bekk.]; διὰ τί λικτώρεις τοὺς ῥαβδούχους ὀνομάζουσι; Plut. quaest. Rom. c. 67.)*

4466   **'Ραγαύ** [so WH] or 'Ραγαῦ [R G L T Tr], (רְעוּ [i. e. 'friend'], Gen. xi. 18), ὁ, *Ragau* [A. V. *Reu*; (once *Rehu*)], one of the ancestors of Abraham: Lk. iii. 35. [B. D. Am. ed. s. v. *Reu*.]*

4467 ῥᾳδιούργημα, -τος, τό, (fr. ῥᾳδιουργέω, and this fr. ῥᾳδιουργός, compounded of ῥᾴδιος and ΕΡΓΩ. A ῥᾳδιουργός is one who does a thing with little effort and adroitly; then, in a bad sense, a man who is facile and forward in the perpetration of crime, a knave, a rogue), a piece of knavery, rascality, villany: πονηρόν, Acts xviii. 14. (Dion. Hal., Plut., Lcian.; eccles. writ.) *

4468 ῥᾳδιουργία, -ας, ἡ, (see ῥᾳδιούργημα, cf. πανουργία); 1. prop. ease in doing, facility. 2. levity or easiness in thinking and acting; love of a lazy and effeminate life (Xen.). 3. unscrupulousness, cunning, mischief, [A. V. villany]: Acts xiii. 10. (Polyb. 12, 10, 5; often in Plut.) *

see 4472 [ῥαίνω; see ῥαντίζω.]

4469 ῥακά (Tdf. ῥαχά; [the better accentuation seems to be -ᾶ; cf. Kautzsch, Gram. d. Bibl.-Aram. p. 8]), a Chald. word רֵיקָא [but acc. to Kautzsch (u. s. p.]10) not the stat. emph. of רֵיק, but shortened fr. רֵיקָן (Hebr. רִיק), empty, i. e. a senseless, empty-headed man, a term of reproach used by the Jews in the time of Christ [B. D. s. v. Raca; Wünsche, Erläuterung u. s. w. p. 47]: Mt. v. 22.*

4470 ῥάκος, -ους, τό, (ῥήγνυμι), a piece torn off; spec. a bit of cloth; cloth: Mt. ix. 16; Mk. ii. 21 [here L Tr mrg. ῥάκκος]. (Hom., Hdt., Arstph., Soph., Eur., Joseph., Sept., al.) *

4471 Ῥαμᾶ [T WH Ῥαμά; cf. B. D. Am. ed. s. v. Ramah, 1 init.], רָמָה i. e. a high place, height), ἡ, [indecl. Win. 61 (60)], Ramah, a town of the tribe of Benjamin, situated six Roman miles north of Jerusalem on the road leading to Bethel; now the village of er Râm: Mt. ii. 18 (fr. Jer. xxxviii. 15). Cf. Win. RWB. s. v.; Graf in the Theol. Stud. u. Krit. for 1854, p. 851 sqq.; Pressel in Herzog xii. p. 515 sq.; Furrer in Schenkel BL. v. p. 37; [BB. DD.].*

4472 ῥαντίζω; (fr. ῥαντός besprinkled, and this fr. ῥαίνω); 1 aor. ἐρράντισα and (so L T Tr WH) ἐράντισα (see P, ρ); [1 aor. mid. subjunc. ῥαντίσωνται (sprinkle themselves), Mk. vii. 4 WH txt. (so Volkmar, Weiss, al.) after codd. א B]; pf. pass. ptcp. ἐρραντισμένος (Tdf. ῥεραντ., L Tr WH ῥεραντ. with smooth breathing; see P, ρ); for ῥαίνω, more com. in class. Grk.; to sprinkle: prop. τινά, Heb. ix. 13 (on the rite here referred to cf. Num. xix. 2–10; Win. RWB. s. v. Sprengwasser; [B. D. s. v. Purification]); ib. 19; τὶ αἵματι, ib. 21; [Rev. xix. 13 WH (see περιρραίνω)]. 2. to cleanse by sprinkling, hence trop. to purify, cleanse: ἐρραντισμένοι τὰς καρδίας (on this acc. see B. § 134, 7) ἀπὸ κτλ. Heb. x. 22. (Athen. 12 p. 521 a.; for Hebr. חָטָא, Ps. l. (li.) 9; for נָזָה, Lev. vi. 27; 2 K. ix. 33.) *

4473 ῥαντισμός, -οῦ, ὁ, (ῥαντίζω, q. v.), used only by bibl. and eccl. writ., a sprinkling (purification): αἷμα ῥαντισμοῦ, blood of sprinkling, i. e. appointed for sprinkling (serving to purify), Heb. xii. 24 (ὕδωρ ῥαντισμοῦ for מֵי הַנִּדָּה, Num. xix. 9, 13, 20 sq.); εἰς ῥαντισμὸν αἵματος Ἰησοῦ Χρ. i. e. εἰς τὸ ῥαντίζεσθαι (or ἵνα ῥαντίζωνται) αἵματι Ἰησ. Χρ., that they may be purified (or cleansed from the guilt of their sins) by the blood of Christ, 1 Pet. i. 2 [W. § 30, 2 a.].*

4474 ῥαπίζω; fut. ῥαπίσω [cf. B. 37 (32 sq.)]; 1 aor. ἐρράπισα and (so L T Tr WH) ἐράπισα (see P, ρ); (fr. ῥαπίς a rod); 1. to smite with a rod or staff (Xenophanes in Diog. Laërt. 8, 36; Hdt., Dem., Polyb., Plut., al.). 2. to smite in the face with the palm of the hand, to box the ear: τινά, Mt. xxvi. 67 (where it is distinguished fr. κολαφίζω [A. V. buffet]; for Suidas says ῥαπίσαι· πατάσσειν τὴν γνάθον ἁπλῇ τῇ χειρί not with the fist; hence the Vulg. renders it palmas in faciem ei dederunt; [A. V. mrg. (R. V. mrg.) adopt sense 1 above]); τινὰ ἐπὶ [L T Tr txt. WH εἰς] τὴν σιαγόνα, Mt. v. 39 (Hos. xi. 4). Cf. Fischer, De vitiis Lexx. etc. p. 61 sqq.; Lob. ad Phryn. p. 175; [Schmidt, Syn. ch. 113, 10; Field, Otium Norv. pars iii. p. 71].*

4475 ῥάπισμα, -τος, τό, (ῥαπίζω, q. v.); 1. a blow with a rod or a staff or a scourge, (Antiph. in Athen. 14 p. 623 b.; Anthol., Lcian.). 2. a blow with the flat of the hand, a slap in the face, box on the ear: ῥαπίσμασιν (see βάλλω, 1), Mk. xiv. 65; διδόναι τινὶ ῥάπισμα, Jn. xviii. 22; ῥαπίσματα, Jn. xix. 3, [but in all three exx. R. V. mrg. recognizes sense 1 (see reff. s. v. ῥαπίζω)].*

4476 ῥαφίς, -ίδος, ἡ, (ῥάπτω to sew), a needle: Mt. xix. 24; Mk. x. 25; Lk. xviii. 25 Rec., [(cf. κάμηλος)]. Class. Grk. more com. uses βελόνη (q. v.); see Lob. ad Phryn. p. 90; [W. 25].*

see 4469 [ῥαχά, see ῥακά.]

4477: see 4460 Ῥαχάβ, see Ῥαάβ.

4478 Ῥαχήλ, (רָחֵל a ewe or sheep), ἡ, Rachel [cf. B. D. s. v.], the wife of the patriarch Jacob: Mt. ii. 18 (fr. Jer. xxxviii. 15).*

4479 Ῥεβέκκα (רִבְקָה, fr. רָבַק unused in Hebrew but in Arabic 'to bind,' 'fasten'; hence the subst. i. q. 'ensnarer,' fascinating the men by her beauty), ἡ, Rebecca, the wife of Isaac: Ro. ix. 10.*

see 4480 St. ῥέδη [al. ῥέδα; on the first vowel cf. Tdf.'s note on Rev. as below; WH. App. p. 151ᵃ], (acc. to Quintil. 1, 5, 57 [cf. 68] a Gallic word [cf. Vaníček; Fremdwörter, s. v. reda])—ης, ἡ, a chariot, "a species of vehicle having four wheels" (Isidor. Hispal. orig. 20, 12 (§ 511), [cf. Rich, Dict. of Antiq. s. v. Rheda]): Rev. xviii. 13.*

4481 Ῥεμφάν (R G), or Ῥεφάν (L Tr), or Ῥομφάν (T), [or Ῥομφά WH, see their App. on Acts as below], Remphan [so A.V.], or Rephan [so R.V.], Romphan, [or Rompha], a Coptic pr. name of Saturn: Acts vii. 43, fr. Amos v. 26 where the Sept. render by Ῥαιφάν [or Ῥεφάν] the Hebr. כִּיּוּן, thought by many to be equiv. to the Syriac ܟܐܘܢ, and the Arabic كَيْوَان, designations of Saturn; but by others regarded as an appellative, signifying 'stand,' 'pedestal' (Germ. Gerüst; so Hitzig), or 'statue' (so Gesenius), formed from כון after the analogy of such forms as פִּנּוּק, חִבּוּק, etc. Cf. Win. RWB. s. v. Saturn; Gesenius, Thes. p. 669ᵇ; J. G. Müller in Herzog xii. 736; Merx in Schenkel i. p. 516 sq.; Schrader in Riehm p. 234; [Baudissin in Herzog ed. 2 s. v. Saturn, and reff. there given; B. D. s. v. Remphan].*

4482 ῥέω: fut. ῥεύσω (in Grk. writ. more com. ῥεύσομαι, see

W. 89 (85); [B. 67 (59)]; cf. *Lob.* ad Phryn. p. 739); [(Skr. sru; cf. Lat. *fluo*; Eng. *stream*; Curtius § 517)]; fr. Hom. down; Sept. for זוּב; *to flow*: Jn. vii. 38.

4483; see [Comp.: παραρρέω.] *
(1512 a) 'ΡΕΩ, see εἶπον.

4484 'Ρήγιον, -ου, τό, *Rhegium* (now *Reggio*), a town and promontory at the extremity of the Bruttian peninsula, opposite Messana [*Messina*] in Sicily; (it seems to have got its name from the Greek verb ῥήγνυμι, because at that point Sicily was believed to have been 'rent away' from Italy; so Pliny observes, hist. nat. 3, 8, (14); [Diod. Sic. 4, 85; Strabo 6, 258; Philo de incorrupt. mund. § 26; al. See *Pape*, Eigennamen, s. v.]): Acts xxviii. 13.*

4485 ῥῆγμα, -τος, τό, (ῥήγνυμι), *what has been broken* or *rent asunder*;   **a.** *a fracture, breach, cleft*: Hippocr., Dem., [Aristot.], Polyb., al.; for בְּקִיעַ, Am. vi. 11 Alex.   **b.** plur. for קְרָעִים, *rent clothes*: 1 K. xi. 30 sq.; 2 K. ii. 12.   **c.** *fall, ruin*: Lk. vi. 49.*

4486 ῥήγνυμι (Mt. ix. 17) and ῥήσσω (Hom. Il. 18, 571; 1 K. xi. 31; Mk. ii. 22 R G L mrg.; ix. 18 [Lk. v. 37 L mrg.; (see below)]); fut. ῥήξω; 1 aor. ἔρρηξα; pres. pass. 3 pers. plur. ῥήγνυνται; fr. Hom. down; Sept. for בָּקַע and קָרַע; *to rend, burst* or *break asunder, break up, break through*;   **a.** univ.: τοὺς ἀσκούς, Mk. ii. 22; Lk. v. 37; pass. Mt. ix. 17; i. q. *to tear in pieces* [A.V. *rend*]: τινά, Mt. vii. 6.   **b.** sc. εὐφροσύνην (previously chained up, as it were), *to break forth into joy*: Gal. iv. 27, after Is. liv. 1 (the full phrase is found in Is. xlix. 13; lii. 9; [cf. B. § 130, 5]; in class. Grk. ῥήγνυνται κλαυθμόν, οἰμωγήν, δάκρυα, esp. φωνήν is used of infants or dumb persons beginning to speak; cf. Passow s. v. 2, vol. ii. p. 1332'; [L. and S. s. v. I. 4 and 5]).   **c.** i. q. σπαράσσω, *to distort, convulse*: of a demon causing convulsions in a man possessed, Mk. ix. 18; Lk. ix. 42; in both pass. many [so R. V. txt.] explain it *to dash down, hurl to the ground*, (a common occurrence in cases of epilepsy); in this sense in Artem. oneir. 1, 60 a wrestler is said ῥῆξαι τὸν ἀντίπαλον. Hesych. gives ῥῆξαι· καταβαλεῖν. Also ῥῆξε· κατέβαλε. Cf. Kuinoel or Fritzsche on Mk. ix. 18. [Many hold that ῥήσσω in this sense is quite a different word from ῥήγνυμι (and its collat. or poet. ῥήσσω), and akin rather to (the onomatopoetic) ἀράσσω, ῥάσσω, to throw or dash down; cf. Lobeck in Bttm. Ausf. Spr. § 114, s. v. ῥήγνυμι; *Curtius*, Das Verbum, pp. 162, 315; *Schmidt*, Syn. ch. 113, 7. See as exx. Sap. iv. 19; Herm. mand. 11, 3; Const. apost. 6, 9 p. 165, 14. Cf. προσρήγνυμι.] (Comp.: δια-, περι-, προσρήγνυμι.) *

[Syn.: ῥ ή γ ν υ μ ι, κ α τ ά γ ν υ μ ι, θ ρ α ύ ω: ῥ. *to rend, rend asunder*, makes pointed reference to the separation of the parts; κ. *to break*, denotes the destruction of a thing's unity or completeness; θ. *to shatter*, is suggestive of many fragments and minute dispersion. Cf. Schmidt ch. 115]

4487 ῥῆμα, -τος, τό, (fr. 'ΡΕΩ, pf. pass. εἴρημαι), fr. Theogn., Hdt., Pind. down; Sept. chiefly for דָּבָר; also for אֹמֶר, אִמְרָה, פֶּה מִלָּה, etc.;   **1.** prop. *that which is* or *has been uttered by the living voice, thing spoken, word*, [cf. ἔπος, also λόγος, I. 1]; i. e.   **a.** *any sound produced*

by the voice and having a definite meaning: Mt. xxvii. 14; ῥ. γλώσσης, Sir. iv. 24; φωνὴ ῥημάτων, a sound of words, Heb. xii. 19; ῥήματα ἄρρητα, [unspeakable words], 2 Co. xii. 4.   **b.** Plur. τὰ ῥήματα, *speech, discourse*, (because it consists of words either few or many [cf. Philo, leg. alleg. 3, 61 τὸ δὲ ῥῆμα μέρος λόγου]): Lk. vii. 1; Acts ii. 14; *words, sayings*, Jn. viii. 20; x. 21; Acts [x. 44]; xvi. 38; τὰ ῥ. τινος, *what one has said*, Lk. xxiv. 8, 11, or *taught*, Ro. x. 18; τὰ ῥ. μου, my teaching, Jn. v. 47; xii. 47 sq.; xv. 7; τὰ ῥ. ἃ ἐγὼ λαλῶ, Jn. vi. 63; xiv. 10; [ἀληθείας κ. σωφροσύνης ῥ. ἀποφθέγγομαι, Acts xxvi. 25]; ῥήματα ζωῆς αἰωνίου ἔχεις, thy teaching begets eternal life, Jn. vi. 68; τὰ ῥ. τοῦ θεοῦ, utterances in which God through some one declares his mind, Jn. viii. 47; λαλεῖ τις τὰ ῥ. τοῦ θ. speaks what God bids him, Jn. iii. 34; λαλεῖν πάντα τὰ ῥήματα τῆς ζωῆς ταύτης, to deliver the whole doctrine concerning this life, i. e. the life eternal, Acts v. 20; τὰ ῥ. ἃ δέδωκάς μοι, what thou hast bidden me to speak, Jn. xvii. 8; ῥήματα λαλεῖν πρός τινα, ἐν οἷς etc. to teach one the things by which etc. Acts xi. 14; τὰ ῥήματα τὰ προειρημένα ὑπὸ τινος, what one has foretold, 2 Pet. iii. 2; Jude 17; λαλεῖν ῥήματα βλάσφημα εἴς τινα, to speak abusively in reference to one [see εἰς, B. II. 2 c. β.], Acts vi. 11; κατά τινος, against a thing, ib. 13 [G L T Tr WH om. βλάσφ.].   **c.** *a series of words joined together into a sentence (a declaration of one's mind made in words)*;   **a.** univ. *an utterance, declaration*, (Germ. *eine Aeusserung*): Mt. xxvi. 75; Mk. ix. 32; xiv. 72; Lk. ii. 50; ix. 45; xviii. 34; xx. 26; Acts xi. 16; xxviii. 25; with adjectives, ῥῆμα ἀργόν, Mt. xii. 36; εἰπεῖν πονηρὸν ῥῆμα κατά τινος, to assail one with abuse, Mt. v. 11 [R G; al. om. ῥ.].   **β.** *a saying of any sort, as a message, a narrative*: concerning some occurrence, λαλεῖν τὸ ῥ. περί τινος, Lk. ii. 17; ῥῆμα τῆς πίστεως, *the word of faith*, i. e. concerning the necessity of putting faith in Christ, Ro. x. 8; *a promise*, Lk. i. 38; ii. 29; καλὸν θεοῦ ῥῆμα, God's gracious, comforting promise (of salvation), Heb. vi. 5 (see καλός, e.); καθαρίσας ... ἐν ῥήματι, acc. to promise (prop. *on the ground of his *word* of promise*, viz. the promise of the pardon of sins; cf. Mk. xvi. 16), Eph. v. 26 [al. take ῥ. here as i. q. 'the gospel,' cf. vi. 17, Ro. x. 8; (see Meyer at loc.)]; *the word by which some thing is commanded, directed, enjoined*: Mt. iv. 4 [cf. W. 389 (364) n.]; Lk. iv. 4 R G L Tr in br.; Heb. xi. 3; *a command*, Lk. v. 5; ἐγένετο ῥῆμα θεοῦ ἐπί τινα, Lk. iii. 2 (Jer. i. 1; πρός τινα, Gen. xv. 1; 1 K. xviii. 1); plur. ῥήματα παρὰ σοῦ, *words from thee*, i. e. to be spoken by thee, Acts x. 22; ῥῆμα τῆς δυνάμεως αὐτοῦ, his omnipotent command, Heb. i. 3.   *doctrine, instruction*, [cf. W. 123 (117)]: (τὸ) ῥῆμα (τοῦ) θεοῦ, divine instruction by the preachers of the gospel, Ro. x. 17 [R G; but L T Tr WH ῥ. Χριστοῦ; others give ῥ. here the sense of *command, commission*; (cf. Meyer)]; *saving truth which has God for its author*, Eph. vi. 17; also τοῦ κυρίου, 1 Pet. i. 25; *words of prophecy, prophetic announcement*, τὰ ῥ. τοῦ θεοῦ, Rev. xvii. 17 Rec. [al. οἱ λόγοι τ. θ.].   **2.** In imitation of the Hebr. דָּבָר, *the subject-matter of speech, thing* spoken of, thing; and that   **a.** so far forth as it is a matter of narration: Lk. ii. 15; Acts x. 37; plur., Lk. i. 65; ii. 19, 51; Acts v. 32; xiii. 42.   **b.** in so far as it is matter of command: Lk. i. 37 [see ἀδυνατέω, b.] (Gen. xviii. 14; Deut. xvii. 8).   **c.** a matter of dispute, case at law: Mt. xviii. 16; 2 Co. xiii. 1 [A. V. retains 'word' here and in the preceding pass.], (Deut. xix. 15).*

4488   'Ρησά [Lchm. -σᾶ (so Pape, Eigennamen, s. v.)], ὁ, Rhesa, the son of Zerubbabel: Lk. iii. 27.*

see 4486   ῥήσσω, see ῥήγνυμι.

4489   ῥήτωρ, -ορος, ὁ, ('ΡΕΩ), a speaker, an orator, (Soph. Eur., Arstph., Xen., Plat., al.): of a forensic orator or advocate, Acts xxiv. 1. [Cf. Thom. Mag. s. v. (p. 324, 15 ed. Ritschl); B. D. s. v. Orator, 2.] *

4490   ῥητῶς, (ῥητός), adv., expressly, in express words: ῥητῶς λέγει, 1 Tim. iv. 1. (Polyb. 3, 23, 5; Strabo 9 p. 426; Plut. Brut. 29; [de Stoic. repugn. 15, 10]; Diog. Laërt. 8, 71; [al.; cf. Wetstein on 1 Tim. l. c.; W. 463 (431)].)*

4491   ῥίζα, -ης, ἡ. (akin to Germ. Reis [cf. Lat. radix; Eng. root; see Curtius § 515; Fick, Pt. iii. 775]), fr. Hom. down; Sept. for שֹׁרֶשׁ;   **1.** a root: prop., Mt. iii. 10; Lk. iii. 9; ἐκ ῥιζῶν, from the roots [cf. W. § 51, 1 d.], Mk. xi. 20; ῥίζαν ἔχειν, to strike deep root, Mt. xiii. 6; Mk. iv. 6; trop. οὐ ῥίζαν ἔχειν ἐν ἑαυτῷ, spoken of one who has but a superficial experience of divine truth, has not permitted it to make its way into the inmost recesses of his soul, Mt. xiii. 21; Mk. iv. 17; Lk. viii. 13; in fig. disc. ῥίζα πικρίας (see πικρία) of a person disposed to apostatize and induce others to commit the same offence, Heb. xii. 15; the progenitors of a race are called ῥίζα, their descendants κλάδοι (see κλάδος, b.), Ro. xi. 16–18. Metaph. cause, origin, source: πάντων τῶν κακῶν, 1 Tim. vi. 10; τῆς σοφίας, Sir. i. 6 (5), 20 (18); τῆς ἀθανασίας, Sap. xv. 3; τῆς ἁμαρτίας, of the devil, Ev. Nicod. 23; ἀρχὴ καὶ ῥίζα παντὸς ἀγαθοῦ, Epicur. ap. Athen. 12, 67 p. 546 sq.; πηγὴ καὶ ῥίζα καλοκαγαθία τὸ νομίζειν τυχεῖν παιδείας, Plut. de puer. educ. c. 7 b.   **2.** after the use of the Hebr. שֹׁרֶשׁ, that which like a root springs from a root, a sprout, shoot; metaph. offspring, progeny: Ro. xv. 12; Rev. v. 5; xxii. 16, (Is. xi. 10).*

4492   ῥιζόω, -ῶ: pf. pass. ptcp. ἐρριζωμένος [see Ρ, ρ]; (ῥίζα); fr. Hom. down; to cause to strike root, to strengthen with roots; as often in class. writ. (see Passow s. v. 3; [L. and S. s. v. I.]), trop. to render firm, to fix, establish, cause a person or a thing to be thoroughly grounded: pass. ἐρριζωμένος (Vulg. radicatus) ἐν ἀγάπη, Eph. iii. 17 (18) [not WH]; ἐν Χριστῷ, in communion with Christ, Col. ii. 7. [Comp. ἐκ-ριζόω.] *

4493   ῥιπή, -ῆς, ἡ, (ῥίπτω), used by the Grk. poets fr. Hom. down; a throw, stroke, beat: ὀφθαλμοῦ (Vulg. ictus oculi [A. V. the twinkling of an eye]), a moment of time, 1 Co. xv. 52 [L mrg. ῥοπή, q. v.].*

4494   ῥιπίζω: pres. pass. ptcp. ῥιπιζόμενος; (fr. ῥιπίς a bellows or fan); hence   **1.** prop. to raise a breeze, put air in motion, whether for the sake of kindling a fire or of cooling one's self; hence   **a.** to blow up a fire: φλόγα, πῦρ, Anthol. 5, 122, 6; Plut. Flam. 21.   **b.** to

fan i. e. cool with a fan (Tertull. flabello): Plut. Anton. 26.   **2.** to toss to and fro, to agitate: of the wind, πρὸς ἀνέμων ῥιπίζεται τὸ ὕδωρ, Philo de incorrupt. mundi § 24; ῥιπιζομένη ἄχνη, Dio Cass. 70, 4; δῆμος ἄστατον, κακὸν καὶ θαλάσσῃ πάνθ' ὅμοιον, ὑπ' ἀνέμου ῥιπίζεται, Dio Chr. 32 p. 368 b.; hence joined w. ἀνεμίζεσθαι it is used of a person whose mind wavers in uncertainty between hope and fear, between doing and not doing a thing, Jas. i. 6.*

ῥιπτέω, see ῥίπτω — — — — — — — 4495; see 4496

4496   ῥίπτω and ῥιπτέω (ῥιπτούντων, Acts xxii. 23; on the diff. views with regard to the difference in meaning betw. these two forms see Passow s. v. ῥίπτω, fin.; [Veitch s. v. ῥίπτω, fin. Hermann held that ῥιπτεῖν differed fr. ῥίπτειν as Lat. jactare fr. jacere, hence the former had a frequent. force (cf. Lob. Soph. Aj. p. 177; Cope, Aristot. rhet. vol. i. p. 91 sq.); some of the old grammarians associate with ῥιπτεῖν a suggestion of earnestness or effort, others of contempt]); 1 aor. ἔρριψα G Tr, ἔρρ. R L, ἔριψα T WH, [ptcp. (Lk. iv. 35) ῥίψαν R G Tr WH, better (cf. Tdf. Proleg. p. 102; Veitch p. 512) ῥῖψαν L T]; pf. pass. 3 pers. sing. ἔρριπται [G Tr; al. ἔρρ.] (Lk. xvii. 2), ptcp. ἐρριμμένος G, ἐριμμένος T Tr WH, ῥερ. (with smooth breathing) Lchm. (Mt. ix. 36); on the doubling of ρ and the use of the breathing see Ρ, ρ; fr. Hom. down; Sept. chiefly for הִשְׁלִיךְ;   to cast, throw; i. q. to throw down: τί, Acts xxvii. 19; τὶ ἔκ τινος, ibid. 29; τινὰ εἰς τὴν θάλασσαν, Lk. xvii. 2.   i. q. to throw off: τὰ ἱμάτια (Plat. rep. 5 p. 474 a.), Acts xxii. 23 (they cast off their garments that they might be the better prepared to throw stones [but cf. Wendt in Mey. 5te Aufl.]); τὰ ὅπλα, 1 Macc. v. 43; vii. 44; xi. 51; Xen. Cyr. 4, 2, 33, and often in other Grk. writ.   i. q. to cast forward or before: τινὰ [or τὶ] εἴς τι, [Mt. xxvii. 5 (but here R G L ἐν τῷ ναῷ)]; Lk. iv. 35; τινὰς παρὰ τοὺς πόδας Ἰησοῦ, to set down (with the suggestion of haste and want of care), of those who laid their sick at the feet of Jesus, leaving them at his disposal without a doubt but that he could heal them, Mt. xv. 30.   i. q. to throw to the ground, prostrate: ἐρριμμένοι, prostrated by fatigue, hunger, etc., [R. V. scattered], Mt. ix. 36 (καταλαβὼν ἐρριμμένους καὶ μεθύοντας, the enemy prostrate on the ground, Polyb. 5, 48, 2; of the slain, Jer. xiv. 16; ἐρριμμένα σώματα, 1 Macc. xi. 4; for other exx. see Wahl, Clavis Apocr. V.T. s. v.; τῶν νεκρῶν ἐρριμμένων ἐπὶ τῆς ἀγορᾶς, Plut. Galb. 28, 1). [Comp. ἀπο-, ἐπι- ῥίπτω.] *

4497   'Ροβοάμ, (רְחַבְעָם i. e. 'enlarging the people', equiv. to Εὐρύδημος in Grk., fr. רְחַב and עָם), ὁ, Roboam, Rehoboam, the son and successor of king Solomon: Mt. i. 7.*

4498   'Ρόδη, -ης, ἡ, Rhoda [i. e. 'rose'], the name of a certain maidservant: Acts xii. 13.*

4499   'Ρόδος, -ου, ἡ, Rhodes, [(cf. Pape, Eigennamen, s. v.)], a well-known island of the Cyclades opposite Caria and Lycia, with a capital of the same name: Acts xxi. 1. ([From Hom. down]; 1 Macc. xv. 23.) *

4500   ῥοιζηδόν, (ῥοιζέω to make a confused noise), adv., 'with a loud noise': 2 Pet. iii. 10. (Nicand. ther. 556; Geop., al.) *

(4500α):
see 4481 ['Ρομφά, 'Ρομφάν, see 'Ρεμφάν.]

4501 ————ῥομφαία, -ας, ἡ, a large sword; prop. a long Thracian javelin [cf. Rich, Dict. of Antiq. s. v. Rhompæa]; also a kind of long sword wont to be worn on the right shoulder, (Hesych. ῥομφαία· Θράκιον ἀμυντήριον, μάχαιρα, ξίφος ἢ ἀκόντιον μακρόν; [Suidas 3223 c. (cf. ῥέμβω to revolve, vibrate)]; cf. Plut. Aemil. 18); [A. V. sword]: Rev. i. 16; ii. 12, 16; vi. 8; xix. 15, 21; σοῦ δὲ αὐτῆς τὴν ψυχὴν διελεύσεται ῥομφαία, a fig. for 'extreme anguish shall fill (pierce, as it were) thy soul', Lk. ii. 35, where cf. Kuinoel. (Joseph. antt. 6, 12, 4; 7, 12, 1; in Ev. Nicod. 26 the archangel Michael, keeper of Paradise, is called ἡ φλογίνη ῥομφαία. Very often in Sept. for חֶרֶב; often also in the O. T. Apocr.) *

see 4493 [ῥοπή, -ῆς, ἡ, (ῥέπω), fr. Aeschyl., Plat., down, inclination downwards, as of the turning of the scale: ἐν ῥοπῇ ὀφθαλμοῦ, 1 Co. xv. 52 L mrg. (cf. Tdf.'s note ad loc.); see ῥιπή.*]

4502 'Ρουβήν (in Joseph. antt. 1, 19, 8 'Ρούβηλος), ὁ, (רְאוּבֵן, i. e. behold ye a son! Gen. xxix. 32 [cf. B. D. s. v.]), Reuben, Jacob's firstborn son by Leah: Rev. vii. 5.*

4503 'Ρούθ (in Joseph. antt. 5, 9, 2 'Ρούθη, -ης), ἡ, (רוּת for רְעוּת, a female friend), Ruth, a Moabitish woman, one of the ancestors of king David, whose history is related in the canonical book bearing her name: Mt. i. 5. [B. D. s. v. Ruth.]*

4504 'Ροῦφος, -ου, ὁ, Rufus [i. e. 'red', 'reddish'], a Lat. proper name of a certain Christian: Mk. xv. 21; Ro. xvi. 13. [B. D. s. v. Rufus.]*

4505 ῥύμη, -ης, ἡ, (fr. ΡΥΩ i. q. ἐρύω 'to draw' [but Curtius § 517; Vaniček p. 1210, al., connect it with ῥέω 'to flow']); 1. in earlier Grk. the swing, rush, force, trail, of a body in motion. 2. in later Grk. a tract of way in a town shut in by buildings on both sides; a street, lane: Mt. vi. 2; Lk. xiv. 21; Acts ix. 11; xii. 10; cf. Is. xv. 3; Sir. ix. 7; Tob. xiii. 18. Cf. Lob. ad Phryn. p. 404; [Rutherford, New Phryn. p. 488; Wetstein on Mt. u. s.; W. 22, 23].*

4506 ῥύομαι; fut. ῥύσομαι; 1 aor. ἐρρυσάμην G (ἐρρυσ- R, so T in 2 Co. i. 10; 2 Pet. ii. 7; L everywh. exc. in 2 Tim. iii. 11 txt.) and ἐρυσάμην (so Tr WH everywh., T in Col. i. 13; 2 Tim. iii. 11; L txt. in 2 Tim. iii. 11); a depon. mid. verb, in later Grk. w. the 1 aor. pass. ἐρρύσθην G (-ρρ- R), and (so L T Tr WH in 2 Tim. iv. 17) ἐρύσθην; (on the doubling of ρ, and the breathing, see in P, ρ); fr. Hom. down; Sept. chiefly for הִצִּיל; also for פָּלַט נָאַל (to cause to escape, to deliver), הָלַץ (to draw out), כָּלַם הוֹשִׁיעַ, etc.; fr. ΡΥΩ to draw, hence prop. to draw to one's self, to rescue, to deliver: τινά, Mt. xxvii. 43; 2 Pet. ii. 7; τινὰ ἀπό τινος [cf. W. § 30, 6 a.], Mt. vi. 13; Lk. xi. 4 R L; 1 Th. i. 10 [here T Tr WH ἐκ; 2 Tim. iv. 18]; 1 aor. pass., Ro. xv. 31; 2 Th. iii. 2; τινὰ ἔκ τινος [W. u. s.]: Ro. vii. 24 [cf. W. § 41 a. 5]; 2 Co. i. 10; Col. i. 13; 2 Tim. iii. 11; 2 Pet. ii. 9; 1 aor. pass., Lk. i. 74; 2 Tim. iv. 17; ὁ ῥυόμενος, the deliverer, Ro. xi. 26 (after Is. lix. 20).*

see 4510 ῥυπαίνω: (ῥύπος, q. v.); to make filthy, befoul; to defile, dishonor, (Xen., Aristot., Dion. Hal., Plut., al.); 1 aor.

pass. impv. 3 pers. sing. ῥυπανθήτω, let him be made filthy, i. e. trop. let him continue to defile himself with sins, Rev. xxii. 11 L T Tr WH txt.*

ῥυπαρεύομαι: 1 aor. (pass.) impv. 3 pers. sing. ῥυπα- see 4510 ρευθήτω; (ῥυπαρός, q. v.); to be dirty, grow filthy; metaph. to be defiled with iniquity: Rev. xxii. 11 G L ed. ster. WH mrg. Found nowhere else; see ῥυπαίνω and ῥυπόω.*

4507 ῥυπαρία, -ας, ἡ, (ῥυπαρός), filthiness (Plut. praecept. conjug. c. 28); metaph. of wickedness as moral defilement: Jas. i. 21. [Of sordidness, in Critias ap. Poll. 3, 116; Plut. de adulat. et amic. § 19; al.]*

4508 ῥυπαρός, -ά, -όν, (ῥύπος, q. v.), filthy, dirty: prop. of clothing [A. V. vile], Jas. ii. 2 (Sept. Zech. iii. 3 sq.; Joseph. antt. 7, 11, 3; Plut. Phoc. 18; Dio Cass. 65, 20; ῥυπαρὰ καὶ ἄπλυτα, Artem. oneir. 2, 3 fin.; χλαμύς, Ael. v. h. 14, 10); metaph. defiled with iniquity, base, [A. V. filthy]: Rev. xxii. 11 G L T Tr WH. [(In the sense of sordid, mean, Dion. Hal., al.)]*

4509 ῥύπος, -ου, ὁ, fr. Hom. down, filth: 1 Pet. iii. 21 [B. § 151, 14; W. § 30, 3 N. 3].*

4510 ῥυπόω, -ῶ; 1 aor. impv. 3 pers. sing. ῥυπωσάτω; 1. to make filthy, defile, soil: Hom. Od. 6, 59. 2. intrans. for ῥυπάω, to be filthy: morally, Rev. xxii. 11 Rec.*

4511 ῥύσις, -εως, ἡ, (fr. an unused pres. ῥύω, from which several of the tenses of ῥέω are borrowed), a flowing, issue: τοῦ αἵματος, Mk. v. 25; Lk. viii. 43, [on the two preced. pass. cf. B. § 147, 11; W. § 29, 3 b.], 44, (Hippocr., Aristot.).*

4512 ῥυτίς, -ίδος, ἡ, (ΡΥΩ, to draw together, contract), a wrinkle: Eph. v. 27. (Arstph., Plat., Diod. 4, 51; Plut., Lcian., Anthol., al.)*

4513 'Ρωμαϊκός, -ή, -όν, Roman, Latin: Lk. xxiii. 38 R G L br. Tr mrg. br. [(Polyb., Diod., Dion. Hal., al.)]*

4514 'Ρωμαῖος, -ου, ὁ, a Roman: Jn. xi. 48; Acts ii. 10 [R. V. here from Rome]; xvi. 21, 37 sq.; xxii. 25–27, 29; xxiii. 27; xxv. 16; xxviii. 17. ([Polyb., Joseph., al.]; often in 1 and 2 Macc.)*

4515 'Ρωμαϊστί, adv., in the Roman fashion or language, in Latin: Jn. xix. 20. [Epictet. diss. 1, 17, 16; Plut., App., al.]*

4516 'Ρώμη, -ης, ἡ [on the art. with it cf. W. § 18, 5 b.; (on its derivation cf. Curtius § 517; Vaniček p. 1212; Pape, Eigennamen, s. v.)], Rome, the renowned capital of Italy and ancient head of the world: Acts xviii. 2; xix. 21; xxiii. 11; xxviii. 14, 16; Ro. i. 7, 15; 2 Tim. i. 17. (1 Macc. i. 10; vii. 1; [Aristot., Polyb., al.].) [On Rome in St. Paul's time cf. BB.DD. s. v.; Conybeare and Howson, Life and Epp. etc. ch. xxiv.; Farrar, Life and Work etc. chh. xxxvii., xliv., xlv.; Lewin, St. Paul, vol. ii. ch. vi.; Hausrath, Neutest. Zeitgesch. iii. 65 sqq.; on the Jews and Christians there, see particularly Schürer, Die Gemeindeverfassung der Juden in Rom in d. Kaiserzeit nach d. Inschriften dargest. (Leipz. 1879); Seyerlen, Entstehung u.s.w. der Christengemeinde in Rom (Tübingen, 1874); Huidekoper, Judaism at Rome, 2d ed., N. Y. 1877; Schaff, Hist. of the Chris. Church (1882) vol. i. § 36.]*

4517 ῥώννυμι: *to make strong, to strengthen*; pf. pass. ἔρρωμαι [see P, ρ], *to be strong, to thrive, prosper*; hence the 2 pers. (sing.) impv. is the usual formula in closing a letter, ἔρρωσο, *farewell*: Acts xxiii. 30 [R G]; ἔρρωσθε, Acts xv. 29 (2 Macc. xi. 21; Xen. Cyr. 4, 5, 33; Artem. oneir. 3, 44, al.; ἔρρωσο καὶ ὑγίαινε, Dio Cass. 61, 13).*

Σ

[Σ, σ, s: the practice (adopted by Griesbach, Knapp, al., after H. Stephanus et al.) of employing the character s in the mid. of a comp. word has been abandoned by the recent crit. editors; cf. W. § 5, 1 c.; *Lipsius*, Gram. Untersuch. p. 122; Matthiae § 1 Anm. 5; *Bttm.* Ausf. Sprchl. § 2 Anm. 3; Kühner § 1 Anm. 1. Tdf. ed. 8 writes σ also even at the end of a word, after the older Mss. On movable final s see ἄχρι(s), μέχρι(s), οὕτω(s). The (Ionic) combinations ρσ for ρρ, and σσ for ττ (cf. *Fischer*, Animadvers. ad Veller. etc. i. pp. 193 sq. 203; Kühner § 31 pp. 124, 127), have become predominant (cf. ἄρσην, θαρσέω, θάρσος, ἀπαλλάσσω etc., γλῶσσα, ἥσσων (q. v.), θάλασσα, κηρύσσω, περισσός, πράσσω (q. v.), τάσσω, τέσσαρες, φυλάσσω, etc.), except in a few words, as κρείττων (q. v.), the derivatives of ἐλάττων (of which word both forms are used indiscriminately), ἥττημα, ἡττάω (yet see 2 Co. xii. 13), etc.; cf. B. 7. Some prop. names are spelled indifferently with one σ or with two; as, Ἐλισ(σ)αῖος. ζ is occasionally substituted for σ, esp. before μ, see σβέννυμι, Σμύρνα (σμύρνα, cf. *Soph.* Gloss. § 58, 3, and Lex. s. v.; *Tdf.* Proleg. p. 80; *WH.* App. p. 148; B. 5; *Bttm.* Ausf. Sprchl. § 3 Anm. 6; Bezae cod., ed. *Scrivener*, p. xlviii.; L. and S. s. v. Z, I. 3, and Σ, II. 14 c.); so also ξ, as ξυμβαίνω 1 Pet. iv. 12 Rᵇᵉᶻ; cf. Kühner § 325, 5; *Bttm.* Ausf. Spr. u. s.; see ξύν.]

4518 σαβαχθανί, -νεί T Tr WH [see *WH.* App. p. 155, and s. v. ει, ι], -κθανί Lchm. [in Mt. only], (שְׁבַקְתַּנִי, fr. the Chald. שְׁבַק), *thou hast forsaken me*: Mt. xxvii. 46; Mk. xv. 34 (fr. Ps. xxi. (xxii.) 2, for the Hebr. עֲזַבְתָּנִי, which is so rendered also by the Chaldee paraphrast). [See *Kautzsch*, Gram. d. Bibl.-Aram. (Leipzig 1884) p. 11.]*

4519 σαβαώθ (Hebr. צְבָאוֹת, plur. of צָבָא an army): κύριος σαβαώθ (יְהוָה צְבָאוֹת), [A. V. *Lord of Sabaoth*], i. e. *lord of the armies* sc. of Israel, as those who under the leadership and protection of Jehovah maintain his cause in war (cf. *Schrader*, Ueber d. ursprüngl. Sinn des Gottesnamens Jahve Zebaoth, in the Jahrbb. f. protest. Theol. for 1875, p. 316 sqq., and in Schenkel v. 702 sq.; cf. *Herm. Schultz*, Alttest. Theol. ii. p. 96 sqq.; [B.D. s. v. Sabaoth, the Lord of. But for the other view, acc. to which the *heavenly* "hosts" are referred to, see Hackett in B. D., Am. ed., s. v. Tsebaoth Lord of, and Delitzsch in the Luth. Zeitschr. for 1874, p. 217 sqq.; so Riehm (HWB s. v. Zebaoth) as respects the use of the phrase by the prophets]. On the diverse interpretations of the word cf. *Oehler* in Herzog xvii. p. 400 sqq. [and in his O. T. Theol. (ed. Day) §§ 195 sq.; cf. *T. K. Cheyne*, Isa., ed. 3, vol. i. 11 sq.]): Ro. ix. 29; Jas. v. 4.*

σαββατισμός, -οῦ, ὁ, (σαββατίζω to keep the sabbath); **1.** *a keeping sabbath.* **2.** *the blessed rest from toils and troubles* looked for in the age to come by the true worshippers of God and true Christians [R. V. *sabbath rest*]: Heb. iv. 9. (Plut. de superstit. c. 3; eccl. writ.)* **4520**

σάββατον, -ου, τό, (Hebr. שַׁבָּת), found in the N. T. only in the historical bks. exc. twice in Paul's Epp.; *sabbath*; i. e. **1.** the seventh day of each week, which was a sacred festival on which the Israelites were required to abstain from all work (Ex. xx. 10; xxxi. 13 sqq.; Deut. v. 14); **a.** sing. σάββατον and τὸ σάββατον: Mk. vi. 2; [xv. 42 L Tr]; xvi. 1; Jn. v. 9 sq., etc.; i. q. the institution of the sabbath, the law for keeping holy every seventh day of the week: Mt. xii. 8; Mk. ii. 27 sq.; Lk. vi. 5; λύειν, Jn. v. 18; τηρεῖν, Jn. ix. 16; ἡ ἡμέρα τοῦ σαββάτου (יוֹם הַשַּׁבָּת, Ex. xx. 8 and often), the day of the sabbath, sabbath-day, Lk. xiii. 16; xiv. 5; ὁδὸς σαββάτου, *a sabbath-day's journey*, the distance it is lawful to travel on the sabbath-day, i. e. acc. to the Talmud two thousand cubits or paces, acc. to Epiphanius (haer. 66, 82) six stadia: Acts i. 12, cf. Mt. xxiv. 20, (the regulation was derived fr. Ex. xvi. 29); cf. *Win.* RWB. s. v. Sabbathsweg; *Oehler* in Herzog xiii. 203 sq. [cf. *Leyrer* in Herzog ed. 2 vol. ix. 379]; *Mangold* in Schenkel v. 127 sq.; [*Ginsburg* in Alexander's Kitto s. v. Sabbath Day's Journey; Lumby on Acts i. 12 (in Cambr. Bible for Schools)]. as dat. of time [W. § 31, 9 b.; B. § 133, 26]: σαββάτῳ, Mt. xxiv. 20 [G L T Tr WH]; Lk. xiv. 1; τῷ σαββάτῳ, Lk. vi. 9 L txt. T Tr WH; xiii. 14 sq.; xiv. 3; Acts xiii. 44; ἐν σαββάτῳ, Mt. xii. 2; Jn. v. 16; vii. 22 [here L WH br. ἐν], 23; ἐν τῷ σαββάτῳ, Lk. vi. 7; Jn. xix. 31. accus. τὸ σάββ. during (on) the sabbath [cf. B. § 131, 11; W. § 32,6]: Lk. xxiii. 56; κατὰ πᾶν σ. every sabbath, Acts xiii. 27; xv. 21; xviii. 4. plur. τὰ σάββατα, of several sabbaths, Acts xvii. 2 [some refer this to 2]. **b.** plur. τὰ σάββ. (for the singular) of a single sabbath, *sabbath-day*, (the use of the plur. being occasioned either by the plur. names of festivals, as τὰ ἐγκαίνια, ἄζυμα, γενέσια, or by the Chaldaic form שַׁבָּתָא [W. 177 (167); B. 23 (21)]): Mt. xxviii. 1; Col. ii. 16, (Ex. xx. 10; Lev. xxiii. 32 etc.; τὴν ἑβδόμην σάββατα καλοῦμεν, Joseph. antt. 3, 6, 6; add, 1, 1, 1; [14, 10, 25; Philo de Abrah. § 5; de cherub. § 26; Plut. de superstitione 8]; τὴν τῶν σαββάτων ἑορτήν, **4521**

Plut. symp. 4, 6, 2; hodie tricesima sabbata, Hor. sat. 1, 9, 69; nowhere so used by John exc. in the phrase μία τῶν σαββάτων, on which see 2 below); ἡ ἡμέρα τῶν σ., Lk. iv. 16; Acts xiii. 14; xvi. 13 (Ex. xx. 8; xxxv. 3; Deut. v. 12; Jer. xvii. 21 sq.); τοῖς σάββασιν and ἐν τοῖς σάββασιν (so constantly [exc. Lchm. in Mt. xii. 1, 12] by metaplasm for σαββάτοις, cf. W. 63 (62); [B. 23 (21)]) on the sabbath-day: Mt. xii. 1 [see above], 5, 10-12 [see above]; Mk. i. 21; ii. 23; iii. 2, 4; Lk. iv. 31; vi. 9 [R G L mrg.], (1 Macc. ii. 38; the Sept. uses the form σαββάτοις, and Josephus both forms). On the precepts of the Jews with regard to the observance of the sabbath, which were for the most part extremely punctilious and minute, cf. Win. RWB. s. v. Sabbath; Oehler in Herzog xiii. 192 sqq. [revised by Orelli in ed. 2 vol. xiii. 156 sqq.]; Schürer, Zeitgesch. 2te Aufl. § 28 II.; Mangold in Schenkel v. p. 123 sq.; [BB.DD. s. v.; Geikie, Life and Words of Christ, ch. xxxviii. vol. ii. p. 95 sqq.; Farrar, Life of Christ, ch. xxxi. vol. i. p. 432 sq.; Edersheim, Jesus the Messiah, vol. ii. p. 56 sqq. and App. xvii.]. 2. seven days, a week: πρώτη σαββάτου, Mk. xvi. 9; δὶς τοῦ σαβ. twice in the week, Lk. xviii. 12. The plur. is used in the same sense in the phrase ἡ μία τῶν σαββάτων, the first day of the week (see εἷς, 5) [Prof. Sophocles regards the gen. (dependent on ἡμέρα) in such exx. as those that follow (cf. Mk. xvi. 9 above) as equiv. to μετά w. an acc., the first day after the sabbath; see his Lex. p. 43 par. 6]: Mt. xxviii. 1; Mk. xvi. 2; Lk. xxiv. 1; Jn. xx. 1, 19; Acts xx. 7; κατὰ μίαν σαββάτων (L T Tr WH -του), on the first day of every week, 1 Co. xvi. 2.

4522   σαγήνη, -ης, ἡ, (σάσσω to load, fill), a large fishing-net, a drag-net (Vulg. sagena [cf. Eng. seine]), used in catching fish that swim in shoals [cf. B. D. s. v. Net; Trench, Syn. § lxiv.]: Mt. xiii. 47. (Sept.; Plut. solert. anim. p. 977 f.; Lcian. pisc. 51; Tim. 22; Artem. oneir. 2, 14; Ael. h. a. 11, 12; [βάλλειν σαγ. Babr. fab. 4, 1; 9, 6].) *

4523   Σαδδουκαῖος, -ον, ὁ, a Sadducee, a member of the party of the Sadducees, who, distinguished for birth, wealth, and official position, and not averse to the favor of the Herod family and of the Romans, hated the common people, were the opponents of the Pharisees, and rejecting tradition (see παράδοσις, 2) acknowledged the authority of the O. T. alone in matters pertaining to faith and morals (Joseph. antt. 13, 10, 6); they denied not only the resurrection of the body (Mt. xxii. 23; Mk. xii. 18; Lk. xx. 27; Acts xxiii. 8), but also the immortality of the soul and future retribution (ψυχῆς τε τὴν διαμονὴν καὶ τὰς καθ' ᾅδου τιμωρίας καὶ τιμὰς ἀναιροῦσι, Joseph. b. j. 2, 8, 14, cf. antt. 18, 1, 4), as well as the existence of angels and spirits (Acts xxiii. 8). They maintained man's freedom in opposition to the doctrine of divine predestination (acc. to Joseph. b. j. 2, 8, 14). They are mentioned in the N. T. (in addition to the pass. already referred to) in Mt. iii. 7; xvi. 1, 6, 11 sq., (in which passages they are associated apparently with the Pharisees contrary to the truth of history [(?) cf. the Comm. ad ll. cc.]); Mt. xxii. 34; Acts iv. 1; v. 17;

xxiii. 6 sq. The Sadducees derived their name apparently not from the Hebr. צַדִּיק, as though they boasted of being pre-eminently 'righteous' or 'upright' (since it cannot be shown that the vowel i ever passed over into u), but, acc. to a more probable conjecture now approved by many, from the Zadok (צָדוֹק, Sept. Σαδδούκ), who was high-priest in the time of David and exhibited special fidelity to the king and his house (2 S. xv. 24 sqq.; 1 K. i. 32 sqq.); hence the posterity of this priest (בְּנֵי צָדוֹק, Ezek. xl. 46; xliii. 19; xliv. 15; xlviii. 11) and all their adherents seem to have been called Σαδδουκαῖοι (צְדוֹקִים). Cf., besides others, Win. RWB. s. v. Sadducäer; Reuss in Herzog xiii. p. 289 sqq.; [Sieffert in Herzog ed. 2 xiii. pp. 210-244]; Geiger, Sadduc. u. Pharisäer (Brsl. 1863); Keim i. p. 273 sqq. [Eng. trans. i. (2d ed.) p. 353 sq.]; Hausrath in Schenkel iv. p. 518 sqq.; Schürer, Ntl. Zeitgesch. 2te Aufl. § 26; Wellhausen, Pharis. u. Sadducäer (Greifsw. 1874); Oort, De oorsprong van den naam Sadducëen, in the Theolog. Tijdschrift for 1876, p. 605 sqq.; [Ginsburg, in Alexander's Kitto s. v.; Edersheim, Jesus the Messiah, bk. iii. ch. ii.; Geikie, Life of Christ, ch. xlv. (cf. ch. v.); and B. D. Am. ed. s. v. for additional references].*

4524   Σαδώκ, (צָדוֹק, a pr. name occurring often in the O. T.), ὁ, Sadoc: Mt. i. 14.*

4525   σαίνω: pres. inf. pass. σαίνεσθαι; (ΣΑΩ, σείω); 1. prop. to wag the tail: of dogs, Hom. Od. 16, 6; Ael. v. h. 13, 41; Aesop. fab. 229 ed. Halm [354 ed. Coray]; with οὐρῇ added, Od. 17, 302; Hes. theog. 771; οὐρήν, Aesop l. c.; al.; see Passow [or L. and S.] s. v. I. 2. metaph. a. to flatter, fawn upon, (Aeschyl., Pind., Soph., al.). b. to move (the mind of one), a. agreeably: pass. ὑπ' ἐλπίδος, Aeschyl., Oppian; ἀληθῆ σαίνει τὴν ψυχήν, Aristot. metaph. 13, 3 p. 1090ᵇ, 37. β. to agitate, disturb, trouble: pass. 1 Th. iii. 3 [here A.V. move (B. 263 (226))] (here Lchm. ἀσαίνω, q. v.); οἱ δὲ σαινόμενοι τοῖς λεγομένοις ἐδάκρυον, Diog. Laërt. 8, 41.*

4526   σάκκος (Attic σάκος), -ον, ὁ, Hebr. שַׂק [cf. Vaniček, Fremdwörter, s. v.], a sack (Lat. saccus) i. e. a. a receptacle made for holding or carrying various things, as money, food, etc. (Gen. xlii. 25, 35; Lev. xi. 32). b. a coarse cloth (Lat. cilicium), a dark coarse stuff made especially of the hair of animals [A. V. sackcloth]: Rev. vi. 12; a garment of the like material, and clinging to the person like a sack, which was wont to be worn (or drawn on over the tunic instead of the cloak or mantle) by mourners, penitents, suppliants, Mt. xi. 21; Lk. x. 13, and also by those who, like the Hebrew prophets, led an austere life, Rev. xi. 3 (cf. what is said of the dress of John the Baptist, Mt. iii. 4; of Elijah, 2 K. i. 8). More fully in Win. RWB. s. v. Sack; Roskoff in Schenkel v. 134; [s. v. Sackcloth in B. D.; also in McClintock and Strong. (From Hdt. down.)]*

4527   Σαλά, (שֶׁלַח a missile), ὁ, Sala [so A. V. (but in Gen. Salah) properly Shelah (so R. V.)], prop. name of a man mentioned in Lk. iii. 35 (Gen. x. 24); [T Tr mrg. WH read Σαλά also in Lk. iii. 32, for Σαλμών, q. v.].*

4528   Σαλαθιήλ, (שְׁאַלְתִּיאֵל whom I asked of God), ὁ, Sala-

thiel [Grk. for *Shealtiel* (so R.V.)], the father of Zerubbabel: Mt. i. 12; [Lk. iii. 27].*

4529 **Σαλαμίς**, [on its deriv. see *Pape*, Eigennamen, s. v.], -ῖνος, ἡ, *Salamis*, the principal city of the island Cyprus: Acts xiii. 5. [BB. DD.; Dict. of Geog. s. v.; *Lewin*, St. Paul, i. 120 sq.]*

4530 **Σαλείμ**, τό, *Salim*, a town which acc. to Eusebius and Jerome [Onomast. (ed. Larsow and Parthey) pp. 28, 11; 29, 14] was eight miles S. of Scythopolis: Jn. iii. 23; cf. *Pressel* in Herzog xiii. 326; [cf. Αἰνών]. See Σαλήμ.*

4531 **σαλεύω**; 1 aor. ἐσάλευσα; Pass., pres. ptcp. σαλευόμενος; pf. ptcp. σεσαλευμένος; 1 aor. ἐσαλεύθην; 1 fut. σαλευθήσομαι; (σάλος, q. v.); fr. Aeschyl. and Arstph. down; in Sept. pass. σαλεύομαι for מוֹט and נוּעַ; **a.** prop. of the motion produced by winds, storms, waves, etc.; *to agitate* or *shake*: κάλαμον, pass., Mt. xi. 7; Lk. vii. 24; *to cause to totter*, τὰς δυνάμεις τῶν οὐρ., pass., Mt. xxiv. 29; Mk. xiii. 25; Lk. xxi. 26; τὴν γῆν, Heb. xii. 26 (Is. xxiv. 20; Am. ix. 5); an edifice, Lk. vi. 48; Acts iv. 31; xvi. 26; τὰ μὴ σαλευόμενα, the things which are not shaken, i. e. the perfect state of things which will exist after the return of Christ from heaven and will undergo no change, opp. to τὰ σαλευόμενα, the present order of things subject to vicissitude and decay, Heb. xii. 27. *to shake thoroughly*, of a measure filled by shaking its contents together, Lk. vi. 38. **b.** *to shake down, overthrow*, i. e. trop. *to cast down from one's* (secure and happy) *state*, Acts ii. 25 (fr. Ps. xv. (xvi.) 8); by a trop. use foreign to prof. auth. *to move* or *agitate* the mind, *to disturb* one: τινα ἀπὸ τοῦ νοός, so as to throw him out of his sober and natural mental state [B. 322 (277)], 2 Th. ii. 2; τοὺς ὄχλους, *to stir up*, Acts xvii. 13.*

4532 **Σαλήμ**, ἡ, (Heb. שָׁלֵם), *Salem*: Heb. vii. 1 sq.; cf. Gen. xiv. 18, which some (as Gesenius, Winer, Hitzig, Knobel, Delitzsch) think is the ancient name of the city of Jerusalem, appealing to the words of Ps. lxxvi. 3 וַיְהִי בְשָׁלֵם סֻכּוֹ, and Joseph. antt. 1, 10, 2 τὴν μέντοι Σόλυμα ὕστερον ἐκάλεσαν Ἱεροσόλυμα; cf. b. j. 6, 10. But more correctly [yet cf. B. D. s. v. Salem, and s. v. Melchizedek sub fin.] others (as Rosenmüller, Bleek, Tuch, Roediger in *Gesen.* Thesaur. s. v. p. 1422, Dillmann), relying on the testimony of Jerome ([Ep. ad Evangelum § 7 i. e.] Ep. 73 in Vallarsi's ed. of his Opp. i. p. 446), hold that it is the same as Σαλείμ (q. v.). For the ancient name of Jerusalem was יְבוּס (Judg. xix. 10; 1 Chr. xi. 4; [cf. B. D. Am. ed. s. v. Jebus]), and the form of the name in Ps. lxxvi. 3 [where Sept. εἰρήνη] is to be regarded as poetical, signifying 'safe.'*

4533 **Σαλμών**, (שַׂלְמוֹן, Ruth iv. 21), ὁ, indecl., *Salmon*, the name of a man: Mt. i. 4 sq.; Lk. iii. 32 [here T WH Tr mrg. Σαλά].*

4534 **Σαλμώνη**, -ης, ἡ, *Salmone, Salmonium*, [also *Sammonium*], an eastern and partly northern promontory of Crete opposite Cnidus and Rhodes [the identification of which is somewhat uncertain; see B. D. Am. ed. s. v. Salmone, and Dict. of Geogr. s. v. Samonium]: Acts xxvii. 7.*

4535 **σάλος**, -ου, ὁ, *the tossing* or *swell of the sea* [R. V. billows]: Lk. xxi. 25. (Soph., Eur., al.)*

4536 **σάλπιγξ**, -ιγγος, ἡ, *a trumpet*: Mt. xxiv. 31 [cf. B. 161 (141); 343 (295)]; 1 Co. xiv. 8; Heb. xii. 19; Rev. i. 10; iv. 1; viii. 2, 6, 13; ix. 14; ἐν σάλπιγγι θεοῦ, a trumpet which sounds at God's command (W. § 36, 3 b.), 1 Th. iv. 16; ἐν τῇ ἐσχάτῃ σάλπιγγι, the trumpet which will sound at the last day, 1 Co. xv. 52, [4 (2) Esdr. vi. 23; see Comm. on 1 Th. u. s.]. (From Hom. down; Sept. for שׁוֹפָר and חֲצֹצְרָה.)*

4537 **σαλπίζω**; fut. σαλπίσω (for the earlier σαλπίγξω, see Lob. ad Phryn. p. 191; Sept. also σαλπιῶ, as Num. x. [3], 5, 8, 10); 1 aor. ἐσάλπισα (also in Sept.; Ael. v. h. 1, 26 and other later writ. [cf. Veitch s. v.], for the earlier ἐσάλπιγξα, Xen. anab. 1, 2, 17) [cf. W. 89 (85); B. 37 (32); WH. App. p. 170]; fr. Hom. down; Sept. chiefly for תָּקַע, also for חָצַר; *to sound a trumpet*, [A.V. (mostly) *sound*]: Rev. viii. 6–10, 12 sq.; ix. 1, 13; x. 7; xi. 15; σαλπίσει (strictly sc. ὁ σαλπιστής or ἡ σάλπιγξ), like our *the trumpet will sound* (cf. W. § 58, 9 b. β.; [B. § 129, 16]), 1 Co. xv. 52; σαλπίζειν ἔμπροσθεν ἑαυτοῦ, i. e. to take care that what we do comes to everybody's ears, make a great noise about it, [cf. our do a thing 'with a flourish of trumpets'], Mt. vi. 2 (Cic. ad div. 16, 21 quod polliceris, te buccinatorem fore nostrae existimationis; Achill. Tat. 8, 10 αὕτη οὐχ ὑπὸ σάλπιγγι μόνον, ἀλλὰ καὶ κήρυκι μοιχεύεται).*

4538 **σαλπιστής**, (a later form, used by Theophr. char. 25; Polyb. 1, 45, 13; Dion. Hal. 4, 18, [al.], for the earlier and better σαλπιγκτής, Thuc. 6, 69; Xen. an. 4, 3, 29; Joseph. b. j. 3, 6, 2; and σαλπικτής, Dem. p. 284, 26; App. hisp. 6, 93; and in the best codd. of Xen., Diod., Plut., al.; [cf. *Rutherford*, New Phryn. p. 279]; fr. σαλπίζω [q. v.]), -οῦ, ὁ, *a trumpeter*: Rev. xviii. 22.*

4539 **Σαλώμη**, [Hebr. 'peaceful'], -ης, ἡ, *Salome*, the wife of Zebedee, and the mother of the apostles James the elder and John: Mk. xv. 40; xvi. 1.*

see 4672 **Σαλωμών**, see Σολομών.

4540 **Σαμάρεια** [on the accent cf. Chandler § 104; B. 17 (15); -ία T WH (see *Tdf.* Proleg. p. 87; cf. I, ι); on the forms see *Abbot* in B.D. Am. ed. s. v.], -ας [cf. B. u. s.], ἡ [cf. W. § 18, 5 a.], (Hebr. שֹׁמְרוֹן, Chald. שָׁמְרָיִן pron. *Schame-ra-in*, Assyr. *Samirina*), [on the deriv. see B. D. s. v.], *Samaria*;   **1.** the name of a city built by Omri king of Israel (1 K. xvi. 24), on a mountain of the same name (הַר שֹׁמְרוֹן, Am. vi. 1), situated in the tribe of Ephraim; it was the capital of the whole region and the residence of the kings of Israel. After having been besieged three years by Shalmaneser [IV.], king of Assyria, it was taken and doubtless devastated by Sargon, his son and successor, B. C. 722, who deported the ten tribes of Israel and supplied their place with other settlers; 2 K. xvii. 5 sq. 24 sq.; xviii. 9 sqq. After its restoration, it was utterly destroyed by John Hyrcanus the Jewish prince and high-priest (see next word). Long afterwards rebuilt once more, it was given by Augustus to Herod [the Great], by whom it was named in honor of Augustus *Sebaste*, i. e. *Augusta*, (Strab. lib. 16,

p. 760; Joseph. antt. 15, 7, 3; 8, 5). It is now an obscure village bearing the name of *Sebustieh* or *Sebastiyeh* (cf. *Bädeker*, Palästina, p. 354 sqq. [Eng. trans. p. 340 sqq.; *Murray*, Hndbk. Pt. ii. p. 329 sqq.]). It is mentioned, Acts viii. 5 L T WH, εἰς τὴν πόλιν τῆς Σαμαρείας (gen. of apposition, cf. W. § 59, 8 a.; [B. § 123, 4]), but acc. to the better reading εἰς πόλιν τῆς Σαμ. the gen. is partitive, and does not denote the city but the Samaritan territory; cf. vs. 9.   2. *the Samaritan territory, the region of Samaria*, of which the city Samaria was the capital: Lk. xvii. 11; Jn. iv. 4 sq. 7; Acts i. 8; viii. 1, 5 (see above), 9; ix. 31; xv. 3; by meton. for the inhabitants of the region, Acts viii. 14. Cf. *Win.* RWB. s. v. Samaria; *Robinson*, Palestine ii. 288 sqq.; *Petermann* in Herzog xiii. 359 sqq.; [esp. *Kautzsch* in (Riehm s. v. Samaritaner, and) Herzog ed. 2, xiii. 340 sqq., and reff. there and in B. D. (esp. Am. ed.) s. v. Samaria].*

4541   **Σαμαρείτης** (-ίτης Tdf.; [see *Tdf.* Proleg. p. 87; *WH.* App. p. 154; cf. I, ι]), (Σαμάρεια), -ου, ὁ, *a Samaritan* (*Samarites*, Curt. 4, 8, 9; Tac. ann. 12, 54; *Samaritanus*, Vulg. [(2 K. xvii. 29 'Samaritae')] and eccl. writ.), i. e. an inhabitant either of the city or of the province of Samaria. The origin of the Samaritans was as follows: After Shalmaneser [al. say Esarhaddon, cf. Ezr. iv. 2, 10; but see *Kautzsch* in Herzog ed. 2, as referred to under the preceding word], king of Assyria, had sent colonists from Babylon, Cuthah, Ava, Hamath, and Sepharvaim into the land of Samaria which he had devastated and depopulated [see Σαμάρεια, 1], those Israelites who had remained in their desolated country [cf. 2 Ch. xxx. 6, 10; xxxiv. 9] associated and intermarried with these heathen colonists and thus produced a mixed race. When the Jews on their return from exile were preparing to rebuild the temple of Jerusalem, the Samaritans asked to be allowed to bear their part in the common work. On being refused by the Jews, who were unwilling to recognize them as brethren, they not only sent letters to the king of Persia and caused the Jews to be compelled to desist from their undertaking down to the second year of Darius [Hystaspis] (B. C. 520), but also built a temple for themselves on Mount Gerizim, a place held sacred even from the days of Moses [cf. Deut. xxvii. 12, etc.], and worshipped Jehovah there according to the law of Moses, recognizing only the Pentateuch as sacred. This temple was destroyed B. C. 129 by John Hyrcanus. Deprived of their temple, the Samaritans have nevertheless continued to worship on their sacred mountain quite down to the present time, although their numbers are reduced to some forty or fifty families. Hence it came to pass that the Samaritans and the Jews entertained inveterate and unappeasable enmity towards each other. Samaritans are mentioned in the foll. N. T. pass.: Mt. x. 5; Lk. ix. 52; x. 33; xvii. 16; Jn. iv. 9 [here T om. WH br. the cl.], 39 sq.; viii. 48; Acts viii. 25. In Hebr. the Samaritans are called שֹׁמְרוֹנִים, 2 K. xvii. 29. Cf. *Juynboll*, Commentarii in historiam gentis Samaritanae (Lugd. Bat. 1846); *Win.* RWB. s. v. Samaritaner; *Petermann* in Herzog xiii. p.

363 sqq.; *Schrader* in Schenkel v. p. 150 sqq.; [esp. *Kautzsch* in Herzog and Riehm u. s.].*

Σαμαρεῖτις (-ίτις Tdf.; [see the preced. word]), -ιδος,   **4542** ἡ, (fem. of Σαμαρείτης), *a Samaritan* woman: Jn. iv. 9. (The Samaritan territory, Joseph. b. j. [1, 21, 2, etc.]; 3, 7, 32; Σαμαρεῖτις χώρα, ib. 3, 3, 4.) *

Σαμοθράκη [-θρά- Rᵇᵉᶻ ᵉˡᶻ G (as here and there in prof.   **4543** auth.; see *Pape*, Eigennamen, s. v.); acc. to some 'height of Thrace', acc. to others 'Thracian Samos' (cf. Σάμος); other opinions see in Pape l. c.], -ης, ἡ, *Samothrace*, an island of the Ægean Sea, about 38 m. distant from the coast of Thrace where the river Hebrus empties into the sea (Plin. h. n. 4, 12, (23)), [now *Samothraki*]: Acts xvi. 11.*

Σάμος, [(prob. 'height'; cf. *Pape*, Eigennamen)], -ου,   **4544** ἡ, *Samos*, an island in that part of the Ægean which is called the Icarian Sea, opposite Ionia and not far from Ephesus; it was the birthplace of Pythagoras; [now Grk. Samo, Turkish *Susam Adassi*]: Acts xx. 15.*

Σαμουήλ (שְׁמוּאֵל, for שְׁמוּעַ אֵל i. e. 'heard of God', fr.   **4545** שָׁמַע and אֵל; cf. 1 S. i. 20, 27 [see B. D. s. v. Samuel]), ὁ, [indecl.; Joseph. (antt. 5, 10, 3) Σαμούηλος, -ου], *Samuel*, the son of Elkanah by his wife Anna [or Hannah], the last of the שֹׁפְטִים or judges, a distinguished prophet, and the founder of the prophetic order. He gave the Jews their first kings, Saul and David: Acts iii. 24; xiii. 20; Heb. xi. 32. (1 S. i.–xxv., cf. xxviii.; Sir. xlvi. 13 sqq.) *

Σαμψών, (שִׁמְשׁוֹן fr. שֶׁמֶשׁ fr. שָׁמַשׁ, 'sun-like', cf. Hebr. אִישׁ   **4546** fr. אֵשׁ), [B. 15 (14)], ὁ, *Samson* (Vulg. *Samson*), one of the Israelite judges (שֹׁפְטִים), famous for his strength and courage, the Hebrew Hercules [cf. BB.DD.; McC. and S. s. v. 2, 4; esp. *Orelli* in Herzog ed. 2 s. v. Simson] (Judg. xiii. sqq.): Heb. xi. 32.*

σανδάλιον, -ου, τό, (dimin. of σάνδαλον [which is prob.   **4547** a Persian word; cf. *Vaniček*, Fremdwörter, s. v.]), *a sandal, a sole made of wood* or *leather, covering the bottom of the foot and bound on with thongs*: Mk. vi. 9; Acts xii. 8. (Hdt., Joseph., Diod., Ael., Hdian., al.; for נַעַל in Is. xx. 2; Judith x. 4; xvi. 9. [In the Sept. and Joseph. σανδ. and ὑπόδημα are used indiscriminately; cf. Is. xx. 2; Josh. v. 15; Joseph. b. j. 6, 1, 8.]) Cf. *Win.* RWB. s. v. Schuhe; *Roskoff* in Schenkel v. 255; [*Kamphausen* in Riehm p. 1435 sqq.; B. D. s. v. Sandal; *Edersheim*, Jesus the Messiah, i. 621].*

σανίς, -ίδος, ἡ, *a board, a plank*: Acts xxvii. 44. (Fr.   **4548** Hom. down; Sept., Cant. viii. 9; Ezek. xxvii. 5.) *

Σαούλ (שָׁאוּל 'asked for'), ὁ, indecl. (in Joseph. Σάου-   **4549** λος), *Saul*;   **1.** the name of the first king of Israel: Acts xiii. 21.   **2.** the Jewish name of the apostle Paul, but occurring only in address [cf. B. 6]: Acts ix. 4, 17; xxii. 7, 13; xxvi. 14; in the other pass. of the Acts the form Σαῦλος (q. v.) with the Grk. term. is used.*

σαπρός, -ά, -όν, (σήπω, 2 aor. pass. σαπῆναι);   **1.**   **4550** *rotten, putrid*, ([Hipponax], Hippcr., Arstph., al.).   **2.** *corrupted by age and no longer fit for use, worn out*, (Arstph., Dio Chr., al.); hence in general, *of poor quality, bad, unfit for use, worthless*, [A. V. *corrupt*], (πᾶν, ὁ

μὴ τὴν ἰδίαν χρείαν πληροῖ, σαπρὸν λέγομεν, Chrys. hom.
4 on 1 Ep. to Tim.): δένδρον, καρπός, opp. to καλός, Mt.
vii. 17 sq.; xii. 33; Lk. vi. 43; fishes, Mt. xiii. 48 [here
A. V. bad]; trop. λόγος, Eph. iv. 29 (cf. Harless ad loc.);
δόγμα, Epict. 3, 22, 61.   Cf. Lob. ad Phryn. p. 377 sq.*

4551   Σαπφείρη, dat. -η (RGTWH), -ᾳ (LTr; cf. [WH.
App. p. 156]; B. 11; [W. 62 (61)]), ἡ, (either Aram.
ספּיראַ i. e. 'beautiful'; Peshitto ܣܰܦܺܝܪܰܐ; or fr. σάπφειρος, q. v.), Sapphira, the name of a woman: Acts v. 1.*

4552   σάπφειρος, -ου, ἡ, Hebr. סַפִּיר, sapphire, a precious
stone [perh. our lapis lazuli, cf. B. D. s. v. Sapphire;
Riehm, HWB. s. v. Edelsteine, 14]: Rev. xxi. 19.   (Theophr., Diosc., al.; Sept.) *

4553   σαργάνη [(prop. 'braided-work', fr. r. tark; Fick, Pt.
iii. p. 598; Vaníček p. 297)], -ης, ἡ;   **1.** a braided
rope, a band, (Aeschyl. suppl. 788).   **2.** a basket, a
basket made of ropes, a hamper [cf. B.D. s. v. Basket]:
2 Co. xi. 33; (Timocl. in Athen. 8 p. 339 e.; 9 p. 407 e.;
[al.]).*

4554   Σάρδεις, dat. -εσιν, αἱ, [fr. Aeschyl., Hdt., down], Sardis [or Sardes], the capital of Lydia, a luxurious city;
now an obscure village, Sart, with extensive ruins: Rev.
4555;   i. 11; iii. 1, 4.   [Cf. McC. and S. s. v.]*
see 4556   σάρδινος, -ου, ὁ, Rev. iv. 3 Rec., i. q. σάρδιον, q. v.*
4556   σάρδιον, -ου, τό, [neut. of σάρδιος, see below], sard, sardius, a precious stone, of which there are two kinds,
concerning which Theophr. de lapid. 16, 5, § 30 ed.
Schneid. says, τοῦ γὰρ σαρδίου τὸ μὲν διαφανὲς ἐρυθρότερον
δὲ καλεῖται θῆλυ, τὸ δὲ διαφανὲς μὲν μελάντερον δὲ καὶ
ἄρσεν, the former of which is called carnelian (because
flesh-colored; Hebr. אֹדֶם, Sept σάρδιον, Ex. xxviii. 17;
xxxvi. 17 (xxxix. 10); Ezek. xxviii. 13; αἱματόεντα σάρδια,
Orph. de lapid. 16, 5), the latter sard: Rev. iv. 3 (Rec.
σαρδίνῳ); xxi. 20 GLTTrWH.   Hence the adj. σάρδιος, -α, -ον, [fr. Σάρδεις, cf. Plin. h. n. 37, 7] sardine sc.
λίθος (the full phrase occurs Ex. xxxv. 8 [var.]): Rev.
xxi. 20 Rec.   [B. D. s. vv. Sardine, Sardius.]*
see 4557   σαρδιόνυξ, i. q. σαρδόνυξ (q. v.): Rev. xxi. 20 Lchm.*
4557   σαρδόνυξ [Lchm. σαρδιόνυξ], -υχος, ὁ, (σάρδιον and ὄνυξ),
sardonyx, a precious stone marked by the red colors of
the carnelian (sard) and the white of the onyx [B. D.
s. v.; Riehm, HWB. s. v. Edelsteine 12]: Rev. xxi. 20.
(Joseph., Plut., Ptol., al.; [Gen. ii. 12 Aq. (Montf.)].)*
4558   Σάρεπτα [Tr mrg. Σάρεφθα; Tdf. in O. T. Σαρεπτά],
(צָרְפַת fr. צָרַף to smelt; hence perh. 'smelting-house'),
-ων [yet cf. B. 15 (14); but declined in Obad.], τά; Sarep-
ta [so A. V.; better with O. T. Zarephath] a Phœnician
town between Tyre and Sidon, but nearer Sidon, [now
Surafend; cf. B. D. s. v. Zarephath], (1 K. xvii. 9; Obad.
20; in Joseph. antt. 8, 13, 2 Σαρεφθά): τῆς Σιδωνίας, in
the land of Sidon, Lk. iv. 26.   Cf. Robinson, Palestine
ii. 474 sqq.; [B. D. u.s.].*

4559   σαρκικός, -ή, -όν, (σάρξ), fleshly, carnal (Vulg. carnalis);
1. having the nature of flesh, i. e. under the control of the
animal appetites (see σάρξ, 3), Ro. vii. 14 Rec. (see σάρκινος, 3); governed by mere human nature (see σάρξ, 4)
not by the Spirit of God, 1 Co. iii. 1, 3, also 4 RG; hav-

ing its seat in the animal nature or roused by the animal
nature, αἱ σαρκικαὶ ἐπιθυμίαι, 1 Pet. ii. 11; i. q. human:
with the included idea of weakness, ὅπλα, 2 Co. x. 4; with
the included idea of depravity, σαρκ. σοφία (i. e. πανουργία, 2 Co. iv. 2), 2 Co. i. 12.   [(Anthol. Pal. 1, 107; cf.
ἀπέχου τῶν σαρκικῶν κ. σωματικῶν ἐπιθυμιῶν, 'Teaching'
etc. 1, 4).   Cf. Trench, Syn. § lxxi.]   **2.** pertaining
to the flesh, i. e. to the body (see σάρξ, 2): relating to
birth, lineage, etc., ἐντολή, Heb. vii. 16 Rec.; τὰ σαρκικά,
things needed for the sustenance of the body, Ro. xv.
27; 1 Co. ix. 11, (Aristot. h. anim. 10, 2 p. 635ᵃ, 11; Plut.
de placit. philos. 5, 3, 7; once in Sept., 2 Chr. xxxii. 8
Compl.).*

4560   σάρκινος, -η, -ον, (σάρξ), [Arstph., Plat., Aristot., al.],
fleshy, Lat. carneus, i. e.   **1.** consisting of flesh, composed of flesh, (for proparoxytones ending in -ινος generally denote the material of which a thing is made,
cf. Fritzsche, Ep. ad Rom. ii. p. 46 sq.; [Donaldson, New
Crat. § 258]); Vulg. carnalis: opp. to λίθινος, 2 Co. iii.
3 (σάρκ. ἰχθύς, opp. to a fish of gold which has been
dreamed of, Theocr. id. 21, 66; the word is also found
in Plato, Aristot., Theophr., Plut.; Sept., al.).   **2.**
pertaining to the body (as earthly and perishable material,
opp. to ζωὴ ἀκατάλυτος): Heb. vii. 16 GLTTrWH (see
σαρκικός, 2).   **3.** it is used where σαρκικός might
have been expected: viz. by GLTTrWH in Ro. vii. 14
and 1 Co. iii. 1; in these pass., unless we decide that Paul
used σαρκικός and σάρκινος indiscriminately, we must
suppose that σάρκινος expresses the idea of σαρκικός with
an emphasis: wholly given up to the flesh, rooted in the
flesh as it were.   Cf. W. §16, 3 γ.; Fritzsche u. s.; Reiche,
Comment. crit. in N. T. i. p. 138 sqq.; Holsten, Zum
Evang. des Paulus u. Petrus p. 397 sqq. (Rostock, 1867);
[Trench, Syn. § lxxii.].*

4561   σάρξ, σαρκός, ἡ, (Aeol. σύρξ; hence it seems to be derived fr. σύρω, akin to σαίρω, 'to draw,' 'to draw off,'
and to signify what can be stripped off fr. the bones [Etym.
Magn. 708, 34; "sed quis subsignabit" (Lob. Paralip.
p. 111)]), fr. Hom. down, Hebr. בָּשָׂר;
1. prop. flesh (the soft substance of the living body,
which covers the bones and is permeated with blood) of
both men and beasts: 1 Co. xv. 39; plur. — of the flesh
of many beings, Rev. xix. 18, 21; of the parts of the
flesh of one, Lk. xxiv. 39 Tdf.; Rev. xvii. 16; accordingly it is distinguished both from blood, σὰρξ καὶ αἷμα
(on which expression see below, 2 a.; 3 bis; 4 fin. [cf.
W. 19]), and from bones, πνεῦμα σάρκα καὶ ὀστέα οὐκ ἔχει,
Lk. xxiv. 39 (οὐ γὰρ ἔτι σάρκας τε καὶ ὀστέα ἶνες ἔχουσιν,
Hom. Od. 11, 219).   φαγεῖν τὰς σάρκας τινός: prop.,
Rev. xvii. 16; xix. 18, (Lev. xxvi. 29; κατεσθίειν, 2 K.
ix. 36, and often in Sept.; in class. Grk. freq. βιβρώσκειν
σάρκας; σαρκῶν ἐδωδή, Plut. septem sap. conviv. c. 16);
trop. to torture one with eternal penal torments, Jas. v. 3,
cf. Mic. iii. 3; Ps. xxvi. (xxvii.) 2; φαγεῖν and τρώγειν
τὴν σάρκα τοῦ υἱοῦ τοῦ ἀνθρώπου, in fig. disc. to appropriate to one's self the saving results of the violent death endured by Christ, Jn. vi. 52–56; ἀπέρχεσθαι or πορεύεσθαι
ὀπίσω σαρκός, to follow after the flesh, is used of those

who are on the search for persons with whom they can gratify their lust [see ὀπίσω, 2 a.], Jude 7; 2 Pet. ii. 10; τὸ σῶμα τῆς σαρκός, the body compacted of flesh [cf. W. 188 (177)], Col. i. 22. Since the flesh is the visible part of the body, σάρξ is

2. i. q. *the body*, not designating it, however, as a skilful combination of related parts ('an organism,' which is denoted by the word σῶμα), but signifying the material or substance of the living body [cf. Aeschyl. Sept. 622 γέροντα τὸν νοῦν σάρκα δ᾽ ἡβῶσαν φέρει]; a. univ.: Jn. vi. 63 (see πνεῦμα, 2 p. 520ᵃ mid.); Acts ii. 26, 30 Rec.; 2 Co. xii. 7; Gal. iv. 14; Eph. v. 29; Heb. ix. 10, 13; [1 Pet. iii. 21]; Jude 8; μία σάρξ, one body, of husband and wife, Mk. x. 8; so εἰς σάρκα μίαν (fr. Gen. ii. 24), Mt. xix. 5; Mk. x. 8; 1 Co. vi. 16; Eph. v. 31; opp. to ψυχή, Acts ii. 31 (ἔδωκεν . . . Ἰησ. Χρ. . . . τὴν σάρκα ὑπὲρ τῆς σαρκὸς ἡμῶν καὶ τὴν ψυχὴν ὑπὲρ τῶν ψυχῶν ἡμῶν, Clem. Rom. 1 Cor. 49, 6 [cf. Iren. 5, 1, 1; but G L T Tr WH drop ἡ ψυχὴ αὐτοῦ in Acts l. c.]); opp. to πνεῦμα (the human), 1 Co. v. 5; 2 Co. vii. 1; Col. ii. 5; 1 Pet. iii. 18; iv. 6; σὰρξ κ. αἷμα, i. q. ψυχικὸν σῶμα, 1 Co. xv. 50, cf. 44; ἡ περιτομὴ ἐν σαρκί, Ro. ii. 28; Eph. ii. 11; τὸ πρόσωπόν μου ἐν σαρκί, [A. V. *my face in the flesh*], my bodily countenance, Col. ii. 1; ἀσθένεια σαρκός, of disease, Gal. iv. 13; ἐν τῇ θνητῇ σαρκὶ ἡμῶν, 2 Co. iv. 11 (cf. ἐν τῷ σώματι ἡμῶν, vs. 10); ἐν τῇ σαρκὶ αὐτοῦ, by giving up his body to death, Eph. ii. 14 (15); also διὰ τῆς σαρκὸς αὐτοῦ, Heb. x. 20, cf. Jn. vi. 51, (προσφέρειν τὴν σάρκα μου, *to offer in sacrifice my flesh* — Christ is speaking, Barn. ep. 7, 5; τὴν σάρκα παραδοῦναι εἰς καταφθοράν, ibid. 5, 1). life on earth, which is passed in the body (*flesh*), is designated by the foll. phrases: ἐν σαρκὶ εἶναι, Ro. vii. 5 (where Paul uses this expression with designed ambiguity in order to involve also the ethical sense, 'to be in the power of the *flesh*,' to be prompted and governed by the *flesh*; see 4 below); ζῆν ἐν σαρκί, Gal. ii. 20; Phil. i. 22; ἐπιμένειν ἐν σαρκί, Phil. i. 24; ὁ ἐν σαρκὶ χρόνος, 1 Pet. iv. 2; αἱ ἡμέραι τῆς σαρκὸς αὐτοῦ, of Christ's life on earth, Heb. v. 7. ἐν σαρκί or ἐν τῇ σαρκί, in things pertaining to the flesh (body), such as circumcision, descent, etc.: Gal. vi. 12 sq.; πεποιθέναι, Phil. iii. 3 sq.; ἔχειν πεποίθησιν, Phil. iii. 4.   b. used of natural or physical origin, generation, relationship: οἱ συγγενεῖς κατὰ σάρκα, Ro. ix. 3 [cf. W. § 20, 2 a.]; τέκνα τῆς σαρκός, children by birth, natural posterity, ibid. 8; ἀδελφὸν ἐν σαρκὶ καὶ ἐν κυρίῳ, a natural brother (as it were) and a Christian brother, Philem. 16; οἱ τῆς σαρκὸς ἡμῶν πατέρες, our natural fathers (opp. to God ὁ πατὴρ τῶν πνευμάτων, see πατήρ, 1 a. and 3 b.), Heb. xii. 9; τὰ ἔθνη ἐν σαρκί, Gentiles by birth, Eph. ii. 11; Ἰσραὴλ κατὰ σάρκα, 1 Co. x. 18 (the opposite term Ἰσραὴλ τοῦ θεοῦ, of Christians, is found in Gal. vi. 16); τὸ κατὰ σάρκα, as respects the flesh i. e. human origin, Ro. ix. 5 [(Clem. Rom. 1 Cor. 32, 2; Iren. haer. 4, 4, 1 and frag. 17 ed. Stieren p. 836)]; γενόμενος ἐκ σπέρματος Δαυεὶδ κατὰ σ. Ro. i. 3; ὁ κατὰ σάρκα γεννηθείς, born by natural generation (opp. to ὁ κατὰ πνεῦμα γενν. i. e. by the supernatural power of God, operating in the promise), Gal. iv. 29, 23; τὸ γεγεννημένον ἐκ

τῆς σαρκὸς σάρξ ἐστιν, that which has been born of the natural man is a natural man (opp. to one who has been born again by the power of the Holy Spirit), Jn. iii. 6; ἡ σάρξ μου, those with whom I share my natural origin, my fellow-countrymen, Ro. xi. 14 (ἰδοὺ ὀστᾶ σου καὶ σάρκες σου, 2 S. v. 1; add, xix. 13; Gen. xxxvii. 27; Judg. ix. 2); εἶναι ἐκ τῆς σαρκὸς κ. ἐκ τῶν ὀστέων τινός, which in its proper use signifies to be '*formed out of one's flesh and bones*' (Gen. ii. 23; to be related to one by birth, Gen. xxix. 14), is transferred metaph. to the church, which spiritually derives its origin from Christ and is united to him, just as Eve drew her origin from her husband Adam, Eph. v. 30 [R G Tr mrg. br.].   c. the sensuous nature of man, 'the animal nature': without any suggestion of depravity, τὸ θέλημα τῆς σαρκός, of sexual desire, Jn. i. 13; *the animal nature with cravings which incite to sin*: Mt. xxvi. 41; Mk. xiv. 38; Ro. vii. 18 (for which τὰ μέλη is used in 22 sq.); xiii. 14; Jude 23; opp. to ὁ νοῦς, Ro. vii. 25; ἡ ἐπιθυμία τῆς σαρκός, 1 Jn. ii. 16 (with its manifestation, ἡ ἐπιθυμία τῶν ὀφθαλμῶν; [al. regard this last as a new specification; cf. Westcott ad loc.]); plur. 2 Pet. ii. 18, (τὰ τῆς σαρκὸς πάθη, 4 Macc. vii. 18; τὸ μὴ δεδουλῶσθαι σαρκὶ καὶ τοῖς πάθεσι ταύτης διάγειν, ὑφ᾽ ὧν κατασπώμενος ὁ νοῦς τῆς θνητῆς ἀναπίμπλαται φλυαρίας, εὐδαίμων τι καὶ μακάριον, Plu'. consol. ad Apoll. c. 13; τῆς σαρκὸς ἡδονή, opp. to ψυχή, Plut. de virt. et vit. c. 3; add, Philo de gigant. § 7; Diog. Laërt. 10, 145; animo cum hac *carne* grave certamen est, Sen. consol. ad Marc. 24; animus liber habitat; nunquam me *caro* ista compellet ad metum, Sen. epp. 65 [7, 3, 22]; non est summa felicitatis nostrae in *carne* ponenda, ibid. 74 [9, 3, 16]). *the physical nature of man as subject to suffering*: παθεῖν σαρκί, 1 Pet. iv. 1; ἐν τῇ σαρκί μου, in that my flesh suffers afflictions, Col. i. 24 (where cf. Meyer and De Wette [and Bp. Lghtft.]); θλίψιν ἔχειν τῇ σαρκί, 1 Co. vii. 28.

3. *a living creature* (because possessed of a body of flesh), whether man or beast: πᾶσα σάρξ (in imitation of the Hebr. כָּל-בָּשָׂר [W. 33]), *every living creature*, 1 Pet. i. 24; with οὐ preceding (qualifying the verb [W. § 26, 1; B. 121 (106)]), *no living creature*, Mt. xxiv. 22; Mk. xiii. 20; spec. *a man* (ἄνθρωπος for בָּשָׂר, Gen. vi. 13), generally with a suggestion of weakness, frailty, mortality: Sir. xxviii. 5; ἐν τῷ θεῷ ἤλπισα, οὐ φοβηθήσομαι τί ποιήσει μοι σάρξ, Ps. lv. (lvi.) 5; cf. Jer. xvii. 5; ἐμνήσθη, ὅτι σάρξ εἰσιν, Ps. lxxvii. (lxxviii.) 39; σὰρξ κ. αἷμα, Eph. vi. 12; γενεὰ σαρκὸς κ. αἵματος, ἡ μὲν τελευτᾷ, ἑτέρα δὲ γεννᾶται, Sir. xiv. 18; ὁ λόγος σὰρξ ἐγένετο, entered into participation in human nature, Jn. i. 14 (the apostle used σάρξ, not ἄνθρωπος, apparently in order to indicate that he who possessed supreme majesty did not shrink from union with extreme weakness); εὑρίσκειν τι κατὰ σάρκα, to attain to anything after the manner of a (weak) man, i. e. by the use of merely human powers, Ro. iv. 1 (for substance equiv. to ἐξ ἔργων in vs. 2); Hebraistically (see above), πᾶσα σάρξ, *all men*, Lk. iii. 6; Jn. xvii. 2 [W. § 30, 1 a.]; Acts ii. 17; Sir. xlv. 4; with οὐ or μή preceding (qualifying the verb [W. and

B. as referred to above]), *no man, no mortal*, Ro. iii. 20; 1 Co. i. 29; Gal. ii. 16. *man as he appears, such as he presents himself to view, man's external appearance and condition*: κατὰ σάρκα κρίνειν, Jn. viii. 15 [cf. W. 583 (542)] (i. q. κρίνειν κατ' ὄψιν, vii. 24); γινώσκειν or εἰδέναι τινὰ κατὰ σάρκα, 2 Co. v. 16; οἱ κατὰ σάρκα κύριοι (see κατά, II. 3 b.), Eph. vi. 5; Col. iii. 22. univ. *human nature, the soul included*: ἐν ὁμοιώματι σαρκὸς ἁμαρτίας, in a visible form, like human nature which is subject to sin, Ro. viii. 3 [cf. ὁμοίωμα, b.]; ἐν σαρκὶ ἔρχεσθαι, to appear clothed in human nature, 1 Jn. iv. 2 and Rec. in 3; 2 Jn. 7, (Barn. ep. 5, 10); φανεροῦσθαι, 1 Tim. iii. 16 (Barn. ep. 5, 6; 6, 7; 12, 10); κεκοινωνηκέναι αἵματος κ. σαρκός, Heb. ii. 14.

4. σάρξ, when either expressly or tacitly opp. to τὸ πνεῦμα (τοῦ θεοῦ), has an **ethical** sense and denotes *mere human nature, the earthly nature of man apart from divine influence, and therefore prone to sin and opposed to God*; accordingly it includes whatever in the **s o u l** is weak, low, debased, tending to ungodliness and vice ("Thou must not understand '*flesh*', therefore, as though that only were '*flesh*' which is connected with unchastity, but St. Paul uses 'flesh' of the whole man, body and soul, reason and all his faculties included, because all that is in him longs and strives after the flesh" (*Luther*, Pref. to the Ep. to the Rom.); "note that '*flesh*' signifies the entire nature of man, sense and reason, without the Holy Spirit" (*Melanchthon*, Loci, ed. of 1535, in Corpus Reform. xxi. p. 277). This definition is strikingly supported by these two utterances of Paul: οὐδεμίαν ἔσχηκεν ἄνεσιν ἡ σ ὰ ρ ξ ἡμῶν, 2 Co. vii. 5; οὐκ ἔσχηκα ἄνεσιν τῷ π ν ε ύ μ α τ ί μου, 2 Co. ii. 13): Ro. viii. 3; Gal. v. 13, 19; opp. to τὸ πνεῦμα (τοῦ θεοῦ), Ro. viii. 6 sq. 12 sq.; Gal. v. 16 sq.; vi. 8; Col. ii. 13 (on which see ἀκροβυστία, c.); 23 (see πλησμονή); ἐπιθυμία σαρκός, Gal. v. 16; αἱ ἐπιθυμίαι and τὰ θελήματα τῆς σαρκός, Eph. ii. 3; ὁ νοῦς τῆς σαρκός, Col. ii. 18; σῶμα τῆς σαρκός, a body given up to the control of the flesh, i. e. a body whose members our nature, estranged from God, used as its instruments (cf. Ro. vi. 19), Col. ii. 11 G L T Tr WH; τὰ τῆς σαρκός (opp. to τὰ τοῦ πνεύματος), the things which please the flesh, which the flesh craves, Ro. viii. 5; σαρκὶ ἐπιτελοῦμαι, to make for one's self an end [see ἐπιτελέω, 1 fin.] by devoting one's self to the flesh, i. e. by gradually losing the Holy Spirit and giving one's self up to the control of the flesh, Gal. iii. 3; σταυροῦν τὴν σάρκα αὐτοῦ (see σταυρόω, 3 b.), Gal. v. 24; ἐν σαρκὶ εἶναι (opp. to ἐν πνεύματι, sc. τοῦ θεοῦ), to be in the power of the flesh, under the control of the flesh, Ro. viii. 8 sq., cf. vii. 5 (see 2 a. above); οἱ κατὰ σάρκα ὄντες, who exhibit the nature of the flesh, i. q. οἱ σαρκικοί (opp. to οἱ κατὰ πνεῦμα ὄντες), Ro. viii. 5; κατὰ σάρκα περιπατεῖν, to live acc. to the standard of the flesh, to comply in conduct with the impulse of the flesh, Ro. viii. 1 Rec.; 2 Co. x. 2; opp. to κατὰ πνεῦμα, Ro. viii. 4; βουλεύεσθαι, 2 Co. i. 17; καυχᾶσθαι, 2 Co. xi. 18 where cf. Meyer; (opp. to κατὰ πνεῦμα) ζῆν, Ro. viii. 12 sq. (ἐν σαρκὶ τυγχάνουσιν, ἀλλ' οὐ κατὰ σάρκα ζῶσιν, of Christians, Ep. ad Diogn. 5, 8); ἐν

σαρκὶ περιπατοῦντες οὐ κατὰ σάρκα στρατευόμεθα, although the nature in which we live is earthly and therefore weak, yet we do not carry on our warfare according to its law, 2 Co. x. 3, (οὐ κατὰ σάρκα γράφειν, ἀλλὰ κατὰ γνώμην θεοῦ, Ignat. ad Rom. 8, 3); with the suggestion of weakness as respects knowledge: σὰρξ κ. αἷμα, a man liable to err, fallible man: Mt. xvi. 17; Gal. i. 16; ἡ ἀσθένεια τῆς σαρκός, Ro. vi. 19; σοφοὶ κατὰ σάρκα, 1 Co. i. 26. Cf. *Tholuck*, Ueber *σάρξ* als Quelle der Sünde, in the Theol. Stud. u. Krit. for 1855, p. 477 sqq.; *C. Holsten*, Die Bedeut. des Wortes *σάρξ* im Lehrbegriffe des Paulus, 4to, Rostock 1855 [reprinted in his Zum Evang. des Paul. u. Petr. p. 365 sqq. (Rostock, 1867); see also (with esp. ref. to Holsten) *Lüdemann*, Die Anthropologie des Apost. Paul. (Kiel, 1872)]; *Ritschl*, Entstehung der altkathol. Kirche, ed. 2, p. 66 sqq.; *Baur* in the Theol. Jahrbb. for 1857, p. 96 sqq., and in his Bibl. Theol. des N. T. p. 142 sqq., etc.; *Wieseler*, Br. an die Galater, pp. 443 sqq. 448 sqq. [cf. *Riddle* in Schaff's Lange's Com. on Rom. p. 235 sq.]; *Weiss*, Bibl. Theol. des N. T. (ed. 3) § 68 p. 243 sqq., § 100 p. 414 sq.; *Rich. Schmidt*, Paulin. Christologie, p. 8 sqq.; *Eklund*, *σάρξ* vocabulum quid ap. Paulum apost. significet (Lund, 1872); *Pfleiderer*, Paulinismus, p. 47 sqq. [Eng. trans. vol. i. p. 47 sqq.]; *Wendt*, Die Begriffe Fleisch u. Geist im bibl. Sprachgebr. (Gotha, 1878); [*Cremer* in Herzog ed. 2 s. v. Fleisch, but esp. in his Bibl.-theol. Wörterbuch, 3te (or 4te) Aufl. s. v.; *Laidlaw*, The Bible Doctr. of Man (Edinb. 1879), pp. 74 sqq. 373 sq.; *Philippi*, Glaubensl. ed. 2, vol. iii. pp. 231–250; esp. *Dickson*, St. Paul's use of the terms Flesh and Spirit (Glasgow, 1883)]; and the reff. in Meyer on Ro. iv. 1 (6te Aufl.).*

Σαρούχ (Rec.), more correctly (G L T Tr WH) Σερούχ, (שְׂרוּג i. q. שָׂרִיג, 'vine-shoot'), ὁ, *Serug* [so R. V.; but A. V. in the N. T. *Saruch*], the name of a man (Gen. xi. 20 sq. etc.): Lk. iii. 35.* **4562**

σαρόω (for the earlier σαίρω, cf. *Lob.* ad Phryn. p. 83 [W. 24, 91 (87)]), -ῶ; pf. pass. ptcp. σεσαρωμένος; (σάρον a broom); *to sweep, clean by sweeping*: τί, Lk. xv. 8; pass. Mt. xii. 44; Lk. xi. 25. (Artem. oneir. 2, 33; [Apoll. Dysk. p. 253, 7]; Geop.)* **4563**

Σάρρα, -ας, ἡ, (שָׂרָה 'princess', Gen. xvii. 15), *Sarah*, wife of Abraham: Ro. iv. 19; ix. 9; Heb. xi. 11; 1 Pet. iii. 6.* **4564**

Σάρων, -ωνος [so Tdf.; but L WH acc. -ῶνα, Tr -ωνᾶ; cf. B. 16 (14)], ὁ, (Hebr. שָׁרוֹן for שָׁרוֹן fr. יָשַׁר 'to be straight'; [in Hebr. always with the art. הַשָּׁרוֹן 'the level']), *Sharon* [so R. V.; but A. V. *Saron*], a level region extending from Cæsarea of Palestine (Strato's Tower) as far as Joppa [about 30 miles]; it abounded in pasturage and was famous for its fertility (Is. xxxiii. 9; lxv. 10; 1 Chr. xxvii. 29): Acts ix. 35. [Cf. B. D. s. v. Sharon; *Robinson*, Phys. Geogr. etc. p. 126.]* **4565**

σατᾶν indecl. (2 Co. xii. 7 R G [Tdf. in 1 K. xi. 14 accents -τάν (Lagarde leaves it unaccented)]), ὁ, and ὁ σατανᾶς [i. e. with the art. (exc. in Mk. iii. 23; Lk. xxii. 3)], -ᾶ [cf. B. 20 (18); W. § 8, 1], ([Aram. סָטָנָא, **4566 & 4567**

stat. emph. of סָטָן] Hebr. שָׂטָן), *adversary* (one who opposes another in purpose or act); the appellation is given to **1.** the prince of evil spirits, the inveterate adversary of God and of Christ (see διάβολος, and in πονηρός, 2 b.): Mk. iii. [23], 26; iv. 15; Lk. x. 18; xi. 18; 1 Co. v. 5; 2 Co. xi. 14; 1 Th. ii. 18; 1 Tim. i. 20; Rev. ii. 9, 13, 24; iii. 9; he incites to apostasy from God and to sin, Mt. iv. 10; Mk. i. 13; Lk. iv. 8 R L in br.; xxii. 31; Acts v. 3; 1 Co. vii. 5; 2 Co. ii. 11 (10); 1 Tim. v. 15; circumventing men by stratagems, 2 Co. xi. 14; 2 Th. ii. 9; the worshippers of idols are said to be under his control, Acts xxvi. 18; Rev. xii. 9; he is said both himself εἰσέρχεσθαι εἰς τινα, in order to act through him, Lk. xxii. 3; Jn. xiii. 27; and by his demons to take possession of the bodies of men and to afflict them with diseases, Lk. xiii. 16, cf. Mt. xii. 26; 2 Co. xii. 7; by God's assistance he is overcome, Ro. xvi. 20; on Christ's return from heaven he will be bound with chains for a thousand years, but when the thousand years are finished he will walk the earth in yet greater power, Rev. xx. 2, 7, but shortly after will be given over to eternal punishment, ibid. 10. **2.** *a Satan-like man*: Mt. xvi. 23; Mk. viii. 33. [Cf. *Delitzsch* in Riehm s. v.; *Schenkel* in his BL. s. v.; *Hamburger*, Real-Encycl. i. 897 sq.; *Edersheim*, Jesus the Messiah, App. xiii. § ii.; and BB.DD. s. v.]*

4568 σάτον, (Hebr. סְאָה, Chald. סָאתָא, Syr. ܣܐܬܐ), -ου, τό, a kind of dry measure, *a modius and a half* [equiv. to about *a peck and a half* (cf. μόδιος)], (Joseph. antt. 9, 4, 5 ἰσχύει δὲ τὸ σάτον μόδιον καὶ ἥμισυ ἰταλικόν; cf. Gen. xviii. 6 [see Aq. and Symm.]; Judg. vi. 19): Mt. xiii. 33; Lk. xiii. 21, [in both exx. A.V. 'three *measures* of meal' i. e. the common quantity for 'a baking' (cf. Gen. xviii. 6; Judg. vi. 19; 1 S. i. 24)].*

4569 Σαῦλος, -ου, ὁ, (see Σαούλ, 2), *Saul*, the Jewish name of the apostle Paul [cf. *Woldemar Schmidt* in Herzog ed. 2 xi. p. 357 sq.; *Conybeare and Howson*, St. Paul, i. 150 sqq. (Am. ed.); *Farrar*, St. Paul, ch. xix. fin.; B. D. Am. ed. s. v. Names]: Acts vii. 58; viii. 1, 3; ix. 1, 8, 11, 19 Rec., 22, 24, 26 Rec.; xi. 25, 30; xii. 25; xiii. 1 sq. 7, 9.*

4570 σβέννυμι (ζβέννυμι, 1 Th. v. 19 Tdf. [cf. Σ, σ, ς]) and [in classics] σβεννύω; fut. σβέσω; 1 aor. ἔσβεσα; Pass., pres. σβέννυμαι; fr. Hom. down; Sept. for כָּבָה and
* דָּעַךְ, to extinguish, *quench*; **a.** prop.: τί, fire or things on fire, Mt. xii. 20; Eph. vi. 16; Heb. xi. 34; pass. (Sept. for כָּבָה) *to be quenched, to go out*: Mt. xxv. 8; Mk. ix. 44, 46, [both which vss. T WH om. Tr br.], 48. **b.** metaph. *to quench* i. e. *to suppress, stifle*: τὸ πνεῦμα, divine influence, 1 Th. v. 19 (ἀγάπην, Cant. viii. 7; τὰ πάθη, 4 Macc. xvi. 4; χόλον, Hom. Il. 9, 678; ὕβριν, Plat. legg. 8, 835 d.; τὸν θυμόν, ibid. 10, 888 a.).*

4572 σεαυτοῦ, -ῆς, -οῦ, reflex. pron. of the 2d pers., used only in the gen., dat., and acc.; in the N. T. only in the masc.; gen. (*of*) *thyself*, (*of*) *thee*: Jn. viii. 13; xviii. 34 L Tr WH; Acts xxvi. 1; 2 Tim. iv. 11; dat. σεαυτῷ, (*to*) *thyself*, (*to*) *thee*: Jn. xvii. 5; Acts xvi. 28; Ro. ii.

5; 1 Tim. iv. 16; acc. σεαυτόν, *thyself, thee*: Mt. iv. 6; Mk. xii. 31; Lk. iv. 23; Jn. viii. 53; Ro. xiv. 22; Gal. vi. 1; 1 Tim. iv. 7; 2 Tim. ii. 15; Jas. ii. 8; etc. [Cf. B. § 127, 13.]

σεβάζομαι: (σέβας reverence, awe); **1.** *to fear, be afraid*: Hom. Il. 6, 167. 417. **2.** in later auth. i. q. σέβομαι [W. § 2, 1 b.], *to honor religiously, to worship*: with 1 aor. pass. ἐσεβάσθην in an act. sense, Ro. i. 25 (Orph. Argon. 554; eccl. writ.).* **4573**

σέβασμα, -τος, τό, (σεβάζομαι), *whatever is religiously honored, an object of worship*: 2 Th. ii. 4 (Sap. xiv. 20); used of temples, altars, statues, etc., Acts xvii. 23; of idolatrous images, Bel and the Dragon 27; Sap. xv. 17, (Dion. Hal. antt. 1, 30).* **4574**

σεβαστός, -ή, -όν, (σεβάζομαι); **1.** *reverend, venerable.* **2.** ὁ σεβαστός, Lat. *augustus*, the title of the Roman emperors: Acts xxv. 21, 25, (Strabo, Lcian., Hdian., Dio Cass., al.); adj. -ός, -ή, -όν, *Augustan* i. e. taking its name fr. the emperor; a title of honor which used to be given to certain legions, or cohorts, or battalions, "for valor" (ala augusta o b v i r t u t e m appellata. Corpus inscr. Lat. vii. n. 340, 341, 344): σπείρη σεβ. *the Augustan cohort*, Acts xxvii. 1 (λεγεὼν σεβαστή, Ptol. 2, 3, 30; 2, 9, 18; 4, 3, 30). The subject is fully treated by *Schürer* in the Zeitschr. für wissensch. Theol. for 1875, p. 413 sqq.* **4575**

σέβω, and (so everywh. in the Scriptures) σέβομαι; fr. Hom. down; *to revere, to worship*: τινά (a deity), Mt. xv. 9; Mk. vii. 7; Acts xviii. 13; xix. 27, (Sap. xv. 18 etc.; for יָרֵא, Josh. iv. 24; xxii. 25; Jon. i. 9). In the Acts, "proselytes of the gate" (see προσήλυτος, 2) are called σεβόμενοι τὸν θεόν, ['men that worship God'], Acts xvi. 14; xviii. 7, (Joseph. antt. 14, 7, 2); and simply οἱ σεβόμενοι, [A. V. *the devout persons*], Acts xvii. 17; σεβόμενοι προσήλυτοι, [R. V. *devout proselytes*], Acts xiii. 43; σεβόμεναι γυναῖκες, ib. 50; οἱ σεβ. Ἕλληνες, [A. V. *the devout Greeks*], Acts xvii. 4; in the Latin church, *metuentes, verecundi, religiosi, timorati*; Vulg. [exc. Acts xiii. 50] *colentes*; cf. *Thilo* in his Cod. apocr. Nov. Test. p. 521.* **see 4576 St.**

σειρά, -ᾶς, ἡ, (εἴρω, to fasten, bind together, [akin to Lat. *sero, series, servus*, etc.]; cf. Curtius § 518), fr. Hom. down; **a.** *a line, a rope.* **b.** *a chain*: σειραῖς ζόφου, [A.V. *to chains of darkness*, i. e.] to darkness as if to chains, 2 Pet. ii. 4 R G [but Tr WH have σειροῖς, L T σιροῖς, which see in their place]; μιᾷ ἁλύσει σκότους πάντες ἐδέθησαν, Sap. xvii. 17 (18).* **4577**

σειρός, -οῦ, ὁ, i. q. σειρά, q. v.: 2 Pet. ii. 4 Tr WH. But σειρός, Lat. *sirus*, in prof. writ. is *a pit, an underground granary*, [e. g. Dem. p. 100 fin. (where the Schol. τ. θησαυροὺς κ. τ. ὀρύγματα ἐν οἷς κατετίθεντο τὰ σπέρματα σιροὺς ἐκάλουν οἱ Θρᾶκες κ. οἱ Λίβυες); Diod. Sic. 19, 44; cf. Suidas s. v. σειροί; *Valesius* on Harpocr. Lex. s. v. Μελίνη. See *Field*, Otium Norv. Pars iii. ad loc. Accordingly R. V. txt. follows the crit. edd. (cf. σιρός) and renders "*pits* of darkness"].* **see 4577**

σεισμός, -οῦ, ὁ, (σείω), *a shaking, a commotion*: ἐν τῇ θαλάσσῃ, *a tempest*, Mt. viii. 24; as often in Grk. writ. **4578** fr. [Hdt. 4, 28], Soph., Arstph. down, pre-eminently *an earthquake*: Mt. xxiv. 7; xxvii. 54; xxviii. 2; Mk. xiii. 8; Lk. xxi. 11; Acts xvi. 26; Rev. vi. 12; viii. 5; xi. 13, 19; xvi. 18; Sept. for רָעַשׁ.*

4579   σείω; fut. σείσω (Heb. xii. 26 L T Tr WH); Pass., pres. ptcp. σειόμενος; 1 aor. ἐσείσθην; fr. Hom. down; Sept. chiefly for רָעַשׁ; *to shake, agitate, cause to tremble*: Rev. vi. 13; τὴν γῆν, Heb. xii. 26 after Hag. ii. 6; ἐσείσθη ἡ γῆ, Mt. xxvii. 51 (Judg. v. 4; 2 S. xxii. 8); σεισθῆναι ἀπὸ φόβου, of men, to be thrown into a tremor, *to quake for fear*, Mt. xxviii. 4; metaph. *to agitate the mind*: ἐσείσθη ἡ πόλις, [R. V. *was stirred*] i. e. its inhabitants, Mt. xxi. 10. [Comp.: ἀνα-, δια-, κατα- σείω.]*

4580   Σεκοῦνδος, T WH Σέκουνδος [Chandler §§ 233, 235], -ου, ὁ, (a Lat. word), *Secundus*, a certain man of Thessalonica: Acts xx. 4.*

4581   Σελεύκεια [T WH -κία (see I, ι)], -ας, ἡ, *Seleucia*, a city of Syria on the Mediterranean, about 5 m. (40 stadia, Strabo 16 p. 750) N. of the mouth of the river Orontes, about 15 m. (120 stadia) distant fr. Antioch, and opposite Cyprus: Acts xiii. 4 (1 Macc. xi. 8). [Lewin, St. Paul, i. 116 sqq.; *Conyb. and Howson*, ditto, i. 136 sq.]*

4582   σελήνη, -ης, ἡ, (fr. σέλας brightness), fr. Hom. down, Hebr. יָרֵחַ, *the moon*: Mt. xxiv. 29; Mk. xiii. 24; Lk. xxi. 25; Acts ii. 20; 1 Co. xv. 41; Rev. vi. 12; viii. 12; xii. 1; xxi. 23.*

4583   σεληνιάζομαι; (σελήνη); [lit. *to be moon-struck* (cf. *lunatic*); see Wetstein on Mt. iv. 24; Suicer, Thesaur. ii. 945 sq.; BB. DD. s. v. Lunatic] *to be epileptic* (epilepsy being supposed to return and increase with the increase of the moon): Mt. iv. 24; xvii. 15. (Manetho carm. 4, 81 and 217; [Lcian., al.]; eccles. writ.)*

4584   Σεμεΐ, L mrg. Σεμεΐν, T Tr WH Σεμεεΐν [see *WH*. App. p. 155; cf. ει, ι], (שִׁמְעִי i. e. famous), *Semein* [so R. V. but A. V. *Semei*], the name of a man: Lk. iii. 26.*

4585   σεμίδαλις, acc. -ιν, ἡ, *the finest wheaten flour*: Rev. xviii. 13. (Hippocr., Arstph., Joseph., al.; Sept. often for סֹלֶת.)*

4586   σεμνός, -ή, -όν, (σέβω), fr. [Hom. h. Cer., al.], Aeschyl., Pind. down, *august, venerable, reverend*; *to be venerated for character, honorable*: of persons [A.V. *grave*], 1 Tim. iii. 8, 11; Tit. ii. 2; of deeds, Phil. iv. 8. [Cf. Trench § xcii.; Schmidt ch. 173, 5.]*

4587   σεμνότης, -ητος, ἡ, (σεμνός), that characteristic of a pers. or a thing which entitles to reverence or respect, *dignity, gravity, majesty, sanctity*: ἡ τοῦ ἱεροῦ σεμνότης, 2 Macc. iii. 12; in an ethical sense, *gravity* [so R. V. uniformly (cf. Trench p. 347)], *honor, probity, purity*: 1 Tim. ii. 2; iii. 4; Tit. ii. 7. (Eur., Plat., Dem., al.)*

4588   Σέργιος, -ου, ὁ, *Sergius*, surnamed Paulus, proconsul of Cyprus, converted to Christianity by the apostle Paul; otherwise unknown [cf. *Lghtft.* in Contemp. Rev. for 1878, p. 290; *Farrar*, St. Paul, vol. i. Excurs. xvi.; *Renan*, Saint Paul, p. 14 sq.]: Acts xiii. 7.*

see 4562   Σερούχ, see Σαρούχ.

4589   Σήθ, ὁ, (שֵׁת 'put' [A. V. 'appointed'], fr. שִׁית to put [i. e. in place of the murdered Abel; cf. B. D. s. v. Seth], Gen. iv. 25), *Seth*, the third son of Adam: Lk. iii. 38.*

4590   Σήμ (in Joseph. Σήμας), ὁ, (שֵׁם ['name,' 'sign,' 'celebrity'; but variously explained]), *Shem*, the eldest son of Noah: Lk. iii. 36.*

4591   σημαίνω; impf. ἐσήμαινον (Acts xi. 28 L WH txt.); 1 aor. ἐσήμανα, for ἐσήμηνα which is the more com. form in the earlier and more elegant Grk. writ. (see Matthiae § 185; Kühner § 343 s. v.; [Veitch s. v.]; *Lob.* ad Phryn. p. 24 sq.; W. § 15 s. v.; B. 41 (35)); (fr. σῆμα a sign); fr. [Hom.], Aeschyl., Hdt. down; *to give a sign, to signify, indicate*: τί, Acts xxv. 27; foll. by indir. disc., Jn. xii. 33; xviii. 32; xxi. 19; i. q. *to make known*: absol. Rev. i. 1; foll. by acc. w. inf. Acts xi. 28.*

4592   σημεῖον, -ου, τό, (σημαίνω [or σῆμα]), fr. Aeschyl. and Hdt. down, Hebr. אוֹת, *a sign, mark, token*;   **1.** univ. that by which a pers. or a thing is distinguished from others and known: Mt. xxvi. 48; Lk. ii. 12; 2 Th. iii. 17; σημεῖον περιτομῆς (explanatory gen. [cf. B. § 123, 4]), equiv. to σημεῖον, ὅ ἐστι περιτομή, circumcision which should be a sign of the covenant formed with God, Ro. iv. 11; τὰ σημεῖα τοῦ ἀποστόλου, the tokens by which one is proved to be an apostle, 2 Co. xii. 12; a sign by which anything future is pre-announced, Mk. xiii. 4; Lk. xxi. 7; τὸ σημ. τῆς σῆς παρουσίας, gen. of the obj., Mt. xxiv. 3; τοῦ υἱοῦ τοῦ ἀνθρώπου, the sign which indicates that the Messiah will shortly, or forthwith, come from heaven in visible manifestation, ibid. 30; with a gen. of the subj. τὰ σημεῖα τῶν καιρῶν, i. e. the indications of future events which οἱ καιροί furnish, what οἱ καιροί portend, Mt. xvi. 3 [T br. WH reject the pass.]; a sign by which one is warned, an admonition, 1 Co. xiv. 22. used of noteworthy personages, by whom God forcibly admonishes men and indicates to them what he would have them do: thus σημεῖον ἀντιλεγόμενον is said of Jesus Christ, Lk. ii. 34; Ἰωνᾶς ἐγένετο σημεῖον τοῖς Νινευίταις (Jon. iii. 4), Lk. xi. 30; hence, τὸ σημεῖον Ἰωνᾶ, ib. 29, is i. q. τὸ σημεῖον like to that ὃς ἦν Ἰωνᾶς, i. e. to the sign which was given by the mission and preaching of Jonah, to prompt men to seek salvation [W. 189 (177)]; in the same sense, ὁ υἱὸς τοῦ ἀνθρώπου says that he will be a σημεῖον to the men of his generation, ib. 30; but in Mt. xii. 39; xvi. 4 τὸ σημεῖον Ἰωνᾶ is the miraculous experience which befell Jonah himself, cf. xii. 40; that Luke reproduces Christ's words more correctly than Matthew is shown by De Wette and Bleek on Mt. xii. 40, by *Neander*, Leben Jesu, p. 265 sq. ed. 1 [Eng. trans. (3d ed. N. Y. 1851) § 165 p. 245 sq.], and others; [but that Luke's report is less full than Matthew's, rather than at variance with it, is shown by Meyer, Weiss, Keil, and others (on Mt. l. c.)].   **2.** *a sign, prodigy, portent*, i. e. an unusual occurrence, transcending the common course of nature;   **a.** of signs portending remarkable events soon to happen: Lk. xxi. 11, 25; Acts ii. 19; Rev. xii. 1, 3; xv. 1.   **b.** of miracles and wonders by which God authenticates the men sent by him, or by which men prove that the cause they are pleading is God's: Mt. xii. 38 sq.; xvi. 1, 4; Mk. viii. 11 sq.; xvi. 17, 20; Lk. xi. 16, 29; xxiii. 8; Jn. ii. 11, 18, 23; iii. 2; iv. 54; vi. 2, 14. 26, 30; vii. 31; ix. 16; x. 41; xi. 47; xii.

18, 37; xx. 30; Acts ii. 22, 43; viii. 6; 1 Co. i. 22; but the power διδόναι σημεῖα, by which men are deceived, is ascribed also to false teachers, false prophets, and to demons: Mt. xxiv. 24; Mk. xiii. 22; Rev. xiii. 13 sq.; xvi. 14; xix. 20; 2 Th. ii. 9.   σημεῖα κ. τέρατα (אֹתוֹת וּמֹפְתִים) or (yet less freq.) τέρατα κ. σημεῖα (terms which differ not in substantial meaning but only in origin; cf. Fritzsche, Rom. vol. iii. p. 270 sq.; [Trench § xci.]) are found conjoined: Mt. xxiv. 24; Mk. xiii. 22; Jn. iv. 48; Acts ii. 19, 43; iv. 30; v. 12; vi. 8; vii. 36; xiv. 3; xv. 12; Ro. xv. 19; 2 Th. ii. 9, (Deut. xxviii. 46; xxxiv. 11; Neh. ix. 10; Is. viii. 18; xx. 3; Jer. xxxix. (xxxii.) 20; Sap. viii. 8; x. 16; Polyb. 3, 112, 8; Philo, vit. Moys. i. 16; Joseph. antt. 20, 8, 6; b. j. prooem. 11; Plut. Alex. 75; Ael. v. h. 12, 57); with κ. δυνάμεις added, 2 Co. xii. 12; Heb. ii. 4; σημεῖα κ. δυνάμεις, Acts viii. 13; δυνάμεις κ. τέρατα κ. σημεῖα, Acts ii. 22; διδόναι σημεῖα (see δίδωμι, B. II. 1 a.): Mt. xxiv. 24; Mk. xiii. 22 (here Tdf. ποιεῖν σημ., see ποιέω, I. 1 c.); σημεῖα are said γίνεσθαι διά τινος in Acts ii. 43; iv. [16], 30; v. 12; xiv. 3; xv. 12 [here ποιεῖν σημ., see above]; τὸ σημεῖον τῆς ἰάσεως, the miracle, which was the healing, Acts iv. 22.*

4593 **σημειόω, -ῶ:** (σημεῖον), to mark, note, distinguish by marking; Mid. pres. impv. 2 pers. plur. σημειοῦσθε; to mark or note for one's self [W. § 38, 2 b.; B. § 135, 4]: τινά, 2 Th. iii. 14 [cf. B. 92 (80); W. 119 (113)]. (Theophr., Polyb., Philo, Dion. Hal., al.; [Ps. iv. 7 Sept.].) *

4594 **σήμερον** [Attic τήμερον, i. e. ἡμέρα with pronom. prefix (Skr. sa); cf. Vaniček p. 971], adv., fr. Hom. down, Sept. for הַיּוֹם, to-day, this day: Mt. vi. 11; xxi. 5; Acts iv. 9; xiii. 33, etc.; also where the speaker refers to the night just passed, Mt. xxvii. 19; equiv. to this night (now current), Lk. ii. 11; σήμερον ταύτῃ τῇ νυκτί, Mk. xiv. 30; ἕως σήμερον, 2 Co. iii. 15; opp. to αὔριον, Mt. vi. 30; Lk. xii. 28; xiii. 32 sq.; Jas. iv. 13; χθὲς καὶ σήμερον καὶ εἰς τοὺς αἰῶνας, a rhet. periphrasis for ἀεί, Heb. xiii. 8; ἡ σήμερον ἡμέρα, this (very) day, Acts xxvi. 26; ἕως τῆς σ. ἡμέρας, Ro. xi. 8; μέχρι τῆς σήμερον sc. ἡμέρας, Mt. xi. 23; xxviii. 15; ἕως τῆς σ. Mt. xxvii. 8; ἄχρι τῆς σ. (where L T Tr WH add ἡμέρας), 2 Co. iii. 14; ἡ σήμερον, i. q. what has happened to-day [al. render concerning this day's riot; B. § 133, 9; but see Meyer ad loc.; W. § 30, 9 a.], Acts xix. 40; τὸ σήμερον, the word to-day, Heb. iii. 13; as a subst.: ὁρίζει ἡμέραν, σήμερον, "a to-day" (meaning, 'a time for embracing the salvation graciously offered' [cf. R. V. mrg.]), Heb. iv. 7ᵃ.

4595 **σήπω:** fr. Hom. down; to make corrupt; in the Bible also to destroy, Job xl. 7 (12); pass. to become corrupt or rotten; 2 pf. act. σέσηπα, to (have become i. e. to) be corrupted (cf. Bttm. Ausf. Spr. ii. p. 82): ὁ πλοῦτος σέσηπεν, has perished, Jas. v. 2.*

4596 **σηρικός** (Lchm. ed. maj. T WH σιρικός [cf. WH. App. p. 151]), -ή, -όν, (Σήρ, Σῆρες, the Seres, a people of India [prob. mod. China; yet on the name cf. Pape, Eigen-namen, s. v.; Dict. of Geog. s. v. Serica]);   **1.** prop. pertaining to the Seres.   **2.** silken: τὸ σηρικόν, silk, i. e. the fabric, silken garments, Rev. xviii. 12. ([Strabo,

Plut., Arr., Lcian.]; ἐσθήσεσι σηρικαῖς, Joseph. b. j. 7, 5, 4.) *

4597 **σής, σητός, ὁ,** (Hebr. סָס, Is. li. 8; עָשׁ, Job iv. 19; xiii. 28), a moth, the clothes-moth, [B. D. s. v. Moth; Alex.'s Kitto s. v. Ash]: Mt. vi. 19 sq.; Lk. xii. 33. (Pind., Ar stph., Aristot., Theophr., al.) *

4598 **σητό-βρωτος, -ον,** (fr. σής a moth, and βρωτός fr. βι-βρώσκω), moth-eaten: ἱμάτιον, Jas. v. 2 (ἱμάτια, Job xiii. 28; of idol-images, Sibyll. orac. in Theoph. ad Autol. 2, 36).*

4599 **σθενόω, -ῶ:** (σθένος [allied w. στῆναι, hence prop. stead-fastness; Curtius p. 503 sq.] strength), to make strong, to strengthen: τινά, one's soul, 1 Pet. v. 10, where for 1 aor. opt. act. 3 pers. sing. σθενῶσαι, we must read the fut. σθενώσει, with G L T Tr WH. (Pass. in Rhet. Gr. ed. Walz, vol. i. c. 15.) *

4600 **σιαγών, -όνος, ἡ,** the jaw, the jaw-bone, [A. V. cheek]: Mt. v. 39; Lk. vi. 29. (Soph., Xen., Plat., Aristot., al.; Sept. for לְחִי.) *

4601 **σιγάω, -ῶ;** 1 aor. ἐσίγησα; pf. pass. ptcp. σεσιγημένος; (σιγή); fr. Hom. down; to keep silence, hold one's peace: Lk. ix. 36; xviii. 39 L Tr WH; [xx. 26]; Acts xii. 17; xv. 12 sq.; 1 Co. xiv. 28, 30, 34; pass. to be kept in silence, be concealed, Ro. xvi. 25. [Syn. see ἡσυχάζω.] *

4602 **σιγή, -ῆς, ἡ,** (fr. σίζω [onomatopoetic, Etym. Magn. 712, 29] i. e. to command silence by making the sound st or sch; [yet σιγή prob. has no connection with σίζω, but is of European origin (cf. Germ. schweigen); cf. Fick, Pt. iii. 843; Curtius § 572]), fr. Hom. down, silence: Acts xxi. 40; Rev. viii. 1.*

4603 **σιδήρεος, -έα, -εον,** contr. -οῦς, -ᾶ, -οῦν, (σίδηρος), fr. Hom. down, made of iron: Acts xii. 10; Rev. ii. 27; ix. 9; xii. 5; xix. 15.*

4604 **σίδηρος, -ου, ὁ,** fr. Hom. down, iron: Rev. xviii. 12.*

4605 **Σιδών, -ῶνος** [B. 16 (14)], ἡ, (צִידוֹן and צִידֹן, fr. צוּד 'to hunt', in Aram. also 'to fish'; hence prop. taking its name from its abundance of fish; cf. Justin 18, 3), Sidon, a very ancient Phœnician city, formerly distinguished for wealth and traffic, situated near the Mediterranean on the borders of Judæa; it had been assigned to the tribe of Asher (Josh. xix. 28), but the Jews vainly en-deavored to capture it [Judg. i. 31; iii. 3; x. 12]; now Saida, containing about 10,000 [or 9,000, acc. to Porter in Murray's Handbook p. 376] inhabitants [Baedeker, Palestine p. 433]: Mt. xi. 21 sq.; xv. 21; Mk. iii. 8; vii. 24 (where Tom. WH Tr mrg. br. the words καὶ Σιδῶνος), 31; Lk. iv. 26 (where L T Tr WH Σιδωνίας); vi. 17; x. 13 sq.; Acts xxvii. 3. [Cf. BB. DD. s. v.; Schultz in Herzog ed. 2 vol. xiv. 192 sqq.; Schlottmann in Riehm s. v.] *

4606 **Σιδώνιος, -α, -ον,** (Σιδών), belonging to Sidon, of Sidon: τῆς Σιδωνίας sc. χώρας, [R.V. in the land of Sidon], Lk. iv. 26 L T Tr WH (Hom. Od. 13, 285 [but -δον-]); Σι-δώνιοι, the inhabitants of Sidon, Acts xii. 20.*

4607 **σικάριος, -ου, ὁ,** (a Latin word), an assassin, i. e. one who carries a dagger or short sword [Lat. sica (cf. Jo-seph. as below)] under his clothing, that he may kill secretly and treacherously any one he wishes to (a cut-throat): Acts xxi. 38. (Joseph. b. j. 2, 17, 6 σικαρίους ἐκάλουν τοὺς λῃστὰς ἔχοντας ὑπὸ τοῖς κόλποις τὰ ξίφη [cf. 2, 13, 3]; also antt. 20, 8, 10 σικάριοι λῃσταί εἰσι χρώμενοι ξιφιδίοις παραπλησίοις μὲν τὸ μέγεθος τοῖς τῶν Περσῶν ἀκινάκαις, ἐπικαμπέσι δὲ καὶ ὁμοίοις ταῖς ὑπὸ Ῥωμαίων σίκαις καλουμέναις, ἀφ᾿ ὧν καὶ τὴν προσηγορίαν οἱ λῃστεύοντες ἔλαβον πολλοὺς ἀναιροῦντες.) [Syn. see φονεύς.]*

4608   **σίκερα**, τό, (Hebr. שֵׁכָר [rather, acc. to Kautzsch (Gram. p. 11) for שִׁכְרָא (prop. σίκρα) the stat. emphat. of שֵׁכָר (lit. 'intoxicating' drink)]), indecl. [W. 68 (66); B. 24 (21)], (yet Euseb. praep. evang. 6, 10, 8 has a gen. σίκερος [and Soph. in his Lex. quotes fr. Cyrill. Alex. 1, 1041 d. (ed. Migne) a gen. σίκερατος]), *strong drink*, an intoxicating beverage, different from wine [exc. in Num. xxviii. 7 (cf. Is. xxviii. 7)]; it was a factitious product, made of a mixture of sweet ingredients, whether derived from grain and vegetables, or from the juice of fruits (dates), or a decoction of honey: Lk. i. 15 (Lev. x. 9; Num. vi. 3; Deut. xiv. 25 (26); xxix. 6, etc.; the same Hebr. word is rendered also by μέθυσμα, Judg. xiii. 4, 7, 14; Mic. ii. 11). Cf. *Win.* RWB. s. v. Wein, künstlicher; [B. D. s. v. Drink, Strong].*

4609   **Σίλας**, [gen. not found (exc. Joseph. vita 17 -a)], dat. -ᾳ, acc. -αν, [B. 20 (18)], ὁ, *Silas* (contr. fr. Σιλουανός, q. v.; W. 103 (97)), a Roman citizen (Acts xvi. 37 sq.), the companion of the apostle Paul in several of his journeys, and his associate in preaching the gospel: Acts xv. 22, 27, 32, 34 Rec., 40; xvi. 19, 25, 29; xvii. 4, 10, 14 sq.; xviii. 5. [B. D. s. v. Silas.]*

4610   **Σιλουανός**, -οῦ, ὁ, *Silvanus*, the same man who in Acts is called Σίλας (q. v.): 2 Co. i. 19; 1 Th. i. 1; 2 Th. i. 1; 1 Pet. v. 12. [Not infreq. written in the Mss. Σιλβανός, *Silbanus*; cf. Tdf. on ll. cc.] *

4611   **Σιλωάμ**, (Hebr. שִׁלֹחַ, Is. viii. 6, which in Jn. ix. 7 is translated ἀπεσταλμένος, but more correctly [see below] 'a sending out,' '*gushing forth*' (of water); it is formed after the analogy of אוֹיֵב 'had in hatred', 'persecuted', fr. אָיַב; יִלּוֹד 'born', fr. יָלַד 'to bring forth'; ["the purely passive explanation, ἀπεσταλμένος, Jn. ix. 7, is not so incorrect." *Ewald*, Ausführl. Lehrbuch d. Hebr. Spr. § 150, 2 a.; cf. Meyer on Jn. l. c.]), ὁ (in Joseph. ἡ Σ., sc. πηγή, b. j. 5, 12, 2; 6, 8, 5; but also μέχρι τοῦ Σ. b. j. 2, 16, 2; 6, 7, 2; [B. 21 (19)]), [indecl. ; but in Joseph. b. j. 5, 6, 1 ἀπὸ τῆς Σιλωᾶς], *Siloam*, a fountain of sweet and abundant water (Joseph. b. j. 5, 4, 1), flowing into a basin or pool of the same name (Neh. iii. 15), both of which seem to have been situated in the southern part of Jerusalem, although opinions vary on this point: Lk. xiii. 4; Jn. ix. 11, (Is. viii. 6). Cf. [B. D. s. v. Siloam]; *Win.* RWB. s. v. Siloah; *Rödiger* in Gesen. Thesaur. p. 1416; *Leyrer* in Herzog ed. 1, xiv. p. 371 sqq.; *Robinson*, Palestine, i. 333 sqq.; *Tobler*, Die Siloaquelle u. der Oelberg (St. Gallen, 1852); *Kneucker*, Siloah, Quelle Teich u. Thal in Jerus. (Heidelb. 1873); *Furrer* in Schenkel v. 295 sq.; [*Ritter*, Palestine, etc., Eng. trans. i. 148 sq.; *Wilson*, Ordnance Survey, etc., 1865; esp. *Guthe* in the Zeitschr. d. Deutsch. Pal.-Vereins for 1882, pp. 205 sqq. 229 sqq.; Zeitschr. d. Deutsch. Morgenl.-Gesellsch. for 1882, p. 725 sqq.].*

4612   **σιμικίνθιον** (or σημικίνθιον), -ου, τό, (Lat. *semicinctium* [cf. *Rich*, Dict. of Antiq. s. v.], fr. *semi* and *cingo*), a *narrow apron*, or *linen covering*, which workmen and servants were accustomed to wear: Acts xix. 12 [A. V. *aprons*].*

4613   **Σίμων**, -ωνος [B. 16 (14)], ὁ, (שִׁמְעוֹן, 'a hearing', fr. שָׁמַע 'to hear'; [there was also a Grk. name Σίμων (allied w. σιμός, i. e. 'flat-nosed'; *Fick*, Gr. Personennamen, p. 210), but cf. B. D. s. v. Simon init.; Bp. Lghtft. on Gal. p. 266 sq.]), *Simon*: **1.** *Peter*, the apostle: Mt. xvii. 25; Mk. i. 29 sq. 36; Lk. iv. 38; v. 4 sq. 10, etc.; see Πέτρος. **2.** the brother of Judas Lebbæus [cf. s. v. Ἰούδας, 8], an apostle, who is called Κανανίτης [so RG, but L T Tr WH -ναῖος, q. v.], Mt. x. 4; Mk. iii. 18, and ζηλωτής, Lk. vi. 15; Acts i. 13. **3.** a brother of Jesus [cf. s. v. ἀδελφός, 1]: Mt. xiii. 55; Mk. vi. 3. **4.** a certain Cyrenian, who carried the cross of Jesus: Mt. xxvii. 32; Mk. xv. 21; Lk. xxiii. 26. **5.** the father of Judas Iscariot [and himself surnamed Ἰσκαριώτης (see Ἰούδας, 6)]: Jn. vi. 71; xii. 4; xiii. 2, 26. **6.** a certain Pharisee, Lk. vii. 40, 43 sq., who appears to [some, e. g. Grotius, Schleiermacher, Holtzmann, Schenkel, Ewald, Keim, Hug, Bleek (see his Synopt. Erklär. on Lk. l. c.) to] be the same as *Simon the leper*, Mt. xxvi. 6; Mk. xiv. 3; [but the occurrence recorded by Lk. l. c. is now commonly thought to be distinct fr. that narrated by Mt. and Mk. ll. cc.; cf. Godet or Keil on Lk.]. **7.** a certain tanner, living at Joppa: Acts ix. 43; x. 6, 17, 32. **8.** *Simon* ('*Magus*'), the Samaritan sorcerer: Acts viii. 9, 13, 18, 24. The various eccles. stories about him, as well as the opinions and conjectures of modern theologians, are reviewed at length by *Lipsius* in Schenkel v. pp. 301–321; [cf. *W. Möller* in Herzog ed. 2, vol. xiv. p. 246 sqq.; *Schaff*, Hist. of the Chris. Church, vol. ii. (1883) § 121].

4614   **Σινά** [-νά WH; cf. Chandler §§ 135, 138], τό (sc. ὄρος, cf. B. 21 sq. (19)), indecl., Joseph. τὸ Σιναῖον, antt. 3, 5, 1, and τὸ Σιναῖον ὄρος, antt. 2, 12, 1; Hebr. סִינַי [perh. 'jagged'; al. make it an adj. 'belonging to (the desert of) Sin'], (*Sina* or) *Sinai*, a mountain or, rather, a mountainous region in the peninsula of Arabia Petræa, made famous by the giving of the Mosaic law. There are three summits: one towards the west, which is called חוֹרֵב, a second towards the east, *Sinai* prop. so called, the third towards the south, now Mt. St. Catharine. But the distinction between Horeb and Sinai is given differently by different writers; and some think that they were two different names of one and the same mountain (cf. Sir. xlviii. 7); cf. [*McC. and S.* Cycl. s. v. Sinai]; *Win.* RWB. s. v. Sinai; *Arnold* in Herzog ed. 1 vol. xiv. p. 420 sq.; [*Schultz* in ed. 2 vol. xiv. p. 282 sqq.]; *Furrer* in Schenkel v. p. 326 sqq.; [Eng. Ordnance Survey, 1869; *Palmer*, Desert of the Exodus, 1872; also his Sinai from the Monuments, 1878; *Furrer* commends Holland's "Sketch Map" etc. in the Journ. of the Royal Geog. Soc. vol. xxxix. (Lond. 1869)]. The name occurs in Acts vii. 30, 38; Gal. iv. 24 sq.*

4615   **σίναπι** (also σίνηπι [but not in the N. T.], both later for the Attic νάπυ [so accented in late auth., better νᾶπυ], see *Lob.* ad Phryn. p. 288), [thought to be of Egypt. origin; cf. *Vaniček*, Fremdwörter, s. v. νᾶπυ], -εως [B. 14 (13)], τό, *mustard*, the name of a plant which in oriental countries grows from a very small seed and attains to the height of 'a tree'— ten feet and more; hence a very small quantity of a thing is likened to a κόκκος σινάπεως [A. V. *a grain of mustard seed*], Mt. xvii. 20; Lk. xvii. 6; and also a thing which grows to a remarkable size, Mt. xiii. 31 sq.; Mk. iv. 31; Lk. xiii. 19. [Cf. B. D. s. v. Mustard; *Löw*, Aram. Pflanzennamen, § 134; *Carruthers* in the 'Bible Educator' vol. i. p. 119 sq.; *Tristram*, Nat. Hist. of the Bible, p. 472 sq.; *Thomson*, The Land and the Book, ii. 100 sq.] *

4616 σινδών, -όνος, ἡ, (of uncertain origin; Skr. sindhu [Egypt. 'schenti' or 'sent'; cf. *Vaniček*, Fremdwörter, s. v.]; Sept. for כָּרִין, Judg. xiv. 12 sq.; Prov. xxix. 42 (xxxi. 24)), *fine cloth* (Lat. *sindon*), i. e. **1.** *linen cloth*, esp. that which was fine and costly, in which the bodies of the dead were wrapped: Mt. xxvii. 59; Mk. xv. 46; Lk. xxiii. 53, (cf. Hdt. 2, 86 who says of the Egyptians, κατειλίσσουσι πᾶν τὸ σῶμα σινδόνος βυσσίνης [see *Wilkinson's* note in Rawlinson's Herod. 3d ed. l.c.]). **2.** *thing made of fine cloth*: so of a light and loose garment worn at night over the naked body, Mk. xiv. 51 sq. [others suppose a sheet rather than a shirt to be referred to; A. V. *linen cloth*; cf. B.D. Am. ed. s. v. Sheets]. (Besides Hdt., the writers Soph., Thuc., Strabo, Lcian., al., use the word.) *

4617 σινιάζω: 1 aor. infin. σινιάσαι; (σινίον 'a sieve,' 'winnowing-van'; an eccles. and Byzant. word [cf. Macar. homil. 5 p. 73 sq. (496 a. ed. Migne)]); *to sift, shake in a sieve*: τινὰ ὡς τὸν σῖτον, i. e., dropping the fig., by inward agitation to try one's faith to the verge of overthrow, Lk. xxii. 31. (Eccles. writ. [cf. W. 92 (87), 26 (25), and see above].) *

see 4596 σιρικός, see σηρικός.

see 4577 σιρός, -οῦ, ὁ, i. q. σειρός, q. v.: 2 Pet. ii. 4 L T.*

4618 σιτευτός, -ή, -όν, (σιτεύω, to feed with wheat, to fatten), *fattened, fatted*: Lk. xv. 23, 27, 30. (Jer. xxvi. (xlvi.) 21; 1 K. iv. 23, [etc.]; Xen., Polyb., Athen., [al.].) *

see 4621 σιτίον, -ου, τό, (dimin. of σῖτος); **1.** *corn, grain*: Acts vii. 12 L T Tr WH. In prof. writ. also **2.** *food made from grain* (Hdt. 2, 36). **3.** *eatables, victuals, provisions*, ([Hdt.], Arstph., Xen., Plat., Dem., al.).*

4619 σιτιστός, -ή, -όν, (σιτίζω, to feed with grain, to fatten), *fattened*, [plur. τὰ σιτ. as subst., A. V. *fatlings*], Mt. xxii. 4. (Joseph. antt. 8, 2, 4; Athen. 14 p. 656 e.) *

4620 σιτομέτριον, -ου, τό, (Attic writ. said τὸν σῖτον μετρεῖν: out of which later writ. formed the compound σιτομετρεῖν, Gen. xlvii. 12, [14]; Polyb. 4, 63, 10; Diod. 19, 50; Joseph. c. Ap. 1, 14, 7; σιτομετρία, Diod. 2, 41; [cf. *Lob.* ad Phryn. p. 383; W. 25]), *a measured 'portion of' grain* or '*food*': Lk. xii. 42. (Eccles. and Byzant. writ.) *

4621 σῖτος, -ου, ὁ, [of uncertain origin; cf. *Vaniček*, Fremdwörter, s. v.], fr. Hom. down, Sept. chiefly for דָּגָן, *wheat, corn*: Mt. iii. 12; xiii. 25, 29 sq.; Mk. iv. 28; Lk. iii. 17;

[xii. 18 WH Tr txt.]; xvi. 7; xxii. 31; Jn. xii. 24; Acts xxvii. 38; 1 Co. xv. 37; Rev. vi. 6; xviii. 13; plur. τὰ σῖτα (cf. W. 63 (62)), Acts vii. 12 Rec., and often in Sept.*

Σιχάρ, see Συχάρ.   **see 4965**

Σιών, indecl., (its grammat. gend. in the N. T. does **4622** not appear from the pass. in which it is mentioned; cf. B. 21 sq. (19); in the Sept. when it denotes the c i t y of Jerusalem ἡ Σιών occurs, as Ps. ci. (cii.) 14, 17; cxxxi. (cxxxii.) 13; cxxxvi. (cxxxvii.) 1), Hebr. צִיּוֹן [i. e. acc. to some, 'protected' or 'protecting'; acc. to others, 'sunny'; al. al.]; *Sion* [so A. V., but properly (with R. V.)] *Zion*: **1.** the hill on which the higher and more ancient part of Jerusalem was built (עִיר דָּוִד *city of David*, because David captured it); it was the southwesternmost and highest of the hills on which the city stood; [many now would identify it with the eastern hill, some with the northern; cf. *Furrer* in Schenkel iii. 216 sqq.; *Mühlau* in Riehm s. v.; per contra *Wolcott* in B. D. Am. ed. s. v.; *Schultz* in Herzog ed. 2 vi. p. 543 sq.]. **2.** used very often for the entire city of Jerusalem itself: Ro. ix. 33 and 1 Pet. ii. 6, (after Is. xxviii. 16); Ro. xi. 26 (fr. Is. lix. 20); ἡ θυγάτηρ Σιών (see θυγάτηρ, b. β.), Mt. xxi. 5; Jn. xii. 15. **3.** Since Jerusalem, because the temple stood there, was called the dwelling-place of G o d (cf. Mt. v. 35; κύριος τὴν Σιὼν ᾑρετίσατο εἰς κατοικίαν ἑαυτῷ, Ps. cxxxi. (cxxxii.) 13), the expression τὸ Σιὼν ὄρος is transferred to heaven, as the true dwelling-place of God and heavenly beings, the antitype of the earthly Zion: Heb. xii. 22; Rev. xiv. 1.*

σιωπάω, -ῶ; impf., 3 pers. sing. ἐσιώπα, 3 pers. plur. **4623** ἐσιώπων; fut. σιωπήσω (Lk. xix. 40 L T Tr WH); 1 aor. ἐσιώπησα; (σιωπή silence); fr. Hom. down; *to be silent, hold one's peace*: prop., Mt. xx. 31; xxvi. 63; Mk. iii. 4; ix. 34; x. 48; xiv. 61; Lk. xviii. 39 R G; xix. 40; Acts xviii. 9; used of one silent because dumb, Lk. i. 20; 4 Macc. x. 18; like *sileo* in the Lat. poets, used metaph. of a calm, quiet sea [(in rhetorical command)]: Mk. iv. 39. [SYN. see ἡσυχάζω.] *

σκανδαλίζω; 1 aor. ἐσκανδάλισα; Pass., pres. σκανδαλίζο- **4624** μαι; impf. ἐσκανδαλιζόμην; 1 aor. ἐσκανδαλίσθην [cf. B. 52 (45)]; 1 fut. σκανδαλισθήσομαι; (σκάνδαλον); Vulg. *scandalizo*; Peshitto ܐܟܫܠ; prop. *to put a stumbling-block or impediment in the way*, upon which another may trip and fall; *to be a stumbling-block*; in the N. T. always metaph. [R. V. *to cause* or *make to stumble*; A. V. *to offend* (cause to offend)]; **a.** *to entice to sin* (Luth. *ärgern*, i. e. *arg, bös machen*): τινά, Mt. v. 29, [30]; xviii. 6, 8 sq.; Mk. ix. 42 sq. 45, 47; Lk. xvii. 2; 1 Co. viii. 13; pass. Lat. *offendor*, [A. V. *to be offended*], Vulg. *scandalizor*, Peshitto ܐܟܫܠ: Ro. xiv. 21 [R G L T Tr txt.]; 2 Co. xi. 29 [R. V. *is made to stumble*; cf. W. 153 (145)]. **b.** *to cause a person to begin to distrust and desert one whom he ought to trust and obey*; *to cause to fall away*, and in pass. *to fall away* [R. V. *to stumble* (cf. 'Teaching' etc. 16, 5; Herm. vis. 4, 1, 3; mand. 8, 10)]: τινά, Jn. vi. 61; pass., Mt. xiii. 21; xxiv. 10; xxvi. 33; Mk. iv.

17; xiv. 29; [Jn. xvi. 1]; ἔν τινι [A. V.] *to be offended in one*, [*find occasion of stumbling in*], i. e. to see in another what I disapprove of and what hinders me from acknowledging his authority: Mt. xi. 6; xiii. 57; xxvi. 31; Mk. vi. 3; xiv. 27; Lk. vii. 23; *to cause one to judge unfavorably* or *unjustly of another*, Mt. xvii. 27. Since the man who stumbles or whose foot gets entangled feels annoyed, σκανδαλίζω means **c.** *to cause one to feel displeasure at a thing*; *to make indignant*: τινά, pass. *to be displeased, indignant*, [A. V. *offended*], Mt. xv. 12. The verb σκανδαλίζω is found neither in prof. auth. nor in the Sept., but only in the relics of Aquila's version of the O. T., Ps. lxiii. (lxiv.) 9; Is. viii. 15; [xl. 30]; Prov. iv. 12 for כָּשַׁל; besides in Sir. ix. 5; xxiii. 8; xxxv. (xxxii.) 15; [Psalt. Sal. 16, 7. Cf. W. 33.] *

4625 σκάνδαλον, -ου, τό, a purely bibl. [(occurring some twenty-five times in the Grk. O. T., and fifteen, quotations included, in the New)] and eccles. word for σκανδάληθρον, which occurs occasionally in native Grk. writ.; Sept. for מוֹקֵשׁ (a noose, a snare) and מִכְשׁוֹל; **a.** prop. *the movable stick* or *tricker* ('trigger') *of a trap, trap-stick*; *a trap, snare*; *any impediment placed in the way and causing one to stumble* or *fall*, [*a stumbling-block, occasion of stumbling*]: Lev. xix. 14; πέτρα σκανδάλου [A. V. *a rock of offence*], i. e. a rock which is a cause of stumbling (Lat. *offendiculum*), — fig. applied to Jesus Christ, whose person and career were so contrary to the expectations of the Jews concerning the Messiah, that they rejected him and by their obstinacy made shipwreck of salvation (see πρόσκομμα), Ro. ix. 33 and 1 Pet. ii. 8 (7), (fr. Is. viii. 14). **b.** metaph. *any person* or *thing by which one is* ('entrapped') *drawn into error* or *sin* [cf. W. 32]; **α.** of persons [(Josh. xxiii. 13; 1 S. xviii. 21)]: Mt. xiii. 41; xvi. 23 (where σκάνδαλον "non ex effectu, sed ex natura et condicione propria dicitur," Calov.); so Χριστὸς ἐσταυρωμένος is called (because his ignominious death on the cross roused the opposition of the Jews), 1 Co. i. 23. **β.** of things: τιθέναι τινὶ σκάνδαλον (literally, in Judith v. 1), *to put a stumbling-block in one's way*, i. e. to do that by which another is led to sin, Ro. xiv. 13; the same idea is expressed by βάλλειν σκάνδαλον ἐνώπιόν τινος [*to cast a stumbling-block before one*], Rev. ii. 14; οὐκ ἔστι σκάνδαλον ἔν τινι (see εἰμί, V. 4 e.), 1 Jn. ii. 10; plur. σκάνδαλα, *words or deeds which entice to sin* (Sap. xiv. 11), Mt. xviii. 7 [cf. B. 322 (277) n.; W. 371 (348)]; Lk. xvii. 1; σκάνδαλα ποιεῖν παρὰ τὴν διδαχήν, to cause persons to be drawn away from the true doctrine into error and sin [cf. παρά, III. 2 a.], Ro. xvi. 17; τὸ σκάνδ. τοῦ σταυροῦ, the offence which the cross, i. e. Christ's death on the cross, gives (cf. *a.* fin. above), [R. V. *the stumbling-block of the cross*], Gal. v. 11; i. q. a cause of destruction, Ro. xi. 9, fr. Ps. lxviii. (lxix.) 23.*

4626 σκάπτω, 1 aor. ἔσκαψα; [allied w. it are Eng. 'ship', 'skiff', etc.; Curtius § 109; Fick iv. 267; vii. 336]; *to dig*: Lk. vi. 48 (on which see βαθύνω); xiii. 8 [B. § 130, 5]; xvi. 3. ([Hom. h. Merc.]; Arstph., Eurip., Xen., Plat., Aristot., Theophr., al.) [COMP.: κατα-σκάπτω.] *

σκάφη, -ης, ἡ, (σκάπτω [q. v.]), fr. [Aeschyl. and] Hdt. down, *anything dug out, hollow vessel, trough, tray, tub*; spec. *a boat*: Acts xxvii. 16, 30, 32.* **4627**

σκέλος, -ους, τό, fr. Hom. down, *the leg* i. e. from the hip to the toes inclusive: Jn. xix. 31 sq. 33.* **4628**

σκέπασμα, -τος, τό, (σκεπάζω to cover), *a covering*, spec. *clothing* (Aristot. pol. 7, 17 p. 1336ᵃ, 17; Joseph. b. j. 2, 8, 5): 1 Tim. vi. 8.* **4629**

Σκευᾶς, -ᾶ [W. § 8, 1; B. 20 (18)], ὁ, *Sceva*, a certain chief priest [cf. ἀρχιερεύς, 2 fin.]: Acts xix. 14.* **4630**

σκευή, -ῆς, ἡ, [cf. σκεῦος], fr. [Pind., Soph.], Hdt. down, *any apparatus, equipment*, or *furniture*; used of the utensils [outfit, i. e. furniture (? — so R. V. mrg.), or tackling (? — so A. V., R. V. txt.)] of a ship (Diod. 14, 79): Acts xxvii. 19 (Sept. Jon. i. 5).* **4631**

σκεῦος, -ους, τό, [prob. fr. r. sku 'to cover'; cf. Lat. *scutum, cutis, obscurus*; Curtius § 113; Vaniček p. 1115], fr. [Arstph.], Thuc. down; Sept. for כְּלִי; **1.** *a vessel*: Mk. xi. 16; Lk. viii. 16; Jn. xix. 29; Acts x. 11, 16; xi. 5; 2 Tim. ii. 20; Rev. ii. 27; xviii. 12; τὰ σκ. τῆς λειτουργίας, to be used in performing religious rites, Heb. ix. 21; σκεῦος εἰς τιμήν, unto honor, i. e. for honorable use, Ro. ix. 21; 2 Tim. ii. 21, (καθαρῶν ἔργων δοῦλα σκεύη, Sap. xv. 7); εἰς ἀτιμίαν, unto dishonor, i. e. for a low use (as, a urinal), Ro. ix. 21; σκεύη ὀργῆς, into which wrath is emptied, i. e. men appointed by God unto woe, hence the addition κατηρτισμένα εἰς ἀπώλειαν, Ro. ix. 22; σκεύη ἐλέους, fitted to receive mercy, — explained by the words ἃ προητοίμασεν εἰς δόξαν, ib. 23; τὸ σκεῦος is used of a woman, as the vessel of her husband, 1 Th. iv. 4 (see κτάομαι; [al. take it here (as in 2 Co. iv. 7 below) of *the body*]); the female sex, as being weaker than the male, is likened to a σκεῦος ἀσθενέστερον, in order to commend to husbands the obligations of kindness towards their wives (for the weaker the vessels, the greater must be the care lest they be broken), 1 Pet. iii. 7; ὀστράκινα σκεύη is applied to human bodies, as frail, 2 Co. iv. 7. **2.** *an implement*; plur. *household utensils, domestic gear*: Mt. xii. 29; Mk. iii. 27; Lk. xvii. 31, [in these pass. R. V. *goods*]; as the plur. often in Grk. writ. denotes the tackle and armament of vessels (Xen. oec. 8, 12; Plat. Critias p. 117 d.; Lach. p. 183 e.; Polyb. 22, 26, 13), so the sing. τὸ σκεῦος seems to be used spec. and collectively of the sails and ropes (R. V. *gear*) in Acts xxvii. 17. metaph. of a man: σκεῦος ἐκλογῆς (gen. of quality), a chosen instrument [or (so A. V.) 'vessel'], Acts ix. 15; in a base sense, an assistant in accomplishing evil deeds [cf. Eng. 'tool'], σκεῦος ὑπηρετικόν, Polyb. 13, 5, 7; 15, 25, 1.* **4632**

σκηνή, -ῆς, ἡ, [fr. r. ska 'to cover' etc.; cf. σκιά, σκότος, etc.; Lat. *casa, cassis, castrum*; Eng. *shade*, etc.; Curtius § 112; Vaniček p. 1054 sq.], fr. [Aeschyl.], Soph. and Thuc. down; Sept. chiefly for אֹהֶל, often also for מִשְׁכָּן, also for סֻכָּה; *a tent, tabernacle*, (made of green boughs, or skins, or other materials): Mt. xvii. 4; Mk. ix. 5; Lk. ix. 33; Heb. xi. 9; αἱ αἰώνιοι σκηναί (see αἰώνιος, 3), Lk. xvi. 9 (et dabo iis tabernacula aeterna quae praeparaveram illis, 4 (5) Esdr. ii. 11); of that well **4633** known movable temple of God after the pattern of which the temple at Jerusalem was subsequently built [cf. B. D. s. v. Temple]: Heb. viii. 5; ix. 1 Rec.ˢᵗ, 21; with τοῦ μαρτυρίου added (see μαρτύριον, c. fin.), Acts vii. 44; the temple is called σκηνή in Heb. xiii. 10; σκηνὴ ἡ πρώτη, the front part of the tabernacle (and afterwards of the temple), the Holy place, Heb. ix. 2, 6, 8; of the Holy of holies, Heb. ix. 3; the name is transferred to heaven, as the true dwelling-place of God and the prototype of the earthly 'tabernacle' or sanctuary, Heb. ix. 11; Rev. xiii. 6; hence ἡ σκηνὴ ἡ ἀληθινή, heaven, Heb. viii. 2; with a reference to this use of the word, it is declared that when the kingdom of God is perfectly established ἡ σκηνὴ τοῦ θεοῦ will be μετὰ τῶν ἀνθρώπων (after the analogy of σκηνοῦν μετά τινος), Rev. xxi. 3; ὁ ναὸς τῆς σκηνῆς τοῦ μαρτυρίου (see μαρτύριον, c. fin.), the heavenly temple, in which was the tabernacle of the covenant, i. e. the inmost sanctuary or adytum, Rev. xv. 5. ἡ σκ. τοῦ Μολόχ, the tabernacle i. e. portable shrine of Moloch, Acts vii. 43 (for the Orientals on their journeys and military expeditions used to carry with them their deities, together with shrines for them; hence ἡ ἱερὰ σκηνή of the Carthaginians in Diod. 20, 65, where see Wesseling [but cf. סֻכּוּת in Mühlau and Volck's Gesenius, or the recent Comm. on Am. v. 26]). ἡ σκηνὴ Δαυίδ (fr. Am. ix. 11 for סֻכָּה), the hut (tabernacle) of David, seems to be employed, in contempt, of his house, i. e. family reduced to decay and obscurity, Acts xv. 16 (otherwise אֹהֶל דָּוִד in Is. xvi. 5).*

σκηνοπηγία, -ας, ἡ, (σκηνή and πήγνυμι, cf. Heb. viii. 2); 1. the construction of a tabernacle or tabernacles: ἡ τῆς χελιδόνος σκηνοπηγία, the skill of the swallow in building its nest, Aristot. h. a. 9, 7 [p. 612ᵇ, 22]. 2. the feast of tabernacles: Jn. vii. 2. This festival was observed by the Jews yearly for seven days, beginning with the 15th of the month Tisri [i. e. approximately, Oct.; cf. BB.DD. s. v. Month], partly to perpetuate the memory of the time when their ancestors after leaving Egypt dwelt in tents on their way through the Arabian desert (Lev. xxiii. 43), partly as a season of festivity and joy on the completion of the harvest and the vintage (Deut. xvi. 13) ['the feast of ingathering' (see below)]. In celebrating the festival the Jews were accustomed to construct booths of the leafy branches of trees, — either on the roofs or in the courts of their dwellings, or in the streets and squares (Neh. viii. 15, 16), and to adorn them with flowers and fruits of all kinds (Lev. xxiii. 40), — under which, throughout the period of the festival, they feasted and gave themselves up to rejoicing. This feast is called חַג הַסֻּכּוֹת (ἡ) ἑορτὴ (τῆς) σκηνοπηγίας, Deut. xvi. 16; xxxi. 10; Zech. xiv. 16, 18 sq.; 1 Esdr. v. 50 (51); 1 Macc. x. 21; Joseph. antt. 4, 8, 12; (ἡ) ἑορτὴ (τῶν) σκηνῶν, Lev. xxiii. 34; Deut. xvi. 13; [2 Chr. viii. 13; Ezra iii. 4]; 2 Macc. x. 6; σκηναί, Philo de septenar. § 24; ἡ σκηνοπηγία, 2 Macc. i. 9, 18; once [twice] (Ex. xxiii. 16; [xxxiv. 22]) חַג הָאָסִיף, i. e. 'the feast of ingathering' sc. of fruits. [Cf. BB.DD. (esp. Ginsburg in Alex.'s Kitto); Edersheim, The Temple, ch. xiv.].*

σκηνοποιός, -οῦ, ὁ, (σκηνή and ποιέω), a tent-maker, i. q. σκηνορράφος (Ael. v. h. 2, 1); one that made small portable tents, of leather or cloth of goats' hair (Lat. cilicium) or linen, for the use of travellers: Acts xviii. 3 [cf. Meyer ad loc.; Woldemar Schmidt in Herzog ed. 2 vol. xi. p. 359 sq.].*

σκῆνος, -ους, τό, [Hippocr., Plat., al.], a tabernacle, a tent, everywhere [exc. Boeckh, Corp. inscrr. vol. ii. no. 3071] used metaph. of the human body, in which the soul dwells as in a tent, and which is taken down at death: 2 Co. v. 4; ἡ ἐπίγειος ἡμῶν οἰκία τοῦ σκήνους, i. e. ὅ ἐστι τὸ σκῆνος [W. § 59, 7 d., 8 a.], which is the well-known tent, ibid. 1 [R. V. the earthly house of our tabernacle]. Cf. Sap. ix. 15 and Grimm ad loc.; in the same sense in (Plat.) Tim. Locr. p. 100 sqq. and often in other philosophic writ.; cf. Fischer, Index to Aeschin. dial. Socr.; Passow s. v.; [Field, Otium Norv. pars iii. p. 113 (on 2 Co. v. 1)].*

σκηνόω, -ῶ; fut. σκηνώσω; 1 aor. ἐσκήνωσα; to fix one's tabernacle, have one's tabernacle, abide (or live) in a tabernacle (or tent), tabernacle, (often in Xen.; Dem. p. 1257, 6); God σκηνώσει ἐπ' αὐτούς, will spread his tabernacle over them, so that they may dwell in safety and security under its cover and protection, Rev. vii. 15; univ. i. q. to dwell (Judg. v. 17): foll. by ἐν with a dat. of place, Rev. xii. 12; xiii. 6, (ἐν ταῖς οἰκίαις, Xen. an. 5, 5, 11); ἐν ἡμῖν, among us, Jn. i. 14; μετά τινος, with one, Rev. xxi. 3; σύν τινι, to be one's tent-mate, Xen. Cyr. 6, 1, 49. [COMP.: ἐπι-, κατα- σκηνόω.]*

σκήνωμα, -τος, τό, (σκηνόω), a tent, tabernacle: of the temple as God's habitation, Acts vii. 46 (Ps. xiv. (xv.) 1; xxv. (xxvi.) 8; xlii. (xliii.) 3; xlv. (xlvi.) 5; Pausan. 3, 17, 6; of the tabernacle of the covenant, 1 K. ii. 28); metaph. of the human body as the dwelling of the soul (see σκῆνος): ἐν τῷ σκηνώματι εἶναι, of life on earth, 2 Pet. i. 13; ἀπόθεσις (the author blending the conceptions of a tent and of a covering or garment, as Paul does in 2 Co. v. 2), ibid. 14. (Eur., Xen., Plut., al.; Sept. for אֹהֶל and מִשְׁכָּן.)*

σκιά, -ᾶς, ἡ, [(see σκηνή, init.)], fr. Hom. down, Sept. for צֵל; **a.** prop. shadow, i. e. shade caused by the interception of the light: Mk. iv. 32 (cf. Ezek. xvii. 23); Acts v. 15; σκιὰ θανάτου, shadow of death (like umbra mortis, Ovid. metam. 5, 191, and umbra Erebi, Verg. Aen. 4, 26; 6, 404), 'the densest darkness' (because from of old Hades had been regarded as enveloped in thick darkness), trop. the thick darkness of error [i. e. spiritual death; see θάνατος, 1]: Mt. iv. 16; Lk. i. 79, (fr. Is. ix. 1, where צַלְמָוֶת). **b.** a shadow, i. e. an image cast by an object and representing the form of that object: opp. to σῶμα, the thing itself, Col. ii. 17; hence i. q. a sketch, outline, adumbration, Heb. viii. 5; opp. to εἰκών, the 'express' likeness, the very image, Heb. x. 1 (as in Cic. de off. 3, 17, 69 nos veri juris solidam et expresssam effigiem nullam tenemus, umbra et imaginibus utimur).*

σκιρτάω, -ῶ: 1 aor. ἐσκίρτησα; to leap: Lk. i. 41, 44; vi. 23. (Gen. xxv. 22; Ps. cxiii. (cxiv.) 4, 6; Grk. writ. fr. Hom. down.)*

4641   σκληρο-καρδία, -ας, ἡ, (σκληρός and καρδία), a bibl. word, *the characteristic of one who is* σκληρὸς τὴν καρδίαν (Prov. xxviii. 14), or σκληροκάρδιος (Prov. xvii. 20 ; Ezek. iii. 7) ; *hardness of heart*: Mt. xix. 8 ; Mk. x. 5 ; xvi. 14 ; for עָרְלַת לֵבָב, Deut. x. 16 ; Jer. iv. 4 ; Sir. xvi. 10 ; καρδία σκληρά, Sir. iii. 26, 27. [Cf. W. 26, 99 (94).] *

4642   σκληρός, -ά, -όν, (σκέλλω, σκλῆναι, [to dry up, be dry]), fr. [Hes., Theogn.], Pind., Aeschyl. down ; Sept. for קָשֶׁה, *hard, harsh, rough, stiff*, (τὰ σκληρά κ. τὰ μαλακά, Xen. mem. 3, 10, 1) ; of men, metaph., *harsh, stern, hard*: Mt. xxv. 24 (1 S. xxv. 3 ; Is. xix. 4 ; xlviii. 4 ; many exx. fr. prof. auth. are given by Passow s. v. 2 b. ; [L. and S. s. v. II. 2 ; esp. Trench § xiv.]) ; of things : ἄνεμος, *violent, rough*, Jas. iii. 4 ; ὁ λόγος, offensive and intolerable, Jn. vi. 60, equiv. to ὃς σκανδαλίζει, 61 ; σκληρὰ λαλεῖν κατά τινος, to speak hard and bitter things against one, Jude 15 (σκληρὰ λαλεῖν τινι is also used of one who speaks roughly, Gen. xlii. 7, 30 ; ἀποκρίνεσθαι σκληρά, to reply with threats, 1 K. xii. 13) ; σκληρόν ἐστι foll. by an inf., it is dangerous, turns out badly, [A. V. *it is hard*], Acts ix. 5 Rec. ; xxvi. 14.*

4643   σκληρότης, -ητος, ἡ, (σκληρός), *hardness* ; trop. *obstinacy, stubbornness* : Ro. ii. 5. (Deut. ix. 27 ; [Antipho], Plat., Aristot., Theophr., Plut., al.) *

4644   σκληρο-τράχηλος, -ον, (σκληρός and τράχηλος), prop. *stiff-necked*; trop. *stubborn, headstrong, obstinate* : Acts vii. 51 ; Sept. for קְשֵׁה עֹרֶף, Ex. xxxiii. 3, 5 ; xxxiv. 9 ; [etc.] ; Bar. ii. 30 ; Sir. xvi. 11 ; [cf. σκληροτραχηλία, Test. xii. Patr., test. Sym. § 6]. Not found in prof. auth.; [cf. W. 26, 99 (94)].*

4645   σκληρύνω [cf. W. 92 (88)] ; 1 aor. subjunc. 2 pers. plur. σκληρύνητε ; Pass., impf. ἐσκληρυνόμην ; 1 aor. ἐσκληρύνθην ; (σκληρός, q. v.) ; Sept. for הִקְשָׁה and חִזַּק, *to make hard, to harden*; prop. in Hippocr. and Galen ; metaph. *to render obstinate, stubborn*, [A.V. *to harden*] : τινά, Ro. ix. 18 (in opp. to those who interpret it *to treat harshly*, cf. Fritzsche the vol. ii. p. 323 sq. ; [cf., too, Meyer ad loc.]) ; τὴν καρδίαν τινος, Heb. iii. 8, 15 and iv. 7, (fr. Ps. xciv. (xcv.) 8 ; cf. Ex. vii. 3, 22 ; viii. 19 ; ix. 12) ; pass. (Sept. for קָשָׁה and חָזַק) *to be hardened*, i. e. *become obstinate* or *stubborn* : Acts xix. 9 ; Heb. iii. 13.*

4646   σκολιός, -ά, -όν, (opp. to ὀρθός, ὄρθιος, εὐθύς [cf. σκώληξ]), fr. Hom. down, *crooked, curved* : prop. of a way (Prov. xxviii. 18), τὰ σκολιά, Lk. iii. 5 (opp. to ἡ εὐθεῖα sc. ὁδός, fr. Is. xl. 4) ; metaph. *perverse, wicked* : ἡ γενεά ἡ σκολιά, Acts ii. 40 ; with διεστραμμένη added, Phil. ii. 15 (clearly so Deut. xxxii. 5) ; *unfair, surly, froward*, (opp. to ἀγαθὸς κ. ἐπιεικής), 1 Pet. ii. 18.*

4647   σκόλοψ, -οπος, ὁ, fr. Hom. down, *a pointed piece of wood, a pale, a stake* : ἐδόθη μοι σκόλοψ τῇ σαρκί, *a sharp stake* [al. say *splinter*, A.V. *thorn* ; cf. Num. xxxiii. 55 ; Ezek. xxviii. 24 ; Hos. ii. 6 (8) ; Babr. fab. 122, 1. 10 ; al. (Sir. xliii. 19)] *to pierce my flesh*, appears to indicate some constant bodily ailment or infirmity, which, even when Paul had been caught up in a trance to the third heaven, sternly admonished him that he still dwelt in a frail and mortal body, 2 Co. xii. 7 (cf. 1–4) ; [cf. W. § 31, 10 N. 3 ; B. § 133, 27. On Paul's " thorn in the flesh "

see *Farrar*, St. Paul, i. 652 sqq. (Excursus x.) ; Bp. *Lghtft.* Com. on Gal. p. 186 sqq. ; *Schaff* in his ' Popular Commentary ' on Gal. p. 331 sq.] *

4648   σκοπέω, -ῶ ; (σκοπός, q. v.) ; fr. Hom. down ; *to look at, observe, contemplate.*   *to mark* : absol., foll. by μή with the indic. (see μή, III. 2), Lk. xi. 35 ; τινά, to fix one's eyes upon, direct one's attention to, any one : Ro. xvi. 17 ; Phil. iii. 17 ; σεαυτόν, foll. by μή with the subjunc. *to look to, take heed to thyself, lest* etc. Gal. vi. 1 [see μή, II. 1 b.] ; τί, to look at, i. e. care for, have regard to, a thing : 2 Co. iv. 18 ; Phil. ii. 4, (2 Macc. iv. 5). [COMP. : ἐπι-, κατα-σκοπέω.] *

[SYN. : σκοπεῖν is more pointed than βλέπειν ; often i. q. *to scrutinize, observe.* When the physical sense recedes, i. q. *to fix one's* (mind's) *eye on,* direct one's attention to, a thing in order to get it, or owing to interest in it, or a duty towards it. Hence often equiv. to *aim at, care for*, etc. *Schmidt*, Syn. ch. xi. Cf. θεωρέω, ὁράω.]

4649   σκοπός, -οῦ, ὁ, [(fr. a r. denoting ' to spy,' ' peer,' ' look into the distance ' ; cf. also Lat. *specio, speculum, species*, etc. ; Fick i. 251 sq. ; iv. 279 ; Curtius § 111)] ; fr. Hom. down ;   **1.** *an observer, a watchman.*   **2.** the distant *mark* looked at, the *goal* or *end one has in view* : κατὰ σκοπόν (on this phrase see κατά, II. 1 c.), Phil. iii. 14.*

4650   σκορπίζω ; 1 aor. ἐσκόρπισα ; 1 aor. pass. ἐσκορπίσθην ; [(prob. fr. r. skarp ' to cut asunder,' ' cut to pieces ' ; akin is' σκορπίος ; cf. Lat. *scalpere, scrobs*, etc. ; Fick i. 240 ; iii. 811, etc.)] ; *to scatter* : ὁ λύκος σκορπίζει τὰ πρόβατα, Jn. x. 12 ; ὁ μὴ συνάγων μετ' ἐμοῦ σκορπίζει, Mt. xii. 30 ; Lk. xi. 23, (this proverb is taken from a flock, — to which the body of Christ's followers is likened [al. regard the proverb as borrowed fr. agriculture] ; συνάγει τοὺς ἐσκορπισμένους τὸ ὄργανον [i. e. a trumpet], Artem. oneir. 1, 56 init.) ; τινά, in pass., of those who, routed or terror-stricken or driven by some other impulse, fly in every direction : foll. by εἰς w. acc. of place, Jn. xvi. 32 [cf. W. 516 (481)], (1 Macc. vi. 54 ; φοβηθέντες ἐσκορπίσθησαν, Plut. Timol. 4 ; add, Joseph. antt. 6, 6, 3). i. q. *to scatter abroad* (what others may collect for themselves), of one dispensing blessings liberally : 2 Co. ix. 9 fr. Ps. cxi. (cxii.) 9, [cf. W. 469 (437)]. (Acc. to Phrynichus the word was used by Hecataeus ; it was also used — in addition to the writ. already cited — by Strabo 4 p. 198 ; Lcian. asin. 32 ; Ael. v. h. 13, 45 [here διεσκ. (ed. Hercher) ; λόγους (cf. Lat. *spargere rumores*), Joseph. antt. 16, 1, 2] ; cf. *Lob.* ad Phryn. p. 218 ; [W. 22 ; 92 (87)] ; Sept. for הֵפִיץ, 2 S. xxii. 15 ; Ps. xvii. (xviii.) 15. Attic writers say σκεδάννυμι.) [COMP. : δια-σκορπίζομαι.]

4651   σκορπίος, -ον, ὁ, [(for deriv. see the preceding word) ; from Aeschyl. down ; on its accent, cf. Chandler § 246], *a scorpion*, Sept. for עַקְרָב, the name of a little animal, somewhat resembling a lobster, which in warm regions lurks esp. in stone walls ; it has a poisonous sting in its tail [McC. and S. and BB. DD. s. v.] : Lk. x. 19 ; xi. 12 ; Rev. ix. 3, 5, 10.*

4652   σκοτεινός [WH σκοτινός ; see I, ι], -ή, -όν, (σκότος), *full* *of darkness, covered with darkness*, [fr. Aeschyl. down]: opp. to φωτεινός, Mt. vi. 23; Lk. xi. 34, 36, (τὰ σκοτεινὰ κ. τὰ φωτεινά, Xen. mem. 3, 10, 1; [cf. 4, 3, 4]).*

4653 σκοτία, -ας, ἡ, [on its deriv. cf. σκηνή], (Thom. Mag. ὁ σκότος κ. τὸ σκότος· τὸ δὲ σκοτία οὐκ ἐν χρήσει sc. in Attic [cf. Moeris s. v.; L. and S. s. v. σκότος, fin.]), *darkness*: prop. the darkness due to want of daylight, Jn. vi. 17; xx. 1; ἐν τῇ σκοτίᾳ (λαλεῖν τι), unseen, in secret, (i. q. ἐν κρυπτῷ, Jn. xviii. 20), privily, in private, opp. to ἐν τῷ φωτί, Mt. x. 27; Lk. xii. 3; metaph. used of ignorance of divine things, and its associated wickedness, and the resultant misery: Mt. iv. 16 L Tr WH; Jn. i. 5; vi. 17; viii. 12; xii. 35, 46; 1 Jn. i. 5; ii. 8 sq. 11. (Ap. Rh. 4, 1698; Anth. 8, 187. 190; for חֲשֵׁכָה Mic. iii. 6; for אֹפֶל Job xxviii. 3.) *

4654 σκοτίζω: Pass., pf. ptcp. ἐσκοτισμένος (Eph. iv. 18 RG); 1 aor. ἐσκοτίσθην; 1 fut. σκοτισθήσομαι; (σκότος); *to cover with darkness, to darken*; pass. *to be covered with darkness, be darkened*: prop. of the heavenly bodies, as deprived of light [(Eccl. xii. 2)], Mt. xxiv. 29; Mk. xiii. 24; Lk. xxiii. 45 [T WH ἐκλείπω (q. v. 2)]; Rev. viii. 12; ix. 2 [L T WH σκοτόω, q. v.]; metaph. of the eyes, viz. of the understanding, Ro. xi. 10; ἡ καρδία, the mind [see καρδία, 2 b. β.], Ro. i. 21; men τῇ διανοίᾳ, Eph. iv. 18 R G. (Plut. [adv. Col. 24, 4; Cleomed. 81, 28]; Tzetz. hist. 8, 929; Sept. several times for חָשַׁךְ; [Polyb. 12, 15, 10; 3 Macc. iv. 10; Test. xii. Patr., test. Rub. § 3; test. Levi § 14].) *

4655 σκότος, -ου, ὁ, (cf. σκοτία, init.), fr. Hom. down, *darkness*: Heb. xii. 18 Rec. [cf. WH. App. p. 158; W. 66 (64); B. 22 (20)].*

4655 σκότος, -ους, τό, fr. Pind. down, (see the preceding word, and σκοτία, init.), Sept. chiefly for חֹשֶׁךְ, *darkness*;   a. prop.: Mt. xxvii. 45; Mk. xv. 33; Lk. xxiii. 44; Acts ii. 20; 2 Co. iv. 6; αὕτη ἐστὶν ἡ ἐξουσία τοῦ σκότους, this is the power of (night's) darkness, i. e. it has the power of rendering men bold to commit crimes, Lk. xxii. 53; τὰ κρυπτὰ τοῦ σκότους (see κρυπτός), 1 Co. iv. 5; of darkened eyesight or blindness: σκότος ἐπιπίπτει ἐπί τινα i. e. on one deprived of sight, Acts xiii. 11; in fig. disc. εἰ οὖν . . , τὸ σκότος πόσον; *if the light that is in thee is darkness*, darkened (i. e. if the soul has lost its perceptive power), *how great is the darkness* (how much more deplorable than bodily blindness), Mt. vi. 23; cf. Lk. xi. 35. by meton. put for a dark place: Mt. viii. 12; xxii. 13; xxv. 30, (see ἐξώτερος); ζόφος τοῦ σκότους (see ζόφος), 2 Pet. ii. 17; Jude 13.   b. metaph. of ignorance respecting divine things and human duties, and the accompanying ungodliness and immorality, together with their consequent misery (see σκοτία): Jn. iii. 19; Acts xxvi. 18; 2 Co. vi. 14; Eph. vi. 12; Col. i. 13; 1 Pet. ii. 9; (abstract for the concrete) persons in whom darkness becomes visible and holds sway, Eph. v. 8; τὰ ἔργα τοῦ σκότους, deeds done in darkness, harmonizing with it, Ro. xiii. 12; Eph. v. 11; σκότους εἶναι, to be given up to the power of darkness [cf. W. § 30, 5 a.], 1 Th. v. 5; ἐν σκότει εἶναι, ib. 4; οἱ ἐν σκότει, Lk. i. 79; Ro. ii. 19; ὁ λαὸς ὁ καθήμενος ἐν σκότει, Mt. iv. 16 R G T; ἐν σκότει περιπατεῖν, 1 Jn. i. 6.*

4656 σκοτόω, -ῶ: Pass., pf. ptcp. ἐσκοτωμένος; 1 aor. ἐσκοτώθην; [cf. WH. App. p. 171]; (σκότος); *to darken, cover with darkness*: Rev. ix. 2 L T WH; xvi. 10; metaph. *to darken* or *blind* the mind: ἐσκοτωμένοι τῇ διανοίᾳ, Eph. iv. 18 L T Tr WH. ([Soph.], Plat., Polyb., Plut., al.; Sept.) *

4657 σκύβαλον, -ου, τό, (κυσίβαλόν τι ὄν, τὸ τοῖς κυσὶ βαλλόμενον, Suid. [p. 3347 c.; to the same effect Etym. Magn. p. 719, 53 cf. 125, 44; al. connect it with σκῶρ (cf. scoria, Lat. stercus), al. with a r. meaning 'to shiver', 'shred'; Fick, Pt. i. p. 244]), any *refuse*, as the excrement of animals, offscouring, rubbish, dregs, etc.: [A. V. *dung*] i. e. worthless and detestable, Phil. iii. 8. (Sir. xxvii. 4; Philo; Joseph. b. j. 5, 13, 7; Plut.; Strabo; often in the Anthol.) [See on the word, Bp. Lghtft. on Phil. l. c.; Gataker, Advers. Miscell. Posth., c. xliii. p. 868 sqq.] *

4658 Σκύθης, -ου, ὁ, *a Scythian, an inhabitant of Scythia* i. e. modern Russia: Col. iii. 11. By the more civilized nations of antiquity the Scythians were regarded as the wildest of all barbarians; cf. Cic. in Verr. 2, 5, 58 § 150; in Pison. 8, 18; Joseph. c. Apion. 2, 37, 6; [Philo, leg. ad Gaium § 2]; Lcian. Tox. 5 sq.; 2 Macc. iv. 47; 3 Macc. vii. 5. [See Bp. Lghtft. on Col. l. c.; *Hackett* in B.D. s. v. Scythians; Rawlinson's Herod., App. to bk. iv., Essays ii. and iii.; *Vaniček*, Fremdwörter, s. v.] *

4659 σκυθρωπός, -όν, also of three term.; cf. *Lob.* ad Phryn. p. 105 [W. § 11, 1], (σκυθρός and ὤψ), *of a sad and gloomy countenance* (opp. to φαιδρός, Xen. mem. 3, 10, 4): Lk. xxiv. 17; of one who feigns or affects a sad countenance, Mt. vi. 16. (Gen. xl. 7; Sir. xxv. 23; Grk. writ. fr. Aeschyl. down.) *

4660 σκύλλω: pf. pass. ptcp. ἐσκυλμένος; pres. mid. impv. 2 pers. sing. σκύλλου; (σκῦλον, q. v.);   a. *to skin, flay*, (Anthol.).   b. *to rend, mangle*, (Aeschyl. Pers. 577); *to vex, trouble, annoy*, (Hdian. 7, 3, 9 [4]): τινά, Mk. v. 35; Lk. viii. 49; pass. ἐσκυλμένοι, (Vulg. *vexati*) [R. V. *distressed*], Mt. ix. 36 G L T Tr WH; mid. *to give one's self trouble, trouble one's self*: μὴ σκύλλου, Lk. vii. 6.*

4661 σκῦλον [R^bez G L T WH] also σκύλον ([so R^st elz Tr] cf. *Lipsius*, Gram. Untersuch. p. 44), -ου, τό, (fr. the obsol. σκύω, 'to pull off', allied to ξύω, ξύλον [but cf. Curtius § 113; Vaniček p. 1115]);   a. *a* (beast's) *skin stripped off, a pelt*.   b. *the arms stripped off from an enemy, spoils*: plur. Lk. xi. 22. (Soph., Thuc., sqq.; Sept.) *

4662 σκωληκό-βρωτος, -ον, (σκώληξ and βιβρώσκω), *eaten of worms*: Acts xii. 23, cf. 2 Macc. ix. 9. (of a tree, Theophr. c. pl. 5, 9, 1.) *

4663 σκώληξ, -ηκος, ὁ, [perh. akin to σκολιός], *a worm* (Hom. Il. 13, 654); spec. that kind which preys upon dead bodies (Sir. x. 11; xix. 3; 2 Macc. ix. 9; Anthol. 7, 480, 3; 10, 78, 3): ὁ σκώληξ αὐτῶν οὐ τελευτᾷ, by a fig. borrowed fr. Is. lxvi. 24 (cf. Sir. vii. 17; Judith xvi. 17), 'their punishment after death will never cease' [σκ. symbolizing perh. the loathsomeness of the penalty], Mk. ix. 44, 46, [T WH om. Tr br. these two verses], 48.*

4664   σμαράγδινος, -η, -ον, (σμάραγδος, cf. ἀμεθύστινος, ὑακίνθινος, etc.), *of emerald, made of emerald*, [see the foll. word]: sc. λίθος, Rev. iv. 3. [(Lcian.)]*

4665   σμάραγδος, -ου, ὁ [but apparently fem. in the earlier writ., cf. Theophrast. lap. 4, 23; in Hdt. its gend. cannot be determined; cf. *Steph.* Thesaur. s. v.], Lat. *smaragdus*, [A. V. *emerald*], a transparent precious stone noted esp. for its light green color: Rev. xxi. 19. [From Hdt. down; Sept. On the deriv. of the word see *Vaniček*, Fremdwörter, s. v. On its relation to our '*emerald*' (disputed by *King*, Antique Gems, p. 27 sqq.), see Riehm HWB. s. v. 'Edelsteine', 17; *Deane* in the 'Bible Educator', vol. ii. p. 350 sq.]*

4666   σμύρνα, -ης, ἡ, Hebr. מֹר, מוֹר, *myrrh*, a bitter gum and costly perfume which exudes from a certain tree or shrub in Arabia and Ethiopia, or is obtained by incisions made in the bark: Mt. ii. 11; as an antiseptic it was used in embalming, Jn. xix. 39. Cf. Hdt. 2, 40, 86; 3, 107; Theophr. hist. pl. 9, 3 sq.; Diod. 5, 41; Plin. h. n. 12, 33 sq.; [BB.DD.; *Birdwood* in the 'Bible Educator', vol. ii. p. 151; *Löw*, Aram. Pflanzennam. § 185].*

4667   Σμύρνα, -ης, ἡ, *Smyrna*, an Ionian city, on the Ægean Sea, about 40 miles N. of Ephesus; it had a harbor, and flourished in trade, commerce, and the arts; now *Ismir* [BB.DD.]: Rev. i. 11; ii. 8. Tdf. after cod. א [(cf. cod. Bezae, ed. *Scrivener*, p. xlviii.)] has adopted the form Ζμύρν., found also occasionally on coins and in inscrr.; cf. Kühner i. p. 200 e.; [Tdf.'s note on Rev. i. 11; and see Σ, σ, ς, sub fin.; Bp. *Lghtft.* Ignat. ii. 331 note].*

4668   Σμυρναῖος, -ου, ὁ, ἡ, *of* or *belonging to Smyrna, an inhabitant of Smyrna*: Rev. ii. 8 Rec. [(Pind., Hdt.)]*

4669   σμυρνίζω, -ης; (σμύρνα, q. v.);   **1.** intrans. *to be like myrrh* (Diosc. 1, 79).   **2.** *to mix and so flavor with myrrh*: οἶνος ἐσμυρνισμένος (pf. pass. ptcp.) *wine* [A. V. *mingled*] *with myrrh* (Vulg. *murratum vinum*), i. e. flavored or (Plin. h. n. 14, 15) made fragrant with myrrh: Mk. xv. 23. But since the ancients used to infuse myrrh into wine in order to give it a more agreeable fragrance and flavor, we must in this matter accept Matthew's account (xxvii. 34, viz. 'mingled with gall') as by far the more probable; [but see χολή, 2].*

4670   Σόδομα, -ων, τά, (סְדֹם), *Sodom*, a city respecting the location and the destruction of which see Γόμορρα [and (in addition to reff. there given) McC. and S. s. v. Sodom; Schaff-Herzog ib.]: Mt. x. 15; xi. 23 sq.; Mk. vi. 11 (R L in br.); Lk. x. 12; xvii. 29; Ro. ix. 29; 2 Pet. ii. 6; Jude 7; Rev. xi. 8.*

4672   Σολομών (so [R^{st bez elz} G L in Lk. xii. 27; R L Tr WH in Acts vii. 47 (cf. Tdf. on Mt. vi. 29)]) and Σολομών [so R G L T Tr WH in Mt. i. 7; vi. 29; R^{scriv} T Tr WH in Lk. xii. 27; G in Acts vii. 47; (Σαλωμών Tdf. in Acts vii. 47)], -ῶντος (so Rec. uniformly; [L T WH in Acts iii. 11; v. 12; L in Mt. i. 6 also]), and -ῶνος (so [G L T Tr WH in Mt. xii. 42; Lk. xi. 31; Jn. x. 23; G T Tr WH in Mt. i. 6; G Tr in Acts iii. 11; v. 12]; the forms -ών, -ῶνος, are undoubtedly to be preferred, cf. [Tdf. Proleg. pp. 104, 110; WH. App. p. 158]; W. 67 (65); B. 16 (14 sq.)), ὁ, (שְׁלֹמֹה, i. e. 'pacific', Irenaeus, Germ. *Fried-*

rich, Eng. *Frederick*), *Solomon*, the son of David by Bathsheba the wife of Uriah; he succeeded his father, becoming the third king of Israel (B. C. 1015-975 [acc. to the commonly accepted chronology; but cf. the art. 'Zeitrechnung' in Riehm's HWB. (esp. p. 1823 sq.)]), built the temple at Jerusalem, and was distinguished for his magnificence, splendor, and wisdom: Mt. i. 6 sq.; vi. 29; xii. 42; Lk. xi. 31; xii. 27; Jn. x. 23; Acts iii. 11; v. 12; vii. 47.*

4673   σορός, -οῦ, ἡ, *an urn* or *receptacle for keeping the bones of the dead* (Hom. Il. 23, 91); *a coffin* (Gen. l. 26; Hdt. 1, 68; 2, 78; Arstph., Aeschin., Plut., al.); *the funeral-couch* or *bier on which the Jews carried their dead forth to burial* [see B. D. Am. ed. s. v. Coffin; *Edersheim*, Jesus the Messiah, i. 555 sq.]: Lk. vii. 14.*

4674   σός, -ή, -όν, possess. pron. of the 2d pers.; fr. Hom. down; *thy, thine*: Mt. vii. 3, 22; xiii. 27; xxiv. 3; Mk. ii. 18; Lk. xv. 31; xxii. 42; Jn. iv. 42 [here Tr mrg. WH mrg. read the personal σου]; xvii. 6, 9, 10, 17; xviii. 35; Acts v. 4; xxiv. 2 (3), 4; 1 Co. viii. 11; xiv. 16; Philem. 14; οἱ σοί sc. μαθηταί, Lk. v. 33; absol. οἱ σοί, thy kinsfolk, thy friends, Mk. v. 19; τὸ σόν, what is thine, Mt. xx. 14; xxv. 25; plur. τὰ σά [A. V. *thy goods*; cf. W. 592 (551)], Lk. vi. 30. [Cf. W. § 22, 7 sqq.; B. 115 (101) sqq.]*

4676   σουδάριον, -ου, τό, (a Lat. word, *sudarium*, fr. sudor, sweat; cf. B. 18 (16)), *a handkerchief*, i. e. a cloth for wiping the perspiration from the face and for cleaning the nose: Lk. xix. 20; Acts xix. 12; also used in swathing the head of a corpse [A. V. *napkin*], Jn. xi. 44; xx. 7. [Cf. BB.DD. s. v. Handkerchief.]*

4677   Σουσάννα, -ης [cf. B. 17 (15)], ἡ, (שׁוֹשַׁנָּה a lily), *Susanna*, one of the women that attended Jesus on his journeys: Lk. viii. 3.*

4678   σοφία, -ας, ἡ, (σοφός), Hebr. חָכְמָה, *wisdom, broad and full intelligence*, [fr. Hom. down]; used of the knowledge of very diverse matters, so that the shade of meaning in which the word is taken must be discovered from the context in every particular case.   **a.** the wisdom which belongs to men: univ., Lk. ii. 40, 52; spec. the varied knowledge of things human and divine, acquired by acuteness and experience, and summed up in maxims and proverbs, as was ἡ σοφία τοῦ Σολομῶνος, Mt. xii. 42; Lk. xi. 31; the science and learning τῶν Αἰγυπτίων, Acts vii. 22 [cf. W. 227 (213) n.; B. § 134, 6]; the art of interpreting dreams and always giving the sagest advice, Acts vii. 10; the intelligence evinced in discovering the meaning of some mysterious number or vision, Rev. xiii. 18; xvii. 9; skill in the management of affairs, Acts vi. 3; a devout and proper prudence in intercourse with men not disciples of Christ, Col. iv. 5; skill and discretion in imparting Christian truth, Col. i. 28; iii. 16; [2 Pet. iii. 15]; the knowledge and practice of the requisites for godly and upright living, Jas. i. 5; iii. 13, 17; with which σοφία ἄνωθεν κατερχομένη is put in contrast the σοφία ἐπίγειος, ψυχική, δαιμονιώδης, such as is the craftiness of envious and quarrelsome men. Jas. iii. 15, or σαρκικὴ σοφία (see σαρκικός, 1), craftiness, 2 Co. i. 12 (for the context shows that it does not differ essentially from the πανουργία of iv. 2; in Grk. writ. also σοφία is not infreq. used of shrewdness and cunning; cf. Passow [or L. and S.] s. v. 2); the knowledge and skill in affairs requisite for the successful defence of the Christian cause against hostile accusations, Lk. xxi. 15; an acquaintance with divine things and human duties, joined to a power of discoursing concerning them and of interpreting and applying sacred Scripture, Mt. xiii. 54; Mk. vi. 2; Acts vi. 10; the wisdom or instruction with which John the Baptist and Jesus taught men the way to obtain salvation, Mt. xi. 19; Lk. vii. 35, (on these pass. see δικαιόω, 2). In Paul's Epp.: a knowledge of the divine plan, previously hidden, of providing salvation for men by the expiatory death of Christ, 1 Co. i. 30; ii. 6; Eph. i. 8 [W. 111 (105 sq.)]; hence all the treasures of wisdom are said to be hidden in Christ, Col. ii. 3; w. the addition of θεοῦ (gen. of the author), 1 Co. i. 24; ii. 7; πνευματική, Col. i. 9; πνεῦμα σοφίας κ. ἀποκαλύψεως, Eph. i. 17; λόγος σοφίας, the ability to discourse eloquently of this wisdom, 1 Co. xii. 8; opposed to this wisdom is — the empty conceit of wisdom which men make a parade of, a knowledge more specious than real of lofty and hidden subjects: such as the theosophy of certain Jewish Christians, Col. ii. 23; the philosophy of the Greeks, 1 Co. i. 21 sq.; ii. 1; with τοῦ κόσμου added, 1 Co. i. 20; iii. 19; τοῦ αἰῶνος τούτου, 1 Co. ii. 6; τῶν σοφῶν, 1 Co. i. 19; ἀνθρώπων, 1 Co. ii. 5, (in each of these last pass. the word includes also the rhetorical art, such as is taught in the schools), cf. Fritzsche, Rom. vol. i. p. 67 sq.; σοφία τοῦ λόγου, the wisdom which shows itself in speaking [R. V. wisdom of words], the art of the rhetorician, 1 Co. i. 17; λόγοι (ἀνθρωπίνης [so R in vs. 4 (all txts. in 13)]) σοφίας, discourse conformed to philosophy and the art of rhetoric, 1 Co. ii. 4, 13. b. supreme intelligence, such as belongs to God: Rev. vii. 12, also to Christ, exalted to God's right hand, Rev. v. 12; the wisdom of God as evinced in forming and executing his counsels, Ro. xi. 33; with the addition of τοῦ θεοῦ, as manifested in the formation and government of the world, and to the Jews, moreover, in the Scriptures, 1 Co. i. 21; it is called πολυποίκιλος from the great variety of ways and methods by which he devised and achieved salvation through Christ, Eph. iii. 10. In the noteworthy pass. Lk. xi. 49 (where Christ ascribes to 'the wisdom of God' what in the parallel, Mt. xxiii. 34, he utters himself), the words ἡ σοφία τοῦ θεοῦ εἶπεν seem to denote the wisdom of God which is operative and embodied as it were in Jesus, so that the primitive Christians, when to comfort themselves under persecution they recalled the saying of Christ, employed that formula of quotation [cf. 1 Co. i. 24, 30, etc.]; but Luke, in ignorance of this fact, took the phrase for a part of Christ's saying. So Eusebius (h. e. 3, 32, 8), perhaps in the words of Hegesippus, calls those who had personally heard Christ οἱ αὐταῖς ἀκοαῖς τῆς ἐνθέου σοφίας ἐπακοῦσαι κατηξιωμένοι; cf. Grimm in the Stud. u. Krit. for 1853, p. 332 sqq. [For other

explanations of the phenomenon, see the Comm. on Lk. l. c. Cf. Schürer, Zeitgesch. § 33, V. 1 and reff.] *

[Syn.: on the relation of σοφία to γνῶσις see γνῶσις, fin. " While σοφ. is 'mental excellence in its highest and fullest sense' (Aristot. eth. Nic. 6, 7), σύνεσις and φρόνησις are both derivative and special, — applications of σοφία to details: σύν. critical, apprehending the bearing of things, φρόν. practical, suggesting lines of action" (Bp. Lghtft. on Col. i. 9); but cf. Meyer on Col. l. c.; Schmidt, ch. 13 § 10; ch. 147 § 8. See σοφός, fin.]

σοφίζω: 1 aor. inf. σοφίσαι; (σοφός);   **1.** to make **4679** wise, teach: τινά, 2 Tim. iii. 15 (Ps. xviii. (xix.) 8; ἐσόφισάς με τὴν ἐντολήν σου, Ps. cxviii. (cxix.) 98; οὔτε τι ναυτιλίης σεσοφισμένος, οὔτε τι νηῶν, Hes. opp. 647).   **2.** Mid. in Grk. writ. fr. Hdt. down, mostly as depon. to become wise, to have understanding, (ἐσοφίσατο ὑπὲρ πάντας ἀνθρώπους, 1 K. iv. 27 (31); add, Eccl. ii. 15, etc.; freq. in Sir.); to invent, play the sophist; to devise cleverly or cunningly: pf. pass. ptcp. σεσοφισμένοι μῦθοι, 2 Pet. i. 16. [Comp.: κατα-σοφίζομαι.] *

σοφός, -ή, -όν, (akin to σαφής and to the Lat. sapio, **4680** sapiens, sapor, 'to have a taste', etc.; Curtius § 628; [Vaniček p. 991]), Sept. for חָכָם; [fr. Theogn., Pind., Aeschyl. down]; wise, i. e.   **a.** skilled, expert: εἴς τι, Ro. xvi. 19; of artificers (cf. Grimm, Exeg. Hdbch. on Sap. [vii. 21] p. 151): ἀρχιτέκτων, 1 Co. iii. 10; Is. iii. 3, (δημιουργός, of God, Xen. mem. 1, 4, 7).   **b.** wise, i. e. skilled in letters, cultivated, learned: Ro. i. 14, 22; of the Greek philosophers (and orators, see σοφία, a.), 1 Co. i. 19 sq. 26 sq.; iii. 18 sq. [20]; of the Jewish theologians, Mt. xi. 25; Lk. x. 21; of Christian teachers, Mt. xxiii. 34.   **c.** wise in a practical sense, i. e. one who in action is governed by piety and integrity: Eph. v. 15; Jas. iii. 13; and accordingly is a suitable person to settle private quarrels, 1 Co. vi. 5.   **d.** wise in a philosophic sense, forming the best plans and using the best means for their execution: so of God, Ro. xvi. 27, and Rec. in 1 Tim. i. 17; Jude 25; σοφώτερον, contains more wisdom, is more sagaciously thought out, 1 Co. i. 25.*

[Syn.: σοφός, συνετός, φρόνιμος: σοφός wise, see above; συνετός intelligent, denotes one who can 'put things together' (συνιέναι), who has insight and comprehension; φρόνιμος prudent (A. V. uniformly, wise), denotes primarily one who.has quick and correct perceptions, hence 'discreet,' 'circumspect,' etc.; cf. Schmidt ch. 147. See σοφία, fin.]

Σπανία, -ας, ἡ, Spain, in the apostolic age the whole **4681** peninsula S. of the Pyrenees: Ro. xv. 24, 28. ([W. 25]; the more com. Grk. form is Ἱσπανία, 1 Macc. viii. 3, [apparently the Phoenician or Lat. name for Ἰβηρία; cf. Pape, Eigennamen, s. vv.].) *

σπαράσσω: 1 aor. ἐσπάραξα; to convulse [al. tear]: **4682** τινά, Mk. i. 26; ix. 20 R G Tr txt., 26; Lk. ix. 39; see ῥήγνυμι, c. (τὰς γνάθους, Arstph. ran. 424; τὰς τρίχας, Diod. 19, 34; in various other senses in Grk. writ.) [Comp.: συν- σπαράσσω.] *

σπαργανόω, -ῶ: 1 aor. ἐσπαργάνωσα; pf. pass. ptcp. **4683** ἐσπαργανωμένος: (σπάργανον a swathing band); to wrap *in swaddling-clothes* : an infant just born, Lk. ii. 7, 12. (Ezek. xvi. 4 ; [Eur., Aristot.], Hippocr., Plut., al.) *

4684   **σπαταλάω, -ῶ** ; 1 aor. ἐσπατάλησα ; (σπατάλη, riotous living, luxury) ; *to live luxuriously, lead a voluptuous life,* [*give one's self to pleasure*] : 1 Tim. v. 6 ; Jas. v. 5. (Prov. xxix. 21 ; Am. vi. 4 [in both these pass. κατασπ. ; Ezek. xvi. 49] ; Sir. xxi. 15 ; Barnab. ep. 10, 3 ; Polyb. excrpt. Vat. p. 451 [i. e. 37, 4, 6 (ed. Didot)], and occasionally in later and inferior writ.)*

4685   **σπάω, -ῶ** : 1 aor. mid. ἐσπασάμην ; [cogn. w. ἀσπάζομαι (to draw to one's self, embrace, etc.), Eng. *spasm*, etc.] ; fr. Hom. down ; Sept. chiefly for שָׁלַף ; *to draw*: mid. with μάχαιραν [cf. B. § 135, 4], to draw one's sword, Mk. xiv. 47 ; Acts xvi. 27, (Num. xxii. 31 ; τὴν ῥομφαίαν, 23 ; Judg. ix. 54, etc.). [Comp.: ἀνα-, ἀπο-, δια-, ἐπι-, περι- σπάω.] *

4686   **σπεῖρα** [on the accent cf. B. 11 ; Chandler § 161 ; *Tdf.* Proleg. p. 102],ή, gen. -ης (Acts x. 1 ; xxi. 31 : xxvii. 1 ; see [*Tdf.* Proleg. p. 117 ; *WH.* App. p. 156 ; and] μά- χαιρα, init.), [cogn. w. σπυρίς (q. v.)] ;   **a.** Lat. *spira* ; anything rolled into a circle or ball, anything wound, rolled up, folded together.   **b.** *a military cohort* (Polyb. 11, 23, 1 τρεῖς σπείρας· τοῦτο δὲ καλεῖται τὸ σύν- ταγμα τῶν πεζῶν παρὰ Ῥωμαίοις κοόρτις), i. e. the tenth part of a legion [i. e. about 600 men (i. e. legionaries), or if auxiliaries either 500 or 1000 ; cf. *Marquardt*, Römisch. Alterth. III. ii. p. 371. But surely τοῦτο τὸ σύνταγμα in the quotation comprehends the τρεῖς σπ. ; hence Polyb. here makes a σπ. equal to a maniple, cf. 2, 3, 2 ; 6, 24, 5 ; cf. *Zonaras*, Lex. p. 1664, σπ.· σύνταγμα διακοσίων ἀνδρῶν. On the other hand, "the later Grk. writ. almost uniform- ly employ σπ. as the representative of *cohors*" (*Smith*, Dict. of Antiq., ed. 2, s. v. exercitus, p. 500) ; and the use of χιλίαρχος (which was the equiv. of *tribunus*, the commander of a cohort) in connection with it (Jn. xviii. 12 ; Acts xxi. 31), together with the uniform rendering of the word by *cohors* in the Lat. versions, warrants the marg. "cohort" uniformly added in R.V. to the render- ing *band*] : Mt. xxvii. 27 ; Mk. xv. 16 ; Acts x. 1 ; xxi. 31 ; xxvii. 1, and often in Josephus ; *a maniple*, or the thirtieth part of a legion, often so in Polyb. [(see above)] ; *any band, company,* or *detachment, of soldiers* (2 Macc. viii. 23 ; Jud. ix. 11) : Jn. xviii. 3, 12.*

4687   **σπείρω** ; [impf. 2 pers. sing. ἔσπειρες, Mt. xiii. 27 Tr] ; 1 aor. ἔσπειρα, Pass., pres. σπείρομαι ; pf. pass. ptcp. ἐσπαρμένος ; 2 aor. ἐσπάρην ; [derived fr. the quick, jerky, motion of the hand ; cf. our *spurn* (of the foot) ; Cur- tius § 389] ; fr. Hesiod down ; Sept. for זָרַע ; *to sow, scatter seed,*   **a.** prop.: absol., Mt. vi. 26 ; xiii. 3 sq. 18 sq. ; Mk. iv. 3 sq. 14 ; Lk. viii. 5 ; xii. 24 ; [Jn. v. 36 sq. (see in b.)] ; 2 Co. ix. 10 ; with an acc. of the thing, as σπέρμα ζιζάνια, κόκκον, [cf. B. § 131, 5] : Mt. xiii. 24 sq. [but in 25 L T Tr WH have ἐπισπ.], 27, 37, 39 ; Mk. iv. 32 : Lk. viii. 5 ; 1 Co. xv. 36 sq. ; with specifications of place : εἰς τὰς ἀκάνθας, Mt. xiii. 22 ; Mk. iv. 18 ; ἐν τῷ ἀγρῷ, Mt. xiii. 24, [31] ; ἐπὶ τῆς γῆς, Mk. iv. 31 ; ἐπί w. an acc. of place, Mt. xiii. 20, 23 ; Mk. iv. 16, 20 ; παρὰ τὴν ὁδόν, Mt. xiii. 19.   **b.** in proverbial sayings :

absol., Mt. xxv. 24, 26 ; Lk. xix. 21 sq. ; Jn. iv. 37 ; 2 Co. ix. 6 ; τί, Gal. vi. 7, (on these sayings see θερίζω, b.). in comparisons : σπείρειν εἰς τὴν σάρκα, εἰς τὸ πνεῦμα, (σάρξ and πνεῦμα are likened to fields to be sown), to do those things which satisfy the nature and promptings of the σάρξ or of the πνεῦμα, Gal. vi. 8 ; τὸν λόγον, to scatter the seeds of instruction, i. e. to impart instruction, Mk. iv. 14 sq. ; ὁ λόγος ὁ ἐσπαρμένος ἐν ταῖς καρδίαις αὐτῶν, the ideas and precepts that have been implanted like seed in their hearts, i. e. received in their hearts, ibid. 15 (where Tr txt. WH εἰς αὐτούς into their hearts, T L mrg. ἐν αὐτοῖς) ; οὗτός ἐστιν ὁ παρὰ τὴν ὁδὸν σπαρείς, this one experiences the fate of the seed sown by the wayside, Mt. xiii. 19 ; add, 20-23 ; Mk. iv. 16, 18, 20.   τὸ σῶμα, the body, which after death is committed like seed to the earth, 1 Co. xv. 42-44 ; καρπὸν δικαιοσύνης, i. e. that seed which produces καρπὸν δικαιοσύνης [see καρπός, 2 b.], Jas. iii. 18 ; σπείρειν τινί τι, to give, manifest, something to one, from whom we may subsequently receive something else akin to a harvest (θερίζομεν), 1 Co. ix. 11. [Comp.: δια-, ἐπι- σπείρω.] *

4688   **σπεκουλάτωρ, -ορος** (R G -ωρος [cf. Tdf. on Mk. as be- low]), ὁ, (the Lat. word *speculator*), *a looker-out, spy, scout* ; under the emperors an attendant and member of the body-guard, employed as messengers, watchers, and executioners (Sen. de ira 1, 16 centurio supplicio prae- positus condere gladium speculatorem jubet ; also de benef. 3, 25) ; the name is transferred to an attendant of Herod Antipas that acted as executioner : Mk. vi. 27. Cf. Keim ii. 512 [Eng. trans. iv. 219 ; *J. W. Golling* in Thes. Nov. etc. ii. p. 405 sq.] *

4689   **σπένδω** : pres. pass. σπένδομαι ; (cf. Germ. *spenden* [perh. of the 'tossing away' of a liquid, Curtius § 296 ; but cf. Vaniček p. 1245 sq.]) ; fr. Hom. down ; Sept. for נָסַךְ ; *to pour out as a drink-offering, make a libation* ; in the N. T. σπένδεσθαι, *to be offered as a libation,* is figura- tively used of one whose blood is poured out in a violent death for the cause of God : Phil. ii. 17 (see θυσία, b. fin.) ; 2 Tim. iv. 6.*

4690   **σπέρμα, -τος, τό**, (σπείρω, q. v.), fr. Hom. down, Hebr. זֶרַע, *the seed* (fr. which anything springs) ;   **a.** from which a plant germinates ;   **α.** prop. *the seed* i. e. the grain or kernel which contains within itself the germ of the future plant : plur., Mt. xiii. 32 ; Mk. iv. 31 ; 1 Co. xv. 38, (Ex. xvi. 31 ; 1 S. viii. 15) ; the sing. is used collectively of the *grains* or *kernels sown* : Mt. xiii. 24, 27, 37 sq. ; 2 Co. ix. 10 [here L Tr σπόρος].   **β.** metaph. *a seed* i. e. *a residue,* or a few survivors reserved as the germ of a new race (just as seed is kept from the harvest for the sowing), Ro. ix. 29 after Is. i. 9, where Sept. for שָׂרִיד, (so also Sap. xiv. 6 ; 1 Esdr. viii. 85 (87) ; Joseph. antt. 11, 5, 3 ; 12, 7, 3 ; Plat. Tim. p. 23 c.).   **b.** the *semen virile* ;   **α.** prop. : Lev. xv. 16-18 ; xviii. 20 sq., etc., [prob. also Heb. xi. 11, cf. καταβολή 1, and see below] ; often in prof. writ. By meton. the pro- duct of this semen, *seed, children, offspring, progeny* ; *family, race, posterity,* (so in Grk. chiefly in the tragic poets, cf. Passow s. v. 2 b. ii. p. 1498 [L. and S. s. v. II.

3]; and זֶרַע very often in the O. T. [cf. W. 17, 30]); so in the sing., either of one, or collectively of many: Ro. ix. 7 sq.; εἰς καταβολὴν σπέρματος (see [above, and] καταβολή, 2), Heb. xi. 11; ἀνιστάναι and ἐξανιστάναι σπέρμα τινί, Mt. xxii. 24; Mk. xii. 19; Lk. xx. 28, (Gen. xxxviii. 8); ἔχειν σπέρμα, Mt. xxii. 25; ἀφιέναι σπέρμα τινί, Mk. xii. 20–22; τὸ σπ. τινός, Lk. i. 55; Jn. vii. 42; viii. 33, 37; Acts iii. 25; vii. 5 sq.; xiii. 23; Ro. i. 3; [iv. 13]; ix. 7; xi. 1; 2 Co. xi. 22; 2 Tim. ii. 8; Heb. ii. 16; xi. 18; in plur.: παῖς ἐκ βασιλικῶν σπερμάτων, of royal descent, Joseph. antt. 8, 7, 6; τῶν Ἀβραμιαίων σπερμάτων ἀπόγονοι, 4 Macc. xviii. 1; i. q. tribes, races, ἄνθρωποί τε καὶ ἀνθρώπων σπέρμασι νομοθετοῦμεν τὰ νῦν, Plat. legg. 9 p. 853 c. By a rabbinical method of interpreting, opposed to the usage of the Hebr. זֶרַע, which signifies the offspring whether consisting of one person or many, Paul lays such stress on the singular number in Gen. xiii. 15; xvii. 8 as to make it denote but one of Abraham's posterity, and that the Messiah: Gal. iii. 16, also 19; and yet, that the way in which Paul presses the singular here is not utterly at variance with the genius of the Jewish-Greek language is evident from Ἀβραμιαίων σπερμάτων ἀπόγονοι, 4 Macc. xviii. 1, where the plural is used of many descendants [(cf. Delitzsch, Br. a. d. Röm. p. 16 note²; Bp. Lghtft. on Gal. l. c.)]. τὸ σπ. (Ἀβραὰμ) τὸ ἐκ τοῦ νόμου, the seed which is such according to the decision of the law, physical offspring [see νόμος, 2 p. 428ᵃ], τὸ ἐκ πίστεως Ἀβρ. those who are called Abraham's posterity on account of the faith by which they are akin to him [see πίστις, 1 b. a. p. 513ᵇ and ἐκ, II. 7], Ro. iv. 16; add,̓ 18; ix. 8; Gal. iii. 29; similarly Christians are called, in Rev. xii. 17, the σπέρμα of the church (which is likened to a mother, Gal. iv. 26). β. whatever possesses vital force or life-giving power: τὸ σπέρμα τοῦ θεοῦ [(but anarthrous)], the Holy Spirit, the divine energy operating within the soul by which we are regenerated or made the τέκνα τοῦ θεοῦ, 1 Jn. iii. 9.*

4691 σπερμολόγος, -ον, (σπέρμα, and λέγω to collect); 1. picking up seeds: used of birds, Plut. Demet. 28; Athen. 9 p. 387 f.; esp. of the crow or daw that picks up grain in the fields (Germ. Saatkrähe), Arstph. av. 232, 579; Aristot. h. a. 8, 3 p. 592ᵇ, 28, and other writ. 2. of men: lounging about the market-place and picking up a subsistence by whatever may chance to fall from the loads of merchandise (Eustath. on Hom. Od. 5, 490 σπερμολόγοι· οἱ περὶ τὰ ἐμπόρια κ. ἀγορὰς διατρίβοντες διὰ τὸ ἀναλέγεσθαι τὰ ἐκ τῶν φορτίων ἀπορρέοντα καὶ διὰ ζῆν ἐκ τούτων); hence, beggarly, abject, vile, (a parasite); getting a living by flattery and buffoonery, Athen. 3 p. 85 f.; Plut. mor. p. 456 d.; subst. ὁ σπ. an empty talker, babbler, (Dem. p. 269, 19; Athen. 8 p. 344 c.): Acts xvii. 18.*

4692 σπεύδω; impf. ἔσπευδον; 1 aor. ἔσπευσα; (cogn. w. Germ. sich sputen [cf. Eng. speed, Lat. studeo; Vaniček p. 1163; Fick iv. 279]); fr. Hom. down; Sept. for כָּהַר, also for בָּהַל, etc.; 1. intrans. [cf. W. § 38, 1; B. 130, 4], to hasten: as often in the Grk. writ., foll. by an inf. Acts xx. 16; ἦλθον σπεύσαντες, they came with haste, Lk. ii. 16; σπεύσας κατάβηθι [A. V. make haste

and come down], κατέβη, Lk. xix. 5, 6; σπεῦσον κ. ἔξελθε, [A. V. make haste and get thee quickly out], Acts xxii. 18. 2. to desire earnestly: τί, 2 Pet. iii. 12; (Is. xvi. 5; exx. fr. Grk. auth. are given by Passow s. v 2 vol. ii. p. 1501; [L. and S. s. v. II.]).*

σπήλαιον, -ου, τό, (σπέος [cavern; cf. Curtius § 111]), **4693** a cave, [den]: Mt. xxi. 13; Mk. xi. 17; Lk. xix. 46; Jn. xi. 38; Heb. xi. 38; Rev. vi. 15. (Plat., Plut., Lcian., Ael., al.; Sept. for מְעָרָה.) *

σπιλάς, -άδος, ἡ, a rock in the sea, ledge or reef, (Hom. **4694** Od. 3, 298; 5, 401, and in other poets; Polyb., Diod., Joseph. b. j. 3, 9, 3); plur. trop. of men who by their conduct damage others morally, wreck them as it were, i. q. σκάνδαλα, [R. V. txt. hidden rocks], Jude 12 [here L T Tr WH read οἱ (sc. ὄντες) σπ. Some (so R.V. mrg.) make the word equiv. to the following; see Rutherford as there referred to.]*

σπῖλος [WH σπίλος (so Rutherford, New Phryn. p. 87; **4696** L. and S. s. v.); but see Tdf. Proleg. p. 102; Lipsius, Gram. Untersuch. p. 42], -ου, ὁ, (Phryn. rejects this word in favor of the Attic κηλίς; but σπῖλος is used by Joseph., Dion. Hal., Plut., Lcian., Liban., Artemidor.; see Lob. ad Phryn. p. 28 [cf. W. 25]), a spot: trop. a fault, moral blemish, Eph. v. 27; plur. of base and gluttonous men, 2 Pet. ii. 13.*

σπιλόω, -ῶ; pf. pass. ptcp. ἐσπιλωμένος; (σπῖλος); to **4695** defile, spot: τί, Jas. iii. 6; Jude 23. (Dion. Hal., Lcian., Heliod.; Sept.) *

σπλαγχνίζομαι; 1 aor. ἐσπλαγχνίσθην [cf. B. 52 (45)]; **4697** (σπλάγχνον, q. v.); prop. to be moved as to one's bowels, hence to be moved with compassion, have compassion, (for the bowels were thought to be the seat of love and pity): absol., Lk. x. 33; xv. 20; σπλαγχνισθείς with a finite verb, Mt. xx. 34; Mk. i. 41; τινός, to pity one (cf. W. § 30, 10 a.; [B. § 132, 15; but al. regard σπλ. in the foll. example as used absol. and the gen. as depending on κύριος]), Mt. xviii. 27; ἐπί with dat. of the pers., Mt. xiv. 14 G L T Tr WH; Mk. vi. 34 [R G]; Lk. vii. 13 (where Tdf. ἐπί w. acc.); ἐπί τινα, Mt. xiv. 14 Rec.; xv. 32; Mk. [vi. 34 L T Tr WH]; viii. 2; ix. 22; cf. W. § 33, c.; [B. u.s.]; περί τινος ὅτι, Mt. ix. 36. Besides, several times in Test. xii. Patr. [e. g. test. Zab. §§ 4, 6, 7, etc.]; and in the N. T. Apocr.; in Deut. xiii. 8 Symm.; [Ex. ii. 6 cod. Venet.]; and in 1 S. xxiii. 21 incert.; [Clem. Rom. 2 Cor. 1, 7; Herm. mand. 4, 3, 5]; ἐπισπλαγχνίζομαι, Prov. xvii. 5; the act. σπλαγχνίζω is once used for the Attic σπλαγχνεύω, 2 Macc. vi. 8. Cf. Bleek, Einl. ins N. T. ed. 1, p. 75 [Eng. trans. ibid.; ed. 3 (by Mangold) p. 90; W. 30, 33, 92 (87)].*

σπλάγχνον, -ου, τό, and (only so in the N. T.) plur. **4698** σπλάγχνα, -ων, τά, Hebr. רַחֲמִים, bowels, intestines (the heart, lungs, liver, etc.); a. prop.: Acts i. 18 (2 Macc. ix. 5 sq.; 4 Macc. v. 29, and in Grk. writ. fr. Hom. down). b. in the Grk. poets fr. Aeschyl. down the bowels were regarded as the seat of the more violent passions, such as anger and love; but by the Hebrews as the seat of the tenderer affections, esp. kindness, benevolence, compassion, [cf. Bp. Lghtft. on Phil. i. 8; W. 18];

hence i. q. our *heart*, [*tender mercies, affections,* etc. (cf. B. D. Am. ed. s. v. Bowels)] : 1 Jn. iii. 17 (on which see κλείω) ; 2 Co. vi. 12 ; Phil. ii. 1 [here G L T Tr WH εἴ τις σπλάγχνα ; B. 81 (71), cf. Green 109 ; Bp. Lghtft. ad loc.] ; σπλάγχνα ἐλέους (gen. of quality [cf. W. 611 (568) ; so Test. xii. Patr., test. Zab. §§ 7, 8]), a heart in which mercy resides, [*heart of mercy*], Lk. i. 78 ; also σπλ. οἰκτιρμοῦ [Rec. -μῶν], Col. iii. 12 ; τὰ σπλάγχνα αὐτοῦ περισσοτέρως εἰς ὑμᾶς ἐστίν, his heart is the more abundantly devoted to you, 2 Co. vii. 15 ; ἐπιποθῶ ὑμᾶς ἐν σπλάγχνοις Χριστοῦ Ἰησοῦ, in the heart [R. V. *tender mercies*] of Christ, i. e. prompted by the same love as Christ Jesus, Phil. i. 8 ; ἀναπαύειν τὰ σπλ. τινός, to refresh one's soul or heart, Philem. 7, 20 ; τὰ σπλάγχνα ἡμῶν, my very heart, i. e. whom I dearly love, Philem. 12 (so Darius calls his mother and children *his own bowels* in Curt. 4, 14, 22. *meum corculum,* Plaut. Cas. 4, 4, 14 ; *meum cor,* id. Poen. 1, 2, 154 ; [cf. Bp. Lghtft. on Philem. l. c.]). The Hebr. רַחֲמִים is translated by the Sept. now οἰκτιρμοί, Ps. xxiv. (xxv.) 6 ; xxxix. (xl.) 12, now ἔλεος, Is. xlvii. 6 ; once σπλάγχνα, Prov. xii. 10.*

4699 σπόγγος, -ου, ὁ, [perh. akin is *fungus* ; Curtius § 575], fr. Hom. down, *sponge* : Mt. xxvii. 48 ; Mk. xv. 36 ; Jn. xix. 29.*

4700 σποδός, -οῦ, ἡ, fr. Hom. down, *ashes* : Heb. ix. 13 ; ἐν σάκκῳ κ. σποδῷ κάθημαι, to sit clothed in sackcloth and covered with ashes (exhibiting the tokens of grief, cf. Jon. iii. 6 ; Is. lviii. 5 ; lxi. 3 ; Jer. vi. 26 ; Esth. iv. 1, 3 ; 1 Macc. iii. 47 ; cf. σάκκος, b.) : Mt. xi. 21 ; Lk. x. 13.*

4701 σπορά, -ᾶς, ἡ, (σπείρω, 2 pf. ἔσπορα), *seed* : 1 Pet. i. 23 [(i. q. *a sowing,* fig. *origin,* etc., fr. Aeschyl., Plat., down)].*

4702 σπόριμος, -ον, (σπείρω, 2 pf. ἔσπορα), *fit for sowing, sown,* (Xen., Diod., al.) ; τὰ σπόριμα, *sown fields, growing crops,* [A.V. (exc. in Mt.) *corn-fields*], (Geop. 1, 12, 37) : Mt. xii. 1 ; Mk. ii. 23 ; Lk. vi. 1.*

4703 σπόρος, -ου, ὁ, (σπείρω, 2 pf. ἔσπορα) ; **1.** *a sowing* (Hdt., Xen., Theophr., al.). **2.** *seed* (used in sowing) : Mk. iv. 26 sq. ; Lk. viii. 5, 11 ; 2 Co. ix. 10 [L Tr, 10ᵇ], (Deut. xi. 10 ; Theocr., Plut., al.).*

4704 σπουδάζω ; fut. σπουδάσω (a later form for the early -άσομαι, cf. Krüger § 40 s. v., vol. i. p. 190 ; B. 53 (46) ; [W. 89 (85) ; Veitch s. v.]) ; 1 aor. ἐσπούδασα ; (σπουδή, q. v.) ; fr. Soph. and Arstph. down ; **a.** *to hasten, make haste* : foll. by an inf. (cf. σπεύδω, 1), 2 Tim. iv. 9, 21 ; Tit. iii. 12, [al. refer these exx. to b. ; but cf. *Holtzmann,* Com. on 2 Tim. ii. 15]. **b.** *to exert one's self, endeavor, give diligence* : foll. by an inf., Gal. ii. 10 ; Eph. iv. 3 ; 1 Th. ii. 17 ; 2 Tim. ii. 15 ; Heb. iv. 11 ; 2 Pet. i. 10 ; iii. 14 ; foll. by acc. with inf. 2 Pet. i. 15.*

*4705, **4706,** **4707,** **&4708** σπουδαῖος, -α, -ον, (σπουδή), fr. Hdt. down, *active, diligent, zealous, earnest* : ἔν τινι, 2 Co. viii. 22 ; compar. σπουδαιότερος, ibid. 17 [W. 242 sq. (227)], 22 [W. § 35, 1] ; neut. as adv. (Lat. *studiosius*), *very diligently* [cf. B. § 123, 10], 2 Tim. i. 17 R G.*

4709 σπουδαίως, adv. of the preceding ; **a.** *hastily, with haste* : compar. σπουδαιοτέρως [cf. B. 69 (61) ; W. § 11, 2 c.], Phil. ii. 28 [W. 243 (228)]. **b.** *diligently* : 2 Tim. i. 17 L T Tr WH ; Tit. iii. 13 ; *earnestly,* Lk. vii. 4.*

σπουδή, -ῆς, ἡ, (σπεύδω, [q. v.]), fr. Hom. down ; **1.** *haste* : μετὰ σπουδῆς, *with haste,* Mk. vi. 25 ; Lk. i. 39, (Sap. xix. 2 ; Joseph. antt. 7, 9, 7 ; Hdian. 3, 4, 1 ; 6, 4, 3). **2.** *earnestness, diligence* : univ. earnestness in accomplishing, promoting, or striving after anything, Ro. xii. 11 ; 2 Co. vii. 11, 12 ; viii. 7 sq. ; ἐν σπουδῇ, with diligence, Ro. xii. 8 ; σπουδὴν ἐνδείκνυσθαι, Heb. vi. 11 ; πᾶσαν σπουδὴν ποιεῖσθαι (see ποιέω, I. 3 p. 525ᵇ bot.), to give all diligence, interest one's self most earnestly, Jude 3 ; σπουδὴν παρεισφέρειν, 2 Pet. i. 5 ; ἡ σπ. ὑπέρ τινος, earnest care for one, 2 Co. viii. 16 (περί τινος, [Dem. 90, 10] ; Diod. 1, 75).* **4710**

σπυρίς [L WH σφυρίς, q. v.], -ίδος, ἡ, (allied to σπεῖρα, q. v. ; hence, something wound, twisted, or folded together), *a reed basket,* [i. e. *a plaited basket, a lunch basket, hamper* ; cf. B.D. s. v. Basket] : Mt. xv. 37 ; xvi. 10 ; Mk. viii. 8, 20 ; Acts ix. 25. (Hdt., Theophr., Apollod., Alciphr. 3, ep. 56 ; al.). See σφυρίς.* **4711**

στάδιον, -ου, plur. τὰ στάδια [Jn. vi. 19 Tdf.], and οἱ στάδιοι (so [Mt. xiv. 24 Tr txt. WH txt.] ; Lk. xxiv. 13 ; Jn. vi. 19 [not Tdf.] ; Rev. xxi. 16 [Rᵉˡᶻ G L WH mrg.] ; 2 Macc. xi. 5 ; xii. 10, 29 ; in the other pass. the gend. is not apparent [see *Tdf.* Proleg. p. 117 ; *WH.* App. p. 157] ; Krüger § 19, 2, 1), (ΣΤΑΩ, ἵστημι ; hence prop. 'established,' that which stands fast, a 'stated' distance, a 'fixed standard' of length), *a stadium,* i. e. **1.** a measure of length comprising 600 Grk. feet, or 625 Roman feet, or 125 Roman paces (Plin. h. n. 2, 23 (21), 85), hence one eighth of a Roman mile [i. e. 606¾ Eng. feet (about 15 m. less than one fifth of a kilom.)] ; *the space or distance of that length* [A.V. *a furlong*] : [Mt. xiv. 24 Tr txt. WH txt.] ; Lk. xxiv. 13 ; Jn. vi. 19 ; xi. 18 ; Rev. xiv. 20 ; xxi. 16. **2.** *a race-course,* i. e. place in which contests in running were held ; the one who outstripped the rest, and reached the goal first, receiving the prize : 1 Co. ix. 24 [here A. V. *race*]. Courses of this description were to be found in most of the larger Grk. cities, and were, like that at Olympia, 600 Greek feet in length. Cf. *Win.* RWB. s. v. Stadium ; *Grundt* in Schenkel s. v., vol. v. 375 sq. ; [BB. DD. s. v. Games].* **4712**

στάμνος, -ου, (ὁ,) ἡ, (fr. ἵστημι [cf. Curtius § 216]), among the Greeks *an earthen jar,* into which wine was drawn off for keeping (a process called καταςταμνίζειν), but also used for other purposes. The Sept. employ it in Ex. xvi. 33 as the rendering of the Hebr. צִנְצֶנֶת, that little jar [or "*pot*"] in which the manna was kept, laid up in the ark of the covenant ; hence in Heb. ix. 4, and Philo de congr. erud. grat. § 18. Cf. *Lob.* ad Phryn. p. 400 ; [W. 23].* **4713**

στασιαστής, -οῦ, ὁ, (στασιάζω), *the author of or a participant in an insurrection* : Mk. xv. 7 L T Tr WH ([Diod. fr. 10, 11, 1 p. 171, 6 Dind. ; Dion. Hal. ii. 1199] ; Joseph. antt. 14, 1, 3 ; Ptolem.). The earlier Greeks used στασιώτης [Moeris s. v.].* **see 4955**

στάσις, -εως, ἡ, (ἵστημι) ; **1.** *a standing, station, state* : ἔχειν στάσιν, to stand, exist, have stability, Lat. locum habere, [R. V. *is yet standing*], Heb. ix. 8 (Polyb. 5, 5, 3). **2.** fr. Aeschyl. and Hdt. down, *an insurrection* **4714** (cf. Germ. *Aufstand*): Mk. xv. 7; Lk. xxiii. 19, 25; Acts xix. 40 [see σήμερον, sub fin.]; κινεῖν στάσιν [L T Tr WH στάσεις] τινί, [*a mover of insurrections among* i. e.] against [cf. W. 208 (196)] one, Acts xxiv. 5.   **3.** *strife, dissension,* (Aeschyl. Pers. 738; Diog. Laërt. 3, 51): Acts xv. 2; xxiii. 7, 10.*

4715 στατήρ, -ῆρος, ὁ, (fr. ἵστημι, to place in the scales, weigh out [i. e. 'the weigher' (Vaniček p. 1126)]), *a stater, a coin*; in the N. T. a silver stater equiv. to four Attic or two Alexandrian drachmas, a Jewish shekel (see δίδραχμον): Mt. xvii. 27.*

4716 σταυρός, -οῦ, ὁ, [fr. ἵστημι (root *sta*); cf. Lat. *stauro-*, Eng. *staff* (see *Skeat*, Etym. Dict. s. v.); Curtius § 216; Vaniček p. 1126];   **1.** *an upright stake,* esp. *a pointed one,* (Hom., Hdt., Thuc., Xen.).   **2.** *a cross*;   **a.** the well-known instrument of most cruel and ignominious punishment, borrowed by the Greeks and Romans from the Phœnicians; to it were affixed among the Romans, down to the time of Constantine the Great, the guiltiest criminals, particularly the basest slaves, robbers, the authors and abetters of insurrections, and occasionally in the provinces, at the arbitrary pleasure of the governors, upright and peaceable men also, and even Roman citizens themselves; cf. *Win.* RWB. s. v. Kreuzigung; *Merz* in Herzog ed. 1 [(cf. Schaff-Herzog) also *Schultze* in Herzog ed. 2], s. v. Kreuz; Keim iii. p. 409 sqq. [Eng. trans. vi. 138; BB.DD. s. vv. Cross, Crucifixion; *O. Zöckler*, Das Kreuz Christi (Gütersloh, 1875); Eng. trans. Lond. 1878; *Fulda*, Das Kreuz u. d. Kreuzigung (Bresl. 1878); *Edersheim*, Jesus the Messiah, ii. 582 sqq.]. This horrible punishment the innocent Jesus also suffered: Mt. xxvii. 32, 40, 42; Mk. xv. 21, 30, 32; Lk. xxiii. 26; Jn. xix. 17, 19, 25, 31; Col. ii. 14; Heb. xii. 2; θάνατος σταυροῦ, Phil. ii. 8; τὸ αἷμα τοῦ σταυροῦ, blood shed on the cross, Col. i. 20.   **b.** i. q. *the crucifixion which Christ underwent*: Gal. v. 11 (on which see σκάνδαλον, sub fin.); Eph. ii. 16; with the addition of τοῦ Χριστοῦ, 1 Co. i. 17; the saving power of his crucifixion, Phil. iii. 18 (on which see ἐχθρός, fin.); Gal. vi. 14; τῷ σταυρῷ τοῦ Χριστοῦ διώκεσθαι, to encounter persecution on account of one's avowed belief in the saving efficacy of Christ's crucifixion, Gal. vi. 12; ὁ λόγος ὁ τοῦ σταυροῦ, the doctrine concerning the saving power of the death on the cross endured by Christ, 1 Co. i. 18. The judicial usage which compelled those condemned to crucifixion themselves to carry the cross to the place of punishment (Plut. de sera numinis vindict. c. 9; Artem. oneir. 2, 56, cf. Jn. xix. 17), gave rise to the proverbial expression αἴρειν or λαμβάνειν or βαστάζειν τὸν σταυρὸν αὐτοῦ, which was wont to be used of those who on behalf of God's cause do not hesitate cheerfully and manfully to bear persecutions, troubles, distresses, — thus recalling the fate of Christ and the spirit in which he encountered it (cf. *Bleek*, Synop. Erkl. der drei ersten Evangg. i. p. 429 sq.): Mt. x. 38; xvi. 24; Mk. viii. 34; x. 21 [R L in br.]; xv. 21; Lk. ix. 23; xiv. 27.*

4717 σταυρόω, -ῶ: fut. σταυρώσω; 1 aor. ἐσταύρωσα; Pass., pres. σταυροῦμαι; perfect ἐσταύρωμαι; 1 aor. ἐσταυρώ-

θην; (σταυρός, q. v.);   **1.** *to stake, drive down stakes*: Thuc. 7, 25, 6 [here οἱ Συρακόσιοι ἐσταύρωσαν, which the Scholiast renders σταυροὺς κατέπηξαν].   **2.** *to fortify with driven stakes, to palisade*: a place, Thuc. 6, 100; Diod.   **3.** *to crucify* (Vulg. *crucifigo*): τινά,   **a.** prop.: Mt. xx. 19; xxiii. 34; xxvi. 2; xxvii. 22, [23], 26, 31, 35, 38; xxviii. 5; Mk. xv. 13–15, 20, 24 sq. 27; xvi. 6; Lk. xxiii. 21, 23, 33; xxiv. 7, 20; Jn. xix. 6, 10, 15 sq. 18, 20, 23, 41; Acts ii. 36; iv. 10; 1 Co. i. 13, 23; ii. 2, [8]; 2 Co. xiii. 4; Gal. iii. 1; Rev. xi. 8, (Add. to Esth. viii. 13 [34]; for תָּלָה, to hang, Esth. vii. 9. Polyb. 1, 86, 4; Joseph. antt. 2, 5, 4; 17, 10, 10; Artem. oneir. 2, 53 and 56; in native Grk. writ. ἀνασταυροῦν is more common).   **b.** metaph.: τὴν σάρκα, to crucify the flesh, destroy its power utterly (the nature of the fig. implying that the destruction is attended with intense pain [but note the aor.]), Gal. v. 24; ἐσταύρωμαί τινι, and ἐσταύρωταί μοί τι, I have been crucified to something and it has been crucified to me, so that we are dead to each other all fellowship and intercourse between us has ceased, Gal. vi. 14. [COMP.: ἀνα-, συ(ν)- σταυρόω.]*

σταφυλή, -ῆς, ἡ, fr. Hom. down, Sept. for עֵנָב, *grapes, a bunch of grapes*: Mt. vii. 16; Lk. vi. 44; Rev. xiv. 18 [cf. Sept. as referred to s. v. βότρυς].   **4718**

στάχυς, -υος [cf. B. 14], ὁ, [connected w. the r. *sta*, ἵστημι; Curtius p. 721], fr. Hom. down, Sept. for שִׁבֹּלֶת, *an ear* of corn (or growing grain): Mt. xii. 1; Mk. ii. 23; iv. 28; Lk. vi. 1.*   **4719**

Στάχυς, -υος, ὁ, [cf. the preceding word], *Stachys*, the name of a man [cf. Bp. Lghtft. on Philip. p. 174]: Ro. xvi. 9.*   **4720**

στέγη, -ης, ἡ, (στέγω to cover), fr. Aeschyl. and Hdt. down, *a roof*: of a house, Mk. ii. 4; εἰσέρχεσθαι ὑπὸ τὴν στέγην τινός [see εἰσέρχομαι, 1 p. 187ᵇ bot.], Mt. viii. 8; Lk. vii. 6.*   **4721**

στέγω; [allied w. Lat. *tego, toga*, Eng. *deck, thatch*, etc.; Curtius § 155; Fick Pt. iii. 590]; *to cover*;   **1.** *to protect* or *keep by covering, to preserve*: Soph., Plat., Plut., al.   **2.** *to cover over with silence*; *to keep secret*; *to hide, conceal*: τἀμὰ ἔπη, Eur. Electr. 273; τὸν λόγον, Polyb. 8, 14, 5; for other exx. see Passow s. v. 1 b. β.; [L. and S. s. v. II. 2]; μωρὸς οὐ δυνήσεται λόγον στέξαι, Sir. viii. 17; hence ἡ ἀγάπη πάντα στέγει, 1 Co. xiii. 7, is explained by some, love covereth [so R. V. mrg.], i. e. *hides and excuses, the errors and faults of others*; but it is more appropriately rendered (with other interpreters) *beareth*. For στέγω means   **3.** *by covering to keep off* something which threatens, *to bear up against, hold out against*, and so *to endure, bear, forbear*, (τὰς ἐνδείας, Philo in Flacc. § 9; many exx. fr. Grk. auth. fr. Aeschyl. down are given by Passow s. v. 2; [L. and S. s. v. A. esp. 3]): 1 Co. ix. 12; xiii. 7; 1 Th. iii. 1, 5.*   **4722**

στεῖρος, -α, -ον, (i. q. στέρρος, στερεός q. v.); whence Germ. *starr*, Lat. *sterilis*), *hard, stiff*; of men and animals, *barren*: of a woman who does not conceive, Lk. i. 7, 36; xxiii. 29; Gal. iv. 27. (Hom., Theocr., Orph., Anthol.; Sept. for עֲקָרָה, עָקָר.)*   **4723**

στέλλω: (Germ. *stellen*); [cf. Grk. στήλη, στολή, etc.;   **4724**

Lat. *stlocus* (locus); Eng. *stall*, etc.; Curtius § 218; Fick Pt. i. 246; Pt. iv. 274]); fr. Hom. down; **1.** *to set, place, set in order, arrange*; *to fit out, to prepare, equip*; Mid. pres. στέλλομαι, *to prepare one's self, to fit out for one's self*; *to fit out for one's own use*: στελλόμενοι τοῦτο μή τις etc. *arranging, providing for, this* etc. i. e. *taking care* [A. V. *avoiding*], *that no one* etc. 2 Co. viii. 20 [cf. W. § 45, 6 a.; B. 292 (252)]. **2.** *to bring together, contract, shorten*: τὰ ἱστία, Hom. Od. 3, 11; 16, 353; also in mid. Il. 1, 433; *to diminish, check, cause to cease*; pass. *to cease to exist*: βουλομένη τὴν λύπην τοῦ ἀνδρὸς σταλῆναι, Joseph. antt. 5, 8, 3; ὁ χειμὼν ἐστάλη, ibid. 9, 10, 2; mid. *to remove one's self, withdraw one's self, to depart*, foll. by ἀπό with gen. of the pers., *to abstain from familiar intercourse with one*, 2 Th. iii. 6. [COMP.: ἀπο-, ἐξ-απο-, συν-απο-, δια-, ἐπι-, κατα-, συ(ν)-, ὑπο-στέλλω.]*

4725 στέμμα, -τος, τό, (στέφω, pf. pass. ἔστεμμαι, *to crown, to bind round*), *a fillet, a garland*, put upon victims: Acts xiv. 13 [cf. W. 630 (585); B. D. Am. ed. s. v. Garlands]. (From Hom. down.)*

4726 στεναγμός, -οῦ, ὁ, (στενάζω), *a groaning, a sigh*: Acts vii. 34; Ro. viii. 26; see ἀλάλητος. ([Pind.], Tragg., Plat., Joseph., Plut., al.; Sept. for אֲנָחָה, אֲנָקָה, נְאָקָה.)*

4727 στενάζω; 1 aor. ἐστέναξα; (στένω, akin is Germ. *stöhnen* [cf. *sten*-torian; Vaniček p. 1141; Fick Pt. i. 249]); *to sigh, to groan*: 2 Co. v. 2, 4, [cf. W. 353 (331)]; Heb. xiii. 17; ἐν ἑαυτοῖς, *within ourselves*, i. e. in our souls, inwardly, Ro. viii. 23; *to pray sighing*, Mk. vii. 34; κατά τινος, Jas. v. 9 [here R. V. *murmur*]. (Sept.; Tragg., Dem., Plut., al.) [COMP.: ἀνα-, συ(ν)-στενάζω. SYN. cf. κλαίω, fin.]*

4728 στενός, -ή, -όν, fr. Aeschyl. and Hdt. down, Sept. for צַר, *narrow, strait*: πύλη, Mt. vii. 13, [14 here L Tr br. πύλη)]; Lk. xiii. 24.*

4729 στενο-χωρέω, -ῶ: (στενόχωρος; and this fr. στενός, and χῶρος a space); **1.** intrans. *to be in a strait place* (Machon in Athen. 13 p. 582 b.); *to be narrow* (Is. xlix. 19). **2.** trans. *to straiten, compress, cramp, reduce to straits*, (Vulg. *angustio*), (Diod., Lcian., Hdian., al.; [Sept. Josh. xvii. 15; Judg. xvi. 16; Is. xxviii. 20; 4 Macc. xi. 11]): pass. trop. of one sorely 'straitened' in spirit, 2 Co. iv. 8; οὐ στενοχωρεῖσθε ἐν ἡμῖν, *ye are not straitened in us*, ample space is granted you in our souls, i. e. we enfold you with large affection, 2 Co. vi. 12; στενοχωρεῖσθε ἐν τοῖς σπλάγχνοις ὑμῶν, *ye are straitened in your own affections*, so that there is no room there for us, i. e. *you do not grant a place in your heart for love toward me*, ibid.*

4730 στενοχωρία, -ας, ἡ, (στενόχωρος), *narrowness of place, a narrow space*, (Is. viii. 22 [al. take this as metaph.]; Thuc., Plat., al.); metaph. *dire calamity, extreme affliction*, [A. V. *distress, anguish*]: Ro. ii. 9; viii. 35; 2 Co. vi. 4; xii. 10. (Deut. xxviii. 53, 55, 57; Sir. x. 26; [Sap. v. 3]; 1 Macc. ii. 53; xiii. 3; Polyb. 1, 67, 1; [Artemid. oneir. 3, 14]; Ael. v. h. 2, 41; [al.].) [Cf. Trench § lv.]*

4731 στερεός, -ά, -όν, [Vaniček p. 1131; Curtius § 222], fr. Hom. down, *firm, solid, compact, hard, rigid*: λίθος, Hom. Od. 19, 494; *strong, firm, immovable*, θεμέλιος, 2 Tim. ii.

19; τροφή, *solid food*, Heb. v. 12, 14; στερεωτέρα τροφή, Diod. 2, 4; Epictet. diss. 2, 16, 39; trop., *in a bad sense, cruel, stiff, stubborn, hard*; often so in Grk. writ. fr. Hom. down: κραδίη στερεωτέρη λίθοιο, Od. 23, 103; in a good sense, *firm, steadfast*: τῇ πίστει, as respects faith, firm of faith [cf. W. § 31, 6 a.], 1 Pet. v. 9 (see στερεόω, fin.).*

4732 στερεόω, -ῶ: 1 aor. ἐστερέωσα; impf. 3 pers. plur. ἐστερεοῦντο; 1 aor. pass. ἐστερεώθην; (στερεός); *to make solid, make firm, strengthen, make strong*: τινά, the body of any one, Acts iii. 16; τὰς βάσεις, pass. Acts iii. 7; pass. τῇ πίστει, *as respects faith* (see στερεός, fin.), Acts xvi. 5. (Sept.; Xen., Diod.)*

4733 στερέωμα, -τος, τό, (στερεόω), *that which has been made firm*; **a.** (Vulg. *firmamentum*) *the firmament*; so Sept. for רָקִיעַ, the arch of the sky, which in early times was thought to be solid, Gen. i. 6–8; Ezek. i. 22–26; Sir. xliii. 1, [cf. B. D. (esp. Am. ed.) s. v. Firmament]; *a fortified place*, 1 Esdr. viii. 78 (80). **b.** *that which furnishes a foundation*; *on which a thing rests firmly, support*: Aristot. partt. an. 2, 9, 12 p. 655ᵃ, 22; κύριος στερέωμά μου, Ps. xvii. (xviii.) 3. **c.** *firmness, steadfastness*: τῆς πίστεως, Col. ii. 5 [some take it here metaph. in a military sense, *solid front*; cf. Bp. Lghtft. ad loc. (per contra Meyer)].*

4734 Στεφανᾶς, -ᾶ [cf. B. 20 (18)], ὁ, *Stephanas*, a Christian of Corinth: 1 Co. i. 16; xvi. 15, 17.*

4735 στέφανος, -ου, ὁ, (στέφω [to put round; cf. Curtius § 224]), Sept. for עֲטָרָה, [fr. Hom. down], *a crown* (with which the head is encircled); **a.** prop. as a mark of royal or (in general) exalted rank [such pass. in the Sept. as 2 S. xii. 30; 1 Chr. xx. 2; Ps. xx. (xxi.) 4; Ezek. xxi. 26; Zech. vi. 11, 14, (yet cf. 2 S. i. 10 Compl., Lag.), perhaps justify the doubt whether the distinction betw. στέφανος and διάδημα (q. v.) was strictly observed in Hellenistic Grk.]: Mt. xxvii. 29; Mk. xv. 17; Jn. xix. 2, 5; Rev. iv. 4, 10; vi. 2; ix. 7; xiv. 14; with a gen. of the material, ἀστέρων δώδεκα, Rev. xii. 1; the wreath or garland which was given as a prize to victors in the public games [cf. BB. DD. s. v. Games]: 1 Co. ix. 25, cf. 2 Tim. ii. 5. **b.** metaph. **a.** *the eternal blessedness which will be given as a prize to the genuine servants of God and Christ*: ὁ τῆς δικαιοσύνης στέφανος, the crown (wreath) which is the reward of righteousness, 2 Tim. iv. 8; with an epexeget. gen. in the phrases λαμβάνεσθαι, διδόναι τὸν στέφανον τῆς ζωῆς, equiv. to ζωὴν ὡς τὸν στέφανον, Jas. i. 12; Rev. ii. 10; κομίζεσθαι τὸν τῆς δόξης στέφανον, 1 Pet. v. 4; λαβεῖν τ. στέφανόν τινος, to cause one to fail of the promised and hoped for prize, Rev. iii. 11. **β.** *that which is an ornament and honor to one*: so of persons, Phil. iv. 1; στέφ. καυχήσεως (see καύχησις), 1 Th. ii. 19, (Prov. xii. 4; xvi. 31; xvii. 6, etc.).*

4736 Στέφανος, -ου, ὁ, *Stephen*, one of the seven 'deacons' of the church at Jerusalem who was stoned to death by the Jews: Acts vi. 5, 8 sq.; vii. 59; viii. 2; xi. 19; xxii. 20.*

4737 στεφανόω, -ῶ: 1 aor. ἐστεφάνωσα; pf. pass. ptcp. ἐστεφανωμένος; (στέφανος); fr. Hom. down; **a.** *to en-*

circle with a crown, to crown : the victor in a contest, 2 Tim. ii. 5.   b. univ. to adorn, to honor : τινὰ δόξῃ κ. τιμῇ, Heb. ii. 7, 9, fr. Ps. viii. 6.*

4738 στῆθος, -ους, τό, (fr. ἵστημι; that which stands out, is prominent [Etym. Magn. 727, 19 διότι ἔστηκεν ἀσάλευτον]), fr. Hom. down, the breast : Jn. xiii. 25 ; xxi. 20, (cf. κόλπος, 1) ; Rev. xv. 6. τύπτειν εἰς τὸ στῆθος or τύπτ. τὸ στῆθος, of mourners (see κόπτω), Lk. xviii. 13 ; xxiii. 48.*

4739 στήκω ; (an inferior Grk. word, derived fr. ἔστηκα, pf. of ἵστημι ; see B. 48 (41) ; [W. 24, 26 (25) ; WH. App. p. 169 ; Veitch s. v. ἐστήκω ; Mullach s. v. στέκω (p. 299)]) ; to stand : Mk. [iii. 31 T Tr WH] ; xi. 25 [(cf. ὅταν c. β.)] ; Jn. i. 26 L mrg. T Tr txt. WH ; [Rev. xii. 4 WH (but see below)] ; with an emphasis, to stand firm ; trop. to persist, persevere, [A.V. stand fast] : absol. to persevere in godliness and rectitude, 2 Th. ii. 15 ; ἐν κυρίῳ, in one's fellowship with the Lord, Phil. iv. 1 ; 1 Th. iii. 8 [(cf. ἐάν, I. 2 b.)] ; ἐν τῇ πίστει, 1 Co. xvi. 13 ; ἐν ἑνὶ πνεύματι, Phil. i. 27 ; to keep one's standing (opp. to ζυγῷ ἐνέχομαι), τῇ ἐλευθερίᾳ, maintain your allegiance to freedom [cf. W. § 31, 1 k.; B. § 133, 12 ; but L T Tr WH take στ. here absol.; cf. Bp. Lghtft. ad loc.], Gal. v. 1 ; to stand erect, trop. not to sin (opp. to πίπτειν i. q. to sin), τῷ κυρίῳ, dat. commodi [W. u. s.], Ro. xiv. 4. [In Jn. viii. 44 (ἐν τῇ ἀληθείᾳ οὐκ(χ) ἕστηκεν) WH read the impf. ἔστηκεν (where others adopt ἔστηκεν fr. ἵστημι), owing to the preceding οὐκ (T WH after codd. אּ B* D L etc.) ; see Westcott, Com. on Jn. l.c. 'Additional Note' ; WH. Introd. § 407. But such an impf. is nowhere else found (yet cf. Rev. xii. 4 WH), and respecting confusion in the ancient use of the breathings, and the interchange of οὐκ and οὐχ, see οὐ ad init. and reff. there, esp. Tdf. Proleg. p. 90 ; moreover, the familiar pf. (pres.) of ἵστημι thoroughly suits the context ; see ἵστημι, II. 2 d.] ([Sept., Ex. xiv. 13 Alex., Compl. ; 1 K. viii. 11] ; Alex. Aphr. probl. 1, 49 var. ; eccles. writ.) *

4740 στηριγμός, -οῦ, ὁ, (στηρίζω), firm condition, steadfastness : of mind, 2 Pet. iii. 17. (of a standing still, Diod. 1, 81 ; Plut. mor. p. 76 d.) *

4741 στηρίζω ; fut. στηρίξω (as in the best Grk. writ.), and στηρίσω (in 2 Th. iii. 3 cod. Vat., as in Jer. xvii. 5 ; στηριῶ, Jer. iii. 12 ; xxiv. 6 ; Ezek. xiv. 8 ; Sir. vi. 37 [see reff. below]) ; 1 aor. ἐστήριξα, and ἐστήρισα (στήρισον, Lk. xxii. 32 L T Tr WH ; Rev. iii. 2 G L T Tr WH, as in Judg. xix. 5, 8 ; Ezek. vi. 2 ; Prov. xv. 25, etc. ; cf. [WH. App. p. 170]; Bttm. Ausf. Sprchl. i. p. 372 ; B. 36 (32) ; Kühner § 343, 1. p. 910 ; [Veitch s. v.]) ; Pass., pf. ἐστήριγμαι ; 1 aor. ἐστηρίχθην ; (στήριγξ a support ; akin to στερεός, q. v., στερρός, and Germ. stärken ; cf. Curtius § 222) ; fr. Hom. down ; to make stable, place firmly, set fast, fix : ἐστήρικται (χάσμα), is fixed, Lk. xvi. 26 ; στηρίζω τὸ πρόσωπον, to set one's face steadfastly, keep the face turned (Ezek. vi. 2 ; xiii. 17 ; xv. 7 ; etc.) τοῦ πορεύεσθαι εἰς with an acc. of place, a Hebr. expression (see πρόσωπον, 1 b. [and cf. B. § 140, 16 δ.; W. 33]), Lk. ix. 51.   b. to strengthen, make firm ; trop. (not so in prof. auth.) to render constant, confirm, one's mind [A. V. establish] :

τινά, Lk. xxii. 32 ; [Acts xviii. 23 where R G ἐπιστηρ.]; Ro. i. 11 ; xvi. 25 ; 1 Th. iii. 2 ; 2 Th. iii. 3 ; 1 Pet. v. 10 [here Rec. has 1 aor. opt. 3 pers. sing. στηρίξαι] ; Rev. iii. 2 ; τὴν καρδίαν τινός, 1 Th. iii. 13 ; Jas. v. 8 ; τινὰ ἔν τινι, 2 Th. ii. 17 ; 2 Pet. i. 12. [COMP.: ἐπι-στηρίζω.] *

στιβάς, -άδος, ἡ, (fr. στείβω 'to tread on,' 2 aor. ἔστιβον) ;   a. a spread or layer of leaves, reeds, rushes, soft leafy twigs, straw, etc., serving for a bed (Hesych. στιβάς· ἀπὸ ῥάβδων ἢ χλωρῶν χόρτων στρῶσις κ. φύλλων) ; so in Grk. writ. fr. Hdt. down.   b. that which is used in making a bed of this sort, a branch full of leaves, soft foliage : so Mk. xi. 8 L T Tr WH for στοιβάδας, an orthographical error [see Tdf.'s note ad loc.].*   **(4741α); see 4746**

στίγμα, -τος, τό, (fr. στίζω to prick ; [cf. Lat. stimulus, etc. ; Germ. stechen, Eng. stick, sting, etc. ; Curtius § 226]), a mark pricked in or branded upon the body. Acc. to ancient oriental usage, slaves and soldiers bore the name or stamp of their master or commander branded or pricked (cut) into their bodies to indicate what master or general they belonged to, and there were even some devotees who stamped themselves in this way with the token of their gods (cf. Deyling, Observv. iii. p. 423 sqq.) ; hence τὰ στίγματα τοῦ (κυρίου so Rec.) Ἰησοῦ, the marks of (the Lord) Jesus, which Paul in Gal. vi. 17 says he bears branded on his body, are the traces left there by the perils, hardships, imprisonments, scourgings, endured by him for the cause of Christ, and which mark him as Christ's faithful and approved votary, servant, soldier, [see Bp. Lghtft. Com. on Gal. l. c.]. (Hdt. 7, 233 ; Aristot., Ael., Plut., Lcian., al.) *   **4742**

στιγμή, -ῆς, ἡ, (στίζω ; see στίγμα, init.), a point : στιγμὴ χρόνου, a point (i. e. a moment) of time (Cic. pro Flacco c. 25 ; pro Sest. 24 ; Caes. b. c. 2, 14 ; al.), Lk. iv. 5. (Antonin. 2, 17 ; Plut. puer. educ. 17 ; Is. xxix. 5 ; 2 Macc. ix. 11.) *   **4743**

στίλβω ; to shine, glisten : of garments (as in Hom. Il. 3, 392 ; 18, 596 ; cf. Plat. Phaedo 59 p. 110 d.), Mk. ix. 3.*   **4744**

στοά, -ᾶς, ἡ, a portico, a covered colonnade where people can stand or walk protected from the weather and the heat of the sun : Jn. v. 2 ; σ: οὐ Σολομῶνος, a "porch" or portico built by Solomon in the eastern part of the temple (which in the temple's destruction by the Babylonians was left uninjured, and remained down to the times of king Agrippa, to whom the care of the temple was intrusted by the emperor Claudius, and who on account of its antiquity did not dare to demolish and build it anew ; so Josephus relates, antt. 20, 9, 7 ; [but on 'Solomon's Porch' cf. B.D. s. v. Temple (Solomon's Temple, fin.)]) : Jn. x. 23 ; Acts iii. 11 ; v. 12.*   **4745**

στοιβάς, -άδος, ἡ, see στιβάς, b.   - - - - - - - - - - **4746; see (4741α)**

[Στοϊκός, so Lchm. Tdf. for Στωϊκός, q. v.] - - - - - - - - **see 4770**

στοιχεῖον, -ου, τό, (fr. στοῖχος a row, rank, series ; - - - **4747** hence prop. that which belongs to any στοῖχος, that of which a στοῖχος is composed ; hence), any first thing, from which the others belonging to some series or composite whole take their rise ; an element, first principle. The word denotes spec.   **1.** the letters of the alphabet as the elements of speech, not however the written characters (which are called γράμματα), but the spoken sounds: στοιχεῖον φωνῆς φωνὴ ἀσύνθετος, Plat. defin. p. 414 e.; τὸ ῥῶ τὸ στοιχεῖον, id. Crat. p. 426 d.; στοιχεῖόν ἐστι φωνὴ ἀδιαίρετος, οὐ πᾶσα δέ, ἀλλ᾽ ἐξ ἧς πέφυκε συνετὴ γίγνεσθαι φωνή, Aristot. poet. 20, p. 1456ᵇ, 22. **2.** *the elements from which all things have come, the material causes of the universe* (ἔστι δὲ στοιχεῖον, ἐξ οὗ πρώτου γίνεται τὰ γινόμενα καὶ εἰς ὁ ἔσχατον ἀναλύεται . . . τὸ πῦρ, τὸ ὕδωρ, ὁ ἀήρ, ἡ γῆ, Diog. Laërt. Zeno 69, 137); so very often fr. Plat. down, as in Tim. p. 48 b.; in the Scriptures: Sap. vii. 17; xix. 17; 2 Pet. iii. 10, 12. **3.** *the heavenly bodies*, either as parts of the heavens, or (as others think) because in them the elements of man's life and destiny were supposed to reside; so in the earlier eccles. writ.: Ep. ad Diogn. 7, 2; Justin. M. dial. c. Tryph. 23; τὰ οὐράνια στοιχεῖα in dial. apol. 2, 5; στοιχεῖα θεοῦ, created by God, Theoph. Ant. ad Autol. 1, 4; cf. *Hilgenfeld*, Galaterbrief, pp. 66–77. Hence some interpreters infelicitously understand Paul's phrase τὰ στοιχεῖα τοῦ κόσμου, Gal. iv. 3, 9; Col. ii. 8, 20, of the heavenly bodies, because times and seasons, and so s a c r e d s e a s o n s, were regulated by the course of the sun and moon; yet in unfolding the meaning of the passage on the basis of this sense they differ widely. **4.** *the elements, rudiments, primary and fundamental principles* (cf. our 'alphabet' or 'a b c') *of any art, science, or discipline*; e. g. of mathematics, as in the title of Euclid's well-known work; στοιχεῖα πρῶτα καὶ μέγιστα χρηστῆς πολιτείας, Isocr. p. 18 a.; τῆς ἀρετῆς, Plut. de puer. educ. 16, 2; many exx. are given in Passow s. v. 4, ii. p. 1550ᵇ; [cf. L. and S. s. v. II. 3 and 4]. In the N. T. we have τὰ στ. τῆς ἀρχῆς τῶν λογίων τοῦ θεοῦ (see ἀρχή, 1 b. p. 76ᵇ bot.), Heb. v. 12, such as are taught to νήπιοι, ib. 13; τὰ στοιχεῖα τοῦ κόσμου, the rudiments with which mankind like νήπιοι were indoctrinated before the time of Christ, i. e. the elements of religious training, or the ceremonial precepts common alike to the worship of Jews and of Gentiles, Gal. iv. 3, 9, (and since these requirements on account of the difficulty of observing them are to be regarded as a yoke — cf. Acts xv. 10; Gal. v. 1 — those who rely upon them are said to be δεδουλωμένοι ὑπὸ τὰ στ.); spec. the ceremonial requirements esp. of Jewish tradition, minutely set forth by theosophists and false teachers, and fortified by specious arguments, Col. ii. 8, 20. The phrase τὰ στοιχεῖα τοῦ κόσμου is fully discussed by *Schneckenburger* in the Theolog. Jahrbücher for 1848, Pt. iv. p. 445 sqq.; *Neander* in the Deutsche Zeitschrift f. Christl. Wissenschaft for 1850, p. 205 sqq.; *Kienlen* in Reuss u. Cunitz's Beiträge zu d. theolog. Wissenschaften, vol. ii. p. 133 sqq.; *E. Schaubach*, Comment. qua exponitur quid στοιχεῖα τοῦ κόσμου in N. T. sibi velint. (Meining. 1862).*

4748   στοιχέω, -ῶ; fut. στοιχήσω; (στοῖχος a row, series); **a.** *to proceed in a row, go in order*: Xen. Cyr. 6, 3, 34; metaph. *to go on prosperously, to turn out well*: of things, Eccl. xi. 6 for כָּשֵׁר. **b.** *to walk*: with a local dat. [W. § 31, 1 a. cf. p. 219 (205); yet cf. B. § 133, 22 b.].

τοῖς ἴχνεσί τινος, in the steps of one, i. e. follow his example, Ro. iv. 12; *to direct one's life, to live*, with a dat. of the rule [B. u. s.], εἰ πνεύματι . . . στοιχῶμεν, if the Holy Spirit animates us [see ζάω, I. 3 sub fin.], let us exhibit that control of the Spirit in our life, Gal. v. 25; τῷ κανόνι, acc. to the rule, Gal. vi. 16; τῷ αὐτῷ (where Rec. adds κανόνι), Phil. iii. 16 [W. §43, 5 d.; cf. B. § 140, 18 fin.], (τῷ παραδείγματί τινος, Clem. hom. 10, 15); with a ptcp. denoting the manner of acting, στοιχεῖς τ. νόμον φυλάσσων, so walkest as to keep the law [A. V. *walkest orderly, keeping* etc.], Acts xxi. 24. [On the word and its constr. see Fritzsche on Rom. vol. iii. p. 142. COMP.: συ(ν)- στοιχέω.] *

4749   στολή, -ῆς, ἡ, (στέλλω [q. v.] to prepare, equip, 2 pf. ἔστολα); **1.** *an equipment* (Aeschyl.). **2.** *an equipment in clothes, clothing*; spec. *a loose outer garment for men which extended to the feet* [cf. Eng. *stole* (Dict. of Chris. Antiq. s. v.)], worn by kings (Jon. iii. 6), priests, and persons of rank: Mk. xii. 38; xvi. 5; Lk. xv. 22; xx. 46; Rev. vi. 11; vii. 9, 13, [14ᵃ, 14ᵇ Rec.; xxii. 14 L T Tr WH]. (Tragg., Xen., Plat., sqq.; Sept. chiefly for בֶּגֶד.) [Cf. Trench § l.]*

4750   στόμα, -τος, τό, (apparently i. q. τόμα, with σ prefixed, fr. τέμνω, τέτομα, therefore prop. 'cutting' [or 'cut'; so Etym. Magn. 728, 18; al. 'calling', etc.; but doubtful, cf. Curtius § 226 b.; Vaniček p. 1141 and reff.]); fr. Hom. down; Hebr. פֶּה; *the mouth*; **1.** prop. *the mouth as a part of the body*: of man, Jn. xix. 29; Acts xi. 8; Rev. i. 16; iii. 16, and often; of animals, — as of a fish, Mt. xvii. 27; of a horse, Jas. iii. 3; Rev. ix. 17; of a serpent, Rev. xii. 15 sq.; xiii. 5; the jaws of a lion, 2 Tim. iv. 17; Heb. xi. 33; Rev. xiii. 2. Since the thoughts of man's soul find verbal utterance by his mouth, καρδία ('the heart' or soul) and στόμα 'the mouth' are distinguished: Mt. xii. 34; xv. 8 Rec. fr. Is. xxix. 13; Ro. x. 8, 10; in phrases chiefly of a Hebraistic character, the mouth (as the organ of speech) is mentioned in connection with words and speech, Mt. xxi. 16 (fr. Ps. viii. 3), and words are said to proceed ἐκ τοῦ στόματος, Mt. iv. 4 (fr. Deut. viii. 3); Lk. iv. 22; Eph. iv. 29; Col. iii. 8; Jas. iii. 10; τὸ στόμα λαλεῖ τι, Jude 16; on the Hebr. phrase ἀνοίγειν τὸ στόμα, see ἀνοίγω, p. 48ᵃ bot. ἡ ἄνοιξις τοῦ στ. Eph. vi. 19; στόμα πρὸς στόμα λαλῆσαι, [A. V. face to face], 2 Jn. 12; 3 Jn. 14, (τὸ στόμα πρὸς τὸ στόμα, of a kiss, Xen. mem. 2, 6, 32); God or the Holy Spirit is said to speak διὰ τοῦ στόματός τινος [cf. B. 183 (159)], Lk. i. 70; Acts i. 16; iii. 18, 21; iv. 25; or a person is said to hear a thing διὰ στόματός τ. Acts xv. 7; or ἀπὸ τοῦ στ. τ. *from his own mouth* i. e. what he has just said, Lk. xxii. 71; or ἐκ τ. στ. Acts xxii. 14; θηρεῦσαί τι ἐκ τ. στ. τ. Lk. xi. 54; τὸ πνεῦμα τοῦ στ. [*the breath of his mouth*, see πνεῦμα, 1 b.], 2 Th. ii. 8 (Ps. xxxii. (xxxiii.) 6, cf. Is. xi. 4); ἡ ῥομφαία τοῦ στ. a fig. portraying the destructive power of the words of Christ the judge, Rev. ii. 16; δόλος or ψεῦδος ἐν τῷ στ., 1 Pet. ii. 22 and Rev. xiv. 5, (fr. Is. liii. 9); στόμα is put for 'statements', declarations, in Mt. xviii. 16 and 2 Co. xiii.

1, (Deut. xix. 15); Lk. xix. 22 (Eccl. viii. 2). διδόναι τινὶ στόμα, apt forms of speech (as distinguished from the substance of speech, ἡ σοφία), Lk. xxi. 15; στόμα for one who has begun (or is about) to speak, Ro. iii. 19 (Ps. cvi. (cvii.) 42; cf. πᾶν γόνυ and πᾶσα γλῶσσα, Phil. ii. 10 sq. fr. Is. xlv. 23); metaph. the earth is said to open its mouth and καταπίνειν τι, Rev. xii. 16. **2.** Like Lat. *acies*, στόμα μαχαίρας, the *edge* of the sword (פִּי־חֶרֶב, Gen. xxxiv. 26; [Josh. xix. 48; Jer. xxi. 7, etc.]; Judg. xviii. 27, etc.; 2 S. xv. 14 [but in the last two pass. the Sept. render the Hebr. phrase by στ. ῥομφαίας, which (together with στ. ξίφους) is the more common translation; cf. W. 18, 30; B. 320 (274) n.]): Lk. xxi. 24; Heb. xi. 34, (hence δίστομος, q. v.; אֲכַל of a sword, 2 S. ii. 26; xi. 25).

4751   **στόμαχος**, -ου, ὁ, (στόμα, q. v.); **1.** *the throat*: Hom., al. **2.** *an opening, orifice*, esp. of the stomach, Aristot. **3.** in later writ. (as Plut., al.) *the stomach*: 1 Tim. v. 23.*

4752   **στρατεία**, -ας, ἡ, (στρατεύω), *an expedition, campaign; military service, warfare*: Paul likens his contest with the difficulties that oppose him in the discharge of his apostolic duties to a *warfare*, 2 Co. x. 4 (where Tdf. στρατιᾶς, see his note); 1 Tim. i. 18. [(Hdt., Xen., al.)] *

4753   **στράτευμα**, -τος, τό, (στρατεύω), fr. Aeschyl. and Hdt. down; **a.** *an army*: Mt. xxii. 7; Rev. ix. 16; xix. 14 [cf. W. § 59, 4 a.], 19. **b.** *a band of soldiers* [R.V. soldiers]: Acts xxiii. 10, 27. **c.** *body-guard, guardsmen*: plur. Lk. xxiii. 11 [R. V. soldiers].*

see 4757 St.   **στρατεύω**: Mid., pres. στρατεύομαι; 1 aor. subjunc. 2 pers. sing. στρατεύσῃ (1 Tim. i. 18 T Tr txt. WH mrg.); (στρατός [related to στρώννύω, q. v.], an encampment, an army); fr. Hdt. down; *to make a military expedition, to lead soldiers to war* or *to battle*, (spoken of a commander); *to do military duty, be on active service, be a soldier*; in the N. T. only in the mid. (Grk. writ. use the act. and the depon. mid. indiscriminately; cf. Passow s. v. 1 fin.; [L. and S. s. v. I. 2]): prop. of soldiers, Lk. iii. 14; 1 Co. ix. 7; 2 Tim. ii. 4; *to fight*, [A. V. war]: trop. of the conflicts of the apostolic office, 2 Co. x. 3; with a kindred acc. [W. §32, 2; B. § 131, 5], τὴν καλὴν στρατείαν, 1 Tim. i. 18 (ἱερὰν κ. εὐγενῆ στρατείαν στρατεύσασθαι περὶ τῆς εὐσεβείας, 4 Macc. ix. 23); of passions that disquiet the soul, Jas. iv. 1; 1 Pet. ii. 11. [COMP.: ἀντιστρατεύομαι.] *

4755   **στρατηγός**, -οῦ, ὁ, (στρατός and ἄγω), fr. Hdt. down, Sept. chiefly for כֵּן [only plur. כָּנַנִים]; **1.** *the commander of an army*. **2.** in the N. T. a civic commander, a governor, (the name of the duumviri or highest magistrates in the municipia and colonies; they had the power of administering justice in the less important cases; οἱ τῆς πόλεως στρατηγοί, Artem. oneir. 4, 49; of civil magistrates as early as Hdt. 5, 38; [see reff. in Meyer on Acts xvi. 20; L. and S. s. v. II. 2 sq.; cf. Farrar, St. Paul, i. excurs. xvi.]): plur. [R. V. magistrates (after A.V.), with mrg. Gr. prœtors], Acts xvi. 20, 22, 35 sq. [38]. **3.** στρατ. τοῦ ἱεροῦ, 'captain of the temple' [A.V.], i. e. the commander of the Levites who

kept guard in and around the temple (Joseph. antt. 20, 6, 2; [B. D. s. v. Captain, 3; Edersheim, The Temple etc. ch. vii., 2 ed. p. 119 sq.]) : Acts iv. 1; v. 24; plur. Lk. xxii. 52; simply [A. V. captain], Acts v. 26; Lk. xxii. 4.*

4756   **στρατιά**, -ᾶς, ἡ, (στρατός [cf. στρατεύω]), fr. Aeschyl. and Hdt. down, Sept. for צָבָא; **1.** *an army, band of soldiers*. **2.** sometimes in the poets i. q. στρατεία, as Arstph. eqq. 587 (ἐν στρατιαῖς τε καὶ μάχαις), 2 Co. x. 4 Tdf. after the best codd. ([see his note; cf. L. and S. s. v. II.]; Passow s. v. στρατεία, fin.). **3.** in the N. T. ἡ οὐράνιος στρατιά, or ἡ στρατ. τοῦ οὐρανοῦ (Hebr. צְבָא הַשָּׁמַיִם), *the host of heaven* (see δύναμις, f.), i. e. **a.** *troops of angels* (1 K. xxii. 19; Neh. ix. 6): Lk. ii. 13. **b.** *the heavenly bodies, stars of heaven*, (so called on account of their number and their order): Acts vii. 42 (2 Chr. xxxiii. 3, 5; Jer. viii. 2, etc.).*

4757   **στρατιώτης**, -ου, ὁ, (fr. στρατιός [(cf. στρατεύω)], like ἠλιώτης, κλοιώτης, ἠπειρώτης), fr. Hdt. down, *a (common) soldier*: Mt. viii. 9; Mk. xv. 16; Lk. xxiii. 36; Jn. xix. 2; Acts x. 7; xii. 4, etc.; with the addition of Ἰησοῦ Χριστοῦ, metaph., a champion of the cause of Christ, 2 Tim. ii. 3.

4758   **στρατολογέω**, -ῶ: to be a στρατολόγος (and this fr. στρατός and λέγω), *to gather (collect) an army, to enlist soldiers*: ὁ στρατολογήσας, [he that enrolled (him) as a soldier], of the commander, 2 Tim. ii. 4. (Diod., Dion. Hal., Joseph., Plut., al.) *

4759   **στρατοπεδάρχης**, -ου, ὁ, (στρατόπεδον and ἄρχω), [cf. B. 73 (64)]; **a.** *the commander of a camp and army, a military tribune*: Dion. Hal. 10, 36; Lcian. hist. conscr. 22; [Joseph. b. j. 2, 19, 4]. **b.** *Praetorian prefect*, commander of the praetorian cohorts, i. e. captain of the Roman emperor's body-guard: Acts xxviii. 16 [L T Tr WH om. the cl., see Abbot in B. D., Am. ed., s. v. Captain of the Guard]. There were two praetorian prefects, to whose custody prisoners sent bound to the emperor were consigned: Joseph. antt. 18, 6, 6; Plin. epp. 10, 65 (57). [See B. D. Am. ed. u. s.; Bp. Lghtft. on Phil. p. 7 sq.] *

see 4759   [στρατοπέδ-αρχος, -ου, ὁ; see the preceding word. The dat. -χῳ is the reading of some codd. (cf. WH rejected mrg.) in Acts xxviii. 16; cf. ἑκατοντάρχης, init.*]

4760   **στρατό-πεδον**, -ου, τό, (στρατός, and πέδον a plain), fr. Hdt. down; **a.** *a military camp*. **b.** *soldiers in camp, an army*: Lk. xxi. 20.*

4761   **στρεβλόω**, -ῶ; (στρεβλός [fr. στρέφω] twisted, Lat. tortuosus; hence στρέβλη, fem., an instrument of torture); *to twist, turn awry*, (Hdt.); *to torture, put to the rack*, (Arstph., Plat., Dem., Polyb., Joseph., 3 Macc. iv. 14); metaph. *to pervert*, of one who wrests or tortures language to a false sense, 2 Pet. iii. 16.*

4762   **στρέφω**: 1 aor. ἔστρεψα; Pass., pres. στρέφομαι; 2 aor. ἐστράφην; fr. Hom. down; Sept. for הָפַךְ, also for סָבַב, etc.; *to turn, turn round* : τί τινι, to turn a thing to one, Mt. v. 39, and T Tr WH in xxvii. 3 [for ἀποστρέφω, to bring back; see ἀποστρέφω, 2]; reflexively (W. § 38, 1; B. § 130, 4), *to turn one's self* (i. e. to turn the back to one; used of one who no longer cares for another),

Acts vii. 42 [cf. W. 469 (437)]; τὶ εἴς τι, i. q. μεταστρέφω, to turn one thing into another, Rev. xi. 6. Pass. reflexively, *to turn* one's self: στραφείς foll. by a finite verb, *having turned* etc., Mt. vii. 6; [ix. 22 L T Tr WH]; xvi. 23; Lk. vii. 9; ix. 55; xiv. 25; xxii. 61; Jn. i. 38; xx. 16; στραφεὶς πρός τινα, foll. by a fin. verb, [*turning unto* etc., or *turned unto and* etc.], Lk. vii. 44; x. 21 (22) [Rˢᵗ L T], 23; xxiii. 28; στρέφεσθαι εἰς τὰ ὀπίσω, to turn one's self back, Jn. xx. 14; εἰς τὰ ἔθνη, Acts xiii. 46; ἐστράφησαν (ἐν L T Tr WH) ταῖς καρδίαις αὐτῶν εἰς Αἴγυπτον, [R.V. they *turned back in their hearts unto Egypt*] i. e. to their condition there, Acts vii. 39; absol. and trop. *to turn one's self* sc. from one's course of conduct, i. e. *to change one's mind* [cf. W. u. s.]: Mt. xviii. 3 and L T Tr WH in Jn. xii. 40. [COMP.: ἀνα-, ἀπο-, δια-, ἐκ-, ἐπι-, κατα-, μετα-, συ(ν)-, ὑπο- στρέφω.] *

4763 στρηνιάω, -ῶ: 1 aor ἐστρηνίασα; (fr. στρῆνος, q. v.); a word used in middle and later Comedy for τρυφᾶν (cf. *Lob.* ad Phryn. p. 381; [*Rutherford*, New Phryn. p. 475 sq.; W. 25]); *to be wanton, to live luxuriously*: Rev. xviii. 7, 9. [COMP.: κατα-στρηνιάω.] *

4764 στρῆνος, -ους, τό, [allied w. στερεός, q. v.], *excessive strength which longs to break forth, over-strength*; *luxury*, [R. V. *wantonness* (mrg. *luxury*)]: Rev. xviii. 3 (see δύναμις, d.); for שַׁאֲנָן, *arrogance*, 2 K. xix. 28; *eager desire*, Lycophr. 438.*

4765 στρουθίον, -ου, τό, (dimin. of στρουθός), *a little bird*, esp. of the *sparrow* sort, *a sparrow*: Mt. x. 29, 31; Lk. xii. 6 sq. (Aristot. h. a. 5, 2 p. 539ᵇ, 33; 9, 7 p. 613ᵃ, 33; Sept. for צִפּוֹר.) [Cf. *Tristram* in B.D. s. v. Sparrow; Survey of West. Palest., 'Fauna and Flora', p. 67 sq.] *

see 4766 St. στρωννύω, or στρώννυμι: impf. 3 pers. plur. ἐστρώννυον [cf. B. 45 (39)]; 1 aor. ἔστρωσα; pf. pass. ptcp. ἐστρωμένος; (by metathesis fr. στόρνυμι, στορέννυμι, and this fr. ΣΤΟΡΕΩ; [cf. Lat. sterno, struo, etc.; Eng. strew, straw, etc.]; see Curtius § 227); *to spread*: ἱμάτια ἐν τῇ ὁδῷ, Mt. xxi. 8; εἰς τ. ὁδόν, Mk. xi. 8, (πέδον πεδάσμασι, Aeschyl. Ag. 909; εὔμασι πόρον, ib. 921). sc. τὴν κλίνην (which Grk. writ. fr. Hom. down often add, and also λέχος, λέκτρον, etc. [cf. W. 594 (552); B. § 130, 5]) τινί, Acts ix. 34 [A.V. *make thy bed*]; *to spread with couches* or *divans* τὸ ἀνάγαιον, pass. [A.V. *furnished*], Mk. xiv. 15; Lk. xxii. 12. [COMP.: κατα-, ὑπο- στρώννυμι.] *

see 4767 St. στυγητός, -όν, (στυγέω to hate), *hated*, Aeschyl. Prom. 592; *detestable* [A. V. *hateful*]: Tit. iii. 3; στυγητὸν κ. θεομισητὸν πρᾶγμα, of adultery, Philo de decal. § 24 fin.; ἔρως, Heliod. 5, 29.*

4768 στυγνάζω; 1 aor. ptcp. στυγνάσας; (στυγνός sombre, gloomy); *to be sad, to be sorrowful*: prop. ἐπί τινι [R.V. *his countenance fell at* etc.], Mk. x. 22; metaph. of the sky covered with clouds [A. V. *to be lowering*], Mt. xvi. 3 [T br. WH reject the pass.]. (Schol. on Aeschyl. Pers. 470; Sept. thrice for שָׁמֵם, to be amazed, astonished, ἐπί τινα, Ezek. xxvii. 35; xxxii. 10; στυγνότης, of the gloominess of the sky, Polyb. 4, 21, 1.) *

4769 στῦλος [R G WH (Tr in 1 Tim. iii. 15; Rev. x. 1)], more correctly στύλος [so L T (Tr in Gal. ii. 9; Rev. iii. 12)]; see Passow [or L. and S.] s. v. fin. [cf. Chandler

§§ 274, 275; *Lipsius*, Gram. Untersuch. p. 43], -ου, ὁ, [fr. Aeschyl. and Hdt. down], Sept. often for עַמּוּד, *a pillar, column*: στῦλοι πυρός, *pillars of fire*, i. e. flames rising like columns, Rev. x. 1; ποιήσω αὐτὸν στῦλον ἐν τῷ ναῷ τοῦ θεοῦ μου, i. e. (dropping the fig.) I will assign him a firm and abiding place in the everlasting kingdom of God, Rev. iii. 12; used of persons to whose eminence and strength the stability and authority of any institution or organization are due, Gal. ii. 9 [where cf. Bp. Lghtft.]; Clem. Rom. 1 Cor. 5, 2 and the note in Gebhardt and Harnack, (στῦλοι οἴκων εἰσὶ παῖδες ἄρσενες, Eur. Iph. T. 57; exx. fr. [Jewish writ. are given by Schoettgen (on Gal. l. c.) and fr.] eccles. writ. by *Suicer*, Thes. ii. p. 1045 sq.; *columen reipublicae*, Cic. pro Sest. 8, 19, and often elsewh. in Lat. auth.); *a prop* or *support*: τῆς ἀληθείας, 1 Tim. iii. 15.*

4770 Στωϊκός [(WH Στωικός), L T Στοϊκός, see Tdf.'s note on Acts as below; *WH.* App. p. 152], -ή, -όν, *Stoic*, pertaining to the Stoic philosophy, the author of which, Zeno of Citium, taught at Athens in the portico called ἡ ποικίλη στοά: οἱ Στωϊκοὶ φιλόσοφοι, Acts xvii. 18. [(Diog. Laërt. 7, 5; al.)] *

4771 σύ, pron. of the second pers. (Dor. and Aeol. τύ, Boeot. τού), gen. σοῦ, dat. σοί, acc. σέ (which oblique cases are enclitic, unless a preposition precede; yet πρός σε is written [uniformly in Rec. (exc. Mt. xxvi. 18), in Grsb. (exc. Jn. xxi. 22, 23), in Treg. (exc. Mt. xxvi. 18; Acts xxiii. 30), in Lchm. (exc. Mt. xxvi. 18; Jn. xvii. 11, 13; xxi. 22, 23; Acts xxiii. 30), in Tdf. (exc. Mt. xxvi. 18; Lk. i. 19; Jn. xvii. 11, 13; Jn. xxi. 22; Acts xxiii. 18, 30; 1 Tim. iii. 14; Tit. iii. 12); also by WH in Mt. xxv. 39], see ἐγώ, 2; *Lipsius*, Grammat. Untersuch. p. 62 sq. [W. § 6, 3; B. 31 (27)]); plur. ὑμεῖς, etc.; Lat. *tu*, etc.. *vos*, etc.; *thou*, etc., *ye*, etc. The nominatives σύ and ὑμεῖς are expressed for emphasis — before a vocative, as σὺ Βηθλεέμ, Mt. ii. 6; σὺ παιδίον (Lcian. dial. deor. 2, 1), Lk. i. 76; add, Mt. xvii. 5; Acts i. 24; 1 Tim. vi. 11, etc.; ὑμεῖς οἱ Φαρισαῖοι, Lk. xi. 39; — or when the pron. has a noun or a ptcp. added to it in apposition in order to define it more sharply, as σὺ Ἰουδαῖος ὤν (*thou, being a Jew*), Jn. iv. 9, cf. Gal. ii. 14; ὑμεῖς πονηροὶ ὄντες, Mt. vii. 11; — or when several are addressed who are at the same time particularized, σύ . . . σύ, Jas. ii. 3; also in antithesis, Mt. iii. 14; vi. 17; xi. 3; Mk. xiv. 36; Lk. xvi. 7; Jn. ii. 10; iii. 2; Acts x. 15; 1 Co. iii. 23; Jas. ii. 18, and very often; sometimes the antithetic term is suppressed, but is easily understood from the context: εἰ σὺ εἶ, *if it be thou*, and not an apparition, Mt. xiv. 28; add, Lk. xv. 31; xvii. 8, etc.; — or when a particle is added, as σὺ οὖν (at the close of an argument, when the discourse reverts to the person to be directly addressed), Lk. iv. 7; Jn. viii. 5; Acts xxiii. 21; 2 Tim. ii. 1, 3; σὺ δέ (in contrasts), Lk. ix. 60; 2 Tim. iii. 10; Tit. ii. 1; Heb. i. 11, etc.; ὑμεῖς δέ, Mt. xxi. 13; Jas. ii. 6; καὶ σύ, *and thou, thou also, thou too*, Mt. xi. 23; xxvi. 69, 73; Lk. x. 15; xix. 19, 42; xxii. 58; plur., Mt. xv. 3, 16; Lk. xvii. 10; before the 2d pers. of the verb where the person is to be emphasized (like the Germ. *du, ihr eben, du* da, 'it is *thou*,' '*thou* art the very man,' etc.), σὺ εἶ, Mt. xxvii. 11; Mk. xv. 2; Lk. xxiii. 3; Jn. i. 19; iii. 10; iv. 12; viii. 53; Acts xxiii. 3, etc.; plur. Lk. ix. 55 Rec.; σὺ λέγεις, εἶπας, Mt. xxvi. 25; xxvii. 11; Mk. xv. 2; it is used also without special emphasis ([cf. B. § 129, 12, and] see ἐγώ, 1), Mk. xiv. 68; Jn. viii. 13; Acts vii. 28, etc. The genitives σοῦ and ὑμῶν, joined to substantives, have the force of a possessive, and are placed — sometimes after the noun, as τὸν πόδα σου, Mt. iv. 6; τοὺς ἀδελφοὺς ὑμῶν, Mt. v. 47, and very often; — sometimes before the noun (see ἐγώ, 3 b.), as σοῦ αἱ ἁμαρτίαι, Lk. vii. 48; σοῦ τῆς νεότητος, 1 Tim. iv. 12; ὑμῶν δὲ καὶ τρίχες, Mt. x. 30; add, Mk. x. 43 [here Rec. after]; Lk. xii. 30; Jn. xvi. 6; Ro. xiv. 16; 2 Co. i. 24 [here now before, now after]; — sometimes between the article and noun, as τὴν ὑμῶν ἐπιπόθησιν, 2 Co. vii. 7; add, 2 Co. viii. 14 (13), 14; xiii. 9; Phil. i. 19, 25; ii. 30; Col. i. 8. ἔσται σου πάντα (πᾶσα), Lk. iv. 7 [cf. B. § 132, 11, I. a.]. It is added to the pronoun αὐτός: σοῦ αὐτῆς, Lk. ii. 35. On the phrase τί ἐμοὶ καὶ σοί, see ἐγώ, 4. [(Fr. Hom. on.)]

4772 συγγένεια, -ας, ἡ, (συγγενής), fr. Eur. and Thuc. down; [Sept.]; a. *kinship, relationship*. b. *kindred, relations* collectively, *family*: Lk. i. 61; Acts vii. 3, 14.*

4773 συγγενής, -ές, [acc. sing. συγγενῆ, and in Rom. xvi. 11 Treg. συγγενῆν; see ἄρσην], dat. plur. συγγενέσιν and (in Mk. vi. 4 T Tr [WH, also in Lk. ii. 44 WH] acc. to a barbarous declens., cf. [1 Macc. x. 89] B. 25 (22)) συγγενεῦσιν, (σύν and γένος), [fr. Pind., Aeschyl. down; Sept.], *of the same kin, akin to, related by blood*, (Plin. *congener*): Mk. vi. 4; Lk. ii. 44; xxi. 16; τινός, Lk. [i. 58]; xiv. 12; Jn. xviii. 26; Acts x. 24; Ro. xvi. 7, 11, 21, [see below]; ἡ συγγ. Lk. i. 36 R G Tr (Lev. xviii. 14); in a wider sense, *of the same race, a fellow-countryman*: Ro. ix. 3 [(so some take the word in xvi. 7, 11, 21, above; cf. Bp. Lghtft. on Philippians p. 175)].*

see 4773 συγγενίς, -ίδος, ἡ, (see the preceding word), a later Grk. word ([Plut. quaest. Rom. 6]; like εὐγενίς, cf. *Lob.* ad Phryn. p. 451 sq.; cf. W. 69 (67); Kühner i. p. 419 Anm 8), *a kinswoman*: τινός, Lk. i. 36 L T WH.*

4774 συγ-γνώμη [T WH συνγ., cf. σύν, II. fin.], -ης, ἡ, (συγγιγνώσκω, to agree with, to pardon; see γνώμη), fr. [Soph. and] Hdt. down, *pardon, indulgence*: κατὰ συγγνώμην, οὐ κατ' ἐπιταγήν, by way of concession or permission, not by way of command, 1 Co. vii. 6.*

4775 συγ-κάθημαι [T WH συν- (cf. σύν, II. fin.)]; fr. Hdt. down; [Sept.]; *to sit together, to sit with* another: μετά τινος, Mk. xiv. 54; τινί, with one, Acts xxvi. 30.*

4776 συγ-καθίζω [T WH συν- (cf. σύν, II. fin.)]: 1 aor. συνεκάθισα; (see καθίζω); a. trans. *to cause to sit down together, place together*: τινά, foll. by ἐν with a dat. of the place, Eph. ii. 6. b. intrans. *to sit down together*: Lk. xxii. 55 [where Lchm. txt. περικαθ.]. (Xen., Aristot., Plut., al.; Sept.)*

4777 συγ-κακοπαθέω [T WH συν- (cf. σύν, II. fin.)], -ῶ: 1 aor. impv. συγκακοπάθησον; (see κακοπαθέω); *to suffer hardships together with one*: 2 Tim. ii. 3 L T Tr WH; with a dat. com. added, τῷ εὐαγγελίῳ, for the benefit of the gospel, to further it, 2 Tim. i. 8. (Eccles. writ.)*

4778 συγ-κακουχέω [TWH συν- (cf. σύν, II. fin.)], -ῶ: pres. pass. inf. -χεῖσθαι; *to treat ill with another*; pass. *to be ill-treated* in company *with, share persecutions* or *come into a fellowship of ills*: τινί, with one, Heb. xi. 25. Not found elsewhere.*

4779 συγ-καλέω [T WH συν- (cf. σύν, II. fin.)], -ῶ; 1 aor. συνεκάλεσα; Mid., pres. συγκαλοῦμαι; 1 aor. συνεκαλεσάμην; fr. Hom. down; Sept. for קָרָא; *to call together, assemble*: τινάς, Lk. xv. 6 [here Tr mrg. has pres. mid.]; τὴν σπεῖραν, Mk. xv. 16; τὸ συνέδριον, Acts v. 21; mid. *to call together to one's self* [cf. B. § 135, 5]: τινάς, Lk. ix. 1; xv. [6 Tr mrg.], 9 [R G L Tr txt.]; xxiii. 13; Acts x. 24; xxviii. 17.*

4780 συγ-καλύπτω [(cf. σύν, II. fin.)]: pf. pass. ptcp. συγκεκαλυμμένος; fr. Hom. down; Sept. for כָּסָה; *to cover on all sides, to conceal entirely, to cover up completely*: τί, pass., Lk. xii. 2.*

4781 συγ-κάμπτω [T WH συν- (cf. σύν, II. fin.)]: 1 aor. impv. σύγκαμψον; *to bend together, to bend completely*: τὸν νῶτόν τινος, [A. V. *to bow down* one's *back*] i. e. metaph. *to subject one to error and hardness of heart*, a fig. taken from the bowing of the back by captives compelled to pass under the yoke, Ro. xi. 10, fr. Ps. lxviii. (lxix.) 24. (Xen., Plat., Aristot., al.)*

4782 συγ-κατα-βαίνω [T WH συν- (cf. σύν, II. fin.)]: 2 aor. ptcp. plur. συγκαταβάντες; *to go down with*: of those who descend together from a higher place to a lower, as from Jerusalem to Cæsarea, Acts xxv. 5. (Ps. xlviii. (xlix.) 18; Sap. x. 14; Aeschyl., Eur., Thuc., Polyb., Plut., al.; cf. *Lob.* ad Phryn. p. 398; [*Rutherford*, New Phryn. p. 485].)*

4783 συγ-κατά-θεσις [T WH συν- (cf. σύν, II. fin.)], -εως, ἡ, (συγκατατίθημι, q. v.), prop. *a putting together* or *joint deposit (of votes)*; hence *approval, assent, agreement*, [Cic. acad. 2, 12, 37 *adsensio atque adprobatio*]: 2 Co. vi. 16. (Polyb., Dion. Hal., Plut., al.)*

see 4784 St. συγ-κατα-τίθημι [T WH συν- (cf. σύν, II. fin.)]: Mid., pres. ptcp. συγκατατιθέμενος or pf. ptcp. συγκατατεθειμένος (see below); *to deposit together with* another; Mid. prop. *to deposit one's vote in the urn with* another (ψῆφον τιθέναι), hence *to consent to, agree with, vote for*: τῇ βουλῇ κ. τῇ πράξει τινός, Lk. xxiii. 51 [here L mrg. T Tr mrg. WH mrg. pres. ptcp., al. pf. ptcp.]. (Ex. xxiii. 1, 32; Plat. Gorg. p. 501 c., Isae., Dem., Polyb., Joseph., Plut., al.)*

4785 συγ-κατα-ψηφίζω [T WH συν- (cf. σύν, II. fin.)]: 1 aor. pass. συγκατεψηφίσθην; **1.** by depositing (κατά) a ballot in the urn (i. e. *by voting for*) *to assign one a place among* (σύν), *to vote one a place among*: τινὰ μετά τινων, Acts i. 26. **2.** mid. *to vote against with others*, i. e. *to condemn with others*: Plut. Them. 21. Not found elsewhere.*

4786 συγ-κεράννυμι [T WH συν- (cf. σύν, II. fin.)]: 1 aor. συνεκέρασα; pf. pass. ptcp. συγκεκραμένος and in L T Tr WH συγκεκερασμένος [see κεράννυμι, init.]; fr. [Aeschyl., Soph.], Hdt. down; *to mix together, commingle*; *to unite*: συνεκ. τὸ σῶμα, caused the several parts to combine into an organic structure, which is the body, [A.V. *tempered the body together*], 1 Co. xii. 24; τί τινι, to unite one thing to another: οὐκ ὠφέλησεν ... μὴ συγκεκραμένος [so R G T WH mrg., but L Tr WH txt. -νους] ... ἀκού-σασιν, 'the word heard did not profit them, because it had not united itself by faith to [cf. W. § 31, 10; B. § 133, 13] them that heard,' i. e. because the hearers had not by their faith let it find its way into their minds and made it their own; [or, acc. to the text of L Tr WH (R. V.), 'because they had not been united by faith with them that heard'], Heb. iv. 2.*

4787   συγ-κινέω, -ῶ: 1 aor. 3 pers. plur. συνεκίνησαν; to move together with others [Aristot.]; to throw into commotion, excite, stir up: τὸν λαόν, Acts vi. 12. (Polyb., Plut., Longin., al.) *

4788   συγ-κλείω [T WH συν- (cf. σύν, II. fin.)]: 1 aor. συν-έκλεισα; Pass., pres. ptcp. συγ-(συν-)κλειόμενος, Gal. iii. 23 L T Tr WH; but R G ibid. pf. ptcp. -κεκλεισμένος; fr. Hdt. down; Sept. chiefly for סָגַר and הִסְגִּיר, to shut up, (Lat. concludo), i. e.   **a.** to shut up together, enclose, [so s. v. σύν, II. 2; but others (e. g. Fritzsche as below; Meyer on Gal. iii. 22) would make the σύν- always intensive, as in b.]: a shoal of fishes in a net, Lk. v. 6.   **b.** to shut up on all sides, shut up completely; τινὰ εἴς τινα or τι, so to deliver one up to the power of a person or thing that he is completely shut in, as it were, without means of escape: τινὰ εἰς ἀπείθειαν, Ro. xi. 32 (εἰς ἀγῶνα, Polyb. 3, 63, 3; εἰς τοιαύτην ἀμηχανίαν συγκλεισθεὶς Ἀντίγονος μετεμέλετο, Diod. 19, 19; οὐ συνέ-κλεισάς με εἰς χεῖρας ἐχθροῦ, Ps. xxx. (xxxi.) 9; τὰ κτήνη εἰς θάνατον, Ps. lxxvii. (lxxviii.) 50; cf. Fritzsche, Ep. ad Rom. ii. p. 545 sq.); also τινὰ ὑπό τι, under the power of anything, i. e. so that he is held completely subject to it: ὑπὸ ἁμαρτίαν, Gal. iii. 22 (the Scripture has shut up or subjected, i. e. declared them to be subject); sc. ὑπὸ νόμον, with the addition of εἰς τὴν μέλλουσαν πίστιν ἀποκαλυφθῆναι, ib. 23 (see above ad init.); on these words see εἰς, B. II. 3 c. γ. p. 185ª bot.*

4789   συγ-κληρο-νόμος [T WH συν- (cf. σύν, II. fin.)], -ου, ὁ, ἡ, a fellow-heir, a joint-heir, (ἀνεψιὸς καὶ συγκληρονόμος, Philo, leg. ad Gaium § 10), (see κληρονόμος 1 b.): Ro. viii. 17; Eph. iii. 6; one who obtains something assigned to himself with others, a joint participant (see κληρονόμος, 2): with the gen. of the thing, Heb. xi. 9; 1 Pet. iii. 7. Not found elsewhere.*

4790   συγ-κοινωνέω [T WH συν- (cf. σύν, II. fin.)], -ῶ; 1 aor. subj. 2 pers. plur. συγκοινωνήσητε, ptcp. nom. plur. masc. συγκοινωνήσαντες; to become a partaker together with others, or to have fellowship with a thing: with a dat. of the thing, Eph. v. 11; Phil. iv. 14; Rev. xviii. 4. (with a gen. of the thing, Dem. p. 1299, 20; τινί τινος, Dio Cass. 37, 41; 77, 16.) *

4791   συγ-κοινωνός [T WH συν- (cf. σύν, II. fin.)], -όν, partici-pant with others in (anything), joint partner: with a gen. of the thing [cf. W. § 30, 8 a.], Ro. xi. 17; 1 Co. ix. 23; with the addition of the gen. of the pers. with whom one is partaker of a thing, Phil. i. 7; foll. by ἐν with a dat. of the thing, Rev. i. 9.*

4792   συγ-κομίζω: 1 aor. 3 pers. plur. συνεκόμισαν;   **1.** to carry or bring together, to collect [see σύν, II. 2]; to

house crops, gather into granaries: Hdt., Xen., Diod., Plut., al.; Job v. 26.   **2.** to carry with others, help in carrying out, the dead to be burned or buried (Soph. Aj. 1048; Plut. Sull. 38); to bury: Acts viii. 2.*

4793   συγ-κρίνω [T WH συν- (cf. σύν, II. fin.)]; 1 aor. inf. συγ-κρῖναι;   **1.** to join together fitly, compound, combine, (Epicharm. in Plut. mor. p. 110 a.; Plat., Aristot., al.): πνευματικοῖς πνευματικά, 1 Co. ii. 13 (for Paul, in deliver-ing the things disclosed to him by the Holy Spirit in speech derived not from rhetorical instruction but re-ceived from the same divine Spirit, 'combines spiritual things with spiritual', adapts the discourse to the subject; other interpretations are refuted by Meyer ad loc.; πνευματικοῖς is neut.; [but others would take it as masc. and give συγκ. the meaning to interpret (R. V. marg. interpreting spiritual things to spiritual men); cf. Sept. Gen. xl. 8, 16, 22; xli. 12, 15; Judg. vii. 15; Dan. v. 12, etc.; see Heinrici in Meyer 6te Aufl.]).   **2.** acc. to a use foreign to the earlier Greeks (who used παρα-βάλλω), but freq. fr. the time of Aristotle on (cf. Passow s. v. 2; [L. and S. s. v. II.]; Lob. ad Phryn. p. 278 sq.; [W. 23 (22)]), to compare: ἑαυτοὺς ἑαυτοῖς, 2 Co. x. 12 (Sap. vii. 29; xv. 18).*

4794   συγ-κύπτω [T WH συν- (cf. σύν, II. fin.)]; [fr. Hdt. down]; to bend completely forwards, to be bowed together, [cf. σύν, II. 3]: by disease, Lk. xiii. 11. ([Job ix. 27]; Sir. xii. 11; xix. 26.) *

4795   συγκυρία, -ας, ἡ, (συγκυρεῖν, to happen, turn out), acci-dent, chance: κατὰ συγκυρίαν, by chance, accidentally, Lk. x. 31. (Hippocr.; eccles. and Byzant. writ.; Grk. writ. fr. Polyb. down more com. use συγκύρησις and συγ-κύρημα [W. 24].) *

4796   συγ-χαίρω [T WH συν- (cf. σύν, II. fin.)]; impf. συνέχαι-ρον; 2 aor. συνεχάρην [pass. as act., so Veitch (s. v. χαίρω) etc.; al. act., after the analogy of verbs in -μι]; to rejoice with, take part in another's joy, (Aeschyl., Arstph., Xen, al.): with a dat. of the pers. with whom one rejoices, Lk. i. 58 (cf. 14); xv. 6, 9; with a dat. of the thing, 1 Co. xiii. 6; to rejoice together, of many, 1 Co. xii. 26; to con-gratulate (Aeschin., Polyb., [Plut.; cf. Bp. Lghtft. on Phil. as below; 3 Macc. i. 8; Barn. ep. 1, 3 (and Müller ad loc.)]): with the dat. of the pers. Phil. ii. 17 sq.*

4797   συγ-χέω, συγ-χύνω, and συγ-χύννω, [T WH συν- (cf. σύν, II. fin.)] (see ἐκχέω, init.): impf., 3 pers. sing. συνέ-χυνε (Acts ix. 22 R G L Tr, -χυννεν T WH), 3 pers. plur. συνέχεον (Acts xxi. 27 R G T Tr WH [but some would make this a 2 aor., see reff. s. v. ἐκχέω, init.]); 1 aor. 3 pers. plur. συνέχεαν (Acts xxi. 27 L [see ἐκχέω, init.]); Pass., pres. 3 pers. sing. συγ(T WH συν-)χύννεται (Acts xxi. 31 L T Tr WH); pf. 3 pers. sing. συγκέχυται (Acts xxi. 31 R G), ptcp. fem. συγ(T WH συν-)κεχυμένη (Acts xix. 32 R G L T Tr WH); 1 aor. 3 pers. sing. συνεχύθη (Acts ii. 6 R G L T Tr WH); fr. Hom. down; to pour together, commingle: ἦν ἡ ἐκκλησία συγκεχυμένη, was irreg-ularly assembled [al. 'in confusion'], Acts xix. 32; to disturb, τινά, the mind of one, to stir up to tumult or out-break, Acts xxi. 27, 31; to confound or bewilder, Acts ii. 6; ix. 22.*

4798 συγ-χράομαι [T WH συν-], -ῶμαι ; to use with any one, use jointly, (Polyb., Diod., [Philo]) ; with the dat. of a pers., to associate with, to have dealings with : Jn. iv. 9 [Tdf. om. WH br. the cl. οὐ γὰρ . . . Σαμαρ.].*

see 4797 συγ-χύνω and συγχύννω, see συγχέω.

4799 σύγ-χυσις, -εως, ἡ, (συγχέω), [fr. Eur., Thuc., Plat. down], confusion, disturbance : of riotous persons, Acts xix. 29 (1 S. v. 11).*

4800 συ-ζάω [L T Tr WH συν- (cf. σύν, II. fin.)] ; fut. συζήσω ; to live together with one [cf. σύν, II. 1] : of physical life on earth, opp. to συναποθανεῖν, 2 Co. vii. 3 ; τῷ Χριστῷ, to live a new life in union with the risen Christ, i. e. a life dedicated to God, Ro. vi. 8, cf. De Wette [or Meyer ad loc.] ; to live a blessed life with him after death, 2 Tim. ii. 11. (Plat., Dem., Aristot., al.) *

4801 συ-ζεύγνυμι : 1 aor. συνέζευξα ; fr. Eur. and Xen. down ; prop. to fasten to one yoke, yoke together : ἵππους, Xen. Cyr. 2, 2, 26 ; trop. to join together, unite : τί or τινά, of the marriage tie, Mt. xix. 6 ; Mk. x. 9, (νόμος συζευγνὺς ἄνδρα καὶ γυναῖκα, Xen. oec. 7, 30, and often so in Grk. writ.).*

4802 συ-ζητέω [L T Tr WH συν- (cf. σύν, II. fin.)], -ῶ ; impf. 3 pers. sing. συνεζήτει ; **a.** to seek or examine together (Plat.). **b.** in the N. T. to discuss, dispute, [question (A. V. often)] : absol., [Mk. xii. 28] ; Lk. xxiv. 15 ; τινί, with one, Mk. viii. 11 ; ix. 14 [R G L] ; Acts vi. 9 ; in the same sense πρός τινα, Mk. ix. [14 T Tr WH], 16 (where read πρὸς αὑτούς, not with Rec.bez elz G πρὸς αὐτούς [see αὐτοῦ, p. 87]) ; Acts ix. 29 ; πρὸς ἑαυτούς [L Tr WH mrg. or πρ. αὑτούς Rbez elz G] equiv. to πρὸς ἀλλήλους, Mk. i. 27 [where T WH txt. simply αὐτούς as subj.] ; πρὸς ἑαυτούς with the addition of an indirect quest. τὸ τίς etc. with the optat. [cf. B. § 139, 60 ; W. § 41 b. 4 c.], Lk. xxii. 23 ; τί, with the indic., Mk. ix. 10.*

4803 συ-ζήτησις [συν- L Tr mrg. (cf. σύν, II. fin.)], -εως, ἡ, (συζητέω), mutual questioning, disputation, discussion : Acts xv. 2 Rec., 7 R G L Tr mrg.; xxviii. 29 yet G L T Tr WH om. the vs. (Cic. ad fam. 16, 21, 4 ; Philo, opif. mund. § 17 fin. [(var. lect.) ; quod det. pot. § 1] ; legg. alleg. 3, 45.) *

4804 συ-ζητητής [L T Tr WH συν- (cf. σύν, II. fin.)], -οῦ, ὁ, (συζητέω), a disputer, i. e. a learned disputant, sophist : 1 Co. i. 20. (Ignat. ad Eph. 18 [quotation].) *

4805 σύ-ζυγος [L T Tr WH συν- (cf. σύν, II. fin.)], -ον, (συζεύγνυμι), yoked together ; used by Grk. writ. [fr. Aeschyl. down] of those united by the bond of marriage, relationship, office, labor, study, business, or the like ; hence, a yoke-fellow, consort, comrade, colleague, partner. Accordingly, in Phil. iv. 3 most interpreters hold that by the words γνήσιε σύζυγε Paul addresses some particular associate in labor for the gospel. But as the word is found in the midst of (three) proper names, other expositors more correctly take it that also as a proper name ([WH mrg. Σύνζυγε] ; see Laurent, Ueber Synzygos in the Zeitschr. f. d. Luther. Theol. u. Kirche for 1865, p. 1 sqq. [reprinted in his Neutest. Studien, p. 134 sq.]) ; and Paul, alluding (as in Philem. 11) to the meaning of the word as an appellative, speaks of him as 'a genuine Synzygus', i. e. a colleague in fact as well as in name.

Cf. Meyer and Wiesinger ad loc. ; [Hackett in B. D. Am. ed. s. v. Yoke-fellow].*

4806 συ-ζωο-ποιέω, -ῶ : 1 aor. συνεζωοποίησα ; to make one alive together with another (Vulg. convivifico) : Christians, τῷ Χριστῷ [L br. adds ἐν, so WH mrg.], with Christ, Eph. ii. 5 ; σὺν τῷ Χρ. Col. ii. 13 ; in both these pass. new moral life is referred to.*

4807 συκάμινος, -ου, ἡ, Hebr. שִׁקְמָה (of which only the plur. שִׁקְמִים is found in the O. T., 1 K. x. 27 ; Is. ix. 10 ; Am. vii. 14 ; once שִׁקְמוֹת), a sycamine, a tree having the form and foliage of the mulberry, but fruit resembling the fig (i. q. συκομορέα, q. v. [but Tristram, Nat. Hist. of the Bible, 2d ed. p. 396 sq. ; BB.DD., etc., regard the sycamine as the black-mulberry tree, and the sycomore as the fig-mulberry]) : Lk. xvii. 6. (Often in Theophr.; Strab. 17, p. 823 ; Diod. 1, 34 ; Dioscorid. 1, 22.) [Cf. Vaniček, Fremdwörter, p. 54 ; esp. Löw, Aram. Pflanzennamen, § 332, cf. § 338 ; BB.DD. u. s. ; 'Bible Educator' iv. 343 ; Pickering, Chron. Hist. of Plants, pp. 106, 258.] *

4808 συκῆ, -ῆς, ἡ, (contr. fr. συκέα), fr. Hom. down, Hebr. תְּאֵנָה, a fig-tree : Mt. xxi. 19-21 ; xxiv. 32 ; Mk. xi. 13, 20 sq. ; xiii. 28 ; Lk. xiii. 6 sq. ; xxi. 29 ; Jn. i. 48 (49), 50 (51) ; Jas. iii. 12 ; Rev. vi. 13. [Cf. Löw, Aram. Pflanzennamen, § 335.] *

see 4809 St. συκο-μορέα (Lchm. συκομωρέα, [Rec. st bez -μωραία, cf. Tdf.'s note on Lk. as below ; WH. App. pp. 152 and 151]), -ας, ἡ, (fr. σῦκον and μορέα the mulberry tree), i. q. συκάμινος [but see the word, and reff.], a sycomore-tree : Lk. xix. 4. (Geop. 10, 3, 7.) *

4810 σῦκον, -ου, τό, fr. Hom. down, Hebr. תְּאֵנָה, a fig, the ripe fruit of ἡ συκῆ [q. v.] : Mt. vii. 16 ; Mk. xi. 13 ; Lk. vi. 44 ; Jas. iii. 12.*

4811 συκοφαντέω, -ῶ ; 1 aor. ἐσυκοφάντησα ; (fr. συκοφάντης, and this fr. σῦκον 'fig', and φαίνω 'to show'. At Athens those were called συκοφάνται whose business it was to inform against any one whom they might detect exporting figs out of Attica ; and as sometimes they seem to have extorted money from those loath to be exposed, the name συκοφάντης from the time of Aristophanes down was a general term of opprobrium to designate a malignant informer, a calumniator ; a malignant and base accuser from love of gain, [but cf. L. and S. s. v.] ; hence the verb συκοφαντῶ signifies) **1.** to accuse wrongfully, to calumniate, to attack by malicious devices, (Arstph., Xen., Plat., al.). **2.** to exact money wrongfully ; to extort from, defraud : Lk. iii. 14 [here R. V. marg. accuse wrongfully] ; with a gen. of the pers. and acc. of the thing, Lk. xix. 8 (τριάκοντα μνᾶς παρά τινος· Lys. p. 177, 32. Sept. for עָשַׁק, to oppress, defraud, Job xxxv. 9 ; Eccl. iv. 1 ; Ps. cxviii. (cxix.) 122 ; πένητα, Prov. xiv. 31 ; xxii. 16 ; πτωχούς, Prov. xxviii. 3).*

4812 συλαγωγέω, -ῶ ; (σύλη booty, spoil, [cf. συλάω, init.], and ἄγω) ; to carry off booty : τινά, to carry one off as a captive (and slave), θυγατέρα, Heliod. 10, 35 ; παρθένον, Nicet. hist. 5 p. 96 ; to lead away from the truth and subject to one's sway [R. V. make spoil of], Col. ii. 8 (Tatian. or. ad Gr. c. 22, p. 98 ed. Otto).*

4813 συλάω, -ῶ : 1 aor. ἐσύλησα; ([akin to] σύλη 'spoil' [allied with σκῦλον (q. v., yet cf.) Curtius p. 696]); fr. Hom. down; *to rob, despoil:* τινά, 2 Co. xi. 8.*

4814 συλ-λαλέω, [T WH συν- (cf. σύν, II. fin.; *Tdf.* Proleg. p. 76)], -ῶ; impf. 3 pers. plur. συνελάλουν; 1 aor. συνελάλησα; *to talk with:* τινί, with one, Mk. ix. 4; Lk. ix. 30; xxii. 4, (Ex. xxxiv. 35; Is. vii. 6; Polyb. 4, 22, 8); μετά τινος, Mt. xvii. 3; Acts xxv. 12; πρὸς ἀλλήλους [R.V. *spake together one with another*], Lk. iv. 36. [Cf. W. § 52, 4, 15.]*

4815 συλ-λαμβάνω [sometimes συν- (see below)]: fut. 2 pers. sing. συλλήψῃ (L T Tr WH συλλήμψῃ [see M, μ]), Lk. i. 31; pf. [3d pers. sing. συνείληφεν, Lk. i. 36 Tr txt. WH], ptcp. fem. συνειληφυῖα [ib. R G L T]; 2 aor. συνέλαβον; 1 aor. pass. συνελήφθην (L T Tr WH συνελήμφθην; see M, μ), Mid., pres. impv. 2 pers. sing. συλλαμβάνου (T Tr WH συν-, cf. σύν, II. fin.; *Tdf.* Proleg. p. 76) Phil. iv. 3; 2 aor. συνελαβόμην; fr. Aeschyl. and Hdt. down; Sept. for תָּפַשׂ and לָכַד; **1.** Active, **a.** *to seize, take:* τινά, one as a prisoner, Mt. xxvi. 55; Mk. xiv. 48; Lk. xxii. 54; Jn. xviii. 12 [cf. W. 275 (259)]; Acts i. 16; xii. 3; xxiii. 27; ἄγραν ἰχθύων, Lk. v. 9. **b.** *to conceive,* of a woman (often so in Sept. for הָרָה): absol. Lk. i. 24 (Aristot. h. a. 7, 1 p. 582ᵃ, 19; gen. an. 1, 19 p. 727ᵇ, 8 sq.; [Plut. de vitand. aere alien. 4. 4; cf. W. 593 (552)]; B. § 130, 5]); with ἐν γαστρί added, Lk. i. 31; τινά, a son, [Lk. i. 36]; with ἐν τῇ κοιλίᾳ added, Lk. ii. 21; metaph. of 'lust,' whose impulses a man indulges, Jas. i. 15. **2.** Mid. **a.** *to seize for one's self;* in a hostile sense, *to make* (one a permanent) *prisoner:* τινά, Acts xxvi. 21. **b.** with the dat. of a pers. *to take hold together with* one, *to assist, help:* Lk. v. 7; *to succor,* Phil. iv. 3, (Soph. Phil. 282; Plat. Theag. p. 129 c.; Diod. 11, 40; in this sense in Grk. writ. more commonly in the active).*

4816 συλ-λέγω [cf. σύν, II. fin.; *Tdf.* Proleg. p. 76]; fut. συλλέξω; 1 aor. συνέλεξα; pres. pass. 3 pers. sing. συλλέγεται; fr. Hom. down; Sept. chiefly for לָקַט; *to gather up* [cf. σύν, II. 2]: τὰ ζιζάνια (for removal fr. the field), Mt. xiii. 28 sq. 30; pass. ib. 40; τὶ ἀπό with a gen. of the thing, Mt. vii. 16 [cf. W. § 58, 9 b. a.]; τὶ ἐκ with a gen. of the place, to collect in order to carry off, Mt. xiii. 41; in order to keep, Lk. vi. 44; τὶ εἴς τι, into a vessel, Mt. xiii. 48.*

4817 συλ-λογίζομαι: (impf. συνελογιζόμην Lchm.) 1 aor. συνελογισάμην; **a.** *to bring together accounts, reckon up, compute,* (Hdt. et sqq.). **b.** *to reckon with one's self, to reason,* (Plat., Dem., Polyb., al.): Lk. xx. 5.*

4818 συλ-λυπέω: **1.** *to affect with grief together:* Aristot. eth. Nic. 9, 11, 4 p. 1171ᵇ, 7. **2.** Pass., pres. ptcp. συλλυπούμενος [T WH συν- cf. σύν, II. fin. (*Tdf.* Proleg. p. 76)]; *to grieve with one's self* [see σύν, II. 4 (so Fritz., De Wette, al.; but al. regard the σύν as 'sympathetic'; cf. Meyer, Weiss, Morison, on Mk. as below)], *be inwardly grieved,* (Hdt., Plat., Polyb., Diod.): of the pain of indignation, ἐπί τινι, Mk. iii. 5.*

4819 συμ-βαίνω [ξυμ- Rec.ᵇᵉᶻ in 1 Pet. iv. 12; see Σ, σ, ς fin.]; impf. συνέβαινον; 2 aor. συνέβην, ptcp. συμβάς; pf. συμ-βέβηκα; fr. [Aeschyl.], Hdt. down; **1.** *to walk with the feet near together.* **2.** *to come together, meet* with one; hence **3.** of things which fall out at the same time, *to happen, turn out, come to pass,* (so occasionally in the Sept. for קָרָה and קָרָא); as very often in Grk. writ. (Sept. Gen. xlii. 4; xliv. 29), συμβαίνει τί τινι, something befalls, happens to, one: Mk. x. 32; Acts xx. 19; 1 Co. x. 11; [1 Pet. iv. 12]; 2 Pet. ii. 22; τὸ συμβεβηκός τινι, Acts iii. 10 (Sus. 26); absol. τὰ συμβεβηκότα, the things that had happened, Lk. xxiv. 14 (1 Macc. iv. 26; [Joseph. c. Ap. 1, 22, 17]); συνέβη foll. by an acc. with inf. *it happened* [A. V. *so it was*] *that,* etc.: Acts xxi. 35 [cf. W. 323 (303)], exx. fr. prof. auth. are given by Grimm on 2 Macc. iii. 2.*

4820 συμ-βάλλω [συν- WH (so Tdf. exc. Lk. xiv. 31); cf. σύν, II. fin.]; impf. συνέβαλλον; 2 aor. συνέβαλον; 2 aor. mid. συνεβαλόμην; fr. Hom. down; *to throw together, to bring together*; **a.** λόγους (Lat. *sermones conferre*), to converse, Eur. Iphig. Aul. 830; with λόγους omitted [cf. Eng. *confer*], Plut. mor. p. 222 c. (W. 593 (552); [B. 145 (127)]): τινί, *to dispute with* one, Actᵉ xvii. 18 [where A.V. *encountered* (cf. c. below)]; πρὸς ἀλλήλους, to confer with one another, deliberate among themselves, Acts iv. 15. **b.** *to bring together in one's mind, confer with one's self* [cf. σύν, II. 4], *to consider, ponder:* ἐν τῇ καρδίᾳ, to revolve in the mind, Lk. ii. 19 (συμβαλὼν τῷ λογισμῷ τὸ ὄναρ, Joseph. antt. 2, 5, 3). **c.** intrans. (W. § 38, 1; [B. § 130, 4]), *to come together, meet*: τινί, to meet one (on a journey), Acts xx. 14 (Hom. Od. 21, 15; Joseph. antt. 2, 7, 5); *to encounter* in a hostile sense: τινί, *to fight with* one (1 Macc. iv. 34; 2 Macc. viii. 23; xiv. 17; Polyb. 1, 9, 7; 3, 111, 1, and often), with εἰς πόλεμον added, Lk. xiv. 31 (εἰς μάχην, Polyb. 3, 56, 6; Joseph. antt. 12, 8, 4; πρὸς μάχην, Polyb. 10, 37, 4). Mid. *to bring together of one's property, to contribute, aid, help*: πολύ τινι, one, Acts xviii. 27; often so in Grk. auth. also, esp. Polyb.; cf. *Schweighäuser,* Lex. Polyb. p. 576; *Passow* s. v. 1 b. a.; [L. and S. s. v. I. 2]; *Grimm,* Exeget. Hdbch. on Sap. v. 8.*

4821 συμ-βασιλεύω [T συν- so now WH (in exx. as below); cf. σύν, II. fin.): fut. συμβασιλεύσω; 1 aor. συνεβασίλευσα; *to reign together:* τινί, with one; prop., Polyb. 30, 2, 4; Lcian. dial. deor. 16, 2; often in Plut. [also in Dion. Hal., Strabo]; metaph. to possess supreme honor, liberty, blessedness, with one in the kingdom of God: 1 Co. iv. 8 [cf. W. 41 b. 5 N. 2; B. § 139, 10]; 2 Tim. ii. 12; see βασιλεύω.*

4822 συμ-βιβάζω [WH συν- (so Tdf. in Eph. iv. 16; Col. ii. 19); cf. σύν, II. fin.]; 1 aor. συνεβίβασα (Acts xix. 33 L T Tr WH, but see below); Pass., pres. ptcp. συμβιβαζόμενος; 1 aor. ptcp. συμβιβασθείς; (βιβάζω to mount the female, copulate with her; to leap, cover, of animals; allow to be covered, admit to cover); **1.** *to cause to coalesce, to join together, put together:* τὸ σῶμα, pass., of the parts of the body 'knit together' into one whole, compacted together, Eph. iv. 16; Col. ii. 19; *to unite or knit together* in affection, pass., Col. ii. 2 [cf. W. § 63, 2 a.; B. § 144, 13 a.] (to reconcile one to another, Hdt. 1,

74; Thuc. 2, 29). **2.** *to put together in one's mind, to compare*; by comparison *to gather, conclude, consider*: foll. by ὅτι, Acts xvi. 10 (Plat. Hipp. min. p. 369 d.; de rep. 6 p. 504 a.). **3.** *to cause a person to unite with one in a conclusion or come to the same opinion, to prove, demonstrate*: foll. by ὅτι, Acts ix. 22 ([Aristot. top. 7, 5 p. 151ᵃ, 36]; foll. by ὡς, [Aristot. rhet. Alex. 4 p. 1426ᵃ, 37: etc.]; Jambl. vit. Pyth. c. 13 § 60; foll. by the acc. with inf., Ocell. Lucan. 3, 3); by a usage purely Biblical, w. the acc. of a pers., *to teach, instruct*, one: 1 Co. ii. 16; for הֵבִין, Is. xl. 14; for הוֹדִיעַ, Ex. xviii. 16; Deut. iv. 9; Is. xl. 13 Alex., Ald., etc.; for הוֹרָה, Ex. iv. 12, 15; Lev. x. 11; הִשְׂכִּיל בִּינָה, Theodot. Dan. ix. 22. (The reading συνεβίβασαν in Acts xix. 33, given by codd. א A B etc. [and adopted by L T Tr WH] yields no sense; [but it may be translated (with R. V. mrg.) 'some *of the multitude instructed Alexander*', etc.; R. V. txt. translates it *they brought Alexander out of the multitude*, etc.].) *

4823   **συμ-βουλεύω**; 1 aor. συνεβούλευσα; 1 aor. mid. συνεβουλευσάμην; fr. [Theogn., Soph.], Hdt. down; Sept. for יָעַץ and נוֹעָץ; **1.** *to give counsel*: τινί, Jn. xviii. 14; foll. by an inf. Rev. iii. 18. **2.** Mid. *to take counsel with others, take counsel together, to consult, deliberate*: foll. by ἵνα (see ἵνα, II. 2 a.), Mt. xxvi. 4; Jn. xi. 53 [RG Tr mrg.]; foll. by a telic inf., Acts ix. 23.*

4824   **συμ-βούλιον**, -ου, τό, (σύμβουλος); **1.** *counsel*, which is given, taken, entered upon, (Plut. Romul. 14): λαμβάνω (on this phrase see λαμβάνω, I. 6), Mt. xii. 14; xxii. 15; xxvii. 1, 7; xxviii. 12; ποιῶ, to consult, deliberate, Mk. iii. 6 [Tr txt. WH txt. ἐδίδουν σ.]; xv. 1 [T WH mrg. ἑτοιμάσαντες σ.; cf. Weiss ad loc.]. **2.** *a council*, i. e. *an assembly of counsellors* or *persons in consultation* (Plut. Luc. 26): Acts xxv. 12 (the governors and procurators of provinces had a board of assessors or advisers with whom they took counsel before rendering judgment; see Cic. ad fam. 8, 8; Verr. 2, 13; Sueton. vit. Tiber. 33; Lamprid. vit. Alex. Sever. c. 46; cf. Joseph. b. j. 2, 16, 1).*

4825   **σύμ-βουλος**, -ου, ὁ, (σύν and βουλή), *an adviser, counsellor*: Ro. xi. 34 fr. Is. xl. 13. (Tragg., [Hdt.], Arstph., Xen., Plat., al.) *

4826   **Συμεών**, ὁ, [indecl., B. 16 (14)], (for deriv. see Σίμων), *Simeon* [so A. V. uniformly (on 2 Pet. i. 1 see 5 below)]; **1.** the second son of Jacob by Leah (Gen. xxix. 33): Rev. vii. 7. **2.** [R. V. *Symeon*], one of Abraham's descendants: Lk. iii. 30. **3.** that devout *Simeon* who took the infant Jesus in his arms in the temple: Lk. ii. 25 [here Rec.ᵇᵉᶻ Σιμεών], 34. **4.** *Symeon* [so R. V.] surnamed Niger, one of the teachers of the church at Antioch: Acts xiii. 1. **5.** Peter the apostle: Acts xv. 14 [R. V. *Symeon*]; 2 Pet. i. 1 [here L WH txt. Σίμων, and A. V. (R. V.) *Simon*]; respecting him see Σίμων, 1 and Πέτρος, fin.*

4827   **συμ-μαθητής** [T WH συν- (cf. σύν, II. fin.)], -οῦ, ὁ, *a fellow-disciple*: Jn. xi. 16 (Plat. Euthyd. p. 272 c.; Aesop. fab. 48). (Phrynichus says that σύν is not prefixed to

πολίτης, δημότης, φυλέτης, and the like, but only to those nouns which denote an association which is πρόσκαιρος i. e. temporary, as συνέφηβος, συνθιασώτης, συμπότης. The Latin also observes the same distinction and says *commilito meus*, but not *concivis*, but *civis meus*; see Phryn. ed. *Lob.* p. 471; [cf. p. 172; Win. 25].) *

συμ-μαρτυρέω, -ῶ [T WH συν- (cf. σύν, II. fin.)]; *to bear*   **4828** *witness with, bear joint witness* (with one): συμμαρτυρούσης τῆς συνειδήσεως, their conscience *also* bearing witness, Ro. ii. 15 (i. e. together with the deeds of the Gentiles, which accord with the law of God and so bear witness [cf. W. 580 (539)]); foll. by ὅτι, Ro. ix. 1 (besides the fact that the close fellowship I have with Christ compels me to tell the truth); τῷ πνεύματι ἡμῶν, with our spirit already giving its testimony, Ro. viii. 16. Mid. pres. 1 pers. sing. συμμαρτυροῦμαι, *I testify on my own behalf besides* (i. e. besides those things which I have already testified in this book), Rev. xxii. 18 Rec.; but the true reading here, μαρτυρῶ, was restored by Grsb. (Soph., Eur., Thuc., Plat., al.) *

συμ-μερίζω [WH συν- (cf. σύν, II. fin.)]: *to divide at*   see **4829 St.** *the same time, divide together*; *to assign a portion*; Mid. pres. 3 pers. plur. συμμερίζονται: τινί, *to divide together with one* (so that a part comes to me, a part to him), [R.V. *have their portion with*], 1 Co. ix. 13. [Diod., Dion. Hal., Diog. Laërt.] *

συμ-μέτοχος [T WH συν- (cf. σύν, II. fin.)], -ον, *partaking together with one, a joint-partaker*: τινός, of something, Eph. iii. 6; v. 7. (Joseph. b. j. 1, 24, 6; Just. Mart. apol. 2, 13.) *   **4830**

συμ-μιμητής [T WH συν- (cf. σύν, II. fin.)], -οῦ, ὁ, *an imitator with others*: τινός, of one, Phil. iii. 17. Not found elsewhere.*   **4831**

συμ-μορφίζω [Tdf. συν- (cf. σύν, II. fin.)] : pres. pass.   **(4831α);** ptcp. συμμορφιζόμενος; (σύμμορφος); *to bring to the same*   see **4833** *form with some other pers. or thing, to render like*, (Vulg. *configuro*): τινί [R.V. *becoming conformed unto*], Phil. iii. 10 L T Tr WH. Not found elsewhere.*

σύμ-μορφος, -ον, (σύν and μορφή), *having the same form*   **4832** *as another* [cf. σύν, II. 1], (Vulg. *conformis, configuratus*); *similar, conformed to*, [Lcian. amor. 39]: τινός (cf. Matthiae § 379 p. 864; [W. 195 (184); B. § 132, 23]), Ro. viii. 29 (see εἰκών, a.); τινί (Nicand. th. 321), Phil. iii. 21 [(here Tdf. σύνμ.); cf. W. 624 (580)].*

συμ-μορφόω, -ῶ: pres. pass. ptcp. συμμορφούμενος; i.q.   **4833; see** συμμορφίζω, q. v.: Phil. iii. 10 Rec. Nowhere else.*   **(4831α)**

συμ-παθέω [T WH συν- (cf. σύν, II. fin.)], -ῶ: 1 aor.   **4834** συνεπάθησα; (συμπαθής); **a.** *to be affected with the same feeling as another, to sympathize with*, (Aristot., Plut.). **b.** in reference to the wretched, *to feel for, have compassion on*, (Vulg. *compatior*): τινί, Heb. iv. 15 [A. V. *to be touched with the feeling of*]; x. 34, (Isocr. p. 64 b.; Dion. Hal., Plut.).*

συμπαθής, -ές, (σύν and πάσχω), *suffering* or *feeling the*   **4835** *like with another, sympathetic*: 1 Pet. iii. 8, cf. Ro. xii. 15. (Aristot., Theophr., al.) *

συμ-παρα-γίνομαι [T WH συν- (cf. σύν, II. fin.)] : 2 aor.   **4836** mid. συμπαρεγενόμην; **a.** *to come together*: ἐπί τι,

Lk. xxiii. 48 (Ps. lxxxii. (lxxxiii.) 9 ; Hdt., Thuc., Dem., Diod.).　　**b.** *to come to one's help* : τινί, 2 Tim. iv. 16 R G [al. παραγίν., q. v. fin.]*

4837　συμ-παρα-καλέω [T WH συν- (cf. σύν, II. fin.)], -ῶ : 1 aor. pass. inf. συμπαρακληθῆναι ;　　**1.** *to call upon or invite or exhort at the same time or together* (Xen., Plat., Plut., al.).　　**2.** *to strengthen* [A. V. *comfort*] *with others* (souls ; see παρακαλέω, II. 4) : συμπαρακληθῆναι ἐν ὑμῖν, *that I with you may be comforted among you*, i. e. in your assembly, with you, Ro. i. 12.*

4838　συμ-παρα-λαμβάνω [T WH συν- (cf. σύν, II. fin.)] ; 2 aor. συμπαρέλαβον ; *to take along together with* (Plat., Aristot., Plut., al.) ; in the N. T. *to take with one as a companion* : τινά, Acts xii. 25 ; xv. 37 sq.; Gal. ii. 1.*

4839　συμ-παρα-μένω ; fut. συμπαραμενῶ ; *to abide together with* (Hippocr., Thuc., Dion. Hal., al.) ; *to continue to live together* : τινί, with one, Phil. i. 25 [Rec. ; al. παραμένω, q. v.] (Ps. lxxi. (lxxii.) 5).*

4840　συμ-πάρειμι [T WH συν- (cf. σύν, II. fin.)] ; *to be present together* : τινί, with one, Acts xxv. 24. [(Hippocr., Xen., Dem., al.)]*

4841　συμ-πάσχω [T WH συν- (cf. σύν, II. fin.)] ; *to suffer or feel pain together* (in a medical sense, as in Hippocr. and Galen) : 1 Co. xii. 26 ; *to suffer evils* (troubles, persecutions) *in like manner with another* : Ro. viii. 17.*

4842　συμ-πέμπω : 1 aor. συνέπεμψα ; fr. Hdt. down ; *to send together with* : τινὰ μετά τινος, 2 Co. viii. 18 ; τινί, ibid. 22. [Cf. W. § 52, 4, 15.]*

4843　συμ-περι-λαμβάνω [T WH συν- (cf. σύν, II. fin.)] : 2 aor. ptcp. συμπεριλαβών ; fr. Plat. and Dem. down ;　　**1.** *to comprehend at once.*　　**2.** *to embrace* completely : τινά, Acts xx. 10.*

4844　συμ-πίνω : 2 aor. συνέπιον ; fr. [Hdt., Arstph.], Xen. and Plat. down ; *to drink with* : τινί, one, Acts x. 41.*

see 4098　συμ-πίπτω : 2 aor. συνέπεσον ; fr. Hom. down ; *to fall together, collapse, fall in* : of a house, Lk. vi. 49 T Tr WH.*

4845　συμ-πληρόω [in Acts T WH συν- (cf. σύν, II. fin.)], -ῶ : Pass., pres. inf. συμπληροῦσθαι ; impf. συνεπληρούμην ; fr. Hdt. down ;　　**1.** *to fill completely* : συνεπληροῦντο [R. V. *they were filling* with water], of the navigators, (as sometimes in Grk. writ. what holds of the ship is applied to those on board ; cf. *Kypke*, Observv. i. p. 248), Lk. viii. 23.　　**2.** *to complete entirely, to be fulfilled* : of time (see πληρόω, 2 b. a.), pass., Lk. ix. 51 [R. V. *well nigh come*] ; Acts ii. 1.*

4846　συμ-πνίγω [T WH συν- (cf. σύν, II. fin.)] ; impf. συνέπνιγον ; 1 aor. συνέπνιξα ; pres. pass. 3 pers. plur. συμπνίγονται ; *to choke utterly* : the seed of the divine word sown in the mind, Mt. xiii. 22 ; Mk. iv. 7, 19, (δένδρα συμπνιγόμενα, Theophr. c. plant. 6, 11, 6) ; συμπνίγονται, *they are choked*, i. e. the seed of the divine word in their minds is choked, Lk. viii. 14 ; τινά, to press round or throng one so as almost to suffocate him, Lk. viii. 42 [A. V. *thronged*].*

4847　συμ-πολίτης [T WH συν- (cf. σύν, II. fin.)], -ου, ὁ, (see συμμαθητής and reff.), *possessing the same citizenship with others, a fellow-citizen* : συμπολῖται τῶν ἁγίων, spoken

of Gentiles as received into the communion of the saints i. e. of the people consecrated to God, opp. to ξένοι κ. πάροικοι, Eph. ii. 19. (Eur. Heracl. 826 ; Joseph. antt. 19, 2, 2 ; Ael. v. h. 3, 44.)*

4848　συμ-πορεύομαι [T WH συν- (cf. σύν, II. fin.)] ; impf. συνεπορευόμην ;　　**1.** *to go or journey together* (Eur., Xen., Diod.) : τινί, with one, Lk. vii. 11 ; xiv. 25 ; xxiv. 15, (Tob. v. 3, 9 ; ἡμῶν ἡ ψυχὴ συμπορευθεῖσα θεῷ, Plat. Phaedr. p. 249 c. ; μετά τινος, very often in Sept.).　　**2.** *to come together, to assemble* : πρός τινα, Mk. x. 1 (Polyb., Plut.).*

4849　συμπόσιον, -ου, τό, (συμπίνω), *a drinking-party, entertainment*, (Lat. *convivium*) ; by meton. *the party itself, the guests*, (Plut. mor. p. 157 a. ; 704 d.) ; plur. *rows of guests* : συμπόσια συμπόσια, Hebraistically for κατὰ συμπόσια, *in parties, by companies*, ([B. 30 (27) ; § 129 a. 3 ; W. 229 (214) ; 464 (432)] ; see πρασιά), Mk. vi. 39.*

4850　συμ-πρεσβύτερος [T WH συν- (cf. σύν, II. fin.)], -ου, ὁ, *a fellow-elder*, Vulg. *consenior*, (see πρεσβύτερος, 2 b.) : 1 Pet. v. 1. (Eccles. writ.)*

see 4906　συμ-φάγω, see συνεσθίω.

4851　συμ-φέρω ; 1 aor. ptcp. συνενέγκαντες (Acts xix. 19) ; fr. [Hom. (in mid.)], Aeschyl., Hdt. down ; *to bear or bring together* (Lat. *confero*), i. e.　　**1.** with a reference to the object, *to bring together* : τί, Acts xix. 19.　　**2.** with a reference to the subject, *to bear together or at the same time* ; *to carry with others* ; *to collect or contribute in order to help*, hence *to help, be profitable, be expedient* ; συμφέρει, *it is expedient, profitable*, and in the same sense with a neut. plur. : with the subject πάντα, 1 Co. vi. 12 ; x. 23 ; τί τινι, 2 Co. viii. 10 ; with an inf. of the object (as in Grk. writ.), Mt. xix. 10 ; 2 Co. xii. 1 (where L T Tr WH have συμφέρον) ; with the acc. and inf. Jn. xviii. 14 ; συμφέρει τινί foll. by ἵνα (see ἵνα, II. 2 c. [B. § 139, 45 ; W. 337 (316)]), Mt. v. 29 sq.; xviii. 6 ; Jn. xi. 50 ; xvi. 7. τὸ συμφέρον, *that which is profitable* (Soph., Eur., Xen., Dem., al.) : 1 Co. xii. 7 ; plur. (Plat. de rep. 1 p. 341 e.), Acts xx. 20 ; advantage, *profit*, Heb. xii. 10 ; τὸ συμφ. τινός (often in Grk. writ.) *the advantage of one, one's profit*, 1 Co. vii. 35 ; x. 33, (in both which pass. L T Tr WH read σύμφορον, q. v.).*

4852　συμ-φημι [T WH σύν- (cf. σύν, II. fin.)] ; *to consent, confess* : τινί foll. by ὅτι, Ro. vii. 16. (Tragg., Xen., Plat.)*

see 4851　σύμ-φορος, -ον, (συμφέρω, q. v.), *fit, suitable, useful* ; fr. [Hes., Theogn.], Hdt. down ; 4 Macc. v. 10 ; subst. τὸ σύμφορον, *advantage, profit* : with a gen. of the pers. profited, L T Tr WH in 1 Co. vii. 35 , x. 33, [cf. B. § 127, 19 n.], (plur. τὰ σύμφορα, often in prof. auth. [fr. Soph. down]).*

4853　συμ-φυλέτης, -ου, ὁ, (σύν and φυλή ; see συμμαθητής), *one who is of the same people, a fellow-countryman*, (Vulg. *contribulis*) : 1 Th. ii. 14. (Eccles. writ.)*

4854　σύμ-φυτος, -ον, (συμφύω), *planted together* (Vulg. *complantatus*) ; *born together with, of joint origin*, i. e.　　**1.** *connate, congenital, innate, implanted by birth or nature*, (3 Macc. iii. 22 ; Pind., Plat., Aeschyl., Aeschin., Aristot.,

Philo de Abrah. § 31 init.; Joseph. [as, c. Ap. 1, 8, 5]).   **2.** *grown together, united with*, (Theophr. de caus. plant. 5, 5, 2); *kindred* (Plat. Phaedr. p. 246 a.): εἰ σύμφυτοι γεγόναμεν τῷ ὁμοιώματι τοῦ θανάτου αὐτοῦ, ἀλλὰ καὶ (sc. τῷ ὁμοιώματι [al. supply Χριστῷ, and take the ὁμοιώματι as a dat. of respect; for yet another constr. of the second clause cf. B. § 132, 23]) τῆς ἀναστάσεως ἐσόμεθα, *if we have become united with the likeness of his death* (which likeness consists in the fact that in the death of Christ our former corruption and wickedness has been slain and been buried in Christ's tomb), i. e. if it is part and parcel of the very nature of a genuine Christian to be utterly dead to sin, *we shall be united also with the likeness of his resurrection* i. e. our intimate fellowship with his return to life will show itself in a new life consecrated to God, Ro. vi. 5.*

4855   [σνμ-φύω (T WH σὺν- cf. σύν, II. fin.): 2 aor. pass. ptcp. nom. plur. fem. συμφνεῖσαι;   **1.** trans. *to cause to grow together* (Plat., Aristot.).   **2.** pass. intrans. *to grow together, grow with*: Lk. viii. 7.*]

4856   σνμ-φωνέω, -ῶ; fut. συμφωνήσω ([Mt. xviii. 19 T Tr; Lk. v. 36 L T Tr txt. WH]); 1 aor. συνεφώνησα; 1 aor. pass. συνεφωνήθην; fr. Plat. and Aristot. down; prop. *to sound together, be in accord*; of sounds and of musical instruments. In the N. T. trop. *to be in accord, to harmonize*, i. e.   **a.** *to agree together*: περί (as respects) τινος, Mt. xviii. 19 (Dion. Hal. 2, 47); τινί, with a thing, Acts xv. 15 (often in Grk. auth.); *to agree* i. e. *correspond*, of things congruous in nature, Lk. v. 36; pass. συνεφωνήθη ὑμῖν, foll. by an inf., *it was agreed between you to* etc. Acts v. 9.   **b.** *to agree with one in making a bargain, to make an agreement, to bargain*, (Polyb., Diod.): μετά τινος ἐκ δηναρίου (see ἐκ, II. 4), Mt. xx. 2; w. a dat. of the pers. and gen. of the price, ibid. 13, (συνεφώνησεν μετ' αὐτοῦ τριῶν λιτρῶν ἀσήμου ἀργυρίου, Act. Thom. § 2).*

4857   σνμ-φώνησις, -εως, ἡ, (συμφωνέω), *concord, agreement*: πρός τινα, with one, 2 Co. vi. 15. (Eccl. writ.) *

4858   συμφωνία, -ας, ἡ, (σύμφωνος), [fr. Plat. down], *music*: Lk. xv. 25. (Polyb. 26, 10, 5; [plur. of 'the music of the spheres,' Aristot. de caelo 2, 9 p. 290ᵇ, 22; al.]) *

4859   σύμφωνος, -ον, (σύν and φωνή), fr. [Hom. h. Merc. 51; Soph.], Plat., Aristot. down, *harmonious, accordant, agreeing*; τὸ σύμφωνον, thing agreed upon, compact, (Epict. diss. 1, 19, 27]: ἐκ συμφώνου, by mutual consent, by agreement, 1 Co. vii. 5 [cf. W. 303 (285); B. § 139, 20]*

4860   σνμ-ψηφίζω: 1 aor. συνεψήφισα; *to compute, count up*: τὰς τιμάς, Acts xix. 19.   (Mid. τινί, *to vote with one*, Arstph. Lys. 142.) *

4861   σύμ-ψυχος [T WH σύν- (cf. σύν, II. fin.)], -ον, (σύν and ψυχή), *of one mind* (Vulg. unanimis): *of one accord*, Phil. ii. 2.   (Eccl. writ.) *

4862   σύν [the older form ξύν is still found in some edd. in composition (as ξυμ-βαίνω, 1 Pet. iv. 12 Recᵇᵉᶻ; see L. and S. s. v. init.; cf. Σ, σ, ς)], a preposition; it is never used in the Apocalypse, rarely by Matthew [some four times (texts vary)], Mark [some five times, or John (three times)], (who prefer μετά), more frequently by Luke

[(Gospel and Acts) about 79 times] and Paul [about 39 times; on the comparative frequency of these prepp. in the classics, see L. and S. s. v. ad init.]. It takes the Dative after it, and denotes accompaniment and fellowship, whether of action, or of belief, or of condition and experience; (acc. to the grammarians [cf. *Donaldson*, New Crat. § 181; Krüger § 68, 13, 1; Kühner ii. p. 438]; W. 391 (366), a fellowship far closer and more intimate than that expressed by μετά, although in the N. T. this distinction is much oftener neglected than observed). Latin *cum*, Eng. *with*.

I.   **1.** Passages in which the subject of an active verb is said to be or to do something σύν τινι;   **a.** phrases in which σύν is used of accompaniment: εἰμὶ σύν τινι i. e. — *to be with one, to accompany one*, Lk. vii. 12; viii. 38 (Mk. v. 18 μετ' αὐτοῦ); xxii. 56 (Mt. xxvi. 69 and Mk. xiv. 67 μετά); Acts xxvii. 2; *to associate with one*, Lk. xxiv. 44; Acts iv. 13; xiii. 7; Phil. i. 23; Col. ii. 5; 2 Pet. i. 18; οἱ σύν τινι ὄντες, the attendants of one on a journey, Mk. ii. 26 (Mt. xii. 4 and Lk. vi. 4 τοῖς μετ' αὐτοῦ); Acts xxii. 9; οἱ σύν τινι sc. ὄντες, — either the *companions* of one, Lk. v. 9; ix. 32; xxiv. 24, 33; with the noun added, οἱ σὺν ἐμοὶ πάντες ἀδελφοί, Gal. i. 2; Ro. xvi. 14; or one's *colleagues*, Acts v. 17, 21; οἱ σὺν αὐτῷ τεχνῖται, his fellow-craftsmen, Acts xix. 38; εἰμὶ σύν τινι, *to be on one's side*, Acts xiv. 4 (Xen. Cyr. 7, 5, 77); *to assist one*, ἡ χάρις τοῦ θεοῦ (ἡ) σὺν ἐμοί, 1 Co. xv. 10.   **b.** σύν τινι joined to verbs of standing, sitting, going, etc.: σταθῆναι, Acts ii. 14; στῆναι, Acts iv. 14; ἐπιστῆναι, Lk. xx. 1; Acts xxiii. 27; καθίσαι, Acts viii. 31; μένειν, Lk. i. 56; xxiv. 29; Acts xxviii. 16; ἀναπίπτειν, Lk. xxii. 14; γίνεσθαι, to be associated with, Lk. ii. 13; παραγίνεσθαι, to arrive, Acts xxiv. 24; ἔρχεσθαι, Jn. xxi. 3; Acts xi. 12; 2 Co. ix. 4; ἀπέρχεσθαι, Acts v. 26; εἰσέρχεσθαι, Acts iii. 8; xxv. 23; εἰσιέναι, Acts xxi. 18; συνέρχεσθαι, Acts xxi. 16; ἐξέρχεσθαι, Jn. xviii. 1; Acts x. 23; xiv. 20; xvi. 3; πορεύεσθαι, Lk. vii. 6; Acts x. 20; xxiii. 32 [L T Tr WH ἀπέρχεσθαι]; xxvi. 13; 1 Co. xvi. 4; διοδεύειν, Lk. viii. 1 sq.; ἐκπλεῖν, Acts xviii. 18.   with verbs of living, dying, believing: ζῆν, 1 Th. v. 10; ἀποθνῄσκειν, Mt. xxvi. 35; Ro. vi. 8; πιστεύειν, Acts xviii. 8. with other verbs: Acts v. 1; xiv. 13; xx. 36; xxi. 5; Phil. ii. 22; Jas. i. 11.   **2.** Passages in which one is said to be the recipient of some action σύν τινι, or to be associated with one to whom some action has reference: — dative, τινὶ σύν τινι: as ἔδοξε τοῖς ἀποστόλοις σὺν ὅλῃ τῇ ἐκκλησίᾳ, Acts xv. 22, where if Luke had said καὶ ὅλῃ τῇ ἐκκλησίᾳ he would have claimed for the church the same rank as for the apostles; but he wishes to give to the apostles the more influential position; the same applies also to Acts xxiii. 15; 1 Co. i. 2; 2 Co. i. 1; Phil. i. 1.   Accusative, σύν τινί (which precedes) τινα or τι (the pers. or thing added): Ro. viii. 32 (σὺν αὐτῷ, i. e. since he has given him to us); Mk. xv. 27; 1 Co. x. 13; τινὰ or τὶ σύν τινι (the pers. or thing associated or added): Mt. xxv. 27; Mk. viii. 34; 2 Co. i. 21; Col. ii. 13; iv. 9; τὶ σύν τινι, a thing with its power or result, Gal. v. 24; Col. iii. 9; τὶς or τὶ σύν τινι after passives, as

Mt. xxvii. 38; Mk. ix. 4; Lk. xxiii. 32; 1 Co. xi. 32; Gal. iii. 9; Col. iii. 3 sq.; 1 Th. iv. 17. **3.** It stands where καί might have been used (cf. B. 331 (285)): ἐγένετο ὁρμὴ . . . Ἰουδαίων σὺν τοῖς ἄρχουσιν αὐτῶν (equiv. to καὶ τῶν ἀρχ. αὐτ.), Acts xiv. 5; add, Lk. xxiii. 11; Acts iii. 4; x. 2; xxiii. 15; Eph. iii. 18. **4.** Of that which one has or carries with him, or with which he is furnished or equipped (σὺν ἅρμασιν, 3 Macc. ii. 7; σὺν ὅπλοις, Xen. Cyr. 3, 3, 54; many other exx. fr. Grk. writ. are given by Passow s. v. B. I. 2 a.; [L. and S. I. 4]): σὺν τῇ χάριτι ταύτῃ, carrying with him this gift or bounty, 2 Co. viii. 19 R G T cod. Sin. (L Tr WH ἐν τῇ χάρ. τ. in procuring [R. V. in the matter of] this benefit); σὺν τῇ δυνάμει τοῦ κυρίου ἡμῶν Ἰ. Χρ. equipped with the power of our Lord Jesus Christ, 1 Co. v. 4 (so acc. to many interpreters [cf. W. 391 (366)]; but since the N. T. writers are wont to designate the powers and virtues with which one is equipped by the preposition ἐν, it is more correct to connect σὺν τῇ δυν. with συναχθέντων, so that ἡ δύναμις τ. κυρίου is personified and represented as the third subject in the gathering; cf. Mt. xviii. 20 [see δύναμις, a. sub fin.]). **5.** σὺν Χριστῷ ζῆν, to live with Christ, i. e. united (in spiritual bonds) to him, and to lead a strong life by virtue of this union, 2 Co. xiii. 4; σὺν (Rec.) χειρὶ ἀγγέλου (see χείρ), Acts vii. 35 L T Tr WH. **6.** Of the union which arises from the addition or accession of one thing to another: σὺν πᾶσι τούτοις, our 'beside all this' [W. 391 (366)], Lk. xxiv. 21 (Neh. v. 18; 3 Macc. i. 22; Joseph. antt. 17, 6, 5). **7.** On the combination ἅμα σύν, 1 Th. iv. 17; v. 10, see ἅμα, fin.

II. In composition σύν denotes **1.** association, community, fellowship, participation: συνοικέω, σύνειμι, συγγενής, σύμμορφος, συζῆν, συμπάσχειν, συγχρᾶσθαι, etc. **2.** together, i. e. several persons or things united or all in one; as, συγκεράννυμι, συγκλείω, συγκαλέω, συλλέγω, συγκομίζω, etc. **3.** completely: συγκύπτω, συγκαλύπτω, etc. **4.** with one's self, i. e. in one's mind: συλλυπέομαι [but see the word], σύνοιδα, συνείδησις, συντηρέω; cf. Viger. ed. Herm. p. 642 sq. Once or twice in the N. T. after verbs compounded with σύν the preposition is repeated before the object [W. § 52, 4, 15]: Mt. xxvii. 44 L T Tr WH; Col. ii. 13.

As to its Form, σύν in composition before β, μ, π, φ, ψ, passes into συμ-, before λ into συλ-, before γ, κ, χ into συγ-; before ζ [and σ foll. by a consonant] it is elided, hence συζῆν, συζητέω, συσταυρόω, συστέλλω. But in the older manuscripts assimilation and elision are often neglected (cf. ἐν, III. fin.). Following their authority, L Tr WH write συνζάω, συνζητέω, συνζητητής, σύνζυγος, συνσταυρόω, συνστρατιώτης, σύνσωμος; T WH συνβασιλεύω, συνγνώμη, συνκάθημαι, συνκαθίζω, συνκακοπαθέω, συνκακουχέω, συνκαλέω, συνκάμπτω, συνκαταβαίνω, συνκατάθεσις, συνκατατίθημι, συνκαταψηφίζω, συνκεράννυμι, συνκλείω, συνκληρονόμος, συνκοινωνέω, συνκοινωνός, συνκρίνω, (Ἀσύνκριτος), συνκύπτω, συνλαλέω, συνλυπέομαι, συνμαθητής, συνμαρτυρέω, συνμέτοχος, συνμιμητής, συνπαθέω, συνπαραγίνομαι, συνπαρακαλέω, συνπαραλαμβάνω, συνπάρειμι, συνπάσχω,

συνπεριλαμβάνω, συνπνίγω, συνπολίτης, συνπορεύομαι, συνπρεσβύτερος, συνστενάζω, συνστοιχέω, σύνφημι, συνφύω, συνχαίρω, συνχράομαι, συνχέω, σύνψυχος; L Tr mrg. συνζήτησις; T συνμορφίζω, σύνσημον; Tr συνστατικός; WH συνβάλλω, συνβιβάζω, συνμερίζω, συνσχηματίζω. But L T Tr WH retain συγγένεια, συγγενής, συγκαλύπτω, συγκυρία, σύγχυσις, συλλέγω, συμβαίνω, συμβουλεύω, συμβούλιον, σύμβουλος, συμπαθής, συμπόσιον, συμφέρω, σύμφορος, συμφυλέτης, σύμφυτος, συμφωνέω, συμφώνησις, συμφωνία, σύμφωνος (ἀσύμφωνος), συστρέφω, συστροφή; L T Tr συμμερίζω; L T WH συγγενής, συστατικός; L Tr WH συμμορφίζω, σύμμορφος, σύσσημον; L T συγγνώμη, συγκάθημαι, συγκαθίζω, συγκακοπαθέω, συγκακουχέω, συγκαλέω, συγκάμπτω, συγκαταβαίνω, συγκατάθεσις, συγκατατίθημι, συγκαταψηφίζω, συγκεράννυμι, συγκλείω, συγκληρονόμος, συγκοινωνέω, συγκοινωνός, συγκρίνω, συγκύπτω, συγχαίρω, συγχέω, συγχράομαι, συλλαλέω, συλλυπέω, συμβάλλω, συμβασιλεύω, συμβιβάζω, συμμαθητής, συμμαρτυρέω, συμμέτοχος, συμμιμητής, συμπαθέω, συμπαραγίνομαι, συμπαρακαλέω, συμπαραλαμβάνω, συμπάρειμι, συμπάσχω, συμπεριλαμβάνω, συμπληρόω, συμπνίγω, συμπολίτης, συμπορεύομαι, συμπρεσβύτερος, σύμφημι, συμφύω, σύμψυχος, συστενάζω, συστοιχέω; L συλλαμβάνω, συσχηματίζω. Tdf. is not uniform in συλλαμβάνω, συμβάλλω, συμβιβάζω, σύμμορφος, συμπληρόω, συσχηματίζω; nor Tr in συλλαμβάνω, συσχηματίζω; nor WH in συλλαμβάνω, συμπληρόω. These examples show that assimilation takes place chiefly in those words in which the preposition has lost, more or less, its original force and blends with the word to which it is prefixed into a single new idea; as συμβούλιον, συμφέρει, σύμφορος. Cf. [Alex. Buttmann in the Stud. u. Krit. for 1862, p. 180]; Philip Buttmann (the son) ibid. p. 811 sq. [But see Dr. Gregory's exposition of the facts in the Proleg. to Tdf. p. 73 sq.; Dr. Hort in WH. App. p. 149; Meisterhans, Gram. d. Att. Inschr. § 24.]

συν-άγω; fut. συνάξω; 2 aor. συνήγαγον; Pass., pres. συνάγομαι; pf. ptcp. συνηγμένος; 1 aor. συνήχθην; 1 fut. συναχθήσομαι; fr. Hom. down; Sept. chiefly for אָסַף, קָבַץ, and קָבַץ; **a.** to gather together, to gather: with an acc. of the thing, Lk. xv. 13; Jn. vi. 12 sq.; xv. 6; harvests, ὅθεν, Mt. xxv. 24, 26; with εἰς τι added, Mt. iii. 12; vi. 26; xiii. 30; Lk. iii. 17; ποῦ, Lk. xii. 17; ἐκεῖ, Lk. xii. 18; συνάγειν καρπὸν εἰς ζωὴν αἰώνιον (see καρπός, 2 d.), Jn. iv. 36; συνάγω μετά τινος, Mt. xii. 30; Lk. xi. 23; to draw together, collect: fishes, — of a net in which they are caught, Mt. xiii. 47. **b.** to bring together, assemble, collect: αἰχμαλωσίαν (i. e. αἰχμαλώτους), Rev. xiii. 10 R G; εἰς αἰχμαλωσίαν, i. e. τινάς, οἳ ὦσιν αἰχμάλωτοι, Rev. xiii. 10 L ed. min.; to join together, join in one (those previously separated): τὰ τέκνα τοῦ θεοῦ τὰ διεσκορπισμένα εἰς ἕν, Jn. xi. 52, (συν-άξειν εἰς ἓν τὰ ἔθνη καὶ ποιήσειν φιλίαν, Dion. Hal. 2, 45; ὅπως εἰς φιλίαν συνάξουσι τὰ ἔθνη, ibid.); to gather together by convoking: τινάς, Mt. ii. 4; xxii. 10; συνέδριον, Jn. xi. 47; τὴν ἐκκλησίαν, Acts xiv. 27; τὸ πλῆθος, Acts xv. 30; τινὰς εἰς with an acc. of place, Rev. xvi. 16; εἰς τὸν πόλεμον, in order to engage in war, Rev. xvi. 14; xx. 8; ἐπί τινα, unto one, Mt.

4863

xxvii. 27. Pass. *to be gathered* i. e. *come together, gather, meet*, [cf. B. 52 (45)]: absol., Mt. xxii. 41; xxvii. 17; Mk. ii. 2; Lk. xxii. 66; Acts xiii. 44; xv. 6; xx. 7; 1 Co. v. 4; Rev. xix. 19; with the addition of εἰς and an acc. of place, Mt. xxvi. 3; Acts iv. 5; εἰς δεῖπνον, Rev. xix. 17; ἔμπροσθέν τινος, Mt. xxv. 32; ἐπί τινα, unto one, Mk. v. 21; ἐπὶ τὸ αὐτό [see αὐτός, III. 1], Mt. xxii. 34; Acts iv. 26; ἐπί τινα, against one, Acts iv. 27; πρός τινα, unto one, Mt. xiii. 2; xxvii. 62; Mk. iv. 1; vi. 30; vii. 1; ἐν with dat. of the place, Acts iv. 31; ἐν τῇ ἐκκλησίᾳ, Acts xi. 26; μετά τινος, Mt. xxviii. 12; with adverbs of place: οὗ, Mt. xviii. 20; Acts xx. 8; ὅπου, Mt. xxvi. 57; Jn. xx. 19 R G; ἐκεῖ, Jn. xviii. 2; Mt. xxiv. 28; Lk. xvii. 37 R G L. **c.** *to lead with one's self* sc. unto one's home, i. e. *to receive hospitably, to entertain*, [A.V. *to take in*]: ξένον, Mt. xxv. 35, 38, 43, (with the addition of εἰς τὴν οἰκίαν, εἰς τὸν οἶκον, Deut. xxii. 2; Josh. ii. 18; Judg. xix. 18, etc.). [COMP.: ἐπι-συνάγω.] *

4864 **συν-αγωγή**, -ῆς, ἡ, (συνάγω), Sept. for קָהָל and very often for עֵדָה. In Grk. writ. *a bringing together, gathering* (as of fruits), *a contracting*; *an assembling together* of men. In the N. T. **1.** *an assembly of men*: τοῦ Σατανᾶ, whom Satan governs, Rev. ii. 9; iii. 9. **2.** *a synagogue*, i. e. **a.** *an assembly of Jews formally gathered together to offer prayer and listen to the reading and exposition of the Holy Scriptures*; assemblies of the sort were held every sabbath and feast-day, afterwards also on the second and fifth days of every week [see reff. below]: Lk. xii. 11; Acts ix. 2; xiii. 43; xxvi. 11; the name is transferred to an assembly of Christians formally gathered for religious purposes, Jas. ii. 2 (Epiph. haer. 30, 18 says of the Jewish Christians συναγωγὴν οὗτοι καλοῦσι τὴν ἑαυτῶν ἐκκλησίαν καὶ οὐχὶ ἐκκλησίαν [cf. Bp. Lghtft. on Philip. p. 192]); [cf. Trench, Syn. § 1, and esp. Harnack's elaborate note on Herm. mand. 11, 9 (less fully and accurately in Hilgenfeld's Zeitschr. f. wiss. Theol. for 1876, p. 102 sqq.) respecting the use of the word by the church Fathers of the 2d, 3d, and 4th centuries; cf. Hilgenfeld's comments on the same in his 'Hermae Pastor', ed. alt. p. 183 sq.]. **b.** *the building where those solemn Jewish assemblies are held* (Hebr. בֵּית הַכְּנֶסֶת, i. e. 'the house of assembly'). Synagogues seem to date their origin from the Babylonian exile. In the time of Jesus and the apostles every town, not only in Palestine but also among the Gentiles if it contained a considerable number of Jewish inhabitants, had at least one synagogue, the larger towns several or even many. That the Jews held trials and even inflicted punishments in them, is evident from such pass. as Mt. x. 17; xxiii. 34; Mk. xiii. 9; Lk. xii. 11; xxi. 12; Acts ix. 2; xxii. 19; xxvi. 11. They are further mentioned in Mt. iv. 23; vi. 2, 5; ix. 35; xii. 9; xiii. 54; xxiii. 6; Mk. i. 21, 23, 29, 39; iii. 1; vi. 2; xii. 39; Lk. iv. 15 sq. 20, 28, 33, 38, 44; vi. 6; vii. 5; viii. 41; [xi. 43]; xiii. 10; xx. 46; Jn. vi. 59; xviii. 20 [here the anarthrous (so G L T Tr WH) sing. has an indef. or generic force (R. V. txt. *in synagogues*)]; Acts vi. 9; ix. 20; xiii. 5, 14, 42 Rec.; xiv. 1; xv. 21; xvii. 1, 10, 17; xviii. 4, 7, 19, 26; xix. 8; xxiv. 12; xxvi. 11;

(Joseph. antt. 19, 6, 3; b. j. 2, 14, 4. [5; 7, 3, 3; Philo, quod omn. prob. lib. § 12]). Cf. *Win.* RWB. s. v. Synagogen; *Leyrer* in Herzog ed. 1, xv. p. 299 sqq.; *Schürer,* N. T. Zeitgesch. § 27 (esp. ii.); *Kneucker* in Schenkel v. p. 443 sq.; [*Hamburger*, Real-Encycl. ii. p. 1142 sqq.; *Ginsburg* in Alex.'s Kitto, s. v. Synagogue; *Edersheim,* Jesus the Messiah, bk. iii. ch. x.].*

συν-αγωνίζομαι: 1 aor. mid. inf. συναγωνίσασθαι; fr.   **4865** Thuc. and Xen. down; *to strive together with one, to help one in striving*: τινὶ ἐν ταῖς προσευχαῖς, in prayers, i. e. to offer intense prayers with one, Ro. xv. 30; in what sense intense prayer may be likened to a struggle, see Philippi ad loc. [(cf. ἀγωνίζ. in Col. iv. 12 and Bp. Lghtft.'s note)].*

συν-αθλέω, -ῶ; 1 aor. συνήθλησα; *to strive at the same*   **4866** *time with* another: with a dat. commodi [cf. W. § 31, 4], for something, Phil. i. 27; τινὶ ἔν τινι, together with one in something, Phil. iv. 3. (univ. *to help, assist*, Diod. 3, 4.)*

συν-αθροίζω: 1 aor. ptcp. συναθροίσας; pf. pass. ptcp.   **4867** συνηθροισμένος; fr. [Eur., Arstph., al.], Isocr. down; Sept. chiefly for קָבַץ and קִבֵּץ; *to gather together with others*; *to assemble*: τινάς, Acts xix. 25; pass. *to be gathered together*: i. e. *come together*, Lk. xxiv. 33 R G; Acts xii. 12.*

συν-αίρω: 1 aor. inf. συνᾶραι; **1.** *to take up to-*   **4868** *gether with* another or others. **2.** *to bring together with others*: λόγον, *to cast up* or *settle accounts, to make a reckoning with*, (an expression not found in Grk. auth.), Mt. xviii. 23 sq.; μετά τινος, Mt. xxv. 19.*

συν-αιχμάλωτος, -ου, ὁ, ἡ, *a fellow-prisoner* (Vulg. *concap-*   **4869** *tivus*): Ro. xvi. 7; Col. iv. 10; Philem. 23, (Lcian. asin. 27). [Cf. Bp. Lghtft. on Col. l. c.; *Fritzsche*, Com. on Rom. vol. i. p. xxi. note.] *

συν-ακολουθέω, -ῶ; impf. συνηκολούθουν; 1 aor. συνηκο-   **4870** λούθησα; fr. Arstph., Thuc., Isocr. down; *to follow to-gether with* others, *to accompany*: τινί, one, Mk. v. 37 [where Lchm. ἀκολουθ.]; xiv. 51 L T Tr WH; Lk. xxiii. 49.*

συν-αλίζω: (σύν, and ἁλίζω fr. ἁλής, crowded, in a mass;   **4871** [cf. ἅλυσις, init.]); *to gather together, assemble*; pass. pres. ptcp. συναλιζόμενος; *to be assembled, meet with*: τινί, with one, Acts i. 4, where αὐτοῖς is to be supplied. (Hdt., Xen., [Plut. de placit. phil. 902], Joseph., Lcian., Jambl.) [But Meyer defends the rendering given by some of the ancient versions (cf. Tdf.'s note ad loc.) *eating with* (de-riving the word from σύναλος), so A. V. and R. V. mrg.; such passages as Manetho 5, 339; Clem. hom. 13, 4 (al-though *Dressel* after cod. Ottob. reads here συναλ.— yet the recogn. 7, 29 renders *cibum sumimus*); Chrysost. iii. 88 c. (ed. *Migne* iii. 104 mid.); 89 a. (ibid. bottom); 91 d. (ibid. 107 mid.), seem to give warrant for this in-terpretation; cf. *Valckenaer*, Opusc. ii. p. 277 sq. But see at length *Woolsey* in the Bib. Sacr. for Oct. 1882, pp. 605–618.] *

συν-αλλάσσω: (see καταλλάσσω); *to reconcile* (Thuc.,   **(4871α);** Xen., Plat., Dio Cass.; in diff. senses by diff. prof. auth.):   **see 4900** συνήλλασσεν αὐτοὺς εἰς εἰρήνην, (Vulg. *reconciliabat*, i. e. *sought to reconcile*), conative impf. [cf. B. 205 (178); R. V. *would have set them at one again*], Acts vii. 26 L T Tr WH [see συνελαύνω].*

4864

4872   συν-ανα-βαίνω : 2 aor. συνανέβην; to ascend at the same time, come up together with to a higher place : τινί, with one, foll. by εἰς with the acc. of the place, Mk. xv. 41; Acts xiii. 31. (Hdt., Xen., Dion. Hal., Strabo, al.; Sept. several times for עָלָה.)*

4873   συν-ανά-κειμαι; 3 pers. plur. impf. συνανέκειντο; to recline together, feast together, [A. V. ' sit down with ', ' sit at meat with ', (cf. ἀνάκειμαι)] : τινί, with one, Mt. ix. 10; Mk. ii. 15; Lk. xiv. 10; Jn. xii. 2 Rec.; οἱ συνανακείμενοι, [' they that sat at meat with '], the guests, Mt. xiv. 9; Mk. vi. 22, 26 [R G L]; Lk. vii. 49; xiv. 15. ([3 Macc. v. 39]; eccles. and Byzant. writ.)*

4874   συν-ανα-μίγνυμι: to mix up together; Pass., pres. impv. 2 pers. plur. -μίγνυσθε; inf. -μίγνυσθαι; reflex. and metaph. τινί, to keep company with, be intimate with, one : 1 Co. v. 9, 11; 2 Th. iii. 14 [here R T -σθε, L Tr WH -σθαι]. (Plut. Philop. 21; [Sept. Hos. vii. 8 Alex.].)*

4875   συν-ανα-παύομαι: 1 aor. subj. συναναπαύσωμαι; to take rest together with : τινί, with one, Is. xi. 6; to sleep together, to lie with, of husband and wife (Dion. Hal., Plut.); metaph. τινί, to rest or refresh one's spirit with one (i. e. to give and get refreshment by mutual intercourse), Ro. xv. 32 [Lchm. om.].*

4876   συν-αντάω, -ῶ : fut. συναντήσω; 1 aor. συνήντησα; fr. Hom. down; Sept. for פָּנַע, פָּנַע, קָרָה, קוּם, etc.; to meet with : τινί, Lk. ix. [18 WH mrg.], 37; xxii. 10; Acts x. 25; Heb. vii. 1 [cf. B. 293 (252)], 10; trop. of events, to happen, to befall : Acts xx. 22 (Plut. Sulla 2; mid. τὰ συναντώμενα, Polyb. 22, 7, 14; the Hebr. קָרָה also is used of events, Eccles. ii. 14; ix. 11; etc.).*

4877   συν-άντησις, -εως, ἡ, a meeting with (Eurip. Ion 535; Dion. Hal. antt. 4, 66) : εἰς συνάντησίν τινι, to meet one [B. § 146, 3], Mt. viii. 34 R G (for לִקְרַאת, Gen. xiv. 17; xxx. 16; Ex. iv. 27; xviii. 7).*

4878   συν-αντι-λαμβάνομαι: 2 aor. mid. subj. 3 pers. sing. συναντιλάβηται; to lay hold along with, to strive to obtain with others, help in obtaining, (τῆς ἐλευθερίας, Diod. 14, 8); to take hold with another (who is laboring), hence univ. to help : τινί, one, Lk. x. 40; Ro. viii. 26, (Ps. lxxxviii. (lxxxix.) 22; Ex. xviii. 22; Joseph. antt. 4, 8, 4).*

4879   συν-απ-άγω : Pass., pres. ptcp. συναπαγόμενος; 1 aor. συναπήχθην; to lead away with or together : ἵππον, Xen. Cyr. 8, 3, 21; τριήρεις, Hell. 5, 1, 23; τὸν λαὸν μεθ' ἑαυτοῦ, Sept. Ex. xiv. 6; pass. metaph. to be carried away with : with dat. of the thing, i. e. by a thing, so as to experience with others the force of that which carries away (Zosim. hist. 5, 6, 9 αὐτὴ ἡ Σπάρτη συναπήγετο τῇ κοινῇ τῆς Ἑλλάδος ἁλώσει), to follow the impulse of a thing to what harmonizes with it, Gal. ii. 13; 2 Pet. iii. 17; to suffer one's self to be carried away together with (something that carries away), τοῖς ταπεινοῖς (opp. to τὰ ὑψηλὰ φρονεῖν), i. e. to yield or submit one's self to lowly things, conditions, employments, — not to evade their power, Ro. xii. 16.*

4880   συν-απο-θνήσκω : 2 aor. συναπέθανον; to die together; with dat. of the pers. to die with one (Sir. xix. 10, and often in Grk. auth. fr. Hdt. down) : Mk. xiv. 31; sc. ὑμᾶς ἐμοί, that ye may die together with me, i. e. that my

love to you may not leave me even were I appointed to die, 2 Co. vii. 3; sc. τῷ Χριστῷ [cf. W. 143 (136)], to meet death as Christ did for the cause of God, 2 Tim. ii. 11.*

4881   συν-απ-όλλυμι: 2 aor. mid. συναπωλόμην; fr. Hdt. down; to destroy together (Ps. xxv. (xxvi.) 9); mid. to perish together (to be slain along with) : τινί, with one, Heb. xi. 31.*

4882   συν-απο-στέλλω : 1 aor. συναπέστειλα; to send with : τινά, 2 Co. xii. 18. (Sept.; Thuc., Xen., Dem., Plut., al.)*

4883   συν-αρμολογέω, -ῶ : pres. pass. ptcp. συναρμολογούμενος; (ἁρμολόγος binding, joining; fr. ἁρμός a joint, and λέγω); to join closely together; to frame together : οἰκοδομή, the parts of a building, Eph. ii. 21; σῶμα, the members of the body, Eph. iv. 16. (Eccles. writ.; classic writ. use συναρμόσσειν and συναρμόζειν.)*

4884   συν-αρπάζω : 1 aor. συνήρπασα; plupf. συνηρπάκειν; 1 aor. pass. συνηρπάσθην; to seize by force : τινά, Acts vi. 12; xix. 29; to catch or lay hold of (one, so that he is no longer his own master), Lk. viii. 29; to seize by force and carry away, Acts xxvii. 15. (Tragg., Arstph., Xen., al.)*

4885   συν-αυξάνω : to cause to grow together; pres. inf. pass. συναυξάνεσθαι, to grow together : Mt xiii. 30. (Xen., Dem., Polyb., Plut., al.)*

4862 (see)   συνβ-, see συμβ- and σύν, II. fin.

4862 (see)   συνγ-, see συγγ- and σύν, II. fin.

4886   σύν-δεσμος, -ου, ὁ, (συνδέω);   **1.** that which binds together, a band, bond : of the ligaments by which the members of the human body are united together (Eur. Hipp. 199; Tim. Locr. p. 100 b. [i. e. 3, p. 386 ed. Bekk.]; Aristot. h. a. 10, 7, 3 p. 638ᵇ, 9; Galen), Col. ii. 19 [where see Bp. Lghtft.]; trop. : τῷ συνδέσμῳ τῆς εἰρήνης, i. e. τῇ εἰρήνῃ ὡς συνδέσμῳ, Eph. iv. 3 (σύνδεσμος εὐνοίας κ. φιλίας, Plut. Num. 6); ἥτις ἐστὶ σύνδ. τῆς τελειότητος, that in which all the virtues are so bound together that perfection is the result, and not one of them is wanting to that perfection, Col. iii. 14 [cf. Bp. Lghtft. ad loc.]. εἰς σύνδεσμον ἀδικίας ὁρῶ σε ὄντα, I see that you have fallen into (cf. εἰμί, V. 2 a p. 179ᵃ, and see below) the bond of iniquity, i. e. forged by iniquity to fetter souls, Acts viii. 23 (the phrase σύνδ. ἀδικίας occurs in another sense in Is. lviii. 6).   **2.** that which is bound together, a bundle : prop. σύνδ. ἐπιστολῶν, Hdian. 4, 12, 11 [6 ed. Bekk.]; hence some interpreters think that by σύνδ. ἀδικίας, in Acts viii. 23 above, Simon is described as " a bundle of iniquity ", compacted as it were of iniquity, (just as Cic. in Pison. 9, 21 calls a certain man " animal ex omnium scelerum importunitate ... concretum "); but besides the circumstance that this interpretation is extremely bold, no examples can be adduced of this tropical use of the noun.*

4887   συν-δέω : in Grk. auth. fr. Hom. down;   **1.** to tie together, to bind together.   **2.** to bind or fasten on all sides.   **3.** to bind just as (i. e. jointly with) another : pf. pass. ptcp. ὡς συνδεδεμένοι, as fellow-prisoners [A.V. as bound with them], Heb. xiii. 3 (συνδεδεμένος τῷ οἰνοχόῳ, Joseph. antt. 2, 5, 3).*

4888   **συν-δοξάζω** : 1 aor. pass. συνεδοξάσθην;   **1.** *to approve together, join in approving*: νόμοι συνδεδοξασμένοι ὑπὸ πάντων, Aristot. pol. 5, 7 (9), 20 p. 1310ᵃ, 15.   **2.** *to glorify together* (Vulg. *conglorifico*) : sc. σὺν Χριστῷ, to be exalted to the same glory to which Christ has been raised, Ro. viii. 17.*

4889   **σύν-δουλος, -ου, ὁ,** (σύν and δοῦλος), *a fellow-servant; one who serves the same master with another*; thus used of   **a.** the associate of a servant (or slave) in the proper sense : Mt. xxiv. 49.   **b.** *one who with others serves* (ministers to) *a king*: Mt. xviii. 28, 29, 31, 33.   **c.** *the colleague of one who is Christ's servant in publishing the gospel*: Col. i. 7; iv. 7 [(where cf. Bp. Lghtft.)].   **d.** *one who with others acknowledges the same Lord, Jesus, and obeys his commands*: Rev. vi. 11.   **e.** *one who with others is subject to the same divine authority in the Messianic economy*: so of angels as the fellow-servants of Christians, Rev. xix. 10; xxii. 9. (Moeris says, p. 273, ὁμόδουλος ἀττικῶς, σύνδουλος ἑλληνικῶς. But the word is used by Arstph., Eur., Lysias.) *

4890   **συνδρομή, -ῆς, ἡ,** (συντρέχω), *a running together, concourse,* esp. hostile or riotous : Acts xxi. 30. (Aristot. rhetor. 3, 10 p. 1411ᵃ, 29; Polyb., Diod., al.; 3 Macc. iii. 8.) *

4891   **συν-εγείρω** : 1 aor. συνήγειρα; 1 aor. pass. συνηγέρθην; *to raise together, to cause to rise together*; Vulg. *conresuscito* [also *conresurgo, resurgo*]; (τὰ πεπτωκότα, 4 Macc. ii. 14; pass. *to rise together from their seats,* Is. xiv. 9; trop. λύπας καὶ θρήνους, Plut. mor. p. 117 c.) ; in the N. T. trop. *to raise up together from moral death* (see θάνατος, 2) *to a new and blessed life devoted to God* : ἡμᾶς τῷ Χριστῷ (risen from the dead, because the ground of the new Christian life lies in Christ's resurrection), Eph. ii. 6; Col. iii. 1; ἐν Χριστῷ, Col. ii. 12.*

4892   **συν-έδριον, -ου, τό,** (σύν and ἕδρα) ; hence prop. 'a sitting together'), in Grk. auth. fr. Hdt. down, *any assembly* (esp. *of magistrates, judges, ambassadors*), *whether convened to deliberate* or *to pass judgment*; Vulg. *concilium*; in the Scriptures   **1.** *any session* or *assembly of persons deliberating* or *adjudicating* (Prov. xxii. 10; Ps. xxv. (xxvi.) 4; Jer. xv. 17; 2 Macc. xiv. 5; 4 Macc. xvii. 17): συνήγαγον συνέδριον, [A. V. *gathered a council*], Jn. xi. 47.   **2.** spec.   **a.** *the Sanhedrin, the great council at Jerusalem* (Talm. סַנְהֶדְרִין), consisting of seventy-one members, viz. scribes (see γραμματεύς, 2), elders, prominent members of the high-priestly families (hence called ἀρχιερεῖς; see ἀρχιερεύς, 2), and the high-priest, the president of the body. The fullest periphrasis for Sanhedrin is found in Mt. xxvi. 3 R G; Mk. xiv. 43, 53, (viz. οἱ ἀρχιερεῖς καὶ οἱ γραμματεῖς καὶ οἱ πρεσβύτεροι). The more important causes were brought before this tribunal, inasmuch as the Roman rulers of Judæa had left to it the power of trying such cases, and also of pronouncing sentence of death, with the limitation that a capital sentence pronounced by the Sanhedrin was not valid unless it were confirmed by the Roman procurator (cf. Jn. xviii. 31; Joseph. antt. 20, 9, 1). The Jews trace the origin of the Sanhedrin to Num. xi. 16 sq. The

Sanhedrin [A. V. *council*] is mentioned in Mt. v. 22; xxvi. 59; Mk. xiv. 55; xv. 1; Lk. xxii. 66; Acts iv. 15; v. 21, 27, 34, 41; vi. 12, 15; xxii. 30; xxiii. 1, 6, 15, 20, 28; xxiv. 20; used [(as in class. Grk.)] of t h e p l a c e of meeting in Acts iv. 15.   **b.** the *smaller tribunal* or *council* (so A. V.) which every Jewish town had for the decision of the less important cases (see κρίσις, 4) : Mt. x. 17; Mk. xiii. 9.   Cf. *Win.* RWB. s. v. Synedrium; *Leyrer* in Herzog ed. 1 s. v. Synedrium [*Strack* in ed. 2] ; *Schürer*, Neutest. Zeitgesch. 2te Aufl. § 23, II., III. [and in Riehm p. 1595 sqq.]; *Holtzmann* in Schenkel v. p. 446 sqq.; [BB. DD. s. v. Sanhedrim (esp. *Ginsburg* in Alex.'s Kitto); *Hamburger*, Real-Encycl. ii. pp. 1147–1155; *Edersheim*, Jesus the Messiah, ii. 553 sqq.; *Farrar*, Life of Christ, Excurs. xiii.].*

4893   **συν-είδησις, -εως, ἡ,** (συνείδον), Lat. *conscientia*, [lit. 'joint-knowledge'; see σύν, II. 4], i. e.   **a.** *the consciousness of anything*: with a gen of the obj., τῶν ἁμαρτιῶν, a soul conscious of sins, Heb. x. 2 (τοῦ μύσους, Diod. 4, 65; συνείδησις εὐγενής, consciousness of nobility; a soul mindful of its noble origin, Hdian. 7, 1, 8 [3 ed. Bekk.]).   **b.** *the soul as distinguishing between what is morally good and bad, prompting to do the former and shun the latter, commending the one, condemning the other; c o n s c i e n c e :* with a gen. of the subj., ἡ σ. τινος, Ro. ii. 15 (where the idea of ἡ συνείδησις is further explained by καὶ μεταξὺ . . . ἢ καὶ ἀπολογουμένων [cf. W. 580 (539); see ἀπολογέομαι, 2, and συμμαρτυρέω]); Ro. ix. 1; 1 Co. viii. 7 [cf. W. § 30, 1 a.], 10, 12; x. 29; 2 Co. i. 12; iv. 2; v. 11; Heb. ix. 14 (ἡ τοῦ φαύλου συνείδησις, Philo, fragm., vol. ii. p. 659 ed. Mangey [vi. p. 217 sq. ed. Richter]); ἡ ἰδία συνείδησις, 1 Tim. iv. 2; ἄλλη συνείδ. i. q. ἄλλου τινὸς συν. 1 Co. x. 29; διὰ τὴν συνείδησιν, *for conscience' sake,* because conscience requires it (viz. the conduct in question), Ro. xiii. 5; in order not to occasion scruples of conscience (in another), 1 Co. x. 28; μηδὲν ἀνακρίνειν διὰ τὴν συνείδ. (anxiously) questioning nothing, as though such questioning were demanded by conscience, 1 Co. x. 25, 27; διὰ συνείδησιν θεοῦ, because conscience is impressed and governed by the idea of God (and so understands that griefs are to be borne according to God's will), 1 Pet. ii. 19; ἡ συνείδ. τοῦ εἰδώλου, a conscience impressed and controlled by an idea of the idol (i. e. by a notion of the idol's existence and power), 1 Co. viii. 7 Rec.; τελειῶσαί τινα κατὰ τὴν συνείδησιν (sc. αὐτοῦ), so to perfect one that his own conscience is satisfied, i. e. that he can regard himself as free from guilt, Heb. ix. 9; ἐλέγχεσθαι ὑπὸ τῆς συν. Jn. viii. 9 (ὑπὸ τοῦ συνειδότος, Philo de Josepho § 9 fin.; συνέχεσθαι τῇ συνειδ. Sap. xvii. 10); ἡ συνείδησις ἡ said μαρτυρεῖν, Ro. ix. 1; συμμαρτυρεῖν, Ro. ii. 15; τὸ μαρτύριον τῆς συν. 2 Co. i. 12.   With epithets : ἀσθενής, not strong enough to distinguish clearly between things lawful for a Christian and things unlawful, 1 Co. viii. 7, cf. 10; συνείδ. ἀγαθή, a conscience reconciled to God, 1 Pet. iii. 21; free from guilt, consciousness of rectitude, of right conduct, Acts xxiii. 1; 1 Tim. i. 5, (Hdian. 6, 3, 9 [4 ed. Bekk.]); ἔχειν συνείδ. ἀγαθήν, 1 Tim. i. 19; 1 Pet. iii. 16, (ἐν ἀγαθῇ συνεἰδ. ὑπάρχειν, Clem. Rom. 1 Cor. 41, 1) ; ἔχειν συν. καλήν, Heb. xiii. 18 ; συν. καθαρά, 1 Tim. iii. 9 ; 2 Tim. i. 3, (Clem. Rom. 1 Cor. 45, 7, cf. ἀγνὴ συν. ibid. 1, 3 ; καθαρὸς τῇ συνειδήσει, Ignat. ad Trall. 7, 2) ; ἀπρόσκοπος, Acts xxiv. 16 ; πονηρά, a mind conscic·is of wrong-doing, Heb. x. 22 ([ἐν συνειδήσει πο:ηρᾷ, 'Teaching' etc. 4, 14] ; ἀπρεπής, Lcian. amor. 49). ἡ συνείδησις καθαρίζεται ἀπὸ κτλ. Heb. ix. 14 ; μολύνεται, 1 Co. viii. 7 ; μιαίνεται, Tit. i. 15, (μηδὲν ἑκουσίως ψεύδεσθαι μηδὲ μιαίνειν τὴν αὑτοῦ συνείδησιν, Dion. Hal. jud. Thuc. 8. ἅπασιν ἡμῖν ἡ συνείδησις θεός, Menand. 597 p. 103 ed. Didot ; βροτοῖς ἅπασιν ἡ συνείδησις θεός, ibid. 654 p. 101 ed. Didot ; Epictet. fragm. 97 represents ἡ συνείδησις as filling the same office in adults which a tutor [παιδαγωγός, q. v.] holds towards boys ; with Philo, Plutarch, and others, τὸ συνειδός is more common. In Sept. once for כַּדָּע, Eccl. x. 20 ; [i. q. conscience, Sap. xvii. 11 ; cf. Delitzsch, Brief an d. Röm. p. 11]). Cf. esp. Jahnel, Diss. de conscientiae notione, qualis fuerit apud veteres et apud Christianos usque ad aevi medii exitum. Berol. 1862 [also the same, Ueber den Begr. Gewissen in d. Griech. Philos. (Berlin, 1872)] ; Kähler, Das Gewissen. I. die Entwickelung seiner Namen u. seines Begriffes. i. Alterth. u. N.ʹT. (Halle, 1878) ; [also in Herzog ed. 2, s. v. Gewissen ; Zezschwitz, Profangräcität u.s.w. pp. 52–57 ; Schenkel, s. v. Gewissen both in Herzog ed. 1, and in his BL. ; P. Ewald, De vocis συν. ap. script. Novi Test. vi ac potestate (pp. 91 ; 1883) ; other reff. in Schaff-Herzog, s. v. Conscience].*

see 4894 St.

συν-είδον, ptcp. συνιδών ; pf. σύνοιδα, ptcp. fem. gen. συνειδυίας (Acts v. 2 R G, -ης L T Tr WH ; cf. B. 12 (11) ; [Tdf. Proleg. p. 117 ; WH. App. p. 156]) ; (see εἴδω) ; fr. Hdt. down ; **1.** to see (have seen) together with others. **2.** to see (have seen) in one's mind, with one's self (cf. Fritzsche, Com. on Rom. vol. i. p. 120 ; on Mark pp. 36 and 78 ; [see σύν, II. 1 and 4]), i. e. to understand, perceive, comprehend : συνιδών, when he had understood it, Acts xii. 12 [A.V. considered] ; xiv. 6 [became aware], (2 Macc. iv. 41 ; xiv. 26, 30 ; 3 Macc. v. 50 ; Polyb. 1, 4, 6 ; 3, 6, 9 ; etc. ; Joseph. antt. 7, 15, 1 ; b. j. 4, 5, 4 ; Plut. Them. 7). Perfect σύνοιδα [cf. σύν, u. s.] **1.** to know with another, be privy to [so A.V.] : Acts v. 2. **2.** to know in one's mind or with one's self ; to be conscious of : τὶ ἐμαυτῷ, 1 Co. iv. 4 [R. V. know nothing against myself (cf. Wright, Bible Word-Book, 2d ed., s. v. 'By')] (τὴν ἀδικίαν, Joseph. antt. 1, 1, 4 ; exx. fr. Grk. writ. are given by Passow s. v. σύνοιδα, a. ; [L. and S. s. v. σύνοιδα, 2] ; foll. by ὅτι, [Dion. Hal. ii. 995, 9] ; Barn. ep. 1, (4) 3).*

4895   σύν-ειμι, ptcp. gen. plur. masc. συνόντων ; impf. 3 pers. plur. συνῆσαν ; (σύν, and εἰμί to be) ; fr. Hom. Od. 7, 270 down ; to be with : τινί, one, Lk. ix. 18 [WH mrg. συνήντησαν] ; Acts xxii. 11.*

4896   σύν-ειμι, ptcp. συνιών ; (σύν, and εἶμι to go) ; fr. Hom. down ; to come together : Lk. viii. 4.*

4897   συν-εισ-έρχομαι : 2 aor. συνεισῆλθον ; to enter together : τινί, with one, — foll. by an acc. of the place, Jn. vi. 22 ; xviii. 15. (Eur., Thuc., Xen., al. ; Sept.) *

4898   συν-έκδημος, -ου, ὁ, ἡ, (σύν, and ἔκδημος away from one's people), a fellow-traveller, companion in travel : Acts

xix. 29 ; 2 Co. viii. 19. ([Diod. fr. lib. 37, 5, 1 and 4 ed. Dind.] ; Joseph. vit. 14 ; Plut. Oth. 5 ; Palaeph. fab. 46, 4.)*

συν-εκ-λεκτός, -ή, -όν, (see ἐκλεκτός), elected or chosen (by God to eternal life) together with : 1 Pet. v. 13.*   **4899**

συν-ελαύνω : 1 aor. συνήλασα ; fr. Hom. down ; to drive together, to compel ; trop. to constrain by exhortation, urge : τινὰ εἰς εἰρήνην, to be at peace again, Acts vii. 26 R G (εἰς τὸν τῆς σοφίας ἔρωτα, Ael. v. h. 4, 15).*   **4900**

συν-επι-μαρτυρέω, -ῶ, ptcp. gen. sing. masc. συνεπιμαρτυροῦντος ; to attest together with ; to join in bearing witness, to unite in adding testimony : Heb. ii. 4. (Aristot., Polyb., [Plut.], Athen., Sext. Emp. ; Clem. Rom. 1 Cor. 23, 5 ; 43, 1.) *   **4901**

συν-επι-τίθημι : 2 aor. mid. συνεπεθέμην ; to place upon (or near) together with, help in putting on ; mid. to attack jointly, to assail together, set upon with, (see ἐπιτίθημι, 2 b.) : Acts xxiv. 9 G L T Tr WH [R V. joined in the charge] (so in Thuc. 6, 10 ; Xen. Cyr. 4, 2, 3 ; Plat. Phileb. p. 16 a. ; Polyb. 5, 78, 4 ; Diod. 1, 21).*   **see 2007**

συν-έπομαι : impf. συνειπόμην ; fr. Hom. down ; to follow with, to accompany : τινί, one, Acts xx. 4.*   **4902**

συνεργέω, -ῶ ; impf. 3 pers. sing. συνήργει ; (συνεργός, q. v.) ; fr. Eur., Xen., Dem. down ; Vulg. coöperor [(in 2 Co. vi. 1 adjuvo)] ; to work together, help in work, be a partner in labor : 1 Co. xvi. 16 ; 2 Co. vi. 1 ; to put forth power together with and thereby to assist, Mk. xvi. 20 ; τινί, with one : ἡ πίστις συνήργει τοῖς ἔργοις, faith (was not inactive, but by coworking) caused Abraham to produce works, Jas. ii. 22 [here Tr txt. συνέργει (hardly collat. form of συνείργω to unite, but) a misprint for -γεῖ] ; τινὶ εἴς τι (in prof. writ. also πρός τι, see Passow [or L. and S.] s. v.), to assist, help, (be serviceable to) one for a thing, Ro. viii. 28 [A. V. all things work together for good] ; τί τινι εἴς τι, a breviloquence equiv. to συνεργῶν πορίζω τί τινι, so that acc. to the reading πάντα συνεργεῖ ὁ θεός the meaning is, 'for them that love God, God coworking provides all things for good or so that it is well with them' (Fritzsche), [R. V. mrg. God worketh all things with them for good], Ro. viii. 28 Lchm. [WH in br. ; cf. B. 193 (167)], (ἑαυτοῖς τὰ συμφέροντα, Xen. mem. 3, 5, 16). Cf. Fritzsche, Ep. ad Rom. vol. ii. p. 193 sq.*   **4903**

συνεργός, -όν, (σύν and ΕΡΓΩ), [fr. Pind.], Europ., Thuc. down, a companion in work, fellow-worker, (Vulg. adjutor [Phil. ii. 25 ; 3 Jn. 8 coöperator]) : in the N. T. with a gen. of the pers., one who labors with another in furthering the cause of Christ, Ro. xvi. 3, 9, 21 ; Phil. ii. 25 ; iv. 3 ; [1 Th. iii. 2 Rec.] ; Philem. 1, 24 ; θεοῦ, one whom God employs as an assistant, as it were (a fellow-worker with God), 1 Th. iii. 2 (G L txt. WH mrg. but with τοῦ θεοῦ in br. ; Rec. et al. διάκονον, q. v. 1). plur. : 1 Co. iii. 9 ; with gen. of the thing (a joint-promoter [A. V. helper]), συν. ἐσμεν τῆς χαρᾶς, we labor with you to the end that we may rejoice in your Christian state, 2 Co. i. 24. εἰς ὑμᾶς, (my) fellow-worker to you-ward, in reference to you, 2 Co. viii. 23 ; εἰς τὴν βασ. τ. θεοῦ, for the advancement of the kingdom of God, Col. iv. 11 ; τῇ ἀληθείᾳ, for (the benefit of) the truth, [al. render (so R. V.)   **4904** '*with* the truth'; see Westcott ad loc.], 3 Jn. 8. (2 Macc. viii. 7 ; xiv. 5.) *

4905   **συν-έρχομαι**; impf. συνηρχόμην ; 2 aor. συνῆλθον, once (Acts x. 45 T Tr WH) 3 pers. plur. συνῆλθαν (see ἀπέρχομαι, init.) ; pf. ptcp. συνεληλυθώς ; plupf. 3 pers. plur. συνεληλύθεισαν ; fr. Hom. down (Il. 10, 224 in tmesis) ; **1.** *to come together,* i. e.   **a.** *to assemble* : absol., Mk. iii. 20 ; Acts i. 6 ; ii. 6 ; x. 27 ; xvi. 13 ; xix. 32 ; xxi. 22 ; [xxii. 30 G L T Tr WH] ; xxviii. 17 ; [1 Co. xiv. 20 ; foll. by ἐκ with gen. of place, Lk. v. 17 Lchm. txt.] ; foll. by εἰς with an acc. of the place, Acts v. 16 ; πρός τινα, Mk. vi. 33 Rec. ; ἐπὶ τὸ αὐτό [see ἐπί, C. I. 1 d.], 1 Co. xi. 20 ; xiv. 23 [here L txt. ἔλθῃ] ; with a dat. of the pers. *with one,* which so far as the sense is concerned is equiv. *to unto one* (for exx. fr. Grk. writ. see Passow s. v. 2 ; [L. and S. s. v. II. 1 and 3 ; cf. W. 215 (202)]), Mk. xiv. 53 [here T WH txt. om. Tr mrg. br. the dat.] ; Jn. xi. 33 ; with adverbs of place : ἐνθάδε, Acts xxv. 17 ; ὅπου, Jn. xviii. 20 ; [foll. by an infin. of purpose, Lk. v. 15] ; foll. by εἰς, — indicating either the end, as εἰς τὸ φαγεῖν, 1 Co. xi. 33 ; or the result, 1 Co. xi. 17, 34 ; ἐν ἐκκλησίᾳ, in sacred assembly [R. V. mrg. *in congregation*], 1 Co. xi. 18 (W. § 50, 4 a.).   **b.** Like the Lat. *convenio* i. q. *coeo* : of conjugal cohabitation, Mt. i. 18 [but cf. Weiss ad loc. (and the opinions in Meyer)] (Xen. mem. 2, 2, 4 ; Diod. 3, 58 ; Philo de caritat. § 14 ; de fortitud. § 7 ; de speciall. legg. § 4 ; Joseph. antt. 7, 8, 1 and 7, 9, 5 ; Apollod. bibl. 1, 3, 3) ; with ἐπὶ τὸ αὐτό added, 1 Co. vii. 5 Rec.   **2.** *to go* (*depart*) or *come with* one, *to accompany* one (see ἔρχομαι, II. p. 252ᵃ) : τινί, with one, Lk. xxiii. 55 [Tr txt. br. the dat.] ; Acts i. 21 [here A. V. *company with*] ; ix. 39 ; x. 23, 45 ; xi. 12 ; with εἰς τὸ ἔργον added, Acts xv. 38 ; σύν τινι, Acts xxi. 16.*

4906   **συν-εσθίω** ; impf. συνήσθιον ; 2 aor. συνέφαγον ; *to eat with, take food together with* [cf. σύν, II. 1] : τινί, with one, Lk. xv. 2 ; Acts x. 41 ; xi. 3 ; 1 Co. v. 11, (2 S. xii. 17) ; μετά τινος, Gal. ii. 12 ; Gen. xliii. 31 ; Ex. xviii. 12, [cf. W. § 52, 4, 15]. (Plat., Plut., Lcian.)*

4907   **σύνεσις**, -εως, ἡ, (συνίημι, q. v.) ;   **1.** *a running together,* *a flowing together* : of two rivers, Hom. Od. 10, 515.   **2.**   **a.** fr. Pind. down, *understanding* : Lk. ii. 47 ; 1 Co. i. 19 (fr. Is. xxix. 14) ; Eph. iii. 4 ; Col. ii. 2 ; 2 Tim. ii. 7 ; πνευματική, Col. i. 9.   **b.** *the understanding,* i. e. *the mind so far forth as it understands* : Mk. xii. 33 ; Sap. iv. 11. (Sept. for בִּינָה, תְּבוּנָה, דַּעַת, מַדָּע, שֵׂכֶל, etc. ; also for מַשְׂכִּיל, a poem.) [SYN. see σοφία, fin. ; cf. Bp. Lghtft. on Col. i. 9 ; Schmidt ch. 147, 8.] *

4908   **συνετός**, -ή, -όν, (συνίημι), fr. Pind. down, Sept. for חָכָם, נָבוֹן, etc., *intelligent, having understanding, wise, learned* : Mt. xi. 25 ; Lk. x. 21 ; Acts xiii. 7 ; 1 Co. i. 19 (fr. Is. xxix. 14). [SYN. see σοφός, fin.] *

4909   **συν-ευ-δοκέω**, -ῶ, (see εὐδοκέω, init.) ;   **a.** *to be pleased together with, to approve together* (with others) : absol. (yet so that the thing giving pleasure is evident from the context), Acts xxii. 20 G L T Tr WH ; with a dat. of the thing, Lk. xi. 48 ; Acts viii. 1 ; xxii. 20 Rec. ([Polyb. 24, 4, 13] ; 1 Macc. i. 57 ; 2 Macc. xi. 24).   **b.** *to be pleased at the same time with, consent, agree to,* ([Polyb. 32, 22, 9] ; 2 Macc. xi. 35) ; foll. by an inf. 1 Co. vii. 12 sq. [R.V. here *be content*] ; w. a dat. of a pers. *to applaud* [R. V. *consent with*], Ro. i. 32. (Diod. ; eccles. writ.) *

4910   **συν-ευωχέω**, -ῶ : pres. pass. ptcp. συνευωχούμενος ; (εὐωχέω, to feed abundantly, to entertain ; fr. εὖ and ἔχω) ; *to entertain together* ; pass. *to feast sumptuously with* : Jude 12 ; τινί, with one, 2 Pet. ii. 13. ([Aristot. eth. Eud. 7, 12, 14 p. 1245ᵇ, 5], Joseph., Lcian., al.) *

4911   **συν-εφ-ίστημι** : *to place over or appoint together* ; 2 aor. συνεπέστην ; *to rise up together* : κατά τινος, against one, Acts xvi. 22. [(From Thuc. down.)] *

4912   **συν-έχω** ; fut. συνέξω ; 2 aor. συνέσχον ; Pass., pres. συνέχομαι ; impf. συνειχόμην ; fr. Hom. down ;   **1.** *to hold together* ; any whole, lest it fall to pieces or something fall away from it : τὸ συνέχον τὰ πάντα, the deity as holding all things together, Sap. i. 7 (see Grimm ad loc.).   **2.** *to hold together with constraint, to compress,* i. e.   **a.** *to press together with the hand* : τὰ ὦτα, to stop the ears, Acts vii. 57 (τὸ στόμα, Is. lii. 15 ; τὸν οὐρανόν, to shut, that it may not rain, Deut. xi. 17 ; 1 K. viii. 35).   **b.** *to press on every side* : τινά, Lk. viii. 45 ; with πάντοθεν added, of a besieged city, Lk. xix. 43.   **3.** *to hold completely,* i. e.   **a.** *to hold fast* : prop. a prisoner, Lk. xxii. 63 (τὰ αἰχμάλωτα, Lcian. Tox. 39) ; metaph. in pass. *to be held by, closely occupied with,* any business (Sap. xvii. 19 (20) ; Hdian. 1, 17, 22, (9 ed. Bekk.) ; Ael. v. h. 14, 22) : τῷ λόγῳ, in teaching the word, Acts xviii. 5 G L T Tr WH [here R.V. *constrained by*].   **β.** *to constrain, oppress,* of ills laying hold of one and distressing him ; pass. *to be holden with* i. q. *afflicted with, suffering from* : νόσοις, Mt. iv. 24 ; πυρετῷ, Lk. iv. 38 ; δυσεντερίῳ, Acts xxviii. 8 (many exx. fr. Grk. writ. fr. Aeschyl. and Hdt. down are given in Passow s. v. συνέχω, I. a. ; [L. and S. s. v. I. 4]) ; of affections of the mind : φόβῳ, Lk. viii. 37 (ὀδύρμῷ, Ael. v. h. 14, 22 ; ἀληδόνι, Plut. de fluv. 2, 1 ; ἀθυμίᾳ, ib. 7, 5 ; 19, 1 ; λύπῃ, 17, 3 ; for other exx. see Grimm on Sap. xvii. 10).   **γ.** *to urge, impel* : trop. the soul, ἡ ἀγάπη ... συνέχει ἡμᾶς, 2 Co. v. 14 [A.V. *constraineth*] ; πῶς (how greatly, how sorely) συνέχομαι, Lk. xii. 50 [A. V. *straitened*] ; τῷ πνεύματι, Acts xviii. 5 Rec. συνέχομαι ἐκ τῶν δύο, I am hard pressed on both sides, my mind is impelled or disturbed from each side [R. V. *I am in a strait betwixt the two*], Phil. i. 23.*

συνζ-, see συζ-, and συν, II. sub fin.   **see 4862**

4913   **συν-ήδομαι** ;   **1.** in Grk. writ. chiefly fr. Soph., Eur., Xen. down, *to rejoice together with* (another or others [cf. σύν, II. 1]).   **2.** in the N. T. once *to rejoice or delight with one's self or inwardly* (see σύν, II. 4) : τινί, in a thing, Ro. vii. 22, where cf. Fritzsche ; [al refer this also to 1 ; cf. Meyer].*

4914   **συνήθεια**, -ας, ἡ, (συνήθης, and this fr. σύν and ἦθος), fr. Isocr., Xen., Plat. down, Lat. *consuetudo,* i. e.   **1.** *intercourse* (with one), *intimacy* : 4 Macc. xiii. 21.   **2.** *custom* : Jn. xviii. 39 [cf. B. § 139, 45] ; 1 Co. xi. 16.   **3.** *a being used to* : with a gen. of the object to which one is accustomed, 1 Co. viii. 7 L T Tr WH.*

4915　συν-ηλικιώτης, -ου, ὁ, (fr. σύν, and ἡλικία q. v.), one of the same age, an equal in age: Gal. i. 14. (Diod. 1, 53 fin.; Dion. Hal. antt. 10, 49 init.; but in both pass. the best codd. have ἡλικιώτης; [Corp. inscrr. iii. p. 434 no. 4929]; Alciphr. 1, 12). Cf. συμμαθητής.*

4916　συν-θάπτω: 2 aor. pass. συνετάφην; fr. Aeschyl. and Hdt. down; to bury together with: τῷ Χριστῷ, together with Christ, pass., διὰ τοῦ βαπτίσματος εἰς τὸν θάνατον sc. αὐτοῦ, Ro. vi. 4; ἐν τῷ βαπτίσματι, Col. ii. 12. For all who in the rite of baptism are plunged under the water, thereby declare that they put faith in the expiatory death of Christ for the pardon of their past sins; therefore Paul likens baptism to a burial by which the former sinfulness is buried, i. e. utterly taken away.*

4917　συν-θλάω, -ῶ: 1 fut. pass. συνθλασθήσομαι; to break to pieces, shatter, (Vulg. confringo, conquasso): Mt. xxi. 44 [but T om. L Tr mrg. WH br. the vs.]; Lk. xx. 18. (Sept.; [Manetho, Alex. ap. Athen., Eratosth., Aristot. (v. l.)], Diod., Plut., al.) *

4918　συν-θλίβω; impf. συνέθλιβον; to press together, press on all sides: τινά, of a thronging multitude, Mk. v. 24, 31. (Plat., Aristot., Strab., Joseph., Plut.) *

4919　συν-θρύπτω, ptcp. nom. plur. masc. συνθρύπτοντες; to break in pieces, to crush: metaph. τὴν καρδίαν, to break one's heart, i. e. to deprive of strength and courage, dispirit, incapacitate for enduring trials, Acts xxi. 13. (In eccles. and Byzant. writ.) *

see 4920—σvν-ίέω, see συνίημι.

4920　——— συν-ίημι, 2 pers. plur. συνίετε, 3 pers. plur. συνιοῦσιν (Mt. xiii. 13 R G T; 2 Co. x. 12 Rec., fr. the unused form συνιέω), and συνιᾶσιν (2 Co. x. 12 L T Tr WH), and συνίουσιν (Mt. xiii. 13 L Tr WH fr. the unused συνίω), subjunc. 3 pers. plur. συνιῶσι (R G L T Tr in Mk. iv. 12 and Lk. viii. 10, fr. the unused σύνιέω or fr. συνίημι) and συνίωσι (WH in Mk. and Lk. ll. cc., fr. the unused συνίω), impv. 2 pers. plur. συνίετε, inf. συνιέναι, ptcp. συνιῶν (Ro. iii. 11 R G T fr. συνιέω), and συνίων (ibid. L Tr WH, and often in Sept., fr. συνίω), and συνιείς (Mt. xiii. 23 L T Tr WH; Eph. v. 17 R G; but quite erroneously συνιῶν, Grsb. in Mt. l. c. [Alf. in Ro. iii. 11; cf. WH. App. p. 167; Tdf. Proleg. p. 122]; W. 81 (77 sq.); B. 48 (42); Fritzsche on Rom. vol. i. p. 174 sq.); fut. συνήσω (Ro. xv. 21); 1 aor. συνῆκα; 2 aor. subjunc. συνῆτε, συνῶσι, impv. 2 pers. plur. σύνετε (Mk. vii. 14 L T Tr WH); (σύν, and ἵημι to send); 1. prop. to set or bring together, in a hostile sense, of combatants, Hom. Il. 1, 8; 7, 210. 2. to put (as it were) the perception with the thing perceived; to set or join together in the mind, i. e. to understand, (so fr. Hom. down; Sept. for בִּין and הִשְׂכִּיל): with an acc. of the thing, Mt. xiii. 23, 51; Lk. ii. 50; xviii. 34; xxiv. 45; foll. by ὅτι, Mt. xvi. 12; xvii. 13; foll. by an indirect quest., Eph. v. 17; ἐπὶ τοῖς ἄρτοις, 'on the loaves' as the basis of their reasoning [see ἐπί, B. 2 a. a.], Mk. vi. 52; where what is understood is evident from the preceding context, Mt. xiii. 19; xv. 10; Mk. vii. 14; absol., Mt. xiii. 13-15; xv. 10; Mk. iv. 12; viii. 17, 21; Lk. viii. 10; Acts vii. 25; xxviii. 26 sq.; Ro. xv. 21; 2 Co. x. 12; ὁ συνιῶν or συνίων as subst. [B. 295

(253 sq.); W. 109 (104)], the man of understanding, Hebraistically i. q. a good and upright man (as having knowledge of those things which pertain to salvation; see μωρός): Ro. iii. 11 (fr. Ps. xiii. (xiv.) 2). [SYN. see γινώσκω, fin.] *

συνιστάω and συνιστάω, see the foll. word.　　see 4921

συν-ίστημι (Ro. iii. 5; v. 8; xvi. 1; 2 Co. x. 18; Gal.　4921 ii. 18 Rec.; ptcp. συνιστάντες, 2 Co. iv. 2 L T Tr; vi. 4 L T Tr), or συνιστάνω (2 Co. v. 12; Gal. ii. 18 G L T Tr WH; inf. συνιστάνειν, 2 Co. iii. 1 R G T WH; ptcp. συνιστάνων, 2 Co. iv. 2 WH; vi. 4 WH; x. 12, 18 L T Tr WH), or συνιστάω (inf. συνιστᾶν, 2 Co. iii. 1 L Tr; ptcp. συνιστῶν, 2 Co. iv. 2 R G; vi. 4 R G; x. 18 Rec.; see ἵστημι); 1 aor. συνέστησα; pf. συνέστηκα; 2 pf. ptcp. συνεστώς [nom. plur. neut. -ῶτα, 2 Pet. iii. 5 WH mrg.]; pres. pass. inf. συνίστασθαι; fr. Hom. Il. 14, 96 down; 1. to place together, to set in the same place, to bring or band together; in the 2 aor., pf. and plupf. intransitively, to stand with (or near): συνεστώς τινι, Lk. ix. 32. 2. to set one with another i. e. by way of presenting or introducing him, i. e. to commend (Xen., Plat., Dem., Polyb., Joseph., Plut.): τινά, 2 Co. iii. 1; vi. 4; x. 12, 18; τινά τινι, Ro. xvi. 1; 2 Co. v. 12 [cf. B. 393 (336)]; τινὰ πρὸς συνείδησίν τινος, 2 Co. iv. 2; pass. ὑπό τινος, 2 Co. xii. 11, (1 Macc. xii. 43; 2 Macc. iv. 24). 3. to put together by way of composition or combination, to teach by combining and comparing, hence to show, prove, establish, exhibit, [W. 23 (22)]: τί, Ro. iii. 5; v. 8, (εὔνοιαν, Polyb. 4, 5, 6); ἑαυτοὺς ὥς τινες, 2 Co. vi. 4; with two acc. one of the object, the other of the predicate, Gal. ii. 18 (Diod. 13, 91; συνίστησιν αὐτὸν προφήτην, Philo rer. div. haer. § 52); foll. by an acc. with inf. [cf. B. 274 (236)], 2 Co. vii. 11 (Diod. 14, 45). 4. to put together (i. e. unite parts into one whole), pf., plupf. and 2 aor. to be composed of, consist: ἐξ ὕδατος κ. δι᾽ ὕδατος, 2 Pet. iii. 5 [cf. W. § 45, 6 a.; (see above, init.)]; to cohere, hold together: τὰ πάντα συνέστηκεν ἐν αὐτῷ, Col. i. 17 (Plat. de rep. 7 p. 530 a.; Tim. p. 61 a.; [Bonitz's index to Aristotle (Berlin Acad. ed.) s. v. συνιστάναι], and often in eccles. writ.; [cf. Bp. Lghtft. on Col. l. c.]).*

[συν-κατα-νεύω: 1 aor. ptcp. συνκατανεύσας; to consent to, agree with: Acts xviii. 27 WH (rejected) mrg. (Polyb. 3, 52, 6; al.) *]

συνκ-, see συγκ-
συνλ-, see συλλ-　} cf. σύν, II. fin.　(4921α)
συνμ-, see συμμ-　　　　　　　　　　　　see 4862

συν-οδεύω; to journey with, travel in company with: with　4922 a dat. of the pers., Acts ix. 7. (Hdian. 4, 7, 11 [6 ed. Bekk.], Lcian., Plut., al.; Sap. vi. 25.) *

συνοδία, -ας, ἡ, (σύνοδος), a journey in company; by　4923 meton. a company of travellers, associates on a journey, a caravan, [A. V. company]: Lk. ii. 44. (Strab., Plut., [Epict., Joseph.; ξυνοδεία, Gen. xxxvii. 25 cod. Venet. i. q. family, Neh. vii. 5, 64, Sept.], al.) *

συν-οικέω, -ῶ; to dwell together (Vulg. cohabito): of the　4924 domestic association and intercourse of husband and wife, 1 Pet. iii. 7; for many exx. of this use, see Passow s. v. 1; [L. and S. s. v. I. 2].*

4925 συν-οικοδομέω, -ῶ : pres. pass. συνοικοδομοῦμαι ; (Vulg. coaedifico) ; to build together i. e.   **a.** to build together or with others [1 Esdr. v. 65 (66)].   **b.** to put together or construct by building, out of several things to build up one whole, (οἰκία εὖ συνῳκοδομημένη καὶ συνηρμοσμένη, of the human body, Philo de praem. et poen. § 20) : Eph. ii. 22. (Besides, in Thuc., Diod., Dio Cass., Plut.) *

4926 συν-ομιλέω, -ῶ ; to talk with : τινί, one, Acts x. 27. (to hold intercourse with, [Ceb. tab. 13 ; Joseph. b. j. 5, 13, 1], Epiphan., Tzetz.) *

4927 συν-ομορέω, -ῶ ; (συνόμορος, having joint boundaries, bordering on, fr. σύν and ὅμορος, and this fr. ὁμός joint, and ὅρος a boundary) ; to border on, be contiguous to, [A. V. join hard] : τινί, to a thing, Acts xviii. 7. (Byzant. writ.) *

4928 συν-οχή, -ῆς, ἡ, (συνέχω, q. v.), a holding together, narrowing ; narrows, the contracting part of a way, Hom. Il. 23, 330. Metaph. straits, distress, anguish : Lk. xxi. 25 ; with καρδίας added, 2 Co. ii. 4, (contractio animi, Cic. Tusc. 1, 37, 90 ; opp. to effusio, 4, 31, 66 ; συνοχὴν κ. ταλαιπωρίαν, Job xxx. 3 ; [cf. Judg. ii. 3 ; plur. Ps. xxiv. (xxv.) 17 Aq.]).*

see 4862   συνπ-, see συμπ-
see 4862   [συνσ-, see συσ- and συσσ-]   } cf. σύν, II. fin.
see 4862   συνστ-, see συστ-

4929 συν-τάσσω : 1 aor. συνέταξα ; fr. Hdt. down ;   **a.** to put in order with or together, to arrange ;   **b.** to (put together), constitute, i. e. to prescribe, appoint, (Aeschin., Dem. ; physicians are said συντάσσειν φάρμακον, Ael. v. h. 9, 13 ; [Plut. an sen. sit gerend. resp. 4, 8]) : τινί, Mt. xxi. 6 L Tr WH ; xxvi. 19 ; xxvii. 10 ; Sept. often for צִוָּה.*

4930 συντέλεια, -ας, ἡ, (συντελής), completion, consummation, end, (so in Grk. writ. fr. Polyb. on ; Sept. chiefly for כָּלָה ; for קֵץ in Dan. xii. 4, 13 ; in other senses fr. Aeschyl. down) : αἰῶνος or τοῦ αἰῶνος, Mt. xiii. 39, 40 L T Tr WH, 49 ; xxiv. 3 ; xxviii. 20 ; τοῦ αἰῶνος τούτου, Mt. xiii. 40 R G ; τῶν αἰώνων, Heb. ix. 26 (see αἰών, 3 p. 19ᵇ bot. [cf. Herm. sim. 9, 12, 3 and Hilgenfeld ad loc.]) ; καιροῦ and καιρῶν, Dan. ix. 27 ; xii. 4 ; τῶν ἡμερῶν, ibid. 13 ; ἀνθρώπου, of his death, Sir. xi. 27 (25) ; cf. xxi. 9.*

4931 συν-τελέω, -ῶ ; fut. συντελέσω ; 1 aor. συνετέλεσα ; Pass., pres. inf. συντελεῖσθαι ; 1 aor. συνετελέσθην (Jn. ii. 3 T WH 'rejected' mrg.), ptcp. συντελεσθείς ; fr. Thuc. and Xen. down ; Sept. often for כָּלָה ; also sometimes for תָּמַם, עָשָׂה, etc. ;   **1.** to end together or at the same time.   **2.** to end completely ; bring to an end, finish, complete : τοὺς λόγους, Mt. vii. 28 R G ; τὸν πειρασμόν, Lk. iv. 13 ; ἡμέρας, pass., Lk. iv. 2 ; Acts xxi. 27, (Job i. 5 ; Tob. x. 7).   **3.** to accomplish, bring to fulfilment ; pass. to come to pass, Mk. xiii. 4 ; λόγον, a word, i. e. a prophecy, Ro. ix. 28 (ῥῆμα, Lam. ii. 17).   **4.** to effect, make, [cf. our conclude] : διαθήκην, Heb. viii. 8 (Jer. xli. (xxxiv.) 8, 15).   **5.** to finish, i. e. in a use foreign to Grk. writ., to make an end of : συνετελέσθη ὁ οἶνος τοῦ γάμου, [was at an end with], Jn. ii. 3 Tdf. after cod. Sin. (Ezek. vii. 15 for אָכַל ; to bring to an end, destroy, for כָּלָה, Jer. xiv. 12 ; xvi. 4).*

συν-τέμνω ; pf. pass. ptcp. συντετμημένος ; fr. Aeschyl.   **4932** and Hdt. down ;   **1.** to cut to pieces, [cf. σύν, II. 3].   **2.** to cut short ; metaph. to despatch briefly, execute or finish quickly ; to hasten, (συντέμνειν sc. τὴν ὁδόν, to take a short cut, go the shortest way, Hdt. 7, 123 ; sc. τὸν λόγον, to speak briefly, Eur. Tro. 441 ; τὰς ἀποκρίσεις, to abridge, sum up, Plat. Prot. p. 334 d. ; ἐν βραχεῖ πολλοὺς λόγους, Arstph. Thesm. 178) : λόγον [q. v. I. 2 b. a.], to bring a prophecy or decree speedily to accomplishment, Ro. ix. 28 ; λόγος συντετμημένος, a short word, i. e. an expedited prophecy or decree, ibid. [R G Tr mrg. in br.] (both instances fr. Sept. of Is. x. 23) ; cf. Fritzsche ad loc. vol. ii. p. 350.*

συν-τηρέω, -ῶ : impf. 3 pers. sing. συνετήρει ; pres. pass.   **4933** 3 pers. plur. συντηροῦνται ; [fr. Aristot. de plant. 1, 1 p. 816ᵇ, 8 down] ;   **a.** to preserve (a thing from perishing or being lost) : τί, pass. (opp. to ἀπόλλυσθαι), Mt. ix. 17 ; Lk. v. 38 [T WH om. Tr br. the cl.] ; τινά, to guard one, keep him safe, fr. a plot, Mk. vi. 20 (ἑαυτὸν ἀναμάρτητον, 2 Macc. xii. 42 [cf. Tob. i. 11 ; Sir. xiii. 12]).   **b.** to keep within one's self, keep in mind (a thing, lest it be forgotten [cf. σύν, II. 4]) : πάντα τὰ ῥήματα, Lk. ii. 19 (τὸ ῥῆμα ἐν τῇ καρδίᾳ μου, Dan. vii. 28 Theod. ; τὴν γνώμην παρ' ἑαυτῷ, Polyb. 31, 6, 5 ; [absol. Sir. xxxix. 2]).*

συν-τίθημι : Mid., 2 aor. 3 pers. plur. συνέθεντο ; plpf.   **see 4934 St.** 3 pers. plur. συνετέθειντο ; fr. Hom. down ; to put with or together, to place together ; to join together ; Mid.   **a.** to place in one's mind, i. e. to resolve, determine ; to make an agreement, to engage, (often so in prof. writ. fr. Hdt. down ; cf. Passow s. v. 2 b. ; [L. and S. s. v. B. II.]) : συνετέθειντο, they had agreed together [W. § 38, 3], foll. by ἵνα, Jn. ix. 22 [W. § 44, 8 b.] ; συνέθεντο, they agreed together, foll. by τοῦ with an inf. [B. 270 (232)], Acts xxiii. 20 ; they covenanted, foll. by an inf. [B. u. s.], Lk. xxii. 5.   **b.** to assent to, to agree to : Acts xxiv. 9 Rec. [see συνεπιτίθημι] (τινί, Lys. in Harpocr. [s. v. Καρκίνος] p. 106, 9 Bekk.).*

συν-τόμως, (συντέμνω), [fr. Aeschyl., Soph., Plat. down],   **4935** adv., concisely i. e. briefly, in few words : ἀκοῦσαί τινος, Acts xxiv. 4 (γράψαι, Joseph. c. Ap. 1, 1 ; διδάσκειν, ibid. 1, 6, 2 ; [εἰπεῖν, ibid. 2, 14, 1 ; ἐξαγγέλλειν, Mk. xvi. WH (rejected) 'Shorter Conclusion']) ; for exx. fr. Grk. writ. see Passow [or L. and S.] s. v. fin.*

συν-τρέχω ; 2 aor. συνέδραμον ; fr. [Hom.], Aeschyl.,   **4936** Hdt. down ;   **1.** to run together : of the gathering of a multitude of people, ἐκεῖ, Mk. vi. 33 ; πρός τινα, Acts iii. 11.   **2.** to run along with others ; metaph. to rush with i. e. cast one's self, plunge, 1 Pet. iv. 4. [COMP. : ἐπι-συντρέχω.] *

συν-τρίβω, ptcp. neut. -τρίβον Lk. ix. 39 R G Tr, -τρί-   **4937** βον L T WH (cf. Veitch s. v. τρίβω, fin.) ; fut. συντρίψω ; 1 aor. συνέτριψα ; Pass., pres. συντρίβομαι ; pf. inf. συντετρίφθαι [R G Tr WH ; but -τρίφθαι L T (cf. Veitch u. s.)], ptcp. συντετριμμένος ; 2 fut. συντριβήσομαι ; fr. Hdt. [(?), Eurip.] down ; Sept. very often for שָׁבַר ; to break, to break in pieces, shiver, [cf. σύν, II. 3] : κάλαμον, Mt. xii. 20 ; τὰς πέδας, pass. Mk. v. 4 ; τὸ ἀλάβαστρον (the sealed orifice of the vase [cf. BB. DD. s. v. Alabaster]),

Mk. xiv. 3; ὀστοῦν, pass. Jn. xix. 36 (Ex. xii. 46; Ps. xxxiii. (xxxiv.) 21); τὰ σκεύη, Rev. ii. 27; *to tread down*: τὸν Σατανᾶν ὑπὸ τοὺς πόδας (by a pregn. constr. [W. § 66, 2 d.]), *to put Satan under foot and* (as a conqueror) *trample on him*, Ro. xvi. 20; *to break down, crush*: τινά, to tear one's body and shatter one's strength, Lk. ix. 39. Pass. to suffer extreme sorrow and be, as it were, crushed: οἱ συντετριμμένοι τὴν καρδίαν [cf. W. 229 (215)], i. q. οἱ ἔχοντες τὴν καρδίαν συντετριμμένην, [A. V. *the broken-hearted*], Lk. iv. 18 Rec. fr. Is. lxi. 1 ([cf. Ps. xxxiii. (xxxiv.) 19; cxlvi. (cxlvii.) 3, etc.]; συντριβῆναι τῇ διανοίᾳ, Polyb. 21, 10, 2; 31, 8, 11; τοῖς φρονήμασι, Diod. 11, 78; [ταῖς ἐλπίσιν, 4, 66; ταῖς ψυχαῖς, 16, 81]).*

4938 σύν‑τριμμα, ‑τος, τό, (συντρίβω), Sept. chiefly for שֶׁבֶר; **1.** *that which is broken* or *shattered, a fracture*: Aristot. de audibil. p. 802ᵃ, 34; of a broken limb, Sept. Lev. xxi. 19. **2.** trop. *calamity, ruin, destruction*: Ro. iii. 16, fr. Is. lix. 7, where it stands for שֹׁד, a devastation, laying waste, as in xxii. 4; Sap. iii. 3; 1 Macc. ii. 7; [etc.].*

4939 σύν‑τροφος, ‑ου, ὁ, (συντρέφω), [fr. Hdt. down], *nourished with one* (Vulg. *collactaneus* [Eng. *foster-brother*]); *brought up with one*; univ. *companion of one's childhood and youth*: τινός (of some prince or king), Acts xiii. 1. (1 Macc. i. 6; 2 Macc. ix. 29; Polyb. 5, 9, 4; Diod. 1, 53; Joseph. b. j. 1, 10, 9; Ael. v. h. 12, 26.)*

4941 Συντύχη and (so Tdf. edd. 7, 8; cf. *Lipsius*, Gramm. Untersuch. p. 31; [*Tdf.* Proleg. p. 103; Kühner § 84 fin.; on the other hand, Chandler § 199]) Συντυχή, ή, [acc. ‑ην], *Syntyche*, a woman belonging to the church at Philippi: Phil. iv. 2. (The name occurs several times in Grk. inscrr. [see Bp. Lghtft. on Phil. l. c.].)*

4940 συν‑τυγχάνω: 2 aor. inf. συντυχεῖν; fr. [Soph.], Hdt. down; *to meet with, come to* [A. V. *come at*] one: with a dat. of the pers., Lk. viii. 19.*

4942 συν‑υπο‑κρίνομαι: 1 aor. pass. συνυπεκρίθην, with the force of the mid. [cf. B. 52 (45)]; *to dissemble with*: τινί, one, Gal. ii. 13. (Polyb. 3, 92, 5 and often; see *Schweighaeuser*, Lex. Polyb. p. 604; Plut. Marius, 14, 17.)*

4943 συν‑υπουργέω, ‑ῶ; (ὑπουργέω to serve, fr. ὑπουργός, and this fr. ὑπό and ΕΡΓΩ); *to help together*: τινί, by any thing, 2 Co. i. 11. (Lcian. bis accusat. c. 17 συναγωνιζομένης τῆς ἡδονῆς, ἥπερ αὐτῇ τὰ πολλὰ ξυνυπουργεῖ.)*

see 4862 συνφ‑, see συμφ‑ ⎫
see 4862 συνχ‑, see συνχ‑ ⎬ cf. σύν, II. fin.
see 4862 συνψ‑, see συμψ‑ ⎭

4944 συν‑ωδίνω; **a.** prop. *to feel the pains of travail with, be in travail together*: οἶδε ἐπὶ τῶν ζῴων τὰς ὠδῖνας ὁ σύνοικος καὶ συνωδίνει γε τὰ πολλὰ ὥσπερ καὶ ἀλεκτρυόνες, Porphyr. de abstin. 3, 10; [cf. Aristot. eth. Eud. 7, 6 p. 1240ᵃ, 36]. **b.** metaph. *to undergo agony* (like a woman in childbirth) *along with*: Ro. viii. 22 (where σύν refers to the several parts of which ή κτίσις consists, cf. Meyer ad loc.); κακοῖς, Eur. Hel. 727.*

4945 συνωμοσία, ‑ας, ή, (συνόμνυμι), fr. Arstph. and Thuc. down, *a swearing together*; *a conspiracy*: συνωμοσίαν ποιεῖν (see ποιέω, I. 1 c. p. 525ᵃ top), Acts xxiii. 13 Rec.; ποιεῖσθαι (see ποιέω, I. 3), ibid. L T Tr WH.*

4946 Συράκουσαι [so accented commonly (Chandler §§ 172, 175); but acc. to *Pape*, Eigennamen, s. v., ‑κοῦσαι in Ptol. 3, 4, 9; 8, 9, 4], ‑ῶν, αἱ, *Syracuse*, a large maritime city of Sicily, having an excellent harbor and surrounded by a wall 180 stadia in length [so Strabo 6 p. 270; "but this statement exceeds the truth, the actual circuit being about 14 Eng. miles or 122 stadia" (Leake p. 279); see Dict. of Geogr. s. v. p. 1067ᵇ]; now *Siragosa*: Acts xxviii. 12.*

4947 Συρία, ‑ας, ή, *Syria*; in the N. T. a region of Asia, bounded on the N. by the Taurus and Amanus ranges, on the E. by the Euphrates and Arabia, on the S. by Palestine, and on the W. by Phœnicia and the Mediterranean, [cf. BB.DD. s. v. Syria; *Ryssel* in Herzog ed. 2, s. v. Syrien; cf. also Ἀντιόχεια, 1 and Δαμασκός]: Mt. iv. 24; Lk. ii. 2; Acts xv. 23, 41; xviii. 18; xx. 3; xxi. 3; Gal. i. 21. [On the art. with it cf. W. § 18, 5 a.]*

4948 Σύρος, ‑ου, ὁ, *a Syrian*, i. e. a native or an inhabitant of Syria: Lk. iv. 27; fem. Σύρα, *a Syrian woman*, Mk. vii. 26 Tr WH mrg. [(Hdt., al.)]*

4949 Συροφοίνισσα (so Rec.; a form quite harmonizing with the analogies of the language, for as Κίλιξ forms the fem. Κίλισσα, Θρᾷξ the fem. Θρᾷσσα, ἄναξ the fem. ἄνασσα, so the fem. of Φοῖνιξ is always, by the Greeks, called Φοίνισσα), Συροφοινίκισσα (so L T WH; hardly a pure form, and one which must be derived fr. Φοινίκη; cf. Fritzsche on Mk. p. 296 sq.; W. 95 (91)), Συραφοινίκισσα (Grsb.; a form which conflicts with the law of composition), ‑ης, ή, (Tr WH mrg. Σύρα Φοινίκισσα), *a Syrophœnician* woman, i. e. of Syrophoenice by race, that is, from the Phoenice forming a part of Syria (Σύρο being prefixed for distinction's sake, for there were also Λιβυφοίνικες, i. e. the Carthaginians. The Greeks included both Phœnicia and Palestine under the name ή Συρία; hence Συρία ή Παλαιστίνη in Hdt. 3, 91; 4, 39; Just. Mart. apol. i. 1; and ή Φοινίκη Συρία, Diod. 19, 93; Συροφοινίκη, Just. Mart. dial. c. Tryph. c. 78, p. 305 a.): Mk. vii. 26 [cf. B. D. s. v. Syro-Phœnician]. (The masc. Συροφοῖνιξ is found in Lcian. concil. deor. c. 4; [*Syrophoenix* in Juv. sat. 8, 159 (cf. 160)].)*

4950 Σύρτις [Lchm. σύρτις; cf. *Tdf.* Proleg. p. 103; Chandler § 650], ‑εως, acc. ‑ιν, ή, (σύρω, q. v. [al. fr. Arab. *sert* i. e. 'desert'; al. al., see *Pape*, Eigennamen, s. v.]), *Syrtis*, the name of two places in the African or Libyan Sea between Carthage and Cyrenaica, full of shallows and sandbanks, and therefore destructive to ships; the western *Syrtis*, between the islands Cercina and Meninx [or the promontories of Zeitha and Brachodes], was called *Syrtis minor*, the eastern [extending from the promontory of Cephalae on the W. to that of Boreum on the E.] was called *Syrtis major* (*sinus Psyllicus*); this latter must be the one referred to in Acts xxvii. 17, for upon this the ship in which Paul was sailing might easily be cast after leaving Crete. [Cf. B. D. s. v. Quicksands.]*

4951 σύρω; impf. ἔσυρον; fr. [Aeschyl. and Hdt. (in comp.), Aristot.], Theocr. down; [Sept. 2 S. xvii. 13]; *to draw, drag*: τί, Jn. xxi. 8; Rev. xii. 4; τινά, one (before the judge, to prison, to punishment; ἐπὶ τὰ βασανιστήρια, εἰς

τὸ δεσμωτήριον, Epict. diss. 1, 29, 22; al.), Acts viii. 3;
ἔξω τῆς πόλεως, Acts xiv. 19; ἐπὶ τοὺς πολιτάρχας, Acts
xvii. 6. [COMP.: κατασύρω.]*

4952 συ-σπαράσσω: 1 aor. συνεσπάραξα; to convulse completely (see ῥήγνυμι, c.): τινά, Mk. ix. 20 L T Tr mrg.
WH; Lk. ix. 42. (Max. Tyr. diss. 13, 5.)*

4953 σύσ-σημον [Tdf. συν- (cf. σύν, II. fin.)], -ον, τό, (σύν
and σῆμα), a common sign or concerted signal, a sign given
acc. to agreement: Mk. xiv. 44. (Diod., Strab., Plut., al.;
for סֵן, a standard, Is. v. 26; xlix. 22; lxii. 10.) The
word is condemned by Phrynichus, ed. Lob. p. 418, who
remarks that Menander was the first to use it; cf. Sturz,
De dial. Maced. et Alex. p. 196.*

4954 σύσ-σωμος [L T Tr WH συν- (cf. σύν, II. fin.)], -ον,
(σύν and σῶμα), belonging to the same body (i. e. metaph.
to the same church) [R. V. fellow-members of the body]:
Eph. iii. 6. (Eccles. writ.)*

4955 συ-στασιαστής, -οῦ, ὁ, (see στασιαστής), a companion
in insurrection, fellow-rioter: Mk. xv. 7 R G (Joseph.
antt. 14, 2, 1).*

4956 συ-στατικός [Tr συν- (cf. σύν, II. fin.)], -ή, -όν, (συν-
ίστημι, q. v.), commendatory, introductory: ἐπιστολαὶ συστ.
[A. V. epistles of commendation], 2 Co. iii. 1ᵃ, 1ᵇ R G,
and often in eccles. writ., many exx. of which have been
collected by Lydius, Agonistica sacra (Zutph. 1700), p.
123, 15; [Suicer, Thesaur. Eccles. ii. 1194 sq.]. (γράμματα παρ' αὐτοῦ λαβεῖν συστατικά, Epict. diss. 2, 3, 1; [cf.
Diog. Laërt. 8, 87]; τὸ κάλλος παντὸς ἐπιστολίου συστα-
τικώτερον, Aristot. in Diog. Laërt. 5, 18, and in Stob. flor.
65, 11, ii. 435 ed. Gaisf.)*

4957 συ-σταυρόω [L T Tr WH συν- (cf. σύν, II. fin.)], -ῶ:
Pass., pf. συνεσταύρωμαι; 1 aor. συνεσταυρώθην; to crucify along with; τινά τινι, one with another; prop.:
Mt. xxvii. 44 (σὺν αὐτῷ L T Tr WH); Mk. xv. 32 (σὺν
αὐτῷ L T WH); Jn. xix. 32; metaph.: ὁ παλαιὸς ἡμῶν
ἄνθρωπος συνεσταυρώθη sc. τῷ Χριστῷ, i. e. (dropping the
figure) the death of Christ upon the cross has wrought
the extinction of our former corruption, Ro. vi. 6; Χριστῷ
συνεσταύρωμαι, by the death of Christ upon the cross I
have become utterly estranged from (dead to) my former habit of feeling and action, Gal. ii. 19 (20).*

4958 συ-στέλλω: 1 aor. συνέστειλα; pf. pass. ptcp. συνεσταλμένος; prop. to place together; **a.** to draw together,
contract, (τὰ ἱστία, Arstph. ran. 999; τὴν χεῖρα, Sir. iv.
31; εἰς ὀλίγον συστέλλω, Theophr. de caus. plant. 1, 15,
1); to diminish (τὴν δίαιταν, Isocr. p. 280 d.; Dio Cass.
39, 37); to shorten, abridge, pass. ὁ καιρὸς συνεσταλμένος
ἐστίν, the time has been drawn together into a brief
compass, is shortened, 1 Co. vii. 29. **b.** to roll together, wrap up, wrap round with bandages, etc., to en-
shroud (τινὰ πέπλοις, Eur. Troad. 378): τινά, i. e. his
corpse (for burial), Acts v. 6.*

4959 συ-στενάζω [T WH συν- (cf. σύν, II. fin.)]; to groan
together: Ro. viii. 22, where σύν has the same force as
in συνωδίνω, b. (τινί, with one, Eur. Ion 935; Test. xii.
Patr. (test. Isach. § 7) p. 629).*

4960 συ-στοιχέω [T WH συν- (cf. σύν, II. fin.)], -ῶ; (see στοιχέω); to stand or march in the same row (file) with: so once

prop. of soldiers, Polyb. 10, 21, 7; hence to stand over
against, be parallel with; trop. to answer to, resemble: τινί,
so once of a type in the O. T. which answers to the antitype in the New, Gal. iv. 25 [cf. Bp. Lghtft. ad loc.].*

4961 συ-στρατιώτης [T Tr WH συν- (so Lchm. in Philem.;
cf. σύν, II. fin.)], -ου, ὁ, a fellow-soldier, Xen., Plat., al.;
trop. an associate in labors and conflicts for the cause of
Christ: Phil. ii. 25; Philem. 2.*

4962 συ-στρέφω: 1 aor. ptcp. συστρέψας; pres. pass. ptcp.
συστρεφόμενος; [fr. Aeschyl. and Hdt. down]; **1.**
to twist together, roll together (into a bundle): φρυγάνων
πλῆθος, Acts xxviii. 3. **2.** to collect, combine, unite:
τινάς, pass. [reflexively (?)] of men, to [gather themselves
together,] assemble: Mt. xvii. 22 L T Tr txt. WH, see
ἀναστρέφω, 3 a.*

4963 συ-στροφή, -ῆς, ἡ, (συστρέφω); **a.** a twisting up
together, a binding together. **b.** a secret combination,
a coalition, conspiracy: Acts xxiii. 12 (Ps. lxiii. (lxiv.)
3; [2 K. xv. 15; Am. vii. 10]); a concourse of disorderly
persons, a riot (Polyb. 4, 34, 6), Acts xix. 40.*

4964 συ-σχηματίζω [WH συν- (so T in Ro., Tr in 1 Pet.; cf·
σύν, II. fin.)]: pres. pass. ptcp. συσχηματίζομαι; (σχηματίζω, to
form); a later Grk. word; to conform [(Aristot. top. 6,
14 p. 151ᵇ, 8; Plut. de profect. in virt. 12 p. 83 b.)];
pass. reflexively, τινί, to conform one's self (i. e. one's
mind and character) to another's pattern, [fashion one's
self according to, (cf. Bp. Lghtft. Com. on Phil. p. 130
sq.)]: Ro. xii. 2; 1 Pet. i. 14 [cf. W. 352 (330 sq.)].
(πρός τι, Plut. Num. 20 com. text.)*

4965 Συχάρ (Rec.ᵉˡˢ Σιχάρ), ἡ, Sychar, a town of Samaria,
near to the well of the patriarch Jacob, and not far from
Flavia Neapolis (Συχὰρ πρὸ τῆς Νέας πόλεως, Euseb. in
his Onomast. [p. 346, 5 ed. Larsow and Parthey]) towards the E., the representative of which is to be found
apparently in the modern hamlet al Askar (or 'Asker):
Jn. iv. 5, where cf. Bäumlein, Ewald, Brückner [in De
Wette (4th and foll. edd.)], Godet; add, Ewald, Jahrbb.
f. bibl. Wissensch. viii. p. 255 sq.; Bädeker, Palestine,
pp. 328, 337; [Lieut. Conder in the Palest. Explor. Fund
for July 1877, p. 149 sq. and in Survey of West. Pal.:
'Special Papers', p. 231; Edersheim, Jesus the Messiah,
Appendix xv.]. The name does not seem to differ
from סוכר, a place mentioned by the Talmudists in
עין סוכר 'the fountain Sucar' and בקעת עין סוכר 'the
valley of the fountain Sucar'; cf. Delitzsch in the Zeitschr. f. d. luth. Theol. for 1856, p. 240 sqq. Most interpreters, however, think that Συχάρ is the same as
Συχέμ (q. v. 2), and explain the form as due to a soften-
ing of the harsh vulgar pronunciation (cf. Credner, Einl.
in d. N. T. vol. i. p. 264 sq.), or conjecture that it was
fabricated by way of reproach by those who wished to
suggest the noun שֶׁקֶר, 'falsehood', and thereby brand
the city as given up to idolatry [cf. Hab. ii. 18], or the
word שִׁכֹּר, 'drunken' (on account of Is. xxviii. 1), and
thus call it the abode of μωροί, see Sir. l. 26, where
the Shechemites are called λαὸς μωρός; cf. Test. xii. Patr.
(test. Levi § 7) p. 564 Σικήμ, λεγομένη πόλις ἀσυνέτων.
To these latter opinions there is this objection, among

others, that the place mentioned by the Evangelist was very near Jacob's well, from which Shechem, or Flavia Neapolis, was distant about a mile and a half. [Cf. B.D. s. v. Sychar; also *Porter* in Alex.'s Kitto, ibid.] *

4966 Συχέμ, Hebr. שְׁכֶם [i. e. 'shoulder,' 'ridge'], *Shechem* [A. V. *Sychem* (see below)], prop. name of **1.** a man of Canaan, son of Hamor (see Ἐμμόρ), prince in the city of Shechem (Gen. xxxiii. 19; xxxiv. 2 sqq.): Acts vii. 16 R G. **2.** a city of Samaria (in Sept. sometimes Συχέμ, indecl., sometimes Σίκιμα, gen. -ων, as in Joseph. and Euseb.; once τὴν Σίκιμα τὴν ἐν ὄρει Ἐφραΐμ, 1 K. xii. 25 [for still other var. see B. D. (esp. Am. ed.) s. v. Shechem]), Vulg. *Sichem* [ed. Tdf. *Sychem*; cf. B.D. u. s.], situated in a valley abounding in springs at the foot of Mt. Gerizim (Joseph. antt. 5, 7, 2; 11, 8, 6); laid waste by Abimelech (Judg. ix. 45), it was rebuilt by Jeroboam and made the seat of government (1 K. xii. 25). From the time of Vespasian it was called by the Romans *Neapolis* (on coins *Flavia Neapolis*); whence by corruption comes its modern name, *Nablus* [or *Nabulus*]; acc. to Prof. *Socin* (in Bädeker's Palestine p. 331) it contains about 13,000 inhabitants (of whom 600 are Christians, and 140 Samaritans) together with a few ["about 100"] Jews: Acts vii. 16.*

4967 σφαγή, -ῆς, ἡ, (σφάζω), *slaughter*: Acts viii. 32 (after Is. liii. 7); πρόβατα σφαγῆς, *sheep* destined *for slaughter* (Zech. xi. 4; Ps. xliii. (xliv.) 23), Ro. viii. 36; ἡμέρα σφαγῆς (Jer. xii. 3), i. q. day of destruction, Jas. v. 5. (Tragg., Arstph., Xen., Plat., sqq.; Sept. for הֲרֵגָה, טֶבַח, etc.) *

4968 σφάγιον, -ου, τό, (σφαγή), fr. Aeschyl. and Hdt. down, that which is destined for slaughter, *a victim* [A.V. *slain beast*]: Acts vii. 42 [cf. W. 512 (477)] (Am. v. 25; Ezek. xxi. 10).*

4969 σφάζω, Attic σφάττω: fut. σφάξω, Rev. vi. 4 L T Tr WH; 1 aor. ἔσφαξα; Pass., pf. ptcp. ἐσφαγμένος; 2 aor. ἐσφάγην; fr. Hom. down; very often for שָׁחַט, to *slay*, *slaughter, butcher*: prop., ἀρνίον, Rev. v. 6, 12; xiii. 8; τινά, to put to death by violence (often so in Grk. writ. fr. Hdt. down), 1 Jn. iii. 12; Rev. v. 9; vi. 4, 9; xviii. 24. κεφαλὴ ἐσφαγμένη εἰς θάνατον, mortally wounded [R.V. *smitten unto death*], Rev. xiii. 3. [Comp.: κατα-σφάζω.]*

4970 σφόδρα (properly neut. plur. of σφοδρός, vehement, violent), fr. Pind. and Hdt. down, *exceedingly, greatly*: placed after adjectives, Mt. ii. 10; Mk. xvi. 4; Lk. xviii. 23; Rev. xvi. 21; with verbs, Mt. xvii. 6, 23; xviii. 31; xix. 25; xxvi. 22; xxvii. 54; Acts vi. 7.*

4971 σφοδρῶς, adv., fr. Hom. Od. 12, 124 down, *exceedingly*: Acts xxvii. 18.*

4972 σφραγίζω (Rev. vii. 3 Rec.ˢᵗ); 1 aor. ἐσφράγισα; 1 aor. mid. ptcp. σφραγισάμενος; Pass., pf. ptcp. ἐσφραγισμένος; 1 aor. ἐσφραγίσθην; [in 2 Co. xi. 10 Rec.ˢᵗ gives the form σφραγίσεται "de coniectura vel errore" (Tdf.; see his note ad loc.)]; (σφραγίς, q. v.); Sept. for חָתַם; to set a *seal upon, mark with a seal, to seal*; **a.** for security: τί, Mt. xxvii. 66; sc. τὴν ἄβυσσον, to close it, lest Satan after being cast into it should come out;

hence the addition ἐπάνω αὐτοῦ, over him i. e. Satan, Rev. xx. 3, (ἐν ᾧ —i. e. δώματι — κεραυνός ἐστιν ἐσφραγισμένος, Aeschyl. Eum. 828; mid. σφραγίζομαι τὴν θύραν, Bel and the Dragon 14 Theodot.). **b.** Since things sealed up are concealed (as, the contents of a letter), σφραγίζω means trop. *to hide* (Deut. xxxii. 34), *keep in silence, keep secret*: τί, Rev. x. 4; xxii. 10, (τὰς ἁμαρτίας, Dan. ix. 24 Theodot.; τὰς ἀνομίας, Job xiv. 17; τοὺς λόγους σιγῇ, Stob. flor. 34, 9 p. 215; θαύματα πολλὰ σοφῇ σφρηγίσσατο σιγῇ, Nonn. paraphr. evang. Ioan. 21, 140). **c.** in order to mark a person or thing; hence *to set a mark upon by the impress of a seal, to stamp*: angels are said σφραγίζειν τινὰς ἐπὶ τῶν μετώπων, i. e. with the seal of God (see σφραγίς, c.) to stamp his servants on their foreheads as destined for eternal salvation, and by this means to confirm their hopes, Rev. vii. 3, cf. Ewald ad loc. [B.D. s. vv. Cuttings and Forehead]; hence οἱ ἐσφραγισμένοι, fourteen times in Rec. vss. 4–8, four times by G L T Tr WH, (δεινοῖσι σημάντροισιν ἐσφραγισμένοι, Eur. Iph. Taur. 1372); metaph.: τινὰ τῷ πνεύματι and ἐν τῷ πν., respecting God, who by the gift of the Holy Spirit indicates who are his, pass., Eph. i. 13; iv. 30; absol., mid. with τινά, 2 Co. i. 22. **d.** in order to prove, confirm, or attest a thing; hence trop. *to confirm, authenticate, place beyond doubt*, (a written document τῷ δακτυλίῳ, Esth. viii. 8): foll. by ὅτι, Jn. iii. 33; τινά, to prove by one's testimony to a person that he is what he professes to be, Jn. vi. 27. Somewhat unusual is the expression σφραγισάμενος αὐτοῖς τὸν καρπὸν τοῦτον, when I shall have confirmed (sealed) to them this fruit (of love), meaning apparently, when I shall have given authoritative assurance that this money was collected for their use, Ro. xv. 28. [Comp.: κατα-σφραγίζω.] *

4973 σφραγίς, -ῖδος, ἡ, (akin, apparently, to the verb φράσσω or φράγνυμι), fr. Hdt. down, Sept. for חוֹתָם, *a seal*; i.e. **a.** *the seal placed upon books* [cf. B. D. s. v. Writing, subfin.; *Gardthausen*, Palaeogr. p. 27]: Rev. v. 1; λῦσαι τὰς σφρ., ib. 2, 5 [Rec.]; ἀνοῖξαι, ib. [5 G L T Tr WH], 9; vi. 1, 3, 5, 7, 9, 12; viii. 1. **b.** *a signet-ring*: Rev. vii. 2. **c.** *the inscription* or *impression made by a seal*: Rev. ix. 4 (the name of God and Christ stamped upon their foreheads must be meant here, as is evident from xiv. 1); 2 Tim. ii. 19. **d.** *that by which anything is confirmed, proved, authenticated, as by a seal*, (a token or proof): Ro. iv. 11; 1 Co. ix. 2. [Cf. BB.DD. s. v. Seal.] *

σφυδρόν, -οῦ, τό, i. q. σφυρόν, q. v.: Acts iii. 7 T WH. **see 4974** (Hesych. σφυδρά· ἡ περιφέρεια τῶν ποδῶν.) *

σφυρίς, i. q. σπυρίς, q. v., (cf. *Lob.* ad Phryn. p. 113; **see 4711** Curtius p. 503; [*Steph.* Thesaur. s. vv.]), Lchm. in Mt. xvi. 10 and Mk. viii. 8; WH uniformly (see their App. p. 148).*

σφυρόν, -οῦ, τό, fr. Hom. down, *the ankle* [A.V. *ankle-* **4974** *bone*]: Acts iii. 7 [T WH σφυδρόν, q. v.].*

σχεδόν, (ἔχω, σχεῖν), adv., fr. Hom. down; **1.** *near,* **4975** *hard by*. **2.** fr. Soph. down [of degree, i. e.] *well-nigh, nearly, almost*; so in the N. T. three times before πᾶς:

Acts xiii. 44 ; xix. 26 ; Heb. ix. 22 [but see W. 554 (515)
n.; (R. V. *I may almost say*)]; (2 Macc. v. 2 ; 3 Macc.
v. 14).*

4976 σχῆμα, -τος, τό, (ἔχω, σχεῖν), fr. Aeschyl. down, Lat.
habitus [cf. Eng. *haviour* (fr. *have*)], A. V. *fashion*, Vulg.
figura [but in Phil. *habitus*], (tacitly opp. to the material or substance): τοῦ κόσμου τούτου, 1 Co. vii. 31 ; *the
habitus*, as comprising everything in a person which
strikes the senses, the figure, bearing, discourse, actions,
manner of life, etc., Phil. ii. 7 (8). [Syn. see μορφή
fin., and Schmidt ch. 182, 5.]*

4977 σχίζω [(Lk. v. 36 R G L mrg.)]; fut. σχίσω (Lk. v. 36
L txt. T Tr txt. WH [cf. B. 37 (32 sq.)]) ; 1 aor. ἔσχισα ;
Pass., pres. ptcp. σχιζόμενος ; 1 aor. ἐσχίσθην ; [allied w.
Lat. *scindo, caedo*, etc. (cf. Curtius § 295)]; fr. [(Hom.
h. Merc.)] Hesiod down ; Sept. several times for בָּקַע, Is.
xxxvii. 1 for קָרַע ; *to cleave, cleave asunder, rend*: τί, Lk.
v. 36 ; pass. αἱ πέτραι, Mt. xxvii. 51 ; οἱ οὐρανοί, Mk. i. 10 ;
τὸ καταπέτασμα, Lk. xxiii. 45 ; with εἰς δύο added, into two
parts, *in twain* [(εἰς δύο μέρη, of a river, Polyb. 2, 16,
11)], Mt. xxvii. 51 ; Mk. xv. 38 ; τὸ δίκτυον, Jn. xxi. 11 ;
to divide by rending, τί, Jn. xix. 24. trop. in pass. *to
be split into factions, be divided*: Acts xiv. 4 ; xxiii. 7,
(Xen. conv. 4, 59 ; τοῦ πλήθους σχιζομένου κατὰ αἵρεσιν,
Diod. 12, 66).*

4978 σχίσμα, -τος, τό, (σχίζω), *a cleft, rent* ; **a.** prop.
a rent : Mt. ix. 16 ; Mk. ii. 21, (Aristot., Theophr.). **b.**
metaph. *a division, dissension* : Jn. vii. 43 ; ix. 16 ; x.
19 ; 1 Co. i. 10 ; xi. 18 ; xii. 25, (eccles. writ. [Clem.
Rom. 1 Cor. 2, 6, etc.; ' Teaching ' 4, 3 ; etc.]). [Cf. reff.
s. v. αἵρεσις, 5.]*

4979 σχοινίον, -ου, τό, (dimin. of the noun σχοῖνος, ὁ and ἡ, a
rush), fr. Hdt. down, prop. *a cord* or *rope made of rushes* ;
univ. *a rope* : Jn. ii. 15 ; Acts xxvii. 32.*

4980 σχολάζω ; 1 aor. subjunc. σχολάσω, 1 Co. vii. 5 G L T
Tr WH ; (σχολή, q. v.) ; **1.** *to cease from labor* ;
to loiter. **2.** *to be free from labor, to be at leisure,
to be idle* ; τινί, *to have leisure for a thing*, i. e. *to give one's
self to a thing*: ἵνα σχολάσητε (Rec. σχολάζητε) τῇ προσευχῇ, 1 Co. vii. 5 (for exx. fr. prof. auth. see Passow
s. v.; [L. and S. s. v. III.]). **3.** of things ; e. g. of
places, *to be unoccupied, empty* : οἶκος σχολάζων, Mt. xii.
44 ; [Lk. xi. 25 WH br. Tr mrg. br.], (τόπος, Plut. Gai.
Grac. 12 ; of a centurion's vacant office, Eus. h. e. 7, 15 ;
in eccl. writ. of vacant eccl. offices, [also of officers without charge ; cf. Soph. Lex. s. v.]).*

4981 σχολή, -ῆς, ἡ, (fr. σχεῖν ; hence prop. Germ. *das Anhalten* ; [cf. Eng. 'to hold on,' equiv. to either *to stop* or
to persist]) ; **1.** fr. Pind. down, *freedom from labor,
leisure*. **2.** acc. to later Grk. usage, *a place where
there is leisure for anything, a school* [cf. L. and S. s. v.
III.; W. 23]: Acts xix. 9 (Dion. Hal. de jud. Isocr. 1 ;
de vi Dem. 44 ; often in Plut.).*

4982 σώζω [al. σῴζω (cf. *WH*. Intr. § 410 ; Meisterhans p.
87)] ; fut. σώσω ; 1 aor. ἔσωσα ; pf. σέσωκα ; Pass., pres.
σῴζομαι ; impf. ἐσῳζόμην ; pf. 3 pers. sing. (Acts iv. 9) σέσωσται and (acc. to Tdf.) σέσωται (cf. Kühner i. 912 ; [Photius
s. v.; *Rutherford*, New Phryn. p. 99 ; Veitch s. v.]) ; 1 aor.

ἐσώθην ; 1 fut. σωθήσομαι ; (σῶς 'safe and sound' [cf. Lat.
sanus ; Curtius § 570 ; Vaniček p. 1038]) ; fr. Hom. down ;
Sept. very often for הוֹשִׁיעַ, also for מִלַּט, נָצַל, and הִצִּיל,
sometimes for עָזַר ; *to save, to keep safe and sound, to
rescue from danger* or *destruction* (opp. to ἀπόλλυμι,
q. v.) ; Vulg. *salvumfacio* (or *fio*), *salvo*, [*salvifico, libero*,
etc.];   **a.** univ., τινά, one (from injury or peril) ;
to save a suffering one (from perishing), e. g. one suffering from disease, *to make well, heal, restore to health* : Mt.
ix. 22 ; Mk. v. 34 ; x. 52 ; Lk. vii. 50 [al. understand this
as including s p i r i t u a l healing (see b. below)] ; viii.
48 ; xvii. 19 ; xviii. 42 ; Jas. v. 15 ; pass., Mt. ix. 21 ; Mk.
v. 23, 28 ; vi. 56 ; Lk. viii. 36, 50 ; Jn. xi. 12 ; Acts iv. 9
[cf. B. § 144, 25]; xiv. 9.   *to preserve one who is in
danger of destruction, to save* (i. e. *rescue*) : Mt. viii. 25 ;
xiv. 30 ; xxiv. 22 ; xxvii. 40, 42, 49 ; Mk. xiii. 20 ; xv. 30
sq.; Lk. xxiii. 35, 37, 39 ; pass., Acts xxvii. 20, 31 ; 1 Pet.
iv. 18 ; τὴν ψυχήν, (physical) life, Mt. xvi. 25 ; Mk. iii.
4 ; viii. 35 ; Lk. vi. 9 ; ix. 24 and R G L in xvii. 33 ; σῴζειν
τινὰ ἐκ with gen. of the place, *to bring safe forth from*,
Jude 5 ; ἐκ τῆς ὥρας ταύτης, from the peril of this hour,
Jn. xii. 27 ; with gen. of the state, ἐκ θανάτου, Heb. v. 7 ;
cf. *Bleek*, Brief an d. Hebr. ii. 2 p. 70 sq.; [W. § 30, 6 a.;
see ἐκ, I. 5].   **b.** *to save* in the technical biblical
sense ; — negatively, *to deliver from the penalties of the
Messianic judgment*, Joel ii. 32 (iii. 5) ; *to save from the
evils which obstruct the reception of the Messianic deliverance* : ἀπὸ τῶν ἁμαρτιῶν, Mt. i. 21 ; ἀπὸ τῆς ὀργῆς sc. τοῦ θεοῦ,
from the punitive wrath of God at the judgment of the
last day, Ro. v. 9 ; ἀπὸ τῆς γενεᾶς τῆς σκολιᾶς ταύτης, Acts
ii. 40 ; ψυχὴν ἐκ θανάτου (see θάνατος, 2), Jas. v. 20 ; [ἐκ
πυρὸς ἁρπάζοντες, Jude 23] ; — positively, *to make one a
partaker of the salvation by Christ* (opp. to ἀπόλλυμι, q. v.) :
hence σῴζεσθαι and εἰσέρχεσθαι εἰς τὴν βασ. τοῦ θεοῦ are
interchanged, Mt. xix. 25, cf. 24 ; Mk. x. 26, cf. 25 ; Lk.
xviii. 26, cf. 25 ; so σῴζεσθαι and ζωὴν αἰώνιον ἔχειν, Jn.
iii. 17, cf. 16. Since salvation begins in this life (in deliverance from error and corrupt notions, in moral purity,
in pardon of sin, and in the blessed peace of a soul reconciled to God), but on the visible return of Christ from
heaven will be perfected in the consummate blessings of
ὁ αἰὼν ὁ μέλλων, we can understand why τὸ σῴζεσθαι is
spoken of in some passages as a present possession, in
others as a good yet future : — as a blessing b e g i n n i n g
(or begun) on e a r t h, Mt. xviii. 11 Rec. ; Lk. viii. 12 ;
xix. 10 ; Jn. v. 34 ; x. 9 ; xii. 47 ; Ro. xi. 14 ; 1 Co. i. 21 ;
vii. 16 ; ix. 22 ; x. 33 ; xv. 2 ; 1 Th. ii. 16 ; 2 Th. ii. 10 ;
2 Tim. i. 9 ; Tit. iii. 5 ; 1 Pet. iii. 21 ; τῇ ἐλπίδι (dat. of the
instrument) ἐσώθημεν (aor. of the time when they turned
to Christ), Ro. viii. 24 ; χάριτί ἐστε σεσωσμένοι διὰ τῆς
πίστεως, Eph. ii. 5 [cf. B. § 144, 25], 8 ; — as a thing still
future, Mt. x. 22 ; xxiv. 13 ; [Mk. xiii. 13] ; Ro. v. 10 ;
1 Co. iii. 15 ; 1 Tim. ii. 15 ; Jas. iv. 12 ; τὴν ψυχήν, Mk.
viii. 35 ; Lk. ix. 24 ; ψυχάς, Lk. ix. 56 Rec. ; τὸ πνεῦμα,
pass. 1 Co. v. 5 ; by a pregnant construction (see εἰς, C.
1 p. 185ᵇ bot.), τινὰ εἰς τὴν βασιλείαν τοῦ κυρίου αἰώνιον,
to save and transport *into* etc. 2 Tim. iv. 18 (ἡ εὐσέβεια
ἡ σῴζουσα εἰς τὴν ζωὴν αἰώνιον, 4 Macc. xv. 2 ; many exx.

of this constr. are given in Passow vol. ii. p. 1802ᵃ; [cf. L. and S. s. v. II. 2]).   univ.: [Mk. xvi. 16]; Acts ii. 21; iv. 12; xi. 14; xiv. 9; xv. 1, [11]; xvi. 30 sq.; Ro. ix. 27; x. 9, 13; xi. 26; 1 Tim. ii. 4; iv. 16; Heb. vii. 25; Jas. ii. 14; ἁμαρτωλούς, 1 Tim. i. 15; τὰς ψυχάς, Jas. i. 21; οἱ σωζόμενοι, Rev. xxi. 24 Rec.; Lk. xiii. 23; Acts ii. 47; opp. to οἱ ἀπολλύμενοι, 1 Co. i. 18; 2 Co. ii. 15, (see ἀπόλλυμι, 1 a. β.).   [COMP.: δια-, ἐκ- σώζω.] *

4983   σῶμα, -τος, τό, (appar. fr. σῶς 'entire', [but cf. Curtius § 570; al. fr. r. ska, sko, 'to cover', cf. Vaniček p. 1055; Curtius p. 696]), Sept. for נְוִיָה, בָּשָׂר, etc.; נְבֵלָה (a corpse), also for Chald. דְּשַׁם; a body; and **1.** the body both of men and of animals (on the distinction between it and σάρξ see σάρξ, esp. 2 init.; [cf. Dickson, St. Paul's use of 'Flesh' and 'Spirit', p. 247 sqq.]);   **a.** as everywh. in Hom. (who calls the living body δέμας) and not infreq. in subseq. Grk. writ., a dead body or corpse: univ. Lk. xvii. 37; of a man, Mt. xiv. 12 R G; [Mk. xv. 45 R G]; Acts ix. 40; plur. Jn. xix. 31; τὸ σ. τινος, Mt. xxvii. 58 sq.; Mk. xv. 43; Lk. xxiii. 52, 55; Jn. xix. 38, 40; xx. 12; Jude 9; of the body of an animal offered in sacrifice, plur. Heb. xiii. 11 (Ex. xxix. 14; Num. xix. 3).   **b.** as in Grk. writ. fr. Hesiod down, the living body: — of animals, Jas. iii. 3; — of man: τὸ σῶμα, absol., Lk. xi. 34; xii. 23; 1 Co. vi. 13, etc.; ἐν σώματι εἶναι, of earthly life with its troubles, Heb. xiii. 3; distinguished fr. τὸ αἷμα, 1 Co. xi. 27; τὸ σῶμα and τὰ μέλη of it, 1 Co. xii. 12, 14–20; Jas. iii. 6; τὸ σῶμα the temple of τὸ ἅγιον πνεῦμα, 1 Co. vi. 19; the instrument of the soul, τὰ διὰ τοῦ σώμ. sc. πραχθέντα, 2 Co. v. 10; it is distinguished — fr. τὸ πνεῦμα, in Ro. viii. 10; 1 Co. v. 3; vi. 20 Rec.; vii. 34; Jas. ii. 26, (4 Macc. xi. 11); — fr. ἡ ψυχή, in Mt. vi. 25; x. 28; Lk. xii. 22, (Sap. i. 4; viii. 19 sq.; 2 Macc. vii. 37; xiv. 38; 4 Macc. i. 28, etc.); — fr. ἡ ψυχή and τὸ πνεῦμα together, in 1 Th. v. 23 (cf. Song of the Three, 63); σῶμα ψυχικόν and σ. πνευματικόν are distinguished, 1 Co. xv. 44 (see πνευματικός, 1 and ψυχικός, a.); τὸ σ. τινος, Mt. v. 29 sq.; Lk. xi. 34; Ro. iv. 19; viii. 23 [cf. W. 187 (176)], etc.; ὁ ναὸς τοῦ σώμ. αὐτοῦ, the temple which was his body, Jn. ii. 21; plur., Ro. i. 24; 1 Co. vi. 15; Eph. v. 28; the gen. of the possessor is omitted where it is easily learned from the context, as 1 Co. v. 3; 2 Co. iv. 10; v. 8; Heb. x. 22 (23), etc.; τὸ σῶμα τῆς ταπεινώσεως ἡμῶν, the body of our humiliation (subjective gen.), i. e. which we wear in this servile and lowly human life, opp. to τὸ σ. τῆς δόξης αὐτοῦ (i. e. τοῦ Χριστοῦ), the body which Christ has in his glorified state with God in heaven, Phil. iii. 21; διὰ τοῦ σώμ. τοῦ Χριστοῦ, through the death of Christ's body, Ro. vii. 4; διὰ τῆς προσφορᾶς τοῦ σώμ. Ἰησοῦ Χριστοῦ, through the sacrificial offering of the body of Jesus Christ, Heb. x. 10; τὸ σ. τῆς σαρκός, the body consisting of flesh, i. e. the physical body (tacitly opp. to Christ's spiritual body, the church, see 3 below), Col. i. 22 (differently in ii. 11 [see just below]); σῶμα τοῦ θανάτου, the body subject to death, given over to it [cf. W. § 30, 2 β.], Ro. vii. 24; the fact that the body includes ἡ σάρξ, and in the flesh also the incentives to sin (see σάρξ, 4), gives origin to

the foll. phrases: μὴ βασιλευέτω ἡ ἁμαρτία ἐν τῷ θνητῷ ὑμῶν σώματι, Ro. vi. 12 [cf. W. 524 (488)]; αἱ πράξεις τοῦ σώματος, Ro. viii. 13.   Since the body is the instrument of the soul (2 Co. v. 10), and its members the instruments either of righteousness or of iniquity (Ro. vi. 13, 19), the foll. expressions are easily intelligible: σῶμα τῆς ἁμαρτίας, the body subject to, the thrall of, sin [cf. W. § 30, 2 β.], Ro. vi. 6; τὸ σ. τῆς σαρκός, subject to the incitements of the flesh, Col. ii. 11 (where Rec. has τὸ σ. τῶν ἁμαρτιῶν τῆς σαρκός).   δοξάζετε τὸν θεὸν ἐν τῷ σώματι ὑμῶν, 1 Co. vi. 20; μεγαλύνειν τὸν Χριστὸν ἐν τῷ σώματι, εἴτε διὰ ζωῆς, εἴτε διὰ θανάτου, Phil. i. 20; παραστῆσαι τὰ σώματα θυσίαν ζῶσαν ... τῷ θεῷ (i. e. by bodily purity [cf. Mey. ad loc.]), Ro. xii. 1.   **c.** Since acc. to ancient law in the case of slaves the body was the chief thing taken into account, it is a usage of later Grk. to call slaves simply σώματα; once so in the N. T.: Rev. xviii. 13, where the Vulg. correctly translates by mancipia [A. V. slaves], (σώματα τοῦ οἴκου, Gen. xxxvi. 6; σώματα καὶ κτήνη, Tob. x. 10; Ἰουδαϊκὰ σώματα, 2 Macc. viii. 11; exx. fr. Grk. writ. are given by Lob. ad Phryn. p. 378 sq. [add (fr. Soph. Lex. s. v.), Polyb. 1, 29, 7; 4, 38, 4, also 3, 17, 10 bis]; the earlier and more elegant Grk. writ. said σώματα δοῦλα, οἰκετικά, etc.).   **2.** The name is transferred to the bodies of plants, 1 Co. xv. 37 sq., and of stars [cf. our 'heavenly bodies']; hence Paul distinguishes between σώματα ἐπουράνια, bodies celestial, i. e. the bodies of the heavenly luminaries and of angels (see ἐπουράνιος, 1), and σ. ἐπίγεια, bodies terrestrial (i. e. bodies of men, animals, and plants), 1 Co. xv. 40 (ἅπαν σῶμα τῆς τῶν ὅλων φύσεως ... τὸ σῶμα τοῦ κόσμου, Diod. 1, 11).   **3.** trop. σῶμα is used of a (large or small) number of men closely united into one society, or family as it were; a social, ethical, mystical body; so in the N. T. of the church: Ro. xii. 5; 1 Co. x. 17; xii. 13; Eph. ii. 16; iv. 16; v. 23; Col. i. 18; ii. 19; iii. 15; with τοῦ Χριστοῦ added, 1 Co. x. 16; xii. 27; Eph. i. 23; iv. 12; v. 30; Col. i. 24; of which spiritual body Christ is the head, Eph. iv. 15 sq.; v. 23; Col. i. 18; ii. 19, who by the influence of his Spirit works in the church as the soul does in the body. ἓν σῶμα κ. ἓν πνεῦμα, Eph. iv. 4.   **4.** ἡ σκιά and τὸ σῶμα are distinguished as the shadow and the thing itself which casts the shadow: Col. ii. 17; σκιὰν αἰτησόμενος βασιλείας, ἧς ἥρπασεν ἑαυτῷ τὸ σῶμα, Joseph. b. j. 2, 2, 5; [(Philo de confus. ling. § 37; Lcian. Hermot. 79)].

σωματικός, -ή, -όν, (σῶμα), fr. Aristot. down, corporeal (Vulg. corporalis), bodily;   **a.** having a bodily form   **4984** or nature: σωματικῷ εἴδει, Lk. iii. 22 (opp. to ἀσώματος, Philo de opif. mund. § 4).   **b.** pertaining to the body: ἡ γυμνασία, 1 Tim. iv. 8 (ἕξις, Joseph. b. j. 6, 1, 6; ἐπιθυμίαι σωμ. 4 Macc. i. 32; [ἐπιθυμίαι καὶ ἡδοναί, Aristot. eth. Nic. 7, 7 p. 1149ᵇ, 26; al.; ἀπέχου τῶν σαρκικῶν καὶ σωματικῶν ἐπιθυμιῶν, 'Teaching' etc. 1, 4]).*

σωματικῶς, adv., bodily, corporeally (Vulg. corporaliter),   **4985** i. q. ἐν σωματικῷ εἴδει, yet denoting his exalted and spiritual body, visible only to the inhabitants of heaven, Col. ii. 9, where see Meyer [cf. Bp. Lghtft.].*

4986 Σώπατρος, -ου, ὁ, [cf. W. 103 (97)], *Sopater*, a Christian, one of Paul's companions: Acts xx. 4. [See Σωσί-πατρος.]*

4987 σωρεύω· fut. σωρεύσω ; pf. pass. ptcp. σεσωρευμένος ; (σωρός, a heap) ; [fr. Aristot. down] ; *to heap together, to heap up*: τὶ ἐπί τι, Ro. xii. 20 (fr. Prov. xxv. 22 ; see ἄνθραξ) ; τινά τινι, to overwhelm one with a heap of anything : trop. ἁμαρτίαις, to load one with the consciousness of many sins, pass. 2 Tim. iii. 6. [Comp. : ἐπι-σωρεύω.] *

4988 Σωσθένης, -ους, ὁ, *Sosthenes* ; 1. the ruler of the Jewish synagogue at Corinth, and an opponent of Christianity : Acts xviii. 17. 2. a certain Christian, an associate of the apostle Paul : 1 Co. i. 1. The name was a common one among the Greeks.*

4989 Σωσίπατρος, -ου, ὁ, *Sosipater*, a certain Christian, one of Paul's kinsmen, (perhaps the same man who in Acts xx. 4 is called Σώπατρος [q. v. ; yet the latter was from Berœa, Sosipater in Corinth] ; cf. Σωκράτης and Σωσι-κράτης, Σωκλείδης and Σωσικλείδης, see *Fritzsche*, Ep. ad Rom. vol. iii. p. 316 ; [cf. *Fick*, Gr. Personennamen, pp. 79, 80]) : Ro. xvi. 21.*

4990 σωτήρ, -ῆρος, ὁ, (σώζω), fr. Pind. and Aeschyl. down, Sept. for יֵשַׁע, יְשׁוּעָה, [מוֹשִׁיעַ], *savior, deliverer; preserver*; (Vulg. [exc. Lk. i. 47 (where *salutaris*)] *salvator*, Luth. *Heiland*) [cf. B. D. s. v. Saviour, I.] ; (Cic. in Verr. ii. 2, 63 Hoc quantum est? ita magnum, ut Latine uno verbo exprimi non possit. Is est nimirum 'soter', *qui salutem dedit*. The name was given by the ancients to deities, esp. tutelary deities, to princes, kings, and in general to men who had conferred signal benefits upon their country, and in the more degenerate days by way of flattery to personages of influence ; see Passow [or L. and S.] s. v. ; *Paulus*, Exgt. Hdbch. üb. d. drei erst. Evang. i. p. 103 sq. ; [Wetstein on Lk. ii. 11 ; B. D. u. s.]) In the N. T. the word is applied to God, — σωτ. μου, he who signally exalts me, Lk. i. 47 ; ὁ σωτ. ἡμῶν, the author of our salvation through Jesus Christ (on the Christian conception of 'to save', see σώζω, b. [and on the use of σωτήρ cf. Westcott on 1 Jn. iv. 14]), 1 Tim. i. 1 ; ii. 3 ; Tit. i. 3 ; ii. 10 ; iii. 4 ; with διὰ Ἰησοῦ Χριστοῦ added, Jude 25 [Rec. om. διὰ Ἰ. Χ.] ; σωτὴρ πάντων, 1 Tim. iv. 10 (cf. Ps. xxiii. (xxiv.) 5 ; xxvi. (xxvii.) 1 ; Is. xii. ; xvii. 10 ; xlv. 15, 21 ; Mic. vii. 7, etc.) ; — to the Messiah, and Jesus as the Messiah, through whom God gives salvation : Lk. ii. 11 ; Acts v. 31 ; xiii. 23 ; ὁ σωτ. τοῦ κόσμου, Jn. iv. 42 ; 1 Jn. iv. 14 ; ἡμῶν, 2 Tim. i. 10 ; Tit. i. 4 ; ii. 13 ; iii. 6 ; σωτὴρ Ἰησοῦς Χριστός, 2 Pet. i. [1 where Rec.bez elz inserts ἡμῶν)], 11 ; ii. 20 ; iii. 18 ; ὁ κύριος καὶ σωτήρ, 2 Pet. iii. 2 ; σωτὴρ τοῦ σώματος, univ. ('the savior' i. e.) *preserver* of the body, i. e. of the church, Eph. v. 23 (σωτὴρ ὄντως ἀπάντων ἐστὶ καὶ γενέτωρ, of God the preserver of the world, Aristot. de mundo, c. 6 p. 397ᵇ, 20) ; σωτήρ is used of Christ as the giver of future salvation, on his return from heaven, Phil. iii. 20. ["The title is confined (with the exception of the writings of St Luke) to the later writings of the N. T." (Westcott u. s.)] *

4991 σωτηρία, -ας, ἡ, (σωτήρ), *deliverance, preservation, safety, salvation* : deliverance from the molestation of enemies, Acts vii. 25 ; with ἐξ ἐχθρῶν added, Lk. i. 71 ; preservation (of physical life), safety, Acts xxvii. 34 ; Heb. xi. 7. in an ethical sense, *that which conduces to the soul's safety* or *salvation* : σωτηρία τινὶ ἐγένετο, Lk. xix. 9 ; ἡγεῖσθαί τι σωτηρίαν, 2 Pet. iii. 15 ; in the technical biblical sense, the Messianic *salvation* (see σώζω, b.). a. univ. : Jn. iv. 22 ; Acts iv. 12 ; xiii. 47 ; Ro. xi. 11 ; 2 Th. ii. 13 ; 2 Tim. iii. 15 ; Heb. ii. 3 ; vi. 9 ; Jude 3 ; opp. to ἀπώ-λεια, Phil. i. 28 ; αἰώνιος σωτηρία, Heb. v. 9 (for תְּשׁוּעַת עוֹלָמִים, Is. xlv. 17) ; [add, Mk. xvi. WH in the (rejected) 'Shorter Conclusion'] ; ὁ λόγος τῆς σωτηρίας ταύτης, instruction concerning that salvation which John the Baptist foretold [cf. W. 237 (223)], Acts xiii. 26 ; τὸ εὐαγγέ-λιον τῆς σωτηρίας ὑμῶν, Eph. i. 13 ; ὁδὸς σωτηρίας, Acts xvi. 17 ; κέρας σωτηρίας (see κέρας, b.), Lk. i. 69 ; ἡμέρα σωτηρίας, the time in which the offer of salvation is made, 2 Co. vi. 2 (fr. Is. xlix. 8) ; κατεργάζεσθαι τὴν ἑαυτοῦ σωτηρίαν, Phil. ii. 12 ; κληρονομεῖν σωτηρίαν, Heb. i. 14 ; [ὁ ἀρχηγὸς τῆς σωτηρίας, Heb. ii. 10] ; εἰς σωτηρίαν, *unto* (the attainment of) *salvation*, Ro. [i. 16] ; x. [1], 10 ; 1 Pet. ii. 2 [Rec. om.]. b. *salvation* as the present possession of all true Christians (see σώζω, b.) : 2 Co. i. 6 ; vii. 10 ; Phil. i. 19 ; σωτηρία ἐν ἀφέσει ἁμαρτιῶν, Lk. i. 77 ; σωτηρίας τυχεῖν μετὰ δόξης αἰωνίου, 2 Tim. ii. 10. c. *future salvation*, the sum of benefits and blessings which Christians, redeemed from all earthly ills, will enjoy after the visible return of Christ from heaven in the consummated and eternal kingdom of God : Ro. xiii. 11 ; 1 Th. v. 9 ; Heb. ix. 28 ; 1 Pet. i. 5, 10 ; Rev. xii. 10 ; ἐλπὶς σωτηρίας, 1 Th. v. 8 ; κομίζεσθαι σωτηρίαν ψυχῶν, 1 Pet. i. 9 ; ἡ σωτηρία τῷ θεῷ ἡμῶν (dat. of the possessor, sc. ἐστίν [cf. B. § 129, 22] ; cf. לַיהוָה הַיְשׁוּעָה, Ps. iii. 9), the salvation which is bestowed on us belongs to God, Rev. vii. 10 ; ἡ σωτηρία . . . τοῦ θεοῦ (gen. of the possessor [cf. B. § 132, 11, i. a.], for Rec. τῷ θεῷ) ἡμῶν sc. ἐστίν, Rev. xix. 1. (Tragg., [Hdt.], Thuc., Xen., Plat., al. Sept. for יֵשַׁע, יְשׁוּעָה, פְּלֵיטָה, תְּשׁוּעָה *escape*.) *

4992 σωτήριος, -ον, (σωτήρ), fr. Aeschyl., Eur., Thuc. down, *saving, bringing salvation* : ἡ χάρις ἡ σωτήριος, Tit. ii. 11 (Sap. i. 14 ; 3 Macc. vii. 18) ; ἡ σωτήριος δίαιτα, Clem. Alex. Paedag. p. 48 ed. Sylb.). Neut. τὸ σωτήριον (Sept. often for יְשׁוּעָה, less freq. for יֵשַׁע), as often in Grk. writ., substantively, *safety*, in the N. T. (the Messianic) *salvation* (see σώζω, b. and in σωτηρία) : with τοῦ θεοῦ added, decreed by God, Lk. iii. 6 (fr. Is. xl. 5) ; Acts xxviii. 28 ; Clem. Rom. 1 Cor. 35, 12 ; *he who embodies this salvation*, or *through whom God is about to achieve it* : of the Messiah, Lk. ii. 30 (τὸ σωτ. ἡμῶν Ἰησοῦς Χρ. Clem. Rom. 1 Cor. 36, 1 [where see Harnack]) ; simply, equiv. to *the hope of* (future) *salvation*, Eph. vi. 17. (In the Sept. τὸ σωτ. often for שֶׁלֶם, a thank-offering [or 'peace-offering'], and the plur. occurs in the same sense in Xen., Polyb., Diod., Plut., Lcian., Hdian.) *

4993 σω-φρονέω, -ῶ ; 1 aor. impv. σωφρονήσατε ; (σώφρων, q. v.) ; fr. Tragg., Xen., Plat. down ; *to be of sound* *mind*, i. e. **a.** *to be in one's right mind*: of one who has ceased δαιμονίζεσθαι, Mk. v. 15; Lk. viii. 35; opp. to ἐκστῆναι, 2 Co. v. 13, (the σωφρονῶν and μανείς are contrasted in Plat. de rep. i. p. 331 c.; σωφρονοῦσαι and μανεῖσαι, Phaedr. p. 244 b.; ὁ μεμηνὼς . . . ἐσωφρόνησε, Apollod. 3, 5, 1, 6). **b.** *to exercise self-control*; i. e. **α.** *to put a moderate estimate upon one's self, think of one's self soberly*: opp. to ὑπερφρονεῖν, Ro. xii. 3. **β.** *to curb one's passions*, Tit. ii. 6; joined with νήφω (as in Lcian. Nigrin. 6), [R. V. *be of sound mind* and *be sober*], 1 Pet. iv. 7.*

4994 **σωφρονίζω**, 3 pers. plur. ind. -ζουσιν, Tit. ii. 4 L mrg. T Tr, al. subjunc. -ζωσι; *to make one σώφρων, restore one to his senses; to moderate, control, curb, discipline; to hold one to his duty*; so fr. Eur. and Thuc. down; *to admonish, to exhort earnestly*, [R. V. *train*]: τινά foll. by an inf. Tit. ii. 4.*

4995 **σωφρονισμός**, -οῦ, ὁ, (σωφρονίζω); **1.** *an admonishing* or *calling to soundness of mind, to moderation and self-control*: Joseph. antt. 17, 9, 2; b. j. 2, 1, 3; App. Pun. 8, 65; Aesop. fab. 38; Plut.; [Philo, legg. alleg. 3, 69]. **2.** *self-control, moderation*, (σωφρονισμοί τινες ἡ μετάνοια τῶν νέων, Plut. mor. p. 712 c. i. e. quaest. conviv. 8, 3): πνεῦμα σωφρονισμοῦ, 2 Tim. i. 7, where see Huther; [but Huther, at least in his later edd., takes the word transitively, i. q. *correction* (R. V. *discipline*); see also Holtzmann ad loc.].*

σωφρόνως, (σώφρων), adv., fr. [Aeschyl.], Hdt. down, **4996** *with sound mind, soberly, temperately, discreetly*: Tit. ii. 12 (Sap. ix. 11).*

σωφροσύνη, -ης, ἡ, (σώφρων), fr. Hom. (where σαοφρο- **4997** σύνη) down; **a.** *soundness of mind* (opp. to μανία, Xen. mem. 1, 1, 16; Plat. Prot. p. 323 b.): ῥήματα σωφροσύνης, words of sanity [A. V. *soberness*], Acts xxvi. 25. **b.** *self-control, sobriety*, (ea virtus, cujus proprium est, motus animi appetentes regere et sedare semperque adversantem libidini moderatam in omni re servare constantiam, Cic. Tusc. 3, 8, 17; ἡ σωφροσ. ἐστὶ καὶ ἡδονῶν τινων καὶ ἐπιθυμιῶν ἐγκράτεια, Plat. rep. 4, 430 e.; cf. Phaedo p. 68 c.; sympos. p. 196 c.; Diog. Laërt. 3, 91; 4 Macc. i. 31; σωφροσύνη δὲ ἀρετὴ δι' ἣν πρὸς τὰς ἡδονὰς τοῦ σώματος οὕτως ἔχουσιν ὡς ὁ νόμος κελεύει, ἀκολασία δὲ τοὐναντίον, Aristot. rhet. 1, 9, 9): 1 Tim. ii. 15; joined with αἰδώς (as in Xen. Cyr. 8, 1, 30 sq.) ibid. 9; [cf. *Trench*, N. T. Syn. § xx., and see αἰδώς].*

σώφρων, -ον, (fr. σάος, contr. σῶς [cf. σώζω, init.], and **4998** φρήν, hence the poet. σαόφρων; cf. ἄφρων, ταπεινόφρων, μεγαλόφρων), [fr. Hom. down]; **a.** *of sound mind, sane, in one's senses*, (see σωφρονέω, a. and σωφροσύνη, a.). **b.** *curbing one's desires and impulses, self-controlled, temperate*, [R.V. *soberminded*], ([ἐπιθυμεῖ ὁ σώφρων ὧν δεῖ καὶ ὡς δεῖ καὶ ὅτε, Aristot. eth. Nic. 3, 15 fin.], see σωφροσύνη, b.): 1 Tim. iii. 2; Tit. i. 8; ii. 2, 5.*

T

[T, τ: on the receding of ττ in the vocabulary of the N. T. before σσ, see under Σ, σ, s.]

4999 **ταβέρναι**, -ῶν, αἱ, (a Lat. word [cf. B. 17 (15)]), *taverns*: Τρεῖς Ταβέρναι (gen. Τριῶν Ταβερνῶν), *Three Taverns*, the name of an inn or halting-place on the Appian way between Rome and The Market of Appius [see Ἄππιος]; it was ten Roman miles distant from the latter place and thirty-three from Rome (Cic. ad Attic. 2, 10, (12)) [cf. B.D. s. v. Three Taverns]: Acts xxviii. 15.*

5000 **Ταβιθά** [WH Ταβειθά, see their App. p. 155, and s. v. ει, ι; the better accent seems to be -θᾶ (see Kautzsch as below)], ἡ, (טַבְיְתָא, a Chald. name in the 'emphatic state' [*Kautzsch*, Gram. d. Bibl.-Aram. u. s. w. p. 11, writes it טַבְיְאָה, stat. emphat. of טַבְיָ], Hebr. צְבִי, i. e. δορκάς, q. v.), *Tabitha*, a Christian woman of Joppa, noted for her works of benevolence: Acts ix. 36, 40. [Cf. B. D. s. v. Tabitha.]*

5001 **τάγμα**, -τος, τό, (τάσσω); **a.** prop. *that which has been arranged, thing placed in order.* **b.** spec. *a body*

of soldiers, a corps: 2 S. xxiii. 13; Xen. mem. 3, 1, 11; often in Polyb.; Diod. 17, 80; Joseph. b. j. 1, 9, 1; 3, 4, 2; [esp. for the Roman 'legio' (exx. in *Soph.* Lex. s. v. 3)]; hence univ. *a band, troop, class*: ἕκαστος ἐν τῷ ἰδίῳ τάγματι (the same words occur in Clem. Rom. 1 Cor. 37, 3 and 41, 1), 1 Co. xv. 23, where Paul specifies several distinct bands or classes of those raised from the dead [A. V. *order*. Of the 'order' of the Essenes in Joseph. b. j. 2, 8, 3. 8].*

τακτός, -ή, -όν, (τάσσω), fr. Thuc. (4, 65) down, *or-* **5002** *dered, arranged, fixed, stated*: τακτὴ ἡμέρα (Polyb. 3, 34, 9; Dion. Hal. 2, 74), Acts xii. 21 [A. V. *set*].*

ταλαιπωρέω, -ῶ: 1 aor. impv. ταλαιπωρήσατε; (ταλαί- **5003** πωρος, q. v.); fr. Eur. and Thuc. down; Sept. for שָׁדַד; **a.** *to toil heavily, to endure labors and hardships; to be afflicted; to feel afflicted and miserable*: Jas. iv. 9. **b.** in Grk. writ. and Sept. also transitively [cf. L. and S. s. v. II.], *to afflict*: Ps. xvi. (xvii.) 9; Is. xxxiii. 1.*

ταλαιπωρία, -ας, ἡ, (ταλαίπωρος, q. v.), *hardship, trouble*, **5004**

calamity, misery: Ro. iii. 16 (fr. Is. lix. 7); plur. [*miseries*], Jas. v. 1.   (Hdt., Thuc., Isocr., Polyb., Diod., Joseph., al.; Sept. chiefly for שֹׁד.) *

5005   **ταλαίπωρος, -ον,** (fr. ΤΑΛΑΩ, ΤΛΑΩ, to bear, undergo, and πῶρος a callus [al. πωρός, but cf. Suidas (ed. Gaisf.) p. 3490 c. and note; al. connect the word with περάω, πειράω, cf. Curtius § 466]), *enduring toils and troubles; afflicted, wretched*: Ro. vii. 24; Rev. iii. 17.   (Is. xxxiii. 1; Tob. xiii. 10; Sap. iii. 11; xiii. 10; [Pind.], Tragg., Arstph., Dem., Polyb., Aesop., al.) *

5006   **ταλαντιαῖος, -α, -ον,** (τάλαντον, q. v.; like δραχμιαῖος, στιγμιαῖος, δακτυλιαῖος, λιτριαῖος, etc.; see *Lob.* ad Phryn. p. 544), *of the weight* or *worth of a talent*: Rev. xvi. 21. (Dem., Aristot., Polyb., Diod., Joseph., Plut., al.) *

5007   **τάλαντον, -ου, τό,** (ΤΑΛΑΩ, ΤΛΑΩ [to bear]);   **1.** *the scale of a balance, a balance, a pair of scales* (Hom.).   **2.** *that which is weighed, a talent,* i. e.   **a.** a weight, varying in different places and times.   **b.** a sum of money weighing a talent and varying in different states and acc. to the changes in the laws regulating the currency; the Attic talent was equal to 60 Attic minae or 6000 drachmae, and worth about 200 pounds sterling or 1000 dollars [cf. L. and S. s. v. II. 2 b.].   But in the N. T. probably the Syrian talent is referred to, which was equal to about 237 dollars [but see BB. DD. s. v. Money]: Mt. xviii. 24; xxv. 15 sq. [18 Lchm.], 20, 22, 24 sq. 28.   (Sept. for כִּכָּר, Luth. *Centner*, the heaviest Hebrew weight; on which see *Kneucker* in Schenkel v. p. 460 sq.; [BB. DD. s. v. Weights].)*

5008   **ταλιθά** [WH ταλειθά, see their App. p. 155, and s. v. ει, ι; more correctly accented -θά (see Kautzsch, as below, p. 8; cf. *Tdf.* Proleg. p. 102)], a Chald. word טְלִיתָא [acc. to Kautzsch (Gram. d. Bibl.-Aram. p. 12) more correctly טַלְיְתָא, fem. of טַלְיָא 'a youth'], *a damsel, maiden*: Mk. v. 41.*

5009   **ταμεῖον** [so T WH uniformly], more correctly ταμιεῖον [R G L Tr in Mt. vi. 6], (cf. *Lob.* ad Phryn. p. 493; W. 94 (90); [*Tdf.* Proleg. p. 88 sq.]), -ου, τό, (ταμιεύω), fr. Thuc. and Xen. down;   **1.** *a storechamber, storeroom*: Lk. xii. 24 (Deut. xxviii. 8; Prov. iii. 10 [Philo, quod omn. prob. lib. § 12]).   **2.** *a chamber,* esp. 'an *inner chamber'; a secret room*: Mt. vi. 6; xxiv. 26; Lk. xii. 3, (Xen. Hell. 5, 4, 5; Sir. xxix. 12; Tob. vii. 15, and often in Sept. for חֶדֶר).*

see 3568   **τανῦν,** see νῦν, 1 f. a. p. 430ᵇ top.

5010   **τάξις, -εως, ἡ,** (τάσσω), fr. Aeschyl. and Hdt. down;   **1.** *an arranging, arrangement*.   **2.** *order,* i. e. *a fixed succession observing also a fixed time*: Lk. i. 8.   **3.** *due* or *right order*: κατὰ τάξιν, in order, 1 Co. xiv. 40; *orderly condition*, Col. ii. 5 [some give it here a military sense, '*orderly array*', see στερέωμα, c.].   **4.** the post, rank, or position which one holds in civil or other affairs; and since this position generally depends on one's talents, experience, resources, τάξις becomes equiv. to *character, fashion, quality, style,* (2 Macc. ix. 18; i. 19; οὐ γὰρ ἱστορίας, ἀλλὰ κουρεακῆς λαλιᾶς ἐμοὶ δοκοῦσι τάξιν ἔχειν, Polyb. 3, 20, 5): κατὰ τὴν τάξιν (for which in vii. 15 we have κατὰ τὴν ὁμοιότητα) Μελχισεδέκ, after the manner

of the priesthood [A. V. *order*] of Melchizedek (acc. to the Sept. of Ps. cix. (cx.) 5 עַל־דִּבְרָתִי), Heb. v. 6, 10; vi. 20; vii. 11, 17, 21 (where T Tr WH om. the phrase).*

5011   **ταπεινός, -ή -όν,** fr. [Pind.], Aeschyl., Hdt. down, Sept. for עָנִי, עָנָו, שָׁפָל, etc., *low,* i. e.   **a.** prop. *not rising far from the ground*: Ezek. xvii. 24.   **b.** metaph.   **a.** as to condition, *lowly, of low degree*: with a subst. Jas. i. 9; substantively οἱ ταπεινοί, opp. to δυνάσται, Lk. i. 52; i. q. *brought low with grief, depressed,* (Sir. xxv. 23), 2 Co. vii. 6.   Neut. τὰ ταπεινά, Ro. xii. 16 (on which see συναπάγω, fin.).   **β.** *lowly in spirit, humble*: opp. to ὑπερήφανος, Jas. iv. 6; 1 Pet. v. 5 (fr. Prov. iii. 34); with τῇ καρδίᾳ added, Mt. xi. 29 (τῷ πνεύματι, Ps. xxxiii. (xxxiv.) 19); in a bad sense, *deporting one's self abjectly, deferring servilely to others,* (Xen. mem. 3, 10, 5; Plat. legg. 6 p. 774 c.; often in Isocr.), 2 Co. x. 1. [Cf. reff. s. v. ταπεινοφροσύνη, fin.] *

5012   **ταπεινοφροσύνη, -ης, ἡ,** (ταπεινόφρων; opp. to μεγαλοφροσύνη, ὑψηλοφροσύνη, [cf. W. 99 (94)]), *the having a humble opinion of one's self; a deep sense of one's (moral) littleness; modesty, humility, lowliness of mind*; (Vulg. humilitas, Luth. *Demuth*): Acts xx. 19; Eph. iv. 2; Phil. ii. 3; Col. iii. 12; 1 Pet. v. 5; used of an affected and ostentatious humility in Col. ii. 18, 23.   (The word occurs neither in the O. T., nor in prof. auth.—[but in Joseph. b. j. 4, 9, 2 in the sense of *pusillanimity*; also Epictet. diss. 3, 24, 56 in a bad sense. See Trench, N. T. Syn. §xlii.; Bp. *Lghtft.* on Phil. l. c.; *Zezschwitz,* Profangräcität, u.s.w., pp. 20, 62; W. 26].) *

see 5391   **ταπεινόφρων, -ον,** (ταπεινός and φρήν), *humble-minded,* i. e. *having a modest opinion of one's self*: 1 Pet. iii. 8, where Rec. φιλόφρονες.   (Prov. xxix. 23; in a bad sense, *pusillanimous, mean-spirited,* μικροὺς ἡ τύχη καὶ περιδεεῖς ποιεῖ καὶ ταπεινόφρονας, Plut. de Alex. fort. 2, 4; [de tranquill. animi 17.   See W. § 34, 3 and reff. s. v. ταπεινοφροσύνη, fin.].) *

5013   **ταπεινόω, -ῶ;** fut. ταπεινώσω; 1 aor. ἐταπείνωσα; Pass., pres. ταπεινοῦμαι; 1 aor. ἐταπεινώθην; 1 fut. ταπεινωθήσομαι; (ταπεινός); *to make low, bring low,* (Vulg. humilio);   **a.** prop.: ὄρος, βουνόν, i. e. to level, reduce to a plain, pass. Lk. iii. 5 fr. Is. xl. 4.   **b.** metaph. *to bring into a humble condition, reduce to meaner circumstances*; i. e.   **a.** *to assign a lower rank* or *place to; to abase*; τινά, pass., *to be ranked below others who are honored* or *rewarded* [R. V. *to humble*]: Mt. xxiii. 12; Lk. xiv. 11; xviii. 14.   **β.** ταπεινῶ ἐμαυτόν, *to humble* or *abase myself,* by frugal living, 2 Co. xi. 7; in pass. of one who submits to want, Phil. iv. 12; ἑαυτόν, of one who stoops to the condition of a servant, Phil. ii. 8.   **c.** *to lower, depress,* [Eng. *humble*]: τινά, one's soul, bring down one's pride; ἐμαυτόν, to have a modest opinion of one's self, to behave in an unassuming manner devoid of all haughtiness, Mt. xviii. 4; xxiii. 12; Lk. xiv. 11; xviii. 14; pass. ταπεινοῦμαι ἐνώπιον κυρίου (see ἐνώπιον, 2 b. fin.) in a mid. sense [B. 52 (46)], to confess and deplore one's spiritual littleness and unworthiness, Jas. iv. 10 (in the same sense ταπεινοῦν τὴν ψυχὴν αὐτοῦ, Sir. ii.

17; vii. 17; Sept. for עָנָה נֶפֶשׁ, *he afflicted his soul*, of persons fasting, Lev. xvi. 29, 31; xxiii. 27, 32; Is. lviii. 3, 5, 10; τὴν ψυχήν τινος, to disturb, distress, the soul of one, Protev. Jac. c. 2. 13. 15 [rather, *to humiliate*; see the passages]); ὑπὸ τὴν χεῖρα τ. θεοῦ, to submit one's self in a lowly spirit to the power and will of God, 1 Pet. v. 6 (cf. Gen. xvi. 9); i. q. *to put to the blush*, 2 Co. xii. 21. ([Hippocr.], Xen., Plat., Diod., Plut.; Sept. for עָנָה, שָׁפֵל and הִשְׁפִּיל, דְּכָא, הַכְנִיעַ, etc.) [See reff. s. v. ταπεινοφροσύνη.] *

5014   ταπείνωσις, -εως, ἡ, (ταπεινόω), *lowness, low estate*, [*humiliation*]: Lk. i. 48; Acts viii. 33 (fr. Is. liii. 8); Phil. iii. 21 (on which see σῶμα, 1 b.); metaph. *spiritual abasement*, leading one to perceive and lament his (moral) littleness and guilt, Jas. i. 10, see Kern ad loc. (In various senses, by Plat., Aristot., Polyb., Diod., Plut.; Sept. for עֳנִי.)   [See reff. s. v. ταπεινοφροσύνη.] *

5015   ταράσσω; impf. ἐτάρασσον; 1 aor. ἐτάραξα; Pass., pres. impv. 3 pers. sing. ταρασσέσθω; impf. ἐταρασσόμην; pf. τετάραγμαι; 1 aor. ἐταράχθην; fr. Hom. down; *to agitate, trouble* (a thing, by the movement of its parts to and fro):   **a.** prop.: τὸ ὕδωρ, Jn. v. 4 [R L], 7, (Ezek. xxxii. 2; τὸν πόντον, Hom. Od. 5, 291; τὸ πέλαγος, Eur. Tro. 88; τὸν ποταμόν, Aesop. fab. 87 (25)).   **b.** trop. *to cause one inward commotion, take away his calmness of mind, disturb his equanimity; to disquiet, make restless*, (Sept. for בָּהַל, etc.; pass. ταράσσομαι for רָגַז, to be stirred up, irritated);   **a.** *to stir up*: τὸν ὄχλον, Acts xvii. 8; [τοὺς ὄχλους, Acts xvii. 13 L T Tr WH].   **β.** *to trouble*: τινά, to strike one's spirit with fear or dread, pass., Mt. ii. 3; xiv. 26; Mk. vi. 50; Lk. i. 12; [xxiv. 38]; 1 Pet. iii. 14; ταράσσεται ἡ καρδία, Jn. xiv. 1, 27; to affect with great pain or sorrow: ἑαυτόν (cf. our *to trouble one's self*), Jn. xi. 33 [A. V. *was troubled*] (some understand the word here of **b o d i l y** agitation) (σεαυτὸν μὴ τάρασσε, Antonin. 4, 26); τετάρακται ἡ ψυχή, Jn. xii. 27 (Ps. vi. 4); ἐταράχθη τῷ πνεύματι, Jn. xiii. 21.   **γ.** *to render anxious* or *distressed, to perplex* the mind of one *by suggesting scruples* or *doubts*, (Xen. mem. 2, 6, 17): Gal i. 7; v. 10; τινὰ λόγοις, Acts xv. 24. [COMP.: δια-, ἐκ- ταράσσω.] *

5016   ταραχή, -ῆς, ἡ, (ταράσσω), fr. [Pind.], Hdt. down, *disturbance, commotion*: prop. τοῦ ὕδατος, Jn. v. 4 [R L]; metaph. *a tumult, sedition*: in plur. Mk. xiii. 8 R G.*

5017   τάραχος, -ου, ὁ, (ταράσσω), *commotion, stir* (of mind): Acts xii. 18; *tumult* [A. V. *stir*], Acts xix. 23. (Sept.; Xen., Plut., Lcian.) *

5018   Ταρσεύς, -έως, ὁ, (Ταρσός, q. v.), *belonging to Tarsus, of Tarsus*: Acts ix. 11; xxi. 39.*

5019   Ταρσός, -οῦ, ἡ, [on its accent cf. Chandler §§ 317, 318], in prof. auth. also Ταρσοί, -ῶν, αἱ, *Tarsus*, a maritime city, the capital of Cilicia during the Roman period (Joseph. antt. 1, 6, 1), situated on the river Cydnus, which divided it into two parts (hence the plural Ταρσοί). It was not only large and populous, but also renowned for its Greek learning and its numerous schools of philosophers (Strab. 14 p. 673 [cf. Bp. Lghtft. on Col. p. 303 sq.]). Moreover it was a free city (Plin. 5, 22), and

exempt alike from the jurisdiction of a Roman governor, and the maintenance of a Roman garrison; although it was not a Roman 'colony'. It had received its freedom from Antony (App. b. civ. 5, 7) on the condition that it might retain its own magistrates and laws, but should acknowledge the Roman sovereignty and furnish auxiliaries in time of war. It is now called *Tarso* or *Tersus*, a mean city of some 6000 inhabitants [others set the number very much higher]. It was the birthplace of the apostle Paul: Acts ix. 30; xi. 25; xxii. 3. [BB.DD. s. v.; *Lewin*, St. Paul, i. 78 sq. cf. 2.] *

5020   ταρταρόω, -ῶ: 1 aor. ptcp. ταρταρώσας; (τάρταρος, the name of a subterranean region, doleful and dark, regarded by the ancient Greeks as the abode of the wicked dead, where they suffer punishment for their evil deeds; it answers to the Gehenna of the Jews, see γέεννα); *to thrust down to Tartarus* (sometimes in the Scholiasts) [cf. W. 25 (24) n.]; *to hold captive in Tartarus*: τινὰ σειραῖς [q. v.] ζόφου, 2 Pet. ii. 4 [A. V. *cast down to hell* (making the dat. depend on παρέδωκεν)].*

5021   τάσσω: 1 aor. ἔταξα; pf. inf. τεταχέναι (Acts xviii. 2 T Tr mrg.); Pass., pres. ptcp. τασσόμενος; pf. 3 pers. sing. τέτακται, ptcp. τεταγμένος; 1 aor. mid. ἐταξάμην; fr. [Pind., Aeschyl.], Hdt. down; Sept. for שׂוּם, and occasionally for נָתַן, צִוָּה, שׁוּת, etc.; *to put in place; to station*;   **a.** *to place in a certain order* (Xen. mem. 3, 1, 7 [9]), *to arrange, to assign a place, to appoint*: τινά, pass. αἱ ἐξουσίαι ὑπὸ θεοῦ τεταγμέναι εἰσίν [A. V. *ordained*], Ro. xiii. 1 [καιρούς, Acts xvii. 26 Lchm.]; ἑαυτὸν εἰς διακονίαν τινί, to consecrate [R. V. *set*] one's self to minister unto one, 1 Co. xvi. 15 (ἐπὶ τὴν διακονίαν, Plat. de rep. 2 p. 371 c.; εἰς τὴν δουλείαν, Xen. mem. 2, 1, 11); ὅσοι ἦσαν τεταγμένοι εἰς ζωὴν αἰώνιον, as many as were appointed [A. V. *ordained*] (by God) to obtain eternal life, or to whom God had decreed eternal life, Acts xiii. 48; τινὰ ὑπό τινα, to put one under another's control [A. V. *set under*], pass., Mt. viii. 9 L WH in br., cod. Sin.; Lk. vii. 8, (ὑπό τινα, Polyb. 3, 16, 3; 5, 65, 7; Diod. 2, 26, 8; 4, 9, 5); τινί τι, to assign (appoint) *a thing to one*, pass. Acts xxii. 10 (Xen. de rep. Lac. 11, 6).   **b.** *to appoint, ordain, order*: foll. by the acc. with inf., Acts xv. 2; [xviii. 2 T Tr mrg.]; (foll. by an inf., Xen. Hier. 10, 4; Cyr. 4, 5, 11). Mid. (as often in Grk. writ.) prop. *to appoint on one's own responsibility* or *authority*: οὗ ἐτάξατο αὐτοῖς ὁ Ἰησοῦς sc. πορεύεσθαι, Mt. xxviii. 16; *to appoint mutually*, i. e. *agree upon*: ἡμέραν (Polyb. 18, 19, 1, etc.), Acts xxviii. 23. [COMP.: ἀνα- (-μαι), ἀντι-, ἀπο-, δια-, ἐπι-δια-(-μαι), ἐπι-, προ-, προσ-, συν-, ὑπο- τάσσω. SYN. see κελεύω, fin.] *

5022   ταῦρος, -ου, ὁ, [fr. r. meaning 'thick', 'stout'; allied w. σταυρός, q. v.; cf. Vaniček p. 1127; Fick Pt. i. p. 246. Cf. Eng. *steer*], fr. Hom. down, Sept. for שׁוֹר, *a bull* (*ox*): Mt. xxii. 4; Acts xiv. 13; Heb. ix. 13; x. 4.*

5024; see 3588 &846   ταυτά, by crasis for τὰ αὐτά: 1 Th. ii. 14 R L mrg., and some manuscripts [(but see Tdf. on Lk. as below)] and edd. also in Lk. vi. 23 [L mrg.], 26 [L mrg.]; xvii. 30 G L. [See W. § 5, 3; B. 10; WH. App. p. 145; cf. Meisterhans § 18, 1; αὐτός, III.] *

*For 5023, 5025, & 5026 see 3778 and corresponding nos. in Strong.

5027   **ταφή**, -ῆς, ἡ, (θάπτω), fr. Hdt. down ; Sept. several times for קְבוּרָה and קֶבֶר, *burial* : Mt. xxvii. 7.*

5028   **τάφος**, -ου, ὁ. (θάπτω) ;   **1.** *burial* (so from Hom. down).   **2.** *a grave, sepulchre*, (so fr. Hes. down) : Mt. xxiii. 27, 29 ; xxvii. 61, 64, 66 ; xxviii. 1 ; in a comparison : τάφος ἀνεῳγμένος ὁ λάρυγξ αὐτῶν, their speech threatens destruction to others, it is death to some one whenever they open their mouth, Ro. iii. 13.   Sept. for קֶבֶר, and sometimes for קְבוּרָה.*

5029   **τάχα**, (ταχύς), adv. ;   **1.** *hastily, quickly, soon*, (so fr. Hom. down).   **2.** as often in Grk. writ. fr. [Hes., Aeschyl.], Hdt. down, *perhaps, peradventure* : Ro. v. 7 ; Philem. 15.*

see 5032   [**τάχειον**, WH for τάχιον, q. v. ; and cf. s. v. ει, ι.]

5030   **ταχέως**, (ταχύς), adv., [fr. Hom. down], *quickly, shortly* : Lk. xiv. 21 ; xvi. 6 ; Jn. xi. 31 : 1 Co. iv. 19 ; Gal. i. 6 ; Phil. ii. 19, 24 ; 2 Tim. iv. 9 ; with the added suggestion of inconsiderateness [*hastily*] : 2 Th. ii. 2 ; 1 Tim. v. 22.*

5031   **ταχινός**, -ή, -όν, fr. Theocr. down, *swift, quick* : of events soon to come or just impending, 2 Pet. i. 14 ; ii. 1, (Is. lix. 7 ; Sap. xiii. 2 ; Sir. xviii. 26).*

5032   **τάχιον** [WH τάχειον ; see their App. p. 154 and cf. ει, ι], (neut. of the compar. ταχίων), adv., for which the more ancient writ. used θᾶσσον or θᾶττον, see Lob. ad Phryn. p. 76 sq. ; W. § 11, 2 a. ; [B. 27 (24)] ; *more swiftly, more quickly* : in comparison, Jn. xx. 4 [cf. W. 604 (562)] ; with the suppression of the second member of the comparison [W. 243 (228)] : Heb. xiii. 19 (sooner, sc. than would be the case without your prayers for me), 23 (sc. than I depart) ; Jn. xiii. 27 (sc. than you seem to have resolved to) ; 1 Tim. iii. 14 R G T (sc. than I anticipated).*

5033   **τάχιστα**, (neut. plur. of the superl. τάχιστος, fr. τάχυς), adv., [fr. Hom. down], *very quickly* : ὡς τάχιστα, as quickly as possible [A. V. *with all speed*], Acts xvii. 15.*

5034   **τάχος**, -ους, τό, fr. Hom. down, *quickness, speed* : ἐν τάχει (often in Grk. writ. fr. Aeschyl. and Pind. down), *quickly, shortly*, Acts xii. 7 ; xxii. 18 ; [xxv. 4] ; Ro. xvi. 20 ; *speedily, soon*, (Germ. *in Bälde*), Lk. xviii. 8 ; 1 Tim. iii. 14 L Tr WH ; Rev. i. 1 ; xxii. 6.*

5035   **ταχύ**, (neut. of the adj. ταχύς), adv., [fr. Pind. down], *quickly, speedily, (without delay)* : Mt. v. 25 ; xxviii. 7 sq. ; Mk. xvi. 8 Rec. ; Lk. xv. 22 L Tr br. WH ; Jn. xi. 29 ; ἔρχεσθαι, Rev. ii. 5 Rec.bez elz, 16 ; iii. 11 ; xi. 14 ; xxii. 7, 12, 20 ; forthwith, i. e. while in the use of my name he is performing mighty works, Mk. ix. 39.*

5036   **ταχύς**, -εῖα, -ύ, fr. Hom. down, *quick, fleet, speedy* : opp. to βραδύς (as in Xen. mem. 4, 2, 25), εἰς τὸ ἀκοῦσαι, [A. V. *swift to hear*], Jas. i. 19.*

5037   **τέ**, (as δέ comes fr. δή, μέν fr. μήν, so τέ fr. the adv. τῇ, prop. *as* ; [al. ally it with καί, cf. Curtius §§ 27, 647 ; Vaniček p. 95 ; Fick Pt. i. 32 ; *Donaldson*, New Crat. § 195]), a copulative enclitic particle (on the use of which cf. *Hermann* ad Vig. p. 833 ; *Klotz* ad Devar. II. 2 p. 739 sqq.) ; in the N. T. it occurs most frequently in the Acts, then in the Ep. to the Heb., somewhat rarely in the other bks. (in Mt. three or four times, in Mk. once, viz. xv. 36 R G ; in John's Gospel three times ;

nowhere in the Epp. to the Gal., Thess., or Col., nor in the Epistles of John and Peter ; twice in text. Rec. of Rev., viz. i. 2 ; xxi. 12) ; *and*, Lat. *que*, differing from the particle καί in that the latter is c o n j u n c t i v e, τέ a d j u n c t i v e [W. § 53, 2 ; acc. to *Bäumlein* (Griech. Partikeln, p. 145), καί introduces something new under the same aspect yet as an external addition, whereas τέ marks it as having an inner connection with what precedes ; hence καί is the more general particle, τέ the more special and precise ; καί may often stand for τέ, but not τέ for καί. (Cf. *Ebeling*, Lex. Homer., s. v. καί, init.)].

   1. τέ, standing alone (i. e. not followed by another τέ, or by καί, or other particle), joins   **a.** parts of one and the same sentence, as συναχθέντες συμβούλιόν τε λαβόντες, Mt. xxviii. 12 ; ἐν ἀγάπῃ πνεύματί τε πραότητος, 1 Co. iv. 21 ; add, Acts ii. 33 ; x. 22 ; xi. 26 ; xx. 11 ; xxiii. 10 [WH txt. om.], 24 ; xxiv. 5 ; xxvii. 20 sq. ; xxviii. 23 ; Heb. i. 3 ; vi. 5 ; ix. 1.   **b.** complete sentences : Jn. iv. 42 ; vi. 18 ; Acts ii. 37 ; iv. 33 ; v. 19, 35, 42 ; vi. 7, 12 sq. ; viii. 3, 13, 25, 31 ; x. 28, 33, 48 [here T Tr WH δέ (see 6 below)] ; xi. 21 ; xii. 6, 8 [L Tr WH δέ (see 6 below)], 12 ; xiii. 4, 39 ; xv. 4, 39 ; xvi. 13, 23 [WH txt. δέ (see 6 below)], 34 ; xvii. 5 [R G], 19 [Tr txt. WH δέ (see 6 below)], 26 ; xviii. 11 [R G], 26 ; xix. 11, 18, 29 ; xx. 3, 7 ; xxi. [18ᵃ Tdf.], 18ᵇ, 20 [not Lchm.], 37 ; xxii. 8 ; xxiii. 5 ; xxiv. 27 ; xxvii. 5, 8, 17, 29 [Tr mrg. δέ (see 6 below)], 43 ; Ro. ii. 19 ; Heb. xii. 2 ; introduces a sentence serving to illustrate the matter in hand, Acts i. 15 ; iv. 13.

   2. τέ . . . καί, and τέ καί, *not only . . . but also*, *as well . . . as*, *both . . . and* ; things are thus connected which are akin, or which are united to each other by some inner bond, whether logical or real ; [acc. to W. 439 (408) ; Bäumlein u. s. p. 224 sq., these particles give no intimation respecting the relative value of the two members ; but acc. to *Rost*, Griech. Gram. § 134, 4 ; *Donaldson*, Gr. Gram. § 551 ; Jelf § 758 ; *Klotz* ad Devar. II. 2, p. 740, the member with καί is the more emphatic ;   **a.** parts of one and the same sentence (which is completed by a single finite verb) : ἐσθίειν τε καὶ πίνειν, Lk. xii. 45 ; φοβητρά τε καὶ σημεῖα, Lk. xxi. 11 ; ἀρχιερεῖς τε καὶ γραμματεῖς, Lk. xxii. 66 ; πονηροὺς τε καὶ ἀγαθούς, Mt. xxii. 10 ; Ἡρῴδης τε καὶ Πόντιος Πιλᾶτος, Acts iv. 27 ; ἄνδρες τε καὶ γυναῖκες, Acts viii. 12 ; ix. 2 ; xxii. 4 ; πάντη τε κ. πανταχοῦ, Acts xxiv. 3 ; ἀσφαλῆ τε καὶ βεβαίαν, Heb. vi. 19 ; add, Acts i. 1 ; ii. 9 sq. ; ix. 29 ; xiv. 1, 5 ; xv. 9 ; xviii. 4 ; xix. 10, 17 ; xx. 21 ; xxi. 12 ; xxvi. 22 ; Ro. i. 12, 14, 16 ; iii. 9 ; x. 12 ; 1 Co. i. 2 [R G], 24, 30 ; Heb. iv. 12ᵃ Rec., 12ᵇ ; v. 1 [here L om. Tr WH br.], 7, 14 ; viii. 3 ; ix. 19 ; x. 33 ; xi. 32 ; Jas. iii. 7 ; τέ is annexed to the article, which is — either repeated after the καί before the following noun, Lk. ii. 16 ; xxiii. 12 ; Jn. ii. 15 ; Acts v. 24 ; viii. 38 ; xvii. 10 ; xviii. 5 ; xxi. 25 [R G] ; xxvi. 30 ; — or (less commonly) omitted. Acts i. 13 ; xiii. 1 ; [xxi. 25 L T Tr WH] ; Ro. i. 20.   τέ is annexed to a preposition, which after the following καί is — either repeated, Acts i. 8 where L om. Tr br. the repeated ἐν ; Phil. i. 7 [R om. L br. the second ἐν] ; —

or omitted, Acts x. 39 [Tr txt. WH]; xxv. 23; xxviii. 23. τέ is annexed to a relative pronoun, although it does not belong so much to the pronoun as to the substantive connected with it, Acts xxvi. 22. it is annexed to an adverb, ἔτι τε καί, [and moreover], Acts xxi. 28. When more than two members are joined together, the first two are joined by τέ καί or τέ ... καί, the rest by καί: Lk. xii. 45; Acts i. 13; v. 24 [R G]; xxi. 25; 1 Co. i. 30; Heb. ii. 4.   **b.** τέ ... καί connect whole sentences (each of which has its own finite verb, or its own subject): Acts ii. 3 sq. R G; xvi. 26 R G; τέ ... καὶ ... καί, Acts xxi. 30.   **3.** τέ ... δέ are so combined that τέ adds a sentence to what has been previously said, and δέ introduces something opposed to this added sentence [W. 439 (409)]: Acts xix. 2 L T Tr WH; 3 R G L Tr txt. WH txt.; xxii. 28 R G.   **4.** τέ ... τέ presents as parallel (or coordinate) the ideas or sentences which it connects, as ... so (cf. Kühner § 520; [Jelf § 754, 3; W. § 53, 4]; on the Lat. que ... que cf. Herzog on Sallust, Cat. 9, 3): Acts ii. 46; xvi. 11 sq. R G; xvii. 4; xxvi. 10 L T Tr WH txt., 16; Heb. vi. 2 [Tr br. WH txt. om. second τέ], (Sap. vii. 13; xv. 7); τέ καὶ ... τέ, Acts ix. 15 [L T Tr WH]; τέ καὶ ... τέ ... καί, Acts xxvi. 20 [L T Tr WH].   εἴτε ... εἴτε, see εἰ, III. 15; ἐάν τε ... ἐάν τε, see ἐάν, I. 3 e.   μήτε ... μήτε ... τέ, neither ... nor ... and, Acts xxvii. 20 (Xen. an. 4, 4, 6).   **5.** τέ γάρ (which began to be frequent fr. Aristot. down), Lat. namque, etenim, for also, for indeed, [W. 448 (417)], are so used that the former particle connects, the latter gives the reason: Ro. i. 26 (so that in 27 we must read ὁμοίως δὲ καί [with L Tr mrg.], see in 6 below); vii. 7 (4 Macc. v. 22); τέ γὰρ ... καί, Heb. ii. 11; ἐάν τε γὰρ ... ἐάν τε, for whether ... or (whether), Ro. xiv. 8; ἐάν τε γὰρ καί, for although (Lat. namque etiamsi), 2 Co. x. 8 [R G].   **6.** The reading often varies in codd. and edd. between τέ and δέ; as, Mt. xxiii. 6; Acts iii. 10; iv. 14; viii. 1, 6; xix. 46; Jude 6, etc. [see in 1 b. above]. In Ro. i. 27, following Lchm. [Tr mrg.], we ought certainly to read ὁμοίως δὲ καί; cf. Fritzsche ad loc. p. 77; [B. 361 (309) n.].   **7.** As respects Position (cf. Kühner § 520 Anm. 5; W. 559 sq. (520)), τέ is properly annexed to that word or idea which is placed in parallelism with another (as Ἰουδαῖοί τε καὶ Ἕλληνες); but writers also take considerable liberty in placing it, and readily subjoin it to an article or a preposition; for examples see in 2 a. above.

τεῖχος, -ους, τό, [cf. θιγγάνω; allied with it are Eng. 'dike' and 'ditch'], fr. Hom. down, Sept. very freq. for חוֹמָה 'wall'; the wall round a city, town-wall: Acts ix. 25; 2 Co. xi. 33; Heb. xi. 30; Rev. xxi. 12, 14 sq., 17–19.*

τεκμήριον, -ου, τό, (fr. τεκμαίρω to show or prove by sure signs; fr. τέκμαρ a sign), fr. Aeschyl. and Hdt. down, that from which something is surely and plainly known; an indubitable evidence, a proof, (Hesych. τεκμήριον· σημεῖον ἀληθές): Acts i. 3 (Sap. v. 11; 3 Macc. iii. 24).*

τεκνίον, -ου, τό, (dimin. of τέκνον, q. v.; [on the accent, cf. W. 52; Chandler § 347]), a little child; in the N. T. used as a term of kindly address by teachers to their disciples [always in the plur. little children: Mk. x. 24 Lchm.]; Jn. xiii. 33; Gal. iv. 19 (where L txt. T Tr WH mrg. τέκνα); 1 Jn. ii. 1, 12, 28; iii. 7 [WH mrg. παιδία], 18; iv. 4; v. 21. (Anthol.)*

τεκνογονέω, -ῶ; (τεκνογόνος, and this fr. τέκνον and ΓΕΝΩ); to beget or bear children: 1 Tim. v. 14. (Anthol. 9, 22, 4.)*

τεκνογονία, -ας, ἡ, child-bearing: 1 Tim. ii. 15. (Aristot. h. a. 7, 1, 8 [p.582ᵃ, 28].)*

τέκνον, -ου, τό, (τίκτω, τεκεῖν), fr. Hom. down, Sept. chiefly for בֵּן, sometimes for יֶלֶד, offspring; plur. children;   **a.** prop.   **α.** univ. and without regard to sex, child: Mk. xiii. 12; Lk. i. 7; Acts vii. 5; Rev. xii. 4; plur., Mt. vii. 11; x. 21; xv. 26; Mk. vii. 27; xii. 19; Lk. i. 17; xiv. 26; Acts xxi. 5; 2 Co. xii. 14; Eph. vi. 1; Col. iii. 20 sq.; 1 Th. ii. 7, 11; 1 Tim. iii. 4; Tit. i. 6; 2 Jn. 1, 4, 13, and often; with emphasis: to be regarded as true, genuine children, Ro. ix. 7; τέκνα ἐπαγγελίας, children begotten by virtue of the divine promise, Ro. ix. 8; accounted as children begotten by virtue of God's promise, Gal. iv. 28; τὰ τέκνα τῆς σαρκός, children by natural descent, Ro. ix. 8. in a broader sense (like the Hebr. בָּנִים), posterity: Mt. ii. 18; iii. 9; Lk. iii. 8; Acts ii. 39; xiii. 33 (32). with emphasis: genuine posterity, true offspring, Jn. viii. 39; (of women) to be regarded as children, 1 Pet. iii. 6.   **β.** spec. a male child, a son: Mt. xxi. 28; Acts xxi. 21; Rev. xii. 5; in the voc., in kindly address, Mt. xxi. 28; Lk. ii. 48; xv. 31.   **b.** metaph. the name is transferred to that intimate and reciprocal relationship formed between men by the bonds of love, friendship, trust, just as between parents and children;   **α.** in affectionate address, such as patrons, helpers, teachers, and the like, employ; voc. child (son), my child, children. (Lat. fili, mi fili, etc., for carissime, etc.): Mt. ix. 2; Mk. ii. 5; x. 24 [here Lchm. τεκνία, q. v.].   **β.** just as in Hebrew, Syriac, Arabic, Persian, so in the N. T., pupils or disciples are called children of their teachers, because the latter by their instruction nourish the minds of their pupils and mould their characters (see γεννάω, 2 b.): Philem. 10; 2 Tim. i. 2; 3 Jn. 4; in affectionate address, Gal. iv. 19 L txt. T Tr WH mrg.; 1 Tim. i. 18; 2 Tim. ii. 1; with ἐν κυρίῳ added, 1 Co. iv. 17; ἐν πίστει, 1 Tim. i. 2; κατὰ κοινὴν πίστιν, Tit. i. 4, (בְּנֵי הַנְּבִיאִים, sons i. e. disciples of the prophets, 1 K. xxi. (xx.) 35; 2 K. ii. 3, 5, 7; among the Persians, 'sons of the Magi' i. e. their pupils).   **γ.** τέκνα τοῦ θεοῦ, children of God, — in the O. T. of 'the people of Israel' as especially dear to God: Is. xxx. 1; Sap. xvi. 21; — in the N. T., in Paul's writings, all who are animated by the Spirit of God (Ro. viii. 14) and are closely related to God: Ro. viii. 16 sq. 21; Eph. v. 1; Phil. ii. 15; those to whom, as dearly beloved of God, he has appointed salvation by Christ, Ro. ix. 8; in the writings of John, all who ἐκ θεοῦ ἐγεννήθησαν (have been begotten of God, see γεννάω, 2 d.): Jn. i. 12 sq.; 1 Jn. iii. 1 sq. 10; v. 2; those whom God knows to be qualified to obtain the nature and dignity of his children, Jn. xi. 52. [Cf. Westcott on the Epp. of St.

John, pp. 94, 120; "In St. Paul the expressions 'sons of God', 'children of God', mostly convey the idea of liberty (see however Phil. ii. 15), in St. John of guilelessness and love; in accordance with this distinction St. Paul uses υἱοί as well as τέκνα, St. John τέκνα only" (Bp. Lghtft.); cf. υἱὸς τοῦ θεοῦ, 4.]   δ. τέκνα τοῦ διαβόλου, those who in thought and action are prompted by the devil, and so reflect his character: 1 Jn. iii. 10.   c. metaph. and Hebraistically, one is called τέκνον of anything who depends upon it, is possessed by a desire or affection for it, is addicted to it; or who is liable to any fate; thus in the N. T. we find   a. children of a city, i. e. its citizens, inhabitants, (Jer. ii. 30; Joel ii. 23; 1 Macc. i. 38; υἱοὶ Σιών, Ps. cxlix. 2): Mt. xxiii. 37; Lk. xiii. 34; xix. 44; Gal. iv. 25.   β. τέκνα τῆς σοφίας, the votaries of wisdom, those whose souls have, as it were, been nurtured and moulded by wisdom: Mt. xi. 19 (where T Tr txt. WH have hastily adopted ἔργων for τέκνων; cf. Keim ii. p. 369 [Eng. trans. iv. p. 43 sq.; per contra, see Tdf.'s note and WH. App. ad loc.]); Lk. vii. 35; τέκνα ὑπακοῆς, those actuated by a desire to obey, obedient, 1 Pet. i. 14; τοῦ φωτός, both illumined by the light, and loving the light, Eph. v. 8.   γ. κατάρας τέκνα, exposed to cursing, 2 Pet. ii. 14; τῆς ὀργῆς, doomed to God's wrath or penalty, Eph. ii. 3; cf. Steiger on 1 Pet. i. 14; W. 238 (223); [B. 161 (141)]. In the same way ἔκγονος is used sometimes in Grk. writ.; as, ἔκγ. ἀδικίας, δειλίας, Plat. legg. 3 p. 691 c.; 10 p. 901 e.

[SYN. τέκνον, υἱός: τ. and υἱ. while concurring in pointing to parentage, differ in that τ. gives prominence to the physical and outward aspects, υἱ. to the inward, ethical, legal. Cf. b. γ. above; υἱὸς τοῦ θεοῦ, fin.; παῖς, fin. and reff. (esp. that to Höhne).]

5044   τεκνο-τροφέω, -ῶ: 1 aor. ἐτεκνοτρόφησα; (τεκνοτρόφος, and this from τέκνον and τρέφω); to bring up children: 1 Tim. v. 10. (φέρει ὕδωρ, ὅταν τεκνοτροφῇ, sc. the bee, Aristot. h. a. 9, 40 [27], 14 [p. 625ᵇ, 20].)*

5045   τέκτων, -ονος, ὁ, (τεκεῖν, τίκτω; akin to τέχνη, τεύχω, hence prop. 'begetter' [Curtius § 235]), fr. Hom. down, Sept. for חָרָשׁ; a worker in wood, a carpenter: Mt. xiii. 55; Mk. vi. 3 [see WH. App. on the latter pass.].*

5046   τέλειος, -α, -ον, (τέλος), in classic Grk. sometimes also -ος, -ον, (cf. W. § 11, 1), fr. Hom. down, Sept. several times for שָׁלֵם, תָּמִים, etc.; prop. brought to its end, finished; wanting nothing necessary to completeness; perfect: ἔργον, Jas. i. 4; ἡ ἀγάπη, 1 Jn. iv. 18; ὁ νόμος, Jas. i. 25; [δώρημα, Jas. i. 17]; τελειοτέρα σκηνή, a more perfect (excellent) tabernacle, Heb. ix. 11; τὸ τέλειον, substantively, that which is perfect: consummate human integrity and virtue, Ro. xii. 2 [al. take it here as an adj. belonging to θέλημα]; the perfect state of all things, to be ushered in by the return of Christ from heaven, 1 Co. xiii. 10; of men, full-grown, adult; of full age, mature, (Aeschyl. Ag. 1504; Plat. legg. 11 p. 929c.): Heb. v. 14; τέλ. ἀνήρ (Xen. Cyr. 1, 2, 4 sq.; 8, 7, 6; Philo de cherub. § 32; opp. to παιδίον νήπιον, Polyb. 5, 29, 2; for other exx. fr. other auth. see Bleek, Brief a. d. Hebr. ii. 2 p. 133 sq.), μέχρι ... εἰς ἄνδρα τέλειον, until we rise to the same level of

knowledge which we ascribe to a full-grown man, until we can be likened to a full-grown man, Eph. iv. 13 (opp. to νήπιοι, 14); τέλειοι ταῖς φρεσί (opp. to παιδία and νηπιάζοντες ταῖς φρεσί), 1 Co. xiv. 20 [here A. V. men]; absol. οἱ τέλειοι, the perfect, i. e. the more intelligent, ready to apprehend divine things, 1 Co. ii. 6 [R.V. mrg. full-grown] (opp. to νήπιοι ἐν Χριστῷ, iii. 1; in simple opp. to νήπιος, Philo de legg. alleg. i. § 30; for מֵבִין, opp. to μανθάνων, 1 Chr. xxv. 8; [cf. Bp. Lghtft. on Col. i. 28; Phil. iii. 15]); of mind and character, one who has reached the proper height of virtue and integrity: Mt. v. 48; xix. 21; Phil. iii. 15 [cf. Bp. Lghtft. u. s.]; Jas. i. 4; in an absol. sense, of God: Mt. v. 48; τέλειος ἀνήρ, Jas. iii. 2 (τέλ. δίκαιος, Sir. xliv. 17); as respects understanding and goodness, Col. iv. 12; τέλ. ἄνθρωπος ἐν Χριστῷ, Col. i. 28 [cf. Bp. Lghtft. u. s. SYN. see ὁλόκληρος, and Trench § xxii.].*

5047   τελειότης, -ητος, ἡ, (τέλειος, q. v.), perfection;   a. i. e. the state of the more intelligent: Heb. vi. 1 [here R.V. mrg. full growth].   b. perfection: (τῆς ἀγάπης, Clem. Rom. 1 Cor. 50, 1 [where see Harnack]); absol. moral and spiritual perfection, Col. iii. 14 [A.V. perfectness], on which pass. see σύνδεσμος, 1. (Prov. xi. 3 Alex.; Judg. ix. 16, 19; Sap. vi. 15; xii. 17; Clem. Rom. 1 Cor. 53, 5; Plat. deff. p. 412 b. d.; [Aristot. phys. 3, 6 p. 207ᵃ, 21; 8, 7 p. 261ᵃ, 36]; Antonin. 5, 15.) [Cf. reff. s. v. τέλειος, and B. Hartung, Der Begriff der τελειότης im N. T. (4to. Leipz. 1881).]*

5048   τελειόω (in prof. auth. also τελεόω, which Hdt. uses everywhere [and which is "the prevailing form in Attic prose" (L. and S.)]; other writ. use both forms indifferently), -ῶ: 1 aor. ἐτελείωσα; pf. τετελείωκα; Pass. (or Mid.), pres. τελειοῦμαι; pf. τετελείωμαι; 1 aor. ἐτελειώθην; (τέλειος); fr. Hdt., Soph., Thuc., and Plat. down; equiv. to τέλειον ποιῶ, to make perfect or complete;   1. to carry through completely; to accomplish, finish, bring to an end: τὸν δρόμον, Acts xx. 24; τὸ ἔργον, Jn. iv. 34; v. 36; xvii. 4, (Neh. vi. 16; τὸν οἶκον, 2 Chr. viii. 16); τὰς ἡμέρας, Lk. ii. 43; mid. [pres. cf. B. 38 (33)] τελειοῦμαι, I finish, complete, what was given me to do, Lk. xiii. 32 [some (so A. V.) take it here as pass., I am perfected (understanding of his death; cf. Ellicott, Life of our Lord, Lect. vi. p. 242 n.¹; Keim ii. 615 n.¹)].   2. to complete (perfect), i. e. add what is yet wanting in order to render a thing full: τὴν ἀγάπην, pass., 1 Jn. ii. 5; iv. 12, 17; ἡ δύναμίς μου ἐν ἀσθενείᾳ τελειοῦται, my power shows itself most efficacious in them that are weak, 2 Co. xii. 9 R G; ἐκ τῶν ἔργων ἡ πίστις ἐτελειώθη, by works faith was perfected, made such as it ought to be, Jas. ii. 22; τετελείωταί τις ἐν τῇ ἀγάπῃ, one has been made perfect in love, his love lacks nothing, 1 Jn. iv. 18 (οἱ τελειωθέντες ἐν ἀγάπῃ, Clem. Rom. 1 Cor. 50, 3; [τελειῶσαι τὴν ἐκκλησίαν σου ἐν τῇ ἀγάπῃ σου, 'Teaching' etc. 10, 5]); ἵνα ὦσι τετελειωμένοι εἰς ἕν, that they may be perfected into one, i. e. perfectly united, Jn. xvii. 23. τινά, to bring one's character to perfection: ἤδη τετελείωμαι, I am already made perfect, Phil. iii. 12 (Sap. iv. 13); ὦ ψυχὴ ... ὅταν τελειωθῇς καὶ βραβείων καὶ στεφάνων ἀξιωθῇς, Philo de legg.

alleg. 3, 23; ψυχὴ ... τελειωθεῖσα ἐν ἀρετῶν ἄθλοις καὶ ἐπὶ τὸν ὅρον ἐφικομένη τοῦ καλοῦ, id. de somn. 1, 21; i. q. to be found perfect, Sir. xxxiv. (xxxi.) 10). **3.** to bring to the end (goal) proposed: οὐδέν, Heb. vii. 19; τινά, [to perfect or consummate] i. e. to raise to the state befitting him: so of God exalting Jesus to the state of heavenly majesty, Heb. ii. 10; in pass., Heb. v. 9; vii. 28; to raise to the state of heavenly blessedness those who put their faith in the expiatory death of Christ, pass., Heb. xi. 40; xii. 23, ([Act. Petr. et Paul. § 88, ed. Tdf. p. 39; Act. Barnab. § 9, id. p. 68; cf. 'Teaching' etc. 16, 2]; with μαρτυρίῳ added, of the death of the apost. Paul, Euseb. h. e. 2, 22, 2 [cf. Heinichen's note on 7, 15, 5]); to make one meet for future entrance on this state and give him a sure hope of it even here on earth, Heb. x. 1, 14; τινὰ κατὰ συνείδησιν, Heb. ix. 9; cf. Bleek, Brief an d. Hebr. ii. 1 p. 297 sqq.; C. R. Köstlin, Lehrbegriff des Evang. u. der Briefe Johannis (Berl. 1843) p. 421 sqq.; Riehm, Lehrbegriff des Hebr.-Br., § 42, p. 340 sqq.; Pfleiderer, Paulinismus, p. 344 sq. [Eng. trans. ii. p. 72 sqq.].　　　**4.** to accomplish, i. e. bring to a close or fulfilment by event: τὴν γραφήν, the prophecies of Scripture, pass., Jn. xix. 28 [cf. W. 459 (428); B. § 151, 20].*

5049　　τελείως, (τέλειος), adv., perfectly, completely: 1 Pet. i. 13. [Plat., Isocr., Aristot., etc.; cf. W. 463 (431).]*

5050　　τελείωσις, -εως, ἡ, (τελειόω), a completing, perfecting: **a.** fulfilment, accomplishment; the event which verifies a promise (see τελειόω, 4): Lk. i. 45 [Judith x. 9; Philo de vit. Moys. iii. § 39]. **b.** consummation, perfection, (see τελειόω, 3): Heb. vii. 11. (In various senses in Aristot., Theophr., Diod.) [Cf. reff. s. v. τελειόω, 3.]*

5051　　τελειωτής, -οῦ, ὁ, (τελειόω), (Vulg. consummator), a perfecter: τῆς πίστεως, one who has in his own person raised faith to its perfection and so set before us the highest example of faith, Heb. xii. 2. The word occurs nowhere else.*

5052　　τελεσφορέω, -ῶ; (τελεσφόρος, fr. τέλος and φέρω); to bring to (perfection or) maturity (sc. καρπούς): Lk. viii. 14. (Used alike of fruits, and of pregnant women and animals bringing their young to maturity; 4 Macc. xiii. 19; Theophr., Geop., Philo, Diod., Joseph., al.; [Ps. lxiv. (lxv.) 10 Symm.].)*

5053　　τελευτάω, -ῶ; 1 aor. ἐτελεύτησα; pf. ptcp. τετελευτηκώς (Jn. xi. 39 L T Tr WH); (τελευτή); fr. Hom. down; **1.** trans. to finish; to bring to an end or close: τὸν βίον, to finish life, to die, often fr. Aeschyl. and Hdt. down. **2.** intrans. [cf. B. § 130, 4] to have an end or close, come to an end; hence to die, very often so fr. Aeschyl. and Hdt. down (Sept. for כּוּת), and always in the N. T.: Mt. ii. 19; ix. 18; xxii. 25; Mk. ix. 44, 46 [(these two vss. T WH om. Tr br.)], 48; Lk. vii. 2; Jn. xi. 39 L T Tr WH; Acts ii. 29; vii. 15; Heb. xi. 22; θανάτῳ τελευτάτω (in imitation of the Hebr. מוֹת יוּמַת, Ex. xxi. .12, 15–17, etc.), [A. V. let him die the death i. e.] let him surely die [W. 339 (319); B. § 133, 22], Mt. xv. 4; Mk. vii. 10.*

5054　　τελευτή, -ῆς, ἡ, (τελέω), end [see τέλος, 1 a. init.]; the end of life, decease, death: Mt. ii. 15 (and often in Grk. writ. fr. Pind. and Thuc. down; Sept. for כּוּת): with

βιότοιο added, Hom. Il. 7, 104; τοῦ βίου, Hdt. 1, 30, and often in Attic writ.).*

τελέω, -ῶ; 1 aor. ἐτέλεσα [cf. W. § 13, 3 c.]; pf. τετέλεκα (2 Tim. iv. 7); Pass., pres. 3 pers. sing. τελεῖται (2 Co. xii. 9 L T Tr WH); pf. τετέλεσμαι; 1 aor. ἐτελέσθην; 1 fut. τελεσθήσομαι; (τέλος); fr. Hom. down; **1.** to bring to a close, to finish, to end: ἔτη, pass., passed, finished, Rev. xx. 3, 5, 7, ([so fr. Hom. and Hes. down; Aristot. h. a. 7, 1 init. p. 580ᵇ, 14 ἐν τοῖς ἔτεσι τοῖς δὶς ἑπτὰ τετελεσμένοις]; τριῶν τελουμένων ἡμερῶν, Lcian. Alex. 38); τὸν δρόμον (Hom. Il. 23, 373, 768; Soph. Electr. 726), 2 Tim. iv. 7; τοὺς λόγους, Mt. vii. 28 L T Tr WH; xix. 1; xxvi. 1; τὰς παραβολάς, Mt. xiii. 53; [ἄχρι τελεσθῶσιν αἱ πληγαί, Rev. xv. 8]; a rare use is τελεῖν τὰς πόλεις, i. e. your flight or journey through the cities [R. V. ye shall not have gone through the cities, etc.], Mt. x. 23 (similar are ἀνύειν τοὺς τόπους, Polyb. 5, 8, 1; τὰ ἕλη, 3, 79, 5; consummare Italiam, Flor. 1, (13) 18, 1; explore urbes, Tibull. 1, 4, 69; conficere aequor immensum, Verg. Georg. 2, 541; also xii. signorum orbem, Cic. nat. deor. 2, 20, 52); with the ptcp. of a verb (like ἄρχομαι, παύομαι, cf. W. § 45, 4 a.; B. § 144, 14), Mt. xi. 1. **2.** to perform, execute, complete, fulfil, (so that the thing done corresponds to what has been said, the order, command, etc.), i. e. **a.** with special reference to the subject-matter, to carry out the contents of a command: τὸν νόμον, Ro. ii. 27 [cf. W. 134 (127)]; Jas. ii. 8; τὴν ἐπιθυμίαν (i. e. τὸ ἐπιθυμούμενον), Gal. v. 16. **β.** with reference also to the form, to do just as commanded, and generally involving a notion of time, to perform the last act which completes a process, to accomplish, fulfil: ἅπαντα (πάντα) τὰ κατὰ νόμον, Lk. ii. 39; τὴν μαρτυρίαν, the duty of testifying, Rev. xi. 7; τὸ μυστήριον, pass. Rev. x. 7 [cf. W. 277 (260)]; τὸ βάπτισμα, pass. Lk. xii. 50; πάντα, pass. Jn. xix. 28 [the distinction betw. τελέω and τελειόω may be seen in this vs.]; τοὺς λόγους (τὰ ῥήματα) τοῦ θεοῦ, pass. Rev. xvii. 17; ἅπαντα (πάντα) τὰ γεγραμμένα, Acts xiii. 29; pass., Lk. xviii. 31 [see γράφω, 2 c.]; with ἐν ἐμοί (in me) added, in my experience, Lk. xxii. 37; ἐν πληγαῖς, in the infliction of calamities, Rev. xv. 1; τετέλεσται, [A. V. it is finished] everything has been accomplished which by the appointment of the Father as revealed in the Scriptures I must do and bear, Jn. xix. 30. i. q. τελειόω, 2, q. v. (made perfect): 2 Co. xii. 9 L T Tr WH. **3.** to pay: τὰ δίδραχμα, Mt. xvii. 24; φόρους, Ro. xiii. 6, (τὸν φόρον, Plat. Alc. 1 p. 123 a.; τὰ τέλη, often in Attic writ.). [Comp.: ἀπο-, δια-, ἐκ-, ἐπι-, συν- τελέω.]*

5055

τέλος, -ους, τό, [cf. Curtius § 238], fr. Hom. down, Sept. mostly for קֵץ; **1.** end, i. e. **a.** termination, the limit at which a thing ceases to be, (in the Grk. writ. always the end of some act or state, but not of the end of a period of time, which they call τελευτή; in the Scriptures also of a temporal end; an end in space is everywhere called πέρας): τῆς βασιλείας, Lk. i. 33; ζωῆς, Heb. vii. 3; τοῦ καταργουμένου, 2 Co. iii. 13; τὰ τέλη τῶν αἰώνων, 1 Co. x. 11 (τέλος τῶν ἡμερῶν, Neh. xiii. 6; τῶν ἑπτὰ ἐτῶν, 2 K. viii. 3; ἀρχὴ καὶ τέλος καὶ μεσότης χρόνων.

5056

Sap. vii. 18); i. q. he who puts an end to: τέλος νόμου Χριστός, Christ has brought the law to an end (πᾶσίν ἐστιν ἀνθρώποις τέλος τοῦ βίου θάνατος. Dem. 1306, 25), Ro. x. 4; cf. Fritzsche ad loc., vol. ii. p. 377 sq. πάντων τὸ τέλος, the end of all things (i. e. of the present order of things), 1 Pet. iv. 7; also in the phrases ἕως τέλους, 1 Co. i. 8; 2 Co. i. 13; μέχρι τέλους, Heb. iii. 6 [Tr mrg. WH br. the cl.], 14; ἄχρι τέλους, Heb. vi. 14; Rev. ii. 26. What 'end' is intended the reader must determine by the context; thus, τὸ τέλος denotes the end of the Messianic pangs (dolores Messiae; see ὠδίν) in Mt. xxiv. 6, 14, (opp. to ἀρχὴ ὠδίνων) in Mt. xiii. 7 (cf. 9); Lk. xxi. 9; τὸ τέλος in 1 Co. xv. 24 denotes either the end of the eschatological events, or the end of the resurrection i. e. the last or third act of the resurrection (to include those who had not belonged to the number of οἱ τοῦ Χριστοῦ ἐν τῇ παρουσίᾳ αὐτοῦ), 1 Co. xv. 24 cf. 23; see De Wette ad loc.; Weizel in the Theol. Stud. u. Krit. for 1836, p. 978; Grimm in the Zeitschr. f. wissensch. Theol. for 1873, p. 388 sqq.; [yet cf. Heinrici in Meyer (6te Aufl.) ad loc.]. εἰς τέλος, — to the very end appointed for these evils, Mt. x. 22; xxiv. 13; Mk. xiii. 13; also at the end, at last, finally, Lk. xviii. 5 (Vulg. in novissimo) [i. e. lest at last by her coming she wear me out; but al. take it i. q. Hebr. לָנֶצַח (cf. Job xiv. 20 etc. see Trommius) and connect it with the ptcp., lest by her coming to the last i. e. continually; see ὑπωπιάζω, sub fin.]; Jn. xiii. 1 [al. to the uttermost, completely (cf. our to the very last); see Westcott, and Weiss (in Meyer 6te Aufl.) ad loc.; Grimm on 2 Macc. viii. 29], cf. ἀγαπάω, sub fin., (Xen. oec. 17, 10; Hes. opp. 292; Hdt. 3, 40; 9, 37; Soph. Phil. 409; Eur. Ion 1615; Ael. v. h. 10, 16); to the (procurement of their) end, i. e. to destruction [A. V. to the uttermost (cf. reff. u. s.)], 1 Th. ii. 16 (for לְכָלָה, 2 Chr. xii. 12); τέλος ἔχειν, to have an end, be finished, (often in Grk. writ.), Lk. xxii. 37 [al. give τέλος here the sense of fulfilment (cf. τελέω, 2)]; i. q. to perish, Mk. iii. 26. τὸ δὲ τέλος, adverbially, finally (denique vero): 1 Pet. iii. 8 (Plat. legg. 6 p. 768 b.; καὶ τό γε τέλος, ibid. 5 p. 740 e.; but generally in prof. auth. τέλος in this sense wants the article; cf. Passow ii. p. 1857ª; [L. and S. s. v. I. 4 a.]). **b.** the end i. e. the last in any succession or series: (ἡ) ἀρχὴ καὶ (τὸ) τέλος, of God, who by his perpetuity survives all things, i. e. eternal, Rev. i. 8 Rec.; xxi. 6; xxii. 13. **c.** that by which a thing is finished, its close, issue: Mt. xxvi. 58; final lot, fate, as if a recompense: with a gen. of the thing, Ro. vi. 21 sq.; Heb. vi. 8; 1 Pet. i. 9; with a gen. of the person whom the destiny befalls, 2 Co. xi. 15; Phil. iii. 19; 1 Pet. iv. 17; τοῦ κυρίου (gen. of author), the closing experience which befell Job by God's command, Jas. v. 11 (referring to Job xlii. [esp. 12]). **d.** the end to which all things relate, the aim, purpose: 1 Tim. i. 5 (often so in philos. fr. Plat. de rep. 6 p. 494 a. down; cf. Fritzsche on Rom. ii. p. 378). **2.** toll, custom, [i. e. an indirect tax on goods; see φόρος and κῆνσος]: Mt. xvii. 25; Ro. xiii. 7, (Xen., Plat., Polyb., Aeschin., Dem., al.; 1 Macc. x. 31; xi. 35).*

τελώνης, -ου, ὁ, (fr. τέλος [(q. v. 2)] tax, and ὠνέομαι to buy; cf. δημοσιώνης, ὀψώνης, δεκατώνης), fr. Arstph., Aeschin., Aristot., Polyb. down; **1.** a renter or farmer of taxes (Lat. publicanus); among the Romans usually a man of equestrian rank. **2.** a tax-gatherer, collector of taxes or tolls, (Vulg. publicanus incorrectly: [so A. V. publican]), one employed by a publican or farmer-general in collecting the taxes. The tax-collectors were, as a class, detested not only by the Jews but by other nations also, both on account of their employment and of the harshness, greed, and deception, with which they prosecuted it; (hence they are classed by Artem. oneir. 1, 23; 4, 57, with καπήλοις καὶ τοῖς μετὰ ἀναιδείας ζῶσι καὶ λῃσταῖς καὶ ζυγοκρούσταις καὶ παραλογισταῖς ἀνθρώποις; Lcian. necyom. c. 11 puts together μοιχοί, πορνοβοσκοὶ καὶ τελῶναι καὶ κόλακες καὶ συκοφάνται [Theophr. charact. 6 (περὶ ἀπονοίας) πανδοχεῦσαι, καὶ πορνοβοσκῆσαι, καὶ τελωνῆσαι]): Mt. v. 46, 47 Rec.; x. 3; Lk. iii. 12; v. 27, 29; vii. 29; xviii. 10, 11, 13; the plur. is joined with ἁμαρτωλοί, Mt. ix. 10 sq.; [xi. 19]; Mk. ii. 15 sq.; Lk. v. 30; vii. 34; xv. 1; with πόρναι, Mt. xxi. 31 sq.; ὁ ἐθνικὸς κ. ὁ τελώνης, Mt. xviii. 17. Cf. Win. RWB. s. v. Zoll, Zöllner; [BB. DD. s.v. Publican; Wetstein on Mt. v. 46; Edersheim, Jesus the Messiah, i. 515 sqq.].*

5057

τελώνιον, -ου, τό, (τελώνης, cf. δεκατώνιον): [**1.** customs, toll: Strabo 16, 1, 27. **2.**] toll-house, place of toll, tax-office: the place in which the tax-collector sat to collect the taxes [Wiclif, tolbothe]: Mt. ix. 9; Mk. ii. 14; Lk. v. 27.*

5058

τέρας, gen. τέρατος, pl. τέρατα (cf. κέρας, init.), τό, (apparently akin to the verb τηρέω; accordingly something so strange as to cause it to be 'watched' or 'observed'; [others connect it with ἀστήρ, ἀστραπή, etc., hence 'a sign in the heavens'; Vaniček p. 1146; Curtius § 205]; see Fritzsche, Ep. ad Rom. iii. p. 270), fr. Hom. down, Sept. for מוֹפֵת, a prodigy, portent; miracle [A.V. wonder] performed by any one; in the N. T. it is found only in the plur. and joined with σημεῖα; for the passages see σημεῖον, p. 574ª.

5059

Τέρτιος, -ου, ὁ, Tertius, an amanuensis of the apostle Paul: Ro. xvi. 22. [B. D. s. v.]*

5060

Τέρτυλλος, -ου, ὁ, Tertullus, a Roman orator: Acts xxiv. 1 sq. [See ῥήτωρ.]*

5061

τεσσαράκοντα R G, but several times [i. e. betw. 8 and 14] in Lchm. and everywhere in T WH (and Tr, exc. Rev. xxi. 17) τεσσεράκοντα (a form originally Ionic [yet cf. B. as below]; see Kühner § 187, 5; B. 28 (25) sq.; cf. W. 43; [Tdf. Proleg. p. 80; WH. App. p. 150]), οἱ, αἱ, τά, indecl. numeral, forty: Mt. iv. 2; Mk. i. 13; Lk. iv. 2; Jn. ii. 20; etc.

5062

[τεσσαράκοντα-δύο, forty-two: Rev. xi. 2 Rec.ᵇᵉᶻ; xiii. 5 Rec.ᵇᵉᶻ ᵉˡᶻ.*]

(5062α)

τεσσαρακονταετής (T Tr WH τεσσερ-, see τεσσαράκοντα; L T accent -έτης, see ἑκατονταέτης), -ές, (τεσσαράκοντα, and ἔτος), of forty years, forty years old: Acts vii. 23; xiii. 18. (Hes. opp. 441.)*

5063

[τεσσαρακοντα-τέσσαρες, -ων, forty-four: Rev. xxi. 17 Rec.ᵇᵉᶻ ᵉˡᶻ.*]

(5063α)

5064 τέσσαρες, -ων, οἱ, αἱ, τέσσαρα, τά, gen. τεσσάρων, dat. τέσσαρσιν, ([Lchm. reads τέσσερες 7 times to 33, Tdf. 6 to 35, Tr 6 to 33, WH 6 to 34; Lchm. sometimes has τέσσερα, T Tr WH always; L Tr sometimes have τέσσερας (see WH. App. p. 150)]; but no editor adopts ε in the gen. or dat.; see τεσσαράκοντα and reff.), four : Mt. xxiv. 31; Mk. ii. 3; Lk. ii. 37; Jn. xi. 17; Acts x. 11; Rev. iv. 4, etc.

5065 τέσσαρες-και-δέκατος, -η, -ον, the fourteenth : Acts xxvii. 27, 33.*

see 5064 [τέσσερ- see τεσσαρ- (cf. Meisterhans § 21, 4)]

5066 τεταρταῖος, -α, -ον, (τέταρτος), an ordinal numeral, used in answer to the question on what day? one who does or suffers a thing till the fourth day or on the fourth day : τεταρταῖός ἐστιν, i. e. he has been four days in the tomb, or it is the fourth day since he was buried, [A. V. he hath been dead four days], Jn. xi. 39 (ἤδη γὰρ ἦσαν πεμπταῖοι, already five days dead, Xen. an. 6, 4 (2), 9).*

5067 τέταρτος, -η, -ον, (fr. τέτταρες), the fourth : Mt. xiv. 25; Mk. vi. 48; Acts x. 30; Rev. iv. 7, etc. [From Hom. down.]

see 5064 τετρα-, in composition i. q. τέτορα, Aeolic [Doric rather] for τέσσαρα.

see 5075 [τετρααρχέω, see τετραρχέω.]
see 5076 [τετραάρχης, see τετράρχης.]

5068 τετράγωνος, -ον, (fr. τέτρα, q. v., and γῶνος [i. e. γωνία]), quadrangular, square ; [A. V. four-square] (Vulg. in quadro positus) : Rev. xxi. 16. (Sept.; Hdt., Plat., Aristot., Polyb., Plut., al.) *

5069 τετράδιον, -ου, τό, (τετράς, the number four), a quaternion (τὸ ἐκ τεσσάρων συνεστός, Suid.) : τῶν στρατιωτῶν, a guard consisting of four soldiers (for among the Romans this was the usual number of the guard to which the custody of captives and prisons was intrusted ; two soldiers were confined with the prisoner and two kept guard outside), Acts xii. 4, where the four quaternions mentioned were on guard one at a time during each of the four watches. (Philo in Flacc. § 13 i. e. ed. Mang. vol. ii. p. 533, 25.) *

5070 τετρακισ-χίλιοι, -αι, -α, (τετράκις and χίλιοι), four thousand : Mt. xv. 38 ; xvi. 10 ; Mk. viii. 9, 20 ; Acts xxi. 38. [(Hdt., Arstph., Thuc., al.)] *

5071 τετρακόσιοι, -αι -α, (fr. τετράκις, and the term. -όσιος indicating one hundred ; [cf. G. Meyer, Gr. Gram. § 16 f.]), four hundred : Acts v. 36 ; vii. 6 ; xiii. 20 ; Gal. iii. 17. [(Hdt., Thuc., Xen., al.)] *

5072 τετράμηνος, -ον, (fr. τέτρα, q. v., and μήν ; cf. Lob. ad Phryn. p. 549), of four months, lasting four months : τετράμηνός ἐστιν sc. χρόνος, Jn. iv. 35, where Rec. τετράμηνόν ἐστιν, as in Judg. xix. 2 Alex.; xx. 47. (Thuc., Aristot., Polyb., Plut., al.) *

5073 τετραπλόος, (-οῦς), -όη (-ῆ), -όον (-οῦν), (fr. τέτρα, and πλόος, to which corresponds the Lat. -plus in duplus, triplus, fr. ΠΛΕΩ [but cf. Vaniček p. 501]), quadruple, fourfold : Lk. xix. 8. (Sept. ; Xen., Joseph., Plut., al.) *

5074 τετρά-πους, -ουν, gen. -οδος, (fr. τέτρα, q. v., and πούς a foot), fr. Hdt. and Thuc. down, four-footed : neut. plur. sc. beasts, Acts x. 12; xi. 6 ; Ro. i. 23. (Sept. for בְּהֵמָה.) *

5075 τετραρχέω [T WH τετρααρχ. (see WH. App. p. 145)], -ῶ ; (τετράρχης, q. v.), to be governor of a tetrarchy, be tetrarch : with a gen. of the region, Lk. iii. 1. [(Joseph. b. j. 3, 10, 7.)] *

5076 τετράρχης [T WH τετραάρχης; see the preceding word, and cf. Tdf. Proleg. p. 117], -ου, ὁ, (fr. τέτρα, q. v., and ἄρχω), a tetrarch ; i. e. **1.** a governor of the fourth part of any region. Thus Strabo, 12 p. 567, states that Galatia was formerly divided into three parts, each one of which was distributed into four smaller subdivisions each of which was governed by 'a tetrarch'; again, in lib. 9 p. 430, he relates that Thessaly, before the time of Philip of Macedon, had been divided into four 'tetrarchies' each of which had its own 'tetrarch'. **2.** the word lost its strict etymological force, and came to denote the governor of a third part or half of a country, or even the ruler of an entire country or district provided it were of comparatively narrow limits ; a petty prince [cf. e. g. Plut. Anton. 56, 3, i. p. 942 a.]. Thus Antony made Herod (afterwards king) and Phasael, sons of Antipater, tetrarchs of Palestine, Joseph. antt. 14, 13, 1. After the death of Herod the Great, his sons, Archelaus styled an ethnarch but Antipas and Philip with the title of 'tetrarchs', divided and governed the kingdom left by their father ; Joseph. antt. 17, 11, 4. Cf. Fischer, De vitiis etc. p. 428; Win. RWB. s. v. Tetrarch, and esp. Keim in Schenkel v. p. 487 sqq. The tetrarch Herod Antipas is mentioned in Mt. xiv. 1; Lk. iii. 19 ; ix. 7; Acts xiii. 1.*

see 5177 τεύχω, see τυγχάνω.

5077 τεφρόω, -ῶ : 1 aor. ptcp. τεφρώσας ; (τέφρα ashes) ; to reduce to ashes : 2 Pet. ii. 6. (Aristot. [?], Theophr., Dio Cass., Philo, Antonin., al.) *

5078 τέχνη, -ης, ἡ, (fr. τεκεῖν, see τέκτων), fr. Hom. down, art : univ. Rev. xviii. 22 [here A. V. craft] ; of the plastic art, Acts xvii. 29 ; of a trade (as often in Grk. writ.), Acts xviii. 3.*

5079 τεχνίτης, -ου, ὁ, (τέχνη), fr. Soph. [(?), Plato], Xen. down, Sept. several times for חָרָשׁ, an artificer, craftsman : Acts xix. 24, 38; Rev. xviii. 22 ; of God the framer of the higher and eternal course of things, Heb. xi. 10 (of God the architect of the world, Sap. xiii. 1, where cf. Grimm, Exeget. Hdbch. p. 234 [cf. also Trench, Syn. § cv. ; Piper, Monumentale Theol. § 26]).*

5080 τήκω : fr. Hom. down ; to make liquid ; pass. to become liquid, to melt ; to perish or be destroyed by melting : 2 Pet. iii. 12, where for the pres. 3 pers. sing. τήκεται Lchm. gives the fut. τακήσεται [see WH on the pass. and in their App. p. 171], cf. Is. xxxiv. 4 τακήσονται πᾶσαι αἱ δυνάμεις τῶν οὐρανῶν. [Cf. Veitch s. v.] *

5081 τηλαυγῶς, adv., (fr. the adj. τηλαυγής, far-shining, fr. τῆλε afar, and αὐγή radiance), at a distance and clearly : Mk. viii. 25 [where T WH mrg. δηλαυγῶς, q. v.]. (adj., Job xxxvii. 20 ; Ps. xviii. (xix.) 9 ; and esp. in the Grk. poets fr. Pind. down ; τηλαυγέστερον ὁρᾶν, Diod. 1, 50.)*

5082 τηλικ-οῦτος, -αύτη, -οῦτο, (fr. τηλίκος and οὗτος [but then (it is urged) it should have been τηλιχοῦτος; hence better connected with αὐτός; al. al.   Cf. *Bttm.* Ausf. Spr. § 79 A. 4; Kühner § 173, 6: Vaniček p. 268; L. and S. s.v. οὗτος, init.]), in Attic writ. fr. Aeschyl. down ;   **1.** *of such an age*; used of any age, *of so great an age, so old*; also *so young.*   **2.** *of so great a size,* in bulk: πλοῖα, Jas. iii. 4.   **3.** intensively, *such and so great* (Lat. *tantus talisque*) : 2 Co. i. 10; Heb. ii. 3; Rev. xvi. 18.*

5083   **τηρέω, -ῶ**; impf. ἐτήρουν; fut. τηρήσω; 1 aor. ἐτήρησα; pf. τετήρηκα, 3 pers. plur. τετηρήκασιν (Jn. xvii. 6 R G) and τετήρηκαν (ibid. L T Tr WH, [see γίνομαι, init.]); Pass., pres. τηροῦμαι; impf. ἐτηρούμην; pf. τετήρημαι; 1 aor. ἐτηρήθην; (τηρός, found only once, Aeschyl. suppl. 248, where it is doubtful whether it means 'guarding' or 'watching'), fr. Pind., Soph., Thuc. down; Sept. several times for נָצַר, שָׁמַר, etc.; *to attend to carefully, take care of*; i. e.   **a.** prop. *to guard*: τινά, a prisoner, Mt. xxvii. 36, 54 ; Acts xvi. 23; pass., Acts xii. 5; [xxiv. 23]; xxv. 4, 21 [ᵇ]; τί, xii. 6; οἱ τηροῦντες, [(R.V.) *the watchers*] the guards, Mt. xxviii. 4 (Cant. iii. 3).   **b.** metaph. *to keep*: τινά, one in that state in which he is, τὴν ἑαυτοῦ παρθένον, his own virgin daughter, sc. as a virgin i. e. unmarried, 1 Co. vii. 37 ; ἑαυτόν, himself such as he is, i. e. begotten of God, 1 Jn. v. 18 [but here T Tr WH αὐτόν]; with a pred. accus. added : ἅγνον, 1 Tim. v. 22; ἄσπιλον ἀπὸ τοῦ κόσμου, Jas. i. 27; ἀβαρῆ τινι, 2 Co. xi. 9, (ἁπλοῦν, Antonin. 6, 30; τινὰ ἄμεμπτον τῷ θεῷ, Sap. x. 5); τί with a pred. accus. 1 Tim. vi. 14 [but see in c. below]; pass. τηροῦμαι, with an adv., ἀμέμπτως, 1 Th. v. 23 ; with a dat. of the pers., Χριστῷ, devoted to Christ, [W. 421 (392)], Jude 1 ; τηρεῖν τινα ἔν τινι, *to keep in* i. e. cause one to persevere or stand firm in a thing: ἐν τῷ ὀνόματι θεοῦ (see p. 447ᵇ bot.), Jn. xvii. 11 sq.; ἐν ἀγάπῃ θεοῦ, Jude 21; τινὰ ἔκ τινος, by guarding to cause one to escape in safety out of etc. : ἐκ τοῦ πονηροῦ, out of the power and assaults of Satan, Jn. xvii. 15 [cf. B. 327 (281); W. 410 (383)]; ἐκ τῆς ὥρας τοῦ πειρασμοῦ, Rev. iii. 10.   *to keep*: i. e. not to leave, τὴν ἀρχήν, Jude 6; not to throw away, τὰ ἱμάτια, Rev. xvi. 15. *to hold firmly*: τὴν ἑνότητα τοῦ πνεύματος, Eph. iv. 3; anything as a mental deposit, τὴν πίστιν, 2 Tim. iv. 7; Rev. xiv. 12 [cf. W. 536 (499); B. 78 (68)]. to show one's self to be actually holding a thing fast, i. e.   **c.** *to observe*: sc. πῶς κτλ. Rev. iii. 3; τί, Mt. xxiii. 3; Acts xxi. 25 [Rec.]; τὴν παράδοσιν, Mk. vii. 9 [WH (rejected) mrg. στήσητε] (τὰ ἐκ παραδόσεως τῶν πατέρων, Joseph. antt. 13, 10, 6); τὸν νόμον, Acts xv. 5 and Rec. in 24; Jas. ii. 10; τὸ σάββατον, the command respecting sabbath-keeping, Jn. ix. 16; τὰς ἐντολάς (of either God or Christ), Mt. xix. 17; Jn. xiv. 15, 21 ; xv. 10; 1 Jn. ii. 3 sq.; iii. 22, 24; v. 2 (where L T Tr WH ποιῶμεν); v. 3; Rev. xii. 17; xiv. 12 [see above, b. fin.]; τὴν ἐντολήν, 1 Tim. vi. 14 [see in b. above; πάντα ὅσα ἐνετειλάμην, Mt. xxviii. 20]; τὸν λόγον, either of Christ or of God, Jn. viii. 51 sq. 55; xiv. 23; xv. 20; xvii. 6; 1 Jn. ii. 5; Rev. iii. 8; τοὺς λόγους, of Christ, Jn. xiv. 24; τὸν λόγον τῆς ὑπομονῆς μου (i. e. Ἰησοῦ), Rev. iii. 10; τὰ ἔργα μου, the works that I command, Rev. ii. 26; τοὺς

λόγους τῆς προφητείας, Rev. xxii. 7; τοῦ βιβλίου τούτου, Rev. xxii. 9; τὰ ἐν τῇ προφητείᾳ γεγραμμένα, Rev. i. 3; cf. *Lipsius,* Paulin. Rechtfertigungsl. p. 194 sq.   **d.** *to reserve*: τινὰ εἴς τι, to undergo something, 2 Pet. ii. 4 [cf. W. 342 (321); εἰς τὴν τοῦ Σεβαστοῦ διάγνωσιν, Acts xxv. 21*]; Jude 6; τινὰ εἰς ἡμέραν κρίσεως, 2 Pet. ii. 9; τοὺς οὐρανοὺς πυρὶ (to be burned with fire) εἰς ἡμέραν κρίσεως, 2 Pet. iii. 7; τὶ εἴς τινα, a thing for one's advantage, 1 Pet. i. 4; τὶ εἰς ἡμέραν τινά, to be used some day for some purpose, Jn. xii. 7; τὶ ἕως ἄρτι, Jn. ii. 10; τί with the dat. of the pers., for rewarding or punishing one, pass., 2 Pet. ii. 17; Jude 13.   [COMP. : δια-, παρα-, συν-τηρέω.]*

[SYN. τηρέω, φυλάσσω: τηρ. *to watch* or *keep*, φυλ. *to guard*; τηρ. expresses watchful care and is suggestive of present possession, φυλ. indicates safe custody and often implies assault from without; τηρ. may mark the result of which φυλ. is the means (e. g. Jn. xvii. 12 where the words occur together, cf. Wisd. x. 5). See Westcott on Jn. viii. 51; Schmidt ch. 208, esp. § 4.]

τήρησις, -εως, ἡ, (τηρέω) ;   **a.** *a watching*: of pris-   **5084** oners (Thuc. 7, 86); the place where prisoners are kept, *a prison,* [R. V. *ward*]: Acts iv. 3; v. 18.   **b.** *a keeping,* i. e. complying with, obeying: τῶν ἐντολῶν, 1 Co. vii. 19; Sir. xxxv. (xxxii.) 23; νόμων, Sap. vi. 19.*

Τιβεριάς, -άδος, ἡ, (fr. Τιβέριος), a city of Galilee, near   **5085** the Lake of Gennesaret, which Herod Antipas, tetrarch of Galilee, greatly enlarged [but see BB.DD. s. v. and esp. *Schürer,* Neutest. Zeitgesch. p. 234 note] and beautified, and named Tiberias in honor of Tiberius Caesar (Joseph. antt. 18, 2, 3). It is now called *Tubariyeh,* a poor and wretched town of about 3000 inhabitants, swarming with fleas for which the place is notorious throughout Syria: Jn. vi. 1, 23; xxi. 1. Cf. Robinson ii. 380-394; *Win.* RWB. s. v.; *Rüetschi* in Herzog ed. 1 xvi. 161; *Weizsäcker* in Schenkel v. 526 sq.; [*Mühlau* in Riehm p. 1661 sq.]; Bädeker pp. 367-369.*

Τιβέριος, -ου, ὁ, *Tiberius,* the Roman emperor (fr.   **5086** [Aug. 19] A. D. 14 to [March 16] A. D. 37) in whose reign Christ was crucified: Lk. iii. 1.*

τιθέω, i. q. τίθημι, q. v.   **see 5087**

τίθημι, 3 pers. plur. τιθέασιν (Mt. v. 15; [W. § 14, 1 a.;   **5087** B. 44 (38)]); impf. (fr. τιθέω) 3 pers. sing. ἐτίθει (2 Co. iii. 13), 3 pers. plur. ἐτίθουν (Mk. vi. 56 [R G L]; Acts iii. 2; iv. 35) [and (T Tr WH in Mk. l. c.) ἐτίθεσαν, cf. B. 45 (39); WH. App. p. 167]; fut. θήσω; 1 aor. ἔθηκα; 2 aor. (ἔθην) subj. θῶ, [impv. 2 pers. plur. θέτε, Lk. xxi. 14 L T Tr WH (for R G 2 aor. mid. impv. θέσθε)], inf. θεῖναι, ptcp. θείς; pf. τέθεικα; Pass., pres. 3 pers. sing. τίθεται (Mk. xv. 47 R G); pf. 3 pers. sing. τέθειται (Mk. xv. 47 L T Tr WH); 1 aor. ἐτέθην; 2 aor. mid. ἐθέμην (2 pers. sing. ἔθου, Acts v. 4); (see ἐπιτίθημι); fr. Hom. down; Sept. mostly for שׂוּם and שִׂים, נָתַן and שִׁית and הָנִיחַ, הִשִּׁית, etc.;   **1.** *to set, put, place,* i. e. causative of κεῖσθαι; hence   **a.** *to place* or *lay*: τί, as θεμέλιον, [Lk. vi. 48]; xiv. 29; 1 Co. iii. 10 sq. (θεμείλια, Hom. Il. 12, 29); λίθον, Ro. ix. 33; 1 Pet. ii. 6; τί, opp. to αἴρειν, Lk. xix. 21 sq. (cf. Xen. oec. 8, 2) ; τινὶ πρόσκομμα [or (acc. to WH mrg.) σκάνδαλον], Ro. xiv. 13; τὶ εἴς τι, Lk. xi. 33 [W.

238 (223)] ; τινὰ ποῦ, ὅπου, ἐκεῖ, [ὧς], of the dead laid to rest somewhere, Mk. xv. 47 ; xvi. 6 ; [Lk. xxiii. 55] ; Jn. xi. 34 ; xix. 42 ; xx. 2, 13, 15 ; ἐν with dat. of the place, Mt. xxvii. 60 ; Mk. vi. 29 ; [xv. 46 L Tr WH] ; Lk. xxiii. 53 ; Jn. xix. 41 ; Acts vii. 16 ; ix. 37 ; εἰς μνημεῖον, Acts xiii. 29 ; Rev. xi. 9 ; (in Grk. writ. fr. Hom. down, very often of the laying away or depositing anywhere of the bones or ashes of the dead ; like Lat. ponere i. q. sepelire, cf. Klotz, Handwörterb. d. Lat. Spr. ii. 822ᵇ ; [Harpers' Lat. Dict. s. v. pono, I. B. 10]). τὶ or τινὰ ἐπί τινος, [Lk. viii. 16ᵇ L T Tr WH] ; Acts v. 15 ; Jn. xix. 19 ; [Rev. x. 2 G L T Tr WH] ; ἐπί τι, [Mk. iv. 21 L T Tr WH] ; viii. 25 Tr txt. WH] ; 2 Co. iii. 13 ; Rev. x. 2 [Rec.] ; ἐπί τινα, to put upon one, τὰς χεῖρας, Mk. x. 16 ; [τὴν δεξιάν, Rev. i. 17 G L T Tr WH] ; τὶ ὑπό τι, Mk. v. 15 ; Mk. iv. 21 ; Lk. xi. 33 ; ὑποκάτω τινός, Lk. viii. 16 ; τινὰ ὑπὸ τοὺς πόδας (see πούς), 1 Co. xv. 25 [cf. W. 523 (487)] ; τὶ παρὰ τοὺς πόδας τ. to lay at one's feet, Acts iv. 35, 37 [here Tdf. πρὸς] ; v. 2 ; τινὰ ἐνώπιόν τ. Lk. v. 18 ; metaph. ἐπί τινα τὸ πνεῦμα, i. e. to imbue one with, Mt. xii. 18. Mid. to have one put or placed : τινὰ εἰς φυλακήν, to order one to be put in prison, Acts xii. 4 ; ἐν (τῇ) φυλακῇ, Mt. xiv. 3 [here L T Tr WH ἀπο-τίθ.] ; Acts v. 25, (Gen. xli. 10 ; xlii. 17, 30 ; [B. 329 (283) ; W. 414 (386)]) ; εἰς τήρησιν, Acts iv. 3 ; ἐν τηρή-σει, Acts v. 18. to place for one's self : as βουλήν, to lay a plan [A. V. advised], Acts xxvii. 12 (Judg. xix. 30 ; βουλὰς ἐν ψυχῇ μου, Ps. xii. (xiii.) 3) ; τὰ μέλη, to set, dispose, 1 Co. xii. 18 ; [καιροὺς ἐν τῇ ἰδίᾳ ἐξουσίᾳ, set within his own authority, Acts i. 7 (so R. V. txt. ; but al. refer it to 2 below)] ; τὶ εἰς τὰ ὦτά μου, to receive [A. V. let sink] into the ears, i. e. to fix in the mind, Lk. ix. 44 ; εἰς τὴν καρδίαν, to propose to one's self, to pur-pose, foll. by an inf. Lk. xxi. 14 [R G] ; also τὶ ἐν τῇ καρδίᾳ, to lay a thing up in one's heart to be remembered and pondered, Lk. i. 66 ; [xxi. 14 L T Tr WH], (1 S. xxi. 12 ; [W. § 2, 1 c., and B. as above]) ; to propose to one's self something [A. V. conceived this thing in thine heart], Acts v. 4 ; also ἐν τῷ πνεύματι, foll. by an inf. [A.V. to purpose in the spirit], Acts xix. 21 ; to place (or posit) for the execution of one's purpose, θέμενος ἐν ἡμῖν τὸν λόγον τῆς καταλλαγῆς, since he has placed (deposited) in our minds the doctrine concerning reconciliation (sc. to be made known to others), 2 Co. v. 19. b. to put down, lay down ; i. e. a. to bend downwards : τὰ γόνατα, to bend or bow the knees, to kneel, Mk. xv. 19 ; Lk. xxii. 41 ; Acts vii. 60 ; ix. 40 ; xx. 36 ; xxi. 5, (Lat. genua pono, Ovid. fast. 2, 438 ; Curt. 8, 7, 13). β. like Lat. pono (cf. Klotz s. v. ; [Harpers' Dict. s. v. I. B. 9]), to lay off or aside, to wear or carry no longer : τὰ ἱμάτια (Lat. vestes pono), Jn. xiii. 4 (Plut. Alc. 8) ; τὴν ψυχήν, to lay down, give up, one's life, Jn. x. 17 sq. ; with ὑπέρ τινος added, Jn. x. 11, 15 ; xiii. 37 sq. ; xv. 13 ; 1 Jn. iii. 16, (ἔθηκε [or τέθεικεν] τὴν σάρκα αὐτοῦ κύριος, Barn. ep. 6, 3 [irrelevant ; see the passage] ; unlike the Lat. phrases vitam ponere, Cic. ad fam. 9, 24, 4 ; Propert. eleg. 2, 10, 43 ; [animam ponere], Sil. Ital. 10, 303 ; spiritum ponere, Val. Max. 7, 8, 8, since these phrases mean only to die ;

more like the expression prius animam quam odium de-ponere, Nep. Hann. 1, 3). γ. to lay by, lay aside money : παρ' ἑαυτῷ, 1 Co. xvi. 2. c. to set on (serve) something to eat or drink : οἶνον, Jn. ii. 10 (Xen. mem. 3, 14, 1 ; so also Lat. pono ; cf. Klotz u. s. p. 822ᵃ ; [Har-pers' Dict. s. v. I. B. 8]). d. to set forth, something to be explained by discourse : τὴν βασιλείαν τ. θεοῦ ἐν παραβολῇ, Mk. iv. 30 L txt. T Tr txt. WH (on this pass. see παραβολή, 2). 2. to make (Lat. constituo), τινά with a pred. acc. : τινὰ ὑποπόδιον, Mt. xxii. 44 [where L T Tr WH ὑποκάτω, put underneath] ; Mk. xii. 36 [WH ὑποκάτω] ; Lk. xx. 43 ; Acts ii. 35 ; Heb. i. 13 ; x. 13, (fr. Ps. cix. (cx.) 1) ; add, Ro. iv. 17 (fr. Gen. xvii. 5) ; Heb. i. 2 ; pass., 1 Tim. ii. 7 ; 2 Tim. i. 11 ; τί with a pred. acc. : 1 Co. ix. 18 (in Grk. writ. fr. Hom. down, often in the poets, rarely in prose writ., as Ael. v. h. 13, 6 ; Lcian. dial. marin. 14, 2 ; in the O. T. cf. Gen. xvii. 5 ; Lev. xxvi. 31 ; Is. v. 20 ; Sap. x. 21 ; 2 Macc. v. 21 ; 3 Macc. v. 14). Mid. to make (or set) for one's self or for one's use : τινά with a pred. acc., Acts xx. 28 ; 1 Co. xii. 28, (in Grk. writ. fr. Hom. down, even in prose, to make one one's own, as τινὰ φίλον to make one a friend, see Passow p. 1893ᵃ ; [L. and S. s. v. B. I.]). τιθέναι τινὰ εἴς τι, to appoint one to (destine one to be) anything, pass., 1 Pet. ii. 8 ; w. εἰς τι instead of the pred. acc. (Hebrais-tically [cf. W. 228 (214) ; B. § 131, 7]), Acts xiii. 47 fr. Is. xlix. 6 (Jer. i. 5). Mid. to appoint for one's use : τινὰ εἰς διακονίαν, to appoint one to one's service, 1 Tim. i. 12 [W. § 45, 4 fin.] ; to appoint with one's self or in one's mind : τινὰ εἰς ὀργήν, to decree one to be subject to wrath, 1 Th. v. 9 ; [to this use many refer Acts i. 7, see ἐξουσία 1, and ἐν, I. 5 d. β. ; cf. 1 a. above]. τιθέναι τινὰ ἵνα, Jn. xv. 16 ; τιθέναι τὸ μέρος τινὸς μετά τινος (see μέρος, 1), Mt. xxiv. 51 ; Lk. xii. 46. 3. to set, fix, establish, (Lat. statuo) ; a. to set forth (Germ. auf-stellen) : ὑπόδειγμα, 2 Pet. ii. 6. b. to establish, or-dain, (Germ. festsetzen, anordnen) : νόμον, to enact, Gal. iii. 19 Grsb. (very often in prof. auth. fr. Hdt. down, both in the act. and the mid. ; cf. Passow s. v. III. 3 b. ; [L. and S. s. v. A. III. 5]). [COMP. : ἀνα-, προσ-ανα-, ἀπο-, δια-, ἀντι-δια-, ἐκ-, ἐπι-, συν-επι-, κατα-, συν-κατα-, μετα-, παρα-, περι-, προ-, προσ-, συν-, ὑπο- τίθημι.] *

τίκτω ; fut. τέξομαι ; 2 aor. ἔτεκον ; 1 aor. pass. ἐτέχθην ;   **5088** fr. Hom. down ; Sept. for יָלַד ; to bring forth, bear, produce (fruit from the seed) ; prop., of women giving birth : absol., Lk. i. 57 [B. 267 (230)] ; ii. 6 ; Jn. xvi. 21 ; Gal. iv. 27 ; Heb. xi. 11 Rec. ; Rev. xii. 2, 4 ; υἱόν, Mt. i. 21, 23, 25 ; Lk. i. 31 ; ii. 7 ; Rev. xii. 5, 13 ; pass., Mt. ii. 2 ; Lk. ii. 11 ; of the earth bringing forth its fruits : βοτάνην, Heb. vi. 7 (Eur. Cycl. 333 ; γαῖαν, ἣ τὰ πάντα τίκτεται, Aeschyl. Cho. 127 ; γῆς τῆς πάντα τικτούσης, Philo opif. m. § 45, who draws out at length the comparison of the earth to a mother). metaph. to bear, bring forth : ἁμαρτίαν, in the simile where ἡ ἐπιθυμία is likened to a female, Jas. i. 15 (ἀρετήν, Plat. conv. p. 212 a.).*

τίλλω ; impf. ἔτιλλον ; fr. Hom. down ; to pluck, pluck   **5089** off : στάχυας, Mt. xii. 1 ; Mk. ii. 23 [on this cf. p. 524ᵇ top] ; Lk. vi. 1.*

5090   **Τιμαῖος** (טִמָא fr. Chald. טְמָא, Hebr. טָמֵא, to be unclean), -ου, ὁ, *Timæus*, the name of a man : Mk. x. 46.*

5091   **τιμάω, -ῶ** ; fut. τιμήσω ; 1 aor. ἐτίμησα ; pf. pass. ptcp. τετιμημένος ; 1 aor. mid. ἐτιμησάμην ; (τιμή) ; fr. Hom. down ;   **1.** *to estimate, to fix the value* ; mid. *to fix the value of something belonging to one's self* (Vulg. *appretio* ; cf. *Hagen*, Sprachl. Erörterungen zur Vulgata, Freib. 1863, p. 99) : τινά, [R. V. *to price*], Mt. xxvii. 9 (on which see ἀπό, I. 2) ; Sept. for הֶעֱרִיךְ, Lev. xxvii. 8, 12, 14.   **2.** *to honor* [so uniformly A. V.], *to have in honor, to revere, venerate* ; Sept. for כִּבֵּד : God, Mt. xv. 8 ; Mk. vii. 6 ; Jn. v. 23 ; viii. 49 ; Christ, Jn. v. 23 ; parents, Mt. xv. 4 sq. ; xix. 19 ; Mk. vii. 10 ; x. 19 ; Lk. xviii. 20 ; Eph. vi. 2 ; other men, 1 Tim. v. 3 ; 1 Pet. ii. 17 ; with πολλαῖς τιμαῖς added, *to honor with many honors*, Acts xxviii. 10 ; of God, rewarding Christians with honor and glory in his kingdom, Jn. xii. 26. [COMP.: ἐπιτιμάω.] *

5092   **τιμή, -ῆς, ἡ,** (fr. τίω, to estimate, honor, pf. pass. τέτιμαι), fr. Hom. down, Sept. for עֵרֶךְ (a valuing, rating), הָדָר, יְקָר, כָּבוֹד ;   **1.** *a valuing by which the price is fixed* ; hence *the price* itself : of the price paid or received for a person or thing bought or sold, with a gen. of the pers. Mt. xxvii. 9 ; with a gen. of the thing, Acts v. 2 sq. ; plur., Acts iv. 34 ; xix. 19 ; τιμὴ αἵματος, the price paid for killing, [cf. 'blood-money'], Mt. xxvii. 6 ; ἠγοράσθητε τιμῆς, (not gratis, but) *with a price*, i. e. (contextually, with emphasis) *at a great price* [B. § 132, 13 ; yet see W. 595 (553)], 1 Co. vi. 20 [here Vulg. *magno pretio*] ; vii. 23 ; ὠνεῖσθαι τιμῆς ἀργυρίου, to buy for a price reckoned in silver, i. e. for silver, Acts vii. 16 ; *thing prized* [A. V. *honor*], Rev. xxi. 24 [Rec.], 26.   **2.** *honor* which belongs or is shown to one : the honor of one who outranks others, pre-eminence, δόξα κ. τιμή, Heb. ii. 7, 9 ; 2 Pet. i. 17 ; in the doxologies : τῷ θεῷ (sc. ἔστω [cf. B. § 129, 22 Rem.]) τιμή or ἡ τιμή, 1 Tim. i. 17 ; vi. 16 ; Rev. v. 13 ; vii. 12 ; xix. 1 Rec. ; the honor which one has by reason of the rank and state of the office which he holds, Heb. v. 4 (and often in Grk. writ. ; cf. Bleek on Heb. l. c.) ; *veneration* : διδόναι, λαβεῖν, τιμήν, Rev. iv. 9, 11 ; v. 12 ; *deference, reverence*, Ro. xii. 10 ; xiii. 7 ; 1 Tim. v. 17 ; vi. 1 ; honor appearing in the rewards of the future life, Ro. ii. 7, 10 ; 1 Pet. i. 7 ; praise of which one is judged worthy, 1 Pet. ii. 7 [here R.V. txt. *preciousness* (cf. 1 above)] ; mark of honor, πολλαῖς τιμαῖς τιμᾶν τινα, Acts xxviii. 10 ; univ. in phrases : ἐν τιμῇ, honorably, 1 Th. iv. 4 (on this pass. see κτάομαι) ; οὐκ ἐν τιμῇ τινι, not in any honor, i. e. worthy of no honor, Col. ii. 23 [al. *value* ; see πλησμονή] ; εἰς τιμήν, Ro. ix. 21 ; 2 Tim. ii. 20 sq., (on these pass. see σκεῦος, 1) ; περιτιθέναι τινὶ τιμήν, 1 Co. xii. 23 (see περιτίθημι, b.) ; τιμὴν ἀπονέμειν τινί, to show honor to one, 1 Pet. iii. 7 ; διδόναι τιμήν, 1 Co. xii. 24 ; ἔχειν τιμήν, to have honor, be honored, Jn. iv. 44 ; Heb. iii. 3.*

5093   **τίμιος, -α, -ον,** (τιμή), fr. Hom. down ;   **a.** prop. *held as of great price*, i. e. *precious* : λίθος, Rev. xvii. 4 ; xviii. 12, 16 ; xxi. 19 ; plur. 1 Co. iii. 12 [R. V. *costly* stones] ; compar. τιμιώτερος, 1 Pet. i. 7 Rec. ; superl. τιμιώτατος,

Rev. xviii. 12 ; xxi. 11.   **b.** metaph. *held in honor, esteemed, especially dear* : Heb. xiii. 4 ; τινί, to one, Acts v. 34 ; xx. 24 [here with a gen. also, acc. to the text of T Tr WH (οὐδενὸς λόγου etc. *not worth a word* ; cf. Meyer ad loc.)] ; καρπὸς τῆς γῆς, Jas. v. 7 ; αἷμα, 1 Pet. i. 19 ; ἐπαγγέλματα, 2 Pet. i. 4.*

5094   **τιμιότης, -ητος, ἡ,** (τίμιος) ;   **a.** prop. *preciousness, costliness* ; *an abundance of costly things* : Rev. xviii. 19.   **b.** metaph. *worth, excellence* : Aristot. de partt. an. 1, 5 [p. 644ᵇ, 32] ; eth. Nic. 10, 7 fin. [p. 1178ᵃ, 1] ; διαφέρουσι τιμιότητι αἱ ψυχαὶ καὶ ἀτιμίᾳ ἀλλήλων, de gen. anim. 2, 3 [p. 736ᵇ, 31].*

5095   **Τιμόθεος, -ου, ὁ,** voc. Τιμόθεε (1 Tim. vi. 20 ; cf. Krüger § 16 Anm. 2 ; [W. § 8, 2 c. ; B. 12]), *Timothy*, a resident of Lystra, apparently, whose father was a Greek and mother a Jewess, Acts xvi. 1 sqq. He was Paul's companion in travel, and fellow-laborer : Acts xvii. 14 sq. ; xviii. 5 ; xix. 22 ; xx. 4 ; Ro. xvi. 21 ; 1 Co. iv. 17 ; xvi. 10 ; 2 Co. i. 1, 19 ; Phil. i. 1 ; ii. 19 ; Col. i. 1 ; 1 Th. i. 1 ; iii. 2, 6 ; 2 Th. i. 1 ; 1 Tim. i. 2, 18 ; vi. 20 ; 2 Tim. i. 2 ; Philem. 1 ; Heb. xiii. 23.*

5096   **Τίμων** [on the accent cf. W. § 6, 1, l.], -ωνος, ὁ, *Timon*, one of the seven deacons of the church at Jerusalem : Acts vi. 5.*

5097   **τιμωρέω, -ῶ** ; 1 aor. pass. ἐτιμωρήθην ; (fr. τιμωρός, and this fr. τιμή and οὖρος, see θυρωρός) ; fr. Soph. and Hdt. down ; prop. *to be a guardian* or *avenger of honor* ; hence   **1.** *to succor, come to the help of* : τινί, one, Soph., Hdt., Thuc., al.   **2.** *to avenge* : τινί, one, Hdt., Xen., al.   **3.** in the N. T. τιμωρῶ τινα, *to take vengeance on one, to punish* : Acts xxii. 5 ; xxvi. 11, (Soph. O. R. 107 ; in Grk. writ. the mid. is more com. in this sense).*

5098   **τιμωρία, -ας, ἡ,** (τιμωρός, see τιμωρέω) ;   **1.** *a rendering help* ; *assistance*, [(Hdt., Thuc., al.)].   **2.** *vengeance, penalty, punishment* : Heb. x. 29 (Prov. xix. 29 ; xxiv. 22 ; in the Grk. writ. fr. Aeschyl. and Hdt. down). [SYN. see κόλασις, fin.] *

5099   **τίνω** : fut. τίσω ; fr. Hom. down ; *to pay, to recompense* : δίκην, to pay penalty, suffer punishment, 2 Th. i. 9 (Plat. Phaedo p. 81 d. ; Theaet. p. 177 a. ; Ael. v. h. 13, 2 ; δίκας, id. 1, 24 ; θωήν, Hom. Od. 2, 193 ; ποινάς, Pind. Ol. 2, 106 ; ζημίαν, Sept. Prov. xxvii. 12). [COMP.: ἀποτίνω.] *

5101   **τίς,** neut. **τί,** gen. τίνος, interrogative pronoun, [fr. Hom. down].   **1.** *who, which, what?* Sept. τίς for מִי, τί for מַה ;   **a.** used Adjectively, in a direct question : τίς βασιλεύς, Lk. xiv. 31 ; τίς γυνή, Lk. xv. 8 ; τί περισσόν, Mt. v. 47 ; τί σημεῖον, Jn. ii. 18, and many other passages. in an indirect question, 1 Th. iv. 2, etc. ; τίνα ἢ ποῖον καιρόν, 1 Pet. i. 11 ; used instead of a pred. in a direct quest., τίς (sc. ἐστιν) ἡ αἰτία, Acts x. 21 ; τίς καὶ ποταπὴ ἡ γυνή, Lk. vii. 39 ; add, Ro. iii. 1 ; 1 Co. ix. 18, etc. ; neut., Mt. xxiv. 3 ; Mk. v. 9 ; in an indir. quest. with the optative, Lk. viii. 9 ; τίς foll. by ἄν, Jn. xiii. 24 R G ; Acts xxi. 33 [R G] ; τί with the optative, Lk. xv. 26 [Tr WH add ἄν, so L br.] ; xviii. 36 [L br. Tr br. WH mrg. add ἄν] ; with the indicative, Eph. i. 18 ;   **b.** used alone or Substantively : in a direct quest., τίς

---

*See p. 625 for 5100.

ὑπέδειξεν ὑμῖν φυγεῖν; Mt. iii. 7; Lk. iii. 7; Rev. xviii. 18, etc.; τίνος, Mt. xxii. 20, 28; Mk xii. 16; τίνι, Lk. xiii. 18; τίνα, Jn. xviii. 4, 7; τί θέλετέ μοι δοῦναι; Mt. xxvi. 15; τί in an indirect quest., foll. by the indicative, Mt. vi. 3; Jn. xiii. 12; 1 Co. xiv. 16; Rev. ii. 7, 11, 17, and very often; foll. by the aor. subjunc., Mt. vi. 25; Lk. xii. 11, etc.; foll. by the optative w. ἄν, Lk. i. 62; vi. 11, etc. Emphatic words get prominence by being placed before the pronoun [B. § 151, 16]: ὑμεῖς δὲ τίνα με λέγετε εἶναι, Mt. xvi. 15; Mk. viii. 29; Lk. ix. 20; καὶ ἡμεῖς τί ποιήσομεν (or ποιήσωμεν), Lk. iii. 14; οὗτος δὲ τί, Jn. xxi. 21 [cf. e. β.]; add, Jn. i. 19; viii. 5; ix. 17; Acts xix. 15; Ro. ix. 19ᵇ [cf. W. 274 (257)], 20; xiv. 4, 10; Eph. iv. 9; Jas. iv. 12; exx. fr. Grk. writ. are given in Passow p. 1908ᵇ; [L. and S. s. v. B. I. 1 b.]. A question is often asked by τίς as the leading word, when the answer expected is "no one": Acts viii. 33; Ro. vii. 24; viii. 33 sq.; ix. 19; x. 16; xi. 34 sq.; 1 Co. ix. 7; 2 Co. xi. 29; Heb. i. 5, 13. τίς εἰ μή, who . . . save (or but), (i. e. no one but), Mk. ii. 7; Lk. v. 21; Ro. xi. 15; 1 Co. ii. 11; Heb. iii. 18; 1 Jn. ii. 22; v. 5. c. two questions are blended into one: τίς τί ἄρῃ, what each should take, Mk. xv. 24; τίς τί διεπραγματεύσατο, Lk. xix. 15 [not Tr WH]; ἐγὼ δὲ τίς ἤμην δυνατὸς κωλῦσαι τὸν θεόν; who was I? was I able to withstand God? Acts xi. 17; cf. W. § 66, 5, 3; Passow p. 1909ᵃ; Ast, Lex. Platon. iii. p. 394; Franz V. Fritzsche, Index ad Lcian. dial. deor. p. 164; the same constr. occurs in Lat. writ.; cf. Ramshorn, Lat. Gram. p. 567. τίς is joined with conjunctions: καὶ τίς, Mk. x. 26; Lk. x. 29; xviii. 26; Rev. vi. 17, (see καί, I. 2 g.); τίς ἄρα, see ἄρα, 1; τίς οὖν, Lk. x. 36 [here T WH om. L Tr br. οὖν]; 1 Co. ix. 18. τίς with a partitive gen.: Mt. xxii. 28; Mk. xii. 23; Lk. x. 36; Acts vii. 52; Heb. i. 5, 13; with ἐκ and a gen. of the class, Mt. vi. 27; Lk. xiv. 28; Jn. viii. 46; in an indir. quest. with the optat., Lk. xxii. 23 [cf. W. § 41 b. 4 c.]; with ἄν added, Lk. ix. 46. d. in indir. questions the neuter article is sometimes placed before the pronouns τίς and τί; see ὁ, II. 10 a. e. Respecting the neuter τί the following particulars may be noted: a. τί οὗτοί σου καταμαρτυροῦσιν; a condensed expression for τί τοῦτό ἐστιν, ὃ οὗτοί σου καταμ.; Mt. xxvi. 62; Mk. xiv. 60, (B. 251 (216) explains this expression differently); also τί τοῦτο ἀκούω περὶ σοῦ; [(R.V.)] what is this (that) I hear of thee? (unless preference be given to the rendering, 'why do I hear this of thee' [see under β. below]), Lk. xvi. 2; cf. Bornemann ad loc.; [W. § 66, 5, 3]. β. τί πρὸς ἡμᾶς; sc. ἐστιν, what is that to us? [W. 586 (545); B. 138 (121)], Mt. xxvii. 4; Jn. xxi. 22; τί ἐμοὶ κ. σοί; see ἐγώ, 4; τί μοι etc. what have I to do with etc. 1 Co. v. 12; τί σοι or ὑμῖν δοκεῖ; [what thinkest thou etc.], Mt. xvii. 25; xxii. 17, 42; xxvi. 66; Jn. xi. 56 (here before ὅτι supply in thought δοκεῖ ὑμῖν, to introduce a second question [R. V. What think ye? That he will not come etc.]). τί θέλεις; and τί θέλετε; foll. by a subjunc., our what wilt thou (that) I should etc.: Mt. xx. 32 [here Lchm. br. inserts ἵνα]; Mk. x. 51; xv. 12 [WH om. Tr br. θέλ.]; Lk. xviii. 41; 1 Co. iv. 21; τί with the deliberative subj.:

Mt. vi. 31; xxvii. 22; Mk. iv. 30 [here L mrg. T Tr txt. WH πῶς]; Lk. xii. 17; xiii. 18; Jn. xii. 27; τί foll. by a fut.: Acts iv. 16 (where L ed. ster. T Tr WH ποιήσωμεν); 1 Co. xv. 29; τί (sc. ἐστίν [B. 358 (307); W. § 64, 2 a.]) ὅτι etc., how is it that etc. i. e. why etc., Mk. ii. 16 R G L; Lk. ii. 49; Acts v. 4, 9; τί γέγονεν, ὅτι etc. [R. V. what is come to pass that etc.], Jn. xiv. 22; οὗτος δὲ τί (sc. ἔσται or γενήσεται [W. 586 (546); B. 394 (338)]), what will be his lot? Jn. xxi. 21 (cf. Acts xii. 18 τί ἄρα ὁ Πέτρος ἐγένετο; Xen. Hell. 2, 3, 17 τί ἔσοιτο ἡ πολιτεία). τί i. q. διὰ τί, why? wherefore? (Matthiae § 488, 8; Krüger § 46, 3 Anm. 4; [W. § 21, 3 N. 2]): Mt. vi. 28; vii. 3; Mk. ii. 7 sq.; xi. 3; Lk. ii. 48; vi. 41; xii. 57; xxiv. 38; Jn. vii. 19; xviii. 23; Acts xiv. 15; xxvi. 8; Ro. iii. 7; ix. 19 sq.; 1 Co. iv. 7; x. 30; xv. 29 sq.; Gal. iii. 19; v. 11; Col. ii. 20, and often. ἵνα τί or ἱνατί, see s. v. p. 305ᵃ. διὰ τί [or διατί (see διά, B. II. 2 a. p. 134ᵇ)], why? wherefore? Mt. ix. 11, 14; xiii. 10; Mk. vii. 5; xi. 31; Lk. xix. 23, 31; Jn. vii. 45; xiii. 37; Acts v. 3; 1 Co. vi. 7; 2 Co. xi. 11; Rev. xvii. 7, and often. εἰς τί, to what? to what end? to what purpose? Mt. xiv. 31; xxvi. 8; Mk. xiv. 4; xv. 34, (Sap. iv. 17; Sir. xxxix. 21). τί οὖν, etc. why then, etc.: Mt. xvii. 10; xix. 7; xxvii. 22; Mk. xii. 9; Lk. xx. 15; Jn. i. 25; see also in οὖν, b. a.; τί οὖν ἐροῦμεν, see ibid. τί γάρ; see γάρ, II. 5. γ. Hebraistically for רָה, how, how greatly, how much, with adjectives and verbs in exclamations [W. § 21 N. 3; cf. B. 254 (218)]: Mt. vii. 14 G L Tr; Lk. xii. 49 [on this see εἰ, I. 4 fin.], (Ps. iii. 2; v. 20; Cant. i. 10; τί πολὺ τὸ ἀγαθόν σου; Symm. Ps. xxx. 19). 2. equiv. to πότερος, -α, -ον, whether of two, which of the two: Mt. xxi. 31; xxiii. 17 [here L τί; see below]; xxvii. 17, 21; Lk. xxii. 27; neut. τί, Mt. ix. 5; [xxiii. 17 Lchm., 19]; Mk. ii. 9; Lk. v. 23; Phil. i. 22; cf. Ast, Lex. Plat. iii. p. 394; Matthiae § 488, 4; W. 169 (159). 3. equiv. to ποῖος, -α, -ον, of what sort, what (kind): Mk. i. 27; vi. 2; Lk. iv. 36; viii. 9; xxiv. 17; Jn. vii. 36; Acts xvii. 19; 1 Co. xv. 2; Eph. i. 18 sq. Cf. Hermann on Viger p. 731. 4. By a somewhat inaccurate usage, yet one not unknown to Grk. writ., it is put for the relatives ὅς and ὅστις: thus, τίνα (L T Tr WH τί) με ὑπονοεῖτε εἶναι, οὐκ εἰμὶ ἐγώ (where one would expect ὅν), Acts xiii. 25; δοθήσεται ὑμῖν, τί λαλήσετε [-σητε T Tr WH; L br. the cl.], Mt. x. 19; ἑτοίμασον, τί δειπνήσω, Lk. xvii. 8; [οἶδα τίνας ἐξελεξάμην, Jn. xiii. 18 T Tr txt. WH]; esp. after ἔχειν (as in the Grk. writ.): οὐκ ἔχουσι, τί φάγωσιν, Mt. xv. 32; Mk. vi. 36; viii. 1 sq.; cf. W. § 25, 1; B. 251 (216); on the distinction betw. the Lat. habeo quid and habeo quod cf. Ramshorn, Lat. Gram. p. 565 sq.

τὶς, neut. τὶ, gen. τινός, indefinite (enclitic) pronoun (bearing the same relation to the interrog. τίς that πού, πώς, ποτέ do to the interrogatives ποῦ, πῶς, πότε); 1. a certain, a certain one; used of persons and things concerning which the writer either cannot or will not speak more particularly; a. joined to nouns substantive, as well as to adjectives and to numerals used substantively); as, Σαμαρείτης τις, Lk. x. 33; ἱερεύς, Lk. i. 5; x. 31; ἀνήρ, Lk. viii. 27; Acts iii. 2; viii. 9; xiv. 8; ἄνθρω-

πος, Mt. xviii. 12; Lk. x. 30; Acts ix. 33; plur. Jude 4;
τόπος, Lk. xi. 1; Acts xxvii. 8; κώμη, Lk. x. 38; xvii. 12,
and in many other pass.; with proper names (as τὶς
Σίμων), Mk. xv. 21; Lk. xxiii. 26; Acts ix. 43; xxi. 16;
xxv. 19. δύο τινές with a partit. gen., Lk. vii. 18 (19);
Acts xxiii. 23; ἕτερος, Acts viii. 34; plur. Acts xxvii. 1;
it indicates that the thing with which it is connected
belongs to a certain class and resembles it: ἀπαρχήν
τινα, a kind of firstfruits, Jas. i. 18, cf. W. § 25, 2 a;
joined to adjectives of quality and quantity, it requires
us to conceive of their degree as the greatest possible;
as, φοβερά τις ἐκδοχή, a certain fearful expectation, Heb.
x. 27, where see Delitzsch [or Alford] (δεινή τις δύναμις,
Xen. mem. 1, 3, 12; other exx. fr. the Grk. writ. are
given in W. § 25, 2 c.; [L. and S. s. v. A. II. 8]; Matthiae § 487, 4; [Bnhdy. p. 442]; incredibilis quidam
amor, Cic. pro Lig. c. 2, 5); μέγας τις, Acts viii. 9.   **b.**
it stands alone, or substantively: univ. τὶς one, a certain
one, Mt. xii. 47 [but WH in mrg. only]; Lk. ix. 49, 57;
xiii. 6, 23; Jn. xi. 1; Acts v. 25; xviii. 7; plur. τινές, certain, some: Lk. xiii. 1; Acts xv. 1; Ro. iii. 8; 1 Co. iv.
18; xv. 34; 2 Co. iii. 1; Gal. ii. 12; 2 Th. iii. 11; 1 Tim.
i. 3, 19; iv. 1; v. 15; vi. 10; 2 Pet. iii. 9; τινές ἐν ὑμῖν,
some among you, 1 Co. xv. 12; a participle may be
added, — either with the article, τινές οἱ etc., Lk. xviii.
9; 2 Co. x. 2; Gal. i. 7; or without it, 1 Tim. vi. 21;
τὶς and τινές with a partit. gen.: Lk. xi. 1; xiv. 15; 2 Co.
x. 12.   **2.**   **a.** joined to nouns and signifying
some: χρόνον τινά, some time, a while, 1 Co. xvi. 7; ἡμέραι
τινές, some (or certain) days, Acts ix. 19; x. 48; xv. 36;
xvi. 12; xxiv. 24; xxv. 13; μέρος τι, Lk. xi. 36 [here WH
mrg. br. τι]; Acts v. 2; 1 Co. xi. 18; τὶ βρώσιμον, Lk.
xxiv. 41; add, Mk. xvi. 18; Jn. v. 14; Acts xvii. 21; xxiii.
20; xxviii. 21; Heb. xi. 40; βραχύ τι, Acts v. 34 (where
L T Tr WH om. τι); Heb. ii. 7; περισσότερόν τι, 2 Co. x.
8; μικρόν τι, 2 Co. xi. 16; it serves modestly to qualify
or limit the measure of things, even though that is thought
to be ample or large [cf. 1 a. sub fin.]: κοινωνία τις, a certain contribution, Ro. xv. 26; καρπός, Ro. i. 13; χάρισμα,
ibid. 11. with a participle, ἀθετήσας τις, if any one has
set at nought, Heb. x. 28 [but this ex. belongs rather
under the next head].   **b.** standing alone, or used
substantively, and signifying some one, something; any
one, anything: univ., Mt. xii. 29; Mk. ix. 30; xi. 16; Lk.
viii. 46; Jn. ii. 25; vi. 46; Acts xvii. 25; Ro. v. 7; 1 Co.
xv. 35; 2 Co. xi. 20 sq.; Heb. iii. 4; Jas. ii. 18; 2 Pet. ii.
19, etc.; τὶς ἐξ ὑμῶν, Jas. ii. 16; ἐξ ὑμῶν τις, Heb. iii. 13;
with a partitive gen., Lk. vii. 36; xi. 45; 1 Co. vi. 1;
neut. τὶ with a partit. gen., Acts iv. 32; Ro. xv. 18; Eph.
v. 27.   εἷς τις, see εἷς, 3 p. 187ᵃ. it answers not infrequently to the indefinite one (Germ. man, French on):
Mk. viii. 4; Jn. ii. 25; xvi. 30; Ro. viii. 24; Heb. v. 12
(where some [viz. R G T Tr (cf. W. 169 (160)); R. V.
mrg. which be the rudiments etc.; cf. c. below]) incorrectly read τίνα [yet cf. B. 268 (230) note, cf. 260 (223)
note]), etc.; cf. Matthiae § 487, 2. εἴ τις, see εἰ, III. 16;
ἐάν τις, τινος, etc.: Mt. xxi. 3; xxiv. 23; Mk. xii. 19; Lk.
xvi. 31; Jn. vi. 51; vii. 17; viii. 51 sq.; ix. 22, 31; x. 9;

xi. 9 sq. 57; xii. 26, 47; Acts ix. 2 [here Tdf. ἄν]; xiii.
41; 1 Co. v. 11; viii. 10; x. 28; Col. iii. 13; 1 Tim. i. 8;
2 Tim. ii. 5, 21; Jas. ii. 14; v. 19; 1 Jn. ii. 15; iv. 20; v.
16; Rev. iii. 20; xxii. 18 sq.; ἄν τινων, Jn. xx. 23 [here
Lchm. ἐάν]; ἐὰν μή τις, Jn. iii. 3, 5; xv. 6; Acts viii. 31;
οὐ . . . τις, not . . . any one, i. e. no one, Jn. x. 28; οὔτε
. . . τις, Acts xxviii. 21; οὐδὲ . . . τις, Mt. xi. 27; xii. 19;
οὐκ . . . ὑπό τινος, 1 Co. vi. 12; μή τις, lest any (man), Mt.
xxiv. 4; Mk. xiii. 5; Acts xxvii. 42; 1 Co. i. 15; xvi. 11;
2 Co. viii. 20; xi. 16; xii. 6; Eph. ii. 9; 1 Th. v. 15; Heb.
iv. 11; xii. 15; hath any (one), Jn. iv. 33 [cf. μήτις, 2]; μή
τινα, 2 Co. xii. 17; πρὸς τὸ μή . . . τινα, 1 Th. ii. 9; ὥστε
. . . μή τινα, Mt. viii. 28; like the Lat. aliquis, it is used
with the verb εἶναι emphatically: to be somebody, i. e.
somebody of importance, some eminent personage, [W.
§ 25, 2 c.; B. § 127, 16], Acts v. 36 (see exx. fr. the Grk.
writ. in Passow s. v. B. II. 2 d.; [L. and S. ibid. A. II. 5];
on the phrase τὶ εἶναι see e. β. below).   Plur. τινές,
some (of that number or class of men indicated by the
context): Mk. xiv. 4, 65; Lk. xxi. 5; Jn. xiii. 29; τινές
are distinguished from οἱ πάντες, 1 Co. viii. 7; ix. 22.
τινές with an anarthrous participle, Mk. xiv. 57; Lk.
xiii. 1; ταῦτά τινες ἦτε, such (of this sort) were some of
you, 1 Co. vi. 11 [cf. οὗτος, I. 2 d.]; τινές with a partitive
gen., Mt. ix. 3; xii. 38; xxviii. 11; Mk. vii. 1 sq.; xii.
13; Lk. vi. 2; xix. 39; Acts v. 15; xvii. 18, 28, and
often; foll. by ἐκ and a partit. gen., Lk. xi. 15; Jn. vi.
64; vii. 25, 44; ix. 16; xi. 37, 46; Acts xi. 20; xv. 24,
etc.; Paul employs τινές by meiosis in reference to many,
when he would mention something censurable respecting
them in a mild way: Ro. iii. 3; 1 Co. x. 7-10.   **c.**
Sometimes the subject τὶς, τινές, or the object τινα, τινάς,
is not added to the verb, but is left to be understood by
the reader (cf. B. § 132, 6; [W. §§ 58, 2; 64, 4]): before the partit. gen. Acts xxi. 16; before ἀπό, Mt. xxvii.
9 (1 Macc. vii. 33); before ἐκ, Mt. xxiii. 34; Lk. xxi.
16; [Jn. i. 24 T Tr WH (cf. R. V. mrg.); vii. 40 L T
Tr WH (cf. R. V. mrg.)]; xvi. 17; [2 Jn. 4; Rev. ii.
10]. [Other exx. of its apparent omission are the following: as subject, — of a finite verb (W. § 58, 9 b. β.;
B. § 129, 19): φησί, 2 Co. x. 10 R G T Tr txt. WH txt.;
ὅταν λαλῇ τὸ ψεῦδος, Jn. viii. 44 (acc. to one interpretation; see R. V. marg.); of an infin.: οὐ χρείαν ἔχετε
γράφειν ὑμῖν, 1 Th. iv. 9 R G T Tr txt. WH; χρείαν ἔχετε
τοῦ διδάσκειν ὑμᾶς, τίνα etc. Heb. v. 12 R G T Tr (but see
2 b. above). as object: δός μοι πιεῖν, Jn. iv. 7; cf. Mk.
v. 43. See Kühner § 352 g.; Krüger § 55, 3, 21.]   **d.**
It stands in partitions: τὶς . . . ἕτερος δέ, one . . . and
another, 1 Co. iii. 4; plur. τινές (μὲν) . . . τινὲς (δὲ), Lk.
ix. 7 sq.; Acts xvii. 18; Phil. i. 15; cf. Passow s. v. B.
II. 2 e.; [L. and S. ibid. A. II. 11. c.].   **e.** Besides
what has been already adduced, the foll. should be noticed respecting the use of the neut. τὶ;   **a.** univ.
anything, something: Mt. v. 23; Mk. viii. 23; Lk. xi. 54;
Acts xxv. 5, 11; 1 Co. x. 31, and very often; οὐδὲ . . . τί,
neither . . . anything, 1 Tim. vi. 7.   **β.** like the Lat.
aliquid it is used emphatically, equiv. to something of
consequence, something extraordinary (cf. b. above): in

the phrase εἶναί τι, 1 Co. iii. 7; Gal. ii. 6; vi. 3; cf. Passow s. v. B. II. 2 d.; [L. and S. s. v. A. II. 5]; and on the Lat. *aliquid esse* see *Klotz*, Handwörterb. d. Lat. Spr. i. 298ᵇ; [Harpers' Dict. s. v. aliquis, II. C. 1] (on the other hand, in 1 Co. x. 19 τὶ εἶναι means *to be anything, actually to exist*); εἰδέναι [L T Tr WH ἐγνωκέναι] τι, i. e. much, 1 Co. viii. 2. **3.** As respects the Position of the word, when used adjectively it stands — now before its noun (τὶς ἀνήρ, Acts iii. 2; xiv. 8; τὶς μαθητής, Acts ix. 10; τινὰς ἑτέρους, Acts xxvii. 1; τὶ ἀγαθόν, Jn. i. 47); now, and indeed far more frequently, after it, as ἱερεύς τις, Lk. i. 5; x. 31; ἀνήρ τις, Lk. viii. 27, etc., etc. Τινές, used substantively, is found at the beginning of a sentence in Mt. xxvii. 47; Lk. vi. 2; Jn. xiii. 29; 1 Tim. v. 24; Phil. i. 15; cf. W. § 25, 2 Note, and 559 (520). The particle δέ may stand betw. it and its substantive (as Σαμαρείτης δέ τις), as in Lk. x. 33, 38; Acts viii. 9; Heb. x. 27.

(5100α);   **see 5103**   Τίτιος, -ου, ὁ, the praenomen of a certain Corinthian, a Jewish proselyte, also surnamed *Justus*: Acts xviii. 7 T Tr br. WH (see Τίτος).*

5102   τίτλος, -ου, ὁ, a Lat. word, *a title; an inscription*, giving the accusation or crime for which a criminal suffered: Jn. xix. 19, 20, and after it Ev. Nic. c. 10, 1 fin. (Sueton. Calig. c. 32 praecedente *titulo* qui causam poenae indicaret; again, Domit. c. 10 canibus objecit cum hoc *titulo*: impie locutus parmularius.) *

5103   Τίτος [Rec.ˢᵗ in the subscription, Τῖτος; cf. *Lipsius*, Gram. Unters. p. 42 sq.; *Tdf.* Proleg. p. 103; *Pape*, Eigennamen, s. v.; W. § 6, 1 m.], -ου, ὁ, *Titus*, a Gentile Christian, Paul's companion in some of his journeys and assistant in Christian work: 2 Co. ii. 13; vii. 6, 13 sq.; viii. 6, 16, 23; xii. 18; Gal. ii. 1, 3; 2 Tim. iv. 10; Tit. i. 4. He is not mentioned in the Book of Acts. But since Titus is the praenomen, perhaps he appears in the Acts under his second, or, if he was a Roman, under his third name; cf. Rückert on 2 Cor. p. 410. He is by no means, however, to be identified (after *Wieseler*, Com. ü. d. Brief a. d. Galater, p. 573 sq. [also his Chron. d. apost. Zeit. p. 204]) with the Titus of Acts xviii. 7, even if the reading (of some authorities [see Tdf.'s note ad loc.]) Τίτου [see Τίτιος above] 'Ιούστου be the true one.*

see 5099   τίω, a form from which some N. T. lexicons [e. g. Wahl, Bretschneider, Robinson, Bloomfield, Schirlitz, Harting, al.] incorrectly derive τίσουσιν in 2 Th. i. 9; see τίνω.

5105   τοιγαροῦν, (fr. the enclitic τοί or τῷ, γάρ, and οὖν, Germ. *doch denn nun*; cf. Delitzsch on Heb. xii. 1; [Ellicott on 1 Th. iv. 8]), a particle introducing a conclusion with some special emphasis or formality, and generally occupying the first place in the sentence, *wherefore then, for which reason, therefore, consequently*: 1 Th. iv. 8; Heb. xii. 1, (for לָכֵן, Job xxii. 10; xxiv. 22; 4 Macc. i. 34; vi. 28 var.; xiii. 15; Soph., Xen., Plato, sqq.); cf. *Klotz* **see 1065** ad Devar. ii. 2 p. 738.*
&2544 St. τοίγε in καίτοιγε, see γέ, 3 f.

5106   τοίνυν, (fr. the enclitic τοί and νῦν), fr. Pind. [and

Hdt.] down, *therefore, then, accordingly*; contrary to the use of the more elegant Grk. writ., found at the beginning of the sentence (cf. *Lob.* ad Phryn. p. 342 sq.; [W. 559 (519 sq.); B. § 150, 19]): Heb. xiii. 13 (Is. iii. 10; v. 13); as in the better writ., after the first word: Lk. xx. 25 [yet T Tr WH put it first here also]; 1 Co. ix. 26 and Rec. in Jas. ii. 24, (Sap. i. 11; viii. 9; 4 Macc. i. 13, 15 sqq.).*

5107   τοιόσδε, τοιάδε, τοιόνδε, (τοῖος and δέ), fr. Hom. down, *such*, generally with an implied suggestion of something excellent or admirable: 2 Pet. i. 17.*

5108   τοιοῦτος, τοιαύτη, τοιοῦτο and τοιοῦτον (only this second form of the neut. occurs in the N. T., and twice [but in Mt. xviii. 5 T WH have -το]), (fr. τοῖος and οὗτος [al. say lengthened fr. τοῖος or connected with αὐτός; cf. τηλικοῦτος]), [fr. Hom. down], *such as this, of this kind or sort;* **a.** joined to nouns: Mt. ix. 8; xviii. 5; Mk. iv. 33; vi. 2; vii. 8 [here T WH om. Tr br. the cl.], 13; ix. 37 [here Tdf. τούτων]; Jn. ix. 16; Acts xvi. 24; 1 Co. v. 1; xi. 16; 2 Co. iii. 4, 12; xii. 3; Heb. vii. 26; viii. 1; xii. 3; xiii. 16; Jas. iv. 16. **b.** οἷος . . . τοιοῦτος: Mk. xiii. 19; 1 Co. xv. 48; 2 Co. x. 11; τοιοῦτος . . . ὁποῖος, Acts xxvi. 29; τοιοῦτος ὢν ὡς etc. Philem. 9 [where see Bp. Lghtft.]. **c.** used substantively, **a.** without an article: Jn. iv. 23; neut. μηδὲν τοιοῦτον, Acts xxi. 25 Rec.; plur., Lk. ix. 9; xiii. 2 [here T Tr txt. WH ταῦτα]. **β.** with the article, ὁ τοιοῦτος *one who is of such a character, such a one*, [B. § 124, 5; W. 111 (106); Krüger § 50, 4, 6; Kühner on Xen. mem. 1, 5, 2; Ellicott on Gal. v. 21]: Acts xxii. 22; 1 Co. v. 5, 11; 2 Co. ii. 6 sq.; x. 11; xii. 2, 5; Gal. vi. 1; Tit. iii. 11, plur., Mt. xix. 14; Mk. x. 14; Lk. xviii. 16; Jn. viii. 5; Ro. [ii. 14 Lmrg.]; xvi. 18; 1 Co. vii. 28; xvi. 16, 18; 2 Co. xi. 13; Phil. ii. 29; 2 Th. iii. 12; 1 Tim. vi. 5 Rec.; 3 Jn. 8; neut. plur., Acts xix. 25; Ro. i. 32; ii. 2 sq.; 1 Co. vii. 15; Gal. v. 21, 23; Eph. v. 27; Heb. xi. 14.*

5109   τοῖχος, -ου, ὁ, fr. Hom. down, Sept. often for קִיר, a *wall* [esp. of a house; cf. τεῖχος]: Acts xxiii. 3.*

5110   τόκος, -ου, ὁ, (fr. τίκτω, pf. τέτοκα); **1.** *birth;* **a.** *the act of bringing forth.* **b.** *that which has been brought forth, offspring;* (in both senses from Homer down). **2.** *interest* of money, *usury*, (because it multiplies money, and as it were 'breeds' [cf. e. g. Merchant of Venice i. 3]): Mt. xxv. 27; Lk. xix. 23, (so in Grk. writ. fr. Pind. and Arstph. down; Sept. for נֶשֶׁךְ).*

5111   τολμάω, -ῶ; impf. 3 pers. sing. ἐτόλμα, plur. ἐτόλμων; fut. τολμήσω; 1 aor. ἐτόλμησα; (τόλμα or τόλμη ['daring'; Curtius § 236]); fr. Hom. down; *to dare;* **a.** *not to dread or shun through fear*: foll. by an inf., Mt. xxii. 46; Mk. xii. 34; Lk. xx. 40; Jn. xxi. 12 [W. § 65, 7 b.]; Acts v. 13; vii. 32; Ro. xv. 18; 2 Co. x. 12; Phil. i. 14; Jude 9; τολμήσας εἰσῆλθεν, took courage and went in, Mk. xv. 43 [Hdian. 8, 5, 22; Plut. vit. Cam. 22, 6]. **b.** *to bear, endure; to bring one's self to;* [cf. W. u. s.]: foll. by an inf., Ro. v. 7; 1 Co. vi. 1. **c.** absol. *to be bold; bear one's self boldly, deal boldly*: 2 Co. xi. 21; ἐπί τινα, against one, 2 Co. x. 2. [COMP.: ἀποτολμάω.]*

*For 5104 see 3588

[Syn. τολμάω, θαρρέω: θ. denotes confidence in one's own strength or capacity, τ. boldness or daring in undertaking; θ. has reference more to the character, τ. to its manifestation. Cf. Schmidt ch. 24, 4; ch. 141. The words are found together in 2 Co. x. 2.]

5112 τολμηρότερον, (neut. compar. from the adj. τολμηρός), [Thuc., sqq.], *more boldly*: Ro. xv. 15 [L ed. ster. Tr txt. WH -τέρως; W. 243 (228)].*

5113 τολμητής, -οῦ, ὁ, (τολμάω), *a daring man*: 2 Pet. ii. 10. (Thuc. 1, 70; Joseph. b. j. 3, 10, 2; Philo de Joseph. § 38, Plut., Lcian.) *

5114 τομώτερος, -α, -ον, (compar. fr. τομός cutting, sharp, and this fr. τέμνω), *sharper*: Heb. iv. 12 ([Pseudo-] Phocylid. vs. 116 [(Gnom. Poet. Graec. ed. Brunck p. 116)] ὅπλον τοι λόγος ἀνδρὶ τομώτερόν ἐστι σιδήρου; add, Timon in Athen. 10 p. 445 e.; Lcian. Tox. 11).*

5115 τόξον, -ου, τό, fr. Hom. down, Sept. often for קֶשֶׁת, *a bow*: Rev. vi. 2.*

5116 τοπάζιον, -ου, τό, (neut. of the adj. τοπάζιος, fr. τόπαζος), *topaz*, a greenish-yellow precious stone (our chrysolith [see BB. DD., esp. Riehm s. v. Edelsteine 18]): Rev. xxi. 20 (Diod., Strab.; Sept. for פִּטְדָה, Ex. xxviii. 17; xxxvi. 17 (xxxix. 10); Ezek. xxviii. 13. The Grk. writ. more commonly use the form τόπαζος).*

5117 τόπος, -ου, ὁ, in Attic fr. Aeschyl. and his contemporaries on; Sept. מָקוֹם; *place*; i. e. **1.** prop. any portion of space marked off, as it were, from surrounding space; used of **a.** an inhabited place, as a city, village, district: Lk. iv. 37; x. 1; Acts xii. 17; xvi. 3; xxvii. 2, 8; 1 Co. i. 2; 2 Co. ii. 14; 1 Th. i. 8; Rev. xviii. 17 [G L T Tr WH]; τὸν τόπον καὶ τὸ ἔθνος, the place which the nation inhabit, i. e. the holy land and the Jewish people, Jn. xi. 48 (cf. 2 Macc. v. 19 sq.); τόπος ἅγιος, the temple (which the Sept. of Is. lx. 13 calls ὁ ἅγιος τόπος τοῦ θεοῦ), Mt. xxiv. 15. of a house, Acts iv. 31. of uninhabited places, with adjectives: ἔρημος, Mt. xiv. 13, 15; Mk. i. 35; vi. 31 sq.; Lk. iv. 42; ix. 10 R G L, 12; πεδινός, Lk. vi. 17; ἄνυδρος, plur., Mt. xii. 43; Lk. xi. 24. of any place whatever: κατὰ τόπους, [R.V. in divers places] i. e. the world over [but see κατά, II. 3 a. a.], Mt. xxiv. 7; Mk. xiii. 8; [ἐν παντὶ τόπῳ, 2 Th. iii. 16 Lchm.]; of places in the sea, τραχεῖς τόποι, Acts xxvii. 29 [R.V. rocky ground]; τόπ. διθάλασσος, [A. V. place where two seas met], ibid. 41. of that 'place' where what is narrated occurred: Lk. x. 32; xix. 5; xxii. 40; Jn. v. 13; vi. 10; xviii. 2. of a place or spot where one can settle, abide, dwell: ἑτοιμάζειν τινὶ τόπον, Jn. xiv. 2 sq., cf. Rev. xii. 6; ἔχειν τόπον, a place to dwell in, Rev. l. c.; οὐκ ἦν αὐτοῖς τόπος ἐν τῷ καταλύματι, Lk. ii. 7; διδόναι τινὶ τόπον, to give one place, give way to one, Lk. xiv. 9ᵃ; τόπος οὐχ εὑρέθη αὐτοῖς, Rev. xx. 11; of the seat which one gets in any gathering, as at a feast, Lk. xiv. 10; τὸν ἔσχατον τόπον κατέχειν, ibid. 9ᵇ; of the place or spot occupied by things placed in it, Jn. xx. 7. the particular place referred to is defined by the words appended: — by a genitive, τόπ. τῆς βασάνου, Lk. xvi. 28; τῆς καταπαύσεως, Acts vii. 49; κρανίου, Mt. xxvii. 33; Mk. xv. 22; Jn. xix. 17; [τὸν τόπον τῶν ἥλων, Jn. xx. 25ᵇ L T Tr mrg.]; — by the addition of οὗ, ὅπου,

ἐφ' or ἐν ᾧ, foll. by finite verbs, Mt. xxviii. 6; Mk. xvi. 6; Jn. iv. 20; vi. 23; x. 40; xi. 6, 30; xix. 41; Acts vii. 33; Ro. ix. 26; — by the addition of a proper name: τόπος λεγόμενος, or καλούμενος, Mt. xxvii. 33; Mk. xv. 22; Lk. xxiii. 33; Jn. xix. 13; Rev. xvi. 16; ὁ τόπος τινός, the place which a person or thing occupies or has a right to: Rev. ii. 5; vi. 14; xii. 8; where a thing is hidden, τῆς μαχαίρας i. e. its sheath, Mt. xxvi. 52. the abode assigned by God to one after death wherein to receive his merited portion of bliss or of misery: (ὁ ἴδιος τόπος (τινός), univ. Ignat. ad Magnes. 5, 1 [cf. ὁ αἰώνιος τόπος, Tob. iii. 6]); applied to Gehenna, Acts i. 25 (see ἴδιος, 1 c.); ὁ ὀφειλόμενος τόπος, of heaven, Polyc. ad Philip. 9, 2; Clem. Rom. 1 Cor. 5, 4; also ὁ ἅγιος τόπος, ibid. 5, 7; [ὁ ὡρισμένος τ. Barn. ep. 19, 1; Act. Paul et Thecl. 28; see esp. Harnack's note on Clem. Rom. 1 Cor. 5, 4]. **b.** a place (passage) in a book: Lk. iv. 17 (καὶ ἐν ἄλλῳ τόπῳ φησίν, Xen. mem. 2, 1, 20 [(but this is doubtful; cf. L. and S. s. v. I. 4; yet cf. Kühner ad loc.); Philo de Joseph. § 26; Clem. Rom. 1 Cor. 8, 4]; in the same sense χώρα in Joseph. antt. 1, 8, 3). **2.** metaph. **a.** the condition or station held by one in any company or assembly: ἀναπληροῦν τὸν τόπον τοῦ ἰδιώτου, [R. V. filleth the place of the unlearned], 1 Co. xiv. 16; τῆς διακονίας ταύτης καὶ ἀποστολῆς, [R.V. the place in this ministry, etc.], Acts i. 25 L T Tr WH. **b.** opportunity, power, occasion for acting: τόπον λαμβάνειν τῆς ἀπολογίας, opportunity to make his defence, Acts xxv. 16 (ἔχειν τ. ἀπολογίας, Joseph. antt. 16, 8, 5); τόπον διδόναι τῇ ὀργῇ (sc. τοῦ θεοῦ), Ro. xii. 19; τῷ διαβόλῳ, Eph. iv. 27, (τῷ ἰατρῷ, to his curative efforts in one's case, Sir. xxxviii. 12; νόμῳ ὑψίστου, ibid. xix. 17; τόπον διδόναι τινί, foll. by an inf., ibid. iv. 5); τόπ. μετανοίας εὑρίσκειν, Heb. xii. 17, on this pass. see εὑρίσκω, 3 (διδόναι, Sap. xii. 10; Clem. Rom. 1 Cor. 7, 5; Lat. locum relinquere paenitentiae, Liv. 44, 10; 24, 26; [Plin. ep. ad Trai 96 (97), 10 cf. 2]; ἔχειν τόπον μετανοίας, Tat. or. ad Graec. 15 fin.; διὰ τὸ μὴ καταλείπεσθαί σφισι τόπον ἐλέους μηδὲ συγγνώμης, Polyb. 1, 88, 2); τόπον ἔχειν sc. τοῦ εὐαγγελίζεσθαι, Ro. xv. 23; τ. ζητεῖν, with a gen. of the thing for which influence is sought among men: διαθήκης, pass. Heb. viii. 7 [cf. μέμφομαι].

[Syn. τόπος 1, χώρα, χωρίον: τόπ. place, indefinite; a portion of space viewed in reference to its occupancy, or as appropriated to a thing; χώρα region, country, extensive; space, yet bounded; χωρίον parcel of ground (Jn. iv. 5), circumscribed; a definite portion of space viewed as enclosed or complete in itself; τόπος and χωρίον (plur., R. V. lands) occur together in Acts xxviii. 7. Cf. Schmidt ch. 41.]

5118 τοσοῦτος, -αύτη, -οῦτο (Heb. vii. 22 L T Tr WH) and -οῦτον, (fr. τόσος and οὗτος; [al. say lengthened fr. τόσος; cf. τηλικοῦτος, init.]), so great; with nouns: of quantity, τοσ. πλοῦτος, Rev. xviii. 17 (16); of internal amount, πίστις, Mt. viii. 10; Lk. vii. 9; [ὅσα ἐδόξασεν ἑαυτήν, τοσοῦτον δότε βασανισμόν, Rev. xviii. 7]; of size, νέφος, Heb. xii. 1; plur. so many: ἰχθύες, Jn. xxi. 11; σημεῖα, Jn. xii. 37; γένη φωνῶν, 1 Co. xiv. 10; ἔτη, Lk. xv. 29 [(here A. V. these many)], (in prof. writ., esp. the Attic, we often find τοσοῦτος καὶ τοιοῦτος and the reverse; see Heindorf on Plat. Gorg. p. 34; Passow p. 1923ᵇ; [L. and S. s. vv.]); foll. by ὥστε, *so many as to be able*, etc. [B. 244 (210)], Mt. xv. 33; of time: *so long*, χρόνος, [Jn. xiv. 9]; Heb. iv. 7; of length of space, τὸ μῆκος τοσοῦτόν ἐστιν ὅσον etc. Rev. xxi. 16 Rec.; absol., plur. *so many*, Jn. vi. 9; neut. plur. [*so many things*], Gal. iii. 4; τοσούτου, *for so much* (of price), Acts v. 8 (9); dat. τοσούτῳ, preceded or followed by ὅσῳ (as often in the Grk. writ. fr. Hdt. down [W. § 35, 4 N. 2]), *by so much* : τοσ. κρείττων, *by so much better*, Heb. i. 4; τοσούτῳ μᾶλλον ὅσῳ etc. Heb. x. 25; καθ᾿ ὅσον . . . κατὰ τοσοῦτον, *by how much . . . by so much*, Heb. vii. 22.*

5119   **τότε**, demonstr. adv. of time, (fr. the neut. art. τό, and the enclit. τέ [q. v.]; answering to the relative ὅτε [Kühner § 506, 2 c.]), fr. Hom. down, *then*; *at that time*;   **a.** *then* i. e. at the time when the things under consideration were taking place, (of a concomitant event): Mt. ii. 17 (τότε ἐπληρώθη); iii. 5, 13; xii. 22, 38; xv. 1; xix. 13; xx. 20; xxvii. 9, 16; Ro. vi. 21; foll. by a more precise specification of the time by means of an added participle, Mt. ii. 16; Gal. iv. 8; opp. to νῦν, Gal. iv. 29; Heb. xii. 26; ὁ τότε κόσμος, the world that then was, 2 Pet. iii. 6.   **b.** *then* i. e. when the thing under consideration had been said or done, *thereupon*; so in the historical writers (esp. Matthew), by way of transition from one thing mentioned to another which could not take place before it [W. 540 (503); B. § 151, 31 fin.]: Mt. iv. 1, 5; xxvi. 14; xxvii. 38; Acts i. 12; x. 48; xxi. 33; not infreq. of things which took place immediately afterwards, so that it is equiv. to *which having been done* or *heard* : Mt. ii. 7; iii. 15; iv. 10 sq.; viii. 26; xii. 45; xv. 28; xvii. 19; xxvi. 36, 45; xxvii. 26 sq.; Lk. xi. 26; τότε οὖν, Jn. xi. 14 [Lchm. br. οὖν]; xix. 1, 16; xx. 8; εὐθέως τότε, Acts xvii. 14; τότε preceded by a more definite specification of time, as μετὰ τὸ ψωμίον, Jn. xiii. 27; or by an aor. ptcp. Acts xxviii. 1. ὅτε . . . τότε, etc., *when . . . then*: Mt. xiii. 26; xxi. 1; Jn. xii. 16; ὡς . . . τότε, etc., Jn. vii. 10; xi. 6; preceded by a gen. absol. which specifies time, Acts xxvii. 21. ἀπὸ τότε *from that time on*, see ἀπό, I. 4 b. p. 58ᵇ.   **c.** of things future; *then* (at length) when the thing under discussion takes place (or shall have taken place): τότε simply, Mt. xxiv. 23, 40; xxv. 1, 34, 37, 41, 44 sq.; opp. to ἄρτι, 1 Co. xiii. 12; καὶ τότε, Mt. vii. 23; xvi. 27; xxiv. 10, 14, 30; Mk. xiii. 21, 26 sq.; Lk. xxi. 27; 1 Co. iv. 5; Gal. vi. 4; 2 Th. ii. 8; καὶ τότε preceded by πρῶτον, Mt. v. 24; vii. 5; Lk. vi. 42. ὅταν (with a subjunc. pres.) . . . τότε, etc. *when . . . then*, etc. [W. § 60, 5], 2 Co. xii. 10; 1 Th. v. 3; ὅταν (with an aor. subj. i. q. Lat. fut. pf.) . . . τότε, etc., Mt. ix. 15; xxiv. 16; xxv. 31; Mk. ii. 20; xiii. 14; Lk. v. 35; xxi. 20 sq.; Jn. ii. 10 [T WH om. L Tr br. τότε]; viii. 28; 1 Co. xv. 28, 54; xvi. 2; Col. iii. 4. Of the N. T. writ. Matthew uses τότε most frequently, ninety-one times [(so Holtzmann, Syn. Evang. p. 293); rather, eighty-nine times acc. to R T, ninety times acc. to G L Tr WH]; it is not found in [Eph., Phil., Philem., the Past. Epp., the Epp. of Jn., Jas., Jude], the Rev.

τοὐναντίον (by crasis for τὸ ἐναντίον [B. 10]), [(Arstph., **5121** Thuc., al.)], *on the contrary, contrariwise*, (Vulg. *e contrario*), accus. used adverbially [W. 230 (216)]: 2 Co. ii. 7; Gal. ii. 7; 1 Pet. iii. 9.*

τοὔνομα (by crasis for τὸ ὄνομα [B. 10; WH. App. p. **5122** 145]), [fr. Hom. Il. 3, 235 down], *the name*; accus. absol. [B. § 131, 12; W. 230 (216) cf. ὄνομα, 1] *by name*: Mt. xxvii. 57.*

τουτέστι [cf. W. p. 45; B. 11 (10)] for τοῦτ᾿ ἔστι, and **5123** this for τοῦτό ἐστι, see εἰμί, II. 3.   *

τράγος, -ου, ὁ, fr. Hom. down, *a he-goat*: plur., Heb. **5131** ix. 12 sq. 19; x. 4.*

τράπεζα, -ης, ἡ, (fr. τέτρα, and πέζα a foot), fr. Hom. **5132** down, Sept. for שֻׁלְחָן, *a table*;   **1.**   **a.** a table on which food is placed, an eating-table: Mt. xv. 27; Mk. vii. 28; Lk. xvi. 21; xix. 23; xxii. 21, 30; the table in the temple at Jerusalem on which the consecrated loaves were placed (see πρόθεσις, 1), Heb. ix. 2.   **b.** equiv. to the *food* placed upon the table (cf. Fritzsche on Add. to Esth. iv. 14): παρατιθέναι τράπεζαν, (like the Lat. *mensam apponere* [cf. our 'to set a good table']), *to set a table*, i. e. *food*, before one (Thuc. 1, 130; Ael. v. h. 2, 17), Acts xvi. 34; διακονεῖν ταῖς τραπέζαις (see διακονέω, 3), Acts vi. 2.   **c.** *a banquet, feast*, (fr. Hdt. down): Ro. xi. 9 (fr. Ps. lxviii. (lxix.) 23); μετέχειν τραπέζης δαιμονίων, to partake of a feast prepared by [(?) see below] demons (the idea is this: the sacrifices of the Gentiles inure to the service of demons who employ them in preparing feasts for their worshippers; accordingly one who participates in those feasts, enters into communion and fellowship with the demons); κυρίου, to partake of a feast prepared by [(?) see below] the Lord (just as when he first instituted the supper), 1 Co. x. 21 [but it seems more natural to take the genitives δαιμ. and κυρ. simply as possessive (cf. W. 189 (178); B. § 127, 27), and to modify the above interpretation accordingly].   **2.** *the table* or *stand of a money-changer*, where he sits, exchanging different kinds of money for a fee (agio), and paying back with interest loans or deposits, (Lys., Isocr., Dem., Aristot., Joseph., Plut., al.): Mt. xxi. 12; Mk. xi. 15; Jn. ii. 15; τὸ ἀργύριον διδόναι ἐπὶ (τὴν) τράπεζαν, to put the money into a (the) bank at interest, Lk. xix. 23.*

τραπεζίτης [-ζείτης T WH; see WH. App. p. 154, and **5133** cf. ει, ι], -ου, ὁ, (τράπεζα, q. v.), *a money-changer, broker, banker*, one who exchanges money for a fee, and pays interest on deposits: Mt. xxv. 27.   (Cebet. tab. 31; [Lys.], Dem., Joseph., Plut., Artem., al.) *

τραῦμα, -τος, τό, (ΤΡΑΩ, ΤΡΩΩ, τιτρώσκω, to wound, **5134** akin to θραύω), *a wound*: Lk. x. 34. (From Aeschyl. and Hdt. down; Sept. several times for פֶּצַע.) *

τραυματίζω: 1 aor. ptcp. τραυματίσας; pf. pass. ptcp. **5135** τετραυματισμένος; (τραῦμα); fr. Aeschyl. and Hdt. down, *to wound*: Lk. xx. 12; Acts xix. 16.*

τραχηλίζω: (τράχηλος);   **1.** *to seize and twist the **5136** neck* or *throat*; used of combatants who handle thus their antagonists (Philo, Plut., Diog. Laërt., al.).   **2.** *to bend back the neck* of the victim to be slain, *to lay bare* or *expose by bending back*; hence trop. *to lay bare*, uncover, expose: pf. pass. ptcp. τετραχηλισμένος τινί, laid bare, laid open, made manifest to one, Heb. iv. 13.*

5137   **τράχηλος**, -ου, ὁ, [allied w. τρέχω; named from its movableness; cf. Vaniček p. 304], fr. Eur. and Arstph. down, Sept. chiefly for צַוָּאר, also for יָרֵךְ, etc., the neck: Mt. xviii. 6; Mk. ix. 42; Lk. xv. 20; xvii. 2; Acts xv. 10; xx. 37; τὸν ἑαυτοῦ τράχηλον ὑποτιθέναι (sc. ὑπὸ τὸν σίδηρον), [A.V. to lay down one's own neck i. e.] to be ready to incur the most imminent peril to life, Ro. xvi. 4.*

5138   **τραχύς**, -εῖα, -ύ, fr. Hom. down, rough: ὁδοί, Lk. iii. 5; τόποι, rocky places (in the sea), Acts xxvii. 29.*

5139   **Τραχωνῖτις**, -ιδος, ἡ, Trachonitis, a rough [(Grk. τραχύς)] region, tenanted by robbers, situated between Antilibanus [on the W.] and the mountains of Batanaea [on the E.], and bounded on the N. by the territory of Damascus: Lk. iii. 1 (Joseph. antt. 16, 9, 3 and often). [See Porter in BB.DD.]*

5140   **τρεῖς**, οἱ, αἱ, **τρία**, τά, three: Mt. xii. 40; Mk. viii. 2; Lk. ii. 19, and often. [From Hom. down.]

see 4999 — **Τρεῖς Ταβέρναι**, see ταβέρναι.

5141 ———— **τρέμω**; used only in the pres. and impf.; fr. Hom. down; to tremble: Mk. v. 33; Lk. viii. 47; Acts ix. 6 Rec.; with a ptcp. (cf. W. § 45, 4 a.; [B. § 144, 15 a.]), to fear, be afraid, 2 Pet. ii. 10. [SYN. see φοβέω, fin.]*

5142   **τρέφω**; 1 aor. ἔθρεψα; Pass., pres. τρέφομαι; pf. ptcp. τεθραμμένος; fr. Hom. down; to nourish, support; to feed: τινά, Mt. vi. 26; xxv. 37; Lk. xii. 24; Acts xii. 20; Rev. xii. 6, 14; to give suck, Lk. xxiii. 29 L T Tr WH; to fatten, Jas. v. 5 [here A. V. nourish].   to bring up, nurture, Lk. iv. 16 [here T WH mrg. ἀνατρέφω] (1 Macc. iii. 33; xi. 39, and often in prof. auth.). [COMP.: ἀ ἀ-, ἐκ-, ἐν- τρέφω.]*

5143   **τρέχω**; impf. ἔτρεχον; 2 aor. ἔδραμον; fr. Hom. down; Sept. for רוץ; to run;   **a.** prop.: of persons in haste, Mk. v. 6; Jn. xx. 2, 4; with a telic inf. Mt. xxviii. 8; δραμών with a finite verb, Mt. xxvii. 48; Mk. xv. 36; Lk. xv. 20; τρέχω ἐπί with an acc. of place, Lk. xxiv. 12 [T om. L Tr br. WH reject the vs.]; εἰς πόλεμον, Rev. ix. 9; of those who run in a race-course (ἐν σταδίῳ), 1 Co. ix. 24, 26.   **b.** metaph.: of doctrine rapidly propagated, 2 Th. iii. 1 [R. V. run]; by a metaphor taken from the runners in a race, to exert one's self, strive hard; to spend one's strength in performing or attaining something: Ro. ix. 16; Gal. v. 7; εἰς κενόν, Gal. ii. 2 [W. 504 (470); B. § 148, 10]; Phil. ii. 16; τὸν ἀγῶνα, Heb. xii. 1 (see ἀγών, 2); the same expression occurs in Grk. writ., denoting to incur extreme peril, which it requires the exertion of all one's efforts to overcome, Hdt. 8, 102; Eur. Or. 878; Alc. 489; Electr. 883; Iph. Aul. 1456; Dion. Hal. 7, 48, etc.; miserabile currunt certamen, Stat. Theb. 3, 116. [COMP.: εἰσ-, κατα-, περι-, προ-, προσ-, συν-, ἐπι- συν-, ὑπο- τρέχω.]*

see 5168   **τρῆμα**, -ατος, τό, (τιτράω, τίτρημι, ΤΡΑΩ, to bore through, pierce), a perforation, hole: βελόνης, Lk. xviii. 25 L T Tr WH; [ῥαφίδος, Mt. xix. 24 WH txt.]. (Arstph., Plat., Aristot., Plut., al.)*

5144   **τριάκοντα**, οἱ, αἱ, τά, (τρεῖς), thirty: Mt. xiii. 8; Mk. iv. 8; Lk. iii. 23, etc. [From Hom. down.]

τριακόσιοι, -αι, -α, three hundred: Mk. xiv. 5; Jn. xii. 5. [From Hom. down.]*   **5145**

τρίβολος, -ου, ὁ, (τρεῖς and βάλλω, [(cf. βέλος), three-pointed]), a thistle, a prickly wild plant, hurtful to other plants: Mt. vii. 16; Heb. vi. 8. (Arstph., al.; Sept. for דַּרְדַּר, Gen. iii. 18; Hos. x. 8; for צְנִינִים thorns, Prov. xxii. 5.) [Cf. B. D. s. v. Thorns and Thistles, 4; Löw, Aram. Pflanzennamen, § 302.]*   **5146**

τρίβος, -ου, ἡ, (τρίβω to rub), a worn way, a path: Mt. iii. 3; Mk. i. 3; Lk. iii. 4, fr. Is. xl. 3. (Hom. hymn. Merc. 448; Hdt., Eur., Xen., al.; Sept. for אֹרַח, נְתִיבָה, דֶּרֶךְ, מְסִלָּה, etc.)*   **5147**

τριετία, -ας, ἡ, (τρεῖς and ἔτος), a space of three years: Acts xx. 31. (Theophr., Plut., Artem. oneir. 4, 1; al.)*   **5148**

τρίζω; to squeak, make a shrill cry, (Hom., Hdt., Aristot., Plut., Lcian., al.): trans. τοὺς ὀδόντας, to grind or gnash the teeth, Mk. ix. 18; κατά τινος, Ev. Nicod. c. 5.*   **5149**

τρίμηνος, -ον, (τρεῖς and μήν), of three months (Soph., Aristot., Theophr., al.); neut. used as subst. a space of three months (Polyb., Plut., 2 K. xxiv. 8): Heb. xi. 23.*   **5150**

τρίς, (τρεῖς), adv., thrice: Mt. xxvi. 34, 75; Mk. xiv. 30, 72; Lk. xxii. 34, 61; Jn. xiii. 38; 2 Co. xi. 25; xii. 8; ἐπὶ τρίς [see ἐπί, C. I. 2 d. p. 235ᵃ bot.], Acts x. 16; xi. 10. [From Hom. down.]*   **5151**

τρίστεγος, -ον, (τρεῖς and στέγη), having three roofs or stories: Dion. Hal. 3, 68; [Joseph. b. j. 5, 5, 5]; τὸ τρίστεγον, the third story, Acts xx. 9 (Gen. vi. 16 Symm.); ἡ τριστέγη, Artem. oneir. 4, 46.*   **5152**

τρισχίλιοι, -αι, -α, (τρίς and χίλιοι), three thousand: Acts ii. 41. [From Hom. down.]*   **5153**

τρίτος, -η, -ον, the third: with substantives, Mk. xv. 25; Lk. xxiv. 21; Acts ii. 15; 2 Co. xii. 2; Rev. iv. 7; vi. 5; viii. 10; xi. 14, etc.; τῇ τρίτῃ ἡμέρᾳ, Mt. xvi. 21; xvii. 23; xx. 19; Mk. ix. 31 [Rec.]; x. 34 Rec.; Lk. xxiv. 46; Acts x. 40; 1 Co. xv. 4; τῇ ἡμέρᾳ τῇ τρίτῃ, Lk. xviii. 33; Jn. ii. 1 [L mrg. Tr WH mrg. τῇ τρίτῃ ἡμέρᾳ]; ἕως τῆς τρίτ. ἡμέρας, Mt. xxvii. 64; τρίτον, acc. masc. substantively, a third [(sc. servant)], Lk. xx. 12; neut. τὸ τρίτον with a gen. of the thing, the third part of anything, Rev. viii. 7–12; ix. 15, 18; xii. 4; neut. adverbially, τὸ τρίτον the third time, Mk. xiv. 41; Jn. xxi. 17; also without the article, τρίτον a third time, Lk. xxiii. 22; τοῦτο τρίτον, this is (now) the third time (see οὗτος, II. d.), Jn. xxi. 14; 2 Co. xii. 14 [not Rec.ˢ]; xiii. 1; τρίτον in enumerations after πρῶτον, δεύτερον, in the third place, thirdly, 1 Co. xii. 28; ἐκ τρίτου, a third time [W. § 51, d.], Mt. xxvi. 44 [L Tr mrg. br. ἐκ τρίτου].   **5154**

τρίχινος, -η, -ον, (θρίξ, q. v.), made of hair (Vulg. cilicinus): Rev. vi. 12 [see σάκκος, b.]. (Xen., Plat., Sept., al.)*   **5155**

τριχός, see θρίξ.   see 2359

τρόμος, -ου, ὁ, (τρέμω), fr. Hom. down, a trembling, quaking with fear: Mk. xvi. 8; μετὰ φόβου κ. τρόμου, with fear and trembling, used to describe the anxiety of one who distrusts his ability completely to meet all requirements, but religiously does his utmost to fulfil his duty, 2 Co. vii. 15; Eph. vi. 5; Phil. ii. 12; ἐν φ. κ. ἐν τρ. (Is. xix. 16), 1 Co. ii. 3 (φόβος and τρόμος are joined in   **5156**

Gen. ix. 2; Ex. xv. 16; Deut. [ii. 25]; xi. 25, etc.; ἐν ᾧ. . . . ἐν τρ. Ps. ii. 11). [SYN. cf. φοβέω, fin.] *

5157 τροπή, -ῆς, ἡ, (fr. τρέπω to turn), a turning: of the heavenly bodies, Jas. i. 17 (on this see ἀποσκίασμα); often so in the Grk. writ. fr. Hom. and Hes. down [see L. and S. s. v. 1]; cf. Job xxxviii. 33; Sap. vii. 18; Deut. xxxiii. 14; [Soph. Lex. s. v.].*

5158 τρόπος, -ου, ὁ, (fr. τρέπω, see τροπή), fr. [Pind.], Aeschyl. and Hdt. down; **1.** a manner, way, fashion: ὅν τρόπον, as, even as, like as, [W. § 32, 6; B. § 131, 12]: Mt. xxiii. 37; Lk. xiii. 34; Acts i. 11; vii. 28; 2 Tim. iii. 8, (Gen. xxvi. 29; Ex. xiv. 13; [Deut. xi. 25; Ps. xli. (xlii.) 2]; Ezek. xlii. 7; xlv. 6; Mal. iii. 17; Xen. mem. 1, 2, 59; anab. 6, 1 (3), 1; Plat. rep. 5 p. 466 e.); τὸν ὅμοιον τούτοις τρόπον, [in like manner with these], Jude 7; καθ᾽ ὃν τρόπον, as, Acts xv. 11; xxvii. 25; κατὰ πάντα τρόπον, Ro. iii. 2; κατὰ μηδένα τρόπον, in no wise, 2 Th. ii. 3 (4 Macc. iv. 24; x. 7; κατὰ οὐδένα τρόπον, 2 Macc. xi. 31; 4 Macc. v. 16); παντὶ τρόπῳ, Phil. i. 18 (1 Macc. xiv. 35, and very often in the Grk. writ.); also ἐν παντὶ τρόπῳ, 2 Th. iii. 16 [here Lchm. ἐν π. τόπῳ; cf. W. § 31, 8 d.]. **2.** manner of life, character: Heb. xiii. 5 [R. V. mrg. 'turn of mind'; (cf. τοὺς τρόπους κυρίου ἔχειν, 'Teaching' 11, 8)].*

5159 τροπο-φορέω, -ῶ; 1 aor. ἐτροποφόρησα; (fr. τρόπος, and φέρω to bear); to bear one's manners, endure one's character: τινά, Acts xiii. 18 R Tr txt. WH (see their App. ad loc.), after codd. ℵ B etc.; Vulg. mores eorum sustinuit; (Cic. ad Attic. 13, 29; Schol. on Arstph. ran. 1432; Sept. Deut. i. 31 cod. Vat.; [Orig. in Jer. 248]; Apost. constt. 7, 36 (p. 219, 19 ed. Lagarde)]); see τροφοφορέω.*

5160 τροφή, -ῆς, ἡ, (τρέφω, 2 pf. τέτροφα), food, nourishment: Mt. iii. 4; vi. 25; x. 10; xxiv. 45; Lk. xii. 23; Jn. iv. 8; Acts ii. 46; ix. 19; xiv. 17; xxvii. 33 sq. 36, 38; Jas. ii. 15; of the food of the mind, i. e. the substance of instruction, Heb. v. 12, 14. (Tragg., Xen., Plat., sqq.; Sept. for מָזוֹן, אֹכֶל, לֶחֶם, etc.) *

5161 Τρόφιμος [on its accent cf. W. § 6, 1 l.], -ου, ὁ, Trophimus, an Ephesian Christian, a friend of the apostle Paul: Acts xx. 4; xxi. 29; 2 Tim. iv. 20.*

5162 τροφός, -οῦ, ἡ, (τρέφω; see τροφή), a nurse: 1 Th. ii. 7. (From Hom. down; for מֵינֶקֶת, Gen. xxxv. 8; 2 K. xi. 2; Is. xlix. 23.) *

see 5159 τροφο-φορέω, -ῶ; 1 aor. ἐτροφοφόρησα; (τροφός and φέρω); to bear like a nurse or mother, i. e. to take the most anxious and tender care of: τινά, Acts xiii. 18 G L T Tr mrg. [R. V. mrg. bear as a nursing-father] (Deut. i. 31 cod. Alex. etc.; 2 Macc. vii. 27; Macar. hom. 46, 3 and other eccles. writ.); see τροποφορέω.*

5163 τροχιά, -ᾶς, ἡ, (τροχός, q. v.), a track of a wheel, a rut; a track, a path: τροχιὰς ὀρθὰς ποιήσατε τοῖς ποσὶν ὑμῶν, i. e. follow the path of rectitude, do right, Heb. xii. 13 after Prov. iv. 26 (where מַעְגַּל, as in ii. 15; iv. 11; v. 6, 21; in some of the later poets equiv. to τροχός).*

5164 τροχός, -οῦ, ὁ, (τρέχω), fr. Hom. down, a wheel: Jas. iii. 6 (on this pass. see γένεσις 3; [cf. W. 54 (53)]).*

5165 τρύβλιον [so T (cf. Proleg. p. 102) WH; -βλίον R G L Tr] (on the accent see Passow s. v.; [Chandler § 350;

Göttling p. 408])), -ου, τό, a dish, a deep dish [cf. B. D. s. v. Dish]: Mt. xxvi. 23; Mk. xiv. 20. (Arstph., Plut., Lcian., Ael. v. h. 9, 37; Sept. for קְעָרָה, for which also in Joseph. antt. 3, 8, 10; Sir. xxxiv. (xxxi.) 14.) *

5166 τρυγάω, -ῶ; 1 aor. ἐτρύγησα; (fr. τρύγη [lit. 'dryness'] fruit gathered ripe in autumn, harvest); fr. Hom. down; Sept. several times for בָּצַר, אָרָה, קָצַר; to gather in ripe fruits; to gather the harvest or vintage: as in the Grk. writ., with acc. of the fruit gathered, Lk. vi. 44; Rev. xiv. 18; or of the plant from which it is gathered, Rev. xiv. 19.*

5167 τρυγών, -όνος, ἡ, (fr. τρύζω to murmur, sigh, coo, of doves; cf. γογγύζω), a turtle-dove: Lk. ii. 24. (Arstph., Theocr., al.; Ael. v. h. 1, 15; Sept. for תֹּר.) *

5168 τρυμαλιά, -ᾶς, ἡ, (i. q. τρῦμα, or τρύμη, fr. τρύω to wear away, perforate), a hole, [eye of a needle]: Mk. x. 25, and R G in Lk. xviii. 25. (Judg. xv. 11; Jer. xiii. 4; xvi. 16; Sotad. in Plut. mor. p. 11 a. [i. e. de educ. puer. § 14]; Geop.) *

5169 τρύπημα, -τος, τό, (τρυπάω to bore), a hole, [eye of a needle]: Mt. xix. 24 [here WH txt. τρῆμα, q. v.]. (Arstph., Plut., Geop., al.) *

5170 Τρύφαινα, -ης, ἡ, (τρυφάω, q. v.), Tryphœna, a Christian woman: Ro. xvi. 12. [B. D. s. v.; Bp. Lghtft. on Phil. p. 175 sq.] *

5171 τρυφάω, -ῶ; 1 aor. ἐτρύφησα; (τρυφή, q. v.); to live delicately, live luxuriously, be given to a soft and luxurious life: Jas. v. 5. (Neh. ix. 25; Is. lxvi. 11; Isocr., Eur., Xen., Plat., sqq.) [COMP.: ἐν-τρυφάω. SYN. cf. Trench § liv.] *

5172 τρυφή, -ῆς, ἡ, (fr. θρύπτω to break down, enervate), pass. and mid. to live softly and delicately), softness, effeminacy, luxurious living: Lk. vii. 25; 2 Pet. ii. 13. (Eur., Arstph., Xen., Plato, sqq.; Sept.) *

5173 Τρυφῶσα, -ης, ἡ, (τρυφάω, q. v.), Tryphosa, a Christian woman: Ro. xvi. 12. [See reff. under Τρύφαινα.] *

5174 Τρωάς, and (so L T WH [see I, ι and reff. in Pape, Eigennamen s. v.]) Τρῳάς, -άδος, ἡ, [on the art. with it see W. § 5, b.], Troas, a city near the Hellespont, formerly called Ἀντιγόνεια Τρ. but by Lysimachus Ἀλεξάνδρεια ἡ Τρ. in honor of Alexander the Great; it flourished under the Romans [and with its environs was raised by Augustus to a colonia juris italici, 'the Troad'; cf. Strab. 13, 1, 26; Plin. 5, 33]: Acts xvi. 8, 11; xx. 5 sq.; 2 Co. ii. 12; 2 Tim. iv. 13. [B. D. s. v.]*

5175 Τρωγύλλιον (so Ptolem. 5, 2, 8), or Τρωγίλιον [(better -γύλιον; see WH. App. p. 159)] (so Strab. 14, p. 636), -ου, τό, Trogyllium, the name of a town and promontory of Ionia, not far from the island Samos, at the foot of Mt. Mycale, between Ephesus and the mouth of the river Maeander: Acts xx. 15 R G. [Cf. B. D. s. v.] *

5176 τρώγω; to gnaw, craunch, chew raw vegetables or fruits (as nuts, almonds, etc.): ἄγρωστιν, of mules, Hom. Od. 6, 90, and often in other writers of animals feeding; also of men fr. Hdt. down (as σῦκα, Hdt. 1, 71; βότρυς, Arstph. eqq. 1077; blackberries, Barn. ep. 7, 8 [where see Harnack, Cunningham, Müller]; κρόμυον μετὰ δεῖπνον, Xen. conv. 4, 8); univ. to eat: absol. (δύο τρώγομεν ἀδελφοί, we mess together, Polyb. 32, 9, 9) joined with πίνειν, Mt. xxiv. 38 (so also Dem. p. 402, 21; Plut. symp. 1, 1, 2; Ev. Nicod. c. 15, p. 640 ed. Thilo [p. 251 ed. Tdf.]); τὸν ἄρτον, Jn. xiii. 18 (see ἄρτος 2 and ἐσθίω b.); figuratively, Jn. vi. 58; τὴν σάρκα, the 'flesh' of Christ (see σάρξ, 1), Jn. vi. 54, 56 sq.*

5177 τυγχάνω; 2 aor. ἔτυχον; pf. (Heb. viii. 6) τέτευχα [so cod. B], and (so L T Tr mrg. WH cod. ℵ) τέτυχα a later and rarer form (which not a few incorrectly think is everywhere to be regarded as a clerical error; B. 67 (59); Kühner § 343 s. v.; [Veitch s. v.; Phryn. ed. *Lob.* p. 595; WH. App. p. 171]), in some texts also τετύχηκα (a form com. in the earlier writ. [*Rutherford*, New Phryn. p. 483 sq., and reff. as above]); a verb in freq. use fr. Hom. down; "est Lat. *attingere* et *contingere*; Germ. *treffen*, c. accus. i. q. *etwas erlangen*, neut. *es trifft sich.*" *Ast*, Lex. Platon. s. v.; hence **1.** trans. **a.** prop. *to hit the mark* (opp. to ἁμαρτάνειν to miss the mark), of one discharging a javelin or arrow, (Hom., Xen., Lcian.). **b.** trop. *to reach, attain, obtain, get, become master of*: with a gen. of the thing (W. 200 (188)), Lk. xx. 35 [W. 609 (566)]; Acts xxiv. 2 (3); xxvi. 22; xxvii. 3; 2 Tim. ii. 10; Heb. viii. 6; xi. 35. **2.** intrans. *to happen, chance, fall out*: εἰ τύχοι (*if it so fall out*), it may be, perhaps, (freq. in prof. auth.), 1 Co. xiv. 10, where see Meyer; or, considered in ref. to the topic in hand, it may be i. q. *to specify, to take a case, as, for example*, 1 Co. xv. 37, (Vulg. in each pass. *ut puta*; [cf. Meyer u. s.]); τυχόν adverbially, *perhaps, it may be*, 1 Co. xvi. 6 (cf. B. § 145, 8; [W. § 45, 8 N. 1]; see exx. fr. Grk. writ. in Passow s. v. II. 2 b.; [L. and S. s. v. B. III. 2; *Soph.* Lex. s. v.]). *to meet* one; hence ὁ τυχών, he who meets one or presents himself unsought, any chance, ordinary, common person, (see Passow s. v. II. 2; [L. and S. s. v. A. II. 1 b.; *Soph.* Lex. s. v.]): οὐ τυχών, *not common*, i. e. *eminent, exceptional*, [A. V. *special*], Acts xix. 11; xxviii. 2, (3 Macc. iii. 7); *to chance to be*: ἡμιθανῆ τυγχάνοντα, half dead as he happened to be, just as he was, Lk. x. 30 R G. [Comp.: ἐν-, ὑπερ-εν-, ἐπι-, παρα-, συν- τυγχάνω.]*

5178 τυμπανίζω: (τύμπανον); **1.** *to beat the drum* or *timbrel.* **2.** *to torture with the tympanum*, an instrument of punishment: ἐτυμπανίσθησαν (Vulg. *distenti sunt*), Heb. xi. 35 [R. V. *were tortured* (with marg. Or, *beaten to death*)] (Plut. mor. p. 60 a.; joined with ἀνασκολοπίζεσθαι, Lcian. Jup. trag. 19); the tympanum seems to have been a wheel-shaped instrument of torture, over which criminals were stretched as though they were skins, and then horribly beaten with clubs or thongs [cf. our 'to break upon the wheel'; see Eng. Dicts. s. v. Wheel]; cf. [Bleek on Heb. u. s.]; Grimm on 2 Macc. vi. 19 sq.*

see 5179 τυπικῶς, (fr. the adj. τυπικός, and this fr. τύπος); adv., *by way of example* (*prefiguratively*): ταῦτα τυπικῶς συνέβαινον ἐκείνοις, these things happened unto them as a warning to posterity [R. V. *by way of example*], 1 Co. x. 11 L T Tr WH. (Eccles. writ.)*

5179 τύπος, -ου, ὁ, (τύπτω), fr. [Aeschyl. and] Hdt. down;

1. *the mark of a stroke or blow*; *print*: τῶν ἥλων, Jn. xx. 25ᵃ, 25ᵇ [where L T Tr mrg. τόπον], (Athen. 13 p. 585 c. τοὺς τύπους τῶν πληγῶν ἰδοῦσα). **2.** *a figure formed by a blow or impression*; hence univ. *a figure, image*: of the images of the gods, Acts vii. 43 (Amos v. 26; Joseph. antt. 1, 19, 11; 15, 9, 5). [Cf. κύριοι τύπος θεοῦ, Barn. ep. 19, 7; 'Teaching' 4, 11.] **3.** *form*: διδαχῆς, i. e. the teaching which embodies the sum and substance of religion and represents it to the mind, Ro. vi. 17; i. q. *manner of writing*, the contents and form of a letter, Acts xxiii. 25 (3 Macc. iii. 30). **4.** *an example*; **a.** in the technical sense, viz. *the pattern in conformity to which a thing must be made*: Acts vii. 44; Heb. viii. 5, (Ex. xxv. 40). **β.** in an ethical sense, *a dissuasive example, pattern of warning*: plur. of ruinous events which serve as admonitions or warnings to others, 1 Co. x. 6, 11 R G; *an example to be imitated*: of men worthy of imitation, Phil. iii. 17; with a gen. of the pers. to whom the example is offered, 1 Tim. iv. 12; 1 Pet. v. 3; τύπον ἑαυτὸν διδόναι τινί, 2 Th. iii. 9; γενέσθαι τύπον [τύπους R L mrg. WH mrg.; cf. W. § 27, 1 note] τινί, 1 Th. i. 7; παρέχεσθαι ἑαυτὸν τύπον καλῶν ἔργων, to show one's self an example of good works, Tit. ii. 7. **γ.** in a doctrinal sense, *a type* i. e. a person or thing prefiguring a future (Messianic) person or thing: in this sense Adam is called τύπος τοῦ μέλλοντος sc. Ἀδάμ, i. e. of Jesus Christ, each of the two having exercised a pre-eminent influence upon the human race (the former destructive, the latter saving), Ro. v. 14.*

5180 τύπτω; impf. ἔτυπτον; pres. pass. inf. τύπτεσθαι; fr. Hom. down; Sept. for הִכָּה; *to strike, smite, beat* (with a staff, a whip, the fist, the hand, etc.): τινά, Mt. xxiv. 49; Lk. xii. 45; Acts xviii. 17; xxi. 32; xxiii. 3; τὸ στόμα τινός, Acts xxiii. 2; τὸ πρόσωπόν τινος, Lk. xxii. 64 [here L br. T Tr WH om. the cl.]; τινὰ ἐπὶ [Tdf. εἰς] τὴν σιαγόνα, Lk. vi. 29; εἰς τ. κεφαλήν τινος, Mk. xv. 19; [τὴν κεφαλήν τινος, Mk. xv. 19]; ἑαυτῶν τὰ στήθη (Lat. *plangere pectora*), of mourners, to smite their breasts, Lk. xxiii. 48; also τ. εἰς τὸ στῆθος, Lk. xviii. 13 [but G L T Tr WH om. εἰς]. God is said τύπτειν *to smite* one on whom he inflicts punitive evil, Acts xxiii. 3 (Ex. viii. 2; 2 S. xxiv. 17; Ezek. vii. 9; 2 Macc. iii. 39). *to smite* metaph. i. e. *to wound, disquiet*: τὴν συνείδησίν τινος, one's conscience, 1 Co. viii. 12 (ἵνα τί τύπτει σε ἡ καρδία σου; 1 S. i. 8; τὸν δὲ ἄχος ὀξὺ κατὰ φρένα τύψε βαθεῖαν, Hom. Il. 19, 125; Καμβύσεα ἔτυψε ἡ ἀληθηΐη τῶν λόγων, Hdt. 3, 64).*

5181 Τύραννος, -ου, ὁ, *Tyrannus*, an Ephesian in whose school Paul taught the gospel, but of whom we have no further knowledge [cf. B. D. s. v.]: Acts xix. 9.*

5182 τυρβάζω: pres. pass. τυρβάζομαι; (τύρβη, Lat. *turba*, confusion; [cf. Curtius § 250]); [fr. Soph. down]; *to disturb, trouble*: prop. τὸν πηλόν, Arstph. vesp. 257; trop. in pass. *to be troubled in mind, disquieted*: περὶ πολλά, Lk. x. 41 R G (with the same constr. in Arstph. pax 1007; μὴ ἄγαν τυρβάζου, Nilus epist. 2, 258).*

5183 Τύριος, -ου, ὁ, ἡ, *a Tyrian*, inhabitant of Tyre: Acts xii. 20. [(Hdt., al.)]*

5184   **Τύρος**, -ου, ἡ, (Hebr. צֹור or צֹר; fr. Aram. טוּר a rock), *Tyre*, a Phœnician city on the Mediterranean, very ancient, large, splendid, flourishing in commerce, and powerful by land and sea. In the time of Christ and the apostles it was subject to the Romans, but continued to possess considerable wealth and prosperity down to A. D. 1291. It is at present an obscure little place containing some five thousand inhabitants, part Mohammedans part Christians, with a few Jews (cf. Bädeker's Palestine p. 425 sq.; [Murray's ditto p. 370 sq.]). It is mentioned Acts xxi. 3, 7, and (in company with Sidon) in Mt. xi. 21 sq.; xv. 21; Lk. vi. 17; x. 13 sq.; Mk. iii. 8; vii. 24 (where T om. Tr mrg. WH br. καὶ Σιδῶνος), 31. [BB. DD.]*

5185   **τυφλός**, -οῦ, ὁ, (τύφω, to raise a smoke; hence prop. 'darkened by smoke'), fr. Hom. down, Sept. for עִוֵּר, *blind*;   **a.** prop.: Mt. ix. 27 sq.; xi. 5; Mk. viii. 22 sq.; x. 46; Lk. vii. 21 sq.; xiv. 13, 21; Jn. ix. 1 sq. 13; x. 21, etc.   **b.** as often in prof. auth. fr. Pind. down, mentally *blind*: Mt. xv. 14; xxiii. 17, 19, 24, 26; Jn. ix. 39–41; Ro. ii. 19; 2 Pet. i. 9; Rev. iii. 17.

5186   **τυφλόω**, -ῶ: 1 aor. ἐτύφλωσα; pf. τετύφλωκα; fr. [Pind. and] Hdt. down; *to blind, make blind*; in the N. T. metaph. *to blunt the mental discernment, darken the mind*:

Jn. xii. 40; 1 Jn. ii. 11; τὰ νοήματα, 2 Co. iv. 4, (τὴν ψυχὴν τυφλωθείην, Plat. Phaedo p. 99 e.).*

τυφόω, -ῶ: Pass., pf. τετύφωμαι; 1 aor. ptcp. τυφωθείς; (τύφος, smoke; pride); prop. *to raise a smoke, to wrap in a mist*; used only metaph.   **1.** *to make proud, puff up with pride, render insolent*; pass. *to be puffed up* with haughtiness or pride, 1 Tim. iii. 6 (Strab., Joseph., Diog. Laërt., al.).   **2.** *to blind with pride* or *conceit, to render foolish* or *stupid*: 1 Tim. vi. 4; pf. ptcp. *beclouded, besotted*, 2 Tim. iii. 4, (Dem., Aristot., Polyb., Plut., al.).*   5187

τύφω: (τῦφος, smoke); fr. Hdt. down; *to cause or emit smoke* (Plaut. *fumifico*), *raise a smoke*; pass. (pres. ptcp. τυφόμενος) *to smoke* (Vulg. *fumigo*): Mt. xii. 20.*   5188

τυφωνικός, -ή, -όν, (τυφῶν [cf. Chandler ed. 1 § 659], a whirlwind, hurricane, typhoon), *like a whirlwind, tempestuous*: ἄνεμος, Acts xxvii. 14.*   5189

Τύχικος [so WH; W. § 6, 1 l.] but RGLT Tr Τυχικός (*Lipsius*, Gram. Unters. p. 30; [*Tdf*. Proleg. p. 103; Chandler § 266]), -ου, ὁ, *Tychicus*, an Asiatic Christian, friend and companion of the apostle Paul: Acts xx. 4; Eph. vi. 21; Col. iv. 7; 2 Tim. iv. 12; Tit. iii. 12. [See Bp. Lghtft. on Col. l. c.; B. D. s. v.]*   5190

τυχόν, see τυγχάνω, 2.   see 5177

Υ

[**Υ, υ**: on the use and the omission of the mark of diaeresis with, see *Tdf*. Proleg. p. 108; *Lipsius*, Gram. Untersuch. p. 136 sqq.; cf. *Scrivener*, Collation of Cod. Sin. etc. 2d ed. p. xxxviii.]

5191   **ὑακίνθινος**, -η, -ον, (ὑάκινθος), *of hyacinth, of the color of hyacinth*, i. e. *of a red color bordering on black* (Hesych. ὑακίνθινον· ὑπομελανίζον): Rev. ix. 17 (Hom., Theocr., Lcian., al.; Sept.).*

5192   **ὑάκινθος**, -ου, ὁ, *hyacinth*, the name of a flower (Hom. and other poets; Theophr.), also of a precious stone of the same color, i. e. *dark-blue verging towards black* [A. V. *jacinth* (so R. V. with mrg. *sapphire*); cf. B. D. s. v. Jacinth; Riehm s. v. Edelsteine 9] (Philo, Joseph., Galen, Heliod., al.; Plin. h. n. 37, 9, 41): Rev. xxi. 20.*

5193   **ὑάλινος**, -η, -ον, (ὕαλος, q. v.), in a fragment of Corinna and occasionally in the Grk. writ. fr. Arstph. down, *of glass* or *transparent like glass, glassy*: Rev. iv. 6; xv. 2.*

5194   **ὕαλος**, -ου, ὁ, [prob. allied w. ὕει, ὑετός (q. v.); hence 'rain-drop', Curtius § 604; Vaniček p. 1046; but al. make it of Egypt. origin (cf. L. and S. s. v.)], fr. Hdt. ([3, 24] who writes ὕελος; [cf. W. 22]) down;   **1.** *any stone transparent like glass.*   **2.** *glass*: Rev. xxi. 18, 21.*

ὑβρίζω; 1 aor. ὕβρισα; Pass., 1 aor. ptcp. ὑβρισθείς; 1 fut. ὑβρισθήσομαι; (ὕβρις); fr. Hom. down;   **1.** intrans. *to be insolent*; *to behave insolently, wantonly, outrageously.*   **2.** trans. *to act insolently and shamefully towards one* (so even Hom.), *to treat shamefully*, [cf. W. § 32, 1 b. β.]: Mt. xxii. 6; Lk. xviii. 32; Acts xiv. 5; [1 Th. ii. 2]; of one who injures another by speaking evil of him, Lk. xi. 45. [COMP.: ἐν-υβρίζω.]*   5195

ὕβρις, -εως, ἡ, (fr. ὑπέρ [(see Curtius p. 540); cf. Lat. *superbus*, Eng. 'uppishness']), fr. Hom. down, Sept. for גָּאוֹן, גַּאֲוָה, זָדוֹן, etc.;   **a.** *insolence*; *impudence, pride, haughtiness.*   **b.** *a wrong springing from insolence, an injury, affront, insult* [in Grk. usage the mental injury and the wantonness of its infliction being prominent; cf. *Cope* on Aristot. rhet. 1, 12, 26; 2, 2, 5; see ὑβριστής]: prop., plur. 2 Co. xii. 10 (Hesych. ὕβρεις· τραύματα, ὀνείδη); trop. *injury inflicted by the violence of a tempest*: Acts xxvii. 10, 21, (τὴν ἀπὸ τῶν ὄμβρων ὕβριν, Joseph. antt. 3, 6, 4; δείσασα θαλάττης ὕβριν, Anthol. 7, 291, 3; [cf. Pind. Pyth. 1, 140]).*   5196

ὑβριστής, -οῦ, ὁ, (ὑβρίζω), fr. Hom. down, *an insolent man*, 'one who, uplifted with pride, either heaps insulting language upon others or does them some shameful act of   5197 *wrong'* (Fritzsche, Ep. ad Rom. i. p. 86; [cf. *Trench*, Syn. § xxix.; Schmidt ch. 177; *Cope* on Aristot. rhet. 2, 2, 5 (see ὕβρις)]): Ro. i. 30; 1 Tim. i. 13.*

5198   **ὑγιαίνω**; (ὑγιής); fr. Hdt. down; *to be sound, to be well, to be in good health*: prop., Lk. v. 31; vii. 10; xv. 27; [3 Jn. 2]; metaph. the phrase ὑγιαίνειν ἐν τῇ πίστει [B. § 133, 19] is used of one whose Christian opinions are free from any admixture of error, Tit. i. 13; τῇ πίστει, τῇ ἀγάπῃ, τῇ ὑπομονῇ, [cf. B. u. s.], of one who keeps these graces sound and strong, Tit. ii. 2; ἡ ὑγιαίνουσα διδασκαλία, the sound i. e. true and incorrupt doctrine, 1 Tim. i. 10; 2 Tim. iv. 3; Tit. i. 9; ii. 1; also λόγοι ὑγιαίνοντες (Philo de Abrah. § 38), 1 Tim. vi. 3; 2 Tim. i. 13, (ὑγιαίνουσαι περὶ θεῶν δόξαι καὶ ἀληθεῖς, Plut. de aud. poet. c. 4).*

5199   **ὑγιής**, -ές, acc. ὑγιῆ (four times in the N. T., Jn. v. 11, 15; vii. 23; Tit. ii. 8; for which ὑγιᾶ is more com. in Attic [cf. Meisterhans p. 66]), fr. Hom. down, *sound*: prop. [A. V. *whole*], of a man who is sound in body, Mt. xv. 31 [WH only in mrg., but Tr br. in mrg.]; Acts iv. 10; γίνομαι, Jn. v. 4 [R L], 6, 9, 14; ποιεῖν τινα ὑγιῆ (Hdt., Xen., Plat., al.), *to make one whole* i. e. restore him to health, Jn. v. 11, 15; vii. 23; ὑγιὴς ἀπό etc. *sound* and thus free *from* etc. (see ἀπό, I. 3 d.), Mk. v. 34; of the members of the body, Mt. xii. 13; Mk. iii. 5 Rec.; Lk. vi. 10 Rec.; metaph. λόγος ὑγ. [A. V. *sound speech*] i. e. teaching which does not deviate from the truth (see ὑγιαίνω), Tit. ii. 8 (in the Grk. writ., often equiv. to *wholesome, fit, wise*: μῦθος, Il. 8, 524; λόγος οὐκ ὑγιής, Hdt. 1, 8; see other exx. in Passow s. v. 2; [L. and S. s. v. II. 2 and 3]).*

5200   **ὑγρός**, -ά, -όν, (ὕω to moisten; [but al. fr. a different r. meaning 'to moisten', fr. which also Lat. umor, umidus; cf. Vaniček p. 867; Curtius § 158]), fr. Hom. down, *damp, moist, wet*; opp. to ξηρός (q. v.), *full of sap, green*: ξύλον, Lk. xxiii. 31 (for רטב sappy, in Job viii. 16).*

5201   **ὑδρία**, -ας, ἡ, (ὕδωρ), *a vessel for holding water; a water-jar, water-pot*: Jn. ii. 6 sq.; iv. 28. (Arstph., Athen., al.; Sept. for כַּד. [Cf. *Rutherford*, New Phryn. p. 23.]) *

5202   **ὑδροποτέω**, -ῶ; (ὑδροπότης); *to drink water, [be a drinker of water]*; W. 498 (464)]: 1 Tim. v. 23. (Hdt. 1, 71; Xen., Plat., Lcian., Athen., al.; Ael. v. h. 2, 38.)*

5203   **ὑδρωπικός**, -ή, -όν, (ὕδρωψ, the dropsy, i. e. internal water), *dropsical, suffering from dropsy*: Lk. xiv. 2. (Hipper., [Aristot.], Polyb. 13, 2, 2; [al.].) *

5204   **ὕδωρ**, (ὕω [but cf. Curtius § 300]), gen. ὕδατος, τό, fr. Hom. down, Hebr. מַיִם, *water*: of the water in rivers, Mt. iii. 16; Rev. xvi. 12; in wells, Jn. iv. 7; in fountains, Jas. iii. 12; Rev. viii. 10; xvi. 4; in pools, Jn. v. 3 sq. [R L], 7; of the water of the deluge, 1 Pet. iii. 20; 2 Pet. iii. 6 [W. 604 sq. (562)]; of water in any of earth's repositories, Rev. viii. 10 sq.; xi. 6; ὁ ἄγγελος τῶν ὑδάτων, Rev. xvi. 5; of water as a primary element, out of and through which the world that was before the deluge arose and was compacted, 2 Pet. iii. 5. plur. τὰ ὕδατα, of the waves of the Lake of Galilee, Mt. xiv. 28 sq.; (so also the sing. τὸ ὕδωρ in Lk. viii. 25); of the waves of

the sea, Rev. i. 15; xiv. 2, (on both these pass. see φωνή, 1); πολλὰ ὕδατα, many springs or fountains, Jn. iii. 23; fig. used of many peoples, Rev. xvii. 1, as the seer himself explains it in vs. 15, cf. Nah. ii. 8; of a quantity of water likened to a river, Rev. xii. 15; of a definite quantity of water drawn for drinking, Jn. ii. 7; ποτήριον ὕδατος, Mk. ix. 41; for washing, Mt. xxvii. 24; Lk. vii. 44; Jn. xiii. 5; Heb. x. 22 (23); τὸ λουτρὸν τοῦ ὕδατος, of baptism, Eph. v. 26 [cf. W. 138 (130)]; κεράμιον ὕδατος, Mk. xiv. 13; Lk. xxii. 10. in opp. to other things, whether elements or liquids: opp. to τῷ πνεύματι κ. πυρί [cf. B. § 133, 19; W. 217 (204), 412 (384)], Mt. iii. 11; Lk. iii. 16; to πνεύματι alone, Jn. i. 26, 31, 33; Acts i. 5, (in all these pass. the water of baptism is intended); to τῷ πυρί alone, Mt. xvii. 15; Mk. ix. 22; to τῷ οἴνῳ, Jn. ii. 9; iv. 46; to τῷ αἵματι, Jn. xix. 34; Heb. ix. 19; 1 Jn. v. 6, 8. Allegorically, that which refreshes and keeps alive the soul is likened to water, viz. *the Spirit and truth of God*, Jn. iv. 14 sq. (ὕδωρ σοφίας, Sir. xv. 3); on the expressions ὕδωρ ζῶν, τὸ ὕδωρ τ. ζωῆς, ζῶσαι πηγαὶ ὑδάτων, see ζάω, II. a. and ζωή, 2 b. p. 274*.

5205   **ὑετός**, -οῦ, ὁ, (ὕω to rain), fr. Hom. down, Sept. for גֶּשֶׁם and מָטָר, *rain*: Acts xiv. 17; xxviii. 2; Heb. vi. 7; Jas. v. 7 (where L T Tr WH om. ὑετόν; on this pass. see ὄψιμος and πρώϊμος); ibid. 18; Rev. xi. 6.*

5206   **υἱοθεσία**, -ας, ἡ, (fr. υἱός and θέσις, cf. ὁροθεσία, νομοθεσία; in prof. auth. fr. Pind. and Hdt. down we find θετὸς υἱός or θετὸς παῖς, an adopted son), *adoption, adoption as sons* (Vulg. *adoptio filiorum*): [Diod. l. 31 § 27, 5 (vol. x. 31, 13 Dind.)]; Diog. Laërt. 4, 53; Inscrr. In the N. T. it is used to denote **a.** that relationship which God was pleased to establish between himself and the Israelites in preference to all other nations (see υἱὸς τοῦ θεοῦ, 4 init.): Ro. ix. 4. **b.** the nature and condition of the true disciples of Christ, who by receiving the Spirit of God into their souls become the sons of God (see υἱὸς τοῦ θεοῦ, 4): Ro. viii. 15; Gal. iv. 5; Eph. i. 5; it also includes the blessed state looked for in the future life after the visible return of Christ from heaven; hence ἀπεκδέχεσθαι υἱοθεσίαν, *to wait for adoption*, i. e. the consummate condition of the sons of God, which will render it evident that they are the sons of God, Ro. viii. 23, cf. 19.*

5207   **υἱός**, -οῦ, ὁ, fr. Hom. down, Sept. for בֵּן and Chald. בַּר, *a son (male offspring)*; **1.** prop. **a.** rarely of the young of animals: Mt. xxi. 5 (Ps. xxviii. (xxix.) 1; Sir. xxxviii. 25); generally of the offspring of men, and in the restricted sense, *male issue (one begotten by a father and born of a mother)*: Mt. x. 37; Lk. i. 13; [xiv. 5 L T Tr WH]; Acts vii. 29; Gal. iv. 22, etc.; ὁ υἱός τινος, Mt. vii. 9; Mk. ix. 17; Lk. iii. 2; Jn. i. 42 (43), and very often. as in Grk. writ., υἱός is often to be supplied by the reader [W. § 30, 3 p. 593 (551)]: as τὸν τοῦ Ζεβεδαίου, Mt. iv. 21; Mk. i. 19. plur. υἱοί τινος, Mt. xx. 20 sq.; Lk. v. 10; Jn. iv. 12; Acts i. 17; Heb. xi. 21, etc. with the addition of an adj., as πρωτότοκος, Mt. i. 25 [R G]; Lk. ii. 7; μονογενής, Lk. vii. 12. οἱ υἱοί, *genuine sons*, are distinguished fr. οἱ νόθοι in Heb. xii. 8. i. q. τέκνον with ἄρσην added, *a man child* [B. 80 (70)], Rev. xii. 5; of one (actually or to be) regarded as a son, although properly not one, Jn. xix. 26; Acts vii. 21; Heb. xi. 24; in kindly address, Heb. xii. 5 fr. Prov. iii. 11 (see τέκνον, a. β.).   **b.** in a wider sense (like θυγάτηρ, τέκνον), *a descendant, one of the posterity of any one* : τινός, Mt. i. 20; ὁ υἱὸς Δαυίδ, of the Messiah, Mt. xxii. 42, 45; Mk. xii. 35, 37; Lk. xx. 41, 44; of Jesus the Messiah, Mt. ix. 27; xii. 23; xv. 22; xx. 30 sq.; xxi. 9, 15; Mk. x. 47 sq.; Lk. xviii. 38 sq. plur. υἱοί τινος, Mt. xxiii. 31; Heb. vii. 5; υἱοὶ Ἰσραήλ, Israelites [*the children of Israel*], Mt. xxvii. 9; Acts ix. 15; x. 36; 2 Co. iii. 7, 13; Heb. xi. 21 sq.; Rev. ii. 14; vii. 4; xxi. 12, (see Ἰσραήλ); υἱοὶ Ἀβραάμ, *sons of Abraham*, is trop. applied to those who by their faith in Christ are akin to Abraham, Gal. iii. 7.   **2.** trop. and acc. to the Hebr. mode of speech [W. 33 (32)], υἱός with the gen. of a person : of one who depends on another or is his follower : οἱ υἱοί of teachers, i. q. *pupils* (see τέκνον, b. β. [cf. Iren. haer. 4, 41, 2 qui enim ab aliquo edoctus est, verbo filius docentis dicitur, et ille eius pater]), Mt. xii. 27; Lk. xi. 19; τοῦ πονηροῦ, who in thought and action are prompted by the evil one and obey him, Mt. xiii. 38; υἱὸς διαβόλου, Acts xiii. 10; with the gen. of a thing, one who is connected with or belongs to a thing by any kind of close relationship [W. § 34, 3 N. 2; B. § 132, 10]: υἱοὶ τοῦ νυμφῶνος (see νυμφών), Mt. ix. 15; Mk. ii. 19; Lk. v. 34, (τῆς ἄκρας, the garrison of the citadel, 1 Macc. iv. 2; in Ossian 'a son of the hill' i. e. 'a hunter', 'a son of the sea' i. e. 'a sailor'; cf. Jen. Lit. Zeit. for 1836 No. 58 p. 462 sq.) ; τοῦ αἰῶνος τούτου, those whose character belongs to this age [is ' worldly '], Lk. xvi. 8; xx. 34; τῆς ἀπειθείας, i. e. ἀπειθεῖς, Eph. ii. 2; v. 6; Col. iii. 6 [here T Tr WH om. L br. the cl.], (ἀνομίας, Ps. lxxxviii. (lxxxix.) 23; τῆς ὑπερηφανίας, 1 Macc. ii. 47); βροντῆς, who resemble thunder, thundering, (see Βοανεργές), Mk. iii. 17; τοῦ φωτός, instructed in evangelical truth and devotedly obedient to it, Lk. xvi. 8; Jn. xii. 36; with καὶ τῆς ἡμέρας added, 1 Th. v. 5; τῆς ἀναστάσεως, sharers in the resurrection, Lk. xx. 36; παρακλήσεως, Acts iv. 36; one to whom any thing belongs : as υἱοὶ τῶν προφητῶν κ. τῆς διαθήκης, those to whom the prophetic and covenant promises belong, Acts iii. 25; for whom a thing is destined, as υἱοὶ τῆς βασιλείας, Mt. viii. 12; xiii. 38; τῆς ἀπωλείας, Jn. xvii. 12; 2 Th. ii. 3; one who is worthy of a thing, as γεέννης, Mt. xxiii. 15; εἰρήνης, Lk. x. 6, (θανάτου, 1 S. xx. 31; 2 S. xii. 5; בֶּן הַכּוֹת, Sept. ἄξιος πληγῶν, Deut. xxv. 2). [SYN. see τέκνον.]

υἱὸς τοῦ ἀνθρώπου, Sept. for בֶּן אָדָם, Chald. בַּר אֱנָשׁ, *son of man*; it is   **1.** prop. a periphrasis for 'man', esp. com. in the poet. bks. of the O. T., and usually carrying with it a suggestion of weakness and mortality: Num. xxiii. 19; Job xvi. 21; xxv. 6; Ps. viii. 5; Is. li. 12; Sir. xvii. 30 (25), etc.; often in Ezekiel, where God addresses the prophet by this name, as ii. 1, 3; iii. 1 (ii. 10), etc.; plur. בְּנֵי הָאָדָם (because אָדָם wants the plur.), υἱοὶ τῶν ἀνθρώπων, Gen. xi. 5; 1 S. xxvi. 19; Ps. x. (xi.) 4; Prov. viii. 31, etc. So in the N. T.: Mk. iii. 28; Eph.

iii. 5, (Sap. ix. 6); sing. ὅμοιος υἱῷ ἀνθρ. [*like unto a son of man*], of Christ in the apocalyptic vision, Rev. i. 13 [here υἱόν T WH txt.]; xiv. 14 [υἱόν T WH], (after Dan. vii. 13).   **2.** In Dan. vii. 13 sq., cf. 18, 22, 27, the appellation *son of man* (בַּר אֱנָשׁ) symbolically denotes the fifth kingdom, universal and Messianic; and by this term its *humanity* is indicated in contrast with the barbarity and ferocity of the four preceding kingdoms (the Babylonian, the Median, the Persian, the Macedonian) typified under the form of beasts (vs. 2 sqq.). But in the book of Enoch (written towards the close of the 2d cent. before Christ [but cf. B. D. (esp. Am. ed.); *Lipsius* in Dict. of Chris. Biog. s. v.; *Dillmann* in Herzog (ed. 2, vol. xii. p. 350 sq.); *Schodde*, Book of Enoch, p. 20 sqq.]) the name ' *son of man* ' is employed to designate the person of the Messiah: 46, 2 sq.; 48, 2; 62, 7. 9. 14; 63, 11; 69, 26 sq.; 70, 1; 71, 17. (The chapters in which the name occurs are the work, if not of the first author of the book (as Ewald and Dillmann think [but see B. D. Am. ed. p. 740ᵇ; and Herzog as above p. 351]), at least of a Jewish writer (cf. *Schürer*, Neutest. Zeitgesch. § 32 V. 2 p. 626), certainly not (as Hilgenfeld, Volkmar, Keim, and others imagine) of a Christian interpolator.) In the language of the Jews in Jn. xii. 34 the titles Χριστός and υἱὸς τοῦ ἀνθρώπου are used as synonyms.   **3.** The title ὁ υἱὸς τοῦ ἀνθρώπου, *the Son of Man*, is used by Jesus of himself (speaking in the third person) in Mt. viii. 20; ix. 6; x. 23; xi. 19; xii. 8, 32, 40; xiii. 37, 41; xvi. 13, 27 sq.; xvii. 9, 12, 22; xviii. 11 Rec.; xix. 28; xx. 18, 28; xxiv. 27, 30, 37, 39, 44; xxiv. 30 (twice); xxv. 13 Rec., 31; xxvi. 2, 24, 45, 64; Mk. ii. 10, 28; viii. 31, 38; ix. 9, 12, 31; x. 33, 45; xiii. 26; xiv. 21, 41, 62; Lk. v. 24; vi. 5, 22; vii. 34; ix. 22, 26, 44, 56 Rec., 58; xi. 30; xii. 8, 10, 40; xvii. 22, 24, 26, 30; xviii. 8, 31; xix. 10; xxi. 27, 36; xxii. 22, 48, 69; xxiv. 7; Jn. i. 51 (52); iii. 13 sq.; vi. 27, 53, 62; viii. 28; xii. 23, 34; xiii. 31, (once without the article, Jn. v. 27), doubtless in order that (by recalling Dan. vii. 13 sq. — not, as some suppose, Ps. viii. 5) he might thus intimate his Messiahship (as is plain from such pass. as ὄψεσθε τ. υἱ. τ. ἀνθρ. . . . ἐρχόμενον ἐπὶ τῶν νεφελῶν τοῦ οὐρανοῦ, Mt. xxvi. 64; Mk. xiv. 62, cf. Dan. vii. 13; τὸν υἱ. τ. ἀνθρ. ἐρχόμενον ἐν τῇ βασιλείᾳ αὐτοῦ, Mt. xvi. 28; ὅταν καθίσῃ ὁ υἱ. τ. ἀνθρ. ἐπὶ θρόνου δόξης αὐτοῦ, Mt. xix. 28) ; and also (as appears to be the case at least fr. Mk. ii. 28, where ὁ υἱὸς τοῦ ἀνθρώπου stands in emphatic antithesis to the repeated ὁ ἄνθρωπος preceding), that he might designate himself as the head of the human race, *the* man κατ' ἐξοχήν, the one who both furnished the pattern of the perfect man and acted on behalf of all mankind. Christ seems to have preferred this to the other Messianic titles, because by its lowliness it was least suited to foster the expectation of an earthly Messiah in royal splendor. There are no traces of the application of the name to Jesus in the apostolic age except in the speech of Stephen, Acts vii. 56, and that of James, the brother of Jesus, in a fragment from Hegesippus given in Eus. h. e. 2, 23 (25), 13, each being a reminiscence of the words of Jesus in Mt. xxvi. 64, (to which may be added, fr. the apostolic fathers, Ignat. ad Ephes. 20, 2 ἐν Ἰησοῦ Χριστῷ τῷ κατὰ σάρκα ἐκ γένους Δαυίδ, τῷ υἱῷ ἀνθρώπου καὶ υἱῷ θεοῦ). This disuse was owing no doubt to the fact that the term did not seem to be quite congruous with the divine nature and celestial majesty of Christ; hence in Barn. ep. 12, 10 we read, Ἰησοῦς οὐχ υἱὸς ἀνθρώπου (i. e. like Joshua), ἀλλ' υἱὸς τοῦ θεοῦ [cf. Harnack's note on the pass.]. On this title, see esp. Holtzmann in Hilgenfeld's Zeitschr. für wissenschaftl. Theol., 1865, p. 212 sqq.; Keim ii. p. 65 sqq. [(Eng. trans. vol. iii. p. 79 sqq.); Immer, Theol. d. N. T. p. 105 sqq.; Westcott, Com. on Jn. p. 33 sq.; and other reff. in Meyer on Mt. viii. 20; B. D. Am. ed. s. v. Son of Man].*

υἱὸς τοῦ θεοῦ, *son of God*;   **1.** in a physical sense, in various applications: originating by direct creation, not begotten by man, — as the first man Adam, Lk. iii. 38; Jesus, begotten of the Holy Ghost without the intervention of a human father, Lk. i. 35; in a heathen sense, as uttered by the Roman centurion of Jesus, a 'demigod' or 'hero', Mt. xxvii. 54; Mk. xv. 39.   **2.** in a metaphysical sense, in various applications: plur., of men, who although the issue of human parents yet could not come into being without the volition of God, the primary author of all things, Heb. ii. 10, cf. vss. 11, 13; of men as partaking of immortal life after the resurrection, and thus becoming more closely related to God, Lk. xx. 36; of angels, as beings superior to men, and more closely akin to God, Deut. xxxii. 43; for בְּנֵי אֱלֹהִים in Sept. of Gen. vi. 2, 4; Ps. xxviii. (xxix.) 1; lxxxviii. (lxxxix.) 7 (a phrase which in Job i. 6; ii. 1; xxxviii. 7 is translated ἄγγελοι θεοῦ); in the highest sense Jesus Christ is called ὁ υἱὸς τοῦ θεοῦ as of a nature superhuman and closest to God: Ro. i. 4; viii. 3; Gal. iv. 4; and esp. in the Ep. to the Heb., i. 2 (1), 5, 8; iii. 6; iv. 14; v. 5, 8; vi. 6; vii. 3, 28; x. 29. [Cf. B. D. s.v. Son of God, and reff. in Am. ed.]   **3.** in a theocratic sense: of kings and magistrates, as vicegerents of God the supreme ruler, 2 S. vii. 14; Ps. ii. 7; υἱοὶ ὑψίστου, Ps. lxxxi. (lxxxii.) 6; πρωτότοκος (sc. τοῦ θεοῦ), of the king of Israel, Ps. lxxxviii. (lxxxix.) 28. In accordance with Ps. ii. 7 and 2 S. vii. 14, the Jews called the Messiah ὁ υἱὸς τοῦ θεοῦ pre-eminently, as the supreme representative of God, and equipped for his office with the fulness of the Holy Spirit, i. e. endued with divine power beyond any of the sons of men, Enoch 105, 2. In the N. T. it is used of Jesus — in the utterances of the devil, Mt. iv. 3, 6; Lk. iv. 3, 9; in passages where Jesus is addressed by this title, Mt. viii. 29; xiv. 33; xxvii. 40, 43; Mk. iii. 11; v. 7; Lk. iv. 41; viii. 28; xxii. 70; Jn. xix. 7; Acts viii. 37 Rec.; ix. 20; xiii. 33; υἱὸς τοῦ ὑψίστου, Lk. i. 32; in the language of Jesus concerning himself, Mt. xxviii. 19; Jn. ix. 35; x. 36, cf. Mt. xxi. 37 sq.; Mk. xii. 6; besides, in Rev. ii. 18; ὁ υἱ. τ. θ., (ὁ) βασιλεὺς τοῦ Ἰσραήλ, Jn. i. 49 (50); ὁ Χριστὸς ὁ υἱ. τ. θ., Mt. xxvi. 63; Jn. xi. 27; Ἰησοῦς Χριστὸς υἱ. τ. [L Tr WH marg. om. τοῦ] θ. Mk. i. 1 [here T WH txt. om.

(see WH. App. p. 23)]; ὁ Χριστὸς ὁ υἱὸς τοῦ εὐλογητοῦ, Mk. xiv. 61; with the added e t h i c a l idea of one who enjoys intimate intercourse with God: ὁ Χριστὸς ὁ υἱ. τ. θεοῦ ζῶντος, Mt. xvi. 16, and Rec. in Jn. vi. 69. in the solemn utterances of God concerning Jesus: ὁ υἱός μου ὁ ἀγαπητός, Mt. iii. 17; xvii. 5; Mk. i. 11; ix. 7; Lk. iii. 22; ix. 35 [R G L txt.]; 2 Pet. i. 17, cf. Mt. ii. 15.   **4.** in an e t h i c a l sense with very various reference; *those whom God esteems as sons*, whom he loves, protects and benefits above others: so of the Jews, Deut. xiv. 1; Sap. xii. 19 sqq.; xviii. 4; υἱοὶ καὶ θυγατέρες τοῦ θεοῦ, Is. xliii. 6; Sap. ix. 7; πρωτότοκος τοῦ θεοῦ, Ex. iv. 22; in the N. T. of Christians, Ro. ix. 26; Rev. xxi. 7; *those whose character God, as a loving father, shapes by chastisement*, Heb. xii. 5–8; *those who revere God as their father*, the pious worshippers of God, Sap. ii. 13 [here π α ῖ ς κυρίου], 18; *those who in character and life resemble God* (Sir. v. 10 υἱοὶ ὑψίστου; [cf. Epict. dissert. 1, 9, 6]): Mt. v. 9, 45; υἱοὶ ὑψίστου, Lk. vi. 35; υἱοὶ κ. θυγατέρες, spoken of Christians, 2 Co. vi. 18; *those who are governed by the Spirit of God*, Ro. viii. 14 (ὅσοι πνεύματι θεοῦ ἄγονται, οὗτοι υἱοί εἰσι τοῦ θεοῦ), repose the same calm and joyful trust in God which children do in their parents, Ro. viii. 14 sqq.; Gal. iii. 26; iv. 6 sq., and hereafter in the blessedness and glory of the life eternal will openly wear this dignity of sons of God, Ro. viii. 19 (ἀποκάλυψις τῶν υἱῶν τοῦ θεοῦ), cf. 1 Jn. iii. 2, (see τέκνον, b. γ. [and reff.]). pre-eminently of *Jesus, as enjoying the supreme love of God, united to him in affectionate intimacy, privy to his saving counsels, obedient to the Father's will in all his acts*: Mt. xi. 27; Lk. x. 22; Jn. iii. 35 sq.; v. 19 sq. In many passages of the writings of John and of Paul, this ethical sense so blends with the metaphysical and the theocratic, that it is often very difficult to decide which of these elements is predominant in a particular case: Jn. i. 34; iii. 17; v. 21–23, 25 sq.; vi. 40; viii. 35 sq.; xi. 4; xiv. 13; xvii. 1; 1 Jn. i. 3, 7; ii. 22–24; iii. 8, 23; iv. 10, 14 sq.; v. 5, 9–13, 20; 2 Jn. 3, 9; Ro. i. 3, 9; v. 10; viii. 3, 29, 32; 1 Co. i. 9; xv. 28; 2 Co. i. 19; Gal. i. 16; ii. 20; Eph. iv. 13; 1 Th. i. 10; ὁ υἱὸς τῆς ἀγάπης αὐτοῦ (i. e. God's), Col. i. 13; ὁ Χριστὸς ὁ υἱ. τ. θ. Jn. xx. 31; ὁ μονογενὴς υἱ., Jn. i. 18 [here Tr WH μονογ. θεός, L mrg. ὁ μ. θ. (see μονογ. and reff.)]; iii. 18; ὁ υἱ. τ. θ. ὁ μονογ., iii. 16; 1 Jn. iv. 9, (see μονογενής). It can hardly be doubted that a reverent regard for the transcendent difference which separates Christ from all those who by his grace are exalted to the dignity of sons of God led John always to call Christians τέκνα τοῦ θεοῦ, not as Paul does υἱοί and τέκνα τοῦ θεοῦ indiscriminately; the like reverence moved Luther to translate the plur. υἱοί τ. θ. everywhere by *Kinder Gottes*; [cf., however, τέκνον, b. γ. and reff.].   This appellation is not found in 2 Th., Phil., Philem., the Pastoral Epp., nor in 1 Pet. or in the Ep. of James.*

ὕλη, -ης, ἡ, *a forest, a wood; felled wood, fuel*: Jas. iii. 5. (From Hom. down; Sept.) *

ὑμεῖς, see σύ.

Ὑμέναιος [on its accent cf. W. § 6, 1 l.; Chandler

*For 5209 & 5210 see 4771.

§ 253], -ου, ὁ, ('Υμήν, -ένος, ὁ, the god of marriage), Hymenæus, a heretic, one of the opponents of the apostle Paul: 1 Tim. i. 20; 2 Tim. ii. 17. [B. D. s. v.]*

5212 ὑμέτερος, -α, -ον, (ὑμεῖς), possess. pron. of the 2d pers. plur., *your, yours*; **a.** *possessed by you*: with substantives, Jn. viii. 17; 2 Co. viii. 8 [Rec.ᵉˡᶻ ἡμετ.]; Gal. vi. 13; neut. τὸ ὑμ. substantively, opp. to τὸ ἀλλότριον, Lk. xvi. 12 [(WH txt. τὸ ἡμέτ.); cf. W. § 61, 3 a.]. **b.** *allotted to you*: ὑμ. σωτηρία, Acts xxvii. 34; τὸ ὑμ. ἔλεος, Ro. xi. 31; ὁ καιρὸς ὁ ὑμέτ., the time appointed, opportune, for you, Jn. vii. 6; as a predicate, ὑμετέρα ἐστὶν ἡ βασιλεία τοῦ θεοῦ, Lk. vi. 20. **c.** *proceeding from you*: τὸν ὑμέτ. sc. λόγον, Jn. xv. 20; [1 Co. xvi. 17 L T Tr WH txt.]. **d.** objectively (see ἐμός, c. β.; [W. § 22, 7; B. § 132, 3]): ὑμετέρα (Rec.ˢᵗ ἡμετ.) καύχησις, glorying in you, 1 Co. xv. 31. [On the use of the word in the N. T. cf. B. § 127, 21.]*

5214 ὑμνέω, -ῶ: impf. ὕμνουν; fut. ὑμνήσω; 1 aor. ptcp. ὑμνήσας; (ὕμνος); fr. Hes. down; Sept. often for הָלַל, זָמַר הֵשִׁיר, הוֹרָה; **1.** trans. *to sing the praise of, sing hymns to*: τινά, Acts xvi. 25; Heb. ii. 12. **2.** intrans. *to sing a hymn, to sing*: Mt. xxvi. 30; Mk. xiv. 26, (in both pass. of the singing of the paschal hymns; these were Pss. cxiii.–cxviii. and Ps. cxxxvi., which the Jews call the 'great Hallel', [but see *Ginsburg* in Kitto s. v. Hallel; *Edersheim*, The Temple etc. p. 191 sq.; Buxtorf (ed. Fischer) p. 314 sq.]); Ps. lxiv. (lxv.) 13 (14); 1 Macc. xiii. 47.*

5215 ὕμνος, -ου, ὁ, in Grk. writ. fr. Hom. down, *a song in praise of gods, heroes, conquerors*, [cf. Trench as below, p. 297], but in the Scriptures *of God*; *a sacred song, hymn*: plur., Eph. v. 19; Col. iii. 16. (1 Macc. iv. 33; 2 Macc. i. 30; x. 7; [Jud. xvi. 13], etc.; of the Psalms of David, Joseph. antt. 7, 12, 3; for תְּהִלָּה, Ps. xxxix. (xl.) 4; lxiv. (lxv.) 2; for שִׁיר, Is. xlii. 10.)*

[SYN. ὕμνος, ψαλμός, ᾠδή: ᾠδή is the generic term; ψαλμ. and ὕμν. are specific, the former designating a song which took its general character from the O. T. 'Psalms' (although not restricted to them, see 1 Co. xiv. 15, 26), the latter a song of praise. "While the leading idea of ψαλμ. is a musical accompaniment, and that of ὕμν. praise to God, ᾠδή is the general word for a song, whether accompanied or unaccompanied, whether of praise or on any other subject. Thus it was quite possible for the same song to be at once ψαλμός, ὕμνος and ᾠδή" (Bp. Lghtft. on Col. iii. 16). The words occur together in Col. iii. 16 and Eph. v. 19. See *Trench*, Syn. c. lxxviii.]

5217 ὑπ-άγω; impf. ὑπῆγον; **1.** trans. *to lead under, bring under*, (Lat. *subducere*); so in various applications in the Grk. writ. fr. Hom. down; once in the Scriptures, ὑπήγαγε κύριος τὴν θάλασσαν, for הוֹלִיךְ, he caused to recede, drove back, the sea, Ex. xiv. 21. **2.** in the N. T. always intrans. (less freq. so in prof. auth. fr. Hdt. down), (Lat. *se subducere*) *to withdraw one's self, to go away, depart*, [cf. ἄγω, 4; and see B. 204 (177)]: absol., Mk. vi. 33; Lk. viii. 42 (where L Tr mrg. πορεύεσθαι); xvii. 14; Jn. viii. 21; xiv. 5, 28, (Tob. xii. 5); οἱ ἐρχόμενοι καὶ οἱ ὑπάγοντες, coming and going, Mk. vi. 31; ὑπάγει κ. πωλεῖ, Mt. xiii. 44; ὑπῆγον κ. ἐπίστευον, Jn. xii.

11; [ἵνα ὑπάγητε κ. καρπὸν φέρητε, Jn. xv. 16]; ἀφίημί τινα ὑπάγειν, to permit one to depart freely wherever he wishes, Jn. xi. 44; xviii. 8; ὕπαγε is used by one in dismissing another: Mt. [iv. 10 R T Tr WH]; viii. 13; xx. 14; Mk. [ii. 9 Tdf.]; vii. 29; x. 52; with εἰς εἰρήνην added, Mk. v. 34; ὑπάγετε ἐν εἰρήνῃ, Jas. ii. 16; or in sending one somewhere to do something, Lk. x. 3; plur. Mt. viii. 32; with oriental circumstantiality (see ἀνίστημι, II. 1 c.) ὕπαγε is prefixed to the imperatives of other verbs: Mt. v. 24; viii. 4; [xviii. 15 G L T Tr WH]; xix. 21; xxi. 28; xxvii. 65; xxviii. 10; Mk. i. 44; x. 21; xvi. 7; Jn. iv. 16; ix. 7; Rev. x. 8; with καί inserted, Mt. xviii. 15 Rec.; Mk. vi. 38 [T Tr WH om. T br. καί]; Rev. xvi. 1. Particularly, ὑπάγω is used to denote the final departure of one who ceases to be another's companion or attendant, Jn. vi. 67; euphemistically, of one who departs from life, Mt. xxvi. 24; Mk. xiv. 21. with designations of place: ποῦ (for ποῖ [W. § 54, 7; B. 71 (62)]), Jn. xii. 35; xiv. 5; xvi. 5; 1 Jn. ii. 11; opp. to ἔρχεσθαι, to come, Jn. iii. 8; viii. 14; ὅπου (for ὅποι [W. and B. u. s.]), Jn. viii. 21 sq.; xiii. 33, 36; xiv. 4; Rev. xiv. 4; ἐκεῖ, Jn. xi. 8; πρὸς τὸν πέμψαντά με, πρὸς τὸν πατέρα, πρὸς τὸν θεόν, to depart (from earth) to the father (in heaven) is used by Jesus of himself, Jn. vii. 33; xiii. 3; xvi. 5, 10, 16 [T Tr WH om. L br. the cl.], 17; foll. by εἰς with an acc. of the place, Mt. ix. 6; xx. 4, 7; Mk. ii. 11; xi. 2; xiv. 13; Lk. xix. 30; Jn. vi. 21 [cf. B. 283 (243)]; vii. 3; ix. 11; xi. 31; εἰς αἰχμαλωσίαν, Rev. xiii. 10; εἰς ἀπώλειαν, Rev. xvii. 8, 11; foll. by εἰς w. an acc. of the place and πρός τινα, Mt. xxvi. 18; Mk. v. 19; ὑπάγω ἐπί τινα, Lk. xii. 58; ὑπάγω with an inf. denoting the purpose, Jn. xxi. 3; μετά τινος with an acc. of the way, Mt. v. 41. On the phrase ὕπαγε ὀπίσω μου [Mt. iv. 10 G L br.; xvi. 23; Mk. viii. 33; Lk. iv. 8 R L in br.], see ὀπίσω, 2 a. fin.*

5218 ὑπ-ακοή, -ῆς, ἡ, (fr. ὑπακούω, q. v.), *obedience, compliance, submission*, (opp. to παρακοή): absol. εἰς ὑπακοήν, *unto obedience* i. e. to obey, Ro. vi. 16 [cf. W. 612 (569); B. § 151, 28 d.]; obedience rendered to any one's counsels: with a subject. gen., 2 Co. vii. 15; x. 6; Philem. 21; with a gen. of the object, —of the thing to which one submits himself, τῆς πίστεως (see πίστις, 1 b. a. p. 513ᵇ), Ro. i. 5; xvi. 26; τῆς ἀληθείας, 1 Pet. i. 22; of the person, τοῦ Χριστοῦ, 2 Co. x. 5; the obedience of one who conforms his conduct to God's commands, absol. 1 Pet. i. 2; opp. to ἁμαρτία, Ro. vi. 16; τέκνα ὑπακοῆς, i. e. ὑπήκοοι, 1 Pet. i. 14; with a subjective gen. Ro. xv. 18; an obedience shown in observing the requirements of Christianity, ὑπ. ὑμῶν, i. e. contextually, *the report concerning your obedience*, Ro. xvi. 19; the obedience with which Christ followed out the saving purpose of God, esp. by his sufferings and death: absol. Heb. v. 8; with a gen. of the subject, Ro. v. 19. (The word is not found in prof. auth.; nor in the Sept., except in 2 S. xxii. 36 with the sense of favorable *hearing*; in 2 S. xxiii. 23 Aq. we find ὁ ἐπὶ ὑπακοὴν τινος, Vulg. *qui alicui est a secretis*, where it bears its primary and proper signification of *listening*; see ὑπακούω.)*

*For 5213 & 5216 see 4771.

5219 ὑπ-ακούω; impf. ὑπήκουον; 1 aor. ὑπήκουσα; fr. Hom. down; to listen, hearken; **1.** prop.: of one who on a knock at the door comes to listen who it is, (the duty of the porter), Acts xii. 13 [where A. V. hearken, R. V. answer] (Xen. symp. 1, 11; Plat. Crito p. 43 a.; Phaedo p. 59 e.; Dem., Lcian., Plut., al.). **2.** to hearken to a command, i. e. to obey, be obedient unto, submit to, (so in Grk. writ. fr. Hdt. down): absol. Phil. ii. 12 [cf. W. 594 (552)]; ὑπήκουσεν ἐξελθεῖν, [R. V. obeyed to go out i. e.] went out obediently, Heb. xi. 8; with a dat. of the pers. (in Grk. writ. also w. a gen.), Mt. viii. 27; Mk. i. 27; iv. 41; Lk. viii. 25; xvii. 6; Ro. vi. 16; Eph. vi. 1, 5; Col. iii. 20, 22; Heb. v. 9; 1 Pet. iii. 6; with a dat. of the thing, τῇ πίστει (see πίστις, 1 b. a. p. 513ᵇ near top), Acts vi. 7; ὑπηκούσατε εἰς ὃν παρεδόθητε τύπον διδαχῆς, by attraction for τῷ τύπῳ τῆς διδαχῆς εἰς ὃν κτλ. [W. § 24, 2 b.; cf. τύπος, 3], Ro. vi. 17; τῷ εὐαγγελίῳ, Ro. x. 16; 2 Th. i. 8; τῷ λόγῳ, 2 Th. iii. 14; τῇ ἁμαρτίᾳ (Rec.), ταῖς ἐπιθυμίαις (L T Tr WH), i. e. to allow one's self to be captivated by, governed by, etc., Ro. vi. 12.*

5220 ὕπανδρος, -ον, (ὑπό and ἀνήρ), under i. e. subject to a man: γυνή, married, Ro. vii. 2. (Num. v. [20], 29; Sir. ix. 9; [Prov. vi. 24]; xli. 21; Polyb. 10, 26, 3; [Diod. 32, 10, 4 vol. v. 50, 17 ed. Dind.]; Plut., Artem., Heliod.)*

5221 ὑπ-αντάω, -ῶ: 1 aor. ὑπήντησα; to go to meet, to meet: τινί, Mt. viii. 28; Lk. viii. 27; Jn. xi. 20, 30; xii. 18; also L T Tr WH in Mk. v. 2; Jn. iv. 51; and T Tr WH in Mt. xxviii. 9; Acts xvi. 16; [and T in Lk. xvii. 12 (so WH mrg. but without the dat.)]; in a military reference, of a hostile meeting: Lk. xiv. 31 L T Tr WH. (Pind., Soph., Eur., Xen., Joseph., Plut., Hdian., al.)*

5222 ὑπ-άντησις, -εως, ἡ, (ὑπαντάω), a going to meet: Jn. xii. 13, and L T Tr WH in Mt. viii. 34 [B. § 146, 3] and xxv. 1 [cf. B. l. c.]. (Judg. xi. 34; Joseph. antt. 11, 8, 4; App. b. c. 4, 6.)*

5223 ὕπαρξις, -εως, ἡ, (ὑπάρχω, q. v.), [fr. Aristot. down], possessions, goods, wealth, property, (i. q. τὰ ὑπάρχοντα): Acts ii. 45; Heb. x. 34, (for רְכוּשׁ, 2 Chr. xxxv. 7; Dan. xi. 24 Theodot.; for מִקְנֶה, Ps. lxxvii. (lxxviii.) 48; Jer. ix. 10; for הוֹן, Prov. xviii. 11; xix. 14; Polyb., Dion. Hal., Diod., Plut., Artem.).*

5225 ὑπ-άρχω; impf. ὑπῆρχον; **1.** prop. to begin below, to make a beginning; univ. to begin; (Hom., Aeschyl., Hdt., sqq.). **2.** to come forth, hence to be there, be ready, be at hand, (Aeschyl., Hdt., Pind., sqq.): univ. and simply, Acts xix. 40 [cf. B. § 151, 29 note]; xxvii. 12, 21; ἔν τινι, to be found in one, Acts xxviii. 18; with a dat. of the pers. ὑπάρχει μοί τι, something is mine, I have something: Acts iii. 6; iv. 37; xxviii. 7; 2 Pet. i. 8 (where Lchm. παρόντα; Sir. xx. 16; Prov. xvii. 17; Job ii. 4, etc.); τὰ ὑπάρχοντα, one's substance, one's property, Lk. viii. 3; xii. 15 L txt. T Tr WH; Acts iv. 32, (Gen. xxxi. 18; Tob. iv. 8; Dio C. 38, 40); also τὰ ὑπ. τινος, Mt. xix. 21; xxiv. 47; xxv. 14; Lk. xi. 21; xii. 15 R G L mrg., 33, 44 [here L mrg. Tr mrg. the dat.]; xiv. 33; xvi. 1; xix. 8; 1 Co. xiii. 3; Heb. x. 34, (often in Sept. for מִקְנֶה, רְכוּשׁ; נְכָסִים, Sir. xli. 1; Tob. i. 20, etc.; τὰ ἴδια ὑπάρχοντα, Polyb. 4, 3, 1). **3.** to be.

*For 5224 see 5225.

with a predicate nom. (as often in Attic) [cf. B. § 144, 14, 15 a., 18; W. 350 (328)]: as ἄρχων τῆς συναγωγῆς ὑπῆρχεν, Lk. viii. 41; add, Lk. ix. 48; Acts vii. 55; viii. 16; xvi. 3; xix. 36; xxi. 20; 1 Co. vii. 26; xii. 22; Jas. ii. 15; 2 Pet. iii. 11; the ptcp. with a predicate nom., being i. e. who is etc., since or although he etc. is: Lk. xvi. 14; xxiii. 50; Acts ii. 30; iii. 2; xiv. 8 Rec.; xvii. 24; [xxii. 3]; Ro. iv. 19; 1 Co. xi. 7; 2 Co. viii. 17; xii. 16; Gal. i. 14; ii. 14; plur., Lk. xi. 13; Acts xvi. 20, 37; xvii. 29; 2 Pet. ii. 19. ὑπάρχειν foll. by ἐν w. a dat. of the thing, to be contained in, Acts x. 12; to be in a place, Phil. iii. 20; in some state, Lk. xvi. 23; ἐν τῇ ἐξουσίᾳ τινός, to be left in one's power or disposal, Acts v. 4; ἐν ἱματισμῷ ἐνδόξῳ καὶ τρυφῇ, to be gorgeously apparelled and to live delicately, Lk. vii. 25; ἐν μορφῇ θεοῦ ὑπάρχειν, to be in the form of God (see μορφή), Phil. ii. 6 [here R.V. mrg. Gr. being originally (?; yet cf. 1 Co. xi. 7)]; foll. by ἐν with a dat. plur. of the pers., among, Acts iv. 34 R G; 1 Co. xi. 18. ὑπ. μακρὰν ἀπό τινος, Acts xvii. 27; πρὸς τῆς σωτηρίας, to be conducive to safety, Acts xxvii. 34. [COMP.: προ- ὑπάρχω.] *

5226 ὑπ-είκω; fr. Hom. down; to resist no longer, but to give way, yield, (prop. of combatants); metaph. to yield to authority and admonition, to submit: Heb. xiii. 17.*

5227 ὑπ-εναντίος, -α, -ον; **a.** opposite to; set over against: ἵπποι ὑπεν. ἀλλήλοις, meeting one another, Hes. scut. 347. **b.** trop. (Plat., Aristot., Plut., al.), opposed to, contrary to: τινί, Col. ii. 14 [where see Bp. Lghtft.]; ὁ ὑπεν. as subst. (Xen., Polyb., Plut.), an adversary, Heb. x. 27, cf. Sept. Is. xxvi. 11, (Sept. for אוֹיֵב (צָר); often in the O. T. Apocr.*

5228 ὑπέρ, [cf. Eng. up, over, etc.], Lat. super, over, a preposition, which stands before either the gen. or the acc. according as it is used to express the idea of state and rest or of motion over and beyond a place.

I. with the GENITIVE; cf. W. 382 (358) sq. **1.** prop. of place, i. e. of position, situation, extension: over, above, beyond, across. In this sense it does not occur in the N. T.; but there it always, though joined to other classes of words, has a tropical signification derived from its original meaning. **2.** i. q. Lat. pro, for, i. e. for one's safety, for one's advantage or benefit, (one who does a thing for another, is conceived of as standing or bending 'over' the one whom he would shield or defend [cf. W. u. s.]): προσεύχομαι ὑπέρ τ. Mt. v. 44; Lk. vi. 28 [T Tr mrg. WH περί (see 6 below)]; Col. i. 3 L Tr WH mrg. (see 6 below); [Jas. v. 16 L Tr mrg. WH txt.], 9; εὔχομαι, Jas. v. 16 [R G T Tr txt. WH mrg.]; after δέομαι, Acts viii. 24; and nouns denoting prayer, as δέησις, Ro. x. 1; 2 Co. i. 11; ix. 14; Phil. i. 4; Eph. vi. 19; προσευχή, Acts xii. 5 (here L T Tr WH περί [see 6 below]; Ro. xv. 30; 1 Tim. ii. 1, 2; εἶναι ὑπέρ τ. (opp. to κατά τινος), to be for one i. e. to be on one's side, to favor and further one's cause, Mk. ix. 40; Lk. ix. 50; Ro. viii. 31, cf. 2 Co. xiii. 8; τὸ ὑπέρ τ. that which is for one's advantage, Phil. iv. 10 [but see ἀναθάλλω and φρονέω, fin.]; ἐντυγχάνω and ὑπερεντυγχάνω, Ro. viii. 26 R G, 27, 34; Heb. vii. 25, cf. ix. 24; λέγω, Acts xxvi. 1

R WH txt. [see 6 below]; μεριμνῶ, 1 Co. xii. 25; ἀγρυπνῶ, Heb. xiii. 17; ἀγωνίζομαι ἐν ταῖς προσευχαῖς, Col. iv. 12, cf. Ro. xv. 30; πρεσβεύω, Eph. vi. 20; 2 Co. v. 20; with subst.: ζῆλος, 2 Co. vii. 7; [Col. iv. 13 Rec.]; πόνος, Col. iv. 13 [G L T Tr WH]; σπουδή, 2 Co. vii. 12; viii. 16; διάκονος, Col. i. 7; to offer offerings for, Acts xxi. 26; to enter the heavenly sanctuary for (used of Christ), Heb. vi. 20; ἀρχιερέα καθίστασθαι, Heb. v. 1; after the ideas of suffering, dying, giving up life, etc.: Ro. ix. 3; xvi. 4; 2 Co. xii. 15; after τὴν ψυχὴν τιθέναι (ὑπέρ τινος), in order to avert ruin, death, etc., from one, Jn. x. 11; xiii. 37 sq.; of Christ dying to procure salvation for his own, Jn. x. 15; xv. 13; 1 Jn. iii. 16; Christ is said τὸ αἷμα αὐτοῦ ἐκχύνειν, pass., Mk. xiv. 24 L T Tr WH [see 6 below]; Lk. xxii. 20 [WH reject the pass.]; ἀπολέσθαι, Jn. xviii. 14 Rec.; ἀποθνήσκειν, Jn. xi. 50 sqq.; [xviii. 14 L T Tr WH]; Acts xxi. 13; Ro. v. 7; of Christ undergoing death for man's salvation, Ro. v. 6, 8; xiv. 15; 1 Th. v. 10 [here T Tr WH txt. περί (see 6 below); 1 Pet. iii. 18 L T Tr WH txt.]; γενέσθαι θανάτου, Heb. ii. 9; σταυρωθῆναι, 1 Co. i. 13 (here L txt. Tr mrg. WH mrg. περί [see 6 below]; [of God giving up his Son, Ro. viii. 32]; παραδιδόναι τινὰ ἑαυτόν, Gal. ii. 20; Eph. v. 2, 25; διδόναι ἑαυτόν, Tit. ii. 14; with a predicate accus. added, ἀντίλυτρον, 1 Tim. ii. 6; τὸ σῶμα αὐτοῦ διδόναι, pass. Lk. xxii. 19 [WH reject the pass.], cf. 1 Co. xi. 24; τυθῆναι (θυθῆναι, see θύω, init.), 1 Co. v. 7; παθεῖν, 1 Pet. ii. 21; iii. 18 [R G WH mrg.; iv. 1 R G]; ἁγιάζειν ἑαυτόν, Jn. xvii. 19. Since what is done for one's advantage frequently cannot be done without acting in his stead (just as the apostles teach that the death of Christ inures to our salvation because it has the force of an expiatory sacrifice and was suffered in our stead), we easily understand how ὑπέρ, like the Lat. pro and our for, comes to signify **3.** in the place of, instead of, (which is more precisely expressed by ἀντί; hence the two prepositions are interchanged by Irenaeus, adv. haer. 5, 1, τῷ ἰδίῳ αἵματι λυτρωσαμένου ἡμᾶς τοῦ κυρίου καὶ δόντος τὴν ψυχὴν ὑπὲρ τῶν ἡμετέρων ψυχῶν καὶ τὴν σάρκα τὴν ἑαυτοῦ ἀντὶ τῶν ἡμετέρων σαρκῶν): ἵνα ὑπὲρ σοῦ μοι διακονῇ, Philem. 13; ὑπὲρ τῶν νεκρῶν βαπτίζεσθαι (see βαπτίζω, fin.), 1 Co. xv. 29; [add, Col. i. 7 L txt. Tr txt. WH txt.]; in expressions concerning the death of Christ: εἷς ὑπὲρ πάντων ἀπέθανεν (for the inference is drawn ἄρα οἱ πάντες ἀπέθανον, i. e. all are reckoned as dead), 2 Co. v. 14 (15), 15; add, 21; Gal. iii. 13. [On this debated sense of ὑπέρ, see Meyer and Van Hengel on Ro. v. 6; Ellicott on Gal. and Philem. ll. cc.; Wieseler on Gal. i. 4; Trench, Syn. § lxxxii.; W. 383 (358) note.] Since anything whether of an active or passive character which is undertaken on behalf of a person or thing is undertaken 'on account of' that person or thing, ὑπέρ is used **4.** of the impelling or moving cause; on account of, for the sake of, any person or thing: ὑπὲρ τῆς τοῦ κόσμου ζωῆς, to procure (true) life for mankind, Jn. vi. 51; to do or suffer anything ὑπὲρ τοῦ ὀνόματος θεοῦ, Ἰησοῦ, τοῦ κυρίου: Acts v. 41; ix. 16; xv. 26; xxi. 13; Ro. i. 5; 3 Jn. 7; πάσχειν ὑπὲρ τοῦ Χριστοῦ, Phil. i.

29; ὑπὲρ τῆς βασιλείας τοῦ θεοῦ, 2 Th. i. 5; στενοχωρίαι ὑπὲρ τοῦ Χριστοῦ, 2 Co. xii. 10 [it is better to connect ὑπέρ etc. here with εὐδοκῶ]; ἀποθνήσκειν ὑπὲρ θεοῦ, Ignat. ad Rom. 4. examples with a gen. of the thing are, Jn. xi. 4; Ro. xv. 8; 2 Co. i. 6; xii. 19; ὑπὲρ τῆς εὐδοκίας, to satisfy (his) good-pleasure, Phil. ii. 13; with a gen. of the pers., 2 Co. i. 6; Eph. iii. 1, 13; Col. i. 24; δοξάζειν, εὐχαριστεῖν ὑπέρ τ. (gen. of the thing), Ro. xv. 9; 1 Co. x. 30; ὑπὲρ πάντων, for all favors, Eph. v. 20; εὐχαριστεῖν ὑπέρ with a gen. of the pers., Ro. i. 8 (here L T Tr WH περί [see 6 below]); 2 Co. i. 11; Eph. i. 16; ἀγῶνα ἔχειν ὑπέρ with a gen. of the pers. Col. ii. 1 L T Tr WH [see 6 below]; ὑπὲρ (τῶν) ἁμαρτιῶν (or ἀγνοημάτων), to offer sacrifices, Heb. v. 1, 3 (here L T Tr WH περί [see 6 below]); vii. 27; ix. 7; x. 12; ἀποθανεῖν, of Christ, 1 Co. xv. 3; ἑαυτὸν δοῦναι, Gal. i. 4 R WH txt. [see 6 below]. **5.** Like the Lat. super (cf. Klotz, HWB. d. Lat. Spr. ii. p. 1497b; [Harpers' Lat. Dict. s. v. II. B. 2 b.]), it freq. refers to the object under consideration, concerning, of, as respects, with regard to, ([cf. B. § 147, 21]; exx. fr. prof. auth. are given in W. 383 (358 sq.)); so after καυχᾶσθαι, καύχημα, καύχησις, [R. V. on behalf of]: 2 Co. v. 12; vii. 4, 14; viii. 24; ix. 2 sq.; xii. 5; 2 Th. i. 4 [here L T Tr WH ἐγ- (or ἐν-) καυχᾶσθαι]; φυσιοῦσθαι, 1 Co. iv. 6 [al. refer this to 4 above; see Meyer ed. Heinrici (cf. φυσιόω, 2 fin.)]; ἐλπίς, 2 Co. i. 7 (6); ἀγνοεῖν, 8 (here L T Tr WH mrg. περί [see 6 below]); φρονεῖν, Phil. i. 7 (2 Macc. xiv. 8); ἐρωτᾶν, 2 Th. ii. 1; κράζειν, to proclaim concerning, Ro. ix. 27; [παρακαλεῖν, 1 Th. iii. 2 G L T Tr WH (see 6 below)]; after εἰπεῖν, Jn. i. 30 L T Tr WH [see 6 below]; (so after verbs of saying, writing, etc., 2 S. xviii. 5; 2 Chr. xxxi. 9; Joel i. 3; Judith xv. 4; 1 Esdr. iv. 49; 2 Macc. xi. 35); εἴτε ὑπὲρ Τίτου, whether inquiry be made about Titus, 2 Co. viii. 23; ὑπὲρ τούτου, concerning this, 2 Co. xii. 8. **6.** In the N. T. Mss., as in those of prof. auth. also, the prepositions ὑπέρ and περί are confounded, [cf. W. 383 (358) note; § 50, 3; B. § 147, 21; Kühner § 435, I. 2 e.; Meisterhans § 49, 12; also Wieseler or Ellicott on Gal. as below; Meyer on 1 Co. xv. 3, (see περί I. c. δ.)]; this occurs in the foll. pass.: Mk. xiv. 24; [Lk. vi. 28]; Jn. i. 30; Acts xii. 5; xxvi. 1; Ro. i. 8; 1 Co. i. 13; 2 Co. i. 8; Gal. i. 4; Col. i. 3; ii. 1; [1 Th. iii. 2 v. 10]; Heb. v. 3. [For ὑπὲρ ἐκ περισσοῦ or ὑπὲρ ἐκπερισσοῦ, see ὑπερεκπερισσοῦ.]

II. with the ACCUSATIVE (cf. W. § 49, e.); over, beyond, away over; more than; **1.** prop. of the place 'over' or 'beyond' which, as in the Grk. writ. fr. Hom. down; not thus used in the N. T., where it is always **2.** metaph. of the measure or degree exceeded [cf. B. § 147, 21]; **a.** univ.: εἶναι ὑπέρ τινα, to be above i. e. superior to one, Mt. x. 24; Lk. vi. 40; τὸ ὄνομα τὸ ὑπὲρ πᾶν ὄνομα sc. ὄν, the name superior to every (other) name, Phil. ii. 9; κεφαλὴν ὑπὲρ πάντα sc. οὖσαν, the supreme head or lord [A.V. head over all things], Eph. i. 22; ὑπὲρ δοῦλον ὄντα, more than a servant, Philem. 16; more than [R. V. beyond], ibid. 21; ὑπὲρ πάντα, above (i. e. more and greater than) all, Eph.

iii. 20ᵃ; ὑπὲρ τὴν λαμπρότητα τοῦ ἡλίου, above (i. e. surpassing) the brightness of the sun, Acts xxvi. 13; more (to a greater degree) than, φιλεῖν τινα ὑπέρ τινα, Mt. x. 37 (exx. fr. prof. auth. are given by Fritzsche ad loc.); beyond, 1 Co. iv. 6; 2 Co. xii. 6; ὑπὲρ ὃ δύνασθε, beyond what ye are able, beyond your strength, 1 Co. x. 13 [cf. W. 590 (549)]; also ὑπὲρ δύναμιν, 2 Co. i. 8; opp. to κατὰ δύναμιν (as in Hom. Il. 3, 59 κατ᾽ αἶσαν, οὐδ᾽ ὑπὲρ αἶσαν, cf. 6, 487; 17, 321. 327), 2 Co. viii. 3 (where L T Tr WH παρὰ δύναμιν).   b. with words implying comparison: προκόπτειν, Gal. i. 14; of the measure beyond which one is reduced, ἡττᾶσθαι, 2 Co. xii. 13 [W. § 49 e.], (πλεονάζω, 1 Esdr. viii. 72; περισσεύω, 1 Macc. iii. 30; ὑπερβάλλω, Sir. xxv. 11); after comparatives i. q. than, Lk. xvi. 8; Heb. iv. 12, (Judg. xi. 25; 1 K. xix. 4; Sir. xxx. 17); cf. W. § 35, 2; [B. § 147, 21].   ὑπέρ is used adverbially; as, ὑπὲρ ἐγώ [L ὑπερεγώ (cf. W. 46 (45)), WH ὑπὲρ ἐγώ (cf. W. § 14, 2 Note)], much more (or in a much greater degree) I, 2 Co. xi. 23; cf. Kypke ad loc.; W. 423 (394). [For ὑπὲρ λίαν see ὑπερλίαν.]

III. In Composition ὑπέρ denotes   1. over, above, beyond: ὑπεράνω, ὑπερέκεινα, ὑπερεκτείνω.   2. excess of measure, more than: ὑπερεκπερισσοῦ, ὑπερνικάω.   3. aid, for; in defence of: ὑπερεντυγχάνω. Cf. Viger. ed. Hermann p. 668; Fritzsche on Rom. vol. i. p. 351; [Ellicott on Eph. iii. 20].*

^{see 5229 St.}   **ὑπερ-αίρω**: pres. mid. ὑπεραίρομαι; (ὑπέρ and αἴρω); to lift or raise up over some thing; mid. to lift one's self up, be exalted, be haughty: 2 Co. xii. 7 [R.V. to be exalted overmuch]; ἐπί τινα, above one, 2 Th. ii. 4; with a dat. incom. τινί, to carry one's self haughtily to, behave insolently towards one, 2 Macc. v. 23; (very variously in prof. auth. fr. Aeschyl. and Plato down).*

5230   **ὑπέρακμος, -ον**, (Vulg. superadultus);   1. beyond the ἀκμή or bloom of life, past prime, (Plat. de rep. 5 p. 460 e. ἆρ᾽ οὖν σοι ξυνδοκεῖ μέτριος χρόνος ἀκμῆς τὰ εἴκοσιν ἔτη γυναικί, ἀνδρὶ δὲ τὰ τριάκοντα): Eustath.   2. overripe, plump and ripe, (and so in greater danger of defilement): of a virgin [R. V. past the flower of her age], 1 Co. vii. 36.*

5231   **ὑπερ-άνω**, (ὑπέρ and ἄνω), adv., above: τινός [cf. W. § 54, 6], above a thing, — of place, Eph. iv. 10; Heb. ix. 5; of rank and power, Eph. i. 21. (Sept.; [Aristot.], Polyb., Joseph., Plut., Lcian., Ael., al., [W. § 50, 7 Note 1; B. § 146, 4].) *

5232   **ὑπερ-αυξάνω**; to increase beyond measure; to grow exceedingly: 2 Th. i. 3. [Andoc., Galen, Dio Cass., al.]*

5233   **ὑπερ-βαίνω**; fr. Hom. down; to step over, go beyond; metaph. to transgress: δίκην, νόμους, etc., often fr. Hdt. and Pind. down; absol. to overstep the proper limits i. e. to transgress, trespass, do wrong, sin: joined with ἁμαρτάνειν, Hom. Il. 9, 501; Plat. rep. 2 p. 366 a.; spec. of one who defrauds another in business, overreaches, (Luth. zu weit greifen), with καὶ πλεονεκτεῖν added, 1 Th. iv. 6 [but see πρᾶγμα, b.].*

5234   **ὑπερβαλλόντως**, (fr. the ptcp. of the verb ὑπερβάλλω, as ὄντως fr. ὤν), above measure: 2 Co. xi. 23. (Job xv. 11; Xen., Plat., Polyb., al.) *

ὑπερ-βάλλω; fr. Hom. down;   1. trans. to surpass in throwing; to throw over or beyond any thing.   2. intrans. to transcend, surpass, exceed, excel; ptcp. ὑπερβάλλων, excelling, exceeding; Vulg. [in Eph. i. 19; iii. 19] supereminens; (Aeschyl., Hdt., Eur., Isocr., Xen., Plat., al.): 2 Co. iii. 10; ix. 14; Eph. i. 19; ii. 7; with a gen. of the object surpassed (Aeschyl. Prom. 923; Plat. Gorg. p. 475 b.; cf. Matthiae § 358, 2), ἡ ὑπερβάλλουσα τῆς γνώσεως ἀγάπη Χριστοῦ, the love of Christ which passeth knowledge, Eph. iii. 19 [cf. W. 346 (324) note].*   ⁵²³⁵

ὑπερ-βολή, -ῆς, ἡ, (ὑπερβάλλω, q. v.), fr. Hdt. [8, 112, 4] and Thuc. down;   1. prop. a throwing beyond.   2. metaph. superiority, excellence, pre-eminence, [R. V. exceeding greatness]: with a gen. of the thing, 2 Co. iv. 7; xii. 7; καθ᾽ ὑπερβολήν, beyond measure, exceedingly, pre-eminently: Ro. vii. 13; 1 Co. xii. 31 [cf. W. § 54, 2 b.; B. § 125, 11 fin.]; 2 Co. i. 8; Gal. i. 13, (4 Macc. iii. 18; Soph. O. R. 1196; Isocr. p. 84 d. [i. e. πρὸς Φίλ. 5]; Polyb. 3, 92, 10; Diod. 2, 16; 17, 47); καθ᾽ ὑπ. εἰς ὑπερβολήν, beyond all measure, [R. V. more and more exceedingly], 2 Co. iv. 17.*   ⁵²³⁶

ὑπερ-εγώ [Lchm.], i. q. ὑπὲρ ἐγώ (see ὑπέρ, II. 2 c.): 2 Co. xi. 23. Cf. W. 46 (45).*   ^{see 5228}

ὑπερ-εῖδον; (see εἴδω); fr. Hdt. and Thuc. down; to overlook, take no notice of, not attend to: τί, Acts xvii. 30.*   ^{see 5237 St.}

ὑπερ-έκεινα, (i. q. ὑπὲρ ἐκεῖνα, like ἐπέκεινα, i. q. ἐπ᾽ ἐκεῖνα [W. § 6, 1 l.]), beyond: τὰ ὑπ. τινος, the regions lying beyond the country of one's residence, 2 Co. x. 16 [cf. W. § 54, 6]. (Byzant. and eccles. writ.: ἐπέκεινα ῥήτορες λέγουσι . . . ὑπερέκεινα δὲ μόνον οἱ σύρφακες, Thom. Mag. p. 336 [W. 463 (431)].) *   ⁵²³⁸

ὑπερ-εκ-περισσοῦ, [Rec. ὑπὲρ ἐκπερ. and in Eph. ὑπὲρ ἐκ περ.; see περισσός, 1], adv., (Vulg. [in Eph. iii. 20] superabundanter), superabundantly; beyond measure; exceedingly: 1 Th. v. 13 R G WH txt.; iii. 10; [exceeding abundantly foll. by ὑπέρ i. q.] far more than, Eph. iii. 20 [B. § 132, 21]. Not found elsewhere [exc. in Dan. iii. 22 Ald., Compl. Cf. B. § 146, 4].*   ^{see 4053}

ὑπερ-εκ-περισσῶς, adv., beyond measure: 1 Th. v. 13 L T Tr WH mrg. [R. V. exceeding highly]; see ἐκπερισσῶς. (Clem. Rom. 1 Cor. 20, 11.) *   ^{see 4053}

ὑπερ-εκ-τείνω; to extend beyond the prescribed bounds, stretch out beyond measure, stretch out overmuch: 2 Co. x. 14 [cf. W. 474 (442)]. (Anth. 9, 643, 6 acc. to the emendation of Wm. Dind.; Greg. Naz., Eustath.) *   ⁵²³⁹

ὑπερ-εκ-χύνω (-ύννω, L T Tr WH; see ἐκχέω, init.); to pour out beyond measure; pass. to overflow, run over, (Vulg. supereffluo): Lk. vi. 38; Joel ii. 24 [Alex., etc.]. (Not found elsewhere.)   ⁵²⁴⁰

ὑπερ-εν-τυγχάνω; to intercede for one: ὑπέρ τινος [W. § 52, 4, 17], Ro. viii. 26; on this pass. see πνεῦμα p. 522ᵇ. (Eccl. writ.) *   ⁵²⁴¹

ὑπερ-έχω; fr. Hom. down;   1. trans. to have or hold over one (as τὴν χεῖρα, of a protector, with a gen. of the pers. protected; so in Grk. writ. fr. Hom. down; Joseph. antt. 6, 2, 2).   2. intrans. to stand out, rise above, overtop, (so prop. first in Hom. Il. 3, 210); met-   ⁵²⁴²

aph.   **a.** *to be above, be superior in rank, authority, power*: βασιλεῖ ὡς ὑπερέχοντι, [A. V. as *supreme*], 1 Pet. ii. 13; ἐξουσίαι ὑπερέχουσαι, of magistrates (A. V. *higher powers*), Ro. xiii. 1 (οἱ ὑπερέχοντες, substantively, *the prominent men, rulers*, Polyb. 28, 4, 9; 30, 4, 17; of kings, Sap. vi. 6).   **b.** *to excel, to be superior*: τινός, *better than* [cf. B. § 132, 22], Phil. ii. 3 (Sir. xxxvi. 7; Xen. venat. 1, 11; Plat. Menex. p. 237 d.; Dem. p. 689, 10; Diod. 17, 77); *to surpass*: τινά or τί [cf. B. § 130, 4], Phil. iv. 7; τὸ ὑπερέχον, subst. *the excellency, surpassing worth* [cf. W. § 34, 2], Phil. iii. 8.*

5243   ὑπερηφανία, -ας, ἡ, (ὑπερήφανος, q. v.), *pride, haughtiness, arrogance*, the characteristic of one who, with a swollen estimate of his own powers or merits, looks down on others and even treats them with insolence and contempt: Mk. vii. 22. (From Xen. and Plat. down; Sept. for נָאוָה and גָּאוֹן; often in the O. T. Apocr.) *

5244   ὑπερήφανος, -ον, (fr. ὑπέρ and φαίνομαι, with the connective [or Epic extension (cf. Curtius § 392)] η; cf. ὑπερηφερής, δυσηλεγής, τανηλεγής, εὐηγενής), fr. Hes. down;   **1.** *showing one's self above others, overtopping, conspicuous above others, pre-eminent*, (Plat., Plut., al.).   **2.** especially in a bad sense, *with an overweening estimate of one's means or merits, despising others or even treating them with contempt, haughty*, [cf. Westcott, Epp. of St. John, p. 64^b]: Ro. i. 30; 2 Tim. iii. 2; opp. to ταπεινοί, Jas. iv. 6; 1 Pet. v. 5, (in these two pass. after Prov. iii. 34); with διανοίᾳ καρδίας added, Lk. i. 51. (Sept. for גֵּא, רָם, גָּאוָה, etc.; often in the O. T. Apocr.) [See *Trench*, Syn. § xxix.; Schmidt ch. 176, 8.] *

see 3029   ὑπερλίαν (formed like ὑπεράγαν, ὑπέρευ), and written separately ὑπὲρ λίαν (so R Tr [cf. W. § 50, 7 Note; B. § 146, 4]), *over much*; *pre-eminently*: οἱ ὑπερλίαν ἀπόστολοι, the most eminent apostles, 2 Co. xi. 5; xii. 11.*

5245   ὑπερ-νικάω, -ῶ; (Cyprian *supervinco*); *to be more than a conqueror, to gain a surpassing victory*: Ro. viii. 37. (Leon. tactic. 14, 25 νικᾷ κ. μὴ ὑπερνικᾷ; Socrat. h. e. 3, 21 νικᾶν καλόν, ὑπερνικᾶν δὲ ἐπίφθονον. Found in other eccl. writ. Euseb. h. e. 8, 14, 15, uses ὑπὲρ ἐκ νικᾶν.) *

5246   ὑπέρ-ογκος, -ον, (ὑπέρ, and ὄγκος a swelling), *over-swollen*; metaph. *immoderate, extravagant*: λαλεῖν, φθέγγεσθαι, ὑπέρογκα, [A.V. *great swelling words*] expressive of arrogance, Jude 16; 2 Pet. ii. 18; with ἐπὶ τὸν θεόν added, Dan. xi. 36 Theodot., cf. Sept. Ex. xviii. 22, 26. (Xen., Plat., Joseph., Plut., Lcian., Ael., Arr.) *

5247   ὑπεροχή, -ῆς, ἡ, (fr. ὑπέροχος, and this fr. ὑπερέχω, q. v.), prop. *elevation, pre-eminence, superiority*, (prop. in Polyb., Plut., al.); metaph. *excellence* (Plat., Aristot., Polyb., Joseph., Plut., al.): οἱ ἐν ὑπερ. sc. ὄντες, [R. V. *those that are in high place*], of magistrates, 1 Tim. ii. 2 (ἐν ὑπεροκείσθαι, to have great honor and authority, 2 Macc. iii. 11); καθ᾽ ὑπεροχὴν λόγου ἢ σοφίας, [A.V. *with excellency of speech or of wisdom* i. e.] with distinguished eloquence or wisdom, 1 Co. ii. 1.*

5248   ὑπερ-περισσεύω: 1 aor. ὑπερεπερίσσευσα; Pres. pass. ὑπερπερισσεύομαι; (Vulg. *superabundo*); *to abound beyond measure, abound exceedingly*: Ro. v. 20; pass. (see περισσεύω, 2), *to overflow, to enjoy abundantly*: with a

dat. of the thing, 2 Co. vii. 4. (Moschion de pass. mulier. p. 6, ed. Dewez; Byzant. writ.) *

5249   ὑπερ-περισσῶς, adv., *beyond measure, exceedingly*: Mk. vii. 37. Scarcely found elsewhere.*

5250   ὑπερ-πλεονάζω: 1 aor. ὑπερεπλεόνασα; (Vulg. *superabundo*); *to be exceedingly abundant*: 1 Tim. i. 14 (τὸν ὑπερπλεονάζοντα ἀέρα, Heron. spirit. p. 165, 40; several times also in eccl. writ. [ὑπερπλεονάζει absol. *overflows*, Herm. mand. 5, 2, 5]; *to possess in excess*, ἐὰν ὑπερπλεονάσῃ ὁ ἄνθρωπος, ἐξαμαρτάνει, Ps. Sal. v. 19).*

5251   ὑπερ-υψόω, -ῶ: 1 aor. ὑπερύψωσα; (Ambros. *super-exalto*); metaph.   **a.** *to exalt to the highest rank and power, raise to supreme majesty*: τινά, Phil. ii. 9; pass. Ps. xcvi. (xcvii.) 9.   **b.** *to extol most highly*: Song of the Three etc. 28 sqq.; Dan. iii. (iv.) 34 Theodot.   **c.** pass. *to be lifted up with pride, exalted beyond measure*; *to carry one's self loftily*: Ps. xxxvi. (xxxvii.) 35. (Eccl. and Byzant. writ.) *

5252   ὑπερ-φρονέω, -ῶ; (ὑπέρφρων); fr. Aeschyl. and Hdt. down; *to think more highly of one's self than is proper*: Ro. xii. 3.*

5253   ὑπερῷον, -ον, τό, (fr. ὑπερῷος or ὑπερώϊος, 'upper,' and this fr. ὑπέρ; like πατρῷος, πατρῷος, fr. πατήρ; [cf. W. 96 (91)]), in the Grk. writ. (often in Hom.) *the highest part of the house, the upper rooms or story where the women resided*; in bibl. Grk. (Sept. for עֲלִיָּה), *a room in the upper part of a house*, sometimes built upon the flat roof of the house (2 K. xxiii. 12), whither Orientals were wont to retire in order to sup, meditate, pray, etc.; [R. V. *upper chamber*; cf. B. D. s. v. House; McC. and S. s. v.]: Acts i. 13; ix. 37, 39; xx. 8, (Joseph. vit. 30).*

5254   ὑπ-έχω; prop. *to hold under, to put under, place underneath*; as τὴν χεῖρα, Hom. Il. 7, 188; Dem., Plat., al.; metaph. *to sustain, undergo*: δίκην, *to suffer punishment*, Jude 7 (very often so in prof. auth. fr. Soph. down; also δίκας, κρίσιν, τιμωρίαν, etc.; ζημίαν, Eurip. Ion 1308; 2 Macc. iv. 48).*

5255   ὑπήκοος, -ον, (ἀκοή; see ὑπακούω, 2), fr. Aeschyl. and Hdt. down, *giving ear, obedient*: Phil. ii. 8; with dat. of the pers. Acts vii. 39; εἰς πάντα, 2 Co. ii. 9.*

5256   ὑπηρετέω, -ῶ; 1 aor. ὑπηρέτησα; fr. Hdt. down; *to be ὑπηρέτης* (q. v.), prop.   **a.** *to act as rower, to row*, (Diod., Ael.).   **b.** *to minister, render service*: τινί, Acts xiii. 36; xx. 34; xxiv. 23.*

5257   ὑπηρέτης, -ου, ὁ, (fr. ὑπό, and ἐρέτης fr. ἐρέσσω to row), fr. Aeschyl. and Hdt. down;   **a.** prop. *an under rower, subordinate rower*.   **b.** any one who serves with his hands; *a servant*; in the N. T. of the officers and attendants of magistrates as — of the officer who executes penalties, Mt. v. 25; of the attendants of a king, οἱ ὑπ. οἱ ἐμοί, my servants, retinue, the soldiers I should have if I were a king, Jn. xviii. 36; of the servants or officers of the Sanhedrin, Mt. xxvi. 58; Mk. xiv. 54, 65; Jn. vii. 32, 45 sq.; xviii. 3, 12, 22; xix. 6; Acts v. 22, 26; joined with δοῦλος (Plat. polit. p. 289 c.), Jn. xviii. 18; of the attendant of a synagogue, Lk. iv. 20; of any one ministering or rendering service, Acts xiii. 5.   **c.** *any* one who aids another in any work; an assistant: of a preacher of the gospel [A. V. minister, q. v. in B. D.], Acts xxvi. 16; ὑπηρέται λόγου, Lk. i. 2; Χριστοῦ, 1 Co. iv. 1. [SYN. see διάκονος, fin.]*

5258   ὕπνος, -ου, ὁ, [i. e. σύπνος, cf. Lat. sopnus, somnus; Curtius § 391], fr. Hom. down, Hebr. שֵׁנָה, sleep: prop., Mt. i. 24; Lk. ix. 32; Jn. xi. 13; Acts xx. 9; metaph. ἐξ ὕπνου ἐγερθῆναι (see ἐγείρω, 1), Ro. xiii. 11.*

5259   ὑπό (i. e. Lat. sub [Curtius § 393]), prep., under, in prof. auth. used with the gen. dat. and acc., but in the N. T. with the gen. and acc. only. [On the use and the omission of elision with it before words beginning with a vowel, see WH. App. p. 146ᵇ; Tdf. Proleg. p. iv. (addenda et emendanda).]

I. with the GENITIVE (cf. W. 364 (342), 368 sq. (346); B. § 147, 29), it is used   1. prop. in a local sense, of situation or position under something higher, as ὑπὸ χθονός, often fr. Hom. down; ὁ ἐπὶ γῆς καὶ ὑπὸ γῆς χρυσός, Plat. legg. 5 p. 728 a.; hence   2. metaph. of the efficient cause, as that under the power of which an event is conceived of as being; here the Lat. uses a or ab, and the Eng. by; thus   a. after passive verbs,—with the gen. of a person: Mt. i. 22; ii. 15 sq.; Mk. i. 5; ii. 3; [viii. 31 L T Tr WH]; xiv. 18; [vi. 18 Rec.]; Jn. x. 14 R G; xiv. 21; Acts iv. 11; xv. 4; [xxii. 30 L T Tr WH]; Rom. xv. 15 [R G L]; 1 Co. i. 11; 2 Co. i. 4, 16; Gal. i. 11; Eph. ii. 11; Phil. iii. 12; 1 Th. i. 4; 2 Th. ii. 13; Heb. iii. 4, and in many other pass.; φωνῆς ἐνεχθείσης ὑπὸ τῆς μεγαλοπρεποῦς δόξης, when a voice was brought by the majestic glory [cf. R. V. mrg.], i. e. came down to him from God, 2 Pet. i. 17; after γίνομαι, to be done, effected, Lk. ix. 7 R L in br.; xiii. 17; xxiii. 8; Eph. v. 12; γίνεταί τινι ἐπιβουλή, Acts xx. 3; ἡ ἐπιτιμία ἡ ὑπὸ τῶν πλειόνων, sc. ἐπιτιμηθεῖσα, 2 Co. ii. 6; — with the gen. of a thing: Mt. viii. 24; xi. 7; xiv. 24; Lk. vii. 24; viii. 14 [see πορεύω, fin.]; Jn. viii. 9; Acts xxvii. 41; Ro. iii. 21; xii. 21; 1 Co. x. 29; 2 Co. v. 4; Eph. v. 13; Col. ii. 18; Jas. i. 14; ii. 9; iii. 4, 6; 2 Pet. ii. 7, 17; Jude 12; Rev. vi. 13.   b. with neuter verbs, and with active verbs which carry a passive meaning: πάσχειν ὑπό τινος, Mt. xvii. 12; Mk. v. 26; 1 Th. ii. 14, (Hom. Il. 11, 119; Thuc. 1, 77; Xen. symp. 1, 9; Cyr. 6, 1, 36; Hier. 7, 8); ἀπολέσθαι, to perish, 1 Co. x. 9 sq. (very often in prof. auth. fr. Hdt. 3, 32 on); ὑπομένειν τι, Heb. xii. 3 [cf. ἀντιλογία, 2]; λαμβάνειν sc. πληγάς, to be beaten, 2 Co. xi. 24; after a term purely active, of a force by which something is bidden to be done: ἀποκτεῖναι ἐν ῥομφαίᾳ καὶ ὑπὸ τῶν θηρίων τῆς γῆς, by the wild beasts, Rev. vi. 8 [cf. ix. 18 Rec.], (so ὤλεσε θυμὸν ὑφ' Ἕκτορος, Hom. Il. 17, 616; cf. Matthiae ii. p. 1393; [B. 341 (293)]).

II. with the ACCUSATIVE (W. § 49, k.);   1. of motion, in answer to the question 'whither?': to come ὑπὸ τὴν στέγην, Mt. viii. 8; Lk. vii. 6; ἐπισυνάγειν, Mt. xxiii. 37; Lk. xiii. 34; with verbs of putting or placing: Mt. v. 15; Mk. iv. 21; Lk. xi. 33; 1 Co. xv. 25; of placing under or subjecting, Lk. vii. 8; Ro. vii. 14; xvi. 20; 1 Co. xv. 27; Gal. iii. 22; iv. 3; Eph. i. 22;

1 Pet. v. 6; ἔχω τινὰ ὑπ' ἐμαυτόν, Mt. viii. 9; Lk. vii. 8, γίνεσθαι, born under i. e. subject to, Gal. iv. 4; of fali ing, trop. Jas. v. 12 [where Rᵃᵗ εἰς ὑπόκρισιν].   2. of situation, position, tarrying: after κατασκηνοῦν, Mk. iv. 32; κάθημαι, Jas. ii. 3; with the verb εἶναι (to and under) in a local or prop. sense, Jn. i. 48 (49); Acts iv. 12; Ro. iii. 13; 1 Co. x. 1; ἡ ὑπὸ (τὸν) οὐρανόν sc. χώρα, Lk. xvii. 24; πάσῃ κτίσει τῇ ὑπὸ τὸν οὐρ. sc. οὔσῃ, Col. i. 23; τὰ ὑπὸ τὸν οὐρανόν sc. ὄντα, Acts ii. 5, (τὰ ὑπὸ σελήνην, Philo de vit. Moys. ii. § 12); εἶναι ὑπό τινα or τι, to be under, i. e. subject to the power of, any person or thing: Ro. iii. 9; vi. 14, 15; 1 Co. ix. 20; Gal. iii. 10, 25; iv. 2, 21; v. 18; 1 Tim. vi. 1; ὑπὸ ἐξουσίαν sc. ὤν, Mt. viii. 9 (where L WH br. read ὑπὸ ἐξ. τασσόμενος [set under authority], so also cod. Sin.); οἱ ὑπὸ νόμον ὄντες, 1 Co. ix. 20; Gal. iv. 5, (ὑπὸ ἔκπληξιν εἶναι, Protev. Jac. 18); τηρεῖν τινα, Jude 6; φρουρεῖσθαι, Gal. iii. 23.   3. of time, like the Lat. sub (cf. sub vesperam), i. q. about (see exx. fr. the Grk. writ. in Passow p. 2111ᵇ; [L. and S. s. v. C. III.]): ὑπὸ τὸν ὄρθρον, about daybreak, Acts v. 21.   This prep. occurs with the accus. nowhere else in the N. T.   The apostle John uses it only twice with the acc. (xiv. 21; 3 Jn. 12 — three times, if x. 14 R G is counted [cf. viii. 9]), and once with the accus. (i. 48 (49)).

III. in COMPOSITION ὑπό denotes   1. locality, under: ὑποκάτω, ὑποπόδιον, ὑπωπιάζω, ὑποδέω; of the goal of motion, i. e. ὑπό τι, as ὑποδέχομαι (under one's roof); ὑπολαμβάνω (to receive by standing under); ὑποβάλλω, ὑποτίθημι; trop. in expressions of subjection, compliance, etc., as ὑπακούω, ὑπακοή, ὑπήκοος, ὑπόδικος, ὕπανδρος, ὑπάγω, ὑπολείπω, ὑποχωρέω.   2. small in degree, slightly, as ὑποπνέω.

5260   ὑπο-βάλλω: 2 aor. ὑπέβαλον; [fr. Hom. down];   1. to throw or put under.   2. to suggest to the mind.   3. to instruct privately, instigate, suborn: τινά, Acts vi. 11 (ὑπεβλήθησαν κατήγοροι, App. bell. civ. 1, 74; Μηνυτής τις ὑποβλητός, Joseph. b. j. 5, 10, 4).*

5261   ὑπογραμμός, -οῦ, ὁ, (ὑπογράφω), prop.   1. a writing-copy, including all the letters of the alphabet, given to beginners as an aid in learning to draw them: Clem. Alex. strom. 5, 8, 50.   Hence   2. an example set before one: 1 Pet. ii. 21 (2 Macc. ii. 28; Clem. Rom. 1 Cor. 16, 17; 33, 8; [Philo, fragm. vol. ii. 667 Mang. (vi. 229 Richter)], and often in eccl. writ.; ὁ Παῦλος ὑπομονῆς γενόμενος μέγιστος ὑπογραμμός, Clem. Rom. 1 Cor. 5, 7 [where see Bp. Lghtft.]).*

5262   ὑπό-δειγμα, -τος, τό, (ὑποδείκνυμι, q. v.), a word rejected by the Atticists, and for which the earlier writ. used παράδειγμα; see Lob. ad Phryn. p. 12; [Rutherford, New Phryn. p. 62]. It is used by Xen. r. eq. 2, 2, and among subsequent writ. by Polyb., Philo, Joseph., App., Plut., Hdian., al.; cf. Bleek, Brief a. d. Hebr. ii. 1 p. 554;   a. a sign suggestive of anything, delineation of a thing, representation, figure, copy: joined with σκιά, Heb. viii. 5; with a gen. of the thing represented, Heb. ix. 23.   b. an example: for imitation, διδόναι τινί, Jn. xiii. 15; καταλελοιπέναι, 2 Macc. vi. 28; with a gen. of the thing to be imitated, Jas. v. 10 (Sir. xliv. 16 ; 2 Macc. vi. 31); for warning: with a gen. of the thing to be shunned, τῆς ἀπειθείας, Heb. iv. 11; with a gen. of the pers. to be warned, 2 Pet. ii. 6 (τοὺς Ῥωμαίους . . . εἰς ὑπόδειγμα τῶν ἄλλων ἐθνῶν καταφλέξειν τὴν ἱερὰν πόλιν, Joseph. b. j. 2, 16, 4).*

5263   ὑπο-δείκνυμι : fut. ὑποδείξω ; 1 aor. ὑπέδειξα ; fr. Hdt. and Thuc. down; Sept. several times for הִגִּיד ;   **1.** prop. *to show* by placing *under* (i. e. before) the eyes : ὑπέδειξεν αὐτοῖς τὸν πλοῦτον αὐτοῦ, Esth. v. 11; add, Sir. xlix. 8; [al. give ὑπό in this compound the force of 'privily'; but cf. Fritzsche on Mt. p. 126].   **2.** to show by words and arguments, i. e. *to teach* (for הוֹרָה, 2 Chr. xv. 3) [A.V. freq. *to warn*] : τινί, foll. by an inf. of the thing, Mt. iii. 7; Lk. iii. 7; to teach by the use of a figure, τινί, foll. by indir. disc., Lk. vi. 47 ; xii. 5 ; to show or teach by one's example, foll. by ὅτι, Acts xx. 35; *to show* i. e. *make known* (future things), foll. by indir. disc. Acts ix. 16.*

5264   ὑπο-δέχομαι (see ὑπό, III. 1) : 1 aor. ὑπεδεξάμην ; pf. ὑποδέδεγμαι ; fr. Hom. down; *to receive* as a guest : τινά, Lk. xix. 6 ; Acts xvii. 7 ; Jas. ii. 25 ; εἰς τὸν οἶκον, Lk. x. 38. [Cf. δέχομαι, fin.]*

5265   ὑπο-δέω : 1 aor. ὑπέδησα ; 1 aor. mid. ὑπεδησάμην ; pf. pass. or mid. ptcp. ὑποδεδημένος ; fr. Hdt. down (in Hom. with tmesis) ; *to under-bind*; mostly in the mid. *to bind under one's self, bind on* ; [ptcp. *shod*]; with an acc. of the thing : σανδάλια, Mk. vi. 9 ; Acts xii. 8, (ὑποδήματα, Xen. mem. 1, 6, 6 ; Plat. Gorg. p. 490 e.); with an acc. of the member of the body : τοὺς πόδας with ἐν ἑτοιμασίᾳ added, with readiness [see ἑτοιμασία, 2], Eph. vi. 15 (πόδα σανδάλῳ, σανδαλίοις, Lcian. quom. hist. sit conscrib. 22 ; Ael. v. h. 1, 18). [Cf. B. § 135, 2.]*

5266   ὑπόδημα, -τος, τό, (ὑποδέω), fr. Hom. down, Sept. for נַעַל, *what is bound under, a sandal*, a sole fastened to the foot with thongs: Mt. iii. 11; x. 10; Mk. i. 7; Lk. iii. 16 ; x. 4; xv. 22; xxii. 35 ; Jn. i. 27; with τῶν ποδῶν added, Acts vii. 33 ; xiii. 25, (ποδός, Plat. Alc. 1 p. 128 a.). [See σανδάλιον.]*

5267   ὑπόδικος, -ον, i. q. ὑπὸ δίκην ὤν, *under judgment, one who has lost his suit*; with a dat. of the pers. *debtor to one, owing satisfaction to* : τῷ θεῷ, i. e. liable to punishment from God, Ro. iii. 19 [see Morison, Critical Exposition of Romans Third, p. 147 sq.]. (Aeschyl., Plat., Andoc., Lys., Isae., Dem., al.)*

5268   ὑπο-ζύγιος, -α, -ον, i. q. ὑπὸ ζυγὸν ὤν, *under the yoke*; neut. τὸ ὑπ. as subst. *a beast of burden* (so fr. Theogn. and Hdt. down); in bibl. Grk. (since the ass was the common animal used by the Orientals on journeys and for carrying burdens [cf. B. D. s. v. Ass, 1]) spec. *an ass*: Mt. xxi. 5 (Zech. ix. 9) ; 2 Pet. ii. 16; Sept. for חֲמוֹר, *an ass.*

5269   ὑπο-ζώννυμι ; fr. Hdt. down; *to under-gird* : τὸ πλοῖον, to bind a ship together laterally with ὑποζώματα (Plat. de rep. 10 p. 616 c.), i. e. with girths or cables, to enable it to survive the force of waves and tempest, Acts xxvii. 17 (where see Overbeck [or Hackett; esp. Smith, Voyage and Shipwreck, etc., pp. 107 sq. 204 sqq. (cf. βοήθεια)]). (Polyb. 27, 3, 3.)*

ὑπο-κάτω, *under, underneath* : τινός [W. § 54, 6 ; B. § 146, 1], Mt. xxii. 44 L T Tr WH ; Mk. vi. 11; vii. 28; [xii. 36 WH] ; Lk. viii. 16 ; Jn. i. 50 (51) ; Heb. ii. 8; Rev. v. 3, 13 [Tr mrg. br. the cl.]; vi. 9; xii. 1. (Sept.; Plat., Aristot., Polyb., Diod., Plut., al.) [Cf. W. § 50, 7 N.1; B. § 146, 4.]*   **5270**

ὑπο-κρίνομαι ;   **1.** to take up another's statements in reference to what one has decided for one's self (mid. κρίνομαι), i. e. *to reply, answer*, (Hom., Hdt., al.).   **2.** to make answer (speak) on the stage, i. e. *to personate any one, play a part*, (often so fr. Dem. down). Hence   **3.** *to simulate, feign, pretend*, (fr. Dem. and Polyb. down) : foll. by an acc. with the inf. Lk. xx. 20. (2 Macc. vi. 21, 24 ; 4 Macc. vi. 15 ; Sir. xxxv. (xxxii.) 15 ; xxxvi. (xxxiii.) 2.) [COMP. : συν-υποκρίνομαι.]*   **5271**

ὑπό-κρισις, -εως, ἡ, (ὑποκρίνομαι, q. v.) ;   **1.** *an answering ; an answer* (Hdt.).   **2.** *the acting of a stage-player* (Aristot., Polyb., Dion. Hal., Plut., Lcian., Artem., al.).   **3.** *dissimulation, hypocrisy* : Mt. xxiii. 28 ; Mk. xii. 15; Lk. xii. 1 ; Gal. ii. 13 ; 1 Tim. iv. 2 ; [Jas. v. 12 Rec.ˢᵗ] ; 1 Pet. ii. 1 [cf. B. § 123, 2], (2 Macc. vi. 25 ; Polyb. 35, 2, 13 ; Lcian. am. 3 ; Aesop. fab. 106 (284), [Philo, quis rer. div. haeres § 8; de Josepho § 14]).*   **5272**

ὑπο-κριτής, -οῦ, ὁ, (ὑποκρίνομαι, q. v.) ;   **1.** *one who answers, an interpreter*, (Plat., Lcian.).   **2.** *an actor, stage-player*, (Arstph., Xen., Plat., Ael., Hdian.).   **3.** in bibl. Grk. *a dissembler, pretender, hypocrite*: Mt. vi. 2, 5, 16 ; vii. 5; xv. 7; xvi. 3 Rec.; xxii. 18; xxiii. 13 Rec., 14 (13 Tdf.), 15, 23, 25, 27, 29 ; xxiv. 51; Mk. vii. 6; Lk. vi. 42; xi. 44 R L in br.; xii. 56; xiii. 15. (Job xxxiv. 30; xxxvi. 13, for חָנֵף *profane, impious*.) [Mention is made of Heimsoeth, De voce ὑποκριτής comment. (Bonnae, 1874, 4to.).]*   **5273**

ὑπο-λαμβάνω ; 2 aor. ὑπέλαβον ;   **1.** *to take up* (lit. *under* [cf. ὑπό, III. 1]) *in order to raise, to bear on high*, (Hdt. 1, 24); *to take up and carry away* (ὥσπερ νῆα ἄνεμοι ὑπολαβόντες, Stob. serm. 6 p. 79, 17) : τινά, Acts i. 9 (see ὀφθαλμός, mid.).   **2.** *to receive hospitably, welcome* : τινά, 3 Jn. 8 L T Tr WH (Xen. an. 1, 1, 7).   **3.** *to take up* i. e. *follow in speech*, in order either to reply to or controvert or supplement what another has said (very often so in prof. auth. fr. Hdt. down): ὑπολαβὼν εἶπεν, Lk. x. 30 (for עָנָה, Job ii. 4 ; iv. 1; vi. 1; ix. 1; xi. 1; xii. 1, etc.).   **4.** *to take up in the mind*, i. e. *to assume, suppose*: Acts ii. 15; foll. by ὅτι (sc. πλεῖον ἀγαπήσει), Lk. vii. 43, (Job xxv. 3; Tob. vi. 18; Sap. xvii. 2 ; 3 Macc. iii. 8 ; 4 Macc. v. 17 (18) etc., and often in prof. auth. fr. Xen. and Plat. down).*   **5274**

ὑπό-λειμμα [-λιμμα WH (see their App. p. 154; cf. I, ι)], -τος, τό, *a remnant* (see κατάλειμμα) : Ro. ix. 27 L T Tr WH. (Sept.; Aristot., Theophr., Plut., Galen.)*   **see 2640**

ὑπο-λείπω : 1 aor. pass. ὑπελείφθην ; fr. Hom. down; Sept. for הִשְׁאִיר and הוֹתִיר; *to leave behind* [see ὑπό, III. 1]; pass. *to be left behind, left remaining*, Sept. for נִשְׁאַר and נוֹתַר : used of a survivor, Ro. xi. 3.*   **5275**

ὑπολήνιον, -ον, τό, (i. e. τὸ ὑπὸ τὴν ληνόν, cf. τὸ ὑπο-ζύγιον), *a vessel placed under a press* (and in the Orient   **5276** usually sunk in the earth) to receive the expressed juice of the grapes, a pit : [ὤρυξεν ὑπολήνιον; R. V. he digged a pit for the winepress], Mk. xii. 1 ; see ληνός [and B. D. s. v. Winepress]. (Demiopr. ap. Poll. 10 (29), 130 ; Geop.; Sept. for יֶקֶב, Is. xvi. 10 ; Joel iii. 13 (iv. 18) ; Hagg. ii. 16 ; Zech. xiv. 10 Alex.) *

5277   ὑπο-λιμπάνω; (λιμπάνω, less common form of the verb λείπω); to leave, leave behind : 1 Pet. ii. 21. (Themist.; eccl. and Byzant. writ.; to fail, Dion. Hal. 1, 23.) *

5278   ὑπο-μένω; impf. ὑπέμενον; fut. 2 pers. plur. ὑπομενεῖτε; 1 aor. ὑπέμεινα; pf. ptcp. ὑπομεμενηκώς; fr. Hom. down; Sept. for קָוָה, חָכָה, יָחַל.   **1.** to remain i. e. tarry behind : foll. by ἐν with a dat. of the place, Lk. ii. 43 ; ἐκεῖ, Acts xvii. 14.   **2.** to remain i. e. abide, not recede or flee; trop.   **a.** to persevere : absol. and emphat., under misfortunes and trials to hold fast to one's faith in Christ [R. V. commonly endure], Mt. x. 22 ; xxiv. 13 ; Mk. xiii. 13 ; 2 Tim. ii. 12 [cf. vs. 10 in b.] ; Jas. v. 11 ; with τῇ θλίψει added, when trial assails [A. V. in tribulation (i. e. dat. of circumstances or condition)], (cf. Kühner § 426, 3 [Jelf § 603, 1]), Ro. xii. 12 (quite different is ὑπομένειν τῷ κυρίῳ, הוֹחִיל לַיֲהוָה, Lam. iii. 21, 24 ; Mic. vii. 7 ; 2 K. vi. 33 ; חִכָּה לי״, Ps. xxxii. (xxxiii.) 20, to cleave faithfully to [A. V. wait for] the Lord, where the dat. depends on the verb contrary to Grk. usage [cf. W. § 52, 16]).   **b.** to endure, bear bravely and calmly : absol., ill-treatment, 1 Pet. ii. 20 ; εἰς παιδείαν, i. e. εἰς τὸ παιδεύεσθαι, [for or unto chastening], Heb. xii. 7 acc. to the reading of L T Tr WH which is defended at length by Delitzsch ad loc. [and adopted by Riehm (Lehrbegriff u. s. w. p. 758 note), Alford, Moulton, al.], but successfully overthrown [?] by Fritzsche (De conformatione N. Ti. critica quam Lchm. edidit, p. 24 sqq.) [and rejected by the majority of commentators (Bleek, Lünemann, Kurtz, al.)]. with an acc. of the thing, 1 Co. xiii. 7 ; 2 Tim. ii. 10 ; Heb. x. 32 ; xii. 2 sq. 7 R G ; Jas. i. 12.*

5279   ὑπο-μιμνήσκω; fut. ὑπομνήσω; 1 aor. inf. ὑπομνῆσαι; 1 aor. pass. ὑπεμνήσθην; fr. Hom. down; [cf. our 'suggest', see ἀνάμνησις];   **1.** actively, to cause one to remember, bring to remembrance, recall to mind : τί (to another), 2 Tim. ii. 14 ; τινά τι, Jn. xiv. 26 (Thuc. 7, 64 ; Xen. Hier. 1, 3 ; Plat., Isocr., Dem.); with implied censure, 3 Jn. 10 ; τινὰ περί τινος, to put one in remembrance, admonish, of something : 2 Pet. i. 12 (Plat. Phaedr. p. 275 d.); τινά, foll. by ὅτι, Jude 5 (Xen. mem. 3, 9, 8 ; Plat. de rep. 5 p. 452 c.; Ael. v. h. 4, 17); τινά, foll. by an inf. (indicating what must be done), Tit. iii. 1 (Xen. hipparch. 8, 10).   **2.** passively, to be reminded, to remember : τινός, Lk. xxii. 61.*

5280   ὑπό-μνησις, -εως, ἡ, (ὑπομιμνήσκω), fr. Eur., Thuc., Plat. down;   **a.** transitively, (Vulg. commonitio), a reminding (2 Macc. vi. 17) : ἐν ὑπομνήσει, by putting you in remembrance, 2 Pet. i. 13 ; iii. 1 [W. § 61, 3 b.].   **b.** intrans. remembrance : with a gen. of the obj. 2 Tim. i. 5 [(R. V. having been reminded of etc.); al. adhere to the trans. sense (see Ellicott, Huther, Holtzmann ad loc.). SYN. see ἀνάμνησις, fin.] *

5281   ὑπο-μονή, -ῆς, ἡ, (ὑπομένω);   **1.** steadfastness, constancy, endurance, (Vulg. in 1 Th. i. 3 sustinentia, in Jas. v. 11 sufferentia); in the N. T. the characteristic of a man who is unswerved from his deliberate purpose and his loyalty to faith and piety by even the greatest trials and sufferings : Lk. viii. 15 ; xxi. 19 ; Ro. v. 3 sq.; xv. 4 sq.; 2 Co. vi. 4 ; xii. 12 ; Col. i. 11 ; 2 Th. i. 4 ; 1 Tim. vi. 11 ; 2 Tim. iii. 10 ; Tit. ii. 2 ; Heb. x. 36 ; Jas. i. 3 sq.; v. 11 ; 2 Pet. i. 6 ; Rev. ii. 2 sq. 19 ; xiii. 10 ; xiv. 12, (cf. 4 Macc. i. 11 ; ix. 8, 30 ; xv. 30 (27) ; xvii. 4, 12, 23) ; with a gen. of the thing persevered in [W. § 30, 1 fin.] : τοῦ ἔργου ἀγαθοῦ, Ro. ii. 7 ; τῆς ἐλπίδος, 1 Th. i. 3 [cf. B. 155 (136)] ; δι᾽ ὑπομονῆς, [with patience (cf. W. § 51, 1 b.) i. e.] patiently and steadfastly, Ro. viii. 25 ; Heb. xii. 1.   **2.** a patient, steadfast waiting for; [al. question this sense in the New Test., and render the gen. by 'characterizing', 'in respect to', etc.]: Χριστοῦ (gen. of the obj.), the return of Christ from heaven, 2 Th. iii. 5 ; Rev. i. 9 (where L T Tr WH ἐν Ἰησοῦ [which is in Jesus]) ; iii. 10, (cf. Ps. xxxviii. (xxxix.) 8 ; for מִקְוֶה, expectation, hope, 2 Esdr. x. 2 ; Jer. xiv. 8 ; xvii. 13 ; for תִּקְוָה, hope, Ps. [ix. 19] ; lxi. (lxii.) 6 ; lxx. (lxxi.) 5 ; [Job xiv. 19] ; for תּוֹחֶלֶת, Prov. x. 28 Symm.; ὑπομένειν τινά, Xen. an. 4, 1, 21 ; App. b. civ. 5, 81).   **3.** a patient enduring, sustaining : τῶν παθημάτων, 2 Co. i. 6 (λύπης, Plat. defin. p. 412 c.; θανάτου, Plut. Pelop. 1). [SYN. see μακροθυμία, fin.] *

5282   ὑπο-νοέω, -ῶ; impf. ὑπενόουν; fr. Hdt. down; to suppose, surmise : Acts xxv. 18 ; foll. by an acc. with the inf., Acts xiii. 25 [cf. τίς, 4)] ; xxvii. 27.*

5283   ὑπό-νοια, -ας, ἡ, (ὑπονοέω), fr. Thuc. down, a surmising : 1 Tim. vi. 4.*

see 5299   ὑπο-πιάζω, a later form of ὑποπιέζω, to keep down, keep in subjection : 1 Co. ix. 27 Tdf. ed. 7 after the faulty reading of some Mss. for ὑπωπιάζω, q. v. Cf. Lob. ad Phryn. p. 461 ; [Soph. Lex. s. v.; W. § 5, 1 d. 5 ; see ἀμφιάζω].*

5284   ὑπο-πλέω : 1 aor. ὑπέπλευσα ; (Vulg. subnavigo) ; to sail under, i. e. to sail close by, pass to the leeward of : with the acc. of the place, Acts xxvii. 4, 7. (Dio Cass., Dio Chr., al.) *

5285   ὑπο-πνέω : 1 aor. ὑπέπνευσα ;   **a.** to blow underneath (Aristot.).   **b.** to blow softly [see ὑπό, III. 2] : Acts xxvii. 13.*

5286   ὑπο-πόδιον, -ου, τό, (ὑπό and πούς), a footstool (Lat. suppedaneum) : Mt. v. 35 ; Acts vii. 49 (fr. Is. lxvi. 1) ; Jas. ii. 3 ; τιθέναι τινὰ ὑποπ. τῶν ποδῶν τινος, to make one the footstool of one's feet, i. e. to subject, reduce under one's power, (a metaph. taken from the practice of conquerors who placed their feet on the necks of their conquered enemies) : Mt. xxii. 44 R G ; Mk. xii. 36 [here WH ὑποκάτω τῶν π.]; Lk. xx. 43 ; Acts ii. 35 ; Heb. i. 13 ; x. 13, after Ps. cix. (cx.) 2. (Lcian., Athen., al.; Sept. for הֲדֹם ; [cf. W. 26].) *

5287   ὑπό-στασις, -εως, ἡ, (ὑφίστημι), a word very com. in Grk. auth., esp. fr. Aristot. on, in widely different senses, of which only those will be noticed which serve to illustrate N. T. usage ;   **1.** a setting or placing under; thing put under, substructure, foundation : Ps. lxviii. (lxix.) 3; τοῦ οἴκου, Ezek. xliii. 11; τοῦ τάφου, Diod. 1, 66. **2.** that which has foundation, is firm; hence, **a.** that which has actual existence; a substance, real being : τῶν ἐν ἀέρι φαντασμάτων τὰ μέν ἐστι κατ' ἔμφασιν, τὰ δὲ καθ' ὑπόστασιν, Aristot. de mundo, 4, 19 p. 395ᵃ, 30; φαντασίαν μὲν ἔχειν πλούτου, ὑπόστασιν δὲ μή, Artem. oneir. 3, 14; (ἡ αὐγὴ) ὑπόστασιν ἰδίαν οὐκ ἔχει, γεννᾶται δὲ ἐκ φλογός, Philo de incorruptibil. mundi §18; similarly in other writ. [cf. Soph. Lex. s. v. 5; L. and S. s. v. III. 2]. **b.** the substantial quality, nature, of any pers. or thing : τοῦ θεοῦ [R. V. substance], Heb. i. 3 (Sap. xvi. 21; ἴδε . . . τίνος ὑποστάσεως ἢ τίνος εἴδους τυγχάνουσιν οὓς ἐρεῖτε καὶ νομίζετε θεούς, Epist. ad Diogn. 2, 1; [cf. Suicer, Thesaur. s. v.]). **c.** steadiness of mind, firmness, courage, resolution, (οἱ δὲ 'Ρόδιοι θεωροῦντες τὴν τῶν Βυζαντίνων ὑπόστασιν, Polyb. 4, 50, 10; οὐχ οὕτω τὴν δύναμιν, ὡς τὴν ὑπόστασιν αὐτοῦ καὶ τόλμαν καταπεπληγμένων τῶν ἐναντίων, id. 6, 55, 2; add, Diod. 16, 32 sq.; Joseph. antt. 18, 1, 6); confidence, firm trust, assurance : 2 Co. ix. 4; xi. 17; Heb. iii. 14; xi. 1, (for תִּקְוָה, Ruth i. 12; Ezek. xix. 5; for תּוֹחֶלֶת, Ps. xxxviii. (xxxix.) 8). Cf. Bleek, Br. an d. Hebr. ii. 1 pp. 60 sqq. 462 sqq.; Schlatter, Glaube im N. T. p. 581.*

5288 **ὑπο-στέλλω** : impf. ὑπέστελλον; 1 aor. mid. ὑπεστειλά-μην; **1.** Act. to draw down, let down, lower : ἱστίον, Pind. Isthm. 2, 59; to withdraw, [draw back] : ἐμαυτόν, of a timid person, Gal. ii. 12 ([cf. Bp. Lghtft. ad loc.]; often so in Polyb.). **2.** Mid. to withdraw one's self, i. e. to be timid, to cower, shrink : of those who from timidity hesitate to avow what they believe, Heb. x. 38 (fr. Habak. ii. 4 [cf. W. 523 (487)]); to be unwilling to utter from fear, to shrink from declaring, to conceal, dissemble : foll. by τοῦ with the inf. [W. 325 (305); B. 270 (232)], Acts xx. 27; οὐδέν, ibid. 20, (often so in Dem.; cf. Reiske, Index graecit. Dem. p. 774 sq.; Joseph. vit. § 54; b. j. 1, 20, 1).*

5289 **ὑπο-στολή, -ῆς, ἡ,** (ὑποστέλλω, q. v.), prop. a withdraw-ing (Vulg. subtractio), [in a good sense, Plut. anim. an corp. aff. sint pej. § 3 sub fin.]; the timidity of one stealthi-ly retreating : οὐκ ἐσμὲν ὑποστολῆς (see εἰμί, IV. 1 g.), we have no part in shrinking back etc., we are free from the cowardice of etc. [R.V. we are not of them that shrink back etc.], Heb. x. 39 (λάθρα τὰ πολλὰ καὶ μεθ' ὑποστολῆς ἐκακούργησεν, Joseph. b. j. 2, 14, 2; ὑποστολὴν ποιοῦνται, antt. 16, 4, 3).*

5290 **ὑπο-στρέφω** : impf. ὑπέστρεφον; fut. ὑποστρέψω; 1 aor. ὑπέστρεψα; fr. Hom. down; Sept. for שׁוּב; **1.** trans. to turn back, to turn about : as ἵππους, Hom. Il. 5, 581. **2.** intrans. to turn back i. e. to return : absol. Mk. xiv. 40 [here L WH πάλιν ἐλθών Tr ἐλθών]; Lk. ii. 20 (here Rec. ἐπιστρέφ.), 43; viii. 37, 40; ix. 10; x. 17; xvii. 15; xix. 12; xxiii. 48, 56; Acts viii. 28; foll. by an inf. of purpose, Lk. xvii. 18; foll. by διά with a gen. of place, Acts xx. 3; εἰς with an acc. of place, Lk. i. 56; ii. 39 [here T Tr mrg. WH ἐπιστρέφ.], 45; iv. 14; vii. 10; viii. 39; xi. 24; xxiv. 33, 52; Acts i. 12; viii. 25; xiii. 13; xiv. 21; xxi. 6; xxii. 17; xxiii. 32; Gal. i. 17; εἰς

διαφθοράν, Acts xiii. 34; ἀπό with a gen. of place, Lk. iv. 1; xxiv. 9 [WH br. ἀπό etc.]; ἀπό with a gen. of the business, Heb. vii. 1; ἐκ with a gen. of place, Acts xii. 25; ἐκ τῆς ἁγίας ἐντολῆς, of those who after embrac-ing Christianity apostatize, 2 Pet. ii. 21 T Tr WH, but Lchm. (against the authorities) εἰς τὰ ὀπίσω ἀπὸ τῆς etc.*

5291 **ὑπο-στρώννυμι** and ὑποστρωννύω (later forms, found in Plut., Themist., Athen., al., for the earlier ὑποστορέννυμι and ὑποστόρνυμι) : impf. 3 pers. plur. ὑπεστρώννυον; to strew; spread under : τί, Lk. xix. 36 (Is. lviii. 5).*

5292 **ὑπο-ταγή, -ῆς, ἡ,** **1.** the act of subjecting (Dion. Hal.). **2.** obedience, subjection : 2 Co. ix. 13 (on which see ὁμολογία, b.); Gal. ii. 5; 1 Tim. ii. 11; iii. 4.*

5293 **ὑπο-τάσσω** : 1 aor. ὑπέταξα; Pass., pf. ὑποτέταγμαι; 2 aor. ὑπετάγην; 2 fut. ὑποταγήσομαι; pres. mid. ὑποτάσ-σομαι; to arrange under, to subordinate; to subject, put in subjection : τινί τι or τινα, 1 Co. xv. 27ᶜ; Heb. ii. 5; Phil. iii. 21; pass., Ro. viii. 20 [see διά, B. II. 1 b.]; 1 Co. xv. 27ᵇ sq.; 1 Pet. iii. 22; τινὰ or τὶ ὑπὸ τοὺς πόδας τινός, 1 Co. xv. 27ᵃ; Eph. i. 22; ὑποκάτω τῶν ποδῶν τινος, Heb. ii. 8; mid. to subject one's self, to obey; to submit to one's control; to yield to one's admonition or advice : absol. Ro. xiii. 5; 1 Co. xiv. 34 [cf. B. § 151, 30]; τινί, Lk. ii. 51; x. 17, 20; Ro. viii. 7; xiii. 1; 1 Co. xiv. 32; xvi. 16; Eph. v. 21 sq. [but in 22 G T WH txt. om. Tr mrg. br. ὑποτάσσ.], 24; Col. iii. 18; Tit. ii. 5, 9; iii. 1; 1 Pet. ii. 18; iii. 1, 5; v. 5; 2 aor. pass. with mid. force, to obey [R. V. subject one's self, B. 52 (46)], Ro. x. 3; impv. obey, be subject : Jas. iv. 7; 1 Pet. ii. 13; v. 5; 2 fut. pass. Heb. xii. 9. (Sept.; [Aristot.], Polyb., Plut., Arr., Hdian.) *

5294 **ὑπο-τίθημι** : 1 aor. ὑπέθηκα; pres. mid. ptcp. ὑποτιθέμε-νος; fr. Hom. down; to place under (cf. ὑπό, III. 1) : τί, Ro. xvi. 4 (on which see τράχηλος). Mid. metaph. to supply, suggest, (mid. from one's own resources) ; with a dat. of the pers. and acc. of the thing : ταῦτα, these in-structions, 1 Tim. iv. 6. (Often so in prof. auth. fr. Hom. down.) *

5295 **ὑπο-τρέχω** : 2 aor. ὑπέδραμον; fr. Hom. down; prop. to run under; in N. T. once, viz. of navigators, to run past a place on the shore, and therefore in a higher posi-tion (see ὑποπλέω) : νησίον, Acts xxvii. 16 [R. V. run-ning under the lee of; cf. Hackett ad loc.]. *

5296 **ὑπο-τύπωσις, -εως, ἡ,** (ὑποτυπόω, to delineate, outline); **a.** an outline, sketch, brief and summary exposition, (Sext. Empir., Diog. Laërt., al.). **b.** an example, pattern : πρὸς ὑποτ. τῶν μελλόντων πιστεύειν κτλ. for an example of those who should hereafter believe, i. e. to show by the example of my conversion that the same grace which I had obtained would not be wanting also to those who should hereafter believe, 1 Tim. i. 16; the pattern placed before one to be held fast and copied, model : ὑγιαινόντων λόγων, 2 Tim. i. 13.*

5297 **ὑπο-φέρω** : 1 aor. ὑπήνεγκα; 2 aor. inf. ὑπενεγκεῖν; fr. Hom. down; to bear by being under, bear up (a thing placed on one's shoulders); trop. to bear patiently, to en-dure, (often so fr. Xen. and Plat. down) : τί, 1 Co. x.

13; 2 Tim. iii. 11; 1 Pet. ii. 19.   (Prov. vi. 33; Ps. lxviii. (lxix.) 8; Mic. vii. 9; Job ii. 10.) *

5298   ὑπο-χωρέω, -ῶ; 1 aor. ὑπεχώρησα; fr. Hom. down; *to go back* [see ὑπό, III. 1 fin.]; *to withdraw*: εἰς τόπον ἔρημον, Lk. ix. 10; with ἐν and a dat. of the place (see ἐν, I. 7), Lk. v. 16 [cf. W. § 50, 4 a.; B. 312 (268)].*

5299   ὑπωπιάζω; (fr. ὑπώπιον, compounded of ὑπό and ὤψ, ὠπός, which denotes   a. that part of the face which is under the eyes;   b. a blow in that part of the face; a black and blue spot, a bruise); prop. *to beat black and blue, to smite so as to cause bruises and livid spots*, (Aristot. rhet. 3, 11, 15 p. 1413ᵃ, 20; Plut. mor. p. 921 f.; Diog. Laërt. 6, 89): τὸ σῶμα, like a boxer I buffet my body, handle it roughly, discipline it by hardships, 1 Co. ix. 27; metaph. (πόλεις ὑπωπιασμέναι, cities terribly scourged and afflicted by war, bearing the marks of devastation, Arstph. pax 541) *to give one intolerable annoyance* ['beat one out', 'wear one out'], by entreaties [cf. τέλος, 1 a.], Lk. xviii. 5 (cf. aliquem *rogitando obtundat*, Ter. Eun. 3, 5, 6).*

5300   ὗς, ὑός, ὁ, ἡ, fr. Hom. down, Sept. several times for חֲזִיר, *a swine*: 2 Pet. ii. 22.*

5301   ὕσσωπος [on the breathing see *WH.* App. p. 144ᵃ; Lchm. (in both his edd.) spells it with one σ in Jn.], -ου, ἡ, (Hebr. אֵזוֹב, Ex. xii. 22; Num. xix. 6, 18, etc.), *hyssop*, a plant a bunch of which was used by the Hebrews in their ritual sprinklings: Heb. ix. 19; ὑσσώπῳ, i. q. καλάμῳ ὑσσώπου, Jn. xix. 29. Cf. *Win.* RWB. s. v. Ysop; *Arnold* in Herzog xviii. p. 337 sq.; *Furrer* in Schenkel v. 685 sq.; [Riehm p. 1771 sq.; *Löw*, Aram. Pflanzennamen, § 93; *Tristram*, Nat. Hist. etc. p. 455 sq.; B. D. s. v. (esp. Am. ed.)].*

5302   ὑστερέω, -ῶ; 1 aor. ὑστέρησα; pf. ὑστέρηκα; Pass., pres. ὑστεροῦμαι; 1 aor. ptcp. ὑστερηθείς; (ὕστερος); **1.** Act. *to be ὕστερος* i. e. *behind* i. e.   a. *to come late or too tardily* (so in prof. auth. fr. Hdt. down): Heb. iv. 1; *to be left behind in the race* and so fail to reach the goal, to fall short of the end; with ἀπό and the gen. indicating the end, metaph. *fail to become a partaker*: ἀπὸ τῆς χάριτος, Heb. xii. 15 [al. render here *fall back* (i. e. away) *from*; cf. W. § 30, 6 b.; B. 322 (276) sq. cf. § 132, 5] (Eccl. vi. 2).   b. *to be inferior*, in power, influence, rank, 1 Co. xii. 24 (where L T Tr WH pass. ὑστερουμένῳ); in virtue, τί ἔτι ὑστερῶ; in what am I still deficient [A.V. *what lack I yet* (cf. B. § 131, 10)], Mt. xix. 20 (Sir. li. 24; ἵνα γνῶ τί ὑστερῶ ἐγώ, Ps. xxxviii. (xxxix.) 5; μηδ' ἐν ἄλλῳ μηδενὶ μέρει ἀρετῆς ὑστεροῦντας, Plat. de rep. 6 p. 484 d.); μηδέν or οὐδέν foll. by a gen. (depending on the idea of comparison contained in the verb [B. § 132, 22]) of the person, *to be inferior to* [A.V. *to be behind*] *another in nothing*, 2 Co. xi. 5; xii. 11.   c. *to fail, be wanting*, (Diosc. 5, 86): Jn. ii. 3 [not Tdf.]; ἕν σοι [T WH Tr mrg. σε (cf. B. u. s.)] ὑστερεῖ, Mk. x. 21.   d. *to be in want of, lack*: with a gen. of the thing [W. § 30, 6], Lk. xxii. 35 (Joseph. antt. 2, 2, 1). **2.** Pass. *to suffer want* [W. 260 (244)]: Lk. xv. 14; 2 Co. xi. 9 (8); Heb. xi. 37, (Sir. xi. 11); opp. to περισσεύειν, to abound, Phil. iv. 12; τινός, *to be devoid* [R. V. *fall*

short] of, Ro. iii. 23 (Diod. 18, 71; Joseph. antt. 15, 6, 7); ἔν τινι, to suffer want in any respect, 1 Co. i. 7, opp. to πλουτίζεσθαι ἔν τινι, ibid. 5; *to lack* (be inferior) *in excellence, worth*, opp. to περισσεύειν, [A. V. *to be the worse . . . the better*], 1 Co. viii. 8. [COMP.: ἀφ-υστερέω.] *

ὑστέρημα, -τος, τό, (ὑστερέω);   a. *deficiency, that which is lacking*: plur. with a gen. of the thing whose deficiency is to be filled up, Col. i. 24 (on which see ἀνταναπληρόω, and θλίψις sub fin.); 1 Th. iii. 10; τὸ ὑστ. with a gen. [or its equiv.] of the pers., *the absence of one*, 1 Co. xvi. 17 [ὑμ. being taken objectively (W. § 22, 7; B. § 132, 3); al. take ὑμ. subjectively and render *that which was lacking on your part*]; τὸ ὑμῶν ὑστ. τῆς πρός με λειτουργίας, your absence, owing to which something was lacking in the service conferred on me (by you), Phil. ii. 30.   b. in reference to property and resources, *poverty, want, destitution*: Lk. xxi. 4; 2 Co. viii. 14 (13); ix. 12; xi. 9, (Ps. xxxiii. (xxxiv.) 10; Judg. xviii. 10, etc.; eccl. writ.).*   **5303**

ὑστέρησις, -εως, ἡ, (ὑστερέω), *want, poverty*: Mk. xii. 44; καθ' ὑστέρησιν, on account of want, Phil. iv. 11 [cf. κατά, II. 3 c. γ. p. 328ᵇ bot.]. (Eccl. writ.) *   **5304**

ὕστερος, -α, -ον, *latter, later, coming after*: ἐν ὑστέροις καιροῖς, 1 Tim. iv. 1; ὁ ὕστ. i. q. *the second*, Mt. xxi. 31 L Tr WH, but cf. Fritzsche's and Meyer's crit. notes [esp. *WH.* App.] ad loc.   Neut. ὕστερον, fr. Hom. down, adverbially, *afterward, after this, later, lastly*, used alike of a shorter and of a longer period: Mt. iv. 2; xxi. 29, 32, 37; xxv. 11; xxvi. 60; Mk. xvi. 14; Lk. iv. 2 Rec.; [xx. 32 L T Tr WH]; Jn. xiii. 36; Heb. xii. 11; with a gen. *after one*, Mt. xxii. 27; Lk. xx. 32 [R G].*   **5305 & 5306**

ὑφαίνω; fr. Hom. down; Sept. for אָרַג; *to weave*: Lk. xii. 27 T WH (rejected) mrg.*   **(5306α); see 5307**

ὑφαντός, -ή, -όν, (ὑφαίνω, q. v.), fr. Hom. down; *woven*: Jn. xix. 23. (For אֹרֵג, Ex. xxxvi. 30 (xxxix. 22) xxxvi. 35 (xxxix. 27); for חֹשֵׁב, Ex. xxvi. 31, etc.) *   **5307; see (5306α)**

ὑψηλός, -ή, -όν, (ὕψι on high, ὕψος), [fr. Hom. down], *high; lofty*;   a. prop. of place: ὄρος, Mt. iv. 8; xvii. 1; Mk. ix. 2; Lk. iv. 5 R G L br.; Rev. xxi. 10; τεῖχος, Rev. xxi. 12; neut. τὰ ὑψηλά (the heights of heaven; Sept. for מָרוֹם, Ps. xcii. (xciii.) 4; cxii. (cxiii.) 5; Is. xxxiii. 5; lvii. 15), heaven [A.V. *on high*; cf. B. § 124, 8 d.], Heb. i. 3; *exalted on high*: ὑψηλότερος τῶν οὐρανῶν, [made *higher than the heavens*], of Christ raised to the right hand of God, Heb. vii. 26 (cf. Eph. iv. 10); μετὰ βραχίονος ὑψηλοῦ, *with a high* (uplifted) *arm*, i. e. with signal power, Acts xiii. 17 (Sept. often ἐν βραχίονι ὑψηλῷ for בִּזְרוֹעַ נְטוּיָה, as in Ex. vi. 6; Deut. v. 15).   b. metaph. *eminent, exalted*: in influence and honor, Lk. xvi. 15; ὑψηλὰ φρονεῖν, to set the mind on, to seek, *high things* (as honors and riches), to be aspiring, Ro. xii. 16; also Ro. xi. 20 L mrg. T Tr WH; 1 Tim. vi. 17 T WH mrg.; (Lcian. Icaromen. 11, Hermot. 5).*   **5308**

ὑψηλο-φρονέω, -ῶ; (ὑψηλόφρων, and this fr. ὑψηλός and φρήν); *to be high-minded, proud*: Ro. xi. 20 [R G L txt.]; 1 Tim. vi. 17 [R G L Tr WH txt.], (Schol. ad Pind. Pyth. 2, 91). In Grk. writ. μεγαλοφρονεῖν is more common.*   **5309**

5310   **ὕψιστος, -η, -ον,** (superl.; fr. ὕψι on high), in Grk. writ. mostly poetic, *highest, most high*;   **a.** of place: neut. τὰ ὕψιστα (Sept. for מְרוֹמִים), the highest regions, i. e. heaven (see ὑψηλός, a.), Mt. xxi. 9; Mk. xi. 10; Lk. ii. 14; xix. 38, (Job xvi. 19; Is. lvii. 15).   **b.** of rank: of God, ὁ θεὸς ὁ ὕψιστος, the most high God, Mk. v. 7; Lk. viii. 28; Acts xvi. 17; Heb. vii. 1; [Gen. xiv. 18; Philo de leg. ad Gaium § 23]; and simply ὁ ὕψιστος, *the Most High,* Acts vii. 48; and without the article (cf. B. § 124, 8 b. note; [WH. Intr. § 416]), Lk. i. 32, 35, 76; vi. 35, and very often in Sir.; (Hebr. עֶלְיוֹן, אֵל עֶלְיוֹן, יְהוָֹה עֶלְיוֹן, אֱלֹהִים עֶלְיוֹן; Ζεὺς ὕψιστος, Pind. Nem. 1, 90; 11, 2; Aeschyl. Eum. 28).*

5311   **ὕψος, -ους, τό,** fr. Aeschyl. and Hdt. down, Sept. for מָרוֹם, גֹּבַהּ, קוֹמָה, etc., *height:* prop. of measure, Eph. iii. 18; Rev. xxi. 16; of place, heaven [A.V. *on high*], Eph. iv. 8 (fr. Ps. lxvii. (lxviii.) 19); Lk. i. 78; xxiv. 49; metaph. *rank, high station:* Jas. i. 9 (Job v. 11; 1 Macc. i. 40; x. 24; ὕψος ἀρετῆς, Plut. Popl. 6).*

5312   **ὑψόω, -ῶ;** fut. ὑψώσω; 1 aor. ὕψωσα; Pass., 1 aor. ὑψώθην; 1 fut. ὑψωθήσομαι; (ὕψος); [Batr. 81; Hippocr., al.]; Sept. very often for רוּם, also for נָבַהּ, נָשָׂא, גָּדַל, etc.; *to lift up on high, to exalt,* (Vulg. *exalto*): τινά or τί, prop. of place, Jn. iii. 14ᵃ; used of the elevation of Jesus on the cross, Jn. iii. 14ᵇ; viii. 28; xii. 34; with ἐκ τῆς γῆς added, to remove from (lit. *out of*) the earth by crucifixion (ὑψοῦν τινα foll. by ἐκ, Ps. ix. 14), Jn. xii. 32 (the Evangelist himself interprets the word of the lifting up upon the cross, but a careful comparison of viii. 28 and xii. 32 renders it probable that Jesus spoke of the heavenly exaltation which he was to attain by the crucifixion (cf. xii. 23 sqq., xiii. 31 sqq., Lk. xxiv. 26), and employed the Aramaic word רוּם, the ambiguity of which allowed it to be understood of the crucifixion; cf. *Bleek,*

Beiträge zur Evangelienkritik, p. 231 sq.; [the 'lifting up' includes death and the victory over death; the passion itself is regarded as a glorification; cf. Westcott ad loc.]); τινὰ ἕως τοῦ οὐρανοῦ (opp. to καταβιβάζειν [or καταβαίνειν] ἕως ᾅδου), metaph. *to raise to the very summit of opulence and prosperity,* pass., Mt. xi. 23; Lk. x. 15, [al. understand exaltation in privilege as referred to in these pass. (see vs. 21 in Mt.)];   simply τινά, *to exalt, to raise to dignity, honor, and happiness:* Lk. i. 52 (where opp. to ταπεινῶ); Acts xiii. 17; to that state of mind which ought to characterize a Christian, 2 Co. xi. 7; to raise the spirits by the blessings of salvation, Jas. iv. 10; 1 Pet. v. 6; ἐμαυτόν, *to exalt one's self* (with haughtiness and empty pride), (opp. to ταπεινῶ), Mt. xxiii. 12; Lk. xiv. 11; xviii. 14;—in these same pass. ὑψωθήσεται occurs, *he shall be raised to honor.* By a union of the literal and the tropical senses God is said ὑψῶσαι Christ τῇ δεξιᾷ αὐτοῦ, Acts v. 31; pass. Acts ii. 33; the dative in this phrase, judged according to Greek usage, hardly bears any other meaning than *with* (by means of) *his right hand* (his power) [R. V. txt.]; but the context forbids it to denote anything except *at* (to) *the right hand of God* [so R. V. mrg.]; hence the opinion of those has great probability who regard Peter's phrase as formed on the model of the Aramaean לִימִין; cf. *Bleek,* Einl. in das N. T. ed. 1, p. 346 [but see W. 214 (201), 215 (202); Meyer ad loc. COMP.: ὑπερ-υψόω.]*

5313   **ὕψωμα, -τος, τό,** (ὑψόω), *thing elevated, height:* prop. of space, opp. to βάθος, Ro. viii. 39 (τοῦ ἀέρος, Philo de praem. et poen. § 1; ὅταν ὕψωμα λάβῃ μέγιστον ὁ ἥλιος, Plut. mor. p. 782 d.); spec. elevated structure i. e. *barrier, rampart, bulwark:* 2 Co. x. 5. [Sept. (in Jud. x. 8; xiii. 4, actively); cod. Ven. for 'heave-offering' in Lev. vii. 14, 32; Num. xviii. 24 sqq.]*

Φ

5314   **φάγος, -ου, ὁ,** (φάγω), *a voracious man, a glutton,* (it is a subst., and differs fr. φαγός the adj.; cf. φυγός, φειδός; see Fritzsche on Mark p. 790 sqq., but cf. *Lipsius,* Gram. Untersuch. p. 28; W. § 16, 3 c. a., [and § 6, 1 i.; esp. Chandler § 230]): joined with οἰνοπότης:

5315;   Mt. xi. 19; Lk. vii. 34.*
see 2068   **φάγω,** see ἐσθίω.

(5315a);   **φαιλόνης** (so Rec.ᵉʳᵃˢ ˢᵗᵉᵖʰ) or φελόνης (with most Mss. including cod. Sin., Rec.ᵇᵉᶻ ᵉˡᶻ G L T Tr [WH (cf. their see 5341   Intr. § 404 and App. p. 151ᵃ; W. *Dindorf* in Steph. Thes. s. v. φαινόλης, col. 583)]), by metath. for the more com. φαινόλης (found in [Epict. 4, 8, 24]; Artem. oneir. 2, 3; 5, 29; Pollux 7, (13) 61; Athen. 3 p. 97), -ον, ὁ, Lat.

paenula, a *travelling-cloak,* used for protection against stormy weather: 2 Tim. iv. 13, where others erroneously understand it to mean a case or receptacle for books as even the Syriac renders it ܒܝܬ ܟܬܒܐ.*

5316   **φαίνω;** [1 aor. act. subjunc. 3 pers. sing. φάνῃ, L T WH in Rev. viii. 12; xviii. 23, (see below and ἀναφαίνω; W. § 15 s. v.; B. 41 (35))]; Pass., pres. φαίνομαι; 2 aor. ἐφάνην; 2 fut. φανήσομαι and (in 1 Pet. iv. 18) φανοῦμαι (cf. Kühner § 343 s. v.; [Veitch s. v.]); (φάω); in Grk. writ. fr. Hom. down, *to bring forth into the light, cause to shine; to show.* In bibl. Grk   **1.** Active intransitively, *to shine, shed light,* (which the Grks. [commonly

⟨cf. L. and S. s. v. A. II.)] express by the passive), Sept. for הֵאִיר: τὸ φῶς φαίνει, Jn. i. 5; 1 Jn. ii. 8; ὁ λύχνος, Jn. v. 35; 2 Pet. i. 19, (1 Macc. iv. 50; Gen. i. 17); ὁ ἥλιος, Rev. i. 16; ὁ ἥλ. καὶ ἡ σελήνη, Rev. xxi. 23; ἡ ἡμέρα, Rev. viii. 12 Rec. **2.** Passive, **a.** *to shine, be bright or resplendent*: ἡ ἡμέρα, Rev. viii. 12 Tr [(see above); xviii. 23 R G Tr—but see Veitch s. v.; moreover, the foll. exx. should be brought under the next head; see Meyer on Phil. ii. 15]; ὡς φωστῆρες, Phil. ii. 15; ὁ ἀστήρ, Mt. ii. 7; ἡ ἀστραπή, Mt. xxiv. 27. **b.** *to become evident, to be brought forth into light, come to view, appear*: Mt. xxiv. 30; opp. to ἀφανίζεσθαι, Jas. iv. 14; of the appearance of angels: τινί, Mt. i. 20; ii. 13, 19, (2 Macc. iii. 33; x. 29; xi. 8; of God, Joseph. antt. 7, 7, 3; for נִקְרָה in ref. to the same, Num. xxiii. 3); of those restored to life, Lk. ix. 8; τινί, Mk. xvi. 9; of growing vegetation, *to come to light*, Mt. xiii. 26; univ. *to appear, be seen*: φαινόμενα, Heb. xi. 3; impersonally, φαίνεται, *it is seen, exposed to view*: οὐδέποτε ἐφάνη οὕτως ἐν τῷ Ἰσραήλ, *never was it seen in such* (i. e. so remarkable) *a fashion — never was such a sight seen — in Israel*, Mt. ix. 33. **c.** *to meet the eyes, strike the sight, become clear or manifest*, with a predicate nom. (*be seen to be*) [cf. B. § 144, 15 a., 18]: Mt. vi. 16, 18; xxiii. 27 sq.; 2 Co. xiii. 7; ἵνα (sc. ἡ ἁμαρτία) φανῇ ἁμαρτία (equiv. to ἁμαρτωλός), Ro. vii. 13; with the dat. of the pers. added, Mt. vi. 5 (sc. προσευχόμενοι praying); *to be seen, appear*: ὁ ἁμαρτωλὸς ποῦ φανεῖται; i. e. he will nowhere be seen, will perish, 1 Pet. iv. 18. **d.** *to appear to the mind, seem to one's judgment or opinion*: τί ὑμῖν φαίνεται, [A.V. *what think ye*], Mk. xiv. 64 (1 Esdr. ii. 18 (21)); ἐφάνησαν ἐνώπιον αὐτῶν ὡσεὶ λῆροι, Lk. xxiv. 11 [W. § 33 f.; B. § 133, 3. Syn. see δοκέω, fin.]*

5317   **Φαλέκ** [L txt. Tr WH Φάλεκ (but see Tdf. Proleg. p. 104); L mrg. Φάλεγ], ὁ, *Peleg*, (פֶּלֶג 'division'), son of Eber (Gen. x. 25): Lk. iii. 35.*

5318   **φανερός, -ά, -όν,** (φαίνομαι), fr. [Pind.], Hdt. down, *apparent, manifest, evident, known*, (opp. to κρυπτός and ἀπόκρυφος): Gal. v. 19; ἐν πᾶσιν, among all, 1 Tim. iv. 15 Rec.; ἐν αὐτοῖς, in their minds, Ro. i. 19; τινί, dat. of the pers., manifest to one, of a pers. or thing that has become known, Acts iv. 16; vii. 13; [1 Tim. iv. 15 G L T Tr WH]; φανερὸν γίνεσθαι: Mk. vi. 14; [Lk. viii. 17]; 1 Co. iii. 13; xiv. 25; ἐν ὑμῖν, among you, 1 Co. xi. 19; ἐν with a dat. of the place, Phil. i. 13 [see πραιτώριον, 3]; φανερὸν ποιεῖν τινα, [A. V. *to make one known*, i. e.] disclose who and what he is, Mt. xii. 16; Mk. iii. 12; εἰς φανερὸν ἐλθεῖν, to come to light, come to open view, Mk. iv. 22; Lk. viii. 17; ἐν τῷ φανερῷ, in public, openly (opp. to ἐν τῷ κρυπτῷ), Mt. vi. 4 Rec., 6 R G, [18 Rec.]; Ro. ii. 28 [here A.V. *outward, outwardly*]. *manifest* i. e. to be plainly recognized or known: foll. by ἐν with a dat. of the thing *in* (by) *which*, 1 Jn. iii. 10. [Syn. see δῆλος, fin.]*

5319   **φανερόω, -ῶ;** fut. φανερώσω; 1 aor. ἐφανέρωσα; Pass., pres. φανεροῦμαι; pf. πεφανέρωμαι; 1 aor. ἐφανερώθην; 1 fut. φανερωθήσομαι; (φανερός); *to make manifest or visible or known* what has been hidden or unknown, *to*

manifest, whether by words, or deeds, or in any other way; **a.** with an acc. of the thing: pass., Mk. iv. 22; Eph. v. 13; Rev. iii. 18; τὰ ἔργα τινός, pass. Jn. iii. 21; with ἔν τινι added, Jn. ix. 3; τὴν δόξαν αὐτοῦ, of Christ, Jn. ii. 11; sc. τὴν γνῶσιν, 2 Co. xi. 6 L T Tr WH; τὰς βουλὰς τῶν καρδιῶν, of God as judge, 1 Co. iv. 5; τὴν ὀσμὴν τῆς γνώσεως αὐτοῦ δι' ἡμῶν ἐν παντὶ τόπῳ, 2 Co. ii. 14; τὴν σπουδὴν ὑμῶν ἐνώπιον τοῦ θεοῦ, pass. 2 Co. vii. 12; τὴν ζωὴν τοῦ Ἰησοῦ ἐν τῷ σώματι, ἐν τῇ θνητῇ σαρκί, pass. 2 Co. iv. 10 sq.; χάρις τοῦ θεοῦ φανερωθεῖσα διὰ τῆς ἐπιφανείας τοῦ Χριστοῦ, 2 Tim. i. 10; pass. used of something hitherto non-existent but now *made actual and visible, realized*, 1 Jn. iii. 2 (Germ. *verwirklicht werden, in die Erscheinung treten*); ὁδός, Heb. ix. 8 (cf. *iter per Alpes patefieri volebat*, Caes. bell. gall. 3, 1); to bring to light or make manifest, by the advent, life, death, resurrection, of Jesus Christ: τὸ μυστήριον, pass. Ro. xvi. 26; with τοῖς ἁγίοις added, Col. i. 26; *to make known* by teaching: τὸ ὄνομα τοῦ θεοῦ τοῖς ἀνθρώποις, Jn. xvii. 6; τὸ μυστήριον τοῦ Χριστοῦ, Col. iv. 4; τὸν λόγον αὐτοῦ, of God giving instruction through the preachers of the gospel, Tit. i. 3; τὸ γνωστὸν τοῦ θεοῦ αὐτοῖς, of God teaching the Gentiles concerning himself by the works of nature, Ro. i. 19; pass. δικαιοσύνη θεοῦ (made known in the gospel [cf. δικαιοσύνη, 1 c. p. 149b bot.]), Ro. iii. 21; pass. *to become manifest, be made known*: ἐν τούτῳ sc. ὅτι etc. herein that, etc. [see οὗτος, I. 2 b.], 1 Jn. iv. 9; τὰ δικαιώματα τοῦ θεοῦ, Rev. xv. 4. **b.** with an acc. of the person, *to expose to view, make manifest, show* one: ἑαυτὸν τῷ κόσμῳ, of Christ coming forth from his retirement in Galilee and showing himself publicly at Jerusalem, Jn. vii. 4; τοῖς μαθηταῖς, of the risen Christ, Jn. xxi. 1; pass. *to be made manifest, to show one's self, appear*: ἔμπροσθεν τοῦ βήματος τοῦ Χριστοῦ, 2 Co. v. 10; of Christ risen from the dead, τοῖς μαθηταῖς αὐτοῦ, Jn. xxi. 14; Mk. xvi. 14; with ἐν ἑτέρᾳ μορφῇ added, Mk. xvi. 12 (absol. φανερωθείς, Barn. ep. 15, 9); of Christ previously hidden from view in heaven but after his incarnation made visible on earth as a man among men, Heb. ix. 26 (opp. to δεύτερον ὀφθήσεσθαι, of his future return from heaven, ibid. 28); 1 Pet. i. 20; 1 Jn. iii. 5, 8; with ἐν σαρκί added, 1 Tim. iii. 16, (Barn. ep. 5, 6; 6, 7. 9. 14 etc.); ἡ ζωή (the life embodied in Christ; the centre and source of life) ἐφανερώθη, 1 Jn. i. 2; of Christ now hidden from sight in heaven but hereafter to return visibly, Col. iii. 4 (cf. 3); 1 Pet. v. 4; 1 Jn. ii. 28; [cf. Westcott on the Epp. of St. John p. 79 sq.]. of Christians, who after the Saviour's return will be manifested ἐν δόξῃ [see δόξα, III. 4 b.], Col. iii. 4. Pass. *to become known, to be plainly recognized, thoroughly understood*: who and what one is, τινί, Jn. i. 31; what sort of person one is, τῷ θεῷ, 2 Co. v. 11; ἐν ταῖς συνειδήσεσιν ὑμῶν, ibid.; φανεροῦμαι foll. by ὅτι, 2 Co. iii. 3; 1 Jn. ii. 19; ἐν παντὶ φανερωθέντες ἐν πᾶσιν εἰς ὑμᾶς, in every way made manifest (such as we are) among all men to you-ward, 2 Co. xi. 6 [but L T Tr WH give the act. φανερώσαντες, *we have made it* manifest]. (Hdt., Dion. Hal., Dio Cass., Joseph.) [Syn. see ἀποκαλύπτω, fin.]*

5320   **φανερῶς,** (see φανερός), [fr. Aeschyl. and Hdt. down], adv., *manifestly*; i.e.   **a.** *plainly, clearly*: ἰδεῖν τινα, Acts x. 3.   **b.** *openly*: Mk. i. 45; opp. to ἐν κρυπτῷ, Jn. vii. 10.*

5321   **φανέρωσις, -εως, ἡ,** (φανερόω), *manifestation*: with a gen. of the object, 1 Co. xii. 7; 2 Co. iv. 2. ([Aristot. de plantis 2, 1 and 9; also for אוּרִים (Sept. δήλωσις) Lev. viii. 8 cod. Ven.] Eccles. writ.; Hesych.) (Syn. see ἀποκαλύπτω, fin.] *

5322   **φανός, -οῦ, ὁ,** (φαίνω), *a torch* [A. V. *lantern*; Hesych. Ἀττικοὶ δὲ λυχνοῦκον ἐκάλουν ὃ ἡμεῖς νῦν φανόν; cf. Phryn. p. 59 and Lob.'s note; *Rutherford*, New Phryn. p. 131; Athen. 15 p. 699 d. sqq. and Casaubon's notes ch. xviii. see λαμπάς and reff.]: Jn. xviii. 3. (Arstph., Xen., Dion. Hal., Plut., al.) *

5323   **Φανουήλ,** (פְּנוּאֵל) i. e. πρόσωπον θεοῦ), indecl., *Phanuel*, the father of Anna the prophetess: Lk. ii. 36.*

5324   **φαντάζω**: (φαίνω); pres. pass. ptcp. φανταζόμενος; fr. Aeschyl. and Hdt. down; *to cause to appear, make visible, expose to view, show*: τὸ φανταζόμενον, *the appearance, sight*, Heb. xii. 21.*

5325   **φαντασία, -ας, ἡ,** *show, showy appearance, display, pomp*: Acts xxv. 23. (Polyb. 15, 25, 5, etc.; [Diod. 12, 83]; al.) *

5326   **φάντασμα, -τος, τό,** (φαντάζω), *an appearance*; spec. *an apparition, spectre*: Mt. xiv. 26; Mk. vi. 49. (Aeschyl., Eur., Plat., Dion. Hal., Plut., al.; Sap. xvii. 14 (15).) *

5327   **φάραγξ, -αγγος, ἡ,** a valley shut in by cliffs and precipices; *a ravine*: Lk. iii. 5. (Alcm., Eur., Thuc., Dem., Polyb., al.; Sept.) *

5328   **Φαραώ,** (פַּרְעֹה); in Joseph. antt. 2, 13 and 14 Φαραώθης [also Φαραών, -ῶνος, 8, 6, 2, etc.]), ὁ, [indecl. B. 15 (14)], *Pharaoh*, the common title of the ancient kings of Egypt (ὁ φαραὼν κατ' Αἰγυπτίους βασιλέα σημαίνει, Joseph. antt. 8, 6, 2 [acc. to Ebers (in Riehm s. v. Pharao) the name is only the Hebr. form of the Egyptian per-āa denoting (as even Horapollo 1, 62 testifies) *great house*, a current title of kings akin to the Turkish "sublime porte"; al. al.; see BB. DD. s. v.]): Acts vii. 13, 21; Ro. ix. 17; Heb. xi. 24; Φαραώ with βασιλεὺς Αἰγύπτου added in apposition (as if Φαραώ were a proper name, as sometimes in the O. T.: פַּרְעֹה מֶלֶךְ מִצְרַיִם, 1 K. iii. 1; ix. 16; 2 K. xvii. 7; Is. xxxvi. 6, etc.; 1 Esdr. i. 23), Acts vii. 10. Cf. *Vaihinger* in Herzog xi. p. 490 sqq.; [*Ebers* in Riehm u. s.].*

5329   **Φαρές** [on its accent see Tdf. Proleg. p. 104], ὁ, (פֶּרֶץ) a breach, Gen. xxxviii. 29), *Perez* [A. V. *Phares*], a son of Judah by Tamar his daughter-in-law: Mt. i. 3; Lk. iii. 33.*

5330   **Φαρισαῖος, -ου, ὁ,** *a Pharisee*, a member of the sect or party of the Pharisees (Syr. ܦ̈ܪܝܫܐ, rabbinic פְּרוּשִׁין fr. פָּרַשׁ 'to separate', because deviating in their life from the general usage; Suidas s. v. quotes Cedrenus as follows, Φαρισαῖοι, οἱ ἑρμηνευόμενοι ἀφωρισμένοι· παρὰ τὸ μερίζειν κ. ἀφορίζειν ἑαυτοὺς τῶν ἄλλων ἁπάντων εἴς τε τὸ καθαρώτατον τοῦ βίου καὶ ἀκριβέστατον, καὶ εἰς τὰ τοῦ νόμου

ἐντάλματα). The first and feeble beginnings of this sect seem to be traceable to the age immediately succeeding the return from exile. In addition to the books of the O. T. the Pharisees recognized in oral tradition (see παράδοσις, 2) a standard of belief and life (Joseph. antt. 13, 10, 6; Mt. xv. 1; Mk. vii. 3). They sought for distinction and praise by the observance of external rites and by the outward forms of piety, such as ablutions, fastings, prayers, and alms-giving; and, comparatively negligent of genuine piety, they prided themselves on their fancied good works. They held strenuously to a belief in the existence of good and evil angels, and to the expectation of a Messiah; and they cherished the hope that the dead, after a preliminary experience either of reward or of penalty in Hades, would be recalled to life by him and be requited each according to his individual deeds. In opposition to the usurped dominion of the Herods and the rule of the Romans, they stoutly upheld the theocracy and their country's cause, and possessed great influence with the common people. According to Josephus (antt. 17, 2, 4) they numbered more than 6000. They were bitter enemies of Jesus and his cause; and were in turn severely rebuked by him for their avarice, ambition, hollow reliance on outward works, and affectation of piety in order to gain notoriety: Mt. iii. 7; v. 20; vii. 29 Lchm.; ix. 11, 14, 34; xii. 2, 14, 24, 38 Lchm. om.; xv. 1, 12; xvi. 1, 6, 11 sq.; xix. 3; xxi. 45; [xxii. 15, 34, 41]; xxiii. 2, 13–15, 23, 25–27, 29; xxvii. 62; Mk. ii. 16, 18, 24; iii. 6; vii. 1, 3, 5; viii. 11, 15; [ix. 11 L in br. T]; x. 2; xii. 13; Lk. v. 17, 21, 30, 33; vi. 2, 7; vii. 30, 36 sq. 39; xi. 37–39, 42–44 [but in 44 G T Tr WH om. L br. the cl.], 53; xii. 1; xiii. 31; xiv. 1, 3; xv. 2; xvi. 14; xvii. 20; xviii. 10 sq.; xix. 39; Jn. i. 24; iii. 1; iv. 1; vii. 32, 45, 47 sq.; viii. 3, 13; ix. [13], 15 sq. 40; xi. 46 sq. 57; xii. 19, 42; xviii. 3; Acts v. 34; xv. 5; xxiii. 6–9; xxvi. 5; Phil. iii. 5. Cf. *Win.* RWB. s. v. Pharisäer; *Reuss* in Herzog xi. p. 496, and the works referred to above s. v. Σαδδουκαῖος, fin. [esp. Sieffert's dissertation in Herzog ed. 2 (vol. xiii. p. 210 sqq.) and the copious reff. at its close]. An admirable idea of the opinions and practices of the Pharisees may be gathered also from *Paret*, Ueber d. Pharisäismus des Josephus, in the Theol. Stud. u. Krit. for 1856, No. 4, p. 809 sqq.*

5331   **φαρμακεία** [WH κία, so T (exc. in Gal. v. 20; cf. the Proleg. p. 88); see I, ι], -ας, ἡ, (φαρμακεύω);   **a.** *the use* or *the administering of drugs* (Xen. mem. 4, 2, 17).   **b.** *poisoning* (Plat., Polyb., al.): Rev. ix. 21 [here WH txt. Tr mrg. φαρμάκων; many interpp. refer the pass. to next head].   **c.** *sorcery, magical arts*, often found in connection with idolatry and fostered by it: Gal. v. 20 [where see Bp. Lghtft.] (Sap. xii. 4; xviii. 13; for כְּשָׁפִים, Is. xlvii. 9; for לָטִים, Ex. vii. 22; viii. 18; for לְהָטִים, Ex. vii. 11); trop. of the deceptions and seductions of idolatry, Rev. xviii. 23.*

5332   **φαρμακεύς, -εως, ὁ,** (φάρμακον), *one who prepares* or *uses magical remedies*; *a sorcerer*: Rev. xxi. 8 Rec. (Soph., Plat., Joseph., Lcian., Plut., al.) *

━━━━ 5341: see
(5315α)

(5332α);
see 5331

[**φάρμακον, -ου, τό,** fr. Hom. down, *a drug*; *an enchant-ment*: Tr mrg. WH txt. in Rev. ix. 21 (R.V. *sorceries*), for φαρμακεία, q. v. (in b.).*]

5333   **φαρμακός, -ή, -όν,** (φαρμάσσω [to use a φάρμακον]), [fr. Arstph. down];   **1.** *pertaining to magical arts.*   **2.** ὁ φαρμακός, subst., i. e. φαρμακεύς, q. v.: Rev. xxi. 8 G L T Tr WH; xxii. 15. (Sept. several times for כִּשֵּׁף.)*

5334   **φάσις, -εως, ἡ,** (fr. φαίνω);   **1.** in the Attic ora-tors, *the exposure of (informing against) those who have embezzled the property of the state*, or *violated the laws respecting the importation or exportation of merchandise*, or *defrauded their wards*.   **2.** univ. *a disclosure of secret crime* (κοινῶς δὲ φάσεις ἐκαλοῦντο πᾶσαι αἱ μηνύσεις τῶν λανθανόντων ἀδικημάτων, Pollux 8, 6, 47): Susan. 55 Theod.; *of information by report* [A. V. *tidings*], Acts xxi. 31.*

5335   **φάσκω;** impf. ἔφασκον; (ΦΑΩ, φημί); fr. Hom. down; *to affirm, allege, to pretend* or *profess*: foll. by the acc. with the inf., Acts xxiv. 9; xxv. 19; with the inf. and an acc. referring to the subject, Rev. ii. 2 Rec.; foll. by an inf. with a subject nom., Ro. i. 22.*

5336   **φάτνη, -ης, ἡ,** [(πατέομαι to eat; Vaniček p. 445)], *a crib, manger*: Lk. ii. 7, 12, 16; xiii. 15. (From Hom. down; Sept. for אֵבוּס, Job xxxix. 9; Prov. xiv. 4; Is. i. 3; plur. for רְפָתִים, Hab. iii. 17.)*

5337   **φαῦλος, -η, -ον,** (akin to Germ. *faul* and *flau*), *easy, slight, ordinary, mean, worthless, of no account*; ethically, *bad, wicked, base* (Theogn. [?], Eur., Xen., Plat., Plut.): Jas. iii. 16; φαῦλόν τι λέγειν περί τινος, Tit. ii. 8; φαῦλα πράσσειν, [R.V. *to do ill*], Jn. iii. 20; τὰ φ. πράσσειν opp. to τὰ ἀγαθὰ ποιεῖν, Jn. v. 29; φαῦλον (opp. to ἀγαθόν) πράσσειν, Ro. ix. 11 L T Tr WH; 2 Co. v. 10 T Tr txt. WH. [See *Trench*, Syn. § lxxxiv.]*

5338   **φέγγος, -ους, τό,** (akin to φαίνειν), fr. Aeschyl. and Pind. down, *light*: of the moon, Mt. xxiv. 29; Mk. xiii. 24; of a candle or lamp, Lk. xi. 33 R G T Tr mrg. [cf. ἀστραπή, ib. vs. 36]. (Joel ii. 10; iii. (iv.) 15 (20); Ezek. i. 4, 13, 27; Hos. vii. 6.)*

[SYN. αὐγή, φέγγος, φῶς: φῶς *light*—the general term, (of the light of a fire in Mk. xiv. 54; Lk. xxii. 56); φέγγος a more concrete and emphatic term (cf. Lk. xi. 33), the bright sunshine, the beam of light, etc.; αὐγή a still stronger term, suggesting the fiery nature of the light; used of shoot-ing, heating, rays. A Greek spoke of ἡλίου φῶς, φέγ-γος, αὐγή; or, φωτὸς φέγγος, αὐγή; or, φέγγους αὐγή; but these formulas are not reversible. Schmidt ch. 33; cf. Trench § xlvi.]

5339   **φείδομαι;** fut. φείσομαι; 1 aor. ἐφεισάμην; depon. mid.; fr. Hom. down; Sept. for חָמַל, חוּס, חָשַׂךְ (to keep back); *to spare*: absol. 2 Co. xiii. 2; τινός, to spare one [W. § 30, 10 d.; B. § 132, 15], Acts xx. 29; Ro. viii. 32; xi. 21; 1 Co. vii. 28; 2 Co. i. 23; 2 Pet. ii. 4 sq.; *to abstain* [A. V. *forbear*], an inf. denoting the act abstained from being supplied from the context: καυχᾶσθαι, 2 Co. xii. 6 (μὴ φείδου — sc. διδάσκειν — εἰ ἔχεις διδάσκειν, Xen. Cyr. 1, 6, 35; with the inf. added, λέγειν κακά, Eur. Or. 393; δρᾶσαί τι τῶν τυραννικῶν, Plat. de rep. 9 p. 574 b.).*

5340   **φειδομένως,** (fr. the ptcp. φειδόμενος), adv., *sparingly*: 2 Co. ix. 6 (*mildly*, Plut. Alex. 25).*

φελόνης, see φαιλόνης.━━━━━━━━━━━━━━

φέρω; (allied to Germ. *führen, fahren*, [Eng. *bear*, etc. Scotch *bairn*, etc. etc.; cf. Curtius § 411]); impf. ἔφε-ρον; Pass., pres. φέρομαι; impf. ἐφερόμην; fut. act. οἴσω (Jn. xxi. 18; Rev. xxi. 26); 1 aor. ἤνεγκα, ptcp. ἐνέγκας; 2 aor. inf. ἐνεγκεῖν (Mt. vii. 18 T WH); 1 aor. pass. ἠνέχθην (2 Pet. i. 17, 21); [cf. *WH.* App. p. 164; B. 68 (60); W. 90 (85 sq.); esp. Veitch p. 668 sq.]; fr. Hom. down; Sept. for הֵבִיא and נָשָׂא; *to bear*, i. e.   **1.** *to carry*;   **a.** *to carry some burden*: τὸν σταυρὸν ὄπι-σθέν τινος, Lk. xxiii. 26; *to bear with one's self* (which the Grk. writ. express by the mid.), [A. V. *to bring*]: τί, Lk. xxiv. 1; Jn. xix. 39.   **b.** *to move by bearing*; pass. like the Lat. *feror* i. q. *moveor*, *to be conveyed* or *borne*, with a suggestion of speed or force (often so in prof. auth. fr. Hom. down): of persons borne in a ship over the sea, [A. V. *to be driven*], Acts xxvii. 15, 17; of a gust of wind, *to rush*, Acts ii. 2 (cf. Jer. xviii. 14); φωνὴ ἐνεχθεῖσα, was brought, came, 2 Pet. i. 17, 18 (see ὑπό, I. 2 a.); of the mind, *to be moved inwardly*, prompted, ὑπὸ πνεύματος ἁγίου, 2 Pet. i. 21; φέρομαι ἐπί τι [R. V. *press on*], Heb. vi. 1.   **c.** acc. to a less freq. use *to bear up*, i. e. *uphold* (keep from falling): φέρων τὰ πάντα τῷ ῥήματι τῆς δυνάμεως αὐτοῦ, of God [the Son] *the pre-server* of the universe, Heb. i. 3 (so in the Targums and Rabbinical writ. כָּבַל is often used, e. g. עוֹלָמוֹ סוֹבֵל, of God; οὐ δυνήσομαι ἐγὼ μόνος φέρειν τὸν λαὸν τοῦτον, Num. xi. 14, cf. 11; add, Deut. i. 9, for נָשָׂא; ὁ τὰ μὴ [μὲν] ὄντα φέρων καὶ τὰ πάντα γεννῶν, Philo, rer. div. haer. § 7; fr. native Grk. writ. we have φέρειν τὴν πόλιν, Plut. Lucull. 6; cf. *Bleek*, Brief a. d. Hebr. ii. 1 p. 70 sq.).   **2.** *to bear* i. e. *endure* (exx. without number in Grk. writ. fr. Hom. down; cf. Passow s. v. B. I. 3; [L. and S. s. v. A. III.]): τὸν ὀνειδισμόν, Heb. xiii. 13; τί, to endure the rigor of a thing, Heb. xii. 20; τινά, to bear patiently one's conduct, or to spare one (abstain from punishing or destroying), Ro. ix. 22.   **3.** *to bring, bring to, bring forward*;   **a.** prop.: τινά, Acts v. 16; τι, Mk. [vi. 27 R G T Tr WH]; xi. 2 T Tr WH; xii. 16; Lk. xv. 23; Acts iv. 34, 37; v. 2; 2 Tim. iv. 13; τινὰ πρός τινα, Mk. i. 32; ii. 3 [T Tr mrg. WH]; ix. 17 [W. 278 (262)], 19 sq.; [τινὰ ἐπί τινα, Lk. xii. 11 Tr mrg.]; τινά τινι, Mk. vii. 32; viii. 22; [τινὰ ἐπί τινος, Lk. v. 18]; τί τινι, Mk. xii. 15; Jn. ii. 8; with ὧδε added, Mt. xiv. 18 [here Tr mrg. br. ὧδε]; xvii. 17; τὶ πρός τινα, Mk. xi. 7 [T Tr WH]; τὶ εἰς with an acc. of the place, Rev. xxi. 24, 26; τὶ ἐπὶ πίνακι, Mt. xiv. 11; Mk. vi. [27 Lchm.], 28; ἀπό τινος (a part of [see ἀπό, I. 2]), Jn. xxi. 10; φέρω τινὶ φαγεῖν, Jn. iv. 33.   **b.** *to move to, apply*: τὸν δάκτυ-λον, τὴν χεῖρα, ὧδε, εἰς with an acc. of the place, [A. V. *reach*], Jn. xx. 27.   fig., φέρεται ὑμῖν τι, a thing is offered (lit. 'is being brought') to you: ἡ χάρις, 1 Pet. i. 13.   **c.** *to bring by announcing*: διδαχήν, 2 Jn. 10 (τινὶ ἀγγελίην, μῦθον, λόγον, φήμην, etc., in Hom., Pind., al.); *to announce* (see Passow s. v. p. 2231b; [L. and S. s. v. A. IV. 4]): θάνατον, Heb. ix. 16.   **d.** *to bear* i. e. *bring forth, produce*;   **a.** prop.: καρπόν, [Mt. vii. 18a T WH, 18b T]; Mk. iv. 8 [on ἐν ἑξήκοντα etc. WH txt.,

━━━ 5342

see ἐν, I. 5 f.]; Jn. xii. 24; xv. 2, 4 sq. 8, 16; (Hom. Od. 4, 229; Hes. opp. 117; Xen. mem. 2, 1, 28; al.).　β. *to bring forward in speech*: προφητεία, 2 Pet. i. 21 [A. V. *came*]; κρίσιν κατά τινος, 2 Pet. ii. 11; [κατηγορίαν κατά τινος, Jn. xviii. 29 R G L Tr (but here T WH om. κατά)]; αἰτιώματα κατά τινος, Acts xxv. 7 R G [but G om. κατά τ.]; αἰτίαν, ibid. 18 L T Tr WH; (πάσας αἰτίας, reasons, Dem. p. 1328, 22; ἀπολογισμούς, Polyb. 1, 32, 4).　**e.** *to lead, conduct*, [A. V. *bring, carry*, etc. (Germ. *führen*)]: ἐπί with an acc. of the place, Mk. xv. 22; Acts xiv. 13; (ἐκεῖ) ὅπου, Jn. xxi. 18; metaph. a gate is said φέρειν (Lat. *ferre* [Eng. *lead*]) εἰς τὴν πόλιν, Acts xii. 10 (ὁδὸς φ. εἰς ἱερόν, Hdt. 2, 122; διὰ τῆς ἀγορᾶς ἐς τὸ πρὸς ἠῶ, id. 2, 138 [cf. L. and S. s. v. A. VII.]).　[COMP.: ἀνα-, ἀπο-, δια-, εἰσ-, παρ-εισ-, ἐκ-, ἐπι-, κατα-, παρα-, περι-, προ-, προσ-, συν-, ὑπο-φέρω.　SYN. cf. Schmidt ch. 105.]*

5343　φεύγω; fut. φεύξομαι; 2 aor. ἔφυγον; fr. Hom. down; Sept. for נוּס and בָּרַח; *to flee*, i. e.　**a.** *to flee away, seek safety by flight*: absol., Mt. viii. 33; xxvi. 56; Mk. v. 14; xiv. 50; Lk. viii. 34; Jn. x. 12, [13 (here G T Tr txt. WH om. L Tr mrg. br. the cl.)]; Acts vii. 29; foll. by εἰς with an acc. of the place, Mt. ii. 13; x. 23; [xxiv. 16, here R G T WH mrg. ἐπί]; Mk. xiii. 14; Lk. xxi. 21; [Jn. vi. 15 Tdf.]; Rev. xii. 6; foll. by ἐπί with an acc. of the place, Mt. xxiv. 16 [here L Tr WH txt. εἰς]; ἐκ τοῦ πλοίου, Acts xxvii. 30; foll. by ἀπό with a gen. of the place, in a purely local sense, to leave by fleeing, as in Grk. writ. (cf. W. 223 (210); [B. § 131, 1]), Mk. xvi. 8; by ἀπό with a gen. of the pers. inspiring fear or threatening danger (after the Hebr.), Jn. x. 5; Jas. iv. 7; poetically, φεύξεται ἀπ᾽ αὐτῶν ὁ θάνατος, death shall flee from them, opp. to ζητήσουσι θάνατον, Rev. ix. 6.　**b.** metaph. *to flee* (*to shun* or *avoid by flight*) something abhorrent, esp. vices: with an acc. of the thing, 1 Co. vi. 18 (Sap. i. 5; 4 Macc. viii. 18); opp. to διώκειν, 1 Tim. vi. 11; 2 Tim. ii. 22; Hebraistically foll. by ἀπό with a gen. of the thing, 1 Co. x. 14 (ἀπὸ ἁμαρτίας, Sir. xxi. 2).　**c.** *to be saved by flight, to escape safe out of danger*: absol. Heb. xii. 25 R G; with an acc. of the thing, Heb. xi. 34; Hebraistically foll. by ἀπό with a gen. — of the thing, Mt. iii. 7; xxiii. 33; Lk. iii. 7; of the pers. Mk. xiv. 52 [T Tr txt. WH om. L Tr mrg. br. ἀπ᾽ αὐτῶν].　**d.** poetically, *to flee away* i. q. *vanish*: πᾶσα νῆσος ἔφυγε καὶ ὄρη οὐχ εὑρέθησαν, Rev. xvi. 20; with the Hebraistic addition ἀπὸ προσώπου τινός (as in Deut. xxviii. 7; Josh. viii. 4; viii. 5; 2 Chr. x. 2, etc.; see πρόσωπον, 1 b. p. 551ᵇ mid.), Rev. xx. 11. [COMP. and SYN.: ἀποφ. (emphasizes the inner endeavor or aversion), διαφ. (suggests the space which the flight must traverse), ἐκφ. (looks rather to the physical possibility), καταφ. (points to the place or the person where refuge is sought); *Schmidt*, Syn. ch. 109.]*

5344　Φῆλιξ (Lchm. Φήλιξ, [so Tr in Acts xxiv. 22 (by mistake?)]; cf. *Lipsius*, Grammat. Untersuch. p. 37; B. 13 (12); [*Tdf.* Proleg. p. 104; and reff. s. v. κήρυξ]), [lit. 'happy', 'fortunate'], -ικος, ὁ, (Claudius [but in Tacit. hist. 5, 9 called Antonius]) *Felix*, the eleventh procurator of Judæa, (apparently between A.D. 52 and 60).

He was a freedman of Claudius and his mother Antonia, and the brother of Pallas, the powerful favorite of the emperor. He first married Drusilla [(?) see Dict. of Grk. and Rom. Biogr. s. v. 4], the granddaughter of Cleopatra and Antony; and afterwards Drusilla, the daughter of Herod Agrippa. Acc. to Tacitus "per omnem saevitiam ac libidinem jus regium servili ingenio exercuit", and by his cruelty and injustice he stimulated the rage of the turbulent Jews against the Roman rule. When he had retired from the province and come to Rome, the Jews of Cæsarea accused him before the emperor, but through the intercession of his brother Pallas he was acquitted by Nero (cf. Tacit. hist. 5, 9, 5 sq.; annal. 12, 54; Suet. vit. Claudii, 28; Joseph. antt. 20, 7, 1 sq. and 8, 5 sq.; 7, 9; b. j. 2, 13): Acts xxiii. 24, 26; xxiv. 3, 22, 24 sq. 27; xxv. 14.　Cf. *Win.* RWB. s. v.; *Paret* in Herzog iv. 354; [*V. Schmidt* in Herzog ed. 2, iv. 518 sq.]; *Overbeck* in Schenkel ii. 263 sq.; *Schürer*, Neutest. Zeitgesch. p. 303 sq. § 19, 4; [*Farrar*, St. Paul, ch. xli.].*

5345　φήμη, -ης, ἡ, (φημί), *fame, report*: Mt. ix. 26; Lk. iv. 14.　[(From Hom. down.)]*

5346　φημί; impf. ἔφην; (fr. φάω, to bring forth into the light [cf. Curtius § 407]); hence [fr. Hom. down] prop. *to make known one's thoughts, to declare*; to say: ἔφη, he said (once on a time), Mt. xxvi. 61; historical writers, in quoting the words of any one, prefix φησίν, ἔφη, (Lat. *ait, inquit*): Lk. xxii. 58; Acts viii. 36, and often; φησίν and ἔφη are used of a person replying, Mt. xiii. 29; Lk. vii. 40; Jn. i. 23; ix. 38; Acts vii. 2, etc.; of one who asks a question, Mt. xxvii. 23; Acts xvi. 30; xxi. 37; ἔφη μεγάλη τῇ φωνῇ, Acts xxvi. 24; ἀποκριθεὶς ἔφη, Mt. viii. 8; φησίν is interjected into the recorded speech of another [cf. W. § 61, 6], Mt. xiv. 8; Acts xxv. 5, 22; xxvi. 25; also ἔφη, Acts xxiii. 35; φησίν, like the Lat. *ait, inquit*, is employed esp. in the later Grk. usage with an indefinite subject ('impersonally') [cf. *man sagt, on dit, they say*] (inserted in a sentence containing the words of another [cf. W. u. s.]): 2 Co. x. 10 where L Tr mrg. WH mrg. φασίν (cf. Passow ii. p. 2238ᵃ; [L. and S. s. v. II. 1]; B. § 129, 19; [W. § 58, 9 b. β.; § 64, 3]). φησίν sc. ὁ θεός, 1 Co. vi. 16 [here Lchm. br. φησίν]; Heb. viii. 5; [W. 522 (486 sq.)]. The constructions of the verb are the foll.: ἔφη αὐτῷ, he replied to him, to them, Mt. iv. 7; xiii. 28; xxi. 27, etc.; Mk. [ix. 12 T Tr txt. WH]; xiv. 29; Lk. vii. 44; Acts xxvi. 32; ἀποκριθεὶς αὐτῷ ἔφη, Lk. xxiii. 3; ἔφη πρός τινα, Lk. xxii. 70; Acts x. 28; xvi. 37; xxvi. 1; with an acc. of the thing, 1 Co. xv. 19; foll. by ὅτι, 1 Co. x. 19; τοῦτο etc. ὅτι, 1 Co. vii. 29 [Rec.ᵇᵉᶻ ᵉˡᶻ; al. om. ὅτι]; xv. 50; foll. by an acc. with inf., Ro. iii. 8.　[On its alleged omission, see W. § 64, 7 a.　COMP.: σύμ-φημι.]

see 1310 &5346　φημίζω; 1 aor. pass. 3 pers. sing. ἐφημίσθη; esp. freq. in the poets fr. Hesiod down; *to spread a report, to disseminate by report*: Mt. xxviii. 15 T WH mrg. (after codd. א Δ 33 etc.) for διαφημ. q. v.*

5347　Φῆστος, -ου, ὁ, (Porcius) *Festus*, a procurator of Judæa, the successor of Felix [c. A.D. 60] (see Φῆλιξ [and reff., esp. Schürer p. 308 sq.]) : Acts xxiv. 27 ; xxv. 1, 4, 9, 12–14, 22–24 ; xxvi. 24 sq. 32. (Joseph. antt. 20, 8, 9 and 9, 1 ; b. j. 2, 14, 1.) *

5348 **φθάνω**: 1 aor. ἔφθασα [W. § 15 s. v.] ; pf. ἔφθακα (1 Th. ii. 16 L txt. WH mrg.) ; fr. Hom. down ; **1.** *to come before, precede, anticipate* : ἡμεῖς οὐ μὴ φθάσωμεν (see μή, IV. 2) τοὺς κοιμηθέντας, we shall not get the start of those who have fallen asleep, i. e. we shall not attain to the fellowship of Christ sooner than the dead, nor have precedence in blessedness, 1 Th. iv. 15 ; ἔφθασεν ἐπ' αὐτοὺς ἡ ὀργή, (God's penal) wrath came upon them unexpectedly, 1 Th. ii. 16 ; ἔφθασεν ἐφ' ὑμᾶς ἡ βασιλεία τοῦ θεοῦ, the kingdom of God has come upon you sooner than you expected, Mt. xii. 28 ; Lk. xi. 20 ; [but all the preceding exx. except the first are referred by the majority of recent interpp. to the foll. head ; — a meaning esp. common when the verb is construed with prepositions]. **2.** in the Alex. [and other later] writ. the idea of priority disappears, *to come to, arrive at* : εἴς τι, Phil. iii. 16 ; *to reach, attain to,* a thing, Ro. ix. 31 ; ἄχρι τινός, 2 Co. x. 14 ; (τινί, to a thing, Tob. v. 19 ; ἕως τοῦ οὐρανοῦ, Test. xii. Patr. p. 530 [i. e. test. Rub. 5 fin.] ; ἡ μεγαλωσύνη σου ἐμεγαλύνθη καὶ ἔφθασεν εἰς τὸν οὐρανόν, Dan. 4, 19 Theod. [cf. 17, 25 ; φθ. ἕως τῶν οὐρανῶν, 2 Chr. xxviii. 9 ; ἔφθασεν ὁ μὴν ὁ ἕβδομος, 2 Esdr. iii. 1 ; Philo de mund. opif. § 1 ; de legg. alleg. iii. 76 ; de confus. lingg. § 29 ; Plut. apotheg. Lacon. § 28 ; de Alex. s. virt. s. fort. orat. ii. 5. Cf. *Soph.* Lex. s. v. ; *Geldart,* Mod. Greek, p. 206 ; W. § 2, 1 b.]). [COMP.: προ-φθάνω.] *

5349 **φθαρτός, -ή, -όν,** (φθείρω), *corruptible, perishable,* (Vulg. *corruptibilis*) : 1 Co. ix. 25 ; 1 Pet. i. 23 ; ἄνθρωπος, i. e. mortal, opp. to ὁ ἄφθαρτος θεός, Ro. i. 23 ; οὐ φθαρτοῖς ἀργυρίῳ ἢ χρυσίῳ, not with corruptible things, with silver or gold, 1 Pet. i. 18 [W. § 59, 5 fin.] (χρυσὸς κ. ἄργυρος, οὐσίαι φθαρταί, Philo de cherub. § 14 ; οὐκ ἄργυρον οὐδὲ χρυσόν τινα, ἢ ἄλλο τῶν ἐν ὕλαις φθαρταῖς de congr. erudit. grat. § 20) ; neut. τὸ φθαρτόν, that which is liable to corruption, [τὸ φθαρτὸν τοῦτο this *corruptible* (A.V.)], 1 Co. xv. 53 sq. (Diod. 1, 6 ; Philo de legg. alleg. 2, 1 ; de cherub. § 2 ; [Aristot.], Plut., Sext. Emp., al. ; 2 Macc. vii. 16 ; Sap. ix. 15 ; xiv. 8.) *

5350 **φθέγγομαι** ; 1 aor. ptcp. φθεγξάμενος ; (φέγγος [but cf. Vaniček p. 1176], ΦΑΩ) ; depon. mid. ; fr. Hom. down ; **1.** *to give out a sound, noise,* or *cry* ; used by the Grks. of any sort of sound or voice, whether of man or animal or inanimate object — as of thunder, musical instruments, etc. ; [φθέγγ. denotes sound in its relation to the hearer rather than to its cause ; the μέγα λαλῶν is a braggart, the μέγα φθεγγόμενος is a lofty orator ; *Schmidt,* Syn. ch. 1 § 53]. **2.** *to proclaim ; to speak, utter* : Acts iv. 18 ; ὑπέρογκα, 2 Pet. ii. 18 (ἄδικα. Sap. i. 8) ; ὑποζύγιον ἄφωνον ἐν ἀνθρωπίνῃ φωνῇ φθεγξάμενον, 2 Pet. ii. 16. [COMP.: ἀπο-φθέγγομαι.] *

5351 **φθείρω** ; fut. φθερῶ ; 1 aor. ἔφθειρα ; Pass., pres. φθείρομαι ; 2 aor. ἐφθάρην ; 2 fut. φθαρήσομαι ; (akin to Germ. *verderben*) ; Sept. for שָׁחַת ; [fr. Hom. down] ; *to corrupt, to destroy* : prop. τὸν ναὸν τοῦ θεοῦ (in the opinion of the Jews the temple was corrupted, or 'destroyed',

when any one defiled or in the slightest degree damaged anything in it, or if its guardians neglected their duties ; cf. *Deyling,* Observv. sacrae, vol. ii. p. 505 sqq.), dropping the fig., to lead away a Christian church from that state of knowledge and holiness in which it ought to abide, 1 Co. iii. 17ᵃ ; τινά, to punish with death, 1 Co. iii. 17ᵇ ; i. q. to bring to want or beggary (cf. our *ruin* [A. V. *corrupt*]), 2 Co. vii. 2 ; pass. *to be destroyed, to perish* : ἔν τινι, by a thing, Jude 10 ; ἐν with a dat. denoting the condition, ἐν τῇ φθορᾷ αὐτῶν, 2 Pet. ii. 12 L T Tr WH. in an ethical sense, *to corrupt, deprave* : φθείρουσιν ἤθη χρηστὰ ὁμιλίαι κακαί (a saying of Menander [see ἦθος, 2], which seems to have passed into a proverb [see Wetstein ad loc. ; *Gataker,* Advers. miscel. l. i. c. 1 p. 174 sq.]), 1 Co. xv. 33 ; the character of the inhabitants of the earth, Rev. xix. 2 ; pass. φθείρομαι ἀπό τινος, to be so corrupted as to fall away from a thing [see ἀπό, I. 3 d.], 2 Co. xi. 3 ; φθειρόμενον κατὰ τὰς ἐπιθυμίας, [R. V. *waxeth corrupt* etc.], Eph. iv. 22. [COMP.: δια-, κατα-φθείρω.] *

5352 **φθιν-οπωρινός, -ή, -όν,** (φθινόπωρον, late autumn ; fr. φθίνω to wane, waste away, and ὀπώρα autumn), *autumnal* (Polyb. 4, 37, 2 ; Aristot. h. a. 5, 11 ; [Strab.], Plut.) : δένδρα φθινοπ. *autumn trees,* i. e. trees such as they are at the close of autumn, dry, leafless and without fruit, hence ἄκαρπα is added ; used of unfruitful, worthless men, Jude 12 [cf. Bp. *Lghtft.* A Fresh Revision etc. p. 134 sq.].*

5353 **φθόγγος, -ου, ὁ,** (φθέγγομαι, q. v.), *a musical sound,* whether vocal or instrumental (Sap. xix. 17) : 1 Co. xiv. 7 ; Ro. x. 18, in this latter pass. Paul transfers what is said in Ps. xviii. (xix.) 5 to the voices of the preachers of the gospel. (Hom., Tragg., Xen., Plat., al.) *

5354 **φθονέω, -ῶ,** (φθόνος) ; fr. Hom. down ; *to envy* : τινί, one, Gal. v. 26 [here L txt. Tr mrg. WH mrg. read the accus. ; see B. § 132, 15 Rem. ; W. § 31, 1 b.].*

5355 **φθόνος, -ου, ὁ,** fr. [Pind. and] Hdt. down, *envy* : Ro. i. 29 ; Gal. v. 21 ; 1 Tim. vi. 4 ; Tit. iii. 3 ; 1 Pet. ii. 1 ; διὰ φθόνον, *for envy,* i. e. prompted by envy [see διά. B. II. 2 b.], Mt. xxvii. 18 ; Mk. xv. 10 ; Phil. i. 15, (Dio Cass. 44, 36) ; πρὸς φθόνον ἐπιποθεῖ τὸ πνεῦμα ὃ κατῴκησεν [but see κατοικίζω] ἐν ἡμῖν, doth the Spirit which took up its abode within us (i. e. the Holy Spirit) long *enviously* ? (see πρός, I. 3 g.), Jas. iv. 5 [but T (WH in second mrg.) drop the interrog.] ; see on the pass. *Grimm* in the Theol. Stud. u. Krit. for 1854, p. 934 sqq. [SYN. see ζῆλος, 2 fin.] *

5356 **φθορά, -ᾶς, ἡ,** (φθείρω), fr. Aeschyl. and Hdt. down, **1.** *corruption, destruction, perishing,* (opp. to γένεσις, origin, often in Plat., Aristot., Plut. ; opp. to σωτηρία, Plat. Phileb. p. 35 e. ; for נַחַת, Ps. cii. (ciii.) 4 ; Jon. ii. 7) : Ro. viii. 21 (on which see δουλεία) ; 2 Pet. ii. 12ᵃ [some (cf. R. V. mrg.) take φθ. here actively : εἰς φθοράν, *to destroy*] ; ἐν φθορᾷ, in a state of corruption or decomposition (of the body at burial), 1 Co. xv. 42 ; by meton. *that which is subject to corruption, what is perishable,* opp. to ἀφθαρσία, ibid. 50 ; in the Christian sense, *the loss of* salvation, eternal misery (which elsewhere is called ἀπώ-λεια), Col. ii. 22 (see ἀπόχρησις); opp. to ζωὴ αἰώνιος, Gal. vi. 8, cf. Schott ad loc. **2.** in the N. T. in an ethical sense, *corruption* i. e. *moral decay*: 2 Pet. i. 4; ii. 12ᵇ [some take the word here **actively** (R.V. txt. *in their destroying*), al. refer it to 1 above], 19 ; with τῆς ζωῆς added, Sap. xiv. 12.*

5357 φιάλη, -ης, ἡ, fr. Hom. down, Sept. for מִזְרָק, *a broad, shallow bowl, deep saucer* [Dict. of Antiq. s. v. Patera; B. D. Am. ed. s. v. Vial]: Rev. v. 8; xv. 7; xvi. 1–4, 8, 10, 12, 17; xvii. 1; xxi. 9.*

5358 φιλ-άγαθος, -ον, (fr. φίλος and ἀγαθός), *loving goodness*: Tit. i. 8. (Sap. vii. 22; Plut. praec. conjug. c. 17; also comp. Thes. c. Rom. c. 2; [φιλάγαθος οὐ φίλαυτος, Aristot. magn. mor. ii. 14 p. 1212ᵇ 18; Polyb. 6, 53, 9; Philo de vit. Moys. ii. § 2].)*

5359 Φιλαδέλφεια [T WH -ία (cf. *Tdf.* Proleg. p. 87), see I, ι], -ας, ἡ, *Philadelphia* (now *Alahshar, Allahschir*, [or *Ala-Shehr* i. e. "The White City" (Sayce)]), a city of Lydia in Asia Minor, situated near the eastern base of Mount Tmolus, founded and named by the Pergamene king Attalus II. Philadelphus. After the death of king Attalus III. Philometor, B. C. 133, it together with his entire kingdom came by his will under the jurisdiction of the Romans: Rev. i. 11; iii. 7.*

5360 φιλαδελφία, -ας, ἡ, (φιλάδελφος), *the love of brothers* (or *sisters*), *brotherly love*, (prop., 4 Macc. xiii. 22; xiv. 1; [Philo, leg. ad Gaium § 12]; Joseph. antt. 4, 2, 4; Lcian. dial. deor. 26, 2; Plut. libell. περὶ φιλαδελφίας; [cf. Babrius 47, 15]); in the N. T. *the love which Christians cherish for each other as 'brethren'* (see ἀδελφός, 4); [*love of the brethren*] (Vulg. *caritas* or *amor fraternitatis*): Ro. xii. 10; 1 Th. iv. 9; Heb. xiii. 1; 1 Pet. i. 22; 2 Pet. i. 7, cf. 1 Jn. v. 1.*

5361 φιλ-άδελφος, -ον, (φίλος and ἀδελφός), *loving brother or sister* (Soph., Plut., Anthol.); in a broader sense, *loving one like a brother*, Xen. mem. 2, 3, 17; *loving one's fellow-countrymen*, of an Israelite, 2 Macc. xv. 14; *of a Christian loving Christians*, 1 Pet. iii. 8 [R.V. *loving as brethren*].*

5362 φίλανδρος, -ον, (φίλος and ἀνήρ), [fr. Aeschyl. down (in other senses)], *loving her husband*: Tit. ii. 4 (φίλανδροι καὶ σώφρονες γυναῖκες, Plut. praec. conj. c. 28).*

5363 φιλανθρωπία, -ας, ἡ, (φιλάνθρωπος), fr. Xen. and Plat. down, *love of mankind, benevolence*, (Vulg. *humanitas*), [R.V. *kindness*]: Acts xxviii. 2; Tit. iii. 4. [Cf. *Field, Otium Norv. Pars iii.* ad ll. cc.]*

5364 φιλανθρώπως, adv., *humanely, kindly*: Acts xxvii. 3. (Isocr., Dem., Polyb., Diod., Plut., al.; 2 Macc. ix. 27.)*

5365 φιλαργυρία, -ας, ἡ, (φιλάργυρος), *love of money, avarice*: 1 Tim. vi. 10. (Isocr., Polyb., Ceb. tab. c. 23; Diod. 5, 26; [Diog. Laërt. 6, 50; Stob. flor. 10, 38; Philo de mut. nom. § 40]; Plut., Lcian., Hdian. 6, 9, 17 (8); 4 Macc. i. 26.) [Cf. *Trench*, Syn. § xxiv.]*

5366 φιλ-άργυρος, -ον, (φίλος and ἄργυρος), *loving money, avaricious*: Lk. xvi. 14; 2 Tim. iii. 2. (Soph., Xen., Plat., al.)*

5367 φιλ-αυτος, -ον, (φίλος and αὐτός), *loving one's self*; *too*

intent on one's own interests, selfish: 2 Tim. iii. 2. (Aristot. [(cf. φιλάγαθος); rhet. 1, 11, 26 (where cf. Cope) ἀνάγκη πάντας φιλαύτους εἶναι ἢ μᾶλλον ἢ ἧττον]; Philo, legg. alleg. 1, 15; Plut., [Epict.], Lcian., Sext. Emp.; διὰ τὸ φύσει πάντας εἶναι φιλαύτους, Joseph. antt. 3, 8, 1.) [Cf. *Trench*, Syn. § xciii.]*

5368 φιλέω, -ῶ; impf. 3 pers. sing. ἐφίλει; 1 aor. ἐφίλησα; pf. πεφίληκα; (φίλος); fr. Hom. down; **1.** *to love*; *to be friendly to one*, (Sept. several times for אָהֵב): τινά, Mt. x. 37; Jn. v. 20 [here L mrg. ἀγαπᾷ]; xi. 3, 36; xv. 19; xvi. 27; xx. 2; xxi. 15–17; 1 Co. xvi. 22; Rev. iii. 19; with ἐν πίστει added, with a love founded in and springing from faith, Tit. iii. 15; τί, *to love* i. e. *delight in, long for*, a thing: τὴν πρωτοκλισίαν, Mt. xxiii. 6; ἀσπασμούς, Lk. xx. 46; τὴν ψυχήν, to be desirous of preserving one's life (opp. to μισεῖν, to hate it when it cannot be kept without denying Christ), Jn. xii. 25; with nouns denoting virtues or vices: τὸ ψεῦδος, Rev. xxii. 15 (σοφίαν, Prov. xxix. 3; viii. 17); foll. by an inf., like the Lat. *amo facere, to love to do*, i. e. *to do with pleasure*: Mt. vi. 5 (Is. lvi. 10; Pind. Nem. 1, 15; Aeschyl. septem 619; Agam. 763; Suppl. 769; Eur. Iph. Taur. 1198; Rhes. 394; Xen. hipparch. 7, 9; Ael. v. h. 14, 37). **2.** *to kiss*: τινά, Mt. xxvi. 48; Mk. xiv. 44; Lk. xxii. 47, (often in the Grk. writ.; Sept. for נָשַׁק, Gen. xxvii. 26 sq., and often). **3.** As to the distinction between ἀγαπᾶν and φιλεῖν: the former, by virtue of its connection with ἄγαμαι, properly denotes a love founded in admiration, veneration, esteem, like the Lat. *diligere, to be kindly disposed to one, wish one well*; but φιλεῖν denotes an inclination prompted by sense and emotion, Lat. *amare*: ὁ μὴ τοῦ δεόμενος οὐδέ τι ἀγαπῴη ἄν· ὁ δὲ μὴ ἀγαπῴη [-πῶν (?)], οὐδ' ἂν φιλοῖ, Plat. Lys. p. 215 b.; ἐφιλήσατε αὐτὸν (Julius Caesar) ὡς πατέρα καὶ ἠγαπήσατε ὡς εὐεργέτην, Dio Cass. 44, 48; ut scires, eum a me non *diligi* solum, verum etiam *amari*, Cic. ad fam. 13, 47; L. Clodius valde me *diligit* vel, ut ἐμφατικώτερον dicam, valde me *amat*, id. ad Brut. 1. Hence men are said ἀγαπᾶν God, not φιλεῖν; and God is said ἀγαπῆσαι τὸν κόσμον (Jn. iii. 16), and φιλεῖν the disciples of Christ (Jn. xvi. 27); Christ bids us ἀγαπᾶν (not φιλεῖν) τοὺς ἐχθρούς (Mt. v. 44), because love as an **emotion** cannot be commanded, but only love as a **choice**. Wisdom says, τοὺς ἐμὲ φιλοῦντας ἀγαπῶ, Prov. viii. 17. As a further aid in judging of the difference compare the two words compare the foll. pass.: Jn. xi. 3, 5, 36; xxi. 15–17; [even in some cases where they might appear to be used interchangeably (e. g. Jn. xiv. 23; xvi. 27) the difference can still be traced]. From what has been said, it is evident that ἀγαπᾶν is not, and cannot be, used of sexual love [but it is so used occasionally by the later writers; cf. Pericl. 24, 12 p. 165 e.; symp. 7 p. 180 b. ὁ ἐρώμενος τὸν ἐραστὴν ἀγαπᾷ; cf. *Steph. Thesaur.* i. p. 209 a.; *Soph.* Lex. s. v. ἀγαπάω, 2; *Woolsey* in the Andover Rev. for Aug. 1885, p. 170 sq.]. Cf. *Tittmann*, Syn. N. T. i. p. 50 sqq.; Cremer s. v. ἀγαπάω [4te Aufl. p. 9 sq.]; Trench § xii.; [Schmidt ch. 136, esp. § 6; *Cope*, Aristot. rhet. vol. i. App. A. (also given in the Journ. of Philol. for 1868, p. 88 sqq.) ; also *Höhne* in (Luthardt's) Zeitschr. f. kirchl. Wissensch. u. s. w. for 1882, p. 6 sqq. ; esp. Woolsey u. s..   COMP. : κατα-

(5368a):
see 5384 φιλέω.] *

φίλη, ἡ, see φίλος, 2.

5369 ---- **φιλήδονος**, -ον, (φίλος and ἡδονή), *loving pleasure*: 2 Tim. iii. 4. (Polyb. 40, 6, 10 ; Plut., Lcian., al.) *

5370 **φίλημα**, -τος, τό, fr. Aeschyl. down, *a kiss* (see φιλέω, 2) : Lk. vii. 45 ; xxii. 48, (Prov. xxvii. 6 ; Cant. i. 2) ; ἅγιον, the kiss with which, as a sign of fraternal affection, Christians were accustomed to welcome or dismiss their companions in the faith : Ro. xvi. 16 ; 1 Co. xvi. 20 ; 2 Co. xiii. 12 ; 1 Th. v. 26 ; it is also called φίλημα ἀγάπης, 1 Pet. v. 14. Cf. *Kahle*, De osculo sancto (Regiom. 1867) ; [B. D. s. v. Kiss ; also Dict. of Christ. Antiq. s. v. Kiss].*

5371 **Φιλήμων**, -ονος, ὁ, *Philemon*, of Colossæ, converted to Christianity by Paul (Philem. 19), and the recipient of the lovely little letter which bears his name in the N. T. : Philem. 1. [BB. DD. s. v. ; esp. Bp. *Lghtft.* Com. on Col. and Philem., Intr.] *

5372 **Φίλητος** ([Chandler § 325 ; but] R L T Tr Φιλητός, see Τυχικός [*Tdf.* Proleg. p. 103]), -ου, ὁ, *Philetus*, a heretic : 2 Tim. ii. 17.*

5373 **φιλία**, -ας, ἡ, (φίλος), *friendship* : with a gen. of the object, Jas. iv. 4. [(Theogn., Hdt., al.)] *

5374 **Φιλιππήσιος**, -ου, ὁ, *a Philippian* : Phil. iv. 15.*

5375 **Φίλιπποι**, -ων, οἱ, [on the plur. cf. W. § 27, 3], *Philippi*, a city of Macedonia Prima [see B. D s v. Macedonia], situated on [near] the northern coast of the Ægean Sea, between the rivers Strymon and Nestus, and the cities Neapolis and Amphipolis. It took its name from Philip I. of Macedon, who built it up from a village called Κρηνίδες, and adorned and fortified it : Acts xvi. 12 (on this pass. see κολώνια) ; xx. 6 ; Phil. i. 1 ; 1 Th. ii. 2. [See Bp. *Lghtft.* Com. on Philip., Intr. iii.] *

5376 **Φίλιππος**, -ου, ὁ, *Philip* ;   **1.** a son of Herod the Great by his fifth wife, Cleopatra of Jerusalem (Joseph. antt. 17, 1, 3), and by far the best of his sons. He was tetrarch of Gaulanitis, Trachonitis, Auranitis, Batanæa. and (acc. to the disputed statement of Lk. iii. 1) of Ituræa also [cf. Schürer as below ; but see B. D. Am. ed. s. v. Ituræa] ; and the founder of the cities of Cæsarea Philippi (in the Decapolis) and Julias. After having lived long in celibacy, he married Salome, the daughter of Herod [Philip, the disinherited ; see below] his half-brother (Joseph. antt. 18, 5, 4). He ruled mildly, justly and wisely thirty-seven years, and in A. D. 34 died without issue, leaving a grateful memory of his reign in the minds of his subjects (Joseph. antt. 18, 2, 1 and 4, 6 ; b. j. 2, 9, 1) : Mt. xvi. 13 ; Mk. viii. 27 ; Lk. iii. 1 ; cf. *Keim* in Schenkel iii. p. 40 sqq. ; *Schürer*, Neutest. Zeitgesch. § 17, a. ; [BB. DD.]. In Mt. xiv. 3 ; Mk. vi. 17, and Lk. iii. 19 Rec. it is said that his wife was Herodias (see Ἡρωδιάς) ; thus Herod, the son of Herod the Great by Mariamne the daughter of the high-priest Simon (Joseph. antt. 18, 5, 1 ; b. j. 1, 28, 4), who lived as a private citizen in comparative obscurity and was the first

husband of Herodias (Joseph. antt. 18, 5, 4), seems to have been confounded with Philip, who as a ruler was better known (cf. *Volkmar*, Ueber ein. histor. Irrthum in den Evangg., in Zeller's Theol. Jahrbb. for 1846, p. 363 sqq.). Many interpreters (see esp. *Krebs*, Observv. etc. p. 37 sq. ; [*Deyling*, Observv. sacr. vol. ii. (ed. 2) p. 342 sqq.]), in vindication of the Evangelists, make the somewhat improbable conjecture that the first husband of Herodias had two names, one a family name Herod, the other a proper name Philip ; [yet so *Winer*, RWB. s. v. Philippus, 5 ; BB. DD. ; *Gerlach* in the Zeitschr. f. Luth. Theol. for 1869, p. 32 sq. ; Meyer on Mt. l. c. ; Weiss on Mk. l. c.].   **2.** *Philip* of Bethsaida [in Galilee], one of the apostles : Mt. x. 3 ; Mk. iii. 18 ; Lk. vi. 14 ; Jn. i. 43-48 (44-49) ; vi. 5, 7 ; xii. 21 sq. ; xiv. 8 sq. ; Acts i. 13.   **3.** *Philip*, one of the seven deacons of the church at Jerusalem, and also an 'evangelist' (εὐαγγελιστής. q. v.) : Acts vi. 5 ; viii. 5-40 ; xxi. 8.*

φιλό-θεος, -ον, (φίλος and θεός), *loving* [A.V. *lovers of*] *God* : 2 Tim. iii. 4. ([Aristot. rhet. 2, 17, 6], Philo, Lcian., al.) *   5377

Φιλόλογος, -ου, ὁ, [lit. 'fond of talk'], *Philologus*, a certain Christian : Ro. xvi. 15. [Cf. Bp. *Lghtft.* Com. on Philip., note on "Cæsar's Household" § 10.] *   5378

φιλονεικία, -ας, ἡ, (φιλόνεικος, q. v.), *love of strife, eagerness to contend*, (Plat., Plut., Lcian., al. ; 4 Macc. i. 26) ; *contention* : Lk. xxii. 24. (2 Macc. iv. 4 ; Thuc. 8, 76 ; Joseph. antt. 7, 8, 4 ; Antonin. 3, 4 ; in a good sense, *emulation*, Xen., Plat., Dem., Plut., al.) *   5379

φιλό-νεικος, -ον, (φίλος, and νεῖκος strife), *fond of strife, contentious* : 1 Co. xi. 16. (Pind., Plat., Polyb., Joseph., Plut., al. ; in a good sense, *emulous*, Xen., Plat., Plut., al.) *   5380

φιλο-ξενία, -ας, ἡ, (φιλόξενος, q. v.), *love to strangers, hospitality* : Ro. xii. 13 ; Heb. xiii. 2. (Plat., Polyb., al.) *   5381

φιλό-ξενος, -ον, (φίλος and ξένος), fr. Hom. down, *hospitable, generous to guests*, [*given to hospitality*] : 1 Tim. iii. 2 ; Tit. i. 8 ; 1 Pet. iv. 9.*   5382

φιλο-πρωτεύω ; (φιλόπρωτος, fond of being first, striving after the first place ; fr. φίλος and πρῶτος : Artem. oneir. 2, 32 ; Plut. [Alcib. 2, 2] ; mor. p. 471 e. [i. e. de tranquil. an. 12 ; p. 793 e. i. e. an seni sit etc. 18, 8]) ; *to aspire after pre-eminence, to desire to be first* : 3 Jn. 9. (Several times in eccles. writ.) *   5383

φίλος, -η, -ον, fr. Hom. down, *friendly* [cf. L. and S. s. v. I. and II.] : φίλον εἶναί τινι, *to be friendly to one, wish him well*, Acts xix. 31 ;   **1.** ὁ φίλος, Sept. for רֵעַ, אֹהֵב, subst., *a friend* : Lk. vii. 6 ; xi. 5 ; xv. 6 ; xvi. 9 ; xxiii. 12 ; Acts xxvii. 3 ; 3 Jn. 15 (14) ; joined with συγγενεῖς, Lk. xxi. 16 ; *an associate*, opp. to δοῦλος, Jn. xv. 15 ; φίλοι ἀναγκαῖοι, [A. V. *near friends*] Lat. *necessitate conjuncti*, Acts x. 24 ; φίλε, *friend*, in kindly address, Lk. xiv. 10 ; with a gen. of the subject, ὁ φίλος τινός, Lk. xi. 6, [8] ; xii. 4 ; xiv. 12 ; xv. 29 ; Jn. xi. 11 ; xv. 13 sq. ; spec. *he who associates familiarly with one, a companion*, Mt. xi. 19 ; Lk. vii. 34 ; ὁ φ. τοῦ νυμφίου, the rabbinical שׁוֹשְׁבֵן [q. v. in Buxtorf or Levy] (i. e. 'son of   5384 gladness'), one of the bridegroom's friends who on his behalf asked the hand of the bride and rendered him various services in closing the marriage and celebrating the nuptials [B. D. s. v. Marriage, III.; *Edersheim*, Jewish Social Life, p. 152], Jn. iii. 29; φίλος τοῦ Καίσαρος, on Caesar's side, loyal to his interests, Jn. xix. 12; θεοῦ, esp. dear to God, peculiarly favored with his intimacy, Jas. ii. 23 ([cf. Harnack and Bp. Lghtft. on Clem. Rom. 1 Cor. 10, 1; *Rönsch* in the Zeitschr. f. wissenschaftl. Theol. for 1873, p. 583 sq.]; also in prof. auth. cf. *Grimm*, Exeget. Hdbch. on Sap. vii. 27 p. 164); with a gen. of the thing, *one who finds his pleasure in a thing*, φίλος τοῦ κόσμου, Jas. iv. 4.   **2.** Fem. φίλη, ἡ, *a (female) friend*: Lk. xv. 9.*

5385   φιλο-σοφία, -ας, ἡ, (fr. φιλόσοφος), prop. *love (and pursuit) of wisdom*; used in the Grk. writ. of either zeal for or skill in any art or science, any branch of knowledge, see Passow s. v. [cf. L. and S. s. v.]. Once in the N. T. of the theology, or rather theosophy, of certain Jewish-Christian ascetics, which busied itself with refined and speculative inquiries into the nature and classes of angels, into the ritual of the Mosaic law and the regulations of Jewish tradition respecting practical life: Col. ii. 8; see Grimm on 4 Macc. i. 1 p. 298 sq.; [Bp. Lghtft. on Col. l. c., and Prof. Westcott in B. D. s. v. Philosophy].*

5386   φιλό-σοφος, -ον, ὁ, (φίλος and σοφός), *a philosopher, one given to the pursuit of wisdom or learning* [Xen., Plat., al.]; in a narrower sense, *one who investigates and discusses the causes of things and the highest good*: Acts xvii. 18. [See reff. under the preceding word.]*

5387   φιλόστοργος, -ον, (φίλος, and στοργή the mutual love of parents and children; also of husbands and wives), *loving affection, prone to love, loving tenderly*; used chiefly of the reciprocal tenderness of parents and children: τῇ φιλαδελφίᾳ (dat. of respect) εἰς ἀλλήλους, [R. V. *in love of the brethren tenderly affectioned one to another*], Ro. xii. 10. (Xen., Plut., Lcian., Ael., al.) Cf. *Fritzsche*, Com. on Rom. vol. iii. p. 69.*

5388   φιλότεκνος, -ον, (φίλος and τέκνον), *loving one's offspring or children*: joined with φίλανδρος (as in Plut. mor. p. 769 c.), of women, Tit. ii. 4. (4 Macc. xv. 3–5; Hdt. 2, 66; Arstph., Eur., Aristot., Plut., Lcian., al.) *

5389   φιλοτιμέομαι, -οῦμαι; (φιλότιμος, and this fr. φίλος and τιμή); depon. pass. (with fut. mid.); freq. in Grk. writ. fr. Andoc., Lysias, Xen., Plat. down;   **a.** *to be fond of honor; to be actuated by love of honor; from a love of honor to strive* to bring something to pass.   **b.** foll. by an inf., *to be ambitious to* etc., 1 Th. iv. 11; Ro. xv. 20; *to strive earnestly, make it one's aim*, 2 Co. v. 9.*

5390   φιλοφρόνως, (φιλόφρων, q. v.), adv., *kindly, in a friendly manner*, [A.V. *courteously*]: Acts xxviii. 7. (2 Macc. iii. 9; 4 Macc. viii. 5; occasionally in Grk. writ. fr. [Soph. and] Hdt. down.)*

5391   φιλόφρων, -ον, (φίλος and φρήν), fr. Pind. and Aeschyl. down, *friendly, kind*: 1 Pet. iii. 8 Rec.*

5392   φιμόω, -ῶ, [inf. φιμοῖν 1 Pet. ii. 15 WH (see their App. p. 166 and Intr. § 410; B. 44 (38); see ἀποδεκατόω]; fut. φιμώσω; 1 aor. ἐφίμωσα: Pass., pf. impv. 2 pers. sing. πεφίμωσο; 1 aor. ἐφιμώθην; (φιμός a muzzle); *to close the mouth with a muzzle, to muzzle*: prop. βοῦν, the ox, 1 Co. ix. 9 R G L WH txt. (see κημόω); 1 Tim. v. 18, fr. Deut. xxv. 4 where for חָסַם; (univ. *to fasten, compress*, τῷ ξύλῳ τὸν αὐχένα τινός, Arstph. nub. 592); metaph. *to stop the mouth, make speechless, reduce to silence*: τινά, Mt. xxii. 34; 1 Pet. ii. 15; pass. *to become speechless, hold one's peace*, Mt. xxii. 12; Mk. i. 25; iv. 39; Lk. iv. 35, (Joseph. b. j. prooem. § 5; lib. 1, 22, 3; Lcian. de morte peregr. 15; univ. *to be kept in check*, 4 Macc. i. 35).*

5393   Φλέγων [i. e. 'burning'], -οντος, ὁ, *Phlegon*, a Christian at Rome: Ro. xvi. 14.*

5394   φλογίζω; (φλόξ, q. v.); *to ignite, set on fire*, (Sir. iii. 30; Ex. ix. 24; Ps. xcvi. (xcvii.) 3; *to burn up*, 1 Macc. iii. 5; Soph. Philoct. 1199): in fig. disc. *to operate destructively*, have a most pernicious power, Jas. iii. 6; in the pass. of that in which the destructive influences are kindled, ibid. (see πῦρ, p. 558ᵇ top).*

5395   φλόξ, gen. φλογός, ἡ, (φλέγω [to burn; cf. Lat. 'flagro', etc.]), fr. Hom. down, Sept. for לַהַב and לֶהָבָה, *a flame*: Lk. xvi. 24; on the phrases φλὸξ πυρός and πῦρ φλογός see πῦρ, p. 558ᵃ.

5396   φλυαρέω, -ῶ; (φλύαρος, q. v.); *to utter nonsense, talk idly, prate*, (Hdt., Xen., Plat., Isocr., Plut., al.); *to bring forward idle accusations, make empty charges*, Xen. Hell. 6, 3, 12; joined with βλασφημεῖν, Isocr. 5, 33: τινὰ λόγοις πονηροῖς, to accuse one falsely with malicious words, 3 Jn. 10 [A. V. *prating against* etc.].*

5397   φλύαρος, -ον, (φλύω, 'to boil up,' 'throw up bubbles', of water; and since bubbles are hollow and useless things, 'to indulge in empty and foolish talk'); of persons, *uttering* or *doing silly things, garrulous, babbling*, [A. V. *tattlers*]: 1 Tim. v. 13 [Dion. Hal. de comp. verb. 26, vol. v. 215, 3; al.]; of things, *foolish, trifling, vain*: φιλοσοφία, 4 Macc. v. 10. ([Plat., Joseph. vit. § 31; often in Plut.; Aeschyl. dial. Socr. 3, 13; al.) *

5398   φοβερός, -ά, -όν, (φοβέω), fr. Aeschyl. down, [*fearful* i. e.]   **1.** (actively) *inspiring fear, terrible, formidable*; Sept. for נוֹרָא.   **2.** (passively) *affected with fear, timid*; in the N. T., only in the former (active) sense: Heb. x. 27, 31; xii. 21.*

5399   φοβέω, -ῶ: Pass., pres. ἐφοβούμαι; impf. ἐφοβούμην; 1 aor. ἐφοβήθην; fut. φοβηθήσομαι; (φόβος); fr. Hom. down, *to terrify, frighten*, Sap. xvii. 9; *to put to flight by terrifying* (to scare away). Pass.   **1.** *to be put to flight, to flee*, (Hom.).   **2.** *to fear, be afraid*; Sept. very often for ירא; absol. *to be struck with fear, to be seized with alarm*: of those who fear harm or injury, Mt. x. 31; xiv. 30; xxv. 25; Mk. v. 33, 36; x. 32; xvi. 8; Lk. viii. 50; xii. 7, 32; Jn. xii. 15; xix. 8; Acts xvi. 38; xxii. 29; [Ro. xiii. 4]; Heb. xiii. 6; 1 Jn. iv. 18; opp. to ὑψηλοφρονεῖν, Ro. xi. 20; of those startled by strange sights or occurrences, Mt. xiv. 27; xvii. 7; xxviii. 5, 10; Mk. vi. 50; Lk. i. 13, 30; ii. 10; ix. 34; [xxiv. 36 L in br.]; Jn. vi. 19, 20; Acts xviii. 9; xxvii. 24, [but in the last two pass. perh. the exhortation has a wider ref.];

Rev. i. 17; with σφόδρα added, Mt. xvii. 6; xxvii. 54; of those struck with amazement, [Mt. ix. 8 L T Tr WH]; Mk. v. 15; Lk. v. 10; viii. 25, 35.   with an acc. of the contents [cognate acc.] (see ἀγαπάω, sub fin.) : φόβον μέγαν, lit. to 'fear a great fear,' fear exceedingly, Mk. iv. 41; Lk. ii. 9, (1 Macc. x. 8) ; φόβον αὐτῶν, the fear which they inspire [see φόβος, 1], 1 Pet. iii. 14 (Is. viii. 12 ; τοῦ Ταντάλου, to be filled with the same fear as Tantalus, Schol. ad Eur. Or. 6) ; with the synonymous πτόησιν (q. v.), 1 Pet. iii. 6.   τινά, to fear one, be afraid of one, lest he do harm, be displeased, etc.: Mt. x. 26 ; xiv. 5 ; xxi. 26, 46 ; Mk. xi. 18, 32 [cf. B. § 151, 11] ; xii. 12 ; Lk. xix. 21 ; xx. 19 ; xxii. 2 ; Jn. ix. 22 ; Acts v. 26 [cf. B. § 139, 48 ; W. 505 (471)] ; ix. 26 ; Ro. xiii. 3 ; Gal. ii. 12 ; τὸν θεόν, God, the judge and avenger, Mt. x. 28 ; Lk. xii. 5 ; xxiii. 40, (Ex. i. 17, 21 ; 1 S. xii. 18) ; τί, to fear danger from something, Heb. xi. 23, 27 ; to fear (dread to undergo) some suffering, Rev. ii. 10.   in imitation of the Hebr. (יָרֵא כִּי), foll. by ἀπό τινος (cf. B. § 147, 3) : Mt. x. 28 ; Lk. xii. 4, (Jer. i. 8, 17 ; x. 2 ; Lev. xxvi. 2 ; 1 Macc. ii. 62 ; viii. 12 ; Jud. v. 23).   as in the Grk. writ., φοβοῦμαι μή, to fear lest, with the subjunc. aor. : Acts [xxiii. 10 L T Tr WH] ; xxvii. 17 ; μήπως, lest perchance, Acts xxvii. 29 [here L μήπω (q. v. 2), al. μήπου (q.v.)] ; 2 Co. xi. 3 ; xii. 20 ; φοβηθῶμεν (i. q. let us take anxious care) μήποτέ τις δοκῇ, lest any one may seem [see δοκέω, 2 fin.], Heb. iv. 1 ; φοβοῦμαι ὑμᾶς, μήπως κεκοπίακα, Gal. iv. 11 (see μήπως, 1 b.) ; φοβοῦμαι with an inf. to fear (i. e. hesitate) to do something (for fear of harm), Mt. i. 20 ; ii. 22 ; Mk. ix. 32 ; Lk. ix. 45, (for numerous exx. in the Grk. writ. fr. Aeschyl. down see Passow s. v. 2, vol. ii. p. 2315ᵃ ; [L. and S. s. v. B. II. 4]).   **3.** to reverence, venerate, to treat with deference or reverential obedience : τινά, Mk. vi. 20 ; Eph. v. 33 ; τὸν θεόν, used of his devout worshippers, Lk. i. 50 ; xviii. 2, 4 ; Acts x. 2, 22, 35 ; [Col. iii. 22 Rec.] ; 1 Pet. ii. 17 ; Rev. xiv. 7 ; xix. 5 ; also τὸν κύριον, Col. iii. 22 [G L T Tr WH] ; Rev. xv. 4 ; τὸ ὄνομα τοῦ θεοῦ, Rev. xi. 18, (Deut. iv. 10 ; v. 29 ; vi. 2, 13, 24 ; xiii. 4 ; xiv. 22 (23) ; Prov. iii. 7 ; Ps. xxxiii. (xxxiv.) 10, and many other pass. ; very often in Sir., cf. Wahl, Clavis Apocr. V. T. s. v. fin.) ; οἱ φοβούμενοι τ. θεόν spec. of proselytes : Acts xiii. 16, 26, (see σέβω).   COMP. : ἐκ- φοβέω.*

[SYN. : ἐκπλήσσεσθαι to be astonished, prop. to be struck with terror, of a sudden and startling alarm ; but, like our "astonish" in popular use, often employed on comparatively slight occasions, and even then with strengthening particles (as σφόδρα Mt. xix. 25, ὑπερπερισσῶς Mk. vii. 37) ; πτοεῖν to terrify, to agitate with fear ; τρέμειν to tremble, predominantly physical ; φοβεῖν to fear, the general term ; often used of a protracted state.   Cf. Schmidt ch. 139.]

5400   **φόβητρον** [or -θρον (so L Tr WH ; see WH. App. p. 149)], -ου, τό, (φοβέω), that which strikes terror, a terror, (cause of) fright : Lk. xxi. 11. (Plat. Ax. p. 367 a. ; Hippocr., Lcian., al., ["but always in plur." (L. and S.)] ; for חֲגָא, Is. xix. 17.)*

5401   **φόβος**, -ου, ὁ, (φέβομαι ; like φόρος, τρόμος, πόνος, fr. φέρω, τρέμω, πένομαι), fr. Hom. down, Sept. for יִרְאָה, פַּחַד,

אֵימָה (terror), חִתִּית (id.) ;   **1.** fear, dread, terror; in a subjective sense (οὐδέν ἐστι φόβος εἰ μὴ προδοσία τῶν ἀπὸ λογισμοῦ βοηθημάτων, Sap. xvii. 11 ; προσδοκίαν λέγω κακοῦ τοῦτο, εἴτε φόβον, εἴτε δέος καλεῖτε, Plat. Protag. p. 358 d.) : univ., 1 Jn. iv. 18 ; φόβος ἐπί τινα πίπτει, [Acts xix. 17 L Tr] ; Rev. xi. 11 Rec. ; ἐπιπίπτει, Lk. i. 12 ; Acts xix. 17 [R G T WH ; Rev. xi. 11 L T Tr WH] ; ἐγένετο, Lk. i. 65 ; Acts v. 5, 11 ; λαμβάνει τινά, Lk. vii. 16 (Hom. Il. 11, 402) ; γίνεταί τινι, Acts ii. 43 ; πλησθῆναι φόβου, Lk. v. 26 ; συνέχεσθαι φόβῳ, Lk. viii. 37 ; ἔχειν φόβον, 1 Tim. v. 20 (Hdt. 8, 12) ; κατεργάζεσθαί τινι φόβον, 2 Co. vii. 11 ; φοβεῖσθαι φόβον (see φοβέω, 2), Mk. iv. 41 ; Lk. ii. 9 ; with a gen. of the object added, 1 Pet. iii. 14 [so W. § 32, 2 ; al. subject. gen.] ; ἀπὸ φόβου, for fear, Lk. xxi. 26 ; ἀπὸ τοῦ φόβ. for the fear, with which they were struck, Mt. xiv. 26 ; with a gen. of the object added, Mt. xxviii. 4 ; εἰς φόβον, unto (that ye may) fear, Ro. viii. 15 ; μετὰ φόβου, Mt. xxviii. 8 ; with καὶ τρόμου added, 2 Co. vii. 15 ; Eph. vi. 5 ; Phil. ii. 12 ; ἐν φόβῳ κ. ἐν τρόμῳ (see τρόμος), 1 Co. ii. 3 ; τινὰ ἐν φόβῳ σώζειν (Rec.), ἐλεᾶν (L T Tr WH), with anxious heed lest ye be defiled by the wickedness of those whom ye are rescuing, Jude 23 ; plur. φόβοι, feelings of fear, fears, [W. 176 (166)], 2 Co. vii. 5 ; φόβος τινός, gen. of the obj. (our fear of one) : τῶν Ἰουδαίων, Jn. vii. 13 ; xix. 38 ; xx. 19 ; βασανισμοῦ, Rev. xviii. 10, 15 ; θανάτου, Heb. ii. 15 (Xen. mem. 1, 4, 7).   In an objective sense, that which strikes terror : φόβος ἀγαθῶν ἔργων, or more correctly (with L T Tr WH) τῷ ἀγαθῷ ἔργῳ, a terror to (or for), Ro. xiii. 3.   **2.** reverence, respect, (for authority, rank, dignity) : Ro. xiii. 7 ; 1 Pet. ii. 18 ; iii. 16 (15) ; ἡ ἐν φόβῳ ἀναστροφή, behavior coupled with [cf. ἐν, I. 5 e.] reverence for one's husband, 1 Pet. iii. 2 ; φόβος with a gen. of the obj. : τοῦ κυρίου, Acts ix. 31 ; 2 Co. v. 11 ; Χριστοῦ, Eph. v. 21 [not Rec.] ; θεοῦ, Ro. iii. 18 ; 2 Co. vii. 1 ; [Eph. v. 21 Rec.] ; θεοῦ is omitted as suggested by the context, 1 Pet. i. 17 ; (often in the O. T. יִרְאַת אֱלֹהִים and יִרְאַת יְהוָה). [SYN. see δειλία, δέος, fin. ; cf. φοβέω.] *

5402   **Φοίβη**, -ης, ἡ, [lit. 'bright', 'radiant'], Phœbe or Phebe, a deaconess of the church at Cenchreæ, near Corinth : Ro. xvi. 1 [(see διάκονος, 2 fin.)].*

5403   **Φοινίκη**, -ης, ἡ, Phœnice or Phœnicia, in the apostolic age a tract of the province of Syria, situated on the coast of the Mediterranean between the river Eleutherus and the promontory of Carmel, some thirty miles long and two or three broad, [but see BB. DD. s. v.] : Acts xi. 19 ; xv. 3 ; xxi. 2.*

see 4949   **Φοινίκισσα**, see Συροφοίνισσα.

5404   **φοῖνιξ** (or, as some prefer to write it, φοίνιξ ; cf. W. § 6, 1 c. ; [and reff. s. v. κῆρυξ]), -ικος, ὁ ;   **I.** as an appellative, a palm-tree (fr. Hom. down ; Sept. for תָּמָר) : τὰ βαΐα τῶν φοιν. (see βαΐον), the branches of the palm-trees, Jn. xii. 13 ; but φοίνικες itself [A. V. palms] is put for the branches in Rev. vii. 9 (2 Macc. x. 7 ; xiv. 4 ; [so Aristot. magn. mor. § 34 p. 1196ᵃ, 36]).   **II.** a prop. name, Phœnix, a city and haven of Crete [B. D. (esp. Am. ed.) s. v. Phenice] : Acts xxvii. 12.*

*For 5405 see Strong.

5406 φονεύς, -έως, ὁ, (φόνος), fr. Hom. down, *a murderer, a homicide*: Mt. xxii. 7; Acts vii. 52; xxviii. 4; 1 Pet. iv. 15; Rev. xxi. 8; xxii. 15; ἀνὴρ φονεύς [cf. ἀνήρ, 3], Acts iii. 14.*

[Syn.: φονεύς any *murderer*,—the genus of which σικάριος the *assassin* is a species; while ἀνθρωποκτόνος (q. v.) has in the N. T. a special emphasis. Trench § lxxxiii.]

5407 φονεύω; fut. φονεύσω; 1 aor. ἐφόνευσα; (φονεύς); fr. [Pind., Aeschyl.], Hdt. down; Sept. mostly for רצח, also for הרג, הכּה, etc.; *to kill, slay, murder*; absol. *to commit murder* [A. V. *kill*]: Mt. v. 21; Jas. iv. 2; οὐ (q. v. 6) φονεύσεις, Mt. v. 21; xix. 18; Ro. xiii. 9, (Ex. xx. 15); μὴ φονεύσῃς, Mk. x. 19; Lk. xviii. 20; Jas. ii. 11. τινά: Mt. xxiii. 31, 35; Jas. v. 6.*

5408 φόνος, -ου, ὁ, (ΦΕΝΩ; cf. φόβος, init.), fr. Hom. down, *murder, slaughter*: Mk. xv. 7; Lk. xxiii. 19, 25; Acts ix. 1; Ro. i. 29; ἐν φόνῳ μαχαίρας, Heb. xi. 37 (Ex. xvii. 13; Num. xxi. 24; Deut. xiii. 15; xx. 13); plur. φόνοι, *murders*: Mt. xv. 19; Mk. vii. 21; Gal. v. 21 [T WH om. L Tr br. φόν.]; Rev. ix. 21.*

5409 φορέω, -ῶ; fut. φορέσω [1 Co. xv. 49 R G WH mrg.]; 1 aor. ἐφόρεσα, (later forms for the earlier φορήσω and ἐφόρησα, cf. *Bttm.* Ausf. Spr. ii. 315; *Kühner* [and esp. *Veitch*]s. v.; *W.* §13, 3 c.; [*B.* 37 (32)]); (frequent. of φέρω, and differing from it by denoting not the simple and transient act of bearing, but a continuous or habitual bearing; cf. *Lob.* ad Phryn. p. 585 sq.; *Hermann* on Soph. Electr. 715; [*Trench* § lviii.; *Schmidt*, ch. 105, 6]; accordingly, ἀγγελίην φέρειν means 'to carry a (single) message', Hdt. 3, 53 and 122; ἀγγελίην φορέειν, 'to serve as (fill the office of) a messenger', Hdt. 3, 34; hence we are said φορεῖν those things which we carry about with us or wear, as e. g. our clothing); fr. Hom. down; *to bear constantly, wear*: of clothing, garments, armor, etc., Mt. xi. 8; Jn. xix. 5; Ro. xiii. 4 (on this pass. see μάχαιρα, 2); 1 Co. xv. 49 [see above, and *WH.* Intr. § 404]; Jas. ii. 3, (Sir. xi. 5; xl. 4).*

5410; φόρον, -ου, τό, Lat. *forum*; see Ἄππιος.
see 675

5411 φόρος, -ου, ὁ, (fr. φέρω, hence prop. ὃ φέρεται; cf. φόβος), fr. Hdt. down, Sept. for מַס and (2 Esdr. iv. 20; vi. 8; Neh. v. 4) for מִדָּה, *tribute*, esp. the annual tax levied upon houses, lands, and persons [cf. *Thom. Mag.* ed. Ritschl p. 387, 13; *Grotius* as quoted in *Trench* § cvii. 7; see τέλος, 2]: φόρον, φόρους διδόναι Καίσαρι, Lk. xx. 22; xxiii. 2, (1 Macc. viii. 4, 7); ἀποδιδόναι, Ro. xiii. 7; τελεῖν, Ro. xiii. 6.*

5412 φορτίζω; pf. pass. ptcp. πεφορτισμένος; (φόρτος, q. v.); *to place a burden upon, to load*: φορτίζειν τινὰ φορτίον (on the double acc. see *B.* 149 (130)), to load one with a burden (of rites and unwarranted precepts), Lk. xi. 46; πεφορτισμένος 'heavy laden' (with the burdensome requirements of the Mosaic law and of tradition, and with the consciousness of sin), Mt. xi. 28. (Ezek. xvi. 33; Hes. opp. 692; Lcian. navig. 45; Anthol. 10, 5, 5; eccles. writ.) [Comp.: ἀπο-φορτίζομαι.]*

5413 φορτίον, -ου, τό, (dimin. of φόρτος, but dimin. only in form not in signif.; cf. *Bttm.* Ausf. Spr. ii. p. 440; [*W.* § 2, 1 d. fin.]), fr. Hes. down, Sept. for מַשָּׂא, *a burden, load*: of the freight or lading of a ship (often so in Grk. writ. fr. Hes. opp. 645, 695 down), Acts xxvii. 10 G L T Tr WH. Metaph.: of burdensome rites, plur., [Mt. xxiii. 4]; Lk. xi. 46; of the obligations Christ lays upon his followers, and styles a 'burden' by way of contrast to the precepts of the Pharisees the observance of which was most oppressive, Mt. xi. 30 (αὐτὸς μόνος δύναται βαστάσαι Ζήνωνος φορτίον, Diog. Laërt. 7, 5, 4 (171); see ζυγός, 1 b.); of faults, the consciousness of which oppresses the soul, Gal. vi. 5 [yet cf. Bp. Lghtft. ad loc. Syn. see ὄγκος, fin.]*

5414 φόρτος, -ου, ὁ, (fr. φέρω), fr. Hom. down, *a load, burden*: Acts xxvii. 10 Rec. [of a ship's lading].*

5415 Φορτουνᾶτος (or Φουρτ. R G), -ου, ὁ, [a Lat. name, 'happy'], *Fortunatus*, a Christian of Corinth [cf. Bp. Lghtft. on Clem. Rom. 1 Cor. 59 (65)]: 1 Co. xvi. 17.*

5416 φραγέλλιον, -ου, τό, (Lat. *flagellum*; B. 18 (16)), *a scourge*: Jn. ii. 15.*

5417 φραγελλόω, -ῶ: 1 aor. ptcp. φραγελλώσας; [Lat. *flagello*]; *to scourge*: τινά, Mt. xxvii. 26; Mk. xv. 15. (Eccles. writ.) *

5418 φραγμός, -οῦ, ὁ, (φράσσω to fence round), *a hedge, a fence*: Mt. xxi. 33; Mk. xii. 1; Lk. xiv. 23; trop. that which separates, prevents two from coming together, Eph. ii. 14 [A. V. *partition*], see μεσότοιχον. (Sept. Sir. xxxvi. 30 (27); Hdt., Soph., Thuc., Plut., al.) *

5419 φράζω: 1 aor. impv. φράσον; fr. Hom. down; *to indicate plainly, make known, declare*, whether by gesture (φωνῆσαι μὲν οὐκ εἶχε, τῇ δὲ χειρὶ ἔφραζεν, Hdt. 4, 113), or by writing or speaking, or in other ways; *to explain*: τινὶ τὴν παραβολήν, the thought shadowed forth in the parable, Mt. xiii. 36 [R G T Tr txt.]; vv. 15. (Twice in Sept. for הַבִּין, Job vi. 24; הוֹרָה, xii. 8.) *

5420 φράσσω: 1 aor. ἔφραξα; Pass., 2 aor. subj. 3 pers. sing. φραγῇ; 2 fut. 3 pers. sing. φραγήσεται (2 Co. xi. 10 R^{bez elz} G L T Tr WH); [(allied w. Lat. *farcio*, Germ. *Berg*, Eng. *borough*; cf. Vaniček p. 614); fr. Hom. down]; *to fence in, block up, stop up, close up*, (τὰ ὦτα τοῦ μὴ ἀκοῦσαι, Prov. xxi. 13; τὴν ὁδὸν ἐν σκόλοψιν, Hos. ii. 6; πηγήν, Prov. xxv. 26; στόματα λεόντων, Heb. xi. 33): ἡ καύχησις αὕτη οὐ φραγήσεται, this glorying shall not be stopped, i. e. no one shall get from my conduct an argument to prove that it is empty, 2 Co. xi. 10 [on the reading of Rec.^{st} (σφραγίσεται) see σφραγίζω, init.]; trop. *to put to silence*, [A. V. *stop*]: τὸ στόμα, Ro. iii. 19.*

5421 φρέαρ, -ατος, τό, fr. the Hom. hymn Cer. 99 and Hdt. 6, 119 down; Sept. for בְּאֵר and (in 1 S. xix. 22; 2 S. iii. 26; Jer. xlviii. (xli.) 7, 9) בּוֹר (a pit, cistern), *a well*: Lk. xiv. 5; Jn. iv. 11 sq.; φρ. τῆς ἀβύσσου, the pit of the abyss (because the nether world is thought to increase in size the further it extends from the surface of the earth and so to resemble a cistern, the orifice of which is narrow), Rev. ix. 1 sq.*

5422 φρεν-απατάω, -ῶ; (φρεναπάτης, q. v.): τινά, *to deceive any one's mind*, Gal. vi. 3 ["more is implied by this word than by ἀπατᾶν, for it brings out the idea of **subjective fancies**" Bp. Lghtft. ad loc.]; cf. *Green*, Crit. Notes ad loc.]. (Eccles. and Byzant. writ.)*

5423 **φρεναπάτης, -ου, ὁ,** (φρήν and ἀπάτη), a *mind-deceiver*; Vulg. *seductor*; [A. V. *deceiver*]: Tit. i. 10. (Several times in eccles. writ.)*

5424 **φρήν, φρενός, ἡ,** plur. **φρένες,** fr. Hom. down, Sept. several times in Prov. for לֵב; **1.** *the midriff* or *diaphragm*, the parts about the heart. **2.** *the mind*; *the faculty of perceiving and judging*: also in the plur.; as, 1 Co. xiv. 20.*

5425 **φρίσσω;** very often in Grk. writ. fr. Hom. down; *to be rough*, Lat. *horreo, horresco*, i. e. **1.** *to bristle, stiffen, stand up*: ἔφριξάν μου τρίχες, Job iv. 15 Sept.; with ὀρθαί added, Hes. opp. 510; ὀρθὰς ... φρίσσει τρίχας (cogn. acc. of the part affected), Hes. scut. 391; with cold, διὰ τὸ ψύχος, Plut. quaest. nat. 13, 2 p. 915 b. **2.** *to shudder, to be struck with extreme fear, to be horrified*: absol., Jas. ii. 19; 4 Macc. xiv. 9; like the Lat. *horreo, horresco*, constr. with an acc. of the object exciting the fear, Hom. Il. 11, 383, and often.*

5426 **φρονέω, -ῶ;** impf. 1 pers. sing. ἐφρόνουν, 2 pers. plur. ἐφρονεῖτε; fut. 2 pers. plur. φρονήσετε; pres. pass. impv. 3 pers. sing. φρονείσθω, Phil. ii. 5 R G (see 3 below); (φρήν); fr. Hom. down; **1.** *to have understanding, be wise*, (Hom., al.). **2.** *to feel, to think*: absol. ὡς νήπιος ἐφρόνουν, 1 Co. xiii. 11; *to have an opinion of one's self, think of one's self*: μὴ ὑπερφρονεῖν παρ' ὃ δεῖ φρονεῖν, Ro. xii. 3 (μεῖζον φρονεῖν ἢ κατ' ἄνδρα, Soph. Ant. 768); φρονεῖν εἰς τὸ σωφρονεῖν, [R. V. *so to think as to think soberly*], to be modest, not to let one's opinion (though just) of himself exceed the bounds of modesty, ibid.; ὑπὲρ ὃ γέγραπται, in one's opinion of one's self to go beyond the standard prescribed in Scripture, 1 Co. iv. 6 R G [cf. B. 394 sq. (338); W. § 64, 4]. with an acc. of the thing, *to think, judge*: ἃ φρονεῖς, what your opinion is, Acts xxviii. 22; οὐδὲν ἄλλο, Gal. v. 10; τὶ ἑτέρως, Phil. iii. 15; several persons are said φρονεῖν τὸ αὐτό, *to be of the same mind*, i. e. to agree together, cherish the same views, be harmonious: 2 Co. xiii. 11; Phil. ii. 2; iii. 16 Rec.; iv. 2; with ἐν ἀλλήλοις added, Ro. xv. 5; also τὸ ἓν φρονοῦντες, having that one mind, Phil. ii. 2 (the phrase τὸ ἕν having reference to τὸ αὐτό; see Meyer [but cf. Bp. Lghtft.] ad loc.); τὶ ὑπέρ τινος, to hold some opinion, judge, think, concerning one, Phil. i. 7; τὸ αὐτὸ εἰς ἀλλήλους, to be of the same mind towards one another, Ro. xii. 16. **3.** *to direct one's mind to a thing, to seek* or *strive for*; τά τινος, *to seek one's interests* or *advantage*; *to be of one's party, side with him*, (in public affairs, Add. to Esth. viii. 5; 1 Macc. x. 20; Dio Cass. 51, 4; Hdian. 8, 6, 14 (6); for other exx. fr. Xen. [or Hdt. 1, 162 fin.] down see Passow s. v. II.; [L. and S. II. 2 c.]; hence) τὰ τοῦ θεοῦ and τὰ τῶν ἀνθρ., to be intent on promoting what God wills (spec. his saving purposes), and what pleases men, Mt. xvi. 23; Mk. viii. 33; τὰ τῆς σαρκός and τὰ τοῦ πνεύματος (σάρξ [q. v. 4] and πνεῦμα [q. v. p. 522*] being personified), to pursue those things which gratify the flesh, ... the Holy Spirit, Ro. viii. 5, cf. 6. τὰ ἐπίγεια, Phil. iii. 19; τὰ ἄνω and τὰ ἐπὶ τῆς γῆς, Col. iii. 2, (ἀνθρώπινα, θνητά, Aristot. eth. Nic. 10, 7 p. 1177ᵇ, 32); τοῦτο φρονεῖτε (pres. impv.) ἐν ὑμῖν,

[R. V. *have this mind in you*], be intent within yourselves on this, Phil. ii. 5 L T Tr WH; pass. φρονεῖταί τι ἔν τινι, some habit of thought (expressed by deeds) exists in one, Phil. ii. 5 R G [A. V. *let this mind be in you*]; ὑψηλά (see ὑψηλός, b.). φρονεῖν ἡμέραν, to regard a day, observe it as sacred, Ro. xiv. 6; φρ. ὑπέρ τινος, to take thought, have a care, for one, Phil. iv. 10 [see ἀναθάλλω, fin. COMP. : κατα-, παρα-, περι-, ὑπερ- φρονέω.]*

φρόνημα, -τος, τό, (φρονέω, q. v.), *what one has in mind, the thoughts and purposes*, [A. V. *mind*]: Ro. viii. 6 sq. 27. (Hesych. φρόνημα· βούλημα, θέλημα. In various other senses also fr. Aeschyl. down.)* **5427**

φρόνησις, -εως, ἡ, (φρονέω), *understanding*: joined with σοφία (as 1 K. iv. 25 (29); Dan. i. 17 Theod.; ἡ σοφία ἀνδρὶ τίκτει φρόνησιν, Prov. x. 23), Eph. i. 8 [A. V. *prudence*; see σοφία, fin.]; spec. *knowledge and holy love of the will of God* [A. V. *wisdom*], Lk. i. 17 (Sap. iii. 15; Sept. for בִּינָה, תְּבוּנָה; חָכְמָה; used variously by Grk. writ. fr. Soph. and Eur. down).* **5428**

φρόνιμος, -ον, (φρονέω), **a.** *intelligent, wise* [so A. V. uniformly]: 1 Co. x. 15; opp. to μωρός, 1 Co. iv. 10; opp. to ἄφρων, 2 Co. xi. 19; φρόνιμος παρ' ἑαυτῷ, one who deems himself wise, [A. V. *wise in one's own conceits*], Ro. xi. 25; xii. 16, (Prov. iii. 7). **b.** *prudent*, i. e. *mindful of one's interests*: Mt. x. 16; xxiv. 45; Lk. xii. 42; opp. to μωρός, Mt. vii. 24 (cf. 26); xxv. 2, 4, 8 sq. compar. φρονιμώτερος, Lk. xvi. 8. (From Soph., Xen., Plat. down; Sept. for נָבוֹן, חָכָם, מֵבִין; [Syn. see σοφός, fin.]* **5429**

φρονίμως, adv., *prudently, wisely*: Lk. xvi. 8. [From Arstph. down.]* **5430**

φροντίζω; (φροντίς ['thought', fr. φρονέω]); fr. Theogn. and Hdt. down; *to think, to be careful; to be thoughtful* or *anxious*: foll. by an inf. Tit. iii. 8.* **5431**

φρουρέω, -ῶ; impf. ἐφρούρουν; fut. φρουρήσω; Pass., pres. ptcp. φρουρούμενος; impf. ἐφρουρούμην; (φρουρός, contr. fr. προορός fr. προοράω to see before, foresee); fr. Aeschyl. and Hdt. down; **1.** *to guard, protect by a military guard*, either in order to prevent hostile invasion, or to keep the inhabitants of a besieged city from flight; (often so fr. Thuc. down): τὴν πόλιν, i. e. not *he surrounded the city with soldiers*, but *by posting sentries he kept the gates guarded*, 2 Co. xi. 32 [R.V. *guarded*], cf. Acts ix. 24. **2.** metaph.: τινά, pass., ὑπὸ νόμου, under the control of the Mosaic law, that we might not escape from its power, with συγκεκλεισμένοι [συν(γ)κλειόμενοι L T Tr WH] added, Gal. iii. 23 [R. V. *kept in ward*; cf. Plut. de defect. orac. § 29; Sap. xvii. 15]; *to protect by guarding* (Soph. O. R. 1479), *to keep*: τὰς καρδίας ἐν Χριστῷ, i. e. in close connection with Christ, Phil. iv. 7; τινὰ εἴς τι, by watching and guarding *to preserve* one for the attainment of something [R. V. *guarded unto* etc.], pass. 1 Pet. i. 5.* **5432**

φρυάσσω: 1 aor. 3 pers. plur. ἐφρύαξαν; (everywhere in prof. auth. and also in Macc. as a depon. mid. φρυάσσομαι [W. 24]); *to neigh, stamp the ground, prance, snort; to be high-spirited*: prop. of horses (Anthol. 5, 202, 4; Callim. lav. Pallad. vs. 2); of men, *to take on lofty airs,* **5433**

behave arrogantly, (2 Macc. vii. 34; 3 Macc. ii. 2, Anthol., Diod., Plut., al.; [cf. Wetstein on Acts as below]); active for רָגַשׁ, *to be tumultuous, to rage*, Acts iv. 25 fr. Ps. ii. 1.*

5434 φρύγανον, -ου, τό, (fr. φρύγω or φρύσσω, φρύττω, to dry, parch; cf. Lat. frigo, frux, fructus), *a dry stick, dry twig*; generally in the plur. this word comprises all dry sticks, brush-wood, fire-wood, or similar material used as fuel: Acts xxviii. 3. (Hdt. 4, 62; Arstph., Thuc., Xen., Philo, al.; Sept. for קַשׁ straw, stubble, Is. xl. 24; xli. 2; xlvii. 14; for חָרוּל bramble, Job xxx. 7.)*

5435 Φρυγία, -ας, ἡ, *Phrygia*, a region of Asia Minor, bounded by Bithynia, Galatia, Lycaonia, Pisidia, Lydia, and Mysia. Those of its cities mentioned in the N. T. are Laodicea, Hierapolis, and Colossæ: Acts ii. 10; xvi. 6; xviii. 23. [B. D. s. v.; Bp. Lghtft. on Col., Intr., diss. i. esp. pp. 17 sq. 23 sq.]*

5436 Φύγελλος and (L T Tr WH [see WH. App. p. 159]) Φύγελος, -ου, ὁ, *Phygellus* [better *Phyg'-elus*], a Christian, who was with Paul at Rome and deserted him [see B.D. s. v. and the Comm.]: 2 Tim. i. 15.*

5437 φυγή, -ῆς, ἡ, (φεύγω), fr. Hom. down, *flight*: Mt. xxiv. 20; Mk. xiii. 18 Rec.*

5438 φυλακή, -ῆς, ἡ, (φυλάσσω), fr. Hom. down, Sept. for מַטָּרָה, מִשְׁמָר, מִשְׁמֶרֶת (a prison), כֶּלֶא (enclosure, confinement), *guard, watch*, i. e. **a.** in an act. sense, *a watching, keeping watch*: φυλάσσειν φυλακάς, *to keep watch*, Lk. ii. 8 (often in the Grk. writ. fr. Xen. an. 2, 6, 10, etc.; Plat. legg. 6 p. 758 d. down; [cf. φυλακὰς ἔχειν, etc. fr. Hom. (Il. 9, 1 etc.); often also in Sept. for שָׁמַר מִשְׁמָרוֹת). **b.** like the Lat. *custodia* and more freq. the plur. *custodiae* (see *Klotz*, Hdwrbch. [or Harpers' Lat. Dict.] s. v.), i. q. *persons keeping watch, a guard, sentinels*: Acts xii. 10 [here A. V. *ward*] (and very often in prof. auth. fr. Hom. down). **c.** *the place where captives are kept, a prison*: Mt. xiv. 10; xxv. 36, [39], 43 sq.; Mk. vi. 17, 27 (28); Lk. iii. 20; xxi. 12; xxii. 33; Acts v. 19, 22; viii. 3; xii. 5 sq. 17; xvi. 27, 40; xxii. 4; xxvi. 10; 2 Co. vi. 5 [here, as in Heb. xi. 36, A. V. *imprisonment*]; 2 Co. xi. 23; 1 Pet. iii. 19; Rev. xviii. 2 [twice; rendered in A. V. *hold* and *cage* (R. V. *hold*)]; xx. 7, (Hdt. 3, 152; Thuc. 3, 34; Plut., al.; Sept. for מַטָּרָה, בֵּית כֶּלֶא, and בֵּית הַכֶּלֶא, מִשְׁמָר); βάλλειν or τιθέναι τινὰ εἰς (τ.) φυλακήν or ἐν (τῇ) φυλακῇ: Mt. v. 25; xiv. 3 [R G, al. ἀπέθετο]; xviii. 30; Lk. xii. 58; xxiii. 19, 25; Jn. iii. 24; Acts v. 25; viii. 3 [here παραδιδόναι εἰς φ.]; xii. 4; xvi. 23 sq. 37; Rev. ii. 10. **d.** of the time (of night) during which guard was kept, *a watch* i. e. the period of time during which a part of the guard were on duty, and at the end of which others relieved them. As the earlier Greeks divided the night commonly into three parts [see L. and S. s. v. I. 4], so, previously to the exile, the Israelites also had three watches in a night; subsequently, however, after they became subject to Rome, they adopted the Roman custom of dividing the night into four watches: Mt. xxiv. 43; ἐν τῇ δευτέρᾳ, τρίτῃ, Lk. xii. 38; τετάρτῃ, Mt. xiv. 25; Mk. vi. 48. Cf. Win. RWB.

s. v. Nachtwache; [McC. and S. s. v. Night-watch; B. D. s. v. Watches of Night].*

5439 φυλακίζω; (φυλακή [or φύλαξ]); *to cast into prison, imprison*: Acts xxii. 19. (Sap. xviii. 4; eccles. and Byzant. writ.)*

5440 φυλακτήριον, -ου, τό, (neut. of the adj. φυλακτήριος, -α, -ον, fr. φυλακτήρ ['poetic for φύλαξ']); **1.** *a fortified place provided with a garrison, a station for a guard or garrison.* **2.** *a preservative* or *safeguard, an amulet*: Dem. p. 71, 24; Diosc. 5, 158 (159) sq., often in Plut. The Jews gave the name of φυλακτήρια (in the Talm. תְּפִלִּין *prayer-fillets*, Germ. *Gebetsriemen*; [cf. O. T. 'frontlets']) to small strips of parchment on which were written the foll. pass. from the law of Moses, Ex. xiii. 1–10, 11–16; Deut. vi. 4–9; xi. 13–21, and which, enclosed in little cases, they were accustomed when engaged in prayer to wear fastened by a leather strap to the forehead and to the left arm over against the heart, in order that they might thus be solemnly reminded of the duty of keeping the commands of God in the head and in the heart, acc. to the directions given in Ex. xiii. 16; Deut. vi. 8; xi. 18; (cf. Joseph. antt. 4, 8, 13). These scrolls were thought to have power, like amulets, to avert various evils and to drive away demons (Targ. on Cant. viii. 3); hence their Greek name. [But see *Ginsburg* in Alex.'s Kitto s. vv. Phylacteries (sub fin.) and Mezuza.] The Pharisees were accustomed τὰ φυλακτήρια αὐτῶν πλατύνειν, *to widen, make broad*, their phylacteries, that they might render them more conspicuous and show themselves to be more eager than the majority to be reminded of God's law: Mt. xxiii. 5. Cf. *Win.* RWB. s. v. Phylakterien; *Leyrer* in Herzog xi. 639 sqq.; *Kneucker* in Schenkel i. 601 sqq.; *Delitzsch* in Riehm 270 sq.; [*Edersheim*, Jewish Social Life etc., p. 220 sqq.; B. D. s. v. Frontlets; esp. *Hamburger*, Real-Encycl. s. v. Tephillin, vol. ii. p. 1203 sq.; *Ginsburg* in Alex.'s Kitto u. s.].*

5441 φύλαξ, -ακος, ὁ, (φυλάσσω), *a guard, keeper*: Acts v. 23; xii. 6, 19. (From Hom. down; Sept. for שֹׁמֵר.) *

5442 φυλάσσω; fut. φυλάξω; 1 aor. ἐφύλαξα; Mid., pres. φυλάσσομαι; 1 aor. ἐφυλαξάμην; pres. pass. φυλάσσομαι; fr. Hom. down; Sept. times too many to count for שָׁמַר, occasionally for נָצַר, [etc.]; **1.** Act. *to guard* (Lat. *custodio*); i. e. **a.** *to watch, to keep watch*: with φυλακήν added, Lk. ii. 8 (see φυλακή, a.). **b.** *to guard* or *watch, have an eye upon*: τινά, one, lest he escape, Acts xii. 4; xxviii. 16; pass., Acts xxiii. 35; Lk. viii. 29; τί, any thing, lest it be carried off: τὰ ἱμάτια, Acts xxii. 20. **c.** *to guard* a person (or thing) *that he may remain safe*, i. e. lest he suffer violence, be despoiled, etc., i. q. *to protect*: τὴν αὐλήν, Lk. xi. 21; ἀπό τινος, to protect one from a pers. or thing, 2 Th. iii. 3 [see πονηρός, p. 531ᵃ], (Xen. Cyr. 1, 4, 7; Ps. cxl. (cxli.) 9; cf. B. § 147, 3; [W. 223 (209)]); τὴν παραθήκην (or παρακαταθήκην), to keep from being snatched away, preserve safe and unimpaired, 1 Tim. vi. 20; 2 Tim. i. 14; with the addition of εἴς τινα ἡμέραν, i. e. that it may be forthcoming on that day, 2 Tim. i. 12; *to guard from* being lost or perishing, i. e. (with the predominant idea of a happy issue), to preserve : τινά, Jn. xvii. 12 (where ἐφύλαξα is explained by the foll. οὐδεὶς ἐξ αὐτῶν ἀπώλετο [cf. τηρέω, fin.]) ; 2 Pet. ii. 5 ; τινά with a pred. accus. Jude 24 ; φυλάξει (opp. to ἀπολέσει) τ. ψυχὴν εἰς ζωὴν αἰώ. i. e. will keep it with the result that he will have life eternal, Jn. xii. 25 ; ἑαυτὸν ἀπό τ. to guard one's self from a thing, 1 Jn. v. 21 [where cf. Westcott]. **d.** to guard, i. e. to care for, take care not to violate ; to observe : τὸν νόμον, Acts vii. 53 ; xxi. 24 ; Gal. vi. 13, (Lev. xix. 37, etc.; Soph. Trach. 616 ; al. ; νόμους, Xen. Hell. 1, 7, 30 ; Plat. de rep. 6 p. 484 b. ; polit. p. 292 a.) ; single precepts of the Mosaic law, Mt. xix. 20 L T Tr WH ; Mk. x. 20 Lchm.; Lk. xviii. 21 L T Tr txt. WH ; [τὰ δικαιώματα τοῦ νόμου, Ro. ii. 26] ; τὸν λόγον τοῦ θεοῦ, Lk. xi. 28 ; τὰ ῥήματα of Jesus, Jn. xii. 47 L T Tr WH ; apostolic directions, Acts xvi. 4 ; 1 Tim. v. 21. **2.** Mid. **a.** to observe for one's self something to escape, i. e. to avoid, shun, flee from : by a use com. in Grk. writ. fr. Aeschyl. and Hdt. down, with an acc. of the obj., τί, Acts xxi. 25 [A. V. keep themselves from] ; τινά, 2 Tim. iv. 15 [A.V. be thou ware of] ; ἀπό τινος, to keep one's self from a thing, Lk. xii. 15 (Xen. Cyr. 2, 3, 9 ; [Hell. 7, 2, 10]) ; ἵνα μή, 2 Pet. iii. 17 (ὅπως μή, Xen. mem. 1, 2, 37 ; other exx. in Passow s. v. p. 2360ᵃ ; [L. and S. s. v. C. II.]). **b.** by a usage foreign to Grk. writ. but very freq. in the Sept. (cf. W. 253 (238)), to guard for one's self (i. e. for one's safety's sake) so as not to violate, i. e. to keep, observe : ταῦτα πάντα (the precepts of the Mosaic law), Mt. xix. 20 R G ; Mk. x. 20 R G T Tr WH ; Lk. xviii. 21 R G Tr mrg., (Ex. xiii. 17 ; Lev. xviii. 4 ; xx. 8, 22 ; xxvi. 3, and many other pass.). [Comp. : δια-φυλάσσω. Syn. see τηρέω, fin.] *

5443　**φυλή, -ῆς, ἡ,** (fr. φύω), fr. Pind. and Hdt. down ; **1.** a tribe ; in the N. T. all the persons descended from one of the twelve sons of the patriarch Jacob (Sept. for מַטֶּה and שֵׁבֶט ; also for מִשְׁפָּחָה, see πατριά, 2) : Heb. vii. 13 sq. ; with the addition of the genitives Ἀσήρ, Βενιαμίν, etc., Lk. ii. 36 ; Acts xiii. 21 ; Ro. xi. 1 ; Phil. iii. 5 ; Rev. v. 5 ; vii. 5–8 ; δώδεκα φ. τοῦ Ἰσραήλ, Mt. xix. 28 ; Lk. xxii. 30 ; Jas. i. 1 ; Rev. xxi. 12 ; [πᾶσα φυλὴ υἱῶν Ἰσραήλ, Rev. vii. 4]. **2.** a race, nation, people : Mt. xxiv. 30 ; Rev. [i. 7] ; v. 9 ; vii. 9 ; [xi. 9] ; xiii. 7 ; xiv. 6.*

5444　**φύλλον, -ου, τό,** (φύω), a leaf : Mt. xxi. 19 ; xxiv. 32 ; Mk. xi. 13 ; xiii. 28 ; Rev. xxii. 2. [From Hom. down.]*

5445　**φύραμα, -τος, τό,** (φυράω to mix), any substance mixed with water and kneaded ; a mass, lump : of dough (Num. xv. 20 sq. ; [plur., Ex. viii. 3 ; xii. 34] ; Aristot. probl. 21, 18 p. 929ᵃ, 25 ; Plut. quaest. conv. 6, 7, 2, 15 p. 693 e.), 1 Co. v. 6 sq. ; Gal. v. 9, (on the meaning of which pass. see ζύμη) ; Ro. xi. 16 ; of clay (Plut. praec. ger. reip. 15, 4 p. 811 c.), Ro. ix. 21 [cf. B. § 140, 3 Rem.].*

5446　**φυσικός, -ή, -όν,** (φύσις), natural, i. e. **a.** produced by nature, inborn, (very often so fr. Xen. [mem. 3, 9, 1] down). **b.** agreeable to nature, (Dion. Hal., Plut., al.) : opp. to παρὰ φύσιν, Ro. i. 26, [27]. **c.** governed by (the instincts of) nature : ζῷα γεγεννημένα φυσικά, 2 Pet. ii. 12 [R. V. born mere animals].*

φυσικῶς, adv., in a natural manner, by nature, under the guidance of nature : by the aid of the bodily senses, Jude 10. [(Aristot., Philo, al.)] *　5447

φυσιόω, -ῶ ; Pass., pres. φυσιοῦμαι; pf. ptcp. πεφυσιωμένος ; 1 aor. ἐφυσιώθην ; **1.** (fr. φύσις), to make natural, to cause a thing to pass into nature, (Clem. Alex.; Simplic.). **2.** i. q. φυσάω, φυσιάω (fr. φῦσα a pair of bellows), to inflate, blow up, blow out, to cause to swell up ; trop. to puff up, make proud : 1 Co. viii. 1 ; pass. to be puffed up, to bear one's self loftily, 1 Co. iv. 18 sq. ; v. 2 ; xiii. 4 ; ὑπὸ τοῦ νοὸς τῆς σαρκὸς αὐτοῦ, Col. ii. 18 ; ὑπέρ τινος (see ὑπέρ, I. 2 [and cf. 5]) κατά τινος, 1 Co. iv. 6 [see ἵνα, II. 1 d.]. (Eccles. and Byzant. writ.)*　5448

φύσις, -εως, ἡ, (fr. φύω, q. v., as Lat. natura fr. nascor, ingenium fr. geno, gigno), fr. Hom. Od. 10, 303 down ; nature, i. e. **a.** the nature of things, the force, laws, order, of nature ; as opp. to what is monstrous, abnormal, perverse : ὁ, ἡ, τὸ παρὰ φύσιν, that which is contrary to nature's laws, against nature, Ro. i. 26 (οἱ παρὰ φύσιν τῇ Ἀφροδίτῃ χρώμενοι, Athen. 13 p. 605 ; ὁ παιδεραστὴς ... τὴν παρὰ φύσιν ἡδονὴν διώκει, Philo de spec. legg. i. § 7) ; as opposed to what has been produced by the art of man : οἱ κατὰ φύσιν κλάδοι, the natural branches, i. e. branches by the operation of nature, Ro. xi. 21, 24 [W. 193 (182)], contrasted with οἱ ἐγκεντρισθέντες παρὰ φύσιν, contrary to the plan of nature, cf. 24 ; ἡ κατὰ φύσιν ἀγριέλαιος, ibid. ; as opposed to what is imaginary or fictitious : οἱ μὴ φύσει ὄντες θεοί, who are gods not by nature, but acc. to the mistaken opinion of the Gentiles (λεγόμενοι θεοί, 1 Co. viii. 5), Gal. iv. 8 ; nature, i. e. natural sense, native conviction or knowledge, as opp. to what is learned by instruction and accomplished by training or prescribed by law : ἡ φύσις (i. e. the native sense of propriety) διδάσκει τι, 1 Co. xi. 14 ; φύσει ποιεῖν τὰ τοῦ νόμου, naturâ magistrâ, guided by their natural sense of what is right and proper, Ro. ii. 14. **b.** birth, physical origin : ἡμεῖς φύσει Ἰουδαῖοι, we so far as our origin is considered, i. e. by birth, are Jews, Gal. ii. 15 (φύσει νεώτερος, Soph. O. C. 1295 ; τῷ μὲν φύσει πατρίς, τὸν δὲ νόμῳ πολίτην ἐπεποίηντο, Isocr. Evagr. 21 ; φύσει βάρβαροι ὄντες, νόμῳ δὲ Ἕλληνες, Plat. Menex. p. 245 d. ; cf. Grimm on Sap. xiii. 1) ; ἡ ἐκ φύσεως ἀκροβυστία, who by birth is uncircumcised or a Gentile (opp. to one who, although circumcised, has made himself a Gentile by his iniquity and spiritual perversity), Ro. ii. 27. **c.** a mode of feeling and acting which by long habit has become nature : ἦμεν φύσει τέκνα ὀργῆς, by (our depraved) nature we were exposed to the wrath of God, Eph. ii. 3 (this meaning is evident from the preceding context, and stands in contrast with the change of heart and life wrought through Christ by the blessing of divine grace ; φύσει πρὸς τὰς κολάσεις ἐπιεικῶς ἔχουσιν οἱ Φαρισαῖοι, Joseph. antt. 13, 10, 6. [Others (see Meyer) would lay more stress here upon the constitution in which this 'habitual course of evil' has its origin, whether that constitution be regarded (with some) as already developed at birth, or (better) as undeveloped ; cf. Aristot. pol. 1, 2 p. 1252ᵇ, 32 sq. οἷον ἕκαστόν ἐστι τῆς　　5449 γενέσεως τελεσθείσης, ταύτην φαμὲν τὴν φύσιν εἶναι ἑκάστου, ὥσπερ ἀνθρώπου, etc.; see the exx. in Bonitz's index s. v. Cf. W. § 31, 6 a.]). **d.** *the sum of innate properties and powers by which one person differs from others*, distinctive native peculiarities, natural characteristics : φύσις θηρίων (the natural strength, ferocity and intractability of beasts [A. V. (every) *kind of beasts*]), ἡ φύσις ἡ ἀνθρωπίνη (the ability, art, skill, of men, the qualities which are proper to their nature and necessarily emanate from it), Jas. iii. 7 [cf. W. § 31, 10]; θείας κοινωνοὶ φύσεως, (the holiness distinctive of the divine nature is specially referred to), 2 Pet. i. 4 ('Αμενώφει . . . θείας δοκοῦντι μετεσχηκέναι φύσεως κατά τε σοφίαν καὶ πρόγνωσιν τῶν ἐσομένων, Joseph. c. Ap. 1, 26).*

5450 **φυσίωσις, -εως, ἡ,** (φυσιόω, q. v.), (Vulg. *inflatio*), *a puffing up of soul, loftiness, pride* : plur. [A.V. *swellings*] 2 Co. xii. 20. (Eccles. writ.)*

5451 **φυτεία, -ας, ἡ,** (φυτεύω, q. v.); **1.** *a planting* (Xen., Theophr., Plut., Ael., al.). **2.** *thing planted, a plant,* (i. q. φύτευμα) : Mt. xv. 13, [Athen. 5 p. 207 d.; Boeckh, Corp. inscrr. No. 4521 vol. iii. p. 240].*

5452 **φυτεύω;** impf. ἐφύτευον; 1 aor. ἐφύτευσα; pf. pass. ptcp. πεφυτευμένος; 1 aor. pass. impv. 2 pers. sing. φυτεύθητι; (φυτόν); fr. Hom. down; Sept. for נָטַע, several times for שׁוּל; *to plant* : absol., Lk. xvii. 28; 1 Co. iii. 6–8; φυτείαν, Mt. xv. 13; ἀμπελῶνα, Mt. xxi. 33; Mk. xii. 1; Lk. xx. 9; 1 Co. ix. 7; τὶ ἐν with a dat. of the place, pass., Lk. xiii. 6; xvii. 6.*

5453 **φύω;** 2 aor. pass. (ἐφύην) ptcp. φυέν (for which the Attic writ. more com. use the 2 aor. act. ἔφυν with the ptcp. φύς, φύν, in a pass. or intrans. sense; cf. Bttm. Ausf. Spr. ii. p. 321; Krüger § 40 s. v.; Kühner § 343 s. v.; [Veitch s. v.]; W. § 15 s. v.; [B. 68 (60)]; [cf. Lat. *fui, fore*, etc.; Curtius § 417]; fr. Hom. down; **1.** *to beget, bring forth, produce*; pass. *to be born, to spring up, to grow* : Lk. viii. 6, 8; **2.** intrans. *to shoot forth, spring up* : Heb. xii. 15 [W. 252 (237). Comp. : ἐκ-, συμ-φύω.]*

5454 **φωλεός, -οῦ, ὁ,** *a lurking-hole, burrow;* *a lair* : of animals, Mt. viii. 20; Lk. ix. 58. (Aristot., Ael., Plut., Geop., al.) *

5455 **φωνέω, -ῶ;** impf. 3 pers. sing. ἐφώνει; fut. φωνήσω; 1 aor. ἐφώνησα; 1 aor. inf. pass. φωνηθῆναι; (φωνή); **1.** as fr. Hom. down, intrans. *to sound, emit a sound, to speak* : of a cock, *to crow*, Mt. xxvi. 34, 74 sq.; Mk. xiv. 30, 68 [L br. WH om. the cl. (see the latter's App. ad loc.)], 72; Lk. xxii. 34, 60 sq.; Jn. xiii. 38; xviii. 27, (of the cries of other animals, Is. xxxviii. 14; Jer. xvii. 11; Zeph. ii. 14; rarely so in prof. auth. as [Aristot. (see L. and S. s. v. I. 2)], Aesop. fab. 36 [225 ed. Halm]); of men, *to cry, cry out, cry aloud, speak with a loud voice* : foll. by the words uttered, Lk. viii. 8; with φωνῇ μεγάλῃ added [(cf. W. § 32, 2 fin.), Mk. i. 26 T Tr WH]; Acts xvi. 28; ἐφώνησε λέγων, Lk. viii. 54; φωνήσας εἶπεν, Lk. xvi. 24; φωνήσας φωνῇ μεγ. εἶπεν, Lk. xxiii. 46; ἐφών. κραυγῇ [L T Tr WH φωνῇ] μεγ. λέγων, Rev. xiv. 18; [φωνήσαντες ἐπυνθάνοντο (WH txt. ἐπύθοντο), Acts x. 18]. **2.** as fr. [Hom. Od. 24, 535] Soph. down,

trans. **a.** *to call, call to one's self* : τινά, — either by one's own voice, Mt. xx. 32; xxvii. 47; Mk. ix. 35; x. 49 [cf. B. § 141, 5 fin.]; xv. 35; Jn. i. 48 (49); ii. 9; iv. 16; x. 3 L T Tr WH; xi. 28ᵃ; xviii. 33; Acts ix. 41; x. 7; — or through another; *to send for, summon* : Mk. iii. 31 R G; Lk. xvi. 2; Jn. ix. 18, 24; xi. 28ᵇ; εἶπε φωνηθῆναι αὐτῷ τούς κτλ. Lk. xix. 15; φων. τινα ἐκ, with a gen. of the place, *to call out of* (i. e. bid one to quit a place and come to one), Jn. xii. 17. **b.** *to invite* : Lk. xiv. 12. **c.** i. q. *to address, accost, call* by a name : τινά, foll. by a nom. of the title (see W. § 29, 1; [B. § 131, 8]), Jn. xiii. 13. [Comp. : ἀνα-, ἐπι-, προσ-, συμ-φωνέω.] *

5456 **φωνή, -ῆς, ἡ,** (φάω to shine, make clear, [cf. Curtius § 407; L. and S. s. v. φάω]), fr. Hom. down, Hebr. קוֹל; **1.** *a sound, tone* : of inanimate things, as of musical instruments, Mt. xxiv. 31 [T om. φ., WH give it only in mrg.; cf. B. § 132, 10]; 1 Co. xiv. 7 sq.; Rev. xiv. 2; xviii. 22, (Is. xviii. 3; xxiv. 8; Sir. l. 16; 1 Macc. v. 31); ὀργάνων, Plat. de rep. 3 p. 397 a; συρίγγων, Eur. Tro. 127; ψαλτηρίου καὶ αὐλοῦ, Plut. mor. p. 713 c.); of wind, Jn. iii. 8; Acts ii. 6; of thunder, Rev. vi. 1; xiv. 2; xix. 6, cf. iv. 5; viii. 5; xi. 19; xvi. 18; *noise*, of a millstone, Rev. xviii. 22; of a thronging multitude, Rev. xix. 1, 6; of chariots, Rev. ix. 9; of wings, *whir* (Ezek. i. 24), ibid.; of waters (Ezek. i. 24; 4 Esdr. vi. 17), Rev. i. 15; xiv. 2; xix. 6; also with the gen. of a thing implying speech, *the sound* [A. V. *voice*] : τοῦ ἀσπασμοῦ, Lk. i. 44; ῥημάτων, Heb. xii. 19; *the cry* (of men), φωνὴ μεγάλη, a loud cry, Mk. xv. 37; the clamor of men making a noisy demand, Lk. xxiii. 23, cf. Acts xix. 34; absol. *a cry* i. e. *wailing, lamentation*, Mt. ii. 18 (fr. Jer. xxxviii. (xxxi.) 15). **2.** *a voice*, i. e. *the sound of uttered words* : λαλεῖν φωνάς, Rev. x. 3; those who begin to cry out or call to any one are said τὴν φωνὴν αἴρειν, Lk. xvii. 13; πρός τινα, Acts iv. 24; φωνὴν ἐπαίρειν, Lk. xi. 27; Acts ii. 14; xiv. 11; xxii. 22; [φ. κράζειν (or ἐκκράζειν), Acts xxiv. 21 (cf. B. § 143, 11)]; φωνῇ μεγάλῃ added to verbs : to λέγειν, Rev. v. 12; viii. 13; (ἐν φωνῇ μεγ. Rev. xiv. 7 [Lchm. om. ἐν; xiv. 9]); to εἰπεῖν, Acts viii. 28; Acts xvi. 10; to φάναι, Acts xxvi. 24; to αἰνεῖν τὸν θεόν, Lk. xix. 37; with verbs of crying out, shouting : ἀναβοᾶν, Mt. xxvii. 46 [R G L txt. T]; βοᾶν, [Mt. xxvii. 46 L mrg. Tr WH]; Mk. xv. 34; Acts viii. 7; φωνεῖν, [Mk. i. 26 T Tr WH]; Lk. xxiii. 46; Acts xvi. 28; [Rev. xiv. 18 L T Tr WH]; ἀναφωνεῖν, Lk. i. 42 [R G L Tr mrg.]; κηρύσσειν (ἐν φων. μεγ.), Rev. v. 2 [Rec. om. ἐν]; κραυγάζειν, Jn. xi. 43; ἀνακράζειν, Lk. iv. 33; κράζειν, Mt. xxvii. 50; Mk. i. 26 [R G L]; v. 7; Acts vii. 57, 60; Rev. vi. 10; vii. 2, 10; x. 3; [xviii. 2 Rec.]; xix. 17; κράζ. ἐν φων. μεγ. Rev. xiv. 15; ἐν ἰσχυρᾷ φωνῇ, Rev. xviii. 2 [G L T Tr WH]; μετὰ φωνῆς μεγ. δοξάζειν τὸν θ. Lk. xvii. 15; of declarations from heaven, heard though no speaker is seen : ἰδοὺ φωνὴ λέγουσα, Mt. iii. 17; xvii. 5; ἔρχεται φωνή, Mk. ix. 7 [R G L Tr txt.]; Jn. xii. 28; ἐξέρχεται, Rev. xvi. 17; xix. 5; γίνεται φωνή, Mk. i. 11 [T om. WH br. ἐγέν.; ix. 7 T Tr mrg. WH]; Lk. iii. 22; ix. 35 sq.; Jn. xii. 30; [Acts vii. 31 (where Rec. adds πρὸς αὐτόν)]; πρός τινα, Acts x. 13, 15; [φωνῆς ἐνεχθείσης αὐτῷ, 2 Pet.

5456

i. 17]; ἐγένοντο φωναὶ μεγάλαι, Rev. xi. 15; [ἀπεκρίθη φωνή, Acts xi. 9]; ἀκούειν φωνήν [cf. B. §§ 132, 17; 144, 16 a.], Acts ix. 4; xxii. 9, [14]; xxvi. 14; 2 Pet. i. 18; Rev. i. 10; iv. 1 [B. § 129, 8 b.]; vi. 6 [here L T TrWH insert ὡς], 7 [here G om. Tr br. φων.]; ix. 13 [B. u. s.]; x. 4, 8; xi. 12 [R G L WH mrg.]; xii. 10; xiv. 2; xviii. 4; xix. 6; ἀκούειν φωνῆς [B. § 132, 17; W. § 30, 7 d.], Acts ix. 7; xi. 7; xxii. 7; Rev. [xi. 12 T Tr WH txt.]; xiv. 13; xvi. 1; xxi. 3; βλέπειν τὴν φων. i. e. the one who uttered the voice, Rev. i. 12. φωνή with a gen. of the subject: βοῶντος, Mt. iii. 3; Mk. i. 3; Lk. iii. 4; Jn. i. 23, all fr. Is. xl. 3; [ἀγγέλου ὅταν μέλλῃ σαλπίζειν, Rev. x. 7]; ἡ φ. τινος, the natural (familiar) sound of one's voice, Acts xii. 14; Rev. iii. 20, (Cant. v. 2); the manner of speaking, as a shepherd's (cry or call to his sheep), Jn. x. 3–5; to such 'voices' Jesus likens his precepts approved ('heard') by all the good, Jn. x. 16, 27, cf. xviii. 37; ἀνθρώπου, human utterance, 2 Pet. ii. 16; φ. τινος, the voice of a clamorous person, Mt. xii. 19 (Is. xlii. 2); of one exulting, jubilant, Jn. iii. 29; Rev. xviii. 23; ἀγγέλων πολλῶν, singing the praises of Christ, Rev. v. 11 sq.; the sound of the words of Christ as he shall recall the dead to life (the Resurrection-cry), Jn. v. 25, 28; ἀρχαγγέλου, the awakening shout of the archangel, the leader of the angelic host, 1 Th. iv. 16; τοῦ θεοῦ, of God,—teaching, admonishing, whether in the O. T. Scriptures or in the gospel, Jn. v. 37; Heb. iii. 7, 15; iv. 7; shaking the earth, Heb. xii. 26; the speech, discourse, θεοῦ οὐκ ἀνθρ. Acts xii. 22; [τὰς φωνὰς τῶν προφητῶν, the predictions ('read every sabbath'), Acts xiii. 27]; ἀλλάξαι τὴν φ. (see ἀλλάσσω), Gal. iv. 20. **3.** speech, i. e. a language, tongue: 1 Co. xiv. 10 sq. (Joseph. c. Ap. 1, 1; [1, 9, 2; 1, 14, 1, etc.]; Ceb. tab. 33; Ael. v. h. 12, 48; Diog. Laërt. 8, 3; for other exx. fr. Grk. writ. see Passow s. v. p. 2377ᵇ; [L. and S. s. v. II. 3]; Gen. xi. 1; Deut. xxviii. 49; τῇ ἑβραΐδι φωνῇ, 4 Macc. xii. 7; τῇ πατρίῳ φωνῇ, 2 Macc. vii. 8, 21, 27). [SYN. cf. Schmidt ch. 1 § 27; Trench § lxxxix.; and see λαλέω, ad init.]*

5457 φῶς, φωτός, τό, (contr. fr. φάος, fr. φάω to shine), fr. Hom. (who [as well as Pind.] uses the form φάος) down, Hebr. אוֹר, light (opp. to τὸ σκότος, ἡ σκοτία); **1.** prop. **a.** univ.: ὁ θεὸς ὁ εἰπὼν ἐκ σκότους φῶς λάμψαι, 2 Co. iv. 6 (Gen. i. 3); λευκὰ ὡς τὸ φῶς, Mt. xvii. 2; νεφέλη φωτός [Grsb. txt.] i. e. consisting of light, i. q. φωτεινή in R L T TrWH, Mt. xvii. 5; τὸ φῶς τοῦ κόσμου, of the sun, Jn. xi. 9; τὸ φῶς οὐκ ἔστιν ἐν αὐτῷ, the light (i. e. illumining power) is not in him, consequently he does not see or distinguish the objects about him, Jn. xi. 10; the light emitted by a lamp, Lk. viii. 16; [xi. 33 L Tr txt. WH]. a heavenly light, such as surrounds angels when they appear on earth: hence ἄγγελος φωτός, 2 Co. xi. 14, and illumines the place where they appear, Acts xii. 7; a light of this kind shone around Paul when he was converted to Christ, Acts xxii. 6, [9], 11 [W. 371 (348)]; with the addition of οὐρανόθεν, Acts xxvi. 13; of ἀπὸ [or ἐκ] τοῦ οὐρανοῦ, Acts ix. 3. **b.** by meton. anything emitting light: a heavenly luminary (or star),

plur. Jas. i. 17 [see πατήρ, 3 a.]; fire, because it is light and gives light: Lk. xxii. 56; θερμαίνεσθαι πρὸς τὸ φῶς, Mk. xiv. 54, (1 Macc. xii. 29; Xen. Hell. 6, 2, 29; Cyr. 7, 5, 27); a lamp or torch: plur. φῶτα, Acts xvi. 29 (φῶς ἔχειν, Xen. Hell. 5, 1, 8; in plur. often in Plut.). **c.** light i. e. brightness (Lat. splendor), [see a. above]: ἡλίου, Rev. xxii. 5; of a lamp, Jn. v. 35 (where it symbolizes his rank, influence, worth, mighty deeds); with the addition of λύχνου, Rev. xviii. 23 (Jer. xxv. 10); of the divine Shechinah (see δόξα, III. 1), Rev. xxi. 24 (Ps. lxxxviii. (lxxxix.) 16; Is. lx. 1, 19 sq.). **2.** φῶς is often used in poetic discourse, in metaphor, and in parable; **a.** The extremely delicate, subtile, pure, brilliant quality of light has led to the use of φῶς as an appellation of God, i. e. as by nature incorporeal, spotless, holy, [cf. Westcott, Epp. of St. John, p. 15 sqq.]: 1 Jn. i. 5 (Sap. vii. 26 where cf. Grimm); he is said εἶναι ἐν τῷ φωτί, in a state of supreme sanctity, 1 Jn. i. 7; φῶς οἰκῶν ἀπρόσιτον, a fig. describing his nature as alike of consummate majesty and inaccessible to human comprehension, 1 Tim. vi. 16 (Ps. ciii. (civ.) 2); used of that heavenly state, consummate and free from every imperfection, to which the true disciples of Christ will be exalted, i. q. the kingdom of light, Col. i. 12. **b.** By a fig. freq. in the N. T. [cf. in classic Grk. τῆς ἀληθείας τὸ φῶς, Eur. I. T. 1046 etc.; see L. and S. s. v. II. 2], φῶς is used to denote truth and its knowledge, together with the spiritual purity congruous with it, (opp. to τὸ σκότος b., ἡ σκοτία, q. v.): ἡ ζωὴ ἦν τὸ φῶς τῶν ἀνθρώπων, had the nature of light in men, i. e. became the source of human wisdom, Jn. i. 4; esp. the saving truth embodied in Christ and by his love and effort imparted to mankind, Mt. iv. 16; Jn. i. 5; iii. 19–21; Acts xxvi. 18, 23; 2 Co. vi. 14; Eph. v. 13ᵃ [cf. below]; τὸ φῶς τὸ ἀληθινόν, 1 Jn. ii. 8; τὸ θαυμαστὸν τοῦ θεοῦ φῶς, 1 Pet. ii. 9 (Clem. Rom. 1 Cor. 36, 2 cf. 59, 2); τὸ φῶς ὑμῶν, the divine truth with which ye are imbued, Mt. v. 16; ἔχειν τὸ φ. τῆς ζωῆς, the light by which the true life is gained, Jn. viii. 12; τὰ ὅπλα [Lchm. mrg. ἔργα] τοῦ φωτός, Ro. xiii. 12; καρπὸς τοῦ φωτός, Eph. v. 9 G L T Tr WH; ἐν τῷ φωτὶ περιπατεῖν, to live agreeably to saving wisdom, 1 Jn. i. 7; ἐν τῷ φωτὶ εἶναι, to be imbued with saving wisdom, μένειν, to continue devoted to it, to persevere in keeping it, 1 Jn. ii. 9 sq.; οἱ υἱοὶ τοῦ φωτός (see υἱός, 2 p. 635ᵃ), Lk. xvi. 8; Jn. xii. 36; 1 Th. v. 5; τέκνα τοῦ φ. (see τέκνον, c. β. p. 618ᵃ), Eph. v. 8. by meton. φῶς is used of one in whom wisdom and spiritual purity shine forth, and who imparts the same to others: φῶς ἐν σκότει, Ro. ii. 19; [φῶς ἐθνῶν, Acts xiii. 47]; in a pre-eminent sense is Jesus the Messiah called φῶς and τὸ φῶς: Lk. ii. 32; Jn. i. 7 sq.; xii. 35 sq. 46; τὸ φῶς τοῦ κόσμου, Jn. viii. 12; ix. 5, (τὸ φῶς τοῦ κόσμου τὸ δοθὲν ἐν ὑμῖν εἰς φωτισμὸν παντὸς ἀνθρώπου, Test. xii. Patr. test. Levi § 14); τὸ φῶς τὸ ἀληθινόν, Jn. i. 9; by the same name the disciples of Jesus are distinguished, Mt. v. 14; Christians are called φῶς ἐν κυρίῳ, having obtained saving wisdom in communion with Christ, Eph. v. 8. πᾶν τὸ φανερούμενον φῶς ἐστιν, everything made manifest by the aid of Christian truth has taken on the nature of light, so that its true character and quality are no longer hidden, Eph. v. 13ᵇ [al. take φῶς here in an outward or physical sense, and regard the statement as a general truth confirmatory of the assertion made respecting spiritual 'φωτός' just before (cf. above)].   c. By a fig. borrowed from daylight φῶς is used of *that which is exposed to the view of all*: ἐν τῷ φωτί (opp. to ἐν τῇ σκοτίᾳ), *openly, publicly*, (ἐν φάει, Pind. Nem. 4, 63), Mt. x. 27; Lk. xii. 3.   d. *reason, mind*; *the power of understanding* esp. moral and spiritual truth: τὸ φῶς τὸ ἐν σοί, Mt. vi. 23; Lk. xi. 35. [Syn. see φέγγος, fin.] *

5458   φωστήρ, -ῆρος, ὁ, (φῶς, φώσκω);   **1.** *that which gives light, an illuminator*, (Vulg. *luminar*): of the stars (*luminaries*), Phil. ii. 15 (Sap. xiii. 2; Sir. xliii. 7; Gen. i. 14, 16; Heliod. 2, 24; [Anthol. Pal. 15, 17; of sun and moon, Test. xii. Patr. test. Levi 14]; eccles. writ.).   **2.** *light, brightness*: Rev. xxi. 11 (Anthol. 11, 359) [al. refer this to 1; cf. Trench § xlvi.].*

5459   φωσ-φόρος, -ον, (φῶς and φέρω), *light-bringing, giving light*, (Arstph., Eur., Plat., Plut., al.) ; as subst. ὁ φ. (Lat. *Lucifer*), the planet Venus, the morning-star, *day-star*, (Plat. Tim. Locr. p. 96 e.; Plut., al.): 2 Pet. i. 19, on the meaning of this pass. see λύχνος.*

5460   φωτεινός [WH φωτινός, see I, ι], -ή, -όν, (φῶς), *light*, i. e. *composed of light, of a bright character*: νεφέλη, Mt. xvii. 5 [not Grsb.]; οἱ ὀφθαλμοὶ κυρίου μυριοπλασίως ἡλίου φωτεινότεροι, Sir. xxiii. 19.   *full of light, well lighted*, opp. to σκοτεινός, Mt. vi. 22; Lk. xi. 34, 36, (τὰ σκοτεινὰ καὶ τὰ φωτεινὰ σώματα, Xen. mem. 3, 10, 1).*

5461   φωτίζω; fut. φωτίσω (Rev. xxii. 5 L WH; 1 Co. iv. 5), Attic φωτιῶ (Rev. xxii. 5 G T Tr); 1 aor. ἐφώτισα; pf. pass. ptcp. πεφωτισμένος; 1 aor. pass. ἐφωτίσθην;   **1.** intrans. *to give light, to shine*, (Aristot., Theophr., Plut., al.; Sept. for אוֹר, Num. viii. 2, etc.): ἐπί τινα, Rev. xxii. 5 [Rom. WH br. ἐπί].   **2.** trans.   a. prop. *to enlighten, light up, illumine*: τινά, Lk. xi. 36: τὴν πόλιν,

Rev. xxi. 23 (ἀκτῖσι τὸν κόσμον, of the sun, Diod. 3, 48; Sept. for הָאִיר); ἡ γῆ ἐφωτίσθη ἐκ τῆς δόξης αὐτοῦ, [A.V. *was lightened*] shone with his glory, Rev. xviii. 1.   b. *to bring to light, render evident*: τὰ κρυπτὰ τοῦ σκότους, 1 Co. iv. 5; [Eph. iii. 9 acc. to the reading of T L br. WH txt. (but see c.)], (τὴν αἵρεσίν τινος, the preference, opinion, of one, Polyb. 23, 3, 10; τὴν ἀλήθειαν, Epict. diss. 1, 4, 31; πεφωτισμένων τῶν πραγμάτων ὑπὸ τῆς ἀληθείας, Lcian. cal. non tem. cred. 32); *to cause something to exist and thus to come to light and become clear to all*: ζωὴν κ. ἀφθαρσίαν διὰ τοῦ εὐαγγελίου, opp. to καταργῆσαι τὸν θάνατον, 2 Tim. i. 10.   c. by a use only bibl. and eccles. *to enlighten spiritually, imbue with saving knowledge*: τινά, Jn. i. 9; with a saving knowledge of the gospel: hence φωτισθέντες of those who have been made Christians, Heb. vi. 4; x. 32; foll. by an indir. quest. Eph. iii. 9 [see b. above], (Sir. xlv. 17; for הָאִיר, Ps. cxviii. (cxix.) 130; for הוֹרָה, to instruct, inform, teach, Judg. xiii. 8 Alex.; 2 K. xii. 2; φωτοῦσιν αὐτοὺς τὸ κρίμα τοῦ θεοῦ τῆς γῆς, 2 K. xvii. 27 [cf. 28; al.]); *to give understanding to*: πεφωτισμένοι τοὺς ὀφθαλμοὺς τῆς καρδίας [Rec. διανοίας], as respects the eyes of your soul, Eph. i. 18 [B. § 145, 6]; [(cf. Sir. xxxi. (xxxiv.) 20, etc.).]*

5462   φωτισμός, -οῦ, ὁ, (φωτίζω);   a. *the act of enlightening, illumination*: πρὸς φωτισμὸν τῆς γνώσεως, i. q. πρὸς τὸ φωτίζειν τὴν γνῶσιν, that by teaching we may bring to light etc. 2 Co. iv. 6 (on which pass. see πρόσωπον, 1 a. sub fin. p. 551ᵇ top).   b. *brightness, bright light*, (ἐξ ἡλίου, Sext. Emp. p. 522, 9; ἀπὸ σελήνης, Plut. [de fac. in orb. lun. § 16, 13] p. 929 d. [ib. § 18, 4 p. 931 a.]; Sept. for אוֹר, Ps. xxvi. (xxvii.) 1; xliii. (xliv.) 4; lxxvii. (lxxviii.) 14; Job iii. 9; for מָאוֹר, Ps. lxxxix. (xc.) 8): εἰς τὸ μὴ αὐγάσαι [καταυγάσαι L mrg. Tr mrg.] τὸν φ. τοῦ εὐαγγελίου, that the brightness of the gospel might not shine forth [R. V. *dawn* (upon them)], i. e. (dropping the fig.) that the enlightening truth of the gospel might not be manifest or be apprehended, 2 Co. iv. 4.*

X

5463   χαίρω; impf. ἔχαιρον; fut. χαρήσομαι (Lk. i. 14; Jn. xvi. 20, 22; Phil. i. 18, for the earlier form χαιρήσω, cf. [W. 90 (86); B. 68 (60)]; *Bttm.* Ausf. Spr. ii. 322 sq.; Matthiae § 255 s. v.; Kühner § 343 s. v.; Krüger § 40 s. v.; [Veitch s. v.]), once χαρῶ (Rev. xi. 10 Rec., a form occurring nowhere else); 2 aor. [pass. as act.] ἐχάρην [cf. συγχαίρω, init.]; fr. Hom. down; Sept. for שָׂמַח, גִּיל, שׂושׂ; *to rejoice, be glad*;   a. in the prop. and strict sense: [Mk. xiv. 11]; Lk. xv. 5, [32]; xix. 6, 37; xxii. 5; xxiii. 8; Jn. iv. 36; viii. 56; xx. 20; Acts v. 41;

viii. 39; xi. 23; xiii. 48; 2 Co. [vi. 10]; vii. 7; xiii. 9, 11 [some refer this to b. in the sense of *farewell*]; Phil. ii. 17, 28; Col. ii. 5; 1 Th. v. 16; 1 Pet. iv. 13; 3 Jn. 3; opp. to κλαίειν, Ro. xii. 15; 1 Co. vii. 30; opp. to κλαίειν κ. θρηνεῖν, Jn. xvi. 20; opp. to λύπην ἔχειν, ib. 22; joined with ἀγαλλιᾶσθαι, Mt. v. 12; Rev. xix. 7; with σκιρτᾶν, Lk. vi. 23; χαίρειν ἐν κυρίῳ (see ἐν, I. 6 b. p. 211ᵇ mid. [cf. B. 185 (161)]), Phil. iii. 1; iv. 4, 10; χαίρειν χαρὰν μεγάλην [cf. χαρά, a.], to rejoice exceedingly, Mt. ii. 10; also χαρᾷ χαίρειν (W. § 54, 3; B. § 133, 22), Jn. iii. 29;

ἡ χαρά ᾗ χαίρομεν, 1 Th. iii. 9; χαίρειν ἐπί with a dat. of the object, Mt. xviii. 13; Lk. i. 14; xiii. 17; Acts xv. 31; Ro. xvi. 19 L T Tr WH; 1 Co. xiii. 6; xvi. 17; 2 Co. vii. 13; Rev. xi. 10, (Xen. mem. 2, 6, 35; Cyr. 8, 4, 12; Plat. legg. 5 p. 739 d.; cf. Kühner § 425 Anm. 6; [W. § 33 a.; B. § 133, 23]; in the Grk. writ. generally with a simple dat. of the obj. as Prov. xvii. 19); διά τι, Jn. iii. 29; διά τινα, Jn. xi. 15; 1 Th. iii. 9; ἐν τούτῳ, Phil. i. 18; [ἐν τ. παθήμασί μου, Col. i. 24]; with an acc. of the obj., τὸ αὐτό, Phil. ii. 18 (ταυτά, Dem. p. 323, 6; cf. Matthiae § 414 p. 923; Krüger § 46, 5, 9); τὸ ἐφ᾿ ὑμῖν (see ὁ, II. 8 p. 436ᵃ), Ro. xvi. 19 R G; ἀπό τινος, i. q. χαρὰν ἔχειν, to derive joy from one, 2 Co. ii. 3; χαίρ. foll. by ὅτι, Jn. xiv. 28; 2 Co. vii. 9, 16; 2 Jn. 4; ἐν τούτῳ ὅτι, Lk. x. 20; with a dat. of the cause: τῇ ἐλπίδι χαίροντες, let the hope of future blessedness give you joy, Ro. xii. 12 [yet cf. W. § 31, 1 k., 7 d.].   b. in a broader sense, to be well, to thrive; in salutations, the impv. χαῖρε, hail! Lat. salve, (so fr. Hom. down): Mt. xxvi. 49; xxvii. 29; Mk. xv. 18; Lk. i. 28; Jn. xix. 3; plur. χαίρετε, [A. V. all hail], Mt. xxviii. 9; at the beginning of letters the inf. χαίρειν (sc. λέγει or κελεύει): Acts xv. 23; xxiii. 26; Jas. i. 1, (often in the bks. of Macc.; cf. Grimm on 1 Macc. x. 18; Otto in the Jahrbb. f. deutsch. Theol. for 1867, p. 678 sqq.; cf. Hilgenfeld, Galaterbrief, p. 99 sqq.; Xen. Cyr. 4, 5, 27; Ael. v. h. 1, 25); fully, χαίρειν λέγω, to give one greeting, salute, 2 Jn. 10, [11]. [COMP.: συν-χαίρω.] *

5464 χάλαζα, -ης, ἡ, (χαλάω, q. v. [so Etym. Magn. 805, 1; but Curtius (§ 181) says "certainly has nothing to do with it "]), fr. Hom. down, Sept. for בָּרָד, hail: Rev. viii. 7; xi. 19; xvi. 21.*

5465 χαλάω, -ῶ; fut. χαλάσω; 1 aor. ἐχάλασα; 1 aor. pass. ἐχαλάσθην; fr. Aeschyl. and Pind. down;   a. to loosen, slacken, relax.   b. to let down from a higher place to a lower: τί or τινά, Mk. ii. 4; Lk. v. 4 sq.; Acts xxvii. 17, 30, [in these two pass. in a nautical sense, to lower]; τινὰ ἐν σπυρίδι, Acts ix. 25; pass. 2 Co. xi. 33.*

5466 Χαλδαῖος, -ου, ὁ, a Chaldæan; γῆ Χαλδαίων the land of the Chaldæans, Chaldæa: Acts vii. 4, where a reference to Gen. xi. 28, 31 and xv. 7 seems to show that southern Armenia is referred to. The different opinions of other interpreters are reviewed by Dillmann on Genesis (3te Aufl.) p. 223 sq.; [cf. Schrader in Riehm s. v.; Sayce in Encycl. Brit. s. v. Babylonia].*

5467 χαλεπός, -ή, -όν, (fr. χαλέπτω to oppress, annoy, [(?)]), fr. Hom. down, hard (Lat. difficilis);   a. hard to do, to take, to approach.   b. hard to bear, troublesome, dangerous: καιροὶ χαλεποί, [R.V. grievous], 2 Tim. iii. 1; harsh, fierce, savage: of men, Mt. viii. 28 (Is. xviii. 2 and often in prof. auth. fr. Hom. down).*

5468 χαλιναγωγέω, -ῶ; 1 aor. inf. χαλιναγωγῆσαι; (χαλινός and ἄγω); to lead by a bridle, to guide, (ἵππον, Walz, Rhett. Graec. i. p. 425, 19); trop. to bridle, hold in check, restrain: τὴν γλῶσσαν, Jas. i. 26; τὸ σῶμα, Jas. iii. 2; τὰς τῶν ἡδονῶν ὀρέξεις, Lcian. tyrann. 4. [(Poll. 1 § 215.)] *

5469 χαλινός, -οῦ, ὁ, (χαλάω), a bridle: Jas. iii. 3; Rev. xiv. 20. (From Aeschyl. and Pind. down.) *

χάλκεος, -έα, -εον, contr. -οῦς, -ῆ, -οῦν, (χαλκός), fr. Hom. **5470** down, brazen, [A. V. of brass]: Rev. ix. 20.*

χαλκεύς, -έως, ὁ, (χαλκός), fr. Hom. down, a worker in **5471** copper or iron, a smith: 2 Tim. iv. 14 [A. V. copper-smith].*

χαλκηδών, -όνος, ὁ, chalcedony, a precious stone de- **5472** scribed by Plin. h. n. 37, 5 (18), 72 [see B. D. (esp. Am. ed.) s. v.]: Rev. xxi. 19.*

χαλκίον, -ου, τό, (χαλκός), a (copper or) brazen vessel: **5473** Mk. vii. 4. ([Arstph.], Xen. oec. 8, 19; [al.].) *

χαλκο-λίβανον (so Suidas [but see ed. Gaisf. s. v.]), -ου, **5474** τό, more correctly χαλκολίβανος, -ου, ἡ, (acc. to the read-ing as it ought to be restored [(but see the edd.)]) in Rev. i. 15 ὡς ἐν καμίνῳ πεπυρωμένη; cf. Düsterdieck's crit. note [see B. 80 (69) note]), a word of doubtful meaning, found only in Rev. i. 15, and ii. 18, chalcolibanus, Vulg. aurichalcum or orichalcum (so cod. Amiat., [al. aeric.]; Luther Messing, [R. V. burnished brass]); acc. to the testimony of an ancient Greek [Ansonius] in Salmasius (Exercitt. ad Solin. p. 810 a.: ὁ λίβανος ἔχει τρία εἴδη δένδρων, καὶ ὁ μὲν ἄρρην ὀνομάζεται χαλκολίβανος, ἡλιοειδὴς καὶ πυρρὸς ἤγουν ξανθός), a certain kind of (yellow) frankincense; but both the sense of the passages in Rev. and a comparison of Dan. x. 6 and Ezek. i. 7, which seem to have been in the writer's thought, compel us to understand some metal, like gold if not more precious (cf. Hebr. חַשְׁמַל, a metal composed of gold and silver, Sept. ἤλεκτρον, Vulg. electrum, Ezek. i. 4, 27; viii. 2); this in-terpretation is confirmed by the gloss of Suidas: εἶδος ἠλέκτρου τιμιώτερον χρυσοῦ, ἔστι δὲ τὸ ἤλεκτρον ἀλλότυπον χρυσίον μεμιγμένον ὑέλῳ κ. λιθείᾳ. The word is com-pounded, no doubt, of χαλκός and λίβανος, not of χαλκός and לָבָן 'white.' Cf. Win. RWB. s. v. Metalle; Wetzel in the Zeitschr. f. d. luth. Theol. for 1869, p. 92 sqq.; cf. Ewald, Johann. Schriften, ii. p. 117 sq.; [Lee in the 'Speaker's Com.' ad loc.].*

χαλκός, -οῦ, ὁ, fr. Hom. down, Sept. for נְחֹשֶׁת, brass: **5475** 1 Co. xiii. 1; Rev. xviii. 12; (like the Lat. aes) what is made of brass, money, coins of brass (also of silver and of gold), Mt. x. 9; Mk. vi. 8; xii. 41. [B. D. s. v. Brass; Dict. of Antiq. s. v. aes.]*

χαμαί, adv.   a. on the ground, on the earth.   b. **5476** to the ground; in both senses fr. Hom. down; in the latter sense Jn. ix. 6 [where, however, Eng. idiom re-tains on]; xviii. 6.*

Χαναάν, ἡ, Hebr. כְּנַעַן [lit. 'lowland'], Canaan, the **5477** land of Canaan, indecl. prop. name: in the narrower sense, of that part of Palestine lying west of the Jordan, Acts vii. 11; in a wider sense, of all Palestine, Acts xiii. 19.*

Χαναναῖος, -α, -ον, Hebr. כְּנַעֲנִי, Canaanite; the name **5478** of the ancient inhabitants of Palestine before its con-quest by the Israelites; in Christ's time i. q. Phœnician [R.V. Canaanitish]: Mt. xv. 22.*

χαρά, -ᾶς, ἡ, (χαίρω), fr. Aeschyl. and Soph. down, **5479** Sept. for שִׂמְחָה and שָׂשׂוֹן, joy, gladness;   a: Lk. i. 14; xv. 7, 10; Jn. xv. 11; xvi. 22, 24; xvii. 13; Acts viii. 8; 2 Co. vii. 13; viii. 2; Gal. v. 22; Col. i. 11; Phil. ii.

2; 1 Jn. i. 4 ; 2 Jn. 12 ; opp. to κατήφεια, Jas. iv. 9 ; opp. to λύπη, Jn. xvi. 20 ; 2 Co. ii. 3 ; Heb. xii. 11 ; ὑμῶν, i. e. the joy received from you, 2 Co. i. 24 (opp. to the 'sorrow' which Paul on returning to Corinth would both experience and give, ii. 1–3) ; χαρὰ τῆς πίστεως, springing from faith, Phil. i. 25 ; χαίρειν χαρὰν μεγ. Mt. ii. 10 [W. § 32, 2 ; B. 131, 5] ; ἀγαλλιᾶσθαι χαρᾷ, 1 Pet. i. 8 ; χαρὰν [Rec.ˢᵗ χάριν] πολλὴν ἔχειν ἐπί with a dat. of the thing, Philem. 7 ; πληροῦν τινα χαρᾶς, Ro. xv. 13 ; πληροῦσθαι χαρᾶς, Acts xiii. 52 ; 2 Tim. i. 4 ; ποιεῖν τινι χαρὰν μεγάλην, Acts xv. 3 ; ἀπὸ τῆς χαρᾶς, for joy, Mt. xiii. 44 ; Lk. xxiv. 41 ; Acts xii. 14 ; ἐν χαρᾷ (ἔρχεσθαι), Ro. xv. 32 ; μετὰ χαρᾶς, with joy, Mt. xiii. 20 ; xxviii. 8 ; Mk. iv. 16 ; Lk. viii. 13 ; x. 17 ; xxiv. 52 ; Acts xx. 24 Rec.; Phil. i. 4 ; ii. 29 ; Heb. x. 34 ; xiii. 17, (Polyb. 11, 33, 7 ; 22, 17, 12 ; Xen. Hiero 1, 25) ; with πνεύματος ἁγίου added, joy wrought by the Holy Spirit, 1 Th. i. 6 ; χαρὰ ἐν πνεύματι ἁγίῳ, joyousness caused by [cf. ἐν, I. 6 (p. 211ᵇ bot.) and B. § 133, 23] the Holy Spirit, Ro. xiv. 17 ; χαρὰ ἐπί τινι, 2 Co. vii. 4 ; χαίρειν χαρᾷ διά τι, Jn. iii. 29 [cf. χαίρω, a.] ; also διά τινα (a relative pron. intervening), 1 Th. iii. 9 ; ἡ χαρὰ ὅτι, Jn. xvi. 21 ; χαρὰ ἵνα (see ἵνα, II: 2 d.), 3 Jn. 4.   b. by meton. the cause or occasion of joy : Lk. ii. 10 ; Jas. i. 2 ; [so 2 Co. i. 15 WH txt. Tr mrg. (al. χάρις, q. v. 3 b.)] ; of persons who are one's 'joy': 1 Th. ii. 19 sq.; Phil. iv. 1 ; of a joyful condition or state : ἀντὶ ... χαρᾶς, to attain to blessedness at the right hand of God in heaven, Heb. xii. 2 ; the same idea is expressed in the parable by the words, ἡ χαρὰ τοῦ κυρίου, the blessedness which the Lord enjoys, Mt. xxv. 21, 23.*

5480 χάραγμα, -τος, τό, (χαράσσω to engrave) ;   a. a stamp, an imprinted mark : of the mark stamped on the forehead or the right hand as the badge of the followers of Antichrist, Rev. xiii. 16 sq.; xiv. 9, 11 ; xv. 2 Rec.; xvi. 2 ; xix. 20 ; xx. 4, (πυρός, the mark branded upon horses, Anacr. 26 [55], 2).   b. thing carved, sculpture, graven work : of idolatrous images, Acts xvii. 29. (In various other senses in Grk. writ. fr. Soph. down.) *

5481 χαρακτήρ, -ῆρος, ὁ, (χαράσσω to engrave, cut into), fr. Aeschyl. and Hdt. down ;   1. prop. the instrument used in engraving or carving, (cf. ζωστήρ, λαμπτήρ, λουτήρ, φυσητήρ ; cf. our 'stamp' or 'die').   2. the mark (figure or letters) stamped upon that instrument or wrought out on it ; hence univ. a mark or figure burned in (Lev. xiii. 28) or stamped on, an impression ; the exact expression (the image) of any person or thing, marked likeness, precise reproduction in every respect (cf. facsimile) : χ. τῆς ὑποστάσεως τοῦ θεοῦ, of Christ, acc. to his nature as ὁ θεῖος λόγος, Heb. i. 3 ; σφραγῖδι θεοῦ, ἧς ὁ χαρακτήρ ἐστιν ὁ ἀΐδιος λόγος, Philo de plant. Noë § 5 ; χ. θείας δυνάμεως, of the human mind, Philo, quod det. potiori ins. § 23 ; God τὸν ἄνθρωπον ἔπλασεν τῆς ἑαυτοῦ εἰκόνος χαρακτῆρα, Clem. Rom. 1 Cor. 33, 4 ; οἱ πιστοὶ ἐν ἀγάπῃ χαρακτῆρα θεοῦ πατρὸς διὰ Ἰησοῦ Χριστοῦ (ἔχουσιν), Ignat. ad Magnes. 5, 2. the peculiarity, by which things are recognized and distinguished from each other, [cf. Eng. characteristic] : 2 Macc. iv. 10.*

5482 χάραξ, -ακος, ὁ, (χαράσσω) ;   1. a pale or stake, a palisade, [(Arstph., Dem., al.)].   2. a palisade or rampart (i. e. pales between which earth, stones, trees and timbers are heaped and packed together) : Lk. xix. 43 (Is. xxxvii. 33 ; Ezek. iv. 2 ; xxvi. 8 ; Polyb.; Joseph. vit. 43 ; Arr. exp. Alex. 2, 19, 9 ; Plut., al.).*

5483 χαρίζομαι ; depon. mid.; fut. χαρίσομαι (Ro. viii. 32 ; Lcian. d. mar. 9, 1, for which Grk. writ. com. use the Attic χαριοῦμαι [cf. WH. App. p. 163 sq.; B. 37 (32) ; W. § 15 s. v.]) ; pf. κεχάρισμαι ; 1 aor. ἐχαρισάμην ; 1 aor. pass. ἐχαρίσθην (Acts iii. 14 ; 1 Co. ii. 12 ; Phil. i. 29, [cf. B. 52 (46)]) ; fut. pass. χαρισθήσομαι with a pass. signif. (Philem. 22) ; (χάρις) ; often in Grk. writ. fr. Hom. down ; to do something pleasant or agreeable (to one), to do a favor to, gratify ;   a. univ. to show one's self gracious, kind, benevolent : τινί, Gal. iii. 18 [al. (supply τ. κληρονομίαν and) refer this to c. below].   b. to grant forgiveness, to pardon : 2 Co. ii. 7 ; with a dat. of the pers., Eph. iv. 32 ; Col. iii. 13 ; with an acc. of the thing, 2 Co. ii. 10 [cf. W. § 39, 1 b. and 3 N. 3] ; τινὶ τὴν ἀδικίαν, 2 Co. xii. 13 ; τὰ παραπτώματα, Col. ii. 13.   c. to give graciously, give freely, bestow : τινί τι, Lk. vii. 21 ; Ro. viii. 32 ; Phil. ii. 9 ; pass., 1 Co. ii. 12 ; Phil. i. 29 ; where a debt is referred to, to forgive [cf. b. above], Lk. vii. 42 sq.; τινί τινα, graciously to restore one to another who desires his safety (e. g. a captive [R.V. grant]), pass., Acts iii. 14 ; Philem. 22 ; or to preserve for one a person in peril, Acts xxvii. 24 ; τινά τινι, to give up to another one whom he may punish or put to death, Acts xxv. 11 [(cf. R. V. mrg.)] ; with the addition of εἰς ἀπώλειαν, ib. 16.*

5484 χάριν, acc. of the subst. χάρις used absol.; prop. in favor of, for the pleasure of ; χάριν Ἕκτορος, Hom. Il. 15, 744, al. ; 1 Macc. ix. 10 ; Judith viii. 19 ; like the Lat. abl. gratia, it takes on completely the nature of a preposition, and is joined to the gen., for, on account of, for the sake of : Gal. iii. 19 (on which see παράβασις) ; 1 Tim. v. 14 ; Tit. i. 11 ; Jude 16 ; τούτου χάριν, on this account, for this cause, Eph. iii. 1 (Xen. mem. 1, 2, 54) ; τούτου χ. ἵνα, Eph. iii. 14 [cf. W. 566 (526)] ; Tit. i. 5 ; οὗ χάριν, for which cause, Lk. vii. 47 ; χάριν τίνος ; for what cause ? wherefore ? 1 Jn. iii. 12. Except in 1 Jn. iii. 12, χάριν is everywhere in the N. T. placed after the gen., as it generally is in prof. auth. (cf. Passow s. v. I. 3 a. p. 2416ᵇ ; Herm. ad Vig. p. 701) ; in the O. T. Apocr. it is placed sometimes before, sometimes after ; cf. Wahl, Clavis Apocr. s. v. 6 b.; Grimm on 1 Macc. iii. 29.*

5485 χάρις, -ιτος, acc. χάριν, and twice in L T Tr WH the rarer form χάριτα (Acts xxiv. 27 ; Jude 4) which is also poetic (cf. Bttm. Ausf. Spr. i. § 44 Anm. 1 ; [WH. App. 157ᵇ ; B. 13 (12)]), acc. plur. χάριτας (Acts xxiv. 27 R G), ἡ, (χαίρω), fr. Hom. down, Hebr. חֵן, grace ; i. e.   1. prop. that which affords joy, pleasure, delight, sweetness, charm, loveliness : grace of speech (Eccl. x. 12 ; Sir. xxi. 16 ; xxxvii. 21 ; Hom. Od. 8, 175 ; τῶν λόγων, Dem. 51, 9 ; 1419, 16 ; χάριτες μωρῶν, verbal pleasantries which the foolish affect in order to ingratiate themselves, Sir. xx. 13), λόγοι χάριτος (gen. of quality), Lk. iv. 22 ; χάριν διδόναι τοῖς ἀκούουσιν, Eph. iv.

29; ἐν χάριτι, with grace [the subst. ἅλας being added; see Bp. Lghtft.], Col. iv. 6.   **2.** *good-will, loving-kindness, favor*: in a broad sense, χάρις παρά τινι, Lk. ii. 52; ἔχειν χάριν πρός τινα, to have favor with one, Acts ii. 47; χάρις ἐναντίον τινός, Acts vii. 10; [χάριν κατά τινος αἰτεῖσθαι ὅπως (q. v. II. 2), Acts xxv. 3 (but al. refer this to 3 b. below)]; χάρις (of God) ἐστὶν ἐπί τινα, attends and assists one, Lk. ii. 40; Acts iv. 33; χάριν (χάριτα) χάριτας κατατίθεσθαί τινι (see κατατίθημι), Acts xxiv. 27; xxv. 9; *favor* (i. e. act of *favoring* [cf. W. § 66 fin.]), 2 Co. viii. 4.   χάρις is used of the kindness of a master towards his inferiors or servants, and so esp. of God towards men: εὑρίσκειν χάριν παρὰ τῷ θ. Lk. i. 30; ἐνώπιον τοῦ θεοῦ, Acts vii. 46; τοῦτο χάρις sc. ἐστίν, this wins for us (God's) favor [R.V. *is acceptable*], 1 Pet. ii. 19; with παρὰ θεῷ added, ib. 20; παραδίδοσθαι τῇ χ. τοῦ θεοῦ, to be committed or commended to the protecting and helping favor of God, Acts xiv. 26; xv. 40. The apostles and N. T. writers at the beginning and end of their Epp. crave for their readers the favor ('grace') of God or of Christ, to which all blessings, esp. spiritual, are due: Ro. i. 7; xvi. 20, 24 [R G]; 1 Co. i. 3; xvi. 23; 2 Co. i. 2; xiii. 13 (14); Gal. i. 3; vi. 18; Eph. i. 2; vi. 24; Phil. i. 2; iv. 23; Col. i. 2; iv. 18; 1 Th. i. 1; v. 28; 2 Th. i. 2; iii. 18; 1 Tim. i. 2; vi. 21(22); 2 Tim. i. 2; iv. 22; Tit. i. 4; iii. 15; Philem. 3, 25; Heb. xiii. 25; 1 Pet. i. 2; 2 Pet. i. 2; iii. 18 [cf. 3 a.]; 2 Jn. 3; Rev. i. 4; xxii. 21; cf. *Otto*, Ueber d. apostol. Segensgruss χάρις ὑμῖν etc., in the Jahrbb. f. deutsche Theol. for 1867, p. 678 sqq. Moreover, the word χάρις contains the idea of *kindness which bestows upon one what he has not deserved*: Ro. xi. 6; hence κατὰ χάριν and κατὰ ὀφείλημα are contrasted in Ro. iv. 4, 16; χάριτι and ἐξ ἔργων in Ro. xi. 6; κατ᾽ ἐκλογὴν χάριτος, ib. 5; but the N. T. writers use χάρις pre-eminently of that kindness by which God bestows favors even upon the ill-deserving, and grants to sinners the pardon of their offences, and bids them accept of eternal salvation through Christ: Ro. iii. 24; v. 17, 20 sq.; [vi. 1]; 1 Co. xv. 10; Gal. i. 15; ii. 21; Eph. i. 6, [7]; ii. 5, 7 sq.; Phil. i. 7; Col. i. 6; 2 Th. ii. 16; 1 Tim. i. 14; 2 Tim. i. 9; Heb. ii. 9 [here Treg. mrg. χωρίς]; x. 29; xii. 15; xiii. 9; 1 Pet. i. 10; Jude 4; εὑρίσκειν χάριν, Heb. iv. 16; ἡ χάρις τοῦ θεοῦ ἡ σωτήριος, Tit. ii. 11; ὁ λόγος τῆς χάριτος, the message of his grace, Acts xiv. 3; xx. 32; τὸ εὐαγγέλιον τῆς χάριτος τοῦ θεοῦ, Acts xx. 24; it is styled '*the grace of Christ*,' in that through pity for sinful men Christ left his state of blessedness with God in heaven, and voluntarily underwent the hardships and miseries of human life, and by his sufferings and death procured salvation for mankind: [Acts xv. 11]; 2 Co. viii. 9; Ro. v. 15; Gal. i. 6; [Tit. iii. 7]; Jn. i. 14, 17.   χάρις is used of *the merciful kindness by which God, exerting his holy influence upon souls, turns them to Christ, keeps, strengthens, increases them in Christian faith, knowledge, affection, and kindles them to the exercise of the Christian virtues*: 2 Co. iv. 15; vi. 1; 2 Th. i. 12; οἱ πεπιστευκότες διὰ τῆς χάριτος, Acts xviii. 27; ὑπὸ χάριν εἶναι, to be subject to the power of grace,

opp. to ὑπὸ νόμον εἶναι, Ro. vi. 14 sq.; ἐκπίπτειν τῆς χάρ. Gal. v. 4; προσμένειν τῇ χ. Acts xiii. 43 [G L T Tr WH]; ἐπιμένειν, ibid. Rec.; ἐν τῇ χάριτι (R G WH txt. om. the art.), prompted by grace, Col. iii. 16; the grace of God promoting the progress and blessings of the Christian religion, Acts xi. 23; [prompting its possessors to benefactions, 2 Co. ix. 14]; sustaining and aiding the efforts of the men who labor for the cause of Christ, 1 Co. xv. 10; 2 Co. i. 12; the favor of Christ, assisting and strengthening his followers and ministers to bear their troubles, 2 Co. xii. 9.   **3.** *what is due to grace*;   **a.** *the spiritual condition of one governed by the power of divine grace*, what the theologians call the '*status gratiae*': ἑστηκέναι ἐν τῇ χ. Ro. v. 2; εἰς τὴν χ. 1 Pet. v. 12; αὐξάνειν ἐν χάριτι, 2 Pet. iii. 18; ἐνδυναμοῦσθαι ἐν τῇ χάριτι τῇ ἐν Χριστῷ, 2 Tim. ii. 1.   **b.** *a token* or *proof of grace*, 2 Co. i. 15 [A. V. *benefit* (WH txt. Tr mrg. χαράν, q. v. under b.)]; *a gift of grace; benefaction, bounty*: used of alms, 1 Co. xvi. 3; 2 Co. viii. 6 sq. 19, (Sir. iii. 29 (31); xxix. 15; xxx. 6; 4 Macc. v. 8; Xen. Ages. 4, 3 sq.; Hier. 8, 4); πᾶσα χάρις, all earthly blessings, wealth, etc., which are due to divine goodness, 2 Co. ix. 8; ὁ θεὸς πάσης χάριτος, the author and giver of benefits of every kind, 1 Pet. v. 10. *the aid* or *succor of divine grace*: διδόναι χάριν ταπεινοῖς, 1 Pet. v. 5; Jas. iv. 6; the salvation offered to Christians is called χάρις, *a gift of divine grace*, 1 Pet. i. 10, 13; of the various blessings of Christ experienced by souls: λαβεῖν χάριν ἀντὶ χάριτος (see ἀντί, 2 e. p. 49ᵇ bot.), Jn. i. 16; χάρις ζωῆς, the gift of grace seen in the reception of life [cf. ζωή, 2 b.], 1 Pet. iii. 7; *capacity and ability due to the grace of God* (Germ. *Gnadenausrüstung*), Eph. iv. 7; πλήρης χάριτος, Acts vi. 8 G L T Tr WH; ποικίλη χάρις, the aggregate of the extremely diverse powers and gifts granted to Christians, 1 Pet. iv. 10; used of the power to undertake and administer the apostolic office: λαβεῖν χάριν καὶ ἀποστολήν, i. e. χάριν τῆς ἀποστολῆς, Ro. i. 5; ἡ χ. ἡ δοθεῖσά μοι (Paul), Ro. xii. 3, 6; xv. 15; 1 Co. iii. 10; Gal. ii. 9; Eph. iii. 2, 7; δοθ. ὑμῖν, of the gifts of knowledge and utterance conferred upon Christians, 1 Co. i. 4; ἐδόθη μοι ἡ χ. αὕτη, foll. by an inf., Eph. iii. 8; of the desire to give alms roused by the grace of God, 2 Co. viii. 1.   **4.** *thanks* (for benefits, services, favors); prop.: χάριτι, with thanksgiving, 1 Co. x. 30; χάριν ἔχειν τινί (Lat. *gratiam habere alicui*), to be thankful to one, Lk. xvii. 9; 1 Tim. i. 12; 2 Tim. i. 3; Heb. xii. 28, (2 Macc. iii. 33, and countless times in prof. auth.; cf. Passow s. v. p. 2416ᵃ sub fin.; [L. and S. s. v. II. 2]; *Ast*, Lex. Plat. ii. p. 539 sq.; *Bleek*, Brief a. d. Hebr. ii. 2, p. 975); foll. by ἐπί with a dat. of the thing, Philem. 7; 1 Co. ii 2 and 7, Rec.ˢᵗ ᵇᵉˢ (cf. p. 233ᵃ mid.); χάρις τῷ θεῷ sc. ἔστω, Ro. vii. 25 L T Tr WH txt.; foll. by ὅτι, Ro. vi. 17 (χ. τοῖς θεοῖς, ὅτι etc. Xen. Cyr. 7, 5, 72; 8, 7, 3; an. 3, 3, 14; oec. 8, 16); with a ptcp. added to the dat. (by apposition), 1 Co. xv. 57; 2 Co. ii. 14; viii. 16; foll. by ἐπί with a dat. of the thing [cf. ἐπί, B. 2 a. δ.], 2 Co. ix. 15.   **i. q.** *recompense, reward*, Lk. vi. 32–34 (for which Mt. v. 46 uses μισθός).*

5486   χάρισμα, -τος, τό, (χαρίζομαι), a gift of grace; a favor which one receives without any merit of his own; in the N. T. [where (exc. 1 Pet. iv. 10) used only by Paul] the gift of divine grace (so also in Philo de alleg. legg. iii. § 24 fin. δωρεὰ καὶ εὐεργεσία καὶ χάρισμα θεοῦ τὰ πάντα ὅσα ἐν κόσμῳ καὶ αὐτὸς ὁ κόσμος ἐστίν); used of the natural gift of continence, due to the grace of God as creator, 1 Co. vii. 7; deliverance from great peril to life, τὸ εἰς ἡμᾶς χ. bestowed upon us, 2 Co. i. 11; the gift of faith, knowledge, holiness, virtue, Ro. i. 11; the economy of divine grace, by which the pardon of sin and eternal salvation is appointed to sinners in consideration of the merits of Christ laid hold of by faith, Ro. v. 15 sq.; vi. 23; plur. of the several blessings of the Christian salvation, Ro. xi. 29; in the technical Pauline sense χαρίσματα [A. V. gifts] denote extraordinary powers, distinguishing certain Christians and enabling them to serve the church of Christ, the reception of which is due to the power of divine grace operating in their souls by the Holy Spirit [cf. Cremer in Herzog ed. 2 vol. v. 10 sqq. s. v. Geistesgaben]: Ro. xii. 6; 1 Co. i. 7; xii. 4, 31; 1 Pet. iv. 10; χαρίσματα ἰαμάτων, 1 Co. xii. 9, 28, 30; spec. the sum of those powers requisite for the discharge of the office of an evangelist: 1 Tim. iv. 14; 2 Tim. i. 6. ([Of temporal blessings, 'Teaching' 1, 5 (cf. δώρημα in Herm. mand. 2, 4)]; eccl. writ.) *

5487   χαριτόω, -ῶ: 1 aor. ἐχαρίτωσα; pf. pass. ptcp. κεχαριτωμένος; (χάρις);   1. to make graceful i. e. charming, lovely, agreeable: pass. Sir. xviii. 17; ταῖς διαλόξοις στροφαῖς χαριτούμενος ὀφρύν, Liban. vol. iv. p. 1071, 14.   2. to pursue with grace, compass with favor; to honor with blessings: τινά, Eph. i. 6; pass. Lk. i. 28, [some would take it in these two exx. subjectively (R. V. mrg. endued with grace)]; Ps. xviii. 26 Symm.; [Herm. sim. 9, 24, 3; Test. xii. Patr. test. Joseph. 1]; eccles. and Byzant. writ.*

5488   Χαρράν, (Hebr. חָרָן [i. e. (prob.) 'parched', 'arid'], Gen. xi. 31; xii. 5; xxvii. 43), Haran [so R. V.; A. V. (after the Grk.) Charran], called Κάρραι in Grk. writ. and Carræ in Lat., a city of Mesopotamia, of great antiquity and made famous by the defeat of Crassus: Acts vii. 2, 4. Cf. Win. RWB. s. v.; Vaihinger in Herzog v. 539; [Schultz in Herzog ed. 2, s. v.]; Steiner in Schenkel ii. 592; Schrader in Riehm p. 571.*

5489   χάρτης, -ου, ὁ, (χαράσσω), paper: 2 Jn. 12; Jer. xliii. (xxxvi.) 23. ([Plat. Com. fragm. 10 p. 257 (Didot); cf. inscr. (B.C. 407) in Kirchhoff, Inscrr. Attic. i. No. 324]; Ceb. tab. 4; Diosc. 1, 115.) [Cf. Birt, Antikes Buchwesen, index i. s. v.; Gardthausen, Griech. Palaeographie, p. 23; Edersheim, Jesus the Messiah, ii. p. 270 sq.] *

5490   χάσμα, -τος, τό, (χαίνω to yawn), a gaping opening, a chasm, gulf: i. q. a great interval, Lk. xvi. 26. (Hes. theog. 740; Eur., Plat., Plut., Lcian., Ael., al.) *

5491   χεῖλος, -ους, τό, gen. plur. in the uncontr. form χειλέων (Heb. xiii. 15; see ὄρος), (χέω i. q. ΧΑΩ, χαίνω), fr. Hom. down, Sept. for שָׂפָה, a lip;   a. in the N. T. of the speaking mouth [cf. W. 32]: Mt. xv. 8; Mk. vii. 6; Ro. iii. 13; 1 Co. xiv. 21; Heb. xiii. 15 (on which see καρπός,

2 c.); 1 Pet. iii. 10.   b. metaph.: χεῖλος τῆς θαλάσσης, the sea-shore, Heb. xi. 12 (Gen. xxii. 17; Ex. vii. 15; xiv. 30, etc.; of the shore of a lake, Joseph. b. j. 3, 10, 7; of the banks of rivers, Hdt. 2, [70]. 94; [Aristot. de mirab. aud. 46; 150; cf. hist. an. 6, 16 p. 570ᵃ, 22]; Polyb. 3, 14, 6; [cf. W. pp. 18, 30]).*

5492   χειμάζω: pres. pass. ptcp. χειμαζόμενος; (χεῖμα stormy weather, winter [cf. χειμών]); to afflict with a tempest, to toss about upon the waves: pass. Acts xxvii. 18 [R. V. labored with the storm]. (Aeschyl., Thuc., Plat., Diod., Plut., Lcian., al.) [COMP.: παρα-χειμάζω.] *

5493   χείμαρρος, (for the more com. χειμάρροος [sc. ποταμός], Att. contr. χειμάρρους [q. v. in L. and S. fin.], cf. Lob. ad Phryn. p. 234), -ου, ὁ, (χεῖμα winter, and ῥέω, ῥόος), fr. Hom. down, Sept. very often for נַחַל, lit. flowing in winter, a torrent: Jn. xviii. 1 [where A. V. brook].*

5494   χειμών, -ῶνος, ὁ, (χεῖμα, and this fr. χέω on account of the 'pouring' rains; [al. connect it with χι-ών, snow, frost (cf. Lat. hiems, etc.); see Curtius § 194; L. and S. s. v. χιών, fin.]), winter;   a. stormy or rainy weather, a tempest (so fr. Hom. down): Mt. xvi. 3 [Tdf. br. WH reject the pass.]; Acts xxvii. 20.   b. winter, the winter season, (so fr. Thuc. and Arstph. down): Jn. x. 22; 2 Tim. iv. 21; χειμῶνος, in winter (-time), in the winter (Plat. de rep. 3 p. 415 e.; Xen. mem. 3, 8, 9; al. [cf. W. § 30, 11; B. § 132, 26]), Mt. xxiv. 20; Mk. xiii. 18.*

5495   χείρ, gen. χειρός, acc. χεῖραν (1 Pet. v. 6 Tdf.; see ἄρσην, fin.), ἡ, [fr. r. meaning 'to lay hold of'; cf. Lat. heres, etc.; Curtius § 189; Vaniček p. 249 sq.], fr. Hom. down, Hebr. יָד, the hand: Mt. iii. 12; Mk. iii. 1; Lk. vi. 6; 1 Tim. ii. 8; Heb. xii. 12, and often; the gen. with the verbs ἅπτομαι, ἐπιλαμβάνομαι, κρατέω, πιάζω, etc., which see in their places; the dat. with ἐργάζομαι, ἐσθίω, etc.; ὁ ἀσπασμὸς τῇ ἐμῇ χειρί, 1 Co. xvi. 21; Col. iv. 18; 2 Th. iii. 17; the acc. with the verbs αἴρω, δέω, ἐκπετάννυμι, ἐκτείνω, ἐμβάπτω, ἐπιτίθημι, καθαρίζω, κατασείω, νίπτω, etc. ἡ ἐπίθεσις τῶν χειρῶν [see ἐπίθεσις and reff.], 1 Tim. iv. 14; 2 Tim. i. 6; ἐν χειρί τινος, in imitation of the Hebr. בְּיַד פ [cf. B. § 133, 20 cf. 319 sq. (274); Bp. Lghtft. on Gal. iii. 19], by the help or agency, of any one, by means of any one, Acts vii. 35 Rec.; Gal. iii. 19; σὺν χειρὶ ἀγγέλου, with the aid or service of the angel [cf. B. u. s.], Acts vii. 35 L T Tr WH; those things in the performance of which the hands take the principal part (as e. g. in working miracles), are said to be done διὰ χειρός or χειρῶν or τῶν [cf. B. § 124, 8 d.] χειρῶν τινος, Mk. vi. 2; Acts v. 12; xiv. 3; xix. 11; univ., Acts ii. 23; vii. 25; xi. 30; xv. 23; ἐπὶ χειρῶν, Mt. iv. 6; Lk. iv. 11; ἐπὶ τὴν χ., Rev. xiv. 9; xx. 1 [here Treg. mrg. ἐν τῇ χ.], 4; ἐκ, Acts xxviii. 4; Rev. viii. 4; εἰς τὴν χ. (on his hand), Lk. xv. 22; ἡ χείρ, as an acting subject (see γλῶσσα, 1), Lk. xxii. 21; plur., Acts xvii. 25; xx. 34; 1 Jn. i. 1; τὰ ἔργα τῶν χ., Acts vii. 41; Rev. ix. 20; ἐκδικεῖν τὸ αἷμά τινος ἔκ τινος (see ἐκδικέω, b. and ἐκ I. 7), Rev. xix. 2. By meton. ἡ χείρ is put for power, activity, (for exx. fr. prof. auth. fr. Hom. down see Passow s. v. p. 2431ᵇ; [L. and S. s. v. p. 1720ᵛ]): παραδιδόναι τινὰ εἰς χεῖράς τινων, into the hostile hands (Deut. i. 27; Job xvi.

11), Mt. xvii. 22; xxvi. 45; Mk. ix. 31; Lk. ix. 44; xxiv. 7; Acts xxi. 11; xxviii. 17; διδόναι τι ἐν τῇ χειρί τινος, to commit to one's protecting and upholding power, Jn. iii. 35; also εἰς τ. χεῖράς τινος, Jn. xiii. 3; τινὰ ἐκ τῶν χειρ. or ἐκ χειρός τινος (fr. the hostile power of any one) ἀπάγειν, Acts xxiv. 7 Rec.; ἐξελέσθαι, Acts xii. 11 (Gen. xxxii. 11; Ex. xviii. 8 sq.); ἐξέρχεσθαι, Jn. x. 39; ῥυσθῆναι, Lk. i. 74; σωτηρία, ib. 71; ἐκφεύγειν τὰς χεῖράς τινος, 2 Co. xi. 33. By a fig. use of language χείρ or χεῖρες are attributed to God, symbolizing his *might*, *activity*, *power*; conspicuous **a.** in creating the universe: ἔργα τῶν χειρῶν αὐτοῦ, Heb. i. 10 (Ps. ci. (cii.) 26). **β.** in upholding and preserving: Lk. xxiii. 46; Jn. x. 29 (cf. 28); χεὶρ κυρίου ἐστὶ μετά τινος, God is present, protecting and aiding one, Lk. i. 66; Acts xi. 21. **γ.** in punishing: χεὶρ κυρίου ἐπὶ σέ, Acts xiii. 11 (1 S. xii. 15); ἐμπίπτειν εἰς χ. θεοῦ ζῶντος, Heb. x. 31. **δ.** in determining and controlling the destinies of men: Acts iv. 28; ταπεινοῦσθαι ὑπὸ τὴν κραταιὰν χεῖρα τοῦ θεοῦ, 1 Pet. v. 6.

5496 χειραγωγέω, -ῶ; pres. pass. ptcp. χειραγωγούμενος; (χειραγωγός, q. v.; cf. χαλιναγωγέω); *to lead by the hand*: τινά, Acts ix. 8; xxii. 11. (Anacr., Diod., Plut., Lcian., Artem., al.) *

5497 χειρ-αγωγός, -όν, (χείρ and ἄγω), *leading* one *by the hand*: Acts xiii. 11. (Artem. oneir. 1, 48; Plut., al.) *

5498 χειρόγραφον, -ου, τό, (χείρ and γράφω), *a handwriting*, *what one has written with his own hand* (Polyb. 30, 8, 4; Dion. Hal. 5, 8; al.); spec. *a note of hand, or writing in which one acknowledges that money has either been deposited with him or lent to him by another, to be returned at an appointed time* (Tob. v. 3; ix. 5; Plut. mor. p. 829 a. de vitand. aere al. 4, 3; Artem. oneir. 3, 40); metaph. applied in Col. ii. 14 [(where R.V. *bond*)] to the Mosaic law, which shews men to be chargeable with offences for which they must pay the penalty.*

5499 χειρο-ποίητος, -ον, (χείρ and ποιέω), *made by the hand* i. e. *the skill of man* (see ἀχειροποίητος): of temples, Mk. xiv. 58; Acts vii. 48; xvii. 24; Heb. ix. 11, 24; of circumcision, Eph. ii. 11. (In Sept. of idols; of other things, occasionally in Hdt., Thuc., Xen., Polyb., Diod.) *

5500 χειρο-τονέω, -ῶ: 1 aor. ptcp. χειροτονήσας; 1 aor. pass. ptcp. χειροτονηθείς; (fr. χειροτόνος extending the hand, and this fr. χείρ and τείνω); fr. [Arstph.], Xen., Plat., Isocr. down; **a.** prop. *to vote by stretching out the hand* (cf. Xen. an. 3, 2, 33 ὅτῳ δοκεῖ ταῦτα, ἀνατεινάτω τὴν χεῖρα· ἀνέτειναν ἅπαντες). **b.** *to create* or *appoint by vote*: τινά, one to have charge of some office or duty, pass. 2 Co. viii. 19, and in the spurious subscriptions in 2 Tim. iv. 23; Tit. iii. 15. **c.** with the loss of the notion of extending the hand, *to elect, appoint, create*: τινά, Acts xiv. 23 (see exx. fr. the Grk. writ. in Passow s. v. p. 2440ᵃ; χειροτονεῖσθαι ὑπὸ θεοῦ βασιλέα, Philo de praem. et poen. § 9; [βασιλέως ὕπαρχος ἐχειροτονεῖτο, de Joseph. § 41]; Joseph. antt. 6, 4, 2; [7, 11, 1; of the choice of Jon. as high-priest, 13, 2, 2; cf. Hatch in Dict. of Chris. Antiq. s. v. Ordination, p. 1501ᵇ; Harnack on 'Teaching' etc. 15, 1]). [Comp.: προ-χειροτονέω.] *

χείρων, -ον, (compar. of κακός; derived fr. the obsol. **5501** χέρης, which has been preserved in the dat. χέρηϊ, acc. χέρηα, plur. χέρηες, χέρηα; cf. Bttm. Ausf. Spr. i. p. 268 [cf. Ebeling, Lex. Hom. s. v. χέρης]), [fr. Hom. down], *worse*: Mt. ix. 16; Mk. ii. 21; γίνεται τὰ ἔσχατα χείρονα τῶν πρώτων, Mt. xii. 45; 2 Pet. ii. 20; εἰς τὸ χεῖρον ἔρχεσθαι, [*to grow worse*], of one whose illness increases, Mk. v. 26; ἵνα μὴ χεῖρόν σοί τι γένηται, lest some worse thing befall thee, Jn. v. 14; πόσῳ χείρων τιμωρία, [A.V. *how much sorer punishment*], Heb. x. 29; ἐπὶ τὸ χεῖρον προκόπτειν ([A. V. *wax worse and worse*]; see προκόπτω, 2), 2 Tim. iii. 13; of the moral character, ἀπίστου χείρων, 1 Tim. v. 8.*

Χερουβίμ (R G) and Χερουβείν (L T Tr WH; in Mss. **5502** also Χερουβίν, Χερουβείμ; [cf. Tdf. Proleg. p. 84; WH. App. p. 155ᵃ; and s. v. ει, ι]), τά (neut. gend. also in most places in the Sept.; rarely, as Ex. xxv. 18, 19, οἱ Χερ.; Χερούβεις in Ex. xxv. 18 [but this is a mistake; the form in -εις seems not to occur in the O. T.]; in Philo τὰ Χερουβίμ, in Joseph. οἱ Χερουβεῖς, antt. 3, 6, 5; αἱ Χερουβεῖς, ibid. 8, 3, 3; the use of the neut. gender seemed most suitable, because they were ζῶα; Χερουβεῖς ζῶά ἐστι πετεινά, μορφὴν δ᾽ οὐδενὶ τῶν ὑπ᾽ ἀνθρώπων ἑωραμένων παραπλήσια, Joseph. antt. 3, 6, 5), Hebr. כְּרוּבִים (hardly of Semitic origin, but cognate to the Grk. γρύψ, γρυπός [for the various opinions cf. Gesenius's Hebr. Lex. ed. Mühlau and Volck s. v. כְּרוּב]), *cherubim*, two golden figures of living creatures with two wings; they were fastened to the lid of the ark of the covenant in the Holy of holies (both of the sacred tabernacle and of Solomon's temple) in such a manner that their faces were turned towards each other and down towards the lid, which they overshadowed with their expanded wings. Between these figures God was regarded as having fixed his dwelling-place (see δόξα, III. 1): Heb. ix. 5. In Ezek. i. and x. another and far more elaborate form is ascribed to them; but the author of the Ep. to the Heb. has Ex. xxv. 18–20 in mind. Cf. Win. RWB. s. v. Cherubim; Gesenius, Thes. ii. p. 710 sq.; Dillmann in Schenkel i. 509 sqq.; Riehm, De Natura et Notione Symbolica Cheruborum (Basil. 1864); also his 'Die Cherubim in d. Stiftshütte u. im Tempel' in the Theol. Stud. u. Krit. for 1871 p. 399 sqq.; and in his HWB. p. 227 sqq.; [cf. Lenormant, Beginnings of History, (N. Y. 1882), ch. iii.].*

χήρα, -ας, ἡ, (fem. of the adj. χῆρος, 'bereft'; akin to **5503** χέρσος, sterile, barren, and the Lat. careo, [but cf. Curtius § 192]), fr. Hom. Il. 6, 408 down, Sept. for אַלְמָנָה, *a widow*: Mt. xxiii. 14 (13) Rec.; Mk. xii. 40, 42 sq.; Lk. ii. 37; iv. 25; vii. 12; xviii. 3, 5; xx. 47; xxi. 2 sq.; Acts vi. 1; ix. 39, 41; 1 Co. vii. 8; 1 Tim. v. 3–5, 9, 11, 16; Jas. i. 27; with γυνή added (2 S. xiv. 5, and often in the Grk. writ. fr. Hom. Il. 2, 289 down), Lk. iv. 26; a city stripped of inhabitants and riches is represented under the figure of *a widow*, Rev. xviii. 7.*

χθές (Rec.; also Grsb. in Acts and Heb.), i. q. ἐχθές **5504** (q. v.), *yesterday*; Sept. for תְּמוֹל. [Hom. (h. Merc.), al.]

χιλίαρχος, -ου, ὁ, (χίλιοι and ἄρχω; [on the form of **5506** the word cf. reff. s. v. ἑκατοντάρχης, and L. and S. s. v. χιλιάρχης]), *the commander of a thousand soldiers, a chiliarch*; *the commander of a Roman cohort (a military tribune)*: Jn. xviii. 12; Acts xxi. 31–33, 37; xxii. 24, 26–29; xxiii. 10, 15, 17–19, 22; xxiv. 7 Rec., 22; xxv. 23, (Sept. for שַׂר אֲלָפִים and רֹאשׁ אֲלָפִים). *any military commander* [R. V. *high* or *chief captain, captain*]: Mk. vi. 21; Rev. vi. 15; xix. 18. [(Aeschyl., Xen., al.)]*

5505   χιλιάς, -άδος, ἡ, (χίλιοι), *a thousand, the number one thousand*: plur., Lk. xiv. 31; Acts iv. 4; 1 Co. x. 8; Rev. v. 11; vii. 4–8; xi. 13; xiv. 1–3; xxi. 16; Sept. for אֲלָפִים, אֶלֶף. [Hdt. on.]*

5507   χίλιοι, -αι, -α, *a thousand*: 2 Pet. iii. 8; Rev. xi. 3, etc.

5508   Χίος, -ου, ἡ, *Chios*, an island in the Ægean Sea, between Samos and Lesbos, not far from the shore of Lydia: Acts xx. 15.*

5509   χιτών, -ῶνος, ὁ, fr. Hom. down, Sept. for כֻּתֹּנֶת and כְּתֹנֶת, *a tunic*, an undergarment, usually worn next the skin: Mt. x. 10; Mk. vi. 9; Lk. iii. 11; ix. 3; Jude 23; it is distinguished from τὸ ἱμάτιον (q. v. 2) or τὰ ἱμάτια in Mt. v. 40; Lk. vi. 29; Jn. xix. 23; Acts ix. 39; univ. *a garment, vestment* (Aeschyl. suppl. 903), plur. (Plut. Tib. Gracch. 19), Mk. xiv. 63. [Cf. *Rich*, Dict. of Antiq. s. v. Tunica; and reff. s. v. ἱμάτιον, u. s.]*

5510   χιών, -όνος, ἡ, fr. Hom. down, Sept. for שֶׁלֶג, *snow*: Mt. xxviii. 3; Mk. ix. 3 (where it is omitted by G T Tr WH); Rev. i. 14.*

5511   χλαμύς, -ύδος, ἡ, (acc. to the testimony of Pollux 10, 38, 164, first used by Sappho), *a chlamys*, an outer garment usually worn over the χιτών [q. v.]; spec. the Lat. *paludamentum* [q. v. in *Rich*, Dict. of Antiq. s. v. sub fin.], a kind of short cloak worn by soldiers, military officers, magistrates, kings, emperors, etc. (2 Macc. xii. 35; Joseph. antt. 5, 1, 10; Hdian., Ael., al.; often in Plut.): Mt. xxvii. 28, 31, [A.V. *robe*; see Meyer ad loc.; *Trench*, Syn. § l.; Rich (as above) s. v. Chlamys; and other reff. s. v. ἱμάτιον].*

5512   χλευάζω; impf. ἐχλεύαζον; (χλεύη, jesting, mockery); *to deride, mock, jeer*: Acts ii. 13 Rec.; xvii. 32. (2 Macc. vii. 27; Sap. xi. 15; Arstph., Dem., Polyb., Diod., Plut., Lcian., al.) [COMP.: δια-χλευάζω.]*

5513   χλιαρός, -ά, -όν, (χλίω, to become warm, liquefy, melt), *tepid, lukewarm*: metaph. of the condition of a soul wretchedly fluctuating between a torpor and a fervor of love, Rev. iii. 16. (Hdt., Pind., Diod., Plut., Athen., Geop.)*

5514   Χλόη [(i. e. 'tender verdure'); an appellation of Demeter, 'the Verdant')], -ης, ἡ, *Chloe*, a Christian woman of Corinth: 1 Co. i. 11. [Cf. B. D. s. v.]*

5515   χλωρός, -ά, -όν, (contr. fr. χλοερός, fr. χλόη, tender green grass or corn): **1.** *green*: χόρτος, Mk. vi. 39 (Gen. i. 30); Rev. viii. 7; πᾶν χλωρόν, ix. 4. **2.** *yellowish, pale*: ἵππος, Rev. vi. 8. (In both senses fr. Hom. down.)*

5516   χξϛʹ, *six hundred and sixty-six* (χʹ = 600; ξʹ = 60; ϛʹ = 6), a mystical number the meaning of which is clear when it is written in Hebr. letters, קסר נרון, i. e. Νέρων Καῖσαρ, 'Nero Caesar', (sometimes the Jews write קסר

for the more common קיסר, the Syriac always ܩܣܪ, cf. Ewald, Die Johann. Schriften, ii. p. 263 note; [*Schürer*, N. T. Zeitgesch. ed. 1, § 25 III. p. 449 note]; נ = 50, ר = 200, ו = 6, נ = 50, ק = 100, ס = 60, ר = 200): Rev. xiii. 18 R G T Tr. [For a digest of opinions respecting this much debated number see *Lee* in the 'Speaker's Com.' ad loc.]*

5517   χοϊκός, -ή -όν, (χοῦς, q. v.), *made of earth, earthy*: 1 Co. xv. 47–49. (γυμνοὶ τούτους τοῦ χοϊκοῦ βάρους, Anon. in *Walz*, Rhett. i. p. 613, 4; [Hippol. haer. 10, 9 p. 314, 95].)*

5518   χοῖνιξ, -ικος, ἡ, fr. Hom. Od. 19, 28 down, *a choenix*, a dry measure, containing four cotylae or two sextarii [i. e. less than our 'quart'; cf. L. and S. s. v.] (or as much as would support a man of moderate appetite for a day; hence called in Athen. 3 § 20 p. 98 e. ἡμεροτροφίς [cf. ἡ χοῖνιξ ἡμερησίου τροφῆς, Diog. Laërt. 8, 18]): Rev. vi. 6 [where A.V. *measure* (see Am. appendix ad loc.)].*

5519   χοῖρος, -ου, ὁ, fr. Hom. down, *a swine*: plur., Mt. vii. 6; viii. 30, [31] 32; Mk. v. 11–13, 14 Rec., [16]; Lk. viii. 32 sq.; xv. 15 sq. (Not found in the O. T.)*

5520   χολάω, -ῶ; (χολή, q. v.); **1.** *to be atrabilious*; *to be mad* (Arstph. nub. 833). **2.** *to be angry, enraged*, (for χολοῦμαι, more com. in the earlier Grk. writ. fr. Hom. down): τινί, Jn. vii. 23 (3 Macc. iii. 1; Artem., Nicand., Mosch., Diog. Laërt., al.).*

5521   χολή, -ῆς, ἡ, (i. q. χόλος, fr. χέω to pour out [now thought to be connected with χλόη, χλωρός, etc. 'yellowish green'; cf. Curtius § 200; Vaniček p. 247]), first found in Archilochus (8th cent. B. C.), afterwards in Aeschyl. et sqq. **1.** *bile, gall*: Mt. xxvii. 34 (cf. Sept. Ps. lxviii. (lxix.) 22) [cf. B. D. s. v. Gall]; Acts viii. 23 (on which see πικρία); for מְרֵרָה, Job xvi. 13. **2.** in the O. T. it is also used of other bitter things; for לַעֲנָה, wormwood, Prov. v. 4; Lam. iii. 15; hence some understand the word in Mt. xxvii. 34 to mean *myrrh*, on account of Mk. xv. 23; but see σμυρνίζω, 2; [B. D. u. s.].*

χόος, see χοῦς.----------------------- } 5522; see (5529a)

Χοραζίν [so G L, also Mt. xi. 21 Rec.; Lk. x. 13 Rec.elz]; ---- 5523 Χοραζείν T Tr WH; [Χωραζίν, Lk. x. 13 Rec.st bez; see ει, ι; *Tdf.* Proleg. p. 84; *WH*. App. p. 155a]), ἡ, indecl. *Chorazin*, a town of Galilee, which is mentioned neither in the O. T. nor by Josephus; acc. to Jerome (in his Onomast. [cf. Euseb. onomast. ed. Larsow and Parthey p. 374]) two miles distant from Capernaum; perhaps the same place which in the talmud, Menach. f. 85, 1 is called כרזין [cf. *Edersheim*, Jesus the Messiah, ii. 139], the remains of which Robinson (Biblical Researches, iii. 347, 359 sq.) thinks must be sought for in the ruins of the modern Tell Hûm; but Wilson (Recovery of Jerusalem Am. ed. pp. 270, 292 sqq.; Our Work in Palestine, p. 188), with whom [Thomson (Land and Book, ii. 8)], Socin (in Baedeker's Palestine and Syria, Eng. ed. p. 374), Wolff (in Riehm p. 235), [the Conders (Hdbk. to the Bible, p. 324), and the majority of recent scholars] agree, holds to the more probable opinion which identifies it with *Kerâzeh*, a heap of ruins lying an hour's journey to the N. E. of Tell Hûm: Mt. xi. 21; Lk. x. 13. Cf. *Win.* RWB. s. v.; Keim i. p. 605 [Eng. trans. ii. 367] and ii. 118 [Eng. trans. iii. 143].*

5524 χορηγέω, -ῶ; fut. 3 pers. sing. χορηγήσει (2 Co. ix. 10 G L T Tr WH); 1 aor. opt. 3 pers. sing. χορηγῆσαι (ib. Rec.); (χορηγός, the leader of a chorus; fr. χορός and ἄγω [ἥγέομαι]); fr. [Simon.], Xen., Plat. down; **1.** *to be a chorus-leader, lead a chorus.* **2.** *to furnish the chorus at one's own expense; to procure and supply all things necessary to fit out the chorus* (so very often in the Attic writ.). **3.** in later writ. ([Aristot.], Polyb., Diod., Philo, Joseph., Plut., Ael., al.; 1 K. iv. 7; 1 Macc. xiv. 10; 2 Macc. iii. 3, etc.), *to supply, furnish abundantly:* τί, 2 Co. ix. 10; 1 Pet. iv. 11. [COMP.: ἐπι-χορη-γέω.] *

5525 χορός, -οῦ, ὁ, (by metath. fr. ὄρχος, ὀρχέομαι, [(?)]; prob. related to χόρτος (Lat. *hortus*), χρόνος, etc., denoting primarily 'an enclosure for dancing'; cf. Curtius § 189]), fr. Hom. down, *a band (of dancers and singers), a circular dance, a dance, dancing:* Lk. xv. 25 (for מְחוֹלָה, Ex. xv. 20; Judg. xi. 34, etc.; for מָחוֹל, Lam. v. 15; Ps. cl. 4).*

5526 χορτάζω: 1 aor. ἐχόρτασα; 1 aor. pass. ἐχορτάσθην; fut. pass. χορτασθήσομαι; (χόρτος, q. v.); first in Hesiod (opp. 450); **a.** *to feed with herbs, grass, hay, to fill* or *satisfy with food, to fatten;* animals (so uniformly in the earlier Grk. writ. [cf. Bp. Lghtft. on Phil. iv. 12; W. 23]): ὄρνεα ἐκ τῶν σαρκῶν, pass. Rev. xix. 21 [here A. V. *were filled*]. **b.** in later (cf. Sturz, Dial. Maced. and Alex. p. 200 sqq.) and Biblical Greek, *to fill* or *satisfy men* (Sept. for שָׂבַע and הִשְׂבִּיעַ; with some degree of contempt in Plat. de rep. 9 p. 586 a. κεκυφότες εἰς γῆν καὶ εἰς τραπέζας βόσκονται χορταζόμενοι καὶ ὀχεύοντες). **a.** prop.: τινά, Mt. xv. 33; pass., Mt. xiv. 20; xv. 37; Mk. vi. 42; vii. 27; viii. 8; Lk. ix. 17; Jn. vi. 26; Jas. ii. 16; opp. to πεινᾶν, Phil. iv. 12; τινά τινος (like πίμπλημι [cf. W. § 30, 8 b.]): ἄρτων, with bread, Mk. viii. 4 (Ps. cxxxi. (cxxxii.) 15); τινὰ ἀπό with a gen. of the thing [cf. B. § 132, 12], pass. Lk. xvi. 21 (Ps. ciii. (civ.) 13); [τινὰ ἐκ w. gen. of the thing (B. u. s.), pass. Lk. xv. 16 Tr mrg. WH]. **β.** metaph.: τινά, *to fulfil* or *satisfy the desire of any one*, Mt. v. 6; Lk. vi. 21, (Ps. cvi. (cvii.) 9).*

5527 χόρτασμα, -τος, τό, (χορτάζω), *feed, fodder*, for animals (Sept.; Polyb., Diod., Plut., al.); *food, (vegetable) sustenance*, whether for men or flocks: plur. Acts vii. 11.*

5528 χόρτος, -ου, ὁ: **1.** the place where grass grows and animals graze: Hom. Il. 11, 774; 24, 640. **2.** fr. Hes. down, *grass, herbage, hay, provender*: of green grass, Mt. vi. 30; xiv. 19; Lk. xii. 28; Jn. vi. 10; Jas. i. 10 sq.; 1 Pet. i. 24 (fr. Is. xl. 6 sqq.); Rev. ix. 4; χόρτ. χλωρός, Mk. vi. 39; Rev. viii. 7; χόρτος of growing crops, Mt. xiii. 26; Mk. iv. 28; of hay, 1 Co. iii. 12. (Sept. for חָצִיר grass, and עֵשֶׂב.) *

5529 Χουζᾶς, -ᾶ [Tdf. Proleg. p. 104; B. 20 (18)], ὁ, *Chuzas* [A.V. (less correctly) *Chusa*], the steward of Herod Antipas: Lk. viii. 3.*

(5529a) χοῦς, -οός, acc. -οῦν, ὁ, (contr. for χόος, fr. χέω, to pour),

fr. Hdt. down; **1.** prop. *earth dug out, an earth-heap* (Germ. *Schutt*): ὁ χοῦς ὁ ἐξορυχθείς, Hdt. 2, 150. **2.** *dust* (Sept. for עָפָר): Mk. vi. 11; Rev. xviii. 19, ([Josh. vii. 11; Sap. v. 15; Sir. xliv. 21, etc.]; Plut. mor. p. 1096 b. [i. e. non posse suaviter etc. 13, 7]).*

5530 χράομαι, χρῶμαι; impf. 3 pers. plur. ἐχρῶντο; 1 aor. ἐχρησάμην; pf. κέχρημαι (1 Co. ix. 15 G L T Tr WH); fr. Hom. down; (mid. of χράω [thought to be allied by metath. with χείρ (cf. Curtius § 189)], 'to grant a loan', 'to lend' [but cf. L. and S. s. v.; they regard the radical sense as 'to furnish what is needful']; hence) **1.** prop. *to receive a loan; to borrow*. **2.** *to take for one's use; to use:* τινί [W. § 31, 1 i.], *to make use of a thing*, Acts xxvii. 17; 1 Co. ix. 12, 15; 1 Tim. i. 8; v. 23; τῷ κόσμῳ, the good things of this world, 1 Co. vii. 31 R G (see below); μᾶλλον χρῆσαι, sc. the opportunity of becoming free, ib. 21 (where others, less fitly, supply τῷ κληθῆναι δοῦλον [see reff. s. v. εἰ, III. 6 a.]). contrary to the regular usage of class. Grk. with an acc.: τὸν κόσμον, 1 Co. vii. 31 L T Tr WH; see Meyer ad loc.; B. § 133, 18; W. u. s.; (also in Sap. vii. 14 acc. to some codd.; [L. and S. give (Pseudo-)Aristot. oecon. 2, 22 p. 1350ᵃ, 7]). with the dat. of a virtue or vice describing the mode of thinking or acting: τῇ ἐλαφρίᾳ, [R. V. 'shew fickleness'], 2 Co. i. 17; πολλῇ παρρησίᾳ, ib. iii. 12, (for numerous exx. fr. Grk. writ. fr. Hdt. down, see Passow ii. p. 2497ᵇ; [L. and S. s. v. II. a.]). with adverbs (see Passow ii. p. 2497ᵃ; [L. and S. s. v. IV.]): ἀποτόμως, *to deal sharply, use sharpness*, 2 Co. xiii. 10. of the use of persons: τινί, *to bear one's self towards, to deal with, treat*, one (often so in Grk. writ.; see Passow ii. p. 2496ᵇ; [L. and S. s. v. III. 1 and 2]), Acts xxvii. 3.*

χράω: see κίχρημι.

5531; see (2797a) p. 347

χρεία, -ας, ἡ, (χρή), fr. Aeschyl. and Soph. down; **1.** *necessity, need:* τὰ πρὸς τὴν χρείαν [L T Tr WH πρ. τὰς χρείας (cf. below)], such things as suited the exigency, such things as we needed for sustenance and the journey, Acts xxviii. 10; εἰς τὰς ἀναγκαίας χρείας, [A. V. *for necessary uses*] i. e. to supply what is admittedly necessary for life [cf. Babr. fab. 136, 9); al. understand the 'wants' here as comprising those of charity or of worship], Tit. iii. 14; πρὸς οἰκοδομὴν τῆς χρείας, for the edification of souls, of which there is now special need, Eph. iv. 29 [cf. R. V. and mrg.]; ἔστι χρεία, *there is need*, foll. by an acc. with inf. Heb. vii. 11; ἔστι χρεία τινός, *there is need of something*, Rev. xxii. 5 Grsb.; Lk. x. 42 [(but not WH mrg.)]; ἔχω χρείαν τινός, *to have need of (be in want of) some thing* (often in the Grk. writ. fr. Aeschyl. down, cf. Passow s. v. 1; [L. and S. s. v. II. 1]), Mt. vi. 8; xxi. 3; Mk. xi. 3; Lk. [ix. 11; xv. 7]; xix. 31, 34; xxii. 71; Jn. xiii. 29; 1 Co. xii. 21, 24; 1 Th. iv. 12; Heb. x. 36; Rev. iii. 17 R G (see below); xxi. 23; xxii. 5 (not Grsb.); τοῦ with an inf. Heb. v. 12 [W. § 44, 4 a.; cf. τὶς, 2 b. p. 626ᵃ bot.]; the gen. of the thing is evident fr. the context, Acts ii. 45; iv. 35; with the gen. of a pers. whose aid, testimony, etc., is needed, Mt. ix. 12; xxvi. 65; Mk. ii. 17; xiv. 63; Lk. v. 31; ἔχω χρείαν, foll. by an inf. (cf. B. § 140, 3), *I* etc.

5531; see (2797a) p. 347

5532

have need to etc., Mt. iii. 14; xiv. 16; Jn. xiii. 10; 1 Th. i. 8; **iv. 9** [with which cf. v. 1 (see W. 339 (318); B. § 140, 3)]; foll. by ἵνα (see ἵνα, II. 2 c. [B. § 139, 46; cf. Epictet. diss. 1, 17, 18]), Jn. ii. 25; xvi. 30; 1 Jn. ii. 27; χρείαν ἔχω, absol., *to have need*: Mk. ii. 25; [Eph. iv. 28]; 1 Jn. iii. 17; οὐδὲν χρείαν ἔχω, to have need as to nothing [cf. B. § 131, 10], Rev. iii. 17 L T Tr WH. ἡ χρεία with a gen. of the subj. *the condition of one deprived of those things which he is scarcely able to do without, want, need*: λειτουργὸς τῆς χρείας μου (see λειτουργός, 2 fin.), Phil. ii. 25; πληροῦν τὴν χρείαν τινός (Thuc. 1. 70), Phil. iv. 19; [add, εἰς (Lchm. br. εἰς) τὴν χρείαν μοι ἐπέμψατε, unto (i. e. to relieve, cf. εἰς, B. II. 3 c. γ. p. 185b top) my need, Phil. iv. 16]; plur. *one's necessities*: ὑπηρετεῖν ταῖς χ. to provide for one's necessities, Acts xx. 34; κοινωνεῖν ταῖς χ. [cf. p. 352ᵃ top], Ro. xii. 13. **2.** *duty, business*, (so esp. fr. Polyb. down [cf. Jud. xii. 10; 1 Macc. xii. 45; xiii. 37; 2 Macc. vii. 24, etc.]): Acts vi. 3.*

5533 **χρεωφειλέτης** (L T Tr WH χρεοφ.; cf. Lob. ad Phryn. p. 691; W. § 5, 1 d. 13; [WH. App. p. 152b; Tdf. Proleg. p. 89; T (?; see u. s.) WH -φιλέτης, cf. WH. App. p. 154b (see I, ι)]), -ου, ὁ, (χρέος or χρέως, a loan, a debt, and ὀφειλέτης, q. v.), *a debtor*: Lk. vii. 41; xvi. 5. (Prov. xxix. 13; Job xxxi. 37; Aesop. fab. 289 [ed. Coray, 11 ed. Halm]; several times in Plut.; [also in Diod., Dion. Hal.; see Soph. Lex. s. v.].)*

5534 **χρή**; (fr. χράω, χράει contr. χρῆ); impers. verb, *it is necessary; it behooves*: foll. by an inf. Jas. iii. 10 [(B. §§ 131, 3; 132, 12). From Hom. on. Syn. see δεῖ, fin.]*

5535 **χρῄζω**; (χρή); fr. Hom. down; *to have need of, to be in want of*: with a gen. of the obj. [W. § 30, 8 a.], Mt. vi. 32; Lk. xi. 8; xii. 30; Ro. xvi. 2 [here w. gen. of a pers.]; 2 Co. iii. 1.*

5536 **χρῆμα**, -τος, τό, (χράομαι), in Grk. writ. whatever is for use, whatever one uses, *a thing, matter, affair, event, business*; spec. *money* (rarely so in the sing. in prof. auth., as Hdt. 3, 38; Diod. 13, 106 [cf. L. and S. s. v. I. sub fin.]): Acts iv. 37; plur. *riches* (often in Grk. writ. fr. Hom. Od. 2, 78; 16, 315 etc. down), Mk. x. 24 [T WH om. Tr mrg. br. the cl.]; οἱ τὰ χρήματα ἔχοντες, *they that have riches*, Mk. x. 23; Lk. xviii. 24; *money*, Acts viii. 18, 20; xxiv. 26, (for כֶּסֶף, silver, Job xxvii. 17; for נְכָסִים, riches, Josh. xxii. 8; 2 Chr. i. 11 sq.).*

5537 **χρηματίζω**; fut. χρηματίσω (Ro. vii. 3 [cf. B. 37 (33)]; in Grk. writ. everywh. the Attic -ιῶ, so too Jer. xxxii. 16 (xxv. 30); xxxiii. (xxvi.) 2); 1 aor. ἐχρημάτισα; pf. pass. κεχρημάτισμαι; 1 aor. pass. ἐχρηματίσθην; (χρῆμα business); in prose writ. fr. Hdt. down; **1.** *to transact business*, esp. *to manage public affairs*; *to advise or consult with one about public affairs*; *to make answer to those who ask advice, present inquiries or requests*, etc.; used of judges, magistrates, rulers, kings. Hence in some later Grk. writ. **2.** *to give a response to those consulting an oracle* (Diod. 3, 6; 15, 10; Plut. mor. p. 435 c. [i. e. de defect. oracc. 46]; several times in Lcian.); hence used of God in Joseph. antt. 5, 1, 14; 10, 1, 3; 11, 8, 4; univ. (dropping all ref. to a previous consultation), *to give a divine command or admonition, to teach from heaven*, [(Jer. xxxii. 16 (xxv. 30))]: with a dat. of the pers. Job xl. 3; pass. foll. by an inf. [A. V. revealed etc.], Lk. ii. 26 (χρηματίζειν λόγους πρός τινα, Jer. xxxvii. (xxx.) 2); pass. *to be divinely commanded, admonished, instructed*, [R. V. warned of God], Mt. ii. 12, 22; Acts x. 22; Heb. viii. 5; xi. 7, (this pass. use is hardly found elsewh. exc. in Joseph. antt. 3, 8, 8; [11, 8, 4]; cf. B. § 134, 4; [W. § 39, 1 a.]); *to be the mouthpiece of divine revelations, to promulge the commands of God, (τινί, Jer. xxxiii. (xxvi.) 2; xxxvi. (xxix.) 23): of Moses, Heb. xii. 25 [R. V. warned]. **3.** *to assume or take to one's self a name from one's public business* (Polyb., Diod., Plut., al.); univ. *to receive a name or title, be called*: Acts xi. 26; Ro. vii. 3, (Joseph. antt. [8, 6, 2]; 13, 11, 3; b. j. 2, 18, 7; [c. Apion. 2, 3, 1; Philo, quod deus immut. § 25 fin.; leg. ad Gaium § 43]; Ἀντίοχον τὸν Ἐπιφανῆ χρηματίζοντα, Diod. in Müller's fragm. vol. ii. p. xvii. no. xxi. 4; Ἰάκωβον τὸν χρηματίσαντα ἀδελφὸν τοῦ κυρίου, Acta Philippi init. p. 75 ed. Tdf.; Ἰακώβου ... ὃν καὶ ἀδελφὸν τοῦ Χριστοῦ χρηματίσαι οἱ θεῖοι λόγοι περιέχουσιν, Eus. h. e. 7, 19; [cf. Soph. Lex. s. v. 2]).*

χρηματισμός, -οῦ, ὁ, (χρηματίζω, q. v.), *a divine response, an oracle*: Ro. xi. 4. (2 Macc. ii. 4; cf. Diod. 1, 1; 14, 7; Clem. Rom. 1 Cor. 17, 5; [cf. Artem. oneir. 1, 2 p. 8; Suicer, Thesaur. s. v. (vol. ii. col. 1532)]; in various other senses in the Grk. writ. fr. Xen. and Plat. down.)* **5538**

χρήσιμος, -η, -ον, (χράομαι), first in Theogn. 406, *fit for use, useful*: 2 Tim. ii. 14.* **5539**

χρῆσις, -εως, ἡ, (χράομαι), *use*: of the sexual use of a woman, Ro. i. 26 sq. (παιδική, Lcian. amor. 25; ὀρέξεις παρὰ τὰς χρήσεις, Plut. placit. philos. 5, 5; [cf. Isocr. p. 386 c.; Plat. legg. 8 p. 841 a.; Aristot., al.]).* **5540**

χρηστεύομαι; (χρηστός, q. v.); *to show one's self mild, to be kind, use kindness*: 1 Co. xiii. 4. (Eccles. writ., as Euseb. h. e. 5, 1, 46; τινί, towards one, Clem. Rom. 1 Cor. 13, 2; 14, 3.)* **5541**

χρηστολογία, -ας, ἡ, (fr. χρηστολόγος, and this fr. χρηστός, q. v., and λέγω; cf. Jul. Capitol. in the life of Pertinax c. 13 "Omnes, qui libere fabulas conferebant, male Pertinaci loquebantur, χρηστολόγον eum appellantes, qui bene loqueretur et male faceret"), *fair speaking, the smooth and plausible address which simulates goodness*: Ro. xvi. 18. (Eustath. p. 1437, 27 [on Il. 23, 598]; eccles. writ.)* **5542**

χρηστός, -ή, -όν, (χράομαι), fr. Hdt. down, Sept. for טוֹב; **1.** prop. *fit for use, useful; virtuous, good*: ἤθη χρηστά, 1 Co. xv. 33 ([Treg. χρῆστα (but cf. B. 11)], see ἦθος, 2). **2.** *manageable*, i. e. *mild, pleasant*, (opp. to harsh, hard, sharp, bitter): of things, χρηστότερος οἶνος, pleasanter, Lk. v. 39 [here T Tr txt. χρηστός; so WH in br.] (of wine also in Plut. mor. p. 240 d. [i. e. Lacaen. apophtheg. (Gorg. 2); p. 1073 a. (i. e. de com. notit. 28)]; of food and drink, Plat. de rep. 4 p. 438 a.; σῦκα, Sept. Jer. xxiv. 3, 5); ὁ ζυγός (opp. to burdensome), Mt. xi. 30 [A. V. easy]; of persons, *kind, benevolent*: of God, 1 Pet. ii. 3 [A. V. gracious] fr. Ps. xxxiii. (xxxiv.) **5543**

9; τὸ χρηστὸν τοῦ θεοῦ i. q. ἡ χρηστότης [W. § 34, 2], Ro. ii. 4; of men, εἰς τινα towards one, Eph. iv. 32; ἐπί τινα, Lk. vi. 35 [here of God; in both pass. A. V. kind].*

5544 χρηστότης, -ητος, ἡ, (χρηστός); **1.** moral goodness, integrity: Ro. iii. 12 (fr. Ps. xiii. (xiv.) 3) [A. V. 'doeth good']. **2.** benignity, kindness: Ro. ii. 4; 2 Co. vi. 6; Gal. v. 22; Col. iii. 12; Tit. iii. 4; ἡ χρ. τινὸς ἐπί τινα, Ro. xi. 22 (opp. to ἀποτομία [q. v.]); Eph. ii. 7. (Sept.; Eur., Isae., Diod., Joseph., Ael., Hdian.; often in Plut.) [See Trench, Syn. § lxiii.] *

5545 χρίσμα (so R G L ed. min. WH) and χρῖσμα (L ed. maj. T Tr; on the accent see W. § 6, 1 e.; Lipsius, Grammat. Untersuch. p. 35; [Tdf. Proleg. p. 102]), -τος, τό, (χρίω, q. v.), anything smeared on, unguent, ointment, usually prepared by the Hebrews from oil and aromatic herbs. Anointing was the inaugural ceremony for priests (Ex. xxviii. 37; xl. 13 (15); Lev. vi. 22; Num. xxxv. 25), kings (1 S. ix. 16; x. 1; xv. 1; xvi. 3, 13), and sometimes also prophets (1 K. xix. 16 cf. Is. lxi. 1), and by it they were regarded as endued with the Holy Spirit and divine gifts (1 S. xvi. 13; Is. lxi. 1; Joseph. antt. 6, 8, 2 πρὸς τὸν Δαυίδην — when anointed by Samuel — μεταβαίνει τὸ θεῖον καταλιπὸν Σάουλον· καὶ ὁ μὲν προφητεύειν ἤρξατο, τοῦ θείου πνεύματος εἰς αὐτὸν μετοικισαμένου); [see BB. DD. s. vv. Ointment, Anointing]. Hence in 1 Jn. ii. 20 (where ἀπὸ τοῦ ἁγίου is so used as to imply that this χρίσμα renders them ἁγίους [cf. Westcott ad loc.]) and 27, τὸ χρίσμα is used of the gift of the Holy Spirit, as the efficient aid in getting a knowledge of the truth; see χρίω. (Xen., Theophr., Diod., Philo, al.; for מִשְׁחָה, Ex. xxix. 7; xxx. 25; xxxv. 14; xl. 7 (9).) *

5546 Χριστιανός [cf. Bp. Lghtft. on Philip. p. 16 note], -οῦ, ὁ, (Χριστός), a Christian, a follower of Christ: Acts xi. 26; xxvi. 28; 1 Pet. iv. 16. The name was first given to the worshippers of Jesus by the Gentiles, but from the second century (Justin Mart. [e. g. apol. 1, 4 p. 55 a.; dial. c. Tryph. § 35; cf. 'Teaching' etc. 12, 4]) onward accepted by them as a title of honor. Cf. Lipsius, Ueber Ursprung u. ältesten Gebrauch des Christennamens. 4to pp. 20, Jen. 1873. [Cf. Soph. Lex. s. v. 2; Farrar in Alex.'s Kitto s. v.; on the 'Titles of Believers in the N. T.' see Westcott, Epp. of St. John, p. 125 sq.; cf. Dict. of Chris. Antiqq. s. v. 'Faithful'.] *

5547 χριστός, -ή, -όν, (χρίω), Sept. for מָשִׁיחַ, anointed: ὁ ἱερεὺς ὁ χριστός, Lev. iv. 5; vi. 22; οἱ χριστοὶ ἱερεῖς, 2 Macc. i. 10; the patriarchs are called, substantively, οἱ χριστοὶ θεοῦ, Ps. civ. (cv.) 15; the sing. ὁ χριστὸς τοῦ κυρίου (מְשִׁיחַ יְהֹוָה) in the O. T. often of the king of Israel (see χρίσμα), as 1 S. ii. 10, 35; [xxiv. 11; xxvi. 9, 11, 23]; 2 S. i. 14; Ps. ii. 2; xvii. (xviii.) 51; Hab. iii. 13; [2 Chr. xxii. 7]; also of a foreign king, Cyrus, as sent of God, Is. xlv. 1; of the coming king whom the Jews expected to be the saviour of their nation and the author of their highest felicity: the name ὁ χριστός (מָשִׁיחַ, Chald. מְשִׁיחָא) is not found in the O. T. but is first used of him in the Book of Enoch 48, 10 [cf. Schodde's note]; 52, 4 (for the arguments by which

some have attempted to prove that the section containing these passages is of Christian origin are not convincing [cf. υἱὸς τοῦ ἀνθρώπου, 2 and reff.]), after Ps. ii. 2 referred to the Messiah; [cf. Psalter of Sol. 17, 36; 18, 6. 8]. Cf. Keim ii. 549 [Eng. trans. iv. 263 sq.; Westcott 'Additional Note' on 1 Jn. v. 1. On the general subject see Schürer, Neutest. Zeitgesch. § 29.] In the N. T. it is used **1.** of the Messiah, viewed in his generic aspects [the word, that is to say, being used as an appellative rather than a proper name], ὁ χριστός: Mt. ii. 4; xvi. 16; xxiii. 10; xxiv. 5, 23; xxvi. 63; Mk. viii. 29; xii. 35; xiii. 21; xiv. 61; Lk. iii. 15; iv. 41; xx. 41; xxii. 67 (66); xxiii. 39; xxiv. 26, 46; Jn. i. 20, 25, [41 (42) Rec.]; iii. 28; iv. 29; vi. 69 Rec.; vii. 26, 31, 41; xi. 27; xii. 34; xx. 31; Acts ii. 30 Rec., 31; iii. 18; viii. 5; ix. 22; xvii. 3ᵃ; xviii. 5, 28; xxvi. Jn. ii. 22; v. 1; ὁ χριστὸς κυρίου or τοῦ θεοῦ, Lk. ii. 26; ix. 20; Acts iv. 26; without the article, Lk. ii. 11; xxiii. 2; Jn. i. 41 (42) L T Tr WH; ix. 22; Acts ii. 36; ὁ χριστός, ὁ βασιλεὺς τοῦ Ἰσραήλ, Mk. xv. 32; ὁ χριστός so used as to refer to Jesus, Rev. xx. 4, 6; with τοῦ θεοῦ added, Rev. xi. 15; xii. 10. **2.** It is added, as an appellative ('Messiah', 'anointed'), to the proper name Ἰησοῦς: **a.** Ἰησοῦς ὁ χριστός, Jesus the Christ ('Messiah'): Acts v. 42 R G; ix. 34 [R G]; 1 Co. iii. 11 Rec.; 1 Jn. v. 6 [R G L]; Ἰησοῦς ὁ λεγόμενος χριστός, who they say is the Messiah [(cf. b. below)], Mt. xxvii. 22; without the art. Ἰησοῦς χριστός, Jesus as Christ or Messiah, Jn. xvii. 3; 1 Jn. iv. 2; 2 Jn. 7, [but in all three exx. it seems better to take χρ. as a prop. name (see b. below)]; ὁ χριστὸς Ἰησοῦς, the Christ (Messiah) who is Jesus, [Mt. i. 18 WH mrg. (see b. below)]; Acts v. 42 L T Tr WH [R. V. Jesus as the Christ]; xix. 4 Rec. **b.** ὁ Χριστός is a proper name (cf. W. § 18, 9 N. 1; [as respects the use of a large or a small initial letter the critical edd. vary: Tdf. seems to use the capital initial in all cases; Treg. is inconsistent (using a small letter, for instance, in all the exx. under 1 above, exc. Lk. xxii. 67 and Jn. iv. 29; in Mt. i. 1 a capital, in Mk. i. 1 a small letter, etc.); WH have adopted the principle of using a capital when the art. is absent and avoiding it when the art. is present (1 Pet. being intentionally excepted; the small letter being retained also in such exx. as Lk. ii. 11; xxiii. 2; Acts ii. 36, etc.); see WH. Intr. § 415]): Mt. i. 17; xi. 2; Ro. i. 16 Rec.; vii. 4; ix. 5; xiv. 18 [here L om. Tr br. the art.]; xv. 19; 1 Co. i. 6, etc. without the article, Mk. ix. 41; Ro. vi. 4; viii. 9, 17; 1 Co. i. 12; Gal. ii. 16 sq. 19 (20), 21; iii. 27; Phil. i. 10, 13, 19–21, 23; ii. 16; Col. ii. 5, 8; Heb. iii. 6, and often. Ἰησοῦς Χριστός, Mt. i. 1, 18 [here Tr om. 'I., WH txt. br. 'I.; al ὁ 'I. Χρ. which is unique; see WH. App. ad loc.]; Mk. i. 1; Jn. i. 17; Acts ii. 38; iii. 6; iv. 10; viii. 12; [ix. 34 L T Tr WH]; x. 36; xi. 17; xv. 26; xvi. 18, 31 [R G]; xx. 21 [here L WH txt. om. Tr br. Χρ.]; xxviii. 31 [Tdf. om. Χρ.]; Ro. i. 1 [R G WH txt. (see below)], 6, 8; ii. 16 [R G Tr txt. WH mrg. (see below)]; 1 Co. i. 7–9; iii. 11 [G T Tr WH (Rec. 'I. ὁ Χρ.)]; xv. 57, and very often in the Epp. of Paul and Peter; Heb.

xiii. 8, 21; 1 Jn. i. 3, 7 [R G]; ii. 1; [v. 6 G T Tr WH]; 2 Jn. 7 [(see a. above)]; Jude 4, 17, 21; Rev. i. 1 sq. 5; xxii. 21 [R G (WH br. al. om. Χρ.)]. Χριστὸς Ἰησοῦς, Ro. [i. 1 T Tr WH mrg. (see above); ii. 16 T Tr mrg. WH txt. (see above)]; vi. 3 [WH br. 'I.]; 1 Co. i. 2, 30; [iii. 11 Lchm. (see above)]; Gal. iii. 14 [here Tr txt. WH txt. 'I. X.]; iv. 14; v. 6 [WH br. 'I.]; vi. 15; Phil. ii. 5; iii. 3, 14; Col. ii. 6; 1 Tim. i. 2; ii. 5. Ἰησοῦς ὁ λεγόμενος Χριστός, surnamed 'Christ' [(cf. a. above)], Mt. i. 16.   on the phrases ἐν Χριστῷ, ἐν Χριστῷ Ἰησοῦ, see ἐν, I. 6 b. p. 211ᵇ [cf. W. § 20, 2 a.]. Χριστός and Ἰησοῦς Χρ. ἔν τισιν, preached among, 2 Co. i. 19; Col. i. 27 [al. (so R.V.) would take ἐν here internally (as in the foll. exx.), within; cf. ἐν, I. 2]; Χριστὸς ἔν τισιν is used of the person of Christ, who by his holy power and Spirit lives in the souls of his followers, and so moulds their characters that they bear his likeness, Ro. viii. 10 (cf. 9); 2 Co. xiii. 5; Gal. ii. 20; Eph. iii. 17; a mind conformed to the mind of Christ, Gal. iv. 19.

5548   χρίω: 1 aor. ἔχρισα; (akin to χείρ [(?), see Curtius § 201], χραίνω; prop. 'to touch with the hand', 'to besmear'); fr. Hom. down; Sept. for מָשַׁח; *to anoint* (on the persons who received anointing among the Hebrews, see χρίσμα); in the N. T. only trop. of God   **a.** consecrating Jesus to the Messianic office, and furnishing him with powers necessary for its administration (see χρίσμα): Lk. iv. 18 (after Is. lxi. 1); contrary to common usage with an acc. of the thing, ἔλαιον (like verbs of clothing, putting on, etc. [cf. W. § 32, 4 a.; B. § 131, 6]), Heb. i. 9 (fr. Ps. xliv. (xlv.) 8; in Theoph. ad Autol. 1, 12 we find χρίεσθαι ἔλαιον θεοῦ and χρ. φωτὶ καὶ πνεύματι almost in the same sentence; πνεύματι ἁγίῳ καὶ δυνάμει, Acts x. 38; also χρίειν used absol., Acts iv. 27.   **b.** enduing Christians with the gifts of the Holy Spirit [cf. Westcott on 1 Jn. ii. 20]: 2 Co. i. 21. [COMP.: ἐν-, ἐπι- χρίω. SYN. see ἀλείφω, fin.] *

5549   χρονίζω; fut. χρονίσω (Heb. x. 37 T Tr txt. WH), Attic χρονιῶ (ibid. R G L Tr mrg.); (χρόνος); fr. Aeschyl. and Hdt. down; Sept. for אָחַר; *to linger, delay, tarry*: Mt. xxv. 5; Heb. x. 37; foll. by ἐν with a dat. of the place, Lk. i. 21; foll. by an inf., Mt. xxiv. 48 [L T Tr WH om. inf.]; Lk. xii. 45.*

5550   χρόνος, -ου, ὁ, fr. Hom. down, Sept. for יוֹם, עֵת, etc. *time*: Heb. xi. 32; Rev. x. 6; ὁ χρ. τοῦ φαινομένου ἀστέρος, the time since the star began to shine [cf. φαίνω, 2 a.], Mt. ii. 7; [ὁ χρ. τοῦ τεκεῖν αὐτήν (Gen. xxv. 24), Lk. i. 57 (B. 267 (230); cf. W. § 44, 4 a.)]; τῆς ἐπαγγελίας, Acts vii. 17; τῆς παροικίας, 1 Pet. i. 17; χρόνοι ἀποκαταστάσεως, Acts iii. 21; οἱ χρ. τῆς ἀγνοίας, Acts xvii. 30; χρόνου διαγενομένου, Acts xxvii. 9; πόσος χρόνος ἐστίν, ὡς τοῦτο γέγονεν, Mk. ix. 21; ὁ παρεληλυθὼς χρ. 1 Pet. iv. 3 (where Rec. adds τοῦ βίου); τεσσαρακονταετής, Acts vii. 23; xiii. 18; στιγμὴ χρόνου, Lk. iv. 5; πλήρωμα τοῦ χρόνου, Gal. iv. 4; ποιεῖν ([q. v. II. d.] *to spend*) χρόνον, Acts xv. 33; xviii. 23; βιῶσαι τὸν ἐπίλοιπον χρόνον, 1 Pet. iv. 2; διδόναι χρόνον τινί (i. e. a space of time, respite), ἵνα etc. Rev. ii. 21 [(Joseph. b. j. 4, 3, 10)]; plur. joined with καιροί, Acts i. 7; 1 Th. v. 1, (see καιρός, 2 e. p. 319ᵃ); ἐπ' ἐσχάτων

(L T Tr WH ἐσχάτου) τῶν χρ. (see ἔσχατος, 1 fin.), 1 Pet. i. 20; [add, ἐπ' ἐσχάτου τοῦ (Tr WH om. τοῦ) χρόνου, Jude 18 L T Tr WH].   with prepositions: ἄχρι, Acts iii. 21; διὰ τὸν χρ., on account of the length of time, Heb. v. 12 (Polyb. 2, 21, 2; Alciphr. 1, 26, 9); ἐκ χρόνων ἱκανῶν, for a long time, Lk. viii. 27 [R G L Tr mrg. (see below)]; ἐν χρόνῳ, Acts i. 6, 21; ἐν ἐσχάτῳ χρόνῳ, Jude 18 Rec.; ἐπὶ χρόνον, [A. V. *for a while*], Lk. xviii. 4; ἐπὶ πλείονα χρ. [A. V. *a longer time*], Acts xviii. 20; ἐφ' ὅσον χρ. *for so long time* as, so long as, Ro. vii. 1; 1 Co. vii. 39; Gal. iv. 1; κατὰ τὸν χρόνον, *according to* (the relations of) *the time*, Mt. ii. 16; μετὰ πολὺν χρόνον, Mt. xxv. 19; μετὰ τοσοῦτον χρ. Heb. iv. 7; πρὸ χρόνων αἰωνίων, [R. V. *before times eternal*], 2 Tim. i. 9; Tit. i. 2. the **dative** is used to express the time *during* which something occurs (dat. of *duration* of time, cf. W. § 31, 9; [B. § 133, 26]): [χρόνῳ ἱκανῷ, *for a long time*, Lk. viii. 27 T Tr txt. WH]; ἱκανῷ χρόνῳ, Acts viii. 11; [τοσούτῳ χρόνῳ, Jn. xiv. 9 L T Tr mrg. WH mrg.]; πολλοῖς χρόνοις [R. V. mrg. *of a long time* (A. V. *oftentimes*); cf. πολύς, c.], Lk. viii. 29; αἰωνίοις, [R. V. *through times eternal*], Ro. xvi. 25. The **accus.** is used in answer to the question **how long**: χρόνον, *for a while*, Acts xix. 22; Rev. vi. 11 (where in R L T Tr WH μικρόν is added); also χρ. τινά, [A.V. *a while*], 1 Co. xvi. 7; ὅσον χρ. [A. V *while*], Mk. ii. 19; χρόνους ἱκανούς, *for a long time*, Lk. xx. 9; μικρὸν χρόνον, Jn. vii. 33; xii. 35; Rev. xx. 3; πολὺν χρ. Jn. v. 6; τοσοῦτον χρ. Jn. xiv. 9 [R G Tr txt. WH txt.]; ἱκανόν, [A. V. *long time*], Acts xiv. 3; οὐκ ὀλίγον, [R. V. *no little time*], Acts xiv. 28; τὸν πάντα χρ. Acts xx. 18. [On the ellipsis of χρόνος in such phrases as ἀφ' οὗ, ἐν τῷ ἑξῆς (Lk. vii. 11 L mrg. Tr txt. WH txt.), ἐν τῷ καθεξῆς (Lk. viii. 1), ἐξ ἱκανοῦ, etc., see ἀπό, I. 4 b. p. 58ᵇ top, ἑξῆς, καθεξῆς, ἐκ IV. 1, etc. SYN. see καιρός, fin.; cf. αἰών, fin.]*

5551   χρονοτριβέω, -ῶ: 1 aor. inf. χρονοτριβῆσαι; (χρόνος and τρίβω); *to wear away time, spend time*: Acts xx. 16. (Aristot. rhet. 3, 3, 3 [p. 1406ᵃ, 37]; Plut., Heliod., Eustath., Byz. writ.) *

5552   χρύσεος, -έα, -εον, contr. -οῦς, -ῆ, -οῦν, [but acc. sing. fem. -σᾶν, Rev. i. 13 L T Tr WH]; gen. plur. -σέων, Rev. ii. 1 L Tr; (on its inflection cf. B. 26 (23); Phryn. ed. Lob. p. 207; L. and S. s. v. init.)], (χρυσός), fr. Hom. down, *golden; made of gold*; also *overlaid* or *covered with gold*: 2 Tim. ii. 20; Heb. ix. 4; Rev. i. 12 sq. 20; ii. 1; iv. 4; v. 8; viii. 3; ix. 7 Grsb., 13, 20; xiv. 14; xv. 6 sq.; xvii. 4; xxi. 15.*

5553   χρυσίον, -ου, τό, (dimin. of χρυσός, cf. φορτίον), fr. Hdt. down, Sept. for זָהָב, *gold*, both that which is imbedded in the earth and is dug out of it (Plat. Euthyd. p. 288 e.; Sept. Gen. ii. 11; hence μεταλλευθέν, Lcian. de sacr. 11): χρ. πεπυρωμένον ἐκ πυρός, [R. V. *refined by fire*], Rev. iii. 18; and that which has been smelted and wrought, Heb. ix. 4; [1 Co. iii. 12 T Tr WH]; 1 Pet. i. 7; Rev. xxi. 18, 21; i. q. *gold coin*, 'gold': Acts iii. 6; xx. 33; 1 Pet. i. 18; *golden ornaments, precious things made of gold*, 1 Tim. ii. 9 L WH txt.; 1 Pet. iii. 3; Rev. xvii. 4 G L WH txt.; xviii. 16 G L Tr txt. WH txt. (cf. χρυσός).*

5554   χρυσο-δακτύλιος, -ον, (χρυσός and δακτύλιος), gold-ringed, adorned with gold rings: Jas. ii. 2. (Besides only in Hesych. s. v. χρυσοκόλλητος; [W. 26].) [Cf. B. D. s. v. Ring.]*

5555   χρυσό-λιθος, -ον, ὁ, (χρυσός and λίθος), chrysolith, chrysolite, a precious stone of a golden color; our topaz [cf. BB. DD. s. v. Chrysolite; esp. Riehm, HWB. s. v. Edelsteine 5 and 19]: Rev. xxi. 20. (Diod. 2, 52; Joseph. antt. 3, 7, 5; Sept. for תַּרְשִׁישׁ, Ex. xxviii. 20; xxxvi. 20 (xxxix. 13); [Ezek. i. 16 Aq.].)*

5556   χρυσό-πρασος [-ον Lchm.], -ον, ὁ, (fr. χρυσός, and πράσον a leek), chrysoprase, a precious stone in color like a leek, of a translucent golden-green [cf. BB. DD. s. v.; Riehm, HWB. s. v. Edelsteine 6]: Rev. xxi. 20.*

5557   χρυσός, -οῦ, ὁ, fr. Hom. down, Hebr. זָהָב, gold (ὁ ἐπὶ γῆς καὶ ὁ ὑπὸ γῆς, Plat. legg. 5 p. 728 a.): univ., Mt. ii. 11; 1 Co. iii. 12 [RGL (al. χρυσίον, q. v.)]; Rev. ix. 7; i. q. precious things made of gold, golden ornaments, Mt. xxiii. 16 sq.; 1 Tim. ii. 9 [here LWH txt. χρυσίον]; Jas. v. 3; Rev. xvii. 4 (LWH txt. χρυσίον); xviii. 12, 16 (L Tr txt. WH txt. χρυσίον); an image made of gold, Acts xvii. 29; stamped gold, gold coin, Mt. x. 9.*

see 5552   χρυσοῦς, see χρύσεος.

5558   χρυσόω, -ῶ: pf. pass. ptcp. κεχρυσωμένος; to adorn with gold, to gild: κεχρυσωμένη χρυσῷ, [A.V. decked with gold], Rev. xvii. 4; and ἐν [GLTr om. WH br. ἐν] χρυσῷ, xviii. 16, of a woman ornamented with gold so profusely that she seems to be gilded; Sept. for מְצֻפָּה זָהָב in Ex. xxvi. 32. (Hdt., Arstph., Plat., Diod., Plut., al.)*

5559   χρώς, gen. χρωτός, ὁ, (cf. χροιά, the skin [cf. Curtius § 201]), fr. Hom. down, (who [generally] uses the gen. χροός etc. [cf. Ebeling, Lex. Hom., or L. and S. s. v.]), the surface of the body, the skin: Acts xix. 12; Sept. for בָּשָׂר, twice for עוֹר, Ex. xxxiv. 29 sq. Alex.*

5560   χωλός, -ή, -όν, fr. Hom. down, Sept. for פִּסֵּחַ, lame: Acts iii. 2, 11 Rec.; xiv. 8; plur., Mt. xi. 5; xv. 30 sq.; xxi. 14; Lk. vii. 22; xiv. 13, 21; Jn. v. 3; Acts viii. 7; τὸ χωλόν, Heb. xii. 13 (on which see ἐκτρέπω, 1). deprived of a foot, maimed, [A.V. halt]: Mt. xviii. 8; Mk. ix. 45.*

5561   χώρα, -ας, ἡ, (ΧΑΩ [cf. Curtius § 179], to lie open, be ready to receive), fr. Hom. down, Sept. for מְדִינָה, אֶרֶץ, 'a province'; **1.** prop. the space lying between two places or limits. **2.** a region or country; i. e. a tract of land: ἡ χ. ἐγγὺς τῆς ἐρήμου, Jn. xi. 54; [in an elliptical phrase, ἡ ἀστραπὴ (ἡ) ἀστράπτουσα ἐκ τῆς ὑπὸ τὸν οὐρανὸν εἰς τὴν ὑπ' οὐρανὸν λάμπει, A.V. part . . . part, Lk. xvii. 24 (cf. W. § 64, 5); on the ellipsis of χώρα in other phrases (ἐξ ἐναντίας, ἐν δεξιᾷ, etc.), see W. l. c.; B. 82 (72)]; land as opp. to the sea, Acts xxvii. 27; land as inhabited, a province or country, Mk. v. 10; [vi. 55 L mrg. T Tr WH]; Lk. xv. 13–15; xix. 12; Acts xiii. 49; with a gen. of the name of the region added: Τραχωνίτιδος, Lk. iii. 1; τῆς Ἰουδαίας, Acts xxvi. 20; [(or an equiv. adj.)] Γαλατική, Acts xvi. 6; xviii. 23; τῶν Ἰουδαίων, Acts x. 39; plur. τῆς Ἰουδαίας καὶ Σαμαρείας, [A.V. regions], Acts viii. 1; ἐν χώρᾳ κ. σκιᾷ θανάτου, in a region of densest darkness (see σκιά, a), Mt. iv. 16; τινός,

the country of one, Mt. ii. 12; χ. for its inhabitants, Mk. i. 5; Acts xii. 20; the (rural) region environing a city or village, the country, Lk. ii. 8; Γεργεσηνῶν, Γερασηνῶν, Γαδαρηνῶν, Mt. viii. 28; Mk. v. 1; Lk. viii. 26; the region with towns and villages which surrounds the metropolis, Jn. xi. 55. **3.** land which is ploughed or cultivated, ground: Lk. xii. 16; plur., Lk. xxi. 21 [R.V. country]; Jn. iv. 35 [A.V. fields]; Jas. v. 4 [A. V. fields]. [Syn. see τόπος, fin.]*

{Χωραζίν, see Χοραζίν.}   **see 5523**

5562   χωρέω, -ῶ; fut. inf. χωρήσειν (Jn. xxi. 25 Tr WH); 1 aor. ἐχώρησα; (χῶρος, a place, space, and this fr. ΧΑΩ, cf. χώρα); **1.** prop. to leave a space (which may be occupied or filled by another), to make room, give place, yield, (Hom. Il. 12, 406; 16, 592; al.); to retire, pass: of a thing, εἴς τι, Mt. xv. 17. metaph. to betake one's self, turn one's self: εἰς μετάνοιαν, 2 Pet. iii. 9 [A. V. come; cf. μετάνοια, p. 406ᵃ]. **2.** to go forward, advance, proceed, (prop. νύξ, Aeschyl. Pers. 384); to make progress, gain ground, succeed, (Plat. Eryx. p. 398 b.; legg. 3 p. 684 e.; [χωρεῖ τὸ κακόν, Arstph. nub. 907, vesp. 1483; al.]; Polyb. 10, 35, 4; 28, 15, 12; al.): ὁ λόγος ὁ ἐμὸς οὐ χωρεῖ ἐν ὑμῖν, gaineth no ground among you or within you [R. V. hath not free course (with mrg. hath no place) in you], Jn. viii. 37 [cf. Field, Otium Norv. pars iii. ad loc.]. **3.** to have space or room for receiving or holding something (Germ. fassen); prop.: τί, a thing to fill the vacant space, Jn. xxi. 25 [not Tdf.]; of a space large enough to hold a certain number of people, Mk. ii. 2 (Gen. xiii. 6 [cf. Plut. praec. ger. reipub. 8, 5 p. 804 b.]); of measures, which hold a certain quantity, Jn. ii. 6; 1 K. vii. 24 (38); 2 Chr. iv. 5, and in Grk. writ. fr. Hdt. down. metaph. to receive with the mind or understanding, to understand, (τὸ Κάτωνος φρόνημα, Plut. Cat. min. 64; ὅσον αὐτῷ ἡ ψυχὴ χωρεῖ, Ael. v. h. 3, 9); to be ready to receive, keep in mind, and practise: τὸν λόγον τοῦτον, this saying, Mt. xix. 11 sq. [(cf. Plut. Lycurg. 13, 5)]; τινά, to receive one into one's heart, make room for one in one's heart, 2 Co. vii. 2. [Comp.: ἀνα-, ἀπο-, ἐκ-, ὑπο- χωρέω. Syn. cf. ἔρχομαι.]*

5563   χωρίζω; fut. χωρίσω [B. 37 (33)]; 1 aor. inf. χωρίσαι; pres. mid. χωρίζομαι; pf. pass. ptcp. κεχωρισμένος; 1 aor. pass. ἐχωρίσθην; (χωρίς, q. v.); fr. Hdt. down; to separate, divide, part, put asunder: τί, opp. to συζεύγνυμι, Mt. xix. 6; Mk. x. 9; τινὰ ἀπό τινος, Ro. viii. 35, 39, (Sap. i. 3); pf. pass. ptcp. Heb. vii. 26. Mid. and 1 aor. pass. with a reflex. signif. to separate one's self from, to depart; **a.** to leave a husband or wife: of divorce, 1 Co. vii. 11, 15; ἀπὸ ἀνδρός, ib. 10 (a woman κεχωρισμένη ἀπὸ τοῦ ἀνδρός, Polyb. 32, 12, 6 [al.]). **b.** to depart, go away: [absol. Philem. 15 (euphemism for ἔφυγε), R. V. was parted from thee]; foll. by ἀπό with a gen. of the place, Acts i. 4; ἐκ with a gen. of the place, Acts xviii. 1 sq. ([W. § 36, 6 a.]; εἴς with an acc. of the place, 2 Macc. v. 21; xii. 12; Polyb., Diod., al.). [Comp.: ἀπο-, δια- χωρίζω.]*

5564   χωρίον, -ου, τό, (dimin. of χῶρος or χώρα), fr. Hdt. down; **1.** a space, a place; a region, district. **2.**

a piece of ground, a field, land, (Thuc., Xen., Plat., al.): Mt. xxvi. 36; Mk. xiv. 32; Jn. iv. 5 [A. V. *parcel of ground*]; Acts i. 18 sq.; iv. 34 [plur. *lands*]; v. 3, 8; *a farm, estate* : plur. Acts xxviii. 7. [Syn. see τόπος, fin.] *

5565 χωρίς, (ΧΑΩ, see χώρα [cf. Curtius § 192]), adv., fr. Hom. down;   **1.** *separately, apart* : Jn. xx. 7.   **2.** as a prep. with the gen. [W. § 54, 6];   **a.** *without* any pers. or thing (making no use of, having no association with, apart from, aloof from, etc.) : 1 Co. [iv. 8]; xi. 11; Phil. ii. 14; 1 Tim. ii. 8; v. 21; Heb. [ii. 9 Treg. mrg.]; xi. 40; παραβολῆς, without making use of a parable, Mt. xiii. 34; Mk. iv. 34; ὁρκωμοσίας, Heb. vii. 20 (21), 21; χ. αἵματος, Heb. ix. 7, 18; αἱματεκχυσίας, Heb. ix. 22; *without* i. e. being absent or wanting: Ro. vii. 8 sq. [R.V. *apart from*]; Heb. xi. 6; xii. 8, 14; Jas. ii. 18 (Rec. ἐκ), 20, 26, [in these three exx. R. V. *apart from*]; without connection and fellowship with one, Jn. xv. 5 [R.V.

apart from]; destitute of the fellowship and blessings of one: χωρὶς Χριστοῦ [cf. W. § 54, 2 a.; R. V. *separate from Christ*], Eph. ii. 12; *without the intervention* (participation or co-operation) of one, Jn. i. 3; Ro. iii. 21, [28; iv. 6; x. 14]; χ. θεμελίου, without laying a foundation, Lk. vi. 49; χ. τῆς σῆς γνώμης, without consulting you, [cf. γνώμη, fin. (Polyb. 3, 21, 1. 2. 7)], Philem. 14; 'without leaving room for' : χ. ἀντιλογίας, Heb. vii. 7; οἰκτιρμῶν, x. 28.   χ. τοῦ σώματος, freed from the body, 2 Co. xii. 3 L T Tr WH (Rec. ἐκτός, q. v. b. a.); χωρὶς ἁμαρτίας, without association with sin, i. e. without yielding to sin, without becoming stained with it, Heb. iv. 15; not to expiate sin, Heb. ix. 28.   **b.** *besides* : Mt. xiv. 21; xv. 38; 2 Co. xi. 28. [Syn. cf. ἄνευ.] *

5566 χῶρος, -ου, ὁ, *the north-west wind* (Lat. *Corus* or *Caurus*) : for the quarter of the heavens from which this wind blows, Acts xxvii. 12 (on which see λίψ, 2).*

Ψ

5567 ψάλλω; fut. ψαλῶ; (fr. ψάω, to rub, wipe; to handle, touch, [but cf. Curtius p. 730]);   **a.** *to pluck off, pull out* : ἔθειραν, the hair, Aeschyl. Pers. 1062.   **b.** *to cause to vibrate by touching, to twang* : τόξων νευρὰς χειρί, Eur. Bacch. 784; spec. χόρδην, *to touch* or *strike the chord, to twang the strings* of a musical instrument so that they gently vibrate (Aristot. probl. 19, 23 [p. 919ᵇ, 2]); and absol. *to play on a stringed instrument, to play the harp,* etc. : Aristot., Plut., Arat., (in Plat. Lys. p. 209 b. with καὶ κρούειν τῷ πλήκτρῳ added [but not as explanatory of it; the Schol. ad loc. says ψῆλαι, τὸ ἄνευ πλήκτρου τῷ δακτύλῳ τὰς χορδὰς ἐπαφᾶσθαι]; it is distinguished from κιθαρίζειν in Hdt. 1, 155); Sept. for נגן and much oftener for זמר; *to sing to the music of the harp;* in the N. T. *to sing a hymn, to celebrate the praises of God in song,* Jas. v. 13 [R.V. *sing praise*]; τῷ κυρίῳ, τῷ ὀνόματι αὐτοῦ, (often so in Sept.), in honor of God, Eph. v. 19 [here A. V. *making melody*]; Ro. xv. 9; ψαλῶ τῷ πνεύματι, ψαλῶ δὲ καὶ τῷ νοΐ, 'I will sing God's praises indeed with my whole soul stirred and borne away by the Holy Spirit, but I will also follow reason as my guide, so that what I sing may be understood alike by myself and by the listeners', 1 Co. xiv. 15.*

5568 ψαλμός, -οῦ, ὁ, (ψάλλω), *a striking, twanging,* [(Eur., al.)]; spec. *a striking the chords* of a musical instrument [(Pind., Aeschyl., al.)]; hence *a pious song, a psalm,* (Sept. chiefly for מִזְמוֹר), Eph. v. 19; Col. iii. 16; the phrase ἔχειν ψαλμόν is used of one who has it in his heart to sing or recite a song of the sort, 1 Co. xiv. 26 [cf. Heinrici ad loc., and Bp. Lghtft. on Col. u. s.]; one of the songs of the book of the O. T. which is entitled

ψαλμοί, Acts xiii. 33; plur. the (book of) Psalms, Lk. xxiv. 44; βίβλος ψαλμῶν, Lk. xx. 42; Acts i. 20. [Syn. see ὕμνος, fin.]*

5569 ψευδ-άδελφος, -ου, ὁ, (ψευδής and ἀδελφός), *a false brother,* i. e. one who ostentatiously professes to be a Christian, but is destitute of Christian knowledge and piety: 2 Co. xi. 26; Gal. ii. 4.*

5570 ψευδ-απόστολος, -ου, ὁ, (ψευδής and ἀπόστολος), *a false apostle,* one who falsely claims to be an ambassador of Christ : 2 Co. xi. 13.*

5571 ψευδής, -ές, (ψεύδομαι), fr. Hom. Il. 4, 235 down, *lying, deceitful, false* : Rev. ii. 2; μάρτυρες, Acts vi. 13; substantively οἱ ψευδεῖς, [A. V. *liars*], Rev. xxi. 8 [here Lchm. ψευστής, q. v.].*

5572 ψευδο-διδάσκαλος, -ου, ὁ, (ψευδής and διδάσκαλος), a *false teacher* : 2 Pet. ii. 1.*

5573 ψευδο-λόγος, -ον, (ψευδής and λέγω), *speaking (teaching) falsely, speaking lies* : 1 Tim. iv. 2. (Arstph. ran. 1521; Polyb., Lcian., Aesop, al.) *

5574 ψεύδομαι; 1 aor. ἐψευσάμην; (depon. mid. of ψεύδω [allied w. ψιθυρίζω etc. (Vaniček p. 1195)] 'to deceive', 'cheat'; hence prop. *to show one's self deceitful, to play false*); fr. Hom. down; *to lie, to speak deliberate falsehoods* : Heb. vi. 18; 1 Jn. i. 6; Rev. iii. 9; οὐ ψεύδομαι, Ro. ix. 1; 2 Co. xi. 31; Gal. i. 20; 1 Tim. ii. 7; τινά, *to deceive one by a lie, to lie to,* (Eur., Arstph., Xen., Plut., al.): Acts v. 3; like verbs of saying, with a dat. of the pers. (cf. W. § 31, 5; B. § 133, 1; Green p. 100 sq.), Acts v. 4 (Ps. xvii. (xviii.) 45; lxxvii. (lxxviii.) 36; lxxxviii. (lxxxix.) 36; Josh. xxiv. 27; [Jer. v. 12], etc.); εἴς τινα, Col. iii. 9; κατά τινος, against one, Mt. v. 11 [L G om.

Tr mrg. br. ψευδ.; al. connect καθ' ὑμῶν with εἴπωσι and make ψευδ. a simple adjunct of mode (A. V. *falsely*)]; κατὰ τῆς ἀληθείας, Jas. iii. 14 [here Tdf. makes ψευδ. absol.; cf. W. 470 (438) n.³]. (Sept. for בְּחַשׁ and בָּזָב.)*

5575 ψευδο-μάρτυρ, unless more correctly ψευδομάρτυς or rather ψευδόμαρτυς (as αὐτόμαρτυρ; see Passow s. v. ψευδομάρτυς [esp. *Lob.* Paralip. p. 217; cf. Etym. Magn. 506, 26]), -υρος, ὁ, (ψευδής and μάρτυρ [q. v.]), *a false witness*: Mt. xxvi. 60; τοῦ θεοῦ, false witnesses of i. e. concerning God [W. § 30, 1 a.], 1 Co. xv. 15. (Plat. Gorg. p. 472 b.; Aristot. pol. 2, 9, 8 [p. 1274ᵇ, 6; but the true reading here is ψευδομαρτυριῶν (see Bentley's Works ed. Dyce, vol. i. p. 408); a better ex. is Aristot. rhet. ad Alex. 16 p. 1432ᵃ, 6; cf. Plut. praec. ger. reip. 29, 1; Constt. apost. 5, 9; Pollux 6, 36, 153].) *

5576 ψευδο-μαρτυρέω, -ῶ: impf. ἐψευδομαρτύρουν; fut. ψευδομαρτυρήσω; 1 aor. subj. 2 pers. sing. ψευδομαρτυρήσῃς; *to utter falsehoods in giving testimony, to testify falsely, to bear false witness,* (Xen. mem. 4, 4, 11; Plat. rep. 9, p. 575 b.; legg. 11 p. 937 c.; Aristot. rhet. 1, 14, 6 p. 1375ᵃ, 12; [rhet. ad Alex. 16 p. 1432ᵃ, 6]; Joseph. antt. 3, 5, 5): Mt. xix. 18; [Mk. x. 19]; Lk. xviii. 20; Ro. xiii. 9 Rec.; κατά τινος, Mk. xiv. 56 sq. (as Ex. xx. 16; Deut. v. 20).*

5577 ψευδο-μαρτυρία, -ας, ἡ, (ψευδομαρτυρέω), *false testimony, false witness*: Mt. xv. 19; xxvi. 59. (Plat., Plut.; often in the Attic orators.) *

see 5575 ψευδόμαρτυς, see ψευδομάρτυρ.

5578 ψευδο-προφήτης, -ου, ὁ, (ψευδής and προφήτης), *one who, acting the part of a divinely inspired prophet, utters falsehoods under the name of divine prophecies, a false prophet*: Mt. vii. 15; xxiv. 11, 24; Mk. xiii. 22; Lk. vi. 26; Acts xiii. 6; 2 Pet. ii. 1; 1 Jn. iv. 1; Rev. xvi. 13; xix. 20; xx. 10. (Jer. vi. 13; xxxiii. (xxvi.) 8, 11, 16; xxxiv. (xxvii.) 7; xxxvi. (xxix.) 1, 8; Zech. xiii. 2; Joseph. antt. 8, 13, 1; 10, 7, 3; b. j. 6, 5, 2; [τὸν τοιοῦτον εὐθυβόλω ὀνόματι ψευδοπροφήτην προσαγορεύει, κιβδηλεύοντα τὴν ἀληθῆ προφητείαν κ. τὰ γνήσια νόθοις εὑρήμασι ἐπισκιάζοντα κτλ. Philo de spec. legg. iii. § 8]; eccles. writ. ['Teaching' 11, 5 etc. (where see Harnack)]; Grk. writ. use ψευδόμαντις.) *

5579 ψεῦδος, -ους, τό, fr. Hom. down, Sept. for שֶׁקֶר, כָּזָב, כַּחַשׁ, *a lie; conscious and intentional falsehood*: univ. Rev. xiv. 5 (where Rec. δόλος); opp. to ἡ ἀλήθεια, Jn. viii. 44; Eph. iv. 25; οὐκ ἔστι ψεῦδος, opp. to ἀληθές ἐστιν, is no lie, 1 Jn. ii. 27; τέρατα ψεύδους, [A. V. *lying wonders*] exhibited for the treacherous purpose of deceiving men, 2 Th. ii. 9; in a broad sense, *whatever is not what it professes to be*: so of perverse, impious, deceitful precepts, 2 Th. ii. 11; 1 Jn. ii. 21; of idolatry, Ro. i. 25; ποιεῖν ψεῦδος, to act in accordance with the precepts and principles of idolatry, Rev. xxi. 27; xxii. 15, [cf. xxi. 8, and p. 526ᵇ mid.]. *

5580 ψευδό-χριστος, -ου, ὁ, (ψευδής and χριστός), *a false Christ* (or *Messiah*), (one who falsely lays claim to the name and office of the Messiah): Mt. xxiv. 24; Mk. xiii. 22.*

5581 ψευδώνυμος, -ον, (ψεῦδος [ψευδής, rather] and ὄνομα),

falsely named [A. V. *falsely so called*]: 1 Tim. vi. 20. (Aeschyl., Philo, Plut., Sext. Emp.) *

5582 ψεῦσμα, -τος, τό, (ψεύδω), *a falsehood, a lie*, (Plat. Meno p. 71 d.; Plut., Lcian.; Sept.); spec. the perfidy by which a man by sinning breaks faith with God, Ro. iii. 7.*

5583 ψεύστης, -ου, ὁ, (ψεύδω), fr. Hom. down, *a liar*: Jn. viii. 44, 55; 1 Jn. i. 10; ii. 4, 22; iv. 20; v. 10; 1 Tim. i. 10; Tit. i. 12; [Rev. xxi. 8 Lchm. (al. ψευδής, q. v.)]; one who breaks faith, *a false* or *faithless man* (see ψεῦσμα), Ro. iii. 4 cf. Prov. xix. 22.*

5584 ψηλαφάω, -ῶ: 1 aor. ἐψηλάφησα, optat. 3 pers. plur. ψηλαφήσειαν (Acts xvii. 27, the Æolic form; see ποιέω, init.); pres. pass. ptcp. ψηλαφώμενος; (fr. ψάω, to touch); *to handle, touch, feel*: τί or τινά, Lk. xxiv. 39; Heb. xii. 18 [see R. V. txt. and mrg., cf. B. § 134, 8; W. 343 (322)]; 1 Jn. i. 1; metaph. *mentally to seek after tokens of a person* or *thing*: θεόν, Acts xvii. 27 [A.V. *feel after*]. (Hom., Arstph., Xen., Plat., Polyb., Philo, Plut.; often for מוּשׁ, הֵמִישׁ, מָשַׁשׁ.) [SYN. see ἅπτω, 2 c.] *

5585 ψηφίζω; 1 aor. ἐψήφισα; (ψῆφος, q. v.); *to count with pebbles, to compute, calculate, reckon*: τὴν δαπάνην, Lk. xiv. 28; τὸν ἀριθμόν, to explain by computing, Rev. xiii. 18. (Polyb., Plut., Palaeph., Anthol.; commonly and indeed chiefly in the mid. in the Grk. writ. *to give one's vote by casting a pebble into the urn; to decide by voting*.) [COMP.: συγ-, κατα-, συμ- ψηφίζω.]*

5586 ψῆφος, -ου, ἡ, (fr. ψάω, see ψάλλω), *a small, worn, smooth stone; pebble*, [fr. Pind., Hdt., down; (in Hom. ψηφίς)]; **1.** since in the ancient courts of justice the accused were condemned by black pebbles and acquitted by white (cf. Passow s. v. ψῆφος, 2 c., vol. ii. p. 2574ᵇ; [L. and S. s. v. 4 d.]; Ovid. met. 15, 41; [Plut. Alcib. 22, 2]), and a man on his acquittal was spoken of as νικήσας (Theophr. char. 17 (19), 3) and the ψῆφος acquitting him called νικητήριος (Heliod. 3, 3 sub fin.), Christ promises that to the one who has gained eternal life by coming off conqueror over temptation (τῷ νικοῦντι [A. V. *to him that overcometh*]) he will give ψῆφον λευκήν, Rev. ii. 17; but the figure is explained differently by different interpp.; cf. Düsterdieck [or Lee in the 'Speaker's Com.'] ad loc.; [B. D. s. v. Stones, 8]. Ewald (Die Johann. Schriften, ii. p. 136; [cf. Lee u. s.; Plumptre in B. D. s. v. Hospitality, fin.]) understands it to be the *tessera hospitalis* [cf. *Rich*, Dict. of Antiq. s. v. Tessera, 3; *Becker*, Charicles, sc. i. note 17], which on being shown secures admission to the enjoyment of the heavenly manna; the Greek name, however, for this tessera, is not ψῆφος, but σύμβολον.   **2.** *a vote* (on account of the use of pebbles in voting): καταφέρω (q. v.), Acts xxvi. 10.*

5587 ψιθυρισμός, -οῦ, ὁ, (ψιθυρίζω, to whisper, speak into one's ear), *a whispering*, i. e. secret slandering, (Vulg. susurratio, Germ. Ohrenbläserei): joined w. καταλαλιά [cf. Ro. i. 29 (30)], 2 Co. xii. 20; Clem. Rom. 30, 3; 35, 5. (Plut.; Sept. for לַחַשׁ, of the magical murmuring of a charmer of snakes, Eccl. x. 11.) *

5588 ψιθυριστής, -οῦ, ὁ, (see the preced. word), *a whisperer*, secret slanderer, detractor, (Germ. *Ohrenbläser*): Ro. i. 29 (30). (At Athens an epithet of Hermes, Dem. p. 1358, 6; also of ὁ Ἔρως and Aphrodite, Suidas p. 3957 c.; [cf. W. 24].)*

5589 ψιχίον, -ου, τό, (dimin. of ψίξ, ψιχός, ἡ, a morsel), *a little morsel, a crumb* (of bread or meat): Mt. xv. 27; Mk. vii. 28; Lk. xvi. 21 [T WH om. L Tr br. ψ.]. (Not found in Grk. auth. [cf. W. 24; 96 (91)].)*

5590 ψυχή, -ῆς, ἡ, (ψύχω, to breathe, blow), fr. Hom. down, Sept. times too many to count for נֶפֶשׁ, occasionally also for לֵב and לֵבָב; **1.** *breath* (Lat. *anima*), i. e. **a.** *the breath of life;* the vital force which animates the body and shows itself in breathing: Acts xx. 10; of animals, Rev. viii. 9, (Gen. ix. 4 sq.; xxxv. 18; ἐπιστραφήτω ἡ ψυχὴ τοῦ παιδαρίου, 1 K. xvii. 21); so also in those pass. where, in accordance with the trichotomy or threefold division of human nature by the Greeks, ἡ ψυχή is distinguished from τὸ πνεῦμα (see πνεῦμα, 2 p. 520ᵃ [and reff. s. v. πν. 5]), 1 Th. v. 23; Heb. iv. 12. **b.** *life:* μεριμνᾶν τῇ ψυχῇ, Mt. vi. 25; Lk. xii. 22; τὴν ψυχὴν ἀγαπᾶν, Rev. xii. 11; [μισεῖν, Lk. xiv. 26]; τιθέναι, Jn. x. 11, 15, 17; xiii. 37 sq.; xv. 13; 1 Jn. iii. 16; παραδιδόναι, Acts xv. 26; διδόναι (λύτρον, q. v.), Mt. xx. 28; Mk. x. 45; ζητεῖν τὴν ψυχήν τινος (see ζητέω, 1 a.), Mt. ii. 20; Ro. xi. 3; add, Mt. vi. 25; Mk. iii. 4; Lk. vi. 9; xii. 20, 23; Acts xx. 24; xxvii. 10, 22; Ro. xvi. 4; 2 Co. i. 23; Phil. ii. 30; 1 Th. ii. 8; in the pointed aphorisms of Christ, intended to fix themselves in the minds of his hearers, the phrases εὑρίσκειν, σώζειν, ἀπολλύναι τὴν ψυχὴν αὐτοῦ, etc., designate as ψυχή in one of the antithetic members *the life which is lived on earth,* in the other, *the* (blessed) *life in the eternal kingdom of God:* Mt. x. 39; xvi. 25 sq.; Mk. viii. 35–37; Lk. ix. 24, 56 Rec.; xvii. 33; Jn. xii. 25; the life destined to enjoy the Messianic salvation is meant also in the foll. phrases [(where R. V. soul)]: περιποίησις ψυχῆς, Heb. x. 39; κτᾶσθαι τὰς ψυχάς, Lk. xxi. 19; ὑπὲρ τῶν ψυχῶν, [here A.V. (not R.V.) *for you;* cf. c. below], 2 Co. xii. 15. **c.** *that in which there is life; a living being;* ψυχὴ ζῶσα, *a living soul,* 1 Co. xv. 45; [Rev. xvi. 3 R Tr mrg.], (Gen. ii. 7; plur. i. 20); πᾶσα ψυχὴ ζωῆς, Rev. xvi. 3 [G L T Tr txt. WH] (Lev. xi. 10); πᾶσα ψυχή, *every soul,* i. e. *every one,* Acts ii. 43; iii. 23; Ro. xiii. 1, (so כָּל־נֶפֶשׁ, Lev. vii. 17 (27); xvii. 12); with ἀνθρώπου added, *every soul of man* (נֶפֶשׁ אָדָם, Num. xxxi. 40, 46, [cf. 1 Macc. ii. 38]), Ro. ii. 9. ψυχαί, *souls* (like the Lat. *capita*) i. e. *persons* (in enumerations; cf. Germ. *Seelenzahl*): Acts ii. 41; vii. 14; xxvii. 37; 1 Pet. iii. 20, (Gen. xlvi. 15, 18, 22, 26, 27; Ex. i. 5; xii. 4; Lev. ii. 1; Num. xix. 11, 13, 18; [Deut. x. 22]; the exx. fr. Grk. authors (cf. Passow s. v. 2, vol. ii. p. 2590ᵇ) are of a different sort [yet cf. L. and S. s. v. II. 2]); ψυχαὶ ἀνθρώπων of slaves [A. V. *souls of men* (R.V. with mrg. 'Or *lives*')], Rev. xviii. 13 (so [Num. xxxi. 35]; Ezek. xxvii. 13; see σῶμα, 1 c. [cf. W. § 22, 7 N. 3]). **2.** *the soul* (Lat. *animus*), **a.** *the seat of the feelings, desires, affections, aversions,* (our soul, heart, etc. [R. V. almost uniformly *soul*]; for exx. fr. Grk. writ. see Passow s. v. 2, vol. ii.

p. 2589ᵇ; [L. and S. s. v. II. 3]; Hebr. נֶפֶשׁ, cf. *Gesenius, Thesaur.* ii. p. 901 in 3): Lk. i. 46; ii. 35; Jn. x. 24 [cf. αἴρω, 1 b.]; Acts xiv. 2, 22; xv. 24; Heb. vi. 19; 2 Pet. ii. 8, 14; ἡ ἐπιθυμία τῆς ψ. Rev. xviii. 14; ἀνάπαυσιν ταῖς ψυχαῖς εὑρίσκειν, Mt. xi. 29; Ψυχή, . . . ἀναπαύου, φάγε, πίε [WH br. these three impvs.], εὐφραίνου (personification and direct address), Lk. xii. 19, cf. 18 (ἡ ψυχή ἀναπαύσεται, Xen. Cyr. 6, 2, 28; εὐφραίνειν τὴν ψυχήν, Ael. v. h. 1, 32); εὐδοκεῖ ἡ ψυχή μου (anthropopathically, of God), Mt. xii. 18; Heb. x. 38; περίλυπός ἐστιν ἡ ψυχή μου, Mt. xxvi. 38; Mk. xiv. 34; ἡ ψυχή μου τετάρακται, Jn. xii. 27; ταῖς ψυχαῖς ὑμῶν ἐκλυόμενοι, [*fainting in your souls* (cf. ἐκλύω, 2 b.)], Heb. xii. 3; ἐν ὅλῃ τῇ ψυχῇ σου, *with all thy soul,* Mt. xxii. 37; [Lk. x. 27 L txt. T Tr WH]; ἐξ ὅλης τῆς ψυχῆς σου (Lat. *ex toto animo*), *with* [lit. *from* (cf. ἐκ, II. 12 b.)] *all thy soul,* Mk. xii. 30, 33 [here T WH om. the phrase]; Lk. x. 27 [R G], (Deut. vi. 5; [Epict. diss. 3, 22, 18 (cf. Xen. anab. 7, 7, 43]; Antonin. 3, 4; [esp. 4, 31; 12, 29]; ὅλῃ τῇ ψυχῇ φροντίζειν τινός [rather, with κεχαρίσθαι], Xen. mem. 3, 11, 10); μιᾷ ψυχῇ, *with one soul* [cf. πνεῦμα, 2 p. 520ᵃ bot.], Phil. i. 27; τοῦ πλήθους . . . ἦν ἡ καρδία καὶ ἡ ψυχὴ μία, Acts iv. 32 (ἐρωτηθεὶς τί ἐστι φίλος, ἔφη· μία ψυχὴ δύο σώμασιν ἐνοικοῦσα, Diog. Laërt. 5, 20 [cf. Aristot. eth. Nic. 9, 8, 2 p. 1168ᵇ, 7; on the elliptical ἀπὸ μιᾶς (sc. ψυχῆς?), see ἀπό, III.]); ἐκ ψυχῆς, *from the heart, heartily,* [Eph. vi. 6 (Tr WH with vs. 7)]; Col. iii. 23, (ἐκ τῆς ψυχῆς often in Xen.; τὸ ἐκ ψυχῆς πένθος, Joseph. antt. 17, 6, 5). **b.** *the* (human) *soul in so far as it is so constituted that by the right use of the aids offered it by God it can attain its highest end and secure eternal blessedness, the soul regarded as a moral being designed for everlasting life:* 3 Jn. 2; ἀγρυπνεῖν ὑπὲρ τῶν ψυχῶν, Heb. xiii. 17; ἐπιθυμίαι, αἵτινες στρατεύονται κατὰ τῆς ψυχῆς, 1 Pet. ii. 11; ἐπίσκοπος τῶν ψυχῶν, ib. 25; σώζειν τὰς ψυχάς, Jas. i. 21; ψυχὴν ἐκ θανάτου, *from eternal death,* Jas. v. 20; σωτηρία ψυχῶν, 1 Pet. i. 9; ἁγνίζειν τὰς ψυχὰς ἑαυτῶν, ib. 22; [τὰς ψυχὰς πιστῷ κτίστῃ παρατίθεσθαι, 1 Pet. iv. 19]. **c.** *the soul as an essence which differs from the body and is not dissolved by death* (distinguished fr. τὸ σῶμα, as the other part of human nature [so in Grk. writ. fr. Isocr. and Xen. down; cf. exx. in Passow s. v. p. 2589ᵃ bot.; L. and S. s. v. II. 2]): Mt. x. 28, cf. 14. 14 (it is called ἀθάνατος, Hdt. 2, 123; Plat. Phaedr. p. 245 c., 246 a., al.; ἄφθαρτος, Joseph. b. j. 2, 8, 14; διαλυθῆναι τὴν ψυχὴν ἀπὸ τοῦ σώματος, Epict. diss. 3, 10, 14); the soul freed from the body, a disembodied soul, Acts ii. 27, 31 Rec.; Rev. vi. 9; xx. 4, (Sap. iii. 1; [on the Homeric use of the word, see *Ebeling,* Lex. Hom. s. v. 3 and reff. sub fin., also *Proudfit* in Bib. Sacr. for 1858, pp. 753–805]).*

5591 ψυχικός, -ή, -όν, (ψυχή), (Vulg. *animalis,* Germ. *sinnlich*), *of* or *belonging to the* ψυχή; **a.** *having the nature and characteristics of the* ψυχή i. e. *of the principle of animal life, which men have in common with the brutes* (see ψυχή, 1 a.); [A. V. *natural*]: σῶμα ψυχικόν, 1 Co. xv. 44; substantively, τὸ ψυχικόν [W. 592 (551)], ib. 46; since both these expressions do not differ in substance or conception from σὰρξ καὶ αἷμα in vs. 50, Paul might have also written σαρκικόν; but prompted by the phrase ψυχὴ ζῶσα in vs. 45 (borrowed fr. Gen. ii. 7), he wrote ψυχικόν. **b.** *governed by the* ψυχή i. e. the sensuous nature with its subjection to appetite and passion (as though made up of nothing but ψυχή): ἄνθρωπος (i. q. σαρκικός [or σάρκινος, q. v. 3] in iii. 1), 1 Co. ii. 14; ψυχικοί, πνεῦμα μὴ ἔχοντες, Jude 19 [A. V. *sensual* (R. V. with mrg. 'Or *natural*, Or *animal*'); so in the foll. ex.]; σοφία, a wisdom in harmony with the corrupt desires and affections, and springing from them (see σοφία, a. p. 581[b] bot.), Jas. iii. 15. (In various other senses in prof. auth. fr. Aristot. and Polyb. down.)*

5592 ψύχος (R G Tr WH), more correctly ψῦχος (L T; cf. [*Tdf.* Proleg. p. 102]; *Lipsius*, Grammat. Untersuch. p. 44 sq.), -ους, τό, (ψύχω, q. v), fr. Hom. down, *cold*: Jn. xviii. 18; Acts xxviii. 2; 2 Co. xi. 27; for קֹר, Gen. viii. 22; for קָרָה, Ps. cxlvii. 6 (17); Job xxxvii. 8.*

5593 ψυχρός, -ά, -όν, (ψύχω, q. v.), fr. Hom. down, *cold, cool*: neut. of cold water, ποτήριον ψυχροῦ, Mt. x. 42 ([ψυχρῷ λοῦνται, Hdt. 2, 37]; ψυχρὸν πίνειν, Epict. ench. 29, 2; πλύνεσθαι ψυχρῷ, diss. 4, 11, 19; cf. W. 591 (550)); metaph. like the Lat. *frigidus*, *cold* i. e. *sluggish, inert, in mind* (ψ. τὴν ὀργήν, Lcian. Tim. 2): of

one destitute of warm Christian faith and the desire for holiness, Rev. iii. 15 sq.*

5594 ψύχω: 2 fut. pass. ψυγήσομαι [cf. *Lob.* ad Phryn. p. 318; Moeris ed. Piers. p. 421 s. v.]; fr. Hom. down; *to breathe, blow, cool by blowing*; pass. *to be made* or *to grow cool* or *cold*: trop. of waning love, Mt. xxiv. 12.*

5595 ψωμίζω; 1 aor. ἐψώμισα; (ψωμός, a bit, a morsel; see ψωμίον); **a.** *to feed by putting a bit* or *crumb (of food) into the mouth* (of infants, the young of animals, etc.): τινά τινι (Arstph., Aristot., Plut., Geop., Artem. oneir. 5, 62; Porphyr., Jambl.). **b.** univ. *to feed, nourish*, (Sept. for הֶאֱכִיל [W. § 2, 1 b.]: τινά, Ro. xii. 20; Clem. Rom. 1 Cor. 55, 2; with the acc. of the thing, *to give a thing to feed some one, feed out to*, (Vulg. *distribuo in cibos pauperum* [A. V. *bestow . . . to feed the poor*]): 1 Co. xiii. 3; in the O. T. τινά τι, Sir. xv. 3; Sap. xvi. 20; Num. xi. 4; Deut. xxxii. 13; Ps. lxxix. (lxxx.) 6; Is. lviii. 14, etc.; cf. W. § 32, 4 a. note.*

5596 ψωμίον, -ου, τό, (dimin. of ψωμός), *a fragment, bit, morsel*, [A. V. *sop*]: Jn. xiii. 26 sq. 30. (Ruth ii. 14; Job xxxi. 17, [but in both ψωμός]; Antonin. 7, 3; Diog. Laërt. 6, 37.)*

5597 ψώχω; (fr. obsol. ψώω for ψάω); *to rub, rub to pieces*: τὰς στάχυας ταῖς χερσίν, Lk. vi. 1. [(mid. in Nicand.)]*

Ω

5598 Ω, ω: omega, the last (24th) letter of the Grk. alphabet: ἐγώ εἰμι τὸ Ω [WH 'Ω, L ᾦ, T ω], i. q. τὸ τέλος, i. e. *the last* (see A, *a*, ἄλφα [and B. D. (esp. Am. ed.) s. v. and art. 'Alpha', also art. A and Ω by *Piper* in Herzog (cf. Schaff-Herzog), and by *Tyrwhitt* in Dict. of Chris. Antiq.]), Rev. i. 8, 11 Rec.; xxi. 6; xxii. 13. [On the interchange of ω and ο in Mss. see *Scrivener*, Plain Introduction etc. p. 627; 'Six Lectures' etc. p. 176; *WH*. Intr. § 404; cf. esp. *Meisterhans*, Gram. d. Att. Inschr. p. 10.]*

5599 ᾦ, an interjection, prefixed to vocatives (on its use in the N. T. cf. B. 140 (122); [W. § 29, 3]), *O*; it is used **a.** in address: ᾦ Θεόφιλε, Acts i. 1; add, Acts xviii. 14; xxvii. 21 [here Tdf. ᾧ (ex errore); on the pass. which follow cf. B. u. s.]; Ro. ii. 1, 3; ix. 20; 1 Tim. vi. 20; and, at the same time, reproof, Jas. ii. 20. **b.** in exclamation: and that of admiration, Mt. xv. 28; Ro. xi. 33 [here Rec.[st] Lchm. ᾧ; cf. Chandler §§ 902, (esp.) 904]; of reproof, Lk. xxiv. 25; Acts xiii. 10; Gal. iii. 1; with the nom. (W. § 29, 2), Mt. xvii. 17; Mk. ix. 19; Lk. ix. 41. [(From Hom. down.)]*

5601 'Ωβήδ (R G; see Ἰωβήδ), ὁ, (Hebr. עוֹבֵד [i. e. 'servant' sc. of Jehovah]), *Obed*, the grandfather of king David: Mt. i. 5; Lk. iii. 32, (Ruth iv. 17 sq.; 1 Chr. ii. 12).*

*For 5600 see 1510.

5602 ὧδε, adv., (fr. ὅδε); **1.** *so, in this manner*, (very often in Hom.). **2.** adv. of place; **a.** *hither, to this place* (Hom. Il. 18, 392; Od. 1, 182; 17, 545; cf. B. 71 (62 sq.) [cf. W. § 54, 7; but its use in Hom. of place is now generally denied; see *Ebeling*, Lex. Hom. s. v. p. 484[b]; L. and S. s. v. II.]): Mt. viii. 29; xiv. 18 [Tr mrg. br. ὧδε]; xvii. 17; xxii. 12; Mk. xi. 3; Lk. ix. 41; xiv. 21; xix. 27; Jn. vi. 25; xx. 27; Acts ix. 21; Rev. xi. 1; xi. 12, (Sept. for הֲלֹם, Ex. iii. 5; Judg. xviii. 3; Ruth ii. 14); ἕως ὧδε, [*even unto this place*], Lk. xxiii. 5. **b.** *here, in this place*: Mt. xii. 6, 41 sq.; xiv. 17; Mk. ix. 1, 5; xvi. 6; Lk. ix. 33; xxii. 38; xxiv. 6 [WH reject the cl.]; Jn. vi. 9; xi. 21, 32, and often, (Sept. for פֹּה): τὰ ὧδε, the things that are done here, Col. iv. 9; ὧδε, in this city, Acts ix. 14; in this world, Heb. xiii. 14; opp. to ἐκεῖ (here, i. e. according to the Levitical law still in force; there, i. e. in the passage in Genesis concerning Melchizedek), Heb. vii. 8; ὧδε with some addition, Mt. xiv. 8; Mk. vi. 3; viii. 4; Lk. iv. 23; ὧδε ὁ Χριστός, ἤ ὧδε, here is Christ, or there, [so A. V., but R. V. here is the Christ, or, Here (cf. ὧδε καὶ ὧδε, hither and thither, Ex. ii. 12 etc.)], Mt. xxiv. 23; ὧδε ἤ . . . ἐκεῖ, Mk. xiii. 21 [T WH om. ἤ; Tr mrg. reads καὶ]; Lk. xvii. 21, 23 [here T Tr WH mrg. ἐκεῖ . . . ὧδε (WH txt. ἐκεῖ ἤ . . . ὧδε)]; Jas. ii. 3 [here Rec. ἐκεῖ ἤ . . .

ὧδε; G L T Tr WH om. ὧδε (WH txt. and marg. varying the place of ἐκεῖ)]. Metaph. *in this thing*, Rev. xiii. 10, 18; xiv. 12; xvii. 9, [the phrase ὧδέ ἐστιν in at least two of these pass. (viz. xiii. 18; xiv. 12) seems to be equiv. to 'here there is opportunity for', 'need of' etc. (so in Epict. diss. 3, 22, 105)]; *in this state of things, under these circumstances*, 1 Co. iv. 2 L [who, however, connects it with vs. 1] T Tr WH; cf. Meyer ad loc.

5603 ᾠδή, -ῆς, ἡ, (i. q. ἀοιδή, fr. ἀείδω i. e. ᾄδω, to sing), fr. Soph. and Eur. down, Sept. for שִׁיר and שִׁירָה, *a song, lay, ode*; in the Scriptures a song in praise of God or Christ: Rev. v. 9; xiv. 3; Μωϋσέως κ. τοῦ ἀρνίου, the song which Moses and Christ taught them to sing, Rev. xv. 3; plur. with the epithet πνευματικαί, Eph. v. 19 [here L br. πν.]; Col. iii. 16. [SYN. see ὕμνος, fin.]*

5604 ὠδίν (1 Th. v. 3; Is. xxxvii. 3) for ὠδίς (the earlier form; cf. W. § 9, 2 e. N. 1), -ῖνος, ἡ, fr. Hom. Il. 11, 271 down, *the pain of childbirth, travail-pain, birth-pang*: 1 Th. v. 3; plur. ὠδῖνες ([pangs, throes, R. V. *travail*]; Germ. *Wehen*), i. q. intolerable anguish, in reference to the dire calamities which the Jews supposed would precede the advent of the Messiah, and which were called חֶבְלֵי הַמָּשִׁיחַ [see the Comm. (esp. Keil) on Mt. l. c.], Mt. xxiv. 8; Mk. xiii. 8 (9); ὠδῖνες θανάτου [Tr mrg. ᾅδου], the pangs of death, Acts ii. 24, after the Sept. who translated the words חֶבְלֵי מָוֶת by ὠδῖνες θ., deriving the word חֶבְלֵי not, as they ought, from חֵבֶל, i. e. σχοινίον 'cord', but from חֵבֶל, ὠδίς, Ps. xvii. (xviii.) 5; cxiv. (cxvi.) 3; 2 S. xxii. 6.*

5605 ὠδίνω; fr. Hom. down; Sept. for חוּל, thrice for חָבַל; *to feel the pains of childbirth, to travail*: Gal. iv. 27; Rev. xii. 2; in fig. disc. Paul uses the phrase οὓς πάλιν ὠδίνω, i. e. whose souls I am striving with intense effort and anguish to conform to the mind of Christ, Gal. iv. 19. [COMP.: συν-ωδίνω.]*

5606 ὦμος, -ου, ὁ, (ΟΙΩ i. q. φέρω [(?)]; allied w. Lat. *umerus*, cf. Vaniček p. 38; Curtius § 487]), fr. Hom. down, *the shoulder*: Mt. xxiii. 4; Lk. xv. 5.*

5608 ὠνέομαι, -οῦμαι : 1 aor. ὠνησάμην (which form, as well as ἐωνησάμην, belongs to later Grk., for which the earlier writ. used ἐπριάμην; cf. *Lob.* ad Phryn. p. 137 sqq.; [*Rutherford*, New Phryn. p. 210 sqq.; Veitch s. v.]; W. § 12, 2; § 16 s. v.); fr. Hdt. down; *to buy*: with a gen. of the price, Acts vii. 16.*

5609 ὠόν [so R G Tr, but L T WH ᾠόν; see (Etym. Magn. 822, 40) I, ι], -οῦ, τό, fr. Hdt. down, *an egg*: Lk. xi. 12, (for בֵּיצָה, found only in the plur. בֵּיצִים, Deut. xxii. 6 sq.; Is. x. 14, etc.).*

5610 ὥρα, -ας, ἡ, fr. Hom. down, Sept. for עֵת and in Dan. for שָׁעָה; **1.** *a certain definite time* or *season* fixed by natural law and returning with the revolving year; of the seasons of the year, spring, summer, autumn, winter, as ὥρα τοῦ θέρους, πρώϊμος κ. ὄψιμος, χειμερία, etc.; often in the Grk. writ. [cf. L. and S. s. v. A. I. 1 c., and on the inherent force of the word esp. Schmidt ch. 44 § 6 sq.]. **2.** *the daytime* (bounded by the rising and the setting of the sun), *a day*: ὥρα παρῆλθεν, Mt. xiv. 15; ἤδη ὥρας πολλῆς γενουμένης (or γινομένης), [A. V.

when the day was now far spent], Mk. vi. 35 (see πολύς, c. [but note that in the ex. fr. Polyb. there cited πολλῆς ὥρας means *early*]); ὀψίας [ὀψὲ Τ Tr mrg. WH txt.] ἤδη οὔσης τῆς ὥρας [WH mrg. br. τῆς ὥρας], Mk. xi. 11 (ὀψὲ τῆς ὥρας, Polyb. 3, 83, 7; τῆς ὥρας ἐγίγνετο ὀψέ, Dem. p. 541, 28). **3.** *a twelfth part of the day-time, an hour*, (the twelve hours of the day are reckoned from the rising to the setting of the sun, Jn. xi. 9 [cf. BB. DD. s. v. Hour; Riehm's HWB. s. v. Uhr]): Mt. xxiv. 36; xxv. 13; Mk. xiii. 32; xv. 25, 33; Lk. xxii. 59; xxiii. 44; Jn. i. 39 (40); iv. 6; xix. 14; with τῆς ἡμέρας added, Acts ii. 15; of the hours of the night, Lk. xii. 39; xxii. 59; with τῆς νυκτός added, Acts xvi. 33; xxiii. 23; dat. ὥρᾳ, in stating the time when [W. § 31, 9; B. § 133, 26]: Mt. xxiv. 44; Mk. xv. 34; Lk. xii. 39 sq.; preceded by ἐν, Mt. xxiv. 50; Jn. iv. 52; Acts xvi. 33; accus. to specify when [W. § 32, 6; B. § 131, 11]: Jn. iv. 52; Acts x. 3; 1 Co. xv. 30; Rev. iii. 3; also to express duration [W. and B. ll. cc.]: Mt. xx. 12 [cf. ποιέω, I. 1 a. fin.]; xxvi. 40; Mk. xiv. 37; preceded by prepositions: ἀπό, Mt. xxvii. 45; Acts xxiii. 23; ἕως, Mt. xxvii. 45; μέχρι, Acts x. 30; περί with the accus. Acts x. 9. improp. used for *a very short time*: μιᾷ ὥρᾳ, Rev. xviii. 10 [Rec. ἐν, WH mrg. acc.], 17 (16), 19; πρὸς ὥραν, [A. V. *for a season*], Jn. v. 35; 2 Co. vii. 8; Gal. ii. 5 [here A. V. *for an hour*]; Philem. 15; πρὸς καιρὸν ὥρας, [*for a short season*], 1 Th. ii. 17. **4.** *any definite time, point of time, moment*: Mt. xxvi. 45; more precisely defined — by a gen. of the thing, Lk. i. 10; xiv. 17; Rev. iii. 10; xiv. 7, 15; by a gen. of the pers. *the fit* or *opportune time for one*, Lk. xxii. 53; Jn. ii. 4; by a pronoun or an adj.: ἡ ἄρτι ὥρα, [A. V. *this present hour*], 1 Co. iv. 11; ἐσχάτη ὥρα, the last hour i. e. the end of this age and very near the return of Christ from heaven (see ἔσχατος, 1 p. 253b), 1 Jn. ii. 18 [cf. Westcott ad loc.]; αὐτῇ τῇ ὥρᾳ, that very hour, Lk. ii. 38 [here A.V. (not R.V.) *that instant*]; xxiv. 33; Acts xvi. 18; xxii. 13; ἐν αὐτῇ τῇ ὥρᾳ, in that very hour, Lk. vii. 21 [R G L txt.]; xii. 12; xx. 19; ἐν τῇ ὥρᾳ ἐκείνῃ, Mt. viii. 13; ἐν ἐκείνῃ τῇ ὥρᾳ, Mt. x. 19 [Lchm. br. the cl.]; Mk. xiii. 11; [Lk. vii. 21 L mrg. T Tr WH]; Rev. xi. 13; ἀπ' ἐκείνης τῆς ὥρας, Jn. xix. 27; ἀπὸ τῆς ὥρας ἐκείνης, Mt. ix. 22; xv. 28; xvii. 18; by a conjunction: ὥρα ὅτε, Jn. iv. 21, 23; v. 25; xvi. 25; ἵνα (use ἵνα, II. 2 d.), Jn. xii. 23; xiii. 1; xvi. 2, 32; by καί and a finite verb, Mt. xxvi. 45; by a relative pron. ὥρα ἐν ᾗ, Jn. v. 28; by the addition of an acc. with an inf. Ro. xiii. 11 (οὔπω ὥρα συναχθῆναι τὰ κτήνη, Gen. xxix. 7; see exx. in the Grk. writ., fr. Aeschyl. down, in Passow s. v. vol. ii. p. 2620b; [L. and S. s. v. B. I. 3]; so the Lat. *tempus est*, Cic. Tusc. 1, 41, 99; ad Att. 10, 8). Owing to the context ὥρα sometimes denotes *the fatal hour, the hour of death*: Mt. xxvi. 45; Mk. xiv. 35, 41; Jn. xii. 27; xvi. 4 [here L Tr WH read ἡ ὥρα αὐτῶν i. e. the time when these predictions are fulfilled]; xvii. 1; ἡ ὥρα τινός, 'one's hour', i. e. the time when one must undergo the destiny appointed him by God : so of Christ, Jn. vii. 30; viii. 20, cf. xvi. 21. [On the omission of the word see ἐξαυτῆς, (ἀφ' ἧς? cf.

p. 58ᵇ top), W. § 64, 5 s. v. ; B. 82 (71) ; on the omission of the art. with it (e. g. 1 Jn. ii. 18), see W. § 19 s. v.]

5611   ὡραῖος, -α, -ον, (fr. ὥρα, 'the bloom and vigor of life', 'beauty' in the Grk. writ., who sometimes join the word in this sense with χάρις [which suggests grace of movement] or κάλλος [which denotes, rather, symmetry of form]), fr. Hes. down, *ripe*, *mature*, (of fruits, of human age, etc.) ; hence *blooming*, *beautiful*, (of the human body, Xen., Plat., al. ; with τῇ ὄψει added, Gen. xxvi. 7 ; xxix. 17 ; xxxix. 6 ; 1 K. i. 6) : πόδες, Ro. x. 15 ; of a certain gate of the temple, Acts iii. 2, 10 ; [τάφοι κεκονιαμένοι, Mt. xxiii. 27] ; σκεῦος, 2 Chr. xxxvi. 19. [Cf. Trench, Syn. § cvi.]*

5612   ὠρύομαι ; depon. mid. ; Sept. for אָשַׁג ; *to roar*, *to howl*, (of a lion, wolf, dog, and other beasts) : 1 Pet. v. 8 (Judg. xiv. 5 ; Ps. xxi. (xxii.) 14 ; Jer. ii. 15 ; Sap. xvii. 18 ; Theocr., Plut., al.) ; of men, *to raise a loud and inarticulate cry* : either of grief, Hdt. 3, 117 ; or of joy, id. 4, 75 ; *to sing with a loud voice*, Pind. Ol. 9, 163.*

5613   ὡς [Treg. (by mistake) in Mt. xxiv. 38 ὥς ; cf. W. 462 (431) ; Chandler § 934, and reff. in *Ebeling*, *Lex.* Hom. s. v. p. 494ᵇ bot.], an adverbial form of the relative pron. ὅς, ἥ, ὅ which is used in comparison, *as*, *like as*, *even as*, *according as*, *in the same manner as*, etc. (Germ. *wie*) ; but it also assumes the nature of a conjunction, of time, of purpose, and of consequence. On its use in the Grk. writ. cf. *Klotz* ad Devar. ii. 2, ch. xxxv. p. 756 sqq. ; [L. and S. s. v.].

I. ὡς as an adverb of comparison ; **1.** It answers to some demonstrative word (οὕτως, or the like), either in the same clause or in another member of the same sentence [cf. W. § 53, 5] : οὕτως . . . ὡς, Jn. vii. 46 [L WH om. Tr br. ὡς etc.] ; 1 Co. iii. 15 ; iv. 1 ; ix. 26 ; Eph. v. 28, 33 ; Jas. ii. 12 ; οὕτως . . . ὡς ἐάν [T Tr WH om. ἐάν (cf. Eng. *as should a man cast* etc.)] . . . βάλῃ, so etc. . . . *as if* etc. Mk. iv. 26 ; ὡς . . . οὕτως, Acts viii. 32 ; xxiii. 11 ; 1 Co. vii. 17 ; 2 Co. xi. 3 [R G] ; 1 Th. v. 2 ; ὡς ἄν (ἐάν) foll. by subj. [(cf. ἄν, II. 2 a. fin.)] . . . οὕτως, 1 Th. ii. 7 sq. ; ὡς . . . οὕτω καί, Ro. v. 15 [here WH br. καί], 18 ; 2 Co. i. 7 L T Tr WH ; vii. 14 ; ὡς [T Tr WH καθὼς] . . . κατὰ τὰ αὐτά [L G ταὐτά, Rec. ταῦτα], Lk. xvii. 28–30 ; ἴσος . . . ὡς καί, Acts xi. 17 ; sometimes in the second member of the sentence the demonstrative word (οὕτως, or the like) is omitted and must be supplied by the mind, as Mt. viii. 13 ; Col. ii. 6 ; ὡς . . . καί (where οὕτω καί might have been expected [W. u. s. ; B. § 149, 8 c.]), Mt. vi. 10 ; Lk. xi. 2 [here G T Tr WH om. L br. the cl.] ; Acts vii. 51 [Lchm. καθώς] ; Gal. i. 9 ; Phil. i. 20, (see καί, II. 1 a.) ; to this construction must be referred also 2 Co. xiii. 2 ὡς παρὼν τὸ δεύτερον, καὶ ἀπὼν νῦν, as when I was present the second time, so now being absent [(cf. p. 317* top) ; al. render (cf. R. V. mrg.) *as if I were present the second time, even though I am now absent*]. **2.** ὡς with the word or words forming the comparison is so subjoined to a preceding verb that οὕτως must be mentally inserted before the same. When thus used ὡς refers   **a.** to the manner ('form') of the action expressed by the finite

verb, and is equiv. to *in the same manner as*, *after the fashion of* ; it is joined in this way to the subject (nom.) of the verb : Mt. vi. 29 ; vii. 29 ; xiii. 43 ; 1 Th. ii. 11 ; 2 Pet. ii. 12 ; Jude 10, etc. ; to an acc. governed by the verb : as ἀγαπᾶν τὸν πλησίον σου ὡς σεαυτόν, Mt. xix. 19 ; xxii. 39 ; Mk. xii. 31, 33 ; Lk. x. 27 ; Ro. xiii. 9 ; Gal. v. 14 ; Jas. ii. 8 ; add, Philem. 17 ; Gal. iv. 14 ; [here many (cf. R. V. mrg.) would bring in also Acts iii. 22 ; vii. 37 (cf. c. below)] ; or to another oblique case : as Phil. ii. 22 ; to a subst. with a prep. : as ὡς ἐν κρυπτῷ, Jn. vii. 10 [Tdf. om. ὡς] ; ὡς ἐν ἡμέρᾳ σφαγῆς, Jas. v. 5 [R G ; al. om. ὡς] ; ὡς διὰ ξηρᾶς, Heb. xi. 29 ; add, Mt. xxvi. 55 ; Mk. xiv. 48 ; Lk. xxii. 52 ; Ro. xiii. 13 ; Heb. iii. 8 ; when joined to a nom. or an acc. it can be rendered *like*, (*like*) *as*, (Lat. *instar*, *veluti*) : Mt. x. 16 ; Lk. xxi. 35 ; xxii. 31 ; 1 Co. iii. 10 ; 1 Th. v. 4 ; 2 Tim. ii. 17 ; Jas. i. 10 ; 1 Pet. v. 8 ; 2 Pet. iii. 10 ; καλεῖν τὰ μὴ ὄντα ὡς ὄντα (see καλέω, 1 b. β. sub fin.), Ro. iv. 17.   **b.** ὡς joined to a verb makes reference to the 'substance' of the act expressed by the verb, i. e. the action designated by the verb is itself said to be done ὡς, *in like manner (just) as*, something else : Jn. xv. 6 (for τὸ βάλλεσθαι ἔξω is itself the very thing which is declared to happen [i. e. the unfruitful disciple is 'cast forth' just as the severed branch is 'cast forth']) ; 2 Co. iii. 1 [Lchm. ὡς [περ]] ; generally, however, the phrase ὡς καί is employed [W. § 53, 5], 1 Co. ix. 5 ; xvi. 10 [here WH txt. om. καί] ; Eph. ii. 3 ; 1 Th. v. 6 [L T Tr WH om. καί] ; 2 Tim. iii. 9 ; Heb. iii. 2 ; 2 Pet. iii. 16.   **c.** ὡς makes reference to similarity or equality, in such expressions as εἶναι ὥς τινα, i. e. 'to be like' or 'equal to' one, Mt. xxii. 30 ; xxviii. 3 ; Mk. vi. 34 ; xii. 25 ; Lk. vi. 40 ; xi. 44 ; xviii. 11 ; xxii. 26 sq. ; Ro. ix. 27 ; 1 Co. vii. 7, 29–31 ; 2 Co. ii. 17 ; 1 Pet. i. 24 ; 2 Pet. iii. 8 ; ἵνα μὴ ὡς κατ' ἀνάγκην τὸ ἀγαθόν σου ᾖ, that thy benefaction may not be like something extorted by force, Philem. 14 ; γίνεσθαι ὥς τινα, Mt. x. 25 ; xviii. 3 ; Lk. xxii. 26 ; Ro. ix. 29 ; 1 Co. iv. 13 ; ix. 20–22 [in vs. 22 T Tr WH om. L Tr mrg. br. ὡς] ; Gal. iv. 12 ; μένειν ὥς τινα, 1 Co. vii. 8 ; ποιεῖν τινα ὥς τινα, Lk. xv. 19 ; passages in which ἐστίν, ἦν, ὦν (or ὁ ὤν) is left to be supplied by the reader : as ἡ φωνὴ αὐτοῦ ὡς φωνὴ ὑδάτων, Rev. i. 15 ; ὀφθαλμούς, sc. ὄντας, Rev. ii. 18 ; πίστιν sc. οὖσαν, Mt. xvii. 20 ; Lk. xvii. 6 ; add, Rev. iv. 7 ; ix. 2, 5, 7–9, 17 ; x. 1 ; xii. 15 ; xiii. 2 ; xiv. 2 ; xx. 8 ; xxi. 21 ; Acts iii. 22 ; vii. 37, [many (cf. R. V. mrg.) refer these last two pass. to a. above] ; x. 11 ; xi. 5, etc. ; before ὡς one must sometimes supply τί, 'something like' or 'having the appearance of' this or that : thus ὡς θάλασσα, i. e. something having the appearance of [R. V. *as it were*] a sea, Rev. iv. 6 G L T Tr WH ; viii. 8 ; ix. 7 ; xv. 2, (so in imitation of the Hebr. כְּ, cf. Deut. iv. 32 ; Dan. x. 18 ; cf. *Gesenius*, Thes. p. 648ᵇ [*Soph.* Lex. s. v. 2]) ; passages where the comparison is added to some adjective : as, ὑγιὴς ὡς, Mt. xii. 13 ; λευκὰ ὡς, Mt. xvii. 2 ; Mk. ix. 3 [R L] ; add, Heb. xii. 16 ; Rev. i. 14 ; vi. 12 ; viii. 10 ; x. 9 ; xxi. 2 ; xxii. 1.   **d.** ὡς so makes reference to the quality of a person, thing, or action, as to be equiv. to *such as*, *exactly like*, *as* it were. Germ. als; and **a.** to a quality which really belongs to the person or thing: ὡς ἐξουσίαν ἔχων, Mt. vii. 29; Mk. i. 22; ὡς μονογενοῦς παρὰ πατρός, Jn. i. 14; add, [(L T Tr WH in Mt. v. 48; vi. 5, 16)]; Acts xvii. 22; Ro. vi. 13 [here L T Tr WH ὡσεί]; xv. 15; 1 Co. iii. 1; vii. 25; 2 Co. vi. 4; xi. 16; Eph. v. 1, 8, 15; Col. iii. 12; 1 Th. ii. 4; 1 Tim. v. 1 sq.; 2 Tim. ii. 3; Tit. i. 7; Philem. 9, 16 [where cf. Bp. Lghtft.]; Heb. iii. 5 sq.; vi. 19; xi. 9; xiii. 17; 1 Pet. i. 14, 19; ii. 2, 5, 11; iii. 7; iv. 10, 15 sq. 19 [R G]; 2 Pet. i. 19; 2 Jn. 5; Jas. ii. 12; Rev. i. 17; v. 6; xvi. 21; xvii. 12, etc.; ὡς οὐκ ἀδήλως sc. τρέχων, as one who is not running etc. 1 Co. ix. 26; concisely, ὡς ἐξ εἰλικρινείας and ἐκ θεοῦ sc. λαλοῦντες, borrowed from the neighboring λαλοῦμεν, 2 Co. ii. 17; τινὰ ὡς τινα or τι after verbs of esteeming, knowing, declaring, etc. [W. §§ 32, 4 b.; 59, 6]: as, after λογίζειν, λογίζεσθαι, Ro. viii. 36; 1 Co. iv. 1 (where οὕτως precedes); 2 Co. x. 2; ἡγεῖσθαι, 2 Th. iii. 15; ἔχειν, Mt. xiv. 5; xxi. 26, 46 [but here L T Tr WH read εἰς (cf. ἔχω, I. 1 f.)], (τινὰς ὡς θεούς, Ev. Nicod. c. 5); ἀποδεικνύναι, 1 Co. iv. 9; παραβάλλειν [or ὁμοιοῦν (q. v.)], Mk. iv. 31; διαβάλλειν, pass. Lk. xvi. 1; ἐλέγχειν, pass. Jas. ii. 9; εὑρίσκειν, pass. Phil. ii. 7 (8). **β.** to a quality which is supposed, pretended, feigned, assumed: ὡς ἁμαρτωλὸς κρίνομαι, Ro. iii. 7; ὡς πονηρόν, Lk. vi. 22; add, 1 Co. iv. 7; viii. 7; 2 Co. vi. 8–10; xi. 15 sq.; xiii. 7; 1 Pet. ii. 12; frequently it can be rendered as if, as though, Acts iii. 12; xxiii. 15, 20; xxvii. 30; 1 Co. v. 3; 2 Co. x. 14; xi. 17; Col. ii. 20; Heb. xi. 27; xiii. 3; ἐπιστολῆς ὡς δι' ἡμῶν, sc. γεγραμμένης, 2 Th. ii. 2. **3.** ὡς with the gen. absol. presents the matter spoken of — either as the belief of the writer, 2 Co. v. 20; 2 Pet. i. 3; or as some one's erroneous opinion: 1 Co. iv. 18; 1 Pet. iv. 12; cf. W. § 65, 9; [B. § 145, 7; esp. §144, 22]. In general, by the use of ὡς the matter spoken of is presented — either as a mere matter of opinion: as in ὡς ἐξ ἔργων sc. ὁ Ἰσραὴλ νόμον δικαιοσύνης ἐδίωξεν, Ro. ix. 32 (where it marks the imaginary character of the help the Israelites relied on, they thought to attain righteousness in that way [A. V. as it were by works]); — or as a purpose: πορεύεσθαι ὡς ἐπὶ θάλασσαν, that, as they intended, he might go to the sea, Acts xvii. 14, cf. Meyer ad loc.; W. 617 (573 sq.), [but L T Tr WH read ἕως, as far as to etc.]; — or as merely the thought of the writer: Gal. iii. 16; before ὅτι, 2 Co. xi. 21; — or as the thought and pretence of others: also before ὅτι, 2 Th. ii. 2: cf. W. u. s.; [B. § 149, 3; on ὡς ὅτι in 2 Co. v. 19 (A. V. to wit) see W. and B. ll. cc. (cf. Esth. iv. 14; Joseph. c. Ap. 1, 11, 1 and Müller's note; L. and S. s. v. G. 2; Soph. Lex. s. v. 7)]; ὡς ἄν, as if, as though, 2 Co. x. 9 [cf. W. 310 (291); but cf. Soph. Lex. s. v. 1, and see ἄν, IV.]. **4.** ὡς has its own verb, with which it forms a complete sentence; **a.** ὡς with a finite verb is added by way of illustration, and is to be translated as, just as, (Lat. sicut, eo modo quo): Eph. vi. 20; Col. iii. 18; iv. 4; 1 Pet. iii. 6; 2 Pet. ii. 1; 1 Jn. i. 7; Rev. ii. 28 (27) [this ex. is referred by some (cf. R. V.

mrg.) to 2 a. above]; vi. 13; ix. 3; xviii. 6 [here ὡς καί; the ex. seems to belong under 2 b. above]. in phrases in which there is an appeal — either to the O. T. (ὡς γέγραπται), Mk. i. 2 [here T Tr WH καθώς]; vii. 6; Lk. iii. 4; Acts xiii. 33; or in general to the testimony of others, Acts xvii. 28; xxii. 5; xxv. 10; Ro. ix. 25; 1 Co. x. 7 R G (cf. ὥσπερ, b.). in phrases like ποιεῖν ὡς προσέταξεν or συνέταξεν, etc.: Mt. i. 24; xxvi. 19; xxviii. 15; Lk. xiv. 22 [here T Tr txt. WH ὅ]; Tit. i. 5; likewise, Mt. viii. 13; xv. 28; Rev. x. 7; sc. γενηθήτω μοι, Mt. xxvi. 39. in short parenthetic or inserted sentences: ὡς εἰώθει, Mk. x. 1; ὡς ἐνομίζετο, Lk. iii. 23; ὡς λογίζομαι, 1 Pet. v. 12; ὡς ὑπολαμβάνετε, Acts ii. 15; ὡς λέγουσιν, Rev. ii. 24; ὡς ἂν ἤγεσθε, [R. V. howsoever ye might be led] utcunque agebamini [cf. B. § 139, 13; 383 sq. (329); W. § 42, 3 a.], 1 Co. xii. 2. ὡς serves to add an explanatory extension [and is rendered in A. V. how (that)]: Acts x. 38; τὴν . . . ὑπακοήν, ὡς etc. 2 Co. vii. 15; τοῦ λόγου τοῦ κυρίου, ὡς εἶπεν αὐτῷ, Lk. xxii. 61; τοῦ ῥήματος, ὡς ἔλεγεν, Acts xi. 16, (Xen. Cyr. 8, 2, 14; an. 1, 9, 11); cf. Bornemann, Schol. ad Luc. p. 141. **b.** ὡς is used to present, in the form of a comparison, a motive which is urged upon one, — as ἄφες ἡμῖν τὰ ὀφειλήματα ἡμῶν, ὡς καὶ ἡμεῖς ἀφήκαμεν (R G ἀφίεμεν) κτλ. (for which Lk. xi. 4 gives καὶ γὰρ αὐτοὶ ἀφίομεν), Mt. vi. 12, — or which actuates one, as χάριν ἔχω τῷ θεῷ . . . ὡς ἀδιάλειπτον ἔχω τὴν περὶ σοῦ μνείαν, 2 Tim. i. 3 (for the dear remembrance of Timothy moves Paul's gratitude to God); [cf. Jn. xix. 33 (cf. II. a. below)]; in these examples ὡς has almost the force of a causal particle; cf. Klotz ad Devar. ii. 2 p. 766; [L. and S. s. v. B. IV.; W. 448 (417)]. **c.** ὡς adds in a rather loose way something which serves to illustrate what precedes, and is equiv. to the case is as though [R. V. it is as when]: Mk. xiii. 34, where cf. Fritzsche p. 587; unless one prefer, with Meyer et al., to make it an instance of anantapodoton [cf. A. V. 'For the Son of Man is as a man' etc.]; see ὥσπερ, a. fin. **5.** according as: Ro. xii. 3; 1 Co. iii. 5; Rev. xxii. 12. **6.** ὡς, like the Germ. wie, after verbs of reading, narrating, testifying, and the like, introduces that which is read, narrated, etc.; hence it is commonly said to be equivalent to ὅτι (cf. Klotz ad Devar. ii. 2 p. 765); but there is this difference between the two, that ὅτι expresses the thing itself, ὡς the mode or quality of the thing [hence usually rendered how], (cf. W. § 53, 9; [Meyer on Ro. i. 9; cf. L. and S. s. v. B. I.]): thus after ἀναγινώσκειν, Mk. xii. 26 (where T Tr WH πῶς); Lk. vi. 4 [here T WH br. ὡς; Ltxt. reads πῶς]; cf. μνησθήναι, Lk. xxiv. 6 [L mrg. ὅσα]; θεᾶσθαι, Lk. xxiii. 55; ὑπομνῆσαι, Jude 5 [here ὅτι (not ὡς) is the particle], 7 [al. regard ὡς here as introducing a confirmatory illustration of what precedes (A. V. even as etc.); cf. Huther, or Brückner's De Wette, ad loc.]; εἰδέναι, Acts x. 38; Ro. xi. 2; 1 Th. ij. 11; ἐπίστασθαι, Acts x. 28 [here many (cf. R. V. mrg.) connect ὡς with the adj. immediately following (see 8 below)]; xx. 18, 20; ἀπαγγέλλειν, Lk. viii. 47; ἐξηγεῖσθαι, Lk. xxiv. 35; μάρτυς, Ro. i. 9 [here al. connect ὡς with the word which follows it (cf. 8 below)]; Phil. i. 8.   **7.** ὡς before numerals denotes *nearly, about*: as, ὡς δισχίλιοι, Mk. v. 13; add, Mk. viii. 9; Lk. ii. 37 (here L T Tr WH ἕως); viii. 42; Jn. i. 39 (40); [iv. 6 L T Tr WH]; vi. 19 (here Lchm. ὡσεί); xi. 18; [xix. 39 G L T Tr WH]; xxi. 8; Acts i. 15 [Tdf. ὡσεί]; v. 7, [36 L T Tr WH]; xiii. [18 (yet not WH txt.); cf. καί, I. 2 f.], 20; xix. 34 [WH ὡσεί]; Rev. viii. 1, (ᾳ, 1 S. xi. 1; xiv. 2, etc.); for exx. fr. Grk. writ. see Passow s. v. vol. ii. p. 2631ᵇ; [L. and S. s. v. E; *Soph*. Lex. s. v. 3].   **8.** ὡς is prefixed to adjectives and adverbs, and corresponds to the Lat. *quam, how*, Germ. *wie*, (so fr. Hom. down): ὡς ὡραῖοι, Ro. x. 15; add, Ro. xi. 33; ὡς ὁσίως, 1 Th. ii. 10, (Ps. lxxii. (lxxiii.) 1); with a superlative, *as much as can be*: ὡς τάχιστα, *as quickly as possible* (very often in prof. auth.), Acts xvii. 15; cf. Viger. ed. *Hermann*, pp. 562, 850; Passow ii. 2 p. 2631ᵇ bot.; [L. and S. s. v. Ab. III.].

II. ὡς as a **particle of time;**   **a.** *as, when, since*; Lat. *ut, cum*, [W. § 41 b. 3, 1; § 53, 8]: with the indic., ὡς δὲ ἐπορεύοντο, Mt. xxviii. 8 (9); Mk. ix. 21 [Tr mrg. ἐξ οὗ]; Lk. i. 23, 41, 44; ii. 15, 39; iv. 25; v. 4; vii. 12; xi. 1; xv. 25; xix. 5, 29; xxii. 66; xxiii. 26; xxiv. 32; Jn. ii. 9, 23; iv. 1, 40, [45 Tdf.]; vi. 12, 16; vii. 10; viii. 7; xi. 6, 20, 29, 32 sq.; xviii. 6; [cf. xix. 33 (see I. 4 b. above)]; xx. 11; xxi. 9; Acts i. 10; v. 24; vii. 23; viii. 36; ix. 23; x. 7, 17, 25; xiii. [18 WH txt. (see I. 7 above)], 25, 29; xiv. 5; xvi. 4, 10, 15; xvii. 13; xviii. 5; xix. 9, 21; xx. 14, 18; xxi. 1, 12, 27; xxii. 11, 25; xxv. 14; xxvii. 1, 27; xxviii. 4, (Hom. Il. 1, 600; 2, 321; 3, 21; Hdt. 1, 65, 80; Xen. Cyr. 1, 4, 4. 8. 20; often in the O. T. Apocr. esp. 1 Macc.; cf. *Wahl*, Clavis apocr. V. T., s. v. IV. e. p. 507 sq.).   **b.** *while, when*, (Lat. *dum, quando*): Lk. xx. 37; *as long as, while*, Jn. [ix. 4 Tr mrg. WH mrg. (cf. ἕως, I. 2)]; xii. 35, [36], L T Tr WH [(cf. ἕως, u. s.)]; Lk. xii. 58; Gal. vi. 10 [here A.V. *as* (so R.V. in Lk. l. c.); T WH read the subj. (*as we may have* etc.); Meyer (on Jn. xii. 35; Gal. l. c.) everywhere denies the meaning *while*; but cf. L. and S. s. v. B. V. 2.; Bp. Lghtft. on Gal. l. c.].   **c.** ὡς ἄν, *as soon as*: with the subj. pres. Ro. xv. 24 [A. V. here *whensoever*]; with the 2 aor. subj. having the force of the fut. perf., 1 Co. xi. 34 [R. V. *whensoever*]; Phil. ii. 23. [Cf. B. 232 (200); W. § 42, 5 a.; *Soph*. Lex. s. v. 6.]

III. ὡς as a **final particle** (Lat. *ut*), *in order that, in order to* [cf. *Gildersleeve* in Am. Journ. of Philol. No. 16, p. 419 sq.]: foll. by an inf. [(cf. B. 244 (210); W. 318 (299); Krüger § 65, 3, 4), Lk. ix. 52 L mrg. WH]; Acts xx. 24, (3 Macc. i. 2; 4 Macc. xiv. 1); ὡς ἔπος εἰπεῖν, *so to say* (see εἶπον, 1 a.), Heb. vii. 9 [L mrg. εἶπεν].

IV. ὡς as a **consecutive particle**, introducing a consequence, *so that*: so (acc. to the less freq. usage) with the indic. (Hdt. 1, 163; 2, 135; W. 462 (431)), Heb. iii. 11; iv. 3, (Hebr. רְשֶׁאֲ, Ps. xciv. (xcv.) 11); [but many interpp. question this sense with the indic. (the exx. fr. Hdt. are not parallel), and render ὡς in Heb. ll. cc. *as* (so R. V.)].

ὡσαννά [see *WH*. Intr. § 408; but L T ὡσ.; see *Tdf*.   **5614** Proleg. p. 107], (derived from Ps. cxvii. (cxviii.) 25 אָנָ הָעֲישׁוֹה, i. e. 'save, I pray', Sept. σῶσον δή; [in **form** the word seems to be the Greek reproduction of an abbreviated pronunciation of the Hebr. (אָנ-עֲישׁוֹה); al. would make it אָנֲעֲישׁוֹא ('save us'); cf. *Hilgenfeld*, Evang. sec. Hebraeos (ed. alt. 1884) p. 25 and p. 122; *Kautzsch*, Gram. d. Bibl.-Aram. p. 173]), *hosanna*; *be propitious*: Mt. xxi. 9; Mk. xi. 9 sq.; Jn. xii. 13; with τῷ υἱῷ Δαυΐδ added, be propitious to the Messiah, Mt. xxi. 9, 15, [cf. ὡσαννὰ τῷ θεῷ Δαβίδ, 'Teaching' 10, 6 (where see Harnack's note)].*

ὡσ-αύτως, (ὡς and αὕτως), adv., [as a single word, Post-   **5615** Homeric], *in like manner, likewise*: put after the verb, Mt. xx. 5; xxi. 30, 36; put before the verb, Mk. xiv. 31; Lk. xiii. 3 (here L T Tr WH ὁμοίως), 5 (T Trtxt. WH); Ro. viii. 26; 1 Tim. v. 25; Tit. ii. 6; as often in Grk. writ. the verb must be supplied from the preceding context, Mt. xxv. 17; Mk. xii. 21; Lk. xx. 31; xxii. 20 [WH reject the pass.]; 1 Co. xi. 25; 1 Tim. ii. 9 (sc. βούλομαι, cf. 8); iii. 8 (sc. δεῖ, cf. 7), 11; Tit. ii. 3 (sc. πρέπει εἶναι).*

ὡσ-εί, (ὡς and εἰ [*Tdf*. Proleg. p. 110]), adv., fr. Hom.   **5616** down, prop. *as if*, i. e.   **a.** *as it were (had been), as though, as, like as, like*: Mt. iii. 16; ix. 36 [Treg. ὡς]; Lk. iii. 22 (L T Tr WH ὡς); Acts ii. 3; vi. 15; ix. 18 [L T Tr WH ὡς]; Ro. vi. 13 L T Tr WH; xii. 12; also Rec. in Mk. i. 10; Jn. i. 32; γίνεσθαι ὡσεί, Mt. xxviii. 4 R G; Mk. ix. 26; Lk. xxii. 44 [L br. WH reject the pass.]; εἶναι ὡσεί, Mt. xxviii. 3 [L T Tr WH ὡς], and Rec. in Heb. xi. 12 and Rev. i. 14; φαίνεσθαι ὡσεί τι, to appear like a thing, Lk. xxiv. 11.   **b.** *about, nearly*: **α.** before numerals: Mt. xiv. 21; Lk. i. 56 [R G]; iii. 23; ix. 14, 28; xxii. 41, 59; xxiii. 44; Jn. vi. 10 [R G L (al. ὡς)]; Acts ii. 41; iv. 4 [R G]; x. 3 [in L T Tr WH it is strengthened here by the addition of περί]; xix. 7; also, Rec. in Mk. vi. 44; R G in Jn. iv. 6; xix. 14 [G?], 39; Acts v. 36; Lchm. in Jn. vi. 19, (Judg. iii. 29; Neh. vii. 66; Xen. Hell. 1, 2, 9; 2, 4, 25).   **β.** before a measure of space: ὡσεὶ λίθου βολήν, Lk. xxii. 41.*

Ὡσηέ [G T Tr, but R L 'Ωσ.; see *WH*. Intr. § 408;   **5617** *Tdf*. Proleg. p. 107], (עַשׁוֹה 'deliverance'), ὁ, *Hosea*, a well-known Hebrew prophet, son of Beeri and contemporary of Isaiah (Hos. i. 1 sq.): Ro. ix. 25.*

ὥσ-περ, ([cf. *Tdf*. Proleg. p. 110]; fr. ὡς and the enclit.   **5618** particle πέρ, which, "in its usual way, augments and brings out the force of ὡς" *Klotz* ad Devar. ii. 2 p. 768; see πέρ), adv., [fr. Hom. down], *just as, even as*;   **a.** in a protasis with a finite verb, and followed by οὕτως or οὕτως καί in the apodosis [cf. W. §§ 53, 5; 60, 5]: Mt. xii. 40; xiii. 40; xxiv. 27, 37 sq. 38 (L T Tr [cf. ὡς init.] WH ὡς); Lk. xvii. 24; Jn. v. 21, 26; Ro. v. 19, 21; vi. 4, 19; xi. 30; 1 Co. xi. 12; xv. 22; xvi. 1; 2 Co. i. 7 (here L T Tr WH ὡς); Gal. iv. 29; Eph. v. 24 [L T Tr WH ὡς]; Jas. ii. 26; ὥσπερ . . . ἵνα καί ([cf. W. § 43, 5 a.; B. 241 (208); cf. ἵνα, II. 4 b.]), 2 Co. viii. 7; εὐλογίαν . . . ἑτοίμην εἶναι [cf. W. § 44, 1 c.] οὕτως ὡς εὐλογίαν καὶ μὴ ὥσπερ etc. '**that** your bounty might so be ready as a matter of bounty and not as if' etc. 2 Co. ix. 5 [but only Rec. reads ὥσπερ, and even so the example does not strictly belong under this head] ; the apodosis which should have been introduced by οὕτως is wanting [W. § 64, 7 b.; p. 569 (530) ; cf. B. § 151, 12 and 23 g.] : Ro. v. 12 (here what Paul subjoined in vs. 13 sq. to prove the truth of his statement πάντες ἥμαρτον, prevented him from adding the apodosis, which had it corresponded accurately to the terms of the protasis would have run as follows : οὕτω καὶ δι' ἑνὸς ἀνθρώπου ἡ δικαιοσύνη εἰς τὸν κόσμον εἰσῆλθε καὶ διὰ τῆς δικαιοσύνης ἡ ζωή· καὶ οὕτως εἰς πάντας ἀνθρώπους ἡ ζωὴ διελεύσεται, ἐφ' ᾧ πάντες δικαιωθήσονται; this thought he unfolds in vs. 15 sqq. in another form) ; Mt. xxv. 14 (here the extended details of the parable caused the writer to forget the apodosis which he had in mind at the beginning; [cf. ὡς, I. 4 c.]).   b. it stands in close relation to what precedes : Mt. v. 48 (L T Tr WH ὡς) ; vi. 2, 5 (L T Tr WH ὡς), 7, 16 (L T Tr WH ὡς) ; xx. 28 ; xxv. 32 ; Acts iii. 17 ; xi. 15 ; 1 Co. viii. 5 ; 1 Th. v. 3 ; Heb. iv. 10 ; vii. 27 ; ix. 25 ; Rev. x. 3 ; ὥσπερ γέγραπται, 1 Co. x. 7 L T Tr WH ; εἰμὶ ὥσπερ τις, to be of one's sort or class (not quite identical in meaning with ὡς or ὡσεί τις, to be like one [cf. Bengel ad loc.]), Lk. xviii. 11 [but L Tr WH mrg. ὡς] ; γίνομαι, Acts ii. 2 (the gen. is apparently not to be explained by the omission of ἦχος, but rather as gen. absol.: just as when a mighty wind blows, i. e. just as a sound is made when a mighty wind blows [R.V. as of the rushing of a mighty wind]) ; ἔστω σοι ὥσπερ ὁ ἐθνικός κτλ. let him be regarded by thee as belonging to the number of etc. Mt. xviii. 17.*

5619   ὡσ-περ-εί, (ὥσπερ and εἰ [Tdf. Proleg. p. 110]), adv., fr. Aeschyl. down, as, as it were : 1 Co. xv. 8.*

5620   ὥσ-τε, (fr. ὡς and the enclit. τέ [Tdf. Proleg. p. 110]), a consecutive conjunction, i. e. expressing consequence or result, fr. Hom. down, cf. Klotz ad Devar. ii. 2 p. 770 sqq. ; W. § 41 b. 5 N. 1 p. 301 (282 sq.) ; [B. § 139, 50] ;   1. so that, [A. V. frequently insomuch that] ;   a. with an inf. (or acc. and inf.) [B. § 142, 3; the neg. in this construction is μή, B. § 148, 6 ; W. 480 (447)] : preceded by the demonstr. οὕτως, Acts xiv. 1 ; τοσοῦτος, Mt. xv. 33 (so many loaves as to fill etc.); without a demonstr. preceding (where ὥστε defines more accurately the magnitude, extent, or quantity), Mt. viii. 24, 28 ; xii. 22 ; xiii. 2, 32, 54 ; xv. 31 ; xxvii. 14 ; Mk. i. 27, 45 ; ii. 2, 12 ; iii. 10, 20 ; iv. 1, 32, 37 ; ix. 26 ; xv. 5 ; Lk. v. 7 ; xii. 1 ; Acts i. 19 ; v. 15 ; xv. 39 ; xvi. 26 ; xix. 10, 12, 16 ; Ro. vii. 6 ; xv. 19 ; 1 Co. i. 7 ; v. 1 ; xiii. 2 ; 2 Co. i. 8 ; ii. 7 ; iii. 7 ; vii. 7 ; Phil. i. 13 ; 1 Th. i. 7 sq. ; 2 Th. i. 4 ; ii. 4 ; Heb. xiii. 6 ; 1 Pet. i. 21 ; it is used also of a designed result, so as to i. q. in order to, for to, Mt. x. 1 ; xxiv. 24 [their design] ; xxvii. 1 ; Lk. iv. 29 (Rec. εἰς τό) ; ix. 52 [L mrg. WH ὡς, q. v. III.] ; and L T Tr WH in Lk. xx. 20 [R G εἰς τό], (1 Macc. i. 49 ; iv. 2, 28 ; x. 3 ; 2 Macc. ii. 6 ; Thuc. 4, 23 ; Xen. Cyr. 3, 2, 16 ; Joseph. antt. 13, 5, 10 ; Eus. h. e. 3,

28, 3 [cf. Soph. Lex. s. v. 5]) ; cf. W. 318 (298) ; B. § 139, 50 Rem.   b. so that, with the indicative [B. 244 (210) ; cf. W. 301 (283) ; Meyer or Ellicott on Gal. as below] : Gal. ii. 13, and often in prof. auth. ; preceded by οὕτως, Jn. iii. 16.   2. so then, therefore, wherefore : with the indic. (cf. Passow s. v. II. 1 b., vol. ii. p. 2639ᵇ; [L. and S. s. v. B. II. 2 ; the neg. in this constr. is οὐ, B. § 148, 5]), Mt. xii. 12 ; xix. 6 ; xxiii. 31 ; Mk. ii. 28 ; x. 8 ; Ro. vii. 4, 12 ; xiii. 2 ; 1 Co. iii. 7 ; vii. 38 ; xi. 27 ; xiv. 22 ; 2 Co. iv. 12 ; v. 16 sq.; Gal. iii. 9, 24 ; iv. 7, 16 ; once with a hortatory subj. 1 Co. v. 8 [here L mrg. ind.]. before an imperative : 1 Co. iii. 21 ; [iv. 5] ; x. 12 ; xi. 33 ; xiv. 39 ; xv. 58 ; Phil. ii. 12 ; iv. 1 ; 1 Th. iv. 18 ; Jas. i. 19 [L T Tr WH read ἴστε ; cf. p. 174ᵃ top] ; 1 Pet. iv. 19.*

see 5621   ὠτάριον, -ου, τό, (dimin. of οὖς, ὠτός; cf. γυναικάριον [W. 24, 96 (91)]), i. q. ὠτίον (q. v.), the ear : Mk. xiv. 47 L T Tr WH ; Jn. xviii. 10 T Tr WH. (Anthol. 11, 75, 2 ; Anaxandrides ap. Athen. 3, p. 95 c.) *

5621   ὠτίον, -ου, τό, (dimin. of οὖς, ὠτός, but without the dimin. force; "the speech of common life applied the diminutive form to most of the parts of the body, as τὰ ῥινία the nose, τὸ ὀμμάτιον, στηθίδιον, χελύνιον, σαρκίον the body" Lob. ad Phryn. p. 211 sq. [cf. W. 25 (24)]), a later Greek word, the ear : Mt. xxvi. 51 ; Mk. xiv. 47 [R G (cf. ὠτάριον)] ; Lk. xxii. 51 ; Jn. xviii. 10 [R G L (cf. ὠτάριον)], 26. (Sept. for אֹזֶן, Deut. xv. 17 ; 1 S. ix. 15 ; xx. 2, 13 ; 2 S. xxii. 45 ; Is. l. 4 ; Am. iii. 12.) *

5622   ὠφέλεια [WH -λία (cf. I, ι)], -ας, ἡ, (ὠφελής), fr. [Soph. and] Hdt. down, usefulness, advantage, profit : Ro. iii. 1 ; τῆς ὠφελείας χάριν (Polyb. 3, 82, 8 [yet in the sense of 'booty']), Jude 16. (Job xxii. 3 ; Ps. xxix. (xxx.) 10.)*

5623   ὠφελέω, -ῶ; fut. ὠφελήσω ; 1 aor. ὠφέλησα ; Pass., pres. ὠφελοῦμαι ; 1 aor. ὠφελήθην ; 1 fut. ὠφεληθήσομαι (Mt. xvi. 26 L T Tr WH) ; (ὄφελος) ; fr. Aeschyl. and Hdt. down ; Sept. for הוֹעִיל ; to assist, to be useful or advantageous, to profit : absol. Ro. ii. 25 ; with acc. οὐδέν, to be of no use, to effect nothing, Mt. xxvii. 24 ; Jn. vi. 63 ; xii. 19, [in these exx. (Jn. vi. 63 excepted) A. V. prevail] ; τινά, to help or profit one, Heb. iv. 2 ; τινά τι to help, profit, one in a thing ([but the second acc. is a cognate acc. or the acc. of a neut. adj. or pron.; cf. W. 227 (213)] so fr. Hdt. 3, 126 down) : οὐδέν τινα, 1 Co. xiv. 6 ; Gal. v. 2 ; τί ὠφελήσει [or ὠφελεῖ (τὸν)] ἄνθρωπον, ἐάν κτλ.; [(T WH follow with an inf.)], what will (or 'doth') it profit a man if etc. [(or 'to' etc.)]? Mk. viii. 36 ; pass. ὠφελοῦμαι, to be helped or profited : Heb. xiii. 9 ; with acc. μηδέν, Mk. v. 26 ; οὐδέν, 1 Co. xiii. 3 ; with acc. of the interrog. τί, Mt. xvi. 26 ; Lk. ix. 25 [here WH mrg. gives the act.] ; τὶ ἔκ τινος (gen. of pers.), to be profited by one in some particular [cf. Mey. on Mt. as below ; ἐκ, II. 5], Mt. xv. 5 ; Mk. vii. 11.*

5624   ὠφέλιμος, -ον, (ὠφελέω), profitable : τινί (dat. of advantage), Tit. iii. 8 ; πρός τι (Plat. de rep. 10 p. 6˙7 d. [W. 213 (200)]), 1 Tim. iv. 8 ; 2 Tim. iii. 16.*

APPENDIX

PREFATORY REMARKS

———•———

THE lists of words herewith subjoined, as an aid to researches involving the language of the New Testament, require a few preliminary remarks by way of explanation.

In the attempt to classify the vocabulary of the New Testament, words which occur in secular authors down to and including Aristotle (who died B.C. 322) are regarded as belonging to the classical period of the language, and find no place in the lists.

Words first met with between B.C. 322 and B.C. 150 are regarded as "Later Greek" and registered in the list which bears that heading; but between B.C. 280 and B.C. 150 they have "Sept." appended to them in case they also occur in that version.

Words which first appear in the secular authors between B.C. 150 and B.C. 100 and are also found in the Septuagint are credited to "Biblical Greek" (list 1 p. 693), but with the name of the secular author added.

Words which first appear between B.C. 100 and A.D. 1 are registered solely as "Later Greek."

Words which first occur between A.D. 1 and A.D. 50 are enrolled as "Later Greek," but with the name of the author appended.

Words which appear first in the secular authors of the last half of the first century of our era have an asterisk prefixed to them, and are enrolled both in the list of "Later Greek" and in the list of "Biblical Greek."

A New Testament word credited to Biblical Greek, if not found in the Septuagint but occurring in the Apocryphal books of the Old Testament, is so designated by an appended "Apocr."[1]

Whenever a word given in either the Biblical or the Later Greek list is also found in the Anthologies or the Inscriptions, that fact has been noted (as an intimation that such word may possibly be older than it appears to be); and if the word belong to "Later Greek," the name of the oldest determinate author in which it occurs is also given.

The New Testament vocabulary has thus been classified according to hard and fast chronological lines. But to obviate in some measure the incorrect impression which the rigor of such a method might give, it will be noticed that a twofold recognition has been accorded to words belonging to the periods in which the secular usage and the sacred may be supposed to overlap: viz., for the period covered by the preparation of the Septuagint, for the fifty years which followed its completion, and for the last half of the first Christian century. Nevertheless, the uncertainty inseparable from the results no scholar will overlook. Indeed, the surprises

---

[1] It should be noted that in the following lists the term "Sept." is used in its restricted sense to designate merely the canonical books of the Greek Old Testament; but in the body of the lexicon "Sept." often includes all the books of the Greek version, — as well the apocryphal as the canonical. In the lists of words peculiar to individual writers an appended "fr. Sept." signifies that the word occurs only in a quotation from the Septuagint.

almost every one has experienced in investigating the age of some word in his vernacular which has dropped out of use for whole stretches of time and then reappeared, may admonish him of the precarious character of conclusions respecting the usage of an ancient language, of which only fragmentary relics survive, and those often but imperfectly examined. The rough and problematical results here given are not without interest; but they should not be taken for more than they are worth.

The scheme of distribution adopted will be rendered more distinct by the subjoined

CHRONOLOGICAL CONSPECTUS

Words in use before B.C. 322 . . . . are ranked as classical, and remain unregistered.

Words first used between B.C. 322 and B.C. 280 . . . . are enrolled as Later Greek.

Words first used between B.C. 280 and B.C. 150 . . . . . { receive a single enrolment but double notation, viz. as Later Greek with Sept. usage noted.

Words first used between B.C. 150 and B.C. 100 . . . . . { receive a single enrolment but double notation, viz. as Biblical Greek with secular usage noted.

Words first used between B.C. 100 and A.D. 1 . . . . are enrolled simply as Later Greek.

Words first used between A.D. 1 and A.D. 50 . . . . . { are enrolled as Later Greek but with the name of the author appended.

Words first used between A.D. 50 and A.D. 100 . . . . . { receive a double enrolment, viz. both as Biblical and as Later Greek (with asterisk prefixed and name of secular author appended).

The selection of the distinctive New Testament significations has not been so simple a matter as might be anticipated : —

It is obvious that the employment of a word in a figure of speech cannot be regarded as giving it a new and distinct signification. Accordingly, such examples as ἀνακλίνω in the description of future blessedness (Mt. viii. 11), ἄνεμος to designate the ever-changing doctrinal currents (Eph. iv. 14), ἀπαρχή of first converts (Ro. xvi. 5), πόλις of the consummated kingdom of God (Heb. xiii. 14 etc.), σταυρόω as applied to the σάρξ (Gal. v. 24 etc.), χείρ to denote God's power (Lk. i. 66 etc.), and similar uses, are omitted.

Again, the mere application of a word to spiritual or religious relations does not in general amount to a new signification. Accordingly, such terms as γινώσκειν θεόν, δοῦλος Χριστοῦ, ὑπηρέτης τοῦ λόγου, λύτρον and μαρτυρέω in the Christian reference, μένω in St. John's phraseology, and the like, have been excluded. Yet this restriction has not been so rigorously enforced as to rule out such words as ἐκλέγομαι, καλέω, κηρύσσω, κρίνω, προφητεύω, and others, in what would be confessed on all hands to be characteristic or technical New Testament senses.

In general, however, the list is a restricted rather than an inclusive one.

An appended mark of interrogation indicates uncertainty owing to diversity of text. In the lists of words peculiar to individual New Testament writers —

a. When the use of a word by an author (or book) is unquestioned in any single passage such word is credited to him *without* an interrogation-mark, even though its use be disputed by some edition of the text in every other passage of that author.

b. When a word is found in one author (or book) according to all editions, but though occurring in others is questioned there by some form of the text in every instance, it is credited to the first, and the name of the others is appended in parenthesis with a question-mark.

c. When a word is found in two authors (or books), but in one of them stands in a quotation from the Septuagint, it is credited to the one using it at first hand, and its use by the other is noted with " Sept." or " fr. Sept." appended.

d. A word which is found in but a single author (or book) is credited to the same with a question-mark, even though its use be disputed by one or another form of the text in every instance of its occurrence.

e. A word which is found in two or more authors (or books) yet is disputed by one or another form of the text in every instance, is excluded from the lists altogether.

The monumental misjudgments committed by some who have made questions of authorship turn on vocabulary alone will deter students, it is to be hoped, from misusing the lists exhibiting the peculiarities of the several books.

Explanations which apply only to particular lists are given at the beginning of those lists. Proper names of persons, countries, rivers, places, have been omitted.

In drawing up the lists free use has been made of the collections to be found in Winer's Grammar, the various Introductions and Encyclopædias, the articles by Professor Potwin in the Bibliotheca Sacra for 1875, 1876, 1880, such works as those of Holtzmann on the Synoptical Gospels and the Pastoral Epistles, and especially the copious catalogues given by Zeller in his Theologische Jahrbücher for 1843, pp. 445–525.

In conclusion, a public expression of my thanks is due to W. W. Fenn, A. B., a student in the Theological department of the University, for very efficient and painstaking assistance.

J. H. T.

Cambridge, Mass.,
December, 1885.

CONTENTS

———•———

APPENDIX

I

LATER, *i.e.* POST–ARISTOTELIAN, GREEK WORDS IN THE NEW TESTAMENT

N. B. For explanations see the Prefatory Remarks.

*ἀγαθοποιός Plut.
ἀγνόημα
ἀδηλότης
ἀδιαλείπτως
ἄθεσμος
ἀθέτησις Cicero
ἄθλησις Polyb., Inscr.
ἀκαιρέομαι
ἀκατάλυτος
ἀκατάπαυστος
ἀκρασία
*ἀκροατήριον Plut.
ἀκυρόω
ἀλάβαστρον (-τον Hdt.)
ἀλεκτοροφωνία Aesop
Ἀλεξανδρινός (or -δρῖνος)
ἀλήθω Anthol.
ἀλληγορέω Philo
ἀμαράντινος Inscr.?
ἀμετάθετος
ἀμετανόητος
*ἀναγεννάω Joseph.
ἀνάδειξις
ἀνάθεμα Anthol.
ἀναθεωρέω
ἀναντίρρητος
ἀναντιρρήτως
ἀναπολόγητος
*ἀνατάσσομαι Plut. (Sept.?)
ἀνάχυσις
*ἀνεπαίσχυντος Joseph.
*ἀνθυπατεύω Plut.
ἀνθύπατος Inscr., Polyb.
ἀντιδιατίθημι Philo
*ἀντιλοιδορέω Plut.
Ἀντιοχεύς
*ἄντλημα Plut.
ἀντοφθαλμέω
ἀνυπότακτος
ἀπαράβατος
ἀπαρτισμός
ἀπαύγασμα Philo

*ἀπείραστος Joseph.
*ἀπεκδύομαι Joseph.?
ἀπ(or ἀφ-)ελπίζω
ἀπερισπάστως
*ἀπόδεκτος Plut.
ἀποθησαυρίζω
ἀποκαραδοκία
ἀπόκριμα Polyb., Inscr.
ἀπολείχω
ἀποτομία
ἀπολύτρωσις
ἀποστασία Archim., Sept.
ἀποφορτίζομαι Philo
*ἀπόχρησις Plut.
ἀπρόσιτος
Ἀραψ Strab.
ἀροτριάω
*ἁρπαγμός Plut.
ἀρτέμων Vitruv.
*ἀρχιερατικός Joseph., Inscr.
Ἀσιάρχης Strab., Inscr.
ἀσσάριον Anth., Dion. Hal.,
  Inscr.
ἀστοχέω
ἀφθαρσία Philo
*ἄψινθος Aret. (-θιον Xen.
  on).
βαθέως
*βαπτισμός Joseph.
*βαπτιστής Joseph.
βιαστής Philo (βιατάς Pind.)
*γάγγραινα Plut.
γάζα Theophr., Inscr.
γονυπετέω
γραώδης Strab.
*γυμνητεύω Plut.
δεισιδαιμονία Polyb., Inscr.
*δεσμοφύλαξ Joseph.
*δηνάριον Plut.
διαγνωρίζω Philo
διάταγμα Sap., Inscr.
διαυγάζω

διαφημίζω
διδακτικός Philo
διερμηνεύω
διετία Philo, Inscr.
διθάλασσος
δίψυχος Philo
δουλαγωγέω
δυσεντέριον (-τερία Hippocr.)
δυσερμήνευτος
ἐγκακέω or ἐκκακέω
ἐγκοπή or ἐκκοπή
ἐθνάρχης Philo
ἐθνικός
ἐκδαπανάω
ἔκθαμβος
ἐκθαυμάζω Sir.
ἐκνήφω Anthol.
ἔκπαλαι Philo
ἐκπλήρωσις
ἐκτένεια
*ἐλαφρία Aret.
ἐλεημοσύνη Sept. (Gen.)
ἔλευσις
*ἐμμαίνομαι Joseph.
ἐμπλοκή
*ἐνδόμησις Joseph.
ἐνέργημα
*ἐνορκίζω? Joseph., Inscr.
ἐνώπιον
*ἐξαρτίζω Joseph., Inscr.
ἐξισχύω
*ἐξορκιστής Joseph.
*ἔξυπνος Joseph.
*ἐπαγωνίζομαι Plut., Inscr.
*ἐπαθροίζω Plut.
ἐπάν (B.C. 265)
ἐπαρχία
ἐπαφρίζω
*ἐπενδύω Joseph.(-δύνω Hdt.)
ἐπιβαρέω Dion. Hal., Inscr.
ἐπιθανάτιος
Ἐπικούρειος

ἐπισκηνόω
*ἐπισωρεύω Plut.
ἐπιταγή
ἐπιχορηγέω
ἑτερόγλωσσος
εὐθυδρομέω
εὐκαιρέω
εὔκοπος
*εὐνουχίζω Joseph.
*εὐποιΐα Joseph., Inscr.
*εὐπρόσδεκτος Plut.
*εὐψυχέω Joseph., Anthol.,
  Inscr.
ζεστός
ἡμιθανής Anthol.
ἡμιώριον
ἤρεμος
*Ἡρωδιανοί Joseph.
θειότης Philo
*θεόπνευστος Plut., Orac.
  Sibyl.
*θεότης Plut.
θηριομαχέω
θρησκεία (-κίη Hdt.)
θριαμβεύω
θύϊνος
θυμομαχέω
ἱερουργέω Philo, Inscr.
ἱματισμός
*Ἰουδαϊκός Joseph.
*Ἰουδαϊκῶς Joseph.
ἰσότιμος Philo
*καθεξῆς Plut., Inscr.
καθημερινός
κακουχέω
καταβαρέω
καταβαρύνω
καταγωνίζομαι
κατάκριμα
καταντάω
*κατάρτισις Plut.
κατάστημα

καταυγάζω? Apoll. Rhod., Anthol.
*κατευλογέω? Plut.
κατηχέω
κατοπτρίζομαι Philo
καυματίζω
καυστηριάζω?
κενοδοξία
κενόδοξος
κεντυρίων
κερματιστής
κολώνια (-νία, etc.) Inscr.
*κορβᾶν (-βανᾶς) Joseph.
κράβαττος or κράββατος
κρυπτή
κτήτωρ Diod., Inscr., Anth.
κτίσμα
κωμόπολις
*μαθητεύω Plut.
μαθήτρια
*μάκελλον Plut.
μαργαρίτης
*ματαιολογία Plut.
μεθερμηνεύω
*μεσουράνημα Plut.
μεταμορφόω
μετριοπαθέω Philo
*μιασμός Plut.
μίλιον
μορφόω Anth.
μόρφωσις
νάρδος Anth.
*νεκρόω Plut., Anth., Inscr.
*νέκρωσις Aret.
νεωτερικός
νησίον
*ξέστης? Joseph., Anthol.
ξυράω (ξυρέω Hdt.)
ὁδηγός
οἰκέτεια? Strab., Inscr.
*οἰκιακός Plut.

*οἰκοδεσποτέω Plut.
οἰκτίρμων Theocr., Sept., Anthol.
ὀνάριον
παλιγγενεσία Philo
πανδοχεῖον? (-κεῖον Arstph.)
πανδοχεύς? (-κεύς Plato)
παρατήρησις Epigr.
παραχειμασία
παρείσακτος
παρεισέρχομαι
παρεκτός
πατροπαράδοτος Diod., Inscr.
περιλάμπω
περιοχή
περιπείρω
περπερεύομαι M. Antonin.
πολλαπλασίων
*πολυμερῶς Joseph.
πολυτρόπως Philo
πορισμός
ποταπός (ποδαπός Aeschyl.)
*πραιτώριον Joseph., Inscr.
πραϋπάθεια (-θία)? Philo
*πρόγνωσις Plut., Anthol.
προελπίζω
προευαγγελίζομαι Philo
*προκαταγγέλλω Joseph.
προκοπή
*προσαίτης Plut.
προσανέχω?
πρόσκαιρος
προσκληρόω Philo
πρόσκλισις?
προσκοπή
*προσρήγνυμι Joseph.
προσφάτως
προφητικός Philo
ῥαδιούργημα
ῥητῶς

ῥοιζηδόν
ῥομφαία Sept.
*σαββατισμός Plut.
*Σαδδουκαῖος Joseph.
σαλπιστής Theophr., Inscr. (-πίγκτης Thuc.)
σάπφειρος
σαρόω
σέβασμα
σεβαστός Strab., Inscr.
σημειόω
σηρικός
*σικάριος Joseph.
σίναπι
*σιτιστός Joseph.
σκοτία Apoll. Rhod., Sept., Anthol.
σκύβαλον Anthol., Strab.
σκωληκόβρωτος
σπιλόω
στασιαστής?
στρατολογέω
στρατοπεδάρχης
στρῆνος Lycoph., Sept., Anthol.
*συγγενίς? Plut., Inscr.
συγκατάθεσις
*συγκαταψηφίζω Plut.
συγκληρονόμος Philo
συγχράομαι?
συζήτησις?
συμβασιλεύω
συμβούλιον Inscr.
συμμερίζω
σύμμορφος
συμπνίγω
συναθλέω
συνέκδημος Palaeph.
συνηλικιώτης Inscr.
συγκατανεύω?
*συνοδεύω Plut.

συνυποκρίνομαι
συσπαράσσω
συστατικός (-κώτερον Aristot.)
*συστασιαστής? Joseph.
συστοιχέω
*σωματικῶς Plut.
σωφρονισμός Philo, Aesop
*ταπεινοφροσύνη Joseph.
ταχινός Theocr., Sept.
τάχιον
τελώνιον
τετράδιον Philo
*τετραρχέω Joseph.
τετράρχης
τομώτερος
τριετία
τρίστεγος
τροχιά Nicand., Sept., Anthol.
*τυφωνικός Plut.
υἱοθεσία Diod., Inscr.
ὑπερπλεονάζω
ὑπογραμμός Philo
ὑπολιμπάνω
ὑποπόδιον Chares, Sept.
*ὑποστολή Joseph.
ὑποταγή
ὑποτύπωσις Quint.
*φειδομένως Plut.
φιλαδελφία (Alex.?) Philo
φιλήδονος Anth.
φρυάσσω Callim., Sept., Anth.
χάρισμα Philo
χειρόγραφον Polyb., Inscr.
χόρτασμα Phylarch., Sept.
ψώχω
ὠτίον Sept., Anth.

TOTAL 318 (75*, 16?)

II

BORROWED WORDS

1. Words borrowed from the Hebrew.

N. B. Hebraisms in signification and construction (whether 'proper' or 'improper') are excluded; so, too, are words of Semitic origin which had previously found their way into Greek usage.

Ἀβαδδών
Ἀββᾶ
Ἀκελδαμά

ἀλληλούϊα Sept.
ἀμήν Sept.
Βαάλ Sept.
βάρ
βάτος Apocr.
Βεελζεβούλ (-βούβ)
Βελίαρ (-λίαλ)
Βοανεργές
Γαββαθά
γέεννα (γαιέν. Josh. xviii. 16)
Γολγοθᾶ

Ἑβραϊκός
Ἑβραῖος Sept.
Ἑβραΐς Apocr.
Ἑβραϊστί Apocr.
ἐλωΐ (cf. ἠλί)
Ἐμμανουήλ Sept.
ἐφφαθά
ζιζάνιον
ἠλί or ἠλί or ἠλεί (cf. ἐλωΐ)
Ἰουδαΐζω Sept.
Ἰουδαϊκός Apocr. and -κῶς

Ἰουδαϊσμός Apocr.
Καναναῖος?
Κανανίτης?
κατήγωρ?
κορβᾶν or κορβανᾶς
κύρος Sept.
κούμ or κούμ or κούμ
λαμά or λαμμά or λεμά or λημά, etc.
μαμωνᾶς
μάννα Sept.

μαρὰν ἀθά (μαραναθά)
Μεσσίας
Μολόχ Sept.
(μωρέ?)
πάσχα Sept.
προσάββατον? Sept. Apocr.
ῥαββί, -βεί
ῥαββονί, -βουνί, -νεί
ῥακά or ῥακᾶ or ῥαχά
σαβαχθανί, -νεί
σαβαώθ Sept.
σαββατισμός
σάββατον Sept.
Σαδδουκαῖος
σατᾶν or σατανᾶς Sept.
σάτον Sept.
σίκερα Sept.
ταλιθά

ὕσσωπος Sept.
Φαρισαῖος
Χερουβίμ, -βείν, Sept.
ὡσαννά
TOTAL 57.

2. Words borrowed from the Latin.

N. B. Proper names are excluded, together with Latinisms which had already been adopted by profane authors.

δηνάριον
δίδωμι ἐργασίαν i. q. operam do
ἔχω i. q. aestimo
κῆνσος
κοδράντης

κολωνία etc.
κουστωδία
λαμβάνω (q. v. I. 3 e.) i. q. capto
τὸ ἱκανὸν λαμβάνειν i. q. satis accipere
συμβούλιον λαμβάνειν i. q. consilium capere
λεγεών (through Aram.?)
λέντιον
λιβερτῖνος
μάκελλον
μεμβράνα
μόδιος
ξέστης
πραιτώριον
ῥέδα or -δη? (cf. 3 below.)
σικάριος

σιμικίνθιον
σουδάριον (cf. III. 1)
σπεκουλάτωρ
ταβέρναι (αἱ)
τίτλος
φαινόλης paenula (cf. φαιλόνης in III. 1)
φόρον
φραγέλλιον
φραγελλόω
χῶρος (?)
TOTAL 30.

3. Words borrowed from other Foreign Tongues.

βαΐον (Egyptian)
ῥέδα or -δη (Gallic? cf. 2)

III

BIBLICAL, i. e. NEW TESTAMENT, GREEK

N. B. For explanations see the Prefatory Remarks.

1. Biblical Words.

Ἀβαδδών Sept.
Ἀββᾶ
ἄβυσσος, ἡ, Sept. (as adj. Aeschyl. et sqq.)
ἀγαθοεργέω (-θουργέω?)
ἀγαθοποιέω Sept.
ἀγαθοποιΐα
*ἀγαθοποιός Plut.
ἀγαθωσύνη Sept.
ἀγαλλίασις Sept.
ἀγαλλιάω Sept.
ἀγάπη Sept.
ἀγενεαλόγητος
ἀγιάζω Sept., Anthol.
ἁγιασμός Sept.
ἁγιότης Apocr.
ἁγιωσύνη Sept.
ἄγναφος
ἁγνισμός Sept., Inscr.
ἁγνότης Inscr.
ἀδελφότης Apocr.
ἀδιαφθορία?
ἀθετέω Sept., Polyb., Inscr.
αἱματεκχυσία
αἴνεσις Sept.
αἰσχροκερδῶς
αἰτίωμα?

αἰχμαλωσία Sept., Polyb.
αἰχμαλωτεύω Sept.
αἰχμαλωτίζω Sept., Inscr.
ἀκαθάρτης?
ἀκατάγνωστος Epigr., Inscr., Apocr.
ἀκατακάλυπτος Sept., Polyb.
ἀκατάκριτος
ἀκατάπαστος?
ἀκαταστασία Sept., Polyb.
ἀκατάσχετος Sept.
Ἀκελδαμά
*ἀκροατήριον Plut.
ἀκροβυστία Sept.
ἀκρογωνιαῖος Sept.
ἅλα?
ἀλάλητος Anthol.
ἁλιεύω Sept.
ἁλίσγημα
ἀλληλούϊα Sept.
ἀλλογενής Sept.
ἀλλότρι(ο)επίσκοπος
ἀλόη Sept.? [Apocr.
ἀμάραντος Orac. Sib., Inscr.,
ἀμέθυστος Sept., Anthol.
ἀμήν Sept.
ἀμφιάζω Sept., Anthol.
*ἀναγεννάω Joseph.
ἀναζάω Inscr.

ἀναζώννυμι Sept.
ἀναθεματίζω Sept., Inscr.
ἀνακαινόω
ἀνακαίνωσις
ἀνάπειρος? Apocr. (-πηρος, Plato sqq.)
ἀναστατόω Sept.?
*ἀνατάσσομαι Plut. (Sept.?)
ἀνεκδιήγητος
ἀνεκλάλητος
ἄνελεος?
ἀνεμίζω
ἀνένδεκτος
ἀνεξίκακος
ἀνεξιχνίαστος Sept.
*ἀνεπαίσχυντος Joseph.
ἀνετάζω Sept.?
ἀνεύθετος
ἀνθρωπάρεσκος Sept.
*ἀνθυπατεύω Plut.
ἀνίλεως?
ἀνταπόδομα Sept.
ἀνταποκρίνομαι Sept., Aesop
*ἀντιλοιδορέω Plut.
ἀντίλυτρον Sept., Orph.
ἀντιμετρέω?
ἀντιμισθία
ἀντιπαρέρχομαι Anthol. Apocr.

ἀντίχριστος
*ἄντλημα Plut.
ἀνυπόκριτος Apocr.
ἀπασπάζομαι
*ἀπείραστος Joseph.
ἀπεκδέχομαι
*ἀπεκδύομαι Joseph.?
ἀπέκδυσις
ἀπελεγμός
ἀπελπίζω Sept., Polyb., Anth.
ἀπέναντι Sept., Polyb., Inscr.
ἀπερίτμητος Sept.
ἀποδεκατόω Sept. (-τεύω?)
*ἀπόδεκτος Plut.
ἀποκάλυψις Sept.
ἀποκαταλλάσσω
ἀποκεφαλίζω Sept. (David over Goliath)
ἀποκυλίω Sept.
Ἀπολλύων
ἀποσκίασμα
ἀποσυνάγωγος
ἀποφθέγγομαι Sept.
*ἀπόχρησις Plut.
ἀπρόσμαχος Apocr.
ἀπροσωπολή(μ)πτως
ἀργυρόκοπος Sept., Inscr.
ἀρκετός Chrysipp., Anthol.

Ἀρμαγεδών etc.
*ἁρπαγμός Plut.
ἄρραφος
ἀρσενοκοίτης Anthol., Orac. Sibyl.
ἀρτιγέννητος
οἱ ἄρτοι τῆς προθέσεως Sept.
ἀρχάγγελος
*ἀρχιερατικός Joseph., Inscr.
ἀρχιποίμην
ἀρχισυνάγωγος Inscr.
ἀρχιτελώνης
ἀρχιτρίκλινος
ἀσαίνω? (q. v.)
ἄσπιλος Anthol.
ἀστατέω Anthol.
ἀστήρικτος Anthol.
ἀσφαλίζω Sept., Polyb.
αὐθεντέω
αὐτοκατάκριτος
ἀφεδρών
ἀφελότης
ἀφθορία?
ἀφιλάγαθος
ἀφιλάργυρος
ἀφυπνόω Sept., Anthol.
ἀφυστερέω Sept., Polyb.
ἀχειροποίητος
ἀχρειόω Sept., Polyb.
*ἄψινθος Aret. (-θιον from Xen. on)
Βαάλ Sept.
βαθμός Sept.
βαῖον Sept.? Apocr.
βάπτισμα
*βαπτισμός Joseph.
*βαπτιστής Joseph.
Βάρ
βασιλίσκος? Sept., Polyb., Aesop, Inscr.
βάτος Apocr.
βαττολογέω
βδέλυγμα Sept.
βδελυκτός Sept.
βεβηλόω Sept.
Βεελζεβούλ (-βούβ)
Βελίαρ (-λίαλ)
βήρυλλος Apocr., Anthol.
βιβλαρίδιον
βίωσις Apocr.
βλητέος
Βοανε (or -η-) ργές
βολίζω
βολίς Sept., Anthol.
βραδυπλοέω
βροχή Sept.
βυρσεύς Inscr.
Γαββαθᾶ
*γάγγραινα Plut.
γαζοφυλάκιον Sept.

γαμίζω
γέεννα (Sept. Josh. xviii. 16)
γεώργιον Sept.
γνώστης Sept.
γογγύζω Sept.
γογγυσμός Sept.
γογγυστής
Γολγοθᾶ
*γυμνητεύω Plut.
γυμνότης
δαιμονιώδης
δειγματίζω
δειλιάω Sept.
δεκαδύο Sept.
δεκαέξ Sept.
δεκαοκτώ Sept.
δεκαπέντε Sept., Polyb.
δεκατέσσαρες Sept., Polyb.
δεκατόω Sept.
δεκτός Sept.
δεξιοβόλος (-λάβος)
*δεσμοφύλαξ Joseph.
δευτερόπρωτος?
*δηνάριον Plut.
διαγογγύζω Sept.
διαγρηγορέω
διακαθαρίζω
διακατελέγχομαι
διαλιμπάνω Apocr.
διανεύω Sept., Polyb.
διαπαρατριβή?
διασκορπίζω Sept., Polyb.
διασπορά Apocr.
διαταγή Sept., Inscr.
δίδραχμον Sept.
διδῶμι ἐργασίαν
διενθυμέομαι?
διερμηνεία?
διερμηνευτής?
δικαιοκρισία Sept.?
δίλογος
διοδεύω Sept., Polyb., Inscr., Anthol.
δισμυρίας?
διώκτης
δογματίζω Sept., Anthol.
δοκιμή
δοκίμιον (-μεῖον, Plato)
δολιόω Sept.
δότης Sept.
δυναμόω Sept.
δυνατέω
δυσβάστακτος Sept.
δωδεκάφυλον Orac. Sib.
δωροφορία
ἑβδομηκοντάκις Sept.
ἑβδομηκονταπέντε Sept.
Ἑβραϊκός
Ἑβραῖος Sept.
Ἑβραΐς Apocr.

Ἑβραϊστί Apocr.
ἐγκαίνια Sept.
ἐγκαινίζω Sept.
ἐγκαυχάομαι? Sept., Aesop
ἐγκομβόομαι
ἑδραίωμα
ἐθελοθρησκεία
ἐθνικῶς
εἰδωλεῖον Apocr.
εἰδωλόθυτος Apocr.
εἰδωλολατρεία
εἰδωλολάτρης
εἰρηνοποιέω Sept.
ἐκγαμίζω?
ἐκγαμίσκω?
ἐκδικέω Sept., Inscr.
ἐκδίκησις Sept., Polyb., Inscr.
ἐκζητέω Sept.
ἐκζήτησις?
ἐκθαμβέω Sept.? Apocr., Orph.
ἐκμυκτηρίζω Sept.
ἐκπειράζω Sept.
ἐκπερισσῶς?
ἐκπορνεύω Sept.
ἐκριζόω Sept., Orac. Sib., Inscr.
ἔκτρομος?
ἐλαιών Sept.
*ἐλαφρία Aret.
ἐλαχιστότερος
ἐλεγμός? Sept.
ἔλεγξις Sept.
ἔλεος, τό, Sept., Polyb.
ἐλλογάω (-γέω)
ἐλωΐ Sept. (cf. ἠλί)
*ἐμμαίνομαι Joseph.
Ἐμμανουήλ Sept.
ἐμμέσῳ?
ἐμπαιγμονή?
ἐμπαιγμός Sept.
ἐμπαίκτης Sept.
ἐμπεριπατέω Sept.
ἐναγκαλίζομαι Sept., Anthol.
ἔναντι? Sept.
ἐνδιδύσκω Sept.
*ἐνδόμησις Joseph.
ἐνδοξάζω Sept.
ἔνδυμα Sept.
ἐνδυναμόω Sept.
ἔνεδρον? Sept.
ἐνευλογέω? Sept.
ἐννενηκονταεννέα
*ἐνορκίζω? Joseph., Inscr.
ἔνταλμα Sept.
ἐνταφιάζω Sept., Anthol.
ἐνταφιασμός
ἔντρομος Sept., Anthol.
ἐνωτίζομαι Sept.

ἐξαγοράζω Sept., Polyb.
ἐξακολουθέω Sept., Polyb.
ἐξάπινα Sept.
ἐξαπορέω Sept., Polyb.
*ἐξαρτίζω Joseph., Inscr.
ἐξαστράπτω Sept.
ἐξέραμα
ἐξηχέω Sept., Polyb.
ἐξολοθρεύω Sept.
ἐξομολογέω Sept.
*ἐξορκιστής Joseph.
ἐξουδενέω (-νόω) Sept.
ἐξουθενέω (-νόω) Sept.
ἐξυπνίζω Sept.
*ἔξυπνος Joseph.
ἐξώτερος Sept.
*ἐπαγωνίζομαι Plut., Inscr.
*ἐπαθροίζω Plut.
ἐπαναπαύω Sept.
ἐπάρχειος Inscr.
ἐπαύριον Sept.
*ἐπενδύω Joseph. (-δύνω Hdt.)
ἐπιγαμβρεύω Sept.
ἐπίγνωσις Sept., Polyb.
ἐπιδιατάσσομαι
ἐπιδιορθόω Inscr.
ἐπικατάρατος Sept., Inscr.
Ἐπικούρειος Anthol.
ἐπιλείχω?
ἐπιλησμονή Apocr.
ἐπιούσιος
ἐπιπόθησις
ἐπιπόθητος
ἐπιποθία
ἐπιπορεύομαι Sept., Polyb.
ἐπιρράπτω
ἐπισκοπή Sept.
ἐπισυνάγω Sept., Polyb., Aesop
ἐπισυναγωγή Apocr.
ἐπισυντρέχω
ἐπισύστασις Sept.
*ἐπισωρεύω Plut.
ἐπιφαύσκω Sept.
ἐπιφώσκω Inscr.
ἐπιχορηγία
ἐρήμωσις Sept.
ἐρίφιον? Apocr.
ἑτεροδιδασκαλέω
ἑτεροζυγέω
εὐαγγελιστής
εὐάρεστος Apocr.
εὐδοκέω Sept., Polyb.
εὐδοκία Sept., Inscr.
εὐκοπώτερον (-κοπος Polyb.)
εὐλογητός Sept.
εὐμετάδοτος
*εὐνουχίζω Joseph.
εὐπάρεδρος?

*εὐποιΐα Joseph., Inscr.
*εὐπρόσδεκτος Plut.
εὐπρόσεδρος
εὐπροσωπέω
εὐρακύλων
εὐρο(or-υ-)κλύδων } ?
*εὐψυχέω Joseph., Anthol.,
    Inscr.
ἐφημερία Sept.
ἐφφαθά
ζευκτηρία
ζιζάνιον
ἠλί (cf. ἐλωΐ)
*Ἡρωδιανοί Joseph.
ἥττημα Sept.
θεατρίζω
θειώδης
θέλησις Sept.
θεοδίδακτος
θεομάχος Alleg. Homer.
*θεόπνευστος Plut., Orac.
    Sibyl.
*θεότης Plut.
θορυβάζω?
θρῆσκος
θυσιαστήριον Sept.
ἱεράτευμα Sept.
ἱερατεύω Sept., Inscr.
ἱκανόω Sept.
ἱλαρότης Sept.
ἱλασμός Sept.
ἱλαστήριος Sept.
ἱματίζω
Ἰουδαΐζω Sept.
*Ἰουδαϊκός Apocr.
*Ἰουδαϊκῶς Joseph.
Ἰουδαϊσμός Apocr.
ἰσάγγελος
καθαρίζω Sept. (Hippocr.?)
καθαρισμός Sept.
*καθεξῆς Plut., Inscr.
καλοδιδάσκαλος
καλοποιέω Sept.?
κάμιλος?
Καναναῖος?
Κανανίτης?
καρδιογνώστης
καταγγελεύς
κατάθεμα?
καταθεματίζω?
κατακαυχάομαι Sept.
κατακληροδοτέω? Sept.?
κατακληρονομέω? Sept.
κατακολουθέω Sept., Polyb.
κατάκρισις
καταλαλιά
κατάλαλος
κατάλειμμα? Sept.
καταλιθάζω
κατάλυμα Sept., Polyb.

κατανάθεμα?
καταναθεματίζω?
καταντάω Sept., Polyb.
κατάνυξις Sept.
κατανύσσω Sept.
καταπέτασμα Sept.
*κατάρτισις Plut.
καταρτισμός
κατασκήνωσις Sept., Polyb.,
    Inscr.
κατασοφίζομαι Sept., Inscr.
καταστρηνιάω
κατάσχεσις Sept.
καταφρονητής Sept.
κατείδωλος
κατέναντι Sept., Inscr.
κατενώπιον Sept.
κατεξουσιάζω
*κατευλογέω? Plut.
κατεφίστημι
κατήγωρ?
κατιόω Apocr.
κατοικητήριον Sept.
κατοικία Sept., Polyb.
καυσόω
καύσων Sept.
καύχησις Sept.
κενοφωνία
κεφαλιόω (-λαιόω Thuc.)
κῆνσος Inscr.
κλυδωνίζομαι Sept.
κοδράντης
κόκκινος Sept.
κολαφίζω
κολωνία etc.
*κορβᾶν or κορβανᾶς Joseph.
κόρος Sept.
κοσμοκράτωρ Orph., Inscr.
κοῦμι etc.
κουστωδία
κραταιόω Sept.
κρυσταλλίζω
κύλισμα? or κυλισμός?
κυριακός Inscr.
κυριότης
λαμά etc.
λαξευτός Sept.
λατομέω Sept.
λεγιών etc. (cf. list II. 2)
λειτουργικός Sept.
λέντιον
λιβερτῖνος Inscr.
λιθοβολέω Sept.
λογία (ἡ)
λογομαχέω
λογομαχία
λυτρωτής Sept. (Philo)
λυχνία Sept., Inscr.
*μαθητεύω Plut.
*μάκελλον Plut.

μακρόθεν Sept., Polyb.
μακροθυμέω Sept.
μακροθύμως
μαμωνᾶς
μάννα Sept.
μαρὰν ἀθά (μαραναθά)
*ματαιολογία Plut.
ματαιότης Sept., Inscr.
ματαιόω Sept.
μεγαλειότης Sept., Inscr.
μεγαλωσύνη Sept.
μεγιστάν Sept.
μεθοδεία
μελίσσιος? (-αῖος, Nicand.)
μεμβράνα
μεριστής
μεσίτης Sept., Polyb.
μεσότοιχον (-χος, Eratos.)
*μεσουράνημα Plut.
Μεσσίας
μετοικεσία Sept., Anthol.
*μιασμός Plut.
μισθαποδοσία
μισθαποδότης
μίσθιος Sept., Anthol.
μογ(γ)ιλάλος Sept.
μόδιος
μοιχαλίς Sept.
μολυσμός Sept.
μοσχοποιέω
μυλικός?
μύλινος? Inscr.
μύλος Sept., Anthol., Orac.
    Sibyl.
(μωρέ?)
*νεκρόω Plut., Anthol., In-
    scr.
*νέκρωσις Aret.
νεόφυτος Sept. (lit.; so Ar-
    stph. in Pollux 1, 231)
νῖκος Sept., Anthol., Orph.
νιπτήρ
νομοδιδάσκαλος
νοσσιά? Sept. (νεοσσιά Hdt.,
    al.)
νυμφών Apocr.
νυχθήμερον Orac. Sibyl.
ξενοδοχέω Graec. Ven. (-κέω,
    Hdt.)
*ξέστης? Joseph., Anthol.
*οἰκιακός Plut.
*οἰκοδεσποτέω Plut.
οἰκοδομή Sept. (Aristot.?)
οἰκουργός?
ὀκταήμερος (Graec. Ven.)
ὀλιγοπιστία?
ὀλιγόπιστος
ὀλιγόψυχος Sept.
ὀλίγως Anthol.
ὀλοθρευτής

ὀλο(or -ε-)θρεύω Sept., An-
    thol.
ὁλοκαύτωμα Sept.
ὁλοκληρία Sept.
ὀμείρομαι? Sept.?
ὁμοιάζω?
ὀνειδισμός Sept.
ὀνικός
ὀπτάνω Sept.
ὀπτασία Sept., Anthol.
ὀρθοποδέω
ὀρθοτομέω Sept.
ὀρθρίζω Sept.
ὀρθρινός? Sept., Anthol.
ὁρκωμοσία Sept.
ὁροθεσία
οὐά
οὐαί Sept.
ὀφειλή
ὀφθαλμοδουλεία
ὀχλοποιέω
ὀψάριον
παγιδεύω Sept.
παιδιόθεν
παμπληθεί
παντοκράτωρ Sept., Anthol.,
    Inscr.
παραβιάζομαι Sept., Polyb.
παραβολεύομαι?
παραβουλεύομαι?
παραδιατριβή?
παραδειγματίζω Sept., Polyb.
παραζηλόω Sept.
παραλυτικός
παραπικραίνω Sept.
παραπικρασμός Sept.
παράπτωμα Sept., Polyb.
παραφρονία
παρεπίδημος Sept., Polyb.
παροικία Sept.
παρομοιάζω?
παροργισμός Sept.
πάσχα Sept.
πατριάρχης Sept.
πειθός
πειρασμός Sept.
πεισμονή
πελεκίζω Sept., Polyb.
πεντεκαιδέκατος Sept.
πεποίθησις Sept.
περιαστράπτω Apocr.
περίθεσις
περικάθαρμα Sept.
περικεφαλαία Sept., Polyb.,
    Inscr.
περικρατής Apocr.
περικρύπτω
περιούσιος Sept.
περισσεία Sept., Inscr.
περιτομή Sept.

περίψημα Sept., Inscr.
πλημμύρα etc. Sept., Anthol.
πληροφορία
πνευματικῶς
πολιτάρχης Inscr., Epigr.
*πολυμερῶς Joseph.
πολύσπλαγχνος
πορφυρόπωλις
ποταμοφόρητος
*πραιτώριον Joseph., Inscr.
πρεσβυτέριον Inscr.
προαιτιάομαι
προαμαρτάνω
προβλέπω Sept.
*πρόγνωσις Plut., Anthol.
προενάρχομαι
προεπαγγέλλω
*προκαταγγέλλω Joseph.
πρόκριμα
προκυρόω
προμαρτύρομαι
προμεριμνάω
προορίζω
προσάββατον? Sept.?, Apocrypha
*προσαίτης Plut.
(προσαχέω?)
προσδαπανάω Inscr.
προσεάω
προσεγγίζω? Sept., Polyb., Anthol.
προσευχή Sept., Inscr.
προσήλυτος Sept.
προσκαρτέρησις
πρόσκομμα Sept.
προσκυνητής Inscr.
προσοχθίζω Sept., Orac. Sibyl.
προσπαίω? (Soph.?)
πρόσπεινος
*προσρήγνυμι Joseph.
προσφάγιον Inscr.
πρόσχυσις
προσωπολη(μ)πτέω
προσωπολή(μ)πτης
προσωπολη(μ)ψία
προφητεία Sept., Inscr.
πρωϊνός Sept.
πρωτοκαθεδρία
πρωτοκλισία (ή) Apocr.
πρωτοτόκια (τά) Sept.
πρωτότοκος Sept., Anthol.
(-τόκος, act., Hom. down)
τὸ πῦρ τὸ αἰώνιον etc.
πυρράζω? (-ρίζω Sept.)
ῥαββί, -βεί
ῥαββονί etc.
ῥακά etc.
ῥαντίζω Sept.
ῥαντισμός Sept.

ῥέδη or ῥέδα
ῥυπαρεύομαι?
σαβαχθανί, -νεί
σαβαώθ Sept.
*σαββατισμός Plut.
σάββατον Sept., Anthol.
σαγήνη Sept.
*Σαδδουκαῖος Joseph.
σάρδινος?
σαρδιόνυξ?
σατᾶν or σατανᾶς Sept.
σάτον Sept.
σεληνιάζομαι
σητόβρωτος Sept., Orac. Sibyl.
σθενόω
*σικάριος Joseph.
σίκερα Sept.
σιμικίνθιον
σινιάζω
*σιτιστός Joseph.
σιτομέτριον (-τρον Plut.)
σκανδαλίζω
σκάνδαλον Sept.
σκηνοποιός
σκληροκαρδία Sept.
σκληροτράχηλος Sept.
σκοτίζω Sept., Polyb.
σμαράγδινος
σμυρνίζω
σουδάριον (σωδάριον Hermippus)
σπεκουλάτωρ
σπλαγχνίζομαι Sept.?
στήκω Sept.
στρατοπέδαρχος?
στυγνάζω Sept., Polyb.
*συγγενίς? Plut., Inscr.
συγκακοπαθέω
συγκακουχέω
*συγκαταψηφίζω
συγκοινωνός
συζητητής
συζωοποιέω
συκομορέα
συλαγωγέω   [Inscr.
συλλαλέω Sept., Polyb.,
συμμιμητής
συμμορφίζω?
συμμορφόω?
συμπρεσβύτερος
συμφυλέτης
συμφώνησις
σύμψυχος
συναιχμάλωτος
συνανάκειμαι Apocr.
συναναμίγνυμι Sept.?
συναναπαύομαι? Sept.
συναντιλαμβάνομαι Sept., Inscr.

συναρμολογέω
συνεγείρω Sept.
συνεκλεκτός
συνθρύπτω
*συνοδεύω Plut.
συνομορέω
σύσσημον (Menander in Phryn.), Sept.
σύσσωμος
*συστασιαστής Joseph.
συσταυρόω
σφυδρόν?
*σωματικῶς Plut.
ταβέρναι (αἱ)
ταλιθά
ταπεινόφρων? Sept.
*ταπεινοφροσύνη Joseph.
ταρταρόω
τεκνίον Anthol.
τεκνογονέω Anthol.
τελειωτής
τεσσαρακονταδύο?
τεσσαρακοντατέσσαρες?
*τετραρχέω Joseph.
τίτλος Inscr.
τοπάζιον Sept.
τροποφορέω? Sept.
τροφοφορέω? Sept.?
τρυμαλιά Sept. (Sotad.)
τυπικῶς?
*τυφωνικός Plut.
ὑπακοή Sept.
ὕπανδρος Sept., Polyb.
ὑπάντησις Sept.
ὑπερέκεινα
ὑπερεκπερισσοῦ Sept.?
ὑπερεκπερισσῶς?
ὑπερεκτείνω Anthol.?
ὑπερεκχύνω Sept.?
ὑπερεντυγχάνω
ὑπερνικάω
ὑπερπερισσεύω
ὑπερπερισσῶς
ὑπερυψόω Sept.
ὑπολήνιον Sept.
ὑποπιάζω?
ὑποπλέω Anthol.
*ὑποστολή Joseph.
ὑποστρώννυμι Sept.
ὕσσωπος Sept.
ὑστέρημα Sept.
ὑστέρησις
ὑψηλοφρονέω?
ὕψωμα Sept., Orac. Sib.
φάγος
φαι(or φε-)λόνης (φαινόλης Rhinthon, c. B.C. 300, in Pollux 7, 61)
Φαρισαῖος
*φειδομένως Plut.

φιλοπρωτευω
φόρον
φραγέλλιον
φραγελλόω
φρεναπατάω
φρεναπάτης
φυλακίζω Sept.
φυσίωσις
φωστήρ Sept., Anthol.
φωτισμός Sept.
χαλιναγωγέω
χαλκηδών (Pliny)
χαλκολίβανον
χαριτόω Apocr.
Χερουβίμ etc. Sept.
χοϊκός
χρεωφειλέτης etc. Sept., Aesop
χρηστεύομαι
χρηστολογία
χρυσοδακτύλιος
χρυσόλιθος Sept.
χρυσόπρασος
χῶρος
ψευδάδελφος
ψευδαπόστολος
ψευδοδιδάσκαλος
ψευδοπροφήτης Sept.
ψευδόχριστος
ψιθυρισμός Sept.
ψιχίον
ψωμίον Sept.
ὡσαννά

TOTAL 767, (76*, 89 ?)

2. Biblical Significations.

N. B. "Sept." or "Apocr." is added to a word in case it occur in the same sense in the Septuagint version or (if not there) in the Apocryphal books of the O.T. Moreover, characteristic N. T. significations which also occur in Philo and Josephus but in no other secular authors have been included in the list, with the proper designations appended. See the Prefatory Remarks, p. 688.

ἡ ἄβυσσος (Sept.)
ἀγάπη 2
ἄγγελος 2 (Sept., Philo)
ἀδελφή 2
ἀδελφός 2 (Sept., Philo), 4, 5 (Sept.)
ἀδιάκριτος 2
ἀδρότης
ἀδυνατέω b. (Sept.)
αἵρεσις 5
αἱρετικός 2

αἰών 2 (Apocr.), 3
ἀλήθεια I. 1 c.
ἀληθεύω b.
ἁμαρτία 3, 4
ἀμήτωρ 5 (Philo)
ἀνάθεμα 2 a., b.
(ἀνασταυρόω)
ἀναφέρω 2 (Sept.)
ἀνθομολογέομαι 3 fin. (Sept.)
ἄνομος 1
ἀνόμως
ἀνοχή
ἀντίληψις (Sept.)
ἀντιλογία 2 (Sept.)
ἀντίτυπος 1, 2
ἀπάτωρ
ἀπαύγασμα (Apocr.)
ἁπλότης fin. (Joseph.)
ἀποθνήσκω II.
ἀποκαλύπτω 2 c. (Sept.)
ἀποκάλυψις 2 a.
ἀποκρίνω 2 (Sept.)
ἀπόλλυμι 1 a. β.
ἀπολύτρωσις 2
ἀποστάσιον 1 (Sept.), 2
ἀποστολή 4
ἀπόστολος 2, 3
ἀποστοματίζω
ἀποτάσσω 1
ἀπώλεια 2 b.
ἀρεσκεία (Philo)
ἀρχή 5
ἀσύνετος fin. (Apoc.)
αὐγάζω 2 (Sept.)
αὐτός II. 2 (Sept.)
ἀφυπνόω b.
ἀφυστερέω 2 (Sept.)
βαπτίζω II.
βαπτισμός (Joseph.)
βασιλεία 3
βλέπω 2 c. mid.
γαμέω 2
γένεσις 3
γεννάω 2 b. (Philo), c., d.
γλῶσσα 2 init.
γράμμα 2 c. (Philo, Joseph.)
γραμματεύς 2 (Sept.)
δαίμων 2 (Joseph.)
δέω 2 c.
ὁ διάβολος Sept.
διαθήκη 2 (i. q. בְּרִית)
διακονία 3, 4
διάκονος 2
διακρίνομαι 3
διανοίγω 2
διαπονοῦμαι c. (Apocr.)
διατίθεμαι διαθήκην etc. (Sept.)
δίδωμι IV. 5
δικαιοσύνη 1 c.

δικαιόω 2, 3, (Sept.)
δικαίωσις
δίλογος 2
διώκω 3
δόξα III. (Sept.)
δοξάζω 4 (Sept.)
δύναμις b.
δῶμα 3 (Sept.)
δωρεά b. (Sept.)
ἐγγύς 1 b.
ἐγείρω 2, 4
ἔγερσις fin.
ἐθνικός 3
ἔθνος 4 (Sept.), 5
εἰ I. 5 (Sept.), III. 9 (Sept.)
εἴδω II. 3 (Sept.)
εἴδωλον 2 (Sept.)
εἰμί II. 5 (Sept.)
εἶπον 5 (Sept.)
εἰρήνη 3 (Sept.), 4, 5, 6 (Sept.)
ἐκ I. 7 (Sept.)
ἔκβασις 2 (Apocr.)
ἐκδοχή 4
ἐκκλησία 2 (Sept.), 4
ἐκλέγομαι (Sept.)
ἐκλεκτός (Sept.)
ἐκλογή
ἔκστασις 3 (Sept.)
ἔλεος 2, 3
Ἑλληνίς 2
ἐμβατεύω 2 (Apocr., Philo)
ἐμβριμάομαι fin.
ἐν I. 6 b., 8 b. (Sept.), 8 c.
ἐναντίον 2 fin. (Sept.)
ἐνεργέω 3
ἐξανάστασις fin.
ἔξοδος fin. (Philo)
ἐξομολογέω 2 (Sept.)
ἐξουσία 4 c. ββ., d.
ἐπερωτάω 2 (Sept.)
ἐπερώτημα 3
ἐπιγαμβρεύω 2 (Sept.)
ἐπικαλέω 2 (Sept.)
ἐπισκέπτομαι b. (Sept.)
ἐπισκοπή b. (Sept.), c. (Sept.)
ἐπίσκοπος fin.
ἐπιστροφή Apocr.
ἐπιτιμία Apocr.
ἐρεύγομαι 3 (Sept.)
εὐαγγελίζω III.
εὐαγγέλιον 2 a., b.
εὐδοκέω b.
εὐλογέω 2, 3, 4, (Sept.)
εὐλογία 3 Sept., 4, 5 (Sept.)
εὔσπλαγχνος (Apocr.)
ἔχω I. 1 f.
ζάω I. 2
ζωή 2 a., b.
ζωογονέω 3 (Sept.)
ζωοποιέω 2

ἡμέρα 1 b., 3 (Sept.)
ἡσυχάζω c. (Sept.)
θάνατος 2 (Sept., Philo)
θέλω 4 (Sept.)
θεός 4 (Sept.)
θεωρέω 2 c. sub fin.
θριαμβεύω 2
θροέω fin. (Sept.)
θυγάτηρ b. (Sept.)
θυμιατήριον 2 (Philo, Joseph.)
ἴδιος 1 d. (Apocr.)
ἱερεύς b.
ἱλασμός 2 (Sept.)
ἱλαστήριον, τό, 1 (Sept.), 2 (Sept.)
ἰσχύω 2 a. (Sept.)
καθαρίζω 1 b. (Apocr.), 2 (Sept.)
καθεύδω 2 b. (Sept.)
κακία 3 (Sept.)
κακόω 2 (Sept.)
κακολογέω 2 (Sept.)
καλέω 1 b. β.
καμμύω (Sept.)
κάμπτω b. (Sept.)
κανών 1
καρπός 2 c. (Sept.)
καταισχύνω 2 fin. (Sept.)
κατάπαυσις 2 (Sept.)
καταστολή 2 (Sept.)
κατατομή
κέρας b. (Sept.)
κεφαλαιόω 2
κήρυγμα (Sept.)
κῆρυξ 1 fin.
κηρύσσω b.
κληρονομέω 2 fin.
κληρονομία 2 a., b.
κληρονόμος 1 b., 2 (Sept.)
κληρόω 4 (Apocr.)
κλῆσις 2
κλητός a., b.
κοιλία 5 (Sept.)
κοινός 2 (Apocr.)
κοινόω 2 (Apocr.)
κοινωνία 3
κοπή 2 (Sept.)
κοπιάω 2 (Sept.)
κοσμικός 2, 3
κόσμος 5 (Apocr.), 6, 7, 8 (Sept.)
κρίσις 5 a. β., 6 (Sept.)
κρίσις 3 b., 4 (Sept.), 5 (Sept.)
κριτήριον 1 (Sept.)
κριτής 2 (Sept.)
κτίσις 2 (Apocr.), 3
κτίσμα
κῶλον
λαμβάνω I. 3 e. (cf. list II. 2)
λάσκω 2

λειτουργέω 2 c. (Apocr.)
λειτουργία 3 b.
λιβανωτός 2
λικμάω 3 (Sept.)
λόγος III.
λύτρωσις fin. (Sept.)
μαθητεύω
μακροθυμέω 2 (Sept.)
μακροθυμία 2 (Sept.)
μάρτυς c.
μεσιτεύω 2 (Philo)
μεταίρω 2
μοιχαλίς b. (Sept.)
μοιχός fin.
μυστήριον 2, 3 (Sept.)
μωραίνω 2 (Sept.)
μωρός fin. (Sept.)
νεκρός 2
νεώτερος d.
νόμος 2 (Apocr.), 3, 4 (Sept.)
νύμφη 2 fin. (Sept.)
οἰκοδομέω b. β.
οἰκοδομή 1
ὁμολογέω 4
ὄνομα 2 (Sept.), 3 (Sept.), 4
ὀπίσω 2 (Sept.)
οὐρανός 2 (Sept.)
ὀφειλέτης b.
ὀφείλημα b.
ὀφείλω c.
ὀφθαλμός in phrases (Sept.)
ὀχύρωμα 2 (Sept.)
ἡ ὀψία
ὀψώνιον 2
παιδεία 2 b. (Sept.), c. (Sept.)
παιδεύω 2 b. (Sept.), c. (Sept.)
παῖς 2 fin. (Sept. ; i. q. עֶבֶד)
παράκλητος 3 (Philo)
παραβολή 3, 4, (Sept.)
παράδεισος 3, 4
παρακοή
παρασκευή 3 (Joseph.)
παρθένος 2
πάροικος 2 (Sept.)
παρρησία 3 (Philo)
πατάσσω 2 (Sept.), 3 (Sept.)
πειράζω 2 d. (Sept.)
πειρασμός b., c., (Sept.)
πεντηκοστή (Apocr.)
περιπατέω b.
περιποίησις 2, 3
περισσεία 4
περίσσευμα 2
περισσεύω 2
περιτομή a. γ., b.
πιστεύω 1 b.
πίστις 1 b.
πνεῦμα 3 c., d., 4
πνευματικός 3
πορεία

πορεύω b. (Sept.)
πορνεία b. (Sept.)
πορνεύω 3 (Sept.)
πόρνη 2
ποτήριον b.
πρεσβύτερος 2 a., b., c.
προάγω 2 b.
προσανέχω 2
προσευχή 2 (Philo)
προσήλυτος (Joseph.)
προσκαλέω b.
προστίθημι 2 sub fin. (Sept.)
πρόσωπον 1 b., c., 2, (Sept.)
προφητεύω b., c., d., (Sept.)
προφήτης II. 1 (Sept.)
πρωτότοκος b.
ῥῆμα 2 (Sept.)
ῥίζα 2 (Sept.)

σάββατον 2
σαρκικός 1
σάρκινος 3
σάρξ 2 b. (Sept.), 3 (Sept.), 4
σεβάζομαι 2
σκανδαλίζω (Apocr.)
σκάνδαλον b. (Sept.)
σκηνοπηγία 2 (Sept.)
σκότος b.
σοφία b.
σταυρός 2 b.
στέφανος b. a.
στηρίζω b.
στοιχεῖον 3
στόμα 2 (Sept.)
στρατιά 3 (Sept.)
συζητέω b.
συμβιβάζω 3 fin.

συνάγω c. (Sept.)
συναγωγή 2 (Joseph., Philo)
συναίρω 2
συνδοξάζω 2
συνεγείρω fin.
συνέδριον 2 b.
συντελέω 5 (Sept.)
σύντριμμα 2 (Sept.)
σχίσμα b.
σώζω b. (Sept.)
σῶμα 3
σωτήρ (Sept.)
σωτηρία a. (Sept.), b., c.
σωτήριον, τό (Sept.)
τέκνον c. (Sept.)
τίς 1 e. γ. (Sept.)
τραχηλίζω 2
τύπος 4 γ.

υἱοθεσία a., b.
υἱός 2 (Sept.)
υἱὸς τοῦ ἀνθρώπου 3 (Sept.)
υἱὸς τοῦ θεοῦ 2, 3, (Sept.)
ὑποκριτής 3 (Sept.)
ὑποπνέω b.
ὑποτύπωσις b.
φυλακτήριον 2
φυλάσσω 2 b. (Sept.)
φωτίζω 2 c. (Sept.)
χαρίζομαι b.
χάρις 2 sub fin., 3 a.
χάρισμα (Philo)
χαριτόω 2
χριστός 2
χρίω a., b.
ψυχή 1 c., 2 b.
ψωμίζω b.

IV

WORDS PECULIAR TO INDIVIDUAL NEW TESTAMENT WRITERS

N. B. A word which occurs only in a quotation by the N. T. writer from the Septuagint is so marked. In the Apocalypse, which contains no express quotations, a word is so designated only when the context plainly indicates a (conscious or unconscious) reminiscence on the part of the writer. For other explanations see the Prefatory Remarks, p. 688 sq.

1. To Matthew.

ἀγγεῖον
ἄγγος?
ἄγκιστρον
ἄθῳος
αἷμα ἀθῷον
αἷμα δίκαιον
αἱμορροέω
αἱρετίζω
ἀκμήν
ἀμφίβληστρον (Mk.?)
ἀκριβόω
ἀναβιβάζω
ἀναίτιος
ἄνηθον
ἀπάγχω
ἀπονίπτω
βάρ?
βαρύτιμος?
βασανιστής
(βασιλεία τῶν οὐρανῶν, see οὐρανός)
βαττολογέω
βιαστής
βροχή
δαίμων (Mk.? Lk.? Rev.?)
δάνειον
ὁ δεῖνα

δέσμη
διακαθαρίζω (Lk.?)
διακωλύω
διαλλάσσω
διασαφέω
δίδραχμον
διέξοδος
διετής
διστάζω
διυλίζω
διχάζω
ἑβδομηκοντάκις
ἔγερσις
ἐγκρύπτω (Lk.?)
ὁ ἐθνικός (3 Jn.?)
ἐνθυμέομαι (Acts?)
εἰδέα (ἰδέα)
εἰρηνοποιός
ἐκλάμπω
Ἐμμανουήλ fr. Sept.
ἐμπορία
ἐμπρήθω
ἐξορκίζω
ἐξώτερος
ἐπιγαμβρεύω
ἐπικαθίζω
ἐπιορκέω
ἐπισπείρω?
ἐρεύγομαι

ἐρίζω
ἐρίφιον?
ἑταῖρος
εὐδία?
εὐνοέω
εὐνουχίζω
εὐρύχωρος
ζιζάνιον
ἠλί
θαυμάσιος
(θεέ voc.)
θεριστής
θρῆνος?
θυμόω
(ἰδέα, see εἰδέα)
ἰῶτα
καθά
καθηγητής
καταθεματίζω?
καταμανθάνω
καταναθεματίζω?
καταποντίζω
κῆτος fr. Sept.
κουστωδία
κρυφαῖος?
κύμινον
κώνωψ   [συμβ.)
(λαμβάνειν συμβούλιον, see
μαλακία

μεταίρω
μετοικεσία
μίλιον
μισθόω
μυλών?
νόμισμα
νοσσίον (Lk.?)
οἰκέτεια?
οἰκιακός
ὀλιγοπιστία?
ὄναρ (κατ᾽ ὄναρ)
ὀνικός (Mk.? Lk.?)
οὐδαμῶς
βασιλεία τῶν οὐρανῶ.
παγιδεύω
παραθαλάσσιος
παρακούω (Mk.?)
παρατιθέναι παραβολήν
παρομοιάζω?
παροψίς
πεζός?
πικρῶς (Lk.?)
πλατύς
πληροῦν τὸ ῥηθέν
πολυλογία
προβιβάζω (Acts?)
προσπαίω?
προφθάνω
πυρράζω?

ῥακ(or -χ-)ά (or ῥακᾶ)
ῥαπίζω
σαγήνη
σεληνιάζομαι
σιτιστός
στατήρ
συμβούλιον λαμβάνε:ν
συναίρω (λόγον)
συνάντησις?
συναυξάνω
συντάσσω
τάλαντον
ταφή
τελευτή
τοὔνομα?
τραπεζίτης
τρύπημα?
τύφω
φημίζω?
φράζω
φυγή (Mk.?)
φυλακτήριον
φυτεία
Χαναναῖος
χλαμύς
ψευδομαρτυρία
ψύχω

TOTAL 137 (2 fr. Sept., 21 ?)

2. To Mark.

ἀγρεύω
ἄλαλος
ἀλεκτοροφωνία
ἀλλαχοῦ?
ἀμφιβάλλω?
ἄμφοδον
ἀνακυλίω?
ἄναλος
ἀναπηδάω?
ἀναστενάζω
ἀπόδημος
ἀποστεγάζω
ἀτιμάω }?
ἀτιμόω }
ἀφρίζω
βοανε(or-η)ργες
γναφεύς
δηλαυγῶς? (cf. τηλαυγῶς)
διαρπάζω (Mt.?)
δισχίλιοι
δύσις?
δύσκολος
ἔγγιστα?
εἶτεν?
ἐκθαμβέω
ἐκθαυμάζω?
ἐκπερισσῶς?
ἔκφοβος (Heb. fr. Sept.)

ἐλωΐ
ἐναγκαλίζομαι
ἐνειλέω
ἔννυχος
ἐξάπινα
ἐξουδ(or-θ-)ενόω?
ἐπιβάλλω (intr.)
ἐπικεφάλαιον?
ἐπιρράπτω
ἐπισυντρέχω
ἐσχάτως (ἔχειν)
ἐφφαθά
θαμβέω (Acts?)
θανάσιμος
θυγάτριον
τὸ ἱκανὸν ποιεῖν
καταβαρύνω?
καταδιώκω
κατακόπτω
κατευλογέω?
κατοίκησις
κεντυρίων
κεφαλαιόω }
κεφαλιόω }
κοῦμι etc.
κυλίω
κωμόπολις
μεθόριον?
μηκύνω
μογ(γ)ιλάλος
μυρίζω
νουνεχῶς
ξέστης
ὁδοποιέω?
(ὁδὸν ποιέω?)
ὄμμα (Mt.?)
ὅσπερ?
οὐά
ὀχετός?
ὄψιος (adj.)?
παιδιόθεν
πάμπολυς?
πανταχόθεν?
παρόμοιος
πεζῇ (Mt.?)
περιτρέχω
πρασιά
προαύλιον
προμεριμνάω
προσάββατον?
προσεγγίζω?
προσκεφάλαιον
προσορμίζω
προσπορεύομαι
πυγμή?
σκώληξ fr. Sept.
σμυρνίζω
σπεκουλάτωρ
στασιαστής?
στιβάς (στοιβάς)?

στίλβω
συλλυπέω
συμβούλιον ποιεῖν?
συμπόσιον
συνθλίβω
Συραφοινίκισσα }
Συροφοινίκισσα }
Συροφοίνισσα }
σύσσημον
συστασιαστής?
ταλιθά
τηλαυγῶς? (cf. δηλαυγῶς)
τρίζω
τρυμαλιά (Lk.?)
ὑπερηφανία
ὑπερπερισσῶς
ὑπολήνιον
χαλκίον

TOTAL 102 (1 fr. Sept., 32 ?)

3. To Luke.

N. B. Words found only in the Gospel are followed by a G.; those found only in the Acts, by an A.; those undesignated are common to both.

ἀγαθουργέω A.?
ἀγκάλη G.
ἁγνισμός A.
ἄγνωστος A.
ἀγοραῖος A.
ἄγρα G.
ἀγράμματος A.
ἀγραυλέω G.
ἀγωνία G.?
ἀηδία G.?
'Αθηναῖος A.
ἀθροίζω G.?
αἶνος G. (Mt. fr. Sept.)
αἰσθάνομαι G.
αἴτιον(τό)
αἰτίωμα (-αμα) A.
αἰχμάλωτος G. fr. Sept.
ἀκατάκριτος A.
ἀκρίβεια A.
ἀκριβής G.
ἀκροατήριον A.
ἀκωλύτως A.
'Αλεξανδρεύς A.
'Αλεξανδρῖνος (or -νός) A.
ἀλίσγημα A.
ἀλλογενής G.
ἀλλόφυλος A.
ἀμάρτυρος A.
ἀμπελουργός G.
ἀμύνω A.
ἀμφιά(or -έ-)ζω G.?
ἀναβαθμός A.
ἀναβάλλω A.

ἀνάβλεψις G. fr. Sept.
ἀναβολή A.
ἀναγνωρίζω A.? fr. Sept.
ἀναδείκνυμι
ἀνάδειξις G.
ἀναδίδωμι A.
ἀναζητέω
ἀναθέματι ἀναθεματίζειν A.
ἀνάθημα G.?
ἀναίδεια G.
ἀναίρεσις A.
ἀνακαθίζω A. (G.?)
ἀνάκρισις A.
ἀνάλη(μ)ψις G.
ἀναντίρρητος A.
ἀναντιρρήτως A.
ἀναπείθω A.
ἀνάπειρος }
ἀνάπηρος } G.
ἀναπτύσσω G.?
ἀνασκευάζω A.
ἀνασπάω
ἀνατάσσομαι G.
ἀνατρέφω A. (G.?)
ἀναφαίνω
ἀναφωνέω G.
ἀνάψυξις A.
ἀνέκλειπτος G.
ἀνένδεκτος G.
ἀνετάζω A.
ἀνεύθετος A.
ἀνευρίσκω
ἀνθομολογέομαι G.
ἀνθυπατεύω A.?
ἀνθύπατος A.
ἀνοικοδομέω A. fr. Sept.
ἀντεῖπον
ἀντιβάλλω G.
ἀντικαλέω G.
ἀντικρύ etc. A.
ἀντιπαρέρχομαι G.
ἀντιπέρα(-ν) }
ἀντίπερα } G.
ἀντιπίπτω A.
ἀντοφθαλμέω A.
ἀνωτερικός A.
(ἀξιόω w. inf.)
ἀπαιτέω G.
ἀπαρτισμός G.
ἀπασπάζομαι A.?
ἄπειμι abeo A.
ἀπελαύνω A.
ἀπελεγμός A.
ἀπ(or αφ-)ελπίζω G.
ἀπερίτμητος A. fr. Sept.
ἀπογραφή
ἀποδεκατεύω G.?
ἀποδέχομαι
ἀποθλίβω G.
ἀποκατάστασις A.

ἀποκλείω G.
ἀπολείχω G.?
ἀπομάσσω G.
ἀποπίπτω A.
ἀποπλέω A.
ἀποπλύνω G.?
ἀποπνίγω G. (Mt. ?)
ἀπορία G.
ἀπορρίπτω A.
ἀποσκευάζω A.?
ἀποστοματίζω G.
ἀποτινάσσω
ἀποφθέγγομαι A.
ἀποφορτίζομαι A.
ἀποψύχω G.
ἆράγε (ἆρά γε) A.
ἀργυροκόπος A.
Ἄραψ A.
Ἄρειος πάγος A.
Ἀρεοπαγίτης A.
(ἀρήν) ἀρνός G.
ἄροτρον G.
ἀρτέμων A.
ἀρχιερατικός A.
ἀρχιτελώνης G.
ἄσημος A.
Ἀσιανός A.
Ἀσιάρχης A.
ἀσιτία A.
ἄσιτος A.
ἀσκέω A.
ἀσμένως A.
ἆσσον A.?
ἀστράπτω G.
ἀσύμφωνος A.
ἀσώτως A.
ἄτεκνος G.
ἄτερ G.
αὐγή A.
Αὔγουστος G.
αὐστηρός G.
αὐτόπτης G.
αὐτόχειρ A.
ἄφαντος G.
ἀφελότης A.
ἀφελπίζω (cf. ἀπελπίζω) G.
ἄφιξις A.
ἄφνω A.
ἀφρός G.
ἀφυπνόω.
ἀχλύς A.
βαθέως G.?
βαθύνω G.
βαλ(λ)άντιον G.
βάπτω G. (Jn.? Rev.?)
βαρύνω G.?
τὰ βασίλεια G.
βάσις A.
βάτος (Heb. *Bath*) G.
βελόνη G.?

Βεροιαῖος A.
βία A.
βίαιος A.
βίωσις A.
βολή G.
βολίζω A.
βουνός G. fr. Sept.
βραδυπλοέω A.
βρύχω A.
βρώσιμος G.
βυρσεύς A.
βωμός A.
γάζα A.
Γαλατικός A.
γελάω G.
γερουσία A.
γῆρας G.
γλεῦκος A.
γνώστης A.
δακτύλιος G.
δαν(ε)ιστής G.
δαπάνη G.
δεισιδαιμονία A.
δεισιδαίμων A.
δεκαδύο A.?
δεκαοκτώ G.?
δεξιοβόλος? }
δεξιολάβος } A.
Δερβαῖος A.
δεσμέω A.?
δεσμοφύλαξ A.
δεσμώτης A.
δευτεραῖος A.
δευτερόπρωτος G.?
δημηγορέω A.
δῆμος A.
δημόσιος A.
διαβάλλω G.
διαγγέλλω (Ro. fr. Sept.)
διαγινώσκω A.
διαγνωρίζω G.?
διάγνωσις A.
διαγογγύζω G.
διαγρηγορέω G.
διαδέχομαι A.
διάδοχος A.
διαδίδωμι (Jn.? Rev.?)
διακαθαίρω G.?
διακατελέγχομαι A.
διακούω A.
διαλαλέω G.
διαλείπω G.
διάλεκτος A.
διαλιμπάνω A.?
διαλύω A.
διαμάχομαι A.
διαμερισμός G.
διανέμω G.
διανεύω G.
διανόημα G.

διανυκτερεύω G.
διανύω A.
διαπλέω A.
διαπονέω A.
διαπορέω
διαπραγματεύομαι G.
διαπρίω A.
διασείω G.
διασπείρω A.
διάστημα A.
διαταράσσω G. fr. Sept.
διατελέω A.
διατηρέω
διαφεύγω A.
διαφθορά A.
διαφυλάσσω G. fr. Sept.
διαχειρίζω A.
διαχλευάζω A.?
διαχωρίζω G.
διενθυμέομαι A.?
διεξέρχομαι A.?
διερωτάω A.
διετία A.
διήγησις G.
διθάλασσος A.
διΐστημι
διϊσχυρίζομαι
δικάζω G.?
δικαστής A. (G.?)
διοδεύω
διοπετής A.
διόρθωμα A.?
Διόσκουροι A.
δούλη
δοχή G.
δραχμή G.
δυσβάστακτος G. (Mt.?)
δυσεντερία (-τέριον) A.
δωδεκάφυλον A.
ἔα G. (Mk.?)
ἑβδομήκοντα
ἑβδομηκοντάεξ A.?
ἑβδομηκονταπέντε A.?
Ἑβραϊκός G.?
ἐγκάθετος G.
ἔγκλημα G.
ἔγ(or ἐν-)κυος G.
ἐδαφίζω G. fr. Sept.
ἔδαφος A.
ἐθίζω G.
εἰσκαλέομαι A.
εἰσπηδάω A.
εἰστρέχω A.
ἑκατοντάρχης A. G.? (Mt.?)
ἐκβολή A.
ἐκγαμίσκω G.?
ἐκδιηγέομαι A.
ἔκδοτος A.
ἐκεῖσε A.
ἔκθαμβος A.

ἔκθετος A.
ἐκκολυμβάω A.
ἐκκομίζω G.
ἐκκρέμαμαι (or ἐκκρέμομαι) G.
ἐκλαλέω A.
ἐκλείπω G.? (Heb. fr. Sept.)
ἐκμυκτηρίζω G.
ἐκπέμπω A.
ἐκπηδάω A.?
ἐκπλέω A.
ἐκπληρόω A.
ἐκπλήρωσις A.
ἐκσώζω A.?
ἐκταράσσω A.
ἐκτελέω G.
ἐκτένεια A.
ἐκτενέστερον G.?
ἐκτίθημι A.
ἐκχωρέω A.
ἐκψύχω A.
ἐλαιών A. (G.?)
Ἐλαμ(ε)ίτης A.
ἔλευσις A.
ἑλκόω G.
Ἑλληνιστής A.
ἐμβάλλω G.
ἐμβιβάζω A.
ἐμμαίνομαι A.
ἐμπιπράω A.?
ἐμ(or ἐν-)πνέω A.
ἐμφανής A. (Ro. fr. Sept.)
ἔναντι ?
ἐνδεής A.
ἐνδέχεται (impers.) G.
ἐνδιδύσκω G. (Mk.?)
ἐνέδρα ?
ἐνεδρεύω A. (G.?)
ἔνεδρον A.?
ἐνισχύω A. (G.?)
ἔνκυος cf. ἔγκυος
ἐννέα G.
ἐν(ν)εός A.
ἐννεύω G.
(τὰ) ἐνόντα A.
ἐνοχλέω G.? (Heb. fr. Sept.)
ἐπινέω cf. ἐμπνέω
ἐντόπιος A.
ἔντρομος A. (Heb.?)
ἐνύπνιον A. fr. Sept.
ἐνωτίζομαι A.
ἐξαιτέω G.
ἐξάλλομαι A.
ἐξαστράπτω G.
ἔξειμι A.
ἑξῆς
ἐξολοθρεύω }
ἐξολεθρεύω } A.
ἐξορκιστής A.
ἐξοχή A.
ἔξυπνος A.

ὄρθριος G.?
ὄρνιξ G.?
ὀροθεσία A.
οὐρανόθεν A.
οὐσία G.
ὀφρύς G.
ὀχλέω A. (G.?)
ὀχλοποιέω A.
παθητός A.
παῖς, ἡ, G.
παμπληθεί G.
πανδοχεῖον (or -κίον) G.
πανδοχεύς (or -κεύς) G.
πανοικί (or -κεί) A.
πανταχῇ or πανταχῆ A.?
πάτη (or -τη) A.
παραβάλλω A. (Mk.?)
παραβιάζομαι
παράδοξος G.
παραθεωρέω A.
παραινέω A.
παρακαθέζομαι G.?
παρακαθίζω G.?
παρακαλύπτω G.
παραλέγομαι A.
παράλιος G.
παρανομέω A.
παραπλέω A.
παράσημος A.
παρατείνω A.
παρατήρησις G.
παρατυγχάνω A.
παραχειμασία A.
παρεμβάλλω A.?
παρενοχλέω A.
παρθενία G.
παροίχομαι A.
παροτρύνω A.
πατρῷος A.
πεδινός G.
πεζεύω A.
πειράω A. (Heb.?)
πενιχρός G.
πεντεκαιδέκατος G.
περαιτέρω A.?
περιάπτω G.?
περιαστράπτω A.
περικαθίζω G.?
περικρατής A.
περικρύπτω G.
περικυκλόω G.
περιλάμπω
περιμένω A.
πέριξ A.
περιοικέω G.
περίοικος G.
περιοχή A.
περιρ(ρ)ήγνυμι A.
περισπάω G.
περιτρέπω A.

πήγανον G.
πιέζω G.
πιμπράω A.?
πινακίδιον G.?
πινακίς G.?
πλέω (Rev.?)
πλήμ(μ)υρα (or -ύρα) G.
πλόος A.
πνικτός A.
πνοή A.
πολίτης (Heb.?)
πολλαπλασίων G. (Mt.?)
πολιτάρχης A.
Ποντικός A.   [Sept.)
πόρρω G. (Mt. and Mk. fr.
πορφυρόπωλις A.
πραγματεύομαι G.
πράκτωρ G.
πρεσβεία G.
πρηνής A.
προβάλλω
προκαταγγέλλω A. (2 Co.?)
προκηρύσσω A.
προμελετάω G.
προοράω A.
προπορεύω
προσαναβαίνω G.
προσαναλίσκω G.?
προσανέχω A.?
προσαπειλέω A.
προσαχέω A.?
προσδαπανάω G.
προσδέομαι A.
προσδοκία
προσεάω A.
προσεργάζομαι G.
προσέχειν ἑαυτοῖς
προσκληρόω A.
προσκλίνω A.?
προσλαλέω A.
πρόσπεινος A.
προσπήγνυμι A.
προσποιέω G. (Jn.??)
προσρήγνυμι A. (Mt.?)
προσφάτως A.
προσψαύω A.
προσωπολή(μ)πτης A.
προτάσσω A.?
προτείνω A.
προτρέπω A.
προϋπάρχω
προφέρω G.
προχειρίζω A.
προχειροτονέω A.
πρώ (or -ῶ-, or -ῷ-) ρα A.
πρωτοστάτης A.
πρώτως A.?
πτοέω G.
πτύσσω G.
πύθων A.

πυρά A.
ῥαβδοῦχος A.
ῥαδιούργημα A.
ῥαδιουργία A.
ῥῆγμα G.
ῥήτωρ A.
Ῥωμαϊκός G.?
ῥώννυμι A.
σάλος G.
σανίς A.
σεβαστός A.
Σιδώνιος
σικάριος A.
σίκερα G.
σιμικίνθιον A.
σινιάζω G.
σιτευτός G.
σιτίον A.?
σιτομέτριον G.
σκάπτω G.
σκάφη A.
σκευή A.
σκηνοποιός A.
σκιρτάω G.
σκληροτράχηλος A.
σκῦλον (or σκύλον) G.
σκωληκόβρωτος A.
σορός A.
σπαργανόω G.
σπερμολόγος A.
στέμμα A.
στερεόω A.
στιγμή A.
στρατηγός
στρατιά (cf. 2 Co. x. 4 Tdf.)
στρατοπεδάρχης? }
στρατοπέδαρχος? } A.
στρατόπεδον G.
Στωϊκός A.
συγγένεια
συγγενίς G.?
συγκαλύπτω G.
συγκαταβαίνω A.
συγκατατίθημι G.
συγκαταψηφίζω A.
συγκινέω A.
συγκομίζω A.
συγκύπτω G.
συγκυρία G.
συγχέω A.
σύγχυσις A.
συ(ν)ζήτησις A.?
συκάμινος G.
συκομορέα
 -μωρέα } G.
 -μωραία }
συκοφαντέω A.
συλλογίζομαι G.
συμβάλλω
συμπαραγίνομαι G. (2 Tim.?)

συμπάρειμι A.
συμπεριλαμβάνω A.
συμπίνω A.
συμπίπτω G.?
συμπληρόω
συμφύω G.
συμφωνία G.
συμψηφίζω A.
συναθροίζω A. (G.?)
συνακολουθέω G. (Mk.?)
συναλίζω A.
συναλλάσσω A.?
συναρπάζω
συνδρομή A.
σύνειμι (εἰμί) A. (G.?)
σύνειμι (εἶμι) G.
συνελαύνω A.?
συνεπιτίθημι A.?
συνέπομαι A.
συνεφίστημι A.
συνθλάω G. (Mt.?)
συνθρύπτω A.
συνκατανεύω A.?
συνοδεύω A.
συνοδία G.
συνομιλέω A.
συνομορέω A.
συντόμως A. (Mk.??)
σύντροφος A.
συντυγχάνω G.
συνωμοσία A.
Σύρος G. (Mk.?)
Σύρτις (or σύρτις) A.
συσπαράσσω G. (Mk.?)
συστρέφω A. (Mt.?)
συστροφή A.
σφάγιον A. fr. Sept.
σφοδρῶς A.
σφυδρόν A.?
σφυρόν A.?
σχολή A.
τακτός A.
τανῦν (τὰ νῦν) A.
τάραχος A.
τάχιστα A.
τεκμήριον A.
τελεσφορέω G.
τεσσαρακονταετής A.
τεσσαρεσκαιδέκατος A.
τετράδιον A.
τετραπλόος G.
τετραρχέω G.   [καρδία
τίθεσθαι εἰς τὰ ὦτα or ἐν
τιμωρέω A.
τοῖχος A.
τραῦμα A.
τραυματίζω
τραχύς
τριετία A.
τρίστεγος A.

τρισχίλιοι Α.
τροποφορέω? } Α. fr. Sept.
τροφοφορέω? }
τρυγών G. fr. Sept.
τυρβάζω G.? (cf. θορυβάζω)
Τύριος Α.
τυφωνικός Α.
ὑγρός G.
ὑδρωπικός G.
ὑπερεῖδον Α.
ὑπερεκχύνω G.
ὑπερῷον Α.
ὑπηρετέω Α.
ὑποβάλλω Α.
ὑποζώννυμι Α.
ὑποκρίνομαι G.
ὑπολαμβάνω (3 Jn.?)
ὑπονοέω Α.
ὑποπλέω Α.
ὑποπνέω Α.
ὑποστρώννυμι G.
ὑποτρέχω Α.
ὑποχωρέω G.
ὑφαίνω G.?
φαντασία Α.
φάραγξ G. fr. Sept.
φάσις Α.
φάτνη G.
φιλανθρώπως Α.
φίλη (ἡ) G.
φιλονεικία G.
φιλόσοφος Α.
φιλοφρόνως Α.
φόβηθρον(or -τρον) G.
φόρτος Α.?
φρονίμως G.
φρυάσσω Α. fr. Sept.
φρύγανον Α.
φυλακίζω Α.
φύλαξ Α.
Χαλδαῖος Α.
χάραξ G.
χάσμα G.
χειμάζω Α.
χειραγωγέω Α.
χειραγωγός Α.
χλευάζω Α.
χορός G.
χόρτασμα Α.
χρεωφειλέτης(or χρεοφιλ.) G.
χρονοτριβέω Α.
χρώς Α.
χῶρος Α.
ψώχω G.
ὠνέομαι Α.
ὠόν G.

Gospel 312 (11 fr. Sept., 52?)
Acts 478 (15 fr. Sept., 49?)
Both 61.
TOTAL 851 (26 fr. Sept., 101?)

4. To all three Synoptists.

ἀγανακτέω
ἀγέλη
ἅλα?
ἀλάβαστρον
ἁλιεύς
ἀμὴν λέγω ὑμῖν
ἀναβοάω?
ἀνακλίνω
ἀνεκτός
ἀπαίρω
ἀποδημέω
ἀποκεφαλίζω
ἀποκυλίω
οἱ ἄρτοι τῆς προθέσεως
ἄσβεστος
ἀσκός
βαπτιστής
Βεελζεβούλ (-βούβ)
γαλήνη
γαμίσκω?
διαβλέπω?
διαλογίζομαι (Jn.?)
δυσκόλως
ἑκατονταπλασίων?
ἐκδίδωμι
ἐμπαίζω
ἐμπτύω
ἐπίβλημα
ἐπιγραφή
ἐπισυνάγω
ἐρήμωσις
εὐκοπώτερόν ἐστι
θέρος
θηλάζω
κακῶς ἔχειν
κάμηλος
καταγελάω
κράσπεδον
κρημνός
κωφός
λεγεών (-γιών)
λέπρα
λεπρός
μακρός?
μόδιος
νυμφών
οἰκοδεσπότης
ὀρχέομαι
παραλυτικός?
πενθερά
περίλυπος
πήρα   [Sept.)
(πόρρω Mt. and Mk. fr.
πίναξ
προβαίνω
πρωτοκαθεδρία
πρωτοκλισία
πύργος

ῥαφίς?
ῥήγνυμι (Gal. fr. Sept.)
σίναπι
σινδών
σκύλλα?
σπλαγχνίζομαι
τὰ σπόριμα
στάχυς
στέγη
συμπνίγω
συντηρέω
τελώνης
τελώνιον
τίλλω
τρίβος fr. Sept.
υἱὸς Δαυίδ
ὑποκριτής
φέγγος?
χοῖρος
ψευδομαρτυρέω (Ro.?)
ψιχίον

TOTAL 78 (1 fr. Sept., 10?)

5. To John.

N. B. Words peculiar to the Gospel, or to one or another of the Epistles, are so marked.

ἀγγελία 1 EP.
ἀγγέλλω G.?
ἁλιεύω G.
ἀλλαχόθεν G.
ἀλόη G.
ἁμαρτίαν ἔχειν G., 1 EP.
ἀμὴν ἀμήν G.
ἄν (ἐάν) G.? 1 EP.?
ἀναμάρτητος G. (viii. 7)
ἀνάστασις { ζωῆς / κρίσεως } G.
ἀνθρακιά G.
ἀνθρωποκτόνος G., 1 EP.
ἀντίχριστος 1 EP., 2 EP.
ἀντλέω G.
ἄντλημα G.
ἀπεκρίθη καὶ εἶπε G.
ἀπέρχομαι εἰς τὰ ὀπίσω G.
ἀποσυνάγωγος G.
ἄρ(ρ)αφος G.
ἀρχιτρίκλινος G.
ὁ ἄρχων τοῦ κόσμου(τούτου)G.
αὐτόφωρος G. (viii. 4).
βαΐον G.
βασιλίσκος G.?
βιβρώσκω G.
Γαββαθᾶ G.
γενετή G.
γεννηθῆναι ἄνωθεν G., ἐκ (τοῦ) θεοῦ G. 1 EP., ἐκ (τοῦ) πνεύματος G.

γέρων G.
γλωσσόκομον G.
δακρύω G.
δειλιάω G.
δήποτε G.? (v. 4)
διαζωννύω G.
δίδυμος G.
ἐγκαίνια G.
εἶναι ἐκ τοῦ κόσμου G., 1 EP.
εἶναι { ἐκ τῶν ἄνω / ἐκ τῶν κάτω } G.
ἐκνεύω }
ἐκνέω } G.
ἕλιγμα G.?
ἐμπόριον G.
ἐμφυσάω G.
ἐξέρχεσθαι ἐκ (ἀπὸ, παρὰ) τοῦ θεοῦ G.
ἐξυπνίζω G.
ἐπάρατος G.?
ἐπενδύτης G.
ἐπιδέχομαι 3 EP.
ἐπιχρίω G.
(ἡ) ἐσχάτη ἡμέρα G.
ζώννυμι G. (Acts?)
ἧλος G.
ἤπερ G.?
θεοσεβής G.
θήκη G.
θρέμμα G.
ἱλασμός 1 EP.
καθαίρω G. (Heb.?)
καταγράφω G.? (viii. 6).
κέδρος G.?
κειρία G.
κέρμα G.
κερματιστής G.
κηπουρός G.
κίνησις G. (v. 3)
κλῆμα G.
κοίμησις G.
κολυμβήθρα G.
κομψότερον ἔχειν G.
κρίθινος G.
λέντιον G.
λιθόστρωτος G.
λίτρα G.
λόγχη G.
μεσόω G.
Μεσσίας G.
μετρητής G.
μίγμα G.?
μονή G.
νίκη 1 EP.
νιπτήρ G.
νόσημα G.? (v. 4)
νύσσω G.
ὄζω G.
ὀθόνιον G. (Lk.?)
ὁμοῦ G. (Lk.?)

ὀνάριον G.
οὐκοῦν G.
ὀψάριον G.
παιδάριον G. (Mt.?)
πενθερός G.
περιδέω G.   [3 EP.
περιπατεῖν ἐν ἀληθείᾳ 2 EP.,
περιπατεῖν ἐν τῇ σκοτίᾳ (or
   ἐν τῷ σκότει) G., 1 EP.
περιπατεῖν ἐν τῷ φωτί 1 EP.
ποιεῖν τὴν ἀλήθειαν G., 1 EP.
πότερος G.
προβατική G.
προβάτιον G.?
προσαιτέω G. (Mk.? Lk.?)
προσκυνητής G.
προσφάγιον G.
πτέρνα G.
πτύσμα G.
ῥέω G.
Ῥωμαϊστί G.
σκέλος G.
σκηνοπηγία G.
συγχράομαι G.?
συμμαθητής G.
συνεισέρχομαι G.
τεκνίον G., 1 EP. (Mk.? Gal.?)
τεταρταῖος G.
τετράμηνος G.
τιθέναι ψυχήν G., 1 EP.
τίτλος G.
ὑδρία G.
ὑπάντησις G. (Mt.?)
ὑφαντός G.
φανός G.
φιλοπρωτεύω 3 EP.
φλυαρέω 3 EP.
φραγέλλιον G.
χαμαί G.
χάρτης 2 EP.
χείμαρρος G.
χολάω G.
χρίσμα 1 EP.
ψυχὴν τιθέναι, see τιθέναι ψ.
ψωμίον G.

Gospel 114 (12?)
Epp. 11
Gospel and Epp. 8 (1?)
TOTAL 133 (13?)

6. To Paul.

a. TO THE LONGER EPISTLES AND PHILEMON.

N. B. Words peculiar to any single Epistle are so designated by the appended abbreviation.

ἀβαρής 2 Co.
ἀγαθωσύνη
ἄγαμος 1 Co.

ἀγανάκτησις 2 Co.
ἀγενής 1 Co.
ἁγιωσύνη
ἁγνότης 2 Co.
ἁγνῶς Phil.
ἀγριέλαιος Ro.
ἀγρυπνία 2 Co.
ἀδάπανος 1 Co.
ἀδήλως 1 Co.
ἀδιαλείπτως
ἁδρότης 2 Co.
ἀθά cf. μαρὰν ἀθά
ἄθεος Eph.
ἀθυμέω Col.
αἴνιγμα 1 Co.
αἴσθησις Phil.
αἰσχρολογία Col.
αἰσχρότης Eph.
αἰτιάομαι Ro.
αἰχμαλωτεύω Eph. fr. Sept. (2 T.?)
ἀκαιρέομαι Phil.
ἀκατακάλυπτος 1 Co.
ἄκων 1 Co.
ἀλάλητος Ro.
ἀληθεύω
ἀλληγορέω Gal.
ἄλυπος Phil.
ἀμέμπτως 1 Th.
ἀμετακίνητος 1 Co.
ἀμεταμέλητος
ἀμετανόητος Ro.
ἄμετρος 2 Co.
ἀναθάλλω Phil.
ἀνακαινόω
ἀνακαλύπτω 2 Co.
ἀνακεφαλαιόω
ἀνακόπτω Gal.?
ἀναλογία Ro.
ἀναμένω 1 Th.
ἀνανεόω Eph.
ἀνάξιος 1 Co.
ἀναξίως 1 Co.
ἀναπολόγητος Ro.
ἀνδρίζω 1 Co.
ἀνεκδιήγητος 2 Co.
ἀνελεήμων Ro.
ἀνεξερεύ(or -ραύ-)νητος Ro.
ἀνεξιχνίαστος
ἀνεψιός Col.
ἀνήκω
ἄνθραξ Ro. fr. Sept.
ἀνθρωπάρεσκος
ἀνθρώπινον λέγω Ro.
ἄνοιξις Eph.
ἀνόμως Ro.
ἀνοχή Ro.
ἀνταναπληρόω Col.
ἀνταπόδοσις Col.
ἀντίλη(μ)ψις 1 Co.

ἀντιμισθία
ἀντιστρατεύομαι Ro.
ἀπαλγέω Eph.
ἀπαλλοτριόω
ἀπαρασκεύαστος 2 Co.
ἀπ(or ἀφ-)εῖδον Phil.
ἄπειμι absum
ἀπεῖπον 2 Co.
ἀπεκδύομαι Col.
ἀπέκδυσις Col.
ἀπελεύθερος 1 Co.
ἀπερισπάστως 1 Co.
ἁπλότης
ἀπόδειξις 1 Co.
ἀποκαραδοκία
ἀποκαταλλάσσω
ἀπόκριμα 2 Co.
ἀπορφανίζω 1 Th.
ἀποστυγέω Ro.
ἀποτίνω Philem.
ἀποτολμάω Ro.
ἀπορία Ro.
ἀπουσία Phil.
ἀπόχρησις Col.
ἄρα οὖν
ἀρά Ro.
ἀρραβών
ἀρεσκεία Col.
ἁρμόζω 2 Co.
ἁρπαγμός Phil.
ἄρρητος 2 Co.
ἀρχιτέκτων 1 Co.
ἀσαίνω 1 Th.?
ἀσθένημα Ro.
ἄσοφος Eph.
ἀσπίς Ro.
ἀστατέω 1 Co.
ἀσύνθετος Ro.
ἀσχημονέω 1 Co.
ἀσχήμων 1 Co.
ἀτακτέω 2 Th.
ἄτακτος 1 Th.
ἀτάκτως 2 Th.
ἄτομος 1 Co.
αἰγάζω 2 Co.?
αὐθαίρετος 2 Co.
αὐλός 1 Co.
αὔξησις
αὐτάρκης Phil.
ἀφειδία Col.
ἀφή
ἀφικνέομαι Ro.
Ἀχαϊκός 1 Co.
ἀχρεῖος Ro. fr. Sept.
ἄχρηστος Philem.
ἄψυχος 1 Co.
Βαάλ Ro. fr. Sept.
βασκαίνω Gal.
Βελίαλ or Βελίαρ 2 Co.
βέλος Eph.

βραβεῖον
βραβεύω Col.
βρόχος 1 Co.
βυθός 2 Co.
Γαλάτης Gal.
γεώργιον 1 Co.
γνησίως Phil.
γραπτός Ro.
γυμνητεύω 1 Co.
δάκνω Gal.
Δαμασκηνός 2 Co.
δειγματίζω Col. (Mt.?)
διαίρεσις 1 Co.
διαστολή
διδακτός 1 Co. (Jn. fr. Sept.)
διερμηνεία 1 Co.?
διερμηνευτής 1 Co.?
δικαιοκρισία Ro.
δικαίωσις Ro.
διόπερ 1 Co.
διχοστασία
δίψος 1 Co.
δογματίζω Col.
δοκιμή
δόλιος 2 Co.
δολιόω Ro. fr. Sept.
δολόω 2 Co.
δότης 2 Co.
δουλαγωγέω 1 Co.
δράσσομαι 1 Co.
δυναμόω Col. (Eph.? Heb.?)
δυνατέω 2 Co. (Ro.?)
δυσφημέω 1 Co.?
δυσφημία 2 Co.
δωροφορία Ro.?
ἐγγράφω 2 Co. (Lk.?)
ἐγγύτερον Ro.
ἐγκαυχάομαι 2 Th.?
ἐγκεντρίζω Ro.
ἐγκοπή (or ἐκκ-, or ἐνκ-) 1 Co.
ἐγκρατεύομαι 1 Co.
ἐγκρίνω 2 Co.
ἑδραῖος
ἐθελοθρησκεία Col.
ἐθνάρχης 2 Co.
ἐθνικῶς Gal.
εἰδωλεῖον 1 Co.
εἰκῆ, -κῇ (Mt.?)
εἴκω Gal.
εἰλικρίνεια (or -νία)
εἰρηνοποιέω Col.
εἰσδέχομαι 2 Co.
ἑκατονταέτης Ro.
ἐκδαπανάω 2 Co.
ἐκδημέω 2 Co.
ἔκδικος
ἐκδιώκω 1 Th. (Lk.?)
ἐκκαίω Ro.
ἐκκλάω Ro.
ἐκκλείω

ἐκκοπή cf. ἐγκοπή
ἐκνήφω 1 Co.
ἑκούσιος Philem.
ἐκπετάννυμι Ro. fr. Sept.
ἐκπτύω Gal.
ἐκτρέφω Eph.
ἔκτρωμα 1 Co.
ἐκφοβέω 2 Co.
ἑκών
ἐλαττονέω 2 Co. fr. Sept.
ἐλαφρία 2 Co.
ἐλαχιστότερος Eph.
ἐλλογάω or -γέω
ἐμβατεύω Col.
ἐμπεριπατέω 2 Co. fr. Sept.
ἐνάρχομαι
ἔνδειγμα 2 Th.
ἔνδειξις
ἐνδημέω 2 Co.
ἐνδοξάζω 2 Th.
ἐνέργεια
ἐνέργημα 1 Co.
ἐνκοπή cf. ἐγκοπή
ἐνορκίζω 1 Th. ?
ἑνότης Eph.
ἐντροπή 1 Co.
ἐντυπόω 2 Co.
ἐξαγοράζω
ἐξαίρω 1 Co.? and fr. Sept.
ἐξανάστασις Phil.
ἐξαπατάω (1 Tim. ?)
ἐξαπορέω 2 Co.
ἐξεγείρω
ἐξηχέω 1 Th.
ἐξισχύω Eph.
ἑορτάζω 1 Co.
ἐπακούω 2 Co. fr. Sept.
ἐπαναμιμνήσκω Ro.
ἐπείπερ Ro. ?
ἐπεκτείνω Phil.
ἐπενδύω 2 Co.
ἐπιβαρέω
ἐπιδιατάσσομαι Gal.
ἐπιδύω Eph.
ἐπιθανάτιος 1 Co.
ἐπιθυμητής 1 Co.
ἐπικαλύπτω Ro. fr. Sept.
ἐπικατάρατος Gal. fr. Sept.
  (Jn. ?)
ἐπιπόθησις 2 Co.
ἐπιπόθητος Phil.
ἐπιποθία Ro.
ἐπισκηνόω 2 Co.
ἐπισπάω 1 Co.
ἐπιτιμία 2 Co.
ἐπιφαύσκω Eph.
ἐπιχορηγία
ἐπονομάζω Ro.
ἑπτακισχίλιοι Ro.
ἐρεθίζω 2 Co. (Col.?)

ἑρμηνεία 1 Co.
ἑρμηνευτής 1 Co.?
τί ἐροῦμεν Ro.
ἑτερόγλωσσος 1 Co.
ἑτεροζυγέω 2 Co.
ἑτέρως Phil.
ἑτοιμασία Eph.
εὔνοια Eph. (1 Co. ?)
εὐπάρεδρος ⎫ 1 Co.
εὐπρόσεδρος ⎭
εὐπροσωπέω Gal.
εὔσημος 1 Co.
εὐσχημόνως
εὐσχημοσύνη 1 Co.
εὐτραπελία Eph.
εὐφημία 2 Co.
εὔφημος Phil.
εὐχάριστος Col.
εὐψυχέω Phil.
εὐωδία
ἐφευρετής Ro.
ἐφικνέομαι 2 Co.
ὁ ἠγαπημένος (of Christ)
  Eph.
ἢ ἀγνοεῖτε Ro.
ἥδιστα 2 Co.
ἦθος 1 Co. fr. Menander
ἡνίκα 2 Co.
ἤτοι Ro.
ἥττημα
ἥττων or ἥσσων
ἠχέω 1 Co. (Lk.?)
θειότης Ro.
θέλω ἐν Col.
θεοδίδακτος 1 Th.
θεοστυγής Ro.
θεότης Col.
θήρα Ro.
θηριομαχέω 1 Co.
θνητός
θριαμβεύω
θυρεός Eph.
ἴαμα 1 Co.
ἱερόθυτος 1 Co.?
ἱεροσυλέω Ro.
ἱερουργέω
ἱκανότης 2 Co.
ἱκανόω
ἱλαρός 2 Co.
ἱλαρότης Ro.
ἱμείρομαι (? cf. ὁμείρομαι)
ἵνα ('where') ?
Ἰουδαΐζω Gal.
Ἰουδαϊκῶς Gal.
Ἰουδαϊσμός Gal.
ἰσότης
ἰσόψυχος Phil.
ἱστορέω Gal.
καθαίρεσις 2 Co.
καθό (1 Pet.?)

καθοράω Ro.
καινότης Ro.
κακοήθεια Ro.
καλάμη 1 Co.
καλλιέλαιος Ro.
καλοποιέω 2 Th.
κάλυμμα 2 Co.
κάμπτω
κανών
καπηλεύω 2 Co.
καταβαρέω 2 Co.
καταβραβεύω Col.
καταδουλόω
κατακαλύπτω 1 Co.
κατάκριμα Ro.
κατάκρισις 2 Co.
κατάλαλος Ro.
κατάλειμμα Ro.?
καταλλαγή
καταλλάσσω
καταναρκάω 2 Co.
κατάνυξις Ro. fr. Sept.
κατάρτισις 2 Co.
καταρτισμός Eph.
κατασκοπέω Gal.
καταστρώννυμι 1 Co.
κατατομή Phil.
καταυγάζω 2 Co.?
καταχθόνιος Phil.
καταχράομαι 1 Co.
κατοπτρίζομαι 2 Co.
κατώτερος Eph.
κέλευσμα 1 Th.
κενοδοξία Phil.
κενόδοξος Gal.
κενόω
κημόω 1 Co. ʼ
κίνδυνος
κληρόω Eph.
κλίμα
κλυδωνίζομαι Eph.
κολακεία 1 Th.
κομάω 1 Co.
κόμη 1 Co.
κοσμοκράτωρ Eph.
κρέας
κρυφῇ, -φῆ Eph.
κυβεία Eph.
κυβέρνησις 1 Co.
κύμβαλον 1 Co.
κυριακὸν δεῖπνον 1 Co.
κυρόω
Λαοδικεύς Col. (Rev. ?)
λάρυγξ Ro.
λεῖμμα Ro.
λῆψις Phil.
λογία 1 Co.
λογισμός
λοίδορος 1 Co.
λύσις 1 Co.

μακαρισμός
μάκελλον 1 Co.
μακροχρόνιος Eph.
μαρὰν ἀθά (μαραναθά) 1 Co.
ματαιόω Ro.
μεγάλως Phil.
μέγεθος Eph.
μεθοδεία Eph.
μέθυσος 1 Co.
μεσότοιχον Eph.
μετακινέω Col.
μεταλλάσσω Ro.
μετασχηματίζω
μετοχή 2 Co.
μήτιγε (μήτι γε, μή τι γε) 1
  Co.
μολυσμός 2 Co.
μομφή Col.
μορφόω Gal.
μόχθος
μυέω Phil.
μυκτηρίζω Gal.
μωμάομαι 2 Co.
μωρία 1 Co.
μωρολογία Eph.
νέκρωσις
νή 1 Co.
νηπιάζω 1 Co.
νόημα
νομοθεσία Ro.
νουμηνία Col.
νυχθήμερον 2 Co.
νῶτος Ro. fr. Sept.
οἰκτείρω Ro. fr. Sept.
ὀκταήμερος Phil.
ὀλέθριος 2 Th.?
ὀλιγόψυχος 1 Th.
ὀλοθρευτής 1 Co.
ὀλοτελής 1 Th.
ὁμείρομαι 1 Th.? (cf. ἱμείρ.)
ὁμιλία 1 Co. fr. Menander
ὀνίνημι Philem.
ὁρατός Col.
ὄρεξις Ro.
ὀρθοποδέω Gal.
ὅσγε Ro.
ὁσίως 1 Th.
ὄσφρησις 1 Co.
ὀφθαλμοδουλεία
ὀχύρωμα 2 Co.
πάθος
παιδαγωγός
παίζω 1 Co. fr. Sept.
παλαιότης Ro.
πάλη Eph.
πανοῦργος 2 Co.
παραβολεύομαι ? ⎫ Phil.
παραβουλεύομαι? ⎭
παραζηλόω
παράκειμαι Ro.

45

παραμυθία 1 Co.
παραμύθιον Phil.
παραπλήσιον Phil.
παραυτίκα 2 Co.
παραφρονέω 2 Co.
παρεδρεύω (cf. προσεδρ.) 1 Co.?
παρείσακτος Gal.
παρεισέρχομαι
πάρεσις Ro.
παρηγορία Col.
πάροδος 1 Co.
παροργίζω
παροργισμός Eph.
πατρικός Gal.
πειθός 1 Co.
(Πειθώ 1 Co.?)
πεισμονή Gal.
πένης 2 Co. fr. Sept.
πεντάκις 2 Co.
πεποίθησις
περιεργάζομαι 2 Th.
περικάθαρμα 1 Co.
περικεφαλαία 1 Th. (Eph. fr. Sept.)
περιλείπω 1 Th.
περίψημα 1 Co.
περπερεύομαι 1 Co.
πέρυσι 2 Co.
πιθα·ολογία Col.
πιότης Ro.
πλάσμα Ro.
τὸ πλεῖστον (adv.) 1 Co.
πλεονεκτέω
πλεονέκτης
πλησμονή Col.
πλουτίζω
ποίημα
πολίτευμα Phil.
πολυποίκιλος Eph.
πρεσβεύω
προαιρέω 2 Co.
προαιτιάομαι Ro.
προακούω Col.
προαμαρτάνω 2 Co.
προγίνομαι Ro.
προδίδωμι Ro.
προελπίζω Eph.
προενάρχομαι 2 Co.
προεπαγγέλλω Ro. (2 Co.?)
προετοιμάζω
προευαγγελίζομαι Gal.
προέχω Ro.
προηγέομαι Ro.
προθέσμιος Gal.
προκαλέω Gal.
προκαταρτίζω 2 Co.
προκυρόω Gal.
προλέγω
προπάσχω 1 Th.

προπάτωρ Ro.?
προσαγωγή
προσαναπληρόω 2 Co.
προσανατίθημι Gal.
προσεδρεύω (cf. παρεδρ.) 1 Co.?
προσηλόω Col.
προκαρτέρησις Eph.
προσκοπή 2 Co.
πρόσλη(μ)ψις Ro.
προσοφείλω Philem.
προστάτις Ro.
προσφιλής Phil.
προτίθημι
πρωτεύω Col.
πτηνά (τά) 1 Co.
πτύρω Phil.
πτωχεύω 2 Co.
πυκτεύω 1 Co.
ῥιζόω
ῥιπή ? } 1 Co.
ῥοπή ? }
ῥυτίς Eph.
σαίνεσθαι 1 Th.?
σαργάνη 2 Co.
σατᾶν (not -νᾶς) 2 Co.?
σεβάζομαι Ro.
σημειόω 2 Th.
σκῆνος 2 Co.
σκληρότης Ro.
σκόλοψ 2 Co.
σκοπός Phil.
σκύβαλον Phil.
Σκύθης Col.
σπουδαῖος 2 Co. (2 T.?)
στέγω
στέλλω
στενοχωρέω 2 Co.
στενοχωρία
στερέωμα Col.
στίγμα Gal.
συγγνώμη 1 Co.
συγκαθίζω Eph. (Lk.?)
συγκάμπτω Ro. fr. Sept.
συγκατάθεσις 2 Co.
συγκρίνω
συζητητής 1 Co.
σύζυγος Phil.
συζωοποιέω
συλαγωγέω Col.
συλάω 2 Co.
σύμβουλος Ro. fr. Sept.
συμμαρτυρέω Ro. (Rev.?)
συμμερίζω 1 Co.
συμμέτοχος Eph.
συμμιμητής Phil.
συμμορφίζω Phil.?
σύμμορφος
συμμορφόω Phil.?
συμπαρακαλέω Ro.

συμπαραμένω Phil.?
συμπάσχω
συμπέμπω 2 Co.
συμπολίτης Eph.
σύμφημι Ro.
σύμφορον, τό. 1 Co.?
συμφυλέτης 1 Th.
σύμφυτος Ro.
συμφώνησις 2 Co.
σύμφωνος 1 Co.
σύμψυχος Phil.
συναγωνίζομαι Ro.
συναθλέω Phil.
συναιχμάλωτος
συναναμίγνυμι
συναναπαύομαι Ro.?
συναποστέλλω 2 Co.
συναρμολογέω Eph.
συνδοξάζω Ro.
συνεγείρω
συνήδομαι Ro.
συνηλικιώτης Gal.
συνθάπτω
συνοικοδομέω Eph.
συντέμνω Ro. fr. Sept.
σύντριμμα Ro. fr. Sept.
συνυποκρίνομαι Gal.
συνυπουργέω 2 Co.
συνωδίνω Ro.
σύσσωμος Eph.
συστατικός 2 Co.
συστενάζω Ro.
συστοιχέω Gal.
συστρατιώτης
σχῆμα
σωματικῶς Col.
τάγμα 1 Co.
τάχα
τίνω 2 Th.
τολμηρότερον or -τέρως Ro.
τράχηλον ὑποτιθέναι Ro.
τροφός 1 Th.
τυπικῶς 1 Co.?
εἰ τύχοι, τυχόν, 1 Co.
υἱοθεσία
ὕμνος
ὕπα·δρος Ro.
ὑπεραίρω
ὑπέρακμος 1 Co.
ὑπεραυξάνω 2 Th.
ὑπερβαίνω 1 Th.
ὑπερβαλλόντως 2 Co.
ὑπερβάλλω
ὑπερβολή
ὑπερεγώ 2 Co.?
ὑπερέκεινα 2 Co.
ὑπερεκπερισσοῦ
ὑπερεκπερισσῶς 1 Th.?
ὑπερεκτείνω 2 Co.
ὑπερεντυγχάνω Ro.

ὑπερλίαν 2 Co.
ὑπερνικάω Ro.
ὑπερπερισσεύω
ὑπερυψόω Phil.
ὑπερφρονέω Ro.
ὑπόδικος Ro.
ὑπόλειμμα Ro.?
ὑπολείπω Ro.
ὑποπιάζω 1 Co.?
ὕψωμα
φανέρωσις
φειδομένως 2 Co.
φθόγγος 1 Co. (Ro. fr. Sept.)
φθονέω Gal.
Φιλιππήσιος Phil.
φιλόνεικος 1 Co.
φιλοσοφία Col.
φιλόστοργος Ro.
φιλοτιμέομαι
φρεναπατάω Gal.
φρήν 1 Co.
φρόνημα Ro.
φύραμα
φυσιόω
φυσίωσις 2 Co.
φωτισμός 2 Co.
χειρόγραφον Col.
χοϊκός 1 Co.
χρηματισμός Ro.
χρῆσις Ro.
χρηστεύομαι 1 Co.
χρηστολογία Ro.
ψευδάδελφος
ψευδαπόστολος 2 Co.
ψεῦσμα Ro.
ψιθυρισμός 2 Co.
ψιθυριστής Ro.
ψωμίζω
ὥσπερεί 1 Co.

Ro. 113 (13 fr. Sept., 6?)
1 Co. 110 (2 fr. Sept., 12?)
2 Co. 99 (4 fr. Sept., 4?)
Gal. 34 (1 fr. Sept., 1?)
Eph. 43 (1 fr. Sept.)
Phil. 41 (4?)
Col. 38
1 Thess. 23 (5?)
2 Thess. 11 (2?)
Philem. 5.
Common to two or more Epistles 110.
TOTAL 627 (21 fr. Sept., 34?)

b. TO THE PASTORAL EPISTLES.

N. B. Words peculiar to some single Epistle of the three are so designated.

ἀγαθοεργέω 1 T.
ἁγνεία 1 T.

ἀγωγή 2 T.
ἀδηλότης 1 T.
ἀδιαφθορία Tit.? (cf. ἀφθορία)
ἀθλέω 2 T.
αἰδώς 1 T. (Heb.?)
αἱρετικός Tit.
αἰσχροκερδής
αἰχμαλωτεύω 2 T.? (Eph. fr. Sept.)
ἀκαίρως 2 T.
ἀκατάγνωστος Tit
ἀκρατής 2 T.
ἄλλως 1 T.
ἄμαχος
ἀμοιβή 1 T.
ἀναζωπυρέω 2 T.
ἀνάλυσις 2 T.
ἀνανήφω 2 T.
ἀνατρέπω
ἀναψύχω 2 T.
ἀνδραποδιστής 1 T.
ἀνδρόφονος 1 T.
ἀνεξίκακος 2 T.
ἀνεπαίσχυντος 2 T.
ἀνεπίληπτος 1 T.
ἀνήμερος 2 T.
ἀνόσιος
ἀντιδιατίθημι 2 T.
ἀντίθεσις 1 T.
ἀντίλυτρον 1 T.
ἀπαίδευτος 2 T.
ἀπέραντος 1 T.
ἀπόβλητος 1 T.
ἀπόδεκτος 1 T.
ἀποδοχή 1 T.
ἀποθησαυρίζω 1 T.
ἀποτρέπω 2 T.
ἀπρόσιτος 1 T.
ἄρτιος 2 T.
ἄσπονδος 2 T. (Ro.?)
ἀστοχέω
αὐθεντέω 1 T.
αὐτοκατάκριτος Tit.
ἀφθορία Tit.? (cf. ἀδιαφθορία)
ἀφιλάγαθος 2 T.
ἀψευδής Tit.
βαθμός 1 T.
βασιλεὺς τῶν αἰώνων 1 T.
βδελυκτός Tit.
βελτίων 2 T.
βλαβερός 1 T.
γάγγραινα 2 T.
γενεαλογία
γόης 2 T.
(τὰ) ἱερὰ γράμματα 2 T.
γραώδης 1 T.
γυμνασία 1 T.
γυναικάριον 2 T.

δειλία 2 T.
διαβεβαιόομαι
διάβολος (as adj.)
διάγω
διαπαρατριβή 1 T.? (cf. παραδιατριβή)
διατροφή 1 T.
διδακτικός
δίλογος 1 T.
διώκτης 1 T.
ἐγκρατής Tit.
ἑδραίωμα 1 T.
ἔκγονα (τά) 1 T.
ἔκδηλος 2 T.
ἐκζήτησις 1 T.?
ἐκλεκτοὶ ἄγγελοι 1 T.
ἐκστρέφω Tit.
ἔλαττον (adv.) 1 T.
ἐλεγμός 2 T.?
ἡ μακαρία ἐλπίς Tit.
ἐνδύνω intrans. 2 T.
ἔντευξις 1 T.
ἐντρέφω 1 T.
ἐπανόρθωσις 2 T.
ἐπαρκέω 1 T.
ἐπιδιορθόω Tit.
ἐπίορκος 1 T.
ἐπιπλήσσω 1 T.
ἐπιστομίζω Tit.
ἐπισωρεύω 2 T.
ἑτεροδιδασκαλέω 1 T.
εὐμετάδοτος 1 T.
εὐσεβῶς
ἤρεμος 1 T.
θεόπνευστος 2 T.
θεοσέβεια 1 T.
ἱεροπρεπής Tit.
Ἰουδαϊκός Tit.
καλοδιδάσκαλος Tit.
καταλέγω 1 T.
κατάστημα Tit.
καταστολή 1 T.
καταστρηνιάω 1 T.
καταστροφή 2 T. (2 Pet.?)
καταφθείρω 2 T. (2 Pet.?)
κατηγορία (Lk. and Jn.?)
καυστηριάζω? }
καυτηριάζω ? } 1 T.
κενοφωνία
κνήθω 2 T.
κοινωνικός 1 T.
κόσμιος 1 T.
κοσμίως 1 T.?
λογομαχέω 2 T.
λογομαχία 1 T.
λόγος ὑγιής Tit.
μάμμη
ματαιολογία 1 T.
ματαιολόγος Tit. [Mk.?]
μελετάω 1 T. (Acts fr. Sept.,

μεμβράνα 2 T.
μετάλη(μ)ψις 1 T.
μηδέποτε 2 T.
μητραλῴας? }
μητρολῴας? } 1 T.
μητρόπολις 1 T.
μονόω 1 T.
νεόφυτος 1 T.
νεωτερικός 2 T.
νηφάλεος
νομίμως
νοσέω 1 T.
ξενοδοχέω 1 T.
οἰκοδεσποτέω 1 T.
οἰκοδομία 1 T.?
οἰκουργός? }
οἰκουρός? } Tit.
ἡ καλὴ ὁμολογία 1 T.
ὁμολογουμένως 1 T.
ὀργίλος Tit.
ὀρθοτομέω 2 T.
παραδιατριβή 1 T.? (cf. διαπαρατριβή)
παραθήκη 2 T. (1 T.?)
παρακαταθήκη 2 T. (1 T.?)
πάροινος
πατραλῴας? }
πατρολῴας? } 1 T.
περίστασθαι (" to avoid ")
περιούσιος Tit.
περιπείρω 1 T.
περιφρονέω Tit.
πιστὸς ὁ λόγος (cf. Rev. xxi. 5 etc.)
πιστόω 2 T.
πλέγμα 1 T.
πλήκτης
πορισμός 1 T.
πραγματεία 2 T.
πραϋπάθεια (-θία) 1 T.?
πρεσβῦτις Tit.
πρόγονος
πρόκριμα 1 T.
πρόσκλησις? }
πρόσκλισις? } 1 T.
προφήτης (of a poet) Tit.
ῥητῶς 1 T.
σεμνότης
σκέπασμα 1 T.
στεφανόω 2 T. (Heb. fr. Sept.)
στόμαχος 1 T.
στρατολογέω 2 T.
στυγητός Tit.
συγκακοπαθέω 2 T.
σώζω εἰς τὴν βασιλείαν κτλ. 2 T.
σωτήριος (as adj.) Tit.
σωφρονίζω Tit.
σωφρονισμός 2 T.

σωφρόνως Tit.
σώφρων
τεκνογονέω
τεκνογονία 1 T.
τεκνοτροφέω 1 T.
τυφόω
ὑγιαίνω metaph. (τῇ ἀγάπῃ, πίστει, ὑπομονῇ, etc.)
ὑδροποτέω 1 T.
ὑπερπλεονάζω 1 T.
ὑπόνοια 1 T.
ὑποτύπωσις
φαιλόνης? }
φελόνης? } 2 T. (cf. III. 1)
φιλάγαθος Tit.
φίλανδρος Tit.
φιλαργυρία 1 T.
φίλαυτος 2 T.
φιλήδονος 2 T.
φιλόθεος 2 T.
φιλότεκνος Tit.
φλύαρος 1 T.
φρεναπάτης Tit.
φροντίζω Tit.
χαλκεύς 2 T.
χάρις, ἔλεος, εἰρήνη ἀπὸ θ. (as a salutation)
χρήσιμος 2 T.
ψευδολόγος 1 T.
ψευδώνυμος 1 T.
ὠφέλιμος
1 Tim. 82 (6?)
2 Tim. 53 (2?)
Tit. 33 (2?)
TOTAL 168 (10?)

c. BOTH TO THE PASTORAL AND THE OTHER PAULINE EPISTLES.

ἀδιάλειπτος
ἀθανασία
αἰσχρός
αἰχμαλωτεύω?
ἁλαζών
ἀλοάω
ἀνακαίνωσις
ἀνέγκλητος
ἀποτόμως
ἀρσενοκοίτης
ἄσπονδος?
ἄστοργος
ἀτιμία
αὐτάρκεια
ἀφθαρσία
ἀφορμή
γνήσιος
ἐκκαθαίρω
ἐνοικέω
ἐξαπατάω?

ἐπιταγή
ἐπιφάνεια
ἔρις
εὔχρηστος
ἤπιος?
ἱερός (Mk. ?)
κέρδος
λουτρόν
μνεία
μόρφωσις
ναυαγέω
νουθεσία
ὀδύνη
οἰκεῖος
οἰκέω
ὄλεθρος
ὀστράκιν·
πλάσσω
προΐστημι
προκοπή
προνοέω
σεμνός
σπένδω
στρατεία?
συζάω
συμβασιλεύω
σωρεύω
ὑβριστής
ὑπεροχή
ὑποτονή
ὑποτίθημι
ὑψηλοφρονέω?
χρηστότης

TOTAL 53 (6 ?)

7. To the Epistle to the Hebrews.

ἀγενεαλόγητος
ἁγιότης (2 Co. ?)
ἀγνόημα
ἀθέτησις
ἄθλησις
αἴγειος
αἱματεκχυσία
αἴνεσις
αἰσθητήριον
αἴτιος (ὁ)
ἀκατάλυτος
ἀκλινής
ἀκροθίνιον
ἀλυσιτελής
ἀμετάθετος
ἀμήτωρ
ἀνακαινίζω
ἀναλογίζομαι
ἀναρίθμητος
ἀ·ασταυρόω
ἀνταγωνίζομαι

ἀντικαθίστημι
ἀπαράβατος
ἀπάτωρ
ἀπαύγασμα
ἄπειρος
ἀποβλέπω
ἀπόστολος of Christ
ἁρμός
ἀφανής
ἀφανισμός
ἀφομοιόω
ἀφοράω
βοηθός fr. Sept.
βολίς? fr. Sept.
βοτάνη
γενεαλογέω
γεωργέω
γνόφος
δάμαλις
δεκάτη
δεκατόω
δέος?
δέρμα
δημιουργός
δήπου
διάταγμα?
διαφορώτερος
διηνεκής
διϊκνέομαι
διόρθωσις
δοκιμασία?
δυσερμήνευτος
ἐάνπερ
(ἡ) ἑβδόμη
ἔγγυος
ἐγκαινίζω
εἰ μήν?
ἐκβαίνω?
ἐκδοχή
ἐκλανθάνω
ἔκτρομος?
ἔλεγχος (2 Tim. ?)
ἐμπαιγμός
ἐνυβρίζω
ἕξις
ἐπεισαγωγή
ἐπιλείπω
ἐπισκοπέω (1 Pet. ?)
ἔπος
εὐαρεστέω
εὐαρέστως
εὐθύτης fr. Sept.
εὐλάβεια
εὐλαβέομαι (Acts?)
εὐπερίστατος
εὐποιΐα
ἦ μήν? (cf. εἰ μήν)
θεατρίζω
θέλησις
θεμέλιον καταβάλλομαι

θεράπων
θύελλα
θυμιατήριον
ἱερωσύνη
ἱκετήριος
καθαρότης
καίτοι (Lk. ?)
κακουχέω
καρτερέω
καταγωνίζομαι
κατάδηλος
καταναλίσκω
κατασκιάζω
κατάσκοπος
κατατοξεύω? fr. Sept.
καῦσις
κεφαλίς fr. Sept.
κοπή fr. Sept.
κριτικός
κῶλον fr. Sept.
λειτουργικός
Λευϊτικός
μερισμός
μεσιτεύω
μετάθεσις
μετέπειτα
μετριοπαθέω
μηδέπω
μηλωτή
μισθαποδοσία
μισθαποδότης
μυελός
νέφος
νόθος
νομοθετέω
νωθρός
ὄγκος
ἡ οἰκουμένη ἡ μέλλουσι
ὀλιγωρέω fr. Sept.
ὀλοθρεύω, ὀλεθρεύω
ὁμοιότης
ὁ ὀνειδισμὸς τοῦ Χριστ
ὁρκωμοσία
πανήγυρις
παραδειγματίζω (Mt. ?)
παραπικραίνω
παραπικρασμός fr. Sept
παραπίπτω
παραπλησίως
παραρρέω
παρίημι (Lk. ?)
παροικέω (Lk. ?)
πεῖρα
πήγνυμι
πολυμερῶς
πολυτρόπως
πρίζω (πρίω)
προβλέπω
πρόδρομος
προσαγορεύω

προσοχθίζω fr. Sept.
πρόσφατος
πρόσχυσις
πρωτοτόκια
ῥαντίζω (Mk.? Rev.?)
σαββατισμός
ὁ σκότος?
στάμνος
συγκακουχέω
συμπαθέω
συναπόλλυμι
συνδέω
συνεπιμαρτυρέω
τελειωτής
τιμωρία
τομώτερος
τράγος
τραχηλίζω
τρίμηνος
τροχιά fr. Sept.
τυμπανίζω
ὑπείκω
ὑποστολή
φαντάζω
φοβερός
χαρακτήρ
Χερουβίμ, -βείν

TOTAL 169 (12 fr. Sept., 11 ?)

8. To James.

ἄγε
ἀδιάκριτος
ἀκατάστατος
ἀκατάσχετος?
ἁλυκός
ἀμάω
ἀνέλεος?
ἀνεμίζω
ἀνίλεως?
ἀπείραστος
ἁπλῶς
ἀποκυέω
ἀποσκίασμα
ἀποτελέω (Lk.?)
αὐχέω?
ἀφυστερέω?
βοή
βρύω
γέλως
δαιμονιώδης
δίψυχος
ΕΙΚΩ
ἔμφυτος
ἐνάλιος
ἐξέλκω
ἔοικα (see ΕΙΚΩ)
ἐπιλησμονή
ἐπιστήμων
ἐπιτήδειος

ὁ εὐθύνων
εὐπειθής
εὐπρέπεια
ἐφήμερος
θανατηφόρος
θρῆσκος
ἰός (Ro. fr. Sept.)
κακοπάθεια
κατήφεια
κατιόω
κατοικίζω?
κενῶς
μαραίνω
μεγαλαυχέω?
μετάγω
μετατρέπω?
νομοθέτης
ὀλολύζω
ὁμοίωσις fr. Sept.
ὄψιμος
παραλλαγή
πικρός
ποία?
ποίησις
πολύσπλαγχνος
προσωπολη(μ)πτέω
πρώ(or ό-)ϊμος
ῥιπίζω
ῥυπαρία
ῥυπαρός (Rev. ?)
σήπω
σητόβρωτος
ταλαιπωρέω
ταλαιπωρία (Ro. fr. Sept.)
ταχύς
τροπή
τροχός
τρυφάω
ὕλη
φιλία
φλογίζω
φρίσσω
χαλιναγωγέω
χρή
χρυσοδακτύλιως

Total 73 (1 fr Sept., 9 ?)

9. To Peter.

N. B. Words peculiar to one Epistle or the other are so marked by the numeral which follows them; words unmarked are common to both.

ἀγαθοποιΐα 1
ἀγαθοποιός 1
ἀδελφότης 1
ἀδίκως 1

ἄδολος 1
ἄθεσμος 2
αἰσχροκερδῶς 1
ἀκατάπαστος ? } 2
ἀκατάπαυστος? }
ἀλλοτρι(ο)επίσκοπος 1
ἅλωσις 2
ἀμαθής 2
ἀμαράντινος 1
ἀμάραντος 1
ἀμώμητος 2 (Phil.?)
ἀναγεννάω 1
ἀναγκαστῶς 1
ἀναζώννυμι 1
ἀνάχυσις 1
ἀνεκλάλητος 1
ἀντιλοιδορέω 1
ἀπογίνομαι 1
ἀπόθεσις
ἀπονέμω 1
ἀποφεύγω 2
ἀπροσωπολή(μ)πτως 1
ἀργέω 2
ἀρτιγέννητος 1
ἀρχιποίμην 1
ἀστήρικτος 2
αὐχμηρός 2
βιόω 1
βλέμμα 2
βόρβορος 2
βραδυτής 2
γυναικεῖος 1
διαυγάζω 2
δυσνόητος 2
ἐγκατοικέω 2
ἐγκομβόομαι 1
ἑκάστοτε 2
ἔκπαλαι 2
ἐκτενής 1 (Lk. ?)
ἐκτενῶς 1 (Lk. ?)
ἔλεγξις 2
ἐμπαιγμονή 2
ἐμπλοκή 1
ἔνδυσις 1
ἐντρυφάω 2
ἐξαγγέλλω 1 (Mk. ? ?)
ἐξακολουθέω 2
ἐξέραμα 2
ἐξεραυνάω? } 1
ἐξερευνάω? }
ἐπάγγελμα 2
ἐπερώτημα 1
ἐπικάλυμμα 1
ἐπίλοιπος 1
ἐπίλυσις 2
ἐπιμαρτυρέω 1
ἐποπτεύω 1
ἐπόπτης 2
ἱεράτευμα 1
ἰσότιμος 2

κακοποιός 1 (Jn. ?)
κατακλύζω 2
καυσόω 2
κλέος 1
κραταιός 1
κτίστης 1
κύλισμα ? } 2
κυλισμός ? }
λήθη 2
μεγαλοπρεπής 2
μίασμα 2
μιασμός 2
μνήμη 2
μυωπάζω 2
μώλωψ 1 fr. Sept.
μῶμος 2
οἰνοφλυγία 1
ὀλίγως ? 2
ὀμίχλη ? 2
ὁμόφρων 1
ὁπλίζω 2
παρανομία 2
παραφρονία 2
παρεισάγω 2
παρεισφέρω 2
πατροπαράδοτος 1
περίθεσις 1
πλαστός 2
πότος 1
προθύμως 1
προμαρτύρομαι 1
πτόησις 1
ῥοιζηδόν 2
ῥύπος 1
σειρά ? }
σειρός ? } 2
σιρός ? }
σθενόω 1
σπορά 1
στηριγμός 2
στρεβλόω 2
συμπαθής 1
συμπρεσβύτερος 1
συνεκλεκτός 1
συνοικέω 1
ταπεινόφρων 1 ?
ταρταρόω 2
ταχινός 2
τελείως 1
τεφρόω 2
τήκω 2
τοιόσδε 2
τολμητής 2
ὑπογραμμός 1
ὑποζύγιον 2 (Mt. fr. Sept.)
ὑπολιμπάνω 1
ὗς 2
φιλάδελφος 1
φιλόφρων 1?
φωσφόρος 2

ψευδοδιδάσκαλος 2
ὠρύομαι 1

1 Epistle 63 (1 fr. Sept., 2 ?)
2 Epistle 57 (5 ?)
Common to Both 1
Total 121.

10. To Jude.

εἰς πάντας τοὺς αἰῶνας
πρὸ παντὸς τοῦ αἰῶνος
ἀποδιορίζω
ἄπταιστος
γογγυστής
δεῖγμα
ἐκπορνεύω
ἐνυπνιάζω (Lk. fr. Sept.)
ἐξελέγχω ?
ἐπαγωνίζομαι
ἐπαφρίζω
μεμψίμοιρος
ὀπίσω σαρκός
παρεισδύω
πλανήτης
πρόσωπα θαυμάζω
σπιλάς
ὑπέχω
φθινοπωρινός
φυσικῶς

Total 20 (1 ?)

11. To the Apocalypse.

τὸ Α καὶ τὸ Ω
Ἀβαδδών
αἰχμαλωσία (Eph. fr. Sept.)
ἀκαθάρτης?
ἀκμάζω
ἄκρατος fr. Sept.
ἀλληλούϊα
ἄλφα (see τὸ Α καὶ τὸ Ω)
ἀμέθυστος
ὁ ἀμήν
ἄμωμον?
ἀνὰ εἷς ἕκαστος
Ἀπολλύων
ἄρκος or ἄρκτος
Ἁρμαγεδών etc.
ἄψινθος
βάλλειν σκάνδαλον ἐνώπιον
βασανισμός
βάτραχος
βήρυλλος
βιβλαρίδιον
βιβλιδάριον?
βότρυς
βύσσινος
τὸ δάκρυον?
τὸ δέκατον as subst.

διάδημα
διαυγής?
διαφανής?
διπλόω
δισμυριάς?
δράκων
δωδέκατος
ἐγχρίω
εἱλίσσω?
ἐλεφάντινος
Ἑλληνικός (Lk. ?)
ἐμέω
ἐμμέσῳ?
ἐνδόμησις (ἐνδώμησις)
ἑξακόσιοι
Ἐφεσῖνος?
ζηλεύω?
ξύλον τῆς ζωῆς fr. Sept.,
  ζωῆς πηγαὶ ὑδάτων? fr.
  Sept., (τὸ) ὕδωρ (τῆς)
  ζωῆς fr. Sept.
ζεστός
ἡμιώριον (ἡμίωρον)
ὁ ἦν
ὁ θάνατος ὁ δεύτερος
θαῦμα (2 Co. ?)
θαῦμα (μέγα) θαυμάζειν
θειώδης
θεολόγος?
θύϊνος
ἴασπις
ἱππικός
ἶρις
κατάθεμα? } fr. Sept.
κατανάθεμα? }
κατασφραγίζω
κατήγωρ?
καῦμα

κεραμικός fr. Sept.
κεράννυμι
κιθαρῳδός
κιν(ν)άμωμον
κλέμμα
κολλούριον (κολλύριον)
κριθή
κρυσταλλίζω
κρύσταλλος
κυκλεύω?
κυκλόθεν
ἡ κυριακὴ ἡμέρα
λευκοβύσσινον?
λιβανωτός
λίνον? (Mt. fr. Sept.)
λιπαρός
μαζός? }
μασθός? }
μάρμαρος
μασ(σ)άομαι
μεσουράνημα
μέτωπον
μηρός
μουσικός
μυκάομαι
μύλινος?
νεφρός fr. Sept.
Νικολαΐτης
ὄλυνθος
ὅμιλος?
ὅπου ἐκεῖ (Hebr. אֲשֶׁר שָׁם)
ὀπώρα
ὅρασις (Lk. fr. Sept.)
ὅρμημα
ὄρνεον
ἡ οὐαί
οὐαί w. acc. of pers.?
οὐρά

πάρδαλις
πελεκίζω
πέμπτος
περιρ(ρ)αίνω?
(πετάομαι) πέτομαι
πλήσσω
πλύνω (Lk. ?)
ποδήρης
πόνος (Col. ?)
ποταμοφόρητος
πρωϊνός etc.
ὁ πρῶτος κ. ὁ ἔσχατος
πύρινος
πυρρός
ῥέδη (ῥέδα)
ῥυπαίνω?
ῥυπαρεύομαι?
ῥυπόω?
σαλπιστής
σάπφειρος
σάρδινος?
σάρδιον?
σαρδιόνυξ? }
σαρδόνυξ? }
σεμίδαλις
σηρικός (σιρικός)
σίδηρος
σκοτόω (Eph. ?)
σμαράγδινος
σμάραγδος
Σμυρναῖος?
στρηνιάω
στρῆνος
σώματα slaves
ταλαντιαῖος
τεσσαρακονταδύο?
τεσσαρακο τατέσσαρες?
τετράγωνος

τιμιότης
τόξον
τοπάζιον
τρίχινος
ὑακίνθινος
ὑάκινθος
ὑάλινος
ὕαλος
φαρμακεύς?
φάρμακον?
φαρμακός·
φιάλη
χάλαζα
χάλκεος
χαλκηδών
χαλκολίβανοι
χλιαρός
χοῖνιξ
χρυσόλιθος
χρυσόπρασος
χρυσόω
τὸ Ω (see τὸ Α καὶ τὸ Ω)

TOTAL 156 (7 fr. Sept., 33 ?)

12. To the Apocalypse and the Fourth Gospel.

βροντή (cf. Mk. iii. 17)
δέκατος
Ἑβραϊστί
ἐκκεντέω
κυκλεύω?
ὄψις
πορφυροῦς
σκηνόω
φοίνιξ

TOTAL 9 (1 ?)

V

FORMS OF VERBS

———◆———

The List which follows is not intended to be a mere museum of grammatical curiosities on the one hand, or a catalogue of all the verbal forms occurring in the Greek Testament on the other ; but it is a collection of those forms (or their representatives) which may possibly occasion a beginner some perplexity. The practical end, accordingly, for which the list has been prepared has prescribed a generous liberty as respects admission to it. Yet the following classes of forms have been for the most part excluded : forms which are traceable by means of the cross references given in the body of the Lexicon, or which hold so isolated a position in its alphabet that even a tyro can hardly miss them ; forms easily recognizable as compounded, in case the simple form has been noted ; forms readily explainable by the analogy of some form which is given.

Ordinarily it has been deemed sufficient to give the *representative* form of a tense, viz., the First Person (or in the case of the Imperative the Second Person) Singular, the Nominative Singular Masculine of a Participle, etc. ; but when some other form seemed likely to prove more embarrassing, or was the only one found in the New Testament, it has often been the form selected.

The word "of" in the descriptions introduces not necessarily the stem from which a given form comes, but the entry in the Lexicon under which the form will be found. The epithet "Alex." it is hardly necessary to add, has been employed only for convenience and in its technical sense.

ἀγάγετε, 2 aor. act. impv. 2 pers. plur. of ἄγω.

ἀγάγῃ, 2 aor. act. subj. 3 pers. sing. of ἄγω.

ἁγνίσθητι, 1 aor. pass. impv. of ἁγνίζω.

αἴσθωνται, 2 aor. subj. 3 pers. plur. of αἰσθάνομαι.

αἰτείτω, pres. impv. 3 pers. sing. of αἰτέω.

ἀκήκοα, 2 pf. act. of ἀκούω.

ἀλλαγήσομαι, 2 fut. pass. of ἀλλάσσω.

ἀλλάξαι, 1 aor. act. inf. of ἀλλάσσω.

ἀλλάξει, fut. act. 3 pers. sing. of ἀλλάσσω.

ἁμαρτήσῃ, 1 aor. act. subj. 3 pers. sing. of ἁμαρτάνω.

ἀμησάντων, 1 aor. act. ptcp. gen. plur. of ἀμάω.

ἀνάβα and ἀνάβηθι, 2 aor. act. impv. of ἀναβαίνω.

ἀναβέβηκα, pf. act. of ἀναβαίνω.

ἀναγαγεῖν, 2 aor. act. inf. of ἀνάγω.

ἀναγνούς, 2 aor. act. ptcp. of ἀναγινώσκω.

ἀναγνῶναι, 2 aor. act. inf. of ἀναγινώσκω.

ἀναγνωσθῇ, 1 aor. pass. subj. 3 pers. sing. of ἀναγινώσκω.

ἀνακεκύλισται, pf. pass. 3 pers. sing. of ἀνακυλίω.

ἀναλοῖ, pres. ind. act. 3 pers. sing. of ἀναλίσκω.

ἀναλωθῆτε, 1 aor. pass. subj. 2 pers. plur. of ἀναλίσκω.

ἀναμνήσω, fut. act. of ἀναμιμνήσκω.

ἀναπαήσομαι, fut. mid. of ἀναπαύω (cf. also παύω, init.).

ἀνάπεσαι, 1 aor. mid. impv. of ἀναπίπτω.

ἀνάπεσε, ἀνάπεσον, 2 and 1 aor. act. impv. of ἀναπίπτω.

ἀνάστα and ἀνάστηθι, 2 aor. act. impv. of ἀνίστημι.

ἀνατεθραμμένος, pf. pass. ptcp. of ἀνατρέφω.

ἀνατείλῃ, 1 aor. act. subj. 3 pers. sing. of ἀνατέλλω.

ἀνατέταλκεν, pf. act. 3 pers. sing. of ἀνατέλλω.

ἀναφάναντες, 1 aor. act. ptcp. nom. plur. of ἀναφαίνω.

ἀναφανέντες, 2 aor. pass. ptcp. nom. plur. of ἀναφαίνω.

ἀναχθέντες, 1 aor. pass. ptcp. nom. plur. masc. of ἀνάγω.

ἀνάψαντες, 1 aor. act. ptcp. nom. plur. masc. of ἀνάπτω.

ἀνέγνωτε, 2 aor. act. 2 pers. plur. of ἀναγινώσκω.

ἀνεθάλετε, 2 aor. act. 2 pers. plur. of ἀναθάλλω.

ἀνεθέμην, 2 aor. mid. of ἀνατίθημι.

ἀνέθη, 1 aor. pass. 3 pers. sing. of ἀνίημι.

ἀνεθρέψατο, 1 aor. mid. 3 pers. sing. of ἀνατρέφω.

ἀνείλετο (-ατο, Alex.), 2 aor. mid. 3 pers. sing. of ἀναιρέω.

ἀνεῖλον (-ατε, -αν, Alex.), 2 aor. act. of ἀναιρέω.

ἀνειχόμην, impf. mid. of ἀνέχω.

ἀνελεῖ, fut. act. 3 pers. sing. of ἀναιρέω.

ἀνελεῖν, 2 aor. act. inf. of ἀναιρέω.

ἀνέλωσι, 2 aor. act. subj. 3 pers. plur. of ἀναιρέω.

ἀνενέγκαι, -κας, 1 aor. act. inf. and ptcp. of ἀναφέρω.

ἀνενεγκεῖν, 2 aor. act. inf. of ἀναφέρω.

ἀνέντες, 2 aor. act. ptcp. nom. plur. masc. of ἀνίημι.

ἀνέξομαι, fut. mid. of ἀνέχω.

ἀνέπεσον (-σαν, Alex.), 2 aor. act. 3 pers. plur. of ἀναπίπτω.

ἀνέσεισα, 1 aor. act. of ἀνασείω.

ἀνεστράφημεν, 2 aor. pass. 1 pers. plur. of ἀναστρέφω.

ἀνεσχόμην, 2 aor. mid. of ἀνέχω.

ἀνέτειλα, 1 aor. act. of ἀνατέλλω.

ἀνετράφη, 2 aor. pass. 3 pers. sing. of ἀνατρέφω.

ἀνεῦρον (-αν, Alex.), 2 aor. act. 3 pers. plur. of ἀνευρίσκω.

ἀνέῳγα, 2 pf. act. of ἀνοίγω.

ἀνεῳγμένος, pf. pass. ptcp. of ἀνοίγω.

ἀνεῳγότα, 2 pf. act. ptcp. acc. sing. masc. of ἀνοίγω.

ἀνέῳξα, 1 aor. act. of ἀνοίγω.

ἀνεῳχθῆναι, 1 aor. pass. inf. of ἀνοίγω.

ἀνήγαγον, 2 aor. act. of ἀνάγω.

ἀνήγγειλα, 1 aor. act. of ἀναγγέλλω.

ἀνηγγέλην, 2 aor. pass. of ἀναγγέλλω.

ἀνήνεγκεν, 1 or 2 aor. act. 3 pers. sing. of ἀναφέρω.

ἀνῃρέθην, 1 aor. pass. of ἀναιρεω.

ἀνήφθη, 1 aor. pass. 3 pers. sing. of ἀνάπτω.

ἀνήχθην, 1 aor. pass. of ἀνάγω.

ἀνθέξεται, fut. mid. 3 pers. sing. of ἀντέχω.

ἀνθέστηκε, pf. ind. act. 3 pers. sing. of ἀνθίστημι.

ἀνθίστανται, pres. mid. 3 pers. plur. of ἀνθίστημι.

ἀνθίστατο, impf. mid. 3 pers. sing. of ἀνθίστημι.

ἀνιέντες, pres. act. ptcp. nom. plur. masc. of ἀνίημι.

ἀνοιγήσεται, 2 fut. pass. 3 pers. sing. of ἀνοίγω.

ἀνοιγῶσιν, 2 aor. pass. subj. 3 pers. plur. of ἀνοίγω.

ἀνοῖξαι, 1 aor. act. inf. of ἀνοίγω.

ἀνοίξῃ, 1 aor. act. subj. 3 pers. sing. of ἀνοίγω.

ἄνοιξον, 1 aor. act. impv. of ἀνοίγω.

ἀνοίσω, fut. act. of ἀναφέρω.

ἀνοιχθήσεται, 1 fut. pass. 3 pers. sing. of ἀνοίγω.

ἀνοιχθῶσιν, 1 aor. pass. subj. 3 pers. plur. of ἀνοίγω.

ἀνταποδοῦναι, 2 aor. act. inf. of ἀνταποδίδωμι.

ἀνταποδώσω, fut. act. of ἀνταποδίδωμι.

ἀντέστην, 2 aor. act. of ἀνθίστημι.

ἀντιστῆναι, 2 aor. act. inf. of ἀνθίστημι.

ἀντίστητε, 2 aor. impv. 2 pers. plur. of ἀνθίστημι.

ἀνῶ, 2 aor. act. subj. of ἀνίημι.

ἀπαλλάξῃ, 1 aor. act. subj. 3 pers. sing. of ἀπαλλάσσω.

ἀπαρθῇ, 1 aor. pass. subj. 3 pers. sing. of ἀπαίρω.

ἀπαρνησάσθω, 1 aor. mid. impv. 3 pers. sing. of ἀπαρνέομαι.

ἀπαρνήσῃ, fut. 2 pers. sing. of ἀπαρνέομαι.

ἀπατάτω, pres. act. impv. 3 pers. sing. of ἀπατάω.

ἀπατηθεῖσα, 1 aor. pass. ptcp. nom. sing. fem. of ἀπατάω.

ἀπέβησαν, 2 aor. act. 3 pers. plur. of ἀποβαίνω.

ἀπέδειξεν, 1 aor. act. 3 pers. sing. of ἀποδείκνυμι.

ἀπέδετο, 2 aor. mid. 3 pers. sing. of ἀποδίδωμι.

ἀπεδίδοσαν, ἀπεδίδουν, impf. act. 3 pers. plur. of ἀποδίδωμι.

ἀπέδοτο, -δοσθε, etc., 2 aor. mid. of ἀποδίδωμι.

ἀπέδωκεν, 1 aor. act. 3 pers. sing. of ἀποδίδωμι.

ἀπέθανεν, 2 aor. act. 3 pers. sing. of ἀποθνήσκω.

ἀπειπάμεθα, 1 aor. mid. 1 pers. plur. of ἀπεῖπον.

ἀπεῖχον, impf. act. of ἀπέχω.

ἀπεκατεστάθη, 1 aor. pass. of ἀποκαθίστημι.

ἀπεκατέστην, 2 aor. act. of ἀποκαθίστημι.

ἀπεκρίθην, 1 aor. pass. of ἀποκρίνω.

ἀπεκτάνθην, 1 aor. pass. of ἀποκτείνω.

ἀπεληλύθεισαν, plpf. 3 pers. plur. of ἀπέρχομαι.

ἀπελθών, 2 aor. act. ptcp. of ἀπέρχομαι.

ἀπενεγκεῖν, 2 aor. act. inf. of ἀποφέρω.

ἀπενεχθῆναι, 1 aor. pass. inf. of ἀποφέρω.

ἀπεπνίγη, 2 aor. pass. 3 pers. sing. of ἀποπνίγω.

ἀπέπνιξαν, 1 aor. act. 3 pers. plur. of ἀποπνίγω.

ἀπεστάλην, 2 aor. pass. of ἀποστέλλω.

ἀπέσταλκα, pf. act. of ἀποστέλλω.

ἀπεσταλμένος, pf. pass. ptcp. of ἀποστέλλω.

ἀπέστειλα, 1 aor. act. of ἀποστέλλω.

ἀπέστη (-ησαν), 2 aor. act. 3 pers. sing. (plur.) of ἀφίστημι.

ἀπεστράφησαν, 2 aor. pass. 3 pers. plur. of ἀποστρέφω.

ἀπετάξατο, 1 aor. mid. 3 pers. sing. of ἀποτάσσω.

ἀπῄεσαν, impf. 3 pers. plur. of ἄπειμι.

ἀπήλασεν, 1 aor. act. 3 pers. sing. of ἀπελαύνω.

ἀπηλγηκότες, pf. act. ptcp. nom. plur. masc. of ἀπαλγέω.

ἀπῆλθον (-θαν, Alex. 3 pers. plur.), 2 aor. act. of ἀπέρχομαι.

ἀπηλλάχθαι, pf. pass. inf. of ἀπαλλάσσω.

ἀπηρνησάμην, 1 aor. of ἀπαρνέομαι.

ἀπησπασάμην, 1 aor. of ἀπασπάζομαι.

ἀποβάντες, 2 aor. act. ptcp. of ἀποβαίνω.

ἀποβήσεται, fut. 3 pers. sing. of ἀποβαίνω.

ἀποδεδειγμένον, pf. pass. ptcp. neut. of ἀποδείκνυμι.

ἀποδεικνύντα (-δειγνύοντα), pres. act. ptcp. acc. sing. masc. of ἀποδείκνυμι.

ἀποδεῖξαι, 1 aor. act. inf. of ἀποδείκνυμι.

ἀποδιδόναι, -δότω, pres. act. inf. and impv. (3 pers. sing.) of ἀποδίδωμι.

ἀποδιδοῦν, pres. act. ptcp. neut. of ἀποδίδωμι.

ἀποδοθῆναι, 1 aor. pass. inf. of ἀποδίδωμι.

ἀποδοῖ, -δῷ, 2 aor. act. subj. 3 pers. sing. of ἀποδίδωμι.

ἀπόδος, -δοτε, 2 aor. act. impv. of ἀποδίδωμι.

ἀποδοῦναι, -δούς, 2 aor. act. inf. and ptcp. of ἀποδίδωμι.

ἀποδῴη, 2 aor. act. opt. 3 pers. sing. of ἀποδίδωμι.

ἀποθανεῖν, 2 aor. act. inf. of ἀποθνήσκω.

ἀποκαθιστᾷ, -τάνει, pres. act. 3 pers. sing. of ἀποκαθίστημι.

ἀποκατηλλάγητε, 2 aor. pass. 2 pers. plur. of ἀποκαταλλάσσω.

ἀποκριθείς, 1 aor. pass. ptcp. of ἀποκρίνω.

ἀποκταίνω, -κτείνω, -κτέννω, -κτένω, pres.; see ἀποκτείνω.

ἀποκτανθείς, 1 aor. pass. ptcp. of ἀποκτείνω.

ἀποκτέννυντες, pres. ptcp. nom. plur. masc. of ἀποκτείνω.

ἀποκτενῶ, fut. act. of ἀποκτείνω.

ἀπολέσαι, -λέσω, 1 aor. act. inf. and subj. of ἀπόλλυμι.

ἀπολέσω, fut. act. of ἀπόλλυμι.

ἀπολοῦμαι, fut. mid. of ἀπόλλυμι.

ἀπολῶ, fut. act. of ἀπόλλυμι.

ἀπόλωλα, 2 pf. act. of ἀπόλλυμι.

ἀπο(ρ)ρίψαντας, 1 aor. act. ptcp. acc. plur. masc. of ἀπο(ρ)ρίπτω.

ἀποσταλῶ, 2 aor. pass. subj. of ἀποστέλλω.

ἀποστείλας, 1 aor. act. ptcp. of ἀποστέλλω.

ἀποστῇ, 2 aor. act. subj. 3 pers. sing. of ἀφίστημι.

ἀποστήσομαι, fut. mid. of ἀφίστημι.

ἀπόστητε (-στήτω), 2 aor. act. impv. 2 pers. plur. (3 pers. sing.) of ἀφίστημι.

ἀποστραφῇς, 2 aor. pass. subj. 2 pers. sing. of ἀποστρέφω.

ἀπόστρεψον, 1 aor. act. impv. of ἀποστρέφω.

ἀποταξάμενος, 1 aor. mid. ptcp. of ἀποτάσσω.

ἅπτου, pres. mid. impv. of ἅπτω.

ἀπώλεσα, 1 aor. act. of ἀπόλλυμι.

ἀπωλόμην, 2 aor. mid. of ἀπόλλυμι.

ἀπωσάμενος, 1 aor. mid. ptcp. of ἀπωθέω.

ἆραι, 1 aor. act. inf. of αἴρω.

ἄρας, 1 aor. act. ptcp. of αἴρω.

ἀρέσει, fut. act. 3 pers. sing. of ἀρέσκω.

ἀρέσῃ, 1 aor. act. subj. 3 pers. sing. of ἀρέσκω.

ἄρῃ, 1 aor. act. subj. 3 pers. sing. of αἴρω.

ἀρθῇ (-θῶσιν), 1 aor. pass. subj. 3 pers. sing. (plur.) of αἴρω.

ἀρθήσεται, 1 fut. pass. 3 pers. sing. of αἴρω.

ἄρθητι, 1 aor. pass. impv. of αἴρω.

ἀρκέσῃ, 1 aor. act. subj. 3 pers. sing. of ἀρκέω.

ἆρον, 1 aor. act. impv. of αἴρω.

ἁρπαγέντα, 2 aor. pass. ptcp. acc. sing. masc. of ἁρπάζω.

ἀρῶ (-οῦσιν), fut. act. 1 pers. sing. (3 pers. plur.) of αἴρω.

αὐξηθῇ, 1 aor. pass. subj. 3 pers. sing. of αὐξάνω.

ἀφέθην, 1 aor. pass. of ἀφίημι.

ἀφεῖλεν, 2 aor. act. 3 pers. sing. of ἀφαιρέω.

ἀφεῖναι, 2 aor. act. inf. of ἀφίημι.

ἀφεῖς, pres. ind. act. 2 pers. sing. of (ἀφέω) ἀφίημι.

ἀφείς, 2 aor. act. ptcp. of ἀφίημι.
ἀφελεῖ, fut. act. 3 pers. sing. of ἀφαιρέω.
ἀφελεῖν, 2 aor. act. inf. of ἀφαιρέω.
ἀφέλῃ, 2 aor. act. subj. 3 pers. sing. of ἀφαιρέω.
ἄφες, 2 aor. act. impv. of ἀφίημι.
ἀφέωνται, pf. pass. 3 pers. plur. of ἀφίημι.
ἀφῇ, 2 aor. act. subj. 3 pers. sing. of ἀφίημι.
ἀφῆκα, 1 aor. act. of ἀφίημι.
ἀφίεμεν, pres. act. 1 pers. plur. of ἀφίημι.
ἀφίενται, -ονται, pres. pass. 3 pers. plur. of ἀφίημι.
ἀφίκετο, 2 aor. 3 pers. sing. of ἀφικνέομαι.
ἀφίομεν, pres. act. 1 pers. plur. of (ἀφίω) ἀφίημι.
ἀφιοῦσιν, pres. act. 3 pers. plur. of (ἀφιέω) ἀφίημι.
ἀφίστασο, pres. mid. impv. of ἀφίστημι.
ἀφίστατο, impf. mid. 3 pers. sing. of ἀφίστημι.
ἀφοριεῖ, -οῦσιν, (Attic) fut. 3 pers. sing. and plur. of ἀφορίζω.
ἀφῶμεν, 2 aor. act. subj. 1 pers. plur. of ἀφίημι.
ἀφωμοιωμένος, pf. pass. ptcp. of ἀφομοιόω.
ἀχθῆναι, 1 aor. pass. inf. of ἄγω.
ἀχθήσεσθε, 1 fut. pass. 2 pers. plur. of ἄγω.
ἅψας, 1 aor. act. ptcp. of ἅπτω.
ἅψῃ, 1 aor. act. subj. 3 pers. sing. of ἅπτω.

βαλῶ, fut. act. of βάλλω.
βάλω, -λῃ, (-λε), 2 aor. act. subj. (impv.) of βάλλω.
βαρείσθω, pres. impv. pass. 3 pers. sing. of βαρέω.
βάψῃ, 1 aor. act. subj. 3 pers. sing. of βάπτω.
βεβαμμένον, pf. pass. ptcp. neut. of βάπτω.
βέβληκεν, pf. act. 3 pers. sing. of βάλλω.
βεβλημένος, pf. pass. ptcp. of βάλλω.
βέβληται, pf. pass. 3 pers. sing. of βάλλω.
βληθείς, 1 aor. pass. ptcp. of βάλλω.
βλήθητι, 1 aor. pass. impv. of βάλλω.

γαμησάτωσαν, 1 aor. act. impv. 3 pers. plur. of γαμέω.
γεγένημαι, pf. pass. of γίνομαι.
γεγέννημαι, pf. pass. of γεννάω.
γέγοναν (-νώς), 2 pf. act. 3 pers. plur. (ptcp.) of γίνομαι.
γεγόνει, plpf. act. 3 pers. sing. (without augm.) of γίνομαι.
γενάμενος, 2 aor. mid. ptcp. (Tdf. ed. 7) of γίνομαι.
γενέσθω, 2 aor. impv. 3 pers. sing. of γίνομαι.
γενηθήτω, 1 aor. pass. impv. 3 pers. sing. of γίνομαι.
γένησθε, 2 aor. mid. subj. 2 pers. plur. of γίνομαι.
γένωνται, 2 aor. mid. subj. 3 pers. plur. of γίνομαι.
γήμας, 1 aor. act. ptcp. of γαμέω.
γήμῃς, 1 aor. act. subj. 2 pers. sing. of γαμέω.
γνοῖ, 2 aor. act. subj. 3 pers. sing. of γινώσκω.
γνούς, 2 aor. act. ptcp. of γινώσκω.
γνῶ, γνῷ, 2 aor. act. subj. 1 and 3 pers. sing. of γινώσκω.
γνῶθι, 2 aor. act. impv. of γινώσκω.
γνωριοῦσιν, (Attic) fut. 3 pers. plur. of γνωρίζω.
γνωσθῇ, 1 aor. pass. subj. 3 pers. sing. of γινώσκω.
γνωσθήσεται, 1 fut. pass. 3 pers. sing. of γινώσκω.
γνώσομαι, fut. of γινώσκω.
γνώτω, 2 aor. act. impv. 3 pers. sing. of γινώσκω.

δαρήσομαι, 2 fut. pass. of δέρω.
δέδεκται, pf. 3 pers. sing. of δέχομαι.
δεδεκώς, pf. act. ptcp. of δέω.
δέδεμαι, pf. pass. of δέω.
δεδιωγμένος, pf. pass. ptcp. of διώκω.
δέδοται, pf. pass. 3 pers. sing. of δίδωμι.
δεδώκεισαν, plpf. act. 3 pers. plur. of δίδωμι.
δέῃ, pres. subj. of impers. δεῖ.
δεθῆναι, 1 aor. pass. inf. of δέω.
δείραντες, 1 aor. act. ptcp. nom. plur. masc. of δέρω.
δέξαι, 1 aor. impv. of δέχομαι.
δέξηται (-ωνται), 1 aor. subj. 3 pers. sing. (plur.) of δέχομαι.
δῆσαι, 1 aor. act. inf. of δέω.
δήσῃ, 1 aor. act. subj. 3 pers. sing. of δέω.
διαβάς, 2 aor. act. ptcp. of διαβαίνω.
διαβῆναι, 2 aor. act. inf. of διαβαίνω.
διάδος, 2 aor. act. impv. of διαδίδωμι.
διακαθᾶραι, 1 aor. act. inf. of διακαθαίρω.
διαλλάγηθι, 2 aor. pass. impv. of διαλλάσσω.
διαμείνῃ, 1 aor. act. subj. 3 pers. sing. of διαμένω.
διαμεμενηκότες, pf. act. ptcp. nom. plur. masc. of διαμένω.
διαμένεις, pres. ind. act. 2 pers. sing. of διαμένω.
διαμενεῖς, fut. ind. act. 2 pers. sing. of διαμένω.
διανοίχθητι, 1 aor. pass. impv. of διανοίγω.
διαρ(ρ)ήξας, 1 aor. act. ptcp. of διαρρήγνυμι.
διασπαρέντες, 2 aor. pass. ptcp. nom. plur. masc. of διασπείρω.
διασπασθῇ, 1 aor. pass. subj. 3 pers. sing. of διασπάω.
διαστάσης, 2 aor. act. ptcp. gen. sing. fem. of διΐστημι.
διαστρέψαι, 1 aor. act. inf. of διαστρέφω.
διαταγείς, 2 aor. pass. ptcp. of διατάσσω.
διαταχθέντα, 1 aor. pass. ptcp. neut. of διατάσσω.
διατεταγμένος, pf. pass. ptcp. of διατάσσω.
διατεταχέναι, pf. act. inf. of διατάσσω.
διδόασι, pres. act. 3 pers. plur. of δίδωμι.
διέβησαν, 2 aor. act. 3 pers. plur. of διαβαίνω.
διεῖλον, 2 aor. act. of διαιρέω.
διενέγκῃ, 1 or 2 aor. act. subj. 3 pers. sing. of διαφέρω.
διερ(ρ)ήγνυντο, impf. pass. 3 pers. sing. of διαρρήγνυμι.
διέρ(ρ)ηξεν, 1 aor. act. 3 pers. sing. of διαρρήγνυμι.
διερ(ρ)ήσσετο, impf. pass. 3 pers. sing. of διαρρήγνυμι.
διεσάφησαν, 1 aor. act. 3 pers. plur. of διασαφέω.
διεσπάρησαν, 2 aor. pass. 3 pers. plur. of διασπείρω.
διεσπάσθαι, pf. pass. inf. of διασπάω.
διεστειλάμην, 1 aor. mid. of διαστέλλω.
διέστη, 2 aor. act. 3 pers. sing. of διΐστημι.
διεστραμμένος, pf. pass. ptcp. of διαστρέφω.
διέταξα, 1 aor. act. of διατάσσω.
διεφθάρην, 2 aor. pass. of διαφθείρω.
διεφθαρμένος, pf. pass. ptcp. of διαφθείρω.
διηκόνουν, impf. act. of διακονέω.
διήνοιγεν, impf. act. 3 pers. sing. of διανοίγω.
διήνοιξεν, 1 aor. act. 3 pers. sing. of διανοίγω.
διηνοίχθησαν, 1 aor. pass. 3 pers. plur. of διανοίγω.
διορυγῆναι, 2 aor. pass. inf. of διορύσσω.
διορυχθῆναι, 1 aor. pass. inf. of διορύσσω.
διώδευε, impf. 3 pers. sing. of διοδεύω.
διωξάτω, 1 aor. act. impv. 3 pers. sing. of διώκω.

διώξητε, 1 aor. act. subj. 2 pers. plur. of διώκω.

διωχθήσονται, 1 fut. pass. 3 pers. plur. of διώκω.

δοθεῖσαν, 1 aor. pass. ptcp. acc. sing. fem. of δίδωμι.

δοθῇ, 1 aor. pass. subj. 3 pers. sing. of δίδωμι.

δοθῆναι, 1 aor. pass. inf. of δίδωμι.

δοῖ, 2 aor. act. subj. 3 pers. sing. of δίδωμι.

δός, δότε, δότω, 2 aor. act. impv. of δίδωμι.

δοῦναι, 2 aor. act. inf. of δίδωμι.

δούς, 2 aor. act. ptcp. of δίδωμι.

δύνῃ, pres. ind. 2 pers. sing. of δύναμαι.

δῷ, δώῃ, 2 aor. act. subj. 3 pers. sing. of δίδωμι.

δώῃ, 2 aor. act. opt. 3 pers. sing. of δίδωμι.

δῶμεν, δῶτε, 2 aor. act. subj. 1 and 2 pers. plur. of δίδωμι.

δώσῃ (-σωμεν), 1 aor. act. subj. 3 pers. sing. (1 pers. plur.) of δίδωμι.

ἔβαλον (-αν, Alex. 3 pers. plur.), 2 aor. act. of βάλλω.

ἐβάσκανε, 1 aor. act. 3 pers. sing. of βασκαίνω.

ἐβδελυγμένος, pf. pass. ptcp. of βδελύσσω.

ἐβέβλητο, plpf. pass. 3 pers. sing. of βάλλω.

ἐβλήθην, 1 aor. pass. of βάλλω.

ἐγγιεῖ, (Attic) fut. 3 pers. sing. of ἐγγίζω.

ἐγγίσαι, 1 aor. act. inf. of ἐγγίζω.

ἐγεγόνει, plpf. act. 3 pers. sing. of γίνομαι.

ἔγειραι, 1 aor. mid. impv. of ἐγείρω.

ἐγεῖραι, 1 aor. act. inf. of ἐγείρω.

ἐγείρου, pres. pass. impv. of ἐγείρω.

ἐγενήθην, 1 aor. pass. of γίνομαι.

ἐγεννήθην, 1 aor. pass. of γεννάω.

ἐγερεῖ, fut. act. 3 pers. sing. of ἐγείρω.

ἐγερθείς, 1 aor. pass. ptcp. of ἐγείρω.

ἐγερθήσεται, 1 fut. pass. 3 pers. sing. of ἐγείρω.

ἐγέρθητι, 1 aor. pass. impv. of ἐγείρω.

ἐγήγερμαι, pf. pass. of ἐγείρω.

ἔγημα, 1 aor. act. of γαμέω.

ἐγκρῖναι, 1 aor. act. inf. of ἐγκρίνω.

ἔγνωκαν (i. q. ἐγνώκασιν), pf. act. 3 pers. plur. of γινώσκω.

ἐγνωκέναι, pf. act. inf. of γι·ώσκω.

ἔγνων, 2 aor. act. of γινώσκω.

ἔγνωσται, pf. pass. 3 pers. sing. of γινώσκω.

ἔγχρισαι, 1 aor. mid. impv. of ἐγχρίω.

ἐγχρῖσαι, 1 aor. act. inf. of ἐγχρίω.

ἔγχρισον, 1 aor. act. impv. of ἐγχρίω.

ἐδαφιοῦσιν, (Attic) fut. 3 pers. plur. of ἐδαφίζω.

ἐδέετο, ἐδεῖτο, ἐδεῖτο, impf. 3 pers. sing. of δέομαι.

ἔδει, impf. of impers. δεῖ.

ἔδειραν, 1 aor. act. 3 pers. plur. of δέρω.

ἔδησα, 1 aor. act. of δέω.

ἐδίωξα, 1 aor. act. of διώκω.

ἐδολιοῦσαν, impf. (Alex.) 3 pers. plur. of δολιόω.

ἔδραμον, 2 aor. act. of τρέχω.

ἔδυ, ἔδυσεν, 2 and 1 aor. act. 3 pers. sing. of δύνω.

ἔζην, ἔζῆτε, ἔζων, impf. act. of ζάω.

ἔζησα, 1 aor. act. of ζάω.

ἐθέμην, 2 aor. mid. of τίθημι.

ἔθετο (-εντο), 2 aor. mid. 3 pers. sing. (plur.) of τίθημι.

ἔθηκα, 1 aor. act. of τίθημι.

ἔθου, 2 aor. mid. 2 pers. sing. of τίθημι.

ἔθρεψα, 1 aor. act. of τρέφω.

ἐθύθη, 1 aor. pass. 3 pers. sing. of θύω.

εἴα, impf. act. 3 pers. sing. of ἐάω.

εἴασα, 1 aor. act. of ἐάω.

εἶδα, (Alex.) 2 aor. act. of εἴδω.

εἰθισμένον, pf. pass. ptcp. neut. of ἐθίζω.

εἵλατο (-ετο), aor. mid. 3 pers. sing. of αἱρέω.

εἴληπται, pf. pass. 3 pers. sing. of λαμβάνω.

εἴληφες (-φας), pf. act. 2 pers. sing. of λαμβάνω.

εἶλκον, impf. act. of ἕλκω.

εἱλκωμένος, pf. pass. ptcp. of ἑλκόω.

εἶξαμεν, 1 aor. act. 1 pers. plur. of εἴκω.

εἰσδραμοῦσα, 2 aor. act. ptcp. fem. of εἰστρέχω.

εἰσελήλυθαν (-λύθασιν), pf. 3 pers. plur. of εἰσέρχομαι.

εἰσῄει, impf. 3 pers. sing. of εἴσειμι.

εἰσίασιν, pres. ind. 3 pers. plur. of εἴσειμι.

εἱστήκεισαν, plpf. act. 3 pers. plur. of ἵστημι.

εἶχαν, εἴχοσαν, impf. (Alex.) 3 pers. plur. of ἔχω.

εἴων, impf. of ἐάω.

ἐκάθε(or ά)ρισεν, 1 aor. act. 3 pers. sing. of καθαρίζω.

ἐκάθε(or α)ρίσθη, 1 aor. pass. 3 pers. sing. of καθαρίζω.

ἐκδόσεται, -δώσεται, fut. mid. 3 pers. sing. of ἐκδίδωμι.

ἐκέκραξα and ἔκραξα, 1 aor. act. of κράζω.

ἐκέρασα, 1 aor. act. of κεράννυμι.

ἐκέρδησα, 1 aor. act. of κερδαίνω.

ἐκκαθάρατε, 1 aor. act. impv. 2 pers. plur. of ἐκκαθαίρω.

ἐκκαθάρῃ, 1 aor. act. subj. 3 pers. sing. of ἐκκαθαίρω.

ἐκκεχυμένος, pf. pass. ptcp. of ἐκχέω.

ἐκκοπήσῃ, 2 fut. pass. 2 pers. sing. of ἐκκόπτω.

ἔκκοψον, 1 aor. act. impv. of ἐκκόπτω.

ἔκλασα, 1 aor. act. of κλάω.

ἔκλαυσα, 1 aor. act. of κλαίω.

ἐκλέλησθε, pf. mid. 2 pers. plur. of ἐκλανθάνω.

ἐκλήθην, 1 aor. pass. of καλέω.

ἐκόψασθε, 1 aor. mid. 2 pers. plur. of κόπτω.

ἐκπλεῦσαι, 1 aor. act. inf. of ἐκπλέω.

ἔκραξα, 1 aor. act. of κράζω.

ἐκρύβη, 2 aor. pass. 3 pers. sing. of κρύπτω.

ἐκσῶσαι, 1 aor. act. inf. of ἐκσώζω.

ἐκτενεῖς, fut. act. 2 pers. sing. of ἐκτείνω.

ἐκτησάμην, 1 aor. of κτάομαι.

ἔκτισται, pf. pass. 3 pers. sing. of κτίζω.

ἐκτραπῇ, 2 aor. pass. subj. 3 pers. sing. of ἐκτρέπω.

ἐκτραπήσονται, 2 fut. pass. 3 pers. plur. of ἐκτρέπω.

ἐκφύῃ, pres. subj. or 2 aor. act. subj. 3 pers. sing. of ἐκφύω.

ἐκφυῇ, 2 aor. pass. subj. 3 pers. sing. of ἐκφύω.

ἐκχέαι, 1 aor. act. inf. of ἐκχέω.

ἐκχέατε, 1 aor. act. impv. 2 pers. plur. of ἐκχέω.

ἐκχέετε, pres. (or 2 aor.) act. impv. 2 pers. plur of ἐκχέω.

ἐκχυννόμενος, ἐκχυνόμενος, see ἐκχέω.

ἐλάβατε (-βετε), 2 aor. act. 2 pers. plur. of λαμβάνω.

ἐλάκησε, 1 aor. act. 3 pers. sing. of λάσκω.

ἔλαχε, 2 aor. act. 3 pers. sing. of λαγχάνω.

ἐλέησον, 1 aor. act. impv. of ἐλεέω.

ἐλεύσομαι, fut. of ἔρχομαι.

ἐληλακότες, pf. act. ptcp. nom. plur. masc. of ἐλαύνω.

ἐλήλυθα, pf. of ἔρχομαι.

ἐλιθάσθησαν, 1 aor. pass. 3 pers. plur. of λιθάζω.
ἑλκύσαι or ἑλκῦσαι, 1 aor. act. inf. of ἕλκω.
ἐλλογᾶτο, impf. pass. 3 pers. sing. of ἐλλογέω.
ἑλόμενος, 2 aor. mid. ptcp. of αἱρέω.
ἐλπιοῦσιν, (Attic) fut. 3 pers. plur. of ἐλπίζω.
ἔμαθον, 2 aor. act. of μανθάνω.
ἐμασσῶντο, ἐμασῶντο, impf. 3 pers. plur. of μασ(σ)άομαι.
ἐμβάς, 2 aor. act. ptcp. of ἐμβαίνω.
ἐμβάψας, 1 aor. act. ptcp. of ἐμβάπτω.
ἐμβῆναι, 2 aor. act. inf. of ἐμβαίνω.
ἔμιξε, 1 aor. act. 3 pers. sing. of μίγνυμι.
ἐμπεπλησμένος, pf. pass. ptcp. of ἐμπίπλημι.
ἐμπλακείς, 2 aor. pass. ptcp. of ἐμπλήσσω.
ἐμπλησθῶ, 1 aor. pass. subj. 1 pers. sing. of ἐμπίπλημι.
ἐνεδυναμοῦτο, impf. pass. 3 pers. sing. of ἐνδυναμόω.
ἐνεῖχεν, impf. act. 3 pers. sing. of ἐνέχω.
ἐνένευον, impf. act. of ἐννεύω.
ἐνέπλησεν, 1 aor. act. 3 pers. sing. of ἐμπίπλημι.
ἐνεπλήσθησαν, 1 aor. pass. 3 pers. plur. of ἐμπίπλημι.
ἐνέπρησε, 1 aor. act. 3 pers. sing. of ἐμπρήθω.
ἐνέπτυον, -σαν, impf. and 1 aor. act. 3 pers. plur. of ἐμπτύω.
ἑνεστηκότα, pf. act. ptcp. acc. sing. masc. of ἐνίστημι.
ἐνεστῶτα, -ῶσαν, -ῶτος, pf. act. ptcp. acc. masc. and fem.
and gen. sing. of ἐνίστημι.
ἐνετειλάμην, 1 aor. mid. of ἐντέλλω.
ἐνεφάνισαν, 1 aor. act. 3 pers. plur. of ἐμφανίζω.
ἐνεφύσησε, 1 aor. act. 3 pers. sing. of ἐμφυσάω.
ἐνεχθείς, 1 aor. pass. ptcp. of φέρω.
ἐνήργηκα, pf. act. of ἐνεργέω.
ἐγκρῖναι, 1 aor. act. inf. of ἐγκρίνω.
ἐνοικοῦν, pres. act. ptcp. nom. sing. neut. of ἐνοικέω.
ἐντελεῖται, fut. mid. 3 pers. sing. of ἐντέλλω.
ἐντέταλται, pf. mid. 3 pers. sing. of ἐντέλλω.
ἐντραπῇ, 2 aor. pass. subj. 3 pers. sing. of ἐντρέπω.
ἐντραπήσονται, 2 fut. pass. 3 pers. plur. of ἐντρέπω.
ἔνυξε, 1 aor. act. 3 pers. sing. of νύσσω.
ἐνύσταξαν, 1 aor. act. 3 pers. plur. of νυστάζω.
ἐνῴκησε, 1 aor. act. 3 pers. sing. of ἐνοικέω.
ἐξαλ(ε)ιφθῆναι, 1 aor. pass. inf. of ἐξαλείφω.
ἐξαναστήσῃ, 1 aor. act. subj. 3 pers. sing. of ἐξανίστημι.
ἐξανέστησαν, 2 aor. act. 3 pers. plur. of ἐξανίστημι.
ἐξάρατε, 1 aor. act. impv. 2 pers. plur. of ἐξαίρω.
ἐξαρεῖτε, fut. act. 2 pers. plur. of ἐξαίρω.
ἐξαρθῇ, 1 aor. pass. subj. 3 pers. sing. of ἐξαίρω.
ἐξέδετο or ἐξέδοτο, 2 aor. mid. 3 pers. sing. of ἐκδίδωμι.
ἐξείλατο or ἐξείλετο, 2 aor. mid. 3 pers. sing. of ἐξαιρέω.
ἐξεκαύθησαν, 1 aor. pass. 3 pers. plur. of ἐκκαίω.
ἐξέκλιναν, 1 aor. act. 3 pers. plur. of ἐκκλίνω.
ἐξεκόπης, 2 aor. pass. 2 pers. sing. of ἐκκόπτω.
ἔξελε, 2 aor. act. impv. of ἐξαιρέω.
ἐξελέξω, 1 aor. mid. 2 pers. sing. of ἐκλέγω.
ἐξέληται, 2 aor. mid. subj. 3 pers. sing. of ἐξαιρέω.
ἐξενέγκαντες, 1 aor. act. ptcp. nom. plur. masc. of ἐκφέρω.
ἐξενεγκεῖν, 2 aor. act. inf. of ἐκφέρω.
ἐξένευσα, 1 aor. act. either of ἐκνεύω or ἐκνέω.
ἐξεπέτασα, 1 aor. act. of ἐκπετάννυμι.
ἐξεπλάγησαν, 2 aor. pass. 3 pers. plur. of ἐκπλήσσω.
ἐξέπλει, impf. act. 3 pers. sing. of ἐκπλέω.

ἐξεστακέναι, pf. act. inf. of ἐξίστημι.
ἐξέστραπται, pf. pass. 3 pers. sing. of ἐκστρέφω.
ἐξετάσαι, 1 aor. act. inf. of ἐξετάζω.
ἐξετράπησαν, 2 aor. pass. 3 pers. plur. of ἐκτρέπω.
ἐξέχεε, 1 aor. act. 3 pers. sing. of ἐκχέω.
ἐξεχύθησαν, 1 aor. pass. 3 pers. plur. of ἐκχέω.
ἐξέωσεν, 1 aor. act. 3 pers. sing. of ἐξωθέω.
ἐξῄεσαν, impf. 3 pers. plur. of ἔξειμι.
ἐξηραμμένος, pf. pass. ptcp. of ξηραίνω.
ἐξήρανα and -ράνθην, 1 aor. act. and pass. of ξηραίνω.
ἐξήρανται, pf. pass. 3 pers. sing. of ξηραίνω.
ἐξηρεύνησα, 1 aor. act. of ἐξερευνάω.
ἐξηρτισμένος, pf. pass. ptcp. of ἐξαρτίζω.
ἐξήχηται, pf. pass. 3 pers. sing. of ἐξηχέω.
ἐξιέναι, pres. inf. of ἔξειμι.
ἐξιστάνων, ἐξιστῶν, impf. act. of ἐξίστημι.
ἐξοίσουσι, fut. act. 3 pers. plur. of ἐκφέρω.
ἐξῶσαι, 1 aor. act. inf. of ἐξωθέω.
ἔξωσεν or ἔξῶσεν, 1 aor. act. 3 pers. sing. of ἐξωθέω.
ἑόρακα, pf. act. of ὁράω.
ἐπαγαγεῖν, 2 aor. act. inf. of ἐπάγω.
ἔπαθεν, 2 aor. act. 3 pers. sing. of πάσχω.
ἐπαναπαήσομαι, fut. mid. of ἐπαναπαύω (see παύω).
ἐπάξας, 1 aor. act. ptcp. of ἐπάγω.
ἐπάρας, 1 aor. act. ptcp. of ἐπαίρω.
ἐπειράσω, 1 aor. mid. 2 pers. sing. of πειράζω.
ἐπειρᾶτο (-ρῶντο), impf. mid. 3 pers. sing. (plur.) of πειράω.
ἔπεισα, 1 aor. act. of πείθω.
ἐπείσθησαν, 1 aor. pass. 3 pers. plur. of πείθω.
ἐπεῖχεν, impf. act. 3 pers. sing. of ἐπέχω.
ἐπέκειλαν, 1 aor. act. 3 pers. plur. of ἐπικέλλω.
ἐπεκέκλητο, plpf. pass. 3 pers. sing. of ἐπικαλέω.
ἐπελάθετο (-θοντο), 2 aor. 3 pers. sing. (plur.) of ἐπιλανθάνομαι.
ἐπέλειχον, impf. act. of ἐπιλείχω.
ἐπεποίθει, 2 plpf. act. 3 pers. sing. of πείθω.
ἔπεσα, (Alex.) 2 aor. act. of πίπτω.
ἐπέστησαν, 2 aor. act. 3 pers. plur. of ἐφίστημι.
ἐπέσχεν, 2 aor. act. 3 pers. sing. of ἐπέχω.
ἐπετίμα, impf. 3 pers. sing. of ἐπιτιμάω.
ἐπετράπη, 2 aor. pass. 3 pers. sing. of ἐπιτρέπω.
ἐπεφάνη, 2 aor. pass. 3 pers. sing. of ἐπιφαίνω.
ἐπέχρισεν, 1 aor. act. 3 pers. sing. of ἐπιχρίω.
ἐπηκροῶντο, impf. 3 pers. plur. of ἐπακροάομαι.
ἐπῄνεσεν, 1 aor. act. 3 pers. sing. of ἐπαινέω.
ἔπηξεν, 1 aor. act. 3 pers sing. of πήγνυμι.
ἔπηρα, 1 aor. act. of ἐπαίρω.
ἐπήρθη, 1 aor. pass. 3 pers. sing. of ἐπαίρω.
ἐπῆρκεν, pf. act. 3 pers. sing. of ἐπαίρω.
ἐπῃσχύνθην and ἐπαισχύνθην, 1 aor. of ἐπαισχύνομαι.
ἐπιβλέψαι, 1 aor. mid. impv. of ἐπιβλέπω.
ἐπιβλέψαι, 1 aor. act. inf. of ἐπιβλέπω.
ἐπίβλεψον, 1 aor. act. impv. of ἐπιβλέπω.
ἔπιδε, impv. of ἐπεῖδον.
ἐπίθες, 2 aor. act. impv. of ἐπιτίθημι.
ἐπικέκλησαι, pf. mid. 2 pers. sing. of ἐπικαλέω.
ἐπικέκλητο, plpf. pass. 3 pers. sing. of ἐπικαλέω.
ἐπικληθέντα, 1 aor. pass. ptcp. acc. sing. masc. of ἐπικαλέω.

ἐπικράνθησαν, 1 aor. pass. 3 pers. plur. of πικραίνω.
ἐπιλελησμένος, pf. pass. ptcp. of ἐπιλανθάνομαι.
ἐπιμελήθητι, 1 aor. pass. impv. of ἐπιμελέομαι.
ἔπιον, 2 aor. act. of πίνω.
ἐπιπλήξῃς, 1 aor. act. subj. 2 pers. sing. of ἐπιπλήσσω.
ἐπιποθήσατε, 1 aor. act. impv. 2 pers. plur. of ἐπιποθέω.
ἐπιστᾶσα, 2 aor. act. ptcp. nom. sing. fem. of ἐφίστημι.
ἐπίσταται, pres. ind. mid. 3 pers. sing. of ἐφίστημι.
ἐπίσταται, pres. ind. 3 pers. sing. of ἐπίσταμαι.
ἐπίστηθι, 2 aor. act. impv. of ἐφίστημι.
ἐπιστώθης, 1 aor. pass. 2 pers. sing. of πιστόω.
ἐπιτεθῇ, 1 aor. pass. subj. 3 pers. sing. of ἐπιτίθημι.
ἐπιτιθέασι, pres. act. 3 pers. plur. of ἐπιτίθημι.
ἐπιτίθει, pres. act. impv. of ἐπιτίθημι.
ἐπιτιμῆσαι (-μῆσαι), 1 aor. act. inf. (opt. 3 pers. sing.) of ἐπιτιμάω.
ἐπιφᾶναι, 1 aor. act. inf. of ἐπιφαίνω.
ἐπλανήθησαν, 1 aor. pass. 3 pers. plur. of πλανάω.
ἐπλάσθη, 1 aor. pass. 3 pers. sing. of πλάσσω.
ἐπλήγη, 2 aor. pass. 3 pers. sing. of πλήσσω.
ἔπλησαν, 1 aor. act. 3 pers. plur. of πίμπλημι.
ἐπλήσθη (-θησαν), 1 aor. pass. 3 pers. sing. (plur.) of πίμπλημι.
ἐπλουτήσατε, 1 aor. act. 2 pers. plur. of πλουτέω.
ἐπλουτίσθητε, 1 aor. pass. 2 pers. plur. of πλουτίζω.
ἔπλυναν, 1 aor. act. 3 pers. plur. of πλύνω.
ἔπνευσαν, 1 aor. act. 3 pers. plur. of πνέω.
ἐπνίγοντο, impf. pass. 3 pers. plur. of πνίγω.
ἔπνιξαν, 1 aor. act. 3 pers. plur. of πνίγω.
ἐπράθη, 1 aor. pass. 3 pers. sing. of πιπράσκω.
ἐπρίσθησαν, 1 aor. pass. 3 pers. plur. of πρίζω.
ἐπροφήτευον (-σα), impf. (1 aor.) act. of προφητεύω.
ἔπτυσε, 1 aor. act. 3 pers. sing. of πτύω.
ἐπώκειλαν, 1 aor. act. 3 pers. plur. of ἐποκέλλω.
ἐρ(ρ)άντισε, 1 aor. act. 3 pers. sing. of ῥαντίζω.
ἐρ(ρ)άπισαν, 1 aor. act. 3 pers. plur. of ῥαπίζω.
ἐρριζωμένοι, pf. pass. ptcp. nom. plur. masc. of ῥιζόω.
ἐρ(ρ)ιμμένοι, pf. pass. ptcp. nom. plur. masc. of ῥίπτω.
ἔρ(ρ)ιπται, pf. pass. 3 pers. sing. of ῥίπτω.
ἔρ(ρ)ιψαν, 1 aor. act. 3 pers. plur. of ῥίπτω.
ἐρ(ρ)ύσατο, 1 aor. mid. 3 pers. sing. of ῥύομαι.
ἐρ(ρ)ύσθην, 1 aor. pass. of ῥύομαι.
ἔρρωσο, ἔρρωσθε, pf. pass. impv. of ῥώννυμι.
ἐσάλπισε, 1 aor. act. 3 pers. sing. of σαλπίζω.
ἔσβεσαν, 1 aor. act. 3 pers. plur. of σβέννυμι.
ἐσείσθην, 1 aor. pass. of σείω.
ἐσκυλμένοι, pf. pass. ptcp. nom. plur. masc. of σκύλλω.
ἐσπαρμένος, pf. pass. ptcp. of σπείρω.
ἐστάθην, 1 aor. pass. of ἵστημι.
ἑστάναι, ἑστᾶναι, pf. act. inf. of ἵστημι.
ἑστήκεισαν, -κεσαν, plpf. act. 3 pers. plur. of ἵστημι.
ἕστηκεν, impf. 3 pers. sing. of στήκω.
ἑστηκώς, pf. act. ptcp. of ἵστημι.
ἔστην, 2 aor. act. of ἵστημι.
ἐστηριγμένος, pf. pass. ptcp. of στηρίζω.
ἐστήρικται, pf. pass. 3 pers. sing. of στηρίζω.
ἑστός (-ώς), pf. act. ptcp. neut. (masc. and neut.) of ἵστημι.
ἐστράφησαν, 2 aor. pass. 3 pers. plur. of στρέφω.

ἐστρωμένον, pf. pass. ptcp. neut. of στρωννύω.
ἔστρωσαν, 1 aor. act. 3 pers. plur. of στρωννύω.
ἔστωσαν, impv. 3 pers. plur. of εἰμί.
ἐσφαγμένος, pf. pass. ptcp. of σφάζω.
ἐσφραγισμένος, pf. pass. ptcp. of σφραγίζω.
ἔσχηκα, pf. act. of ἔχω.
ἐσχηκότα, pf. act. ptcp. acc. sing. masc. of ἔχω.
ἔσχον, 2 aor. act. of ἔχω.
ἐτάφη, 2 aor. pass. 3 pers. sing. of θάπτω.
ἐτέθην, 1 aor. pass. of τίθημι.
ἐτεθνήκει, plpf. act. 3 pers. sing. of θνήσκω.
ἔτεκεν, 2 aor. act. 3 pers. sing. of τίκτω.
ἐτέχθη, 1 aor. pass. 3 pers. sing. of τίκτω.
ἐτίθει, impf. act. 3 pers. sing. of τίθημι.
ἐτύθη, 1 aor. pass. 3 pers. sing. of θύω.
εὐηρεστηκέναι (εὐαρεστηκέναι), pf. act. inf. of εὐαρεστέω.
εὐξάμην (εὐξαίμην), 1 aor. (opt.) of εὔχομαι.
εὕραμεν, εὗραν, (Alex.) 2 aor. act. of εὑρίσκω.
εὑράμενος and εὑρόμενος, 2 aor. mid. ptcp. of εὑρίσκω.
εὑρεθῶσιν, 1 aor. pass. subj. 3 pers. plur. of εὑρίσκω.
εὑρηκέναι, pf. act. inf. of εὑρίσκω.
εὐφράνθητι, 1 aor. pass. impv. of εὐφραίνω.
ἔφαγον, 2 aor. act. of ἐσθίω.
ἐφαλλόμενος, ἐφαλόμενος, 2 aor. ptcp. of ἐφάλλομαι.
ἐφάνην, 2 aor. pass. of φαίνω.
ἔφασκεν, impf. act. 3 pers. sing. of φάσκω.
ἐφείσατο, 1 aor. 3 pers. sing. of φείδομαι.
ἐφεστώς, pf. act. ptcp. of ἐφίστημι.
ἔφθακα, -σα, pf. and 1 aor. act. of φθάνω.
ἐφθάρην, 2 aor. pass. of φθείρω.
ἔφιδε (ἔπιδε), impv. of ἐπεῖδον.
ἐφίλει, impf. act. 3 pers. sing. of φιλέω.
ἐφίσταται, pres. mid. 3 pers. sing. of ἐφίστημι.
ἔφραξαν, 1 aor. act. 3 pers. plur. of φράσσω.
ἐφρύαξαν, 1 aor. act. 3 pers. plur. of φρυάσσω.
ἔφυγον, 2 aor. act. of φεύγω.
ἐχάρην, 2 aor. pass. (as act.) of χαίρω.
ἔχρισα, 1 aor. act. of χρίω.
ἐχρῶντο, impf. 3 pers. plur. of χράομαι.
ἐψεύσω, 1 aor. mid. 2 pers. sing. of ψεύδομαι.
ἑώρακαν, -ράκασιν, pf. act. 3 pers. plur. of ὁράω.
ἑώρακαι, plpf. act. 3 pers. sing. of ὁράω.
ἑωρακώς, pf. act. ptcp. of ὁράω.
ἑώρων, impf. act. 3 pers. plur. of ὁράω.

ζβέννυτε, pres. act. impv. 2 pers. plur. (Tdf.) of σβέννυμι.
ζῇ, ζῆν or ζῆν, ζῆς, ζῶ, see ζάω.
ζῶσαι, 1 aor. mid. impv. of ζώννυμι.
ζώσει, fut. act. 3 pers. sing. of ζώννυμι

ἠβουλήθην, etc., see βούλομαι.
ἤγαγον, 2 aor. act. of ἄγω.
ἠγάπα, impf. act. 3 pers. sing. of ἀγαπάω.
ἠγαπηκόσι, pf. act. ptcp. dat. plur. of ἀγαπάω.
ἤγγειλαν, 1 aor. act. 3 pers. plur. of ἀγγέλλω.
ἤγγικα, -σα, pf. and 1 aor. act. of ἐγγίζω.

ἤγειρεν, 1 aor. act. 3 pers. sing. of ἐγείρω.
ἠγέρθην, 1 aor. pass. of ἐγείρω.
ἤγετο (-γοντο), impf. pass. 3 pers. sing. (plur.) of ἄγω.
ἤγημαι, pf. of ἡγέομαι.
ἡγνικότες, pf. act. ptcp. nom. plur. masc. of ἁγνίζω.
ἡγνισμένος, pf. pass. ptcp. of ἁγνίζω.
ἠγνόουν, impf. act. of ἀγνοέω.
ᾔδεισαν, plpf. 3 pers. plur. of οἶδα (see εἴδω, II.).
ἠδύνατο (ἐδύνατο), impf. 3 pers. sing. of δύναμαι.
ἠδυνήθη, ἠδυνάσθη, 1 aor. 3 pers. sing. of δύναμαι.
ἤθελον, impf. of θέλω.
ἥκασι, pf. act. 3 pers. plur. of ἥκω.
ἠκολουθήκαμεν, pf. act. 1 pers. plur. of ἀκολουθέω.
ἥλατο, 1 aor. 3 pers. sing. of ἅλλομαι.
ἠλαττωμένος, pf. pass. ptcp. of ἐλαττόω.
ἠλαύνετο, impf. pass. 3 pers. sing. of ἐλαύνω.
ἠλεήθην, 1 aor. pass. of ἐλεέω.
ἠλεημένος, pf. pass. ptcp. of ἐλεέω.
ἠλέησα, 1 aor. act. of ἐλεέω.
ἤλειψα, 1 aor. act. of ἀλείφω.
ἡλκωμένος, pf. pass. ptcp. of ἑλκόω.
ἤλλαξαν, 1 aor. act. 3 pers. plur. of ἀλλάσσω.
ἤλλετο, impf. 3 pers. sing. of ἅλλομαι.
ἤλπικα, -σα, pf. and 1 aor. act. of ἐλπίζω.
ἡμάρτηκα, pf. act. of ἁμαρτάνω.
ἥμαρτον, 2 aor. act. of ἁμαρτάνω.
ἤμεθα, ἤμεν, impf. 1 pers. plur. of εἰμί.
ἤμελλον and ἔμελλον, impf. of μέλλω.
ἤμην, impf. of εἰμί.
ἠμφιεσμένος, pf. pass. ptcp. of ἀμφιέννυμι.
ἤνεγκα, 1 aor. act. of φέρω.
ἠνειχόμην, impf. mid. of ἀνέχω.
ἠνεσχόμην, 2 aor. mid. of ἀνέχω.
ἠνέχθην, 1 aor. pass. of φέρω.
ἠνεῳγμένος, pf. pass. ptcp. of ἀνοίγω.
ἠνέῳξα (ἠνέῳξα Tr ?), 1 aor. act. of ἀνοίγω.
ἠνεῴχθην, 1 aor. pass. of ἀνοίγω.
ἠνοίγην, 2 aor. pass. of ἀνοίγω.
ἠνοιγμένος, pf. pass. ptcp. of ἀνοίγω.
ἤνοιξα, 1 aor. act. of ἀνοίγω.
ἠνοίχθην, 1 aor. pass. of ἀνοίγω.
ἥξει, fut. act. 3 pers. sing. of ἥκω.
ἥξῃ, 1 aor. act. subj. 3 pers. sing. of ἥκω.
ἠξίου, impf. act. 3 pers. sing. of ἀξιόω.
ἠξίωται, pf. pass. 3 pers. sing. of ἀξιόω.
ἠπατήθη, 1 aor. pass. 3 pers. sing. of ἀπαταω.
ἠπείθησαν, 1 aor. act. 3 pers. plur. of ἀπειθέω.
ἠπείθουν, impf. act. of ἀπειθέω.
ἠπείλει, impf. act. 3 pers. sing. of ἀπειλέω.
ἠπίστουν, impf. act. of ἀπιστέω.
ἠπόρει, impf. act. 3 pers. sing. of ἀπορέω.
ἥπτοντο, impf. mid. 3 pers. plur. of ἅπτω.
ἦρα, 1 aor. act. of αἴρω.
ἠρ-(εἰρ-)γαζόμην, -σάμην, impf. and 1 aor. of ἐργάζομαι.
ἠρέθισα, 1 aor. act. of ἐρεθίζω.
ἤρεσα, 1 aor. act. of ἀρέσκω.
ἤρεσκον, impf. act. of ἀρέσκω.
ἠρημώθη, 1 aor. pass. 3 pers. sing. of ἐρημόω.

ἠρημωμένην, pf. pass. ptcp. acc. sing. fem. of ἐρημόω.
ἤρθην, 1 aor. pass. of αἴρω.
ἦρκεν, pf. act. 3 pers. sing. of αἴρω.
ἠρμένος, pf. pass. ptcp. of αἴρω.
ἠρνεῖτο, impf. 3 pers. sing. of ἀρνέομαι.
ἤρνημαι, pf. pass. of ἀρνέομαι.
ἠρνημένος, pf. pass. ptcp. of ἀρνέομαι.
ἠρνησάμην, 1 aor. of ἀρνέομαι.
ἠρνήσω, 1 aor. 2 pers. sing. of ἀρνέομαι.
ἠρξάμην, 1 aor. mid. of ἄρχω.
ἡρπάγη, 2 aor. pass. 3 pers. sing. of ἁρπάζω.
ἥρπασε, 1 aor. act. 3 pers. sing. of ἁρπάζω.
ἡρπάσθη, 1 aor. pass. 3 pers. sing. of ἁρπάζω.
ἠρτυμένος, pf. pass. ptcp. of ἀρτύω.
ἤρχοντο, impf. 3 pers. plur. of ἔρχομαι.
ἠρώτουν, ἠρώτων, impf. act. 3 pers. plur. of ἐρωτάω.
ἦς, ἦσθα, impf. 2 pers. sing. of εἰμί.
ἤσθιον, impf. act. of ἐσθίω.
ἡσσώθητε, 1 aor. pass. 2 pers. plur. of ἡττάω.
ᾐτήκατε, pf. act. 1 pers. plur. of αἰτέω.
ᾔτησα, -σάμην, 1 aor. act. and mid. of αἰτέω.
ἠτίμασα, 1 aor. act. of ἀτιμάζω.
ἠτίμησα, 1 aor. act. of ἀτιμάω.
ἠτιμωμένος, pf. pass. ptcp. of ἀτιμόω.
ᾐτοῦντο, impf. mid. 3 pers. plur. of αἰτέω.
ἡττήθητε, 1 aor. pass. 2 pers. plur. of ἡττάω.
ἥττηται, pf. pass. 3 pers. sing. of ἡττάω.
ἤτω, pres. impv. 3 pers. sing. of εἰμί.
ηὐδόκησα, 1 aor. act. of εὐδοκέω.
ηὐδοκοῦμεν, impf. act. 1 pers. plur. of εὐδοκέω.
ηὐκαίρουν, impf. act. of εὐκαιρέω.
ηὐλήσαμεν, 1 aor. act. 1 pers. plur. of αὐλέω.
ηὐλόγει, impf. act. 3 pers. sing. of εὐλογέω.
ηὐλόγηκα, -σα, pf. and 1 aor. act. of εὐλογέω.
ηὔξησα, 1 aor. act. of αὔξανω.
ηὐπορεῖτο, impf. mid. 3 pers. sing. of εὐπορέω.
ηὑρίσκετο, impf. pass. 3 pers. sing. of εὑρίσκω.
ηὕρισκον, impf. act. of εὑρίσκω.
ηὐφόρησεν, 1 aor. act. 3 pers. sing. of εὐφορέω.
ηὐφράνθη, 1 aor. pass. 3 pers. sing. of εὐφραίνω.
ηὐχαρίστησαν, 1 aor. act. 3 pers. plur. of εὐχαριστέω.
ηὐχόμην, impf. of εὔχομαι.
ἤφιε, impf. 3 pers. sing. of ἀφίημι (ἀφίω).
ἤχθην, 1 aor. pass. of ἄγω.
ἠχρειώθησαν, 1 aor. pass. 3 pers. plur. of ἀχρειόω.
ἡψάμην, 1 aor. mid. of ἅπτω.

θάψαι, 1 aor. act. inf. of θάπτω.
θεῖναι, θείς, 2 aor. act. inf. and ptcp. of τίθημι.
θέμενος, 2 aor. mid. ptcp. of τίθημι.
θέντες, 2 aor. act. ptcp. nom. plur. masc. of τίθημι.
θέσθε, 2 aor. mid. impv. 2 pers. plur. of τίθημι.
θέτε, 2 aor. act. impv. 2 pers. plur. of τίθημι.
θίγῃς, θίγῃ, 2 aor. act. subj. 2 and 3 pers. sing. of θιγγάνω.
θῶ, 2 aor. act. subj. of τίθημι.

ἰάθη (-θῇ), 1 aor. pass. ind. (subj.) 3 pers. sing. of ἰάομαι.

ἴαται, pf. pass. 3 pers. sing. of ἰάομαι.

ἰᾶται, pres. 3 pers. sing. of ἰάομαι.

ἰᾶτο, impf. 3 pers. sing. ἰάομαι.

ἴδαν, ἴδον, collat. forms of εἶδον.

ἴσασι, 3 pers. plur. of the 2 pf. οἶδα (see εἴδω, II.).

ἴσθι, impv. 2 pers. sing. of εἰμί.

ἱστάνομεν and ἱστῶμεν, pres. ind. 1 pers. plur. of ἵστημι.

ἴστε, 2 pers. plur. ind. or impv. of οἶδα (see εἴδω, II.).

ἱστήκειν, plpf. act. of ἵστημι.

ἰώμενος, pres. ptcp. of ἰάομαι.

καθαριεῖ, (Attic) fut. 3 pers. sing. of καθαρίζω.

καθαρίσαι, 1 aor. act. inf. of καθαρίζω.

καθαρίσῃ, 1 aor. act. subj. 3 pers. sing. of καθαρίζω.

καθαρίσθητι, 1 aor. pass. impv. of καθαρίζω.

καθεῖλε, 2 aor. act. 3 pers. sing. of καθαιρέω.

καθελῶ, fut. act. of καθαιρέω.

κάθῃ, pres. ind. 2 pers. sing. of κάθημαι.

καθῆκαν, 1 aor. act. 3 pers. plur. of καθίημι.

καθήσεσθε, fut. 2 pers. plur. of κάθημαι.

καθῆψε, 1 aor. act. 3 pers. sing. of καθάπτω.

κάθου, pres. impv. of κάθημαι.

καλέσαι, 1 aor. act. inf. of καλέω.

κάλεσον, 1 aor. act. impv. of καλέω.

κάμητε, 2 aor. act. subj. 2 pers. plur. of κάμνω.

κατάβα and κατάβηθι, 2 aor. act. impv. of καταβαίνω.

καταβάς, 2 aor. act. ptcp. of καταβαίνω.

καταβέβηκα, pf. act. of καταβαίνω.

καταβῇ, 2 aor. act. subj. 3 pers. sing. of καταβαίνω.

κατακαήσομαι, 2 fut. pass. of κατακαίω.

κατακαῦσαι, 1 aor. act. inf. of κατακαίω.

κατακαυχῶ, pres. impv. of κατακαυχάομαι.

καταλάβῃ, 2 aor. act. subj. 3 pers. sing. of καταλαμβάνω.

καταπίῃ, 2 aor. act. subj. 3 pers. sing. of καταπίνω.

καταποθῇ, 1 aor. pass. subj. 3 pers. sing. of καταπίνω.

καταρτίσαι, 1 aor. act. inf. or opt. (3 pers. sing.) of καταρτίζω.

κατασκηνοῖν (-νοῦν), pres. act. inf. of κατασκηνόω.

κατάσχωμεν, 2 aor. act. subj. 1 pers. plur. of κατέχω

κατεαγῶσιν, 2 aor. pass. subj. 3 pers. plur. of κατάγνυμι.

κατέαξαν, 1 aor. act. 3 pers. plur. of κατάγνυμι.

κατεάξει, fut. act. 3 pers. sing. of κατάγνυμι.

κατέβη (-ησαν), 2 aor. act. 3 pers. sing. (plur.) of καταβαίνω.

κατεγνωσμένος, pf. pass. ptcp. of καταγινώσκω.

κατειλημμένος, pf. pass. ptcp. of καταλαμβάνω.

κατειληφέναι, pf. act. inf. of καταλαμβάνω.

κατεκάη, 2 aor. pass. 3 pers. sing. of κατακαίω.

κατέκλασε, 1 aor. act. 3 pers. sing. of κατακλάω.

κατέκλεισα, 1 aor. act. of κατακλείω.

κατενεχθείς, 1 aor. pass. ptcp. of καταφέρω.

κατενύγησαν, 2 aor. pass. 3 pers. plur. of κατανύσσω.

κατεπέστησαν, 2 aor. act. 3 pers. plur. of κατεφίστημι.

κατέπιε, 2 aor. act. 3 pers. sing. of καταπίνω.

κατεπόθη, 1 aor. pass. of καταπίνω.

κατεσκαμμένα, pf. pass. ptcp. nom. plur. neut. of κατασκάπτω.

κατεστρεμμένος, -στραμμένος, pf. pass. ptcp. of καταστρέφω.

κατεστρώθησαν, 1 aor. pass. 3 pers. plur. of καταστρώννυμι.

κατευθῦναι, 1 aor. act. inf. of κατευθύνω.

κατευθύναι, 1 aor. act. opt. 3 pers. sing. of κατευθύνω.

κατέφαγον, 2 aor. act. of κατεσθίω.

κατήγγειλα, 1 aor. act. of καταγγέλλω.

κατηγγέλη, 2 aor. pass. 3 pers. sing. of καταγγέλλω.

κατήνεγκα, 1 aor. act. of καταφέρω.

κατήντηκα, -σα, pf. and 1 aor. act. of καταντάω.

κατηράσω, 1 aor. 2 pers. sing. of καταράομαι.

κατήργηται, pf. pass. 3 pers. sing. of καταργέω.

κατηρτισμένος, pf. pass. ptcp. of καταρτίζω.

κατηρτίσω, 1 aor. mid. 2 pers. sing. of καταρτίζω.

κατησχύνθην, 1 aor. pass. of καταισχύνω.

κατήχηνται, pf. pass. 3 pers. plur. of κατηχέω.

κατηχήσω, 1 aor. act. subj. of κατηχέω.

κατίωται, pf. pass. 3 pers. sing. of κατιόω.

κατῴκισεν, 1 aor. act. 3 pers. sing. of κατοικίζω.

καυθήσομαι, καυχήσωμαι, see καίω.

καυχᾶσαι, pres. ind. 2 pers. sing. of καυχάομαι.

κεκαθα(or ε)ρισμένος, pf. pass. ptcp. of καθαρίζω.

κεκαθαρμένος, pf. pass. ptcp. of καθαίρω.

κεκαλυμμένος, pf. pass. ptcp. of καλύπτω.

κεκαυμένος, pf. pass. ptcp. of καίω.

κεκερασμένου, pf. pass. ptcp. gen. sing. masc. of κεράννυμι.

κέκλεισμαι, pf. pass. of κλείω.

κέκληκα, pf. act. of καλέω.

κέκληται, pf. pass. 3 pers. sing. of καλέω.

κέκλικεν, pf. act. 3 pers. sing. of κλίνω.

κέκμηκας, pf. act. 2 pers. sing. of κάμνω.

κεκορεσμένος, pf. pass. ptcp. of κορέννυμι.

κέκραγε, 2 pf. act. 3 pers. sing. of κράζω.

κεκράξονται, fut. mid. 3 pers. plur. of κράζω.

κεκρατηκέναι, pf. act. inf. of κρατέω.

κεκράτηνται, pf. pass. 3 pers. plur. of κρατέω.

κέκρικει, plpf. act. 3 pers. sing. of κρίνω.

κέκριμαι, pf. pass. of κρίνω.

κεκρυμμένος, pf. pass. ptcp. of κρύπτω.

κεράσατε, 1 aor. act. impv. 2 pers. plur. of κεράννυμι.

κερδανῶ, κερδήσω, fut. act. of κερδαίνω.

κερδάνω, 1 aor. act. subj. of κερδαίνω.

κεχάρισμαι, pf. of χαρίζομαι.

κεχαριτωμένη, pf. pass. ptcp. nom. sing. fem. of χαριτόω.

κέχρημαι, pf. of χράομαι.

κεχωρισμένος, pf. pass. ptcp. of χωρίζω.

κηρύξαι (al. κηρῦξαι), 1 aor. act. inf. of κηρύσσω.

κλάσαι, 1 aor. act. inf. of κλάω.

κλαύσατε, 1 aor. act. impv. 2 pers. plur. of κλαίω.

κλαύσω, κλαύσομαι, fut. of κλαίω.

κλεισθῶσιν, 1 aor. pass. subj. 3 pers. plur. of κλείω.

κληθῇς, κληθῶμεν, κληθῆναι, κληθέν, 1 aor. pass. of καλέω.

κλῶμεν, pres. ind. 1 pers. plur. of κλάω.

κλώμενον, pres. pass. ptcp. neut. of κλάω.

κλῶντες, pres. act. ptcp. nom. plur. masc. of κλάω.

κοιμώμενος, pres. pass. ptcp. of κοιμάω.

κολλήθητι, 1 aor. pass. impv. of κολλάω.

κομιεῖται, (Attic) fut. mid. 3 pers. sing. of κομίζω.

κομίσασα, 1 aor. act. ptcp. nom. sing. fem. of κομίζω.

κορεσθέντες, 1 aor. pass. ptcp. nom. plur. masc. of κορέννυμι.
κόψας, 1 aor. act. ptcp. of κόπτω.
κράζον (not κράζον), pres. ptcp. neut. of κράζω.
κράξας, 1 aor. act. ptcp. of κράζω.
κράξουσιν, fut. act. 3 pers. plur. of κράζω.
κράτει, pres. impv. of κρατέω.
κριθήσεσθε, 1 fut. pass. 2 pers. plur. of κρίνω.
κριθῶσιν, 1 aor. pass. subj. 3 pers. plur. of κρίνω.
κρυβῆναι, 2 aor. pass. inf. of κρύπτω.
κτήσασθε, 1 aor. mid. impv. 2 pers. plur. of κτάομαι.
κτήσησθε, 1 aor. mid. subj. 2 pers. plur. of κτάομαι.

λάβε(-βη), 2 aor. act. impv. (subj. 3 pers. sing.) of λαμβάνω.
λαθεῖν, 2 aor. act. inf. of λανθάνω.
λαχοῦσι, 2 aor. act. ptcp. dat. plur. of λαγχάνω.
λάχωμεν, 2 aor. act. subj. 1 pers. plur. of λαγχάνω.
λελου(σ)μένος, pf. pass. ptcp. of λούω.
λέλυσαι, pf. pass. 2 pers. sing. of λύω.
λη(μ)φθῇ, 1 aor. pass. subj. 3 pers. sing. of λαμβάνω.
λή(μ)ψομαι, fut. of λαμβάνω.
λίπῃ, 2 aor. act. subj. 3 pers. sing. of λείπω.

μάθετε, 2 aor. act. impv. 2 pers. plur. of μανθάνω.
μάθητε, 2 aor. act. subj. 2 pers. plur. of μανθάνω.
μαθών, 2 aor. act. ptcp. of μανθάνω.
μακαριοῦσι, (Attic) fut. 3 pers. plur. of μακαρίζω.
μακροθύμησον, 1 aor. act. impv. of μακροθυμέω.
μεθιστάναι, pres. act. inf. of μεθίστημι.
μεθυσθῶσιν, 1 aor. pass. subj. 3 pers. plur. of μεθύσκω.
μεῖναι, 1 aor. inf. of μένω.
μείναντες, 1 aor. ptcp. nom. plur. masc. of μένω.
μείνατε, μεῖνον, 1 aor. impv. of μένω.
μείνῃ, -ητε, -ωσιν, 1 aor. subj. of μένω.
μελέτα, pres. act. impv. of μελετάω.
μεμαθηκώς, pf. act. ptcp. of μανθάνω.
μεμενήκεισαν, plpf. act. 3 pers. plur. of μένω.
μεμιαμμένος or -σμένος, pf. pass. ptcp. of μιαίνω.
μεμίανται, pf. pass. 3 pers. sing. or plur. of μιαίνω.
μεμιγμένος, pf. pass. ptcp. of μίγνυμι.
μέμνησθε, pf. mid. 2 pers. plur. of μιμνήσκω.
μεμύημαι, pf. pass. of μυέω.
μενεῖτε, fut. ind. 2 pers. plur. of μένω.
μένετε, pres. ind. or impv. 2 pers. plur. of μένω.
μετάβα, μετάβηθι, 2 aor. act. impv. of μεταβαίνω.
μετασταθῶ, 1 aor. pass. subj. of μεθίστημι.
μεταστραφήτω, 2 aor. pass. impv. 3 pers. sing. of μεταστρέφω.
μετέθηκεν, 1 aor. act. 3 pers. sing. of μετατίθημι.
μετέστησεν, 1 aor. act. 3 pers. sing. of μεθίστημι.
μετέσχηκεν, pf. act. 3 pers. sing. of μετέχω.
μετετέθησαν, 1 aor. pass. 3 pers. plur. of μετατίθημι.
μετήλλαξαν, 1 aor. act. 3 pers. plur. of μεταλλάσσω.
μετῆρεν, 1 aor. act. 3 pers. sing. of μεταίρω.
μετοικιῶ, (Attic) fut. act. of μετοικίζω.
μετῴκισεν, 1 aor. act. 3 pers. sing. of μετοικίζω.

μιανθῶσιν, 1 aor. pass. subj. 3 pers. plur. of μιαίνω.
μνησθῆναι, 1 aor. pass inf. of μιμνήσκω.
μνήσθητι, -τε, 1 aor. pass. impv. of μιμνήσκω.
μνησθῶ, -θῇς, 1 aor. pass. subj. of μιμνήσκω.

νενίκηκα, pf. act. of νικάω.
νενομοθέτητο, plpf. pass. 3 pers. sing. of νομοθετέω.
νήψατε, 1 aor. impv. 2 pers. plur. of νήφω.
νόει, pres. act. impv. of νοέω.
νοούμενα, pres. pass. ptcp. neut. plur. of νοέω.

ὀδυνᾶσαι, pres. ind. mid. 2 pers. sing. of ὀδυνάω.
οἴσω, fut. act. of φέρω.
ὀμνύναι, ὀμνύειν, pres. act. inf. of ὀμνύω.
ὀμόσαι, -ας, 1 aor. act. inf. and ptcp. of ὀμνύω.
ὀμόσῃ, 1 aor. act. subj. 3 pers. sing. of ὀμνύω.
ὀναίμην, 2 aor. mid. opt. of ὀνίνημι.
ὀρῶσαι, pres. act. ptcp. nom. plur. fem. of ὁράω.
ὀφθείς, 1 aor. pass. ptcp. of ὁράω.
ὄψει, ὄψῃ, fut. 2 pers. sing. of ὁράω.
ὄψεσθε, fut. 2 pers. plur. of ὁράω.
ὄψησθε, 1 aor. mid. subj. 2 pers. plur. of ὁράω.

παθεῖν, 2 aor. act. inf. of πάσχω.
πάθῃ, 2 aor. act. subj. 3 pers. sing. of πάσχω.
παίσῃ, 1 aor. act. subj. 3 pers. sing. of παίω.
παραβολευσάμενος, 1 aor. ptcp. of παραβολεύομαι.
παραβουλευσάμενος, 1 aor. ptcp. of παραβουλεύομαι.
παραδεδώκεισαν, plpf. 3 pers. plur. of παραδίδωμι.
παραδιδοῖ, παραδιδῷ, pres. subj. 3 pers. sing. of παραδίδωμι.
παραδιδούς (παραδούς), pres. (2 aor.) ptcp. of παραδίδωμι.
παραδῷ (-δοῖ), 2 aor. act. subj. 3 pers. sing. of παραδίδωμι.
παραθεῖναι, 2 aor. act. inf. of παρατίθημι.
παράθου, 2 aor. mid. impv. of παρατίθημι.
παραθῶσιν, 2 aor. act. subj. 3 pers. plur. of παρατίθημι.
παραιτοῦ, pres. impv. of παραιτέομαι.
παρακεκαλυμμένος, pf. pass. ptcp. of παρακαλύπτω.
παρακεχειμακότι, pf. act. ptcp. dat. sing. of παραχειμάζω.
παρακληθῶσιν, 1 aor. pass. subj. 3 pers. plur. of παρακαλέω.
παρακύψας, 1 aor. act. ptcp. of παρακύπτω.
παραλη(μ)φθήσεται, 1 fut. pass. 3 pers. sing. of παραλαμβάνω.
παραπλεῦσαι, 1 aor. act. inf. of παραπλέω.
παραρ(ρ)υῶμεν, 2 aor. pass. subj. 1 pers. plur. of παραρρέω.
παραστῆσαι, 1 aor. act. inf. of παρίστημι.
παραστήσατε, 1 aor. act. impv. 2 pers. plur. of παρίστημι.
παραστῆτε, 2 aor. act. subj. 2 pers. plur. of παρίστημι.
παρασχών, 2 aor. act. ptcp. of παρέχω.
παρατιθέσθωσαν, pres. impv. 3 pers. plur. of παρατίθημι.
παρεδίδοσαν, impf. (Alex.) 3 pers. plur. of παραδίδωμι.
παρέθεντο, 2 aor. mid. 3 pers. plur. of παρατίθημι.
πάρει, pres. ind. 2 pers. sing. of πάρειμι.
παρειμένος, pf. pass. ptcp. of παρίημι.
παρεῖναι, 2 aor. act. inf. of πάρημι and pres. inf. of πάρειμι.
παρεισάξουσιν, fut. act. 3 pers. plur. of παρεισάγω.

παρεισεδύησαν, 2 aor. pass. 3 pers. plur. of παρεισδύω.

παρεισέδυσαν, 1 aor. act. 3 pers. plur. of παρεισδύω.

παρεισενέγκαντες, 1 aor. act. ptcp. nom. plur. masc. of παρεισφέρω.

παρειστήκεισαν, plpf. act. 3 pers. plur. of παρίστημι.

παρεῖχαν, impf. (Alex.) 3 pers. plur. of παρέχω.

παρειχόμην, impf. mid. of παρέχω.

παρέκυψεν, 1 aor. act. 3 pers. sing. of παρακύπτω.

παρελάβοσαν, 2 aor. act. (Alex.) 3 pers. plur. of παραλαμβάνω.

παρελεύσονται, fut. 3 pers. plur. of παρέρχομαι.

παρεληλυθέναι (-θώς), pf. act. inf. (ptcp.) of παρέρχομαι.

παρελθάτω (-θέτω), 2 aor. act. impv. 3 pers. sing. of παρέρχομαι.

παρενεγκεῖν, 2 aor. act. inf. of παραφέρω.

παρέξει, fut. act. 3 pers. sing. of παρέχω.

παρέξῃ, fut. mid. 2 pers. sing. of παρέχω.

παρεπίκραναν, 1 aor. act. 3 pers. plur. of παραπικραίνω.

παρεσκεύασται, pf. pass. 3 pers. sing. of παρασκευάζω.

παρεστηκότες and παρεστῶτες, pf. act. ptcp. nom. plur. masc. of παρίστημι.

παρεστήσατε, 1 aor. act. 2 pers. plur. of παρίστημι.

παρέτεινε, 1 aor. act. 3 pers. sing. of παρατείνω.

παρετήρουν, impf. act. 3 pers. plur. of παρατηρέω.

παρήγγειλαν, 1 aor. act. 3 pers. plur. of παραγγέλλω.

παρηκολούθηκας (-σας), pf. (1 aor.) act. 2 pers. sing. of παρακολουθέω.

παρῄνει, impf. act. 3 pers. sing. of παραινέω.

παρῃτημένος, pf. pass. ptcp. of παραιτέομαι.

παρῃτήσαντο, 1 aor. mid. 3 pers. plur. of παραιτέομαι.

παρῴκησεν, 1 aor. act. 3 pers. sing. of παροικέω.

παρωξύνετο, impf. pass. 3 pers. sing. of παροξύνω.

παρώτρυναν, 1 aor. act. 3 pers. plur. of παροτρύνω.

παρῳχημένος, pf. ptcp. of παροίχομαι.

παυσάτω, 1 aor. act. impv. 3 pers. sing. of παύω.

πεῖν, 2 aor. act. inf. of πίνω.

πείσας, 1 aor. act. ptcp. of πείθω.

πείσω, fut. act. of πείθω.

πέπαυται, pf. mid. 3 pers. sing. of παύω.

πεπειραμένος, pf. pass. ptcp. of πειράω.

πεπειρασμένος, pf. pass. ptcp. of πειράζω.

πέπεισμαι, -μένος, pf. pass. ind. and ptcp. of πείθω.

πεπιεσμένος, pf. pass. ptcp. of πιέζω.

πεπιστεύκεισαν, plpf. act. 3 pers. plur. of πιστεύω.

πεπιστευκόσι, pf. act. ptcp. dat. plur. of πιστεύω.

πεπλάνησθε, pf. pass. 2 pers. plur. of πλανάω.

πεπλάτυνται, pf. pass. 3 pers. sing. of πλατύνω.

πεπληρωκέναι, pf. act. inf. of πληρόω.

πέποιθα, 2 pf. of πείθω.

πέπονθα, 2 pf. of πάσχω.

πεπότικεν, pf. act. 3 pers. sing. of ποτίζω.

πέπρακε, pf. act. 3 pers. sing. of πιπράσκω.

πεπραμένος, pf. pass. ptcp. of πιπράσκω.

πέπραχα, pf. act. of πράσσω.

πέπτωκα, -κες, -καν, pf. act. 3 pers. plur. of πίπτω.

πεπυρωμένος, pf. pass. ptcp. of πυρόω.

πέπωκε (-καν), pf. act. 3 pers. sing. (plur.) of πίνω.

πεπωρωμένος, pf. pass. ptcp. of πωρόω.

περιάψας, 1 aor. act. ptcp. of περιάπτω.

περιδραμόντες, 2 aor. act. ptcp. nom. plur. of περιτρέχω.

περιεδέδετο, plpf. pass. 3 pers. sing. of περιδέω.

περιεζωσμένος, pf. pass. ptcp. of περιζώννυμι.

περιέκρυβον, 2 aor. of περικρύπτω (or impf. of περικρύβω).

περιελεῖν, 2 aor. act. inf. of περιαιρέω.

περιέπεσον, 2 aor. act. of περιπίπτω.

περιεσπᾶτο, impf. pass. 3 pers. sing. of περισπάω.

περιέσχον, 2 aor. act. of περιέχω.

περιέτεμον, 2 aor. act. of περιτέμνω.

περιζῶσαι, 1 aor. mid. impv. of περιζώννυμι.

περιῃρεῖτο, impf. pass. 3 pers. sing. of περιαιρέω.

περιθέντες, 2 aor. act. ptcp. nom. plur. of περιτίθημι.

περιΐστασο, pres. mid. (pass.) impv. of περιΐστημι.

περιπέσητε, 2 aor. act. subj. 2 pers. plur. of περιπίπτω.

περιρεραμμένον, pf. pass. ptcp. neut. of περιρραίνω.

περιρ(ρ)ήξαντες, 1 aor. act. ptcp. nom. plur. of περιρρήγνυμι.

περισσεῦσαι 1 aor. act. inf., and περισσεύσαι 1 aor. act. opt. 3 pers. sing., of περισσεύω.

περιτετμημένος, pf. pass. ptcp. of περιτέμνω.

περιτιθέασιν, pres. act. 3 pers. plur. of περιτίθημι.

περιτμηθῆναι, 1 aor. pass. inf. of περιτέμνω.

πεσεῖν, 2 aor. act. inf. of πίπτω.

πεσεῖται (-οῦνται), fut. 3 pers. sing. (plur.) of πίπτω.

πέσετε, 2 aor. act. impv. 2 pers. plur. of πίπτω.

πέτηται, pres. subj. 3 pers. sing. of πέτομαι.

πετώμενος, pres. ptcp. of πετάομαι.

πεφανέρωται (-νερῶσθαι), pf. pass. (inf.) of φανερόω.

πεφίμωσο, pf. pass. impv. of φιμόω.

πιάσαι, 1 aor. act. inf. of πιάζω.

πίε, 2 aor. act. impv. of πίνω.

πιεῖν, 2 aor. act. inf. of πίνω.

πίεσαι, πίεσθε, fut. 2 pers. sing. and plur. of πίνω.

πίῃ, 2 aor. act. subj. 3 pers. sing. of πίνω.

πικρανεῖ, fut. act. 3 pers. sing. of πικραίνω.

πῖν, 2 aor. act. inf. of πίνω.

πίω, 2 aor. act. subj. of πίνω.

πλάσας, 1 aor. act. ptcp. of πλάσσω.

πλέξαντες, 1 aor. act. ptcp. nom. plur. masc. of πλέκω.

πλεονάσαι, 1 aor. act. opt. 3 pers. sing. of πλεονάζω.

πληθῦναι, 1 aor. act. opt. 3 pers. sing. of πληθύνω.

πληθύνει, pres. act. 3 pers. sing. of πληθύνω.

πληθυνεῖ, fut. 3 pers. sing. of πληθύνω.

πληθυνθῆναι, 1 aor. pass. inf. of πληθύνω.

πληρωθῇ, -θῆτε, -θῶ, -θῶσιν, 1 aor. pass. subj. of πληρόω.

πληρῶσαι 1 aor. inf., and πληρώσαι 1 aor. opt. 3 pers. sing., of πληρόω.

πλήσας, 1 aor. act. ptcp. of πίμπλημι.

πλησθείς, 1 aor. pass. ptcp. of πίμπλημι.

πλησθῇς, 1 aor. pass. subj. 2 pers. sing. of πίμπλημι.

πνέῃ, pres. act. subj. 3 pers. sing. of πνέω.

ποιήσειαν, (Aeolic) 1 aor. opt. 3 pers. plur. of ποιέω.

ποιμαίνει, pres. act. 3 pers. sing. of ποιμαίνω.

ποιμάνατε, 1 aor. act. impv. 2 pers. plur. of ποιμαίνω.

ποιμανεῖ, fut. act. 3 pers. sing. of ποιμαίνω.

πορεύου, pres. mid. impv. of πορεύομαι.

πραθέν, 1 aor. pass. ptcp. neut. of πιπράσκω.

πραθῆναι, 1 aor. pass. inf. of πιπράσκω.

προβάς, 2 aor. act. ptcp. of προβαίνω.

προβεβηκυῖα, pf. act. ptcp. fem. of προβαίνω.

προγεγονότων, pf. act. ptcp. gen. plur. of προγίνομαι.

προεβίβασαν, 1 aor. act. 3 pers. plur. of προβιβάζω.

προεγνωσμένος, pf. pass. ptcp. of προγινώσκω.

προελεύσεται, fut. 3 pers. sing. of προέρχομαι.

προενήρξατο (-ασθε), 1 aor. 3 pers. sing. (2 pers. plur.) of προενάρχομαι.

προεπηγγείλατο, 1 aor. mid. 3 pers. sing. of προεπαγγέλλω.

προεπηγγελμένος, pf. pass. ptcp. of προεπαγγέλλω.

προεστῶτες, pf. act. ptcp. nom. plur. masc. of προΐστημι.

προέτειναν, 1 aor. act. 3 pers. plur. of προτείνω.

προεφήτευον, impf. act. of προφητεύω.

προέφθασεν, 1 aor. act. 3 pers. sing. of προφθάνω.

προεωρακότες, pf. act. ptcp. nom. plur. masc. of προοράω.

προῆγεν, impf. act. 3 pers. sing. of προάγω.

προηλπικότας, pf. act. ptcp. acc. plur. masc. of προελπίζω.

προημαρτηκώς, pf. act. ptcp. of προαμαρτάνω.

προητιασάμεθα, 1 aor. 1 pers. plur. of προαιτιάομαι.

προητοίμασα, 1 aor. act. of προετοιμάζω.

προκεκηρυγμένος, pf. pass. ptcp. of προκηρύσσω.

προκεχειρισμένος, pf. pass. ptcp. of προχειρίζω.

προκεχειροτονημένος, pf. pass. ptcp. of προχειροτονέω.

προορώμην and προωρώμην, impf. mid. of προοράω.

προσανέθεντο, 2 aor. mid. 3 pers. plur. of προσανατίθημι.

προσειργάσατο, 1 aor. mid. 3 pers. sing. of προσεργάζομαι.

προσεκλίθη, 1 aor. pass. 3 pers. sing. of προσκλίνω.

προσεκολλήθη, 1 aor. pass. 3 pers. sing. of προσκολλάω.

προσεκύνουν, impf. act. of προσκυνέω.

προσενήνοχεν, pf. act. 3 pers. sing. of προσφέρω.

προσέπεσε, -σαν, -σον, 2 aor. act. of προσπίπτω.

προσέρ(ρ)ηξα, 1 aor. act. of προσρήγνυμι.

προσέσχηκα, pf. act. of προσέχω.

προσεφώνει, impf. act. 3 pers. sing. of προσφωνέω.

προσεῶντος, pres. act. ptcp. gen. sing. of προσεάω.

προσήνεγκα (-κον), 1 aor. (2 aor.) act. of προσφέρω.

προσηνέχθη, 1 aor. pass. 3 pers. sing. of προσφέρω.

προσηργάσατο, 1 aor. 3 pers. sing. of προσεργάζομαι.

προσηύξατο, 1 aor. 3 pers. sing. of προσεύχομαι.

προσηύχετο, impf. 3 pers. sing. of προσεύχομαι.

πρόσθες, 2 aor. act. impv. of προστίθημι.

προσκύνησον, 1 aor. act. impv. of προσκυνέω.

προσλαβοῦ, 2 aor. mid. impv. of προσλαμβάνω.

προσμεῖναι, 1 aor. act. inf. of προσμένω.

προσπήξας, 1 aor. act. ptcp. of προσπήγνυμι.

προστῆναι, 2 aor. act. inf. of προΐστημι.

προσωρμίσθησαν, 1 aor. pass. 3 pers. plur. of προσορμίζω.

προσώχθισα, 1 aor. act. of προσοχθίζω.

προτρεψάμενος, 1 aor. mid. ptcp. of προτρέπω.

προϋπῆρχον, impf. act. of προϋπάρχω.

πταίσητε, 1 aor. act. subj. 2 pers. plur. of πταίω.

πτοηθέντες, 1 aor. pass. ptcp. nom. plur. masc. of πτοέω.

πτοηθῆτε, 1 aor. pass. impv. 2 pers. plur. of πτοέω.

πτύξας, 1 aor. act. ptcp. of πτύσσω.

πτύσας, 1 aor. act. ptcp. of πτύω.

πυθόμενος, 2 aor. ptcp. of πυνθάνομαι.

ῥαντίσωνται, 1 aor. mid. subj. 3 pers. plur. of ῥαντίζω.

ῥεραντισμένοι (or ῥεραντ. or ἐρραντ.), pf. pass. ptcp. nom. plur. masc. of ῥαντίζω.

ῥεριμμένος (or ἐρριμμένος or ἐριμμ.), pf. pass. ptcp. of ῥίπτω.

ῥεύσουσιν, fut. 3 pers. plur. of ῥέω.

ῥῆξον, 1 aor. act. impv. of ῥήγνυμι.

ῥήξωσιν, 1 aor. act. subj. 3 pers. plur. of ῥήγνυμι.

ῥίψαν (better ῥῖψαν), 1 aor. act. ptcp. neut. of ῥίπτω.

ῥυπανθήτω, 1 aor. pass. impv. 3 pers. sing. of ῥυπαίνω.

ῥυπαρευθήτω, 1 aor. pass. impv. 3 pers. sing. of ῥυπαρεύομαι.

ῥῦσαι, -σάσθω, 1 aor. mid. impv. of ῥύομαι.

ῥυσθῶ (-θῶμεν), 1 aor. pass. subj. 1 pers. sing. (plur.) of ῥύομαι.

σαροῖ, pres. ind. 3 pers. sing. of σαρόω.

σβέσαι, 1 aor. act. inf. of σβέννυμι.

σβέσει, fut. act. 3 pers. sing. of σβέννυμι.

σβεσθήσεται, 1 fut. pass. 3 pers. sing. of σβέννυμι.

σεσαλευμένος, pf. pass. ptcp. of σαλεύω.

σεσαρωμένος, pf. pass. ptcp. of σαρόω.

σέσηπε, 2 pf. act. 3 pers. sing. of σήπω.

σεσιγημένος, pf. pass. ptcp. of σιγάω.

σέσωκα, pf. act. of σώζω.

σέσωσται and σέσωται, pf. pass. 3 pers. sing. of σώζω.

σημᾶναι, 1 aor. act. inf. of σημαίνω.

σθενώσαι, 1 aor. act. opt. 3 pers. sing. of σθενόω.

σθενώσει, fut. act. 3 pers. sing. of σθενόω.

σιγήσῃ, 1 aor. act. subj. 3 pers. sing. of σιγάω.

σκύλλου, pres. mid. impv. of σκύλλω.

σπαρείς, 2 aor. pass. ptcp. of σπείρω.

σπεῦσον, 1 aor. act. impv. of σπεύδω.

σταθῇ, 1 aor. pass. subj. 3 pers. sing of ἵστημι.

σταθῆναι, 1 aor. pass. inf. of ἵστημι.

στάς, 2 aor. act. ptcp. of ἵστημι.

στῆθι (στῆναι), 2 aor. act. impv. (inf.) of ἵστημι.

στηρίξαι, 1 aor. act. inf. or 1 aor. opt. 3 pers. sing of στηρίζω.

στήριξον and στήρισον, 1 aor. act. impv. of στηρίζω.

στηρίξω, στηρίσω, στηριῶ, fut. act. of στηρίζω.

στήσῃ, στήσῃς, στήσητε, etc., 1 aor. act. subj. of ἵστημι.

στήσομαι, 1 fut. mid. of ἵστημι.

στραφείς -φέντες, 2 aor. pass. ptcp. of στρέφω.

στραφῆτε, 2 aor. pass. subj. 2 pers. plur. of στρέφω.

στρῶσον, 1 aor. act. impv. of στρωννύω.

συγκατατεθειμένος, pf. mid. ptcp. of συγκατατίθημι.

συγκατατιθέμενος, pres. mid. ptcp. of συγκατατίθημι.

συγκεκερασμένος and συγκεκραμένος, pf. pass. ptcp. of συγκεράννυμι.

συγκέχυται, pf. pass. 3 pers. sing. of συγχέω.

συλλαβοῦσα, 2 aor. act. ptcp. nom. sing. fem. of συλλαμβάνω.

συλλή(μ)ψῃ, fut. 2 pers. sing. of συλλαμβάνω.

συμπαρακληθῆναι, 1 aor. pass. inf. of συμπαρακαλέω.

συμπαρόντες, pres. ptcp. nom. plur. masc. of συμπάρειμι.

συμφυεῖσα, 2 aor. pass. ptcp. nom. plur. fem. of συμφύω.

συναγάγετε, 2 aor. act. impv. 2 pers. plur. of συνάγω.

46

συνανέκειντο, impf. 3 pers. plur. of συνανάκειμαι.
συναπαχθέντες, 1 aor. pass. ptcp. nom. plur. masc. of συναπάγω.
συναπέθανον, 2 aor. act. of συναποθνήσκω.
συναπήχθη, 1 aor. pass. 3 pers. sing. of συναπάγω.
συναπώλετο, 2 aor. mid. 3 pers. sing. of συναπόλλυμι.
συνᾶραι, 1 aor. act. inf. of συναίρω.
συναχθήσομαι, 1 fut. pass. of συνάγω.
συνδεδεμένοι, pf. pass. ptcp. nom. plur. masc. of συνδέω.
συνέζευξεν, 1 aor. act. 3 pers. sing. of συζεύγνυμι.
συνέθεντο, 2 aor. mid. 3 pers. plur. of συντίθημι.
συνειδυίης (or -ας), pf. act. ptcp. gen. sing. fem. of συνεῖδον.
συνειληφυῖα, pf. act. ptcp. fem. of συλλαμβάνω.
συνείπετο, impf. 3 pers. sing. of συνέπομαι.
συνείχετο, impf. pass. 3 pers. sing. of συνέχω.
συνεκόμισαν, 1 aor. act. 3 pers. plur. of συγκομίζω.
συνεληλύθεισαν, plpf. 3 pers. plur. of συνέρχομαι.
συνεληλυθυῖαι, pf. ptcp. nom. plur. fem. of συνέρχομαι.
συνεπέστη, 2 aor. act. 3 pers. sing. of συνεφίστημι.
συνέπιον, 2 aor. act. of συμπίνω.
συνεσπάραξεν, 1 aor. act. 3 pers. sing. of συσπαράσσω.
συνεσταλμένος, pf. pass. ptcp. of συστέλλω.
συνεστῶσα (-τῶτα), 2 pf. ptcp. nom. sing. fem. (neut. plur.) of συνίστημι.
συνέταξα, 1 aor. act. of συντάσσω.
συνετάφημεν, 2 aor. pass. 1 pers. plur. of συνθάπτω.
σύνετε, 2 aor. act. ind. or impv. 2 pers. plur. of συνίημι.
συνετέθειντο, plpf. mid. 3 pers. plur. of συντίθημι.
συνετήρει, impf. act. 3 pers. sing. of συντηρέω.
συνέφαγες, 2 aor. act. 2 pers. sing. of συνεσ ϑ.
συνέχεαν, 1 aor. act. 3 pers. plur. of συγχέω.
συνέχεον, impf. (2 aor.? cf. ἐκχέω) 3 pers. plur. of συγχέω.
συνεχύθη, 1 aor. pass. 3 pers. sing. of συγχέω.
συνεψήφισαν, 1 aor. act. 3 pers. plur. of συμψηφίζω.
συνηγέρθητε, 1 aor. pass. 2 pers. plur. of συνεγείρω.
συνηγμένος, pf. pass. ptcp. of συνάγω.
συνήθλησαν, 1 aor. act. 3 pers. plur. of συναθλέω.
συνηθροισμένος, pf. pass. ptcp. of συναθροίζω.
συνῆκαν, 1 aor. act. 3 pers. plur. of συνίημι.
συνήλασεν, 1 aor. act. 3 pers. sing. of συνελαύνω.
συνήλλασσεν, impf. act. 3 pers. sing. of συναλλάσσω.
συνήντησεν, 1 aor. act. 3 pers. sing. of συναντάω.
συνήργει, impf. 3 pers. sing. of συνεργέω.
συνηρπάκει, plpf. act. 3 pers. sing. of συναρπάζω.
συνήρπασαν, 1 aor. act. 3 pers. plur. of συναρπάζω.
συνῆσαν, impf. 3 pers. plur. of σύνειμι.
συνήσθιεν, impf. 3 pers. sing. of συνεσθίω.
συνῆτε, 2 aor. act. subj. 2 pers. plur. of συνίημι.
συνήχθη (-ησαν), 1 aor. pass. 3 pers. sing. (plur.) of συνάγω.
συνιᾶσι, συνιοῦσι, συνίουσι, pres. act. 3 pers. plur. of συνίημι.
συνιδών, ptcp. of συνεῖδον.
συνιείς, συνίων, συνιῶν (not -ιών), pres. ptcp. of συνίημι.
συνίετε, pres. ind. or impv. 2 pers. plur. of συνίημι.
συνιόντος, ptcp. gen. sing. of σύνειμι (εἰμί).
συνιστᾶν, -ῶν, pres. inf. and ptcp. of συνίστημι.
συνίωσι and συνιῶσι, pres. subj. 3 pers. plur. of συνίημι.
συνόντων, ptcp. gen. plur. of σύνειμι (εἰμί).

συνταφέντες, 2 aor. pass. ptcp. nom. plur. masc. of συνθάπτω.
συντελεσθείς, 1 aor. pass. ptcp. of συντελέω.
συντετμημένος, pf. pass. ptcp. of συντέμνω.
συντετριμμένος, pf. pass. ptcp. of συντρίβω.
συντετρίφθαι or -τρῖφθαι, pf. pass. inf. of συντρίβω.
συντρίβον or -τρῖβον, pres. act. ptcp. neut. of συντρίβω.
συνυπεκρίθησαν, 1 aor. pass. 3 pers. plur. of συνυποκρίνομαι.
συνῶσι, 2 aor. act. subj. 3 pers. plur. of συνίημι.
σωθῇ, -θῆναι, -θῆτε, -θῶσιν, 1 aor. pass. of σώζω.
σῶσαι, 1 aor. act. inf. of σώζω.

τακήσεται, fut. pass. 3 pers. sing. of τήκω, q. v.
ταραχθῆναι, 1 aor. pass. inf. of ταράσσω.
τεθέαται, pf. 3 pers. sing. of θεάομαι.
τέθεικα, pf. act. of τίθημι.
τεθεμελίωτο, plpf. pass. 3 pers. sing. of θεμελιόω.
τεθῇ, 1 aor. pass. subj. 3 pers. sing. of τίθημι.
τεθλιμμένος, pf. pass. ptcp. of θλίβω.
τεθνάναι, 2 pf. act. inf. of θνήσκω.
τεθνηκέναι, pf. act. inf. of θνήσκω.
τεθραμμένος, pf. pass. ptcp. of τρέφω.
τεθραυσμένος, pf. pass. ptcp. of θραύω.
τεθυμένα, pf. pass. ptcp. neut. of θύω.
τεθῶσιν, 1 aor. pass. subj. 3 pers. plur. of τίθημι.
τέκῃ, 2 aor. act. subj. 3 pers. sing. of τίκτω.
τελεσθῶσιν, 1 aor. pass. subj. 3 pers. plur. of τελέω.
τέξῃ, fut. 2 pers. sing. of τίκτω.
τεταγμένος, pf. pass. ptcp. of τάσσω.
τέτακται, pf. pass. 3 pers. sing. of τάσσω.
τεταραγμένος, pf. pass. ptcp. of ταράσσω.
τετάρακται, pf. pass. 3 pers. sing. of ταράσσω.
τεταχέναι, pf. act. inf. of τάσσω.
τετέλεσται, pf. pass. 3 pers. sing. of τελέω.
τέτευχα, pf. act. of τυγχάνω.
τετήρηκαν, -ασιν, pf. act. 3 pers. plur. of τηρέω.
τετιμημένος, pf. pass. ptcp. of τιμάω.
τετραχηλισμένος, pf. pass. ptcp. of τραχηλίζω.
τετύφωται, pf. pass. 3 pers. sing. of τυφόω.
τέτυχα, τετύχηκα, pf. act. of τυγχάνω.
τεχθείς, 1 aor. pass. ptcp. of τίκτω.
τιθέασιν, pres. ind. act. 3 pers. plur. of τίθημι.
τίσουσιν, fut. act. 3 pers. plur. of τίνω.

ὑπέδειξα, 1 aor. act. of ὑποδείκνυμι.
ὑπέθηκα, 1 aor. act. of ὑποτίθημι.
ὑπέλαβεν, 2 aor. act. 3 pers. sing. of ὑπολαμβάνω.
ὑπελείφθην, 1 aor. pass. of ὑπολείπω.
ὑπέμεινα, 1 aor. act. of ὑπομένω.
ὑπέμενον, impf. of ὑπομένω.
ὑπεμνήσθην, 1 aor. pass. of ὑπομιμνήσκω.
ὑπενεγκεῖν, 2 aor. act. inf. of ὑποφέρω.
ὑπενόουν, impf. act. of ὑπονοέω.
ὑπεπλεύσαμεν, 1 aor. act. 1 pers. plur. of ὑποπλέω.
ὑπεριδών, ptcp. of ὑπερεῖδον.

ὑπέστρεψα, 1 aor. act. of ὑποστρέφω.
ὑπεστρώννυον, impf. 3 pers. plur. of ὑποστρώννυμι.
ὑπετάγη, 2 aor. pass. 3 pers. sing. of ὑποτάσσω.
ὑπέταξα, 1 aor. act. of ὑποτάσσω.
ὑπῆγον, impf. act. of ὑπάγω.
ὑπήκουον, impf. act. of ὑπακούω.
ὑπήνεγκα, 1 aor. act. of ὑποφέρω.
ὑπῆρχον, impf. act. of ὑπάρχω.
ὑποδέδεκται, pf. 3 pers. sing. of ὑποδέχομαι.
ὑποδεδημένος, pf. pass. ptcp. of ὑποδέω.
ὑπόδησαι, 1 aor. mid. impv. of ὑποδέω.
ὑποδραμόντες, 2 aor. act. ptcp. nom. plur. masc. of ὑποτρέχω.
ὑπομείνας, 1 aor. act. ptcp. of ὑπομένω.
ὑπομεμενηκότα, pf. act. ptcp. acc. sing. masc. of ὑπομένω.
ὑπομνῆσαι, 1 aor. act. inf. of ὑπομιμνήσκω.
ὑπομνήσω, fut. act. of ὑπομιμνήσκω.
ὑποπνεύσαντος, 1 aor. act. ptcp. gen. sing. of ὑποπνέω.
ὑποστείληται, 1 aor. mid. subj. 3 pers. sing. of ὑποστέλλω.
ὑποταγῇ, 2 aor. pass. subj. 3 pers. sing of ὑποτάσσω.
ὑποταγήσομαι, 2 fut. pass. of ὑποτάσσω.
ὑποτάγητε, 2 aor. pass. impv. 2 pers. plur. of ὑποτάσσω.
ὑποτάξαι, 1 aor. act. inf. of ὑποτάσσω.
ὑποτασσέσθωσαν, pres. mid. impv. 3 pers. plur. of ὑποτάσσω.
ὑποτέτακται, pf. pass. 3 pers. sing. of ὑποτάσσω.
ὑστερηκέναι, pf. act. inf. of ὑστερέω.
ὑψωθῶ, 1 aor. pass subj. of ὑψόω.

φάγεσαι, fut. 2 pers. sing. of ἐσθίω.
φάνῃ, 1 aor. act. subj. 3 pers. sing. of φαίνω.
φανῇ, -νῇς, -νῶσιν, 2 aor. pass. subj. of φαίνω.
φανήσομαι and φανοῦμαι, 2 fut. pass. of φαίνω.
φείσομαι, fut. of φείδομαι.
φεύξομαι, fut. of φεύγω.
φθαρῇ, 2 aor. pass. subj. 3 pers. sing. of φθείρω.
φθαρήσομαι, 2 fut. pass. of φθείρω.
φθάσωμεν, 1 aor. subj. 1 pers. plur. of φθάνω.
φθερεῖ, fut. act. 3 pers. sing. of φθείρω.
φιμοῖν, -μοῦν, pres. act. inf. of φιμόω.
φιμώθητι, 1 aor. pass. impv. 2 pers. sing. of φιμόω.
φραγῇ, 2 aor. pass. subj. 3 pers. sing. of φράσσω.
φραγήσομαι, 2 fut. pass. of φράσσω.
φράσον, 1 aor. impv. of φράζω.
φρονείσθω, pres. pass. impv. 3 pers. sing. of φρονέω.

φυέν, 2 aor. pass. ptcp. neut. of φύω.
φύλαξον, 1 aor. act. impv. of φυλάσσω.
φύς, 2 aor. act. ptcp. of φύω.
φυτεύθητι, 1 aor. pass. impv. of φυτεύω.
φωτιεῖ, (Attic) fut. 3 pers. sing. of φωτίζω.

χαλῶσιν, pres. act. 3 pers. plur. of χαλάω.
χαρῆναι, 2 aor. pass. inf. of χαίρω.
χαρήσομαι, fut. mid. of χαίρω.
χάρητε, 2 aor. impv. 2 pers. plur. of χαίρω.
χαρῆτε, 2 aor. subj. 2 pers. plur. of χαίρω.
χαροῦσιν, fut. 3 pers. plur. of χαίρω (Rev. xi. 10 unique).
χρῆσαι, 1 aor. mid. impv. of χράομαι.
χρήσηται, 1 aor. subj. 3 pers. sing. of χράομαι.
χρῆσον, 1 aor. act. impv. of κίχρημι.
χρῆται, pres. subj. 3 pers. sing. of χράομαι.
χρονιεῖ, (Attic) fut. 3 pers. sing. of χρονίζω.
χρῶ, pres. impv. of χράομαι.
χωρῆσαι, 1 aor. act. inf. of χωρέω.
χωρίσαι, 1 aor. act. inf. of χωρίζω.
χωροῦσαι, pres. act. ptcp. nom. plur. fem. of χωρέω.
χωροῦσι, pres. act. 3 pers. plur. of χωρέω.

ψηλαφήσειαν, (Aeolic) 1 aor. opt. 3 pers. plur. of ψηλαφάω.
ψυγήσεται, 2 fut. pass. 3 pers. sing. of ψύχω.
ψωμίσω, 1 aor. act. subj. of ψωμίζω.

ᾠκοδόμητο, plpf. pass. 3 pers. sing. of οἰκοδομέω.
ᾠκοδόμουν, impf. act. of οἰκοδομέω.
ὡμίλει, impf. act. 3 pers. sing. of ὁμιλέω.
ὡμολόγουν, impf. act. of ὁμολογέω.
ὤμοσα, 1 aor. act. of ὄμνυμι.
ὠνείδισε, 1 aor. act. 3 pers. sing. of ὀνειδίζω.
ὠνόμασα, 1 aor. act. of ὀνομάζω.
ὤρθριζεν, impf. 3 pers. sing. of ὀρθρίζω.
ὥρισα, 1 aor. act. of ὁρίζω.
ὡρισμένος, pf. pass. ptcp. of ὁρίζω.
ὥρμησα, 1 aor. act. of ὁρμάω.
ὤρυξεν, 1 aor. act. 3 pers. sing. of ὀρύσσω.
ὠρχήσασθε, 1 aor. 2 pers. plur. of ὀρχέομαι.
ὤφειλον, impf. of ὀφείλω.
ὤφθην, 1 aor. pass. of ὁράω.

ADDITIONS AND CORRECTIONS

———◆———

THE printing of the Lexicon was nearly finished before the plan of the Appendix, as respects its details, had been decided on. Consequently facts respecting a word's use are occasionally assumed there which are not expressly stated under the word itself. Professor Grimm held it to be unnecessary to refer to profane usage in the case of familiar and current words. And although the number of classic vouchers for the age of a word has been greatly multiplied, they have not been given with that invariable completeness which the chronological distribution of the vocabulary in the Appendix renders desirable. Consistency would require that it be expressly noted that the following words are in use as early as Homer or Hesiod : ἄγκιστρον, ἀγνῶς, ἄγρα, ἀδρότης, ἀθέμι(σ)τος, Ἀθηναῖος, Αἰγύπτιος, Αἰθίοψ, αἰσχρός, δή, δια(or η)κόσιοι, εἶμι, ἐκεῖθεν, ἐκεῖσε, Ἑλλάς, Ἕλλην, ἕνεκα, ἐντεῦθεν, ἕξ, ἐξάγω, ἐξαίρω, ἔξειμι, ἐξέρχομαι, ἑξήκοντα, ἔξω, ἐπεγείρω, ἐπεί, ἐπειδή, ἐπεῖδον, ἔπειτα, ἐπικαλύπτω, ἔπος, ἑπτά, ἥλιος, θαρσέω, θάρσος, Κρής, κτῆμα, μηκέτι, μῆτις (μήτι), νίπτω, χίλιοι ; that the following are as old as Pindar, Herodotus, or the Tragedians : ἀγνωσία, αἱμορροέω, ἐκδοχή, ἐνοικέω, ἐξακόσιοι, ἔξωθεν, ἔπαινος, Ἐφέσιος, θροέω, κοινόω, κολάζω, κράσπεδον, Μακεδών, μάταιος, μέντοι, μετέχω, μηδέποτε, μηδέπω, Μῆδος, μωραίνω, νή, οὐκοῦν, οὐχί, ὀχετός, παράσημος, πάροικος, πόμα, προστάτις, στάδιον, στατήρ, στοά, συνοικέω, Χαλδαῖος ; that the following may be found in Thucydides, Aristophanes, Plato, or Xenophon : ἀγράμματος, ἀδάπανος, ἀλήθω, Ἀχαΐα, ἔγγιστα, ἐγγύτερον, ἐπίθεσις, ἐπικαθίζω, ἐπισκευάζω, καταλαλέω, ματαιολόγος, μήτιγε, μνᾶ, μουσικός, νυνί, ὀθόνιον, πάροινος, ῥαφίς, σπουδαίως, στάμνος, συναγωγή, συναίρω, σφυρίς, φάσις, φιλοσοφία ; that the following are in use from Aristotle on : ἐπεκτείνω, ἐπιστηρίζω, εὐθύτης, ἦχος, κεράτιον, κοπή, μαργαρίτης (Theophr.), νάρδος (Theophr.), πρώτως ; that the following may be found in the 3d century before Christ : βαθέως, ἐπάν (inscr. B. C. 265), — δεκαέξ and δεκαοκτώ in the Sept. ; that the following appear in Polybius : Ἀλεξανδρῖνος, Ἀντιοχεύς, προσανέχω ; while Diod. Sic., Dion. Hal., or Strabo vouch for Ἄραψ, Ἀσιάρχης, Ἐπικούρειος, τάχιον.

Other words without vouchers either first make their appearance in the New Testament writings, or are so treated in the Lexicon as to furnish a student with the means of tracing their history.

Many interesting facts relative to noteworthy New Testament forms, and even constructions, will be found in *Meisterhans*, Grammatik der Attischen Inschriften, Berlin, 1885 (2d much "enlarged and improved" edition 1888). See, for example, on the various forms of δίδωμι, ἵημι, ἵστημι, τίθημι, § 74 ; on the intrusion into the 2 aor. of the α of the 1 aor. (ἤνεγκαν, εἶπας, εὑράμενος, etc.) § 66, 6. 7. 8 ; on γί(γ)νομαι, γι(γ)νώσκω, § 63, 20. 21 ; on ἔνι and ἔνεστι, § 74, 12 ; on (ἐ)θέλω, § 63, 23 ; on the fut. χαρήσομαι, § 64, 7. On anomalies or variations in augment, § 62 ; on ἐλπίς, καθ' ἰδίαν, § 32, 2. 4 ; on ἕνεκεν, εἵνεκεν, § 83, 26 ; on the use of the cases and prepositions, §§ 82, 83 ; of the art. with πᾶς, § 84, 41 ; etc., etc. References to it (of necessity restricted to the first edition, 1885) have been introduced into the body of the Lexicon where the plates easily permitted.

p. 1ᵇ, s. v. Ἀββᾶ ; respecting its accent see *Tdf.* Proleg. p. 102 ; *Kautzsch*, Grammatik d. Biblisch-Aramäischen u. s. w. (Leipzig, 1884) p. 8.

p. 4ᵇ, line 1, add " See *Westcott*, Epp. of St. John, p. 48 sq."

p. 7ᵇ, first paragraph, add to the reff. E. *Issel*, Der Begriff der Heiligkeit im N. T. (Leiden, 1887).

p. 13ᵇ, s. v. ἄθεος, l. 8 ; on the application of the term to Christians by the heathen see Bp. *Lghtft.*'s note on Ign. ad Trall. 3, vol. ii. p. 160.

p. 19ᵃ, line 13 from bot. *before* Longin. *insert* οἱ ἀπ' αἰῶνος Ῥωμαῖοι, Dion Cass. 63, 20, 2 cf. 5 ;

p. 27ᵃ, s. v. ἀληθής, fin., add to the reff. A. *Schlatter*, Der Glaube im Neuen Testament (Leiden, 1885), p. 169.

p. 72ᵇ, last line but one, after " Arabian king " insert Aretas IV., styled Φιλόπατρις 'lover of his country,' who reigned B. C. 9 (or 8) to A. D. 39 (or 40) (see Gutschmid's List of Nabathaean kings in J. *Euting*, Nab. Inschriften aus Arabien, Berlin 1885, p. 84 sq.)

p. 74ᵃ, s. v. Ἁρμαγεδών, fin., add But see WH u. s.

p. 74ᵇ, s. v. ἁρπαγμός, fin., add to the reff. *Wetzel* in Stud. u. Krit. for 1887, pp. 535–552.

p. 78ᵃ, s. v. ἀρχιερεύς 3, for the application of the term to Christ by the early writers see Bp. *Lghtft.* on

Clem. Rom. 1 Cor. 36 p. 118 sq., and on Ign. ad Philad. 9 vol. ii. p. 274.

p. 82ᵃ, s. v. 'Ασύγκριτος, line 1, after 'Ασύνκρ. add (cf. σύν, II. last paragraph)

p. 87ᵇ, first paragraph, last line, *for* Rev. viii. 6, etc.). *read* Rev. viii. 6; xviii. 7; cf. Scrivener's Greek Testament (1887) p. v. note). Tr reads αὐτῶν in Rev. vii. 11.

ibid. after "Cf." insert Meisterhans ed. 2 § 59, 4. 5;

p. 97ᵃ, line 15, מַלְכוּת הַשֵּׁ — probably the *article* should be stricken out; cf. Prof. Geo. F. Moore in the Andover Review for July 1887, p. 105.

p. 98ᵃ, s. v. βασιλεία, fin., to the reff. add *Edersheim*, Jesus the Messiah, i. 264 sqq.

p. 98ᵇ, s. v. βαστάζω, line 1, *before* fut. *insert* impf. 3 pers. sing. ἐβάσταζεν; *and after* 1 aor. ἐβάστασα; add, Pass., pres. inf. βαστάζεσθαι; impf. 3 pers. sing. ἐβαστάζετο;

p. 100ᵃ, s. v. Βεελζεβούλ, last line but one, add (within the brackets) But see *Baudissin* in Herzog ed. 2, vol. ii. p. 209 sq.; *Kautzsch*, Gram. d. Bibl.-Aram. p. 9.

p. 101ᵃ, top, — On the recent identification of the pool ('twin pools') of Bethesda, near the church of St. Anne, see Pal. Explor. Fund for July, 1888.

p. 107ᵃ, line 1, *for* -θά WH *read* -θά Tr WH

p. 107ᵇ, s. v. Γάζα, line 7, *for* 16, 30 *read* 16, 2, 30

p. 108ᵇ, s. v. Γαλιλαία, last line but four, *for* 16, 34 *read* 16, 2, 34

p. 111ᵇ, s. v. γέεννα, line 29, *for* 2 K. i. *read* 2 K. i. 10–12

p. 128ᵃ, line 2, add to the reff. (within the brackets) *Caspari*, Chron.-geogr. Einl. pp. 83–90; *Schürer*, Neutest. Zeitgesch. §23, I. vol. ii. p. 83 (Eng. trans. ii.¹ p. 94)

p. 131ᵃ, Sʏɴ. *add* The words are associated in 2 Co. xi. 4.

p. 164ᵃ, s. v. Ἑβραΐς fin., add to the reff. Kautzsch p. 17 sq.; *Neubauer* in Studia Biblica (Oxford, 1885) pp. 39–74.

p. 198ᵇ, insert in its place "ἐκ-περισσοῦ, see ἐκπερισσῶς and ὑπερεκπερισσοῦ."

p. 256ᵃ, s. v. εὖ, line 3 — "contrary to ordinary Grk. usage" etc.; yet cf. Schmidt, vol. iv. p. 398.

p. 268ᵇ, s. v. ἕως, II. 2 c., for ἕως πρός in Lk. xxiv. 50, note the rendering given in R. V.: *until they were over against* etc.

p. 274ᵃ, s. v. ζωή, fin., to the works referred to add "Westcott, Epp. of St. John, p. 204 sqq."

p. 276ᵇ, s. v. ἡδύοσμος, fin., add to the reff. "Löw, Aram. Pflanzennamen, § 200."

p. 287ᵇ, s. v. θεός, 1 fin., add to the reff. "For θεοί in application to (deceased) Christians, see Theoph. ad Autol. 2, 27; Hippol. refut. omn. haer. 10, 34; Iren. haer. 3, 6, 1 fin.; 4, 1, 1; 4, 38, 4; cf. esp. *Harnack*, Dogmengesch. i. p. 82 note."

s. v. θεός 2, add "On patristic usage cf. *Harnack*, Dogmengesch. i. pp. 131, 695; Bp. *Lghtft*. Ignat. vol. ii. p. 26."

s. v. θεός 3, add "On ὁ θεός and θεός, esp. in the writings of John, see *Westcott*, Epp. of St. John, p. 165 sqq."

p. 292ᵃ, s. v. θριαμβεύω, add to the reff. at the close "*Findlay* in the Expositor, vol. x. p. 403 sqq.; xi. 78; *Waite* in the 'Speaker's Com.' on 2 Co. l. c. p. 404 sq."

p. 297ᵃ, first paragraph, last line but six, κατ' ἰδίαν — add, On κατ' ἰδίαν (WH's 'alt.' in Mt. xiv. 23; xvii. 1, 19; xx. 17; xxiv. 3; Mk. iv. 34; vi. 31; ix. 28; xiii. 3), see their App. pp. 143, 145; Meisterhans n. ³⁰⁶

p. 300ᵃ, s. v. Ἰησοῦς, line 10, *read* "in the Zeitschr. f. d. Luth. Theol. 1876, p. 209 sq.; [Keim i. 384 sq. (Eng. trans. ii. 97 sq.)]."

p. 306ᵃ, Sʏɴ., last line, add to the reff. E. Höhne in the Ztschrft. f. kirchl. Wissensch. u. s. w. 1886, pp. 607–617.

p. 314ᵇ, s. v. καθολικός, line 5, after "Smyrn. c. 8" insert "[see esp. Bp. Lghtft.'s note]"

p. 319ᵇ, s. v. καίω, line 7, to the reff. on καυχήσωμαι add "Bp. Lghtft. on Col., 7th ed., p. 395 n."

p. 354ᵃ, line 15, the words εἰς τοὺς κόλπους αὐτῶν are wanting in good Mss.

p. 358ᵃ, s. v. κοῦμι; add "See *Edersheim*, Jesus the Messiah, i. 631 note."

p. 365ᵇ, line 18, on this use of κύριος add ref. to Bp. Lghtft. on Ign., mart. Polyc. 8, p. 959.

p. 376ᵃ, s. v. λέπρα, add to the reff. *Clark* in the 'Speaker's Com.' on Lev. pp. 559 sqq. 570 sqq.; Sir *Risdon Bennett*, Diseases of the Bible. 1887. ("By-Paths of Bible Knowledge" vol. ix.)

p. 382ᵃ, first paragraph, line 15, add For a translation of Lücke's discussion see Christian Examiner for 1849 pp. 165 sqq. 412 sqq. To the reff. given may be added *Mansel* in Alex.'s Kitto s. v. Philosophy; *Zeller*, Philos. der Griechen, 3te Theil, 2², p. 369 sq. (1881); *Drummond*, Philo Judaeus, vol. ii. pp. 156–273.

p. 402ᵃ, line 18 sq., on ἐν μέσῳ and ἀνὰ μέσον cf. R. F. *Weymouth* in Journ. of Philol. 1869, ii. pp. 318–322.

p. 417ᵇ, insert in its place (before μονή) μόνας, see καταμόνας.

p. 420ᵇ, s. v. Μωσῆς, line 1, "constantly so in the text. Rec." — not quite correct; Rec.ˢᵗ uses Μωϋσῆς in Acts vi. 14; vii. 35, 37; xv. 1, 5; 2 Tim. iii. 8; Heb. ix. 19.

p. 421ᵃ, line 20, "by L Tr WH"—Tr does not seem to be consistent; see the diæresis, for example, in Acts xv. 1, 5; 2 Tim. iii. 8; Heb. ix. 19.

p. 425ᵇ, s. v. νηστεύω, line 6, after xviii. 12 insert [(cf. 'Teaching' 8, 1 and Harnack or Schaff ad loc.)]

p. 433ᵃ, introduce as line 1 (*before* ὁ, ἡ, τό) — O, o: — on its interchange with omega see Ω, ω.

p. 445ᵇ, s. v. ὁμοίωμα, last line "p. 301 sqq." — add *Dickson*, St. Paul's Use of the Terms 'Flesh' and 'Spirit' (Glasgow, 1883), p. 322 sqq.

p. 465ᵇ, line 32 mid., add see H. Gebhardt, Der Himmel im N. T., in Ztschr. f. kirchl. Wissensch. u. kirchl. Leben, 1886 pp. 555–575.

p. 474ᵃ, Syn. sub fin., on the elasticity of the term παῖς as respects age, see Bp. *Lghtft.* Apostolic Fathers, Pt. II. vol. i. p. 432 note.

p. 501ᵇ, under c. δ., after Ro. viii. 3 add [al. find here the same idiom as in Heb. x. 6 below (cf. R. V. txt.)]

p. 508ᵃ, line 18 sq., add to the reff. *Lipsius*, Apokr. Apostelgesch. ii.¹ (1887) p. 1 sqq.

p. 512ᵇ, s. v. πιστικός, line 9, add [but see Rev. *Wm. Houghton* in Proc. of Soc. of Bibl. Archaeol. Jan. 10, 1888]

p. 514ᵃ, to the reff. s. v. πίστις add *A. Schlatter*, Der Glaube im Neuen Testament (Leiden, 1885).

p. 521ᵃ, paragraph 4 a., line 4, "the Sept. renders by " etc. — not correct; the rendering of the Sept. in both passages is τὸ πν. τὸ ἅγιον.

p. 529ᵇ, par. c., line 5 sq., "so πολλῆς ὥρας, Polyb. 5, 8, 3 " — but see p. 679ᵇ, line 2.

p. 536ᵃ, line 15, after 1 Pet. v. 1 sq. insert [T WH om.]

p. 537ᵇ, s. v. προβατικός fin. — see under Βηθεσδά, p. 101ᵃ above.

p. 566ᵇ, s. v. Σαλά insert [Lchm. Σάλα]

p. 568ᵇ, line 2, add "On the Christology of the Samaritans see *Westcott*, Introd. to the Study of the Gospels, 5th ed., p. 159 sq."

p. 572ᵃ, first paragraph, end; add to the reff. "*Dorner.* System d. Christ. Glaubenslehre, § 85, vol. ii. 1 p. 188

sqq.; *Woldemar Schmidt* in Herzog ed. 2, xv. 358 sq.; esp. *Weser* in Stud. u. Krit. for 1882 pp. 284–303.

p. 584ᵃ, line 24, for "*Delitzsch*, Br. a. d. Röm. p. 16 note² " read *Geiger*, in Zeitschr. d. deutsch. Morgenl. Gesellsch. 1858, pp. 307–309; *Delitzsch* in Luth. Zeitschr. 1877 p. 603 sq.; *Driver* in the Expositor for Jan. 1889 p. 18 sq.

p. 608ᵇ, s. v. συστρατιώτης. line 1, *for* T Tr WH συν- (so Lchm. in Philem.; *read* L T Tr WH συν- (

p. 619ᵇ, s. v. τέλος 1 a., line 2, — "in the Grk. writ." etc. add cf. Schmidt ch. 193 esp. §§ 3 and 9.

p. 626ᵇ, line 38, *before* 2 Jn. 4 *insert* Acts xix. 33 R.V. mrg. (cf. συμβιβάζω, 3 fin.) ;

p. 653ᵃ, s. v. Φιλαδέλφεια, line 3, " The White City " (Sayce), add, al. "the pied or striped city " (cf. Bp. *Lghtft.* Apost. Fathers, Pt. II. sect. i. p. 245)

p. 665ᵇ, s. v. χαρίζομαι, last line, after ib. 16 add [but G L T Tr WH om. εἰς ἀπ.]

p. 669ᵇ, line 7, add to ref. *Schaff*, Hist. i. 841 sqq.; the Expositor for Nov. 1885, p. 381 sq.; *Salmon*, Introd., Lect. xiv.

p. 672ᵃ, s. v. Χριστιανός, line 7 sqq., add — yet see Bp. *Lghtft.* Apost. Fathers, Pt. II. vol. i. p. 400 sqq.

p. 678ᵇ, s. v. ψύχω, fin., add [Comp. : ἀνα-, ἀπο-, ἐκ-, κατα-, also εὐ-ψύχω.]

p. 708, col. 2, insert (in its place) " ἐνοχλέω fr. Sept. (Lk.?) "

SUPPLEMENTARY ADDITIONS AND CORRECTIONS, 1895

p. 43ᵃ, s. v. ἀνα-τρέπω, line 1, *insert after* ἀνα-τρέπω ; [1 aor. ἀνέτρεψα :] and *after* the definitions, [τὰς τραπέζας, Jn. ii. 15 WH txt.]; ethically, etc.

p. 64ᵃ, s. v. ἀπόκρυφος, fin., *read* [cf. Bp. Lghtft. on the word, Col. l. c.; and Ign. i. 351 sq.]

p. 241ᵇ, line 7, *read food for* (i.e. necessary or sufficient for) the morrow.

p. 281ᵃ, line 7, *after* Mk. vi. 17, 19, 22, *insert* [here WHR mg. read αὐτοῦ (for αὐτῆς τῆς), and thus make the *daughter's* name Herodias (as well as the mother's) ; but see *Schürer*, Gesch. § 17 b. n. 29.]

p. 354ᵇ, s. v. κομψότερον, line 4, *for* κόμψος *read* κομψῶς (yet cf. *Chandler*, § 885 fin.)

p. 365ᵃ, s. v. κυριακός, line 9, *after* Harnack *add* Harris, p. 105 sq.

p. 423ᵇ, line 6, *add to the reff.* Meisterhans, p. 8.

p. 507ᵃ, s. v. περπερεύομαι, line 4 sq., *read* is used of self-display, employing rhetorical embellishments in extolling one's self excessively, in Cic. ad Attic. 1, 14.

p. 708ᵇ, insert between ἐμπαιγμός and ἐνυβρίζω, " ἐνοχλέω fr. Sept. (Zk.?) "

p. 712ᵃ, s. v. ἀπαρνήσῃ, *after* fut. *add* and 1 aor. mid. subj.

p. 712ᵃ, delete the word ἀπεδίδοσαν.

p. 712ᵃ, delete the line beginning ἀπηρνησάμην.